The Complete Index
to
Literary Sources
in Film

Edited by
Alan Goble

London • Melbourne • Munich • New Providence, NJ

British Library Cataloguing in Publication Data
A catalogue record for this title is available from the British Library

Library of Congress Cataloging-in-Publication Data
A catalog record for this book is available from the Library of Congress

Published by Bowker-Saur, Windsor Court, East Grinstead House, East Grinstead, West Sussex RH19 1XA, UK
Tel: +44(0)1342 326972 Fax: +44(0)1342 335612
Email: lis@bowker-saur.com
Web site: www.bowker-saur.co.uk

Bowker-Saur is part of REED BUSINESS INFORMATION.

ISBN 1-85739-229-9   24345784

Cover design by Downland Creative Services
Printed on acid-free paper
Printed and bound in Great Britain by Antony Rowe, Wiltshire

To Valerie

To Valerie

Contents

Contents

Foreword

Alan Goble is unique. It is not too much to say that in the whole history of the cinema he is unequalled for the extent of the data he has gathered and recorded, single-handed. His vast filmographical volumes and CD-ROMs can only be compared with the Herculean enterprises of the great pioneer bibliographers, like Alexander Cruden who compiled the first concordance of the *Bible* in the eighteenth century.

Only those who do not understand the process would say that his achievement has been made possible by the availability of digital technology. It is true that computers and databases enable him and us to do much more with the data, to sort it this way and that, to extract new meanings and illuminations from it. But the basic business of collecting it all together in the first place remains the same as it always was, a dogged labour for the eye and the mind and the memory and the hand – even if the hand now manipulates a keyboard rather than a pen. The names, the titles, the dates and all the other facts that now so obediently perform their permutations on our computer screens, thanks to Goble's CD-ROMs, had first to be painstakingly gathered and sifted from a vast amorphous mass of pre-digital records. The process which has ended in these neat and easy reference tools began with endless trawls through old books, filmographies, magazines, programmes, cuttings – never letting a fragment of ephemera go by without scrutiny, in case it yielded a lost credit.

In this new book, Alan Goble reorganises his data and enlarges his scope to record the literary sources of more than a hundred years of films. It is probably true to say that ever since 1896, when the Biograph company filmed Joseph Jefferson in scenes from his stage success Rip Van Winkle, the majority of films have owed their themes to a previous play or book, short story or poem. Mostly – but not always – filmmakers have acknowledged their sources. Alan Goble now sets out to identify, date and record as many of these as he can.

The job has been undertaken before, but never with such ambition as in the present book. Tom Costello's *International Guide to Literature on Film* is essentially the work of a bibliographer and is precise in the assembly of its data, but he records only sound films (on his own principle that without speech, literary sources are less

relevant), which can be frustrating if you are trying to discover how many times *Les Miserables* or *David Copperfield* have been filmed. Moreover he is rigorous in insisting on his interpretation of "literary". Alan Goble's work, however, includes any book, play or story. All of them, in his opinion, are "literary" and the penny-dreadful writers of Westerns and Romance take their place alongside Tolstoy and Shakespeare.

Alan Goble's greatest quality distinguishes him both from the journalist and the academic. The journalist deals in the instantly available. The academic traces around himself circumscribed limits within which he can be safe and certain. In contrast, Alan Goble's temperament always takes him to the very limit. The user of his CD-ROMs, searching in the more rarefied fields, sometimes encounters the frustration of finding a thoroughly obscure title with little more information than a date or a single name attached to it. He can be reassured that if this is all that Alan Goble has found, no-one else is likely to discover more. Other filmographers might not even bother to retain such fragments; but Goble loves information far too much ever to heartlessly abandon an orphan fact. If he finds it, he records it.

No doubt in this new adventure too the researcher will sometimes find himself accompanying the author to the unmapped outer regions of filmographic knowledge. Back on terra firma though, in the recorded territories of film history, it will take real doggedness to find omissions. (Quite the reverse: I would not for example have included Auden's *Night Mail* commentary, commissioned for the film rather than a source in the true sense. But a questionable inclusion here or there is a far better fault than omission).

It is a reference book like no other, and a marvellous playground into the bargain. Only see what pleasurable and curious distractions overtake you when you embark on a search through these pages for the most-often adapted book or the most-filmed author or the writer the filmmakers missed.

David Robinson
Film critic and historian

Preface

That one of the great passions of my life is books is confirmed by the ten thousand plus books that populate my house. Films and books have been a source of unending interest to me since I was old enough to read and go to the cinema and I have enjoyed compiling this book. It has brought back memories of books long forgotten and the pleasure they gave at the time I read them.

David Lean's Great Expectations, which I saw when I was ten, was instrumental in me reading Dickens and over the years, several other films of novels have been the reason for me to seek that author out, to read more of his or her work. The film of John Buchan's *The Thirty-Nine Steps* started me reading Buchan but as this book shows, very little of his work has been filmed.

Occasionally, one reads a book and says, "What a good film that would make!", but it never happens. Many years ago, I remember thinking that about Vina Delmar's novel, *Beloved*, and waited in vain. What I did not know at the time was that Delmar had provided many stories for Hollywood, but unfortunately *Beloved* was not to be one of them. Another, George R. Stewart's *Earth Abides* appeared ideal film material to me, although science fiction films were not popular at the time of its publication in 1949. It is still in publication and it has a great number of devotees. Somebody could film it now!

Films of books do not alway live up to expectations either. Although John Ford was praised for his version of *How Green Was My Valley*, and it also attracted several Oscars, to me it never quite captured the flavour of Richard Llewellyn's magnificent saga of the Welsh valleys. However, a favourite book, Sinclair Lewis's Elmer Gantry, was filmed to perfection, in my opinion, with Burt Lancaster and Jean Simmons presenting their characters exactly as I had imagined them.

This introduction also gives me the opportunity to promote one author whose name is not well known and his contribution to literature virtually ignored. I speak of James Hilton. How many authors in this book would have been proud to have written *Goodbye, Mr. Chips*, *Lost Horizon* and *Random Harvest*? Quite a few, I think.

All these books are entirely different and all made memorable films. How many authors of these authors have introduced a new word into the language? We have Hilton to thank for "Shangri-La". Whatever his literary merit may be considered to be, he has shown he was a master storyteller.

It was common to film plays, especially during the 1920s to 1940s, mostly following the play's structure and just opening them out a little. As television began to widen it audience in the fifties, plays regularly formed part of its schedule and the cinema quickly reduced the number of plays filmed. Only the best, such as Tennessee Williams's *A Streetcar Named Desire* and William Inge's *Picnic* could entice the customers. Figures for the plays detailed in this book show 1755 plays filmed in the 1930s, 736 in the 1950s and 283 in the 1980s which illustrates the point.

The theatre has provided me with some great nights of entertainment, many with a film connection. Great ones that spring to mind were seeing James Stewart in *Harvey*, Henry Fonda as Clarence Darrow and Bela Lugosi in *Dracula*. These were opportunities to see masters of one medium performing in another and not one disappointed.

Great novels, plays and stories invariably make excellent films and if they don't, the fault more likely lies with the film production company for failing to dramatise them properly. The constantly filmed authors like Shakespeare, Chekhov, Dickens, de Maupassant, Poe and Zola are testimony to this, yet these days we see seven figure sums being paid for film rights for novels that have very little literary merit. I hope this book will help producers to identify which great novels, plays and stories have not yet been filmed and consider filming them. Chances are the story would be more interesting and the script a lot cheaper!

Alan Goble
October 1999
(E-mail: Alan.Goble@compuserve.com)

Introduction

This index contains 30 572 literary sources of film covering the period 1895 to 1999 from 83 countries. There are credits for 12 122 authors. It is culled from *The Complete Index to World Film since 1895*, a CD-ROM published in 1998, together with data that has been added since to the database in preparation for a new edition in 2000. As such, it is a work in progress, but this book should invariably produce the information required.

Documentation on film is often contradictory and the literary origin of a film is sometimes unverifiable. A common problem is a source that states 'from a story by ...'. This may be a story by O.Henry, which is then likely to be one of the many short stories he wrote. If it is by an unrecognised name, though, it is often not clear whether it was a published story or a story outline that was produced by the studio. It is also rarely clear whether the name of the story was the same as the film title. For the purpose of this book I have assumed it was so unless I have been able to confirm that it was not that title, or I have established it was named something else.

Another difficulty is determining what literary form the source takes. I have not used the word 'novella', only 'story','short story', 'serial story', 'novel' and 'book'. For example, sources call Merimee's *Carmen* both novel and short story and I have followed the novel interpretation. Instances such as these can be debatable, but what you will find in this index are details of the various film productions of the story. 'Book' usually refers to a non-fictional work. Where available, I have given the date and place of first publication.

For plays I have endeavoured to find the place and date of the first production. For Shakespeare's plays, I have use the estimated dates of production given in *Benet's Readers Encyclopedia*.

Explanatory Notes

Author Index
The following may be given for an author.
Name
Year of birth
Year of death
Other names
Title of literary source
    Film title
        Year

Director(s)
Actors
Type of film
Origin of film
Alternative film titles
Prod/Rel. company

Film Index
Film title
Year
Director(s)
Country of origin
Literary source
Author
Place and date of publication or production
Literary form

Literary Source Index
Title
Place and date of publication or production
Literary form
Author

Country of Origin

ALG	Algeria
ARG	Argentina
ASL	Australia
AUS	Austria
BLG	Belgium
BRK	Burkino Faso
BRZ	Brazil
BUL	Bulgaria
CHL	Chile
CHN	China
CLM	Columbia
CMB	Cambodia
CMR	Cameroon
CND	Canada
CNG	Congo
CPV	Cape Verde Islands
CRT	Croatia
CUB	Cuba
CZC	Czechoslovakia
CZE	Czech Republic
DNM	Denmark
EGY	Egypt
FNL	Finland
FRN	France

GDR	German Democratic Republic	SPN	Spain
GRC	Greece	SVK	Slovakia
GRM	Germany	SWD	Sweden
HKG	Hong Kong	SWT	Switzerland
HNG	Hungary	SYR	Syria
ICL	Iceland	THL	Thailand
IND	India	TNS	Tunisia
INN	Indonesia	TRK	Turkey
IRL	Ireland	TWN	Taiwan
IRN	Iran	UKN	United Kingdom
ISR	Israel	USA	United States
ITL	Italy	USS	Union of Soviet Republics
JMC	Jamaica	VNZ	Venezuela
JPN	Japan	VTN	Vietnam
KOR	Korea	YGS	Yugoslavia
KZK	Kazakhstan	ZIM	Zimbabwe
LBN	Lebanon		
LCH	Lichtenstein		
LXM	Luxembourg		
MLI	Mali		
MNG	Mongolia		
MRC	Morocco		
MXC	Mexico		
MZM	Mozambique		
NCR	Nicaragua		
NGR	Nigeria		
NRW	Norway		
NTH	The Netherlands		
NZL	New Zealand		
PHL	The Philippines		
PKS	Pakistan		
PLN	Poland		
PNM	Panama		
PRC	Puerto Rico		
PRT	Portugal		
PRU	Peru		
RMN	Romania		
RSS	Russia		
SAF	South Africa		
SKR	South Korea		
SLN	Sri Lanka		
SLO	Slovenia		
SNL	Senegal		

Abbreviations

ANM	animated
ANS	animated short
CMP	compilation
d	Director
DCS	short documentary
DOC	documentary
EXP	experimental
f	feet
lps.	leading players
m	metres
M	minutes
MTV	made for television
r	reel
SER	series
SHS	short series
SIL	silent
SND	sound
SRL	serial
SSF	short sound film
TVM	television film
UNF	unfinished

Acknowledgements

My thanks are due to all those who provide me with corrections and information in order to make *The Complete Index to World Film since 1895* the most accurate record of the world's film production available. Those benefits should show within this book. Special thanks to John Walker, editor of the Halliwell film books, whose interest is sincerely appreciated; my agent Rosemary Scoular, for her enthusiam and Steven Warriner of Bowker-Saur for making our working relationship a pleasurable and productive one. Lastly, my thanks to George Wead, for showing faith in this product.

Author Index

A

AAKJAER, JEPPE (1866–1930), DNM
Jens Langkniv, 1915, Novel
   Jens Langkniv 1940 d: Peter Knutzon, Peter Lind. lps: Poul Reichhardt, Bjarne Henning-Jensen, Asbjorn Andersen. 57M DNM. prod/rel: Cimbria Film

Livet Paa Hegnsgaard, 1907, Play
   Livet Paa Hegnsgaard 1939 d: Arne Weel. lps: Erik Henning-Jensen, Karin Nellemose, Holger Reenberg. 100M DNM. *Life on the Hegn Farm* (USA) prod/rel: ASA Film

Naar Bender Elsker, 1911, Play
   Naar Bonder Elsker 1942 d: Arne Weel. lps: Axel Frische, Inge Hvid-Moller, Jorn Jeppesen. 88M DNM. prod/rel: Palladium Film

AANRUD, HANS
Short Stories
   Storfolk Og Smafolk 1951 d: Tancred Ibsen. 92M NRW.

ABATI, JOAQUIN
La Meraviglia Di Damasco, Musical Play
   Accadde a Damasco E Febbre 1943 d: Primo Zeglio, Jose Luis Lopez Rubio. lps: Paola Barbara, Germana Paolieri, Miguel Liguero. 90M ITL/SPN. *Sucedio En Damasco* (SPN); *La Meraviglia Di Damasco*; *Accadde a Damasco*; *Febbre*; *Fiebre* prod/rel: U.F.I.S.A., E.I.a.

El Orgullo de Albacete, Play
   Orgullo de Albacete, El 1928 d: Luis R. Alonso. lps: Jose Montenegro, Soledad Franco Rodriguez, Alfonso Orozco Romero. SPN. prod/rel: Producciones Hornemann (Madrid)

ABBEY, EDWARD (1927–1989), USA
Brave Cowboy, New York 1956, Novel
   Lonely are the Brave 1962 d: David Miller. lps: Kirk Douglas, Gena Rowlands, Walter Matthau. 107M USA. *The Last Hero* prod/rel: Joel Productions

Fire on the Mountain, Book
   Fire on the Mountain 1981 d: Donald Wrye. lps: Ron Howard, Buddy Ebsen, Julie Carmen. TVM. 104M USA. prod/rel: NBC, Bonnard

ABBOT, ANTHONY
Article
   Boomerang! 1947 d: Elia Kazan. lps: Dana Andrews, Lee J. Cobb, Jane Wyatt. 88M USA. prod/rel: 20th Century-Fox

ABBOTT, ANTHONY
About the Murder of a Circus Queen, New York 1932, Novel
   Circus Queen Murder, The 1933 d: R. William Neill. lps: Adolphe Menjou, Greta Nissen, Donald Cook. 65M USA. *About the Murder of the Circus Queen* prod/rel: Columbia Pictures Corp.

About the Murder of the Night Club Lady, New York 1931, Novel
   Night Club Lady, The 1932 d: Irving Cummings. lps: Adolphe Menjou, Mayo Methot, Skeets Gallagher. 70M USA. prod/rel: Columbia Pictures Corp.©

ABBOTT, ELEANOR HALLOWELL
Little Eve Egerton, New York 1914, Novel
   Little Eve Edgarton 1916 d: Robert Z. Leonard. lps: Herbert Rawlinson, Ella Hall, Doris Pawn. 5r USA. *Little Eva Egerton* prod/rel: Bluebird Photoplays, Inc.©

Molly Make-Believe, New York 1910, Novel
   Molly Make-Believe 1916 d: J. Searle Dawley. lps: Marguerite Clark, Mahlon Hamilton, Master Dick Gray. 5r USA. prod/rel: Famous Players Film Co.©, Paramount Pictures Corp.

Old Dad, New York 1919, Novel
   Old Dad 1920 d: Lloyd Ingraham. lps: Mildred Harris Chaplin, Irving Cummings, Hazel Howell. 5r USA. prod/rel: Chaplin-Mayer Pictures Co.©, Associated First National Pictures, Inc.

ABBOTT, GEORGE (1887–1995), USA
Broadway a Play, New York 1927, Play
   Broadway 1929 d: Paul Fejos. lps: Glenn Tryon, Evelyn Brent, Merna Kennedy. 9661f USA. prod/rel: Universal Pictures
   Broadway 1942 d: William A. Seiter. lps: George Raft, Pat O'Brien, Janet Blair. 91M USA. prod/rel: Universal

Coquette, New York 1928, Play
   Coquette 1929 d: Sam Taylor. lps: Mary Pickford, Johnny Mack Brown, Matt Moore. 6993f USA. prod/rel: Pickford Corp., United Artists

The Fall Guy, New York 1924, Play
   Fall Guy, The 1930 d: A. Leslie Pearce. lps: Jack Mulhall, Mae Clarke, Ned Sparks. 70M USA. *Trust Your Wife* (UKN) prod/rel: RKO Productions

Four Walls, New York 1927, Play
   Four Walls 1928 d: William Nigh. lps: John Gilbert, Joan Crawford, Vera Gordon. 6620f USA. prod/rel: Metro-Goldwyn-Mayer Pictures
   Straight Is the Way 1934 d: Paul Sloane. lps: Karen Morley, Franchot Tone, Gladys George. 65M USA. *Four Walls* prod/rel: Metro-Goldwyn-Mayer Corp.©

Heat Lightning, New York 1933, Play
   Heat Lightning 1934 d: Mervyn Leroy. lps: Aline MacMahon, Preston Foster, Lyle Talbot. 63M USA. prod/rel: Warner Bros. Pictures©
   Highway West 1941 d: William McGann. lps: Brenda Marshall, Arthur Kennedy, William Lundigan. 62M USA. prod/rel: Warner Bros.

A Holy Terror, New York 1925, Play
   Hills of Peril 1927 d: Lambert Hillyer. lps: Buck Jones, Georgia Hale, Albert J. Smith. 4983f USA. prod/rel: Fox Film Corp.

Lilly Turner, New York 1932, Play
   Lilly Turner 1933 d: William A. Wellman. lps: Ruth Chatterton, George Brent, Frank McHugh. 65M USA. prod/rel: First National Pictures©

Love 'Em and Leave 'Em, New York 1926, Play
   Love 'Em and Leave 'Em 1926 d: Frank Tuttle. lps: Evelyn Brent, Lawrence Gray, Louise Brooks. 6r USA. prod/rel: Famous Players-Lasky, Paramount Pictures

On Your Toes, New York 1936, Musical Play
   On Your Toes 1939 d: Ray Enright. lps: Vera Zorina, Eddie Albert, Frank McHugh. 93M USA. prod/rel: Warner Bros. Pictures©, First National Picture

Ringside, New York 1928, Play
   Night Parade 1929 d: Malcolm St. Clair. lps: Hugh Trevor, Lloyd Ingraham, Dorothy Gulliver. 74M USA. *Sporting Life* (UKN) prod/rel: RKO Productions

Those We Love, New York 1930, Play
   Those We Love 1932 d: Robert Florey. lps: Kenneth MacKenna, Mary Astor, Lilyan Tashman. 77M USA. prod/rel: K.B.S. Film Corp., World Wide Pictures©

Three Men on a Horse, New York 1935, Play
   Three Men on a Horse 1936 d: Mervyn Leroy. lps: Frank McHugh, Sam Levene, Joan Blondell. 88M USA. prod/rel: Warner Bros. Pictures©

ABBOTT, SHEPARD
C.H.U.D., Novel
   C.H.U.D. 1984 d: Douglas Cheek. lps: Laure Mattos, John Heard, Kim Greist. 110M USA. prod/rel: New World Pictures, Bonime Associates

ABDULLAH, ACHMED
Bucking the Tiger, New York 1917, Novel
   Bucking the Tiger 1921 d: Henry Kolker. lps: Conway Tearle, Winifred Westover, Gladden James. 5550f USA. prod/rel: Selznick Pictures, Select Pictures

The Honorable Mr. Wong, Play
   Hatchet Man, The 1932 d: William A. Wellman. lps: Edward G. Robinson, Loretta Young, Dudley Digges. 74M USA. *The Honourable Mr. Wong* (UKN) prod/rel: First National Pictures©

The Honourable Gentleman, 1919, Short Story
   Pagan Love 1920 d: Hugo Ballin. lps: Togo Yamamoto, Mabel Ballin, Rockliffe Fellowes. 6r USA. *The Honourable Gentleman* prod/rel: Hugo Ballin Productions, Inc.©, W. W. Hodkinson Corp.

The Remittance Woman, Garden City, Ny. 1924, Novel
   Remittance Woman, The 1923 d: Wesley Ruggles. lps: Ethel Clayton, Rockliffe Fellowes, Mario Carillo. 6500f USA. prod/rel: R-C Pictures, Film Booking Offices of America

ABEL, ROBERT
The Samson Slasher, Play
   Breakdown 1952 d: Edmund Angelo. lps: Ann Richards, William Bishop, Anne Gwynne. 77M USA. prod/rel: Realart

ABERG, JOHN EINAR
Anglar, Finns Dom, Pappa?, Uppsala 1955, Novel
   Anglar, Finns Dom? 1961 d: Lars-Magnus Lindgren. lps: Jarl Kulle, Christina Schollin, Edvin Adolphson. 110M SWD. *Do You Believe in Angels?* (UKN); *Love Mates* (USA) prod/rel: Sandrews

Mats-Peter, Novel
   Mats-Peter 1972 d: Jarl Kulle. lps: Ingvar Kjellson, Per Nygren, Bertil Norstrom. 90M SWD. prod/rel: Sandrew

ABOUT, EDMOND
Germaine, Novel
   Per un Figlio 1920 d: Mario Bonnard. lps: Nini Dinelli, Mina d'Orvella, Dillo Lombardi. 1316m ITL. *Germana* prod/rel: Celio Film

L' Homme a l'Oreille Cassee, 1862, Short Story
   Homme a l'Oreille Cassee, L' 1934 d: Robert Boudrioz. lps: Thomy Bourdelle, Jacqueline Daix, Alice Tissot. 75M FRN. prod/rel: Realisations d'Art Cinematographique
   Uomo Dall'Orecchio Mozzato, L' 1916 d: Ubaldo Maria Del Colle. lps: Ubaldo Maria Del Colle, Clarette Sabatelli. 1000m ITL. prod/rel: Riviera Film

Le Roi Des Montagnes, 1857, Short Story
   Voleur de Femmes, Le 1963 d: Willy Rozier. lps: Felix Marten, Lucille Saint-Simon, Claude Rollet. 90M FRN. *Le Roi Des Montagnes* prod/rel: Sport Films

Trente Et Quarante, 1859, Novel
   Trente Et Quarante 1945 d: Gilles Grangier. lps: Georges Guetary, Martine Carol, Jeanne Fusier-Gir. 105M FRN. prod/rel: Gaumont, S.N.E.G.

ABRAHAM, EDWARD
Story
   Murder Elite 1985 d: Claude Whatham. lps: Ali MacGraw, Billie Whitelaw, Hywel Bennett. TVM. 95M UKN. prod/rel: Tyburn Entertainment

ABRAHAM, PAUL
Die Blume von Hawaii, Opera
   Blume von Hawaii, Die 1933 d: Richard Oswald. lps: Marta Eggerth, Hans Junkermann, Ivan Petrovich. F GRM.
   Blume von Hawaii, Die 1953 d: Geza von CziffrA. lps: Maria Litto, William Stelling, Ursula Justin. 95M GRM. *The Flower of Hawaii* prod/rel: Arion, Deutsche London

Viktoria Und Ihr Husar, Opera
   Viktoria Und Ihr Husar 1954 d: Rudolf Schundler. lps: Eva Bartok, Frank Felder, Friedrich Schonfelder. 95M GRM. *Victoria and Her Hussar* prod/rel: Allfram, Sonor

ABRAHAM, PETER
Das Schulgespenst, Novel
   Schulgespenst, Das 1986 d: Rolf Losansky. lps: Nicole Lichtenheldt, Ricardo Roth, Karin Duwel. 92M GDR. *The School Ghost* prod/rel: Defa

ABRAHAM, VALERIE
Story
   Murder Elite 1985 d: Claude Whatham. lps: Ali MacGraw, Billie Whitelaw, Hywel Bennett. TVM. 95M UKN. prod/rel: Tyburn Entertainment

ABRAHAMS, DR. JOHNSON
Night Nurse, Novel
   Irish Hearts 1934 d: Brian Desmond Hurst. lps: Nancy Burne, Lester Matthews, Patric Knowles. 71M UKN. *Norah O'Neale* (USA) prod/rel: Clifton-Hurst, MGM

ABRAHAMS, PETER
The Fan, Novel
   Fan, The 1996 d: Anthony Scott. lps: Robert de Niro, Wesley Snipes, Ellen Barkin. 117M USA. prod/rel: Wendy Ferman and Scott Free Production

ABRAHAMSON, MARTIN
The Trial of Chaplain Jensen, Book
   Trial of Chaplain Jensen, The 1975 d: Robert Day. lps: James Franciscus, Charles Durning, Joanna Miles. TVM. 78M USA. prod/rel: 20th Century-Fox, Monash/Pressman Production

ABRAMS, LEON
Heat Lightning, New York 1933, Play
   Heat Lightning 1934 d: Mervyn Leroy. lps: Aline MacMahon, Preston Foster, Lyle Talbot. 63M USA. prod/rel: Warner Bros. Pictures©
   Highway West 1941 d: William McGann. lps: Brenda Marshall, Arthur Kennedy, William Lundigan. 62M USA. prod/rel: Warner Bros.

ABRAMS, MARGARET
The Uncle, Boston 1962, Novel
   Uncle, The 1964 d: Desmond Davis. lps: Rupert Davies, Brenda Bruce, Maurice Denham. 87M UKN. prod/rel: Play-Pix Films, British Lion Films

ABU-BAKAR, A.
Novel
   Ozerele Dlja Moej Ljubimoj 1972 d: Tengiz Abuladze. lps: Ramas Giorgobjani, Nani Bregwadse, Georgi Gegetschkori. 75M USS. *Samkauli Satr Posatvis; A Necklace for My Beloved* prod/rel: Grusija

ACCURSI, MICHELE
Don Pasquale, Opera
   Don Pasquale 1940 d: Camillo Mastrocinque. lps: Armando Falconi, Laura Solari, Greta GondA. 98M ITL. prod/rel: Cinecitta S.A., Generalcine

ACHARD, MARCEL (1899–, FRN
L' Alibi, Novel
   Alibi 1942 d: Brian Desmond Hurst. lps: Margaret Lockwood, Hugh Sinclair, James Mason. 82M UKN. prod/rel: Corona Productions, British Lion

La Belle Mariniere, 1930, Play
   Belle Mariniere, La 1932 d: Harry Lachman. lps: Pierre Blanchar, Jean Gabin, Madeleine Renaud. 80M FRN. prod/rel: Films Paramount

Domino, 1932, Play
   Domino 1943 d: Roger Richebe. lps: Fernand Gravey, Aime Clariond, Bernard Blier. 100M FRN. prod/rel: Films Roger Richebe

L' Idiot, Paris 1960, Play
   Shot in the Dark, A 1964 d: Blake Edwards. lps: Peter Sellers, Elke Sommer, George Sanders. 101M UKN/USA. prod/rel: Mirisch-Geoffrey Productions, United Artists

Jean de la Lune, 1929, Play
   Jean de la Lune 1931 d: Jean Choux. lps: Rene Lefevre, Madeleine Renaud, Michel Simon. 84M FRN. prod/rel: Productions Georges Marret
   Jean de la Lune 1948 d: Marcel Achard. lps: Claude Dauphin, Danielle Darrieux, Jeannette Batti. 94M FRN. prod/rel: Films Roger Richebe

Mistigri, 1931, Play
   Mistigri 1931 d: Harry Lachman. lps: Noel-Noel, Madeleine Renaud, Simone Heliard. 80M FRN. prod/rel: Films Paramount

Noix de Coco, 1936, Play
   Noix de Coco 1938 d: Jean Boyer. lps: Raimu, Marie Bell, Suzet Mais. 80M FRN. prod/rel: a.C.E.

Patate, Paris 1957, Play
   Patate 1964 d: Robert Thomas. lps: Jean Marais, Danielle Darrieux, Anne Vernon. 95M FRN/ITL. *Friend of the Family* (USA); *L' Amico Di Famiglia* (ITL) prod/rel: Belstar Productions, Les Films Du Siecle

Petrus, 1934, Play
   Petrus 1946 d: Marc Allegret. lps: Fernandel, Pierre Brasseur, Simone Simon. 95M FRN/SWT. *Freibeuter Der Liebe; Quello Che M'e Costato Amare; Monsieur Petrus* prod/rel: Films Imperia (Paris), C.C. Co-Production Cinematographique

ACHARD, PAUL
La Croix du Sud, Novel
   Croix du Sud, La 1931 d: Andre Hugon. lps: Charles de Rochefort, Kaissa-Robba, Alexandre Mihalesco. 66M FRN. prod/rel: Pathe-Natan

ACHARYA, GUNWANTRAI
Allabeli, Play
   Mulu Manek 1955 d: Manhar Rangildas Raskapur. lps: Shanta Apte, Arvind Pandya, Champsibhai NagdA. 137M IND. *Moolu Manek* prod/rel: Vikram Chitra

ACHILLE, GIUSEPPE
Novel
   Harlem 1943 d: Carmine Gallone. lps: Elisa Cegani, Vivi Gioi, Massimo Girotti. 80M ITL. *Knock-Out* prod/rel: Cines, E.N.I.C.

Inventiamo l'Amore, Play
   Inventiamo l'Amore 1938 d: Camillo Mastrocinque. lps: Evi Maltagliati, Gino Cervi, Sergio Tofano. 71M ITL. prod/rel: Scalera Film

Il Pozzo Dei Miracoli, Play
   Pozzo Dei Miracoli, Il 1941 d: Gennaro Righelli. lps: Vivi Gioi, Antonio Centa, Elena Altieri. 83M ITL. prod/rel: Imperial Film, I.C.I.

Traversata Nera, Play
   Traversata Nera 1939 d: Domenico M. Gambino. lps: Mario Ferrari, Germana Paolieri, Dria PaolA. 88M ITL. prod/rel: Sovrania Film, Generalcine

ACKER, EDWARD
An Unseen Enemy, Play
   Unseen Enemy, An 1912 d: D. W. Griffith. lps: Walter Miller, Lillian Gish, Dorothy Gish. 999f USA. prod/rel: Biograph Co.

ACKERLEY, J. R.
We Think the World of You, Novel
   We Think the World of You 1989 d: Colin Gregg. lps: Alan Bates, Gary Oldman, Frances Barber. 94M UKN. prod/rel: Gold Screen, Film Four International

ACOSTA, IVAN
El Super, Play
   Super, El 1979 d: Leon Ichaso, Orlando Jimenez Leal. lps: Raymundo Hidalgo-Gato, Zully Montero, Reynaldo MedinA. 90M USA/CUB. *El Super* prod/rel: Arce, Ichaso Prod.

ACREMANT, GERMAINE
Ces Dames aux Chapeaux Verts, Novel
   Ces Dames aux Chapeaux Verts 1929 d: Andre Berthomieu. lps: Rene Lefevre, Alice Tissot, Simone Mareuil. 2750m FRN. prod/rel: Etoile Films
   Ces Dames aux Chapeaux Verts 1937 d: Maurice Cloche. lps: Micheline Cheirel, Alice Tissot, Pierre Larquey. 109M FRN. *The Ladies in the Green Hats* (USA) prod/rel: C.I.C.C.
   Ces Dames aux Chapeaux Verts 1948 d: Fernand Rivers. lps: Marguerite Pierry, Colette Richard, Henri Guisol. 95M FRN. prod/rel: Films Fernand Rivers

La Sarrazine, Novel
   Tourbillon de Paris, Le 1928 d: Julien Duvivier. lps: Lil Dagover, Leon Bary, Gaston Jacquet. F FRN. prod/rel: Film d'Art (Vandal Et Delac)

ACREMONT, A.
La Mome, Play
   Nipper, The 1930 d: Louis Mercanton. lps: Betty Balfour, John Stuart, Anne Grey. 84M UKN. *The Brat* prod/rel: Betty Balfour Pictures, United Artists

ACUNA, MANUEL
El Pasado, 1890, Play
   Her Sacrifice 1926 d: Wilfred Lucas. lps: Gaston Glass, Bryant Washburn, Herbert Rawlinson. 6100f USA. prod/rel: Sanford Productions

ADAIR, BRYANT
It's Always the Woman, Play
   It's Always the Woman 1916 d: Wilfred Noy. lps: Hayden Coffin, Barbara Hoffe, Daisy Burrell. 5050f UKN. prod/rel: Clarendon

ADAIR, GILBERT
Love and Death on Long Island, Novel
   Love and Death on Long Island 1997 d: Richard Kwietniowski. lps: John Hurt, Jason Priestley, Fiona Loewi. 93M UKN/CND. prod/rel: Skyline Films (U.K.), Imagex (Nova Scotia)

ADAM, ADOLPHE (1803–1856), FRN
Le Postillon de Lonjumeau, Paris 1836, Opera
   Postillon von Lonjumeau, Der 1935 d: Carl Lamac. lps: Alfred Neugebauer, Thekla Ahrens, Leo Slezak. 95M AUS/SWT. *Der Konig Lachelt - Paris Lacht; Le Postillon de Lonjumeau; Postillon Im Hochzeitsrock* prod/rel: Thekla-Film, Atlantis-Film

ADAM, ALFRED
Capitaine Pantoufle, Play
   Capitaine Pantoufle 1953 d: Guy Lefranc. lps: Francois Perier, Pierre Mondy, Marthe Mercadier. 90M FRN. prod/rel: Gaumont, Paul Wagner

Sylvie Et le Fantome, Play
   Sylvie Et le Fantome 1946 d: Claude Autant-LarA. lps: Odette Joyeux, Francois Perier, Julien Carette. 102M FRN. *Sylvie and the Phantom* (USA); *Sylvia and the Ghost* (UKN) prod/rel: Discina

ADAM, PAUL (1862–1920), FRN
Le Serpent Noir, Play
   Mouettes, Les 1916 d: Maurice Mariaud. lps: Paul Vermoyal, Lionel Clement, Yvonne Sergyl. FRN. prod/rel: Film d'Art

ADAMI, GIUSEPPE
Fanny Ballerina Della Scala, Novel
   Ballerine 1936 d: Gustav Machaty. lps: Silvana Jachino, Olivia Fried, Laura Nucci. 77M ITL. *Fanny -Ballerina Della Scala* prod/rel: Anonima Film Internazionali, E.N.I.C.

Felicita Colombo, Play
   Felicita Colombo 1937 d: Mario Mattoli. lps: Dina Gali, Armando Falconi, Roberta Mari. 78M ITL. prod/rel: Capitani, Icar

Nonna Felicita, Play
   Nonna Felicita 1938 d: Mario Mattoli. lps: Dina Galli, Armando Falconi, Maurizio d'AncorA. 76M ITL. prod/rel: I.C.A.R., Generalcine

L' Olmo E l'Edera, Novel
   Lupo E la Sirenetta, Il 1918 d: Emilio Graziani-Walter. lps: Dolly Morgan, Emilio Graziani-Walter. 1499m ITL. prod/rel: Savoia Film

ADAMOVICH, ALEXEI
Books
   Idi I Smotri 1986 d: Elem Klimov. lps: Alexei Kravchenko, Olga Mironova, Liubomiras Lauciavicus. 142M USS. *Come and See* (UKN) prod/rel: Byelarusfilm, Mosfilm

ADAMS, CLIFTON
The Dangerous Days of Kiowa Jones, Novel
   Dangerous Days of Kiowa Jones, The 1966 d: Alex March. lps: Robert Horton, Diane Baker, Sal Mineo. TVM. 100M USA. prod/rel: MGM

The Desperado, Novel
   Cole Younger, Gunfighter 1958 d: R. G. Springsteen. lps: Frank Lovejoy, James Best, Abby Dalton. 78M USA. prod/rel: Allied Artists
   Desperado, The 1954 d: Thomas Carr. lps: Wayne Morris, Jimmy Lydon, Beverly Garland. 81M USA. prod/rel: Allied Artists, Silvermine Prods.

Gambling Man, Novel
   Outlaw's Son, The 1957 d: Lesley Selander. lps: Dane Clark, Ben Cooper, Lori Nelson. 89M USA. prod/rel: United Artists, Bel-Air

ADAMS, EUSTACE L.
Loot Below, Story
   Desperate Cargo 1941 d: William Beaudine. lps: Ralph Byrd, Carol Hughes, Julie Duncan. 69M USA. prod/rel: P.R.C.

Sixteen Fathoms Under, 1932, Short Story
   16 Fathoms Deep 1948 d: Irving Allen. lps: Lon Chaney Jr., Arthur Lake, Lloyd Bridges. 82M USA. prod/rel: Lake, Monogram
   Sixteen Fathoms Deep 1934 d: Armand Schaefer. lps: Sally O'Neil, Lon Chaney Jr., George Regas. 59M USA. *16 Fathoms Deep; Sixteen Fathoms Under* prod/rel: Monogram Pictures Corp.©, Paul Malvern Production

ADAMS, FRANK
The Time the Place and the Girl, New York 1907, Musical Play
   Time the Place and the Girl, The 1929 d: Howard Bretherton. lps: Grant Withers, Betty Compson, Gertrude Olmstead. 6339f USA. prod/rel: Warner Brothers Pictures

ADAMS, FRANK R., Adams, Frank Ramsay
The American Sex, 1925, Short Story
   Meet the Prince 1926 d: Joseph Henabery. lps: Joseph Schildkraut, Marguerite de La Motte, Vera Steadman. 5929f USA. prod/rel: Metropolitan Pictures Corp. of Calif.

Blind Justice, Short Story
   Last Hour, The 1923 d: Edward Sloman. lps: Milton Sills, Carmel Myers, Pat O'Malley. 6658f USA. *Blind Justice* prod/rel: Mastodon Films

Friend Wife, Story
   Galloping Fish 1924 d: Thomas H. Ince, Del Andrews. lps: Louise Fazenda, Sydney Chaplin, Ford Sterling. 5559f USA. prod/rel: Thomas H. Ince Corp., Associated First National Pictures

Happiness Preferred, 1936, Short Story
   Outcast 1936 d: Robert Florey. lps: Warren William, Karen Morley, Lewis Stone. 73M USA. *Happiness Preferred* prod/rel: Paramount Pictures©, Major Pictures Corp.

Manhandling Ethel, 1921, Short Story
Enchantment 1921 d: Robert G. VignolA. lps: Marion Davies, Forrest Stanley, Edith Shayne. 6982f USA. prod/rel: Cosmopolitan Productions, Paramount Pictures

Miles Brewster and the Super Sex, 1921, Short Story
Super-Sex, The 1922 d: Lambert Hillyer. lps: Robert Gordon, Charlotte Pierce, Tully Marshall. 5749f USA. prod/rel: Frank R. Adams Productions, American Releasing Corp.

Molly and I and the Silver Ring, Boston 1915, Novel
Molly and I 1920 d: Howard M. Mitchell. lps: Shirley Mason, Alan Roscoe, Harry Dunkinson. 5250f USA. prod/rel: Fox Film Corp., William Fox©
My Unmarried Wife 1918 d: George Siegmann. lps: Carmel Myers, Kenneth Harlan, Beatrice Van. 5r USA. *Molly and I* prod/rel: Bluebird Photoplays, Inc.©

No Experience Required, 1917, Short Story
Pointing Finger, The 1919 d: Edward Kull, Edward Morrisey. lps: Mary MacLaren, Johnnie Cooke, Carl Stockdale. 5r USA. *No Experience Required* prod/rel: Universal Film Mfg. Co.©

Proxies, 1920, Short Story
Proxies 1921 d: George D. Baker. lps: Norman Kerry, Zena Keefe, Raye Dean. 6283f USA. prod/rel: Cosmopolitan Productions, Famous Players-Lasky

Skin Deep, Short Story
Almost a Lady 1926 d: E. Mason Hopper. lps: Marie Prevost, Harrison Ford, George K. Arthur. 5702f USA. prod/rel: Metropolitan Pictures Corp. of Calif., Producers Distributing Corp.

There are No Villains, Story
There are No Villains 1921 d: Bayard Veiller. lps: Viola Dana, Gaston Glass, Edward Cecil. 4410f USA. prod/rel: Metro Pictures

Unexpected Places, Novel
Unexpected Places 1918 d: E. Mason Hopper. lps: Bert Lytell, Rhea Mitchell, Colin Kenny. 5r USA. prod/rel: Metro Pictures Corp.©

Without the Net, 1922, Short Story
Circus Girl 1937 d: John H. Auer. lps: Donald Cook, June Travis, Betty Compson. 64M USA. *Without a Net* prod/rel: Republic Pictures Corp.

ADAMS, FREDERICK UPHAM
The Bottom of the Well, New York 1906, Novel
Bottom of the Well, The 1917 d: John S. Robertson. lps: Evart Overton, Agnes Ayres, Adele de Garde. 5r USA. prod/rel: Vitagraph Co. of America©

John Burt, Philadelphia 1903, Novel
When Men are Tempted 1918 d: William Wolbert. lps: Mary Anderson, Alfred Whitman, Ronald Bradbury. 5r USA. prod/rel: Vitagraph Co. of America©, Greater Vitagraph

ADAMS, GERALD DRAYSON (1904–, ASL, Adams, Gerald
Star Sapphire, Story
His Kind of Woman 1951 d: John Farrow, Richard Fleischer (Uncredited). lps: Robert Mitchum, Jane Russell, Vincent Price. 120M USA. prod/rel: RKO Radio, Howard Hughes Presentation

Wings of the Hawk, Novel
Wings of the Hawk 1953 d: Budd Boetticher. lps: Van Heflin, Julie Adams, Abbe Lane. 81M USA. prod/rel: Universal-International

ADAMS, H. AUSTIN
'Ception Shoals, New York 1917, Play
Out of the Fog 1919 d: Albert Capellani. lps: Alla Nazimova, Charles Bryant, Henry Harmon. 7r USA. *'Ception Shoals* prod/rel: Metro Pictures Corp.©

ADAMS, HUNTER DOHERTY
Gesundheit: Good Health Is a Laughing Matter, 1993, Book
Patch Adams 1998 d: Tom Shadyac. lps: Robin Williams, Daniel London, Monica Potter. 115M USA. prod/rel: Universal City Studios©, Blue Wolf

ADAMS, JUSTIN
Quincy Adams Sawyer, New York 1902, Play
Quincy Adams Sawyer and Mason's Corner Folks 1912. 4r USA. *Quincy Adams Sawyer* prod/rel: Puritan Special Features Corp.©, State Rights

ADAMS, RICHARD (1920–, UKN
Girl in a Swing, Novel
Girl on the Swing, The 1989 d: Gordon Hessler. lps: Meg Tilly, Rupert Frazer, Nicholas Le Prevost. 112M USA/UKN. *The Girl in a Swing* prod/rel: Panorama

The Plague Dogs, Novel
Plague Dogs, The 1984 d: Martin Rosen. ANM. 103M UKN/USA. prod/rel: Nepenthe Productions

Watership Down, Novel
Watership Down 1978 d: Martin Rosen. ANM. 92M UKN. prod/rel: Nepenthe

ADAMS, SAMUEL HOPKINS (1871–1958), USA
The Clarion, Boston 1914, Novel
Clarion, The 1916 d: James Durkin. lps: Carlyle Blackwell, Howard Hall, Marion Dentler. 5r USA. prod/rel: Equitable Motion Pictures Corp.©, World Film Corp.

Enter d'Arcy, 1917, Short Story
Wanted - a Husband 1919 d: Lawrence C. Windom. lps: Billie Burke, James L. Crane, Margaret Linden. 4596f USA. prod/rel: Famous Players-Lasky Corp.©, Paramount-Artcraft Pictures

The Gorgeous Hussy, Boston 1934, Novel
Gorgeous Hussy, The 1936 d: Clarence Brown. lps: Lionel Barrymore, Joan Crawford, Robert Taylor. 105M USA. prod/rel: Metro-Goldwyn-Mayer Corp.©

The Harvey Girls, 1942, Novel
Harvey Girls, The 1945 d: George Sidney. lps: Judy Garland, John Hodiak, Ray Bolger. 101M USA. prod/rel: MGM

Night Bus, 1933, Short Story
Eve Knew Her Apples 1945 d: Will Jason. lps: Ann Miller, William Wright, Robert Williams. 64M USA.
It Happened One Night 1934 d: Frank CaprA. lps: Clark Gable, Claudette Colbert, Walter Connolly. 105M USA. *Night Bus* prod/rel: Columbia Pictures Corp.©
You Can't Run Away from It 1956 d: Dick Powell. lps: June Allyson, Jack Lemmon, Charles Bickford. 95M USA. *It Happened One Night* prod/rel: Columbia

Orpheus, 1916, Short Story
Love Sublime, A 1917 d: Tod Browning, Wilfred Lucas. lps: Wilfred Lucas, Carmel Myers, F. A. Turner. 5r USA. *Orpheus* prod/rel: Fine Arts Film Co., Triangle Distributing Corp.

The Perfect Specimen, New York 1936, Novel
Perfect Specimen, The 1937 d: Michael Curtiz. lps: Errol Flynn, Joan Blondell, Hugh Herbert. 88M USA. prod/rel: Warner Bros. Pictures©, First National Picture

Siege, New York 1924, Novel
Siege 1925 d: Svend Gade. lps: Virginia Valli, Eugene O'Brien, Mary Alden. 6424f USA. prod/rel: Universal Pictures

Triumph, 1916, Short Story
Triumph 1917 d: Joseph de Grasse. lps: Dorothy Phillips, Lon Chaney, William Stowell. 5r USA. prod/rel: Bluebird Photoplays, Inc.©

ADAMSON, EWART
The Adventuress, Story
Desert Bride, The 1928 d: Walter Lang. lps: Betty Compson, Allan Forrest, Edward Martindel. 5400f USA. prod/rel: Columbia Pictures

The Scourge of Fate, Story
Flaming Fury 1926 d: James P. Hogan. lps: Charles Delaney, Betty May, Boris Karloff. 4464f USA. prod/rel: R-C Pictures, Film Booking Offices of America

ADAMSON, HANS C.
Hellcats of the Sea, 1955, Book
Hellcats of the Navy 1957 d: Nathan Juran. lps: Ronald Reagan, Nancy Davis, Arthur Franz. 81M USA. prod/rel: Columbia, Morningside

ADAMSON, JOY (1910–1980), GRM, Adamson, Joy Friederike Victoria Gessner
Born Free, London 1960, Book
Born Free 1965 d: James Hill. lps: Virginia McKenna, Bill Travers, Geoffrey Keen. 95M UKN. prod/rel: Columbia, Open Road

Living Free, Book
Living Free 1972 d: Jack Couffer. lps: Nigel Davenport, Susan Hampshire, Geoffrey Keen. 91M UKN. prod/rel: Columbia, Open Road

ADDEYMAN, ELIZABETH
The Secret Tent, Play
Secret Tent, The 1956 d: Don Chaffey. lps: Donald Gray, Andree Melly, Jean Anderson. 69M UKN. prod/rel: Forward Films, British Lion

ADDINGTON, SARAH
Bless Their Hearts, 1936, Short Story
And So They Were Married 1936 d: Elliott Nugent. lps: Melvyn Douglas, Mary Astor, Edith Fellows. 75M USA. *Bless Their Hearts* prod/rel: Columbia Pictures Corp.

Dance Team, New York 1931, Novel
Dance Team 1932 d: Sidney Lanfield. lps: James Dunn, Sally Eilers, Ralph Morgan. 83M USA. prod/rel: Fox Film Corp.

ADDISON, SMITH
The Rise and Fall of Officer 13, Story
Rise and Fall of Officer 13, The 1915 d: Horace Davey. lps: Lee Moran. SHT USA. prod/rel: Nestor

ADDISON, THOMAS
The Boss of Powderville, 1916, Short Story
Grand Passion, The 1918 d: Ida May Park. lps: Dorothy Phillips, William Stowell, Jack Mulhall. 7r USA. *The Boss of Powderville* prod/rel: Universal Film Mfg. Co., Jewel Productions, Inc.©

ADE, GEORGE (1866–1944), USA
Artie, New York 1907, Play
Artie, the Millionaire Kid 1916 d: Harry Handworth. lps: Ernest Truex, Dorothy Kelly, John T. Kelly. 5r USA. prod/rel: Vitagraph Co. of America©, Blue Ribbon Feature

Betty's Dream Hero, Story
Betty's Dream Hero 1915 d: Robert Z. Leonard. lps: Robert Leonard, Ella Hall, Harry Carter. 2r USA. prod/rel: Laemmle

The College Widow, New York 1904, Play
College Widow, The 1915 d: Barry O'Neil. lps: Ethel Clayton, George Soule Spencer, Rosetta Brice. 5-6r USA. prod/rel: Lubin Mfg. Co.©, V-L-S-E, Inc.
College Widow, The 1927 d: Archie Mayo. lps: Dolores Costello, William Collier Jr., Douglas Gerrard. 6616f USA. prod/rel: Warner Brothers Pictures
Freshman Love 1936 d: William McGann. lps: Frank McHugh, Patricia Ellis, Warren Hull. 65M USA. *Rhythm on the River* (UKN) prod/rel: Warner Bros. Pictures©

The County Chairman, New York 1903, Play
County Chairman, The 1914 d: Allan Dwan. lps: Harold Lockwood, MacLyn Arbuckle, William Lloyd. 4-5r USA. prod/rel: Famous Players Film Co., Paramount Pictures Corp.
County Chairman, The 1935 d: John G. Blystone. lps: Will Rogers, Evelyn Venable, Mickey Rooney. 85M USA. prod/rel: Fox Film Corp.

The Fair Co-Ed, New York 1909, Play
Fair Co-Ed, The 1927 d: Sam Wood. lps: Marion Davies, Johnny Mack Brown, Jane Winton. 6408f USA. *The Varsity Girl* prod/rel: Metro-Goldwyn-Mayer Pictures

Father and the Boys, New York 1908, Play
Father and the Boys 1915 d: Joseph de Grasse. lps: Digby Bell, Harry Ham, Colin Chase. 5r USA. prod/rel: Universal Film Mfg. Co.©
Young As You Feel 1931 d: Frank Borzage. lps: Will Rogers, Fifi d'Orsay, Lucien Littlefield. 78M USA. *Father and the Boys*; *Cure for the Blues* prod/rel: Fox Film Corp.©, Frank Borzage's Production

Just Out of College, New York 1905, Play
Just Out of College 1915 d: George Irving. lps: Eugene O'Brien, Amelia Summerville, Marie Edith Wells. 5r USA. prod/rel: Frohman Amusement Corp., State Rights
Just Out of College 1920 d: Alfred E. Green. lps: Jack Pickford, Molly Malone, George Hernandez. 5r USA. prod/rel: Goldwyn Pictures Corp.©, Goldwyn Distributing Corp.

Making the Grade, 1928, Short Story
Making the Grade 1929 d: Alfred E. Green. lps: Edmund Lowe, Lois Moran, Lucien Littlefield. 5903f USA. prod/rel: Fox Film Corp.

Marse Covington, 1906, Play
Marse Covington 1915 d: Edwin Carewe. lps: Edward Connelly, Louise Huff, John J. Williams. 5r USA. prod/rel: Rolfe Photoplays Inc., Metro Pictures Corp.©

The Slim Princess, 1906, Short Story
Slim Princess, The 1915 d: E. H. Calvert. lps: Francis X. Bushman, Ruth Stonehouse, Wallace Beery. 4r USA. prod/rel: Essanay Film Mfg. Co.©, V-L-S-E, Inc.
Slim Princess, The 1920 d: Victor Schertzinger. lps: Mabel Normand, Hugh Thompson, Tully Marshall. 4990f USA. prod/rel: Goldwyn Pictures Corp.©, Goldwyn Distributing Corp.

ADES, GEORGES
Le Livre de Goha le Simple, Novel
Goha 1958 d: Jacques Baratier. lps: Omar Sharif, Zina Bouzaiane, Lauro Gazzolo. 83M FRN/TNS. prod/rel: U.G.C., Films Franco-Africains

ADKINS, ELLA
Second Chance, Play
Time Is My Enemy 1954 d: Don Chaffey. lps: Dennis Price, Renee Asherson, Susan Shaw. 64M UKN. prod/rel: Vandyke, Independent Film Distributors

ADLEMAN, ROBERT H.
The Devil's Brigade, Philadelphia 1966, Novel
Devil's Brigade, The 1968 d: Andrew V. McLaglen. lps: William Holden, Cliff Robertson, Vince Edwards. 130M USA. prod/rel: United Artists

3

ADLER, HANS
Folies-Bergere, Play
Folies-Bergere 1935 d: Marcel Achard. lps: Maurice Chevalier, Nathalie Paley, Sim VivA. 75M FRN. prod/rel: 20th Century-Fox

Madchen Fur Alles, Play
Madchen Fur Alles 1937 d: Carl Boese. lps: Grethe Weiser, Ralph Arthur Roberts, Ellen Frank. 88M GRM. prod/rel: Majestic, Terra

Meine Nichte Susanne, Play
Meine Nichte Susanne 1950 d: Wolfgang Liebeneiner. lps: Hilde Krahl, Inge Meysel, Ingrid Pankow. 92M GRM. *My Niece Susanne* prod/rel: Sphinx, UFA

The Red Cat, New York 1934, Play
Folies Bergere de Paris 1935 d: Roy Del Ruth. lps: Maurice Chevalier, Merle Oberon, Ann Sothern. 85M USA. *The Man from the Folies Bergere* (UKN); *Folies Bergere*; *Folies-Bergere* prod/rel: 20th Century Pictures©, Darryl Zanuck Production

On the Riviera 1951 d: Walter Lang. lps: Danny Kaye, Gene Tierney, Corinne Calvet. 90M USA. prod/rel: 20th Century-Fox

That Night in Rio 1941 d: Irving Cummings. lps: Alice Faye, Don Ameche, Carmen MirandA. 90M USA. *Road to Rio* prod/rel: 20th Century-Fox

ADLER, JOSEF
Krasna Vyzvedacka, Novel
Krasna Vyzvedacka 1927 d: M. J. Krnansky. lps: Bronislava Livia, Jan W. Speerger, Luigi Hofman. 2067m CZC. *The Beautiful Spy* prod/rel: Borsky a Sulc, la Tricolore

ADLER, POLLY
A House Is Not a Home, New York 1953, Autobiography
House Is Not a Home, A 1964 d: Russell Rouse. lps: Shelley Winters, Robert Taylor, Cesar Romero. 97M USA. prod/rel: Embassy Pictures

ADLER, WARREN
War of the Roses, Novel
War of the Roses 1989 d: Danny Devito. lps: Michael Douglas, Kathleen Turner, Danny Devito. 116M USA. prod/rel: 20th Century Fox, Gracie Films

ADLERSFELD-BALLESTREM
Die Weissen Rosen von Ravensberg, Novel
Weissen Rosen von Ravensberg, Die 1919 d: Nils Chrisander. lps: Nils Chrisander, Uschi Elleot, Robert Scholz. 1262m GRM. prod/rel: Deutsche Bioscop

Weissen Rosen von Ravensberg, Die 1929 d: Rudolf Meinert. lps: Diana Karenne, Viola Garden, Jack Trevor. 2296m GRM. prod/rel: Omnia-Film

ADONIAS FILHO
Um Anjo Mal, 1968, Short Story
Anjo Mau, Um 1972 d: Roberto Santos. lps: Adriana Prieto, Flavio Portho, Francisco Di Franco. 109M BRZ. *The Evil Angel*; *Bad Angel*

O Forte, 1965, Novel
Forte, O 1974 d: Olney Sao Paulo. 85M BRZ.

ADRIAN, GUNTER
Make Love Not War - Die Liebesgeschichte Unserer Zeit, Novel
Make Love Not War - Die Liebesgeschichte Unserer Zeit 1968 d: Werner Klett. lps: Gibson Kemp, Claudia Bremer, Heinz-Karl Diesing. 82M GRM. *Make Love Not War - the Love Story of Our Time* prod/rel: Werner Klett, Eckelkamp

AESCHYLUS (525–456bc), GRC
Prometheus Vinctus, c468 bc, Play
Prometheus Bound -the Illiac Passion 1966 d: Gregory J. Markopoulos. lps: Richard Beauvais, David Beauvais, Robert Alvarez. EXP. 90M USA. *The Illiac Passion*; *The Iliac Passion*; *The Markopoulos Passion*

Promitheas Se Deftero Prosopo 1975 d: Kostas Ferris. lps: Yannis Kanoupakis, Myrto Parashi, Vangelis Maniatis. 90M GRC. *Prometheus Second Person Singular*; *Prometheas Se Theftero Prosopo*; *Prometheas Se Deftero Prosopo*

AGAMEMNON
Oresteia, Play
Mourning Becomes Electra 1947 d: Dudley Nichols. lps: Rosalind Russell, Michael Redgrave, Raymond Massey. 173M USA. prod/rel: RKO Radio

AGARBICEANU, ION
Arhangelii, 1914, Novel
Flacari Pe Comori 1988 d: Nicolae Margineanu. lps: Remus Margineanu, Claudiu Bleont, Mircea Albulescu. 102M RMN. *Will O'The Wisp*; *Flames Above Treasures*; *Flames on the Treasures*

Fefeleaga, 1908, Short Story
Nunta de Piatra 1972 d: Mircea Veroiu, Dan PitA. lps: Leopoldina Balanuta, Radu Boruzescu, George Calboreanu Jr. 88M RMN. *The Stone Wedding*

Jandarmul, 1941, Short Story
Intoarcerea Din Iad 1984 d: Nicolae Margineanu. 98M RMN. *Return from Hell*; *Coming Back from Hell*

La O Nunta, 1909, Short Story
Nunta de Piatra 1972 d: Mircea Veroiu, Dan PitA. lps: Leopoldina Balanuta, Radu Boruzescu, George Calboreanu Jr. 88M RMN. *The Stone Wedding*

Lada, 1910, Short Story
Duhul Aurului 1974 d: Mircea Veroiu, Dan PitA. lps: Eliza Petrachescu, Dora Ivanciuc, Liviu RozoreA. 96M RMN. *Lust for Gold*; *Gold Fever*; *Gold's Ghost*

Vilva Bailor, 1909, Short Story
Duhul Aurului 1974 d: Mircea Veroiu, Dan PitA. lps: Eliza Petrachescu, Dora Ivanciuc, Liviu RozoreA. 96M RMN. *Lust for Gold*; *Gold Fever*; *Gold's Ghost*

AGEE, JAMES (1909–1955), USA, Agee, James Rufus
A Death in the Family, New York 1957, Novel
All the Way Home 1963 d: Alex Segal. lps: Jean Simmons, Robert Preston, Pat Hingle. 103M USA. prod/rel: Paramount, Talent Associates

All the Way Home 1981 d: Delbert Mann. lps: Sally Field, William Hurt, Ned Beatty. TVM. 98M USA. prod/rel: NBC, Paramount

A Mother's Tale, 1952, Short Story
Mother's Tale, A 1977 d: Rex Goff. 18M USA.

AGUIRRE, JULIEN
Operazione Ogro, Book
Ogro 1979 d: Gillo Pontecorvo. lps: Gian Maria Volonte, Jose Sacristan, Eusebio PoncelA. 113M ITL/SPN/FRN. *Operacion Ogro* (SPN); *Operation Ogre*; *Tunel*; *Tunnel* prod/rel: Vides Cin.Ca (Roma), Sabre Film (Madrid)

AGUSTI, IGNACIO
Mariona Rebull, 1944, Novel
Mariona Rebull 1947 d: Jose Luis Saenz de HerediA. lps: Blanca de Silos, Jose Maria Seoane, Sara Montiel. 91M SPN.

El Viudo Rius, 1945, Novel
Mariona Rebull 1947 d: Jose Luis Saenz de HerediA. lps: Blanca de Silos, Jose Maria Seoane, Sara Montiel. 91M SPN.

AHLSEN, LEOPOLD
Philemon Und Baucis, Play
Am Galgen Hangt Die Liebe 1960 d: Edwin Zbonek. lps: Carl Wery, Annie Rosar, Sieghardt Rupp. 93M GRM. *On the Gallows Hangs Their Love* prod/rel: Rex, Bloemer

AHMAD, SHAHNON
Ranju Sepanjang Jalan, Novel
Neak Sri 1992 d: Rithy Panh. lps: Peng Phan, Mom Soth, Chhim Naline. 130M CMB/FRN. *Les Gens de la Riziere* (FRN); *People of the Rice Fields*; *Rice People*; *Neak Sre* prod/rel: Ba, Thelma

AHN, DUYEN
La Coline de Fanta, Novel
Poussieres de Vie 1996 d: Rachid Bouchareb. lps: Daniel Guyant, Gilles Chitlaphone, Jehan Pages. F ALG. *Living Dust* prod/rel: 3B Productions

AHO, JUHANI (1861–1921), FNL, Brofelt, Johannes
Juha, 1911, Novel
Juha 1937 d: Nyrki TapiovaarA. lps: Irma Seikkula, Hannes Narhi, Tuulikki Paananen. 101M FNL.

Juha 1956 d: Toivo SarkkA. lps: Eino Kaipainen, Elina Pohjanpaa, Veikko Uusimaki. 115M FNL.

Juha 1999 d: Aki Kaurismaki. lps: Sakari Kuosmanen, Kati Outinen, Andre Wilms. 77M FNL. prod/rel: Sputnik Oy, Yle-Tv1

AICARD, JEAN
Le Diamant Noir, 1895, Novel
Diamant Noir 1940 d: Jean Delannoy. lps: Charles Vanel, Maurice Escande, Guy Denancy. 98M FRN. *Black Diamond* prod/rel: Minerva

Diamant Noir, Le 1922 d: Andre Hugon. lps: Henry Krauss, Claude Merelle, Ginette Maddie. 3270m FRN. prod/rel: Films Andre Hugon

Gaspard de Besse, Novel
Gaspard de Besse 1935 d: Andre Hugon. lps: Antonin Berval, Raimu, Nicole Vattier. 110M FRN. *Dawn Over France* (USA) prod/rel: Hugon-Films

L' Ibis Bleu, Novel
Ibis Bleu, L' 1918 d: Camille de Morlhon. lps: Pierre Magnier, Raoul Praxy, MaxA. 1425m FRN. prod/rel: Films Valetta

L' Illustre Maurin, 1908, Novel
Illustre Maurin, L' 1933 d: Andre Hugon. lps: Antonin Berval, Nicole Vattier, Jean Aquistapace. 122M FRN. *Maurin the Illustrious* prod/rel: Hugon-Films, Gaumont-Franco-Films-Aubert

Maurin Des Maures, 1905, Novel
Maurin Des Maures 1932 d: Andre Hugon. lps: Nicole Vattier, Antonin Berval, Jean Aquistapace. 100M FRN.

Notre-Dame d'Amour, 1896, Novel
Notre-Dame d'Amour 1922 d: Andre Hugon. lps: Jean Toulout, Claude Merelle, Charles de Rochefort. 1900m FRN. prod/rel: Films Andre Hugon

Notre-Dame d'Amour 1936 d: Pierre Caron. lps: Antonin Berval, Raymond Cordy, Lise Delamare. 84M FRN. prod/rel: Productions Claude Dolbert

Le Pere Lebonnard, 1889, Play
Papa Lebonnard 1920 d: Mario Bonnard. lps: Ugo Piperno, Maria Caserini Gasparini, Nini Dinelli. 1705m ITL. prod/rel: Celio Film

Pere Lebonnard, Le 1938 d: Jean de Limur, Marcello Albani. lps: Ruggero Ruggeri, Jean Murat, Madeleine Sologne. 92M FRN/ITL. *Papa Lebonnard* (ITL) prod/rel: Scalera Film

Le Roi de Camargue, 1890, Novel
Gardian, Le 1945 d: Jean de Marguenat. lps: Tino Rossi, Edouard Delmont, Lilia Vetti. 90M FRN. prod/rel: Lutetia

Roi de Camargue 1934 d: Jacques de Baroncelli. lps: Antonin Berval, Simone Bourday, Paul Azais. 75M FRN. *King of Camargue* prod/rel: General Film

Roi de Camargue, Le 1921 d: Andre Hugon. lps: Charles de Rochefort, Elmire Vautier, Jean Toulout. F FRN. prod/rel: Films Andre Hugon

La Rue du Pave d'Amour, Novel
Rue du Pave d'Amour, La 1923 d: Andre Hugon. lps: Jean Toulout, Sylvette Fillacier, Adrienne Duriez. 1900m FRN. prod/rel: Hugon Films

AIKEN, CONRAD (1889–1973), USA
Secret Snow Silent Snow, 1934, Short Story
Silent Snow, Secret Snow 1966 d: Gene Kearney. 17M USA.

AIKEN, JOAN
Mort un Dimanche de Pluie, Novel
Mort un Dimanche de Pluie 1986 d: Joel Santoni. lps: Nicole Garcia, Dominique Lavanant, Jean-Pierre Bacri. 110M FRN/SWT. prod/rel: Incite, Fr 3

The Wolves of Willoughby Chase, Novel
Wolves of Willoughby Chase, The 1989 d: Stuart Orme. lps: Stephanie Beacham, Mel Smith, Geraldine James. 89M UKN. prod/rel: Entertainment, Subatomnic

AIMATOV, CHINGIZ
Voskhozhdeniye Na Fudziyamu, 1978, Play
Voshozdenie Na Fudzijamu 1988 d: Bolotbek Shamshiev. 129M USS. *Climbing Mount Fuji*; *The Ascent of Fujiyama*; *Voskohzhdeniye Na Fudziyama*; *The Ascent of Mount Fuji*

AINSWORTH, HARRISON (1805–1882), UKN, Ainsworth, William Harrison
Guy Fawkes, Novel
Guy Fawkes 1923 d: Maurice Elvey. lps: Matheson Lang, Nina Vanna, Hugh Buckler. 6600f UKN. prod/rel: Stoll

Jack Sheppard, London 1839, Novel
Jack Sheppard 1912 d: Percy Nash. 3200f UKN. prod/rel: London Films, Cosmopolitan

Jack Sheppard 1923 d: Henry C. Taylor. lps: William West, May Lavelle, John F. Pearson. 2000f UKN. prod/rel: Broadoak Picture Productions

King Charles, Novel
King Charles 1913 d: Wilfred Noy. lps: P. G. Ebbutt, Dorothy Bellew. 4120f UKN. prod/rel: Clarendon

Old St. Paul's, Novel
Old St. Paul's 1914 d: Wilfred Noy. lps: Lionelle Howard, R. Juden, P. G. Ebbutt. 3077f UKN. *When London Burned* (USA) prod/rel: Clarendon

Rookwood, London 1834, Novel
Dick Turpin 1933 d: John Stafford, Victor Hanbury. lps: Victor McLaglen, Jane Carr, Frank Vosper. 79M UKN. prod/rel: Stoll-Stafford, Gaumont-British

Dick Turpin's Ride to York 1922 d: Maurice Elvey. lps: Matheson Lang, Isobel Elsom, Cecil Humphreys. 7660f UKN. prod/rel: Stoll

The Tower of London, Novel
Tower of London, The 1909 d: James Williamson ?. 1125f UKN. prod/rel: Williamson

AINSWORTH, LEONORA
Dear Little Old Time Girl, Story
Dear Little Old Time Girl 1915 d: William C. Dowlan. lps: William C. Dowlan, Violet MacMillan. SHT USA. prod/rel: Laemmle

AIRD, CATHERINE
Novel
Prooi, de 1984 d: Vivian Pieters. lps: Maayke Bouten, Johan Leysen, Marlous FluitsmA. 95M NTH. *The Prey* prod/rel: Frans Rasker Prod.

AIRTH, RENNIE
Le Grand Escogriffe, Novel
Grand Escogriffe, Le 1976 d: Claude Pinoteau. lps: Yves Montand, Agostina Belli, Claude Brasseur. 100M FRN/ITL. *Il Genio* (ITL) prod/rel: Da.Ma Film, Productions 2000

AITKEN, ROBERT
A Million a Minute: a Romance of Modern New York and Paris, New York 1908, Novel
Million a Minute, A 1916 d: John W. Noble. lps: Francis X. Bushman, Beverly Bayne, Robert W. Cummings. 5r USA. prod/rel: Quality Pictures Corp.©, Metro Pictures Corp.

AITMATOV, CHINGIZ (1928–, KRG
Belyi Parokhod, 1970, Short Story
Byeli Parokhod 1976 d: Bolotbek Shamshiev. lps: Nurgazy Sydygaliyev, Assankal Kuttubajev, Drosbek Kutmanaliyev. 101M USS. *The White Steamer; The White Ship; Belyi Parokhod; The White Boat; Belyj Parohod*
Dzhamilia, 1958, Short Story
Jamilya 1969 d: Irina PoplavskayA. lps: Natalia Arinbasarova, Suymenkul Chokmorov, Nasreddin Dibashev. 95M USS. *Djamila; Dzhamilia*
Krasnoe Jabloko, 1963, Short Story
Krasnoye Yabloko 1975 d: Tolomush Okeyev. lps: Suymenkul Chokmorov. 83M USS. *The Red Apple; Krasnoe Jabloko*
Materinskoe Pole, 1963, Short Story
Materinskoye Polye 1968 d: Gennadi Bazarov. lps: Baken Kadykeyeva, Raushan Sarmurzina, Bolot Beyshenaliyev. 81M USS. *The Mother's Field; Materinskoe Pole; Materinskaya Polye*
Pervyi Uchitel, 1963, Short Story
Pervyi Uchitel 1965 d: Andrei Konchalovsky. lps: Natalia Arinbasarova, Bolot Beyshenaliyev, Idris Nogaibayev. 98M USS. *The First Teacher* (UKN); *Pervyj Ucitel; Pervji Oetsjitel* prod/rel: Kirgisfilm, Mosfilm
Gul'sary Proshchay, 1966, Short Story
Prashnai Gulsara 1969 d: Sergei Urusevsky. lps: Nurmukhan Zhanturin, Farida SharipovA. 71M USS. *The Ambler's Race; The Trotter's Gait; Byeg Inokhodtsa*
Rannie Zhuravli, 1975, Short Story
Rannie Zhuravli 1979 d: Bolotbek Shamshiev. lps: Suymenkul Chokmorov. 95M USS. *Early Cranes; Rannie Zuravli; The Cranes Fly Early*
Topoliok Moi V Krasnoi Kosynke, 1961, Short Story
Ya-Tyan'-Shan 1972 d: Irina PoplavskayA. 133M USS. *I Am Tien-Shan*
Verblyuzhii Glaz, 1961, Short Story
Znoi 1963 d: Larissa Shepitko. lps: Bolotbek Shamshiev, Klara Joesoepzjanova, Noermoekhan Zjanturin. 84M USS. *The Heat Wave; Heat; Znoj*

AJAR, EMILE
Madame Rosa, Novel
Vie Devant Soi, La 1977 d: Moshe Mizrahi. lps: Simone Signoret, Claude Dauphin, Samy Ben Youb. 105M FRN. *Madame Rosa* (USA) prod/rel: Lira Films

AKAE, BAKU
Sekatomu Rai Gishi, Novel
Sekatomu Rai Gishi 1982 d: Yoichi Takabayashi. lps: Masayo Utsunomiya, Tomisaburo Wakayama, Yusuke TakitA. 109M JPN. *Irezumi - Spirit of the Tattoo* prod/rel: Daiei Co.
Sekka Tomurai Zashi Irezumi, Novel
Sekka Tomurai Zashi Irezumi 1981 d: Yoichi Takabayashi. lps: Tomisaburo Wakayama, Masayo Utsunomiya, Yusuke TakitA. 108M JPN. *Irezumi (Spirit of Tattoo)* (USA); *Irezumi: the Spirit of Tattoo* prod/rel: Daiei International, Daiichi Kazumi

AKAGAWA, JIRO
Futari, Novel
Futari 1991 d: Nobuhiko Obayashi. lps: Hikari Ishida, Tomoko Nakajima, Toshinori Omi. 150M JPN. *Chizuko's Younger Sister* prod/rel: Psc Co.

AKINS, ZOE (1886–1958), USA
Daddy's Gone a-Hunting, New York 1921, Play
Daddy's Gone a-Hunting 1925 d: Frank Borzage. lps: Alice Joyce, Percy Marmont, Virginia Marshall. 5851f USA. *A Man's World* prod/rel: Metro-Goldwyn Pictures
Women Love Once 1931 d: Edward Goodman. lps: Eleanor Boardman, Paul Lukas, Juliette Compton. 74M USA. *Daddy's Gone a-Hunting* prod/rel: Paramount Publix Corp.©
Declassee, New York 1921, Play
Declassee 1925 d: Robert G. VignolA. lps: Lloyd Hughes, Corinne Griffith, Clive Brook. 7733f USA. *The Social Exile* prod/rel: Corinne Griffith Productions, First National Pictures

Declassee, New York 1923, Play
Her Private Life 1929 d: Alexander KordA. lps: Billie Dove, Walter Pidgeon, Holmes Herbert. 6488f USA. prod/rel: First National Pictures
The Furies, New York 1928, Play
Furies, The 1930 d: Alan Crosland. lps: Lois Wilson, H. B. Warner, Theodore von Eltz. 6606f USA. prod/rel: First National Pictures
The Greeks Had a Word for It, New York 1930, Play
Greeks Had a Word for Them, The 1932 d: Lowell Sherman. lps: Joan Blondell, Ina Claire, Madge Evans. 77M USA. *Three Broadway Girls; The Greeks Had a Word for It* prod/rel: United Artists Corp., Feature Productions©
How to Marry a Millionaire 1953 d: Jean Negulesco. lps: Marilyn Monroe, Betty Grable, Lauren Bacall. 95M USA. prod/rel: 20th Century-Fox
The Moon-Flower, New York 1924, Play
Eve's Secret 1925 d: Clarence Badger. lps: Betty Compson, Jack Holt, William Collier Jr. 6305f USA. prod/rel: Famous Players-Lasky, Paramount Pictures
Morning Glory, Los Angeles 1939, Play
Morning Glory 1933 d: Lowell Sherman. lps: Katharine Hepburn, Adolphe Menjou, Douglas Fairbanks Jr. 74M USA. prod/rel: RKO Radio Pictures©
Stage Struck 1958 d: Sidney Lumet. lps: Henry Fonda, Susan Strasberg, Joan Greenwood. 95M USA. prod/rel: RKO Radio, Buena Vista
The Sad Horse, Unpublished, Novel
Sad Horse, The 1959 d: James B. Clark. lps: David Ladd, Chill Wills, Rex Reason. 78M USA. prod/rel: 20th Century-Fox, Associated Producers

AKSYONOV, VASILI (1932–, RSS
Papa Slozhi!, 1962, Short Story
Puteshestviye 1967 d: Inessa Selezneva, Inna Tumanyan. lps: Vladimir Retsepter, Svetlana Skoraya, Alexey Eibozhenko. 102M USS. *Journey*
Zavtraki Sorok Tret'ego Godo, 1962, Short Story
Puteshestviye 1967 d: Inessa Selezneva, Inna Tumanyan. lps: Vladimir Retsepter, Svetlana Skoraya, Alexey Eibozhenko. 102M USS. *Journey*
Zvyozdny Bilet, 1961, Novel
Moi Mladshii Brat 1962 d: Alexander Zarkhi. 85M USS. *My Younger Brother; Moj Mladsij Brat*

AKU, YU
Setouchi Moonlight Serenade, Novel
Setouchi Moonlight Serenade 1997 d: Masahiro ShinodA. lps: Kyozo Nagatsuka, Hideyuki Kasahara, Jun TobA. 117M JPN. *Moonlight Serenade* prod/rel: Shochiku Co., Office Two
Setouchi Shonen Yakyu Dan, Novel
Setouchi Shonen Yakyu Dan Seishunhen Saigo No Rakuen 1987 d: Haruhiko MimurA. lps: Toshihiko Tahara, Isako Waisio, Hikaru Kurosaki. 112M JPN. *MacArthur's Children - Part II* prod/rel: Herald Ace, Inc.
Setouchi Shonen Yakyudan 1984 d: Masahiro ShinodA. lps: Masako Natsume, Shima Iwashita, Hiromi Go. 117M JPN. *Boys' Baseball Team of Setouchi; MacArthur's Children* (USA) prod/rel: Shochiku Co.

AKUTAGAWA, RYUNOSUKE (1892–1927), JPN
Jigoku-Hen, 1918, Novel
Jigoku-Hen 1969 d: Shiro ToyodA. lps: Kinnosuke Nakamura, Tatsuya Nakadai, Yoko Naito. 95M JPN. *Portrait of Hell* (USA); *The Hell Screen; A Story of Hell* prod/rel: Toho Co.
Rashomon, 1915, Short Story
Outrage, The 1964 d: Martin Ritt. lps: Paul Newman, Laurence Harvey, Claire Bloom. 97M USA. *Judgment in the Sun* prod/rel: KHF Productions, MGM
Rashomon 1950 d: Akira KurosawA. lps: Toshiro Mifune, MacHiko Kyo, Masayuki Mori. 88M JPN. *In the Woods* prod/rel: Daiei Motion Picture Co.
Yabu No Naka, 1922, Short Story
Iron Maze 1991 d: Hiroaki YoshidA. lps: Jeff Fahey, Bridget Fonda, Hiroaki Murakami. 102M USA/JPN. prod/rel: First Independent, Trans-Tokyo Film Partners
Outrage, The 1964 d: Martin Ritt. lps: Paul Newman, Laurence Harvey, Claire Bloom. 97M USA. *Judgment in the Sun* prod/rel: KHF Productions, MGM
Rashomon 1950 d: Akira KurosawA. lps: Toshiro Mifune, MacHiko Kyo, Masayuki Mori. 88M JPN. *In the Woods* prod/rel: Daiei Motion Picture Co.
Yoba, Short Story
Yoba 1976 d: Tadashi Imai. lps: MacHiko Kyo, Kazuko Inano, Shinjiro EbarA. 96M JPN. *The Old Woman Ghost; The Witch; The Possessed* prod/rel: Nagata Productions, Daiei Motion Picture Co.

ALARINI, FULBERTO
L' Rimedi Par le Done, Play
Rimedio Per le Donne, Il 1914 d: Ernesto Vaser. lps: Ernesto Vaser, Ada Marangoni. 690m ITL. prod/rel: Itala Film

ALAS, LEOPOLDO (1852–1901), SPN, Alas Y Urena, Clarin
Cordera! Adios, 1892, Short Story
Adios, Cordera 1966 d: Pedro Mario Herrero. lps: Carlos Estrada, Jose Maria Prada, Emilio Gutierrez CabA. 87M SPN. *Goodbye Lamb*
La Regenta, 1884, Novel
Regenta, La 1974 d: Gonzalo Suarez. lps: Emma Penella, Keith Baxter, Nigel Davenport. 109M SPN. *The Regent's Wife; The Regent*

ALBARET, CELESTE
Monsieur Proust, Book
Celeste 1981 d: Percy Adlon. lps: Eva Mattes, Jurgen Arndt, Norbert WarthA. 107M GRM. prod/rel: Pelemele, Bayerische Rundfunk

ALBEE, EDWARD (1928–, USA, Albee, Edward Franklin
A Delicate Balance, 1966, Play
Delicate Balance, A 1973 d: Tony Richardson. lps: Katharine Hepburn, Paul Scofield, Lee Remick. 134M USA. prod/rel: American Express, Ely Landau
Who's Afraid of Virginia Wolf?, New York 1962, Play
Who's Afraid of Virginia Woolf? 1966 d: Mike Nichols. lps: Richard Burton, Elizabeth Taylor, George Segal. 132M USA. prod/rel: Warner Bros. Pictures, Chenault Productions

ALBERT, KATH
Loco, New York 1946, Play
How to Marry a Millionaire 1953 d: Jean Negulesco. lps: Marilyn Monroe, Betty Grable, Lauren Bacall. 95M USA. prod/rel: 20th Century-Fox

ALBERT, MARVIN H.
Apache Rising, Greenwich, Ct. 1957, Novel
Duel at Diablo 1966 d: Ralph Nelson. lps: James Garner, Sidney Poitier, Bibi Andersson. 103M USA. prod/rel: Rainbow Productions, Brien Productions
The Bounty Killer, Greenwich, Ct. 1958, Novel
Precio de un Hombre, El 1966 d: Eugenio Martin. lps: Richard Wyler, Tomas Milian, John Ireland. 89M SPN/ITL. *The Bounty Killer* (ITL); *The Ugly Ones* (USA); *The Price of a Man* prod/rel: Tecisa, Discobolo Film (Roma)
The Law and Jake Wade, 1956, Novel
Law and Jake Wade, The 1958 d: John Sturges. lps: Richard Widmark, Robert Taylor, Patricia Owens. 86M USA. prod/rel: MGM
The Man in Black, Story
Rough Night in Jericho 1967 d: Arnold Laven. lps: Dean Martin, George Peppard, Jean Simmons. 104M USA. prod/rel: Martin Rackin Production
Renegade Posse, Novel
Bullet for a Badman 1964 d: R. G. Springsteen. lps: Audie Murphy, Darren McGavin, Ruta Lee. 80M USA. *Renegade Posse* prod/rel: Universal

ALBERT-JEAN
Six Cent Mille Francs Par Mois, Play
Six Cent Mille Francs Par Mois 1933 d: Leo Joannon. lps: Germaine Michel, Georges Biscot, Pierre de Guingand. 75M FRN. prod/rel: Norma-Film

ALBERTON, BRUNO
Story
Ciao, Pais. 1956 d: Osvaldo Langini. lps: Leonora Ruffo, Lyla Rocco, Maria Grazia FranciA. F ITL. prod/rel: Astory Film

ALBINATI, E.
The Polish Car Window Cleaner, Novel
Ballata Dei Lavavetri, La 1998 d: Peter Del Monte. lps: Olek Mincer, Agata Buzek, Kim Rossi Stuart. 93M ITL. *The Ballad of the Windshield Washers* prod/rel: Mikado, P.F.A. Films

ALBRAND, MARTHA (1914–1981), GRM, Lambert, Christine, Holland, Katrin
Desperate Moment, Novel
Desperate Moment 1953 d: Compton Bennett. lps: Dirk Bogarde, Mai Zetterling, Philip Friend. 88M UKN. prod/rel: General Film Distributors, Fanfare

ALCOFORADO, MARIA
Liebesbriefe Einer Portugiesischen Nonne, Novel
Liebesbriefe Einer Portugiesischen Nonne, Die 1977 d: Jesus Franco. lps: Susan Hemingway, William Berger, Herbert Fux. 85M SWT/GRM. *Cartas de Amor de Uma Freira Portuguesa; Love Letters from a Portuguese Nun; Lettres d'Amour d'une Nonne Portugaise; Love Letters of a Portuguese Nun* prod/rel: Cinemec, Ascot

ALCOTT, LOUISA MAY (1832–1888), USA
Little Men, Boston 1871, Novel
   Little Men 1934 d: Phil Rosen. lps: Junior Durkin, Frankie Darro, David Durand. 77M USA. prod/rel: Mascot Pictures Corp.©
   Little Men 1940 d: Norman Z. McLeod. lps: Kay Francis, Jack Oakie, George Bancroft. 84M USA. prod/rel: RKO Radio Pictures©, the Play's the Thing Productions
   Louisa May Alcott's Little Men 1998 d: Rodney Gibbons. lps: Michael Caloz, Mariel Hemingway, Ben Cook. 98M CND. prod/rel: Legacy, Brainstorm Media
Little Women, Boston 1868, Novel
   Little Women 1917 d: G. B. Samuelson, Alexander Butler. lps: Daisy Burrell, Mary Lincoln, Minna Grey. 5000f UKN. prod/rel: G. B. Samuelson, Moss
   Little Women 1919 d: Harley Knoles. lps: Dorothy Bernard, Isabel Lamon, Lillian Hall. 5433f USA. prod/rel: William A. Brady, State Rights
   Little Women 1933 d: George Cukor. lps: Katharine Hepburn, Joan Bennett, Paul Lukas. 117M USA. prod/rel: RKO Radio Pictures©
   Little Women 1948 d: Mervyn Leroy. lps: June Allyson, Peter Lawford, Margaret O'Brien. 122M USA. prod/rel: MGM
   Little Women 1978 d: David Lowell Rich. lps: Meredith Baxter, Susan Dey, Ann Dusenberry. TVM. 200M USA. prod/rel: Universal TV
   Little Women 1994 d: Gillian Armstrong. lps: Winona Ryder, Gabriel Byrne, Trini Alvarado. 118M USA. prod/rel: Columbia Tristar, Di Novi Pictures
An Old Fashioned Girl, 1870, Novel
   Old-Fashioned Girl, An 1949 d: Arthur Dreifuss. lps: Gloria Jean, Frances Rafferty, Jimmy Lydon. 82M USA. prod/rel: Eagle-Lion

ALDECOA, IGNACIO
Con El Viento Solano, 1956, Novel
   Con El Viento Solano 1968 d: Mario Camus. lps: Antonio Gades, Maria Jose Alfonso, Erasmo Pascual. 100M SPN. *With the Wind in Hot Sunlight; With the Hot Easterly Wind; In the Torrid Wind*
Los Pajaros de Baden-Baden, 1965, Short Story
   Pajaros de Baden-Baden, Los 1974 d: Mario Camus. lps: Catherine Spaak, Frederic de Pasquale, Jose Luis Alonso. 120M SPN. *The Birds of Baden-Baden*
Young Sanchez, 1959, Short Story
   Joven Sanchez, El 1963 d: Mario Camus. lps: Julian Mateos, Carlos Otero, Consuelo de NievA. 92M SPN. *Young Sanchez*

ALDERMAN, TOM
Hit and Run, Novel
   Hitting Home 1988 d: Robin Spry. lps: Kerrie Keane, Daniel Pilon, Saul Rubinek. 100M CND. *Obsessed; Hit and Run* prod/rel: Telescene

ALDINGTON, RICHARD (1892–1962), UKN
All Men are Enemies, New York 1933, Novel
   All Men are Enemies 1934 d: George Fitzmaurice. lps: Helen Twelvetrees, Mona Barrie, Hugh Williams. 79M USA. prod/rel: Fox Film Corp.

ALDRICH, BESS STREETER (1881–1954), USA
Miss Bishop, Novel
   Cheers for Miss Bishop 1941 d: Tay Garnett. lps: Martha Scott, William Gargan, Edmund Gwenn. 95M USA. prod/rel: United Artists
The Woman Who Was Forgotten, 1926, Short Story
   Woman Who Was Forgotten, The 1930 d: Richard Thomas. lps: Leroy Mason, Belle Bennett, Jack Mower. 7800f USA. prod/rel: Woman Who Was Forgotten, Inc., States Cinema Corp.

ALDRICH, DARRAGH
Enchanted Hearts, Garden City, N.Y. 1917, Novel
   Prince There Was, A 1921 d: Tom Forman. lps: Thomas Meighan, Mildred Harris, Charlotte Jackson. 5553f USA. prod/rel: Famous Players-Lasky, Paramount Pictures

ALDRICH, THOMAS BAILEY (1836–1907), USA
Judith of Bethulia, 1904, Play
   Judith of Bethulia 1914 d: D. W. Griffith. lps: Blanche Sweet, Henry B. Walthall, Kate Bruce. 4r USA. *Her Condoned Sin* prod/rel: Biograph Co.©, General Film Co.

ALDRIN, EDWIN E. "BUZZ"
Return to Earth, Book
   Return to Earth 1976 d: Jud Taylor. lps: Cliff Robertson, Shirley Knight, Charles Cioffi. TVM. 90M USA. prod/rel: King-Hitzig Production

ALECSANDRI, VASILE
Cucoana Chirita in Iasi, 1852, Play
   Chirita la Lasi 1988 d: Mircea Dragan. 83M RMN. *Ma'am Chiritza Goes to Jassy; Madam Chirita in Jassy*

Cucoana Chirita in Provincie, 1852, Play
   Cucoana Chirita 1987 d: Mircea Dragan. 94M RMN. *Ma'am Chiritza; Madam Chirita*

ALEICHEM, SHALOM (1859–1916), RSS, Rabinowitz, Solomon J.
Story
   Evreiskoie Schastie 1925 d: Alexis Granowsky. lps: Solomon Mikhoels, I. Rogaler, S. Epstein. 87M USS. prod/rel: Goskino
   Tuviyah Ve Sheva Benotaiv 1968 d: Menahem Golan. lps: Shmuel Rodensky, Ninette Dinar, Tikvah Mor. 120M ISR/GRM. *Tevye Und Seine Sieben Tochter* (GRM); *Tevye and His Seven Daughters; Tuvia Ve'sheva B'notav* prod/rel: C.C.C., Noah
Khavah, Short Story
   Broken Barriers 1919 d: Charles E. Davenport. lps: Philip Sanford, Alice Hastings, Alexander Tenenholtz. 7r USA. *Khavah* prod/rel: Zion Films, Inc.©, National Film Distributors
Tevye and His Daughters, Short Story
   Fiddler on the Roof 1971 d: Norman Jewison. lps: Topol, Norma Crane, Leonard Frey. 180M USA. prod/rel: Mirisch, United Artists
Tevye Der Milkhiker, New York 1919, Play
   Tevya 1939 d: Maurice Schwartz. lps: Maurice Schwartz, Rebecca Weintraub, Miriam Riselle. 93M USA. *Tevya the Milkman* prod/rel: Maymon Film

ALESSI, RINO
L'Argine, Play
   Argine, L' 1938 d: Corrado d'Errico. lps: Luisa Ferida, Gino Cervi, Guglielmo Sinaz. 84M ITL. prod/rel: Scalera Film, C. Consorzio Adriatico
Il Conte Aquila, Play
   Conte Aquila, Il 1956 d: Guido Salvini. lps: Valentina Cortese, Rossano Brazzi, Paolo StoppA. 95M ITL. prod/rel: Salvini Film, Dear Film
   Teresa Confalonieri 1934 d: Guido Brignone. lps: Marta Abba, Nerio Bernardi, Luigi Carini. 88M ITL. *L' Angelo Della Rivolta; Love and Loyalty* (USA) prod/rel: S.A.P.F., Anonima Pittaluga

ALEXAKIS, VASSILIS
Talgo, Novel
   Xafnikos Erotas 1984 d: Yorgos Tseberopoulos. lps: Betty Livanou, Antonis Theodoracopoulos, Nikitas Tsakiroglou. 100M GRC. *Sudden Love; Talgo* prod/rel: Yorgos Tseberopoulos, Greek Film Centre

ALEXANDER, ARNO
Morgen Werde Ich Verhaftet, Novel
   Morgen Werde Ich Verhaftet 1939 d: Karl H. Stroux. lps: Ferdinand Marian, Kathe Dorsch, Gisela Uhlen. 85M GRM. prod/rel: Euphono, a.K.a.

ALEXANDER, ELIZABETH
Fifty-Two Weeks for Florette, 1921, Short Story
   You Belong to Me 1934 d: Alfred L. Werker. lps: Lee Tracy, Helen Morgan, Helen Mack. 67M USA. *Honor Bright* prod/rel: Paramount Productions
Roles, Boston 1924, Novel
   Changing Husbands 1924 d: Frank Urson, Paul Iribe. lps: Leatrice Joy, Victor Varconi, Raymond Griffith. 6799f USA. prod/rel: Famous Players-Lasky, Paramount Pictures
Second Choice, New York 1928, Novel
   Second Choice 1930 d: Howard Bretherton. lps: Dolores Costello, Chester Morris, Jack Mulhall. 6150f USA. prod/rel: Warner Brothers Pictures
The Self-Made Wife, 1922, Short Story
   Self-Made Wife, The 1923 d: John Francis Dillon. lps: Ethel Grey Terry, Crauford Kent, Virginia Ainsworth. 4960f USA. prod/rel: Universal Pictures

ALEXANDER, KARL
A Private Investigation, Novel
   Missing Pieces 1983 d: Mike Hodges. lps: Elizabeth Montgomery, John Reilly, David Haskell. TVM. 96M USA. *A Private Investigation* prod/rel: Entheoz Unlimited Prods.

ALEXANDER, LLOYD (1924–, USA, Alexander, Lloyd Chudley
The Chronicles of Prydainby, Novel
   Black Cauldron, The 1985 d: Ted Berman, Richard Rich. ANM. 80M USA. prod/rel: Buena Vista, Walt Disney Productions

ALEXANDER, PATRICK
Death of a Thin-Skinned Animal, Novel
   Professionnel, Le 1981 d: Georges Lautner. lps: Jean-Paul Belmondo, Robert Hossein, Jean Desailly. 109M FRN. *The Professional* (USA) prod/rel: Les Films Ariane, Cerito

ALEXANDER, RONALD
Holiday for Lovers, New York 1957, Play
   Holiday for Lovers 1959 d: Henry Levin. lps: Jane Wyman, Clifton Webb, Jill St. John. 103M USA. prod/rel: 20th Century-Fox

Time Out for Ginger, 1952, Play
   Billie 1965 d: Don Weis. lps: Patty Duke, Jim Backus, Billy de Wolfe. 87M USA. prod/rel: Chrislaw Productions

ALEXANDER, SHANA
Decision to Die, 1964, Short Story
   Slender Thread, The 1965 d: Sydney Pollack. lps: Sidney Poitier, Anne Bancroft, Telly Savalas. 98M USA. prod/rel: Athene Productions
Money, Madness & Murder Money, Novel
   Money, Madness & Murder 1987 d: Paul Bogart. lps: Lee Remick, John Glover, Tate Donovan. TVM. 279M USA. *Nutcracker: Money, Madness and Murder*

ALEXIE, SHERMAN
The Lone Ranger and Tonto Fistfight in Heaven, Book
   Smoke Signals 1998 d: Chris Eyre. lps: Adam Beach, Evan Adams, Irene Bedard. 88M USA. prod/rel: Shadow Catcher Entertainment

ALEY, MAXWELL
Son of Mama Posita, Story
   You're Not So Tough 1940 d: Joe May. lps: Billy Halop, Huntz Hall, Bobby Jordan. 71M USA. prod/rel: Universal Pictures Co.©

ALFAYATE, LUIS
Mia Moglie Mi Piace Di Piu, Play
   Mi Mujer Me Gusta Mas 1960 d: Antonio Roman. lps: Walter Chiari, Yvonne Bastien, Franco Fabrizi. 99M SPN/ITL. *La Moglie Di Mio Marito* (ITL); *I Prefer My Wife; My Husband's Wife* prod/rel: Wanguard Film, Explorer Film

ALFRIEND, EDWARD M.
The Great Diamond Robbery, New York 1895, Play
   Great Diamond Robbery, The 1914 d: Edward A. Morange, Daniel V. Arthur (Spv). lps: Wallace Eddinger, Gail Kane, Dorothy Arthur. 6r USA. prod/rel: Playgoers Film Co.

ALFVEN, INGER
S/Y Gladjen, Novel
   S/Y Gladjen 1989 d: Goran Du Rees. lps: Viveka Seldahl, Lena Olin, Stellan Skarsgard. TVM. 100M SWD. *S/Y Joy*

ALGREN, NELSON (1909–1981), USA
The Man With the Golden Arm, 1949, Novel
   Man With the Golden Arm, The 1955 d: Otto Preminger. lps: Frank Sinatra, Eleanor Parker, Kim Novak. 119M USA. prod/rel: United Artists, Carlyle Prods.
A Walk on the Wild Side, New York 1956, Novel
   Walk on the Wild Side 1962 d: Edward Dmytryk. lps: Laurence Harvey, Capucine, Jane FondA. 114M USA. prod/rel: Famous Artists Productions, Columbia

ALI, MUHAMMAD (1942–, USA, Clay, Cassius
Autobiography
   Greatest, The 1977 d: Tom Gries. lps: Muhammad Ali, Herbert Muhammad, Ernest Borgnine. 101M USA/UKN. prod/rel: Columbia, EMI

ALIBERT, HENRI
Au Pays Des Cigales, Opera
   Au Pays Des Cigales 1945 d: Maurice Cam. lps: Henri Alibert, Gorlett, Francine Bessy. 85M FRN. prod/rel: D.U.C.
Au Pays du Soleil, Opera
   Au Pays du Soleil 1933 d: Robert Peguy. lps: Henri Alibert, Lisette Lanvin, Fernand Flament. 79M FRN. prod/rel: Films Tellus
Les Gangsters du Chateau d'If, Opera
   Gangsters du Chateau d'If, Les 1939 d: Rene Pujol. lps: Henri Alibert, Pierre Larquey, Germaine Roger. 95M FRN. prod/rel: Vondas Films
Trois de la Canebiere, Opera
   Trois de la Canebiere 1955 d: Maurice de Canonge. lps: Jeannette Batti, Colette Dereal, Marcel Merkes. 102M FRN. prod/rel: Films Tellus, Cocinex
Trois de la Marine, Opera
   Trois de la Marine 1934 d: Charles Barrois. lps: Armand Bernard, Henri Alibert, Rivers Cadet. 90M FRN. prod/rel: Metropa-Film
   Trois de la Marine 1956 d: Maurice de Canonge. lps: Jeannette Batti, Marcel Merkes, Henri Genes. 95M FRN. prod/rel: Cocinex, L.P.C.
Un de la Canebiere, Opera
   Un de la Canebiere 1938 d: Rene Pujol. lps: Henri Alibert, Rellys, Germaine Roger. 98M FRN. prod/rel: Vondas Films
Zou le Midi Bouge, Opera
   Arenes Joyeuses 1935 d: Karl Anton. lps: Betty Stockfeld, Lisette Lanvin, Lucien Baroux. 90M FRN. prod/rel: Metropa-Film

ALIBRANDI, TOM
Privileged Information, Book
Sworn to Silence 1987 d: Peter Levin. lps: Peter Coyote, Dabney Coleman, Caroline McWilliams. TVM. 100M USA.

ALISON, JOAN
Everybody Comes to Rick's, Play
Casablanca 1942 d: Michael Curtiz. lps: Humphrey Bogart, Ingrid Bergman, Paul Henreid. 102M USA. prod/rel: Warner Bros.

ALIX, BLANCHE
L' As, Play
Ceux du Ciel 1940 d: Yvan Noe. lps: Pierre Renoir, Jean Galland, Aimos. 86M FRN. prod/rel: Fana Films

ALLAIN, MARCEL
Coeur d'Heroine, Novel
Coeur d'Heroine 1918. FRN. prod/rel: Pathe Frere
Fantomas, Novel
Fantomas 1913 d: Louis Feuillade. lps: Rene Navarre, Georges Melchior, Renee Carl. 1115m FRN. *Fantomas Under the Shadow of the Guillotine* prod/rel: Gaumont
Fantomas 1964 d: Andre Hunebelle. lps: Jean Marais, Louis de Funes, Mylene Demongeot. 105M FRN. *Fantomas 70* prod/rel: P.A.C., S.N.E.G.
Juve Contre Fantomas, Novel
Juve Contre Fantomas 1913 d: Louis Feuillade. lps: Rene Navarre, Edmond Breon, Renee Carl. SRL. 1227m FRN. *Juve Vs. Fantomas; Fantomas II*
Le Magistrat Cambrioleur, Novel
Faux Magistrat, Le 1914 d: Louis Feuillade. lps: Rene Navarre, Edmond Breon, Suzanne Le Bret. 1881m FRN. *The False Magistrate; Fantomas V* prod/rel: Gaumont
Monsieur Personne, Novel
Monsieur Personne 1936 d: Christian-Jaque. lps: Jules Berry, Josseline Gael, Andre Berley. 90M FRN. *Mr. Nobody* prod/rel: Productions Sigma
Le Policier Apache, Novel
Fantomas Contre Fantomas 1914 d: Louis Feuillade. lps: Rene Navarre, Edmond Breon, Renee Carl. 1274m FRN. *Fantomas the Crook Detective; Fantomas IV* prod/rel: Gaumont

ALLAIS, ALPHONSE
L' Affaire Blaireau, 1899, Novel
Affaire Blaireau, L' 1923 d: Louis Osmont. lps: Andre Brunot, Emile Saint-Ober, Marcelle Duval. 1800m FRN. prod/rel: Pathe-Consortium-Cinema
Affaire Blaireau, L' 1931 d: Henry Wulschleger. lps: Bach, Alice Tissot, Charles Montel. 100M FRN. prod/rel: Alex Nalpas
Ni Vu, Ni Connu. 1958 d: Yves Robert. lps: Louis de Funes, Pierre Mondy, Noelle Adam. 95M FRN. *Vive Monsieur Blaireau; L' Affaire Blaireau* prod/rel: Champs-Elysees Production

ALLAN, JANET
Little Big Shot, Play
Little Big Shot 1952 d: Jack Raymond. lps: Ronald Shiner, Marie Lohr, Derek Farr. 90M UKN. prod/rel: Byron, Associated British Film Distributors

ALLAN, TED
Lies My Father Told Me, Short Story
Lies My Father Told Me 1960 d: Don Chaffey. lps: Harry Brogan, Betsy Blair, Eddie Golden. 60M UKN. prod/rel: Emmet Dalton
Lies My Father Told Me 1975 d: Jan Kadar. lps: Yossi Yadin, Len Birman, Marilyn Lightstone. 102M CND. *Les Mensonges Que Mon Pere Me Contait* prod/rel: Pentimento Productions, Pentacle VIIi Productions Ltd.
Love Streams, Play
Love Streams 1983 d: John Cassavetes. lps: John Cassavetes, Gena Rowlands, Diahnne Abbott. 141M USA. prod/rel: MGM, United Artists
The Woman Luli Sent Me, Novel
Sept Fois Par Jour. 1971 d: Denis Heroux. lps: Rosanna Schiaffino, Jean Coutu, Dalia Friedland. 87M CND/ISR. *Seven Times a Day; 7 Fois. (Par Jour); 7 Times a Day; Adam and Eva* prod/rel: Les Productions Heroux Ltee., Minotaur Film Productions Inc.

ALLARDICE, JAMES B.
At War With the Army, New York 1949, Play
At War With the Army 1950 d: Hal Walker. lps: Dean Martin, Jerry Lewis, Polly Bergen. 93M USA. prod/rel: Paramount, York Picture Corp.

ALLBEURY, TED (1917–, UKN
Novel
Blue Ice 1992 d: Russell Mulcahy. lps: Michael Caine, Sean Young, Ian Holm. 105M USA. prod/rel: M & M Productions

No Place to Hide, Novel
Hostage 1992 d: Robert Young. lps: Sam Neill, Talisa Soto, James Fox. TVM. 104M UKN/ARG. prod/rel: Portman Entertainment, Independent Image

ALLEGRETTO, MICHAEL
Night of Reunion, Book
Terror in the Shadows 1995 d: William A. Graham. lps: Leigh McCloskey, Marcy Walker, Jacob Loyst. TVM. 87M USA. prod/rel: Freyda Rothstein Prods., Lois Luger Prods.

ALLEINS, MADELEINE
Vers l'Extase, Novel
Vers l'Extase 1960 d: Rene Wheeler. lps: Pascale Petit, Gianni Esposito, Serge Sauvion. 86M FRN. *L' Extase* prod/rel: Films Matignon

ALLEN, AUSTEN
Pleasure Cruise, London 1932, Play
No Dejes la Puerta Abierta 1933 d: Lewis Seiler. lps: Raul Roulien, Mona Maris, Romualdo Tirado. 8r USA. *Don't Leave the Door Open; Trip to Nowhere; Donde Has Pasado la Noche?; Viaje de Placer*
Pleasure Cruise 1933 d: Frank Tuttle. lps: Roland Young, Genevieve Tobin, Ralph Forbes. 72M USA. prod/rel: Fox Film Corp.©

ALLEN, FRANCIS K.
Murder Stole My Missing Hours, Short Story
Road to Alcatraz 1945 d: Nick Grinde. lps: Robert Lowery, June Storey, Grant Withers. 60M USA. prod/rel: Republic

ALLEN, GRANT
The Scallywag, Novel
Scallywag, The 1921 d: Challis Sanderson. lps: Fred Thatcher, Muriel Alexander, Ann Elliott. 4400f UKN. prod/rel: Master, Butcher's Film Service
What's Bred in the Bone, Novel
What's Bred.. Comes Out in the Flesh 1916 d: Sidney Morgan. lps: Janet Alexander, Lauderdale Maitland, Frank Tennant. 3374f UKN. prod/rel: Master, Kino Exclusives
The Woman Who Did, Novel
Woman Who Did, The 1915 d: Walter West. lps: Eve Balfour, Thomas H. MacDonald, George Foley. 6000f UKN. prod/rel: Broadwest, Gerrard

ALLEN, HERVEY (1889–1949), USA, Allen, William Hervey
Anthony Adverse, New York 1933, Novel
Anthony Adverse 1936 d: Mervyn Leroy. lps: Fredric March, Olivia de Havilland, Donald Woods. 139M USA. prod/rel: Warner Bros. Pictures, Inc.

ALLEN, IRVING ROSS
The Money Maker, New York 1918, Novel
Beating the Odds 1919 d: Paul Scardon. lps: Harry T. Morey, Betty Blythe, Jean Paige. 5r USA. prod/rel: Vitagraph Co. of America©

ALLEN, JANE
A Girl's Best Friend Is Wall Street, Book
She Knew All the Answers 1941 d: Richard Wallace. lps: Joan Bennett, Franchot Tone, John Hubbard. 85M USA. *A Girl's Best Friend Is Wall Street* prod/rel: Columbia
Thanks God I'll Take It from Here, Novel
Without Reservations 1946 d: Mervyn Leroy. lps: Claudette Colbert, John Wayne, Don Defore. 107M USA. prod/rel: RKO Radio

ALLEN, JAY PRESSON
The First Wife, Play
Wives and Lovers 1963 d: John Rich. lps: Van Johnson, Janet Leigh, Shelley Winters. 103M USA. *First Wife* prod/rel: Hal Wallis Productions, Paramount
Just Tell Me What You Want, Novel
Just Tell Me What You Want 1979 d: Sidney Lumet. lps: Ali MacGraw, Alan King, Myrna Loy. 112M USA. prod/rel: Warner Bros.

ALLEN, JOHANNES
Nu, Copenhagen 1967, Novel
Tumult 1969 d: Hans Abramson. lps: Gertie Jung, Bjorn Puggaard-Muller, Paul Glargaard. 91M DNM. *Relations (ITL); Tumult -Sonja Age 16; Sonja - 16 Ar* prod/rel: Athena Film
Ung Leg, Novel
Ung Leg 1956 d: Johannes Allen. lps: Gitta Norby, Anne Werner Thomsen, Frits Helmuth. 82M DNM. *The Young Have No Time* prod/rel: Dansk

ALLEN, ROBERT SHARON
Washington Merry-Go-Round, New York 1931, Book
Washington Merry-Go-Round 1932 d: James Cruze. lps: Lee Tracy, Constance Cummings, Walter Connolly. 78M USA. *Invisible Power (UKN)* prod/rel: Columbia Pictures Corp.©

ALLEN, WOODY (1935–, USA, Konigsberg, Allen Stewart
Don't Drink the Water, New York 1966, Play
Don't Drink the Water 1969 d: Howard Morris. lps: Jackie Gleason, Estelle Parsons, Ted Bessell. 98M USA. prod/rel: Jack Rollins-Charles H. Joffe Production
Play It Again Sam, Play
Play It Again Sam 1972 d: Herbert Ross. lps: Woody Allen, Diane Keaton, Tony Roberts. 86M USA. prod/rel: Apjac

ALLENDE, ISABEL (1942–, CHL
The House of the Spirits, Novel
House of the Spirits, The 1993 d: Bille August. lps: Jeremy Irons, Meryl Streep, Glenn Close. 138M DNM/GRM/PRT. *The House of Spirits*

ALLERTON, MARK
John Hinte - Gentleman in Blue, Novel
Gentleman in Blue, The 1917. 4000f UKN. prod/rel: Kinematograph Concessions, Monopol

ALLHOFF, FRED
Tracking New York's Crime Barons, 1936, Short Story
I Am the Law 1938 d: Alexander Hall. lps: Edward G. Robinson, Barbara O'Neil, John Beal. 83M USA. *Outside the Law* prod/rel: Columbia Pictures Corp. of California©

ALLINGHAM, MARGERY (1904–1966), UKN
Room to Let, Radio Play
Room to Let 1950 d: Godfrey Grayson. lps: Jimmy Hanley, Valentine Dyall, Christine Silver. 68M UKN. prod/rel: Hammer, Exclusive
Tiger in the Smoke, 1952, Novel
Tiger in the Smoke 1956 d: Roy Ward Baker. lps: Donald Sinden, Muriel Pavlow, Tony Wright. 94M UKN. prod/rel: Rank, Rank Film Distributors

ALLISTER, RAY
Friese-Greene, Book
Magic Box, The 1951 d: John Boulting. lps: Robert Donat, Margaret Johnston, Maria Schell. 118M UKN. prod/rel: Festival Films, British Lion

ALMAGOR, GILA
Book
Hakayitz Shel Aviya 1988 d: Eli Cohen. lps: Gila Almagor, Kaipo Cohen, Eli Cohen. 96M ISR. *Avia's Summer; Hakaitz Shel Avia; The Summer of Aviya*

ALMEIDA, GERMANO
Mr. Napumoceno's Last Will and Testament, Novel
Testamento 1998 d: Francisco Manso. lps: Nelson Xavier, Maria Ceica, Chico Diaz. 108M PRT/BRZ/CPV. prod/rel: Portuguese National Television, Adr Prods.

ALONSO MILLAN, JUAN JOSE
Estado Civile: Marta, Novel
Marta 1971 d: Jose Antonio Nieves Conde. lps: Marisa Mell, Stephen Boyd, Isa MirandA. 91M SPN/ITL. *...Dopo Di Che Uccide Il Maschio E Lo Divora (ITL); Bloodbath; ..and Then Kills the Male and Eats It; Estado Civil: Marta; Stato Civile: Marta* prod/rel: Atlantida Film (Madrid), Cinemar (Roma)

ALPHONSUS, JOAO
Totonia Pacheco, 1935, Novel
Predileto, O 1975 d: Roberto Palmari. lps: Jofre Soares. 95M BRZ. *The Favorite*

ALSBERG, MAX
Voruntersuchung, Play
Autour d'une Enquete 1931 d: Henri Chomette, Robert Siodmak. lps: Annabella, Florelle, Jean Perier. 93M FRN. prod/rel: U.F.a., a.C.E.
Voruntersuchung 1931 d: Robert Siodmak. lps: Albert Bassermann, Gustav Frolich, Hans Brausewetter. 95M GRM. *Preliminary Investigation; Inquest* prod/rel: UFA

ALTENDORF, WOLFGANG
Der Transport, Novel
Transport, Der 1961 d: Jurgen Roland. lps: Hannes Messemer, Armin Dahlen, Inge Langen. 92M GRM. *Destination Death; The Transport* prod/rel: Fono, U.F.H.

ALTENKIRCH, FERDINAND
Man Braucht Kein Geld, Play
Man Braucht Kein Geld 1931 d: Carl Boese. lps: Hedy Lamarr, Heinz Ruhmann, Hans Moser. 96M GRM. prod/rel: Allianz
Onkel Aus Amerika, Der 1953 d: Carl Boese. lps: Georg Thomalla, Hans Moser, Grethe Weiser. 100M GRM. prod/rel: C.C.C., Prisma
Pas Besoin d'Argent, Play
Pas Besoin d'Argent 1933 d: Jean-Paul Paulin. lps: Claude Dauphin, Lisette Lanvin, Jeanne Lion. 75M FRN. prod/rel: Films P.A.D.

ALTHEER, PAUL
Die Flucht in Den Harem, Zurich 1927, Play
Was Isch Denn I Mym Harem Los? 1937 d: Rene Guggenheim. lps: Rudolf Bernhard, Max Haufler, Alfred Rasser. 90M SWT. *Mais Qu'est-Ce Qui Se Passe Dans Mon Harem?* prod/rel: A.B.C. Film Bale

ALTIERI, MAJOR JAMES
Darby's Rangers, 1945, Book
Darby's Rangers 1958 d: William A. Wellman. lps: James Garner, Etchika Choureau, Jack Warden. 121M USA. *The Young Invaders* (UKN) prod/rel: Warner Bros.

ALTIMUS, HENRY
The Microbe, 1919, Short Story
Microbe, The 1919 d: Henry Otto. lps: Viola Dana, Kenneth Harlan, Arthur Maude. 5r USA. prod/rel: Metro Pictures Corp.©

ALVAREZ ACOSTA, MIGUEL
El Rio Y la Muerte, Novel
Rio Y la Muerte, El 1954 d: Luis Bunuel. lps: Columba Dominguez, Miguel Torruco, Joaquin Cordero. 93M MXC. *The River and Death* (USA); *Death and the River* prod/rel: Clasa Films Mudiales

ALVAREZ, ENRIQUE G.
Los Cuatro Robinsones, Play
Cuatro Robinsones, Los 1926 d: Reinhardt Blothner. lps: Guillermo Munoz Custodio, Ricardo Vargas, Jose Arguelles. SPN. prod/rel: Omnia Film (Madrid)

ALVAREZ QUINTERO, JOAQUIN (1873–1944), SPN
Cabrita Que Tira Al Monte, Play
Cabrita Que Tira Al Monte 1925 d: Fernando Delgado. lps: Consuelo Reyes, Manuel Soriano, Maria Comendador. 77M SPN. prod/rel: Santiago Solo De Zaldivar (Madrid)
Malvaloca, Play
Malvaloca 1926 d: Benito Perojo. lps: Lydia Gutierrez, Manuel San German, Javier de RiverA. 1614m SPN. *Hollyhock* prod/rel: Goya Film (Madrid)

ALVAREZ QUINTERO, SERAFIN (1871–1938), SPN
Cabrita Que Tira Al Monte, Play
Cabrita Que Tira Al Monte 1925 d: Fernando Delgado. lps: Consuelo Reyes, Manuel Soriano, Maria Comendador. 77M SPN. prod/rel: Santiago Solo De Zaldivar (Madrid)
Malvaloca, Play
Malvaloca 1926 d: Benito Perojo. lps: Lydia Gutierrez, Manuel San German, Javier de RiverA. 1614m SPN. *Hollyhock* prod/rel: Goya Film (Madrid)

ALVORD, LOUISE
Sally Ann's Strategy, Story
Sally Ann's Strategy 1912 d: Walter Edwin. lps: Alice Washburn, Mary Fuller, Charles Ogle. 675f USA. prod/rel: Edison

ALVUS
Il Treno Delle 21.15, Play
Treno Delle 21.15, Il 1933 d: Amleto Palermi. lps: Romano Calo, Laura Adani, Sandro Ruffini. 70M ITL. prod/rel: Caesar Film

AMACKER, HAROLD
The Death Rider, Story
No Name on the Bullet 1959 d: Jack Arnold. lps: Audie Murphy, Charles Drake, Joan Evans. 77M USA. prod/rel: Universal-International

AMADA, KINGEN
Konchu Dai Senso, Short Story
Konchu Daisenso 1968 d: Kazui Nihonmatsu. lps: Keisuke Sonoi, Yusuke Kawazu, Emi Shindo. 84M JPN. *War of Insects; Genocide* (USA) prod/rel: Shochiku Co.

AMADO, JORGE (1912–, BRZ
Capitaes Da Areia, 1937, Novel
Wild Pack, The 1971 d: Hall Bartlett. lps: Kent Lane, Tisha Sterling, John Rubenstein. 102M USA. *The Sandpit Generals; The Defiant*
Dona Flor E Sue Dois Maridos, 1966, Novel
Dona Flor E Seus Dois Maridos 1978 d: Bruno Barreto. lps: Sonia Braga, Jose Wilker, Mauro MendocA. 110M BRZ. *Dona Flor and Her Two Husbands* (USA) prod/rel: Carnaval, Luis Carlos Barreto
Cravo E Canela Gabriela, 1958, Novel
Gabriela 1984 d: Bruno Barreto. lps: Sonia Braga, Marcello Mastroianni, Antonio CantaforA. 104M BRZ/ITL. *Cravo E Canela Gabriela* prod/rel: The Sultana Corp.
Jubiaba, 1935, Novel
Jubiaba 1986 d: Nelson Pereira Dos Santos. lps: Francois Goussard, Zeze Mota, Betty FariA. 101M BRZ/FRN. *Bahia de Tous Les Saints* (FRN)
Seara Vermelha, 1946, Novel
Seara Vermelha 1963 d: Alberto d'AversA. 116M BRZ. *The Violent Land*

Tenda Dos Milagres, 1969, Novel
Tenda Dos Milagres 1977 d: Nelson Pereira Dos Santos. lps: Hugo Carvana, Sonia Dias, Anecy RochA. 132M BRZ. *Tent of Miracles* (USA); *La Boutique Des Miracles* prod/rel: Regina
Tieta Do Agreste, Novel
Tieta Do Agreste 1996 d: Carlos Diegues. lps: Sonia Braga, Marilia Pera, Esteves Chico Anysio. 141M BRZ/UKN. *Tieta of Agreste* prod/rel: Columbia, Sky Light Cinema

AMANAT, SAYED AGA HASAN
Indrasabha, 1853, Play
Indra Sabha 1932 d: J. J. Madan. lps: Kajjan, Nissar, Jehan ArA. 211M IND. *Indrasabha* prod/rel: Madan Theatres

AMATEAU, ROD (1923–, USA
The Operator, Novel
Where Does It Hurt? 1972 d: Rod Amateau. lps: Peter Sellers, Jo Ann Pflug, Rick Lenz. 85M USA/UKN. prod/rel: Hemdale

AMATO, PEPPINO
Sera Di Pioggia, Story
Seven Hills of Rome, The 1957 d: Roy Rowland, Mario Russo. lps: Mario Lanza, Renato Rascel, Marisa Allasio. 103M USA/ITL. *Arrivederci Roma* (ITL) prod/rel: MGM, Lecloud Prods. (Usa)

AMBAI
Milechan, Short Story
Pehla Adhyay 1981 d: Vishnu Mathur. lps: Dinesh Shakul, Jyoti Ranadive, Madan Jain. 130M IND. *Pahala Adhyay* prod/rel: Dhwanyalok Films

AMBERG, CHARLES
Clivia, Opera
Clivia 1954 d: Karl Anton. lps: Claude Farrell, Peter Pasetti, Hans Richter. 98M GRM. prod/rel: Central-Europa, Prisma

AMBIENT, MARK
The Arcadians, London 1909, Musical Play
Arcadians, The 1927 d: Victor Saville. lps: Ben Blue, Jeanne de Casalis, Vesta SylvA. 7000f UKN. *Land of Heart's Desire* prod/rel: Gaumont

AMBLER, ERIC (1909–, UKN
Epitaph for a Spy, 1938, Novel
Hotel Reserve 1944 d: Lance Comfort, Max Greene. lps: James Mason, Lucie Mannheim, Raymond Lovell. 89M UKN. prod/rel: RKO-Radio British
Journey Into Fear, Novel
Journey Into Fear 1942 d: Norman Foster, Orson Welles (Uncredited). lps: Joseph Cotten, Ruth Warrick, Orson Welles. 69M USA. prod/rel: RKO Radio
Journey Into Fear 1975 d: Daniel Mann. lps: Sam Waterston, Zero Mostel, Yvette Mimieux. 103M CND. *Burn Out; Le Voyage de la Peur* prod/rel: New World Productions Ltd., International Film Distributors
The Light of Day, London 1962, Novel
Topkapi 1964 d: Jules Dassin. lps: Peter Ustinov, Melina Mercouri, Maximilian Schell. 120M USA/FRN. *The Light of Day* prod/rel: Filmways, Inc., F-H Productions
The Mask of Dimitrios, 1939, Novel
Mask of Dimitrios, The 1944 d: Jean Negulesco. lps: Sydney Greenstreet, Peter Lorre, Zachary Scott. 95M USA. prod/rel: Warner Bros.
The October Man, Novel
October Man, The 1947 d: Roy Ward Baker. lps: John Mills, Joan Greenwood, Edward Chapman. 110M UKN. *Hangman's Noose* prod/rel: General Film Distributors, Two Cities
Uncommon Danger, Novel
Background to Danger 1943 d: Raoul Walsh. lps: George Raft, Brenda Marshall, Sydney Greenstreet. 80M USA. prod/rel: Warner Bros.

AMBROGI, SILVANO
Neurotandem, Novel
Sculacciata, La 1974 d: Pasquale Festa Campanile. lps: Antonio Salinas, Sydne Rome, Gino Pernice. 90M ITL. prod/rel: Filmes Cin.Ca, Titanus

AMEN, CAROL
The Last Testament, Story
Testament 1983 d: Lynne Littman. lps: Jane Alexander, William Devane, Ross Harris. 90M USA. prod/rel: Paramount

AMENDOLA, MARIO
Il Miracola, Play
Diavolo in Convento, Il 1951 d: Nunzio MalasommA. lps: Gilberto Govi, Mariella Lotti, Georges Galley. 85M ITL. prod/rel: Taurus Film
Scandalo Al Collegio, Musical Play
Innocente Casimiro, L' 1945 d: Carlo Campogalliani. lps: Erminio MacArio, Ada Dondini, Lea Padovani. 83M ITL. prod/rel: Ars Societa Produzioni Cin.Che, Lux Film

AMERMAN, LOCKHART
Guns in the Heather, Novel
Guns in the Heather 1969 d: Robert Butler. lps: Glenn Corbett, Alfred Burke, Kurt Russell. 90M UKN. *Spy Busters; The Secret of Boyne Castle* prod/rel: Walt Disney

AMES, CHRISTINE
The Human Side, Los Angeles 1933, Play
Human Side, The 1934 d: Edward Buzzell. lps: Adolphe Menjou, Doris Kenyon, Charlotte Henry. 70M USA. prod/rel: Universal Pictures Corp.©

AMES, DELANO
She Shall Have Murder, Novel
She Shall Have Murder 1950 d: Daniel Birt. lps: Rosamund John, Derrick de Marney, Mary Jerrold. 90M UKN. prod/rel: Concanen Recordings, Independent Film Distributors

AMES, JOHN
Book
Second Serve 1986 d: Anthony Page. lps: Vanessa Redgrave, Martin Balsam, William Russ. TVM. 100M USA. *I Change My Life; The Renee Richards Story* prod/rel: Linda Yellen, Lorimar

AMES, JOSEPH BUSHNELL
Shoe Bar Stratton, New York 1922, Novel
Catch My Smoke 1922 d: William Beaudine. lps: Tom Mix, Lillian Rich, Claude Peyton. 4070f USA. prod/rel: Fox Film Corp.

AMICHES, CARLOS
Play
Chica Del Gato, La 1926 d: Antonio Calvache. lps: Josefina Ochoa, Elena Salvador, Carlos Diaz de MendozA. 74M SPN. prod/rel: Film Numancia (Madrid)
Es Mi Hombre!, Play
Es Mi Hombre 1928 d: Carlos Fernandez CuencA. lps: Carmen Salvatierra Redondo, Rosario Velazquez, Manuel Montenegro. 80M SPN. *He's My Man* prod/rel: Cosmos Film (Madrid)

AMIEL, DENYS
Trois Et une, Play
Romance a Trois 1942 d: Roger Richebe. lps: Fernand Gravey, Simone Renant, Denise Grey. 98M FRN. prod/rel: Richebe

AMILA, JEAN
Le Boucher Des Hurlus, Novel
Sortez Des Rangs 1996 d: Jean-Denis Robert. lps: Stanislas Crevillen, Laure Duthilleul, Pierre-Arnaud Crespeau. 97M FRN. *Fall Out* prod/rel: Sfp Cinema, la Gueville

AMILA, JOHN
La Bonne Tisane, Novel
Bonne Tisane, La 1957 d: Herve Bromberger. lps: Raymond Pellegrin, Madeleine Robinson, Bernard Blier. 104M FRN. *Kill Or Cure* prod/rel: Contact Org., Rene Thevenet/ Contact Org.
Langes Radieux, Novel
Fleur d'Oseille 1967 d: Georges Lautner. lps: Mireille Darc, Anouk Ferjac, Maurice Biraud. 110M FRN. *Le Fric Met Les Voiles; Fleur d'Epine; Langes Radieux* prod/rel: Speva Films
La Loups Dans la Bergerie, Novel
Loups Dans la Bergerie, Les 1959 d: Herve Bromberger. lps: Jean Babilee, Jean-Marc Bory, Pierre Mondy. 80M FRN. *The Damned and the Daring* (UKN) prod/rel: Madeleine Films, Francitel
Sans Attendre Godot, Novel
Quand la Femme S'en Mele 1957 d: Yves Allegret. lps: Edwige Feuillere, Jean Servais, Bernard Blier. 90M FRN/ITL/GRM. *When a Woman Meddles* (USA); *Killer Lassen Bitten* (GRM); *The Killers* prod/rel: Regina, Royal Films

AMIR, ELI
Book
Tarnagol Kaparot 1991 d: Dan Wolman. lps: Nir Sadeh, Efrat Lavie, Bobby Ne'eman. F ISR. *The Scapegoat* prod/rel: Israel Television

AMIS, KINGSLEY (1922–1995), UKN
Lucky Jim, 1953, Novel
Lucky Jim 1957 d: John Boulting. lps: Ian Carmichael, Terry-Thomas, Hugh Griffith. 95M UKN. prod/rel: British Lion, Charter
The Old Devils, 1986, Novel
Old Devils, The 1991 d: Tristram Powell. lps: John Stride, James Grant, Ray Smith. TVM. 180M UKN. prod/rel: BBC Wales
Stanley and the Women, 1984, Novel
Stanley and the Women 1991 d: David Tucker. lps: John Thaw, Geraldine James, Sheila Gish. TVM. 205M UKN. prod/rel: Central Television

Take a Girl Like You, London 1960, Novel
 Take a Girl Like You 1969 d: Jonathan Miller. lps: Hayley Mills, Oliver Reed, Noel Harrison. 101M UKN. prod/rel: Albion Film Group, Columbia

That Uncertain Feeling, London 1955, Novel
 Only Two Can Play 1962 d: Sidney Gilliat. lps: Peter Sellers, Mai Zetterling, Virginia Maskell. 106M UKN. *That Uncertain Feeling* prod/rel: Vale Film Productions, British Lion

AMIS, MARTIN (1949–, UKN
The Rachel Papers, 1973, Novel
 Rachel Papers, The 1989 d: Damian Harris. lps: Dexter Fletcher, Ione Skye, Jonathan Pryce. 91M UKN. prod/rel: Virgin, Initial Film & Television

AMITAI, LILY PERRY
Book
 Golem Bema'agal 1993 d: Aner Preminger. lps: Hagit Dasberg, Nicole Castel, Gedalia Besser. F ISR. *Blindman's Bluff; Blind Man's Bluff; Dummy in a Circle*

AMMANITI, NICCOLO
L' Ultimo Capodanna Dell'Umanita, Novel
 Ultimo Capodanno, L' 1998 d: Marco Risi. lps: Monica Bellucci, Alessandro Haber, Francesca d'AlojA. 106M ITL. *The Last New Year's Eve* prod/rel: Sorpasso Film, Istituto Luce

AMMER, PETER
Pudelnackt in Oberbayern, Novel
 Pudelnackt in Oberbayern 1968 d: Hans Albin. lps: Hans von Borsody, Ini Assmann, Anke Syring. 85M GRM. *Stark Naked in Upper Bavaria* prod/rel: Top, Romano

AMORY, RICHARD
Song of the Loon, New York 1966, Novel
 Song of the Loon 1970 d: Andrew Herbert. lps: Jon Iverson, Morgan Royce, Lancer Ward. 79M USA. prod/rel: Sawyer Productions

AMPARO ESCANDON, MARIA
Santitos, Novel
 Santitos 1999 d: Alejandro Springall. lps: Dolores Heredia, Demian Bichir, Alberto EstrellA. 105M MXC. *Traveling Saints* prod/rel: Instituto Mexicano de Cinematografia, Tabasco Films

AMSTEIN, JURG
Feuerwerk, Play
 Feuerwerk 1956 d: Kurt Hoffmann. lps: Lilli Palmer, Karl Schonbock, Romy Schneider. 90M GRM. *Oh! My Papa; Oh Mein Papa* prod/rel: N.D.F., Bavaria

AN BO
Chun Feng Cui Dao Nuoming He, Play
 Chun Feng Cui Dao Nuoming He 1954 d: Ling Zhifeng. lps: Bi XIng, Jiang Li, Zhang Xuecheng. 1r CHN. *The Spring Wind Blows Over the Nuoming River* prod/rel: Northeast Film Studio

ANAND, MULK RAJ (1905–, IND
Two Leaves and a Bud, 1937, Novel
 Rahi 1953 d: Khwaya Ahmad Abbas. lps: Dev Anand, Balraj Sahni, Nalini Jaywant. 139M IND. *The Wayfarer* prod/rel: Naya Sansar
 Two Leaves and a Bud 1952 d: Khwaya Ahmad Abbas. lps: Dev Anand, Balraj Sahni, Nalini Jaywant. 139M IND. prod/rel: Naya Sansar

ANANTHAMURTHY, U. R. (1932–, IND, Anantha Murthy, Udipi R.
Bara, Story
 Bara 1981 d: M. S. Sathyu. lps: Anant Nag, Lavlin Madhu, Nitin Sethi. 135M IND. *The Famine; Sookha; The Arid Earth; The Drought; Dushkal*
Samskara, 1966, Novel
 Samskara 1970 d: Pattabhi Rama Reddy. lps: Girish Karnad, Snehalata Reddy, P. Lankesh. 113M IND. *Funeral Rites; Last Rites* prod/rel: Ramamanohara Chitra

ANDAM, F. D.
..Und Wer Kusst Mich?, Novel
 Ragazza Dal Livido Azzurro, La 1933 d: E. W. Emo. lps: Hilda Springher, Sergio Tofano, Renato Cialente. 65M ITL. *La Signorina Dal Livido Azzurro* prod/rel: Persic, Itala

ANDERBERG, BENGT
Story
 Svara Provningen, Den 1969 d: Torgny Wickman. lps: Jarl Borssen, Diana Kjaer, Margit Carlqvist. 83M SWD. prod/rel: Swedish Film Investment

ANDERS, KAREL
Novel
 Kariera Matky Lizalky 1937 d: Ladislav Brom. lps: Antonie Nedosinska, Theodor Pistek, Eva GerovA. 2822m CZC. *The Career of Mother Lizalka* prod/rel: Reiter

ANDERSCH, ALFRED
Die Rote, 1960, Novel
 Rote, Die 1962 d: Helmut Kautner. lps: Ruth Leuwerik, Rossano Brazzi, Giorgio Albertazzi. 100M GRM/ITL. *La Rossa* (ITL); *The Redhead* (USA) prod/rel: Magid Film, Compagnia Cin.Ca Champion (Roma)
Winterspelt, 1974, Novel
 Winterspelt 1944 1977 d: Eberhard Fechner. lps: Ulrich von Dobschutz, Katharina Thalbach, Hans Christian Blech. 110M GRM. *Winterspelt* prod/rel: Ullstein Av, S.F.B.
Zanzibar, Novel
 Sansibar Oder Der Letzte Grund 1986 d: Bernhard Wicki. lps: Peter Kremer, Cornelia Schmaus, Gisela Stein. MTV. 163M GRM/GDR. *Zanzibar*

ANDERSEN, BENNY
Orfeus I Undergrunden, 1979, Play
 Danmark Er Lukket 1981 d: Dan TscherniA. lps: Christoffer Bro, Anne Linnet, Ove Sprogoe. 91M DNM. *Denmark Is Closed*
Svantes Viser, 1972, Verse
 Da Svante Forsvandt 1975 d: Henning Carlsen. lps: Poul Dissing, Benny E. Andersen, Fritze Hedemann. 87M DNM. *When Svante Disappeared*

ANDERSEN, CHRISTOPHER
Madonna: Unauthorized, Book
 Madonna: Innocence Lost 1994 d: Bradford May. lps: Terumi Matthews, Wendie Malick, Jeff Yagher. TVM. 87M USA.

ANDERSEN, HANS CHRISTIAN (1805–1875), DNM
Story
 Angelo Del Miracolo, L' 1945 d: Piero Ballerini. lps: Emma Gramatica, Attilio Dottesio, Milena Penovich. F ITL. prod/rel: Vittoria Film (Venezia)
Short Story
 Emperor's New Clothes, The 1987 d: David Irving. lps: Robert Morse, Jason Carter, Lysette Anthony. 80M USA. *Cannon Movie Tales: the Emperor's New Clothes* prod/rel: Cannon
Autobiography
 Mr. H. C. Andersen 1950 d: Ronald Haines. lps: Ashley Glynne, Constance Lewis, Terence Noble. 62M UKN. *Hans Christian Andersen* (USA) prod/rel: British Foundation
Short Story
 Roi Et l'Oiseau, Le 1979 d: Paul Grimault. ANM. 84M FRN. *The King and the Bird; The King and Mister Bird; Mister Bird to the Rescue* prod/rel: Les Films Paul Grimault, Les Films Gibe
Short Stories
 Stories from a Flying Trunk 1980 d: Christine Edzard. lps: Murray Melvin, Ann Firbank, Tasneem Maqsood. 87M UKN. prod/rel: Emi, Sands
Fyrtojet, Copenhagen 1835, Short Story
 Der Kom En Soldat 1969 d: Peer Guldbrandsen. lps: Willy Rathnov, Hanne Borchsenius, Poul Bundgaard. 98M DNM. *The Tinderbox Or the Story of a Lighter; Scandal in Denmark* (USA) prod/rel: Novaris Film
 Feuerzeug, Das 1959 d: Siegfried Hartmann. lps: Rolf Ludwig, Bella Waldritter, Hannes Fischer. 81M GDR. *The Tinder Box* (USA) prod/rel: Defa
 Fyrtojet 1946 d: Allan Johnsen, Sven Methling. ANM. 73M DNM. *Magic Lighter* (USA); *The Tinder Box*
Der Grimme Aelling, 1844, Short Story
 Udiwitjelnaja Istorija, Pochoshaja Na Skasku 1966 d: Boris Dolin. lps: O. Schakov, J. Maklanschin, Sascha Chotojewitsch. 68M USS. *Udivitel'naja Istozijz Pokhozhaja Na Skazhu* prod/rel: Film Studio Mosnautschfilm
Histoiren Om En Moder, 1848, Short Story
 Historien Om En Moder 1979 d: Claus Weeke. lps: Anna Karina, Tove Maes, Bodil Udsen. 21M DNM. *Story of a Mother*
Den Lille Haufrue, 1837, Short Story
 Little Mermaid, The 1989 d: John Musker, Ron Clements. ANM. 82M USA. prod/rel: Buena Vista, Disney
 Mala Morska Vila 1975 d: Karel KachynA. lps: Miroslava Safrankova, Radovan Lukavsky, Marie RosulkovA. 104M CZC. *The Little Mermaid; The Little Sea Nymph; Mal Morska Vila* prod/rel: Filmstudio Barrandov
 Rusalochka 1976 d: Vladimir Bychkov. 82M USS/BUL. *Malkata Roussalka; The Little Mermaid; Rusalotchka*
Den Lille Pige Med Svovlstikkerne, 1846, Short Story
 Fetita Cu Chibrituri 1967 d: Aurel Miheles. lps: Ana Szeles. 18M RMN. *Match Girl; The Little Match Girl*
 Lille Pige Med Svovlstikkerne, Den 1953 d: Johan Jacobsen. 14M DNM. *The Little Match Girl*

 Little Match Girl, The 1914 d: Percy Nash?. lps: John East. 500f UKN. prod/rel: Neptune, Browne
 Little Match Girl, The 1983 d: Wally Broodbent, Mark Hoeger. lps: Nancy Duncan, Dan Hays, Matt McKim. USA.
 Little Match Girl, The 1987 d: Michael Constance. lps: Twiggy, Roger Daltrey, Natalie Morse. TVM. 90M UKN.
 Little Match Girl, The 1987 d: Michael Lindsay-Hogg. lps: Keshia Knight Pulliam, William Daniels, John Rhys-Davies. TVM. 100M USA.
 Madchen Mit Den Schwefelholzern, Das 1953 d: Fritz Genschow. lps: Johanna Wichmann, Fritz Genschow, Sabine Eggerth. 38M GRM. prod/rel: Europaische Television, Jugendfilm
 Petite Marchande d'Allumettes, La 1928 d: Jean Renoir, Jean Tedesco. lps: Catherine Hessling, Manuel Rabinovitch, Amy Wells. 1500m FRN. *La Petite Fille aux Allumettes; The Little Match Girl* prod/rel: Jean Renoir, Jean Tedesco
Nattergalen, 1844, Short Story
 Cisaruv Slavik 1948 d: Jiri Trnka, Milos Makovec. ANM. 68M CZC. *The Emperor and the Nightingale; The Emperor's Nightingale* prod/rel: Loutkovy
Prinsessen Pa Aerten, 1835, Short Story
 Princess and the Pea, The 1979 d: Keith Goddard. 10M UKN.
 Princess and the Pea, The 1983 d: Tony Bill. lps: Liza Minnelli, Tom Conti, Nancy Allen. MTV. 60M USA.
 Printzessa Na Goroshine 1976 d: Boris Rytsarev. 89M USS.
 Prinzessa Na Goroschine 1976 d: Boris Ryazarev. lps: Andrej Podoschian, Irina Jurewitsch, Irina MalyschewA. 91M USS. prod/rel: Gorki-Studio
 Svinedrengen Og Prinsessen Pa Aerten 1962 d: Poul Ilsoe. ANM. 50M DNM.
De Rode Skoe, 1845, Short Story
 Red Shoes, The 1948 d: Michael Powell, Emeric Pressburger. lps: Anton Walbrook, Moira Goring, Moira Shearer. 134M UKN. prod/rel: General Film Distributors, the Archers
The Seven Swans, Short Story
 Seven Swans, The 1918 d: J. Searle Dawley. lps: Marguerite Clark, Richard Barthelmess, William Danforth. 5r USA. prod/rel: Famous Players Film Co.©, Paramount Pictures Corp.
Skyggen, 1847, Short Story
 Shadow, The 1976 d: Don Ham. 27M USA.
Snedronningen, 1845, Short Story
 Lumikuningatar 1986 d: Paivi Hartzell. lps: Satu Silvo, Outi Vainionkulma, Sebastian Kaatrasalo. 88M FNL. *The Snow Queen* prod/rel: Neofilmi Oy
 Snyezhnaya Korolyeva 1967 d: Gennadi Kazansky. lps: Valeri Nikitenko, Lena Proklova, Slava TsyupA. 85M USS. *The Snow Queen; Snezhnaya Koroleva; Snejnaia Koroleva*
Den Standhaftige Tinsoldat, 1838, Short Story
 Petit Soldat, Le 1947 d: Paul Grimault. ANM. 11M FRN. *The Little Soldier*
 Petite Parade, La 1930 d: Ladislas Starevitch. lps: Nina Star. 1480f FRN. *The Little Parade* (USA)
Svinedrengen, 1842, Short Story
 Prinzessin Und Der Schweinehirt, Die 1953 d: Herbert B. Fredersdorf. lps: Liane Croon, Dieter Ansbach, Victor Janson. 81M GRM. *The Princess and the Swineherd* prod/rel: Infa, Jugendfilm
 Svinopas 1941 d: Alexander MacHeret. 24M USS.
Tommelise, 1835, Short Story
 Oyayubime 19— d: Yugo SerikawA. ANM. 65M JPN. *Thumbelina* prod/rel: Toei Animation Co.
 Thumbelina 1970 d: Barry Mahon. lps: Shay Garner, Pat Morell, Bob O'Connell. 62M USA. prod/rel: Cinetron Corp.
De Vilde Svaner, 1838, Short Story
 Dikie Lebedi 1988 d: Helle Karis. 86M USS.

ANDERSON, DAVID WOLF
A Tale of the Flatwoods Blue Moon, Indianapolis 1919, Novel
 Blue Moon, The 1920 d: George L. Cox. lps: Pell Trenton, Elinor Field, Harry Northrup. 6r USA. prod/rel: American Film Co.©, Pathe Exchange, Inc.

ANDERSON, EDWARD
Thieves Like Us, 1937, Novel
 They Live By Night 1948 d: Nicholas Ray. lps: Farley Granger, Cathy O'Donnell, Howard Da SilvA. 95M USA. *The Twisted Road; Your Red Wagon* prod/rel: RKO Radio
 Thieves Like Us 1973 d: Robert Altman. lps: Keith Carradine, Shelley Duvall, John Schuck. 122M USA. prod/rel: United Artists

ANDERSON, FREDERICK IRVING
Short Stories
Return of Sophie Lang, The 1936 d: George Archainbaud. lps: Gertrude Michael, Guy Standing, Ray Milland. 68M USA. prod/rel: Paramount Productions©

Golden Fleece, 1918, Short Story
Golden Fleece, The 1918 d: G. P. Hamilton. lps: Joe Bennett, Peggy Pearce, Jack Curtis. 5r USA. prod/rel: Triangle Film Corp., Triangle Distributing Corp.

The Notorious Sophie Lang, London 1925, Novel
Notorious Sophie Lang, The 1934 d: Ralph Murphy. lps: Gertrude Michael, Paul Cavanagh, Alison Skipworth. 64M USA. prod/rel: Paramount Productions©

ANDERSON, JANE
The Baby Dance, Play
Baby Dance, The 1998 d: Jane Anderson. lps: Laura Dern, Stockard Channing, Peter Riegert. TVM. 95M USA. prod/rel: Egg Pictures, Pacific Motion Pictures

ANDERSON, MAXWELL (1888–1959), USA
Anne of the Thousand Days, New York 1948, Play
Anne of the Thousand Days 1969 d: Charles Jarrott. lps: Richard Burton, Genevieve Bujold, Irene Papas. 146M UKN. *Anne of a Thousand Days* prod/rel: Rank Film Distributors, Universal

The Devil's Hornpipe, Unproduced, Play
Never Steal Anything Small 1959 d: Charles Lederer. lps: James Cagney, Shirley Jones, Roger Smith. 115M USA. prod/rel: Universal-International

Elizabeth the Queen, New York 1930, Play
Private Lives of Elizabeth and Essex, The 1939 d: Michael Curtiz. lps: Bette Davis, Errol Flynn, Olivia de Havilland. 106M USA. *Elizabeth the Queen; Elizabeth and Essex; The Knight and the Lady* prod/rel: Warner Bros. Pictures©

The Eve of St. Mark, 1942, Play
Eve of St. Mark, The 1944 d: John M. Stahl. lps: Anne Baxter, William Eythe, Michael O'SheA. 96M USA. prod/rel: 20th Century-Fox

Joan of Lorraine, New York 1946, Play
Joan of Arc 1948 d: Victor Fleming. lps: Ingrid Bergman, Jose Ferrer, Francis L. Sullivan. 145M USA. prod/rel: RKO Radio

Key Largo, 1939, Play
Key Largo 1948 d: John Huston. lps: Edward G. Robinson, Claire Trevor, Humphrey Bogart. 101M USA. prod/rel: Warner Bros.

Knickerbocker Holiday, New York 1938, Musical Play
Knickerbocker Holiday 1944 d: Harry J. Brown. lps: Nelson Eddy, Charles Coburn, Constance Dowling. 85M USA. prod/rel: United Artists

Mary of Scotland, New York 1933, Play
Mary of Scotland 1936 d: John Ford. lps: Katharine Hepburn, Fredric March, Florence Eldridge. 123M USA. prod/rel: RKO Radio Pictures©

Saturday's Children, New York 1927, Play
Maybe It's Love 1935 d: William McGann. lps: Gloria Stuart, Ross Alexander, Frank McHugh. 69M USA. *Halfway to Heaven* prod/rel: First National Productions Corp., Warner Bros. Pictures©
Saturday's Children 1929 d: Gregory La CavA. lps: Corinne Griffith, Grant Withers, Albert Conti. 7920f USA. prod/rel: First National Pictures, Walter Morosco Productions
Saturday's Children 1940 d: Vincent Sherman. lps: John Garfield, Anne Shirley, Claude Rains. 101M USA. *Married Pretty and Poor* prod/rel: Warner Bros. Pictures©
Saturday's Children 1950. lps: John Ericson, Joan Caulfield. MTV. USA. prod/rel: Lux Video Theatre
Saturday's Children 1952. lps: Shirley Standee, Mickey Rooney. MTV. USA. prod/rel: Celanese Theater
Saturday's Children 1962 d: Leland Hayward. lps: Cliff Robertson, Inger Stevens. MTV. USA.

The Story of Christopher Emmanuel Balestrero, Book
Wrong Man, The 1957 d: Alfred Hitchcock. lps: Henry Fonda, Vera Miles, Anthony Quayle. 105M USA. prod/rel: Warner Bros.

Tropical Twins, Play
Cock-Eyed World, The 1929 d: Raoul Walsh. lps: Victor McLaglen, Edmund Lowe, Lili DamitA. 115M USA. prod/rel: Fox Film Corp.

What Price Glory, New York 1924, Play
What Price Glory 1926 d: Raoul Walsh. lps: Victor McLaglen, Edmund Lowe, Dolores Del Rio. 12r USA. prod/rel: Fox Film Corp.
What Price Glory 1952 d: John Ford. lps: James Cagney, Dan Dailey, Corinne Calvet. 111M USA. prod/rel: 20th Century-Fox

Winterset, New York 1935, Play
Winterset 1936 d: Alfred Santell. lps: Burgess Meredith, Margo, Eduardo Ciannelli. 78M USA. prod/rel: RKO Radio Pictures©, Pandro S. Berman Production
Winterset 1951. lps: Richard Carlyle, Eduardo Ciannelli. MTV. USA. prod/rel: ABC
Winterset 1959. lps: Don Murray, Piper Laurie, George C. Scott. MTV. USA. prod/rel: NBC, Hallmark Hall of Fame

ANDERSON, PATRICK
The President's Mistress, Novel
President's Mistress, The 1978 d: John Llewellyn Moxey. lps: Beau Bridges, Susan Blanchard, Joel Fabiani. TVM. 100M USA. prod/rel: Stephen Friedman/Kings Road Production

ANDERSON, PEGGY
Nurse, Book
Nurse 1980 d: David Lowell Rich. lps: Michael Learned, Robert Reed, Tom Aldredge. TVM. 105M USA.

ANDERSON, ROBERT
Silent Night Lonely Night, Play
Silent Night, Lonely Night 1969 d: Daniel Petrie. lps: Lloyd Bridges, Shirley Jones, Lynn Carlin. TVM. 100M USA. prod/rel: Universal

Unfaithful, Book
Unfaithful 1992 d: Steven Schachter. lps: Tom Skerritt, Blythe Danner, Roma Downey. TVM. 89M USA. *Getting Up and Going Home* prod/rel: Hearst Entertainment Prods.©, the Polone Company

ANDERSON, ROBERT WOODRUFF (1917–, USA, Anderson, Robert W.
I Never Sang for My Father, New York 1968, Play
I Never Sang for My Father 1970 d: Gilbert Cates. lps: Melvyn Douglas, Gene Hackman, Estelle Parsons. 92M USA. *Strangers* prod/rel: Jamel Productions

Tea and Sympathy, New York 1953, Play
Tea and Sympathy 1956 d: Vincente Minnelli. lps: Deborah Kerr, John Kerr, Leif Erickson. 122M USA. prod/rel: MGM

ANDERSON, SHERWOOD (1876–1941), USA
I'm a Fool, 1923, Short Story
I'm a Fool 1977 d: Noel Black. lps: Ron Howard, Santiago Gonzalez. MTV. 36M USA. prod/rel: Learning in Focus

ANDERSON, VERILY
Beware of Children, London 1958, Novel
No Kidding 1960 d: Gerald Thomas. lps: Leslie Phillips, Geraldine McEwan, Julia Lockwood. 87M UKN. *Beware of Children* (USA) prod/rel: Gregory, Hake & Walker, Anglo-Amalgamated

ANDERSON, WILL
Take It from Me, Play
Take It from Me 1926 d: William A. Seiter. lps: Reginald Denny, Blanche Mehaffey, Ben Hendricks Jr. 6649f USA. prod/rel: Universal Pictures

ANDERSON, WILLIAM C.
*Bat*21*, Book
Bat*21 1988 d: Peter Markle. lps: Gene Hackman, Danny Glover, Jerry Reed. 105M USA. *Bat.21* prod/rel: Tri-Star

Hurricane Hunters, Novel
Hurricane 1974 d: Jerry Jameson. lps: Larry Hagman, Martin Milner, Jessica Walter. TVM. 78M USA. prod/rel: Metromedia Productions

ANDOM, R.
We Three and Troddles, Novel
Four Men in a Van 1921 d: Hugh Croise. lps: Manning Haynes, Donald Searle, Johnny Butt. 7000f UKN. prod/rel: Direct Film Traders, Titan

ANDRADE, JORGE
Vereda Da Salvacao, 1965, Play
Vereda Da Salvacao 1965 d: Anselmo Duarte. lps: Raul Cortez, Jose Parisi, Lelia Abramo. 100M BRZ. *Salvation Road; Path of Salvation* prod/rel: Anselmo Duarte

ANDRE, MICHEL
Play
Virginie 1962 d: Jean Boyer. lps: Roger Pierre, Michele Girardon, Mireille Darc. 73M FRN. prod/rel: Films Corona, Films de la Pleiade

ANDREAS, FRED
Einer Zuviel an Bord, Novel
Einer Zuviel an Bord 1935 d: Gerhard Lamprecht. lps: Albrecht Schoenhals, Lida Baarova, Ernst Karchow. 83M GRM. prod/rel: Universum-Film, Transit

Die Gelbe Flagge, Novel
Gelbe Flagge, Die 1937 d: Gerhard Lamprecht. lps: Hans Albers, Dorothea Wieck, Olga TschechowA. 93M GRM. prod/rel: Euphono, Panorama

Das Gesetz Der Liebe, Novel
Gesetz Der Liebe, Das 1945 d: Hans Schweikart. lps: Hilde Krahl, Ferdinand Marian, Paul Hubschmid. 96M GRM. *Law of Love* prod/rel: Bavaria, Union

Die Hexe, Novel
Hexe, Die 1954 d: Gustav Ucicky. lps: Anita Bjorg, Karlheinz Bohm, Attila Horbiger. 97M GRM. *The Witch* prod/rel: Capitol, Prisma

Un Homme de Trop a Bord, Novel
Homme de Trop a Bord, Un 1935 d: Roger Le Bon, Gerhard Lamprecht. lps: Thomy Bourdelle, Jacques Dumesnil, Annie Ducaux. 80M FRN. prod/rel: U.F.a., a.C.E.

Ein Mann Will Nach Deutschland, Novel
Mann Will Nach Deutschland, Ein 1934 d: Paul Wegener. lps: Karl Ludwig Diehl, Brigitte Horney, Siegfried Schurenberg. 97M GRM. *Ein Mann Will in Die Heimat* prod/rel: UFA

Die Sache Mit Schorrsiegel, Novel
Sache Mit Schorrsiegel, Die 1928 d: Jaap Speyer. lps: Walter Rilla, Anita Dorris, Ernst Prockl. 2659m GRM. *Conscience* prod/rel: Terra-Film

Das Schone Fraulein Schragg, Novel
Schone Fraulein Schragg, Das 1937 d: Hans Deppe. lps: Hansi Knoteck, Paul Klinger, Otto Gebuhr. 97M GRM. prod/rel: Tonlicht

ANDREOTA, PAUL
Les Suspects, Novel
Suspects, Les 1974 d: Michel Wyn. lps: Mimsy Farmer, Paul Meurisse, Michel Bouquet. 90M FRN. *La Polizia Indaga: Siamo Tutti Sospettati* (ITL); *La Pieuvre* prod/rel: Cite, Telecip

ANDREWS, CHARLTON
Ladies' Night in a Turkish Bath, Play
Ladies' Night in a Turkish Bath 1928 d: Eddie Cline. lps: Dorothy MacKaill, Jack Mulhall, Sylvia Ashton. 6592f USA. *Ladies' Night* (UKN) prod/rel: Asher-Small-Rogers, First National Pictures

ANDREWS, CLARENCE EDWARD
Innocents of Paris, New York 1928, Novel
Innocents of Paris 1929 d: Richard Wallace. lps: Maurice Chevalier, Sylvia Beecher, Russell Simpson. 69M USA. prod/rel: Paramount Famous Lasky Corp.

ANDREWS, DAISY H.
Drifting, New York 1910, Play
Drifting 1923 d: Tod Browning. lps: Priscilla Dean, Matt Moore, Wallace Beery. 7394f USA. prod/rel: Universal Pictures
Shanghai Lady 1929 d: John S. Robertson. lps: Mary Nolan, James Murray, Lydia Yeamans Titus. 5926f USA. *The Girl from China* (UKN) prod/rel: Universal Pictures

ANDREWS, MARY RAYMOND SHIPMAN
The Courage of the Commonplace, New York 1911, Novel
Courage of the Commonplace, The 1917 d: Ben Turbett. lps: Leslie Austen, William Calhoun, Mildred Havens. 4620f USA. prod/rel: Thomas A. Edison, Inc.©, Perfection Pictures

The Three Things, Boston 1915, Novel
Unbeliever, The 1918 d: Alan Crosland. lps: Raymond McKee, Marguerite Courtot, Kate Lester. 6468f USA. prod/rel: Thomas A. Edison, Inc.©, Perfection Pictures

ANDREWS, ROBERT D.
Story
Mayor of 44th Street 1942 d: Alfred E. Green. lps: George Murphy, Anne Shirley, Richard Barthelmess. 86M USA. prod/rel: RKO

Three Girls Lost, 1930, Story
Three Girls Lost 1931 d: Sidney Lanfield. lps: Loretta Young, John Wayne, Lew Cody. 72M USA. prod/rel: Fox Film Corp.©, Sidney Lanfield Production

Windfall, New York 1931, Novel
If I Had a Million 1932 d: Stephen Roberts, James Cruze. lps: Gary Cooper, George Raft, Mary Boland. 88M USA. prod/rel: Paramount Publix Corp.©

ANDREWS, ROBERT HARDY
Story
King's Thief, The 1955 d: Robert Z. Leonard. lps: Edmund Purdom, David Niven, George Sanders. 78M USA. prod/rel: MGM
Wyoming Mail 1950 d: Reginald Le Borg. lps: Stephen McNally, Alexis Smith, Howard Da SilvA. 87M USA. prod/rel: Universal-International

Great Day in the Morning, 1950, Novel
Great Day in the Morning 1956 d: Jacques Tourneur. lps: Virginia Mayo, Robert Stack, Ruth Roman. 92M USA. prod/rel: RKO Radio, Edmund Grainger Prods.

Kid from Texas, Novel
Kid from Texas, The 1950 d: Kurt Neumann. lps: Audie Murphy, Gale Storm, Albert Dekker. 78M USA. *Texas Kid -Outlaw* (UKN) prod/rel: Universal-International

ANDREWS, STANLEY
Story
Pigeon, The 1969 d: Earl Bellamy. lps: Sammy Davis Jr., Dorothy Malone, Victoria Vetri. TVM. 74M USA. prod/rel: Thomas/Spelling Productions

ANDREWS, VIRGINIA (1924–1986), USA
Flowers in the Attic, Novel
Flowers in the Attic 1987 d: Jeffrey Bloom. lps: Louise Fletcher, Victoria Tennant, Kristy Swanson. 92M USA. prod/rel: New World

ANDREYEV, LEONID NIKOLAEVICH (1871–1919), RSS
Kto Poluchaet Poshchechiny Tot, Play
He Who Gets Slapped 1924 d: Victor Sjostrom. lps: Lon Chaney, Norma Shearer, John Gilbert. 6953f USA. prod/rel: Metro-Goldwyn-Mayer Corp., Metro-Goldwyn Distributing Corp.

ANDRIC, IVO (1892–1975), SRB
Anikina Vremena, 1931, Short Story
Anikina Vremena 1954 d: Vladimir Pogacic. lps: Milena Dapcevic, Bratislav Grbic, Ljubinka Bobic. 97M YGS. *Legends About Anika*
Gospodica, 1945, Novel
Gospodjica 1980 d: Vojtech Jasny. lps: Heidelide Weiss, Rade Serbedzija, Jelisaveta Sablic. 110M YGS/GRM. *Das Fraulein; The Maiden; Gospodica; Young Lady*
Zeko, 1948, Short Story
I to Ce Proci 1985 d: Nenad Dizdarevic. lps: Fabijan Sovagovic, Olivera Markovic, Velimir Zivojinovic. 99M YGS. *That to Will Pass; It Will Pass Also*

ANDRIS, COLETTE
Le Danseuse Nue, Novel
Danseuse Nue, La 1952 d: Pierre-Louis. lps: Catherine Erard, Jean Debucourt, Pierre Larquey. 105M FRN. prod/rel: Compagnie Francaise De Prod. Cinematogr.

ANDRZEJEWSKI, JERZY (1909–1983), PLN
Bramu Raju, 1960, Novel
Vrata Raja 1967 d: Andrzej WajdA. lps: Lionel Stander, Ferdy Mayne, Mathieu Carriere. 89M UKN/YGS. *Bramy Raju* (YGS); *Gates to Paradise; Gates of Paradise* prod/rel: Jointex
Popiol I Diament, 1948, Novel
Popiol I Diament 1958 d: Andrzej WajdA. lps: Zbigniew Cybulski, Ewa Krzyzewska, Adam Pawlikowski. 105M PLN. *Ashes and Diamonds* (UKN) prod/rel: Kadr Film Unit, Film Polski

ANET, CLAUDE
Ariane, Novel
Ariane 1931 d: Paul Czinner. lps: Elisabeth Bergner, Rudolf Forster, Annemarie Steinsieck. 85M GRM. prod/rel: Nero
Ariane 1931 d: Paul Czinner. lps: Elisabeth Bergner, Percy Marmont, Oriel Ross. 70M UKN. *The Loves of Ariane* prod/rel: Nerofilm, Pathe Natan
Love in the Afternoon 1957 d: Billy Wilder. lps: Audrey Hepburn, Maurice Chevalier, Gary Cooper. 130M USA. *Fascination* prod/rel: Allied Artists
Ariane, Jeune Fille Russe 1931 d: Paul Czinner. lps: Gaby Morlay, Victor Francen, Jean Dax. 85M FRN. prod/rel: Pathe-Nathan
La Fin d'une Idylle, Novel
Mayerling 1936 d: Anatole Litvak. lps: Danielle Darrieux, Charles Boyer, Jean Dax. 101M FRN. prod/rel: Concordia Production Cinematographique
Mayerling, Paris 1931, Book
Mayerling 1968 d: Terence Young. lps: Omar Sharif, Catherine Deneuve, James Mason. 141M UKN/FRN. prod/rel: Les Films Corona, Winchester Film Production

ANGEL, WALTER
Manege, Novel
Manege 1927 d: Max Reichmann. lps: Raimondo Van Riel, Ernest Van Duren, Kurt Gerron. 2799m GRM. prod/rel: Deutsche Film-Union Ag

ANGELOTTI, MARION POLK
The Firefly of France, New York 1918, Novel
Firefly of France, The 1918 d: Donald Crisp. lps: Wallace Reid, Anna Little, Charles Ogle. 5r USA. prod/rel: Famous Players-Lasky Corp.©, Paramount Pictures

ANGELOU, MAYA (1928–, USA, Johnson, Marguerite
I Know Why the Caged Bird Sings, 1969, Autobiography
I Know Why the Caged Bird Sings 1979 d: Fielder Cook. lps: Diahann Carroll, Constance Good, Ruby Dee. TVM. 100M USA. prod/rel: Tomorrow Entertainment

ANGERMAYER, FRED A.
Strich Durch Die Rechnung, Play
Rivaux de la Piste 1932 d: Serge de Poligny. lps: Albert Prejean, Jim Gerald, Suzet Mais. 98M FRN. prod/rel: U.F.a., a.CE.

ANGOT, MICHELE
Amelie Boule, Novel
Amelie Ou le Temps d'Aimer 1961 d: Michel Drach. lps: Marie-Jose Nat, Jean Sorel, Clotilde Joano. 110M FRN. *Amelia Or the Time for Love; Amelie; A Time to Die* prod/rel: Port-Royal Films, Indus Films

ANGUS, BERNADINE
Angel Island, Play
Fog Island 1945 d: Terry O. Morse. lps: George Zucco, Lionel Atwill, Jerome Cowan. 72M USA. prod/rel: Universal

ANHALT, EDNA
Quarantine, Short Story
Panic in the Streets 1950 d: Elia Kazan. lps: Richard Widmark, Paul Douglas, Barbara Bel Geddes. 96M USA. prod/rel: 20th Century-Fox
Some Like 'Em Cold, Short Story
Panic in the Streets 1950 d: Elia Kazan. lps: Richard Widmark, Paul Douglas, Barbara Bel Geddes. 96M USA. prod/rel: 20th Century-Fox

ANHALT, EDWARD
Quarantine, Short Story
Panic in the Streets 1950 d: Elia Kazan. lps: Richard Widmark, Paul Douglas, Barbara Bel Geddes. 96M USA. prod/rel: 20th Century-Fox
Some Like 'Em Cold, Short Story
Panic in the Streets 1950 d: Elia Kazan. lps: Richard Widmark, Paul Douglas, Barbara Bel Geddes. 96M USA. prod/rel: 20th Century-Fox

ANICET-BOURGEOIS, A.
La Signora Di Saint Tropez, Play
Appassionatamente 1954 d: Giacomo Gentilomo. lps: Amedeo Nazzari, Myriam Bru, Isa BarzizzA. 102M ITL. prod/rel: Rizzoli Film, Dear Film

ANNADURAI, C. N.
Velaikkari, Play
Velaikkari 1949 d: A. S. A. Sami. lps: K. R. Ramaswamy, M. N. Nambiar, T. S. Baliah. 186M IND. *Maid Servant* prod/rel: Jupiter Pictures

ANNESLEY, MAUDE
Wind Along the Waste, New York 1910, Novel
Shattered Dreams 1922 d: Paul Scardon. lps: Miss Du Pont, Bertram Grassby, Herbert Heyes. 4878f USA. *Clay* prod/rel: Universal Film Mfg. Co.
The Wine of Life, Novel
Wine of Life, The 1924 d: Arthur Rooke. lps: Betty Carter, Clive Brook, James Carew. 5600f UKN. prod/rel: Stoll

ANNIXTER, PAUL
Swiftwater, New York 1950, Novel
Those Calloways 1965 d: Norman Tokar. lps: Brian Keith, Vera Miles, Brandon de Wilde. 131M USA. *Those Crazy Calloways* prod/rel: Walt Disney Productions, Buena Vista

ANON
Beowulf, c750, Verse
Beowulf 1976 d: Don Fairservice. 60M UKN.
Le Chanson de Roland, c1125, Verse
Chanson de Roland, La 1979 d: Frank Cassenti. lps: Klaus Kinski, Alain Cuny, Pierre Clementi. 110M FRN.
Elckerlijc, c1485, Play
Elckerlyc 1975 d: Jos Stelling. lps: George Bruens, Lucie Singeling, Geert Tijssens. 94M NTH. *Everyman; Elckerlijc*
Lazarillo de Tormes, 1554, Novel
Lazarillo de Tormes, El 1925 d: Florian Rey. lps: Alfredo Hurtado, Manuel Montenegro, Carmen Viance. 71M SPN. *The Blindman's Guide to Tormes* prod/rel: Atlantida
Lazarillo de Tormes, El 1959 d: Cesar Ardavin. lps: Marco Paoletti, Juanjo Menendez, Carlos CasaravillA. 109M SPN. *Lazarillo* (USA); *Lazzarillo de Tomes; The Blind Man's Guide to Tormes* prod/rel: Hesperia Films
Maria Marten, London 1840, Play
Maria Marten 1928 d: Walter West. lps: Trilby Clark, Warwick Ward, James Knight. 7430f UKN. prod/rel: QTS, Ideal
Maria Marten; Or, the Murder at the Red Barn 1902 d: Dicky Winslow. lps: A. W. Fitzgerald, Mrs. Fitzgerald. 400f UKN. prod/rel: Harrison
Maria Marten; Or, the Murder at the Red Barn 1913 d: Maurice Elvey. lps: Elisabeth Risdon, Fred Groves, Douglas Payne. 2850f UKN. prod/rel: Motograph

Maria Marten; Or, the Murder in the Red Barn 1935 d: Milton Rosmer. lps: Tod Slaughter, Sophie Stewart, Eric Portman. 67M UKN. *Murder in the Old Red Barn* (USA); *Maria Marten* prod/rel: George King, MGM
Mariken Van Nieumeghen, c1485-1510, Play
Mariken Van Nieumeghen 1974 d: Jos Stelling. lps: Ronni Montagne, Sander Bals, Lucie Singeling. 83M NTH. *Mariken from Nijmegen*
Sir Gawain and the Green Knight, c1375, Verse
Gawain and the Green Knight 1973 d: Stephen Weeks. lps: Murray Head, Ciaran Madden, Nigel Green. 93M UKN. prod/rel: United Artists, Sancrest

ANOUILH, JEAN (1910–1987), FRN
Becket Ou l'Honneur de Dieu, 1959, Play
Becket 1964 d: Peter Glenville. lps: Richard Burton, Peter O'Toole, John Gielgud. 165M UKN. prod/rel: Paramount Film Service, Keep Films
Ornifle; Ou le Courant d'Air, 1956, Play
Ornifle Oder Erzurnte Himmel 1972 d: Helmut Kautner. 113M GRM.
Le Rendez-Vous de Senlis, Play
Quartieri Alti 1944 d: Mario Soldati. lps: Adriana Benetti, Nerio Bernardi, Enzo Biliotti. 82M ITL. prod/rel: Industrie Cin.Che Italiane
Romeo Et Jeannette, 1946, Play
Monsoon 1953 d: Rod Amateau. lps: Ursula Thiess, Diana Douglas, George Nader. 79M USA/IND. prod/rel: United Artists, C.F.G. (Films) Ltd.
La Valse Des Toreadors, Paris 1952, Play
Waltz of the Toreadors 1962 d: John Guillermin. lps: Peter Sellers, Dany Robin, John Fraser. 104M UKN. *The Amorous General* prod/rel: Independent Artists, Rank Film Distributors
Le Voyageur Sans Bagage, 1936, Play
Voyageur Sans Bagages, Le 1943 d: Jean Anouilh. lps: Pierre Fresnay, Blanchette Brunoy, Marguerite Deval. 99M FRN. prod/rel: Eclair-Journal

ANSARIAN, MAHNAZ
Story
Leila 1998 d: Dariush Mehrjui. lps: Leila Hatami, Ali Mosaffa, Jamileh Sheikhi. 124M IRN. prod/rel: Farazmand Film, Hubert Bals Fund, Rotterdam

AN-SKI, SOLOMON
Der Dibuk, 1916, Play
Dybbuk 1937 d: Michael Waszynski. lps: Leon Liebgold, Lili Liliana, Max Bozyk. 125M PLN. *The Dybbuk*
Hadybbuk 1968 d: Ilan Eldad, Shraga Friedman. lps: David Opatoshu, Tina Wodetzky, Tutte Lemkow. 90M ISR/GRM. *The Dybbuk; Between Two Worlds*

ANSON, HARRIS
Mary Keep Your Feet Still, Short Story
Her Soul's Inspiration 1917 d: Jack Conway. lps: Ella Hall, Marc Robbins, R. Hasset Ryan. 5r USA. *Mary Keep Your Feet Still* prod/rel: Bluebird Photoplays, Inc.©

ANSON, JAY (1924–1980), USA
Book
Amityville Horror, The 1979 d: Stuart Rosenberg. lps: James Brolin, Margot Kidder, Rod Steiger. 126M USA. prod/rel: Cinema 77

ANSPACHER, LOUIS K.
The Embarrassment of Riches, New York 1906, Play
Embarrassment of Riches, The 1918 d: Eddie Dillon. lps: Lillian Walker, Carleton Brickett, Henry Sedley. 5r USA. prod/rel: Lillian Walker Pictures Corp., W. W. Hodkinson Corp.
The Unchastened Woman, New York 1915, Play
Unchastened Woman, The 1918 d: William Humphrey. lps: Grace Valentine, Frank Mills, Victor Sutherland. 7r USA. *Two Men and a Woman(?)* prod/rel: Rialto de Luxe Productions, Perfection Pictures
Unchastened Woman, The 1925 d: James Young. lps: Theda Bara, Wyndham Standing, Dale Fuller. 6800f USA. prod/rel: Chadwick Pictures
A Woman of Impulse, New York 1909, Play
Woman of Impulse, A 1918 d: Edward Jose. lps: Lina Cavalieri, Gertrude Robinson, Raymond Bloomer. 4440f USA. prod/rel: Famous Players-Lasky Corp.©, Paramount Pictures

ANSTEY, F. (1856–1934), UKN, Guthrie, Thomas Anstey
The Brass Bottle, London 1900, Novel
Brass Bottle, The 1914 d: Sidney Morgan. lps: E. Holman Clark, Alfred Bishop, Doris Lytton. 3600f UKN. prod/rel: Theatre & General
Brass Bottle, The 1923 d: Maurice Tourneur. lps: Harry Myers, Ernest Torrence, Tully Marshall. 5290f USA. prod/rel: Maurice Tourneur Productions, Associated First National Pictures

11

Brass Bottle, The 1964 d: Harry Keller. lps: Tony Randall, Burl Ives, Barbara Eden. 89M USA. prod/rel: Randall-Greshler

The Man from Blankleys, 1893, Short Story
Guest of Honour 1934 d: George King. lps: Henry Kendall, Edward Chapman, Margaret Yarde. 53M UKN. prod/rel: Warner Bros., First National
Man from Blankleys, The 1930 d: Alfred E. Green. lps: John Barrymore, Loretta Young, William Austin. 67M USA. prod/rel: Warner Brothers Pictures

The Tinted Venus, 1885, Novel
One Touch of Venus 1948 d: William A. Seiter. lps: Robert Walker, Ava Gardner, Dick Haymes. 81M USA. prod/rel: Universal
Tinted Venus, The 1921 d: Cecil M. Hepworth. lps: Alma Taylor, George Dewhurst, Maud Cressall. 5200f UKN. prod/rel: Hepworth

Vice Versa, 1882, Novel
Vice Versa 1916 d: Maurice Elvey. lps: Charles Rock, Douglas Munro, Edward O'Neill. 3900f UKN. prod/rel: London, Jury
Vice Versa 1948 d: Peter Ustinov. lps: Roger Livesey, Kay Walsh, Anthony Newley. 111M UKN. prod/rel: General Film Distributors, Two Cities

ANSTRUTHER, GERALD
Dangerous Afternoon, Play
Dangerous Afternoon 1961 d: Charles Saunders. lps: Ruth Dunning, Nora Nicholson, Joanna Dunham. 62M UKN. prod/rel: Bryanston, Theatrecraft

They Also Serve, Short Story
Master Spy 1963 d: Montgomery Tully. lps: Stephen Murray, June Thorburn, Alan Wheatley. 74M UKN. prod/rel: Eternal Films, Grand National

The Third Visitor, London 1945, Play
Third Visitor, The 1951 d: Maurice Elvey. lps: Sonia Dresdel, Guy Middleton, Hubert Gregg. 85M UKN. prod/rel: Elvey-Gartside, Eros

ANTEQUIL, GEORGES
La Maitresse Legitime, Book
Ehe in Not 1929 d: Richard Oswald. lps: Elga Brink, Walter Rilla, Evelyn Holt. 2273m GRM. *Ehen Zu Dritt* prod/rel: Nero-Film

ANTHELME, PAUL
Nos Deux Consciences, 1902, Play
I Confess 1953 d: Alfred Hitchcock. lps: Montgomery Clift, Anne Baxter, Karl Malden. 95M USA. prod/rel: Warner Bros., Alfred Hitchcock Prods.

ANTHONY, C. L.
Autumn Crocus, London 1931, Play
Autumn Crocus 1934 d: Basil Dean. lps: Ivor Novello, Fay Compton, Jack Hawkins. 86M UKN. prod/rel: Associated Talking Pictures, Associated British Film Disributors
Service, London 1932, Play
Looking Forward 1933 d: Clarence Brown. lps: Lionel Barrymore, Lewis Stone, Benita Hume. 82M USA. *Service* (UKN); *The New Deal*; *Yesterday's Rich* prod/rel: Metro-Goldwyn-Mayer Corp.©

ANTHONY, EDWARD S.
The Big Cage, New York 1933, Book
Big Cage, The 1933 d: Kurt Neumann. lps: Clyde Beatty, Anita Page, Andy Devine. 77M USA. prod/rel: Universal Pictures Corp.
Wild Cargo, New York 1932, Book
Wild Cargo 1934 d: Armand Denis. lps: Frank Buck. DOC. 96M USA. prod/rel: the Van Beuren Corp.©, RKO Radio Pictures

ANTHONY, EVELYN (1928–, UKN, Thomas, Evelyn Ward
The Tamarind Seed, Novel
Tamarind Seed, The 1974 d: Blake Edwards. lps: Julie Andrews, Omar Sharif, Anthony Quayle. 125M UKN. prod/rel: Avco Embassy, Jewel

ANTHONY, JOSEPH
The Man Without a Past, Short Story
Wheel of Destiny, The 1927 d: Duke Worne. lps: Forrest Stanley, Georgia Hale, Percy Challenger. 5869f USA. prod/rel: Duke Worne Productions, Rayart Pictures

ANTIER, BENJAMIN
L' Auberge Des Adrets, Play
Auberge Sanglante ,L' 1913 d: Emile Chautard. lps: Andre Liabel, Charles Krauss, Mevisto. FRN. prod/rel: Acad

ANTOINE, ANDRE-PAUL
L' Ennemie, Play
Tendre Ennemie, La 1935 d: Max Ophuls. lps: Georges Vitray, Marc Valbel, Simone Berriau. 85M FRN. *The Tender Enemy* (USA); *L' Ennemie* prod/rel: Eden-Productions

Metier de Femme, Play
Inevitable Monsieur Dubois, L' 1943 d: Pierre Billon. lps: Andre Luguet, Annie Ducaux, Felicien Tramel. 99M FRN. prod/rel: P.A.C.

ANTON, EDOARDO
La Fidanzata Del Bersagliere, Play
Ragazza Del Bersagliere, La 1967 d: Alessandro Blasetti. lps: Graziella Granata, Antonio Casagrande, Vittorio Caprioli. 107M ITL. *The Bersagliere's Girl*; *The Sharpshooter's Girl* prod/rel: Rizzoli Film, Cineriz
Il Serpente a Sonagli, Play
Serpente a Sonagli, Il 1935 d: Raffaello Matarazzo. lps: Nino Besozzi, Andreina Pagnani, Lilla Brignone. 74M ITL. prod/rel: Tiberia Film, S.a.N.G.R.a.F.

ANTONA-TRAVERSI, CAMILLO
La Torre Di Pietra, 1913, Play
Torre Di Pietra, La 1914 d: Roberto Troncone. lps: Ottone Merckel, Iole Bertini, Eugenio RennA. 800m ITL. prod/rel: Partenope Film

ANTONELLI, LUIGI
Il Barone Di Corbo, Play
Barone Di Corbo, Il 1939 d: Gennaro Righelli. lps: Laura Nucci, Enrico Glori, Vanna Vanni. 75M ITL. prod/rel: Juventus Film, Artisti Associati

ANTONIA (LIDIA RAVERA)
Porci Con le Ali, Book
Porci Con le Ali 1977 d: Paolo Pietrangeli. lps: Cristiana Mancinelli, Franco Bianchi, Lou Castel. 105M ITL. **If Pigs Had Wings** prod/rel: Eidoscope, Uski Film

ANTONIO, JOAO
Perus E Bacanaco Malagueta, 1963, Short Story
Jogo Da Vida, O 1977 d: Maurice CapovillA. lps: Lima Duarte, Gianfrancesco Guarnieri, Mauricio Do Valle. 95M BRZ. *The Game of Life*

ANTROBUS, JOHN
The Bed Sitting Room, 1963, Play
Bed Sitting Room, The 1969 d: Richard Lester. lps: Ralph Richardson, Rita Tushingham, Michael Hordern. 91M UKN. prod/rel: Oscar Lewenstein Productions, United Artists

ANZENGRUBER, LUDWIG (1839–1889), AUS
Doppelselbstmord, 1876, Play
Doppelselbstmord 1937 d: Max W. Kimmich. 21M GRM. *Double Suicide*
Hochzeit Im Heu 1951 d: Arthur M. Rabenalt. lps: Oskar Sima, Dagny Servaes, Fritz Lehmann. 89M GRM/AUS. *Wedding in the Hay* prod/rel: Cordial, Schonbrunn
Der G'wissenswurm, 1905, Novel
Jugendsunde, Die 1936 d: Franz Seitz. lps: Max Schultes, Bert Schultes, Maria Stadler. 81M GRM. prod/rel: Majestic, Commerz
Die Kreuzelschreiber, 1892, Play
Kreuzlschreiber, Der 1950 d: Eduard von Borsody. lps: Emil Hess, Charlotte Schellhorn, Fritz Kampers. 95M GRM. *The Crossers*; *The Cross-Makers* prod/rel: Tobis, Donau
Weiberkrieg, Der 1928 d: Franz Seitz. lps: Liane Haid, Fritz Kampers, Lotte Lorring. 2226m GRM. prod/rel: Munchener Lichtspielkunst Ag
Der Meineidbauer, 1891, Play
Meineidbauer, Der 1926 d: Jacob Fleck, Luise Fleck. lps: Arthur Ranzenhofer, Eduard von Winterstein, Elisabeth Markus. 2416m GRM. prod/rel: Hegewald-Film
Meineidbauer, Der 1941 d: Leopold Hainisch. lps: Eduard Kock, O. W. Fischer, Anna Exl. 94M GRM. prod/rel: Euphono, Doring
Meineidbauer, Der 1956 d: Rudolf Jugert. lps: Heidemarie Hatheyer, Carl Wery, Hans von Borsody. 106M GRM. *Die Sunderin Vom Fernerhof*; *The Perjured Farmer* prod/rel: Eichberg, Gloria
Der Pfarrer von Kirchfeld, 1897, Play
Madchen Vom Pfarrhof, Das 1955 d: Alfred Lehner. lps: Waltraut Haas, Erich Auer, Franziska Kinz. 95M AUS. *Der Kirchfeldpfarrer* prod/rel: Zenith, Sonor
Pfarrer von Kirchfeld, Der 1926 d: Jacob Fleck, Luise Fleck. lps: Wilhelm Dieterle, Margarete Lanner, Fritz Kampers. 2513m GRM. *The Pastor of Kirchfeld*
Pfarrer von Kirchfeld, Der 1937 d: Jacob Fleck, Luise Fleck. lps: Hans Jaray, Frieda Richard, Karl ParylA. 85M AUS. *The Pastor of Kirchfeld* prod/rel: Excelsior
Pfarrer von Kirchfeld, Der 1955 d: Hans Deppe. lps: Claus Holm, Ulla Jacobsson, Annie Rosar. 94M GRM. *The Pastor of Kirchfeld* prod/rel: H.D., Constantin
Der Schandfleck, 1904, Novel
Schandfleck, Der 1956 d: Herbert B. Fredersdorf. lps: Hans von Borsody, Lotte Ledl, Gerlinde Locker. 99M AUS/GRM. prod/rel: Rex, Schonbrunn

Der Sternsteinhof, 195-, Novel
Sternsteinhof 1976 d: Hans W. Geissendorfer. lps: Katja Rupe, Tilo Pruckner, Peter Kern. 125M GRM. *The Sternstein Manor*; *Sternstein Estate* prod/rel: Roxy, Bayerischer Rundfunk
Das Vierte Gebot, 1891, Play
Vierte Gebot, Das 1920 d: Richard Oswald. lps: Cornelius Kirschner, Hans Homma, Emmy Schleinitz. 1945m GRM. prod/rel: Richard Oswald-Film
Vierte Gebot, Das 1950 d: Eduard von Borsody. lps: Attila Horbiger, Dagny Servaes, Hans Putz. 100M AUS. *Der Weg Abwarts* prod/rel: Donau-Berna

AO RAN
Yan Yang Tian, Novel
Yan Yang Tian 1973 d: Lin Nong. lps: Zhang Lianwen, Ma Jingwu, Guo Zhenqing. 10r CHN. *Bright Sunny Skies* prod/rel: Changchun Film Studio

APESTEGUY, PIERRE
La Dame d'Onze Heures, Novel
Dame d'Onze Heures, La 1947 d: Jean Devaivre. lps: Micheline Francey, Junie Astor, Paul Meurisse. 97M FRN. prod/rel: Neptune

APITZ, BRUNO
Nackt Unter Wolfen, Halle 1958, Novel
Nackt Unter Wolfen 1962 d: Frank Beyer. lps: Erwin Geschonneck, Gerry Wolff, Armin Mueller-Stahl. 125M GDR. *Naked Among the Wolves* (USA); *Naked Among Wolves* prod/rel: Defa

APPEL, BENJAMIN
Fortress in the Rice, Indianapolis 1951, Novel
Cry of Battle 1963 d: Irving Lerner. lps: Van Heflin, James MacArthur, Rita Moreno. 99M USA/PHL. *To Be a Man* prod/rel: Allied Artists

APPEL, DAVID
Comanche, 1951, Novel
Tonka 1958 d: Lewis R. Foster. lps: Philip Carey, Jerome Courtland, Rafael Campos. 97M USA. *A Horse Called Comanche*; *A Horse Named Comanche* prod/rel: Buena Vista, Walt Disney Prods.

APPLEBY, JOHN
The Captive City, New York 1955, Novel
Citta Prigionera, La 1962 d: Joseph Anthony, Mario Chiari. lps: David Niven, Ben Gazzara, Michael Craig. 108M ITL. *Conquered City* (USA); *Captive City* prod/rel: Lux Film, Maxima Cin.Ca

APPLIN, ARTHUR
The Girl Who Saved His Honour, 1913, Novel
Madame Pinkette & Co. 1917 d: Maurits H. Binger. lps: Annie Bos, Cecil Ryan, Jan Van Dommelen. 2200m NTH. *Om Zijn Eer*; *For His Honour*; *The Girl Who Saved His Honour* (UKN) prod/rel: Filmfabriek-Hollandia
The Lure of London, Play
Lure of London, The 1914 d: Bert Haldane?. lps: Ivy Close, Edward Viner, M. Gray Murray. 5250f UKN. prod/rel: Barker, Co-Operative
The Whirlpool, Novel
London Love 1926 d: Manning Haynes. lps: Fay Compton, John Stuart, Miles Mander. 7560f UKN. *The Whirlpool* prod/rel: Gaumont
Wicked, Novel
All the Winners 1920 d: Geoffrey H. Malins. lps: Owen Nares, Maudie Dunham, Sam Livesey. 6000f UKN. prod/rel: G. B. Samuelson, General

APTE, HARI NARAYAN
Gad Aala Pan Sinha Gela, Novel
Sinhagad 1923 d: Baburao Painter. lps: Balasaheb Yadav, Kamaladevi, Miss Nalini. 6880f IND. prod/rel: Maharashtra Film
Sinhagad 1933 d: V. Shantaram. lps: Keshavrao Dhaiber, Shinde, Shankarrao Bhosle. 135M IND. prod/rel: Prabhat Film

APTE, NARAYAN HARI
Amritmanthan, Novel
Amritmanthan 1934 d: V. Shantaram. lps: Chandramohan, Shanta Apte, Shuresh Babu. 155M IND. *Churning for Nectar*; *Amrit Manthan*; *The Churning of the Oceans* prod/rel: Prabhat Film
Hridayachi Shrimanti, Novel
Pratibha 1937 d: Baburao Painter. lps: Durga Khote, Keshavrao Date, Miss HeerA. 124M IND. prod/rel: Shalini Cinetone
Na Patnari Goshta, 1923, Novel
Duniya Na Mane 1937 d: V. Shantaram. lps: Raja Mene, Shanta Apte, Keshavrao Date. 166M IND. *Unwilling Society*; *The Vermilon Mark*; *The Unexpected* prod/rel: Prabhat Film
Kunku 1937 d: V. Shantaram. lps: Shanta Apte, Keshavrao Date, Raja Nene. 163M IND. *The Unexpected* prod/rel: Prabhat Film

ARLEY, CATHERINE
La Femme de Paille, Paris 1956, Novel
   Woman of Straw 1964 d: Basil Dearden. lps: Gina Lollobrigida, Sean Connery, Ralph Richardson. 117M UKN. prod/rel: Novus Films, United Artists

ARLINGTON, ADRIAN
These Our Strangers, Novel
   Those Kids from Town 1942 d: Lance Comfort. lps: Shirley Lenner, Jeanne de Casalis, Percy Marmont. 82M UKN. prod/rel: British National, Anglo-American

ARLISS, GEORGE
Hamilton, New York 1917, Play
   Alexander Hamilton 1931 d: John G. Adolfi. lps: George Arliss, Doris Kenyon, Montagu Love. 73M USA. prod/rel: Warner Bros. Pictures

ARLT, ROBERTO
Noche Terrible, 1933, Short Story
   Noche Terrible 1967 d: Rodolfo Kuhn. lps: Jorge Rivera Lopez, Susana Rinaldi, Federico Luppi. 48M ARG. *The Terrible Night*
Los Siete Locos, 1929, Novel
   Siete Locos, Los 1973 d: Leopoldo Torre-Nilsson. lps: Alfredo Alcon, Norma Aleandro, Hector Alterio. 119M ARG. *Seven Mad Men* (USA); *The Seven Madmen*

ARMAN DE CAILLAVET, GASTON
L' Amour Veille, Paris 1907, Play
   Amour Veille, L' 1937 d: Henry Roussell. lps: Henri Garat, Robert Pizani, Jacqueline Francell. 109M FRN. prod/rel: Societe Des Films Osso, Societe Du Film Amour Veille
   Love Watches 1918 d: Henry Houry. lps: Corinne Griffith, Denton Vane, Edmund Burns. 5r USA. prod/rel: Vitagraph Co. of America©, Blue Ribbon Feature
L' Ane de Buridan, 1909, Play
   Ane de Buridan, L' 1916?.
   Ane de Buridan, L' 1932 d: Alexandre Ryder. lps: Colette Darfeuil, Mona Goya, Rene Lefevre. 77M FRN. prod/rel: Pathe-Natan
   Asino Di Buridano, L' 1917 d: Eleuterio Rodolfi. lps: Eleuterio Rodolfi, Fernanda Negri-Pouget, Lydia QuarantA. 1588m ITL. prod/rel: Veritas
L' Ange du Foyer, Play
   Ange du Foyer, L' 1936 d: Leon Mathot. lps: Betty Stockfeld, Lucien Baroux, Roger Duchesne. 95M FRN. prod/rel: Societe Nouvelle De Cinematographie
La Belle Aventure, Paris 1914, Play
   Beautiful Adventure, The 1917 d: Dell Henderson. lps: Ann Murdock, Ada Boshell, Edward Fielding. 5-6r USA. prod/rel: Empire All Star Corp.©, Mutual Film Corp.
   Belle Aventure, La 1932 d: Roger Le Bon, Reinhold Schunzel. lps: Kathe von Nagy, Michele Alfa, Jean Perier. 80M FRN. prod/rel: U.F.a., a.CE.
   Belle Aventure, La 1942 d: Marc Allegret. lps: Claude Dauphin, Louis Jourdan, Micheline Presle. 92M FRN. *Twilight* (USA) prod/rel: Films Imperia
Le Bois Sacre, Play
   Bois Sacre, Le 1939 d: Leon Mathot, Robert Bibal. lps: Gaby Morlay, Elvire Popesco, Marcel Dalio. 80M FRN. prod/rel: Bervia Films
L' Habit Vert, Play
   Habit Vert, L' 1937 d: Roger Richebe. lps: Elvire Popesco, Meg Lemonnier, Victor Boucher. 109M FRN. prod/rel: Societe Des Films Roger Richebe
Miquette Et Sa Mere, Play
   Miquette 1940 d: Jean Boyer. lps: Lilian Harvey, Lucien Baroux, Andre Lefaur. F FRN. *La Demoiselle du Tabac*; *Miquette Et Sa Mere* prod/rel: U.F.P.C.
   Miquette Et Sa Mere 1914 d: Henri Pouctal. lps: Eve Lavalliere, Henri Germain. 1200m FRN. prod/rel: le Film d'Art
   Miquette Et Sa Mere 1933 d: Henri Diamant-Berger, D. B. Maurice. lps: Blanche Montel, Marcelle Monthil, Roland Toutain. 85M FRN. prod/rel: Films Diamant
   Miquette Et Sa Mere 1949 d: Henri-Georges Clouzot. lps: Daniele Delorme, Mireille Perrey, Louis Jouvet. 96M FRN. *Miquette* (USA) prod/rel: Alcina, C.I.C.C.
Monsieur Brotonneau, Play
   Monsieur Brotonneau 1939 d: Alexander Esway. lps: Raimu, Josette Day, Saturnin Fabre. 100M FRN. prod/rel: Films Marcel Pagnol
Papa, 1911, Play
   Derniere Aventure 1941 d: Robert Peguy. lps: Jean Max, Pierre Dux, Annie Ducaux. 104M FRN. prod/rel: Fernand Rivers
   Papa 1915 d: Nino OxiliA. lps: Ruggero Ruggeri, Amleto Novelli, Pina Menichelli. 594m ITL. prod/rel: Cines

Primerose, 1911, Play
   Primerose 1919 d: Mario Caserini. lps: Thea, Ugo Piperno, Elena Sangro. 2085m ITL. prod/rel: Cines
   Primerose 1933 d: Rene Guissart. lps: Henri Rollan, Madeleine Renaud, Marguerite Moreno. 80M FRN. prod/rel: Edmond Pingrin
Le Roi, 1908, Play
   King on Main Street, The 1925 d: Monta Bell. lps: Adolphe Menjou, Bessie Love, Greta Nissen. 6229f USA. prod/rel: Famous Players-Lasky, Paramount Pictures
   Roi, Le 1936 d: Piere Colombier. lps: Victor Francen, Raimu, Gaby Morlay. 113M FRN. *Le Roi S'amuse* prod/rel: Films Modernes, Emile Natan
   Roi, Le 1949 d: Marc-Gilbert Sauvajon. lps: Maurice Chevalier, Sophie Desmarets, Annie Ducaux. 95M FRN. *A Royal Affair* (USA) prod/rel: Speva Films, Michel Safra

ARMAND, J.
U Svateho Antonicka, Opera
   U Sveteho Antonicka 1933 d: Svatopluk Innemann. lps: Ota Bubenicek, Hana Vitova, Jara Pospisil. 2686m CZC. *By St. Anthony*; *At St. Anthony's* prod/rel: Elekta

ARMANDY, ANDRE
Le Paradis de Satan, Novel
   Paradis de Satan, Le 1938 d: Felix Gandera, Jean Delannoy. lps: Jean-Pierre Aumont, Pierre Renoir, Jany Holt. 85M FRN. prod/rel: Productions Georges Legrand
Rapa-Nui, Novel
   Goldene Abgrund, Der 1927 d: Mario Bonnard. lps: Liane Haid, Andre Roanne, Robert Leffler. 2229m GRM/FRN. *Rapa-Nui* (FRN); *Welt Und Halwelt* prod/rel: Societe Des Cineromans, Films De France
Le Renegat, Paris 1929, Novel
   Renegades 1930 d: Victor Fleming. lps: Warner Baxter, Myrna Loy, Noah Beery. 84M USA. prod/rel: Fox Film Corp.
Les Reprouves, Novel
   Reprouves, Les 1936 d: Jacques Severac. lps: Jean Servais, Pierre Mingand, Janine Crispin. 90M FRN. prod/rel: Hades Films
Silverbell Ou la Nuit Sans Astres, Novel
   Barranco, Ltd. 1932 d: Andre Berthomieu. lps: Rosine Derean, Felicien Tramel, Julien Bertheau. 95M FRN. prod/rel: Nicaea Films Production
La Voie Sans Disque, Novel
   Voie Sans Disque, La 1933 d: Leon Poirier. lps: Gina Manes, Daniel Mendaille, Camille Bert. 109M FRN. prod/rel: Comptoir Francais Du Film Documentaire

ARMANI, FRANK H.
Privileged Information, Book
   Sworn to Silence 1987 d: Peter Levin. lps: Peter Coyote, Dabney Coleman, Caroline McWilliams. TVM. 100M USA.

ARMAT
The Hotel Mouse, Play
   Hotel Mouse, The 1923 d: Fred Paul. lps: Lillian Hall-Davis, Campbell Gullan, Warwick Ward. 6500f UKN. prod/rel: British Super, Jury

ARMONT, PAUL
L' Amoureuse Aventure, Play
   Amoureuse Aventure, L' 1931 d: Wilhelm Thiele. lps: Marie Glory, Jeanne Boitel, Albert Prejean. 84M FRN. prod/rel: Vandal Et Delac
Ces Messieurs de la Sante, Play
   Ces Messieurs de la Sante 1933 d: Piere Colombier. lps: Edwige Feuillere, Pauline Carton, Raimu. 115M FRN. prod/rel: Pathe-Nathan
Le Chevalier Au Masques, Play
   Purple Mask, The 1955 d: H. Bruce Humberstone. lps: Tony Curtis, Colleen Miller, Dan O'Herlihy. 82M USA. prod/rel: Universal-International
Un Chien Qui Rapporte, Play
   Chien Qui Rapporte, Un 1931 d: Jean Choux. lps: Arletty, Rene Lefevre, Medy. 87M FRN. prod/rel: Superfilm
Coiffeur Pour Dames, Play
   Coiffeur Pour Dames 1931 d: Rene Guissart. lps: Fernand Gravey, Mona Goya, Irene Brillant. 80M FRN. *Artist With the Ladies* (USA) prod/rel: Films Paramount
Dicky, Play
   Monsieur Breloque a Disparu 1937 d: Robert Peguy. lps: Lucien Baroux, Junie Astorm, Marcel Simon. 95M FRN. prod/rel: B.A.P. Films
   Trappola d'Amore 1940 d: Raffaello Matarazzo. lps: Giuseppe Porelli, Carla Candiani, Paolo StoppA. 80M ITL. *Le Prodezze Di Dicky*; *Dicky* prod/rel: Oceano Film, Generalcine
L' Ecole Des Cocottes, Play
   Ecole Des Cocottes, L' 1935 d: Piere Colombier. lps: Renee Saint-Cyr, Pauline Carton, Raimu. 106M FRN. prod/rel: Pathe-Natan

The French Doll, New York 1922, Play
   French Doll, The 1923 d: Robert Z. Leonard. lps: Mae Murray, Orville Caldwell, Rod La Rocque. 7028f USA. prod/rel: Tiffany Productions, Metro Pictures
Le Mari Garcon, Play
   Mari Garcon, Le 1933 d: Alberto Cavalcanti. lps: Jean Debucourt, Yvonne Garat, Jeanne Cheirel. 85M FRN. *Le Garcon Divorce* prod/rel: Amax-Films
Souris d'Hotel, Play
   Souris d'Hotel 1927 d: Adelqui Millar. lps: Ica de Lenkeffy, Arthur Pusey, Suzanne Delmas. 2500m FRN. prod/rel: Albatros
Le Tailleur Au Chateau, Paris 1924, Play
   Love Me Tonight 1932 d: Rouben Mamoulian. lps: Maurice Chevalier, Jeanette MacDonald, Charlie Ruggles. 104M USA. prod/rel: Paramount Publix Corp.©, Rouben Mamoulian Production
Le Truc du Bresilien, Play
   Truc du Bresilien, Le 1932 d: Alberto Cavalcanti. lps: Robert Arnoux, Colette Darfeuil, Yvonne Garat. 87M FRN. prod/rel: Films Tenax
Le Valet Maitre, Play
   Valet Maitre, Le 1941 d: Paul Mesnier. lps: Elvire Popesco, Marguerite Deval, Henri Garat. 90M FRN. prod/rel: S.P.C.
Le Zebre, Play
   Glad Eye, The 1920 d: Kenelm Foss. lps: James Reardon, Dorothy Minto, Hayford Hobbs. 6000f UKN. prod/rel: Reardon British Films, IFT
   Glad Eye, The 1927 d: Maurice Elvey, Victor Saville. lps: Estelle Brody, Hal Sherman, John Stuart. 7700f UKN. prod/rel: Gaumont

ARMONT, ROBERT
Theodore Et Cie, 1909, Play
   Mare Di Guai, Un 1940 d: Carlo Ludovico BragagliA. lps: Umberto Melnati, Junie Astor, Luigi Almirante. 76M ITL. prod/rel: Atlas Film, I.C.I.
   Teodoro E Socio 1925 d: Mario Bonnard. lps: Mario Bonnard, Marcel Levesque, Alexiane. 2076m ITL. prod/rel: Bonnard
   Theodore Et Cie 1933 d: Piere Colombier. lps: Raimu, Albert Prejean, Alice Field. 97M FRN. prod/rel: Pathe-Natan

ARMSTRONG, ANTHONY
The Case of Mr. Pelham, Novel
   Man Who Haunted Himself, The 1970 d: Basil Dearden. lps: Roger Moore, Hildegard Knef, Olga Georges-Picot. 94M UKN. prod/rel: Excalibur, Warner-Pathe
He Was Found in the Road, Novel
   Man in the Road, The 1956 d: Lance Comfort. lps: Derek Farr, Ella Raines, Donald Wolfit. 84M UKN. prod/rel: Gibraltar, Grand National
Orders are Orders, London 1932, Play
   Orders are Orders 1954 d: David Paltenghi. lps: Brian Reece, Margot Grahame, Raymond Huntley. 78M UKN. prod/rel: Group 3, British Lion
   Orders Is Orders 1933 d: Walter Forde. lps: Charlotte Greenwood, James Gleason, Cyril Maude. 88M UKN. prod/rel: Gaumont British, Ideal
Ten Minute Alibi, London 1933, Play
   Ten Minute Alibi 1935 d: Bernard Vorhaus. lps: Phillips Holmes, Aileen Marson, Theo Shall. 64M UKN. prod/rel: British Lion, Transatlantic
The Wide Guy, Novel
   Don't Ever Leave Me 1949 d: Arthur Crabtree. lps: Jimmy Hanley, Petula Clark, Hugh Sinclair. 85M UKN. prod/rel: Triton, General Film Distributors

ARMSTRONG, CHARLOTTE (1906–1969), USA
The Case of the Three Weird Sisters, Novel
   Three Weird Sisters, The 1948 d: Daniel Birt. lps: Nancy Price, Mary Clare, Mary Merrall. 82M UKN. prod/rel: British National, Pathe
The Enemy, Short Story
   Talk About a Stranger 1952 d: David Bradley. lps: George Murphy, Nancy Davis, Billy Gray. 65M USA. *The Enemy*; *The Next Door Neighbor* prod/rel: MGM
Le Jour Des Parques, Novel
   Rupture, La 1970 d: Claude Chabrol. lps: Stephane Audran, Michel Bouquet, Jean-Claude Drouot. 125M FRN/ITL/BLG. *All'ombra Del Delitto* (ITL); *The Breakup* (USA); *Le Jour Des Parques*; *Hallucination* prod/rel: Films la Boetie, Cinevog Films
Mischief, 1950, Novel
   Don't Bother to Knock 1952 d: Roy Ward Baker. lps: Richard Widmark, Marilyn Monroe, Anne Bancroft. 76M USA. prod/rel: 20th Century-Fox
   Sitter, The 1991 d: Rick Berger. lps: Kim Myers, Brett Cullen, Susan Barnes. TVM. 100M USA.

The Unsuspected, Novel
  Unsuspected, The 1947 d: Michael Curtiz. lps: Claude Rains, Joan Caulfield, Audrey Totter. 103M USA. prod/rel: Warner Bros.

ARMSTRONG, H. C.
Hidden, Novel
  Dead Men are Dangerous 1939 d: Harold French. lps: Robert Newton, Betty Lynne, John Warwick. 69M UKN. prod/rel: Pathe, Welwyn

ARMSTRONG, HARRY
Sweet Adeline, 1903, Song
  Sweet Adeline 1926 d: Jerome Storm. lps: Charles Ray, Gertrude Olmstead, Jack Clifford. 7r USA. prod/rel: Chadwick Pictures

ARMSTRONG, PAUL
Alias Jimmy Valentine, New York 1910, Play
  Alias Jimmy Valentine 1915 d: Maurice Tourneur. lps: Robert Warwick, Ruth Shepley, Johnny Hines. 5r USA. prod/rel: World Film Corp.©, Peerless Pictures
  Alias Jimmy Valentine 1920 d: Edmund Mortimer. lps: Bert Lytell, Vola Vale, Eugene Pallette. 6r USA. prod/rel: Metro Pictures Corp.©, Screen Classics, Inc.
  Alias Jimmy Valentine 1929 d: Jack Conway. lps: William Haines, Lionel Barrymore, Leila Hyams. 7803f USA. prod/rel: Metro-Goldwyn-Mayer Pictures
  Return of Jimmy Valentine, The 1936 d: Lewis D. Collins. lps: Roger Pryor, Charlotte Henry, Lois Wilson. 72M USA. prod/rel: Republic Pictures Corp.©
The Bludgeon, New York 1914, Novel
  Bludgeon, The 1915 d: Webster Cullison. lps: Kathryn Osterman, John Dunn, Frank Beamish. 5r USA. prod/rel: Equitable Motion Pictures Corp.©, World Film Corp.
Blue Grass, New York 1908, Play
  Blue Grass 1915 d: Charles M. Seay. lps: Thomas A. Wise, Clara Whipple, George Soule Spencer. 5r USA. prod/rel: Equitable Motion Pictures Corp.©, World Film Corp.
The Deep Purple, Chicago 1910, Play
  Deep Purple, The 1915 d: James Young. lps: Clara Kimball Young, Milton Sills, Edward M. Kimball. 5r USA. prod/rel: World Film Corp.©
  Deep Purple, The 1920 d: Raoul Walsh. lps: Miriam Cooper, Helen Ware, Vincent Serrano. 6661f USA. prod/rel: Mayflower Photoplay Corp.©, Realart Pictures Corp.
The Escape, New York 1913, Play
  Escape, The 1914 d: D. W. Griffith. lps: Blanche Sweet, Mae Marsh, Robert Harron. 7r USA. prod/rel: Majestic Motion Picture Co., Mutual Film Corp.
  Escape, The 1928 d: Richard Rosson. lps: William Russell, Virginia Valli, Nancy Drexel. 5109f USA. prod/rel: Fox Film Corp.
Going Some, New York 1909, Play
  Going Some 1920 d: Harry Beaumont. lps: Cullen Landis, Helen Ferguson, Lillian Hall. 5453f USA. prod/rel: Eminent Authors Pictures, Inc., Goldwyn Distributing Corp.
The Greyhound, New York 1912, Play
  Greyhound, The 1914 d: Lawrence McGill. lps: Catherine Carter, Elita Proctor Otis, Anna Laughlin. 5r USA. prod/rel: Life Photo Film Corp.©, State Rights
The Heart of a Thief, New York 1914, Play
  Hold That Blonde! 1945 d: George Marshall. lps: Veronica Lake, Eddie Bracken, Frank Fenton. 76M USA. Good Intentions prod/rel: Paramount
  Paths of Flame 1926. lps: Art Mix, Dorothy Lee. 4750f USA. prod/rel: Denver Dixon Productions, Aywon Film Corp.
  Paths to Paradise 1925 d: Clarence Badger. lps: Betty Compson, Raymond Griffith, Thomas Santschi. 6741f USA. prod/rel: Famous Player-Lasky, Paramount Pictures
The Heir to the Hoorah, New York 1905, Play
  Ever Since Eve 1934 d: George Marshall. lps: George O'Brien, Mary Brian, Betty Blythe. 75M USA. The Heir to the Hoorah prod/rel: Fox Film Corp.
  Heir to the Hoorah, The 1916 d: William C. de Mille. lps: Thomas Meighan, Anita King, Edythe Chapman. 5r USA. The Heir to the Hurrah prod/rel: Jesse L. Lasky Feature Play Co.©, Paramount Pictures Corp.
The Renegade, New York C.1910, Play
  Lure of Woman, The 1915 d: Travers Vale. lps: Alice Brady, June Elvidge, George Ralph. 5r USA. The Lure of Women prod/rel: World Film Corp.©
A Romance of the Underworld, New York 1911, Play
  Romance of the Underworld 1928 d: Irving Cummings. lps: Mary Astor, Ben Bard, Robert Elliott. 6162f USA. Romance and Bright Lights prod/rel: Fox Film Corp.

Romance of the Underworld, A 1918 d: James Kirkwood. lps: Catherine Calvert, Eugene O'Brien, David Powell. 6-7r USA. prod/rel: Frank A. Keeney Pictures Corp.©, William L Sherry Service
Via Wireless, New York 1908, Play
  Via Wireless 1915 d: George Fitzmaurice. lps: Gail Kane, Bruce McRae, Brandon Hurst. 5r USA. prod/rel: Pathe Exchange, Inc., Gold Rooster Play

ARMSTRONG, RICHARD
Passage Home, Novel
  Passage Home 1955 d: Roy Ward Baker. lps: Anthony Steel, Peter Finch, Diane Cilento. 102M UKN. prod/rel: General Film Distributors, Group Films

ARMSTRONG, THOMAS
The Crowthers of Bankdam, Novel
  Master of Bankdam, The 1947 d: Walter Forde. lps: Anne Crawford, Dennis Price, Tom Walls. 105M UKN. prod/rel: Group Film Distributors, Holbein

ARMSTRONG, WILLIAM
Sounder, 1969, Novel
  Part 2 Sounder 1976 d: William A. Graham. lps: Harold Sylvester, Ebony Wright, Taj Mahal. 98M USA. Sounder II
  Sounder 1972 d: Martin Ritt. lps: Cicely Tyson, Paul Winfield, Kevin Hooks. 105M USA. prod/rel: 20th Century Fox, Radnitz-Mattel

ARNAC, M.
Heinz Im Mond, Novel
  Heinz Im Mond 1934 d: R. A. Stemmle. lps: Heinz Ruhmann, Annemarie Sorensen, Rudolf Platte. 84M GRM. prod/rel: Cicero-Filmprod.

ARNAC, MARCEL
Novel
  Steppin' in Society 1945 d: Alexander Esway. lps: Edward Everett Horton, Gladys George, Ruth Terry. 72M USA. prod/rel: Republic
A l'Heritage Ou Les Vacances Singulieres, Novel
  Circonstances Attenuantes 1939 d: Jean Boyer. lps: Michel Simon, Arletty, Marie-Jose. 87M FRN. prod/rel: Ste Francaise De Production Et D'edition
Deux Paillassons un Coeur, Novel
  Tombeur, Le 1957 d: Rene Delacroix. lps: Marthe Mercadier, Genevieve Cluny, Jacques Jouanneau. 86M FRN. prod/rel: Films De L'abeille, Cocinor

ARNAUD, ETIENNE
Manoeuvres de Nuit, Play
  Mam'zelle Spahi 1934 d: Max de Vaucorbeil. lps: Noel-Noel, Raymond Cordy, Mady Berry. 85M FRN.
La Mariee du Regiment, Play
  Mariee du Regiment, La 1935 d: Maurice Cammage. lps: Pierre Larquey, Suzanne Dehelly, Andre Berley. 90M FRN. prod/rel: Maurice Cammage

ARNAUD, G. J.
Un Petit Paradis, Novel
  Petit Paradis, Un 1981 d: Michel Wyn. lps: Yolande Folliot, Richard Berry, Francois Chaumette. 92M FRN. prod/rel: TF 1

ARNAUD, G. V.
Le Coucou, Novel
  Nuit du Coucou, La 1987 d: Michel Favart. lps: Florent Pagny, Marie Riviere, Isabelle Otero. TVM. 90M FRN.

ARNAUD, GEORGES
Le Salaire de la Peur, 1950, Novel
  Salaire de la Peur, Le 1953 d: Henri-Georges Clouzot. lps: Yves Montand, Charles Vanel, Vera Clouzot. 156M FRN/ITL. Vite Vendute (ITL); The Wages of Fear (USA); Il Salario Della Paura prod/rel: C.I.C.C., Filmsonor
  Sorcerer 1977 d: William Friedkin. lps: Roy Scheider, Bruno Cremer, Francisco Rabal. 122M USA. The Wages of Fear (UKN) prod/rel: Film Properties International

ARNAUD, G.-J.
L' Eternite Pour Nous, Paris 1960, Novel
  Cri de la Chair, Le 1963 d: Jose Benazeraf. lps: Monique Just, Silvia Sorente, Michel Lemoine. 92M FRN. Sin on the Beach (USA); L' Eternite Pour Nous; Eternity for Us; Romance on the Beach prod/rel: Les Films Univers
Les Longs Manteaux, Novel
  Longs Manteaux, Les 1985 d: Gilles Behat. lps: Bernard Giraudeau, Claudia Ohana, Robert Charlebois. 105M FRN/ARG. prod/rel: Les Films de la Tour, a.K.F.

ARNAUD, JEAN-JACQUES
Zone Rouge, Novel
  Zone Rouge 1986 d: Robert Enrico. lps: Richard Anconina, Sabine Azema, Helene Surgere. 110M FRN. prod/rel: Revcom, TF 1

ARNICHES, CARLOS
Alma de Dios, Opera
  Alma de Dios 1923 d: Manuel NoriegA. lps: Elisa Ruiz Romero, Irene Alba, Juan Bonafe. 2167m SPN. prod/rel: Atlantida
Los Aparecidos, Opera
  Aparecidos, Los 1927 d: Jose Buchs. lps: Amelia Munoz, Jose Maria Jimeno, Jose Montenegro. F SPN. The Ghosts prod/rel: Ediciones Forns-Buchs (Madrid)
Los Chicos de la Escuela, Opera
  Chicos de la Escuela, Los 1925 d: Florian Rey. lps: Isabel Alemany, Maria Luz Callejo, Manuel San German. 59M SPN. The Schoolboys prod/rel: Atlantida
Doloretes, Opera
  Doloretes 1922 d: Jose Buchs. lps: Elisa Ruiz Romero, Manuel San German, Maria Comendador. 2100m SPN. prod/rel: Atlantida
Don Quintin El Amargao, Opera
  Don Quintin El Amargao 1925 d: Manuel NoriegA. lps: Lina Moreno, Consuelo Reyes, Jose Arguelles. 80M SPN. prod/rel: Cartago Films (Madrid)
Las Estrellas, Play
  Estrellas, Las 1927 d: Luis R. Alonso. lps: Isabel Alemany, Juan de Orduna, Jose Montenegro. SPN. prod/rel: Producciones Hornemann (Madrid)
Los Granujas, Play
  Granujas, Los 1924 d: Fernando Delgado, Manuel NoriegA. lps: Alfredo Hurtado, Elisa Ruiz Romero, Clotilde Romero. 42M SPN. The Rogues prod/rel: Ediciones Maricampo (Madrid)
Los Guapos, Play
  Guapos O Gente Brava, Los 1923 d: Manuel NoriegA. lps: Eugenia Zuffoli, Manuel Rusell, Javier de RiverA. 2205m SPN. prod/rel: Atlantida
El Pobre Valbuena, Opera
  Pobre Valbuena, El 1923 d: Jose Buchs. lps: Antonio Gil, Alfonso Aguilar, Manuel San German. F SPN. Poor Valbueno prod/rel: Film Espanola (Madrid)
El Punao de Rosas, Opera
  Punao de Rosas, El 1923 d: Rafael Salvador. lps: Angeles Ortiz, Pedro Fernandez Cuenca, Jose OrtegA. SPN. prod/rel: Rafael Salvador Films (Madrid)

ARNOLD, ELLIOTT
Blood Brother, Novel
  Broken Arrow 1950 d: Delmer Daves. lps: James Stewart, Jeff Chandler, Debra Paget. 93M USA. prod/rel: 20th Century-Fox
The Commandos, Novel
  First Comes Courage 1943 d: Dorothy Arzner. lps: Merle Oberon, Brian Aherne, Carl Esmond. 88M USA. Attack By Night prod/rel: Columbia
Deep in My Heart, 1949, Book
  Deep in My Heart 1954 d: Stanley Donen. lps: Jose Ferrer, Merle Oberon, Helen Traubel. 132M USA. prod/rel: MGM
Flight from Ashiya, New York 1959, Novel
  Flight from Ashiya 1964 d: Michael Anderson. lps: Yul Brynner, Richard Widmark, George Chakiris. 102M USA/JPN. Ashiya Kara No Hiko (JPN) prod/rel: Harold Hecht Films, Daiei Motion Picture Co.

ARNOLD, FRANK
Rendez-Vous Champs-Elysees, Short Story
  Rendez-Vous Champs-Elysees 1937 d: Jacques Houssin. lps: Jules Berry, Pierre Larquey, Micheline Cheirel. 92M FRN. Le Controleur Des Champs-Elysees; Rendez-Vous aux Champs-Elysees prod/rel: Jean Berton

ARNOLD, FRANZ ROBERT
Der Furst von Pappenheim, Opera
  Furst von Pappenheim, Der 1927 d: Richard Eichberg. lps: Curt Bois, Mona Maris, Dina GrallA. 2306m GRM. The Prince of Pappenheim prod/rel: Eichberg-Film
  Furst von Pappenheim, Der 1952 d: Hans Deppe. lps: Hannelore Schroth, Viktor de Kowa, Grethe Weiser. 104M GRM. prod/rel: Central, Prisma
Hurra - Ein Junge!, Play
  Ach, Egon 1961 d: Wolfgang Schleif. lps: Heinz Erhardt, Rudolf Vogel, Gunther Philipp. 90M GRM. Oh Egon prod/rel: Kurt Ulrich, Europa
  Hurra - Ein Junge! 1931 d: Georg Jacoby. lps: Max Adalbert, Georg Alexander, Lucie Englisch. F GRM. Hooray - It's a Boy
  Hurra - Ein Junge! 1953 d: Ernst MarischkA. lps: Walter Muller, Theo Lingen, Grethe Weiser. 90M GRM. Hooray - It's a Boy! prod/rel: Berolina, Constantin
It's a Boy, New York 1922, Play
  It's a Boy 1933 d: Tim Whelan. lps: Leslie Henson, Edward Everett Horton, Heather Thatcher. 80M UKN. prod/rel: Gainsborough, Woolf & Freedman

Der Keusche Lebemann, Play
Keusche Lebemann, Der 1952 d: Carl Boese. lps: Georg Thomalla, Joe Stockel, Gerthe Weiser. 94M GRM. *The Virgin Playboy* prod/rel: Central Cinema, Prisma

Die Spanische Fliege, Play
Spanische Fliege, Die 1955 d: Carl Boese. lps: Joe Stockel, Rudolf Platte, Hans Leibelt. 94M GRM. *The Spanish Fly* prod/rel: Deutsche Spielfilm, Victor von Struve

Stopsel, Play
Tausend Fur Eine Nacht 1932 d: Max Mack. lps: Jakob Tiedtke, Claire Rommer, Johanna Terwin. 1972m GRM/CZC. *A Thousand for One Night* prod/rel: Wolframfilm, Avanti-Tonfilm Berlin
Tisic Za Jednu Noc 1932 d: Jaroslav SvarA. lps: Theodor Pistek, Ruzena Slemrova, Marie GrossovA. 1841m CZC. *A Thousand for One Night* prod/rel: Wolframfilm

Unter Geschaftsaufsicht, Play
Keusche Josef, Der 1953 d: Carl Boese. lps: Renate Mannhardt, Ludwig Schmitz, Lucie Englisch. 94M GRM. *Joseph the Pure* prod/rel: Algefa, Falken
To Neznate Hadimrsku 1931 d: Martin Fric, Carl Lamac. lps: Vlasta Burian, Meda Valentova, Otto Rubik. 2599m CZC. *You Don't Know Hadimrska; Hadimrsku Doesn't Know; Don't You Know Mrs. Hadimrska?* prod/rel: Elekta
Wehe, Wenn Er Losgelassen 1931 d: Martin Fric, Carl Lamac. lps: Vlasta Burian, Mabel Hariot, Harry Frank. 2251m GRM/CZC. *Unter Geschaftsaufsicht* prod/rel: Elekta, Ondra-Lamac-Film

Die Vertagte Hochzeitsnacht, Play
Interrupted Honeymoon, The 1936 d: Leslie Hiscott. lps: Claude Hulbert, Francis L. Sullivan, Hugh Wakefield. 72M UKN. prod/rel: British Lion
Vertagte Hochzeitsnacht, Die 1953 d: Karl G. Kulb. lps: Theo Lingen, Steffie Strouk, Hans Leibelt. 85M GRM. *The Postponed Wedding Night* prod/rel: Ariston, N.F.

Der Wahre Jakob, Play
Nacht Im Separee, Eine 1950 d: Hans Deppe. lps: Kurt Seifert, Olga Tschechowa, Sonja Ziemann. 95M GRM. *A Night in a Separate Chamber* prod/rel: Berolina, Gloria
Wahre Jakob, Der 1960 d: Rudolf Schundler. lps: Willy Millowitsch, Renate Ewert, Jane Tilden. 88M GRM. *The Real Jacob* prod/rel: Corona, U.F.H.

A Warm Corner, Play
Warm Corner, A 1930 d: Victor Saville. lps: Leslie Henson, Heather Thatcher, Connie Ediss. 104M UKN. prod/rel: Gainsborough, Ideal

Weekend Im Paradies, Play
Liebe Im Finanzamt 1952 d: Kurt Hoffmann. lps: Paul Dahlke, Carola Hohn, Christiane Jansen. 85M GRM. *Wochenend Im Paradies; Love in the Tax Office* prod/rel: Standard, N.W.D.F.

ARNOLD, GEORGES
Esprit Es-Tu la, Play
Esprit Es-Tu la 1917 d: Fernand Rivers. lps: Fernand Rivers, Louis Maurel, Madeleine Guitty. 260m FRN.

ARNOLD, JESS
A Mission for General Houston, Story
Eagle and the Hawk, The 1950 d: Lewis R. Foster. lps: John Payne, Rhonda Fleming, Dennis O'Keefe. 104M USA. *Spread Eagle* prod/rel: Paramount, Pine-Thomas

ARNOLD, LAWRENCE
La Tempete, Short Story
Fiancailles Rouges, Les 1926 d: Roger Lion. lps: Jean Murat, Dolly Davis, Gil Clary. F FRN. prod/rel: Films Roger Lion

ARNOLD, MICHAEL
The Archduke, New York 1967, Book
Mayerling 1968 d: Terence Young. lps: Omar Sharif, Catherine Deneuve, James Mason. 141M UKN/FRN. prod/rel: Les Films Corona, Winchester Film Production

ARNOW, HARRIETTE
The Doll Maker, 1954, Novel
Doll Maker, The 1983 d: Daniel Petrie. lps: Jane Fonda, Levon Helm, Amanda Plummer. TVM. 150M USA. *The Dollmaker* prod/rel: ABC, Finnegan Associates

AROZARENA, RAFAEL
Mararia, Novel
Mararia 1998 d: Antonio Jose Betancor. lps: Carmelo Gomez, Ian Glen, Goya Toledo. 109M SPN. prod/rel: Aiete Films, Ariane Films

ARPINO, GIOVANNI
Anima Persa, Novel
Anima Persa 1976 d: Dino Risi. lps: Catherine Deneuve, Vittorio Gassman, Anicee AlvinA. 111M ITL/FRN. *Ames Perdues; Lost Soul* prod/rel: Dean Film (Roma), Fox Production (Paris)

Il Buio E Il Miele, Novel
Profumo Di Donna 1974 d: Dino Risi. lps: Vittorio Gassman, Alessandro Momo, Agostina Belli. 100M ITL. *Scent of a Woman* (USA); *That Female Scent* (UKN); *Scent of Woman* prod/rel: Dean Film, Fida Cin.Ca
Scent of a Woman 1992 d: Martin Brest. lps: Al Pacino, Chris O'Donnell, James Rebhorn. 156M USA. prod/rel: Universal, City Lights

ARRABAL, FERNANDO (1932–, MRC
Baal Babylone, 1959, Novel
Viva la Muerte 1970 d: Fernando Arrabal. lps: Nuria Espert, Anouk Ferjac, Mahdi Chaouch. 100M FRN/TNS. *Hurrah for Death* prod/rel: Isabelle, S.a.T.P.E.C.

Fando Et Lis, Paris 1958, Play
Fando Y Lis 1968 d: Alejandro Jodorowsky. lps: Sergio Klainer, Diana Mariscal, Maria Teresa Rivas. 100M MXC. *Fando and Lis* (USA); *Tar Babies* (UKN); *Fando Y Lys* prod/rel: Producciones Panic

Le Grand Ceremonial, 1965, Play
Grand Ceremonial, Le 1968 d: Pierre-Alain Jolivet. lps: Michel Tureau, Marcella Saint-Amant, Ginette Leclerc. 110M FRN. *Weird Weirdo* (UKN) prod/rel: Alcinter

Guernica, 1961, Play
Guernica -Jede Stunde Verletzt Und Die Leute Totet 1963 d: Peter Lilienthal. lps: Heinz Meier, Annemarie Schradiek, Friedrich Mertel. 30M GRM. *Jede Stunde Verletzt Und Die Letzte Totet*

ARRIAGA, GUILLERMO
Un Dulce Olor a Muerte, Novel
Dulce Olor a Muerte, Un 1999 d: Gabriel Retes. lps: Karra Elejalde, Ana Alvarez, Diego LunA. 98M MXC/SPN/ARG. *A Sweet Scent of Death* prod/rel: Mirador Films, Ivania Films

ARRIGHI, CLETTO
Dal Tecc Alla Cantina, Play
Scena a Soggetto Musicale 1914 d: Arnaldo Giacomelli. lps: Eduardo Ferravilla, Maria FerravillA. ITL. prod/rel: Comerio

ARRIGHI, MEL
Alter Ego, Novel
Murder By the Book 1987 d: Mel Damski. lps: Robert Hays, Catherine Mary Stewart, Celeste Holm. TVM. 100M USA. *Alter Ego* prod/rel: Peter Nelson Prod., Orion Television

ARSAN, EMMANUELLE
Emmanuelle, Novel
Emmanuelle 1974 d: Just Jaeckin. lps: Sylvia Kristel, Marika Green, Daniel Sarky. 94M FRN. prod/rel: Trinacra, Orphee

ARSENIEVA, VLADIMIR K.
Okhotnik Dersu, Book
Derzu Uzala 1975 d: Akira KurosawA. lps: Yuri Solomin, Maxim Munsuk, M. Bechkov. 141M JPN/USS. *Dersu Uzala* prod/rel: Mosfilm, Atelie-41

ARTEMAS (MASON, ARTHUR T.)
A Dear Fool, Novel
Dear Fool, A 1921 d: Harold Shaw. lps: George K. Arthur, Edna Flugrath, Edward O'Neill. 6454f UKN. prod/rel: Stoll

ARTEMOWSKY, SEMEN
Zaporozheta Za Dunayem, St. Petersburg 1863, Opera
Cossacks in Exile 1939 d: Edgar G. Ulmer. lps: Maria Sokil, Michael Shvetz, Nicholas Harlash. 82M USA. *Cossacks Across the Danube; Cossacks in Exile* prod/rel: Avramenko Film Co.
Zaporozets Za Dunayem 1938 d: Y. P. Kavaledge. F USS. *Cossacks Beyond the Danube*

ARTHUR, ART
Rhino!, Novel
Rhino! 1964 d: Ivan Tors. lps: Harry Guardino, Shirley Eaton, Robert Culp. 91M USA/SAF. prod/rel: Ivan Tors, MGM

ARTHUR, BURT
Ride Out for Revenge, Novel
Ride Out for Revenge 1957 d: Bernard Girard. lps: Rory Calhoun, Gloria Grahame, Lloyd Bridges. 78M USA. prod/rel: United Artists, Bryna Prods.

ARTHUR, JOSEPH
Blue Jeans, New York 1890, Play
Blue Jeans 1917 d: John H. Collins. lps: Viola Dana, Robert Walker, Sally Crute. 7r USA. prod/rel: Metro Pictures Corp.©

The Still Alarm, New York 1887, Play
Still Alarm, The 1918 d: Colin Campbell. lps: Thomas Santschi, Bessie Eyton, Frank Clark. 6r USA. prod/rel: Selig Polyscope Co., State Rights
Still Alarm, The 1926 d: Edward Laemmle. lps: Helene Chadwick, William Russell, Richard C. Travers. 7207f USA. prod/rel: Universal Pictures

ARTHUR, LEE
The Auctioneer, New York 1913, Play
Auctioneer, The 1927 d: Alfred E. Green. lps: George Sidney, Marion Nixon, Gareth Hughes. 5500f USA. prod/rel: Fox Film Corp.

Cohen's Luck, Play
Cohen's Luck 1915 d: John H. Collins. lps: Viola Dana, William Wadsworth, Lillian Devere. 4r USA. prod/rel: Thomas A. Edison, Inc.©, General Film Co.

ARTHUR, MACK
The Isle of Destiny, Short Story
Isle of Destiny, The 1920 d: Tamar Lane. lps: Paul Gilmore, Hazel Hudson, Frank Williams. 6r USA. prod/rel: Character Pictures Corp., Rialto Productions

ARTHUR, TIMOTHY SHAY
Ten Nights in a Bar- Room and What I Saw There, Philadelphia 1839, Novel
Ten Nights in a Bar Room 1911 d: Frank Boggs. lps: Charles Clary, Kathlyn Williams. 2000f USA. prod/rel: Selig Polyscope Co.

Ten Nights in a Bar-Room and What I Saw There, Philadelphia 1839, Novel
Ten Nights in a Bar Room 1921 d: Oscar Apfel. lps: Ivy Ward, John Lowell, Nell Clark Keller. 8r USA. prod/rel: Blazed Trail Productions, Arrow Film Corp.
Ten Nights in a Barroom 1913 d: Lee Beggs. lps: Robert Vaughn, Violet Horner, Robert Lawrence. 5r USA. prod/rel: Photo Drama Co.©
Ten Nights in a Bar-Room 1926 d: Roy Calnek. lps: Charles Gilpin, Myra Burwell, Lawrence Chenault. 6700f USA. prod/rel: Colored Players Film Corp.

ARTHURS, GEORGE
Marry the Girl, London 1930, Play
Marry the Girl 1935 d: MacLean Rogers. lps: Sonnie Hale, Winifred Shotter, Hugh Wakefield. 69M UKN. prod/rel: British Lion

Their Night Out, Play
Their Night Out 1933 d: Harry Hughes. lps: Claude Hulbert, Renee Houston, Gus McNaughton. 74M UKN. *His Night Out* prod/rel: British International Pictures, Wardour

ARTINGER ANNEMARIE
Okay Mama, Novel
Solang' Es Hubsche Madchen Gibt 1955 d: Arthur M. Rabenalt. lps: Grethe Weiser, Georg Thomalla, Alice Kessler. 106M GRM. *As Long As There are Pretty Girls* prod/rel: Carlton, Gloria

ARTINGER, ANNEMARIE
Anonyme Briefe, Novel
Anonyme Briefe 1949 d: Arthur M. Rabenalt. lps: Kathe Haack, Tilly Lauenstein, O. E. Hasse. 95M GRM. *Anonymous Letters* prod/rel: Cordial, Europa

ARTU (RICCARDO ARTUFFO)
Il Trattato Scomparso, Play
Masque Qui Tombe, Le 1933 d: Mario Bonnard. lps: Jean Worms, Tania Fedor, Lucienne Le Marchand. 85M FRN.
Trattato Scomparso, Il 1933 d: Mario Bonnard. lps: Leda Gloria, Giuditta Rissone, Nini Dinelli. 78M ITL. prod/rel: Cines, Anonima Pittaluga

ARUNDEL, EDITH
Persistent Warrior, Novel
Green Fingers 1947 d: John Harlow. lps: Robert Beatty, Carole Raye, Nova Pilbeam. 83M UKN. prod/rel: British National, Anglo-American

ARUNDEL, REX HOWARD
Over the Odds, Play
Over the Odds 1961 d: Michael Forlong. lps: Marjorie Rhodes, Glenn Melvyn, Thora Hird. 65M UKN. prod/rel: Rank Film Distributors, Jermyn

ASBJORNSEN, PEDER CHRISTEN (1812–1885), NRW, Asbjornsen, Peter Christian
Princessen Som Ingen Kunde Malbinde Felgesvenden, 1910, Short Story
Princessen Som Ingen Kunne Malbinde 1932 d: Walter Fyrst. 36M NRW.

ASBURY, HERBERT (1891–1963), USA
Gangs of New York, New York 1936, Novel
Gangs of New York 1938 d: James Cruze. lps: Charles Bickford, Ann Dvorak, Alan Baxter. 67M USA. prod/rel: Republic Pictures Corp.©

ASCANIO
Le Film du Poilu, Short Story
 Film du Poilu, Le 1928 d: Henri Desfontaines. lps: Ninon Gilles, Daniel Mendaille, Roby Guichard. 2400m FRN.

ASCH, SHOLOM
Uncle Moses, New York 1918, Novel
 Uncle Moses 1932 d: Sidney M. Goldin, Aubrey Scotto. lps: Maurice Schwartz, Rubin Goldberg, Judith Abarbanel. 88M USA. prod/rel: Yiddish Talking Pictures

ASCHE, OSCAR
Chu Chin Chow, London 1916, Musical Play
 Chu Chin Chow 1923 d: Herbert Wilcox. lps: Betty Blythe, Herbert Langley, Randle Ayrton. 13r UKN. prod/rel: Graham-Wilcox
 Chu Chin Chow 1934 d: Walter Forde. lps: George Robey, Fritz Kortner, Anna May Wong. 102M UKN. prod/rel: Gaumont-British, Gainsborough

ASHBROOK, HARRIETTE
The Murder of Steven Kester, New York 1931, Novel
 Green Eyes 1934 d: Richard Thorpe. lps: Charles Starrett, John Wray, Shirley Grey. 68M USA. prod/rel: Chesterfield Motion Pictures Corp.©

ASHELBE, DETECTIVE
Le Club Des Aristocrates, Novel
 Club Des Aristocrates, Le 1937 d: Piere Colombier. lps: Jules Berry, Elvire Popesco, Viviane Romance. 89M FRN. prod/rel: Productions Claude Dolbert
Dedee d'Anvers, Novel
 Dedee d'Anvers 1947 d: Yves Allegret. lps: Simone Signoret, Bernard Blier, Marcello Pagliero. 100M FRN. *Dedee* (USA); *Woman of Antwerp* prod/rel: Sacha Gordine
Pepe le Moko, Paris 1937, Novel
 Algiers 1938 d: John Cromwell. lps: Charles Boyer, Sigrid Gurie, Hedy Lamarr. 96M USA. prod/rel: Walter Wanger Productions, Inc.
 Casbah 1948 d: John Berry. lps: Tony Martin, Yvonne de Carlo, Marta Toren. 94M USA. prod/rel: Universal
 Pepe le Moko 1936 d: Julien Duvivier. lps: Jean Gabin, Lucas Gridoux, Mireille Balin. 93M FRN. *Les Nuits Blanches*; *Casbah* prod/rel: Paris-Films-Production

ASHFORD, J.
Kurzer Prozess, Novel
 Kurzer Prozess 1967 d: Michael Kehlmann. lps: Helmut Qualtinger, Alexander Kerst, Gudrun Thielemann. 101M GRM. *Short Work*; *Short Trial* prod/rel: U.F.P., Inter

ASHFORD, JEFFREY
Novel
 Hit and Run 1965 d: Paddy Russell. lps: John Tillinger, Joseph O'Conor. MTV. UKN. prod/rel: BBC

ASHLEY, BERNARD
Terry on the Fence, Novel
 Terry on the Fence 1987 d: Frank Godwin. lps: Jack McNicholl, Neville Watson, Tracey Ann Morris. 70M UKN. prod/rel: Eyline Film and Video, Children's Film and Tv Foundation

ASHTON, HELEN
Yeoman's Hospital, Novel
 White Corridors 1951 d: Pat Jackson. lps: Googie Withers, James Donald, Godfrey Tearle. 102M UKN. prod/rel: General Film Distributors, Vic Films

ASHTON JR., HERBERT
Brothers, Play
 Brothers 1930 d: Walter Lang. lps: Bert Lytell, Dorothy Sebastian, William Morris. 6843f USA. *Blood Brothers* (UKN) prod/rel: Columbia Pictures

ASHTON-WARNER, SYLVIA (1908–1984), NZL
I Passed This Way, Book
 Sylvia 1985 d: Michael Firth. lps: Eleanor David, Nigel Terry, Tom Wilkinson. 98M NZL. prod/rel: Southern Light Pictuers, Cinepro
Spinster, London 1958, Novel
 Two Loves 1961 d: Charles Walters. lps: Shirley MacLaine, Laurence Harvey, Jack Hawkins. 100M USA. *Spinster* (UKN); *I'll Save My Love* prod/rel: Julian Blaustein Productions, MGM
Teacher, Book
 Sylvia 1985 d: Michael Firth. lps: Eleanor David, Nigel Terry, Tom Wilkinson. 98M NZL. prod/rel: Southern Light Pictuers, Cinepro

ASIMOV, ISAAC (1920–1992), RSS
Story
 Nightfall 1988 d: Paul Mayersberg. lps: David Birney, Sarah Douglas, Alexis Kanner. 82M USA. prod/rel: Concorde
The Ugly Little Boy, 1966, Short Story
 Ugly Little Boy, The 1978 d: Barry Morse. 26M USA.

ASINOF, ELIOT
Eight Men Out, Book
 Eight Men Out 1989 d: John Sayles. lps: John Cusack, Clifton James, Michael Lerner. 119M USA. prod/rel: Orion

ASKEW, ALICE
God's Clay, Novel
 God's Clay 1919 d: Arthur Rooke. lps: Janet Alexander, Humberston Wright, Arthur Rooke. 4500f UKN. prod/rel: Arthur Rooke
 God's Clay 1928 d: Graham Cutts. lps: Anny Ondra, Trilby Clark, Franklyn Bellamy. 6301f UKN. prod/rel: First National, First National-Pathe
John Heriot's Wife, Novel
 Vrouw Van Den Minister, de 1920 d: B. E. Doxat-Pratt, Maurits H. Binger. lps: Mary Odette, Henry Victor, Adelqui Millar. 5600f NTH/UKN. *John Heriot's Wife* (UKN); *The Minister's Wife* prod/rel: Anglo-Hollandia Film
Poison, Novel
 Pleydell Mystery, The 1916 d: Albert Ward. lps: Cecil Humphreys, Christine Silver, Richard Lindsay. 5000f UKN. prod/rel: British Empire
Testimony, Novel
 Testimony 1920 d: Guy Newall. lps: Ivy Duke, David Hawthorne, Lawford Davidson. 7189f UKN. prod/rel: George Clark, Stoll

ASKEW, CLAUDE
God's Clay, Novel
 God's Clay 1919 d: Arthur Rooke. lps: Janet Alexander, Humberston Wright, Arthur Rooke. 4500f UKN. prod/rel: Arthur Rooke
 God's Clay 1928 d: Graham Cutts. lps: Anny Ondra, Trilby Clark, Franklyn Bellamy. 6301f UKN. prod/rel: First National, First National-Pathe
John Heriot's Wife, Novel
 Vrouw Van Den Minister, de 1920 d: B. E. Doxat-Pratt, Maurits H. Binger. lps: Mary Odette, Henry Victor, Adelqui Millar. 5600f NTH/UKN. *John Heriot's Wife* (UKN); *The Minister's Wife* prod/rel: Anglo-Hollandia Film
Poison, Novel
 Pleydell Mystery, The 1916 d: Albert Ward. lps: Cecil Humphreys, Christine Silver, Richard Lindsay. 5000f UKN. prod/rel: British Empire
The Shulamite, London 1906, Play
 Shulamite, The 1915 d: George Loane Tucker. lps: Norman McKinnel, Manora Thew, Gerald Ames. 4805f UKN. prod/rel: London, Jury
 Under the Lash 1921 d: Sam Wood. lps: Gloria Swanson, Mahlon Hamilton, Russell Simpson. 5675f USA. *The Shulamite* (UKN) prod/rel: Famous Players-Lasky, Paramount Pictures
Testimony, Novel
 Testimony 1920 d: Guy Newall. lps: Ivy Duke, David Hawthorne, Lawford Davidson. 7189f UKN. prod/rel: George Clark, Stoll

ASSOLLANT, ALFRED
Les Aventures du Capitaine Corcoran, Novel
 Aventures Deu Capitaine Corcoran, Les 1914 d: Charles Krauss. 943m FRN. prod/rel: Eclair

ASTAFJEW, VIKTOR
Story
 Svesdopad 1981 d: Igor Talankin. lps: Pyotr Fyodorov, Pjotr Jurtschenkow, Darya MichailovA. 92M USS. *Zvezdopad*; *Falling Stars*; *The Starfall* prod/rel: Mosfilm

ASTURIAS, MIGUEL ANGEL (1899–1974), GTM
El Senor Presidente, 1946, Novel
 Sr. Presidente, El 1983 d: Manuel Octavio Gomez. lps: Michel Auclair, Reynaldo Miravalles, Bruno Garcin. 100M CUB/NCR/FRN. *El Senor Presidente*; *Mr. President*

ASZTALOS, NIKOLAS
Die Nacht in Siebenburgen, Play
 Tanz Mit Dem Kaiser, Der 1941 d: Georg Jacoby. lps: Marika Rokk, Maria Eis, Axel von Ambesser. 102M GRM. prod/rel: UFA, Central-Europaischer

ATHANAS, VERNE
The Proud Ones, 1952, Novel
 Proud Ones, The 1956 d: Robert D. Webb. lps: Robert Ryan, Virginia Mayo, Jeffrey Hunter. 94M USA. prod/rel: 20th Century-Fox

ATHERTON, GERTRUDE FRANKLIN
The Avalanche: a Mystery Story, New York 1919, Play
 Avalanche, The 1919 d: George Fitzmaurice. lps: Elsie Ferguson, Lumsden Hare, Zeffie Tilbury. 5273f USA. prod/rel: Famous Players-Lasky Corp.©, Artcraft Pictures

Black Oxen, New York 1923, Novel
 Black Oxen 1924 d: Frank Lloyd. lps: Corinne Griffith, Conway Tearle, Tom Ricketts. 7937f USA. prod/rel: Frank Lloyd Productions, Associated First National Pictures
The Crystal Cup, New York 1925, Novel
 Crystal Cup, The 1927 d: John Francis Dillon. lps: Dorothy MacKaill, Rockliffe Fellowes, Jack Mulhall. 6386f USA. prod/rel: Henry Hobart Productions, First National Pictures
Mrs. Balfame, New York 1906, Novel
 Mrs. Balfame 1917 d: Frank Powell. lps: Nance O'Neil, Frank Belcher, Robert Elliott. 6r USA. prod/rel: Frank Powell Producing Corp., Mutual Film Corp.
Patience Sparhawk and Her Times, New York 1897, Novel
 Panther Woman, The 1919 d: Ralph Ince. lps: Olga Petrova, Rockliffe Fellowes, Vernon Steele. 6r USA. *Patience Sparhawk* prod/rel: Petrova Picture Co., First National Exhibitors Circuit
Perch of the Devil, New York 1914, Novel
 Perch of the Devil 1927 d: King Baggot. lps: Mae Busch, Pat O'Malley, Jane Winton. 6807f USA. prod/rel: Universal Pictures
Tower of Ivory, New York 1910, Novel
 Out of the Storm 1920 d: William Parke. lps: Barbara Castleton, John Bowers, Sidney Ainsworth. 5r USA. *The Tower of Ivory* prod/rel: Eminent Authors Pictures, Inc., Goldwyn Distributing Corp.

ATHIS, ALFRED
Le Costaud Des Epinettes, Play
 Amants Et Voleurs 1935 d: Raymond Bernard. lps: Pierre Blanchar, Michel Simon, Florelle. 105M FRN. prod/rel: Productions Odeon
 Costaud Des Epinettes, Le 1922 d: Raymond Bernard. lps: Germaine Fontanes, Henri Debain, Henri Collen. 1405m FRN. prod/rel: Films Tristan Bernard
Les Deux Canards, Play
 Deux Canards, Les 1933 d: Erich Schmidt. lps: Rene Lefevre, Saturnin Fabre, Florelle. 78M FRN. prod/rel: Artia-Film

ATHREYA, ACHARYA
Ngo, Play
 Gumasta 1953 d: R. M. Krishnaswamy. lps: Chittor V. Nagaiah, Sivaram, Pandharibai. 187M IND. prod/rel: Aruna Pictures

ATIYAH, EDWARD
The Thin Line, Novel
 Juste Avant la Nuit 1971 d: Claude Chabrol. lps: Michel Bouquet, Stephane Audran, Francois Perier. 107M FRN/ITL. *Just Before Nightfall* (UKN); *Le Visiteur de la Nuit* prod/rel: Films la Boetie, Columbia Films

ATKEY, BERTRAM
After Dark, Short Story
 After Dark 1924 d: Thomas Bentley. lps: Eric Bransby Williams, Joyce Dearsley, John Hamilton. 1580f UKN. prod/rel: Stoll
Hidden Fires, Novel
 Secret Kingdom, The 1925 d: Sinclair Hill. lps: Matheson Lang, Stella Arbenina, Eric Bransby Williams. 5930f UKN. *Beyond the Veil* prod/rel: Stoll

ATKINSON, ALEX
Wheel of Fate, Play
 Wheel of Fate 1953 d: Francis Searle. lps: Patric Doonan, Sandra Dorne, Bryan Forbes. 70M UKN. *Road House Girl* (USA) prod/rel: Kenilworth, General Film Distributors

ATKINSON, ELEANOR
Greyfriars Bobby, New York 1912, Novel
 Challenge to Lassie 1949 d: Richard Thorpe. lps: Edmund Gwenn, Donald Crisp, Geraldine Brooks. 76M USA. prod/rel: MGM
 Greyfriars Bobby 1961 d: Don Chaffey. lps: Donald Crisp, Laurence Naismith, Alex MacKenzie. 91M UKN/USA. prod/rel: Walt Disney Productions

ATKINSON, HUGH
The Games, London 1967, Novel
 Games, The 1969 d: Michael Winner. lps: Michael Crawford, Stanley Baker, Ryan O'Neal. 97M UKN. prod/rel: 20th Century-Fox
The Reckoning, Novel
 Weekend of Shadows 1978 d: Tom Jeffrey. lps: John Waters, Melissa Jaffer, Wyn Roberts. 95M ASL. prod/rel: Samson Productions Pty Ltd.©, South Australia Film Corp.

The Music of Chance, Novel
   Music of Chance, The 1993 d: Philip Haas. lps: James
   Spader, Mandy Patinkin, M. Emmet Walsh. 97M USA.

AUSTIN, ANNE
Wicked Woman, New York 1933, Novel
   Wicked Woman, A 1934 d: Charles J. Brabin. lps: Jean
   Parker, Charles Bickford, Mady Christians. 76M USA.
   prod/rel: Metro-Goldwyn-Mayer Corp.©

AUSTIN, F. BRITTEN
Buried Treasure, Short Story
   Buried Treasure 1921 d: George D. Baker. lps: Marion
   Davies, Norman Kerry, Anders Randolf. 6964f USA.
   prod/rel: Cosmopolitan Productions, Famous
   Players-Lasky
The Drum, 1923, Short Story
   Drum, The 1924 d: Sinclair Hill. lps: James Carew,
   Jameson Thomas, Molly Johnson. 1731f UKN. prod/rel:
   Stoll
   Last Outpost, The 1935 d: Charles T. Barton, Louis J.
   Gasnier. lps: Cary Grant, Claude Rains, Gertrude
   Michael. 75M USA. *Jungle* prod/rel: Paramount
   Productions©
The Fining Pot Is for Silver, Novel
   Woman Redeemed, A 1927 d: Sinclair Hill. lps: Joan
   Lockton, Brian Aherne, Stella ArbeninA. 7800f UKN.
   prod/rel: Stoll, New Era
The Last Witness, Novel
   Last Witness, The 1925 d: Fred Paul. lps: Isobel
   Elsom, Fred Paul, Stella ArbeninA. 6100f UKN.
   prod/rel: Stoll

AUSTIN, MAY
The King's Romance, Play
   King's Romance, The 1914 d: Ernest G. Batley. lps:
   Fred Morgan, Ethel Bracewell, Henry Victor. 4074f
   UKN. *The Revolutionist* (USA); *Revolution* prod/rel:
   British and Colonial, Kinematograph Trading Co.

AUTIER, PAUL
Gardiens de Phare, Play
   Gardiens de Phare 1928 d: Jean Gremillon. lps:
   Gabrielle Fontan, Geymond Vital, Fromet. 2000m FRN.
   Guardians of Phare prod/rel: Societe Des Films Du
   Grand Guignol

AVERY, STEPHEN MOREHOUSE
Stuffed Shirt, 1932, Short Story
   Hard to Get 1938 d: Ray Enright. lps: Dick Powell,
   Olivia de Havilland, Charles Winninger. 80M USA.
   Head Over Heels; *Hot Heiress*; *For Lovers Only* prod/rel:
   Warner Bros. Pictures©
Target, Short Story
   Annapolis Farewell 1935 d: Alexander Hall. lps:
   Richard Cromwell, Tom Brown, Guy Standing. 75M
   USA. *Gentlemen of the Navy* (UKN); *Target* prod/rel:
   Paramount Productions, Inc.

AXELROD, GEORGE (1922–, USA
Goodbye Charlie, New York 1960, Play
   Goodbye Charlie 1964 d: Vincente Minnelli. lps:
   Debbie Reynolds, Tony Curtis, Walter Matthau. 117M
   USA. prod/rel: Venice Productions, 20th Century Fox
Phffft, Unproduced, Play
   Phffft! 1954 d: Mark Robson. lps: Judy Holliday, Jack
   Lemmon, Jack Carson. 91M USA. prod/rel: Columbia
The Seven Year Itch, New York 1952, Play
   Seven Year Itch, The 1955 d: Billy Wilder. lps:
   Marilyn Monroe, Tom Ewell, Evelyn Keyes. 105M USA.
   prod/rel: 20th Century-Fox
Will Success Spoil Rock Hunter?, New York 1955,
Play
   Will Success Spoil Rock Hunter? 1957 d: Frank
   Tashlin. lps: Jayne Mansfield, Tony Randall, Betsy
   Drake. 95M USA. *Oh! for a Man!* (UKN) prod/rel: 20th
   Century-Fox

AXELSON, MARY MCDOUGAL
Life Begins, New York 1932, Play
   Child Is Born, A 1940 d: Lloyd Bacon. lps: Geraldine
   Fitzgerald, Jeffrey Lynn, Gladys George. 79M USA.
   Give Me a Child prod/rel: Warner Bros. Pictures, Inc.
   Life Begins 1932 d: James Flood, Elliott Nugent. lps:
   Loretta Young, Aline MacMahon, Glenda Farrell. 72M
   USA. *The Dawn of Life* (UKN); *Give Me a Child*;
   Woman's Day prod/rel: First National Pictures©
   Storia d'Amore, Una 1942 d: Mario Camerini. lps:
   Piero Lulli, Carlo Campanini, Guido Notari. 88M ITL.
   prod/rel: Lux Film

AXT, MARIA
Book
   Whopper-Punch 777 1988 d: Jurgen Troster. lps:
   Burkhard Ronnefarth, Manfred Krug, Gunther
   Kaufmann. 68M GRM. prod/rel: Troster Film, Roxy

AYALA, JUAN DEL RIO
Tyrma, Novel
   Principessa Delle Canarie, La 1956 d: Paolo Moffa,
   Carlos Serrano de OsmA. lps: Silvana Pampanini,
   Marcello Mastroianni, Gustavo Rojo. 105M ITL/SPN.
   Tyrma (SPN); *Isola*; *The Island Princess*; *Tirma*;
   Princess of the Canary Islands prod/rel: Film
   Costellazione (Roma), F.I.E.S. (Madrid)

AYCKBOURN, ALAN (1939–, UKN
A Chorus of Disapproval, 1986, Play
   Chorus of Disapproval, A 1989 d: Michael Winner.
   lps: Jeremy Irons, Anthony Hopkins, Prunella Scales.
   100M UKN. prod/rel: Hobo, Curzon
Intimate Exchanges, Play
   Smoking/No Smoking 1993 d: Alain Resnais. lps:
   Sabine Azema, Pierre Arditi. 285M FRN. prod/rel:
   Arena, Camera One
The Norman Conquests, 1974, Play
   Norman Conquests, The 1977 d: Herbert Wise. lps:
   Richard Briers, Penelope Keith, Tom Conti. MTV. 300M
   UKN. prod/rel: Thames Tv
The Revengers' Comedies, Play
   Revengers' Comedies, The 1998 d: Malcolm
   Mowbray. lps: Sam Neill, Helena Bonham-Carter,
   Kristin Scott-Thomas. 82M UKN/FRN. prod/rel: J&m
   Entertainment, BBC Films
Way Upstream, 1983, Play
   Way Upstream 1989 d: Terry Johnson. lps: Barry
   Rutter, Marion Bailey, Nick Dunning. TVM. 105M
   UKN.
   Way Upstream 1991 d: Sandor Francken. lps: Geert de
   Jong, Gees Linnebank, Celia Van Den Boogert. 90M
   NTH.

AYERS, CAPT. JOHN H.
Missing Men, New York 1932, Book
   Bureau of Missing Persons 1933 d: Roy Del Ruth. lps:
   Bette Davis, Lewis Stone, Pat O'Brien. 78M USA.
   Missing Persons prod/rel: First National Pictures, Inc.

AYME, MARCEL (1902–1967), FRN
La Belle Image, 1941, Novel
   Belle Image, La 1950 d: Claude Heymann. lps: Frank
   Villard, Pierre Larquey, Francoise Christophe. 90M
   FRN. *The Beautiful Image* prod/rel: S.N.E.G., C.G.C.
Le Chemin Des Ecoliers, 1946, Novel
   Chemin Des Ecoliers, Le 1959 d: Michel Boisrond.
   lps: Francoise Arnoul, Bourvil, Lino VenturA. 82M
   FRN/ITL. *Furore Di Vivere* (ITL); *The Way of Youth*
   (USA) prod/rel: S.P.C.E., F.L.F.
Clerambard, 1950, Play
   Clerambard 1969 d: Yves Robert. lps: Philippe Noiret,
   Dany Carrel, Martine Sarcey. 100M FRN. prod/rel:
   Productions De La Gueville, Gaumont International
La Grace, Novel
   Gueule de l'Autre, La 1979 d: Pierre TcherniA. lps:
   Jean Poiret, Michel Serrault, Andrea Parisy. TVM.
   100M FRN. *La Grace* prod/rel: Antenne 2
La Jument Verte, Paris 1933, Novel
   Jument Verte, La 1959 d: Claude Autant-LarA. lps:
   Bourvil, Francis Blanche, Sandra Milo. 105M FRN/ITL.
   La Giumenta Verde (ITL); *The Green Mare's Nest*
   (UKN); *The Green Mare* (USA); *Bedroom Vendetta*
   prod/rel: S.N.E. Gaumont, S.O.P.A.C.
Le Passe-Muraille, Paris 1943, Short Story
   Garou-Garou le Passe-Muraille 1950 d: Jean Boyer.
   lps: Bourvil, Gerard Oury, Raymond Souplex. 90M FRN.
   Mr. Peek-a-Boo (USA); *Le Passe-Muraille* prod/rel: Cite
   Films
   Mann Geht Durch Die Wand, Ein 1959 d: Ladislao
   VajdA. lps: Heinz Ruhmann, Nicole Courcel, Rudolf
   Rhomberg. 99M GRM. *The Man Who Walked Through
   the Wall* (USA); *A Man Goes Through the Wall*; *The Man
   Who Could Walk Through Walls* prod/rel: Pen Films,
   D.F.H.
Rue Saint-Sulpice, Short Story
   Favour, the Watch and the Very Big Fish, The
   1991 d: Ben Lewin. lps: Bob Hoskins, Jeff Goldblum,
   Natasha Richardson. 89M UKN/FRN. *Rue
   Saint-Sulpice* (FRN) prod/rel: Films Ariane, Fildebroc
   (Paris)
La Rue Sans Nom, Novel
   Rue Sans Nom, La 1934 d: Pierre Chenal. lps:
   Constant Remy, Pola Illery, Gabriel Gabrio. 82M FRN.
   prod/rel: Les Productions Pellegrin
La Table-aux-Creves, 1929, Novel
   Table aux Creves, La 1951 d: Henri Verneuil. lps:
   Fernandel, Maria Mauban, Fernand Sardou. 92M FRN.
   The Village Feud prod/rel: Films Marceau, Films
   Vendome

La Traversee de Paris, 1946, Short Story
   Traversee de Paris, La 1956 d: Claude Autant-LarA.
   lps: Jean Gabin, Bourvil, Jeannette Batti. 82M
   FRN/ITL. *Pig Across Paris* (UKN); *Four Bags Full*
   (USA) prod/rel: Continentale Prod., Franco-London
   Film
Uranus, 1948, Novel
   Uranus 1990 d: Claude Berri. lps: Philippe Noiret,
   Gerard Depardieu, Jean-Pierre Marielle. 100M FRN.
   prod/rel: Renn Productions, Films a2
La Vouivre, Novel
   Vouivre, La 1988 d: Georges Wilson. lps: Lambert
   Wilson, Suzanne Flon, Kathye Kriegel. 102M FRN.

AYRES, HERBERT
The Common Touch, Novel
   Common Touch, The 1941 d: John Baxter. lps: Greta
   Gynt, Geoffrey Hibbert, Joyce Howard. 104M UKN.
   prod/rel: British National, Anglo-Amalgamated

AYRES, RUBY M., Ayres, Ruby Mildred
Short Story
   Model's Confession, The 1918 d: Ida May Park. lps:
   Mary MacLaren, Kenneth Harlan, Edna Earle. 6r USA.
   prod/rel: Universal Film Mfg. Co.©
A Bachelor Husband, Novel
   Bachelor Husband, A 1920 d: Kenelm Foss. lps: Lyn
   Harding, Renee Mayer, Hayford Hobbs. 5000f UKN.
   prod/rel: Astra Films
The Black Sheep, Novel
   Black Sheep, The 1920 d: Sidney Morgan. lps:
   Margaret Blanche, George Keene, Eve Balfour. 5000f
   UKN. prod/rel: Progress, Butcher's Film Service
Castles in Spain, Novel
   Castles in Spain 1920 d: H. Lisle Lucoque. lps: C.
   Aubrey Smith, Lilian Braithwaite, Bertie Gordon. 5000f
   UKN. prod/rel: Lucoque-Taylor, Gaumont
The Man Without a Heart, New York 1924, Novel
   Man Without a Heart, The 1924 d: Burton L. King.
   lps: Kenneth Harlan, Jane Novak, David Powell. 6000f
   USA. prod/rel: Banner Productions
None But the Brave, Novel
   Somewhere in France 1915 d: Tom Watts. lps: Vera
   Cornish. 3000f UKN. prod/rel: Regal, Yorkshire
   Cinematograph Co.
The Second Honeymoon, New York 1921, Novel
   Second Honeymoon 1930 d: Phil Rosen. lps:
   Josephine Dunn, Edward Earle, Ernest Hilliard. 5586f
   USA. prod/rel: Continental Talking Pictures

AZA, V.
El Rey Que Rabio, Opera
   Rey Que Rabio, El 1929 d: Jose Buchs. lps: Juan de
   Orduna, Amelia Munoz, Jose Montenegro. F SPN. *The
   King Had Rabies* prod/rel: Ediciones Forns-Buchs
   (Madrid)

AZCONA, RAFAEL
Nel Giorno Dell'Onomastico Della Mamma, Story
   **Alla Mia Cara Mamma Nel Giorno Del Suo
   Compleanno** 1974 d: Luciano Salce. lps: Paolo
   Villaggio, Lila Kedrova, Eleonora Giorgi. 105M ITL.
   prod/rel: Rusconi Film, C.I.C.
El Pisito, Novel
   Pisito, El 1957 d: Marco Ferreri, Isidoro Martinez
   Ferry. lps: Jose Luis Lopez Vazquez, Mari Carrillo,
   Concha Lopez-SilvA. 87M SPN. *The Little Apartment*
   prod/rel: Documento

AZUELA, MARIANO (1873–1952), MXC
Mala Yerba, 1909, Novel
   Mala Yerba 1940 d: Gabriel SoriA. lps: Arturo de
   Cordova, Lupita Gallardo, Rene CardonA. 81M MXC.

B

BAAR, JINDRICH SIMON
Cestou Krizovou, Novel
   Cestou Krizovou 1938 d: Jiri Slavicek. lps: Hana
   Vitova, Frantisek Kreuzmann, Zdenek Stepanek.
   2663m CZC. *The Way of the Cross* prod/rel: Monopol
Jan Cimbura, Novel
   Jan Cimbura 1941 d: Frantisek Cap. lps: Gustav
   Nezval, Jirina Stepnickova, Vilem Pfeiffer. 2388m CZC.
   prod/rel: Lucernafilm

BABAY, JOSEF
Zwei Blaue Augen, Novel
   Zwei Blaue Augen 1955 d: Gustav Ucicky. lps:
   Marianne Koch, Claus Holm, Camilla SpirA. 96M GRM.
   Christine (UKN); *Two Blue Eyes* prod/rel: Real, Rank

BABBITT, NATALIE
The Eyes of the Amaryllis, Novel
  Eyes of the Amaryllis, The 1982 d: Frederick King Keller. lps: Ruth Ford, Martha Byrne, Jonathan Bolt. 94M USA. prod/rel: the Amaryllis Company

Tuck Everlasting, Novel
  Tuck Everlasting 1980 d: Frederick King Keller. lps: Fred A. Keller, James McGuire, Paul FlessA. 114M USA. prod/rel: Vestron

BABCOCK, DWIGHT
Chautauqua, New York 1960, Novel
  Trouble With Girls, The 1969 d: Peter Tewkesbury. lps: Elvis Presley, Marlyn Mason, Nicole Jaffe. 97M USA. *Chautauqua* prod/rel: Metro-Goldwyn-Mayer, Inc.

BABER, DOUGLAS
My Death Is a Mockery, Novel
  My Death Is a Mockery 1952 d: Tony Young. lps: Donald Houston, Kathleen Byron, Bill Kerr. 75M UKN. prod/rel: Park Lane, Adelphi

BABERSKE, ROBERT
Spione Am Werk, Novel
  On Secret Service 1933 d: Arthur Woods. lps: Greta Nissen, Carl Ludwig Diehl, Don Alvarado. 91M UKN. *Secret Agent* (USA); *Spy 77* prod/rel: British International Pictures, Wardour

BACCHELLI, ALFREDO
La Via Della Luce, Novel
  Via Della Luce, La 1917 d: Baldassarre Negroni. lps: Hesperia, Tullio Carminati, Diomira Jacobini. 1673m ITL. prod/rel: Tiber Film

BACCHELLI, RICCARDO (1891–, ITL
Il Brigante Di Tacca Del Lupo, 1942, Novel
  Brigante Di Tacca Del Lupo, Il 1952 d: Pietro Germi. lps: Amedeo Nazzari, Saro Urzi, Fausto Tozzi. 103M ITL. *The Brigand of Tacca Del Lupo* prod/rel: Rovere Film, Cines

Il Mulino Del Po, 1938-46, Novel
  Mulino Del Po, Il 1949 d: Alberto LattuadA. lps: Carla Del Poggio, Jacques Sernas, Leda GloriA. 107M ITL. *The Mill on the Po; Mill on the River* prod/rel: Lux Film

BACH, ERNST
Der Furst von Pappenheim, Opera
  Furst von Pappenheim, Der 1927 d: Richard Eichberg. lps: Curt Bois, Mona Maris, Dina GrallA. 2306m GRM. *The Prince of Pappenheim* prod/rel: Eichberg-Film

  Furst von Pappenheim, Der 1952 d: Hans Deppe. lps: Hannelore Schroth, Viktor de Kowa, Grethe Weiser. 104M GRM. prod/rel: Central, Prisma

Hurra - Ein Junge!, Play
  Ach, Egon 1961 d: Wolfgang Schleif. lps: Heinz Erhardt, Rudolf Vogel, Gunther Philipp. 90M GRM. *Oh Egon* prod/rel: Kurt Ulrich, Europa

  Hurra - Ein Junge! 1931 d: Georg Jacoby. lps: Max Adalbert, Georg Alexander, Lucie Englisch. F GRM. *Hooray - It's a Boy*

  Hurra - Ein Junge! 1953 d: Ernst MarischkA. lps: Walter Muller, Theo Lingen, Grethe Weiser. 90M GRM. *Hooray - It's a Boy!* prod/rel: Berolina, Constantin

It's a Boy, New York 1922, Play
  It's a Boy 1933 d: Tim Whelan. lps: Leslie Henson, Edward Everett Horton, Heather Thatcher. 80M UKN. prod/rel: Gainsborough, Woolf & Freedman

Der Keusche Lebemann, Play
  Keusche Lebemann, Der 1952 d: Carl Boese. lps: Georg Thomalla, Joe Stockel, Gerthe Weiser. 94M GRM. *The Virgin Playboy* prod/rel: Central Cinema, Prisma

Die Spanische Fliege, Play
  Spanische Fliege, Die 1955 d: Carl Boese. lps: Joe Stockel, Rudolf Platte, Hans Leibelt. 94M GRM. *The Spanish Fly* prod/rel: Deutsche Spielfilm, Victor von Struve

Stopsel, Play
  Tausend Fur Eine Nacht 1932 d: Max Mack. lps: Jakob Tiedtke, Claire Rommer, Johanna Terwin. 1972m GRM/CZC. *A Thousand for One Night* prod/rel: Wolframfilm, Avanti-Tonfilm Berlin

  Tisic Za Jednu Noc 1932 d: Jaroslav SvarA. lps: Theodor Pistek, Ruzena Slemrova, Marie GrossovA. 1841m CZC. *A Thousand for One Night* prod/rel: Wolframfilm

Unter Geschaftsaufsicht, Play
  Keusche Josef, Der 1953 d: Carl Boese. lps: Renate Mannhardt, Ludwig Schmitz, Lucie Englisch. 94M GRM. *Joseph the Pure* prod/rel: Algefa, Falken

  To Neznate Hadimrsku 1931 d: Martin Fric, Carl Lamac. lps: Vlasta Burian, Meda Valentova, Otto Rubik. 2599m CZC. *You Don't Know Hadimrsku; Hadimrsku Doesn't Know; Don't You Know Mrs. Hadimrska?* prod/rel: Elekta

  Wehe, Wenn Er Losgelassen 1931 d: Martin Fric, Carl Lamac. lps: Vlasta Burian, Mabel Hariot, Harry Frank. 2251m GRM/CZC. *Unter Geschaftsaufsicht* prod/rel: Elekta, Ondra-Lamac-Film

Die Vertagte Hochzeitsnacht, Play
  Interrupted Honeymoon, The 1936 d: Leslie Hiscott. lps: Claude Hulbert, Francis L. Sullivan, Hugh Wakefield. 72M UKN. prod/rel: British Lion

  Vertagte Hochzeitsnacht, Die 1953 d: Karl G. Kulb. lps: Theo Lingen, Steffie Strouk, Hans Leibelt. 85M GRM. *The Postponed Wedding Night* prod/rel: Ariston, N.F.

Der Wahre Jakob, Play
  Nacht Im Separee, Eine 1950 d: Hans Deppe. lps: Kurt Seifert, Olga Tschechowa, Sonja Ziemann. 95M GRM. *A Night in a Separate Chamber* prod/rel: Berolina, Gloria

  Wahre Jakob, Der 1960 d: Rudolf Schundler. lps: Willy Millowitsch, Renate Ewert, Jane Tilden. 88M GRM. *The Real Jacob* prod/rel: Corona, U.F.H.

A Warm Corner, Play
  Warm Corner, A 1930 d: Victor Saville. lps: Leslie Henson, Heather Thatcher, Connie Ediss. 104M UKN. prod/rel: Gainsborough, Ideal

Weekend Im Paradies, Play
  Liebe Im Finanzamt 1952 d: Kurt Hoffmann. lps: Paul Dahlke, Carola Hohn, Christiane Jansen. 85M GRM. *Wochenend Im Paradies; Love in the Tax Office* prod/rel: Standard, N.W.D.F.

BACH, RICHARD (1936–, USA
Jonathan Livingston Seagull, Novel
  Jonathan Livingstone Seagull 1973 d: Hall Bartlett. 120M USA. prod/rel: Paramount, Jls Partnership

BACHE, ELLEN
Safe Passage, Novel
  Safe Passage 1994 d: Robert Allan Ackerman. lps: Susan Sarandon, Sam Shepard, Robert Sean Leonard. 96M USA. prod/rel: Pacific Western

BACHELLER, IRVING ADDISON (1859–1950), USA
Keeping Up With Lizzie, New York 1911, Novel
  Keeping Up With Lizzie 1921 d: Lloyd Ingraham. lps: Enid Bennett, Otis Harlan, Leo White. 6r USA. prod/rel: Rockett Film Corp., W. W. Hodkinson Corp.

The Light in the Clearing, Indianapolis 1917, Novel
  Light in the Clearing, The 1921 d: T. Hayes Hunter. lps: Eugenie Besserer, Clara Horton, Eddie Sutherland. 7r USA. prod/rel: Dial Film Co., W. W. Hodkinson Corp.

BACHMANN, INGEBORG (1926–1973), AUS
Der Junge Lord: Komische Oper in Zwei Akten, Berlin 1965, Opera
  Junge Lord, Der 1965 d: Gustav Rudolf Sellner. lps: Edith Mathis, Donald Grobe, Loren Driscoll. 137M GRM. *The Young Lord* (USA) prod/rel: Beta Film, United Film

BACHMANN, KAREL
Der Spieler, Play
  Duvod K Rozvodu 1937 d: Carl Lamac. lps: Anny Ondra, Oldrich Novy, Adina MandlovA. 2713m CZC. *Grounds for Divorce* prod/rel: Moldavia

  Scheidungsgrund, Der 1937 d: Carl Lamac. lps: Anny Ondra, Paul Horbiger, Ruth Eweler. GRM/CZC. prod/rel: Moldavia, Ondra-Lamac-Film

BACHMANN, LAWRENCE P.
The Lorelei, Novel
  Whirlpool 1959 d: Lewis Allen. lps: Juliette Greco, O. W. Fischer, Muriel Pavlow. 95M UKN. prod/rel: Rank, Rank Film Distributors

The Phoenix, 1955, Novel
  Ten Seconds to Hell 1959 d: Robert Aldrich. lps: Jeff Chandler, Jack Palance, Martine Carol. 93M UKN/USA. prod/rel: Hammer, Seven Arts

BACHWITZ, HANS
The Critical Year, Story
  For Wives Only 1926 d: Victor Heerman. lps: Marie Prevost, Victor Varconi, Charles Gerrard. 5800f USA. prod/rel: Metropolitan Pictures Corp. of Calif., Producers Distributing Corp.

Jennys Bummel, Berlin 1926, Play
  Stranded in Paris 1926 d: Arthur Rosson. lps: Bebe Daniels, James Hall, Ford Sterling. 6106f USA. *You Never Can Tell* prod/rel: Famous Players-Lasky, Paramount Pictures

Liebe Und Trompetenblasen, Play
  Liebe Und Trompetenblasen 1925 d: Richard Eichberg. lps: Lilian Harvey, Harry Liedtke, Harry Halm. 2190m GRM. *Love and Trumpets* prod/rel: Eichberg-Film

  Liebe Und Trompetenblasen 1954 d: Helmut Weiss. lps: Marianne Koch, Hans Holt, Nadja Tiller. 93M GRM. *Love and Trumpets* prod/rel: Oska, Union

BACON, FRANK
Lightnin', New York 1918, Play
  Lightnin' 1925 d: John Ford. lps: Jay Hunt, Madge Bellamy, Wallace MacDonald. 8050f USA. prod/rel: Fox Film Corp.

  Lightnin' 1930 d: Henry King. lps: Will Rogers, Louise Dresser, Joel McCreA. 8500f USA. prod/rel: Fox Film Corp.

BACON, JOSEPHINE DASKAM
The Ghost of Rosy Taylor, 1917, Short Story
  Ghost of Rosy Taylor, The 1918 d: Edward Sloman. lps: Mary Miles Minter, Allan Forrest, George Periolat. 4148f USA. *The Ghost of Rosie Taylor* prod/rel: American Film Co., Mutual Film Corp.

BACRI, JEAN-PIERRE
Un Air de Famille, Play
  Air de Famille, Un 1996 d: Cedric Klapisch. lps: Jean-Pierre Bacri, Agnes Jaoui, Jean-Pierre Darroussin. 107M FRN. prod/rel: Telema©, le Studio Canal©©

BAEHR, NICHOLAS
Ride With Terror, 1963, Play
  Incident, The 1967 d: Larry Peerce. lps: Tony Musante, Martin Sheen, Beau Bridges. 107M USA. prod/rel: Moned Associated, Inc.

BAERLEIN, HENRY
Mariposa, London 1924, Novel
  Charmer, The 1925 d: Sidney Olcott. lps: Pola Negri, Wallace MacDonald, Robert Frazer. 5988f USA. prod/rel: Famous Players-Lasky, Paramount Pictures

BAGLEY, DESMOND (1923–, UKN
The Freedom Trap, Novel
  MacKintosh Man, The 1973 d: John Huston. lps: Paul Newman, Dominique Sanda, James Mason. 99M UKN/USA. prod/rel: Warner Bros., Newman-Foreman

BAGNI, GWEN
Story
  Captain China 1949 d: Lewis R. Foster. lps: John Payne, Gail Russell, Jeffrey Lynn. 97M USA. prod/rel: Paramount

BAGNI, JOHN
  Captain China 1949 d: Lewis R. Foster. lps: John Payne, Gail Russell, Jeffrey Lynn. 97M USA. prod/rel: Paramount

BAGNOLD, EDITH (1878–1961), UKN
The Chalk Garden, London 1956, Play
  Chalk Garden, The 1963 d: Ronald Neame. lps: Deborah Kerr, Hayley Mills, John Mills. 106M UKN. prod/rel: Universal-International, Quota Rentals

National Velvet, 1935, Novel
  International Velvet 1978 d: Bryan Forbes. lps: Nanette Newman, Tatum O'Neal, Christopher Plummer. 127M UKN. prod/rel: MGM

  National Velvet 1944 d: Clarence Brown. lps: Mickey Rooney, Donald Crisp, Anne Revere. 125M USA. prod/rel: MGM

BAHR, HERMANN
Das Konzert, 1909, Play
  Concert, The 1921 d: Victor Schertzinger. lps: Lewis Stone, Myrtle Stedman, Raymond Hatton. 6r USA. prod/rel: Goldwyn Pictures

  Delphine 1931 d: Roger Capellani, Jean de Marguenat. lps: Henri Garat, Jacques Louvigny, Alice CoceA. 77M FRN. prod/rel: Films Paramount

  Fashions in Love 1929 d: Victor Schertzinger. lps: Adolphe Menjou, Fay Compton, Miriam Seegar. 6592f USA. prod/rel: Paramount Famous Lasky Corp.

  Konzert, Das 1931 d: Leo Mittler. lps: Olga Tschechowa, Oskar Karlweis, Ursula Grabley. 79M FRN.

  Konzert, Das 1944 d: Paul Verhoeven. lps: Harry Liedtke, Kathe Haack, Gustav Frohlich. 86M GRM. prod/rel: Tobis, Awus

  Nichts Als Arger Mit Der Liebe 1956 d: Thomas Engel. lps: Sonja Ziemann, Winnie Markus, Viktor de KowA. 95M AUS. prod/rel: Wiener Mundus, Heinrich Bauer-Film

Die Gelbe Nachtigall, Berlin 1907, Play
  Lied Der Nachtigall, Das 1943 d: Theo Lingen. lps: Elfie Mayerhofer, Paul Kemp, Theo Lingen. 89M GRM. prod/rel: Bavaria, Dietz

  Romance in the Dark 1938 d: H. C. Potter. lps: Gladys Swarthout, John Barrymore, John Boles. 80M USA. *The Yellow Nightingale* prod/rel: Paramount Pictures©

Der Meister, 1909, Play
  Skandal in Ischl 1957 d: Rolf Thiele. lps: O. W. Fischer, Elisabeth Muller, Ivan Desny. 94M AUS. prod/rel: Vienna

BAHRE, JENS
Der Dicke Und Ich, Short Story
　　Dicke Und Ich, Der 1981 d: Karl-Heinz Lotz. lps: Carmen-Maja Antoni, Petr Skarke, Wolfgang Winkler. 80M GDR. *The Fatty and Me* prod/rel: Defa

BAI HUA
The Bell-Less Pack Train, Novel
　　Shen Mi de Lu Ban 1955 d: Lin Nong, Zhu Wenshun. lps: Yin Zhiming, Liu Zengqing, Li Jie. 10r CHN. *Mysterious Traveling Companion* prod/rel: Changchun Film Studio

BAI REN
Bing Lin Cheng XIa, Play
　　Bing Lin Cheng XIa 1964 d: Lin Nong. lps: Hao Haiquan, Zhong Shuhuang, Zhang Ran. 10r CHN. *City Under Siege* prod/rel: Changchun Film Studio

BAI XIANYONG
Zuihoude Guizu, Novel
　　Zuihoude Guizu 1989 d: XIe Jin. lps: Pan Hong, Pu Cunxin, Li Kechun. 12r CHN/HKG. *Visitors to New York*; *The Last Aristocrats* prod/rel: Shanghai Film Studio, Sil-Metropole Organisation Ltd.

BAI XIAOWEN
Father Liu Shihai's Wallet, Novel
　　Pi Bao 1956 d: Wang Lan. lps: Su Liqun, Ouyang Mingde, Wang Guangru. 4r CHN. *Wallet* prod/rel: Changchun Film Studio

BAILAC, GENEVIEVE
La Famille Hernandez, Play
　　Famille Hernandez, La 1964 d: Genevieve Bailac. lps: Frederic de Pasquale, Anne Berger, Nicole Mirel. 92M FRN. prod/rel: Films Etienne Bailac

BAILEY, ANNE HOWARD
The Bloody Brood, Story
　　Bloody Brood, The 1959 d: Julian Roffman. lps: Peter Falk, Hunt Powers, Ronald Hartmann. 70M CND. prod/rel: Key Film Productions Ltd., Meridian Films Ltd.

BAILEY, CHARLES WALDO
Seven Days in May, New York 1962, Novel
　　Seven Days in May 1964 d: John Frankenheimer. lps: Burt Lancaster, Kirk Douglas, Ava Gardner. 120M USA. prod/rel: Seven Arts Productions, Joel Productions

BAILEY II, CHARLES W.
The Enemy Within, Novel
　　Enemy Within, The 1994 d: Jonathan Darby. lps: Forest Whitaker, Jason Robards Jr., Sam Waterston. TVM. 100M USA. prod/rel: Vincent Picture Productions, Home Box Office

BAILEY, LESLIE
The Gilbert and Sullivan Book, Book
　　Story of Gilbert and Sullivan, The 1953 d: Sidney Gilliat. lps: Robert Morley, Maurice Evans, Eileen Herlie. 109M UKN. *The Great Gilbert and Sullivan* (USA); *Gilbert and Sullivan*; *Mr. Gilbert and Mr. Sullivan* prod/rel: London Films, British Lion Production Assets

BAILEY, OLIVER D.
Branded, New York 1917, Play
　　Branded Woman, The 1920 d: Albert Parker. lps: Norma Talmadge, Percy Marmont, Vincent Serrano. 5r USA. prod/rel: Norma Talmadge Film Corp., First National Exhibitors Circuit
Liza Ann, Play
　　In Walked Mary 1920 d: George Archainbaud. lps: June Caprice, Thomas J. Carrigan, Stanley Walpole. 4833f USA. *Little Mother Hubbard* prod/rel: Albert Capellani Productions, Inc., Pathe Exchange, Inc.[©]
Pay-Day, New York 1916, Play
　　Pay Day 1918 d: Sidney Drew, Mrs. Sidney Drew. lps: Sidney Drew, Mrs. Sidney Drew, Florence Short. 5r USA. prod/rel: Metro Pictures Corp.[©], Screen Classics, Inc.
A Stitch in Time, New York 1918, Play
　　Stitch in Time, A 1919 d: Ralph Ince. lps: Gladys Leslie, Eugene Strong, Agnes Ayres. 5r USA. prod/rel: Vitagraph Co. of America[©]

BAILEY, ROBERT B.
The Big Rainbow, Story
　　Underwater! 1955 d: John Sturges. lps: Richard Egan, Jane Russell, Gilbert Roland. 99M USA. prod/rel: RKO Radio, Howard Hughes

BAILEY, T. G.
Jenny Omroyd of Oldham, Play
　　Jenny Omroyd of Oldham 1920 d: Frank Etheridge. lps: Nelly Freeland. 5000f UKN. prod/rel: Success Films

BAILEY, TEMPLE
Peacock Feathers, Novel
　　Peacock Feathers 1925 d: Svend Gade. lps: Jacqueline Logan, Cullen Landis, Ward Crane. 6747f USA. prod/rel: Universal Pictures

---

Wallflowers, Philadelphia 1927, Novel
　　Wallflowers 1928 d: James Leo Meehan. lps: Hugh Trevor, Mabel Julienne Scott, Charles A. Stevenson. 6339f USA. prod/rel: Fbo Pictures

BAILLARGE, F. A.
Marie-Madeleine de Vercheres Et Les Siens, Novel
　　Madeleine de Vercheres 1922 d: J.-Arthur Homier. lps: Estelle Belanger, Adrien Lefebvre. 5/6r CND. prod/rel: le Bon Cinema Compagnie Ltee.

BAILLY, AUGUSTE
La Carcasse Et le Tord-Cou, Novel
　　Carcasse Et le Tord-Cou, La 1947 d: Rene Chanas. lps: Michel Simon, Michele Martin, Madeleine Suffel. 100M FRN. prod/rel: Silver-Films
Le Desir Et l'Amour, Novel
　　Desir Et l'Amour, Le 1951 d: Henri Decoin, Luis Maria Delgado. lps: Martine Carol, Francoise Arnoul, Albert Prejean. 89M FRN/SPN. *El Deseo Y El Amor* (SPN) prod/rel: Ste Gle De Cinematographie, L.A.I.S.
Naples Au Baiser de Feu, Novel
　　Flame and the Flesh, The 1954 d: Richard Brooks. lps: Lana Turner, Carlos Thompson, Pier Angeli. 104M USA. prod/rel: MGM
　　Naples Au Baiser de Feu 1925 d: Serge Nadejdine, Jacques Robert. lps: Gaston Modot, Gina Manes, Lilian Constantini. 1880m FRN. prod/rel: Films Legrand
　　Naples Au Baiser de Feu 1937 d: Augusto GeninA. lps: Tino Rossi, Mireille Balin, Michel Simon. 92M FRN. *Kiss of Fire* prod/rel: Paris-Films-Production

BAILY, WALDRON
The Heart of the Blue Ridge, New York 1915, Novel
　　Heart of the Blue Ridge, The 1915 d: James Young. lps: Clara Kimball Young, Chester Barnett, Robert W. Cummings. 5r USA. *The Savage Instinct* prod/rel: World Film Corp.[©], Shubert Feature

BAINBRIDGE, BERYL (1933–, UKN, Bainbridge, Beryl Margaret)
An Awfully Big Adventure, 1989, Novel
　　Awfully Big Adventure, An 1995 d: Mike Newell. lps: Hugh Grant, Alan Rickman, Georgina Cates. 110M UKN. prod/rel: Portman, British Screen
The Dressmaker, Novel
　　Dressmaker, The 1988 d: Jim O'Brien. lps: Joan Plowright, Billie Whitelaw, Peter Postlethwaite. 89M UKN. prod/rel: Rank, Film Four International
Sweet William, 1975, Novel
　　Sweet William 1980 d: Claude Whatham. lps: Sam Waterston, Jenny Agutter, Anna Massey. 92M UKN. prod/rel: Kendon

BAIRD, EDWIN
The City of Purple Dreams, Chicago 1913, Novel
　　City of Purple Dreams, The 1918 d: Colin Campbell. lps: Thomas Santschi, Bessie Eyton, Fritzi Brunette. 7r USA. prod/rel: Selig Polyscope Co., State Rights

BAIRD, MARIE-TERESE
A Lesson in Love, Novel
　　Circle of Two 1980 d: Jules Dassin. lps: Richard Burton, Tatum O'Neal, Nuala Fitzgerald. 105M CND. prod/rel: Film Consortium of Canada Inc., Circle of Two Productions Ltd.

BAIRNSFATHER, BRUCE
The Better 'Ole; Or the Romance of Old Bill, Oxford 1917, Play
　　Better 'Ole; Or, the Romance of Old Bill, The 1918 d: George Pearson. lps: Charles Rock, Arthur Cleave, Hugh E. Wright. 6600f UKN. *Carry on* prod/rel: Welsh, Pearson
　　Better 'Ole, The 1926 d: Charles F. Reisner. lps: Sydney Chaplin, Doris Hill, Harold Goodwin. 8469f USA. prod/rel: Warner Brothers Pictures

BAITZ, JON ROBIN
The Substance of Fire, Play
　　Substance of Fire, The 1996 d: Daniel Sullivan. lps: Ron Rifkin, Sarah Jessica Parker, Tony Goldwyn. 101M USA.

BAKEER, DONALD
Crips, Novel
　　South Central 1992 d: Steve Anderson. lps: Glenn Plummer, Byron Keith Minns, Carl Lumbly. 99M USA. *South Central L.a.* (UKN) prod/rel: Monument, Enchantment

BAKER, ANTONIA
The Ghosts, Story
　　Amazing Mr. Blunden, The 1972 d: Lionel Jeffries. lps: Laurence Naismith, Lynne Frederick, Garry Miller. 98M UKN. prod/rel: Hemdale, Hemisphere

BAKER, DOROTHY (1907–1968), USA, Baker, Dorothy Dodds
Young Man With a Horn, 1938, Novel
　　Young Man With a Horn 1950 d: Michael Curtiz. lps: Kirk Douglas, Lauren Bacall, Doris Day. 112M USA. *Young Man of Music* (UKN) prod/rel: Warner Bros.

BAKER, EDNA MAE
Chicago After Midnight, Short Story
　　Underworld 1937 d: Oscar Micheaux. lps: Sol Johnson, Oscar Polk, Bee Freeman. 8697f USA. prod/rel: Micheaux Pictures Corp., Sack Amusement Enterprises

BAKER, ELLIOTT
A Fine Madness, New York 1964, Novel
　　Fine Madness, A 1966 d: Irvin Kershner. lps: Sean Connery, Joanne Woodward, Jean Seberg. 104M USA. prod/rel: Pan Arts Co., Warner Bros.

BAKER, GEORGE D.
As the Sun Went Down, Play
　　As the Sun Went Down 1919 d: E. Mason Hopper. lps: Edith Storey, Lew Cody, Harry Northrup. 5r USA. prod/rel: Metro Pictures Corp.[©]

BAKER, GLADYS
Labyrinth, Novel
　　Labyrinth 1959 d: Rolf Thiele. lps: Nadja Tiller, Peter Van Eyck, Amedeo Nazzari. 90M GRM/ITL. *Neurose* (ITL); *Labyrinth Der Leidenschaften* prod/rel: Universum, C.E.I. Incom

BAKER, JANE
Moment of Blindness, Play
　　Third Alibi, The 1961 d: Montgomery Tully. lps: Laurence Payne, Patricia Dainton, Jane Griffiths. 68M UKN. prod/rel: Grand National, Eternal

BAKER, LOUISE
Snips and Snails, Novel
　　Her Twelve Men 1954 d: Robert Z. Leonard. lps: Greer Garson, Robert Ryan, Barry Sullivan. 91M USA. *Her 12 Men* prod/rel: MGM

BAKER, PIP
Moment of Blindness, Play
　　Third Alibi, The 1961 d: Montgomery Tully. lps: Laurence Payne, Patricia Dainton, Jane Griffiths. 68M UKN. prod/rel: Grand National, Eternal

BAKER, ROBERT
Arms and the Girl, New York 1916, Play
　　Arms and the Girl 1917 d: Joseph Kaufman. lps: Billie Burke, Thomas Meighan, Louise Emerald Bates. 5r USA. *Delicate Situation* prod/rel: Famous Players Film Co.[©], Paramount Pictures Corp.

BAKER, ROBERT B.
The Conspiracy, New York 1912, Play
　　Conspiracy, The 1914 d: Allan Dwan. lps: John Emerson, Lois Meredith, Francis Byrne. 4-5r USA. prod/rel: Famous Players Film Co., Paramount Pictures Corp.

BAKER, ROBERT MELVILLE
Conspiracy, New York 1913, Novel
　　Conspiracy 1930 d: W. Christy Cabanne. lps: Bessie Love, Ned Sparks, Hugh Trevor. 69M USA. prod/rel: RKO Productions

BAKER, SHARLENE
Finding Signs, Novel
　　Love Always 1996 d: Jude Pauline Eberhard. lps: Marisa Ryan, Moon Zappa, James Victor. 90M USA. prod/rel: Cinewest

BAKER, W. HOWARD
Crime Is My Business, Novel
　　Murder at Site Three 1959 d: Francis Searle. lps: Geoffrey Toone, Barbara Shelley, Jill Melford. 67M UKN. prod/rel: Exclusive Films, Francis Searle

BAKKER, PIET
Ciske de Rat, Amsterdam 1941, Novel
　　Ciske de Rat 1985 d: Guido Pieters. lps: Danny de Munk, Willeke Van Ammelrooy, Herman Van Veen. 105M NTH. *Ciske the Rat* prod/rel: Omega, Amsterdam-Film
　　Ciske, Ein Kind Braucht Liebe 1955 d: Wolfgang Staudte. lps: Dick Van Der Velde, Kees Brusse, Rick Schagen. 96M GRM/NTH. *Ciske* (USA); *Ciske de Rat*; *Ciske the Rat*; *Ciske -a Child Wants Love*; *Ciske -a Child Needs Love*

BALACHANDER, K.
Major Chandrakant, Play
　　Oonche Log 1965 d: Phani Majumdar. lps: Ashok Kumar, Raaj Kumar, Feroz Khan. 144M IND. *Big People*; *High Class People* prod/rel: Chitrakala (Madras)
Server Sundaram, Play
　　Server Sundaram 1964 d: R. Krishnan, S. Panju. lps: Nagesh, Muthuraman, Major Sundarrajan. 165M IND. *Servar Sundaram* prod/rel: Guhan Films

BALASKO, JOSIANE
Un Grand Cri d'Amour, Play
　　Grand Cri d'Amour, Un 1998 d: Josiane Balasko. lps: Josiane Balasko, Richard Berry, Daniel Ceccaldi. 92M FRN. *A Great Shout of Love* prod/rel: Katharina/Renn, Tf1 Films

BALAZ, ANTON
Tabor Padlych Zien, Novel
Tabor Padlych Zien 1998 d: Laco HalamA. lps: Juraj Kukura, Dana Dinkova, Stefan Kvietik. F SVK/GRM/CZE. *The Camp of Fallen Women* prod/rel: Studio Kobila (Bratislava), Inafilm (Munich)

BALAZS, BELA
Almodo Ifjusag, 1946, Novel
Almodo Ifjusag 1974 d: Janos RozsA. lps: Zoltan Csoma, Csaba Domenija, Eva Ras. 81M HNG. *Dreaming Youth*

Heinrich Beginnt Den Kampf, 194-, Short Story
Veszelyes Jatekok 1979 d: Tamas Fejer. 91M HNG/GDR. *Ernste Spiele*; *Dangerous Games*

BALCH, GLENN
Indian Paint, New York 1942, Novel
Indian Paint 1967 d: Norman Foster. lps: Johnny Crawford, Jay Silverheels, Pat Hogan. 91M USA. prod/rel: Tejas Productions

BALCHIN, NIGEL (1908–1970), UKN
Novel
Elf Jahre Und Ein Tag 1963 d: Gottfried Reinhardt. lps: Ruth Leuwerik, Bernhard Wicki, Paul Hubschmid. 100M GRM. *Eleven Years and a Day* prod/rel: Roxy, Nora

Mine Own Executioner, 1945, Novel
Mine Own Executioner 1947 d: Anthony Kimmins. lps: Burgess Meredith, Dulcie Gray, Kieron Moore. 108M UKN. prod/rel: London Films, Harefield

The Small Back Room, 1943, Novel
Small Back Room, The 1948 d: Michael Powell, Emeric Pressburger. lps: David Farrar, Kathleen Byron, Jack Hawkins. 108M UKN. *Hour of Glory* (USA) prod/rel: London Films, the Archers

Sort of Traitors, London 1949, Novel
Suspect 1960 d: Roy Boulting, John Boulting. lps: Tony Britton, Peter Cushing, Virginia Maskell. 81M UKN. *The Risk* (USA) prod/rel: Charter Film Productions, British Lion

BALDA, JIRI
Lojzicka, Opera
Lojzicka 1936 d: Miroslav Cikan. lps: Jarmila Berankova, Jara Kohout, Bozena SvobodovA. 2608m CZC. prod/rel: Gloria

Na Svatem Kopecku, Opera
Na Svatem Kopecku 1934 d: Miroslav Cikan. lps: Jaroslav Vojta, Marie Grossova, Jirina SteimarovA. 2364m CZC. *On Holy Hill* prod/rel: Lepka

U Svateho Antonicka, Opera
U Sveteho Antonicka 1933 d: Svatopluk Innemann. lps: Ota Bubenicek, Hana Vitova, Jara Pospisil. 2686m CZC. *By St. Anthony*; *At St. Anthony's* prod/rel: Elekta

BALDER-OLDEN
Annette Hat Zuviel Geld, Play
Anita V Raji 1934 d: Jan Svitak. lps: Truda Grosslichtova, Zdenka Baldova, Vladimir Borsky. 2091m CZC. *Anita in Paradise* prod/rel: Wolframfilm

Annette Im Paradies 1934 d: Max Obal. lps: Ursula Grabley, Hans Sohnker, Ida Wust. 2270m GRM/CZC. *Ein Kuss Nach Ladenschluss*; *Anita V Raji* prod/rel: Georg Witt Film, Wolframfilm

BALDERSTON, JOHN L.
Berkeley Square, London 1926, Play
Berkeley Square 1933 d: Frank Lloyd. lps: Leslie Howard, Heather Angel, Irene Browne. 90M USA. prod/rel: Fox Film Corp.

Berkeley Square 1949 d: Paul Nickell. lps: William Prince, Leueen MacGrath. MTV. F USA.

Berkeley Square 1951 d: Donald Davis. lps: Richard Greene, Grace Kelly. MTV. F USA.

Berkeley Square 1959 d: George Schaefer. lps: John Kerr, Edna Best. MTV. F USA.

House in the Square, The 1951 d: Roy Ward Baker. lps: Tyrone Power, Ann Blyth, Michael Rennie. 91M UKN/USA. *I'll Never Forget You* (USA); *Man of Two Worlds*; *Journey to the Past*; *The House on the Square* prod/rel: 20th Century Productions, 20th Century-Fox

Red Planet, 1933, Play
Red Planet Mars 1952 d: Harry Horner. lps: Peter Graves, Andrea King, Marvin Miller. 87M USA. *Miracle from Mars* prod/rel: United Artists, Melaby Pictures

BALDUCCI, DAVID
Absolute Power, Novel
Absolute Power 1997 d: Clint Eastwood. lps: Clint Eastwood, Gene Hackman, Ed Harris. 121M USA. prod/rel: Malpaso, Castle Rock Entertainment

BALDWIN, EARL
My Irish Molly, Story
Lullaby of Broadway 1951 d: David Butler. lps: Doris Day, Gene Nelson, S. Z. Sakall. 92M USA. prod/rel: Warner Bros.

BALDWIN, FAITH (1893–1978), USA
Story
Apartment for Peggy 1948 d: George Seaton. lps: Jeanne Crain, William Holden, Edmund Gwenn. 99M USA. prod/rel: 20th Century-Fox Film Corp.

August Week-End, 1933, Short Story
August Week-End 1936 d: Charles Lamont. lps: Betty Compson, Claire McDowell, Valerie Hobson. 70M USA. *Week-End Madness* (UKN) prod/rel: Chesterfield Motion Pictures Corp.

Beauty, New York 1933, Novel
Beauty for Sale 1933 d: Richard Boleslawski. lps: Madge Evans, Alice Brady, Otto Kruger. 87M USA. *Beauty!* (UKN); *Beauty Parlor*; *Beauty* prod/rel: Metro-Goldwyn-Mayer Corp.

Comet Over Broadway, 1937, Story
Comet Over Broadway 1938 d: Busby Berkeley. lps: Kay Francis, Ian Hunter, John Litel. 69M USA. prod/rel: Warner Bros. Pictures

Men are Such Fools, New York 1936, Novel
Men are Such Fools 1938 d: Busby Berkeley. lps: Humphrey Bogart, Priscilla Lane, Wayne Morris. 69M USA. prod/rel: Warner Bros. Pictures©

The Moon's Our Home, New York 1936, Novel
Moon's Our Home, The 1936 d: William A. Seiter. lps: Margaret Sullavan, Henry Fonda, Charles Butterworth. 83M USA. prod/rel: Walter Wanger Productions, Paramount Productions©

The Office Wife, New York 1930, Novel
Office Wife, The 1930 d: Lloyd Bacon. lps: Dorothy MacKaill, Lewis Stone, Hobart Bosworth. 5390f USA. prod/rel: Warner Brothers Pictures

Office Wife, The 1934 d: George King. lps: Nora Swinburne, Chili Bouchier, Cecil Parker. 43M UKN. prod/rel: Warner Bros., First National

Second Chance, Short Story
Second Chance 1950 d: William Beaudine. lps: Ruth Warrick, John Hubbard, Hugh Beaumont. 72M USA. prod/rel: Protestant Film Commission

Skyscraper, New York 1931, Novel
Skyscraper Souls 1932 d: Edgar Selwyn. lps: Warren William, Maureen O'Sullivan, Gregory Ratoff. 99M USA. *Skyscraper* prod/rel: Metro-Goldwyn-Mayer Corp., Metro-Goldwyn-Mayer Dist. Corp.©

Spinster Dinner, 1934, Short Story
Love Before Breakfast 1936 d: Walter Lang. lps: Carole Lombard, Preston Foster, Janet Beecher. 70M USA. *Spinster Dinner* prod/rel: Universal Productions©, Edmund Grainger Production

Weekend Marriage, New York 1932, Novel
Week-End Marriage 1932 d: Thornton Freeland. lps: Loretta Young, Norman Foster, Aline MacMahon. 66M USA. *Working Wives* (UKN); *Weekend Lives* prod/rel: First National Pictures

Wife Versus Secretary, 1935, Short Story
Wife Vs. Secretary 1936 d: Clarence Brown. lps: Clark Gable, Jean Harlow, Myrna Loy. 88M USA. prod/rel: Metro-Goldwyn-Mayer Corp.©

BALDWIN, JAMES (1924–1987), USA, Baldwin, James Arthur
Go Tell It on the Mountain, 1953, Novel
Go Tell It on the Mountain 1985 d: Stan Lathan. lps: Paul Winfield, Rosalind Cash, James Bond III. TVM. 96M USA. prod/rel: Learning in Focus

BALDWIN, THOMAS
Story
Reactor, The 1989 d: David Heavener. lps: David Heavener, Stuart Whitman, Darwyn Swalve. 90M USA. *Deadly Reactor* prod/rel: Action International

BALESTIER, CHARLES W.
Naulahka: a Story of West and East, London 1892, Novel
Naulahka, The 1918 d: George Fitzmaurice. lps: Antonio Moreno, Doraldina, Helene Chadwick. 6r USA. prod/rel: Astra Film Corp., Pathe Exchange, Inc.©

BALESTIER, ELLIOT
Under the Fiddler's Elm, Story
Under the Fiddler's Elm 1915 d: Edgar Jones. lps: Edgar Jones, Justina Huff, Louis Mortelle. 2r USA. prod/rel: Lubin

BALFE, MICHAEL WILLIAM (1808–1870), IRL
The Bohemian Girl, London 1843, Opera
Bohemian Girl, The 1922 d: Harley Knoles. lps: Gladys Cooper, Ivor Novello, C. Aubrey Smith. 7700f UKN. prod/rel: Alliance, Astra

Bohemian Girl, The 1927 d: H. B. Parkinson. lps: Herbert Langley, Pauline Johnson. 1472f UKN. prod/rel: Song Films

Bohemian Girl, The 1936 d: James W. Horne, Charles Rogers. lps: Stan Laurel, Oliver Hardy, Thelma Todd. 80M USA. prod/rel: Hal Roach Studios, Inc., MGM

BALFOUR, LADY EVELYN
Anything Might Happen, Novel
Anything Might Happen 1934 d: George A. Cooper. lps: John Garrick, Judy Kelly, Martin Walker. 66M UKN. prod/rel: Real Art, Radio

BALL, JOHN DUDLEY (1911–1988), USA, Ball, John, Ball Jr., John Dudley
In the Heat of the Night, New York 1965, Novel
In the Heat of the Night 1967 d: Norman Jewison. lps: Rod Steiger, Sidney Poitier, Warren Oates. 110M USA. prod/rel: Mirisch Corporation

In the Heat of the Night 1988 d: David Hemmings. lps: Carroll O'Connor, Howard E. Rollins Jr., Alan Autry. TVM. 96M USA.

BALL, OONA
Barbara Comes to Oxford, Novel
City of Youth, The 1928 d: Charles Calvert. lps: Betty Faire, Lillian Oldland, J. Fisher White. UKN. prod/rel: British University Films

BALL, ZACHARY
Joe Panther, Novel
Joe Panther 1976 d: Paul Krasny. lps: Brian Keith, Ricardo Montalban, Ray Tracey. 110M USA. prod/rel: Artists Creation & Associates Inc.

BALLARD, J. G. (1930–, CHN, Ballard, James Graham
Crash, Novel
Crash 1996 d: David Cronenberg. lps: James Spader, Holly Hunter, Elias Koteas. 100M CND. prod/rel: Alliance Communications, Telefilm Canada

Empire of the Sun, 1984, Novel
Empire of the Sun 1987 d: Steven Spielberg. lps: John Malkovich, Miranda Richardson, Christian Bale. 153M USA. prod/rel: Warner, Robert Shapiro

BALLARD, JOHN FREDERICK, Ballard, Frederick, Ballard, Fred
Believe Me Xantippe, New York 1913, Play
Believe Me, Xantippe 1918 d: Donald Crisp. lps: Wallace Reid, Anna Little, Ernest Joy. 5r USA. prod/rel: Famous Players-Lasky Corp.©, Paramount Pictures

Ladies of the Jury, New York 1929, Play
Ladies of the Jury 1932 d: Lowell Sherman. lps: Edna May Oliver, Jill Esmond, Roscoe Ates. 65M USA. *Women of the Jury* prod/rel: RKO Radio Pictures©

We're on the Jury 1937 d: Ben Holmes. lps: Victor Moore, Helen Broderick, Robert McWade. 71M USA. *We the Jury* prod/rel: RKO Radio Pictures©

When's Your Birthday?, 1935, Play
When's Your Birthday? 1937 d: Harry Beaumont. lps: Joe E. Brown, Marian Marsh, Edgar Kennedy. 77M USA. prod/rel: David L. Loew Productions, RKO Radio Pictures

Young America, New York 1915, Play
Young America 1922 d: Arthur Berthelet. lps: Charles Frohman Everett, Jasper, Madelyn Clare. 5r USA. prod/rel: Essanay Film Mfg. Co., Elk Photo Plays

Young America 1932 d: Frank Borzage. lps: Spencer Tracy, Doris Kenyon, Tommy Conlon. 71M USA. *We Humans* (UKN) prod/rel: Fox Film Corp.©, Frank Borzage Production

BALLARD, TODHUNTER
Two-Edged Vengeance, Novel
Outcast, The 1954 d: William Witney. lps: John Derek, Joan Evans, Jim Davis. 90M USA. *The Fortune Hunter* (UKN) prod/rel: Republic

BALLESTER, GONZALO TORRENTE
Cronica de un Rey Pasmado, Novel
Rey Pasmado, El 1991 d: Imanol Uribe. lps: Gabino Diego, Juan Diego, Laura Del Sol. 110M SPN/FRN/PRT. *Le Roi Ebahi* (FRN); *O Rei Pasmado*; *The Astonished King*

BALLINGER, WILLIAM S.
Portrait in Smoke, Novel
Wicked As They Come 1956 d: Ken Hughes. lps: Arlene Dahl, Philip Carey, Herbert Marshall. 94M UKN. *Portrait in Smoke* (USA) prod/rel: Film Locations, Columbia

Rafferty, Novel
Pushover 1954 d: Richard Quine. lps: Fred MacMurray, Kim Novak, Philip Carey. 88M USA. prod/rel: Columbia

BALMER, EDWIN
The Blind Man's Eyes, Boston 1916, Novel
Blind Man's Eyes 1919 d: John Ince. lps: Bert Lytell, Naomi Childers, Frank Currier. 5r USA. prod/rel: Metro Pictures Corp.©

The Breath of Scandal, Boston 1922, Novel
Breath of Scandal, The 1924 d: Louis J. Gasnier. lps: Betty Blythe, Patsy Ruth Miller, Jack Mulhall. 6900f USA. prod/rel: B. P. Schulberg Productions

Dangerous Business, New York 1927, Novel
   Party Girl 1930 d: Victor Hugo Halperin. lps: Douglas
   Fairbanks Jr., Jeanette Loff, Judith Barrie. 7401f USA.
   Dangerous Business prod/rel: Victory Pictures, Tiffany
   Productions

That Royle Girl, New York 1925, Novel
   "That Royle Girl" 1925 d: D. W. Griffith. lps: Carol
   Dempster, W. C. Fields, James Kirkwood. 10r USA. *D.
   W. Griffith's "That Royle Girl"* prod/rel: Famous
   Players-Lasky, Paramount Pictures

When Worlds Collide, 1950, Novel
   When Worlds Collide 1951 d: Rudolph Mate. lps:
   Richard Derr, Barbara Rush, Larry Keating. 81M USA.
   prod/rel: Paramount

BALMER, EMIL
D'glogge Vo Wallere Schwarzenburger Gschichte,
Berne 1924, Short Story
   Gluckshoger, Der 1942 d: Richard Brewing. lps: Trudi
   Jauch-Gaschen, Kurt Wirth, Elisabeth Ramser. 102M
   SWT. *La Colline du Bonheur* prod/rel: Turicia-Film

BALUCKI, MICHAL
Klub Kawalerow, 1890, Play
   Klub Kawalerow 1962 d: Jerzy Zarzycki. lps:
   Bronislaw Pawlik, Lidia KorsakownA. 95M PLN. *Club
   of Bachelors; Bachelor's Club*

BALZER, GEORGE
Are You With It?, Play
   Are You With It? 1948 d: Jack Hively. lps: Donald
   O'Connor, Olga San Juan, Martha Stewart. 90M USA.
   prod/rel: Universal-International

BANCEY, ANDRE
Roi Des Detectives William Baluchet, Novel
   William Baluchet, Roi Des Detectives 1920 d:
   Gaston Leprieur. lps: Georges Mauloy, Suzanne Talba,
   Armand Numes. 3270m FRN. prod/rel: Monat Films

BANCROFT, GEORGE PLEYDELL
The Ware Case, London 1915, Play
   Ware Case, The 1917 d: Walter West. lps: Matheson
   Lang, Violet Hopson, Ivy Close. 6191f UKN. prod/rel:
   Broadwest, Film Booking Offices

   Ware Case, The 1928 d: Manning Haynes. lps: Stewart
   Rome, Betty Carter, Ian Fleming. 7689f UKN. prod/rel:
   Film Manufacturing Co., Nfp

   Ware Case, The 1938 d: Robert Stevenson. lps: Clive
   Brook, Jane Baxter, Barry K. Barnes. 79M UKN.
   prod/rel: Ealing Studios, C.a.P.A.D.

BANDELLO, MATTEO MARIA (1485–1562), ITL
*Dui Gentiluomini Veneziani Onoratamente Da le
Moglie Sono.*, Novel
   Scandalo Per Bene 1940 d: Esodo Pratelli. lps: Evi
   Maltagliati, Carlo Ninchi, Maurizio d'AncorA. 92M ITL.
   prod/rel: Produzione Associata Cinecitta, Generalcine

BANDISCH
Le Signal Rouge, Novel
   Signal Rouge, Le 1948 d: Ernst Neubach. lps: Erich
   von Stroheim, Frank Villard, Denise Vernac. 105M
   FRN. prod/rel: Pen Films, Ernest Neubach

BANDYOPADHYAY, BIBHUTI BHUSHAN
Aparajita, 1931, Novel
   Aparajito 1956 d: Satyajit Ray. lps: Pinaki Sengupta,
   Smaran Ghoshal, Karuna Banerji. 127M IND. *The
   Unvanquished* (UKN) prod/rel: Epic Films

BANDYOPADHYAY, TARASANKAR
Abhiyan, 1946, Novel
   Abhiyan 1962 d: Satyajit Ray. lps: Soumitra Chatterjee,
   Waheeda Rehman, Robi Ghosh. 150M IND. *The
   Expedition* (UKN); *Abhiyan* prod/rel: Abhijatrik

BANDYYOPADHYAY, MANIK
Padma Nadir Majhi, Novel
   Padma Nadir Majhi 1992 d: Gautam Ghose. lps:
   Utpal Dutt, Mamata Shankar, Humayun Faridi. 126M
   IND. *Boatman of River Padma*; *Padma Nadir Majhi*;
   Boatman of the River Padma prod/rel: West Bengal Film
   Development Corp.

BANERJEE, TARASHANKAR (1898–1971), IND
Ganadevata, 1942, Novel
   Ganadevata 1978 d: Tarun Majumdar. lps: Soumitra
   Chatterjee, Sandhya Roy, Madhabi Mukherjee. 172M
   IND. *The God of the Masses; The People* prod/rel: West
   Bengal Government

Jalsagar, Calcutta 1937, Novel
   Jalsaghar 1958 d: Satyajit Ray. lps: Chhabi Biswas,
   Gangapada Basu, Kali Sarkar. 100M IND. *The Music
   Room* (UKN) prod/rel: Satyajit Ray Productions

Kavi, 1942, Novel
   Kavi 1949 d: Debaki Bose. lps: Nilima Das, Anubha
   Gupta, Robin Majumdar. 151M IND. *The Poet; Kewi*
   prod/rel: Chitramaya

BANG, HERMAN
De Fire Djaevle, Kristiania 1895, Novel
   Four Devils 1929 d: F. W. Murnau. lps: Farrell
   MacDonald, Anders Randolf, Claire McDowell. 9496f
   USA. prod/rel: Fox Film Corp.

Sommerglaeder, 1902, Novel
   Sommerglaeder 1940 d: Sven Methling. lps: Henry
   Nielsen, Ellen Margrethe Stein, Helge
   Kjaerulff-Schmidt. 98M DNM. *Happy Summer* prod/rel:
   Palladium Film

Tine, 1889, Novel
   Tine 1964 d: Knud Leif Thomsen. lps: Lone Hertz.
   137M DNM. *Maid Tine*

Ved Vejen, 1886, Novel
   Ved Vejen 1988 d: Max von Sydow. lps: Tine
   Miehe-Renard, Tammi Ost, Kurt Ravn. 96M
   SWD/DNM/UKN. *Katinka*

BANG, PER
Ute Blaser Sommarvind, Novel
   Ute Blaser Sommarvind 1955 d: Ake Ohberg. lps:
   Margit Carlqvist, Lars Nordrum, Edvin Adolphson. 72M
   SWD/NRW. *Ute Blaser Sommarvind (NRW)*; *Where the
   Summer Wind Blows* prod/rel: Ab Europa, Norsk

BANHAM, DEREK
The Gap, Play
   1917 1970 d: Stephen Weeks. lps: Timothy Bateson,
   David Leland, Geoffrey Davis. 34M UKN. prod/rel:
   Tigon British, Tigon

BANKS, LYNNE REID (1929–, UKN
The L-Shaped Room, London 1960, Novel
   L-Shaped Room, The 1962 d: Bryan Forbes. lps:
   Leslie Caron, Tom Bell, Bernard Lee. 142M UKN.
   prod/rel: Romulus Films, British Lion

BANKS, MRS. LINNAEUS
The Manchester Man, Novel
   Manchester Man, The 1920 d: Bert Wynne. lps:
   Hayford Hobbs, Aileen Bagot, Warwick Ward. 5000f
   UKN. prod/rel: Ideal

BANKS, POLAN
Carriage Entrance, 1947, Novel
   My Forbidden Past 1951 d: Robert Stevenson. lps:
   Ava Gardner, Robert Mitchum, Melvyn Douglas. 81M
   USA. *Carriage Entrance* prod/rel: RKO Radio

January Heights, Novel
   Great Lie, The 1941 d: Edmund Goulding. lps: Mary
   Astor, Bette Davis, George Brent. 107M USA. prod/rel:
   Warner Bros.

The Street of Women, New York 1931, Novel
   Street of Women 1932 d: Archie Mayo. lps: Kay
   Francis, Alan Dinehart, Marjorie Gateson. 70M USA.
   prod/rel: Warner Bros. Pictures©

The Woman Accused, 1933, Story
   Woman Accused, The 1933 d: Paul Sloane. lps: Nancy
   Carroll, Cary Grant, Louis Calhern. 73M USA. prod/rel:
   Paramount Productions©

BANKS, RUSSELL
Affliction, 1989, Novel
   Affliction 1997 d: Paul Schrader. lps: Nick Nolte, Sissy
   Spacek, James Coburn. 114M USA. prod/rel: Largo
   Entertainment Inc.©, Reisman/Kingsgate

The Sweet Hereafter, Novel
   Sweet Hereafter, The 1997 d: Atom Egoyan. lps: Ian
   Holm, Sarah Polley, Bruce Greenwood. 110M CND.
   prod/rel: Ego Film Arts, Alliance Communications

BANKSON, RUSSELL A.
Feud of the Rocking U, Short Story
   Feud of the West 1936 d: Harry L. Fraser. lps: Hoot
   Gibson, Joan Barclay, Buzz Barton. 62M USA. *The
   Vengeance of Gregory Walters* (UKN); *Feud of the Range*
   prod/rel: the Futter Corp., State Rights

BANNAUER, ADOLF
On Parole, Story
   Western Wallop, The 1924 d: Cliff Smith. lps: Jack
   Hoxie, Margaret Landis, J. Gordon Russell. 4662f USA.
   On Parole prod/rel: Universal Pictures

BANNERJEE, BIBHUTIBHUSHAN (1894–1950),
IND, Banerji, Bibhuti Bhusan
Adarsha Hindu Hotel, 1940, Novel
   Adarsha Hindu Hotel 1957 d: Ardhendu Sen. lps:
   Chhabi Biswas, Dhiraj Bhattacharya, Jahar Ganguly.
   141M IND. prod/rel: Sreelekha Pictures

Aparajito, Novel
   Apu Sansar 1958 d: Satyajit Ray. lps: Soumitra
   Chatterjee, Sharmila Tagore, S. Alok Chakravarty.
   117M IND. *The World of Apu* (UKN); *Apur Sansar*
   prod/rel: Satyajit Ray Prod.

Ashani Sanket, 1959, Novel
   Ashani Sanket 1973 d: Satyajit Ray. lps: Soumitra
   Chatterjee, Babita, Sandhya Roy. 101M IND. *Distant
   Thunder* (USA); *Asani Sanket* prod/rel: Balaka Movies

Pather Pancali, 1929, Novel
   Pather Panchali 1955 d: Satyajit Ray. lps: Kanu
   Banerji, Karuna Banerji, Runki Banerji. 115M IND. *The
   Song of the Road; The Lament of the Path; The Saga of
   the Road; Song of the Little Road* prod/rel: West Bengal
   Government

BANNERJEE, SARADINDU
Chidiakhana, Novel
   Chidiakhana 1967 d: Satyajit Ray. lps: Uttam Kumar,
   Kanika Majumdar, Sailen Mukherjee. 135M IND. *Zoo;
   Chiriakhana* prod/rel: Star Prod.

BANNERMAN, KAY
All for Mary, London 1954, Play
   All for Mary 1955 d: Wendy Toye. lps: Nigel Patrick,
   Kathleen Harrison, David Tomlinson. 79M UKN.
   prod/rel: Rank, Rank Film Distributors

Handful of Tansy (Don't Tell Father), 1959, Play
   No, My Darling Daughter! 1961 d: Ralph Thomas.
   lps: Michael Redgrave, Michael Craig, Roger Livesey.
   96M UKN. prod/rel: Five Star Films, Rank

How Say You?, London 1959, Play
   Pair of Briefs, A 1962 d: Ralph Thomas. lps: Michael
   Craig, Mary Peach, Brenda de Banzie. 90M UKN.
   prod/rel: Rank Organisation, Rank Film Distributors

BANNING, MARGARET CULKIN
Enemy Territory, 1937, Short Story
   Woman Against Woman 1938 d: Robert B. Sinclair.
   lps: Herbert Marshall, Mary Astor, Virginia Bruce. 61M
   USA. *Enemy Territory; One Woman's Answer* prod/rel:
   Metro-Goldwyn-Mayer Corp., Loew's, Inc.©

BANNISTER, MAYELL
The Cunninghames Economise, Story
   Cunninghames Economise, The 1922 d: George A.
   Cooper. lps: Sydney N. Folker, Joan McLean, Donald
   Searle. 2614f UKN. prod/rel: Quality Plays, Walturdaw

Geraldine's First Year, Story
   Geraldine's First Year 1922 d: George A. Cooper. lps:
   Sydney N. Folker, Joan McLean, Mrs. L. March. 1365f
   UKN. prod/rel: Quality Plays, Walturdaw

Her Dancing Partner, Story
   Her Dancing Partner 1922 d: George A. Cooper. lps:
   Sydney N. Folker, Joan McLean. 2000f UKN. prod/rel:
   Quality Plays, Walturdaw

Keeping Man Interested, Story
   Keeping Man Interested 1922 d: George A. Cooper.
   lps: Sydney N. Folker, Joan McLean. 2140f UKN.
   prod/rel: Quality Plays, Walturdaw

A Question of Principle, Story
   Question of Principle, A 1922 d: George A. Cooper.
   lps: Sydney N. Folker, Joan McLean, Frank Stanmore.
   1987f UKN. prod/rel: Quality Plays, Walturdaw

BANTI, ANNA
Le Donne Muoiono, Novel
   Equinozio 1971 d: Maurizio Ponzi. lps: Claudine
   Auger, Carla Gravina, Paola PitagorA. 98M ITL.
   Equinox prod/rel: San Diego Cin.Ca

BANVILLE, JOHN (1945–, IRL
The Newton Letter, 1982, Novel
   Reflections 1984 d: Kevin Billington. lps: Gabriel
   Byrne, Donal McCann, Harriet Walter. 103M UKN.
   prod/rel: Film Four

BAO TIANXIAO
Ku'er Liulang Ji, Novel
   Xiao Pengyou 1925 d: Zhang Shichuan. lps: Xuan
   Jinglin, Zheng XIaoqiu, Huang Junfu. 11r CHN. *Young
   Friend* prod/rel: Mingxing Film Company

BARABAS, PAUL
Frau Am Steuer, Play
   Frau Am Steuer 1939 d: Paul Martin. lps: Lilian
   Harvey, Willy Fritsch, Leo Slezak. 84M GRM. prod/rel:
   UFA, Jugendfilm

BARAK, MICHAEL
Enigma Sacrifice, Novel
   Enigma 1982 d: Jeannot Szwarc. lps: Martin Sheen,
   Sam Neill, Brigitte Fossey. 101M UKN/FRN. prod/rel:
   Embassy, Filmcrest

BARANGA, AUREL
Iarba Rea, 1949, Play
   Viata Invinge 1951 d: Dinu Negreanu. lps: Fory
   Etterle, George VracA. 98M RMN. *Life Triumphs*

Travesti, 1971, Play
   Premiera 1976 d: Mihai Constantinescu. lps: Radu
   Beligan. 97M RMN. *Premiere*

BARASCH, NORMAN
Send Me No Flowers, New York 1960, Play
   Send Me No Flowers 1964 d: Norman Jewison. lps:
   Rock Hudson, Doris Day, Tony Randall. 100M USA.
   prod/rel: Martin Melcher Productions

BARBER, ELSIE OAKES
Jenny Angel, New York 1954, Book
Angel Baby 1961 d: Paul Wendkos, Hubert Cornfield. lps: Salome Jens, George Hamilton, Mercedes McCambridge. 97M USA. prod/rel: Madera Productions

BARBER, NOEL
The Other Side of Paradise, Novel
Other Side of Paradise, The 1991 d: Renny Rye. lps: Jason Connery, Josephine Byrnes, Richard Wilson. TVM. 206M UKN/ASL/NZL.

Tanamera, Novel
Tanamera 1989 d: Kevin Dobson, John Power. lps: Christopher Bowen, Lewis Fiander, Kay Tong Lim. TVM. 335M ASL.

BARBER, ROWLAND
The Night They Raided Minsky's, New York 1960, Novel
Night They Raided Minsky's, The 1969 d: William Friedkin. lps: Jason Robards Jr., Norman Wisdom, Thomas Wiseman. 100M USA. *The Night They Invented Striptease* prod/rel: Tandem Productions

BARBIER, EUGENE
L' Abandonne, Novel
Secret d'une Mere, Le 1926 d: Georges Pallu. lps: Marise Maia, Pierre Batcheff, Olga Noel. 2000m FRN. prod/rel: Isis Films

Le Dernier Des Capendu, Novel
Dernier Des Capendu, Le 1923 d: Jean Manoussi. lps: Jean Dehelly, Arlette Strazzi, Laurette Clody. F FRN. prod/rel: Agence Generale Cinematographique

Florine la Fleur du Valois, Novel
Florine, la Fleur du Valois 1926 d: E. B. Donatien. lps: E. B. Donatien, Lucienne Legrand, Berthe Jalabert. 3500m FRN. prod/rel: Nicoea Films

La Legende de la Primitive Eglise, Novel
Martyre de Sainte Maxence, Le 1927 d: E. B. Donatien. lps: Thomy Bourdelle, Lucienne Legrand, Pierre Simon. F FRN. prod/rel: Nicaea Films

Les Mufles, Novel
Mufles, Les 1929 d: Robert Peguy. lps: Pierre Stephen, Suzanne Bianchetti, Edouard Hardoux. 2500m FRN. prod/rel: Nicoea Films Production

Pardonnee, Short Story
Pardonnee 1927 d: Jean Cassagne. lps: Simone Vaudry, Georges Peclet, Gaston Jacquet. 2200m FRN. prod/rel: Nicaea-Film Production

Rapacite, Novel
Rapacite 1929 d: Andre Berthomieu. lps: Florence Gray, Gaston Jacquet, Rene Lefevre. F FRN. prod/rel: Nicea Film Production

BARBIER, JULES
Memorial de Sainte-Helene, Play
Memorial de Saint-Helene Ou la Captivite de Napoleon, Le 1911 d: Michel Carre, Barbier. lps: Georges Treville, Laroche, Roger Monteaux. 610m FRN. prod/rel: Scagl

BARBIERI, ENZO
La Banda Del Sole, Novel
Whisky a Mezzogiorno 1962 d: P. V. Oscar de FinA. lps: Corrado Pani, Nino Besozzi, Lida Ferro. 90M ITL. prod/rel: Oscar Cin.Ca (Milano)

BARBOUR, EDWIN
The Fire Patrol, Worcester 1891, Play
Fire Patrol, The 1924 d: Hunt Stromberg. lps: Anna Q. Nilsson, Will Jeffries, Spottiswoode Aitken. 6600f USA. prod/rel: Hunt Stromberg Productions, Chadwick Pictures

Northern Lights, New York 1895, Play
Northern Lights 1914 d: Edgar Lewis. lps: Iva Shepard, William H. Tooker, Harry Spingler. 5r USA. prod/rel: Life Photo Film Corp., State Rights

BARBU, EUGEN
Domnisoara Aurica, 1962, Short Story
Domnisoara Aurica 1986 d: Serban Marinescu. 98M RMN. *The Old Maid*

Facerea Lumii, 1964, Novel
Facerea Lumii 1971 d: Gheorghe Vitanidis. lps: Irina Petrescu, Colea Rautu, Liviu Ciulei. 111M RMN. *The Making of the World*

Oaie Si Ai Sai, 1958, Short Story
Tatal Risipitor 1974 d: Adrian Petringenaru. lps: Marga Barbu, Toma Caragiu, Leopoldina BalanutA. 92M RMN. *The Prodigal Father*

Soseaua Nordului, 1959, Novel
Procesul Alb 1966 d: Iulian Mihu. lps: Iurie Darie, Marga Barbu, Gheorghe DinicA. 127M RMN. *The White Trial*

BARBUSSE, HENRI
L' Enfer, Novel
Vue Sur l'Enfer 1990 d: Michel Mitrani. lps: Jacques Bonnaffe, Andrea Ferreol. MTV. 85M FRN.

BARCHINA, FRANCISCO
La Barraqueta Del Nano, Play
Barraqueta Del Nano, La 1924 d: Juan Andreu Moragas. lps: Jose Fernandez Bayot, Luis Bori. SPN. prod/rel: Film Artistica Valenciana (Valencia)

BARCLAY, FLORENCE L.
The Mistress of Shenstone, New York 1910, Novel
Mistress of Shenstone, The 1921 d: Henry King. lps: Pauline Frederick, Roy Stewart, Emmett King. 5900f USA. prod/rel: Robertson-Cole Pictures

Le Rosaire, Novel
Rosaire, Le 1934 d: Gaston Ravel, Tony Lekain. lps: Andre Luguet, Louisa de Mornand, Helene Robert. 95M FRN. prod/rel: Florcal Films

BARCUS, JAMES S.
The Governor's Boss, New York 1914, Novel
Governor's Boss, The 1915 d: Charles E. Davenport. lps: William Sulzer, Pauline Hall, Anna Logan. 4400f USA. prod/rel: the Governor's Boss Photoplay Co., State Rights

BARCYNSKA, COUNTESS, Barcynska, Countess Helene
The Honeypot, Novel
Honeypot, The 1920 d: Fred Leroy Granville. lps: Peggy Hyland, Campbell Lindsay, James Lindsay. 6000f UKN. prod/rel: G. B. Samuelson, Granger

Jackie, New York 1921, Novel
Jackie 1921 d: John Ford. lps: Shirley Mason, William Scott, Harry Carter. 4943f USA. prod/rel: Fox Film Corp.

Love Maggy, Novel
Love Maggy 1921 d: Fred Leroy Granville. lps: Peggy Hyland, Campbell Gullan, James Lindsay. 6000f UKN. prod/rel: Samuelson, Granger

Rose O' the Sea, New York 1920, Novel
Rose O' the Sea 1922 d: Fred Niblo. lps: Anita Stewart, Rudolph Cameron, Thomas Holding. 6837f USA. prod/rel: Anita Stewart Productions, Associated First National Pictures

Tesha, Novel
Tesha 1928 d: Victor Saville. lps: Maria Corda, Jameson Thomas, Paul Cavanagh. 7826f UKN. *A Woman in the Night* (USA) prod/rel: British International Pictures, Burlington Films

We Women, Novel
We Women 1925 d: W. P. Kellino. lps: Dollie, Billie, John Stuart. 5000f UKN. prod/rel: Stoll

BARD, MARY
The Doctor Wears Three Faces, 1949, Book
Mother Didn't Tell Me 1950 d: Claude Binyon. lps: Dorothy McGuire, William Lundigan, June Havoc. 88M USA. prod/rel: 20th Century-Fox

BARDAWIL, GEORGES
Aimez-Vous Les Femmes?, Paris 1961, Novel
Aimez-Vous Les Femmes? 1964 d: Jean Leon. lps: Edwige Feuillere, Sophie Daumier, Guy Bedos. 100M FRN/ITL. *A Taste for Women* (USA); *Do You Like Women?* prod/rel: Les Films Number One, Francinex

BARDE, ANDRE
Arthur, Opera
Arthur 1930 d: Leonce Perret. lps: Louis-Jacques Boucot, Lily Zevaco, Edith MerA. F FRN. *Le Culte de la Beaute* prod/rel: Societe Des Films Osso

Le Comte Obligado, Opera
Comte Obligado, Le 1934 d: Leon Mathot. lps: Georges Milton, Jean Aquistapace, Germaine Aussey. 97M FRN. prod/rel: Eureka Films

Pas Sur la Bouche, Opera
Pas Sur la Bouche 1931 d: Nicolas Rimsky, Nicolas Evreinoff. lps: Mireille Perrey, Jeanne Marny, Nicolas Rimsky. 80M FRN. prod/rel: Luna Film

BARDIN, JOHN FRANKLIN
The Last of Philip Banter, Novel
Last of Philip Banter, The 1986 d: Herve Hachuel. lps: Tony Curtis, Scott Paulin, Irene Miracle. 101M SPN/SWT. *Banter* prod/rel: Tesauro-Banter, Herve Hachuel Prod.

BARFOOT, JOAN
Dancing in the Dark, Novel
Dancing in the Dark 1986 d: Leon G. Marr. lps: Martha Henry, Neil Munro, Rosemary Dunsmore. 98M CND. prod/rel: Bright Star, Film Arts

BARGATE, VERITY
Children Crossing, Novel
Children Crossing 1990 d: Angela Pope. lps: Peter Firth, Saskia Reeves, Bob Peck. TVM. 100M UKN. prod/rel: BBC

BARICCO, ALESSANDRO
Novecento, Play
Leggenda Del Pianista Sull'oceano, La 1998 d: Giuseppe Tornatore. lps: Tim Roth, Pruitt Taylor Vince, Melanie Thierry. 170M ITL. *The Legend of the Pianist on the Ocean* prod/rel: Medusa Film, Sciarlo

BARILLET, PIERRE
Ami-Ami
Femmes Sont Marrantes, Les 1958 d: Andre Hunebelle. lps: Micheline Presle, Yves Robert, Pierre Dudan. 75M FRN. *Women are Talkative* (USA) prod/rel: P.A.C., U.G.C./ P.A.C.

Le Don d'Adele, Play
Don d'Adele, Le 1950 d: Emile Couzinet. lps: Charles Dechamps, Marguerite Pierry, Marcel Vallee. 93M FRN. prod/rel: Burgus Films

Forty Carats, Play
Forty Carats 1973 d: Milton Katselas. lps: Liv Ullmann, Edward Albert, Gene Kelly. 108M USA. *40 Carats* prod/rel: Frankovich

BARKEN, ADAM
The Drive, Play
Drive, The 1997 d: Romy Goulem. lps: Daniel Brochu, Fab Filippo, Alain Goulem. 76M CND. prod/rel: Industry Entertainment, David Reckziegel

BARKER, CLIVE (1952–, UKN
Story
Candyman: Farewell to the Flesh 1995 d: Bill Condon. lps: Tony Todd, Kelly Rowan, Timothy Carhart. 94M USA. prod/rel: Polygram, Propaganda

Cabal, Novel
Nightbreed 1989 d: Clive Barker. lps: Craig Sheffer, Anne Bobby, David Cronenberg. 101M UKN/CND. *Night Breed* prod/rel: Morgan Creek

The Forbidden, Story
Candyman 1992 d: Bernard Rose. lps: Virginia Madsen, Kasi Lemmons, Xander Berkeley. 99M USA. prod/rel: Columbia Tristar, Polygram

The Hellbound Heart, Novel
Hellraiser 1987 d: Clive Barker. lps: Andrew Robinson, Clare Higgins, Ashley Laurence. 93M UKN/USA. prod/rel: Cannon, Film Futures

Rawhead Rex, Short Story
Rawhead 1987 d: George Pavlou. lps: David Dukes, Kelly Piper, Niall Toibin. 103M UKN/IRL. *Rawhead Rex* prod/rel: Empire, Alpine

BARKER, HOWARD
No One Was Saved, 1970, Play
Made 1972 d: John MacKenzie. lps: Carol White, John Castle, Roy Harper. 104M UKN.

BARKER, PAT (1943–, UKN
Regeneration, 1991, Novel
Regeneration 1997 d: Gillies MacKinnon. lps: Jonathan Pryce, James Wilby, Jonny Lee Miller. 114M UKN/CND. prod/rel: Rafford Films, BBC Films

Union Street, Novel
Stanley and Iris 1989 d: Martin Ritt. lps: Jane Fonda, Robert de Niro, Swoosie Kurtz. 102M USA. *Letters*; *Union Street* prod/rel: MGM, Lantana

BARKER, RALPH
The Thousand Plan, London 1965, Novel
Thousand Plane Raid, The 1969 d: Boris Sagal. lps: Christopher George, Laraine Stephens, J. D. Cannon. 94M USA. *The 1000 Plane Raid* prod/rel: Oakmont Productions

BARKER, RON
Der Tod Ritt Dienstags, 1963, Novel
Giorni Dell'ira, I 1967 d: Tonino Valerii. lps: Giuliano Gemma, Lee Van Cleef, Walter RillA. 115M ITL/GRM. *Der Tod Ritt Dienstags* (GRM); *Day of Anger* (UKN); *Death Rode on Tuesdays*; *Day of Wrath*; *Gun Law* prod/rel: Sacrosiap (Roma), Corona Film

BARKLEY, DEANNE
Freeway, Novel
Freeway 1988 d: Francis DeliA. lps: Darlanne Fluegel, James Russo, Billy Drago. 91M USA. prod/rel: New World

BARLOW, JAMES
The Burden of Proof, Novel
Villain 1971 d: Michael Tuchner. lps: Richard Burton, Ian McShane, Nigel Davenport. 98M UKN. prod/rel: Emi, Kastner

Term of Trial, London 1961, Novel
Term of Trial 1962 d: Peter Glenville. lps: Laurence Olivier, Simone Signoret, Sarah Miles. 130M UKN. prod/rel: Romulus, Remus

BARNARD, CHARLES
The County Fair, New York 1889, Play
County Fair, The 1920 d: Maurice Tourneur, Edmund Mortimer. lps: Edythe Chapman, David Butler, Wesley Barry. 5r USA. prod/rel: Maurice Tourneur Productions, State Rights

BARNES, GEOFFREY
Party Husband, New York 1930, Novel
Party Husband 1931 d: Clarence Badger. lps: James Rennie, Dorothy MacKaill, Mary Doran. 74M USA. prod/rel: First National Pictures©

BARNES, HOWARD MCKENT
Her Unborn Child, New York 1928, Play
Her Unborn Child 1930 d: Charles McGrath, Albert Ray. lps: Adele Ronson, Elisha Cook Jr., Frances Underwood. 7609f USA. *Her Child* prod/rel: Windsor Picture Plays

The Little Shepherd of Bargain Row, Chicago 1915, Novel
Little Shepherd of Bargain Row, The 1916 d: Fred E. Wright. lps: Sallie Fisher, Richard C. Travers, John Junior. 5r USA. prod/rel: Essanay Film Mfg. Co.©, V-L-S-E, Inc.

Mother's Millions, Play
Mother's Millions 1931 d: James Flood. lps: May Robson, James Hall, Lawrence Gray. 90M USA. *The She-Wolf of Wall Street*; *The She-Wolf* prod/rel: Liberty Productions Co., Universal Pictures Co.©

BARNES, JULIAN (1946-, UKN, Barnes, Julian Patrick
Metroland, 1980, Novel
Metroland 1997 d: Philip Saville. lps: Christian Bale, Lee Ross, Emily Watson. 101M UKN/FRN/SPN. prod/rel: Blue Horizon (London)©, Mact Prods.©

Talking It Over, Novel
Love Etc. 1996 d: Marion Vernoux. lps: Charlotte Gainsbourg, Yvan Attal, Charles Berling. 105M FRN. prod/rel: Aliceleo©, France 3 Cinema©

BARNES, MARGARET ANNE
Murder in Coweta County, Book
Murder in Coweta County 1982 d: Gary Nelson. lps: Johnny Cash, Andy Griffith, Earl Hindman. TVM. 100M USA. *Last Blood* prod/rel: CBS

BARNES, MARGARET AYER (1886–1967), USA
Dishonored Lady, New York 1930, Play
Dishonored Lady 1947 d: Robert Stevenson. lps: Hedy Lamarr, Dennis O'Keefe, Natalie Schafer. 85M USA. prod/rel: United Artists

Westward Passage, Boston 1931, Novel
Westward Passage 1932 d: Robert Milton. lps: Ann Harding, Laurence Olivier, Irving Pichel. 73M USA. prod/rel: RKO Pathe Pictures©

BARNES, PETER
Leonardo's Last Supper, 1970, Play
Leonardo's Last Supper 1976 d: Peter Barnes. 55M UKN.

The Ruling Class, 1969, Play
Ruling Class, The 1972 d: Peter Medak. lps: Peter O'Toole, Alastair Sim, Arthur Lowe. 156M UKN. prod/rel: Keep Films

Spaghetti House, Play
Spaghetti House 1983 d: Giulio Paradisi. lps: Nino Manfredi, Rudolph Walker, Rita Tushingham. 195M ITL. prod/rel: Vides

BARNETT, S. H.
A Place of Dragons, Short Story
Father Goose 1964 d: Ralph Nelson. lps: Cary Grant, Leslie Caron, Trevor Howard. 116M USA. prod/rel: Granox Co.

BARNIER, LUCIEN
Les Clandestins
Clandestins, Les 1945 d: Andre Chotin. lps: Georges Rollin, Suzy Carrier, Constant Remy. 95M FRN. *Danger de Mort* prod/rel: Cine Selection

BAROCCO, ROBERTO
Avventura Di Viaggio, 1887, Short Story
Avventura Di Viaggio 1916 d: Camillo de Riso. lps: Camillo de Riso. 480m ITL. prod/rel: Caesar Film

BAROJA Y NESSI, PIO (1872–1956), SPN, Baroja, Pio
La Busca, 1904, Novel
Busca, La 1967 d: Angelino Fons. lps: Jacques Perrin, Emma Penella, Hugo Blanco. 94M SPN. *The Search*

Las Inquietudes de Shanti Andia, 1911, Novel
Inquietudes de Shanti Andia, Las 1946 d: Arturo Ruiz-Castillo. lps: Jorge Mistral, Josita Hernan, Milagros Leal. 112M SPN. *Las Inquietudes de Santi-Andia*; *The Worries of Shanti Andia*; *Adventures of Shanti-Andia*

Zalacain El Aventurero, 1909, Novel
Zalacain, El Aventurero 1929 d: Francisco Camacho. lps: Pedro Larranaga, Maria Luz Callejo, Andres Carranque de Rios. 64M SPN. prod/rel: C.I.D.E. (Madrid)

Zalacain, El Aventurero 1954 d: Juan de OrdunA. lps: Virgilio Teixeira, Jesus Tordesillas, Elena Espejo. 90M SPN. *Zalacain the Adventurer*

BARON, ALEXANDER
The Human Kind; a Sequence, New York 1953, Novel
Victors, The 1963 d: Carl Foreman. lps: Vince Edwards, Albert Finney, George Hamilton. 175M UKN/USA. prod/rel: Highroad Productions, Open Road Films

BARR, GEORGE
Epitaph for an Enemy, New York 1959, Novel
Up from the Beach 1965 d: Robert Parrish. lps: Cliff Robertson, Red Buttons, Irina Demick. 99M USA. *The Day After* prod/rel: Panoramic Productions

BARR, ROBERT
The Premature Compromise, Short Story
Premature Compromise, The 1914 d: Charles J. Brabin. lps: Marc McDermott, Duncan McRae. 2r USA. prod/rel: Edison

To Tell You the Truth, Radio Play
Oracle, The 1953 d: C. M. Pennington-Richards. lps: Robert Beatty, Joseph Tomelty, Mervyn Johns. 84M UKN. *The Horse's Mouth* (USA); *To Tell the Truth* prod/rel: Associated British Film Distributors, Group Three

Young Lord Stranleigh, Story
Invitation and an Attack, An 1915 d: Charles J. Brabin., Marc MacDermott, Yale Benner. 2r USA. prod/rel: Edison

BARRE
La Toison d'Or, Play
Toison d'Or, La 1916. lps: Cesar, Alice de Tender. 860m FRN. prod/rel: Eclair

BARRE, ALBERT
Une Nuit de Noces, Play
Nuit de Noces 1935 d: Georges Monca, Maurice Keroul. lps: Armand Bernard, Florelle, Claude May. 90M FRN. prod/rel: Films Eclat, Hausmann-Films

Nuit de Noces 1949 d: Rene Jayet. lps: Martine Carol, Mona Goya, Jean Paredes. 85M FRN. *Une Nuit de Noces*; *Wedding Night* prod/rel: Paral Films

Nuit de Noces, Une 1920 d: Marcel Simon. lps: Fernand Rivers, Yvonne Chazel, Annette Grange. 1500m FRN. prod/rel: Pathe

BARRESE, ORAZIO
I Complici: Gli Anni Dell'Antimafia, Book
Corleone 1978 d: Pasquale Squitieri. lps: Giuliano Gemma, Francisco Rabal, Claudia Cardinale. 115M ITL. *Corleone: Father of the Godfathers* prod/rel: Capital Film, Cineriz

BARRETO, AFONSO HENRIQUES DE LIMA
A Nova California, 1948, Short Story
Osso, Amor E Papagaios 1957 d: Carlos Alberto de Souza Barros. lps: Raquel Forner, Luciano Gregory. 102M BRZ. *Bones Love and Parrots*

BARRETT, ALFRED
Cash on Delivery, Short Story
Cash on Delivery 1926 d: Milton Rosmer. lps: Moore Marriott, Forrester Harvey, Gabrielle Casartelli. 2077f UKN. prod/rel: Gaumont

BARRETT, FRANK
The Woman of the Iron Bracelets, Novel
Woman of the Iron Bracelets, The 1920 d: Sidney Morgan. lps: Eve Balfour, George Keene, Margaret Blanche. 5376f UKN. prod/rel: Progress, Butcher's Film Service

BARRETT, HURD
Miss I.Q., Story
Pardon My Rhythm 1944 d: Felix E. Feist. lps: Gloria Jean, Patric Knowles, Marjorie Weaver. 62M USA. prod/rel: Universal

BARRETT, JAMES LEE
The D.I., Television Play
D.I., The 1957 d: Jack Webb. lps: Jack Webb, Don Dubbins, Jackie Loughery. 106M USA. *Drill Instructor* prod/rel: Warner Bros., Mark VII Ltd.

Tribes 1970 d: Joseph Sargent. lps: Darren McGavin, Earl Holliman, Jan-Michael Vincent. 74M USA. *The Soldier Who Declared Peace* (UKN) prod/rel: 20th Century-Fox

BARRETT, MICHAEL
Appointment in Zahrain, London 1960, Novel
Escape from Zahrain 1962 d: Ronald Neame. lps: Yul Brynner, Jack Warden, Sal Mineo. 93M USA. prod/rel: Paramount Pictures

The Heroes of Yuka, London 1968, Novel
Invincible Six, The 1970 d: Jean Negulesco. lps: Stuart Whitman, Elke Sommer, Curd Jurgens. 103M USA/IRN. *The Heroes* prod/rel: Moulin Rouge Productions

The Reward, London 1955, Novel
Reward, The 1965 d: Serge Bourguignon. lps: Max von Sydow, Yvette Mimieux, Efrem Zimbalist Jr. 94M USA/FRN. *La Recompense* (FRN) prod/rel: Arcola Pictures, Twentieth Century-Fox

BARRETT, RICHARD
The Heartbreak Kid, Play
Heartbreak Kid, The 1992 d: Michael Jenkins. lps: Claudia Karvan, Alex Dimitriades, Steve Bastoni. F ASL. prod/rel: View Films

BARRETT, WILLIAM E. (1900–1986), USA, Barrett, William Edmund
The Left Hand of God, 1951, Novel
Left Hand of God, The 1955 d: Edward Dmytryk. lps: Humphrey Bogart, Gene Tierney, Lee J. Cobb. 87M USA. prod/rel: 20th Century-Fox

The Lilies of the Field, New York 1962, Novel
Lilies of the Field 1963 d: Ralph Nelson. lps: Sidney Poitier, Lilia Skala, Lisa Mann. 97M USA. prod/rel: Rainbow Productions

The Wine and the Music, New York 1968, Novel
Pieces of Dreams 1970 d: Daniel Haller. lps: Robert Forster, Lauren Hutton, Will Geer. 100M USA. *The Wine and the Music* prod/rel: Rfb Enterprises

BARRETT, WILSON
Hoodman Blind, London 1885, Play
Hoodman Blind 1913 d: James Gordon. lps: Betty Harte, Herbert Barrington, Mrs. Guy Standing. 5r USA. prod/rel: Pilot Films Corp., State Rights

Hoodman Blind 1923 d: John Ford. lps: David Butler, Gladys Hulette, Regina Connelly. 5434f USA. prod/rel: Fox Film Corp.

Man of Sorrow, A 1916 d: Oscar Apfel. lps: William Farnum, Dorothy Bernard, Dorothea Wolbert. 6r USA. *Hoodman Blind* prod/rel: Fox Film Corp., William Fox©

The Sign of the Cross, London 1895, Play
Sign of the Cross, The 1904 d: William Haggar. lps: Will Haggar Jr., Jenny Linden, James Haggar. 700f UKN. prod/rel: Haggar & Sons, Gaumont

Sign of the Cross, The 1914 d: Frederick A. Thompson. lps: William Farnum, Rosina Henley, Sheridan Block. 4-5r USA. prod/rel: Famous Players Film Co., Paramount Pictures Corp.

Sign of the Cross, The 1932 d: Cecil B. de Mille. lps: Fredric March, Elissa Landi, Claudette Colbert. 125M USA. prod/rel: Paramount Publix Corp.©

BARRETTO, LARRY
Children of Pleasure, New York 1932, Novel
Crash, The 1932 d: William Dieterle. lps: George Brent, Ruth Chatterton, Peter Cavanagh. 65M USA. *Children of Pleasure* prod/rel: First National Pictures, Inc.

BARREYRE, JEAN
Le Navire Aveugle, Novel
Navire Aveugle, Le 1927 d: Joseph Guarino, Adelqui Millar. lps: Adelqui Millar, Colette Darfeuil, Marthe Mellot. F FRN. prod/rel: J. Millet (Consortium Central De Paris)

BARRICELLI, MICHELANGELO
L' Albergo Degli Assenti, Novel
Albergo Degli Assenti, L' 1939 d: Raffaello Matarazzo. lps: Carla Candiani, Maurizio d'Ancora, Camillo Pilotto. 87M ITL. prod/rel: Oceano Film, Artisti Associati

BARRIE, J. M. (1860–1937), UKN, Barrie, James M.
The Admirable Crichton, London 1902, Play
Admirable Crichton, The 1918 d: G. B. Samuelson. lps: Basil Gill, Mary Dibley, James Lindsay. 7817f UKN. prod/rel: G. B. Samuelson, Jury

Admirable Crichton, The 1957 d: Lewis Gilbert. lps: Kenneth More, Diane Cilento, Cecil Parker. 93M UKN. *Paradise Lagoon* (USA) prod/rel: Columbia, Modern Screenplays

Dao Ziren Qu 1936 d: Sun Yu. lps: Jin Yan, Li Lili, Bai Lu. CHN. *Back to Nature* prod/rel: Lianhua Film Company

Male and Female 1919 d: Cecil B. de Mille. lps: Thomas Meighan, Gloria Swanson, Lila Lee. 9r USA. *The Admirable Crichton* (UKN) prod/rel: Famous Players-Lasky Corp.©, Paramount-Artcraft Pictures

Shipwrecked 1913. lps: Anna Q. Nilsson, Guy Coombs. 2000f USA. prod/rel: Kalem

We're Not Dressing 1934 d: Norman Taurog. lps: Bing Crosby, Carole Lombard, George Burns. 80M USA. prod/rel: Paramount Productions©

Alice Sit-By-the-Fire, London 1905, Play
Darling, How Could You? 1951 d: Mitchell Leisen. lps: Joan Fontaine, John Lund, Mona Freeman. 96M USA. *Rendezvous* (UKN) prod/rel: Paramount

Half an Hour, New York 1913, Play
Doctor's Secret, The 1930 d: William C. de Mille. lps: Ruth Chatterton, H. B. Warner, John Loder. 5832f USA. *Half an Hour* prod/rel: Paramount Famous Lasky Corp.

Half an Hour 1920 d: Harley Knoles. lps: Dorothy Dalton, Charles Richman, Albert L. Barrett. 4667f USA. prod/rel: Famous Players-Lasky Corp.©, Paramount Pictures

Segreto Del Dottore, Il 1930 d: Jack Salvatori. lps: Soava Gallone, Alfredo Robert, Lamberto Picasso. 67M FRN. prod/rel: Paramount

Tajemstvi Lekarovo 1930 d: Julius Lebl. lps: Anna Sedlackova, Vaclav Vryda St., Karel Jicinsky. 1700m CZC. *The Doctor's Secret* prod/rel: Paramount

Secret du Docteur, Le 1930 d: Charles de Rochefort. lps: Marcelle Chantal, Leon Bary, Jean Bradin. 67M FRN/USA. prod/rel: Films Paramount, Paramount-Publix Corp.

A Kiss for Cinderella, New York 1920, Play
Kiss for Cinderella, A 1926 d: Herbert Brenon. lps: Betty Bronson, Tom Moore, Esther Ralston. 9686f USA. prod/rel: Famous Players-Lasky, Paramount Pictures

The Little Minister, 1891, Novel
Little Gypsy, The 1915 d: Oscar Apfel. lps: Dorothy Bernard, Julia Hurley, William Riley Hatch. 5r USA. prod/rel: Fox Film Corp., William Fox©

Little Minister, The 1913 d: James Young. lps: Clara Kimball Young, James Young, Mrs. Kimball. 3r USA. prod/rel: Vitagraph Co. of America

Little Minister, The 1915 d: Percy Nash. lps: Joan Ritz, Gregory Scott, Henry Vibart. 3920f UKN. prod/rel: Neptune, Jury

Little Minister, The 1921 d: Penrhyn Stanlaws. lps: Betty Compson, George Hackathorne, Edwin Stevens. 6031f USA. prod/rel: Famous Players-Lasky, Paramount Pictures

Little Minister, The 1922 d: David Smith. lps: Alice Calhoun, James Morrison, Henry J. Hebert. 5800f USA. prod/rel: Vitagraph Co. of America

Little Minister, The 1934 d: Richard Wallace. lps: Katharine Hepburn, John Beal, Donald Crisp. 110M USA. prod/rel: RKO Radio Pictures©

The Old Lady Shows Her Medals, New York 1918, Play
Seven Days Leave 1930 d: Richard Wallace, John Cromwell. lps: Gary Cooper, Beryl Mercer, Daisy Belmore. 83M USA. *Medals* (UKN) prod/rel: Paramount Famous Lasky Corp.

Seven Days Leave 1942 d: Tim Whelan. lps: Lucille Ball, Victor Mature, Harold Peary. 87M USA. prod/rel: RKO Radio

Peter Pan, London 1904, Play
Hook 1991 d: Steven Spielberg. lps: Dustin Hoffman, Robin Williams, Julia Roberts. 144M USA. prod/rel: Amblin Entertainment

Peter Pan 1924 d: Herbert Brenon. lps: Betty Bronson, Ernest Torrence, Cyril Chadwick. 9593f USA. prod/rel: Famous Players-Lasky, Paramount Pictures

Peter Pan 1953 d: Hamilton Luske, Clyde Geronimi. ANM. 77M USA. prod/rel: RKO, Walt Disney Prods.

Peter Pan 1960 d: Vincent J. Donehue. lps: Mary Martin, Cyril Ritchard, Margalo Gillmore. 100M USA.

Peter Pan 1976 d: Dwight Hemion. lps: Danny Kaye, Mia Farrow, Virginia McKennA. MTV. 100M UKN.

Peter Pan 1988. ANM. 50M ASL.

Quality Street, New York 1901, Play
Quality Street 1927 d: Sidney A. Franklin. lps: Marion Davies, Conrad Nagel, Helen Jerome Eddy. 7193f USA. prod/rel: Cosmopolitan Productions, Metro-Goldwyn-Mayer Distributing Corp.

Quality Street 1937 d: George Stevens. lps: Katharine Hepburn, Franchot Tone, Fay Bainter. 84M USA. prod/rel: RKO Radio Pictures©, Pandro S. Berman Production

Rosalind, London 1912, Play
Forever Female 1953 d: Irving Rapper. lps: Ginger Rogers, Paul Douglas, William Holden. 93M USA. prod/rel: Paramount

Sentimental Tommy, 1895, Novel
Sentimental Tommy 1921 d: John S. Robertson. lps: Gareth Hughes, May McAvoy, Mabel Taliaferro. 7876f USA. prod/rel: Famous Players-Lasky, Paramount Pictures

The Twelve Pound Look, 1910, Play
Twelve Pound Look, The 1920 d: Jack Denton. lps: Milton Rosmer, Jessie Winter, Ann Elliott. 5100f UKN. prod/rel: Ideal

What Every Woman Knows, London 1908, Play
What Every Woman Knows 1917 d: Fred W. Durrant. lps: Hilda Trevelyan, A. B. Imeson, Maud Yates. 5100f UKN. prod/rel: Barker, Neptune

What Every Woman Knows 1921 d: William C. de Mille. lps: Lois Wilson, Conrad Nagel, Charles Ogle. 6772f USA. prod/rel: Famous Players-Lasky, Paramount Pictures

What Every Woman Knows 1934 d: Gregory La CavA. lps: Helen Hayes, Brian Aherne, Madge Evans. 92M USA. prod/rel: Metro-Goldwyn-Mayer Corp.©

The Will, London 1913, Play
Will, The 1921 d: A. V. Bramble. lps: Milton Rosmer, Evangeline Hilliard, J. Fisher White. 5000f UKN. prod/rel: Ideal

BARRIERE, THEODORE
La Comtesse de Sommerive, Play
Comtesse de Sommerive, La 1917 d: Jean Kemm, Georges DenolA. lps: Emilienne Dux, Renee Falconetti, Madeleine SoriA. 1266m FRN. prod/rel: Scagl

BARRIGA RIVAS, ROGELIO
La Mayordomia, Mexico City 1952, Novel
Animas Trujano, El Hombre Importante 1961 d: Ismael Rodriguez. lps: Toshiro Mifune, Columba Dominguez, Pepito Romay. 100M MXC. *The Important Man* (USA); *El Hombre Importante*; *El Mayordomo* prod/rel: Peiculas Rodriguez

BARRILI, ANTON GIULIO
Santa Cecilia, 1866, Novel
Santa Cecilia 1919 d: Vasco Salvini. lps: Mary Bayma-Riva, Vasco Salvini, Guido Guiducci. 1836m ITL. prod/rel: Vitrix Film

Val d'Olivi, 1873, Novel
Val d'Olivi 1916 d: Eleuterio Rodolfi. lps: Tullio Carminati, Helena Makowska, Francois-Paul Donadio. 1372m ITL. prod/rel: S.A. Ambrosio

BARRINGER, EMILY DUNNING
Bowery to Bellevue, 1950, Autobiography
Girl in White, The 1952 d: John Sturges. lps: June Allyson, Arthur Kennedy, Gary Merrill. 93M USA. *So Bright the Flame* (UKN) prod/rel: MGM

BARRINGER, MICHAEL
Inquest, Play
Inquest 1931 d: G. B. Samuelson. lps: Mary Glynne, Campbell Gullan, Sydney Morgan. 95M UKN. prod/rel: Majestic, New Era

Inquest 1939 d: Roy Boulting. lps: Elizabeth Allan, Herbert Lomas, Hay Petrie. 60M UKN. prod/rel: Charter, Grand National

BARRINGTON, E.
The Divine Lady; a Romance of Nelson and Lady Hamilton, New York 1924, Novel
Divine Lady, The 1929 d: Frank Lloyd. lps: Corinne Griffith, Victor Varconi, H. B. Warner. 9914f USA. prod/rel: First National Pictures

BARRINGTON, PAMELA
Account Rendered, Novel
Account Rendered 1957 d: Peter Graham Scott. lps: Griffith Jones, Ursula Howells, Honor Blackman. 61M UKN. prod/rel: Rank Film Distributors, Major Productions

The Big Chance, Novel
Big Chance, The 1957 d: Peter Graham Scott. lps: Adrienne Corri, William Russell, Ian Colin. 61M UKN. prod/rel: Major, Rank Film Distributors

BARRON, ELWYN ALFRED
Marcel Levignet, New York 1906, Novel
House of Silence, The 1918 d: Donald Crisp. lps: Wallace Reid, Anna Little, Adele Farrington. 5r USA. prod/rel: Famous Players-Lasky Corp.©, Paramount Pictures

BARROSO, MARIA ALICE
Quem Matou Pacifico, 1969, Novel
Quem Matou Pacifico 1977 d: Renato Santos PereirA. 90M BRZ.

BARROW, HENRY
Story
Chu Chu and the Philly Flash 1981 d: David Lowell Rich. lps: Alan Arkin, Carol Burnett, Jack Warden. 100M USA. prod/rel: Twentieth Century Fox

BARROW, P.
A Daughter of England, Play
Daughter of England, A 1915 d: Leedham Bantock. lps: Marga Rubia Levy, Frank Randall, Frank Dane. 3500f UKN. prod/rel: British Empire

BARROWS, LESLIE S.
The Singing Fool, Story
Singing Fool, The 1928 d: Lloyd Bacon. lps: Al Jolson, Betty Bronson, Josephine Dunn. 9557f USA. prod/rel: Warner Brothers Pictures

BARROWS, THOMAS
Two Weeks Off, New York 1927, Novel
Two Weeks Off 1929 d: William Beaudine. lps: Dorothy MacKaill, Jack Mulhall, Gertrude Astor. 8081f USA. prod/rel: First National Pictures

BARROWS, WAYNE GROVES
The Law of the Range, Novel
Law of the Range, The 1914 d: Henry McRae. lps: Marie Walcamp, William Clifford, Sherman Bainbridge. 3r USA. prod/rel: Bison

BARRY, DAVID
Thunder Road, Article
King of the Mountain 1981 d: Noel Nosseck. lps: Harry Hamlin, Joseph Bottoms, Deborah Van Valkenburgh. 90M USA. prod/rel: Universal

BARRY, DONALD
This Guy Gideon, Story
Red Light 1949 d: Roy Del Ruth. lps: George Raft, Virginia Mayo, Gene Lockhart. 83M USA. prod/rel: United Artists

BARRY, JOHN
Saturn 3, Short Story
Saturn 3 1980 d: Stanley Donen. lps: Farrah Fawcett, Kirk Douglas, Harvey Keitel. 88M UKN. prod/rel: Itc, Transcontinental

BARRY, JULIAN
Lenny, Play
Lenny 1974 d: Bob Fosse. lps: Dustin Hoffman, Valerie Perrine, Jan Miner. 111M USA. prod/rel: United Artists

BARRY, PHILIP (1896–1949), USA
The Animal Kingdom, New York 1932, Play
Animal Kingdom, The 1932 d: Edward H. Griffith, George Cukor (Uncredited). lps: Ann Harding, Leslie Howard, Myrna Loy. 90M USA. *The Woman in His House* (UKN) prod/rel: RKO Radio

One More Tomorrow 1946 d: Peter Godfrey. lps: Ann Sheridan, Dennis Morgan, Alexis Smith. 89M USA. *The Animal Kingdom* prod/rel: Warner Bros.

Holiday, New York 1928, Play
Holiday 1930 d: Edward H. Griffith. lps: Ann Harding, Mary Astor, Edward Everett Horton. 89M USA. prod/rel: Pathe Exchange, Inc.

Holiday 1938 d: George Cukor. lps: Cary Grant, Katharine Hepburn, Doris Nolan. 93M USA. *Free to Live* (UKN); *Unconventional Linda*; *Vacation Bound* prod/rel: Columbia Pictures Corp.©

Paris Bound, New York 1927, Play
Paris Bound 1929 d: Edward H. Griffith. lps: Ann Harding, Fredric March, George Irving. 6687f USA. prod/rel: Pathe Exchange, Inc.

Philadelphia Story, New York 1939, Play
High Society 1956 d: Charles Walters. lps: Bing Crosby, Grace Kelly, Frank SinatrA. 107M USA. prod/rel: MGM, Sol C. Siegel Prods.

Philadelphia Story, The 1940 d: George Cukor. lps: Cary Grant, Katharine Hepburn, James Stewart. 112M USA. prod/rel: Metro-Goldwyn-Mayer Corp., Loew's, Inc.©

Spring Dance, New York 1936, Play
Spring Madness 1938 d: S. Sylvan Simon. lps: Maureen O'Sullivan, Lew Ayres, Ruth Hussey. 67M USA. *Spring Dance*; *Sorority House* prod/rel: Metro-Goldwyn-Mayer Corp., Loew's, Inc.©

Tomorrow and Tomorrow, New York 1931, Play
Tomorrow and Tomorrow 1932 d: Richard Wallace. lps: Ruth Chatterton, Paul Lukas, Robert Ames. 73M USA. prod/rel: Paramount Publix Corp.©

Without Love, New York 1943, Play
Without Love 1945 d: Harold S. Bucquet. lps: Spencer Tracy, Katharine Hepburn, Keenan Wynn. 111M USA. prod/rel: MGM

You and I, New York 1923, Play
Bargain, The 1931 d: Robert Milton. lps: Lewis Stone, John Darrow, Evalyn Knapp. 76M USA. *You and I*; *Fame* prod/rel: First National Pictures, Inc.

BARRY, TOM
Play
Habit 1921 d: Edwin Carewe. lps: Mildred Harris, William E. Lawrence, Ethel Grey Terry. 6r USA. prod/rel: Chaplin-Mayer Pictures Co.©, Associated First National Pictures

Courage, New York 1928, Play
Courage 1930 d: Archie Mayo. lps: Belle Bennett, Marion Nixon, Rex Bell. 6630f USA. prod/rel: Warner Brothers Pictures

My Bill 1938 d: John Farrow. lps: Kay Francis, Bonita Granville, Anita Louise. 65M USA. *In Every Woman's Life*; *Every Woman's Life* prod/rel: Warner Bros. Pictures©

The Upstart, New York 1910, Play
   Upstart, The 1916 d: Edwin Carewe. lps: Marguerite Snow, George Le Guere, James Lackaye. 5r USA. prod/rel: Rolfe Photoplays Inc.©, Metro Pictures Corp.

BARRYMORE, DIANA (1921–1960), USA
Too Soon Too Much, 1957, Autobiography
   Too Much, Too Soon 1958 d: Art Napoleon. lps: Dorothy Malone, Errol Flynn, Efrem Zimbalist Jr. 121M USA. prod/rel: Warner Bros.

BARRYMORE, JEAN
The Black Wolf, Short Story
   Black Wolf, The 1916 d: Frank Reicher. lps: Lou Tellegen, Nell Shipman, Henry J. Hebert. 5r USA. prod/rel: Jesse L. Lasky Feature Play Co.©, Paramount Pictures Corp.

BARSTOW, STAN (1928–, UKN
A Brother's Tale, Novel
   Brother's Tale, A 1983 d: Les Chatfield. lps: Trevor Eve, Kevin McNally. MTV. 156M UKN. prod/rel: Granada

A Kind of Loving, London 1960, Novel
   Kind of Loving, A 1962 d: John Schlesinger. lps: Alan Bates, June Ritchie, Thora Hird. 112M UKN. prod/rel: Vic Films, Waterhall Productions

BART, JEAN
Europolis, 1933, Novel
   Porto-Franco 1961 d: Paul Calinescu. lps: Stefan Ciubotarasu, Geo Barton, Fory Etterle. 82M RMN.

The Man Who Reclaimed His Head, New York 1932, Play
   Man Who Reclaimed His Head, The 1934 d: Edward Ludwig. lps: Claude Rains, Joan Bennett, Lionel Atwill. 82M USA. prod/rel: Universal Pictures Corp.©

The Squall, New York 1926, Play
   Squall, The 1929 d: Alexander KordA. lps: Myrna Loy, Richard Tucker, Alice Joyce. 105M USA. prod/rel: First National Pictures

BART, LIONEL
Lock Up Your Daughters, London 1959, Play
   Lock Up Your Daughters! 1969 d: Peter Coe. lps: Christopher Plummer, Susannah York, Glynis Johns. 103M UKN. prod/rel: Domino Productions, Columbia

BARTA, JAN
Roman Hloupeho Honzy, Novel
   Roman Hloupeho Honzy 1926 d: Frantisek Hlavaty. lps: Zdenek Stepanek, Marta Majova, Libuse FreslovA. 2261m CZC. *The Story of Simple Simon*; *Reditel Sklarny*; *The Director of a Glassworks* prod/rel: Pronax-Film, Josip

BARTH, JOHN (1930–, USA, Barth, John Simmons
End of the Road, New York 1958, Novel
   End of the Road 1970 d: Aram Avakian. lps: Stacy Keach, Harris Yulin, Dorothy Tristan. 111M USA. prod/rel: Allied Artists

BARTH, RICHARD
The Rag Bag Clan, Novel
   Small Killing, A 1981 d: Steven Hilliard Stern. lps: Edward Asner, Jean Simmons, Sylvia Sidney. TVM. 100M USA. prod/rel: CBS, Orgolini-Nelson

BARTHEL, JOAN
A Death in California, Book
   Death in California, A 1986 d: Delbert Mann. lps: Cheryl Ladd, Sam Elliott, Alexis Smith. TVM. 200M USA. prod/rel: ABC, Lorimar

A Death in Canaan, Book
   Death in Canaan, A 1978 d: Tony Richardson. lps: Stefanie Powers, Paul Clemens, Tom Atkins. TVM. 120M USA. prod/rel: Warner Bros., Chris-Rose Productions

BARTHOLOMAE, PHILIP
All Night Long, Play
   Outside Woman, The 1921. lps: Wanda Hawley, Clyde Fillmore, Sidney Bracey. 4225f USA. prod/rel: Realart Pictures

Barnum Was Right, New York 1923, Play
   Barnum Was Right 1929 d: Del Lord. lps: Glenn Tryon, Merna Kennedy, Otis Harlan. 5140f USA. prod/rel: Universal Pictures

Daredevil Kate, Play
   Daredevil Kate 1916 d: Kenean Buel. lps: Virginia Pearson, Mary Martin, Kenneth Hunter. 6r USA. *Dare-Devil Kate* prod/rel: Fox Film Corp., William Fox©

Little Miss Brown, New York 1912, Play
   Little Miss Brown 1915 d: James Young. lps: Vivian Martin, W. J. Ferguson, Julia Stuart. 4r USA. prod/rel: William A. Brady Picture Plays, Inc., World Film Corp.©

Over Night, New York 1911, Play
   Over Night 1915 d: James Young. lps: Vivian Martin, Sam Hardy, Herbert Yost. 5r USA. prod/rel: World Film Corp.©, William A. Brady Feature

BARTLETT, FREDERICK ORIN
The Lady in the Library, Short Story
   Lady in the Library, The 1917 d: Edgar Jones. lps: Jack Vosburgh, Vola Vale, Robert Weycross. 4r USA. prod/rel: Falcon Features, General Film Co.©

The Lion's Den, 1919, Short Story
   Lion's Den, The 1919 d: George D. Baker. lps: Bert Lytell, Alice Lake, Joseph Kilgour. 4900f USA. prod/rel: Metro Pictures Corp.©

Open Sesame, 1918, Short Story
   Alias Mike Moran 1919 d: James Cruze. lps: Wallace Reid, Anna Little, Emory Johnson. 5r USA. prod/rel: Famous Players-Lasky Corp.©, Paramount Pictures

The Seventh Noon, New York 1910, Novel
   Seventh Noon, The 1915. lps: Ernest Glendinning, Winifred Kingston, George Le Guere. 5r USA. prod/rel: Mutual Film Corp.

The Spender, 1916, Short Story
   Spender, The 1919 d: Charles Swickard. lps: Bert Lytell, Mary Anderson, Thomas Jefferson. 5r USA. prod/rel: Metro Pictures Corp.©

The Triflers, Boston 1917, Novel
   Triflers, The 1924 d: Louis J. Gasnier. lps: Mae Busch, Elliott Dexter, Frank Mayo. 6626f USA. prod/rel: B. P. Schulberg Productions

BARTLETT, LANIER
Adios!, New York 1929, Novel
   Lash, The 1930 d: Frank Lloyd. lps: Richard Barthelmess, Mary Astor, Fred Kohler. 75M USA. *Adios* (UKN) prod/rel: First National Pictures

BARTLETT, SY
Story
   Princess and the Pirate, The 1944 d: David Butler. lps: Bob Hope, Virginia Mayo, Victor McLaglen. 94M USA. prod/rel: RKO Radio

Save My Child Fireman, Story
   Sandy Gets Her Man 1940 d: Otis Garrett, Paul Gerard Smith. lps: Baby Sandy, Stuart Erwin, Una Merkel. 74M USA. *Fireman Save My Child* prod/rel: Universal Pictures Co.©

Twelve O'Clock High, Novel
   Twelve O'Clock High 1949 d: Henry King. lps: Gregory Peck, Hugh Marlowe, Gary Merrill. 132M USA. prod/rel: 20th Century-Fox

BARTLETT, VERNON
Calf Love, Novel
   Calf Love 1966 d: Gilchrist Calder. lps: Simon Ward, Isobel Black, Warren Mitchell. MTV. 75M UKN. prod/rel: BBC

BARTLETT, VIRGINIA S.
Adios!, New York 1929, Novel
   Lash, The 1930 d: Frank Lloyd. lps: Richard Barthelmess, Mary Astor, Fred Kohler. 75M USA. *Adios* (UKN) prod/rel: First National Pictures

BARTLEY, MRS. NALBRO ISADORAH
The Bargain True, Boston 1918, Novel
   Lure of Luxury, The 1918 d: Elsie Jane Wilson. lps: Ruth Clifford, Harry Van Meter, Edward Hearn. 5r USA. *The Bargain True* prod/rel: Bluebird Photoplays, Inc.©

BARTLEY, NALBRO
The Bramble Bush, 1914, Serial Story
   Bramble Bush, The 1919 d: Tom Terriss. lps: Corinne Griffith, Frank Mills, Julia Swayne Gordon. 5r USA. prod/rel: Vitagraph Co. of America©

The Cynic Effect, 1920, Short Story
   Country Flapper, The 1922 d: F. Richard Jones. lps: Dorothy Gish, Glenn Hunter, Mildred Marsh. 5000f USA. *The Cynic Effect*; *Oh Jo!*; *Her First Love*; *Old Jo* prod/rel: Dorothy Gish Productions, State Rights

Devil's Lottery, New York 1931, Novel
   Devil's Lottery 1932 d: Sam Taylor. lps: Elissa Landi, Victor McLaglen, Alexander Kirkland. 78M USA. prod/rel: Fox Film Corp.

Miss Antique, 1919, Short Story
   Amateur Wife, The 1920 d: Eddie Dillon. lps: Irene Castle, William P. Carleton, Arthur Rankin. 5r USA. prod/rel: Famous Players-Lasky Corp.©, Paramount-Artcraft Pictures

The Vanity Pool, Novel
   Vanity Pool, The 1918 d: Ida May Park. lps: Mary MacLaren, Thomas Holding, Anna Q. Nilsson. 6r USA. prod/rel: Universal Film Mfg. Co.©

A Woman's Woman, Boston 1919, Novel
   Woman's Woman, A 1922 d: Charles Giblyn. lps: Mary Alden, Louise Lee, Dorothy MacKaill. 7900f USA. prod/rel: Albion Productions, Allied Producers and Distributors

BARTOLINI, ELIO
La Bellezza d'Ippolita, Novel
   Bellezza d'Ippolita, La 1962 d: Giancarlo Zagni. lps: Gina Lollobrigida, Enrico Maria Salerno, MilvA. 90M ITL/FRN. *La Beaute d'Hyppolite* (FRN); *She Got What She Asked for* prod/rel: Arco Film (Roma), Francinex Pathe (Paris)

BARTOLINI, LUIGI
Ladri Di Biciclette, 1948, Novel
   Ladri Di Biciclette 1948 d: Vittorio de SicA. lps: Lamberto Maggiorani, Lianella Carell, Gino SaltamerendA. 88M ITL. *Bicycle Thieves* (UKN); *The Bicycle Thief* prod/rel: Produzioni de Sica, E.N.I.C.

BARTON, BRUCE (1886–1967), USA
The Man Nobody Knows; a Discovery of Jesus, Indianapolis 1925, Book
   Man Nobody Knows, The 1925 d: Errett Leroy Kenepp. 6r USA. prod/rel: Pictorial Clubs

BARTON, RAYNER
Envy My Simplicity, Novel
   Killer Walks, A 1952 d: Ronald Drake. lps: Laurence Harvey, Susan Shaw, Trader Faulkner. 57M UKN. prod/rel: Leontine Entertainments, Grand National

BARTSCH, RUDOLF HANS
Die Geschichte von Der Hannerl Und Ihren Liebhabern, Leipzig 1913, Novel
   Love Me and the World Is Mine 1928 d: E. A. Dupont. lps: Mary Philbin, Norman Kerry, Betty Compson. 6813f USA. *Implacable Destiny* prod/rel: Universal Pictures

Hannerl Und Ihre Liebhaber, Novel
   Hannerl Und Ihre Liebhaber 1921 d: Felix Basch. lps: Grete Freund, Felix Basch, Rosa Valetti. 1787m GRM. prod/rel: Frankfurter Film-Co.

   Hannerl Und Ihre Liebhaber 1935 d: Werner Hochbaum. lps: Olly von Flint, Albrecht Schoenhals, Olga TschechowA. 86M AUS. prod/rel: Favorit

Schwammerl, Leipzig 1916, Novel
   Drei Maderl Um Schubert 1936 d: E. W. Emo. lps: Maria Andergast, Gretl Theimer, Else Elster. 93M GRM. *Dreimaderlhaus* prod/rel: Algefa, Syndikat

   Dreimaderlhaus, Das 1958 d: Ernst MarischkA. lps: Karlheinz Bohm, Gustav Knuth, Magda Schneider. 102M AUS. *The House of the Three Girls* (USA) prod/rel: Erma Film, Aspa Film

BARUCH, ADAM
Story
   Indiani Ba Shemesh 1981 d: Ram Loevy. lps: Doron Nesher, Haim Garfi, Moshe IVgi. TVM. F ISR. *Indiani in the Sun* prod/rel: Israel Television

BARYLLI, GABRIEL
Butterbrot, Play
   Butterbrot 1989 d: Gabriel Barylli. lps: Uwe Ochsenknecht, Heinz Hoenig, Gabriel Barylli. 92M GRM. *Bread and Butter* prod/rel: Bavaria, Iduna Film

Honigmond, Play
   Honigmond 1996 d: Gabriel Barylli. lps: Veronica Ferres, Anica Dobra, Julia Stemberger. 84M GRM. *Honeymoon* prod/rel: Roxy Film, Mtm Cineteve

BARZINI, LUIGI (1908–1984), ITL, Barzini, Luigi Giorgio
Quello Che Non T'aspetti, Play
   Fabbrica Dell'imprevisto, La 1943 d: Jacopo Comin. lps: Maurizio d'Ancora, Vera Bergman, Oretta Fiume. 75M ITL. *Quello Che Non T'aspetti* prod/rel: Atesia Film, Kino Film

BARZMAN, BEN
Don't Ever Leave Me, Story
   Never Say Goodbye 1946 d: James V. Kern. lps: Errol Flynn, Eleanor Parker, Patti Brady. 97M USA. prod/rel: Warner Bros.

BARZMAN, NORMA
   Never Say Goodbye 1946 d: James V. Kern. lps: Errol Flynn, Eleanor Parker, Patti Brady. 97M USA. prod/rel: Warner Bros.

BASCHKIRTZEFF, MARIA
Journal, 1885, Book
   Diario Di Una Donna Amata, Il 1936 d: Henry Koster. lps: Isa Miranda, Hans Jaray, Ennio Cerlesi. 84M ITL. prod/rel: Astra Film (Roma), Panta Film (Vienna)

   Tagebuch Der Geliebten, Das 1936 d: Henry Koster. lps: Isa Miranda, Hans Jaray, Attila Horbiger. F GRM/AUS. *The Affairs of Maupassant*; *Marie Baschkirtzeff*

BASHFORD, H. H.
Back to the Trees, Short Story
   Back to the Trees 1926 d: Edwin Greenwood. lps: Janet Alexander, John Stuart, Gladys Jennings. 1960f UKN. prod/rel: Gaumont

BASS, EDUARD
Klapzubova Jedenactka, Short Story
  Klapzubova Jedenactka 1938 d: Ladislav Brom. lps: Theodor Pistek, Antonie Nedosinska, Fandaa Mrazek. 2536m CZC. *The Klabzuba's Eleven*; *Klapzubova XI* prod/rel: Reiter

BASS, RONALD
The Emerald Illusion, Novel
  Code Name: Emerald 1985 d: Jonathan Sanger. lps: Ed Harris, Max von Sydow, Horst Buchholz. 95M USA. *Codename Emerald*; *Emerald* prod/rel: MGM, United Artists

BASSAN, JEAN
Les Distractions, Novel
  Distractions, Les 1960 d: Jacques Dupont. lps: Jean-Paul Belmondo, Alexandra Stewart, Claude Brasseur. 105M FRN/ITL. *Le Distrazioni* (ITL); *Trapped By Fear* (USA) prod/rel: Societe Francaise De Cinematographique, France Cinema

BASSANI, GIORGIO (1916–, ITL
Il Giardino Dei Finzi-Contini, 1962, Novel
  Giardino Dei Finzi-Contini, Il 1970 d: Vittorio de SicA. lps: Dominique Sanda, Lino Capolicchio, Helmut Berger. 95M ITL/GRM. *Der Garten Der Finzi Contini* (GRM); *The Garden of the Finzi-Continis* (UKN) prod/rel: Documento Film (Roma), C.C.C. Filmkunst (Berlin)

Una Notte Del '43, 1960, Novel
  Lunga Notte Del '43, La 1960 d: Florestano Vancini. lps: Belinda Lee, Gabriele Ferzetti, Enrico Maria Salerno. 106M ITL. *The Long Night of '43* prod/rel: Ajace Prod. Cin.Che, Euro International Film

Gli Occhiali d'Oro, 1956, Novel
  Occhiali d'Oro, Gli 1987 d: Giuliano Montaldo. lps: Philippe Noiret, Rupert Everett, Valeria Golino. 110M ITL/FRN/YGS. *Les Lunettes d'Or* (FRN); *The Gold-Rimmed Glasses*; *The Golden Glasses* prod/rel: L.P., D.M.V.

BASSANO, ENRICO
L' Uomo Sull'acqua, Novel
  E Sbarcato un Marinaio 1940 d: Piero Ballerini. lps: Amedeo Nazzari, Doris Duranti, Germana Paolieri. 74M ITL. prod/rel: Manenti Film, Cine Tirrenia

BASSET, SERGE
Les Grands, Play
  Grands, Les 1916 d: Georges DenolA. lps: Jean Silvestre, Maurice Lagrenee, Simone Frevalles. 1580m FRN. prod/rel: Scagl
  Grands, Les 1924 d: Henri Fescourt. lps: Jeanne Helbling, Max de Rieux, Georges Gauthier. 1900m FRN. prod/rel: Les Films De France
  Grands, Les 1936 d: Felix Gandera, Robert Bibal. lps: Charles Vanel, Gaby Morlay, Pierre Larquey. 85M FRN. prod/rel: Productions Felix Gandera

BASSETT, JAMES
Harm's Way, Cleveland 1962, Novel
  In Harm's Way 1965 d: Otto Preminger. lps: John Wayne, Kirk Douglas, Patricia Neal. 167M USA. prod/rel: Sigma Productions

BASSETT, RONALD
Witchfinder General, London 1966, Novel
  Witchfinder General 1968 d: Michael Reeves. lps: Vincent Price, Ian Ogilvy, Rupert Davies. 87M UKN. *Edgar Allan Poe's Conqueror Worm*; *Conqueror Worm* (USA) prod/rel: Tigon, American-International Pictures

BASSETT, SARA WARE
The Harbor Road, Philadelphia 1919, Novel
  Danger Ahead 1921 d: Rollin S. Sturgeon. lps: Mary Philbin, James Morrison, Jack Mower. 4353f USA. prod/rel: Universal Mfg. Co.

The Taming of Zenas Henry, New York 1915, Novel
  Captain Hurricane 1935 d: John S. Robertson. lps: James Barton, Helen Westley, Helen Mack. 72M USA. *Cape Cod* prod/rel: RKO Radio Pictures, Inc.

BASSING, EILEEN
Home Before Dark, 1957, Novel
  Home Before Dark 1958 d: Mervyn Leroy. lps: Jean Simmons, Dan O'Herlihy, Rhonda Fleming. 136M USA. prod/rel: Warner Bros., Mervy Leroy

BASSO, HAMILTON (1904–1964), USA
Days Before Lent, 1939, Novel
  Holiday for Sinners 1952 d: Gerald Mayer. lps: Gig Young, Janice Rule, Keenan Wynn. 72M USA. *Days Before Lent* prod/rel: MGM

The View from Pompey's Head, 1954, Novel
  View from Pompey's Head, The 1955 d: Philip Dunne. lps: Richard Egan, Dana Wynter, Cameron Mitchell. 97M USA. *Secret Interlude* (UKN) prod/rel: 20th Century-Fox

BASTIANI, ANGE
Caltez Volailles, Novel
  Mefiez-Vous, Mesdames! 1963 d: Andre Hunebelle. lps: Paul Meurisse, Danielle Darrieux, Gaby SylviA. 90M FRN/ITL. *Chi Vuol Dormire Nel Mio Letto?* (ITL) prod/rel: P.A.C., S.N.E.G.

Folle a Lier, Novel
  Ammazzatina, L' 1975 d: Ignazio Dolce. lps: Pino Caruso, Paola Quattrini, Leopoldo Trieste. 100M ITL. prod/rel: Bi.Di.A. Film

Le Pain Des Jules, Play
  Pain Des Jules, Le 1959 d: Jacques Severac. lps: Christian Mery, Bella Darvi, Francoise Vatel. 97M FRN. prod/rel: Films Artistiques Francais, Jad Films

BASTIAN-KLINGER, VINETA
Novel
  Paradies Der Matrosen 1959 d: Harald Reinl. lps: Margit Saad, Boy Gobert, Mara Lane. 102M GRM. *Sailor's Paradise* prod/rel: Kurt Ulrich, U.F.H.

BASURTO, LUIS G.
Cada Quien Su Vida, Play
  Cada Quien Su Vida 1959 d: Julio Bracho. lps: Ana Luisa Peluffo, Kitty de Hoyos, Emma Fink. 100M MXC. prod/rel: Peliculas Rodriguez

BATAILLE, GEORGES (1897–1962), FRN
Histoire de l'Oeil, 1928, Novel
  Simona 1974 d: Patrick Longchamps. lps: Laura Antonelli, Margot Saint-Ange, Maurizio Degli Esposti. 88M ITL/BLG. *L' Histoire de l'Oeil* (BLG); *The Story of the Eye* prod/rel: Rolfilm (Torino), Les Films De L'oeil (Bruxelles)

BATAILLE, HENRY
L' Enchantement, 1900, Play
  Incantesimo 1919 d: Ugo Gracci. lps: Pepa Bonafe, Gianna Terribili-Gonzales, Ugo Gracci. 1308m ITL. prod/rel: Medusa Film

L' Enfant de l'Amour, 1911, Play
  Enfant de l'Amour, L' 1916 d: Emilio Ghione. lps: Emilio Ghione, Alda Borelli, Diomira Jacobini. 1550m ITL. prod/rel: Tiber
  Enfant de l'Amour, L' 1930 d: Marcel L'Herbier. lps: Jaque Catelain, Jean Angelo, Emmy Lynn. F FRN. prod/rel: Pathe-Natan
  Enfant de l'Amour, L' 1944 d: Jean Stelli. lps: Francois Perier, Gaby Morlay, Aime Clariond. 100M FRN. prod/rel: Consortium De Productions De Films

La Femme Nue, 1908, Play
  Donna Nuda, La 1914 d: Carmine Gallone. lps: Lyda Borelli, Lamberto Picasso, Ugo Piperno. 1600m ITL. *The Naked Truth* (UKN) prod/rel: Cines
  Donna Nuda, La 1922 d: Roberto Leone Roberti. lps: Francesca Bertini, Angelo Ferrari, Jole Gerli. 1851m ITL. prod/rel: Bertini
  Femme Nue, La 1926 d: Leonce Perret. lps: Louise Lagrange, Ivan Petrovitch, Andre Nox. 3750m FRN. *The Model from Montmartre* (USA); *Bohemian Love* prod/rel: Natan
  Femme Nue, La 1932 d: Jean-Paul Paulin. lps: Florelle, Alice Field, Raymond Rouleau. 91M FRN. prod/rel: P.A.D.
  Femme Nue, La 1949 d: Andre Berthomieu. lps: Giselle Pascal, Michele Philippe, Yves Vincent. 95M FRN. *The Naked Woman* (USA) prod/rel: Sigma

Les Flambeaux, Play
  Flambeaux, Les 1914 d: Henri Pouctal. lps: Jules Leitner, Dumeny, Nelly Cormon. FRN. prod/rel: le Film d'Art

L' Homme a la Rose, 1921, Play
  Private Life of Don Juan, The 1934 d: Alexander KordA. lps: Douglas Fairbanks Jr., Merle Oberon, Benita Hume. 90M UKN. prod/rel: London Films, United Artists

Maman Colibri, 1904, Play
  Maman Colibri 1918 d: Alfredo de Antoni. lps: Tilde Teldi, Guido Trento, Giorgio Di Chambryl. 1530m ITL. prod/rel: Caesar Film
  Maman Colibri 1929 d: Julien Duvivier. lps: Maria Jacobini, Franz Lederer, Jeanne Dax. 3145m FRN. prod/rel: Film d'Art (Vandal Et Delac)
  Maman Colibri 1937 d: Jean Dreville. lps: Huguette Duflos, Jean-Pierre Aumont, Jean Worms. 99M FRN. prod/rel: Badalo-Film

La Marche Nuptiale, 1905, Play
  Marche Nuptiale, La 1928 d: Andre Hugon. lps: Louise Lagrange, Pierre Blanchar, Paul Guide. F FRN. prod/rel: F.A. Hugon
  Marche Nuptiale, La 1934 d: Mario Bonnard. lps: Henri Rollan, Madeleine Renaud, Jean Marchat. 95M FRN. prod/rel: Paris-Rome Films

  Marcia Nuziale, La 1915 d: Carmine Gallone. lps: Lyda Borelli, Amleto Novelli, Leda Gys. 1550m ITL. prod/rel: Cines
  Marcia Nuziale, La 1934 d: Mario Bonnard. lps: Kiki Palmer, Tullio Carminati, Enrico Viarisio. 92M ITL. prod/rel: Manderfilm

La Masque, 1908, Play
  Maschera, La 1921 d: Ivo Illuminati. lps: Silvana, Nerio Bernardi, Eugenia Masetti. 1340m ITL. prod/rel: Medusa Film

La Phalene, 1913, Play
  Falena, La 1916 d: Carmine Gallone. lps: Lyda Borelli, Andrea Habay, Francesco Cacace. 1748m ITL. prod/rel: Cines

Poliche, 1906, Play
  Narr Seiner Liebe, Der 1929 d: Olga TschechowA. lps: Michael Tschechow, Dolly Davis, Oskar Wullhusq. 2302m GRM. prod/rel: Tschechowa-Film
  Poliche 1934 d: Abel Gance. lps: Constant Remy, Alexandre Darcy, Marie Bell. 90M FRN. prod/rel: Films Criterium

La Possession, Play
  Possession, La 1929 d: Leonce Perret. lps: Francesca Bertini, Pierre de Guingand, Andre Nox. F FRN. prod/rel: Franco-Film

Le Scandale, 1909, Play
  Scandal, The 1923 d: Arthur Rooke. lps: Hilda Bayley, Henry Victor, Edward O'Neill. 6370f UKN/FRN. *Le Scandale* (FRN) prod/rel: Films Legrand, I. B. Davidson
  Scandale, Le 1916 d: Jacques de Baroncelli. lps: Denise Lorys, Paul Escoffier, Berthe Jalabert. 1450m FRN. prod/rel: Film d'Art
  Scandale, Le 1934 d: Marcel L'Herbier. lps: Henri Rollan, Jean Galland, Gaby Morlay. 106M FRN. prod/rel: Ayres D'agular, Eureka-Film

La Tendresse, 1921, Play
  Tendresse, La 1930 d: Andre Hugon. lps: Jean Toulout, Jose Noguero, Marcelle Chantal. 89M FRN. prod/rel: Pathe-Natan, Hugon-Films

La Vierge Folle, 1910, Play
  Vergine Folle, La 1920 d: Gennaro Righelli. lps: Maria Jacobini, Andrea Habay, Alberto Collo. 2083m ITL. prod/rel: Tiber Film
  Vierge Folle, La 1913. lps: Marie-Louise Iribe. FRN.
  Vierge Folle, La 1928 d: Luitz-Morat. lps: Suzy Vernon, Jean Angelo, Maurice Schutz. F FRN. prod/rel: Eclair
  Vierge Folle, La 1938 d: Henri Diamant-Berger. lps: Victor Francen, Michel Andre, Annie Ducaux. 90M FRN. prod/rel: Film d'Art

BATAILLE, MICHEL
L' Arbre de Noel, Paris 1967, Novel
  Arbre de Noel, L' 1969 d: Terence Young. lps: William Holden, Virna Lisi, Bourvil. 110M FRN/ITL. *L' Albero Di Natale* (ITL); *The Christmas Tree* (USA); *When Wolves Cry* prod/rel: Films Corona, Jupiter Generale Cinematografica

BATEMAN, COLIN
Cycle of Violence, Novel
  Crossmaheart 1998 d: Henry Herbert. lps: Gerard Rooney, Maria Lennon, Desmond Cave. 94M UKN. *Cycle of Violence* prod/rel: Lexington Films

Divorcing Jack, Novel
  Divorcing Jack 1998 d: David Caffrey. lps: David Thewlis, Rachel Griffiths, Robert Lindsay. 110M UKN/FRN. prod/rel: BBC Films, Winchester Films

BATES, H. E. (1905–1974), UKN, Bates, Herbert Ernest
The Darling Buds of May, 1958, Novel
  Mating Game, The 1958 d: George Marshall. lps: Debbie Reynolds, Tony Randall, Paul Douglas. 96M USA. prod/rel: MGM

Dulcima, 1953, Short Story
  Dulcima 1971 d: Frank Nesbitt. lps: John Mills, Carol White, Stuart Wilson. 89M UKN. prod/rel: Emi

Fair Stood the Wind for France, 1944, Novel
  Fair Stood the Wind for France 1981. lps: David Beames, Cecile Paoli, Bernard Kay. MTV. 240M UKN. prod/rel: BBC

The Feast of July, Novel
  Feast of July 1995 d: Christopher Menaul. lps: Embeth Davidtz, Ben Chaplin, Tom Bell. 116M UKN/USA. prod/rel: Merchant Ivory Production

The Little Farm, Short Story
  Under Solen 1998 d: Colin Nutley. lps: Rolf Lassgard, Helena Bergstrom, Johan Widerberg. 130M SWD. *Under the Sun* prod/rel: Svensk Filmindustri, Sweetwater

Love for Lydia, Novel
  Love for Lydia 1977 d: Tony Wharmby. lps: Mel Martin, Christopher Blake, Jeremy Irons. MTV. 650M UKN. prod/rel: Lwt

A Month By the Lake, Novel
   Month By the Lake, A 1994 d: John Irvin. lps: Vanessa Redgrave, James Fox, Uma Thurman. 92M USA/UKN. prod/rel: Anuline, Miramax

The Purple Plain, 1947, Novel
   Purple Plain, The 1954 d: Robert Parrish. lps: Gregory Peck, Win Min Than, Brenda de Banzie. 100M UKN. prod/rel: Two Cities, General Film Distributors

The Triple Echo, 1970, Novel
   Triple Echo, The 1972 d: Michael Apted. lps: Glenda Jackson, Oliver Reed, Brian Deacon. 94M UKN. *Soldiers in Skirts* (USA) prod/rel: Hemdale, Senta

BATES, HARRY
Farewell to the Master, Story
   Day the Earth Stood Still, The 1950 d: Robert Wise. lps: Michael Rennie, Patricia Neal, Hugh Marlowe. 92M USA. prod/rel: 20th Century-Fox

BATES, WILLIAM
The Open House
   Loin du Foyer 1917 d: Pierre Bressol. lps: Pierre Bressol, Paul Hubert, Andree Divonne. 1050m FRN. prod/rel: Pathe Consortium

BATTIN, B. W.
Smithereens, Novel
   Hell Hath No Fury 1991 d: Thomas J. Wright. lps: Loretta Swit, Barbara Eden, David Ackroyd. TVM. 100M USA. prod/rel: Bar-Gene Prods. Inc.©, the Finnegan-Pinchuk Company

BATY, GASTON
Dulcinea, Novel
   Dulcinea 1962 d: Vicente EscrivA. lps: Millie Perkins, Folco Lulli, Cameron Mitchell. 103M SPN/ITL/GRM. *Girl from la Mancha*; *Incantesimo d'Amore*; *Enchantment of Love* prod/rel: Aspa Film (Madrid), Nivi Film (Roma)

BAUCHE, HENRI
Le Chateau de la Mort Lente, Play
   Chateau de la Mort Lente, Le 1925 d: E. B. Donatien. lps: E. B. Donatien, Lucienne Legrand, Pierre Etchepare. F FRN. prod/rel: Donatien

BAUER, WOLFGANG
Change, 1969, Play
   Change 1974 d: Bernd Fischerauer. lps: Reiner Schone, Axel Wagner, Sylvia Manas. 101M GRM. prod/rel: Divina, Lisa

BAUM, L. FRANK (1856–1919), USA, Baum, Lyman Frank
The Land of Oz, 1904, Novel
   Return to Oz 1964 d: Arthur Rankin Jr.. ANM. 52M USA.
   Return to Oz 1985 d: Walter Murch. lps: Nicol Williamson, Jean Marsh, Piper Laurie. 110M USA. prod/rel: Buena Vista, Walt Disney Productions

The Last Egyptian, Philadelphia 1908, Novel
   Last Egyptian, The 1914 d: L. Frank Baum. lps: J. Farrell MacDonald, Vivian Reed, May Wells. 5r USA. prod/rel: Oz Film Manufacturing Co., Alliance Films Corp.

The Marvelous Land of Oz, Chicago 1904, Novel
   Wonderful Land of Oz, The 1969 d: Barry Mahon. lps: Joy Webb, Channy Mahon. 72M USA. *The Land of Oz* prod/rel: Cinetron Corp.

The New Wizard of Oz, Chicago 1903, Novel
   His Majesty, the Scarecrow of Oz 1914 d: L. Frank Baum. lps: Frank Moore, Vivian Reed, Fred Woodward. 5r USA. *The New Wizard of Oz*; *The Scarecrow of Oz*; *His Majesty the Scarecrow* prod/rel: Oz Film Manufacturing Co., Alliance Films Corp.

Ozma of Oz, 1907, Novel
   Return to Oz 1964 d: Arthur Rankin Jr.. ANM. 52M USA.
   Return to Oz 1985 d: Walter Murch. lps: Nicol Williamson, Jean Marsh, Piper Laurie. 110M USA. prod/rel: Buena Vista, Walt Disney Productions

Queen Zixi of Oz, Novel
   Magic Cloak of Oz, The 1914 d: L. Frank Baum. lps: Mildred Harris, Violet MacMillan, Fred Woodward. 5r USA. prod/rel: Oz Film Manufacturing Co., Paramount Pictures Corp.

The Wizard of Oz, 1903, Play
   His Majesty, the Scarecrow of Oz 1914 d: L. Frank Baum. lps: Frank Moore, Vivian Reed, Fred Woodward. 5r USA. *The New Wizard of Oz*; *The Scarecrow of Oz*; *His Majesty the Scarecrow* prod/rel: Oz Film Manufacturing Co., Alliance Films Corp.

The Wonderful Wizard of Oz, Chicago 1900, Novel
   Wiz, The 1978 d: Sidney Lumet. lps: Diana Ross, Mabel King, Michael Jackson. 140M USA.
   Wizard of Oz 1910 d: Otis Turner. lps: Hobart Bosworth, Eugenie Besserer, Robert Leonard. 1000f USA. prod/rel: Selig Polyscope Co.

   Wizard of Oz, The 1908. lps: Frank Burns, Joseph Schrode, Grace Elder. SHS. USA. prod/rel: Frank L. Baum (P)
   Wizard of Oz, The 1925 d: Larry Semon. lps: Larry Semon, Bryant Washburn, Dorothy Dwan. 6300f USA. prod/rel: Chadwick Pictures
   Wizard of Oz, The 1939 d: Victor Fleming, King Vidor (Uncredited). lps: Judy Garland, Frank Morgan, Ray Bolger. 101M USA. prod/rel: Metro-Goldwyn-Mayer Corp., Loew's, Inc.©
   Wizard of Oz, The 1982. ANM. 78M USA.

BAUM, VICKI (1888–1960), AUS
Novel
   Hotel Shanghai 1997 d: Peter Patzak. lps: Agnieszka Wagner, Annie Girardot, James McCaffrey. 94M GRM. prod/rel: Manfred Durniok Produktion, Mdr Oriental Communications

La Belle Que Voila, Novel
   Belle Que Voila, La 1949 d: Jean-Paul Le Chanois. lps: Michele Morgan, Ludmilla Tcherina, Henri Vidal. 95M FRN. prod/rel: Films Gibe

Eingang Zur Buhne, Novel
   Futures Vedettes 1955 d: Marc Allegret. lps: Brigitte Bardot, Jean Marais, Isabelle PiA. 95M FRN. *School for Love* (USA); *Sweet Sixteen* (UKN); *Joy of Loving* prod/rel: Regie Du Film, Del Duca

Feme, Novel
   Feme 1927 d: Richard Oswald. lps: Eduard Rothauser, Mathilde Sussin, Hans Stuwe. 2576m GRM. prod/rel: Richard Oswald Film-Prod.

Das Grosse Einmaleins, Novel
   Chateau de Verre, Le 1950 d: Rene Clement. lps: Jean Marais, Jean Servais, Michele Morgan. 95M FRN/ITL. *L' Amante Di Una Notte* (ITL) prod/rel: Franco London Films, Universalia

Helene Wilfur, Novel
   Helene 1936 d: Jean Benoit-Levy, Marie Epstein. lps: Constant Remy, Madeleine Renaud, Helena Manson. 101M FRN. prod/rel: Les Films Marquis

Hell in Frauensee, Novel
   Drei Frauen von Urban Hell, Die 1928 d: Jaap Speyer. lps: Fred Doderlein, Mona Maris, Hilde Maroff. 2087m GRM. *Hell in Frauensee* prod/rel: Terra-Film

Das Joch, Novel
   Aiguille Rouge, L' 1950 d: Emile Edwin Reinert. lps: Michel Auclair, Michele Philippe, Jean Marchat. 85M FRN. prod/rel: Alcina
   Vertraumte Tage 1951 d: Emile Edwin Reinert, Franz Zimmermann. lps: Aglaja Schmid, O. W. Fischer, Axel von Ambesser. 78M GRM/FRN. *Dreamy Days* prod/rel: Alcina, N.F.

Lac aux Dames, Novel
   Lac aux Dames 1934 d: Marc Allegret. lps: Jean-Pierre Aumont, Rosine Derean, Simone Simon. 106M FRN. prod/rel: Sopra

Menschen Im Hotel, Berlin 1929, Novel
   Grand Hotel 1932 d: Edmund Goulding. lps: Greta Garbo, John Barrymore, Joan Crawford. 115M USA. prod/rel: Metro-Goldwyn-Mayer Corp., Metro-Goldwyn-Mayer Dist. Corp.©
   Hotel Berlin 1945 d: Peter Godfrey. lps: Helmut Dantine, Andrea King, Raymond Massey. 98M USA. prod/rel: Warner Bros.
   Menschen Im Hotel 1959 d: Gottfried Reinhardt. lps: O. W. Fischer, Heinz Ruhmann, Michele Morgan. 107M GRM/FRN. *Grand Hotel* (FRN); *People in the Hotel* prod/rel: C.C.C., Modernes
   Weekend at the Waldorf 1945 d: Robert Z. Leonard. lps: Ginger Rogers, Lana Turner, Walter Pidgeon. 130M USA. prod/rel: Metro-Goldwyn-Mayer Corp.

Mortgage of Life, Novel
   Woman's Secret, A 1949 d: Nicholas Ray. lps: Maureen O'Hara, Melvyn Douglas, Gloria Grahame. 85M USA. prod/rel: RKO Radio

Six a Six, Short Story
   Retour a l'Aube 1938 d: Henri Decoin. lps: Danielle Darrieux, Pierre Dux, Therese Dorny. 90M FRN. *She Returned at Dawn* (USA) prod/rel: Production U.D.I.F.

Stud. Chem. Helene Willfuer, Novel
   Stud. Chem. Helene Willfuer 1929 d: Fred Sauer. lps: Olga Tschechowa, Igo Sym, Ernst Stahl-Nachbaur. 2542m GRM. prod/rel: Idealfilm
   Studentin Helen Willfuer 1956 d: Rudolf Jugert. lps: Ruth Niehaus, Hans Sohnker, Elma KarlowA. 102M GRM. *Student Helen Willfuer* prod/rel: C.C.C., Constantin

Vor Rehen Wird Gewarnt, Novel
   Liebe 1956 d: Horst Haechler. lps: Maria Schell, Raf Vallone, Eva Kotthaus. 97M GRM/ITL. *Uragano Sul Po* (ITL); *Love* prod/rel: C.C.C., UFA

BAUMER, MARIE
Penny Arcade, New York 1930, Play
   Sinner's Holiday 1930 d: John G. Adolfi. lps: Grant Withers, Evalyn Knapp, James Cagney. 60M USA. *Women in Love* prod/rel: Warner Brothers Pictures

BAUMGARTEN, HARALD
Funf Millionen Suchen Einen Erben, Novel
   Funf Millionen Suchen Einen Erben 1938 d: Carl Boese. lps: Heinz Ruhmann, Leny Marenbach, Vera von Langen. 87M GRM. *Five Millions Seek an Heir* (USA) prod/rel: Majestic, Turck

Oberarzt Dr. Solm, Novel
   Oberarzt Dr. Solm 1955 d: Paul May. lps: Hans Sohnker, Sybil Werden, Antje Weisgerber. 95M GRM. *Head Doctor Solm* prod/rel: Delos, Alcron

BAVIO, LIBERO
'A Mala Nova, 1902
   Mala Nova, 'A 1920 d: Eduardo Notari, Elvira Notari. lps: Rose Angione, Eduardo Notari, Oreste Tesorone. 1145m ITL. prod/rel: Gennariello Film

BAWDEN, NINA (1925–, UKN
On the Run, Novel
   On the Run 1969 d: Pat Jackson. lps: Dennis Conoley, Robert Kennedy, Tracey Collins. 56M UKN. prod/rel: Children's Film Foundation, Derick Williams

The Solitary Child, Novel
   Solitary Child, The 1958 d: Gerald Thomas. lps: Philip Friend, Barbara Shelley, Rona Anderson. 64M UKN. prod/rel: British Lion, Beaconsfield

BAX, CLIFFORD
Upstream, London 1923, Novel
   Gateway of the Moon, The 1928 d: John Griffith Wray. lps: Dolores Del Rio, Walter Pidgeon, Anders Randolf. 5038f USA. *Upstream* prod/rel: Fox Film Corp.

BAX, ROGER
Came the Dawn, 1949, Novel
   Never Let Me Go 1953 d: Delmer Daves. lps: Clark Gable, Gene Tierney, Bernard Miles. 94M UKN/USA. prod/rel: MGM British

BAXTER, GEORGE OWEN
Donnegan, New York 1923, Novel
   Vagabond Trail, The 1924 d: William A. Wellman. lps: Buck Jones, Marian Nixon, Charles Coleman. 4302f USA. prod/rel: Fox Film Corp.

Free Range Lanning, New York 1921, Novel
   Fighting Streak, The 1922 d: Arthur Rosson. lps: Tom Mix, Patsy Ruth Miller, Gerald Pring. 4888f USA. prod/rel: Fox Film Corp.

Three Who Paid, 1922, Short Story
   Three Who Paid 1923 d: Colin Campbell. lps: Dustin Farnum, Fred Kohler, Bessie Love. 4859f USA. prod/rel: Fox Film Corp.

BAXTER, JAMES K.
Jack Winter's Dream, 1959, Play
   Jack Winter's Dream 1980 d: David Sims. 59M NZL.

BAYARD
Le Mari a la Campagne, 1844, Play
   Marito in Campagna, Il 1912. lps: Mercedes Brignone, Umberto Mozzato, Cesare Quest. 350m ITL. prod/rel: Milano Films
   Marito in Campagna, Il 1920 d: Mario Almirante. lps: Mercedes Brignone, Domenico Serra, Lola Visconti-Brignone. 1151m ITL. prod/rel: Rodolfi Film

BAYARD, JEAN-FRANCOIS
La Fille du Regiment, Paris 1840, Opera
   Figlia Del Reggimento, La 1911. 243m ITL. *Daughter of the Regiment* (USA) prod/rel: Cines
   Figlia Del Reggimento, La 1920 d: Enrico Vidali. lps: Liliane de Rosny, Umberto Mozzato. 1000m ITL. prod/rel: Subalpina
   Fille du Regiment, La 1933 d: Pierre Billon, Carl Lamac. lps: Anny Ondra, Marfa Dhervilly, Pierre Richard-Willm. 90M FRN. prod/rel: Vandor-Film

Le Gamin de Paris, 1836, Play
   Birichino Di Parigi, Il 1916 d: Ugo FalenA. lps: Bianca Bellincioni-Stagno, Silvia Malinverni, Eric Oulton. 1790m ITL. *Il Birichino Di Parigi* prod/rel: Tespi Film
   Gamin de Paris, Le 1923 d: Louis Feuillade. lps: Rene Poyen, Sandra Milowanoff, Adolphe Cande. 1800m FRN. prod/rel: Gaumont
   Gamin de Paris, Le 1932 d: Gaston Roudes. lps: Alice Tissot, Arielle, Pierre Arnac. 73M FRN. prod/rel: Consortium Cinematographique Francais

BAYER, OLIVER WELD
Paper Chase, Story
   Dangerous Partners 1945 d: Edward L. Cahn. lps: James Craig, Signe Hasso, Edmund Gwenn. 74M USA. prod/rel: MGM

BAYER, PAUL
Ball Der Nationen, Opera
Ball Der Nationen 1954 d: Karl Ritter. lps: Zsa Zsa Gabor, Gustav Frohlich, Paul Henckels. 100M GRM. *International Ball* prod/rel: Buhne Und Film, Panorama

BAYER, WILLIAM
Switch, Novel
Doubletake 1985 d: Jud Taylor. lps: Richard Crenna, Beverly d'Angelo, Vincent BaggettA. TVM. 200M USA. prod/rel: CBS, Titus

BAYLE, GEORGES
Du Raisine Dans le Gas-Oil, Novel
Gas-Oil 1955 d: Gilles Grangier. lps: Jean Gabin, Jeanne Moreau, Ginette Leclerc. 90M FRN. *Hi-Jack Highway* (USA) prod/rel: Intermondia

BAYLEY, E. T.
The Mistletoe Bough, Poem
Mistletoe Bough, The 1904 d: Percy Stow. 500f UKN. prod/rel: Clarendon, Gaumont

BAYLY, JAIME
No Se Lo Digas a Nadie, Novel
No Se Lo Digas a Nadie 1998 d: Francisco Lombardi. lps: Santiago Magill, Lucia Jimenez, Christian Meier. 109M SPN/PRU. *Don't Tell Anyone* prod/rel: Lolafilms (Madrid), Inca Films (Lima)

BAZAN, NOELLE
Calvaire d'Amour, Novel
Calvaire d'Amour 1923 d: Victor Tourjansky. lps: Nathalie Lissenko, Charles Vanel, Nicolas Rimsky. 2000m FRN. prod/rel: Films Albatros

BAZIN, HERVE
La Tete Contre Les Murs, 1949, Novel
Tete Contre Les Murs, La 1958 d: Georges Franju. lps: Jean-Pierre Mocky, Pierre Brasseur, Anouk Aimee. 92M FRN. *The Keepers* (UKN) prod/rel: Atica, Elpenor Films

BAZIN, RENE
Donatienne, Novel
Donatienne 1908-13. lps: Jeanne Marie-Laurent. FRN.
Madame Corentine, Novel
Madame Corentine 1914 d: Maurice Mariaud. lps: Armand Dutertre, Kessler, Berthe Jalabert. 1433m FRN. prod/rel: Gaumont
La Terre Qui Meurt, 1899, Novel
Terre Qui Meurt, La 1926 d: Jean Choux. lps: Georges Melchior, Madeleine Renaud, Gilbert Dalleu. 2300m FRN. prod/rel: Etoile Film
Terre Qui Meurt, La 1936 d: Jean Vallee. lps: Pierre Larquey, Simone Bourday, Line Noro. 88M FRN. prod/rel: Paris-Color-Films

BEACH, COM. EDWARD L. (1918–, USA
Run Deep Run Silent, 1955, Novel
Run Silent, Run Deep 1958 d: Robert Wise. lps: Clark Gable, Burt Lancaster, Jack Warden. 93M USA. prod/rel: United Artists, Jeffrey Prods.

BEACH, LEWIS
The Goose Hangs High, New York 1924, Play
Goose Hangs High, The 1925 d: James Cruze. lps: Constance Bennett, Myrtle Stedman, George Irving. 6186f USA. prod/rel: Famous Players-Lasky Corp., Paramount Pictures
This Reckless Age 1932 d: Frank Tuttle. lps: Richard Bennett, Frances Starr, Charles "Buddy" Rogers. 80M USA. *Second Chances; The Goose Hangs High; The Reckless Age* prod/rel: Paramount Publix Corp.©
Merry Andrew, New York 1929, Play
Handy Andy 1934 d: David Butler. lps: Will Rogers, Peggy Wood, Mary Carlisle. 81M USA. *Merry Andrew* prod/rel: Fox Film Group©
Young As You Feel 1940 d: Malcolm St. Clair. lps: Jed Prouty, Spring Byington, Joan Valerie. 60M USA. *The Jones Family in As Young As You Feel* prod/rel: 20th Century-Fox Film Corp.©
A Square Peg, New York 1923, Play
Denial, The 1925 d: Hobart Henley. lps: Claire Windsor, Bert Roach, William Haines. 4791f USA. *The Square Peg* prod/rel: Metro-Goldwyn Pictures

BEACH, REX
The Auction Block; a Novel of New York Life, New York 1914, Novel
Auction Block, The 1917 d: Larry Trimble. lps: Rubye de Remer, Alec B. Francis, Florence Deshon. 7r USA. prod/rel: Rex Beach Film Corp., Goldwyn Distributing Corp.
Auction Block, The 1926 d: Hobart Henley. lps: Charles Ray, Eleanor Boardman, Sally O'Neil. 6239f USA. prod/rel: Metro-Goldwyn-Mayer Pictures

The Barrier, New York 1908, Novel
Barrier, The 1917 d: Edgar Lewis. lps: Mitchell Lewis, Howard Hall, Victor Sutherland. 10r USA. prod/rel: Rex Beach Pictures Co., State Rights
Barrier, The 1926 d: George W. Hill. lps: Norman Kerry, Henry B. Walthall, Lionel Barrymore. 6480f USA. prod/rel: Metro-Goldwyn-Mayer Pictures
Barrier, The 1937 d: Lesley Selander. lps: Leo Carrillo, Jean Parker, James Ellison. 93M USA. prod/rel: Harry Sherman Productions, Inc.
Big Brother, 1923, Short Story
Big Brother 1923 d: Allan Dwan. lps: Tom Moore, Edith Roberts, Raymond Hatton. 7080f USA. prod/rel: Famous Players-Lasky Corp., Paramount Pictures
Young Donovan's Kid 1931 d: Fred Niblo. lps: Jackie Cooper, Richard Dix, Marion Shilling. 77M USA. *Donovan's Kid* (UKN); *Big Brother; Born to the Racket* prod/rel: RKO Radio Pictures©
The Brand, 1913, Short Story
Brand, The 1919 d: Reginald Barker. lps: Kay Laurell, Russell Simpson, Robert McKim. 6433f USA. prod/rel: Goldwyn Pictures Corp., Rex Beach©
The Crimson Gardenia, New York 1916, Short Story
Crimson Gardenia, The 1919 d: Reginald Barker. lps: Owen Moore, Hedda Nova, Tully Marshall. 5400f USA. prod/rel: Rex Beach Pictures Co., Goldwyn Pictures Corp.
Don Careless, 1930, Novel
Avengers, The 1950 d: John H. Auer. lps: Fernando Lamas, Adele Mara, John Carroll. 90M USA/ARG. prod/rel: Republic Pictures Corp.
The Elusive Graft, Story
Kid from the Klondyke 1911 d: Harold Shaw. lps: Harold M. Shaw, Reeva Greenwood, John R. Cumpson. SHT USA. prod/rel: Edison
Flowing Gold, New York 1922, Novel
Flowing Gold 1924 d: Joseph de Grasse. lps: Anna Q. Nilsson, Milton Sills, Alice Calhoun. 8076f USA. prod/rel: Richard Walton Tully Productions, Associated First National Pictures
Flowing Gold 1940 d: Alfred E. Green. lps: John Garfield, Frances Farmer, Pat O'Brien. 82M USA. prod/rel: Warner Bros. Pictures©, First National Pictures
Going Some, New York 1909, Play
Going Some 1920 d: Harry Beaumont. lps: Cullen Landis, Helen Ferguson, Lillian Hall. 5453f USA. prod/rel: Eminent Authors Pictures, Inc., Goldwyn Distributing Corp.
The Goose Woman, 1925, Short Story
Goose Woman, The 1925 d: Clarence Brown. lps: Louise Dresser, Jack Pickford, Constance Bennett. 7500f USA. prod/rel: Universal Pictures
Past of Mary Holmes, The 1933 d: Harlan Thompson, Slavko Vorkapich. lps: Helen Mackellar, Eric Linden, Jean Arthur. 70M USA. *The Goose Woman* prod/rel: RKO Radio Pictures©
Heart of the Sunset, New York 1913, Novel
Heart of the Sunset 1918 d: Frank Powell. lps: Anna Q. Nilsson, Herbert Heyes, Robert Tabor. 7r USA. prod/rel: Rex Beach Pictures Co., Goldwyn Distributing Corp.
The Iron Trail, New York 1913, Novel
Iron Trail, The 1921 d: R. William Neill. lps: Wyndham Standing, Thurston Hall, Reginald Denny. 7r USA. prod/rel: Bennett Pictures, United Artists
Laughing Bill Hyde, 1917, Short Story
Laughing Bill Hyde 1918 d: Hobart Henley. lps: Will Rogers, Anna Lehr, John Sainpolis. 5790f USA. prod/rel: Rex Beach Pictures, Goldwyn Distributing Corp.
The Mating Call, New York 1927, Novel
Mating Call, The 1928 d: James Cruze. lps: Thomas Meighan, Evelyn Brent, Renee Adoree. 6352f USA. prod/rel: Caddo Co., Paramount Pictures
The Michigan Kid, 1925, Short Story
Michigan Kid, The 1928 d: Irvin V. Willat. lps: Renee Adoree, Frederick Esmelton, Virginia Grey. 6030f USA. *The Gambler* prod/rel: Universal Pictures
Michigan Kid, The 1947 d: Ray Taylor. lps: Jon Hall, Victor McLaglen, Rita Johnson. 69M USA. prod/rel: Universal
The Ne'er-Do-Well, New York 1911, Novel
Ne'er-Do-Well, The 1915 d: Colin Campbell. lps: Kathlyn Williams, Wheeler Oakman, Harry Lonsdale. 10r USA. *The Ne'er Do Well* prod/rel: Selig Polyscope Co.©, State Rights
Ne'er-Do-Well, The 1923 d: Alfred E. Green. lps: Thomas Meighan, Lila Lee, Gertrude Astor. 7414f USA. prod/rel: Famous Players-Lasky, Paramount Pictures

The Net, New York 1912, Novel
Fair Lady 1922 d: Kenneth Webb. lps: Betty Blythe, Thurston Hall, Robert Elliott. 6400f USA. prod/rel: Bennett Pictures, United Artists
The North Wind's Malice, 1917, Short Story
North Wind's Malice, The 1920 d: Paul Bern, Carl Harbaugh. lps: Joe King, Thomas Santschi, Henry West. 6275f USA. prod/rel: Eminent Authors Pictures, Inc., Goldwyn Distributing Corp.
Padlocked, New York 1926, Novel
Padlocked 1926 d: Allan Dwan. lps: Lois Moran, Noah Beery, Louise Dresser. 6700f USA. prod/rel: Famous Players-Lasky, Paramount Pictures
Pardners, New York 1905, Novel
Pardners 1910 d: Edwin S. Porter. lps: J. Barney Sherry. 995f USA. prod/rel: Edison
Pardners 1917. lps: Charlotte Walker, Richard Tucker, Leo Gordon. 5r USA. prod/rel: Thomas A. Edison, Inc., Mutual Film Corp.©
Recoil, 1922, Short Story
Recoil, The 1924 d: T. Hayes Hunter. lps: Mahlon Hamilton, Betty Blythe, Clive Brook. 7089f USA. prod/rel: Goldwyn Pictures, Metro-Goldwyn Distributing Corp.
White Shoulders 1931 d: Melville Brown. lps: Mary Astor, Jack Holt, Ricardo Cortez. 81M USA. *Disillusioned* prod/rel: RKO Radio Pictures©
Rope's End, 1913, Short Story
Sainted Devil, A 1924 d: Joseph Henabery. lps: Rudolph Valentino, Nita Naldi, Helena d'Algy. 8633f USA. prod/rel: Famous Players-Lasky, Paramount Pictures
The Silver Horde, New York 1909, Novel
Silver Horde, The 1920 d: Frank Lloyd. lps: Curtis Cooksey, Myrtle Stedman, Robert McKim. 6-7r USA. prod/rel: Eminent Authors Pictures, Inc., Goldwyn Distributing Corp.
Silver Horde, The 1930 d: George Archainbaud. lps: Evelyn Brent, Louis Wolheim, Joel McCreA. 75M USA. prod/rel: RKO Radio Pictures
Son of the Gods, 1929, Serial Story
Son of the Gods 1930 d: Frank Lloyd. lps: Richard Barthelmess, Constance Bennett, Dorothy Mathews. 82M USA. *Thunder of the Gods* (UKN) prod/rel: First National Pictures
The Spoilers, New York 1906, Novel
Spoilers, The 1914 d: Colin Campbell. lps: William Farnum, Kathlyn Williams, Bessie Eyton. 9r USA. prod/rel: Selig Polyscope Co.©
Spoilers, The 1923 d: Lambert Hillyer. lps: Milton Sills, Anna Q. Nilsson, Barbara Bedford. 8020f USA. prod/rel: Jesse D. Hampton Productions, Goldwyn Distributing Corp.
Spoilers, The 1930 d: Edwin Carewe. lps: Gary Cooper, Kay Johnson, Betty Compson. 84M USA. prod/rel: Paramount-Publix Corp.
Spoilers, The 1942 d: Ray Enright. lps: Marlene Dietrich, Randolph Scott, John Wayne. 87M USA. prod/rel: Universal
Spoilers, The 1955 d: Jesse Hibbs. lps: Rory Calhoun, Jeff Chandler, Anne Baxter. 84M USA. prod/rel: Universal-International
The Thaw at Sliscos, Story
Mine on the Yukon, The 1912. 1000f USA. prod/rel: Edison
Too Fat to Fight, Short Story
Too Fat to Fight 1918 d: Hobart Henley. lps: Frank McIntyre, Florence Dixon, Henrietta Floyd. 5457f USA. prod/rel: Rex Beach Pictures Co., Goldwyn Distributing Corp.
The Vengeance of Durand, Novel
Vengeance of Durand, The 1919 d: Tom Terriss. lps: Alice Joyce, Percy Marmont, Gustav von Seyffertitz. 6411f USA. prod/rel: Vitagraph Co. of America©
The Wag Lady, 1916, Short Story
Girl from Outside, The 1919 d: Reginald Barker. lps: Clara Horton, Cullen Landis, Wilton Taylor. 6157f USA. *The Girl from the Outside* prod/rel: Eminent Authors Pictures, Inc., Rex Beach Production
The Winds of Chance, New York 1918, Novel
Winds of Chance 1925 d: Frank Lloyd. lps: Anna Q. Nilsson, Ben Lyon, Viola DanA. 9554f USA. prod/rel: First National Pictures
With Bridges Burned, Story
With Bridges Burned 1915 d: Ashley Miller. lps: Mabel Trunnelle, Augustus Phillips. 3r USA. prod/rel: Edison
The World in His Arms, 1946, Novel
World in His Arms, The 1952 d: Raoul Walsh. lps: Gregory Peck, Ann Blyth, Anthony Quinn. 104M USA. prod/rel: Universal-International

BEAGLE, PETER S.
The Last Unicorn, Novel
　Last Unicorn, The 1982 d: Arthur Rankin Jr., Jules Bass. ANM. 93M USA. prod/rel: Itc

BEAHAN, CHARLES
Don't Fall in Love, 1931, Play
　One Night of Love 1934 d: Victor Schertzinger. lps: Grace Moore, Tullio Carminati, Lyle Talbot. 84M USA. prod/rel: Columbia Pictures Corp.©
Night Court, Play
　Night Court 1932 d: W. S. Van Dyke. lps: Phillips Holmes, Walter Huston, Anita Page. 95M USA. *Justice for Sale* (UKN) prod/rel: Metro-Goldwyn-Mayer Corp., Metro-Goldwyn-Mayer Dist. Corp.©
Society Girl, New York 1931, Play
　Society Girl 1932 d: Sidney Lanfield. lps: James Dunn, Peggy Shannon, Spencer Tracy. 74M USA. prod/rel: Fox Film Corp.©
The Victoria Docks at Eight, Novel
　White Tie and Tails 1946 d: Charles T. Barton. lps: Dan Duryea, William Bendix, Ella Raines. 81M USA. prod/rel: Universal

BEAIRD, DAVID
Scorchers, Play
　Scorchers 1991 d: David Beaird. lps: Faye Dunaway, Denholm Elliott, James Earl Jones. 82M USA. prod/rel: Nova, Goldcrest Films

BEALE, JACK
Ring for Catty, London 1954, Play
　Carry on Nurse 1959 d: Gerald Thomas. lps: Shirley Eaton, Kenneth Connor, Charles Hawtrey. 86M UKN. prod/rel: Anglo-Amalgamated, Beaconsfield
　Twice Round the Daffodils 1962 d: Gerald Thomas. lps: Juliet Mills, Donald Sinden, Donald Houston. 89M UKN. prod/rel: Anglo-Amalgamated, Gregory, Hake & Walker

BEARDSLEY, HELEN
Who Gets the Drumstick, New York 1965, Novel
　Yours, Mine and Ours 1968 d: Melville Shavelson. lps: Henry Fonda, Lucille Ball, Van Johnson. 111M USA. *His Hers and Theirs* prod/rel: Desilu-Walden Productions

BEATON, WELFORD
Behind the Wheel, Story
　Speeding Venus, The 1926 d: Robert T. Thornby. lps: Priscilla Dean, Robert Frazer, Dale Fuller. 5560f USA. prod/rel: Metropolitan Pictures Corp. of Calif., Producers Distributing Corp.

BEATTIE, ANN (1947–, USA
Head Over Heals, Novel
　Head Over Heels 1979 d: Joan Micklin Silver. lps: John Heard, Mary Beth Hurt, Peter Riegert. 98M USA. *Chilly Scenes of Winter* prod/rel: United Artists, Triple Play

BEATTIE, TASMAN
A Thousand Skies, Novel
　Thousand Skies, A 1985 d: David Stevens. lps: John Walton. TVM. F ASL. prod/rel: Thousand Skies

BEATTY, CLYDE
The Big Cage, New York 1933, Book
　Big Cage, The 1933 d: Kurt Neumann. lps: Clyde Beatty, Anita Page, Andy Devine. 77M USA. prod/rel: Universal Pictures Corp.

BEATY, DAVID
Cone of Silence, London 1959, Novel
　Cone of Silence 1960 d: Charles Frend. lps: Michael Craig, Peter Cushing, Bernard Lee. 92M UKN. *Trouble in the Sky* (USA) prod/rel: Bryanston Film, Aubrey Baring Productions
Une Femme Fatale, Novel
　Femme Fatale, Une 1976 d: Jacques Doniol-Valcroze. lps: Anicee Alvina, Heinz Bennent, Jacques Weber. 112M FRN/GRM. *Opfer Der Leidenschaft* (GRM); *Victim of Passion* prod/rel: Bavaria, Les Films de la Seine

BEAUCHAMP, D. D.
A Hunting We Will Go, Story
　Father's Wild Game 1950 d: Herbert I. Leeds. lps: Raymond Walburn, Walter Catlett, Gary Gray. 61M USA. prod/rel: Monogram
Enough for Happiness, Story
　She Couldn't Say No 1954 d: Lloyd Bacon. lps: Jean Simmons, Robert Mitchum, Arthur Hunnicutt. 89M USA. *Beautiful But Dangerous* (UKN); *She Had to Say Yes* prod/rel: RKO Radio
Journey at Sunrise, Short Story
　Father Makes Good 1950 d: Jean Yarbrough. lps: Walter Catlett, Raymond Walburn, Gary Gray. 61M USA. prod/rel: Monogram

BEAUCHEMIN, YVES
Le Matou, Novel
　Matou, Le 1985 d: Jean Beaudin. lps: Guillaume Lemay-Thivierge, Serge Dupire, Justine Carmet. 141M CND/FRN/ITL. *The Alley Cat* prod/rel: Cine le Matou Inc. (Montreal), Initial Groupe (Paris)

BEAUMONT, CHARLES
The Intruder, New York 1959, Novel
　Intruder, The 1961 d: Roger Corman. lps: William Shatner, Frank Maxwell, Beverly Lunsford. 84M USA. *The Stranger* (UKN); *I Hate Your Guts*; *Shame* prod/rel: Filmgroup, Inc.

BEAUMONT, GERALD
133 at 3, 1921, Short Story
　Winner Take All 1932 d: Roy Del Ruth. lps: James Cagney, Virginia Bruce, Marian Nixon. 68M USA. prod/rel: Warner Bros. Pictures©
Betty's a Lady, 1925, Short Story
　Count of Ten, The 1928 d: James Flood. lps: Charles Ray, James Gleason, Jobyna Ralston. 5557f USA. *Betty's a Lady* prod/rel: Universal Pictures
Common Ground, 1936, Short Story
　Frisco Jenny 1933 d: William A. Wellman. lps: Ruth Chatterton, Louis Calhern, Helen Jerome Eddy. 76M USA. *The Common Ground* (UKN) prod/rel: First National Pictures©
Dixie, Short Story
　Dixie Handicap, The 1924 d: Reginald Barker. lps: Claire Windsor, Frank Keenan, Lloyd Hughes. 6509f USA. prod/rel: Metro-Goldwyn Pictures
Even Stephen, 1925, Short Story
　Just Another Blonde 1926 d: Alfred Santell. lps: Dorothy MacKaill, Jack Mulhall, Louise Brooks. 5603f USA. *The Girl from Coney Island* prod/rel: Al Rockett Productions, First National Pictures
The Flower of Napoli, 1924, Short Story
　Man in Blue, The 1925 d: Edward Laemmle. lps: Herbert Rawlinson, Madge Bellamy, Nick de Ruiz. 5634f USA. prod/rel: Universal Pictures
Heavenbent, Short Story
　Rainmaker, The 1926 d: Clarence Badger. lps: William Collier Jr., Georgia Hale, Ernest Torrence. 6055f USA. prod/rel: Famous Players-Lasky, Paramount Pictures
Jack O' Clubs, 1923, Short Story
　Jack O' Clubs 1924 d: Robert F. Hill. lps: Herbert Rawlinson, Ruth Dwyer, Eddie Gribbon. 4717f USA. prod/rel: Universal Pictures
Referee John McArdle, 1921, Short Story
　Referee, The 1922 d: Ralph Ince. lps: Conway Tearle, Anders Randolf, Gladys Hulette. 4665f USA. prod/rel: Selznick Pictures, Select Pictures
The Lady Who Played Fidele, 1925, Short Story
　Scarlet Saint, The 1925 d: George Archainbaud. lps: Mary Astor, Lloyd Hughes, Frank Morgan. 6784f USA. prod/rel: First National Pictures
The Lord's Referee, 1923, Short Story
　Blue Eagle, The 1926 d: John Ford. lps: George O'Brien, Janet Gaynor, William Russell. 6200f USA. prod/rel: Fox Film Corp.
　Silk Hat Kid 1935 d: H. Bruce Humberstone. lps: Lew Ayres, Mae Clarke, Paul Kelly. 70M USA. *The Lord's Referee* prod/rel: Fox Film Corp.©
The Making of O'Malley, 1924, Short Story
　Great O'Malley, The 1937 d: William Dieterle. lps: Pat O'Brien, Humphrey Bogart, Ann Sheridan. 71M USA. *The Making of O'Malley* prod/rel: Warner Bros. Pictures©
　Making of O'Malley, The 1925 d: Lambert Hillyer. lps: Milton Sills, Dorothy MacKaill, Helen Rowland. 7496f USA. prod/rel: First National Pictures
The Money Rider, 1924, Short Story
　Down the Stretch 1927 d: King Baggot. lps: Robert Agnew, Marian Nixon, Virginia True Boardman. 6910f USA. prod/rel: Universal Pictures
My Own Pal, Story
　My Own Pal 1926 d: John G. Blystone. lps: Tom Mix, Olive Borden, Thomas Santschi. 6r USA. prod/rel: Fox Film Corp.
Pride of the Marines, 1921, Story
　Pride of the Marines 1936 d: D. Ross Lederman. lps: Charles Bickford, Florence Rice, Billy Burrud. 66M USA. prod/rel: Columbia Pictures Corp.©
Riders Up, New York 1922, Novel
　Reckless Living 1938 d: Frank McDonald. lps: Robert Wilcox, Nan Grey, Jimmy Savo. 68M USA. *The Winner's Circle* prod/rel: Universal Pictures Co.©
　Riders Up 1924 d: Irving Cummings. lps: Creighton Hale, George Cooper, Kate Price. 4904f USA. *When Johnny Comes Marching Home* prod/rel: Universal Pictures

The Rose of Kildare, 1922, Short Story
　Rose of Kildare, The 1927 d: Dallas M. Fitzgerald. lps: Helene Chadwick, Pat O'Malley, Henry B. Walthall. 6875f USA. *Forgotten Vows* (UKN) prod/rel: Gotham Productions, Lumas Film Corp.
Said With Soap, 1925, Short Story
　Babe Comes Home 1927 d: Ted Wilde. lps: Babe Ruth, Anna Q. Nilsson, Louise Fazenda. 5761f USA. prod/rel: First National Pictures
The Sporting Venus, 1924, Short Story
　Sporting Venus, The 1925 d: Marshall Neilan. lps: Blanche Sweet, Ronald Colman, Lew Cody. 5938f USA. *His Supreme Moment* prod/rel: Metro-Goldwyn Pictures
Two Bells for Pegasus, 1922, Short Story
　Victor, The 1923 d: Edward Laemmle. lps: Herbert Rawlinson, Dorothy Manners, Frank Currier. 4880f USA. prod/rel: Universal Pictures

BEAUMONT, GERMAINE
Agnes de Rien, Novel
　Agnes de Rien 1949 d: Pierre Billon. lps: Paul Meurisse, Daniele Delorme, Yvonne de Bray. 95M FRN. prod/rel: Codo-Cinema

BEBAN, GEORGE
The Sign of the Rose, New York 1911, Play
　Alien, The 1915 d: Thomas H. Ince. lps: George Beban, Edward Gillespie, Hayward Ginn. 8r USA. *The Sign of the Rose* prod/rel: New York Motion Picture Corp.©, Select Film Booking Agency, Inc.
　Sign of the Rose, The 1915 d: Thomas H. Ince. lps: George Beban, Blanche Schwed, Thelma Salter. SHT USA. prod/rel: George Beban Productions, American Releasing Corp.

BECCARI, L. D.
Marghere Di Cavouret, Play
　Lattivendole, Le 1914 d: Ernesto Vaser. lps: Ernesto Vaser, Ada Marangoni, Dante TestA. 633m ITL. *Le Marghere Di Cavouret*; *The Milk Girl* (UKN) prod/rel: Itala Film

BECHDOLF, FREDERICK R.
Back to the Right Trail, Short Story
　Thieves' Gold 1918 d: John Ford. lps: Harry Carey, Molly Malone, Vester Pegg. 5r USA. prod/rel: Universal Film Mfg. Co.©
The Hard Rock Man, New York 1910, Novel
　Hard Rock Breed, The 1918 d: Raymond Wells. lps: Jack Livingston, Margery Wilson, Jack Curtis. 5r USA. prod/rel: Triangle Film Corp., Triangle Distributing Corp.

BECHDOLT, JACK
Broken Chains, 1921, Short Story
　Caught Bluffing 1922 d: Lambert Hillyer. lps: Frank Mayo, Edna Murphy, Wallace MacDonald. 4717f USA. prod/rel: Universal Film Mfg. Co.
Fog Bound, 1921, Short Story
　Fog Bound 1923 d: Irvin V. Willat. lps: Dorothy Dalton, David Powell, Martha Mansfield. 5692f USA. prod/rel: Famous Players-Lasky, Paramount Pictures

BECHER, JOHANNES R.
Abschied, 1940, Novel
　Abschied 1968 d: Egon Gunther. lps: Rolf Ludwig, Katharina Lind, Jan Spitzer. 106M GDR. *Adieu*; *Farewell* prod/rel: Defa

BECHER, ULRICH
Der Bockerer, Play
　Bockerer, Der 1981 d: Franz Antel. lps: Karl Merkatz, Ida Krottendorf, Alfred Bohm. 104M AUS/GRM. *The Obstinate Man*; *The Fusspot*; *Herr Bockerer* prod/rel: T.I.T., Neue Delta

BECHHOFER-ROBERTS, C. E.
Don Chicago, Novel
　Don Chicago 1945 d: MacLean Rogers. lps: Jackie Hunter, Eddie Gray, Joyce Heron. 80M UKN. prod/rel: British National, Anglo-American

BECK, BEATRIX
Leon Morin - Pretre, 1952, Novel
　Leon Morin, Pretre 1961 d: Jean-Pierre Melville. lps: Jean-Paul Belmondo, Emmanuelle Riva, Patricia Gozzi. 130M FRN/ITL. *Leon Morin -Prete* (ITL); *Leon Morin -Priest*; *The Forgiven Sinner* (USA) prod/rel: Rome-Paris Films, Champion

BECKER, BENOIT
La Nuit Des Traques, Novel
　Nuit Des Traques, La 1959 d: Bernard-Roland. lps: Philippe Clay, Juliette Mayniel, Folco Lulli. 84M FRN/BLG. *Men Without Morals* (UKN) prod/rel: Paris Elysees, Gallina Films

BECKER, JUREK
Jakob Der Lugner, 1969, Novel
　Jakob Der Lugner 1975 d: Frank Beyer. lps: Vlastimil Brodsky, Erwin Geschonneck, Manuela Simon. 104M GDR. *Jacob the Liar* (USA)

BECKER, MARIA
Mijnheer Hat Lauter Tochter, Book
  Mijnheer Hat Lauter Tochter 1967 d: Volker Vogeler. lps: Julia Lindig, Guus Verstaete, Ingeborg Uyt Den Bogaard. 50M GRM. *The Gentleman Has Only Daughters* prod/rel: Houwer

BECKER, ROLF
Gestatten Mein Name Is Cox, Radio Play
  Gestatten, Mein Name Ist Cox 1955 d: Georg Jacoby. lps: Johannes Heesters, Claude Borelli, Nadja Tiller. 90M GRM. **If You Please: My Name Is Cox** prod/rel: Eichberg, Panorama

BECKER, STEPHEN
A Covenant With Death, New York 1964, Novel
  Covenant With Death, A 1966 d: Lamont Johnson. lps: George Maharis, Laura Devon, Katy Jurado. 97M USA. prod/rel: Warner Bros.

BECKER, TERRY
Blade in Hong Kong, Novel
  Blade in Hong Kong 1985 d: Reza Badiyi. lps: Terry Lester, Keye Luke, Mike Preston. TVM. 91M USA. prod/rel: Terry Becker Prods.

BECKER-RIEPEN
Haie an Bord, Novel
  Haie an Bord 1970 d: Arthur M. Rabenalt. lps: Freddy Quinn, Karin Dor, Werner Pochath. 100M GRM. *Freddy - Ein Mann Kehrt Heim*; *Sharks on Board* prod/rel: Reginald Puhl, Inter

BECKETT, SAMUEL (1906–1989), IRL
Acte Sans Paroles, 1957, Play
  Act Without Words 1983 d: Margaret Jordan. 17M UKN.
  Acte Sans Paroles 1964 d: Bruno Bettiol, Guido Bettiol. ANM. 11M FRN. *Act Without Words* (USA)
Dis Joe, 1966, Play
  Eh Joe! 1986 d: Alan Gilsenan. 38M IRL.
Va Et Vient, 1966, Play
  Come and Go 1986 d: Nik Houghton. 5M UKN.

BECKLES, GORDON
East of Piccadilly, Novel
  East of Piccadilly 1939 d: Harold Huth. lps: Judy Campbell, Sebastian Shaw, Henry Edwards. 79M UKN. *The Strangler* (USA) prod/rel: Associated British Picture Corporation, Pathe

BECKWITH, REGINALD
Boys in Brown, London 1940, Play
  Boys in Brown 1949 d: Montgomery Tully. lps: Jack Warner, Richard Attenborough, Dirk Bogarde. 85M UKN. prod/rel: Gainsborough, General Film Distributors
A Soldier for Christmas, London 1944, Play
  This Man Is Mine 1946 d: Marcel Varnel. lps: Tom Walls, Glynis Johns, Jeanne de Casalis. 103M UKN. *Christmas Weekend* prod/rel: Columbia British

BECQUE, HENRI
La Parisienne, 1885, Play
  Parisienne, Une 1957 d: Michel Boisrond. lps: Charles Boyer, Henri Vidal, Brigitte Bardot. 86M FRN/ITL. *Una Parigina* (ITL); *La Parisienne* (USA) prod/rel: Films Ariane, Filmsonor

BECQUER, GUSTAVO ADOLFO
La Cruz Del Diablo, 1860, Short Story
  Cruz Del Diablo, La 1974 d: John Gilling. lps: Carmen Sevilla, Ramiro Oliveros, Adolfo Marsillach. 104M SPN. *The Devil's Cross*
El Miserere, 1862, Short Story
  Cruz Del Diablo, La 1974 d: John Gilling. lps: Carmen Sevilla, Ramiro Oliveros, Adolfo Marsillach. 104M SPN. *The Devil's Cross*
El Monte de Las Animas, 1860, Short Story
  Cruz Del Diablo, La 1974 d: John Gilling. lps: Carmen Sevilla, Ramiro Oliveros, Adolfo Marsillach. 104M SPN. *The Devil's Cross*

BEDEL, MAURICE
Molinoff Indre-Et-Loire, Paris 1928, Novel
  Along Came Youth 1930 d: Lloyd Corrigan, Norman Z. McLeod. lps: Charles "Buddy" Rogers, Frances Dee, Stuart Erwin. 6623f USA. prod/rel: Paramount-Publix Corp.

BEDFORD-JONES, H.
Garden of the Moon, 1937, Short Story
  Garden of the Moon 1938 d: Busby Berkeley. lps: Pat O'Brien, Margaret Lindsay, John Payne. 94M USA. prod/rel: Warner Bros. Pictures©

BEEDING, FRANCIS
The House of Dr. Edwardes, Novel
  Spellbound 1945 d: Alfred Hitchcock. lps: Ingrid Bergman, Gregory Peck, Jean Acker. 111M USA. *The House of Dr. Edwardes* prod/rel: United Artists

The Norwich Victims, Novel
  Dead Men Tell No Tales 1938 d: David MacDonald. lps: Emlyn Williams, Hugh Williams, Sara Seegar. 80M UKN. prod/rel: British National, Associated British Picture Corporation

BEER, OTTO F.
Man Ist Nur Zweim Jung, Play
  Man Ist Nur Zweimal Jung 1958 d: Helmut Weiss. lps: Wolf Albach-Retty, Winnie Markus, Heidi Bruhl. 96M AUS. prod/rel: Mundus, Excelsior

BEER, THOMAS
Little Eva Ascends, 1921, Short Story
  Little Eva Ascends 1922 d: George D. Baker. lps: Gareth Hughes, Eleanor Fields, May Collins. 4901f USA. *On Tour* prod/rel: S-L Pictures, Metro Pictures

BEERBOHM, MAX (1876–1956), UKN
Death in the Hand, Short Story
  Death in the Hand 1948 d: A. Barr-Smith. lps: Esme Percy, Ernest Jay, Cecile Chevreau. 43M UKN. prod/rel: Four Star, General Film Distributors

BEERS, ETHEL LYNN
No One to Spare Or Which Shall It Be?, Story
  Which Shall It Be? 1924 d: Renaud Hoffman. lps: Willis Marks, Ethel Wales, David Torrence. 4600f USA. *Not One to Spare* prod/rel: Renaud Hoffman Productions, W. W. Hodkinson Corp.

BEERS, ETHELIN ELLIOT
The Picket Guard, Poem
  Picket Guard, The 1913 d: Allan Dwan. lps: Wallace Reid, Pauline Bush, Marshall Neilan. 2r USA. prod/rel: Bison

BEESTON, L. J.
The Cavern Spider, Short Story
  Cavern Spider, The 1924 d: Thomas Bentley. lps: Jameson Thomas, Fred Raynham, Winifred Izard. 1750f UKN. prod/rel: Stoll

BEGAG, AZOUZ
Le Gone du Chaaba, Novel
  Gone du Chaaba, Le 1998 d: Christophe RuggiA. lps: Bouzid Negnoug, Mohamed Fellag, Francois Morel. 102M FRN. *The Kid from Chaaba* prod/rel: Vertigo Prods., Films Christiani

BEGOVIC, MILAN
Americka Jachta Ve Splitu, Short Story
  Bila Jachta Ve Splitu 1939 d: Ladislav Brom. lps: Theodor Pistek, Jirina Sedlackova, Leopolda DostalovA. 2094m CZC. *The White Yacht in Split* prod/rel: Sun

BEHAN, BRENDAN (1923–1964), IRL
The Quare Fellow, 1956, Play
  Quare Fellow, The 1962 d: Arthur Dreifuss. lps: Patrick McGoohan, Sylvia Syms, Walter MacKen. 90M UKN/IRL. prod/rel: Bryanston, Liger
  Quare Fellow, The 1967 d: Harvey Hart. MTV. CND.

BEHAN, CHARLES
Dangerously Yours, 1929, Play
  Murder By the Clock 1931 d: Edward Sloman. lps: William "Stage" Boyd, Lilyan Tashman, Irving Pichel. 76M USA. prod/rel: Paramount Publix Corp.©

BEHM, MARC
Mortelle Randonnee, Novel
  Mortelle Randonnee 1983 d: Claude Miller. lps: Michel Serrault, Isabelle Adjani, Guy Marchand. 121M FRN. *Deadly Run* (UKN) prod/rel: Telema, Levallois
The Unsuspecting Wife, Story
  Charade 1963 d: Stanley Donen. lps: Audrey Hepburn, Cary Grant, Walter Matthau. 116M USA. prod/rel: Universal

BEHN, NOEL
Big Stick-Up at Brink's, Book
  Brink's Job, The 1978 d: William Friedkin. lps: Peter Falk, Peter Boyle, Allen Garfield. 103M USA. *Big Stickup at Brink's* prod/rel: Universal
The Kremlin Letter, New York 1966, Novel
  Kremlin Letter, The 1970 d: John Huston. lps: Bibi Andersson, Richard Boone, Nigel Green. 123M USA. prod/rel: 20th Century-Fox Film Corporation

BEHRENBERG, BRUCE
My Little Brother Is Coming Tomorrow, Book
  Grambling's White Tiger 1981 d: Georg Stanford Brown. lps: Bruce Jenner, Harry Belafonte, Levar Burton. TVM. 100M USA. *The Grumbling White Tiger* prod/rel: NBC, Interplanetary Productions

BEHREND, ARTHUR
The House of the Spaniard, Novel
  House of the Spaniard, The 1936 d: Reginald Denham. lps: Brigitte Horney, Peter Haddon, Jean Galland. 70M UKN. prod/rel: Independent Film Producers, Phoenix

BEHRMAN, S. N. (1893–1973), USA
Biography, New York 1932, Play
  Biography of a Bachelor Girl 1934 d: Edward H. Griffith. lps: Ann Harding, Robert Montgomery, Edward Everett Horton. 85M USA. *Biography of a Bachelor* prod/rel: Metro-Goldwyn-Mayer Corp.
Brief Moment, New York 1931, Play
  Brief Moment 1933 d: David Burton. lps: Carole Lombard, Gene Raymond, Monroe Owsley. 71M USA. prod/rel: Columbia Pictures Corp.
No Time for Comedy, Indianapolis 1939, Play
  No Time for Comedy 1940 d: William Keighley. lps: James Stewart, Rosalind Russell, Genevieve Tobin. 98M USA. *Guy With a Grin* prod/rel: Warner Bros. Pictures©
The Pirate, New York 1942, Play
  Pirate, The 1948 d: Vincente Minnelli. lps: Gene Kelly, Judy Garland, Walter Slezak. 102M USA. prod/rel: MGM
Second Man, New York 1927, Play
  He Knew Women 1930 d: F. Hugh Herbert, Lynn Shores. lps: Lowell Sherman, Alice Joyce, David Manners. 67M USA. prod/rel: RKO Productions

BEIJE, INGRID
Het Ar Min Langtan, Novel
  Het Ar Min Langtan 1956 d: Bengt Logardt. lps: Margit Carlqvist, Alf Kjellin, Bengt Logardt. 89M SWD. *My Hot Desire* prod/rel: Ab Europa

BEINHART, LARRY
American Hero, Novel
  Wag the Dog 1997 d: Barry Levinson. lps: Dustin Hoffman, Robert de Niro, Anne Heche. 97M USA. prod/rel: Tribeca, Baltimore Pictures

BEISSIER
Le Champion du Regiment, Play
  Champion du Regiment, Le 1932 d: Henry Wulschleger. lps: Bach, Charles Montel, Germaine Charley. 91M FRN. prod/rel: Alex Nalpas

BEISSIER, FERNAND
Histoire d'un Pierrot, 1893
  Histoire d'un Pierrot 1914 d: Baldassarre Negroni. lps: Francesca Bertini, Leda Gys, Emilio Ghione. 1200m ITL. *Pierrot the Prodigal* (USA) prod/rel: Celio Film, Italica Ars

BEKEFFI, STEFAN
Die Unentschuldigte Stunde, Play
  Unentschuldigte Stunde, Die 1957 d: Willi Forst. lps: Adrian Hoven, Erika Remberg, Rudolf Forster. 95M AUS. prod/rel: Sascha

BEKEFFY, ISTVAN
Play
  Assenza Ingiustificata 1939 d: Max Neufeld. lps: Alida Valli, Amedeo Nazzari, Lilia Silvi. 90M ITL. prod/rel: Era Film, Minerva Film
Kozmetika, 1933, Play
  Kiss and Make Up 1934 d: Harlan Thompson. lps: Cary Grant, Genevieve Tobin, Helen Mack. 80M USA. *Cosmetics* prod/rel: Paramount Productions©, A. B. P. Schulberg Production

BELASCO, DAVID (1859–1931), USA
La Belle Russe, New York 1882, Play
  Belle Russe, La 1914 d: William J. Hanley. lps: Evelyn Russell, Lawrence Gordon, Frank Wood. 5r USA. prod/rel: Regent Feature Film Co.©
  Belle Russe, La 1919 d: Charles J. Brabin. lps: Theda Bara, Warburton Gamble, Marian Stewart. 5400f USA. prod/rel: Fox Film Corp., William Fox©
Du Barry, New York 1901, Play
  Du Barry, La 1914 d: Eduardo BencivengA. lps: Leslie Carter, Richard Thornton, Hamilton Revelle. 11r ITL. *La Dubarry* prod/rel: S.A. Ambrosio, Photodrama Prod. Co.
  Du Barry 1915 d: George Kleine. lps: Mrs. Leslie Carter, Richard Thornton, Campbell Gollan. 6r USA. *Dubarry* prod/rel: George Kleine©
  Du Barry, Woman of Passion 1930 d: Sam Taylor. lps: Norma Talmadge, William Farnum, Conrad Nagel. 90M USA. *Du Barry* (UKN); *Deception; Flame of the Flesh* prod/rel: Art Cinema Corp., United Artists
The Girl I Left Behind Me, New York 1893, Play
  Girl I Left Behind Me, The 1915 d: Lloyd B. Carleton. lps: Robert Edeson, Claire Whitney, Stuart Holmes. 5r USA. prod/rel: Box Office Attraction Co., William Fox©
Girl of the Golden West, New York 1905, Play
  Girl of the Golden West, The 1914 d: Cecil B. de Mille. lps: Mabel Van Buren, House Peters, Theodore Roberts. 5r USA. prod/rel: Jesse L. Lasky Feature Play Co.©, Paramount Pictures Corp.
  Girl of the Golden West, The 1923 d: Edwin Carewe. lps: Sylvia Breamer, J. Warren Kerrigan, Russell Simpson. 6800f USA.

Girl of the Golden West, The 1930 d: John Francis Dillon. lps: Ann Harding, James Rennie, Harry Bannister. 81M USA. prod/rel: First National Pictures
Girl of the Golden West, The 1938 d: Robert Z. Leonard. lps: Jeanette MacDonald, Nelson Eddy, Walter Pidgeon. 120M USA. prod/rel: Metro-Goldwyn-Mayer Corp., Loew's, Inc.©

The Heart of Maryland, New York 1895, Play
Heart of Maryland, The 1915 d: Herbert Brenon. lps: Mrs. Leslie Carter, William F. Shay, Matt Snyder. 6r USA. prod/rel: Tiffany Film Corp., Metro Pictures Corp.©
Heart of Maryland, The 1921 d: Tom Terriss. lps: Catherine Calvert, Crane Wilbur, Felix Krembs. 6r USA. prod/rel: Vitagraph Co. of America
Heart of Maryland, The 1927 d: Lloyd Bacon. lps: Dolores Costello, Jason Robards, Warner Richmond. 5868f USA. prod/rel: Warner Brothers Pictures

The Honorable Mr. Wong, Play
Hatchet Man, The 1932 d: William A. Wellman. lps: Edward G. Robinson, Loretta Young, Dudley Digges. 74M USA. *The Honourable Mr. Wong* (UKN) prod/rel: First National Pictures©

Laugh, Clown, Laugh!, New York 1923, Play
Laugh, Clown, Laugh 1928 d: Herbert Brenon. lps: Lon Chaney, Bernard Siegel, Loretta Young. 7045f USA. prod/rel: Metro-Goldwyn-Mayer Pictures

Lord Chumley, New York 1888, Play
Forty Winks 1925 d: Frank Urson, Paul Iribe. lps: Viola Dana, Raymond Griffith, Theodore Roberts. 6293f USA. prod/rel: Famous Players-Lasky, Paramount Pictures
Lord Chumley 1914 d: James Kirkwood. lps: Henry B. Walthall, Walter Miller, Lillian Gish. 4r USA. prod/rel: Biograph Co., Klaw & Erlanger©

May Blossom, New York 1884, Play
May Blossom 1915 d: Allan Dwan. lps: Gertrude Robinson, Russell Bassett, Marshall Neilan. 4r USA. prod/rel: Famous Players Film Co., Paramount Pictures Corp.

Men and Women, Play
Men and Women 1925 d: William C. de Mille. lps: Richard Dix, Claire Adams, Neil Hamilton. 6223f USA. prod/rel: Famous Players-Lasky, Paramount Pictures

Pawn Ticket No. 210, Play
Pawn Ticket 210 1922 d: Scott R. Dunlap. lps: Shirley Mason, Irene Hunt, Jake Abraham. 4871f USA. prod/rel: Fox Film Corp.

The Return of Peter Grimm, New York 1911, Play
Return of Peter Grimm, The 1926 d: Victor Schertzinger. lps: Alec B. Francis, John Roche, Janet Gaynor. 6961f USA. prod/rel: Fox Film Corp.
Return of Peter Grimm, The 1935 d: George Nicholls Jr. lps: Lionel Barrymore, Helen Mack, Edward Ellis. 83M USA. prod/rel: RKO Radio Pictures©

Rose of the Rancho, New York 1906, Play
Rose of the Rancho 1914 d: Cecil B. de Mille, Wilfred Buckland. lps: Bessie Barriscale, Monroe Salisbury, Jane Darwell. 5r USA. prod/rel: Jesse L. Lasky Feature Play Co.©, Paramount Pictures Corp.
Rose of the Rancho 1936 d: Marion Gering, Robert Florey (Uncredited). lps: John Boles, Gladys Swarthout, Charles Bickford. 85M USA. prod/rel: Paramount Pictures

The Son-Daughter, New York 1919, Play
Son-Daughter, The 1932 d: Clarence Brown. lps: Helen Hayes, Ramon Novarro, Lewis Stone. 80M USA. prod/rel: Metro-Goldwyn-Mayer Corp., Metro-Goldwyn-Mayer Dist. Corp.©

Sweet Kitty Bellairs, New York 1903, Play
Sweet Kitty Bellairs 1916 d: James Young. lps: Mae Murray, Tom Forman, Belle Bennett. 5r USA. prod/rel: Jesse L. Lasky Feature Play Co.©, Paramount Pictures Corp.
Sweet Kitty Bellairs 1930 d: Alfred E. Green. lps: Claudia Dell, Ernest Torrence, Walter Pidgeon. 5772f USA.

BELBEL, SERGI
Caricies, Play
Caricies 1998 d: Ventura Pons. lps: David Selvas, Laura Conejero, Julieta Serrano. 94M SPN. *Caresses* prod/rel: Els Films de la Rambla©, Television Espanola

BELIERES, LEON
Le Concierge Revient de Suite, Play
Concierge Revient de Suite, Le 1937 d: Fernand Rivers. lps: Jean Kolb, Andre Simeon, C. P. Cousin. SHT FRN.

BELL, CHARLES W.
Parlor, Bedroom and Bath, New York 1917, Play
Buster Se Marie 1931 d: Edward Brophy, Claude Autant-LarA. lps: Buster Keaton, Jeanne Helbling, Andre Luguet. 80M USA. prod/rel: Metro-Goldwyn-Mayer
Casanova Wider Willen 1931 d: Edward Brophy. lps: Buster Keaton, Marion Lessing, Paul Morgan. F USA.
Parlor, Bedroom and Bath 1920 d: Eddie Dillon. lps: Ruth Stonehouse, Eugene Pallette, Kathleen Kirkham. 6r USA. prod/rel: Metro Pictures Corp.©
Parlor, Bedroom and Bath 1931 d: Edward Sedgwick. lps: Buster Keaton, Charlotte Greenwood, Reginald Denny. 72M USA. *A Romeo in Pyjamas* (UKN) prod/rel: Metro-Goldwyn-Mayer Corp., Metro-Goldwyn-Mayer Dist. Corp.©

BELL, CHRISTINE
The Perez Family, Novel
Perez Family, The 1995 d: Mira Nair. lps: Anjelica Huston, Marisa Tomei, Alfred MolinA. 112M USA. prod/rel: Samuel Goldwyn Company

BELL, J. J., Bell, John Joy
Courting Christina, Short Story
Wee MacGregor's Sweetheart, The 1922 d: George Pearson. lps: Betty Balfour, Donald McCardle, Nora Swinburne. 5300f UKN. prod/rel: Welsh-Pearson, Jury
Dancing Days, Story
Dancing Days 1926 d: Albert Kelley. lps: Helene Chadwick, Forrest Stanley, Gloria Gordon. 5900f USA. prod/rel: Preferred Pictures
Kitty Carstairs, London 1917, Novel
Beyond London Lights 1928 d: Tom Terriss. lps: Adrienne Dore, Lee Shumway, Bill Elliott. 5583f USA. *Kitty Carstairs* (UKN) prod/rel: Fbo Pictures
Oh Christina, Short Story
Wee MacGregor's Sweetheart, The 1922 d: George Pearson. lps: Betty Balfour, Donald McCardle, Nora Swinburne. 5300f UKN. prod/rel: Welsh-Pearson, Jury
Thou Fool, Novel
Thou Fool 1926 d: Fred Paul. lps: Stewart Rome, Marjorie Hume, Mary Rorke. 5100f UKN. prod/rel: Stoll, Equity British
Thread O' Scarlet, Play
Thread O' Scarlet 1930 d: Peter Godfrey. lps: George Merritt, Arthur Goullet, William Freshman. 35M UKN. prod/rel: Gaumont

BELL, MARY HAYLEY (1914–, CHN
Whistle Down the Wind, London 1958, Novel
Whistle Down the Wind 1961 d: Bryan Forbes. lps: Hayley Mills, Bernard Lee, Alan Bates. 99M UKN. prod/rel: Beaver Films, Allied Film Makers

BELL, PEARL DOLES
Her Elephant Man, New York 1919, Novel
Her Elephant Man 1920 d: Scott R. Dunlap. lps: Shirley Mason, Alan Roscoe, Henry J. Hebert. 5r USA. prod/rel: Fox Film Corp., William Fox©
His Harvest, New York 1915, Novel
Love's Harvest 1920 d: Howard M. Mitchell. lps: Shirley Mason, Raymond McKee, Edwin Booth Tilton. 5r USA. *His Harvest* prod/rel: Fox Film Corp., William Fox©
Just Mary, Story
For Another Woman 1924 d: David Kirkland. lps: Kenneth Harlan, Florence Billings, Henry Sedley. 5637f USA. prod/rel: Rayart Pictures
Sandra, New York 1924, Novel
Sandra 1924 d: Arthur H. Sawyer. lps: Barbara La Marr, Bert Lytell, Leila Hyams. 7794f USA. prod/rel: Associated Pictures, First National Pictures

BELL, ROBERT
This Same Garden, Play
While I Live 1947 d: John Harlow. lps: Tom Walls, Sonia Dresdel, Clifford Evans. 85M UKN. *Dream of Olwen* prod/rel: Edward Dryhurst, 20th Century-Fox

BELL, SAM HANNA
December Bride, 1951, Novel
December Bride, The 1989 d: Thaddeus O'Sullivan. lps: Donal McCann, Saskia Reeves, Ciaran Hinds. 91M IRL/UKN. prod/rel: Bfi, Film Four

BELL, THOMAS
All Brides are Beautiful, Novel
From This Day Forward 1946 d: John Berry. lps: Joan Fontaine, Mark Stevens, Rosemary de Camp. 95M USA. *All Brides are Beautiful* prod/rel: RKO Radio

BELL, VEREEN (1911–1944), USA
Swamp Water, Novel
Lure of the Wilderness 1952 d: Jean Negulesco. lps: Jeffrey Hunter, Jean Peters, Constance Smith. 93M USA. *Cry of the Swamp* prod/rel: 20th Century-Fox

Swamp Water 1941 d: Jean Renoir. lps: Walter Brennan, Walter Huston, Anne Baxter. 90M USA. *The Man Who Came Back* (UKN); *L' Etang Tragique* (FRN) prod/rel: 20th Century-Fox

BELLAH, JAMES WARNER (1899–1976), USA
Big Hunt, Short Story
She Wore a Yellow Ribbon 1949 d: John Ford. lps: John Wayne, Joanne Dru, John Agar. 104M USA. prod/rel: RKO Radio
Bug Out, Story
Target Zero 1955 d: Harmon Jones. lps: Richard Conte, Peggie Castle, Charles Bronson. 92M USA. prod/rel: Warner Bros.
Dancing Lady, New York 1932, Novel
Dancing Lady 1933 d: Robert Z. Leonard. lps: Joan Crawford, Clark Gable, Franchot Tone. 90M USA. prod/rel: Metro-Goldwyn-Mayer Corp.
Massacre, Story
Fort Apache 1948 d: John Ford. lps: Henry Fonda, John Wayne, Shirley Temple. 127M USA. prod/rel: RKO Radio
Mission Without a Record, Story
Rio Grande 1950 d: John Ford. lps: John Wayne, Maureen O'Hara, Claude Jarman Jr. 105M USA. prod/rel: Republic, Argosy
War Party, Short Story
She Wore a Yellow Ribbon 1949 d: John Ford. lps: John Wayne, Joanne Dru, John Agar. 104M USA. prod/rel: RKO Radio
The White Invader, Novel
Command, The 1953 d: David Butler. lps: Guy Madison, Joan Weldon, James Whitmore. 88M USA. *Rear Guard* prod/rel: Warner Bros.

BELLAMANN, HENRY
King's Row, Novel
Kings Row 1942 d: Sam Wood. lps: Ann Sheridan, Robert Cummings, Ronald Reagan. 127M USA. prod/rel: Warner Bros.

BELLEGARDE, SOLANGE
Gloria, Novel
Gloria 1977 d: Claude Autant-LarA. lps: Valerie Jeannet, Valerie Mokhazni, Alain Marcel. 120M FRN. prod/rel: Productions 2000

BELLI, PINO
Beta Som, Novel
Finche Dura la Tempesta 1962 d: Charles Frend, Bruno Vailati. lps: James Mason, Gabriele Ferzetti, Lilli Palmer. 105M ITL/FRN. *Defi a Gibraltar* (FRN); *Torpedo Bay* (USA); *Beta Som* prod/rel: Galatea, Panorama

BELLINI, VINCENZO (1801–1835), ITL
Norma, Milan 1831, Opera
Norma (Episodio Della Gallia Sotto Il Dominio Di Roma Imperiale) 1911 d: Romolo Bacchini. 332m ITL. prod/rel: Vesuvio Films
Norma, La 1911. lps: Rina Agozzino-Alessio, Bianca Lorenzoni, Alfredo Robert. 267m ITL. *Norma* (UKN) prod/rel: Film d'Arte Italiana
La Sonnambula, Milan 1831, Opera
Sonnambula, La 1952 d: Cesare Barlacchi. lps: Gino Sininberghi, Paola Bertini, Alfredo ColellA. 85M ITL. prod/rel: Lessicum Film

BELLOC, DENIS
Les Ailes de Julien, Novel
Victor. Pendant Qu'il Est Trop Tard 1998 d: Sandrine Veysset. lps: Jeremy Chaix, Lydia Andrei, Mathieu Lane. 86M FRN. *Victor. While It's Too Late* prod/rel: Pyramide, Ognon Pictures

BELLOMO, BINO
Cenomila Lettere Di Guerra - Censura Militare, Book
Lettere Dal Fronte 1975 d: Vittorio Schiraldi. DOC. 95M ITL. prod/rel: Istituto Luce

BELLOTO, RENE
Sur la Terre Comme Au Ciel, Novel
Peril En la Demeure 1985 d: Michel Deville. lps: Christophe Malavoy, Nicole Garcia, Anais Jeanneret. 101M FRN. *Death in a French Garden* (UKN); *Peril* (USA) prod/rel: Gaumont, Elefilm

BELLOW, SAUL (1915–, CND
Seize the Day, 1956, Short Story
Seize the Day 1986 d: Fielder Cook. lps: Robin Williams, Joseph Wiseman, Jerry Stiller. 93M USA. prod/rel: Learning in Focus

BELMONT, ELEANOR ROBESON
The Case of the Black Parrot, Novel
Case of the Black Parrot, The 1941 d: Noel Smith. lps: William Lundigan, Maris Wrixon, Eddie Foy Jr. 60M USA. prod/rel: Warner Bros.

BELOHRADSKA, HANA
Bez Limce Bez Krasy, Prague 1962, Novel
..a Paty Jezdec Je Strach 1964 d: Zbynek Brynych. lps: Miroslav MacHacek, Olga Scheinpflugova, Jiri AdamirA. 95M CZC. *The Fifth Rider Is Fear* (UKN); *..and the Fifth Rider Is Fear*; *The Fifth Horseman Is Fear* (USA) prod/rel: Barrandov Films

BELOT, ADOLPHE
Les Etrangleurs, Paris 1879, Novel
Grip of Iron, The 1913 d: Arthur Charrington. lps: Fred Powell, Nell Emerald, H. Agar Lyons. 3250f UKN. prod/rel: Brightonia, Andrews
Grip of Iron, The 1920 d: Bert Haldane. lps: George Foley, Malvina Longfellow, James Lindsay. 5000f UKN. prod/rel: Famous Pictures, General
Stranglers of Paris, The 1913 d: James Gordon. lps: James Gordon, Jane Fearnley, Anna Lehr. 6r USA. prod/rel: Motion Drama Co., Victory Film Co.

BEMBENEK, LAWRENCIA
Woman on Trial, Autobiography
Woman on the Run: the Lawrencia Bembenek Story 1993 d: Sandor Stern. lps: Tatum O'Neal, Bruce Greenwood, Peggy McCay. TVM. 200M USA.

BEMELMANS, LUDWIG (1898–1962), AUS
Madeline, Book
Madeline 1998 d: Daisy von Scherler Mayer. lps: Frances McDormand, Nigel Hawthorne, Hatty Jones. 90M USA/GRM. prod/rel: Sony Pictures Entertainment, Tristar Pictures

BENAICHA, BRAHIM
Book
Vivre Au Paradis 1998 d: Bourlem Guerdjou. lps: Roschdy Zem, Fadila Belkebla, Omar Bekhaled. 104M FRN/BLG/ALG. *Living in Paradise* prod/rel: 3B Prods.(Paris), Alinea Film (Brussels)

BEN-AMOTZ, DAN
Novel
Lo Sam Zayin 1987 d: Shmuel Imberman. lps: Ika Zohar, Anat Wachsmann, Liora Grossman. 89M ISR. *I Don't Give a Damn*; *Don't Give a Damn* prod/rel: Roll Films

BENASSAR, BARTHOLOME
Le Dernier Saut, Novel
Dernier Saut, Le 1969 d: Edouard Luntz. lps: Maurice Ronet, Michel Bouquet, Cathy Rosier. 105M FRN/ITL. *Indagine Su un Para Accusato Di Omicida* (ITL) prod/rel: Fida Cin.Ca, Lira Films

BENAVENTE Y MARTINEZ, JACINTO (1866–1954), SPN
Alma Triunfante, 1902, Play
De Mujer a Mujer 1950 d: Luis LuciA. lps: Amparo Rivelles, Ana Mariscal, Manuel LunA. 96M SPN. *Woman to Woman*
La Fuerza Bruta, 1908, Play
Forza Bruta, La 1941 d: Carlo Ludovico BragagliA. lps: Juan de Landa, Rossano Brazzi, Germana Paolieri. 80M ITL/SPN. *La Force Brutale* (SPN); *Serata Di Gala* prod/rel: Lux Film
La Honradez de la Cerradura, 1943, Play
Honradez de la Cerradura, La 1950 d: Luis Escobar. lps: Mayrata O'Wisiedo, Ramon Elias, Francisco Rabal. 95M SPN. *Fake Integrity*
Lecciones de Buen Amor, 1924, Play
Lecciones de Buen Amor 1943 d: Rafael Gil. lps: Rafael Rivelles, Pastora Pena, Mercedes Vecino. 91M SPN. *Lessons of Good Love*
La Malquerida, 1913, Play
Malquerida, La 1940 d: Jose Luis Lopez Rubio. lps: Tarsila Criado, Jesus Tordesillas, Luchy Soto. 93M SPN. *The Ill-Loved*
Malquerida, La 1949 d: Emilio Fernandez. lps: Dolores Del Rio, Pedro Armendariz, Columba Dominguez. 86M MXC. prod/rel: Francisco De P. Cabrera
La Mariposa Que Volo Sobre El Mar, 1926, Play
Mariposa Que Volo Sobre El Mar, La 1951 d: Antonio Obregon. lps: Nini Montian, Luis Hurtado, Guillermina Grin. 84M SPN. *The Butterfly That Flew Over the Sea*
Mas Alla de la Muerte, Novel
Mas Alla de la Muerte 1924 d: Benito Perojo, Jacinto Benavente. lps: Andree Brabant, Georges Lannes, Frank Dane. 83M SPN/FRN. *Au-Dela de la Mort* (FRN); *Beyond Death* prod/rel: Films Benavente (Madrid)
Nadie Sabe Lo Que Quiere; O El Bailarin Y El Trabajador, 1925, Play
Bailarin Y El Trabajador, El 1936 d: Luis MarquinA. lps: Ana Maria Custodio, Roberto Rey, Pepe Isbert. 94M SPN. *The Dancer and the Worker*

No Quiero No Quiero!, 1928, Play
No Quiero, No Quiero 1938 d: Francisco Elias. lps: Fred Galiana, Enrique Guitart, Enriqueta Soler. 106M SPN. *I Don't.! I Don't!*
La Noche Del Sabado, 1903, Play
Noche Del Sabado, La 1950 d: Rafael Gil. lps: Maria Felix, Rafael Duran, Jose Maria Seoane. 79M SPN. *Saturday Night*
Pepa Doncel, 1928, Play
Pepa Doncel 1969 d: Luis LuciA. lps: Aurora Bautista, Juan Luis Galiardo, Maribel Martin. 97M SPN.
Pour Toute la Vie, Novel
Pour Toute la Vie 1924 d: Benito Perojo. lps: Paul Menant, Simone Vaudry, Rachel Devirys. 3200m FRN/SPN. *Para Toda la Vida* (SPN); *For an Entire Life* prod/rel: Societe Des Films Benavente, Films Benavente (Madrid)
Rosas de Otono, 1914, Play
Rosas de Otono 1943 d: Juan de OrdunA. lps: Maria F. Ladron de Guevara, Julia Lajos, Luis Prendes. 72M SPN. *Autumn Roses*
Senora Ama, 1908, Play
Senora Ama 1954 d: Julio Bracho. lps: Dolores Del Rio, Jose Suarez, Maria Luz GaliciA. 85M MXC/SPN.
Vidas Cruzadas, 1929, Play
Vidas Cruzadas 1942 d: Luis MarquinA. lps: Ana Mariscal, Luis Pena, Isabel de Pomes. 70M SPN. *Crossed Lives*

BENCEY, ANDRE
L' Affaire du Train 24, Novel
Affaire du Train 24, L' 1921 d: Gaston Leprieur. lps: Jeanne Brindeau, Eugenie Nau, Adolphe Cande. SRL. 8EP FRN.

BENCHLEY, NATHANIEL (1915–1981), USA, Benchley, Nathaniel Goddard
The Off-Islanders, New York 1961, Novel
Russians are Coming, the Russians are Coming, The 1966 d: Norman Jewison. lps: Carl Reiner, Eva Marie Saint, Alan Arkin. 126M USA. prod/rel: Mirisch Corporation
Sail a Crooked Ship, New York 1960, Novel
Sail a Crooked Ship 1961 d: Irving S. Brecher. lps: Robert Wagner, Ernie Kovacs, Dolores Hart. 88M USA. prod/rel: Philip Barry Productions
The Visitors, New York 1964, Novel
Spirit Is Willing, The 1967 d: William Castle. lps: Sid Caesar, Vera Miles, Barry Gordon. 94M USA. prod/rel: William Castle Enterprises
Welcome to Xanadu, Novel
Sweet Hostage 1975 d: Lee Philips. lps: Linda Blair, Martin Sheen, Jeanne Cooper. TVM. 100M USA. *Welcome to Xanadu* prod/rel: Brut Productions

BENCHLEY, PETER (1940–, USA, Benchley, Peter Bradford
Creature, Novel
Peter Benchley's Creature 1998 d: Stuart Gillard. lps: Craig T. Nelson, Kim Cattrall, Colm Feore. TVM. 240M USA. prod/rel: MGM Television, Trilogy Entertainment
The Deep, 1976, Novel
Deep, The 1977 d: Peter Yates. lps: Robert Shaw, Jacqueline Bisset, Nick Nolte. 123M USA. prod/rel: Columbia
The Island, 1979, Novel
Island, The 1980 d: Michael Ritchie. lps: Michael Caine, David Warner, Angela Punch-McGregor. 115M USA. prod/rel: Universal
Jaws, 1974, Novel
Jaws 1975 d: Steven Spielberg. lps: Robert Shaw, Roy Scheider, Richard Dreyfuss. 125M USA. prod/rel: Universal

BENDER, L.
Spatzen in Gottes Hand, Play
Gluck Aus Ohio 1951 d: Heinz Paul. lps: Hermann Brix, Edith Prager, Loni Heuser. 85M GRM. *Spatzen in Gottes Hand*; *Good Fortune from Ohio* prod/rel: Merkur, Danubia

BENDL, EDMUND JOSEF
Der Sonnblick Ruft, Novel
Sonnblick Ruft, Der 1952 d: Eberhard Frowein. lps: Eduard Kock, Marianne Wischmann, Sepp Rist. 75M GRM/AUS. *The Call of the Sun Watch* prod/rel: Telos, Augusta

BENDOW, PETTER
Die Frau Im Talar, Novel
Frau Im Talar, Die 1929 d: Adolf Trotz. lps: Aud Egede Nissen, Paul Richter, Mona Martenson. 2400m GRM. prod/rel: Mondial-Film

BENE, CARMELO
Nostra Signora Dei Turchi, Novel
Nostra Signora Dei Turchi 1968 d: Carmelo Bene. lps: Carmelo Bene, Lydia Mancinelli, Salvatore Sinicalchi. 125M ITL. *Our Lady of the Turks* prod/rel: Giorgio Patara, Carmelo Bene

BENEDETTI, MARIO (1920–, URG
La Tregua, 1960, Novel
Tregua, La 1974 d: Sergio Renan. lps: Hector Alterio, Ana Maria Picchio, Ditto Oscar Martinez. 105M ARG. *The Truce*

BENEDETTI, SILVIO
Se Quell'Idiota Ci Pensasse., Play
Ma Chi Te Lo Fare? 1948 d: Ignazio Ferronetti. lps: Fanny Marchio, Antonio Gandusio, Annibale Betrone. 90M ITL. *La Sirena Del Golfo* prod/rel: Organizzazione Vincenzo Di Pea
Se Quell'idiota Ci Pensasse. 1939 d: Nino Giannini. lps: Annibale Betrone, Fanny Marchio, Roberto VillA. 88M ITL. prod/rel: Comoedia Film, Romulus Film

BENEDICT, CHARLES
The Lily of Killarney, Opera
Lily of Killarney 1927 d: H. B. Parkinson. lps: Herbert Langley, Kathlyn Hilliard. 1690f UKN. prod/rel: Song Films
Lily of Killarney, The 1922 d: Challis Sanderson. lps: Betty Farquhar, Bertram Burleigh, Booth Conway. 1067f UKN. prod/rel: Master Films, Gaumont

BENEDICTUS, DAVID (1938–, UKN
You're a Big Boy Now, London 1963, Novel
You're a Big Boy Now 1966 d: Francis Ford CoppolA. lps: Elizabeth Hartman, Geraldine Page, Julie Harris. 97M USA. prod/rel: Phil Feldman, Seven Arts Productions

BENEDIX, PETER
Documents
Fall Lena Christ, Der 1968 d: Hans W. Geissendorfer. lps: Heidi Stroh, Edith Volksmann, Eberhard Peiker. 95M GRM. *The Case of Lena Christ* prod/rel: B.R.

BENEFIELD, BARRY
Valiant Is the Word for Carrie, New York 1935, Novel
Valiant Is the Word for Carrie 1936 d: Wesley Ruggles. lps: Gladys George, Arline Judge, John Howard. 110M USA. *With Banners Blowing* prod/rel: Paramount Pictures

BENEFIELD, JOHN BARRY
The Chicken-Wagon Family, New York 1925, Novel
Chicken Wagon Family 1939 d: Herbert I. Leeds. lps: Jane Withers, Leo Carrillo, Marjorie Weaver. 64M USA. prod/rel: Twentieth Century-Fox Film Corp.
Dixie Merchant, The 1926 d: Frank Borzage. lps: J. Farrell MacDonald, Madge Bellamy, Jack Mulhall. 5126f USA. prod/rel: Fox Film Corp.

BENELLI, SEM
L' Arzigogolo, 1922, Play
Arzigogolo, L' 1924 d: Mario Almirante. lps: Italia Almirante Manzini, Annibale Betrone, Alberto Collo. 2419m ITL. prod/rel: Alba Film
La Cena Delle Beffe, 1909, Play
Cena Delle Beffe, La 1941 d: Alessandro Blasetti. lps: Amedeo Nazzari, Osvaldo Valenti, Clara Calamai. 86M ITL. *The Jokers Banquet* prod/rel: Cines, E.N.I.C.
La Gorgona, 1913, Play
Gorgona, La 1915 d: Mario Caserini. lps: Madeleine Celiat, Annibale Ninchi, Cesare Zocchi. 1200m ITL. prod/rel: S.A. Ambrosio
Gorgona, La 1942 d: Guido Brignone. lps: Mariella Lotti, Rossano Brazzi, Camillo Pilotto. 85M ITL. prod/rel: Artisti Associati, Florentia

BENES, JARA
Parizanka, Opera
Slecna Matinka 1938 d: Vladimir Slavinsky. lps: Vera Ferbasova, Stanislav Strnad, Theodor Pistek. 2832m CZC. *Miss Mother* prod/rel: Lucernafilm

BENES, KAREL J.
Kouzelny Dum, Novel
Kouzelny Dum 1939 d: Otakar VavrA. lps: Adina Mandlova, Ruzena Naskova, Leopolda DostalovA. 2897m CZC. *The Enchanted House*; *The Magic House*; *The Enchanting House* prod/rel: Elekta
Stolen Life, Novel
Stolen Life 1939 d: Paul Czinner. lps: Elisabeth Bergner, Michael Redgrave, Wilfred Lawson. 91M UKN. prod/rel: Orion Productions, Paramount
Stolen Life, A 1946 d: Curtis Bernhardt. lps: Bette Davis, Glenn Ford, Dane Clark. 107M USA. prod/rel: Warner Bros.

BENESOVA, BOZENA
Don Pablo Don Pedro a Vera Lukasova, Novel
  Vera Lukasova 1939 d: E. F. Burian. lps: Jirina
  Stranska, Rudolf Hrusinsky, Lola SkrbkovA. 2508m
  CZC. prod/rel: Elekta

BENES-TREBIZSKY, VACLAV
Bludne Duse, Novel
  Bludne Duse 1926 d: Jan W. Speerger. lps: Theodor
  Pistek, Bozena Svobodova, Mana ZeniskovA. 2115m
  CZC. *The Lost Soul* prod/rel: Jaroslav Pesout, Jan
  Sourek

BENET I JORNET, JOSEP M.
Amic/Amat, Play
  Amic/Amat 1999 d: Ventura Pons. lps: Josep Maria
  Pou, Rosa Maria Sarda, Mario Gas. 91M SPN.
  Beloved/Friend prod/rel: Lauren Films, Els Films de la
  Rambla

E.R., Play
  Actrius 1996 d: Ventura Pons. lps: Nuria Espert, Rosa
  Maria Sarda, Anna Lizaran. 88M SPN. *Actresses*
  prod/rel: Els Films de la Rambla S.a.©, Tve Television
  Espanola

BENET, STEPHEN VINCENT (1898–1953), USA
The Devil and Daniel Webster, 1937, Short Story
  All That Money Can Buy 1941 d: William Dieterle.
  lps: Edward Arnold, Walter Huston, James Craig. 112M
  USA. *The Devil and Daniel Webster; Daniel and the
  Devil; Here Is a Man* prod/rel: RKO Radio

Everybody Was Very Nice, 1936, Short Story
  Love, Honor and Behave 1938 d: Stanley Logan. lps:
  Wayne Morris, Priscilla Lane, John Litel. 70M USA.
  Everybody Was Very Nice prod/rel: Warner Bros.
  Pictures©

Famous, 1946, Short Story
  Just for You 1952 d: Elliott Nugent. lps: Bing Crosby,
  Jane Wyman, Ethel Barrymore. 104M USA. prod/rel:
  Paramount

The Sobbin' Women, 1937, Short Story
  Seven Brides for Seven Brothers 1954 d: Stanley
  Donen. lps: Howard Keel, Jane Powell, Jeff Richards.
  102M USA. prod/rel: MGM

Uriah's Son, 1924, Short Story
  Necessary Evil, The 1925 d: George Archainbaud. lps:
  Ben Lyon, Viola Dana, Frank Mayo. 6307f USA.
  prod/rel: First National Pictures

BENEVENTE Y MARTINEZ, JACINTO
La Malquerida, 1913, Play
  Passion Flower, The 1921 d: Herbert Brenon. lps:
  Norma Talmadge, Courtenay Foote, Eulalie Jensen.
  6755f USA. prod/rel: Norma Talmadge Film Co.,
  Associated First National Pictures

BEN-EZER, EHUD
Story
  Hamachtzayya 1990 d: Ron Ninio. lps: Uri Gavrieli,
  Sasson Gabai, Hannah Azoulai-Hasfari. F ISR. *The
  Quarry*

BEN-GAVRIEL, M. Y.
Das Haus in Der Karpfengasse, Novel
  Haus in Der Karpfengasse, Das 1964 d: Kurt
  Hoffmann. lps: Jana Brejchova, Edith
  Schultze-Westrum, Rudolf Deyl. 109M GRM. *The House
  in the Karpfengasse; The House on Carp Lane* prod/rel:
  Independent

BENGTSSON, FRANS GUNNAR
Rode Orm Sjofarara I Vasterled, Stockholm 1941,
Novel
  Long Ships, The 1964 d: Jack Cardiff. lps: Richard
  Widmark, Sidney Poitier, Russ Tamblyn. 125M
  UKN/YGS. *Dugi Brodovi* (YGS) prod/rel: Warwick Film
  Productions, Avala Film

BENIERES, LOUIS
Papillon Dit Lyonnais le Juste, Play
  Bach Millionnaire 1933 d: Henry Wulschleger. lps:
  Bach, Georges Treville, Roger Treville. 97M FRN.
  Papillon Dit Lyonnais le Juste prod/rel: Alex Nalpas

BENJAMIN, PHILIP
Quick Before It Melts, New York 1964, Novel
  Quick, Before It Melts 1965 d: Delbert Mann. lps:
  George Maharis, Robert Morse, Anjanette Comer. 98M
  USA. prod/rel: Biography Productions, MGM

BENNET, ROBERT AMES
His Temporary Wife, 1917, Short Story
  His Temporary Wife 1920 d: Joseph Levering. lps:
  Mary Boland, Edmund Breese, Rubye de Remer. 6r
  USA. prod/rel: Joseph Levering Productions, W. W.
  Hodkinson Corp.

Into the Primitive, Chicago 1908, Novel
  Into the Primitive 1916 d: Thomas N. Heffron. lps:
  Kathlyn Williams, Guy Oliver, Harry Lonsdale. 5r USA.
  prod/rel: Selig Polyscope Co.©

BENNETT, ALAN (1934–, UKN
The Madness of George III, Play
  Madness of King George, The 1994 d: Nicholas
  Hytner. lps: Nigel Hawthorne, Helen Mirren, Ian Holm.
  110M UKN/USA. prod/rel: Rank, Samuel Goldwyn Co.

A Question of Attribution, Play
  Question of Attribution, A 1991 d: John Schlesinger.
  lps: James Fox, Gregory Floy, Geoffrey Palmer. TVM.
  70M UKN. prod/rel: BBC Tv, BBC Films for Screen One

BENNETT, ARNOLD (1867–1931), UKN, Bennett, E.
  Arnold, Bennett, Enoch Arnold
Novel
  Clayhanger 1976 d: John Davies, David Reid. lps:
  Harry Andrews, Janet Suzman, Peter McEnery. MTV.
  1300M UKN. prod/rel: Atv

Buried Alive, London 1908, Novel
  Great Adventure, The 1921 d: Kenneth Webb. lps:
  Lionel Barrymore, Doris Rankin, Octavia Broske. 5627f
  USA. prod/rel: Whitman Bennett Productions,
  Associated First National Pictures

  His Double Life 1933 d: Arthur Hopkins, William C. de
  Mille. lps: Roland Young, Lillian Gish, Montagu Love.
  68M USA. prod/rel: Eddie Dowling Pictures Corp.©,
  Paramount Pictures

  Holy Matrimony 1943 d: John M. Stahl. lps: Monty
  Woolley, Gracie Fields, Laird Cregar. 87M USA.
  prod/rel: 20th Century-Fox

The Card, 1912, Novel
  Card, The 1922 d: A. V. Bramble. lps: Laddie Cliff,
  Hilda Cowley, Joan Barry. 5080f UKN. prod/rel: Ideal

  Card, The 1952 d: Ronald Neame. lps: Alec Guinness,
  Glynis Johns, Valerie Hobson. 91M UKN. *The Promoter*
  (USA) prod/rel: General Film Distributors, British Film
  Makers

The Grand Babylon Hotel, Novel
  Grand Babylon Hotel, The 1916 d: Frank Wilson. lps:
  Fred Wright, Margaret Blanche, Gerald Lawrence.
  5275f UKN. prod/rel: Hepworth, Shaftesbury

The Great Adventure, London 1913, Play
  Great Adventure, The 1915 d: Larry Trimble. lps:
  Henry Ainley, Esme Hubbard, Rutland Barrington.
  5500f UKN. prod/rel: Turner Films, Ideal

  His Double Life 1933 d: Arthur Hopkins, William C. de
  Mille. lps: Roland Young, Lillian Gish, Montagu Love.
  68M USA. prod/rel: Eddie Dowling Pictures Corp.©,
  Paramount Pictures

Milestones, London 1912, Play
  Milestones 1916 d: Thomas Bentley. lps: Isobel Elsom,
  Owen Nares, Campbell Gullan. 8640f UKN. prod/rel: G.
  B. Samuelson, Moss

  Milestones 1920 d: Paul Scardon. lps: Lewis Stone,
  Alice Hollister, Gertrude Robinson. 5782f USA.
  prod/rel: Goldwyn Pictures Corp.©, Goldwyn
  Distributing Corp.

Mr. Prohack, 1922, Novel
  Dear Mr. Prohack 1949 d: Thornton Freeland. lps:
  Cecil Parker, Glynis Johns, Hermione Baddeley. 91M
  UKN. *Mr. Prohack* prod/rel: General Film Distributors,
  Wessex

The Old Wives' Tale, 1908, Novel
  Old Wives' Tale, The 1921 d: Denison Clift. lps: Fay
  Compton, Florence Turner, Henry Victor. 5000f UKN.
  prod/rel: Ideal

Sacred and Profane Love, London 1919, Play
  Sacred and Profane Love 1921 d: William D. Taylor.
  lps: Elsie Ferguson, Conrad Nagel, Thomas Holding.
  4964f USA., Famous Players-Lasky

La Ville Des Milles Joies, Novel
  Stadt Der Tausend Freuden, Die 1927 d: Carmine
  Gallone. lps: Paul Richter, Adele Sandrock, Langhorne
  Burton. 2245m GRM/FRN. *La Ville Des Mille Joies*
  (FRN) prod/rel: Lothar Stark Gmbh, Societe Des Films
  Art

BENNETT, CHARLES
After Midnight, 1929, Play
  Midnight 1931 d: George King. lps: John Stuart, Eve
  Gray, George Bellamy. 45M UKN. prod/rel: George
  King, Fox

Blackmail, London 1928, Play
  Blackmail 1929 d: Alfred Hitchcock. lps: Anny Ondra,
  John Longden, Donald Calthrop. 96M UKN. prod/rel:
  British International Pictures, Wardour

The Last Hour, Play
  Last Hour, The 1930 d: Walter Forde. lps: Stewart
  Rome, Richard Cooper, Kathleen Vaughan. 75M UKN.
  prod/rel: Nettlefold, Butcher's Film Service

BENNETT, DOROTHEA
The Jigsaw Man, Novel
  Jigsaw Man, The 1984 d: Terence Young. lps: Michael
  Caine, Laurence Olivier, Susan George. 98M UKN.
  prod/rel: J & M, Evangrove

BENNETT, DOROTHY
Fly Away Home, Play
  Always in My Heart 1942 d: Jo Graham. lps: Kay
  Francis, Walter Huston, Gloria Warren. 92M USA.
  prod/rel: Warner Bros.

BENNETT, EMERSON
The Forest Rose, Novel
  Forest Rose, The 1912 d: Theodore Marston. lps:
  Marguerite Snow, Frederick Vroom, William Russell. 2r
  USA. prod/rel: Thanhouser

BENNETT, JAY
Catacombs, New York 1959, Novel
  Catacombs 1964 d: Gordon Hessler. lps: Gary Merrill,
  Jane Merrow, Georgina Cookson. 90M UKN. *The
  Woman Who Wouldn't Die* (USA) prod/rel:
  Parroch-Mccallum Productions, Associated Producers,
  Inc.

BENNETT, JOHN
Barnaby Lee, 1902, Short Story
  Barnaby Lee 1917 d: Edward H. Griffith. lps: John
  Tansey, Samuel Niblack, Hugh Thompson. 4r USA.
  prod/rel: Thomas A. Edison, Inc.

BENNETT, KEM
Death at Attention, Novel
  Time Bomb 1952 d: Ted Tetzlaff. lps: Glenn Ford,
  Anne Vernon, Maurice Denham. 72M UKN. *Terror on a
  Train* (USA) prod/rel: MGM-British

The Queer Fish, Novel
  Doublecross 1956 d: Anthony Squire. lps: Donald
  Houston, William Hartnell, Fay Compton. 71M UKN.
  Double Cross prod/rel: Beaconsfield, British Lion

BENNETT, ROLFE
Bachelor's Baby, Novel
  Bachelor's Baby 1932 d: Harry Hughes. lps: Ann
  Casson, William Freshman, Henry Wenman. 58M UKN.
  prod/rel: British International Pictures, Pathe

  Bachelor's Baby, A 1922 d: Arthur Rooke. lps:
  Constance Worth, Malcolm Tod, Tom Reynolds. 5200f
  UKN. prod/rel: I. B. Davidson, Granger

BENNETT-THOMPSON, LILLIAN
Short Story
  Gauntlet, The 1920 d: Edwin L. Hollywood. lps: Harry
  T. Morey, Louiszita Valentine, Frank Hagney. 4629f
  USA. *The Gauntlet of Greed* prod/rel: Vitagraph Co. of
  America©

Where the Heat Lies, 1922, Short Story
  Love Gambler, The 1922 d: Joseph J. Franz. lps: John
  Gilbert, Carmel Myers, Bruce Gordon. 4682f USA.
  prod/rel: Fox Film Corp.

Without Compromise, New York 1922, Novel
  Without Compromise 1922 d: Emmett J. Flynn. lps:
  William Farnum, Lois Wilson, Robert McKim. 5173f
  USA. prod/rel: Fox Film Corp.

BEN-NIR, YITZHAK
Roman Be'hemshachim, Novel
  Roman Be'hemshachim 1985 d: Oded Kotler. lps:
  Topol, Galia Topol, Efrat Lavie. ISR. *Forever Again*

BENOIT, PIERRE
Novel
  Signora Dell'ovest, Una 1942 d: Carl Koch. lps:
  Michel Simon, Isa Pola, Rossano Brazzi. 85M ITL.
  Carovane; Carovana prod/rel: Scalera Film

L' Atlantide, Paris 1919, Novel
  Antinea, l'Amante Della Citta Sepolta 1961 d:
  Edgar G. Ulmer, Giuseppe Masini. lps: Haya Harareet,
  Jean-Louis Trintignant, James Westmoreland. 100M
  ITL/FRN. *Journey Beneath the Desert* (USA); *Atlantis
  the Lost Continent*; *L' Atlantide* (FRN); *The Lost
  Kingdom*; *End of Atlantis* prod/rel: C.C.M. (Roma),
  Fides (Paris)

  Atlantide, L' 1921 d: Jacques Feyder. lps: Stacia
  Napierkowska, Jean Angelo, Georges Melchior. 4000m
  FRN. *Lost Atlantis*; *Missing Husbands* prod/rel: Ste
  Generale Pour Le Dev. De La Cinema.

  Atlantide, L' 1932 d: G. W. Pabst. lps: Pierre Blanchar,
  Brigitte Helm, Jean Angelo. 94M FRN. prod/rel:
  Nero-Film, Societe Internationale Cinematographique

  Atlantide, L' 1991 d: Bob Swaim. lps: Jean Rochefort,
  Victoria Mahoney, Tcheky Karyo. 110M FRN.

  Herrin von Atlantis, Die 1932 d: G. W. Pabst. lps:
  Brigitte Helm, Gustav Diessl, Tela (Tela-Tchai) Tschai.
  88M GRM. *The Mistress of Atlantis*; *Lost Atlantis*
  prod/rel: Romain Pines, Nero

  Siren of Atlantis 1948 d: Gregg R. Tallas. lps: Maria
  Montez, Jean-Pierre Aumont, Dennis O'Keefe. 75M
  USA. *Atlantis the Lost Continent*; *Queen of Atlantis*;
  Atlantis prod/rel: United Artists

Axelle, Paris 1928, Novel
   Surrender 1931 d: William K. Howard. lps: Warner Baxter, Leila Hyams, Ralph Bellamy. 69M USA. *I Surrender; The Surrender* prod/rel: Fox Film Corp.©, William K. Howard Production

Bethsabee, Novel
   Bethsabee 1947 d: Leonide Moguy. lps: Danielle Darrieux, Georges Marchal, Paul Meurisse. 90M FRN. prod/rel: C.I.C.C.

Boissiere, Novel
   Boissiere 1937 d: Fernand Rivers. lps: Pierre Renoir, Lucien Nat, Spinelly. 91M FRN. prod/rel: Films Fernand Rivers

C'est Arrive a Aden, Novel
   C'est Arrive a Aden 1956 d: Michel Boisrond. lps: Dany Robin, Andre Luguet, Jean Bretonniere. 88M FRN. *It Happened in Aden* prod/rel: Jb Films

La Chatelaine du Liban, Novel
   Chatelaine du Liban, La 1926 d: Marco de Gastyne. lps: Arlette Marchal, Ivan Petrovitch, Gaston Modot. F FRN. prod/rel: Natan
   Chatelaine du Liban, La 1933 d: Jean Epstein. lps: Jean Murat, Spinelly, George Grossmith. 95M FRN. prod/rel: Vandal Et Delac
   Chatelaine du Liban, La 1956 d: Richard Pottier. lps: Jean-Claude Pascal, Jean Servais, Gianna Maria Canale. 105M FRN/ITL. *La Castellana Del Libano* (ITL); *The Woman from Lebanon* (UKN); *The Lebanese Mission* (USA); *Lady of Lebanon*; *Desert Retour* prod/rel: C.T.I., Jeanvic Films

La Chaussee Des Geants, Novel
   Chaussee Des Geants, La 1926 d: Jean Durand, Robert Boudrioz. lps: Armand Tallier, Philippe Heriat, Jeanne Helbling. 3400m FRN. prod/rel: Sphinx, Rene Fernand

Les Compagnons d'Ulysse, Novel
   Angelica 1939 d: Jean Choux. lps: Viviane Romance, Georges Flamant, Marcelle Yrven. 95M FRN/ITL. *Rosa Di Sangue* (ITL); *La Rose de Sang* prod/rel: Scalera Film

Koenigsmark, Novel
   Koenigsmark 1923 d: Leonce Perret. lps: Jaque Catelain, Huguette Duflos, Georges Vaultier. 3750m FRN. prod/rel: Films Radia
   Koenigsmark 1935 d: Maurice Tourneur. lps: Elissa Landi, John Lodge, Pierre Fresnay. 96M UKN. prod/rel: Capitol, General Film Distributors
   Koenigsmark 1935 d: Maurice Tourneur. lps: Pierre Fresnay, John Lodge, Jean Max. 115M FRN. *The Crimson Dynasty* prod/rel: Societe Des Films Roger Richebe
   Koenigsmark 1953 d: Solange Bussi, Christian-Jaque. lps: Silvana Pampanini, Jean-Pierre Aumont, Renee Faure. 90M FRN/ITL. prod/rel: Sigma, Vog

Lunegarde, Novel
   Lunegarde 1944 d: Marc Allegret. lps: Gaby Morlay, Jean Tissier, Giselle Pascal. 90M FRN. prod/rel: Lux-Films, Pathe Cinema

Mademoiselle de la Ferte, Novel
   Mademoiselle de la Ferte 1949 d: Roger Dallier. lps: Jany Holt, Pierre Cressoy, Jean Servais. 98M FRN. prod/rel: Comptoir Francais De Prods. Cinematog.

Les Nuits de Moscou, Novel
   Moscow Nights 1935 d: Anthony Asquith. lps: Harry Baur, Laurence Olivier, Penelope Dudley-Ward. 75M UKN. *I Stand Condemned* (USA); *Natacha* prod/rel: London Films, Capitol Films
   Nuits Moscovites, Les 1934 d: Alexis Granowsky. lps: Harry Baur, Pierre Richard-Willm, AnnabellA. 95M FRN. prod/rel: G.G. Film

L' Oublie, Short Story
   Princesse Mandane 1927 d: Germaine Dulac. lps: Edmonde Guy, Edmond Van Duren, Jacques ArnnA. F FRN. *L' Oublie* prod/rel: Alex Nalpas

Pour Don Carlos, Novel
   Pour Don Carlos 1921 d: Musidora, Jacques Lasseyne. lps: Musidora, Marguerite Greyval, Abel Tarride. 3000m FRN. prod/rel: Films Musidora

Le Puits de Jacobs, Novel
   Puits de Jacob, Les 1925 d: Edward Jose. lps: Betty Blythe, Leon Mathot, Andre Nox. 4500m FRN. *Daughter of Israel* (USA) prod/rel: Markus Et Steger

Le Soleil de Minuit, Novel
   Soleil de Minuit, Le 1943 d: Bernard-Roland. lps: Josseline Gael, Jules Berry, Saturnin Fabre. 88M FRN. prod/rel: S.U.F.

BEN-PORAT, Y.
Story
   Chavura She'ka'zot 1962 d: Ze'ev Havatzelet. lps: Yossi Banai, Bomba Tzur, Oded Teomi. F ISR. *What a Gang!*

BENRIMO, J. H.
The Willow Tree, New York 1917, Play
   Willow Tree, The 1920 d: Henry Otto. lps: Viola Dana, Edward Connelly, Pell Trenton. 6r USA. prod/rel: Screen Classics, Metro Pictures Corp.©

BENSON, E. F. (1867–1940), UKN
Novel
   Mapp and Lucia 1985 d: Donald McWhinnie. lps: Geraldine McEwan, Prunella Scales, Nigel Hawthorne. MTV. 300M UKN. prod/rel: Lwt

BENSON, FLETCHER D.
La Nuit Des Perverses, Novel
   Cousines, Les 1969 d: Louis Soulanes. lps: Nicole Debonne, Robert Lombard, Solange Pradel. 97M FRN. *From Ear to Ear* (USA); *The French Cousins*; *The Coffin* prod/rel: Claude Capra, Les Activites Cinematographiques

BENSON, JAMES
Above Us the Waves, Book
   Above Us the Waves 1955 d: Ralph Thomas. lps: John Mills, John Gregson, Donald Sinden. 99M UKN. prod/rel: General Film Distributors, London Independent Producers

BENSON, ROBERT
The Necromancers, Novel
   Spellbound 1941 d: John Harlow. lps: Derek Farr, Vera Lindsay, Frederick Leister. 82M UKN. *The Spell of Amy Nugent* (USA); *Passing Clouds* prod/rel: Pyramid Amalgamated, United Artists

BENSON, SALLY (1900–1972), USA
Junior Miss, Novel
   Junior Miss 1945 d: George Seaton. lps: Peggy Ann Garner, Allyn Joslyn, Stephen Dunne. 94M USA. prod/rel: 20th Century-Fox
Meet Me in St. Louis, 1942, Short Story
   Meet Me in St. Louis 1944 d: Vincente Minnelli. lps: Judy Garland, Margaret O'Brien, Mary Astor. 113M USA. prod/rel: MGM

BENTHAM, JOSEPHINE
A Bride for Henry, 1937, Short Story
   Bride for Henry, A 1937 d: William Nigh. lps: Anne Nagel, Warren Hull, Henry Mollison. 58M USA. prod/rel: Monogram Pictures Corp.
Janie, New York 1942, Play
   Janie 1944 d: Michael Curtiz. lps: Joyce Reynolds, Robert Hutton, Edward Arnold. 106M USA. prod/rel: Warner Bros.

BENTLEY, E. C. (1875–1956), UKN, Bentley, Edmund Clerihew
Trent's Last Case, London 1913, Novel
   Trent's Last Case 1920 d: Richard Garrick. lps: Gregory Scott, Pauline Peters, Clive Brook. 5500f UKN. prod/rel: Broadwest, Walturdaw
   Trent's Last Case 1929 d: Howard Hawks. lps: Donald Crisp, Raymond Griffith, Raymond Hatton. 5834f USA. prod/rel: Fox Film Corp.
   Trent's Last Case 1952 d: Herbert Wilcox. lps: Margaret Lockwood, Michael Wilding, Orson Welles. 90M UKN. prod/rel: Imperadio, Wilcox-Neagle

BENTLEY, JOHN
Rendezvous With Death, Novel
   Night Invader, The 1943 d: Herbert Mason. lps: Anne Crawford, David Farrar, Carl Jaffe. 81M UKN. prod/rel: Warner Bros., First National

BENTLEY, NICOLAS
The Floating Dutchman, Novel
   Floating Dutchman, The 1953 d: Vernon Sewell. lps: Dermot Walsh, Sydney Tafler, Mary Germaine. 76M UKN. prod/rel: Merton Park, Anglo-Amalgamated
Third Party Risk, Novel
   Third Party Risk 1955 d: Daniel Birt. lps: Lloyd Bridges, Finlay Currie, Maureen Swanson. 70M UKN. *The Deadly Game*; *Big Deadly Game* prod/rel: Hammer, Exclusive

BENZONNI, JULIETTE
Catherine Il Suffit d'un Amour, Novel
   Catherine, Il Suffit d'un Amour 1968 d: Bernard Borderie. lps: Olga Georges-Picot, Francine Berge, Roger Van Hool. 102M FRN/ITL/GRM. *Catherine un Solo Impossibile Amore* (ITL); *Catherine*; *Catherine -Ein Leben Fur Die Liebe* (GRM); *Catherine -a Live for Love*; *Catherine Il Suffit d'Amour* prod/rel: Lira Films, Iduna Films

BERAUD, HENRI
Le Martyre de l'Obese, Novel
   Martyre de l'Obese, Le 1932 d: Pierre Chenal. lps: Suzet Mais, Andre Berley, Jacques Maury. 87M FRN. prod/rel: Aster-Film

BERBEROVA, NINA
L' Accompagnatrice, Novel
   Accompagnatrice, L' 1992 d: Claude Miller. lps: Richard Bohringer, Elena Safonova, Romane Bohringer. 111M FRN. *The Accompanist* (UKN) prod/rel: Film Par Film, de la Boissiere Orly

BERCOVICI, ERIC
So Little Cause for Caroline, Novel
   One Shoe Makes It Murder 1982 d: William Hale. lps: Robert Mitchum, Angie Dickinson, Mel Ferrer. TVM. 100M USA. prod/rel: Fellows-Keegan Company, Lorimar Prods.

BERCOVICI, KONRAD
The Bear Tamer's Daughter, 1921, Short Story
   Revenge 1928 d: Edwin Carewe. lps: Dolores Del Rio, James Marcus, Sophia OrtigA. 6541f USA. prod/rel: Edwin Carewe Productions, United Artists
The Law of the Lawless, 1921, Short Story
   Law of the Lawless, The 1923 d: Victor Fleming. lps: Dorothy Dalton, Theodore Kosloff, Charles de Roche. 6387f USA. prod/rel: Famous Players-Lasky, Paramount Pictures
The Volga Boatman, New York 1926, Novel
   Volga Boatman, The 1926 d: Cecil B. de Mille. lps: William Boyd, Elinor Fair, Robert Edeson. 11r USA. prod/rel: de Mille Pictures, Producers Distributing Corp.

BERCOVICI, MARIE M.
Strangers All; Or Separate Lives, 1934, Play
   Strangers All 1935 d: Charles Vidor. lps: May Robson, Preston Foster, William Bakewell. 70M USA. prod/rel: RKO Radio Pictures©

BERCOVITCH, REUBEN
Story
   Hell in the Pacific 1968 d: John Boorman. lps: Lee Marvin, Toshiro Mifune. 103M USA/JPN. *Taiheiyo No Jigoku* (JPN); *Two Soldiers East and West*; *The Enemy*; *Pacific War* prod/rel: Selmur Pictures Corporation, Henry G. Saperstein Enterprises

BEREL, PIERRE
Amica, Monte Carlo 1905, Opera
   Amica 1916 d: Enrico Guazzoni. lps: Leda Gys, Amleto Novelli, Nella MontagnA. 1212m ITL. prod/rel: Cines

BEREND, ALICE
Die Brautigame Der Babette Bomberling, Novel
   Brautigame Der Babette Bomberling 1927 d: Victor Janson. lps: Xenia Desni, Walter Rilla, Egon von Jordan. 2237m GRM. prod/rel: Alfred Sittarz
Herr Funf, Novel
   Homme Qui Ne Sait Pas Dire Non, L' 1932 d: Heinz Hilpert. lps: Lisette Lanvin, Paulette Dubost, Willi Domgraf-Fassbaender. 82M FRN. prod/rel: Societe Des Films Osso

BERENDT, JOHN
Midnight in the Garden of Good and Evil, Book
   Midnight in the Garden of Good and Evil 1997 d: Clint Eastwood. lps: Kevin Spacey, John Cusack, Jack Thompson. 155M USA. prod/rel: Malpaso, Silver Pictures

BERGAMIN, JOSE
Los Naufragos de la Calle de la Providencia, Play
   Angel Exterminador, El 1962 d: Luis Bunuel. lps: Silvia Pinal, Jacqueline Andere, Augusto Benedico. 95M MXC. *The Exterminating Angel* (USA) prod/rel: Uninci, S.a., Films 59

BERGER, CYRIL
Lucile, Short Story
   Lucile 1923 d: Georges MoncA. lps: Georges Gauthier, Marise Dauvray, Jean Lorette. 1710m FRN. prod/rel: J. Boudet

BERGER, HENNING
Syndafloden, Play
   Maske Fallt, Die 1930 d: William Dieterle. lps: Lissi Arna, Anton Pointner, Karl Etlinger. 7r USA. prod/rel: First National Pictures
   Sin Flood, The 1922 d: Frank Lloyd. lps: Richard Dix, Helene Chadwick, James Kirkwood. 6500f USA. prod/rel: Goldwyn Pictures
   Way of All Men, The 1930 d: Frank Lloyd. lps: Douglas Fairbanks Jr., Dorothy Revier, Robert Edeson. 6032f USA. *Sin Flood* (UKN) prod/rel: First National Pictures

BERGER, JOHN (1926–, UKN
Play Me Something, 1987, Short Story
   Play Me Something 1989 d: Timothy Neat. lps: Tilda Swinton, John Berger, Liz Lockhead. TVM. 74M UKN. prod/rel: British Film Institute, Film Four International

BERGER, JOSEF
Ehe Fur Eine Nacht, Play
    Ehe Fur Eine Nacht 1953 d: Victor Tourjansky. lps: Gustav Frohlich, Adrian Hoven, Hans Leibelt. 92M GRM. *Marriage for a Night* prod/rel: Ariston, N.F.

BERGER, THOMAS (1924–, USA, Berger, Thomas Louis
Little Big Man, New York 1964, Novel
    Little Big Man 1970 d: Arthur Penn. lps: Dustin Hoffman, Faye Dunaway, Jeff Corey. 150M USA. prod/rel: Hiller Productions, Stockbridge Productions

Neighbors, 1980, Novel
    Neighbors 1981 d: John G. Avildsen. lps: John Belushi, Kathryn Walker, Cathy Moriarty. 95M USA. prod/rel: Columbia

BERGERAT, EMILE
Capitaine Blomet, Play
    Capitaine Blomet 1947 d: Andree Feix. lps: Fernand Gravey, Gaby Sylvia, Jean Meyer. 90M FRN. *N'ecrivez Jamais* prod/rel: Pathe-Cinema

BERGMAN, HJALMAR (1883–1931), SWD
Dollar, 1926, Play
    Dollar 1938 d: Gustaf Molander. lps: Ingrid Bergman, Hakan Westergren, Georg Rydeberg. 78M SWD.

Frickan I Frack, 1925, Novel
    Flickan I Frack 1956 d: Arne Mattsson. lps: Maj-Britt Nilsson, Folke Sundquist, Anders Henrikson. 99M SWD. *Girl in a Dress-Coat* prod/rel: Ab Sandrew-Produktion

Hans Nads Testamente, 1910, Novel
    Hans Nads Testamente 1919 d: Victor Sjostrom. lps: Karl Mantzius, Carl Browallius, Greta Almroth. 1543m SWD. *His Grace's Last Testament* (UKN); *His Grace's Will* (USA); *The Will of His Grace* prod/rel: Ab Svenska Biografteatern
    Hans Nads Testamente 1940 d: Per Lindberg. lps: Olof Sandborg, Barbro Kollberg, Hjordis Petterson. 92M SWD. *His Grace's Will* prod/rel: Ab Svensk Filmindustri

Markurells I Wadkoping, 1919, Novel
    Markurells I Wadkoping 1930 d: Victor Sjostrom. lps: Victor Sjostrom, Pauline Brunius, Sture Lagerwall. 96M SWD/GRM. *Vater Und Sohn* (GRM); *Father and Son* (USA); *The Markurells of Wadkoping* prod/rel: Film Ab Minerva, Terra Film Ag (Germany)

Swedenhielms, 1925, Play
    Familien Swedenhjelm 1947 d: Lau Lauritzen Jr. lps: Ebbe Rode, Else Jarlbak, Mogens Brandt. 93M DNM. *Familie Swedenhielm* prod/rel: Asa
    Glucklicher Mensch, Ein 1943 d: Paul Verhoeven. lps: Ewald Balser, Viktor de Kowa, Maria Landrock. 94M GRM. *Schule Des Lebens* prod/rel: Tobis, D.F.V.
    Swedenhielms 1935 d: Gustaf Molander. lps: Gosta Ekman, Bjorn Berglund, Hakan Westergren. 92M SWD. prod/rel: Svensk Filmindustri

BERGMAN, PETER
Americathon 1998, Play
    Americathon 1979 d: Neal Israel. lps: Peter Riegert, Harvey Korman, Fred Willard. 85M USA/GRM. *1998 - Die Vier Milliarden Dollar Show*; *Americathon 1998* prod/rel: United Artists

BERGSTAEDT, G.
Novel
    Prazdnik Svyatovo Iorgene 1930 d: Yakov Protazanov. lps: Anatol Ktorov, Igor Iliinski, Mikhail Klimov. 84M USS. *The Holiday of St. Jorgen*; *The Feast of St. Jorgen*; *Festival at St. Jurgen*; *Prazdnik Sviatogo Yorgena* prod/rel: Meschrabpom-Film

BERKELEY, MARTIN
Kangaroo, Novel
    Kangaroo 1952 d: Lewis Milestone. lps: Peter Lawford, Richard Boone, Maureen O'HarA. 84M ASL/USA. prod/rel: 20th Century-Fox

The Penalty, Play
    Penalty, The 1941 d: Harold S. Bucquet. lps: Edward Arnold, Lionel Barrymore, Marsha Hunt. 79M USA. *Roosty* prod/rel: MGM

BERKELEY, REGINALD
Dawn, New York 1928, Novel
    Dawn 1928 d: Herbert Wilcox. lps: Sybil Thorndike, Marie Ault, Mary Brough. 7300f UKN. prod/rel: British & Dominions, Woolf & Freedman
    Nurse Edith Cavell 1939 d: Herbert Wilcox. lps: Anna Neagle, Edna May Oliver, George Sanders. 98M USA. prod/rel: RKO Radio Pictures, Imperadio Pictures, Ltd.©

French Leave, London 1920, Play
    Amour Et Discipline 1931 d: Jean Kemm. lps: Mona Goya, Mme. Rauzena, Maurice Jacquelin. 80M FRN. *La Fuite a l'Anglaise* prod/rel: Etablissements Jacques Haik

    French Leave 1930 d: Jack Raymond. lps: Madeleine Carroll, Sydney Howard, Arthur Chesney. 92M UKN. prod/rel: D and H Productions, Sterling
    French Leave 1937 d: Norman Lee. lps: Betty Lynne, Edmund Breon, John Longden. 86M UKN. prod/rel: Welwyn, Pathe

The Lady With a Lamp, London 1929, Play
    Lady With a Lamp, The 1951 d: Herbert Wilcox. lps: Anna Neagle, Michael Wilding, Gladys Young. 110M UKN. *The Lady With the Lamp* prod/rel: British Lion, Imperadio

Mr. Abdulla, Play
    Lucky Girl 1932 d: Gene Gerrard, Frank Miller. lps: Gene Gerrard, Molly Lamont, Gus McNaughton. 75M UKN. prod/rel: British International Pictures, Wardour

Speed, Play
    Man from Chicago, The 1930 d: Walter Summers. lps: Bernard Nedell, Dodo Watts, Joyce Kennedy. 88M UKN. prod/rel: British International Pictures, Wardour

BERKEY, BRIAN FAIR
Keys to Tulsa, Novel
    Keys to Tulsa 1997 d: Leslie Greif. lps: Eric Stoltz, Cameron Diaz, Randy Graff. 113M USA. prod/rel: Polygram Film Entertainment, Itc Entertainment Group

BERKEY, RALPH
Time Limit!, New York 1956, Play
    Time Limit 1957 d: Karl Malden. lps: Richard Widmark, Richard Basehart, Dolores Michaels. 95M USA. prod/rel: United Artists, Heath Prods.

BERKHOFS, ASTER
Het Spook Van Monniksveer, Novel
    Spook Van Monniksveer, Het 1989 d: Eddy Asselbergs, Frank Van Mechelen. lps: Frank Dingenen, Marilou Mermans, Hilde Heijnen. TVM. 65M BLG.

BERKMAN, TED
Cast a Giant Shadow, New York 1962, Biography
    Cast a Giant Shadow 1966 d: Melville Shavelson. lps: Kirk Douglas, Senta Berger, Angie Dickinson. 141M USA. *Evasive Peace* prod/rel: United Artists

BERKOFF, STEVEN (1937–, UKN
Decadence, Play
    Decadence 1993 d: Steven Berkoff. lps: Steven Berkoff, Joan Collins, Christopher Biggins. 108M UKN/GRM. prod/rel: Mayfair, Vendetta

BERLANGA, LUIS (1921–, SPN
Nel Giorno Dell'Onomastico Della Mamma, Story
    Alla Mia Cara Mamma Nel Giorno Del Suo Compleanno 1974 d: Luciano Salce. lps: Paolo Villaggio, Lila Kedrova, Eleonora Giorgi. 105M ITL. prod/rel: Rusconi Film, C.I.C.

BERLIN, IRVING (1888–1989), USA, Baline, Israel
The Cocoanuts, New York 1925, Musical Play
    Cocoanuts, The 1929 d: Robert Florey, Joseph Santley. lps: Groucho Marx, Harpo Marx, Chico Marx. 96M USA. prod/rel: Paramount Famous Lasky Corp.

Mr. Bones, Musical Play
    Mammy 1930 d: Michael Curtiz. lps: Al Jolson, Lois Moran, Louise Dresser. 84M USA. prod/rel: Warner Brothers Pictures

Stop Look and Listen, Play
    Stop, Look and Listen 1926 d: Larry Semon. lps: Larry Semon, Dorothy Dwan, Mary Carr. 5305f USA. prod/rel: Larry Semon Productions

BERLYN, ALFRED
Coming Home, Poem
    Coming Home 1913 d: Wilfred Noy. 1000f UKN. prod/rel: Clarendon

The Hand of a Child, Poem
    Hand of a Child, The 1913 d: Wilfred Noy. 1000f UKN. prod/rel: Clarendon

BERMAN, BEN LUCIEN
Mississippi, New York 1929, Novel
    Heaven on Earth 1931 d: Russell MacK. lps: Lew Ayres, Anita Louise, Harry Beresford. 78M USA. *Mississippi* prod/rel: Universal Pictures Corp.©

BERNA, PAUL
A Hundred Million Francs, Novel
    Horse Without a Head, The 1963 d: Don Chaffey. lps: Jean-Pierre Aumont, Herbert Lom, Leo McKern. 89M UKN. prod/rel: Walt Disney

BERNANOS, GEORGES (1888–1948), FRN
Journal d'un Cure de Campagne, 1936, Novel
    Journal d'un Cure de Campagne, Le 1950 d: Robert Bresson. lps: Claude Laydu, Jean Riveyre, Armand Guibert. 110M FRN. *Diary of a Country Priest* (USA) prod/rel: U.G.C.

Novelle Histoire de Mouchette, Paris 1937, Novel
    Mouchette 1966 d: Robert Bresson. lps: Nadine Nortier, Jean-Claude Guilbert, Maria Cardinal. 90M FRN. prod/rel: Argos Films, Parc Film

Sous le Soleil de Satan, 1926, Novel
    Sous le Soleil de Satan 1987 d: Maurice Pialat. lps: Gerard Depardieu, Sandrine Bonnaire, Maurice Pialat. 98M FRN. *Under Satan's Sun* (USA); *Under the Sun of Satan* prod/rel: Erato, Antenne 2

BERNARD
Le Meurtrier de Theodore, Play
    Meurtrier de Theodore, Le 1908-18 d: Georges MoncA. lps: Gorby, Prince, Irma Genin. FRN. prod/rel: Pathe

BERNARD, JEAN-JACQUES
L'Absolution, Short Story
    Absolution, L' 1922 d: Jean Kemm. lps: Genevieve Felix, Paul Jorge, Marion Darcy. 1720m FRN.

BERNARD, TRISTAN
Short Story
    Poignard Malais, Le 1930 d: Roger Goupillieres. lps: Jean Marchat, Gaby Basset, Charlotte Barbier-Krauss. 60M FRN. prod/rel: Pathe-Natan

L' Anglais Tel Qu'on le Parle, Play
    Anglais Tel Qu'on le Parle, L' 1930 d: Robert Boudrioz. lps: Wera Engels, Felicien Tramel, Gustave Hamilton. F FRN. prod/rel: Gaumont, Franco-Film-Aubert

Cordon-Bleu, Play
    Cordon-Bleu 1931 d: Karl Anton. lps: Pierre Bertin, Louis Baron Fils, Jeanne Helbling. 70M FRN. prod/rel: Films Paramount

Le Costaud Des Epinettes, Play
    Amants Et Voleurs 1935 d: Raymond Bernard. lps: Pierre Blanchar, Michel Simon, Florelle. 105M FRN. prod/rel: Productions Odeon
    Costaud Des Epinettes, Le 1922 d: Raymond Bernard. lps: Germaine Fontanes, Henri Debain, Henri Collen. 1405m FRN. prod/rel: Films Tristan Bernard

La Course a la Vertu, Play
    Course a la Vertu, La 1936 d: Maurice Gleize. lps: Colette Darfeuil, Alice Tissot, Andre Berley. 82M FRN. prod/rel: Max Lerel

Le Danseur Inconnu, France 1909, Play
    Danseur Inconnu, Le 1928 d: Rene Barberis. lps: Andre Roanne, Janet Young, Andre Nicolle. 2200m FRN. prod/rel: Societe Des Cineromans, Films De France
    Love Cheat, The 1919 d: George Archainbaud. lps: June Caprice, Creighton Hale, Edwards Davis. 4640f USA. *The Unknown Dancer* prod/rel: Albert Capellani Productions, Inc., Pathe Exchange, Inc.

Les Deux Canards, Play
    Deux Canards, Les 1933 d: Erich Schmidt. lps: Rene Lefevre, Saturnin Fabre, Florelle. 78M FRN. prod/rel: Artia-Film

Embrassez-Moi, Play
    Embrassez-Moi 1928 d: Robert Peguy, Max de Rieux. lps: Prince-Rigadin, Suzanne Bianchetti, Jacques ArnnA. F FRN. prod/rel: Alex Nalpas
    Embrassez-Moi 1932 d: Leon Mathot. lps: Georges Milton, Tania Fedor, Jeanne Helbling. 89M FRN. prod/rel: Gaumont-Franco-Film-Aubert

Jeanne Dore, Play
    Jeanne Dore 1915 d: Louis Mercanton, Rene Hervil. lps: Sarah Bernhardt, Raymond Bernard, Jean Marie de L'isle. 1600m FRN. prod/rel: Eclipse, Transatlantic
    Jeanne Dore 1938 d: Mario Bonnard. lps: Emma Gramatica, Evi Maltagliati, Sergio Tofano. 88M ITL. prod/rel: Scalera Film

Mathilde Et Ses Mitaines, Novel
    Dernier Metro 1945 d: Maurice de Canonge. lps: Alexandre Rignault, Gaby Morlay, Fernand Fabre. 98M FRN. prod/rel: C.F.D.F.

Le Peintre Exigeant, Play
    Peintre Exigeant, Le 1929 d: Maurice Champreux, Robert Beaudoin. lps: Max Lerel, Derigal, Martell. 1100m FRN. prod/rel: Gaumont

Le Petit Cafe, Paris 1912, Play
    Petit Cafe, Le 1919 d: Max Linder, Raymond Bernard. lps: Max Linder, Jean Joffre, Wanda Lyon. 1800m FRN. prod/rel: Films Diamant
    Petit Cafe, Le 1931 d: Ludwig Berger. lps: Maurice Chevalier, Yvonne Valle, Tania Fedor. 83M USA. prod/rel: Films Paramount, Paramount Publix Corp.
    Playboy of Paris 1930 d: Ludwig Berger. lps: Maurice Chevalier, Frances Dee, O. P. Heggie. 6512f USA. prod/rel: Paramount-Publix Corp.

Que le Monde Est Petit!, Play
    Fortune, La 1931 d: Jean Hemard. lps: Claude Dauphin, Daniel Lecourtois, Jeanne Marny. 102M FRN. prod/rel: Felix Merio

Le Seul Bandit du Village, Play
  Seul Bandit du Village, Le 1931 d: Robert Bossis. lps: Georges Bever, Germaine Risse, Lise HestiA. SHT FRN. prod/rel: Paramount

Triplepatte, Play
  Triplepatte 1922 d: Raymond Bernard. lps: Henri Debain, Pierre Palau, Edith Jehanne. 1700m FRN. prod/rel: Societe Des Films Tristan Bernard

Le Voyage Imprevu, Novel
  Runaway Ladies 1935 d: Jean de Limur. lps: Betty Stockfeld, Hugh Wakefield, Edna Searle. 56M UKN. prod/rel: International Players, Exclusive
  Voyage Imprevu, Le 1934 d: Jean de Limur. lps: Roger Treville, Betty Stockfeld, Jean Tissier. 87M FRN/SWT. *Die Schule Der Liebe* prod/rel: Production Helgal

BERNARD, V.
Le Bapteme du Petit Oscar, Play
  Bapteme du Petit Oscar, Le 1932 d: Jean Dreville. lps: Rene Donnio, Charles Lorrain, A. Ternet. 1200m FRN.

BERNARDINI, ALBINO
Un Anno a Pietralata, Book
  Diario Di un Maestro 1973 d: Vittorio de SetA. lps: Bruno Cirino, Marisa Fabbri, Mico Cundari. MTV. 135M ITL. *Diary of a Schoolteacher; Diary of a Teacher* prod/rel: Miro Film, Rai Radiotelevisione Italiana

BERNARI, CARLO
Per Cause Imprecisate, Short Story
  Amore Amaro 1974 d: Florestano Vancini. lps: Lisa Gastoni, Leonard Mann, Rita Livesi. 110M ITL. *Bitter Love* prod/rel: Fral, Alpherat

BERNAUER, RUDOLF
Der Garten Eden, Berlin 1926, Play
  Garden of Eden, The 1928 d: Lewis Milestone. lps: Corinne Griffith, Louise Dresser, Lowell Sherman. 7300f USA. prod/rel: Feature Productions, United Artists

Konto X, Play
  Duchacek to Zaridi 1938 d: Carl Lamac. lps: Vlasta Burian, Ladislav Hemmer, Milada GampeovA. 2446m CZC. *Duchacek Will Fix It* prod/rel: Metropolitan

The Lilac Domino, Play
  Lilac Domino, The 1937 d: Friedrich Zelnik. lps: June Knight, Michael Bartlett, Athene Seyler. 79M UKN. prod/rel: Grafton-Capitol-Cecil, United Artists

Southern Roses, Play
  Southern Roses 1936 d: Friedrich Zelnik. lps: George Robey, Neil Hamilton, Gina Malo. 78M UKN. prod/rel: Grafton, General Film Distributors

Die Tolle Komtess, Opera
  Tolle Komtess, Die 1928 d: Richard Lowenbein. lps: Dina Gralla, Werner Fuetterer, Ralph Arthur Roberts. 2349m GRM. *The Crazy Countess* prod/rel: Richard Eichberg-Film

Das Zweite Leben, 1927, Play
  Once a Lady 1931 d: Guthrie McClintic. lps: Ruth Chatterton, Ivor Novello, Jill Esmond. 80M USA. prod/rel: Paramount Publix Corp.©
  Three Sinners 1928 d: Rowland V. Lee. lps: Pola Negri, Warner Baxter, Paul Lukas. 7092f USA. prod/rel: Paramount Famous Lasky Corp.

BERND, ART
Story
  Ruth 1983 d: Jerzy Hoffman. lps: Sharon Brauner, Anna Dymna, Gunter Lamprecht. 94M PLN/GRM. *Blutiger Schnee (Zu Freiwild Verdammt)* (GRM); *Wedle Wyrokow Twoich*; *Zu Freiwild Verdammt*; *After Your Decrees* prod/rel: C.C.C.-Filmkunst, S.F.B.

BERNDORFF, HANS RUDOLF
Das Schwarz-Weiss-Rote Himmelbett, Novel
  Schwarz-Weiss-Rote Himmelbett, Das 1962 d: Rolf Thiele. lps: Daliah Lavi, Martin Held, Thomas Fritsch. 100M GRM. *The Black, White and Red Fourposter; The Black, White and Red Wedding Bed* prod/rel: Franz Seitz, Schorcht

BERNEDE, ARTHUR
Chantecoq, Novel
  Chantecoq 1916 d: Henri Pouctal. lps: Pougaud, Gaston Michel, Edmee Pichard. FRN. *Coeur de Francaise* prod/rel: Film d'Art

Coeur de Francaise, Play
  Coeur de Francaise 1916 d: Gaston Leprieur. lps: Maxime Desjardins, Albert Dieudonne, Andree Pascal. FRN. prod/rel: Les Grands Films Lordier

La Loupiote, Novel
  Loupiote, La 1908-18. FRN.
  Loupiote, La 1922 d: Georges Hatot. lps: Regine Dumien, Lucien Dalsace, Jacques Normand. SRL. 6260m FRN.

Loupiote, La 1936 d: Jean Kemm, Jean-Louis Bouquet. lps: Pierre Larquey, Robert Pizani, Suzanne Rissler. 87M FRN. prod/rel: Films Artistiques Francais

Poker d'As, Novel
  Poker d'As 1928 d: Henri Desfontaines. lps: Rene Navarre, Suzanne Delmas, Simone Mareuil. SRL. 8EP FRN. prod/rel: Societe Des Cineromans

Sous l'Epaulette, Play
  Sous l'Epaulette 1908-18. lps: Leon Mathot, Louise Colliney. FRN.

Vidocq, Novel
  Vidocq 1923 d: Jean Kemm. lps: Rene Navarre, Elmire Vautier, Genica Missirio. SRL. 10EP FRN. prod/rel: Societe Des Cineromans

BERNERI, GIUSEPPE
Meo Patacca, Poem
  Meo Patacca 1972 d: Marcello Ciorciolini. lps: Luigi Proietti, Enzo Cerusico, Marilu Tolo. 124M ITL. prod/rel: Explorer Film '58, Euro International Film

BERNIER, ALFRED
Le Trait d'Union, Short Story
  Trait d'Union, Le 1910 d: Emile Chautard. lps: Karlmos, Suzanne Goldstein, Eugenie Nau. 225m FRN. prod/rel: Eclair, Acad

BERNSTEIN, CARL (1944–, USA
All the President's Men, 1974, Book
  All the President's Men 1976 d: Alan J. PakulA. lps: Robert Redford, Dustin Hoffman, Jack Warden. 138M USA. prod/rel: Warner Bros., Wildwood

BERNSTEIN, HENRI
Plays
  Traumende Mund, Der 1932 d: Paul Czinner. lps: Elisabeth Bergner, Rudolf Forster, Anton Edthofer. 86M GRM. *Dreaming Mouth* prod/rel: Matador, Pathe

L' Assaut, Play
  Assaut, L' 1936 d: Pierre-Jean Ducis. lps: Charles Vanel, Alice Field, Andre Alerme. 80M FRN. prod/rel: Henry Ullmann

Le Bonheur, Play
  Bonheur, Le 1935 d: Marcel L'Herbier. lps: Charles Boyer, Michel Simon, Gaby Morlay. 110M FRN. prod/rel: Pathe-Cinema

Le Detour, 1902, Play
  Via Piu Lunga, La 1918 d: Mario Caserini. lps: Maria Jacobini, Tullio Carminati, Andrea Habay. 1621m ITL. prod/rel: Tiber Film

L' Elevation, 1917, Play
  Elevazione 1920 d: Telemaco Ruggeri. lps: Linda Pini, Luigi Cimara, Cesare Carini. 1486m ITL. prod/rel: S.A. Ambrosio

La Griffe, Paris 1906, Play
  Washington Masquerade, The 1932 d: Charles J. Brabin. lps: Lionel Barrymore, Karen Morley, Nils Asther. 86M USA. *Mad Masquerade* (UKN); *Public Life; Washington Whirlpool; The Washington Show* prod/rel: Metro-Goldwyn-Mayer Corp., Metro-Goldwyn-Mayer Corp.©

Israel, 1908, Play
  Israel 1919 d: Andre Antoine. lps: Vittoria Lepanto, Alberto Collo, Vittorio Rossi Pianelli. 1525m ITL. prod/rel: Tiber Film

Jou-Jou, 1902, Play
  Jou-Jou 1916 d: Baldassarre Negroni. lps: Hesperia, Alberto Collo, Diana d'Amore. 2165m ITL. prod/rel: Tiber Film

Melo, Play
  Dreaming Lips 1935 d: Lee Garmes, Paul Czinner. lps: Elisabeth Bergner, Raymond Massey, Romney Brent. 94M UKN. prod/rel: Trafalgar, United Artists
  Melo 1932 d: Paul Czinner. lps: Pierre Blanchar, Gaby Morlay, Victor Francen. 95M FRN.
  Melo 1986 d: Alain Resnais. lps: Sabine Azema, Pierre Arditi, Andre Dussollier. 112M FRN. prod/rel: Mk2 Productions, Films a2
  Melodramma 1934 d: Robert Land, Giorgio C. Simonelli. lps: Elsa Merlini, Renato Cialente, Corrado RaccA. 65M ITL. prod/rel: S.a.P.F., Anonima Pittaluga
  Traumende Mund, Der 1953 d: Josef von Baky. lps: Maria Schell, O. W. Fischer, Frits Van Dongen. 90M GRM. *Dreaming Lips* (USA); *Dreaming Mouth* prod/rel: Fama, N.W.D.F.

Le Messager, Play
  Messager, Le 1937 d: Raymond Rouleau. lps: Jean Gabin, Jean-Pierre Aumont, Gaby Morlay. 98M FRN. prod/rel: Films Albatros

La Rafale, 1905, Play
  Rafale, La 1920 d: Jacques de Baroncelli. lps: Fannie Ward, Jean Joffre, Jean Dax. 1650m FRN. prod/rel: Film d'Art (Vandal Et Delac)

Raffiche 1920 d: Enrico RomA. lps: Tullio Carminati, Sigrid Lind, Vivina Ungari Schmitz. 1517m ITL. prod/rel: Carminati Film

Samson, New York 1908, Play
  Samson 1915 d: Edgar Lewis. lps: William Farnum, Maude Gilbert, Edgar L. Davenport. 5r USA. prod/rel: Box Office Attraction Co., William Fox©
  Samson 1936 d: Maurice Tourneur. lps: Harry Baur, Gaby Morlay, Gabrielle Dorziat. 88M FRN. prod/rel: Paris-Films-Production
  Sansone 1922 d: Torello Rolli. lps: Angelo Ferrari, Elena Sangro, Franco Gennaro. 1735m ITL. prod/rel: Caesar Film
  Shackles of Gold 1922 d: Herbert Brenon. lps: William Farnum, Al Loring, Marie Shotwell. 5957f USA. prod/rel: Fox Film Corp.

Le Venin, Play
  Orage 1937 d: Marc Allegret. lps: Charles Boyer, Jean-Louis Barrault, Michele Morgan. 98M FRN. *Le Venin* prod/rel: Andre Daven

Victor, Play
  Victor 1951 d: Claude Heymann. lps: Jean Gabin, Francoise Christophe, Jacques Castelot. 90M FRN. prod/rel: M.A.I.C.

Le Voleur, Paris 1907, Play
  Thief, The 1914 d: Edgar Lewis. lps: Dorothy Donnelly, Edgar L. Davenport, Iva Shepard. 5r USA. prod/rel: Box Office Attraction Co., Fox Film Corp.©
  Thief, The 1920 d: Charles Giblyn. lps: Pearl White, Charles Waldron, Wallace McCutcheon. 6r USA. prod/rel: Fox Film Corp., William Fox©
  Voleur, Le 1914 d: Adrien Caillard. lps: Paul Escoffier, Gaston Dubosc, Jeanne Provost. 1090m FRN. prod/rel: Scagl
  Voleur, Le 1933 d: Maurice Tourneur. lps: Victor Francen, Madeleine Renaud, Yolande Laffon. 60M FRN. prod/rel: Vandal Et Delac

BERNSTEIN, ISADORE
Tugboat Princess, Story
  Tugboat Princess 1936 d: David Selman. lps: Walter C. Kelly, Valerie Hobson, Edith Fellows. 68M CND. prod/rel: Central Films Ltd.

BERNSTEIN, LEONARD
On the Town, Musical Play
  On the Town 1949 d: Gene Kelly, Stanley Donen. lps: Gene Kelly, Frank Sinatra, Jules Munshin. 98M USA. prod/rel: MGM

West Side Story, New York 1957, Play
  West Side Story 1961 d: Robert Wise, Jerome Robbins. lps: Natalie Wood, Richard Beymer, Russ Tamblyn. 155M USA. prod/rel: Mirisch Pictures, Seven Arts Productions

BERNSTEIN, MOREY
The Search for Bridey Murphy, Book
  Search for Bridie Murphy, The 1956 d: Noel Langley. lps: Teresa Wright, Louis Hayward, Nancy Gates. 84M USA. prod/rel: Paramount

BERR DE TURIQUE, J.
Chateau Historique, Play
  Chateau Historique 1923 d: Henri Desfontaines. lps: Emile Drain, Eva Raynal, Pauline Carton. 1600m FRN. prod/rel: Gaumont
  Femmes Sont Folles, Les 1950 d: Gilles Grangier. lps: Raymond Rouleau, Noel Roquevert, Gaby SylviA. 90M FRN. prod/rel: Cinephonic, S.G.G.C.

La Route du Devoir, Novel
  Route de Devoir, La 1915 d: Georges MoncA. lps: Henry Mayer, Garay, Gabrielle Robinne. 1480m FRN. prod/rel: Scagl

BERR, GEORGES
Play
  Cross My Heart 1946 d: John Berry. lps: Betty Hutton, Sonny Tufts, Michael Chekhov. 83M USA. prod/rel: Paramount

Arlette Et Ses Papas, Play
  Arlette Et Ses Papas 1934 d: Henry Roussell. lps: Renee Saint-Cyr, Christiane Delyne, Jules Berry. 85M FRN. *Avril* prod/rel: Pathe-Nathan

Azais, Play
  Azais 1931 d: Rene Hervil. lps: Max Dearly, Simone Rouviere, Jeanne Saint-Bonnet. 102M FRN. prod/rel: Etablissements Jacques Haik

La Carotte, Play
  Carotte, La 1914. lps: Charles Lamy, Lucien Cazalis, Catherine Fonteney. 780m FRN. prod/rel: Scagl

Un Coup de Telephone, Play
  Coup de Telephone, Un 1931 d: Georges Lacombe. lps: Jean Weber, Colette Darfeuil, Jeanne Boitel. 88M FRN. prod/rel: Films Albatros

L' Ecole Des Contribuables, Play
Ecole Des Contribuables, L' 1934 d: Rene Guissart. lps: Armand Bernard, Paul Pauley, Mireille Perrey. 75M FRN. prod/rel: France Univers-Films

Un Jeune Homme Qui Se Tue, Play
Chourinette 1933 d: Andre Hugon. lps: Frederic Duvalles, Mireille, Yvonne Hebert. 95M FRN. *Un Jeune Homme Qui Se Tue* prod/rel: Hugon-Films, Gaumont-Franco-Film-Aubert

Ma Soeur Et Moi, Play
Caprice de Princesse 1933 d: Henri-Georges Clouzot, Karl Hartl. lps: Albert Prejean, Armand Bernard, Marie Bell. 85M FRN. prod/rel: U.F.a., a.C.E.
Meine Schwester Und Ich 1929 d: Manfred NoA. lps: Mady Christians, Jack Trevor, Igo Sym. 2475m GRM. *My Sister and I* prod/rel: National-Film Ag
Meine Schwester Und Ich 1954 d: Paul Martin. lps: Sonja Ziemann, Adrian Hoven, Herta Staal. 90M GRM. *My Sister and I* prod/rel: C.C.C., Gloria

Maitre Bolbec Et Son Mari, Play
Maitre Bolbec Et Son Mari 1934 d: Jacques Natanson. lps: Madeleine Soria, Lucien Baroux, Jean Debucourt. 80M FRN. prod/rel: Acta Film
World at Her Feet, The 1927 d: Luther Reed. lps: Florence Vidor, Lido Manetti, Margaret Quimby. 5691f USA. prod/rel: Paramount Famous Lasky Corp.

Le Million, Paris 1910, Play
Milione, Il 1920 d: Wladimiro Apolloni. lps: Elsa d'Auro, Fernando Ribacchi, Rinaldo Rinaldi. 1651m ITL. prod/rel: Celio Film
Million, Le 1931 d: Rene Clair. lps: Rene Lefevre, Annabella, Wanda Greville. 91M FRN. prod/rel: Societe Des Films Sonores Tobis
Million, The 1915 d: Thomas N. Heffron. lps: Edward Abeles, Ruby Hoffman, William Roselle. 4r USA. prod/rel: Famous Players Savage Co., Famous Players Film Co.

Mon Crime, Paris 1934, Play
True Confession 1937 d: Wesley Ruggles. lps: Carole Lombard, Fred MacMurray, John Barrymore. 85M USA. *Mon Crime* prod/rel: Paramount Pictures©

Parlez-Moi d'Amour, Play
Parlez-Moi d'Amour 1935 d: Rene Guissart. lps: Roger Treville, Paul Pauley, Germaine Aussey. 75M FRN. prod/rel: Flores-Films

Train to Venice, Play
My Life With Caroline 1941 d: Lewis Milestone. lps: Ronald Colman, Anna Lee, Charles Winninger. 81M USA. prod/rel: RKO Radio, United Producers

Le Train Pour Venise, Play
Train Pour Venise, Le 1938 d: Andre Berthomieu. lps: Victor Boucher, Huguette Duflos, Madeleine Suffel. F FRN. prod/rel: B.U.P.

BERRINI, NINO
I Tre Sentimentali, 1918, Play
Tre Sentimentali, I 1921 d: Augusto GeninA. lps: Lydia Quaranta, Angelo Ferrari, Carlo Tedeschi. 1791m ITL. prod/rel: U.C.I., Photodrama

BERROYER, JACKIE
Femme de Berroyer Est Plus Belle Que Toi - Connasse!, Novel
Tempete Dans un Verre d'Eau 1997 d: Arnold Barkus. lps: Jackie Berroyer, Arnold Barkus, Maria de Medeiros. 88M FRN/USA. *Tempest (in a Teapot)* (USA) prod/rel: Paris New York Prod., Double a Films

BERRY, DAVID
The Whales of August, Play
Whales of August, The 1987 d: Lindsay Anderson. lps: Bette Davis, Lillian Gish, Vincent Price. 91M USA. prod/rel: Circle, Nelson

BERSEZIO, VITTORIO
Le Miserie Di Monsu Travet, 1871, Play
Miserie Del Signor Travet, Le 1946 d: Mario Soldati. lps: Carlo Campanini, Gino Cervi, Vera Carmi. 100M ITL. *His Young Wife* (USA) prod/rel: Pan Film, Lux Film

BERSTEL, JULIUS
Calais-Douvres, Novel
Calais - Douvres 1931 d: Jean Boyer, Anatole Litvak. lps: Lilian Harvey, Andre Roanne, Armand Bernard. 87M FRN. prod/rel: U.F.a., a.C.E.

Nie Wieder Liebe, Play
Nie Wieder Liebe 1931 d: Anatole Litvak. lps: Lilian Harvey, Harry Liedtke, Felix Bressart. 88M GRM. *No More Love* (USA) prod/rel: UFA

BERTATI, GIOVANNI
Il Matrimonio Segreto, Opera
Matrimonio Segreto, Il 1943 d: Camillo Mastrocinque. lps: Laura Solari, Hilde Petri, Nerio Bernardi. UNF. ITL. prod/rel: Appia, S.a.F.a.

BERTAUT, SIMONE
Book
Piaf 1973 d: Guy Casaril. lps: Brigitte Ariel, Pascale Christophe, Guy Trejean. 104M FRN/USA. *Piaf - the Early Years* (USA); *The Sparrow of Pigalle*; *La Mome Piaf* prod/rel: Films Feuer Et Martin

BERTHOLD, WILL
Kriegsgericht, Munich 1959, Novel
Kriegsgericht 1959 d: Kurt Meisel. lps: Karlheinz Bohm, Christian Wolff, Klaus Kammer. 85M GRM. *Court Martial* (USA); *Military Court*

Munchner Illustrierten, Book
Spion Fur Deutschland 1956 d: Werner Klinger. lps: Martin Held, Nadja Tiller, Walter Giller. 110M GRM. *Spy for Germany* prod/rel: Berolina, D.F.H.

BERTO, GIUSEPPE
Il Brigante, 1951, Novel
Brigante, Il 1961 d: Renato Castellani. lps: Adelmo Di Fraia, Francesco Seminario, Serena Vergano. 143M ITL. *The Brigand* prod/rel: Cineriz

Il Cielo E Rosso, 1947, Novel
Cielo E Rosso, Il 1950 d: Claudio GorA. lps: Marina Berti, Jacques Sernas, Mischa Auer Jr. 95M ITL. *Le Ciel Est Rouge* (FRN) prod/rel: Acta Film

La Cosa Buffa, 1966, Novel
Cosa Buffa, La 1972 d: Aldo Lado. lps: Ottavia Piccolo, Gianni Morandi, Angela Goodwin. 108M ITL/FRN. prod/rel: Euro International Film (Roma), Carlton Filmexport (Paris)

Oh Serafina!, 1973, Novel
Oh, Serafina! 1976 d: Alberto LattuadA. lps: Renato Pozzetto, Dalila Di Lazzaro, Angelica IppolitA. 100M ITL. *O Serafina!* prod/rel: Rizzoli Film, Cineriz

La Ragazza Va in Calabria, Short Story
Togli le Gambe Dal Parabrezza 1969 d: Massimo FranciosA. lps: Alberto Lionello, Carole Andre, Leopoldo Trieste. 110M ITL. *Play Italy* prod/rel: Turis Film

BERTOLAZZI, CARLO
La Gibigianna, 1898, Play
Gibigianna, La 1919 d: Luigi Maggi. lps: Lucy Di San Germano, Sandro Ruffini, Maria Roasio. 1271m ITL. prod/rel: Ambrosio Film
Vanita 1947 d: Giorgio PastinA. lps: Liliana Laine, Walter Chiari, Ruggero Ruggeri. F ITL. *Vanity*; *La Gibigianna* prod/rel: Fauno Film, Generalcine

La Principessina, 1908
Amanda 1916 d: Giuseppe Sterni. lps: Lina Millefleurs, Esperia Sperani, Alfonso Trouche. 1320m ITL. prod/rel: Milano Film

BERTON, PIERRE
Zaza, Paris 1898, Play
Zaza 1910. lps: Lydia de Roberti. 232m ITL. prod/rel: Pasquali E C.
Zaza 1913 d: Adrien Caillard. lps: Georges Grand, Marie Ventura, Jules Mondos. 550m FRN. prod/rel: Scagl
Zaza 1915 d: Edwin S. Porter, Hugh Ford. lps: Pauline Frederick, Julian L'Estrange, Ruth Cummings. 5r USA. prod/rel: Famous Players Film Co., Charles Frohman Co.
Zaza 1923 d: Allan Dwan. lps: Gloria Swanson, H. B. Warner, Ferdinand Gottschalk. 7076f USA. prod/rel: Famous Players-Lasky, Paramount Pictures
Zaza 1938 d: George Cukor. lps: Claudette Colbert, Herbert Marshall, Bert Lahr. 87M USA. prod/rel: Paramount Pictures©
Zaza 1942 d: Renato Castellani. lps: Isa Miranda, Antonio Centa, Aldo Silvani. 88M ITL. prod/rel: Lux Film
Zaza 1955 d: Rene Gaveau. lps: Lilo, Maurice Teynac, Pauline Carton. 82M FRN. prod/rel: U.E.C., General Productions

BERTRAM, ARTHUR
The Wolf Wife, Play
Esther Redeemed 1915 d: Sidney Morgan. lps: Fanny Tittell-Brune, Julian Royce, Cecil Fletcher. 3000f UKN. prod/rel: Renaissance, Standard

BERTRAM, EWALD
Ultimatum, Novel
Ultimatum 1938 d: Robert Wiene, Robert Siodmak (Uncredited). lps: Erich von Stroheim, Abel Jacquin, Bernard Lancret. 83M FRN. prod/rel: Films Ultimatum

BERTUCH, MAX
Gluckliche Reise, Opera
Gluckliche Reise 1933 d: Alfred Abel. lps: Paul Henckels, Adele Sandrock, Magda Schneider. 78M GRM. *Happy Voyage*
Gluckliche Reise 1954 d: Thomas Engel. lps: Paul Hubschmid, Inge Egger, Paul Klinger. 87M GRM. *Happy Voyage* prod/rel: Capitol, Prisma

BESANT, SIR WALTER (1836–1901), UKN
All Sorts and Conditions of Men, Novel
All Sorts and Conditions of Men 1921 d: Georges Treville. lps: Renee Kelly, Rex Davis, James Lindsay. 4880f UKN. prod/rel: Ideal

Beyond the Dreams of Avarice, Novel
Beyond the Dreams of Avarice 1920 d: Thomas Bentley. lps: Henry Victor, Joyce Dearsley, Alban Atwood. 5900f UKN. prod/rel: Ideal

The Children of Gibeon, Novel
Children of Gibeon, The 1920 d: Sidney Morgan. lps: Joan Morgan, Langhorne Burton, Eileen Magrath. 5000f UKN. prod/rel: Progress, Butcher's Film Service

BESIER, RUDOLF
The Barretts of Wimpole Street, London 1930, Play
Barretts of Wimpole Street, The 1934 d: Sidney A. Franklin. lps: Norma Shearer, Fredric March, Charles Laughton. 111M USA. *A Forbidden Alliance* prod/rel: Metro-Goldwyn-Mayer Corp.
Barretts of Wimpole Street, The 1950 d: Donald Davis. lps: Helen Hayes, Robert Pastene. MTV. F USA.
Barretts of Wimpole Street, The 1953 d: Fielder Cook. lps: Valerie Cossart, Alexander Scourby. MTV. F USA.
Barretts of Wimpole Street, The 1955 d: James Sheldon. lps: Geraldine Fitzgerald, Robert Douglas. MTV. F USA.
Barretts of Wimpole Street, The 1956 d: Vincent J. Donehue. lps: Katharine Cornell, Anthony Quayle. MTV. F USA.
Barretts of Wimpole Street, The 1957 d: Sidney A. Franklin. lps: Jennifer Jones, John Gielgud, Bill Travers. 105M UKN/USA. prod/rel: Metro-Goldwyn-Mayer British

The Prude's Fall, London 1920, Play
Prude's Fall, The 1924 d: Graham Cutts. lps: Jane Novak, Julanne Johnson, Warwick Ward. 5675f UKN. prod/rel: Gainsborough, Woolf & Freedman

Secrets, London 1922, Play
Secrets 1924 d: Frank Borzage. lps: Norma Talmadge, Eugene O'Brien, Patterson Dial. 8363f USA. prod/rel: Joseph M. Schenck, Associated First National Pictures
Secrets 1933 d: Frank Borzage, Marshall Neilan (Uncredited). lps: Mary Pickford, Leslie Howard, C. Aubrey Smith. 85M USA. prod/rel: United Artists Corp., the Pickford Corp.©

BESNARD, LUCIEN
Dans l'Ombre du Harem, Play
Dans l'Ombre du Harem 1928 d: Leon Mathot. lps: Leon Mathot, Louise Lagrange, Jackie Monnier. F FRN. prod/rel: Paris International Film

BESSA-LUIS, AGUSTINA
Fanny Owen, 1979, Novel
Francisca 1981 d: Manoel de OliveirA. lps: Teresa Menezes, Diogo Doria, Mario Barroso. 166M PRT. *Francesca* prod/rel: V.O. Filmes

Vale Abraao, Novel
Vale Abraao 1993 d: Manoel de OliveirA. lps: Mario Barroso, Leonor Silveira, Cecile Sanz de AlbA. 189M PRT/FRN/SWT. *Abraham Valley* (UKN); *El Valle Abraham*; *Val Abraham* prod/rel: Artificial Eye, Mandragoa

BESSIE, ALVA
Bread and a Stone, Novel
Hard Traveling 1986 d: Dan Bessie. lps: J. E. Freeman, Ellen Geer, Barry Corbin. 107M USA. prod/rel: Shire

The Symbol, 1966, Novel
Sex Symbol, The 1974 d: David Lowell Rich. lps: Connie Stevens, Shelley Winters, Jack Carter. TVM. 110M USA. prod/rel: the Douglas Cramer Company, Columbia Pictures

BESSON, RENE
Vacances, Play
Vacances 1931 d: Robert Boudrioz. lps: Lucien Galas, Florelle, Georges CharliA. 82M FRN. prod/rel: Gaumont-Franco-Film-Aubert

BESTE, KONRAD
Das Vergnugliche Leben Der Doktorin Lohnefin, Short Story
Dieser Mann Gehort Mir 1950 d: Paul Verhoeven. lps: Winnie Markus, Heidemarie Hatheyer, Gustav Frohlich. 96M GRM. *This Man Belongs to Me* prod/rel: Junge Film-Union

BETAAB, NARAYAN PRASAD
Zehari Saap, Play
Zehari Saap 1933 d: J. J. Madan. lps: Patience Cooper, Kajjan, Sorabji KerawalA. 156M IND. *Poisonous Snake*; *Zahari Saap* prod/rel: Madan Theatres

BETHEA, JACK
Bed Rock, Boston 1924, Novel
  Coming Through 1925 d: A. Edward Sutherland. lps: Thomas Meighan, Lila Lee, John Miltern. 6522f USA. prod/rel: Famous Players-Lasky, Paramount Pictures
Honor Bound, Boston 1927, Novel
  Honor Bound 1928 d: Alfred E. Green. lps: George O'Brien, Estelle Taylor, Leila Hyams. 6188f USA. prod/rel: Fox Film Corp.

BETJEMAN, JOHN (1906–1984), UKN
Agricultural Caress, 1966, Poem
  Late Flowering 1981 d: Charles Wallace. 21M UKN.
Indoor Games Near Newbury, 1948, Verse
  Indoor Games Near Newbury 1976 d: Chris Clough. 5M UKN.
Myfanwy, 1940, Poems
  Late Flowering 1981 d: Charles Wallace. 21M UKN.
Subaltern's Love Song, 1940, Poem
  Late Flowering 1981 d: Charles Wallace. 21M UKN.

BETSCH, ROLAND
Narren Im Schnee, Novel
  Narren Im Schnee 1938 d: Hans Deppe. lps: Anny Ondra, Paul Klinger, Gisela Schluter. 80M GRM. prod/rel: Cinephon, Globus

BETTAUER, HUGO
La Rue Sans Joie, Novel
  Rue Sans Joie, La 1938 d: Andre Hugon. lps: Albert Prejean, Dita Parlo, Valery Inkijinoff. 87M FRN. prod/rel: Productions Andre Hugon

BETTI, UGO (1892–1953), ITL
Corruzione Al Palazzo Di Giustizia, Play
  Corruzione Al Palazzo Di Giustizia 1975 d: Marcello Aliprandi. lps: Franco Nero, Martin Balsam, Fernando Rey. 110M ITL. *Corruption in the Halls of Justice*; *Streets of Eternity* prod/rel: Filmes, Ital Noleggio Cin.Co
Delitto All'isola Della Capre, 1946, Play
  Possedees, Les 1955 d: Charles Brabant. lps: Raf Vallone, Madeleine Robinson, Magali Noel. 90M FRN/ITL. *L' Isola Delle Donne Sole* (ITL); *Passionate Summer* (USA); *The Possessed* prod/rel: Films Marceau, Laetitia
I Nostri Sogni, Play
  Nostri Sogni, I 1943 d: Vittorio Cottafavi. lps: Vittorio de Sica, Maria Mercader, Paolo StoppA. 83M ITL. prod/rel: Iris Film, E.N.I.C.

BEUCLER, ANDRE
Gueule d'Amour, Novel
  Gueule d'Amour 1937 d: Jean Gremillon. lps: Jean Gabin, Mireille Balin, Rene Lefevre. 90M FRN. prod/rel: U.F.a., a.C.E.

BEVAN, A. C.
The Story of Zarak Khan, Book
  Zarak 1957 d: Terence Young, Yakima Canutt. lps: Victor Mature, Michael Wilding, Anita Ekberg. 95M UKN. prod/rel: Columbia, Warwick

BEVAN, DONALD
Stalag 17, New York 1951, Play
  Stalag 17 1953 d: Billy Wilder. lps: William Holden, Don Taylor, Otto Preminger. 120M USA. prod/rel: Paramount

BEVILACQUA, ALBERTO
Short Story
  Tutto Suo Padre 1978 d: Maurizio Lucidi. lps: Enrico Montesano, Marilu Prati, Cristiano Censi. 88M ITL. prod/rel: Variety Film
Attenti Al Buffone, Novel
  Attenti Al Buffone 1975 d: Alberto BevilacquA. lps: Mariangela Melato, Nino Manfredi, Eli Wallach. 110M ITL. *The Female Is the Deadliest of the Species*; *Eye of the Cat* prod/rel: Medusa Distribuzione
La Califfa, Novel
  Califfa, La 1970 d: Alberto BevilacquA. lps: Ugo Tognazzi, Romy Schneider, Marina Berti. 99M ITL/FRN. *The Lady Caliph* prod/rel: Fair Film (Roma), Les Films Corona (Paris)

BEYERLEIN
Le Retraite, Play
  Retraite, La 1910 d: Andre Calmettes, Henri Pouctal. lps: Roger Monteaux, Roger Vincent, Marthe Mellot. FRN. prod/rel: Film d'Art
Suona la Ritirata, Novel
  Silenzio, Il 1921 d: Luciano DoriA. lps: Cecyl Tryan, Alberto Collo, Carlo Benetti. 1653m ITL. prod/rel: Fert

BEYERLEIN, FRANZ ADAM
Der Zapfenstreich, Play
  Grosse Zapfenstreich, Der 1952 d: Georg Hurdalek. lps: Johanna Matz, Jan Hendriks, Friedrich Domin. 100M GRM. *Last Taps* prod/rel: Comc, Danubia

BEZBARUAH, LAKHINDRANATH
Joymati Kunwari, Play
  Joymati 1935 d: Jyoti Prasad Agarwal. lps: Phani Sarma, Phanu Barua, Asaideo Handige. 4267m IND. prod/rel: Chitralekha Movietone

BEZZERIDES, ALBERT ISAAC
Long Haul, New York 1938, Novel
  They Drive By Night 1940 d: Raoul Walsh. lps: George Raft, Ann Sheridan, Ida Lupino. 93M USA. *The Road to 'Frisco* (UKN) prod/rel: Warner Bros. Pictures©
Thieves' Market, Novel
  Thieves' Highway 1949 d: Jules Dassin. lps: Richard Conte, Valentina Cortese, Lee J. Cobb. 94M USA. *Collision*; *Hard Bargain*; *Thieves' Market* prod/rel: 20th Century Fox

BHANDARI, MANU
Yeh Sach Hai, Short Story
  Rajanigandha 1974 d: Basu Chatterjee. lps: Amol Palekar, Vidya Sinha, Dinesh Thakur. 110M IND. *Tuberoses*; *Rajnigandha*; *Tube Rose* prod/rel: Devki Chitra

BHARATI, DHARAMVIR
Suraj Ka Satwan Ghoda, Novel
  Suraj Ka Satwan Ghoda 1992 d: Shyam Benegal. lps: Amrish Puri, Neena Gupta, K. K. RainA. 130M IND. *Seventh Horse of the Sun's Chariot*; *Suraj Ka Satva Ghoda*; *The Seventh Horse of the Sun* prod/rel: Nfdc

BHATTACHARYA, BIJON
Jabanbandi, Play
  Dharti Ke Lal 1946 d: Khwaya Ahmad Abbas. lps: Sombhu Mitra, Balraj Sahni, Usha DuttA. 125M IND. *Children of the Earth* prod/rel: Ipta
Nabanna, Play
  Dharti Ke Lal 1946 d: Khwaya Ahmad Abbas. lps: Sombhu Mitra, Balraj Sahni, Usha DuttA. 125M IND. *Children of the Earth* prod/rel: Ipta

BIALK, ELISA
The Sainted Sisters of Sandy Creek, Story
  Sainted Sisters, The 1948 d: William D. Russell. lps: Veronica Lake, Joan Caulfield, Barry Fitzgerald. 89M USA. prod/rel: Paramount

BIANCIARDI, LUCIANO
Il Complesso Di Loth, Novel
  Merlo Maschio, Il 1971 d: Pasquale Festa Campanile. lps: Laura Antonelli, Lando Buzzanca, Lino Toffolo. 113M ITL. prod/rel: Clesi Cin.Ca, Euro International Film
La Vita Agra, Novel
  Vita Agra, La 1964 d: Carlo Lizzani. lps: Ugo Tognazzi, Giovanna Ralli, Rossana Martini. 120M ITL. *Bitter Life* prod/rel: Film Napoleon (Roma), Euro International Film

BIANCOLI, ORESTE
Alla Moda!, Play
  Frenesia 1939 d: Mario Bonnard. lps: Dina Galli, Antonio Gandusio, Betty Stockfeld. 85M ITL. *Frenzy* prod/rel: E.I.a., Amato

BIBIYAN, SIMON
Terror in Beverly Hills, Novel
  Terror in Beverly Hills 1988 d: John Myhers. lps: Frank Stallone, Behruz Vosughi, Cameron Mitchell. 89M USA. prod/rel: Peacock Films

BICKERTON, DEREK
Payroll, London 1959, Novel
  Payroll 1961 d: Sidney Hayers. lps: Michael Craig, Francoise Prevost, Billie Whitelaw. 105M UKN. *I Promise to Pay* prod/rel: Lynx Films, Independent Artists

BICKHAM, JACK
Baker's Hawk, Novel
  Baker's Hawk 1976 d: Lyman D. Dayton. lps: Clint Walker, Burl Ives, Diane Baker. 105M USA. prod/rel: Doty-Dayton

BICKHAM, JAMES M.
The Apple Dumpling Gang, Novel
  Apple Dumpling Gang, The 1975 d: Norman Tokar. lps: Bill Bixby, Susan Clark, Don Knotts. 100M USA. prod/rel: Buena Vista, Walt Disney

BIDDLE, FRANCIS
Mr. Justice Holmes, Book
  Magnificent Yankee, The 1950 d: John Sturges. lps: Louis Calhern, Ann Harding, Eduard Franz. 88M USA. *The Man With Thirty Sons* (UKN) prod/rel: MGM

BIDERMAN, ANN
Story
  American Dreamer 1984 d: Rick Rosenthal. lps: Jobeth Williams, Tom Conti, Giancarlo Giannini. 105M USA. prod/rel: Warner Bros., CBS Theatrical Films

BIELEN, OTTO
Kleines Bezirksgericht, Play
  Kleines Bezirksgericht 1938 d: Alwin Elling. lps: Hans Moser, Ida Wust, Gusti Wolf. 107M GRM. prod/rel: Astra

BIELER, MANFRED
Madchenkrieg, 1975, Novel
  Madchenkrieg, Der 1977 d: Bernhard Sinkel, Alf Brustellin. lps: Hans Christian Blech, Adelheid Arndt, Antonia Reininghaus. 143M GRM. *Girl's War*; *The Three Sisters*; *Girls at War*; *The Girls' War* prod/rel: Independent, a.B.S.
Maria Morzeck Oder Das Kaninchen Bin Ich, 1965, Novel
  Kaninchen Bin Ich, Das 1965 d: Kurt Maetzig. lps: Angelika Waller, Alfred Muller, Irma Munch. 110M GDR. *The Rabbit Is Me* prod/rel: Defa-Studio Fur Spielfilme, Arbeitsgruppe Roter Kreis
  Maria Morzek 1976 d: Horst Flick. 92M GRM.

BIENEK, HORST
Die Erste Polka, 1975, Novel
  Erste Polka, Die 1978 d: Klaus Emmerich. lps: Maria Schell, Erland Josephson, Guido Wieland. 105M GRM. *The First Polka* prod/rel: N.D.F., Bavaria
Schloss Konigswald, Novel
  Schloss Konigswald 1987 d: Peter Schamoni. lps: Camilla Horn, Carola Hohn, Marianne Hoppe. 89M GRM. *Die Letzte Geschichte von Schloss Konigswald*; *Last Tale of Konigswald Castle* prod/rel: Peter Schamoni Prod., Allianz
Die Zelle, 1968, Novel
  Zelle, Die 1971 d: Horst Bienek. lps: Robert Naegele, Helmut Pick, Wolf Martienzen. 87M GRM. *The Cell* prod/rel: Syrinx

BIERCE, AMBROSE (1842–1914?), USA
Short Story
  Oiseau Moqueur, L' 1962 d: Robert Enrico. lps: Stephane Fey, Francois Frankiel, Eric Frankiel. 40M FRN. prod/rel: Filmartic, Les Films Du Centaure
Boarded Window, 1891, Short Story
  Boarded Window 1973 d: Alan Beattie. 17M USA.
George Thurston, 1891, Short Story
  Amerikai Anziksz 1976 d: Gabor Body. lps: Gyorgy Cserhalmi. 104M HNG. *American Torso*; *Amerikai Anzix*; *A View of America*
The Man and the Snake, 1891, Short Story
  Man and the Snake, The 1972 d: Sture Rydman. lps: John Fraser, Andre Morell, Clive Morton. 26M UKN.
Mockingbird, 1891, Short Story
  Au Coeur de la Vie 1968 d: Robert Enrico. lps: Stephane Fey, Francois Frankiel, Eric Frankiel. 95M FRN. prod/rel: Franco-London Films, Sinfonia Films
Occurrence at Owl Creek Bridge, 1891, Short Story
  Au Coeur de la Vie 1968 d: Robert Enrico. lps: Stephane Fey, Francois Frankiel, Eric Frankiel. 95M FRN. prod/rel: Franco-London Films, Sinfonia Films
Parker Adderson, Philosopher, 1891, Short Story
  Parker Adderson, Philosopher 1977 d: Arthur Barron. lps: Harris Yulin, Douglas Watson. MTV. 37M USA. prod/rel: Learning in Focus

BIERNATH, HORST
Vater Sein Dagegen Sehr, Novel
  Vater Sein Dagegen Sehr 1957 d: Kurt Meisel. lps: Heinz Ruhmann, Marianne Koch, Hans Leibelt. 95M GRM. *It's Hard to Be a Father* prod/rel: Berolina, D.F.H.

BIGGERS, EARL DERR (1884–1933), USA
The Agony Column, Indianapolis 1916, Novel
  Blind Adventure, The 1918 d: Wesley Ruggles. lps: Edward Earle, Betty Howe, Frank Norcross. 5r USA. *The Agony Column* prod/rel: Vitagraph Co. of America©, Blue Ribbon Feature
  Passage from Hong Kong 1941 d: D. Ross Lederman. lps: Douglas Kennedy, Lucille Fairbanks, Richard Ainley. 61M USA. prod/rel: Warner Bros.
  Second Floor Mystery, The 1930 d: Roy Del Ruth. lps: Grant Withers, Loretta Young, H. B. Warner. 5628f USA. *The Second Story Mystery*; *The Second Story Murder* prod/rel: Warner Brothers Pictures
Behind That Curtain, Indianapolis 1928, Novel
  Behind That Curtain 1929 d: Irving Cummings. lps: Warner Baxter, Lois Moran, Gilbert Emery. 8320f USA. prod/rel: Fox Film Corp.
  Charlie Chan's Chance 1932 d: John G. Blystone. lps: Warner Oland, Alexander Kirkland, H. B. Warner. 73M USA. prod/rel: Fox Film Corp.
The Black Camel, Indianapolis 1929, Novel
  Black Camel, The 1931 d: Hamilton MacFadden. lps: Warner Oland, Sally Eilers, Bela Lugosi. 71M USA. prod/rel: Fox Film Corp.

Broadway Broke, 1922, Short Story
Broadway Broke 1923 d: J. Searle Dawley. lps: Mary Carr, Percy Marmont, Gladys Leslie. 5923f USA. prod/rel: Murray W. Garsson Productions, Selznick Distributing Corp.

Charlie Chan Carries on, Indianapolis 1930, Novel
Charlie Chan Carries on 1931 d: Hamilton MacFadden. lps: Warner Oland, John Garrick, Marguerite Churchill. 69M USA. prod/rel: Fox Film Corp.

Charlie Chan's Murder Cruise 1940 d: Eugene J. Forde. lps: Sidney Toler, Marjorie Weaver, Lionel Atwill. 75M USA. *Charlie Chan's Oriental Cruise*; *Charlie Chan's Cruise*; *Chan's Cruise*; *Chan's Murder Cruise* prod/rel: 20th Century-Fox Film Corp.

Eran Trece 1932 d: David Howard. lps: Manuel Arbo, Juan Torena, Ana Maria Custodio. 9r USA. prod/rel: Fox Film Corp.

The Chinese Parrot, Indianapolis 1926, Novel
Chinese Parrot, The 1927 d: Paul Leni. lps: Marian Nixon, Florence Turner, Hobart Bosworth. 7304f USA. prod/rel: Universal Pictures

The Deuce of Hearts, Short Story
Take the Stand 1934 d: Phil Rosen. lps: Jack La Rue, Thelma Todd, Russell Hopton. 78M USA. *The Great Radio Mystery* (UKN) prod/rel: Liberty Pictures Corp.©

Each According to His Gifts, Short Story
Gown of Destiny, The 1918 d: Lynn Reynolds. lps: Herrera Tejedde, Alma Rubens, Allan Sears. 5r USA. prod/rel: Triangle Film Corp., Triangle Distributing Corp.

Fifty Candles, Indianapolis 1926, Novel
Fifty Candles 1921 d: Irvin V. Willat. lps: Bertram Grassby, Marjorie Daw, Ruth King. 5r USA. prod/rel: Willat Productions, W. W. Hodkinson Corp.

The Girl Who Paid Dividends, 1921, Short Story
Her Face Value 1921 d: Thomas N. Heffron. lps: Wanda Hawley, Lincoln Plummer, Dick Rosson. 4718f USA. prod/rel: Realart Pictures, Paramount Pictures

Honeymoon Flats, 1927, Short Story
Honeymoon Flats 1928 d: Millard Webb. lps: George Lewis, Dorothy Gulliver, Kathlyn Williams. 6057f USA. prod/rel: Universal Pictures

The House Without a Key, Indianapolis 1925, Novel
Charlie Chan's Greatest Case 1933 d: Hamilton MacFadden. lps: Warner Oland, Heather Angel, John Warburton. 70M USA. prod/rel: Fox Film Corp.

Idle Hands, 1921, Short Story
Millionaire, The 1931 d: John G. Adolfi. lps: George Arliss, Evalyn Knapp, David Manners. 82M USA. *The Ruling Passion* prod/rel: Warner Bros. Pictures©

That Way With Women 1947 d: Frederick de CordovA. lps: Sydney Greenstreet, Dane Clark, Martha Vickers. 84M USA. *A Very Rich Man* prod/rel: Warner Bros.

Inside the Lines, New York 1915, Play
Inside the Lines 1918 d: David M. Hartford. lps: Lewis Stone, Marguerite Clayton, Carl Herlinger. 6r USA. prod/rel: Delcah Photoplays, Inc., Pyramid Film Corp.

Inside the Lines 1930 d: Roy J. Pomeroy. lps: Betty Compson, Ralph Forbes, Montagu Love. 76M USA. prod/rel: RKO Productions

John Henry and the Restless Sex, 1921, Short Story
Too Much Business 1922 d: Jess Robbins. lps: Edward Everett Horton, Ethel Grey Terry, Tully Marshall. 6100f USA. prod/rel: Vitagraph Co. of America

Love Insurance, Indianapolis 1914, Novel
Love Insurance 1920 d: Donald Crisp. lps: Bryant Washburn, Lois Wilson, Theodore Roberts. 5r USA. prod/rel: Famous Players-Lasky Corp.©, Paramount Pictures

One Night in the Tropics 1940 d: A. Edward Sutherland. lps: Allan Jones, Nancy Kelly, Bud Abbott. 92M USA. *Caribbean Holiday*; *Moonlight in the Tropics* prod/rel: Universal Pictures Co.©

Reckless Age, The 1924 d: Harry Pollard. lps: Reginald Denny, Ruth Dwyer, John Steppling. 6954f USA. prod/rel: Universal Pictures

BIGGERS, EARL DERR
The Man Upstairs, Indianapolis 1916, Novel
Man Upstairs, The 1926 d: Roy Del Ruth. lps: Monte Blue, Dorothy Devore, Helen Dunbar. 7r USA. prod/rel: Warner Brothers Pictures

BIGGERS, EARL DERR (1884–1933), USA
The Ruling Passion, 1922, Short Story
Ruling Passion, The 1922 d: F. Harmon Weight. lps: George Arliss, Doris Kenyon, Edmund Burns. 7000f USA. prod/rel: Distinctive Productions, United Artists

Seven Keys to Baldpate, Indianapolis 1913, Novel
House of the Long Shadows 1983 d: Pete Walker. lps: Vincent Price, Christopher Lee, Peter Cushing. 101M UKN. *House of Long Shadows* prod/rel: Cannon

Seven Keys to Baldpate 1917 d: Hugh Ford. lps: George M. Cohan, Anna Q. Nilsson, Hedda Hopper. 5r USA. prod/rel: Artcraft Pictures Corp.©, Cohan Feature Film Corp.

Seven Keys to Baldpate 1925 d: Fred Newmeyer. lps: Douglas MacLean, Edith Roberts, Anders Randolf. 6648f USA. prod/rel: Famous Players-Lasky, Paramount Pictures

Seven Keys to Baldpate 1929 d: Reginald Barker. lps: Richard Dix, Miriam Seegar, Crauford Kent. 6742f USA. prod/rel: RKO Productions

Seven Keys to Baldpate 1935 d: William Hamilton, Edward Killy. lps: Gene Raymond, Mary Callahan, Eric Blore. 80M USA. prod/rel: RKO Radio Pictures©

Seven Keys to Baldpate 1947 d: Lew Landers. lps: Jimmy Conlin, Tony Barrett, Tom Keene. 66M USA. prod/rel: RKO Radio Pictures

Trouping With Ellen, 1922, Short Story
Trouping With Ellen 1924 d: T. Hayes Hunter. lps: Helene Chadwick, Mary Thurman, Gaston Glass. 6452f USA. *Pity the Chorus Girl* prod/rel: Eastern Productions, Producers Distributing Corp.

BIGIARETTI, LIBERO
La Controfigura, Novel
Controfigura, La 1971 d: Romolo Guerrieri. lps: Jean Sorel, Ewa Aulin, Lucia Bose. 94M ITL. prod/rel: Claudia Cin.Ca, C.I.D.I.F.

BILHAUD, PAUL
Le Paradis, Play
Belle de Montparnasse, La 1937 d: Maurice Cammage. lps: Jeanne Aubert, Colette Darfeuil, Frederic Duvalles. 87M FRN. prod/rel: Cinereve

Paradis, Le 1914 d: Gaston Leprieur. lps: Raoul Villot, Charles Reschal, Pierre Etchepare. FRN. prod/rel: Grands Films Populaires, G. Lordier

Le Pillole Di Ercole, Play
Pillole Di Ercole, Le 1960 d: Luciano Salce. lps: Nino Manfredi, Sylva Koscina, Vittorio de SicA. 85M ITL. *Hercules' Pills*; *Le Pillole d'Ercole* prod/rel: Dino de Laurentiis Cin.Ca, Maxima Film

BILHAUD, PIERRE
La Gueule du Loup, 1904, Play
Gola Del Lupo, La 1923 d: Torello Rolli. lps: Camillo de Riso, Francesco Amodio, Fernanda Negri-Pouget. 1336m ITL. prod/rel: Caesar Film

BILIANOVA, POPELKA
Do Panskeho Stavu, Novel
Do Panskeho Stavu 1925 d: Karl Anton. lps: Antonie Nedosinska, Karel Noll, Jarmila VackovA. 2972m CZC. *Becoming Middle-Class*; *To the Lord's Estate*; *Matka Kracmerka I.*; *Into the Genteel State of Life*; *Mother Kracmerka I, The* prod/rel: Karel Spelina, Chicago

Matka Kracmerka 1934 d: Vladimir Slavinsky. lps: Antonie Nedosinska, Theodor Pistek, Hana VitovA. 3096m CZC. *Mother Kracmerka* prod/rel: Osvald Kosek, Julius Schmitt

V Panskem Stavu, Novel
Matka Kracmerka 1934 d: Vladimir Slavinsky. lps: Antonie Nedosinska, Theodor Pistek, Hana VitovA. 3096m CZC. *Mother Kracmerka* prod/rel: Osvald Kosek, Julius Schmitt

V Panskem Stavu 1927 d: Vaclav Kubasek. lps: Karel Noll, Antonie Nedosinska, Karel Lamac. 1270m CZC. *A Lordly Estate*; *Matka Kracmerka II*; *Mother Kracmerka II* prod/rel: Vaclav Bayer, Bavafilm

BILLETDOUX, RAPHAELLE
Mes Nuits Sont Plus Belles Que Vos Jours, Novel
Mes Nuits Sont Plus Belles Que Vos Jours 1988 d: Andrzej Zulawski. lps: Sophie Marceau, Jacques Dutronc, Valerie Lagrange. 89M FRN. *My Nights are More Beautiful Than Your Days* prod/rel: Sara

BILLINGER, RICHARD
Gabriele Dambrone, Play
Gabriele Dambrone 1943 d: Hans Steinhoff. lps: Gusti Huber, Siegfried Breuer, Ewald Balser. 101M GRM. prod/rel: Terra, Gloria

Der Gigant, Play
Goldene Stadt, Die 1942 d: Veit Harlan. lps: Kristina Soderbaum, Rudolf Prack, Paul Klinger. 109M GRM. prod/rel: UFA, Turck

Wen Die Gotter Lieben, Novel
Wen Die Gotter Lieben 1942 d: Karl Hartl. lps: Hans Holt, Irene von Meyendorff, Winnie Markus. 112M GRM. *The Mozart Story* (USA); *Mozart* prod/rel: Wien-Film

BINCHY, MAEVE (1940–, IRL
Circle of Friends, Novel
Circle of Friends 1994 d: Pat O'Connor. lps: Chris O'Donnell, Minnie Driver, Geraldine O'Rawe. 102M IRL/USA. prod/rel: Rank, Price

BINDING, RUDOLF GEORG
Moselfahrt Aus Liebeskummer, 1932, Short Story
Moselfahrt Aus Liebeskummer 1953 d: Kurt Hoffmann. lps: Lisabeth Muller, Will Quadflieg, Renate Mannhardt. 90M GRM. *Lovesick on the Moselle* prod/rel: Ariston, Columbia

Der Opfergang, 1911, Short Story
Opfergang 1944 d: Veit Harlan. lps: Carl Raddatz, Kristina Soderbaum, Irene von Meyendorff. 95M GRM. *The Great Sacrifice* (UKN) prod/rel: UFA, N.W.D.F.

BINGHAM, JOHN (1911–, UKN
Fragment of Fear, Novel
Fragment of Fear 1970 d: Richard C. Sarafian. lps: David Hemmings, Gayle Hunnicutt, Flora Robson. 95M UKN. prod/rel: Columbia British, Columbia

BIOY CASARES, ADOLFO (1914–1984), ARG
Novel
Sueno de Los Heroes, El 1997 d: Sergio Renan. F ARG. *The Dream of Heroes*

La Invencion Di Morel, 1940, Novel
Invenzione Di Morel, L' 1974 d: Emidio Greco. lps: Giulio Brogi, Anna Karina, John Steiner. 110M ITL. *Morel's Invention* prod/rel: Alga Cin.Ca, Mount Street Film

Otra Esperanza, 1978, Short Story
Otra Esperanza 1991 d: Mercedes Frutos. 90M ARG.

El Perjurio de la Nieve, 1945, Novel
Crimen de Oribe, El 1950 d: Leopoldo Torre-Nilsson, Leopoldo Torres-Rios. lps: Roberto Escalada, Carlos Thomson, Raul de Lange. 85M ARG. *Oribe's Crime*

BIRABEAU, ANDRE
La Chaleur du Sein, Play
Chaleur du Sein, La 1938 d: Jean Boyer. lps: Arletty, Gabrielle Dorziat, Jeanne Lion. 85M FRN. prod/rel: Heraut Films

C.H.F.R. 35, Short Story
A Vos Ordres, Madame 1942 d: Jean Boyer. lps: Jean Tissier, Suzanne Dehelly, Jacqueline Gauthier. 91M FRN. prod/rel: Pathe-Cinema

Cote d'Azur, Play
Cote d'Azur 1931 d: Roger Capellani. lps: Robert Burnier, Simone Heliard, Yvonne Hebert. 80M FRN. prod/rel: Films Paramount

Un Dejeuner de Soleil, Play
Ai Vostri Ordini, Signora! 1939 d: Mario Mattoli. lps: Elsa Merlini, Vittorio de Sica, Giuditta Rissone. 70M ITL. *Madame at Your Orders* (USA); *Orgia Di Sole*; *Al Vostri Ordina Signora!*; *Giochi Di Societa* prod/rel: Aurora-Fona Roma, I.C.I.

Dejeuner de Soleil, Un 1937 d: Marcel Cravenne. lps: Jules Berry, Gaby Morlay, Jacques Baumer. 100M FRN. prod/rel: Societe Des Films Roger Richebe

La Femme Fatale, Play
Femme Fatale, La 1945 d: Jean Boyer. lps: Gaby Sylvia, Pierre Brasseur, Jacques Louvigny. 95M FRN. prod/rel: Metzger Et Woog

Le Fille Et le Garcon, Play
Fille Et le Garcon, La 1931 d: Wilhelm Thiele, Roger Le Bon. lps: Lilian Harvey, Henri Garat, Lucien Baroux. 85M FRN. *The Girl and the Boy* prod/rel: U.F.a., a.C.E.

Fiori d'Arancio, Play
Fiori d'Arancio 1945 d: Dino Hobbes Cecchini. lps: Toti Dal Monte, Laura Carli, Luigi Tosi. F ITL. prod/rel: Scalera Film

La Fleur d'Oranger, Play
Fleur d'Oranger, La 1932 d: Henry Roussell. lps: Andre Lefaur, Simone Deguyse, Helene Robert. 87M FRN. prod/rel: Pathe-Natan

On a Trouve une Femme Nue, Play
On a Trouve une Femme Nue 1934 d: Leo Joannon. lps: Jean Aquistapace, Mireille Balin, Jeanne Loury. 90M FRN. *On a Perdu une Femme Nue* prod/rel: Metropa Films

Votre Sourire, Play
Votre Sourire 1934 d: Pierre Caron, Monty Banks. lps: Victor Boucher, Marie Glory, Renee Devilder. 85M FRN. prod/rel: Compagnie Francaise Cinematographique

Le Voyage a l'Ombre, Play
Voyage d'Agrement 1935 d: Christian-Jaque. lps: Felicien Tramel, Yvonne Garat, Nane Germon. 80M FRN. prod/rel: Amax-Films

BIRD, CAROL
Missing Men, New York 1932, Book
Bureau of Missing Persons 1933 d: Roy Del Ruth. lps: Bette Davis, Lewis Stone, Pat O'Brien. 78M USA. *Missing Persons* prod/rel: First National Pictures, Inc.

BIRD, SARAH
The Boyfriend School, Novel
Don't Tell Her It's Me 1990 d: Malcolm Mowbray. lps: Steve Guttenberg, Jami Gertz, Shelley Long. 102M USA. *The Boyfriend School; The Two of Gus* prod/rel: Sovereign Pictures

BIRD, T. H.
Gamblers Sometimes Win, Novel
March Hare, The 1956 d: George M. O'Ferrall. lps: Peggy Cummins, Terence Morgan, Wilfrid Hyde-White. 85M UKN. prod/rel: Achilles, British Lion

BIRDWELL, RUSSELL G.
Jim Thorpe - All American, Autobiography
Jim Thorpe - All American 1951 d: Michael Curtiz. lps: Burt Lancaster, Charles Bickford, Steve Cochran. 107M USA. *Man of Bronze* (UKN) prod/rel: Warner Bros.

BIRMINGHAM, GEORGE A.
General John Regan, London 1913, Play
General John Regan 1921 d: Harold Shaw. lps: Milton Rosmer, Madge Stuart, Edward O'Neill. 6300f UKN. prod/rel: Stoll

General John Regan 1933 d: Henry Edwards. lps: Henry Edwards, Chrissie White, Ben Welden. 74M UKN. prod/rel: British and Dominions, United Artists

BIRNEY, HOFFMAN
The Dice of God, New York 1956, Novel
Glory Guys, The 1965 d: Arnold Laven. lps: Andrew Duggan, Tom Tryon, Harve Presnell. 112M USA. prod/rel: Bristol Pictures

BIRO, LAJOS
A Carno Szinmu: Harom Felvonasban, Budapest 1913, Play
Forbidden Paradise 1924 d: Ernst Lubitsch. lps: Pola Negri, Rod La Rocque, Adolphe Menjou. 7543f USA. prod/rel: Famous Players-Lasky, Paramount Pictures
Royal Scandal, A 1945 d: Otto Preminger, Ernst Lubitsch. lps: Tallulah Bankhead, William Eythe, Anne Baxter. 94M USA. *Czarina* (UKN) prod/rel: 20th Century-Fox

The Czarina, Play
Catherine the Great 1934 d: Paul Czinner. lps: Elisabeth Bergner, Douglas Fairbanks Jr., Flora Robson. 96M UKN. *The Rise of Catherine the Great* prod/rel: United Artists, London Films

Der Legioner, Play
Silent Lover, The 1926 d: George Archainbaud. lps: Milton Sills, Natalie Kingston, William Humphrey. 6500f USA. *Men of the Dawn* prod/rel: First National Pictures

The Moon-Flower, New York 1924, Play
Eve's Secret 1925 d: Clarence Badger. lps: Betty Compson, Jack Holt, William Collier Jr. 6305f USA. prod/rel: Ffamous Players-Lasky, Paramount Pictures

A Rabolovag, Budapest 1912, Novel
Heart Thief, The 1927 d: Nils Chrisander. lps: Joseph Schildkraut, Lya de Putti, Robert Edeson. 6035f USA. prod/rel: Metropolitan Pictures Corp. of Calif., Producers Distributing Corp.

Szinmu Negy Felvonasban, Budapest 1917, Play
Five Graves to Cairo 1943 d: Billy Wilder. lps: Franchot Tone, Anne Baxter, Akim Tamiroff. 96M USA. prod/rel: Paramount

Hotel Imperial 1927 d: Mauritz Stiller. lps: Pola Negri, James Hall, George Siegmann. 7091f USA. prod/rel: Famous Players-Lasky, Paramount Pictures

Hotel Imperial 1939 d: Robert Florey. lps: Isa Miranda, Ray Milland, Reginald Owen. 78M USA. *Invitation to Happiness; I Loved a Soldier* prod/rel: Paramount Pictures©

Hotel Sahara 1951 d: Ken Annakin. lps: Yvonne de Carlo, Peter Ustinov, David Tomlinson. 96M UKN. prod/rel: General Film Distributors, Tower

BIRO, LUDWIG
Don Juans Drei Nachte, Berlin 1917, Novel
Don Juan's Three Nights 1926 d: John Francis Dillon. lps: Lewis Stone, Shirley Mason, Malcolm McGregor. 6374f USA. prod/rel: Henry Hobart Productions, First National Pictures

BIRON, HERVE
Nuages Sur Les Brules, Novel
Brules, Les 1958 d: Bernard Devlin. lps: Felix Leclerc, Aime Major, Roland d'Amour. 111M CND. *The Promised Land* prod/rel: Office National Du Film

BISCHOFF, BENGTA
Das Gelbe Haus Am Pinnasberg, Novel
Gelbe Haus Am Pinnasberg, Das 1970 d: Alfred Vohrer. lps: Eddi Arent, Siegfried Schurenberg, Tilly Lauenstein. 94M GRM. *The Yellow House on Mt. Pinnas* prod/rel: Roxy, Inter

BISHOP, CASEY
Sisterhood, Novel
Ladies Club, The 1986 d: Janet Greek. lps: Karen Austin, Diana Scarwid, Christine Belford. 90M USA. *Violated; The Sisterhood* prod/rel: New Line Cinema

BISHOP, CURTIS
Shadow Range, 1947, Novel
Cow Country 1953 d: Lesley Selander, Curtis Bishop. lps: Edmond O'Brien, Bob Lowry, Helen Westcott. 82M USA. prod/rel: Allied Artists

BISHOP, HENRY
Sweet Home Home, 1823, Song
Home, Sweet Home 1914 d: D. W. Griffith. lps: Henry B. Walthall, Lillian Gish, Dorothy Gish. 6r USA. prod/rel: Majestic Motion Picture Co., Reliance Motion Picture Co.

BISHOP, JIM (1907–1987), USA, Bishop, James Alonzo
F.D.R.: the Last Year, Book
F.D.R., the Last Year 1980 d: Anthony Page. lps: Jason Robards Jr., Eileen Heckart, Edward Binns. TVM. 153M USA. prod/rel: NBC, Columbia

BISHOP, LEONARD
Against Heaven's Hand, Novel
Seven in Darkness 1969 d: Michael Caffey. lps: Milton Berle, Sean Garrison, Dina Merrill. TVM. 75M USA. prod/rel: Paramount

BISS, GERALD
Branded, Novel
Branded 1920 d: Charles Calvert. lps: Josephine Earle, Dallas Anderson, Nora Swinburne. 5835f UKN. prod/rel: Gaumont, British Screencraft

BISSELL, RICHARD
7½ Cents, Novel
Pajama Game, The 1957 d: George Abbott, Stanley Donen. lps: Doris Day, John Raitt, Carol Haney. 101M USA. *What Lola Wants* prod/rel: Warner Bros., Abbott-Donen

BISSON, ALEXANDRE
Le Bon Juge, Play
Bon Juge, Le 1913 d: Georges MoncA. lps: Prince, Yvonne Maelec, Gabrielle Lange. 720m FRN. prod/rel: Pathe Freres

Chateau Historique, Play
Chateau Historique 1923 d: Henri Desfontaines. lps: Emile Drain, Eva Raynal, Pauline Carton. 1600m FRN. prod/rel: Gaumont

Femmes Sont Folles, Les 1950 d: Gilles Grangier. lps: Raymond Rouleau, Noel Roquevert, Gaby SylviA. 90M FRN. prod/rel: Cinephonic, S.G.G.C.

Le Controleur Des Wagons-Lits, 1898, Play
Controllore Dei Vagoni-Letto, Il 1922 d: Mario Almirante. lps: Oreste Bilancia, Leonie Laporte, Vittorio Pieri. 1681m ITL. prod/rel: Alba Film

Schlafwagenkontrolleur, Der 1935 d: Richard Eichberg. lps: Danielle Darrieux, Alice Tissot, Albert Prejean. 90M GRM/FRN. *Le Controleur Des Wagon-Lits* (FRN) prod/rel: Bavaria-Film

La Famille Pont-Biquet, Play
Famille Pont-Biquet, La 1935 d: Christian-Jaque. lps: Armand Bernard, Paul Pauley, Gina Manes. 90M FRN. prod/rel: Films U.D.

La Femme X, Paris 1908, Play
Madame X 1916 d: George F. Marion. lps: Dorothy Donnelly, Edwin Fosberg, Ralph Morgan. 6r USA. prod/rel: Henry W. Savage, Inc.©, Pathe Exchange, Inc.

Madame X 1920 d: Frank Lloyd. lps: Pauline Frederick, William Courtleigh Jr., Casson Ferguson. 6475f USA. prod/rel: Goldwyn Pictures Corp.©, Goldwyn Distributing Corp.

Madame X 1929 d: Lionel Barrymore. lps: Lewis Stone, Ruth Chatterton, Raymond Hackett. 95M USA. *Absinthe* prod/rel: Metro-Goldwyn-Mayer Pictures

Madame X 1937 d: Sam Wood, Gustav Machaty (Uncredited). lps: Gladys George, John Beal, Warren William. 75M USA. prod/rel: Metro-Goldwyn-Mayer Corp.©

Madame X 1966 d: David Lowell Rich. lps: Lana Turner, Keir Dullea, John Forsythe. 100M USA. prod/rel: Universal Pictures, Ross Hunter Productions

Madame X 1981 d: Robert Ellis Miller. lps: Tuesday Weld, Len Cariou, Eleanor Parker. TVM. 100M USA.

Mujer X, La 1931 d: Carlos Borcosque. lps: Maria F. Landon de Guevara, Rafael Rivelles, Jose Crespo. 78M USA. prod/rel: Metro-Goldwyn-Mayer Corp., Culver Export

Trial of Madame X, The 1948 d: Paul England. lps: Mara Russell-Tavernan, Paul England, Eddie Leslie. 54M UKN. prod/rel: Invicta, Wyndham T. Vint

Feu Toupinel, Play
Feu Toupinel 1933 d: Roger Capellani. lps: Colette Darfeuil, Simone Deguyse, Mauricet. 86M FRN. prod/rel: Societe Universelle De Films

Jalouse, Play
Etes-Vous Jalouse? 1937 d: Henri Chomette. lps: Suzy Prim, Gabrielle Dorziat, Andre Luguet. 100M FRN. prod/rel: F.R.D.

Monsieur le Directeur, Play
Monsieur le Directeur 1913 d: Georges MoncA. lps: Prince, Paul Numa, Yvonne Maelec. 720m FRN. prod/rel: Pathe Freres

Monsieur le Directeur 1924 d: Robert Saidreau. lps: Jean Dax, Claire Nobis, Andre Dubosc. 1800m FRN.

Le Roi Koko, Play
Roi Koko, Le 1913 d: Georges MoncA. lps: Prince. 570m FRN. prod/rel: Pathe Freres

Les Surprises du Divorce, 1888, Play
Sorprese Del Divorzio, Le 1923 d: Guido Brignone. lps: Lia Miari, Leonie Laporte, Alberto Collo. 1774m ITL. prod/rel: Alba Film

Sorprese Del Divorzio, Le 1939 d: Guido Brignone. lps: Armando Falconi, Filippo Scelzo, Sergio Tofano. 84M ITL. prod/rel: Scalera Film

Surprises du Divorce, Les 1912 d: Georges MoncA. lps: Prince, Leon Bernard, Suzanne Demay. 710m FRN. prod/rel: Scagl

Surprises du Divorce, Les 1933 d: Jean Kemm. lps: Mauricet, Nadine Picard, Maximilienne. 87M FRN. prod/rel: Alex Nalpas

La Veglione, Paris 1893, Play
Her Beloved Villain 1920 d: Sam Wood. lps: Wanda Hawley, Harrison Ford, Tully Marshall. 5r USA. *La Veglione* prod/rel: Realart Pictures Corp.©

Voyage d'Agrement, 1881, Play
Viaggio Di Piacere, Un 1922 d: Ermanno Geymonat. lps: Camillo de Riso, Silvana Morello, Umberto Zanuccoli. 1531m ITL. prod/rel: Caesar Film

BISTOLFI, EMO
L' Eredita Della Zio Nicola, Play
Uomini E Nobiluomini 1959 d: Giorgio Bianchi. lps: Vittorio de Sica, Silvia Pinal, Antonio Cifariello. 90M ITL. prod/rel: Cineproduzioni Bistolfi, Cineriz

BIZET, RENE
La Bateau de Verre, Short Story
Brennende Schiff, Das 1927 d: Constantin J. David. lps: Kathe von Nagy, Eric Barclay, Mary Kid. 2593m GRM/FRN. *Le Bateau de Verre* (FRN) prod/rel: Productions Milliet, Goron-Film

BJERKE, ANDRE
De Dodes Tjern, 1942, Novel
Dodes Tjern, de 1958 d: Kare Bergstrom. lps: Georg Richter, Inger Teien, Henki Kolstad. 77M NRW.

BJORNEBOE, JENS (1920–1976), NRW
Den Onde Hyrde, 1960, Novel
Tonny 1962 d: Nils R. Muller. 87M NRW.

Uten En Trad, Oslo 1966, Novel
Uden En Traevl 1968 d: Annelise Meineche. lps: Anne Grete, Ib Mossin, Niels Borksand. 98M DNM. *Without a Stitch* (USA) prod/rel: Palladium

BJORNSON, BJORNSTJERNE (1832–1910), NRW
En Glad Gutt, 1859, Short Story
Glad Gutt, En 1932 d: John W. Brunius. lps: Hauk Aabel. 96M NRW.

Synnove Solbakken, 1857, Novel
Synnove Solbakken 1934 d: Tancred Ibsen. lps: Karin Ekelund, John Ekman. 81M SWD.

Synnove Solbakken 1957 d: Gunnar Hellstrom. lps: Synnove Strigen, Gunnar Helstrom, Harriet Andersson. 86M SWD. *Girl of Solbakken* prod/rel: Sandrew-Bauman, Artist

BLACK, ARTHUR
Life Is Pretty Much the Same, Play
Plaything, The 1929 d: Castleton Knight. lps: Estelle Brody, Heather Thatcher, Nigel Barrie. 78M UKN. prod/rel: British International Pictures, Wardour

BLACK, ARTHUR JARVIS
The Village Squire, Play
Village Squire, The 1935 d: Reginald Denham. lps: David Horne, Leslie Perrins, Moira Lynd. 66M UKN. prod/rel: British and Dominions, Paramount British

BLACK, BETTY
Sisterhood, Novel
Ladies Club, The 1986 d: Janet Greek. lps: Karen Austin, Diana Scarwid, Christine Belford. 90M USA. *Violated; The Sisterhood* prod/rel: New Line Cinema

BLACK, IAN STUART
The High Bright Sun, London 1962, Novel
High Bright Sun, The 1964 d: Ralph Thomas. lps: Dirk Bogarde, George Chakiris, Susan Strasberg. 114M UKN. *McGuire Go Home* (USA); *A Date With Death* prod/rel: Rank Organisation, Rank Film Distributors

In the Wake of a Stranger, Novel
In the Wake of a Stranger 1959 d: David Eady. lps: Tony Wright, Shirley Eaton, Danny Green. 64M UKN. prod/rel: Butcher's Film Service, Crest

We Must Kill Toni, London 1954, Play
She'll Have to Go 1962 d: Robert Asher. lps: Bob Monkhouse, Alfred Marks, Hattie Jacques. 90M UKN. *Maid for Murder* (USA) prod/rel: Asher Brothers Production, Anglo-Amalgamated

BLACK, LADBROOKE
A Cinema Girl's Romance, Novel
Cinema Girl's Romance, A 1915 d: George Pearson. lps: Agnes Glynne, Fred Paul, Alice de Winton. 3500f UKN. prod/rel: G. B. Samuelson, Royal

BLACKBURN, JOHN
The Giant Woman, Novel
Destiny of a Spy 1969 d: Boris Sagal. lps: Lorne Greene, Rachel Roberts, Anthony Quayle. TVM. 100M USA. *The Gaunt Woman* prod/rel: NBC, Universal TV

Nothing But the Night, Novel
Nothing But the Night 1972 d: Peter Sasdy. lps: Christopher Lee, Peter Cushing, Diana Dors. 90M UKN. *The Resurrection Syndicate*; *The Devil's Undead* (USA) prod/rel: Rank, Charlemagne

BLACKBURN, THOMAS W., Blackburn, Tom W.
Story
Cattle Queen of Montana 1954 d: Allan Dwan. lps: Barbara Stanwyck, Ronald Reagan, Gene Evans. 88M USA. prod/rel: RKO

Range War, 1949, Novel
Short Grass 1950 d: Lesley Selander. lps: Rod Cameron, Cathy Downs, Johnny Mack Brown. 82M USA. prod/rel: Allied Artists, Monogram

Raton Pass, 1950, Novel
Raton Pass 1951 d: Edwin L. Marin. lps: Dennis Morgan, Patricia Neal, Steve Cochran. 84M USA. *Canyon Pass* (UKN) prod/rel: Warner Bros.

Sierra Baron, 1955, Novel
Sierra Baron 1958 d: James B. Clark, Raphael J. SevillA. lps: Brian Keith, Rick Jason, Rita Gam. 82M USA. prod/rel: 20th Century-Fox

BLACKE, WILLIAM
The Miracle of Hate, Story
Man Who Fights Alone, The 1924 d: Wallace Worsley. lps: William Farnum, Lois Wilson, Edward Everett Horton. 6337f USA. prod/rel: Famous Players-Lasky, Paramount Pictures

BLACKMORE, PETER
Miranda, Play
Miranda 1948 d: Ken Annakin. lps: Googie Withers, Glynis Johns, Griffith Jones. 80M UKN. prod/rel: General Film Distributors, Gainsborough

BLACKMORE, R. D. (1825–1900), UKN, Blackmore, Richard Doddridge
Lorna Doone, 1869, Novel
Lorna Doone 1911 d: Theodore Marston. lps: Frank Crane, Marguerite Snow, William Garwood. SHT USA. prod/rel: Thanhouser
Lorna Doone 1912 d: Wilfred Noy. lps: Dorothy Bellew. 4300f UKN. prod/rel: Clarendon, Gaumont
Lorna Doone 1915 d: J. Farrell MacDonald. lps: Vola Smith, Edward Cecil, G. Raymond Nye. 2r USA. prod/rel: Biograph Co.
Lorna Doone 1920 d: H. Lisle Lucoque. lps: Dennis Wyndham, Bertie Gordon, Roy Raymond. 5150f UKN. prod/rel: Butcher's Film Service
Lorna Doone 1922 d: Maurice Tourneur. lps: Madge Bellamy, John Bowers, Frank Keenan. 6200f USA. prod/rel: Thomas H. Ince Corp., Associated First National Pictures
Lorna Doone 1935 d: Basil Dean. lps: Victoria Hopper, John Loder, Margaret Lockwood. 90M UKN. prod/rel: Associated Talking Pictures, Associated British Film Distributors
Lorna Doone 1951 d: Phil Karlson. lps: Barbara Hale, Richard Greene, Carl Benton Reid. 88M USA. prod/rel: Columbia
Lorna Doone 1990 d: Andrew Grieve. lps: Clive Owen, Sean Bean, Polly Walker. TVM. 105M UKN. prod/rel: Working Title, Thames Tv

BLACKWELL, NELL
The Wound Stripe, 1925, Play
Man from Yesterday, The 1932 d: Berthold Viertel. lps: Claudette Colbert, Clive Brook, Charles Boyer. 71M USA. *The Woman of Flame* prod/rel: Paramount Publix Corp.©

BLACKWOOD, ALGERNON (1869–1951), UKN
Short Stories
Algernon Blackwood Stories 1949 d: Anthony Gilkison. lps: Algernon Blackwood. SHS. UKN. prod/rel: Rayant Pictures, 20th Century-Fox

BLACKWOOD, DAVID
Fools Die Fast, Play
Fools Die Fast 1996 d: James Purcell. lps: Peter Outerbridge, Kate Greenhouse, Victor Ertmanis. 86M CND. prod/rel: New Film Co.

BLACKWOOD, JOHN H.
Come Again Smith, Play
Come Again Smith 1919 d: E. Mason Hopper. lps: J. Warren Kerrigan, Lois Wilson, Henry A. Barrows. 5027f USA. prod/rel: Jesse D. Hampton Productions, W. W. Hodkinson Corp.

BLAIR, CHARLES
Thunder Above, Novel
Beyond the Curtain 1960 d: Compton Bennett. lps: Richard Greene, Eva Bartok, Marius Goring. 88M UKN. prod/rel: Rank Film Distributors, Welbeck

BLAIR, GWENDA
Almost Golden, Biography
Almost Golden - the Jessica Savitch Story 1995 d: Peter Werner. lps: Sela Ward, Ron Silver, Judith Ivey. TVM. 100M USA. prod/rel: Safronski Productions, ABC Productions

BLAIR, JOAN
Return from the River Kwai, Book
Return from the River Kwai 1989 d: Andrew V. McLaglen. lps: Chris Penn, Edward Fox, Denholm Elliott. 98M UKN/USA. prod/rel: Rank, Screenlife Establishment

BLAIR JR., CLAY
Return from the River Kwai, Book
Return from the River Kwai 1989 d: Andrew V. McLaglen. lps: Chris Penn, Edward Fox, Denholm Elliott. 98M UKN/USA. prod/rel: Rank, Screenlife Establishment

BLAIR, NAN
Humanity, Short Story
Whom the Gods Would Destroy 1919 d: Frank Borzage. lps: Jack Mulhall, Pauline Starke, Kathryn Adams. 7r USA. *Whom the Gods Destroy*; *Humanity* prod/rel: C. R. Macauley Photoplays, First National Exhibitors Circuit

BLAIS, MARIE-CLAIRE (1939–, CND
Le Sourd Dans la Ville, Novel
Sourd Dans la Ville, Le 1986 d: Mireille Dansereau. lps: Beatrice Picard, Guillaume Lemay-Thivierge, Angele Coutu. 97M CND. *Deaf to the City*

BLAISDELL, ANNE
Nightmare, New York 1961, Novel
Fanatic 1965 d: Silvio Narizzano. lps: Tallulah Bankhead, Stefanie Powers, Peter Vaughan. 97M UKN. *Die! Die! My Darling* (USA) prod/rel: Hammer, Seven Arts

BLAKE, GEORGE
The Shipbuilders, 1935, Novel
Shipbuilders, The 1943 d: John Baxter. lps: Clive Brook, Morland Graham, Nell Ballantyne. 89M UKN. prod/rel: British National, Anglo-American

BLAKE, JAMES W.
Sidewalks of New York, Song
Sidewalks of New York 1923 d: Lester Park. lps: Hanna Lee, Bernard Siegel, King Bradley. 6r USA. prod/rel: Lester Park

BLAKE, NICHOLAS (1904–1972), UKN, Day-Lewis, Cecil
The Beast Must Die, London 1938, Novel
Que la Bete Meure 1969 d: Claude Chabrol. lps: Michel Duchaussoy, Caroline Cellier, Jean Yanne. 115M FRN/ITL. *Uccidero un Uomo* (ITL); *This Man Must Die* (USA); *Killer!* (UKN) prod/rel: Les Films la Boetie, Rizzoli Films

BLANC, HENRI-FREDERIC
Combat de Fauves Au Crepuscule, Novel
Combat de Fauves 1997 d: Benoit Lamy. lps: Richard Bohringer, Ute Lemper, Papa WembA. 88M BLG/GRM/FRN. *Wild Games* prod/rel: Lamy Film, Rtbf (Belgium)

BLANCO, JOSE J.
Santo, Book
Latino Bar 1991 d: Paul Leduc. lps: Dolores Pedro, Roberto Sosa, Milagros Carias. 90M SPN/VNZ/CUB.

BLANEY, CHARLES E.
Across the Pacific, New York 1904, Play
Across the Pacific 1914 d: Edwin Carewe. lps: Dorothy Dalton, Sam Hines, Millar. 5r USA. prod/rel: Charles E. Blaney Productions, World Film Corp.©

The Curse of Drink, 1904, Play
Curse of Drink, The 1922 d: Harry O. Hoyt. lps: Harry T. Morey, Edmund Breese, Marguerite Clayton. 5900f USA. prod/rel: Weber & North

The Dancer and the King, Play
Dancer and the King, The 1914 d: E. Arnaud. lps: Cecil Spooner, Victor Sutherland, Howard Lang. 5r USA. prod/rel: Charles E. Blaney Productions, World Film Corp.

The Girl Who Came Back, Hoboken 1920, Play
Girl Who Came Back, The 1923 d: Tom Forman. lps: Miriam Cooper, Gaston Glass, Kenneth Harlan. 6100f USA. prod/rel: B. P. Schulberg Productions, Preferred Pictures

The Love Bandit, 1921, Play
Love Bandit, The 1924 d: Dell Henderson. lps: Doris Kenyon, Victor Sutherland, Jules Cowles. 5800f USA. prod/rel: Charles E. Blaney Productions, Vitagraph Co. of America

More to Be Pitied Than Scorned; Or Death Before Dishonor, 1903, Novel
More to Be Pitied Than Scorned 1922 d: Edward J. Le Saint. lps: J. Frank Glendon, Rosemary Theby, Philo McCullough. 5800f USA. prod/rel: Waldorf Productions, C. B. C. Film Sales

Only a Shopgirl, Play
Only a Shop Girl 1922 d: Edward J. Le Saint. lps: Estelle Taylor, Mae Busch, Wallace Beery. 6400f USA. prod/rel: C. B. C. Film Sales

Red Kisses, Play
Picture Brides 1934 d: Phil Rosen. lps: Dorothy MacKaill, Alan Hale, Regis Toomey. 68M USA. prod/rel: Allied Pictures Corp.©

BLANEY, HARRY CLAY
Picture Brides 1934 d: Phil Rosen. lps: Dorothy MacKaill, Alan Hale, Regis Toomey. 68M USA. prod/rel: Allied Pictures Corp.©

BLANK-EISMANN, MARIE
Sissi, Novel
Sissi 1956 d: Ernst MarischkA. lps: Romy Schneider, Karlheinz Bohm, Magda Schneider. 147M AUS. *Forever My Love* prod/rel: Erma, UFA

BLANKFORT, MICHAEL
The Juggler, Novel
Juggler, The 1953 d: Edward Dmytryk. lps: Kirk Douglas, Milly Vitale, Paul Stewart. 86M USA. prod/rel: Columbia, Stanley Kramer Prods.

The Widow Makers, Novel
See How They Run 1965 d: David Lowell Rich. lps: John Forsythe, Senta Berger, Jane Wyatt. TVM. 100M USA. *The Widow Makers* prod/rel: Universal

BLAS, TONY
Le Picador, Novel
Picador, Le 1932 d: Jaquelux. lps: Jean Mauran, Ginette d'Yd, Madeleine Guitty. 91M FRN. prod/rel: M.B. Films

BLASCO IBANEZ, VICENTE (1867–1928), SPN
La Barraca, 1898, Novel
Barraca, La 1944 d: Roberto Gavaldon. lps: Luana Alcaniz, Jose Baviera, Pascual Guillot. 118M MXC. *The Cottage*

La Bodega, Novel
Bodega, La 1930 d: Benito Perojo. lps: Gabriel Gabrio, Conchita Piquer, Colette Darfeuil. F SPN/FRN. *The Wine Cellar* prod/rel: Cie Generale De Prod. Cinematografique, Julio Cesar, S.A. (Madrid)

Canas Y Barro, 1902, Novel
Palude Tragica 1953 d: Juan de OrdunA. lps: Anna Amendola, Delia Scala, Erno CrisA. 100M SPN/ITL. *La Palude Del Peccato* (ITL); *Amore E Fango*; *Canas Y Barro*; *Mud and Reeds*

Los Cuatro Jinetes Del Apocalipsis, Valencia 1916, Novel
Debout Les Morts 1915 d: Henri Pouctal, Leonce Perret. lps: Jean Daragon, Paul Hubert, Lise Laurent. FRN.

Four Horsemen of the Apocalypse, The 1921 d: Rex Ingram. lps: Rudolph Valentino, Alice Terry, Pomeroy Cannon. 11r USA. prod/rel: Metro Pictures

Four Horsemen of the Apocalypse, The 1961 d: Vincente Minnelli. lps: Glenn Ford, Ingrid Thulin, Charles Boyer. 153M USA. prod/rel: Julian Blaustein, MGM

Los Enemigos de la Mujer, Novel
Enemies of Women, The 1923 d: Alan Crosland. lps: Lionel Barrymore, Alma Rubens, Pedro de CordobA. 11r USA. prod/rel: Cosmopolitan Productions, Goldwyn Distributing Corp.

Entre Naranjos, Novel
Torrent, The 1926 d: Monta Bell. lps: Ricardo Cortez, Greta Garbo, Gertrude Olmstead. 6769f USA. *Ibanez' Torrent* prod/rel: Cosmopolitan Pictures, Metro-Goldwyn-Mayer Distributing Corp.

Flor de Mayo, 1895, Novel
Flor de Mayo 1957 d: Roberto Gavaldon. lps: Jack Palance, Pedro Armendariz, Maria Felix. 100M MXC. *Beyond All Limits* (USA); *Spoilers of the Sea*; *Flowers of May*; *A Mexican Affair* prod/rel: Cinematografica Latino Americana

Mare Nostrum, 1916, Novel
Mare Nostrum 1925 d: Rex Ingram. lps: Uni Apollon, Alex Nova, Kada-Abd-El-Kader. 11r USA. *Our Sea* prod/rel: Metro-Goldwyn-Mayer Pictures
Mare Nostrum 1948 d: Rafael Gil. lps: Maria Felix, Fernando Rey, Jose Nieto. 104M SPN/ITL. *Albi Di Sangue* (ITL); *Tragic Dawn*

Sangre Y Arena, Buenos Aires 1908, Novel
Arenes Sanglantes 1917 d: Max Andre. 2000m FRN.
Blood and Sand 1922 d: Fred Niblo. lps: Rudolph Valentino, Lila Lee, Nita Naldi. 8110f USA. prod/rel: Paramount Pictures, Famous Players-Lasky
Blood and Sand 1941 d: Rouben Mamoulian. lps: Tyrone Power, Linda Darnell, Rita Hayworth. 124M USA. prod/rel: 20th Century-Fox

La Tierra de Todos, Novel
Temptress, The 1926 d: Fred Niblo, Mauritz Stiller. lps: Greta Garbo, Antonio Moreno, Roy d'Arcy. 8221f USA. prod/rel: Cosmopolitan Productions, Metro-Goldwyn-Mayer Distributing Corp.

BLATTY, WILLIAM PETER (1928–, USA
The Exorcist, Novel
Exorcist, The 1973 d: William Friedkin. lps: Ellen Burstyn, Max von Sydow, Lee J. Cobb. 122M USA. prod/rel: Warner Bros., Hoya

Legion, Novel
Exorcist III: the Legion 1990 d: William Peter Blatty. lps: George C. Scott, Ed Flanders, Brad Dourif. 109M USA. prod/rel: Fox, Morgan Creek

The Ninth Configuration, Novel
Ninth Configuration, The 1980 d: William Peter Blatty. lps: Stacy Keach, Scott Wilson, Jason Miller. 118M USA. *Twinkle Twinkle Killer Kane* prod/rel: Warner, Lorimar

BLAVET, E.
Mio Zio Barbassous, 1891, Play
Mio Zio Barbassous 1921 d: Riccardo Cassano. lps: Elena Sangro, Nino Camarda, Myosa de Coudray. 2306m ITL. *Mon Oncle Barbassous*; *Barbassous* prod/rel: Chimera Film

BLAZKOVA, MARIE
Rozvod Na Zhousku, Novel
Klatovsti Dragouni 1937 d: Karel SpelinA. lps: Bedrich Veverka, Truda Grosslichtova, Zita KabatovA. 2722m CZC. *The Dragoons of Klatovy* prod/rel: Dafa

Spodni Tony, Novel
Manzelstvi Na Uver 1936 d: Oldrich Kminek. lps: Zita Kabatova, Eva Gerova, Vera FerbasovA. 2359m CZC. *Marriage on Credit* prod/rel: Nationalfilm

BLEAKNEY, CORNELIA
Playing the Same Game, Story
Playing the Same Game 1915 d: Edwin McKim. lps: Davy Don, Florence Williams, Carrie Reynolds. SHT USA. prod/rel: Lubin

BLEASDALE, ALAN (1946–, UKN
Boys from the Blackstuff, 1983, Play
Black Stuff, The 1978 d: Jim Goddard. lps: Bernard Hill, Michael Angelis, Tom Georgeson. TVM. 107M UKN.

BLEDSOE, JERRY
Blood Games, Novel
Honor Thy Mother 1992 d: David Greene. lps: Sharon Gless, William McNamara, Brian Wimmer. TVM. 90M USA. *Honour Thy Mother* prod/rel: Point of View Productions, Mte Inc.

BLEECK, OLIVER
The Procane Chronicle, Novel
St. Ives 1976 d: J. Lee Thompson. lps: Charles Bronson, Jacqueline Bisset, John Houseman. 94M USA. prod/rel: Warner Bros.

BLEIER, ROCKY
Biography
Fighting Back 1980 d: Robert Lieberman. lps: Robert Urich, Art Carney, Bonnie BedeliA. TVM. 100M USA. prod/rel: ABC, Mtm

BLENEAU, ADELE
The Nurse's Story: in Which Reality Meets Romance, Indianapolis 1915, Novel
Adele 1919 d: Wallace Worsley. lps: Kitty Gordon, Mahlon Hamilton, Wedgewood Nowell. 6r USA. *The Nurse* prod/rel: United Picture Theatres of America

BLETTENBERG, DETLEF
Killing Drugs, Novel
Killing Drugs 1988 d: Rolf von Sydow. lps: Heiner Lauterbach, Gunther Maria Halmer, Christiner Garner. 110M GRM. *Bangkok Story* prod/rel: Manfred Durniok Prod., Bayerischer Rundfunk

BLICHER, STEEN STEENSEN
Hosekraemmeren, 1829, Short Story
Hosekraemmeren 1963 d: Max Hellner, Johannes Vaabensted. lps: Henry Jessen. 50M DNM.
Hosekraemmeren 1971 d: Knud Leif Thomsen. lps: Frans Andersson, Lily Broberg, Pia Gronning. 84M DNM.

Praesten I Vejlby, 1829, Novel
Praesten I Vejlby 1931 d: George Schneevoigt. lps: Holger Madsen, Henrik Malberg, Karin Nellemore. 107M DNM. prod/rel: Nordisk Tonefilm
Praesten I Vejlby 1972 d: Claus Orsted. lps: Peter Steen, Annelise Gabold, Karl Stegger. 90M DNM. *The Works of the Devil*

Praesten I Vejlby, 1829, Novel
Praesten I Vejlby 1920 d: August Blom. lps: Gunnar Tolnaes. 94M DNM. *The Vicar of Vejlby*; *The Land of Fate*

Sildig Opvaagnen, 1828, Short Story
Filmen Og Elise 1986 d: Claus Ploug. lps: Kirsten Olesen, Frits Helmuth, Ann-Mari Max Hansen. 106M DNM. *Film About Elise*; *Elise*

De Tre Helligaftener, 1840, Novel
Bejleren -En Jysk Roverhistorie 1975 d: Knud Leif Thomsen. lps: Troels Moller, Inge Margrethe Svendsen, Grethe Thordahl. 101M DNM.

BLICKENSDORFER, WALTER
Aux Abois, Zurich 1953, Novel
Gejagten, Die 1960 d: Max Michel. lps: Heinrich Gretler, Claude Farell, Helen VitA. 94M SWT. *Die Heuchler*; **Aux Abois**; *Les Hypocrites* prod/rel: Urania-Film

BLIER, BERTRAND
Beau-Pere, Novel
Beau-Pere 1981 d: Bertrand Blier. lps: Patrick Dewaere, Ariel Besse, Maurice Ronet. 120M FRN. *Stepfather* prod/rel: Sara, Antenne 2

BLISH, JAMES (1921–1975), USA, Blish, James Benjamin
There Shall Be No Darkness, Novel
Beast Must Die, The 1974 d: Paul Annett. lps: Calvin Lockhart, Peter Cushing, Charles Gray. 92M UKN. *Black Werewolf* prod/rel: British Lion, Amicus

BLIXEN, KAREN (1885–1962), DNM, Dinesen, Isak, Andrezel, Pierre
Afrikanske Farm, 1937, Short Story
Out of Africa 1985 d: Sydney Pollack. lps: Meryl Streep, Robert Redford, Klaus Maria Brandauer. 162M USA/UKN. prod/rel: Universal, Mirage

Babette's Feast, 1950, Short Story
Babettes Gaestebud 1987 d: Gabriel Axel. lps: Stephane Audran, Jean-Philippe Lafont, Gudmar Wivesson. 105M DNM/FRN. *Le Festin de Babette* (FRN); *Babette's Feast* (UKN) prod/rel: Panorama, Nordisk

Breve Fra Africa, 1960, Short Story
Out of Africa 1985 d: Sydney Pollack. lps: Meryl Streep, Robert Redford, Klaus Maria Brandauer. 162M USA/UKN. prod/rel: Universal, Mirage

Skibsdrengens Fortaelling, Copenhagen 1942, Short Story
Histoire Immortelle 1968 d: Orson Welles. lps: Orson Welles, Roger Coggio, Jeanne Moreau. 63M FRN. *Immortal Story* prod/rel: O.R.T.F., Albina Films

Skygger Paa Graesset, 1978, Short Story
Out of Africa 1985 d: Sydney Pollack. lps: Meryl Streep, Robert Redford, Klaus Maria Brandauer. 162M USA/UKN. prod/rel: Universal, Mirage

BLOCH, BERT
Oh, What a Nurse!, Play
Oh, What a Nurse! 1926 d: Charles F. Reisner. lps: Sydney Chaplin, Patsy Ruth Miller, Gayne Whitman. 6930f USA. prod/rel: Warner Brothers Pictures

Dark Victory, New York 1934, Play
Dark Victory 1939 d: Edmund Goulding. lps: Bette Davis, George Brent, Humphrey Bogart. 105M USA. prod/rel: Warner Bros. Pictures, Inc.
Dark Victory 1976 d: Robert Butler. lps: Elizabeth Montgomery, Anthony Hopkins, Michele Lee. TVM. 150M USA. prod/rel: Universal

Stolen Hours 1963 d: Daniel Petrie. lps: Susan Hayward, Michael Craig, Diane Baker. 100M UKN/USA. *Summer Flight* prod/rel: Mirisch Films, Barbican Films

BLOCH, PEDRO
Os Pais Abstratos, 1965, Play
Ate Que O Casamento Nos Separe 1968 d: Flavio Tambellini. 90M BRZ. *Until Marriage Separates Us*; *Till Marriage Does Us Apart*; *Till Marriage Do Us Part*

BLOCH, ROBERT (1917–1994), USA
Enoch, 1965, Short Story
Torture Garden 1967 d: Freddie Francis. lps: Jack Palance, Burgess Meredith, Beverly Adams. 93M UKN. prod/rel: Amicus Productions, Columbia

Method for Murder, Short Story
House That Dripped Blood, The 1970 d: Peter Duffell. lps: John Bennett, John Bryans, Denholm Elliott. 102M UKN. prod/rel: Amicus, Cinerama

Mr. Steinway, 1954, Short Story
Torture Garden 1967 d: Freddie Francis. lps: Jack Palance, Burgess Meredith, Beverly Adams. 93M UKN. prod/rel: Amicus Productions, Columbia

Psycho, 1959, Novel
Psycho 1960 d: Alfred Hitchcock. lps: Anthony Perkins, Janet Leigh, Vera Miles. 108M USA. prod/rel: Paramount, Alfred Hitchcock

Psycho, 1959, Novel
Psycho 1998 d: Gus Van Sant. lps: Vince Vaughn, Anne Heche, Julianne Moore. 109M USA. prod/rel: Universal Pictures, Imagine Entertainment

The Skull of the Marquis de Sade, New York 1965, Short Story
Skull, The 1965 d: Freddie Francis. lps: Peter Cushing, Patrick Wymark, Christopher Lee. 83M UKN. prod/rel: Amicus Productions, Paramount

Sweets to the Sweet, Short Story
House That Dripped Blood, The 1970 d: Peter Duffell. lps: John Bennett, John Bryans, Denholm Elliott. 102M UKN. prod/rel: Amicus, Cinerama

Terror Over Hollywood, 1957, Short Story
Torture Garden 1967 d: Freddie Francis. lps: Jack Palance, Burgess Meredith, Beverly Adams. 93M UKN. prod/rel: Amicus Productions, Columbia

Waxworks, Short Story
House That Dripped Blood, The 1970 d: Peter Duffell. lps: John Bennett, John Bryans, Denholm Elliott. 102M UKN. prod/rel: Amicus, Cinerama

BLOCHMAN, LAWRENCE G.
Bombay Mail, Boston 1934, Novel
Bombay Mail 1934 d: Edwin L. Marin. lps: Edmund Lowe, Shirley Grey, Onslow Stevens. 68M USA. prod/rel: Universal Pictures Corp.

Golden Goose Wild Goose, Story
Pursuit 1935 d: Edwin L. Marin. lps: Chester Morris, Sally Eilers, Scotty Beckett. 82M USA. prod/rel: Metro-Goldwyn-Mayer Corp.©

BLOCK, ANITA ROWE
Love and Kisses, New York 1963, Play
Love and Kisses 1965 d: Ozzie Nelson. lps: Ricky Nelson, Kristin Harmon Nelson, Jack Kelly. 87M USA. prod/rel: Universal Pictures

BLOCK, LAWRENCE
Book
Burglar 1987 d: Hugh Wilson. lps: Whoopi Goldberg, Bob Goldthwait, G. W. Bailey. 102M USA. prod/rel: Warner

Nightmare Honeymoon, Novel
Nightmare Honeymoon 1972 d: Elliot Silverstein. lps: Dack Rambo, Rebecca Dianna Smith, Pat Hingle. 115M USA. *Deadly Honeymoon* prod/rel: MGM

BLOCK, LIBBIE
Wild Calendar, Novel
Caught 1949 d: Max Ophuls. lps: Robert Ryan, Barbara Bel Geddes, James Mason. 88M USA. prod/rel: MGM

BLODGETT, MICHAEL
Hero and the Terror, Novel
Hero and the Terror 1982 d: William Tannen. lps: Chuck Norris, Brynn Thayer, Steve James. 96M USA. prod/rel: Cannon

BLONDEL, ROGER
Mouton Enrage le, Novel
Mouton Enrage, Le 1974 d: Michel Deville. lps: Jane Birkin, Jean-Louis Trintignant, Romy Schneider. 104M FRN/ITL. *Il Montone Infuriato* (ITL); *Love at the Top* (USA); *The Enraged Sheep*; *The French Way*; *Seducer, The* prod/rel: Trac.Fra, Viaduc

BLONDIN, ANTOINE
Un Singe En Hiver, Paris 1959, Novel
Singe En Hiver, Un 1962 d: Henri Verneuil. lps: Jean-Paul Belmondo, Jean Gabin, Suzanne Flon. 102M FRN. *A Monkey in Winter* (USA); *It's Hot in Hell* prod/rel: Cipra, Cite Films

BLOOM, JOHN
Evidence of Love, Book
Killing in a Small Town, A 1990 d: Stephen Gyllenhaal. lps: Barbara Hershey, Brian Dennehy, John Terry. TVM. 100M USA. *Evidence of Love*

BLOOM, MURRAY TEIGH
The 13th Man, Novel
Last Embrace 1979 d: Jonathan Demme. lps: Roy Scheider, Janet Margolin, John Glover. 101M USA. prod/rel: United Artists

BLOOMFIELD, ROBERT
When Strangers Meet, New York 1956, Novel
Einer Frisst Den Anderen 1964 d: Ray Nazarro, Gustav Gavrin. lps: Cameron Mitchell, Jayne Mansfield, Elisabeth Flickenschildt. 95M GRM/ITL/USA. *La Morte Vestita Di Dollari* (ITL); *Dog Eat Dog* (USA); *When Strangers Meet*; *They Eat Each Other Up*; *Ora Di Uccidere, L'* prod/rel: Ernst Neubach-Filmproduktion, Unione Cin.Ca Internazionale

BLOSSOM, HENRY MARTYN
Checkers: a Hard Luck Story, Chicago 1896, Novel
Checkers 1913 d: Augustus Thomas. lps: Thomas W. Ross, Jack Regan, Gertrude Shipman. 6r USA. prod/rel: All Star Feature Corp., State Rights
Checkers 1919 d: Richard Stanton. lps: Thomas J. Carrigan, Jean Acker, Ellen Cassidy. 7r USA. prod/rel: Fox Film Corp., William Fox©
Gold Heels 1924 d: W. S. Van Dyke. lps: Robert Agnew, Peggy Shaw, Lucien Littlefield. 6020f USA. prod/rel: Fox Film Corp.
Mademoiselle Modiste; a Comic Opera, New York 1905, Musical Play
Kiss Me Again 1931 d: William A. Seiter. lps: Walter Pidgeon, Bernice Clair, Frank McHugh. 76M USA. *Toast of the Legion* (UKN); *Mademoiselle Modiste* prod/rel: First National Pictures©
Mademoiselle Modiste 1926 d: Robert Z. Leonard. lps: Corinne Griffith, Norman Kerry, Willard Louis. 6230f USA. prod/rel: Corinne Griffith Productions, First National Pictures
The Red Mill, New York 1906, Musical Play
Red Mill, The 1926 d: Roscoe Arbuckle. lps: Marion Davies, Owen Moore, Louise FazendA. 6337f USA. prod/rel: Cosmopolitan Productions, Metro-Goldwyn-Mayer Distributing Corp.
The Yankee Consul, New York 1904, Musical Play
Yankee Consul, The 1924 d: James W. Horne. lps: Arthur Stuart Hull, Douglas MacLean, Patsy Ruth Miller. 6148f USA. prod/rel: Douglas Maclean Productions, Associated Exhibitors

BLOW, SIDNEY
The Double Event, 1917, Play
Double Event, The 1921 d: Kenelm Foss. lps: Mary Odette, Roy Travers, Lionelle Howard. 5000f UKN. prod/rel: Astra Films
Double Event, The 1934 d: Leslie H. Gordon. lps: Jane Baxter, Ruth Taylor, O. B. Clarence. 68M UKN. prod/rel: Triumph, Producers Distributing Corporation
The Officer's Mess, London 1918, Play
Officer's Mess, The 1931 d: Manning Haynes. lps: Richard Cooper, Harold French, Elsa Lanchester. 98M UKN. prod/rel: Harry Rowson, Paramount
Peaches, 1915, Play
Weddings are Wonderful 1938 d: MacLean Rogers. lps: June Clyde, Esmond Knight, Rene Ray. 79M UKN. prod/rel: Canterbury, RKO Radio

BLUHMEN, DAVID
Nerone E Messalina, Novel
Nerone E Messalina 1953 d: Primo Zeglio. lps: Gino Cervi, Yvonne Sanson, Paola BarbarA. 85M ITL. *Nero and the Burning of Rome* (USA) prod/rel: Spettacolo Film, Tiber

BLUM
Chauffeur Antoinette, Play
Love Contract, The 1932 d: Herbert Selpin. lps: Winifred Shotter, Owen Nares, Sunday Wilshin. 80M UKN. prod/rel: British and Dominions, Woolf & Freedman
Conduisez-Moi Madame, Play
Conduisez-Moi, Madame 1932 d: Herbert Selpin. lps: Armand Bernard, Rolla Norman, Jeanne Boitel. 80M FRN. *Antoinette* prod/rel: Les Comedies Filmees

BLUME, JUDY (1938–, USA, Blume, Judy Sussman
Forever, Novel
Forever 1978 d: John Korty. lps: Stephanie Zimbalist, Dean Butler, John Friedrich. 100M USA. prod/rel: Emi Television, Roger Gimbel Productions

BLUNT, GILES
Cold Eye, Novel
Couleurs du Diable, Les 1997 d: Alain JessuA. lps: Ruggero Raimondi, Wadeck Stanczak, Isabelle Pasco. 83M FRN/ITL. *The Devil's Colors* prod/rel: Les Films De L'astre, Aj Films (France)

BLUTHGEN, VICTOR
Gensdarm Mobius, Novel
Gensdarm Mobius 1913 d: Stellan Rye. lps: Georg Molenar, Lucie Hoflich, Lothar Korner. 1066m GRM. prod/rel: Deutsche Bioscop

BLY, CAROL
Short Stories
Rachel River 1987 d: Sandy Smolan. lps: Zeljko Ivanek, Pamela Reed, Craig T. Nelson. 90M USA. prod/rel: Taurus

BLYTHE, RONALD
Akenfield, Book
Akenfield 1975 d: Peter Hall. lps: Garrow Shand, Peggy Cole, Barbara Tilney. 95M UKN. prod/rel: Angle Films, Lwt

BLYTON, ENID (1897–1968), UKN, Blyton, Enid Mary
Novel
Fem Og Spionerne, de 1969 d: Trine Hedman. lps: Ove Sprogoe, Astrid Villaume, Lily Broberg. 84M DNM/GRM. *Five Go Adventuring*; **De 5 Og Spionerne**; *Funf Freunde in Der Tinte* (GRM); *Five Friends in a Jam* prod/rel: Terra, Panorama
The Castle of Adventure, Novel
Castle of Adventure, The 1990 d: Terry Marcel. lps: Susan George, Gareth Hunt, Isobel Black. TVM. 118M UKN.
Five Have a Mystery to Solve, Novel
Five Have a Mystery to Solve 1964 d: Ernest Morris. lps: David Palmer, Darryl Read, Amanda Coxell. SRL. 96M UKN. prod/rel: Children's Film Foundation, Rayant
Five on a Treasure Island, Novel
Five on a Treasure Island 1957 d: Gerald Landau. lps: Rel Grainer, Richard Palmer, Gillian Harrison. SRL. 126M UKN. prod/rel: Rank Screen Services, Children's Film Foundation

BOBROWSKI, JOHANNES (1917–1965), GRM
Levins Muhle, 1964, Novel
Levins Muhle 1980 d: Horst Seemann. lps: Erwin Geschonneck, Katja Paryla, Christian Grashof. 121M GDR. *Levin's Mill* prod/rel: Defa

BOCCA, AL
Requiem for a Redhead, London 1953, Novel
Assignment Redhead 1956 d: MacLean Rogers. lps: Richard Denning, Carole Mathews, Ronald Adam. 79M UKN. *Million Dollar Manhunt* (USA); *Undercover Girl* prod/rel: Butcher's Film Service

BOCCACCIO, GIOVANNI (1313–1375), ITL
Il Decameron, 1349-50, Book
Andreuccio Da Perugia 1910. 228m ITL. prod/rel: Cines
Boccaccio '70 1962 d: Federico Fellini, Luchino Visconti. lps: Anita Ekberg, Peppino de Filippo, Dante Maggio. 225M ITL/FRN. *Boccace 70* prod/rel: Concordia Compagnia Cin.Ca, Cineriz (Roma)
Decameron Nights 1924 d: Herbert Wilcox. lps: Lionel Barrymore, Ivy Duke, Werner Krauss. 9650f UKN/GRM. *Dekameron-Nachte* (GRM) prod/rel: Graham-Wilcox Productions, Decla
Decameron Nights 1953 d: Hugo Fregonese. lps: Joan Fontaine, Louis Jourdan, Binnie Barnes. 94M UKN/USA. prod/rel: Film Locations, Eros
Decamerone, Il 1912 d: Gennaro Righelli. lps: Gennaro Righelli, Maria Righelli, Ruffo Geri. 1500m ITL. prod/rel: Vesuvio Films
Decamerone, Il 1971 d: Pier Paolo Pasolini. lps: Franco Citti, Ninetto Davoli, Silvana Mangano. 111M ITL/FRN/GRM. *The Decameron* (USA) prod/rel: P.E.A. (Roma), Les Productions Artistes (Paris)

BOCK, CHRISTIAN
Ich Und Du, Play
Ich Und Du 1953 d: Alfred Weidenmann. lps: Hardy Kruger, Liselotte Pulver, Doris Kirchner. 90M GRM. *You and I* prod/rel: Neue Emelka, Zeyn
Das Madchen Ohne Pyjama, Play
Madchen Ohne Pyjama, Das 1957 d: Hans Quest. lps: Gunther Philipp, Elma Karlowa, Bum Kruger. 94M GRM. *The Girl Without Pajamas* prod/rel: Arca, Constantin

BODANSKY, ROBERT
Gipsy Love, London 1912, Operetta
Rogue Song, The 1929 d: Lionel Barrymore. lps: Lawrence Tibbett, Catherine Dale Owen, Nance O'Neil. 115M USA. prod/rel: Metro-Goldwyn-Mayer Pictures

Tanz Ins Gluck, Opera
Tanz Ins Gluck 1951 d: Alfred Stoger. lps: Johannes Heesters, Waltraut Haas, Lucie Englisch. 101M AUS. prod/rel: Mundus, UFA

BODELSEN, ANDERS
Guldregn, Novel
Guldregn 1988 d: Soren Kragh-Jacobsen. lps: Ricki Rasmussen, Ken Vedsegaard, Tania Frydensberg. 97M DNM. *Shower of Gold* prod/rel: Metronome, Danisches Fernsehen
Handeligt Uheld, 1968, Novel
Haendeligt Uheld 1971 d: Erik Balling. lps: Judy Geeson, Roy Dotrice, Zena Walker. 106M DNM. *One of Those Things* (UKN)
Signalet, 1965, Short Story
Signalet 1966 d: Ole Gammeltoft. 29M DNM.
Taenk Pa Et Tal (Think of a Number), 1968, Novel
Silent Partner, The 1978 d: Daryl Duke. lps: Elliott Gould, Susannah York, Christopher Plummer. 105M CND. *L' Argent de la Banque*; *Double Deadly* prod/rel: Silent Partner Film Productions Ltd., Tiberius Film Production Ltd.
Taenk Pa Et Tal 1969 d: Palle Kjarulff-Schmidt. lps: Henning Moritzen, Bibi Andersson, Peter Ronild. 102M DNM. *Think of a Number*

BODER, ADAM
Novel
Plusz Minusz Egy Nap 1972 d: Zoltan Fabri. lps: Anatol Constantin, Ferenc Bencze, Marton Andrassi. 91M HNG. *One Day Less One Day More*; *One Day More Or Less*; *A Day More Or Less* prod/rel: Mafilm

BODET, ROBERT
Mon Depute Et Sa Femme, Play
Mon Depute Et Sa Femme 1937 d: Maurice Cammage. lps: Paul Pauley, Mireille Perrey, Suzanne Dehelly. 95M FRN. prod/rel: Maurice Cammage

BOEHEIM, OLLY
Philine, Novel
Komodianten 1941 d: G. W. Pabst. lps: Kathe Dorsch, Hilde Krahl, Gustav Diessl. 112M GRM. *The Players*; *The Actors* prod/rel: Bavaia, Bejohr

BOEHM, DAVID
Play
Employee's Entrance 1933 d: Roy Del Ruth. lps: Warren William, Loretta Young, Wallace Ford. 75M USA. prod/rel: First National Pictures©

BOEHM, SYDNEY
Legend of the Incas, Story
Secret of the Incas 1954 d: Jerry Hopper. lps: Charlton Heston, Thomas Mitchell, Robert Young. 101M USA. prod/rel: Paramount

BOEHME, MARGARETHE, Bohme, Margarethe
Tagebuch Einer Verlorenen, Novel
Tagebuch Einer Verlorenen 1929 d: G. W. Pabst. lps: Louise Brooks, Josef Rovensky, Fritz Rasp. 94M GRM. *Diary of a Lost Girl* (UKN); *Diary of a Lost One* prod/rel: G. W. Pabst

BOERNER, CLAUS ERICH
Gefahrtin Meines Sommers, Novel
Gefahrtin Meines Sommers 1943 d: Fritz Peter Buch. lps: Anna Dammann, Paul Hartmann, Wolfgang Lukschy. 92M GRM. prod/rel: Berlin, Central Europaischer

BOERNER, KLAUS ERICH
Ursula, Short Story
Primanerinnen 1951 d: Rolf Thiele. lps: Ingrid Andree, Walter Giller, Christiane Jansen. 95M GRM. *Twelfth Grade Girls* prod/rel: Filmaufbau, D.F.H.

BOGARDE, DIRK (1921–1999), UKN, Van Den Bogaerde, Derek
Voices in the Garden, Short Story
Voices in the Garden 1992 d: Pierre Boutron. lps: Anouk Aimee, Joss Ackland, Samuel West. TVM. 86M UKN/FRN. prod/rel: Gaumont Television, Picture Base International

BOGART, FRANK
The Virgin of Nuremberg, Novel
Vergine Di Norimberga, La 1963 d: Antonio Margheriti. lps: Rossana Podesta, Georges Riviere, Christopher Lee. 85M ITL. *Castle of Terror* (UKN); *Horror Castle* (USA); *The Virgin of Nuremburg*; *Horror Castle (Where the Blood Flows)*; *Terror Castle* prod/rel: Gladiator Productions, Atlantica Cin.Ca

BOGGS, RUSSELL A.
Dan Kurrie's Inning, Short Story
Sand! 1920 d: Lambert Hillyer. lps: William S. Hart, Mary Thurman, G. Raymond Nye. 4869f USA. prod/rel: William S. Hart Co.©, Famous Players-Lasky Corp.

BOGHEN, ANDRE
Le Film du Poilu, Short Story
Film du Poilu, Le 1928 d: Henri Desfontaines. lps: Ninon Gilles, Daniel Mendaille, Roby Guichard. 2400m FRN.

BOGNER, NORMAN
Seventh Avenue, Novel
Seventh Avenue 1977 d: Richard Irving. lps: Steven Keats, Dori Brenner, Jane Seymour. TVM. 300M USA. prod/rel: Universal TV

BOGOMOLOV, VLADIMIR OSIPOVICH
Ivan, Moscow 1959, Short Story
Ivanovo Detstvo 1962 d: Andrei Tarkovsky. lps: Kolya Burlyaev, Valentin Zubkov, Evgenij Zharikov. 97M USS. *My Name Is Ivan* (USA); *Ivan's Childhood*; *The Youngest Spy*; *Detstvo Ivana*; *Childhood of Ivan* prod/rel: Mosfilm

BOGOSIAN, ERIC (1953–, USA
Suburbia, Play
Suburbia 1996 d: Richard Linklater. lps: Jayce Bartok, Amie Carey, Nicky Katt. 121M USA. prod/rel: Detour Filmproduction, Castle Rock Entertainment

BOGZA, GEO
Sfirsitul Lui Iacob Onisia, 1949, Short Story
Iacob 1988 d: Mircea Daneliuc. lps: Dorel Visan. 115M RMN. *Jacob*

BOILEAU, PIERRE
A Coeur Perdu, Paris 1959, Novel
Meurtre En 45 Tours 1960 d: Etienne Perier. lps: Danielle Darrieux, Michel Auclair, Jean Servais. 110M FRN. *Murder at 45 Rpm* prod/rel: Cite Films

Celle Qui N'etait Plus, Novel
Diabolique 1996 d: Jeremiah Chechik. lps: Sharon Stone, Isabelle Adjani, Chazz Palminteri. 107M USA. prod/rel: Morgan Creek Productions
Diaboliques, Les 1954 d: Henri-Georges Clouzot. lps: Simone Signoret, Vera Clouzot, Paul Meurisse. 110M FRN. *The Fiends* (UKN); *Diabolique* (USA) prod/rel: Filmsonor
Reflections of Murder 1974 d: John Badham. lps: Tuesday Weld, Sam Waterston, Joan Hackett. TVM. 100M USA. prod/rel: ABC Circle Films

D'entre Les Morts, 1954, Novel
Vertigo 1958 d: Alfred Hitchcock. lps: James Stewart, Kim Novak, Barbara Bel Geddes. 128M USA. prod/rel: Paramount, Alfred Hitchcock Prods.

Les Louves, Novel
Letters to an Unknown Lover 1985 d: Peter Duffell. lps: Cherie Lunghi, Yves Beneyton, Ralph Bates. TVM. 100M UKN/FRN. *Les Louves* (FRN) prod/rel: Portman Prods., Channel Four
Louves, Les 1956 d: Luis Saslavsky. lps: Francois Perier, Micheline Presle, Jeanne Moreau. 101M FRN. *The She-Wolves* (UKN); *Demoniaque*; *Demoniac*; *Las Lobas* prod/rel: Zodiaque Films

Les Magiciennes, Novel
Magiciennes, Les 1960 d: Serge Friedman. lps: Jacques Riberolles, Alice Kessler, Ellen Kessler. 97M FRN. *Double Deception* (USA); *Frantic*; *The Magicians* prod/rel: Speva Films, Intertele Films

Maldonne, Novel
Maldonne 1968 d: Sergio Gobbi. lps: Pierre Vaneck, Elsa Martinelli, Robert Hossein. 98M ITL/FRN. prod/rel: Paris Cannes Production, Mega Films

Malefices, Paris 1961, Novel
Malefices 1961 d: Henri Decoin. lps: Juliette Greco, Jean-Marc Bory, Liselotte Pulver. 104M FRN. *Where the Truth Lies* (USA); *Evil Spell*; *Sorcery*; *Evil Spirits* prod/rel: Marianne Productions, S.N.E.G.
Malefices 1990 d: Carlo RolA. lps: Pierre Malet, Iris Berben, Susanne Lothar. TVM. 90M FRN.

Terminus, Novel
Ruckfahrt in Den Tod 199- d: Hans-Jurgen Togel. lps: Peter Bongartz, Wolfgang Wahl, Iris Berben. TVM. 90M GRM.

Les Victimes, Novel
Victimes, Les 1996 d: Patrick Grandperret. lps: Vincent Lindon, Jacques Dutronc, Karin Viard. 95M FRN. *Victims* prod/rel: Gaumont International

Les Visages de l'Ombre, Paris 1953, Novel
Faces in the Dark 1960 d: David Eady. lps: John Gregson, Mai Zetterling, John Ireland. 85M UKN. prod/rel: Pennington-Eady Productions, Rank Film Distributors

BOITO, ARRIGO (1842–1918), ITL, Boito, Enrico
La Gioconda, Milan 1876, Opera
Gioconda, La 1953 d: Giacinto Solito. lps: Alba Arnova, Paolo Carlini, Virginia Loy. F ITL. prod/rel: Org. Cin.Ca Internazionale

BOITO, CAMILLO
Senso, Milan 1883, Novel
Senso 1954 d: Luchino Visconti. lps: Alida Valli, Farley Granger, Massimo Girotti. 120M ITL. *The Wanton Countess* (UKN); *The Wanton Contessa*; *Sentiment* prod/rel: Lux Film

BOJER, JOHAN
The Power of a Lie, London 1908, Novel
Power of a Lie, The 1922 d: George Archainbaud. lps: Mabel Julienne Scott, David Torrence, Maude George. 4910f USA. prod/rel: Universal Pictures

Sigurd Braa, 1916, Play
Sangen Till Livet 1943 d: Leif Sinding. 108M NRW.

Verdens Ansigt, Copenhagen 1917, Novel
Face of the World 1921 d: Irvin V. Willat. lps: Edward Hearn, Barbara Bedford, Harry Duffield. 5800f USA. prod/rel: Willat Productions, W. W. Hodkinson Corp.

BOLAND, BRIDGET
Cockpit, 1948, Play
Lost People, The 1949 d: Bernard Knowles, Muriel Box. lps: Dennis Price, Mai Zetterling, Richard Attenborough. 88M UKN. *The Cockpit* prod/rel: General Film Distributors, Gainsborough

The Prisoner, London 1954, Play
Prisoner, The 1955 d: Peter Glenville. lps: Alec Guinness, Jack Hawkins, Wilfred Lawson. 95M UKN. prod/rel: Facet, London Independent Producers

BOLAND, JOHN
The League of Gentlemen, London 1958, Novel
League of Gentlemen, The 1960 d: Basil Dearden. lps: Jack Hawkins, Nigel Patrick, Roger Livesey. 113M UKN. prod/rel: Allied Film Makers, Rank Film Distributors

BOLDREWOOD, ROLF
Robbery Under Arms, 1888, Novel
Robbery Under Arms 1957 d: Jack Lee. lps: Peter Finch, Ronald Lewis, Maureen Swanson. 99M UKN/ASL. prod/rel: Rank, Rank Film Distributors
Robbery Under Arms 1985 d: Ken Hannam, Donald Crombie. lps: Sam Neill, Steven Vidler, Christopher Cummins. 141M ASL. prod/rel: Itc Entertainment, South Australia Film Corp. Prods.©

BOLDT, GERHARDT
The Last Days of the Chancellery, Book
Ultimi Dieci Giorni Di Hitler, Gli 1973 d: Ennio de Concini. lps: Alec Guinness, Doris Kunstmann, John Bennett. 104M ITL/UKN. *Hitler: the Last Ten Days* (UKN) prod/rel: West Film (Roma), W. Reinhardt Production (London)

BOLDT, JOHANNES
Paradies Der Junggesellen, Novel
Paradies Der Junggesellen 1939 d: Kurt Hoffmann. lps: Heinz Ruhmann, Hans Brausewetter, Josef Sieber. 84M GRM. *Bachelor's Paradise* (USA) prod/rel: Terra, Turck

BOLL, HEINRICH (1917–1985), GRM
Ansichten Eines Clowns, 1963, Novel
Ansichten Eines Clowns 1975 d: Vojtech Jasny. lps: Helmut Griem, Hanna Schygulla, Eva-Maria Meineke. 120M GRM. *The Clown* (USA); *Opinions of a Clown*; *Faces of a Clown* prod/rel: Independent Film, Constantin

Billard Um Halb Zehn, Cologne 1959, Novel
Nicht Versohnt Oder "Es Hilft Nur Gewalt, Wo Gewalt Herrscht" 1965 d: Jean-Marie Straub, Daniele Huillet. lps: Heinrich Hargesheimer, Carlheinz Hargesheimer, Martha Standner. 53M GRM. *Es Hilft Nicht Wo Gewalt Herrscht*; *Unreconciled*; *Not Reconciled Or "Only Violence Helps Where It Rules"*; *Nicht Versohnt* prod/rel: Straub-Huillet

Das Brot Der Fruhen Jahre, 1955, Novel
Brot Der Fruhen Jahre, Das 1962 d: Herbert Vesely. lps: Christian Doermer, Karen Blanguernon, Vera TschechowA. 89M GRM. *The Bread of Our Early Years*; *The Bread of the Early Years* prod/rel: Modern Art, Atlas

Dr. Murkes Gesammeles Schweigen, 1958, Short Story
Doktor Murkes Samlade Tystnad 1968 d: Per Berglund. 29M SWD. *Dr. Murkes Samlade Tystnad*; *Dr. Murkes Collected Silences*

Gruppenbild Mit Dame, 1971, Novel
Gruppenbild Mit Dame 1977 d: Aleksandar Petrovic. lps: Romy Schneider, Brad Dourif, Michel Galabru. 107M GRM/FRN/YGS. *Portrait de Groupe Avec Dame* (FRN); *Group Portrait With a Lady* (USA) prod/rel: Stella, Cinema 77

Hauptstadtisches Journal, 1957, Short Story
MacHorka-Muff 1962 d: Jean-Marie Straub, Daniele Huillet. lps: Erich von Kuby, Renate Lang, Rolf Thiede. 18M GRM.

Die Verlorene Ehre Der Katharina Blum, 1974, Novel
Act of Passion 1984 d: Simon Langton. lps: Marlo Thomas, Kris Kristofferson, George DzundzA. TVM. 104M USA. *The Lost Honor of Kathryn Beck* prod/rel: CBS, Comworld
Verlorene Ehre Der Katharina Blum, Die 1975 d: Volker Schlondorff, Margarethe von TrottA. lps: Angela Winkler, Mario Adorf, Dieter Laser. 105M GRM. *The Lost Honor of Katharina Blum* (USA) prod/rel: Bioskop, Paramount-Orion

BOLLA, NINO
La Grande Tragica, Book
Eleonora Duse 1950 d: Filippo Walter Ratti. lps: Elisa Cegani, Andrea Checchi, Rossano Brazzi. 90M ITL. prod/rel: San Giorgio Film, Artisti Associati

BOLNICK, PASTER
Winnie: My Life in the Institution, Book
Winnie 1988 d: John Korty. lps: Meredith Baxter, David Morse, Jenny O'HarA. TVM. 100M USA.

BOLOGNA, JOSEPH
Lovers and Other Strangers, New York 1968, Play
Lovers and Other Strangers 1970 d: Cy Howard. lps: Gig Young, Bonnie Bedelia, Beatrice Arthur. 106M USA. prod/rel: ABC Pictures

BOLT, BEN
Diana of the Islands, Novel
Mutiny 1925 d: F. Martin Thornton. lps: Nigel Barrie, Doris Lytton, Walter Tennyson. 4250f UKN. *Diana of the Islands* prod/rel: George Clark, Ducal

The Gay Corinthian, Novel
Gay Corinthian, The 1924 d: Arthur Rooke. lps: Victor McLaglen, Betty Faire, Cameron Carr. 5300f UKN. *The Three Wagers* prod/rel: I. B. Davidson, Butcher's Film Service

BOLT, CAROL
One Night Stand, Play
One Night Stand 1978 d: Allan King. lps: Chapelle Jaffe, Brent Carver, Dinah Christie. 93M CND. *One-Night Stand* prod/rel: Canadian Broadcasting Corp., Allan King Associates Ltd.

BOLT, NEVILLE
Hollow Reed, Short Story
Hollow Reed 1995 d: Angela Pope. lps: Martin Donovan, Joely Richardson, Ian Hart. 104M UKN/GRM. prod/rel: Channel 4 Tv, Scala (Hollow Reed) Ltd

BOLT, PETER
Die Braut Nr. 68, Novel
Land Ohne Frauen, Das 1929 d: Carmine Gallone. lps: Conrad Veidt, Elga Brink, Ernes Verebes. 3220m GRM. *Terra Senza Donne* prod/rel: F.P.S. Film

BOLT, ROBERT (1924–1995), UKN, Bolt, Robert Oxton
A Man for All Seasons, London 1960, Play
Man for All Seasons, A 1966 d: Fred Zinnemann. lps: Paul Scofield, Wendy Hiller, Leo McKern. 120M UKN. prod/rel: Highland Films, Columbia
Man for All Seasons, A 1988 d: Charlton Heston. lps: Charlton Heston, Vanessa Redgrave, John Gielgud. TVM. 150M USA.

BOLTON, GUY
Adam and Eva, New York 1923, Play
Adam and Eva 1923 d: Robert G. VignolA. lps: Marion Davies, T. Roy Barnes, Tom Lewis. 7153f USA. prod/rel: Paramount, Cosmopolitan Productions

Anything Goes, New York 1934, Musical Play
Anything Goes 1936 d: Lewis Milestone. lps: Bing Crosby, Ethel Merman, Charles Ruggles. 92M USA. *Tops Is the Limit* prod/rel: Paramount Productions, Inc.
Anything Goes 1956 d: Robert Lewis. lps: Bing Crosby, Donald O'Connor, Zizi Jeanmaire. 106M USA. prod/rel: Paramount

The Cave Girl, New York 1920, Play
Cave Girl, The 1921 d: Joseph J. Franz. lps: Teddie Gerard, Charles Meredith, Wilton Taylor. 4405f USA. prod/rel: Inspiration Pictures, Associated First National Pictures

Chicken Feed; Or Wages for Wives, New York 1923, Play
Wages for Wives 1925 d: Frank Borzage. lps: Jacqueline Logan, Creighton Hale, Earle Foxe. 6650f USA. prod/rel: Fox Film Corp.

The Dark Angel, New York 1925, Play
Dark Angel, The 1925 d: George Fitzmaurice. lps: Ronald Colman, Vilma Banky, Wyndham Standing. 7311f USA. prod/rel: Samuel Goldwyn Productions, First National Pictures
Dark Angel, The 1935 d: Sidney A. Franklin. lps: Fredric March, Merle Oberon, Herbert Marshall. 105M USA. prod/rel: Samuel Goldwyn, Inc., United Artists

BOOTH, HILLIARD
Short Story
Black Gate, The 1919 d: Theodore Marston. lps: Earle Williams, Ruth Clifford, Clarissa Selwynne. 5r USA. prod/rel: Vitagraph Co. of America©

BOOTH, JOHN HUNTER
The Masquerader, New York 1917, Play
Masquerader, The 1933 d: Richard Wallace. lps: Ronald Colman, Elissa Landi, Halliwell Hobbes. 78M USA. prod/rel: United Artists Corp., Samuel Goldwyn, Inc.

Rolling Home, Play
Rolling Home 1926 d: William A. Seiter. lps: Reginald Denny, Marian Nixon, E. J. Ratcliffe. 6993f USA. prod/rel: Universal Pictures

BOOTHBY, GUY
A Bid for Fortune, Novel
Bid for Fortune, A 1917 d: Sidney Morgan. lps: A. Harding Steerman, Violet Graham, Sydney Vautier. 4000f UKN. prod/rel: Unity-Super

BOOTHE, CLARE
Kiss the Boys Goodbye, New York 1938, Play
Kiss the Boys Goodbye 1941 d: Victor Schertzinger. lps: Mary Martin, Don Ameche, Oscar Levant. 85M USA. prod/rel: Paramount

Margin for Error, New York 1939, Play
Margin for Error 1943 d: Otto Preminger. lps: Joan Bennett, Milton Berle, Otto Preminger. 74M USA. prod/rel: 20th Century-Fox

BOOTHROYD, DERRICK
Value for Money, Novel
Value for Money 1955 d: Ken Annakin. lps: John Gregson, Diana Dors, Susan Stephen. 93M UKN. prod/rel: Rank Film Distributors, Group Films

BORCHERT, WOLFGANG (1921–1947), GRM
Draussen von Der Tur, 1947, Play
Liebe 47 1949 d: Wolfgang Liebeneiner. lps: Hilde Krahl, Karl John, Dieter Horn. 118M GRM. *Love in 47*; *Love 47* prod/rel: Filmaufbau, Panorama

BORDEAUX, HENRI (1870–1963), FRN
Book
Chasse aux Chamois Dans Les Alpes Fribourgeoises, Une 1926 d: Pierre Lebrun. lps: Eduard Buchs, Moser, Egger. DOC. 90M SWT. *Eine Gemsjagd in Den Freiburger Alpen* prod/rel: Film-Artes

Le Calvaire de Cimiez, Novel
Calvaire de Cimiez, Le 1934 d: Jacques de Baroncelli, Rene Dalliere. lps: Marie-Ange Rivain, Marie-Louise Sarky, Francois Chatenay. 80M FRN. prod/rel: Cinereve, Films Armor

Le Chemin de Roselande, Short Story
Chemin de Roseland, Le 1924 d: Maurice Gleize. lps: Regine Dumien, Louis Roller. 1450m FRN. prod/rel: Super Film

La Croisee Des Chemins, Novel
Croisee Des Chemins, La 1942 d: Andre Berthomieu. lps: Pierre Richard-Willm, Pierre Brasseur, Josette Day. 90M FRN. prod/rel: Marcel Pagnol

L' Ecran Brise, Novel
Ecran Brise, L' 1922 d: Raoul d'Auchy. lps: Georges Mauloy, Andree Lionel, Therese Vasseur. 1265m FRN. prod/rel: E. D'auchy Film

La Neige Sur Les Pas, Novel
Neige Sur Les Pas, La 1923 d: Henri Etievant. lps: Victor Francen, Germaine Fontanes, M. Borin. 2000m FRN. prod/rel: Films Legrand

Neige Sur Les Pas, La 1941 d: Andre Berthomieu. lps: Pierre Blanchar, Georges Lannes, Michele AlfA. 91M FRN. prod/rel: F.P.D.F.

Les Roquevilard, Novel
Roquevillard, Les 1943 d: Jean Dreville. lps: Charles Vanel, Aime Clariond, Jean Paqui. 95M FRN. prod/rel: Sirius

Yamile Sous Les Cedres, Novel
Yamile Sous Les Cedres 1939 d: Charles d'Espinay. lps: Jose Noguero, Denise Bosc, Georges Peclet. 95M FRN. prod/rel: Imperial Film Production

BORDEN, MARY
Action for Slander, Novel
Action for Slander 1937 d: Tim Whelan, Victor Saville. lps: Clive Brook, Ann Todd, Margaretta Scott. 83M UKN. prod/rel: London Films, Victor Saville Productions

BORDEWIJK, F.
Karakter, Novel
Karakter 1997 d: Mike Van Diem. lps: Fedja Van Huet, Jan Decleir, Betty Schuurman. 120M NTH. *Character* prod/rel: Almerica Film B.V.©, Nps

BORDY, MAX
Sybil, Play
Duchess of Buffalo, The 1926 d: Sidney A. Franklin. lps: Constance Talmadge, Tullio Carminati, Edward Martindel. 6940f USA. *Sybil* prod/rel: Constance Talmadge Productions, First National Pictures

BORENSTEIN, TAMAR
Kofiko, Novel
Going Bananas 1987 d: Boaz Davidson. lps: Dom Deluise, Jimmie Walker, David Mendenhall. 94M USA. *My African Adventure* prod/rel: Cannon

BORER, MARY CATHCART
Story
Eagle Rock 1964 d: Henry Geddes. lps: Pip Rolls, Christine Thomas, Stephen Morris. 62M UKN. prod/rel: World Safari, Children's Film Foundation

The House With the Blue Door, Novel
Secret Tunnel, The 1947 d: William C. Hammond. lps: Anthony Wager, Ivor Bowyer, Murray Matheson. 49M UKN. prod/rel: Merton Park, General Film Distributors

Tabitha, London 1956, Play
Who Killed the Cat? 1966 d: Montgomery Tully. lps: Mary Merrall, Ellen Pollock, Amy Dalby. 76M UKN. prod/rel: Grand National, Eternal

BORETZ, ALLAN
Room Service, Play
Step Lively 1944 d: Tim Whelan. lps: Frank Sinatra, George Murphy, Adolphe Menjou. 88M USA. prod/rel: RKO

BORG, WASHINGTON
Leggenda Per Violino in 4 Tempi
Bimbi Lontani 1939 d: Baldassarre Negroni. lps: Hesperia, Tullio Carminati, Guido Guiducci. 1207m ITL. prod/rel: Film d'Arte Italiana

Le Quattro Stagioni
Notturni 1919 d: Guido Di Sandro. lps: Clarette Rosaj, Guido Graziosi, Georgette Faraboni. 1762m ITL. prod/rel: Quirinus Film

BORGES, JORGE LUIS (1899–1986), ARG
Emma Zunz, 1949, Short Story
Dias de Odio 1954 d: Leopoldo Torre-Nilsson. lps: Raul Del Valle, Nicolas Fregues, Elisa Galve. 70M ARG. *Days of Hate* (USA); *Days of Hatred*

La Intrusa, 1952, Short Story
Intrusa, A 1979 d: Carlos Hugo Christensen. lps: Jose de Abreu, Arlindo Barreto, Palmira BarbosA. 100M BRZ/ARG. *The Intruder*; *The Intrusion*

Tema Del Traidor Y Del Heroe, 1944, Short Story
Strategia Del Ragno, La 1969 d: Bernardo Bertolucci. lps: Giulio Brogi, Alida Valli, Tino Scotti. 110M ITL. *The Spider's Strategy*; *The Spider's Stratagem* prod/rel: Red Film, Rai Tv

BORK, TEDA
Im Namen Einer Mutter, Novel
Im Namen Einer Mutter 1960 d: Erich Engels. lps: Ulla Jacobsson, Claus Holm, Dietmar Schonherr. 90M GRM. *In the Name of a Mother* prod/rel: D.F.H.

BORLAND, HAL
When the Legends Die, Novel
When the Legends Die 1972 d: Stuart Millar. lps: Richard Widmark, Frederic Forrest, Luana Anders. 107M USA. prod/rel: 20th Century Fox

BORN, NICHOLAS
Die Falschung, 1979, Novel
Falschung, Die 1981 d: Volker Schlondorff. lps: Bruno Ganz, Hanna Schygulla, Jean Carmet. 110M GRM/FRN. *Circle of Deceit* (UKN); *Le Faussaire* (FRN); *False Witness*; *The Forgery*; *Deception, The* prod/rel: Bioskop, Artemis

BORNEMANN, ERNEST
Face the Music, Novel
Face the Music 1954 d: Terence Fisher. lps: Alex Nicol, Eleanor Summerfield, John Salew. 84M UKN. *The Black Glove* (USA) prod/rel: Hammer, Exclusive

BORNICHE, ROGER
Flic Story, Novel
Flic Story 1975 d: Jacques Deray. lps: Alain Delon, Jean-Louis Trintignant, Renato Salvatori. 110M FRN/ITL. prod/rel: Mondial Te.Fi., Adel

L' Ultima Invasione, Novel
Rene la Canne 1976 d: Francis Girod. lps: Michel Piccoli, Gerard Depardieu, Sylvia Kristel. 105M FRN/ITL. *Tre Simpatiche Carogne*; *Tre Simpatiche Carogne. E Vissero Insieme Felici Imbrogliando E Truffando* (ITL) prod/rel: Presidents (Paris), Rizzoli Film (Roma)

BOROWIAK, SIMONE
Frau Rettich Die Czerni Und Ich, Novel
Frau Rettich, Die Czerni Und Ich 1998 d: Markus Imboden. lps: Iris Berben, Martina Gedeck, Jeanette Hain. 96M GRM. *Mrs. Rettich Czerny and Me* prod/rel: Jugendfilm, Bavaria Film

BOROWSKI, TADEUSZ (1922–1951), PLN
Krajobraz Po Bitwie, Novel
Krajobraz Po Bitwie 1970 d: Andrzej WajdA. lps: Daniel Olbrychski, Tadeusz Janczar, Stanislawa CelinskA. 110M PLN. *Landscape After the Battle*; *Landscape After Battle* prod/rel: Film Polski

BOROWSKY, MARVIN
The Long Journey, Story
Somewhere in the Night 1946 d: Joseph L. Mankiewicz. lps: John Hodiak, Lloyd Nolan, Richard Conte. 108M USA. prod/rel: 20th Century-Fox

BORROW, GEORGE (1803–1881), UKN
Romany Rye, London 1857, Novel
Broken Law, The 1915 d: Oscar Apfel. lps: William Farnum, Dorothy Bernard, Nicholas Dunaew. 5r USA. prod/rel: Fox Film Corp., William Fox©

BORSHCHAGOVSKIY, A.
Trevoshnyye Oblaka
Tretiy Taym 1963 d: Yevgyeni Karelov. lps: Yuri Volkov, Vladimir Kashpur, Leonid Kuravlyov. 88M USS. *The Last Game* (USA); *The Third Time* prod/rel: Mosfilm

BOSBOOM-TOUSSAINT, ANNA L. G.
Majoor Frans, 1874, Novel
Majoor Frans 1916 d: Maurits H. Binger. lps: Annie Bos, Louis H. Chrispijn, Frederick Vogeding. 1970m NTH. *Major Frans*; **De Soldatendochter** prod/rel: Filmfabriek-Hollandia

BOSCO, WALLY
Story
Mr. Horatio Knibbles 1971 d: Robert Hird. lps: Lesley Roach, Gary Smith, Rachel Brennock. 55M UKN. prod/rel: C.F.F. Productions

BOSE, RAJASEKHAR
Birinchi Baba
Mahapurush 1965 d: Satyajit Ray. lps: Charuprakash Ghosh, Prasad Mukherjee, Robi Ghosh. 65M IND. *The Holy Man* prod/rel: R.D.B.

BOSE, SAMARESH
Paar, Short Story
Paar 1984 d: Gautam Ghose. lps: Naseeruddin Shah, Shabana Azmi, Utpal Dutt. 141M IND. *Saahil*; *The Crossing* prod/rel: Orchid Films

BOSETZKY, HORST
Kein Reihenhaus Fur Robin Hood, Novel
Kein Reihenhaus Fur Robin Hood 1980 d: Wolfgang Gremm. lps: Hermann Lause, Jutta Speidel, Rudolf Waldemar Brem. 100M GRM. *No Townhouse for Robin Hood* prod/rel: Regina Ziegler Filmprod.

BOSHER, KATE LANGLEY
"*Frequently Martha*" *Mary Cary*, New York 1910, Novel
Nobody's Kid 1921 d: Howard Hickman. lps: Mae Marsh, Kathleen Kirkham, Anne Schaefer. 5r USA. *Little Miss Somebody*; *Mary Cary* prod/rel: Robertson-Cole Pictures

BOSSE, MALCOLM
Angent Trouble, Novel
Agent Trouble 1987 d: Jean-Pierre Mocky. lps: Catherine Deneuve, Richard Bohringer, Tom Novembre. 86M FRN. *Trouble Agent* prod/rel: Canal Plus, a.F.C.

BOST, PIERRE
Monsieur Ladmiral Va Bientot Mourir, 1945, Novel
Dimanche a la Compagne, Un 1984 d: Bertrand Tavernier. lps: Louis Ducreux, Sabine Azema, Michel Aumont. 94M FRN. *Sunday in the Country* (UKN) prod/rel: Sara Films, Films a2

BOSWORTH, ALLAN R.
The Crows of Edwina Hill, New York 1961, Novel
Nobody's Perfect 1968 d: Alan Rafkin. lps: Doug McClure, David Hartman, James Whitmore. 103M USA. *The Winning Position* prod/rel: Universal Pictures

BOTTCHER, MAXIMILIAN
Krach Im Hinterhaus, Play
Krach Im Hinterhaus 1935 d: Veit Harlan. lps: Henny Porten, Eduard von Winterstein. F GRM. *Trouble Back Stairs* (USA)

Krach Im Hinterhaus 1949 d: Erich Kobler. lps: Paul Dahlke, Fita Benkhoff, Ursula Herking. 85M GRM. *Trouble in the Back House* prod/rel: Zeyn, Bavaria

Krach Im Vorderhaus, Play
Krach Im Vorderhaus 1941 d: Paul Heidemann. lps: Ernst Waldow, Grethe Weiser, Mady Rahl. 75M GRM. prod/rel: Tobis

BOTTOME, PHYLLIS (1884–1963), UKN, Forbes-Dennis, Mrs. Ernan
Danger Signal, Novel
Danger Signal 1945 d: Robert Florey. lps: Faye Emerson, Zachary Scott, Richard Erdman. 78M USA. prod/rel: Warner Bros.

Heart of a Child, Novel
Heart of a Child 1958 d: Clive Donner. lps: Jean Anderson, Donald Pleasence, Richard Williams. 77M UKN. prod/rel: Beaconsfield, Rank Film Distributors

The Mortal Storm, London 1937, Novel
Mortal Storm, The 1940 d: Frank Borzage. lps: Margaret Sullavan, James Stewart, Robert Young. 100M USA. prod/rel: Metro-Goldwyn-Mayer Corp., Loew's, Inc.©

Private Worlds, Boston 1934, Novel
Private Worlds 1935 d: Gregory La CavA. lps: Claudette Colbert, Charles Boyer, Joan Bennett. 84M USA. prod/rel: Walter Wanger Productions, Paramount Productions©

BOUBER, HERMAN
Bleeke Bet, 1917, Play
Bleeke Bet 1923 d: Alex Benno. lps: Alida Gijtenbeek, Beppie de Vries, Rika Kloppenburg. 2200m NTH. *Pale Bet* prod/rel: Alex Benno, Actueel-Film

Bleeke Bet 1934 d: Alex Benno, Richard Oswald. lps: Aaf Bouber, Johan Elsensohn, Jopie Koopman. 102M NTH. *Pale Betty* prod/rel: Monopol-Dls

De Jantjes, 1920, Play
Jantjes, de 1922 d: Maurits H. Binger, B. E. Doxat-Pratt. lps: Beppie de Vries, Greta Meyer, Maurits de Vries. 1766m NTH. *The Jack-Tars* prod/rel: Filmfabriek-Hollandia

Oranje Hein, 1918, Play
Oranje Hein 1925 d: Alex Benno. lps: Johan Elsensohn, Aaf Bouber-Ten Hoope, Maurits de Vries. 2272m NTH. *Orange Hein* prod/rel: Alex Benno, Actueel-Film

Oranje Hein 1936 d: Max Nosseck. lps: Herman Bouber, Aaf Bouber, Max Croiset. 78M NTH.

Zeemansvrouwen, 1928, Play
Zeemansvrouwen 1930 d: Henk Kleinmann. lps: Harry Boda, Jos Schetzer, Raas Luijben. 2360m NTH. *Seamen's Wives* prod/rel: N.V. Filmfabriek "Holland"

BOUCHARD, MICHEL MARC
Les Feluettes; Ou la Repetition d'un Drame Romantique, 1987, Play
Lilies 1996 d: John Greyson. lps: Brent Carver, Marcel Sabourin, Aubert Pallascio. 92M CND. prod/rel: Galafilm©, Triptych Media©

BOUCHARD, ROBERT
Matricule 33, Play
Matricule 33 1933 d: Karl Anton. lps: Edwige Feuillere, Andre Luguet, Abel Tarride. 91M FRN. prod/rel: S.a.P.E.C.

BOUCHARDY, JEAN
Jean le Coucher, 1852, Novel
Vetturale Del Moncenisio, Il 1916 d: Leopoldo Carlucci. lps: Achille Majeroni, Lina Millefleurs, Elda Bruni-De Negri. 1811m ITL. prod/rel: Milano Film

Vetturale Del Moncenisio, Il 1927 d: Baldassarre Negroni. lps: Bartolomeo Pagano, Rina de Liguoro, Umberto Casilini. 2499m ITL. prod/rel: S.A. Pittaluga

Vetturale Del Moncenisio, Il 1956 d: Guido Brignone. lps: Roldano Lupi, Elisa Cegani, Virna Lisi. 88M ITL. prod/rel: Produzioni Alberto Manca, Radius Prod. (Paris)

BOUCHERON, MAXIME
Miss Helyett, Opera
Miss Helyett 1927 d: Georges Monca, Maurice Keroul. lps: Marie Glory, Pierre Hot, Fernand Fabre. 2100m FRN. prod/rel: G.P.C. Phocea

Miss Helyett 1933 d: Hubert Bourlon, Jean Kemm. lps: Josette Day, Jim Gerald, Germaine Reuver. 75M FRN. prod/rel: Societe Des Films Vega

BOUCICAULT, DION (1820?–1890), IRL
Across the Continent, New York 1871, Play
Across the Continent 1913. lps: Herbert Barrington, Herbert L. Barry, Wilbur Hudson. 4r USA. prod/rel: Pilot Films Corp., State Rights

After Dark, London 1868, Play
After Dark 1915 d: Frederick A. Thompson. lps: Alec B. Francis, Dorothy Green, Eric Maxon. 5r USA. prod/rel: William A. Brady Picture Plays, Inc., World Film Corp.©

After Dark 1915 d: Warwick Buckland. lps: Flora Morris, Harry Royston, Harry Gilbey. 3000f UKN. prod/rel: Buckland Films, a1

Arrah-Na-Pogue, 1865, Play
Arrah-Na-Pogue 1911 d: Sidney Olcott. lps: Gene Gaunthier, Sidney Olcott, Agnes Mapes. 3000f USA.

The Colleen Bawn, London 1860, Play
Colleen Bawn, The 1911 d: Sidney Olcott. lps: Gene Gaunthier, Jack J. Clark, Sidney Olcott. 3000f USA. prod/rel: Kalem

Colleen Bawn, The 1924 d: W. P. Kellino. lps: Henry Victor, Colette Brettel, Stewart Rome. 6650f UKN. *The Loves of Colleen Bawn* prod/rel: Stoll

Lily of Killarney 1929 d: George Ridgwell. lps: Cecil Landeau, Pamela Parr, Dennis Wyndham. SIL. 6100f UKN. prod/rel: British International Pictures, Wardour

Lily of Killarney 1934 d: Maurice Elvey. lps: John Garrick, Gina Malo, Stanley Holloway. 88M UKN. *The Bride of the Lake* (USA) prod/rel: Twickenham, Associated Producers and Distributors

Conn the Shaugraun, Play
Murphy's Wake 1906. 335f UKN. prod/rel: Walturdaw

Erin's Isle, Play
O'Neil, The 1911 d: Sidney Olcott. lps: Jack J. Clark, Gene Gaunthier, Robert VignolA. 1000f IRL/USA. *The O'Neill* prod/rel: Kalem

Grimaldi, Play
Grimaldi 1914 d: Charles Vernon. lps: Bransby Williams, Sidney Kearns. 1000f UKN. prod/rel: Planet Films, Hibbert

Kathleen Mavourneen, Play
Kathleen Mavourneen 1913 d: Charles J. Brabin. lps: Mary Fuller, Marc McDermott, Augustus Phillips. 1050f USA. prod/rel: Edison

Kathleen Mavourneen 1913 d: Herbert Brenon. lps: Jane Fearnley, William E. Shay, Frank Smith. 3r USA. prod/rel: Imp

Kathleen Mavourneen 1930 d: Albert Ray. lps: Sally O'Neil, Charles Delaney, Robert Elliott. 5196f USA. *The Girl from Ireland* (UKN) prod/rel: Tiffany Productions

London Assurance, London 1841, Play
London Assurance 1913 d: Lawrence McGill. lps: Edgena de Lespine, E. P. Sullivan, Ethel Phillips. SHT USA. prod/rel: Reliance

The Long Strike, Story
Long Strike, The 1912 d: Herbert Brenon. lps: Vivian Prescott, Frank Smith, William E. Shay. 2r USA. prod/rel: Imp

Onawanda, Play
Onawanda; Or, an Indian's Devotion 1909 d: J. Stuart Blackton (Spv). lps: Edith Storey. 545f USA. *An Indian's Devotion* prod/rel: Vitagraph Co. of America

The Shaughraun, London 1875, Play
My Wild Irish Rose 1922 d: David Smith. lps: Pat O'Malley, Helen Howard, Maud Emery. 7r USA. prod/rel: Vitagraph Co. of America

Shaughraun, The 1912 d: Sidney Olcott. lps: Sidney Olcott, Jack J. Clark, Robert Melville. 3000f USA. prod/rel: Kalem

The Streets of London, London 1864, Play
Streets of London, The 1929 d: Norman Lee. lps: David Dunbar, Jack Rutherford, James Lincoln. SIL. 3600f UKN. prod/rel: H. B. Parkinson, Pioneer

The Streets of New York, Play
Streets of New York, The 1913 d: Travers Vale. lps: Madge Orlamond, J. H. Roberts, Herbert Barrington. 3r USA. prod/rel: Pilot

BOUCICAULT, RUTH HOLT
The Substance of His House, Boston 1914, Novel
House Divided, A 1919 d: J. Stuart Blackton. lps: Sylvia Breamer, Herbert Rawlinson, Lawrence Grossmith. 5-6r USA. *Love Marriage and Divorce* prod/rel: J. Stuart Blackton Productions, Inc., Independent Sales Corp.

BOUDARD, ALPHONSE
Gegene le Tatoue, Novel
Tatoue, Le 1968 d: Denys de La Patelliere. lps: Jean Gabin, Louis de Funes, Dominique Davray. 90M FRN/ITL. *Nemici Per la Pelle -Il Tatuato* (ITL); *Million Dollar Legs*; *Comme En 14* prod/rel: Films Copernic, Films Corona

La Metamorphose Des Cloportes, Paris 1962, Novel
Metamorphose Des Cloportes 1965 d: Pierre Granier-Deferre. lps: Lino Ventura, Charles Aznavour, Irina Demick. 102M FRN/ITL. *Sotto Il Tallone* (ITL); *Cloportes* (USA) prod/rel: Films Du Siecle, Produzioni Artistic Internazionali

BOUDRIOZ, ROBERT
L' Apre Lutte, Play
Apre Lutte, L' 1917 d: Robert Boudrioz, Jacques de Feraudy. lps: Jean Duval, Maurice Lagrenee, Andre Marnay. 1400m FRN.

BOUGH, JACKIE
Why Have They Taken Our Children?, Book
Vanished Without a Trace 1993 d: Vern Gillum. lps: Karl Malden, Tim Ransom, Travis Fine. TVM. 89M USA.

BOULLE, PIERRE (1912–, FRN, Boulle, Pierre Francois Marie-Louis
La Planete Des Singes, Paris 1963, Novel
Planet of the Apes 1968 d: Franklin J. Schaffner. lps: Charlton Heston, Roddy McDowall, Kim Hunter. 112M USA. prod/rel: Apjac Productions

Le Pont de la Riviere Kwai, 1952, Novel
Bridge on the River Kwai, The 1957 d: David Lean. lps: William Holden, Alec Guinness, Jack Hawkins. 161M UKN/USA. prod/rel: Columbia, Horizon

BOULTON, MATTHEW
The Burglar and the Girl, Play
Burglar and the Girl, The 1928 d: Hugh Croise. lps: Moore Marriott, Dorothy Boyd. SND. 12M UKN. prod/rel: de Forest Phonofilms

The Corduroy Diplomat, Play
King of Hearts 1936 d: Oswald Mitchell, Walter Tennyson. lps: Will Fyffe, Gwenllian Gill, Richard Dolman. 82M UKN. prod/rel: Butcher's Film Service

His Rest Day, Play
His Rest Day 1927 d: George A. Cooper. lps: Matthew Boulton. SND. 9M UKN. prod/rel: de Forest Phonofilms

BOURBON, DIANA
Atlantic Adventurer, 1934, Short Story
Atlantic Adventure 1935 d: Albert S. Rogell. lps: Lloyd Nolan, Nancy Carroll, Harry Langdon. 70M USA. prod/rel: Columbia Pictures Corp.

Roaring Lady, 1933, Short Story
Roaming Lady 1936 d: Albert S. Rogell. lps: Fay Wray, Ralph Bellamy, Thurston Hall. 68M USA. prod/rel: Columbia Pictures Corp.©

BOURDEAUX, HENRI
Les Roquevillard, Novel
Roquevillard, Les 1922 d: Julien Duvivier. lps: Maxime Desjardins, Jeanne Desclos, Edmond Van Daele. 1960m FRN. prod/rel: Societe Regionale De Cinematographie

BOURDET, EDOUARD
Fric-Frac, 1937, Play
Fric-Frac 1939 d: Maurice Lehmann, Claude Autant-LarA. lps: Fernandel, Arletty, Michel Simon. 120M FRN. prod/rel: Productions Maurice Lehmann

Hymenee, 1941, Play
Hymenee 1946 d: Emile Couzinet. lps: Gaby Morlay, Maurice Escande, Bernard Lancret. 95M FRN. prod/rel: Burgus Films

Le Sexe Faible, 1931, Play
Sexe Faible, Le 1934 d: Robert Siodmak. lps: Jeanne Cheirel, Marguerite Moreno, Victor Boucher. 95M FRN. *The Weaker Sex* prod/rel: Nero-Film

Vient de Paraitre, 1928, Play
Vient de Paraitre 1949 d: Jacques Houssin. lps: Pierre Fresnay, Blanchette Brunoy, Helene Petit. 97M FRN. prod/rel: Sideral Films

BOURGAIN, A.
Le Drame du 23, Play
Drame du 23, Le 1914. FRN.

BOURGEOIS
La Mendicante Di Sassonia, Novel
Mendicante Di Sassonia, Il 1921 d: Giovanni PezzingA. lps: Mary Dumont, Mara Gall, Maria Pasquali. 1784m ITL. prod/rel: Tiziano Film

BOURGEOIS, ANICET
L' Aveugle, Play
Aveugle, L' 1914. lps: Louis Gauthier. 627m FRN. prod/rel: Acad

La Bouquetiere Des Innocents, Play
Bouquetiere Des Innocents, La 1922 d: Jacques Robert. lps: Jacques Guilhene, Lilian Constantini, Simone Vaudry. 2000m FRN. prod/rel: Gaumont - Serie Pax

La Fille Des Chiffonniers, Play
Fille Des Chiffonniers, La 1911 d: Albert Capellani, Georges MoncA. lps: Paul Capellani, Jean Kemm, Andree Pascal. 655m FRN. prod/rel: Scagl

Fille Des Chiffonniers, La 1922 d: Henri Desfontaines. lps: Jacques Gretillat, Blanche Montel, Madeleine Guitty. 2800m FRN. prod/rel: Gaumont - Serie Pax

Le Medecin Des Enfants, Play
Medecin Des Enfants, Le 1916 d: Georges DenolA. lps: Maxime Desjardins, Henry Roussell, Vera Sergine. 830m FRN. prod/rel: Scagl

BOURGEOIS, GERARD
Mam'zelle Bonaparte, Novel
Mam'zelle Bonaparte 1941 d: Maurice Tourneur. lps: Raymond Rouleau, Edwige Feuillere, Monique Joyce. 100M FRN. prod/rel: Continental-Films

BOURGET, PAUL (1852–1935), FRN, Bourget, Paul Charles Joseph
Andre Cornelis, Novel
Andre Cornelis 1915 d: Henri Pouctal. lps: Jane Hading. FRN. prod/rel: le Film d'Art

Andre Cornelis 1918 d: Jean Kemm, Georges DenolA. lps: Romuald Joube, Marie-Louise Derval, Pierre Magnier. 1500m FRN. prod/rel: Scagl

Andre Cornelis 1927 d: Jean Kemm. lps: Malcolm Tod, Claude France, Georges Lannes. SRL. FRN. *Sins of Desire* prod/rel: Jacques Haik

Anomalies, Short Story
Ma Maison de Saint-Cloud 1926 d: Jean Manoussi. lps: Andre Nox, Sabine Landray, Paul Jorge. 1550m FRN. prod/rel: Agence Generale Cinematographique

Cosmopolis, Novel
Cosmopolis 1919 d: Gaston Ravel. lps: Mina d'Orvella, Alberto A. Capozzi, Elena Sangro. 2885m ITL. *Life* (UKN) prod/rel: Cines

Le Disciple, 1889, Novel
Discepolo, Il 1917 d: Giuseppe Giusti. lps: Fabienne Fabreges, Dante Testa, Mary Cleo Tarlarini. 1690m ITL. prod/rel: Corona Film

L' Echeance, Short Story
Tout Se Paie 1920 d: Henry Houry. lps: Berthe Jalabert, Rolla Norman, Georges Saillard. 1740m FRN. prod/rel: Societe D'editions Cinematographiques

L' Ecuyere, Novel
Ecuyere, L' 1922 d: Leonce Perret. lps: Jean Angelo, Marcya Capri, Valentine Petit. 1900m FRN. prod/rel: Leonce Perret

Une Idylle Tragique, 1896
Dama S Barzojem 1912 d: Max Urban. lps: Andula Sedlackova, Rudolf Matucha, Jaroslav Hurt. CZC. *The Lady With the Borzoi; The Lady and the Watchdog* prod/rel: Asum

Idillio Tragico 1922 d: Gaston Ravel. lps: Helena Makowska, Guido Trento, Ferruccio Lado. 2156m ITL. prod/rel: Medusa Film

Monique, 1920, Novel
Monique 1921 d: Lucio d'AmbrA. lps: Lia Formia, Nera Badaloni, Umberto Zanuccoli. 1647m ITL. prod/rel: D'ambra Film

Le Sens de la Mort, Novel
Sens de la Mort, Le 1922 d: Yakov Protazanov. lps: Andre Nox, Rene Clair, Yanova Koghen. 1600m FRN. prod/rel: Ermolieff-Cinema

BOUSQUET, JACQUES
L' Amour Chante, Novel
Profesor de Mi Mujer, El 1930 d: Robert Florey. lps: Imperio Argentina, J. Ortiz de Zarate, Julia Lajos. F SPN. *El Professor Di Mi Senora; El Amor Solfeando* prod/rel: Cinaes (Barcelona), Renacimiento Films (Madrid)

Un Ange Passe, 1924, Short Story
Blonde Or Brunette 1927 d: Richard Rosson. lps: Adolphe Menjou, Greta Nissen, Arlette Marchal. 5872f USA. prod/rel: Famous Players-Lasky Corp., Paramount Pictures

Le Champion du Regiment, Play
Champion du Regiment, Le 1932 d: Henry Wulschleger. lps: Bach, Charles Montel, Germaine Charley. 91M FRN. prod/rel: Alex Nalpas

Chou-Chou Poids-Plume, Play
Chouchou Poids Plume 1932 d: Robert Bibal. lps: Geo Laby, Colette Broido, Wanda Greville. 87M FRN. prod/rel: Films Leon Poirier

Chou-Chou Poids-Plume 1925 d: Gaston Ravel. lps: Andre Roanne, Olga Day, Andre Lefaur. F FRN.

Mannequins, Opera
Mannequins 1933 d: Rene Hervil. lps: Noel-Noel, Paul Amiot, Edmee Favart. 80M FRN. prod/rel: Etablissements Jacques Haik

BOUSSENARD, LUIGI
Il Giro Del Mondo Di un Biricchino Di Parigi, Novel
Giro Del Mondo Di un Biricchino Di Parigi, Il 1921 d: Luigi Maggi, Dante Cappelli. lps: Franco Cappelli, Lola Romanos, Dante Cappelli. 1504m ITL. prod/rel: Ambrosio-Zanolla Film

BOUSSINOT, ROGER
Le Treizieme Caprice, Novel
13E Caprice, Le 1967 d: Roger Boussinot. lps: Pierre Brice, Marie Laforet, Pascale Roberts. 90M FRN. *Le Treizieme Caprice* prod/rel: Terra Films

BOUTET, FREDERIC
Gribiche, Short Story
Gribiche 1925 d: Jacques Feyder. lps: Francoise Rosay, Jean Forest, Rolla Norman. 2500m FRN. *Mother of Mine* prod/rel: Films Albatros

Le Reflet de Claude Mercoeur, Novel
Reflet de Claude Mercoeur, Le 1923 d: Julien Duvivier. lps: Gaston Jacquet, Maud Richard, Camille Beuve. 2135m FRN. prod/rel: Films J.D.

Le Spectre de Monsieur Imberger, Play
Mystere Imberger, Le 1935 d: Jacques Severac. lps: Simone Deguyse, Jean Galland, Gaston Modot. 82M FRN. *Le Spectre de M. Imberger* prod/rel: Compagnie Autonome De Cinematographie

BOUVE, WINSTON
The Girl on the Stairs, 1924, Short Story
Girl on the Stairs, The 1924 d: William Worthington. lps: Patsy Ruth Miller, Frances Raymond, Arline Pretty. 6214f USA. prod/rel: Peninsula Studios, Producers Distributing Corp.

BOUVIER, ALEXIS
Detresse, Short Story
Detresse 1929 d: Jean Durand. lps: Alice Roberte, Harry Pilcer, Philippe Heriat. F FRN. prod/rel: Franco-Films

BOWEN, CATHERINE D. (1897–1973), USA, Bowen, Catherine Drinker
Beloved Friend, Book
Music Lovers, The 1970 d: Ken Russell. lps: Richard Chamberlain, Glenda Jackson, Max Adrian. 123M UKN. *The Lonely Heart* prod/rel: United Artists, Russfilms

BOWER, B. M., Sinclair, Bertha Muzzy
The Flying U Ranch, New York 1914, Novel
Flying U Ranch, The 1927 d: Robert de Lacy. lps: Tom Tyler, Nora Lane, Bert Hadley. 4924f USA. prod/rel: R-C Pictures, Film Booking Offices of America

The Happy Family, New York 1910, Novel
Galloping Devil, The 1920 d: Nate Watt. lps: Franklyn Farnum, Vester Pegg, Genevieve Berte. 5500f USA. *Andy of the Flying U; Galloping Devils* prod/rel: Canyon Pictures Corp.©, State Rights

Jean of the Lazy a, Boston 1915, Novel
Ridin' Thunder 1925 d: Cliff Smith. lps: Jack Hoxie, Katherine Grant, Jack Pratt. 4358f USA. *Riding Thunder* prod/rel: Universal Pictures

The Lonesome Trail, Book
Lonesome Trail, The 1914 d: Colin Campbell. lps: Wheeler Oakman, Gertrude Ryan. SHT USA. prod/rel: Selig Polyscope Co.

Points West, Boston 1928, Novel
Points West 1929 d: Arthur Rosson. lps: Hoot Gibson, Alberta Vaughn, Frank Campeau. 5491f USA. prod/rel: Universal Pictures

The Ranch at the Wolverine, Boston 1914, Novel
Wolverine, The 1921 d: William Bertram. lps: Helen Gibson, Jack Connolly, Leo Maloney. 5r USA. prod/rel: Spencer Productions, Associated Photoplays

BOWER, MARION
The Chinese Puzzle, London 1918, Play
Chinese Puzzle, The 1919 d: Fred Goodwins. lps: Leon M. Lion, Lilian Braithwaite, Milton Rosmer. 5000f UKN. prod/rel: Ideal

Chinese Puzzle, The 1932 d: Guy Newall. lps: Leon M. Lion, Lilian Braithwaite, Elizabeth Allan. 81M UKN. prod/rel: Twickenham, Woolf & Freedman

BOWERS, WILLIAM
Jungle Patrol, Play
Jungle Patrol 1948 d: Joseph M. Newman. lps: Kristine Miller, Arthur Franz, Ross Ford. 72M USA. prod/rel: 20th Century Fox

BOWKER, FANNY
Priscilla the Rake, Play
She Was Only a Village Maiden 1933 d: Arthur Maude. lps: Anne Grey, Lester Matthews, Carl Harbord. 61M UKN. *Priscilla the Rake* prod/rel: Sound City, MGM

BOWKETT, SYDNEY
Squire the Audacious, Play
Audacious Mr. Squire, The 1923 d: Edwin Greenwood. lps: Jack Buchanan, Valia, Russell Thorndike. 4770f UKN. prod/rel: British & Colonial

BOWLES, PAUL (1910–, USA
The Sheltering Sky, 1949, Novel
Sheltering Sky, The 1989 d: Bernardo Bertolucci. lps: Debra Winger, John Malkovich, Campbell Scott. 137M UKN/ITL. *Il Te Nel Deserto* (ITL) prod/rel: Sahara Company, Tao Film

BOWMAN, EARL WAYLAND
High Stakes, 1920, Short Story
Big Stakes 1922 d: Clifford S. Elfelt. lps: J. B. Warner, Elinor Fair, Les Bates. 4650f USA. prod/rel: Metropolitan Pictures, East Coast Productions

The Ramblin' Kid, Indianapolis 1920, Novel
Long, Long Trail, The 1929 d: Arthur Rosson. lps: Hoot Gibson, Sally Eilers, Walter Brennan. 5331f USA. prod/rel: Universal Pictures

Ramblin' Kid, The 1923 d: Edward Sedgwick. lps: Hoot Gibson, Laura La Plante, Harold Goodwin. 6395f USA. *Long Trail, the Long* prod/rel: Universal Pictures

BOWMAN, PETER
Beach Red, New York 1945, Book
Beach Red 1967 d: Cornel Wilde. lps: Cornel Wilde, Rip Torn, Burr Debenning. 105M USA. prod/rel: Theodora Productions

BOWNE, ALAN
Beirut, Play
Bloodstream 1993 d: Stephen Tolkin. lps: Cuba Gooding Jr., Moira Kelly, Omar Epps. 90M USA. prod/rel: Hbo

BOWSER, AUBREY
The Man Who Would Be White, Story
Call of His People, The 1922. lps: George Edward Brown, Edna Morton, Mae Kemp. 6r USA. prod/rel: Reol Productions

BOYD, HUTCHESON
Sauce for the Goose, New York 1911, Play
Sauce for the Goose 1918 d: Walter Edwards. lps: Constance Talmadge, Harrison Ford, Harland Tucker. 5r USA. prod/rel: Select Pictures Corp.©

BOYD, JEROLD HAYDEN
Story
Holle von Manitoba, Die 1965 d: Sheldon Reynolds. lps: Lex Barker, Pierre Brice, Marianne Koch. 92M GRM/SPN. *Un Lugar Llamada "Glory"* (SPN); *A Place Called Glory* (USA); *Place Called Glory City; Hell in Manitoba* prod/rel: C.C.C., Midega

BOYD, THOMAS ALEXANDER
The Long Shot, New York 1925, Short Story
Blaze O' Glory 1929 d: Renaud Hoffman, George J. Crone. lps: Eddie Dowling, Betty Compson, Frankie Darro. 8333f USA. prod/rel: Sono-Art Productions

Sombras de Gloria 1930 d: Andrew L. Stone. lps: Jose Bohr, Mona Rico, Francisco Maran. 9500f USA. prod/rel: Sono-Art Productions

BOYD, WILLIAM
Stars and Bars, Novel
Stars and Bars 1988 d: Pat O'Connor. lps: Daniel Day-Lewis, Martha Plimpton, Harry Dean Stanton. 94M USA. prod/rel: Columbia

BOYER, DAVID
The Sidelong Glances of a Pigeon Kicker, New York 1968, Novel
Sidelong Glances of a Pigeon Fancier 1971 d: John Dexter. lps: Jordan Christopher, Jill O'Hara, Robert Walden. 106M USA. *Pigeons* prod/rel: Saturn Pictures

BOYER, FRANCOIS
Bebert Et l'Omnibus, Novel
Bebert Et l'Omnibus 1963 d: Yves Robert. lps: Martin Lartigue, Jacques Higelin, Jean Richard. 95M FRN. *The Holy Terror; Bebert and the Train* prod/rel: Films de la Gueville

BOYESEN, ALGERNON
The Greater Woman, Play
Greater Woman, The 1917 d: Frank Powell. lps: Marjorie Rambeau, Hassan Mussalli, Aubrey Beattie. 5r USA. prod/rel: Frank Powell Producing Corp.©, Mutual Film Corp.

BOYLE, BILL
Crossbar, Story
Crossbar 1979 d: John Trent. lps: Brent Carver, Kim Cattrall, Kate Reid. TVM. 77M CND. *Plus Loin Plus Haut* prod/rel: Canadian Broadcasting Corp., Crossbar Productions Ltd.

BOYLE, G. COGRAGHESSAN
The Road to Wellville, Novel
Road to Wellville, The 1994 d: Alan Parker. lps: Anthony Hopkins, Bridget Fonda, Matthew Broderick. 120M USA. prod/rel: Beacon, Dirty Hands

BOYLE, GEORGE
Convention Girl, New York 1933, Novel
Convention Girl 1934 d: Luther Reed. lps: Rose Hobart, Weldon Heyburn, Sally O'Neil. 67M USA. *Atlantic City Romance* (UKN) prod/rel: Falcon Pictures Corp.

BOYLE, JACK
An Answer in Grand Larceny, 1919, Short Story
Missing Millions 1922 d: Joseph Henabery. lps: Alice Brady, David Powell, Frank Losee. 5870f USA. prod/rel: Famous Players-Lasky, Paramount Pictures

Boomerang Bill, Story
Boomerang Bill 1922 d: Tom Terriss. lps: Lionel Barrymore, Marguerite Marsh, Margaret Seddon. 5489f USA. prod/rel: Cosmopolitan Productions, Paramount Pictures

Boston Blackie, New York 1920, Novel
Blackie's Redemption 1919 d: John Ince. lps: Bert Lytell, Alice Lake, Henry Kolker. 5r USA. *Powers That Pray* prod/rel: Metro Pictures Corp.©

Boston Blackie's Little Pal, 1918, Short Story
Boston Blackie's Little Pal 1918 d: E. Mason Hopper. lps: Bert Lytell, Rhea Mitchell, Joey Jacobs. 5r USA. prod/rel: Metro Pictures Corp.©

The Daughter of Mother McGinn, Story
 Through the Dark 1924 d: George W. Hill. lps: Colleen Moore, Forrest Stanley, Margaret Seddon. 7999f USA. prod/rel: Cosmopolitan Corp., Goldwyn-Cosmopolitan Distributing Corp.

Debt of Dishonor, Short Story
 Soiled 1924 d: Fred Windermere. lps: Kenneth Harlan, Vivian Martin, Mildred Harris. 6800f USA. prod/rel: Phil Goldstone Productions, Truart Film Corp.

The Face in the Fog, 1920, Short Story
 Face in the Fog, The 1922 d: Alan Crosland. lps: Lionel Barrymore, Seena Owen, Lowell Sherman. 6095f USA. prod/rel: Cosmopolitan Productions, Paramount Pictures

Miss Doris - Safe-Cracker, 1918, Short Story
 Silk Lined Burglar, The 1919 d: John Francis Dillon. lps: Priscilla Dean, Ashton Dearholt, Sam de Grasse. 6r USA. prod/rel: Universal Film Mfg. Co.©

The Poppy Girl's Husband, 1919, Short Story
 Poppy Girl's Husband, The 1919 d: William S. Hart, Lambert Hillyer. lps: William S. Hart, Juanita Hansen, Walter Long. 4806f USA. *Poppy Girl* (UKN) prod/rel: William S. Hart Productions, Inc.©, Famous Players-Lasky Corp.

A Problem in Grand Larceny, 1919, Short Story
 Missing Millions 1922 d: Joseph Henabery. lps: Alice Brady, David Powell, Frank Losee. 5870f USA. prod/rel: Famous Players-Lasky, Paramount Pictures

The Water Cross, 1919, Short Story
 Boston Blackie 1923 d: Scott R. Dunlap. lps: William Russell, Eva Novak, Frank Brownlee. 4522f USA. prod/rel: Fox Film Corp.

BOYLE, JIMMY
A Sense of Freedom, Autobiography
 Sense of Freedom, A 1979 d: John MacKenzie. lps: David Hayman, Alex Norton, Fulton MacKay. TVM. 104M UKN. prod/rel: Stv

BOYLE, KAY (1903–1992), USA
Avalanche, 1944, Novel
 Avalanche 1946 d: Irving Allen. lps: Bruce Cabot, Roscoe Karns, Helen Mowery. 70M USA. prod/rel: Producers Releasing Corp.

Maiden Maiden, 1957, Short Story
 Five Days One Summer 1982 d: Fred Zinnemann. lps: Sean Connery, Betsy Brantley, Lambert Wilson. 108M USA. prod/rel: Warner Bros., the Ladd Company

BOYSS, FRANK
Wir Fahren Mit Der U-Bahn Nach St. Pauli, Play
 Wir Fahren Mit Der U-Bahn Nach St. Pauli 1970 d: Claus Muras. lps: Otto Lutje, Michael Korrontay. 91M GRM. *With the Subway to St. Paul's* prod/rel: Saturn

BRAATEN, OSKAR
Bak Hokerens Disk, 1918, Novel
 Godvakker Maren 1940 d: Knut Hergel. 89M NRW.
 Kjaere Maren 1976 d: Jan Erik During. lps: Inger Lise Rypdal, Gisle Straume, Karin Helene Haugen. 91M NRW.
 Ungen 1974 d: Barthold Halle. lps: Britt Langlie, Rolv Wesenlund, Solvi Wang. 122M NRW. *The Baby*

Bra Mennesker, 1930, Play
 Bra Manninskor 1937 d: Leif Sinding. 92M NRW. *Bra Mennesker*
 Det Regnar Pa Var Karlek 1946 d: Ingmar Bergman. lps: Birger Malmsten, Barbro Kollberg, Gosta Cederlund. 95M SWD. *Man With an Umbrella* (UKN); *It Rains on Our Love* (USA) prod/rel: Nordisktonefilm

Godvakker - Maren, 1927, Play
 Godvakker Maren 1940 d: Knut Hergel. 89M NRW.

Den Store Barnedapen, 1926, Play
 Store Barnedapen, Den 1931 d: Einer Sissener, Tancred Ibsen. lps: Hauk Aabel. 105M NRW.

Ungen, 1911, Play
 Ungen 1938 d: Rasmus Breistein. lps: Hauk Aabel. 101M NRW.
 Ungen 1974 d: Barthold Halle. lps: Britt Langlie, Rolv Wesenlund, Solvi Wang. 122M NRW. *The Baby*

BRABANT, CHARLES
Carillons Sans Joie, Novel
 Carillons Sans Joie 1962 d: Charles Brabant. lps: Paul Meurisse, Raymond Pellegrin, Dany Carrel. 100M FRN/ITL. *Vento Caldo Di Battaglia* (ITL) prod/rel: Lisa Films, Unidex

BRACCO, ROBERTO
Il Diritto Di Vivere, 1900, Play
 Diritto Di Vivere, Il 1912 d: Roberto Troncone. ITL. prod/rel: Partenope Film

Don Pietro Caruso, 1895, Play
 Don Pietro Caruso 1914 d: Emilio Ghione. lps: Emilio Ghione, Francesca Bertini, Alberto Collo. 1200m ITL. prod/rel: Caesar Film

Una Donna, 1892, Play
 Donna, Una 1917 d: Mario Gargiulo. lps: Tina Xeo, Dillo Lombardi, Raffaello Mariani. 1400m ITL. prod/rel: Flegrea Film

Maternita, 1903, Play
 Maternita 1917 d: Ugo de Simone. lps: Italia Almirante Manzini, Giuseppe Ciabattini, Guido Trento. 1700m ITL. prod/rel: Gladiator Film

Nellina, 1908, Play
 Nellina 1920 d: Gustavo SerenA. lps: Gustavo Serena, Tilde Kassay, Cia Fornaroli. 1540m ITL. prod/rel: Caesar Film

Notte Di Neve, 1906, Play
 Notte Di Neve 1921 d: Giulio Tanfani-Moroni. lps: Maria Caserini Gasparini, Giovanni Schettini, Sara Long. 1618m ITL. prod/rel: Excelsior Film

Oucchie Cunzacrate, 1916, Play
 Occhi Consacrati 1919 d: Luigi Mele. lps: Bianchina de Crescenzo, Luigi Mele, Maria Almari. 1220m ITL. prod/rel: Cyrius Film

Il Perfetto Amore, 1910, Play
 Perfetto Amore, Il 1918 d: Guido Brignone. lps: Armando Falconi, Mercedes Brignone, Armand Pouget. 1575m ITL. prod/rel: Cines

La Piccola Fonte, 1905, Play
 Piccola Fonte, La 1917 d: Roberto Leone Roberti. lps: Francesca Bertini, Annibale Ninchi, Olga Benetti. 1900m ITL. prod/rel: Caesar Film

La Principessa
 Principessa, La 1917 d: Camillo de Riso. lps: Leda Gys, Camillo de Riso, Lido Manetti. 1536m ITL. prod/rel: Caesar Film

Sperduti Nel Buio, 1901, Play
 Sperduti Nel Buio 1914 d: Nino Martoglio, Roberto Danesi. lps: Giovanni Grasso, Virginia Balistrieri, Dillo Lombardi. 1870m ITL. prod/rel: Morgana Film
 Sperduti Nel Buio 1947 d: Camillo Mastrocinque. lps: Vittorio de Sica, Jacqueline Plessis, Nello Mele. 105M ITL. *La Ragazza Perduta* prod/rel: Edi Film, Romana Film

Uocchie Cunzacrate, 1916, Play
 Occhi Consacrati 1918 d: Luigi Mele. lps: Olga Paradisi, Luigi Mele, Maria Almari. 1090m ITL. prod/rel: Cyrius Film

BRACE, BLANCHE
The Adventure of a Ready Letter Writer, 1920, Short Story
 Don't Write Letters 1922 d: George D. Baker. lps: Gareth Hughes, Bartine Burkette, Herbert Hayes. 4800f USA. prod/rel: S-L Pictures, Metro Pictures
 Letter for Evie, A 1945 d: Jules Dassin. lps: John Carroll, Hume Cronyn, Marsha Hunt. 89M USA. *All the Things You are* prod/rel: MGM

BRACKETT, CHARLES WILLIAM
Interlocutory, 1924, Short Story
 Tomorrow's Love 1925 d: Paul Bern. lps: Agnes Ayres, Pat O'Malley, Raymond Hatton. 5842f USA. prod/rel: Famous Players-Lasky, Paramount Pictures

Pearls Before Cecily, 1923, Short Story
 Risky Business 1926 d: Alan Hale. lps: Vera Reynolds, Ethel Clayton, Kenneth Thomson. 6594f USA. prod/rel: de Mille Pictures, Producers Distributing Corp.

Pointed Heels, 1929, Short Story
 Pointed Heels 1929 d: A. Edward Sutherland. lps: William Powell, Fay Wray, Helen Kane. 61M USA. prod/rel: Paramount Famous Lasky Corp.

BRACKETT, LEIGH (1915–1978), USA
The Tiger Among Us, New York 1957, Novel
 13 West Street 1962 d: Philip Leacock. lps: Alan Ladd, Rod Steiger, Michael Callan. 80M USA. *13 East Street; The Tiger Among Us* prod/rel: Ladd Enterprises

BRADBURY, MALCOLM (1932–, UKN, Bradbury, Malcolm Stanley
The History Man, Novel
 History Man, The 1981 d: Robert Knights. lps: Isla Blair, Nigel Stock, Antony Sher. MTV. 300M UKN. prod/rel: BBC

BRADBURY, RAY (1920–, USA, Bradbury, Ray Douglas
Banshee, 1988, Short Story
 Ray Bradbury's Nightmares Volume 2 1985 d: Douglas Jackson, Ralph L. Thomas. lps: Charles Martin Smith, Peter O'Toole, Jennifer Dale. TVM. 70M USA.

The Crowd, 1943, Short Story
 Ray Bradbury's Nightmares Volume 2 1985 d: Douglas Jackson, Ralph L. Thomas. lps: Charles Martin Smith, Peter O'Toole, Jennifer Dale. TVM. 70M USA.

Fahrenheit 451, New York 1953, Novel
 Fahrenheit 451 1966 d: Francois Truffaut. lps: Oskar Werner, Julie Christie, Cyril Cusack. 112M UKN. prod/rel: Vineyard Productions, Anglo-Enterprise Film Productions

The Foghorn, 1951, Play
 Beast from 20,000 Fathoms, The 1953 d: Eugene Lourie. lps: Paul Hubschmid, Paula Raymond, Cecil Kellaway. 80M USA. prod/rel: Warner Bros.

I Sing the Body Electric!, Short Story
 Ray Bradbury's the Electric Grandmother 1981 d: Noel Black. lps: Maureen Stapleton, Edward Herrmann, Paul Benedict. TVM. 48M USA. *The Electric Grandmother*

The Last Night in the World, 1951, Short Story
 Illustrated Man, The 1969 d: Jack Smight. lps: Rod Steiger, Claire Bloom, Robert Drivas. 103M USA. prod/rel: Warner Bros., Seven Arts, Inc.

The Long Rain, 1950, Short Story
 Illustrated Man, The 1969 d: Jack Smight. lps: Rod Steiger, Claire Bloom, Robert Drivas. 103M USA. prod/rel: Warner Bros., Seven Arts, Inc.

The Magic White Suit, 1957, Short Story
 Wonderful Ice Cream Suit, The 1998 d: Stuart Gordon. lps: Joe Mantegna, Esai Morales, Edward James Olmos. 77M USA. prod/rel: Walt Disney Pictures

The Meteor, Short Story
 It Came from Outer Space 1953 d: Jack Arnold. lps: Richard Carlson, Barbara Rush, Charles Drake. 81M USA. prod/rel: Universal-International

The Murderer, 1953, Short Story
 Murderer, The 1976 d: Andrew Silver. 28M USA.

The Playground, 1953, Short Story
 Ray Bradbury's Nightmares Volume 1 1985 d: Bruce Pittman, William Fruet. lps: Drew Barrymore, Janet Laine-Green, Roger Dunn. TVM. 70M USA.

The Screaming Woman, 1951, Short Story
 Ray Bradbury's Nightmares Volume 1 1985 d: Bruce Pittman, William Fruet. lps: Drew Barrymore, Janet Laine-Green, Roger Dunn. TVM. 70M USA.
 Screaming Woman, The 1972 d: Jack Smight. lps: Olivia de Havilland, Joseph Cotten, Walter Pidgeon. TVM. 73M USA. prod/rel: Universal

The Silver Locusts, Short Story
 Martian Chronicles, The 1979 d: Michael Anderson. lps: Rock Hudson, Gayle Hunnicutt, Darren McGavin. TVM. 300M USA. prod/rel: Charles Fries Productions, Stonehenge Productions

Something Wicked This Way Comes, 1962, Novel
 Something Wicked This Way Comes 1983 d: Jack Clayton. lps: Jonathan Pryce, Jason Robards Jr., Diane Ladd. 95M USA. prod/rel: Buena Vista

The Veldt, 1951, Short Story
 Illustrated Man, The 1969 d: Jack Smight. lps: Rod Steiger, Claire Bloom, Robert Drivas. 103M USA. prod/rel: Warner Bros., Seven Arts, Inc.

BRADDELL, MAURICE
It's You I Want, London 1933, Play
 It's You I Want 1936 d: Ralph Ince. lps: Seymour Hicks, Marie Lohr, Hugh Wakefield. 73M UKN. prod/rel: British Lion

BRADDON, MARY ELIZABETH (1837–1915), UKN
Aurora Floyd, Novel
 Aurora Floyd 1912 d: Theodore Marston. lps: Florence Labadie, Harry Benham, William Garwood. 2r USA. prod/rel: Thanhouser
 Aurora Floyd 1915 d: Travers Vale. lps: Louise Vale, Franklin Ritchie, Jack Drumier. 2r USA. prod/rel: Biograph Co.
 Her Bitter Lesson 1912 d: Hardee Kirkland. lps: Adrienne Kroell. 1000f USA. prod/rel: Selig Polyscope Co.

Lady Audley's Secret, London 1862, Novel
 Lady Audley's Secret 1906. UKN. prod/rel: Walturdaw
 Lady Audley's Secret 1912 d: Otis Turner. lps: Jane Fearnley, King Baggot. 1000f USA. prod/rel: Imp
 Lady Audley's Secret 1915 d: Marshall Farnum. lps: Theda Bara, Clifford Bruce, William Riley Hatch. 5r USA. *The Secrets of Society* prod/rel: Fox Film Corp., William Fox©
 Lady Audley's Secret 1920 d: Jack Denton. lps: Margaret Bannerman, Manning Haynes, Betty Farquhar. 5150f UKN. prod/rel: Ideal

BRADDON, RUSSELL
Night of the Lepus, Novel
 Night of the Lepus 1972 d: William F. Claxton. lps: Stuart Whitman, Janet Leigh, Rory Calhoun. 88M USA. *Rabbits* prod/rel: A. C. Lyles

BRADFIELD, SCOTT
The History of Luminous Motion, Novel
 Luminous Motion 1998 d: Bette Gordon. lps: Eric Lloyd, Deborah Kara Unger, Terry Kinney. 94M USA. prod/rel: Fiona Films, Good Machine

BRADFORD, BARBARA TAYLOR
Act of Will, Novel
   Act of Will 1989 d: Don Sharp. lps: Victoria Tennant, Peter Coyote, Elizabeth Hurley. TVM. 203M USA. prod/rel: Portman, Tyne Tees Tv
Remember, Novel
   Remember 1993 d: John Herzfeld. lps: Donna Mills, Stephen Collins, Derek de Lint. MTV. 200M USA. *Barbara Taylor Bradford's Remember*
To Be the Best, Novel
   To Be the Best 1991 d: Tony Wharmby. lps: Lindsay Wagner, Anthony Hopkins, Stephanie Beacham. TVM. 200M UKN/USA.
Voice of the Heart, Novel
   Voice of the Heart 1989 d: Tony Wharmby. lps: Lindsay Wagner, James Brolin, Victoria Tennant. TVM. 192M USA. prod/rel: Portman, Htv
A Woman of Substance, Novel
   Hold the Dream 1986 d: Don Sharp. lps: Jenny Seagrove, Stephen Collins, Deborah Kerr. MTV. 200M UKN/USA. *Hold That Dream*
   Woman of Substance, A 1984 d: Don Sharp. lps: Jenny Seagrove, Barry Bostwick, Deborah Kerr. TVM. 300M UKN/USA. prod/rel: Operation Prime Time, Artemis Portman

BRADLE JR., BEN
The Ambush Murders, Book
   Ambush Murders, The 1982 d: Steven Hilliard Stern. lps: James Brolin, Dorian Harewood, Alfre Woodard. TVM. 100M USA. prod/rel: CBS, Charles Fries

BRADLEY, ALICE
The Governor's Lady, New York 1912, Play
   Governor's Lady, The 1915 d: George Melford. lps: Edith Wynne Mathison, James Neill, Theodore Roberts. 5r USA. prod/rel: Jesse L. Lasky Feature Play Co.©, Paramount Pictures Corp.
The Governor's Lady, New York 1912, Novel
   Governor's Lady, The 1923 d: Harry Millarde. lps: Robert T. Haines, Jane Grey, Anna Luther. 7669f USA. prod/rel: Fox Film Corp.

BRADLEY, LILLIAN T.
What Happened Then?, Play
   What Happened Then? 1934 d: Walter Summers. lps: Richard Bird, Lorna Storm, Francis L. Sullivan. 62M UKN. prod/rel: British International Pictures, Wardour
The Woman on the Index, New York 1918, Novel
   Woman on the Index, The 1919 d: Hobart Henley. lps: Pauline Frederick, Wyndham Standing, Jere Austin. 5r USA. prod/rel: Goldwyn Pictures Corp.©, Goldwyn Distributing Corp.
The Wonderful Thing, New York 1920, Play
   Wonderful Thing, The 1921 d: Herbert Brenon. lps: Norma Talmadge, Harrison Ford, Julia Hoyte. 6880f USA. prod/rel: Norma Talmadge Productions, Associated First National Pictures

BRADLEY, MARY HASTINGS
The Fortieth Door, New York 1920, Novel
   40th Door, The 1924 d: George B. Seitz. lps: Allene Ray, Bruce (4) Gordon, David Dunbar. 6000f USA. prod/rel: Pathe Exchange, Inc.
The Palace of Darkened Windows, New York 1914, Novel
   Palace of Darkened Windows, The 1920 d: Henry Kolker. lps: Claire Anderson, Arthur Edmund Carewe, Jay Belasco. 6r USA. *The Palace of the Darkened Windows* prod/rel: National Pictures Theatres, Inc.©, Select Pictures Corp.

BRADSHAW, GEORGE
Old Mrs. Leonard and the machine Guns, 1937, Short Story
   Lady and the Mob, The 1939 d: Ben Stoloff. lps: Lee Bowman, Ida Lupino, Henry ArmettA. 65M USA. *Old Mrs. Leonard and the machine Guns*; *Mrs. Leonard Misbehaves*; *Old Mrs. Leonard and Her machine Guns* prod/rel: Columbia Pictures Corp. of California©
Shoestring, 1933, Short Story
   New Faces of 1937 1937 d: Leigh Jason. lps: Joe Penner, Milton Berle, Parkyakarkus. 100M USA. *Young People* prod/rel: RKO Radio Pictures©
Venus Rising, London 1962, Short Story
   How to Steal a Million 1966 d: William Wyler. lps: Audrey Hepburn, Peter O'Toole, Eli Wallach. 127M USA.; *How to Steal a Million Dollars and Live Happily Ever After* prod/rel: World Wide Productions

BRADY, CYRUS TOWNSEND
As the Sparks Fly Upwards, Story
   Hearts Adrift 1914 d: Edwin S. Porter. lps: Mary Pickford, Harold Lockwood. 4-5r USA. prod/rel: Famous Players Film Co., State Rights

The Better Man, New York 1910, Novel
   Better Man, The 1914 d: Mr. Powers. lps: William Courtleigh Jr., Robert Broderick, Alice Claire Elliott. 4r USA. prod/rel: Famous Players Film Co., State Rights
Britton of the Seventh, Chicago 1914, Novel
   Britton of the Seventh 1916 d: Lionel Belmore. lps: Darwin Karr, Charles Kent, Bobby Connelly. 4r USA. prod/rel: Vitagraph Co. of America©, V-L-S-E, Inc.
By the World Forgot, Chicago 1917, Novel
   By the World Forgot 1918 d: David Smith. lps: Hedda Nova, J. Frank Glendon, Edward Alexander. 4006f USA. prod/rel: Vitagraph Co. of America©, Blue Ribbon Feature
The Chalice of Courage: a Romance of Colorado, New York 1912, Novel
   Chalice of Courage, The 1915 d: Rollin S. Sturgeon. lps: Myrtle Gonzales, William Duncan, George Holt. 5-6r USA. prod/rel: Vitagraph Co. of America©, Blue Ribbon Feature
Colton U.S.N., Play
   Colton, U.S.N. 1915 d: Paul Scardon. lps: Charles Richman, Eleanor Woodruff, James Morrison. SHT USA. prod/rel: Vitagraph Co. of America
Hearts on the Highway, New York 1911, Novel
   Hearts and the Highway 1915 d: Wilfred North. lps: Lillian Walker, Darwin Karr, Donald Hall. 5r USA. prod/rel: Vitagraph Co. of America©, Blue Ribbon
The Heights of Hazard, Story
   Heights of Hazard, The 1915 d: Harry Lambart. lps: Charles Richman, Eleanor Woodruff, Charles Kent. 5r USA. prod/rel: Vitagraph Co. of America©, Blue Ribbon Feature
The Island of Regeneration: a Story of What Ought to Be, New York 1909, Novel
   Island of Regeneration, The 1915 d: Harry Davenport. lps: Edith Storey, Antonio Moreno, S. Rankin Drew. 6r USA. prod/rel: Vitagraph Co. of America©, Broadway Star Features Co.
The Island of Surprise, New York 1915, Novel
   Island of Surprise, The 1916 d: Paul Scardon. lps: William Courtenay, Charles Kent, Anders Randolf. 5r USA. prod/rel: Vitagraph Co. of America©, V-L-S-E, Inc.
The Little Angel of Canyon Creek, New York 1914, Novel
   Little Angel of Canyon Creek, The 1914 d: Rollin S. Sturgeon. lps: Gertrude Short, George Stanley, Violet Malone. 5r USA. prod/rel: Vitagraph Co. of America©, Broadway Star Feature
The Man Who Won, Chicago 1919, Novel
   Man Who Won, The 1919 d: Paul Scardon. lps: Harry T. Morey, Maurice Costello, Betty Blythe. 4333f USA. prod/rel: Vitagraph Co. of America©
Richard the Brazen, New York 1906, Novel
   Richard the Brazen 1917 d: Perry N. Vekroff. lps: Harry T. Morey, Alice Joyce, William Frederic. 5r USA. prod/rel: Vitagraph Co. of America©, Blue Ribbon Feature
The Ring and the Man, New York 1909, Novel
   Ring and the Man, The 1914 d: Francis Powers. lps: Bruce McRae, Robert Broderick, Helen Aubrey. 4r USA. prod/rel: Famous Players Film Co., State Rights
The Southerners, Novel
   Southerners, The 1914 d: Richard Ridgely, John H. Collins. lps: Mabel Trunnelle, Bigelow Cooper, Herbert Prior. 3r USA. prod/rel: Edison

BRADY, LEO
Edge of Doom, 1949, Novel
   Edge of Doom 1950 d: Mark Robson. lps: Farley Granger, Dana Andrews, Joan Evans. 99M USA. *Stronger Than Fear* (UKN) prod/rel: RKO Radio

BRADY, MICHAEL
To Gillian on Her 37th Birthday, Play
   To Gillian on Her 37th Birthday 1996 d: Michael Pressman. lps: Peter Gallagher, Claire Danes, Kathy Baker. 92M USA. prod/rel: David E. Kelley, Rastar

BRAGARD, RENE
Le Feu Dans la Peau, Novel
   Feu Dans la Peau, Le 1953 d: Marcel Blistene. lps: Giselle Pascal, Raymond Pellegrin, Philippe Lemaire. 107M FRN/ITL. *Fire Under Her Skin* (USA); *Fire in the Skin* (UKN) prod/rel: S.L.P.F., Lutetia

BRAGG, MELVYN (1939–, UKN
A Time to Dance, Novel
   Time to Dance, A 1991 d: Kevin Billington. lps: Ronald Pickup, Dervla Kirwan, Rosemary McHale. TVM. 180M UKN. prod/rel: BBC Scotland

BRAHMS, CARYL
The Elephant Is White, Novel
   Give Us the Moon 1944 d: Val Guest. lps: Margaret Lockwood, Vic Oliver, Peter Graves. 95M UKN. prod/rel: General Film Distributors, Gainsborough

No Nightingales, Novel
   Ghosts of Berkeley Square, The 1947 d: Vernon Sewell. lps: Robert Morley, Felix Aylmer, Yvonne Arnaud. 89M UKN. prod/rel: British National, Pathe
Trottie True, Novel
   Trottie True 1948 d: Brian Desmond Hurst. lps: Jean Kent, James Donald, Hugh Sinclair. 96M UKN. *The Gay Lady* (USA) prod/rel: General Film Distributors, Two Cities

BRAINE, JOHN (1922–1986), UKN, Braine, John Gerard
Life at the Top, London 1962, Novel
   Life at the Top 1965 d: Ted Kotcheff. lps: Laurence Harvey, Jean Simmons, Honor Blackman. 117M UKN. prod/rel: Romulus Films, Columbia
Room at the Top, 1957, Novel
   Room at the Top 1959 d: Jack Clayton. lps: Simone Signoret, Laurence Harvey, Heather Sears. 117M UKN. prod/rel: Independent Film Distributors, Remus

BRAINERD, ELEANOR HOYT
Jean? How Could You, Garden City N.Y. 1917, Novel
   How Could You, Jean? 1918 d: William D. Taylor. lps: Mary Pickford, Casson Ferguson, Herbert Standing. 4750f USA. prod/rel: Mary Pickford Production, Famous Players-Lasky Corp.©
Pegeen, New York 1915, Novel
   Pegeen 1920 d: David Smith. lps: Bessie Love, Edmund Burns, Ruth Fuller Golden. 5-6r USA. prod/rel: Vitagraph Co. of America©

BRAITHWAITE, E. R.
To Sir, With Love, London 1957, Novel
   To Sir, With Love 1966 d: James Clavell. lps: Sidney Poitier, Christian Roberts, Judy Geeson. 105M UKN/USA. prod/rel: Columbia British, Columbia

BRAITHWAITE, MAX
Why Shoot the Teacher?, Novel
   Why Shoot the Teacher? 1976 d: Silvio Narizzano. lps: Bud Cort, John Friesen, Samantha Eggar. 99M CND. *Pitie Pour le Prof!* prod/rel: Fraser Films Ltd., W.S.T.T. Ltd.

BRALY, MALCOLM (1925–1980), USA
On the Yard, Novel
   On the Yard 1978 d: Raphael D. Silver. lps: John Heard, Thomas G. Waites, Mike Kellin. 102M USA. prod/rel: Midwest Film Productions

BRAM, CHRISTOPHER
Father of Frankenstein, Novel
   Gods and Monsters 1998 d: Bill Condon. lps: Ian McKellen, Brendan Fraser, Lynn Redgrave. 105M USA. prod/rel: Regent Entertainment, BBC Films

BRAMI, CLAUDE
Rocca: Mortels Rendez-Vous, Novel
   Rocca: Mortels Rendez-Vous 1994 d: Paul Planchon. lps: Raymond Pellegrin, Jan Rouiller, Henri Guybet. TVM. 91M FRN.

BRAMMER, JULIUS
Hoheit Tanzt Walzer, Operetta
   Hoheit Tanzt Walzer 1935 d: Max Neufeld. lps: Hans Homma, Anna Kallina, Phillis Fehr. 103M AUS/CZC. *Tanacek Panny Marinky* (CZC) prod/rel: Elekta
   Valse Eternelle 1936 d: Max Neufeld. lps: Pierre Brasseur, Jean Servais, Renee Saint-Cyr. 102M FRN/CZC. prod/rel: Elekta
Grafin Maritza, Vienna 1924, Operetta
   Grafin Mariza 1925 d: Hans Steinhoff. lps: Vivian Gibson, Harry Liedtke, Colette Brettel. 2324m GRM. *Countess Mariza* prod/rel: Terra-Film Ag
   Grafin Mariza 1932 d: Richard Oswald. lps: Dorothea Wieck, Hubert Marischka, Charlotte Ander. 113M GRM. *Countess Mariza* prod/rel: Roto, Sud-Film
   Grafin Mariza 1958 d: Rudolf Schundler. lps: Christine Gorner, Rudolf Schock, Renate Ewert. 110M GRM. *Countess Mariza* prod/rel: Carlton, Constantin

BRANALD, ADOLF
Vizita, Novel
   Pozor, Vizita! 1981 d: Karel KachynA. lps: Rudolf Hrusinsky, Ludovit Gresso, Veronika JenikovA. 84M CZC. *Watch Out the Doctors' Rounds*; *Look Out the Doctor's About!*; *Doctor's Round*; *Vizita* prod/rel: Barrandov Film Studios

BRANCATI, VITALIANO (1907–1954), ITL
Il Bell'Antonio, 1949, Novel
   Bell'antonio, Il 1960 d: Mauro Bolognini. lps: Marcello Mastroianni, Claudia Cardinale, Pierre Brasseur. 105M ITL/FRN. *Bel Antonio*; *Handsome Antonio*; *Handsome Tony* prod/rel: Cino Del Duco, Arco Film (Roma)
Don Giovanni in Sicilia, 1941, Novel
   Don Giovanni in Sicilia 1967 d: Alberto LattuadA. lps: Lando Buzzanca, Katia Moguy, Carletto Sposito. 104M ITL. *Don Giovanni in Sicily* prod/rel: Adelphia Compagnia Cin.Ca, Interfilm

Paolo Il Caldo, 1955, Novel
  Paolo Il Caldo 1973 d: Marco Vicario. lps: Rossana Podesta, Giancarlo Giannini, Lionel Stander. 102M ITL. *The Sensuous Sicilian; The Sensual Man* prod/rel: Medusa Distribuzione, Atlantica Cin.Ca Produzione

Il Vecchio Con Gli Stivali, 1944, Short Story
  Anni Difficili 1948 d: Luigi ZampA. lps: Umberto Spadero, Ave Ninchi, Massimo Girotti. 89M ITL. *Difficult Years* (USA); *The Little Man* (UKN) prod/rel: Briguglio Film

BRANCH, HOUSTON
Story
  Wild Harvest 1947 d: Tay Garnett. lps: Alan Ladd, Robert Preston, Dorothy Lamour. 92M USA. *Big Haircut* prod/rel: Paramount

River Lady, Novel
  River Lady 1948 d: George Sherman. lps: Yvonne de Carlo, Rod Cameron, Dan DuryeA. 78M USA. prod/rel: Universal-International

Wildcat, New York 1921, Play
  Showdown, The 1928 d: Victor Schertzinger. lps: George Bancroft, Evelyn Brent, Neil Hamilton. 7616f USA. prod/rel: Paramount Famous Lasky Corp.

BRAND, CHRISTIANNA (1907–, UKN
Death in High Heels, Novel
  Death in High Heels 1947 d: Lionel Tomlinson. lps: Don Stannard, Bill Hodge, Veronica Rose. 47M UKN. prod/rel: Marylebone, Exclusive

Green for Danger, Novel
  Green for Danger 1946 d: Sidney Gilliat. lps: Sally Gray, Trevor Howard, Rosamund John. 91M UKN. prod/rel: General Film Distributors, Individual

BRAND, ERIC D.
The Love Doctor, Play
  Realities 1930 d: Bernerd Mainwaring. lps: Dodo Watts, Laurence Ireland, Ian Harding. 13M UKN. prod/rel: British International Pictures, Wardour

BRAND, MAX (1892–1944), USA, Faust, Frederick Schiller
Above the Law, 1918, Short Story
  Lawless Love 1918 d: Robert T. Thornby. lps: Jewel Carmen, Henry Woodward, Edward Hearn. 5r USA. prod/rel: Fox Film Corp., William Fox©

The Adopted Son, 1917, Short Story
  Adopted Son, The 1917 d: Charles J. Brabin. lps: Francis X. Bushman, Beverly Bayne, J. W. Johnston. 6r USA. prod/rel: Metro Pictures Corp.©, Rolfe Photodrama

Alcatraz, New York 1923, Novel
  Just Tony 1922 d: Lynn Reynolds. lps: Tom Mix, Claire Adams, J. P. Lockney. 5233f USA. prod/rel: Fox Film Corp.

The Black Rider, Story
  Cavalier, The 1928 d: Irvin V. Willat. lps: Richard Talmadge, Barbara Bedford, Nora Cecil. 6775f USA. prod/rel: Tiffany-Stahl Productions

Champion of Lost Causes, 1924, Short Story
  Champion of Lost Causes 1925 d: Chester Bennett. lps: Edmund Lowe, Barbara Bedford, Walter McGrail. 5115f USA. prod/rel: Fox Film Corp.

Children of the Night, 1919, Short Story
  Children of the Night 1921 d: John Francis Dillon. lps: William Russell, Ruth Renick, Maurice B. Flynn. 5011f USA. prod/rel: Fox Film Corp.

Clung, 1920, Serial Story
  Shame 1921 d: Emmett J. Flynn. lps: John Gilbert, Mickey Moore, Frankie Lee. 8322f USA. prod/rel: Fox Film Corp.

Dark Rosaleen, 1925, Short Story
  Flying Horseman, The 1926 d: Orville O. Dull. lps: Buck Jones, Gladys McConnell, Bruce Covington. 4971f USA. *White Eagle* prod/rel: Fox Film Corp.

Darkness, Short Story
  Darkness 1923 d: George A. Cooper. lps: Hugh Miller, Hilda Sims, Gordon Craig. 2000f UKN. prod/rel: Quality Plays, Gaumont

Destry Rides Again, New York 1930, Novel
  Destry 1954 d: George Marshall. lps: Audie Murphy, Mari Blanchard, Lyle Bettger. 95M USA. prod/rel: Universal-International

  Destry Rides Again 1932 d: Ben Stoloff, Alan James. lps: Tom Mix, Claudia Dell, Zasu Pitts. 53M USA. *Justice Rides Again; When Destry Rides* prod/rel: Universal Picture Corp.

  Destry Rides Again 1939 d: George Marshall. lps: Marlene Dietrich, James Stewart, Charles Winninger. 94M USA. *The Man from Montana* prod/rel: Universal Pictures Co., Joe Pasternak Production

Fate's Honeymoon, 1917, Short Story
  Thousand to One, A 1920 d: Rowland V. Lee. lps: Hobart Bosworth, Ethel Grey Terry, Charles West. 6-7r USA. prod/rel: J. Parker Read, Jr. Productions, Associated Producers, Inc.

Gun Gentlemen, Short Story
  Mile-a-Minute Romeo 1923 d: Lambert Hillyer. lps: Tom Mix, Betty Jewel, J. Gordon Russell. 5306f USA. prod/rel: Fox Film Corp.

Hired Guns, 1923, Short Story
  Gunfighter, The 1923 d: Lynn Reynolds. lps: William Farnum, Doris May, L. C. Shumway. 4700f USA. prod/rel: Fox Film Corp.

Internes Can't Take Money, 1936, Story
  Internes Can't Take Money 1937 d: Alfred Santell. lps: Barbara Stanwyck, Joel McCrea, Lloyd Nolan. 79M USA. *You Can't Take Money* (UKN) prod/rel: Paramount Pictures©

Mr. Cinderella, 1917, Novel
  Kiss Or Kill 1918 d: Elmer Clifton. lps: Herbert Rawlinson, Priscilla Dean, Alfred Allen. 5r USA. prod/rel: Universal Film Mfg. Co.©

The Night Horseman, New York 1920, Novel
  Night Horsemen, The 1921 d: Lynn Reynolds. lps: Tom Mix, May Hopkins, Harry Lonsdale. 4970f USA. prod/rel: Fox Film Corp.

Powder Town, Novel
  Powder Town 1942 d: Rowland V. Lee. lps: Victor McLaglen, Edmond O'Brien, June Havoc. 79M USA. prod/rel: RKO Radio

The Secret of Dr. Kildare, 1939, Story
  Secret of Dr. Kildare, The 1939 d: Harold S. Bucquet. lps: Lew Ayres, Lionel Barrymore, Lionel Atwill. 83M USA. prod/rel: Metro-Goldwyn-Mayer Corp., Loew's, Inc.©

Senor Jingle Bells, 1925, Short Story
  Best Bad Man, The 1925 d: John G. Blystone. lps: Tom Mix, Buster Gardner, Cyril Chadwick. 4983f USA. prod/rel: Fox Film Corp.

Singing Guns, Novel
  Singing Guns 1950 d: R. G. Springsteen. lps: Vaughn Monroe, Ella Raines, Walter Brennan. 91M USA. prod/rel: Republic, Palomar Pictures

South of the Rio Grande, 1936, Novel
  My Outlaw Brother 1951 d: Elliott Nugent. lps: Mickey Rooney, Wanda Hendrix, Robert Preston. 82M USA. *My Brother the Outlaw* prod/rel: Eagle-Lion

Tiger, 1921, Serial Story
  Tiger True 1921 d: J. P. McGowan. lps: Frank Mayo, Fritzi Brunette, Elinor Hancock. 4689f USA. prod/rel: Universal Film Mfg. Co.

Trailin', New York 1920, Novel
  Holy Terror, A 1931 d: Irving Cummings. lps: George O'Brien, Sally Eilers, Rita La Roy. 53M USA. *Wyoming Wonder* prod/rel: Fox Film Corp.©, Irving Cummings Production

  Trailin' 1921 d: Lynn Reynolds. lps: Tom Mix, Eva Novak, Bert Sprotte. 4355f USA. prod/rel: Fox Film Corp.

The Untamed, New York 1919, Novel
  Fair Warning 1931 d: Alfred L. Werker. lps: George O'Brien, Louise Huntington, Mitchell Harris. 74M USA. prod/rel: Fox Film Corp.©

  Untamed, The 1920 d: Emmett J. Flynn. lps: Tom Mix, Pauline Starke, George Siegmann. 5r USA. prod/rel: Fox Film Corp., William Fox©

Who Am I?, 1918, Short Story
  Who Am I? 1921 d: Henry Kolker. lps: Claire Anderson, Gertrude Astor, Niles Welch. 4943f USA. prod/rel: Selznick Pictures, Select Pictures

BRANDAO, IGNACIO DE LOYOLA
Ascensao Ao Mundo de Anuska, 1965, Short Story
  Anuska, Manequim E Muhler 1968 d: Francisco Ramalho Jr. lps: Marilia Branco, Francisco Cuoco, Ivan MesquitA. 95M BRZ. *Anushka Model and Woman; Anuska -Manikine and Woman*

Bebel Que a Cidade Comeu, 1960, Novel
  Bebel, Garota Propaganda 1968 d: Maurice CapovillA. lps: Rossana Ghessa, John Herbert, Paulo Jose. 103M BRZ. *Bebel - Propaganda Girl; Advertising Girl Bebel*

BRANDE, DOROTHEA
Wake Up and Live, New York 1936, Book
  Wake Up and Live 1937 d: Sidney Lanfield. lps: Walter Winchell, Ben Bernie, Alice Faye. 91M USA. prod/rel: Twentieth Century-Fox Film Corp.©

BRANDEL, MARC
The Lizard's Tail, Novel
  Hand, The 1981 d: Oliver Stone. lps: Michael Caine, Andrea Marcovicci, Annie McEnroe. 108M USA. prod/rel: Orion, Warner

BRANDEN, BARBARA
The Passion of Any Rand, Book
  Passion of Any Rand, The 1999 d: Christopher Menaul. lps: Helen Mirren, Eric Stoltz, Julie Delpy. 104M USA. prod/rel: Showtime, Producers Entertainment Group

BRANDNER, GARY
Cameron's Closett, Novel
  Cameron's Closet 1988 d: Armand Mastroianni. lps: Cotter Smith, Mel Harris, Scott Curtis. 86M USA. prod/rel: Smart Egg Pictures

The Howling II, Novel
  Howling II. Your Sister Is a Werewolf 1984 d: Philippe MorA. lps: Christopher Lee, Annie McEnroe, Reb Brown. 90M USA/ITL/FRN. *The Howling 2* prod/rel: Emi

Howling III, Novel
  Howling III, The 1987 d: Philippe MorA. lps: Barry Otto, Imogen Annesley, Dasha BlahovA. 94M ASL. *Howling 3: the Marsupials; The Marsupials: the Howling 3* prod/rel: Square Pictures, Bancannia Holdings

The Howling, Novel
  Howling, The 1981 d: Joe Dante. lps: Dee Wallace Stone, Patrick MacNee, Dennis Dugan. 90M USA. prod/rel: Avco Embassy

BRANDON, CURT
Bugle's Wake, 1952, Novel
  Seminole Uprising 1955 d: Earl Bellamy. lps: George Montgomery, Karin Booth, William Fawcett. 74M USA. prod/rel: Columbia, Eros Films Ltd.

BRANDON, DOROTHY
The Outsider, London 1923, Play
  Outsider, The 1926 d: Rowland V. Lee. lps: Jacqueline Logan, Lou Tellegen, Walter Pidgeon. 5424f USA. *Daybreak* prod/rel: Fox Film Corp.

  Outsider, The 1931 d: Harry Lachman. lps: Joan Barry, Harold Huth, Norman McKinnel. 93M UKN. prod/rel: Cinema House, MGM

  Outsider, The 1939 d: Paul L. Stein. lps: George Sanders, Mary Maguire, Barbara Blair. 90M UKN. prod/rel: Associated British Picture Corporation

Wild Heather, Play
  Wild Heather 1921 d: Cecil M. Hepworth. lps: Chrissie White, Gerald Ames, G. H. Mulcaster. 5735f UKN. prod/rel: Hepworth

BRANDON, JOHN G.
The Silent House, London 1927, Play
  Silent House, The 1929 d: Walter Forde. lps: Mabel Poulton, Gibb McLaughlin, Arthur Pusey. SIL. 9376f UKN. prod/rel: Nettlefold, Butcher's Film Service

BRANDON-THOMAS, JEVAN
Passing Brompton Road, London 1928, Play
  Her Reputation 1931 d: Sidney Morgan. lps: Iris Hoey, Frank Cellier, Malcolm Tearle. 67M UKN. prod/rel: London Screenplays, Paramount

BRANDYS, KAZIMIERZ
Jak Byc Kochana, 1960, Short Story
  Jak Byc Kochana 1962 d: Wojciech J. Has. lps: Zbigniew Cybulski, Barbara Krafftowna, Artur Mlodnicki. 100M PLN. *How to Be Loved* (USA) prod/rel: Kamera Film Unit

Matka Krolow, 1957, Novel
  Matka Krolow 1982 d: Janusz Zaorski. lps: Zbigniew Zapasiewicz, Boguslaw Linda, Magda Teresa Wojcik. 126M PLN. *Mother of Krols; The Mother of Kings; Mother of the Krol Family*

Samson, 1948, Novel
  Samson 1961 d: Andrzej WajdA. lps: Beata Tyszkiewicz, Serge Merlin, Alina JanowskA. 118M PLN.

Sposob Bycia, 1963, Novel
  Sposob Bycia 1966 d: Jan Rybkowski. lps: Andrzej Lapicki, Jerzy Skolimowski, Lucyna WinnickA. 81M PLN. *A Frame of Mind; A Manner of Behaving*

BRANNER, HANS CHRISTIAN
Soskende, 1952, Play
  Soskende 1966 d: Johan Jacobsen. lps: Asbjorn Andersen, Viggo Bro, Birgitte Federspiel. 99M DNM. *The Judge* prod/rel: Flamingo Film

BRANSCOMBE, ARTHUR
The Cradle of the Washingtons, Book
  Romance and Reality 1921 d: Harry Lambart. lps: Cora Goffin, Isabel Jeans. UKN. prod/rel: Lambart Films

BRANSTEN, RICHARD
Short Stories
  Margie 1946 d: Henry King. lps: Jeanne Crain, Alan Young, Glenn Langan. 94M USA. prod/rel: 20th Century-Fox

53

BRASCH, THOMAS
Story
  Vor Den Vatern Sterben Die Sohne 1981 d: Claudia
  Holldack. lps: Klaus Pohl, Peter Seum, Eva Mattes. 83M
  GRM. prod/rel: Ullstein Av-Prod., ZDF

BRASSEUR, PIERRE (1903–1972), FRN
Grisou, Play
  Grisou 1938 d: Maurice de Canonge. lps: Madeleine
  Robinson, Odette Joyeux, Pierre Brasseur. 87M FRN.
  Les Hommes Sans Soleil prod/rel: Films Albatros

BRATT, ANATOL
Novel
  **Bel Ami 2000 Oder: Wie Verfuhrt Man Einen
  Playboy?** 1966 d: Michael Pfleghar. lps: Peter
  Alexander, Linda Christian, Antonella Lualdi. 101M
  FRN/AUS/ITL. *100 Ragazze Per un Playboy* (ITL); *How
  to Seduce a Playboy* (USA); *Cento Ragazze Per un
  Playboy*; *Bel Ami 66* prod/rel: Intercontinental
  Produktion (Vienna), Metheus Film (Roma)

BRATT, HARALD
Alexa, Play
  Rausch Einer Nacht 1951 d: Eduard von Borsody. lps:
  Paul Dahlke, Christl Mardayn, Gertrud Kuckelmann.
  100M GRM. *One Night's Intoxication* prod/rel: Allegro,
  Globus
Die Insel, Play
  Vers l'Abime 1934 d: Serge Veber, Hans Steinhoff. lps:
  Brigitte Helm, Francoise Rosay, Raymond Rouleau.
  94M FRN. prod/rel: U.F.a., a.CE.
Operation North Star, Television Play
  Master Plan, The 1954 d: Cy Endfield. lps: Wayne
  Morris, Tilda Thamar, Norman Wooland. 78M UKN.
  prod/rel: Gibraltar, Grand National
Schutzenfest, Play
  Schwarze Schaf, Das 1943 d: Friedrich Zittau, Walter
  Janssen. lps: Lotte Koch, Ernst von Klipstein,
  Waldemar Leitgeb. 87M GRM. *The Black Sheep*
  prod/rel: Prag, Sudwest

BRAUN, CURT J.
Warum Lugt Fraulein Kathe?, Novel
  Warum Lugt Fraulein Kathe? 1935 d: Georg Jacoby.
  lps: Dolly Haas, Albrecht Schoenhals, Ida Wust. 89M
  GRM. prod/rel: Majestic-Film

BRAUN, CURT JOHANNES
Der Fluchtling Aus Chikago, Novel
  Fluchtling Aus Chikago, Der 1934 d: Johannes
  Meyer. lps: Gustav Frohlich, Luise Ullrich, Lil Dagover.
  108M GRM. prod/rel: Atlanta, Bavaria
Die Frau Ohne Vergangenheit, Novel
  Frau Ohne Vergangenheit, Die 1939 d: Nunzio
  MalasommA. lps: Sybille Schmitz, Albrecht Schoenhals,
  Maria von Tasnady. 91M GRM. prod/rel: Euphono,
  Bavaria
Der Frauendiplomat, Play
  How's Chances 1934 d: Anthony Kimmins. lps: Harold
  French, Tamara Desni, Davy Burnaby. 73M UKN. *The
  Diplomatic Lover* prod/rel: Sound City, Fox
Die Grosse Kurve, Play
  Musik Bei Nacht 1953 d: Kurt Hoffmann. lps: Paul
  Hubschmid, Gertrud Kuckelmann, Curd Jurgens. 86M
  GRM. *Music By Night* prod/rel: Helios, Bavaria
Die Stadt Ist Voller Geheimnisse, Play
  Stadt Ist Voller Geheimnisse, Die 1955 d: Fritz
  Kortner. lps: Annemarie Duringer, Erich Schellow,
  Walther Sussenguth. 105M GRM. *City of Secrets* (USA);
  Secrets of the City; *The City Is Full of Secrets* prod/rel:
  Real, Europa
Das Verschlossene Haus, Book
  Seltsame Leben Des Herrn Bruggs, Das 1951 d:
  Erich Engel. lps: Gustav Knuth, Christl Mardayn,
  Adrian Hoven. 89M GRM. *Mr. Bruggs' Strange Life*
  prod/rel: Trianon, Deutsche London

BRAUN, FRANK F.
Akte Fabreani, Novel
  Dein Leben Gehort Mir 1939 d: Johannes Meyer. lps:
  Karin Hardt, Dorothea Wieck, Karl Martell. 80M GRM.
  prod/rel: Cine Allianz, Bavaria
Das Madchen Mit Der Mundharmonika, Novel
  Arlette Erobert Paris 1953 d: Victor Tourjansky. lps:
  Johanna Matz, Karlheinz Bohm, Paul Dahlke. 99M
  GRM. *Arlette Conquers Paris* prod/rel: Rotary, Alcron
Von Der Liebe Reden Wir Spater, Novel
  Von Der Liebe Reden Wir Spater 1953 d: Karl
  Anton. lps: Gustav Frohlich, Maria Holst, Liselotte
  Pulver. 97M GRM. *Von Liebe Reden Wir Spater*; *We'll
  Talk About Love Later* prod/rel: Apollo, Deutsche
  London

BRAUN, M. G.
Les Caids, Novel
  Caids, Les 1972 d: Robert Enrico. lps: Serge Reggiani,
  Michel Constantin, Juliet Berto. 100M FRN. *The Hell
  Below* (UKN) prod/rel: Les Belles-Rives

Le Sang Des Mattioli, Novel
  En Plein Cirage 1961 d: Georges Lautner. lps: Martine
  Carol, Felix Marten, Francis Blanche. 104M FRN/ITL.
  Operazione Gold Ingot (ITL); *Operation Gold Ingot*
  (USA) prod/rel: Films de la Bourdonnaye, Delbar Films

BRAUN, WILHELM
Dirnentragodie, Play
  Dirnentragodie 1927 d: Bruno Rahn. lps: Asta
  Nielsen, Oscar Homolka, Hilde Jennings. 2388m GRM.
  Women Without Men (USA); *Tragedy of the Street*
  prod/rel: Pantomim-Film

BRAUNE, RUDOLF
Junge Leute in Der Stadt, Novel
  Junge Leute in Der Stadt 1985 d: Karl-Heinz Lotz.
  lps: Mirko Haninger, Ulrike Krumbiegel, Maria
  Probosz. 88M GDR. *Young People in the City* prod/rel:
  Defa

BRAUNER, ARTUR
Story
  Spur Fuhrt Nach Berlin, Die 1952 d: Frantisek Cap.
  lps: Irina Garden, Gordon Howard, Kurt Meisel. 95M
  GRM/USA. *International Counterfeiters* (USA); *The
  Track Leads to Berlin*; *The Trail Leads to Berlin*;
  Adventure in Berlin prod/rel: Republic, Ccc Prods.

BRAVETTA, VITTORIO EMANUELE
Umanita, Poem
  Umanita 1919 d: Elvira GiallanellA. 730m ITL.
  prod/rel: Liana Film

BRAWLEY, ERNEST
The Rap, Novel
  Fast-Walking 1981 d: James B. Harris. lps: James
  Woods, Tim McIntire, Kay Lenz. 115M USA. prod/rel:
  Lorimar

BRAY, ISOBEL
The Shuttle of Life, Novel
  Shuttle of Life, The 1920 d: D. J. Williams. lps: C.
  Aubrey Smith, Evelyn Brent, Jack Hobbs. 4256f UKN.
  prod/rel: British Actors, Phillips

BRDECKA, JIRI
Story
  Faunovo Velmi Pozdni Odpoledne 1984 d: Vera
  ChytilovA. lps: Leos Sucharipa, Vlasta Spicnerova,
  Libuse PospisilovA. 103M CZC. *The Late Afternoon of a
  Faun*; *A Faun's Very Late Afternoon* prod/rel: Kratky
  Film
Limonadovy Joe, Prague 1958, Novel
  Limonadovy Joe 1964 d: Oldrich Lipsky. lps: Karel
  Fiala, Milos Kopecky, Kveta FialovA. 99M CZC.
  Lemonade Joe (USA); *Konska Opera* prod/rel:
  Barrandov Film Studio

BRE, SILVIA
Snack Bar Budapest, Novel
  Snack Bar Budapest 1988 d: Tinto Brass. lps:
  Giancarlo Giannini, Raffaella Baracchi, Philippe
  Leotard. 102M ITL. prod/rel: San Francisco, Metro

BREAKSTON, GEORGE P.
Nightmare
  Manster, The 1962 d: George Breakston, Kenneth L.
  Crane. lps: Peter Dyneley, Jane Hylton, Satoshi
  NakamurA. 72M USA/JPN. *The Manster -Half Man
  Half Monster*; *The Split* (UKN); *The Two-Headed
  Monster*; *Nightmare* prod/rel: Shaw-Breakston
  Enterprises, United Artists of Japan, Inc.

BREAL, PIERRE-ARISTIDE
Les Femmes Sont Des Anges, Novel
  Femmes Sont Des Anges, Les 1952 d: Marcel
  Aboulker. lps: Viviane Romance, Jeanne Fusier-Gir,
  Jacques Grello. 95M FRN. *Edmee* prod/rel: Films De La
  Tour, C.a.P.A.C.
Les Hussards, Play
  Hussards, Les 1955 d: Alex Joffe. lps: Bourvil, Bernard
  Blier, Giovanna Ralli. 102M FRN. prod/rel: Cocinor,
  Cocinex

BREBAN, NICOLAE
Animale Bolnave, 1968, Novel
  Printre Colinele Verzi 1971 d: Nicolae Breban. lps:
  Dan Nutou, Mircea Albulescu, Emilia Dobrin. 95M
  RMN. *In the Green Hills*; *Sick Animals*

BRECHT, BERTOLT (1898–1956), GRM
*Arbeitsplatz Oder Im Schweisse Deines Angesichts
Sollst Du.*, 1962, Short Story
  Tod Und Auferstehung Des Wilheim Hausmann
  1977 d: Christa Muhl. 76M GDR. *Death and
  Resurrection of Wilhelm Hausmann*
Der Aufhaltsame Aufstieg Der Arturo Ui, 1958,
Play
  Karyera Arturo Ui: Novaya Vyersiya 1996 d: Boris
  Blank. lps: Alexander Filippenko, Vyacheslav Nivenny,
  Alexej Zharkov. 103M RSS. prod/rel: Studio Evrazia
Baal, 1922, Play
  Life Story of Baal ,the 1978 d: Edward Bennett. 57M
  UKN.

Die Dreigroschenoper, Berlin 1928, Play
  Dreigroschenoper, Die 1930 d: G. W. Pabst. lps:
  Rudolf Forster, Carola Neher, Reinhold Schunzel. 112M
  GRM. *The Threepenny Opera* (USA); *The Beggar's
  Opera* prod/rel: Tobis
  Dreigroschenoper, Die 1963 d: Wolfgang Staudte.
  lps: Sammy Davis Jr., Curd Jurgens, June Ritchie. 124M
  GRM/FRN. *L' Opera de Quat'sous* (FRN); *The
  Threepenny Opera* prod/rel: Kurt Ulrich, C.E.C.
  Opera de Quat' Sous, L' 1930 d: G. W. Pabst. lps:
  Albert Prejean, Florelle, Gaston Modot. 90M GRM. *The
  Threepenny Opera* prod/rel: Warner Bros., First
  National
Furchte Und Elend Des Dritten Reiches, 1941, Play
  Ubitzi Vykhodyat Na Dorogu 1942 d: V. I. Pudovkin,
  Yuri Tarich. 70M USS. *Murderers are on Their Way*; *The
  Murderers are Coming*
Die Geschafte Des Herrn Julius Caesar, 1957,
Novel
  Geschichtsunterricht 1972 d: Jean-Marie Straub,
  Daniele Huillet. lps: Gottfried Bold, Benedikt Zulauf,
  Johann Unterpertinger. 90M GRM. *History Lessons*
  (USA); *History Instruction* prod/rel: Janus
Herr Puntila Und Sein Knecht Matti, 1948, Play
  Herr Puntila Und Sein Knecht Matti 1955 d:
  Alberto Cavalcanti. lps: Curt Bois, Heinz Engelmann,
  Maria Emo. 97M AUS. *Mr. Puntila and His Valet Matti*;
  Puntila; *Herr Puntila and His Servant Matti* prod/rel:
  Wien-Film
  Herra Puntila Ja Hanen Renkinsa Matti 1979 d:
  Ralf LangbackA. lps: Lasse Poysti, Pekka Laiho, Arja
  SaijonmaA. 109M FNL/SWD. *Mr. Puntila and His
  Servant Matti*; *Herr Puntila Och Hans Drang* (SWD)
Leben Des Galilei, 1949, Play
  Galileo 1975 d: Joseph Losey. lps: Topol, Edward Fox,
  Colin Blakely. 145M UKN/CND. prod/rel: Ely Landau,
  Cinevision
Mutter Courage Und Ihre Kinder, 1949, Play
  Mutter Courage Und Ihre Kinder 1960 d: Peter
  Palitzsch, Manfred Wekwerth. lps: Helene Weigel,
  Angelika Hurwicz, Ekkehard Schall. 149M GDR.
  Mother Courage and Her Children prod/rel: Defa
Die Unwurdige Greisin, Berlin 1948, Short Story
  Vieille Dame Indigne, La 1964 d: Rene Allio. lps:
  Sylvie, Malka Ribovska, Victor Lanoux. 88M FRN. *The
  Shameless Old Lady* (USA) prod/rel: S.P.A.C.-Cinema

BREDES, DON
Hard Feelings, Novel
  Hard Feelings 1982 d: Daryl Duke. lps: Carl Marotte,
  Charlaine Woodard, Grand L. Bush. 105M CND/USA.
  Sneakers; *Cent Rancunes* prod/rel: Drah Productions
  (Astra) Ltd. (Montreal), Astral Bellevue Pathe Inc.
  (Montreal)

BREEN JR., JOSEPH I.
Story
  Breakthrough 1950 d: Lewis Seiler. lps: David Brian,
  John Agar, Frank Lovejoy. 91M USA. prod/rel: Warner
  Bros.

BREESE, EDMUND
A Man's Home, Albany, Ny. 1917, Play
  Man's Home, A 1921 d: Ralph Ince. lps: Harry T.
  Morey, Kathlyn Williams, Faire Binney. 6235f USA.
  prod/rel: Selznick Pictures, Select Pictures

BREFFORT, ALEXANDRE
Irma la Douce, Paris 1956, Play
  Irma la Douce 1963 d: Billy Wilder. lps: Shirley
  MacLaine, Jack Lemmon, Lou Jacobi. 149M USA.
  prod/rel: Mirisch Co., Phalanx Productions

BREIDAHL, AXEL
Aufruhr Im Damenstift, Play
  Aufruhr Im Damenstift 1941 d: F. D. Andam. lps:
  Maria Landrock, Hedwig Bleibtreu, Pepi Glockner. 82M
  GRM. prod/rel: Algefa, Siegel Monopol

BREILLAT, CATHERINE
36 Fillette, Novel
  36 Fillette 1987 d: Catherine Breillat. lps: Delphine
  Zentout, Etienne Chicot, Olivier Parniere. 88M FRN.
  Virgin; *Virgin - 36 Fillette*; *Size 36 Girls* prod/rel:
  French Prod., C.B. Films

BREINERSDORFER, FRED
Der Hammermorder, Book
  Hammermorder, Der 1990 d: Bernd Schadewald. lps:
  Christian Redl, Ulrike Kriener, Silvan Oesterle. TVM.
  90M GRM. prod/rel: Ccc-Television Artur Brauner, ZDF

BREINHOLST, WILLY
Sommar Och Syndare, Novel
  Sommar Och Syndare 1960 d: Arne Mattsson. lps:
  Elsa Prawitz, Karl Arne Holsten, Yvonne Lombard.
  84M SWD/DNM. *Summer and Sinners* prod/rel: Lorens
  Marmstedt

Vergiss Nicht Deine Frau Zu Kussen, Novel
   Vergiss Nicht Deine Frau Zu Kussen 1967 d: Egil
   Kolsto. lps: Walter Giller, Ghita Norby, Christina
   Schollin. 90M GRM/DNM. *Don't Forget to Kiss Your
   Wife; Els. Din Naeste!* (DNM) prod/rel: Nfg, Merry

BREN, J. ROBERT
Cry Copper, Story
   Naked Alibi 1954 d: Jerry Hopper. lps: Sterling
   Hayden, Gloria Grahame, Gene Barry. 86M USA.
   prod/rel: Universal-International

BRENDA
Froggy's Little Brother, Novel
   Froggy's Little Brother 1921 d: A. E. Coleby. lps:
   Maurice Thompson, Stephen Frayne, Henry Doyle.
   5250f UKN. *Children of Courage* prod/rel: Stoll

BRENNAN, FREDERICK HAZLITT
God's Gift to Women, 1930, Short Story
   Play Girl 1932 d: Ray Enright. lps: Loretta Young,
   Norman Foster, Winnie Lightner. 7r USA. *Playgirl*;
   Eight to Five; Love on a Budget prod/rel: Warner Bros.
   Pictures©

He Follows the Sun Again, Article
   Follow the Sun 1951 d: Sidney Lanfield. lps: Glenn
   Ford, Anne Baxter, Dennis O'Keefe. 96M USA. prod/rel:
   20th Century-Fox

Horse Flesh, 1930, Short Story
   Sporting Blood 1931 d: Charles J. Brabin. lps: Clark
   Gable, Ernest Torrence, Madge Evans. 84M USA.
   Horseflesh prod/rel: Metro-Goldwyn-Mayer Corp.,
   Metro-Goldwyn-Mayer Dist. Corp.©

The Matron's Report, 1928, Short Story
   Blue Skies 1929 d: Alfred L. Werker. lps: Helen
   Twelvetree, Frank Albertson, Rosa Gore. 5408f USA.
   prod/rel: Fox Film Corp.
   Little Miss Nobody 1936 d: John G. Blystone. lps:
   Jane Withers, Jane Darwell, Ralph Morgan. 72M USA.
   The Matron's Report; Public Nuisance No.1 prod/rel:
   Twentieth Century-Fox Film Corp.©

Miss Pacific Fleet, 1934, Short Story
   Miss Pacific Fleet 1935 d: Ray Enright. lps: Joan
   Blondell, Glenda Farrell, Hugh Herbert. 66M USA.
   prod/rel: Warner Bros. Pictures©

One Night at Susie's, Story
   One Night at Susie's 1930 d: John Francis Dillon. lps:
   Billie Dove, Douglas Fairbanks Jr., Helen Ware. 5760f
   USA. prod/rel: First National Pictures

A Perfect Weekend, 1934, Short Story
   St. Louis Kid, The 1934 d: Ray Enright. lps: James
   Cagney, Patricia Ellis, Allen Jenkins. 67M USA. *A
   Perfect Weekend* (UKN) prod/rel: Warner Bros.
   Production Corp., Warner Bros. Pictures©

Shanghai Madness, 1932, Short Story
   Shanghai Madness 1933 d: John G. Blystone. lps:
   Spencer Tracy, Fay Wray, Ralph Morgan. 63M USA.
   prod/rel: Fox Film Corp.©

They Sell Sailors Elephants, Story
   Girl in Every Port, A 1952 d: Chester Erskine. lps:
   Groucho Marx, William Bendix, Marie Wilson. 86M
   USA. prod/rel: RKO Radio

BRENNAN, GEORGE HUGH
Anna Malleen, New York 1911, Novel
   Luring Lights, The 1915 d: Robert G. VignolA. lps:
   Stella Hoban, Corinne Malvern, Helen Lindroth. 5r
   USA. prod/rel: Kalem Co., General Film Co.

BRENNAN, MATTHEW
The Big Sweep, Play
   Lucky Loser 1934 d: Reginald Denham. lps: Richard
   Dolman, Aileen Marson, Anna Lee. 68M UKN. prod/rel:
   British and Dominions, Paramount British

BRENNAN, PETER
Razorback, Novel
   Razorback 1983 d: Russell Mulcahy. lps: Gregory
   Harrison, Arkie Whiteley, Bill Kerr. 95M ASL. prod/rel:
   U.aA. Films Ltd.©, Western Film Productions (No. 1)

BRENON, ROBERT
The Secret, Play
   Secret, The 1955 d: Cy Endfield. lps: Sam Wanamaker,
   Mandy Miller, Andre Morell. 80M UKN. prod/rel:
   Laureate, Golden Era

BRENT, WILLIAM
Yesterday's Heroes, 1939, Novel
   Yesterday's Heroes 1940 d: Herbert I. Leeds. lps: Jean
   Rogers, Robert Sterling, Ted North. 66M USA. prod/rel:
   20th Century-Fox Film Corp.©

BRENTANO, LOWELL
Danger - Men Working, Baltimore, Md. 1936, Play
   Crime Nobody Saw, The 1937 d: Charles T. Barton.
   lps: Lew Ayres, Vivienne Osborne, Eugene Pallette. 60M
   USA. *Danger -Men Working* prod/rel: Paramount
   Pictures, Inc.

The Spider, New York 1927, Play
   Spider, The 1931 d: William Cameron Menzies,
   Kenneth MacKennA. lps: Edmund Lowe, Lois Moran,
   Howard Phillips. 65M USA. *The Midnight Cruise*
   prod/rel: Fox Film Corp.©

BRERA, GIANNI
Il Corpo Della Ragassa, Novel
   Corpo Della Ragazza, Il 1979 d: Pasquale Festa
   Campanile. lps: Enrico Maria Salerno, Clara Colosimo,
   Nino Bignamini. 104M ITL. *The Young Girl's Body*
   prod/rel: Filmauro, Titanus

BRESLIN, HOWARD
Story
   Platinum High School 1960 d: Charles Haas. lps:
   Mickey Rooney, Terry Moore, Dan DuryeA. 93M USA.
   Young and Deadly Rich (UKN); *Trouble at 16* prod/rel:
   MGM

Bad Time at Hondo, Story
   Bad Day at Black Rock 1955 d: John Sturges. lps:
   Spencer Tracy, Robert Ryan, Anne Francis. 81M USA.
   prod/rel: Metro-Goldwyn-Mayer Corp.

BRESLIN, JIMMY
The Gang That Couldn't Shoot Straight, Novel
   Gang That Couldn't Shoot Straight, The 1971 d:
   James Goldstone. lps: Jerry Orbach, Leigh
   Taylor-Young, Jo Van Fleet. 96M USA. prod/rel: MGM

BRETON, TOMAS
La Dolores, Opera
   Dolores, La 1923 d: Maximiliano Thous. lps: Ana Giner
   Soler, Leopoldo Pitarch, Jose Latorre. 2575m SPN.
   prod/rel: Compania Cin.Ca Hispano-Portuguesa,
   P.A.C.E.

La Verbena de la Paloma, Opera
   Verbena de la Paloma, La 1921 d: Jose Buchs. lps:
   Elisa Ruiz Romero, Florian Rey, Julia Lozano. 57M
   SPN. *The Feast of the Dove; The Paloma Fair* prod/rel:
   Atlantida (Madrid)

BRETT, SIMON (1945–, UKN, Brett, Simon Anthony
Lee
Dead Romantic, Novel
   Dead Romantic 1992 d: Patrick Lau. lps: Janet
   McTeer, Clive Wood, Jonny Lee Miller. TVM. 89M UKN.
   prod/rel: BBC Pebble Mill, Screen Two

A Shock to the System, Novel
   Shock to the System, A 1990 d: Jan Egleson. lps:
   Michael Caine, Elizabeth McGovern, Peter Riegert.
   91M USA. prod/rel: Medusa, Corsair

BRETTSCHNEIDER, RUDOLF
Prinzessin Dagmar, Play
   Madchenpensionat 1936 d: Geza von Bolvary. lps:
   Attila Horbiger, Hilde Krahl, Leopoldine Konstantin.
   93M AUS/HNG. *Leanyintezet* (HNG); *Prinzessin
   Dagmar* prod/rel: Styria

BREUER, BESSIE
Memory of Love, New York 1934, Novel
   In Name Only 1939 d: John Cromwell. lps: Carole
   Lombard, Cary Grant, Kay Francis. 94M USA. *The Kind
   Men Marry; Memory of Love* prod/rel: RKO Radio
   Pictures©

BREWER, GIL
Hell's Our Destination, Novel
   Lure of the Swamp, The 1957 d: Hubert Cornfield.
   lps: Marshall Thompson, Willard Parker, Joan Vohs.
   75M USA. prod/rel: 20th Century-Fox, Regal Films

BREWER JR., GEORGE EMERSON
Dark Victory, New York 1934, Play
   Dark Victory 1939 d: Edmund Goulding. lps: Bette
   Davis, George Brent, Humphrey Bogart. 105M USA.
   prod/rel: Warner Bros. Pictures, Inc.
   Dark Victory 1976 d: Robert Butler. lps: Elizabeth
   Montgomery, Anthony Hopkins, Michele Lee. TVM.
   150M USA. prod/rel: Universal
   Stolen Hours 1963 d: Daniel Petrie. lps: Susan
   Hayward, Michael Craig, Diane Baker. 100M
   UKN/USA. *Summer Flight* prod/rel: Mirisch Films,
   Barbican Films

BREZAN, JURIJ
Story
   Schwarze Muhle, Die 1975 d: Celino Bleiweiss. lps:
   Leon Niemczyk, Klaus Brasch, Wolfgang Penz. 90M
   GDR. prod/rel: Fernsehen Der D.D.R.

BRIANT, ROY
When Jerry Comes Home, Play
   Itching Palms 1923 d: James W. Horne. lps: Tom
   Gallery, Herschal Mayall, Virginia Fox. 6100f USA.
   prod/rel: R-C Pictures, Film Booking Offices of America

BRICKER, GEORGE
The Dancing Masters, Novel
   Dancing Masters, The 1943 d: Malcolm St. Clair. lps:
   Stan Laurel, Oliver Hardy, Trudy Marshall. 64M USA.
   prod/rel: 20th Century-Fox

BRICKHILL, PAUL (1916–1991), ASL, Brickhall, Paul
Chester Jerome
Enemy Coast Ahead, Book
   Dam Busters, The 1955 d: Michael Anderson. lps:
   Richard Todd, Michael Redgrave, Derek Farr. 125M
   UKN. prod/rel: Associated British Picture Corporation,
   Ab-Pathe

The Great Escape, 1950, Novel
   Great Escape, The 1963 d: John Sturges. lps: Steve
   McQueen, James Garner, Richard Attenborough. 168M
   USA. prod/rel: Mirisch Corporation, Alpha Corporation

Reach for the Sky, 1954, Novel
   Reach for the Sky 1956 d: Lewis Gilbert. lps: Kenneth
   More, Muriel Pavlow, Lyndon Brook. 135M UKN.
   prod/rel: Rank Film Distributors, Pinnacle

BRICUSSE, LESLIE (1931–, UKN
Stop the World - I Want to Get Off, London 1961,
Play
   Stop the World - I Want to Get Off 1966 d: Philip
   Saville. lps: Tony Tanner, Millicent Martin, Leila Croft.
   100M UKN. prod/rel: Warner Bros. Pictures,
   Warner-Pathe

BRIDGERS, ANNE P.
Coquette, New York 1928, Play
   Coquette 1929 d: Sam Taylor. lps: Mary Pickford,
   Johnny Mack Brown, Matt Moore. 6993f USA. prod/rel:
   Pickford Corp., United Artists

BRIDGES, VICTOR
Another Man's Shoes, New York 1913, Novel
   Another Man's Shoes 1922 d: Jack Conway. lps:
   Herbert Rawlinson, Barbara Bedford, Una Trevelyn.
   4251f USA. prod/rel: Universal Film Mfg. Co.
   Phantom Buccaneer, The 1916 d: J. Charles Haydon.
   lps: Richard C. Travers, Gertrude Glover, Thurlow
   Brewer. 5r USA. prod/rel: Essanay Film Mfg. Co.©,
   K-E-S-E Service

Greensea Island, Novel
   Through Fire and Water 1923 d: Thomas Bentley.
   lps: Clive Brook, Flora Le Breton, Lawford Davidson.
   6188f UKN. prod/rel: Ideal

The Lady from Longacre, New York 1919, Novel
   Greater Than a Crown 1925 d: R. William Neill. lps:
   Edmund Lowe, Dolores Costello, Margaret Livingston.
   5r USA. prod/rel: Fox Film Corp.
   Lady from Longacre, The 1921 d: George Marshall.
   lps: William Russell, Mary Thurman, Mathilde
   Brundage. 5r USA. prod/rel: Fox Film Corp.

Mr. Lyndon at Liberty, Novel
   Mr. Lyndon at Liberty 1915 d: Harold Shaw. lps:
   Edna Flugrath, Fred Groves, Harry Welchman. 5130f
   UKN. prod/rel: London, Jury

BRIDIE, JAMES
The Anatomist, 1931, Play
   Anatomist, The 1961 d: Leonard William. lps: Alastair
   Sim, George Cole, Jill Bennett. 73M UKN. prod/rel: Dola
   Films

Daphne Laureola, Play
   Daphne Laureola 1978 d: Waris Hussein. lps: Joan
   Plowright, Laurence Olivier, Arthur Lowe. MTV. 94M
   UKN. prod/rel: Granada

The Golden Legend of Shults, 1939, Play
   There Was a Crooked Man 1960 d: Stuart Burge. lps:
   Norman Wisdom, Alfred Marks, Andrew Cruickshank.
   107M UKN. prod/rel: Knightsbridge Productions,
   United Artists

It Depends What You Mean, London 1944, Play
   Folly to Be Wise 1952 d: Frank Launder. lps: Alastair
   Sim, Roland Culver, Elizabeth Allan. 91M UKN.
   prod/rel: London Films, British Lion Production Assets

A Sleeping Clergyman, London 1933, Play
   Flesh and Blood 1951 d: Anthony Kimmins. lps:
   Richard Todd, Glynis Johns, Joan Greenwood. 102M
   UKN. prod/rel: British Lion, Harefield

What Say They?, 1939, Play
   You're Only Young Twice! 1952 d: Terry Bishop. lps:
   Duncan MacRae, Joseph Tomelty, Patrick Barr. 81M
   UKN. prod/rel: Group Three, Associated British Film
   Distributors

BRIEUX, EUGENE
Les Avaries, Liege 1902, Play
   Damaged Goods 1915 d: Thomas Ricketts. lps:
   Richard Bennett, Adrienne Morrison, Maud Milton. 7r
   USA. prod/rel: American Film Mfg. Co.©, State Rights
   Damaged Goods 1919 d: Alexander Butler. lps:
   Campbell Gullan, Marjorie Day, J. Fisher White. 5000f
   UKN. prod/rel: G. B. Samuelson, Woolf & Freedman
   Marriage Forbidden 1936 d: Phil Goldstone. lps:
   Pedro de Cordoba, Phyllis Barry, Douglas Walton. 61M
   USA. *Damaged Goods* prod/rel: Criterion Pictures Corp.

L' Avocat, 1922, Play
   Avocat, L' 1925 d: Gaston Ravel. lps: Rolla-Norman,
   Mirales, Jeanne MeA. F FRN.

Coup de Feu Dans la Nuit 1942 d: Robert Peguy. lps: Mary Morgan, Henri Rollan, Jean Debucourt. 87M FRN. *Un Coup de Feu Dans la Nuit; Secrets de Famille* prod/rel: Societe Des Films Fernand Rivers

Le Berceau, Paris 1908, Play
Cradle, The 1922 d: Paul Powell. lps: Ethel Clayton, Charles Meredith, Mary Jane Irving. 4698f USA. prod/rel: Famous Players-Lasky, Paramount Pictures

Blanchette, 1892, Play
Blanchette 1912 d: Henri Pouctal. lps: Leon Bernard, Armand Tallier, Rosni-Derys. 600m FRN. prod/rel: Film d'Art

Blanchette 1921 d: Rene Hervil. lps: Pauline Johnson, Leon Mathot, Therese Kolb. 1800m FRN. prod/rel: Films Andre Legrand

Blanchette 1936 d: Pierre Caron. lps: Marie Bell, Mady Berry, Jean Martinelli. 89M FRN. prod/rel: J.L.S.

La Petite Amie, Play
Petite Amie, La 1916 d: Marcel Simon. lps: Felix Huguenet, Roger Gaillard, Jane Renouardt. 1203m FRN. prod/rel: Cinedrama

La Robe Rouge, 1900, Play
Robe Rouge, La 1912 d: Henri Pouctal. lps: Felix Huguenet, Georges Grand, Jeanne Delvair. 850m FRN. prod/rel: le Film d'Art

Robe Rouge, La 1933 d: Jean de Marguenat. lps: Constant Remy, Jacques Gretillat, Suzanne Rissler. 95M FRN. prod/rel: Europa-Films

Simone, Novel
Simone 1918 d: Camille de Morlhon. lps: Duquesne, Armand Tallier, Lilian Greuze. 1525m FRN. prod/rel: Films Valetta

Simone 1926 d: E. B. Donatien. lps: Jean Dehelly, Lucienne Legrand, E. B. Donatien. SRL. 7EP FRN. prod/rel: Establissements Louis Aubert

BRIGADERE, ANNA
Story
Pohadka O Malickovi 1985 d: Gunar Piesis. lps: Rolands Neilands, Elza Radzina, Astrida KairisA. 83M CZC/USS. *The Fairy Tale of Malicek; Maltschik-S-Paltschik* prod/rel: Filmove Studio Barrandov, Studio Riga

BRIGGS, RAYMOND
Father Christmas, Book
Father Christmas 1992 d: Dave Unwin. ANM. UKN.

The Snowman, Book
Snowman, The 1983 d: Dianne Jackson. ANM. 30M UKN. prod/rel: Snowman Enterprises

When the Wind Blows, Book
When the Wind Blows 1986 d: Jimmy T. Murakami. ANM. 85M UKN. prod/rel: Meltdown, Film Four International

BRIGHOUSE, HAROLD
Hobson's Choice, London 1916, Play
Hobson's Choice 1920 d: Percy Nash. lps: Joe Nightingale, Joan Ritz, Arthur Pitt. 5547f UKN. prod/rel: Master, British Exhibitors' Films

Hobson's Choice 1931 d: Thomas Bentley. lps: Viola Lyel, James Harcourt, Frank Pettingell. 65M UKN. prod/rel: British International Pictures, Wardour

Hobson's Choice 1954 d: David Lean. lps: Charles Laughton, John Mills, Brenda de Banzie. 107M UKN. prod/rel: London Films, British Lion Production Assets

Hobson's Choice 1983 d: Gilbert Cates. lps: Richard Thomas, Sharon Gless, Jack Warden. TVM. 100M USA. prod/rel: CBS, Blue-Greene

Other Times, Play
Children of Jazz 1923 d: Jerome Storm. lps: Theodore Kosloff, Ricardo Cortez, Robert Cain. 6080f USA. prod/rel: Famous Players-Lasky, Paramount Pictures

The Winning Goal, Play
Winning Goal, The 1920 d: G. B. Samuelson. lps: Harold Walden, Maudie Dunham, Tom Reynolds. 5000f UKN. prod/rel: G. B. Samuelson, General

BRILANT, ARTHUR M.
Play
Strange Case of Clara Deane, The 1932 d: Louis J. Gasnier, Max Marcin. lps: Wynne Gibson, Pat O'Brien, Frances Dee. 78M USA. *Clara Deane; Case of Clara Deane* prod/rel: Paramount Publix Corp.©

BRIMMER, GABRIELLA
Gaby, Book
Gaby 1987 d: Luis Mandoki. lps: Norma Aleandro, Rachel Levin, Liv Ullmann. 114M MXC/UKN/USA. *Gaby; a True Story; Gaby -Una Historia Verdadera* prod/rel: Tri-Star

BRIN, DAVID
The Postman, Novel
Postman, The 1997 d: Kevin Costner. lps: Kevin Costner, Will Patton, Larenz Tate. 178M USA. prod/rel: Tig, Warner Bros.©

BRINGUIER, PAUL
Au Nom de la Loi, Novel
Au Nom de la Loi 1931 d: Maurice Tourneur. lps: Marcelle Chantal, Regine Dancourt, Gabriel Gabrio. 77M FRN. prod/rel: Pathe-Nathan

BRINIG, MYRON
The Sisters, New York 1937, Novel
Sisters, The 1938 d: Anatole Litvak. lps: Errol Flynn, Bette Davis, Anita Louise. 99M USA. prod/rel: Warner Bros. Pictures©, Anatole Litvak Production

BRINISTOL, E. A.
Story
Ballyhoo's Story, The 1913 d: Rollin S. Sturgeon. 1000f USA. prod/rel: Vitagraph Co. of America

BRINK, ANDRE (1935–, SAF
A Dry White Season, 1979, Novel
Dry White Season, A 1988 d: Euzhan Palcy. lps: Donald Sutherland, Janet Suzman, Zakes Mokae. 107M USA. prod/rel: MGM, United Artists

BRINK, CAROL (1895–1981), USA, Brink, Carol Ryrie
Stopover, Novel
All I Desire 1953 d: Douglas Sirk. lps: Barbara Stanwyck, Richard Carlson, Lyle Bettger. 70M USA. prod/rel: Universal-International

BRINKLEY, WILLIAM
Don't Go Near the Water, Novel
Don't Go Near the Water 1957 d: Charles Walters. lps: Glenn Ford, Gia Scala, Earl Holliman. 107M USA. prod/rel: MGM, Avon Prod.

BRINKMAN, BO
Ice House, Play
Ice House 1989 d: Eagle Pennell. lps: Melissa Gilbert, Bo Brinkman, Buddy Quaid. 86M USA. prod/rel: Monarch H

BRIQUET
Alma - Where Do You Live?, Musical Play
Alma, Where Do You Live? 1917 d: Hal Clarendon. lps: Ruth MacTammany, George Larkin, Jack Newton. 6r USA. prod/rel: Newfields Producing Corp., State Rights

BRISBARRE
Les Pauvres de Paris, Play
Pauvres de Paris, Les 1913 d: Georges DenolA. lps: Jules Mondos, Louis Ravet, Gina Barbieri. 1095m FRN. prod/rel: Scagl

BRISKIN, MORT
Story
Man Alone, A 1955 d: Ray Milland. lps: Ray Milland, Mary Murphy, Ward Bond. 96M USA. prod/rel: Republic

BRISKIN, SAMUEL J.
The Millionaire Policeman, Story
Millionaire Policeman, The 1926 d: Edward J. Le Saint. lps: Herbert Rawlinson, Eva Novak, Eugenie Besserer. 5189f USA. prod/rel: Banner Productions, Ginsberg-Kann Distributing Corp.

BRISTOW, GWEN
Jubilee Trail, Novel
Jubilee Trail 1954 d: Joseph Kane. lps: Vera Ralston, Joan Leslie, Forrest Tucker. 103M USA. prod/rel: Republic

The Ninth Guest, New Orleans 1930, Novel
Ninth Guest, The 1934 d: R. William Neill. lps: Donald Cook, Genevieve Tobin, Hardie Albright. 69M USA. prod/rel: Columbia Pictures Corp.©

Tomorrow Is Forever, Novel
Tomorrow Is Forever 1946 d: Irving Pichel. lps: Orson Welles, Claudette Colbert, George Brent. 105M USA. prod/rel: RKO Radio

BRITTAIN, VERA (1896–1970), ULM, Catlin, Mrs. George Edward Gordon
Testament of Youth, 1933, Autobiography
Testament of Youth 1979 d: Moira Armstrong. lps: Cheryl Campbell, Jane Wenham, Emrys James. MTV. 250M UKN.

BRIZZI, ENRICO
Jack Frusciante E Uscito Dal Gruppo, Novel
Jack Frusciante Uscito Dal Gruppo 1996 d: Enza Negroni. lps: Stefano Accorsi, Violante Placido, Alessandro Zamattio. 100M ITL. *Jack Frusciante Has Left the Band; Jack Frusciante Left the Band* prod/rel: Brosfilm, Medusa Film

BRIZZOLARA, CARLO
Temporale Rosy, Novel
Temporale Rosy 1979 d: Mario Monicelli. lps: Gerard Depardieu, Faith Minton, Roland Bock. 120M ITL/FRN/GRM. *Rosy la Bourrasque* (FRN); *Hurricane Rosy* (GRM); *Hurricane Rosie* prod/rel: P.E.A. (Roma), Les Prods. Artistes Associes (Paris)

BROADBRIDGE, HUGH
Moorland Terror, Novel
Road to Fortune, The 1930 d: Arthur Varney-Serrao. lps: Guy Newall, Doria March, Florence Desmond. 60M UKN. prod/rel: Starcraft, Paramount

BROADHURST, GEORGE, Broadhurst, George H., Broadhurst, George Howells
Bought and Paid for, New York 1911, Play
Bought and Paid for 1916 d: Harley Knoles. lps: Alice Brady, Montagu Love, Francis X. Conlan. 5r USA. *The Faun* (UKN) prod/rel: William A. Brady Picture Plays, Inc., World Film Corp.

Bought and Paid for 1922 d: William C. de Mille. lps: Agnes Ayres, Jack Holt, Walter Hiers. 5601f USA. prod/rel: Famous Players-Lasky, Paramount Pictures

The Call of the North, New York 1908, Play
Call of the North, The 1914 d: Cecil B. de Mille, Oscar Apfel. lps: Robert Edeson, Winifred Kingston, Theodore Roberts. 5r USA. prod/rel: Jesse L. Lasky Feature Play Co.©, State Rights

The Dollar Mark, New York 1909, Play
Dollar Mark, The 1914 d: O. A. C. Lund. lps: Robert Warwick, Barbara Tennant, Eric Mayne. 5r USA. prod/rel: William A. Brady Picture Plays, Inc., World Film Corp.©

Innocent, New York 1914, Play
Innocent 1918 d: George Fitzmaurice. lps: Fannie Ward, John Miltern, Armand Kaliz. 5r USA. *Innocence* prod/rel: Astra Film Corp., Pathe Exchange, Inc.

The Law of the Land, New York 1914, Play
Law of the Land, The 1917 d: Maurice Tourneur. lps: Olga Petrova, Wyndham Standing, Mahlon Hamilton. 5r USA. prod/rel: Jesse L. Lasky Feature Play Co.©, Paramount Pictures Corp.

The Man of the Hour, New York 1906, Play
Man of the Hour, The 1914 d: Maurice Tourneur. lps: Robert Warwick, Ned Burton, Eric Mayne. 5r USA. prod/rel: William A. Brady Picture Plays, Inc., World Film Corp.©

The Mills of the Gods, New York 1907, Play
Man Who Found Himself, The 1915 d: Frank H. Crane. lps: Robert Warwick, Paul McAllister, Arline Pretty. 5r USA. *The Coward* prod/rel: William A. Brady Picture Plays, Inc., World Film Corp.©

The Price, New York 1911, Play
Price, The 1915 d: Joseph A. Golden. lps: Helen Ware, Wilmuth Merkyl, James Cooley. 5r USA. prod/rel: Equitable Motion Pictures Corp., World Film Corp.

Wife Against Wife 1921 d: Whitman Bennett. lps: Pauline Starke, Percy Marmont, Edward Langford. 5864f USA. prod/rel: Whitman Bennett Productions, Associated First National Pictures

Today, New York 1913, Play
Today 1930 d: William Nigh. lps: Conrad Nagel, Catherine Dale Owen, Sarah Padden. 6660f USA. prod/rel: Majestic Pictures

Today 1917 d: Ralph Ince. lps: Florence Reed, Alice Gale, Gus Weinberg. 5r USA. prod/rel: Today Feature Film Corp., Ralph Ince Production

What Happened to Jones, New York 1897, Play
What Happened to Jones 1915 d: Fred MacE. lps: Fred MacE, Josie Sadler, Mary Charleson. 5r USA. prod/rel: William A. Brady Picture Plays, Inc., World Film Corp.©

What Happened to Jones 1920 d: James Cruze. lps: Bryant Washburn, Margaret Loomis, Morris Foster. 4539f USA. prod/rel: Famous Players-Lasky Corp.©, Paramount-Artcraft Pictures

What Happened to Jones 1926 d: William A. Seiter. lps: Reginald Denny, Marian Nixon, Melbourne MacDowell. 6726f USA. prod/rel: Universal Pictures

What Money Can't Buy, New York 1915, Play
What Money Can't Buy 1917 d: Lou Tellegen. lps: Jack Pickford, Louise Huff, Theodore Roberts. 5r USA. prod/rel: Jesse L. Lasky Feature Play Co.©, Paramount Pictures Corp.

Why Smith Left Home, New York 1899, Play
Why Smith Left Home 1919 d: Donald Crisp. lps: Bryant Washburn, Lois Wilson, Mayme Kelso. 4155f USA. prod/rel: Famous Players-Lasky Corp.©, Paramount-Artcraft Pictures

Wild Oats Lane, New York 1922, Play
Wild Oats Lane 1926 d: Marshall Neilan. lps: Viola Dana, Robert Agnew, John MacSweeney. 6900f USA. prod/rel: Marshall Neilan Productions, Producers Distributing Corp.

Wildfire, New York 1908, Play
Wildfire 1915 d: Edwin Middleton. lps: Lillian Russell, Lionel Barrymore, Sam J. Ryan. 5r USA. prod/rel: World Film Corp.©, Shubert Feature

Wildfire 1925 d: T. Hayes Hunter. lps: Aileen Pringle, Edna Murphy, Holmes Herbert. 6550f USA. prod/rel: Distinctive Pictures, Vitagraph Co. of America

The Woman on the Index, New York 1918, Novel
Woman on the Index, The 1919 d: Hobart Henley. lps: Pauline Frederick, Wyndham Standing, Jere Austin. 5r USA. prod/rel: Goldwyn Pictures Corp.©, Goldwyn Distributing Corp.

The Wrong Mr. Wright, Play
Wrong Mr. Wright, The 1927 d: Scott Sidney. lps: Jean Hersholt, Enid Bennett, Dorothy Devore. 6459f USA. prod/rel: Universal Pictures

BROADHURST, THOMAS WILLIAM
Our Pleasant Sins, New York 1919, Play
Damaged Love 1930 d: Irvin V. Willat. lps: June Collyer, Charles Starrett, Eloise Taylor. 6333f USA. prod/rel: Superior Talking Pictures, Sono Art-World Wide Pictures

BROD, MAX
Nach Der Man Sich Sehnt, Die Frau, Novel
Frau, Nach Der Man Sich Sehnt, Die 1929 d: Curtis Bernhardt. lps: Marlene Dietrich, Fritz Kortner, Uno Henning. 2360m GRM. *Enigma; Three Loves* prod/rel: Terra

Prozess Bunterbart, Play
Sensations-Prozess 1928 d: Friedrich Feher. lps: Magda Sonja, Anton Pointner, Carl Goetz. 3368m GRM. prod/rel: National-Film Ag

BRODIE, JULIAN
Beauty and the Beat, 1936, Short Story
Love on the Run 1936 d: W. S. Van Dyke. lps: Joan Crawford, Clark Gable, Franchot Tone. 80M USA. prod/rel: Metro-Goldwyn-Mayer Corp.©

BRODKEY, HAROLD (1930–1996), USA
Story
First Love 1977 d: Joan Darling. lps: William Katt, Susan Dey, John Heard. 92M USA. prod/rel: Paramount

BRODY, ALEXANDER
Die Geliebte, Play
Geliebte, Die 1927 d: Robert Wiene. lps: Edda Croy, Harry Liedtke, Adele Sandrock. 2168m GRM. *The Beloved* prod/rel: Pan Europa-Film

Lea Lyon, Play
Surrender 1927 d: Edward Sloman. lps: Mary Philbin, Ivan Mosjoukine, Otto Matieson. 8249f USA. *The President* (UKN) prod/rel: Universal Pictures

BRODY, SANDOR
A Tanitono, 1908, Play
Tanitono, A 1945 d: Marton Keleti. lps: Eva Szorenyi, Pal Javor, Kalman Rozsahegyi. 69M HNG. *The Schoolmistress*

BROEHL-DELHAES, CHRISTEL
Kamerad Mutter, Novel
Aus Erster Ehe 1940 d: Paul Verhoeven. lps: Franziska Kinz, Ferdinand Marian, Maria Landrock. 89M GRM. prod/rel: Tobis, Knevels

BROGGER, SUZANNE
Fri Os Fra Kaerligheden, 1973, Novel
Violer Er Bla 1974 d: Peter Refn. lps: Lisbeth Lundquist, Annika Hoydal, Lisbeth Dahl. 120M DNM. *Violets are Blue*

BROMFIELD, LOUIS (1896–1956), USA
Story
Brigham Young - Frontiersman 1940 d: Henry Hathaway. lps: Tyrone Power, Linda Darnell, Dean Jagger. 114M USA. *Brigham Young* (UKN) prod/rel: Twentieth Century-Fox Film Corp.

Better Than Life, 1936, Short Story
It All Came True 1940 d: Lewis Seiler. lps: Ann Sheridan, Humphrey Bogart, Jeffrey Lynn. 97M USA. *The Roaring Nineties*; *And It All Came True* prod/rel: Warner Bros. Pictures©

McLeod's Folly, 1939, Short Story
Johnny Come Lately 1943 d: Edward Jose. lps: James Cagney, Grace George, Marjorie Main. 97M USA. *Johnny Vagabond* (UKN) prod/rel: United Artists

A Modern Hero, New York 1932, Novel
Modern Hero, A 1934 d: G. W. Pabst. lps: Richard Barthelmess, Jean Muir, Marjorie Rambeau. 71M USA. prod/rel: Warner Bros. Pictures©

Mrs. Parkington, 1943, Novel
Mrs. Parkington 1944 d: Tay Garnett. lps: Greer Garson, Walter Pidgeon, Edward Arnold. 124M USA. prod/rel: MGM

The Rains Came, New York 1937, Novel
Rains Came, The 1939 d: Clarence Brown. lps: Myrna Loy, Tyrone Power, George Brent. 103M USA. prod/rel: Twentieth Century-Fox Film Corp.

Rains of Ranchipur, The 1955 d: Jean Negulesco. lps: Lana Turner, Richard Burton, Fred MacMurray. 104M USA. prod/rel: 20th Century-Fox

A Scarlet Woman, 1929, Short Story
Life of Vergie Winters, The 1934 d: Alfred Santell. lps: Ann Harding, John Boles, Helen Vinson. 82M USA. *Vergie Winters* prod/rel: RKO Radio Pictures©

Single Night, 1932, Story
Night After Night 1932 d: Archie Mayo. lps: George Raft, Mae West, Constance Cummings. 76M USA. prod/rel: Paramount Publix Corp.©

Twenty-Four Hours, New York 1930, Novel
24 Hours 1931 d: Marion Gering. lps: Clive Brook, Miriam Hopkins, Regis Toomey. 68M USA. *The Hours Between* (UKN); *Twenty-Four Hours* prod/rel: Paramount Publix Corp.©

BRONDER, LUCIA
Rockabye, 1924, Play
Rockabye 1932 d: George Cukor. lps: Constance Bennett, Joel McCrea, Paul Lukas. 75M USA. prod/rel: RKO Radio Pictures©

BRONSON, MRS. OWEN
Story
Barefoot Boy 1914 d: Robert G. VignolA. lps: Marguerite Courtot, Alice Hollister, Tom Moore. 3r USA. prod/rel: Kalem

The Charming Deceiver, Story
Charming Deceiver, The 1921 d: George L. Sargent. lps: Alice Calhoun, Jack McLean, Charles Kent. 5r USA. prod/rel: Vitagraph Co. of America

BRONTE, ANNE (1820–1849), UKN
The Tenant of Wildfell Hall, 1848, Novel
Tenant of Wildfell Hall, The 1996 d: Mike Barker. lps: Tara Fitzgerald, Rupert Graves, Toby Stephens. MTV. 159M UKN.

BRONTE, CHARLOTTE (1816–1855), UKN
Jane Eyre, London 1847, Novel
Jane Eyre 1910. 304m ITL. *The Mad Lady of Chester* (USA)

Jane Eyre 1910 d: Theodore Marston. lps: Frank Crane, Irma Taylor, Amelia Barleon. 1000f USA. prod/rel: Thanhouser

Jane Eyre 1914 d: Frank H. Crane. lps: Irving Cummings, Ethel Grandin, Miss Hazelton. 2r USA. prod/rel: Imp

Jane Eyre 1914 d: Martin J. Faust. lps: Alberta Roy, Lisbeth Blackstone, Mary Frye Clements. 4r USA. prod/rel: Whitman Features Co.©, Blinkhorn Photoplays Corp.

Jane Eyre 1915 d: Travers Vale. lps: Louise Vale, Franklin Ritchie, Gretchen Hartman. 3r USA. prod/rel: Biograph Co.

Jane Eyre 1921 d: Hugo Ballin. lps: Norman Trevor, Mabel Ballin, Crauford Kent. 6550f USA. prod/rel: Hugo Ballin Productions, W. W. Hodkinson Corp.

Jane Eyre 1934 d: W. Christy Cabanne. lps: Virginia Bruce, Colin Clive, Beryl Mercer. 70M USA. prod/rel: Monogram Pictures Corp.©

Jane Eyre 1944 d: Robert Stevenson. lps: Joan Fontaine, Orson Welles, Margaret O'Brien. 96M USA. prod/rel: 20th Century-Fox

Jane Eyre 1968 d: Giorgos Lois. lps: Manos Katrakis, Hristina Silva, Elektra Papathanasiou. 80M GRC.

Jane Eyre 1970 d: Delbert Mann. lps: George C. Scott, Susannah York, Ian Bannen. TVM. 110M UKN/USA. prod/rel: Omnibus, Sagittarius

Jane Eyre 1983 d: Julian Amyes. lps: Timothy Dalton, Zelah Clarke, Judy Cornwell. MTV. 238M UKN.

Jane Eyre 1996 d: Franco Zeffirelli. lps: William Hurt, Charlotte Gainsbourg, Joan Plowright. 112M USA. prod/rel: Cineritmo, Rochester Films

Memorie Di Una Istitutrice, Le 1917 d: Riccardo Tolentino. lps: Valentina Frascaroli, Dillo Lombardi, Fernanda Sinimberghi. 1605m ITL. *L' Orfanella Di Londra; Jane Eyre* prod/rel: Latina-Ars

Woman and Wife 1918 d: Edward Jose. lps: Alice Brady, Elliott Dexter, Helen Greene. 5r USA. *The Lifted Cross* prod/rel: Select Pictures Corp.©

Shirley, 1849, Novel
Shirley 1922 d: A. V. Bramble. lps: Carlotta Breese, Clive Brook, Harvey Braban. 5584f UKN. prod/rel: Ideal

BRONTE, EMILY JANE (1818–1948), UKN
Wuthering Heights, London 1847, Novel
Cumbres Borrascosas 1953 d: Luis Bunuel. lps: Irasema Dilian, Jorge Mistral, Lilia Prado. 90M MXC. *Wuthering Heights* (USA); *Abismo de Pasion; Abyss of Passion* prod/rel: Tepeyas

Hurlevent 1986 d: Jacques Rivette. lps: Fabienne Babe, Lucas Belvaux, Sandra Montaigu. 130M FRN. *Wuthering Heights* prod/rel: la Cecilia, Renn

Wuthering Heights 1920 d: A. V. Bramble. lps: Milton Rosmer, Colette Brettel, Warwick Ward. 6230f UKN. prod/rel: Ideal

Wuthering Heights 1939 d: William Wyler. lps: Merle Oberon, Laurence Olivier, David Niven. 103M USA. prod/rel: United Artists Corp., Samuel Goldwyn, Inc.

Wuthering Heights 1970 d: Robert Fuest. lps: Anna Calder-Marshall, Timothy Dalton, Julian Glover. 105M USA/UKN. prod/rel: American International Pictures, Anglo-Emi

Wuthering Heights 1992 d: Peter Kosminsky. lps: Juliette Binoche, Ralph Fiennes, Janet McTeer. 106M USA. *Emily Bronte's Wuthering Heights* prod/rel: Paramount

BROOKE, ELEANOR
The King of Hearts, New York 1954, Play
That Certain Feeling 1956 d: Norman Panama, Melvin Frank. lps: Bob Hope, Eva Marie Saint, George Sanders. 103M USA. prod/rel: Paramount, P & F Prods.

BROOKE, HAROLD
All for Mary, London 1954, Play
All for Mary 1955 d: Wendy Toye. lps: Nigel Patrick, Kathleen Harrison, David Tomlinson. 79M UKN. prod/rel: Rank, Rank Film Distributors

Handful of Tansy (Don't Tell Father), 1959, Play
No, My Darling Daughter! 1961 d: Ralph Thomas. lps: Michael Redgrave, Michael Craig, Roger Livesey. 96M UKN. prod/rel: Five Star Films, Rank

How Say You?, London 1959, Play
Pair of Briefs, A 1962 d: Ralph Thomas. lps: Michael Craig, Mary Peach, Brenda de Banzie. 90M UKN. prod/rel: Rank Organisation, Rank Film Distributors

BROOKE, HUGH
Fear Has Black Wings, Novel
This Is My Love 1954 d: Stuart Heisler. lps: Faith Domergue, Linda Darnell, Dan DuryeA. 91M USA. prod/rel: RKO Radio, Allan Dowling Pictures

Saturday Island, Novel
Saturday Island 1951 d: Stuart Heisler. lps: Linda Darnell, Tab Hunter, Donald Gray. 102M UKN. *Island of Desire* (USA) prod/rel: Coronado, RKO-Radio

BROOKNER, ANITA (1928–, UKN
Hotel du Lac, Novel
Hotel du Lac 1985 d: Giles Foster. lps: Anna Massey, Denholm Elliott, Julia McKenzie. TVM. 75M UKN. prod/rel: BBC

BROOKS, ALDEN
Escape, New York 1924, Novel
Exquisite Sinner, The 1926 d: Josef von Sternberg, Phil Rosen. lps: Conrad Nagel, Renee Adoree, Paulette Duval. 5977f USA. prod/rel: Metro-Goldwyn-Mayer Pictures

BROOKS, MARION
Ashes, Story
Ashes 1913 d: Oscar Apfel, Edgar Lewis. lps: Irving Cummings, Rosemary Theby, Edgena de Lespine. 2r USA. prod/rel: Reliance

BROOKS, NORMAN
Fragile Fox, New York 1954, Play
Attack! 1956 d: Robert Aldrich. lps: Jack Palance, Eddie Albert, Lee Marvin. 107M USA. prod/rel: United Artists Corp., Associates and Aldrich Co., Inc.

BROOKS, RICHARD
The Brick Foxhole, Novel
Crossfire 1947 d: Edward Dmytryk. lps: Robert Young, Robert Ryan, Robert Mitchum. 86M USA. prod/rel: RKO Radio

The Night the World Folded, Novel
Deadline, U.S.A. 1952 d: Richard Brooks. lps: Humphrey Bogart, Ethel Barrymore, Kim Hunter. 87M USA. *Deadline* (UKN) prod/rel: 20th Century-Fox

BROOKS, VIRGINIA
Little Lost Sister, Chicago 1914, Novel
Little Lost Sister 1917 d: Alfred E. Green. lps: Vivian Reed, Bessie Eyton, Marion Warner. 5r USA. prod/rel: Selig Polyscope Co.©, Red Seal Play

BROPHY, JOHN
The Day They Robbed the Bank of England, Novel
Day They Robbed the Bank of England, The 1960 d: John Guillermin. lps: Aldo Ray, Elizabeth Sellars, Peter O'Toole. 85M UKN. prod/rel: MGM, Summit

Fixed Bayonets, Novel
Fixed Bayonets 1951 d: Samuel Fuller. lps: Richard Basehart, Gene Evans, Michael O'SheA. 92M USA. *Old Soldiers Never Die* prod/rel: 20th Century-Fox

The Immortal Sergeant, Novel
Immortal Sergeant, The 1943 d: John M. Stahl. lps: Henry Fonda, Maureen O'Hara, Thomas Mitchell. 91M USA. prod/rel: 20th Century-Fox

Turn the Key Softly, Novel
Turn the Key Softly 1953 d: Jack Lee. lps: Yvonne Mitchell, Terence Morgan, Joan Collins. 81M UKN. prod/rel: Chiltern, General Film Distributors

Waterfront, Novel
Waterfront 1950 d: Michael Anderson. lps: Robert Newton, Kathleen Harrison, Susan Shaw. 80M UKN. *Waterfront Women* (USA) prod/rel: General Film Distributors, Conqueror

BROSNAN, JOHN
Slimmer, Novel
Proteus 1995 d: Bob Keen. lps: Craig Fairbrass, Toni Barry, William Marsh. 96M UKN.

BROT
Le Meurtrier de Theodore, Play
Meurtrier de Theodore, Le 1908-18 d: Georges MoncA. lps: Gorby, Prince, Irma Genin. FRN. prod/rel: Pathe

BROWN, ALICE FARWELL
John of the Woods, Story
Prince of a King, A 1923 d: Albert Austin. lps: Dinky Dean, Virginia Pearson, Eric Mayne. 5217f USA. prod/rel: Z. A. Stegmuller, Selznick Distributing Corp.

BROWN, BETH
Applause, New York 1928, Novel
Applause 1929 d: Rouben Mamoulian. lps: Helen Morgan, Joan Peers, Fuller Mellish Jr. 78M USA. prod/rel: Paramount Famous Lasky Corp.

BROWN, CAMPBELL RAE
Kissing Cup's Race, Poem
Kissing Cup's Race 1920 d: Walter West. lps: Violet Hopson, Gregory Scott, Clive Brook. 6337f UKN. prod/rel: Hopson Productions, Butcher's Film Service
Kissing Cup's Race 1930 d: Castleton Knight. lps: Stewart Rome, Madeleine Carroll, John Stuart. 75M UKN. prod/rel: Butcher's Film Service

BROWN, CARTER (1923–1985), UKN, Yates, Alan Geoffrey
A Palir la Nuit, Novel
Touchez Pas aux Blondes! 1960 d: Maurice Cloche. lps: Philippe Clay, Dario Moreno, Jany Clair. 93M FRN. prod/rel: C.F.P.C.

Blague Dans le Coin, Novel
Blague Dans le Coin 1963 d: Maurice Labro. lps: Fernandel, Perrette Pradier, Francois Maistre. 100M FRN. prod/rel: Societe Francaise de Cinematographie

BROWN, CHARLES
The Fates and Flora Fourflush, Story
Fates and Flora Fourflush, The 1914 d: Wally Van. lps: Clara Kimball Young, L. Rogers Lytton, Templer Saxe. SRL. USA. *The Ten Billion Dollar Vitagraph Mystery Serial* prod/rel: Vitagraph Co. of America

BROWN, CHARLES MOLYNEAUX
Death Hops the Bells, 1938, Short Story
Irish Luck 1939 d: Howard Bretherton. lps: Frankie Darro, Dick Purcell, Lillian Elliott. 58M USA. *Amateur Detective* (UKN) prod/rel: Monogram Pictures Corp.©

BROWN, CHRISTY
My Left Foot, Book
My Left Foot 1989 d: Jim Sheridan. lps: Daniel Day-Lewis, Ray McAnally, Brenda Fricker. 103M UKN/IRL. prod/rel: Palace, Ferndale Films

BROWN, DANIEL
Heading for Heaven, Play
Heading for Heaven 1947 d: Lewis D. Collins. lps: Stuart Erwin, Glenda Farrell, Russ Vincent. 71M USA. prod/rel: Eagle-Lion

BROWN, FREDERICK
Screaming Mimi, 1949, Novel
Screaming Mimi 1958 d: Gerd Oswald. lps: Anita Ekberg, Philip Carey, Gypsy Rose Lee. 79M USA. prod/rel: Columbia, Sage Prods.

BROWN, GRACE DREW
Spring Fever, Story
Nancy from Nowhere 1922 d: Chester M. Franklin. lps: Bebe Daniels, Eddie Sutherland, Vera Lewis. 5167f USA. prod/rel: Realart Pictures, Paramount Pictures

BROWN, HARRY PETER M'NAB
A Sound of Hunting, New York 1945, Play
Eight Iron Men 1953 d: Edward Dmytryk. lps: Bonar Colleano, Arthur Franz, Lee Marvin. 80M USA. *The Dirty Dozen* prod/rel: Columbia, Stanley Kramer Co.

The Stars in Their Courses, New York 1960, Novel
El Dorado 1967 d: Howard Hawks. lps: John Wayne, Robert Mitchum, James Caan. 127M USA. prod/rel: Laurel Productions, Paramount

A Walk in the Sun, 1944, Novel
Walk in the Sun, A 1946 d: Lewis Milestone. lps: Dana Andrews, Richard Conte, Sterling Holloway. 117M USA. *Salerno Beachhead* prod/rel: 20th Century Fox, Lewis Milestone Prods.

BROWN, HELEN GURLEY
Sex and the Single Girl, New York 1962, Novel
Sex and the Single Girl 1964 d: Richard Quine. lps: Tony Curtis, Natalie Wood, Henry FondA. 114M USA. prod/rel: Reynard Productions

BROWN, J. E.
Incident at 125th St., Story
Incident in San Francisco 1970 d: Don Medford. lps: Richard Kiley, Leslie Nielsen, Dean Jagger. TVM. 100M USA. prod/rel: Quinn Martin Productions

BROWN, J. P. S.
Pocket Money, Novel
Pocket Money 1972 d: Stuart Rosenberg. lps: Paul Newman, Lee Marvin, Strother Martin. 102M USA. prod/rel: First Artists, Coleytown

BROWN, JOE DAVID
Addie Pray, Novel
Paper Moon 1973 d: Peter Bogdanovich. lps: Ryan O'Neal, Tatum O'Neal, Madeline Kahn. 103M USA. prod/rel: Paramount

Kings Go Forth, Novel
Kings Go Forth 1958 d: Delmer Daves. lps: Frank Sinatra, Tony Curtis, Natalie Wood. 109M USA. prod/rel: United Artists, Ross-Elton

Stars in My Crown, 1947, Novel
Stars in My Crown 1950 d: Jacques Tourneur. lps: Joel McCrea, Ellen Drew, Dean Stockwell. 89M USA. prod/rel: MGM

BROWN, KARL
Decision to Kill, Novel
Vanquished, The 1953 d: Edward Ludwig. lps: John Payne, Coleen Gray, Lyle Bettger. 84M USA. *Gallant Rebel* prod/rel: Paramount, Pine-Thomas

They Creep in the Dark, Story
Ape Man, The 1943 d: William Beaudine. lps: Bela Lugosi, Louise Currie, Wallace Ford. 64M USA. *Lock Your Doors* (UKN); *Lock Up Your Daughters*; *The Gorilla Strikes* prod/rel: Monogram Pictures Corp.

BROWN, KENNETH H.
The Brig, New York 1963, Play
Brig, The 1965 d: Jonas Mekas, Adolfas Mekas. lps: Warren Finnerty, James Anderson, Henry Howard. 68M USA.

BROWN, LEE RENICK
Sin Cargo, Story
Sin Cargo 1926 d: Louis J. Gasnier. lps: Shirley Mason, Robert Frazer, Earl Metcalfe. 6147f USA. prod/rel: Tiffany Productions

BROWN, LEW
Flying High, New York 1930, Musical Play
Flying High 1931 d: Charles F. Reisner. lps: Bert Lahr, Charlotte Greenwood, Pat O'Brien. 80M USA. *Happy Landing* (UKN) prod/rel: Metro-Goldwyn-Mayer Corp., Metro-Goldwyn-Mayer Dist. Corp.©

Follow Thru, New York 1929, Musical Play
Follow Thru 1930 d: Laurence Schwab, Lloyd Corrigan. lps: Charles "Buddy" Rogers, Nancy Carroll, Zelma O'Neal. 8386f USA. prod/rel: Paramount-Publix Corp.

Good News, New York 1927, Musical Play
Good News 1930 d: Nick Grinde, Edgar J. MacGregor. lps: Mary Lawlor, Stanley Smith, Bessie Love. 8100f USA. prod/rel: Metro-Goldwyn-Mayer Pictures
Good News 1947 d: Charles Walters. lps: June Allyson, Peter Lawford, Patricia Marshall. 95M USA. prod/rel: MGM

Hold Everything, New York 1928, Musical Play
Hold Everything 1930 d: Roy Del Ruth. lps: Joe E. Brown, Winnie Lightner, Georges Carpentier. 7513f USA. prod/rel: Warner Brothers Pictures

Yokel Boy, New York 1939, Musical Play
Yokel Boy 1942 d: Joseph Santley. lps: Albert Dekker, Joan Davis, Eddie Foy Jr. 69M USA. *Hitting the Headlines* (UKN) prod/rel: Republic

BROWN, LIONEL
The Price of Wisdom, 1932, Play
Price of Wisdom, The 1935 d: Reginald Denham. lps: Mary Jerrold, Roger Livesey, Mary Newland. 64M UKN. prod/rel: British and Dominions, Paramount British

To Have and to Hold, London 1937, Play
To Have and to Hold 1951 d: Godfrey Grayson. lps: Avis Scott, Patrick Barr, Robert Ayres. 63M UKN. prod/rel: Hammer, Exclusive

BROWN, MARTIN
Cobra, New York 1924, Play
Cobra 1925 d: Joseph Henabery. lps: Rudolph Valentino, Nita Naldi, Casson Ferguson. 6895f USA. prod/rel: Ritz-Carlton Pictures, Paramount Pictures

The Exciters, Story
Exciters, The 1923 d: Maurice Campbell. lps: Bebe Daniels, Antonio Moreno, Burr McIntosh. 5939f USA. prod/rel: Famous Players-Lasky

Great Music, New York 1924, Play
Soul-Fire 1925 d: John S. Robertson. lps: Richard Barthelmess, Bessie Love, Percy Ames. 8262f USA. prod/rel: Inspiration Pictures, First National Pictures

The Idol, Great Neck, N.Y. 1929, Play
Mad Genius, The 1931 d: Michael Curtiz. lps: John Barrymore, Marian Marsh, Donald Cook. 81M USA. prod/rel: Warner Bros. Pictures©

The Lady, New York 1923, Play
Lady, The 1925 d: Frank Borzage. lps: Norma Talmadge, Wallace MacDonald, Brandon Hurst. 7357f USA. *Lady* prod/rel: Norma Talmadge Productions, First National Pictures
Secret of Madame Blanche, The 1933 d: Charles J. Brabin. lps: Irene Dunne, Lionel Atwill, Phillips Holmes. 83M USA. *The Lady* prod/rel: Metro-Goldwyn-Mayer Corp., Metro-Goldwyn-Mayer Dist. Corp.©

Paris, New York 1928, Musical Play
Paris 1929 d: Clarence Badger. lps: Irene Bordoni, Jack Buchanan, Louise Closser Hale. 88M USA. prod/rel: First National Pictures

A Very Good Young Man, New York 1918, Play
Very Good Young Man, A 1919 d: Donald Crisp. lps: Bryant Washburn, Helene Chadwick, Julia Faye. 4350f USA. prod/rel: Famous Players-Lasky Corp.©, Paramount Pictures

BROWN, OLGA HALL
The Slave Bracelet, Story
Other Woman, The 1931 d: G. B. Samuelson. lps: Isobel Elsom, David Hawthorne, Eva Moore. 64M UKN. prod/rel: Majestic, United Artists

BROWN, PORTER EVERSON
A Fool There Was, 1909, Play
Fool There Was, A 1915 d: Frank Powell. lps: Theda Bara, Edward Jose, Runa Hodges. 6r USA. *The Vampire* prod/rel: William Fox Vaudeville Co., Box Office Attraction Co.

BROWN, RAY
The Tintype, Novel
Timestalkers 1987 d: Michael Schultz. lps: William Devane, Lauren Hutton, Klaus Kinski. TVM. 100M USA.

BROWN, ROSELLEN
Before and After, Novel
Before and After 1996 d: Barbet Schroeder. lps: Meryl Streep, Liam Neeson, Edward Furlong. 107M USA. prod/rel: Buena Vista, Hollywood

BROWN, ROWLAND
A Handful of Clouds, Story
Doorway to Hell, The 1930 d: Archie Mayo. lps: Lew Ayres, Charles Judels, Dorothy Mathews. 78M USA. *A Handful of Clouds* (UKN) prod/rel: Warner Brothers Pictures

BROWN, ROYAL
The Final Close-Up, 1918, Short Story
Final Close-Up, The 1919 d: Walter Edwards. lps: Shirley Mason, Francis McDonald, James Gordon. 5r USA. prod/rel: Famous Players-Lasky Corp.©, Paramount Pictures

From Four to Eleven-Three, 1920, Short Story
Kiss in Time, A 1921 d: Thomas N. Heffron. lps: Wanda Hawley, T. Roy Barnes, Bertram Johns. 4351f USA. prod/rel: Realart Pictures

Peggy Does Her Darndest, 1918, Short Story
Peggy Does Her Darndest 1919 d: George D. Baker. lps: May Allison, Robert Ellis, Rosemary Theby. 5r USA. prod/rel: Metro Pictures Corp.©

BROWN, T. K.
Story
Haunts of the Very Rich 1972 d: Paul Wendkos. lps: Lloyd Bridges, Cloris Leachman, Edward Asner. TVM. 73M USA. prod/rel: ABC Circle Films

BROWN, V. D.
Jerry's Mother-in-Law, Play
Jerry's Mother-in-Law 1913 d: James Young. lps: Sidney Drew, Clara Kimball Young, Kate Price. 2000f USA. prod/rel: Vitagraph Co. of America

BROWN, VERA
Redhead, New York 1933, Novel
Redhead 1934 d: Melville Brown. lps: Bruce Cabot, Grace Bradley, Regis Toomey. 76M USA. prod/rel: Monogram Pictures Corp.©, Dorothy Reid Production
Redhead 1941 d: Edward L. Cahn. lps: June Lang, Johnny Downs, Eric Blore. 64M USA. prod/rel: Monogram

BROWN, WALTER C.
Prelude to Murder, Short Story
House in the Woods, The 1957 d: Maxwell Munden. lps: Ronald Howard, Patricia Roc, Michael Gough. 60M UKN. prod/rel: Archway, Film Workshop

BROWN, WILL C.
The Border Jumpers, 1955, Novel
Man of the West 1958 d: Anthony Mann. lps: Gary Cooper, Julie London, Lee J. Cobb. 100M USA. prod/rel: United Artists, Ashton Prods.

BROWNE, ALAN
Forty Deuce, Play
Forty Deuce 1981 d: Paul Morrissey. lps: Orson Bean, Kevin Bacon, Mark Keyloun. 89M USA. prod/rel: Island

BROWNE, ELEANOR
Highway to Romance, New York 1937, Novel
Cross-Country Romance 1940 d: Frank Woodruff. lps: Gene Raymond, Wendy Barrie, Hedda Hopper. 68M USA. *Cross Country Romance* prod/rel: RKO Radio Pictures, Inc.

BROWNE, GERALD A.
Green Ice, Novel
Green Ice 1980 d: Ernest Day. lps: Ryan O'Neal, Anne Archer, Omar Sharif. 115M USA/UKN. prod/rel: Itc Entertainments, Lew Grade
Harrowhouse, Novel
11 Harrowhouse 1974 d: Aram Avakian. lps: Charles Grodin, Candice Bergen, John Gielgud. 95M UKN. *Anything for Love; Fast Fortune; Eleven Harrowhouse* prod/rel: 20th Century Fox, Harrowhouse

BROWNE, JOHN BARTON
Garden of the Moon, 1937, Short Story
Garden of the Moon 1938 d: Busby Berkeley. lps: Pat O'Brien, Margaret Lindsay, John Payne. 94M USA. prod/rel: Warner Bros. Pictures©

BROWNE, K. R. G.
Easy Money, Novel
Forging Ahead 1933 d: Norman Walker. lps: Margot Grahame, Garry Marsh, Antony Holles. 49M UKN. prod/rel: Harry Cohen, Fox
Please Teacher, London 1935, Play
Please Teacher 1937 d: Stafford Dickens. lps: Bobby Howes, Rene Ray, Wylie Watson. 76M UKN. prod/rel: Associated British Picture Corporation, Wardour
The White Rat, Story
White Rat, The 1922 d: George A. Cooper. lps: Sydney N. Folker, Ernest A. Douglas, Adeline Hayden Coffin. 1300f UKN. prod/rel: Quality Plays, Walturdaw
Yes Madam?, Novel
Yes, Madam? 1938 d: Norman Lee. lps: Bobby Howes, Diana Churchill, Wylie Watson. 77M UKN. prod/rel: Associated British Picture Corp.
Yes, Madam 1933 d: Leslie Hiscott. lps: Frank Pettingell, Kay Hammond, Harold French. 46M UKN. prod/rel: British Lion, Fox

BROWNE, LEWIS ALLEN
The Bigamists, Story
Naughty But Nice 1927 d: Millard Webb. lps: Colleen Moore, Donald Reed, Claude Gillingwater. 6520f USA. prod/rel: John Mccormick Productions, First National Pictures
Circumstances Alter Divorce Cases, Short Story
Innocence 1923 d: Edward J. Le Saint. lps: Anna Q. Nilsson, Freeman Wood, Earle Foxe. 5923f USA. prod/rel: Columbia Pictures, C. B. C. Film Sales
Please Get Married, New York 1919, Play
Please Get Married 1919 d: John Ince. lps: Viola Dana, Antrim Short, Margaret Campbell. 5-7r USA. prod/rel: Screen Classics, Inc., Metro Pictures Corp.©
The Woman Hater, Short Story
Sooner Or Later 1920 d: Wesley Ruggles. lps: Owen Moore, Seena Owen, Clifford Gray. 5r USA. *Plans of Men; The Woman Hater; Who's Who?* prod/rel: Selznick Pictures Corp.©, Select Pictures Corp.

BROWNE, PORTER EMERSON
The Bad Man, New York 1920, Play
Bad Man, The 1923 d: Edwin Carewe. lps: Holbrook Blinn, Jack Mulhall, Walter McGrail. 6404f USA. prod/rel: Edwin Carewe Productions, Associated First National Pictures
Bad Man, The 1930 d: Clarence Badger. lps: Walter Huston, Dorothy Revier, Sidney Blackmer. 90M USA. prod/rel: First National Pictures
Bad Man, The 1941 d: Richard Thorpe. lps: Wallace Beery, Lionel Barrymore, Laraine Day. 70M USA. *Two-Gun Cupid* (UKN) prod/rel: MGM
Lopez, le Bandit 1930 d: John Daumery. lps: Geymond Vital, Jeanne Helbling, Suzy Vernon. 71M FRN. prod/rel: Warner Bros, First National
West of Shanghai 1937 d: John Farrow. lps: Boris Karloff, Gordon Oliver, Beverly Roberts. 65M USA. *War Lord; China Bandit; The Adventures of Chang; Cornered* prod/rel: Warner Bros. Pictures©, First National Picture

A Fool There Was, New York 1909, Play
Fool There Was, A 1922 d: Emmett J. Flynn. lps: Estelle Taylor, Lewis Stone, Irene Rich. 6604f USA. prod/rel: Fox Film Corp.
Someone and Somebody, New York 1917, Novel
Too Many Millions 1918 d: James Cruze. lps: Wallace Reid, Ora Carew, Tully Marshall. 4517f USA. prod/rel: Famous Players-Lasky Corp.©, Paramount Pictures
The Spendthrift, New York 1910, Play
Spendthrift, The 1915 d: Walter Edwin. lps: Cyril Keightley, Irene Fenwick, Mattie Ferguson. 5829f USA. prod/rel: George Kleine©

BROWNE, ROBERT GORDON
The Cheerful Fraud, New York 1925, Novel
Cheerful Fraud, The 1927 d: William A. Seiter. lps: Reginald Denny, Gertrude Olmstead, Otis Harlan. 6945f USA. prod/rel: Universal Pictures

BROWNE, WALTER
Everywoman, New York 1911, Play
Everywoman 1919 d: George Melford. lps: Violet Heming, Monte Blue, Wanda Hawley. 6854f USA. prod/rel: Famous Players-Lasky Corp.©, Paramount-Artcraft Super Special

BROWNE, WYNARD
The Holly and the Ivy, London 1950, Play
Holly and the Ivy, The 1952 d: George M. O'Ferrall. lps: Ralph Richardson, Celia Johnson, Margaret Leighton. 83M UKN. prod/rel: British Lion Production Assets, London Films

BROWNELL, JOHN C.
The Nut Farm, New York 1929, Play
Nut Farm, The 1935 d: Melville Brown. lps: Wallace Ford, Florence Roberts, Oscar Apfel. 68M USA. prod/rel: Monogram Pictures Corp.©
The Ultimate Good, Story
Bad Company 1925 d: Edward H. Griffith. lps: Madge Kennedy, Bigelow Cooper, Conway Tearle. 5551f USA. prod/rel: St. Regis Pictures, Associated Exhibitors

BROWNING, ELIZABETH BARRETT (1806–1861), UKN
The Cry of the Children, Poem
Cry of the Children, The 1912. lps: James Cruze, Marie Eline, Ethel Wright. SHT USA. prod/rel: Thanhouser

BROWNING, H. V.
A Member of Tattersalls, Play
Member of Tattersalls, A 1919 d: Albert Ward. lps: Isobel Elsom, Malcolm Cherry, Campbell Gullan. 6000f UKN. prod/rel: G. B. Samuelson, Granger

BROWNING, RICOU
Story
Flipper 1963 d: James B. Clark. lps: Chuck Connors, Luke Halpin, Kathleen Maguire. 90M USA. prod/rel: Ivan Tors, MGM

BROWNING, ROBERT (1812–1889), UKN
A Blot in the 'Scutcheon, Poem
Blot in the 'Scutcheon, A 1912 d: D. W. Griffith. lps: Dorothy Bernard, Edwin August, Miriam Cooper. SHT USA. prod/rel: Biograph Co.
The Flight of the Duchess, 1845, Poem
Flight of the Duchess, The 1916 d: Eugene Nowland. lps: Gladys Hulette, Wayne Arey, Robert Gray. 5r USA. prod/rel: Thanhouser Film Corp., Mutual Film Corp.
A Light Woman, 1855, Short Story
Light Woman, A 1920 d: George L. Cox. lps: Helen Jerome Eddy, Hallam Cooley, Claire Du Brey. 6r USA. prod/rel: American Film Co.©, Pathe Exchange, Inc.
The Pied Piper of Hamelin, 1842, Poem
Pied Piper of Hamelin, The 1911 d: Theodore Marston. lps: Frank Crane, Marguerite Snow, James Cruze. SHT USA. prod/rel: Thanhouser
Pied Piper of Hamelin, The 1911. 900f FRN. prod/rel: Pathe
Pied Piper of Hamelin, The 1913 d: George A. Lessey. lps: Herbert Prior, Robert Brower, Mary Fuller. 1000f USA. prod/rel: Edison
Pied Piper of Hamelin, The 1916. 1r USA. prod/rel: Edison
Pied Piper of Hamelin, The 1926 d: Frank Tilley. lps: Edward Sorley, Judd Green. 2000f UKN. prod/rel: British Projects, Bsc
Pied Piper of Hamelin, The 1957 d: Bretaigne Windust. lps: Van Johnson, Claude Rains, Lori Nelson. MTV. 90M USA.
Pied Piper of Hamelin, The 1960 d: Lotte Reiniger. ANS. UKN.
Pied Piper of Hamelin, The 1982 d: Brian Cosgrove, Mark Hall. ANM. 87M UKN. prod/rel: Hall-Cosgrove
Pied Piper of Hamelin, The 1985 d: Nicholas Meyer. lps: Eric Idle. MTV. 49M USA. *The Pied Piper*

Pied Piper, The 1907 d: Percy Stow. 755f UKN. prod/rel: Clarendon
Pied Piper, The 1972 d: Jacques Demy. lps: Donovan, Donald Pleasence, Jack Wild. 90M UKN/GRM. *The Pied Piper of Hamelin* prod/rel: Sagittarius, Goodtimes
Pippa Passes, London 1841, Poem
Child of M'sieu 1919 d: Harrish Ingraham. lps: Marie Osborne, Philo McCullough, Harrish Ingraham. 5r USA. prod/rel: Triangle Film Corp., Triangle Distributing Corp.
Pippa Passes Or the Song of Conscience 1909 d: D. W. Griffith. lps: Gertrude Robinson, George Nicholls, Adele de Garde. 983f USA. prod/rel: Biograph Co.
The Ring and the Book, Poem
Ring and the Book, The 1914. 2r USA. prod/rel: Biograph Co.
Women and Roses, Poem
Women and Roses 1914 d: Wallace Reid. lps: Wallace Reid, Dorothy Davenport, Lillian Brockwell. SHT USA. prod/rel: Nestor

BROZIK, EMANUEL
Tulak, Opera
Anicko, Vrat Se! 1926 d: Theodor Pistek. lps: Anny Ondra, Theodor Pistek, Karel Lamac. 1502m CZC. *Tulak; Come Back! Anicka; The Tramp* prod/rel: Fiserfilm, Filmove Zavody

BRUANT, ARISTIDE
Coeur de Francaise, Play
Coeur de Francaise 1916 d: Gaston Leprieur. lps: Maxime Desjardins, Albert Dieudonne, Andree Pascal. FRN. prod/rel: Les Grands Films Lordier
La Loupiote, Novel
Loupiote, La 1908-18. FRN.
Loupiote, La 1922 d: Georges Hatot. lps: Regine Dumien, Lucien Dalsace, Jacques Normand. SRL. 6260m FRN.
Loupiote, La 1936 d: Jean Kemm, Jean-Louis Bouquet. lps: Pierre Larquey, Robert Pizani, Suzanne Rissler. 87M FRN. prod/rel: Films Artistiques Francais

BRUCE, GEORGE
Story
Mask of the Avenger 1951 d: Phil Karlson. lps: John Derek, Anthony Quinn, Jody Lawrance. 83M USA. prod/rel: Columbia
Born to Hang, Short Story
Born to Hang 1934 d: Aubrey Scotto. F USA. prod/rel: Goldsmith Productions, Ltd.
Kit Carson, Short Story
Frontier Uprising 1961 d: Edward L. Cahn. lps: Jim Davis, Nancy Hadley, Ken Mayer. 68M USA. prod/rel: Zenith Pictures
Navy Blue and Gold, New York 1937, Novel
Navy Blue and Gold 1937 d: Sam Wood. lps: Robert Young, James Stewart, Florence Rice. 93M USA. prod/rel: Metro-Goldwyn-Mayer Corp.

BRUCE, J. CAMPBELL
Escape from Alcatraz, Novel
Escape from Alcatraz 1979 d: Don Siegel. lps: Clint Eastwood, Patrick McGoohan, Roberts Blossom. 112M USA. prod/rel: Paramount

BRUCE, JEAN
Bonne Mesure, Paris 1953, Novel
Vicomte Regle Ses Comptes, Le 1967 d: Maurice Cloche. lps: Kerwin Mathews, Edmond O'Brien, Jean Yanne. 100M FRN/ITL/SPN. *The Viscount Furto Alla Banca Mondiale* (ITL); *Atraco Al Hampa* (SPN); *Las Aventuras Del Vizconde; Les Aventures du Vicomte; The Viscount* prod/rel: Criterion Film, Producciones Cin.Ca D.I.A. (Madrid)
Cinq Gars Pour Singapour, Paris 1959, Novel
Cinq Gars Pour Singapour 1967 d: Bernard Toublanc-Michel. lps: Sean Flynn, Marika Green, Terry Downes. 105M FRN/ITL. *Cinque Marines Per Singapore* (ITL); *Singapore Singapore* (USA); *Five Ashore in Singapore* (Paris), Poste Parisien
Le Dernier Quart d'Heure, Paris 1955, Novel
Furia a Bahia Pour Oss 117 1965 d: Andre Hunebelle, Jacques Besnard. lps: Frederick Stafford, Mylene Demongeot, Raymond Pellegrin. 110M FRN/ITL. *Oss 117 Furia a Bahia* (ITL); *Mission for a Killer; Oss 117 -Mission for a Killer* (USA); *Trouble in Bahia for Oss 117* prod/rel: P.A.C., P.C.M.
Documents a Vendre, Novel
Bal Des Espions, Le 1960 d: Michel Clement, Umberto Scarpelli. lps: Francoise Arnoul, Michel Piccoli, Charles Regnier. 96M FRN/ITL. *Le Schiave Bianche* (ITL); *Danger in the Middle East* (USA) prod/rel: Generale Francaise Du Film, C.F.P.C. (Paris)

Lila de Calcutta, Paris 1960, Novel
Banco a Bangkok 1964 d: Andre Hunebelle. lps: Kerwin Mathews, Robert Hossein, Pier Angeli. 118M FRN/ITL. *Oss 117 Minaccia Bangkok* (ITL); *Shadow of Evil* (USA); *Banco a Bangkok Pour Oss 117*; *Jackpot in Bangkok for Oss 117* prod/rel: P.A.C., C.I.C.C.

O.S.S. 117 N'est Pas Mort, Novel
O.S.S. 117 N'est Pas Mort 1956 d: Jean SachA. lps: Ivan Desny, Magali Noel, Yves Vincent. 80M FRN. *O.S.S. 117 Is Not Dead*; *Oss 117 N'est Pas Mort* prod/rel: Omnium Films, Globe

O.S.S. 117 Prend le Maquis, Novel
O.S.S. 117 Se Dechaine 1963 d: Andre Hunebelle. lps: Kerwin Mathews, Irina Demick, Nadia Sanders. 110M FRN/ITL. *Oss 117 Segretissimo* (ITL); *Oss 117* (USA) prod/rel: P.A.C., Films Borderie

Pas de Roses a Ispahan Pour O.S.S. 117, Novel
Niente Rose Per Oss 117 1968 d: Jean-Pierre Desagnat, Renzo Cerrato. lps: John Gavin, Margaret Lee, Curd Jurgens. 110M FRN/ITL. *Pas de Roses Pour Oss 117* (FRN); *Oss 117 -Double Agent* (USA); *No Roses for Oss 117*; *Oss 117 Murder for Sale* (UKN) prod/rel: P.A.C., Da.Ma Cin.Ca (Roma)

Vacances Pour O.S.S. 117, Novel
O.S.S. 117 Prend Des Vacances 1969 d: Pierre Kalfon. lps: Luc Merenda, Norma Bengell, Edwige Feuillere. 90M FRN/BRZ. *Oss 117 Takes a Vacation* prod/rel: Films Number One, Vera Cruz Films

BRUCK, EDITH
Andremo in Citta, Novel
Andremo in Citta 1966 d: Nelo Risi. lps: Geraldine Chaplin, Nino Castelnuovo, Stefania Careddu. 95M ITL/YGS. prod/rel: Aica Cin.Ca, Romor Film (Roma)

BRUCKNER, PASCAL
Lune de Fiel, Novel
Lune de Fiel 1992 d: Roman Polanski. lps: Hugh Grant, Kristin Scott-Thomas, Emmanuelle Seigner. 139M FRN/UKN. *Bitter Moon* (UKN) prod/rel: Les Films Alain Sarde, Canal©

BRUHL, HANS
Willkommen in Mergenthal, Play
Ehesanatorium 1955 d: Franz Antel. lps: Adrian Hoven, Maria Emo, Gunther Philipp. 90M AUS. *So Ein Madchen Mit 16 Ja* prod/rel: Ofra, Schonbrunn

BRUNEL, HENRI
La Verte Moisson, Novel
Verte Moisson, La 1959 d: Francois Villiers. lps: Claude Brasseur, Dany Saval, Jacques Perrin. 95M FRN. prod/rel: Films Caravelle, Gaumont

BRUNN, LAURIDAS
The Midnight Sun, Story
Midnight Sun, The 1926 d: Dimitri Buchowetzki. lps: Laura La Plante, Pat O'Malley, Raymond Keane. 8767f USA. prod/rel: Universal Pictures

BRUNNGRABER, RUDOLF
Prozesz Auf Leben Und Tod, Novel
Prozess, Der 1948 d: G. W. Pabst. lps: Ewald Balser, Ernst Deutsch, Maria Eis. 108M AUS. *In Name Der Menschlichkeit*; *The Trial* prod/rel: Hubler-Kahla

BRUNS, URSULA
Dick Und Dalli Und Die Ponies, Novel
Madels Vom Immenhof, Die 1955 d: Wolfgang Schleif. lps: Angelika Meissner, Heidi Bruhl, Margarete Haagen. 91M GRM. *The Girls from Immen Farm* prod/rel: Arca, N.F.

BRUNSWICK, LEON
Le Postillon de Lonjumeau, Paris 1836, Opera
Postillon von Lonjumeau, Der 1935 d: Carl Lamac. lps: Alfred Neugebauer, Thekla Ahrens, Leo Slezak. 95M AUS/SWT. *Der Konig Lachelt - Paris Lacht*; *Le Postillon de Lonjumeau*; *Postillon Im Hochzeitsrock* prod/rel: Thekla-Film, Atlantis-Film

BRUSH, KATHARINE
Footlights and Fools, Story
Footlights and Fools 1929 d: William A. Seiter. lps: Colleen Moore, Raymond Hackett, Fredric March. 6952f USA. prod/rel: First National Pictures

Free Woman, 1936, Short Story
Honeymoon in Bali 1939 d: Edward H. Griffith. lps: Fred MacMurray, Madeleine Carroll, Allan Jones. 95M USA. *Husbands Or Lovers* (UKN); *Husbands and Lovers*; *My Love for Yours*; **Are Husbands Necessary?** prod/rel: Paramount Pictures©

Maid of Honor, 1932, Short Story
Lady of Secrets 1936 d: Marion Gering. lps: Ruth Chatterton, Otto Kruger, Lionel Atwell. 73M USA. *No More Yesterdays*; *Maid of Honor* prod/rel: Columbia Pictures Corp.©

Red-Headed Woman, New York 1931, Novel
Red Headed Woman 1932 d: Jack Conway. lps: Jean Harlow, Chester Morris, Una Merkel. 75M USA. *Red-Headed Woman* prod/rel: Metro-Goldwyn-Mayer Corp., Metro-Goldwyn-Mayer Dist. Corp.©

Young Man of Manhattan, New York 1930, Novel
Young Man of Manhattan 1930 d: Monta Bell. lps: Claudette Colbert, Norman Foster, Ginger Rogers. 7306f USA. prod/rel: Paramount-Publix Corp.

BRUUN, LAURIDS
Eine Seltsame Nacht, Novel
Seltsame Nacht Der Helga Wangen, Die 1928 d: Holger-Madsen. lps: Lee Parry, Franz Lederer, Gertrud de Lalsky. 2301m GRM. prod/rel: National-Film Ag

BRUYERE, CHRISTIAN
Walls, Play
Walls 1984 d: Thomas Shandel. lps: Winston Rekert, Andree Pelletier, Alan Scarfe. 88M CND. *Lock Up* prod/rel: Jericho Films Ltd.

BRYAN, ALFRED
I Didn't Raise My Boy to Be a Soldier, 1915, Song
I'm Glad My Boy Grew Up to Be a Soldier 1915 d: Frank Beal. lps: Harry Mestayer, Eugenie Besserer, Harry de Vere. 4r USA. *I Didn't Raise My Boy to Be a Soldier* prod/rel: Selig Polyscope Co.©

BRYAN, C. D. B.
Friendly Fire, Book
Friendly Fire 1979 d: David Greene. lps: Carol Burnett, Ned Beatty, Sam Waterston. TVM. 145M USA. prod/rel: ABC, Marble Arch Productions

BRYAN, ERNEST E.
The Last Coupon, Play
Last Coupon, The 1932 d: Thomas Bentley. lps: Leslie Fuller, Mary Jerrold, Molly Lamont. 84M UKN. prod/rel: British International Pictures, Wardour
Spring Handicap 1937 d: Herbert Brenon. lps: Will Fyffe, Maire O'Neill, Billy Milton. 68M UKN. prod/rel: Associated British Picture Corporation

BRYAN, GRACE LOVELL
Class, 1919, Short Story
You Never Can Tell 1920 d: Chester M. Franklin. lps: Bebe Daniels, Jack Mulhall, Edward Martindel. 5302f USA. prod/rel: Realart Pictures Corp.©

You Never Can Tell, 1919, Short Story
You Never Can Tell 1920 d: Chester M. Franklin. lps: Bebe Daniels, Jack Mulhall, Edward Martindel. 5302f USA. prod/rel: Realart Pictures Corp.©

BRYAN, MICHAEL
Intent to Kill, Novel
Intent to Kill 1958 d: Jack Cardiff. lps: Richard Todd, Betsy Drake, Herbert Lom. 89M UKN. prod/rel: 20th Century-Fox, Zonic

BRYAN, PETER
Short Story
Morte Negli Occhi Del Gatto, La 1973 d: Antonio Margheriti. lps: Doris Kunstmann, Konrad Georg, Jane Birkin. 96M ITL/FRN/GRM. *Sieben Tote in Den Augen Der Katze* (GRM); *Seven Deaths in the Cat's Eye*; *Seven Dead in the Cat's Eye*; *Les Diablesses* (FRN); *Corringa -Sept Morts Dans Les Yeux du Chat* prod/rel: Starkiss, Falcon International Film (Roma)

BRYANT, MARGUERITE
Richard, New York 1922, Novel
Breathless Moment, The 1924 d: Robert F. Hill. lps: William Desmond, Charlotte Merriam, Alfred Fisher. 5556f USA. *Sentenced to Soft Labor* prod/rel: Universal Pictures
Railroaded 1923 d: Edmund Mortimer. lps: Herbert Rawlinson, Esther Ralston, Alfred Fisher. 5390f USA. *Thicker Than Water* prod/rel: Universal Pictures

BRYSON, JOHN
Evil Angels, Book
Cry in the Dark, A 1988 d: Fred Schepisi. lps: Meryl Streep, Sam Neill, Bruce Myles. 121M USA/ASL. *Evil Angels* (ASL); *Guilty By Suspicion* prod/rel: Warner Bros., Evil Angel Films©

BUARQUE, CHICO
Opera Do Malandro, Play
Opera Do Malandro 1985 d: Ruy GuerrA. lps: Edson Celulari, Claudia Ohana, Elba Ramalho. 105M FRN/BRZ/MZM. *Malandro* (USA); *The Rogue's Opera* prod/rel: Mk2 Productions (Paris), Austra (Brazil)

BUBER, MARTIN
Short Story
Goldstein 1965 d: Philip Kaufman, Benjamin Manaster. lps: Lou Gilbert, Ellen Madison, Thomas Erhart. 115M USA. prod/rel: Montrose Film Productions

BUCCI, VINCENZO
Strana, Play
Strana 1917 d: Alfredo Robert. lps: Mercedes de Personali-Galeotti, Antonio Gandusio, Igino Iaccarino. 1334m ITL. prod/rel: Mercedes Film

BUCH, FRITZ PETER
Ganzer Kerl, Ein, Play
Ganzer Kerl, Ein 1939 d: Fritz Peter Buch. lps: Heidemarie Hatheyer, Albert Matterstock, Truus Van Alten. 87M GRM. prod/rel: ABC

Vertrag Um Karakat, Play
Mit Versiegelter Order 1938 d: Karl Anton. lps: Viktor de Kowa, Paul Hartmann, Suse Graf. 95M GRM. *Under Sealed Orders* (USA) prod/rel: Majestic, Deustchland

BUCHAN, JOHN (1875–1940), UKN, Tweedsmuir, Baron
Huntingtower, 1922, Novel
Huntingtower 1927 d: George Pearson. lps: Harry Lauder, Vera Voronina, Pat Aherne. 7192f UKN. prod/rel: Welsh-Pearson-Elder, Paramount

The Thirty-Nine Steps, 1915, Novel
39 Steps, The 1935 d: Alfred Hitchcock. lps: Robert Donat, Madeleine Carroll, Godfrey Tearle. 86M UKN. *The Thirty-Nine Steps* prod/rel: Gaumont British
39 Steps, The 1959 d: Ralph Thomas. lps: Kenneth More, Taina Elg, Brenda de Banzie. 93M UKN. *The Thirty-Nine Steps* prod/rel: Rank, Rank Film Distributors
Thirty-Nine Steps, The 1978 d: Don Sharp. lps: Robert Powell, David Warner, Eric Porter. 102M UKN. *The 39 Steps* prod/rel: Rank, Norfolk International

The Three Hostages, Novel
Three Hostages, The 1977 d: Clive Donner. lps: Barry Foster, Diana Quick, John Castle. TVM. 85M UKN. prod/rel: BBC

BUCHANAN, MADELEINE SHARPE
The Chessboard, Short Story
Dangerous Business 1920 d: R. William Neill. lps: Constance Talmadge, Kenneth Harlan, George Fawcett. 5718f USA. *The Human Chess Board* prod/rel: Norma Talmadge Film Corp., Associated First National Pictures

BUCHANAN, PETER
High Rise Donkey, Novel
High Rise Donkey 1979 d: Michael Forlong. lps: Leigh Gotch, Wendy Cook, Linda Frith. 57M UKN. prod/rel: Children's Film Foundation

BUCHANAN, ROBERT
Alone in London, London 1885, Play
Alone in London 1915 d: Larry Trimble. lps: Florence Turner, Henry Edwards, Edward Lingard. 4525f UKN. prod/rel: Turner Films, Ideal

The Charlatan, Play
Charlatan, The 1916 d: Sidney Morgan. lps: Eille Norwood, Violet Graham, Anna Mather. 4363f UKN. prod/rel: Famous Authors, Crown

The English Rose, London 1890, Play
English Rose, The 1920 d: Fred Paul. lps: Fred Paul, Humberston Wright, Sydney N. Folker. 4890f UKN. prod/rel: British Standard, Whincup

Fra Giacone, Poem
Fra Giacone 1913. lps: Eric Williams. UKN. prod/rel: Eric Williams Speaking Pictures, Searchlight

God and the Man, Novel
God and the Man 1918 d: Edwin J. Collins. lps: Langhorne Burton, Joyce Carey, Bert Wynne. 6935f UKN. prod/rel: Ideal

The Lights of Home, London 1892, Play
Lights of Home, The 1920 d: Fred Paul. lps: George Foley, Nora Hayden, Jack (3) Raymond. 5500f UKN. prod/rel: Screen Plays, British Exhibitors' Films

The Little Milliner, Poem
Love in an Attic 1923 d: Edwin Greenwood. lps: Nina Vanna, Russell Thorndike, Walter Tennyson. 1796f UKN. prod/rel: British & Colonial, Walturdaw

A Man's Shadow, London 1889, Play
Man's Shadow, A 1920 d: Sidney Morgan. lps: Langhorne Burton, Violet Graham, Gladys Mason. 5500f UKN. prod/rel: Progress, Butcher's Film Service

Matt, Novel
Matt 1918 d: A. E. Coleby. lps: Greta MacDonald, A. E. Coleby, Ernest A. Douglas. 5128f UKN. prod/rel: I. B. Davidson, Tiger

Phil Blood's Leap, Poem
Phil Blood's Leap 1913 d: Wilfred Noy. 1000f UKN. prod/rel: Clarendon

The Trumpet Call, London 1891, Play
Trumpet Call, The 1915 d: Percy Nash. lps: Gregory Scott, Joan Ritz, Douglas Payne. 4480f UKN. prod/rel: Neptune, Gaumont

BUCHANAN, THOMPSON
As Good As New, New York 1930, Play
As Good As New 1933 d: Graham Cutts. lps: Winna Winifried, John Batten, Sunday Wilshin. 48M UKN. prod/rel: Warner Bros., First National

Easy to Love 1934 d: William Keighley. lps: Adolphe Menjou, Genevieve Tobin, Mary Astor. 70M USA. prod/rel: Warner Bros. Pictures©

The Bridal Path, New York 1913, Play
All's Fair in Love 1921 d: E. Mason Hopper. lps: May Collins, Richard Dix, Marcia Manon. 5r USA. *The Bridal Path*; *Look Before You Leap* prod/rel: Goldwyn Pictures Corp.

Civilian Clothes, New York 1919, Play
Civilian Clothes 1920 d: Hugh Ford. lps: Thomas Meighan, Martha Mansfield, Maude Turner Gordon. 5267f USA. prod/rel: Famous Players-Lasky Corp.©, Paramount Pictures

The Cub, New York 1910, Play
Cub, The 1915 d: Maurice Tourneur. lps: Dorothy Farnum, Martha Hedman, Johnny Hines. 5r USA. prod/rel: William A. Brady Picture Plays, Inc., World Film Corp.©

Rainbow Riley 1926 d: Charles Hines. lps: Johnny Hines, Brenda Bond, Bradley Barker. 7057f USA. prod/rel: Burr and Hines Enterprises, First National Pictures

Life, New York 1914, Play
Life 1920 d: Travers Vale. lps: Jack Mower, Arline Pretty, J. H. Gilmour. 5r USA. prod/rel: William A. Brady, Famous Players-Lasky Corp.

The Rack, New York 1911, Play
Rack, The 1916 d: Emile Chautard. lps: Alice Brady, Milton Sills, June Elvidge. 5r USA. prod/rel: William A. Brady Picture Plays, Inc., World Film Corp.©

Thirty a Week, Play
Thirty a Week 1918 d: Harry Beaumont. lps: Tom Moore, Tallulah Bankhead, Alec B. Francis. 5r USA. prod/rel: Goldwyn Pictures Corp.©, Goldwyn Distributing Corp.

A Woman's Way, New York 1909, Play
Woman's Way, A 1916 d: Barry O'Neil. lps: Carlyle Blackwell, Ethel Clayton, Montagu Love. 5r USA. prod/rel: World Film Corp.©

BUCHBINDER, BERNHARD
Die Forsterchristl, Opera
Forsterchristl, Die 1926 d: Friedrich Zelnik. lps: Lya Mara, Harry Liedtke, Wilhelm Dieterle. 2623m GRM. *Flower of the Forest*; *The Forester's Daughter* prod/rel: Sudfilm

Forsterchristl, Die 1931 d: Friedrich Zelnik. lps: Paul Horbiger, Paul Richter, Adele Sandrock. 80M GRM. *The Forester's Daughter*

Forsterchristl, Die 1952 d: Arthur M. Rabenalt. lps: Johanna Matz, Angelika Hauff, Kathe von Nagy. 104M GRM. *The Forester's Daughter* prod/rel: Carlton, Panorama

Forsterchristl, Die 1962 d: Franz J. Gottlieb. lps: Sabine Sinjen, Peter Weck, Sieghardt Rupp. 104M GRM. *The Forester's Daughter* prod/rel: Carlton, Constantin

On a Jeho Sestra, Play
Er Und Sein Schwester 1931 d: Carl Lamac. lps: Vlasta Burian, Anny Ondra, Berthe Ostyn. 2191m GRM/SWT. prod/rel: Elekta, Ondra-Lamac-Film

On a Jeho Sestra 1931 d: Martin Fric, Carl Lamac. lps: Vlasta Burian, Anny Ondra, Otto Rubik. 2538m CZC. *He and His Sister*; *Him and His Sister* prod/rel: Elekta

BUCHHEIM, LOTHAR GUNTHER
Das Boot, Novel
Boot, Das 1981 d: Wolfgang Petersen. lps: Jurgen Prochnow, Herbert Gronemeyer, Klaus Wennemann. 149M GRM. *The Boat* (UKN) prod/rel: Bavarian Tv, Wdr

BUCHHOLTZ, JOHANNES
Susanne, 1931, Novel
Susanne 1950 d: Torben Anton Svendsen. lps: Erik Mork, Astrid Villaume. 102M DNM.

BUCHMAN, HAROLD
Snafu, New York 1944, Play
Snafu 1945 d: Jack Moss. lps: Robert Benchley, Vera Vague, Conrad Janis. 82M USA. *Welcome Home* (UKN) prod/rel: Columbia, George Abbott Prods.

BUCHNER, GEORG (1813–1837), GRM
Lenz, 1839, Short Story
Lenz 1971 d: Georg Moorse. lps: Michael Konig, Louis Waldon, Sigurd Bischoff. 130M GRM. prod/rel: Literarisches Colloquium, Workshop B. Moorse

Lenz 1981 d: Alexandre Rockwell. lps: Cody Maher, Kim Radonovich, Alexander Rockwell. 93M USA. prod/rel: Alexandre Rockwell

Lenz 1987 d: Andras Szirtes. 99M HNG.

Woyzeck, 1879, Play
Franz 1974 d: John Sweeney, Paul Aspland. lps: John Sweeney, Paul Aspland, Graham Harley. UNF. CND. prod/rel: House of Canterbury Motion Picts. Prods., Sun-Owl Productions Ltd.

Wodzeck 1984 d: Oliver Herbrich. lps: Detlef Kugow, Ariane Erdelt, Johannes HablA. 82M GRM. *Wodzek*; *Woyzeck*

Woyzeck 1967 d: Rudolf Noelte. 90M GRM.

Wozzeck 1947 d: Georg C. Klaren. lps: Kurt Meisel, Helga Zulch, Arno Paulsen. 97M GDR. *Der Fall Wozzeck*; *Woyzeck* prod/rel: Defa

Woyzeck 1979 d: Werner Herzog. lps: Klaus Kinski, Eva Mattes, Wolfgang Reichmann. 82M GRM. *Woyzeck* (USA)

BUCHWALD, ART
A Gift from the Boys, Novel
Surprise Package 1960 d: Stanley Donen. lps: Yul Brynner, Mitzi Gaynor, Noel Coward. 99M UKN. prod/rel: Columbia, Donen Enterprises

BUCK, CHARLES NEVILLE
The Battle Cry, New York 1914, Novel
Call of the Cumberlands, The 1916 d: Julia Crawford Ivers. lps: Dustin Farnum, Myrtle Stedman, Winifred Kingston. 5r USA. prod/rel: Pallas Pictures, Paramount Pictures Corp.

Her Man 1918 d: Ralph Ince, John Ince. lps: Elaine Hammerstein, W. Lawson Butt, George Anderson. 6r USA. *The Battle Cry*; *The Woman Eternal* prod/rel: Advanced Motion Picture Corp., Pathe Exchange, Inc.©

The Call of the Cumberlands, 1913, Novel
Call of the Cumberlands, The 1916 d: Julia Crawford Ivers. lps: Dustin Farnum, Myrtle Stedman, Winifred Kingston. 5r USA. prod/rel: Pallas Pictures, Paramount Pictures Corp.

The Code of the Mountains, New York 1915, Novel
Woman's Power, A 1916 d: Robert T. Thornby. lps: Mollie King, Douglas MacLean, Charles Mitchell. 5r USA. *The Code of the Mountains* prod/rel: William A. Brady Picture Plays, Inc., World Film Corp.©

Destiny, New York 1916, Novel
Destiny 1919 d: Rollin S. Sturgeon. lps: Dorothy Phillips, William Stowell, Stanhope Wheatcroft. 5475f USA. prod/rel: Universal Film Mfg. Co.©, Jewel Productions, Inc.

The Flight to the Hills, Garden City, Ny. 1926, Novel
Runaway, The 1926 d: William C. de Mille. lps: Clara Bow, Warner Baxter, William Powell. 6218f USA. prod/rel: Famous Players-Lasky, Paramount Pictures

The Key to Yesterday, New York 1910, Novel
Key to Yesterday, The 1914 d: John Francis Dillon. lps: Carlyle Blackwell, Edna Mayo, John Francis Dillon. 4r USA. prod/rel: Favorite Players Film Co.©, Alliance Film Corp.

The Roof Tree, New York 1921, Novel
Roof Tree, The 1921 d: John Francis Dillon. lps: William Russell, Florence Deshon, Sylvia Breamer. 4409f USA. prod/rel: Fox Film Corp.

The Tyranny of Weakness, 1917, Novel
Love, Honor and Obey 1920 d: Leander de CordovA. lps: Wilda Bennett, Claire Whitney, Henry Harmon. 5840f USA. prod/rel: Metro Pictures Corp.©

When Bear Cat Went Dry, New York 1918, Novel
When Bearcat Went Dry 1919 d: Oliver L. Sellers. lps: Vangie Valentine, Walt Whitman, Bernard Durning. 6r USA. prod/rel: C. R. Macauley Photoplays, Inc.©, World Film Corp.

BUCK, FRANK
Fang and Claw, New York 1935, Book
Fang and Claw 1935 d: Frank Buck, Ray Taylor. lps: Frank Buck. DOC. 74M USA. prod/rel: Van Beuren Corp.©, RKO Radio Pictures

Wild Cargo, New York 1932, Book
Wild Cargo 1934 d: Armand Denis. lps: Frank Buck. DOC. 96M USA. prod/rel: the Van Beuren Corp.©, RKO Radio Pictures

BUCK, PEARL (1892–1973), USA, Buck, Pearl
The Big Wave, New York 1948, Short Story
Big Wave, The 1962 d: Tad Danielewski. lps: Sessue Hayakawa, Ichizo Itami, Mickey Curtis. 98M USA/JPN. prod/rel: Stratton Productions, Toho Co.

China Sky, 1942, Novel
China Sky 1945 d: Ray Enright. lps: Randolph Scott, Ruth Warrick, Ellen Drew. 78M USA. prod/rel: RKO Radio

The Dragon Seed, 1942, Novel
Dragon Seed 1944 d: Jack Conway, Harold S. Bucquet. lps: Katharine Hepburn, Walter Huston, Aline MacMahon. 145M USA. *Dragonseed* prod/rel: MGM

The Good Earth, New York 1931, Novel
Good Earth, The 1937 d: Sidney A. Franklin, Victor Fleming (Uncredited). lps: Paul Muni, Luise Rainer, Walter Connolly. 138M USA. prod/rel: Metro-Goldwyn-Mayer Corp.©

Satan Never Sleeps, New York 1952, Novel
Satan Never Sleeps 1962 d: Leo McCarey. lps: William Holden, Clifton Webb, France Nuyen. 126M USA/UKN. *The Devil Never Sleeps*; *Flight from Terror*; *China Story* prod/rel: 20th Century-Fox, Leo Mccarey

BUCKLEY, FRANK R.
Peg Leg and the Kidnapper, 1925, Short Story
Gentle Cyclone, The 1926 d: W. S. Van Dyke. lps: Buck Jones, Rose Blossom, William Walling. 4825f USA. prod/rel: Fox Film Corp.

BUCKNER, ROBERT
The Man Behind the Mask, Short Story
Man Behind the Gun, The 1952 d: Felix E. Feist. lps: Randolph Scott, Patrice Wymore, Dick Wesson. 82M USA. prod/rel: Warner Bros.

Moon Pilot, 1960, Short Story
Moon Pilot 1962 d: James Neilson. lps: Tom Tryon, Brian Keith, Edmond O'Brien. 98M USA. prod/rel: Walt Disney Production

Safari, Novel
Safari 1956 d: Terence Young. lps: Victor Mature, Janet Leigh, John Justin. 92M UKN. prod/rel: Warwick, Columbia

BUCKSTONE, J. B.
Married Life, London 1834, Play
Married Life 1921 d: Georges Treville. lps: Gerald McCarthy, Peggy Hathaway, Roger Treville. 5000f UKN. prod/rel: Ideal

Single Life, London 1839, Play
Single Life 1921 d: Edwin J. Collins. lps: Campbell Gullan, Kathleen Vaughan, Sydney Paxton. 4750f UKN. prod/rel: Ideal

BUDD, JACKSON
A Convict Has Escaped, Novel
They Made Me a Fugitive 1947 d: Alberto Cavalcanti. lps: Sally Gray, Trevor Howard, Griffith Jones. 103M UKN. *I Became a Criminal* (USA); *They Made Me a Criminal* prod/rel: Warner Bros., Alliance

BUDRYS, ALGIS (1931–, USA
Master of the Hounds, Novel
To Kill a Clown 1972 d: George Bloomfield. lps: Alan Alda, Blythe Danner, Heath Lamberts. 104M USA. prod/rel: Palomar

Who?
Who? 1974 d: Jack Gold. lps: Elliott Gould, Trevor Howard, Joseph BovA. 93M UKN. *The Man in the Steel Mask*; *Man Without a Face*; *Robo Man*; *Prisoner of the Skull*; *Man in the Skull Mask, The* prod/rel: British Lion, Hemisphere

BUECHLER, JOHN
Story
Demonwarp 1988 d: Emmett Alston. lps: George Kennedy, David Michael O'Neill, Pamela Gilbert. 91M USA. prod/rel: Vidmark-Design

BUELL, JOHN
The Pyx, Novel
Pyx, The 1973 d: Harvey Hart. lps: Karen Black, Christopher Plummer, Donald Pilon. 107M CND. *The Hooker Cult Murders*; *La Lunule* prod/rel: Host Productions Quebec Ltd., Cinepix

BUERO VALLEJO, ANTONIO (1916–, SPN
Historia de Una Escalera, 1950, Play
Historia de Una Escalera 1950 d: Ignacio F. Iquino. lps: Maruchi Fresno, Leonor Maria, Juny Orly. 87M SPN. *The Story of a Staircase*

Madrugada, 1954, Play
Madrugada 1957 d: Antonio Roman. lps: Luis Pena, Zully Moreno, Antonio Prieto. 88M SPN. *Dawn*

BUFFIEL, DR.
Srazka Vlaku a Uz Mou Milou, Play
Funebrak 1932 d: Carl Lamac. lps: Vlasta Burian, Josef Rovensky, Theodor Pistek. 2534m CZC. *The Undertaker* prod/rel: Elekta

BUFFINGTON, STEPHANIE
Three on a Date, Book
Three on a Date 1978 d: Bill Bixby. lps: June Allyson, Loni Anderson, Ray Bolger. TVM. 100M USA. prod/rel: ABC Circle Films

BUFORD, GORDON
Story
My Dog, the Thief 1969 d: Robert Stevenson. lps: Dwayne Hickman, Mary Ann Mobley, Elsa Lanchester. 88M USA. prod/rel: Walt Disney

BUGLIOSI, VINCENT (1934–, USA
And the Sea Will Tell, Book
  And the Sea Will Tell 1991 d: Tommy Lee Wallace. lps: Richard Crenna, Rachel Ward, Hart Bochner. TVM. 200M USA.

Helter Skelter, Book
  Helter Skelter 1976 d: Tom Gries. lps: Steve Railsback, George Dicenzo, Nancy Wolfe. TVM. 194M USA. *Massacre in Hollywood* prod/rel: Lorimar Productions

Till Death Us Do Part, Book
  Till Death Us Do Part 1991 d: Yves Simoneau. lps: Treat Williams, Arliss Howard, Rebecca Jenkins. TVM. 94M USA. *'Til Death Us Do Part; Married for Murder*

BUKOWSKI, CHARLES (1920–1994), GRM
California, the Copulating Mermaid of Venice, Short Story
  Crazy Love 1986 d: Dominique Deruddere. lps: Josse de Pauw, Geert Hunaerts, Florence Beliard. 90M BLG/FRN. *Amour Est un Chien de l'Enfer* (FRN); *Love Is a Dog from Hell* (USA) prod/rel: Mainline, Multimedia

Erections, Ejaculations, Exhibitions and Tales of Ordinary., Book
  Storie Di Ordinaria Follia 1981 d: Marco Ferreri. lps: Ben Gazzara, Ornella Muti, Susan Tyrrell. 101M ITL/FRN. *Conte de la Folie Ordinaire* (FRN); *Tales of Ordinary Madness* prod/rel: 23 Giugno, Ginis

Short Story
  Killers, The 1984 d: Patrick Roth. lps: Jack Kehoe, Raymond Mayo, Allan Magicovsky. 60M USA. prod/rel: Roth Film

BULGAKOV, MIKHAIL (1891–1940), RSS
Master I Margarita, 1967, Novel
  Majstor I Margarita 1973 d: Aleksandar Petrovic. lps: Ugo Tognazzi, Mimsy Farmer, Alain Cuny. 101M YGS/ITL. *Il Maestro E Margherita* (ITL); *The Master and Margarita* prod/rel: Euro International Film (Roma), Dunav Film (Belgrado)

Sobach'e Serdtse, 1968, Short Story
  Cuore Di Cane 1975 d: Alberto LattuadA. lps: Mario Adorf, Cochi Ponzoni, Max von Sydow. 113M ITL/GRM. *Warum Bell Herr Bobikow?* (GRM); *Dog's Heart; Why Is Mr. Bobikow Barking?* prod/rel: Filmalpha (Roma), Corona Filmproduktion (Munich)

The White Guard, Play
  White Guard, The 1982 d: Don Taylor. MTV. F UKN. prod/rel: BBC

BULL, JACOB BREDA
Jorund Smed, 1924, Novel
  Dit Vindarna Bar 1948 d: Ake Ohberg. lps: George Fant, Eva Strom, Elof Ahrle. 88M SWD/NRW. *Jorund Smed* (NRW); *Where the Winds Lead* prod/rel: Ab Svea Film, Europa Film a/S

BULL, LOIS
Broadway Virgin, New York 1931, Novel
  Manhattan Butterfly 1935 d: Lewis D. Collins. lps: William Bakewell, Dorothy Burgess, Kenneth Thomson. 73M USA. *Midnight Butterfly* (UKN); *Broadway Virgin* prod/rel: Major Pictures Corp., Cameo Pictures Corp.

BULLETT, GERALD
The Jury, Novel
  Last Man to Hang, The 1956 d: Terence Fisher. lps: Tom Conway, Elizabeth Sellars, Eunice Gayson. 75M UKN. prod/rel: Act Films, Columbia

BULLIVANT, CECIL H.
Blood Money, Novel
  Blood Money 1921 d: Fred Goodwins. lps: Adelqui Millar, Dorothy Fane, Frank Dane. 4722f UKN/NTH. *Bloedgeld* (NTH); *The Harper's Mystery* prod/rel: Granger-Binger Film

The Wife Whom God Forgot, Novel
  Wife Whom God Forgot, The 1920 d: William J. Humphrey. lps: Gertrude McCoy, G. H. Mulcaster, R. Henderson Bland. 5500f UKN. *Tangled Hearts* prod/rel: Alliance Film Corp., Anchor

The Woman Wins, Novel
  Woman Wins, The 1918 d: Frank Wilson. lps: Violet Hopson, Trevor Bland, Cameron Carr. 5500f UKN. prod/rel: Broadwest, Granger

BULLRICH, SILVINA (1915–1992), ARG
Un Momento Muy Largo, Novel
  Vuoto, Il 1964 d: Piero Vivarelli. lps: Venantino Venantini, Elsa Daniel, Rafael Pisareff. 85M ITL/ARG. prod/rel: Virtus Film (Roma), Federico J. Aicardi Prod. (Buenos Aires)

BULMER, FRED
When Woman Hates, Play
  When Woman Hates 1916 d: Albert Ward. lps: Henry Lonsdale, Mercy Hatton, Jose Brookes. 5500f UKN. prod/rel: British Empire Films

BUNGEY, E. NEWTON
The Autumn of Pride, Novel
  Autumn of Pride, The 1921 d: W. P. Kellino. lps: Nora Swinburne, David Hawthorne, Mary Dibley. 6300f UKN. prod/rel: Gaumont, Westminster

Class and No Class, Novel
  Class and No Class 1921 d: W. P. Kellino. lps: Judd Green, Pauline Johnson, David Hawthorne. 6207f UKN. prod/rel: Gaumont, Westminster

The Squire of Long Hadley, Novel
  Squire of Long Hadley, The 1925 d: Sinclair Hill. lps: Marjorie Hume, Brian Aherne, G. H. Mulcaster. 6250f UKN. *A Romance of Riches* prod/rel: Stoll

BUNING, ARNOLD WERUMEUS
Mottige Janus, Play
  Mottige Janus 1922 d: Maurits H. Binger. lps: Maurits de Vries, August Van Den Hoeck, Kitty Kluppell. 1800m NTH. *Pock-Marked Janus* prod/rel: Filmfabriek-Hollandia

BUNJE, KARL
Der Etappenhase, Play
  Etappenhase, Der 1937 d: Joe Stockel. lps: Gunther Luders, Leny Marenbach, Erich Fiedler. 109M GRM. prod/rel: Astra, Super

  Etappenhase, Der 1956 d: Wolfgang Becker. lps: Beppo Brem, Michael Cramer, Wera Frydtberg. 90M GRM. *Rear Echelon Man* prod/rel: Hoela, Panorama

Familienanschluss, Play
  Familienanschluss 1941 d: Carl Boese. lps: Karin Hardt, Hermann Speelmans, Ludwig Schmitz. 86M GRM. prod/rel: Terra, Fortuna

BUNKER, EDWARD
Straight Time, Novel
  Straight Time 1978 d: Ulu Grosbard. lps: Dustin Hoffman, Theresa Russell, Harry Dean Stanton. 114M USA. *No Beast So Fierce* prod/rel: First Artists

BUNN, ALFRED (1798–1860), UKN
The Bohemian Girl, London 1843, Opera
  Bohemian Girl, The 1922 d: Harley Knoles. lps: Gladys Cooper, Ivor Novello, C. Aubrey Smith. 7700f UKN. prod/rel: Alliance, Astra

  Bohemian Girl, The 1927 d: H. B. Parkinson. lps: Herbert Langley, Pauline Johnson. 1472f UKN. prod/rel: Song Films

  Bohemian Girl, The 1936 d: James W. Horne, Charles Rogers. lps: Stan Laurel, Oliver Hardy, Thelma Todd. 80M USA. prod/rel: Hal Roach Studios, Inc., MGM

BUNNER, HENRY C.
Zenobia's Infidelity, 1925, Short Story
  Zenobia 1939 d: Gordon Douglas. lps: Oliver Hardy, Harry Langdon, Billie Burke. 71M USA. *Elephants Never Forget* (UKN); *It's Spring Again*; *Zenobia's Infidelity* prod/rel: United Artists Corp., Hal Roach Studios©

BUNYAN, JOHN (1628–1688), UKN
The Pilgrim's Progress, 1684, Allegory
  Pellegrino, Il 1912 d: Mario Caserini. lps: Vitale de Stefano, Antonio Grisanti, Filippo CostamagnA. 1067m ITL. *The Life of John Bunyan* (USA); *The Pilgrim's Progress* (UKN); *The Pilgrim* prod/rel: S.A. Ambrosio

BURCHARD, PETER
One Gallant Rush, Book
  Glory 1989 d: Edward Zwick. lps: Matthew Broderick, Denzel Washington, Cary Elwes. 122M USA. prod/rel: Tri-Star

BURDICK, EUGENE (1918–1965), USA, Burdick, Eugene Leonard
Fail-Safe, New York 1962, Novel
  Fail-Safe 1964 d: Sidney Lumet. lps: Dan O'Herlihy, Walter Matthau, Frank Overton. 111M USA. prod/rel: Columbia Pictures

The Ugly American, New York 1958, Novel
  Ugly American, The 1963 d: George Englund. lps: Marlon Brando, Eiji Okada, Sandra Church. 120M USA. *The Quiet American* prod/rel: Universal Pictures

BURGER, GOTTFRIED
Baron Prasil, Novel
  Baron Prasil 1961 d: Karel Zeman. lps: Jana Brejchova, Jan Werich, Milos Kopecky. 84M CZC. *The Fabulous Baron Munchausen* (USA); *Baron Munchausen* (UKN); *Baron Munchhausen* prod/rel: Ceskoslovensky Film

BURGER, GOTTFRIED AUGUST
Lenore, Poem
  Lenore 1913. GRM. prod/rel: Eiko-Film

BURGER, HERMANN
Schilten, Novel
  Schilten 1980 d: Beat Kuert. lps: Michael Maassen, Gudrun Geier, Norbert Schwientek. 92M SWT. *Schilten - "Mit Dem Nebel Davongekommen"* prod/rel: Beat Kuert, Barbara Riesen

BURGESS, ALAN
The Small Woman, Book
  Inn of the Sixth Happiness 1958 d: Mark Robson. lps: Ingrid Bergman, Curd Jurgens, Robert Donat. 159M UKN/USA. prod/rel: 20th Century-Fox

BURGESS, ANTHONY (1917–1994), UKN
A Clockwork Orange, 1962, Novel
  Clockwork Orange, A 1971 d: Stanley Kubrick. lps: Malcolm McDowell, Patrick Magee, Warren Clarke. 137M UKN. prod/rel: Warner Bros., Polaris

BURGESS, GELETT (1866–1951), USA, Burgess, Frank Gelett
The Cave Man, New York 1911, Play
  Cave Man, The 1915 d: Theodore Marston. lps: Robert Edeson, Fay Wallace, Lillian Burns. 5r USA. *The Caveman* prod/rel: Vitagraph Co. of America©, Blue Ribbon Feature

  Caveman, The 1926 d: Lewis Milestone. lps: Matt Moore, Marie Prevost, John Patrick. 6741f USA. prod/rel: Warner Bros.

Find the Woman, Indianapolis 1911, Novel
  Manhattan Knight, A 1920 d: George A. Beranger. lps: George Walsh, Virginia Hammond, William H. Budd. 4855f USA. *Find the Woman* prod/rel: Fox Film Corp., William Fox

The Heart Line, Indianapolis 1907, Novel
  Heart Line, The 1921 d: Frederick A. Thompson. lps: Leah Baird, Jerome Patrick, Frederick Vroom. 6r USA. prod/rel: Leah Baird Productions, Pathe Exchange, Inc.

Two O'Clock Courage, Indianapolis 1934, Novel
  Two in the Dark 1936 d: Ben Stoloff. lps: Walter Abel, Margot Grahame, Wallace Ford. 74M USA. *Two O'Clock Courage* prod/rel: RKO Radio Pictures©

  Two O'Clock Courage 1945 d: Anthony Mann. lps: Tom Conway, Ann Rutherford, Richard Lane. 68M USA. prod/rel: RKO Radio

The White Cat, New York 1907, Novel
  Two-Soul Woman, The 1918 d: Elmer Clifton. lps: Priscilla Dean, Joseph Girard, Ashton Dearholt. 5r USA. *The White Cat* prod/rel: Bluebird Photoplays, Inc.©

  Untameable, The 1923 d: Herbert Blache. lps: Gladys Walton, Malcolm McGregor, John Sainpolis. 4776f USA. *The White Cat; The Two Souled Woman* prod/rel: Universal Pictures

BURKE, COLIN
The Diamond Walkers, Novel
  Jagd Auf Blaue Diamanten 1966 d: Paul Martin. lps: Harald Leipnitz, Joachim Hansen, Marisa Mell. 92M SAF/GRM. *The Diamond Walkers* prod/rel: S.a., Constantin

BURKE, EDMUND LAWRENCE
Johnny Get Your Gun, New York 1917, Novel
  Johnny Get Your Gun 1919 d: Donald Crisp. lps: Fred Stone, Mary Anderson, Casson Ferguson. 4501f USA. prod/rel: Famous Players-Lasky Corp.©, Artcraft Pictures

BURKE, EDWIN
Brothers, Play
  Woman Trap 1929 d: William A. Wellman. lps: Hal Skelly, Chester Morris, Evelyn Brent. 6168f USA. prod/rel: Paramount Famous Lasky Corp.

This Thing Called Love, New York 1928, Play
  This Thing Called Love 1929 d: Paul L. Stein. lps: Edmund Lowe, Constance Bennett, Roscoe Karns. 6697f USA. prod/rel: Pathe Exchange, Inc.

  This Thing Called Love 1940 d: Alexander Hall. lps: Melvyn Douglas, Rosalind Russell, Allyn Joslyn. 98M USA. *Married But Single* (UKN) prod/rel: Columbia Pictures Corp.©

BURKE, JAMES LEE
Two for Texas, Novel
  Two for Texas 1997 d: Rod Hardy. lps: Kris Kristofferson, Scott Bairstow, Tom Skerritt. TVM. 120M USA. prod/rel: Bleeker Street Films

BURKE, JONATHAN
Echo of Barbara, Novel
  Echo of Barbara 1961 d: Sidney Hayers. lps: Mervyn Johns, Maureen Connell, Paul Stassino. 58M UKN. prod/rel: Rank Film Distributors, Independent Artists

BURKE, RICHARD
The Dead Take No Bows, Novel
  Dressed to Kill 1941 d: Eugene J. Forde. lps: Lloyd Nolan, Mary Beth Hughes, Sheila Ryan. 75M USA. prod/rel: 20th Century Fox

BURKE, THOMAS
Beryl and the Croucher, Short Story
  No Way Back 1949 d: Stefan Osiecki. lps: Terence de Marney, Eleanor Summerfield, Jack Raine. 72M UKN. prod/rel: Concanen Recordings, Eros

The Chink and the Child, 1916, Short Story
Broken Blossoms 1919 d: D. W. Griffith. lps: Lillian Gish, Richard Barthelmess, Donald Crisp. 6r USA. *The Chink and the Child; Broken Blossoms; Or the Yellow Man and the Girl* prod/rel: United Artists Corp., D. W. Griffith©
Broken Blossoms 1936 d: John Brahm. lps: Dolly Haas, Emlyn Williams, Arthur Margetson. 78M UKN. prod/rel: Twickenham, Twickenham Film Distributors

Gina of Chinatown, 1916, Short Story
Dream Street 1921 d: D. W. Griffith. lps: Carol Dempster, Ralph Graves, Charles Emmett MacK. 10r USA. prod/rel: D. W. Griffith, United Artists

The Lamp in the Window, 1916, Short Story
Dream Street 1921 d: D. W. Griffith. lps: Carol Dempster, Ralph Graves, Charles Emmett MacK. 10r USA. prod/rel: D. W. Griffith, United Artists

Twelve Golden Curls, Short Story
Curlytop 1924 d: Maurice Elvey. lps: Shirley Mason, Wallace MacDonald, Warner Oland. 5828f USA. prod/rel: Fox Film Corp.

Twinkletoes, London 1917, Novel
Twinkletoes 1926 d: Charles J. Brabin. lps: Colleen Moore, Kenneth Harlan, Tully Marshall. 7833f USA. prod/rel: John Mccormick Productions, First National Pictures

BURLINGTON, CHARLES
Meyer l'Ipocrita, Novel
Erede Di Jago, L' 1913 d: Alberto Carlo Lolli. lps: Ubaldo Maria Del Colle, Adriana Costamagna, Giovanni Spano. 850m ITL. *L'Ipocrita; Jago's Inheritance* (UKN) prod/rel: Savoia Film

BURMAN, BEN LUCIEN
Steamboat 'Round the Bend, New York 1933, Novel
Steamboat Round the Bend 1935 d: John Ford. lps: Will Rogers, Anne Shirley, Irvin S. Cobb. 90M USA. *Steamboat Bill* prod/rel: Fox Film Corp., Twentieth Century-Fox Film Corp.©

BURMEISTER, JON
Tigers Don't Cry, Novel
Tigers Don't Cry 1976 d: Peter Collinson. lps: Anthony Quinn, John Phillip Law, Simon SabelA. 102M SAF. *Target for an Assassin* (USA); *Target of an Assassin; The Long Shot; African Rage; The Tiger Doesn't Cry* prod/rel: Heynz Films

BURNET, DANA
Blindness, 1919, Serial Story
Eyes of the Heart 1920 d: Paul Powell. lps: Mary Miles Minter, Edmund Burns, Lucien Littlefield. 5084f USA. *Blindness* prod/rel: Realart Pictures Corp.©

Four Walls, New York 1927, Play
Four Walls 1928 d: William Nigh. lps: John Gilbert, Joan Crawford, Vera Gordon. 6620f USA. prod/rel: Metro-Goldwyn-Mayer Pictures
Straight Is the Way 1934 d: Paul Sloane. lps: Karen Morley, Franchot Tone, Gladys George. 65M USA. *Four Walls* prod/rel: Metro-Goldwyn-Mayer Corp.©

Mr. Billings Spends His Dime, 1920, Short Story
Mr. Billings Spends His Dime 1923 d: Wesley Ruggles. lps: Walter Hiers, Jacqueline Logan, George Fawcett. 5585f USA. *Mr. Billings Puts Things Right* prod/rel: Famous Players-Lasky, Paramount Pictures

Pettigrew's Girl, 1918, Short Story
Pettigrew's Girl 1919 d: George Melford. lps: Ethel Clayton, Monte Blue, James Mason. 5r USA. *Private Pettigrew's Girl* prod/rel: Famous Players-Lasky Corp.©, Paramount Pictures
Shopworn Angel, The 1928 d: Richard Wallace. lps: Nancy Carroll, Gary Cooper, Paul Lukas. 7377f USA. prod/rel: Paramount Famous Lasky Corp.
Shopworn Angel, The 1938 d: H. C. Potter. lps: Margaret Sullavan, James Stewart, Walter Pidgeon. 85M USA. prod/rel: Metro-Goldwyn-Mayer Corp., Loew's, Inc.©
That Kind of Woman 1959 d: Sidney Lumet. lps: Sophia Loren, Tab Hunter, George Sanders. 92M USA. prod/rel: Paramount, Ponti-Girosi

Sadie Goes to Heaven, 1917, Short Story
Sadie Goes to Heaven 1917 d: W. S. Van Dyke. lps: Mary McAllister, Jenny St. George, Russell McDermott. 5r USA. prod/rel: Essanay Film Mfg. Co.©, Perfection Pictures

The Shining Adventure, New York 1916, Novel
Shining Adventure, The 1925 d: Hugo Ballin. lps: Percy Marmont, Mabel Ballin, Ben Alexander. 5148f USA. prod/rel: Madeline Brandeis Productions, Astor Pictures

Technic, 1925, Short Story
Marriage Clause, The 1926 d: Lois Weber. lps: Francis X. Bushman, Billie Dove, Warner Oland. 7680f USA. *The Star Maker* prod/rel: Universal Pictures

Those High Society Blues, 1925, Short Story
High Society Blues 1930 d: David Butler. lps: Janet Gaynor, Charles Farrell, William Collier Sr. 102M USA. prod/rel: Fox Film Corp.

Wandering Daughters, 1922, Short Story
Wandering Daughters 1923 d: James Young. lps: Marguerite de La Motte, William V. Mong, Mabel Van Buren. 5547f USA. prod/rel: Sam E. Rork, Associated First National Pictures

BURNETT, FRANCES HODGSON (1849–1924), USA, Burnett, Frances Eliza Hodgson
The Dawn of a Tomorrow, New York 1906, Novel
Dawn of a Tomorrow, The 1915 d: James Kirkwood. lps: Mary Pickford, David Powell, Forrest Robinson. 5r USA. prod/rel: Famous Players Film Co., Paramount Pictures Corp.
Dawn of a Tomorrow, The 1924 d: George Melford. lps: Jacqueline Logan, David Torrence, Raymond Griffith. 6084f USA. prod/rel: Famous Players-Lasky, Paramount Pictures

Edith's Burglar, Boston 1878, Novel
Family Secret, The 1924 d: William A. Seiter. lps: Baby Peggy Montgomery, Gladys Hulette, Edward Earle. 5676f USA. prod/rel: Universal Pictures

Esmeralda, 1877, Short Story
Esmeralda 1915 d: James Kirkwood. lps: Mary Pickford, Fuller Mellish, Ida Waterman. 4-5r USA. prod/rel: Famous Players Film Co.©, Paramount Pictures Corp.

The Fair Barbarian, New York 1880, Novel
Fair Barbarian, The 1917 d: Robert T. Thornby. lps: Vivian Martin, Clarence Geldart, Douglas MacLean. 5r USA. prod/rel: Pallas Pictures, Paramount Pictures Corp.

A Lady of Quality, New York 1896, Novel
Lady of Quality, A 1913 d: J. Searle Dawley. lps: Cecilia Loftus, House Peters, Hal Clarendon. 5r USA. prod/rel: Famous Players Film Co., State Rights
Lady of Quality, A 1924 d: Hobart Henley. lps: Virginia Valli, Lionel Belmore, Margaret Seddon. 8640f USA. prod/rel: Universal Pictures

Little Lord Fauntleroy, New York 1886, Novel
Little Lord Fauntleroy 1914 d: F. Martin Thornton. lps: Gerald Royston, Jane Wells, H. Agar Lyons. 5280f UKN. prod/rel: Natural Colour Kinematograph Co.
Little Lord Fauntleroy 1921 d: Alfred E. Green, Jack Pickford. lps: Mary Pickford, Claude Gillingwater, Joseph J. Dowling. 9984f USA. prod/rel: Mary Pickford Co., United Artists
Little Lord Fauntleroy 1936 d: John Cromwell. lps: Freddie Bartholomew, C. Aubrey Smith, Guy Kibbee. 102M USA. prod/rel: United Artists Corp, Selznick International Pictures©
Little Lord Fauntleroy 1976 d: Paul Annett. lps: Glenn Anderson, Paul Rogers, Jennie Linden. MTV. 300M UKN.
Little Lord Fauntleroy 1980 d: Jack Gold. lps: Alec Guinness, Ricky Schroder, Eric Porter. TVM. 103M UKN. prod/rel: Norman Rosemont
Little Lord Fauntleroy 1994 d: Andrew Morgan. lps: George Baker, Betsy Brantley, Michael Benz. MTV. 158M UKN. prod/rel: BBC
Ultimo Lord, L' 1926 d: Augusto GeninA. lps: Carmen Boni, Bonaventura Ibanez, Lido Manetti. 2170m ITL. prod/rel: Films Pittaluga

Louisiana, New York 1919, Novel
Louisiana 1919 d: Robert G. VignolA. lps: Vivian Martin, Robert Ellis, Noah Beery. 4611f USA. prod/rel: Famous Players-Lasky Corp.©, Paramount Pictures

The Pretty Sister of Jose, New York 1889, Novel
Pretty Sister of Jose, The 1915 d: Allan Dwan. lps: Marguerite Clark, Jack Pickford, Rupert Julian. 5r USA. prod/rel: Famous Players Film Co., Paramount Pictures Corp.

Sara Crewe, New York 1888, Novel
Little Princess, A 1986 d: Carol Wiseman. lps: Amelia Shankley, Nigel Havers, Maureen Lipman. MTV. 174M UKN.
Little Princess, A 1995 d: Alfonso Cuaron. lps: Eleanor Bron, Liam Cunningham, Liesel Matthews. 97M USA.
Little Princess, The 1917 d: Marshall Neilan, Howard Hawks (Uncredited). lps: Mary Pickford, Norman Kerry, Theodore Roberts. 5r USA.
Little Princess, The 1939 d: Walter Lang. lps: Shirley Temple, Richard Greene, Anita Louise. 93M USA. *Sara Crewe*
Principessina 1943 d: Tulio Gramantieri. lps: Rosanna Dal, Nerio Bernardi, Roberto VillA. 78M ITL. prod/rel: Bassoli Film, Tirrenia Cin.Ca

The Secret Garden, New York 1909, Novel
Secret Garden, The 1919 d: Gustav von Seyffertitz. lps: Lila Lee, Dick Rosson, Spottiswoode Aitken. 5r USA. prod/rel: Famous Players-Lasky Corp.©, Paramount Pictures
Secret Garden, The 1949 d: Fred M. Wilcox. lps: Margaret O'Brien, Dean Stockwell, Brian Roper. 105M USA. prod/rel: MGM
Secret Garden, The 1975 d: Dorothea Brooking. lps: Sarah Hollis Andrews, David Patterson, John Woodnutt. MTV. 210M UKN.
Secret Garden, The 1984 d: Katrina Murray. MTV. 107M UKN.
Secret Garden, The 1987 d: Alan Grint. lps: Gennie James, Barret Oliver, Jadrien Steele. TVM. 100M UKN.
Secret Garden, The 1993 d: Agnieszka Holland. lps: Kate Maberly, Heydon Prowse, Andrew Knott. 101M USA.

The Shuttle, New York 1906, Novel
Shuttle, The 1918 d: Rollin S. Sturgeon. lps: Constance Talmadge, Alan Roscoe, Edith Johnson. 5r USA. prod/rel: Select Pictures Corp.©

That Lass O' Lowrie's, New York 1877, Novel
Secret Love 1916 d: Robert Z. Leonard. lps: Helen Ware, Harry Carey, Ella Hall. 6r USA. *That Lassie O' Lowrie's; That Lass O' Lowrie's* prod/rel: Bluebird Photoplays, Inc., Universal Film Mfg. Co.©

BURNETT, MURRAY
Everybody Comes to Rick's, Play
Casablanca 1942 d: Michael Curtiz. lps: Humphrey Bogart, Ingrid Bergman, Paul Henreid. 102M USA. prod/rel: Warner Bros.

BURNETT, WILLIAM RILEY (1899–, USA, Burnett, W. R.
Story
Bullet Scars 1942 d: D. Ross Lederman. lps: Regis Toomey, Adele Longmire, Howard Da SilvA. 50M USA. prod/rel: Warner Bros.

1935, Story
Dr. Socrates 1935 d: William Dieterle. lps: Paul Muni, Ann Dvorak, Barton MacLane. 74M USA. prod/rel: Warner Bros. Pictures, Inc.

Story
King of the Underworld 1939 d: Lewis Seiler. lps: Humphrey Bogart, Kay Francis, James Stephenson. 69M USA. *Unlawful* prod/rel: Warner Bros. Pictures©
Yellow Sky 1949 d: William A. Wellman. lps: Gregory Peck, Richard Widmark, Anne Baxter. 99M USA. prod/rel: 20th Century-Fox

Across the Aisle, 1936, Short Story
36 Hours to Kill 1936 d: Eugene J. Forde. lps: Brian Donlevy, Gloria Stuart, Douglas Fowley. 65M USA. *36 Hours to Live; Across the Aisle* prod/rel: Twentieth Century-Fox Film Corp.

Adobe Walls, 1953, Novel
Arrowhead 1953 d: Charles Marquis Warren. lps: Charlton Heston, Jack Palance, Katy Jurado. 105M USA. prod/rel: Paramount

Asphalt Jungle, New York 1949, Novel
Asphalt Jungle, The 1950 d: John Huston. lps: Sterling Hayden, Louis Calhern, James Whitmore. 112M USA. prod/rel: MGM
Badlanders, The 1958 d: Delmer Daves. lps: Alan Ladd, Ernest Borgnine, Katy Jurado. 85M USA. prod/rel: Metro-Goldwyn-Mayer Corp., Arcola Productions
Cairo 1963 d: Wolf RillA. lps: George Sanders, Richard Johnson, Fatin HamamA. 91M USA. prod/rel: MGM
Cool Breeze 1972 d: Barry Pollack. lps: Thalmus Rasulala, Judy Pace, Jim Watkins. 102M USA. prod/rel: MGM

Captain Lightfoot, 1954, Novel
Captain Lightfoot 1955 d: Douglas Sirk. lps: Rock Hudson, Barbara Rush, Jeff Morrow. 91M USA. prod/rel: Universal-International

Dark Command: a Kansas Iliad, New York 1938, Novel
Dark Command 1940 d: Raoul Walsh. lps: Claire Trevor, John Wayne, Walter Pidgeon. 94M USA. prod/rel: Republic Pictures Corp.

Dark Hazard, New York 1933, Novel
Dark Hazard 1934 d: Alfred E. Green. lps: Edward G. Robinson, Genevieve Tobin, Glenda Farrell. 72M USA. prod/rel: First National Pictures, Inc.
Wine, Women and Horses 1937 d: Louis King. lps: Barton MacLane, Ann Sheridan, Dick Purcell. 64M USA. *Lady Luck* prod/rel: Warner Bros. Pictures©

Giant Swing, 1932, Novel
Dance Hall 1941 d: Irving Pichel. lps: Carole Landis, Cesar Romero, William Henry. 74M USA. prod/rel: 20th-Century-Fox

High Sierra, 1940, Novel
  Colorado Territory 1949 d: Raoul Walsh. lps: Joel McCrea, Virginia Mayo, Dorothy Malone. 94M USA. prod/rel: Warner Bros.

  High Sierra 1941 d: Raoul Walsh. lps: Humphrey Bogart, Ida Lupino, Alan Curtis. 100M USA. prod/rel: Warner Bros.

  I Died a Thousand Times 1955 d: Stuart Heisler. lps: Jack Palance, Shelley Winters, Lori Nelson. 109M USA. *Jagged Edge* prod/rel: Warner Bros.

The Iron Man, New York 1930, Novel
  Iron Man 1931 d: Tod Browning. lps: Lew Ayres, Robert Armstrong, Jean Harlow. 73M USA. prod/rel: Universal Pictures Corp.©, Tod Browning Production

  Iron Man 1951 d: Joseph Pevney. lps: Jeff Chandler, Evelyn Keyes, Stephen McNally. 82M USA. prod/rel: Universal-International

  Some Blondes are Dangerous 1937 d: Milton Carruth. lps: William Gargan, Dorothea Kent, Nan Grey. 68M USA. *Blonde Dynamite* prod/rel: Universal Pictures Co.©

Jail Breaker, 1932, Story
  Whole Town's Talking, The 1935 d: John Ford. lps: Edward G. Robinson, Jean Arthur, Arthur Hohl. 95M USA. *Passport to Fame* (UKN); *Jail Breaker* prod/rel: Columbia Pictures Corp.©, John Ford Production

Little Caesar, New York 1929, Novel
  Little Caesar 1931 d: Mervyn Leroy. lps: Edward G. Robinson, Douglas Fairbanks Jr., Glenda Farrell. 80M USA. prod/rel: First National Pictures©

Nobody Lives Forever, 1943, Novel
  Nobody Lives Forever 1946 d: Jean Negulesco. lps: John Garfield, Geraldine Fitzgerald, Walter Brennan. 100M USA. prod/rel: Warner Bros.

Saint Johnson, New York 1930, Novel
  Law and Order 1932 d: Edward L. Cahn. lps: Walter Huston, Harry Carey, Raymond Hatton. 73M USA. *Guns A'blazing*; *Saint Johnson*; *Bullet Proof* prod/rel: Universal Pictures Corp.©

  Law and Order 1940 d: Ray Taylor. lps: Johnny Mack Brown, Fuzzy Knight, Nell O'Day. 57M USA. *Lucky Ralston* (UKN); *The Law*; *The Man from Cheyenne* prod/rel: Universal Pictures Co.©

  Law and Order 1953 d: Nathan Juran. lps: Ronald Reagan, Dorothy Malone, Alex Nicol. 80M USA. prod/rel: Universal-International

  Wild West Days 1937 d: Ford Beebe, Cliff Smith. lps: Johnny Mack Brown, Lynn Gilbert, Russell Simpson. SRL. 265M USA.

Vanity Row, 1952, Novel
  Accused of Murder 1956 d: Joseph Kane. lps: David Brian, Vera Ralston, Sidney Blackmer. 74M USA. prod/rel: Republic Pictures Corp.

BURNFORD, SHEILA (1918–1984), UKN
The Incredible Journey, Boston 1961, Novel
  Incredible Journey, The 1963 d: Fletcher Markle. lps: Emile Genest, John Drainie, Tommy Tweed. 80M USA. prod/rel: Walt Disney Productions, Buena Vista

  Homeward Bound: the Incredible Journey 1993 d: Duwayne Dunham. lps: Don Adler, Ed Bernard, Kevin Timothy ChevaliA. 85M USA. prod/rel: Buena Vista, Walt Disney

BURNHAM, CLARA LOUISE
Heart's Haven, Boston 1918, Novel
  Heart's Haven 1922 d: Benjamin B. Hampton. lps: Robert McKim, Claire Adams, Carl Gantvoort. 5275f USA. prod/rel: Benjamin B. Hampton Productions, W. W. Hodkinson Corp.

Jewel; a Chapter in Her Life, Boston 1903, Novel
  Chapter in Her Life, A 1923 d: Lois Weber. lps: Claude Gillingwater, Jane Mercer, Jacqueline Gadsdon. 6330f USA. *Jewel* prod/rel: Universal Pictures

  Jewel 1915 d: Phillips Smalley, Lois Weber. lps: Ella Hall, Rupert Julian, Hilda Hollis Sloman. 5r USA. prod/rel: Universal Film Mfg. Co.©, Broadway Universal Feature

The Opened Shutters, New York 1906, Novel
  Opened Shutters, The 1914 d: Otis Turner. lps: Herbert Rawlinson, Anna Little, Betty Schade. 4r USA. prod/rel: Universal Film Mfg. Co., Gold Seal

BURNS, BERNARD K.
The Woman on the Jury, New York 1923, Play
  Love Racket, The 1929 d: William A. Seiter. lps: Dorothy MacKaill, Sidney Blackmer, Edmund Burns. 6118f USA. *Such Things Happen* (UKN) prod/rel: First National Pictures

  Woman on the Jury, The 1924 d: Harry O. Hoyt. lps: Sylvia Breamer, Frank Mayo, Lew Cody. 7408f USA. prod/rel: Associated First National Pictures

BURNS, COM. HARRY A.
Case of the Blind Pilot, Short Story
  Men of the Fighting Lady 1954 d: Andrew Marton. lps: Van Johnson, Walter Pidgeon, Louis Calhern. 80M USA. prod/rel: MGM

BURNS, KEN
Lewis & Clark, Book
  Lewis & Clark - the Journey of the Corps of Discovery 1997 d: Ken Burns. DOC. 240M USA. prod/rel: Florentine Films, Weta-Tv

BURNS, NEAL
A Looney Love Affair, Story
  Looney Love Affair, A 1915 d: Horace Davey. lps: Ray Gallagher, Billie Rhodes, Harry Rattenberry. SHT USA. prod/rel: Nestor

Saved By a Skirt, Story
  Saved By a Skirt 1915 d: Horace Davey. lps: Billie Rhodes, Neal Burns, Ray Gallagher. SHT USA. prod/rel: Nestor

BURNS, REX
The Avenging Angel, Novel
  Messenger of Death 1988 d: J. Lee Thompson. lps: Charles Bronson, Trish Van Devere, Laurence Luckinbill. 91M USA. *Avenging Angels* prod/rel: Cannon

BURNS, ROBERT E.
I Am a Fugitive from a Georgia Chain Gang!, 1932, Autobiography
  I Am a Fugitive from a Chain Gang 1932 d: Mervyn Leroy. lps: Paul Muni, Glenda Farrell, Helen Vinson. 93M USA. *I Am a Fugitive*; *I Am a Fugitive from a Georgia Chain Gang* prod/rel: Warner Bros. Pictures©

BURNS, VINCENT GODFREY
Book
  Man Who Broke 1,000 Chains, The 1987 d: Daniel Mann. lps: Val Kilmer, Charles Durning, Sonia BragA. TVM. 115M USA. *Unchained* prod/rel: Hbo Pictures, Journey Entertainment

BURNS, WALTER NOBLE
The Robin Hood of El Dorado, New York 1932, Book
  Robin Hood of El Dorado 1936 d: William A. Wellman. lps: Warner Baxter, Bruce Cabot, Margo. 88M USA. *Born to Die*; *I Am Joaquin*; *In Old California*; *Murietta* prod/rel: Metro-Goldwyn-Mayer Corp.©

The Saga of Billy the Kid, Garden City, N.Y. 1926, Novel
  Billy the Kid 1930 d: King Vidor. lps: Johnny Mack Brown, Wallace Beery, Kay Johnson. 92M USA. *The Highwayman Rides* prod/rel: Metro-Goldwyn-Mayer Pictures

  Billy the Kid 1941 d: David Miller. lps: Robert Taylor, Brian Donlevy, Ian Hunter. 95M USA. prod/rel: Metro-Goldwyn-Mayer Corp.

BURRESS, JOHN
The Missouri Traveler, 1955, Novel
  Missouri Traveler, The 1958 d: Jerry Hopper. lps: Brandon de Wilde, Lee Marvin, Gary Merrill. 103M USA. prod/rel: Buena Vista, Cornelius V. Whitney Pictures

BURRI, EMIL
Die Kleine Trafik, Play
  Tochter Ihrer Exzellenz, Die 1934 d: Reinhold Schunzel. lps: Kathe von Nagy, Dagny Servaes, Willy Fritsch. 92M GRM. prod/rel: UFA

BURROUGH, BRYAN
Barbarians at the Gates, Book
  Barbarians at the Gate 1993 d: Glenn Jordan. lps: James Garner, Jonathan Pryce, Peter Riegert. TVM. 113M USA. prod/rel: Home Box Office©, Hbo Pictures

BURROUGHS, EDGAR RICE (1875–1950), USA
At the Earth's Core, 1922, Novel
  At the Earth's Core 1976 d: Kevin Connor. lps: Peter Cushing, Doug McClure, Caroline Munro. 90M UKN. prod/rel: Amicus

The Lad and the Lion, 1917, Short Story
  Lad and the Lion, The 1917 d: Alfred E. Green. lps: Vivian Reed, Will MacHin, Charles Le Moyne. 5r USA. prod/rel: Selig Polyscope Co.©, Red Seal Plays

The Land That Time Forgot, 1924, Novel
  Land That Time Forgot, The 1974 d: Kevin Connor. lps: Doug McClure, John McEnery, Susan Penhaligon. 90M UKN/USA. prod/rel: Amicus

The Oakdale Affair, 1918, Novel
  Oakdale Affair, The 1919 d: Oscar Apfel. lps: Evelyn Greeley, Corene Uzzell, Charles MacKay. 5-6r USA. prod/rel: World Film Corp.©

The Revenge of Tarzan, New York 1915, Novel
  Return of Tarzan, The 1920 d: Harry Revier. lps: Gene Pollar, George Romain, Estelle Taylor. 7r USA. *The Revenge of Tarzan* prod/rel: Numa Pictures Corp.©, Goldwyn Distributing Corp.

Tarzan and the Golden Lion, Chicago 1923, Novel
  Tarzan and the Golden Lion 1927 d: J. P. McGowan. lps: James Pierce, Frederic Peters, Edna Murphy. 5807f USA. prod/rel: R-C Pictures, Film Booking Offices of America

Tarzan of the Apes, Chicago 1914, Novel
  Greystoke: the Legend of Tarzan, Lord of the Apes 1983 d: Hugh Hudson. lps: Christopher Lambert, Andie MacDowell, Ian Holm. 129M UKN. *Greystoke* prod/rel: Warner Bros., Wea Records

  Romance of Tarzan, The 1918 d: Wilfred Lucas. lps: Elmo Lincoln, Enid Markey, Cleo Madison. 6481f USA. prod/rel: National Film Corp. of America, First National Exhibitors Circuit

  Tarzan of the Apes 1918 d: Scott Sidney. lps: Elmo Lincoln, Enid Markey, Gordon Griffith. 10r USA. prod/rel: National Film Corp. of America, First National Exhibitors Circuit

  Tarzan the Ape Man 1959 d: Joseph M. Newman. lps: Denny Miller, Joanna Barnes, Cesare DanovA. 82M USA. prod/rel: MGM

  Tarzan the Ape Man 1981 d: John Derek. lps: Bo Derek, Richard Harris, John Phillip Law. 112M USA. prod/rel: MGM, United Artists

  Tarzan, the Ape Man 1932 d: W. S. Van Dyke. lps: Johnny Weissmuller, Maureen O'Sullivan, C. Aubrey Smith. 101M USA. prod/rel: Metro-Goldwyn-Mayer Corp., Metro-Goldwyn-Mayer Dist. Corp.©

BURROUGHS, WILLIAM S. (1914–1997), USA, Burroughs, William Seward
The Naked Lunch, Novel
  Naked Lunch, The 1991 d: David Cronenberg. lps: Peter Weller, Judy Davis, Ian Holm. 115M CND/UKN. prod/rel: Record Picture Company (London), Naked Lunch Productions (Toronto)

BURROWS, ABE (1910–1985), USA, Burrows, Abram Solman
Cactus Flower, New York 1964, Play
  Cactus Flower 1969 d: Gene Saks. lps: Walter Matthau, Ingrid Bergman, Goldie Hawn. 103M USA. prod/rel: Columbia

Can-Can, Play
  Can-Can 1960 d: Walter Lang. lps: Shirley MacLaine, Frank Sinatra, Maurice Chevalier. 131M USA. prod/rel: 20th Century-Fox

BURSA, ANDRZEJ
Zabicie Ciotki, Novel
  Zabicie Ciotki 1984 d: Grzegorz Krolikiewicz. lps: Robert Herubin, Maria Kleydysz, Miroslawa ZaborowskA. 106M PLN. *Killing the Aunt*; *The Killing of the Aunt*

BURT, KATHARINE NEWLIN
Body and Soul, 1919, Short Story
  Body and Soul 1927 d: Reginald Barker. lps: Aileen Pringle, Norman Kerry, Lionel Barrymore. 5902f USA. *The Branding Iron* prod/rel: Metro-Goldwyn-Mayer Pictures

The Branding Iron, New York 1919, Novel
  Branding Iron, The 1920 d: Reginald Barker. lps: Barbara Castleton, James Kirkwood, Russell Simpson. 7r USA. prod/rel: Goldwyn Pictures Corp.©, Reginald Barker Productions

The Leopardess, Story
  Leopardess, The 1923 d: Henry Kolker. lps: Alice Brady, Edward Langford, Montagu Love. 5621f USA. prod/rel: Famous Players-Lasky, Paramount Pictures

The Red-Headed Husband, 1926, Short Story
  Silent Rider, The 1927 d: Lynn Reynolds. lps: Hoot Gibson, Blanche Mehaffey, Ethan Laidlaw. 5808f USA. prod/rel: Universal Pictures

Singed Wings, Story
  Singed Wings 1922 d: Penrhyn Stanlaws. lps: Bebe Daniels, Conrad Nagel, Adolphe Menjou. 7788f USA. prod/rel: Famous Players-Lasky, Paramount Pictures

Snowblind, 1921, Short Story
  Snowblind 1921 d: Reginald Barker. lps: Russell Simpson, Mary Alden, Cullen Landis. 6r USA. *Snow Blindness* prod/rel: Goldwyn Pictures

Summoned, 1923, Short Story
  Way of a Girl, The 1925 d: Robert G. VignolA. lps: Eleanor Boardman, Matt Moore, William Russell. 5025f USA. prod/rel: Metro-Goldwyn Pictures

BURT, KENDALL
The One That Got Away, Book
  One That Got Away, The 1957 d: Roy Ward Baker. lps: Hardy Kruger, Colin Gordon, Michael Goodliffe. 111M UKN. prod/rel: Rank, Rank Film Distributors

BURT, MAXWELL STRUTHERS (1882–1954), USA
The Interpreter's House, New York 1924, Novel
  I Want My Man 1925 d: Lambert Hillyer. lps: Doris Kenyon, Milton Sills, Phyllis Haver. 6172f USA. prod/rel: First National Pictures

BURTIS, THOMAS
War of the Wildcats, Short Story
War of the Wildcats 1943 d: Albert S. Rogell. lps: John Wayne, Martha Scott, Albert Dekker. 102M USA. *In Old Oklahoma* prod/rel: Republic

BURTIS, THOMSON
New Guinea Gold, Novel
Crosswinds 1951 d: Lewis R. Foster. lps: John Payne, Rhonda Fleming, Forrest Tucker. 93M USA. *Jungle Attack* prod/rel: Paramount, Pine-Thomas

BURTON, BEATRICE
The Flapper Wife, New York 1925, Novel
His Jazz Bride 1926 d: Herman C. Raymaker. lps: Marie Prevost, Matt Moore, Gayne Whitman. 6420f USA. prod/rel: Warner Brothers Pictures
Footloose, Novel
Footloose Widows 1926 d: Roy Del Ruth. lps: Louise Fazenda, Jacqueline Logan, Jason Robards. 7163f USA. *Fine Feathers* (UKN) prod/rel: Warner Brothers Pictures
Sally's Shoulders, New York 1927, Novel
Sally's Shoulders 1928 d: Lynn Shores. lps: Lois Wilson, George Hackathorne, Huntley Gordon. 6279f USA. prod/rel: Fbo Pictures

BURTON, G. MARION
Born of the Cyclone, Play
Untamed Youth 1924 d: Emile Chautard. lps: Derelys Perdue, Lloyd Hughes, Ralph Lewis. 4558f USA. *Beware the Woman*; *Born of the Cyclone* prod/rel: R-C Pictures, Film Booking Offices of America

BURTON, SHELLY
Story
Electric Horseman, The 1979 d: Sydney Pollack. lps: Robert Redford, Jane Fonda, Valerie Perrine. 121M USA. prod/rel: Columbia Pictures, Wildwood Enterprises

BURTON, VAL
Romance Incorporated, Story
Honeymoon Ahead 1945 d: Reginald Le Borg. lps: Allan Jones, Grace McDonald, Raymond Walburn. 60M USA. *Incorporated Romance* prod/rel: Universal

BUSCH, NIVEN
Duel in the Sun, Novel
Duel in the Sun 1946 d: King Vidor, Josef von Sternberg (Uncredited). lps: Joseph Cotten, Jennifer Jones, Lionel Barrymore. 138M USA. prod/rel: Selznick Releasing, Vanguard Prods.
The Furies, 1948, Novel
Furies, The 1950 d: Anthony Mann. lps: Barbara Stanwyck, Walter Huston, Wendell Corey. 109M USA. prod/rel: Paramount, Wallis-Hazen Inc.
They Dream of Home, Novel
Till the End of Time 1946 d: Edward Dmytryk. lps: Dorothy McGuire, Guy Madison, Robert Mitchum. 105M USA. *The Dream of Home* prod/rel: RKO Radio

BUSCH, WILHELM
Abenteuer Eines Junggesellen, 1875, Short Story
Tobias Knopp, Abenteuer Eines Junggesellen 1950 d: Walter Pentzlin. ANM. 76M GRM.
Die from Helene, 1872, Short Story
From Helene, Die 1965 d: Axel von Ambesser. lps: Simone Rethel, Theo Lingen, Friedrich von Thun. 91M GRM. *Pious Helen* prod/rel: Franz Seitz
Max Und Moritz: Eine Bubengeschichte in Sieben Streichen, 1865, Short Story
Max Und Moritz 1956 d: Norbert Schultze. lps: Norbert Schultze, Christian Schultze, Edith Elsholtz. 73M GRM.
Spuk Mit Max Und Moritz 1951 d: Ferdinand Diehl. lps: Anni Fahrnberger, Renate Deppisch. 60M GRM.

BUS-FEKETE, LADISLAUS
Birthday, Play
Heaven Can Wait 1943 d: Ernst Lubitsch. lps: Don Ameche, Gene Tierney, Charles Coburn. 112M USA. prod/rel: 20th Century-Fox
Du Haut En Bas, Play
Du Haut En Bas 1933 d: G. W. Pabst. lps: Jean Gabin, Mauricet, Janine Crispin. 79M FRN. *High and Low* prod/rel: Societe Des Fils Sonores Tobis
Heartbeat, Story
Appointment for Love 1941 d: William A. Seiter. lps: Charles Boyer, Margaret Sullavan, Rita Johnson. 89M USA. prod/rel: Universal
Jean, Vienna 1936, Play
Baroness and the Butler, The 1938 d: Walter Lang. lps: William Powell, Annabella, Helen Westley. 80M USA. *Jean* prod/rel: Twentieth Century-Fox Film Corp.
Three Girls, Play
Ladies in Love 1936 d: Edward H. Griffith. lps: Janet Gaynor, Loretta Young, Constance Bennett. 97M USA. *Three Girls* prod/rel: Twentieth Century-Fox Film Corp.©

Twelve in a Box, 1938, Play
Perfect Strangers 1949 d: Bretaigne Windust. lps: Ginger Rogers, Dennis Morgan, Thelma Ritter. 88M USA. *Too Dangerous to Love* (UKN) prod/rel: Warner Bros.

BUSHNELL, ADELYN
Glory, Play
Laughing at Trouble 1937 d: Frank Strayer. lps: Jane Darwell, Sara Haden, Lois Wilson. 67M USA. *Laughing at Death*; *Glory* prod/rel: Twentieth Century-Fox Film Corp.©

BUSSY, RENE
La Fille du Bouif, Play
Fille du Bouif, La 1931 d: Rene Bussy. lps: Felicien Tramel, Henri Leoni, Loulou Hegoburu. 60M FRN. prod/rel: Franco-Belge Cinema

BUTLER, ELLIS PARKER
The Jack-Knife Man, New York 1913, Novel
Jack-Knife Man, The 1920 d: King Vidor. lps: Florence Vidor, F. A. Turner, Harry Todd. 6r USA. *The Jack Knife Man* prod/rel: King Vidor Productions, First National Exhibitors Circuit
Pigs Is Pigs, Book
Pigs Is Pigs 1914 d: George D. Baker. lps: John Bunny, Etienne Girardot, Courtlandt Van Deusen. SHT USA. prod/rel: Vitagraph Co. of America

BUTLER, FRANK
Hangman's Whip, New York 1933, Play
Island of Lost Men 1939 d: Kurt Neumann. lps: Anna May Wong, J. Carrol Naish, Eric Blore. 63M USA. *North of Singapore*; *King of the River* prod/rel: Paramount Pictures©

BUTLER, GEORGE
Pumping Iron II: the Unprecedented Woman, Book
Pumping Iron II: the Women 1985 d: George Butler. lps: Rachel McLish, Bev Francis. DOC. 107M USA. prod/rel: Bar Belle Productions, White Mountain

BUTLER, GERALD
Kiss the Blood Off My Hands, Novel
Kiss the Blood Off My Hands 1948 d: Norman Foster. lps: Burt Lancaster, Joan Fontaine, Robert Newton. 80M USA. *Blood on My Hands* (UKN); *The Unafraid* prod/rel: Universal, Norma Prods.
Mad With Much Heart, 1945, Novel
On Dangerous Ground 1951 d: Nicholas Ray. lps: Robert Ryan, Ward Bond, Ida Lupino. 82M USA. prod/rel: RKO Radio
They Cracked Her Glass Slipper, Novel
Third Time Lucky 1949 d: Gordon Parry. lps: Glynis Johns, Dermot Walsh, Charles Goldner. 91M UKN. *They Cracked Her Glass Slipper* prod/rel: Alliance, Kenilworth

BUTLER, RACHEL BURTON
Mama's Affair, New York 1920, Play
Mama's Affair 1921 d: Victor Fleming. lps: Constance Talmadge, Effie Shannon, Katherine Kaelred. 5950f USA. prod/rel: Constance Talmadge Film Co., Associated First National Pictures

BUTLER, WILLIAM
Story
Butterfly Revolution 1985 d: Penelope Spheeris. lps: Charles Stratton, Harold P. Pruett, Adam Carl. 85M USA. *Summer Camp Nightmare*; *Summer Camp Massacre* prod/rel: Manson International
The Butterfly Revolution, Novel
Summer Camp Nightmare 1987 d: Bert L. Dragin. lps: Chuck Connors, Charles Stratton, Adam Carl. 87M USA. *The Butterfly Revolution* prod/rel: Concorde

BUTOR, MICHEL (1926–, FRN
La Modification, 1957, Novel
Modification, La 1970 d: Michel Worms. lps: Maurice Ronet, Emmanuelle Riva, Sylva KoscinA. 88M FRN/ITL. *La Moglie Nuova* (ITL) prod/rel: Fono Roma, Rene Thevenet

BUTTERFIELD, ROGER
Story
Pride of the Marines 1945 d: Delmer Daves. lps: John Garfield, Eleanor Parker, Dane Clark. 120M USA. *Forever in Love* (UKN); *Body and Soul* prod/rel: Warner Bros.

BUTTITTA, PIETRO
Il Volantino, Novel
Sbandata, La 1974 d: Alfredo Malfatti. lps: Domenico Modugno, Eleonora Giorgi, Pippo Franco. 100M ITL. prod/rel: Mondial Te.Fi., Titanus

BUXTON, HENRY J.
Wanted: a Blemish, 1919, Short Story
Amateur Devil, An 1920 d: Maurice Campbell. lps: Bryant Washburn, Charles Wyngate, Ann May. 4464f USA. *Wanted -a Blemish* prod/rel: Famous Players-Lasky Corp.©, Paramount Pictures

BUYSSE, CYRIEL
Lente, Book
Lente 1983 d: Dre Poppe. lps: Chris Thijs, Jo de Meyere, Blanka Heirman. TVM. 55M BLG.
Tantes, 1924, Novel
Tantes 1984 d: Juul Claes. lps: Dora Van Der Groen, Denise de Weerdt, Emmy Leemans. MTV. 64M BLG.

BUZO, ALEXANDER
Coralie Lansdowne Says No, Play
Coralie Lansdowne Say No 1980 d: Michael Carson. lps: Wendy Hughes, David Waters, Brian Blain. TVM. F ASL. prod/rel: Australian Broadcasting Corp.
Rooted, Play
Rooted 1985 d: Ron Way. lps: James Laurie, Genevieve Mooy, Terry Serio. TVM. F ASL. prod/rel: Australian Broadcasting Corp.

BUZURA, AUGUSTIN
Orgolii, 1977, Novel
Orgolii 1981 d: Manole Marcus. 116M RMN. *Pride*

BUZZATI, DINO
Un Amore, 1963, Novel
Amore, Un 1965 d: Gianni Vernuccio. lps: Agnes Spaak, Rossano Brazzi, Gerard Blain. 95M ITL/FRN. *Une Garce Inconsciente* (FRN); *Elle Aime Ca* prod/rel: Produzioni Vernuccio (Milano), Prima Film (Roma)
Barnabo Delle Montagne, Novel
Barnabo Delle Montagne 1993 d: Mario BrentA. lps: Marco Pauletti, Duilio Fontana, Alessandra Milan. 125M ITL/FRN/SWT. *Barnabo from the Mountains*; *Barnabo of the Mountains* prod/rel: Nautilus, Number One
Il Deserto Dei Tartari, 1940, Novel
Deserto Dei Tartari, Il 1976 d: Valerio Zurlini. lps: Jacques Perrin, Vittorio Gassman, Max von Sydow. 140M ITL/FRN/GRM. *Le Desert Des Tartares* (FRN); *Die Tatarenwuste* (GRM); *The Desert of the Tartars* prod/rel: Cinema Due (Roma), Regane Films (Paris)
Sette Piani, Short Story
Fischio Al Naso, Il 1967 d: Ugo Tognazzi. lps: Ugo Tognazzi, Olga Villi, Alicia Brandet. 110M ITL. *The Seventh Floor* (USA); *The Whistling in the Nose*; *The Man With the Whistling Nose* prod/rel: Sancro International, Cineriz

BYASS, B. O.
Things Hidden, Short Story
Fools Step in 1938 d: Nigel Byass. lps: Betty Dorian, Douglas Vine. 13M UKN. prod/rel: Fraternity Films, British Screen Services

BYATT, A. S. (1936–, UKN, Byatt, Antonia Susan
Morpho Eugenia, Novel
Angels and Insects 1995 d: Philip Haas. lps: Mark Rylance, Kristin Scott-Thomas, Patsy Kensit. 117M USA/UKN. *Angels & Insects* prod/rel: Film Four, Samuel Goldwyn

BYFORD, JOAN
The Haunted Light, 1928, Play
Phantom Light, The 1935 d: Michael Powell. lps: Binnie Hale, Gordon Harker, Ian Hunter. 75M UKN. prod/rel: Gaumont British, Gainsborough

BYINGTON, ROBERT
Javelkemeiche, Story
Olympia 1998 d: Robert Byington. lps: Carmen Nogales, Jason Andrews, Damian Young. 76M USA. prod/rel: Big Tomato

BYKOV, VALENTIN
Kar'yer, Novel
Kar'yer 1990 d: Nikolai Skuibin. lps: Igor Bochkin, Yuriy Stupakov, Svetlana KopylovA. 107M USS.

BYRAPPA, S. L.
Vamsha Vriksha, Novel
Vamsha Vriksha 1971 d: Girish Karnad, B. V. Karanth. lps: Venkata Rao Talegiri, L. V. Sharada Rao, B. V. Karanth. 166M IND. *The Family Tree*; *Vamsha Vruksha*

BYRNE, DONN
Fiddler's Green, 1918, Short Story
All Man 1918 d: Paul Scardon. lps: Harry T. Morey, Betty Blythe, James Gaillord. 4471f USA. prod/rel: Vitagraph Co. of America©, Blue Ribbon Feature
A Prodigal in Utopia, Short Story
Dangerous Hours 1920 d: Fred Niblo. lps: Lloyd Hughes, Barbara Castleton, Claire Du Brey. 7r USA. *Americanism (Versus Bolshevism)* prod/rel: Thomas H. Ince Productions, Famous Players-Lasky Corp.
The Tale of a Gypsy Horse, Short Story
Wings of the Morning 1937 d: Harold Schuster. lps: Annabella, Henry Fonda, Leslie Banks. 85M UKN/USA. prod/rel: New World, 20th Century-Fox

BYRNE, DOROTHEA DONN
Irish and Proud of It, Story
Irish and Proud of It 1936 d: Donovan Pedelty. lps: Richard Hayward, Dinah Sheridan, Gwenllian Gill. 72M UKN. prod/rel: Crusade, Paramount

BYRNE, JOHN
Cuttin' a Rug, Play
Slab Boys, The 1997 d: John Byrne. lps: Robin Laing, Duncan Ross, Russell Barr. 97M UKN. prod/rel: Skreba Film, Wanderlust Films

The Slab Boys, Play
Slab Boys, The 1997 d: John Byrne. lps: Robin Laing, Duncan Ross, Russell Barr. 97M UKN. prod/rel: Skreba Film, Wanderlust Films

BYRNE, JOHN F.
Eight Bells, 1891, Play
Eight Bells 1916 d: John F. Byrne. lps: Andrew Byrne, John Kearney, Dorothy Graham. 5r USA. prod/rel: Eight Bells Film Co.©, World Film Corp.

BYRON, GEORGE
The Two Foscari, Play
Due Foscari, I 1942 d: Enrico Fulchignoni. lps: Carlo Ninchi, Rossano Brazzi, Elli Parvo. 85M ITL. prod/rel: Scalera Film

BYRON, H. J.
Our Boys, London 1875, Play
Our Boys 1915 d: Sidney Morgan. lps: Maitland Marler, Compton Coutts, Kathleen Harrison. 2450f UKN. prod/rel: Cherry Kearton, Standard

Uncle Dick's Darling, London 1869, Play
Uncle Dick's Darling 1920 d: Fred Paul. lps: George Bellamy, Humberston Wright, Ronald Power. 4890f UKN. prod/rel: British Standard, Anchor

BYRON, LORD (1788–1824), UKN, Byron, George Gordon
Cain, 1821, Poem
Caino 1910. 177m ITL. prod/rel: Milano Films

The Corsair, London 1814, Poem
Corsair, The 1914 d: Frank Powell. lps: Crane Wilbur, Anna Rose, Edward Jose. 4r USA. prod/rel: Pathe Freres, Eclectic Film Co.©

Mazeppa, Poem
Mazeppa 1908 d: Frank Dudley. 500f UKN. prod/rel: Walturdaw

BYRON, OLIVER DOUD
Across the Continent, New York 1871, Play
Across the Continent 1913. lps: Herbert Barrington, Herbert L. Barry, Wilbur Hudson. 4r USA. prod/rel: Pilot Films Corp., State Rights

C

CAB, MARCO
Au Pays Des Cigales, Opera
Au Pays Des Cigales 1945 d: Maurice Cam. lps: Henri Alibert, Gorlett, Francine Bessy. 85M FRN. prod/rel: D.U.C.

Au Soleil de Marseille, Opera
Au Soleil de Marseille 1937 d: Pierre-Jean Ducis. lps: Mireille Ponsard, Henri Garat, Gorlett. F FRN. prod/rel: Henri Ullmann

Marseilles Mes Amours, Opera
Marseille Mes Amours 1939 d: Jacques Daniel-Norman. lps: Leon Belieres, Mireille Ponsard, Janine Roger. 102M FRN. prod/rel: G.a.R.B.

CABALLERO, AGUSTIN
A Orillas Del Jucar, Story
Voluntad! 1928 d: Mario Roncoroni. lps: Silvia de Silva, Agustin Caballero, Purita Andreu. SPN. prod/rel: Ediciones Caballero (Valencia)

CABALLERO, FERNAN (1796–1877), SPN, Bohl de Faber, Cecilia
La Familia Alvareda, 1856, Novel
Luna de Sangre 1950 d: Francisco Rovira BeletA. lps: Paquita Rico, Francisco Rabal, Isabel de Pomes. 93M SPN. *Bloody Moon*

CABEZA DE VACA, ALVAR NUNEZ
Naufragios, Book
Cabeza de Vaca 1990 d: Nicolas EchevarriA. lps: Juan Diego, Daniel Jimenez Cacho, Carlos Castanon. 112M MXC/SPN/UKN. prod/rel: Iguana Productions

CABIERI, RENALDO
Amanti, Play
Amanti 1968 d: Vittorio de SicA. lps: Faye Dunaway, Marcello Mastroianni, Caroline Mortimer. 88M ITL/FRN. *Le Temps Des Amants* (FRN); *A Place for Lovers* (USA); *Lovers* prod/rel: C.C. Champion (Roma), Les Films Concordia (Paris)

CADIEUX, PAULINE
La Lampe Dans la Fenetre, Novel
Cordelia 1980 d: Jean Beaudin. lps: Louise Portal, Gaston Lepage, Raymond Cloutier. 116M CND. prod/rel: Office National Du Film

CAEN, HENRI
Un Petit Trou Pas Cher, Play
Petit Trou Pas Cher, Un 1934 d: Pierre-Jean Ducis. lps: Jules Berry, Albert Malbert, Suzy Prim. 45M FRN. prod/rel: Alliance Cinematographique Europeenne, Pierre-Jean Ducis

CAESAR, ARTHUR
The Butter and Egg Man, Novel
Tenderfoot's Triumph, The 1910 d: Frank Powell, D. W. Griffith. lps: Arthur Johnson, Lottie Pickford, Dell Henderson. 989f USA. prod/rel: Biograph Co.

CAESAR, IRVING
Saratoga Chips, Play
Straight Place and Show 1938 d: David Butler. lps: The Ritz Brothers, Richard Arlen, Ethel Merman. 68M USA. *They're Off* (UKN) prod/rel: Twentieth Century-Fox Film Corp.©

CAGE, WILLIAM
Appuntamento Col Disonore, Novel
Appuntamento Col Disonore 1970 d: Adriano Bolzoni. lps: Michael Craig, Klaus Kinski, Eva Renzi. 100M ITL/GRM/YGS. *Special Kommando Wildganse* (GRM); *The Night of the Assassin* prod/rel: Roberto Cin.Ca (Roma), Lisa Film (Munich)

CAGLIERI, EMILIO
Play
Toto Cerca Pace 1954 d: Mario Mattoli. lps: Toto, Ave Ninchi, Isa BarzizzA. 2473m ITL. prod/rel: Rosa Film, Titanus
Lo Smemorato, Play
Smemorato, Lo 1936 d: Gennaro Righelli. lps: Angelo Musco, Paola Borboni, Luisa FeridA. 79M ITL. prod/rel: Capitani, I.C.A.R.

CAHAN, ABRAHAM (1860–1951), RSS
Yekl, 1896, Novel
Hester Street 1975 d: Joan Micklin Silver. lps: Steven Keats, Carol Kane, Paul Freedman. 86M USA. prod/rel: Midwest Film Prods.

CAHUET, ALBERIC
Colonel d'Empire Pontcarral, Novel
Pontcarral, Colonel d'Empire 1942 d: Jean Delannoy. lps: Pierre Blanchar, Annie Ducaux, Suzy Carrier. 125M FRN. prod/rel: Pathe-Cinema

CAIDIN, MARTIN
Cyborg, Novel
Six Million Dollar Man, The 1973 d: Richard Irving. lps: Lee Majors, Barbara Anderson, Martin Balsam. TVM. 73M USA. *Cyborg* prod/rel: Universal

Marooned, New York 1964, Novel
Marooned 1969 d: John Sturges. lps: Gregory Peck, Richard Crenna, David Janssen. 133M USA. prod/rel: Frankovich Productions

CAILLAVA, RAYMOND
Les Clandestines, Paris 1954, Novel
Clandestines, Les 1954 d: Raoul Andre. lps: Nicole Courcel, Dominique Wilms, Maria Mauban. 93M FRN. *Vice Dolls* (USA); *Secret Women* prod/rel: Vascos Films

CAILLOU, ALAN
The Cheetahs, Novel
Cheetah 1989 d: Jeff Blyth. lps: Keith Coogan, Lucy Deakins, Colin Mothupi. 84M USA. prod/rel: Buena Vista, Walt Disney

Khartoum, Book
Khartoum 1966 d: Basil Dearden. lps: Charlton Heston, Laurence Olivier, Richard Johnson. 134M UKN. prod/rel: United Artists, Julian Blaustein

Rampage, New York 1961, Novel
Rampage 1963 d: Phil Karlson, Henry Hathaway (Uncredited). lps: Robert Mitchum, Jack Hawkins, Elsa Martinelli. 98M USA. *Jungle Rampage* prod/rel: Talbot Productions, Seven Arts Productions

CAIN, JAMES M. (1892–1977), USA, Cain, James Mallahan
Baby in the Icebox, 1933, Short Story
She Made Her Bed 1934 d: Ralph Murphy. lps: Richard Arlen, Sally Eilers, Robert Armstrong. 78M USA. *Baby in the Ice Box* prod/rel: Paramount Productions©

Butterfly, 1947, Novel
Butterfly 1981 d: Matt Cimber. lps: Stacy Keach, Pia Zadora, Orson Welles. 107M USA. prod/rel: Analysis
Career in C Major, 1938, Short Story
Everybody Does It 1949 d: Edmund Goulding. lps: Celeste Holm, Paul Douglas, Linda Darnell. 98M USA.
Wife, Husband and Friend 1939 d: Gregory Ratoff. lps: Loretta Young, Warner Baxter, Binnie Barnes. 80M USA. *Women are Dangerous*; *Career in C Major* prod/rel: Twentieth Century-Fox Film Corp.©
Double Indemnity, 1943, Novel
Double Indemnity 1944 d: Billy Wilder. lps: Barbara Stanwyck, Fred MacMurray, Edward G. Robinson. 106M USA. prod/rel: Paramount
Double Indemnity 1973 d: Jack Smight. lps: Richard Crenna, Lee J. Cobb, Samantha Eggar. TVM. 100M USA. prod/rel: Universal
The Embezzler, 1940, Short Story
Money and the Woman 1940 d: William K. Howard. lps: Jeffrey Lynn, Brenda Marshall, John Litel. 80M USA. prod/rel: Warner Bros. Pictures©, First National Picture
Love's Lovely Counterfeit, 1942, Novel
Slightly Scarlet 1956 d: Allan Dwan. lps: John Payne, Rhonda Fleming, Arlene Dahl. 99M USA. prod/rel: RKO, Filmcrest Prods.
Mildred Pierce, 1941, Novel
Mildred Pierce 1945 d: Michael Curtiz. lps: Joan Crawford, Jack Carson, Zachary Scott. 113M USA. prod/rel: Warner Bros.
The Postman Always Rings Twice, 1934, Novel
Dernier Tournant, Le 1939 d: Pierre Chenal. lps: Fernand Gravey, Michel Simon, Corinne Luchaire. 90M FRN. *The Postman Always Rings Twice*; *The Last Bend* prod/rel: Gladiator Films
Ossessione 1943 d: Luchino Visconti. lps: Clara Calamai, Massimo Girotti, Dhia Cristiani. 140M ITL. *The Postman Always Rings Twice* prod/rel: Industrie Cinematografiche Italiane
Postman Always Rings Twice, The 1946 d: Tay Garnett. lps: Lana Turner, John Garfield, Cecil Kellaway. 113M USA. prod/rel: MGM
Postman Always Rings Twice, The 1981 d: Bob Rafelson. lps: Jack Nicholson, Jessica Lange, John Colicos. 125M USA. prod/rel: Paramount
Szenvedely 1998 d: Gyorgy Feher. lps: Ildiko Bansagi, Janos Derzsi, Dzsoko Roszics. 149M HNG. *Passion* prod/rel: Magyar Tv Drama Studio, Budapest Film Studio
Serenade, 1937, Novel
Interlude 1957 d: Douglas Sirk. lps: June Allyson, Rossano Brazzi, Marianne Koch. 89M USA. prod/rel: Universal-International
Interlude 1967 d: Kevin Billington. lps: Oskar Werner, Barbara Ferris, Virginia Maskell. 114M UKN. *When Tomorrow Comes* prod/rel: Columbia, Domino
Serenade 1956 d: Anthony Mann. lps: Mario Lanza, Joan Fontaine, Sara Montiel. 121M USA. prod/rel: Warner Bros.
When Tomorrow Comes 1939 d: John M. Stahl. lps: Irene Dunne, Charles Boyer, Barbara O'Neil. 90M USA. *The Modern Cinderella*; *Give Us the Night* prod/rel: Universal Pictures Co.©

CAIN, JONATHAN
Saigon Commandos - Mad Minute, Novel
Saigon Commandos 1987 d: Clark Henderson. lps: Richard Young, P. J. Soles, John Allen Nelson. 91M USA. prod/rel: Concorde

CAIN, PAUL
Fast One, 1932, Short Story
Gambling Ship 1933 d: Louis J. Gasnier, Max Marcin. lps: Cary Grant, Benita Hume, Glenda Farrell. 72M USA. prod/rel: Paramount Productions©
Lead Party, 1932, Short Story
Gambling Ship 1933 d: Louis J. Gasnier, Max Marcin. lps: Cary Grant, Benita Hume, Glenda Farrell. 72M USA. prod/rel: Paramount Productions©
Velvet, 1932, Short Story
Gambling Ship 1933 d: Louis J. Gasnier, Max Marcin. lps: Cary Grant, Benita Hume, Glenda Farrell. 72M USA. prod/rel: Paramount Productions©

CAINE, HALL (1853–1931), UKN, Caine, Sir Thomas Henry Hall
The Bondman, London 1890, Novel
Bondman, The 1916 d: Edgar Lewis. lps: William Farnum, Harry Spingler, Carey Lee. 5-6r USA. prod/rel: Fox Film Corp., William Fox©
Bondman, The 1929 d: Herbert Wilcox. lps: Norman Kerry, Frances Cuyler, Donald McCardle. SIL. 8660f UKN. prod/rel: British & Dominions, Woolf & Freedman

The Christian: a Story, London 1897, Novel
Christian, The 1914 d: Frederick A. Thompson. lps: Earle Williams, Edith Storey, Edward M. Kimball. 8r USA. prod/rel: Vitagraph Co. of America©, Liebler Co.

Christian, The 1915 d: George Loane Tucker. lps: Derwent Hall Caine, Elisabeth Risdon, Gerald Ames. 9170f UKN. prod/rel: London, Jury

Christian, The 1923 d: Maurice Tourneur. lps: Richard Dix, Mae Busch, Gareth Hughes. 8000f USA. prod/rel: Goldwyn Pictures

The Deemster, London 1887, Novel
Deemster, The 1917 d: Howell Hansel. lps: Derwent Hall Caine, Marian Swayne, Sidney Bracey. 7-9r USA. *The Bishop's Son* prod/rel: Arrow Film Corp.©, State Rights

The Eternal City, London 1901, Novel
Eternal City, The 1915 d: Edwin S. Porter, Hugh Ford. lps: Pauline Frederick, Thomas Holding, Kittens Reichert. 8r USA. prod/rel: Famous Players Film Co., Select Film Booking Agency

Eternal City, The 1923 d: George Fitzmaurice. lps: Barbara La Marr, Bert Lytell, Lionel Barrymore. 7800f USA. prod/rel: Madison Productions, Associated First National Pictures

The Manxman, 1894, Novel
Manxman, The 1916 d: George Loane Tucker. lps: Henry Ainley, Elisabeth Risdon, Fred Groves. 9000f UKN. prod/rel: London, Jury

Manxman, The 1929 d: Alfred Hitchcock. lps: Carl Brisson, Anny Ondra, Malcolm Keen. SIL. 8163f UKN. prod/rel: British International Pictures, Wardour

The Prodigal Son, 1904, Novel
Prodigal Son, The 1923 d: A. E. Coleby. lps: Stewart Rome, Henry Victor, Edith Bishop. 17r UKN. prod/rel: Stoll

The Woman of Knockaloe, New York 1923, Novel
Barbed Wire 1927 d: Mauritz Stiller, Rowland V. Lee. lps: Pola Negri, Clive Brook, Einar Hanson. 6951f USA. prod/rel: Paramount Famous Lasky Corp.

The Woman Thou Gavest Me, London 1913, Novel
Woman Thou Gavest Me, The 1919 d: Hugh Ford. lps: Katherine MacDonald, Milton Sills, Jack Holt. 6001f USA. prod/rel: Famous Players-Lasky Corp.©, Paramount-Artcraft Special

CAINE, JEFFREY
The Cold Room, Novel
Cold Room, The 1983 d: James Dearden. lps: George Segal, Amanda Pays, Renee Soutendijk. TVM. 95M UKN/USA. *Behind the Wall* prod/rel: Hbo, Jethro

CAINE, LYNN
Widow, Novel
Widow 1976 d: J. Lee Thompson. lps: Michael Learned, Bradford Dillman, Farley Granger. TVM. 100M USA. prod/rel: Lorimar Productions

CAINE, WILLIAM
Great Snakes, Novel
Great Snakes 1920 d: Gerald James, Gaston Quiribet. lps: Eileen Dennes, Frank Stanmore, Hugh Clifton. 7093f UKN. prod/rel: Hepworth

CALANCHI, S.
Una Leggera Euforia, Short Story
Ultima Volta, L' 1976 d: Aldo Lado. lps: Joe Dallesandro, Eleonora Giorgi, Massimo Ranieri. 105M ITL. *Born Winner* prod/rel: Marzia Cin.Ca, European Inc.

CALDERON DE LA BARCA, PEDRO (1600–1681), SPN
El Alcalde de Zalamea, 1651, Play
Alcalde de Zalamea, El 1953 d: Jose Gutierrez Maesso. lps: Manuel Luna, Jose Marco Davo, Isabel de Pomes. 87M SPN.

Richter von Zalamea, Der 1920 d: Ludwig Berger. lps: Albert Steinruck, Agnes Straub, Lil Dagover. 2186m GRM. prod/rel: Decla-Bioscop Ag

Richter von Zalamea, Der 1955 d: Martin Hellberg. lps: J. J. Buttner, Gudrun Schmidt-Ahrens, Albert Garbe. 106M GDR. *The Judge of Zalamea* prod/rel: Defa

La Dama Duende, 1647, Play
Dama Duende, La 1945 d: Luis Saslavsky. lps: Delia Garces, Antonia HerrerA. 101M ARG. *The Phantom Lady*

El Gran Teatro Del Mundo, 1645
MacHtrausch - Aber Die Liebe Siegt 1942 d: Ernst Biller. lps: Hans Fehrmann, Max Knapp, Ernst Stiefel. 95M SWT. *La Fievre du Pouvoir*; *Das Grosse Welttheater*; *Welttheater Einsiedeln - Geld Oder Glaube*; *Welt Und Theater*; *Grosse Liebe Um Das Welttheater* prod/rel: Film-Kunst-Zurich Ag

El Moro de la Alpujarra
Moro Dell'apuxarra (Il Tuxani), Il 1911 d: Mario Caserini. lps: Amleto Novelli, Gianna Terribili-Gonzales. 302m ITL. *Il Tuxani*; *Moorish Bride* (UKN) prod/rel: Cines

La Vida Es Sueno, 1647, Play
Memoire Des Apparences 1986 d: Raul Ruiz. lps: Sylvain Thirolle, Roch Leibovici, Benedicte Dire. 105M FRN. *Memoire Des Apparences: la Vie Est un Songe*; *Life Is a Dream*

Principe Encadenado, El 1960 d: Luis LuciA. lps: Javier Escriva, Antonio Vilar, Luis Prendes. 103M SPN. *The Prince in Bondage*; *The Prince in Chains*; *The Chained Prince*

CALDERONI, PIETRO
L' Avventura Di un Uomo Tranquillo, Book
Testimone a Rischio 1997 d: Pasquale Pozzessere. lps: Fabrizio Bentivoglio, Claudio Amendola, Margherita Buy. 97M ITL. *Witness in Danger*; *Risking Witness* prod/rel: Taodue Film, Istituto Luce

CALDWELL, ANNE
Dixiana, Story
Dixiana 1930 d: Luther Reed. lps: Bebe Daniels, Everett Marshall, Bert Wheeler. 99M USA. prod/rel: RKO Productions

The Nest Egg, New York 1910, Play
Marry Me 1925 d: James Cruze. lps: Florence Vidor, Edward Everett Horton, John Roche. 5526f USA. prod/rel: Famous Players-Lasky, Paramount Pictures

Top O' the Mornin', c1913, Play
Top O' the Morning, The 1922 d: Edward Laemmle. lps: Gladys Walton, Harry Myers, Doreen Turner. 4627f USA. prod/rel: Universal Film Mfg. Co.

CALDWELL, ERSKINE (1903–1987), USA, Caldwell, Erskine Preston
Claudelle Inglish, Boston 1959, Novel
Claudelle Inglish 1961 d: Gordon Douglas. lps: Diane McBain, Arthur Kennedy, Will Hutchins. 99M USA. *Young and Eager* (UKN) prod/rel: Warner Bros.

God's Little Acre, 1933, Novel
God's Little Acre 1958 d: Anthony Mann. lps: Robert Ryan, Tina Louise, Aldo Ray. 110M USA. prod/rel: United Artists

Tobacco Road, 1932, Novel
Tobacco Road 1941 d: John Ford. lps: Charley Grapewin, Marjorie Rambeau, Gene Tierney. 84M USA. prod/rel: 20th Century-Fox

CALDWELL, TAYLOR (1900–1985), UKN, Caldwell, Janet Miriam Taylor
Captains and the Kings, Novel
Captains and the Kings 1976 d: Douglas Heyes, Allen Reisner. lps: Richard Jordan, Perry King, Patty Duke. TVM. 450M USA. prod/rel: Mca, Universal TV

Testimony of Two Men, Novel
Testimony of Two Men 1977 d: Larry Yust, Leo Penn. lps: David Birney, Barbara Parkins, Steve Forrest. TVM. 300M USA. prod/rel: Universal

CALEF, NOEL
Ascenseur Pour l'Echafaud, Paris 1956, Novel
Ascenseur Pour l'Echafaud, L' 1957 d: Louis Malle. lps: Jeanne Moreau, Maurice Ronet, Georges Poujouly. 88M FRN. *Lift to the Scaffold* (UKN); *Frantic* (USA); *Elevator to the Gallows* prod/rel: Nouvelles Editions De Films

La Bouteille de Lait, Story
Imbarco a Mezzanotte 1952 d: Joseph Losey. lps: Paul Muni, Joan Lorring, Vittorio ManuntA. 87M ITL/USA. *Stranger on the Prowl* (USA); *Encounter* prod/rel: Consorzio Produttori Cin. Tirrenia, Riviera Film

Echec Au Porteur, Novel
Echec Au Porteur 1957 d: Gilles Grangier. lps: Gert Frobe, Paul Meurisse, Jeanne Moreau. 86M FRN. prod/rel: Orex Films, Corona

Recours En Grace, Novel
Recours En Grace 1960 d: Laslo Benedek. lps: Raf Vallone, Emmanuelle Riva, Annie Girardot. 97M FRN/ITL. *Tra Due Donne* (ITL) prod/rel: Marceau, Cocinor

Rodolphe Et le Revolveur, Novel
Tiger Bay 1959 d: J. Lee Thompson. lps: John Mills, Horst Buchholz, Hayley Mills. 105M UKN. prod/rel: Rank Film Distributors, Independent Artists

CALHOUN, D. D.
The Arab, Story
One Stolen Night 1923 d: Robert Ensminger. lps: Alice Calhoun, Herbert Heyes, Otto Hoffman. 4900f USA. prod/rel: Vitagraph Co. of America

One Stolen Night 1929 d: Scott R. Dunlap. lps: Betty Bronson, William Collier Jr., Mitchell Lewis. 5243f USA. prod/rel: Warner Brothers Pictures

CALINESCU, GEORGE
Bietul Ioanide, 1953, Novel
Bietul Ioanide 1979 d: Dan PitA. lps: Marga Barbu, Leopoldina Balanuta, Ion Caramitru. 121M RMN. *Memories from an Old Chest of Drawers*; *Ioanide*

Enigma Otiliei, 1938, Novel
Felix Si Otilia 1972 d: Iulian Mihu. lps: Radu Boruzescu, Julieta Szonyi. 146M RMN. *Felix and Otilia*

Scrinul Negru, 1960, Novel
Bietul Ioanide 1979 d: Dan PitA. lps: Marga Barbu, Leopoldina Balanuta, Ion Caramitru. 121M RMN. *Memories from an Old Chest of Drawers*; *Ioanide*

CALLADO, ANTONIO
Madona de Cedro, 1957, Novel
Madona de Cedro, A 1968 d: Carlos CoimbrA. lps: Leonardo Vilar, Leila Diniz, Anselmo Duarte. 110M BRZ. *The Cedar Madonna*; *The Virgin of Cedar*

Zumbi Do Catacumba Pedro Mico, 1957, Play
Pedro Mico 1985 d: Ipojuca Fontes. lps: Pele, Tereza Rachel, Jorge DoriA. 99M BRZ. *Peter Monkey*; *Monkey Pete*

Quarup, 1967, Novel
Kuarup 1988 d: Ruy GuerrA. lps: Taumaturgo Ferreira, Fernanda Torres, Claudia RaiA. 116M BRZ.

CALLAGHAN, MORLEY (1903–1990), CND, Callagan, Morley Edward
Short Stories
Now That April's Here 1958 d: William Davidson. lps: Don Borisenko, Judy Welch, Beth Amos. 84M CND. prod/rel: Klenman-Davidson Productions Ltd.

CALLAHAN, ROBERT E.
Daughter of the West, Novel
Daughter of the West 1949 d: Harold Daniels. lps: Martha Vickers, Philip Reed, Donald Woods. 77M USA. prod/rel: Film Classics

CALTHROP, DION CLAYTON
The Old Country, Play
Old Country, The 1921 d: A. V. Bramble. lps: Gerald McCarthy, Kathleen Vaughan, Haidee Wright. 5000f UKN. prod/rel: Ideal

Out to Win, London 1921, Play
Out to Win 1923 d: Denison Clift. lps: Catherine Calvert, Clive Brook, Irene Norman. 6000f UKN. prod/rel: Ideal

Perpetua; Or the Way to Treat a Woman, New York 1911, Novel
Love's Boomerang 1916 d: P. C. Hartigan. lps: O. C. Jackson, Yvette Mitchell, Harry Depp. SHT USA. prod/rel: Famous Players-Lasky, Paramount Pictures

Perpetua 1922 d: John S. Robertson, Tom Geraghty. lps: David Powell, Ann Forrest, Geoffrey Kerr. 6200f UKN/USA. *Love's Boomerang* (USA) prod/rel: Famous Players-Lasky, Paramount

A Southern Maid, London 1920, Musical Play
Southern Maid, A 1933 d: Harry Hughes. lps: Bebe Daniels, Clifford Mollison, Harry Welchman. 85M UKN. prod/rel: British International Pictures, Wardour

CALVINO, ITALO (1923–1985), ITL
Il Cavaliere Inesistente, 1959, Novel
Cavaliere Inesistente, Il 1970 d: Pino Zac. lps: Hana Ruzickova, Stefano Oppedisano, Evelina Vermigli Gori. 110M ITL. *The Non-Existent Knight*; *The Imaginary Knight* prod/rel: Istituto Nazionale Luce, Ital Noleggio

Ultimo Viene Il Corvo, Short Stories
Palookaville 1995 d: Alan Taylor. lps: William Forsythe, Vincent Gallo, Adam Trese. 93M USA. prod/rel: Public Television Playhouse, Playhouse International Pictures

CALVINO, VITTORIO
La Torre Sul Pollaio, Play
Strano Appuntamento 1951 d: D. Akos HamzA. lps: Umberto Spadaro, Marina Bonfigli, Leda GloriA. F ITL. *Strange Appointment* prod/rel: Ardire Film (Genova), Minerva Film

CALVO SOTELO, JOAQUIN
Cartas Credenciales, 1961, Play
Operacion Embajada 1964 d: Fernando Palacios. lps: Alberto Closas, Analia Gade, Jose Luis Lopez Vazquez. 89M SPN. *Operation Embassy*

Cuando Llegue la Noche, 1944, Play
Cuando Llegue la Noche 1946 d: Jeronimo MihurA. lps: Irasema Dilian, Julio Pena, Juana Manso. 109M SPN. *When the Night Comes*

Milagro En la Plaza Del Progreso, 1954, Play
Angel Tuvo la Culpa, Un 1959 d: Luis LuciA. lps: Emma Penella, Jose Luis Ozores, Amparo Rivelles. 111M SPN. *Blame It on an Angel*; *An Angel Was to Blame*

Una Muchachita de Valladolid, 1957, Play
Muchachita de Valladolid, Una 1958 d: Luis Cesar Amadori. lps: Alberto Closas, Analia Gade, Lina Rosales. 93M SPN.

La Muralla, 1955, Play
  Muralla, La 1958 d: Luis LuciA. lps: Armando Calvo, Irasema Dilian, Pepita Serrador. 96M SPN. *The Wall*

Operacion Embajada, 1962, Play
  Operacion Embajada 1964 d: Fernando Palacios. lps: Alberto Closas, Analia Gade, Jose Luis Lopez Vazquez. 89M SPN. *Operation Embassy*

Plaza de Oriente, 1947, Play
  Plaza de Oriente 1962 d: Mateo Cano. lps: Maria Luz Galicia, Luis Prendes, Carlos EstradA. 92M SPN.

La Visita Que No Toco El Timbre, 1951, Play
  Visita Que No Toco El Timbre, La 1964 d: Mario Camus. lps: Alberto Closas, Jose Luis Lopez Vazquez, Laura ValenzuelA. 92M SPN. *The Visitor Who Did Not Ring the Bell*; *La Visita Que No Llamo Al Timbre*

Viva Lo Imposible!, 1951, Play
  Viva Lo Imposible! 1957 d: Rafael Gil. lps: Paquita Rico, Manolo Moran, Jose Maria Rodero. 98M SPN. *Live the Impossible*; *Family Adventure*; *Let's Make the Impossible!*

CALZA-BINI, GINO
Mia Moglie Si E Fidanzata, 1914, Play
  Mia Moglie Si E Fidanzata 1921 d: Gero Zambuto. lps: Leda Gys, Carlo Reiter, Gian Paolo Rosmino. 1552m ITL. prod/rel: Lombardo Film

CAMARGO, JORACY
O Bobo Do Rei, 1932, Play
  Bobo Do Rei, O 1936 d: MesquitinhA. 92M BRZ. *The King's Jester*

Deus Lhe Pague, 193-, Play
  Dios Lhe Pague 1947 d: Luis Cesar Amadori. lps: Arturo de Cordova, Zully Moreno, Enrice Chaico. 103M ARG. *God Will Pay You*

CAMASIO, SANDRO
Addio Giovinezza, 1911, Play
  Addio Giovinezza! 1913 d: Sandro Camasio. lps: Alessandro Bernard, Lydia Quaranta, Amerigo Manzini. 1012m ITL. prod/rel: Itala Film
  Addio Giovinezza 1918 d: Augusto GeninA. lps: Maria Jacobini, Lido Manetti, Helena MakowskA. 2038m ITL. prod/rel: Itala Film
  Addio Giovinezza 1927 d: Augusto GeninA. lps: Carmen Boni, Walter Slezak, Elena Sangro. 2352m ITL. prod/rel: S.A. Pittaluga
  Addio, Giovinezza! 1940 d: Ferdinando M. Poggioli. lps: Maria Denis, Adriano Rimoldi, Carlo Campanini. 88M ITL. prod/rel: I.C.I., S.a.F.I.C.

I Tre Sentimentali, 1918, Play
  Tre Sentimentali, I 1921 d: Augusto GeninA. lps: Lydia Quaranta, Angelo Ferrari, Carlo Tedeschi. 1791m ITL. prod/rel: U.C.I., Photodrama

La Zingara, 1909, Play
  Zingara, La 1912 d: Sandro Camasio. lps: Adriana Costamagna, Maria Jacobini, Wanda Hejmann. 620m ITL. prod/rel: Savoia Film

CAMBON, RENE
Combat de Negres, Novel
  Train d'Enfer 1965 d: Gilles Grangier. lps: Jean Marais, Marisa Mell, Howard Vernon. 92M FRN/SPN/ITL. *Danger Dimensione Morte* (ITL); *Trampa Bajo El Sol* (SPN); *Operation Double Cross* prod/rel: Marceau-Cocinor, Ceres Films

Le Fou du Labo 4, Novel
  Fou du Labo 4, Le 1967 d: Jacques Besnard. lps: Jean Lefebvre, Bernard Blier, Pierre Brasseur. 90M FRN. *The Madman of Lab 4* prod/rel: Gaumont International

CAMERON, ANNE
Green Dice, 1926, Short Story
  Mr. Skitch 1933 d: James Cruze. lps: Will Rogers, Rochelle Hudson, Zasu Pitts. 70M USA. *Green Dice*; *There's Always Tomorrow* prod/rel: Fox Film Corp.©

CAMERON, GEORGE
Agnes, New York 1908, Play
  Million Bid, A 1914 d: Ralph Ince. lps: Anita Stewart, Julia Swayne Gordon, Charles Kent. 4-5r USA. prod/rel: Vitagraph Co. of America©, Broadway Star Features
  Million Bid, A 1927 d: Michael Curtiz. lps: Dolores Costello, Warner Oland, Malcolm McGregor. 6310f USA. prod/rel: Warner Brothers Pictures

CAMERON, IAN
The Island at the Top of the World, Novel
  Island at the Top of the World, The 1974 d: Robert Stevenson. lps: David Hartman, Donald Sinden, Jacques Marin. 94M USA. prod/rel: Walt Disney

CAMERON, LADY MARY
Often a Bridegroom, Short Story
  Many Happy Returns 1934 d: Norman Z. McLeod. lps: George Burns, Gracie Allen, Joan Marsh. 65M USA. prod/rel: Paramount Productions©

CAMILLE, L.
Alsace, Play
  Alsace 1916 d: Henri Pouctal. lps: Dieudonne, Barbier, Camille Bardou. 1650m FRN. prod/rel: le Film d'Art

CAMMARANO, SALVATORE
Lucia Di Lammermoor, 1835, Opera
  Lucia Di Lammermoor 1948 d: Piero Ballerini. lps: Nelly Corradi, Loretta Di Lelio, Italo Tajo. 92M ITL. prod/rel: Opera Film

CAMOLETTI, LUIGI
Suor Teresa, Play
  Grande Rinuncia, La 1951 d: Aldo Vergano. lps: Lea Padovani, Luigi Tosi, Vanda Carr. 90M ITL. *Suor Teresa* prod/rel: C.M. Produzione Film

CAMOLETTI, MARC
Boeing-Boeing, 1960, Play
  Boeing Boeing 1965 d: John Rich. lps: Tony Curtis, Jerry Lewis, Dany Saval. 102M USA. prod/rel: Hal Wallis, Paramount

La Difficulte d'Etre Infidele, Play
  Difficulte d'Etre Infidele, La 1963 d: Bernard Toublanc-Michel. lps: Gisele Hauchecorne, Bernard Tiphaine, Dany Boy. 108M FRN/ITL. *I Piaceri Coniugali* (ITL) prod/rel: la Pleiade, Cocinor-Marceau

CAMP, WADSWORTH, Camp, Charles Wadsworth
The Abandoned Room, New York 1917, Novel
  Love Without Question 1920 d: B. A. Rolfe. lps: Olive Tell, James Morrison, Peggy Parr. 6-7r USA. prod/rel: Jans Pictures, Inc.©, State Rights

The Black Cap, 1920, Short Story
  Daughter of the Law, A 1921 d: Jack Conway. lps: Carmel Myers, Jack O'Brien, Fred Kohler. 4752f USA. prod/rel: Universal Film Mfg. Co.

The Gray Mask, 1915, Short Story
  Gray Mask, The 1915 d: Frank H. Crane. lps: Edwin Arden, Barbara Tennant, Johnny Hines. 5r USA. *The Grey Mask* prod/rel: Shubert Film Corp., World Film Corp.©

Hate, Short Story
  Hate 1922 d: Maxwell Karger. lps: Alice Lake, Conrad Nagel, Harry Northrup. 5500f USA. prod/rel: Metro Pictures

The House of Fear, New York 1916, Novel
  House of Fear, The 1939 d: Joe May. lps: William Gargan, Irene Hervey, Dorothy Arnold. 67M USA. prod/rel: Crime Club Productions, Universal Pictures Co.©

The Signal Tower, 1920, Short Story
  Signal Tower, The 1924 d: Clarence Brown. lps: Virginia Valli, Rockliffe Fellowes, Frankie Darro. 6714f USA. prod/rel: Universal Pictures

CAMP, WILLIAM
Idol on Parade, Novel
  Idol on Parade 1959 d: John Gilling. lps: William Bendix, Anne Aubrey, Anthony Newley. 92M UKN. prod/rel: Columbia, Warwick

CAMPANA, DOMENICO
Novel
  Stanza Dello Scirocco, La 1998 d: Maurizio SciarrA. lps: Giancarlo Giannini, Tiziana Lodato, Francesco Benigno. 93M ITL. *Scirocco* prod/rel: Fandango

CAMPANELLA, ROY
It's Good to Be Alive, Book
  It's Good to Be Alive 1974 d: Michael Landon. lps: Paul Winfield, Louis Gossett Jr., Ruby Dee. TVM. 100M USA. prod/rel: Metromedia Productions

CAMPAUX, FRANCOIS
Story
  Blue Veil, The 1951 d: Curtis Bernhardt. lps: Jane Wyman, Charles Laughton, Joan Blondell. 113M USA. prod/rel: RKO Radio, Wald-Krasna Prod.

Cherie Noire, Play
  Tesoro Mio 1979 d: Giulio Paradisi. lps: Johnny Dorelli, Sandra Milo, Renato Pozzetto. 108M ITL. *My Darling*; *My Dearest Treasure*; *Tesoromio* prod/rel: Vides Cin.Ca, Cineriz

CAMPBELL, ALAN
The Dust of Egypt, London 1912, Play
  Dust of Egypt, The 1915 d: George D. Baker. lps: Antonio Moreno, Edith Storey, Hughie MacK. 6r USA. prod/rel: Vitagraph Co. of America©, Blue Ribbon Feature

CAMPBELL, ALICE
Juggernaut, Novel
  Juggernaut 1936 d: Henry Edwards. lps: Boris Karloff, Mona Goya, Arthur Margetson. 74M UKN. *The Demon Doctor* prod/rel: Jh Productions, Wardour
  Temptress, The 1949 d: Oswald Mitchell. lps: Joan Maude, Arnold Bell, Don Stannard. 85M UKN. prod/rel: Bushey, Ambassador

---

CAMPBELL, ARGYLE
Spring 3100, New York 1928, Play
  Jealousy 1934 d: R. William Neill. lps: Nancy Carroll, George Murphy, Donald Cook. 68M USA. *Spring Three Thousand One Hundred*; *Spring 3100* prod/rel: Columbia Pictures Corp. of California©

CAMPBELL, BARTLEY
Fairfax, New York 1879, Play
  Crucible of Life, The 1918 d: Harry Lambart. lps: Grace Darmond, Frank O'Connor, Jack Sherrill. 7r USA. prod/rel: Authors Film Co., State Rights

The Galley Slave, New York 1879, Play
  Galley Slave, The 1915 d: J. Gordon Edwards. lps: Theda Bara, Stuart Holmes, Claire Whitney. 5r USA. prod/rel: Fox Film Corp., William Fox©

My Partner, New York 1879, Play
  My Partner 1916 d: Mr. Sanger. lps: Burr McIntosh, Mary Mantell, James Ryan. 5r USA. prod/rel: Gaumont Co., Mutual Film Corp.

Siberia, New York 1911, Play
  Siberia 1926 d: Victor Schertzinger. lps: Alma Rubens, Edmund Lowe, Lou Tellegen. 6950f USA. prod/rel: Fox Film Corp.

The White Slave, Play
  White Slave, The 1913. lps: Clara Kimball Young, Lillian Walker, Earle Williams. 2000f USA. prod/rel: Vitagraph Co. of America

CAMPBELL, EVELYN
Short Story
  Masked Angel 1928 d: Frank O'Connor. lps: Betty Compson, Erick Arnold, Wheeler Oakman. 5632f USA. *Her Love Cottage* (UKN) prod/rel: Chadwick Pictures, First Division Distributors

Barter, 1917, Novel
  Soul for Sale, A 1918 d: Allen Holubar. lps: Dorothy Phillips, Alan Roscoe, Catherine Kirkwood. 5586f USA. prod/rel: Universal Film Mfg. Co., Bluebird Photoplays, Inc.

Empty Hearts, 1924, Short Story
  Empty Hearts 1924 d: Alfred Santell. lps: John Bowers, Charlie Murray, John Miljan. 6r USA. prod/rel: Banner Productions

A Harp in Hock, Story
  Harp in Hock, A 1927 d: Renaud Hoffman. lps: Rudolf Schildkraut, Junior Coghlan, May Robson. 5996f USA. *The Samaritan* prod/rel: de Mille Pictures, Pathe Exchange, Inc.

Nobody's Bride, Novel
  Which Woman? 1918 d: Tod Browning, Harry Pollard. lps: Ella Hall, Priscilla Dean, Eddie Sutherland. 5r USA. *Woman Against Woman*; *Nobody's Bride* prod/rel: Bluebird Photoplays, Inc.©

Splurge, 1924, Short Story
  Early to Wed 1926 d: Frank Borzage. lps: Matt Moore, Kathryn Perry, Albert Gran. 5912f USA. prod/rel: Fox Film Corp.

Yesterday's Wife, 1920, Short Story
  Yesterday's Wife 1923 d: Edward J. Le Saint. lps: Irene Rich, Eileen Percy, Lottie Williams. 5800f USA. prod/rel: Columbia Pictures, C. B. C. Film Sales

CAMPBELL, GEORGE
Cry for Happy, New York 1958, Novel
  Cry for Happy 1961 d: George Marshall. lps: Glenn Ford, Donald O'Connor, Miiko TakA. 110M USA. prod/rel: William Goetz, Columbia Pictures Corp.

CAMPBELL, HELEN
Wilderness, Story
  Love's Wilderness 1924 d: Robert Z. Leonard. lps: Corinne Griffith, Holmes Herbert, Ian Keith. 7037f USA. *Wilderness* prod/rel: Corinne Griffith Productions, First National Pictures

CAMPBELL, JAMES A.
The Little Breadwinner, Play
  Little Breadwinner, The 1916 d: Wilfred Noy. lps: Kitty Atfield, Maureen O'HarA. 4875f UKN. prod/rel: Clarendon

The Queen Mother, Play
  Queen Mother, The 1916 d: Wilfred Noy. lps: Owen Roughwood, Gladys Mason, Barbara Rutland. 4500f UKN. prod/rel: Clarendon

CAMPBELL, PHYLLIS
The White Hen, Novel
  White Hen, The 1921 d: Frank Richardson. lps: Mary Glynne, Leslie Faber, Pat Somerset. 5000f UKN. prod/rel: Zodiac, Walker

CAMPBELL, R. WRIGHT
Where Pigeons Go to Die, Book
  Where Pigeons Go to Die 1990 d: Michael Landon. lps: Michael Landon, Art Carney, Robert Hy Gorman. TVM. 100M USA.

CAMPBELL, REGINALD
Tiger Valley, New York 1931, Novel
Girl from Mandalay, The 1936 d: Howard Bretherton. lps: Esther Ralston, Donald Cook, Conrad Nagel. 68M USA. prod/rel: Republic Pictures Corp.©

CAMPBELL, SCOTT
Below the Deadline, Short Story
Banker's Double, The 1915 d: Langdon West. lps: Robert Conness, Bigelow Cooper. SHT USA. prod/rel: Edison
Case of the Vanished Bonds, The 1914 d: Langdon West. lps: Robert Conness, Yale Boss. SHT USA. prod/rel: Edison
The Under Secretary, Story
Unpaid Ransom, An 1915. lps: Augustus Phillips, Bessie Learn, Carlton King. SHT USA. prod/rel: Edison

CAMPBELL, SIR MALCOLM
Salute to the Gods, New York 1935, Novel
Burn 'Em Up O'Connor 1938 d: Edward Sedgwick. lps: Dennis O'Keefe, Cecilia Parker, Harry Carey. 70M USA. *Skids* prod/rel: Metro-Goldwyn-Mayer Corp.

CAMPION, CYRIL
The Admiral's Secret, 1928, Play
Admiral's Secret, The 1934 d: Guy Newall. lps: Edmund Gwenn, Hope Davy, James Raglan. 63M UKN. prod/rel: Real Art, Radio
Ask Beccles, London 1926, Play
Ask Beccles 1933 d: Redd Davis. lps: Garry Marsh, Mary Newland, Abraham Sofaer. 68M UKN. prod/rel: British and Dominions, Paramount British
The Lash, London 1926, Play
Lash, The 1934 d: Henry Edwards. lps: Lyn Harding, John Mills, Joan Maude. 63M UKN. prod/rel: Real Art, Radio
The Masqueraders, Play
Four Masked Men 1934 d: George Pearson. lps: John Stuart, Judy Kelly, Miles Mander. 81M UKN. *Behind the Masks* prod/rel: Real Art, Universal
The Sentence of Death, Play
Sentence of Death, The 1927 d: Miles Mander. lps: Owen Nares, Dorothy Boyd, Peter Evan Thomas. SND. 9M UKN. *His Great Moment* prod/rel: de Forest Phonofilms
A Touch of the Moon, Play
Touch of the Moon, A 1936 d: MacLean Rogers. lps: John Garrick, Dorothy Boyd, Joyce Bland. 67M UKN. prod/rel: GS Enterprises, Radio
Trust Berkely, London 1933, Play
Adventure Limited 1934 d: George King. lps: Harry Milton, Pearl Argyle, Sebastian Shaw. 69M UKN. prod/rel: British and Dominions, Paramount British
Watch Beverly, 1930, Play
Watch Beverly 1932 d: Arthur Maude. lps: Henry Kendall, Dorothy Bartlam, Francis X. Bushman. 80M UKN. *Watch Beverley* prod/rel: Sound City, Butcher's Film Service

CAMPION, NARDI REEDER
Bringing Up the Brass, 1951, Book
Long Gray Line, The 1955 d: John Ford. lps: Tyrone Power, Maureen O'Hara, Robert Francis. 138M USA. prod/rel: Columbia, Rotha Prods.

CAMPO, ROSSANA
In Principio Erano le Mutande, Novel
In Principio Erano le Mutande 1999 d: Anna Negri. lps: Teresa Saponangelo, Stefania Rocca, Bebo Storti. 92M ITL. *In the Beginning There Was Underwear* prod/rel: Medusa Film, Mastrofilm

CAMUS, ALBERT (1913–1960), ALG
La Chute, 1956, Novel
Val, de 1974 d: Adriaan Ditvoorst. lps: Peter Oosthoek, Jules Hamel, Henny AlmA. 30M NTH. *The Fall*
L' Etranger, Paris 1942, Novel
Straniero, Lo 1967 d: Luchino Visconti. lps: Marcello Mastroianni, Anna Karina, Georges Wilson. 104M ITL/FRN/ALG. *L' Etranger* (FRN); *The Stranger* (USA); *The Outsider* prod/rel: Dino de Laurentiis Cin.Ca, Master Film (Roma)
Les Muets, 1957, Short Story
Parole a Venire, Le 1970 d: Peter Del Monte. lps: Natalino Longo, Mario Cellupica, Ennio Di Stefano. MTV. 54M ITL. prod/rel: Rai-Tv
La Peste, Paris 1947, Novel
Peste, La 1991 d: Luis Puenzo. lps: William Hurt, Sandrine Bonnaire, Jean-Marc Barr. 140M FRN/ARG/UKN. *The Plague* (UKN) prod/rel: Cyril de Rouvre, the Pepper Prince Company

CANFIELD, DOROTHY
The Eternal Masculine, Short Story
Two Heads on a Pillow 1934 d: William Nigh. lps: Miriam Jordan, Hardie Albright, Lona Andre. 71M USA. *Love Can't Wait* prod/rel: Liberty Pictures Corp.©

The Home-Maker, New York 1924, Novel
Home Maker, The 1925 d: King Baggot. lps: Alice Joyce, Clive Brook, Billy Kent Schaeffer. 7755f USA. prod/rel: Universal Pictures

CANFIELD, MARK
Beware of Bachelors, Short Story
Beware of Bachelors 1928 d: Roy Del Ruth. lps: Audrey Ferris, William Collier Jr., Clyde Cook. 5778f USA. *No Questions Asked* prod/rel: Warner Brothers Pictures

CANKAR, IVAN
Martin Kacur, 1906, Novel
Idealist 1976 d: Igor Pretnar. lps: Radko Polic, Milena Zupancic, Dare UlagA. 121M YGS. *The Idealist*
Na Klancu, 1902, Novel
Na Klancu 1971 d: Vojko Duletic. lps: Stefka Drolc, Janez Bermez, Ivan Jezernik. 100M YGS. *In the Gorge; At the Ravine*

CANNAN, DENIS
Us, Play
Benefit of the Doubt 1967 d: Peter Whitehead. lps: Eric Allan, Mary Allen, Hugh Armstrong. 70M UKN. *Us* prod/rel: Lorrimer, Saga
Tell Me Lies 1968 d: Peter Brook. lps: Mark Jones, Pauline Munro, Eric Allan. 116M UKN. *Make and Break* prod/rel: London Continental, Ronorus

CANNING, VICTOR (1911–, UKN
Castle Minerva, London 1955, Novel
Masquerade 1964 d: Basil Dearden. lps: Cliff Robertson, Jack Hawkins, Marisa Mell. 102M UKN. *Operation Masquerade; The Shabby Tiger* prod/rel: Novus Films, United Artists
Chance at the Wheel, Short Story
Man on the Beach, A 1956 d: Joseph Losey. lps: Donald Wolfit, Michael Medwin, Michael Ripper. 29M UKN. prod/rel: Hammer, Exclusive
Family Plot, Novel
Family Plot 1976 d: Alfred Hitchcock. lps: Bruce Dern, Karen Black, Barbara Harris. 121M USA. prod/rel: Universal Pictures
Golden Salamander, Novel
Golden Salamander, The 1950 d: Ronald Neame. lps: Trevor Howard, Anouk Aimee, Herbert Lom. 87M UKN. prod/rel: General Film Distributors, Pinewood
His Bones are Coral, London 1955, Novel
Shark! 1969 d: Samuel Fuller, Rafael Portillo. lps: Burt Reynolds, Barry Sullivan, Arthur Kennedy. 92M USA/MXC. *Un Arma de Dos Filos* (MXC); *Maneater; Caine* prod/rel: Heritage Enterprises, Cinematografica Calderon
The House of the Seven Flies, Novel
House of the Seven Hawks, The 1959 d: Richard Thorpe. lps: Robert Taylor, Nicole Maurey, Linda Christian. 92M UKN/USA. prod/rel: MGM, Coronado
The Limbo Line, Novel
Limbo Line, The 1968 d: Samuel Gallu. lps: Craig Stevens, Kate O'Mara, Vladek Sheybal. 99M UKN. prod/rel: London Independent Producers, Trio-Group W
Panther's Moon, 1948, Novel
Spy Hunt 1950 d: George Sherman. lps: Howard Duff, Marta Toren, Philip Friend. 75M USA. *Panther's Moon* (UKN); *Spy Ring* prod/rel: Universal-International
The Runaways, Novel
Runaways, The 1975 d: Harry Harris. lps: Dorothy McGuire, Van Williams, John Randolph. TVM. 78M USA. prod/rel: Lorimar Productions
The Scorpio Letters, Novel
Scorpio Letters, The 1968 d: Richard Thorpe. lps: Alex Cord, Shirley Eaton, Laurence Naismith. TVM. 98M USA. prod/rel: MGM
Venetian Bird, Novel
Venetian Bird 1952 d: Ralph Thomas. lps: Richard Todd, Eva Bartok, John Gregson. 95M UKN. *The Assassin* (USA) prod/rel: General Film Distributors, British Film Makers

CANNON, NORMAN
Spendlove Hall, Play
Annie, Leave the Room! 1935 d: Leslie Hiscott. lps: Eva Moore, Morton Selten, Jane Carr. 76M UKN. prod/rel: Twickenham, Universal

CANNON, RAYMOND
Loco Weed, Story
Broncho Buster, The 1927 d: Ernst Laemmle. lps: Fred Humes, Gloria Grey, George Connors. 4687f USA. prod/rel: Universal Pictures

CANTINI, ARTURO
Turbamento, Play
Turbamento 1942 d: Guido Brignone. lps: Renzo Ricci, Mariella Lotti, Luisella Beghi. 86M ITL. prod/rel: E.I.a.

CANTINI, GUIDO
E Tornato Carnevale, Play
E Tornato Carnevale 1937 d: Raffaello Matarazzo. lps: Armando Falconi, Clara Tabody, Hilda Springher. 87M ITL. prod/rel: Tiberia Films, S.a.N.G.R.a.F.
Ho Sognato Il Paradiso, Play
Ho Sognato Il Paradiso 1950 d: Giorgio PastinA. lps: Geraldine Brooks, Vittorio Gassman, Franca Marzi. 95M ITL. *Streets of Sorrow* (USA) prod/rel: Itala Film, Artisti Associati
La Signora Paradiso, Play
Signora Paradiso, La 1934 d: Enrico Guazzoni. lps: Memo Benassi, Elsa de Giorgi, Mino Doro. 75M ITL. prod/rel: Tirrenia Film
L' Uomo Del Romanzo, Play
Uomo Del Romanzo, L' 1941 d: Mario Bonnard. lps: Conchita Montenegro, Amedeo Nazzari, Carla Candiani. 70M ITL. prod/rel: Produzione Associata Sovrania, I.C.A.R.

CANTOR, ELI
The Nest, Novel
Nest, The 1988 d: Terence H. Winkless. lps: Robert Lansing, Lisa Langlois, Franc Luz. 88M USA. prod/rel: Concorde

CANTU, CESARE
Margherita Pusterla, 1838, Novel
Margherita Pusterla 1910 d: Mario Caserini. 324m ITL. prod/rel: Cines

CANUDO
L' Autre Aile, Novel
Autre Aile, L' 1924 d: Henri Andreani. lps: Jean Murat, Marthe Ferrare, Mary Harald. 2068m FRN. prod/rel: Dal-Film

CANWAY, W. H.
Sammy Going South, London 1961, Novel
Sammy Going South 1963 d: Alexander MacKendrick. lps: Edward G. Robinson, Constance Cummings, Harry H. Corbett. 128M UKN. *A Boy Ten Feet Tall* (USA); *A Boy Is Ten Feet Tall* prod/rel: Bryanston, Seven Arts

CAO ZHAN, Cao Xueqin
Hong Lou Meng, c1750-92, Novel
Hong Lou Er You 1951 d: Yang XIao-Zhong. lps: Yan Huizhu, Lin Muyu, Jin Chuan. 12r CHN. *The Two You Sisters in the Red Mansion* prod/rel: Guotai Film Studio
Hong Lou Meng 1962 d: Chen Fan. 169M CHN. *Dream of the Red Chamber*
Hong Lou Meng 1988-89 d: XIe Tieli. lps: XIa Qin, Tao Huiming, Fu Yiwei. 480M CHN. *Dreams of the Red Chamber; A Dream of Red Mansions* prod/rel: Beijing Film Studio
Wang XIfeng Danao Ning-Kuofu 1939 d: Yueh Feng. 90M CHN.; *Lady Wang XIfeng Makes Trouble in the Mansion House*
You San Jie 1963 d: Wu Yong-Gang. 129M CHN. *The Third Lady You*

CAPEK, KAREL (1890–1938), CZC
Bila Nemoc, 1937, Play
Bila Nemoc 1937 d: Hugo Haas. lps: Hugo Haas, Bedrich Karen, Karla OlicovA. 78M CZC. *Skeleton on Horseback; The White Illness; The White Disease; The White Sickness* prod/rel: Moldavia
Hordubal, 1933, Novel
Hordubal 1937 d: Martin Fric. lps: Jaroslav Vojta, Palo Bielik, Suzanne Marwille. 2695m CZC. *The Hordubal Brothers; The Hordubals* prod/rel: Lloyd
Krakatit, 1924, Novel
Krakatit 1948 d: Otakar VavrA. lps: Karel Hoger, Florence Marly. 110M CZC.
Temne Slunce 1980 d: Otakar VavrA. lps: Radoslav Brzobohaty, Magda Vasaryova, Rudolf Hrusinsky. 135M CZC. *Krakatit; Dark Sun; Cerne Slunce; Black Sun* prod/rel: Filmove Studio Barrandov
Loupeznik, Play
Loupeznik 1931 d: Josef Kodicek. lps: Theodor Pistek, Marta Majova, Marta TrojanovA. 2411m CZC. *The Brigand; The Robber* prod/rel: Ab Vinohrady
Prvni Parta, 1937, Novel
Prvni Parta 1959 d: Otakar VavrA. lps: Eduard Cupak, Marie Tomasova, Jaroslav VojtA. 95M CZC. *The First Rescue Party*

CAPEK-CHOD, KAREL MATEJ
Experiment, Novel
Experiment 1943 d: Martin Fric. lps: Zdenek Stepanek, Vlasta Matulova, Vitezslav VejrazkA. 2652m CZC. prod/rel: Nationalfilm
Humoreska, Novel
Humoreska 1939 d: Otakar VavrA. lps: Rudolf Hrusinsky, Jaroslav Prucha, Vladimir Salac. 2453m CZC. *Humoresque; Humorous Sketch* prod/rel: Lucernafilm

Turbina, Novel
Turbina 1941 d: Otakar VavrA. lps: Frantisek Smolik, Lida Baarova, Vlasta MatulovA. 2808m CZC. *The Turbine* prod/rel: Slavia-Film

CAPELLUPO, MICHAEL
Aaron Gillespie Will Make You a Star, Play
Aaron Gillespie Will Make You a Star 1996 d: Massimo Mazzucco. lps: Scott Caan, Holly Gagnier, Scott Trust. 94M USA. prod/rel: Maga

CAPETANOS, LEON
Novel
My Palikari 1982 d: Dezso Magyar, Charles S. Dubin. lps: Telly Savalas, Keith Gordon, Dora Volonaki. TVM. 90M USA. *Silent Rebellion; Big Shot*

CAPITE, DON
A Lost King, Novel
Harry and Son 1983 d: Paul Newman. lps: Paul Newman, Robby Benson, Ellen Barkin. 118M USA. *Harry & Son* prod/rel: Orion

CAPO, GIAN
Nina Non Far la Stupida, Play
Nina, Non Far la Stupida 1937 d: Nunzio MalasommA. lps: Assia Noris, Nino Besozzi, Vanna Vanni. 76M ITL. prod/rel: S.P.E.C.I.

CAPON, PAUL
Murder at Shinglestrand, Novel
Hidden Homicide 1959 d: Tony Young. lps: Griffith Jones, James Kenney, Patricia Laffan. 72M UKN. prod/rel: Rank Film Distributors, Bill & Michael Luckwell

CAPOTE, TRUMAN (1924–1984), USA
Among the Paths to Eden, 1960, Short Story
Trilogy 1969 d: Frank Perry. lps: Mildred Natwick, Susan Dunfee, Carol Gustafson. TVM. 110M USA. *Truman Capote's Trilogy* prod/rel: American Broadcasting Co., Xerox Corporation
Breakfast at Tiffany's, New York 1958, Novel
Breakfast at Tiffany's 1961 d: Blake Edwards. lps: Audrey Hepburn, George Peppard, Patricia Neal. 115M USA. prod/rel: Paramount
A Christmas Memory, 1946, Short Story
Trilogy 1969 d: Frank Perry. lps: Mildred Natwick, Susan Dunfee, Carol Gustafson. TVM. 110M USA. *Truman Capote's Trilogy* prod/rel: American Broadcasting Co., Xerox Corporation
The Glass House, Story
Glass House, The 1972 d: Tom Gries. lps: Vic Morrow, Alan Alda, Clu Gulager. TVM. 73M USA. *Truman Capote's the Glass House* prod/rel: CBS, Tomorrow Entertainment
The Grass Harp, 1951, Novel
Grass Harp, The 1995 d: Charles Matthau. lps: Piper Laurie, Sissy Spacek, Walter Matthau. 107M USA. prod/rel: Grass Harp Productions, Fine Line Features
In Cold Blood, New York 1966, Book
In Cold Blood 1967 d: Richard Brooks. lps: Robert Blake, Scott Wilson, John Forsythe. 134M USA. prod/rel: Pax Enterprises
In Cold Blood 1996 d: Jonathan Kaplan. lps: Anthony Edwards, Eric Roberts, Sam Neill. TVM. 240M USA. prod/rel: Pacific Motion Pictures, Hallmark Entertainment
Miriam, 1944, Short Story
Trilogy 1969 d: Frank Perry. lps: Mildred Natwick, Susan Dunfee, Carol Gustafson. TVM. 110M USA. *Truman Capote's Trilogy* prod/rel: American Broadcasting Co., Xerox Corporation

CAPRANICA, LUIGI
Giovanni Dalle Bande Nero, Novel
Giovanni Dalle Bande Nere 1957 d: Sergio Grieco. lps: Vittorio Gassman, Anna Maria Ferrero, Constance Smith. 85M ITL. *Jean Des Bandes Noires* (FRN); *The Violent Patriot* prod/rel: P.O. Film

CAPRIOLI, GINO
Una Lampada Alla Finestra, Play
Lampada Alla Finestra, Una 1940 d: Gino Talamo. lps: Ruggero Ruggeri, Laura Solari, Luigi Almirante. 84M ITL. prod/rel: Europa Film

CAPUANA, LUIGI (1839–1915), ITL
Short Story
Malia 1946 d: Giuseppe Amato. lps: Anna Proclemer, Maria Denis, Rossano Brazzi. 98M ITL. prod/rel: Titanus, G. Amato
Cardello, Short Story
Girovaghi, I 1956 d: Hugo Fregonese. lps: Peter Ustinov, Carla Del Poggio, Abbe Lane. 88M ITL. *The Wanderers* prod/rel: Villani, Rossini
Lu Cavalieri Pidagna, 1909, Play
Cavalier Petagna, Il 1926 d: Mario Gargiulo. lps: Giovanni Grasso Sr., Soava Gallone, Gustavo SerenA. 1599m ITL. prod/rel: Pittaluga

Zaganella E Il Cavaliere 1932 d: Gustavo Serena, Giorgio Mannini. lps: Arturo Falconi, Marcella Albani, Carlo Lombardi. 80M ITL. prod/rel: Caesar Film
Lu Paraninfu, Play
Paraninfo, Il 1934 d: Amleto Palermi. lps: Angelo Musco, Enrica Fantis, Rosina Anselmi. 80M ITL. *The Matchmaker* (USA) prod/rel: Ventura Film, Artisti Associati
Malia, 1895, Play
Malia 1912. lps: Enna Saredo, Augusto Mastripietri, Mariano Bottino. 1071m ITL. *Witchcraft* (UKN) prod/rel: Cines
Il Marchese Di Roccaverdina, 1901, Novel
Gelosia 1943 d: Ferdinando M. Poggioli. lps: Luisa Ferida, Roldano Lupi, Elena Zareschi. 88M ITL. prod/rel: Cines, Universalcine
Gelosia 1953 d: Pietro Germi. lps: Marisa Belli, Erno Crisa, Liliana Gerace. 95M ITL. *Jealousy* prod/rel: Excelsa Film, Minerva Film

CAPUS, ALFRED
L' Aventurier, Play
Aventurier, L' 1916 d: Maurice Mariaud. lps: Louis Leubas, Louise Colliney, Jeanne Marie-Laurent. 950m FRN. prod/rel: Gaumont
Aventurier, L' 1924 d: Maurice Mariaud, Louis Osmont. lps: Jean Angelo, Jeanne Helbling, Monique Chryses. 1925m FRN. prod/rel: Les Films De France
Aventurier, L' 1934 d: Marcel L'Herbier. lps: Victor Francen, Blanche Montel, Alexandre Rignault. 92M FRN. prod/rel: Pathe-Nathan
La Chatelaine, Play
Chatelaine, La 1914 d: Louis Feuillade. lps: Armand Dutertre, Maurice Vinot, Marie Dorly. 1350m FRN. prod/rel: Gaumont
Leontines Ehemanner, Play
Leontines Ehemanner 1928 d: Robert Wiene. lps: Claire Rommer, Georg Alexander, Adele Sandrock. 2265m GRM. prod/rel: Max Glass-Film
Les Maris de Leontine, Play
Maris de Leontine, Les 1947 d: Rene Le Henaff. lps: Pierre Jourdan, Gil Roland, Robert Murzeau. 90M FRN. *T'en Souviens-Tu Mon Amour?* prod/rel: Berton Et Cie
L' Oiseau Blesse, Play
Oiseau Blesse, L' 1914 d: Leonce Perret?, Maurice Mariaud?. lps: Laurent Morlas, Luitz-Morat, Jeanne Marie-Laurent. 975m FRN. prod/rel: Gaumont
La Petite Fonctionnaire, Play
Petite Fonctionnaire, La 1912 d: Rene Leprince. lps: Emile Duard, Girier, Suzanne Goldstein. 745m FRN. prod/rel: Scagl
Petite Fonctionnaire, La 1926 d: Roger Goupillieres. lps: Andre Roanne, Yvette Armel, Pauline Carton. F FRN. prod/rel: Films De France, Societe Des Cineromans
La Veine, Play
Veine, La 1928 d: Rene Barberis. lps: Sandra Milowanoff, Rolla Norman, Paulette Berger. F FRN. prod/rel: Societe Des Cineromans

CARAGIALE, ION LUCA
Arenasul Roman, 1893, Short Story
Arendasul Roman 1952 d: Jean Georgescu. lps: Marcel Angelescu, Radu Beligan, Grigore Vasiliu-Birlic. 7M RMN. *The Romanian Farmer*
C.F.R., 1899-1909, Short Story
Mofturi 1900 1965 d: Jean Georgescu. lps: Iurie Darie, Geo Barton, Grigore Vasiliu-Birlic. 75M RMN. *Trifles 1900*
O Conferenta, 1899-1909, Short Story
Mofturi 1900 1965 d: Jean Georgescu. lps: Iurie Darie, Geo Barton, Grigore Vasiliu-Birlic. 75M RMN. *Trifles 1900*
Conul Leonida Fata Cu Reactiunea, 1880, Play
D-Ale Carnavalului 1958 d: Gheorghe Naghi, Aurel Miheles. lps: Grigore Vasiliu-Birlic, Alexandru Giugaru. 82M RMN. *Carnival Stories; Carnival Scenes*
D-Ale Carnavalului, 1885, Play
D-Ale Carnavalului 1958 d: Gheorghe Naghi, Aurel Miheles. lps: Grigore Vasiliu-Birlic, Alexandru Giugaru. 82M RMN. *Carnival Stories; Carnival Scenes*
De Ce Trag Clopotele, Mitica 1981 d: Lucian Pintilie. lps: Gheorghe Dinica, Tora Vasilescu, Stefan Iordache. 125M RMN. *Mitica? Why are the Bells Ringing; Carnival Stories; Mitica? Why Do the Bells Toll*
Diplomatie, 1899-1909, Short Story
Mofturi 1900 1965 d: Jean Georgescu. lps: Iurie Darie, Geo Barton, Grigore Vasiliu-Birlic. 75M RMN. *Trifles 1900*
Doua Loturi, 1901, Short Story
Doua Lozuri 1957 d: Gheorghe Naghi, Aurel Miheles. lps: Margareta Pogonat, Marcel Angelescu, Grigore Vasiliu-Birlic. 63M RMN. *Two Lottery Tickets*

O Faclie de Paste, 1890, Short Story
Furchte Dich Nicht, Jakob! 1981 d: Radu GabreA. lps: Andre Heller, Aviva Gaire, Dan Nutzu. 101M GRM/PRT. *Jacob! Have No Fear; Jacob! Don't Be Afraid* prod/rel: Galla, Neue-Telecontact
Leiba Zibal 1930 d: Alexandru Stefanescu, Ion BrunA. 56M RMN.
In Vreme de Razboi, 1898-99, Short Story
Inainte de Tacere 1979 d: Alexa Visarion. lps: Ion Caramitru, Valeria Seciu, Liviu RozoreA. 101M RMN. *Ahead of the Silence; Before Silence*
La Hanul Lui Minjoala, 1898, Short Story
Hanul Dintre Dealuri 1988 d: Cristiana Nicolae. lps: Dana Dogaru, Alexandru Repan, Forin Busuioc. 112M RMN. *The Inn Among the Hills; The Inn in the Hills*
Lantiu Slabiciunilor, 1901, Short Story
Lantul Slabiciunilor 1952 d: Jean Georgescu. lps: Marcel Angelescu, Radu Beligan, Grigore Vasiliu-Birlic. 8M RMN. *Chain of Weakness*
Napasta, 1890, Play
Napasta 1982 d: Alexa Visarion. 98M RMN.
O Noapte Furtunoasa, 1879, Play
Noapte Furtunoasa, O 1943 d: Jean Georgescu. lps: Stefan Baroi, Radu Beligan, George Demetru. 68M RMN. *Stormy Night*
O Scrisoare Pierduta, 1885, Play
Scrisoare Pierduta, O 1956 d: Victor Iliu, Sica Alexandrescu. lps: Marcel Angelescu, Radu Beligan, Ion Fintesteanu. 138M RMN. *A Lost Letter*
Telegrame, 1899, Short Story
Telegrame 1959 d: Gheorghe Naghi, Aurel Miheles. lps: Grigore Vasiliu-Birlic, Alexandru Giugaru, Stefan Ciubotarasu. 77M RMN. *Telegrams*
Vizita, 1901, Short Story
Vizita 1952 d: Jean Georgescu. lps: Marcel Angelescu, Radu Beligan, Grigor Vasilu-Birlic. 8M RMN. *A Visit*

CARB, DAVID
Long Ago Ladies, Boston 1934, Play
Chatterbox 1936 d: George Nicholls Jr. lps: Anne Shirley, Phillips Holmes, Edward Ellis. 68M USA. *Long Ago Ladies* prod/rel: RKO Radio Pictures, Inc.

CARBALLIDO, EMILIO
Las Visitaciones Del Diablo, 1965, Novel
Visitaciones Del Diablo, Las 1968 d: Alberto Isaac. lps: Ignacio Lopez Tarso, Gloria Marin, Enrique Lizalde. 95M MXC. *The Visitations of the Devil; The Devil's Visitations*

CARCATERRA, LORENZO
Sleepers, Book
Sleepers 1996 d: Barry Levinson. lps: Kevin Bacon, Robert de Niro, Dustin Hoffman. 147M USA. prod/rel: Warner Bros., Polygram Film Productions

CARCO, FRANCIS (1886–1958), FRN, Carcopino-Tusoli, Francois Marie
L' Homme Traque, 1922, Novel
Homme Traque, L' 1946 d: Robert Bibal. lps: Marcel Herrand, Louise Carletti, Antonin Berval. 100M FRN. prod/rel: Codo-Cinema
Les Innocents, Novel
Apachen von Paris, Die 1927 d: Nikolai Malikoff. lps: Ruth Weyher, Lia Eibenschutz, Jaque Catelain. 2661m GRM/FRN. *Paname N'est Pas Paris* (FRN); *Apaches of Paris* (USA); *Paname* prod/rel: a.C.E.
Jesus la Caille, 1914, Novel
M'sieur la Caille 1955 d: Andre Pergament. lps: Jeanne Moreau, Philippe Lemaire, Roger Pierre. 82M FRN. *Jesus la Caille; Monsieur la Caille; The Parasites* (UKN) prod/rel: S.P.I.C., Paris-Nice Productions
Mon Homme, Paris 1921, Play
Shadows of Paris 1924 d: Herbert Brenon. lps: Pola Negri, Charles de Roche, Huntley Gordon. 6549f USA. prod/rel: Famous Players-Lasky, Paramount Pictures
L' Ombre, 1933, Novel
Ombre, L' 1948 d: Andre Berthomieu. lps: Fernand Ledoux, Pierre Louis, Renee Faure. 100M FRN. prod/rel: M.A.I.C., U.G.C.
Prisons de Femmes, 1930, Novel
Prisons de Femmes 1938 d: Roger Richebe. lps: Viviane Romance, Renee Saint-Cyr, Francis Carco. 94M FRN. prod/rel: Societe Des Films Roger Richebe
Prisons de Femmes 1958 d: Maurice Cloche. lps: Daniele Delorme, Jacques Duby, Vega Vinci. 100M FRN. prod/rel: Comptoir Francais De Prod. Cinematograph
Tva Kvinnor 1947 d: Arnold Sjostrand. lps: Eva Dahlbeck, Cecile Ossbahr, Gunnar Bjornstrand. 96M SWD. *Two Women*

CARDINAL, MARIE
La Cle Sur la Porte, Novel
Cle Sur la Porte, La 1978 d: Yves Boisset. lps: Annie Girardot, Patrick Dewaere, Stephane Jobert. 102M FRN. prod/rel: Cineproductions, S.F.P.

Les Mots Pour le Dire, Novel
Mots Pour le Dire, Les 1983 d: Jose Pinheiro. lps: Nicole Garcia, Marie-Christine Barrault, Daniel Mesguich. 92M FRN. *Words to Say It* prod/rel: Stephan Films, Filmedis

CARDOSO, LUCIO
Cronica Da Casa Assassinada, 1959, Novel
Casa Assassinada, A 1971 d: Paulo Cesar Saraceni. lps: Norma Bengell, Carlos Kroeber, Nelson Dantas. 103M BRZ. *Murder Case*

O Desconhecido, 1940, Short Story
Desconhecido, O 1980 d: Ruy Santos. lps: Luiz Linhares, Isolda Cresta, Sonia OiticicA. 85M BRZ. *O Desconhecido Delmiro Gouveia; The Unknown*

Maos Vazias, 1938, Short Story
Maos Vazias 1971 d: Luiz Carlos LacerdA. 90M BRZ.

CARE, HARRY
The Sob Sister, Story
Sob Sister, The 1914 d: Otis Turner. lps: Anna Little, Herbert Rawlinson, Frank Lloyd. 2r USA. prod/rel: Rex

CARETTE, LOUIS
Concierto Barroco, 1974, Novel
Barroco 1988 d: Paul Leduc. lps: Angela Molina, Francisco Rabal, Roberto SosA. 108M MXC.

CAREY, ERNESTINE G. (1908–, USA, Carey, Ernestine Moller Gilbreth)
Belles on Their Toes, Book
Belles on Their Toes 1952 d: Henry Levin. lps: Myrna Loy, Jeanne Crain, Edward Arnold. 89M USA. prod/rel: 20th Century-Fox

Cheaper By the Dozen, Book
Cheaper By the Dozen 1950 d: Walter Lang. lps: Clifton Webb, Myrna Loy, Jeanne Crain. 85M USA. prod/rel: 20th Century-Fox

CAREY, GABRIELLE
Puberty Blues, Novel
Puberty Blues 1982 d: Bruce Beresford. lps: Nell Schofield, Jad Capelja, Geoff Rhoe. 87M ASL. prod/rel: Limelight Productions Pty Ltd.©, Australian Film Commission

CAREY, HENRY (1687?–1743), UKN
Sally in Our Alley, c1715, Song
Sally in Our Alley 1913 d: Colin Campbell. lps: Wheeler Oakman, Thomas Santschi, Bessie Eyton. 1000f USA. prod/rel: Selig Polyscope Co.

Sally in Our Alley 1916 d: Travers Vale. lps: Carlyle Blackwell, Muriel Ostriche, Patrick Foy. 5r USA. *Mollie O' Pigtail Alley* prod/rel: Peerless Features Producing Co., World Film Corp.©

CAREY, PETER
Short Story
Vom Anderen Stern 1982 d: Petra Haffter. lps: Julia Lindig, Claude Oliver Rudolph, Volker Spengler. 80M GRM. *From Another Planet* prod/rel: C© H Film

Bliss, Novel
Bliss 1985 d: Ray Lawrence. lps: Barry Otto, Lynette Curran, Helen Jones. 111M ASL. prod/rel: the Quantum Group, Window III Productions©

Crabs, Short Story
Dead-End Drive-in 1986 d: Brian Trenchard-Smith. lps: Ned Manning, Natalie McCurry, Peter Whitford. 92M ASL. *Dead End Drive in* prod/rel: Springvale Productions©, New South Wales Film Corp.©

Oscar and Lucinda, Novel
Oscar and Lucinda 1997 d: Gillian Armstrong. lps: Ralph Fiennes, Cate Blanchett, Ciaran Hinds. 132M USA/ASL. prod/rel: Dalton Films, Fox Searchlight Pictures

CARGILL, PATRICK (1918–1996), UKN
Ring for Catty, London 1954, Play
Carry on Nurse 1959 d: Gerald Thomas. lps: Shirley Eaton, Kenneth Connor, Charles Hawtrey. 86M UKN. prod/rel: Anglo-Amalgamated, Beaconsfield

Twice Round the Daffodils 1962 d: Gerald Thomas. lps: Juliet Mills, Donald Sinden, Donald Houston. 89M UKN. prod/rel: Anglo-Amalgamated, Gregory, Hake & Walker

CARLE, RICHARD
Mary's Lamb, New York 1908, Play
Mary's Lamb 1915 d: Donald MacKenzie. lps: Richard Carle, Jessie Ralph, Marie Wayne. 5r USA. prod/rel: Pathe Exchange, Inc., Gold Rooster Plays

The Tenderfoot, Chicago 1903, Play
Tenderfoot, The 1932 d: Ray Enright. lps: Joe E. Brown, Ginger Rogers, Lew Cody. 73M USA. prod/rel: First National Pictures©

CARLET DE MARIVAUX, PIERRE
Le Jeu de l'Amour Et du Hasard, 1730, Play
Amoureux du France, Les 1963 d: Pierre Grimblat, Francois Reichenbach. lps: Catherine Rouvel, Marie-France Pisier, Olivier Despax. 96M FRN/ITL. *Il Gioco Degli Innamorati* (ITL); *Humour Et France Amour* prod/rel: Boreal, Stella Films

Nostri Figli, I 1914 d: Ugo FalenA. lps: Paola Monti, Guido Brignone, Lola Visconti-Brignone. 750m ITL. prod/rel: Film d'Arte Italiana

CARLETON, HENRY GUY
A Gilded Fool, New York 1892, Play
Gilded Fool, A 1915 d: Edgar Lewis. lps: William Farnum, Agnes Everett, George de Carlton. 5r USA. prod/rel: William Fox Vaudeville Co., Box Office Attraction Co.

CARLETON, MARJORIE
Cry Wolf, Novel
Cry Wolf 1947 d: Peter Godfrey. lps: Barbara Stanwyck, Errol Flynn, Geraldine Brooks. 84M USA. prod/rel: Warner Bros.

CARLETON, WILL
Farm Festivals, Book
First Settler's Story, The 1912. lps: James Gordon, Laura Sawyer. 1000f USA. prod/rel: Edison

Over the Hill from the Poorhouse, 1873, Poem
Over the Hill 1931 d: Henry King. lps: Mae Marsh, James Kirkwood, James Dunn. 94M USA. prod/rel: Fox Film Corp.©

Over the Hill to the Poorhouse 1920 d: Harry Millarde. lps: Mary Carr, William Welsh, Sherry Tansey. 11r USA. *Over the Hill* prod/rel: Fox Film Corp.©, William Fox©

Over the Hill to the Poorhouse, 1873, Poem
Over the Hill 1931 d: Henry King. lps: Mae Marsh, James Kirkwood, James Dunn. 94M USA. prod/rel: Fox Film Corp.©

Over the Hill to the Poorhouse 1920 d: Harry Millarde. lps: Mary Carr, William Welsh, Sherry Tansey. 11r USA. *Over the Hill* prod/rel: Fox Film Corp.©, William Fox©

Over the Hills 1911 d: Joseph Smiley, George Loane Tucker. lps: Lucille Younge, King Baggot, Robert Leonard. 1000f USA. prod/rel: Imp

CARLILE, C. DOUGLAS
The Kidnapped King, Play
Kidnapped King, The 1909. lps: Carlotta de Yonson, C. Douglas Carlile, Lee Gilbert. 820f UKN. prod/rel: Manufacturer's Film Agency

Sexton Blake, Play
Sexton Blake 1909 d: C. Douglas Carlile. lps: C. Douglas Carlile, Russell Barry. 1280f UKN. prod/rel: Gaumont

CARLILE, CLANCY
Honkytonk Man, Novel
Honkytonk Man 1983 d: Clint Eastwood. lps: Clint Eastwood, Kyle Eastwood, John McIntire. 123M USA. prod/rel: Warner Bros.

CARLINI, O.
L' Importuno Vince l'Avaro, 1887, Play
Importuno Vince l'Avaro, L' 1916. lps: Il Piccolo Bob, Cav. Enrico Tovagliari, Contessina de Windermer. 502m ITL. prod/rel: Bob-Film

CARLISLE, HELEN GRACE
Mother's Cry, New York 1930, Novel
Mother's Cry 1930 d: Hobart Henley. lps: Dorothy Peterson, David Manners, Helen Chandler. 6860f USA. prod/rel: First National Pictures

CARLSON, RICHARD (1912–1977), USA
Story
Johnny Rocco 1958 d: Paul Landres. lps: Stephen McNally, Coleen Gray, James Flavin. 85M USA. prod/rel: Allied Artists, Scott R. Dunlap

CARLUCCI, ANTONIO
Io Il Tebano, Book
Altri Uomini 1997 d: Claudio Bonivento. lps: Claudio Amendola, Ennio Fantastichini, Veronica Pivetti. 91M ITL. *Other Men* prod/rel: International Dean Film

CARLYLE, ANTHONY
The Alley Cat, Novel
Alley Cat, The 1929 d: Hans Steinhoff. lps: Mabel Poulton, Jack Trevor, Clifford McLaglen. SIL. 7229f UKN. prod/rel: British & Foreign Films
Nachtgestalten 1929 d: Hans Steinhoff. lps: Margit Manstad, Jack Trevor, Mabel Poulton. 2653m GRM. *Nur Ein Gassenmadel* prod/rel: Orplid-Film

A Gamble With Hearts, Novel
Gamble With Hearts, A 1923 d: Edwin J. Collins. lps: Milton Rosmer, Madge Stuart, ValiA. 5000f UKN. prod/rel: Master, W & F

CARNEGIE, MARGARET
Mad Dog, Novel
Mad Dog 1976 d: Philippe MorA. lps: Dennis Hopper, Jack Thompson, David Gulpilil. 102M ASL. *Mad Dog Morgan* (USA) prod/rel: Mad Dog

CARNES, CONRAD D.
Book
Brainwash 1981 d: Bobby Roth. lps: Yvette Mimieux, Christopher Allport, Cindy Pickett. 97M USA. *The Naked Weekend; Circle of Power; Mystique* prod/rel: Mehlman, Qui Productions

CARNEY, DANIEL
The Square Circle, Novel
Wild Geese II 1985 d: Peter Hunt. lps: Scott Glenn, Barbara Carrera, Edward Fox. 125M UKN/USA. prod/rel: Thorn Emi, Frontier Film Productions

Whispering Death, Novel
Whispering Death 1975 d: Jurgen Goslar. lps: James Faulkner, Christopher Lee, Trevor Howard. 96M SAF/GRM. *Der Flusternde Tod* (GRM); *Night of the Askari; Albino* (USA); *Death in the Sun; Blind Spot* prod/rel: Lord, Eichberg

The Wild Geese, Novel
Wild Geese, The 1978 d: Andrew V. McLaglen. lps: Richard Burton, Roger Moore, Richard Harris. 134M UKN. prod/rel: Rank, Richmond

CARNEY, JACK
Plunder Road, Novel
Plunder Road 1957 d: Hubert Cornfield. lps: Gene Raymond, Jeanne Cooper, Wayne Morris. 72M USA. prod/rel: 20th Century-Fox, Regal Films

CAROFF, ANDRE
Le Battant, Novel
Battant, Le 1982 d: Alain Delon. lps: Alain Delon, Francois Perier, Pierre Mondy. 120M FRN. prod/rel: Adel

CARPENTER, EDWARD CHILDS
The Bachelor Father, New York 1928, Play
Bachelor Father, The 1931 d: Robert Z. Leonard. lps: Marion Davies, Ralph Forbes, C. Aubrey Smith. 84M USA. *The Lion's Share* prod/rel: Metro-Goldwyn-Mayer Corp.

Pere Celibataire, Le 1930 d: Arthur Robison. lps: Andre Luguet, Lili Damita, Jeanne Helbling. 88M FRN. prod/rel: Metro-Goldwyn-Mayer

Captain Courtesy, Philadelphia 1906, Novel
Captain Courtesy 1915 d: Hobart Bosworth. lps: Dustin Farnum, Herbert Standing, Winifred Kingston. 5r USA. prod/rel: Bosworth, Inc.©, Oliver Morosco Photoplay Co.

The Challenge, Play
Challenge, The 1916 d: Donald MacKenzie. lps: Charles Gotthold, Montagu Love, Helene Chadwick. 5r USA. prod/rel: Astra Film Corp., Pathe Exchange, Inc.©

The Cinderella Man, New York 1916, Play
Cinderella Man, The 1918 d: George Loane Tucker. lps: Tom Moore, Mae Marsh, Alec B. Francis. 6r USA. prod/rel: Goldwyn Pictures Corp.©, Goldwyn Distributing Corp.

The Code of Victor Jallot, Philadelphia 1907, Novel
Love Mart, The 1927 d: George Fitzmaurice. lps: Billie Dove, Gilbert Roland, Raymond Turner. 7388f USA. *Louisiana* prod/rel: First National Pictures

Connie Goes Home, Play
Major and the Minor, The 1942 d: Billy Wilder. lps: Ginger Rogers, Ray Milland, Diana Lynn. 100M USA. prod/rel: Paramount

The Leopard Lady, Play
Leopard Lady, The 1928 d: Rupert Julian. lps: Jacqueline Logan, Alan Hale, Robert Armstrong. 6650f USA. prod/rel: de Mille Pictures, Pathe Exchange, Inc.

Polly in the Pantry, Story
Pardon My French 1921 d: Sidney Olcott. lps: Vivian Martin, George Spink, Thomas Meegan. 5500f USA. prod/rel: Goldwyn Pictures

The Tongues of Men, New York 1913, Play
Tongues of Men 1916 d: Frank Lloyd. lps: Constance Collier, Forrest Stanley, Herbert Standing. 5r USA. *The Tongues of Men* prod/rel: Oliver Morosco Photoplay Co.©, Paramount Pictures Corp.

Whistling in the Dark, New York 1932, Play
Whistling in the Dark 1932 d: Elliott Nugent. lps: Ernest Truex, Una Merkel, Edward Arnold. 78M USA. *Scared!* (UKN) prod/rel: Metro-Goldwyn-Mayer Corp., Metro-Goldwyn-Mayer Dist. Corp.

Whistling in the Dark 1941 d: S. Sylvan Simon. lps: Red Skelton, Ann Rutherford, Virginia Grey. 77M USA. prod/rel: Metro-Goldwyn-Mayer Corp.

CARPENTER, JO
The Reluctant Hangman, Story
Good Day for a Hanging 1958 d: Nathan Juran. lps: Fred MacMurray, Margaret Hayes, Robert Vaughn. 85M USA. prod/rel: Columbia

CARPENTER, JOHN
The Eyes of Laura Mars, Novel
Eyes of Laura Mars, The 1978 d: Irvin Kershner. lps: Faye Dunaway, Tommy Lee Jones, Brad Dourif. 104M USA. prod/rel: Jon Peters, Columbia

CARPENTER, MARGARET
Experiment Perilous, Novel
Experiment Perilous 1944 d: Jacques Tourneur. lps: George Brent, Hedy Lamarr, Paul Lukas. 91M USA. prod/rel: RKO Radio

CARPENTIER, ALEJO (1904–, CUB
El Recurso Del Metodo, 1974, Novel
Recurso Del Metodo, El 1978 d: Miguel Littin. lps: Nelson Villagra, Katy Jurado, Alain Cuny. 150M MXC/CUB/FRN. *The Resort of the Method; Reasons of State; Viva El Presidente; El Dictador; Recourse to the Method, The*

CARPI, PIERO
Cagliostro Il Taumauturgo, Book
Cagliostro 1975 d: Daniele Pettinari. lps: Bekim Fehmiu, Rosanna Schiaffino, Curd Jurgens. 108M ITL. prod/rel: R. Putignani Produzioni, 20th Century Fox
Un' Ombra Nell'Ombra, Novel
Ombra Nell'ombra, Un' 1979 d: Pier Carpi. lps: Anne Heywood, Valentina Cortese, Frank Finlay. 106M ITL. prod/rel: Rassy Film, Aretusa Film

CARR, A. H. Z.
Finding Maubee, Novel
Mighty Quinn, The 1989 d: Carl Schenkel. lps: Denzel Washington, Robert Townsend, James Fox. 98M USA. *Finding Maubee* prod/rel: MGM
Return from Limbo, 1936, Short Story
Women are Like That 1938 d: Stanley Logan. lps: Kay Francis, Pat O'Brien, Ralph Forbes. 78M USA. *Return from Limbo; This Woman Is Dangerous* prod/rel: Warner Bros. Pictures©, First National Picture

CARR, ALBERT Z.
The Trial of Johnny Nobody, 1950, Short Story
Johnny Nobody 1961 d: Nigel Patrick. lps: Nigel Patrick, Yvonne Mitchell, Aldo Ray. 88M UKN. prod/rel: Viceroy Films, Columbia

CARR, ALEXANDER
An April Shower, 1915, Play
April Fool 1926 d: Nat Ross. lps: Alexander Carr, Duane Thompson, Mary Alden. 7100f USA. prod/rel: Chadwick Pictures

CARR, CHARLES P.
Ecce Homo, Play
Westminster Passion Play - Behold the Man, The 1951 d: Walter RillA. lps: Charles P. Carr. 75M UKN. prod/rel: Film Reports, Companions of the Cross

CARR, DAVID
Touch Wood, Play
Nearly a Nasty Accident 1961 d: Don Chaffey. lps: Jimmy Edwards, Kenneth Connor, Shirley Eaton. 91M UKN. prod/rel: Marlow Productions, Britannia

CARR, J. L.
Story
Day in Summer, A 1989 d: Bob Mahoney. lps: Jack Shepherd, Peter Egan, Suzanne Bertish. TVM. 120M UKN. prod/rel: Ytv
A Month in the Country, Novel
Month in the Country, A 1987 d: Pat O'Connor. lps: Colin Firth, Kenneth Branagh, Natasha Richardson. 96M UKN. prod/rel: Euston Films, Film Four International

CARR, JOHN DICKSON (1906–1977), USA
Short Story
Appointment With Fear 1946 d: Ronald Haines. SHS. UKN. prod/rel: British Foundation, 20th Century-Fox
The Burning Court, New York 1959, Novel
Chambre Ardente, La 1961 d: Julien Duvivier. lps: Nadja Tiller, Jean-Claude Brialy, Perrette Pradier. 110M FRN/ITL/GRM. *I Peccatori Della Foresta Nera* (ITL); *Das Brennende Gericht* (GRM); *The Curse and the Coffin* (UKN); *The Burning Court* prod/rel: International Production, UFA Comacico
Cabin B-16, Radio Play
Dangerous Crossing 1953 d: Joseph M. Newman. lps: Jeanne Crain, Michael Rennie, Max Showalter. 75M USA. prod/rel: 20th Century-Fox
Treacherous Crossing 1992 d: Tony Wharmby. lps: Lindsay Wagner, Angie Dickinson, Grant Show. TVM. 100M USA.

The Clock Strikes Eight, Short Story
Clock Strikes Eight, The 1946 d: Ronald Haines. lps: Mary Shaw, Millicent Wolf, Mona Wynne. 27M UKN. *Appointment With Fear: the Clock Strikes Eight* prod/rel: British Foundation, 20th Century-Fox
The Emperor's Snuffbox, Novel
That Woman Opposite 1957 d: Compton Bennett. lps: Phyllis Kirk, Dan O'Herlihy, Wilfrid Hyde-White. 85M UKN. *City After Midnight* (USA); *Woman Opposite* prod/rel: Monarch, British Lion
Gentleman from Paris, Novel
Man With a Cloak, The 1951 d: Fletcher Markle. lps: Joseph Cotten, Barbara Stanwyck, Louis Calhern. 81M USA. prod/rel: MGM
The Gong Cried Murder, Short Story
Gong Cried Murder, The 1946 d: Ronald Haines. lps: Ivan Wilmot, Diana Decker, Keith Shepherd. 29M UKN. *Appointment With Fear: the Gong Cried Murder* prod/rel: British Foundation, 20th Century-Fox
The House in Rue Rapp, Short Story
House in Rue Rapp, The 1946 d: Ronald Haines. lps: Mary Waterman, Herbert C. Walton, Robert Bradfield. 31M UKN. *Appointment With Fear: the House in Rue Rapp* prod/rel: British Foundation, 20th Century-Fox

CARR, MARY JANE
Children of the Covered Wagon, 1934, Novel
Westward Ho the Wagons! 1957 d: William Beaudine. lps: Fess Parker, Jeff York, Kathleen Crowley. 90M USA. prod/rel: Buena Vista, Walt Disney Prods.

CARR, RICHARD
MacHo Callahan, Novel
MacHo Callahan 1970 d: Bernard L. Kowalski. lps: David Janssen, Jean Seberg, Lee J. Cobb. 99M USA. prod/rel: Avco Embassy Pictures

CARR, ROGER VAUGHAN
Dead Man's Float, Novel
Dead Man's Float 1980 d: Peter Maxwell. lps: Sally Boyden, Greg Rowe, Jacqui Gordon. TVM. 75M ASL. prod/rel: Andromeda Productions

CARRE, ALBERT
Feu Toupinel, Play
Feu Toupinel 1933 d: Roger Capellani. lps: Colette Darfeuil, Simone Deguyse, Mauricet. 86M FRN. prod/rel: Societe Universelle De Films
Le Mari Sans Femme, Play
Mariti Allegri, I 1914 d: Camillo de Riso. lps: Camillo de Riso, Lydia Quaranta, Letizia QuarantA. ITL. prod/rel: Film Artistica Gloria
La Veglione, Paris 1893, Play
Her Beloved Villain 1920 d: Sam Wood. lps: Wanda Hawley, Harrison Ford, Tully Marshall. 5r USA. *La Veglione* prod/rel: Realart Pictures Corp.©

CARRE, FABRICE
Josephine Vendue Par Ses Soeurs, Opera
Josephine Vendue Par Ses Soeurs 1913 d: Georges DenolA. lps: Baron Fils, Louis Blanche, Mado Floreal. 725m FRN. prod/rel: Pathe Freres
Mio Zio Barbassous, 1891, Play
Mio Zio Barbassous 1921 d: Riccardo Cassano. lps: Elena Sangro, Nino Camarda, Myosa de Coudray. 2306m ITL. *Mon Oncle Barbassous; Barbassous* prod/rel: Chimera Film
Monsieur le Directeur, Play
Monsieur le Directeur 1913 d: Georges MoncA. lps: Prince, Paul Numa, Yvonne Maelec. 720m FRN. prod/rel: Pathe Freres
Monsieur le Directeur 1924 d: Robert Saidreau. lps: Jean Dax, Claire Nobis, Andre Dubosc. 1800m FRN.

CARRE, MICHEL
Memorial de Sainte-Helene, Play
Memorial de Saint-Helene Ou la Captivite de Napoleon, Le 1911 d: Michel Carre, Barbier. lps: Georges Treville, Laroche, Roger Monteaux. 610m FRN. prod/rel: Scagl
La Mome, Play
Nipper, The 1930 d: Louis Mercanton. lps: Betty Balfour, John Stuart, Anne Grey. 84M UKN. *The Brat* prod/rel: Betty Balfour Pictures, United Artists

CARRENO Y SEVILLA, ANSELMO
La Del Soto Del Parral, Opera
Del Soto Del Parral, La 1927 d: Leon ArtolA. lps: Teresita Zaza, Jose Nieto, Ana Tur. F SPN. prod/rel: Leon Artola

CARRETERO, JOSE-MARIA
El Caballero Audaz, Novel
Sin Ventura, La 1923 d: Benito Perojo, E. B. Donatien. lps: Lucienne Legrand, Madeleine Guitty, E. B. Donatien. 2497m SPN/FRN. *La Malchanceuse* (FRN); *The Unlucky Woman* prod/rel: Films Donatien, Hispania Rubens Films

Venenosa, La 1928 d: Roger Lion. lps: Cecile Tryant, Raquel Meller, Warwick Ward. F FRN. *Superstition* prod/rel: Plus-Altra Films
El Jefe Politico, Novel
Reponse du Destin, La 1924 d: Andre Hugon. lps: Colette Darfeuil, Rene Navarre, James DevesA. F FRN. *L' Homme Des Baleares* prod/rel: Films Andre Hugon

CARRIERE, JEAN-CLAUDE
L' Alliance, Novel
Alliance, L' 1970 d: Christian de Chalonge. lps: Jean-Claude Carriere, Anna Karina, Isabelle Sadoyan. 90M FRN. *The Wedding Ring* prod/rel: C.a.P.A.C.

CARRIERI, RAFFAELE
Un Milionario Si Ribella, Novel
Miliardi, Che Follia! 1942 d: Guido Brignone. lps: Giuseppe Lugo, Mara Landi, Kia Legnani. 85M ITL. prod/rel: S.a.F.a., Minerva Film

CARRIGAN, NORMAN
Raiders of the Golden Triangle, Novel
Raiders of the Golden Triangle 1985 d: Tom Saichur. lps: Sarah Chapter, Manny Ashley, Peter RamwA. 93M HKG. prod/rel: Intercontinental-Film

CARRIGHAR, SALLY
Icebound Summer, Novel
Two Against the Arctic 1974 d: Robert Clouse. lps: Susie Silouk, Marty Smith, Rossman Peetock. TVM. 90M USA. prod/rel: Walt Disney Productions

CARRINGTON, E.S.
Nightstick, New York 1927, Play
Alibi 1929 d: Roland West. lps: Chester Morris, Harry Stubbs, Mae Busch. 90M USA. *The Perfect Alibi* (UKN); *Nightstick* prod/rel: Feature Productions, United Artists

CARRION, MIGUEL RAMOS
La Bruja, Opera
Bruja, La 1923 d: Maximiliano Thous. lps: Lola Paris, Concha Gorge, Leopoldo Pitarch. SPN. prod/rel: Compania Cin.Ca Hispano-Portuguesa

CARROL, SIDNEY
Gambit, Novel
Gambit 1966 d: Ronald Neame. lps: Michael Caine, Shirley MacLaine, Herbert Lom. 108M USA. prod/rel: Universal

CARROLL
So Long Letty, New York 1916, Musical Play
So Long Letty 1920 d: Al Christie. lps: T. Roy Barnes, Colleen Moore, Grace Darmond. 6r USA. prod/rel: Christie Film Co., Robertson-Cole Distributing Corp.©

CARROLL, CURT
San Antone, Short Story
San Antone 1952 d: Joseph Kane. lps: Rod Cameron, Forrest Tucker, Arleen Whelan. 53M USA. prod/rel: Republic

CARROLL, EARL
Bavu, New York 1922, Play
Bavu 1923 d: Stuart Paton. lps: Wallace Beery, Estelle Taylor, Forrest Stanley. 6968f USA. *The Attic of Felix Bavu; Thundering Dawn* prod/rel: Universal Pictures
Murder at the Vanities, New York 1933, Play
Murder at the Vanities 1934 d: Mitchell Leisen. lps: Jack Oakie, Kitty Carlisle, Carl Brisson. 89M USA. prod/rel: Paramount Productions©
So Long Letty, New York 1916, Musical Play
So Long Letty 1929 d: Lloyd Bacon. lps: Charlotte Greenwood, Claude Gillingwater, Grant Withers. 5865f USA. prod/rel: Warner Brothers Pictures

CARROLL, GLADYS HASTY (1904–, USA
As the Earth Turns, New York 1933, Novel
As the Earth Turns 1934 d: Alfred E. Green. lps: Donald Woods, Jean Muir, Russell Hardie. 73M USA. prod/rel: Warner Bros Pictures, Inc.

CARROLL, JIM
The Basketball Diaries, Book
Basketball Diaries, The 1995 d: Scott Kalvert. lps: Leonardo Dicaprio, Bruno Kirby, Lorraine Bracco. 102M USA. prod/rel: New Line, Island
Curtis's Charm, Short Story
Curtis's Charm 1995 d: John L'Ecuyer. lps: Maurice Dean Wint, Callum Keith Rennie, Rachael Crawford. 80M CND. prod/rel: Rapid Dog Films

CARROLL, LEWIS (1832–1898), UKN, Dodgson, Charles Lutwidge
Alice's Adventures in Wonderland, London 1865, Book
Alice 1980 d: Jerzy Gruza, Yacek Bromski. lps: Sophie Barjac, Jean-Pierre Cassel, Susannah York. 90M BLG/PLN/UKN. *Alicja* (PLN)
Alice in Wonderland 1951 d: Clyde Geronimi, Hamilton Luske. ANM. 75M USA. prod/rel: RKO Radio, Walt Disney

Alice in Wonderland 1903 d: Cecil M. Hepworth, Percy Stow. lps: May Clark, Cecil Hepworth, Mrs. Hepworth. 800f UKN. prod/rel: Hepworth

Alice in Wonderland 1915 d: W. W. Young. lps: Viola Savoy. 5r USA. prod/rel: Nonpareil Feature Film Corp.

Alice in Wonderland 1931 d: Bud Pollard. lps: Gus Alexander, Lillian Ardell, Meyer Berensen. 55M USA. prod/rel: Bud Pollard Production

Alice in Wonderland 1933 d: Norman Z. McLeod. lps: Charlotte Henry, Richard Arlen, Gary Cooper. 76M USA. prod/rel: Paramount Productions, Inc.

Alice in Wonderland 1951 d: Louis Bunin. ANM. 75M USA.

Alice in Wonderland 1951 d: Dallas Bower. lps: Carol Marsh, Stephen Murray, Pamela Brown. 83M UKN/FRN/USA. prod/rel: Lou Bunin (New York), Union Generale Cinematographie (Paris)

Alice in Wonderland 1967 d: Jonathan Miller. lps: Ann-Marie Mallik, Freda Dowie, Jo Maxwell-Muller. MTV. 80M UKN. prod/rel: BBC

Alice in Wonderland 1976 d: Bud Townsend. lps: Kristine Debell, Juliet Graham, John Lawrence. 88M USA. prod/rel: Cruiser

Alice in Wonderland 1986 d: Harry Harris. lps: Telly Savalas, Red Buttons, Carol Channing. TVM. 208M USA. prod/rel: CBS, Irwin Allen Prods.

Alice in Wonderland 1999 d: Nick Willing. lps: Tina Majorino, Martin Short, Miranda Richardson. TVM. 180M USA. prod/rel: Hallmark Entertainment, NBC Entertainment

Alice's Adventures in Wonderland 1972 d: William Sterling. lps: Fiona Fullerton, Hywel Bennett, Michael Crawford. 101M UKN. prod/rel: Josef Shaftel

Neco Z Alenky 1987 d: Jan Svankmajer. lps: Kristyna KohoutovA. ANM. 85M SWT/GRM/UKN. *Something for Alice; Alice; Nakoz Alenky*

Jabberwocky, 1872, Verse
Jabberwocky 1977 d: Terry Gilliam. lps: Michael Palin, Max Wall, Deborah Fallender. 101M UKN. prod/rel: Umbrella Entertainment

Through the Looking Glass, London 1870, Book
Alice 1980 d: Jerzy Gruza, Yacek Bromski. lps: Sophie Barjac, Jean-Pierre Cassel, Susannah York. 90M BLG/PLN/UKN. *Alicja (PLN)*

Alice in Wonderland 1915 d: W. W. Young. lps: Viola Savoy. 5r USA. prod/rel: Nonpareil Feature Film Corp.

Alice in Wonderland 1933 d: Norman Z. McLeod. lps: Charlotte Henry, Richard Arlen, Gary Cooper. 76M USA. prod/rel: Paramount Productions, Inc.

Alice in Wonderland 1951 d: Dallas Bower. lps: Carol Marsh, Stephen Murray, Pamela Brown. 83M UKN/FRN/USA. prod/rel: Lou Bunin (New York), Union Generale Cinematographie (Paris)

Alice in Wonderland 1986 d: Harry Harris. lps: Telly Savalas, Red Buttons, Carol Channing. TVM. 208M USA. prod/rel: CBS, Irwin Allen Prods.

CARROLL, RICHARD
The Romantic Mr. Hinklin, Story
You Can't Fool Your Wife 1940 d: Ray McCarey. lps: Lucille Ball, James Ellison, Robert Coote. 68M USA. *The Romantic Mr. Hinklin* prod/rel: RKO Radio Pictures©

CARROLL, SIDNEY
Big Deal in Laredo, 1962, Play
Big Hand for the Little Lady, A 1966 d: Fielder Cook. lps: Henry Fonda, Joanne Woodward, Jason Robards Jr. 96M USA. *Big Deal at Dodge City* (UKN) prod/rel: Eden Productions

CARSON, MURRAY
Rosemary, London 1896, Play
Rosemary 1915 d: William J. Bowman, Fred J. Balshofer. lps: Marguerite Snow, Paul Gilmore, Virginia Kraft. 5r USA. prod/rel: Quality Pictures Corp., Metro Pictures Corp.©

CARSON, RACHEL (1907–1964), USA, Carson, Rachel Louise
The Sea Around Us, 1951, Book
Sea Around Us, The 1952 d: Irwin Allen. DOC. 61M USA. prod/rel: RKO

CARSON, ROBERT (1909–1983), USA
Aloha Means Goodbye, Serial Story
Across the Pacific 1942 d: John Huston. lps: Humphrey Bogart, Mary Astor, Sydney Greenstreet. 97M USA. prod/rel: Warner Bros.

Come Be My Love, Short Story
Once More My Darling 1949 d: Robert Montgomery. lps: Robert Montgomery, Ann Blyth, Jane Cowl. 94M USA. prod/rel: Universal-International, Neptune Prods.

Third Girl from the Right, Story
Ain't Misbehavin' 1955 d: Edward Buzzell. lps: Rory Calhoun, Piper Laurie, Jack Carson. 82M USA. prod/rel: Universal

You Gotta Stay Happy, Serial Story
You Gotta Stay Happy 1948 d: H. C. Potter. lps: James Stewart, Joan Fontaine, Eddie Albert. 100M USA. prod/rel: Universal-International, Rampart Prods.

CARSON, SONNY
Autobiography
Education of Sonny Carson, The 1974 d: Michael Campus. lps: Rony Clanton, Don Gordon, Joyce Walker. 105M USA. prod/rel: Paramount

CARSTAIRS, JOHN PADDY
Solid Said the Earl, Novel
Yank in Ermine, A 1955 d: Gordon Parry. lps: Peter Thompson, Noelle Middleton, Harold Lloyd Jr. 85M UKN. prod/rel: Monarch

CARTEN, AUDREY
Gay Love, London 1933, Play
Gay Love 1934 d: Leslie Hiscott. lps: Florence Desmond, Sophie Tucker, Sydney Fairbrother. 76M UKN. prod/rel: British Lion

CARTEN, WAVENEY
Gay Love 1934 d: Leslie Hiscott. lps: Florence Desmond, Sophie Tucker, Sydney Fairbrother. 76M UKN. prod/rel: British Lion

CARTER, ANGELA (1940–, UKN
Short Story
Company of Wolves, The 1984 d: Neil Jordan. lps: David Warner, Angela Lansbury, Graham Crowden. 95M UKN. prod/rel: Itc, Palace

The Magic Toyshop, 1967, Novel
Magic Toyshop, The 1986 d: David Wheatley. lps: Tom Bell, Caroline Milmoe, Kilian McKennA. TVM. 103M UKN. prod/rel: Palace Pictures, Granada

A Rather English Marriage, Novel
Rather English Marriage, A 1998 d: Paul Seed. lps: Albert Finney, Tom Courtenay, Joanna Lumley. 104M UKN. prod/rel: Wall to Wall Television, BBC

CARTER, ARTHUR
The Mad Ball, Play
Operation Mad Ball 1957 d: Richard Quine. lps: Jack Lemmon, Ernie Kovacs, Kathryn Grant. 105M USA. prod/rel: Columbia, Jed Harris Prods.

CARTER, AUDREY
Fame, London 1929, Play
Notorious Affair, A 1930 d: Lloyd Bacon. lps: Billie Dove, Basil Rathbone, Kay Francis. 6218f USA. *Faithful* prod/rel: First National Pictures

CARTER, DAN T.
Scottsboro - a Tragedy of the American South, Book
Judge Horton and the Scottsboro Boys 1976 d: Fielder Cook. lps: Arthur Hill, Vera Miles, Lewis J. Stadlen. TVM. 100M USA. prod/rel: Tomorrow Entertainment Productions

CARTER, DANIEL D.
The Master Mind, New York 1913, Play
Master Mind, The 1914 d: Oscar Apfel, Cecil B. de Mille. lps: Edmund Breese, Mabel Van Buren, Robert Edeson. 5-6r USA. prod/rel: Jesse L. Lasky Feature Play Co.©, State Rights

Master Mind, The 1920 d: Kenneth Webb. lps: Lionel Barrymore, Gypsy O'Brien, Ralph Kellard. 6r USA. *The Mastermind; Sinners Three* prod/rel: Whitman Bennett Productions, Associated First National Pictures, Inc.

CARTER, DESMOND
Little Tommy Tucker, Play
Out of the Blue 1931 d: Gene Gerrard, John Orton. lps: Gene Gerrard, Jessie Matthews, Kay Hammond. 88M UKN. prod/rel: British International Pictures, Pathe

CARTER, FORREST
The Education of Little Tree, Novel
Education of Little Tree, The 1997 d: Richard Friedenberg. lps: James Cromwell, Tantoo Cardinal, Joseph Ashton. 112M USA. prod/rel: Jake Eberts, Allied Films

Gone to Texas, Novel
Outlaw Josey Wales, The 1976 d: Clint Eastwood. lps: Clint Eastwood, Chief Dan George, Sondra Locke. 136M USA. prod/rel: Warner Bros.

CARTER, LINCOLN J.
The Eleventh Hour, Play
Eleventh Hour, The 1923 d: Bernard J. Durning. lps: Shirley Mason, Buck Jones, Richard Tucker. 6820f USA. prod/rel: Fox Film Corp.

The Fast Mail, Play
Fast Mail, The 1922 d: Bernard J. Durning. lps: Buck Jones, Eileen Percy, James Mason. 6r USA. prod/rel: Fox Film Corp.

The Tornado, 1891, Play
Tornado, The 1924 d: King Baggot. lps: House Peters, Ruth Clifford, Richard Tucker. 6375f USA. prod/rel: Universal Pictures

CARTER, MARY
Tell Me My Name, Book
Tell Me My Name 1977 d: Delbert Mann. lps: Arthur Hill, Barbara Barrie, Barnard Hughes. TVM. 100M USA/CND. prod/rel: Talent Associates Ltd. (New York), Reid-Cowan Productions Inc. (Toronto)

CARTER, RICHARD
The Man Who Rocked the Boat, 1956, Novel
Slaughter on Tenth Avenue 1957 d: Arnold Laven. lps: Richard Egan, Jan Sterling, Dan DuryeA. 103M USA. prod/rel: Universal-International

CARTER, ROBERT
The Sugar Factory, Novel
Sugar Factory, The 1998 d: Robert Carter. lps: Matt Day, Rhondda Findleton, John Waters. 91M ASL. prod/rel: Imagine Films, Australian Film Commission

CARTER, ROBERT P.
The Deserters, New York 1910, Play
Sacred Silence 1919 d: Harry Millarde. lps: William Russell, George MacQuarrie, Mabel Julienne Scott. 6r USA. prod/rel: Fox Film Corp., William Fox©

CARTER, SARA FLANIGAN
Sudie and Simpson, Novel
Sudie and Simpson 1990 d: Joan Tewkesbury. lps: Louis Gossett Jr., Sara Gilbert, John Jackson. TVM. 100M USA.

CARTER, WAVERLY
Fame, London 1929, Play
Notorious Affair, A 1930 d: Lloyd Bacon. lps: Billie Dove, Basil Rathbone, Kay Francis. 6218f USA. *Faithful* prod/rel: First National Pictures

CARTER, WINIFRED
Princess Fitz, Novel
Mrs. Fitzherbert 1947 d: Montgomery Tully. lps: Peter Graves, Joyce Howard, Leslie Banks. 99M UKN. prod/rel: British National, Pathe

CARTIER, RUDOLPH
Story
Man from Morocco, The 1945 d: Max Greene. lps: Anton Walbrook, Margaretta Scott, Mary Morris. 115M UKN. prod/rel: Pathe, Associated British Picture Corporation

CARTLAND, BARBARA (1901–, UKN, Cartland, Mary Barbara Hamilton
Cupid Rides Pillion, Novel
Lady and the Highwayman, The 1988 d: John Hough. lps: Emma Samms, Oliver Reed, Claire Bloom. TVM. 100M UKN. prod/rel: Parkfield

Duel of Hearts, Novel
Duel of Hearts 1992 d: John Hough. lps: Alison Doody, Michael York, Geraldine Chaplin. TVM. 100M UKN.

The Flame Is Love, Novel
Flame Is Love, The 1979 d: Michael O'Herlihy. lps: Linda Purl, Shane Briant, Timothy Dalton. TVM. 100M USA/UKN. prod/rel: NBC, Friendly-O'herlihy

The Ghost in Monte Carlo, Novel
Ghost in Monte Carlo, The 1990 d: John Hough. lps: Oliver Reed, Christopher Plummer, Samantha Eggar. TVM. 100M UKN.

A Hazard of Hearts, Novel
Hazard of Hearts, A 1987 d: John Hough. lps: Helena Bonham-Carter, Edward Fox, Fiona Fullerton. TVM. 92M UKN. prod/rel: MGM

CARTON, JACQUES
Edouard, Novel
Belle Revanche, La 1938 d: Paul Mesnier. lps: Roger Karl, Maurice Escande, Christiane Delyne. 100M FRN. prod/rel: S.I.F.a.

Le Mistral, Novel
Mistral, Le 1942 d: Jacques Houssin. lps: Fernand Charpin, Andrex, Orane Demazis. 75M FRN. prod/rel: S.P.D.F.

CARTON, R. C.
The Ashes of Revenge, Novel
Ashes of Revenge, The 1915 d: Harold Shaw. lps: Edna Flugrath, Philip Hewland, Gwynne Herbert. 3600f UKN. prod/rel: London, Jury

Liberty Hall, London 1892, Play
Liberty Hall 1914 d: Harold Shaw. lps: Ben Webster, Edna Flugrath, O. B. Clarence. 3600f UKN. prod/rel: London, Jury

Lord and Lady Algy, New York 1903, Play
  Lord and Lady Algy 1919 d: Harry Beaumont. lps: Tom Moore, Naomi Childers, Leslie Stuart. 5834f USA. prod/rel: Goldwyn Pictures Corp.©, Goldwyn Distributing Corp.

Mr. Hopkinson, London 1905, Play
  Rolling in Money 1934 d: Albert Parker. lps: Isabel Jeans, Leslie Sarony, Horace Hodges. 85M UKN. prod/rel: Fox British

Mr. Preedy and the Countess, London 1909, Play
  Mr. Preedy and the Countess 1925 d: George Pearson. lps: Frank Stanmore, Mona Maris, W. Cronin Wilson. F UKN. prod/rel: Welsh-Pearson, Woolf & Freedman

The Tree of Knowledge, London 1897, Play
  Tree of Knowledge, The 1920 d: William C. de Mille. lps: Robert Warwick, Kathlyn Williams, Wanda Hawley. 5r USA. prod/rel: Famous Players-Lasky Corp.©, Paramount-Artcraft Pictures

CARTOUX, LOUIS
Le Fils du Flibustier
  Fils du Flibustier, Le 1922 d: Louis Feuillade. lps: Aime Simon-Girard, Sandra Milowanoff, Georges Biscot. SRL. 9220m FRN. *The Son of a Buccaneer* prod/rel: Gaumont

CARTOUX, PAUL
Le Roi de la Pedale, Novel
  Roi de la Pedale, Le 1925 d: Maurice Champreux. lps: Georges Biscot, Blanche Montel, Jean Murat. FRN. prod/rel: Gaumont

CARTWRIGHT, JIM
The Rise and Fall of Little Voice, Play
  Little Voice 1998 d: Mark Herman. lps: Brenda Blethyn, Jane Horrocks, Michael Caine. 96M UKN. prod/rel: Scala Productions, Miramax Film

Road, Play
  Road 1987 d: Alan Clarke. lps: Jane Horrocks, Mossie Smith, Lesley Sharp. TVM. 60M UKN. prod/rel: BBC

CARUSO, DOROTHY
His Life and Death Enrico Caruso, 1945, Biography
  Great Caruso, The 1951 d: Richard Thorpe. lps: Mario Lanza, Ann Blyth, Dorothy Kirsten. 109M USA. prod/rel: MGM

CARY, FALKLAND
The Hypnotist, 1956, Play
  Hypnotist, The 1957 d: Montgomery Tully. lps: Roland Culver, Patricia Roc, Paul Carpenter. 88M UKN. *Scotland Yard Dragnet* (USA) prod/rel: Anglo-Amalgamated, Merton Park

Madame Tictac, 1950, Play
  No Road Back 1957 d: Montgomery Tully. lps: Skip Homeier, Paul Carpenter, Patricia Dainton. 83M UKN. prod/rel: Gibraltar, RKO

Watch It Sailor!, London 1960, Play
  Watch It Sailor! 1961 d: Wolf RillA. lps: Dennis Price, Marjorie Rhodes, Irene Handl. 81M UKN. prod/rel: Columbia, Cormorant

CARY, JOYCE (1888–1957), IRL
The Horse's Mouth, 1944, Novel
  Horse's Mouth, The 1959 d: Ronald Neame. lps: Alec Guinness, Kay Walsh, Renee Houston. 95M UKN. prod/rel: United Artists, Knightsbridge

Mister Johnson, 1939, Novel
  Mister Johnson 1990 d: Bruce Beresford. lps: Pierce Brosnan, Edward Woodward, Maynard Eziashi. 101M USA. prod/rel: Mister Johnson Enterprises

CARY, LUCIAN
The Duke Comes Back, Garden City, N.Y. 1933, Novel
  Duke Comes Back, The 1937 d: Irving Pichel. lps: Allan Lane, Genevieve Tobin, Heather Angel. 64M USA. *The Call of the Ring* (UKN) prod/rel: Republic Pictures Corp.©
  Duke of Chicago 1949 d: George Blair. lps: Tom Brown, Audrey Long, Grant Withers. 59M USA. prod/rel: Republic

Johnny Gets His Gun, 1934, Short Story
  Straight from the Shoulder 1936 d: Stuart Heisler. lps: Ralph Bellamy, Katherine Locke, David Holt. 67M USA. *Johnny Gets His Gun* prod/rel: Paramount Pictures©

White Flannels, 1925, Short Story
  White Flannels 1927 d: Lloyd Bacon. lps: Louise Dresser, Jason Robards, Virginia Brown Faire. 6820f USA. prod/rel: Warner Brothers Pictures

CASANOVA, GIACOMO (1725–1798), ITL
Memoires de Jacques Casanova de Seingalt, 1826-38, Autobiography
  Casanova 1976 d: Federico Fellini. lps: Donald Sutherland, Tina Aumont, Cicely Browne. 158M ITL. *Casanova de Fellini* (FRN); *Fellini's Casanova*; *Il Casanova Di Federico Fellini* prod/rel: P.E.a., Titanus

  Infanzia, Vocazione E Prima Esperienze Di Giacomo Casanova, Veneziano 1969 d: Luigi Comencini. lps: Leonard Whiting, Maria Grazia Buccella, Claudio de Kunert. 132M ITL. *Casanova* prod/rel: Mega Film, Panta

CASARES, ADOLFO BIOY
Short Story
  Otra Esperanza 1996 d: Mercedes Frutos. lps: Pepe Soriano, Hector Bidonde, Constanza Maral. F ARG. *Another Hope*

CASE, DAVID
Fengriffen, Novel
  And Now the Screaming Starts! 1973 d: Roy Ward Baker. lps: Peter Cushing, Herbert Lom, Patrick Magee. 91M UKN. *I Have No Mouth But I Must Scream*; *Fengriffen* prod/rel: Amicus

CASELLA, ALBERTO
La Morte in Vacanza, Play
  Death Takes a Holiday 1934 d: Mitchell Leisen. lps: Fredric March, Evelyn Venable, Guy Standing. 78M USA. *Strange Holiday* prod/rel: Paramount Productions, Inc.
  Death Takes a Holiday 1971 d: Robert Butler. lps: Yvette Mimieux, Monte Markham, Myrna Loy. TVM. 74M USA. prod/rel: Universal
  Meet Joe Black 1998 d: Martin Brest. lps: Brad Pitt, Anthony Hopkins, Claire Forlani. 181M USA. prod/rel: Universal Pictures, City Light Films

CASERO, ANTONIO
Estudiantas Y Modistillas, Play
  Estudiantes Y Modistillas 1927 d: Juan Antonio Cabero. lps: Elisa Ruiz Romero, Juan de Orduna, Felipe Fernansuar. SPN. prod/rel: Film Madrilena (Madrid)

CASEY, ROSEMARY
Return Engagement, 1936, Play
  Fools for Scandal 1938 d: Mervyn Leroy. lps: Carole Lombard, Fernand Gravey, Ralph Bellamy. 85M USA. *Food for Scandal* prod/rel: Warner Bros. Pictures©

CASEY, WARREN
Grease, Musical Play
  Grease 1978 d: Randall Kleiser. lps: John Travolta, Olivia Newton-John, Stockard Channing. 111M USA. prod/rel: Paramount

CASONA, ALEJANDRO
La Barca Sin Pescador, 1945, Play
  Barca Sin Pescador, La 1964 d: Jose Maria Forn. lps: Gerard Landry, Amparo Soler Leal, Mabel Karr. 83M SPN. *The Boat Without the Fisherman*; *A Boat Without a Fisherman*

La Dama Del Alba, 1944, Play
  Dama Del Alba, La 1965 d: Francisco Rovira BeletA. lps: Juliette Villard, Daniel Martin, Dolores Del Rio. 104M SPN. *The Lady of the Dawn*

Nuestra Natacha, 1936, Play
  Nuestra Natacha 1936 d: Benito Perojo. lps: Ana Maria Custodio, Rafael Rivelles, Pastora PenA. 90M SPN. *Our Natacha*

Las Tres Perfectas Casadas, 1941, Play
  Tres Perfectas Casadas, Las 1972 d: Benito Alazraki. lps: Mauricio Garces, Teresa Gimpera, Saby Kamalich. 94M SPN/MXC. *Las 3 Perfectas Casadas*

CASPARY, VERA (1904–, USA
Bedelia, Novel
  Bedelia 1946 d: Lance Comfort. lps: Margaret Lockwood, Ian Hunter, Barry K. Barnes. 90M UKN. prod/rel: John Corfield, General Film Distributors

Blind Mice, New York 1930, Play
  Working Girls 1931 d: Dorothy Arzner. lps: Charles "Buddy" Rogers, Frances Dee, Paul Lukas. 77M USA. prod/rel: Paramount Publix Corp.©

Gardenia, Story
  Blue Gardenia, The 1953 d: Fritz Lang. lps: Richard Conte, Anne Baxter, Ann Sothern. 90M USA. prod/rel: Warner Bros., Blue Gardenia Productions

Laura, Novel
  Laura 1944 d: Otto Preminger. lps: Gene Tierney, Dana Andrews, Clifton Webb. 88M USA. prod/rel: 20th Century Fox
  Laura 1955 d: John Brahm. lps: Dana Wynter, George Sanders, Robert Stack. MTV. 50M USA.

Les Girls, Novel
  Les Girls 1957 d: George Cukor. lps: Gene Kelly, Kay Kendall, Taina Elg. 114M USA. prod/rel: MGM

CASSAGNE, JEAN
La Justiciere, Play
  Justiciere, La 1925 d: Maurice Gleize. lps: Rene Navarre, Marianne Lauf, Albert Prejean. SRL. 6EP FRN. prod/rel: Maurice De Marsan

CASSIDY, CAROLYN
Autobiography
  Heart Beat 1979 d: John Byrum. lps: Sissy Spacek, John Heard, Nick Nolte. 108M USA. *Heartbeat* prod/rel: Pressman, Further Prod.

CASSOLA, CARLO (1917–, ITL
La Ragazza Di Bube, 1960, Novel
  Ragazza Di Bube, La 1963 d: Luigi Comencini. lps: Claudia Cardinale, George Chakiris, Marc Michel. 111M ITL/FRN. *La Ragazza* (FRN); *Bebo's Girl* (USA) prod/rel: Lux Film (Roma), Vides Cin.Ca

La Visita, 1942, Short Story
  Visita, La 1963 d: Antonio Pietrangeli. lps: Sandra Milo, Francois Perier, Mario Adorf. 105M ITL/FRN. *Annonces Matrimoniales*; *The Visit*; *La Entrevista* prod/rel: Zebra Film (Roma), Aera Film (Paris)

CASTANS, RAYMOND
Auguste, Play
  Auguste 1961 d: Pierre Chevalier. lps: Fernand Raynaud, Jean Poiret, Valerie Lagrange. 90M FRN. prod/rel: Marceau, Cocinor

CASTELL, ALEXANDER
Unfug Der Liebe, Novel
  Unfug Der Liebe 1928 d: Robert Wiene. lps: Maria Jacobini, Jack Trevor, Betty Astor. 2088m GRM. prod/rel: Max Glass-Film

CASTELLANO (1928–, ITL, Castellano, Franco
In Arte Fuhrer Zio Adolfo, Novel
  Zio Adolfo in Arte Fuhrer 1978 d: Castellano, Pipolo. lps: Adriano Celentano, Claudio Bigagli, Francoise Bastien. 96M ITL. *Adolfo Hitler Alias Il Mio Zio* prod/rel: Dania Film, Medusa Distribuzione

CASTELLO BRANCO, CAMILO
Amor de Perdicao, 1862, Novel
  Amor de Perdicao 1943 d: Antonio Lopes Ribeiro. lps: Carmen Dolores, Antonio Silva, Antonio Vilar. 128M PRT. *Doomed Love*
  Amor de Perdicao 1977 d: Manoel de OliveirA. lps: Antonio Sequeira Lopes, Cristina Hauser, Elsa Wallenkamp. 270M PRT. *Love of Perdition*; *Doomed Love*; *Ill-Fated Love* prod/rel: Instituto Portugues de Cinema, Centro Portugues de Cinema

CASTELLVI Y OLIVERAS
El Relicario, Song
  Relicario, El 1926 d: Miguel Contreras Torres. lps: Miguel Contreras Torres, Sally Rand, Judy King. 7r SPN. *El Relicario de Joseito*; *La Novela de un Torero* prod/rel: Miguel Contreras Torres

CASTELOT, ANDRE
Napoleon II l'Aiglon, Novel
  Napoleon II l'Aiglon 1961 d: Claude Boissol. lps: Marianne Koch, Sabine Sinjen, Bernard Verley. 100M FRN. *L'Aiglon* prod/rel: Films Matignon

CASTILLO, JOSE
Armiamoci E. Partite, Play
  Armiamoci E. Partite 1915 d: Camillo de Riso. lps: Camillo de Riso, Emilio Petacci, Fanny Ferrari. 560m ITL. prod/rel: Film Artistica Gloria

CASTILLOU, HENRI
La Fievre Monte a El Pao, Novel
  Fievre Monte a El Pao, La 1959 d: Luis Bunuel. lps: Gerard Philipe, Maria Felix, Jean Servais. 110M FRN/MXC. *Los Ambiciosos* (MXC); *Republic of Sin* (UKN); *The Fever Mounts at El Pao* prod/rel: Groupe Des Quatre, Cinematografica Filmex

CASTLE, AGNES
The Bath Comedy, 1900, Novel
  Incomparable Bellairs, The 1914 d: Harold Shaw. lps: Edna Flugrath, Gregory Scott, Mercy Hatton. 3400f UKN. *The Incomparable Mistress Bellairs* (USA) prod/rel: London, Renters

Rose of the World, New York 1905, Novel
  Rose of the World, The 1918 d: Maurice Tourneur. lps: Elsie Ferguson, Wyndham Standing, Percy Marmont. 5r USA. prod/rel: Famous Players-Lasky Corp., Artcraft Pictures Corp.©

CASTLE, CHRISTINE
The Big Strong Man, Story
  Big Strong Man, The 1922 d: George A. Cooper. lps: George Turner, Wyn Richmond, Frank Stanmore. 1707f UKN. prod/rel: Quality Plays, Walturdaw

CASTLE, EGERTON (1858–1920), UKN
The Bath Comedy, 1900, Novel
  Incomparable Bellairs, The 1914 d: Harold Shaw. lps: Edna Flugrath, Gregory Scott, Mercy Hatton. 3400f UKN. *The Incomparable Mistress Bellairs* (USA) prod/rel: London, Renters

Rose of the World, New York 1905, Novel
Rose of the World, The 1918 d: Maurice Tourneur. lps: Elsie Ferguson, Wyndham Standing, Percy Marmont. 5r USA. prod/rel: Famous Players-Lasky Corp., Artcraft Pictures Corp.©

Young April, New York 1899, Novel
Young April 1926 d: Donald Crisp. lps: Joseph Schildkraut, Rudolf Schildkraut, Bessie Love. 6858f USA. prod/rel: de Mille Pictures, Producers Distributing Corp.

CASTLE, IRENE
My Husband, New York 1919, Book
Story of Vernon and Irene Castle, The 1939 d: H. C. Potter. lps: Fred Astaire, Ginger Rogers, Edna May Oliver. 93M USA. *The Life of Vernon and Irene Castle; The Castles; The Romantic Vernon Castles* prod/rel: RKO Radio Pictures©, Pandro S. Berman Production

My Memories of Vernon Castle, 1919, Short Story
Story of Vernon and Irene Castle, The 1939 d: H. C. Potter. lps: Fred Astaire, Ginger Rogers, Edna May Oliver. 93M USA. *The Life of Vernon and Irene Castle; The Castles; The Romantic Vernon Castles* prod/rel: RKO Radio Pictures©, Pandro S. Berman Production

CASTLE, JOHN
The Password Is Courage, 1955, Biography
Password Is Courage, The 1962 d: Andrew L. Stone. lps: Dirk Bogarde, Maria Perschy, Alfred Lynch. 116M UKN. prod/rel: Andrew L. Stone, Virginia Stone

CASTLE, SHIRLEY
Story
From Nine to Nine 1936 d: Edgar G. Ulmer. lps: Ruth Roland, Roland Drew, Doris Covert. 75M CND. *Death Strikes Again; The Man With the Umbrella* prod/rel: Coronet Pictures Ltd.

CASTLETON, PAUL A.
Son of Robin Hood, Novel
Bandit of Sherwood Forest, The 1946 d: George Sherman, Henry Levin. lps: Cornel Wilde, Anita Louise, Jill Esmond. 85M USA. prod/rel: Columbia

CATALA, JORDI
L' Abric de Pell, Story
Fermin Y Paulina 1927. SPN. prod/rel: Films Sancho (Barcelona)

CATES, TORY
Cloud Waltz, Novel
Cloud Waltz 1987 d: Gordon Flemyng. lps: Kathleen Beller, Francois Eric Gedron, David Baxt. TVM. 97M UKN/USA. *Cloud Waltzing; Cloud Waltzer* prod/rel: Yorkshire Television

CATHALA, SOPHIE
Meurtre d'un Serin, Novel
Faibles Femmes 1959 d: Michel Boisrond. lps: Mylene Demongeot, Pascale Petit, Jacqueline Sassard. 92M FRN. *Le Donne Sono Deboli* (ITL); *Three Murderesses* (USA); *Women are Weak* (UKN) prod/rel: Transcontinental Films

CATHCART, COUNTESS VERA
The Woman Tempted, Novel
Woman Tempted, The 1926 d: Maurice Elvey. lps: Juliette Compton, Warwick Ward, Nina VannA. 7417f UKN. prod/rel: M.E. Productions, Wardour

CATHER, WILLA (1873–1947), USA
Jack-a-Boy, 1965, Short Story
Jack-a-Boy 1980 d: Carl Colby. 28M USA.

A Lost Lady, New York 1923, Novel
Lost Lady, A 1924 d: Harry Beaumont. lps: Irene Rich, Matt Moore, June Marlowe. 7111f USA. prod/rel: Warner Brothers Pictures

Lost Lady, A 1934 d: Alfred E. Green. lps: Barbara Stanwyck, Frank Morgan, Ricardo Cortez. 61M USA. *Courageous* (UKN) prod/rel: Warner Bros. Production Corp., First National Pictures©

My Antonia, 1918, Novel
My Antonia 1995 d: Joseph Sargent. lps: Jason Robards Jr., Eva Marie Saint, Neil Patrick Harris. TVM. 120M USA.

O Pioneers, 1913, Novel
O Pioneers! 1992 d: Glenn Jordan. lps: Jessica Lange, David Strathairn, Tom Aldredge. TVM. 100M USA. prod/rel: Craig Anderson Prods., Lorimar

Paul's Case, 1905, Short Story
Paul's Case 1977 d: Lamont Johnson. lps: Eric Roberts, Michael Higgins. MTV. 52M USA. prod/rel: Learning in Focus

CATO, NANCY
All the Rivers Run, Novel
All the Rivers Run 1983 d: George Miller, Pino AmentA. lps: John Waters, Sigrid Thornton, Charles Tingwell. TVM. 274M ASL. prod/rel: Crawford

CATTO, MAX (1907–1992), UKN
The Devil at Four O'Clock, London 1958, Novel
Devil at 4 O'Clock, The 1961 d: Mervyn Leroy. lps: Spencer Tracy, Frank Sinatra, Gregoire Aslan. 126M USA. prod/rel: Mervyn Leroy, Fred Kohlmar

Ferry to Hongkong, London 1957, Novel
Ferry to Hong Kong 1959 d: Lewis Gilbert. lps: Curd Jurgens, Orson Welles, Sylvia Syms. 113M UKN. prod/rel: Rank Organisation, Rank Film Distributors

Fire Down Below, Novel
Fire Down Below 1957 d: Robert Parrish. lps: Rita Hayworth, Robert Mitchum, Jack Lemmon. 115M UKN. prod/rel: Warwick, Columbia

The Flanagan Boy, Novel
Flanagan Boy, The 1953 d: Reginald Le Borg. lps: Barbara Payton, Frederick Valk, John Slater. 81M UKN. *Bad Blonde* (USA); *This Woman Is Trouble* prod/rel: Hammer, Exclusive

French Salad, 1934, Play
Happy Family, The 1936 d: MacLean Rogers. lps: Hugh Williams, Leonora Corbett, Eve Gray. 67M UKN. prod/rel: British Lion

A Hill in Korea, Novel
Hill in Korea, A 1956 d: Julian Amyes. lps: George Baker, Stanley Baker, Harry Andrews. 81M UKN. *Hell in Korea* (USA) prod/rel: British Lion, Wessex

The Killing Frost, Novel
Trapeze 1956 d: Carol Reed. lps: Burt Lancaster, Gina Lollobrigida, Tony Curtis. 105M USA. prod/rel: United Artists, Susan Prods.

Mister Moses, London 1961, Novel
Mister Moses 1964 d: Ronald Neame. lps: Robert Mitchum, Carroll Baker, Ian Bannen. 116M UKN. prod/rel: Talbot Productions, Frank Ross Productions

Murphy's War, Novel
Murphy's War 1970 d: Peter Yates. lps: Peter O'Toole, Sian Phillips, Philippe Noiret. 106M UKN. prod/rel: London Screenplays, Deeley-Yates

A Prize of Gold, Novel
Prize of Gold, A 1955 d: Mark Robson. lps: Richard Widmark, Mai Zetterling, Nigel Patrick. 100M UKN. prod/rel: Warwick, Columbia

Seven Thieves, Novel
Seven Thieves 1960 d: Henry Hathaway. lps: Edward G. Robinson, Rod Steiger, Joan Collins. 102M USA. prod/rel: 20th Century Fox

They Walk Alone, London 1938, Play
Daughter of Darkness 1948 d: Lance Comfort. lps: Anne Crawford, Maxwell Reed, Siobhan McKennA. 91M UKN. prod/rel: Kenilworth-Alliance, Paramount

CATTOPADHYAY, SARAT CANDRA
Biraj Bau, 1914, Novel
Biraj Bahu 1954 d: Bimal Roy. lps: Kamini Kaushal, Abhi Bhattacharya, ShakuntalA. 145M IND. *The Daughter-in-Law* prod/rel: Hiren Choudhury Prod.

Debdas, 1910, Novel
Devdas 1955 d: Bimal Roy. lps: Dilip Kumar, Suchitra Sen, VyjayanthimalA. 159M IND. *Debdas* prod/rel: Bimal Roy Prod.

Mej-Didi, 1915, Short Story
Manjhli Didi 1968 d: Hrishikesh Mukherjee. lps: Meena Kumari, Dharmendra, Lalita Pawar. 150M IND. *Second Sister; Middle Sister; Majhli Didi*

Parinita, 1914, Short Story
Parineeta 1952 d: Bimal Roy. lps: Ashok Kumar, Meena Kumari, Asit Baran. 151M IND. prod/rel: Ashok Kumar Prod.

CAUTE, DAVID (1936–, UKN
Comrade Jacob, 1961, Novel
Winstanley 1975 d: Kevin Brownlow. lps: Miles Halliwell, Jerome Willis, Terry Higgins. 95M UKN.

CAUVIN, PATRICK
A Little Romance, Novel
Little Romance, A 1979 d: George Roy Hill. lps: Laurence Olivier, Arthur Hill, Sally Kellerman. 108M USA/FRN. prod/rel: Orion, Warner

CAVALLOTTI, FELICE
Lea, 1888, Play
Lea 1910 d: Giuseppe de Liguoro (Uncredited). 300m ITL. prod/rel: Croce E C.

Lea 1916 d: Diana Karenne, Salvatore Aversano (Uncredited). lps: Diana Karenne, Umberto Casilini, Alfonsina Pieri. 1713m ITL. prod/rel: Sabaudo Film

Il Povero Piero, 1884, Play
Povero Piero, Il 1921 d: Umberto Mozzato. lps: Umberto Mozzato, Enrica Massola, Daisy Ferrero. 1590m ITL. prod/rel: Itala Film

CAVANAUGH, ARTHUR
The Deadly Trap, Novel
Maison Sous Les Arbres, La 1971 d: Rene Clement. lps: Faye Dunaway, Frank Langella, Barbara Parkins. 95M FRN/ITL. *Unico Indizio Una Sciarpa Gialla* (ITL); *The Deadly Trap* (UKN); *Death Scream* prod/rel: Oceania P.I.C.

CAVAZZONI, ERMANNO
La Voce Della Luna, Novel
Voce Della Luna, La 1990 d: Federico Fellini. lps: Roberto Benigni, Paolo Villaggio, Nadia Ottaviani. 120M ITL/FRN. *The Voice of the Moon; Voices of the Moon; Le Voci Della Luna* prod/rel: Cecchi Gori Group, Tiger Cin.Ca

CAVETT, FRANK
Forsaking All Others, New York 1933, Play
Forsaking All Others 1934 d: W. S. Van Dyke. lps: Clark Gable, Joan Crawford, Robert Montgomery. 84M USA. prod/rel: Metro-Goldwyn-Mayer Corp.©

CAYLOR, ROSE
Man-Eating Tiger, Allentown, PA. 1927, Play
Spring Tonic 1935 d: Clyde Bruckman. lps: Lew Ayres, Claire Trevor, Jack Haley. 55M USA. *Man-Eating Tiger; Hold That Tiger* prod/rel: Fox Film Corp.©

CECH, SVATOPLUK (1846–1908), CZC
Lesetinsky Kovar, Poem
Lesetinsky Kovar 1924 d: Ferry Seidl, Rudolf Mestak. lps: Frantisek V. Kucera, Marie Jaksova, Jiri Hron. 2199m CZC. *The Blacksmith of Lesetin* prod/rel: Ferry Seidl, Svetofilm

Vylet Pana Broucka Na Mars, Novel
Vylet Pana Broucka Na Mars 1921. CZC. *Mr. Broucek's Excursion to Mars* prod/rel: Tatrafilm, Iris-Film

CECH-STRAN, VACLAV
Chuda Holka, Novel
Chuda Holka 1929 d: Martin Fric. lps: Suzanne Marwille, Bozena Svobodova, Karel FialA. 2333m CZC. *Poor Girl* prod/rel: Fortuna Film

CECIL, HENRY (1902–1976), UKN, Leon, Henry Cecil
Brothers in Law, Novel
Brothers in Law 1957 d: Roy Boulting. lps: Richard Attenborough, Ian Carmichael, Terry-Thomas. 94M UKN. prod/rel: British Lion, Tudor

CELA, CAMILO JOSE (1916–, SPN
La Colmena, 1951, Novel
Colmena, La 1983 d: Mario Camus. lps: Victoria Abril, Jose Sacristan, Francisco AlgorA. 112M SPN. *The Bee-Hive* prod/rel: Agata Films

La Familia de Pascual Duarte, 1945, Novel
Pascual Duarte 1975 d: Ricardo Franco. lps: Jose Luis Gomez, Paco Ojea, Hector Alterio. 100M SPN. prod/rel: Elias Querejeta

CELESTIN, JACK
Crime on the Hill, 1932, Play
Crime on the Hill 1933 d: Bernard Vorhaus. lps: Sally Blane, Nigel Playfair, Lewis Casson. 69M UKN. prod/rel: British International Pictures, Wardour

Jury's Evidence, Play
Jury's Evidence 1936 d: Ralph Ince. lps: Hartley Power, Margaret Lockwood, Nora Swinburne. 74M UKN. prod/rel: British Lion

Line Engaged, 1934, Play
Line Engaged 1935 d: Bernerd Mainwaring. lps: Bramwell Fletcher, Jane Baxter, Arthur Wontner. 68M UKN. prod/rel: British Lion

The Man at Six, London 1928, Play
Gables Mystery, The 1938 d: Harry Hughes. lps: Francis L. Sullivan, Antoinette Cellier, Leslie Perrins. 66M UKN. prod/rel: Welwyn, MGM

Man at Six, The 1931 d: Harry Hughes. lps: Anne Grey, Lester Matthews, Gerald Rawlinson. 70M UKN. *The Gables Mystery* (USA) prod/rel: British International Pictures, Wardour

The Silent Witness, New York 1931, Play
Silent Witness, The 1932 d: Marcel Varnel, R. Lee Hough. lps: Lionel Atwill, Greta Nissen, Weldon Heyburn. 73M USA. prod/rel: Fox Film Corp.©

CELVAL, FELIX
Le Champion du Regiment, Play
Champion du Regiment, Le 1932 d: Henry Wulschleger. lps: Bach, Charles Montel, Germaine Charley. 91M FRN. prod/rel: Alex Nalpas

CENDRARS, BLAISE (1887–1961), SWT, Sauser, Frederic-Louis
Books
Film 100% Brasileiro, Um 1986 d: Jose de Barros. lps: Paulo Cesar Pereio, Odete Lara, Maria Gladys. 84M BRZ. *A 100% Brazilian Film* prod/rel: Grupo Nuvo de Cinema, Embrafilme

Or. la Merveilleuse Histoire du General Johann August Suter, Paris 1925, Novel
　Sutter's Gold 1936 d: James Cruze. lps: Edward Arnold, Lee Tracy, Binnie Barnes. 94M USA. prod/rel: Universal Productions©

CENZATO, GIOVANNI
Ho Perduto Mio Marito!, Play
　Ho Perduto Mio Marito! 1937 d: Enrico Guazzoni. lps: Paola Borboni, Nino Besozzi, Enrico Viarisio. 75M ITL. prod/rel: Astra Film, E.N.I.C.

Il Ladro Sono Io!, Play
　Ladro Sono Io!, Il 1940 d: Flavio CalzavarA. lps: Nelly Corradi, Carlo Tamberlani, Dina Perbellini. 75M ITL. prod/rel: Mediterranea Film, C.I.N.F.

CERAM, C. W.
Graves and Scholars Gods, Article
　Valley of the Kings 1954 d: Robert Pirosh. lps: Robert Taylor, Eleanor Parker, Carlos Thompson. 86M USA. prod/rel: MGM

CERAMI, VINCENZO
Un Borghese Piccolo Piccolo, Novel
　Borghese Piccolo Piccolo, Un 1977 d: Mario Monicelli. lps: Alberto Sordi, Shelley Winters, Vincenzo Crocitti. 122M ITL. *An Average Man* prod/rel: Auro Cin.Ca, Cineriz

Il Casotto, Short Story
　Casotto, Il 1977 d: Sergio Citti. lps: Ugo Tognazzi, Mariangela Melato, Catherine Deneuve. 102M ITL. *The Beach Hut* (USA) prod/rel: Parva Cin.Ca, Medusa

CERDA, ENRIQUE
Moros Y Cristianos, Opera
　Moros Y Cristianos 1926 d: Maximiliano Thous. lps: Anita Giner Soler, Leopoldo Pitarch, Ramon Serneguet. 71M SPN. prod/rel: Produccion Artista Cin.Ca Espanola

CERIO, FERRUCCIO
La Casa Sul Mare, Story
　Aurora Sul Mare 1935 d: Giorgio C. Simonelli. lps: Renzo Ricci, Giovanna Scotto, Norma Redivo. 68M ITL. prod/rel: Manenti Film

CERVENA, ADELA
Kantor Ideal, Novel
　Kantor Ideal 1932 d: Martin Fric. lps: Carl Lamac, Anny Ondra, Oskar Marion. 2562m CZC/GRM. *Betragen Ungenugend* (GRM); *Conduct Unsatisfactory*; *Master Ideal*; *The Ideal Schoolmaster* prod/rel: Vladimir Kabelik, Moldavia

CERVENKA, JAN
Pisne Zavisovy, Verse
　Za Tichych Noci 1940 d: Gina Hasler. lps: Karel Hoger, Lida Baarova, Svetla SvozilovA. 2430m CZC. *During Quiet Nights* prod/rel: Lucernafilm

CESARO, CHRIS
Home Fires Burning, Play
　Home Fires Burning 1992 d: L. A. Puopolo. lps: Karen Allen, Raymond J. Barry, Michael Dolan. 103M USA. *The Turning* prod/rel: White Deer, L. A. Puopolo

CESBRON, GILBERT
Il Est Minuit Dr. Schweitzer, Play
　Il Est Minuit, Dr. Schweitzer 1952 d: Andre Haguet. lps: Pierre Fresnay, Jeanne Moreau, Raymond Rouleau. 95M FRN. *The Story of Doctor Schweitzer* (UKN) prod/rel: Nordia Films

CHABER, M. E.
The Man Inside, Novel
　Man Inside, The 1958 d: John Gilling. lps: Jack Palance, Anita Ekberg, Nigel Patrick. 97M UKN. prod/rel: Columbia, Warwick

CHABOT, ADRIEN
Marielle Thibaut
　Bete Traquee, La 1922 d: Rene Le Somptier, Michel Carre. lps: Edmond Van Daele, France Dhelia, Jeanne Marie-Laurent. 2000m FRN.

CHABROL, JEAN-PIERRE
Un Homme de Trop, Paris 1958, Novel
　Homme de Trop, Un 1967 d: Costa-Gavras. lps: Charles Vanel, Bruno Cremer, Jean-Claude Brialy. 115M FRN/ITL. *Il 13° Uomo* (ITL); *One Man Too Many*; *Shock Troops* (USA) prod/rel: Terra Films, Les Productions Artistes Associes

CHACE, M. HAILE
Sellout, Novel
　Hot Cars 1956 d: Don McDougall. lps: John Bromfield, Joi Lansing, Mark DanA. 60M USA. prod/rel: United Artists, Bel-Air

CHAINE, PIERRE
Bagnes d'Enfants, Play
　Bagnes d'Enfants 1914 d: Emile Chautard. lps: Josette Andriot, Georges Dorival, Henri Gouget. 880m FRN. prod/rel: Acad

　Bagnes d'Enfants 1933 d: Georges Gauthier. lps: Germaine Dermoz, Leonie Balme, Andre Marnay. F FRN. *Gosses de Misere* prod/rel: Artisans Du Film

CHAIS, PAMELA HERBERT
Six Weeks in August, Play
　Guess Who's Sleeping in My Bed? 1973 d: Theodore J. Flicker. lps: Barbara Eden, Dean Jones, Kenneth Mars. TVM. 73M USA. prod/rel: ABC Circle Films

CHAKRAVARTY, AMALENDU
Abiroto Chen Mukh, Story
　Ek Din Pratidin 1979 d: Mrinal Sen. lps: Satya Bannerjee, Geeta Sen, Mamata Shankar. 95M IND. *And Still Breaks the Dawn*; *And Quiet Rolls the Dawn*; *Quiet Rolls the Day*; *Every Day One Day*; *Edkin Pratidin* prod/rel: Mrinal Sen Prod.

CHAKRBORTY, AMALENDU
Story
　Akaler Sandhaney 1980 d: Mrinal Sen. lps: Dhritiman Chatterjee, Smita Patil, Sreela Majumdar. 125M IND. *In Search of Famine*; *Aakaler Sandhane* prod/rel: D.K. Films

CHAMALES, TOM T.
Go Naked in the World, New York 1959, Novel
　Go Naked in the World 1960 d: Ranald MacDougall. lps: Gina Lollobrigida, Anthony Franciosa, Ernest Borgnine. 103M USA. prod/rel: Arcola Pictures, MGM

New So Few, 1957, Novel
　Never So Few 1959 d: John Sturges. lps: Frank Sinatra, Gina Lollobrigida, Paul Henreid. 124M USA. *Campaign Burma* prod/rel: MGM, Canterbury

CHAMBE, RENE
Sous le Casque de Cuir, Novel
　Sous le Casque de Cuir 1931 d: Albert de Courville, Francisco Elias. lps: Pierre Richard-Willm, Gina Manes, Gaston Modot. 95M FRN. prod/rel: Cinemasques

CHAMBERLAIN, GEORGE AGNEW
Home, New York 1914, Novel
　Call of Home, The 1922 d: Louis J. Gasnier. lps: Leon Bary, Irene Rich, Ramsey Wallace. 5523f USA. prod/rel: R-C Pictures

Lovely Reason, 1916, Serial Story
　Upside Down 1919 d: Lawrence C. Windom. lps: Taylor Holmes, Anna Lehr, Roy Applegate. 5r USA. prod/rel: Triangle Film Corp., Triangle Distributing Corp.

The Phantom Filly, Novel
　April Love 1957 d: Henry Levin. lps: Pat Boone, Shirley Jones, Dolores Michaels. 99M USA. prod/rel: 20th Century-Fox Film Corp.

　Home in Indiana 1944 d: Henry Hathaway. lps: Walter Brennan, Charlotte Greenwood, Lon McAllister. 103M USA. prod/rel: 20th Century-Fox

Scudda Hoo Scudda Hay, Novel
　Scudda-Hoo! Scudda Hay! 1948 d: F. Hugh Herbert. lps: June Haver, Lon McCallister, Walter Brennan. 95M USA. *Summer Lightning* (UKN); *Scudda Hoo Scudda Hay* prod/rel: 20th Century-Fox

Taxi!, 1919, Short Story
　Taxi 1919 d: Lawrence C. Windom. lps: Taylor Holmes, Lillian Hall, Irene Tams. 5r USA. prod/rel: Triangle Film Corp.

The White Man, Indianapolis 1919, Novel
　White Man 1924 d: Louis J. Gasnier. lps: Kenneth Harlan, Alice Joyce, Walter Long. 6337f USA. prod/rel: B. P. Schulberg Productions

CHAMBERLAIN, LUCIA
The Other Side of the Door, Indianapolis 1909, Novel
　Other Side of the Door, The 1916 d: Thomas Ricketts. lps: Harold Lockwood, May Allison, William Stowell. 5r USA. prod/rel: American Film Co.©, Mutual Film Corp.

The Underside, 1917, Short Story
　Blackmail 1920 d: Dallas M. Fitzgerald. lps: Viola Dana, Alfred Allen, Wyndham Standing. 6r USA. prod/rel: Screen Classics, Inc., Metro Pictures Corp.©

CHAMBERS, C. HADDON (1860–1921), ASL, Chambers, Charles Haddon
Captain Swift, London 1888, Play
　Captain Swift 1914 d: Edgar Lewis. lps: Iva Shepard, David Wall, George de Carlton. 5r USA. prod/rel: Life Photo Film Corp., State Rights

　Captain Swift 1920 d: Tom Terriss. lps: Earle Williams, Alice Calhoun, Florence Dixon. 5r USA. prod/rel: Vitagraph Co. of America©

The Fatal Card, London 1894, Play
　Fatal Card, The 1915 d: James Kirkwood. lps: John Mason, Hazel Dawn, Russell Bassett. 5r USA. prod/rel: Famous Players Film Co., Charles Frohman Co.

The Idler, New York 1890, Play
　Idler, The 1915 d: Lloyd B. Carleton. lps: Charles Richman, Catherine Countiss, Claire Whitney. 5r USA. prod/rel: Box Office Attraction Co., William Fox Photoplays Supreme

A Modern Magdalen, New York 1902, Play
　Modern Magdalen, A 1915 d: Will S. Davis. lps: Catherine Countiss, Lionel Barrymore, William H. Tooker. 5r USA. prod/rel: Life Photo Film Corp., State Rights

Passers-By, London 1911, Play
　Passers By 1916 d: Stanner E. V. Taylor. lps: Charles Cherry, Mary Charleson, Marguerite Skirvin. 5r USA. *Passers-By* prod/rel: Equitable Motion Pictures Corp.©, World Film Corp.

　Passers-By 1920 d: J. Stuart Blackton. lps: Herbert Rawlinson, Leila Valentine, Ellen Cassidy. 6r USA. *Passers By* prod/rel: J. Stuart Blackton Feature Pictures, Inc, Pathe Exchange, Inc.©

CHAMBERS, ELWYN WHITMAN
Once Too Often, Novel
　Blonde Ice 1948 d: Jack Bernhard. lps: Leslie Brooks, Robert Paige, Walter Sande. 78M USA. prod/rel: Film Classics

CHAMBERS, KELLETT
An American Widow, New York 1909, Play
　American Widow, An 1918 d: Frank Reicher. lps: Ethel Barrymore, Irving Cummings, Dudley Hawley. 5r USA. prod/rel: Metro Pictures Corp.©, Metro Wonderplay

CHAMBERS, ROBERT W.
Anne's Bridge, New York 1914, Novel
　Fettered Woman, The 1917 d: Tom Terriss. lps: Alice Joyce, Webster Campbell, Donald MacBride. 5r USA. prod/rel: Vitagraph Co. of America©, Greater Vitagraph (V-L-S-E)

Athalie, New York 1915, Novel
　Unseen Forces 1920 d: Sidney A. Franklin. lps: Sylvia Breamer, Conrad Nagel, Sam de Grasse. 6r USA. *Athalie* prod/rel: Mayflower Photoplay Corp.©, Associated First National Pictures, Inc.

Between Friends, New York 1914, Novel
　Between Friends 1924 d: J. Stuart Blackton. lps: Lou Tellegen, Anna Q. Nilsson, Norman Kerry. 6936f USA. prod/rel: Vitagraph Co. of America

　Woman Between Friends, The 1918 d: Tom Terriss. lps: Alice Joyce, Marc McDermott, Robert Walker. 5r USA. prod/rel: Vitagraph Co. of America©, Blue Ribbon Feature

The Business of Life, New York 1913, Novel
　Business of Life, The 1918 d: Tom Terriss. lps: Alice Joyce, Walter McGrail, Betty Blythe. 5r USA. prod/rel: Vitagraph Co. of America©

The Cambric Mask, New York 1899, Novel
　Cambric Mask, The 1919 d: Tom Terriss. lps: Alice Joyce, Maurice Costello, Herbert Pattee. 5r USA. prod/rel: Vitagraph Co. of America©

Cardigan, New York 1901, Novel
　Cardigan 1922 d: John W. Noble. lps: William Collier Jr., Betty Carpenter, Thomas Cummings. 6788f USA. prod/rel: Messmore Kendall, American Releasing Corp.

The Common Law, New York 1911, Novel
　Common Law, The 1916 d: Albert Capellani. lps: Clara Kimball Young, Conway Tearle, Barry Whitcomb. 7r USA. prod/rel: Clara Kimball Young Film Corp.©, Lewis J. Selznick Enterprises, Inc.

　Common Law, The 1923 d: George Archainbaud. lps: Corinne Griffith, Conway Tearle, Elliott Dexter. 7527f USA. prod/rel: Selznick Pictures

　Common Law, The 1931 d: Paul L. Stein. lps: Constance Bennett, Lew Cody, Joel McCreA. 77M USA. prod/rel: RKO Pathe Pictures, Inc.

The Danger Mark, New York 1909, Novel
　Danger Mark, The 1918 d: Hugh Ford. lps: Elsie Ferguson, Mahlon Hamilton, Gertrude McCoy. 5r USA. prod/rel: Famous Players-Lasky Corp.©, Artcraft Pictures

The Dark Star, New York 1917, Novel
　Dark Star, The 1919 d: Allan Dwan. lps: Marion Davies, Norman Kerry, Matt Moore. 7r USA. prod/rel: Cosmopolitan Productions, International Film Service©

The Fighting Chance, New York 1906, Novel
　Fighting Chance, The 1916?. lps: E. K. Lincoln, Violet Horner. 5r USA. prod/rel: Mutual Film Corporation

　Fighting Chance, The 1920 d: Charles Maigne. lps: Anna Q. Nilsson, Conrad Nagel, Clarence Burton. 5894f USA. prod/rel: Famous Players-Lasky Corp.©, Paramount-Artcraft Pictures

The Firing Line, New York 1908, Novel
Firing Line, The 1919 d: Charles Maigne. lps: Irene Castle, David Powell, Irene West. 5483f USA. prod/rel: Famous Players-Lasky Corp.©, Paramount-Artcraft Special

The Hidden Children, New York 1914, Novel
Hidden Children, The 1917 d: Oscar Apfel. lps: Harold Lockwood, May Allison, Lillian West. 5r USA. prod/rel: Yorke Film Corp.©, Metro Pictures Corp.

My Girl Philippa, New York 1916, Novel
Girl Philippa, The 1917 d: S. Rankin Drew. lps: Anita Stewart, S. Rankin Drew, Frank Morgan. 8r USA. prod/rel: Vitagraph Co. of America©, Blue Ribbon Feature

The Restless Sex, New York 1918, Novel
Restless Sex, The 1920 d: Robert Z. Leonard. lps: Marion Davies, Ralph Kellard, Carlyle Blackwell. 6505f USA. prod/rel: Cosmopolitan Productions, International Screen Service Co.©

Secret Service Operator, New York 1934, Novel
Operator 13 1934 d: Richard Boleslawski. lps: Marion Davies, Gary Cooper, Katharine Alexander. 86M USA. *Spy 13* (UKN) prod/rel: Metro-Goldwyn-Mayer Corp.©

The Shining Band, London 1901, Novel
Even As Eve 1920 d: B. A. Rolfe, Chester M. de Vonde. lps: Grace Darling, Ramsey Wallace, E. J. Radcliffe. 6r USA. *The Shining Band; The Amazing Lovers* prod/rel: A. H. Fischer Features, Inc., First National Exhibitors Circuit

The Turning Point, 1912, Novel
Turning Point, The 1920 d: J. A. Barry. lps: Katherine MacDonald, Leota Lorraine, Nigel Barrie. 5-6r USA. prod/rel: Katherine Macdonald Pictures Corp., First National Exhibitors Circuit, Inc.

Who Goes There, New York 1915, Novel
Who Goes There! 1917 d: William P. S. Earle. lps: Harry T. Morey, Corinne Griffith, Arthur Donaldson. 5r USA. prod/rel: Vitagraph Co. of America©, Blue Ribbon Feature

CHAMBERS, WHITMAN
Cabaret, Short Story
Sensation Hunters 1933 d: Charles Vidor. lps: Arline Judge, Preston Foster, Marion Burns. 74M USA. prod/rel: Monogram Pictures Corp.©, Robert Welsh Production

The Campanile Murders, New York 1933, Novel
Murder on the Campus 1934 d: Richard Thorpe. lps: J. Farrell MacDonald, Edward Van Sloan, Dewey Robinson. 73M USA. *At the Stroke of Nine* (UKN); *On the Stroke of Nine* prod/rel: Chesterfield Motion Pictures Corp.©

The Come on, Novel
Come on, The 1956 d: Russell J. Birdwell. lps: Anne Baxter, Sterling Hayden, John Hoyt. 83M USA. *The Come-on* prod/rel: Allied Artists

Murder of a Wanton, New York 1934, Novel
Sinner Take All 1936 d: Errol Taggart. lps: Joseph Calleia, Margaret Lindsay, Bruce Cabot. 78M USA. prod/rel: Metro-Goldwyn-Mayer Corp.©

CHAMBLAIN DE MARIVAUX, PIERRE
Caribia, Play
Caribia 1977 d: Arthur M. Rabenalt. lps: Rossano Brazzi, Gaby Herbst, Ti-Corn. 89M GRM. prod/rel: Interarzt, Azor

CHAMPION, BOB
Champion's Story, Book
Champions 1983 d: John Irvin. lps: John Hurt, Edward Woodward, Jan Francis. 115M UKN. prod/rel: Embassy, Archerwest

CHAMPLY, HENRI
L' Homme Qui Mourra Demain, Novel
Quand Sonnera Midi 1957 d: Edmond T. Greville. lps: Dany Robin, Georges Marchal, Jose Lewgoy. 96M FRN/ITL. *Plotone Di Esecuzione* (ITL); *L' Homme Qui Mourra Demain* prod/rel: Sigma, Italia Films

CHAMPSAUR, FELICIEN
L' Arriviste, Novel
Arriviste, L' 1914 d: Gaston Leprieur. lps: Jean Toulout, Jacques Guilhene, Romuald Joube. 1600m FRN. prod/rel: Lordier, Gfp

Arriviste, L' 1924 d: Andre Hugon. lps: Henri Baudin, Ginette Maddie, Pierre Blanchar. 2500m FRN. prod/rel: Films Andre Hugon

L' Empereur Des Pauvres, Novel
Empereur Des Pauvres, L' 1921 d: Rene Leprince. lps: Leon Mathot, Henry Krauss, Gina Relly. SRL. 6EP FRN. prod/rel: Pathe-Consortium-Cinema

CHAMSON, ANDRE (1900–, FRN
L' Auberge de l'Abime, 1933, Novel
Auberge de l'Abime, L' 1942 d: Willy Rozier. lps: Aime Clariond, Roger Duchesne, Janine Darcey. 99M FRN. prod/rel: Sport Films

La Crime Des Justes, 1928, Novel
Crime Des Justes, Le 1948 d: Jean Gehret. lps: Jean Debucourt, Claudine Dupuis, Jean-Marc Lambert. 90M FRN. prod/rel: Les Gemeaux, Andre Sarrut

Tabusse, 1928, Novel
Tabusse 1948 d: Jean Gehret. lps: Rellys, Marcel Levesque, Paulette Andrieux. 95M FRN. prod/rel: Les Gemeaux, Andre Sarrut

CHANCE, JOHN NEWTON
Crosstrap, Novel
Crosstrap 1962 d: Robert Hartford-Davis. lps: Laurence Payne, Jill Adams, Gary Cockrell. 61M UKN. prod/rel: Unifilms, Newbery Clyne Avon

The Flying Eye, Novel
Flying Eye, The 1955 d: William C. Hammond. lps: David Hannaford, Julia Lockwood, Harcourt Williams. 53M UKN. prod/rel: British Films, Children's Film Foundation

CHANCEL, JULES
Le Prince Consort, 1919, Play
Love Parade, The 1929 d: Ernst Lubitsch. lps: Maurice Chevalier, Jeanette MacDonald, Lupino Lane. 110M USA. *Parade d'Amour* prod/rel: Paramount Famous Lasky Corp.

CHANCELLOR, JOHN
King of the Damned, Play
King of the Damned 1936 d: Walter Forde. lps: Conrad Veidt, Helen Vincent, Noah Beery. 76M UKN. prod/rel: Gaumont-British

Open All Night, Play
Open All Night 1934 d: George Pearson. lps: Frank Vosper, Margaret Vines, Gillian Lind. 61M UKN. prod/rel: Real Art, Radio

CHANDER, KRISHNAN
Jab Khet Jaage, 1948, Novel
Maabhoomi 1979 d: Gautam Ghose. lps: Saichand, Bhopal Reddy, Yadagini. 152M IND. *Our Land; Maa Bhoomi; The Motherland* prod/rel: Chaitanya Chitra

CHANDLEE, HARRY
The Labyrinth, Story
Labyrinth, The 1915 d: E. Mason Hopper. lps: Gail Kane, Dolly Larkin, Richard Neill. 5r USA. prod/rel: Equitable Motion Pictures Corp.©, World Film Corp.

CHANDLER, JEROME GREER
Fire and Rain, Book
Fire and Rain 1989 d: Jerry Jameson. lps: Charles Haid, John Beck, Tom Bosley. TVM. 100M USA. prod/rel: Paramount

CHANDLER, RAYMOND (1888–1959), USA, Chandler, Raymond Thornton
Story
Blue Dahlia, The 1946 d: George Marshall. lps: Alan Ladd, William Bendix, Veronica Lake. 99M USA. prod/rel: Paramount

The Big Sleep, 1939, Novel
Big Sleep, The 1946 d: Howard Hawks. lps: Humphrey Bogart, Lauren Bacall, John Ridgely. 114M USA. prod/rel: Warner Bros.

Big Sleep, The 1978 d: Michael Winner. lps: Robert Mitchum, Sarah Miles, Richard Boone. 99M UKN/USA. prod/rel: United Artists, Winkast

Farewell My Lovely, 1940, Novel
Falcon Takes Over, The 1942 d: Irving Reis. lps: George Sanders, Lynn Bari, James Gleason. 63M USA.

Farewell My Lovely 1975 d: Dick Richards. lps: Robert Mitchum, Charlotte Rampling, John Ireland. 95M USA. prod/rel: Avco Embassy, Itc

Murder, My Sweet 1945 d: Edward Dmytryk. lps: Dick Powell, Claire Trevor, Anne Shirley. 95M USA. *My Lovely Farewell* (UKN) prod/rel: RKO Radio

The High Window, 1942, Novel
Brasher Doubloon, The 1947 d: John Brahm. lps: George Montgomery, Nancy Guild, Conrad Janis. 73M USA. *The High Window* (UKN) prod/rel: 20ᵗʰ Century-Fox

Time to Kill 1942 d: Herbert I. Leeds. lps: Lloyd Nolan, Heather Angel, Doris Merrick. 61M USA. prod/rel: 20ᵗʰ Century-Fox

The Lady in the Lake, 1943, Novel
Lady in the Lake 1946 d: Robert Montgomery. lps: Robert Montgomery, Audrey Totter, Lloyd Nolan. 103M USA. prod/rel: MGM

The Little Sister, Boston 1949, Novel
Marlowe 1969 d: Paul Bogart. lps: James Garner, Sharon Farrell, Gayle Hunnicutt. 95M USA. *The Little Sister* prod/rel: Katzka-Berne Productions, Cherokee Productions

The Long Goodbye, 1953, Novel
Long Goodbye, The 1973 d: Robert Altman. lps: Elliott Gould, Nina Van Pallandt, Sterling Hayden. 111M USA. prod/rel: E-K-Corporation, United Artists

Poodle Springs, Novel
Poodle Springs 1998 d: Bob Rafelson. lps: James Caan, Dina Meyer, David Keith. TVM. 95M USA. prod/rel: Universal TV Entertainment/Mca, Mirag

CHANFRAU, FRANK
Kit, the Arkansaw Traveler, Play
Kit, the Arkansaw Traveler 1914 d: Kenean Buel. lps: Alice Hollister, Marguerite Courtot, Jere Austin. 3r USA. prod/rel: Kalem

CHANG CHANG HSI-KUO
Qi Wang, 1982, Novel
King of Chess 1991 d: Yim Ho, Tsui Hark. 111M HKG.

CHANG, EILEEN
Bun Sang Yun, Novel
Bun Sang Yun 1997 d: Hsu An-HuA. lps: Leon Lai, Wu Chien-Lien, Anita Mui. 123M HKG. *Eighteen Springs* prod/rel: Mandarin Films

Qingchengzhi Lian, Novel
Qingchengzhi Lian 1984 d: Hsu An-HuA. lps: Cora Miao, Chou Jun-Fa, Chiang Chung Ping. 94M HKG. *Love in a Fallen City* prod/rel: Run Run Shaw

CHANLAINE, PIERRE
Mam'zelle Bonaparte, Novel
Mam'zelle Bonaparte 1941 d: Maurice Tourneur. lps: Raymond Rouleau, Edwige Feuillere, Monique Joyce. 100M FRN. prod/rel: Continental-Films

CHANSLOR, ROY
Story
Gambling on the High Seas 1940 d: George Amy. lps: Wayne Morris, Jane Wyman, Gilbert Roland. 56M USA. *Floating Trouble* prod/rel: Warner Bros. Pictures©, First National Pictures

The Ballad of Cat Ballou, Boston 1956, Novel
Cat Ballou 1965 d: Elliot Silverstein. lps: Jane Fonda, Lee Marvin, Michael Callan. 96M USA. prod/rel: Columbia

Hi Nellie, Story
Hi Nellie! 1934 d: Mervyn Leroy. lps: Paul Muni, Glenda Farrell, Ned Sparks. 75M USA. prod/rel: Warner Bros. Pictures©

House Across the Street, The 1949 d: Richard L. Bare. lps: Bruce Bennett, Janis Paige, James Holden. 69M USA. prod/rel: Warner Bros.

Love Is on the Air 1937 d: Nick Grinde. lps: Ronald Reagan, June Travis, Eddie Acuff. 61M USA. *The Radio Murder Mystery* (UKN); *Inside Story* prod/rel: Warner Bros. Pictures©

You Can't Escape Forever 1942 d: Jo Graham. lps: George Brent, Brenda Marshall, Paul Harvey. 77M USA. prod/rel: Warner Bros.

Johnny Guitar, Novel
Johnny Guitar 1954 d: Nicholas Ray. lps: Joan Crawford, Mercedes McCambridge, Sterling Hayden. 110M USA. prod/rel: Republic

CHANTEPLEURE, GUY
La Passagere, Novel
Passagere, La 1948 d: Jacques Daroy. lps: Georges Marchal, Henri Bosc, Dany Robin. 112M FRN. prod/rel: Societe Mediterraneenne

CHAPI, RUPERTO (1851–1909), SPN, Chapi Y Lorente, Ruperto
La Bruja, Opera
Bruja, La 1923 d: Maximiliano Thous. lps: Lola Paris, Concha Gorge, Leopoldo Pitarch. SPN. prod/rel: Compania Cin.Ca Hispano-Portuguesa

Curro Vargas, Opera
Curro Vargas 1923 d: Jose Buchs. lps: Ricardo Galache, Angelina Breton, Maria Comendador. 3200m SPN. prod/rel: Film Espanola (Madrid)

El Punao de Rosas, Opera
Punao de Rosas, El 1923 d: Rafael Salvador. lps: Angeles Ortiz, Pedro Fernandez Cuenca, Jose OrtegA. SPN. prod/rel: Rafael Salvador Films (Madrid)

La Revoltosa, Opera
Revoltosa, La 1924 d: Florian Rey. lps: Josefina Tapias, Juan de Orduna, Jose Moncayo. 71M SPN. *The Mischievous One; The Riotous Girl* prod/rel: Goya Film (Madrid)

El Rey Que Rabio, Opera
Rey Que Rabio, El 1929 d: Jose Buchs. lps: Juan de Orduna, Amelia Munoz, Jose Montenegro. F SPN. *The King Had Rabies* prod/rel: Ediciones Forns-Buchs (Madrid)

Rosario la Cortijera, Opera
Rosario la Cortijera 1923 d: Jose Buchs. lps: Elisa Ruiz Romero, Miguel Cuchet, Manuel San German. 2200m SPN. *Rosario the Girl of the Farm* prod/rel: Films Espanola (Madrid)

CHAPIN, ANNA ALICE
The Deserters, New York 1910, Play
   Sacred Silence 1919 d: Harry Millarde. lps: William
   Russell, George MacQuarrie, Mabel Julienne Scott. 6r
   USA. prod/rel: Fox Film Corp., William Fox©

The Eagle's Mate, New York 1914, Novel
   Eagle's Mate, The 1914 d: James Kirkwood. lps: Mary
   Pickford, James Kirkwood, Ida Waterman. 5165f USA.
   prod/rel: Famous Players Film Co., Paramount Pictures
   Corp.

The Girl of Gold, 1920, Short Story
   Girl of Gold, The 1925 d: John Ince. lps: Florence
   Vidor, Malcolm McGregor, Alan Roscoe. 4969f USA.
   prod/rel: Regal Pictures, Producers Distributing Corp.

Mountain Madness, New York 1917, Novel
   Mountain Madness 1920 d: Lloyd B. Carleton. lps:
   Mignon Anderson, Ed Coxen, Jack Lott. 5-6r USA.
   prod/rel: Lloyd Carleton Productions, Clermont
   Photoplays Corp.

CHAPIN, ANNE MORRISON
Love Flies in the Window, Stockbridge, MA. 1933,
Play
   This Man Is Mine 1934 d: John Cromwell. lps: Irene
   Dunne, Ralph Bellamy, Constance Cummings. 76M
   USA. *Transient Love; Husbands Come and Go* prod/rel:
   RKO Radio Pictures©, Pandro S. Berman Production

CHAPIN, CARL
The Test, Short Story
   Fire-Fighter's Love, The 1912 d: Oscar Eagle. lps:
   Charles Clary, William Stowell, Adrienne Kroell. 1000f
   USA. prod/rel: Selig Polyscope Co.

CHAPIN, FREDERIC
C.O.D., New York 1912, Play
   C.O.D. 1915 d: Tefft Johnson. lps: Harry Davenport,
   Hughie MacK, Charles Brown. 4r USA. prod/rel:
   Vitagraph Co. of America©, Broadway Star Features

The Lost City, Short Story
   Jungle Princess, The 1920. lps: Juanita Hansen,
   George Chesebro, Frank Clark. 7r USA. prod/rel: Selig
   Polyscope Co., State Rights

CHAPIN, ROBERT
G.I. Honeymoon, Play
   G.I. Honeymoon 1945 d: Phil Karlson. lps: Gale Storm,
   Peter Cookson, Arline Judge. 70M USA. prod/rel:
   Monogram

CHAPLIN, CHARLES (1889–1977), UKN, Chaplin,
Charles Spencer
My Biography, Book
   Chaplin 1992 d: Richard Attenborough. lps: Robert
   Downey Jr., Geraldine Chaplin, Dan Aykroyd. 145M
   UKN. prod/rel: Guild, Lambeth

CHAPLIN, PATRICE
Siesta, Novel
   Siesta 1988 d: Mary Lambert. lps: Ellen Barkin,
   Gabriel Byrne, Julian Sands. 100M USA/UKN. prod/rel:
   Palace, Lorimar

CHAPMAN, EDDIE
Joey Boy, Novel
   Joey Boy 1965 d: Frank Launder. lps: Harry H.
   Corbett, Stanley Baxter, Bill Fraser. 91M UKN.
   prod/rel: British Lion, Temgrange

CHAPMAN, JOHN
Dry Rot, London 1954, Play
   Dry Rot 1956 d: Maurice Elvey. lps: Ronald Shiner,
   Brian Rix, Peggy Mount. 87M UKN. prod/rel: Romulus,
   Remus

CHAPMAN, ROBERT
Behind the Headlines, Novel
   Behind the Headlines 1956 d: Charles Saunders. lps:
   Paul Carpenter, Hazel Court, Adrienne Corri. 67M
   UKN. prod/rel: Kenilworth, Rank Film Distributors

Murder for the Millions, Novel
   Murder Reported 1957 d: Charles Saunders. lps: Paul
   Carpenter, Melissa Stribling, Patrick Holt. 58M UKN.
   prod/rel: Fortress, Columbia

One Jump Ahead, Novel
   One Jump Ahead 1955 d: Charles Saunders. lps: Paul
   Carpenter, Diane Hart, Jill Adams. 66M UKN. prod/rel:
   Kenilworth, Fortress

Winter Wears a Shroud, Novel
   Delavine Affair, The 1954 d: Douglas Pierce. lps:
   Peter Reynolds, Honor Blackman, Gordon Jackson.
   64M UKN. *Murder Is News* prod/rel:
   Croydon-Passmore, Monarch

CHAPMAN, TOM
Story
   Hangar 18 1980 d: James L. Conway. lps: Darren
   McGavin, Robert Vaughn, Gary Collins. 99M USA.
   Invasion Force prod/rel: Sunn Classics

CHAPMAN, VERA
The King's Damosel, Novel
   Quest for Camelot 1998 d: Frederick Du Chan. ANM.
   86M USA. *The Magic Sword Quest for Camelot* prod/rel:
   Warner Bros.©

CHARAND, GABRIEL
Ames Nostalgiques, Novel
   Danzatrice Mascherata, La 1916 d: Pier Antonio
   Gariazzo. lps: Cecyl Tryan, Mario CimarrA. 1623m ITL.
   Anima Nostalgica prod/rel: Gloria Film

CHAREF, MEHDI
Le the Au Harem d'Archimede, Novel
   The Au Harem d'Archimede, Le 1984 d: Mehdi
   Charef. lps: Kader Boukhanef, Remi Martin, Laure
   Duthilleul. 110M FRN. *Tea in the Harem* (USA)
   prod/rel: K.G. Prod., Ministere de la Culture

CHARELL, ERIK (1895–1974), GRM
Feuerwerk, Play
   Feuerwerk 1956 d: Kurt Hoffmann. lps: Lilli Palmer,
   Karl Schonbock, Romy Schneider. 90M GRM. *Oh! My
   Papa; Oh Mein Papa* prod/rel: N.D.F., Bavaria

CHARLES, MOIE
Scarlet Thread, 1949, Play
   Scarlet Thread 1951 d: Lewis Gilbert. lps: Kathleen
   Byron, Laurence Harvey, Sydney Tafler. 84M UKN.
   prod/rel: Nettlefold, International Realist

CHARLES, THERESA
Happy Now I Go, Novel
   Woman With No Name, The 1950 d: Ladislao Vajda,
   George M. O'Ferrall. lps: Phyllis Calvert, Edward
   Underdown, Helen Cherry. 83M UKN. *Her Panelled
   Door* (USA) prod/rel: Independent Film Producers,
   Ab-Pathe

CHARLES-ROUX, EDMONDE
Oublier Palermo, Novel
   Dimenticare Palermo 1990 d: Francesco Rosi. lps:
   James Belushi, Mimi Rogers, Joss Ackland. 100M
   ITL/FRN. *Oublier Palermo* (FRN); *To Forget Palermo*
   prod/rel: C.G. Group Leopard, Gaumont

CHARPENTIER, GUSTAVE (1860–1956), FRN
Louise, Paris 1900, Opera
   Louise 1939 d: Abel Gance. lps: Grace Moore, Suzanne
   Despres, Georges Thill. 85M FRN. prod/rel: Societe
   Parisienne De Production De Film

CHARPENTIER, JULES
Das Haus Auf Dem Hugel, Novel
   Haus Auf Dem Hugel, Das 1964 d: Werner Klinger.
   lps: Ron Randell, Paul Esser, Bum Kruger. 91M AUS.
   prod/rel: Hoela

CHARRIERE, HENRI (1906–1973), FRN
Papillon, Book
   Papillon 1973 d: Franklin J. Schaffner. lps: Steve
   McQueen, Dustin Hoffman, Victor Jory. 150M USA.
   prod/rel: Papillon Partnership, Corona

CHARTERIS, LESLIE (1907–1993), SNG, Yin, Leslie
Charles Bowyer
Novel
   Saint Prend l'Affut, Le 1966 d: Christian-Jaque. lps:
   Jean Marais, Maria Brockerhoff, Jess Hahn. 90M
   FRN/ITL. *Il Santo Prende la Mira* (ITL); *The Saint
   Versus.* (USA) prod/rel: Intermondia Films, S.N.C.

Angels of Doom, New York 1931, Novel
   Saint Strikes Back, The 1939 d: John Farrow. lps:
   George Sanders, Wendy Barrie, Jonathan Hale. 67M
   USA. *The Saint Strikes Twice* prod/rel: RKO Radio
   Pictures©

Getaway, Short Story
   Saint's Vacation, The 1941 d: Leslie Fenton. lps:
   Hugh Sinclair, Sally Gray, Arthur MacRae. 75M UKN.
   prod/rel: RKO-Radio British

Lady on a Train, Novel
   Lady on a Train 1945 d: Charles David. lps: Deanna
   Durbin, Ralph Bellamy, David Bruce. 94M USA.
   prod/rel: Universal

Meet the Tiger, Novel
   Saint Meets the Tiger, The 1941 d: Paul L. Stein. lps:
   Hugh Sinclair, Jean Gillie, Clifford Evans. 79M UKN.
   prod/rel: RKO-Radio British

The Million Pound Day, Short Story
   Saint in London, The 1939 d: John Paddy Carstairs.
   lps: George Sanders, Sally Gray, Ballard Berkeley. 77M
   UKN. prod/rel: RKO-Radio

Le Saint a Palm Springs, Novel
   Saint Mene la Danse, Le 1960 d: Jacques Nahum. lps:
   Felix Marten, Jean Desailly, Michele Mercier. 90M
   FRN. *The Dance of Death* (USA); *Le Saint Conduit le Bal*
   prod/rel: Films Du Cyclope, Lux

The Saint in New York, London 1935, Novel
   Saint in New York, The 1938 d: Ben Holmes. lps:
   Louis Hayward, Kay Sutton, Sig Ruman. 72M USA.
   prod/rel: RKO Radio Pictures©

CHARTRETTES, PAUL
Le Gars du Milieu, Play
   Nuit de Folies, Une 1934 d: Maurice Cammage. lps:
   Fernandel, Jacques Varennes, Marcelle Parysis. 90M
   FRN. prod/rel: Fortuna-Film-Production

CHARVAY, ROBERT
L' Enfant du Miracle, Play
   Enfant du Miracle, L' 1932 d: D. B. Maurice. lps:
   Armand Bernard, Marcel Vallee, Blanche Montel. 79M
   FRN. prod/rel: Societe Des Films Diamant

Mademoiselle Josette, Ma Femme, Play
   Mademoiselle Josette, Ma Femme 1914 d: Andre
   Liabel. lps: Keppens, Cesar, Renee Sylvaire. 605m FRN.
   prod/rel: Eclair

   Mademoiselle Josette, Ma Femme 1926 d: Gaston
   Ravel. lps: Livio Pavanelli, Dolly Davis, Agnes
   Esterhazy. 2462m FRN. prod/rel: Alga-Films, Films De
   France

   Mademoiselle Josette, Ma Femme 1932 d: Andre
   Berthomieu. lps: Annabella, Jean Murat, Jean Marconi.
   84M FRN. prod/rel: Films De France

   Mademoiselle Josette, Ma Femme 1950 d: Andre
   Berthomieu. lps: Odile Versois, Fernand Gravey,
   Georges Lannes. 92M FRN. prod/rel: Majestic-Films

CHASE, BORDEN (1900–1971), USA
Blue White and Perfect, Novel
   Blue, White and Perfect 1941 d: Herbert I. Leeds. lps:
   Lloyd Nolan, Mary Beth Hughes, Helene Reynolds. 74M
   USA. prod/rel: 20th Century Fox

The Chisholm Trail, Short Story
   Red River 1948 d: Howard Hawks. lps: John Wayne,
   Montgomery Clift, Walter Brennan. 133M USA.
   prod/rel: United Artists

   Red River 1988 d: Richard Michaels. lps: James
   Arness, Bruce Boxleitner, Gregory Harrison. TVM.
   100M USA. prod/rel: MGM, Ua Telecommunications

Concerto, Story
   I've Always Loved You 1946 d: Frank Borzage. lps:
   Philip Dorn, Catherine McLeod, William Carter. 117M
   USA. *Concerto* (UKN) prod/rel: Republic

East River, New York 1935, Novel
   Under Pressure 1935 d: Raoul Walsh. lps: Edmund
   Lowe, Victor McLaglen, Florence Rice. 70M USA.
   Bed-Rock; Man Lock; East River prod/rel: Fox Film
   Corp.©

Hell's Kitchen Has a Pantry, Novel
   Devil's Party, The 1938 d: Ray McCarey. lps: Victor
   McLaglen, William Gargan, Paul Kelly. 70M USA.
   Hell's Kitchen; Riot Patrol prod/rel: Universal Pictures
   Co.

Life of Gerard Graham Dennis, Story
   Great Jewel Robber, The 1950 d: Peter Godfrey. lps:
   David Brian, Marjorie Reynolds, John Archer. 91M
   USA. *After Nightfall* prod/rel: Warner Bros.

The Man from Colorado, Novel
   Man from Colorado, The 1949 d: Henry Levin. lps:
   Glenn Ford, Ellen Drew, William Holden. 99M USA.
   prod/rel: Columbia

Pay to Learn, Story
   Navy Comes Through, The 1942 d: A. Edward
   Sutherland. lps: Pat O'Brien, George Murphy, Jane
   Wyatt. 82M USA. prod/rel: RKO Radio

CHASE, DAVID
The Hunter, Story
   Scream of the Wolf 1974 d: Dan Curtis. lps: Peter
   Graves, Clint Walker, Jo Ann Pflug. TVM. 73M USA.
   prod/rel: Metromedia Productions

La Tumba Des Vampiro, Novel
   Tumba Des Vampiro, La 1974 d: Leon Klimovsky. lps:
   William Smith, Mike Pataki, Lyn Peters. 89M SPN/ITL.
   prod/rel: Leon Klimovsky, Classic

CHASE, JAMES HADLEY (1906–, UKN, Raymond,
Rene
Novel
   Lotosbluten Fur Miss Quon 1966 d: Jurgen Roland.
   lps: Lang Jeffries, Francisca Tu, Daniel Emilfork. 95M
   GRM/FRN/ITL. *Coup de Gong a Hong-Kong* (FRN);
   Trappola Per 4 (ITL); *A Lotus for Miss Quon* (USA);
   Lotus Blossoms for Miss Quon prod/rel: Rapid, Pea

   Pas Folle la Guepe 1972 d: Jean Delannoy. lps:
   Francoise Rosay, Anny Duperey, Bruno Pradal. 100M
   FRN/GRM/ITL. *Nur Eine Frage Der Zeit* (GRM)
   prod/rel: Filmsonor, Marceau-Fides

   Pittsville - Eine Safe Voll Blut 1974 d: Krzysztof
   Zanussi. lps: Horst Buchholz, Ann Wedgeworth, Chip
   Taylor. 95M GRM/USA. *The Catamount Killing* (USA);
   Longhelder Fur Pittsville; Pittsville prod/rel: Manfred
   Durniok Prod., Starlight

Sarg Aus Hongkong, Ein 1964 d: Manfred R. Kohler. lps: Heinz Drache, Elga Andersen, Sabina Sesselmann. 86M GRM/FRN. *A Coffin from Hong Kong* (USA) prod/rel: Urania, Rapid

Wartezimmer Zum Jenseits 1964 d: Alfred Vohrer. lps: Hildegard Knef, Gotz George, Richard Munch. 90M GRM. *Waiting Room to the Beyond* prod/rel: Rialto, Constantin

A Tenir Au Frais, Novel
Demoniaque, Le 1968 d: Rene Gainville. lps: Anne Vernon, Francois Gabriel, Claude Cerval. 90M FRN. *Le Contempteur*; *La Mort En Liberte* prod/rel: C.E.P.C.

Ca N'arrive Qu'aux Vivants, Novel
Ca N'arrive Qu'aux Vivants 1958 d: Tony Saytor. lps: Raymond Pellegrin, Giselle Pascal, Magali Noel. 78M FRN. prod/rel: S.N.C., Films Marivaux

Come Easy - Go Easy, London 1960, Novel
Chair de Poule 1964 d: Julien Duvivier. lps: Robert Hossein, Jean Sorel, Catherine Rouvel. 110M FRN/ITL. *Pelle d'Oca* (ITL); *Highway Pickup* (UKN) prod/rel: Paris-Films Production, Interopa Film

Crime and Passion, Novel
Crime and Passion 1975 d: Ivan Passer. lps: Omar Sharif, Karen Black, Joseph Bottoms. 92M USA/UKN/GRM. *There's an Ace Up My Sleeve*; *Ace Up Your Sleeve*; *Ace Up My Sleeve*; *Frankensteins Spukschloss* (GRM); *Frankenstein's Haunted Castle* prod/rel: Film-Cine

Eve, London 1945, Novel
Eva 1962 d: Joseph Losey, Guidarino Guidi. lps: Jeanne Moreau, Stanley Baker, Virna Lisi. 155M FRN/ITL. *Eva (the Devil's Woman)*; *Eve* prod/rel: Interopa Film (Roma), Paris-Films Production (Paris)

Fais-Moi Confiance, Novel
Canailles, Les 1959 d: Maurice Labro. lps: Marina Vlady, Robert Hossein, Scilla Gabel. 102M FRN/ITL. *Le Canaglie* (ITL); *Take Me As I Am* (UKN); *Riff-Raff* (USA); *The Ruffians* prod/rel: Societe Princia, Transmonde Films

The Grissom Gang, Novel
Grissom Gang, The 1971 d: Robert Aldrich. lps: Kim Darby, Scott Wilson, Tony Musante. 128M USA. prod/rel: Associates & Aldrich

High Stakes, Novel
I'll Get You for This 1951 d: Joseph M. Newman. lps: George Raft, Coleen Gray, Charles Goldner. 85M UKN/USA. *Lucky Nicky Cain* (USA) prod/rel: Independent Film Distributors, Kaydor-Romulus

Hit and Run, Novel
Delit de Fuite 1958 d: Bernard Borderie. lps: Antonella Lualdi, Felix Marten, Folco Lulli. 100M FRN/ITL/YGS. *Sangue Sull'asfalto* (ITL) prod/rel: C.I.C.C., Aurelia Film

Hit and Run 1985 d: Claudio Cutry. lps: Ken Roberson, George Kennedy, Pamela Bryant. 90M USA. *Rigged* prod/rel: Cinestar

L' Homme a l'Impermeable, Novel
Homme a l'Impermeable, L' 1957 d: Julien Duvivier. lps: Fernandel, Bernard Blier, Jacques Duby. 106M FRN/ITL. *L' Uomo Dall'Impermeabile* (ITL); *The Man in the Raincoat* (UKN); *Fugue Pour Clarinette*; *Partie Fine* prod/rel: Jacques Bar, Cite Films

Just Another Sucker, Novel
Palmetto 1998 d: Volker Schlondorff. lps: Woody Harrelson, Elisabeth Shue, Gina Gershon. 114M USA/GRM. prod/rel: Columbia Pictures, Castle Rock Entertainment©

The Last Page, Play
Last Page, The 1952 d: Terence Fisher. lps: George Brent, Marguerite Chapman, Raymond Huntley. 84M UKN. *Manbait* (USA) prod/rel: Exclusive, Hammer

Une Manche Et la Belle, Novel
Manche Et la Belle, Une 1957 d: Henri Verneuil. lps: Henri Vidal, Mylene Demongeot, Isa MirandA. 98M FRN. *What Price Murder* (USA); *The Evil That Is Eve*

Mefiez-Vous Fillettes, Novel
Mefiez-Vous, Fillettes 1957 d: Yves Allegret. lps: Antonella Lualdi, Robert Hossein, Michele Cordoue. 87M FRN/ITL. *Young Girls Beware* (USA); *La Casa Di Madame Kora* (ITL) prod/rel: Agens Delahaie, Silver Films

Mise En Caisse, Novel
Dans la Gueule du Loup 1961 d: Jean-Charles Dudrumet. lps: Felix Marten, Magali Noel, Pascale Roberts. 73M FRN. prod/rel: Panda Films, Robert Ciriez Daubigny

Miss Shumway Waves a Wand, Novel
Miss Shumway Jette un Sort 1962 d: Jean Jabely. lps: Taina Beryll, Jess Hahn, Harold Kaye. 94M FRN/ARG. *Une Blonde Comme Ca!*; *Miss Shumway Casts a Spell* prod/rel: Metzger and Woog, Paris-Elysee Films

Rough Magic 1995 d: Clare Peploe. lps: Bridget Fonda, Russell Crowe, Jim Broadbent. 104M UKN/FRN. *Miss Shumway Jette un Sort* (FRN) prod/rel: 20th Century Fox, Ugc

Mission to Venice, Novel
Voir Venise Et Crever 1966 d: Andre Versini. lps: Sean Flynn, Madeleine Robinson, Karin Baal. 100M FRN/GRM/ITL. *Mord Am Canale Grande* (GRM); *Murder on the Grand Canal*; *La Spia Che Venne Dall'Ovest* (ITL) prod/rel: Metzger Et Woog, Marceau-Cocinor

No Orchids for Miss Blandish, Novel
No Orchids for Miss Blandish 1948 d: St. John L. Clowes. lps: Jack La Rue, Linden Travers, Hugh McDermott. 104M UKN. prod/rel: Alliance, Tudor

Par un Beat Matin d'Ete, Novel
Par un Beau Matin d'Ete 1964 d: Jacques Deray. lps: Jean-Paul Belmondo, Sophie Daumier, Geraldine Chaplin. 93M FRN/ITL/SPN. *Rapina Al Sole* (ITL); *Secuestro Bajo El Sol* (SPN) prod/rel: Sud Pacifique, C.I.C.C.

La Petite Vertu, Novel
Petite Vertu, La 1968 d: Serge Korber. lps: Dany Carrel, Jacques Perrin, Robert Hossein. 90M FRN. prod/rel: Gaumont International

Retour de Manivelle, Novel
Retour de Manivelle 1957 d: Denys de La Patelliere. lps: Michele Morgan, Daniel Gelin, Peter Van Eyck. 118M FRN/ITL. *There's Alway's a Price Tag* (USA) prod/rel: Intermondia Films, Cinematografica Associata

This Way for the Shroud, Novel
Morte a Contratto 1993 d: Gianni Lepre. lps: Giampiero Bianchi, Eleonora Brigliadori, Andrea Prodan. TVM. 200M ITL.

Try This One for Size, Novel
Try This One for Size 1989 d: Guy Hamilton. lps: Michael Brandon, David Carradine, Arielle Dombasle. 107M USA/FRN/ITL. *La Grande Fauche* (FRN); *Sauf Votre Respect* prod/rel: Candice Prod., S.G.G.C.

The Way the Cookie Crumbles, Novel
Trop Petit, Mon Ami 1969 d: Eddy Matalon. lps: Michael Dunn, Jane Birkin, Bernard Fresson. 95M FRN. prod/rel: Films Corona, Films Du Quadrangle

What's Better Than Money
Requiem Per Voce E Pianoforte 1993 d: Tomaso Sherman. lps: Simona Cavallari, Massimo Popolizio, Lara Wendel. TVM. 200M ITL.

The World in My Pocket, London 1959, Novel
An Einem Freitag Um Halb Zwolf 1961 d: Alvin Rakoff. lps: Rod Steiger, Nadja Tiller, Peter Van Eyck. 103M GRM/FRN/ITL. *Il Mondo Nella Mia Tasca* (ITL); *The World in My Pocket* (USA); *Die Toten Tabula Rasa-Funf*; *Vendredi 13 Heures* (FRN); *Pas de Mentalite* prod/rel: Corona Filmproduktion, Criterion Film

You Have Yourself a Deal, London 1966, Novel
Blonde de Pekin, La 1968 d: Nicolas Gessner. lps: Mireille Darc, Georgia Moll, Claudio Brook. 95M FRN/ITL/GRM. *Die Blonde von Peking* (GRM); *Peking Blonde* (USA); *La Bionda Di Pechino* (ITL); *The Blonde from Peking*; *Professional Blonde* prod/rel: Hans Eckelkamp Film Produktion, Copernic Films

CHASE, MARY COYLE (1907–, USA
Bernardine, 1953, Play
Bernardine 1957 d: Henry Levin. lps: Pat Boone, Terry Moore, Janet Gaynor. 95M USA. prod/rel: 20th Century-Fox

Chi House, 1939, Play
Sorority House 1939 d: John Farrow. lps: Anne Shirley, James Ellison, J. M. Kerrigan. 63M USA. *That Girl from College* (UKN); *Chi House* prod/rel: RKO Radio Pictures©

Harvey, New York 1944, Play
Harvey 1950 d: Henry Koster. lps: James Stewart, Josephine Hull, Cecil Kellaway. 104M USA. prod/rel: Universal-International

Harvey 1972 d: Fielder Cook. lps: James Stewart, Helen Hayes, Arleen Francis. TVM. 74M USA.

Harvey 1996 d: George Schaefer. lps: Harry Anderson, Brendan Beiser, Lynda Boyd. TVM. F USA. prod/rel: Pmp Productions

CHASTAIN, THOMAS
Death Stalk, Novel
Death Stalk 1975 d: Robert Day. lps: Vic Morrow, Neville Brand, Vince Edwards. TVM. 78M USA. prod/rel: David Wolper Pictures

CHATEAUBRIAND, FRANCOIS RENE
Aventures du Dernier Abencerage, 1826
Ultimo Degli Abenceragi, L' 1911. 284m ITL. *The Last of His Race* (UKN) prod/rel: Cines

CHATFIELD-TAYLOR, HOBART C.
The Crimson Wing, Chicago 1902, Novel
Crimson Wing, The 1915 d: E. H. Calvert. lps: E. H. Calvert, Ruth Stonehouse, Beverly Bayne. 6r USA. prod/rel: Essanay Film Mfg. Co.©, V-L-S-E, Inc.

CHATRIAN, ALEXANDRE
L' Ami Fritz, Novel
Ami Fritz, L' 1933 d: Jacques de Baroncelli. lps: Simone Bourday, Lucien Duboscq, Jacques de Feraudy. 90M FRN. prod/rel: Les Films Artistiques Francais

The Bells, Play
Bells, The 1913 d: Oscar Apfel. lps: E. P. Sullivan, Irving Cummings, Gertrude Robinson. 2r USA. prod/rel: Reliance

Le Juif Polonais, Paris 1869, Play
Bells, The 1918 d: Ernest C. Warde. lps: Frank Keenan, Lois Wilson, Joseph J. Dowling. 5r USA. prod/rel: Anderson-Brunton Co., Pathe Exchange, Inc.©

Bells, The 1926 d: James Young. lps: Lionel Barrymore, Fred Warren, Boris Karloff. 6300f USA. prod/rel: Chadwick Pictures

Bells, The 1931 d: Harcourt Templeman, O. M. Werndorff. lps: Donald Calthrop, Jane Welsh, Edward Sinclair. 75M UKN/GRM. prod/rel: Producers Distributing Corporation, British Sound Films Productions

Juif Polonais, Le 1931 d: Jean Kemm. lps: Harry Baur, Simone Mareuil, Georges La Cressonniere. 95M FRN. prod/rel: Establissements Jacques Haik

Les Rantzau, Play
Rantzau, Les 1924 d: Gaston Roudes. lps: France Dhelia, Georges Melchior, Maurice Schutz. 1900m FRN. prod/rel: Gaston Roudes, Sphinx

CHATTERJEE, BANKIMCHANDRA (1838–1894), IND, Chatterji, Bankimchandra
Anandmath, 1884, Novel
Anandmath 1952 d: Hemen GuptA. lps: Prithviraj Kapoor, Geeta Bali, RanjanA. 176M IND. prod/rel: Filmistan

CHATTERJEE, SARATCHANDRA (1876–1938), IND, Chatterji, Saratchandra
Boikunther Will, 1916, Novel
Sautela Bhai 1962 d: Mahesh Kaul. lps: Guru Dutt, Pronoti Bhattacharya, Bipin GuptA. 165M IND. *The Stepbrother* prod/rel: Alok Bharati

Dena Paona, Novel
Pujarin 1936 d: Prafulla Roy. lps: K. L. Saigal, Chandra, Pahadi Sanyal. 137M IND. prod/rel: International Filmcraft, New Theatres

Devdas, 1917, Novel
Devdas 1935 d: Pramathesh Chandra BaruA. lps: Pramathesh Chandra Barua, Jamuna, K. C. Dey. 139M IND. *Debbas* prod/rel: New Theatres

Devdas 1941 d: Pramathesh Chandra BaruA. lps: K. L. Saigal, Jamuna, K. C. Dey. 141M IND. prod/rel: New Theatres

Swami, 1918, Novel
Swami 1977 d: Basu Chatterjee. lps: Girish Karnad, Shabana Azmi, Vikram. 129M IND. *The Husband*; *Lord and Master* prod/rel: Jaya Sarathy Combine

CHATTERTON, RUTH
The Man in Evening Clothes, Story
She Wolves 1925 d: Maurice Elvey. lps: Alma Rubens, Jack Mulhall, Bertram Grassby. 5783f USA. prod/rel: Fox Film Corp.

CHATTOPADHYAY, JALADHAR
Reetimata Natak, 1936, Play
Talkie of Talkies 1937 d: Sisir Kumar Bhaduri. lps: Sisir Kumar Bhaduri, Ahindra Choudhury, Jahar Ganguly. 135M IND. *Dasturmoto Talkie* prod/rel: Kali Films

CHATWIN, BRUCE
On the Black Hill, 1982, Novel
On the Black Hill 1987 d: Andrew Grieve. lps: Mike Gwilym, Robert Gwilym, Bob Peck. 117M UKN. prod/rel: Bfi, Channel 4

Utz, Novel
Utz 1992 d: George Sluizer. lps: Armin Mueller-Stahl, Brenda Fricker, Peter Riegert. 91M UKN/GRM/ITL. prod/rel: Viva Pictures, BBC Films

The Viceroy of Ouidah, Novel
Cobra Verde 1987 d: Werner Herzog. lps: Klaus Kinski, King Ampaw, Jose Lewgoy. 110M GRM. prod/rel: Concorde, Werner Herzog Film Production

CHAUCER, GEOFFREY (c1343–1400), UKN
The Canterbury Tales, c1400, Verse
Racconti Di Canterbury, I 1972 d: Pier Paolo Pasolini. lps: Pier Paolo Pasolini, Hugh Griffith, Josephine Chaplin. 111M ITL/FRN. *The Canterbury Tales* (UKN) prod/rel: P.E.A. (Roma), Productions Artistes Associes (Paris)

CHAYEFSKY, PADDY (1923–1981), UKN, Chayefsky, Paddy Sidney
Story
As Young As You Feel 1951 d: Harmon Jones. lps: Monty Woolley, Thelma Ritter, David Wayne. 77M USA. prod/rel: 20th Century-Fox
Altered States, 1978, Novel
Altered States 1980 d: Ken Russell. lps: William Hurt, Blair Brown, Bob Balaban. 103M USA. prod/rel: Warner Bros.
The Bachelor Party, 1955, Television Play
Bachelor Party, The 1957 d: Delbert Mann. lps: Don Murray, E. G. Marshall, Jack Warden. 87M USA. prod/rel: United Artists, Norma Productions
The Catered Affair, 1955, Television Play
Catered Affair, The 1956 d: Richard Brooks. lps: Ernest Borgnine, Bette Davis, Debbie Reynolds. 93M USA. *Wedding Breakfast* (UKN) prod/rel: MGM
Holiday Song
Zug Nach Manhattan, Der 1981 d: Rolf von Sydow. lps: Heinz Ruhmann, Ulrike Bliefert, Hans Hessling. MTV. 60M GRM. *Holiday Song*
Marty, 1953, Television Play
Marty 1953 d: Delbert Mann. lps: Rod Steiger, Nancy Marchand. MTV. 53M USA.
Marty 1955 d: Delbert Mann. lps: Ernest Borgnine, Betsy Blair, Esther Minciotti. 99M USA. prod/rel: United Artists, Hecht-Lancaster-Steven Prods.
Middle of the Night, 1954, Television Play
Middle of the Night 1959 d: Delbert Mann. lps: Kim Novak, Glenda Farrell, Fredric March. 118M USA. prod/rel: Columbia, Sudan Co.

CHEEVER, JOHN (1912–1982), USA
The Five Forty-Eight, 1955, Short Story
5:48, The 1979 d: James Ivory. TVM. 58M USA. *The Five Forty-Eight*
The Swimmer, 1964, Short Story
Swimmer, The 1968 d: Frank Perry, Sydney Pollack (Uncredited). lps: Burt Lancaster, Janet Landgard, Janice Rule. 94M USA. prod/rel: Horizon Dover, Inc.

CHEKHOV, ANTON (1860–1904), RSS
Short Stories
Toto E Il Re Di Roma 1952 d: Steno, Mario Monicelli. lps: Toto, Anna Carena, Giovanna PalA. 95M ITL. prod/rel: Golden Film, Humanitas Film
Novel
Uberflussige Menschen 1926 d: Alexander Rasumny. lps: Bruno Arno, Hans Brausewetter, Wilhelm Diegelmann. 2693m GRM. *Superfluous People* (USA) prod/rel: Prometheus
Weidenbaum, Der 1984 d: Sohrab Shahid Saless. lps: Josef Stehlik, Peter Stanik, Milan Drotar. MTV. 90M GRM/CZC. *The Willow Tree* prod/rel: Radio Bremen, Slovensky Film
Anna Na Shee, 1895, Short Story
Anna Na Shee 1954 d: Isider Annensky. lps: Alla Larionova, A. Sashin-Nikolsky, Petya Maltsev. 86M USS. *The Anna Cross*
Anyuta, 1886, Short Story
Aniuta 1960 d: Marija Andjaparidze. 20M USS. *Anyuta*
Baby, 1891, Short Story
Glavnyj Svidetel 1969 d: Aida ManasarovA. 69M USS. *The Main Witness; Glavnye Svidetel*
Bezzakonie, 1887, Short Story
Bezzakonie 1953 d: Konstantin Yudin. 15M USS.
Chayka, St. Petersburg 1896, Play
Chaika 1971 d: Yuli Karasik. lps: Ludmila Savelieva, Vladimir Chetverikov, Alla DemidovA. 98M USS. *The Seagull* (UKN); *Cajka; Chayka*
Gabbiano, Il 1977 d: Marco Bellocchio. lps: Laura Betti, Giulio Brogi, Pamela Villoresi. MTV. 132M ITL. *The Sea Gull* (USA); *The Seagull* prod/rel: Italtelevision, Rai Tv
Sea Gull, The 1969 d: Sidney Lumet. lps: James Mason, Vanessa Redgrave, Simone Signoret. 141M UKN/USA. prod/rel: Sidney Lumet Productions, Warner-Pathe
Chelovek V Futlyare, 1898, Short Story
Chelovek V Futlyare 1939 d: Isider Annensky. 95M USS.
Chelovek V Futlyare 1983 d: Leonid Zarubin. ANM. 19M USS.
Chernyi Monakh, 1894, Short Story
Tchiorni Monak 1988 d: Ivan Dykhovichny. lps: Stanislas Lioubchine, Tatyana Droubitch, Piotr Fomienko. 90M USS. *Le Moine Noir; Chernyi Monakh; The Black Monk*
The Cherry Orchard, Play
Vishnevyj Sad 1993 d: Anna ChernakovA. lps: Tatjana Lavrova, Alexander Feklistov, Elena KolchuginA. 78M RSS. *The Cherry Garden; The Cherry Orchard* prod/rel: Ao Vima, Vgik

Le Contrebasse, Short Story
Contrebasse, La 1962 d: Maurice Fasquel. lps: Nicole Gueden, Christian Marin. 30M FRN. prod/rel: Tadie Cinema
Dama S Sobachkoy, 1899, Short Story
Dama S Sobachkoi 1960 d: Josif Heifitz. lps: Alexei Batalov, Iya Savvina, Ala ChostakovA. 90M USS. *The Lady With the Dog* (USA); *The Lady With the Little Dog; Lady With a Little Dog; Dama S Sobackoj* prod/rel: Lenfilm
Oci Ciornie 1987 d: Nikita Mikhalkov. lps: Marcello Mastroianni, Silvana Mangano, Marthe Keller. 118M ITL. *Dark Eyes* (USA); *Black Eyes* prod/rel: Rai
Damy, 1886, Short Story
Damy 1954 d: Lev Kulidjanov, Genrikh Oganisyan. 18M USS. *Ladies*
Dom S Mezoninom, 1896, Short Story
Dom S Mezoninom 1961 d: Yakov Bazelyan. lps: Sergei Yakovlev, Ninel Myshkova, Lyudmila Gordeychik. 86M USS. *House With an Attic* (USA) prod/rel: Yalta Film Studio
Una Domanda Dim Matrimonio, Play
Matrimonio, Il 1954 d: Antonio Petrucci. lps: Vittorio de Sica, Silvana Pampanini, Renato Rascel. F ITL. prod/rel: Film Costellazione, Cei-Incom
Drama Na Okhote, 1884, Short Story
Moj Laskovyj I Neznyj Zver 1978 d: Emil Lotyanu. lps: Galina Belyayeva, Oleg Yankovsky, Kirill Lavrov. 105M USS. *The Shooting Party* (USA); *The Hunting Accident; Moi Laskovei I Nezhnei Zver; Drama Na Okhote; My Sweet and Tender Animal*
Summer Storm 1944 d: Douglas Sirk. lps: George Sanders, Linda Darnell, Anna Lee. 106M USA. prod/rel: United Artists
Duel, 1891, Short Story
Duel 1961 d: Tatyana Berezantseva, Lev Rudnik. lps: Lyudmila Shagalova, Oleg Strizhenov, Vladimir Druzhnikov. 88M USS. prod/rel: Mosfilm
Plokhoy Khoroshyi Chelovek 1974 d: Josif Heifitz. 90M USS. *The Good Bad Man; Plohoj Horosij Celovek; A Bad Goody; The Duel*
Dyadya Vanya, 1899, Play
Dyadya Vanya 1971 d: Andrei Konchalovsky. lps: Innokenti Smoktunovsky, Irina Kupchenko, Sergei Bondarchuk. 102M USS. *Uncle Vanya; Diadia Vanya; Djadja Vanja* prod/rel: Mosfilm
Uncle Vanya 1958 d: John Goetz, Franchot Tone. lps: Franchot Tone, Dolores Dorn-Heft, George Voscovec. 98M USA. prod/rel: Continental Distributing, the "Uncle Vanya" Company
Uncle Vanya 1963 d: Stuart Burge. 117M UKN.
Ionych, 1898, Short Story
V Gorode "S" 1966 d: Josif Heifitz. lps: Anatoli Papanov, Andrey Popov, Nonna TerentievA. 106M USS. *In the Town of "S"* prod/rel: Lenfilm
Istoriya Odnoy Poyezdki, 1888, Novel
Steppa, La 1962 d: Alberto LattuadA. lps: Daniele Spallone, Pavle Vuisic, Charles Vanel. 110M ITL/FRN. *La Steppe* (FRN); *The Steppe* (USA) prod/rel: Zebra Film (Roma), Aera Films (Paris)
Iubelei, 1891, Play
Iubelei 1944 d: Vladimir Petrov. 40M USS. *Jubilee; Jubilej*
Kalkhas, 1896, Short Story
Lebedinaya Pesnya 1966 d: Juri Mogilevtzev. 18M USS.
Kashtanka, 1887, Short Story
Kashtanka 1952 d: M. M. Tsekhanovsky. ANM. 32M USS.
Khirurgia, 1884, Short Story
Khirurgia 1939 d: Jan Frid. 38M USS.
Khorista, 1886, Short Story
Khoristka 1978 d: Alexander Muratov. 19M USS.
Khudozhestvo, 1886, Short Story
Khudozhestvo 1960 d: Mark Kovalyov. 10M USS. *A Work of Art: Satirical Shorts; A Work of Art*
Leshii, 1890, Play
Wood Demon, The 1974 d: Donald McWhinnie. 110M UKN.
Medved, 1888, Play
Boor, The 1955 d: Nathan Zucker. 15M USA.
Medved 1938 d: Isider Annensky. 45M USS.
Mest, 1886, Short Story
Revenge 1960 d: Irina PoplavskayaA. 26M USS. *Vengeance*
Mstitel, Short Story
Semejnoe Scaste 1969 d: Andrei Ladynin. USS.
Na Dache, 1886, Short Story
Na Dache 1954 d: Georgy Lomidze. 18M USS.
Nalim, 1885, Short Story
Nalim 1938 d: Sergei Sploshnov. 12M USS. *The Fish*

Nalim 1953 d: Alexei Zolotnitzkie. 54M USS.
Nervy, Short Story
Semejnoe Scaste 1969 d: Sergei Soloviev, Alexander Shein. 89M USS. *Happy Family; Family Happiness; Semeinoe Schaste*
Nesut Menya Koni, Novel
Nesut Menya Koni 1997 d: Vladimir Motyl. lps: Andrej Sokolov, G. Pechnikov, A. Vagner. F RSS. *Horses Fly Me* prod/rel: Arion, Kinocentre
Nevesta, 1902, Short Story
Nevesta 1956 d: Grigori Nikulin, Vladimir Shredel. 87M USS.
L' Orso, Play
Matrimonio, Il 1954 d: Antonio Petrucci. lps: Vittorio de Sica, Silvana Pampanini, Renato Rascel. F ITL. prod/rel: Film Costellazione, Cei-Incom
Ot Nechego Delat, 1885-1888, Short Story
Semejnoe Scaste 1969 d: Sergei Soloviev, Alexander Shein. 89M USS. *Happy Family; Family Happiness; Semeinoe Schaste*
Palata No.6, 1892, Short Story
Paviljon Vi 1979 d: Lucian Pintilie. lps: Slobodan Perovic, Zoran Radmilovic, Pavle Vuisic. 97M YGS. *Pavilion Vi*
Pari, 1888, Short Story
Bet, The 1969 d: Ron Waller. 24M USA.
Perepolokh, 1886, Short Story
Perepoloh 1955 d: Vassily Ordynsky, Yakov Segel. SHT USS. *Hullabaloo; Confusion; Alarm; Perepolokh*
Peresolil, 1885, Short Story
Peresolil 1959 d: Vladimir Degtyarov. ANM. 16M USS.
Platonov, c1890, Play
Neokontchennia Piessa Dlia Mekanitcheskovo Pianina 1977 d: Nikita Mikhalkov. lps: Aleksandr Kalaigin, Yelena Solovei, Yevgenia Glushenko. 100M USS. *Unfinished Work for Mechanical Piano; The Mechanical Piano; Unfinished Piece for Player-Piano; Neokoncennaja Pesa Dlja Mehaniceskogo Pianino; Neokonchennaya Pyesa Dlya Mekhanicheskovo Pianino*
Poprygunya, 1892, Short Story
Poprygunya 1955 d: Samson Samsonov. lps: Sergei Bondarchuk, Ludmila Tselikovskaya, Vladimir Druzhnikov. 103M USS. *The Grasshopper* (USA); *The Gadfly; Poprigunya; The Fidget* prod/rel: Mosfilm
Il Pranzo Di Nozze, Play
Matrimonio, Il 1954 d: Antonio Petrucci. lps: Vittorio de Sica, Silvana Pampanini, Renato Rascel. F ITL. prod/rel: Film Costellazione, Cei-Incom
Preloyheniye, Short Story
Semejnoe Scaste 1969 d: Andrei Ladynin. USS.
Proisshestviye, 1886, Short Story
Dogadjaj 1969 d: Vatroslav MimicA. lps: Pavle Vuisic, Serdo Mimica, Boris Dvornik. 93M YGS. *An Event* (USA); *Dogadaj* prod/rel: Jadran Film
Proizvedeniye Iskusstva, 1886, Short Story
Proizvedeniye Iskusstva 1959 d: Mark Kovalyov. 10M USS.
Rasskaz Neizvestnogo Cheloveka, 1893, Short Story
Rasskaz Neizvestnogo Celoveka 1980 d: Vitautus Zalakevicius. 99M USS. *The Unknown Man's Story; The Story of a Stranger; Story of an Unknown Man*
Roman I Kontrabasom, 1886, Short Story
Romance With a Double Bass 1976 d: Robert Young. lps: Connie Booth, John Cleese, Graham Crowden. 41M UKN.
Sapogi, 1884-85, Short Story
Sapogi 1957 d: Vladimir Niemoliaiev. 25M USS.
Shvedskaya Spichka, 1883, Short Story
Svedskaya Spicka 1954 d: Konstantin Yudin. 61M USS. *The Safety Match* (UKN); *Svedskaya Spichka; The Swedish Match*
Step, 1888, Short Story
Step 1978 d: Sergei Bondarchuk. lps: Stanislav Lyubshin, Ivan Lapikov, Innokenti Smoktunovsky. 131M USS. *The Steppes; Styep; The Steppe*
The Steppe, Short Story
Steppe, La 1989 d: Jean-Jacques Goron. lps: Catherine Rouvel, Jean-Marc Thibault, Matthieu Gain. TVM. 120M FRN.
Svadba, 1889, Play
Svadba 1944 d: Isider Annensky. 47M USS. *Wedding; The Marriage*
Toska, 1885, Short Story
Father, The 1970 d: Mark Fine. 28M USA.
Toska 1969 d: Aleksandr Blank. 21M USS. *Grief*
Tri Sestry, Moscow 1901, Play
Paura E Amore 1987 d: Margarethe von TrottA. lps: Fanny Ardant, Greta Scacchi, Valeria Golino. 114M ITL/GRM/FRN. *Furchten Und Lieben* (GRM); *Trois Soeurs; Love and Fear* (USA); *Peur Et Amour* (FRN); *Three Sisters* prod/rel: Erre Produzione, Bioskop

Three Sisters, The 1966 d: Lee Strasberg, Paul Bogart. lps: Kim Stanley, Geraldine Page, Shelley Winters. TVM. 168M USA.

Three Sisters, The 1968 d: Cedric MessinA. lps: Janet Suzman, Eileen Atkins, Michele Dotrice. MTV. 125M UKN.

Three Sisters, The 1970 d: Laurence Olivier, John Sichel. lps: Jeanne Watts, Joan Plowright, Louise Purnell. 165M UKN. prod/rel: British Lion, Alan Clore Films

Tri Sestry 1964 d: Samson Samsonov. lps: Lyubov Sokolova, Margarita Volodina, Tatyana Malchenko. 118M USS. *Three Sisters*

Tri Sestry 1994 d: Sergei Soloviev. lps: Otto Zander, Ksenija Kachalina, Olga BelyaevA. 98M RSS/GRM. *The Three Sisters*

Tzvety Zapozdalye, 1882, Short Story
Chveti Zapozdalie 1969 d: Abram Room. 101M USS. *Belated Flowers* (USA); *Tzvety Zapozdalye*

Uncle Vanya, 1900, Play
August 1996 d: Anthony Hopkins. lps: Anthony Hopkins, Kate Burton, Leslie Phillips. 99M USA/UKN. prod/rel: Majestic, Granada Films
Country Life 1994 d: Michael Blakemore. lps: Sam Neill, Greta Scacchi, John Hargreaves. 117M ASL. prod/rel: Metro Tartan, Affc

V Ovrage, 1900, Short Story
Beneficiary, The 1979 d: Carlo Gebler. lps: Marian Richardson, Desmond Fenell, Siobhan Ni Shuilleabhain. 100M UKN. prod/rel: Calro Gebler
Kasba 1990 d: Kumar Shahani. lps: Shatrughan Sinha, Mita Vasisht, Manohar Singh. 121M IND. *The Township*; *Kasbah* prod/rel: Nfdc, Doordarshan

V Sude, 1886, Short Story
Sud 1967 d: David Kocharyan. 20M USS.

Vanka, 1884, Short Story
Vanka 1960 d: Edvard Bocharov. 32M USS.
Vanka Zhukov 1981 d: Leonid Zarubin. ANM. 10M USS.

Vedma, 1886, Short Story
Vedma 1956 d: Alexander Abramov. 31M USS. *The Witch*

Vint, 1884, Short Story
Karty 1965 d: Rollan Sergienko. 18M USS.

Vragi, 1887, Short Story
Vragi 1960 d: Yuri Yegorov. 22M USS. *Enemies*

CHELIEU, ARMAN
Novel
Cantante de Napoles, El 1935 d: Howard Bretherton. lps: Enrico Caruso Jr., Carmen Rio, Mona Maris. 77M USA. *The Singer of Naples* prod/rel: Warner Bros. Pictures, Inc.

CHELLI, GAETANO CARLO
L' Eredita Ferramonti, Novel
Eredita Ferramonti, L' 1976 d: Mauro Bolognini. lps: Anthony Quinn, Dominique Sanda, Fabio Testi. 119M ITL. *The Inheritance* (USA); *The Inheritors* prod/rel: Flag Productions, Titanus

CHEN BAICHEN
Qun Mo, 1947, Play
Qun Mo 1948 d: Xu Changlin. 90M CHN.

CHEN DUNDE
The Soul of Kunlun Pass, Novel
Tie Xue Kun Lun Guan 1994 d: Yang Guangyuan. lps: Gao Zhang, Liu Dawei, Tan Feng. 14r CHN. *Bloody Battle at Kunlun Pass* prod/rel: Guangxi Film Studio

CHEN LENGXUE
Huoli Zuiren, Novel
Jiushi Wo 1928 d: Zhu Shouju. lps: Wang Naidong, Wang Yizhi, Wang Yiman. 9r CHN. *It's Me* prod/rel: Da Zhonghua Baihe Film Company

CHEN QITONG
Ke Shan Hong Ri, Opera
Ke Shan Hong Ri 1960 d: Dong Zhaoqi. lps: Li Bing, Jiang Honggang, Dong Zhiyuan. 12r CHN. *The Red Sun Over the Ke Mountains* prod/rel: August First Film Studio

Wan Shui-Qian Shan, Play
Wan Shui-Qian Shan 1959 d: Cheng Yin, Hua Chun. lps: Lan Ma, Huang Kai, Liang Yuru. 10r CHN.; *Across Ten Thousand Rivers and One Thousand Mountains* prod/rel: August First Film Studio

CHEN RUOXI
Geng Er in Beijing, Novel
Shi Lian Zhe 1987 d: Qin Zhiyu. lps: Liu Yan, Xu Lili, Li Jing. 10r CHN. *The Disappointed Lover* prod/rel: Beijing Film Studio

CHEN YUANBIN
Quiju Da Guanshi, Novel
Qiuju Da Guansi 1992 d: Zhang Yimou. lps: Gong Li, Liu Peiqi, Yang Liuchun. 100M HKG/CHN. *The Story of Qiu Ju*; *Qui Ju Da Guanshi*; *Qiu Ju Goes to Court* prod/rel: Beijing Youth Film Studio, Sil-Metropole Organization Ltd.

CHEN YUN
Nian Qing de Yi Dai, Play
Nian Qing de Yi Dai 1965 d: Zhao Ming. lps: Yang Zaibao, Da Shichang, Cao Lei. 12r CHN. *The Younger Generation* prod/rel: Tianma Film Studio
Nian Qing de Yi Dai 1976 d: Ling Zhiao, Zhang Huijun. lps: Bi Jiancang, Zhang Ruifang, Li Yan. 9r CHN. *The Younger Generation* prod/rel: Shanghai Film Studio

CHENG SHUZHENG
Steel Giant, Novel
Gang Tie Ju Ren 1974 d: Yan Gong. lps: Li Yalin, Wang Wenlin, Guo Zhenqing. 11r CHN. *Steel Giant* prod/rel: Changchun Film Studio

CHERAU, GASTON
Champi-Tortu, Novel
Champi-Tortu 1920 d: Jacques de Baroncelli. lps: Henri Janvier, Maria Kouznetzoff, Mme. Trefeuil. 1685m FRN. prod/rel: Film d'Art

CHERBULIEZ, VICTOR
Le Comte Kostia, Novel
Comte Kostia, Le 1924 d: Jacques Robert. lps: Conrad Veidt, Genica Athanasiou, Andre Nox. 2800m FRN/GRM. *Graf Kostja* prod/rel: Jacques Robert
La Ferme du Choquart, Novel
Ferme du Choquart, La 1921 d: Jean Kemm. lps: Genevieve Felix, Mevisto, Maurice Escande. 1840m FRN. prod/rel: Scagl
Miss Rovel, Novel
Miss Rovel 1921 d: Jean Kemm. lps: Jane Faber, Jean Worms, Jean Devalde. 1770m FRN. prod/rel: Scagl

CHERRIER, J.-B.
Le Secret d'Helene Marimon, Novel
Secret d'Helene Marimon, Le 1953 d: Henri Calef. lps: Isa Miranda, Carla Del Poggio, Frank Villard. 100M FRN/ITL. *Il Tradimento Di Elena Marimon* (ITL) prod/rel: S.N.C., Willemetz

CHESSMAN, CARYL
Book
Cell 2455, Death Row 1955 d: Fred F. Sears. lps: William Campbell, Robert Campbell, Marian Carr. 77M USA. prod/rel: Columbia

CHESTER, GEORGE RANDOLPH (1869–1924), USA
Short Stories
New Adventures of Get Rich Quick Wallingford, The 1931 d: Sam Wood. lps: William Haines, Leila Hyams, Jimmy Durante. 96M USA. *Get-Rich-Quick Wallingford*; *The New Wallingford* prod/rel: Metro-Goldwyn-Mayer Corp., Metro-Goldwyn-Mayer Dist. Corp.©
The Enemy, New York 1915, Novel
Enemy, The 1916 d: Paul Scardon. lps: Evart Overton, Peggy Hyland, Charles Kent. 7r USA. prod/rel: Vitagraph Co. of America©, Blue Ribbon Feature
Five Thousand an Hour, New York 1912, Novel
Five Thousand an Hour 1918 d: Ralph Ince. lps: Hale Hamilton, Lucille Lee Stewart, Florence Short. 5r USA. prod/rel: Metro Pictures Corp.©
The Head of the Family, 1912, Short Story
Head of the Family, The 1928 d: Joseph C. Boyle. lps: William Russell, Mickey Bennett, Virginia Lee Corbin. 6250f USA. prod/rel: Gotham Productions, Lumas Film Corp.
The Making of Bobby Burnit, New York 1909, Novel
Making of Bobby Burnit, The 1914 d: Oscar Apfel. lps: Edward Abeles, Theodore Roberts, Bessie Barriscale. 4r USA. *Bobby Burnit* prod/rel: Jesse L. Lasky Feature Play Co., Paramount Pictures Corp.
The Mission and the Maid, the Man, Story
Man, the Mission and the Maid, The 1915 d: Theodore Marston. lps: Dorothy Kelly, James Morrison, George Cooper. SHT USA. prod/rel: Vitagraph Co. of America
The Other Woman, Novel
Fools of Fashion 1926 d: James C. McKay. lps: Mae Busch, Marceline Day, Theodore von Eltz. 6484f USA. prod/rel: Tiffany Productions
Quarantined Rivals, 1906, Short Story
Quarantined Rivals 1927 d: Archie Mayo. lps: Robert Agnew, Kathleen Collins, John Miljan. 6806f USA. prod/rel: Gotham Productions, Lumas Film Corp.
Shadows of the Past, Story
Shadows of the Past 1914 d: Ralph Ince. lps: E. K. Lincoln, Anita Stewart, L. Rogers Lytton. 3r USA. prod/rel: Broadway Star

A Tale of Red Roses, Indianapolis 1914, Novel
My Man 1924 d: David Smith. lps: Patsy Ruth Miller, Dustin Farnum, Niles Welch. 6800f USA. prod/rel: Vitagraph Co. of America

CHESTER, LILLIAN
The Enemy, New York 1915, Novel
Enemy, The 1916 d: Paul Scardon. lps: Evart Overton, Peggy Hyland, Charles Kent. 7r USA. prod/rel: Vitagraph Co. of America©, Blue Ribbon Feature

CHESTERTON, G. K. (1874–1936), UKN, Chesterton, Gilbert Keith
Short Stories
Er Kann's Nicht Lassen 1962 d: Axel von Ambesser. lps: Heinz Ruhmann, Grit Bottcher, Rudolf Forster. 94M GRM. *Pater Brown: Er Kann's Nicht Lassen*; *He Just Can't Stop It* prod/rel: Bavaria
Story
Schwarze Schaf, Das 1960 d: Helmut Ashley. lps: Heinz Ruhmann, Siegfried Lowitz, Lina Carstens. 95M GRM. *The Black Sheep* prod/rel: Bavaria
The Blue Cross, 1929, Short Story
Father Brown 1954 d: Robert Hamer. lps: Alec Guinness, Joan Greenwood, Peter Finch. 91M UKN. *The Detective* (USA) prod/rel: Columbia, Facet
Detective Father Brown, Novel
Sanctuary of Fear 1979 d: John Llewellyn Moxey. lps: Barnard Hughes, Kay Lenz, Michael McGuire. TVM. 100M USA. *Girl in the Park*; *Father Brown -Detective*; *Father Brown* prod/rel: NBC, Marble Arch Productions
Man Alive, 1912, Novel
Revolver aux Cheveux Rouges, Le 1973 d: Frederic Geilfus. lps: Pierre Vernier, Anna Gael, Gisele Oudart. 90M BLG/FRN. *De Revolver Met Het Rode Haar*; *Man Alive*
The Man Who Knew Too Much, 1922, Short Story
Man Who Knew Too Much, The 1934 d: Alfred Hitchcock. lps: Leslie Banks, Edna Best, Peter Lorre. 75M UKN. prod/rel: Gaumont-British
Man Who Knew Too Much, The 1956 d: Alfred Hitchcock. lps: James Stewart, Doris Day, Bernard Miles. 120M USA. prod/rel: Paramount, Hitchcock Prods.
The Wisdom of Father Brown, New York 1915, Short Story
Father Brown, Detective 1935 d: Edward Sedgwick. lps: Walter Connolly, Paul Lukas, Gertrude Michael. 67M USA. prod/rel: Paramount Productions©

CHESTNUT, J. HERBERT
The Love of Pierre Larosse, Story
Love of Pierre Larosse, The 1914 d: Theodore Marston. lps: Dorothy Kelly, James Morrison, George Cooper. SHT USA. prod/rel: Vitagraph Co. of America

CHESTNUTT, CHARLES
Behind the Hills, Novel
Deceit 1923 d: Oscar Micheaux. lps: Evelyn Preer, William E. Fontaine, George Lucas. 6r USA. prod/rel: Micheaux Film Corp.
The Conjure Woman, Novel
Conjure Woman, The 1926 d: Oscar Micheaux. lps: Evelyn Preer, Percy Verwayen. F USA. prod/rel: Micheaux Film Corp.
Veiled Aristocrats, Novel
Veiled Aristocrats 1932 d: Oscar Micheaux. lps: Lorenzo Tucker, Barrington Guy, Laura Bowman. F USA. prod/rel: Micheaux Pictures Corp., Micheaux Production

CHETWYND-HAYES, RONALD
Story
Monster Club, The 1980 d: Roy Ward Baker. lps: Vincent Price, John Carradine, Donald Pleasence. 97M UKN. prod/rel: Itc, Chips

CHEVALIER, ALBERT
My Old Dutch, Poem
My Old Dutch 1911 d: George D. Baker. lps: Maurice Costello, Van Dyke Brooke, Mary Maurice. 1000f USA. prod/rel: Vitagraph Co. of America
My Old Dutch, London 1919, Play
My Old Dutch 1926 d: Larry Trimble. lps: May McAvoy, Pat O'Malley, Cullen Landis. 7750f USA. prod/rel: Universal Pictures

CHEVALIER, PAUL
More Deadly Than the Male, London 1960, Novel
More Deadly Than the Male 1959 d: Robert Bucknell. lps: Jeremy White, Ann Davy, Edna Dore. 60M UKN. prod/rel: U.N.a., Cross Channel

CHEVALIER, GABRIEL (1895–1969), FRN
Clochemerle, Novel
Clochemerle 1947 d: Pierre Chenal. lps: Jean Brochard, Simone Michels, Maximilienne. 90M FRN. *The Scandals of Clochemerle* (USA) prod/rel: Cinema Production

CHEYNEY, PETER (1896–1951), UKN
Novel
A Toi de Faire, Mignonne 1963 d: Bernard Borderie.
lps: Eddie Constantine, Henri Cogan, Gaia Germani.
93M FRN/ITL. *L' Agente Federale Lemmy Caution*
(ITL); *Your Turn Darling* (USA) prod/rel: C.I.C.C.,
Films Borderie
Lemmy Pour Les Dames 1961 d: Bernard Borderie.
lps: Eddie Constantine, Françoise Brion, Claudine
Coster. 97M FRN. *Lemmy for the Women* (USA); *Ladies'*
Man prod/rel: C.I.C.C., Films Borderie
Callaghan a Toi de Jouer, Novel
A Toi de Jouer, Callaghan 1954 d: Willy Rozier. lps:
Tony Wright, Lysiane Rey, Colette Ripert. 88M FRN.
prod/rel: Sport Films
Cet Homme Est Dangereux, Novel
Cet Homme Est Dangereux 1953 d: Jean SachA. lps:
Eddie Constantine, Gregoire Aslan, Colette Dereal. 92M
FRN. *Dangerous Agent* (USA); *This Man Is Dangerous*
prod/rel: Lutetia, Sonofilms
Comment Qu'elle Est, Novel
Comment Qu'elle Est? 1960 d: Bernard Borderie. lps:
Eddie Constantine, Andre Luguet, Francoise Brion.
92M FRN. *Women are Like That* (USA) prod/rel:
C.I.C.C., Films Borderie
Les Femmes S'en Balancent, Novel
Femmes S'en Balancent, Les 1953 d: Bernard
Borderie. lps: Eddie Constantine, Nadia Gray,
Dominique Wilms. 115M FRN. prod/rel: C.I.C.C., S.N.
Pathe-Cinema
La Mome Vert-de-Gris, Novel
Mome Vert-de-Gris, La 1952 d: Bernard Borderie. lps:
Eddie Constantine, Dominique Wilms, Howard Vernon.
90M FRN. *Poison Ivy* (USA); *Gun Moll* prod/rel:
C.I.C.C., Pathe Cinema
Plus de Whisky Pour Callaghan, Novel
Plus de Whisky Pour Callaghan 1955 d: Willy
Rozier. lps: Tony Wright, Magali de Vendeuil, Robert
Berri. 89M FRN. prod/rel: Sport Film
Sinister Errand, 1945, Novel
Diplomatic Courier 1952 d: Henry Hathaway. lps:
Tyrone Power, Patricia Neal, Stephen McNally. 97M
USA. prod/rel: 20th Century-Fox
Uneasy Terms, Novel
Uneasy Terms 1948 d: Vernon Sewell. lps: Michael
Rennie, Moira Lister, Faith Brook. 91M UKN. prod/rel:
British National, Pathe
The Urgent Hangman, Novel
Meet Mister Callaghan 1954 d: Charles Saunders.
lps: Derrick de Marney, Harriette Johns, Peter Neil.
88M UKN. prod/rel: Pinnacle, Eros
Vous Pigez?, Novel
Vous Pigez? 1955 d: Pierre Chevalier. lps: Eddie
Constantine, Maria Frau, Luisa Rivelli. 98M FRN/ITL.
Il Maggiorato Fisico (ITL); *The Diamond machine*
(USA) *You Dig?*; *You Get It?*; *Donne Danni E Diamanti*
prod/rel: Dismage, Transalpina

CHIARA, PIERO
La Banca Di Monate, Short Story
Banca Di Monate, La 1976 d: Francesco Massaro. lps:
Paolo Bonicelli, Quinto Parmeggiani, Walter Chiari.
106M ITL. *The Bank in Monate* prod/rel: Euro
International Film
Il Cappotto Di Astrakan, Novel
Cappotto Di Astrakan, Il 1979 d: Marco Vicario. lps:
Johnny Dorelli, Andrea Ferreol, Marcel Bozzuffi. 105M
ITL. *The Astrakan Coat* prod/rel: Vides Cin.Ca (Roma),
Les Films Ariane (Paris)
Il Piatto Piange, Novel
Piatto Piange, Il 1974 d: Paolo Nuzzi. lps: Aldo
MacCione, Agostina Belli, Andrea Ferreol. 110M ITL.
prod/rel: Clodio Cin.Ca, Euro International Film
La Spartizione, Novel
Venga a Prendere Il Caffe Da Noi 1970 d: Alberto
LattuadA. lps: Ugo Tognazzi, Francesca Romana
Coluzzi, Milena Vukotic. 113M ITL. *Come Have Coffee*
With Us (USA); *The Man Who Came for Coffee* prod/rel:
Mars Film, Paramount
La Stanza Del Vescovo, Novel
Stanza Del Vescovo, La 1977 d: Dino Risi. lps: Ugo
Tognazzi, Ornella Muti, Patrick Dewaere. 110M
ITL/FRN. *La Chambre de l'Eveque* (FRN); *The Bishop's*
Room; *The Forbidden Room*; *The Bishop's Bedroom*
prod/rel: Merope, Carlton Film Export (Roma)

CHIARELLI, LUIGI
Extra Dry - Carnevale 1910 - Carnevale 1913, 1914,
Play
Extra-Dry - Carnevale 1910 - Carnevale 1913 1914
d: Gino Calza-Bini. lps: Fernanda Sinimberghi, Dante
Cappelli, Carolina CatenA. ITL. prod/rel: Film Artistica
Gloria

Fuochi d'Artificio, Play
Fuochi d'Artificio 1938 d: Gennaro Righelli. lps:
Amedeo Nazzari, Linda Pini, Vanna Vanni. 74M ITL.
prod/rel: Juventus Film, I.C.I.
La Maschera E Il Volto, 1916, Play
Maschera E Il Volto, La 1919 d: Augusto GeninA. lps:
Italia Almirante Manzini, Vittorio Rossi Pianelli, Ettore
Piergiovanni. 1900m ITL. prod/rel: Itala Film
Maschera E Il Volto, La 1942 d: Camillo
Mastrocinque. lps: Laura Solari, Nino Besozzi, Sergio
Tofano. 85M ITL. prod/rel: Kinofilm, a.C.I.
La Scala Di Seta, 1917, Play
Scala Di Seta, La 1920 d: Arnaldo Frateili. lps: Elena
Wronowska, Luciano Molinari, Memo Benassi. 2074m
ITL. prod/rel: Tespi Film
La Venere Orgiasta, Short Story
Circe Moderna 1914 d: Alberto Degli Abbati. lps: Elisa
Severi, Mario Bonnard, Dante Cappelli. 1400m ITL.
Turbine Fatale prod/rel: Film Artistica Gloria

CHIAROMONTE, ADRIANA
I Sogni Nel Cassetto, Novel
Sogni Nel Cassetto, I 1957 d: Renato Castellani. lps:
Lea Massari, Enrico Pagani, Cosetta Greco. 101M ITL.
Dreams in the Drawer prod/rel: Rizzoli Film (Roma),
Francinex (Paris)

CHIESA, FRANCESCO (1871–1973), SWT
L' Innocenza, Novel
Innocenza, L' 1986 d: Villi Herman. lps: Enrica Maria
Modugno, Alessandro Haber, Teco Celio. 90M SWT.
prod/rel: Imago, S.S.R.

CHIKAMATSU, MONZAEMON (1653–1725), JPN
Daikyoji Sekireki, 1715, Play
Chikamatsu Monogatari 1954 d: Kenji Mizoguchi.
lps: Kazuo Hasegawa, Kyoko Kagawa, Eitaro Shindo.
102M JPN. *A Story from Chikamatsu* (USA); *The*
Crucified Lovers prod/rel: Daiei Motion Picture Co.
Meido No Hikyaku (the Courier to Hell), Play
Lover's Exile, The 1980 d: Marty Gross. lps: Tamao
Yoshida, Minnosuke Yoshida, Kanjuro Kiritake. 86M
CND. prod/rel: Marty Gross Film Productions Inc., New
Cinema
Onna Goroshi Abura No Jigoku, 1721, Play
Onna Goroshi Abura Jigoku 1958 d: Hiromichi
HorikawA. lps: Senjaku Nakamura, Ganjiro Nakamura,
Eiko Miyoshi. 99M JPN. *The Prodigal Son* (USA)
prod/rel: Toho Co.
Shinju Ten No Amijima, 1720, Play
Shinju Ten No Amijima 1969 d: Masahiro ShinodA.
lps: Kichiemon Nakamura, Shima Iwashita, Hosei
Komatsu. 142M JPN. *Double Suicide at Amijima*;
Double Suicide (USA) prod/rel: Hyogensha, Nippon Art
Theatre Guild
Sonezaki Shinju, 1703, Play
Sonezaki Shinju 1978 d: Yasuzo MasumurA. lps:
Meiko Kaji, Ryudo Uzaki, Hisashi IgawA. 112M JPN.
Lovers' Suicide in Sonezaki; *Double Suicide*; *Double*
Suicide at Sonezaki prod/rel: Kodasha Co., Kimura
Productions
Yari No Gonza, Play
Yari No Gonza 1985 d: Masahiro ShinodA. lps: Hiromi
Goh, Shima Iwashita, Shohei Hino. 126M JPN. *The*
Spearman Gonza; *Yari No Gonza Kazane Katabira*
prod/rel: Daiei Motion Picture Co.

CHILD, LINCOLN
The Relic, Novel
Relic, The 1997 d: Peter Hyams. lps: Penelope Ann
Miller, Tom Sizemore, Linda Hunt. 110M USA.
prod/rel: Pacific Western, Paramount Pictures
Corporation

CHILD, RICHARD WASHBURN
The Game of Light, 1914, Short Story
Live Wire, The 1925 d: Charles Hines. lps: Johnny
Hines, Edmund Breese, Mildred Ryan. 6850f USA.
prod/rel: First National Pictures
The Hands of Nara, New York 1922, Novel
Hands of Nara, The 1922 d: Harry Garson. lps: Clara
Kimball Young, Count John Orloff, Elliott Dexter. 6000f
USA. prod/rel: Samuel Zierler Photoplay Corp., Metro
Pictures
Here's How, 1924, Short Story
Mad Whirl, The 1925 d: William A. Seiter. lps: May
McAvoy, Jack Mulhall, Myrtle Stedman. 6184f USA.
Jazz Parents prod/rel: Universal Pictures
The Man Who Disappeared, Story
Man Who Disappeared, The 1914 d: Charles J.
Brabin. lps: Marc McDermott, Barry O'Moore, Miriam
Nesbitt. SRL. 10r USA. prod/rel: Edison
That's Good, 1915, Short Story
That's Good 1919 d: Harry L. Franklin. lps: Hale
Hamilton, Grace La Rue, Herbert Prior. 5r USA.
prod/rel: Metro Pictures Corp.©

A Whiff of Heliotrope, 1918, Short Story
Forgotten Faces 1928 d: Victor Schertzinger. lps:
Clive Brook, Mary Brian, Olga BaclanovA. 7640f USA.
prod/rel: Paramount Famous Lasky Corp.
Forgotten Faces 1936 d: E. A. Dupont. lps: Herbert
Marshall, Gertrude Michael, Robert Cummings. 72M
USA. *Something to Live for*; *Heliotrope* prod/rel:
Paramount Productions©
Gentleman After Dark, A 1942 d: Edwin L. Marin.
lps: Brian Donlevy, Miriam Hopkins, Preston Foster.
77M USA. prod/rel: United Artists, Edward Small
Heliotrope 1920 d: George D. Baker. lps: Diana Allen,
Wilfred Lytell, Frederick Burton. 7r USA. *A Whiff of*
Heliotrope prod/rel: Cosmopolitan Productions,
International Film Service Co.©

CHILDERS, ERSKINE (1870–1922), IRL
The Riddle of the Sands, 1903, Novel
Riddle of the Sands, The 1978 d: Tony Maylam. lps:
Simon MacCorkindale, Michael York, Jenny Agutter.
102M UKN/USA. prod/rel: Rank, Worldmark

CHILDS, HERBERT
Way of a Gaucho, 1948, Novel
Way of a Gaucho 1952 d: Jacques Tourneur. lps: Rory
Calhoun, Gene Tierney, Richard Boone. 91M USA.
prod/rel: 20th Century-Fox

CHILTON, CHARLES
Long Trail, the Long, Play
Oh! What a Lovely War 1969 d: Richard
Attenborough. lps: Dirk Bogarde, Phyllis Calvert,
Jean-Pierre Cassel. 144M UKN. *War and Peace Season*
prod/rel: Accord Films, Paramount

CHINMOKU
Shusaku Endo, 1966, Novel
Chinmoku 1972 d: Masahiro ShinodA. lps: David
Lampson, Mako, Tetsuro TambA. 126M JPN. *Silence*
(USA)

CHINODYA, SHIMMER
Short Story
Everyone's Child 1996 d: Tsitsi DsangarembgA. lps:
Nomsa Mlambo, Thulani Sandhla, Walter MuparutsA.
90M ZIM. prod/rel: Media for Development Trust
(Harare)

CHIOSSONE, DAVIDE
La Suonatrice d'Arpa, 1848, Novel
Suonatrice d'Arpa, La 1917 d: Mario Ceccatelli. lps:
Elvira Redaelli, Lola Visconti-Brignone, Bruna
Ceccatelli. 1922m ITL. prod/rel: Italo-Egiziana Film

CHIPP, ELINOR
Whose Widow, Short Story
Amazing Wife, The 1919 d: Ida May Park. lps: Mary
MacLaren, Frank Mayo, Stanhope Wheatcroft. 6r USA.
prod/rel: Universal Film Mfg. Co.©

CHIRGWIN, GEORGE H.
The Blind Boy, Play
Blind Boy, The 1917 d: Edwin J. Collins, Jack Clare.
lps: G. H. Chirgwin, Ivy Montford, Evelyn Sydney. 4130f
UKN. prod/rel: British Photoplay Productions, Ruffells

CHITI, UGO
Alegretto. Per Bene Ma Non Troppo, Play
Albergo Roma 1996 d: Ugo Chiti. lps: Alessandro
Benvenuti, Tcheky Karyo, Claudio Bisio. 98M ITL.
prod/rel: Union Pn

CHITTENDEN, FRANK
The Uninvited, Novel
Stranger in Town 1957 d: George Pollock. lps: Alex
Nicol, Anne Page, Mary Laura Wood. 73M UKN.
prod/rel: Tempean, Eros

CHIVOT
La Mascotte, Opera
Mascotte, La 1935 d: Leon Mathot. lps: Lucien Baroux,
Germaine Roger, Armand Dranem. 100M FRN.
prod/rel: Films Mascottes

CHODERLOS DE LACLOS, PIERRE AMBROSE
(1741–1803), FRN
Les Liaisons Dangereuses, 1782, Novel
Cruel Intentions 1999 d: Roger Kumble. lps: Sarah
Michelle Gellar, Ryan Phillippe, Reese Witherspoon.
95M USA. prod/rel: Sony Pictures Entertainment,
Columbia Pictures
Dangerous Liaisons 1988 d: Stephen Frears. lps:
Glenn Close, John Malkovich, Michelle Pfeiffer. 120M
UKN/USA. *Les Liaisons Dangereuses* prod/rel: Warner
Bros.
Femme Fidele, Une 1976 d: Roger Vadim. lps: Sylvia
Kristel, Jon Finch, Nathalie Delon. 90M FRN. *When a*
Woman in Love. (UKN); *When a Woman Is in Love*
Liaisons Dangereuses, Les 1959 d: Roger Vadim. lps:
Gerard Philipe, Jeanne Moreau, Jeanne Valerie. 105M
FRN/ITL. *Relazioni Pericolose* (ITL); *Dangerous Love*
Affairs; *Les Liaisons Dangereuses 1960* prod/rel: Films
Marceau

Valmont 1989 d: Milos Forman. lps: Colin Firth, Annette Bening, Meg Tilly. 137M FRN/UKN. prod/rel: Renn Productions (Paris), Timothy Burrill Productions (London)

CHODOROV, EDWARD
Kind Lady, New York 1935, Play
Kind Lady 1935 d: George B. Seitz. lps: Aline MacMahon, Basil Rathbone, Mary Carlisle. 76M USA. *House of Menace* prod/rel: Metro-Goldwyn-Mayer Corp.©

Oh Men! Oh Women!, Play
Oh, Men! Oh, Women! 1957 d: Nunnally Johnson. lps: David Niven, Dan Dailey, Ginger Rogers. 90M USA. prod/rel: 20th Century-Fox

CHODOROV, JEROME
Anniversary Waltz, New York 1954, Play
Happy Anniversary 1959 d: David Miller. lps: David Niven, Mitzi Gaynor, Carl Reiner. 81M USA. prod/rel: United Artists, Fields

Junior Miss, New York 1941, Play
Junior Miss 1945 d: George Seaton. lps: Peggy Ann Garner, Allyn Joslyn, Stephen Dunne. 94M USA. prod/rel: 20th Century-Fox

Those Endearing Young Charms, Play
Those Endearing Young Charms 1945 d: Lewis Allen. lps: Robert Young, Laraine Day, Bill Williams. 81M USA. prod/rel: RKO Radio

CHOLMONDELEY, MARY
Moth and Rust, Novel
Moth and Rust 1921 d: Sidney Morgan. lps: Sybil Thorndike, Malvina Longfellow, Langhorne Burton. 4796f UKN. prod/rel: Progress, Butcher's Film Service

Red Pottage, Novel
Red Pottage 1918 d: Meyrick Milton. lps: C. Aubrey Smith, Mary Dibley, Gerald Ames. 4825f UKN. prod/rel: Ideal

CHONZ, SELINA
Uorsin de la S-Chella, 1945, Book
Cloche Pour Ursli, Un 1964 d: Ulrich Kundig, Nicolas Gessner. lps: Gianni Cantoni. 19M SWT. *Schellen-Ursli* prod/rel: Condor-Film

CHOPIN, KATE (1851–1904), USA, Chopin, Kate O'Flaherty
The Awakening, 1899, Novel
End of August, The 1981 d: Bob Graham. lps: Sally Sharp, Lilia Skala, David Marshall Grant. 107M USA. prod/rel: Quartet
Grand Isle 1991 d: Mary Lambert. lps: Kelly McGillis, Jon de Vries, Adrian Pasdar. TVM. 112M USA.

CHORELL, WALENTIN
Kattorna, Helsinki 1963, Play
Kattorna 1965 d: Henning Carlsen. lps: Eva Dahlbeck, Gio Petre, Monica Nielsen. 93M SWD. *The Cats* prod/rel: Lorens Marstedt

Miriam, 1954, Novel
Miriam 1957 d: William Markus. lps: Anneli Sauli, Pentti Siimes, Irma SeikkulA. 88M FNL. prod/rel: Suomen Filmiteollisuus

CHOROMANSKI, MICHAL
Zazdrosc I Medycyna, 1932, Novel
Zazdrosc I Medycyna 1973 d: Janusz Majewski. lps: Mariusz Dmochowski, Ewa KrzyzewskA. 99M PLN. *Jealousy and Medicine*

CHOUDHURY, ARUN
Pasher Bari
Pakkainti Ammayi 1953 d: Chittajalu PullayyA. lps: Anjali Devi, V. Kamaladevi, MohanakrishnA. 164M IND. *The Girl Next Door*; *Pakka Inti Ammayi* prod/rel: East India Films

CHRIST, LENA
Documents
Fall Lena Christ, Der 1968 d: Hans W. Geissendorfer. lps: Heidi Stroh, Edith Volksmann, Eberhard Peiker. 95M GRM. *The Case of Lena Christ* prod/rel: B.R.

CHRISTENSEN, WILFRIED
Die Forelle, Novel
Weg in Die Vergangenheit, Der 1954 d: Karl Hartl. lps: Paula Wessely, Attila Horbiger, Josef Meinrad. 90M AUS. prod/rel: Paula Wessely

CHRISTIAN, TINA CHAD
Baby Love, London 1968, Novel
Baby Love 1968 d: Alastair Reid. lps: Ann Lynn, Keith Barron, Linda Hayden. 98M UKN. prod/rel: Avton Film Productions, Avco Embassy

CHRISTIANSEN, SIGURD WESLEY
To Levende Og En Dod, Oslo 1925, Novel
Mrtvy Mezi Zivymi 1947 d: Borivoj Zeman. lps: Karel Hoger, Zdenka ProchazkovA. 90M CZC. *Dead Among the Living*
To Levende Og En Dod 1937 d: Tancred Ibsen. 83M NRW. *Two Living and One Dead*

Tva Levande Och En Dod 1961 d: Anthony Asquith. lps: Virginia McKenna, Bill Travers, Patrick McGoohan. 92M SWD/UKN. *One Dead Two Living* (UKN); *Two Living and One Dead* prod/rel: Swan Productions, Wera Film

CHRISTIE, AGATHA (1890–1976), UKN
Novel
Murder Is Easy 1982 d: Claude Whatham. lps: Bill Bixby, Lesley-Anne Down, Olivia de Havilland. TVM. 100M USA. prod/rel: CBS, Warner Bros.

4.50 from Paddington, London 1957, Novel
Murder She Said 1961 d: George Pollock. lps: Margaret Rutherford, Arthur Kennedy, Muriel Pavlow. 86M UKN/USA. *Meet Miss Marple* prod/rel: MGM British

The A.B.C. Murders, London 1936, Novel
ABC Murders, The 1966 d: Frank Tashlin. lps: Tony Randall, Anita Ekberg, Robert Morley. 90M UKN. *The Alphabet Murders*; *Amanda* prod/rel: MGM British
ABC Murders, The 1992 d: Andrew Grieve. lps: David Suchet, Hugh Fraser, Philip Jackson. TVM. 105M UKN.

After the Funeral, London 1953, Novel
Murder at the Gallop 1963 d: George Pollock. lps: Margaret Rutherford, Robert Morley, Flora Robson. 81M UKN. prod/rel: MGM British

Appointment With Death, Novel
Appointment With Death 1987 d: Michael Winner. lps: Peter Ustinov, Lauren Bacall, Piper Laurie. 108M UKN.; *Agatha Christie's Hercule Poirot: Appointment With Death* prod/rel: Cannon

Black Coffee, Novel
Black Coffee 1931 d: Leslie Hiscott. lps: Austin Trevor, Adrianne Allen, Richard Cooper. 78M UKN. prod/rel: Twickenham, Woolf & Freedman
Coffret de Laque, Le 1932 d: Jean Kemm. lps: Alice Field, Danielle Darrieux, Isabelle Anderson. 85M FRN. prod/rel: Etablissements Jacques Haik

The Body in the Library, Novel
Miss Marple: the Body in the Library 1985 d: Silvio Narizzano. lps: Joan Hickson, Gwen Watford, Trudie Styler. TVM. 154M UKN. *The Body in the Library* prod/rel: BBC

A Caribbean Mystery, Novel
Caribbean Mystery, A 1983 d: Robert Lewis. lps: Helen Hayes, Barnard Hughes, Jameson Parker. TVM. 100M USA. *Agatha Christie's a Caribbean Mystery* prod/rel: CBS, Warner
Miss Marple: a Caribbean Mystery 1989 d: Christopher Petit. lps: Joan Hickson, Donald Pleasence, Sophie Ward. TVM. 115M UKN. *A Caribbean Mystery* prod/rel: BBC

Dead Man's Folly, Novel
Agatha Christie's Dead Man's Folly 1986 d: Clive Donner. lps: Peter Stapleton, Jean Stapleton, Constance Cummings. TVM. 100M USA/UKN. *Dead Man's Folly* prod/rel: Warner Bros. Tv.

Death on the Nile, Novel
Death on the Nile 1978 d: John Guillermin. lps: Peter Ustinov, Jane Birkin, Lois Chiles. 140M USA/UKN. *Agatha Christie's Death on the Nile* prod/rel: Emi

Endless Night, Novel
Endless Night 1971 d: Sidney Gilliat. lps: Hywel Bennett, Hayley Mills, Britt Ekland. 99M UKN. *Agatha Christie's Endless Night* prod/rel: British Lion, Emi

Evil Under the Sun, Novel
Evil Under the Sun 1982 d: Guy Hamilton. lps: Peter Ustinov, Jane Birkin, Colin Blakely. 117M UKN. *Agatha Christie's Evil Under the Sun* prod/rel: Emi, Mersham

Lord Edgware Dies, Novel
Lord Edgware Dies 1934 d: Henry Edwards. lps: Austin Trevor, Jane Carr, Richard Cooper. 81M UKN. prod/rel: Real Art, Radio

The Mirror Crack'd from Side to Side, Novel
Mirror Crack'd, The 1980 d: Guy Hamilton. lps: Angela Lansbury, Geraldine Chaplin, Tony Curtis. 106M UKN/USA. prod/rel: Emi, John Brabourne

Mrs. McGinty's Dead, London 1952, Novel
Murder Most Foul 1964 d: George Pollock. lps: Margaret Rutherford, Ron Moody, Dennis Price. 90M UKN. prod/rel: MGM British

Murder in Three Acts, Play
Agatha Christie's Murder in Three Acts 1986 d: Gary Nelson. lps: Peter Ustinov, Tony Curtis, Emma Samms. TVM. 104M USA. *Murder in Three Acts* prod/rel: CBS

A Murder Is Announced, Novel
Miss Marple: a Murder Is Announced 1984 d: David Giles. lps: Joan Hickson, Ursula Howells, Renee Asherson. TVM. 154M UKN. *A Murder Is Announced* prod/rel: BBC

The Murder of Roger Ackroyd, 1926, Novel
Alibi 1931 d: Leslie Hiscott. lps: Austin Trevor, Franklin Dyall, Elizabeth Allan. 75M UKN. prod/rel: Twickenham, Woolf & Freedman

Murder on the Orient Express, Novel
Murder on the Orient Express 1974 d: Sidney Lumet. lps: Albert Finney, Lauren Bacall, Martin Balsam. 128M UKN. prod/rel: Emi, Gw Films

Murder With Mirrors, Novel
Murder With Mirrors 1985 d: Dick Lowry. lps: Helen Hayes, Bette Davis, John Mills. TVM. 100M USA. *Agatha Christie's Murder With Mirrors* prod/rel: CBS, Warner Bros. Tv

The Mysterious Affair at Styles, Novel
Mysterious Affair at Styles, The 1990 d: Ross Devenish. lps: David Suchet, Hugh Fraser, David Rintoul. TVM. 103M UKN.; *Agatha Christie's Hercule Poirot: the Mysterious Affair at Styles*

Ordeal By Innocence, Novel
Ordeal By Innocence 1984 d: Desmond Davis. lps: Donald Sutherland, Christopher Plummer, Faye Dunaway. 90M UKN. *Agatha Christie's Ordeal By Innocence* prod/rel: London Cannon Films

The Passing of Mr. Quin, Novel
Passing of Mr. Quin, The 1928 d: Leslie Hiscott. lps: Stewart Rome, Trilby Clark, Ursula Jeans. 8520f UKN. prod/rel: Strand, Cecil Cattermoul

Philomel Cottage, Story
Love from a Stranger 1937 d: Rowland V. Lee. lps: Ann Harding, Basil Rathbone, Binnie Hale. 90M UKN. prod/rel: Trafalgar, United Artists
Love from a Stranger 1947 d: Richard Whorf. lps: Sylvia Sidney, John Hodiak, John Howard. 81M USA. *A Stranger Walked in* (UKN) prod/rel: Eagle-Lion

A Pocketful of Rye, Story
Miss Marple: a Pocketful of Rye 1985 d: Guy Slater. lps: Joan Hickson, Peter Davison, Clive Merrison. TVM. 100M UKN. *A Pocketful of Rye* prod/rel: BBC

The Secret Adversary, Novel
Abenteuer G.M.B.H., Die 1929 d: Fred Sauer. lps: Carlo Aldini, Eve Grey, Elfriede Borodin. 2600m GRM. prod/rel: Orplid-Film

The Seven Dials Mystery, Novel
Seven Dials Mystery, The 1980 d: Tony Wharmby. lps: John Gielgud, Harry Andrews, Cheryl Campbell. TVM. 140M UKN.

Sparkling Cyanide, Novel
Sparkling Cyanide 1983 d: Robert Lewis. lps: Anthony Andrews, Deborah Raffin, Pamela Bellwood. TVM. 100M USA. *Agatha Christie's Sparkling Cyanide* prod/rel: CBS, Stan Margulies Prods.

The Spider's Web, London 1954, Play
Spider's Web, The 1960 d: Godfrey Grayson. lps: Glynis Johns, John Justin, Jack Hulbert. 89M UKN. prod/rel: United Artists, Danzigers

Ten Little Niggers, London 1939, Novel
And Then There Were None 1945 d: Rene Clair. lps: Barry Fitzgerald, Louis Hayward, Walter Huston. 98M USA. *Ten Little Niggers* (UKN); *Les Dix Petits Indiens* prod/rel: 20th Century-Fox
And Then There Were None 1974 d: Peter Collinson. lps: Oliver Reed, Richard Attenborough, Elke Sommer. 98M UKN/SPN/GRM. *Diez Negritos* (SPN); *Death in Persepolis*; *Ten Little Indians*; *Ten Little Niggers*; *Ein Unbekannter Rechnet Ab* (GRM) prod/rel: Emi
Ten Little Indians 1965 d: George Pollock. lps: Hugh O'Brian, Shirley Eaton, Fabian. 91M UKN. prod/rel: Tenlit Films, Warner-Pathe

Witness for the Prosecution, London 1953, Play
Witness for the Prosecution 1957 d: Billy Wilder. lps: Charles Laughton, Tyrone Power, Marlene Dietrich. 116M USA. prod/rel: United Artists, Edward Small-Arthur Hornblow Pictures
Witness for the Prosecution 1983 d: Alan Gibson. lps: Ralph Richardson, Deborah Kerr, Diana Rigg. TVM. 94M UKN. prod/rel: CBS Entertainment

CHRISTIE, CAMPBELL (1893–, IND, Christie, Campbell Manning
Carrington V.C., London 1953, Play
Carrington V.C. 1954 d: Anthony Asquith. lps: David Niven, Margaret Leighton, Noelle Middleton. 106M UKN. *Court Martial* (USA) prod/rel: Independent Film Distributors, Romulus

Grand National Night, London 1946, Play
Grand National Night 1953 d: Bob McNaught. lps: Nigel Patrick, Moira Lister, Beatrice Campbell. 81M UKN. *Wicked Wife* (USA) prod/rel: Talisman, Renown

His Excellency, London 1950, Play
His Excellency 1952 d: Robert Hamer. lps: Eric Portman, Cecil Parker, Helen Cherry. 84M UKN. prod/rel: Ealing Studios, General Film Distributors

Someone at the Door, London 1935, Play
  Someone at the Door 1936 d: Herbert Brenon. lps:
  Billy Milton, Aileen Marson, Noah Beery. 74M UKN.
  prod/rel: British International Pictures, Wardour
  Someone at the Door 1950 d: Francis Searle. lps:
  Michael Medwin, Garry Marsh, Yvonne Owen. 65M
  UKN. prod/rel: Hammer, Exclusive

CHRISTIE, DOROTHY (1896–, IND, Walker, Dorothy
Casson
Carrington V.C., London 1953, Play
  Carrington V.C. 1954 d: Anthony Asquith. lps: David
  Niven, Margaret Leighton, Noelle Middleton. 106M
  UKN. *Court Martial* (USA) prod/rel: Independent Film
  Distributors, Romulus
Grand National Night, London 1946, Play
  Grand National Night 1953 d: Bob McNaught. lps:
  Nigel Patrick, Moira Lister, Beatrice Campbell. 81M
  UKN. *Wicked Wife* (USA) prod/rel: Talisman, Renown
His Excellency, London 1950, Play
  His Excellency 1952 d: Robert Hamer. lps: Eric
  Portman, Cecil Parker, Helen Cherry. 84M UKN.
  prod/rel: Ealing Studios, General Film Distributors
Someone at the Door, London 1935, Play
  Someone at the Door 1936 d: Herbert Brenon. lps:
  Billy Milton, Aileen Marson, Noah Beery. 74M UKN.
  prod/rel: British International Pictures, Wardour
  Someone at the Door 1950 d: Francis Searle. lps:
  Michael Medwin, Garry Marsh, Yvonne Owen. 65M
  UKN. prod/rel: Hammer, Exclusive

CHRISTINE, HENRI
Arthur, Opera
  Arthur 1930 d: Leonce Perret. lps: Louis-Jacques
  Boucot, Lily Zevaco, Edith MerA. F FRN. *Le Culte de la
  Beaute* prod/rel: Societe Des Films Osso
Dede, Opera
  Dede 1934 d: Rene Guissart. lps: Danielle Darrieux,
  Albert Prejean, Rene Bergeron. 75M FRN. prod/rel:
  France Univers-Film
Phi-Phi, Opera
  Phi-Phi 1926 d: Georges Pallu. lps: Andre Deed,
  Georges Gauthier, Rita Jolivet. F FRN. prod/rel: Natan

CHRISTMAN, ELIZABETH
A Nice Italian Girl, Novel
  Black Market Baby 1977 d: Robert Day. lps: Linda
  Purl, Desi Arnaz Jr., Jessica Walter. TVM. 100M USA.
  Don't Steal My Baby; *A Dangerous Love* prod/rel: ABC,
  Brut Productions

CHRISTOPHER, JOHN (1922–, UKN
Novel
  Tripods, The 1986 d: Graham Theakston, Christopher
  Barry. lps: John Shackely, Jim Baker, Roderick Horn.
  TVM. 225M UKN/ASL. prod/rel: BBC, Channel 7
The Death of Grass, London 1956, Novel
  No Blade of Grass 1970 d: Cornel Wilde. lps: Nigel
  Davenport, Jean Wallace, Anthony May. 96M UKN.
  prod/rel: Symbol Productions, MGM

CHRISTOPHER, MICHAEL
The Shadow Box, Play
  Shadow Box, The 1980 d: Paul Newman. lps: Joanne
  Woodward, Christopher Plummer, Valerie Harper.
  TVM. 103M USA. prod/rel: Shadow Box Film Company

CHU, LOUIS
Eat a Bowl of Tea, Novel
  Eat a Bowl of Tea 1989 d: Wayne Wang. lps: Cora
  Miao, Russell Wong, Victor Wong. 104M USA. prod/rel:
  American Playhouse Theatre, Columbia

CHUGHTAI, ISMAT
Garam Hawa, Short Story
  Garam Hawa 1973 d: M. S. Sathyu. lps: Balraj Sahni,
  Dinanath Zutshi, Badar Begum. 146M IND. *Hot Wind*;
  Hot Winds; *Warm Wind*; *Garam Hava*; *Garm Hawa*
  prod/rel: Unit 3 Mm

CHURCH, JEAN
Book
  Brainwash 1981 d: Bobby Roth. lps: Yvette Mimieux,
  Christopher Allport, Cindy Pickett. 97M USA. *The
  Naked Weekend*; *Circle of Power*; *Mystique* prod/rel:
  Mehlman, Qui Productions

CHURCHILL, WINSTON (1871–1947), USA
The Crisis, New York 1901, Novel
  Crisis, The 1916 d: Colin Campbell. lps: Thomas
  Santschi, Bessie Eyton, Sam Drane. 7-12r USA.
  prod/rel: Selig Polyscope Co.©, Super Film
The Dwelling-Place of Light, New York 1917, Novel
  Dwelling Place of Light, The 1920 d: Jack Conway.
  lps: Claire Adams, King Baggot, Robert McKim. 7r USA.
  prod/rel: Benjamin B. Hampton Productions, W. W.
  Hodkinson Corp.

The Inside of the Cup, New York 1912, Novel
  Inside of the Cup, The 1921 d: Albert Capellani. lps:
  William P. Carleton, David Torrence, Edith Hallor. 7r
  USA. prod/rel: Cosmopolitan Productions, Paramount
  Pictures
Richard Carvel, New York 1899, Novel
  Richard Carvel 1915?. USA. prod/rel: Quality
  Pictures Corp., Metro Picture Corp.

CHURCHILL, WINSTON SPENCER (1874–1965),
UKN
My Early Life, Autobiography
  Young Winston 1972 d: Richard Attenborough. lps:
  Simon Ward, Peter Cellier, Ronald Hines. 157M UKN.
  prod/rel: Columbia, Open Road

CHUTE, CAROLYN
Maine, the Beans of Egypt, Novel
  Beans of Egypt, Maine 1994 d: Jennifer Warren. lps:
  Martha Plimpton, Kelly Lynch, Rutger Hauer. 109M
  USA. *Forbidden Choices*

CIBOTTO, G. A.
Scano Boa, Novel
  Scano Boa 1961 d: Renato Dall'arA. lps: Carla Gravina,
  Jose Suarez, Alain Cuny. 95M ITL/SPN. prod/rel:
  Cin.Ca Lombarda, Ara Cin.Ca (Milano)

CICONI, TEOBALDO
La Figlia Unica, 1853
  Figlia Unica, La 1919 d: Camillo de Riso. lps: Tilde
  Kassay, Amleto Novelli, Camillo de Riso. 1711m ITL.
  prod/rel: Caesar Film
La Statua Di Carne, 1862, Play
  Amore d'Oltretomba, L' 1912. lps: Dora Baldanello,
  Alessandro Bernard, Giovanni Casaleggio. 824m ITL.
  Light After Darkness (UKN) prod/rel: Itala Film
  Statua Di Carne, La 1912 d: Giuseppe de Liguoro. lps:
  Clara Vendtme, Arturo Pirovano, Wladimiro de
  Liguoro. 585m ITL. prod/rel: Milano Films
  Statua Di Carne, La 1912 d: Attilio Fabbri. lps: Pina
  Fabbri, Luciano David, Paolo Continelli. 895m ITL.
  prod/rel: Latium Film
  Statua Di Carne, La 1921 d: Mario Almirante. lps:
  Italia Almirante Manzini, Lido Manetti, Alberto Collo.
  2190m ITL. prod/rel: Fert
  Statua Vivente, La 1943 d: Camillo Mastrocinque. lps:
  Laura Solari, Fosco Giachetti, Camilla Pilotto. 85M ITL.
  La Statua Di Carne prod/rel: Kino Film, a.C.I.

CIMAROSA, DOMENICO
Il Matrimonio Segreto, Opera
  Matrimonio Segreto, Il 1943 d: Camillo
  Mastrocinque. lps: Laura Solari, Hilde Petri, Nerio
  Bernardi. UNF. ITL. prod/rel: Appia, S.a.F.a.

CINELLI, DELFINO
Calafuria, Novel
  Calafuria 1943 d: Flavio CalzavarA. lps: Doris Duranti,
  Gustav Diessl, Aldo Silvani. 75M ITL. prod/rel:
  Nazionalcine, Manenti Film
La Trappola, Novel
  Tragica Notte 1942 d: Mario Soldati. lps: Doris
  Duranti, Carlo Ninchi, Andrea Checchi. 80M ITL. *La
  Trappola* prod/rel: Scalera Film

CINO, BEPPE
La Casa Del Buon Ritorno, Novel
  Casa Del Buon Ritorno, La 1986 d: Giuseppina
  Marotta, Beppe Cino. lps: Amanda Sandrelli, Stefano
  Gabrini, Francesco CostA. 87M ITL. prod/rel: Movie
  Machine

CIPRELLI, LEONE
Santo Disonore, Play
  Santo Disonore 1949 d: Guido Brignone. lps: Antonio
  Vilar, Elli Parvo, Otello Toso. 90M ITL. prod/rel:
  Romana Film

CLAER, HANS HENNING
Das Bullenkloster, Novel
  Lass Jucken, Kumpel : Das Bullenkloster 1972 d:
  Franz MarischkA. lps: Birgit Bergen, Elke Boltenhagen,
  Andre Eismann. 92M GRM. *Das Bullenkloster*; *Bull
  Monastery* prod/rel: Deutsche Dynamic, Victoria
Kumpel Lass Jucken, Novel
  Lass Jucken, Kumpel 1972 d: Franz MarischkA. lps:
  Michel Jacot, Anne Graf, Walter Kraus. 96M GRM. *The
  Itch* prod/rel: Deutsche Dynamic, Barny Bornhauser
Kumpel! Lass Laufen, Novel
  Lass Jucken, Kumpel (6): Lass Laufen, Kumpel!
  1981 d: Franz MarischkA. lps: Hans Henning Claer,
  Sibylle Rauch, Zachi Noy. 87M GRM. *Kumpel! Lass
  Laufen*; *Let 'Em Run Buddy* prod/rel: Planet, Scotia

CLAES, ERNEST
Novel
  Witte Van Sichem, de 1980 d: Robbe de Hert. lps: Eric
  Clerckx, Paul 's Jongers, Willy Vandermeulen. 108M
  BLG. *Filasse* (FRN); *Tow*; **De Witte** prod/rel: New Star
  Visie

Fanfare de Sint-Jansvrienden, Novel
  Uilenspiegel Leeft Nog 1935 d: Jan Vanderheyden.
  lps: Frits Vaerewijck, Serre Van Eeckhoudt, Nand Buyl.
  100M BLG.

CLAIRVILLE
La Fille de Madame Angot, Brussels 1872, Operetta
  Fille de Madame Angot, La 1935 d: Jean
  Bernard-Derosne. lps: Andre Bauge, Jean Aquistapace,
  MoniquellA. 85M FRN. prod/rel: Ste Francaise De Prod.
  Cinematographique
Le Meurtrier de Theodore, Play
  Meurtrier de Theodore, Le 1908-18 d: Georges
  MoncA. lps: Gorby, Prince, Irma Genin. FRN. prod/rel:
  Pathe

CLANCEY, VERNON
Man Hunt, Novel
  Dangerous Fingers 1937 d: Norman Lee. lps: James
  Stephenson, Betty Lynne, Leslie Perrins. 79M UKN.
  Wanted By Scotland Yard (USA) prod/rel: Rialto, Pathe

CLANCY, TOM (1947–, USA, Clancy Jr., Thomas L.)
Clear and Present Danger, Novel
  Clear and Present Danger 1994 d: Phil Noyce. lps:
  Harrison Ford, Willem Dafoe, Anne Archer. 141M USA.
  prod/rel: Paramount
The Hunt for Red October, Novel
  Hunt for Red October, The 1990 d: John McTiernan.
  lps: Sean Connery, Alec Baldwin, Scott Glenn. 137M
  USA. prod/rel: Paramount
Op Center, Novel
  Tom Clancy's Op Center 1995 d: Lewis Teague. lps:
  Harry Hamlin, Lindsay Frost, Carl Weathers. TVM.
  240M USA. *Op Center*
Patriot Games, Novel
  Patriot Games 1992 d: Phil Noyce. lps: Harrison Ford,
  Anne Archer, Patrick Bergin. 117M USA. prod/rel:
  Paramount

CLAREL, PIERRE
Le Club Des 400 Coups, Novel
  Club Des 400 Coups, Le 1952 d: Jacques Daroy. lps:
  Henri Vilbert, Gerard Landry, Michele Philippe. 91M
  FRN. *Le Club Des Quatre Cent Coups* prod/rel: Films
  Paradis, Films Fernand Rivers

CLARETIE, JULES
L'Accusateur, Novel
  Accusateur, L' 1920 d: Edouard-Emile Violet. lps:
  Felix Ford, Julio de Romero. 1567m FRN. prod/rel:
  Films Lucifer
Un Assassin, 1866, Novel
  Roberto Burat 1920 d: Mario Almirante. lps: Lola
  Visconti-Brignone, Domenico Serra, Giuseppe
  Brignone. 1545m ITL. *L'Inganno* prod/rel: Rodolfi Film
Boum-Boum, Short Story
  Boum-Boum 1908 d: Maurice de Feraudy. lps: Maurice
  de Feraudy, Mme Daumerie, Petite Testard. 141m FRN.
  prod/rel: Gaumont
Le Petit Jacques, 1881, Novel
  Ninna Nanna 1914 d: Guglielmo Zorzi. lps: Pina
  Menichelli, Annibale Ninchi, Ida Carloni-Talli. 370m
  ITL. *Il Sorriso Dell'inncenza*; *The Smile of a Child*
  (UKN) prod/rel: Cines
  Petit Jacques, Le 1912 d: Georges MoncA. lps:
  Georges Saillard, Germaine Dermoz, Henri Etievant.
  1085m FRN. prod/rel: Pathe Freres
  Petit Jacques, Le 1923 d: Georges Lannes, Georges
  Raulet. lps: Andre Rolane, Henri Baudin, Violette Jyl.
  3300m FRN. prod/rel: Phocea Film
  Petit Jacques, Le 1934 d: Gaston Roudes. lps:
  Constant Remy, Line Noro, Annie Ducaux. 108M FRN.
  prod/rel: le Consortium Cinematographique Francais
Le Prince Zilah, Paris 1885, Play
  Her Final Reckoning 1918 d: Emile Chautard. lps:
  Pauline Frederick, John Miltern, Robert Cain. 5r USA.
  prod/rel: Famous Players-Lasky Corp.©, Paramount
  Pictures
  Prince Zilah, Le 1926 d: Gaston Roudes. lps: Genica
  Missirio, France Dhelia, Arlette Verlaine. 2687m FRN.
  prod/rel: Films Gaston Roudes
  Principe Zilah, Il 1919 d: Ugo de Simone. lps: Helena
  Makowska, Francois-Paul Donadio, Guido Trento.
  1349m ITL. prod/rel: Gladiator

CLARK, ALAN R.
High Wall, Play
  High Wall 1947 d: Curtis Bernhardt. lps: Robert
  Taylor, Audrey Totter, Herbert Marshall. 99M USA.
  prod/rel: MGM

CLARK, BRIAN
Whose Life Is It Anyway?, 1978, Play
  Whose Life Is It Anyway? 1981 d: John Badham. lps:
  Richard Dreyfuss, John Cassavetes, Christine Lahti.
  119M USA. prod/rel: MGM, United Artists

CLARK, EDWARD
De Luxe Annie, New York 1917, Play
De Luxe Annie 1918 d: Roland West. lps: Norma Talmadge, Eugene O'Brien, Frank Mills. 7065f USA. prod/rel: Norma Talmadge Film Corp.©, Select Pictures Corp.

CLARK, ELLERY HARDING
Carib Gold, 1926, Novel
Caribbean 1952 d: Edward Ludwig. lps: John Payne, Arlene Dahl, Cedric Hardwicke. 97M USA. *Caribbean Gold* (UKN) prod/rel: Paramount, Pine-Thomas
Loaded Dice, Indianapolis 1909, Novel
Loaded Dice 1918 d: Herbert Blache. lps: Frank Keenan, Florence Billings, Guy Coombs. 5r USA. prod/rel: Pathe Exchange, Inc.©

CLARK, FRANK HOWARD
American Aristocracy, Story
Blue Blood 1925 d: Scott R. Dunlap. lps: George Walsh, Cecille Evans, Philo McCullough. 5600f USA. prod/rel: Chadwick Pictures

CLARK, J. FRANK
The Bird Man, Story
High Flyer, The 1926 d: Harry J. Brown. lps: Reed Howes, Ethel Shannon, James Bradbury. 5610f USA. prod/rel: Harry J. Brown Productions, Rayart Pictures

CLARK, MARY HIGGINS
Novel
Weep No More My Lady 1994 d: Michel Andrieu. lps: Daniel J. Travanti, Kristin Scott-Thomas, Shelley Winters. TVM. 90M FRN/GRM. *Rivalinnen*
Stillwatch, Novel
Stillwatch 1987 d: Rod Holcomb. lps: Lynda Carter, Angie Dickinson, Don Murray. TVM. 100M USA.
A Stranger Is Watching, Novel
Stranger Is Watching, A 1982 d: Sean S. Cunningham. lps: Kate Mulgrew, Rip Torn, James Naughton. 92M USA. prod/rel: MGM, United Artists
Where are the Children, Novel
Where are the Children? 1986 d: Bruce Malmuth. lps: Jill Clayburgh, Max Gail, Harley Cross. 92M USA. prod/rel: Columbia

CLARK, OLGA PRINTZLAU
The Scarlet Sin, Story
Scarlet Sin, The 1915 d: Otis Turner, Hobart Bosworth. lps: Hobart Bosworth, Jane Novak, Hart Hoxie. 4r USA. *The Shepherd of the Mines* prod/rel: Universal Film Mfg. Co.©, Broadway Universal Feature

CLARK, RUTH
Bonny the Pony, Novel
Riders of the New Forest 1946 d: Philip Leacock. lps: Ivor Bowyer, Jill Gibbs, Michael Cabon. SRL. 75M UKN. prod/rel: Gb Instructional, General Film Distributors

CLARK, VALMA
Judgement of the West, Story
Slander the Woman 1923 d: Allen Holubar. lps: Dorothy Phillips, Lewis Dayton, Robert Anderson. 7040f USA. *The White Frontier* prod/rel: Universal Pictures

CLARK, WALTER VAN TILBURG (1908–1973), USA
The Ox-Bow Incident, 1940, Novel
Ox-Bow Incident, The 1943 d: William A. Wellman. lps: Henry Fonda, Dana Andrews, Mary Beth Hughes. 75M USA. *Strange Incident* (UKN) prod/rel: 20th Century-Fox
Ox-Bow Incident, The 1956 d: Gerd Oswald. lps: Robert Wagner, Cameron Mitchell, E. G. Marshall. MTV. 50M USA.
The Track of the Cat, 1949, Novel
Track of the Cat 1954 d: William A. Wellman. lps: Robert Mitchum, Teresa Wright, Diana Lynn. 102M USA. prod/rel: Warner Bros., Wayne-Fellows Prods.

CLARKE, ARTHUR C. (1917–, UKN
2010: Odyssey Two, 1982, Novel
2010 1984 d: Peter Hyams. lps: Roy Scheider, John Lithgow, Helen Mirren. 116M USA. *2010: the Year We Make Contact* prod/rel: MGM, United Artists
Breaking Strain, Short Story
Trapped in Space 1994 d: Arthur Allan Seidelman. lps: Jack Wagner, Jack Coleman, Kay Lenz. 87M USA. prod/rel: Wilshire Court Prods.©, Village Roadshow Pictures
The Sentinel, 1951, Short Story
2001: a Space Odyssey 1968 d: Stanley Kubrick. lps: Keir Dullea, Gary Lockwood, William Sylvester. 160M UKN/USA. *Journey Beyond the Stars* prod/rel: MGM, Hawk

CLARKE, DONALD HENDERSON
Female, New York 1932, Novel
Female 1933 d: Michael Curtiz, William Dieterle (Uncredited). lps: Ruth Chatterton, George Brent, Ferdinand Gottschalk. 65M USA. prod/rel: First National Pictures©

The Housekeeper's Daughter, New York 1938, Novel
Housekeeper's Daughter, The 1939 d: Hal Roach. lps: Joan Bennett, John Hubbard, Adolphe Menjou. 81M USA. prod/rel: United Artists Corp., Hal Roach Studios©
The Impatient Maiden, New York 1931, Novel
Impatient Maiden, The 1932 d: James Whale. lps: Lew Ayres, Mae Clarke, Una Merkel. 80M USA. prod/rel: Universal Pictures Corp.©
Louis Beretti, New York 1929, Novel
Born Reckless 1930 d: John Ford. lps: Edmund Lowe, Catherine Dale Owen, Warren Hymer. 7400f USA. prod/rel: Fox Film Corp.
Millie, New York 1930, Novel
Millie 1931 d: John Francis Dillon. lps: Helen Twelvetrees, Lilyan Tashman, Robert Ames. 85M USA. prod/rel: Charles R. Rogers Productions, RKO Radio Pictures©
Millie's Daughter, Novel
Millie's Daughter 1947 d: Sidney Salkow. lps: Gladys George, Gay Nelson, Paul Campbell. 70M USA. prod/rel: Columbia

CLARKE, GRANT
Second Hand Rose, 1921, Song
Second Hand Rose 1922 d: Lloyd Ingraham. lps: Gladys Walton, George B. Williams, Eddie Sutherland. 4433f USA. prod/rel: Universal Film Mfg. Co.

CLARKE, JOSEPH I. C.
Heartease, New York 1897, Play
Heartsease 1919 d: Harry Beaumont. lps: Tom Moore, Helene Chadwick, Larry Steers. 4950f USA. prod/rel: Goldwyn Pictures Corp.©, Goldwyn Distributing Corp.

CLARKE, KENNETH B.
The Blue Tattooing, 1915, Short Story
Faith Endurin' 1918 d: Cliff Smith. lps: Roy Stewart, Fritzi Ridgeway, Will Jeffries. 5r USA. *Faith and Endurin'* prod/rel: Triangle Film Corp., Triangle Distributing Corp.
The Girl Who Wasn't Wanted, 1928, Short Story
Rough Romance 1930 d: A. F. Erickson. lps: George O'Brien, Helen Chandler, Antonio Moreno. 55M USA. prod/rel: Fox Film Corp.
Immediate Lee, Short Story
Immediate Lee 1916 d: Frank Borzage. lps: Frank Borzage, Anna Little, Chick Morrison. 5r USA. *Hair Trigger Cassidy; Hair Trigger Casey* prod/rel: American Film Co., Mutual Film Corp.
The Sea Panther, Short Story
Sea Panther, The 1918 d: Thomas N. Heffron. lps: William Desmond, Mary Warren, Jack Richardson. 5r USA. prod/rel: Triangle Film Corp., Triangle Distributing Corp.

CLARKE, MARCUS (1846–1881), ASL
For the Term of His Natural Life, Novel
For the Term of His Natural Life 1927 d: Norman Dawn. lps: Eva Novak, George Fisher, Dunstan Webb. F ASL.
For the Term of His Natural Life 1983 d: Rob Stewart. lps: Colin Friels, Anthony Perkins, Patrick MacNee. TVM. 390M ASL. prod/rel: Patty Payne, Wilton Schiller

CLARKE-HOOK, S.
Short Stories
Jack, Sam and Pete 1919 d: Percy Moran. lps: Percy Moran, Eddie Willey, Ernest A. Trimingham. 5000f UKN. prod/rel: Pollock-Daring Productions

CLAUDE, CATHERINE
Le Magot de Josefa, Novel
Magot de Josefa, Le 1963 d: Claude Autant-LaraA. lps: Anna Magnani, Bourvil, Pierre Brasseur. 90M FRN/ITL. *La Pila Della Peppa* (ITL) prod/rel: Raimbourg Productions Star Presse, Arco Film

CLAUDE, PIERRE
Paix Sur le Rhin, Novel
Paix Sur le Rhin 1938 d: Jean Choux. lps: Dita Parlo, Francoise Rosay, John Loder. F FRN. prod/rel: P.S.R. Production

CLAUDEL, PAUL (1868–1955), FRN, Claudel, Paul Louis Charles Marie
Jeanne d'Arc Au Bucher, 1939, Play
Giovanna d'Arco Al Rogo 1954 d: Roberto Rossellini. lps: Ingrid Bergman, Tullio Carminati, Giancinto Prandelli. 76M ITL/FRN. *Jeanne d'Arc Au Bucher* (FRN); *Joan at the Stake; Jeanne Au Bucher; Joan of Arc at the Stake* prod/rel: Produzioni Cin.Che Associate

CLAUS, HUGO, Claus, Hugo Maurice Julien
De Dans Van de Reiger, 1962, Play
Dans Van de Reiger, de 1966 d: Fons Rademakers. lps: Gunnel Lindblom, Jean Desailly, Mien Duymaer Van Twist. 92M NTH. *Dance of the Heron* (UKN) prod/rel: Fons Rademakers

Het Jaar Van de Kreeft, 1972, Novel
Jaar Van de Kreeft, Het 1975 d: Herbert Curiel. lps: Willeke Van Ammelrooy, Rutger Hauer, Piet Romer. 96M NTH. *Year of the Cancer; Cancer Rising*
Het Mes, Novel
Mes, Het 1960 d: Fons Rademakers. lps: Reitze Van Der Linden, Ellen Vogel, Paul Cammermans. 92M NTH. *The Knife* prod/rel: Maatschappij
Omtrent Deedee, Novel
Sacrament, Het 1989 d: Hugo Claus. lps: Frank Aendenboom, Jan Decleir, Hugo Van Den Berghe. 100M BLG. *The Sacrament*

CLAUSEN, CARL
A Perfect Crime, 1920, Short Story
Perfect Crime, A 1921 d: Allan Dwan. lps: Monte Blue, Jacqueline Logan, Stanton Heck. 5r USA. prod/rel: Allan Dwan Productions, Associated Producers
Poker Face, 1926, Short Story
Killer at Large 1936 d: David Selman. lps: Mary Brian, Russell Hardie, Betty Compson. 58M USA. *Poker Face; Killers on the Loose* prod/rel: Columbia Pictures Corp. of California©

CLAUSER, SUZANNE
A Girl Named Sooner, Novel
Girl Named Sooner, A 1975 d: Delbert Mann. lps: Lee Remick, Richard Crenna, Don Murray. 100M USA. prod/rel: 20th Century-Fox

CLAUZEL, RAYMOND
La Maison Au Soleil, Novel
Maison Au Soleil, La 1929 d: Gaston Roudes. lps: France Dhelia, Gaston Jacquet, Georges Melchior. 2950m FRN. *Gueule Cassee* prod/rel: Franco Film
Mon Oncle d'Arles, Play
Coup de Mistral, Un 1933 d: Gaston Roudes. lps: Jane Maguenat, France Dhelia, Fortune. 80M FRN. *Mon Oncle d'Arles* prod/rel: Productions Cinegraphiques

CLAVEL, BERNARD
Le Tonnerre de Dieu, Novel
Tonnerre de Dieu, Le 1965 d: Denys de La Patelliere. lps: Jean Gabin, Michele Mercier, Lilli Palmer. 95M FRN/ITL/GRM. *Matrimonio Alla Francese* (ITL); *Herr Auf Schloss Brassac* (GRM); *God's Thunder* (UKN); *Auch Eine Franzosische Ehe; Even a French Marriage* prod/rel: Les Films Copernic, Finda Cinematografica
Le Voyage du Pere, Novel
Voyage du Pere, Le 1966 d: Denys de La Patelliere. lps: Fernandel, Lilli Palmer, Laurent Terzieff. 90M FRN/ITL. *Destinazione Marciapiede* (ITL) prod/rel: Films Copernic, Gafer

CLAVEL, MAURICE
Une Fille Pour l'Ete, Paris 1957, Novel
Fille Pour l'Ete, Une 1960 d: Edouard Molinaro. lps: Pascale Petit, Micheline Presle, Michel Auclair. 80M FRN/ITL. *A Mistress for the Summer* (USA); *Una Ragazza Per l'Estate* (ITL); *Girls for the Summer* (UKN); *A Girl for the Summer; Lover for the Summer, A* prod/rel: Boreal Films, Filmsonor

CLAVELL, JAMES (1924–1994), ASL, Clavell, James Dumaresq
King Rat, London 1963, Novel
King Rat 1965 d: Bryan Forbes. lps: Alex Segal, Patrick O'Neal, Todd Armstrong. 135M USA. prod/rel: Coleytown Productions
The Last Valley, Novel
Last Valley, The 1970 d: James Clavell. lps: Michael Caine, Omar Sharif, Florinda Bolkan. 125M UKN. prod/rel: Cinerama, Season
Shogun, Novel
Shogun 1981 d: Jerry London. lps: Richard Chamberlain, Toshiro Mifune, Yoko ShimadA. TVM. 580M USA/JPN. *James Clavell's Shogun* prod/rel: Paramount Television, Paramount Pictures Corporation
Tai-Pan, Novel
Tai-Pan 1986 d: Daryl Duke. lps: Bryan Brown, Joan Chen, John Stanton. 127M USA. *James Clavell's Tai-Pan* prod/rel: de Laurentiis

CLAWSON, ELLIOTT J.
His Wife in Arizona, Novel
Hungry Eyes 1918 d: Rupert Julian. lps: Ruth Clifford, Monroe Salisbury, Rupert Julian. 5r USA. *His Wife from Arizona* prod/rel: Bluebird Photoplays, Inc.©
The Tragedy of Whispering Creek, Story
Tragedy of Whispering Creek, The 1914 d: Allan Dwan. lps: Pauline Bush, Murdock MacQuarrie, Lon Chaney. 2000f USA. prod/rel: Bison

CLAXTON, OLIVER
Lucky Night, 1935, Short Story
Lucky Night 1939 d: Norman Taurog. lps: Myrna Loy, Robert Taylor, Henry O'Neill. 90M USA. prod/rel: Metro-Goldwyn-Mayer Corp., Loew's, Inc.©

CLAY, BERTHA M., Brame, Charlotte M.
Dora Thorne, New York 1880, Novel
Dora Thorne 1910. lps: Harry Benham. 900f USA. prod/rel: Selig Polyscope Co.
Dora Thorne 1915 d: Lawrence Marston. lps: Lionel Barrymore, William Russell, Millicent Evans. 4r USA. prod/rel: Biograph Co.©, General Film Co.
My Poor Wife, Novel
His Wife 1915 d: George Foster Platt. lps: Geraldine O'Brien, Holmes Herbert, Lorraine Huling. 5r USA. *My Wife* prod/rel: Thanhouser Film Corp., Mutual Film Corp.
Thorns and Orange Blossoms, New York 1883, Novel
Thorns and Orange Blossoms 1922 d: Louis J. Gasnier. lps: Estelle Taylor, Kenneth Harlan, Arthur Stuart Hull. 6971f USA. prod/rel: Preferred Pictures, Al Lichtman Corp.
Wife in Name Only, Story
Wife in Name Only 1923 d: George W. Terwilliger. lps: Mary Thurman, Arthur Housman, Edmund Lowe. 4868f USA. prod/rel: Pyramid Pictures, Selznick Distributing Corp.

CLEARY, JON (1917–), ASL
The Green Helmet, London 1957, Novel
Green Helmet, The 1961 d: Michael Forlong. lps: Bill Travers, Ed Begley, Sidney James. 88M UKN. prod/rel: MGM British
The High Commissioner, London 1966, Novel
Nobody Runs Forever 1968 d: Ralph Thomas. lps: Rod Taylor, Christopher Plummer, Lilli Palmer. 101M UKN. *The High Commissioner* (USA) prod/rel: Rank Organisation, Selmur Pictures
High Road to China, Novel
High Road to China 1982 d: Brian G. Hutton. lps: Tom Selleck, Bess Armstrong, Jack Weston. 104M USA. prod/rel: Warner Bros.
The Sundowners, Novel
Sundowners, The 1960 d: Fred Zinnemann. lps: Deborah Kerr, Robert Mitchum, Peter Ustinov. 124M UKN/USA/ASL. prod/rel: Warner Bros., Warner-Pathe

CLEAVER, BILL
Where the Lilies Bloom, Book
Where the Lilies Bloom 1974 d: William A. Graham. lps: Julie Gholson, Jan Smithers, Matthew Burrill. 96M USA. prod/rel: Mattel Productions

CLEAVER, VERA (1919–, USA, Cleaver, Vera Allen
Where the Lilies Bloom 1974 d: William A. Graham. lps: Julie Gholson, Jan Smithers, Matthew Burrill. 96M USA. prod/rel: Mattel Productions

CLECKLEY M.D., HERVEY M.
A Case of Multiple Personality, Book
Three Faces of Eve, The 1957 d: Nunnally Johnson. lps: Joanne Woodward, David Wayne, Lee J. Cobb. 95M USA. prod/rel: 20th Century-Fox

CLELAND, JOHN (1709–1789), UKN
Fanny Hill; Or Memoirs of a Woman of Pleasure, London 1749, Novel
Fanny Hill 1964 d: Russ Meyer. lps: Miriam Hopkins, Leticia Roman, Walter Giller. 105M GRM/USA. *Fanny Hill: Memoirs of a Woman of Pleasure* (USA); *Romp of Fanny Hill* prod/rel: Famous Players Corporation, Ccc-Filmkunst
Fanny Hill 1968 d: Mac Ahlberg. lps: Diana Kjaer, Hans Ernback, Keve Hjelm. 101M SWD. *The Swedish Fanny Hill*
Fanny Hill 1983 d: Gerry O'HarA. lps: Lisa Raines, Oliver Reed, Wilfrid Hyde-White. 92M UKN. prod/rel: Fh Prods., Brent Walker Film

CLEMENCEAU, GEORGES
Les Plus Forts, Paris 1898, Novel
Strongest, The 1920 d: Raoul Walsh. lps: Renee Adoree, Carlo Liten, Harrison Hunter. 5-6r USA. prod/rel: Fox Film Corp., William Fox©
Le Voile du Bonheur, Play
Voile du Bonheur, Le 1910 d: Albert Capellani. lps: Henry Krauss, Georges Treville, Madeleine Carlier. 870m FRN. prod/rel: Scagl
Voile du Bonheur, Le 1923 d: Edouard-Emile Violet. lps: Sussie Wata, Shu Hou, Liao Sze Tchin. 2000m FRN. *The Veil of Happiness*

CLEMENS, LEROY
Alias the Deacon, New York 1925, Play
Alias the Deacon 1928 d: Edward Sloman. lps: Jean Hersholt, June Marlowe, Ralph Graves. 6869f USA. prod/rel: Universal Pictures
Half a Sinner 1934 d: Kurt Neumann. lps: Sally Blane, Joel McCrea, Berton Churchill. 73M USA. *Alias the Deacon* prod/rel: Universal Pictures Corp.©

Aloma of the South Seas, New York 1925, Play
Aloma of the South Seas 1926 d: Maurice Tourneur. lps: Gilda Gray, Percy Marmont, Warner Baxter. 8514f USA. prod/rel: Famous Players-Lasky Corp., Paramount Pictures
Aloma of the South Seas 1941 d: Alfred Santell. lps: Dorothy Lamour, Jon Hall, Lynne Overman. 77M USA. prod/rel: Paramount
The Deacon, New York 1925, Play
Alias the Deacon 1940 d: W. Christy Cabanne. lps: Bob "Bazooka" Burns, Mischa Auer, Peggy Moran. 74M USA. prod/rel: Universal Pictures Co.
The Hurdy-Gurdy Man, 1922, Play
Love, Live and Laugh 1929 d: William K. Howard. lps: George Jessel, Lila Lee, David Rollins. 8090f USA. prod/rel: Fox Film Corp.

CLEMENTS, COLIN
Borrowed Love, Story
Call of the West 1930 d: Albert Ray. lps: Dorothy Revier, Matt Moore, Tom O'Brien. 70M USA. prod/rel: Columbia Pictures
June Mad, Play
Her First Beau 1941 d: Theodore Reed. lps: Jackie Cooper, Jane Withers, Edith Fellows. 76M USA. prod/rel: Columbia
Notorious Gentleman, Story
Smooth As Silk 1946 d: Charles T. Barton. lps: Kent Taylor, Virginia Grey, Jane Adams. 65M USA. *Notorious Gentleman*

CLERC, HENRI
Le Spectre de Monsieur Imberger, Play
Mystere Imberger, Le 1935 d: Jacques Severac. lps: Simone Deguyse, Jean Galland, Gaston Modot. 82M FRN. *Le Spectre de M. Imberger* prod/rel: Compagnie Autonome De Cinematographie

CLERK, ERNIE
Le Judoka Dans la Ville, Novel
Judoka, Agent Secret, Le 1966 d: Pierre Zimmer. lps: Jean-Claude Bercq, Marilu Tolo, Perrette Pradier. 95M FRN/ITL. *Carnet Per un Morto* (ITL) prod/rel: France Cinema Productions, Tigielle 33
Judoka En Enfer, Novel
Casse-Tete Chinois Pour le Judoka 1968 d: Maurice Labro. lps: Marc Briand, Marilu Tolo, Heinz Drache. 100M FRN/ITL/GRM. *Die Sieben Masken Des Judoka* (GRM); *Chinese Puzzle for Judoka*; *Ore Violente* (ITL); *Le Judoka Dans l'Enfer* prod/rel: G.R.K., Films Corona

CLEVELAND, JOHN
Article
Mayor of 44th Street 1942 d: Alfred E. Green. lps: George Murphy, Anne Shirley, Richard Barthelmess. 86M USA. prod/rel: RKO

CLEVELY, HUGH
Archer Plus 20, Novel
Meet Maxwell Archer 1939 d: John Paddy Carstairs. lps: John Loder, Leueen McGrath, Marta Labarr. 74M UKN. *Detective Maxwell Archer* (USA) prod/rel: RKO Radio

CLEWES, HOWARD
Green Grow the Rushes, Novel
Green Grow the Rushes 1951 d: Derek Twist. lps: Roger Livesey, Honor Blackman, Richard Burton. 79M UKN. *Brandy Ashore* prod/rel: Act Films, British Lion
The Long Memory, Novel
Long Memory, The 1953 d: Robert Hamer. lps: John Mills, John McCallum, Elizabeth Sellars. 96M UKN. prod/rel: General Film Distributors, Europa

CLEWLOW, CAROL
A Woman's Guide to Adultery, Novel
Woman's Guide to Adultery, A 1993 d: David Hayman. lps: Theresa Russell, Sean Bean, Amanda Donohue. MTV. 160M UKN.

CLIFFORD, CHARLES L.
Army Girl, 1935, Short Story
Army Girl 1938 d: George Nicholls Jr. lps: Madge Evans, Preston Foster, Heather Angel. 90M USA. prod/rel: Republic Pictures Corp.
The Real Glory, London 1938, Novel
Real Glory, The 1939 d: Henry Hathaway. lps: Gary Cooper, David Niven, Andrea Leeds. 96M USA. *The Last Frontier* prod/rel: United Artists Corp., Samuel Goldwyn, Inc.

CLIFFORD, FRANCIS (1917–1975), UKN
Act of Mercy, London 1959, Novel
Guns of Darkness 1962 d: Anthony Asquith. lps: Leslie Caron, David Niven, James Robertson Justice. 102M UKN. *Act of Mercy* prod/rel: Concorde, Cavalcade Films

The Grosvenor Square Goodbye, 1974, Novel
Goodbye & Amen 1978 d: Damiano Damiani. lps: Tony Musante, Claudia Cardinale, John Forsythe. 105M ITL. *The Uomo Della C.I.a.*; *Goodbye and Amen* prod/rel: Capital Film, Rizzoli Film
The Naked Runner, London 1966, Novel
Naked Runner, The 1967 d: Sidney J. Furie. lps: Frank Sinatra, Peter Vaughan, Derren Nesbitt. 102M UKN. prod/rel: Artanis Productions, Warner-Pathe

CLIFFORD, MRS. W. K.
The Likeness of the Night, London 1908, Play
Likeness of the Night, The 1921 d: Percy Nash. lps: Renee Kelly, Minna Grey, Harold Deacon. 5434f UKN. prod/rel: Screen Plays, British Exhibitors' Films

CLIFFORD, W. K.
Eve's Lovers, 1924, Short Story
Eve's Lover 1925 d: Roy Del Ruth. lps: Irene Rich, Bert Lytell, Clara Bow. 7237f USA. prod/rel: Warner Brothers Pictures

CLIFFORD, WILLIAM H.
See You in Jail, Story
See You in Jail 1927 d: Joseph Henabery. lps: Jack Mulhall, Alice Day, MacK Swain. 5800f USA. prod/rel: Ray Rockett Productions

CLIFT, DENISON (1892–1961), USA
Man About Town, New York 1932, Novel
Man About Town 1932 d: John Francis Dillon. lps: Warner Baxter, Karen Morley, Conway Tearle. 76M USA. prod/rel: Fox Film Corp.©
Room 40 O. B., Novel
Secrets of Scotland Yard 1944 d: George Blair. lps: Edgar Barrier, Stephanie Bachelor, C. Aubrey Smith. 68M USA. prod/rel: Republic
Scotland Yard, New York 1929, Play
Impostor, El 1931 d: Lewis Seiler. lps: Juan Torena, Blanca de Castejon, Carlos Villarias. 9r USA. prod/rel: Fox Film Corp.
Scotland Yard 1930 d: William K. Howard. lps: Edmund Lowe, Joan Bennett, Donald Crisp. 6750f USA. *Bart. "Detective Clive"* (UKN) prod/rel: Fox Film Corp.
Scotland Yard 1941 d: Norman Foster. lps: Nancy Kelly, Edmund Gwenn, John Loder. 68M USA. prod/rel: 20th Century Fox
Warn London, Novel
Warn London 1934 d: T. Hayes Hunter. lps: Edmund Gwenn, John Loder, Leonora Corbett. 68M UKN. prod/rel: British Lion

CLIFTON, ETHEL
The Doormat, New York 1922, Play
Honeymoon Express, The 1926 d: James Flood. lps: Willard Louis, Irene Rich, Holmes Herbert. 6768f USA. prod/rel: Warner Brothers Pictures

CLIFTON, FRANK M.
The Wild Bull's Lair, Story
Wild Bull's Lair, The 1925 d: Del Andrews. lps: Fred Thomson, Catherine Bennett, Herbert Prior. 5280f USA. prod/rel: R-C Pictures, Film Booking Offices of America

CLIFTON-JAMES, M. E.
I Was Monty's Double, Book
I Was Monty's Double 1958 d: John Guillermin. lps: John Mills, Cecil Parker, M. E. Clifton-James. 100M UKN. *Monty's Double* prod/rel: Film Traders, Setfair

CLINE, EDWARD
High Spirits, Story
Ghost Catchers 1944 d: Eddie Cline. lps: Ole Olsen, Chic Johnson, Gloria Jean. 68M USA. prod/rel: Universal

CLOETE, STUART (1897–1976), FRN, Cloete, Edward Fairly Stuart Graham
The Fiercest Heart, Boston 1960, Novel
Fiercest Heart, The 1961 d: George Sherman. lps: Stuart Whitman, Juliet Prowse, Ken Scott. 91M USA. prod/rel: 20th Century-Fox Film Corp.

CLOONEY, ROSEMARY
This for Remembrance, Autobiography
Rosie: the Rosemary Clooney Story 1982 d: Jackie Cooper. lps: Sondra Locke, Tony Orlando, Penelope Milford. TVM. 100M USA.

CLOQUEMIN
Gardiens de Phare, Play
Gardiens de Phare 1928 d: Jean Gremillon. lps: Gabrielle Fontan, Geymond Vital, Fromet. 2000m FRN. *Guardians of Phare* prod/rel: Societe Des Films Du Grand Guignol

CLORK, HARRY
The Milky Way, New York 1934, Play
Kid from Brooklyn, The 1946 d: Norman Z. McLeod. lps: Danny Kaye, Virginia Mayo, Vera-Ellen. 114M USA. prod/rel: Samuel Goldwyn, RKO

Milky Way, The 1936 d: Leo McCarey. lps: Harold Lloyd, Adolphe Menjou, Verree Teasdale. 85M USA. prod/rel: Paramount Productions©

CLOSTERMANN, PIERRE (1921–, FRN
Le Grand Cirque
Grand Cirque, Le 1949 d: Georges Peclet. lps: Pierre Cressoy, Pierre Larquey, Pamela Skiff. 120M FRN. prod/rel: Imperator Film

CLOU, JOHN
A Caravan to Camul, Book
Conqueror, The 1956 d: Dick Powell. lps: John Wayne, Susan Hayward, Pedro Armendariz. 111M USA. prod/rel: RKO Radio

CLOUSTON, J. STORER (1870–1944), UKN, Clouston, Joseph Storer
Short Stories
Lunatic at Large, The 1927 d: Fred Newmeyer. lps: Leon Errol, Dorothy MacKaill, Jack Raymond. 5521f USA. prod/rel: First National Pictures
His First Offence, Novel
Drole de Drame 1937 d: Marcel Carne. lps: Louis Jouvet, Michel Simon, Francoise Rosay. 109M FRN. *Bizarre Bizarre* (USA); *L' Affaire Molyneux* prod/rel: Productions Corniglion-Molinier
The Lunatic at Large, Novel
Lunatic at Large, The 1921 d: Henry Edwards. lps: Henry Edwards, Chrissie White, Lyell Johnston. 5120f UKN. prod/rel: Hepworth
The Mystery of Number 47, New York 1911, Novel
Mystery of Number 47, The 1917 d: Otis B. Thayer. lps: Ralph Herz, Nellie Hartley, Louiszita Valentine. 5r USA. prod/rel: Selig Polyscope Co.©, Red Seal Play
The Spy in Black, Novel
Spy in Black, The 1939 d: Michael Powell. lps: Conrad Veidt, Sebastian Shaw, Valerie Hobson. 82M UKN. *U-Boat 29* (USA) prod/rel: Harefield, Columbia

CLOWES, ST. JOHN LEIGH
Dear Murderer, Play
Dear Murderer 1947 d: Arthur Crabtree. lps: Eric Portman, Greta Gynt, Dennis Price. 94M UKN. prod/rel: General Film Distributors, Gainsborough

CLUCHEY, RICK
The Cage, Play
Weeds 1987 d: John Hancock. lps: Nick Nolte, Rita Taggart, Lane Smith. 115M USA. *Honour Among Thieves* prod/rel: Kingsgate, de Laurentiis Entertainment Group

CLUGSTON, KATHARINE
The Head of the Family, 1924, Play
Last Gentleman, The 1934 d: Sidney Lanfield. lps: George Arliss, Edna May Oliver, Charlotte Henry. 78M USA. *Head of the Family* prod/rel: United Artists Corp., 20th Century Pictures©

CLUM, WOODWORTH
Apache Agent, 1936, Biography
Walk the Proud Land 1956 d: Jesse Hibbs. lps: Audie Murphy, Anne Bancroft, Pat Crowley. 88M USA. prod/rel: Universal-International

CLUMEZ, LUIGI
Mio Dio!. Pace, Novel
Pace, Mio Dio!. 1914 d: Carlo Simoneschi. lps: Lola Visconti-Brignone, Ignazio Mascalchi, Carlo Simoneschi. 1200m ITL. prod/rel: Volsca Film

CLYMER, JOHN B.
Don't Fall in Love, Short Story
Thanks for Listening 1937 d: Marshall Neilan. lps: Pinky Tomlin, Maxine Doyle, Aileen Pringle. 60M USA. *Partly Confidential* (UKN) prod/rel: Conn Productions, Ambassador Pictures
Mind Your Feet Kitty, Short Story
Delicious Little Devil, The 1919 d: Robert Z. Leonard. lps: Mae Murray, Harry Rattenberry, Richard Cummings. 5650f USA. prod/rel: Universal Film Mfg. Co.©

COATES, JOHN
True As a Turtle, Novel
True As a Turtle 1957 d: Wendy Toye. lps: John Gregson, June Thorburn, Cecil Parker. 96M UKN. prod/rel: Rank, Rank Film Distributors

COATES, ROBERT M. (1897–, USA, Coates, Robert Myron
Wisteria Cottage, 1948, Novel
Edge of Fury 1958 d: Irving Lerner, Robert Gurney Jr. lps: Michael Higgins, Lois Holmes, Jean Allison. 77M USA. prod/rel: United Artists, Wisteria

COBB, ELISABETH
She Was a Lady, Indianapolis 1934, Novel
She Was a Lady 1934 d: Hamilton MacFadden. lps: Helen Twelvetrees, Donald Woods, Ralph Morgan. 77M USA. prod/rel: Fox Film Corp.©

COBB, HUMPHREY (1889–1944), USA
Paths of Glory, 1935, Novel
Paths of Glory 1957 d: Stanley Kubrick. lps: Kirk Douglas, Ralph Meeker, Adolphe Menjou. 87M USA. prod/rel: United Artists, Bryna Pictures

COBB, IRVIN S. (1876–1944), USA, Cobb, Irvin Shrewsbury
Boys Will Be Boys, 1917, Short Story
Boys Will Be Boys 1921 d: Clarence Badger. lps: Will Rogers, Irene Rich, Charles Mason. 4300f USA. prod/rel: Goldwyn Pictures
Field of Honor, 1916, Short Story
Fields of Honor 1918 d: Ralph Ince. lps: Mae Marsh, Marguerite Marsh, George Cooper. 5r USA. *Field of Honor* prod/rel: Goldwyn Pictures Corp.©
The Life of the Party, 1919, Short Story
Life of the Party, The 1920 d: Joseph Henabery. lps: Roscoe Arbuckle, Winnifred Greenwood, Roscoe Karns. 5944f USA. prod/rel: Famous Players-Lasky Corp.©
The Lord Provides, Short Story
Sun Shines Bright, The 1953 d: John Ford. lps: Charles Winninger, Arleen Whelan, John Russell. 92M USA. prod/rel: Republic, Argosy
The Mob from Massac, Short Story
Sun Shines Bright, The 1953 d: John Ford. lps: Charles Winninger, Arleen Whelan, John Russell. 92M USA. prod/rel: Republic, Argosy
The Sun Shines Bright, Short Story
Sun Shines Bright, The 1953 d: John Ford. lps: Charles Winninger, Arleen Whelan, John Russell. 92M USA. prod/rel: Republic, Argosy
Under Sentence, New York 1916, Play
Fighting Odds 1917 d: Allan Dwan. lps: Maxine Elliott, Henry Clive, Charles Dalton. 6r USA. prod/rel: Goldwyn Pictures Corp., Goldwyn Distributing Corp.
The Web, Short Story
Face in the Dark, The 1918 d: Hobart Henley. lps: Mae Marsh, Niles Welch, Alec B. Francis. 6r USA. prod/rel: Goldwyn Pictures Corp.©, Goldwyn Distributing Corp.
The Woman Accused, 1933, Story
Woman Accused, The 1933 d: Paul Sloane. lps: Nancy Carroll, Cary Grant, Louis Calhern. 73M USA. prod/rel: Paramount Productions©
The Young Nuts of America, 1923, Short Story
New School Teacher, The 1924 d: Gregory La CavA. lps: Doris Kenyon, Charles "Chic" Sale, Mickey Bennett. 5284f USA. prod/rel: C. C. Burr Pictures

COBB, THOMAS
Mrs. Erricker's Reputation, Novel
Mrs. Erricker's Reputation 1920 d: Cecil M. Hepworth. lps: Alma Taylor, Gerald Ames, James Carew. 5780f UKN. prod/rel: Hepworth

COBURN, ANDREW
Un Dimanche de Flics, Novel
Dimanche de Flics, Un 1982 d: Michel Vianey. lps: Jean Rochfort, Victor Lanoux, Barbara SukowA. 99M FRN/GRM. *Zwei Profis Steigen Aus*; *Two Pros Call It Quits* prod/rel: Filmax, K.F. Kinofilm
Sweetheart
Toutes Peines Confondues 1991 d: Michel Deville. lps: Patrick Bruel, Jacques Dutronc, Mathilda May. 107M FRN.
Widow's Walk, Novel
Noyade Interdite 1987 d: Pierre Granier-Deferre. lps: Philippe Noiret, Guy Marchand, Elisabeth Bourgine. 100M FRN. prod/rel: Paradis Film, Fr 3

COBURN, WALLACE G.
Yellowstone Pete's Only Daughter, Poem
Sunset Princess, The 1918. lps: Marjorie Daw, Wallace Coburn, C. M. Giffen. 5r USA. *The Golden Goddess* prod/rel: Great West Film Co., State Rights

COBURN, WALTER J.
Barb Wire, New York 1931, Novel
Rawhide Halo, The 1960 d: Roger Kay. lps: Walter Brennan, Leif Erickson, Luana Patten. 64M USA. *Barb Wire (the Rawhide Halo)*; *Shoot Out at Big Sag* prod/rel: Brennan Productions
Burnt Ranch, 1933, Short Story
Westerner, The 1934 d: David Selman. lps: Tim McCoy, Marion Shilling, Joseph Sawyer. 60M USA. prod/rel: Columbia Pictures Corp.©
Ride 'Im Cowboy, Short Story
Between Dangers 1927 d: Richard Thorpe. lps: Buddy Roosevelt, Alma Rayford, Rennie Young. 4533f USA. prod/rel: Action Pictures, Pathe Exchange, Inc.
The Sun Dance Kid, Story
Fightin' Comeback, The 1927 d: Tenny Wright. lps: Buddy Roosevelt, Clara Horton, Sidney M. Goldin. 4415f USA. prod/rel: Action Pictures, Pathe Exchange, Inc.

Triple Cross for Danger, Story
Fighting Fury 1924 d: Cliff Smith. lps: Jack Hoxie, Helen Holmes, Fred Kohler. 4491f USA. prod/rel: Universal Pictures

COCHRAN, RICE E.
Be Prepared, 1952, Novel
Mister Scoutmaster 1953 d: Henry Levin. lps: Clifton Webb, Edmund Gwenn, George Winslow. 87M USA. *Mr. Scoutmaster* prod/rel: 20th Century-Fox

COCKRELL, EUSTACE
Rocky's Rose, Story
Fast Company 1953 d: John Sturges. lps: Polly Bergen, Howard Keel, Marjorie Main. 68M USA. prod/rel: MGM
The World in His Corner, Short Story
Tennessee Champ 1953 d: Fred M. Wilcox. lps: Dewey Martin, Keenan Wynn, Shelley Winters. 73M USA. prod/rel: MGM

COCKRELL, FRANCIS M.
Count Pete, 1935, Short Story
Walking on Air 1936 d: Joseph Santley. lps: Ann Sothern, Gene Raymond, Henry Stephenson. 70M USA. *Count Pete* prod/rel: RKO Radio Pictures©

COCKRELL, FRANK
Dark Waters, Story
Dark Waters 1944 d: Andre de Toth. lps: Merle Oberon, Franchot Tone, Thomas Mitchell. 90M USA. prod/rel: United Artists

COCKRELL, MARIAN
Dark Waters 1944 d: Andre de Toth. lps: Merle Oberon, Franchot Tone, Thomas Mitchell. 90M USA. prod/rel: United Artists

COCTEAU, JEAN (1889–1963), FRN
L' Aigle a Deux Tetes, 1946, Play
Aigle a Deux Tetes, L' 1948 d: Jean Cocteau. lps: Edwige Feuillere, Jean Marais, Silvia Monfort. 95M FRN. *The Eagle With Two Heads* (UKN); *The Eagle Has Two Heads* prod/rel: Films Ariane-Sirius
Mistero Di Oberwald, Il 1979 d: Michelangelo Antonioni. lps: Monica Vitti, Franco Branciaroli, Paolo Bonacelli. 128M ITL/GRM. *Das Geheimnis von Oberwald* (GRM); *The Oberwald Mystery*; *The Mystery of Oberwald*; *The Secret of Oberwald* prod/rel: Rai-Tv (Roma), Polytel International (Hamburg)
Le Bel Indifferent, 1949, Play
Bel Indifferent, Le 1957 d: Jacques Demy. 29M FRN.
Les Enfants Terribles, 1925, Novel
Enfants Terribles, Les 1949 d: Jean-Pierre Melville. lps: Nicole Stephane, Edouard Dhermitte, Renee CosimA. 107M FRN. *The Strange Ones* (UKN) prod/rel: Melville Productions
Orphee, 1927, Play
Orphee 1950 d: Jean Cocteau. lps: Jean Marais, Marie Dea, Maria Casares. 112M FRN. *Orpheus* (USA) prod/rel: Andre Paulve
Les Parents Terribles, 1938, Play
Intimate Relations 1953 d: Charles H. Frank. lps: Harold Warrender, Elsy Albiin, Marian Spencer. 86M UKN. *Disobedient* prod/rel: Advance, Adelphi
Parents Terribles, Les 1948 d: Jean Cocteau. lps: Yvonne de Bray, Gabrielle Dorziat, Marcel Andre. 100M FRN. *The Storm Within* (USA) prod/rel: Ariane
Thomas l'Imposteur, 1923, Novel
Thomas l'Imposteur 1964 d: Georges Franju. lps: Emmanuelle Riva, Jean Servais, Fabrice Rouleau. 100M FRN. *Thomas the Imposter* prod/rel: Filmel
La Voix Humaine, 1930, Play
Amore 1948 d: Roberto Rossellini. lps: Anna Magnani, Federico Fellini, Peparuolo. 78M ITL. *La Voix Humaine*; *Woman*; *Miracle*; *L' Amore*; *Ways of Love* prod/rel: Tevere Film, Ceiad

CODY, LIZA
Anna Lee: Headcase, Novel
Anna Lee: Headcase 1993 d: Colin Bucksey. lps: Imogen Stubbs, Alan Howard, Michael Bryant. TVM. 105M UKN. prod/rel: Lwt

CODY, WILLIAM F. (1846–1917), USA, Cody, William Frederick, Cody, Buffalo Bill
The Great West That Was, Book
Indians are Coming, The 1930 d: Henry McRae. lps: Tim McCoy, Allene Ray, Edmund Cobb. SRL. 12EP USA. prod/rel: Universal

COE, CHARLES FRANCIS
Gangster Me, New York 1927, Novel
Me, Gangster 1928 d: Raoul Walsh. lps: June Collyer, Don Terry, Anders Randolf. 6042f USA. prod/rel: Fox Film Corp.
Ransom, Philadelphia 1934, Novel
Nancy Steele Is Missing! 1937 d: George Marshall. lps: Victor McLaglen, Walter Connolly, Peter Lorre. 86M USA. *The Lost Nancy Steele* prod/rel: Twentieth Century-Fox Film Corp.©

Repeal, 1934, Novel
Gay Bride, The 1934 d: Jack Conway. lps: Carole Lombard, Chester Morris, Zasu Pitts. 82M USA. *Repeal* prod/rel: Metro-Goldwyn-Mayer Corp.©

The River Pirate, New York 1928, Novel
River Pirate, The 1928 d: William K. Howard. lps: Victor McLaglen, Lois Moran, Nick Stuart. 6937f USA. prod/rel: Fox Film Corp.

COETZEE, J. M. (1940–, SAF, Coetzee, John Michael
In the Heart of the Country, 1977, Novel
Dust 1985 d: Marion Hansel. lps: Jane Birkin, Trevor Howard, John MatshikizA. 88M BLG/FRN. prod/rel: Man's Films (Brussels), Daska Films (Ghent)

COFFEE, LENORE (1900–1984), USA
Age of Indiscretion, Story
Age of Indiscretion 1935 d: Edward Ludwig. lps: Helen Vinson, Paul Lukas, David Holt. 90M USA. prod/rel: MGM

Weep No More, Novel
Another Time, Another Place 1958 d: Lewis Allen. lps: Lana Turner, Barry Sullivan, Glynis Johns. 95M UKN/USA. prod/rel: Paramount, Kaydor

COFFINET, CHRISTIAN
La Fille de Proie, Paris 1953, Novel
Moucharde, La 1958 d: Guy Lefranc. lps: Dany Carrel, Pierre Vaneck, Yves Deniaud. 100M FRN. *Woman of Sin* (USA) prod/rel: Films Artistiques Francais, Films Marius Bouchet

COGHLAN, CHARLES
The Royal Box, New York 1897, Play
Royal Box, The 1914 d: Oscar Eagle. lps: Gertrude Coghlan, Thomas Carrigan, Clifford Bruce. 4r USA. prod/rel: Selig Polyscope Co.©, General Film Co.
Royal Box, The 1930 d: Bryan Foy. lps: Alexander Moissi, Camilla Horn, Lew Hearn. 8000f USA. prod/rel: Warner Brothers Pictures

COGNETTI, GOFFREDO
A Santa Lucia, 1887, Play
A Santa Lucia 1917 d: Ugo FalenA. lps: Bianca Stagno-Bellincioni, Ettore Piergiovanni, Rina CalabriA. 1291m ITL. prod/rel: Tespi Film

COHAN, GEORGE M. (1878–1942), USA, Cohan, George Michael
The Baby Cyclone, Play
Baby Cyclone, The 1928 d: A. Edward Sutherland. lps: Lew Cody, Aileen Pringle, Robert Armstrong. 5053f USA. prod/rel: Metro-Goldwyn-Mayer Pictures

Broadway Jones, New York 1912, Play
Broadway Jones 1917 d: Joseph Kaufman. lps: George M. Cohan, Marguerite Snow, Russell Bassett. 6r USA. prod/rel: Cohan Feature Film Co., Artcraft Pictures Corp.©

Elmer the Great, New York 1928, Play
Cowboy Quarterback, The 1939 d: Noel Smith. lps: Bert Wheeler, Gloria Dickson, Marie Wilson. 56M USA. *Lighthorse Harry* prod/rel: Warner Bros. Pictures, Inc.
Elmer the Great 1933 d: Mervyn Leroy. lps: Joe E. Brown, Patricia Ellis, Claire Dodd. 70M USA. prod/rel: First National Pictures©
Fast Company 1929 d: A. Edward Sutherland. lps: Evelyn Brent, Jack Oakie, Skeets Gallagher. 6863f USA. prod/rel: Paramount Famous Lasky

Forty-Five Minutes from Broadway, 1906, Musical Play
Forty-Five Minutes from Broadway 1920 d: Joseph de Grasse. lps: Charles Ray, Dorothy Devore, Hazel Howell. 5548f USA. *45 Minutes from Broadway* prod/rel: Charles Ray Productions, Inc., Arthur S. Kane Pictures Corp.

Gambling, New York 1929, Play
Gambling 1934 d: Rowland V. Lee. lps: George M. Cohan, Dorothy Burgess, Wynne Gibson. 82M USA. prod/rel: Harold B. Franklin, Fox Film Corp.©

Jr. George Washington, New York 1906, Play
George Washington, Jr. 1924 d: Malcolm St. Clair. lps: Wesley Barry, Gertrude Olmstead, Leon Bary. 6100f USA. prod/rel: Warner Brothers Pictures

Get-Rich-Quick Wallingford, New York 1910, Play
Get-Rich-Quick Wallingford 1921 d: Frank Borzage. lps: Sam Hardy, Norman Kerry, Doris Kenyon. 7381f USA. prod/rel: Cosmopolitan Productions, Paramount Pictures

Hit-the-Trail-Holliday, New York 1915, Play
Hit-the-Trail Holliday 1918 d: Marshall Neilan. lps: George M. Cohan, Marguerite Clayton, Robert Broderick. 5r USA. prod/rel: Famous Players-Lasky Corp.©, Artcraft Pictures

The Hometowners, New York 1926, Play
Home Towners, The 1928 d: Bryan Foy. lps: Richard Bennett, Doris Kenyon, Robert McWade. 5693f USA. prod/rel: Warner Brothers Pictures

Ladies Must Live 1940 d: Noel Smith. lps: Wayne Morris, Rosemary Lane, Roscoe Karns. 58M USA. *Hometowners* prod/rel: Warner Bros. Pictures©
Times Square Playboy 1936 d: William McGann. lps: Gene Lockhart, Kathleen Lockhart, Warren William. 62M USA. *His Best Man* (UKN); *Broadway Playboy*; *The Gentleman from Big Bend* prod/rel: Warner Bros. Pictures©

The House of Glass, New York 1915, Play
Lure of Jade, The 1921 d: Colin Campbell. lps: Pauline Frederick, Thomas Holding, Arthur Rankin. 5935f USA. prod/rel: Robertson-Cole Co., R-C Pictures
Seltsame Vergangenheit Der Thea Carter, Die 1929 d: Josef Levigard. lps: June Marlowe, Olaf Fonss, Hermann Vallentin. 2188m GRM. prod/rel: Universal Pictures Corp.

Little Johnny Jones, New York 1904, Play
Little Johnny Jones 1923 d: Arthur Rosson, Johnny Hines. lps: Johnny Hines, Wyndham Standing, Margaret Seddon. 7165f USA. prod/rel: Warner Brothers Pictures
Little Johnny Jones 1929 d: Mervyn Leroy. lps: Eddie Buzzell, Alice Day, Edna Murphy. 6621f USA. prod/rel: First National Pictures

Little Nellie Kelly, New York 1922, Musical Play
Little Nellie Kelly 1940 d: Norman Taurog. lps: Judy Garland, George Murphy, Charles Winninger. 100M USA. prod/rel: Metro-Goldwyn-Mayer Corp., Loew's, Inc.©

The Meanest Man in the World, 1920, Play
Meanest Man in the World, The 1923 d: Eddie Cline. lps: Bert Lytell, Blanche Sweet, Bryant Washburn. 5600f USA. prod/rel: Principal Pictures, Associated First National Pictures

The Meanest Man in the World, New York 1920, Play
Meanest Man in the World, The 1943 d: Sidney Lanfield. lps: Jack Benny, Priscilla Lane, Eddie "Rochester" Anderson. 57M USA. prod/rel: 20th Century-Fox

The Song and Dance Man, New York 1923, Play
Song and Dance Man 1936 d: Allan Dwan. lps: Claire Trevor, Paul Kelly, Michael Whalen. 72M USA. prod/rel: Twentieth Century-Fox Film Corp.©
Song and Dance Man, The 1926 d: Herbert Brenon. lps: Tom Moore, Bessie Love, Harrison Ford. 6997f USA. prod/rel: Famous Players-Lasky, Paramount Pictures

COHEN, LESTER
Sweepings, New York 1926, Novel
Sweepings 1933 d: John Cromwell. lps: Lionel Barrymore, William Gargan, Gloria Stuart. 80M USA. prod/rel: RKO Radio Pictures©
Three Sons 1939 d: Jack Hively. lps: Edward Ellis, Kent Taylor, Virginia Vale. 72M USA. prod/rel: RKO Radio Pictures©

COHEN, OCTAVUS ROY (1891–1959), USA
Story
Curtain at Eight 1934 d: E. Mason Hopper. lps: Dorothy MacKaill, Jack Mulhall, Russell Hopton. 74M USA. prod/rel: Majestic Pictures Corp.

False Fires, Story
Law and the Man 1928 d: Scott Pembroke. lps: Thomas Santschi, Gladys Brockwell, Robert Ellis. 5916f USA. prod/rel: Trem Carr Productions, Rayart Pictures

The House in the Mist, 1917, Short Story
Eyes of Mystery, The 1918 d: Tod Browning. lps: Edith Storey, Bradley Barker, Harry Northrup. 5r USA. prod/rel: Metro Pictures Corp.

I Love You Again, New York 1937, Novel
I Love You Again 1940 d: W. S. Van Dyke. lps: William Powell, Myrna Loy, Frank McHugh. 99M USA. prod/rel: Metro-Goldwyn-Mayer Corp., Loew's, Inc.©

The Iron Chalice, Boston 1925, Novel
Big Gamble, The 1931 d: Fred Niblo. lps: William Boyd, Warner Oland, Dorothy Sebastian. 63M USA. *The Iron Chalice* prod/rel: RKO Pathe Pictures, Inc.
Red Dice 1926 d: William K. Howard. lps: Rod La Rocque, Marguerite de La Motte, Ray Hallor. 7257f USA. prod/rel: Demille Productions, Producers Distributing Corp.

Kid Tinsel, Novel
Pittsburgh Kid, The 1942 d: Jack Townley. lps: Billy Conn, Jean Parker, Dick Purcell. 76M USA. prod/rel: Republic

Marco Himself, 1929, Short Story
Social Lion, The 1930 d: A. Edward Sutherland. lps: Jack Oakie, Mary Brian, Skeets Gallagher. 5403f USA. *High Society* prod/rel: Paramount-Publix Corp.

The Outer Gate, Boston 1927, Novel
Outer Gate, The 1937 d: Raymond Cannon. lps: Ralph Morgan, Kay Linaker, Ben Alexander. 64M USA. *Behind Prison Bars*; *Beyond Prison Gates* prod/rel: Monogram Pictures Corp.©

Transient Lady, 1934, Short Story
Transient Lady 1935 d: Edward Buzzell. lps: Gene Raymond, Henry Hull, Frances Drake. 72M USA. *False Witness* (UKN)

The Triple Cross, 1918, Serial Story
Kaiser's Shadow, The 1918 d: R. William Neill. lps: Dorothy Dalton, Thurston Hall, Edward Cecil. 4379f USA. *The Kaiser's Shadow Or the Triple Cross* prod/rel: Thomas H. Ince Corp.©, Famous Players-Lasky Corp.

COHN, ART
The Life of Joe E. Lewis, Biography
Joker Is Wild, The 1957 d: Charles Vidor. lps: Frank Sinatra, Mitzi Gaynor, Jeanne Crain. 126M USA. *All the Way* prod/rel: Paramount, a.M.B.L. Prod.

COHN, BEN
The Trap That Failed, Story
Trap That Failed, The 1915 d: Murdock MacQuarrie. lps: Duke Aldis, Murdock MacQuarrie, Arthur Moon. SHT USA. prod/rel: Big U

COHN, NIK
Story
Saturday Night Fever 1977 d: John Badham. lps: John Travolta, Karen Lynn Gorney, Barry Miller. 119M USA. prod/rel: Paramount Pictures

COKE, PETER
Breath of Spring, London 1958, Play
Make Mine Mink 1960 d: Robert Asher. lps: Terry-Thomas, Athene Seyler, Hattie Jacques. 101M UKN. prod/rel: Rank, Rank Film Distributors

COLANTUONI, ALBERTO
Il Destino in Tasca, Play
Destino in Tasca, Il 1938 d: Gennaro Righelli. lps: Enrico Viarisio, Vanna Vanni, Romolo CostA. 63M ITL. *La Fortuna in Tasca* prod/rel: Juventus Film, C.I.N.F.

I Fratelli Castiglioni, Play
Fratelli Castiglioni, I 1937 d: Corrado d'Errico. lps: Camillo Pilotto, Ugo Ceseri, Amedeo Nazzari. 66M ITL. prod/rel: Amato Film, E.I.a.

COLE, BERT
Olimpia, Play
Bobo, The 1967 d: Robert Parrish. lps: Peter Sellers, Britt Ekland, Rossano Brazzi. 103M UKN. prod/rel: Gina, Warner-Pathe

COLE, BRANDON
Illuminata, Play
Illuminata 1998 d: John Turturro. lps: John Turturro, Katherine Borowitz, Christopher Walken. 120M USA. prod/rel: Overseas Filmgroup, Greenstreet Films

COLE, SOPHIE
Money Isn't Everything, Novel
Money Isn't Everything 1925 d: Thomas Bentley. lps: Olive Sloane, Arthur Burne, Gladys Hamer. 4960f UKN. prod/rel: Stoll

COLEBY, WILFRED T.
The Headmaster, London 1913, Play
Headmaster, The 1921 d: Kenelm Foss. lps: Cyril Maude, Margot Drake, Miles Malleson. 5500f UKN. prod/rel: Astra Films

COLEGATE, ISABEL
The Shooting Party, Novel
Shooting Party, The 1984 d: Alan Bridges. lps: James Mason, Edward Fox, Dorothy Tutin. 108M UKN. prod/rel: Edenflow, Geoff Reeve Film & Television

COLEMAN, CARYL
The Main Street Kid, Radio Play
Main Street Kid, The 1948 d: R. G. Springsteen. lps: Al Pearce, Janet Martin, Alan Mowbray. 64M USA. prod/rel: Republic

COLEMAN, CY
Sweet Charity, New York 1966, Play
Sweet Charity 1969 d: Bob Fosse. lps: Shirley MacLaine, Sammy Davis Jr., Ricardo Montalban. 152M USA. prod/rel: Universal Pictures

COLEMAN, GILBERT P.
Brown of Harvard, New York 1906, Play
Brown of Harvard 1911 d: Colin Campbell. lps: Hobart Bosworth, Bessie Eyton, Kempton Greene. 1000f USA. prod/rel: Selig Polyscope Co.
Brown of Harvard 1918 d: Harry Beaumont. lps: Tom Moore, Hazel Daly, Warner Richmond. 6r USA. *Tom Brown of Harvard* prod/rel: Selig Polyscope Co.©, Perfection Pictures
Brown of Harvard 1926 d: Jack Conway. lps: Jack Pickford, Mary Brian, Francis X. Bushman Jr. 7941f USA. prod/rel: Metro-Goldwyn-Mayer Pictures

COLEMAN, JOHN R.
Blue Collar Journal, Book
  Secret Life of John Chapman, The 1976 d: David Lowell Rich. lps: Ralph Waite, Susan Anspach, Pat Hingle. TVM. 78M USA. prod/rel: the Jozak Company
COLEMAN, LONNIE (1920–1982), USA, Coleman, Lonnie William
Novel
  Beulah Land 1980 d: Virgil W. Vogel, Harry Falk. lps: Lesley Ann Warren, Paul Rudd, Meredith Baxter. TVM. 267M USA. prod/rel: NBC, Columbia
Next of Kin, Play
  Hot Spell 1958 d: Daniel Mann, George Cukor (Uncredited). lps: Shirley Booth, Anthony Quinn, Shirley MacLaine. 86M USA. prod/rel: Paramount, Hal Wallis
COLERIDGE, SAMUEL TAYLOR (1772–1834), UKN
The Rime of the Ancient Mariner, 1857, Poem
  Ancient Mariner, The 1925 d: Henry Otto, Chester Bennett. lps: Clara Bow, Earle Williams, Leslie Fenton. 5548f USA. prod/rel: Fox Film Corp.
COLET, JEAN
Chanson Flamenca, Novel
  Epave, L' 1949 d: Willy Rozier. lps: Andre Le Gall, Aime Clariond, Francoise Arnoul. 94M FRN. prod/rel: Sport-Films
COLETTE, SIDONIE GABRIELLE (1873–1954), FRN, Colette
Le Ble En Herbe, 1923, Novel
  Ble En Herbe, Le 1953 d: Claude Autant-LarA. lps: Edwige Feuillere, Nicole Berger, Pierre-Michel Beck. 106M FRN. *The Game of Love* (USA); *The Ripening Seed* (UKN) prod/rel: Franco-London Films
Cheri, 1920, Novel
  Cheri 1950 d: Pierre Billon. lps: Jean Desailly, Marcelle Chantal, Yvonne de Bray. 90M FRN. prod/rel: Codo-Cinema
Claudine a l'Ecole, 1900, Novel
  Claudine a l'Ecole 1937 d: Serge de Poligny. lps: Pierre Brasseur, Max Dearly, Blanchette Brunoy. 109M FRN. prod/rel: Films Regent
Duo, Short Story
  Viaggio in Italia 1953 d: Roberto Rossellini. lps: Ingrid Bergman, George Sanders, Anna Proclemer. 97M ITL/FRN. *L' Amour Est le Plus Fort* (FRN); *The Lonely Woman* (UKN); *The Strangers* (USA); *Journey to Italy*; *A Trip to Italy* prod/rel: Sveva Film, Junior Film
L' Envers du Music-Hall, 1913, Novel
  Divine 1935 d: Max Ophuls. lps: Jorge Rigaud, Philippe Heriat, Simone Berriau. 82M FRN. prod/rel: Eden-Productions
Gigi, 1945, Novel
  Gigi 1948 d: Jacqueline Audry. lps: Frank Villard, Daniele Delorme, Gaby Morlay. 105M FRN. prod/rel: Codo-Cinema
  Gigi 1958 d: Vincente Minnelli. lps: Leslie Caron, Louis Jourdan, Maurice Chevalier. 115M USA. prod/rel: MGM, Arthur Freed Prods.
L' Ingenue Libertine, 1909, Novel
  Minne 1916 d: Andre Hugon. lps: MusidorA. 1250m FRN. prod/rel: Lumina
  Minne l'Ingenue Libertine 1950 d: Jacqueline Audry. lps: Daniele Delorme, Frank Villard, Roland Armontel. 90M FRN. *Minne* (USA); *L' Ingenue Libertine* prod/rel: Codo-Cinema
Julie de Carneilhan, 1941, Novel
  Julie de Carneilhan 1949 d: Jacques Manuel. lps: Edwige Feuillere, Pierre Brasseur, Jacques Dumesnil. 95M FRN. prod/rel: Ariane, Sirius
Comment l'Esprit Vient aux Filles Mitsou; Ou, 1919, Novel
  Mitsou 1956 d: Jacqueline Audry. lps: Daniele Delorme, Fernand Gravey, Francois Guerin. 98M FRN. *Mitsou Ou Comment l'Esprit Vient aux Filles* prod/rel: General Productions, Ardennes Films
La Vagabonde, 1910, Novel
  Vagabonda, La 1919 d: Ugo FalenA. lps: Musidora, Enrico Roma, Luigi Maggi. 974m ITL. prod/rel: Film d'Arte Italiana
  Vagabonda, La 1931 d: Solange Bussi. lps: Fernand Fabre, Marcelle Chantal, Jean Wall. 85M FRN. prod/rel: Exclusivites Artistiques
COLIN
Il Treno Delle 21.15, Play
  Treno Delle 21.15, Il 1933 d: Amleto Palermi. lps: Romano Calo, Laura Adani, Sandro Ruffini. 70M ITL. prod/rel: Caesar Film

COLLARD, ROBERT
L' Aventure Commencera Ce Soir, Novel
  Soir. Par Hasard, Un 1964 d: Yvan Govar. lps: Annette Stroyberg, Pierre Brasseur, Jean Servais. 95M FRN/BLG. *Agent of Doom* (USA); *One Night. By Accident* prod/rel: G.R.K., Japa Films
COLLEE, JOHN
Paper Mask, Novel
  Paper Mask 1989 d: Christopher Morahan. lps: Paul McGann, Amanda Donohue, Frederick Treves. 105M UKN. prod/rel: Enterprise, Film Four International
COLLIER, CONSTANCE (1880–1955), UKN, Hardie, Laura Constance
Downhill, London 1926, Play
  Downhill 1927 d: Alfred Hitchcock. lps: Ivor Novello, Isabel Jeans, Ian Hunter. 7600f UKN. *When Boys Leave Home* (USA) prod/rel: Gainsborough, Woolf & Freedman
The Rat, London 1924, Play
  Rat, The 1925 d: Graham Cutts. lps: Ivor Novello, Mae Marsh, Isabel Jeans. 7323f UKN. prod/rel: Gainsborough, Woolf & Freedman
  Rat, The 1937 d: Jack Raymond. lps: Ruth Chatterton, Anton Walbrook, Rene Ray. 72M UKN. prod/rel: Imperator, Radio
COLLIER SR., WILLIAM
The Hottentot, New York 1920, Play
  Going Places 1939 d: Ray Enright. lps: Dick Powell, Anita Louise, Allen Jenkins. 84M USA. prod/rel: Warner Bros. Pictures©
  Hottentot, The 1922 d: James W. Horne, Del Andrews. lps: Douglas MacLean, Madge Bellamy, Lilie Leslie. 5953f USA. prod/rel: Thomas H. Ince Productions, Associated First National Pictures
  Hottentot, The 1929 d: Roy Del Ruth. lps: Edward Everett Horton, Patsy Ruth Miller, Douglas Gerrard. 77M USA. prod/rel: Warner Brother Pictures
Never Say Die, New York 1912, Play
  Never Say Die 1924 d: George J. Crone. lps: Douglas MacLean, Lillian Rich, Helen Ferguson. 5891f USA. prod/rel: Douglas Maclean Productions, Associated Exhibitors
  Never Say Die 1939 d: Elliott Nugent. lps: Martha Raye, Bob Hope, Andy Devine. 80M USA. prod/rel: Paramount Pictures
COLLIER, WILLIAM
Going Crooked, New York 1926, Play
  Going Crooked 1926 d: George Melford. lps: Bessie Love, Oscar Shaw, Gustav von Seyffertitz. 5345f USA. prod/rel: Fox Film Corp.
COLLIGNON, ILSE
Unruhige Tochter, Novel
  Unruhige Tochter 1967 d: Hansjorg Amon. lps: Brigitte Skay, Jorns Andersson, Ruedi Walter. 100M SWT/GRM. *Restless Daughters* prod/rel: Urania, Afiba
COLLIN, PAUL
Amica, Monte Carlo 1905, Opera
  Amica 1916 d: Enrico Guazzoni. lps: Leda Gys, Amleto Novelli, Nella MontagnA. 1212m ITL. prod/rel: Cines
COLLINGHAM, G. C.
A Royal Divorce, London 1891, Play
  Royal Divorce, A 1923 d: Alexander Butler. lps: Gwylim Evans, Gertrude McCoy, Lillian Hall-Davis. 10r UKN. prod/rel: Napoleon
COLLINS, CHARLES
The Sins of St. Anthony, Short Story
  Sins of St. Anthony, The 1920 d: James Cruze. lps: Bryant Washburn, Margaret Loomis, Lorenza Lazzarini. 4575f USA. *The Sin of St. Anthony* prod/rel: Famous Players-Lasky Corp.©, Paramount-Artcraft Pictures
COLLINS, DALE
Ordeal, New York 1924, Novel
  Ship from Shanghai, The 1929 d: Charles J. Brabin. lps: Conrad Nagel, Kay Johnson, Carmel Myers. 66M USA. prod/rel: Metro-Goldwyn-Mayer Pictures
Rich and Strange, Novel
  Rich and Strange 1931 d: Alfred Hitchcock. lps: Henry Kendall, Joan Barry, Percy Marmont. 92M UKN. *East of Shanghai* prod/rel: British International Pictures, Wardour
The Sentimentalists, Boston 1927, Novel
  His Woman 1931 d: Edward Sloman. lps: Gary Cooper, Claudette Colbert, Douglas Dumbrille. 80M USA. *Blind Cargo*; *Sal of Singapore* prod/rel: Paramount Publix Corp.©
  Sal of Singapore 1929 d: Howard Higgin. lps: Phyllis Haver, Alan Hale, Fred Kohler. 6389f USA. prod/rel: Pathe Exchange, Inc.

COLLINS, FRANK L.
The Mouthpiece, New York 1929, Play
  Illegal 1955 d: Lewis Allen. lps: Edward G. Robinson, Nina Foch, Hugh Marlowe. 88M USA. prod/rel: Warner Bros.
  Man Who Talked Too Much, The 1940 d: Vincent Sherman. lps: George Brent, Virginia Bruce, Brenda Marshall. 75M USA. *The Sentence*; *Broadway Lawyer* prod/rel: Warner Bros. Pictures©
  Mouthpiece, The 1932 d: James Flood, Elliott Nugent. lps: Warren William, Sidney Fox, Mae Madison. 90M USA. prod/rel: Warner Bros. Pictures©
COLLINS, JACKIE (1939–, UKN, Collins, Jacqueline Jill
The Bitch, Novel
  Bitch, The 1979 d: Gerry O'HarA. lps: Joan Collins, Kenneth Haigh, Antonio CantaforA. 93M UKN. prod/rel: Brent Walker
The Stud, Novel
  Stud, The 1978 d: Quentin Masters. lps: Joan Collins, Oliver Tobias, Sue Lloyd. 90M UKN. prod/rel: Brent Walker, Artoc
The World Is Full of Married Men, Novel
  World Is Full of Married Men, The 1979 d: Robert Young. lps: Anthony Franciosa, Carroll Baker, Gareth Hunt. 107M UKN. prod/rel: New Realm, Married Men Productions
COLLINS, LARRY
Is Paris Burning?, New York 1965, Novel
  Paris Brule-T-Il? 1966 d: Rene Clement. lps: Jean-Paul Belmondo, Charles Boyer, Leslie Caron. 175M FRN. *Is Paris Burning?* (UKN) prod/rel: Transcontinental Films, Marianne Productions
COLLINS, MAYNARD
Hank Williams the Show He Never Gave, Play
  Hank Williams "the Show He Never Gave" 1982 d: David AcombA. lps: Sneezy Waters, Dixie Seatle, Sean McCann. 86M CND. *Stranger in the Night* prod/rel: Fcc Films Ltd., Film Consortium of Canada Inc.
COLLINS, NORMAN
Story
  Invasion Quartet 1961 d: Jay Lewis. lps: Bill Travers, Spike Milligan, Gregoire Aslan. 87M UKN. prod/rel: MGM British
London Belongs to Me, Novel
  London Belongs to Me 1948 d: Sidney Gilliat. lps: Richard Attenborough, Alastair Sim, Fay Compton. 112M UKN. *Dulcimer Street* (USA) prod/rel: General Film Distributors, Individual
COLLINS, SEWELL
Bracelets, Play
  Bracelets 1931 d: Sewell Collins. lps: Bert Coote, Joyce Kennedy, D. A. Clarke-Smith. 50M UKN. prod/rel: Gaumont
Nine Forty-Five, Play
  Nine Forty-Five 1934 d: George King. lps: Binnie Barnes, Donald Calthrop, Violet Farebrother. 59M UKN. prod/rel: Warner Bros., First National
COLLINS, WILKIE (1824–1889), UKN, Collins, William Wilkie
Armadale, Novel
  Armadale 1916 d: Richard Garrick. lps: Alexander Gaden, Iva Shepard, John E. MacKin. 3r USA. prod/rel: Gaumont
The Dead Secret, Novel
  Dead Secret, The 1913 d: Stanner E. V. Taylor. lps: Marion Leonard. SHT USA. prod/rel: Monopol Films
The Dream-Woman, Boston 1873, Novel
  Dream Woman, The 1914 d: Alice Blache. lps: Claire Whitney, Fraunie Fraunholz. 4r USA. prod/rel: Blache Features, Inc.©
The Moonstone, London 1868, Novel
  Moonstone, The 1909. 1000f USA. prod/rel: Selig Polyscope Co.
  Moonstone, The 1915 d: Frank H. Crane. lps: Eugene O'Brien, Elaine Hammerstein, Ruth Findlay. 5r USA. prod/rel: World Film Corp.©
  Moonstone, The 1934 d: Reginald Barker. lps: David Manners, Phyllis Barry, Gustav von Seyffertitz. 62M USA. prod/rel: Monogram Pictures Corp.©, Paul Malvern Production
  Pierre de Lune, La 1911. lps: Georges Flateau, Habay, Madeleine Barjac. 405m FRN. prod/rel: Eclipse, Radios
The New Magdalen, 1873, Novel
  New Magdalen, The 1910 d: Joseph A. Golden. lps: Pearl White, Paul Panzer. 900f USA. prod/rel: Powers
  New Magdalen, The 1912 d: Herbert Brenon. lps: Vivian Prescott, Jane Fearnley, William E. Shay. 2r USA. prod/rel: Imp

New Magdalen, The 1914 d: Travers Vale. lps: Louise Vale, Charles Hill Mailes. 2r USA. prod/rel: Biograph Co.

She Loves and Lies, 1885, Short Story
She Loves and Lies 1920 d: Chet Withey. lps: Norma Talmadge, Conway Tearle, Octavia Broske. 5555f USA. *Two Women* prod/rel: Norma Talmadge Film Corp., Select Pictures Corp.©

The Woman in White, London 1860, Novel
Crimes at the Dark House 1940 d: George King. lps: Tod Slaughter, Hilary Eaves, Sylvia Marriott. 69M UKN. prod/rel: Pennant, British Lion
Tangled Lives 1917 d: J. Gordon Edwards. lps: Genevieve Hamper, Stuart Holmes, Robert B. Mantell. 5r USA. prod/rel: Fox Film Corp., William Fox©
Twin Pawns, The 1919 d: Leonce Perret. lps: Mae Murray, J. W. Johnston, Warner Oland. 6r USA. *The Curse of Greed* prod/rel: Acme Pictures Corp., Leonce Perret Production
Woman in White, The 1912. 2r USA. prod/rel: Thanhouser
Woman in White, The 1912. lps: Janet Salisbury, Charles Craig, Alec Frank. 2r USA. prod/rel: Gem
Woman in White, The 1917 d: Ernest C. Warde. lps: Florence Labadie, Richard Neill, Gertrude Dallas. 5-6r USA. prod/rel: Thanhouser Film Corp., Pathe Exchange, Inc.
Woman in White, The 1929 d: Herbert Wilcox. lps: Blanche Sweet, Haddon Mason, Cecil Humphreys. SIL 6702f UKN. prod/rel: British & Dominions, Woolf & Freedman
Woman in White, The 1948 d: Peter Godfrey. lps: Alexis Smith, Eleanor Parker, Sydney Greenstreet. 109M USA. prod/rel: Warner Bros.

COLLISON, WILSON
Blonde Baby, New York 1931, Book
Three Wise Girls 1932 d: William Beaudine. lps: Jean Harlow, Mae Clarke, Walter Byron. 68M USA. *Blonde Baby* prod/rel: Columbia Pictures Corp.©

Congo Landing, New York 1934, Novel
Congo Maisie 1939 d: H. C. Potter. lps: Ann Sothern, John Carroll, Shepperd Strudwick. 70M USA. prod/rel: Metro-Goldwyn-Mayer Corp.

Dark Dame, New York 1935, Novel
Maisie 1939 d: Edwin L. Marin. lps: Ann Sothern, Robert Young, Ruth Hussey. 74M USA. *Maisie Was a Lady*; *Broadway to Wyoming* prod/rel: Metro-Goldwyn-Mayer Corp., Loew's, Inc.©

Expensive Women, New York 1931, Novel
Expensive Women 1931 d: Hobart Henley. lps: Dolores Costello, Warren William, Anthony Bushell. 63M USA. prod/rel: Warner Bros. Pictures©

Get That Girl, Story
Woman Wanted 1935 d: George B. Seitz. lps: Maureen O'Sullivan, Joel McCrea, Lewis Stone. 70M USA. *Manhattan Madness* prod/rel: Metro-Goldwyn-Mayer Corp.©

Getting Gertie's Garter, New York 1921, Play
Getting Gertie's Garter 1927 d: E. Mason Hopper. lps: Marie Prevost, Charles Ray, Harry Myers. 6859f USA. prod/rel: Metropolitan Pictures Corp. of Calif., Producers Distributing Corp.
Getting Gertie's Garter 1945 d: Allan Dwan. lps: Dennis O'Keefe, Marie McDonald, Barry Sullivan. 72M USA. prod/rel: United Artists, Edward Small
Night of the Garter 1933 d: Jack Raymond. lps: Sydney Howard, Winifred Shotter, Elsie Randolph. 86M UKN. prod/rel: British and Dominions, United Artists

The Girl in the Limousine, New York 1919, Play
Girl in the Limousine, The 1924 d: Larry Semon. lps: Larry Semon, Claire Adams, Charlie Murray. 5630f USA. prod/rel: Chadwick Pictures, Associated First National Pictures

The Girl in Upper C, Play
Girl in the Pullman, The 1927 d: Erle C. Kenton. lps: Marie Prevost, Harrison Ford, Franklin Pangborn. 5867f USA. *The Girl on the Train* (UKN) prod/rel: de Mille Pictures, Pathe Exchange, Inc.

Red Dust, New York 1928, Play
Mogambo 1953 d: John Ford. lps: Grace Kelly, Clark Gable, Ava Gardner. 115M USA. prod/rel: MGM
Red Dust 1932 d: Victor Fleming. lps: Clark Gable, Jean Harlow, Mary Astor. 86M USA. prod/rel: Metro-Goldwyn-Mayer Corp., Metro-Goldwyn-Mayer Dist. Corp.©

Red-Haired Alibi, New York 1932, Novel
Red Haired Alibi 1932 d: W. Christy Cabanne. lps: Merna Kennedy, Grant Withers, Arthur Hoyt. 77M USA. *Red-Haired Alibi* prod/rel: Premier Attractions, Tower Productions

There's Always a Woman, 1937, Short Story
There's Always a Woman 1938 d: Alexander Hall. lps: Joan Blondell, Melvyn Douglas, Mary Astor. 82M USA. prod/rel: Columbia Pictures Corp. of California©

Up in Mabel's Room, New York 1919, Play
Up in Mabel's Room 1926 d: E. Mason Hopper. lps: Marie Prevost, Harrison Ford, Phyllis Haver. 6345f USA. prod/rel: Christie Film Co., Producers Distributing Corp.
Up in Mabel's Room 1944 d: Allan Dwan. lps: Marjorie Reynolds, Dennis O'Keefe, Gail Patrick. 76M USA. prod/rel: United Artists

The Woman in Purple Pajamas, New York 1931, Novel
Scarlet Week-End, A 1932 d: George Melford. lps: Dorothy Revier, Theodore von Eltz, Phyllis Barrington. 63M USA. prod/rel: Willis Kent Productions, State Rights

COLLO, LUIGI
Una Leggera Euforia, Short Story
Ultima Volta, L' 1976 d: Aldo Lado. lps: Joe Dallesandro, Eleonora Giorgi, Massimo Ranieri. 105M ITL. *Born Winner* prod/rel: Marzia Cin.Ca, European Inc.

COLLODI, CARLO (1826–1890), ITL, Lorenzini, Carlo
Le Avventure Di Pinocchio, 1883, Short Story
Adventures of Pinocchio, The 1996 d: Steve Barron. lps: Martin Landau, Jonathan Taylor Thomas (Voice), Genevieve Bujold. 96M UKN/FRN/GRM. prod/rel: New Line, Savoy
Avventure Di Pinocchio, Le 1935 d: Umberto Spano. ANM. ITL. prod/rel: Cartoni Animati Italiani Roma
Avventure Di Pinocchio, Le 1947 d: Giannetto Guardone. lps: Mariella Lotti, Alessandro Tomei, Vittorio Gassman. 92M ITL. prod/rel: Excelsa Film, Fiaba Film
Avventure Di Pinocchio, Le 1968 d: Giuliano Cenci. ANM. 98M ITL. *The Adventures of Pinocchio*; *Pinocchio*
Avventure Di Pinocchio, Le 1972 d: Luigi Comencini. lps: Nino Manfredi, Franco Franchi, Andrea Balestri. 135M ITL/FRN/GRM. *Les Aventures de Pinocchio* (FRN); *Pinocchio* prod/rel: San Paolo Film, Cinepat
Pinocchio 1911 d: Giulio Antamoro. lps: Ferdinand Guillaume, Augusto Mastripietri, Lea Giunchi. 1350m ITL. *Le Avventure Di Pinocchio* prod/rel: Cines
Pinocchio 1940 d: Hamilton Luske, Ben Sharpsteen. ANM. 88M USA. prod/rel: RKO Radio Pictures, Walt Disney Productions©
Pinocchio 1968 d: Sidney Smith. lps: Burl Ives, Peter Noone, Anita Gilette. MTV. 74M USA.
Pinocchio 1976 d: Ron Field, Sidney Smith. lps: Danny Kaye, Sandy Duncan, Flip Wilson. TVM. 75M USA.
Pinocchio 1983 d: Peter Medak. lps: James Coburn, Carl Reiner, Paul Reubens. MTV. 50M USA.
Pinocchio 1985 d: Barry Letts. lps: Derek Smith, Rhoda Lewis, Roy McCready. MTV. 108M UKN.
Pinocchio 1991 d: Hiroshi Saito. ANM. 90M JPN.
Pinocchio E le Sue Avventure 1958 d: Attilio Giovannini. lps: Armando Sviato, Luisa Vallisi, A. Caporali. F ITL. prod/rel: Bruno Ditz
Turlis Abenteuer 1967 d: Walter Beck, Ron Merk. lps: Martin Florchinger, Alfred Muller, Vera Oelschlegel. 75M GDR. *Pinocchio* (USA); *Turli's Adventure* prod/rel: Defa

COLOMA, LUIS (1851–1915), SPN, Coloma, Padre Luis
Boy, 1910, Novel
Boy 1925 d: Benito Perojo. lps: Juan de Orduna, Manuel San German, Suzy Vernon. SRL. SPN/FRN. *Grand Gosse* (FRN); *Big Boy*; *Boy (O El Marino Espanol)* prod/rel: Goya-Films (Madrid)
Boy 1940 d: Antonio Calvache. lps: Luis Pena, Antonio Vico, Mary EmmA. 100M SPN.

Jeromin, 1905-07, Novel
Jeromin 1953 d: Luis LuciA. lps: Ana Mariscal, Jaime Blanch, Rafael Duran. 97M SPN.

Pequeneces, 1890, Novel
Pequeneces 1949 d: Juan de OrdunA. lps: Aurora Bautista, Jorge Mistral, Sara Montiel. 137M SPN.
Trifles

COLOS, LEN
The Electric Man, Story
Man Made Monster 1941 d: George Waggner. lps: Lionel Atwill, Lon Chaney Jr., Anne Nagel. 60M USA. *The Electric Man* (UKN); *The Atomic Monster*; *Mysterious Dr. R.*; *Man-Made Monster* prod/rel: Universal

COLSON, CHARLES W.
Born Again, Novel
Born Again 1978 d: Irving Rapper. lps: Dean Jones, Anne Francis, Jay Robinson. 110M USA. prod/rel: Avco Embassy

COLTON, JOHN
The Cat That Walked Alone, Story
Woman Who Walked Alone, The 1922 d: George Melford. lps: Dorothy Dalton, Milton Sills, E. J. Radcliffe. 5947f USA. prod/rel: Famous Players-Lasky, Paramount Pictures

Drifting, New York 1910, Play
Drifting 1923 d: Tod Browning. lps: Priscilla Dean, Matt Moore, Wallace Beery. 7394f USA. prod/rel: Universal Pictures
Shanghai Lady 1929 d: John S. Robertson. lps: Mary Nolan, James Murray, Lydia Yeamans Titus. 5926f USA. *The Girl from China* (UKN) prod/rel: Universal Pictures

The Shanghai Gesture, New York 1929, Play
Shanghai Gesture, The 1941 d: Josef von Sternberg. lps: Gene Tierney, Walter Huston, Victor Mature. 106M USA. prod/rel: United Artists

COLTON, JOSEPH
The Gay Dog, London 1951, Play
Gay Dog, The 1954 d: Maurice Elvey. lps: Wilfred Pickles, Petula Clark, Megs Jenkins. 87M UKN. prod/rel: Coronet, Eros

COLVER, ALICE ROSS
The Dear Pretender, Philadelphia 1924, Novel
On Thin Ice 1925 d: Malcolm St. Clair. lps: Tom Moore, Edith Roberts, William Russell. 6675f USA. prod/rel: Warner Brothers Pictures

COLWELL, HENRY CLIFFORD
The Penalty, New York 1910, Play
Tattlers, The 1920 d: Howard M. Mitchell. lps: Madlaine Traverse, Howard Scott, Jack Rollins. 5r USA. *The Penalty* prod/rel: Fox Film Corp., William Fox©

COMANDINI, ADELE
The Mating of Millie, Novel
Mating of Millie, The 1948 d: Henry Levin. lps: Glenn Ford, Evelyn Keyes, Ron Randell. 87M USA. prod/rel: Columbia

Rebel Island, Story
Flame of the Islands 1955 d: Edward Ludwig. lps: Yvonne de Carlo, Howard Duff, Zachary Scott. 90M USA. prod/rel: Republic Pictures Corp.

COMDEN, BETTY
The Bells are Ringing, Musical Play
Bells are Ringing, The 1960 d: Vincente Minnelli. lps: Judy Holliday, Dean Martin, Fred Clark. 125M USA. prod/rel: Metro-Goldwyn-Mayer Corp.

On the Town, Musical Play
On the Town 1949 d: Gene Kelly, Stanley Donen. lps: Gene Kelly, Frank Sinatra, Jules Munshin. 98M USA. prod/rel: MGM

COMFORT, ALEX (1920–, UKN, Comfort, Alexander
The Joy of Sex, Book
Joy of Sex, The 1984 d: Martha Coolidge. lps: Cameron Dye, Michelle Meyrink, Colleen Camp. 93M USA. *National Lampoon's Joy of Sex* prod/rel: Paramount, Cinema Group Venture

COMFORT, WILL LEVINGTON
The Sheriff of Contention, Short Story
Angel of Contention, The 1914 d: John B. O'Brien. lps: Lillian Gish, Spottiswoode Aitken, George Siegmann. 2r USA. prod/rel: Majestic

Somewhere in Sonora, Boston 1925, Novel
Somewhere in Sonora 1927 d: Albert S. Rogell. lps: Ken Maynard, Kathleen Collins, Frank Leigh. 5718f USA. prod/rel: Charles R. Rogers Productions, First National Pictures
Somewhere in Sonora 1933 d: MacK V. Wright. lps: John Wayne, Shirley Palmer, Henry B. Walthall. 59M USA. prod/rel: Warner Bros. Pictures©, Vitagraph, Inc.©

COMISSO, GIOVANNI
La Donna Del Lago, Novel
Donna Del Lago, La 1965 d: Luigi Bazzoni, Franco Rossellini. lps: Peter Baldwin, Virna Lisi, Valentina Cortese. 84M ITL. *The Possessed* (UKN); *The Lady of the Lake* prod/rel: B.R.C. Produzioni, Istituto Nazionale Luce

COMMANDINI, ADELE
Night Life, Story
Night Club Girl 1944 d: Eddie Cline. lps: Vivian Austin, Edward Norris, Billy Dunn. 61M USA. *Night Club*; *Night Life* prod/rel: Universal

COMPANEEZ, JACQUES
Adieu Cherie, Short Story
Adieu Cherie 1945 d: Raymond Bernard. lps: Danielle Darrieux, Gabrielle Dorziat, Louis Salou. 115M FRN. prod/rel: Osso Roitfeld

Un Ami Viendra Ce Soir, Play
Ami Viendra Ce Soir, Un 1945 d: Raymond Bernard. lps: Michel Simon, Madeleine Sologne, Paul Bernard. 125M FRN. *A Friend Will Come Tonight* (USA) prod/rel: Francinex

Le Destin S'amuse, Short Story
Destin S'amuse, Le 1946 d: Emile Edwin Reinert. lps: Dany Robin, Andre Claveau, Robert Murzeau. 85M FRN. *Coup de Maitre* prod/rel: Films Ariane

Schweigepflicht, Short Story
Du Mein Stilles Tal 1955 d: Leonard Steckel. lps: Winnie Markus, Curd Jurgens, Ingeborg Schoner. 92M GRM. *Schweigepflicht* prod/rel: C.C.C., Gloria

COMPTON, DAVID
Death Watch, Novel
Death Watch 1979 d: Bertrand Tavernier. lps: Romy Schneider, Harvey Keitel, Harry Dean Stanton. 128M UKN/FRN/GRM. *La Mort En Direct* (FRN); *Deathwatch*; *Death in Full View*; *Death Watch -Der Gekaufte Tod* (GRM) prod/rel: Tv 13, Corona

COMSTOCK, HARRIET T., Comstock, Harriet Theresa
Janet of the Dunes, Novel
Janet of the Dunes 1913 d: Richard Ridgely. lps: Mabel Trunnelle, Herbert Prior, Charles Ogle. 2000f USA. prod/rel: Edison

Joyce of the North Woods, Novel
Joyce of the North Woods 1913 d: Ashley Miller. lps: Mary Fuller, Augustus Phillips. 2000f USA. prod/rel: Edison

Mam'selle Jo, Garden City, N.Y. 1918, Novel
Silent Years 1921 d: Louis J. Gasnier. lps: Rose Dione, Tully Marshall, George McDaniel. 6056f USA. *Ma'mselle Jo* prod/rel: R-C Pictures

The Drummer Boy Molly, Novel
Molly, the Drummer Boy 1914 d: George A. Lessey. lps: Viola Dana, John Sturgeon, Mrs. William Bechtel. SHT USA. prod/rel: Edison

The Place Beyond the Winds, Garden City, N.Y. 1914, Novel
Place Beyond the Winds, The 1916 d: Joseph de Grasse. lps: Dorothy Phillips, Lon Chaney, Jack Mulhall. 5r USA. prod/rel: Universal Film Mfg. Co.©, Red Feather Photoplays

A Son of the Hills, New York 1913, Novel
Son of the Hills, A 1917 d: Harry Davenport. lps: Antonio Moreno, Robert Gaillord, Julia Swayne Gordon. 5r USA. prod/rel: Vitagraph Co. of America©, Greater Vitagraph (V-L-S-E)

The Tenth Woman, Garden City, N.Y. 1923, Novel
Tenth Woman, The 1924 d: James Flood. lps: Beverly Bayne, John Roche, June Marlowe. 6900f USA. prod/rel: Warner Brothers Pictures

COMSTOCK, HOWARD WARREN
Stepping Sisters, New York 1930, Play
Stepping Sisters 1932 d: Seymour Felix. lps: Louise Dresser, Minna Gombell, William Collier Sr. 60M USA. prod/rel: Fox Film Corp.©

The Terror, New York 1931, Play
Doctor X 1932 d: Michael Curtiz. lps: Lionel Atwill, Preston Foster, Fay Wray. 80M USA. prod/rel: First National Pictures, Inc., Warner Bros.

CONCHON, GEORGES
Les Honneurs de la Guerre, Novel
Horizon, L' 1967 d: Jacques Rouffio. lps: Jacques Perrin, Macha Meril, Rene Dary. 99M FRN. prod/rel: Production Internationale Cinevision, Cinetel

CONDE, JOSE
Um Ramo Para Luisa, 1959, Short Story
Ramo Para Luiza, Um 1965 d: J. B. Tanko. 105M BRZ.

CONDE, NICHOLAS
The Religion, Novel
Believers, The 1987 d: John Schlesinger. lps: Martin Sheen, Helen Shaver, Harley Cross. 113M USA. prod/rel: Orion

CONDON, FRANK
The Alibi, Story
Alibi, The 1915 d: Clem Easton. lps: William Garwood, Violet Mersereau. SHT USA. prod/rel: Imp

The Legend of Hollywood, 1924, Short Story
Legend of Hollywood, The 1924 d: Renaud Hoffman. lps: Percy Marmont, Zasu Pitts, Alice Davenport. 5414f USA. prod/rel: Charles R. Rogers Productions, Producers Distributing Corp.

Speed But No Control, 1924, Short Story
No Control 1927 d: Scott Sidney, E. J. Babille. lps: Harrison Ford, Phyllis Haver, Jack Duffy. 5573f USA. prod/rel: Metropolitan Pictures Corp. of Calif., Producers Distribution Corp.

CONDON, RICHARD (1915–1996), USA, Condon, Richard Thomas
The Manchurian Candidate, New York 1959, Novel
Manchurian Candidate, The 1962 d: John Frankenheimer. lps: Frank Sinatra, Laurence Harvey, Janet Leigh. 127M USA. prod/rel: M.C. Productions, United Artists

The Oldest Confession, New York 1958, Novel
Happy Thieves, The 1962 d: George Marshall. lps: Rex Harrison, Rita Hayworth, Joseph Wiseman. 89M USA. *The Oldest Confession*; *Once a Thief* prod/rel: Hillworth Productions

Prizzi's Honor, 1982, Novel
Prizzi's Honor 1985 d: John Huston. lps: Jack Nicholson, Kathleen Turner, Robert LoggiA. 129M USA. prod/rel: 20th Century-Fox, ABC Motion Pictures

Winter Kills, 1974, Novel
Winter Kills 1979 d: William Richert. lps: Jeff Bridges, John Huston, Anthony Perkins. 97M USA. prod/rel: Winter Gold Productions

CONFORTES, CLAUDE
Le Roi Des Cons, Play
Roi Des Cons, Le 1981 d: Claude Confortes. lps: Francis Perrin, Marie-Christine Descouard, Bernadette Lafont. 99M FRN. prod/rel: C.a.P.A.C., Films de la Colombe

CONG SHEN
Qian Wan Buy Yao Wang Ji, Play
Qian Wan Buy Yao Wang Ji 1964 d: XIe Tieli, Cong Shen. lps: Luo Yupu, Peng Yu, Qin Wen. 10r CHN. *Never Forget* prod/rel: Beijing Film Studio

CONLIN, RICHARD
Angels in the Outfield, Radio Play
Angels in the Outfield 1951 d: Clarence Brown. lps: Paul Douglas, Janet Leigh, Keenan Wynn. 102M USA. *Angels and Pirates* (USA); *Angels and the Pirates* prod/rel: Metro-Goldwyn-Mayer Corp.

CONN, MAURICE
The Girl and the Gorilla, Story
Zamba 1949 d: William Berke. lps: Jon Hall, June Vincent, George Cooper. 75M USA. *Zamba the Gorilla* (UKN); *The Girl and the Gorilla* prod/rel: Eagle-Lion

CONNAUGHTON, SHANE
The Run of the Country, Novel
Run of the Country, The 1995 d: Peter Yates. lps: Albert Finney, Matt Keeslar, Victoria Smurfit. 109M UKN/IRL. prod/rel: Rank, Castle Rock

CONNELL, EVAN S. (1924–, USA, Connell, E. S.
Mr. Bridge, 1969, Novel
Mr. & Mrs. Bridge 1990 d: James Ivory. lps: Paul Newman, Joanne Woodward, Blythe Danner. 127M USA. *Mr. and Mrs. Bridge* prod/rel: Merchant-Ivory, Miramax

Mrs. Bridge, 1959, Novel
Mr. & Mrs. Bridge 1990 d: James Ivory. lps: Paul Newman, Joanne Woodward, Blythe Danner. 127M USA. *Mr. and Mrs. Bridge* prod/rel: Merchant-Ivory, Miramax

CONNELL, RICHARD, Connell, Richard Edward Story
Meet John Doe 1941 d: Frank CaprA. lps: Gary Cooper, Barbara Stanwyck, Edward Arnold. 132M USA. *John Doe Dynamite* (UKN) prod/rel: Warner Bros.

$100.00, 1928, Short Story
New Year's Eve 1929 d: Henry Lehrman. lps: Mary Astor, Charles Morton, Earle Foxe. 5984f USA. prod/rel: Fox Film Corp.

Brother Orchid, 1938, Short Story
Brother Orchid 1940 d: Lloyd Bacon. lps: Edward G. Robinson, Ann Sothern, Humphrey Bogart. 91M USA. prod/rel: Warner Bros. Pictures, Inc.

A Friend of Napoleon, 1923, Short Story
Seven Faces 1929 d: Berthold Viertel. lps: Paul Muni, Marguerite Churchill, Lester Lonergan. 7750f USA. prod/rel: Fox Film Corp.

If I Was Alone With You, 1929, Short Story
Cheer Up and Smile 1930 d: Sidney Lanfield. lps: Dixie Lee, Arthur Lake, Olga BaclanovA. 5730f USA. prod/rel: Fox Film Corp.

Isles of Romance, 1924, Short Story
No Place to Go 1927 d: Mervyn Leroy. lps: Mary Astor, Lloyd Hughes, Hallam Cooley. 6431f USA. *Her Primitive Mate* (UKN) prod/rel: Henry Hobart Productions, First National Pictures

A Little Bit of Broadway, 1924, Short Story
Bright Lights 1925 d: Robert Z. Leonard. lps: Charles Ray, Pauline Starke, Lilyan Tashman. 6153f USA. *A Little Bit of Broadway* prod/rel: Metro-Goldwyn-Mayer Pictures

The Most Dangerous Game, 1930, Short Story
Bloodlust 1961 d: Ralph Brooke. lps: Wilton Graff, Lilyan Chauvin, Robert Reed. 68M USA. prod/rel: Crown International

Game of Death, A 1946 d: Robert Wise. lps: John Loder, Audrey Long, Edgar Barrier. 72M USA. *Dangerous Adventure*; *The Most Dangerous Game* prod/rel: RKO Radio Pictures

Most Dangerous Game, The 1932 d: Ernest B. Schoedsack, Irving Pichel. lps: Joel McCrea, Fay Wray, Leslie Banks. 63M USA. *The Hounds of Zaroff* (UKN); *Skull Island* prod/rel: RKO Radio Pictures©

Run for the Sun 1956 d: Roy Boulting. lps: Richard Widmark, Jane Greer, Trevor Howard. 99M USA. prod/rel: United Artists, Russ-Field Corp.

The Solid Gold Article, 1929, Short Story
Not Damaged 1930 d: Chandler Sprague. lps: Lois Moran, Walter Byron, Robert Ames. 6500f USA. prod/rel: Fox Film Corp.

The Swamp Angel, 1923, Short Story
Painted People 1924 d: Clarence Badger. lps: Colleen Moore, Ben Lyon, Charlotte Merriam. 6820f USA. prod/rel: Associated First National Pictures

CONNELLY, MARC (1890–1980), USA, Connelly, Marcus Cook
Beggar on Horseback, New York 1924, Play
Beggar on Horseback 1925 d: James Cruze. lps: Edward Everett Horton, Esther Ralston, Erwin Connelly. 7197f USA. prod/rel: Famous Players-Lasky Corp., Paramount Pictures

Dulcy, New York 1921, Play
Dulcy 1923 d: Sidney A. Franklin. lps: Constance Talmadge, Claude Gillingwater, Jack Mulhall. 6859f USA. prod/rel: Constance Talmadge Film Co., Associated First National Pictures

Dulcy 1940 d: S. Sylvan Simon. lps: Ann Sothern, Ian Hunter, Roland Young. 67M USA. prod/rel: Metro-Goldwyn-Mayer Corp.©

Not So Dumb 1930 d: King Vidor. lps: Marion Davies, Elliott Nugent, Raymond Hackett. 7650f USA. *Rosalie* (UKN); *Dulcy* prod/rel: Metro-Goldwyn-Mayer Pictures

The Green Pastures, New York 1930, Play
Green Pastures, The 1936 d: William Keighley, Marc Connelly. lps: Rex Ingram, Oscar Polk, Eddie "Rochester" Anderson. 93M USA. prod/rel: Warner Bros. Pictures©

To the Ladies!, New York 1922, Play
Elmer and Elsie 1934 d: Gilbert Pratt. lps: George Bancroft, Frances Fuller, Roscoe Karns. 65M USA. *Ladies First* prod/rel: Paramount Productions©

To the Ladies 1923 d: James Cruze. lps: Edward Everett Horton, Theodore Roberts, Helen Jerome Eddy. 6268f USA. prod/rel: Famous Players-Lasky, Paramount Pictures

The Wild Man of Borneo, New York 1927, Play
Wild Man of Borneo, The 1941 d: Robert B. Sinclair. lps: Frank Morgan, Mary Howard, Billie Burke. 78M USA. prod/rel: MGM

CONNERS, BARRY
Applesauce, New York 1925, Play
Always a Bride 1940 d: Noel Smith. lps: George Reeves, Rosemary Lane, John Eldredge. 58M USA. prod/rel: Warner Bros. Pictures

Brides are Like That 1936 d: William McGann. lps: Ross Alexander, Anita Louise, Dick Purcell. 67M USA. *Applesauce*; *Every Girl for Herself*; *Red Apples* prod/rel: Warner Bros. Pictures, Inc.

CONNOLLY, MYLES
Lady Smith, 1936, Short Story
Palm Springs 1936 d: Aubrey Scotto. lps: Frances Langford, Smith Ballew, Guy Standing. 72M USA. *Palm Springs Affair* (UKN) prod/rel: Walter Wanger Productions, Paramount Productions©

CONNOR, MARIE
Convict 99, Play
Convict 99 1909 d: Arthur Gilbert. lps: Frank Beresford. 1060f UKN. prod/rel: Gaumont

Convict 99 1919 d: G. B. Samuelson. lps: C. M. Hallard, Daisy Burrell, Wee Georgie Wood. 6075f UKN. prod/rel: G. B. Samuelson, Granger

CONNOR, RALPH (1860–1937), CND, Gordon, Charles William
Corporal Cameron of the North West Mounted Police, Novel
Cameron of the Royal Mounted 1921 d: Henry McRae. lps: Gaston Glass, Irving Cummings, Vivienne Osborne. 6r CND. prod/rel: Winnipeg Productions Ltd.

The Doctor: a Tale of the Rockies, New York 1906, Novel
Heart of a Lion, The 1918 d: Frank Lloyd. lps: William Farnum, Wanda Hawley, Mary Martin. 5r USA. prod/rel: Fox Film Corp., William Fox©

The Foreigner; a Tale of Saskatchewan, New York 1909, Novel
God's Crucible 1921 d: Henry McRae. lps: Gaston Glass, Gladys Coburn, Wilton Lackaye. 7r CND/USA. *The Foreigner* prod/rel: Winnipeg Productions Ltd., W. W. Hodkinson Corp.

Glengarry School Days, Novel
Glengarry School Days 1923 d: Henry McRae. lps: Pauline Garon, James Harrison, Harlan E. Knight. 5r CND. *The Critical Age* (USA); *The Good-for-Nothin'*; *The Good Fer Nothin'* prod/rel: Ottawa Film Productions Ltd.

Man from Glengarry, Chicago 1901, Novel
Man from Glengarry, The 1922 d: Henry McRae. lps: Anders Randolf, Warner Richmond, Harlan Knight. 5200f CND/USA. prod/rel: Ernest Shipman Film Service, W. W. Hodkinson Corp.

The Sky Pilot, Chicago 1899, Novel
Sky Pilot, The 1921 d: King Vidor. lps: John Bowers, Colleen Moore, David Butler. 6305f USA. prod/rel: Cathrine Curtis Corp., Associated First National Pictures

CONNOR, REARDON
Shake Hands With the Devil, Novel
Shake Hands With the Devil 1959 d: Michael Anderson. lps: James Cagney, Don Murray, Dana Wynter. 111M UKN/IRL. prod/rel: United Artists, Troy Films

CONNORS, BARRY
The Patsy, New York 1925, Play
Patsy, The 1928 d: King Vidor. lps: Marion Davies, Orville Caldwell, Marie Dressler. 7289f USA. *The Politic Flapper* (UKN) prod/rel: Metro-Goldwyn-Mayer Pictures

CONRAD, CARL
Play
Centomila Dollari 1940 d: Mario Camerini. lps: Assia Noris, Amedeo Nazzari, Lauro Gazzolo. 83M ITL. prod/rel: Astra Film, E.N.I.C.

CONRAD, JOSEPH (1857–1924), PLN, Korzeniowski, Jozef
Novel
Des Teufels Paradies 1987 d: Vadim GlownA. lps: Jurgen Prochnow, Sam Waterston, Susanna Hamilton. 96M GRM. *The Devil's Paradise* prod/rel: Atossa, ZDF

Amy Foster, Short Story
Swept from the Sea 1997 d: Beeban Kidron. lps: Vincent Perez, Rachel Weisz, Ian McKellen. 115M UKN. *Swept from the Sea - the Story of Amy Foster*; *Amy Foster* prod/rel: Phoenix Pictures, Tapson Steel Films©

Between the Tides, Short Story
Laughing Anne 1953 d: Herbert Wilcox. lps: Margaret Lockwood, Wendell Corey, Forrest Tucker. 90M UKN. prod/rel: Imperadio, Wilcox-Neagle

The Duel, 1908, Short Story
Duellists, The 1977 d: Ridley Scott. lps: Keith Carradine, Harvey Keitel, Albert Finney. 101M UKN. prod/rel: Scott Free, Nffc

Heart of Darkness, 1899, Novel
Apocalypse Now 1979 d: Francis Ford CoppolA. lps: Marlon Brando, Robert Duvall, Martin Sheen. 153M USA. prod/rel: United Artists, Omni Zoetrope

Lord Jim, London 1900, Novel
Lord Jim 1925 d: Victor Fleming. lps: Percy Marmont, Shirley Mason, Noah Beery. 6702f USA. prod/rel: Famous Players-Lasky, Paramount Pictures
Lord Jim 1965 d: Richard Brooks. lps: Peter O'Toole, James Mason, Curd Jurgens. 154M UKN/USA. prod/rel: Columbia Pictures, Keep Films

Nostromo, 1904, Novel
Nostromo 1996 d: Alastair Reid. lps: Albert Finney, Colin Firth, Serena Scott Thomas. MTV. 321M UKN. *Joseph Conrad's Nostromo* prod/rel: BBC
Silver Treasure, The 1926 d: Rowland V. Lee. lps: George O'Brien, Jack Rollins, Helena d'Algy. 5386f USA. *Nostromo* prod/rel: Fox Film Corp.

An Outcast of the Islands, 1896, Novel
Outcast of the Islands 1951 d: Carol Reed. lps: Ralph Richardson, Trevor Howard, Robert Morley. 102M UKN. prod/rel: London Films, British Lion Production Assets

The Rescue, London 1920, Novel
Rescue, The 1929 d: Herbert Brenon. lps: Ronald Colman, Lili Damita, Alfred Hickman. 7980f USA. prod/rel: Samuel Goldwyn, Inc., United Artists

Romance, 1903, Novel
Road to Romance, The 1927 d: John S. Robertson. lps: Ramon Novarro, Marceline Day, Marc MacDermott. 6544f USA. *Romance* (UKN) prod/rel: Metro-Goldwyn-Mayer Pictures

The Rover, 1923, Novel
Avventuriero, L' 1967 d: Terence Young. lps: Anthony Quinn, Rosanna Schiaffino, Rita Hayworth. 105M ITL/UKN. *The Rover* (USA) prod/rel: Arco Film (Roma), Selmur Prods. (London)

The Secret Agent, 1907, Novel
Joseph Conrad's the Secret Agent 1996 d: Christopher Hampton. lps: Bob Hoskins, Patricia Arquette, Gerard Depardieu. 95M UKN/USA. prod/rel: Capitol Films©, Heyman/Hoskins
Sabotage 1936 d: Alfred Hitchcock. lps: Sylvia Sidney, Oscar Homolka, John Loder. 76M UKN. *A Woman Alone* (USA); *The Woman Alone* prod/rel: Gaumont British

The Secret Sharer, 1910, Short Story
Face to Face 1952 d: John Brahm, Bretaigne Windust. lps: James Mason, Michael Pate, Gene Lockhart. 92M USA. prod/rel: RKO Radio, Theasquare Prods.

The Shadow Line, 1916, Novel
Smuga Cienia 1976 d: Andrzej WajdA. lps: Marek Kondrat, Graham Lines, Tom Wilkinson. MTV. 105M PLN/UKN. *The Shadow Line* (UKN) prod/rel: Film Polski - Gruppe X, Thames Television

Tomorrow, 1903, Short Story
Naufragio 1977 d: Jaime Humberto Hermosillo. lps: Maria Rojo, Ana Ofelia Murguia, Jose Alonso. F MXC. *Shipwreck*; *Shipwrecked*

Under Western Eyes, 1911, Novel
Sous Les Yeux d'Occident 1936 d: Marc Allegret. lps: Pierre Fresnay, Michel Simon, Daniele ParolA. 95M FRN. *Rasumoff*; *Rasumov* prod/rel: Daven, Andre

Victory, London 1915, Novel
Dangerous Paradise 1930 d: William A. Wellman. lps: Nancy Carroll, Richard Arlen, Warner Oland. 5244f USA. *Flesh of Eve* prod/rel: Paramount-Famous Lasky Corp.
Dans une Ile Perdue 1930 d: Alberto Cavalcanti. lps: Enrique de Rivero, Daniele Parola, Philippe Heriat. 73M FRN. prod/rel: Films Paramount
Riva Dei Bruti, La 1930 d: Mario Camerini. lps: Camillo Pilotto, Carlo Lombardi, Carmen Boni. 73M FRN. prod/rel: Paramount
Tropennachte 1930 d: Leo Mittler. lps: Dita Parlo, Robert Thoeren, Fritz Greiner. 65M FRN.
Victory 1919 d: Maurice Tourneur. lps: Jack Holt, Seena Owen, Wallace Beery. 4735f USA. prod/rel: Maurice Tourneur Productions, Inc.©, Famous Players-Lasky Corp.
Victory 1940 d: John Cromwell. lps: Fredric March, Betty Field, Cedric Hardwicke. 78M USA. prod/rel: Paramount Pictures©
Victory 1997 d: Mark Peploe. lps: Willem Dafoe, Sam Neill, Irene Jacob. 99M UKN/FRN/GRM. prod/rel: Telescope Films, Recorded Picture Company Ltd.©

CONRAN, SHIRLEY
Lace, Novel
Lace 1984 d: William Hale. lps: Bess Armstrong, Brooke Adams, Arielle Dombasle. TVM. 240M USA/UKN. prod/rel: ABC, Lorimar Prods.

CONROY, ALBERT
Estouffade a la Caraibe, Novel
Estouffade a la Caraibe 1966 d: Jacques Besnard. lps: Jean Seberg, Frederick Stafford, Serge Gainsbourg. 102M FRN/ITL. *Pagati Per Morire* (ITL); *The Looters* (UKN); *Gold Robbers* prod/rel: P.A.C., C.M.V. Cin.Ca

CONROY, PAT
The Great Santini, Novel
Great Santini, The 1980 d: Lewis John Carlino. lps: Robert Duvall, Michael O'Keefe, Blythe Danner. 115M USA. *The Ace*; *Gift of Fury* prod/rel: Orion, Warner Bros.

The Lords of Discipline, Novel
Lords of Discipline, The 1983 d: Franc Roddam. lps: David Keith, Mark Breland, Robert Prosky. 103M UKN/USA. prod/rel: Paramount

The Prince of Tides, Novel
Prince of Tides, The 1991 d: Barbra Streisand. lps: Nick Nolte, Barbra Streisand, Blythe Danner. 132M USA. prod/rel: Columbia, Barwood/Longfellow

The Water Is Wide, Novel
Conrack 1974 d: Martin Ritt. lps: Jon Voight, Hume Cronyn, Paul Winfield. 107M USA. prod/rel: Twentieth Century-Fox

CONSCIENCE, HENDRIK (1812–1883), BLG
De Loteling, 1850, Novel
Loteling, de 1974 d: Roland Verhavert. lps: Jan Decleir, Ansje Beentjes, Gaston Vandermeulen. 90M BLG. *Le Conscrit*; *The Conscript* prod/rel: Kunst En Kino N.V., Elan Film

CONSIDINE, ROBERT
Ladies' Day, Play
Ladies' Day 1943 d: Leslie Goodwins. lps: Lupe Velez, Eddie Albert, Patsy Kelly. 62M USA. prod/rel: RKO Radio

CONSIGLI, A.
L' Importuno Vince l'Avaro, 1887, Play
Importuno Vince l'Avaro, L' 1916. lps: Il Piccolo Bob, Cav. Enrico Tovagliari, Contessina de Windermer. 502m ITL. prod/rel: Bob-Film

CONSTANDUROS, DENIS
Acacia Avenue, London 1943, Play
29 Acacia Avenue 1945 d: Henry Cass. lps: Gordon Harker, Carla Lehmann, Jimmy Hanley. 83M UKN. *The Facts of Love* (USA); *The Facts of Life* prod/rel: Boca, Columbia

CONSTANDUROS, MABEL
29 Acacia Avenue 1945 d: Henry Cass. lps: Gordon Harker, Carla Lehmann, Jimmy Hanley. 83M UKN. *The Facts of Love* (USA); *The Facts of Life* prod/rel: Boca, Columbia

CONSTANT DE REBEQUE, HENRI-BENJAMIN (1767–1830), SWT, Constant, Benjamin
Adolphe, 1816, Novel
Adolphe Ou l'Age Tendre 1968 d: Bernard Toublanc-Michel. lps: Ulla Jacobsson, Jean-Claude Dauphin, Philippe Noiret. 103M FRN/GRM/PLN. *The Tender Age* (UKN); *Adolphe Or the Awkard Age* prod/rel: Prisma Films

CONSTANT, JACQUES
Leur Derniere Nuit, Novel
Leur Derniere Nuit 1953 d: Georges Lacombe. lps: Madeleine Robinson, Jean Gabin, Michel Barbey. 98M FRN. *Their Last Night* (USA); *Hold-Up*; *Une Chambre En Ville* prod/rel: C.C.F.C.

CONSTANTIN-WEYER, MAURICE
Un Homme Se Penche Sur Son Passe, Novel
Homme Se Penche Sur Son Passe, Un 1957 d: Willy Rozier. lps: Barbara Rutting, Hans Christian Blech, Jacques Bergerac. 96M FRN/GRM. *Schwarzer Stern in Weissen Nacht* (GRM); *Black Star in a White Night* prod/rel: Sport-Films, Pallas Films

Un Sourire Dans la Tempete, Novel
Sourire Dans la Tempete, Un 1950 d: Rene Chanas. lps: Michele Martin, Richard Ney, Roger Pigaut. 95M FRN/GRM/AUS. *Ein Lacheln Im Sturm* (GRM) prod/rel: Acteurs Et Techniciens Francais

Telle Qu'elle Etait En Son Vivant, Novel
Piste du Nord, La 1939 d: Jacques Feyder. lps: Michele Morgan, Charles Vanel, Louis Dumontier. 110M FRN. *La Loi du Nord* prod/rel: Filmos

CONTY, PIERRE
Monsieur Suzuki, Novel
Monsieur Suzuki 1959 d: Robert Vernay. lps: Jacques Thielment, Ivan Desny, Claude Farell. 98M FRN. *The Versailles Affair* prod/rel: Elysee Films

CONWAY, HUGH
Called Back, London 1884, Novel
Called Back 1912. lps: James Cruze, Florence Labadie. 2r USA. prod/rel: Thanhouser
Called Back 1914 d: George Loane Tucker. lps: Henry Ainley, Jane Gail, Charles Rock. 3536f UKN. prod/rel: London, Fenning
Called Back 1914 d: Otis Turner. lps: Herbert Rawlinson, Anna Little, William Worthington. 4r USA. prod/rel: Universal Film Mfg. Co.©, Gold Seal
Called Back 1933 d: Reginald Denham, Jack Harris. lps: Franklin Dyall, Lester Matthews, Dorothy Boyd. 50M UKN. prod/rel: Real Art, Radio

The Last Rose of Summer, Novel
Last Rose of Summer, The 1920 d: Albert Ward. lps: Daisy Burrell, Owen Nares, Minna Grey. 6500f UKN. prod/rel: G. B. Samuelson, Granger

Slings and Arrows, Novel
Mystere 1919 d: Serrador. lps: Jeanne Brindeau, Georges Treville, Henri Maillard. 2200m FRN.

CONY, CARLOS HEITOR
O Verao Antes, 1964, Novel
Antes, O Verao 1968 d: Gerson Tavares. lps: Jardel Filho, Norma Bengell, Gilda Grillo. 80M BRZ. *Before the Summer*; *The Summer Before*; *The Summer First*

Materia de Memoria, 1962, Novel
Homem E Sua Jaula, Um 1969 d: Fernando Cony Campos, Paulo Gil Soares. lps: Hugo Carvana, Esmeralda de Barros. 80M BRZ. *A Man and His Prison*

COOK, DAVID
Second Best, Novel
Second Best 1994 d: Chris Menges. lps: William Hurt, Chris Cleary Miles, Keith Allen. 105M USA/UKN. prod/rel: Warner, Regency

Winter Doves, Novel
Walter 1982 d: Stephen Frears. lps: Ian McKellen, Sarah Miles, Barbara Jefford. TVM. 120M UKN. *Loving Walter* (USA) prod/rel: Central, Randel Evans Productions

COOK, EDWARD
The Life of Florence Nightingale, Book
Florence Nightingale 1915 d: Maurice Elvey. lps: Elisabeth Risdon, Fred Groves, A. V. Bramble. 3570f UKN. prod/rel: British & Colonial, Ideal

COOK, KENNETH
Wake in Fright, Novel
Outback 1971 d: Ted Kotcheff. lps: Donald Pleasence, Gary Bond, Chips Rafferty. 109M ASL. *Wake in Fright* prod/rel: Nit, Group W

COOK, ROBIN (1940–, USA
Coma, Novel
Coma 1978 d: Michael Crichton. lps: Genevieve Bujold, Michael Douglas, Elizabeth Ashley. 113M USA. prod/rel: MGM

Invasion, Novel
Robin Cook's "Invasion" 1997 d: Armand Mastroianni. lps: Luke Perry, Kim Cattrall, Rebecca Gayheart. TVM. 240M USA. prod/rel: von Zerneck/Serter Films

Mortal Fear, Novel
Mortal Fear 1994 d: Larry Shaw. lps: Joanna Kerns, Gregory Harrison, Max Gail. TVM. 90M USA. *Robin Cook's Mortal Fear* prod/rel: von Zerneck Sertner Films

Outbreak, Novel
Robin Cook's Formula for Death 1995 d: Robin Cook. lps: William Devane, Nicollette Sheridan, Barry Corbin. TVM. 90M USA. *Formula for Death*

Sphinx, Novel
Sphinx 1981 d: Franklin J. Schaffner. lps: Lesley-Anne Down, Frank Langella, Maurice Ronet. 119M USA. prod/rel: Warner Bros.

COOK, WILL
Comanche Captives, New York 1960, Novel
Two Rode Together 1961 d: John Ford. lps: James Stewart, Richard Widmark, Shirley Jones. 109M USA. prod/rel: John Ford Productions, Shpetner Productions

Frontier Feud, Novel
Quincannon, Frontier Scout 1956 d: Lesley Selander. lps: Tony Martin, Peggie Castle, John Bromfield. 83M USA. *Frontier Scout* (UKN) prod/rel: United Artists, Bel-Air

Guns of North Texas, New York 1958, Novel
Uomini Dal Passo Pesante, Gli 1966 d: Alfredo Antonini, Mario Sequi. lps: Joseph Cotten, Gordon Scott, James Mitchum. 105M ITL. *The Tramplers* (USA) prod/rel: Anna Marie Chretien, Alvaro Mancori

COOK, WILLIAM WALLACE
After His Own Heart, 1920, Short Story
After Your Own Heart 1921 d: George Marshall. lps: Tom Mix, Ora Carew, George Hernandez. 4244f USA. prod/rel: Fox Film Corp.

A Knight of the Range, Story
Sonora Kid, The 1927 d: Robert de Lacy. lps: Tom Tyler, Peggy Montgomery, Billie Bennett. 4565f USA. prod/rel: R-C Pictures, Film Booking Offices of America

The Old West Per Contract, Short Story
'49 - '17 1917 d: Ruth Ann Baldwin. lps: Joseph Girard, Donna Drew, Leo Pierson. 5r USA. *The Old West Per Contract* prod/rel: Universal Film Mfg. Co.©, Butterfly Picture

COOKE, BALDWIN G.
His Last Dollar, New York 1904, Play
His Last Dollar 1914. lps: David Higgins, Betty Gray, Hal Clarendon. 4r USA. prod/rel: Famous Players Film Co., Paramount Pictures Corp.

COOKE, MARJORIE BENTON
Cinderella Jane, Garden City, N.Y. 1917, Novel
Mad Marriage, The 1921 d: Rollin S. Sturgeon. lps: Carmel Myers, Truman Van Dyke, William Brunton. 4531f USA. prod/rel: Universal Film Mfg. Co.

The Girl Who Lived in the Woods, Chicago 1910, Novel
Little 'Fraid Lady, The 1920 d: John G. Adolfi. lps: Mae Marsh, Tully Marshall, Kathleen Kirkham. 6r USA. *The Girl Who Lived in the Woods* prod/rel: Robertson-Cole Co., Robertson-Cole Distributing Corp.©

The Incubus, New York 1915, Novel
Her Husband's Friend 1920 d: Fred Niblo. lps: Enid Bennett, Rowland Lee, Tom Chatterton. 5r USA. *The Incubus* prod/rel: Thomas H. Ince Productions, Famous Players-Lasky Corp.

The Love Call, Short Story
Love Call, The 1919 d: Louis W. Chaudet. lps: Billie Rhodes, Lloyd Whitlock, Hart Hoxie. 5r USA. prod/rel: National Film Corp. of America, Robertson-Cole Co.

COOKSON, CATHERINE (1906–, UKN
The Black Candle, Novel
Black Candle, The 1991 d: Roy Battersby. lps: Samantha Bond, Denholm Elliott, Nathaniel Parker. TVM. 102M UKN. prod/rel: World Wide Tv International, Tyne Tees Tv

The Black Velvet Gown, Novel
Black Velvet Gown, The 1991 d: Norman Stone. lps: Janet McTeer, Bob Peck, Geraldine Somerville. TVM. 102M UKN. prod/rel: World Wide Tv International, Tyne Tees Tv

The Cinder Path, Novel
Cinder Path, The 1994 d: Simon Langton. lps: Lloyd Owen, Catherine Zeta Jones, Maria Miles. MTV. 165M UKN.

The Dwelling Place, Novel
Dwelling Place, The 1990 d: Gavin Millar. lps: Tracy Whitwell, Ray Stevenson, Luke Conway. MTV. 305M UKN.

The Fifteen Streets, Novel
Fifteen Streets, The 1989 d: David Wheatley. lps: Owen Teale, Clare Holman, Ian Bannen. TVM. 105M UKN. prod/rel: World Wide Tv International, Tyne Tees Tv

The Gambling Man, Novel
Gambling Man, The 1994. lps: Robson Green, Bernard Hill. MTV. 152M UKN.

The Mallen Trilogy, Novel
Mallens: Part 1 - the Mallen Streak, The 1978 d: Richard (5) Martin, Ronald Wilson. lps: John Duttine. MTV. 171M UKN.

Mallens: Part 2 - the Mallen Girls, The 1978 d: Richard (5) Martin, Ronald Wilson. lps: John Duttine. MTV. 177M UKN.

Mallens: Part 3 - the Mallen Secret, The 1980 d: Roy Roberts, Mary McMurray. lps: Juliet Stevenson, Gerry Sundquist, Caroline Blakiston. MTV. 140M UKN.

Mallens: Part 4 - the Mallen Curse, The 1980 d: Mary McMurray, Brian Mills. lps: Juliet Stevenson, Gerry Sundquist, Caroline Blakiston. MTV. 147M UKN.

The Moth, Novel
Moth, The 1996 d: Roy Battersby. lps: Juliet Aubrey, Jack Davenport, David (4) Bradley. TVM. 150M UKN.

Rooney, Novel
Rooney 1958 d: George Pollock. lps: John Gregson, Muriel Pavlow, Barry Fitzgerald. 88M UKN. prod/rel: Rank, Rank Film Distributors

The Tide of Life, Novel
Tide of Life, The 1995 d: David Wheatley. lps: Gillian Kearney, Ray Stevenson, Patricia Dunn. MTV. 150M UKN.

The Wingless Bird, Novel
Wingless Bird, The 1996. lps: Claire Skinner, Julian Wadham, Edward Atterton. MTV. 146M UKN.

COOLEN, ANTON
Dorp Aan de Rivier, Novel
Dorp Aan de Rivier 1958 d: Fons Rademakers. lps: Max Croiset, Mary Dresselhuys, Bernard Droog. 92M NTH. *Doctor in the Village* (UKN); *Village on the River* prod/rel: Nationale Film Productie

COOLIDGE, DANE (1873–1940), USA
The Land of the Broken Promise, 1913, Novel
Yaqui, The 1916 d: Lloyd B. Carleton. lps: Hobart Bosworth, Golda Coldwell, Dorothy Love Clark. 5r USA. prod/rel: Bluebird Photoplays, Inc.©

Rimrock Jones, New York 1917, Novel
Rimrock Jones 1918 d: Donald Crisp. lps: Wallace Reid, Anna Little, Charles Ogle. 5r USA. prod/rel: Jesse L. Lasky Feature Play Co.©, Paramount Pictures

COOLUS, ROMAIN
Antoinette Sabrier, Play
Antoinette Sabrier 1927 d: Germaine Dulac. lps: Eve Francis, Gabriel Gabrio, Yvette Armel. F FRN. prod/rel: Ste Des Cineromans

Les Bleus de l'Amour, Play
Bleus de l'Amour, Les 1917 d: Henri Desfontaines. lps: Henry Laverne, Baron Fils, Guyon Fils. FRN. prod/rel: Film d'Art

Bleus de l'Amour, Les 1932 d: Jean de Marguenat. lps: Fernand Charpin, Nina Myral, Roger Bourdin. 97M FRN. prod/rel: Lutece-Film

Le Chien de Montargis, Play
Chien de Montagis, Le 1909 d: Georges MoncA. 235m FRN. prod/rel: Scagl

Diane Au Bain, Play
Cercasi Modella 1932 d: E. W. Emo. lps: Elsa Merlini, Gianfranco Giachetti, Nino Besozzi. 80M ITL. prod/rel: Itala, S.a.P.F.

Petite Peste, Play
Petite Peste 1938 d: Jean de Limur. lps: Rene Lefevre, Henri Rollan, Genevieve Callix. 80M FRN. prod/rel: Aime Frapin

La Reine de Biarritz, Play
Reine de Biarritz, La 1934 d: Jean Toulout. lps: Jean Dax, Andre Burgere, Alice Field. 80M FRN. prod/rel: Vega Films

La Sonnette d'Alarme, Play
Sonnette d'Alarme, La 1935 d: Christian-Jaque. lps: Jean Murat, Josette Day, Pierre Stephen. 70M FRN. prod/rel: Productions Sigma

COONEY, CAROLINE B.
The Face on the Milk Carton, Novel
Face on the Milk Carton, The 1995 d: Waris Hussein. lps: Kellie Martin, Sharon Lawrence, Edward Herrmann. TVM. 92M USA. prod/rel: Family Productions

Rearview Mirror, Novel
Rearview Mirror 1984 d: Lou Antonio. lps: Michael Beck, Lee Remick, Tony Musante. TVM. 100M USA. prod/rel: Simon/Asher Entertainments

Whatever Happened to Janie, Novel
Face on the Milk Carton, The 1995 d: Waris Hussein. lps: Kellie Martin, Sharon Lawrence, Edward Herrmann. TVM. 92M USA. prod/rel: Family Productions

COONEY, MICHAEL
Murder in Mind, Play
Murder in Mind 1997 d: Andy Morahan. lps: Nigel Hawthorne, Mary-Louise Parker, Jimmy Smits. 88M USA/UKN. prod/rel: Lakeshore International, BBC

COONEY, RAY (1932–, UKN
Comrade Chase Me, Play
Not Now, Comrade 1976 d: Harold Snoad, Ray Cooney. lps: Leslie Phillips, Roy Kinnear, Windsor Davies. 90M UKN. prod/rel: Emi, Not Now

Darling Not Now, Play
Not Now, Darling 1972 d: Ray Cooney, David Croft. lps: Leslie Phillips, Ray Cooney, Moira Lister. 97M UKN. prod/rel: Sedgemoor, Not Now Films

Out of Order, Play
Miniszter Felrelep, A 1998 d: Andras Kern, Robert Koltai. lps: Andras Kern, Robert Koltai, Sandor Gasnar. 100M HNG. *Out of Order* prod/rel: Inter-Com

There Goes the Bride, Play
There Goes the Bride 1980 d: Terry Marcel. lps: Tom Smothers, Twiggy, Martin Balsam. 90M UKN. prod/rel: Lonsdale

Why Not Stay for Breakfast?, Play
Why Not Stay for Breakfast? 1979 d: Terry Marcel. lps: George Chakiris, Gemma Craven, Yvonne Wilder. 95M UKN. prod/rel: Artgrove

COOPER, COURTNEY RYLEY
Christmas Eve at Pilot Butte, 1921, Short Story
Desperate Trails 1921 d: John Ford. lps: Harry Carey, Irene Rich, George E. Stone. 4577f USA. *Christmas Eve at Pilot Butte* prod/rel: Universal Film Mfg. Co.

The Land of the Lost, Story
Step on It! 1922 d: Jack Conway. lps: Hoot Gibson, Edith Yorke, Frank Lanning. 4225f USA. prod/rel: Universal Film Mfg. Co.

The Last Frontier, Boston 1923, Novel
Last Frontier, The 1926 d: George B. Seitz. lps: William Boyd, Marguerite de La Motte, Jack Hoxie. 7800f USA. prod/rel: Metropolitan Pictures Corp. of Calif., Producers Distributing Corp.

The White Desert, New York 1922, Novel
White Desert, The 1925 d: Reginald Barker. lps: Claire Windsor, Pat O'Malley, Robert Frazer. 6464f USA. prod/rel: Metro-Goldwyn Pictures

COOPER, DENNIS
Frisk, Novel
Frisk 1995 d: Todd Verow. lps: Michael Gunther, Craig Chester, Parker Posey. 83M USA. prod/rel: Strand Releasing©, Industrial Eye

COOPER, EDMUND
Story
Invisible Boy, The 1957 d: Herman Hoffman. lps: Richard Eyer, Philip Abbott, Diane Brewster. 82M USA. prod/rel: MGM, Pan Prods.

COOPER, ELIZABETH
Drusilla With a Million, New York 1916, Novel
  Drusilla With a Million 1925 d: F. Harmon Weight. lps: Mary Carr, Priscilla Bonner, Kenneth Harlan. 7391f USA. prod/rel: Associated Arts Corp., Film Booking Offices of America

COOPER, GILES
Wittering and Zigo Unman, Television Play
  Unman, Wittering and Zigo 1971 d: John MacKenzie. lps: David Hemmings, Douglas Wilmer, Tony Haygarth. 102M UKN. prod/rel: Paramount, Mediarts

COOPER, HENRY ST. JOHN
Sunny Ducrow, New York 1920, Novel
  Sunny Side Up 1926 d: Donald Crisp. lps: Vera Reynolds, Edmund Burns, George K. Arthur. 5994f USA. *Footlights* prod/rel: de Mille Pictures, Producers Distributing Corp.

COOPER, JAMES A.
Cap'n Abe Storekeeper: a Story of Cape Cod, New York 1917, Novel
  Captain's Captain, The 1918 d: Tom Terriss. lps: Alice Joyce, Arthur Donaldson, Maurice Costello. 4251f USA. *Cap'n Abe's Niece* prod/rel: Vitagraph Co. of America©, Blue Ribbon Feature

COOPER, JAMES FENIMORE (1789–1851), USA
Novel
  Wildtoter, Der 1966 d: Richard Groschopp. lps: Gojko Mitic, Rolf Romer, Helmut Schreiber. 90M GDR. prod/rel: Defa

The Deerslayer, 1841, Novel
  Chingachgock - Die Grosse Schlange 1967 d: Richard Groschopp. lps: Gojko Mitic, Rolf Romer, Lilo Grahn. 91M GDR. *Chingachgock - the Big Snake* prod/rel: Defa
  Deerslayer 1943 d: Lew Landers. lps: Bruce Kellogg, Jean Parker, Larry Parks. 67M USA. prod/rel: Republic, Cardinal Pictures
  Deerslayer, The 1913 d: Hal Reid, Larry Trimble. lps: Hal Reid, Wallace Reid, Florence Turner. 2000f USA. prod/rel: Vitagraph Co. of America
  Deerslayer, The 1957 d: Kurt Neumann. lps: Lex Barker, Rita Moreno, Forrest Tucker. 78M USA. prod/rel: 20th Century-Fox, Regal Films
  Deerslayer, The 1978 d: Richard Friedenberg. lps: Steve Forrest, Ned Romero, John Anderson. TVM. 78M USA. prod/rel: NBC, Schick Sunn Classics

The Last of the Mohicans, Boston 1826, Novel
  Dernier Des Mohicans, Le 1968 d: Jean Dreville, Sergiu Nicolaescu. MTV. 82M FRN/RMN. *Ultimul Mohican* (RMN); *The Last of the Mohicans*
  In the Days of the Six Nations 1911. 2r USA. prod/rel: Republic
  Last of the Mohicans 1932 d: Ford Beebe, B. Reeves Eason. lps: Harry Carey, Hobart Bosworth, Junior Coghlan. SRL. 250M USA.
  Last of the Mohicans, The 1911 d: Theodore Marston. lps: Frank Crane, William Russell, Alphonse Ethier. SHT USA. prod/rel: Thanhouser
  Last of the Mohicans, The 1911. SHT USA. prod/rel: Powers
  Last of the Mohicans, The 1920 d: Maurice Tourneur, Clarence Brown. lps: Wallace Beery, Barbara Bedford, Alan Roscoe. 6r USA. prod/rel: Maurice Tourneur Productions, Inc., Associated Producers, Inc.
  Last of the Mohicans, The 1936 d: George B. Seitz, Wallace Fox. lps: Randolph Scott, Binnie Barnes, Henry Wilcoxon. 91M USA. prod/rel: United Artists Corp., Reliance Productions of California©
  Last of the Mohicans, The 1977 d: James L. Conway. lps: Steve Forrest, Ned Romero, Andrew Prine. TVM. 100M USA. prod/rel: Schick Sunn Classics
  Last of the Mohicans, The 1992 d: Michael Mann. lps: Daniel Day-Lewis, Madeleine Stowe, Russell Means. 122M USA. prod/rel: Morgan Creek
  Last of the Redmen 1947 d: George Sherman. lps: Jon Hall, Michael O'Shea, Evelyn Ankers. 77M USA. *Last of the Redskins* (UKN) prod/rel: Columbia
  Letzte Mohikaner, Der 1965 d: Harald Reinl. lps: Anthony Steffen, Karin Dor, Daniel Martin. 90M GRM/ITL/SPN. *La Valle Delle Ombre Rosse* (ITL); *The Last Tomahawk*; *El Ultimo Mohicano* (SPN); *The Last of the Mohicans*; *L' Ultimo Dei Mohicani* prod/rel: International Germania, Balcazar
  Uncas, El Fin de Una Raza 1964 d: Mateo Cano. lps: Jack Taylor, Paul Muller, Sara LezanA. 85M SPN/ITL/GRM. *L' Ultimo Dei Mohicani* (ITL); *Fall of the Mohicans*; *Lederstrumpf -Der Letzte Mohaniker* (GRM); *The Last of the Mohicans*

The Leather Stocking Tales, Novel
  Leather Stocking 1909 d: D. W. Griffith. lps: James Kirkwood, Linda Arvidson, Marion Leonard. 996f USA. prod/rel: Biograph Co.

The Pathfinder, 1840, Novel
  Aventure En Ontario 1968 d: Jean Dreville, Sergiu Nicolaescu. MTV. 97M FRN/RMN. *Aventuri in Ontario* (RMN); *Adventures in Ontario*; *The Pathfinder*
  Iroquois Trail, The 1950 d: Phil Karlson. lps: George Montgomery, Brenda Marshall, Glenn Langan. 85M USA. *The Tomahawk Trail* (UKN) prod/rel: United Artists, Edward Small
  Pathfinder, The 1952 d: Sidney Salkow. lps: George Montgomery, Helena Carter, Jay Silverheels. 78M USA. prod/rel: Columbia
  Pathfinder, The 1994 d: Donald Shebib. lps: Kevin Dillon, Laurie Holden, Graham Greene. 105M CND.
  Sledopyt 1987 d: Pavel Lyubimov. lps: Andreis Zhagars, Anastasia Niemolieva, Ehmmanuil Vitorgan. 105M USS.

The Pioneers, 1823, Novel
  Pioneers, The 1941 d: Al Herman. lps: Tex Ritter, Slim Andrews, Red Foley. 58M USA. prod/rel: Monogram

The Prairie, 1827, Novel
  Prairie, La 1968 d: Pierre Gaspard-Huit, Sergiu Nicolaescu. MTV. 95M FRN/RMN. *Preria* (RMN); *The Prairie*
  Prairie, The 1947 d: Frank Wisbar. lps: Lenore Aubert, Alan Baxter, Russ Vincent. 80M USA. prod/rel: Screen Guild

The Spy, New York 1821, Novel
  Spy, The 1914 d: Otis Turner. lps: Herbert Rawlinson, Edna Maison, William Worthington. 4r USA. prod/rel: Universal Film Mfg. Co.

COOPER, JILLY (1937–, UKN
Riders, Novel
  Jilly Cooper's Riders 1993 d: Gabrielle Beaumont. lps: Marcus Gilbert, Michael Praed, Arabella Tjve. TVM. 205M UKN. *Riders* prod/rel: Anglia

COOVER, ROBERT (1932–, USA
The Babysitter, Short Story
  Babysitter, The 1995 d: Guy Ferland. lps: Alicia Silverstone, J. T. Walsh, Lois Chiles. 91M USA. prod/rel: Spelling Films International©, Joel Schumacher Productions

COPIC, BRANKO
Dozivljaji Nikoletine Bursaca, 1956, Short Story
  Nikoletina Bursac 1964 d: Branko Bauer. lps: Dragomir Pajic, Milan Srdoc, Olga Vujadinovic. 102M YGS. *Dozivljaji Nikoletine Bursaca*; *Adventures of Nikoletina Bursac*

Orlovi Rano Lete, 1957, Novel
  Orlovi Rano Lete 1966 d: Soja Jovanovic. lps: Miodrag Petrovic-Ckalja, Ljubisa Samardzic, Dragutin Dobricanin. 90M YGS. *The Eagles Fly Early*

COPPEE, FRANCOIS
Le Coupable, Paris 1896, Play
  Coupable, Le 1908-18. lps: Henry Krauss, Philippe Garnier, Jeanne Delvair. FRN.
  Coupable, Le 1917 d: Andre Antoine. lps: Sylvie, Romuald Joube, Mona Gondre. 1690m FRN. prod/rel: Scagl
  Coupable, Le 1936 d: Raymond Bernard. lps: Pierre Blanchar, Gabriel Signoret, Madeleine Ozeray. 107M FRN. prod/rel: Filmor
  Guilty Man, The 1918 d: Irvin V. Willat. lps: Gloria Hope, Vivian Reed, William Garwood. 5144f USA. prod/rel: Thomas H. Ince, Inc., Paramount Pictures Corp.

Le Luthier de Cremone, Play
  Luthier de Cremone, Le 1909 d: Andre Calmettes. lps: Claude Garry, Jean Dax, Amelie Dieterle. 235m FRN. prod/rel: Pathe Freres

Pour la Couronne, Play
  Pour la Couronne 1912 d: Henri Pouctal. lps: Philippe Garnier, Jean Marie de L'isle, Jeanne Delvair. 260m FRN. prod/rel: Film d'Art

Severo Torelli, Play
  Severo Torelli 1914 d: Louis Feuillade. lps: Fernand Herrmann, Laurent Morlas, Renee Carl. 1208m FRN. prod/rel: Gaumont

The Violin Maker of Cremona, Story
  Violin Maker of Cremona, The 1909 d: D. W. Griffith. lps: Mary Pickford, David Miles, Owen Moore. 963f USA. prod/rel: Biograph Co.

COPPEL, ALEC
A Bird in the Nest, Play
  Bliss of Mrs. Blossom, The 1968 d: Joseph McGrath. lps: Shirley MacLaine, Richard Attenborough, James Booth. 93M UKN. prod/rel: Paramount

Chip, Chip Chip, Play
  Statue, The 1970 d: Rod Amateau. lps: David Niven, Virna Lisi, Robert Vaughn. 89M UKN. prod/rel: Cinerama, Josef Shaftel

The Gazebo, New York 1958, Play
  Gazebo, The 1959 d: George Marshall. lps: Glenn Ford, Debbie Reynolds, Carl Reiner. 102M USA. prod/rel: MGM

I Killed the Count, London 1937, Play
  I Killed the Count 1938 d: Friedrich Zelnik. lps: Syd Walker, Ben Lyon, Terence de Marney. 89M UKN. *Who Is Guilty?* prod/rel: Grafton, Grand National

Laughs With a Stranger, Short Story
  Moment to Moment 1966 d: Mervyn Leroy. lps: Jean Seberg, Honor Blackman, Sean Garrison. 108M USA. prod/rel: Mervyn Leroy Productions, Universal

A Man About a Dog, Novel
  Obsession 1948 d: Edward Dmytryk. lps: Robert Newton, Sally Gray, Naunton Wayne. 98M UKN. *The Hidden Room* (USA) prod/rel: General Film Distributors, Independent Sovereign

Mr. Denning Drives North, Novel
  Mr. Denning Drives North 1951 d: Anthony Kimmins. lps: John Mills, Phyllis Calvert, Sam Wanamaker. 93M UKN. prod/rel: London Films, British Lion

CORARITO, GREG
The Sadistic Hypnotist
  Wanda (the Satanic Hypnotist) 1969 d: Greg Corarito. lps: Katharine Shubeck, Dick Dangerfield, Janine Sweet. 75M USA. prod/rel: Falu Productions

CORBALEY, KATE
The Fire Brigade, Story
  Fire Brigade, The 1926 d: William Nigh. lps: May McAvoy, Charles Ray, Holmes Herbert. 8716f USA. *Fire!* prod/rel: Metro-Goldwyn-Mayer Pictures

CORBETT, JAMES
Man-Eaters of Kumaon, Story
  Man-Eater of Kumaon 1948 d: Byron Haskin. lps: Wendell Corey, Sabu, Joanne Page. 79M USA. prod/rel: Universal

CORBETT, JAMES J.
The Roar of the Crowd, Book
  Gentleman Jim 1942 d: Raoul Walsh. lps: Errol Flynn, Alexis Smith, Jack Carson. 104M USA. prod/rel: Warner Bros.

CORBETT, SCOTT (1913–, USA, Corbett, Winfield Scott
The Reluctant Landlord, 1950, Novel
  Love Nest 1951 d: Joseph M. Newman. lps: June Haver, William Lundigan, Frank Fay. 84M USA. prod/rel: 20th Century-Fox

CORBUCCI, BRUNO (1931–, ITL
Aragoste Di Sicilia, Play
  Prima Notte Del Dr. Danieli, Industriale Col Complesso Del Giocattolo 1970 d: Gianni Grimaldi. lps: Francoise Prevost, Lando Buzzanca, Katia ChristinA. 93M ITL/FRN. *La Prima Notte Del Dottore Danieli*; *La Toubib En Delire*; *Beaucoup de Nuits Pour Rien* prod/rel: Princeps Cin.Ca, Medusa Distribuzione

CORCORAN, JAMES
Bitter Harvest: Murder in the Heartland, Book
  In the Line of Duty: the Twilight Murders 1991 d: Dick Lowry. lps: Rod Steiger, Michael Gross, Gary BasarabA. TVM. 91M USA. *In the Line of Duty: Manhunt in the Dakotas*; *In the Line of Duty 3: Time to Kill*; *Time to Kill: in the Line of Duty 3* prod/rel: Patchett Kauman Entertainment

CORCORAN, WILLIAM
Trail Street, Novel
  Trail Street 1947 d: Ray Enright. lps: Randolph Scott, Robert Ryan, Anne Jeffreys. 84M USA. prod/rel: RKO

CORDAY, MICHEL
Le Lynx, Novel
  Lynx, Le 1914 d: Bernard-Deschamps. 900m FRN. prod/rel: Cosmograph

CORDELIER, JEANNE
La Derobade, Novel
  Derobade, La 1979 d: Daniel Duval. lps: Miou-Miou, Maria Schneider, Daniel Duval. 114M FRN. *Memoirs of a French Whore* (USA); *The Getaway Life*; *The Life* (UKN); *The Getaway*; *The Evasion* prod/rel: a.T.C. 3000 Prodis

CORDIER, CHARLES
Story
  Nacht Der Entscheidung 1956 d: Falk Harnack. lps: Carl Raddatz, Hilde Krahl, Albert Lieven. 104M GRM. *Night of Decision* prod/rel: Filmaufbau

CORELLI, MARIE (1854–1924), UKN, MacKay, Mary
God's Good Man, Novel
  God's Good Man 1919 d: Maurice Elvey. lps: Basil Gill, Peggy Carlisle, Barry Bernard. 5777f UKN. prod/rel: Stoll

Holy Orders, Novel
  Holy Orders 1917 d: A. E. Coleby, Arthur Rooke. lps: Malvina Longfellow, A. E. Coleby, Arthur Rooke. 4744f UKN. prod/rel: I. B. Davidson, Ruffells

Innocent, Novel
  Innocent 1921 d: Maurice Elvey. lps: Madge Stuart, Basil Rathbone, Lawrence Anderson. 5933f UKN. prod/rel: Stoll

The Sorrows of Satan, New York 1895, Novel
  Sorrows of Satan, The 1917 d: Alexander Butler. lps: Gladys Cooper, Owen Nares, Cecil Humphreys. 5000f UKN. prod/rel: G. B. Samuelson, Walker
  Sorrows of Satan, The 1926 d: D. W. Griffith. lps: Adolphe Menjou, Ricardo Cortez, Lya de Putti. 8691f USA. prod/rel: Famous Players-Lasky, Paramount Pictures

Temporal Power, Novel
  Potere Sovrano, Il 1916 d: Baldassarre Negroni, Percy Nash. lps: Hesperia, Emilio Ghione, Diana d'Amore. 2257m ITL. *Temporal Power* prod/rel: Tiber

Thelma - a Norwegian Princess, London 1887, Novel
  Modern Thelma, A 1916 d: John G. Adolfi. lps: Vivian Martin, Harry Hilliard, William H. Tooker. 5r USA. prod/rel: Fox Film Corp., William Fox©
  Thelma 1910 d: Theodore Marston. lps: Miss Rosamonde, Alphonse Ethier. 1000f USA. prod/rel: Thanhouser
  Thelma 1911. SHT USA. prod/rel: Selig Polyscope Co.
  Thelma 1918 d: A. E. Coleby, Arthur Rooke. lps: Malvina Longfellow, Arthur Rooke, Maud Yates. 5794f UKN. prod/rel: I. B. Davidson, Ruffells
  Thelma 1922 d: Chester Bennett. lps: Jane Novak, Barbara Tennant, Gordon Mullen. 6497f USA. prod/rel: Chester Bennett Productions, Film Booking Offices of America

The Treasure of Heaven, Novel
  Treasure of Heaven, The 1916 d: A. E. Coleby. lps: Janet Alexander, A. E. Coleby, Langhorne Burton. 5000f UKN. prod/rel: I. B. Davidson, Tiger

Vendetta, 1886, Novel
  Marma Yogi 1951 d: K. Ramnoth. lps: Anjali Devi, M. G. Ramachandran, S. V. Sahasranaman. 175M IND. *Marmayogi*; *Ej Tha Raja* prod/rel: Jupiter Pictures

Wormwood: a Drama of Paris, London 1890, Novel
  Wormwood 1915 d: Marshall Farnum. lps: Ethel Kaufman, John Sainpolis, Charles Arthur. 5r USA. prod/rel: Fox Film Corp., William Fox©

The Young Diana, 1918, Novel
  Young Diana, The 1922 d: Albert Capellani, Robert G. VignolA. lps: Marion Davies, MacLyn Arbuckle, Forrest Stanley. 6744f USA. prod/rel: Cosmopolitan Productions, Paramount Pictures

CORINTH, CURT
Die Unheimliche Wandlung Des Alex Roscher, Novel
  Unheimliche Wandlung Des Alex Roscher, Die 1943 d: Paul May. lps: Anneliese Reinhold, Viktoria von Ballasko, Rudolf Prack. 89M GRM. *Der Spiegel Der Helena* prod/rel: Bavaria

CORLISS, ALLENE
Summer Lightning, New York 1936, Novel
  I Met My Love Again 1938 d: Joshua Logan, Arthur Ripley. lps: Joan Bennett, Henry Fonda, Dame May Whitty. 80M USA. *Summer Lightning*; *Carelessly We Love* prod/rel: United Artists Corp., Walter Wanger Productions©

CORMACK, BARTLETT
The Racket, New York 1927, Play
  Racket, The 1928 d: Lewis Milestone. lps: Thomas Meighan, Marie Prevost, Louis Wolheim. 7646f USA. prod/rel: Caddo Co., Paramount Famous Lasky Corp.
  Racket, The 1951 d: John Cromwell, Nicholas Ray (Uncredited). lps: Robert Mitchum, Lizabeth Scott, Robert Ryan. 88M USA. prod/rel: RKO, Howard Hughes

CORMAN, AVERY
Kramer Vs. Kramer, Novel
  Kramer Vs. Kramer 1979 d: Robert Benton. lps: Dustin Hoffman, Meryl Streep, Jane Alexander. 105M USA. prod/rel: Stanley R. Jaffe

Oh God!, Novel
  Oh, God! 1977 d: Carl Reiner. lps: George Burns, John Denver, Teri Garr. 104M USA. prod/rel: Warner Bros.

CORMIER, ROBERT
I Am the Cheese, Novel
  I Am the Cheese 1983 d: Robert Jiras. lps: Robert MacNaughton, Hope Lange, Don Murray. 100M USA. prod/rel: Almi

CORMON, EUGENE
Une Cause Celebre, Paris 1877, Play
  Celebrated Case, A 1914 d: George Melford. lps: Alice Joyce, Guy Coombs, Alice Hollister. 4r USA. prod/rel: Kalem Co., General Film Co.

Les Crochets du Pere Martin, 1858, Play
  Gerla Di Papa Martin, La 1909 d: Mario Caserini. 314m ITL. *A Father's Heart* (UKN); *Honour Thy Father* prod/rel: Cines
  Gerla Di Papa Martin, La 1914 d: Eleuterio Rodolfi. lps: Ermete Novelli, Gigetta Morano, Umberto Scalpellini. 823m ITL. prod/rel: S.A. Ambrosio
  Gerla Di Papa Martin, La 1923 d: Mario Bonnard. lps: Francesco Amodio, Amalia Raspantini, Giuseppe Amato. 1795m ITL. prod/rel: Caesar Film
  Gerla Di Papa Martin, La 1940 d: Mario Bonnard. lps: Ruggero Ruggeri, Germana Paolieri, Bella Starace Sainati. 94M ITL. prod/rel: Lux Film

Les Deux Orphelines, 1874, Novel
  Deux Orphelines, Les 1932 d: Maurice Tourneur. lps: Gabriel Gabrio, Rosine Derean, Renee Saint-Cyr. 87M FRN. *The Two Orphans* prod/rel: Pathe-Natan
  Due Orfanelle, Le 1918 d: Eduardo BencivengA. lps: Enna Saredo, Olga Benetti, Irma Berrettini. 2658m ITL. prod/rel: Caesar Film
  Due Orfanelle, Le 1942 d: Carmine Gallone. lps: Alida Valli, Maria Denis, Osvaldo Valenti. 85M ITL. *The Two Orphans* prod/rel: Grandi Film Storici, S.a.F.I.C.
  Due Orfanelle, Le 1966 d: Riccardo FredA. lps: Mike Marshall, Sophie Dares, Valeria Giangottini. 90M ITL/FRN. *Les Deux Orphelines* (FRN); *The Two Orphans* (USA) prod/rel: Comptoir Francais Du Film Production, Cine Italia Film
  Due Orfanelle, Le 1978 d: Leopoldo SavonA. lps: Isabella Savona, Patrizia Gori, Evelyn Stewart. 90M ITL/SPN. *Unidos Por El Destino* (SPN) prod/rel: Cine Uno (Roma), Copercines (Madrid)
  Duel Scene from "the Two Orphans" 1902 d: William Haggar. 100f UKN. prod/rel: Haggar & Sons
  It Happened in Paris 1932 d: M. J. Weisfeldt. lps: Ranny Weeks, Eva Lorraine, Taylor Holmes. F USA. prod/rel: Picture Classics
  Orphans of the Storm 1921 d: D. W. Griffith. lps: Lillian Gish, Dorothy Gish, Joseph Schildkraut. 14r USA. *The Two Orphans* prod/rel: D. W. Griffith, Inc., United Artists
  Povere Bimbe! 1923 d: Gero Zambuto. lps: Linda Pini, Fernanda Fassy, Lido Manetti. 4296m ITL. prod/rel: Itala
  Two Orphans, The 1911 d: Otis Turner. lps: Kathlyn Williams, Winnifred Greenwood, Myrtle Stedman. 3061f USA. prod/rel: Selig Polyscope Co.
  Two Orphans, The 1915 d: Herbert Brenon. lps: Theda Bara, Jean Sothern, Herbert Brenon. 5-7r USA. prod/rel: Fox Film Corp., William Fox©

CORNEILLE, PIERRE (1606–1684), FRN
Le Cid, 1637, Play
  Cid, Il 1910 d: Mario Caserini. lps: Amleto Novelli, Enna Saredo, Maria Caserini Gasparini. 289m ITL. *Triumphant Hero* (UKN) prod/rel: Cines
  El Cid 1961 d: Anthony Mann, Giovanni Paolucci. lps: Charlton Heston, Sophia Loren, Raf Vallone. 184M USA/ITL. prod/rel: Allied Artists, Dear Film (Roma)

Horace, 1641, Play
  Horace 62 1962 d: Andre Versini. lps: Charles Aznavour, Raymond Pellegrin, Giovanna Ralli. 92M FRN/ITL. *Unn Appuntamento Per Uccidere* (ITL) prod/rel: France London Films, David Film

Othon, 1665, Play
  Yeux Ne Veulent Pas En Tout Temps Se Fermer Ou Peut-Etre Qu'un Jour Rome Se Permettra de Choisir a. 1970 d: Jean-Marie Straub, Daniele Huillet. lps: Adriano Apra, Ennio Lauricella, Olimpia Carlisi. 90M GRM/ITL. *Othon* (UKN); *Eyes Do Not Want to Close at All Times Or Perhaps One Day Rome Will Permit Herself to Choose in H..* prod/rel: Janus, Straub-Huillet

CORNELL, EVAN S.
Son of the Morning Star
  Son of the Morning Star 1991 d: Mike Robe. lps: Gary Cole, Rosanna Arquette, Terry O'Quinn. TVM. 192M USA.

CORNELL, HUGHES
Born Rich, Philadelphia 1924, Novel
  Born Rich 1924 d: William Nigh. lps: Claire Windsor, Bert Lytell, Cullen Landis. 7389f USA. prod/rel: Garrick Pictures, First National Pictures

CORNWELL, BERNARD (1944–, UKN
Sharpe's Battle, Novel
  Sharpe's Battle 1995 d: Tom Clegg. lps: Sean Bean, Daragh O'Malley, Allie Byrne. MTV. 101M UKN.

Sharpe's Company, Novel
  Sharpe's Company 1992 d: Tom Clegg. lps: Sean Bean, Assumpta Serna, Brian Cox. MTV. 101M UKN.

Sharpe's Eagles, Novel
  Sharpe's Eagles 1993 d: Tom Clegg. lps: Sean Bean, Brian Cox, Daragh O'Malley. TVM. 104M UKN. prod/rel: Celtic Pictures

Sharpe's Enemy, Novel
  Sharpe's Enemy 1994 d: Tom Clegg. lps: Sean Bean, Daragh O'Malley, Michael Byrne. MTV. 101M UKN.

Sharpe's Gold, Novel
  Sharpe's Gold 1995 d: Tom Clegg. lps: Sean Bean, Daragh O'Malley, Jayne Linehan. MTV. 103M UKN.

Sharpe's Honour, Novel
  Sharpe's Honour 1992 d: Tom Clegg. lps: Sean Bean, Diana Perez, Feodor Atkine. MTV. 101M UKN.

Sharpe's Mission, Novel
  Sharpe's Mission 1996 d: Tom Clegg. lps: Sean Bean, Daragh O'Malley, Abigail Cruttenden. TVM. 101M UKN.

Sharpe's Regiment, Novel
  Sharpe's Regiment 1996 d: Tom Clegg. lps: Sean Bean, Daragh O'Malley, Abigail Cruttenden. MTV. 102M UKN.
  Sharpe's Rifles 1993 d: Tom Clegg. lps: Sean Bean, Brian Cox, Daragh O'Malley. TVM. 104M UKN. prod/rel: Celtic Pictures

Sharpe's Siege, Novel
  Sharpe's Siege 1996 d: Tom Clegg. lps: Sean Bean, Daragh O'Malley, Abigail Cruttenden. MTV. 102M UKN.

Sharpe's Sword, Novel
  Sharpe's Sword 1995 d: Tom Clegg. lps: Sean Bean, Daragh O'Malley, Emily Mortimer. MTV. 102M UKN.

CORONER, CLET
Echappement Libre, Novel
  Echappement Libre 1964 d: Jean Becker. lps: Jean-Paul Belmondo, Jean Seberg, Gert Frobe. 105M FRN/ITL/SPN. *Scappamento Aperto* (ITL); *A Escape Libre* (SPN); *Backfire* (USA); *Der Boss Hat Sich Was Ausgedacht* (GRM); *Boss Came Up With Something, The* prod/rel: Sud Pacifique Films, Capitole Films

CORR, ETT
Story
  White Masks, The 1921 d: George Holt. lps: Franklyn Farnum, Albert Hart, Virginia Lee. 5r USA. prod/rel: William M. Smith Productions, Merit Film Corp.

CORRA, BRUNO
Inventiamo l'Amore, Play
  Inventiamo l'Amore 1938 d: Camillo Mastrocinque. lps: Evi Maltagliati, Gino Cervi, Sergio Tofano. 71M ITL. prod/rel: Scalera Film

Il Passatore, Novel
  Passatore, Il 1947 d: Duilio Coletti. lps: Rossano Brazzi, Valentina Cortese, Carlo Ninchi. 96M ITL. *A Bullet for Stefano* (USA) prod/rel: Lux Film, R.D.L.

Il Pozzo Dei Miracoli, Play
  Pozzo Dei Miracoli, Il 1941 d: Gennaro Righelli. lps: Vivi Gioi, Antonio Centa, Elena Altieri. 83M ITL. prod/rel: Imperial Film, I.C.I.

Traversata Nera, Play
  Traversata Nera 1939 d: Domenico M. Gambino. lps: Mario Ferrari, Germana Paolieri, Dria PaolA. 88M ITL. prod/rel: Sovrania Film, Generalcine

CORRIEM
Le Roi Pandore, Novel
  Roi Pandore, Le 1949 d: Andre Berthomieu. lps: Bourvil, Georges Lannes, Mathilde Casadesus. 95M FRN. prod/rel: Hoche Productions

CORRINGTON, JOHN WILLIAM
Decoration Day, Novel
  Decoration Day 1990 d: Robert Markowitz. lps: James Garner, Judith Ivey, Ruby Dee. TVM. 100M USA. prod/rel: Marian Rees Associates, Vantage Entertainment©

CORRIS, PETER
The Empty Beach, Novel
  Empty Beach, The 1985 d: Chris Thomson. lps: Bryan Brown, Anna Jemison, Belinda Giblin. 89M ASL. prod/rel: Jethro Films Pty. Ltd.©, Hoyts

CORRODI, AUGUST
Wie d'Wahrheit Wurkt, Zurich 1886, Play
  Wie d'Warret Wurkt 1933 d: Walter Lesch, Richard Schweizer. lps: Hans Rehmann, Denyse Navazza, Heinrich Gretler. 102M SWT. *Les Effets de la Verite*; *Wie d'Warret Wurkt* prod/rel: Praesens-Film

CORSARI, WILLI
Het Mysterie Van de Monscheinsonate, Novel
  Mysterie Van de Mondschein Sonate, Het 1935 d: Kurt Gerron. lps: Wiesje Van Tuinen, Louis Saalborn, Annie Verhulst. 84M NTH. *The Mystery of the Moonlight Sonata* prod/rel: Loet C. Barnstijn Prod.

CORSTON, MICHAEL
Don't Panic Chaps, Radio Play
  Don't Panic Chaps! 1959 d: George Pollock. lps: Dennis Price, George Cole, Thorley Walters. 85M UKN. prod/rel: Columbia, Hammer

CORT, H. L.
Listen Lester, Play
  Listen Lester 1924 d: William A. Seiter. lps: Louise Fazenda, Harry Myers, Eva Novak. 6242f USA. prod/rel: Sacramento Pictures, Principal Pictures

CORT, VAN
Mail-Order Bride, 1951, Short Story
  Mail Order Bride 1963 d: Burt Kennedy. lps: Keir Dullea, Buddy Ebsen, Lois Nettleton. 85M USA. *West of Montana* (UKN) prod/rel: Metro-Goldwyn-Mayer, Inc.

CORTAN, F. B.
Am Abend Auf Der Heide, Novel
  Am Abend Auf Der Heide 1941 d: Jurgen von Alten. lps: Magda Schneider, Heinz Engelmann, Gunther Luders. 98M GRM. prod/rel: Cine Allianz, Falken
Hochzeitsreis Ohne Mann, Novel
  Hochzeitsreise Zu Dritt 1939 d: Hubert MarischkA. lps: Maria Andergast, Johannes Riemann, Paul Horbiger. 93M GRM. prod/rel: Algefa, Carmi

CORTAZAR, JULIO (1914–1984), ARG
Story
  Glaserne Himmel, Der 1987 d: Nina Grosse. lps: Helmut Berger, Sylvie Orcier, Agnes Fink. 87M GRM. *The Glass Sky*; *The Glass Heaven* prod/rel: Avista Film, Voissfilm
Final Del Juego, 1964, Short Story
  Blow-Up 1966 d: Michelangelo Antonioni. lps: Vanessa Redgrave, David Hemmings, Sarah Miles. 111M UKN/ITL. prod/rel: MGM, Bridge Film (London)

CORTHIS, ANDRE
Le Criminel, Novel
  Criminel, Le 1926 d: Alexandre Ryder. lps: Andre Nox, Teresina Boronat, Madeleine Barjac. 2400m FRN. prod/rel: Majestic-Film
Son Fils, Novel
  Calvaire de Dona Pia, Le 1925 d: Henry Krauss. lps: Dolly Davis, Max Maxudian, Jean-Louis Allibert. 1800m FRN. prod/rel: Film d'Art (Vandal Et Delac)

CORWIN, NORMAN
My Client Curly, Radio Play
  Once Upon a Time 1944 d: Alexander Hall. lps: Cary Grant, Janet Blair, James Gleason. 89M USA. *Yes Sir That's My Baby!*; *Curly* prod/rel: Columbia

CORY, DESMOND
Deadfall, London 1965, Novel
  Deadfall 1967 d: Bryan Forbes. lps: Michael Caine, Giovanna Ralli, Eric Portman. 120M UKN/USA. prod/rel: 20th Century-Fox, Salamanda

CORYELL, JOHN RUSSELL (1848–1924), USA
Denman Thompson's the Old Homestead, New York 1889, Novel
  Old Homestead, The 1922 d: James Cruze. lps: Theodore Roberts, George Fawcett, T. Roy Barnes. 7696f USA. prod/rel: Famous Players-Lasky, Paramount Pictures
  Old Homestead, The 1935 d: William Nigh. lps: Mary Carlisle, Lawrence Gray, Dorothy Lee. 73M USA. prod/rel: Liberty Pictures Corp.©

COSBY, V.
Trick for Trick, New York 1932, Play
  Trick for Trick 1933 d: Hamilton MacFadden. lps: Ralph Morgan, Victor Jory, Sally Blane. 69M USA. prod/rel: Fox Film Corp.©

COSIC, DOBRICA
Daleko Je Sunce, 1951, Novel
  Daleko Je Sunce 1953 d: Rados Novakovic. lps: Branko Plesa, Dragomir Felba, Rade Markovic. 100M YGS. *The Sun Is Far Away*

COSTA, CARL
Bruder Martin, Play
  Und Der Himmel Lacht Dazu 1954 d: Axel von Ambesser. lps: Paul Horbiger, Marianne Koch, Carl Wery. 105M AUS. *Bruder Martin* prod/rel: Neue Wiener Filmproduktion

COSTA, MARTIN
Fiakermilli, Play
  Fiakermilli, Die 1953 d: Arthur M. Rabenalt. lps: Gretl Schorg, Paul Horbiger, Karl Schonbock. 90M AUS. *Fiakermilli - Liebling von Wien* prod/rel: Schonbrunn
Mariandl, Play
  Mariandl 1961 d: Werner Jacobs. lps: Conny Froboess, Rudolf Prack, Waltraut Haas. 88M AUS. prod/rel: Sascha

COSTAIN, THOMAS B. (1885–1965), CND, Costain, Thomas Bertram
The Black Rose, 1945, Novel
  Black Rose, The 1950 d: Henry Hathaway. lps: Tyrone Power, Orson Welles, Cecile Aubrey. 121M UKN/USA. prod/rel: 20th Century Productions, 20th Century-Fox
The Silver Chalice, 1952, Novel
  Silver Chalice, The 1954 d: Victor Saville. lps: Virginia Mayo, Jack Palance, Pier Angeli. 144M USA. prod/rel: Warner Bros.

COSTELLO, MARY
Titanic Town, Novel
  Titanic Town 1998 d: Roger Michell. lps: Julie Walters, Ciaran Hinds, Nuala O'Neill. 102M UKN. prod/rel: Pandora Cinema, BBC Films

COTLER, GORDON
The Bottletop Affair, New York 1959, Novel
  Horizontal Lieutenant, The 1962 d: Richard Thorpe. lps: Jim Hutton, Paula Prentiss, Jack Carter. 90M USA. prod/rel: Euterpe, Inc.

COTTE, JEAN-LOUIS
La Longue Piste, Novel
  Tetes Brulees, Les 1967 d: Willy Rozier. lps: Lang Jeffries, Philippe Clay, Jacques Dufilho. 100M FRN/SPN. *Cabezas Quemadas* (SPN) prod/rel: Valoria Films, Sport Films

COTTERELL, GEOFFREY
Tiari Tahiti, London 1960, Novel
  Tiara Tahiti 1962 d: Ted Kotcheff. lps: James Mason, John Mills, Claude Dauphin. 100M UKN. prod/rel: Rank Organisation, Rank Film Distributors

COTTRELL, H. D.
Half Breed, 1906, Play
  Half Breed, The 1922 d: Charles A. Taylor. lps: Wheeler Oakman, Ann May, Mary Anderson. 5484f USA. prod/rel: Oliver Morosco Productions, Associated First National Pictures

COUDERC, PIERRE
The Gay Caballero, Story
  Captain Thunder 1930 d: Alan Crosland. lps: Fay Wray, Victor Varconi, Charles Judels. 66M USA. *The Gay Caballero* prod/rel: Warner Brothers Pictures

COUFFER, JACK (1922–, USA
The Concrete Wilderness, New York 1967, Novel
  Medium Cool 1969 d: Haskell Wexler. lps: Robert Forster, Verna Bloom, Peter Bonerz. 111M USA. *Concrete Wilderness* prod/rel: H & J Pictures

COUPON, HENRI
Le Verdict, Novel
  Verdict, Le 1974 d: Andre Cayatte. lps: Sophia Loren, Jean Gabin, Julien Bertheau. 98M FRN/ITL. *L' Accusa E: Violenza Carnale E Omicido* (ITL); *Le Testament*; *Jury of One*; *Verdict* prod/rel: Concordia, P.E.C.F.

COURTELINE, GEORGES
L' Article 330, 1900, Play
  Article 330, L' 1934 d: Marcel Pagnol. lps: Robert Le Vigan, Andre Robert, Jean d'Yd. 40M FRN. prod/rel: Les Auteurs Associes
Boubouroche, Play
  Boubouroche 1911 d: Georges MoncA. lps: Muffat, Georges Treville, Henri Bosc. 260m FRN. prod/rel: Scagl
  Boubouroche 1933 d: Andre Hugon. lps: Jean Brochard, Claude Dauphin, Robert Le Vigan. 45M FRN. prod/rel: Les Productions Andre Hugon
Les Boulingrin, 1914, Play
  Scenes de Menage 1954 d: Andre Berthomieu. lps: Sophie Desmarets, Francois Perier, Bernard Blier. 80M FRN. prod/rel: Franco-London Films
Un Client Serieux, 1897, Play
  Client Serieux, Un 1918 d: Jacques Gretillat. lps: Leon Bernard, Charles Lamy, Alexandre Vargas. 800m FRN. prod/rel: Pathe Consortium
  Client Serieux, Un 1932 d: Claude Autant-LarA. lps: Paul Faivre, Pre Fils, Henri Niel. 22M FRN. prod/rel: Paramount
Le Commissaire Est Bon Enfant, 1899, Play
  Commissaire Est Bon Enfant, le Gendarme Est Sans Pitie, le 1934 d: Jacques Becker, Pierre Prevert. lps: Marcelle Monthil, Jacques Becker, Pierre Palau. 40M FRN. *Pitiless Gendarme* prod/rel: Oberon Films, Andre H. Des Fontaines

Les Gaietes de l'Escadron, 1886, Play
  Allegro Squadrone, L' 1954 d: Paolo MoffA. lps: Vittorio de Sica, Daniel Gelin, Alberto Sordi. 90M ITL/FRN. *Les Gaites de l'Escadron* (FRN); *Un Giorno in Caserna*; *Alberto Il Marmittone* prod/rel: Film Costellazione, Zebra Film (Roma)
  Gaietes de l'Escadron, Les 1932 d: Maurice Tourneur. lps: Raimu, Jean Gabin, Mady Berry. 85M FRN. prod/rel: Pathe-Natan
Le Gendarme Est Sans Pitie, 1899, Play
  Gendarme Est San Pitie, Le 1932 d: Claude Autant-LarA. lps: Louis Ravet, Georges Cahuzac, Charles Camus. 20M FRN. prod/rel: Paramount
Lidoire, 1892, Play
  Lidoire 1913 d: Andre Liabel. 530m FRN. prod/rel: Eclair
  Lidoire 1933 d: Maurice Tourneur. lps: Jean-Francois Martial, Marcel Magnat, Germaine Michel. 20M FRN. prod/rel: Pathe-Natan
Messieurs Les Ronds-de-Cuir, 1893, Novel
  Messieurs Les Ronds de Cuir 1914 d: Andre Liabel. lps: Marchal, Cesar, Mlle Gallet. 490m FRN. prod/rel: Eclair
  Messieurs Les Ronds de Cuir 1936 d: Yves Mirande. lps: Lucien Baroux, Pierre Larquey, Josette Day. 100M FRN. prod/rel: Paris Cine Film
  Messieurs Les Ronds-de-Cuir 1959 d: Henri Diamant-Berger. lps: Noel-Noel, Micheline Dax, Pierre Brasseur. 85M FRN. prod/rel: Film d'Art, Discifilm
Monsieur Badin, Play
  Monsieur Badin 1912. FRN. prod/rel: Gaumont
  Monsieur Badin 1947 d: Georges Regnier. lps: Jean Tissier, Guy Favieres, Sylvain. 13M FRN. prod/rel: Pantheon Production
Monsieur Vernet, Play
  Monsieur Vernet 1916. lps: Jeanne Cheirel. FRN.
La Paix Chez Soi, 1903, Play
  Paix Chez Soi, La 1929. lps: Beatrix Dussane, Jacques Guilhene. SHT FRN. prod/rel: Gaumont
  Scenes de Menage 1954 d: Andre Berthomieu. lps: Sophie Desmarets, Francois Perier, Bernard Blier. 80M FRN. prod/rel: Franco-London Films
La Peur Des Coups, 1895, Play
  Peur Des Coups, La 1932 d: Claude Autant-LarA. lps: Fernand Frey, Henriette Delannoy, Jean Guillet. 600m FRN. prod/rel: Paramount
  Scenes de Menage 1954 d: Andre Berthomieu. lps: Sophie Desmarets, Francois Perier, Bernard Blier. 80M FRN. prod/rel: Franco-London Films
Theodore Cherche Des Allumettes, Play
  Theodore Cherche Des Allumettes 1923 d: Andrew F. Brunelle. lps: Rene Hieronimus, Herendt, Serval. 1000m FRN.
Le Train de 8H.47, 1891, Novel
  Train de 8H.47, Le 1925 d: Georges Pallu. lps: Georges Gauthier, Max Lerel, Louis Moret. F FRN. prod/rel: Isis Films
  Train de 8H.47, Le 1934 d: Henry Wulschleger. lps: Bach, Fernandel, Fernand Charpin. 80M FRN. *The 8.47 Train* prod/rel: Alex Nalpas, Cie Francaise Cinematographique Lux

COURTENAY, BRYCE
The Power of One, Novel
  Power of One, The 1992 d: John G. Avildsen. lps: Stephen Dorff, Armin Mueller-Stahl, Morgan Freeman. 127M USA. prod/rel: Warner Bros.

COURTENAY, SYD
The Idol of Moolah, Play
  Kiss Me Sergeant 1930 d: Monty Banks. lps: Leslie Fuller, Gladys Cruickshank, Gladys Frazin. 56M UKN. prod/rel: British International Pictures, Wardour

COUSINS, MARGARET (1905–, USA
The Life of Lucy Gallant, Novel
  Lucy Gallant 1955 d: Robert Parrish. lps: Jane Wyman, Charlton Heston, Claire Trevor. 104M USA. *Oil Town* prod/rel: Paramount, Pine-Thomas

COUSINS, NORMAN
Anatomy of an Illness, Autobiography
  Anatomy of an Illness 1984 d: Richard T. Heffron. lps: Eli Wallach, Edward Asner, Millie Perkins. TVM. 98M USA. prod/rel: CBS, Twentieth Century Fox

COUTEAUX, ANDRE
Un Monsieur de Compagnie, Paris 1961, Novel
  Monsieur de Compagnie, Un 1964 d: Philippe de BrocA. lps: Jean-Pierre Cassel, Catherine Deneuve, Jean-Pierre Marielle. 94M FRN/ITL. *Poi Ti Sposero* (ITL); *Male Companion* (USA); *I Was a Male Sex Bomb* prod/rel: P.E.C.F., Ultra Film

COUTTIE, EARLE
Something About a Sailor, Play
Watch Your Stern 1960 d: Gerald Thomas. lps: Kenneth Connor, Eric Barker, Leslie Phillips. 88M UKN. prod/rel: Gregory, Hake & Walker, Anglo-Amalgamated

COUVREUR, ANDRE
Le Lynx, Novel
Lynx, Le 1914 d: Bernard-Deschamps. 900m FRN. prod/rel: Cosmograph

COWAN, SADA
Playing the Game, Play
Woman Under Cover, The 1919 d: George Siegmann. lps: Fritzi Brunette, George McDaniel, Harry Spingler. 5645f USA. prod/rel: Universal Film Mfg. Co.©

COWAN, SAM K.
War Diary of Sergeant York, Book
Sergeant York 1941 d: Howard Hawks. lps: Gary Cooper, Walter Brennan, Joan Leslie. 134M USA. prod/rel: Warner Bros.

COWARD, NOEL (1899–1973), UKN, Coward, Noel Pierce
The Astonished Heart, 1936, Play
Astonished Heart, The 1950 d: Anthony Darnborough, Terence Fisher. lps: Noel Coward, Celia Johnson, Margaret Leighton. 89M UKN. prod/rel: Gainsborough, General Film Distributors

Bitter Sweet, London 1929, Operetta
Bitter Sweet 1933 d: Herbert Wilcox. lps: Anna Neagle, Fernand Gravey, Ivy St. Helier. 93M UKN. prod/rel: British and Dominions, United Artists
Bitter Sweet 1940 d: W. S. Van Dyke. lps: Jeanette MacDonald, Nelson Eddy, George Sanders. 92M USA. prod/rel: Metro-Goldwyn-Mayer Corp.

Blithe Spirit, London 1941, Play
Blithe Spirit 1945 d: David Lean. lps: Rex Harrison, Constance Cummings, Kay Hammond. 96M UKN. prod/rel: Two Cities, Cineguild

Cavalcade, London 1931, Play
Cavalcade 1933 d: Frank Lloyd. lps: Diana Wynyard, Clive Brook, Herbert Mundin. 110M USA. prod/rel: Fox Film Corp.
Cavalcade 1955 d: Lewis Allen. lps: Michael Wilding, Merle Oberon. MTV. 44M USA.

Design for Living, New York 1933, Play
Design for Living 1933 d: Ernst Lubitsch. lps: Fredric March, Gary Cooper, Miriam Hopkins. 90M USA. prod/rel: Paramount Productions, Inc.

Easy Virtue, London 1926, Play
Easy Virtue 1927 d: Alfred Hitchcock. lps: Isabel Jeans, Robin Irvine, Franklin Dyall. 7392f UKN. prod/rel: Gainsborough, Woolf & Freedman

Fumed Oak, 1936, Play
Meet Me Tonight 1952 d: Anthony Pelissier. lps: Valerie Hobson, Nigel Patrick, Jack Warner. 85M UKN. *Tonight at 8.30* (USA) prod/rel: British Film Makers, General Film Distributors

Hochzeitsnacht, Play
Letzte Nacht, Die 1927 d: Graham Cutts. lps: Lili Damita, Harry Liedtke, Paul Richter. 2335m GRM. *The Last Night* prod/rel: F.P.G. Film-Prod., UFA

Me and the Girls, 1965, Short Story
Me and the Girls 1985 d: Jack Gold. lps: Tom Courtenay, Nicola McAuliffe, Robert Glenister. MTV. 54M UKN.

Mister and Mrs. Edgehill, 1951, Short Story
Mister and Mrs. Edgehill 1985 d: Gavin Millar. lps: Judi Dench, Ian Holm, Rachel Gurney. MTV. 82M UKN.

Mrs. Capper's Birthday, 1965, Short Story
Mrs. Capper's Birthday 1985 d: Mike Ockrent. lps: Patricia Hayes, Max Wall, Paula Wilcox. MTV. 59M UKN.

Pretty Polly Barlow, London 1964, Short Story
Pretty Polly 1966 d: Bill Bain. lps: Lynn Redgrave, Donald Houston, Dandy Nichols. MTV. UKN. prod/rel: ABC
Pretty Polly 1967 d: Guy Green. lps: Hayley Mills, Trevor Howard, Shashi Kapoor. 102M UKN. *A Matter of Innocence* (USA) prod/rel: Mariana Productions, Universal Pictures, Ltd.

Private Lives, London 1930, Play
Amants Terribles, Les 1936 d: Marc Allegret. lps: Gaby Morlay, Marie Glory, Andre Luguet. 86M FRN. prod/rel: Pan Films
Private Lives 1931 d: Sidney A. Franklin. lps: Norma Shearer, Robert Montgomery, Una Merkel. 87M USA. prod/rel: Metro-Goldwyn-Mayer Corp., Metro-Goldwyn-Mayer Dist. Corp.©

The Queen Was in the Parlour, London 1926, Play
Queen Was in the Parlour, The 1927 d: Graham Cutts. lps: Lili Damita, Paul Richter, Harry Leichke. 7250f UKN. *Forbidden Love; Forbidden Cargo* prod/rel: Gainsborough, Piccadilly
Tonight Is Ours 1933 d: Stuart Walker, Mitchell Leisen (Uncredited). lps: Claudette Colbert, Fredric March, Edwin Maxwell. 76M USA. *The Queen Was in the Parlor* prod/rel: Paramount Productions©

Red Peppers, 1936, Play
Meet Me Tonight 1952 d: Anthony Pelissier. lps: Valerie Hobson, Nigel Patrick, Jack Warner. 85M UKN. *Tonight at 8.30* (USA) prod/rel: British Film Makers, General Film Distributors

Still Life, London 1936, Play
Brief Encounter 1945 d: David Lean. lps: Celia Johnson, Trevor Howard, Stanley Holloway. 86M UKN. prod/rel: General Film Distributors, Cineguild
Brief Encounter 1974 d: Alan Bridges. lps: Richard Burton, Sophia Loren, Jack Hedley. TVM. 115M UKN/ITL/USA. *Breve Incontro* (ITL) prod/rel: Cin.Ca Champion, Itc

This Happy Breed, London 1943, Play
This Happy Breed 1944 d: David Lean. lps: Robert Newton, Celia Johnson, John Mills. 114M UKN. prod/rel: Eagle-Lion, Two Cities

Tonight at 8.30, Play
We Were Dancing 1941 d: Robert Z. Leonard. lps: Norma Shearer, Melvyn Douglas, Gail Patrick. 94M USA. prod/rel: MGM

The Vortex, London 1924, Play
Vortex, The 1927 d: Adrian Brunel. lps: Ivor Novello, Willette Kershaw, Frances Doble. 6281f UKN. prod/rel: Gainsborough, Woolf & Freedman

Waiting in the Wings, Play
Sidste Akt 1987 d: Edward Fleming. lps: Birgitte Federspiel, Mime Fonss, Kirsten Rolffes. 101M DNM.

Ways and Means, 1936, Play
Meet Me Tonight 1952 d: Anthony Pelissier. lps: Valerie Hobson, Nigel Patrick, Jack Warner. 85M UKN. *Tonight at 8.30* (USA) prod/rel: British Film Makers, General Film Distributors

What Mad Pursuit?, 1939, Short Story
What Mad Pursuit? 1985 d: Tony Smith. lps: Carroll Baker, Paul Daneman, Neil Cunningham. MTV. 55M UKN.

COWDEN, JACK
Story
Flipper 1963 d: James B. Clark. lps: Chuck Connors, Luke Halpin, Kathleen Maguire. 90M USA. prod/rel: Ivan Tors, MGM

COWEN, LAWRENCE
The World the Flesh and the Devil, Play
World, the Flesh and the Devil, The 1914 d: F. Martin Thornton. lps: Frank Esmond, Stella St. Audrie, Warwick Wellington. 5125f UKN. prod/rel: Natural Colour Kinematograph Co., Union Jack Photoplays
World, the Flesh and the Devil, The 1932 d: George A. Cooper. lps: Harold Huth, Isla Bevan, Victor Stanley. 53M UKN. prod/rel: Real Art, Radio

COWEN, WILLIAM JOYCE
They Gave Him a Gun, New York 1936, Novel
They Gave Him a Gun 1937 d: W. S. Van Dyke. lps: Spencer Tracy, Gladys George, Franchot Tone. 97M USA. prod/rel: Metro-Goldwyn-Mayer Corp.©

COWL, JANE
Daybreak, New York 1917, Play
Daybreak 1918 d: Albert Capellani. lps: Emily Stevens, Julien L'Estrange, Augustus Phillips. 5r USA. prod/rel: Metro Pictures Corp.©

Information Please, New York 1918, Play
Temperamental Wife, A 1919 d: David Kirkland. lps: Constance Talmadge, Wyndham Standing, Ben Hendricks. 6221f USA. prod/rel: Constance Talmadge Film Co., John Emerson-Anita Loos Production

Lilac Time, New York 1917, Play
Lilac Time 1928 d: George Fitzmaurice. lps: Colleen Moore, Gary Cooper, Burr McIntosh. 9108f USA. *Love Never Dies* (UKN) prod/rel: First National Pictures

Smilin' Through, New York 1919, Play
Smilin' Through 1922 d: Sidney A. Franklin. lps: Norma Talmadge, Wyndham Standing, Harrison Ford. 8000f USA. *Smiling Through* prod/rel: Norma Talmadge Productions, Associated First National Pictures
Smilin' Through 1932 d: Sidney A. Franklin. lps: Norma Shearer, Fredric March, Leslie Howard. 100M USA. prod/rel: Metro-Goldwyn-Mayer Corp., Metro-Goldwyn-Mayer Dist. Corp.©

Smilin' Through 1941 d: Frank Borzage. lps: Jeanette MacDonald, Gene Raymond, Brian Aherne. 100M USA. prod/rel: MGM

COWLES, VIRGINIA SPENCER
Looking for Trouble, Book
Ladies Courageous 1944 d: John Rawlins. lps: Loretta Young, Geraldine Fitzgerald, Diana Barrymore. 88M USA. *When Ladies Fly* prod/rel: Universal

COWLEY, JOY
Nest in a Falling Tree, Novel
Night Digger, The 1971 d: Alastair Reid. lps: Patricia Neal, Pamela Brown, Nicholas Clay. 100M UKN. *The Road Builder* prod/rel: MGM

The Silent One, Novel
Silent One, The 1984 d: Yvonne MacKay. lps: George Henare, Pat Evison, Anzac Wallace. 95M NZL. prod/rel: Gibson Film

COWPER, WILLIAM (1731–1800), UKN
John Gilpin, 1782, Poem
John Gilpin 1908 d: Percy Stow. 495f UKN. prod/rel: Clarendon
John Gilpin's Ride 1908 d: Lewin Fitzhamon. 575f UKN. prod/rel: Hepworth

COXE, GEORGE HARMON (1901–1984), USA
Return Engagement, 1934, Short Story
Here's Flash Casey 1938 d: Lynn Shores. lps: Eric Linden, Boots Mallory, Cully Richards. 63M USA. prod/rel: Grand National Films©, Alexander Bros. Production

COXEN, MURIEL HINE
The Best in Life, New York 1918, Novel
Fifth Avenue Models 1925 d: Svend Gade. lps: Mary Philbin, Norman Kerry, Josef Swickard. 6581f USA. prod/rel: Universal Pictures

COXHEAD, ELIZABETH
The Friend in Need, Novel
Cry from the Streets, A 1958 d: Lewis Gilbert. lps: Max Bygraves, Barbara Murray, Colin Petersen. 100M UKN. prod/rel: Eros, Film Traders

COZZENS, JAMES GOULD (1903–1978), USA
By Love Possessed, New York 1957, Novel
By Love Possessed 1961 d: John Sturges. lps: Lana Turner, Efrem Zimbalist Jr., Jason Robards Jr. 115M USA. prod/rel: United Artists, Mirisch

The Last Adam, New York 1933, Novel
Doctor Bull 1933 d: John Ford. lps: Will Rogers, Marian Nixon, Ralph Morgan. 77M USA. *Life's Worth Living; The Last Adam* prod/rel: Fox Film Corp.

CRAIG, DAVID
The Squeeze, Novel
Squeeze, The 1977 d: Michael Apted. lps: Stacy Keach, Edward Fox, Stephen Boyd. 106M UKN. prod/rel: Warner Bros., Martinat

CRAIG, DORIN
The Key of the World, Novel
Key of the World, The 1918 d: J. L. V. Leigh. lps: Eileen Molyneux, Heather Thatcher, Eric Harrison. 6202f UKN. prod/rel: Gaumont

Mist in the Valley, Novel
Mist in the Valley 1923 d: Cecil M. Hepworth. lps: Alma Taylor, G. H. Mulcaster, James Carew. 6715f UKN. prod/rel: Hepworth

CRAIG, JAMES
If You Want to See Your Wife Again, Novel
Your Money Or Your Wife 1972 d: Allen Reisner. lps: Ted Bessell, Elizabeth Ashley, Jack Cassidy. TVM. 73M USA. prod/rel: Brentwood Productions

CRAIK, DINAH MARIA (1826–1887), UKN
John Halifax - Gentleman, 1857, Novel
John Halifax, Gentleman 1910 d: Theodore Marston. lps: Frank Crane, William Russell. 1000f USA. prod/rel: Thanhouser
John Halifax, Gentleman 1915 d: George Pearson. lps: Fred Paul, Peggy Hyland, Harry Paulo. 5350f UKN. prod/rel: G. B. Samuelson, Moss
John Halifax, Gentleman 1938 d: George King. lps: John Warwick, Nancy Burne, Ralph Michael. 69M UKN. prod/rel: George King, MGM

CRAM, MILDRED
Short Story
Wings Over Honolulu 1937 d: H. C. Potter. lps: Wendy Barrie, Ray Milland, William Gargan. 78M USA. prod/rel: Universal Pictures Co.©
The Feeder, 1926, Short Story
Behind the Make-Up 1930 d: Robert Milton, Dorothy Arzner. lps: Hal Skelly, William Powell, Fay Wray. 6364f USA. prod/rel: Paramount Famous Lasky Corp.
Maquillage 1932 d: Karl Anton. lps: Rosine Derean, Edwige Feuillere, Saint-Granier. 80M FRN. *Je T'attendrai* prod/rel: Films Paramount

Girls Together, 1931, Short Story
This Modern Age 1931 d: Nick Grinde, Clarence Brown (Uncredited). lps: Joan Crawford, Neil Hamilton, Marjorie Rambeau. 68M USA. *Girls Together* prod/rel: Metro-Goldwyn-Mayer Corp., Metro-Goldwyn-Mayer Dist. Corp.©

Sadie of the Desert, 1925, Short Story
Subway Sadie 1926 d: Alfred Santell. lps: Dorothy MacKaill, Jack Mulhall, Charlie Murray. 6727f USA. prod/rel: Al Rockett Productions, First National Pictures

Scotch Valley, New York 1928, Novel
Amateur Daddy 1932 d: John G. Blystone. lps: Warner Baxter, Marian Nixon, Rita La Roy. 74M USA. *Scotch Valley; Bachelor Affairs* prod/rel: Fox Film Corp.

Thin Air, 1934, Short Story
Stars Over Broadway 1935 d: William Keighley. lps: James Melton, Jane Froman, Pat O'Brien. 89M USA. *Radio Jamboree* prod/rel: Warner Bros. Pictures©

CRANE, MACK
Bombshell, Play
Bombshell 1933 d: Victor Fleming. lps: Jean Harlow, Lee Tracy, Frank Morgan. 97M USA. *Blonde Bombshell* (UKN) prod/rel: Metro-Goldwyn-Mayer Corp.

CRANE, STEPHEN (1871–1900), USA, Crane, Stephen Townley
The Blue Hotel, 1899, Short Story
Blue Hotel, The 1977 d: Jan Kadar. lps: David Warner, James Keach, John Bottoms. MTV. 52M USA. prod/rel: Learning in Focus

The Bride Comes to Yellow Sky, 1898, Short Story
Face to Face 1952 d: John Brahm, Bretaigne Windust. lps: James Mason, Michael Pate, Gene Lockhart. 92M USA. prod/rel: RKO Radio, Theasquare Prods.

The Monster, 1899, Short Story
Mannen Utan Ansikte 1959 d: Albert Band. lps: Cameron Mitchell, James Whitmore, Bettye Ackerman. 83M SWD/USA. *Face of Fire* (USA) prod/rel: Allied Artists, Mardi Gras

The Red Badge of Courage, 1895, Novel
Red Badge of Courage, The 1951 d: John Huston. lps: Audie Murphy, Bill Maudlin, John Dierkes. 69M USA. prod/rel: MGM

Red Badge of Courage, The 1974 d: Lee Philips. lps: Richard Thomas, Michael Brandon, Wendell Burton. TVM. 78M USA. prod/rel: 20th Century-Fox

Three Miraculous Soldiers, 1896, Short Story
Three Miraculous Soldiers 1977 d: Bernard Selling. 17M USA.

CRANSTON, J. HERBERT
Etienne Brule - Immortal Scoundrel, Book
Etienne Brule Gibier de Potence 1952 d: Melburn E. Turner. lps: Paul Dupuis, Jacques Auger, Ginette Letondal. 102M CND. prod/rel: Carillon Pictures Ltd.

CRAVEN, FRANK
The First Year, New York 1920, Play
First Year, The 1926 d: Frank Borzage. lps: Matt Moore, Kathryn Perry, John Patrick. 6038f USA. prod/rel: Fox Film Corp.

First Year, The 1932 d: William K. Howard. lps: Janet Gaynor, Charles Farrell, Minna Gombell. 80M USA. prod/rel: Fox Film Corp.©, William K. Howard Production

New Brooms, New York 1925, Play
New Brooms 1925 d: William C. de Mille. lps: Neil Hamilton, Bessie Love, Phyllis Haver. 5443f USA. prod/rel: Famous Players-Lasky, Paramount Pictures

Salt Water, New York 1929, Play
Her First Mate 1933 d: William Wyler. lps: Slim Summerville, Zasu Pitts, Una Merkel. 70M USA. prod/rel: Universal Pictures Corp.©

That's Gratitude, New York 1930, Play
That's Gratitude 1934 d: Frank Craven. lps: Frank Craven, Mary Carlisle, Arthur Byron. 70M USA. prod/rel: Foy Productions, Columbia Pictures Corp.©

Too Many Cooks, New York 1914, Play
Too Many Cooks 1931 d: William A. Seiter. lps: Bert Wheeler, Dorothy Lee, Roscoe Ates. 77M USA. prod/rel: RKO Radio Pictures©

CRAVEN, MARGARET
I Heard the Owl Call My Name, Book
I Heard the Owl Call My Name 1973 d: Daryl Duke. lps: Tom Courtenay, Dean Jagger, Paul Stanley. TVM. 73M USA. prod/rel: Tomorrow Entertainment

CRAWFORD, ANNIE
Kathleen Mavourneen, 1840, Song
Kathleen Mavourneen 1919 d: Charles J. Brabin. lps: Theda Bara, Raymond McKee, Marc McDermott. 5-6r USA. prod/rel: Fox Film Corp., William Fox©

CRAWFORD, CHRISTINA (1939–, USA
Mommie Dearest, Book
Mommie Dearest 1981 d: Frank Perry. lps: Faye Dunaway, Diana Scarwid, Steve Forrest. 129M USA. prod/rel: Paramount

CRAWFORD, CLIFTON
My Best Girl, New York 1912, Musical Play
My Best Girl 1915. lps: Max Figman, Lois Meredith, Lawrence Peyton. 5r USA. prod/rel: Rolfe Photoplays, Inc., Metro Pictures Corp.©

CRAWFORD, F. MARION (1854–1909), USA
In the Palace of the King; a Love Story of Old Madrid, New York 1900, Novel
In the Palace of the King 1915 d: Fred E. Wright. lps: E. J. Ratcliffe, Richard C. Travers, Arline Hackett. 6r USA. prod/rel: Essanay Film Mfg. Co.©, V-L-S-E, Inc.

In the Palace of the King 1923 d: Emmett J. Flynn. lps: Blanche Sweet, Edmund Lowe, Hobart Bosworth. 8657f USA. prod/rel: Goldwyn Pictures, Goldwyn-Cosmopolitan Distributing Corp.

Mr. Isaacs, New York 1882, Novel
Son of India 1931 d: Jacques Feyder. lps: Ramon Novarro, Conrad Nagel, C. Aubrey Smith. 75M USA. *The Son of the Rajah* prod/rel: Metro-Goldwyn-Mayer Corp., Metro-Goldwyn-Mayer Dist. Corp.©

Sant'Ilario, Novel
Sant'ilario 1923 d: Henry Kolker. lps: Edy Darclea, Sandro Salvini, Elena LundA. 1992m ITL. *S. Ilario* prod/rel: Ultra Film

The White Sister, New York 1909, Novel
White Sister, The 1915 d: Fred E. Wright. lps: Viola Allen, Richard C. Travers, Arline Hackett. 6r USA. prod/rel: Essanay Film Mfg. Co.©, V-L-S-E, Inc.

White Sister, The 1923 d: Henry King. lps: Lillian Gish, Ronald Colman, Gail Kane. 13r USA. prod/rel: Inspirational Pictures, Metro Pictures

White Sister, The 1933 d: Victor Fleming. lps: Helen Hayes, Clark Gable, Lewis Stone. 105M USA. prod/rel: Metro-Goldwyn-Mayer Corp., Victor Fleming Production

CRAWFORD, MARION
A Cigarette-Maker's Romance, Novel
Cigarette-Maker's Romance, A 1920 d: Tom Watts. lps: R. Henderson Bland, Dorothy Vernon, William Parry. 5000f UKN. prod/rel: International Producers Federation

Cigarette-Maker's Romance, A 1913 d: Frank Wilson. lps: John Martin-Harvey, Nell de Silva, Margaret Yarde. 4000f UKN. prod/rel: Hepworth, Gaumont

Whosoever Shall Offend, Novel
Whosoever Shall Offend 1919 d: Arrigo Bocchi. lps: Kenelm Foss, Odette Goimbault, Mary Marsh Allen. 5900f UKN. prod/rel: Windsor, Walturdaw

CRAWFORD, OLIVER
Blood on the Branches, Novel
Girl in the Woods 1958 d: Tom Gries. lps: Forrest Tucker, Margaret Hayes, Barton MacLane. 71M USA. prod/rel: Republic Pictures Corp., Ab-Pt Pictures

The Execution, Novel
Execution, The 1985 d: Paul Wendkos. lps: Loretta Swit, Rip Torn, Valerie Harper. TVM. 104M USA. prod/rel: NBC, Newland-Raynor Productions

CRAWSHAY-WILLIAMS, ELIOT
Une Nuit a l'Hotel, Novel
Nuit a l'Hotel, La 1931 d: Leo Mittler. lps: Jean Perier, Marcelle Romee, Betty Stockfeld. 84M FRN. prod/rel: Films Paramount

CREAMER, ROBERT W.
Babe: the Legend Comes to Life, Book
Babe Ruth 1991 d: Mark Tinker. lps: Stephen Lang, Bruce Weitz, Brian Doyle-Murray. TVM. 100M USA. *The Babe*

CREANGA, ION
Amintiri Din Copilarie, 1881-92, Autobiography
Amintiri Din Copilarie 1964 d: Elisabeta Bostan. 59M RMN. *Recollections from Childhood*

Capra Cu Trei Iezi, 1875, Short Story
Ma-Ma 1977 d: Elisabeta Bostan. lps: George Mihaita, Florian Pittis, Ludmila Gurcenko. 89M RMN/USS/FRN. *Mama; Mummy; Rock 'N' Roll Wolf*

Povestea Lui Harap Alb, 1877, Short Story
de-As Fi Harap Alb 1965 d: Ion Popescu-Gopo. lps: Irina Petrusca, Florin Piersic, Chistea Avram. 91M RMN. *White Moor; Harap Alb;* **If I Were Harap Alb**

Povestea Porcului, 1876, Short Story
Povestea Dragostei 1976 d: Ion Popescu-Gopo. lps: Eugenia Popovici, Mircea Bogdan, Nicolae Ifrim. 83M RMN. *The Story of Love; Love's Story*

Punguta Cu Doi Bani, 1876, Short Story
Ramasagul 1985 d: Ion Popescu-Gopo. 87M RMN. *The Bet*

CREASEY, JOHN (1908–1973), UKN, Marric, J. J., Deane, Norman
Gideon's Day, Novel
Gideon's Day 1959 d: John Ford. lps: Jack Hawkins, Dianne Foster, Cyril Cusack. 91M UKN. *Gideon of Scotland Yard* (USA) prod/rel: Columbia British

Hammer the Toff, Novel
Hammer the Toff 1952 d: MacLean Rogers. lps: John Bentley, Patricia Dainton, Valentine Dyall. 71M UKN. prod/rel: Nettlefold, Butcher's Film Service

Salute the Toff, Novel
Salute the Toff 1952 d: MacLean Rogers. lps: John Bentley, Carol Marsh, Valentine Dyall. 75M UKN. *Brighthaven Express* (USA) prod/rel: Nettlefold, Butcher's Film Service

CREED, GERALDINE
The Sun the Moon and the Stars, Short Story
Sun the Moon and the Stars, The 1996 d: Geraldine Creed. lps: Jason Donovan, Gina Moxley, Angie Dickinson. 92M IRL. prod/rel: Blue Light Productions

CREELMAN, JAMES ASHMORE
Jazz King, 1928, Play
Dancers in the Dark 1932 d: David Burton. lps: Miriam Hopkins, Jack Oakie, George Raft. 74M USA. *Jazz King; Dance Palace* prod/rel: Paramount Publix Corp.

CRESSE, R. W.
Hot Spur, Novel
Hot Spur 1968 d: R. L. Frost. lps: James Arena, Virginia Gordon, Joseph Mascolo. 91M USA. *The Naked Spur; Fiery Spur; The Longest Spur* prod/rel: Olympic International

CRESSWELL, HELEN
Moondial, Novel
Moondial 1990 d: Colin Grant. lps: Helen Cresswell, Siri Neal. TVM. 113M UKN.

CRICHTON, KYLE
The Happiest Millionaire, New York 1956, Play
Happiest Millionaire, The 1967 d: Norman Tokar. lps: Fred MacMurray, Tommy Steele, Greer Garson. 164M USA. prod/rel: Walt Disney Productions

CRICHTON, MICHAEL (1942–, USA, Hudson, Jeffrey, Lange, John
The Andromeda Strain, Novel
Andromeda Strain, The 1971 d: Robert Wise. lps: Arthur Hill, David Wayne, James Olson. 137M USA. prod/rel: Universal, Robert Wise

Binary, Novel
Pursuit 1972 d: Michael Crichton. lps: Ben Gazzara, E. G. Marshall, William Windom. TVM. 73M USA. *Binary; Explosion* prod/rel: ABC Circle Films

A Case of Need, Novel
Carey Treatment, The 1972 d: Blake Edwards. lps: James Coburn, Jennifer O'Neill, Pat Hingle. 101M USA. *Emergency Ward* prod/rel: MGM

Congo, Novel
Congo 1995 d: Frank Marshall. lps: Dylan Walsh, Laura Linney, Ernie Hudson. 108M USA. prod/rel: Paramount

Dealing, Novel
Dealing: Or the Berkeley-to-Boston Forty-Brick Lost-Bag Blues 1972 d: Paul Williams. lps: Robert F. Lyons, Barbara Hershey, John Lithgow. 99M USA. prod/rel: Warner Bros.

The Great Train Robbery, Novel
First Great Train Robbery, The 1979 d: Michael Crichton. lps: Sean Connery, Donald Sutherland, Lesley-Anne Down. 110M UKN/USA. *The Great Train Robbery* (USA) prod/rel: United Artists Corp., Starling

The Lost World, Novel
Lost World: Jurassic Park, The 1997 d: Steven Spielberg. lps: Jeff Goldblum, Julianne Moore, Peter Postlethwaite. 134M USA. prod/rel: Amblin Entertainment, Universal City Studios

Rising Sun, Novel
Rising Sun 1993 d: Philip Kaufman. lps: Sean Connery, Wesley Snipes, Harvey Keitel. 129M USA. prod/rel: Twentieth Century-Fox

Sphere, Novel
Sphere 1998 d: Barry Levinson. lps: Dustin Hoffman, Sharon Stone, Samuel L. Jackson. 134M USA. prod/rel: Baltimore Pictures, Constant C

The Terminal Man, Novel
Terminal Man, The 1973 d: Mike Hodges. lps: George Segal, Joan Hackett, Richard Dysart. 107M USA. prod/rel: Warner Bros.

CRICHTON, ROBERT (1925–, USA
The Great Impostor, New York 1959, Novel
Great Impostor, The 1960 d: Robert Mulligan. lps: Tony Curtis, Edmond O'Brien, Arthur O'Connell. 112M USA. prod/rel: Universal Pictures

The Secret of Santa Vittoria, New York 1966, Novel
Secret of Santa Vittoria, The 1969 d: Stanley Kramer. lps: Anthony Quinn, Hardy Kruger, Anna Magnani. 140M USA. prod/rel: Stanley Kramer Corporation, United Artists

CRIDER, DOROTHY
I Married a Dog, Short Story
Wild and Wonderful 1964 d: Michael Anderson. lps: Tony Curtis, Christine Kaufmann, Larry Storch. 88M USA. *Monsieur Cognac* prod/rel: Harold Hecht, Universal Pictures

CRISP, FRANK
The Night Callers, London 1960, Novel
Night Caller, The 1966 d: John Gilling. lps: John Saxon, Maurice Denham, Patricia Haines. 84M UKN. *Blood Beast from Outer Space* (USA); *Night Caller from Outer Space* prod/rel: Butcher's Film Service, New Art

CRISP, LYNDALL
Article
Army Wives 1986 d: Denny Lawrence. lps: Julie Nihill, Lian Lunson, Shane Connor. TVM. 97M ASL. *When Duty Calls* (UKN) prod/rel: Roadshow, Coote & Carroll

CRISP, N. J.
Dangerous Obsession, Play
Darkness Falls 1998 d: Gerry Lively. lps: Sherilyn Fenn, Ray Winstone, Tim Dutton. F UKN. prod/rel: Hoseplace Ltd.©, Film Development Corporation

CRISP, QUENTIN (1908–, UKN, Pratt, Denis
The Naked Civil Servant, Autobiography
Naked Civil Servant, The 1975 d: Jack Gold. lps: John Hurt, Liz Gebhardt, Stanley Lebor. TVM. 78M UKN. prod/rel: Thames Television

CRISSEY, FORREST
Gumshoes 4-B, 1919, Short Story
Bab's Candidate 1920 d: Edward H. Griffith. lps: Corinne Griffith, George Fawcett, Webster Campbell. 4894f USA. *Gumshoes 4-B* prod/rel: Vitagraph Co. of America©, Corinne Griffith Production

CROCE, GIULIO CESARE
Bertoldo Bertoldino E Cacasenno, Poem
Bertoldo, Bertoldino E Cacasenno 1936 d: Giorgio C. Simonelli. lps: Cesco Bassegio, Olga Capri, Fausto Guerzoni. 2439m ITL. prod/rel: Consorzio Autori Prod. Filmi Italiani, C.a.P.F.I.

Bertoldo, Bertoldino E Cacasenno 1954 d: Mario Amendola, Ruggero MacCari. lps: Vinicio Sofia, Alberto Sorrentino, Fulvia Franco. 85M ITL. prod/rel: Felix Nova Film, Minerva Film

Bertoldo, Bertoldino E Cacasenno 1984 d: Mario Monicelli, Maurizio Nichetti. lps: Ugo Tognazzi, Alberto Sordi, Maurizio Nichetti. 121M ITL.

CROCKETT, LUCY HERNDON
The Magnificent Bastards, 1954, Novel
Proud and the Profane, The 1956 d: George Seaton. lps: Deborah Kerr, William Holden, Thelma Ritter. 111M USA. prod/rel: Paramount, Perlberg-Seaton

CROCKETT, S. R.
The Lilac Sunbonnet, Novel
Lilac Sunbonnet, The 1922 d: Sidney Morgan. lps: Joan Morgan, Warwick Ward, Pauline Peters. 5180f UKN. prod/rel: Progress, Butcher's Film Service

A Lowland Cinderella, Novel
Lowland Cinderella, A 1921 d: Sidney Morgan. lps: Joan Morgan, George Foley, Ralph Forbes. 5300f UKN. prod/rel: Progress, Butcher's Film Service

CROFT, MICHAEL
Spare the Rod, Novel
Spare the Rod 1961 d: Leslie Norman. lps: Max Bygraves, Donald Pleasence, Geoffrey Keen. 93M UKN. prod/rel: Bryanston, Weyland

CROFT-COOKE, RUPERT (1903–1979), UKN
Clash By Night, London 1962, Novel
Clash By Night 1963 d: Montgomery Tully. lps: Terence Longdon, Jennifer Jayne, Harry Fowler. 75M UKN. *Escape By Night* (USA) prod/rel: Eternal Film, Grand National

Seven Thunders, Novel
Seven Thunders 1957 d: Hugo Fregonese. lps: Stephen Boyd, James Robertson Justice, Kathleen Harrison. 100M UKN. *The Beasts of Marseilles* (USA) prod/rel: Dial, Rank Film Distributors

CROMMELYNCK, FERNAND
Le Cocu Magnifique, Paris 1920, Play
Cocu Magnifique, Le 1946 d: E. G. de Meyst. lps: Jean-Louis Barrault, Maria Mauban, Berthe Charmal. 90M FRN/BLG. prod/rel: Belnapro

Magnifico Cornuto, Il 1964 d: Antonio Pietrangeli. lps: Claudia Cardinale, Ugo Tognazzi, Bernard Blier. 124M ITL/FRN. *Le Cocu Magnifique* (FRN); *The Magnificent Cuckold* (USA) prod/rel: Sancro Film (Roma), Les Films Copernic (Paris)

Le Sculpteur de Masques, Play
Sculpteur de Masques, Le 1910. lps: Armand Bour, Gina Barbieri. 180m FRN. prod/rel: Pathe

CROMPTON, RICHMAL (1890–1969), UKN
Short Stories
Just William 1939 d: Graham Cutts. lps: Dicky Lupino, Fred Emney, Basil Radford. 72M UKN. prod/rel: Associated British Picture Corporation

Short Story
Just William's Luck 1947 d: Val Guest. lps: William Graham, Leslie Bradley, A. E. Matthews. 92M UKN. prod/rel: Alliance, Diadem

William Comes to Town 1948 d: Val Guest. lps: William Graham, Garry Marsh, Jane Welsh. 89M UKN. *William at the Circus* prod/rel: Diadem, Alliance

CRONIN, A. J. (1896–1981), UKN, Cronin, Archibald Joseph
Beyond This Place, 1953, Novel
Beyond This Place 1959 d: Jack Cardiff. lps: Van Johnson, Vera Miles, Emlyn Williams. 90M UKN. *Web of Evidence* (USA) prod/rel: Renown, Georgefield

The Citadel, 1937, Novel
Citadel, The 1938 d: King Vidor. lps: Robert Donat, Rosalind Russell, Ralph Richardson. 110M UKN/USA. prod/rel: MGM British

Citadel, The 1983 d: Peter Jeffries, Mike Vardy. lps: Ben Cross, Gareth Thomas, Michael Cunningham. MTV. 300M UKN. prod/rel: BBC

Tere Mere Sapne 1971 d: Vijay Anand. lps: Vijay Anand, Dev Anand, Mumtaz. 175M IND. *Our Dreams* prod/rel: Navketan, Vijay Anand Prod.

The Grand Canary, London 1933, Novel
Grand Canary 1934 d: Irving Cummings. lps: Warner Baxter, Madge Evans, Marjorie Rambeau. 78M USA. prod/rel: Fox Film Corp.©, Jesse L. Lasky Production

The Green Years, 1944, Novel
Green Years, The 1946 d: Victor Saville. lps: Charles Coburn, Tom Drake, Beverly Tyler. 128M USA. prod/rel: MGM

Hatters Castle, 1931, Novel
Hatter's Castle 1941 d: Lance Comfort. lps: Robert Newton, Deborah Kerr, Emlyn Williams. 102M UKN. prod/rel: Paramount British

Jupiter Laughs, 1940, Play
Ich Suche Dich 1953 d: O. W. Fischer. lps: O. W. Fischer, Anouk Aimee, Nadja Tiller. 95M GRM. prod/rel: O. W. Fischer, N.F.

Shining Victory 1941 d: Irving Rapper. lps: James Stephenson, Geraldine Fitzgerald, Donald Crisp. 80M USA. *Winged Victory* prod/rel: Warner Bros.

Kaleidoscope in K, 1933, Short Story
Once to Every Woman 1934 d: Lambert Hillyer. lps: Ralph Bellamy, Fay Wray, Walter Connolly. 70M USA. prod/rel: Columbia Pictures Corp.©

The Keys of the Kingdom, 1941, Novel
Keys of the Kingdom, The 1944 d: John M. Stahl. lps: Gregory Peck, Thomas Mitchell, Vincent Price. 137M USA. prod/rel: 20th Century-Fox

The Spanish Gardener, 1950, Novel
Spanish Gardener, The 1956 d: Philip Leacock. lps: Dirk Bogarde, Jon Whiteley, Michael Hordern. 97M UKN. prod/rel: Rank, Rank Film Distributors

The Stars Look Down, 1935, Novel
Stars Look Down, The 1939 d: Carol Reed. lps: Michael Redgrave, Margaret Lockwood, Emlyn Williams. 104M UKN. prod/rel: Grafton, Grand National

Vigil in the Night, Cleveland 1941, Novel
Vigil in the Night 1940 d: George Stevens. lps: Carole Lombard, Brian Aherne, Anne Shirley. 96M USA. prod/rel: RKO Radio Pictures©

CRONIN, MICHAEL
Paid in Full, Novel
Johnny on the Spot 1954 d: MacLean Rogers. lps: Hugh McDermott, Elspet Gray, Paul Carpenter. 72M UKN. prod/rel: E. J. Fancey, New Realm

You Pay Your Money, Novel
You Pay Your Money 1957 d: MacLean Rogers. lps: Hugh McDermott, Jane Hylton, Honor Blackman. 67M UKN. prod/rel: Butcher's Film Service

CRONLEY, JAY
Funny Farm, Book
Funny Farm 1988 d: George Roy Hill. lps: Chevy Chase, Madolyn Smith, Joseph Maher. 101M USA. prod/rel: Warner Bros.

Good Vibes, Novel
Let It Ride 1989 d: Joe Pytka. lps: Richard Dreyfuss, Teri Garr, David Johansen. 86M USA. prod/rel: Paramount

Quick Change, Novel
Hold-Up 1985 d: Alexandre Arcady. lps: Jean-Paul Belmondo, Guy Marchand, Kim Cattrall. 114M FRN/CND. *Quick Change* prod/rel: Cerito Films (Paris), Les Films Ariane (Paris)

Quick Change 1990 d: Howard Franklin, Bill Murray. lps: Bill Murray, Geena Davis, Randy Quaid. 88M USA. prod/rel: Warner Bros., Devoted

CROSBY, PERCY LEE
Dear Sooky, New York 1929, Novel
Sooky 1931 d: Norman Taurog. lps: Jackie Cooper, Robert Coogan, Robert Coogan, Robert Searl. 85M USA. prod/rel: Paramount Publix Corp.©

Skippy, New York 1929, Novel
Skippy 1931 d: Norman Taurog. lps: Jackie Cooper, Robert Coogan, Mitzi Green. 88M USA. prod/rel: Paramount Publix Corp.©

CROSS, RUTH
The Golden Cocoon, New York 1924, Novel
Golden Cocoon, The 1926 d: Millard Webb. lps: Huntley Gordon, Helene Chadwick, Richard Tucker. 7200f USA. prod/rel: Warner Brothers Pictures

A Question of Honor, 1920, Short Story
Question of Honor, A 1922 d: Edwin Carewe. lps: Anita Stewart, Edward Hearn, Arthur Stuart Hull. 6500f USA. prod/rel: Anita Stewart Productions, Associated First National Pictures

CROSS, VICTORIA
Novel
Notte Di Tentazione 1919 d: Giuseppe Pinto. lps: Aurele Sydney, Clelia Antici Mattei, Juliette d'Arienzo. 1806m ITL. *A Night of Tempation* (UKN) prod/rel: Medusa Film

Five Nights, London 1908, Novel
Five Nights 1915 d: Bert Haldane ?. lps: Eve Balfour, Thomas H. MacDonald, Sybil de Bray. 5718f UKN. prod/rel: Barker, Imperial

Five Nights 1918. 6r USA. prod/rel: Classical Motion Picture Co., State Rights

Life's Shop Window, New York 1907, Novel
Life's Shop Window 1914 d: Herbert Brenon, Henry Belmar. lps: Claire Whitney, Stuart Holmes, Henry Belmar. lps: Box Office Attraction Co., William Fox©

Paula, Novel
Paula 1915 d: Cecil Birch. lps: Hettie Payne, Frank McClellan. 6000f UKN. prod/rel: Holmfirth, Initial

CROSSLEY, ROSEMARY
Annie's Coming Out, Book
Annie's Coming Out 1984 d: Gil Brealey. lps: Angela Punch-McGregor, Drew Forsythe, Tina Arhondis. 96M ASL. *A Test of Love* (USA) prod/rel: Film Australia©, Australian Film Commission©

CROTHERS, RACHEL (1878–1958), USA
39 East, New York 1919, Play
39 East 1920 d: John S. Robertson. lps: Constance Binney, Reginald Denny, Alison Skipworth. 5r USA. prod/rel: Realart Pictures Corp.©, Star Productions

As Husbands Go, New York 1931, Play
As Husbands Go 1934 d: Hamilton MacFadden. lps: Warner Baxter, Helen Vinson, Catherine Doucet. 80M USA. prod/rel: Fox Film Corp., Jesse L. Lasky Productions

Let Us Be Gay, New York 1929, Play
Let Us Be Gay 1930 d: Robert Z. Leonard. lps: Norma Shearer, Rod La Rocque, Marie Dressler. 7121f USA. prod/rel: Metro-Goldwyn-Mayer Pictures

Soyons Gais 1931 d: Arthur Robison, Andre Luguet. lps: Adolphe Menjou, Marcel Andre, Lili DamitA. 88M USA. *Gai Gai Demarions-Nous* prod/rel: Metro-Goldwyn-Mayer Corp., Culver Export

A Little Journey, New York 1923, Play
Little Journey, A 1926 d: Robert Z. Leonard. lps: Claire Windsor, William Haines, Harry Carey. 6088f USA. prod/rel: Metro-Goldwyn-Mayer Pictures

A Man's World, New York 1910, Play
Man's World, A 1918 d: Herbert Blache. lps: Emily Stevens, John Merkyl, Frederick C. Truesdell. 4891f USA. prod/rel: Metro Pictures Corp.©

Mary the Third, Boston 1923, Play
Wine of Youth 1924 d: King Vidor. lps: Eleanor Boardman, James Morrison, Johnny Walker. 6600f USA. prod/rel: Metro-Goldwyn Pictures

Nice People, New York 1921, Play
Nice People 1922 d: William C. de Mille. lps: Wallace Reid, Bebe Daniels, Conrad Nagel. 6244f USA. prod/rel: Famous Players-Lasky, Paramount Pictures

Old Lady 31, New York 1916, Play
Captain Is a Lady, The 1940 d: Robert B. Sinclair. lps: Charles Coburn, Beulah Bondi, Virginia Grey. 63M USA. *Old Lady Thirty-One*; *Old Lady 31* prod/rel: Metro-Goldwyn-Mayer Corp.

Old Lady 31 1920 d: John Ince. lps: Emma Dunn, Henry Harmon, Clara Knott. 6r USA. prod/rel: Screen Classics, Inc., Metro Pictures Corp.©

Susan and God, Princeton N.J. 1937, Play
Susan and God 1940 d: George Cukor. lps: Joan Crawford, Fredric March, Ruth Hussey. 115M USA. *The Gay Mrs. Trexel* (UKN) prod/rel: Metro-Goldwyn-Mayer Corp., Loew's, Inc.©
Susan and God 1951 d: Alex Segal. lps: Pamela Brown, Albert Dekker. MTV. USA. prod/rel: ABC

The Three of Us, New York 1906, Play
Three of Us, The 1915 d: John W. Noble. lps: Mabel Taliaferro, Creighton Hale, Edwin Carewe. 5r USA. prod/rel: B. A. Rolfe Photo Plays Co., Alco Film Corp.

When Ladies Meet, New York 1932, Play
When Ladies Meet 1933 d: Harry Beaumont. lps: Ann Harding, Robert Montgomery, Myrna Loy. 85M USA. *Truth Is Stranger*; *Strange Skirts* prod/rel: Metro-Goldwyn-Mayer Corp.©
When Ladies Meet 1941 d: Robert Z. Leonard. lps: Joan Crawford, Robert Taylor, Greer Garson. 108M USA. *Strange Skirts* prod/rel: Metro-Goldwyn-Mayer Corp.

CROUCH, FREDERICK
Kathleen Mavourneen, 1840, Song
Kathleen Mavourneen 1919 d: Charles J. Brabin. lps: Theda Bara, Raymond McKee, Marc McDermott. 5-6r USA. prod/rel: Fox Film Corp., William Fox©

CROUSE, RUSSEL (1893–1966), USA
Call Me Madam, New York 1950, Musical Play
Call Me Madam 1953 d: Walter Lang. lps: Ethel Merman, Donald O'Connor, Vera-Ellen. 117M USA. prod/rel: 20th Century-Fox

Life With Father, Play
Life With Father 1947 d: Michael Curtiz. lps: Irene Dunne, William Powell, Elizabeth Taylor. 118M USA. prod/rel: Warner Bros.

Remains to Be Seen, New York 1951, Play
Remains to Be Seen 1953 d: Don Weis. lps: June Allyson, Van Johnson, Louis Calhern. 89M USA. prod/rel: MGM

State of the Union, New York 1945, Play
State of the Union 1948 d: Frank CaprA. lps: Spencer Tracy, Katharine Hepburn, Angela Lansbury. 124M USA. *The World and His Wife* (UKN) prod/rel: MGM

Tall Story, New York 1959, Play
Tall Story 1960 d: Joshua Logan. lps: Anthony Perkins, Jane Fonda, Ray Walston. 91M USA. prod/rel: Warner Bros.

CROUZAT, HENRI
L' Ile du Bout du Monde, Paris 1954, Novel
Ile du Bout du Monde, L' 1958 d: Edmond T. Greville. lps: Magali Noel, Dawn Addams, Rossana PodestA. 104M FRN. *Temptation Island* (UKN); *Temptation* (USA) prod/rel: Riviera International Films, Jean Joannon

CROWE, CAMERON (1957–, USA
Fast Times at Ridgemont High, Novel
Fast Times at Ridgemont High 1982 d: Amy Heckerling. lps: Sean Penn, Jennifer Jason Leigh, Judge Reinhold. 92M USA. *Fast Times* prod/rel: Universal

CROWLEY, MART
The Boys in the Band, New York 1968, Play
Boys in the Band, The 1970 d: William Friedkin. lps: Kenneth Nelson, Leonard Frey, Cliff Gorman. 120M USA. prod/rel: Cinema Center, Leo

CROY, HOMER (1883–, USA
Article
Baron of Arizona, The 1950 d: Samuel Fuller. lps: Vincent Price, Ellen Drew, Beulah Bondi. 97M USA. prod/rel: Lippert, Deputy Corp.

Family Honeymoon, Novel
Family Honeymoon 1948 d: Claude Binyon. lps: Fred MacMurray, Claudette Colbert, Rita Johnson. 90M USA. prod/rel: Universal

Lady Tubbs, Novel
Lady Tubbs 1935 d: Alan Crosland. lps: Alice Brady, Douglass Montgomery, Anita Louise. 69M USA. *The Gay Lady* (UKN); *Mom* prod/rel: Universal Pictures Corp.©

Sixteen Hands, New York 1938, Novel
I'm from Missouri 1939 d: Theodore Reed. lps: Bob "Bazooka" Burns, Gladys George, Gene Lockhart. 77M USA. prod/rel: Paramount Pictures©

They Had to See Paris, New York 1926, Novel
They Had to See Paris 1929 d: Frank Borzage. lps: Will Rogers, Irene Rich, Owen Davis Jr. 8602f USA. prod/rel: Fox Film Corp.

West of the Water Tower, New York 1923, Novel
West of the Water Tower 1924 d: Rollin S. Sturgeon. lps: Glenn Hunter, May McAvoy, Ernest Torrence. 7432f USA. prod/rel: Famous Players-Lasky, Paramount Pictures

CRUGER, PAUL A.
Easy Pickings, Play
Easy Pickings 1927 d: George Archainbaud. lps: Anna Q. Nilsson, Kenneth Harlan, Philo McCullough. 5400f USA. prod/rel: First National Pictures

CRUTCHFIELD, LES
Showdown, Story
Last Train from Gun Hill 1959 d: John Sturges. lps: Kirk Douglas, Anthony Quinn, Carolyn Jones. 94M USA. prod/rel: Paramount, Bryna

CRYPTOS
Our Miss Gibbs, London 1909, Musical Play
Gaiety Duet, A 1909 d: Arthur Gilbert. lps: George Grossmith, Madge Melbourne, Edmund Payne. 610f UKN. prod/rel: Gaumont

CSATHO, KALMAN
Pokhalo, Novel
Pokhalo 1936 d: Maria Balazs. lps: Ella Gombaszogi, Imre Radai, Mici Erdelyi. 73M HNG. prod/rel: Csaba Filmgyarto

CSERES, TIBOR
Hideg Napok, 1965, Novel
Hideg Napok 1966 d: Andras Kovacs. lps: Zoltan Latinovits, Ivan Darvas, Adam Szirtes. 101M HNG. *Cold Days* (UKN) prod/rel: Mafilm

CUEL, ANDRE
Oeil de Lynx Detective, Play
Oeil de Lynx Detective 1936 d: Pierre-Jean Ducis. lps: Armand Bernard, Alice Tissot, Janine Merrey. 73M FRN. prod/rel: Ullman, Henri

CUEL, GEORGES-ANDRE
Barocco, Novel
Barocco 1925 d: Charles Burguet. lps: Jean Angelo, Charles Vanel, Nilda Duplessy. 2750m FRN. prod/rel: Grandes Productions Cinematographiques

Cafe Noir, Novel
Auberge du Peche, L' 1949 d: Jean de Marguenat. lps: Jean-Pierre Kerien, Jean Paredes, Ginette Leclerc. 108M FRN. prod/rel: Simoun, Films Pathe

Le Marchand de Sable, Novel
Marchand de Sable, Le 1931 d: Andre Hugon. lps: Jean Toulout, Kaissa-Robba, Jean Worms. 88M FRN. *Marchand de Sable El Guelmouna* prod/rel: Pathe-Natan

Le Meneur de Joies, Novel
Meneur de Joies, Le 1929 d: Charles Burguet. lps: Rene Navarre, Evelyn Holt, Carl de Vogt. 2100M FRN/GRM. *Die Schleiertanzerin* (GRM) prod/rel: Rene Navarre, Maxim-Film-Ges.

Tamara la Complaisante, Novel
Tamara la Complaisante 1937 d: Felix Gandera, Jean Delannoy. lps: Vera Korene, Victor Francen, Lucas Gridoux. 87M FRN. prod/rel: Productions Talac

CUENI, CLAUDE
Quicker Than the Eye, Novel
Quicker Than the Eye 1988 d: Nicolas Gessner. lps: Ben Gazzara, Mary Crosby, Catherine Jarrett. 89M SWT/AUS/GRM. *Schneller Als Das Auge* (GRM) prod/rel: Condor Prods.

CULICCHIA, GIUSEPPE
Tutti Giu Per Terra, Novel
Tutti Giu Per Terra 1997 d: Davide Ferrario. lps: Valerio Mastandrea, Carlo Monni, Benedetta Mazzini. 88M ITL. *We All Fall Down* prod/rel: Hera Intl. Film

CULLEN, JAMES
Please Get Married, New York 1919, Play
Please Get Married 1919 d: John Ince. lps: Viola Dana, Antrim Short, Margaret Campbell. 5-7r USA. prod/rel: Screen Classics, Inc., Metro Pictures Corp.©

CULLINAN, THOMAS
The Beguiled, Novel
Beguiled, The 1971 d: Don Siegel. lps: Clint Eastwood, Geraldine Page, Elizabeth Hartman. 109M USA. prod/rel: Universal, Malpaso

CULLUM, RIDGWELL
The Forfeit, Philadelphia 1917, Novel
Forfeit, The 1919 d: Frank Powell. lps: House Peters, Jane Miller, Billy Human. 5r USA. prod/rel: Sunset Pictures Corp., W. W. Hodkinson Corp.

The Night Riders: a Romance of Western Canada, London 1911, Novel
Night Riders, The 1920 d: Alexander Butler. lps: Albert Ray, Maudie Dunham, Andre Beaulieu. 5780f UKN/USA. prod/rel: G. B. Samuelson, General

The One Way Trail, London 1911, Novel
Yosemite Trail, The 1922 d: Bernard J. Durning. lps: Dustin Farnum, Irene Rich, Walter McGrail. 4735f USA. prod/rel: Fox Film Corp.

The Son of His Father, London 1915, Novel
Son of His Father, The 1917 d: Victor Schertzinger. lps: Charles Ray, Vola Vale, Robert McKim. 5r USA. prod/rel: Thomas H. Ince Corp.©, Paramount Pictures Corp.

Twins of Suffering Creek, London 1912, Novel
Man Who Won, The 1923 d: William A. Wellman. lps: Dustin Farnum, Jacqueline Gadsdon, Lloyd Whitlock. 5050f USA. prod/rel: Fox Film Corp.
Twins of Suffering Creek 1920 d: Scott R. Dunlap. lps: William Russell, Louise Lovely, E. Alyn Warren. 5r USA. prod/rel: Fox Film Corp., William Fox©

The Way of the Strong, London 1914, Novel
Way of the Strong, The 1919 d: Edwin Carewe. lps: Anna Q. Nilsson, Joe King, Harry Northrup. 5r USA. prod/rel: Metro Pictures Corp.©

CULOTTA, NINO
They're a Weird Mob, Book
They're a Weird Mob 1966 d: Michael Powell. lps: Walter Chiari, Clare Dunne, Chips Rafferty. 112M UKN/ASL. prod/rel: Rank Film Distributors, Williamson-Powell International

CULVAN, DORIS
Rookie Hey, Play
Hey, Rookie 1944 d: Charles T. Barton. lps: Larry Parks, Ann Miller, Joe Besser. 77M USA. prod/rel: Columbia

CULVAN, K. E. B.
Rookie Hey, Play
Hey, Rookie 1944 d: Charles T. Barton. lps: Larry Parks, Ann Miller, Joe Besser. 77M USA. prod/rel: Columbia

CUMBERLAND, MARTEN
Inside the Room, Play
Inside the Room 1935 d: Leslie Hiscott. lps: Austin Trevor, Dorothy Boyd, Garry Marsh. 66M UKN. prod/rel: Twickenham, Universal

CUMMINGS, DWIGHT
The Reckoning, Story
Reckoning, The 1908 d: D. W. Griffith. lps: Florence Lawrence, MacK Sennett, Harry Salter. 462f USA. prod/rel: Biograph Co.

CUMMINS, MARIE SUSANNA
The Lamplighter, Boston 1854, Novel
Lamplighter, The 1921 d: Howard M. Mitchell. lps: Shirley Mason, Raymond McKee, Albert Knott. 6050f USA. prod/rel: Fox Film Corp.

CUMMINS, RALPH
The Badge of Fighting Hearts, 1921, Short Story
Fire Eater, The 1921 d: B. Reeves Eason. lps: Hoot Gibson, Louise Lorraine, Walter Perry. 4341f USA. prod/rel: Universal Film Mfg. Co.

Cherub of Seven Bar, 1921, Short Story
Loaded Door, The 1922 d: Harry Pollard. lps: Hoot Gibson, Gertrude Olmstead, William Ryno. 4430f USA. prod/rel: Universal Film Mfg. Co.

Laramie Ladd, Story
Lone Hand, The 1922 d: B. Reeves Eason, Nat Ross. lps: Hoot Gibson, Marjorie Daw, Helen Holmes. 4570f USA. *False Play* prod/rel: Universal Film Mfg. Co.

The Princess of the Desert Dream, Story
Where Men are Men 1921 d: William Duncan. lps: William Duncan, Edith Johnson, George Stanley. 5r USA. prod/rel: Vitagraph Co. of America

Rattler Rock, 1923, Short Story
Rarin' to Go 1924 d: Richard Thorpe. lps: Buffalo Bill Jr., Olin Francis, L. J. O'Connor. 4641f USA. *Eager to Work* prod/rel: Action Pictures

CUNHAL, ALVARO
Cinco Noites Cinco Dias, Novel
Cinco Dias, Cinco Noites 1997 d: Jose Fonseca CostA. lps: Victor Norte, Paulo Pires, Ana Padrao. 101M PRT/FRN. *Five Days Five Nights* prod/rel: Madragoa Filmes (Lisbon), Gemini Films

CUNNINGHAM, JACK
See No Evil, Play
Peep 1974 d: Jack Cunningham. lps: Donald Harron, Lois Maxwell, Allan McRae. 77M CND. *L' Oeil de l'Ombre* prod/rel: Image Control Productions Inc.

CUNNINGHAM, JERE
Hunter's Blood, Novel
Hunter's Blood 1986 d: Robert C. Hughes. lps: Sam Bottoms, Kim Delaney, Clu Gulager. 102M USA. prod/rel: Concorde, Cineventure

CUNNINGHAM, JOHN M.
Raiders Die Hard, Novel
Day of the Bad Man 1958 d: Harry Keller. lps: Fred MacMurray, Joan Weldon, John Ericson. 81M USA. prod/rel: Universal-International
Yankee Gold, Novel
Stranger Wore a Gun, The 1953 d: Andre de Toth. lps: Randolph Scott, Claire Trevor, Joan Weldon. 83M USA. prod/rel: Columbia, Scott-Brown

CUNNINGHAM, JOHN W.
The Tin Star, Short Story
High Noon 1952 d: Fred Zinnemann. lps: Gary Cooper, Thomas Mitchell, Lloyd Bridges. 85M USA. prod/rel: United Artists, Stanley Kramer Productions

CURCIO, ARMANDO
A Che Servono Questi Quattrini?, Play
A Che Servono Questi Quattrini? 1942 d: Esodo Pratelli. lps: Eduardo de Filippo, Peppino de Filippo, Paolo StoppA. 85M ITL. prod/rel: Juventus Film, E.N.I.C.
Casanova Farebbe Cosi, Play
Casanova Farebbe Cosi! 1942 d: Carlo Ludovico BragagliA. lps: Eduardo de Filippo, Peppino de Filippo, Clelia MataniA. 62M ITL. prod/rel: Juventus Film, E.N.I.C.

CURIE, EVE (1904–, FRN
Madame Curie, 1937, Biography
Madame Curie 1943 d: Mervyn Leroy. lps: Greer Garson, Walter Pidgeon, Henry Travers. 124M USA. prod/rel: MGM

CURRAN, CHARLES
Ad-Man, 1932, Play
No Marriage Ties 1933 d: J. Walter Ruben. lps: Richard Dix, Elizabeth Allan, Doris Kenyon. 73M USA. *The Public Be Sold*; *Ad-Man* prod/rel: RKO Radio Pictures©

CURRAN, PEARL LENORE
Entrante Rosa Alvaro, 1919, Short Story
What Happened to Rosa 1920 d: Victor Schertzinger. lps: Mabel Normand, Hugh Thompson, Doris Pawn. 5r USA. *Romantic Rosa*; *Rosa Alvaro* prod/rel: Goldwyn Pictures Corp.©, Goldwyn Distributing Corp.

CURRIE, SHELDON
The Glace Bay Miner's Museum, Short Story
Margaret's Museum 1995 d: Mort Ransen. lps: Helena Bonham-Carter, Clive Russell, Craig Olejnik. 114M CND/UKN. *The Glace Bay Miner's Museum* prod/rel: Ranfilm, Imagex

CURROS ENRIQUEZ, MANUEL
A Virxen Do Cristal, Poem
Virgen de Cristal, La 1925 d: Jose Buchs, Saturio Luis Pineiro. lps: Amelia Munoz, Maruja Retana, Julio Rodriguez. F SPN. *The Glass Madonna* prod/rel: Sol Film (Madrid)

CURRY, MAURICE
La Route de Salina, Novel
Sur la Route de Salina 1969 d: Georges Lautner. lps: Robert (3) Walker, Rita Hayworth, Mimsy Farmer. 97M FRN/ITL. *Quando Il Sole Scotta* (ITL); *Road to Salina* (USA); *La Route de Salina* prod/rel: Films Corona, Transinter

CURTIS, JAMES
There Ain't No Justice, Novel
There Ain't No Justice 1939 d: Pen Tennyson. lps: Jimmy Hanley, Edward Rigby, Mary Clare. 83M UKN. prod/rel: Ealing Studios, C.a.P.A.D.
They Drive By Night, Novel
They Drive By Night 1938 d: Arthur Woods. lps: Emlyn Williams, Ernest Thesiger, Anna Konstam. 84M UKN. prod/rel: Warner Bros., First National

CURTIS, JEAN-LOUIS (1917–, FRN
L' Ephebe de Subiaco, 1969, Short Story
Chere Louise 1971 d: Philippe de BrocA. lps: Jeanne Moreau, Julian Negulesco, Didi Perego. 105M FRN/ITL. *La Lunga Notte Di Louise* (ITL); *Louise* (UKN) prod/rel: Compagnia Cin.Ca Champion
Gibier de Potence, 1949, Novel
Gibier de Potence 1951 d: Roger Richebe. lps: Arletty, Georges Marchal, Nicole Courcel. 106M FRN. prod/rel: Films Roger Richebe
Un Jeune Couple, 1967, Novel
Jeune Couple, Un 1968 d: Rene Gainville. lps: Anna Gael, Alain Libolt, Jean-Francois Calve. 85M FRN. *A Young Couple* (USA) prod/rel: Films De L'epee, Terra Films

CURTIS, MICHAEL
Don't Answer the Phone, Novel
Don't Answer the Phone! 1980 d: Robert Hammer. lps: James Westmoreland, Flo Gerrish, Ben Frank. 93M USA. *The Hollywood Strangler* prod/rel: Scorpion, Crown

CURTIS, PETER
The Devil's Own, London 1960, Novel
Witches, The 1966 d: Cyril Frankel. lps: Joan Fontaine, Alec McCowen, Kay Walsh. 91M UKN. *The Devil's Own* (USA) prod/rel: Hammer, Seven Arts
You're Best Alone, Novel
Guilt Is My Shadow 1950 d: Roy Kellino. lps: Patrick Holt, Elizabeth Sellars, Lana Morris. 86M UKN. *The Intruder* prod/rel: Associated British Picture Corporation, Ab-Pathe

CURTIS, TOM
The Throwdown
Killing of Randy Webster, The 1981 d: Sam Wanamaker. lps: Hal Holbrook, Dixie Carter, James Whitmore Jr. TVM. 100M USA. prod/rel: CBS

CURTIS, WALT
Mala Noche, Story
Mala Noche 1987 d: Gus Van Sant Jr. lps: Tim Streeter, Doug Cooeyate, Ray Monge. 78M USA. *Bad Night* prod/rel: Northern Film Co., Frameline

CURTISS, URSULA
The Forbidden Garden, New York 1962, Novel
What Ever Happened to Aunt Alice? 1969 d: Lee H. Katzin. lps: Geraldine Page, Ruth Gordon, Rosemary Forsyth. 101M USA. prod/rel: Associates & Aldrich Co.
I Saw What You Did, New York 1964, Novel
I Saw What You Did 1987 d: Fred Walton. lps: Shawnee Smith, Tammy Lauren, Candace Cameron. TVM. 100M USA. prod/rel: Universal
Out of the Dark, New York 1964, Novel
I Saw What You Did 1965 d: William Castle. lps: Joan Crawford, John Ireland, Leif Erickson. 82M USA. prod/rel: Universal Pictures

CURVERS, ALEXIS
La Ville Eternelle, Novel
Tempo Di Roma 1964 d: Denys de La Patelliere. lps: Charles Aznavour, Serena Vergano, Gregor von Rezzori. 93M FRN/ITL. *Esame Di Giuda* (ITL) prod/rel: Les Films Du Cyclope (Paris), Da.MA. Cinematografica (Roma)

CURWOOD, JAMES OLIVER (1878–1927), USA
Story
Awakening, The 1915 d: Ralph Ince. lps: Anita Stewart, Earle Williams, William Dangman. 2r USA. prod/rel: Vitagraph Co. of America
Broken Silence, The 1922 d: Dell Henderson. lps: Zena Keefe, Robert Elliott, J. Barney Sherry. 5929f USA. prod/rel: Pine Tree Pictures, Arrow Film Corp.
Fangs of the Arctic 1953 d: Rex Bailey. lps: Kirby Grant, Lorna Hansen, Warren Douglas. 62M USA. prod/rel: Monogram, Allied Artists
Novel
Northwest Territory 1951 d: Frank McDonald. lps: Kirby Grant, Gloria Saunders, Chinook A Dog. 61M USA. prod/rel: Monogram
Story
Paid in Advance 1919 d: Allen Holubar. lps: Dorothy Phillips, Joseph Girard, Lon Chaney. 6r USA. *The Girl Who Dared* prod/rel: Universal Film Mfg. Co.©, Jewel Productions, Inc.
Thundergod 1928 d: Charles J. Hunt. lps: Cornelius Keefe, Lila Lee, Walter Long. 5917f USA. prod/rel: Morris R. Schlank Productions, Anchor Film Distributors
Short Story
Vengeance of Rannah 1936 d: Bernard B. Ray. lps: Bob Custer, Rin-Tin-Tin Jr., John Elliott. 56M USA. prod/rel: Reliable Pictures Corp.
Vengeance of Rannah, The 1915 d: Thomas Santschi. lps: George Larkin, Leo Pierson, Lafe McKee. 2r USA.
Story
Wild Horse Round-Up 1936 d: Alan James. lps: Kermit Maynard, Betty Lloyd, Dickie Jones. 58M USA. *Wild Horse Roundup* prod/rel: Ambassador Pictures
Short Story
Yukon Manhunt 1951 d: Frank McDonald. lps: Kirby Grant, Gail Davis, Chinook The Wonder Dog. 63M USA. prod/rel: Monogram
Story
Yukon Vengeance 1954 d: William Beaudine. lps: Kirby Grant, Chinook The Wonder Dog, Monte Hale. 68M USA. prod/rel: Allied Artists
The Alaskan, New York 1923, Novel
Alaskan, The 1924 d: Herbert Brenon. lps: Thomas Meighan, Estelle Taylor, John Sainpolis. 6736f USA. prod/rel: Famous Players-Lasky Corp., Paramount Pictures

The Ancient Highway: a Novel of High Hearts and Open Roads, New York 1925, Novel
Ancient Highway, The 1925 d: Irvin V. Willat. lps: Jack Holt, Billie Dove, Montagu Love. 6034f USA. prod/rel: Famous Players-Lasky Corp., Paramount Pictures
Back to God's Country and Other Stories, New York 1920, Book
Back to God's Country 1927 d: Irvin V. Willat. lps: Renee Adoree, Robert Frazer, Walter Long. 5751f USA. prod/rel: Universal Pictures
Back to God's Country 1953 d: Joseph Pevney. lps: Rock Hudson, Steve Cochran, Marcia Henderson. 78M USA. prod/rel: Universal-International
Baree - Son of Kazan, Garden City, Ny. 1917, Novel
Baree, Son of Kazan 1918 d: David Smith. lps: Nell Shipman, Alfred Whitman, Al GarciA. prod/rel: Vitagraph Co. of America©, Blue Ribbon Feature
Baree, Son of Kazan 1925 d: David Smith. lps: Anita Stewart, Donald Keith, Jack Curtis. 6800f USA. prod/rel: Vitagraph Co. of America
The Battle of Frenchman's Run, Story
Battle of Frenchman's Run, The 1915 d: Theodore Marston. SHT USA. prod/rel: Vitagraph Co. of America
Caryl of the Mountains, Short Story
Caryl of the Mountains 1936 d: Bernard B. Ray. lps: Rin-Tin-Tin Jr., Francis X. Bushman Jr., Lois Wilde. 68M USA. *Get That Girl* (UKN) prod/rel: Reliable Pictures Corp.
Trails of the Wild 1935 d: Sam Newfield. lps: Kermit Maynard, Billie Seward, Fuzzy Knight. 65M USA. *Arrest at Sundown* (UKN); *Caryl of the Mountains* prod/rel: Ambassador Pictures©
Children of Fate, Short Story
Children of Fate 1914 d: Wallace Reid. lps: Wallace Reid, Dorothy Davenport, Joe King. SHT USA. *Love's Western Flight* prod/rel: Nestor
The Country Beyond, New York 1922, Short Story
Country Beyond, The 1926 d: Irving Cummings. lps: Olive Borden, Ralph Graves, Gertrude Astor. 5363f USA. prod/rel: Fox Film Corp.
Country Beyond, The 1936 d: Eugene J. Forde. lps: Rochelle Hudson, Paul Kelly, Robert Kent. 73M USA. prod/rel: Twentieth Century-Fox Film Corp.
The Courage of Marge O'Doone, Garden City, N.Y. 1918, Novel
Courage of Marge O'Doone, The 1920 d: David Smith. lps: Pauline Starke, Niles Welch, George Stanley. 6447f USA. prod/rel: Vitagraph Co. of America©
The Coyote, Short Story
Hawk, The 1935 d: Edward Dmytryk. lps: Yancie Lane, Dickie Jones, Betty Jordan. 60M USA. *Trail of the Hawk*; *Pride of Triple X* prod/rel: Affiliated Pictures Corp., Jay Dee Kay Productions
The Danger Trail, Indianapolis 1910, Novel
Danger Trail, The 1917 d: Frederick A. Thompson. lps: H. B. Warner, Violet Heming, W. Lawson Butt. 5r USA. prod/rel: Selig Polyscope Co.©, K-E-S-E Service
Duty and the Man, Novel
Duty and the Man 1913 d: Oscar Apfel. lps: James Ashley, Gertrude Robinson, Charles Elliott. 2r USA. prod/rel: Reliance
The Fatal Noise, Short Story
Phantom Patrol 1936 d: Charles Hutchison. lps: Kermit Maynard, Joan Barclay, Dick Curtis. 58M USA. prod/rel: Ambassador Pictures
The Fifth Man, Short Story
Fifth Man, The 1914 d: Francis J. Grandon. lps: Bessie Eyton, Charles Clary, Lafe McKee. 3r USA. prod/rel: Selig Polyscope Co.
Whistling Bullets 1937 d: John English. lps: Kermit Maynard, Harley Wood, Jack Ingram. 58M USA. prod/rel: Ambassador Pictures
A Fighting Chance, Story
Fighting Chance, A 1913 d: Ralph Ince. lps: Anita Stewart, Rosemary Theby, Ned Finley. 1000f USA. prod/rel: Vitagraph Co. of America
The Flaming Forest; a Novel of the Canadian Northwest, New York 1921, Novel
Flaming Forest, The 1926 d: Reginald Barker. lps: Antonio Moreno, Renee Adoree, Gardner James. 6567f USA. prod/rel: Cosmopolitan Productions, Metro-Goldwyn-Mayer Distributing Corp.
The Flower of the North, New York 1912, Novel
Flower of the North 1921 d: David Smith. lps: Henry B. Walthall, Pauline Starke, Harry Northrup. 7130f USA. prod/rel: Vitagraph Co. of America

Footprints, Short Story
Fighting Trooper, The 1934 d: Ray Taylor. lps: Kermit Maynard, Barbara Worth, Walter Miller. 63M USA. *The Trooper* (UKN) prod/rel: Ambassador Pictures©

Four Minutes Late, Short Story
Northern Frontier 1935 d: Sam Newfield. lps: Kermit Maynard, Eleanor Hunt, J. Farrell MacDonald. 59M USA. prod/rel: Ambassador Pictures©

Game of Life, Story
Valley of Terror 1937 d: Al Herman. lps: Kermit Maynard, Harley Wood, John Merton. 57M USA. prod/rel: Ambassador Pictures

Getting a Start in Life, Short Story
Rough Riding Rhythm 1937 d: J. P. McGowan. lps: Kermit Maynard, Beryl Wallace, Ralph Peters. 66M USA. *Rough Ridin' Rhythm* prod/rel: Conn Productions, Ambassador Pictures

God of Her People, Story
Man from Hell's River, The 1922 d: Irving Cummings. lps: Irving Cummings, Eva Novak, Wallace Beery. 5r USA. *Hell's River* prod/rel: Irving Cummings Productions, Western Pictures Exploitation Co.

God's Country - and the Woman, New York 1915, Novel
God's Country 1946 d: Robert Tansey. lps: Robert Lowery, Helen Gilbert, William Farnum. 64M USA. prod/rel: Screen Guild Productions, Action Pictures

God's Country and the Law 1921 d: Sidney Olcott. lps: Fred C. Jones, Gladys Leslie, William H. Tooker. 6r USA. prod/rel: Arrow Film Corp., Pine Tree Pictures

God's Country and the Woman 1916 d: Rollin S. Sturgeon. lps: William Duncan, Nell Shipman, George Holt. 8r USA. prod/rel: Vitagraph Co. of America©, Blue Ribbon Feature

God's Country and the Woman 1937 d: William Keighley. lps: George Brent, Beverly Roberts, Barton MacLane. 90M USA. prod/rel: Warner Bros. Pictures©

The Gods Redeem, Story
Gods Redeem, The 1915 d: Van Dyke Brooke. lps: Maurice Costello, Leah Baird, Van Dyke Brooke. 2r USA. prod/rel: Vitagraph Co. of America

The Gold Hunters, Indianapolis 1909, Novel
Gold Hunters, The 1925 d: Paul C. Hurst. lps: David Butler, Hedda Nova, Mary Carr. 6500f USA. prod/rel: Guaranteed Pictures, Davis Distributing Division

Trail of the Yukon 1949 d: William X. Crowley, William Beaudine. lps: Kirby Grant, Suzanne Dalbert, Bill Edwards. 67M USA. prod/rel: Monogram

Yukon Gold 1952 d: Frank McDonald. lps: Kirby Grant, Martha Hyer, Chinook. 62M USA. prod/rel: Monogram

The Golden Snare, New York 1921, Novel
Golden Snare, The 1921 d: David M. Hartford. lps: Lewis Stone, Wallace Beery, Melbourne MacDowell. 5900f USA. prod/rel: David Hartford Productions, Associated First National Pictures

The Grizzly King, Novel
Ours, L' 1988 d: Jean-Jacques Annaud. lps: Jack Wallace, Tcheky Karyo, Andre Lacombe. 100M FRN/CND. *The Bear* (UKN) prod/rel: Tri-Star, Wrenn

Hearts of Men, Story
Hearts of Men 1928 d: James P. Hogan. lps: Mildred Harris, Thelma Hill, Cornelius Keefe. 5800f USA. prod/rel: Morris R. Schlank Productions, Anchor Film Distributors

Hell's Gulch, Short Story
Timber War 1936 d: Sam Newfield. lps: Kermit Maynard, Lucille Lund, Lawrence Gray. 58M USA. prod/rel: Ambassador Pictures©

His Fight, Short Story
His Fight 1914 d: Colin Campbell. lps: Eugenie Besserer, Wheeler Oakman, Henry Otto. SHT USA. prod/rel: Selig Polyscope Co.

Roaring Six Guns 1937 d: J. P. McGowan. lps: Kermit Maynard, Mary Hayes, Sam Flint. 58M USA. prod/rel: Ambasssador Pictures

His Fighting Blood, Short Story
His Fighting Blood 1935 d: James W. English. lps: Kermit Maynard, Polly Ann Young, Ted Adams. 60M USA. prod/rel: Ambassador Pictures©

Honor of the Big Snows, Indianapolis 1911, Novel
Jan of the Big Snows 1922 d: Charles M. Seay. lps: Warner Richmond, Louise Prussing, William Peavy. 4531f USA. prod/rel: Charles M. Seay, American Releasing Corp.

The Hunted Woman, New York 1916, Novel
Hunted Woman, The 1916 d: S. Rankin Drew. lps: Virginia Pearson, S. Rankin Drew, Frank Currier. 5r USA. prod/rel: Vitagraph Co. of America©, V-L-S-E, Inc.

Hunted Woman, The 1925 d: Jack Conway. lps: Seena Owen, Earl Schenck, Diana Miller. 4954f USA. prod/rel: Fox Film Corp.

In the Days of Fanny, Story
In the Days of Fanny 1915 d: Theodore Marston. lps: James Morrison, George Cooper, Dorothy Kelly. 3r USA. prod/rel: Broadway Star, Vitagraph Co. of America

Isobel: a Romance of the Northern Trail, Novel
Isobel 1920 d: Edwin Carewe. lps: House Peters, Jane Novak, Edward Peil. 6r USA. *The Trail's End Isobel; Or; The Trail's End* prod/rel: George H. Davis©, State Rights

Jacqueline, 1918, Short Story
Jacqueline, Or Blazing Barriers 1923 d: Dell Henderson. lps: Marguerite Courtot, Helen Rowland, Gus Weinberg. 6400f USA. *Blazing Barriers* prod/rel: Pine Tree Pictures, Arrow Film Corp.

The Wolf Dog Kazan, Indianapolis 1914, Novel
Kazan 1921 d: Bertram Bracken. lps: Jane Novak, Ben Deely, William Ryno. 6900f USA. prod/rel: Col. William N. Selig, Export & Import Film Co.

Kazan 1949 d: Will Jason. lps: Stephen Dunne, Lois Maxwell, Joseph Sawyer. 66M USA. prod/rel: Columbia

Looking Forward, Short Story
Looking Forward 1910 d: Theodore Marston. lps: Frank Crane, William Russell. 1000f USA. prod/rel: Thanhouser

The Lost Millionaire, Story
Lost Millionaire, The 1913 d: Ralph Ince. lps: E. K. Lincoln, Anita Stewart, Charles Kent. 2000f USA. prod/rel: Vitagraph Co. of America

The Man from Ten Strike, Story
Gold Madness 1923 d: Robert T. Thornby. lps: Guy Bates Post, Cleo Madison, Mitchell Lewis. 5860f USA. *The Man from Ten Strike* prod/rel: Perfect Pictures, Principal Pictures

Man's Law, Story
Man's Law 1915 d: Colin Campbell. 2r USA. prod/rel: Selig Polyscope Co.

The Midnight Call, Story
Midnight Call, The 1914 d: Fred W. Huntley. lps: Harold Lockwood, Mabel Van Buren, Henry Otto. SHT USA. prod/rel: Selig Polyscope Co.

Wildcat Trooper 1936 d: Elmer Clifton. lps: Kermit Maynard, Hobart Bosworth, Fuzzy Knight. 60M USA. *Wild Cat* (UKN) prod/rel: Ambassador Pictures

Mystery of Dead Man's Isle, Short Story
Galloping Dynamite 1937 d: Harry L. Fraser. lps: Kermit Maynard, Ariane Allen, John Merton. 58M USA. *Dawn Rider* prod/rel: Ambassador Pictures

Nomads of the North, New York 1919, Novel
Nikki, Wild Dog of the North 1961 d: Jack Couffer, Don Haldane. lps: Jean Coutu, Emile Genest, Uriel Luft. 72M USA/CND. *Nomades du Nord*; *Nomads of the North* prod/rel: Walt Disney Productions, Cangary, Ltd. (Calgary)

Nomads of the North 1920 d: David M. Hartford. lps: Lewis Stone, Betty Blythe, Lon Chaney. 6r USA. prod/rel: James Oliver Curwood Productions, Inc.©, Associated First National Pictures, Inc.

The Old Code, Story
Old Code, The 1915. lps: William Stowell, Edwin Wallock. 2r USA. prod/rel: Selig Polyscope Co.

The Other Man's Wife, 1920, Short Story
My Neighbor's Wife 1925 d: Clarence Geldert. lps: E. K. Lincoln, Helen Ferguson, Edwards Davis. 6r USA. prod/rel: Clifford S. Elfelt Productions, Davis Distributing Division

Peter God, Short Story
Destroyers, The 1916 d: Ralph Ince. lps: Lucille Lee Stewart, Huntley Gordon, John Robertson. 5r USA. prod/rel: Vitagraph Co. of America©, Blue Ribbon Feature

Playing With Fire, Story
Song of the Trail 1936 d: Russell Hopton. lps: Kermit Maynard, Evelyn Brent, Fuzzy Knight. 68M USA. prod/rel: Ambassador Pictures

The Poetic Justice of Uko San, 1910, Short Story
I Am the Law 1922 d: Edwin Carewe. lps: Alice Lake, Kenneth Harlan, Rosemary Theby. 6800f USA. prod/rel: Edwin Carewe Productions, Affiliated Distributors

Polishing Up, Story
Polishing Up 1914 d: George D. Baker. lps: John Bunny, Flora Finch, William Humphrey. SHT USA. prod/rel: Vitagraph Co. of America

Prejudice of Pierre Marie, Story
Prejudice of Pierre Marie 1911 d: Larry Trimble. lps: Tefft Johnson, Florence Turner, William Humphrey. SHT USA. prod/rel: Vitagraph Co. of America

The Queen of Jungle Land, Story
Queen of Jungle Land, The 1915 d: Joseph J. Franz. lps: Wellington Playter, Edythe Sterling, Lule Warrenton. 3r USA. prod/rel: Bison

The Quest of Joan, Short Story
Girl Who Wouldn't Quit, The 1918 d: Edgar Jones. lps: Louise Lovely, Henry A. Barrows, Mark Fenton. 5r USA. prod/rel: Universal Film Mfg. Co.©

Prisoners of the Storm 1926 d: Lynn Reynolds. lps: House Peters, Peggy Montgomery, Walter McGrail. 6102f USA. prod/rel: Universal Pictures

Red Blood of Courage, Short Story
Red Blood of Courage 1935 d: John English. lps: Kermit Maynard, Ann Sheridan, Reginald Barlow. 55M USA. prod/rel: Ambassador Pictures©

Retribution, Short Story
Timber Fury 1950 d: Bernard B. Ray. lps: David Bruce, Laura Lee, Nicla Di Bruno. 61M USA. prod/rel: Eagle-Lion, Jack Schwarz

The River's End: a New Story of God's Country, New York 1919, Novel
River's End 1930 d: Michael Curtiz. lps: Charles Bickford, Evalyn Knapp, J. Farrell MacDonald. 75M USA. prod/rel: Warner Brothers Pictures

River's End 1940 d: Ray Enright. lps: Dennis Morgan, Elizabeth Earl, George Tobias. 69M USA. *Double Identity* prod/rel: Warner Bros. Pictures©

River's End, The 1920 d: Marshall Neilan, Victor Heerman. lps: Lewis Stone, Marjorie Daw, Jane Novak. 5750f USA. prod/rel: Marshall Neilan Productions, First National Exhibitors Circuit

Some Liar, 1918, Short Story
Some Liar 1919 d: Henry King. lps: William Russell, Eileen Percy, Haywood MacK. 5r USA. prod/rel: American Film Co.©, Pathe Exchange, Inc.

The Speck on the Wall, Novel
Law of the Timber 1941 d: Bernard B. Ray. lps: Marjorie Reynolds, Monte Blue, J. Farrell MacDonald. 63M USA. prod/rel: P.R.C.

Speck on the Wall, The 1914 d: Colin Campbell. lps: Kathlyn Williams, Wheeler Oakman. 2r USA. prod/rel: Selig Polyscope Co.

Steele of the Royal Mounted, New York 1911, Novel
Steele of the Royal Mounted 1925 d: David Smith. lps: Bert Lytell, Stuart Holmes, Charlotte Merriam. 5700f USA. prod/rel: Vitagraph Co. of America

The Story of the Blood-Red Rose, Story
Story of the Blood-Red Rose, The 1914 d: Colin Campbell. lps: Kathlyn Williams, Wheeler Oakman, Charles Clary. 3r USA. prod/rel: Selig Polyscope Co.

The Strength of Men, Story
Strength of Men, The 1913. lps: Ned Finley, Herbert L. Barry, Edith Storey. 2000f USA. prod/rel: Vitagraph Co. of America

Swift Lightning, New York 1926, Novel
Call of the Yukon 1938 d: B. Reeves Eason, John T. Coyle (Uncredited). lps: Richard Arlen, Beverly Roberts, Lyle Talbot. 70M USA. *Thunder in Alaska*; *Swift Lightning* prod/rel: Republic Pictures Corp.

Tentacles of the North, 1915, Short Story
Snow Dog 1950 d: Frank McDonald. lps: Kirby Grant, Elena Verdugo, Rick Vallin. 63M USA. prod/rel: Monogram

Tentacles of the North 1926 d: Louis W. Chaudet. lps: Gaston Glass, Alice Calhoun, Al Roscoe. 5998f USA. prod/rel: Ben Wilson Productions, Rayart Pictures

Lord of the Jungles Thor, Story
Thor, Lord of the Jungles 1913 d: Colin Campbell. lps: Kathlyn Williams, Charles Clary, Thomas Santschi. 3r USA. prod/rel: Selig Polyscope Co.

Till Death Us Do Part, Story
Till Death Us Do Part 1914 d: Colin Campbell. lps: Kathlyn Williams, Wheeler Oakman, Charles Clary. 2r USA. prod/rel: Selig Polyscope Co.

The Tragedy That Lived, Short Story
Fighting Texan, The 1937 d: Charles Abbott. lps: Kermit Maynard, Elaine Shepard, Frank Larue. 58M USA. prod/rel: Ambassador Pictures

Tragedy That Lived, The 1914 d: Colin Campbell. lps: Kathlyn Williams, Wheeler Oakman, Charles Clary. SHT USA. prod/rel: Selig Polyscope Co.

The Trail's End, Novel
In Defiance of the Law 1914 d: Colin Campbell. lps: Wheeler Oakman, Tom Mix. 3r USA. prod/rel: Selig Polyscope Co.

The Treasure of Desert Isle, Story
Treasure of Desert Isle, The 1913 d: Ralph Ince. lps: Charles Kent, Anita Stewart, E. K. Lincoln. 1000f USA. prod/rel: Vitagraph Co. of America

Two Women, Story
Two Women 1915 d: Ralph Ince. lps: Anita Stewart, Earle Williams, Julia Swayne Gordon. 3r USA. prod/rel: Broadway Star Feature, General Film Co.

The Valley of Silent Men, New York 1920, Novel
Valley of Silent Men, The 1922 d: Frank Borzage. lps: Alma Rubens, Lew Cody, Joe King. 7r USA. prod/rel: Cosmopolitan Productions, Paramount Pictures

Wapi the Walrus, Story
Back to God's Country 1919 d: David M. Hartford, Bert Van Tuyle (Uncredited). lps: Nell Shipman, Wheeler Oakman, Wellington Playter. 6r CND/USA. *L' Instinct Qui Veille*; *The Pulse of the Earth*; *Our Lady of the Big Snows* prod/rel: Curwood-Carver Productions Inc., Canadian Photoplays Ltd.

Wheels of Fate
Code of the Mounted 1935 d: Sam Newfield. lps: Kermit Maynard, Robert Warwick, Lillian Miles. 60M USA. prod/rel: Ambassador Pictures, Inc.

When the Door Opened, 1920, Short Story
When the Door Opened 1925 d: Reginald Barker. lps: Jacqueline Logan, Walter McGrail, Margaret Livingston. 6515f USA. prod/rel: Fox Film Corp.

The White Mouse, Story
White Mouse, The 1914 d: Colin Campbell. lps: Bessie Eyton, Wheeler Oakman. 2r USA. prod/rel: Selig Polyscope Co.

Why I Am Here, Story
Why I Am Here 1913 d: Ralph Ince. lps: Sidney Drew, Anita Stewart, Charles Eldridge. SHT USA. prod/rel: Vitagraph Co. of America

The Wilderness Mail, Short Story
Wilderness Mail 1935 d: Forrest Sheldon. lps: Kermit Maynard, Fred Kohler, Doris Brook. 58M USA. prod/rel: Ambassador Pictures
Wilderness Mail, The 1914 d: Colin Campbell. lps: Bessie Eyton, Tom Mix. 2r USA. prod/rel: Selig Polyscope Co.

The Wolf Hunters; a Tale of Adventure in the Wilderness, Indianapolis 1908, Novel
Trail Beyond, The 1934 d: Robert North Bradbury. lps: John Wayne, Noah Beery Jr., Verna Hillie. 55M USA. prod/rel: Lone Star Productions, Monogram Pictures Corp.©
Wolf Hunters, The 1926 d: Stuart Paton. lps: Robert McKim, Virginia Brown Faire, Alan Roscoe. 5976f USA. prod/rel: Ben Wilson Productions, Rayart Pictures
Wolf Hunters, The 1949 d: Budd Boetticher. lps: Kirby Grant, Jan Clayton, Chinook. 70M USA. prod/rel: Monogram

CUSACK, DYMPHNA (1902–1981), ASL, Cusack, Ellen Dympha
Red Sky at Morning, 1942, Play
Red Sky at Morning 1944 d: Hartney Arthur. 55M ASL. *Escape at Dawn* (UKN)

CUSHING, CATHERINE CHISHOLM
Jerry, Play
Don't Call Me Little Girl 1921 d: Joseph Henabery. lps: Mary Miles Minter, Winnifred Greenwood, Ruth Stonehouse. 4212f USA. prod/rel: Realart Pictures

Kitty MacKay, New York 1914, Play
Kitty MacKay 1917 d: Wilfred North. lps: Lillian Walker, Jewell Hunt, Charles Kent. 4950f USA. prod/rel: Vitagraph Co. of America©, Greater Vitagraph (V-L-S-E, Inc.)

Topsy and Eva, New York 1924, Play
Topsy and Eva 1927 d: Del Lord, D. W. Griffith (Uncredited). lps: Rosetta Duncan, Vivian Duncan, Noble Johnson. 7456f USA. prod/rel: Feature Productions, United Artists

Widow By Proxy, New York 1913, Play
Widow By Proxy 1919 d: Walter Edwards. lps: Marguerite Clark, Agnes Vernon, Gertrude Norman. 4444f USA. prod/rel: Famous Players-Lasky Corp.©, Paramount-Artcraft Pictures

CUSHING, TOM
La Gringa, New York 1928, Play
South Sea Rose 1929 d: Allan Dwan. lps: Lenore Ulric, Charles Bickford, Kenneth MacKennA. 6500f USA. prod/rel: Fox Film Corp.

Laugh Clown Laugh!, New York 1923, Play
Laugh, Clown, Laugh 1928 d: Herbert Brenon. lps: Lon Chaney, Bernard Siegel, Loretta Young. 7045f USA. prod/rel: Metro-Goldwyn-Mayer Pictures

Thank You, New York 1921, Play
Thank You 1925 d: John Ford. lps: Alec B. Francis, Jacqueline Logan, George O'Brien. 6900f USA. prod/rel: Fox Film Corp.

CUSHMAN, CLARISSA FAIRCHILD
Young Widow, Novel
Young Widow 1946 d: Edwin L. Marin. lps: Jane Russell, Louis Hayward, Faith Domergue. 100M USA. prod/rel: United Artists

CUSHMAN, DAN
Joe Stay Away, New York 1953, Novel
Stay Away, Joe 1968 d: Peter Tewkesbury. lps: Elvis Presley, Burgess Meredith, Joan Blondell. 102M USA. prod/rel: Metro-Goldwyn-Mayer, Inc.

Timberjack, Novel
Timberjack 1955 d: Joseph Kane. lps: Sterling Hayden, David Brian, Vera Ralston. 94M USA. prod/rel: Republic

CUSSLER, CLIVE (1931–, USA
Raise the Titanic!, Novel
Raise the Titanic 1980 d: Jerry Jameson. lps: Jason Robards Jr., Richard Jordan, David Selby. 113M USA/UKN. prod/rel: Lord Grade, Martin Starger

CUSTOT, PIERRE
Chichinette Et Cie, Novel
Chichinette Et Cie 1921 d: Henri Desfontaines. lps: Blanche Montel, Jeanne Grumbach, Jean Devalde. 1800m FRN. prod/rel: Gaumont - Serie Pax

CUTCLIFFE-HYNE, C. J.
The Adventures of Captain Kettle, Novel
Adventures of Captain Kettle, The 1922 d: Meyrick Milton. lps: Charles Kettle, Nina Grudgeon, Austin Leigh. 5500f UKN. prod/rel: Captain Kettle Films

CVETIC, MATT
I Posed As a Communist for the F.B.I., Book
I Was a Communist for the F.B.I. 1951 d: Gordon Douglas. lps: Frank Lovejoy, Dorothy Hart, Philip Carey. 83M USA. prod/rel: Warner Bros.

CYRIL
Les Yeux Qui Changent, Play
Mains Vengeresses, Les 1911 d: Georges MoncA. lps: Georges Grand, Jeanne Delvair. 405m FRN. prod/rel: Scagl

CYRIL, VICTOR
La Proie, Play
Proie, La 1917 d: Georges MoncA. lps: Henry Mayer, Jacques Gretillat, Gabrielle Robinne. 1340m FRN. prod/rel: Scagl

CZESZKO, BOHDAN
Pokolenie, 1951, Novel
Pokolenie 1954 d: Andrzej WajdA. lps: Zbigniew Cybulski, Tadeusz Janczar, Tadeusz Lomnicki. 88M PLN. *A Generation* (USA); *Light in the Darkness*

D

DA FONSECA, MANUEL
Cerromaior, 1943, Novel
Cerromaior 1981 d: Luis Filipe RochA. lps: Carlos Paulo, Titus de Faria, Elsa Wallenkamp. 90M PRT. prod/rel: Prole Films

DA PONTE, LORENZO (1749–1838), ITL
Cosi Fan Tutte, Vienna 1790, Opera
Cosi Fan Tutte 1970 d: Vaclav Kaslik. lps: Gundula Janowitz, Christa Ludwig, Olivera Miljakovic. 159M AUS/GRM.
Cosi Fan Tutte 1991 d: Tinto Brass. lps: Claudia Koll, Franco Branciaroli, Paolo LanzA. 105M ITL. *Thus Do They All*

Don Giovanni, Prague 1787, Opera
Don Giovanni 1955 d: Paul Czinner, Alfred Travers. lps: Cesare Siepi, Otto Edelmann, Elizabeth Grummer. 170M UKN. *Don Juan* prod/rel: Harmony, Maxwell
Don Giovanni 1979 d: Joseph Losey. lps: Ruggero Raimondi, Kiri Te Kanawa, Edda Moser. 184M ITL/FRN/GRM. prod/rel: Opera Film (Roma), Films a.2.
Don Juan 1922 d: Edwin J. Collins. lps: Pauline Peters, J. R. Tozer, Lillian Douglas. 1000f UKN. prod/rel: Master Films, Gaumont

DA VERONA, GUIDO
Robes Et Manteaux Cleo, Novel
Cleo, Robes Et Manteaux 1933 d: Nunzio MalasommA. lps: Carmen Boni, Arturo Falconi, Franco Coop. 65M ITL. prod/rel: Caesar Film

La Donna Che Invento l'Amore, Novel
Donna Che Invento l'Amore, La 1952 d: Ferruccio Cerio. lps: Rossano Brazzi, Silvana Pampanini, Juan de LandA. 102M ITL. prod/rel: Produzione B.B.

Mimi Bluette Fiore Del Mio Giardino, Novel
Mimi Bluette Fiore Del Mio Giardino 1976 d: Carlo Di PalmA. lps: Monica Vitti, Shelley Winters, Tommy Tune. 105M ITL. prod/rel: P.I.C. (Roma), P.E.C.F. (Paris)

DAAB, H.
Ringside, New York 1928, Play
Night Parade 1929 d: Malcolm St. Clair. lps: Hugh Trevor, Lloyd Ingraham, Dorothy Gulliver. 74M USA. *Sporting Life* (UKN) prod/rel: RKO Productions

D'ABADIE, CHARLES
Les Nouveaux Riches, Play
Nouveaux Riches, Les 1938 d: Andre Berthomieu. lps: Raimu, Betty Stockfeld, Michel Simon. 89M FRN. prod/rel: Grands Films Artistiques, Fernand Weill

Pomme d'Amour, Play
Pomme d'Amour 1932 d: Jean Dreville. lps: Andre Perchichot, Raymond Cordy, Christiane Dor. 87M FRN. prod/rel: a.P.E.C.

D'ABBES, INGRAM
The Laughing Lady, Musical Play
Laughing Lady, The 1946 d: Paul L. Stein. lps: Anne Ziegler, Webster Booth, Peter Graves. 93M UKN. prod/rel: Anglo-American, British National

Shadow Man, Play
Terror on Tiptoe 1936 d: Louis Renoir. lps: Bernard Nedell, Mabel Poulton, Jasper Maskeleyne. 58M UKN. prod/rel: Mb Productions, New Realm

DABIT, EUGENE (1898–1936), FRN
L' Hotel du Nord, 1929, Novel
Hotel du Nord 1938 d: Marcel Carne. lps: Louis Jouvet, Arletty, Jean-Pierre Aumont. 97M FRN. prod/rel: Imperial Film

DABROWSKA, MARIA
Noce I Dnie, 1934-35, Novel
Noce I Dnie 1975 d: Jerzy Antczak. lps: Jadwiga Baranska, Jerzy Binczycki. 274M PLN. *Night and Day*; *Bogumil I Barbara*; *Nights and Days*; *Wiatr W Oczy*

DADONE, CARLO
Il Delitto Del Commendatore, Novel
Delitto Del Commendatore, Il 1921 d: Amedeo Mustacchi. lps: Dante Cappelli, Lilian Dorry, Nina Ferrero. 2157m ITL. prod/rel: Tiziano Film

DAENINCKX, DIDIER
Le Croise de l'Ordre, Novel
Novacek: le Croise de l'Ordre 1994 d: Marco Pico. lps: Patrick Catafilo, Ann-Gisel Glass, Jean-Paul Roussillon. TVM. 98M BLG/FRN/PRT. *Le Croise de l'Ordre*

Playback, Novel
Heroines 1998 d: Gerard Krawczyk. lps: Virginie Ledoyen, Maidi Roth, Marc Duret. 110M FRN. prod/rel: Gaumont, France 2 Cinema

D'AGATA, GIUSEPPE
Novel
Esercito Di Scipione, L' 1978 d: Giuliana Berlinguer. lps: Pietro Biondi, Pier Luigi Giorgio, Gianna Piaz. MTV. F ITL.

Il Medico Della Mutua, Novel
Medico Della Mutua, Il 1968 d: Luigi ZampA. lps: Alberto Sordi, Bice Valori, Sara Franchetti. 98M ITL. *Be Sick. It's Free*; *The Panel Doctor*; *Get Sick. It's Free!* prod/rel: Euro International Film, Explorer Film '58

DAGERMAN, STIG (1923–1954), SWD, Dagerman, Stig Halvard
Brant Barn, 1948, Novel
Brant Barn 1967 d: Hans Abramson. lps: Bente Dessau, Keve Hjelm, Marie Goranzon. 103M SWD. *The Sinning Urge* (UKN); *Burnt Child* prod/rel: Minerva

Brollopsbesvar, Stockholm 1949, Novel
Brollopsbesvar 1964 d: Ake Falck. lps: Jarl Kulle, Margaretha Krook, Lena Hansson. 100M SWD. *Swedish Wedding Night* (USA); *Wedding -Swedish Style* (UKN) prod/rel: Minerva Film Produktion
Natt Pa Glimmingehus, En 1954 d: Torgny Wickman. lps: Edvard Persson, Bengt Logardt, Bibi Andersson. 99M SWD. *Night at Glimminge Castle* prod/rel: Ab Europa Film

Ormen, 1945, Novel
Ormen 1966 d: Hans Abramson. lps: Christina Schollin, Harriet Andersson, Hans Ernback. 90M SWD. *The Serpent* prod/rel: Minerva

D'AGOSTINO, RUTH
The Revelations of a Woman's Heart, Novel
Woman's Heart, A 1926 d: Phil Rosen. lps: Enid Bennett, Gayne Whitman, Edward Earle. 5800f USA. prod/rel: Sterling Pictures

DAHL, ANDRE
Quand Te Tues-Tu?, Novel
Quand Te Tues-Tu? 1931 d: Roger Capellani. lps: Robert Burnier, Noel-Noel, Simone Vaudry. 80M FRN. prod/rel: Films Paramount

DAHL, ROALD (1916–1990), UKN
Beware of the Dog, 1944, Short Story
   36 Hours 1964 d: George Seaton. lps: James Garner, Eva Marie Saint, Rod Taylor. 115M USA. *Thirty-Six Hours* prod/rel: Perlberg-Seaton Productions, Cherokee Productions
Bfg, Novel
   Bfg 1990 d: Brian Cosgrove. ANM. 105M UKN. *Big Friendly Giant* prod/rel: Cosgrove Hall
Danny the Champion of the World, Novel
   Danny, Champion of the World 1989 d: Gavin Millar. lps: Jeremy Irons, Samuel Irons, Robbie Coltrane. 94M UKN/USA. *Danny the Champion of the World; Roald Dahl's Danny the Champion of the World* prod/rel: Portobello Productions, British Screen
James and the Giant Peach, Book
   James and the Giant Peach 1996 d: Henry Selick. lps: Joanna Lumley, Miriam Margolyes, Peter Postlethwaite. ANM. 80M USA. prod/rel: Disney Enterprises
Matilda, Novel
   Matilda 1996 d: Danny Devito. lps: Mara Wilson, Danny Devito, Rhea Perlman. 98M USA. *Roald Dahl's Matilda* (UKN) prod/rel: Tristar Pictures, Jersey Films
The Witches, Novel
   Witches, The 1989 d: Nicolas Roeg. lps: Anjelica Huston, Mai Zetterling, Jasen Fisher. 92M UKN/USA. *Sweet Bird of Youth* prod/rel: Warner Bros., Lorimar

DAHN, FELIX (1834–1912), GRM
Kampf Um Rom, Novel
   Kampf Um Rom, Teil 1: Komm Nur, Mein Liebstes Vogelein 1968 d: Robert Siodmak. lps: Laurence Harvey, Orson Welles, Sylva KoscinA. 103M GRM/ITL/RMN. *The Struggle for Rome; Battle for Rome* prod/rel: C.C.C., Pegaso
   Kampf Um Rom, Teil 2: Der Verrat 1969 d: Robert Siodmak. lps: Laurence Harvey, Orson Welles, Sylva KoscinA. 84M GRM/ITL/RMN. prod/rel: C.C.C., Pegaso

DAISNE, JOHAN
Short Story
   Soir, un Train, Un 1968 d: Andre Delvaux. lps: Yves Montand, Anouk Aimee, Adriana Bogdan. 90M BLG/FRN. *One Night. a Train; A Night. a Train; One Evening on a Train* prod/rel: Parc Films, Films Europa
De Man Die Zijn Haar Liet Knippen, 1947, Novel
   Man Die Zijn Haar Kort Liet Knippen 1966 d: Andre Delvaux. lps: Beata Tyszkiewicz, Senne Rouffaer, Hector Camerlynck. 94M BLG. *The Man Who Had His Hair Cut Short* (UKN); *The Man With a Shaven Head; L' Homme Au Crane Rase* prod/rel: Belgisches (Flamisches)

DAIX, DIDIER
Il Faut Tuer Julie, Play
   How to Murder a Rich Uncle 1957 d: Nigel Patrick, Max Varnel. lps: Nigel Patrick, Charles Coburn, Wendy Hiller. 79M UKN. prod/rel: Warwick, Columbia

D'ALBERT, EUGEN
Tiefland, Opera
   Tiefland 1954 d: Leni Riefenstahl. lps: Leni Riefenstahl, Franz Eichberger, Bernhard Minetti. 98M GRM. *Lowland* prod/rel: Leni Riefenstahl

DALBY, EDMUND
Lend Me Your Wife, Play
   Lend Me Your Wife 1935 d: W. P. Kellino. lps: Henry Kendall, Kathleen Kelly, Cyril Smith. 61M UKN. prod/rel: Grafton, MGM

DALBY, LIZA
Geisha, Book
   American Geisha 1986 d: Lee Philips. lps: Pam Dawber, Richard Narita, Robert Ito. TVM. 104M USA. *Geisha* prod/rel: CBS, Stonehenge Productions

DALE, JAMES
Wild Justice, 1933, Play
   Case of Gabriel Perry, The 1935 d: Albert de Courville. lps: Henry Oscar, Olga Lindo, Margaret Lockwood. 78M UKN. prod/rel: British Lion

DALE, SEPTIMUS
Short Story
   Bruder, Die 1976 d: Wolfgang Gremm. lps: Klaus Lowitsch, Erika Pluhar, Doris Kunstmann. 99M GRM. *The Brothers* prod/rel: Regina Ziegler, C.I.C.

DALEY, ROBERT
Hands of a Stranger, Novel
   Hands of a Stranger 1987 d: Larry Elikann. lps: Armand Assante, Blair Brown, Beverly d'Angelo. TVM. 200M USA. prod/rel: Edgar J. Sherick Associated Prod., Taft Enterntainment
Prince of the City, Book
   Prince of the City 1981 d: Sidney Lumet. lps: Treat Williams, Jerry Orbach, Richard Foronjy. 167M USA. prod/rel: Warner Bros., Orion Pictures

Tainted Evidence, Novel
   Night Falls on Manhattan 1997 d: Sidney Lumet. lps: Andy Garcia, Lena Olin, Richard Dreyfuss. 114M USA. prod/rel: Mount/Kramer, Spelling Films Inc.
To Kill a Cop, Book
   To Kill a Cop 1978 d: Gary Nelson. lps: Joe Don Baker, Louis Gossett Jr., Patrick O'Neal. TVM. 200M USA. prod/rel: David Gerber Productions, Columbia Pictures
Year of the Dragon, Novel
   Year of the Dragon 1985 d: Michael Cimino. lps: Mickey Rourke, John Lone, Ariane. 134M USA. prod/rel: MGM, United Artists

DALIO, MARCEL
Grisou, Play
   Grisou 1938 d: Maurice de Canonge. lps: Madeleine Robinson, Odette Joyeux, Pierre Brasseur. 87M FRN. *Les Hommes Sans Soleil* prod/rel: Films Albatros

DALLAYRAC, DOMINIQUE
Dossier Prostitution, Book
   Dossier Prostitution 1969 d: Jean-Claude Roy. lps: Jean-Philippe Ancelle, Line Arnel, Adaly Bayle. 90M FRN. *Secret French Prostitution Report* (UKN); *Girls for Pleasure* prod/rel: Rene Thevenet, Tanagra Productions

DALL'ONGARO, FRANCESCO
Il Fornaretto, 1846, Play
   Fornaretto Di Venezia, Il 1907 d: Mario Caserini. lps: Ubaldo Maria Del Colle, Fernanda Negri-Pouget. 228m ITL. *The Venetian Baker* (USA) prod/rel: Cines
   Fornaretto Di Venezia, Il 1914 d: Luigi Maggi. lps: Alberto Nepoti, Umberto Mozzato, Eugenia Tettoni. 1400m ITL. prod/rel: Leonardo Film
   Fornaretto Di Venezia, Il 1923 d: Mario Almirante. lps: Alberto Collo, Amleto Novelli, Nini Dinelli. 1875m ITL. *Il Povero Fornaretto Di Venezia* prod/rel: Alba Film
   Fornaretto Di Venezia, Il 1939 d: Duilio Coletti. lps: Elsa de Giorgi, Roberto Villa, Clara Calamai. 73M ITL. prod/rel: Vi-Va Film, Artisti Associati
   Fornaretto Di Venezia, Il 1963 d: Duccio Tessari. lps: Jacques Perrin, Enrico Maria Salerno, Sylva KoscinA. 100M ITL/FRN. *Les Proces Des Doges* (FRN); *The Scapegoat* prod/rel: Ultra Film, Lux Film (Roma)

D'ALPUGET, BLANCHE
Turtle Beach, Novel
   Turtle Beach 1991 d: Stephen Wallace. lps: Greta Scacchi, Joan Chen, Jack Thompson. 90M ASL. prod/rel: Village Roadshow Pictures (Australia)©, Australian Film Finance Corp.©

DALRYMPLE, ANDREW ANGUS
A Quiet Day in Belfast, Play
   Quiet Day in Belfast, A 1974 d: Milad BessadA. lps: Margot Kidder, Barry Foster, Sean McCann. 88M CND. prod/rel: Twinbay Media International, Vision IV Productions Ltd.

DALRYMPLE, LEONA
Diane of the Green Van, Chicago 1914, Novel
   Diane of the Green Van 1919 d: Wallace Worsley. lps: Alma Rubens, Nigel Barrie, Lamar Johnstone. 4800f USA. prod/rel: Winsome Stars Corp., Robertson-Cole Co.

DALTON, EMMETT
Beyond the Limit, New York 1916, Novel
   Beyond the Law 1918 d: Theodore Marston. lps: Emmett Dalton, Virginia Lee, Bobby Connelly. 6r USA. prod/rel: Southern Feature Film Corp., State Rights
When the Daltons Rode, New York 1931, Book
   When the Daltons Rode 1940 d: George Marshall. lps: Randolph Scott, Kay Francis, Brian Donlevy. 80M USA. prod/rel: Universal Pictures Co.©

D'ALTON, LOUIS
They Got What They Wanted, Play
   Talk of a Million 1951 d: John Paddy Carstairs. lps: Jack Warner, Barbara Mullen, Noel Purcell. 78M UKN. *You Can't Beat the Irish* (USA) prod/rel: Associated British Picture Corporation, Ab-Pathe
This Other Eden, 1954, Play
   This Other Eden 1959 d: Muriel Box. lps: Audrey Dalton, Leslie Phillips, Niall MacGinnis. 81M UKN. prod/rel: Regal Films International, Emmett Dalton

DALVI, JAYWANT
Chakra, 1963, Novel
   Chakra 1979 d: Rabindra Dharmaraj. lps: Smita Patil, Naseeruddin Shah, Kulbhushan KharbandA. 140M IND. *Wheel; Vicious Circle* prod/rel: Neo Films

DALY, AUGUSTIN
Under the Gaslight; Or Life and Love in These Times, New York 1867, Play
   Under the Gaslight 1914 d: Lawrence Marston. lps: William Russell, Lionel Barrymore, Hector V. Sarno. 4r USA. prod/rel: Biograph Co., Klaw & Erlanger©

DAM, HENRY J. W.
The Red Mouse, Philadelphia 1903, Play
   Her Silent Sacrifice 1917 d: Edward Jose. lps: Alice Brady, Henry Clive, Robert Paton Gibbs. 5r USA. *The Red Mouse* prod/rel: Select Pictures Corp.©
The Silver Shell, Novel
   Suspect, The 1916 d: S. Rankin Drew. lps: Anita Stewart, S. Rankin Drew, Anders Randolf. 5-6r USA. prod/rel: Vitagraph Co. of America©, Blue Ribbon Feature

D'AMBRA, LUCIO
Mater Admirabilis, Novel
   Luce Del Mondo, La 1935 d: Gennaro Righelli. lps: Kiki Palmer, Corrado Racca, Letizia Bonini. 65M ITL. *Il Padrone Del Mondo* prod/rel: Lobi Film, Lo Bianco Films

DAN, URI
Meyer Lansky: Mogul of the Mob, Book
   Lansky 1999 d: John McNaughton. lps: Richard Dreyfus, Eric Roberts, Anthony LapagliA. TVM. 120M USA. prod/rel: Hbo Pictures, Frederick Zollo Prods.

DANA, R. H. (1815–1882), USA, Dana Jr., Richard Henry
Two Years Before the Mast, 1840, Novel
   Two Years Before the Mast 1946 d: John Farrow. lps: Alan Ladd, Brian Donlevy, Howard Da SilvA. 98M USA. prod/rel: Paramount

DANAILOW, GEORGI
Zabravete Tozi Slouchai, Play
   Zabravete Tozi Slouchai 1984 d: Krassimir Spassov. lps: Filip Trifonov, Boris Lukanov, Ljubomir Kabakchiev. 97M BUL. *The Case of the Investigating Magistrate; Just Forget That Case* prod/rel: Filmbulgaria

DANBY, FRANK
The Heart of a Child, London 1908, Novel
   Heart of a Child, The 1915 d: Harold Shaw. lps: Edna Flugrath, Edward Sass, Hayford Hobbs. 4590f UKN. prod/rel: London, Jury
   Heart of a Child, The 1920 d: Ray C. Smallwood. lps: Alla Nazimova, Charles Bryant, Ray Thompson. 7r USA. prod/rel: the Nazimova Productions, Metro Pictures Corp.©

DANDOLO, MILLY
E Caduta Una Donna, Novel
   E Caduta Una Donna 1941 d: Alfredo Guarini. lps: Isa Miranda, Rossano Brazzi, Vittorina Benvenuti. 72M ITL. prod/rel: Scalera Film
La Fuggitiva, Novel
   Fuggitiva, La 1941 d: Piero Ballerini. lps: Jole Voleri, Anna Magnani, Clelia MataniA. 81M ITL. prod/rel: Industrie Cin.Che Italiane

D'ANDREA, GOFFREDO
Ventimila Leghe Sopra I Mari, Novel
   Due Cuori Fra le Belve 1943 d: Giorgio C. Simonelli. lps: Toto, Vera Carmi, Enrico Glori. 90M ITL. *Toto Nella Fossa Dei Leoni* prod/rel: Bassoli Film, Tirrenia Cin.

DANE, CLEMENCE (1888–1965), UKN, Ashton, Winifred
A Bill of Divorcement, London 1921, Play
   Bill for Divorcement, A 1922 d: Denison Clift. lps: Constance Binney, Fay Compton, Malcolm Keen. 6109f UKN. *A Bill of Divorcement* prod/rel: Ideal
   Bill of Divorcement, A 1932 d: George Cukor. lps: John Barrymore, Katharine Hepburn, Billie Burke. 75M USA. prod/rel: RKO Radio Pictures, Inc.
   Bill of Divorcement, A 1940 d: John Farrow. lps: Maureen O'Hara, Adolphe Menjou, Fay Bainter. 74M USA. *Not for Each Other; Never to Love* prod/rel: RKO Radio
Enter Sir John, London 1928, Play
   Murder 1930 d: Alfred Hitchcock. lps: Herbert Marshall, Norah Baring, Phyllis Konstam. 108M UKN. *Mary* prod/rel: British International Pictures, Wardour

DANGERFIELD, YVES
La Petite Sirene, Novel
   Petite Sirene, La 1980 d: Roger Andrieux. lps: Laura Alexis, Philippe Leotard, Evelyne Dress. 104M FRN. prod/rel: Apple, Fr 3

DANIEL, BELA
La Femme Et le Rossignol, Short Story
   Femme Et le Rossignol, La 1930 d: Andre Hugon. lps: Kaissa Robba, Rolla France, Jean Marconi. 102M FRN. prod/rel: Hugon-Films, Union-Film

DANIEL, H. B.
A Girl in Bohemia, Play
   Girl in Bohemia, A 1919 d: Howard M. Mitchell. lps: Peggy Hyland, Josef Swickard, L. C. Shumway. 4800f USA. prod/rel: Fox Film Corp., William Fox©

DANIEL, ROLAND
The Man With the Magnetic Eyes, Novel
  Man With the Magnetic Eyes, The 1945 d: Ronald Haines. lps: Robert Bradfield, Henry Norman, Joan Carter. 51M UKN. prod/rel: British Foundation

A Wife Or Two, Play
  Wife Or Two, A 1936 d: MacLean Rogers. lps: Henry Kendall, Nancy Burne, Betty Astell. 63M UKN. prod/rel: British Lion

DANIELL, DAVID SCOTT
By Jiminy, Novel
  Treasure in Malta 1963 d: Derek Williams. lps: Mario Debono, Aidan Mompalao de Piro, Charles Thake. SRL. 93M UKN. prod/rel: Children's Film Foundation, Anvil

DANIELS, HAROLD R.
The House on Greenapple Road, Novel
  House on Greenapple Road, The 1970 d: Robert Day. lps: Christopher George, Janet Leigh, Julie Harris. TVM. 113M USA. prod/rel: Quinn Martin Productions

DANIGER, MARGOT
Winterkuhle Hochzeitsreise, Novel
  Ich Hab Mich So an Dich Gewohnt 1952 d: Eduard von Borsody. lps: Inge Egger, O. W. Fischer, Robert Lindner. 97M AUS. *Geschiedenes Fraulein* prod/rel: Donau

DANINOS, PIERRE (1913–, FRN
Les Carnets du Major Thompson, Novel
  Carnets du Major Thompson, Les 1955 d: Preston Sturges. lps: Jack Buchanan, Martine Carol, Noel-Noel. 105M FRN. *The Diary of Major Thompson* (AUK); *The French They are a Funny Race* prod/rel: S.N.E.G., Paul Wagner

DANN, PATTY
Mermaids, Novel
  Mermaids 1990 d: Richard Benjamin. lps: Cher, Bob Hoskins, Winona Ryder. 111M USA. prod/rel: Orion Pictures

D'ANNUNZIO, GABRIELE (1863–1938), ITL
La Chevrefeuille, 1914
  Ferro, Il 1918 d: Ugo FalenA. lps: Bianca Bellincioni-Stagno, Ernesto Sabbatini, Bruno Emanuel Palmi. 1302m ITL. prod/rel: Tespi Film

La Fiaccola Sotto Il Moggio, 1904, Play
  Fiaccola Sotto Il Moggio, La 1911 d: Luigi Maggi. lps: Antonietta Calderari, Norina Rasero, Mary Cleo Tarlarini?. 233m ITL. *Blood Vengeance* (USA) prod/rel: S.A. Ambrosio
  Fiaccola Sotto Il Moggio, La 1916 d: Eleuterio Rodolfi. lps: Helena Makowska, Umberto Mozzato, Linda Pini. 1085m ITL. prod/rel: S.A. Ambrosio

La Figlia Di Jorio, 1904, Play
  Figlia Di Jorio, La 1911. lps: Mary Cleo Tarlarini, Mario Voller Buzzi, Luigi Maggi. 573m ITL. *Jorio's Daughter* (UKN) prod/rel: S.A. Ambrosio
  Figlia Di Jorio, La 1917 d: Eduardo BencivengA. lps: Mario Bonnard, Irene-Saffo Momo, Giovanna Scotto. 1203m ITL. prod/rel: Caesar Film

Forse Che No Forse Che Si, Novel
  Forse Che Si, Forse Che No 1921 d: Gaston Ravel. lps: Maria Carmi, Ettore Piergiovanni, Eugenia Masetti. 2317m ITL. prod/rel: Medusa Film

La Gioconda, Palermo 1899, Play
  Devil's Daughter, The 1915 d: Frank Powell. lps: Theda Bara, Paul Doucet, Victor Benoit. 5r USA. prod/rel: Fox Film Corp., William Fox©
  Gioconda, La 1912 d: Luigi Maggi. lps: Rina Albry, Mary Cleo Tarlarini, Mario Voller Buzzi. 205m ITL. *Love Re-Conquered* (UKN) prod/rel: S.A. Ambrosio
  Gioconda, La 1916 d: Eleuterio Rodolfi. lps: Helena Makowska, Umberto Mozzato, Mercedes Brignone. 1381m ITL. prod/rel: S.A. Ambrosio

Giovanni l'Episcopo, 1891, Novel
  Delitto Di Giovanni Episcopo, Il 1947 d: Alberto LattuadA. lps: Aldo Fabrizi, Yvonne Sanson, Roldano Lupi. 94M ITL. *Flesh Will Surrender* (USA); *Giovanni Episcopo*; *Giovanni Episcopo's Crime* prod/rel: Lux Film, Pao
  Giovanni Episcopo 1916 d: Mario Gargiulo. lps: Achille Vitti, Tina Xeo, Alberto CasanovA. 1245m ITL. prod/rel: Flegrea Film

L' Innocente, 1891, Novel
  Innocente, L' 1912 d: Eduardo BencivengA. lps: Febo Mari, Fernanda Negri-Pouget, Mary Cleo Tarlarini. 148m ITL. prod/rel: S.A. Ambrosio
  Innocente, L' 1976 d: Luchino Visconti. lps: Giancarlo Giannini, Laura Antonelli, Jennifer O'Neill. 125M ITL/FRN. *L' Innocent* (FRN); *The Intruder*; *The Innocent* (USA) prod/rel: Rizzoli Film (Roma), Les Films Jacques Leitienne (Paris)

Leda Senza Cigno, Novel
  Leda Senza Cigno 1918 d: Giulio Antamoro. lps: Leda Gys, Ignazio Lupi, Enrico RomA. 1521m ITL. prod/rel: Polifilm

La Nave, 1908, Play
  Nave, La 1912 d: Eduardo BencivengA. lps: Antonietta Calderari, Vitale de Stefano, Alberto A. Capozzi. 508m ITL. *The Venetian Tribune Marcus* (USA); *The Ship* (UKN) prod/rel: S.A. Ambrosio
  Nave, La 1921 d: Gabriellino d'Annunzio, Mario Roncoroni. lps: Ida Rubinstein, Ciro Galvani, Alfredo Boccolini. 1742m ITL. prod/rel: Ambrosio-Zanotta

Il Piacere, 1889, Novel
  Piacere, Il 1918 d: Amleto Palermi. lps: Vittorina Lepanto, Enrico Roma, Alberto CasanovA. 1390m ITL. prod/rel: Teatro-Lombardo Film

Sogno Di un Tramonto d'Autunno, 1898
  Sogno Di un Tramonto d'Autunno 1911 d: Luigi Maggi. lps: Antonietta Calderari, Mary Cleo Tarlarini, Mario Voller Buzzi. 309m ITL. *An Autumn Sunset Dream* (USA); *A Blind Retribution* (UKN) prod/rel: S.A. Ambrosio

DANSKZKYS, EDUARD PAUL
Ferdinand Raimund, Biography
  Bruderlein Fein 1942 d: Hans Thimig. lps: Marte Harell, Hans Holt, Winnie Markus. 104M GRM. prod/rel: Wien

DANTE ALIGHIERI
La Divina Commedia, 1310, Verse
  Inferno, L' 1911 d: Adolfo Padovan, Francesco Bertolini. lps: Salvatore Papa, Arturo Pirovano, Giuseppe de Liguoro. 1200m ITL. *La Divina Commedia: l'Inferno*; *L' Inferno Dantesco*; *Dante's Inferno* (UKN) prod/rel: Milano Films
  Inferno, L' 1911 d: Giuseppe Berardi, Arturo Busnengo. lps: Giuseppe Berardi, Armando Novi. 400m ITL. *Visioni Dell'inferno*; *Dante's Inferno* (USA) prod/rel: Helios Film
  Paolo E Francesca 1950 d: Raffaello Matarazzo. lps: Odile Versois, Armando Francioli, Andrea Checchi. 97M ITL. *La Storia Di Francesca Da Rimini*; *Francesca Da Rimini* prod/rel: Lux Film
  Paradiso (Visioni Dantesche), Il 1912. 700m ITL. *Dante's Paradise* (UKN); *Paradise and Purgatory* (USA); *Il Paradiso E Il Purgatorio* prod/rel: Psiche Films
  Purgatorio, Il 1911. 408m ITL. prod/rel: S.A. Ambrosio
  Purgatorio, Il 1911 d: Giuseppe Berardi, Arturo Busnengo. lps: Giuseppe Berardi, Armando Novi. 700m ITL. *Dante's Purgatorio* (UKN); *Paradise and Purgatory* (USA); *Purgatory and Paradise* prod/rel: Helios Film
  Saggi Dell'inferno Dantesco 1909 d: Adolfo Padovan, Francesco Bertolini. lps: Salvatore Papa, Arturo Pirovano, Giuseppe de Liguoro. ITL. prod/rel: Saffi-Comerio
  Skarseld 1975 d: Michael Meschke. lps: Jan Blomberg, Ake Nygren, Inger Jalmert-Maritz. 86M SWD. *A Divine Comedy -Purgatory*; *Purgatorio*; *Purgatory*

DANTE, NICHOLAS
A Chorus Line, Play
  Chorus Line, A 1985 d: Richard Attenborough. lps: Michael Douglas, Terrence Mann, Alyson Reed. 118M USA. prod/rel: Columbia, Embassy Film Associates

DANVERS, DENNIS
Wilderness, Novel
  Wilderness 1996 d: Ben Bolt. lps: Amanda Ooms, Owen Teale, Michael Kitchen. TVM. 150M UKN. prod/rel: Red Rooster

D'ARCY, HUGH ANTOINE
The Face on the Barroom Floor, Poem
  Face on the Barroom Floor, The 1908 d: Edwin S. Porter. lps: Charles Inslee, William V. Ranous. 550f USA. prod/rel: Edison
  Face on the Barroom Floor, The 1923 d: John Ford. lps: Henry B. Walthall, Ruth Clifford, Walter Emerson. 5787f USA. *The Love Image* (UKN); *Drink* prod/rel: Fox Film Corp.
  Face on the Barroom Floor, The 1936 d: Bertram Bracken. lps: Dulcie Cooper, Bramwell Fletcher, Walter Miller. 66M USA. prod/rel: Aubrey Kennedy Pictures Corp., State Rights

Madeleine's Christmas, Story
  Madeleine's Christmas 1912 d: Joseph Smiley. lps: Ormi Hawley, Guy d'Ennery, O'Beck. 1000f USA. prod/rel: Lubin

DARD, FREDERIC
L' Accident, Novel
  Accident, L' 1963 d: Edmond T. Greville. lps: Magali Noel, Danik Patisson, Georges Riviere. 91M FRN. *The Accident* (USA) prod/rel: Films Univers, Felix Films

Beru Et Ces Dames, Novel
  Beru Et Ces Dames 1968 d: Guy Lefranc. lps: Gerard Barray, Jean Richard, Paul Preboist. 100M FRN. prod/rel: Jacques Roitfeld

Le Bras de la Nuit, Novel
  Bras de la Nuit, Les 1961 d: Jacques Guymont. lps: Danielle Darrieux, Roger Hanin, Eva Damien. 85M FRN. prod/rel: Ares, Transfilm G.M.

C'est Toi le Venin., Novel
  Toi le Venin 1958 d: Robert Hossein. lps: Marina Vlady, Robert Hossein, Odile Versois. 92M FRN. *Night Is Not for Sleep* (UKN); *Nude in a White Car* (USA); *Blonde in a White Car* prod/rel: Jules Borkon, Champs-Elysees Productions

Cette Mort Dont Tu Parlais, Paris 1957, Novel
  Menteurs, Les 1961 d: Edmond T. Greville. lps: Dawn Addams, Claude Brasseur, Francis Blanche. 90M FRN. *House of Sin* (UKN); *The Liars* (UKN); *Twisted Lives* prod/rel: Mediterranee Cinema

Delivrez-Nous du Mal, Novel
  Dos Au Mur, Le 1958 d: Edouard Molinaro. lps: Gerard Oury, Jeanne Moreau, Philippe Nicaud. 93M FRN. *Evidence in Concrete*; *Back to the Wall* (USA) prod/rel: S.N.E.G., Cinephonic

Les Magiciens, Novel
  Magiciens, Les 1975 d: Claude Chabrol. lps: Franco Nero, Stefania Sandrelli, Gert Frobe. 90M FRN/GRM/ITL. *Profezia Di un Delitto* (ITL); *Initiation a la Mort* prod/rel: Mondial Te.Fi.

Les Mariolles, Novel
  Menace, La 1960 d: Gerard Oury. lps: Robert Hossein, Marie-Jose Nat, Elsa Martinelli. 80M FRN/ITL. *La Minaccia* (ITL); *The Menace* (USA); *Les Mariolles* prod/rel: S.N.E.G., Franco-London Films

Le Monte-Charge, Paris 1961, Novel
  Mort a l'Etage 1993 d: Philippe Venault. lps: Didier Bezace, Anne Roussel, Philippe Dormoy. TVM. 90M FRN/CZC.

La Monte-Charge, Paris 1961, Novel
  Monte-Charge, Le 1961 d: Marcel Bluwal. lps: Robert Hossein, Lea Massari, Robert Dalban. 85M FRN/ITL. *La Morte Sale in Ascensore* (ITL); *Paris Pick-Up* (USA) prod/rel: S.N.E. Gaumont, Marianne Productions

Les Salauds Vont En Enfer, Play
  Salauds Vont En Enfer, Les 1955 d: Robert Hossein. lps: Serge Reggiani, Henri Vidal, Marina Vlady. 91M FRN. *The Wicked Go to Hell* (UKN) prod/rel: Jules Borkon, Champs-Elysees Productions

San Antonio Ne Pense Qu'a Ca, Novel
  San Antonio Ne Pense Qu'a Ca 1981 d: Joel SeriA. lps: Philippe Gaste, Pierre Doris, Jacques Francois. 90M FRN. prod/rel: Uranium

Toi Qui Vivais, Novel
  Premedition 1959 d: Andre Berthomieu. lps: Jean-Claude Pascal, Pascale Roberts, Jean Desailly. 90M FRN. *Premeditated* (USA) prod/rel: Bertho Films, Filmel

DARE, FRANK
The Claim, New York 1917, Play
  Claim, The 1918 d: Frank Reicher. lps: Edith Storey, Wheeler Oakman, Mignon Anderson. 5r USA. prod/rel: Metro Pictures Corp.©

DARIEN, GEORGES
Biribi, Novel
  Biribi 1970 d: Daniel Moosmann. lps: Michel Tureau, Bruno Cremer, Georges Geret. 105M FRN/TNS. prod/rel: Mog Films, Satpec

Le Voleur, Paris 1898, Novel
  Voleur, Le 1967 d: Louis Malle. lps: Jean-Paul Belmondo, Genevieve Bujold, Marie Dubois. 120M FRN/ITL. *The Thief of Paris* (USA); *The Thief* (UKN) prod/rel: Nouvelles Editions De Films, Productions Artistes Associes

DARK, ALICE ELLIOTT
In the Gloaming, 1993, Short Story
  In the Gloaming 1997 d: Christopher Reeve. lps: Glenn Close, Bridget Fonda, David Strathairn. TVM. 60M USA. prod/rel: Frederick Zollo Prods., Hbo Nyc Prods.

DARLING, W. SCOTT
Story
  Bush Pilot 1947 d: Sterling Campbell. lps: Jack La Rue, Rochelle Hudson, Austin Willis. 60M CND. prod/rel: Dominion Productions Ltd.

The Bride Said No, Story
   I'm Nobody's Sweetheart Now 1940 d: Arthur Lubin. lps: Dennis O'Keefe, Constance Moore, Helen Parrish. 64M USA. prod/rel: Universal Pictures Co.©

DARLINGTON, CHARLES
The Mystery of Jack Hilton, Novel
   Mistero Di Jack Hilton, Il 1913 d: Ubaldo Maria Del Colle. lps: Ubaldo Maria Del Colle, Adriana Costamagna, Arturo Garzes. 1100m ITL. *By Power of Attorney* (USA); *The Mystery of Jack Hilton* (UKN) prod/rel: Savoia Film

DARLINGTON, W. A. (1890–, UKN, Darlington, William Aubrey
Alf's Button, 1919, Novel
   Alf's Button 1920 d: Cecil M. Hepworth. lps: Leslie Henson, Alma Taylor, Gerald Ames. 7050f UKN. prod/rel: Hepworth
   Alf's Button 1930 d: W. P. Kellino. lps: Tubby Edlin, Alf Goddard, Nora Swinburne. 96M UKN. prod/rel: Gaumont
   Alf's Button Afloat 1938 d: Marcel Varnel. lps: Bud Flanagan, Chesney Allen, Jimmy Nervo. 89M UKN. prod/rel: Gainsborough, General Film Distributors
Alf's Carpet, 1928, Novel
   Alf's Carpet 1929 d: W. P. Kellino. lps: Carl Schenstrom, Harald Madsen, Janice Adair. 65M UKN. *The Rocket Bus* prod/rel: British International Pictures, Wardour

DARNLEY, JAMES H.
Facing the Music, London 1899, Play
   Smith's Wives 1935 d: Manning Haynes. lps: Ernie Lotinga, Beryl de Querton, Tyrrell Davis. 60M UKN. prod/rel: Fox British

D'ARQUILLIERE
La Branche Morte, Play
   Branche Morte, La 1926 d: Joseph Guarino. lps: Dolly Davis, Firmin Gemier, Henry Richard. 2000m FRN. prod/rel: Scenario

DARRELL, CHARLES
From Shopgirl to Duchess, Play
   From Shopgirl to Duchess 1915 d: Maurice Elvey. lps: Elisabeth Risdon, Fred Groves, A. V. Bramble. 3600f UKN. prod/rel: British & Colonial, Ideal
Her Luck in London, Play
   Her Luck in London 1914 d: Maurice Elvey. lps: Elisabeth Risdon, Fred Groves, A. V. Bramble. 3900f UKN. prod/rel: British and Colonial, Ashley
The Idol of Paris, Play
   Idol of Paris, The 1914 d: Maurice Elvey. lps: Elisabeth Risdon, Fred Groves, A. V. Bramble. 3400f UKN. prod/rel: British and Colonial, Ideal
When London Sleeps, Play
   When London Sleeps 1914 d: Ernest G. Batley. lps: Lillian Wiggins, Douglas Mars, George Foley. 3357f UKN. prod/rel: British and Colonial, Ideal
   When London Sleeps 1932 d: Leslie Hiscott. lps: Harold French, Francis L. Sullivan, Rene Ray. 78M UKN. prod/rel: Twickenham, Associated Producers and Distributors
When Paris Sleeps, Play
   When Paris Sleeps 1917 d: A. V. Bramble. lps: A. V. Bramble, Ivy Martinek, Pauline Peters. 4652f UKN. prod/rel: British & Colonial, Kineto

DART, IRIS RAINER
Beaches, Novel
   Beaches 1988 d: Garry Marshall. lps: Bette Midler, Barbara Hershey, John Heard. 123M USA. *Friends* prod/rel: Warner, Touchstone

D'ARVILLE, BARONESS
Faithless Lover, Story
   Faithless Lover, The 1928 d: Lawrence C. Windom. lps: Eugene O'Brien, Gladys Hulette, Raymond Hackett. 5626f USA. *The Pasteboard Lover* prod/rel: Krelbar Pictures

DASH, UPENDRA KISHORE
Malajanha, Novel
   Malajanha 1965 d: Nitai Palit. lps: Jharana Das, Manimala, GeetA. 164M IND. *The Dead Moon* prod/rel: Raja Saheb of Ali

D'ASTLER, HENRI
Le Picador, Novel
   Picador, Le 1932 d: Jaquelux. lps: Jean Mauran, Ginette d'Yd, Madeleine Guitty. 91M FRN. prod/rel: M.B. Films

DATALLER, ROGER
Steel Saraband, Novel
   Hard Steel 1942 d: Norman Walker. lps: Wilfred Lawson, Betty Stockfeld, John Stuart. 86M UKN. *What Shall It Profit* prod/rel: General Film Distributors, Gregory, Hake & Walker

DAUBIGNY, B.
Les Deux Sergents, 1823, Play
   Due Sergenti, I 1909. 269m ITL. *The Two Sergeants* (UKN) prod/rel: Itala Film
   Due Sergenti, I 1913 d: Ubaldo Maria Del Colle. lps: Alberto A. Capozzi, Ugo Pardi, Orlando Ricci. 1800m ITL. *The Two Sergeants* (USA); *I Due Sergenti Al Cordone Sanitario Di Porto Vandre* prod/rel: Pasquali E C.

DAUDET, ALPHONSE (1840–1897), FRN
L' Arlesienne, 1872, Play
   Arlesienne, L' 1908 d: Albert Capellani. lps: Henri Desfontaines, Paul Capellani, Henry Krauss. 355m FRN. prod/rel: Scagl
   Arlesienne, L' 1922 d: Andre Antoine. lps: Lucienne Breval, Gabriel de Gravone, Louis Ravet. 2010m FRN. prod/rel: Ste D'editions Cinematographiques
   Arlesienne, L' 1930 d: Jacques de Baroncelli. lps: Blanche Montiel, Jose Noguero, Charles Vanel. F FRN. prod/rel: Pathe-Nathan
   Arlesienne, L' 1941 d: Marc Allegret. lps: Raimu, Gaby Morlay, Edouard Delmont. 105M FRN. prod/rel: Films Imperia
La Belle Nivernaise, Short Story
   Belle Nivernaise, La 1923 d: Jean Epstein. lps: Blanche Montel, Maurice Touze, Pierre Hot. 1800m FRN. *The Beauty from Nivernaise*
Eheskandal Im Hause from Jun. Und Risler Sen., Novel
   Eheskandal Im Hause from Jun. Und Risler Sen. 1927 d: Anders W. Sandberg. lps: Lucy Doraine, Karina Bell, Nora Gregor. 2308m GRM. prod/rel: Deutsche Film-Union Ag
L' Elixir du Pere Gaucher, 1869, Short Story
   Lettres de Mon Moulin, Les 1954 d: Marcel Pagnol. lps: Henri Vilbert, Daxely, Rene Sarvil. 160M FRN. *Letters from My Windmill* (UKN) prod/rel: Cie Mediterraneenne De Films, Eminente Films
From Jeune Et Risler Aine, 1874, Novel
   From Jeune Et Risler Aine 1921 d: Henry Krauss. lps: Maurice Escande, Andree Pascal, Henry Krauss. 2000m FRN. prod/rel: Scagl, Pathe
   From Jeune Et Risler Aine 1941 d: Leon Mathot. lps: Bernard Lancret, Mireille Balin, Junie Astor. 104M FRN. prod/rel: U.F.P.C.
Jack, Novel
   Jack 1913 d: Andre Liabel. lps: Villeneuve, Damores, Olga Demidoff. 1250m FRN. prod/rel: Eclair
   Jack 1925 d: Robert Saidreau. lps: Jean Yonnel, Yane Exiane, Madeleine Carlier. 2200m FRN. prod/rel: Robert Saidreau
La Lutte Pour la Vie, 1889, Novel
   Lotta Per la Vita, La 1921 d: Guido Brignone. lps: Giovanni Cimara, Mercedes Brignone, Lola Visconti-Brignone. 1351m ITL. *Maria Antonia* prod/rel: Rodolfi Film
Le Nabab, Novel
   Nabab, Le 1913 d: Albert Capellani. lps: Leon Bernard, Jean Dax, Pierre Larquey. 1130m FRN. prod/rel: Scagl
Le Petit Chose, 1868, Novel
   Last Lesson, The 1942 d: Allan Kenward. 10M USA.
   Petit Chose, Le 1912 d: Rene Leprince. lps: Pierre Pradier, Henri Bosc, Gabrielle Robinne. 795m FRN. prod/rel: Scagl
   Petit Chose, Le 1923 d: Andre Hugon. lps: Max de Rieux, Jean Debucourt, Gilbert Dalleu. 2660m FRN. prod/rel: Films Andre Hugon
   Petit Chose, Le 1938 d: Maurice Cloche. lps: Robert Lynen, Jean Mercanton, Arletty. 95M FRN. prod/rel: C.I.C.C.
La Petite Paroisse, 1901, Novel
   Piccola Parrocchia, La 1923 d: Mario Almirante. lps: Italia Almirante Manzini, Amleto Novelli, Alberto Collo. 2176m ITL. prod/rel: Alba Film
Les Rois En Exil, Paris 1879, Novel
   Confessions of a Queen 1925 d: Victor Sjostrom. lps: Alice Terry, Lewis Stone, John Bowers. 5820f USA. prod/rel: Metro-Goldwyn Pictures
   Federica d'Illiria 1919 d: Eleuterio Rodolfi. lps: Mercedes Brignone, Domenico Serra, Lola Visconti-Brignone. 1798m ITL. *I Re in Esilio* prod/rel: Rodolfi Film
Sapho, Paris 1884, Novel
   Inspiration 1930 d: Clarence Brown. lps: Greta Garbo, Robert Montgomery, Lewis Stone. 74M USA. prod/rel: Metro-Goldwyn-Mayer Corp., Metro-Goldwyn-Mayer Dist. Corp.©
   Safo, Historia de Una Pasion 1943 d: Carlos Hugo Christensen. lps: Guillermo Battaglia, Miguel Gomez Bao, Mirtha Legrand. 98M ARG. *Sappho -Story of a Passion*

   Sapho 1913 d: W. Christy Cabanne. lps: Florence Roberts, Shelly Hull. 6r USA. *Sappho* prod/rel: Majestic Motion Picture Co., Sapho Feature Film Co.
   Sapho 1917 d: Hugh Ford. lps: Pauline Frederick, Thomas Meighan, Frank Losee. 5r USA. prod/rel: Famous Players Film Co.©, Paramount Pictures Corp.
   Sapho 1934 d: Leonce Perret. lps: Jean Max, Mary Marquet, Marcelle Praince. 90M FRN. prod/rel: Pathe-Natan
   Sapho Ou la Fureur d'Aimer 1970 d: Georges Farrel. lps: Marina Vlady, Renaud Verley, Dawn Addams. 95M FRN/ITL. *Sex Is My Game* (UKN); *Sapho* prod/rel: Cosefa, Mediterranee Productions
   Sappho 1913. lps: Florence Roberts, Shelly Hull. SHT USA. prod/rel: Sappho Feature Film, Majestic
   Sappho 1922. lps: Hilda Moore. 1216f UKN. prod/rel: Master Films, British Exhibitors' Films
Tartarin de Tarascon, 1872, Novel
   Tartarin de Tarascon 1934 d: Raymond Bernard. lps: Raimu, Fernand Charpin, Milly Mathis. 95M FRN. prod/rel: Pathe-Natan
   Tartarin de Tarascon 1962 d: Francis Blanche. lps: Francis Blanche, Alfred Adam, Jacqueline Maillan. 105M FRN. prod/rel: Princia, Djinn Films
Tartarin Sur Les Alpes, Novel
   Tartarin Sur Les Alpes 1921 d: Henri Vorins, Paul Barlatier. lps: Paulette Landais, Vilbert, Emilien Richaud. 3400m FRN. prod/rel: Laurea Films
Les Trois Messes Basses, 1869, Short Story
   Lettres de Mon Moulin, Les 1954 d: Marcel Pagnol. lps: Henri Vilbert, Daxely, Rene Sarvil. 160M FRN. *Letters from My Windmill* (UKN) prod/rel: Cie Mediterraneenne De Films, Eminente Films

DAUDET, ERNEST
Le Crime de Jean Malory, Novel
   Nuit du 11 Septembre, La 1923 d: Bernard-Deschamps. lps: Severin Mars, Vera Karalli, Eugenie Boldireff. 1325m FRN. prod/rel: Ermolieff-Cinema
Par la Verite, Short Story
   Pas la Verite 1917 d: Gaston Leprieur?, Maurice de Feraudy?. lps: Paul Mounet, Jean Worms, Paule Andral. 1845m FRN. prod/rel: Films Moliere

D'AUNIA, MARINA
La Cicala, Novel
   Cicala, La 1980 d: Alberto LattuadA. lps: Virna Lisi, Anthony Franciosa, Clio Goldsmith. 101M ITL. *The Cricket; La Cicada* prod/rel: N.I.R Film, P.I.C.

D'AUREVILLY, BARBEY
Le Rideau Cramosi, Short Story
   Rideau Cramoisi, Le 1952 d: Alexandre Astruc. lps: Jean-Claude Pascal, Anouk Aimee, Jim Gerald. 45M FRN. *The Crimson Curtain* prod/rel: Como, Argos

DAUTHENDEY, MAX
Spielereien Einer Kaiserin, Play
   Spielereien Einer Kaiserin 1929 d: Wladimir von Strischewski. lps: Lil Dagover, Peter Voss, Dimitri Smirnoff. 2619m GRM. prod/rel: Greenbaum-Film

D'AUTHEVILLE, FRANCIS
Echee Au Destin, 1950, Novel
   Saadia 1953 d: Albert Lewin. lps: Cornel Wilde, Mel Ferrer, Rita Gam. 82M USA. prod/rel: MGM

DAVEES, ZELDA
Wearing the Pants, Play
   Those People Next Door 1953 d: John Harlow. lps: Jack Warner, Charles Victor, Marjorie Rhodes. 77M UKN. prod/rel: Film Studios Manchester, Eros

DAVEILLANT, C.
Les Degourdis de la 11E, Play
   Degourdis de la 11E, Les 1937 d: Christian-Jaque. lps: Fernandel, Pauline Carton, Andre Lefaur. 91M FRN. prod/rel: Productions Maurice Lehmann

DAVENPORT, GWEN
Belvedere, Novel
   Sitting Pretty 1948 d: Walter Lang. lps: Robert Young, Maureen O'Hara, Clifton Webb. 84M USA. prod/rel: 20th Century-Fox

DAVENPORT, MARCIA (1903–1996), USA
East Side - West Side, Novel
   East Side, West Side 1949 d: Mervyn Leroy. lps: Barbara Stanwyck, James Mason, Van Heflin. 108M USA. prod/rel: MGM
The Valley of Decision, Novel
   Valley of Decision, The 1945 d: Tay Garnett. lps: Greer Garson, Gregory Peck, Donald Crisp. 111M USA. prod/rel: MGM

D'AVESNE, JEAN
La Vocation, Novel
   Vocation, La 1928 d: Jean Bertin. lps: Jaque Catelain, Rachel Devirys, Eric Barclay. F FRN. prod/rel: Astor-Film

DAVET, MICHEL
Douce, Novel
> **Douce** 1943 d: Claude Autant-LarA. lps: Odette Joyeux, Madeleine Robinson, Marguerite Moreno. 104M FRN. *Love Story* prod/rel: Pierre Guerlais

DAVIDSON, ANDREA
Out of the Shadows, Novel
> **Out of the Shadows** 1988 d: Willi Patterson. lps: Charles Dance, Alexandra Paul, Michael J. Shannon. TVM. 105M USA.

DAVIDSON, BILL
Indict and Convict, Book
> **Indict and Convict** 1974 d: Boris Sagal. lps: George Grizzard, Reni Santoni, Susan Howard. TVM. 100M USA. prod/rel: Universal

DAVIDSON, LIONEL (1922–, UKN)
Night of Wenceslas, London 1960, Novel
> **Hot Enough for June** 1963 d: Ralph Thomas. lps: Dirk Bogarde, Sylva Koscina, Robert Morley. 98M UKN. *Agent 8 3/4* (USA) prod/rel: Rank, Rank Film Distributors

DAVIDSON, RONALD
The Young and the Brave, Novel
> **Young and the Brave, The** 1963 d: Francis D. Lyon. lps: Rory Calhoun, William Bendix, Richard Jaeckel. 84M USA. *Attong* prod/rel: MGM

DAVIDSON, SARA
Loose Change, Novel
> **Loose Change** 1978 d: Jules Irving. lps: Cristina Raines, Season Hubley, Laurie Heineman. TVM. 300M USA. *Those Restless Years* prod/rel: Universal

DAVIES, ANDREW
B. Monkey, Novel
> **B Monkey** 1998 d: Michael Radford. lps: Asia Argento, Jared Harris, Jonathon Rhys-Meyer. 115M UKN. prod/rel: Buena Vista Intl., Miramax

Getting Hurt, Novel
> **Getting Hurt** 1998 d: Ben Bolt. lps: Ciaran Hinds, Amanda Ooms, David Hayman. TVM. 90M UKN. prod/rel: BBC

DAVIES, BATTY
Duet, Play
> **House of Darkness** 1948 d: Oswald Mitchell. lps: Laurence Harvey, Lesley Brook, John Stuart. 77M UKN. prod/rel: International Motion Pictures, British Lion

DAVIES, HARRY PARR
The Glorious Days, London 1953, Musical Play
> **Lilacs in the Spring** 1954 d: Herbert Wilcox. lps: Anna Neagle, Errol Flynn, David Farrar. 94M UKN. *Let's Make Up* (USA) prod/rel: Everest, Wilcox-Neagle

Lisbon Story, London 1943, Play
> **Lisbon Story** 1946 d: Paul L. Stein. lps: Patricia Burke, David Farrar, Walter RillA. 103M UKN. prod/rel: British National, Anglo-American

DAVIES, HUBERT HENRY
Cousin Kate, Boston 1910, Play
> **Cousin Kate** 1920 d: Mrs. Sidney Drew. lps: Alice Joyce, Gilbert Emery, Beth Martin. 4800f USA. prod/rel: Vitagraph Co. of America
> **Strictly Modern** 1930 d: William A. Seiter. lps: Dorothy MacKaill, Sidney Blackmer, Julanne Johnston. 5632f USA. prod/rel: First National Pictures

Outcast, New York 1914, Play
> **Girl from 10th Avenue, The** 1935 d: Alfred E. Green. lps: Bette Davis, Ian Hunter, Colin Clive. 69M USA. *Men on Her Mind* (UKN); *The Girl from Tenth Avenue* prod/rel: First National Productions Corp., First National Pictures©
> **Outcast** 1917 d: Dell Henderson. lps: Ann Murdock, David Powell, Catherine Calvert. 6r USA. prod/rel: Empire All-Star Corp.©, Mutual Film Corp.
> **Outcast** 1922 d: Chet Withey. lps: Elsie Ferguson, David Powell, William David. 7309f USA. prod/rel: Famous Players-Lasky, Paramount Pictures
> **Outcast** 1928 d: William A. Seiter. lps: Corinne Griffith, James Ford, Edmund Lowe. 6854f USA. prod/rel: First National Pictures

A Single Man, London 1910, Play
> **Single Man, A** 1928 d: Harry Beaumont. lps: Lew Cody, Aileen Pringle, Marceline Day. 5596f USA. prod/rel: Metro-Goldwyn-Mayer Pictures
> **Single Man, The** 1919 d: A. V. Bramble. lps: Cecil Mannering, Doris Lytton, George Mallett. 5000f UKN. prod/rel: British Lion, Ideal

DAVIES, HUNTER
Here We Go Round the Mulberry Bush, London 1965, Novel
> **Here We Go Round the Mulberry Bush** 1967 d: Clive Donner. lps: Barry Evans, Judy Geeson, Angela Scoular. 96M UKN. prod/rel: Giant Film Production, Ltd., United Artists

DAVIES, J. RALEIGH
The Comeback, Story
> **No Defense** 1921 d: William Duncan. lps: William Duncan, Edith Johnson, Jack Richardson. 5700f USA. prod/rel: Vitagraph Co. of America

Locked Out, Story
> **Girl in His Room, The** 1922 d: Edward Jose. lps: Alice Calhoun, Warner Baxter, Robert Anderson. 4523f USA. *Locked Out* prod/rel: Vitagraph Co. of America

DAVIES, JACK
Story
> **High Flight** 1957 d: John Gilling. lps: Ray Milland, Anthony Newley, Helen Cherry. 102M UKN. prod/rel: Columbia, Warwick

Esther, Ruth and Jennifer, Novel
> **North Sea Hijack** 1980 d: Andrew V. McLaglen. lps: Roger Moore, James Mason, Anthony Perkins. 99M UKN. *Ffolkes* (USA); *Assault Force; Esther, Ruth & Jennifer* prod/rel: Universal, Cinema Seven

DAVIES, L. P.
The Artificial Man, London 1965, Novel
> **Project X** 1968 d: William Castle. lps: Christopher George, Greta Baldwin, Henry Jones. 97M USA. prod/rel: Paramount Pictures, Hanna-Barbera Productions

The Groundstar Conspiracy, Novel
> **Groundstar Conspiracy, The** 1972 d: Lamont Johnson. lps: Michael Sarrazin, George Peppard, Christine Belford. 96M USA/CND. prod/rel: Universal, Hal Roach

Pyschogeist, London 1966, Novel
> **Project X** 1968 d: William Castle. lps: Christopher George, Greta Baldwin, Henry Jones. 97M USA. prod/rel: Paramount Pictures, Hanna-Barbera Productions

DAVIES, MARIA THOMPSON
The Daredevil, New York 1916, Novel
> **Daredevil, The** 1918 d: Francis J. Grandon. lps: Gail Kane, Norman Trevor, William W. Crimans. 5r USA. prod/rel: Gail Kane Productions, Mutual Film Corp.©

The Golden Bird, New York 1918, Novel
> **Little Miss Hoover** 1918 d: John S. Robertson. lps: Marguerite Clark, Eugene O'Brien, Alfred Hickman. 4909f USA. *The Golden Bird* prod/rel: Famous Players-Lasky Corp.©, Paramount Pictures

Out of a Clear Sky, New York 1917, Novel
> **Out of a Clear Sky** 1918 d: Marshall Neilan. lps: Marguerite Clark, Thomas Meighan, E. J. Radcliffe. 5r USA. prod/rel: Famous Players-Lasky Corp., Paramount Pictures

DAVIES, NAUNTON
The Cobweb, Play
> **Cobweb, The** 1917 d: Cecil M. Hepworth. lps: Henry Edwards, Alma Taylor, Stewart Rome. 5700f UKN. prod/rel: Hepworth, Harma
> **Strangling Threads** 1923 d: Cecil M. Hepworth. lps: Alma Taylor, Campbell Gullan, James Carew. 6648f UKN. prod/rel: Hepworth, Ideal

DAVIES, VALENTINE (1905–1961), USA
Story
> **Miracle on 34th Street** 1947 d: George Seaton. lps: Maureen O'Hara, John Payne, Edmund Gwenn. 96M USA. *The Big Heart* (UKN) prod/rel: Twentieth Century-Fox
> **Miracle on 34th Street** 1973 d: Fielder Cook. lps: Jane Alexander, David Hartman, Roddy McDowall. TVM. 100M USA. prod/rel: 20th Century-Fox
> **Miracle on 34th Street** 1994 d: Les Mayfield. lps: Richard Attenborough, Elizabeth Perkins, Dylan McDermott. 114M USA. prod/rel: Twentieth Century-Fox

D'AVINO, MICHELE
Il Materasso Di Maria Ricchezza, Novel
> **Operazione Ricchezza** 1968 d: Vittorio Musy Glori. lps: Gabriella Giorgelli, Raul Cabrera, Regina Bianchi. 89M ITL. prod/rel: Golfo Cin.Ca

DAVIS
Gretchen, Play
> **Sechs Madchen Suchen Nacht Quartier** 1928 d: Hans Behrendt. lps: Jenny Jugo, Truus Van Aalten, Ellen Muller. 2663m GRM. prod/rel: Felsom-Film, Defa

DAVIS, AARON
The Golden Calf, 1926, Short Story
> **Golden Calf, The** 1930 d: Millard Webb. lps: Jack Mulhall, Sue Carol, El Brendel. 6800f USA. *Her Golden Calf* prod/rel: Fox Film Corp.

DAVIS, ALFRED
Last Curtain, 1933, Play
> **Till We Meet Again** 1936 d: Robert Florey. lps: Herbert Marshall, Gertrude Michael, Lionel Atwill. 80M USA. *'Til We Meet Again; Reunion* prod/rel: Paramount Pictures©

DAVIS, ARTHUR L.
Article
> **Death in Small Doses** 1957 d: Joseph M. Newman. lps: Peter Graves, Mala Powers, Chuck Connors. 79M USA. prod/rel: Allied Artists

DAVIS, BEALE
One Way Street, New York 1924, Novel
> **One Way Street** 1925 d: John Francis Dillon. lps: Ben Lyon, Anna Q. Nilsson, Marjorie Daw. 5600f USA. prod/rel: First National Pictures

DAVIS, BILL C.
Mass Appeal, Play
> **Mass Appeal** 1984 d: Glenn Jordan. lps: Jack Lemmon, Zeljko Ivanek, Charles Durning. 100M USA. prod/rel: Universal, Turman-Foster Company

DAVIS, CHARLES BELMONT
The Escape, Story
> **Studio Escapade, A** 1915 d: Lloyd B. Carleton. lps: Bessie Eyton, Lillian Hayward, Edward Peil. 2r USA. prod/rel: Selig Polyscope Co.

Handle With Care, Story
> **Handle With Care** 1922 d: Phil Rosen. lps: Grace Darmond, Harry Myers, James Morrison. 5r USA. prod/rel: Rockett Film Corp., Associated Exhibitors

Nothing a Year, New York 1915, Novel
> **Woman's Business, A** 1920 d: B. A. Rolfe. lps: Olive Tell, Edmund Lowe, Lucille Lee Stewart. 4994f USA. *Nothing a Year* prod/rel: Jans Pictures, Inc., State Rights

The Octopus, 1917, Short Story
> **Mother O' Mine** 1921 d: Fred Niblo. lps: Lloyd Hughes, Betty Ross Clark, Betty Blythe. 6004f USA. prod/rel: Thomas H. Ince Productions, Associated Producers

When Johnny Comes Marching Home, 1914, Short Story
> **Home Stretch, The** 1921 d: Jack Nelson. lps: Douglas MacLean, Beatrice Burnham, Walt Whitman. 4602f USA. prod/rel: Thomas H. Ince Productions, Paramount Pictures

DAVIS, CHRIS
The Fighting Parson, Play
> **Fighting Parson, The** 1912 d: Bert Haldane, George Gray. lps: George Gray. 3000f UKN. prod/rel: Barker, Jury

DAVIS, CLYDE BRION (1894–1962), USA
Adventure, Novel
> **Adventure** 1945 d: Victor Fleming. lps: Clark Gable, Greer Garson, Joan Blondell. 126M USA. prod/rel: MGM

DAVIS, DORRANCE
Apron Strings, 1930, Play
> **Virtuous Husband, The** 1931 d: Vin Moore. lps: Elliott Nugent, Betty Compson, Jean Arthur. 75M USA. *What Wives Don't Want* (UKN); *Apron Strings* prod/rel: Universal Pictures Corp.©

DAVIS, ED
Me Too, Novel
> **All of Me** 1984 d: Carl Reiner. lps: Steve Martin, Lily Tomlin, Victoria Tennant. 93M USA. prod/rel: Universal, Old Time Productions

DAVIS, ELIZABETH
Revenge, Novel
> **Revenge** 1971 d: Jud Taylor. lps: Shelley Winters, Bradford Dillman, Stuart Whitman. TVM. 74M USA. *There Once Was a Woman; One Woman's Revenge* prod/rel: Mark Carliner Productions

DAVIS, ELMER HOLMES (1890–1958), USA, Davis, Elmer
Friends of Mr. Sweeney, New York 1925, Novel
> **Friends of Mr. Sweeney** 1934 d: Edward Ludwig. lps: Charles Ruggles, Eugene Pallette, Berton Churchill. 68M USA. prod/rel: Warner Bros. Pictures©

I'll Show You the Town, New York 1924, Novel
> **I'll Show You the Town** 1925 d: Harry Pollard. lps: Reginald Denny, Marion Nixon, Edward M. Kimball. 7440f USA. prod/rel: Universal Pictures

Old-Timer, 1935, Short Story
> **My American Wife** 1936 d: Harold Young. lps: Francis Lederer, Ann Sothern, Fred Stone. 75M USA. *The Old-Timer; The Count of Arizona* prod/rel: Paramount Productions©

Times Have Changed, New York 1923, Novel
Times Have Changed 1923 d: James Flood. lps: William Russell, Mabel Julienne Scott, Charles West. 5082f USA. prod/rel: Fox Film Corp.

White Pants Willie, Novel
White Pants Willie 1927 d: Charles Hines. lps: Johnny Hines, Leila Hyams, Henry A. Barrows. 6350f USA. prod/rel: B & H Enterprises, First National Pictures

DAVIS, FOREST
Smashing the Rackets, 1937-38, Article
Smashing the Rackets 1938 d: Lew Landers. lps: Chester Morris, Frances Mercer, Rita Johnson. 69M USA. prod/rel: RKO Radio Pictures©

DAVIS, FRANK FOSTER
The Phantom of the Forest, Story
Phantom of the Forest, The 1926 d: Henry McCarty. lps: Betty Francisco, Eddie Phillips, James Mason. 5800f USA. prod/rel: Gotham Productions, Lumas Film Corp.

The Silent Pal, Story
Silent Pal 1925 d: Henry McCarty. lps: Eddie Phillips, Shannon Day, Colin Kenny. 5452f USA. prod/rel: Gotham Productions, Lumas Film Corp.

DAVIS, FREDERICK C.
Meet the Executioner, Story
Lady in the Death House 1944 d: Steve Sekely. lps: Jean Parker, Lionel Atwill, Douglas Fowley. 64M USA. *Her Last Mile; The Executioner* prod/rel: P.R.C.

DAVIS, GUSTAV
Musketyri Z Katakomb, Play
Katakomby 1940 d: Martin Fric. lps: Vlasta Burian, Jaroslav Marvan, Cenek Slegl. 2287m CZC. *Catacombs* prod/rel: UFA

DAVIS, HASSOLDT
The Sorcerer's Village, Book
Sorcerer's Village, The 1958 d: Hassoldt Davis. DOC. 70M USA. *Voodoo Village* prod/rel: Continental Distributing, Grand Prize Films

DAVIS, IRVING KAYE
Madame Julie, 1930, Play
Fils de l'Autre, Le 1931 d: Henri de La Falaise. lps: Jeanne Helbling, Geymond Vital, Emile Chautard. 70M USA. *Une Femme Libre; Madame Julie* prod/rel: RKO-Radio Pictures

Woman Between, The 1931 d: Victor Schertzinger. lps: Lili Damita, O. P. Heggie, Lester Vail. 73M USA. *Madame Julie* (UKN) prod/rel: RKO Radio Pictures©

DAVIS, JOSEPH E.
Mission to Moscow, Book
Mission to Moscow 1943 d: Michael Curtiz. lps: Walter Huston, Ann Harding, Oscar HomolkA. 123M USA. prod/rel: Warner Bros.

DAVIS, LUTHER
Article
Mayor of 44th Street 1942 d: Alfred E. Green. lps: George Murphy, Anne Shirley, Richard Barthelmess. 86M USA. prod/rel: RKO

DAVIS, MARY EVELYN MOORE
The Little Chevalier, New York 1903, Novel
Little Chevalier, The 1917 d: Alan Crosland. lps: Shirley Mason, Ray McKee, Richard Tucker. 4r USA. prod/rel: Thomas A. Edison, Inc.©, K-E-S-E Service

DAVIS, MEREDITH
When Smith Meets Smith, Story
Beyond the Border 1925 d: Scott R. Dunlap. lps: Harry Carey, Mildred Harris, Thomas Santschi. 4469f USA. prod/rel: Rogstrom Productions, Producers Distributing Corp.

DAVIS, NORAH
The Other Woman, New York 1920, Novel
Other Woman, The 1921 d: Edward Sloman. lps: Jerome Patrick, Jane Novak, Helen Jerome Eddy. 5000f USA. prod/rel: J. L. Frothingham Productions, W. W. Hodkinson Corp.

DAVIS, NORBERT
A Gunsmoke Case for Major Cain, Story
Hands Across the Rockies 1941 d: Lambert Hillyer. lps: Bill Elliott, Mary Daily, Dub Taylor. 58M USA. prod/rel: Columbia

DAVIS, OSSIE
Purlie Victorious, New York 1961, Play
Gone are the Days! 1963 d: Nicholas Webster. lps: Ruby Dee, Ossie Davis, Sorrell Booke. 100M USA. *The Man from C.O.T.T.O.N.; Purlie Victorious; The Man from C.O.T.T.O.N. Or How I Stopped Worrying and Learned to Love the Boll Weevil* prod/rel: Hammer Film Corporation

DAVIS, OWEN (1874–1956), USA
At the Switch; Or Her Marriage Vow, Play
Her Marriage Vow 1924 d: Millard Webb. lps: Monte Blue, Willard Louis, Beverly Bayne. 6800f USA. prod/rel: Warner Brothers Pictures

Big Jim Garrity, New York 1914, Play
Big Jim Garrity 1916 d: George Fitzmaurice. lps: Robert Edeson, Eleanor Woodruff, Carl Harbaugh. 5r USA. prod/rel: Pathe Exchange, Inc.©, Gold Rooster Plays

Blow Your Own Horn, Play
Blow Your Own Horn 1923 d: James W. Horne. lps: Warner Baxter, Ralph Lewis, Derelys Perdue. 6315f USA. prod/rel: R-C Pictures, Film Booking Offices of America

Broadway After Dark, Play
Broadway After Dark 1924 d: Monta Bell. lps: Adolphe Menjou, Norma Shearer, Anna Q. Nilsson. 6300f USA. prod/rel: Warner Brothers Pictures

Confession of a Wife; Or from Mill to Millions, Story
Confessions of a Wife 1928 d: Albert Kelley. lps: Helene Chadwick, Arthur Clayton, Ethel Grey Terry. 6047f USA. prod/rel: Excellent Pictures

The Donovan Affair, New York 1926, Play
Donovan Affair, The 1929 d: Frank CaprA. lps: Jack Holt, Dorothy Revier, William Collier Jr. 83M USA. prod/rel: Columbia Pictures

Driftwood, Play
Driftwood 1916 d: Marshall Farnum. lps: Vera Michelena, Clarissa Selwynne, Dora Heritage. 5r USA. prod/rel: Ocean Film Corp., State Rights

Easy Come Easy Go, New York 1925, Play
Easy Come, Easy Go 1928 d: Frank Tuttle. lps: Richard Dix, Nancy Carroll, Charles Sellon. 5364f USA. prod/rel: Paramount Famous Lasky Corp.

Only Saps Work 1930 d: Cyril Gardner, Edwin H. Knopf. lps: Leon Errol, Richard Arlen, Mary Brian. 6644f USA. *Social Errors* prod/rel: Paramount-Publix Corp.

The Family Cupboard, New York 1913, Play
Family Cupboard, The 1915 d: Frank H. Crane. lps: Holbrook Blinn, Frances Nelson, Johnny Hines. 5r USA. prod/rel: William A. Brady Picture Plays, Inc., World Film Corp.©

Forever After, Play
Forever After 1926 d: F. Harmon Weight. lps: Lloyd Hughes, Mary Astor, Hallam Cooley. 6330f USA. prod/rel: First National Pictures

The Gambler of the West, New York 1906, Play
Gambler of the West, The 1915. lps: William J. Butler, Violet Reid, George Pearce. 4r USA. prod/rel: Biograph Co.©, General Film Co.

The Haunted House, New York 1926, Play
Haunted House, The 1928 d: Benjamin Christensen. lps: Larry Kent, Thelma Todd, Edmund Breese. 5755f USA. prod/rel: First National Pictures

Icebound, Boston 1923, Novel
Icebound 1924 d: William C. de Mille. lps: Richard Dix, Lois Wilson, Helen Du Bois. 6471f USA. prod/rel: Famous Players-Lasky, Paramount Pictures

Lazybones, New York 1924, Play
Lazybones 1925 d: Frank Borzage. lps: Buck Jones, Madge Bellamy, Virginia Marshall. 7234f USA. prod/rel: Fox Film Corp.

Life at Yale, Play
Hold 'Em Yale! 1928 d: Edward H. Griffith. lps: Rod La Rocque, Jeanette Loff, Hugh Allan. 7056f USA. *At Yale* prod/rel: de Mille Pictures, Pathe Exchange, Inc.

The Lighthouse By the Sea, 1920, Play
Lighthouse By the Sea, The 1924 d: Malcolm St. Clair. lps: William Collier Jr., Louise Fazenda, Charles Hill Mailes. 6900f USA. prod/rel: Warner Brothers Pictures

Lola, New York 1911, Play
Lola 1914 d: James Young. lps: Clara Kimball Young, Frank Holland, Alec B. Francis. 5r USA. *Without a Soul* prod/rel: World Film Corp.©, Shubert Feature

Marry the Poor Girl, New York 1920, Play
Marry the Poor Girl 1921 d: Lloyd Ingraham. lps: Flora Parker de Haven, Carter de Haven. 5500f USA. prod/rel: Carter de Haven Productions, Associated Exhibitors

Mile-a-Minute Kendall, New York 1916, Play
Mile-a-Minute Kendall 1918 d: William D. Taylor. lps: Jack Pickford, Louise Huff, Charles Arling. 5r USA. *Half-a-Minute Kendall* prod/rel: Famous Players-Lasky Corp.©, Oliver Morosco Photoplay Co.

Mrs. and Mrs. North, New York 1941, Play
Mr. and Mrs. North 1941 d: Robert B. Sinclair. lps: Gracie Allen, William Post Jr., Paul Kelly. 67M USA. prod/rel: MGM

Nellie the Beautiful Cloak Model, Play
Nellie, the Beautiful Cloak Model 1924 d: Emmett J. Flynn. lps: Claire Windsor, Betsy Ann Hisle, Edmund Lowe. 6533f USA. prod/rel: Goldwyn Pictures, Goldwyn-Cosmopolitan Distributing Corp.

The Nervous Wreck, New York 1926, Play
Nervous Wreck, The 1926 d: Scott Sidney. lps: Harrison Ford, Phyllis Haver, Chester Conklin. 6730f USA. prod/rel: Christie Film Co., Producers Distributing Corp.

Up in Arms 1944 d: Elliott Nugent. lps: Danny Kaye, Constance Dowling, Dinah Shore. 105M USA. prod/rel: RKO, Avalon Prods.

Whoopee! 1930 d: Thornton Freeland. lps: Eddie Cantor, Eleanor Hunt, Paul Gregory. 93M USA. prod/rel: Samuel Goldwyn, Inc., United Artists

Nine Forty-Five, Play
Nine Forty-Five 1934 d: George King. lps: Binnie Barnes, Donald Calthrop, Violet Farebrother. 59M UKN. prod/rel: Warner Bros., First National

The Sentimental Lady, Play
Sentimental Lady, The 1915 d: Walter Edwin, Sidney Olcott. lps: Irene Fenwick, Frank Belcher, John Davidson. 4420f USA. prod/rel: George Kleine©, Kleine-Edison Feature Service

The Shamrock and the Rose, Play
Shamrock and the Rose, The 1927 d: Jack Nelson. lps: MacK Swain, Olive Hasbrouck, Edmund Burns. 6700f USA. prod/rel: Chadwick Pictures

Sinners, New York 1915, Play
Sinners 1920 d: Kenneth Webb. lps: Alice Brady, James L. Crane, Agnes Everett. 4833f USA. prod/rel: Realart Pictures Corp.©

Spring Is Here, New York 1929, Musical Play
Spring Is Here 1930 d: John Francis Dillon. lps: Lawrence Gray, Alexander Gray, Bernice Claire. 6386f USA. prod/rel: First National Pictures

Through the Breakers, Play
Through the Breakers 1928 d: Joseph C. Boyle. lps: Holmes Herbert, Margaret Livingston, Clyde Cook. 5035f USA. prod/rel: Gotham Productions, Lumas Film Corp.

Tonight at 12, New York 1928, Play
Tonight at Twelve 1929 d: Harry Pollard. lps: Madge Bellamy, Robert Ellis, Margaret Livingston. 74M USA. prod/rel: Universal Pictures

Up the Ladder, New York 1922, Play
Up the Ladder 1925 d: Edward Sloman. lps: Virginia Valli, Forrest Stanley, Margaret Livingston. 5922f USA. prod/rel: Universal Pictures

The Wishing Ring, New York 1910, Play
Wishing Ring; an Idyll of Old England, The 1914 d: Maurice Tourneur. lps: Vivian Martin, Alec B. Francis, Chester Barnett. 5r USA. *The Wishing Ring* prod/rel: Shubert Feature, World Film Corp.©

The Woman Next Door, Play
Woman Next Door, The 1915 d: Walter Edwin. lps: Irene Fenwick, Camilla Dalberg, Della Connor. 5r USA. prod/rel: George Kleine, Kleine-Edison Feature Service

DAVIS, PHILIP
Skullduggery, Play
Skullduggery 1989 d: Philip Davis. lps: David Thewlis, Steve Sweeney, Paul McKenzie. TVM. 90M UKN. prod/rel: BBC

DAVIS, RHYS
The Safecracker, Book
Safecracker, The 1957 d: Ray Milland. lps: Ray Milland, Barry Jones, Jeannette Sterke. 96M UKN/USA. prod/rel: MGM, Coronado

DAVIS, RICHARD HARDING (1864–1916), USA
Adventures of the Scarlet Car, New York 1907, Novel
Scarlet Car, The 1923 d: Stuart Paton. lps: Herbert Rawlinson, Claire Adams, Edward Cecil. 4417f USA. prod/rel: Universal Pictures

The Adventures of Van Bibber, Story
Van Bibber's Experiment 1911 d: J. Searle Dawley. lps: Charles Ogle, Mabel Trunnelle. 1000f USA. prod/rel: Edison

Andy M'gee's Chorus Girl, 1892, Short Story
Cupid's Fireman 1923 d: William A. Wellman. lps: Buck Jones, Marian Nixon, Brooks Benedict. 4204f USA. prod/rel: Fox Film Corp.

The Bar Sinister, Novel
It's a Dog's Life 1955 d: Herman Hoffman. lps: Jeff Richards, Jarma Lewis, Edmund Gwenn. 88M USA. *The Bar Sinister; Wildfire* prod/rel: MGM

Billy and the Big Stick, 1914, Short Story
Billy and the Big Stick 1917 d: Edward H. Griffith. lps: Raymond McKee, Yona Landowska, William Wadsworth. 4r USA. prod/rel: Thomas A. Edison, Inc.©, K-E-S-E Service

Captain MacKlin: His Memoirs, New York 1902, Novel
Captain MacKlin 1915 d: John B. O'Brien. lps: Jack Conway, Lillian Gish, Spottiswoode Aitken. 4r USA. prod/rel: Majestic Motion Picture Co., Mutual Film Corp.

The Dictator, New York 1904, Play
Dictator, The 1915 d: Oscar Eagle. lps: John Barrymore, Charlotte Ives, Ruby Hoffman. 5r USA. prod/rel: Famous Players Film Co., Paramount Pictures Corp.

Dictator, The 1922 d: James Cruze. lps: Wallace Reid, Theodore Kosloff, Lila Lee. 5221f USA. prod/rel: Famous Players-Lasky, Paramount Pictures

Driftwood, Story
Driftwood 1928 d: W. Christy Cabanne. lps: Don Alvarado, Marceline Day, Alan Roscoe. 6267f USA. prod/rel: Columbia Pictures

The Exiles, 1894, Short Story
Exiles, The 1923 d: Edmund Mortimer. lps: John Gilbert, Betty Bouton, John Webb Dillon. 4719f USA. prod/rel: Fox Film Corp.

Fugitives, 1894, Short Story
Fugitives 1929 d: William Beaudine. lps: Madge Bellamy, Don Terry, Arthur Stone. 5356f USA. *Wise Baby* prod/rel: Fox Film Corp.

Gallegher, Short Story
Gallegher 1910 d: Edwin S. Porter. 985f USA. prod/rel: Edison

The Galloper, New York 1906, Play
Galloper, The 1915 d: Donald MacKenzie. lps: Clifton Crawford, Melville Stewart, Fania Marinoff. 5r USA. prod/rel: Pathe Exchange, Inc., Gold Rooster Plays

The Grand Cross of the Desert, 1927, Short Story
Stephen Steps Out 1923 d: Joseph Henabery. lps: Douglas Fairbanks Jr., Theodore Roberts, Noah Beery. 5652f USA. prod/rel: Famous Players-Lasky, Paramount Pictures

Her First Appearance, Story
Her First Appearance 1910 d: Edwin S. Porter. lps: Robert Conness. 990f USA. prod/rel: Edison

In the Fog, Short Story
How Sir Andrew Lost His Vote 1911. lps: Marc McDermott, Charles Ogle, Camilla Dalberg. SHT USA. prod/rel: Edison

The King's Jackal, New York 1898, Novel
Honor Among Men 1924 d: Denison Clift. lps: Edmund Lowe, Claire Adams, Sheldon Lewis. 4600f USA. prod/rel: Fox Film Corp.

The Lost House, 1911, Short Story
Lost House, The 1915 d: W. Christy Cabanne. lps: Lillian Gish, Wallace Reid, F. A. Turner. 4r USA. prod/rel: Majestic Motion Picture Co., Mutual Film Corp.

The Man Who Could Not Lose, New York 1911, Novel
Man Who Could Not Lose, The 1914 d: Carlyle Blackwell. lps: Carlyle Blackwell, Ruth Hartman, Hal Clements. 5r USA. prod/rel: Favorite Players Film Co.©, Alliance Films Corp.

The Men of Zanzibar, 1913, Short Story
Men of Zanzibar, The 1922 d: Rowland V. Lee. lps: William Russell, Ruth Renick, Claude Peyton. 4999f USA. prod/rel: Fox Film Corp.

Playing Dead, 1915, Short Story
Playing Dead 1915 d: Sidney Drew. lps: Sidney Drew, Mrs. Sidney Drew, Donald Hall. 5r USA. prod/rel: Vitagraph Co. of America©, Blue Ribbon Feature
Restless Souls 1922 d: Robert Ensminger. lps: Earle Williams, Francelia Billington, Arthur Hoyt. 4080f USA. prod/rel: Vitagraph Co. of America

Ranson's Folly, New York 1902, Novel
Ranson's Folly 1910 d: Edwin S. Porter. lps: Herbert Prior, Florence Turner. 1000f USA. prod/rel: Edison

Ranson's Folly 1915 d: Richard Ridgely. lps: Marc McDermott, Mabel Trunnelle, Miriam Ellison. 4r USA. prod/rel: Thomas A. Edison, Inc.©, General Film Co.

Ranson's Folly 1926 d: Sidney Olcott. lps: Richard Barthelmess, Dorothy MacKaill, Anders Randolf. 7322f USA. prod/rel: Inspiration Pictures, First National Pictures

The Scarlet Car, New York 1907, Novel
Scarlet Car, The 1918 d: Joseph de Grasse. lps: Franklyn Farnum, Edith Johnson, Al W. Filson. 5r USA. prod/rel: Bluebird Photoplays, Inc.©

Soldiers of Fortune, New York 1897, Novel
Soldiers of Fortune 1914 d: William F. Haddock, Augustus Thomas. lps: Dustin Farnum, John Sainpolis, Jack Pratt. 6r USA. prod/rel: All Star Feature Corp., State Rights

Soldiers of Fortune 1919 d: Allan Dwan. lps: Norman Kerry, Pauline Starke, Anna Q. Nilsson. 7r USA. prod/rel: Mayflower Photoplay Corp.©, Allan Dwan Production

Somewhere in France, New York 1915, Novel
Somewhere in France 1916 d: Charles Giblyn. lps: Louise Glaum, Howard Hickman, Fannie Midgley. 5r USA. prod/rel: New York Motion Picture Corp., Kay-Bee

The Trap, New York 1915, Play
Trap, The 1919 d: Frank Reicher. lps: Olive Tell, Sidney Mason, Jere Austin. 6r USA. *A Woman's Law* (UKN) prod/rel: Universal Film Mfg. Co.©

The Unfinished Story, Novel
Last Chapter, The 1915 d: William D. Taylor. lps: Carlyle Blackwell, Ruth Hartman, John Sheehan. SHT USA. prod/rel: Favorite Players

Vera the Medium, New York 1908, Novel
Vera the Medium 1916 d: G. M. Anderson. lps: Kitty Gordon, Frank Goldsmith, Lowell Sherman. 5r USA. prod/rel: Kitty Gordon Film Corp., Lewis J. Selznick Enterprises, Inc.©

White Mice, New York 1909, Novel
White Mice 1926 d: Edward H. Griffith. lps: Jacqueline Logan, William Powell, Ernest Hilliard. 5412f USA. prod/rel: Pinella Films, Associated Exhibitors

DAVIS, ROBERT HOBART
The Stain, Novel
Stain, The 1914 d: Frank Powell. lps: Edward Jose, Thurlow Bergen, Virginia Pearson. 6r USA. prod/rel: Eclectic

We are French!, New York 1914, Novel
Bugler of Algiers, The 1916 d: Rupert Julian. lps: Ella Hall, Rupert Julian, Kingsley Benedict. 5r USA. *Comrades* (UKN); *We are French* prod/rel: Bluebird Photoplays, Inc.©

Love and Glory 1924 d: Rupert Julian. lps: Charles de Roche, Wallace MacDonald, Madge Bellamy. 7094f USA. prod/rel: Universal Pictures

DAVIS, ROBERT P.
The Pilot, Novel
Pilot, The 1979 d: Cliff Robertson. lps: Cliff Robertson, Frank Converse, Diane Baker. 92M USA. *Danger in the Skies* prod/rel: New Line, Summit Features

DAVIS SR., OWEN
Jezebel, New York 1933, Play
Jezebel 1938 d: William Wyler. lps: Bette Davis, Henry Fonda, George Brent. 104M USA. prod/rel: Warner Bros. Pictures©, William Wyler Production

DAVIS, STEPHEN
Love Field, Play
Ruby 1992 d: John MacKenzie. lps: Danny Aiello, Sherilyn Fenn, Arliss Howard. 110M USA. prod/rel: Propaganda Films

DAVIS, TERRY
Vision Quest, Novel
Vision Quest 1985 d: Harold Becker. lps: Matthew Modine, Linda Fiorentino, Michael Schoeffling. 105M USA. *Crazy for You* prod/rel: Warner

DAVIS, WILL S.
Labor, Story
Destruction 1915 d: Will S. Davis. lps: Theda Bara, James A. Furey, Esther H. Hoier. 5r USA. prod/rel: Fox Film Corp., William Fox©

DAVISON, FRANK DALBY
Dusty, Novel
Dusty 1982 d: John Richardson. lps: Bill Kerr, Noel Trevarthen, Carol Burns. 88M ASL. prod/rel: Kestrel Films (Australia), Dusty Productions©

DAWE, CARLTON
The Black Spider, London 1911, Novel
Black Spider, The 1920 d: William J. Humphrey. lps: Lydia Kyasht, Bertram Burleigh, Sam Livesey. 5800f UKN. prod/rel: British & Colonial, Butcher's Film Service

Foolish Monte Carlo 1922 d: William Humphrey. lps: Mary Clare, Sam Livesey, Robert Corbins. 4235f USA. prod/rel: Wid Gunning, Inc., R-C Pictures

Shadow of Evil, Novel
Shadow of Evil 1921 d: James Reardon. lps: Cecil Humphreys, Mary Dibley, Reginald Fox. 5694f UKN. prod/rel: British Art, Regent

DAWLEY, J. SEARLE
The Dancer and the King, Play
Dancer and the King, The 1914 d: E. Arnaud. lps: Cecil Spooner, Victor Sutherland, Howard Lang. 5r USA. prod/rel: Charles E. Blaney Productions, World Film Corp.

The Daughter of the People, Play
Daughter of the People, A 1915 d: J. Searle Dawley. lps: Laura Sawyer, Frederic de Belleville, Robert Broderick. 5r USA. prod/rel: Dyreda Art Film Corp.©, World Film Corp.

DAWSON, ANTHONY
The Snorkel, Novel
Snorkel, The 1958 d: Guy Green. lps: Peter Van Eyck, Betta St. John, Mandy Miller. 90M UKN. prod/rel: Columbia, Hammer

DAWSON, CONIGSBY WILLIAM
The Coast of Folly, New York 1924, Novel
Coast of Folly, The 1925 d: Allan Dwan. lps: Gloria Swanson, Anthony Jowitt, Alec B. Francis. 6974f USA. prod/rel: Famous Players-Lasky, Paramount Pictures

DAWSON, PETER
Long Gone, 1956, Short Story
Face of a Fugitive 1959 d: Paul Wendkos. lps: Fred MacMurray, Lin McCarthy, Dorothy Green. 81M USA. prod/rel: Columbia, Morningside

DAY, ARNOLD
Chacals, Novel
Chacals 1917 d: Andre Hugon. lps: Andre Nox, Louis Paglieri, MusidorA. 1525m FRN. prod/rel: Films A. Hugon, Succes

DAY, BETH
I'm Alive! Hey, Book
Hey, I'm Alive! 1975 d: Lawrence Schiller. lps: Edward Asner, Sally Struthers, Milton Selzer. TVM. 78M USA. prod/rel: Charles Fries Productions, Worldvision

DAY, DOROTHY
The Eleventh Virgin, New York 1924, Novel
Woman Hater, The 1925 d: James Flood. lps: Helene Chadwick, Clive Brook, John Harron. 6591f USA. prod/rel: Warner Brothers Pictures

DAY, EDMUND
The Round Up, New York 1907, Play
Round-Up, The 1920 d: George Melford. lps: Roscoe Arbuckle, Mabel Julienne Scott, Irving Cummings. 6417f USA. *The Round Up* prod/rel: Famous Players-Lasky Corp.©, George Melford Production

DAY, ESTHER LYND
Novel
Beggars in Ermine 1934 d: Phil Rosen. lps: Lionel Atwill, Henry B. Walthall, Betty Furness. 72M USA. prod/rel: Monogram Pictures

DAY, HOLMAN FRANCIS
Clothes Make the Pirate, New York 1925, Novel
Clothes Make the Pirate 1925 d: Maurice Tourneur. lps: Leon Errol, Dorothy Gish, Nita Naldi. 8000f USA. prod/rel: Sam E. Rork Productions, First National Pictures

King Spruce, New York 1908, Novel
King Spruce 1920 d: Roy Clements. lps: Mitchell Lewis, Mignon Anderson, Melbourne MacDowell. 7r USA. prod/rel: Dial Film Co., W. W. Hodkinson Corp.

The Landloper; the Romance of a Man on Foot, New York 1915, Novel
Landloper, The 1918 d: George Irving. lps: Harold Lockwood, Pauline Curley, Stanton Heck. 5r USA. prod/rel: Yorke Film Corp., Metro Pictures Corp.©

The Red Lane; a Romance of the Border, New York 1912, Novel
Red Lane, The 1920 d: Lynn Reynolds. lps: Frank Mayo, Lillian Rich, James Mason. 4890f USA. prod/rel: Universal Film Mfg. Co.©

The Rider of the King Log, New York 1919, Novel
Rider of the King Log, The 1921 d: Harry O. Hoyt. lps: Frank Sheridan, Irene Boyle, Richard C. Travers. 7r USA. prod/rel: Associated Exhibitors, Pathe Exchange, Inc.

DAY JR., CLARENCE
Memoirs
Life With Father 1947 d: Michael Curtiz. lps: Irene Dunne, William Powell, Elizabeth Taylor. 118M USA. prod/rel: Warner Bros.

DAY, LILLIAN
Living Up to Lizzie, 1934, Short Story
Personal Maid's Secret 1935 d: Arthur G. Collins. lps: Ruth Donnelly, Margaret Lindsay, Warren Hull. 60M USA. *Living Up to Lizzie* prod/rel: Warner Bros. Pictures©

The Youngest Profession, 1940, Book
Youngest Profession, The 1943 d: Edward Buzzell. lps: Virginia Weidler, Jean Porter, Edward Arnold. 82M USA. prod/rel: MGM

DAY, PRICE
Old Mrs. Leonard and the machine Guns, 1937, Short Story
  Lady and the Mob, The 1939 d: Ben Stoloff. lps: Lee Bowman, Ida Lupino, Henry ArmettA. 65M USA. *Old Mrs. Leonard and the machine Guns; Mrs. Leonard Misbehaves; Old Mrs. Leonard and Her machine Guns* prod/rel: Columbia Pictures Corp. of California©

DAY-HELVEG, ANNE
Liane Das Madchen Aus Dem Urwald, Novel
  Liane, Das Madchen Aus Dem Urwald 1956 d: Eduard von Borsody. lps: Marion Michael, Hardy Kruger, Irene Galter. 88M GRM. *Liane Jungle Goddess* (USA); *Liane -Girl of the Jungle* prod/rel: Arca, N.F.
Liane Die Weisse Sklavin, Novel
  Liane, Die Weisse Sklavin 1957 d: Hermann Leitner, Gino Talamo. lps: Marion Michael, Adrian Hoven, Saro Urzi. 86M GRM/ITL. *Liana la Schiava Bianca* (ITL); *Jungle Girl and the Slaver; Liane the White Slave* prod/rel: Arca, N.F.

DAYLIS, GILBERT
What Would a Gentleman Do?, Play
  What Would a Gentleman Do? 1918 d: Wilfred Noy. lps: Stanley Logan, Queenie Thomas, A. B. Imeson. 5220f UKN. prod/rel: Butcher's Film Service

DAYTON, JAMES
In Slavery Days, Story
  In Slavery Days 1913 d: Otis Turner. lps: Robert Leonard, Margarita Fischer, Jane Ainsley. 2r USA. prod/rel: Rex

DAYTON, KATHARINE
First Lady, New York 1935, Play
  First Lady 1937 d: Stanley Logan. lps: Kay Francis, Anita Louise, Verree Teasdale. 82M USA. prod/rel: Warner Bros. Pictures©

D'AZEGLIO, MASSIMO
Ettore Fieramosca O la Disfida Di Barletta, 1833, Novel
  Ettore Fieramosca 1915 d: Umberto Paradisi. lps: Giovanni Cimara, Laura Darville, Nello Carotenuto. 1575m ITL. *La Disfida Di Barletta* prod/rel: Pasquali E C.
  Ettore Fieramosca 1938 d: Alessandro Blasetti. lps: Gino Cervi, Elisa Cegani, Mario Ferrari. 110M ITL. prod/rel: Nembo Film, E.N.I.C.
  Ettore Fieramosca, Ovvero la Disfida Di Barletta 1909 d: Ernesto Maria Pasquali. lps: Domenico Gambino. 260m ITL. prod/rel: Pasquali E Tempo
Niccolo De' Lapi, 1841, Novel
  Niccolo De' Lapi 1909. 316m ITL. prod/rel: Itala Film

DAZEY, CHARLES T.
In Old Kentucky, Pittsburgh 1893, Play
  In Old Kentucky 1919 d: Marshall Neilan, Alfred E. Green. lps: Anita Stewart, Mahlon Hamilton, Ed Coxen. 7r USA. prod/rel: Anita Stewart Productions, Inc., Louis B. Mayer Productions
  In Old Kentucky 1927 d: John M. Stahl. lps: James Murray, Helene Costello, Wesley Barry. 6646f USA. prod/rel: Metro-Goldwyn-Mayer Pictures
  In Old Kentucky 1935 d: George Marshall. lps: Will Rogers, Dorothy Wilson, Bill Robinson. 86M USA. prod/rel: Fox Film Corp.©, Twentieth Century-Fox Film Corp.
The Sign of the Rose, New York 1911, Play
  Alien, The 1915 d: Thomas H. Ince. lps: George Beban, Edward Gillespie, Hayward Ginn. 8r USA. *The Sign of the Rose* prod/rel: New York Motion Picture Corp.©, Select Film Booking Agency, Inc.
  Sign of the Rose, The 1915 d: Thomas H. Ince. lps: George Beban, Blanche Schwed, Thelma Salter. SHT USA. prod/rel: George Beban Productions, American Releasing Corp.
The Suburban, 1902, Play
  Kentucky Derby, The 1922 d: King Baggot. lps: Reginald Denny, Lillian Rich, Emmett King. 5398f USA. *The Suburban Handicap; They're Off* prod/rel: Universal Film Mfg. Co.
  Suburban, The 1915 d: George A. Lessey. lps: King Baggot, Brinsley Shaw, Frank Smith. 4r USA. prod/rel: Universal Film Mfg. Co.©
The Three Lights, New York 1911, Play
  Night Out, A 1916 d: George D. Baker. lps: May Robson, Flora Finch, Kate Price. 5r USA. prod/rel: Vitagraph Co. of America©, Blue Ribbon Feature
The Winning of Denise, Story
  Mating, The 1915 d: Raymond B. West. lps: Bessie Barriscale, Lew Cody, Enid Markey. 4460f USA. prod/rel: New York Motion Picture Corp., Mutual Film Corp.

Women Men Love, Short Story
  Women Men Love 1920 d: Samuel R. Bradley. lps: William Desmond, Marguerite Marsh, Martha Mansfield. 6r USA. prod/rel: Bradley Feature Film Co., State Rights

DAZEY, FRANK
Sky High, Short Story
  Flirting With Death 1917 d: Elmer Clifton. lps: Agnes Vernon, Herbert Rawlinson, Frank MacQuarrie. 5r USA. prod/rel: Bluebird Photoplays, Inc.©
Sky Life, 1929, Short Story
  Under 18 1931 d: Archie Mayo. lps: Marian Marsh, Warren William, Regis Toomey. 81M USA. *Under Eighteen* prod/rel: Warner Bros. Pictures©

DE ALARCON, PEDRO ANTONIO (1833–1891), SPN
El Capitan Veneno, 1881, Novel
  Capitan Veneno, El 1950 d: Luis MarquinA. lps: Fernando Fernan Gomez, Sara Montiel, Manolo Moran. 94M SPN. *Captain Poison; Captain Venom*
El Clavo, 1854, Short Story
  Clavo, El 1944 d: Rafael Gil. lps: Rafael Duran, Amparo Rivelles, Milagros Leal. 99M SPN. *The Nail*
El Escandalo, 1875, Novel
  Escandalo, El 1943 d: Jose Luis Saenz de HerediA. lps: Armando Calvo, Mercedes Vecino, Trinidad Montero. 114M SPN. *The Scandal*
  Escandalo, El 1963 d: Javier Seto. lps: Espartaco Santoni, Mara Cruz, Lorena Velazquez. 86M SPN.
La Prodiga, 1882, Novel
  Prodiga, La 1946 d: Rafael Gil. lps: Rafael Duran, Paola Barbara, Fernando Rey. 92M SPN. *The Prodigal; The Prodigal Woman*
El Sombrero de Tres Picos, 1874, Short Story
  Bella Mugnaia, La 1955 d: Mario Camerini. lps: Sophia Loren, Vittorio de Sica, Marcello Mastroianni. 95M ITL. *The Miller's Beautiful Wife* (USA); *The Miller's Wife* (UKN) prod/rel: Lux Film
  Cappello a Tre Punte, Il 1935 d: Mario Camerini. lps: Eduardo de Filippo, Peppino de Filippo, Leda GloriA. 85M ITL. *The Three-Cornered Hat* prod/rel: Lido Film
  It Happened in Spain 1935 d: Harry d'Abbadie d'Arrast. 65M UKN/SPN. *The Three-Cornered Hat*
  Picara Molinera, La 1955 d: Leon Klimovsky. lps: Carmen Sevilla, Francisco Rabal, Mischa Auer. 91M SPN/FRN. *Le Moulin Des Amours* (FRN)
  Traviesa Molinera, La 1935 d: Harry d'Abbadie d'Arrast, Ricardo Soriano. lps: Eleanor Boardman, Hilda Moreno, Victor Varconi. 71M SPN. *El Sombrero de Tres Picos*

DE ALENCAR, JOSE MARTINIANO (1829–1877), BRZ
O Gaucho, 1870, Novel
  Paixao de Gaucho 1958 d: Walter George Durst. lps: Victor Merinov. 100M BRZ. *Gaucho Passion*
O Guarani, 1857, Novel
  Guarani, O 1979 d: Fauze Mansur. 90M BRZ. *The Guarani Indian*
  Guarany, Il 1923 d: Salvatore Aversano. lps: Elisenda Annovazzi, Gino Soldarelli, Vittorio Simbalotti. 1984m ITL.
Lenda Do Ceara Iracema, 1865, Novel
  Iracema, a Virgem Dos Labios de Mel 1979 d: Carlos CoimbrA. 95M BRZ.
Luciola, 1862, Short Story
  Anjo Do Lodo 1951 d: Luiz de Barros. 78M BRZ.
  Luciola, O Anjo Pecador 1975 d: Alfredo Sternheim. 95M BRZ.
Lenda Tupi Ubirajara, 1875, Novel
  Lenda de Ubirajara, A 1975 d: Andre Luiz de OliveirA. 110M BRZ. *The Legend of Ubirajara*

DE ALMEIDA, JOSE AMERICO
A Bagaceira, 1928, Novel
  Soledade 1976 d: Paulo Thiago. 90M BRZ.

DE AMICIS, EDMONDO (1846–1908), ITL Story
  Amore E Ginnastica 1973 d: Luigi Filippo d'Amico. lps: Senta Berger, Lino Capolicchio, Adriana Asti. 112M ITL. prod/rel: Documento Film, I.N.C.
Cuore, 1886, Short Story
  Cuore 1948 d: Duilio Coletti. lps: Vittorio de Sica, Maria Mercader, Giorgio de Lullo. 95M ITL. *Heart and Soul* (USA) prod/rel: S.a.F.I.R., E.N.I.C.
  Cuore 1974 d: Romano Scavolini. lps: Renato Cestie, Domenico Santoro, Duilio Cruciani. 80M ITL. prod/rel: Lido Cin.Ca
  Dagli Appennini Alle Ande 1916 d: Umberto Paradisi. lps: Ermanno Roveri, Antonio Monti, Signora Monti. 916m ITL. prod/rel: Gloria Film
  Dagli Appennini Alle Ande 1943 d: Flavio CalzavarA. lps: Cesarino Barbetti, Leda Gloria, Nino Pavese. 85M ITL. prod/rel: Incine, Scalera Film

  Dagli Appennini Alle Ande 1959 d: Folco Quilici. lps: Eleonora Rossi-Drago, Marco Paoletti, Fausto Tozzi. 95M ITL/ARG. prod/rel: David Film, Mondial Cin.Ca (Roma)
  Infermiere Di Tata, L' 1916 d: Leopoldo Carlucci. lps: Guido Petrungaro. 422m ITL. prod/rel: Gloria Film
  Naufragio 1916 d: Umberto Paradisi. lps: Ermanno Roveri, Lavinia Roveri. 521m ITL. prod/rel: Gloria Film
  Piccola Vedetta Lombarda, La 1915 d: Vittorio Rossi Pianelli. lps: Luigino Petrungaro, Antonio Monti. 290m ITL. prod/rel: Film Artistica Gloria
  Piccolo Patriota Padovano, Il 1915 d: Leopoldo Carlucci. lps: Ermanno Roveri, Emilio Petacci. 380m ITL. prod/rel: Film Artistica Gloria
  Piccolo Scrivano Fiorentino, Il 1915 d: Leopoldo Carlucci. lps: Ermanno Roveri, Antonio Monti. 530m ITL. prod/rel: Film Artistica Gloria
  Sangue Romagnolo 1916 d: Leopoldo Carlucci. lps: Luigi Petrungaro. 270m ITL. prod/rel: Gloria Film
  Tamburino Sardo, Il 1911. 220m ITL. *Besieged* (USA); *Sardinian Drummer Boy* (UKN) prod/rel: Cines
  Tamburino Sardo, Il 1915 d: Vittorio Rossi Pianelli. lps: Luigi Petrungaro, Telemaco Ruggeri. 555m ITL. prod/rel: Film Artistica Gloria
  Valor Civile 1916 d: Umberto Paradisi. lps: Ermanno Roveri, Antonio Monti. 440m ITL. prod/rel: Gloria Film
Vita Militare, 1869, Short Story
  Carmela 1942 d: Flavio CalzavarA. lps: Doris Duranti, Pal Javor, Aldo Silvani. 90M ITL. prod/rel: Nazionalcine

DE ANDRADE, MARIO (1893–1945), BRZ, De Morais Andrade, Mario Raul
Verbo Intransitivo Amor, 1927, Novel
  Licao de Amor 1975 d: Eduardo Escorel. lps: Lilian Lemmertz, Rogelio Froes, Irene Revache. 90M BRZ. *Lesson in Love*
O Heroi Sem Nenhum Carater MacUnaima, 1928, Novel
  MacUnaima 1969 d: Joaquim Pedro de Andrade. lps: Grande Otelo, Paulo Jose, Dina Sfat. 102M BRZ. *Jungle Freaks*

DE ANDRADE, OSWALD
Os Condenados, 1922, Novel
  Condenados, Os 1974 d: Zelito VianA. lps: Isabel Ribeiro, Claudio Marzo, Roberto Bataglin. 90M BRZ. *Alma; The Condemned; Perdition*
O Rei Da Vela, Play
  Rei Da Vela, O 1982 d: Jose Celso Martinez Correa, Noilton Nunes. lps: Renato Berghi, Jose Wilker, Ester Goes. 160M BRZ. *King of the Candle* prod/rel: Teatro Oficina, Associacao de Engergias E Trabalhos

DE ANGELIS, R. T.
Il Cantante Misterioso, Novel
  Cantante Misterioso, Il 1955 d: Marino Girolami. lps: Luciano Tajoli, Marcella Mariani, Laura Carli. F ITL. prod/rel: Ariel Film, Zeus Film

DE ARPE, CELEDONIO JOSE
El Capote de Paseo, Novel
  Capote de Paseo, El 1927 d: Carlos de Arpe. lps: Elisa Ruiz Romero, Maria Anaya, Agripina OrtegA. SPN. prod/rel: Arpe (Madrid)

DE ASSIS, JOAQUIM MARIA MACHADO
O Alienista, 1881, Short Story
  Azylo Muito Louco 1970 d: Nelson Pereira Dos Santos. lps: Nildo Parente, Isabel Ribeiro, Arduino Colasanti. 100M BRZ. *Um Asilo Muito Louco; L' Alieniste; O Alienista; The Alienist* prod/rel: Nelson Pereira Dos Santos, Luis Carlos Barreto
Um Apologo, 1885, Short Story
  Apologo, Um 1936 d: Mauro-Humberto, Lucia Miguel PereirA. 7M BRZ.
  Apologo, Um 1939 d: Mauro-Humberto, Roquette Pinto. 15M BRZ.
A Cartomante, 1884, Short Story
  Cartomante, A 1974 d: Marcos FariA. 85M BRZ.
Confissoes de Uma Viuva Moca, 1870, Short Story
  Confissoes de Uma Viuva Moca 1975 d: Adnor PitangA. 90M BRZ.
Dom Casmurro, 1899, Novel
  Capitu 1968 d: Paulo Cesar Saraceni. lps: Isabella, Othon Bastos, Raul Cortez. 105M BRZ.
Um Homem Celebre, 1888, Short Story
  Homem Celebre, O 1974 d: Miguel Faria Junior. 90M BRZ. *A Famous Man*
Memorias Postumas de Bras Cubas, 1881, Novel
  Viagem Ao Fim Do Mundo 1968 d: Fernando Cony Campos. lps: Fabio Porchat, Talula Campos, Jofre Soares. 90M BRZ. *Voyage to the End of the World*
Noite de Almirante, 1884, Short Story
  Esse Rio Que Eu Amo 1961 d: Carlos Hugo Christensen. lps: Jardel Filho, Tonia Carrero, Odete LarA. 104M BRZ.

DE AZEVEDO, ALUISIO
O Cortico, 1890, Novel
Cortico, O 1945 d: Luiz de Barros. 111M BRZ. *The Tenement*
Cortico, O 1978 d: Francisco Ramalho Jr.. 105M BRZ.

DE BALZAC, HONORE (1799–1850), FRN
Story
Black Venus 1983 d: Claude Mulot. lps: Jacqueline Josephine Jones, Jose Antonio Ceinos, Emiliano Redondo. 95M USA/SPN. prod/rel: Film Accounting Services, Playboy Enterprises
Country Parson, The 1915. lps: Louise Vale, Clairette Claire, Jack Drumier. 3r USA. prod/rel: Biograph Co.
Short Story
Liebe 1927 d: Paul Czinner. lps: Elisabeth Bergner, Leopold von Ledebur, Hans Rehmann. 2697m GRM. *Die Herzogin von Langeais*; *Histoire Des Treize*; *Love* prod/rel: Phoebus-Film Ag
Novel
Passion in the Desert 1997 d: Lavinia Currier. lps: Ben Daniels, Michel Piccoli, Paul Meston. 93M USA. prod/rel: Roland Films
Short Stories
Underbara Lognen, Den 1955 d: Michael Road. lps: Michael Road, Stig Olin, Signe Hasso. 95M SWD/USA. *Gentle Thief of Love*; *The True and the False* prod/rel: Davies, Sandrew

L' Amour Masque, Short Story
Amore E la Maschera, L' 1920 d: Mario Gargiulo. lps: Tina Xeo, Dillo Lombardi, Angelo Calabresi. 1200m ITL. prod/rel: Flegrea Film
Maskovana Milenka 1940 d: Otakar VavrA. lps: Lida Baarova, Gustav Nezval, Ladislav Pesek. 2335m CZC. *The Masked Lover*; *Sweetheart in Mask* prod/rel: Lucernafilm

Argow Il Pirata, 1831, Short Story
Per Il Passato 1921 d: Toddi. lps: Maria Carmi, Gleb Zborominsky, Tatiana GorkA. 1686m ITL. prod/rel: Medusa Film

L' Auberge Rouge, 1831, Short Story
Auberge Rouge, L' 1912. lps: Jean Worms, Georges Saillard, Clement. FRN. prod/rel: Films D'art
Auberge Rouge, L' 1923 d: Jean Epstein. lps: Gina Manes, Jean-David Evremond, Leon Mathot. 1800m FRN. *The Red Inn* (USA) prod/rel: Pathe-Consortium-Cinema
Auberge Rouge, L' 1951 d: Claude Autant-LarA. lps: Fernandel, Lud Germain, Julien Carette. 95M FRN. *The Red Inn* prod/rel: Memnon Film

Le Bal Des Sceaux
Reginetta Isotta 1918. lps: Thea, Livio Pavanelli, Eugenia Masetti. 1209m ITL. prod/rel: Cines

La Canne
Ted l'Invisibile 1922 d: Carlo Campogalliani. lps: Carlo Campogalliani, Letizia Quaranta, Arnaldo Firpo. 1584m ITL. prod/rel: Campogalliani E C.

Cesar Birotteau, Novel
Cesar Birotteau 1911 d: Emile Chautard. lps: Georges Saillard, Charles Krauss, Juliette Clarens. 286m FRN. prod/rel: Acad

Le Chef d'Oeuvre Inconnu, 1831, Short Story
Belle Noiseuse -Divertimento 1991 d: Jacques Rivette. lps: Michel Piccoli, Jane Birkin, Emmanuelle Beart. TVM. 240M FRN. *La Belle Noiseuse*
Belle Noiseuse, La 1991 d: Jacques Rivette. lps: Michel Piccoli, Jane Birkin, Emmanuelle Beart. 245M FRN. prod/rel: Pierre Grise Productions

Les Chouans, 1834, Novel
Chouans, Les 1946 d: Henri Calef. lps: Jean Marais, Madeleine Robinson, Marcel Herrand. 99M FRN. *Le Courrier du Roi* prod/rel: Georges Legrand
Revoltes de Lomanach, Les 1953 d: Richard Pottier. lps: Amedeo Nazzari, Dany Robin, Carla Del Poggio. 88M FRN/ITL. *L' Eroe Della Vandea* (ITL); *The Lon Manach Rebels*; *Les Revoltes de Lon Manach* prod/rel: Francois Chavane, S.N.E.G.

Le Club Des Treize, Novel
Club Des Treize, Le 1914 d: Henri Andreani. FRN. prod/rel: Cosmographe

Le Colonel Chabert, 1844, Novel
Colonel Chabert, Le 1911 d: Andre Calmettes, Henri Pouctal. lps: Claude Garry, Aimee de Raynal, Romuald Joube. FRN. prod/rel: le Film d'Art
Colonel Chabert, Le 1943 d: Rene Le Henaff. lps: Raimu, Aime Clariond, Marie Bell. 102M FRN. prod/rel: C.C.F.C.
Colonel Chabert, Le 1994 d: Yves Angelo. lps: Gerard Depardieu, Fanny Ardant, Fabrice Luchini. 110M FRN. *Colonel Chabert*

Colonnello Chabert, Il 1920 d: Carmine Gallone. lps: Charles Le Bargy, Rita Pergament, Umberto Zanuccoli. 1564m ITL. prod/rel: Lucio D'ambra
Homme Sans Nom, Un 1932 d: Roger Le Bon, Gustav Ucicky. lps: Firmin Gemier, Yvonne Hebert, Paul Amiot. 81M FRN. prod/rel: U.Fa., a.C.E.
Mensch Ohne Namen 1932 d: Gustav Ucicky. lps: Werner Krauss, Mathias Wieman, Helene Thimig. 92M GRM. *Man Without a Name*
Oberst Chabert 1914 d: Rudolf Meinert. lps: Heinz Salfner. GRM. prod/rel: Phoebus-Film

Les Contes Drolatiques, 1832-37, Short Stories
Tolldreisten Geschichten - Nach Honore de Balzac, Die 1969 d: Jozef Zachar. lps: Joachim Hansen, Francy Fair, Katherina Alt. 84M GRM. *The Brazen Women of Balzac* (USA); *Sex Is a Pleasure* (UKN); *Komm Liebe Mald Und MacHe*; *The Bawdy Women of Balzac*; *Balzac Stories* prod/rel: Lisa, Gloria

Le Cousin Pons, Novel
Cousin Pons 1914 d: Travers Vale. lps: Charles Hill Mailes, Edward Cecil, A. C. Marston. 2r USA. prod/rel: Biograph Co.
Cousin Pons, Le 1923 d: Jacques Robert. lps: Maurice de Feraudy, Paulette Pax, Claire Darcas. F FRN. prod/rel: Films Art Et Cinema

La Cousine Bette, 1846, Novel
Cousin Bette 1972 d: Gareth Davies. lps: Colin Baker, Ursula Howells, Thorley Walters. MTV. F UKN. prod/rel: BBC
Cousin Bette 1998 d: Des McAnuff. lps: Bob Hoskins, Elisabeth Shue, Jessica Lange. 108M USA/UKN. prod/rel: Fox Searchlight, Twentieth Century-Fox Film Corp.©
Cousine Bette, La 1928 d: Max de Rieux. lps: Henri Baudin, Germaine Rouer, Alice Tissot. 4000m FRN.
Cousine Bette, La 1964 d: Yves-Andre Hubert. lps: Alice Sapritch, Claudine Coster, Jacques Castelot. TVM. 115M FRN.

Un Drame Au Bord de la Mer
Homme du Large, L' 1920 d: Marcel L'Herbier. lps: Jaque Catelain, Roger Karl, Charles Boyer. 1890m FRN. *The Man of the Wide-Open Spaces*; *Man of the Open Seas* prod/rel: Gaumont - Serie Pax

La Duchesse de Langeais, 1839, Novel
Duchesse de Langeais, La 1942 d: Jacques de Baroncelli. lps: Edwige Feuillere, Pierre Richard-Willm, Aime Clariond. 99M FRN. *The Wicked Duchess* (USA) prod/rel: Films Orange
Eternal Flame, The 1922 d: Frank Lloyd. lps: Norma Talmadge, Adolphe Menjou, Wedgewood Nowell. 7453f USA. *The Duchess of Langeais* prod/rel: Norma Talmadge Film Co., Associated First National Pictures
Storia Dei Tredici, La 1917 d: Carmine Gallone. lps: Lyda Borelli, Ugo Piperno, Sandro Salvini. 1679m ITL. prod/rel: Cines

Eugenie Grandet, 1833, Novel
Eugene Grandet 1960 d: Sergei Alexeyev. 100M USS.
Eugenia Grandet 1947 d: Mario Soldati. lps: Alida Valli, Gualtiero Tumiati, Giorgio de Lullo. 105M ITL. prod/rel: Excelsa Film, Minerva Film
Eugenia Grandet 1952 d: Emilio Gomez Muriel. 117M MXC.
Eugenia Grandet 1977 d: Pilar Miro. MTV. F SPN. *Eugenie Grandet*
Eugenie Grandet 1910 d: Emile Chautard. lps: Jacques Guilhene, Germaine Dermoz, Suzanne Revonne. 295m FRN. prod/rel: Acad
Figlia Dell'avaro, La 1913. lps: Goffredo Mateldi, Enna Saredo, Vittoria MonetA. 950m ITL. prod/rel: Roma Film

Le Faiseur, Play
Faiseur, Le 1908-18. FRN.

La Fausse Maitresse, 1841, Short Story
Falsa Amante, La 1920 d: Carmine Gallone. lps: Lia Formia, Umberto Zanuccoli, Renato Piacenti. 1910m ITL. prod/rel: D'ambra Film
Fausse Maitresse, La 1942 d: Andre Cayatte. lps: Danielle Darrieux, Lise Delamare, Bernard Lancret. 85M FRN. prod/rel: Continental-Films

La Femme de Trente Ans, 1831, Short Story
Donna Di Trent'anni, La 1920 d: Riccardo Molinari, Alessandro Des Varennes. lps: Gianna Terribili-Gonzales, Carlo Gervasio, Paolo Nocito. 1308m ITL. *Una Donna Di 30 Anni* prod/rel: Paris Film

Gobseck, 1830, Short Story
Gobsec 1987 d: Alexandr Orlov. lps: Vladimir Tatosov, Sergej Bekhterev, Boris Plotnikov. 100M USS. *Gobsek*
Gobsek 1936 d: Konstantin V. Eggert. 73M USS. *Gobseck*

Un Grand Homme de Province a Paris, 1839, Novel
Elveszett Illuziok 1983 d: Gyula Gazdag. lps: Dorottya Udvaros, Gabor Mate, Robert East. 102M HNG. *Lost Illusions*

La Grande Breteche Ou Les Trois Vengeances, 1837, Novel
Grande Breteche, La 1909 d: Andre Calmettes. lps: Philippe Garnier, Andre Calmettes, Henri Pouctal. 290m FRN. prod/rel: le Film d'Art
Seul Amour, Un 1943 d: Pierre Blanchar. lps: Micheline Presle, Pierre Blanchar, Robert Vattier. 101M FRN. prod/rel: S.N.E.G.
Spergiura! 1909 d: Luigi Maggi, Arturo Ambrosio. lps: Mary Cleo Tarlarini, Alberto A. Capozzi, Luigi Maggi. 253m ITL. prod/rel: S.A. Ambrosio

Grandeur Et Decadence de Cesar Birotteau, 1837, Novel
Cesare Birotteau 1921 d: Arnaldo Frateili. lps: Gustavo Salvini, Rina Calabria, Paula Paxi. 2133m ITL. prod/rel: Tespi Film

L' Histoire Des Treize, Paris 1835, Short Story
Ferragus 1920 d: Enrico Vidali. lps: Lydianne, Enrico Vidali. 1380m ITL. prod/rel: Vidali, Select-Lydianne
Ferragus 1923 d: Gaston Ravel. lps: Elmire Vautier, Rene Navarre, Lucien Dalsace. 2250m FRN. prod/rel: Films Rene Navarre
Fille aux Yeux d'Or, La 1961 d: Jean-Gabriel Albicocco. lps: Marie Laforet, Paul Guers, Francoise Prevost. 92M FRN. *The Girl With the Golden Eyes* (USA) prod/rel: Madeleine Films

Jeanne la Pale, Novel
Giovanna la Pallida 1911 d: Mario Caserini. lps: Maria Righelli, Gennaro Righelli. 505m ITL. *Due Matrimoni*; *The Two Marriages* prod/rel: Cines
Quando la Primavera Ritorno 1916 d: Ivo Illuminati. lps: Maria Jacobini, Amedeo Ciaffi, Angelo GallinA. 1561m ITL. prod/rel: Cines

Madame Firmiani, Short Story
Test, The 1923 d: Edwin Greenwood. lps: Madge Stuart, Russell Thorndike. 2196f UKN. prod/rel: British & Colonial, Walturdaw

Maitre Cornelius
Argentier du Roi Louis XI, L' 1910. lps: Charles Krauss, Dupont-Morgan, Georges Saillard. 295m FRN. prod/rel: Eclair, Acad

La Maratre
Maratre, La 1918 d: Jacques Gretillat. lps: Jean Worms, Dauvilliers, Germaine Dermoz. 1485m FRN. prod/rel: Pathe Consortium

Mercadet, 1851, Play
Faiseur, Le 1936 d: Andre Hugon. lps: Paul Pauley, Philippe Janvier, Janine Borelli. 66M FRN. prod/rel: Productions Andre Hugon
Lovable Cheat, The 1949 d: Richard Oswald. lps: Charlie Ruggles, Peggy Ann Garner, Richard Ney. 75M USA. prod/rel: Film Classics

Les Paysans, Novel
Paysans, Les 1909 d: Charles Decroix. lps: Bahier, Mlle Laurent. 170m FRN. prod/rel: Scagl

La Peau de Chagrin, Paris 1831, Novel
Desire 1920 d: George Edwardes Hall. lps: Dennis Neilson-Terry, Yvonne Arnaud, Christine Maitland. 4460f UKN. *The Magic Skin* prod/rel: British & Colonial, Butcher's Film Service
Dream Cheater, The 1920 d: Ernest C. Warde. lps: J. Warren Kerrigan, Sam Sothern, Wedgewood Nowell. 5r USA. prod/rel: Robert Brunton Productions, W. W. Hodkinson Corp.
Magic Skin, The 1915 d: Richard Ridgely. lps: Everett Butterfield, Mabel Trunnelle, Bigelow Cooper. 4922f USA. prod/rel: Thomas A. Edison, Inc.©, Kleine-Edison Feature Service
Narayana 1920 d: Leon Poirier. lps: Edmond Van Daele, Laurence Myrga, Charles Norville. 1686m FRN. prod/rel: Gaumont - Serie Pax
Peau de Chagrin, La 1911 d: Georges Denola ?, Albert Capellani ?. lps: Paul Capellani, Rene Leprince, Gilberte Sergy. 325m FRN. *The Wild Ass's Skin* (USA) prod/rel: Scagl
Sagrenska Koza 1960 d: Vlado Kristl, Ivo Vrbanic. ANM. 10M YGS. *La Peau de Chagrin*; *The Skin of Sorrow*
Slave of Desire 1923 d: George D. Baker. lps: George Walsh, Bessie Love, Carmel Myers. 6673f USA. *The Magic Skin* prod/rel: Goldwyn Pictures, Goldwyn-Cosmopolitan Distributing Corp.
Unheimlichen Wunsche, Die 1939 d: Heinz Hilpert. lps: Olga Tschechowa, Kathe Gold, Elisabeth Flickenschildt. 98M GRM. *The Unholy Wish*; *The Sinister Wish* prod/rel: Tobis

Le Pere Goriot, Paris 1834, Novel
Karriere in Paris 1951 d: Georg C. Klaren. lps: Ernst Legal, Wolfgang Kuhne, Ursula Burg. 95M GDR. *Career in Paris* prod/rel: Defa

Paris at Midnight 1926 d: E. Mason Hopper. lps: Jetta Goudal, Lionel Barrymore, Mary Brian. 6995f USA. prod/rel: Metropolitan Pictures, Producers Distributing Corp.

Pere Goriot 1915 d: Travers Vale. lps: Edward Cecil, Kate Toncray, A. C. Marston. 2r USA. prod/rel: Biograph Co.

Pere Goriot, Le 1921 d: Jacques de Baroncelli. lps: Gabriel Signoret, Claude France, Jacques Gretillat. 1885m FRN. prod/rel: Film d'Art

Pere Goriot, Le 1944 d: Robert Vernay. lps: Pierre Renoir, Claude Genia, Pierre Larquey. 103M FRN. prod/rel: Pierre O'connell, Arys Nissoti

Pere Goriot, Le 1972 d: Guy Jorre. lps: Charles Vanel, Bruno Garcin, Roger Jacquet. 106M FRN.

La Physiologie du Mariage, Paris 1830, Novel
If Women Only Knew 1921 d: Edward H. Griffith. lps: Robert Gordon, Blanche Davenport, Harold Vosburgh. 6r USA. prod/rel: J. N. Haulty-Gardner Hunting, Robertson-Cole Distributing Corp.

La Rabouilleuse, Paris 1842, Novel
Arrivistes, Les 1960 d: Louis Daquin. lps: Madeleine Robinson, Jean-Claude Pascal, Clara Gansard. 110M FRN/GDR. *La Rabouilleuse*; *Trube Wasser* (GRM) prod/rel: Societe Nouvelle Pathe-Cinema, D.E.F.a.

Colonnello Brideau, Il 1917 d: Giuseppe Pinto. lps: Raffaello Mariani, Pepa Bonafe, Giuseppe Pinto. 1680m ITL. *L' Intorbidotrice* prod/rel: Cosmopoli Film

Honor of the Family 1931 d: Lloyd Bacon. lps: Warren William, Bebe Daniels, Alan Mowbray. 66M USA. prod/rel: First National Pictures©, the Vitaphone Corp.

Rabouilleuse, La 1943 d: Fernand Rivers. lps: Fernand Gravey, Pierre Larquey, Suzy Prim. 100M FRN. prod/rel: Rivers

I Racconti Licenziosi, Book
Tuo Piacere E Il Mio, Il 1973 d: Claudio RaccA. lps: Ewa Aulin, Femi Benussi, Barbara Bouchet. 97M ITL. prod/rel: Naxos Film, Panta

Ursula Mirouet, 1843, Novel
Orsola Mirouet 1914. lps: Adriana Costamagna, Dillo Lombardi. 1150m ITL. prod/rel: Savoia Film

Ursule Mirouet, 1843, Novel
Ursule Mirouet 1912. lps: Rolla Norman, Armand Bour, Louise Sylvie. 1348m FRN. prod/rel: Pathe Freres

Vautrin, 1840, Play
Bagnostrafling, Der 1949 d: Gustav Frohlich. lps: Paul Dahlke, Winnie Markus, Kathe Dorsch. 106M GRM. *The Prisoner* prod/rel: Junge Filmunion, Bavaria

Vautrin 1943 d: Pierre Billon. lps: Michel Simon, Madeleine Sologne, Georges Marchal. 120M FRN. *Vautrin the Thief*; *This Man-Vautrin* prod/rel: S.N.E.G.

DE BARONCELLI, JACQUES
La Maison de l'Espion, Novel
Maison de l'Espion, La 1915 d: Jacques de Baroncelli. lps: Edmond Duquesne, Georges Treville. 600m FRN. prod/rel: Lumina Films

DE BEAUMARCHAIS, PIERRE-AUGUSTIN CARON (1732-1999), FRN, Beaumarchais
Le Barbier de Seville, 1775, Play
Barbero de Sevilla, El 1938 d: Benito Perojo. lps: Miguel Ligero, Raquel Rodrigo, Roberto Rey. 106M SPN/GRM. *Der Barbier von Sevilla* (GRM); *The Barber of Seville*

Barbier de Seville, Le 1933 d: Hubert Bourlon, Jean Kemm. lps: Andre Bauge, Fernand Charpin, Helene Robert. 93M FRN. prod/rel: Societe Des Films Vega

Barbiere Di Siviglia 1913 d: Luigi Maggi. lps: Gigetta Morano, Eleuterio Rodolfi, Ubaldo Stefani. 747m ITL. *The Barber of Seville* (USA) prod/rel: S.A. Ambrosio

Barbiere Di Siviglia, Il 1946 d: Mario CostA. lps: Ferruccio Tagliavini, Tito Gobbi, Nelly Corradi. 110M ITL. *The Barber of Seville* (USA) prod/rel: Tespi Film, Ates Film

Figaro Il Barbiere Di Siviglia 1955 d: Camillo Mastrocinque. lps: Tito Gobbi, Irene Genna, Giulio Neri. 95M ITL. *Barbiere Di Siviglia Figaro* prod/rel: Camillo Mastrocinque

Le Mariage de Figaro, Paris 1784, Play
Figaro 1928 d: Gaston Ravel. lps: Edmond Van Duren, Marie Bell, Genica Missirio. 2000m FRN. prod/rel: Franco-Film

Hochzeit Des Figaro, Die 1968 d: Joachim Hess. lps: Tom Krause, Arlene Saunders, Heinz Blankenburg. MTV. 189M GRM. *The Marriage of Figaro* (USA); *Figaros Hochzeit* prod/rel: Polyphon Film & Tv Productions

Mariage de Figaro, Le 1959 d: Jean Meyer. lps: Georges Descrieres, Yvonne Gaudeau, Jean Piat. 105M FRN. *The Marriage of Figaro* (USA) prod/rel: Les Productions Cinematographiques

Nozze Di Figaro, Le 1911. 317m ITL. *The Marriage of Figaro* (UKN) prod/rel: Cines

Nozze Di Figaro, Le 1913 d: Luigi Maggi. lps: Eleuterio Rodolfi, Gigetta Morano, Ernesto Vaser. 581m ITL. *Il Matrimonio Di Figaro*; *The Marriage of Figaro* (UKN) prod/rel: S.A. Ambrosio

Toller Tag, Ein 1945 d: Oscar F. Schuh. lps: Ilse Werner, Paul Hartmann, Lola Muthel. 74M GRM. *A Crazy Day* prod/rel: UFA, Prisma

DE BEAUVOIR, SIMONE (1908–1986), FRN
Story
Leat Yoter 1967 d: Avram Heffner. lps: Fanny Lubitsch, Avraham Ben-Yosef. SHT ISR. *Slow Down*

All Men are Mortal, Novel
All Men are Mortal 1995 d: Ate de Jong. lps: Irene Jacob, Stephen Rea, Marianne Sagebrecht. 94M NTH/UKN/FRN. prod/rel: Nova, Sigma

Le Sang Des Autres, Novel
Sang Des Autres, Le 1983 d: Claude Chabrol. lps: Jodie Foster, Michael Ontkean, Sam Neill. TVM. 177M FRN/CND. *The Blood of Others* (CND) prod/rel: Cine-Simone, Inc. (Montreal), Filmax (Paris)

DE BELAVALLE, MADELEINE MASSON
Servant of God, Play
Maddalena 1954 d: Augusto GeninA. lps: Marta Toren, Gino Cervi, Charles Vanel. 84M ITL. *Une Fille Nommee Madeleine* (FRN) prod/rel: Titanus

DE BENAVIDES, ALFONSO
Ethel Fue Una Mujer Ingenua, Novel
Ethel Fue Una Mujer Ingenua 1926 d: Alfonso de Benavides. lps: Estrella Garvayo Bermudez de Castro, Alfonso de Benavides. SPN. prod/rel: Alfonso De Benavides (Madrid)

DE BENEDETTI, ALDO
Story
Marito E Mio E l'Ammazzo Quando Mi Pare, Il 1967 d: Pasquale Festa Campanile. lps: Catherine Spaak, Hywel Bennett, Hugh Griffith. 97M ITL. *He's My Husband and I'll Kill Him When I Like*; *Drop Dead My Love* prod/rel: Clesi Cin.Ca, Ital Noleggio Cin.Co

Short Story
Wanda la Peccatrice 1952 d: Duilio Coletti. lps: Frank Villard, Yvonne Sanson, Giulietta MasinA. 93M ITL/FRN. *Wanda la Pecheresse* (FRN) prod/rel: Itala Film, Labor Film (Roma)

La Dama Bianca, Play
Dama Bianca, La 1938 d: Mario Mattoli. lps: Elsa Merlini, Nino Besozzi, Enrico Viarisio. 80M ITL. *The Lady in White* (USA) prod/rel: Aurora Film, Fono Roma

Due Dozzine Di Rose Scarlatte, Play
Rose Scarlatte 1940 d: Vittorio de SicA. lps: Vittorio de Sica, Renee Saint-Cyr, Umberto Melnati. 64M ITL. *Due Dozzine Di Rose Scarlatte* prod/rel: E.R.A. Film, Minerva Film

Lohengrin, Play
Lohengrin 1936 d: Nunzio MalasommA. lps: Vittorio de Sica, Sergio Tofano, Giuditta Rissone. 75M ITL. prod/rel: Ventura Film, E.I.a.

Militizia Territoriale, Play
Milizia Territoriale 1935 d: Mario Bonnard. lps: Antonio Gandusio, Leda Gloria, Enrico Viarisio. 75M ITL. prod/rel: G.A.I., E.I.a.

Il Mondo Vuole Cosi, Play
Mondo Vuole Cosi, Il 1946 d: Giorgio Bianchi. lps: Clara Calamai, Vittorio de Sica, Massimo Serato. 88M ITL. prod/rel: Aura Film, Excelsa

Non Ti Conosco Piu, Play
Non Ti Conosco Piu 1936 d: Nunzio MalasommA. lps: Elsa Merlini, Vittorio de Sica, Nini Gordini Cervi. 65M ITL. prod/rel: Amato Film, E.I.a.

La Resa Di Titi, Play
Resa Di Titi, La 1946 d: Giorgio Bianchi. lps: Clara Calamai, Nino Besozzi, Rossano Brazzi. F ITL. prod/rel: Excelsa Film, Alba Cin.Ca

Lo Sbaglio Di Essere Vivo, Play
Sbaglio Di Essere Vivo, Lo 1945 d: Carlo Ludovico BragagliA. lps: Isa Miranda, Vittorio de Sica, Gino Cervi. F ITL. *My Widow and I* (USA) prod/rel: Fauno Film, Aquila Cin.Ca

Sette Giorni All'altro Mondo, Play
Sette Giorni All'altro Mondo 1936 d: Mario Mattoli. lps: Armando Falconi, Leda Gloria, Mimi Aylmer. 66M ITL. prod/rel: Etrusca Fin., Artisti Associati

Trenta Secondi d'Amore, Play
Trenta Secondi d'Amore 1936 d: Mario Bonnard. lps: Elsa Merlini, Nino Besozzi, Enrico Viarisio. 66M ITL. prod/rel: Amato Film, E.I.a.

DE BENEDETTO, ALDO
Play
Ultimi Cinque Minuti, Gli 1955 d: Giuseppe Amato. lps: Linda Darnell, Vittorio de Sica, Peppino de Filippo. 89M ITL/FRN. *Les Cinq Dernieres Minutes* (FRN); *It Happens in Roma* (USA) prod/rel: Giuseppe Amato, Excelsa Film

L' Uomo Che Sorride, Play
Uomo Che Sorride, L' 1936 d: Mario Mattoli. lps: Vittorio de Sica, Assia Noris, Umberto Melnati. 72M ITL. prod/rel: Amato Film, E.I.a.

DE BOISGOBEY
Il Delitto Dell'Opera, Novel
Delitto Dell'Opera, Il 1917 d: Eleuterio Rodolfi. lps: Mercedes Brignone, Eleuterio Rodolfi, Armand Pouget. 3002m ITL. prod/rel: Jupiter Film

DE BRISAY, HENRI
La Condamnee, Play
Ainsi Va la Vie 1918 d: Pierre Bressol. lps: Paul Escoffier, Andre Lefaur, Marcelle Geniat. 940m FRN. prod/rel: Cgmc

Master Bob Gagnant du Prix de l'Avenir, Play
Master Bob, Gagnant du Prix de l'Avenir 1913. lps: Max Charlier, Gervais, Blanchard. 1210m FRN. prod/rel: Eclair

DE BRUYN, GUNTER
Gluck Im Hinterhaus, Novel
Gluck Im Hinterhaus 1979 d: Hermann Zschoche. lps: Dieter Mann, Jutta Wachowiak, Ute Lubosch. 98M GDR. *Happiness in the Outbuilding* prod/rel: Defa, Gruppe Berlin

Markische Forschungen, Novel
Markische Forschungen 1982 d: Roland Graf. lps: Hermann Beyer, Kurt Bowe, Jutta Wachowiak. 98M GRM. *Explorations in the March of Brandenburg*; *Exploring the Marches of Brandenberg* prod/rel: Defa, Dramaturgengruppe Roter Kreis

DE BUYSIEULX, GEORGES
Le Mont Maudit, Play
Mont Maudit, Le 1920 d: Paul Garbagny. lps: Adolphe Cande, Germaine Sablon, Paulette Berger. F FRN. *The Accursed Mountain*

DE CAMPOAMOR, RAMON
El Tren Expreso, 1872-74, Verse
Tren Expreso, El 1954 d: Leon Klimovsky. lps: Jorge Mistral, Laura Hidalgo, Evangelina Elizondo. 92M SPN.

DE CARVALHO, JOSE CANDIDO
O Coronel E O Lobisomem, 1964, Novel
Coronel E O Lobisomem, O 1980 d: Alcino Diniz. lps: Mauricio Do Valle, Maria Claudia, Jofre Soares. 103M BRZ. *The Colonel and the Wolfman*; *The Colonel and the Werewolf*

DE CASTRO, VIRGINIA
Obra Do Domonio, Novel
Sirene de Pierre 1922 d: Roger Lion, Virginia de Castro. lps: Max Maxudian, Maria Emilia Castelo-Branco, Gil Clary. 1600m FRN/PRT. *Le Fantome d'Amour* prod/rel: Fortuna Film

DE CERVANTES SAAVEDRA, MIGUEL (1547–1616), SPN
La Gitanilla, 1613, Short Story
Gitanilla, La 1940 d: Fernando Delgado. lps: Estrellita Castro, Antonio Vico, Manuel Arbo. 86M SPN. *The Little Gypsy*

La Ilustre Fregona
Ilustre Fregona, La 1927 d: Armando Pou. lps: Maria Muniaian, Angel de Zomeno, Matilde Artero. SPN. prod/rel: Venus Film Espanola (Madrid)

El Ingenioso Hidalgo Don Quijote de la Mancha, 1605-15, Novel
Curioso Impertinente, El 1948 d: Flavio CalzavarA. lps: Jose Maria Seoane, Aurora Bautista, Roberto Rey. 106M SPN.

Diablo Baja la Almohada, Un 1968 d: Jose Maria Forque. lps: Ingrid Thulin, Maurice Ronet, Gabriele Ferzetti. 105M SPN/FRN/ITL. *Le Diable Sous l'Oreiller* (FRN); *Calda E Infedele* (ITL); *Devil Under Your Pillow*; *A Devil Under the Pillow*

Don Chisciotte 1911. 314m ITL. *Don Chisciotte Della Mancia*; *Don Quixote* (UKN) prod/rel: Cines

Don Chisciotte 1984 d: Maurizio Scaparro. 275M ITL. *Don Quixote*

Don Chisciotte E Sancho Panza 1968 d: Gianni Grimaldi. lps: Franco Franchi, Ciccio Ingrassia, Fulvia Franco. 105M ITL. *Don Quixote and Sancho Panza* prod/rel: Claudia Cin.Ca

Don Quichotte 1913 d: Camille de Morlhon. lps: Claude Garry, Vallez, Leontine Massart. 1150m FRN. prod/rel: Pathe Freres

Don Quijote 1961 d: Eino Ruutsalo. FNL.

Don Quijote 1966 d: Carlo-Rim. lps: Josef Meinrad, Roger Carel, Fernando Rey. 97M SPN/FRN/GRM. *Don Quichotte; Don Quixote*

Don Quijote Ayer Y Hoy 1964 d: Cesar Ardavin. 64M SPN. *El Quijote Ayer Y Hoy; Don Quixote Then and Now*

Don Quixote 1916 d: Eddie Dillon. lps: De Wolf Hopper, Fay Tincher, Max Davidson. 5r USA. prod/rel: Fine Arts Film Co., Triangle Film Corp.©

Man of la Mancha 1972 d: Arthur Hiller. lps: Peter O'Toole, Sophia Loren, James Coco. 132M USA/ITL. *L' Uomo Della Mancha* (ITL) prod/rel: P.E.A. (Roma)

Trapalhadas de Dom Quixote & Sancho Panca, As 1980 d: Ary Fernandes. lps: Turibio Ruiz, Ivan Taborda, Osvaldo Barreto. 110M BRZ. *The Misadventures of Don Quixote and Sancho Panza*

Don Kikhot 1957 d: Grigori Kozintsev. lps: Nikolai Cherkassov, Yuri Tolubeyev, Serafima Birman. 110M USS. *Don Quixote* (USA) prod/rel: Lenfilm

Don Quichotte 1932 d: G. W. Pabst. lps: Feodor Chaliapin, Dorville, Renee Vallier. 89M FRN. *Adventures of Don Quixote; Don Quixote* prod/rel: Vandor-Film

Don Quixote 1923 d: Maurice Elvey. lps: George Robey, Jerrold Robertshaw, Bertram Burleigh. 4200f UKN. prod/rel: Stoll

Don Quixote 1932 d: John Farrow, G. W. Pabst. lps: Feodor Chaliapin, George Robey, Sidney Fox. 80M UKN. prod/rel: Neslon-Vandor, United Artists

Don Quixote 1972 d: Alvin Rakoff. lps: Rex Harrison, Frank Finlay, Rosemary Leach. TVM. 100M UKN/USA. *The Adventures of Don Quixote* (USA) prod/rel: BBC, Universal

Don Quixote 1973 d: Robert Helpmann, Rudolf Nureyev. lps: Rudolf Nureyev, Ray Powell, Francis Croese. 111M ASL. prod/rel: John Hargreaves

Don Quixote Cabalga de Nueva 1972 d: Roberto Gavaldon. lps: Cantinflas, Fernando Fernan Gomez, Maria Fernanda d'Ocon. 145M MXC. *Don Quixote Cabalga de Nueva; Don Quixote Rides Again*

Don Quixote de la Mancha 1947 d: Rafael Gil. lps: Rafael Rivelles, Juan Calvo, Fernando Rey. 135M SPN. *Don Quijote de la Mancha; Don Quixote; Don Quixote of la Mancha*

DE CESPEDES, ALBA (1911–, ITL

La Bambolona, Novel
Bambolona, La 1968 d: Franco Giraldi. lps: Ugo Tognazzi, Isabella Rey, Lilla Brignone. 107M ITL. *The Big Doll; Baby Doll* prod/rel: Mega Film, Panta

Suo Padre Io, Novel
Io, Suo Padre 1939 d: Mario Bonnard. lps: Erminio Spalla, Evi Maltagliati, Mariella Lotti. 92M ITL. prod/rel: Scalera Film

Nessuno Torna Indietro, Novel
Nessuno Torna Indietro 1943 d: Alessandro Blasetti. lps: Elisa Cegani, Valentina Cortese, Maria Denis. 75M ITL. *Istituto Grimaldi* prod/rel: Artisti Associati, Quartafilm

Nessuno Torna Indietro 1988 d: Franco Giraldi. lps: Federica Moro, Anne Parillaud, Jacques Perrin. TVM. 360M ITL.

DE CESSE, RAYMOND

Pomme d'Amour, Play
Pomme d'Amour 1932 d: Jean Dreville. lps: Andre Perchichot, Raymond Cordy, Christiane Dor. 87M FRN. prod/rel: a.P.E.C.

DE CESSE, ROBERT

Les Nouveaux Riches, Play
Nouveaux Riches, Les 1938 d: Andre Berthomieu. lps: Raimu, Betty Stockfeld, Michel Simon. 89M FRN. prod/rel: Grands Films Artistiques, Fernand Weill

DE CHANTEPLEURE, GUY

Malencontre, Novel
Malencontre 1920 d: Germaine Dulac. lps: Jeanne Brindeau, Jacques Roussel, Djemil Anik. 1588m FRN. prod/rel: D.H. Films

DE CHANTEPLEURE, MADAME GUY

La Passegere, Novel
Passeggera, La 1918 d: Gero Zambuto. lps: Pina Menichelli, Luciano Molinari, Alberto Nepoti. 1604m ITL. prod/rel: Itala Film

DE CHATEAUBRIANT, ALPHONSE

La Briere, Novel
Briere, La 1924 d: Leon Poirier. lps: Leon Davert, Laurence Myrga, Jeanne Marie-Laurent. 2500m FRN. prod/rel: Jacques Haik

Monsieur Des Lourdines, 1911, Novel
Monsieur Des Lourdines 1942 d: Pierre de Herain. lps: Claude Genia, Mila Parely, Constant Remy. 109M FRN. prod/rel: Pathe Cinema

DE COSTA, LEON

Kosher Kitty Kelly, New York 1925, Play
Kosher Kitty Kelly 1926 d: James W. Horne. lps: Viola Dana, Tom Forman, Vera Gordon. 6103f USA. prod/rel: R-C Pictures, Film Booking Offices of America

DE COSTER, CHARLES

Les Aventures de Till Espiegle, Novel
Aventures de Till l'Espiegle, Les 1956 d: Gerard Philipe, Joris Ivens. lps: Gerard Philipe, Jean Vilar, Fernand Ledoux. 90M FRN/GRM. *The Bold Adventure* (USA); *Thyl l'Espiegle; Till Eulenspiegel* (GRM); *The Adventures of Till Eulenspiegel; Die Abenteuer Des Til Ulenspiegel* prod/rel: D.C.F.a., Films Ariane

DE COTTENS, VICTOR

Trois Cents a l'Heure, Play
Trois Cents a l'Heure 1934 d: Willy Rozier. lps: Dorville, Georges Treville, Mona GoyA. 90M FRN. prod/rel: Lumi-Films

DE CRESCENZO, LUCIANO

Cosi Parlo Bellavista, Novel
Cosi Parlo Bellavista 1984 d: Luciano de Crescenzo. lps: Luciano de Crescenzo, Renato Scarpa, Sergio Solli. 105M ITL. *Thus Spake Bellavista* prod/rel: Eidoscope, Rete Quattro

DE CRESPIGNY, MRS. CHAMPION

Tangled Evidence, Novel
Tangled Evidence 1934 d: George A. Cooper. lps: Sam Livesey, Joan Marion, Michael Hogan. 57M UKN. prod/rel: Real Art, Radio

DE CROISSET, FRANCIS

Ciboulette, Opera
Ciboulette 1933 d: Claude Autant-LarA. lps: Simone Berriau, Robert Burnier, Armand Dranem. 100M FRN. *La Valse Miraculeuse* prod/rel: Cipar-Films

Le Coeur Dispose, Play
Coeur Dispose, Le 1936 d: Georges Lacombe. lps: Raymond Rouleau, Renee Saint-Cyr, Christian Gerard. 70M FRN. prod/rel: a.C.E.

La Dame de Malacca, Novel
Dame de Malacca, La 1937 d: Marc Allegret. lps: Edwige Feuillere, Pierre Richard-Willm, Jacques Copeau. 113M FRN. prod/rel: Regina

L' Epervier, 1914, Play
Epervier, L' 1924 d: Robert Boudrioz. lps: Silvio de Pedrelli, Nilda Du Plessy, Marie-Laure. F FRN. prod/rel: Films Trianon

Epervier, L' 1933 d: Marcel L'Herbier. lps: Charles Boyer, Nathalie Paley, Marguerite Templey. 106M FRN. *Les Amoureux; Bird of Prey* prod/rel: Imperial-Film

Hawk, The 1917 d: Paul Scardon. lps: Earle Williams, Ethel Grey Terry, Denton Vane. 5r USA. prod/rel: Vitagraph Co. of America©, Greater Vitagraph (V-L-S-E, Inc.)

Il Etait une Fois, Play
Il Etait une Fois 1933 d: Leonce Perret. lps: Andre Luguet, Jean Max, Gaby Morlay. 95M FRN. prod/rel: Pathe-Natan

Kvinnas Ansikte, En 1938 d: Gustaf Molander. lps: Ingrid Bergman, Anders Henriksson, Georg Rydeberg. 104M SWD. *A Woman's Face*

Woman's Face, A 1941 d: George Cukor. lps: Joan Crawford, Melvyn Douglas, Conrad Veidt. 105M USA. prod/rel: MGM

Les Nouveaux Messieurs, Play
Nouveaux Messieurs, Les 1928 d: Jacques Feyder. lps: Albert Prejean, Gaby Morlay, Henry Roussell. 1800m FRN. *The New Gentlemen* (USA) prod/rel: Albatros, Sequana Films

La Passerelle, Paris 1902, Play
Afraid to Love 1927 d: Edward H. Griffith. lps: Florence Vidor, Clive Brook, Norman Trevor. 6199f USA. prod/rel: Paramount Famous Lasky Corp.

Marriage of Kitty, The 1915 d: George Melford. lps: Fannie Ward, Cleo Ridgely, Jack Dean. 5r USA. prod/rel: Jesse L. Lasky Feature Play Co.©, Paramount Pictures Corp.

Pierre Ou Jac, Play
Head Over Heels 1937 d: Sonnie Hale. lps: Jessie Matthews, Louis Borell, Robert Flemyng. 81M UKN. *Head Over Heels in Love* (USA) prod/rel: Gaumont-British

Les Vignes du Seigneur, Play
Vignes du Seigneur, Les 1932 d: Rene Hervil. lps: Victor Boucher, Simone Cerdan, Jacqueline Made. 102M FRN. prod/rel: Etablissements Jacques Haik

Vignes du Seigneur, Les 1958 d: Jean Boyer. lps: Fernandel, Pierre Dux, Simone Valere. 94M FRN. prod/rel: F.I.D.E.S., C.O.C.I.N.O.R.

DE CUREL, FRANCOIS (1854–1928), FRN

La Figurante, 1889, Play
Figurante, La 1922 d: Gian Bistolfi. 2063m ITL. prod/rel: Caesar Film

La Fille Sauvage, Paris 1902, Play
Savage Woman, The 1918 d: Edmund Mortimer, Robert G. VignolA. lps: Clara Kimball Young, Milton Sills, Edward M. Kimball. 4680f USA. prod/rel: Clara Kimball Young Picture Co., Select Pictures Corp.©

Terre Inhumaine, Paris 1923, Play
Bois Des Amants, Le 1960 d: Claude Autant-LarA. lps: Francoise Rosay, Horst Frank, Laurent Terzieff. 96M FRN/ITL. *Il Bosco Degli Amanti* (ITL); *Between Love and Duty; Between Love and Desire* (UKN) prod/rel: Hoche Productions, Dama Cinematografica

This Mad World 1930 d: William C. de Mille. lps: Kay Johnson, Basil Rathbone, Louise Dresser. 70M USA. prod/rel: Metro-Goldwyn-Mayer Pictures

DE CURTIS, G. B.

Voce 'E Notte, Song
Voce 'E Notte 1919 d: Oreste Gherardini. lps: Tina Somma, Rita Almanova, Mario GambardellA. 1440m ITL. *Canto Nella Notte* prod/rel: Flegrea Film

DE ECA DE QUEIROS, JOSE MARIA

O Primo Basilio, Novel
Primo Basilio, O 1959 d: Antonio Lopes Ribeiro. lps: Costa Ferreira, Cecilia Guimaraes, Fernando Gusmao. 138M PRT. *Cousin Basilio*

DE ERCILLA Y ZUNIGA, ALONSO

La Araucana, 1589, Verse
Araucana, La 1970 d: Julio Coll. lps: Venantino Venantini, Elsa Martinelli, Julio PenA. 106M SPN/ITL/CHL. *L' Araucana Massacro Degli Dei* (ITL); *The Araucanian Girl; The Araucana; Conquest of Chile; La AraucanA. Conquista de Gigantes* (Roma) prod/rel: M.G.B.

DE FELITTA, FRANK

Audrey Rose, Novel
Audrey Rose 1977 d: Robert Wise. lps: Marsha Mason, John Beck, Anthony Hopkins. 113M USA. prod/rel: United Artists Corp.

DE FILIPPO, EDUARDO

Filumena Marturano, Naples 1946, Play
Filumena Marturano 1951 d: Eduardo de Filippo. lps: Titina de Filippo, Eduardo de Filippo, Tamara Lees. 98M ITL. prod/rel: Arco Film, Variety Film

Matrimonio All'italiana 1964 d: Vittorio de SicA. lps: Sophia Loren, Marcello Mastroianni, Aldo Puglisi. 104M ITL/FRN. *Mariage a l'Italienne* (FRN); *Marriage Italian Style* (USA) prod/rel: Compagnia Cin.Ca Champion (Roma), Les Films Concordia (Paris)

Gennareniello, Play
Marito E Moglie 1952 d: Eduardo de Filippo. lps: Eduardo de Filippo, Titina de Filippo, Tina PicA. 90M ITL. *Husband and Wife* prod/rel: Film Costellazione

Napoli Milionaria!, 1945, Play
Napoli, Milionaria 1950 d: Eduardo de Filippo. lps: Eduardo de Filippo, Leda Gloria, Delia ScalA. 102M ITL. *Side Street Story* (USA) prod/rel: Teatri Della Farnesia, Eduardo de Filippo

Non Ti Pago!, Play
Non Ti Pago! 1942 d: Carlo Ludovico BragagliA. lps: Eduardo de Filippo, Peppino de Filippo, Titina de Filippo. 72M ITL. prod/rel: Cines, Juventus Film

Non Ti Pago! 1954 d: Eduardo de Filippo. lps: Ugo d'Alessio, Eduardo de Filippo, Luisa Conte. MTV. 120M ITL.

Questi Fantasmi!, 1946, Play
Questi Fantasmi 1954 d: Eduardo de Filippo. lps: Renato Rascel, Erno Crisa, Ugo d'Alessio. 90M ITL. *These Ghosts* prod/rel: San Ferdinando Film, Titanus

Questi Fantasmi 1967 d: Renato Castellani. lps: Sophia Loren, Vittorio Gassman, Mario Adorf. 104M ITL/FRN. *Fantomes a l'Italienne* (FRN); *Three Ghosts; These Ghosts; Ghosts -Italian Style* (UKN) prod/rel: Compagnia Cin.Ca Champion (Roma), Les Films Concordia (Paris)

Sabato Domenica E Lunedi, 1959, Play
Sabato, Domenica E Lunedi 1990 d: Lina Wertmuller. lps: Sophia Loren, Luca de Filippo, Luciano de Crescenzo. TVM. 115M ITL. *Sunday and Monday Saturday*

Sik Sik l'Artifice Magico, Play
Quei Due 1935 d: Gennaro Righelli. lps: Eduardo de Filippo, Peppino de Filippo, Assia Noris. 75M ITL. prod/rel: G.A.I., Amato Film

Il Sindaco Del Rione Sanita, 1960, Play
Sindaco, Il 1997 d: Ugo Fabrizio Giordani. lps: Anthony Quinn, Anna Bonaiuto, Raoul BovA. 87M ITL. *The Mayor* prod/rel: Duea Film, Istituto Luce

Le Voci Di Dentro, Milan 1948, Play
Spara Forte, Piu Forte. Non Capisco 1966 d: Eduardo de Filippo. lps: Marcello Mastroianni, Raquel Welch, Guido Alberti. 100M ITL. *Louder. I Don't Understand Shoot Loud* (USA) prod/rel: Master Film, Titanus

DE FILIPPO, PEPPINO
A Coperchia E Caduta Una Stella, Play
In Campagna E Caduta Una Stella 1940 d: Eduardo de Filippo. lps: Eduardo de Filippo, Peppino de Filippo, Rosina Lawrence. 86M ITL. prod/rel: Defilm S.a., Cine Tirrenia

Casanova Farebbe Cosi, Play
Casanova Farebbe Cosi! 1942 d: Carlo Ludovico BragagliA. lps: Eduardo de Filippo, Peppino de Filippo, Clelia MataniA. 62M ITL. prod/rel: Juventus Film, E.N.I.C.

Non E Vero. Ma Ci Credo, Play
Non E Vero. Ma Ci Credo 1952 d: Sergio Grieco. lps: Peppino di Filippo, Titina di Filippo, Carlo Croccolo. F ITL. prod/rel: Gladio Film, Api Film

Quel Bandito Sono Io!, Play
Her Favourite Husband 1950 d: Mario Soldati. lps: Jean Kent, Robert Beatty, Gordon Harker. 79M UKN/ITL. *Quel Bandito Sono Io!* (ITL); *The Taming of Dorothy* (USA) prod/rel: Lux Film (Roma), Renown (London)

DE FLAVIIS, PIO
L'ha Fatto Una Signora, Play
L'ha Fatto Una Signora 1938 d: Mario Mattoli. lps: Rosina Anselmi, Michele Abbruzzo, Alida Valli. 75M ITL. prod/rel: I.C.A.R., Generalcine

DE FLERS, ROBERT
L' Amour Veille, Paris 1907, Play
Amour Veille, L' 1937 d: Henry Roussell. lps: Henri Garat, Robert Pizani, Jacqueline Francell. 109M FRN. prod/rel: Societe Des Films Osso, Societe Du Film Amour Veille
Love Watches 1918 d: Henry Houry. lps: Corinne Griffith, Denton Vane, Edmund Burns. 5r USA. prod/rel: Vitagraph Co. of America©, Blue Ribbon Feature

L' Ane de Buridan, 1909, Play
Ane de Buridan, L' 1916?.
Ane de Buridan, L' 1932 d: Alexandre Ryder. lps: Colette Darfeuil, Mona Goya, Rene Lefevre. 77M FRN. prod/rel: Pathe-Natan
Asino Di Buridano, L' 1917 d: Eleuterio Rodolfi. lps: Eleuterio Rodolfi, Fernanda Negri-Pouget, Lydia QuarantA. 1588m ITL. prod/rel: Veritas

L' Ange du Foyer, Play
Ange du Foyer, L' 1936 d: Leon Mathot. lps: Betty Stockfeld, Lucien Baroux, Roger Duchesne. 95M FRN. prod/rel: Societe Nouvelle De Cinematographie

La Belle Aventure, Paris 1914, Play
Beautiful Adventure, The 1917 d: Dell Henderson. lps: Ann Murdock, Ada Boshell, Edward Fielding. 5-6r USA. prod/rel: Empire All Star Corp.©, Mutual Film Corp.
Belle Aventure, La 1932 d: Roger Le Bon, Reinhold Schunzel. lps: Kathe von Nagy, Michele Alfa, Jean Perier. 80M FRN. prod/rel: U.F.a., a.C.E.
Belle Aventure, La 1942 d: Marc Allegret. lps: Claude Dauphin, Louis Jourdan, Micheline Presle. 92M FRN. *Twilight* (USA) prod/rel: Films Imperia

Le Bois Sacre, Play
Bois Sacre, Le 1939 d: Leon Mathot, Robert Bibal. lps: Gaby Morlay, Elvire Popesco, Marcel Dalio. 80M FRN. prod/rel: Bervia Films

Ciboulette, Opera
Ciboulette 1933 d: Claude Autant-LarA. lps: Simone Berriau, Robert Burnier, Armand Dranem. 100M FRN. *La Valse Miraculeuse* prod/rel: Cipar-Films

L' Habit Vert, Play
Habit Vert, L' 1937 d: Roger Richebe. lps: Elvire Popesco, Meg Lemonnier, Victor Boucher. 109M FRN. prod/rel: Societe Des Films Roger Richebe

Miquette Et Sa Mere, Play
Miquette 1940 d: Jean Boyer. lps: Lilian Harvey, Lucien Baroux, Andre Lefaur. F FRN. *La Demoiselle du Tabac*; *Miquette Et Sa Mere* prod/rel: U.F.P.C.
Miquette Et Sa Mere 1914 d: Henri Pouctal. lps: Eve Lavalliere, Henri Germain. 1200m FRN. prod/rel: le Film d'Art
Miquette Et Sa Mere 1933 d: Henri Diamant-Berger, D. B. Maurice. lps: Blanche Montel, Marcelle Monthil, Roland Toutain. 85M FRN. prod/rel: Films Diamant
Miquette Et Sa Mere 1949 d: Henri-Georges Clouzot. lps: Daniele Delorme, Mireille Perrey, Louis Jouvet. 96M FRN. *Miquette* (USA) prod/rel: Alcina, C.I.C.C.

Monsieur Brotonneau, Play
Monsieur Brotonneau 1939 d: Alexander Esway. lps: Raimu, Josette Day, Saturnin Fabre. 100M FRN. prod/rel: Films Marcel Pagnol

Les Nouveaux Messieurs, Play
Nouveaux Messieurs, Les 1928 d: Jacques Feyder. lps: Albert Prejean, Gaby Morlay, Henry Roussell. 1800m FRN. *The New Gentlemen* (USA) prod/rel: Albatros, Sequana Films

Papa, 1911, Play
Derniere Aventure 1941 d: Robert Peguy. lps: Jean Max, Pierre Dux, Annie Ducaux. 104M FRN. prod/rel: Fernand Rivers
Papa 1915 d: Nino OxiliA. lps: Ruggero Ruggeri, Amleto Novelli, Pina Menichelli. 594m ITL. prod/rel: Cines

Primerose, 1911, Play
Primerose 1919 d: Mario Caserini. lps: Thea, Ugo Piperno, Elena Sangro. 2085m ITL. prod/rel: Cines
Primerose 1933 d: Rene Guissart. lps: Henri Rollan, Madeleine Renaud, Marguerite Moreno. 80M FRN. prod/rel: Edmond Pingrin

Le Roi, 1908, Play
King on Main Street, The 1925 d: Monta Bell. lps: Adolphe Menjou, Bessie Love, Greta Nissen. 6229f USA. prod/rel: Famous Players-Lasky, Paramount Pictures
Roi, Le 1936 d: Piere Colombier. lps: Victor Francen, Raimu, Gaby Morlay. 113M FRN. *Le Roi S'amuse* prod/rel: Films Modernes, Emile Natan
Roi, Le 1949 d: Marc-Gilbert Sauvajon. lps: Maurice Chevalier, Sophie Desmarets, Annie Ducaux. 95M FRN. *A Royal Affair* (USA) prod/rel: Speva Films, Michel Safra

Les Vignes du Seigneur, Play
Vignes du Seigneur, Les 1932 d: Rene Hervil. lps: Victor Boucher, Simone Cerdan, Jacqueline Made. 102M FRN. prod/rel: Etablissements Jacques Haik
Vignes du Seigneur, Les 1958 d: Jean Boyer. lps: Fernandel, Pierre Dux, Simone Valere. 94M FRN. prod/rel: F.I.D.E.S., C.O.C.I.N.O.R.

DE FOREST, MARIAN
Erstwhile Susan, New York 1916, Play
Erstwhile Susan 1919 d: John S. Robertson. lps: Constance Binney, Jere Austin, Alfred Hickman. 5380f USA. prod/rel: Realart Pictures Corp.©

DE FRANCHEVILLE, ROBERT
De Nachtronde, Play
Tusschen Liefde En Plicht 1912. lps: Caroline Van Dommelen, Jan Van Dommelen. NTH. **De Nachtronde**; *Plicht En Liefde*; *Between Love and Duty*; *The Night-Round*; *Duty Stronger Than Love* (UKN) prod/rel: Film-Fabriek F. A. Noggerath

DE FRECE, LADY
Recollections of Vesta Tilley, Book
After the Ball 1957 d: Compton Bennett. lps: Laurence Harvey, Pat Kirkwood, Clive Morton. 89M UKN. prod/rel: Beaconsfield, Romulus

DE GARROS, PAUL
Le Drame de Villesauge, Novel
Drame de Villesauge, Le 1909 d: Victorin Jasset. 215m FRN. prod/rel: Eclair

DE GASPERI, OLIMPIA
Il Racconto Del Piccolo Vetraio, Novel
Piccolo Vetraio, Il 1955 d: Giorgio Capitani. lps: Georges Poujouly, Armando Francioli, Olga Solbelli. F ITL/FRN. *Les Vitriers* (FRN) prod/rel: Filmex, Franca Film

DE GASTYNE, JULES
Le Fils de la Nuit, Novel
Fils de la Nuit, Le 1919 d: Gerard Bourgeois. lps: Fernand Mailly, Mlle. Farnese, Nadette Darson. SRL. FRN. prod/rel: Eclair

DE GIRARDIN, MME
La Joie Fait Peur, Play
Joie Fait Peur, La 1914 d: Jacques Roullet. lps: Pierre Magnier, Georges Le Roy, Aimee Tessandier. 1220m FRN. prod/rel: Meteor Film
Joie Qui Tue, La 1912. lps: Georges Saillard, Pierre Daltour, Jeanne Grumbach. FRN. prod/rel: Eclipse

DE GOBINEAU, JOSEPH ARTHUR
Adelaide, Paris 1913, Play
Adelaide 1968 d: Jean-Daniel Simon. lps: Ingrid Thulin, Jean Sorel, Sylvie Fennec. 100M FRN/ITL. *Fino a Farti Male* (ITL); *The Depraved* (USA) prod/rel: Poste Parisien, Les Films Number One

DE GONCOURT, EDMOND (1822–1896), FRN
La Fille Elisa, 1877, Novel
Fille Elisa, La 1921 d: Edmond Epardaud. lps: Mara Tchoukleva, Ferruccio Biancini. 1435m ITL. prod/rel: Vay Film

Fille Elisa, La 1956 d: Roger Richebe. lps: Dany Carrel, Serge Reggiani, Valentine Tessier. 90M FRN. *Elisa*; *That Girl Elisa* (UKN) prod/rel: Overseas Films, Films Roger Richebe

Les Freres Zemganno, Novel
Freres Zemganno, Les 1925 d: Alberto Francis Bertoni. lps: Constant Remy, Stacia Napierkowska, Roger San JuanA. 2000m FRN. prod/rel: Argus-Film

DE GORSSE, HENRI
La Gamine, 1911, Play
Avventure Di Colette, Le 1916 d: R. Savarese. lps: Anna Fougez, Renato Fabiani, Angelo GallinA. 1741m ITL. prod/rel: Cines
Monella, La 1914 d: Nino OxiliA. lps: Dina Galli, Amerigo Guasti, Stanislao Ciarli. 1107m ITL. prod/rel: Cines
Studio Girl, The 1918 d: Charles Giblyn. lps: Constance Talmadge, Earle Foxe, Johnny Hines. 5r USA. prod/rel: Select Pictures Corp.©

DE GOURIADEC, LOIC
Le Mort En Fuite, Novel
Break the News 1938 d: Rene Clair. lps: Jack Buchanan, Maurice Chevalier, June Knight. 78M UKN. *Fausses Nouvelles* prod/rel: General Film Distributors, Jack Buchanan

DE GRAMONT, J.
A Moi Les Femmes, Play
A Moi Les Femmes 1915. FRN. prod/rel: Pathe Freres

DE GRECE, MICHEL
La Nuit de Serail, Novel
Favorite, The 1989 d: Jack (4) Smith. lps: F. Murray Abraham, Maud Adams, Amber O'SheA. 104M USA/SWT. *La Nuit de Serail* (SWT) prod/rel: Ascona Films

DE GRESAC, FRED
Cora, Play
Cora 1915 d: Edwin Carewe. lps: Emily Stevens, Edwin Carewe, Ethel Stewart. 5r USA. prod/rel: Rolfe Photoplays, Inc., Metro Pictures Corp.©

La Passerelle, Paris 1902, Play
Afraid to Love 1927 d: Edward H. Griffith. lps: Florence Vidor, Clive Brook, Norman Trevor. 6199f USA. prod/rel: Paramount Famous Lasky Corp.
Marriage of Kitty, The 1915 d: George Melford. lps: Fannie Ward, Cleo Ridgely, Jack Dean. 5r USA. prod/rel: Jesse L. Lasky Feature Play Co.©, Paramount Pictures Corp.

Sweethearts, New York 1913, Opera
Sweethearts 1938 d: W. S. Van Dyke. lps: Jeanette MacDonald, Nelson Eddy, Frank Morgan. 114M USA. prod/rel: Metro-Goldwyn-Mayer Corp., Loew's, Inc.©

DE GUIMARAES, FRANCISCO VAZ
Acto Da Primavera, Play
Acto Da Primavera 1963 d: Manoel de OliveirA. lps: Nicolau Da Silva, Ermelinda Pires, Maria MadalenA. 94M PRT. *The Passion of Jesus*; *The Spring Play* prod/rel: Lusomondo, Cinefil

DE HARTOG, JAN (1914–, NTH
The Fourposter, New York 1951, Play
Fourposter, The 1952 d: Irving Reis. lps: Rex Harrison, Lilli Palmer. 103M USA. prod/rel: Columbia, Stanley Kramer Co.

The Inspector, New York 1960, Novel
Inspector, The 1962 d: Philip Dunne. lps: Stephen Boyd, Dolores Hart, Leo McKern. 111M UKN. *Lisa* prod/rel: Red Lion Productions, 20th Century-Fox

The Little Ark, Novel
Little Ark, The 1972 d: James B. Clark. lps: Theodore Bikel, Philip Frame, Genevieve Ambas. 100M USA. prod/rel: Cinema Center

Maitre Apres Dieu, Play
Maitre Apres Dieu 1950 d: Louis Daquin. lps: Pierre Brasseur, Loleh Bellon, Yvette Etievant. 92M FRN. *Skipper Next to God* prod/rel: C.G.C.F., Silver Films

Das Riesenrad, Play
Riesenrad, Das 1961 d: Geza von Radvanyi. lps: Maria Schell, O. W. Fischer, Adrienne Gessner. 109M GRM. *Ferris Wheel* prod/rel: C.C.C., Gloria

The Spiral Road, New York 1957, Novel
Spiral Road, The 1962 d: Robert Mulligan. lps: Rock Hudson, Burl Ives, Gena Rowlands. 145M USA. prod/rel: Universal Pictures

Stella, Novel
Key, The 1958 d: Carol Reed. lps: William Holden, Sophia Loren, Trevor Howard. 134M UKN. prod/rel: Columbia, Open Road

DE JAGERS, DOROTHY
The Average Woman, 1922, Short Story
Average Woman, The 1924 d: W. Christy Cabanne. lps: Pauline Garon, David Powell, Harrison Ford. 6021f USA. prod/rel: C. C. Burr Pictures

DE JANVIER, F. H.
The Sleeping Sentinel, Poem
  Sleeping Sentinel, The 1914. 1000f USA. prod/rel: Lubin

DE KRUIF, PAUL
The Fight for Life, Book
  Fight for Life, The 1940 d: Pare Lorentz. lps: Myron McCormick, Will Geer, Storrs Haynes. DOC. 72M USA. prod/rel: Columbia Pictures Corp., United States Film Service©
Yellow Jack, New York 1934, Play
  Yellow Jack 1938 d: George B. Seitz. lps: Robert Montgomery, Virginia Bruce, Lewis Stone. 83M USA. prod/rel: Metro-Goldwyn-Mayer Corp., Loew's, Inc.©

DE LA FONTAINE, JEAN (1621–1695), FRN
La Cigale, Story
  Cigale, La 1913 d: Elwin Neame. lps: Ivy Close. 2600f UKN. prod/rel: Ivy Close Films, Walturdaw

DE LA FOUCHARDIERE, GEORGES
Les Aventures Cocasses de Boulot Aviateur, Novel
  Boulot Aviateur 1937 d: Maurice de Canonge. lps: Robert Arnoux, Marguerite Moreno, Michel Simon. 89M FRN. *Voleurs Et Cie Fripons* prod/rel: Trianon Film
Le Bouif Errant, Novel
  Bouif Errant, Le 1926 d: Rene Hervil. lps: Felicien Tramel, Albert Prejean, Janine Merrey. SRL. 6EP FRN. prod/rel: Film d'Art (Vandal Et Delac)
La Chienne, Play
  Scarlet Street 1945 d: Fritz Lang. lps: Edward G. Robinson, Joan Bennett, Dan DuryeA. 103M USA. prod/rel: Universal, Diana Prods.-Walter Wangre
Le Crime du Bouif, Novel
  Crime du Bouif, Le 1921 d: Henri Pouctal. lps: Felicien Tramel, Therese Kolb, Jeanne Saint-Bonnet. 1995m FRN. prod/rel: Henri Pouctal
  Crime du Bouif, Le 1932 d: Andre Berthomieu. lps: Felicien Tramel, Marcel Vibert, Mady Berry. 91M FRN. prod/rel: Films De France
La Fille du Bouif, Play
  Fille du Bouif, La 1931 d: Rene Bussy. lps: Felicien Tramel, Henri Leoni, Loulou Hegoburu. 60M FRN. prod/rel: Franco-Belge Cinema

DE LA PARELLE, MAURICE
Little Mr. Fixer, Story
  Little Mr. Fixer 1915 d: Frank Lloyd. lps: Millard K. Wilson, Olive Fuller Golden, Gordon Griffith. SHT USA. *Billy's Cupidity* prod/rel: Laemmle

DE LA PASTURE, MRS. HENRY
The Lonely Lady of Grosvenor Square, Novel
  Lonely Lady of Grosvenor Square, The 1922 d: Sinclair Hill. lps: Betty Faire, Jack Hobbs, Eileen Magrath. 4600f UKN. prod/rel: Ideal

DE LA ROCHE, MAZO (1885–1961), CND
Jalna, Boston 1927, Novel
  Jalna 1935 d: John Cromwell. lps: Ian Hunter, Kay Johnson, C. Aubrey Smith. 78M USA. prod/rel: RKO Radio Pictures©
  Jalna 1994 d: Philippe Monnier. lps: Danielle Darrieux, Serge Dupire, Catherine Mouchet. TVM. 720M FRN/CND.

DE LA VALLIERES, JEAN
L' Irresistible Catherine, Novel
  Irresistible Catherine, L' 1955 d: Andre Pergament. lps: Marie Daems, Michel Auclair, Fernand Sardou. 80M FRN. prod/rel: Jacques Santu, Compagnie D'art Technique

DE LA VARENDE, JEAN
Nez de Cuir, Novel
  Nez-de-Cuir 1952 d: Yves Allegret, Jacques Sigurd. lps: Jean Marais, Massimo Girotti, Francoise Christophe. 92M FRN/ITL. *Nez de Cuir Gentilhomme d'Amour*; *Naso Di Cuoio* (ITL); *Gentiluomo d'Amore*; *Nez de Cuir* prod/rel: Ed. Decharme, Alcina

DE LA VEGA, RICARDO
La Verbena de la Paloma, Opera
  Verbena de la Paloma, La 1921 d: Jose Buchs. lps: Elisa Ruiz Romero, Florian Rey, Julia Lozano. 57M SPN. *The Feast of the Dove*; *The Paloma Fair* prod/rel: Atlantida (Madrid)

DE LA VEGA, VENTURA
El Diablo Cojuelo, 1641, Novel
  Diablo Cojuelo, El 1970 d: Ramon Fernandez. lps: Alfredo Landa, Diana Lorys, Rafael Alonso. 104M SPN. *The Lame Devil*; *The Crippled Devil*
El Hombre de Mundo, 1845, Play
  Hombre de Mundo, El 1948 d: Manuel Tamayo. lps: Maria Martin, Francisco Melgares, Manolo Moran. 104M SPN.

DE LACOMBE, MADAME A.
Gisele Et Son Destin, Short Story
  Etrange Destin 1945 d: Louis Cuny. lps: Henri Vidal, Renee Saint-Cyr, Denise Grey. 110M FRN. prod/rel: Discina

DE LAMARTINE, ALPHONSE
Graziella, 1852, Poem
  Graziella 1917 d: Mario Gargiulo. lps: Tina Xeo, Franco Piersanti, Paolo Poggi. 1475m ITL. prod/rel: Flegrea Film
  Graziella 1926 d: Marcel Vandal. lps: Jean Dehelly, Nina Vanna, Sylviane de Castillo. F FRN. prod/rel: Vandal Et Delac
  Graziella 1955 d: Giorgio Bianchi. lps: Maria Fiore, Jean-Pierre Mocky, Tina PicA. 95M ITL. prod/rel: Trionfalcine, Cei-Incom
Jocelyn, 1836, Verse
  Jocelyn 1922 d: Leon Poirier. lps: Armand Tallier, Suzanne Bianchetti, Roger Karl. 2400m FRN. prod/rel: Gaumont - Serie Pax
  Jocelyn 1933 d: Pierre Guerlais. lps: Samson Fainsilber, Marguerite Weintenberger, Jacqueline Carlier. 86M FRN. prod/rel: Productions Pierre Guerlais
  Jocelyn 1951 d: Jacques de Casembroot. lps: Jean Desailly, Simone Valere, Jean Vilar. 92M FRN. prod/rel: Pantheon Production

DE LANA
Garden of Sleep, Poem
  Poppies 1914 d: Stuart Kinder. 1250f UKN. prod/rel: Climax Films, Browne

DE LASSAGNE, PATRICK
Zonzon, Play
  Zonzon 1998 d: Laurent Bouhnik. lps: Pascal Greggory, Gael Morel, Jamel Debbouze. 100M FRN. prod/rel: Mk2 Diffusion, Playtime

DE LEON, JACK
Crime on the Hill, 1932, Play
  Crime on the Hill 1933 d: Bernard Vorhaus. lps: Sally Blane, Nigel Playfair, Lewis Casson. 69M UKN. prod/rel: British International Pictures, Wardour
Jury's Evidence, Play
  Jury's Evidence 1936 d: Ralph Ince. lps: Hartley Power, Margaret Lockwood, Nora Swinburne. 74M UKN. prod/rel: British Lion
Line Engaged, 1934, Play
  Line Engaged 1935 d: Bernerd Mainwaring. lps: Bramwell Fletcher, Jane Baxter, Arthur Wontner. 68M UKN. prod/rel: British Lion
The Man at Six, London 1928, Play
  Gables Mystery, The 1938 d: Harry Hughes. lps: Francis L. Sullivan, Antoinette Cellier, Leslie Perrins. 66M UKN. prod/rel: Welwyn, MGM
  Man at Six, The 1931 d: Harry Hughes. lps: Anne Grey, Lester Matthews, Gerald Rawlinson. 70M UKN. *The Gables Mystery* (USA) prod/rel: British International Pictures, Wardour
The Silent Witness, New York 1931, Play
  Silent Witness, The 1932 d: Marcel Varnel, R. Lee Hough. lps: Lionel Atwill, Greta Nissen, Weldon Heyburn. 73M USA. prod/rel: Fox Film Corp.©

DE LERA, ANGEL MARIA
Bochorno, 1960, Short Story
  Bochorno 1962 d: Juan de OrdunA. lps: Maria Mahor, Jose Moreno, Gina Romand. 112M SPN. *Sultry Weather*
La Boda, 1959, Novel
  Boda, La 1963 d: Lucas Demare. lps: Jose Suarez, Graciela Borges, Susana Campos. 89M ARG/SPN.
Los Clarines Del Miedo, 1958, Novel
  Clarines Del Miedo, Los 1958 d: Antonio Roman. lps: Francisco Rabal, Rogelio Madrid, Silvia Solar. 95M SPN.

DE LETRAZ, JEAN
Bichon, Play
  Bichon 1935 d: Fernand Rivers. lps: Victor Boucher, Marcel Vallee, Marguerite Deval. 105M FRN. prod/rel: Films Fernand Rivers
  Bichon 1947 d: Rene Jayet. lps: Armand Bernard, Andre Alerme, Jeanne Fusier-Gir. 80M FRN. prod/rel: U.T.C.
  Hurra - Die Firma Hat Eine Kind 1956 d: Hans Richter. lps: Walter Muller, Wera Frydtberg, Loni Heuser. 93M GRM. *Hooray - the Company Has a Child* prod/rel: Rialto, Defir
  Papa Per Una Notte 1939 d: Mario Bonnard. lps: Sergio Tofano, Carlo Romano, Clelia MataniA. 80M ITL. prod/rel: Scalera Film
Conduisez-Moi Madame, Play
  Conduisez-Moi, Madame 1932 d: Herbert Selpin. lps: Armand Bernard, Rolla Norman, Jeanne Boitel. 80M FRN. *Antoinette* prod/rel: Les Comedies Filmees

Descendez on Vous Demande, Play
  Descendez, on Vous Demande 1951 d: Jean Laviron. lps: Jean Tissier, Noelle Norman, Paulette Dubost. 89M FRN. prod/rel: Eole Films
Epousez-Nous Monsieur, Play
  Frederica 1942 d: Jean Boyer. lps: Elvire Popesco, Charles Trenet, Rellys. 92M FRN. prod/rel: Danis, Pierre
L' Extravagante Theodora, Play
  Extravagante Theodora, L' 1949 d: Henri Lepage. lps: Robert Murzeau, Jacqueline Gauthier, Lucienne Le Marchand. 86M FRN. prod/rel: Les Prisonniers Associes
La Fessee, Play
  Fessee, La 1937 d: Pierre Caron. lps: Mireille Perrey, Marguerite Moreno, Albert Prejean. 88M FRN. prod/rel: S.P.a.F.
Nous Avons Tout Fait la Meme Chose, Play
  Nous Avons Tout Fait la Meme Chose 1949 d: Rene Sti. lps: Jose Noguero, Luce Feyrer, Pierre Louis. 92M FRN. prod/rel: Prisonniers Associes, Artistes Et Techniciens Associes
Une Nuit a Megeve, Play
  Nuit a Megeve, Une 1953 d: Raoul Andre. lps: Paul Cambo, Michele Philippe, Jeannette Batti. 91M FRN. prod/rel: Coprocit, a.T.I.C.a
On Demande un Menage, Play
  On Demande un Menage 1945 d: Maurice Cam. lps: Saturnin Fabre, Denise Grey, Marguerite Deval. 90M FRN. prod/rel: Miramar
Voyage a Trois, Play
  Voyage a Trois 1949 d: Jean-Paul Paulin. lps: Jeannette Batti, Maria Riquelme, Pierre Louis. 82M FRN. prod/rel: Francinalp

DE LIGUORO, GIUSEPPE
Murat O la Fine Di un Re, 1901
  Gioacchino Murat (Dalla Locanda Al Trono) 1910 d: Giuseppe de Liguoro. lps: Giuseppe de Liguoro. 276m ITL. *Joachim Murat; from the Tavern to the Throne* (UKN); *Dalla Locana Al Trono* prod/rel: Milano Films

DE LINARES, MARI-LUISA
Short Story
  Comment Epouser un Premier Ministre 1964 d: Michel Boisrond. lps: Jean-Claude Brialy, Pascale Petit, Claude Gensac. 82M FRN/ITL. *Come Sposare un Primo Ministro* (ITL) prod/rel: Films Agiman, Films Champion

DE LISE, NICOLA
Gabriele Il Lampionaro Di Porto, 1853, Play
  Gabriele Il Lampionaro Di Porto 1919 d: Elvira Notari. lps: Oreste Tesorone, Mary Cavaliere, Signora Pappone. 1300m ITL. *Rosa la Pazza* prod/rel: Films Dora

DE L'ISLE-ADAM, VILLIERS
La Torture Par l'Esperance, Short Story
  Conte Cruel 1930 d: Gaston Modot. lps: Gaston Modot. SHT FRN. prod/rel: Natan

DE LORDE, ANDRE
Attaque Nocturne, Play
  Attaque Nocturne 1931 d: Marc Allegret. lps: Fernandel, Madeleine Guitty, Emile Saint-Ober. 25M FRN. prod/rel: Braunberger-Richebe
L' Attentat de la Maison Rouge, Play
  Attentat de la Maison Rouge, L' 1917 d: Gaston Silvestre. lps: Jean Worms, Andre Marnay, Guerard. 1297m FRN. prod/rel: Films Gaston Silvestre
Au Telephone, Play
  Lonely Villa, The 1909 d: D. W. Griffith. lps: Marion Leonard, Mary Pickford, Adele de Garde. 750f USA. prod/rel: Biograph Co.
Bagnes d'Enfants, Play
  Bagnes d'Enfants 1914 d: Emile Chautard. lps: Josette Andriot, Georges Dorival, Henri Gouget. 880m FRN. prod/rel: Acad
  Bagnes d'Enfants 1933 d: Georges Gauthier. lps: Germaine Dermoz, Leonie Balme, Andre Marnay. F FRN. *Gosses de Misere* prod/rel: Artisans Du Film
Le Chateau de la Mort Lente, Play
  Chateau de la Mort Lente, Le 1925 d: E. B. Donatien. lps: E. B. Donatien, Lucienne Legrand, Pierre Etchepare. F FRN. prod/rel: Donatien
La Double Existence du Docteur Morart, Play
  Double Existence du Docteur Morart, La 1919 d: Jacques Gretillat. lps: Jacques Gretillat, Jeanne Delvair, Jean Debucourt. 1230m FRN. prod/rel: Films Pierrot
Figures de Cire, Play
  Figures de Cire 1912 d: Maurice Tourneur. lps: Henri Gouget, Henry Roussell. 290m FRN. *L' Homme aux Figures de Cire*; *The Man With Wax Faces* prod/rel: Eclair

DE LUCIO, JOSE LUIS
La Malcasada, Play
  Malcasada, La 1926 d: Francisco Gomez Hidalgo. lps: Maria Banquer, Jose Nieto, Jose Calle. 4373m SPN. prod/rel: Latino Films (Madrid)

DE LUSSAC, VICTOR
Leggenda Siracusana Dell'Anno 1000
  Christus 1914 d: Giuseppe de Liguoro. lps: Giulia Cassini-Rizzotto, Alessandro Rocca, Lia Monesi-Passaro. 1550m ITL. *La Sfinge Dello Jonio* prod/rel: Etna Film

DE MACEDO, JOAQUIM MANUEL
A Moreninha, 1844, Novel
  Moreninha, A 1970 d: Glauco Mirko Laurelli. 96M BRZ. *The Little Brunette*

DE MAJO, MATTEO
Casa NovA. Vita Nova, Play
  Arrangiatevi! 1959 d: Mauro Bolognini. lps: Toto, Peppino de Filippo, Laura Adani. 105M ITL. prod/rel: Cineriz

DE MANDIARGUEW, ANDRE PIEYRE
La Motocyclette, Paris 1963, Novel
  Girl on a Motorcycle 1968 d: Jack Cardiff. lps: Marianne Faithfull, Alain Delon, Roger Mutton. 91M UKN/FRN. *La Motocyclette* (FRN); *Naked Under Leather* prod/rel: Mid-Atlantic Films, Ares Productions

DE MARCHI, EMILIO (1851–1901), ITL
Il Cappello Del Prete, Novel
  Cappello Da Prete, Il 1944 d: Ferdinando M. Poggioli. lps: Roldano Lupi, Lida Baarova, Luigi Almirante. 90M ITL. *Castigo* prod/rel: Universalcine, Cines
Giacomo l'Idealista, 1897, Novel
  Giacomo l'Idealista 1943 d: Alberto LattuadA. lps: Marina Berti, Massimo Serato, Andrea Checchi. 90M ITL. prod/rel: Artisti Tecnici Associati Milano, Artisti Associati

DE MARCHI, LUIGI
Odissea Verde, Novel
  Indios a Nord-Ovest 1964 d: Luigi de Marchi. lps: Dan Harrison, Marisa Solinas, Pierre Gerard. 90M ITL. *Furia Selvaggia a Maracaibo* prod/rel: Cine Kronos (Bologna)

DE MARIA, NINO
Cuori Negli Abissi, Novel
  Cammino Della Speranza, Il 1950 d: Pietro Germi. lps: Raf Vallone, Elena Varzi, Saro Urzi. 99M ITL. *The Path of Hope*; *The Road to Hope* prod/rel: Lux Film

DE MARNEY, TERENCE (1909–1971), UKN
Wanted for Murder, London 1937, Play
  Wanted for Murder 1946 d: Lawrence Huntington. lps: Eric Portman, Dulcie Gray, Derek Farr. 103M UKN. *A Voice in the Night* prod/rel: Excelsior, 20th Century-Fox

DE MARSAN, MAURICE
Le Petite Radjah, Short Story
  Petit Radjah, Le 1918 d: Paul Barlatier. lps: Max Claudet, Raymond Lyon, Andre Polack. 650m FRN. prod/rel: Phocea Film

DE MARTHOLD, JULES
Le Juge d'Instruction, Play
  Juge d'Instruction, Le 1923 d: Marcel Dumont. lps: Pierre Blanchar, Violette Jyl, Pierre Magnier. 1800m FRN.

DE MARTINO, EMILIO
La Danza Delle Lancette, Novel
  Danza Delle Lancette, La 1936 d: Mario Baffico. lps: Barbara Monis, Ugo Ceseri, Marcello SpadA. 80M ITL. prod/rel: B.M. Societa Cin.Ca, C.I.F.

DE MAUPASSANT, GUY (1850–1893), FRN
Story
  Bird of Prey, The 1918 d: Edward J. Le Saint. lps: Gladys Brockwell, Herbert Heyes, L. C. Shumway. 5r USA. prod/rel: Fox Film Corp., William Fox©
Short Story
  Coward, A 1909 d: Edwin S. Porter. 784f USA. prod/rel: Edison

DE MAUPASSANT, GUY
  Jour de Noces 1971 d: Claude GorettA. lps: Arnold Walter, Dora Doll, Andre Schmidt. MTV. 71M SWT. *The Wedding Day* prod/rel: Westschweizer Fernsehen

DE MAUPASSANT, GUY (1850–1893), FRN
Novel
  Madame Und Ihre Nichte 1969 d: Eberhard Schroeder. lps: Edwige Fenech, Ruth Maria Kubitschek, Fred Williams. 87M GRM. *House of Pleasure* (UKN); *Madame and Her Niece* prod/rel: Rapid, Hape
Short Stories
  Underbara Lognen, Den 1955 d: Michael Road. lps: Michael Road, Stig Olin, Signe Hasso. 95M SWD/USA. *Gentle Thief of Love*; *The True and the False* prod/rel: Davies, Sandrew

L'Auberge, Short Story
  Auberge, L' 1922 d: E. B. Donatien, Edouard-Emile Violet. lps: E. B. Donatien, Edouard-Emile Violet, Mlle. de Wilhems. 1200m FRN. prod/rel: Films Rene Fernand
Bel-Ami, 1885, Novel
  Bel Ami 1939 d: Willi Forst. lps: Willi Forst, Olga Tschechowa, Ilse Werner. 100M GRM. *Der Liebling Schoner Frauen* prod/rel: Willi Forst-Film, Tranocean
  Bel Ami 1955 d: Louis Daquin. lps: Jean Danet, Renee Faure, Anne Vernon. 86M FRN/AUS. prod/rel: Andre Cultet, Films Malesherbes
  Bel Ami 1975 d: Mac Ahlberg. lps: Maria Lynn, Christa Linder, Harry Reems. 104M SWD. *For Men Only*; *L'Empire Des Caresses*; *Bel Ami Profession Play-Boy*; *Rhapsodie Des Sens* prod/rel: Film Invest
  Private Affairs of Bel Ami, The 1947 d: Albert Lewin. lps: George Sanders, Angela Lansbury, Ann Dvorak. 112M USA. prod/rel: United Artists
Les Bijoux, 1884, Short Story
  Romanze in Moll 1943 d: Helmut Kautner. lps: Marianne Hoppe, Paul Dahlke, Ferdinand Marian. 100M GRM. *Romance in a Minor Key* prod/rel: Tobis, Nordwest
Boule de Suif, 1880, Short Story
  Boule-de-Suif 1945 d: Christian-Jaque. lps: Berthe Bovy, Louise Conte, Mona Dol. 103M FRN. *Angel and Sinner* (USA); *Madame Fifi* prod/rel: Artes-Films
  Mademoiselle Fifi 1944 d: Robert Wise. lps: Simone Simon, John Emery, Kurt Kreuger. 69M USA. *The Silent Bell* prod/rel: RKO Radio
  Maria No Oyuki 1935 d: Kenji Mizoguchi. lps: Isuzu Yamada, Komako Hara, Daijiro NatsukawA. 78M JPN. *Oyuki the Madonna* (USA); *Oyuki the Virgin* (UKN); *The Virgin from Oyuki* prod/rel: Daiichi Film Co.
  Pyshka 1934 d: Mikhail Romm. lps: Galina Sergeyeva, Andrei Fayt, Faina RanevskaiA. 65M USS. *A Ball of Suet* (USA); *Boule de Suif*; *Puishka*; *Pushka*; *Psychka* prod/rel: Mosfilm
  Woman Disputed, The 1928 d: Henry King, Sam Taylor. lps: Norma Talmadge, Gilbert Roland, Lido Manetti. 8129f USA. prod/rel: United Artists
Ce Cochon de Morin, 1883, Short Story
  Ce Cochon de Morin 1932 d: Georges Lacombe. lps: Rosine Derean, Colette Darfeuil, Jacques Baumer. 87M FRN. prod/rel: Compagnie Continentale Cinematographique
  Terreur Des Dames, La 1956 d: Jean Boyer. lps: Noel-Noel, Yves Robert, Jean Poiret. 93M FRN. *Ce Cochon de Morin* prod/rel: Eminente, Compagnie Mediterraneenne
La Chevelure, 1885, Short Story
  Chevelure, La 1961 d: Ado Kyrou. 19M FRN.
  Golden Braid 1991 d: Paul Cox. lps: Chris Haywood, Gosia Dobrowolska, Paul Chubb. 91M ASL. prod/rel: Australian Film Commission©, Film Victoria©
Le Collier, Short Story
  Gioielli, I 1913. 345m ITL. *The Jewels* (UKN) prod/rel: Savoia Film
  Necklace, The 1909 d: D. W. Griffith. lps: Rose King, Charles Inslee, MacK Sennett. 969f USA. prod/rel: Biograph Co.
Deux Amis, 1883, Short Story
  Deux Amis, Les 1946 d: Dimitri Kirsanoff. lps: Henri Villemur, Richard Francoeur. 26M FRN. prod/rel: Films Azur
Falsche Perlen, Short Story
  Perlenkette, Die 1951 d: Karl G. Kulb. lps: Winnie Markus, Richard Haussler, Rolf von Nauckhoff. 105M GRM. *Begierde*; *The Chain of Pearls* prod/rel: Allegro, Sudwest
La Femme de Paul, 1881, Short Story
  Masculin-Feminin 1966 d: Jean-Luc Godard. lps: Chantal Goya, Jean-Pierre Leaud, Marlene Jobert. 110M FRN/SWD. *Maskulinum-Femininum* (SWD); *Masculine-Feminine*; *Masculin-Feminin 15 Faits Precis* prod/rel: Anouchka Films, Argos Films
Fini, Short Story
  Finished 1923 d: George A. Cooper. lps: Daisy Campbell, Eileen Magrath, Chris Walker. 1808f UKN. prod/rel: Quality Plays, Gaumont
La Fourmi, Short Story
  Umorismo Nero 1965 d: Giancarlo Zagni, Jose Maria Forque. lps: Sylvie, Pierre Brasseur, Jean Richard. 112M ITL/SPN/FRN. *La Muerte Viaja Demasiado* (SPN); *Humorismo Negro*; *Black Humor*
Histoire d'une Fille de Femme, 1881, Short Story
  Am Anfang War Es Sunde 1954 d: Frantisek Cap. lps: Ruth Niehaus, Viktor Staal, Hansi Knoteck. 96M GRM/YGS. *The Beginning Was Sin* (USA); *V Zacetku Je Bil Greh*; *Greh*; *At First It Was Sin* prod/rel: Saphir Film, Triglav Film

La Horla, 1886, Short Story
  Diary of a Madman 1963 d: Reginald Le Borg. lps: Vincent Price, Nancy Kovack, Chris Warfield. 97M USA. *The Horla* prod/rel: Admiral, United Artists
  Hantises 1997 d: Michel Ferry. lps: John Berry, Francois Negret, Marina Golovine. 80M FRN. *Hauntings* prod/rel: Sammler, Nef
Mademoiselle Fifi, 1881, Short Story
  Boule-de-Suif 1945 d: Christian-Jaque. lps: Berthe Bovy, Louise Conte, Mona Dol. 103M FRN. *Angel and Sinner* (USA); *Madame Fifi* prod/rel: Artes-Films
  Mademoiselle Fifi 1944 d: Robert Wise. lps: Simone Simon, John Emery, Kurt Kreuger. 69M USA. *The Silent Bell* prod/rel: RKO Radio
La Maison Tellier, 1881, Short Story
  Commerce Tranquile, Un 1964 d: Mel Welles, Guido Franco. lps: Frank Wolff, Georgia Moll, Mel Welles. 120M SWT/UKN. *A Quiet Business* prod/rel: Compas-Films, Centre Romand De Cinematographie
  Plaisir, Le 1951 d: Max Ophuls. lps: Gaby Bruyere, Gaby Morlay, Claude Dauphin. 95M FRN. *House of Pleasure* (USA) prod/rel: C.C.F.C.
Le Masque, 1890, Short Story
  Plaisir, Le 1951 d: Max Ophuls. lps: Gaby Bruyere, Gaby Morlay, Claude Dauphin. 95M FRN. *House of Pleasure* (USA) prod/rel: C.C.F.C.
La Modele, 1888, Short Story
  Plaisir, Le 1951 d: Max Ophuls. lps: Gaby Bruyere, Gaby Morlay, Claude Dauphin. 95M FRN. *House of Pleasure* (USA) prod/rel: C.C.F.C.
Musotte, 1891
  Musotte 1920 d: Mario Corsi. lps: Olimpia Barroero, Bruno Emanuel Palmi, Ludovico Bendiner. 1996m ITL. *Musette Fra le Spire Del Destino*; *Fra le Spire Del Destino* prod/rel: Tespi Film
Die Nichten Der Frau Oberst, Short Story
  Nichten Der Frau Oberst, Die 1968 d: Erwin C. Dietrich, Edoardo MulargiA. lps: Tamara Baroni, Heidrun Van Hoven, Kai Fischer. 94M GRM/ITL. *Guess Who's Coming for Breakfast* (UKN); *The Nieces of Frau Oberst*; *The Nieces of the Colonel's Wife*; *Le Nipoti Della Colonnella* (ITL) prod/rel: Urania Filmproduktion (Berlino), Cineproduzioni Associate (Roma)
  Nichten Der Frau Oberst, Die 1980 d: Erwin C. Dietrich. lps: Karine Gambier, Brigitte Lahaie, France Lomay. 90M SWT. prod/rel: Elite
L'Ordonnance, 1889, Short Story
  Ordonnance, L' 1921 d: Victor Tourjansky. lps: Nathalie Kovanko, Alexandre Colas, Paul Hubert. 1550m FRN. prod/rel: Ermolieff-Films
  Ordonnance, L' 1933 d: Victor Tourjansky. lps: Jean Worms, Marcelle Chantal, Paulette Dubost. 76M FRN. *The Orderly* (USA); *Helene* prod/rel: Capitole Film, Films R.P.
Une Partie de Campagne, 1881, Short Story
  Partie de Campagne, Une 1936 d: Jean Renoir. lps: Sylvia Bataille, Georges Saint-Saens, Jane Marken. 39M FRN. *A Day in the Country*; *Country Excursion* prod/rel: Pierre Braunberger
La Parure, Short Story
  Diamond Necklace, The 1921 d: Denison Clift. lps: Milton Rosmer, Jessie Winter, Sara Sample. 5900f UKN. prod/rel: Ideal
Le Pere Milon, Short Story
  Pere Milon, Le 1909 d: Firmin Gemier, Henry Houry. lps: Firmin Gemier. 195m FRN. prod/rel: Film d'Art
The Piece of String, Novel
  Piece of String, The 1911 d: Joseph Smiley, George Loane Tucker. lps: King Baggot, Lucille Younge, Robert Leonard. 1000f USA. prod/rel: Imp
Pierre Et Jean, 1888, Novel
  Mujer Sin Amor, Una 1951 d: Luis Bunuel. lps: Julio Villareal, Rosario Granados, Tito Junco. 91M MXC. *A Woman Without Love* (USA); *A Loveless Woman*; *Cuando Los Hijos Nos Juzgan*; *A Woman Without Pity*
  Pierre Et Jean 1924 d: E. B. Donatien. lps: E. B. Donatien, Georges Charlia, Lucienne Legrand. 1800m FRN. prod/rel: Films Donatien
  Pierre Et Jean 1943 d: Andre Cayatte. lps: Renee Saint-Cyr, Noel Roquevert, Jacques Dumesnil. 72M FRN. prod/rel: Continental Films
La Question du Latin, 1900, Short Story
  Petit Prof', Le 1958 d: Carlo-Rim. lps: Darry Cowl, Yves Robert, Beatrice AltaribA. 88M FRN. prod/rel: Films Marceau
Le Rosier de Madame Husson, 1888, Short Story
  Rosier de Madame Husson, Le 1931 d: Bernard-Deschamps. lps: Fernandel, Francoise Rosay, Mady Berry. 80M FRN. *The Virtuous Isadore* prod/rel: Les Films Ormuzd

Rosier de Madame Husson, Le 1950 d: Jean Boyer. lps: Bourvil, Jacqueline Pagnol, Suzanne Dehelly. 84M FRN. *The Prize* (USA); *The Virtuous Isadore* prod/rel: Agiman, Eminente

Le Signe, 1887, Short Story
Femme Coquette, Une 1955 d: Jean-Luc Godard. lps: Maria Lysandre, Roland Tolma, Jean-Luc Godard. 10M SWT.

Masculin-Feminin 1966 d: Jean-Luc Godard. lps: Chantal Goya, Jean-Pierre Leaud, Marlene Jobert. 110M FRN/SWD. *Maskulinum-Femininum* (SWD); *Masculine-Feminine; Masculin-Feminin 15 Faits Precis* prod/rel: Anouchka Films, Argos Films

The Son's Return, Short Story
Son's Return, The 1909 d: D. W. Griffith. lps: Mary Pickford, Charles West, Tony O'Sullivan. 993f USA. prod/rel: Biograph Co.

A String of Pearls, Short Story
At the Eleventh Hour 1912 d: William V. Ranous. lps: Zena Keefe, Lillian Walker, Herbert L. Barry. 1000f USA. prod/rel: Vitagraph Co. of America

Her Hour of Triumph 1912. lps: Martha Russell, Francis X. Bushman, Lily Branscombe. 1000f USA. prod/rel: Essanay

Tonio, Short Story
Marito E Moglie 1952 d: Eduardo de Filippo. lps: Eduardo de Filippo, Titina de Filippo, Tina PicA. 90M ITL. *Husband and Wife* prod/rel: Film Costellazione

Une Vie: l'Humble Verite, Paris 1883, Novel
Naiskohtaloita 1948 d: Toivo SaakkA. lps: Eeva-Kaarina Volanen. 95M FNL. *Destinies of Women; Une Vie*

Onna No Issho 1967 d: Yoshitaro NomurA. lps: Shima Iwashita, Sachiko Hidari. 138M JPN. *Un Vie; Life of a Woman; One Life*

Vie, Une 1958 d: Alexandre Astruc. lps: Maria Schell, Christian Marquand, Ivan Desny. 86M FRN/ITL. *End of Desire* (USA); *Una Vita; One Life* (UKN); *Una Vita (Il Dramma Di Una Sposa)* prod/rel: Agnes Delahaie Productions, Nepi Film

A Voice from the Fireplace, Short Story
Voice from the Fireplace, A 1910. 486f USA. prod/rel: Essanay

Yvette, 1885, Short Story
Yvette 1927 d: Alberto Cavalcanti. lps: Catherine Hessling, Ica de Lenkeffy, Pauline Carton. 80M FRN. prod/rel: Neo-Film

Yvette 1938 d: Wolfgang Liebeneiner. 98M GRM. *Die Tochter Einer Kurtisane*

Yvette 1990 d: Jean-Pierre Marchand. lps: France Dougnac, Marc Michel, Henri Serre. TVM. 100M FRN.

DE MELO NETO, JOAO CABRAL
Morte E Vida Severina, 1955, Verse
Morte E Vida Severina 1976 d: Zelito VianA. 85M BRZ. *Life and Death of Severina*

O Rio, 1954, Verse
Morte E Vida Severina 1976 d: Zelito VianA. 85M BRZ. *Life and Death of Severina*

DE MILLE, CECIL B. (1881–1959), USA
After Five, New York 1913, Play
After Five 1915 d: Oscar Apfel, Cecil B. de Mille. lps: Edward Abeles, Theodore Roberts, Sessue HayakawA. 5r USA. prod/rel: Jesse L. Lasky Feature Play Co.©, Paramount Pictures Corp.

Night Club, The 1925 d: Frank Urson, Paul Iribe. lps: Raymond Griffith, Wallace Beery, Louise FazendA. 5732f USA. prod/rel: Famous Players-Lasky, Paramount Pictures

Lord Chumley, New York 1888, Play
Forty Winks 1925 d: Frank Urson, Paul Iribe. lps: Viola Dana, Raymond Griffith, Theodore Roberts. 6293f USA. prod/rel: Famous Players-Lasky, Paramount Pictures

Lord Chumley 1914 d: James Kirkwood. lps: Henry B. Walthall, Walter Miller, Lillian Gish. 4r USA. prod/rel: Biograph Co., Klaw & Erlanger©

DE MILLE, HENRY C.
Men and Women, Play
Men and Women 1914 d: James Kirkwood. lps: Lionel Barrymore, Blanche Sweet, Gertrude Robinson. 3r USA. prod/rel: Biograph Co., Klaw & Erlanger

Men and Women 1925 d: William C. de Mille. lps: Richard Dix, Claire Adams, Neil Hamilton. 6223f USA. prod/rel: Famous Players-Lasky, Paramount Pictures

DE MILLE, WILLIAM C.
After Five, New York 1913, Play
After Five 1915 d: Oscar Apfel, Cecil B. de Mille. lps: Edward Abeles, Theodore Roberts, Sessue HayakawA. 5r USA. prod/rel: Jesse L. Lasky Feature Play Co.©, Paramount Pictures Corp.

Night Club, The 1925 d: Frank Urson, Paul Iribe. lps: Raymond Griffith, Wallace Beery, Louise FazendA. 5732f USA. prod/rel: Famous Players-Lasky, Paramount Pictures

Braveheart, Story
Braveheart 1925 d: Alan Hale. lps: Rod La Rocque, Lillian Rich, Robert Edeson. 7256f USA. prod/rel: Cinema Corp. of America

Classmates, New York 1907, Play
Classmates 1914 d: James Kirkwood. lps: Blanche Sweet, Henry B. Walthall, Lionel Barrymore. 4r USA. prod/rel: Klaw & Erlanger©, Biograph Co.

The Land of the Free, New York 1917, Play
One More American 1918 d: William C. de Mille. lps: George Beban, Jack Holt, Helen Jerome Eddy. 5r USA. *The Land of the Free* prod/rel: Jesse L. Lasky Feature Play Co.©, Famous Players-Lasky Corp.

Strongheart, Play
Strongheart 1914 d: James Kirkwood. lps: Henry B. Walthall, Lionel Barrymore, Alan Hale. 3r USA. prod/rel: Biograph Co., Klaw & Erlanger

The Warrens of Virginia, New York 1907, Play
Warrens of Virginia, The 1915 d: Cecil B. de Mille. lps: Blanche Sweet, James Neill, House Peters. 5r USA. prod/rel: Jesse L. Lasky Feature Play Co.©, Paramount Pictures Corp.

Warrens of Virginia, The 1924 d: Elmer Clifton. lps: George Backus, Rosemary Hill, Martha Mansfield. 6536f USA. prod/rel: Fox Film Corp.

The Wild Goose Chase, Play
Wild Goose Chase, The 1915 d: Cecil B. de Mille. lps: Ina Claire, Tom Forman, Theodore Roberts. 4-5r USA. prod/rel: Jesse L. Lasky Feature Play Co.©, Paramount Pictures Corp.

The Woman, New York 1911, Play
Secret Call, The 1931 d: Stuart Walker. lps: Richard Arlen, Peggy Shannon, Claire Dodd. 73M USA. prod/rel: Paramount Publix Corp.©

Telephone Girl, The 1927 d: Herbert Brenon. lps: Madge Bellamy, Holbrook Blinn, Warner Baxter. 5455f USA. prod/rel: Famous Players-Lasky

Woman, The 1915 d: George Melford. lps: Lois Meredith, Theodore Roberts, Mabel Van Buren. 5r USA. prod/rel: Jesse L. Lasky Feature Play Co.©, Paramount Pictures Corp.

Young Romance, Play
Young Romance 1915 d: George Melford. lps: Edith Taliaferro, Tom Forman, Frederick Wilson. 4r USA. prod/rel: Jesse L. Lasky Feature Play Co.©, Paramount Pictures Corp.

DE MIOMANDRE, FRANCIS
La Cabane d'Amour, Novel
Cabane d'Amour, La 1923 d: Jane Bruno-Ruby. lps: Malcolm Tod, Arlette Marchal, Paquerette. 2000m FRN. *Cabin of Love* prod/rel: Films Radia

DE MOLINA, TIRSO, de Molina, Thyrso
Don Gil Dalle Calze Verdi, Novel
Falco d'Oro, Il 1956 d: Carlo Ludovico BragagliA. lps: Anna Maria Ferrero, Nadia Gray, Massimo Serato. 90M ITL. prod/rel: P.O. Film

Don Gil von Den Grunen Hosen, Story
Dona Juana 1928 d: Paul Czinner. lps: Elisabeth Bergner, Walter Rilla, Max Schreck. 3081m GRM. prod/rel: Poetic-Film, UFA

DE MONTEPIN, XAVIER
Le Fiacre N. 13, 1881, Novel
Fiacre 13 1947 d: Raoul Andre, Andre Hugon. lps: Ginette Leclerc, Therese Dulac, Marcel Herrand. 180M FRN. prod/rel: Andre Hugon, Minerva

Fiacre N. 13, Il 1917 d: Alberto A. Capozzi, Gero Zambuto. lps: Alberto A. Capozzi, Helena Makowska, Gigetta Morano. 4070m ITL. prod/rel: S.A. Ambrosio

Fiacre N. 13, Il 1947 d: Mario Mattoli. lps: Marcel Herrand, Ginette Leclerc, Henri Nassiet. F ITL/FRN. prod/rel: Excelsa Film (Roma), Cinematographie de France

La Joueuse d'Orgue, Novel
Joueuse d'Orgue, La 1913 d: Georges DenolA. lps: Jacques Volnys, Jean Ayme, Rose Dione. 1211m FRN.

Joueuse d'Orgue, La 1924 d: Charles Burguet. lps: Eugenie Buffet, Regine Dumien, Edmond Van Daele. 4000m FRN.

Joueuse d'Orgue, La 1936 d: Gaston Roudes. lps: Pierre Larquey, Jacques Varennes, Marcelle Geniat. 85M FRN. prod/rel: Trius Films

Le Medecin Des Folles, 1891, Novel
Medico Delle Pazze, Il 1919 d: Mario Roncoroni. lps: Alfredo Boccolini, Romilde Toschi, Angelo Vianello. 4542m ITL. prod/rel: Ambrosio Film

La Mendiante de Saint-Sulpice, Novel
Mendiante de Saint-Suplice, La 1923 d: Charles Burguet. lps: Maxime Desjardins, Gaby Morlay, Charles Vanel. 4000m FRN. prod/rel: Films Charles Burguet

L' Or Maudit
Oro Maledetto, L' 1911. 480m ITL. *L' Argento Maledetto* prod/rel: Aquila Films

Paoline, 1850
Paolina 1915 d: Vitale de Stefano. lps: Jeanne Nolly, Vitale de Stefano, Lydia QuarantA. 1123m ITL. prod/rel: Savoia Film

La Porteuse de Pain, 1884, Novel
Portatrice Di Pane, La 1911 d: Romolo Bacchini. lps: Gennaro Righelli, Maria Righelli, Ruffo Geri. 1200m ITL. prod/rel: Vesuvio Films

Portatrice Di Pane, La 1916 d: Enrico Vidali. lps: Maria Gandini, Enrico Vidali, Sig. Rodani. 2102m ITL. prod/rel: Vidali

Porteuse de Pain, La 1912 d: Georges DenolA. lps: Henri Etievant, Milo, Jeanne Grumbach. 970m FRN. prod/rel: Scagl

Porteuse de Pain, La 1923 d: Rene Le Somptier. lps: Suzanne Despres, Henri Baudin, Genevieve Felix. SRL 4EP FRN. prod/rel: Film d'Art (Vandal Et Delac)

Porteuse de Pain, La 1934 d: Rene Sti. lps: Jacques Gretillat, Francois Rozet, Germaine Dermoz. 100M FRN. prod/rel: Films Albatros

Porteuse de Pain, La 1949 d: Maurice Cloche. lps: Philippe Lemaire, Vivi Gioi, Nicole Francis. 97M FRN/ITL. *La Portatrice Di Pane* (ITL) prod/rel: Minerva Films, O.I.F.

Porteuse de Pain, La 1963 d: Maurice Cloche. lps: Suzanne Flon, Philippe Noiret, Jeanne Valerie. 120M FRN/ITL. *La Portatrice Di Pane* (ITL); *The Bread Peddler* (USA) prod/rel: C.F.F.P., Euro International Film

Trois Millions de Dot
Tre Milioni Di Dote 1920 d: Camillo de Riso. lps: Elena Lunda, Alfredo Bertone, Raoul Maillard. 3387m ITL. prod/rel: U.C.I., Caesar

DE MONTHERLANT, HENRY (1896–1972), FRN
Malatesta, Play
Malatesta 1964 d: Christopher Morahan. lps: Patrick Wymark, Jessica Dunning, Cyril Shaps. MTV. 90M UKN. prod/rel: BBC

DE MORAES, VINICIUS
Balada Das Duas Mocinhas de Botafogo, 1959, Verse
Marilia E Marina 1976 d: Luis Fernando Goulart. 90M BRZ.

Orfeu Dea Conceicao, 1956, Play
Orfeu Negro 1958 d: Marcel Camus. lps: Bruno Mello, Marpessa Dawn, Lourdes de OliveirA. 106M FRN/ITL. *Orfeo Negro* (ITL); *Black Orpheus* (USA) prod/rel: Dispat Films, Gemma Cinematografica

DE MORGAN, WILLIAM (1839–1917), UKN
Somehow Good, Novel
Somehow Good 1927 d: Jack Raymond. lps: Fay Compton, Stewart Rome, Dorothy Boyd. 7900f UKN. prod/rel: Film Manufacturing Co., Pathe

DE MUSSET, ALFRED (1810–1857), FRN
Barberine, Play
Barberine 1910 d: Emile Chautard. lps: Bruniere, Joe Saint-Bonnet, Germaine Dermoz. 340m FRN. *La Quenouille de Barberine* prod/rel: Acad

Un Caprice, Play
Caprice, Un 1946 d: Lucien Gasnier-Raymond. lps: Jean-Francois Laley, Max Francois, Jacques Morange. 26M FRN. prod/rel: C.G.C.

Les Caprices de Marianne, 1834, Play
Regle du Jeu, La 1939 d: Jean Renoir. lps: Marcel Dalio, Nora Gregor, Mila Parely. 113M FRN. *Les Caprices de Marianne; La Chasse En Sologne; The Rules of the Game* (UKN); *Fair Play* prod/rel: Nouvelle Edition Francaise

Le Chandelier, Play
Chandelier, Le 1912. lps: Nelly Cormon. FRN.

Mesaventure du Capitaine Clavaroche, La 1910. 260m FRN. prod/rel: Pathe Freres

La Confession d'un Enfant du Siecle, 1836, Novel
Confessioni Di un Figlio Del Secolo, Le 1921 d: Gian Bistolfi. lps: Lia Formia, Riccardo Bertacchini, Mario Cusmich. 1862m ITL. prod/rel: D'ambra Film

Spowiedz Dzieciecia Wieku 1985 d: Marek Nowicki. lps: Marek Cichucki, Hanna Mikuc. 100M PLN. *A Confession of a Child of the Century*

Gamiani, Novel
   Pourvu Qu'on Ait l'Ivresse 1974 d: Rinaldo Bassi. lps: Alain Noury, Denyse Roland, Paul Guers. 95M FRN/ITL. *I Piaceri Della Contessa Gamiani* (ITL); *Gamiani*; *Qu'importe le Flacon Pourvu Qu'on Ait l'Ivresse* prod/rel: Erka Cin.Ca
Il Faut Qu'une Porte Soit Ouverte Ou Fermee, 1848, Play
   Il Faut Qu'une Porte Soit Ouverte Ou Ferme 1949 d: Louis Cuny. 19M FRN.
Lorenzaccio, 1834, Novel
   Lorenzaccio 1911. lps: Amelia Cattaneo. 260m ITL/FRN. *Lorenzo Il Magnifico*; *Lorenzo* (UKN) prod/rel: Pathe Freres, Film d'Arte Italiana
   Lorenzaccio 1918 d: Giuseppe de Liguoro. lps: Irene-Saffo Momo, Camillo de Rossi, Camillo Talamo. 2402m ITL. prod/rel: Lux-Artis
   Lorenzaccio 1989 d: Jean-Paul Carrere. lps: Francis Huster, Genevieve Casile, Louis Seigner. TVM. 185M FRN.
   Lorenzaccio 1989 d: Alexandre TartA. lps: Redjep Mirovitsa, Richard Fontana, Jean-Luc Boutte. TVM. 70M FRN.
   Lorenzaccio 1991 d: Georges Lavaudant. lps: Redjep Mitrovitsa, Richard Fontana, Jean-Luc Boutte. TVM. 115M FRN.
Mademoiselle Mimi Pinson, 1853, Short Story
   Mimi Pinson 1957 d: Robert Darene. lps: Dany Robin, Raymond Pellegrin, Andre Luguet. 95M FRN. prod/rel: Films Hergi
Margot, 1838, Short Story
   Margot 1914 d: Ubaldo Maria Del Colle. lps: Lydia Quaranta, Ubaldo Maria Del Colle, Vittorina MonetA. 900m ITL. prod/rel: Savoia Film
La Mouche, 1854, Short Story
   Schonheitsfleckchen, Das 1936 d: Rolf Hansen. lps: Lil Dagover, Susi Lanner, Wolfgang Lebeneiner. 30M GRM.
On Ne Badine Pas Avec l'Amour, 1834, Play
   On Ne Badine Pas Avec l'Amour 1909. lps: Rene Alexandre, Berthe Bovy, Nelly Cormon. 190m FRN. prod/rel: Scagl
   On Ne Badine Pas Avec l'Amour 1961 d: Jean Dessailly. 87M FRN.
La Quenouille de Barbarine, 1835
   Arcolaio Di Barberina, L' 1919 d: Lucio d'AmbrA. lps: Rosetta d'Aprile, Romano Calo, Romano Zampieri. 1553m ITL. prod/rel: D'ambra Film

DE MYLIO, M.
Redempta, Short Story
   Redempta 1917 d: Servaes. lps: Raphael Duflos, Raymonde Lyon, Madeleine Lely. 1150m FRN. prod/rel: Films Servaes

DE NAJAC, EMILE
Cyprienne Or Divorcons, Paris 1883, Play
   Divorcons 1915 d: Dell Henderson. lps: Dell Henderson, Gertrude Bambrick, Dave Morris. 4r USA. prod/rel: Biograph Co.©, General Film Co.
   Don't Tell the Wife 1927 d: Paul L. Stein. lps: Irene Rich, Huntley Gordon, Lilyan Tashman. 6972f USA. prod/rel: Warner Brothers Pictures
   Kiss Me Again 1925 d: Ernst Lubitsch. lps: Marie Prevost, Monte Blue, John Roche. 6722f USA. prod/rel: Warner Brothers Pictures
   Let's Get a Divorce 1918 d: Charles Giblyn. lps: Billie Burke, John Miltern, Pinna Nesbit. 5r USA. prod/rel: Famous Players-Lasky Corp.©
   That Uncertain Feeling 1941 d: Ernst Lubitsch. lps: Merle Oberon, Melvyn Douglas, Burgess Meredith. 84M USA. prod/rel: United Artists

DE NAVARRE, MARGUERITE
L' Heptameron, Novel
   Ah! Si Mon Moine Voulait. 1973 d: Claude Pierson. lps: Marcel Sabourin, Gilles Latulippe, Jean-Marie Proslier. 93M FRN/CND. *Vertudieu!* prod/rel: Citel Inc. (Montreal), Cinepix Inc. (Montreal)

DE NERVAL, GERARD (1808–1855), FRN, Labrunie, Gerard
La Main de Gloire, 1832, Short Story
   Main du Diable, La 1942 d: Maurice Tourneur. lps: Pierre Fresnay, Pierre Palau, Josseline Gael. 82M FRN. *The Devil's Hand* (USA); *La Main Enchantee*; *Carnival of Sinners* prod/rel: Continental-Films

DE OLIVEIRA, JOSE CARLOS
Terror E Extase, 1978, Novel
   Terror E Extase 1980 d: Antonio Calmon. 95M BRZ.

DE PERRODIL, ED
Le Roman de Carpentier
   Roman de Carpentier, Le 1913. lps: Georges Charpentier, Deschamps, Berthe Bovy. 1080m FRN. prod/rel: Les Grands Films Populaires

DE PILLECYN, FILIP
Monsieur Hawarden, 1935, Short Story
   Monsieur Hawarden 1968 d: Harry Kumel. lps: Ellen Vogel, Joan Remmelts, Senne Rouffaer. 109M NTH/BLG. *Mister Hawarden*

DE POLNAY, PETER
Novel
   Julie Pot-de-Colle 1977 d: Philippe de BrocA. lps: Marlene Jobert, Jean-Claude Brialy, Alexandra Stewart. 90M FRN. *Julie Pot de Colle* prod/rel: Film de L'alma, S.F.P.

DE QUEIROS, DINAH SILVEIRA
Floradas Na Serra, 1939, Novel
   Floradas Na Serra 1954 d: Luciano Salce. lps: Cacilda Becker, Lola Brah. 98M BRZ. *Mountain Flowers*

DE QUEIROZ, ECA (1845–1900), PRT, De Queiroz, Jose Maria de Eca
Alves & Cia, Novel
   Amor & Cia 1999 d: Helvecio Ratton. lps: Marco Nanini, Patricia Pillar, Alexandre Borges. 100M BRZ. *Love Inc.* prod/rel: Quimera Filmes

DE QUEVEDO Y VILLEGAS, FRANCISCO GOMEZ (1580–1645), SPN, De Quevedo, Francisco Gomez
La Historia de la Vida Del Buscon, 1626, Novel
   Buscon, El 1974 d: Luciano BerriatuA. lps: Francisco Rabal, Ana Belen, Francisco AlgorA. 99M SPN.

DE QUINCEY, THOMAS (1785–1859), UKN
Confessions of an English Opium Eater, 1821, Short Story
   Confessions of an Opium Eater 1962 d: Albert Zugsmith. lps: Vincent Price, Linda Ho, Philip Ahn. 85M USA. *Evils of Chinatown* (UKN); *Secrets of a Soul*; *Souls for Sale*

DE REGNIER, HENRI (1864–1936), FRN
Short Story
   Bijin Aishu 1931 d: Yasujiro Ozu. lps: Tokihiko Okada, Tatsuo Saito, Yukiko Inoue. 158M JPN. *The Beauty's Sorrows* prod/rel: Shochiku Co.

DE REPIDE, PEDRO
El Madrid de Los Abuelos, Novel
   En Las Entranas de Madrid 1923 d: Rafael Salvador. lps: Herminia Mans, Jose Martin Caro, Jose Perez. SPN. *Las Entranas de Madrid* prod/rel: Rafael Salvador Film (Madrid)

DE REYS, GILLES
Story
   Terzo Occhio, Il 1966 d: Mino Guerrini. lps: Franco Nero, Gioia Pascal, Diana Sullivan. 87M ITL. *The Killer With the Third Eye*; *The Third Eye* prod/rel: Panda Cin.Ca, Medusa

DE RICHTER, CHARLES
Mon Phoque Et Elles, Novel
   Mon Phoque Et Elles 1951 d: Pierre Billon. lps: Francois Perier, Moira Lister, Marie Daems. 95M FRN/SWD. *Min Van Oscar* (SWD); *Akes Lilla Felsteg*; *Mon Phoque*; *The Seal* prod/rel: Terra Film

DE RIVOYRE, CHRISTINE
Le Petit Matin, Novel
   Petit Matin, Le 1971 d: Jean-Gabriel Albicocco. lps: Catherine Jourdan, Mathieu Carriere, Madeleine Robinson. 120M FRN. *The Virgin and the Soldier* prod/rel: Awa Films Production, Pathe Sirius
Les Sultans, Novel
   Sultans, Les 1966 d: Jean Delannoy. lps: Louis Jourdan, Gina Lollobrigida, Daniel Gelin. 96M FRN/ITL. *L' Amante Italiana* (ITL) prod/rel: Cineurop Productions, Mancori Films

DE ROCHEFORT, PAUL
Justice de Singe, Novel
   Sotterraneo Fatale, Il 1920 d: Domenico M. Gambino. lps: Domenico Gambino, Bianca Maria Hubner, Giovanni Paximadi. 1260m ITL. *Giustizia Di Scimmia* prod/rel: Delta Film

DE ROJAS, FERNANDO (1475–1541), SPN
La Celestina, 1500, Play
   Celestina 1977 d: Miguel Sabido. 88M MXC.
   Celestina, La 1968 d: Cesar Ardavin. lps: Julian Mateos, Elisa Ramirez, Amelia de La Torre. 127M SPN/GRM. *The Wanton of Spain -la Celestina*; *The Wanton of Spain* (UKN)
   Celestina, La 1996 d: Gerardo VerA. lps: Penelope Cruz, Juan Diego Botto, Maribel Verdu. 96M SPN. *Celestina* prod/rel: Sogetel, Lola Films
   Celestina P. R., La 1965 d: Carlo Lizzani. lps: Assia Noris, Venantino Venantini, Beba Loncar. 105M ITL. prod/rel: Aston Film

DE ROSSELLI, REX
The Jungle Master, Story
   Jungle Master, The 1914 d: Henry McRae. lps: Marie Walcamp, Rex de Rosselli, William Clifford. 2r USA. prod/rel: Bison

DE ROTSCHILD, HENRI
La Rampe, 1909, Play
   Ribalta, La 1912 d: Mario Caserini. lps: Febo Mari, Maria Caserini Gasparini, Oreste Grandi. 754m ITL. *The Stage* (UKN) prod/rel: S.A. Ambrosio

DE SAINT-COLOMBE, PAUL
Secret Lives, Novel
   Secret Lives 1937 d: Edmond T. Greville. lps: Brigitte Horney, Neil Hamilton, Gyles Isham. 80M UKN. *I Married a Spy* (USA) prod/rel: Independent Films, Phoenix

DE SAINT-EXUPERY, ANTOINE (1900–1944), FRN
Courrier Sud, 1929, Novel
   Courrier-Sud 1936 d: Pierre Billon. lps: Pierre Richard-Willm, Charles Vanel, Jany Holt. 95M FRN. prod/rel: Pan-Cine
Le Petit Prince, 1943, Novel
   Little Prince, The 1973 d: Stanley Donen. lps: Richard Kiley, Steven Warner, Bob Fosse. 89M USA/UKN. prod/rel: Paramount
   Malenki Prints 1966 d: Arunas Zhebriunas. lps: Evaldas Mikaliunas, Donatas Banionis, Otar Koberidze. 68M USS. *The Little Prince*; *Mazazis Princas*; *Malenkij Princ*; *Malenky Prince*
Vol de Nuit, Paris 1931, Novel
   Night Flight 1933 d: Clarence Brown. lps: John Barrymore, Lionel Barrymore, Clark Gable. 91M USA. *Dark to Dawn* prod/rel: Metro-Goldwyn-Mayer Corp.©

DE SAINT-PIERRE, BERNARDIN
Paul Et Virginie, Novel
   Paul Et Virginie 1926 d: Robert Peguy. lps: Jean Bradin, Simone Jacquemin, Jeanne Berangere. F FRN. prod/rel: Compagnie Mauricienne

DE SAINT-PIERRE, MICHEL
Les Aristocrates, Novel
   Aristocrates, Les 1955 d: Denys de La Patelliere. lps: Pierre Fresnay, Brigitte Auber, Jacques Dacqmine. 100M FRN. *The Aristocrats* (UKN) prod/rel: Ste Francaise De Cinematographie, S.N.E.G.
Les Nouveaux Aristocrates, Novel
   Nouveaux Aristocrates, Les 1961 d: Francis Rigaud. lps: Paul Meurisse, Maria Mauban, Charles Belmont. 95M FRN. prod/rel: Chronos Films

DE SANCTIS, CARLO
Il Ponte Della Concordia, Novel
   Nessuno Ha Tradito 1954 d: Roberto Bianchi Montero. lps: Virginia Belmont, Aldo Silvani, Sandro Ruffini. 93M ITL. *Il Ponte Della Concordia* prod/rel: Daunia Film, C.I.F.E.S.

DE SEGONZAC, EDOUARD
Catherine Et Cie, Novel
   Catherine Et Cie 1975 d: Michel Boisrond. lps: Jane Birkin, Patrick Dewaere, Jean-Pierre Aumont. 99M FRN/ITL. *Catherine & Co.* prod/rel: Produzione Intercontinentale Cin.Ca

DE SEGUR, LA COMTESSE
Un Bon Petit Diable, Novel
   Bon Petit Diable, Un 1924 d: Rene Leprince. lps: Jean Rauzena, Jeanne Berangere, Madeleine Erickson. 1350m FRN. prod/rel: Pathe-Consortium-Cinema
Les Malheurs de Sophie, Novel
   Malheurs de Sophie, Les 1945 d: Jacqueline Audry. lps: Madeleine Bousset, Michel Auclair, Andre Alerme. 95M FRN. prod/rel: O.T.C., Pathe-Cinema
   Malheurs de Sophie, Les 1979 d: Jean-Claude Brialy. lps: Paprika Bommenel, Frederic Mestre, Carine Richard. 112M FRN. prod/rel: Franco-American Films, Antenna 2
Les Petites Filles Modeles, Novel
   Petites Filles Modeles, Les 1972 d: Jean-Claude Roy. lps: Michele Girardon, Bella Darvi, Beatrice Arnac. 90M FRN. prod/rel: Tanagra, Planfilm

DE STEFANI, ALESSANDRO
Play
   Al Buio Insieme 1933 d: Gennaro Righelli. lps: Sandra Ravel, Olga Vittoria Gentilli, Maurizio d'AncorA. 67M ITL. *Amiamoci Cosi* prod/rel: Cines, Anonima Pittaluga
I Capricci Di Susanna, Play
   Follie Del Secolo 1939 d: Amleto Palermi. lps: Armando Falconi, Paola Barbara, Sergio Tofano. 90M ITL. prod/rel: Scalera Film
Casanova a Parma, Play
   Arma Bianca 1936 d: Ferdinand M. Poggioli. lps: Leda Gloria, Mimi Aylmer, Nerio Bernardi. 69M ITL. prod/rel: Negroni Film, E.N.I.C.
La Dinamo Dell'Eroismo, Radio Play
   O la Borsa O la Vita 1933 d: Carlo Ludovico BragagliA. lps: Sergio Tofano, Rosetta Tofano, Luigi Almirante. 68M ITL. *La Dinamo Dell'eroismo* prod/rel: Cines, Anonima Pittaluga

Equatore, Play
Equatore 1939 d: Gino Valori. lps: Milena Penovich, Cesare Fantoni, Tino Erler. 75M ITL. prod/rel: Roma Film, Generalcine

Il Triangolo Magico, Play
Brivido 1941 d: Giacomo Gentilomo. lps: Umberto Melnati, Maria Mercader, Clara Calamai. 82M ITL. *Il Triangolo Magico* prod/rel: Incine, E.N.I.C.

Gli Uomini Non Sono Igrati, Play
Uomini Non Sono Ingrati, Gli 1937 d: Guido Brignone. lps: Isa Pola, Gino Cervi, Amelia Chellini. 74M ITL. prod/rel: Imperator Film

DE SYLVA, BUDDY (1895–1950), USA, de Sylva, B. G.
Du Barry Was a Lady, New York 1939, Musical Play
Du Barry Was a Lady 1943 d: Roy Del Ruth. lps: Red Skelton, Lucille Ball, Gene Kelly. 101M USA. prod/rel: MGM

Flying High, New York 1930, Musical Play
Flying High 1931 d: Charles F. Reisner. lps: Bert Lahr, Charlotte Greenwood, Pat O'Brien. 80M USA. *Happy Landing* (UKN) prod/rel: Metro-Goldwyn-Mayer Corp., Metro-Goldwyn-Mayer Dist. Corp.©

Follow Thru, New York 1929, Musical Play
Follow Thru 1930 d: Laurence Schwab, Lloyd Corrigan. lps: Charles "Buddy" Rogers, Nancy Carroll, Zelma O'Neal. 8386f USA. prod/rel: Paramount-Publix Corp.

Hold Everything, New York 1928, Musical Play
Hold Everything 1930 d: Roy Del Ruth. lps: Joe E. Brown, Winnie Lightner, Georges Carpentier. 7513f USA. prod/rel: Warner Brothers Pictures

Manhattan Mary, New York 1927, Musical Play
Follow the Leader 1930 d: Norman Taurog. lps: Ed Wynn, Ginger Rogers, Stanley Smith. 6851f USA. *Manhattan Mary* prod/rel: Paramount-Publix Corp.

Panama Hattie, New York 1940, Musical Play
Panama Hattie 1942 d: Norman Z. McLeod, Vincente Minnelli (Uncredited). lps: Ann Sothern, Red Skelton, Rags Ragland. 79M USA. prod/rel: MGM

Take a Chance, New York 1932, Musical Play
Take a Chance 1933 d: Monte Brice, Laurence Schwab. lps: James Dunn, Cliff Edwards, June Knight. 84M USA. prod/rel: Paramount Productions©

DE TERAMOND, GUY
Le Crime de Monique, Novel
Crime de Monique, Le 1924 d: Robert Peguy. lps: Simone Sandre, Yvette Andreyor, Lucien Dalsace. 1625m FRN. prod/rel: Films Y. Barbaza

DE TIERE, NESTOR
Of Het Treurspel de Smeden Roze Kate, 1893, Play
Roze Kate 1912 d: Oscar Tourniaire. lps: Caroline Van Dommelen, Louis Van Dommelen, Jan Van Dommelen. 800m NTH. *Het Treurspel Der Smeden*; *Red-Haired Kate*; *The Tragedy of the Blacksmiths*; *A Race for Life* (UKN) prod/rel: Film-Fabriek F. A. Noggerath

DE TOLEDO, MARC
Rue de la Paix, Play
Rue de la Paix 1926 d: Henri Diamant-Berger. lps: Henri Mathot, Andree Lafayette, Suzy Pierson. 2000m FRN. *Sins of Fashion*

DE TROYES, CHRETIEN
Conte du Graal, 1181, Verse
Perceval le Gallois 1978 d: Eric Rohmer. lps: Fabrice Luchini, Marc Eyraud, Arielle Dombasle. 140M FRN/GRM/SWT. *Perceval* (USA); *Perceval 1978* prod/rel: Les Films Du Losange, Barbet Schroeder

DE TURIQUE, BERR
Le Double Piege, Play
Double Piege, Le 1923 d: Gaston Roudes. lps: Pierre Stephen. 1400m FRN.

DE UNAMUNO, MIGUEL (1864–1936), SPN, De Unamuno Y Jugo, Miguel
Abel Sanchez: Una Historia de Pasion, 1917, Novel
Abel Sanchez 1946 d: Carlos Serrano de OsmA. lps: Alicia Romay, Mercedes Marino, Rosita Valero. 67M SPN.

Nada Menos Que Todo un Hombre, 1916, Short Story
Entrega, La 1954 d: Julian Soler. lps: Marga Lopez, Arturo de Cordova, Enrique Rambal. 106M MXC. *The Delivery*

Nada Menos Que Todo un Hombre 1971 d: Rafael Gil. lps: Francisco Rabal, Analia Gade, Angel Del Pozo. 132M SPN/USA. *Nothing Less Than a Man*; *No Less Than a Real Man*

Todo un Hombre 1943 d: Pierre Chenal. lps: Guillermo Battaglia, Amelia Bence, Florindo Ferrario. 94M ARG. *A Whole Man*

Todo un Hombre 1983 d: Rafael Villasenor. lps: Amparo Munoz, Vicente Fernandez, Felipe ArriagA. 102M MXC/SPN.

Niebla, 1914, Novel
Niebla 1975 d: Jose JarA. lps: Charo Lopez, Fernando Fernan Gomez, Maximo Valverde. 98M SPN. *Las Cuatro Novias de Augusto Perez*

La Tia Tula, Madrid 1921, Novel
Tia Tula, La 1964 d: Miguel Picazo. lps: Aurora Bautista, Carlos Estrada, Mari Loli Cobos. 118M SPN. *Aunt Tula* prod/rel: Eco Films

DE VAL, LUIS
Los Martires Del Arroyo, Novel
Martires Del Arroyo, Los 1924 d: Enrique Santos. lps: Juanita Diaz, Ramon Orrico Vidal, Angel CarratalA. 2000m SPN. prod/rel: Novella Films (Valencia)

DE VALLY
Le Mari a la Campagne, 1844, Play
Marito in Campagna, Il 1912. lps: Mercedes Brignone, Umberto Mozzato, Cesare Quest. 350m ITL. prod/rel: Milano Films

Marito in Campagna, Il 1920 d: Mario Almirante. lps: Mercedes Brignone, Domenico Serra, Lola Visconti-Brignone. 1151m ITL. prod/rel: Rodolfi Film

DE VARGAS, LUIS
Los Lagarteranos, Opera
Lagarteranos, Los 1928 d: Armando Pou. lps: Josefina Ochoa, Isabel Alemany, Jose Maria Jimeno. SPN.

DE VEGA, LOPE
Fuenteovejuna, 1619, Play
Fuenteovejuna 1947 d: Antonio Roman. lps: Manuel Luna, Amparo Rivelles, Carlos Munoz. 107M SPN.

Alcalde, El Rey, El Mejor, 1620-23, Play
Mejor Alcalde, El Rey, El 1973 d: Rafael Gil. lps: Ray Lovelock, Simonetta Stefanelli, Fernando Sancho. 103M SPN/ITL. *The King, the Best Mayor*; *The Best Mayor Is the King*; *Il Re, Il Miglior Sindico*

La Moza Del Cantaro, 1646, Play
Moza Del Cantaro, La 1953 d: Florian Rey. lps: Paquita Rico, Peter Damon, Rafael Arcos. 88M SPN. *La Mordaza Del Cantaro*; *The Girl With the Pitcher*

DE VIGNY, ALFRED (1797–1863), FRN, De Vigny, Comte Alfred Victor
Le Cor, Poem
Cor, Le 1931 d: Jean Epstein. 205m FRN. prod/rel: Charles-Felix Tavano, Andre H. Des Fontaines

Servitude Et Grandeur Militaires, Short Story
Laurette Ou le Cachet Rouge 1931 d: Jacques de Casembroot. lps: Kissa Kouprine, Jim Gerald, Andre Allehaut. 67M FRN. prod/rel: Nicaea Films Production

DE VILLENEUVE, MADAME
Beauty and the Beast, Story
Beauty and the Beast 1987 d: Eugene Marner. lps: Rebecca de Mornay, John Savage, Yossi Graber. TVM. 90M USA/ISR. prod/rel: Cannon

DE VILLIERS, GERALD
S.a.S. a San Salvador, Novel
S.a.S. a San Salvador 1982 d: Raoul Coutard. lps: Miles O'Keeffe, Raimund Harmstorf, Anton Diffring. 95M FRN/GRM. *S. A. S. Malko - Im Auftrag Des Pentagon*; *Sas a San Salvador*; *Terminate With Extreme Prejudice*; *On Pentagon Business* prod/rel: Elephant, Ugc Top 1

DE VILMORIN, LOUISE (1902–, FRN
Julietta, Novel
Julietta 1953 d: Marc Allegret. lps: Jean Marais, Jeanne Moreau, Dany Robin. 99M FRN. prod/rel: Indus Films, Braunberger, Pierre

Le Lit a Colonnes, Novel
Lit a Colonnes, Le 1942 d: Roland Tual. lps: Fernand Ledoux, Jean Marais, Odette Joyeux. 103M FRN. prod/rel: Synops

Madame de., Novel
Madame de. 1953 d: Max Ophuls. lps: Danielle Darrieux, Vittorio de Sica, Charles Boyer. 100M FRN/ITL. *I Gioielli Di Madame de.* (ITL); *The Diamond Earrings*; *The Earrings of Madame de.* (USA) prod/rel: Franco-London Films, Indus Films

DE VOGUE, MELCHIOR
Jean d'Agreve, Novel
Jean d'Agreve 1922 d: Rene Leprince. lps: Leon Mathot, Nathalie Kovanko, Camille Bert. 1880m FRN. prod/rel: Pathe-Consortium-Cinema

DE VOLTAIRE, FRANCOIS-MARIE AROUET
Ou le Monde Comme Il Va Babouc, 1750, Short Story
Or Et le Plomb, L' 1966 d: Alain Cuniot. lps: Alain Cuniot, Emmanuelle Riva, Max Paul Fouchet. 78M FRN. *Gold and Lead*; *Paris Comme Il Va* prod/rel: S.I.P.A.C., Films J. Willemetz

Candide, 1759, Short Story
Candide, Ou l'Optimisme Au XXeme Siecle 1960 d: Norbert Carbonnaux. lps: Jean-Pierre Cassel, Daliah Lavi, Pierre Brasseur. 88M FRN. *Candide* prod/rel: C.L.M.

Ingenuo, L' 1921 d: Giorgio Ricci. lps: Goffredo d'Andrea, Silvia Malinverni, Ignazio Mascalchi. 2405m ITL. prod/rel: Bernini Film

Mondo Candido 1975 d: Gualtiero Jacopetti, Franco Prosperi. lps: Christopher Brown, Michelle Miller, Jose Quaglio. 110M ITL. prod/rel: Perugia Cin.Ca, Euro International Film

L' Ingenu, 1767, Short Story
Ingenu, L' 1971 d: Norbert Carbonnaux. lps: Renaud Verley, Corinne Marchand, Jean Lefevre. 85M FRN.

DE VONDE, CHESTER
Kongo, New York 1926, Play
Kongo 1932 d: William J. Cowen. lps: Walter Huston, Lupe Velez, Conrad Nagel. 86M USA. prod/rel: Metro-Goldwyn-Mayer Corp., Metro-Goldwyn-Mayer Dist. Corp.©

DE VOTO, BERNARD (1897–1955), USA, de Voto, Bernard Augustine
Across the Wide Missouri, 1947, Novel
Across the Wide Missouri 1951 d: William A. Wellman. lps: Clark Gable, Ricardo Montalban, John Hodiak. 78M USA. prod/rel: MGM

DE VRIES, PETER (1910–1993), USA
The Cat's Pajamas, 1968, Novel
Pete 'N' Tillie 1972 d: Martin Ritt. lps: Walter Matthau, Carol Burnett, Geraldine Page. 100M USA. prod/rel: Universal

Let Me Count the Ways, Boston 1965, Novel
How Do I Love Thee? 1970 d: Michael Gordon. lps: Jackie Gleason, Maureen O'Hara, Shelley Winters. 109M USA. prod/rel: Freeman-Enders Productions

Reuben Reuben, 1964, Novel
Reuben, Reuben 1983 d: Robert Ellis Miller. lps: Tom Conti, Kelly McGillis, Roberts Blossom. 101M USA. prod/rel: 20th Century Fox

Tunnel of Love, 1954, Novel
Tunnel of Love, The 1958 d: Gene Kelly. lps: Doris Day, Richard Widmark, Gig Young. 98M USA. prod/rel: MGM, Joseph Fields Prods.

Witches Milk, 1968, Novel
Pete 'N' Tillie 1972 d: Martin Ritt. lps: Walter Matthau, Carol Burnett, Geraldine Page. 100M USA. prod/rel: Universal

DE VRIES, THEUN
Het Meisje Met Het Rode Haar, Novel
Meisje Met Het Rode Haar, Het 1981 d: Ben Verbong. lps: Renee Soutendijk, Peter Tuinman, Loes LucaA. 116M NTH. *The Girl With the Red Hair* (USA) prod/rel: Movies

DE VYLARS, CELIA
L' Angoisse, Play
House of Mystery 1961 d: Vernon Sewell. lps: Jane Hylton, Peter Dyneley, Nanette Newman. 56M UKN. *The Unseen* prod/rel: Anglo-Amalgamated, Independent Artists

Latin Quarter 1945 d: Vernon Sewell. lps: Derrick de Marney, Frederick Valk, Joan Greenwood. 80M UKN. *Frenzy* (USA) prod/rel: British National, Anglo-American

Medium, The 1934 d: Vernon Sewell. lps: Nancy O'Neil, Shayle Gardner, Barbara Gott. 38M UKN. prod/rel: Film Tests, MGM

DE WINTER, LEON
Zoeken Naar Eileen, Book
Zoeken Naar Eileen 1987 d: Rudolf Van Den Berg. lps: Thom Hoffman, Lysette Anthony, Gary Whelan. 100M NTH. *Searching for Eileen*; *Looking for Eileen*

DE WITT, JACK
Story
Beyond the Blue Horizon 1942 d: Alfred Santell. lps: Dorothy Lamour, Richard Denning, Jack Haley. 76M USA. *Malaya* prod/rel: Paramount

DE WOHL, LOUIS (1903–1961), GRM, von Wohl-Musciny, Ludwig
House of a Thousand Windows, Novel
Crime Over London 1936 d: Alfred Zeisler. lps: Margot Grahame, Paul Cavanagh, Joseph Cawthorn. 80M UKN. prod/rel: United Artists, Criterion

The Joyful Beggar, Philadelphia 1958, Novel
Francis of Assisi 1961 d: Michael Curtiz. lps: Bradford Dillman, Dolores Hart, Stuart Whitman. 106M USA. prod/rel: Perseus Productions

DE WYTTENBACH, MME M. L.
Printemps, Short Story
Manouche - Jeunesse d'Aujourd'hui 1942 d: Fred Surville. lps: Yves Bella, Pierre Dudan, Andre Talmes. 95M SWT. *Manouche Das Madchen Das Den Weg Verlor*; *Jugend von Heute*; *Printemps* prod/rel: Sarco-Films

DE ZANGER, JAN
Novel
   Violence: the Last Resort 1992 d: Rainer Kaufmann.
   lps: Jurgen Vogel, Thomas Heinze, Jasmin Tabatabai.
   TVM. 85M GRM.

DE ZILAHY, LOUIS
L' Oiseau de Feu, Play
   Cette Nuit-la 1933 d: Marc Sorkin. lps: Madeleine
   Soria, Colette Darfeuil, Lucien Rozenberg. 80M FRN.
   prod/rel: Via Film

DE ZUNZUNEGUI, JUAN ANTONIO
Dos Hombres Y Dos Mujeres En Medio, 1944, Novel
   Dos Hombres Y En Medio Dos Mujeres 1977 d:
   Rafael Gil. lps: Alberto Closas, Nadiuska, Gemma
   Cuervo. 101M SPN. *And Two Women Among Them Two
   Men*
El Mundo Sigue, 1960, Novel
   Mundo Sigue, El 1963 d: Fernando Fernan Gomez.
   lps: Fernando Fernan Gomez, Lina Canalejas, Gemma
   Cuervo. 109M SPN. *Life Goes on*

DEAL, BABS H.
The Walls Came Tumbling Down, Novel
   Friendships, Secrets Amd Lies 1979 d: Ann Zane
   Shanks, Marlena Laird. lps: Stella Stevens, Paula
   Prentiss, Tina Louise. TVM. 100M USA. prod/rel: NBC,
   Warner

DEAN, BASIL (1888–1978), UKN
Murder Gang, London 1935, Play
   Sensation 1937 d: Brian Desmond Hurst. lps: John
   Lodge, Diana Churchill, Francis Lister. 67M UKN.
   prod/rel: British International Pictures, Associated
   British Picture Corporation

DEAN, JEAN
Blind Ambition, Book
   Blind Ambition 1979 d: George Schaefer. lps: Martin
   Sheen, Theresa Russell, Michael Callan. TVM. 400M
   USA. prod/rel: CBS, Time-Life Television

DEAN, MAUREEN
Mo, Book
   Blind Ambition 1979 d: George Schaefer. lps: Martin
   Sheen, Theresa Russell, Michael Callan. TVM. 400M
   USA. prod/rel: CBS, Time-Life Television

DEARDEN, HAROLD
Interference, London 1927, Play
   Interference 1929 d: Lothar Mendes, Roy J. Pomeroy.
   lps: William Powell, Evelyn Brent, Clive Brook. 75M
   USA. prod/rel: Paramount Famous Lasky Corp.
   Without Regret 1935 d: Harold Young. lps: Elissa
   Landi, Paul Cavanagh, Kent Taylor. 75M USA. prod/rel:
   Paramount Productions©
Two White Arms, London 1928, Play
   Two White Arms 1932 d: Fred Niblo. lps: Adolphe
   Menjou, Margaret Bannerman, Claud Allister. 81M
   UKN. *Wives Beware* (USA) prod/rel: Cinema House,
   MGM

DEARSLEY, A. P.
The Chigwell Chicken, Play
   And the Same to You 1960 d: George Pollock. lps:
   Brian Rix, Leo Franklyn, William Hartnell. 70M UKN.
   prod/rel: Eros, Monarch
Come Back Peter, Play
   Come Back Peter 1952 d: Charles Saunders. lps:
   Patrick Holt, Peter Hammond, Humphrey Lestocq.
   80M UKN. prod/rel: Present Day, Apex
Fly Away Peter, London 1947, Play
   Fly Away Peter 1948 d: Charles Saunders. lps:
   Frederick Piper, Kathleen Boutall, Margaret Barton.
   60M UKN. prod/rel: Production Facilities, General Film
   Distributors
It Won't Be a Stylish Marriage, Play
   Alf's Baby 1953 d: MacLean Rogers. lps: Jerry
   Desmonde, Pauline Stroud, Olive Sloane. 75M UKN.
   prod/rel: Act Films, Adelphi

DEAVER, JEFFREY
Book
   Dead Silence 1997 d: Daniel Petrie Jr. lps: James
   Garner, Marlee Matlin, Lolita Davidovich. 99M
   CND/USA. prod/rel: Maiden Prods., Hbo

DEBLASIO, EDWARD
The Legend of Lylah Clare, 1963, Play
   Legend of Lylah Clare, The 1968 d: Robert Aldrich.
   lps: Kim Novak, Peter Finch, Ernest Borgnine. 130M
   USA. prod/rel: Associates & Aldrich Co.

DEBRETT, HAL
Before I Wake, Novel
   Before I Wake 1954 d: Albert S. Rogell. lps: Mona
   Freeman, Jean Kent, Maxwell Reed. 78M UKN. *Shadow
   of Fear* (USA) prod/rel: Gibraltar, Grand National

DECAUX, LUCILE
Katia, Novel
   Katia 1938 d: Maurice Tourneur. lps: Danielle
   Darrieux, John Loder, Aime Clariond. 91M FRN.
   prod/rel: Metropa-Film
Katia le Demon Bleu du Tsar Alexandre, Paris
   1938, Novel
   Katja 1959 d: Robert Siodmak. lps: Romy Schneider,
   Curd Jurgens, Pierre Blanchar. 93M GRM/FRN. *Une
   Jeune Fille un Seul Amour* (FRN); *Adorable Sinner*
   (USA); *Magnificent Sinner*; *Katia* prod/rel: Speva Films

DECOIN, DIDIER
La Femme de Chambre du Titanic, Novel
   Camarera Del Titanic, La 1997 d: Bigas LunA. lps:
   Olivier Martinez, Aitana Sanchez-Gijon, Richard
   Bohringer. 98M SPN/FRN/ITL. *La Femme de Chambre
   du Titanic*; *The Chambermaid and the Titanic* prod/rel:
   Mate Prod., Tornasol Films (Spain)

DECOIN, HENRI (1896–1969), FRN
Le Roi de la Pedale, Play
   Roi de la Pedale, Le 1925 d: Maurice Champreux. lps:
   Georges Biscot, Blanche Montel, Jean Murat. FRN.
   prod/rel: Gaumont

DECORI
La Fille du Garde-Chasse, Story
   Fille du Garde-Chasse, La 1912 d: Alexandre
   Devarennes. lps: Jean Kemm, Damores, Darcet. 1000m
   FRN. prod/rel: Odeon Films

DECOURCELLE, PIERRE
Le Crime d'une Sainte
   Crime d'une Sainte, Le 1923 d: Charles Maudru. lps:
   Gaston Jacquet, Noelle Rolland, Maurice Lagrenee.
   2402m FRN. prod/rel: Societe D'edition
   Cinematographique
Les Deux Gosses, Novel
   Deux Gosses, Les 1912 d: Adrien Caillard. lps: Louis
   Gauthier, Pierre Renoir, Madeleine Fromet. 1956m
   FRN. prod/rel: Optima, Pathe
   Deux Gosses, Les 1914 d: Albert Capellani. lps: Paul
   Capellani, Romuald Joube, Andree Pascal. 2660m FRN.
   prod/rel: Scagl
   Deux Gosses, Les 1924 d: Louis Mercanton. lps:
   Edouard Mathe, Gabriel Signoret, Yvette Guilbert.
   SRL. 8EP FRN.
   Deux Gosses, Les 1936 d: Fernand Rivers. lps:
   Germaine Rouer, Serge Grave, Dorville. 115M FRN.
   prod/rel: Films Fernand Rivers
Due Derelitti, I 1952 d: Flavio CalzavarA. lps: Lea
   Padovani, Massimo Serato, Yves Deniaud. 90M ITL.
   prod/rel: Raffaele Colamonici, Umberto Montesi
Gigolette, Novel
   Gigolette 1921 d: Henri Pouctal. lps: Sephora Mosse,
   Georges Colin, Pierre Stephen. F FRN. prod/rel: Societe
   D'editions Cinematographique
   Gigolette 1936 d: Yvan Noe. lps: Paul Azais, Florelle,
   Gabriel Gabrio. 87M FRN. prod/rel: Productions
   Pellegrin Cinema
Plus Que Reine, Novel
   Plus Que Reine 1915 d: Rene Leprince. lps: Jean Dax,
   Rene Alexandre, Gabriel Signoret. FRN. prod/rel: Pathe
   Freres

DECSEY, ERNST
Sissy's Brautfahrt, Play
   King Steps Out, The 1936 d: Josef von Sternberg. lps:
   Grace Moore, Franchot Tone, Walter Connolly. 85M
   USA. *Poor Sister*; *Cissy* prod/rel: Columbia Pictures
   Corp. of California©

DEEPING, WARWICK (1877–1950), UKN, Deeping,
   George Warwick
Doomsday, London 1927, Novel
   Doomsday 1928 d: Rowland V. Lee. lps: Florence Vidor,
   Gary Cooper, Lawrence Grant. 5652f USA. prod/rel:
   Paramount Famous Lasky Corp.
Fox Farm, Novel
   Fox Farm 1922 d: Guy Newall. lps: Guy Newall, Ivy
   Duke, A. Bromley Davenport. 5850f UKN. prod/rel:
   George Clark, Stoll
Kitty, Novel
   Kitty 1929 d: Victor Saville. lps: Estelle Brody, John
   Stuart, Dorothy Cumming. SIL. 8100f UKN. prod/rel:
   British International Pictures, Burlington
Sorrell and Son, 1925, Novel
   Sorrell and Son 1927 d: Herbert Brenon. lps: H. B.
   Warner, Anna Q. Nilsson, Mickey McBan. 9000f USA.
   prod/rel: Feature Productions, United Artists
   Sorrell and Son 1933 d: Jack Raymond. lps: H. B.
   Warner, Hugh Williams, Winifred Shotter. 97M UKN.
   prod/rel: British and Dominions, United Artists
   Sorrell and Son 1984 d: Derek Bennett. lps: Richard
   Pasco, Peter Chelsom, Stephanie Beacham. MTV. 300M
   UKN. prod/rel: Ytv

Two Black Sheep, New York 1933, Novel
   Two Sinners 1935 d: Arthur Lubin. lps: Otto Kruger,
   Martha Sleeper, Cora Sue Collins. 72M USA. *Two Black
   Sheep* (UKN) prod/rel: Republic Pictures Corp.©
Unrest, Novel
   Unrest 1920 d: Dallas Cairns. lps: Dallas Cairns, Mary
   Dibley, Maud Yates. 6000f UKN. prod/rel: Cairns
   Torquay Films, Allied Exporters

DEFILITTA, FRANK
The Entity, Novel
   Entity, The 1982 d: Sidney J. Furie. lps: Barbara
   Hershey, Don Silver, David LabiosA. 125M USA.
   prod/rel: 20th Century-Fox

DEFOE, DANIEL (1660–1731), UKN
Moll Flanders, 1722, Novel
   Amorous Adventures of Moll Flanders, The 1965
   d: Terence Young. lps: Kim Novak, Richard Johnson,
   Angela Lansbury. 126M UKN. prod/rel: Paramount,
   Winchester Film Productions
   Moll Flanders 1996 d: David Attwood. lps: Alex
   Kingston, Daniel Craig, Diana Rigg. TVM. 240M
   USA/UKN. *The Fortunes and Misfortunes of Moll
   Flanders* prod/rel: Granada Television, Wgbh-Boston
   Sex in Sweden 1977 d: Mac Ahlberg. lps: Christopher
   Chittell, Peter Loury, Maria Lynn. 100M SWD.
   Molly-Familjeflickan; *Molly*; *Entreintes Suedoises*;
   Molly l'Ingenue Perverse; *Folles Etreintes de Jennifer*
Robinson Crusoe, 1719, Novel
   Aventuras de Robinson Crusoe, As 1978 d: Mozael
   SilveirA. 90M BRZ.
   Aventuras de Robinson Crusoe, Las 1952 d: Luis
   Bunuel. lps: Dan O'Herlihy, James Fernandez, Felipe de
   AlbA. 90M MXC/USA. *The Adventures of Robinson
   Crusoe*; *Robinson Crusoe* prod/rel: Tepeyac
   Aventures de Robinson Crusoe, Les 1921 d: Gaston
   Leprieur, Mario Gargiulo. lps: Mario Dani, Armand
   Numes, Claude Merelle. 3800m FRN/ITL. *L' Avventure
   Di Robinson Crusoe* (ITL); *Robinson Crusoe* prod/rel:
   Flegrea Film, Monat Films
   Crusoe 1989 d: Caleb Deschanel. lps: Aidan Quinn, Ade
   Sapara, Warren Clarke. 91M USA/UKN. prod/rel:
   Island Pictures
   Naufrago, Il 1909. lps: Alberto A. Capozzi, Gigetta
   Morano. 164m ITL. *The Sailor's Broken Vow* (UKN);
   The Shipwrecked Man (USA) prod/rel: S.A. Ambrosio
   Racconto Della Giungla, Il 1973 d: GibbA. ANM.
   86M ITL. prod/rel: International Film Enterprise,
   Corona Cin.Ca
   Robinson Crusoe 1910 d: August Blom. lps: Einar
   Zangenberg, Franz Skondrup. DNM. prod/rel: Nordfilm
   Robinson Crusoe 1913 d: Otis Turner. lps: Robert
   Leonard, Edward Alexander, Charles W. Travis. 3r
   USA. prod/rel: Bison
   Robinson Crusoe 1916 d: George F. Marion. lps:
   Robert Paton Gibbs. 5r USA. prod/rel: Henry W. Savage,
   Inc.©, Warner Bros.
   Robinson Crusoe 1927 d: M. A. Wetherell. lps: M. A.
   Wetherell, Fay Compton, Herbert Waithe. 6500f UKN.
   prod/rel: Epic Films
   Robinson Crusoe 1946 d: Alexander Andrievski. 74M
   USS.
   Robinson Crusoe 1950 d: Jeff Musso, Amasi Damiani.
   lps: Georges Marchal, Nadia Marlowa, Mauro
   Sambucini. 94M FRN/ITL. *Il Naufrago Del Pacifico*
   (ITL); *Le Naufrage du Pacifique* prod/rel: P.W.T.
   (Roma), Creole Film (Paris)
   Robinson Crusoe 1972 d: GibbA. ANM. 86M ASL.
   Robinson Crusoe 1974 d: James MacTaggart. lps:
   Stanley Baker, Ram John Holder, Jerome Willis. MTV.
   100M UKN. prod/rel: BBC
   Robinson Crusoe on Mars 1964 d: Byron Haskin. lps:
   Paul Mantee, Vic Lundin, Adam West. 110M USA.
   prod/rel: Devonshire Pictures, Paramount Pictures
   Robinson Y Viernes En la Isla Encantada 1969 d:
   Rene Cardona Jr. lps: Hugo Stiglitz, Ahui. 110M MXC.
   Robinson Crusoe and the Tiger; *Robinson Crusoe*
   Tu Imagines Robinson 1968 d: Jean-Daniel Pollet.
   lps: Tobias Engel, Maria LinariA. 90M FRN. *Imagine
   Robinson*
   Vendredi Ou la Vie Sauvage 1981 d: Gerard Vergez.
   lps: Michael York, Roger Blin, Robert Rimbaud. MTV.
   255M FRN.
   **Zhizn I Udivitelnie Prikluchenia Robinzona
   Cruzo** 1973 d: Stanislav Govorukhin. lps: Leonide
   Kouraliev, Irakli Khizanichvili. 92M USS. *Life and
   Amazing Adventures of Robinson Crusoe*; *Robinson
   Crusoe*; *The Life and Remarkable Adventures of
   Robinson Crusoe*

Zivot a Podivuhodna Dobrodruzstvi Robinsona Crusoe, Namornika Z Yorku 1982 d: Stanislav Latal. ANM. 72M CZC/GRM. *Adventures of Robinson Crusoe, the Sailor of York*; *Dobrodruzstvi Robinsona Crusoe*; *The Life and Incredible Adventures of Robinson Crusoe, the Sailor from York*; *Robinson Crusoe*

DEFORD, FRANK
Everybody's All American, Novel
Everybody's All-American 1988 d: Taylor Hackford. lps: Jessica Lange, Dennis Quaid, Timothy Hutton. 127M USA. *When I Fall in Love* prod/rel: Warner Bros.

DEGENHARDT, FRANZ-JOSEF
Brandstellen, Novel
Brandstellen 1977 d: Horst E. Brandt. lps: Dieter Mann, Heidemarie Wenzel, Petra Hinze. 95M GDR. prod/rel: Defa, Unidoc

DEHAN, RICHARD
The Dop Doctor, Novel
Dop Doctor, The 1915 d: Fred Paul, L. C. MacBean. lps: Fred Paul, Agnes Glynne, Bertram Burleigh. 5766f UKN. *The Terrier and the Child*; *The Love Trail* prod/rel: G. B. Samuelson, Pathe

DEIGHTON, LEN (1929–, UKN, Deighton, Leonard Cyril
Billion Dollar Brain, London 1966, Novel
Billion Dollar Brain 1967 d: Ken Russell. lps: Michael Caine, Karl Malden, Francoise Dorleac. 111M UKN/USA. prod/rel: Lowndes Productions, United Artists
Bullet to Beijing, Novel
Len Deighton's Bullet to Beijing 1995 d: George MihalkA. lps: Michael Caine, Jason Connery, Mia SarA. 122M UKN/CND/RSS.
Funeral in Berlin, London 1964, Novel
Funeral in Berlin 1966 d: Guy Hamilton. lps: Michael Caine, Paul Hubschmid, Oscar HomolkA. 102M UKN. *Harry Palmer Returns* prod/rel: Lowndes Productions, Jovera, S.a.
The Ipcress File, London 1962, Novel
Ipcress File, The 1965 d: Sidney J. Furie. lps: Michael Caine, Nigel Green, Guy Doleman. 109M UKN. prod/rel: Steven, S.a., Lowndes Productions
Midnight in St. Petersburg, Novel
Midnight in St. Petersburg 1995 d: Douglas Jackson. lps: Michael Caine, Jason Connery, Michael Gambon. 86M UKN/CND/RSS.
Only When I Larf, London 1968, Novel
Only When I Larf 1968 d: Basil Dearden. lps: Richard Attenborough, David Hemmings, Alexandra Stewart. 105M UKN. prod/rel: Beecord Productions, Paramount

DEJEANS, ELIZABETH
Romance of a Million Dollars, Indianapolis 1922, Novel
Romance of a Million Dollars, The 1926 d: Tom Terriss. lps: Glenn Hunter, Alyce Mills, Gaston Glass. 5300f USA. prod/rel: J. G. Bachmann, Preferred Pictures
The Tiger's Coat, Indianapolis 1917, Novel
Tiger's Coat, The 1920 d: Roy Clements. lps: Myrtle Stedman, W. Lawson Butt, Tina Modotti. 5r USA. prod/rel: Dial Film Co., W. W. Hodkinson Corp.

DEKOBRA, MAURICE (1885–1973), FRN
Furst Odre Clown, Novel
Furst Oder Clown 1927 d: Alexander Rasumny. lps: Arthur Roberts, Marcella Albani, Iwan Petrovich. 2365m GRM. *Prince Or Clown* (USA) prod/rel: Phoebus-Film Ag
Fusille a l'Aube, Novel
Fusille a l'Aube 1950 d: Andre Haguet. lps: Frank Villard, Howard Vernon, Renee Saint-Cyr. 90M FRN. *Secret Document -Vienna* (USA) prod/rel: Societe Mediterraneenne De Production
La Girl aux Mains Fines, Short Story
Liebe Geht Seltsame Wege 1927 d: Fritz Kaufmann, Jean Rosen. lps: Maly Delschaft, Walter Slezak, Fritz Alberti. 2338m GRM/FRN. *La Girl aux Mains Fines* (FRN) prod/rel: Majestic Films, Fritz Kaufmann Film
La Gondole aux Chimeres, Novel
Gondola Delle Chimere, La 1936 d: Augusto GeninA. lps: Marcelle Chantal, Roger Karl, Paul Bernard. 85M ITL/FRN. *La Gondole aux Chimeres* (FRN) prod/rel: Tiberia Film (Roma), Helianthe-Film (Paris)
Hell Is Sold Out, Novel
Hell Is Sold Out 1951 d: Michael Anderson. lps: Richard Attenborough, Mai Zetterling, Herbert Lom. 84M UKN. prod/rel: Zelstro, Eros
MacAo - l'Enfer du Jeu, Novel
MacAo, l'Enfer du Jeu 1939 d: Jean Delannoy. lps: Erich von Stroheim, Sessue Hayakawa, Roland Toutain. 90M FRN. *Mask of Korea* (USA); *Gambling Hell* (UKN); *L' Enfer du Jeu* prod/rel: Demo Films

---

La Madone Des Sleepings, Novel
Madone Des Sleepings, La 1928 d: Maurice Gleize, Marco de Gastyne. lps: Claude France, Olaf Fjord, Henri Valbel. F FRN. prod/rel: Natan
Madone Des Sleepings, La 1955 d: Henri Diamant-Berger. lps: Erich von Stroheim, Giselle Pascal, Katherine Kath. 98M FRN. prod/rel: le Film d'Art
Minuit Place Pigalle, Novel
Minuit, Place Pigalle 1928 d: Rene Hervil. lps: Nicolas Rimsky, Renee Heribel, Francois Rozet. F FRN. prod/rel: International Standard Films
Minuit, Place Pigalle 1934 d: Roger Richebe. lps: Raimu, Helene Robert, Colette Darfeuil. 100M FRN. prod/rel: Societe Parisienne Du Film Parlant
Mon Coeur Au Ralenti, Novel
Mon Coeur Au Ralenti 1927 d: Marco de Gastyne. lps: Philippe Heriat, Annette Benson, Olaf Fjord. F FRN. prod/rel: Editions Natan
Agent K8 Passeport Diplomatique, Novel
Passeport Diplomatique, Agent K8 1965 d: Robert Vernay. lps: Roger Hanin, Christiane Minazzoli, Lucien Nat. 105M FRN/ITL. *Agente Tigre: Sfida Infernale* (ITL) prod/rel: Carmina Films, S.N.C.
Quartier Latin, Novel
Quartier Latin 1929 d: Augusto GeninA. lps: Ivan Petrovitch, Carmen Boni, Gaston Jacquet. 3053m GRM. *Latin Quarter* prod/rel: Films Art Sofar
La Rue Des Bouches Peintes, Novel
Rue Des Bouches Peintes, La 1955 d: Robert Vernay. lps: Francoise Christophe, Paul Bernard, Henri Genes. 87M FRN. prod/rel: Ste Nouvelle Films Dispa, Carmina Films
Soupcons, Novel
Soupcons 1956 d: Pierre Billon. lps: Anne Vernon, Frank Villard, Jacques Castelot. 93M FRN. *La Pavane Des Poisons* prod/rel: Onyx, Licome Films
Le Sphinx a Parles, Paris 1930, Novel
Friends and Lovers 1931 d: Victor Schertzinger. lps: Adolphe Menjou, Laurence Olivier, Lili DamitA. 68M USA. *The Sphinx Has Spoken*; *Wine in the Blood* prod/rel: RKO Radio Pictures©
Yoshiwara, Novel
Yoshiwara 1937 d: Max Ophuls. lps: Pierre Richard-Willm, Sessue Hayakawa, Michiko TanakA. 102M FRN. *Kohana* prod/rel: Milo Film Productions

DEL MORAL, IGNACIO
La Mirada Del Hombre Oscuro, Play
Bwana 1996 d: Imanol Uribe. lps: Andres Pajares, Maria Barranco, Emilio Buale. 82M SPN. prod/rel: Cartel, Aurum Prods.

DEL RIO, JUAN
Three Legionnaires, Novel
Three Legionnaires 1937 d: Hamilton MacFadden. lps: Lyle Talbot, Robert Armstrong, Fifi d'Orsay. 65M USA. *Three Crazy Legionnaires* (UKN) prod/rel: General Pictures Corp., Robert E. Welsh Production

DEL RIVO, LAURA
The Furnished Room, Novel
West 11 1963 d: Michael Winner. lps: Alfred Lynch, Kathleen Breck, Eric Portman. 93M UKN. *West Eleven* prod/rel: Dial Films, Warner-Pathe

DEL SIGNORE, CAMILLO
Story
Clandestino a Trieste 1952 d: Guido Salvini. lps: Jacques Sernas, Doris Duranti, Edda Albertini. 90M ITL. prod/rel: Astor Film

DEL VALLE-INCLAN, RAMON MARIA (1869–1936), SPN
Femeninas, 1895, Short Story
Beatriz 1976 d: Gonzalo Suarez. lps: Carmen Sevilla, Nadiuska, Jorge Rivero. 99M SPN.
Flor de Santidad, 1904, Novel
Flor de Santidad 1972 d: Adolfo Marsillach. lps: Eliana de Santis, Francisco Balcells, Ismael Merlo. 108M SPN. *The Devil's Saint*
Mi Hermana Antonia, 1909, Short Story
Beatriz 1976 d: Gonzalo Suarez. lps: Carmen Sevilla, Nadiuska, Jorge Rivero. 99M SPN.

DELACORTA
Diva, Novel
Diva 1981 d: Jean-Jacques Beineix. lps: Richard Bohringer, Frederic Andrei, Thuy An Luu. 123M FRN. prod/rel: Greenwich, Films Galaxie

DELACOUR, A.
La Cagnotte, 1864, Play
Trois Jours de Bringue a Paris 1953 d: Emile Couzinet. lps: Lucien Baroux, Milly Mathis, Catherine Cheiney. 84M FRN. prod/rel: Burgus Films

---

Le Courrier de Lyon, London 1877, Play
Midnight Stage, The 1919 d: Ernest C. Warde. lps: Frank Keenan, Mignon Anderson, Charles Gunn. 5r USA. prod/rel: Anderson-Brunton Co., Pathe Exchange, Inc.©

DELACOUR, GIRAOUDIN
Midnight Stage, The 1919 d: Ernest C. Warde. lps: Frank Keenan, Mignon Anderson, Charles Gunn. 5r USA. prod/rel: Anderson-Brunton Co., Pathe Exchange, Inc.©

DELAMARE, MAXIME
Vengeance a Rio, Novel
Vengeance a Rio 1991 d: Murilo Salles. lps: Leopoldo Serran, Paulo Jose, Jose de Breu Abreu. TVM. 80M FRN/BRZ/GRM.

DELAND, EDMOND
Dangerous Medicine, Novel
Dangerous Medicine 1938 d: Arthur Woods. lps: Elizabeth Allan, Cyril Ritchard, Edmund Breon. 72M UKN. prod/rel: Warner Bros., First National

DELAND, MARGARET (1857–1945), USA
The Awakening of Helena Richie, New York 1906, Novel
Awakening of Helena Richie, The 1916 d: John W. Noble. lps: Ethel Barrymore, Robert W. Cummings, Frank Montgomery. 5r USA. prod/rel: Rolfe Photoplays, Inc.©, Metro Pictures Corp.
The Iron Woman, New York 1911, Novel
Iron Woman, The 1916 d: Carl Harbaugh. lps: Nance O'Neil, Einar Linden, Alfred Hickman. 6r USA. prod/rel: Popular Plays and Players, Inc.©, Metro Pictures Corp.

DELANEY, SHELAGH (1939–, UKN
A Taste of Honey, Stratford 1958, Play
Taste of Honey, A 1961 d: Tony Richardson. lps: Rita Tushingham, Dora Bryan, Robert Stephens. 100M UKN. prod/rel: Woodfall Film Productions, Bryanston
White Bus, Short Story
White Bus, The 1967 d: Lindsay Anderson. lps: Patricia Healey, Arthur Lowe, John Sharp. 41M UKN. prod/rel: United Artists, Holly

DELANO, EDITH BARNARD
The Flaming Ramparts, 1914, Short Story
Prodigal Wife, The 1918 d: Frank Reicher. lps: Mary Boland, Raymond Bloomer, Lucy Cotton. 5722f USA. prod/rel: Screencraft Pictures, State Rights
Gossip, Story
Gossip 1923 d: King Baggot. lps: Gladys Walton, Ramsey Wallace, Albert Prisco. 4488f USA. prod/rel: Universal Pictures
Rags, Story
Rags 1915 d: James Kirkwood. lps: Mary Pickford, Marshall Neilan, J. Farrell MacDonald. 5r USA. prod/rel: Famous Players Film Co.©, Paramount Pictures Corp.
When Carey Came to Town, 1915, Serial Story
All Woman 1918 d: Hobart Henley. lps: Mae Marsh, Jere Austin, Arthur Housman. 6r USA. prod/rel: Goldwyn Pictures Corp.©
Glorious Adventure, The 1918 d: Hobart Henley. lps: Mae Marsh, Wyndham Standing, Paul Stanton. 4951f USA. prod/rel: Goldwyn Pictures Corp.©, Goldwyn Distributing Corp.
The White Pearl, Story
White Pearl, The 1915 d: George Irving. lps: Marie Doro, Thomas Holding, Walter Craven. 5r USA. prod/rel: Famous Players Film Co., Paramount Pictures Corp.

DELANY, A. ELIZABETH
Having Our Say, 1993, Book
Having Our Say: the Delany Sisters' First 100 Years 1999 d: Lynne Littman. lps: Diahann Carroll, Ruby Dee, Amy Madigan. TVM. 120M USA. prod/rel: Kraft Premiere Movie, Tele Vest

DELANY, SARAH L.
Having Our Say: the Delany Sisters' First 100 Years 1999 d: Lynne Littman. lps: Diahann Carroll, Ruby Dee, Amy Madigan. TVM. 120M USA. prod/rel: Kraft Premiere Movie, Tele Vest

DELARUE-MARDRUS, LUCIE
La Cigale, Novel
Chair Ardente 1932 d: Rene Plaissetty. lps: Jean Marchat, Jean Wall, Mary SertA. 84M FRN. prod/rel: Isis-Film
Graine Au Vent, Novel
Graine Au Vent 1928 d: Maurice Keroul, Jacques Mills. lps: Henri Baudin, Claudie Lombard, Celine James. F FRN. prod/rel: Omega
Graine Au Vent 1943 d: Maurice Gleize. lps: Jacques Dumesnil, Marcelle Geniat, Lise Delamare. 90M FRN. prod/rel: Lux

Les Trois Lys, Novel
Trois Lys, Les 1921 d: Henri Desfontaines. lps: Maurice Escande, Jeanne Grumbach, Paul Baissac. 1470m FRN. prod/rel: Gaumont - Serie Pax

DELAVIGNE, CASIMIR (1793-1843), FRN
Don Juan d'Autriche, Play
Fils de Charles Quint, Le 1912 d: Henri Andreani, Adrien Caillard. lps: Claude Garry, Jean Kemm, Marie VenturA. 605m FRN. prod/rel: Scagl

Les Enfants d'Edouard, Play
Enfants d'Edouard, Les 1909 d: Andre Calmettes. lps: Emile Dehelly, Philippe Garnier, Olga Demidoff. 245m FRN. prod/rel: Film d'Art

Enfants d'Edouard, Les 1914 d: Henri Andreani. lps: Georges Wague, Jean Toulout, Jeanne Delvair. 1200m FRN. prod/rel: Cosmograph

La Muette de Portici, Paris 1828, Opera
Dumb Girl of Portici, The 1916 d: Lois Weber, Phillips Smalley. lps: Anna Pavlova, Rupert Julian, Wadsworth Harris. 8r USA. *Masaniello* prod/rel: Universal Film Mfg. Co.©, State Rights

DELAVIGNE, CASIMIR (1793-1843), FRN, Scribe, Augustin Eugene
Muta Di Portici, La 1911. lps: Mary Cleo Tarlarini. 272m ITL. *Il Trionfo Di Masaniello* prod/rel: S.A. Ambrosio

DELAVIGNE, CASIMIR (1793-1843), FRN
Muta Di Portici, La 1924 d: Telemaco Ruggeri. lps: Livio Pavanelli, Cecyl Tryan. 1400m ITL. prod/rel: a.G. Film

DELAVIGNE, GERMAIN
Le Diplomate, Play
Ambasciatore, L' 1936 d: Baldassarre Negroni. lps: Leda Gloria, Luisa Ferida, Maurizio d'AncorA. 75M ITL. prod/rel: Negroni Film, E.N.I.C.

DELAVIGNETTE, ROGER
Paysans Noirs, Novel
Paysans Noirs 1947 d: Georges Regnier. lps: Louis Arbessier, Antoine Balpetre, Georges Hubert. 99M FRN. *Famoro le Tyran* prod/rel: S.D.a.C., U.G.C.

DELBES
Jeanne la Maudite, Play
Jeanne la Maudite 1913 d: Georges DenolA. lps: Jacquinet, Mosnier, Rachel Behrendt. 935m FRN. prod/rel: Scagl

DELDERFIELD, R. F.
The Bull Boys, Play
Carry on Sergeant 1958 d: Gerald Thomas. lps: William Hartnell, Bob Monkhouse, Shirley Eaton. 83M UKN. prod/rel: Anglo-Amalgamated, Insignia

Diana, Novel
Diana 1983 d: David Tucker. lps: Kevin McNally, Jenny Seagrove. MTV. 550M UKN. prod/rel: BBC

Glad Tidings, Play
Glad Tidings 1953 d: Wolf RillA. lps: Barbara Kelly, Raymond Huntley, Ronald Howard. 67M UKN. prod/rel: Insignia, Eros

The Orchard Walls, 1953, Play
Now and Forever 1956 d: Mario Zampi. lps: Janette Scott, Vernon Gray, Kay Walsh. 91M UKN. prod/rel: Anglofilm, Ab-Pathe

Stop at a Winner, London 1961, Novel
On the Fiddle 1961 d: Cyril Frankel. lps: Alfred Lynch, Sean Connery, Cecil Parker. 97M UKN. *Operation Snafu* (USA); *Operation War Head*; *War Head* prod/rel: S. Benjamin Fisz, Anglo-Amalgamated

To Serve Them All My Days, Novel
To Serve Them All My Days 1980 d: Ronald Wilson. lps: John Duttine, Frank Middlemass, Alan MacNaughton. MTV. 650M UKN. prod/rel: BBC

Where There's a Will, 1954, Play
Where There's a Will 1955 d: Vernon Sewell. lps: Kathleen Harrison, George Cole, Leslie Dwyer. 79M UKN. prod/rel: Film Locations, Eros

Worm's Eye View, London 1945, Play
Worm's Eye View 1951 d: Jack Raymond. lps: Ronald Shiner, Garry Marsh, Diana Dors. 77M UKN. prod/rel: Associated British Film Distributors, Byron

DELEDDA, GRAZIA (1871-1936), ITL
Cenere, 1904, Novel
Cenere 1916 d: Febo Mari. lps: Eleonora Duse, Febo Mari, Misa Mordeglia Mari. 914m ITL. prod/rel: S.A. Ambrosio

Dramma, Short Story
Vie Del Peccato, Le 1946 d: Giorgio PastinA. lps: Jacqueline Laurent, Leonardo Cortese, Andrea Checchi. 90M ITL. prod/rel: Re.Ci.Te. Cin.Ca, Ilaria Film

L' Edera, Novel
Edera, L' 1950 d: Augusto GeninA. lps: Columba Dominquez, Roldano Lupi, Juan de LandA. 95M ITL. *Devotion*; *Delitto Per Amore* prod/rel: Cines

La Madre, 1920, Novel
Proibito 1955 d: Mario Monicelli. lps: Mel Ferrer, Amedeo Nazzari, Lea Massari. 90M ITL/FRN. *Forbidden*; *Du Sang Dans le Soleil* (FRN); *La Madre* prod/rel: Documento Film (Roma), Cormoran Film (Paris)

Marianna Sirca, Novel
Amore Rosso 1953 d: Aldo Vergano. lps: Marina Berti, Massimo Serato, Arnoldo FoA. 98M ITL. *Marianna Sirca* prod/rel: C.M. Film, Regionale

La Notte, Short Story
Grazia, La 1929 d: Aldo de Benedetti. lps: Carmen Boni, Giorgio Bianchi, Ruth Weyher. 2524m ITL. prod/rel: a.D.I.a.

DELETH, AUGUST
The Shuttered Room, Sauk City 1959, Short Story
Shuttered Room, The 1967 d: David Greene. lps: Gig Young, Carol Lynley, Oliver Reed. 99M UKN. prod/rel: Seven Arts Productions, Troy-Schenck Productions

DELF, HARRY
The Family Upstairs, Atlantic City 1925, Play
Family Upstairs, The 1926 d: John G. Blystone. lps: Virginia Valli, Allan Simpson, J. Farrell MacDonald. 5971f USA. prod/rel: Fox Film Corp.

Harmony at Home 1930 d: Hamilton MacFadden. lps: Marguerite Churchill, Rex Bell, Charlotte Henry. 6295f USA. *She Steps Out* prod/rel: Fox Film Corp.

Stop, Look and Love 1939 d: Otto Brower. lps: Jean Rogers, William Frawley, Robert Kellard. 57M USA. *Harmony at Home* prod/rel: Twentieth Century-Fox Film Corp.©

DELGADO, FERNANDO G.
La Mirada Del Otro, Novel
Mirada Del Otro, La 1998 d: Vicente ArandA. lps: Laura Morante, Jose Coronado, Miguel GarciA. 102M SPN. *The Naked Eye*; *The Other Man's Look* prod/rel: Lolafilms

DELIBES, MIGUEL (1920-, SPN
El Camino, 1950, Novel
Camino, El 1963 d: Ana Mariscal. lps: Julia Caba Alba, Joaquin Roa, Mary Delgado. 100M SPN. *The Road*

Mi Idolatrado Hijo Sisi, 1953, Novel
Retrato de Familia 1976 d: Antonio Gimenez-Rico. lps: Antonio Ferrandis, Amparo Soler Leal, Monica Randall. 99M SPN. *Family Portrait*

Las Ratas, Novel
Ratas, Las 1997 d: Antonio Gimenez-Rico. lps: Alvaro Monje, Jose Caride, Juan Jesus Valverde. 97M SPN. *The Rats* prod/rel: Teja Films, Canal Plus Spain

Los Santos Inocentes, 1981, Novel
Santos Inocentes, Los 1984 d: Mario Camus. lps: Alfredo Landa, Francisco Rabal, Terele Pavez. 108M SPN. *The Holy Innocents* prod/rel: Ganesh Producciones Cinematograficas, Television Espanola

DELICADO, FRANCISCO
El Retrato de la Lozana Andaluza, 1528, Novel
Lozana Andaluza, La 1976 d: Vicente EscrivA. lps: Maria Rosaria Omaggio, Enzo Cerusico, Diana Lorys. 97M SPN. *The Belle from Andalusia*

DELION, JEAN
Pouce, Novel
Pacha, Le 1968 d: Georges Lautner. lps: Jean Gabin, Dany Carrel, Felix Marten. 90M FRN/ITL. *La Fredda Alba Del Commissario Joss* (ITL); *Showdown* prod/rel: Gaumont International, Rizzoli

DELL, ETHEL M. (1881-1939), UKN, Savage, Ethel Mary
Bars of Iron, Novel
Bars of Iron 1920 d: F. Martin Thornton. lps: Madge White, Roland Myles, J. R. Tozer. 6053f UKN. prod/rel: Stoll

A Debt of Honour, Novel
Debt of Honour, A 1922 d: Maurice Elvey. lps: Isobel Elsom, Clive Brook, Sydney Seaward. 4787f UKN. prod/rel: Stoll

The Eleventh Hour, Novel
Eleventh Hour, The 1922 d: George Ridgwell. lps: Madge White, Dennis Wyndham, Philip Simmons. 5248f UKN. *The Purple Phial* prod/rel: Stoll

The Experiment, Novel
Experiment, The 1922 d: Sinclair Hill. lps: Evelyn Brent, Clive Brook, Templar Powell. 4900f UKN. prod/rel: Stoll

Greatheart, Novel
Greatheart 1921 d: George Ridgwell. lps: Cecil Humphreys, Madge Stuart, Ernest Benham. 5551f UKN. prod/rel: Stoll

Her Own Free Will, 1922, Short Story
Her Own Free Will 1924 d: Paul Scardon. lps: Helene Chadwick, Holmes Herbert, Allan Simpson. 5959f USA. prod/rel: Eastern Productions, W. W. Hodkinson Corp.

The Hundredth Chance, Novel
Hundredth Chance, The 1920 d: Maurice Elvey. lps: Dennis Neilson-Terry, Mary Glynne, Eille Norwood. 6585f UKN. prod/rel: Stoll

Keeper of the Door, Novel
Keeper of the Door 1919 d: Maurice Elvey. lps: Basil Gill, Peggy Carlisle, Hamilton Stewart. 5466f UKN. prod/rel: Stoll

The Knave of Diamonds, Novel
Knave of Diamonds, The 1921 d: Rene Plaissetty. lps: Mary Massart, Alec Fraser, Cyril Percival. 5569f UKN. prod/rel: Stoll

The Knight Errant, Novel
Knight Errant, The 1922 d: George Ridgwell. lps: Madge Stuart, Rex McDougall, Olaf Hytten. 5290f UKN. prod/rel: Stoll

Lamp in the Desert, Novel
Lamp in the Desert 1922 d: F. Martin Thornton. lps: Gladys Jennings, Lewis Willoughby, George K. Arthur. 5820f UKN. prod/rel: Stoll

The Place of Honour, Novel
Place of Honour, The 1921 d: Sinclair Hill. lps: Hugh Buckler, Madge White, Pardoe Woodman. 5060f UKN. prod/rel: Stoll

The Prey of the Dragon, Novel
Prey of the Dragon, The 1921 d: F. Martin Thornton. lps: Victor McLaglen, Gladys Jennings, Harvey Braban. 5305f UKN. prod/rel: Stoll

A Question of Trust, Novel
Question of Trust, A 1920 d: Maurice Elvey. lps: Madge Stuart, Harvey Braban, Teddy Arundell. 4549f UKN. prod/rel: Stoll

The Rocks of Valpre, Novel
Rocks of Valpre, The 1919 d: Maurice Elvey. lps: Basil Gill, Peggy Carlisle, Cowley Wright. 6272f UKN. prod/rel: Stoll

Rocks of Valpre, The 1935 d: Henry Edwards. lps: John Garrick, Winifred Shotter, Leslie Perrins. 73M UKN. *High Treason* (USA) prod/rel: Real Art, Radio

The Safety Curtain, 1917, Short Story
Safety Curtain, The 1918 d: Sidney A. Franklin. lps: Norma Talmadge, Eugene O'Brien, Anders Randolf. 6r USA. prod/rel: Norma Talmadge Film Corp.©, Select Pictures Corp.

The Swindler, Novel
Swindler, The 1919 d: Maurice Elvey. lps: Cecil Humphreys, Marjorie Hume, Neville Percy. 5436f UKN. prod/rel: Stoll

The Tidal Wave, Novel
Tidal Wave, The 1920 d: Sinclair Hill. lps: Poppy Wyndham, Sydney Seaward, Pardoe Woodman. 6226f UKN. prod/rel: Stoll

The Top of the World, London 1920, Novel
Top of the World, The 1925 d: George Melford. lps: James Kirkwood, Anna Q. Nilsson, Joseph Kilgour. 7167f USA. prod/rel: Famous Players-Lasky, Paramount Pictures

The Way of an Eagle, Novel
Way of an Eagle, The 1918 d: G. B. Samuelson. lps: Isobel Elsom, Andre Beaulieu, Odette Goimbault. 6300f UKN. prod/rel: G. B. Samuelson, Sun

The Woman of His Dreams, Novel
Woman of His Dreams, The 1921 d: Harold Shaw. lps: Mary Dibley, Alec Fraser, Sydney Seaward. 4320f UKN. prod/rel: Stoll

DELL, FLOYD (1887-, USA
Bachelor Father, Play
Casanova Brown 1944 d: Sam Wood. lps: Gary Cooper, Teresa Wright, Frank Morgan. 99M USA. prod/rel: International, Christie

An Unmarried Father, New York 1927, Novel
Little Accident 1939 d: Charles Lamont. lps: Sandra Lee Henville, Hugh Herbert, Florence Rice. 63M USA. prod/rel: Universal Pictures Co.©

Little Accident, The 1930 d: William James Craft. lps: Douglas Fairbanks Jr., Anita Page, Sally Blane. 82M USA. *Unexpected Father* prod/rel: Universal Pictures

Papa Sans le Savoir 1931 d: Robert Wyler. lps: Noel-Noel, Francoise Rosay, Pierre Brasseur. 99M FRN. *Fils a Papa* prod/rel: Universal-Film

DELL, JEFFREY (1904-1985), UKN
Blondie White, Play
Footsteps in the Dark 1941 d: Lloyd Bacon. lps: Errol Flynn, Brenda Marshall, Ralph Bellamy. 96M USA. prod/rel: Warner Bros.

Night Alone, London 1937, Play
Night Alone 1938 d: Thomas Bentley. lps: Emlyn Williams, Leonora Corbett, Lesley Brook. 76M UKN. prod/rel: Welwyn, Pathe

Official Secret, London 1938, Play
Spies of the Air 1939 d: David MacDonald. lps: Barry K. Barnes, Roger Livesey, Joan Marion. 77M UKN. *Official Secret* prod/rel: British National, Associated British Picture Corporation

DELLUC, LOUIS (1892–1924), FRN
Novel
Millionenraub Im Rivieraexpress, Der 1927 d: Joseph Delmont. lps: Gina Manes, Georg Charlies. 1945m GRM. prod/rel: Liberty-Film

Le Train Sans Yeux, Short Story
Train Sans Yeux, Le 1926 d: Alberto Cavalcanti. lps: Gina Manes, Georges Charlia, Hans Mierendorff. F FRN. prod/rel: Neo-Films, Films Legrand

DELLY
Mitsi, Paris 1922, Novel
Rose of Paris, The 1924 d: Irving Cummings. lps: Mary Philbin, Robert Cain, John Sainpolis. 6362f USA. prod/rel: Universal Pictures

DELMAN, DAVID
Conspiracy of Terror, Book
Conspiracy of Terror 1975 d: John Llewellyn Moxey. lps: Michael Constantine, Barbara Rhoades, Mariclare Costello. TVM. 78M USA. prod/rel: Lorimar Productions

DELMAR, EUGENE
Bad Girl, New York 1928, Novel
Bad Girl 1931 d: Frank Borzage. lps: Sally Eilers, James Dunn, Minna Gombell. 90M USA. prod/rel: Fox Film Corp.

DELMAR, THOMAS
The Bravest of the Brave, Story
Bravest of the Brave 1915 d: Allen Curtis. lps: Max Asher. SHT USA. prod/rel: Joker

Those Kids and Cupid, Story
Those Kids and Cupid 1915. lps: Ray Gallagher, Billie Rhodes, Harry Rattenberry. SHT USA. prod/rel: Nestor

DELMAR, VINA (1905–, USA, Delmar, Vina Croter
Story
Great Man's Lady, The 1942 d: William A. Wellman. lps: Barbara Stanwyck, Joel McCrea, Brian Donlevy. 90M USA. prod/rel: Paramount

About Mrs. Leslie, Novel
About Mrs. Leslie 1954 d: Daniel Mann. lps: Shirley Booth, Robert Ryan, Alex Nicol. 104M USA. prod/rel: Paramount

Angie - Uptown Woman, 1929, Short Story
Uptown New York 1932 d: Victor Schertzinger. lps: Jack Oakie, Shirley Grey, Leon Ames. 80M USA. *Uptown Woman* prod/rel: K.B.S. Film Co., World Wide Pictures©

Bad Girl, New York 1928, Novel
Bad Girl 1931 d: Frank Borzage. lps: Sally Eilers, James Dunn, Minna Gombell. 90M USA. prod/rel: Fox Film Corp.

Manhattan Heartbeat 1940 d: David Burton. lps: Robert Sterling, Virginia Gilmore, Joan Davis. 72M USA. *Rain Or Shine; Marriage in Transit; Bad Girl* prod/rel: 20th Century-Fox Film Corp.

A Chance at Heaven, 1932, Short Story
Chance at Heaven 1933 d: William A. Seiter. lps: Ginger Rogers, Joel McCrea, Marian Nixon. 71M USA. prod/rel: RKO Radio Pictures, Inc.

Dance Hall, 1929, Short Story
Dance Hall 1929 d: Melville Brown. lps: Olive Borden, Arthur Lake, Margaret Seddon. 69M USA. prod/rel: RKO Productions

Pick-Up, 1928, Short Story
Pick-Up 1933 d: Marion Gering. lps: Sylvia Sidney, George Raft, Lillian Bond. 76M USA. *Pick Up* prod/rel: Paramount Productions©

Pretty Sadie McKee, 1933, Short Story
Sadie McKee 1934 d: Clarence Brown. lps: Joan Crawford, Franchot Tone, Gene Raymond. 95M USA. prod/rel: Metro-Goldwyn-Mayer Corp.©

The Rich Full Life, New York 1945, Play
Cynthia 1947 d: Robert Z. Leonard. lps: Elizabeth Taylor, George Murphy, S. Z. Sakall. 98M USA. *The Rich Full Life* (UKN) prod/rel: MGM

Sheba, Story
Playing Around 1930 d: Mervyn Leroy. lps: Alice White, Chester Morris, William Bakewell. 5972f USA. *The Furies* prod/rel: First National Pictures

DELORBE, C.
Montmartre, Play
Lulu O un Rendez-Vous a Montmartre 1914 d: Augusto GeninA. lps: Ruggero Ruggeri, Tilde Teldi, Pina Menichelli. 759m ITL. *Lulu* prod/rel: Monopol Film

DELORME, HUGUES
Le Coup de Minuit, Play
Coup de Minuit, Le 1916 d: Maurice Poggi. lps: Maurice Poggi, Pierre Etchepare, Alice de Tender. 450m FRN. prod/rel: Films Lordier

DELPEY, ROGER
Parias de la Gloire, Novel
Parias de la Gloire 1963 d: Henri Decoin. lps: Curd Jurgens, Maurice Ronet, Folco Lulli. 100M FRN/ITL/SPN. *I Disperati Della Gloria* (ITL); *Parias de la Gloria* (SPN); *Pariahs of Glory* (USA) prod/rel: Paris France Films, Films Marly

DELPHI-FABRICE
Le Prince Curacao, Novel
Son Altesse 1922 d: Henri Desfontaines. lps: Jean Devalde, Marguerite Madys, Blanche Montel. 1550m FRN. prod/rel: Gaumont - Serie Pax

DEMARIS, OVID
Candyleg, New York 1961, Novel
Intoccabili, Gli 1969 d: Giuliano Montaldo. lps: John Cassavetes, Britt Ekland, Peter Falk. 115M ITL/USA. *MacHine Gun McCain* (USA); *The Untouchables; At Any Price* prod/rel: Atlantica S.P.a., Euro International Film

The Hoods Take Over, Novel
Gang War 1958 d: Gene Fowler Jr. lps: Charles Bronson, Kent Taylor, Jennifer Holden. 75M USA. prod/rel: 20th Century-Fox, Regal Films

DEMESSE, HENRI
Le Drame Des Charmettes
Drame Des Charmettes, Le 1909. lps: Henri Etievant, Charlet, Catherine Fonteney. 245m FRN. prod/rel: Scagl

La Femme Blonde, Play
Femme Blonde, La 1916 d: Henry Roussell. lps: Andre Liabel, Emmy Lynn, Pepa Bonafe. FRN.

La Petite Fifi, Novel
Petite Fifi, La 1913 d: Henri Pouctal. lps: Marcel Vibert, Rousseau, Marcilly. 950m FRN. prod/rel: Film d'Art

DEMI, JAKUB
Zapomenute Svetlo, Novel
Zapomenute Svetlo 1997 d: Vladimir Michalek. lps: Boleslav Polivka, Veronika Zilkova, Peter Kavan. 101M CZE. *Forgotten Light* prod/rel: Studio Fama 92, Czech Television

DEMING, RICHARD
The Careful Man, London 1962, Novel
Drop Dead, Darling 1966 d: Ken Hughes. lps: Tony Curtis, Rosanna Schiaffino, Lionel Jeffries. 100M UKN. *Baby Arrivederci* (USA); *My Last Duchess* prod/rel: Seven Arts Productions, Paramount

DEMOUZON, ALAIN
Monsieur Abel, Novel
Monsieur Abel 1983 d: Jacques Doillon. lps: Pierre Dux, Zouc, Jacques Denis. TVM. 89M FRN/SWT.

DEMPSEY, BARBARA PIATTELI
Dempsey, Autobiography
Dempsey 1983 d: Gus Trikonis. lps: Treat Williams, Sam Waterston, Sally Kellerman. TVM. 150M USA. prod/rel: CBS, Charles Fries

DEMPSEY, JACK (1895–1983), USA
Dempsey
Dempsey 1983 d: Gus Trikonis. lps: Treat Williams, Sam Waterston, Sally Kellerman. TVM. 150M USA. prod/rel: CBS, Charles Fries

DEMPSTER, DEREK
The Narrow Margin, London 1961, Book
Battle of Britain 1969 d: Guy Hamilton. lps: Laurence Olivier, Robert Shaw, Christopher Plummer. 132M UKN. prod/rel: Spitfire Productions, United Artists

DENEVI, MARCO
Ceremonia Secreta, 1955, Short Story
Secret Ceremony 1968 d: Joseph Losey. lps: Elizabeth Taylor, Mia Farrow, Robert Mitchum. 109M UKN. prod/rel: Universal Pictures, Ltd., World Films

Rosaura a Las Diez, 1955, Novel
Rosaura a Las Diez 1958 d: Mario Soffici. lps: Susana Campos, Maria Luisa Robledo. 100M ARG. *Rosaura at 10:00*

DENHAM, REGINALD (1894–1983), UKN
Ladies in Retirement, London 1939, Play
Ladies in Retirement 1941 d: Charles Vidor. lps: Louis Hayward, Ida Lupino, Evelyn Keyes. 92M USA. prod/rel: Columbia

Mad Room, The 1969 d: Bernard Girard. lps: Stella Stevens, Shelley Winters, Skip Ward. 93M USA. prod/rel: Norman Maurer Productions

Trunk Crime, Play
Trunk Crime 1939 d: Roy Boulting. lps: Manning Whiley, Barbara Everest, Michael Drake. 51M UKN. *Design for Murder* (USA) prod/rel: Charter, Anglo

Wallflower, New York 1944, Play
Wallflower 1948 d: Frederick de CordovA. lps: Joyce Reynolds, Janis Paige, Robert Hutton. 77M USA. prod/rel: Warner Bros.

DENISON, MURIEL
Susannah a Little Girl of the Mounties, New York 1936, Novel
Susannah of the Mounties 1939 d: William A. Seiter. lps: Shirley Temple, Randolph Scott, Margaret Lockwood. 78M USA. *Susannah* prod/rel: 20th Century-Fox Film Corp.©

DENKER, HENRY
Time Limit!, New York 1956, Play
Time Limit 1957 d: Karl Malden. lps: Richard Widmark, Richard Basehart, Dolores Michaels. 95M USA. prod/rel: United Artists, Heath Prods.

D'ENNERY, ADOLPHE-P. (1811–1899), FRN, Dennery, Adolph Philippe, D'ennery, Adolphe
L' Aieule, 1863, Play
Avo, L' 1909. 253m ITL. *L' Avo Avvelenatore; The Grandfather* (UKN) prod/rel: Cines

L' Aveugle, Play
Aveugle, L' 1914. lps: Louis Gauthier. 627m FRN. prod/rel: Acad

Une Cause Celebre, Paris 1877, Play
Celebrated Case, A 1914 d: George Melford. lps: Alice Joyce, Guy Coombs, Alice Hollister. 4r USA. prod/rel: Kalem Co., General Film Co.

Les Deux Orphelines, 1874, Novel
Due Orfanelle, Le 1978 d: Leopoldo SavonA. lps: Isabella Savona, Patrizia Gori, Evelyn Stewart. 90M ITL/SPN. *Unidos Por El Destino* (SPN) prod/rel: Cine Uno (Roma), Copercines (Madrid)

Deux Orphelines, Les 1932 d: Maurice Tourneur. lps: Gabriel Gabrio, Rosine Derean, Renee Saint-Cyr. 87M FRN. *The Two Orphans* prod/rel: Pathe-Natan

Due Orfanelle, Le 1918 d: Eduardo BencivengA. lps: Enna Saredo, Olga Benetti, Irma Berrettini. 2658m ITL. prod/rel: Caesar Film

Due Orfanelle, Le 1942 d: Carmine Gallone. lps: Alida Valli, Maria Denis, Osvaldo Valenti. 85M ITL. *The Two Orphans* prod/rel: Grandi Film Storici, S.a.F.I.C.

Due Orfanelle, Le 1955 d: Giacomo Gentilomo. lps: Myriam Bru, Milly Vitale, Andre Luguet. 95M ITL/FRN. *Les Deux Orphelines* prod/rel: Rizzoli Film (Roma), Francinex (Paris)

Due Orfanelle, Le 1966 d: Riccardo FredA. lps: Mike Marshall, Sophie Dares, Valeria Giangottini. 90M ITL/FRN. *Les Deux Orphelines* (FRN); *The Two Orphans* (USA) prod/rel: Comptoir Francais Du Film Production, Cine Italia Film

Duel Scene from "the Two Orphans" 1902 d: William Haggar. 100f UKN. prod/rel: Haggar & Sons

It Happened in Paris 1932 d: M. J. Weisfeldt. lps: Ranny Weeks, Eva Lorraine, Taylor Holmes. F USA. prod/rel: Picture Classics

Orphans of the Storm 1921 d: D. W. Griffith. lps: Lillian Gish, Dorothy Gish, Joseph Schildkraut. 14r USA. *The Two Orphans* prod/rel: D. W. Griffith, Inc., United Artists

Povere Bimbe! 1923 d: Gero Zambuto. lps: Linda Pini, Fernanda Fassy, Lido Manetti. 4296m ITL. prod/rel: Itala

Two Orphans, The 1911 d: Otis Turner. lps: Kathlyn Williams, Winnifred Greenwood, Myrtle Stedman. 3061f USA. prod/rel: Selig Polyscope Co.

Two Orphans, The 1915 d: Herbert Brenon. lps: Theda Bara, Jean Sothern, Herbert Brenon. 5-7r USA. prod/rel: Fox Film Corp., William Fox

Don Cesar de Bazan, 1844, Play
Don Cesare Di Bazan 1942 d: Riccardo FredA. lps: Gino Cervi, Anneliese Uhlig, Enrico Glori. 76M ITL. *La Lamadel Giustiziere* prod/rel: Elica, Artisti Associati

Rosita 1923 d: Ernst Lubitsch. lps: Mary Pickford, Holbrook Blinn, Irene Rich. 8800f USA. prod/rel: Mary Pickford Co., United Artists

Spanish Dancer, The 1923 d: Herbert Brenon. lps: Pola Negri, Antonio Moreno, Wallace Beery. 8434f USA. prod/rel: Famous Players-Lasky, Paramount Pictures

Martyre!, Novel
Martire! 1917 d: Camillo de Riso. lps: Tilde Kassay, Olga Benetti, Gustavo SerenA. 2661m ITL. prod/rel: Caesar Film

Le Medecin Des Enfants, Play
Medecin Des Enfants, Le 1916 d: Georges DenolA. lps: Maxime Desjardins, Henry Roussell, Vera Sergine. 830m FRN. prod/rel: Scagl

Paillasse, Play
Femme du Saltimbanque, La 1910 d: Georges DenolA. lps: Georges Dorival, Georges Treville, Marthe Mellot. 385m FRN. prod/rel: Scagl

La Signora Di Saint Tropez, Play
 Appassionatamente 1954 d: Giacomo Gentilomo. lps:
 Amedeo Nazzari, Myriam Bru, Isa BarzizzA. 102M ITL.
 prod/rel: Rizzoli Film, Dear Film

DENNIS, CHARLES
The Next to Last Train Ride, Novel
 Finders Keepers 1984 d: Richard Lester. lps: Michael
 O'Keefe, Beverly d'Angelo, Louis Gossett Jr. 96M USA.
 prod/rel: Warner Bros.

DENNIS, GERARD GRAHAM
Life of Gerard Graham Dennis, Story
 Great Jewel Robber, The 1950 d: Peter Godfrey. lps:
 David Brian, Marjorie Reynolds, John Archer. 91M
 USA. *After Nightfall* prod/rel: Warner Bros.

DENNIS, PATRICK (1921–1976), USA, Tanner III,
 Edward Everett
Auntie Mame, Novel
 Auntie Mame 1958 d: Morton Da CostA. lps: Rosalind
 Russell, Forrest Tucker, Coral Browne. 143M USA.
 prod/rel: Warner Bros.
 Mame 1974 d: Gene Saks. lps: Lucille Ball, Robert
 Preston, Beatrice Arthur. 131M USA. prod/rel: Warner,
 ABC

DENNY, ERNEST
All-of-a-Sudden-Peggy, London 1906, Play
 All-of-a-Sudden-Peggy 1920 d: Walter Edwards. lps:
 Marguerite Clark, Jack Mulhall, Lillian Leighton. 4448f
 USA. prod/rel: Famous Players-Lasky Corp.©,
 Paramount-Artcraft Pictures
The Irresistible Marmaduke, London 1918, Play
 Oh, What a Night! 1935 d: Frank Richardson. lps:
 Molly Lamont, James Carew, Valerie Hobson. 58M
 UKN. prod/rel: British Sound Film Productions,
 Universal
Lazybones, 1930, Play
 Lazybones 1935 d: Michael Powell. lps: Claire Luce,
 Ian Hunter, Sara Allgood. 65M UKN. prod/rel: Real Art,
 Radio
Summer Lightning, Play
 Troublesome Wives 1928 d: Harry Hughes. lps: Mabel
 Poulton, Lillian Oldland, Eric Bransby Williams. 5870f
 UKN. *Summer Lightning* prod/rel: Nettlefold,
 Butcher's Film Service
Vanity, London 1913, Play
 Vanity 1935 d: Adrian Brunel. lps: Jane Cain, Percy
 Marmont, John Counsell. 76M UKN. prod/rel: GS
 Enterprises, Columbia

DENTICE, LUDOVICO
MacChie Di Belletto, Milan 1968, Novel
 Detective, Un 1969 d: Romolo Guerrieri. lps: Franco
 Nero, Florinda Bolkan, Adolfo Celi. 104M ITL. *Detective
 Belli* (USA); *A Detective*; *Ring of Death*; *MacChie Di
 Belletto* prod/rel: Fair Film, Interfilm

DENUZIERE, MAURICE
Fausse Riviere, Book
 Louisiana 1984 d: Philippe de Broca, Jacques Demy
 (Uncredited). lps: Margot Kidder, Ian Charleson, Len
 Cariou. TVM. 206M FRN/CND/ITL. *Louisiana* (USA)
 prod/rel: Cine Louisiana Inc. (Montreal), Films
 Antenne-2 (Paris)
Louisiane, Book
 Louisiana 1984 d: Philippe de Broca, Jacques Demy
 (Uncredited). lps: Margot Kidder, Ian Charleson, Len
 Cariou. TVM. 206M FRN/CND/ITL. *Louisiana* (USA)
 prod/rel: Cine Louisiana Inc. (Montreal), Films
 Antenne-2 (Paris)

DENVER, JOSEPH
Rosaleen Dhu, Play
 Rosaleen Dhu 1920 d: William Powers. lps: William
 Powers. 4000f UKN. prod/rel: Celtic Producing Co.

DENVILLE, ALFRED
The Romance of Annie Laurie, Play
 Romance of Annie Laurie, The 1920 d: Gerald
 Somers. lps: Joan Gray, Allan McKelvin. 5000f UKN.
 prod/rel: Lancashire Film Studios

DEON, MICHEL
Un Taxi Mauve, 1973, Novel
 Taxi Mauve, Un 1977 d: Yves Boisset. lps: Charlotte
 Rampling, Philippe Noiret, Agostina Belli. 107M
 FRN/IRL/ITL. *Purple Taxi* (USA); *Un Taxi Colo Malva*
 (ITL) prod/rel: Sofracinema Tfi (Paris), National Film
 Studios of Ireland

DEPREND, JEFFREY
The White Frontier, Story
 Skyscraper 1928 d: Howard Higgin. lps: William Boyd,
 Alan Hale, Sue Carol. 7040f USA. prod/rel: de Mille
 Pictures, Pathe Exchange, Inc.

DERIBERS
Per Essere Piu Libero, Play
 Per Essere Piu Libero 1915 d: Camillo de Riso. lps:
 Camillo de Riso, Daisy Ferrero, Antonio Monti. 340m
 ITL. prod/rel: Film Artistica Gloria

D'ERRICO, CORRADO
Novel
 Fanciulla Dell'altro Mondo, La 1934 d: Gennaro
 Righelli. lps: Odoardo Spadaro, Dria Paola, Mino Doro.
 62M ITL. prod/rel: S.I.C., Anonima Pittaluga

DERY, TIBOR (1894–1978), HNG
A Befejezetien Mondat, 1947, Novel
 148 Perc a Befejezetlen Mondatbol 1974 d: Zoltan
 Fabri. lps: Andras Balint, Mari Csomos, Zoltan
 Latinovits. 128M HNG. *148 Minutes from the
 Unfinished Sentence*; *The Unfinished Sentence*; *The
 Unfinished Sentence in 148 Minutes*
Ket Asszony, 1962, Short Story
 Szerelem 1970 d: Karoly Makk. lps: Lili Darvas, Mari
 Torocsik, Ivan Darvas. 92M HNG. *Love* prod/rel: Mafilm
Az Orias, 1948, Short Story
 Orias, Az 1984 d: Erika Szanto. 84M HNG.
Pesti Felhojatek, 1946, Short Story
 Felhojatek! 1984 d: Gyula Maar. lps: Jiri Menzel,
 Miklos Tonay, Jiri AdamirA. 99M HNG. *Passing Fancy*;
 Budapest Cloudplay
Szerelem, 1956, Short Story
 Szerelem 1970 d: Karoly Makk. lps: Lili Darvas, Mari
 Torocsik, Ivan Darvas. 92M HNG. *Love* prod/rel: Mafilm
Vidam Temetes, 1963, Short Story
 Utolso Kezirat, Az 1986 d: Karoly Makk. lps: Jozef
 Kroner, Aleksander Bardini, Eszter Nagykaloczy. 114M
 HNG. *The Last Manuscript*

DES CARS, GUY
The Brute, Novel
 Green Scarf, The 1954 d: George M. O'Ferrall. lps:
 Michael Redgrave, Leo Genn, Ann Todd. 96M UKN.
 prod/rel: B & a Productions, British Lion
Las Hermanas, Novel
 Hermanas, Las 1962 d: Daniel Tinayre. lps: Mirtha
 Legrand, Silvia Legrand, Jorge Mistral. 89M ARG.
 prod/rel: Argentino Sono

DES LIGNERIS, FRANCOISE
Psyche 58, Paris 1958, Novel
 Psyche 63 1963 d: Alexander Singer. lps: Patricia Neal,
 Curd Jurgens, Samantha Eggar. 95M UKN. *Psyche 59*
 prod/rel: Troy-Schenk Productions, Columbia

DESARBRES, N.
Une Tasse de the, 1860
 Tazza Di the, Una 1923 d: Toddi. lps: Diomira
 Jacobini, Giuseppe Pierozzi, Clara Zambonelli. 745m
 ITL. prod/rel: Selecta-Toddi

DESCAVES, LUCIEN
Le Coeur Ebloui, 1926, Play
 Coeur Ebloui, Le 1938 d: Jean Vallee. lps: Max Dearly,
 Henri Rollan, Huguette Duflos. 90M FRN. prod/rel:
 Productions Claude Dolbert
Oiseaux de Passage, Novel
 Oiseaux de Passage 1925 d: Gaston Roudes. lps:
 France Dhelia, Lucien Dalsace, Mevisto. 2700m FRN.
 prod/rel: Grandes Productions Cinematographiques

DESMARETS, ANNE-MARIE
Torrents, Novel
 Torrents 1946 d: Serge de Poligny. lps: Georges
 Marchal, Renee Faure, Helen VitA. 100M FRN.
 prod/rel: C.P.F.

DESNOES, EDMUNDO
Memorias Del Subdesarrollo, 1965, Novel
 Memorias Del Subdesarrollo 1968 d: Tomas
 Gutierrez AleA. lps: Sergio Corrieri, Daisy Granados,
 Eslinda Nunez. 104M CUB. *Memories of
 Underdevelopment* (USA); *Memorias Del Desarrollo*
 prod/rel: I.C.A.I.C. Havanna

D'ESPARBES, GEORGES
Les Demi-Soldes, Novel
 Agonie Des Aigles, L' 1921 d: Julien Duvivier,
 Bernard-Deschamps. lps: Gaby Morlay, Gilbert Dalleu,
 Severin-Mars. 3200m FRN. prod/rel: Societe Francaise
 D'art Et Cinematograph
 Agonie Des Aigles, L' 1933 d: Roger Richebe. lps:
 Pierre Renoir, Constant Remy, Annie Ducaux. 125M
 FRN. prod/rel: Societe Des Film Roger Richebe
 Agonie Des Aigles, L' 1951 d: Jean Alden-Delos. lps:
 Roger Pigaut, Noel Roquevert, Charles Moulin. 83M
 FRN. *Les Demi-Soldes* prod/rel: Trianon Film

DESPREZ, FRANK
Lasca, Poem
 Lasca 1919 d: Norman Dawn. lps: Edith Roberts, Frank
 Mayo, Veola Harty. 5r USA. prod/rel: Universal Film
 Mfg. Co.©
 Lasca of the Rio Grande 1931 d: Edward Laemmle.
 lps: Leo Carrillo, Johnny Mack Brown, Dorothy
 Burgess. 65M USA. prod/rel: Universal Pictures Corp.©

DESTY, SUZETTE
Chauffeur Antoinette, Play
 Conduisez-Moi, Madame 1932 d: Herbert Selpin. lps:
 Armand Bernard, Rolla Norman, Jeanne Boitel. 80M
 FRN. *Antoinette* prod/rel: Les Comedies Filmees
 Love Contract, The 1932 d: Herbert Selpin. lps:
 Winifred Shotter, Owen Nares, Sunday Wilshin. 80M
 UKN. prod/rel: British and Dominions, Woolf &
 Freedman

DESVALLIERES, JEAN
Les Hommes Sans Nom
 Hommes Sans Nom, Les 1937 d: Jean Vallee. lps:
 Constant Remy, Thomy Bourdelle, Tania Fedor. 94M
 FRN. prod/rel: Votre Film
Le Ranch Des Hommes Forts, Novel
 Fort-Dolores 1938 d: Rene Le Henaff. lps: Roger Karl,
 Pierre Larquey, Alina de SilvA. 93M FRN. *A l'Ombre
 d'une Femme* prod/rel: Film Fort-Dolores

DESVALLIERES, MAURICE
Champignol Malgre Lui, Play
 Champignol Malgre Lui 1933 d: Fred Ellis. lps: Aime
 Simon-Girard, Janine Guise, Lulu Vattier. 96M FRN.
 prod/rel: Hesge
 Champignol Malgre Lui 1913. lps: Madeleine
 Aubrey, Semery, Fernand Rivers. 1050m FRN. prod/rel:
 L. Aubert
Le Fils a Papa, Play
 Fils a Papa, Le 1913 d: Georges MoncA. lps: Prince,
 Gabrielle Lange, Pepa Bonafe. 680m FRN. prod/rel:
 Pathe Freres
L' Hotel du Libre-Echange, Paris 1894, Play
 Aktenskapsbrottaren 1964 d: Hasse Ekman. 93M
 SWD. *The Marriage Wrestler*
 Hotel de Libre Echange, L' 1916 d: Marcel Simon.
 lps: Marcel Simon, Armand Lurville, Jane Faber. 1240m
 FRN. prod/rel: Cinedrama Paz
 Hotel du Libre Echange, L' 1934 d: Marc Allegret.
 lps: Fernandel, Mona Lys, Raymond Cordy. 106M FRN.
 prod/rel: Or-Films
 Hotel Paradiso 1966 d: Peter Glenville. lps: Alec
 Guinness, Gina Lollobrigida, Robert Morley. 99M
 UKN/USA/FRN. *Paradiso -Hotel du Libre-Exchange*
 (FRN) prod/rel: MGM Pictures, Trianon Productions
Prete-Moi Ta Femme, Play
 Prete-Moi Ta Femme 1914 d: Jacques Roullet. lps:
 Hardoux, Pierre Etchepare, Jane Faber. 782m FRN.
 prod/rel: Grand Films Populaires, G. Lordier
 Prete-Moi Ta Femme 1936 d: Maurice Cammage. lps:
 Pierre Brasseur, Pierre Larquey, Suzanne Dehelly. 90M
 FRN. prod/rel: Maurice Cammage

DETHA, VIJAYDAN
Duvidha, Short Story
 Duvidha 1973 d: Mani Kaul. lps: Ravi Menon, Raisa
 Padamsee, Hardan. 83M IND. *Dilemma*; *In Two Minds*;
 Two Roads prod/rel: Mani Kaul Prod.

DETZER, CARL
Hue and Cry, 1933, Short Story
 Car No.99 1935 d: Charles T. Barton. lps: Fred
 MacMurray, Guy Standing, Ann Sheridan. 75M USA.
 Car 99 prod/rel: Paramount Productions, Inc.
One Good Turn, 1933, Short Story
 Car No.99 1935 d: Charles T. Barton. lps: Fred
 MacMurray, Guy Standing, Ann Sheridan. 75M USA.
 Car 99 prod/rel: Paramount Productions, Inc.
Still Small Voice, 1933, Short Story
 Car No.99 1935 d: Charles T. Barton. lps: Fred
 MacMurray, Guy Standing, Ann Sheridan. 75M USA.
 Car 99 prod/rel: Paramount Productions, Inc.

DEVAL, ABEL
Oeil de Lynx Detective, Play
 Oeil de Lynx, Detective 1936 d: Pierre-Jean Ducis.
 lps: Armand Bernard, Alice Tissot, Janine Merrey. 73M
 FRN. prod/rel: Ullman, Henri

DEVAL, JACQUES
L' Amant Reve, 1925, Play
 Her Cardboard Lover 1942 d: George Cukor. lps:
 Norma Shearer, Robert Taylor, George Sanders. 93M
 USA. prod/rel: MGM
Dans Sa Candeur Naive, Paris 1927, Play
 Cardboard Lover, The 1928 d: Robert Z. Leonard. lps:
 Marion Davies, Jetta Goudal, Nils Asther. 7108f USA.
 Her Cardboard Lover prod/rel: Cosmopolitan
 Productions, Metro-Goldwyn-Mayer Distributing Corp.
Etienne, 1930, Play
 Etienne 1933 d: Jean Tarride. lps: Marthe Regnier,
 Vera Markels, Jacques Baumer. 105M FRN. prod/rel:
 Lumina
Une Faible Femme, Play
 Faible Femme, Une 1932 d: Max de Vaucorbeil. lps:
 Andre Luguet, Meg Lemonnier, Betty Daussmond. 73M
 FRN. prod/rel: Films Paramount

La Femme de Ta Jeunesse, Play
Invite du Mardi, L' 1949 d: Jacques Deval. lps: Madeleine Robinson, Bernard Blier, Michel Auclair. 100M FRN. *Du the Pour Monsieur Jose* prod/rel: Films Raoul Ploquin, S.N.E.G.

Marie Galante, Paris 1931, Novel
Marie Galante 1934 d: Henry King. lps: Spencer Tracy, Ketti Gallian, Helen Morgan. 90M USA. prod/rel: Fox Film Corp.©

Le Mauvais Garcon, Play
Mauvais Garcon, Le 1921 d: Henri Diamant-Berger. lps: Maurice Chevalier, Marguerite Moreno, Pierre de Guingand. 1415m FRN. prod/rel: Films Diamant

Oh! Brother, Play
Miss Tatlock's Millions 1948 d: Richard Haydn. lps: John Lund, Wanda Hendrix, Barry Fitzgerald. 101M USA. prod/rel: Paramount

Le Rayon Des Jouets, 1951, Play
Ragazza Di Mille Mesi, La 1961 d: Steno. lps: Ugo Tognazzi, Danielle de Metz, Raimondo Vianello. 105M ITL. *Tognazzi E la Minorenne* prod/rel: Amato Film, Cineriz

Romancero, Novel
Altra Meta Del Cielo, L' 1977 d: Franco Rossi. lps: Adriano Celentano, Monica Vitti, Venantino Venantini. 100M ITL. prod/rel: Plexus Film, P.I.C.

Soubrette, Vienna 1938, Play
Say It in French 1938 d: Andrew L. Stone. lps: Ray Milland, Olympe Bradna, Irene Hervey. 70M USA. prod/rel: Paramount Pictures©

Tovarich, Paris 1933, Play
Tovarich 1937 d: Anatole Litvak. lps: Charles Boyer, Claudette Colbert, Basil Rathbone. 94M USA. *Tonight's Our Night* prod/rel: Warner Bros. Pictures©, Anatole Litvak Production

Tovaritch 1935 d: Jacques Deval, Jean Tarride. lps: Andre Lefaur, Pierre Renoir, Irene de Zilahy. 100M FRN. prod/rel: Productions Cinegraphiques Jacques Deval

DEVI, MAHASHWETA
Sangharsh, Story
Sangharsh 1968 d: H. S. Rawail. lps: Dilip Kumar, Vyjayanthimala, Balraj Sahani. 165M IND. *Conflict; The Battle; Sunghursh* prod/rel: Rahul Theatres

DEVIGNE, ROGER
Menilmontant, Novel
Menilmontant 1936 d: Rene Guissart. lps: Gabriel Signoret, Josette Day, Pierre Larquey. 89M FRN. prod/rel: Paris Cine Films

DEVINE, D. M.
The Fifth Cord, Novel
Giornata Nera Per l'Ariete 1971 d: Luigi Bazzoni. lps: Franco Nero, Pamela Tiffin, Maurizio BonugliA. 100M ITL. *Evil Fingers* (UKN); *Desiderio Perverso; The Fifth Cord* prod/rel: B.R.C. Prod. Cin.Che, Dario Film

DEVITT, HAL
The Gay Caballero, Story
Captain Thunder 1930 d: Alan Crosland. lps: Fay Wray, Victor Varconi, Charles Judels. 66M USA. *The Gay Caballero* prod/rel: Warner Brothers Pictures

DEVKULE, JAYANT
Asha Parat Yete, Novel
Pathlaag 1964 d: Raja Paranjape. lps: Bhavana, Kashinath Ghanekar, Ishwar Agarwal. 123M IND. *The Following; Pathlag* prod/rel: Shripad Chitra

DEWETTER, KAREL
Mrtvi Ziji, Novel
Mrtvi Ziji 1922 d: J. S. Kolar. lps: Karel Fiala, Theodor Pistek, Vojtech Zahorik. CZC. *The Dead are Alive; The Dead are Living; Tajemny Prazsky Doktor; The Mysterious Doctor of Prague* prod/rel: Ab, Biografia

DEWLEN, AL
The Night of the Tiger, New York 1956, Novel
Ride Beyond Vengeance 1966 d: Bernard McEveety. lps: Chuck Connors, Michael Rennie, Kathryn Hays. 100M USA. *The Night of the Tiger* prod/rel: Tiger Co., Sentinal Films

Twilight of Honour, New York 1961, Novel
Twilight of Honor 1963 d: Boris Sagal. lps: Richard Chamberlain, Joey Heatherton, Nick Adams. 104M USA. *The Charge Is Murder* (UKN) prod/rel: Perlberg-Seaton Productions, MGM

DEXTER, COLIN
The Dead of Jericho, Novel
Inspector Morse: the Dead of Jericho 1989 d: Alastair Reid. lps: John Thaw, Kevin Whately, Gemma Jones. TVM. 104M UKN. *The Dead of Jericho* prod/rel: Central Tv, Pickwick

Death Is Now My Neighbour, Novel
Inspector Morse: Death Is Now My Neighbour 1997 d: Charles Beeson. lps: John Thaw, Kevin Whately, Judy Loe. TVM. 104M UKN. *Death Is Now My Neighbour* prod/rel: Carlton Tv, Wgbh Boston

Fat Chance, Novel
Inspector Morse: Fat Chance 1989 d: Roy Battersby. lps: John Thaw, Kevin Whately, Maurice Denham. TVM. 104M UKN. *Fat Chance* prod/rel: Zenith Productions

Greeks Bearing Gifts, Novel
Inspector Morse: Greeks Bearing Gifts 1989 d: Adrian Shergold. lps: John Thaw, Kevin Whately, James Hazeldine. TVM. 104M UKN. *Greeks Bearing Gifts* prod/rel: Zenith Productions

Last Bus to Woodstock, Novel
Inspector Morse: Last Bus to Woodstock 1991 d: Peter Duffell. lps: John Thaw, Kevin Whately, Anthony Bate. TVM. 102M UKN. *Last Bus to Woodstock* prod/rel: Zenith Productions

Promised Land, Novel
Inspector Morse: Promised Land 1989 d: John Madden. lps: John Thaw, Kevin Whately, James Grout. TVM. 103M UKN. *Promised Land* prod/rel: Zenith Productions

The Silent World of Nicholas Quinn, Novel
Inspector Morse: the Silent World of Nicholas Quinn 1987 d: Brian Parker. lps: John Thaw, Kevin Whately, Michael Gough. TVM. 101M UKN. *The Silent World of Nicholas Quinn* prod/rel: Zenith Productions

Who Killed Harry Field?, Novel
Inspector Morse: Who Killed Harry Field? 1989 d: Colin Gregg. lps: John Thaw, Kevin Whately, Trevor Byfield. TVM. 104M UKN. *Who Killed Harry Field?* prod/rel: Zenith Productions

DEXTER, PETER
Paris Trout, Novel
Paris Trout 1991 d: Stephen Gyllenhaal. lps: Dennis Hopper, Barbara Hershey, Ed Harris. 100M USA. prod/rel: Viacom Pictures

DEY, FREDERIC VAN RENSSELAER
A Gentleman of Quality, New York 1909, Novel
Gentleman of Quality, A 1919 d: James Young. lps: Earle Williams, Kathryn Adams, Joyce Moore. 5r USA. prod/rel: Vitagraph Co. of America©

The Last Woman, Short Story
Human Collateral 1920 d: Lawrence C. Windom. lps: Corinne Griffith, Webster Campbell, Maurice Costello. 5r USA. prod/rel: Vitagraph Co. of America©

The Three Keys, New York 1909, Novel
Master Stroke, A 1920 d: Chester Bennett. lps: Earle Williams, Vola Vale, Henry A. Barrows. 4436f USA. *The Three Keys* prod/rel: Vitagraph Co. of America©

Three Keys 1925 d: Edward J. Le Saint. lps: Edith Roberts, Jack Mulhall, Gaston Glass. 5800f USA. prod/rel: Banner Productions

DEYGLUN, HENRY
L' Esprit du Mal, Play
Esprit du Mal, L' 1954 d: Jean-Yves Bigras. lps: Rosanna Seaborn, Denyse St.-Pierre, Roger Garceau. 92M CND. *Le Triomphe du Coeur* prod/rel: Frontier Films Ltd.

D'HEE, LOUIS
L' Agadadza, Short Story
Papoul 1929 d: Marc Allegret. lps: Alex Allin, Madame Abdalla, Marcel La Montagne. 59M FRN. prod/rel: Pierre Braunberger, Neo Films

D'HERBEVILLE, MME
Prete-Moi Ton Habit, Play
Prete-Moi Ton Habit 1917 d: Georges MoncA. lps: Jacques Louvigny, Gaby Morlay, Cocyte. 390m FRN. prod/rel: Scagl

D'HERVILLIEZ, GABRIEL
Transigeons, Play
Transigeons 1936 d: Hubert de Rouvres. lps: Robert Darthez, Henri Cremieux, Rene Blancard. 34M FRN.

DI BELMONTE, LUIGI BRUNO
Mani Aperte Sull'acqua, Play
Roma Bene 1971 d: Carlo Lizzani. lps: Senta Berger, Vittorio Caprioli, Virna Lisi. 100M ITL/GRM/FRN. *Roma Bene -Liebe Und Sex in Rom* (GRM); *Love and Sex in Rome; Scandale a Rome* (FRN) prod/rel: Castoro Film (Roma), Marianne Production (Paris)

DI CASTELNUOVO, LEO
Bere O Affogare
Curiosa Eredita, Una 1914. 263m ITL. *A Conditional Bequest* (UKN) prod/rel: Cines

DI CIAULA, TOMMASO
Tommaso Blu, Novel
Tommaso Blu 1986 d: Florian Furtwangler. lps: Alessandro Haber. 90M GRM. prod/rel: Florian Furtwangler, B.R.

DI DONATO, PIETRO
Christ in Concrete, Novel
Give Us This Day 1949 d: Edward Dmytryk. lps: Sam Wanamaker, Lea Padovani, Kathleen Ryan. 120M UKN. *Salt to the Devil* (USA) prod/rel: Plantagenet, General Film Distributors

DI GIACOMO, SALVATORE
A San Francisco, 1896, Play
A San Francisco 1915 d: Gustavo SerenA. lps: Gustavo Serena, Carlo Benetti, Camillo de Riso. 1100m ITL. prod/rel: Caesar Film

Assunta Spina, 1909, Play
Assunta Spina 1915 d: Gustavo Serena, Francesca Bertini (Uncredited). lps: Francesca Bertini, Gustavo Serena, Carlo Benetti. 1690m ITL. prod/rel: Caesar Film

Assunta Spina 1929 d: Roberto Leone Roberti. lps: Rina de Liguoro, Febo Mari, Elio Steiner. 2009m ITL. prod/rel: Julius Caesar Di Giuseppe Barattolo

Assunta Spina 1948 d: Mario Mattoli. lps: Anna Magnani, Antonio Centa, Eduardo de Filippo. 100M ITL. prod/rel: Ora Film, Titanus

Mese Mariano, 1898, Play
Mese Mariano 1909 d: Ubaldo Pittei. lps: Rina de Liguoro, Febo Mari, Andreina Pagnani. 2132m ITL. prod/rel: Giuseppe Barattolo

'O Voto, 1889, Play
Voto, Il 1907 d: Roberto Troncone. 220m ITL. prod/rel: Fratelli Troncone

Voto, Il 1918 d: Mario Gargiulo. lps: Tina Xeo, Mario Gambardella, Rita AlmanovA. 973m ITL. prod/rel: Flegrea Film

Voto, Il 1951 d: Mario Bonnard. lps: Doris Duranti, Maria Grazia Francia, Giorgio Di Lullo. 94M ITL. *The Vote* prod/rel: Ara Film

DI GUIDA, GIULIANO
L' Immortale, Novel
Immortale, L' 1921 d: Guido Schamberg. lps: Marcella Albani, Roberto Villani, G. M. de Vivo. 1463m ITL. prod/rel: S.A. Ambrosio

DI LAMPEDUSA, GIUSEPPE (1896–1957), ITL, Lampedusa, Giuseppe Tomasi, Prince of
Il Gattopardo, Milan 1958, Novel
Gattopardo, Il 1963 d: Luchino Visconti. lps: Burt Lancaster, Alain Delon, Claudia Cardinale. 205M ITL/FRN. *The Leopard* (USA); *Le Guepard* (FRN) prod/rel: Titanus (Roma), S.N.Pathe Cinema

DI MEANA, MARINA RIPA
I Miei Primi Quarant'anni, Novel
Miei Primi Quarant'anni, I 1988 d: Carlo VanzinA. lps: Carol Alt, Elliott Gould, Jean Rochefort. 107M ITL. *My First Forty Years* (UKN) prod/rel: Cg Silver Film, Reteitalia

DI MEGLIO, C.
Book
Sesso in Confessionale 1974 d: Vittorio de Sisti. lps: Alberto Spinoglio, Pier Maria Rossi, Gloria Serbo. 95M ITL. prod/rel: Supernova

DI VORAZA, JACOPO
Leyenda Aurea, Novel
Genoveva de Brabante 1967 d: Jose Luis Monter. lps: Maria Jose Alfonso, Alberto Lupo, Stephen Forsyth. 85M SPN/ITL. *Genoveffa Di Brabante* (ITL) prod/rel: Imprecine (Roma), Hispamer Film (Madrid)

DIAMANT-BERGER, MAURICE
Paris-Paris
Voyage-Surprise 1946 d: Pierre Prevert. lps: Martine Carol, Rene Bourbon, Sinoel. 85M FRN. *Voyage Surprise* prod/rel: Cooperative Generale Du Cinema, Synops

DIAMOND, PAUL
The Chicken Chronicles, Novel
Chicken Chronicles, The 1977 d: Francis Simon. lps: Steve Guttenberg, Ed Lauter, Lisa Reeves. 95M CND/USA. prod/rel: Avco-Embassy

DIAZ CANEJA, GUILLERMO
Pilar Guerra, Novel
Pilar Guerra 1926 d: Jose Buchs. lps: Maria Antonieta Monterreal, Juan de Orduna, Juan Calvo. 42M SPN. prod/rel: Film Linares (Madrid)

DIAZ, P. R.
El Valle de Las Espadas, Novel
Valle de Las Espadas, El 1963 d: Javier Seto. lps: Espartaco Santoni, Cesar Romero, Frankie Avalon. 129M SPN/USA. *The Castilian* (USA); *Valley of the Swords* prod/rel: Cinemagic, M.D.

DIBDIN-PITT, GEORGE
Sweeney Todd; Or the Fiend of Fleet Street, London 1847, Play
Sweeney Todd, the Demon Barber of Fleet Street 1936 d: George King. lps: Tod Slaughter, Bruce Seton, Eve Lister. 68M UKN. *The Demon Barber of Fleet Street* (USA) prod/rel: George King, MGM

DIBNER, MARTIN
The Deep Six, 1953, Novel
Deep Six, The 1958 d: Rudolph Mate. lps: Alan Ladd, Dianne Foster, William Bendix. 110M USA. prod/rel: Warner Bros., Jaguar

DICENTA, JOAQUIN
Curro Vargas, Opera
Curro Vargas 1923 d: Jose Buchs. lps: Ricardo Galache, Angelina Breton, Maria Comendador. 3200m SPN. prod/rel: Film Espanola (Madrid)
Juan Jose, Novel
Life 1928 d: Adelqui Millar. lps: Adelqui Millar, Marie Ault, Manuela Del Rio. 7147f UKN. *Juan Jose* prod/rel: Whitehall Films, New Era
El Lobo, Play
Lobo, El 1928 d: Joaquin DicentA. lps: Pablo Zapico, Carmen Rico, Modesto Rivas. SPN. prod/rel: Ediciones Dicenta Y Garces De Marcilla
Rosario la Cortijera, Opera
Rosario la Cortijera 1923 d: Jose Buchs. lps: Elisa Ruiz Romero, Miguel Cuchet, Manuel San German. 2200m SPN. *Rosario the Girl of the Farm* prod/rel: Films Espanola (Madrid)
El Senor Feudal, Play
Senor Feudal, El 1925 d: Agustin Carrasco. lps: Javier de Rivera, Ramon Meca, Angelina Breton. SPN. prod/rel: la Nacional (Madrid)

DICK, PHILIP K. (1928–1982), USA
Do Androids Dream of Electric Sheep?, 1969, Novel
Blade Runner 1982 d: Ridley Scott. lps: Harrison Ford, Rutger Hauer, Sean Young. 114M USA. prod/rel: Warner Bros.
Second Variety, Short Story
Screamers 1995 d: Christian Duguay. lps: Peter Weller, Roy Dupuis, Charles Powell. 109M USA/CND/JPN. prod/rel: Jaffa Road XXxi Ltd, 3009122 Canada
We Can Remember It for You Wholesale, 1966, Short Story
Total Recall 1990 d: Paul Verhoeven. lps: Arnold Schwarzenegger, Rachel Ticotin, Sharon Stone. 109M USA. prod/rel: Carolco Pictures

DICK, R. A.
The Ghost and Mrs. Muir, Novel
Ghost and Mrs. Muir, The 1947 d: Joseph L. Mankiewicz. lps: Gene Tierney, Rex Harrison, George Sanders. 104M USA. prod/rel: 20ᵗʰ Century-Fox

DICKENS, C. STAFFORD
The Command Performance, New York 1928, Play
Command Performance 1931 d: Walter Lang. lps: Thelma Todd, Neil Hamilton, Mischa Auer. 80M USA. prod/rel: James Cruze Productions, Inc.
Command Performance 1937 d: Sinclair Hill. lps: Arthur Tracy, Lilli Palmer, Mark Daly. 84M UKN. prod/rel: Grosvenor, General Film Distributors
Intimate Relations, 1932, Play
Intimate Relations 1937 d: Clayton Hutton. lps: June Clyde, Garry Marsh, Vera Bogetti. 66M UKN. prod/rel: Tudor Films, Associated British Film Distributors
Plunder in the Air, Play
Live Wire, The 1937 d: Herbert Brenon. lps: Bernard Nedell, Jean Gillie, Hugh Wakefield. 69M UKN. prod/rel: Tudor, Olympic
The Second Mr. Bush, London 1938, Play
Second Mr. Bush, The 1940 d: John Paddy Carstairs. lps: Derrick de Marney, Kay Walsh, Barbara Everest. 56M UKN. prod/rel: British National, Anglo-American

DICKENS, CHARLES (1812–1870), UKN, Dickens, Charles John Huffam
Barnaby Rudge, London 1841, Novel
Barnaby Rudge 1915 d: Thomas Bentley. lps: Tom Powers, Violet Hopson, Stewart Rome. 5325f UKN. prod/rel: Hepworth, Kinematograph Trading Co.
Dolly Varden 1913 d: Charles J. Brabin. lps: Mabel Trunnelle, Willis Secord, Robert Brower. 1000f USA. prod/rel: Edison
Bleak House, London 1853, Novel
Bleak House 1920 d: Maurice Elvey. lps: Constance Collier, Berta Gellardi, E. Vivian Reynolds. 6400f UKN. prod/rel: Ideal
Bleak House 1922 d: H. B. Parkinson. lps: Sybil Thorndike, Betty Doyle, Stacey Gaunt. 3100f UKN. prod/rel: Master Films, British Exhibitors' Films
Bleak House 1985 d: Ross Devenish. lps: Diana Rigg, Denholm Elliott, Fiona Walker. MTV. 390M UKN. prod/rel: BBC
Jo the Crossing Sweeper 1910. 450f UKN. prod/rel: Walturdaw
Jo the Crossing Sweeper 1918 d: Alexander Butler. lps: Unity More, Dora de Winton, Andre Beaulieu. 5000f UKN. prod/rel: Barker, Bolton

The Chimes, London 1845, Short Story
Chimes, The 1914 d: Thomas Bentley. lps: Stewart Rome, Violet Hopson, Warwick Buckland. 2500f UKN. prod/rel: Hepworth, Renters
Chimes, The 1914 d: Herbert Blache. lps: Tom Terriss, Alfred Hemming, Clarence Harvey. 5r USA. prod/rel: U.S. Amusement Corp., World Film Corp.
Christmas Books, 1848
Sogno Dell'usuraio, Il 1910. 206m ITL. *Dream of Old Scrooge* (UKN) prod/rel: Cines
A Christmas Carol, London 1843, Novel
Christmas Carol, A 1908. lps: Tom Ricketts. 1000f USA. prod/rel: Essanay
Christmas Carol, A 1911 d: John H. Collins, J. Searle Dawley (Spv). lps: Charles Ogle, William Bechtel, Carey Lee. 1000f USA. prod/rel: Edison
Christmas Carol, A 1914 d: Harold Shaw. lps: Charles Rock, Edna Flugrath, George Bellamy. 1340f UKN. prod/rel: London, Fenning
Christmas Carol, A 1938 d: Edwin L. Marin. lps: Reginald Owen, Gene Lockhart, Kathleen Lockhart. 69M USA. prod/rel: Metro-Goldwyn-Mayer Corp.
Christmas Carol, A 1956 d: Ralph Levy. lps: Fredric March, Basil Rathbone, Ray Middleton. MTV. 55M USA.
Christmas Carol, A 1960 d: Robert Hartford-Davis. lps: John Hayter, Stewart Brown, Gordon Mulholland. 28M UKN. prod/rel: Anglo-Amalgamated, Alpha
Christmas Carol, A 1979 d: Jean Tych. ANM. 72M ASL.
Christmas Carol, A 1984 d: Clive Donner. lps: George C. Scott, Nigel Davenport, Frank Finlay. TVM. 100M USA. prod/rel: Entertainment Partners
Christmas Carol: Being a Ghost Story of Christmas, A 19— d: Moira Armstrong. lps: Michael Hordern, John Le Mesurier, Bernard Lee. MTV. 58M UKN.
Dickensian Fantasy, A 1933 d: Aveling Ginever. lps: Lawrence Hanray. 10M UKN. prod/rel: Gee Films, Mackane
Ms. Scrooge 1997 d: John Korty. lps: Cicely Tyson, Katherine Helmond, Michael Beach. TVM. 120M USA. prod/rel: Power Pictures, Wilshire Court Prods.
Muppet Christmas Carol, The 1992 d: Brian Henson. lps: Michael Caine, Steven MacKintosh, Meredith Braun. 86M USA. prod/rel: Buena Vista, Walt Disney
Non E Mai Troppo Tadri 1953 d: Filippo Walter Ratti. lps: Paolo Stoppa, Isa Barzizza, Marcello Mastroianni. 90M ITL. *Una Meravigliosa Notte* prod/rel: Olympic Film
Right to Be Happy, The 1916 d: Rupert Julian. lps: Rupert Julian, John Cook, Claire McDowell. 5r USA. *Scrooge the Skinflint* (UKN); *A Christmas Carol* prod/rel: Bluebird Photoplays, Inc.©
Scrooge 1913 d: Leedham Bantock. lps: Seymour Hicks, William Lugg, Leedham Bantock. 2500f UKN. prod/rel: Zenith Films
Scrooge 1922 d: George Wynn. lps: H. V. Esmond. 1280f UKN. prod/rel: Master Films, British Exhibitors' Films
Scrooge 1923 d: Edwin Greenwood. lps: Russell Thorndike, Nina Vanna, Jack Denton. 1600f UKN. prod/rel: British & Colonial, Walturdaw
Scrooge 1928 d: Hugh Croise. lps: Bransby Williams. SND. 9M UKN. prod/rel: British Sound Film Productions
Scrooge 1935 d: Henry Edwards. lps: Seymour Hicks, Donald Calthrop, Robert Cochran. 78M UKN. prod/rel: Twickenham, Twickenham Film Distributors
Scrooge 1951 d: Brian Desmond Hurst. lps: Alastair Sim, Kathleen Harrison, Jack Warner. 86M UKN. *A Christmas Carol* (USA) prod/rel: Renown
Scrooge 1970 d: Ronald Neame. lps: Albert Finney, Alec Guinness, Edith Evans. 118M UKN. prod/rel: Waterbury Films, 20ᵗʰ Century-Fox
Scrooge; Or, Marley's Ghost 1901 d: W. R. Booth. 620f UKN. prod/rel: R. W. Paul
Scrooged 1988 d: Richard Donner. lps: Bill Murray, Karen Allen, John Forsythe. 101M USA. prod/rel: Paramount
Stingiest Man in Town, The 1956 d: Jules Bass, Arthur Rankin Jr.. ANM. 51M USA.
The Cricket on the Hearth, London 1845, Novel
Cricket on the Hearth, The 1909 d: D. W. Griffith. lps: Charles Inslee, Owen Moore, Violet Mersereau. 985f USA. prod/rel: Biograph Co.

Cricket on the Hearth, The 1914 d: Lawrence Marston. lps: Jack Drumier, Alan Hale, Marie Newton. 2r USA. prod/rel: Biograph Co.
Cricket on the Hearth, The 1914 d: Lorimer Johnston. lps: Sydney Ayres, Vivian Rich, Jack Richardson. 2000f USA. prod/rel: American
Cricket on the Hearth, The 1923 d: Lorimer Johnston. lps: Josef Swickard, Fritzi Ridgeway, Paul Gerson. 7r USA. prod/rel: Paul Gerson Pictures, Selznick Distributing Corp.
Grillon du Foyer, Le 1933 d: Robert Boudrioz. lps: Jim Gerald, Gustave Hamilton, Jeanne Boitel. 90M FRN. prod/rel: Acropole-Cine-Coop
David Copperfield, London 1850, Novel
David Copperfield 1911 d: Theodore Marston. lps: Flora Foster, Anna Seer, Frank Crane. 3r USA. prod/rel: Thanhouser
David Copperfield 1913 d: Thomas Bentley. lps: Kenneth Ware, Eric Desmond, Len Bethel. 7500f UKN. prod/rel: Hepworth, Walturdaw
David Copperfield 1922 d: Anders W. Sandberg. DNM.
David Copperfield 1935 d: George Cukor. lps: Freddie Bartholomew, Frank Lawton, W. C. Fields. 133M USA. *David Copperfield; The Personal History Adventures Experience and Observation of David Copperfield the Younger* prod/rel: Metro-Goldwyn-Mayer, Inc.
David Copperfield 1965 d: Marcel Cravenne. lps: Didier Haudepin, Bernard Verley, Michel Duchaussoy. MTV. 140M FRN.
David Copperfield 1969 d: Delbert Mann. lps: Richard Attenborough, Cyril Cusack, Edith Evans. TVM. 118M UKN. prod/rel: Omnibus Prods., Sagittarius Prods.
David Copperfield 1983 d: Alex Nicholas, Ian MacKenzie. ANM. 72M ASL.
Little Emily 1911 d: Frank Powell. lps: Florence Barker. 1254f UKN. prod/rel: Britannia Films, Pathe
Love and the Law 1910 d: Edwin S. Porter. 1000f USA. prod/rel: Edison
Dombey and Son, London 1848, Novel
Dombey and Son 1917 d: Maurice Elvey. lps: Norman McKinnel, Lilian Braithwaite, Hayford Hobbs. 6800f UKN. prod/rel: Ideal
Rich Man's Folly 1931 d: John Cromwell. lps: George Bancroft, Frances Dee, Robert Ames. 80M USA. prod/rel: Paramount Publix Corp.©
Great Expectations, London 1861, Novel
Great Expectations 1917 d: Robert G. Vignola, Joseph Kaufman. lps: Louise Huff, Jack Pickford, Frank Losee. 5r USA. prod/rel: Famous Players Film Co.©, Paramount Pictures Corp.
Great Expectations 1934 d: Stuart Walker. lps: Henry Hull, Phillips Holmes, Jane Wyatt. 102M USA. prod/rel: Universal Pictures Corp.©
Great Expectations 1946 d: David Lean. lps: John Mills, Valerie Hobson, Bernard Miles. 118M UKN. prod/rel: General Film Distributors, Cineguild
Great Expectations 1975 d: Joseph Hardy. lps: Michael York, Sarah Miles, James Mason. TVM. 124M UKN/USA. prod/rel: Itc, Transcontinental Film Productions
Great Expectations 1982 d: Jean Tych. ANM. 84M ASL.
Great Expectations 1982 d: Julian Amyes. lps: Stratford Johns, Gerry Sundquist, Joan Hickson. MTV. 289M UKN.
Great Expectations 1989 d: Kevin Connor. lps: Anthony Hopkins, Jean Simmons, Anthony Calf. MTV. F USA. prod/rel: Harlech Tv, Channel 3
Great Expectations 1998 d: Alfonso Cuaron. lps: Ethan Hawke, Gwyneth Paltrow, Hank AzariA. 111M USA. prod/rel: Art Linson, Twentieth Century Fox Film Corp.©
Le Grillon du Foyer, Short Story
Grillon du Foyer, Le 1922 d: Jean Manoussi. lps: Marcel Vibert, Sabine Landray, Suzanne Dantes. 1800m FRN. prod/rel: Eclipse
Hard Times, London 1854, Novel
Hard Times 1915 d: Thomas Bentley. lps: Bransby Williams, Leon M. Lion, Dorothy Bellew. 4000f UKN. prod/rel: Transatlantic
Hard Times 1977 d: John Irvin. lps: Patrick Allen, Timothy West, Alan Dobie. MTV. 200M UKN. prod/rel: Granada, Wnet
Hard Times 1995 d: Peter Barnes. lps: Alan Bates, Bob Peck, Bill Paterson. TVM. 120M UKN/USA.

Tempos Dificeis 1988 d: Joao Botelho. lps: Henrique Viana, Julia Britton, Eunice Munoz. 96M PRT/UKN. *Hard Times*; *Tempo Dificeis Este Tempo*; *Tiempos Dificiles* prod/rel: Joao Botelho, Artificial Eye

The Life and Adventures of Martin Chuzzlewit, London 1844, Novel
Martin Chuzzlewit 1912 d: Oscar Apfel, J. Searle Dawley. lps: Guy Hedlund, Harold M. Shaw, Marion Brooks. 3r USA. prod/rel: Edison
Martin Chuzzlewit 1914 d: Travers Vale. lps: Alan Hale. 2r USA. prod/rel: Biograph Co.
Martin Chuzzlewit 1995 d: Pedr James. lps: Paul Scofield, Pauline Turner, Tom Wilkinson. TVM. 325M UKN/USA. prod/rel: BBC Pebble Mill, Wgbh Boston

Little Dorrit, London 1857, Novel
Klein Dorrit 1934 d: Carl Lamac. lps: Anny Ondra, Gustav Waldau, Hilde Hildebrand. 93M GRM. prod/rel: Ondra, Karp
Little Dorrit 1913 d: James Kirkwood. lps: Maude Fealy, Alphonse Ethier, Harry Benham. SHT USA. prod/rel: Thanhouser
Little Dorrit 1920 d: Sidney Morgan. lps: Lady Tree, Langhorne Burton, Joan Morgan. 6858f UKN. prod/rel: Progress, Butcher's Film Service
Little Dorrit 1987 d: Christine Edzard. lps: Derek Jacobi, Alec Guinness, Cyril Cusack. 360M UKN. prod/rel: Sands, Cannon

The Mystery of Edwin Drood, London 1870, Novel
Mystery of Edwin Drood 1935 d: Stuart Walker. lps: Claude Rains, Douglass Montgomery, Heather Angel. 87M USA. prod/rel: Universal Pictures Corp.©
Mystery of Edwin Drood, The 1909 d: Arthur Gilbert. lps: Cooper Willis, Nancy Bevington, James Annand. 1030f UKN. prod/rel: Gaumont
Mystery of Edwin Drood, The 1914 d: Tom Terriss, Herbert Blache. lps: Tom Terriss, Faye Cusick, Alfred Hemming. 5r USA. prod/rel: World Film Corp., Shubert Feature
Mystery of Edwin Drood, The 1993 d: Timothy Forder. lps: Robert Powell, Nanette Newman, Gemma Craven. 112M UKN. prod/rel: Mayfair, First Standard Media

Nicholas Nickleby, London 1870, Novel
Dotheboys Hall; Or, Nicholas Nickleby 1903 d: Alf Collins. lps: William Carrington. 225f UKN. prod/rel: Gaumont
Life and Adventures of Nicholas Nickleby, The 1982 d: Jim Goddard. lps: Roger Rees, David Threlfall, Emily Richard. MTV. 540M UKN. prod/rel: Primetime, Channel Four
Nicholas Nickleby 1912 d: George Nicholls. lps: Harry Benham, Mignon Anderson, Frances Gibson. 2r USA. prod/rel: Thanhouser
Nicholas Nickleby 1948 d: Alberto Cavalcanti. lps: Cedric Hardwicke, Stanley Holloway, Alfred Drayton. 105M UKN. *The Life and Adventures of Nicholas Nickleby* prod/rel: Ealing Studios, General Film Distributors
Yorkshire School, A 1910. 800f USA. prod/rel: Edison

The Old Curiosity Shop, London 1841, Novel
Bottega Dell'antiquario, La 1921 d: Mario Corsi. lps: Gustavo Salvini, Egle Valery, Renato ViscA. 1387m ITL. prod/rel: G. Salvini
Mister Quilp 1974 d: Michael Tuchner. lps: Anthony Newley, David Hemmings, Mona Washbourne. 119M UKN. *The Old Curiosity Shop*; *Quilp* prod/rel: Reader's Digest
Old Curiosity Shop, The 1909. 1000f USA. prod/rel: Essanay
Old Curiosity Shop, The 1911 d: Theodore Marston. lps: Frank Crane, Harry Benham, Marguerite Snow. 1000f USA. prod/rel: Thanhouser
Old Curiosity Shop, The 1912 d: Frank Powell. 990f UKN. prod/rel: Britannia Films, Pathe
Old Curiosity Shop, The 1913 d: Thomas Bentley. lps: Mai Deacon, Warwick Buckland, E. Felton. 5300f UKN. prod/rel: Hepworth, Renters
Old Curiosity Shop, The 1921 d: Thomas Bentley. lps: Mabel Poulton, William Lugg, Hugh E. Wright. 6587f UKN. prod/rel: Welsh-Pearson, Jury
Old Curiosity Shop, The 1934 d: Thomas Bentley. lps: Ben Webster, Elaine Benson, Hay Petrie. 95M UKN. prod/rel: British International Pictures, Wardour
Old Curiosity Shop, The 1989 d: Warwick Gilbert. ANM. 75M ASL.
Old Curiosity Shop, The 1995 d: Kevin Connor. lps: Peter Ustinov, Tom Courtenay, Sally Walsh. TVM. 240M USA/UKN.

Oliver Twist, London 1838, Novel
Fagin 1922 d: H. B. Parkinson. lps: Ivan Berlyn. 1260f UKN. prod/rel: Master Films, British Exhibitors' Films
Mrs. Corney Makes Tea 1913 d: Wilfred Noy. 1000f UKN. prod/rel: Clarendon
Nancy 1922 d: H. B. Parkinson. lps: Sybil Thorndike, Ivan Berlyn. 1578f UKN. prod/rel: Master Films, British Exhibitors' Films
Oliver! 1968 d: Carol Reed. lps: Ron Moody, Shani Wallis, Oliver Reed. 146M UKN. prod/rel: Warwick Film Productions, Romulus Films
Oliver & Company 1989 d: George Scribner. ANM. 72M USA. prod/rel: Disney
Oliver and the Artful Dodger 1972 d: William Hanna, Joseph BarberA. ANM. 95M USA. prod/rel: Hanna-Barbera
Oliver Twist 1909 d: J. Stuart Blackton. lps: Elita Proctor Otis, William Humphrey. 995f USA. prod/rel: Vitagraph Co. of America
Oliver Twist 1912 d: Thomas Bentley. lps: Ivy Millais, John McMahon, Harry Royston. 3700f UKN. prod/rel: Hepworth
Oliver Twist 1912. lps: Nat C. Goodwin, Lillian Delesque, Charles Rogers. 5r USA. prod/rel: General Film Publicity & Sales Co., State Rights
Oliver Twist 1916 d: James Young. lps: Marie Doro, Hobart Bosworth, Tully Marshall. 5r USA. prod/rel: Jesse L. Lasky Feature Play Co.©, Paramount Pictures Corp.
Oliver Twist 1922 d: Frank Lloyd. lps: Jackie Coogan, Lon Chaney, Gladys Brockwell. 7761f USA. prod/rel: Jackie Coogan Productions, Associated First National Pictures
Oliver Twist 1933 d: William J. Cowen. lps: Dickie Moore, Irving Pichel, William "Stage" Boyd. 80M USA. prod/rel: Monogram Pictures Corp.©
Oliver Twist 1940 d: David Bradley. F USA. prod/rel: Brandon
Oliver Twist 1948 d: David Lean. lps: Robert Newton, Alec Guinness, Kay Walsh. 116M UKN. prod/rel: General Film Distributors, Cineguild
Oliver Twist 1974 d: Hal Sutherland. ANM. 75M USA.
Oliver Twist 1982 d: Richard Slapczynski. ANM. 72M ASL.
Oliver Twist 1982 d: Clive Donner. lps: George C. Scott, Tim Curry, Michael Hordern. TVM. 103M USA. prod/rel: Claridge Group Ltd., Grafton
Oliver Twist 1985 d: Gareth Davies. lps: Lysette Anthony, Michael Attwell, Scott Funnell. MTV. 333M UKN.
Oliver Twist, Jr. 1921 d: Millard Webb. lps: Harold Goodwin, Lillian Hall, George Nichols. 5r USA. *The Fortunate Fugitive* prod/rel: Fox Film Corp.
Olivier Twist 1908-10 d: Camille de Morlhon. 280m FRN.
Olivier Twist 1910 d: Andre Calmettes. lps: Baron Fils, Jean Perier, Madeleine Guitty. FRN. prod/rel: le Film d'Art
Storia Di un Orfano 1911. 435m ITL. *Oliver Twist* prod/rel: Cines

Our Mutual Friend, London 1864, Novel
Eugene Wrayburn 1911. lps: Darwin Karr, Richard Ridgeley, Bliss Milford. 1000f USA. prod/rel: Edison

The Pickwick Papers, London 1836, Novel
Adventures of Mr. Pickwick, The 1921 d: Thomas Bentley. lps: Frederick Volpe, Mary Brough, Bransby Williams. 6000f UKN. prod/rel: Ideal
Mr. Pickwick in a Double Bedded Room 1913 d: Wilfred Noy. 1000f UKN. prod/rel: Clarendon
Mr. Pickwick's Predicament 1912 d: J. Searle Dawley. lps: Charles Ogle, Mary Fuller, Marc McDermott. 1000f USA. prod/rel: Edison
Pickwick Papers Parts 1 & 2, The 1912 d: Larry Trimble. lps: John Bunny, James Pryor, Sidney Hunt. 2000f UKN/USA. prod/rel: Vitagraph Co.
Pickwick Papers, The 1952 d: Noel Langley. lps: James Hayter, Nigel Patrick, James Donald. 115M UKN. prod/rel: Renown
Pickwick Papers, The 1985 d: Brian Lighthill. lps: Nigel Stock. MTV. 148M UKN.
Pickwick Papers, The 1985 d: Warwick Gilbert. ANM. 73M ASL.
Pickwick Versus Bardell 1913 d: Wilfred Noy. 1000f UKN. prod/rel: Clarendon

Sparkins, Short Story
Horatio Sparkins 1913 d: Van Dyke Brooke. lps: Courtenay Foote, Flora Finch. 1000f USA. prod/rel: Vitagraph

A Tale of Two Cities, London 1859, Novel
Only Way, The 1925 d: Herbert Wilcox. lps: John Martin-Harvey, Madge Stuart, Betty Faire. 11r UKN. *A Tale of Two Cities* prod/rel: Herbert Wilcox, First National Pictures
Tale of Two Cities, A 19— d: Michael E. Briant. lps: Paul Shelley, Nigel Stock, Ralph Michael. MTV. 172M UKN.
Tale of Two Cities, A 1911 d: William Humphrey. lps: Florence Turner, Maurice Costello, Norma Talmadge. 3021f USA. prod/rel: Vitagraph Co. of America
Tale of Two Cities, A 1917 d: Frank Lloyd. lps: William Farnum, Jewel Carmen, Charles Clary. 7r USA. prod/rel: Fox Film Corp., William Fox©
Tale of Two Cities, A 1922 d: W. C. Rowden. lps: J. Fisher White, Clive Brook, Ann Trevor. 1174f UKN. prod/rel: Master Films, British Exhibitors' Films
Tale of Two Cities, A 1936 d: Jack Conway, W. S.Van Dyke (Uncredited). lps: Ronald Colman, Elizabeth Allan, Edna May Oliver. 123M USA. prod/rel: Metro-Goldwyn-Mayer Corp.©
Tale of Two Cities, A 1958 d: Ralph Thomas. lps: Dirk Bogarde, Dorothy Tutin, Cecil Parker. 117M UKN. prod/rel: Rank, Rank Film Distributors
Tale of Two Cities, A 1980 d: Jim Goddard. lps: Chris Sarandon, Peter Cushing, Kenneth More. TVM. 156M USA.
Tale of Two Cities, A 1984 d: Warwick Gilbert, Di Rudder. ANM. 72M ASL.
Tale of Two Cities, A 1989 d: Philippe Monnier. lps: James Wilby, John Mills, Xavier Deluc. TVM. 188M UKN/FRN. *Un Conte de Deux Villes* (FRN) prod/rel: Granada Tv, Dune Prouction

DICKENS, MONICA (1915–, UKN, Dickens, Monica Enid)
One Pair of Feet, Novel
Lamp Still Burns, The 1943 d: Maurice Elvey. lps: Rosamund John, Stewart Granger, Godfrey Tearle. 90M UKN. prod/rel: General Film Distributors, Two Cities

DICKEY, JAMES (1923–, USA
Deliverance, 1970, Novel
Deliverance 1972 d: John Boorman. lps: Jon Voight, Burt Reynolds, Ned Beatty. 108M USA. prod/rel: Warner Bros.

DICKEY, PAUL
The Broken Wing, New York 1920, Play
Broken Wing, The 1923 d: Tom Forman. lps: Kenneth Harlan, Miriam Cooper, Walter Long. 6216f USA. prod/rel: B. P. Schulberg Productions, Preferred Pictures
Broken Wing, The 1932 d: Lloyd Corrigan. lps: Lupe Velez, Leo Carrillo, Melvyn Douglas. 74M USA. prod/rel: Paramount Publix Corp.
Cape Smoke, 1925, Play
Black Magic 1929 d: George B. Seitz. lps: Josephine Dunn, Earle Foxe, John Holland. 5855f USA. prod/rel: Fox Film Corp.
The Ghost Breaker, New York 1909, Play
Ghost Breaker, The 1914 d: Cecil B. de Mille, Oscar Apfel. lps: H. B. Warner, Theodore Roberts, Rita Stanwood. 5r USA. prod/rel: Jesse L. Lasky Feature Play Co.©, Paramount Pictures Corp.
Ghost Breaker, The 1922 d: Alfred E. Green. lps: Wallace Reid, Lila Lee, Walter Hiers. 5130f USA. prod/rel: Famous Players-Lasky, Paramount Pictures
Ghost Breakers, The 1940 d: George Marshall. lps: Bob Hope, Paulette Goddard, Richard Carlson. 82M USA. prod/rel: Paramount Pictures©
Scared Stiff 1953 d: George Marshall. lps: Dean Martin, Jerry Lewis, Lizabeth Scott. 108M USA. prod/rel: Paramount
Lights Out, New York 1922, Play
Crashing Hollywood 1938 d: Lew Landers. lps: Lee Tracy, Paul Guilfoyle, Joan Woodbury. 61M USA. *Lights Out* prod/rel: RKO Radio Pictures, Inc.
Lights Out 1923 d: Alfred Santell. lps: Ruth Stonehouse, Walter McGrail, Marie Astaire. 6938f USA. prod/rel: R-C Pictures, Film Booking Offices of America
The Lincoln Highwayman, New York 1917, Play
Lincoln Highwayman, The 1920 d: Emmett J. Flynn. lps: William Russell, Lois Lee, Frank Brownlee. 5r USA. prod/rel: Fox Film Corp., William Fox©
The Misleading Lady, New York 1913, Play
Misleading Lady, The 1916 d: Arthur Berthelet. lps: Henry B. Walthall, Edna Mayo, Sidney Ainsworth. 5r USA. prod/rel: Essanay Film Mfg. Co.©, V-L-S-E, Inc.
Misleading Lady, The 1920 d: George Irving, George W. Terwilliger. lps: Bert Lytell, Lucy Cotton, Cyril Chadwick. 6r USA. prod/rel: Metro Pictures Corp.©

Misleading Lady, The 1932 d: Stuart Walker. lps: Claudette Colbert, Edmund Lowe, Stuart Erwin. 75M USA. *Sensation* prod/rel: Paramount Publix Corp.©

DICKINSON, THOMAS W.
The Unbroken Road, Providence, R.I. 1909, Play
Unbroken Road, The 1915. lps: Mary Nash, William H. Tooker, Alexander Gaden. 5r USA. prod/rel: Life Photo Film Corp., State Rights

DICKSON, JUDGE HARRIS
The Kangaroo, 1913, Short Story
Kangaroo, The 1914. 5r USA. prod/rel: Eclair Film Co., World Film Corp.

DIDELOT, FRANCIS
Adam Est Eve, Novel
Adam Est Eve 1953 d: Rene Gaveau. lps: Jean Carmet, Michel Carvel, Jean Tissier. 92M FRN. *Adam Est Eve -la Nouvelle Legende Des Sexes*; *Adam Is Eve -the New Legend of the Sexes* prod/rel: Orex, Fernand Rivers
Les Gosses Menent l'Enquete, Novel
Gosses Menent l'Enquete, Les 1946 d: Maurice Labro. lps: Constant Remy, Lise Topart, Rene Genin. 85M FRN. *L' Etrange Mort de Monsieur Crauqual*; *Le Criminel a Peur Des Gosses*; *Drame Au College* prod/rel: France Production
Le Septieme Jure, Paris 1958, Novel
Septieme Jure, Le 1962 d: Georges Lautner. lps: Bernard Blier, Daniele Delorme, Maurice Biraud. 105M FRN. *The Seventh Juror* (USA) prod/rel: Orexfilm

DIDELOT, ROGER-F.
La machine a Predire la Mort, Novel
Monde Tremblera, Le 1939 d: Richard Pottier. lps: Claude Dauphin, Roger Duchesne, Erich von Stroheim. 108M FRN. *Les Revolte Des Vivants*; *The Death Predicter*; *The Revolt of the Living*; *The World Will Shake* prod/rel: C.I.C.C.

DIDEROT, DENIS (1713–1784), FRN
Jacques le Fataliste Et Son Maitre, 1797, Novel
Dames du Bois de Boulogne, Les 1945 d: Robert Bresson. lps: Paul Bernard, Maria Casares, Elina Labourdette. 90M FRN. *The Ladies of the Bois de Boulogne*; *Ladies of the Park* (USA); *Les Dames de Port Royal* prod/rel: Films Raoul Ploquin
La Religieuse, 1796, Novel
Suzanne Simonin, la Religieuse de Diderot 1965 d: Jacques Rivette. lps: Anna Karina, Liselotte Pulver, Micheline Presle. 120M FRN. *La Religieuse* (UKN); *La Religieuse de Diderot*; *The Nun* (USA) prod/rel: Georges De Beauregard, Rome-Paris Films

DIDION, JOAN (1934–, USA
Play It As It Lays, 1970, Novel
Play It As It Lays 1972 d: Frank Perry. lps: Tuesday Weld, Anthony Perkins, Tammy Grimes. 99M USA.

DIDRIKSON, BABE (1914–1956), USA, Didrikson, Mildred Ella
This Life I've Led, Autobiography
Babe 1975 d: Buzz Kulik. lps: Susan Clark, Alex Karras, Slim Pickens. TVM. 100M USA. prod/rel: MGM

DIEHL, MARGARET
Men, Novel
Men 1997 d: Zoe Clarke-Williams. lps: Sean Young, John Heard, Dylan Walsh. 92M USA. prod/rel: Shonderosa Prods., Hillman/Williams Prods.

DIEHL, WILLIAM
Sharky's machine, Novel
Sharky's machine 1981 d: Burt Reynolds. lps: Burt Reynolds, Vittorio Gassman, Brian Keith. 122M USA. prod/rel: Warner Bros.

DIESEL, EUGEN
Rudolf Diesel, Biography
Diesel 1942 d: Gerhard Lamprecht. lps: Willy Birgel, Paul Wegener, Hilde Weissner. 110M GRM. prod/rel: UFA

DIETRICH, NOAH
Howard: the Amazing Mr. Hughes, Book
Amazing Howard Hughes, The 1977 d: William A. Graham. lps: Tommy Lee Jones, Ed Flanders, James Hampton. TVM. 215M USA. prod/rel: Emi, Roger Gimbel Productions

DIETS, HANS EMIL
Das Bekenntnis Der Ina Kahr, Novel
Bekenntnis Der Ina Kahr, Das 1954 d: G. W. Pabst. lps: Curd Jurgens, Elisabeth Muller, Margot Trooger. 102M GRM. *The Confessions of Ina Kahr* (USA); *Afraid to Love*; *Afraid to Live*; *Ina Kahr's Confession* prod/rel: Omega, N.F.

DIETZ, CURT REINHARD
Heimkehr Ins Leben, Novel
Roman Eines Arztes 1939 d: Jurgen von Alten. lps: Albrecht Schoenhals, Camilla Horn, Maria Andergast. 96M GRM. prod/rel: Aca, Adler

DIETZ, HOWARD
The Band Wagon, New York 1931, Play
Dancing in the Dark 1949 d: Irving Reis. lps: William Powell, Betsy Drake, Mark Stevens. 92M USA. prod/rel: 20th Century Fox

DIETZ, LEW
A Seal Called Andre, Novel
Andre 1994 d: George Miller. lps: Tina Majorino, Chelsea Field, Shane Meier. 95M USA. prod/rel: Kushner-Locke

DIETZENSCHMIDT
Die Kleine Sklavin, Play
Kleine Sklavin, Die 1928 d: Jacob Fleck, Luise Fleck. lps: Grete Mosheim, Fred Louis Lerch, Fritz Richard. 2021m GRM. prod/rel: Essem-Film

DIEUDONNE, ALBERT
Un Lache, Play
Gloire Rouge, La 1917 d: Albert Dieudonne. lps: Pierre Pradier, Maillard, Cebron Norbens. 900m FRN. prod/rel: Film a.D.
Son Crime 1922 d: Albert Dieudonne. lps: Jean Dax, Suzy Pierson, Armand Numes. 1800m FRN. prod/rel: Devallee
La Saisie, Play
Saisie, La 1932 d: Jean Margueritte. lps: Robert Arnoux, Arielle, Fernand Frey. SHT FRN. prod/rel: Paramount

DIEUDONNE, ROBERT
Novel
Finisce Sempre Cosi 1939 d: Enrique T. Susini. lps: Vittorio de Sica, Nedda Francy, Roberto Rey. 68M ITL. prod/rel: Excelsior Film, Minerva Film
La Guitare Et le Jazz-Band, Play
Guitare Et le Jazz-Band, La 1923 d: Gaston Roudes. lps: Violette Trezel, France Dhelia, Jean Devalde. 1725m FRN. prod/rel: Films Sphynx

DIEZ PEYDRO, VICENTE
Rejas Y Votos, Opera
Rejas Y Votos 1925 d: Rafael Salvador. lps: Pablo Alvarez Rubio, Coppelia, Senor Valle. SPN. prod/rel: Rafael Salvador Film (Madrid)

DIFRANCO, ANTHONY
Short Story
Garden of Redemption, The 1997 d: Thomas Michael Donnelly. lps: Anthony Lapaglia, Embeth Davidtz, Dan HedayA. 100M USA. prod/rel: Showtime Networks, Paramount

DIGHTON, JOHN
The Happiest Days of Your Life, London 1947, Play
Happiest Days of Your Life, The 1950 d: Frank Launder. lps: Alastair Sim, Margaret Rutherford, Joyce Grenfell. 91M UKN. prod/rel: British Lion Production Assets, Individual
Who Goes There!, London 1951, Play
Who Goes There! 1952 d: Anthony Kimmins. lps: Nigel Patrick, Valerie Hobson, Peggy Cummins. 85M UKN. *The Passionate Sentry* (USA) prod/rel: British Lion Production Assets, London Films

DIGNON, EDWARD
The Admiral's Secret, 1928, Play
Admiral's Secret, The 1934 d: Guy Newall. lps: Edmund Gwenn, Hope Davy, James Raglan. 63M UKN. prod/rel: Real Art, Radio
Ask Beccles, London 1926, Play
Ask Beccles 1933 d: Redd Davis. lps: Garry Marsh, Mary Newland, Abraham Sofaer. 68M UKN. prod/rel: British and Dominions, Paramount British
The Lion and the Lamb, Play
River Wolves, The 1934 d: George Pearson. lps: Helga Moray, Michael Hogan, John Mills. 56M UKN. prod/rel: Real Art, Radio
The Sentence of Death, Play
Sentence of Death, The 1927 d: Miles Mander. lps: Owen Nares, Dorothy Boyd, Peter Evan Thomas. SND. 9M UKN. *His Great Moment* prod/rel: de Forest Phonofilms

DIJAN, PHILIPPE
37°2 le Matin, Novel
37°2 le Matin 1985 d: Jean-Jacques Beineix. lps: Jean-Hugues Anglade, Beatrice Dalle, Gerard Darmon. 184M FRN. *Betty Blue* (UKN); *37.2 Degrees in the Morning* prod/rel: Gaumont, Constellation

DILLON, BARBARA
A Mom for Christmas, Novel
Mom for Christmas, A 1990 d: George Miller. lps: Olivia Newton-John, Doug Sheehan, Juliet Sorcey. TVM. 100M USA. *A Mom By Magic*

DILLON, BOB
Amateur Night, Story
I'll Remember April 1945 d: Harold Young. lps: Gloria Jean, Kirby Grant, Milburn Stone. 63M USA. prod/rel: Universal

DIMITRIJEVIC, BRANKO
Oktoberfest, Novel
Oktoberfest 1987 d: Dragan KresojA. lps: Svetislav Bule Goncic, Zoran Cvijanovic, Zarko Lausevic. 103M YGS. prod/rel: Inex Film

DIMITROVA, BLAGA
Lavina, 1971, Novel
Lavina 1981 d: Hristo Piskov, Irina AktashevA. lps: Ivan Ivanov, Vanya Tsvetkova, Lyuben Chatalov. 153M BUL. *Avalanche*
Patuvane Kam Sebe Si, 1965, Novel
Otklonenie 1967 d: Grisha Ostrovski, Todor Stoyanov. lps: Ivan Andonov, Nevena Kokanova, Stefan Iliev. 90M BUL. *Side Track*; *Sidetrack*; *Malko Otklonenie*

DIMOV, DIMITAR
Osadeni Dushi, 1945, Novel
Osadeni Dushi 1975 d: Vulo Radev. lps: Edith Szalai, Jan Englert, Russi Chanev. 137M BUL. *Ossudeni Dushu*; *Damned Souls*; *Doomed Souls*
Tyutyun, 1951, Novel
Tyutyun 1962 d: Nicolai Korabov. lps: Nevena Kokanova, Stefan Peichev, Peter Slabakov. 150M BUL. *Tobacco*; *Tiutiun*; *Tutune*; *Tjutjun*; *Tiutun*

DIN, JALAL
The Wild Elephant, Short Story
Maya 1966 d: John Berry. lps: Clint Walker, Jay North, I. S. Johar. 91M USA. prod/rel: King Brothers Production

DINELLI, MEL
The Man, Play
Beware My Lovely 1952 d: Harry Horner. lps: Ida Lupino, Robert Ryan, Taylor Holmes. 77M USA. *Day Without End* prod/rel: RKO Radio

DINGWELL, JOYCE
The House in the Timberwoods, Novel
Winds of Jarrah, The 1983 d: Mark Egerton. lps: Terence Donovan, Susan Lyons, Harold Hopkins. 80M ASL. prod/rel: Film Corporation of Western Australia©, Australian Film Commission

DINIS, JULIO
Os Fidalgos Da Casa Mourisca, 1871, Novel
Fidalgos Da Casa Mourisca, Os 1938 d: Arthur Duarte. lps: Henrique Campos. 117M PRT. *The Noblemen from Casa Mourisca*
A Morgadinha Dos Canaviais, 1868, Novel
Morgadinha Dos Canaviais, A 1949 d: Caetano Bonucci. lps: Eunice Munoz. 93M PRT.
As Pupilas Do Senhor Reitor, 1867, Novel
Pupilas Do Senhor Reitor, As 1960 d: Perdigao QueirogA. lps: Isabel de Castro, Americo Coimbra, Humberto MadeirA. 110M PRT. *The Pupils of the Dean*
Pupilas Do Senhor Reitor, As 1935 d: Jose Leitao de Barros. lps: Raul Solnado, Isabel de Castro. 102M PRT. *The Students of Mr. Reitor*; *The Pupils of the Dean*

DINNEEN, JOSEPH F.
500.000 - and Got Away With It They Stole $2, Story
Six Bridges to Cross 1955 d: Joseph Pevney. lps: Tony Curtis, Julie Adams, George Nader. 96M USA. prod/rel: Universal-International

DINNER, WILLIAM
Alive and Kicking, Play
Alive and Kicking 1958 d: Cyril Frankel. lps: Sybil Thorndike, Kathleen Harrison, Estelle Winwood. 94M UKN. prod/rel: Diador, Ab-Pathe
The Late Edwina Black, London 1949, Play
Late Edwina Black, The 1951 d: Maurice Elvey. lps: David Farrar, Geraldine Fitzgerald, Roland Culver. 78M UKN. *Obsessed* (USA) prod/rel: Independent Film Distributors, Elvey-Gartside

DIPEGO, GERALD
Keeper of the City, Novel
Keeper of the City 1992 d: Bobby Roth. lps: Louis Gossett Jr., Peter Coyote, Renee Soutendijk. TVM. 95M USA. prod/rel: Viacom Pictures

DISCH, THOMAS M.
The Brave Little Toaster, Novel
Brave Little Toaster, The 1987 d: Jerry Rees. ANM. 90M USA. prod/rel: Hyperion, Kushner

DISNEY, DORIS MILES (1907–1976), USA
Do Not Fold Spindle Or Mutilate, Novel
Do Not Fold, Spindle Or Mutilate 1971 d: Ted Post. lps: Helen Hayes, Myrna Loy, Mildred Natwick. TVM. 74M USA. prod/rel: Lee Rich Productions
Family Skeleton, 1949, Novel
Stella 1950 d: Claude Binyon. lps: Ann Sheridan, Victor Mature, David Wayne. 83M USA. prod/rel: 20th Century-Fox
Fugitive Lady, Novel
Strada Buia, La 1949 d: Sidney Salkow, Marino Girolami. lps: Janis Paige, Binnie Barnes, Antonio CentA. 85M ITL/USA. *Fugitive Lady* (USA) prod/rel: Republic Pictures Corp., Venus Prods.

Night of Clear Choice, Novel
Yesterday's Child 1977 d: Corey Allen, Bob Rosenbaum. lps: Shirley Jones, Ross Martin, Claude Akins. TVM. 78M USA. prod/rel: Paramount

Only Couples Need Apply, Novel
Betrayal 1974 d: Gordon Hessler. lps: Amanda Blake, Tisha Sterling, Dick Haymes. TVM. 78M USA. prod/rel: Metromedia Productions

The Straw Man, Novel
Straw Man, The 1953 d: Donald Taylor. lps: Dermot Walsh, Clifford Evans, Lana Morris. 74M UKN. prod/rel: United Artists, Hedgerley

DISRAELI, BENJAMIN (1804–1881), UKN
Sybil, 1846, Novel
Sybil 1921 d: Jack Denton. lps: Evelyn Brent, Cowley Wright, Hubert Gordon Hopkirk. 5300f UKN. prod/rel: Ideal

DITLEVSON, TOVE (1918–1976), DNM
Barndommens Gade, 1943, Novel
Barndommens Gade 1986 d: Astrid Henning-Jensen. lps: Sofie Grabol, Kirsten Lehfeldt, Vigga Bro. 90M DNM. *Street of My Childhood; Early Spring; Street of Childhood*

DITRICHSTEIN, LEO
Are You a Mason?, New York 1901, Play
Are You a Mason? 1915 d: Thomas N. Heffron. lps: John Barrymore, Alfred Hickman, Charles Dixon. 5r USA. *The Joiner* prod/rel: Famous Players Film Co., Paramount Pictures Corp.
Are You a Mason? 1934 d: Henry Edwards. lps: Sonnie Hale, Robertson Hare, Davy Burnaby. 85M UKN. prod/rel: Real Art, Universal

The Great Lover, New York 1915, Play
Great Lover, The 1920 d: Frank Lloyd. lps: John Sainpolis, Claire Adams, John Davidson. 5202f USA. prod/rel: Goldwyn Pictures Corp.©, Frank Lloyd Productions
Great Lover, The 1931 d: Harry Beaumont. lps: Adolphe Menjou, Irene Dunne, Neil Hamilton. 79M USA. prod/rel: Metro-Goldwyn-Mayer Corp., Metro-Goldwyn-Mayer Dist. Corp.©

Mlle. Fifi, New York 1899, Play
Divorce Game, The 1917 d: Travers Vale. lps: Alice Brady, John Bowers, Arthur Ashley. 5r USA. prod/rel: World Film Corp.©, Peerless

Die Thur Ins Freis, Berlin 1908, Play
Is Matrimony a Failure? 1922 d: James Cruze. lps: T. Roy Barnes, Lila Lee, Lois Wilson. 5612f USA. prod/rel: Famous Players-Lasky, Paramount Pictures

DIVINE, DAVID
Boy on a Dolphin, 1955, Novel
Boy on a Dolphin 1957 d: Jean Negulesco. lps: Sophia Loren, Alan Ladd, Clifton Webb. 112M USA. prod/rel: 20th Century-Fox

D'IVOI, PAUL
Les Cinq Sous de Lavarede, Novel
Cinq Sous de Lavarede, Les 1913 d: Henri Andreani. lps: Paul Lack, Godeau, Suzanne Goldstein. 2000m FRN. prod/rel: Les Grands Films Populaires
Cinq Sous de Lavarede, Les 1928 d: Maurice Champreux. lps: Georges Biscot, Carlos Avril, Janine Liezer. SRL. FRN. prod/rel: Films Luminor, Ste Des Cineromans
Cinq Sous de Lavarede, Les 1939 d: Maurice Cammage. lps: Fernandel, Josette Day, Marcel Vallee. 125M FRN. prod/rel: Ste. De Prod. Du Film Les Cinq Sous

Jalma la Double, Novel
Jalma la Double 1927 d: Roger Goupillieres. lps: Lucien Dalsace, Groza Wesco, Acho Chakatouny. F FRN. prod/rel: Societe Des Cineromans

DIX, BEULAH MARIE
The Breed of the Trenshams, London 1905, Play
Breed of the Treshams, The 1920 d: Kenelm Foss. lps: John Martin-Harvey, Mary Odette, Hayford Hobbs. 6000f UKN. prod/rel: Astra Films

The Road to Yesterday, New York 1906, Play
Road to Yesterday, The 1925 d: Cecil B. de Mille. lps: Joseph Schildkraut, Jetta Goudal, Vera Reynolds. 9980f USA. prod/rel: de Mille Pictures, Producers Distributing Corp.

Sucker, New York 1933, Play
Life of Jimmy Dolan, The 1933 d: Archie Mayo. lps: Douglas Fairbanks Jr., Loretta Young, Guy Kibbee. 89M USA. *The Kid's Last Fight* (UKN); *Sucker* prod/rel: Warner Bros. Pictures
They Made Me a Criminal 1939 d: Busby Berkeley. lps: John Garfield, Claude Rains, Gloria Dickson. 92M USA. prod/rel: Warner Bros. Pictures©

DIXON, MORT
That Old Gang of Mine, 1923, Song
That Old Gang of Mine 1925 d: May Tully. lps: MacLyn Arbuckle, Brooke Johns, Tommy Brown. 5r USA. prod/rel: Kerman Films

DIXON, PETER
Novel
Attention Les Enfants Regardent 1977 d: Serge Leroy. lps: Alain Delon, Sophie Renoir, Richard Constantini. 102M FRN. *Careful the Children are Watching* prod/rel: Adel

DIXON, ROSIE
Confessions of a Night Nurse, Novel
Rosie Dixon: Night Nurse 1977 d: Justin Cartwright. lps: Debbie Ash, Caroline Argyle, Beryl Reid. 88M UKN.

DIXON, THOMAS (1864–1946), USA
The Clansman: an Historical Romance of the Ku Klux Klan, New York 1906, Novel
Birth of a Nation, The 1915 d: D. W. Griffith. lps: Lillian Gish, Mae Marsh, Henry B. Walthall. 12r USA. *The Clansman* prod/rel: Epoch Producing Corp.©, David W. Griffith Corp.
Comrades, New York 1909, Novel
Bolshevism on Trial 1919 d: Harley Knoles. lps: Robert Frazer, Leslie Stowe, Howard Truesdell. 6r USA. *Red Republic; Shattered Dreams* prod/rel: Mayflower Photoplay Corp.©, Select Pictures Corp.
The Fall of a Nation: a Sequel to Birth of a Nation, Chicago 1916, Novel
Fall of a Nation, The 1916 d: Thomas Dixon. lps: Arthur Shirley, Lorraine Huling, Flora MacDonald. 7-8r USA. prod/rel: National Drama Corp.©, V-L-S-E, Inc.
The Foolish Virgin, New York 1915, Novel
Foolish Virgin, The 1917 d: Albert Capellani. lps: Clara Kimball Young, Conway Tearle, Catherine Proctor. 5-7r USA. prod/rel: Clara Kimball Young Film Corp.©, Lewis J. Selznick Enterprises
Foolish Virgin, The 1924 d: George W. Hill. lps: Elaine Hammerstein, Robert Frazer, Gladys Brockwell. 5900f USA. prod/rel: Columbia Pictures, C. B. C. Film Sales
The One Woman, New York 1903, Novel
One Woman, The 1918 d: Reginald Barker. lps: W. Lawson Butt, Clara Williams, Adda Gleason. 5260f USA. prod/rel: Mastercraft Photoplay Corp., Select Pictures Corp.

DO REGO, JOSE LINS (1901–1957), BRZ
Fogo Morto, 1943, Novel
Fogo Morto 1976 d: Marcos FariA. 90M BRZ. *The Last Plantation*
Menino de Engenho 1966 d: Walter Lima Jr.. 86M BRZ. *The Boy from the Plantations; Plantation Boy*
Menino de Engenho, 1932, Novel
Menino de Engenho 1966 d: Walter Lima Jr.. 86M BRZ. *The Boy from the Plantations; Plantation Boy*
Pureza, 1937, Novel
Pureza 1940 d: Eduardo Chianca de GarciA. 140M BRZ. *Purity*

DOBBS, MICHAEL
House of Cards, Novel
House of Cards 1991 d: Paul Seed. lps: Ian Richardson, Susannah Harker, Diane Fletcher. TVM. 181M UKN. prod/rel: BBC
To Play the King, Novel
To Play the King 1993 d: Paul Seed. lps: Ian Richardson, Michael Kitchen, Kitty Aldridge. MTV. 210M UKN.

DOBIE, CHARLES CALDWELL
The Blood Red Dawn, New York 1920, Novel
Inner Chamber, The 1921 d: Edward Jose. lps: Alice Joyce, Jane Jennings, Pedro de CordobA. 6r USA. prod/rel: Vitagraph Co. of America

DOBIE, LAURENCE
The Tinker, Stratford 1960, Play
Wild and the Willing, The 1962 d: Ralph Thomas. lps: Virginia Maskell, Paul Rogers, Ian McShane. 122M UKN. *Young and Willing* (USA); *The Young and the Willing* prod/rel: Rank Organisation, Rank Film Distributors

DOBLIN, ALFRED (1878–1957), GRM
Berlin-Alexanderplatz, 1929, Novel
Berlin-Alexanderplatz 1931 d: Phil Jutzi. lps: Heinrich George, Maria Bard, Bernhard Minetti. 121M GRM. prod/rel: Allianz-Tonfilm

DOBYNS, STEPHEN (1941–, USA
Cold Dog Soup, Book
Cold Dog Soup 1989 d: Alan Metter. lps: Randy Quaid, Frank Whaley, Christine Harnos. 90M USA/UKN. prod/rel: Handmade, Aspen
The Two Deaths of Senora Puccini, Novel
Two Deaths 1995 d: Nicolas Roeg. lps: Michael Gambon, Sonia Braga, Patrick Malahide. 96M UKN. prod/rel: BBC

DOCTOROW, E. L. (1931–, USA, Doctorow, Edgar Lawrence
Billy Bathgate, 1989, Novel
Billy Bathgate 1991 d: Robert Benton. lps: Dustin Hoffman, Nicole Kidman, Loren Dean. 107M USA. prod/rel: Warner Bros., Touchstone
The Book of Daniel, 1971, Novel
Daniel 1983 d: Sidney Lumet. lps: Timothy Hutton, Lindsay Crouse, Mandy Patinkin. 129M USA. prod/rel: Paramount
Ragtime, 1971, Novel
Ragtime 1981 d: Milos Forman. lps: James Cagney, Brad Dourif, Moses Gunn. 155M USA. prod/rel: Paramount, Ragtime
Welcome to Hard Times, New York 1960, Novel
Welcome to Hard Times 1967 d: Burt Kennedy. lps: Henry Fonda, Janice Rule, Keenan Wynn. 105M USA. *Killer on a Horse* (UKN) prod/rel: Metro-Goldwyn-Mayer, Inc.

DODD, LEE WILSON
The Return of Eve, New York 1909, Play
Return of Eve, The 1916 d: Arthur Berthelet. lps: Edna Mayo, Eugene O'Brien, Edward Mawson. 5r USA. *When Eve Came Back* prod/rel: Essanay Film Mfg. Co.©, K-E-S-E Service

DODGE, DAVID
Plunder of the Sun, 1949, Novel
Plunder of the Sun 1953 d: John Farrow. lps: Glenn Ford, Diana Lynn, Patricia MedinA. 81M USA. prod/rel: Warner Bros., Wayne-Fellows
To Catch a Thief, 1952, Novel
To Catch a Thief 1955 d: Alfred Hitchcock. lps: Cary Grant, Grace Kelly, Jessie Royce Landis. 97M USA. prod/rel: Paramount

DODGE, HENRY IRVING
Counsel for the Defense, Play
Thirteenth Juror, The 1927 d: Edward Laemmle. lps: Anna Q. Nilsson, Francis X. Bushman, Walter Pidgeon. 5598f USA. prod/rel: Universal Pictures
Skinner's Baby, New York 1917, Novel
Skinner's Baby 1917 d: Harry Beaumont. lps: Bryant Washburn, Hazel Daly, James C. Carroll. 5r USA. prod/rel: Essanay Film Mfg. Co.©, K-E-S-E Service
Skinner's Big Idea, New York 1918, Novel
Skinner's Big Idea 1928 d: Lynn Shores. lps: Bryant Washburn, William Orlamond, James Bradbury. 5967f USA. prod/rel: Fbo Pictures
Skinner's Dress Suit, 1916, Short Story
Skinner Steps Out 1929 d: William James Craft. lps: Glenn Tryon, Merna Kennedy, E. J. Ratcliffe. 70M USA. prod/rel: Universal Pictures
Skinner's Dress Suit 1917 d: Harry Beaumont. lps: Bryant Washburn, Hazel Daly, Harry Dunkinson. 5r USA. prod/rel: Essanay Film Mfg. Co.©, K-E-S-E Service
Skinner's Dress Suit 1926 d: William A. Seiter. lps: Reginald Denny, Laura La Plante, Ben Hendricks Jr. 6887f USA. prod/rel: Universal Pictures
The Yellow Dog, 1918, Short Story
Yellow Dog, The 1918 d: Colin Campbell. lps: Arthur Hoyt, Clara Horton, Ralph Graves. 6r USA. prod/rel: Universal Film Mfg. Co., Jewel Productions, Inc.©

DODGE, LOUIS
Bonnie May, New York 1916, Novel
Bonnie May 1920 d: Joseph de Grasse, Ida May Park. lps: Bessie Love, W. H. Bainbridge, Charles Gordon. 5r USA. prod/rel: Andrew J. Callaghan Productions, Inc.©, Federated Film Exchanges of America, Inc
Gret'n Ann, 1922, Short Story
Dangerous Game, A 1922 d: King Baggot. lps: Gladys Walton, Spottiswoode Aitken, Otto Hoffman. 5087f USA. prod/rel: Universal Pictures

DODSON, KENNETH M.
Away All Boats, 1954, Novel
Away All Boats 1956 d: Joseph Pevney. lps: Jeff Chandler, George Nader, Julie Adams. 114M USA. prod/rel: Universal-International

DOEL, FRANCES
Avalanche, Novel
Avalanche 1978 d: Corey Allen. lps: Rock Hudson, Mia Farrow, Robert Forster. 91M USA. prod/rel: New World Pictures

DOERHOFF, MARTIN
Das Verzauberte Madchen, Play
Was Will Brigitte? 1940 d: Paul Martin. lps: Leny Marenbach, Albert Matterstock, Fita Benkhoff. 96M GRM. prod/rel: Bavaria, Panorama

DOERR, HARRIET
Stones for Ibarra, Novel
Stones for Ibarra 1988 d: Jack Gold. lps: Glenn Close, Keith Carradine, Alfonso Arau. TVM. 100M USA. prod/rel: Titus Productions

DOFF, NEEL
Jours de Famine Et Detresse, Autobiography
Keetje Tippel 1975 d: Paul Verhoeven. lps: Monique Van de Ven, Rutger Hauer, Eddy Brugman. 107M NTH. *Cathy Tippel* (USA); *Katie's Passion; Hot Sweat*

Keetje, Autobiography
Keetje Tippel 1975 d: Paul Verhoeven. lps: Monique Van de Ven, Rutger Hauer, Eddy Brugman. 107M NTH. *Cathy Tippel* (USA); *Katie's Passion; Hot Sweat*

Keetje Trottin, Autobiography
Keetje Tippel 1975 d: Paul Verhoeven. lps: Monique Van de Ven, Rutger Hauer, Eddy Brugman. 107M NTH. *Cathy Tippel* (USA); *Katie's Passion; Hot Sweat*

DOGUET, THERESE
L' Ile Sans Rivage, Novel
Transfuge, Le 1976 d: Yves Prigent. lps: Michele Perollo, Bernard Altmann, Thizon Durand. 82M FRN.

DOHERTY, EDWARD
East River, New York 1935, Novel
Under Pressure 1935 d: Raoul Walsh. lps: Edmund Lowe, Victor McLaglen, Florence Rice. 70M USA. *Bed-Rock; Man Lock; East River* prod/rel: Fox Film Corp.©

DOILLET, LAURENT
Bourrachon, Play
Bourrachon 1935 d: Rene Guissart. lps: Gabriel Signoret, Meg Lemonnier, Marguerite Moreno. 87M FRN. prod/rel: Flores Films

DOLEZALOVA, MARIE
Kdo Jsi Bez Viny, Novel
Osmnactileta 1939 d: Miroslav Cikan. lps: Hana Vitova, Bolek Prchal, Ladislav Bohac. 1812m CZC. *Eighteen-Year Old Girl; Eighteen Years Old* prod/rel: Nationalfilm

DOLLEY, GEORGES
Cote d'Azur, Play
Cote d'Azur 1931 d: Roger Capellani. lps: Robert Burnier, Simone Heliard, Yvonne Hebert. 80M FRN. prod/rel: Films Paramount

Un Drole de Numero, Short Story
Drole de Numero, Un 1933 d: Jean Gourguet. lps: Jean Duvaleix, Jane Pierson, Rosen. 1500m FRN. prod/rel: Synchro-Cine

L' Enfant Prodige, Novel
Boule de Gomme 1931 d: Georges Lacombe. lps: Janine Perrini, Antoine Stacquet, Albert Broquin. 45M FRN. prod/rel: Syncho-Cine

Le Fille Et le Garcon, Play
Fille Et le Garcon, La 1931 d: Wilhelm Thiele, Roger Le Bon. lps: Lilian Harvey, Henri Garat, Lucien Baroux. 85M FRN. *The Girl and the Boy* prod/rel: U.F.a., a.C.E.

La Fleur d'Oranger, Play
Fleur d'Oranger, La 1932 d: Henry Roussell. lps: Andre Lefaur, Simone Deguyse, Helene Robert. 87M FRN. prod/rel: Pathe-Natan

Le Mage du Carlton, Play
Fakir du Grand Hotel, Le 1933 d: Pierre Billon. lps: Armand Bernard, Paulette Dubost, Annie Ducaux. 100M FRN. prod/rel: Dana-Film

Le Mirage du Coeur, Short Story
Mirage du Coeur, Le 1916 d: Georges Treville. lps: Georges Treville, Lise Laurent. 1240m FRN. prod/rel: Formosa Film

Le Soleil a l'Ombre, Novel
Prison En Folie, La 1930 d: Henry Wulschleger. lps: Helene Hallier, Suzanne Dehelly, Noel-Noel. 80M FRN. *Le Soleil a l'Ombre* prod/rel: Star Film

Votre Sourire, Play
Votre Sourire 1934 d: Pierre Caron, Monty Banks. lps: Victor Boucher, Marie Glory, Renee Devilder. 85M FRN. prod/rel: Compagnie Francaise Cinematographique

DOMELA, HARRY
Der Falsche Prinz, Book
Falsche Prinz, Der 1927 d: Heinz Paul. lps: Harry Domela, Ekkehard Arendt, Jack Mylong-Munz. 2769m GRM. prod/rel: Lothar Stark Gmbh, Bayerische Film

DOMINIQUE, ANTOINE
Le Gorille a Mordu l'Archeveque, Novel
Gorille a Mordu l'Archeveque, Le 1962 d: Maurice Labro. lps: Roger Hanin, Jean Le Poulain, Roger Dumas. 88M FRN. *The Deadly Decoy* (USA); *The Bite of the Gorilla* prod/rel: Progefi

Le Gorille Vous Salue Bien, Novel
Gorille Vous Salue Bien, Le 1957 d: Bernard Borderie. lps: Charles Vanel, Pierre Dux, Bella Darvi. 102M FRN. *The Gorilla Salutes You; The Gorilla Greets You* prod/rel: S.N. Pathe-Cinema, Films Raoul Ploquin

Le Pave du Gorille, Novel
Pave du Gorille, Le 1990 d: Roger Hanin. lps: Karim Allaoui, Francois Perier, Robert Hossein. TVM. 90M FRN/GRM/ITL.

La Valse du Gorille, Novel
Valse du Gorille, La 1959 d: Bernard Borderie. lps: Roger Hanin, Charles Vanel, Wolfgang Preiss. 100M FRN. *The Waltz of the Gorilla* prod/rel: Societe Nouvelle Pathe-Cinema, Films Raoul Ploquin

DOMOJAKOV, NIKOLAI
In a Remote Village, Novel
Posledny God Berkoeta 1978 d: Vadim Lisenko. lps: Oleg Kortsjikov, Noerzjoeman Ichimbajev, Alexei Arasjtajev. 101M USS. *Last Year of Berkut*

DONALD, HENRY
Hal 5 and the Haywards, Novel
Adventures of Hal 5, The 1958 d: Don Sharp. lps: Peter Godsell, William Russell, John Glyn-Jones. 59M UKN. prod/rel: Bushey, Children's Film Foundation

DONAT, STEFAN
Kitty Und Die Weltkonferenz, Play
Kitty Und Die Grosse Welt 1956 d: Alfred Weidenmann. lps: Romy Schneider, Karlheinz Bohm, O. E. Hasse. 94M GRM. *Kitty and the Great Big World* prod/rel: Rhombus, UFA

Kitty Und Die Weltkonferenz 1939 d: Helmut Kautner. lps: Hannelore Schroth, Fritz Odemar, Paul Horbiger. 98M GRM. *Kitty and the World Conference* prod/rel: Terra, Lloyd

DONATI, HERMANI
Chao Bruto, 1956, Novel
Chao Bruto 1959 d: Dionizio de Azevedo. 98M BRZ.

Selva Tragica, 1959, Novel
Selva Tragica 1964 d: Roberto Farias. lps: Paulo Copacabana, Mario Petraglia, Dinorah Brillanti. 95M BRZ. *Fieras Humanas*

DONATI, SERGIO
L' Altra Faccia Della Luna, Novel
Tre Notti Violente 1966 d: Nick Nostro. lps: Brett Halsey, Margaret Lee, Jose Calvo. 90M ITL/SPN. *Tres Noches Violentas* (SPN); *Web of Violence* (USA); *3 Noches Violentas* prod/rel: Liber Film (Roma), Hesperia Films (Madrid)

Il Sepolcro Di Carta, Story
Col Cuore in Gola 1967 d: Tinto Brass. lps: Jean-Louis Trintignant, Ewa Aulin, Roberto Bisacco. 107M ITL/FRN. *La Coeur aux Levres* (FRN); *With Heart in Mouth; With Bated Breath; Heart Beat; Deadly Sweet* (USA) prod/rel: Panda Cin.Ca (Roma), Les Films Corona (Paris)

DONCHEV, ANTON
Vreme Razdelno, 1964, Novel
Vreme Na Nasilie 1988 d: Lyudmil Staikov. lps: Iossif Surchadzhiev. 164M BUL. *Time of Parting; Time of Violence; Vreme Razdelno*

DONG-CHUL LEE
Pabo Sunon, Novel
Pabo Sunon 1983 d: Chang-Ho Lee. lps: Bo-Hee Lee, Myung-Kon Kim, Hui-Sung Lee. 87M KOR. prod/rel: Chong-Chan Park, Hwa Chun Trading Co.

DONINI, ALBERTO
L' Orologio a Cucu, Play
Orologio a Cucu, L' 1938 d: Camillo Mastrocinque. lps: Vittorio de Sica, Oretta Fiume, Ugo Ceseri. 82M ITL. *The Cuckoo Clock* prod/rel: Era Film, M.G.M. Italiana

Il Passatore, Play
Notte Delle Beffe, La 1940 d: Carlo Campogalliani. lps: Amedeo Nazzari, Dria Paola, Maurizio d'AncorA. 68M ITL. *Il Passatore* prod/rel: Iris Film, Generalcine

DONIZETTI, GAETANO (1797–1848), ITL
Don Pasquale, Paris 1843, Opera
Don Pasquale 1940 d: Camillo Mastrocinque. lps: Armando Falconi, Laura Solari, Greta GondA. 98M ITL. prod/rel: Cinecitta S.A., Generalcine

L' Elisir d'Amore, Milan 1832, Opera
Elisir d'Amore, L' 1941 d: Amleto Palermi. lps: Armando Falconi, Margherita Carosio, Roberto VillA. 85M ITL. *The Elixir of Love* prod/rel: Fono Roma, Lux Film

Elisir d'Amore, L' 1947 d: Mario CostA. lps: Nelly Corradi, Loretta Di Lelio, Italo Tajo. 85M ITL. *This Wine of Love* (USA) prod/rel: Prora Film, Zeus Film

La Fille du Regiment, Paris 1840, Opera
Daughter of the Regiment 1927 d: H. B. Parkinson. lps: Kitty Barling, Oscar Sosander, Algernon Hicks. 1764f UKN. prod/rel: Song Pictures

Figlia Del Reggimento, La 1920 d: Enrico Vidali. lps: Liliane de Rosny, Umberto Mozzato. 1000m ITL. prod/rel: Subalpina

Regimentstochter, Die 1928 d: Hans Behrendt. lps: Betty Balfour, Alexander d'Arcy, Kurt Gerron. 2406m GRM. prod/rel: Hom-Film

Regimentstochter, Die 1953 d: Georg C. Klaren, Gunther Haenel. lps: Aglaja Schmid, Robert Lindner, Hermann Erhardt. 100M AUS. prod/rel: Nova

Linda Di Chamounix, 1842, Opera
Linda Di Chamounix 1921 d: Luigi Ferraro. lps: Nella Serravezza, Eda Villarosa, Antonio Solinas. 1566m ITL. *La Perla Della Savoia* prod/rel: Eden-Ferrario

Lucia Di Lammermoor, 1835, Opera
Lucia Di Lammermoor 1948 d: Piero Ballerini. lps: Nelly Corradi, Loretta Di Lelio, Italo Tajo. 92M ITL. prod/rel: Opera Film

DONNAY, CHARLES MAURICE
Education de Prince, 1895, Play
Education de Prince 1926 d: Henri Diamant-Berger. lps: Edna Purviance, Pierre Batcheff, Armand Bernard. F FRN. prod/rel: Natan

Education de Prince 1938 d: Alexander Esway. lps: Louis Jouvet, Elvire Popesco, Josette Day. 95M FRN. *The Barge-Keeper's Daughter* prod/rel: C.I.C.C.

DONNAY, MAURICE (1859–1945), FRN
La Douloureuse, 1897, Novel
Douloureuse, La 1921 d: Augusto GeninA. lps: Ria Bruna, Francesco Cacace-Galeota, Pina Orsini. 1738m ITL. prod/rel: U.C.I., Photodrama

Oiseaux de Passage, Novel
Oiseaux de Passage 1925 d: Gaston Roudes. lps: France Dhelia, Lucien Dalsace, Mevisto. 2700m FRN. prod/rel: Grandes Productions Cinematographiques

Paraitre, 1906, Play
Paraitre 1917 d: Maurice Challiot. lps: Armand Tallier, Louis Ravet, Andree Pascal. 1283m FRN. prod/rel: Natura Films

DONN-BYRNE, BRIAN OSWALD
The Bride's Play, Short Story
Bride's Play, The 1921 d: George W. Terwilliger. lps: Marion Davies, Jack O'Brien, Frank Shannon. 6476f USA. prod/rel: Cosmopolitan Productions, Paramount Pictures

Changeling, New York 1923, Short Story
His Captive Woman 1929 d: George Fitzmaurice. lps: Milton Sills, Dorothy MacKaill, Gladden James. 8305f USA. *Stranded in Paradise* prod/rel: First National Pictures

The Foolish Matrons, New York 1920, Novel
Foolish Matrons, The 1921 d: Maurice Tourneur, Clarence Brown. lps: Hobart Bosworth, Doris May, Mildred Manning. 6544f USA. *Is Marriage a Failure?* (UKN) prod/rel: Maurice Tourneur Productions

Hangman's House, New York 1926, Novel
Hangman's House 1928 d: John Ford. lps: June Collyer, Larry Kent, Earle Foxe. 6518f USA. prod/rel: Fox Film Corp.

In Praise of John Carabine, 1925, Short Story
Blarney 1926 d: Marcel de Sano. lps: Renee Adoree, Ralph Graves, Paulette Duval. 6055f USA. *In Praise of James Carabine* prod/rel: Metro-Goldwyn-Mayer Pictures

The Stranger's Banquet, New York 1919, Novel
Stranger's Banquet, The 1922 d: Marshall Neilan. lps: Hobart Bosworth, Claire Windsor, Rockliffe Fellowes. 8800f USA. prod/rel: Marshall Neilan Productions, Goldwyn Distributing Corp.

The Woman God Changed, 1921, Short Story
Woman God Changed, The 1921 d: Robert G. VignolA. lps: Seena Owen, E. K. Lincoln, Henry Sedley. 6502f USA. prod/rel: Cosmopolitan Productions, Paramount Pictures

DONN-BYRNE, DOROTHEA
Enter Madame!, New York 1920, Play
Enter Madame! 1935 d: Elliott Nugent. lps: Elissa Landi, Cary Grant, Lynne Overman. 83M USA. prod/rel: Paramount Productions©

Enter Madame 1922 d: Wallace Worsley. lps: Clara Kimball Young, Elliott Dexter, Louise Dresser. 6500f USA. prod/rel: Samuel Zierler Photoplay Corp., Metro Pictures

DONNELL, ANNIE HAMILTON
'Twas the Night Before Christmas, Story
'Twas the Night Before Christmas 1914 d: Ashley Miller. lps: Harry Eytinge. SHT USA. prod/rel: Edison

DONNELLY, DOROTHY
Poppy, New York 1923, Play
Sally of the Sawdust 1925 d: D. W. Griffith. lps: Carol Dempster, W. C. Fields, Alfred Lunt. 9500f USA. prod/rel: D. W. Griffith, Inc., United Artists

Poppy Comes to Town, New York 1923, Musical Play
Poppy 1936 d: A. Edward Sutherland, Stuart Heisler (Uncredited). lps: W. C. Fields, Rochelle Hudson, Richard Cromwell. 73M USA. prod/rel: Paramount Productions©

DONNELLY, ELFIE
Der Rote Strumpf, Book
  Rote Strumpf, Der 1980 d: Wolfgang Tumler. lps: Inge Meysel, Julie Tumler, Ulrike Bliefert. 92M GRM. *The Red Stocking* prod/rel: Aspekt Telefilm, ZDF

DONNELLY, H. GRATTAN
Darkest Russia, New York 1894, Play
  Darkest Russia 1917 d: Travers Vale. lps: Alice Brady, John Bowers, J. Herbert Frank. 5r USA. prod/rel: World Film Corp.©
The End of the Road, Play
  End of the Road, The 1915 d: Thomas Ricketts. lps: Harold Lockwood, May Allison, Helene Rosson. 5r USA. prod/rel: American Film Co., Mutual Film Corp.
The Woman in Black, New York 1897, Play
  Woman in Black, The 1914 d: Lawrence Marston. lps: Lionel Barrymore, Millicent Evans, Alan Hale. 5r USA. prod/rel: Biograph Co., Klaw and Erlanger©

DONOHER, ELIZABETH ETHEL
The Romany Call, Short Story
  Heart of a Gypsy, The 1919 d: Charles Miller, Harry McRae Webster. lps: Florence Billings, Aida Horton, Mathilde Brundage. 5r USA. *The Heart of a Gipsy* prod/rel: Charles Miller Productions, Hallmark Pictures Corp.

DONOHER, ETHEL
The Black Panther's Cub, Story
  Black Panther's Cub, The 1921 d: Emile Chautard. lps: Florence Reed, Norman Trevor, Henry Stephenson. 6-7r USA. prod/rel: Ziegfeld Cinema Corp., Equity Pictures
The Luxury Tax, Story
  Other Women's Clothes 1922 d: Hugo Ballin. lps: Mabel Ballin, Raymond Bloomer, Crauford Kent. 5600f USA. prod/rel: Hugo Ballin Productions, W. W. Hodkinson Corp.
Silver Lanterns, Story
  Princess on Broadway, The 1927 d: Dallas M. Fitzgerald. lps: Pauline Garon, Dorothy Dwan, Johnny Walker. 5705f USA. prod/rel: Dallas M. Fitzgerald Productions, Pathe Exchange, Inc.

DONOVAN, ROBERT J.
John F. Kennedy in World War II Pt 109, New York 1961, Biography
  Pt 109 1963 d: Leslie H. Martinson. lps: Cliff Robertson, Ty Hardin, James Gregory. 140M USA. prod/rel: Warner Bros. Pictures

DOOLING, RICHARD
Critical Care, Novel
  Critical Care 1997 d: Sidney Lumet. lps: James Spader, Kyra Sedgwick, Helen Mirren. 105M USA. prod/rel: Live Entertainment, Mediaworks

DOR, MILO
Romeo Und Julia in Wien, Novel
  Nina 1956 d: Rudolf Jugert. lps: Karlheinz Bohm, Anouk Aimee, Peter Carsten. 89M GRM. *Romeo Und Julia in Wien* prod/rel: Corona, Bavaria

DOREMUS, MRS. CHARLES A.
Nell Gwynne, New York 1901, Play
  Nell Gwynne 1914. lps: Nellie Stuart. 5r USA. prod/rel: Sawyer, Inc.

DORFMAN, ARIEL (1942–, CHL
Death and the Maiden, Play
  Death and the Maiden 1994 d: Roman Polanski. lps: Sigourney Weaver, Ben Kingsley, Stuart Wilson. 103M USA/FRN/UKN. prod/rel: Electric, Capitol

DORGELES, ROLAND
Les Croix de Bois, Novel
  Croix de Bois, Les 1931 d: Raymond Bernard. lps: Pierre Blanchar, Aimos, Antonin Artaud. 110M FRN. *Wooden Crosses* (USA) prod/rel: Pathe-Natan
Partir, Novel
  Partir. 1931 d: Maurice Tourneur. lps: Jean Marchat, Simone Cerdan, Ginette d'Yd. 95M FRN. *Partir!* prod/rel: Pathe-Natan

DORIN, FRANCOIS
Les Bonshommes, Play
  Pane, Burro E Marmellata 1977 d: Giorgio Capitani. lps: Enrico Montesano, Rossana Podesta, Claudine Auger. 100M ITL. prod/rel: Italian International Film

DORMANN, FELIX
Der Unsterbliche Lump, Novel
  Unsterbliche Lump, Der 1953 d: Arthur M. Rabenalt. lps: Karlheinz Bohm, Ingrid Stenn, Heliane Bei. 105M GRM. *The Undying Bum* prod/rel: Carlton, N.F.
Ein Waltzertraum, Leipzig 1907, Opera
  Smiling Lieutenant, The 1931 d: Ernst Lubitsch. lps: Maurice Chevalier, Claudette Colbert, Miriam Hopkins. 88M USA. prod/rel: Paramount Publix Corp.©, Ernst Lubitsch Production

DORN, DOMINIQUE
Le Parfum de la Peur, Paris 1960, Novel
  Drogue du Vice, La 1963 d: Jose Benazeraf. lps: Hans Verner, Jean-Pierre Kalfon, Marcel Champel. 75M FRN. *Night of Lust* (USA); *La Concerto de la Peur*; *Notte Erotique*; *Night of Love* prod/rel: Les Films Univers, Aurora Films

DORR, NICOLAS
Violeta, Play
  Violeta 1998 d: Alberto Cortes. lps: Blanca Guerra, David Ramy, Katia Elnecave. 90M CUB/MXC. prod/rel: Tabasco Films (Mexico), ICAIC (Cuba)

DORRANCE, ETHEL
His Robe of Honor, New York 1916, Novel
  His Robe of Honor 1918 d: Rex Ingram. lps: Henry B. Walthall, Mary Charleson, Lois Wilson. 6224f USA. prod/rel: Paralta Plays, Inc., W. W. Hodkinson Corp.
Whitewashed Walls, Short Story
  Whitewashed Walls 1919 d: Park Frame. lps: William Desmond, Fritzi Brunette, Carmen Phillips. 5r USA. prod/rel: Jesse D. Hampton Productions, Robertson-Cole Co.
Who Knows?, 1916, Short Story
  Who Knows? 1917 d: Jack Pratt. lps: Betty Brice, Jay Morley, Charles Arling. 6r USA. prod/rel: Bernstein Film Productions, State Rights

DORRANCE, JAMES
His Robe of Honor, New York 1916, Novel
  His Robe of Honor 1918 d: Rex Ingram. lps: Henry B. Walthall, Mary Charleson, Lois Wilson. 6224f USA. prod/rel: Paralta Plays, Inc., W. W. Hodkinson Corp.
Whitewashed Walls, Short Story
  Whitewashed Walls 1919 d: Park Frame. lps: William Desmond, Fritzi Brunette, Carmen Phillips. 5r USA. prod/rel: Jesse D. Hampton Productions, Robertson-Cole Co.
Who Knows?, 1916, Short Story
  Who Knows? 1917 d: Jack Pratt. lps: Betty Brice, Jay Morley, Charles Arling. 6r USA. prod/rel: Bernstein Film Productions, State Rights

DOS LAGOS, CALISTO
Memoria E Massacre Mueda, Play
  Mueda, Memoria E Massacre 1980 d: Ruy GuerrA. lps: Filipe Gunoguacala, Romao Canapoquele, Baltasar NchilemA. 80M MZM. *Mueda Memory and Massacre* prod/rel: Instituto Nacional de Cinema

DOS SANTOS, JOAO FELICIO
Cristo No Lama, 1964, Novel
  Historia Da Numismatica 1954 d: Wilson SilvA. DCS. BRZ.
Rei Dos Palmares Ganga Zumba, 1961, Novel
  Ganga Zumba 1963 d: Carlos Diegues. lps: Antonio Sampaio, Lea Garcia, Eliezer Gomes. 105M BRZ. *Ganga Zumba O Rei Dos Palmares* prod/rel: Studio

DOSS, HELEN
The Family Nobody Wanted, 1954, Book
  Family Nobody Wanted, The 1975 d: Ralph Senensky. lps: Shirley Jones, James Olson, Katherine Helmond. TVM. 78M USA. prod/rel: ABC, Universal

DOSSICK, PHILIP
Transplant, Book
  Transplant 1979 d: William A. Graham. lps: Kevin Dobson, Granville Van Dusen, Ronny Cox. TVM. 100M USA. prod/rel: Time-Life Television

DOSTAL, NICO
Clivia, Opera
  Clivia 1954 d: Karl Anton. lps: Claude Farrell, Peter Pasetti, Hans Richter. 98M GRM. prod/rel: Central-Europa, Prisma

DOSTOYEVSKY, FYODOR
Belye Nochi, St. Petersburg 1848, Short Story
  Notti Bianche, Le 1957 d: Luchino Visconti. lps: Maria Schell, Marcello Mastroianni, Jean Marais. 95M ITL/FRN. *Nuits Blanches* (FRN); *White Nights* (USA); *Sleepless Nights* prod/rel: Ci.As., Vides (Roma)
  Peterburgskaya Noch 1934 d: Grigori Roshal, Vera StroyevA. 75M USS. *Petersburg Nights*; *Saint Petersburg*; *Peterburgskaja Noc*
  Quatre Nuits d'un Reveur 1971 d: Robert Bresson. lps: Isabelle Weingarten, Guillaume Des Forets, Jean-Maurice Monnayer. 90M FRN/ITL. *Four Nights of a Dreamer* (USA) prod/rel: Victoria, Albino Del Orso
Besy, 1872, Novel
  Nella Morsa Della Colpa 1921 d: Aleksandr Uralsky. lps: Mara Tchoukleva, Enrico Piacentini, Lidia Pozzone. 1444m ITL. prod/rel: Triumphalis Film
  Possedes, Les 1988 d: Andrzej WajdA. lps: Jean-Philippe Ecoffey, Lambert Wilson, Omar Sharif. 114M FRN. *The Possessed* prod/rel: Films Du Losange, Gaumont

Bratya Karamazovy, 1880, Novel
  Bratya Karamazovy 1968 d: Ivan Pyriev. lps: Mikhail Ulianov, Lionella Pyrieva, Kirill Lavrov. 227M USS. *The Murder of Dimitri Karamazov*; *The Brothers Karamazov*; *Bratia Karamazov*
  Brothers Karamazov, The 1958 d: Richard Brooks. lps: Yul Brynner, Maria Schell, Claire Bloom. 146M USA. prod/rel: MGM
  Fratelli Karamazoff, I 1948 d: Giacomo Gentilomo. lps: Fosco Giachetti, Mariella Lotti, Elli Parvo. 101M ITL. *The Brothers Karamazov* prod/rel: Cormiran, Pax Film
  Freres Karamazoff, Les 1931 d: Fedor Ozep. lps: Fritz Kortner, Anna Sten, Hanna Waag. 85M FRN. prod/rel: Pathe-Natan
  Maltchiki 1990 d: Yuri Grigoriev, Renita GrigorievA. 86M USS. *Boys*
  Morder Dimitri Karamasoff, Der 1931 d: Fedor Ozep. lps: Fritz Kortner, Anna Sten, Fritz Rasp. 93M GRM. *The Murderer Dimitri Karamasoff* (USA); *Karamazof*; *The Crime of Dimitri Karamazov*; *The Brothers Karamazov* prod/rel: Terra-Film
Dvoynik, 1846, Novel
  Partner 1968 d: Bernardo Bertolucci. lps: Pierre Clementi, Tina Aumont, Stefania Sandrelli. 106M ITL. prod/rel: Red Film, I.N.C.
Dyadyushkin Son, 1859, Short Story
  Dyadyushkin Son 1967 d: Konstantin Voinov. lps: Sergei Martinson, Lidia Smirnova, Zhanna Prokhorenko. 86M USS. *An Uncle's Dream*
Idiot, 1868, Novel
  Ahmaq 1992 d: Mani Kaul. lps: Ayub Khan Din, Shah Rukh Khan, Mita Vashisht. 180M IND. *The Idiot*
  Hakuchi 1951 d: Akira KurosawA. lps: Masayuki Mori, Toshiro Mifune, Setsuko HarA. 265M JPN. *The Idiot* prod/rel: Shochiku Co.
  Idiot 1991 d: Mani Kaul. lps: Ayub Khan Din, Shah Rukh Khan, Mita Vasisht. 180M IND. prod/rel: Doordarshan
  Idiot, L' 1945 d: Georges Lampin. lps: Gerard Philipe, Edwige Feuillere, Marguerite Moreno. 95M FRN. *The Idiot* (UKN) prod/rel: Sacha Gordine
  Idiota, L' 1919 d: Salvatore Aversano. lps: Fernanda Negri-Pouget, Sergio Mari, Fernanda Fassy. 1073m ITL. prod/rel: Cuccari Film
  Nastasia Filipovna 1958 d: Ivan Pyriev. lps: Julia Borisov, Yuri Yakovlev, Nikita Podgorny. 122M USS. *The Idiot* (USA); *The Idiot: Part One*
  Principe Idiota, Il 1919 d: Eugenio Perego. lps: Fernanda Fassy, Lamberto Picasso, Paola Borboni. 1628m ITL. prod/rel: Sabaudo Film
Igrok, 1866, Novel
  Great Sinner, The 1949 d: Robert Siodmak, Mervyn Leroy. lps: Gregory Peck, Ava Gardner, Melvyn Douglas. 110M USA. prod/rel: MGM
  Igrok 1972 d: Alexei Batalov. lps: Nikolai Bourlijayev, Ludmila Dobjenskaya, Jitka ZelenohorskA. 95M USS/CZC. *The Gambler*
  Joueur, Le 1938 d: Louis Daquin, Gerhard Lamprecht. lps: Pierre Blanchar, Roger Karl, Viviane Romance. 95M FRN. prod/rel: Films Sonores Tobis
  Joueur, Le 1958 d: Claude Autant-LarA. lps: Gerard Philipe, Liselotte Pulver, Bernard Blier. 102M FRN/ITL. *Il Giocatore* (ITL); *The Gambler* prod/rel: Franco-London Films, Zebra Films
  Spieler, Der 1938 d: Gerhard Lamprecht. lps: Lida Baarova, Albrecht Schoenhals, Hannes Stelzer. 90M GRM. *Roman Eines Spielers* prod/rel: Euphono, Panorama
Krotkaya, 1876, Short Story
  Femme Douce, Une 1969 d: Robert Bresson. lps: Dominique Sanda, Guy Frangin, Jane Lobre. 105M FRN. *A Gentle Creature* (UKN) prod/rel: Parc Films, Marianne Productions
  Krotkaya 1960 d: Alexander Borisov. 71M USS. *The Humble One*
The Meek Creature, Story
  Nazar 1990 d: Mani Kaul. lps: Shekhar Kapur, Shambhavi, Pervez Merchant. 124M IND. *Eye*; *The Gaze* prod/rel: Infrakino
Memorie Del Sottosuolo, Short Story
  Lungo Viaggio, Il 1974 d: Franco Giraldi. lps: Jan Englert, Ivan Darvas, Flavio Bucci. MTV. F ITL. prod/rel: a1.Fran Cin.Ca, Rai 1 (Roma)
Netochka Nezvanova, 1849, Short Story
  Peterburgskaya Noch 1934 d: Grigori Roshal, Vera StroyevA. 75M USS. *Petersburg Nights*; *Saint Petersburg*; *Peterburgskaja Noc*

Prestupleniye I Nakazaniye, 1867, Novel
  Brott Och Straff 1945 d: Erik Faustman. lps: Erik Faustman, Gunn Wallgren, Sigurd Wallen. 106M SWD. *Crime and Punishment* (UKN)

  Crime and Punishment 1917 d: Lawrence McGill. lps: Derwent Hall Caine, Marguerite Courtot, Sidney Bracey. 5r USA. prod/rel: Arrow Film Corp., Pathe Exchange, Inc.

  Crime and Punishment 1935 d: Josef von Sternberg. lps: Edward Arnold, Peter Lorre, Marian Marsh. 88M USA. prod/rel: Columbia Pictures Corp.

  Crime and Punishment U.S.A. 1959 d: Denis Sanders. lps: Mary Murphy, Frank Silvera, Marian Seldes. 96M USA. prod/rel: Allied Artists, Sanders Associates

  Crime Et Chatiment 1935 d: Pierre Chenal. lps: Harry Baur, Pierre Blanchar, Madeleine Ozeray. 110M FRN. *Crime and Punishment* (USA) prod/rel: General Production

  Crime Et Chatiment 1956 d: Georges Lampin. lps: Robert Hossein, Jean Gabin, Marina Vlady. 108M FRN. *The Most Dangerous Sin* (USA); *Crime and Punishment* (UKN) prod/rel: Champs-Elysees Productions, Jules Borkon

  Crimen Y Castigo 1950 d: Fernando de Fuentes. lps: Roberto Canedo, Lilia Prado, Carlos Lopez MoctezumA. 120M MXC. *Crime and Punishment*

  Phir Subah Hogi 1958 d: Ramesh Saigal. lps: Raj Kapoor, Mala Sinha, Rehman. 168M IND. *It Will Dawn Again*; *Phir Subha Hogi* prod/rel: Parijat Pictures

  Pickpocket 1959 d: Robert Bresson. lps: Martin Lassalle, Pierre Leymarie, Marika Green. 75M FRN. prod/rel: Agnes Delahaie

  Prestuplenie I Nakazanie 1970 d: Lev Kulidjanov. lps: Georgij Taratorkin, Innokenti Smoktunovsky, Tatjana BedovA. 200M USS. *Crime and Punishment*

  Raskolnikow 1923 d: Robert Wiene. lps: Gregori Chmara, Pawel Pawloff, Michael Tarschanow. 3168m GRM. *Crime and Punishment*; *Schuld Und Suhne*

  Rikos Ja Rangaistus 1983 d: Aki Kaurismaki. lps: Markku Toikka, Aino Seppo, Esko Nikkari. 94M FNL. *Crime and Punishment* (USA)

  Sin Compasion 1994 d: Francisco Lombardi. lps: Diego Bertie, Adriana Davila, Jorge ChiarellA. 120M PRU/MXC/FRN. *Sans Pitie* (FRN); *No Mercy* prod/rel: Inca Films, Amaranta (Mexico)

Skverny Anekdot, 1862, Short Story
  Skvenei Anekdot 1965 d: Alexander Alov, Vladimir Naumov. lps: Yevgyeni Yevstigneyev, Viktor Sergachov, Aleksandr Grusinski. 101M USS. *An Ugly Story*; *Bad Joke*; *Skvernyj Anekdot*; *Skwernyj Anekdot* prod/rel: Mosfilm

Il Sosia, Short Story
  Lungo Viaggio, Il 1974 d: Franco Giraldi. lps: Jan Englert, Ivan Darvas, Flavio Bucci. MTV. F ITL. prod/rel: a1.Fran Cin.Ca, Rai 1 (Roma)

Unizhenniye Oskorblennie, Novel
  Unizhenniei Oskorblennie 1996 d: Andrei A. Eshpay. lps: Nastassja Kinski, Nikita Mikhalkov, Sergei Perelygin. 104M RSS/ITL. *The Insulted and the Humiliated* prod/rel: Leila Film Sa, Globus Film

Vechnyi Muzh, 1870, Short Story
  Homme Au Chapeau Rond, L' 1946 d: Pierre Billon. lps: Raimu, Aime Clariond, Micheline Boudet. 95M FRN. *The Eternal Husband* (USA)

  Vengeance d'une Femme, La 1989 d: Jacques Doillon. lps: Isabelle Huppert, Beatrice Dalle, Jean-Louis Murat. 133M FRN. prod/rel: Sara Films

Zapiski Iz Myortvogo Doma, 1864, Short Story
  Myortvyi Dom 1932 d: Vasiliy Fyodorov. 91M USS. *House of the Dead*; *The Dead House*

Zapiski Iz Podpolya, 1864, Short Story
  Memorias Del Subsuelo 1981 d: Nicolas Sarquis. lps: Alberto de Mendoza, Miguel Ligero, Regina Duarte. 106M ARG. *Memories from the Underground*; *El Hombre Del Subsuelo*; *The Man from the Subsoil*

DOUGHERTY, RICHARD
The Commissioner, New York 1962, Novel
  Madigan 1968 d: Don Siegel. lps: Richard Widmark, Henry Fonda, Inger Stevens. 101M USA. prod/rel: Universal Pictures

DOUGLAS, FELICITY
It's Never Too Late, London 1952, Play
  It's Never Too Late 1956 d: Michael McCarthy. lps: Phyllis Calvert, Guy Rolfe, Patrick Barr. 95M UKN. prod/rel: Park Lane, Ab-Pathe

  Liebe Familie, Die 1957 d: Helmut Weiss. lps: Luise Ullrich, Hans Nielsen, Karl Schonbock. 105M AUS. prod/rel: Cosmopol

DOUGLAS, J. MACGREGOR
The Early Bird, Play
  Early Bird, The 1936 d: Donovan Pedelty. lps: Richard Hayward, Jimmy Mageean, Charlotte Tedlie. 69M UKN. prod/rel: Crusade, Paramount

DOUGLAS, LLOYD C. (1877–1951), USA, Douglas, Lloyd Cassel
The Big Fisherman, Novel
  Big Fisherman, The 1959 d: Frank Borzage. lps: Howard Keel, Susan Kohner, John Saxon. 166M USA. prod/rel: Centurion-Rowland V. Lee Prods., Buena Vista

Disputed Passage, Boston 1939, Novel
  Disputed Passage 1939 d: Frank Borzage. lps: Dorothy Lamour, Akim Tamiroff, John Howard. 89M USA. prod/rel: Paramount Pictures, Inc.

Green Light, Boston 1935, Novel
  Green Light 1937 d: Frank Borzage. lps: Errol Flynn, Anita Louise, Margaret Lindsay. 85M USA. prod/rel: Warner Bros. Pictures©, Frank Borzage Production

Magnificent Obsession, New York 1933, Novel
  Magnificent Obsession 1935 d: John M. Stahl. lps: Irene Dunne, Robert Taylor, Charles Butterworth. 110M USA. prod/rel: Universal Productions©

  Magnificent Obsession 1954 d: Douglas Sirk. lps: Jane Wyman, Rock Hudson, Barbara Rush. 112M USA. prod/rel: Universal

The Robe, 1946, Novel
  Robe, The 1953 d: Henry Koster. lps: Richard Burton, Jean Simmons, Victor Mature. 135M USA. prod/rel: 20th Century-Fox

White Banners, Boston 1936, Novel
  White Banners 1938 d: Edmund Goulding. lps: Claude Rains, Fay Bainter, Jackie Cooper. 90M USA. prod/rel: Warner Bros. Pictures©, Cosmopolitan Production

DOUWES DEKKER, EDUARD
Max Havelaar, 1859, Novel
  Max Havelaar 1976 d: Fons Rademakers. lps: Peter Faber, Sacha Bulthuis, Elang Mohamad Soesilaningrat. 170M NTH/INN.; *Max Havelaar of de Koffieveilingen Der Nederlandse Handelsmaatschappij*

DOWD, NANCY
Story
  Coming Home 1978 d: Hal Ashby. lps: Jane Fonda, Jon Voight, Bruce Dern. 128M USA. prod/rel: United Artists

DOWLAN, LEONORA
Lord Barrington's Estate, Story
  Lord Barrington's Estate 1915 d: William C. Dowlan. lps: William C. Dowlan, Violet MacMillan. 3r USA. prod/rel: Victor

DOWLING, EDWARD
Honeymoon Lane, New York 1926, Play
  Honeymoon Lane 1931 d: William James Craft. lps: Eddie Dowling, Ray Dooley, June Collyer. 8r USA. prod/rel: a V & D Production, Sono Art Productions

Sally Irene and Mary, New York 1922, Play
  Sally, Irene and Mary 1925 d: Edmund Goulding. lps: Constance Bennett, Joan Crawford, Sally O'Neil. 5564f USA. prod/rel: Metro-Goldwyn-Mayer Pictures

  Sally, Irene and Mary 1938 d: William A. Seiter. lps: Alice Faye, Tony Martin, Fred Allen. 86M USA. prod/rel: Twentieth Century-Fox Film Corp.©

DOWNES, DONALD C.
The Easter Dinner, New York 1960, Novel
  Pigeon That Took Rome, The 1962 d: Melville Shavelson. lps: Charlton Heston, Elsa Martinelli, Harry Guardino. 101M USA. *The Easter Dinner* prod/rel: Llenroc Productions, Paramount

DOWNEY, ROBERT
The Comeuppance, Play
  Pound 1970 d: Robert Downey. lps: Joe Madden, James Greene, Marie-Claire CharbA. 92M USA. prod/rel: Pound Films

DOWNING, SYBIL
Lady Tetley's Decree, Play
  Lady Tetley's Decree 1920 d: Fred Paul. lps: Marjorie Hume, Hamilton Stewart, Philip Hewland. 4797f UKN. prod/rel: London, Jury

DOWNING, W. F.
  Lady Tetley's Decree 1920 d: Fred Paul. lps: Marjorie Hume, Hamilton Stewart, Philip Hewland. 4797f UKN. prod/rel: London, Jury

DOWNS, ROBERT C. S.
Going Gently, Novel
  Going Gently 1981 d: Stephen Frears. lps: Norman Wisdom, Judi Dench, Fulton MacKay. TVM. 68M UKN. prod/rel: BBC

Peoples, Book
  Billy: Portrait of a Street Kid 1977 d: Steve Gethers. lps: Levar Burton, Ossie Davis, Dolph Sweet. TVM. 100M USA. prod/rel: CBS, Mark Carliner Productions

DOWST, HENRY PAYSON
Story
  Honest Man, An 1918 d: Frank Borzage. lps: William Desmond, Ann Kroman, Mary Warren. 5r USA. prod/rel: Triangle Film Corp., Triangle Distributing Corp.

Alice in Wonderland, Short Story
  Smiling All the Way 1920 d: Fred J. Butler, Hugh McClung. lps: David Butler, Leatrice Joy, Frances Raymond. 4979f USA. prod/rel: D. N. Schwab Productions, Inc.©, State Rights

The Dancin' Fool, 1919, Short Story
  Dancin' Fool, The 1920 d: Sam Wood. lps: Wallace Reid, Bebe Daniels, Raymond Hatton. 4124f USA. prod/rel: Famous Players-Lasky Corp.©, Paramount-Artcraft Pictures

The Man from Ashaluna, Boston 1920, Novel
  On the Stroke of Three 1924 d: F. Harmon Weight. lps: Kenneth Harlan, Madge Bellamy, Mary Carr. 6767f USA. *Sold for Cash* prod/rel: Associated Arts Corp., Film Booking Offices of America

DOYLE, ARTHUR CONAN (1859–1930), UKN
Short Story
  Tiger of San Pedro, The 1921 d: Maurice Elvey. lps: Eille Norwood, Hubert Willis, Lewis Gilbert. 2080f UKN. prod/rel: Stoll

The Abbey Grange, Short Story
  Abbey Grange, The 1922 d: George Ridgwell. lps: Eille Norwood, Hubert Willis, Teddy Arundell. 2200f UKN. prod/rel: Stoll

  Return of Sherlock Holmes: the Abbey Grange, The 1986 d: Peter Hammond. lps: Jeremy Brett, Edward Hardwicke, Paul Williamson. MTV. 52M UKN. *The Abbey Grange* prod/rel: Granada

Adventure of the Dancing Man, 1903, Short Story
  Sherlock Holmes and the Secret Weapon 1942 d: R. William Neill. lps: Basil Rathbone, Nigel Bruce, Kaaren Verne. 68M USA. *Sherlock Holmes Fights Back*; *Secret Weapon* prod/rel: Universal

Adventure of the Empty House, 1903, Short Story
  Woman in Green, The 1945 d: R. William Neill. lps: Basil Rathbone, Nigel Bruce, Hillary Brooke. 68M USA. *Sherlock Holmes and the Woman in Green*; *Invitation to Death* prod/rel: Universal

Adventure of the Final Problem, 1894, Short Story
  Sleeping Cardinal, The 1931 d: Leslie Hiscott. lps: Arthur Wontner, Norman McKinnel, Jane Welsh. 84M UKN. *Sherlock Holmes' Fatal Hour* (USA); *Sherlock Holmes' Final Hour* prod/rel: Twickenham, Warner Bros.

Adventure of the Musgrave Ritual, 1893, Short Story
  Sherlock Holmes Faces Death 1943 d: R. William Neill. lps: Basil Rathbone, Nigel Bruce, Dennis Hoesy. 68M USA. prod/rel: Universal

Adventure of the Six Napoleons, 1904, Short Story
  Pearl of Death, The 1944 d: R. William Neill. lps: Basil Rathbone, Nigel Bruce, Dennis Hoey. 69M USA. *Sherlock Holmes and the Pearl of Death* prod/rel: Universal

The Beryl Coronet, Short Story
  Beryl Coronet, The 1912 d: Georges Treville. lps: Georges Treville, Mr. Moyse. 2300f UKN. prod/rel: Franco British Film Co., Eclair

  Beryl Coronet, The 1921 d: Maurice Elvey. lps: Eille Norwood, Hubert Willis, Henry Vibart. 2340f UKN. prod/rel: Stoll

Black Peter, Short Story
  Black Peter 1922 d: George Ridgwell. lps: Eille Norwood, Hubert Willis, Teddy Arundell. 1800f UKN. prod/rel: Stoll

The Blue Carbuncle, Short Story
  Adventures of Sherlock Holmes: the Blue Carbuncle, The 1984 d: David Carson. lps: Jeremy Brett, David Burke, Rosalind Knight. MTV. 52M UKN. *The Blue Carbuncle* prod/rel: Granada Tv

  Blue Carbuncle, The 1923 d: George Ridgwell. lps: Eille Norwood, Hubert Willis, Douglas Payne. 2000f UKN. prod/rel: Stoll

The Boscombe Valley Mystery, Short Story
  Boscombe Valley Mystery, The 1922 d: George Ridgwell. lps: Eille Norwood, Hubert Willis, Hal Martin. 2450f UKN. prod/rel: Stoll

  Casebook of Sherlock Holmes: the Boscombe Valley Mystery, The 1990 d: June Howson. lps: Jeremy Brett, Edward Hardwicke, Peter Vaughan. MTV. 50M UKN. prod/rel: Granada Tv

The Bruce Partington Plans, Short Story
  Bruce Partington Plans, The 1922 d: George Ridgwell. lps: Eille Norwood, Hubert Willis, Teddy Arundell. 2196f UKN. prod/rel: Stoll

Return of Sherlock Holmes: the Bruce Partington Plans, The 1986 d: John Gorrie. lps: Jeremy Brett, Edward Hardwicke, Charles Gray. MTV. 52M UKN. *The Bruce Partington Plans* prod/rel: Granada

The Cardboard Box, Short Story
Cardboard Box, The 1923 d: George Ridgwell. lps: Eille Norwood, Hubert Willis, Tom Beaumont. 1800f UKN. prod/rel: Stoll

A Case of Identity, Short Story
Case of Identity, A 1921 d: Maurice Elvey. lps: Eille Norwood, Hubert Willis, Edna Flugrath. 2610f UKN. prod/rel: Stoll

Charles Augustus Milverton, 1904, Short Story
Adventures of Sherlock Holmes: the Master Blackmailer, The 1991 d: Peter Hammond. lps: Jeremy Brett, Edward Hardwicke, Robert Hardy. TVM. 104M UKN. *Sherlock Holmes: the Master Blackmailer; The Master Blackmailer*

Charles Augustus Milverton 1922 d: George Ridgwell. lps: Eille Norwood, Hubert Willis, Teddy Arundell. 1900f UKN. prod/rel: Stoll

Missing Rembrandt, The 1932 d: Leslie Hiscott. lps: Arthur Wontner, Jane Welsh, Miles Mander. 84M UKN. *Sherlock Holmes and the Missing Rembrandt* (USA); *The Strange Case of the Missing Rembrandt* prod/rel: Twickenham, Producers Distributing Corporation

The Copper Beeches, Short Story
Adventures of Sherlock Holmes: the Copper Beeches, The 1985 d: Paul Annett. lps: Jeremy Brett, David Burke, Joss Ackland. MTV. 52M UKN. *The Copper Beeches* prod/rel: Granada Tv

Copper Beeches, The 1912 d: Georges Treville. lps: Georges Treville, Mr. Moyse. 1700f UKN. prod/rel: Franco-British Film Co., Eclair

Copper Beeches, The 1921 d: Maurice Elvey. lps: Eille Norwood, Hubert Willis, Madge White. 2193f UKN. prod/rel: Stoll

The Creeping Man, Short Story
Casebook of Sherlock Holmes: the Creeping Man, The 1991 d: Tim Sullivan. lps: Jeremy Brett, Edward Hardwicke, Charles Kay. MTV. 50M UKN. prod/rel: Granada Tv

The Crooked Man, Short Story
Adventures of Sherlock Holmes: the Crooked Man, The 1983 d: Alan Grint. lps: Jeremy Brett, David Burke, Norman Jones. MTV. 55M UKN. *The Crooked Man* prod/rel: Granada Tv

Crooked Man, The 1923 d: George Ridgwell. lps: Eille Norwood, Hubert Willis, Jack Hobbs. 2228f UKN. prod/rel: Stoll

The Croxley Master, Novel
Croxley Master, The 1921 d: Percy Nash. lps: Dick Webb, Dora Lennox, Jack Stanley. 3900f UKN. prod/rel: Screen Plays, British Exhibitors' Films

The Dancing Men, Short Story
Adventures of Sherlock Holmes: the Dancing Men, The 1984 d: John Bruce. lps: Jeremy Brett, David Burke, Terry Evans. MTV. 52M UKN. *The Dancing Men* prod/rel: Granada Tv

Mystery of the Dancing Men, The 1923 d: George Ridgwell. lps: Eille Norwood, Hubert Willis, Frank Goldsmith. 2600f UKN. prod/rel: Stoll

The Devil's Foot, Short Story
Devil's Foot, The 1921 d: Maurice Elvey. lps: Eille Norwood, Hubert Willis, Harvey Braban. 2514f UKN. prod/rel: Stoll

Return of Sherlock Holmes: the Devil's Foot, The 1986 d: Ken Hannam. lps: Jeremy Brett, Edward Hardwicke, Peter Barkworth. MTV. 55M UKN. *The Devil's Foot* prod/rel: Granada

The Disappearance of Lady Frances Carfax, Short Story
Casebook of Sherlock Holmes: the Disappearance of Lady Carfax, The 1990 d: John Madden. lps: Jeremy Brett, Edward Hardwicke, Cheryl Campbell. MTV. 50M UKN. prod/rel: Granada Tv

Disappearance of Lady Frances Carfax, The 1923 d: George Ridgwell. lps: Eille Norwood, Hubert Willis, Tom Beaumont. 1800f UKN. prod/rel: Stoll

The Dying Detective, Short Story
Dying Detective, The 1921 d: Maurice Elvey. lps: Eille Norwood, Hubert Willis, Cecil Humphreys. 2273f UKN. prod/rel: Stoll

The Empty House, 1903, Short Story
Empty House, The 1921 d: Maurice Elvey. lps: Eille Norwood, Hubert Willis, Austin Fairman. 1800f UKN. prod/rel: Stoll

Return of Sherlock Holmes: the Empty House, The 1986 d: Howard Baker. lps: Jeremy Brett, Edward Hardwicke, Patrick Allen. MTV. 52M UKN. *The Empty House* prod/rel: Granada

Sleeping Cardinal, The 1931 d: Leslie Hiscott. lps: Arthur Wontner, Norman McKinnel, Jane Welsh. 84M UKN. *Sherlock Holmes' Fatal Hour* (USA); *Sherlock Holmes' Final Hour* prod/rel: Twickenham, Warner Bros.

Terror By Night 1946 d: R. William Neill. lps: Basil Rathbone, Nigel Bruce, Alan Mowbray. 69M USA. *Sherlock Holmes in Terror By Night* prod/rel: Universal

The Engineer's Thumb, Short Story
Engineer's Thumb, The 1923 d: George Ridgwell. lps: Eille Norwood, Hubert Willis, Bertram Burleigh. 2000f UKN. prod/rel: Stoll

The Exploits of Brigadier Gerard, London 1896, Novel
Adventures of Gerard, The 1970 d: Jerzy Skolimowski. lps: Peter McEnery, Claudia Cardinale, Eli Wallach. 91M UKN/ITL/SWT. *Le Avventure Di Gerard* (ITL) prod/rel: United Artists, Nigel Films

Brigadier Gerard 1915 d: Bert Haldane. lps: Lewis Waller, Madge Titheradge, A. E. George. 5260f UKN. prod/rel: Barker, Walturdaw

Fighting Eagle, The 1927 d: Donald Crisp. lps: Rod La Rocque, Phyllis Haver, Sam de Grasse. 8002f USA. *Brigadier Gerard* prod/rel: de Mille Pictures, Pathe Exchange, Inc.

The Final Problem, Short Story
Adventures of Sherlock Holmes: the Final Problem, The 1985 d: Alan Grint. lps: Jeremy Brett, David Burke, Eric Porter. MTV. 52M UKN. *The Final Problem* prod/rel: Granada Tv

Final Problem, The 1923 d: George Ridgwell. lps: Eille Norwood, Hubert Willis, Percy Standing. 1686f UKN. prod/rel: Stoll

The Firm of Girdlestone, Novel
Firm of Girdlestone, The 1915 d: Harold Shaw. lps: Edna Flugrath, Fred Groves, Charles Rock. 5100f UKN. prod/rel: London, Jury

The Five Orange Pips, 1892, Short Story
House of Fear, The 1945 d: R. William Neill. lps: Basil Rathbone, Nigel Bruce, Aubrey Mather. 69M USA. prod/rel: Universal

The Gloria Scott, Short Story
Gloria Scott, The 1923 d: George Ridgwell. lps: Eille Norwood, Hubert Willis, Reginald Fox. 2070f UKN. prod/rel: Stoll

The Golden Pince-Nez, Short Story
Golden Pince-Nez, The 1922 d: George Ridgwell. lps: Eille Norwood, Hubert Willis, Teddy Arundell. 1675f UKN. prod/rel: Stoll

The Greek Interpreter, Short Story
Adventures of Sherlock Holmes: the Greek Interpreter, The 1985 d: Derek Marlowe. lps: Jeremy Brett, David Burke, Charles Gray. MTV. 52M UKN. *The Greek Interpreter* prod/rel: Granada Tv

Greek Interpreter, The 1922 d: George Ridgwell. lps: Eille Norwood, Hubert Willis, J. R. Tozer. 1862f UKN. prod/rel: Stoll

His Last Bow, 1917, Short Story
His Last Bow 1923 d: George Ridgwell. lps: Eille Norwood, Hubert Willis, Nelson Ramsey. 1600f UKN. prod/rel: Stoll

Sherlock Holmes and the Voice of Terror 1942 d: John Rawlins. lps: Basil Rathbone, Nigel Bruce, Evelyn Ankers. 65M USA. *Sherlock Holmes Saves London*; *The Voice of Terror* prod/rel: Universal

The Hound of the Baskervilles, London 1902, Novel
Hound of the Baskervilles, The 1921 d: Maurice Elvey. lps: Eille Norwood, Catina Campbell, Rex McDougall. 5500f UKN. prod/rel: Stoll

Hound of the Baskervilles, The 1931 d: V. Gareth Gundrey. lps: John Stuart, Robert Rendel, Reginald Bach. 75M UKN. prod/rel: Gaumont, Ideal

Hound of the Baskervilles, The 1939 d: Sidney Lanfield. lps: Richard Greene, Basil Rathbone, Wendy Barrie. 80M USA. prod/rel: Twentieth Century-Fox Film Corp.©

Hound of the Baskervilles, The 1959 d: Terence Fisher. lps: Peter Cushing, Andre Morell, Christopher Lee. 87M UKN. prod/rel: United Artists, Hammer

Hound of the Baskervilles, The 1972 d: Barry Crane. lps: Stewart Granger, Bernard Fox, William Shatner. TVM. 73M USA. *Sherlock Holmes: Hound of the Baskervilles* prod/rel: Universal

Hound of the Baskervilles, The 1978 d: Paul Morrissey. lps: Peter Cook, Dudley Moore, Denholm Elliott. 85M UKN. prod/rel: Hemdale, Michael White Ltd.

Hound of the Baskervilles, The 1983 d: Douglas Hickox. lps: Ian Richardson, Martin Shaw, Denholm Elliott. 101M UKN. prod/rel: Mapleton, Weintraub

Hund von Baskerville 1, Der 1914 d: Rudolf Meinert. lps: Alwin Neuss, Friedrich Kuhne, Hanni Weisse. 1337m GRM. prod/rel: Vitascope

Hund von Baskerville 2, Der 1914 d: Rudolf Meinert. lps: Alwin Neuss, Friedrich Kuhne, Hanni Weisse. 1040m GRM. prod/rel: Vitascope

Hund von Baskerville 3, Der 1915 d: Richard Oswald. lps: Alwin Neuss, Friedrich Kuhne, Erwin Fichtner. GRM. *The Hound of the Baskervilles* (USA); *Das Unheimliche Zimmer*

Hund von Baskerville, Der 1929 d: Richard Oswald. lps: Carlyle Blackwell, Georg Seroff, Alexander Murski. 2382m GRM. *The Hound of the Baskervilles* prod/rel: Erda-Film-Prod.

Hund von Baskerville, Der 1936 d: Carl Lamac. lps: Fritz Rasp, Anneliese Brand, Peter Voss. 79M GRM. *The Hound of the Baskervilles* (USA)

Return of Sherlock Holmes: the Hound of the Baskervilles, The 1988 d: Brian Mills. lps: Jeremy Brett, Edward Hardwicke, Raymond Adamson. TVM. 105M UKN. *The Hound of the Baskervilles* prod/rel: Granada

Sherlock Holmes: the Baskerville Curse 1983 d: Alex Nicholas. ANM. 67M UKN. *Sherlock Holmes and the Baskerville Curse; The Baskerville Curse*

How It Happened, Short Story
How It Happened 1925 d: Alexander Butler. lps: Sydney Seaward. 750f UKN. prod/rel: Riciprocity Films

The Illustrious Client, Short Story
Casebook of Sherlock Holmes: the Illustrious Client, The 1991 d: Tim Sullivan. lps: Jeremy Brett, Edward Hardwicke, Anthony Valentine. MTV. 50M UKN. prod/rel: Granada Tv

The Lost World, London 1912, Novel
Lost World, The 1925 d: Harry O. Hoyt. lps: Bessie Love, Lloyd Hughes, Lewis Stone. 9700f USA. prod/rel: First National Pictures

Lost World, The 1960 d: Irwin Allen. lps: Claude Rains, Michael Rennie, Jill St. John. 97M USA. *The Origin of Man* prod/rel: Twentieth Century-Fox

Lost World, The 1992 d: Timothy Bond. lps: John Rhys-Davies, David Warner, Eric McCormack. 95M USA.

Lot 29, Story
Tales from the Darkside: the Movie 1990 d: John Harrison. lps: Deborah Harry, Matthew Lawrence, Christian Slater. 93M USA. prod/rel: Paramount

The Man With the Twisted Lip, 1892, Short Story
Man With the Twisted Lip, The 1921 d: Maurice Elvey. lps: Eille Norwood, Hubert Willis, Robert Vallis. 2412f UKN. prod/rel: Stoll

Man With the Twisted Lip, The 1951 d: Richard M. Grey. lps: John Longden, Campbell Singer, Hector Ross. 35M UKN. prod/rel: Telecine Films, Grand National

Return of Sherlock Holmes: the Man With the Twisted Lip, The 1986 d: Patrick Lau. lps: Jeremy Brett, Edward Hardwicke, Clive Francis. MTV. 52M UKN. *The Man With the Twisted Lip* prod/rel: Granada

The Missing Three Quarter, Short Story
Missing Three Quarter, The 1923 d: George Ridgwell. lps: Eille Norwood, Hubert Willis, Hal Martin. 2200f UKN. prod/rel: Stoll

The Musgrave Ritual, Short Story
Musgrave Ritual, The 1912 d: Georges Treville. lps: Georges Treville, Mr. Moyse. 1290f UKN. prod/rel: Franco-British Film Co., Eclair

Musgrave Ritual, The 1922 d: George Ridgwell. lps: Eille Norwood, Hubert Willis, Geoffrey Wilmer. 1750f UKN. prod/rel: Stoll

Return of Sherlock Holmes: the Musgrave Ritual, The 1986 d: David Carson. lps: Jeremy Brett, Edward Hardwicke, Michael Culver. MTV. 55M UKN. *The Musgrave Ritual* prod/rel: Granada

The Mystery of Boscombe Vale, Short Story
Mystery of Boscombe Vale, The 1912 d: Georges Treville. lps: Georges Treville, Mr. Moyse. 1700f UKN. prod/rel: Franco-British Film Co., Eclair

The Naval Treaty, Short Story
Adventures of Sherlock Holmes: the Naval Treaty, The 1984 d: Alan Grint. lps: Jeremy Brett, David Burke, David Gwillim. MTV. 52M UKN. *The Naval Treaty* prod/rel: Granada Tv

Naval Treaty, The 1922 d: George Ridgwell. lps: Eille Norwood, Hubert Willis, Jack Hobbs. 1600f UKN. prod/rel: Stoll

The Noble Bachelor, Short Story
  Adventures of Sherlock Holmes: the Eligible Bachelor 1993 d: Peter Hammond. lps: Jeremy Brett, Edward Hardwicke, Rosalie Williams. TVM. 105M UKN. *The Eligible Bachelor*
  Noble Bachelor, The 1921 d: Maurice Elvey. lps: Eille Norwood, Hubert Willis, Arthur Bell. 2100f UKN. *The Lonely Bachelor* prod/rel: Stoll

The Norwood Builder, Short Story
  Adventures of Sherlock Holmes: the Norwood Builder, The 1985 d: Ken Grieve. lps: Jeremy Brett, David Burke, Rosalie Crutchley. MTV. 52M UKN. *The Norwood Builder* prod/rel: Granada Tv
  Norwood Builder, The 1922 d: George Ridgwell. lps: Eille Norwood, Hubert Willis, Teddy Arundell. 2100f UKN. prod/rel: Stoll

Oncle Bernac, Novel
  Drame Sous Napoleon, Un 1921 d: Gerard Bourgeois. lps: Emile Drain, Rex Davis, Germaine Rouer. 2000m FRN. prod/rel: Film-Eclair, Interexchange Ltd

The Priory School, Short Story
  Priory School, The 1921 d: Maurice Elvey. lps: Eille Norwood, Hubert Willis, Leslie English. 2100f UKN. prod/rel: Stoll
  Return of Sherlock Holmes: the Priory School, The 1986 d: John Madden. lps: Jeremy Brett, Edward Hardwicke, Christopher Benjamin. MTV. 52M UKN. *The Priory School* prod/rel: Granada

The Red Circle, Short Story
  Red Circle, The 1922 d: George Ridgwell. lps: Eille Norwood, Hubert Willis, Teddy Arundell. 1780f UKN. prod/rel: Stoll

The Red-Headed League, 1891, Short Story
  Adventures of Sherlock Holmes: the Red-Headed League, The 1985 d: John Bruce. lps: Jeremy Brett, David Burke, Roger Hammond. MTV. 52M UKN. *The Red-Headed League* prod/rel: Granada Tv
  Red-Headed League, The 1921 d: Maurice Elvey. lps: Eille Norwood, Hubert Willis, Teddy Arundell. 2140f UKN. prod/rel: Stoll
  Sherlock Holmes 1932 d: William K. Howard. lps: Clive Brook, Ernest Torrence, Miriam Jordan. 68M USA. prod/rel: Fox Film Corp.©

The Reigate Squires, Short Story
  Reigate Squires, The 1912 d: Georges Treville. lps: Georges Treville, Mr. Moyse. 1800f UKN. prod/rel: Franco-British Film Co., Eclair
  Reigate Squires, The 1922 d: George Ridgwell. lps: Eille Norwood, Hubert Willis, Teddy Arundell. 1900f UKN. prod/rel: Stoll

The Resident Patient, Short Story
  Adventures of Sherlock Holmes: the Resident Patient, The 1985 d: David Carson. lps: Jeremy Brett, David Burke, Nicholas Clay. MTV. 52M UKN. *The Resident Patient* prod/rel: Granada Tv
  Resident Patient, The 1921 d: Maurice Elvey. lps: Eille Norwood, Hubert Willis, Arthur Bell. 2404f UKN. prod/rel: Stoll

Rodney Stone, 1896, Novel
  House of Temperley, The 1913 d: Harold Shaw. lps: Charles Maude, Ben Webster, Lillian Logan. 4500f UKN. prod/rel: London, Jury
  Rodney Stone 1920 d: Percy Nash. lps: Rex Davis, Lionel d'Aragon, Cecil Morton York. F UKN. prod/rel: Screen Plays, British Exhibitors' Films

A Scandal in Bohemia, Short Story
  Adventures of Sherlock Holmes: a Scandal in Bohemia, The 1984 d: Paul Annett. lps: Jeremy Brett, David Burke, Gayle Hunnicutt. MTV. 52M UKN. *A Scandal in Bohemia* prod/rel: Granada Tv
  Scandal in Bohemia, A 1921 d: Maurice Elvey. lps: Eille Norwood, Hubert Willis, Joan Beverley. 2100f UKN. prod/rel: Stoll

The Second Stain, Short Story
  Return of Sherlock Holmes: the Second Stain, The 1986 d: John Bruce. lps: Jeremy Brett, Edward Hardwicke, Patricia Hodge. MTV. 52M UKN. *The Second Stain* prod/rel: Granada
  Second Stain, The 1922 d: George Ridgwell. lps: Eille Norwood, Hubert Willis, Teddy Arundell. 2200f UKN. prod/rel: Stoll

Shoscombe Old Place, Short Story
  Casebook of Sherlock Holmes: the Shoscombe Old Place, The 1990 d: Patrick Lau. lps: Jeremy Brett, Edward Hardwicke, Robin Ellis. MTV. 50M UKN. prod/rel: Granada Tv

The Sign of Four, London 1890, Novel
  Adventures of Sherlock Holmes: the Sign of Four, The 1987 d: Peter Hammond. lps: Jeremy Brett, Edward Hardwicke, Jenny Seagrove. TVM. 105M UKN. *The Sign of Four*

Sherlock Holmes Solves "the Sign of the Four" 1913. lps: Harry Benham. 2r USA. prod/rel: Thanhouser
Sherlock Holmes' the Sign of Four 1983 d: Desmond Davis. lps: Ian Richardson, David Healy, Cherie Lunghi. 103M UKN. *The Sign of Four* (USA) prod/rel: Embassy, Marpleton
  Sign of Four, The 1923 d: Maurice Elvey. lps: Eille Norwood, Isobel Elsom, Fred Raynham. 6750f UKN. prod/rel: Stoll
  Sign of Four, The 1932 d: Rowland V. Lee, Graham Cutts. lps: Arthur Wontner, Isla Bevan, Ian Hunter. 75M UKN. prod/rel: Associated Talking Pictures, Radio

Silver Blaze, 1894, Short Story
  Return of Sherlock Holmes: Silver Blaze, The 1986 d: Brian Mills. lps: Jeremy Brett, Edward Hardwicke, Peter Barkworth. MTV. 52M UKN. *Silver Blaze* prod/rel: Granada
  Silver Blaze 1912 d: Georges Treville. lps: Georges Treville, Mr. Moyse. 1300f UKN. prod/rel: Franco-British Film Co., Eclair
  Silver Blaze 1923 d: George Ridgwell. lps: Eille Norwood, Hubert Willis, Knighton Small. 2100f UKN. prod/rel: Stoll
  Silver Blaze 1937 d: Thomas Bentley. lps: Arthur Wontner, Lyn Harding, Judy Gunn. 70M UKN. *Murder at the Baskervilles* (USA) prod/rel: Twickenham, Associated British Picture Corporation

The Six Napoleons, Short Story
  Return of Sherlock Holmes: the Six Napoleons, The 1986 d: David Carson. lps: Jeremy Brett, Edward Hardwicke, Colin Jeavons. MTV. 52M UKN. *The Six Napoleons* prod/rel: Granada
  Six Napoleons, The 1922 d: George Ridgwell. lps: Eille Norwood, Hubert Willis, Teddy Arundell. 1790f UKN. prod/rel: Stoll

The Solitary Cyclist, Short Story
  Adventures of Sherlock Holmes: the Solitary Cyclist, The 1984 d: Paul Annett. lps: Jeremy Brett, David Burke, Barbara Wilshire. MTV. 52M UKN. *The Solitary Cyclist* prod/rel: Granada Tv
  Solitary Cyclist, The 1921 d: Maurice Elvey. lps: Eille Norwood, Hubert Willis, R. D. Sylvester. 2140f UKN. prod/rel: Stoll

The Speckled Band, 1892, Short Story
  Adventures of Sherlock Holmes: the Speckled Band, The 1984 d: John Bruce. lps: Jeremy Brett, David Burke, Jeremy Kemp. MTV. 52M UKN. *The Speckled Band* prod/rel: Granada Tv
  Speckled Band, The 1912 d: Georges Treville. lps: Georges Treville, Mr. Moyse. 1700f UKN. prod/rel: Franco-British Film Co., Eclair
  Speckled Band, The 1923 d: George Ridgwell. lps: Eille Norwood, Hubert Willis, Lewis Gilbert. 1800f UKN. prod/rel: Stoll
  Speckled Band, The 1931 d: Jack Raymond. lps: Lyn Harding, Raymond Massey, Athole Stewart. 90M UKN. prod/rel: British and Dominions, Woolf & Freedman

The Stockbroker's Clerk, Short Story
  Stockbroker's Clerk, The 1922 d: George Ridgwell. lps: Eille Norwood, Hubert Willis, Olaf Hytten. 1830f UKN. prod/rel: Stoll

The Stolen Papers, Short Story
  Stolen Papers, The 1912 d: Georges Treville. lps: Georges Treville, Mr. Moyse. 1400f UKN. prod/rel: Franco-British Film Co., Eclair

The Stone of Mazarin, Short Story
  Stone of Mazarin, The 1923 d: George Ridgwell. lps: Eille Norwood, Hubert Willis, Tom Beaumont. 1878f UKN. *The Mazarin Stone* prod/rel: Stoll

A Story of Waterloo, London 1894, Play
  Veteran of Waterloo, The 1933 d: A. V. Bramble. lps: Jerrold Robertshaw, Roger Livesey, Joan Kemp-Welch. 48M UKN. prod/rel: National Talkies, Paramount

A Study in Scarlet, London 1887, Novel
  Study in Scarlet, A 1914 d: George Pearson. lps: Fred Paul, Agnes Glynne, Harry Paulo. 5749f UKN. prod/rel: G. B. Samuelson, Moss
  Study in Scarlet, A 1914. lps: Francis Ford, Jack Francis. 2r USA. prod/rel: Gold Seal
  Study in Scarlet, A 1933 d: Edwin L. Marin. lps: Reginald Owen, Anna May Wong, June Clyde. 73M USA. *The Scarlet Ring* prod/rel: K.B.S. Productions©, World Wide Pictures

The Sussex Vampire, Novel
  Sherlock Holmes: the Last Vampyre 1993 d: Tim Sullivan. lps: Jeremy Brett, Edward Hardwicke, Keith Barron. TVM. 105M UKN. *Sherlock Holmes: Vampire of Lamberley*

Thor Bridge, Short Story
  Casebook of Sherlock Holmes: the Problem of Thor Bridge, The 1990 d: Michael Simpson. lps: Jeremy Brett, Edward Hardwicke, Daniel Massey. MTV. 50M UKN. prod/rel: Granada Tv
  Mystery of Thor Bridge, The 1923 d: George Ridgwell. lps: Eille Norwood, Hubert Willis, A. B. Imeson. 2200f UKN. prod/rel: Stoll

The Three Students, Short Story
  Three Students, The 1923 d: George Ridgwell. lps: Eille Norwood, Hubert Willis, William Lugg. 2500f UKN. prod/rel: Stoll

The Tragedy of the Korosko, London 1898, Novel
  Desert Sheik, The 1924 d: Tom Terriss. lps: Wanda Hawley, Nigel Barrie, Pedro de CordobA. 5700f USA. prod/rel: Truart Film Corp., Film Booking Offices of America
  Fires of Fate 1923 d: Tom Terriss. lps: Wanda Hawley, Nigel Barrie, Pedro de CordobA. 7185f UKN. prod/rel: Gaumont, Westminster
  Fires of Fate 1932 d: Norman Walker. lps: Lester Matthews, Dorothy Bartlam, Kathleen O'Regan. 74M UKN. prod/rel: British International Pictures, Wardour

The Valley of Fear, London 1914, Novel
  Triumph of Sherlock Holmes, The 1935 d: Leslie Hiscott. lps: Arthur Wontner, Lyn Harding, Jane Carr. 84M UKN. prod/rel: Real Art, Gaumont-British
  Valley of Fear, The 1916 d: Alexander Butler. lps: H. A. Saintsbury, Daisy Burrell, Booth Conway. 6500f UKN. prod/rel: G. B. Samuelson, Moss

Wisteria Lodge, Short Story
  Return of Sherlock Holmes: Wisteria Lodge, The 1986 d: Peter Hammond. lps: Jeremy Brett, Edward Hardwicke, Freddie Jones. MTV. 55M UKN. *Wisteria Lodge* prod/rel: Granada

The Yellow Face, Short Story
  Yellow Face 1921 d: Maurice Elvey. lps: Eille Norwood, Hubert Willis, Clifford Heatherley. 2020f UKN. prod/rel: Stoll

DOYLE, BRIAN
Angel Square, Novel
  Angel Square 1991 d: Anne Wheeler. lps: Jeremy Radick, Ned Beatty, Nicola Cavendish. 106M CND. *Angel Street* prod/rel: Rendez-Vous, Wheeler-Hendren

DOYLE, LAIRD
Hard Luck Dame, Story
  Dangerous 1935 d: Alfred E. Green. lps: Bette Davis, Franchot Tone, Margaret Lindsay. 80M USA. *Hard Luck Dame* prod/rel: Warner Bros. Pictures, Inc.
  Singapore Woman 1941 d: Jean Negulesco. lps: Brenda Marshall, David Bruce, Virginia Field. 64M USA. prod/rel: Warner Bros.

DOYLE, MONTE
Signpost to Murder, London 1962, Play
  Signpost to Murder 1964 d: George Englund. lps: Joanne Woodward, Stuart Whitman, Edward Mulhare. 77M USA. prod/rel: Marten Productions, MGM

DOYLE, RODDY (1958–, IRL
The Snapper, Novel
  Snapper, The 1993 d: Stephen Frears. lps: Tina Kellegher, Colm Meaney, Ruth McCabe. TVM. 90M UKN. prod/rel: BBC Films for Screen Two

The Van, Novel
  Van, The 1996 d: Stephen Frears. lps: Colm Meaney, Donal O'Kelly, Ger Ryan. 100M UKN/IRL. prod/rel: 20th Century Fox, Deadly Films

DOYLE, WILLIAM R.
Carnival, New York 1924, Play
  Young Desire 1930 d: Lewis D. Collins. lps: Mary Nolan, William Janney, Ralf Harolde. 69M USA. *Carnival Girl* prod/rel: Universal Pictures

DOZIER, ROBERT
Deal a Blow, 1955, Television Play
  Young Stranger, The 1957 d: John Frankenheimer. lps: James MacArthur, Kim Hunter, James Daly. 84M USA. prod/rel: Universal-International

DRABBLE, JOHN
The Windmill, Novel
  Windmill, The 1937 d: Arthur Woods. lps: Hugh Williams, Glen Alyn, Henry Mollison. 62M UKN. prod/rel: Warner Bros., First National

DRABBLE, MARGARET (1939–, UKN
The Millstone, London 1964, Novel
  Touch of Love, A 1969 d: Waris Hussein. lps: Sandy Dennis, Ian McKellen, Michael Coles. 107M UKN. *Thank You All Very Much* (USA); *The Millstone* prod/rel: Palomar Pictures International, Amicus Productions

DRABO, ADAMA
Taafe Fanga, Play
Taafe Fanga 1997 d: Adama Drabo. lps: Fanta Berete, Ramata Drabo, Ibrahim S. KoitA. 100M MLI/GRM. prod/rel: Cnpc (Mali), ZDF

DRACHMAN, HOLGER (1846–1908), DNM
Der Var Engang, 1885, Play
Der Var Engang 1922 d: Carl T. Dreyer. lps: Clara Pontoppidan, Svend Methling, Peter Jerndorff. DNM. *Once Upon a Time*
Der Var Engang 1966 d: John Price. lps: Vigga Bro, Birgitte Bruun, Marianne Flor. 102M DNM. prod/rel: Merry Film
Kirk Og Orgel, 1904, Short Story
Kirke Og Orgel 1932 d: George Schneevoigt. lps: Svend Methling, Clara Pontoppidan, Holger Reenberg. 96M DNM. prod/rel: Nordisk Film

DRAGO, HARRY SINCLAIR
Buckskin Empire, Novel
Buckskin Frontier 1943 d: Lesley Selander. lps: Richard Dix, Lee J. Cobb, Jane Wyatt. 74M USA. *The Iron Road* (UKN) prod/rel: United Artists, George Sherman
Playthings of Desire, New York 1934, Novel
Playthings of Desire 1934 d: George Melford. lps: Linda Watkins, James Kirkwood, Reed Howes. 58M USA. *Murder in the Library* (UKN) prod/rel: Pinnacle Productions, State Rights
Whispering Sage, New York 1922, Novel
Whispering Sage 1927 d: Scott R. Dunlap. lps: Buck Jones, Natalie Joyce, Emile Chautard. 4783f USA. prod/rel: Fox Film Corp.

DRAKE, MAURICE
The Salving of a Derelict, Novel
Nets of Destiny 1924 d: Arthur Rooke. lps: Stewart Rome, Mary Odette, Gertrude McCoy. 5600f UKN. prod/rel: I. B. Davidson, Butcher's Film Service

DRAKE, OLIVER
Story
Dragoon Wells Massacre 1957 d: Harold Schuster. lps: Barry Sullivan, Dennis O'Keefe, Mona Freeman. 88M USA. prod/rel: Allied Artists

DRATLER, JAY
Las Vegas Story, The 1952 d: Robert Stevenson. lps: Victor Mature, Jane Russell, Vincent Price. 88M USA. prod/rel: RKO Radio, Howard Hughes
The Pitfall, Novel
Pitfall 1948 d: Andre de Toth. lps: Dick Powell, Lizabeth Scott, Jane Wyatt. 84M USA. prod/rel: Regal, United Artists

DRAULT, JEAN
600.000 Francs Par Mois, Novel
Six Cent Mille Francs Par Mois 1925 d: Robert Peguy, Nicolas Koline. lps: Nicolas Koline, Madeleine Guitty, Andree Standart. 2200m FRN. *000 Franc Par Mois 600* prod/rel: Cine-France-Films

DRAWBELL, J. W.
Love Story, Novel
Love Story 1944 d: Leslie Arliss. lps: Margaret Lockwood, Stewart Granger, Patricia Roc. 108M UKN. *A Lady Surrenders* (USA) prod/rel: Eagle-Lion, Gainsborough
The Milky Way, Play
Innocents of Chicago, The 1932 d: Lupino Lane. lps: Henry Kendall, Betty Norton, Margot Grahame. 68M UKN. *Why Saps Leave Home* (USA); *The Milky Way* prod/rel: British International Pictures, Wardour
Who Goes Next?, Play
Who Goes Next? 1938 d: Maurice Elvey. lps: Barry K. Barnes, Sophie Steward, Jack Hawkins. 85M UKN. prod/rel: Fox British

DRDA, JAN
Short Stories
Princezne Jasnence a Letajicim Sevci 1987 d: Zdenek TroskA. lps: Michaela Kuklova, Jan Potmesil, Lubor Tokos. 90M CZC. *Princess Jasna and the Flying Cobbler* prod/rel: Filmove Studio Barrandov
Story
Vyssi Princip 1960 d: Jiri Krejcik. lps: Jana Brejchova, Frantisek Smolik, Marie VasovA. 100M CZC. *A Higher Principle* prod/rel: Barrandov
Mestecko Na Dlani, Novel
Mestecko Na Dlani 1942 d: Vaclav Binovec. lps: Frantisek Smolik, Gustav Hilmar, Marie BlazkovA. 2724m CZC. *The Village in Your Palm; Our Little Town; The Town in the Palm of His Hand* prod/rel: Nationalfilm
Stribrna Oblaka, Novel
Stribrna Oblaka 1938 d: Cenek Slegl. lps: Jan S. Kolar, Jaroslav Marvan, Marie BlazkovA. 2410m CZC. *Silver Skies* prod/rel: Espo

DREGELY, GABOR
Der Gatte Des Frauleins, Vienna 1916, Play
Her Wedding Night 1930 d: Frank Tuttle. lps: Clara Bow, Ralph Forbes, Charles Ruggles. 6294f USA. prod/rel: Paramount-Publix Corp.
Miss Bluebeard 1925 d: Frank Tuttle. lps: Bebe Daniels, Robert Frazer, Kenneth MacKennA. 6453f USA. prod/rel: Famous Players-Lasky, Paramount Pictures
A Szerencse Fia, Budapest 1908, Play
Tailor Made Man, A 1922 d: Joseph de Grasse. lps: Charles Ray, Tom Ricketts, Ethel Grandin. 8469f USA. prod/rel: United Artists Corp., Charles Ray Productions
Tailor Made Man, A 1931 d: Sam Wood. lps: William Haines, Dorothy Jordan, Joseph Cawthorn. 80M USA. *The Impostor; A Tailor-Made Man* prod/rel: Metro-Goldwyn-Mayer Corp., Metro-Goldwyn-Mayer Dist. Corp.©

DREISER, THEODORE (1871–1945), USA
An American Tragedy, New York 1925, Novel
American Tragedy, An 1931 d: Josef von Sternberg. lps: Phillips Holmes, Sylvia Sidney, Frances Dee. 95M USA. prod/rel: Paramount Publix Corp.
Place in the Sun, A 1951 d: George Stevens. lps: Elizabeth Taylor, Montgomery Clift, Shelley Winters. 122M USA. prod/rel: Paramount
Jennie Gerhardt, New York 1911, Novel
Jennie Gerhardt 1933 d: Marion Gering. lps: Sylvia Sidney, Donald Cook, Mary Astor. 85M USA. prod/rel: Paramount Productions©, A. B. P. Schulberg Production
The Lost Phoebe, 1916, Short Story
Lost Phoebe, The 1983 d: Mel Damski. 30M USA.
My Brother Paul, 1919, Short Story
My Gal Sal 1942 d: Irving Cummings. lps: Rita Hayworth, Victor Mature, John Sutton. 103M USA. prod/rel: 20th Century Fox
The Prince Who Was a Thief, 1927, Short Story
Prince Who Was a Thief, The 1951 d: Rudolph Mate. lps: Tony Curtis, Piper Laurie, Everett Sloane. 88M USA. prod/rel: Universal-International
Sister Carrie, 1900, Novel
Carrie 1952 d: William Wyler. lps: Jennifer Jones, Laurence Olivier, Miriam Hopkins. 118M USA. prod/rel: Paramount

DRESSER, PAUL
On the Banks of the Wabash, Song
On the Banks of the Wabash 1923 d: J. Stuart Blackton. lps: Mary Carr, Burr McIntosh, James Morrison. 7156f USA. *Banks of the Wabash* prod/rel: Vitagraph Co. of America

DREYER, MAX
Der Ammenkonig, Play
Ammenkonig, Der 1935 d: Hans Steinhoff. lps: Kathe Gold, Richard Romanowsky, Gustav Knuth. 103M GRM. *Das Tal Des Lebens* prod/rel: Centropa, D.F.H.
Die Reifeprufung, Play
Reifende Jugend 1933 d: Carl Froelich. lps: Heinrich George, Peter Voss, Paul Henckels. 115M GRM. *Ripening Youth* prod/rel: Carl Froelich
Reifende Jugend 1955 d: Ulrich Erfurth. lps: Mathias Wieman, Albert Lieven, Christine Keller. 97M GRM. prod/rel: Concordia
Die Siebzehnjahrigen, 1904, Play
Eta Critica, L' 1921 d: Amleto Palermi. lps: Pina Menichelli, Livio Pavanelli, Giorgio Fini. 2135m ITL. prod/rel: Rinascimento Film
Siebzehnjahrigen, Die 1919 d: Hanna Henning. lps: Hanni Weisse, Kurt Vespermann, Bruno Harprecht. 1777m GRM. prod/rel: Doktram-Film
Siebzehnjahrigen, Die 1928 d: Georg Asagaroff. lps: Grete Mosheim, Hans Adalbert Schlettow, Martin Herzberg. 2280m GRM. prod/rel: Terra-Film

DRIANT, COLONEL
Alerte!, Novel
Alerte! 1912 d: Georges Pallu, E. Berny. lps: Gaston Rieffler, Damores, Marc Gerard. 1225m FRN. prod/rel: Gfp Lordier

DRIEU LA ROCHELLE, PIERRE
Une Femme a Sa Fenetre, 1930, Novel
Femme a Sa Fenetre, Une 1976 d: Pierre Granier-Deferre. lps: Romy Schneider, Philippe Noiret, Victor Lanoux. 115M FRN/ITL/GRM. *A Woman at Her Window* (USA); *Una Donna Alla Finestra* (ITL); *Die Frau Am Fenster* (GRM); *Woman at the Window* prod/rel: Cinema 77, Rizzoli Film (Roma)

Le Feu Follet, Paris 1931, Novel
Feu Follet, Le 1963 d: Louis Malle. lps: Maurice Ronet, Jeanne Moreau, Alexandra Stewart. 121M FRN/ITL. *Fuoco Fatuo* (ITL); *The Fire Within* (USA); *Fox Fire; Will O' the Wisp; A Time to Live and a Time to Die* (UKN) prod/rel: Nouvelles Editions De Films, Arco Film

DRIGO, PAOLA
Maria Zef, 1936, Novel
Condannata Senza Colpa 1954 d: Luigi de Marchi. lps: Eva Vanicek, Piero Lulli, Silvana Jachino. 90M ITL. *Maria Zef* prod/rel: Cine Associati

DRILLING, ERIC
River Red, Play
River Red 1998 d: Eric Drilling. lps: Tom Everett Scott, David Moscow, Cara Buono. 104M USA. prod/rel: Drilling Films, Miller Entertainment Group

DRISCOLL, PETER (1942–), SAF
The Wilby Conspiracy, Novel
Wilby Conspiracy, The 1975 d: Ralph Nelson. lps: Michael Caine, Sidney Poitier, Prunella Gee. 106M UKN/USA. prod/rel: United Artists, Optimus

DROGE, E. W.
Ohne Sorge in Sanssouci, Novel
Junge Herzen 1944 d: Boleslav Barlog. lps: Harald Holberg, Lisca Malbran, Ingrid Lutz. 91M GRM. prod/rel: UFA, Atlantic

DROOP, MARIE-LUISE
Kwa Heri, Novel
Reiter von Deutsch-Ostafrika, Die 1934 d: Herbert Selpin. lps: Ilse Stobrawa, Sepp Rist, Peter Voss. 89M GRM. prod/rel: Terra-Film

DROUET, ANNE
Ces Sacrees Vacances, Novel
Ces Sacrees Vacances 1955 d: Robert Vernay. lps: Pierre Destailles, Sophie Desmarets, Pauline Carton. 102M FRN. prod/rel: Globe, Omnium Film

DROUGHT, JAMES
The Gypsy Moths, Norwalk, Ct. 1964, Novel
Gypsy Moths, The 1969 d: John Frankenheimer. lps: Burt Lancaster, Deborah Kerr, Gene Hackman. 110M USA. prod/rel: Metro-Goldwyn-Mayer

DROUILLY, JOSE GERMAIN
Maman, Paris 1924, Play
Magnificent Flirt, The 1928 d: Harry d'Abbadie d'Arrast. lps: Florence Vidor, Albert Conti, Loretta Young. 7r USA. prod/rel: Paramount Famous Lasky Corp.

DRUMMOND DE ANDRADE, CARLOS
O Indio, 1962, Short Story
Cronica Da Cidade Amada 1965 d: Carlos Hugo Christensen. lps: Artur Semedo. 116M BRZ.
Luzia, 1962, Short Story
Cronica Da Cidade Amada 1965 d: Carlos Hugo Christensen. lps: Artur Semedo. 116M BRZ.
A Moca, O Padre, 1959-62, Verse
Padre E a Moca, O 1966 d: Joaquim Pedro de Andrade. lps: Helena Ignez. 102M BRZ. *The Priest and the Girl*

DRUMMOND, JOHN
But for These Men, London 1962, Book
Heroes of Telemark, The 1965 d: Anthony Mann. lps: Kirk Douglas, Richard Harris, Ulla Jacobsson. 131M UKN. *The Unknown Battle* prod/rel: Benton Film Productions, Rank Film Distributors

DRUON, MAURICE (1918–), FRN
Les Grandes Familles, 1948, Novel
Grandes Familles, Les 1959 d: Denys de La Patelliere. lps: Jean Gabin, Pierre Brasseur, Jean Desailly. 92M FRN. *The Possessors* (USA) prod/rel: Filmsonor, Intermondia Films
La Volupte d'Etre, 1954, Novel
Matter of Time, A 1976 d: Vincente Minnelli. lps: Liza Minnelli, Ingrid Bergman, Charles Boyer. 99M USA/UKN/ITL. *Nina* (ITL) prod/rel: American International Production, General International Films

DRURY, ALLEN (1918–, USA, Drury, Allen Stuart
Advise and Consent, New York 1959, Novel
Advise and Consent 1962 d: Otto Preminger. lps: Charles Laughton, Walter Pidgeon, Lew Ayres. 140M USA. prod/rel: Columbia, Alpha - Alpina S.a.

DRURY, MAJ. W. P.
The Flag Lieutenant, London 1908, Play
Flag Lieutenant, The 1919 d: Percy Nash. lps: Ivy Close, George Wynn, Dorothy Fane. 5200f UKN. prod/rel: Barker, Jury
Flag Lieutenant, The 1926 d: Maurice Elvey. lps: Henry Edwards, Dorothy Seacombe, Fred Raynham. 8500f UKN. prod/rel: Astra-National
Flag Lieutenant, The 1932 d: Henry Edwards. lps: Henry Edwards, Anna Neagle, Joyce Bland. 85M UKN. prod/rel: British and Dominions, Woolf & Freedman

DSCHASI DAWA
Ba Sang Ta-Te Ti-Me-Meng, Novel
  Ba Sang Ta-Te Ti-Me-Meng 1985 d: P'an Hsiao-Yang. lps: Ishi Tsosia, Paidan Yuzen, Hai Sang. 105M CHN.

DU BOIS, WILLIAM (1868–1963), USA, Du Bois, William Edward Burghardt
The Pagan Lady, New York 1930, Play
  Pagan Lady, The 1931 d: John Francis Dillon. lps: Evelyn Brent, Conrad Nagel, Charles Bickford. 77M USA. prod/rel: Columbia Pictures Corp.©

DU MAURIER, DAPHNE (1907–1989), UKN
The Birds, 1952, Short Story
  Birds, The 1963 d: Alfred Hitchcock. lps: Rod Taylor, Tippi Hedren, Jessica Tandy. 120M USA. prod/rel: Alfred J. Hitchcock Productions
The Breakthrough, Short Story
  Lifeforce Experiment, The 1993 d: Piers Haggard. lps: Donald Sutherland, Mimi Kuzyk, Corin Nemec. TVM. 120M CND/USA. *Breakthrough*
Don't Look Now, 1971, Short Story
  Don't Look Now 1973 d: Nicolas Roeg. lps: Julie Christie, Donald Sutherland, Hilary Mason. 110M UKN/ITL. *A Venezia un Dicembre Rosso Shocking* (ITL) prod/rel: Casey Production (London), Eldorado Film (Roma)
Frenchman's Creek, 1941, Novel
  Frenchman's Creek 1944 d: Mitchell Leisen. lps: Joan Fontaine, Arturo de Cordova, Basil Rathbone. 113M USA. prod/rel: Paramount
  Frenchman's Creek 1998 d: Ferdinand Fairfax. lps: Tara Fitzgerald, Anthony Delon, James Fleet. TVM. 100M UKN. prod/rel: Carlton Television©, Wgbh Boston
Hungry Hill, 1943, Novel
  Hungry Hill 1947 d: Brian Desmond Hurst. lps: Margaret Lockwood, Dennis Price, Cecil Parker. 109M UKN. prod/rel: General Film Distributors, Two Cities
Jamaica Inn, 1936, Novel
  Jamaica Inn 1939 d: Alfred Hitchcock. lps: Maureen O'Hara, Leslie Banks, Emlyn Williams. 107M UKN. prod/rel: Mayflower, Associated British Picture Corporation
  Jamaica Inn 1985 d: Lawrence Gordon Clark. lps: Patrick McGoohan, Jane Seymour, Trevor Eve. TVM. 200M UKN. prod/rel: Htv
My Cousin Rachel, 1951, Novel
  My Cousin Rachel 1952 d: Henry Koster. lps: Olivia de Havilland, Richard Burton, Audrey Dalton. 98M USA. prod/rel: 20th Century-Fox
  My Cousin Rachel 198- d: Brian Farnham. lps: Geraldine Chaplin, Christopher Guard. MTV. 176M UKN.
Rebecca, London 1938, Novel
  Kohraa 1964 d: Biren Nag. lps: Waheeda Rehman, Biswajit, Manmohan KrishnA. 154M IND. prod/rel: Geetanjali Pictures
  Rebecca 1940 d: Alfred Hitchcock. lps: Laurence Olivier, Joan Fontaine, George Sanders. 130M USA. prod/rel: United Artists Corp., Selznick International Pictures
  Rebecca 1979 d: Simon Langton. lps: Jeremy Brett, Joanna David, Anna Massey. SRL. UKN. prod/rel: BBC
  Rebecca 1995. lps: Charles Dance, Diana Rigg, Faye Dunaway. MTV. 206M UKN.
The Scapegoat, 1957, Novel
  Scapegoat, The 1959 d: Robert Hamer. lps: Alec Guinness, Bette Davis, Nicole Maurey. 92M UKN/USA. prod/rel: MGM, Du Maurier-Guinness
The Years Between, London 1945, Play
  Years Between, The 1946 d: Compton Bennett. lps: Michael Redgrave, Valerie Hobson, Flora Robson. 100M UKN. prod/rel: General Film Distributors, Sydney Box

DU MAURIER, GEORGE (1834–1896), UKN
Peter Ibbetson, New York 1891, Novel
  Forever 1921 d: George Fitzmaurice. lps: Wallace Reid, Elsie Ferguson, Montagu Love. 7236f USA. *The Great Romance*; *Peter Ibbetson* prod/rel: Famous Players-Lasky, Paramount Pictures
  Peter Ibbetson 1935 d: Henry Hathaway. lps: Gary Cooper, Ann Harding, John Halliday. 88M USA. prod/rel: Paramount Productions©
Trilby, London 1894, Novel
  Svengali 1927 d: Gennaro Righelli. lps: Paul Wegener, Anita Dorris, Alexander Granach. 2839m GRM. prod/rel: Terra-Film
  Svengali 1931 d: Archie Mayo. lps: John Barrymore, Marian Marsh, Donald Crisp. 79M USA. prod/rel: Warner Bros. Pictures©
  Svengali 1954 d: Noel Langley. lps: Hildegard Knef, Donald Wolfit, Terence Morgan. 82M UKN. prod/rel: Alderdale, Renown

  Svengali 1982 d: Anthony Harvey. lps: Peter O'Toole, Jodie Foster, Elizabeth Ashley. TVM. 100M USA. prod/rel: Robert Halmi Productions
  Trilby 1914 d: Harold Shaw. lps: Sir Herbert Beerbohm Tree, Viva Birkett, Ion Swinley. 3400f UKN. prod/rel: London, Jury
  Trilby 1915 d: Maurice Tourneur. lps: Clara Kimball Young, Wilton Lackaye, Phyllis Neilson-Terry. 5r USA. prod/rel: Equitable Motion Pictures Corp.©, World Film Corp.
  Trilby 1922. lps: Phyllis Neilson-Terry, Charles Garry. 1300f UKN. prod/rel: Master Films, British Exhibitors' Films
  Trilby 1923 d: James Young. lps: Andree Lafayette, Creighton Hale, Arthur Edmund Carewe. 7321f USA. prod/rel: Richard Walton Tully Productions, Associated First National Pictures

DU MAURIER, GUY
An Englishman's Home, London 1909, Play
  Englishman's Home, An 1914 d: Ernest G. Batley. lps: George Foley, Ernest G. Batley, Dorothy Batley. 2200f USA. prod/rel: British and Colonial, Davison Film Sales Agency
  Englishman's Home, An 1939 d: Albert de Courville. lps: Edmund Gwenn, Mary Maguire, Paul Henreid. 79M UKN. *Madmen of Europe* (USA); *Mad Men of Europe* prod/rel: United Artists, Aldwych

DU PRE, HILARY
A Genius in the Family, Biography
  Hilary and Jackie 1998 d: Anand Tucker. lps: Emily Watson, Rachel Griffiths, James Frain. 122M UKN. prod/rel: Intermedia Films©, Film Four©

DU PRE, PIERS
  Hilary and Jackie 1998 d: Anand Tucker. lps: Emily Watson, Rachel Griffiths, James Frain. 122M UKN. prod/rel: Intermedia Films©, Film Four©

DU SOUCHET, HENRY A.
The Man from Mexico, New York 1897, Play
  Let's Get Married 1926 d: Gregory La CavA. lps: Richard Dix, Lois Wilson, Nat Pendleton. 6800f USA. prod/rel: Famous Players-Lasky, Paramount Pictures
  Man from Mexico, The 1914 d: Thomas N. Heffron. lps: John Barrymore, Wellington Playter, Harold Lockwood. 5145f USA. prod/rel: Famous Players Film Co., Paramount Pictures Corp.
My Friend from India, New York 1912, Play
  My Friend from India 1914 d: Ashley Miller, Harry Beaumont. lps: Walter E. Perkins, Robert Brower, Harry Beaumont. 3r USA. prod/rel: Edison
  My Friend from India 1927 d: E. Mason Hopper. lps: Franklin Pangborn, Elinor Fair, Ben Hendricks Jr. 5750f USA. prod/rel: de Mille Pictures, Pathe Exchange, Inc.
Who Goes There?, Play
  Who Goes There? 1914 d: Ashley Miller. lps: Walter E. Perkins, Viola Dana, Harry Eytinge. 2r USA. prod/rel: Edison

DU TERRAIL, PONSON
Les Amours de Rocambole, Novel
  Amours de Rocambole, Les 1924 d: Charles Maudru. lps: Maurice Thoreze, Claude Merelle, Germaine Fontaines. F FRN. prod/rel: Societe D'editions Cinematographiques
La Capinera Del Mulino, Novel
  Capinera Del Mulino, La 1957 d: Angio Zane. lps: Marisa Belli, Franco Andrei, Giulio Cali. 120M ITL. prod/rel: Onda Film
Les Mysteres Des Bois
  Mysteres Des Bois, Les 1908-18. lps: Claude Merelle. FRN.
Les Premieres Armes de Rocambole, Novel
  Premieres Armes de Rocambole, Les 1924 d: Charles Maudru. lps: Maurice Thoreze, Claude Merelle, Albert Decoeur. 2080m FRN. prod/rel: Societe D'editions Cinematographiques
Le Trompette de la Beresina, Novel
  Si le Roi Savait Ca 1956 d: Caro Canaille, Edoardo Anton. lps: Roberto Risso, Henri Vilbert, Mireille Granelli. 92M FRN/ITL. *Al Servizio Dell'imperatore* (ITL) prod/rel: Medionfilm (Roma), S.N. Films Dispa (Paris)
Les Voleurs du Grand Monde
  Heritage de Cabestan, L' 1913 d: Adrien Caillard. lps: Leon Bernard, Rene Maupre, Germaine Dermoz. 1090m FRN. prod/rel: Scagl

DU XUAN
Wu Ming Ying XIong, Play
  Wu Ming Ying XIong 1958 d: Gao Heng. lps: Mu Hong, Ji Ming, Li Wei. 11r CHN. *Nameless Heroes* prod/rel: Jiangnan Film Studio

DUBE, MARCEL
Les Beaux Dimanches, Play
  Beaux Dimanches, Les 1974 d: Richard Martin. lps: Jean Duceppe, Denise Filiatrault, Luce Guilbeault. 93M CND. prod/rel: Mojack Film Ltee., Cine-Art

DUBERMAN, MARTIN
Stonewall, Book
  Stonewall 1995 d: Nigel Finch. lps: Guillermo Diaz, Frederick Weller, Brendan Corbalis. 99M UKN/USA. prod/rel: BBC

DUBOIS, WILLIAM (1868–1963), USA
I Loved You Wednesday, New York 1932, Play
  I Loved You Wednesday 1933 d: Henry King, William Cameron Menzies. lps: Warner Baxter, Elissa Landi, Victor Jory. 77M USA. prod/rel: Fox Film Corp.©

DUBOIS-JOLLET, AYME
Les Folies d'Elodie, Novel
  Folies d'Elodie, Les 1981 d: Andre Genoves. lps: Marcha Grant, Andre Genoves, Caroline Aguilar. 90M FRN. *Secrets of the Satin Blues*; *Naughty Blue Knickers*; *The Follies of Elodie* prod/rel: Cine 7, a.G.C.

DUBSKA, MANA
Manzelka Neco Tusi, Novel
  Manzelka Neco Tusi 1938 d: Karel SpelinA. lps: Jara Kohout, Ruzena Slemrova, Zita KabatovA. 2245m CZC. *The Wife Smells a Rat* prod/rel: Excelsior

DUCHARME, REJEAN (1942–, CND
Le Nez Qui Vogue, Novel
  Grand Sabordage, Le 1972 d: Alain Perisson. lps: Luce Guilbeault, Nathalie Drivet, Pascal Bressy. 85M CND/FRN. *Milles Et Chateaugue* prod/rel: Dovidis (Paris), Marianne Productions (Paris)

DUCHE, JEAN
Elle Et Moi, Novel
  Elle Et Moi 1952 d: Guy Lefranc. lps: Francois Perier, Dany Robin, Jacqueline Gauthier. 101M FRN. prod/rel: Jacques Roitfeld, Sirius

DUCKETT, ELEANOR SHIPLEY
Alfred the Great, Chicago 1956, Book
  Alfred the Great 1969 d: Clive Donner. lps: David Hemmings, Michael York, Prunella Ransome. 122M UKN. prod/rel: Bernard Smith Films, MGM British

DUCKWORTH, MADGE
Her Nameless(?) Child, Play
  Her Nameless(?) Child 1915 d: Maurice Elvey. lps: Elisabeth Risdon, Fred Groves, A. V. Bramble. 3450f UKN. prod/rel: British and Colonial, Ideal

DUDER, TESSA
Alex, Book
  Alex 1992 d: Megan Simpson. lps: Lauren Jackson, Chris Haywood, Josh Picker. 90M ASL/NZL. prod/rel: Isambard Productions©, New Zealand on Air©

DUDLEY, E. LAWRENCE
Novel
  Voltaire 1933 d: John G. Adolfi. lps: George Arliss, Margaret Lindsay, Doris Kenyon. 72M USA. prod/rel: Warner Bros. Pictures©

DUDLEY, ERNEST
The Harassed Hero, Novel
  Harassed Hero, The 1954 d: Maurice Elvey. lps: Guy Middleton, Joan Winmill, Elwyn Brook-Jones. 61M UKN. prod/rel: Corsair, Ab-Pathe

DUER, CAROLINE
A Lady in Love, Play
  Lady in Love, A 1920 d: Walter Edwards. lps: Ethel Clayton, Harrison Ford, Boyd Irwin. 4607f USA. prod/rel: Famous Players-Lasky Corp.©, Paramount-Artcraft Pictures

DUFF, ALAN
Once Were Warriors, Novel
  Once Were Warriors 1994 d: Lee Tamahori. lps: Temuera Morrison, Rena Owen, Cliff Curtis. 103M NZL. *Once Were Heroes* prod/rel: Communicado, New Zealand Film Commission

DUFF, JAMES
Homefront, Play
  War at Home, The 1996 d: Emilio Estevez. lps: Kathy Bates, Martin Sheen, Kimberly Williams. 124M USA. prod/rel: Avatar Entertainment©, Touchstone Pictures

DUFFY, ALBERT
Queen's Local, Play
  Hunted Men 1938 d: Louis King. lps: Lloyd Nolan, J. Carrol Naish, Lynne Overman. 65M USA. *Crime Gives Orders* prod/rel: Paramount Pictures©

DUFFY, CLINTON T.
The San Quentin Story, 1950, Book
  Duffy of San Quentin 1954 d: Walter Doniger. lps: Louis Hayward, Joanne Dru, Paul Kelly. 78M USA. *Men Behind Bars* (UKN) prod/rel: Warner Bros.

Steel Cage, The 1954 d: Walter Doniger. lps: Paul Kelly, Maureen O'Sullivan, Walter Slezak. 80M USA. prod/rel: United Artists, Phoenix Films

DUFFY, GERALD C.
Sure Fire Flint, 1922, Short Story
  Sure Fire Flint 1922 d: Dell Henderson. lps: Johnny Hines, Edmund Breese, Robert Edeson. 6423f USA. prod/rel: Mastodon Films

DUFTY, WILLIAM
Lady Sings the Blues, Autobiography
  Lady Sings the Blues 1972 d: Sidney J. Furie. lps: Diana Ross, Billy Dee Williams, Richard Pryor. 125M USA. prod/rel: Paramount

DUGANNE, PHYLLIS
Nice Girl?, Play
  Nice Girl? 1941 d: William A. Seiter. lps: Deanna Durbin, Franchot Tone, Walter Brennan. 91M USA. *Love at Last* prod/rel: Universal

DUGUE, FERDINAND
La Bouquetiere Des Innocents, Play
  Bouquetiere Des Innocents, La 1922 d: Jacques Robert. lps: Jacques Guilhene, Lilian Constantini, Simone Vaudry. 2000m FRN. prod/rel: Gaumont - Serie Pax
La Fille Des Chiffonniers, Play
  Fille Des Chiffonniers, La 1911 d: Albert Capellani, Georges MoncA. lps: Paul Capellani, Jean Kemm, Andree Pascal. 655m FRN. prod/rel: Scagl
  Fille Des Chiffonniers, La 1922 d: Henri Desfontaines. lps: Jacques Gretillat, Blanche Montel, Madeleine Guitty. 2800m FRN. prod/rel: Gaumont - Serie Pax

DUHAMEL, GEORGES (1884–1966), FRN, Thevenin, Denis
Confession de Minuit, 1920, Novel
  Aventures de Salavin, Les 1963 d: Pierre Granier-Deferre. lps: Maurice Biraud, Christiane Minazzoli, Julien Carette. 103M FRN. *La Confession de Minuit* prod/rel: Horizons Cinematographiques

DUKOVSKI, DEJAN
Bure Baruta, Play
  Bure Baruta 1998 d: Goran Paskaljevic. lps: Miki Manojlovic, Nebojsa Glogovac, Ana Sofrenovic. 102M YGS/FRN/GRC. prod/rel: Mact Prods. (Paris), Stefi S.A. (Athens)

DULAY, CLAUDE
Chanel Solitaire, Novel
  Chanel Solitaire 1981 d: George Kaczender. lps: Marie-France Pisier, Timothy Dalton, Rutger Hauer. 120M USA/FRN. *Coco Chanel* prod/rel: Gardenia, Todrest

DULUD, MICHEL
Monseigneur, Play
  Banco de Prince 1950 d: Michel Dulud. lps: Lucien Baroux, Meg Lemonnier, Jacqueline Pierreux. 85M FRN. *Le Dauphin Sur la Plage* prod/rel: Techniciens Associes

DUMAS, ALEXANDRE (FILS) (1824–1895), FRN
L' Affaire Clemenceau, Paris 1866, Novel
  Clemenceau Case, The 1915 d: Herbert Brenon. lps: Theda Bara, William E. Shay, Stuart Holmes. 5-6r USA. *Infidelity* (UKN) prod/rel: Fox Film Corp., William Fox©
  Processo Clemenceau, Il 1917 d: Alfredo de Antoni. lps: Francesca Bertini, Gustavo Serena, Alfredo de Antoni. 2433m ITL. prod/rel: Caesar Film
L' Ami Des Femmes, Play
  Amico Delle Donne, L' 1943 d: Ferdinando M. Poggioli. lps: Miria Di San Servolo, Luigi Cimara, Laura Adani. 80M ITL. prod/rel: Viralalba Film, E.N.I.C.
La Dame aux Camelias, Paris 1848, Novel
  Bella Lola, La 1962 d: Alfonso Balcazar. lps: Sara Montiel, Antonio Cifariello, German Cobos. 125M SPN/ITL/FRN. *Quel Nostro Impossibile Amore* (ITL); *Une Dame aux Camelias* (FRN); *Lovely Lola*; *La Belle Lola*
  Camelia 1953 d: Roberto Gavaldon. lps: Maria Felix, Jorge Mistral, Carlos Navarro. 110M MXC/SPN. *Passion Sauvage*
  Camille 1907 d: Viggo Larsen. DNM.
  Camille 1912 d: Herbert Brenon. lps: Gertrude Shipman, Irving Cummings, Arthur Evers. 2000f USA. prod/rel: Champion
  Camille 1915 d: Albert Capellani. lps: Clara Kimball Young, Paul Capellani, Lillian Cook. 5r USA. *A Modern Camille* prod/rel: Shubert Film Corp., World Film Corp.©
  Camille 1917 d: J. Gordon Edwards. lps: Theda Bara, Alan Roscoe, Walter Law. 5r USA. prod/rel: Fox Film Corp., William Fox©

Camille 1921 d: Ray C. Smallwood. lps: Alla Nazimova, Rudolph Valentino, Arthur Hoyt. 5600f USA. prod/rel: Nazimova Productions, Metro Pictures
  Camille 1927 d: Fred Niblo. lps: Norma Talmadge, Gilbert Roland, Lilyan Tashman. 8700f USA. prod/rel: Norma Talmadge Productions, First National Pictures
  Camille 1937 d: George Cukor. lps: Greta Garbo, Robert Taylor, Lionel Barrymore. 108M USA. prod/rel: Metro-Goldwyn-Mayer Corp.
  Camille 1984 d: Desmond Davis. lps: Greta Scacchi, Colin Firth, John Gielgud. TVM. 100M UKN. prod/rel: CBS, Viacom
  Camille 2000 1969 d: Radley H. Metzger. lps: Daniele Gaubert, Nino Castelnuovo, Eleonora Rossi-Drago. 119M ITL/USA. *Camille* prod/rel: Radley Metzger, Spear Produzioni
  Cha Hua Nu 1938 d: Li Pingqian. 98M CHN. *The Lady With Camellias*
  Dame aux Camelias, La 1911 d: Andre Calmettes, Henri Pouctal. lps: Sarah Bernhardt, Lou Tellegen, Paul Capellani. 700m FRN. *Camille*
  Dame aux Camelias, La 1934 d: Fernand Rivers, Abel Gance. lps: Pierre Fresnay, Yvonne Printemps, Jane Marken. 118M FRN. prod/rel: Films Fernand Rivers
  Dame aux Camelias, La 1953 d: Raymond Bernard. lps: Micheline Presle, Gino Cervi, Roland Alexandre. 111M FRN/ITL. *La Signora Dalle Camelie* (ITL); *Camille* (USA) prod/rel: C.C.F.C., Royalty Films
  Dame aux Camelias, La 1981 d: Mauro Bolognini. lps: Isabelle Huppert, Gian Maria Volonte, Bruno Ganz. 115M FRN/ITL/GRM. *La Vera Storia Della Signore Dalle Camelie* (ITL); *The Lady of the Camelias*; *The True Story of Camille*; *Die Kamelien Dame* (GRM); *Signora Dalle Camilie, La* prod/rel: Les Films Du Losange, Fr 3
  Lady of the Camelias, The 1922 d: Edwin J. Collins. lps: Sybil Thorndike, Ward McAllister, Booth Conway. 970f UKN. prod/rel: Master Films, British Exhibitors' Films
  Lady of the Camelias, The 1958 d: George M. O'Ferrall. lps: Ann Todd, David Knight, Pamela Buck. MTV. UKN. prod/rel: ABC
  Signora Dalle Camelie, La 1909 d: Ugo FalenA. lps: Vittoria Lepanto, Alberto Nepoti, Dante Cappelli. 150m ITL. *La Traviata*; *La Signora Delle Camelie*; *Camille* (USA); *The Lady With the Camelias* (UKN) prod/rel: Film d'Arte Italiana
  Signora Dalle Camelie, La 1915 d: Baldassarre Negroni. lps: Hesperia, Alberto Collo, Ida Carloni-Talli. 1600m ITL. prod/rel: Tiber Film
  Signora Dalle Camelie, La 1915 d: Gustavo SerenA. lps: Francesca Bertini, Gustavo Serena, Olga Benetti. 1800m ITL. prod/rel: Caesar Film
  Traviata '53 1953 d: Vittorio Cottafavi. lps: Barbara Laage, Armando Francioli, Eduardo de Filippo. 82M ITL/FRN. *The Lost One*; *Fille d'Amour* (FRN) prod/rel: Produzione Venturini (Roma), E.N.I.C.
La Dame aux Perles, Novel
  Signora Delle Perle, La 1918 d: Gennaro Righelli. lps: Vittorina Lepanto, Andrea Habay, Enrico RomA. 1608m ITL. prod/rel: Tiber Film
Denise, 1885, Novel
  Dionisia 1921 d: Eduardo BencivengA. lps: Fernanda Fassy, Gustavo Serena, Luigi Duse. 1452m ITL. prod/rel: Chimera Film
L' Etrangere, 1877, Play
  Etrangere, L' 1930 d: Gaston Ravel. lps: Elvire Popesco, Fernand Fabre, Henri Debain. 88M FRN. prod/rel: Jean De La Cour, Hegewald-Film
  Straniera, La 1930 d: Amleto Palermi, Gaston Ravel. lps: Ruggero Lupi, Tina Lattanzi, Mimi Aylmer. 88M FRN. prod/rel: Hegewald Film
La Femme de Claude, 1873, Play
  Femme de Claude, La 1918 d: M. Maurice?. lps: Claude Merelle. 1290m FRN. prod/rel: Acad
  Moglie Di Claudio, La 1918 d: Gero Zambuto. lps: Pina Menichelli, Vittorio Rossi Pianelli, Alberto Nepoti. 1798m ITL. prod/rel: Itala Film
Le Fils Naturel, Play
  Fils Naturel, Le 1917 d: Jacques de Baroncelli. lps: Renee Sylvaire. 1280m FRN. prod/rel: Empir's Film
La Princesse de Bagdad, 1881, Play
  Principessa Di Bagdad, La 1918 d: Baldassarre Negroni. lps: Hesperia, Andrea Habay, Goffredo d'AndreA. 1850m ITL. prod/rel: Tiber Film
La Principessa Georges, 1871, Novel
  Principessa Giorgio, La 1920 d: Roberto Leone Roberti. lps: Francesca Bertini, Livio Pavanelli, Gemma de Sanctis. 1528m ITL.

DUMAS, ALEXANDRE (PERE) (1802–1870), FRN
Novel
  Henry, King of Navarre 1924 d: Maurice Elvey. lps: Matheson Lang, Gladys Jennings, Henry Victor. 5250f UKN. prod/rel: Stoll
  Juramento de Lagardere, El 1954 d: Leon Klimovsky. lps: Elsa Daniel, Carlos Cores, Andres Mejuto. 82M ARG. prod/rel: Argentina Sono
Story
  Rose Rosse Per Angelica 1966 d: Steno. lps: Jacques Perrin, Raffaella Carra, Cris HuertA. 110M ITL/SPN/FRN. *El Aventurero de la Rosa Roja* (SPN); *El Caballero de la Rosa Roja*; *Le Chevalier a la Rose Rouge* (FRN) prod/rel: Flora Film, West Film (Roma)
Novel
  Tajna Korolevy Anny Ili Mushketery Tridcat Let Spustja 1993 d: Georgij Jungvald-Khilkevich. lps: M. Bojarskij, V. Smekhov, Valentin Smirnitskij. 143M RSS.; *Queen Anne's Secret or Musketeers Thirty Years Later* prod/rel: Katran, Finist-Bank
Antony, 1831, Novel
  Bastardo, Il 1915 d: Emilio Graziani-Walter. lps: Piero Schiavazzi, Myriam, Vittorio Piacentini. 1300m ITL. prod/rel: Walter Film
The Story of a Dog Black, 1868, Short Story
  Where Is My Father? 1916 d: Joseph Adelman. lps: May Ward, William Sorelle, Edward Roseman. 7r USA. prod/rel: Exclusive Features, Inc.©, State Rights
A Romance of the Reign of Don Carlos Brigand, Novel
  Brigand, The 1952 d: Phil Karlson. lps: Anthony Dexter, Jody Lawrance, Gale Robbins. 93M USA. prod/rel: Columbia
El Caballero de Harmental, Novel
  Conde de Maravillas, El 1927 d: Jose Buchs. lps: Pedro Larranaga, Carmen de Toledo, Modesto Rivas. F SPN. *The Count Maravillas* prod/rel: Ediciones Forns-Buch (Madrid)
Le Chevalier de Maison Rouge, 1846, Novel
  Cavaliere Di Maison Rouge, Il 1953 d: Vittorio Cottafavi. lps: Armando Francioli, Renee Saint Clair, Yvette Lebon. 89M ITL. prod/rel: Prod. Venturini
  Reign of Terror 1914. 6r USA. prod/rel: Eclectic Film Co.©
Le Collier de la Reine, 1849-50, Novel
  Affaire du Collier de la Reine, L' 1945 d: Marcel L'Herbier, Jean Dreville (Uncredited). lps: Maurice Escande, Viviane Romance, Marion Dorian. 118M FRN. *The Queen's Necklace* (USA) prod/rel: Ile De France-Films
  Collier de la Reine, Le 1929 d: Gaston Ravel, Tony Lekain., Marcelle Chantal, Georges Lannes. F FRN. *L' Affaire du Collier de la Reine* prod/rel: Gaumont-Franco-Film-Aubert
Les Compagnons de Jehu, 1857, Novel
  Fighting Guardsman, The 1945 d: Henry Levin. lps: Willard Parker, Anita Louise, Janis Carter. 84M USA. prod/rel: Columbia
Le Comte de Monte-Cristo, Paris 1845, Novel
  Comte de Monte-Cristo, Le 1917 d: Henri Pouctal. lps: Leon Mathot, Nelly Cormon, Alexandre Colas. SRL. 9200m FRN. *Monte-Cristo* prod/rel: le Film d'Art, Pathe Consortium
  Comte de Monte-Cristo, Le 1942 d: Robert Vernay, Ferruccio Cerio. lps: Pierre Richard-Willm, Alexandre Rignault, Michele AlfA. 184M FRN/ITL. *Il Conte Di Montecristo* (ITL); *The Count of Monte Cristo*; *La Rivincita Di Montecristo* (ITL) prod/rel: Regina Film, Excelsa Film
  Comte de Monte-Cristo, Le 1953 d: Robert Vernay. lps: Jean Marais, Lia Amanda, Noel Roquevert. 183M FRN/ITL. *Il Tesoro Di Montecristo* (ITL); *The Count of Monte Cristo* prod/rel: Roitfeld, Sirius
  Comte de Monte-Cristo, Le 1961 d: Claude Autant-LarA. lps: Louis Jourdan, Yvonne Furneaux, Pierre Mondy. 180M FRN/ITL. *The Story of the Count of Monte Cristo* (USA); *Il Conte Di Montecristo* (ITL); *The Story of Monte Cristo*; *The Count of Monte Cristo* prod/rel: Les Films J.-J. Vital, Les Productions Rene Mondiano
  Comte de Monte-Cristo, Le 1979 d: Denys de La Patelliere. lps: Jacques Weber, Carla Romanelli, Manuel TejadA. MTV. 246M FRN.
  Conde de Montecristo, El 1941 d: Chano UruetA. lps: Arturo de Cordova, Mapy Cortes, Consuelo Frank. 193M MXC.
  Conde de Montecristo, El 1953 d: Leon Klimovsky. lps: Jorge Mistral, Elina Colomer, Santiago Gomez Cou. 103M ARG/SPN. prod/rel: Argentina-Sono

Conte Di Montecristo, Il 1908 d: Luigi Maggi. lps: Umberto Mozzato. 297m ITL. *Monte Cristo* (USA) prod/rel: S.A. Ambrosio

Count of Monte Cristo, The 1913 d: Edwin S. Porter, Joseph A. Golden. lps: James O'Neill, Murdock MacQuarrie, Nance O'Neill. 5r USA. prod/rel: Famous Players Film Co.©, State Rights

Count of Monte Cristo, The 1934 d: Rowland V. Lee. lps: Robert Donat, Elissa Landi, Louis Calhern. 115M USA. prod/rel: Reliance Pictures, Inc., United Artists

Count of Monte Cristo, The 1973 d: William Hanna, Joseph BarberA. ANM. 47M USA/ASL.

Count of Monte Cristo, The 1975 d: David Greene. lps: Richard Chamberlain, Tony Curtis, Trevor Howard. TVM. 103M USA/UKN. prod/rel: Itc, Norman Rosemont Productions

Count of Monte Cristo, The 1987 d: Georgij Jungvald-Khilkevich. F USS.

Grafin von Monte Christo, Die 1932 d: Karl Hartl. lps: Brigitte Helm, Lucie Englisch, Gustaf Grundgens. 98M GRM. *The Countess of Monte Cristo*

Monte Cristo 1911. SHT USA. prod/rel: Powers

Monte Cristo 1912 d: Colin Campbell. lps: Hobart Bosworth, Thomas Santschi, Herbert Rawlinson. 3000f USA. *The Count of Monte Cristo* prod/rel: Selig Polyscope Co.

Monte Cristo 1922 d: Emmett J. Flynn. lps: John Gilbert, Estelle Taylor, Robert McKim. 9828f USA. prod/rel: Fox Film Corp.

Monte-Cristo 1928 d: Henri Fescourt. lps: Jean Angelo, Lil Dagover, Marie Glory. 5740m FRN. *Le Comte de Monte-Cristo* prod/rel: Louis Nalpas

Secret de Monte-Cristo, Le 1948 d: Albert Valentin. lps: Pierre Brasseur, Robert Dalban, Marcelle Derrien. 85M FRN. prod/rel: Codo-Cinema

Sous le Signe de Monte-Cristo 1968 d: Andre Hunebelle, Jean-Pierre Desagnat. lps: Michel Auclair, Paul Barge, Pierre Brasseur. 100M FRN/ITL. *Montecristo '70* (ITL) prod/rel: P.A.C. Pathe Cinema, U.G.C. Sirius

Treasure of Monte Cristo, The 1961 d: Robert S. Baker. lps: Rory Calhoun, Patricia Bredin, John Gregson. 95M UKN. *The Secret of Monte Cristo* (USA) prod/rel: Mid-Century, Regal Films International

Uznik Zam if 1988 d: Georgy Jangvald-Khilkevitch. lps: Victor Avilov, Eugeni Dvorzhetsky, Alexei Petrenko. 234M USS/FRN. *Uznik Zamka if*

Le Conte Hermann, 1849, Novel

Hermann 1920 d: Orlando Ricci. lps: Dolly Morgan, Orlando Ricci, Giulio Bellantese. 1516m ITL. *Le Conte Hermann* prod/rel: Etrusca Film

Credits, Story

Prince of Thieves, The 1948 d: Howard Bretherton. lps: Jon Hall, Patricia Morison, Adele Jergens. 72M USA. prod/rel: Columbia

La Dame de Monsoreau, 1856, Novel

Dame de Monsoreau, La 1913 d: Emile Chautard?, Charles Krauss?. lps: Jacques Guilhene, Henri Bosc, Marie-Louise Derval. 2055m FRN. prod/rel: Acad

Dame de Monsoreau, La 1923 d: Rene Le Somptier. lps: Rolla Norman, Gina Manes, Madeleine Erickson. SRL. 6EP FRN. prod/rel: Film d'Art (Vandal Et Delac)

Signora Di Monserau, La 1909 d: Mario Caserini. lps: Ida Dolfini. 420m ITL. *La Dama Di Monsereau*; *La Dama Di Monsoreau*; *The Lady of Monsoreau* (USA) prod/rel: Cines

Les Demoiselles de Saint-Cyr, Play

Educande Di Saint-Cyr, Le 1941 d: Gennaro Righelli. lps: Vanna Vanni, Silvana Jachino, Elio Steiner. 88M ITL. prod/rel: Mediterraneo Film, C.I.N.F.

Une Fille du Regent, 1845, Novel

King's Daughter, The 1916 d: Maurice Elvey. lps: Gerald Ames, Janet Ross, Edward O'Neill. 4414f UKN. prod/rel: London, Jury

Les Freres Corses, 1845, Short Story

Apoorva Sahodarargal 1949 d: T. G. RaghavacharyA. lps: Paluvayi Bhanumathi, M. K. Radha, R. Nagendra Rao. 151M IND. *Strange Brothers* prod/rel: Gemini

Apoorva Sahodharalu 1949 d: Chittajalu PullayyA. lps: Paluvayi Bhanumathi, R. Nagendra Rao, G. Pattu Iyer. 151M IND. *Strange Brothers* prod/rel: Gemini

Corsican Brothers, The 1902 d: Dicky Winslow. lps: A. W. Fitzgerald. 300f UKN. prod/rel: Harrison

Corsican Brothers, The 1912 d: Oscar Apfel, J. Searle Dawley. lps: George Lessey, Miriam Nesbitt, Bigelow Cooper. 1000f USA. prod/rel: Edison

Corsican Brothers, The 1915 d: George A. Lessey. lps: King Baggot, Jane Gail, Hal Clarendon. 3r USA. prod/rel: Imp

Corsican Brothers, The 1920 d: Colin Campbell. lps: Dustin Farnum, Wedgewood Nowell, Winifred Kingston. 6r USA. *The Honor of the Family* prod/rel: United Picture Theatres of America

Corsican Brothers, The 1941 d: Gregory Ratoff. lps: Douglas Fairbanks Jr., Ruth Warrick, Akim Tamiroff. 112M USA. prod/rel: United Artists

Corsican Brothers, The 1985 d: Ian Sharp. lps: Trevor Eve, Geraldine Chaplin, Olivia Hussey. TVM. 100M UKN.

Fratelli Corsi, I 1961 d: Anton Giulio Majano. lps: Geoffrey Horne, Valerie Lagrange, Gerard Barray. 115M ITL/FRN. *Les Freres Corses* (FRN); *The Corsican Brothers* (USA) prod/rel: Flora Film, Variety Film (Roma)

Freres Corses 1938 d: Geo Kelber. lps: Jean Aquistapace, Lucienne Le Marchand, Jacqueline Daix. 81M FRN. prod/rel: Distribution Europeenne

Freres Corses, Les 1917 d: Andre Antoine. lps: Henry Krauss, Romuald Joube, Rose Dione. 1185m FRN. *The Corsican Brothers* (USA) prod/rel: Scagl

Hermanos Corsos, Los 1954 d: Leo Fleider. lps: Antonio Vilar, Analia Gade, Tomas Blanco. 94M ARG. *The Corsican Brothers* prod/rel: Sono

Nishan 1949 d: S. S. Vasan. lps: Paluvayi Bhanumathi, Ranjan, R. Nagendra Rao. 151M IND. *The Mark* prod/rel: Gemini

Joseph Balsamo, 1846-48, Novel

Black Magic 1949 d: Gregory Ratoff. lps: Orson Welles, Nancy Guild, Akim Tamiroff. 105M USA/ITL. *Cagliostro* (ITL); *Gli Spadaccini Della Serenissima* prod/rel: Edward Small Productions

Kean; Ou Desordre du Genie, 1836, Play

Kean 1922 d: Alexander Volkov. lps: Ivan Mosjoukine, Nathalie Lissenko, Otto Detlefsen. 2600m FRN. *Desordre Et Genie* prod/rel: Films Albatros

Kean 1940 d: Guido Brignone. lps: Rossano Brazzi, Germana Paolieri, Mariella Lotti. 78M ITL. *Kean Gli Amori Di un Artista* prod/rel: Scalera Film

Kean, Genio E Sregolatezza 1957 d: Vittorio Gassman, Francesco Rosi (Uncredited). lps: Vittorio Gassman, Anna Maria Ferrero, Eleonora Rossi-Drago. 82M ITL. *Kean Genius Or Scoundrel* prod/rel: Vides Cin.Ca, Lux Film

Kean, Ovvero Genio E Sregolatezza 1916 d: Armando Brunero. lps: Ciro Galvani, Delia Bicchi, Camillo de Rossi. 2452m ITL. *Kean* prod/rel: Brunestelli

Mann, Der Nicht Liebt, Der 1929 d: Guido Brignone. lps: Gustav Diessl, Agnes Esterhazy, Harry Hardt. 2581m GRM. prod/rel: Hom-Ag

Stage Romance, A 1922 d: Herbert Brenon. lps: William Farnum, Peggy Shaw, Holmes Herbert. 6416f USA. prod/rel: Fox Film Corp.

Memoirs d'un Medecin, Paris 1848, Novel

Du Barry 1918 d: J. Gordon Edwards. lps: Theda Bara, Charles Clary, Fred Church. 7r USA. *Madame du Barry* prod/rel: Fox Film Corp., Fox Standard Picture

Les Mohicans de Paris, 1864, Novel

Mohicani Di Parigi, I 1917 d: Leopoldo Carlucci. lps: Irene-Saffo Momo, Achille Majeroni, Giuseppe Sterni. 2395m ITL. prod/rel: Milano Film

Paoline, 1850

Paolina 1915 d: Vitale de Stefano. lps: Jeanne Nolly, Vitale de Stefano, Lydia QuarantA. 1123m ITL. prod/rel: Savoia Film

La Reine Margot, 1845, Novel

Reine Margot, La 1910 d: Camille de Morlhon. lps: Pierre Magnier, Berthe Bovy, Paul Amiot. 750m FRN. prod/rel: Pathe Freres

Reine Margot, La 1914 d: Henri Desfontaines. lps: Leontine Massart, Romuald Joube, Leon Bernard. 2165m FRN. prod/rel: Scagl, Eclectic Films

Reine Margot, La 1954 d: Jean Dreville. lps: Jeanne Moreau, Armando Francioli, Robert Porte. 93M FRN/ITL. *La Regina Margot* (ITL); *A Woman of Evil* prod/rel: Lux Films, Films Vendome

Reine Margot, La 1961 d: Rene Lucot. lps: Alain Quercy, Robert Porte, William Sabatier. MTV. 132M FRN.

Reine Margot, La 1994 d: Patrice Chereau. lps: Isabelle Adjani, Daniel Auteuil, Jean-Hugues Anglade. 162M FRN/GRM/ITL. prod/rel: Renn, France 2

Le Salteador, 1854, Novel

Brigand Gentilhomme, Le 1942 d: Emile Couzinet. lps: Jean Weber, Robert Favart, Michel Vitold. 98M FRN. prod/rel: Burgus-Films

La Tour de Nesle, 1832, Play

Tour de Nesle, La 1912 d: Albert Capellani. lps: Henry Krauss, Paul Capellani, Jeanne Delvair. FRN. prod/rel: Scagl

Tour de Nesle, La 1937 d: Gaston Roudes. lps: Jean Weber, Tania Fedor, Jacques Varennes. 95M FRN. prod/rel: Edmond Ratisbonne

Tour de Nesle, La 1954 d: Abel Gance. lps: Pierre Brasseur, Silvana Pampanini, Paul Guers. 130M FRN/ITL. *La Torre Del Piacere* (ITL); *The Tower of Lust* (UKN) prod/rel: Fernand Rivers

Turm Der Verbotenen Liebe, Der 1968 d: Franz Antel. lps: Terry Torday, Jean Piat, Uschi Glas. 92M GRM/ITL/FRN. *Le Dolcezze Del Peccato* (ITL); *The Tower of Forbidden Love*; *Tower of Screaming Virgins* (USA); *She Lost Her You Know What*; *The Sweetness of Sin* prod/rel: Rapid, Films Cin.Ca

Les Trois Mousquetaires, Paris 1844, Novel

Avventure Dei Tre Moschettieri, Le 1957 d: Joseph Lerner. lps: Paul Campbell, Sebastian Cabot, Domenico Modugno. F ITL. prod/rel: Thetis Film, Juventus Film

Boia Di Lilla, Il 1953 d: Vittorio Cottafavi. lps: Rossano Brazzi, Yvette Lebon, Armando Francioli. 78M ITL/FRN. *Milady Et Les Mousquetaires* (FRN); *La Vita Avventurosa Di Milady*; *Milady and the Musketeers* (USA) prod/rel: Produzione Venturini, Nino Martegani (Milano)

Cavalieri Della Regina, I 1955 d: Mauro Bolognini. lps: Jeffrey Stone, Marina Berti, Domenico Modugno. 82M ITL. prod/rel: Thetis Film, Cei-Incom

Chandika 1940 d: Raghupathy S. PrakasA. lps: P. Kannamba, Vemuri Gaggaiah, Ballari RaghavA. 184M IND. prod/rel: Bhawani Pictures

D'artagnan 1916 d: Charles Swickard. lps: Orrin Johnson, Dorothy Dalton, Louise Glaum. 5r USA. *The Three Musketeers* prod/rel: New York Motion Picture Corp., Kay-Bee

D'artagnan and the Three Musketeers 1978 d: Georgij Jungvald-Khilkevich. MTV. F USS.

Four Musketeers, The 1975 d: Richard Lester. lps: Oliver Reed, Raquel Welch, Richard Chamberlain. 105M UKN/SPN/PNM. *Four Musketeers: the Revenge of Milady*; *The Revenge of Milady* prod/rel: 20th Century Fox, Film Trust

Spada Imbattibile, La 1957 d: Hugo Fregonese. lps: Jeffrey Stone, Paul Campbell, Sebastian Cabot. 83M ITL. prod/rel: Thetis Film, Meyer Bros.

Sparvieri Del Re, Gli 1954 d: Joseph Lerner. lps: Jeffrey Stone, Sebastian Cabot, Domenico Modugno. 80M ITL. prod/rel: Thetis Film

Three Musketeers (Parts I & Ii), The 1911 d: J. Searle Dawley. lps: Sydney Booth, Herbert Delmar, Jack Chagnon. 1000f USA. prod/rel: Edison

Three Musketeers, The 1914 d: Charles V. Henkel. 6r USA. prod/rel: Film Attractions Co.©, State Rights

Three Musketeers, The 1921 d: Fred Niblo. lps: Douglas Fairbanks, Leon Bary, George Siegmann. 12r USA. prod/rel: Douglas Fairbanks Pictures, United Artists

Three Musketeers, The 1935 d: Rowland V. Lee. lps: Walter Abel, Paul Lukas, Ian Keith. 97M USA. prod/rel: RKO Radio Pictures©

Three Musketeers, The 1939 d: Allan Dwan. lps: Don Ameche, The Ritz Brothers, Binnie Barnes. 71M USA. *The Singing Musketeer* (UKN) prod/rel: Twentieth Century-Fox Film Corp.©

Three Musketeers, The 1948 d: George Sidney. lps: Gene Kelly, Van Heflin, June Allyson. 125M USA. prod/rel: Metro-Goldwyn-Mayer Corp.

Three Musketeers, The 1974 d: Richard Lester. lps: Oliver Reed, Raquel Welch, Richard Chamberlain. 107M UKN/PNM. *The Queen's Diamonds* prod/rel: Film Trust

Three Musketeers, The 1993 d: Stephen Herek. lps: Charlie Sheen, Kiefer Sutherland, Chris O'Donnell. 105M USA.

Tre Moschettieri, I 1909 d: Mario Caserini?. lps: Fanny Delisle, Maria Caserini Gasparini. 475m ITL. *The Three Musketeers* (UKN) prod/rel: Cines

Tres Mosquetaros. Y Medio, Los 1956 d: Gilberto Martinez Solares. lps: Tin Tan, Aurora Segura, Rosita Arenas. 100M MXC. *Three & One-Half Musketeers*; *Three and a Half Musketeers*

Tres Mosqueteros, Los 1942 d: Miguel M. Delgado. lps: Cantinflas, Angel Garasa, Consuelo Frank. 130M MXC.

Trois Mousquetaires, Les 1912 d: Andre Calmettes. lps: Emile Dehelly, Nelly Cormon, Marcel Vibert. FRN. prod/rel: Film d'Art

Trois Mousquetaires, Les 1921 d: Henri Diamant-Berger. lps: Aime Simon-Girard, Henri Rollan, Charles Martinelli. SRL. FRN. *The Three Musketeers* prod/rel: Films Diamant

Trois Mousquetaires, Les 1932 d: Henri Diamant-Berger. lps: Aime Simon-Girard, Henri Rollan, Thomy Bourdelle. 246M FRN. prod/rel: Films Diamant

Trois Mousquetaires, Les 1953 d: Andre Hunebelle. lps: Yvonne Sanson, Gino Cervi, Steve Barclay. 120M FRN/ITL. *Fate Largo Ai Moschettieri!* (ITL); *The Three Musketeers* (USA) prod/rel: P.A.C., S.N. Pathe-Cinema

Trois Mousquetaires, Les 1961 d: Bernard Borderie. lps: Gerard Barray, Georges Descrieres, Mylene Demongeot. 202M FRN/ITL. *I Tre Moschettieri* (ITL); *The Three Musketeers* (USA); *Vengeance of the Three Musketeers* prod/rel: Films Borderie, Les Films Modernes

La Tulipe Noire, 1846, Novel
Black Tulip, The 1921 d: Frank Richardson, Maurits H. Binger. lps: Zoe Palmer, Gerald McCarthy, Frank Dane. 5500f UKN/NTH. **De Zwarte Tulp** (NTH); **De Moord Op de Gebroeders Johan En Cornelis de Witt 1672**; *Murder of the Brothers Johan and Cornelis de Witt* prod/rel: Granger-Binger Film

Black Tulip, The 1937 d: Alex Bryce. lps: Patrick Waddington, Ann Soreen, Campbell Gullan. 57M UKN. prod/rel: Fox British

Tulipe Noire, La 1963 d: Christian-Jaque. lps: Alain Delon, Virna Lisi, Francis Blanche. 115M FRN/ITL/SPN. *Il Tulipano Nero* (ITL); *The Black Tulip*; *El Tulipan Negro* (SPN) prod/rel: Mediterranee Cinema, Agata

Le Vicomte de Bragelonne, Paris 1847, Novel
Fifth Musketeer, The 1977 d: Ken Annakin. lps: Sylvia Kristel, Beau Bridges, Ursula Andress. 103M UKN/AUS. *Behind the Iron Mask*

Iron Mask, The 1929 d: Allan Dwan. lps: Douglas Fairbanks, Marguerite de La Motte, Dorothy Revier. 87M USA. prod/rel: United Artists, Elton Corp.

Man in the Iron Mask, The 1939 d: James Whale. lps: Louis Hayward, Joan Bennett, Warren William. 119M USA. prod/rel: United Artists Corp., Edward Small Productions

Man in the Iron Mask, The 1977 d: Mike Newell. lps: Richard Chamberlain, Patrick McGoohan, Louis Jourdan. TVM. 100M USA/UKN. prod/rel: Norman Rosemont Productions, Itc Entertainment Ltd.

Man in the Iron Mask, The 1998 d: William Richert. lps: Edward Albert, Dana Barron, Timothy Bottoms. 85M USA. prod/rel: Invisible Studio, the Fastest Cheapest Best Film Corp.

Man in the Iron Mask, The 1998 d: Randall Wallace. lps: Leonardo Dicaprio, Jeremy Irons, John Malkovich. 132M USA. prod/rel: MGM, United Artists Pictures©

Masque de Fer, Le 1962 d: Henri Decoin. lps: Jean Marais, Jean-Francois Poron, Enrico Maria Salerno. 127M FRN/ITL. *L' Uomo Dalla Maschera Di Ferro* (ITL) prod/rel: Ceres, Gaumont International

Prigioniero Del Re, Il 1954 d: Giorgio Rivalta, Richard Pottier. lps: Pierre Cressoy, Andree Debar, Armando Francioli. 88M ITL. *La Masque de Fer* (FRN); *La Maschera Di Ferro* (ITL) prod/rel: Venturini Produzioni Film

Vengeance du Masque de Fer 1962 d: Francesco de Feo. lps: Michel Lemoine, Wandisa Guida, Andrea Bosic. 89M FRN/ITL. *Vendetta Della Maschera Di Ferro* (ITL); *Prisoner of the Iron Mask* prod/rel: Cineproduzioni Associate, Mida Film (Roma)

Vicomte de Bragelonne, Le 1954 d: Fernando Cerchio. lps: Georges Marchal, Dawn Addams, Franco SilvA. 90M FRN/ITL. *Il Visconte Di Bragelonne* (ITL); *The Last Musketeer* (USA); *The Viscount of Bragelonne*; *The Count of Bragelonne* prod/rel: Comptoir Francais De Prod. Cinematograph, Orso Films

Vingt Ans Apres; Suite de Trois Mousquetaires, 1845, Novel
At Sword's Point 1951 d: Lewis Allen. lps: Cornel Wilde, Maureen O'Hara, Robert Douglas. 81M USA. *Sons of the Musketeers* (UKN) prod/rel: RKO Radio

Return of the Musketeers, The 1989 d: Richard Lester. lps: Michael York, Oliver Reed, Frank Finlay. 101M UKN/FRN/SPN. prod/rel: Entertainment, Timothy Burrell Productions

Vingt Ans Apres 1922 d: Henri Diamant-Berger. lps: Jean Yonnel, Henri Rollan, Pierre de Guingand. SRL. FRN. prod/rel: Pathe-Consortium-Cinema

DUMAS, CHARLES
Lone Wolves, Novel
Secret Journey, The 1939 d: John Baxter. lps: Basil Radford, Sylvie St. Claire, Thorley Walters. 72M UKN. *Among Human Wolves* prod/rel: British National, Anglo

DUMAS, CHARLES-ROBERT
Le Capitaine Benoit, Novel
Capitaine Benoit, Le 1938 d: Maurice de Canonge. lps: Jean Murat, Jean Mercanton, Mireille Balin. 95M FRN. prod/rel: Societe Des Films Vega, Compagnie Cinematographique

Ceux du Deuxieme Bureau, Novel
Loups Entre Eux, Les 1936 d: Leon Mathot. lps: Roger Duchesne, Renee Saint-Cyr, Suzanne Despres. 103M FRN. prod/rel: Compagnie Francaise Cinematographique

Face Au Destin, Novel
Face Au Destin 1939 d: Henri Fescourt. lps: Jorge Rigaud, Jules Berry, Gaby SylviA. 84M FRN. prod/rel: Diffusions Intellectuelles

L' Homme a Abattre, Novel
Homme a Abattre, L' 1936 d: Leon Mathot. lps: Jean Murat, Viviane Romance, Jules Berry. 102M FRN. *The Marked Man* prod/rel: Compagnie Francaise Cinematographique

DUMAS, ROBERT-CLAUDE
Deuxieme Bureau, Novel
Deuxieme Bureau 1935 d: Pierre Billon. lps: Jean Murat, Jean Max, Vera Korene. 110M FRN. prod/rel: Societe Des Films Vega

Second Bureau 1936 d: Victor Hanbury. lps: Marta Labarr, Charles Oliver, Arthur Wontner. 76M UKN. prod/rel: Premier, Stafford

La machine a Predire la Mort, Novel
Monde Tremblera, Le 1939 d: Richard Pottier. lps: Claude Dauphin, Roger Duchesne, Erich von Stroheim. 108M FRN. *Les Revolte Des Vivants*; *The Death Predicter*; *The Revolt of the Living*; *The World Will Shake* prod/rel: C.I.C.C.

DUMESTRE, GASTON
Rose de Nice, Play
Rose de Nice 1921 d: Maurice Challiot, Alexandre Ryder. lps: Suzanne Delve, Paulette Ray, Ivan Hedquist. 1830m FRN. prod/rel: Natura Film (Nice)

Simple Erreur, Play
Simple Erreur 1922 d: Maurice Challiot. lps: Paulette Ray, Therizot, Servatius. 1300m FRN. prod/rel: Natura Film

DUNBAR, ANDREA
The Arbour, Play
Rita, Sue and Bob Too 1987 d: Alan Clarke. lps: Siobhan Finneran, Michelle Holmes, George Costigan. 93M UKN. prod/rel: Mainline, Umbrella Entertainment Productions

Rita, Sue and Bob Too!, Play
Rita, Sue and Bob Too 1987 d: Alan Clarke. lps: Siobhan Finneran, Michelle Holmes, George Costigan. 93M UKN. prod/rel: Mainline, Umbrella Entertainment Productions

DUNBAR, PAUL LAURENCE (1872–1906), USA
The Sport of the Gods, New York 1902, Novel
Sport of the Gods, The 1921 d: Henry J. Vernot. lps: Elizabeth Boyer, Edward R. Abrams, George Edward Brown. 7r USA. prod/rel: Reol Productions

DUNCAN, ALEX
It's a Vet's Life, London 1961, Novel
In the Doghouse 1961 d: Darcy Conyers. lps: Leslie Phillips, Peggy Cummins, Hattie Jacques. 93M UKN. *Vet in the Doghouse* prod/rel: Rank Organisation, Rank Film Distributors

DUNCAN, DAVID (1913–, USA
Story
Monster That Challenged the World, The 1957 d: Arnold Laven. lps: Tim Holt, Audrey Dalton, Hans Conried. 83M USA. prod/rel: United Artists, Gramercy

Lost Treasure of the Andes, Story
Jivaro 1954 d: Edward Ludwig. lps: Fernando Lamas, Rhonda Fleming, Brian Keith. 91M USA. *Lost Treasure of the Amazon* (UKN) prod/rel: Paramount, Pine-Thomas

DUNCAN, DAYTON
Lewis & Clark, Book
Lewis & Clark - the Journey of the Corps of Discovery 1997 d: Ken Burns. DOC. 240M USA. prod/rel: Florentine Films, Weta-Tv

DUNCAN, ISADORA
My Life, New York 1927, Autobiography
Isadora 1968 d: Karel Reisz. lps: Vanessa Redgrave, James Fox, Jason Robards Jr. 138M UKN. *The Loves of Isadora*; *Love Honor and Goodbye* prod/rel: Universal Pictures, Ltd., Rank Film Distributors

DUNCAN, LOIS
I Know What You Did Last Summer, Novel
I Know What You Did Last Summer 1997 d: Jim Gillespie. lps: Jennifer Love Hewitt, Sarah Michelle Gellar, Ryan Phillippe. 101M USA. prod/rel: Columbia Pictures, Mandalay Entertainment©

Summer of Fear, Novel
Stranger in Our House 1978 d: Wes Craven. lps: Linda Blair, Lee Purcell, Jeremy Slate. TVM. 100M USA. *Summer of Fear* (UKN) prod/rel: Inter Planetary Pictures Inc., Finnegan Associates

DUNCAN, NORMAN
The Measure of a Man, New York 1911, Novel
Measure of a Man, The 1924 d: Arthur Rosson. lps: William Desmond, Albert J. Smith, Francis Ford. 4979f USA. prod/rel: Universal Pictures

DUNCAN, SARA J.
The Gold Cure, Novel
Gold Cure, The 1925 d: W. P. Kellino. lps: Queenie Thomas, Gladys Hamer, Eric Bransby Williams. 5700f UKN. prod/rel: Stoll

DUNN, CESAR
The Four-Flusher, New York 1925, Play
Fourflusher, The 1928 d: Wesley Ruggles. lps: George Lewis, Marion Nixon, Eddie Phillips. 6193f USA. *Collegians in Business* prod/rel: Universal Pictures

DUNN, ELIZABETH
Something Borrowed, Story
Meet the Stewarts 1942 d: Alfred E. Green. lps: William Holden, Frances Dee, Grant Mitchell. 72M USA. prod/rel: Columbia

DUNN, J. ALLEN
Beyond the Rim, 1916, Short Story
Island of Desire, The 1917 d: Otis Turner. lps: George Walsh, Anna Luther, Willard Louis. 5r USA. prod/rel: Fox Film Corp., William Fox©

Dead Man's Gold, New York 1920, Novel
No Man's Gold 1926 d: Lewis Seiler. lps: Tom Mix, Eva Novak, Frank Campeau. 5745f USA. prod/rel: Fox Film Corp.

The Mascotte of the Three Star, 1921, Short Story
Action 1921 d: John Ford. lps: Hoot Gibson, Francis Ford, J. Farrell MacDonald. 4509f USA. *Let's Go* prod/rel: Universal Film Mfg. Co.

DUNN, NELL (1936–, UKN
Poor Cow, London 1967, Novel
Poor Cow 1967 d: Kenneth Loach. lps: Carol White, Terence Stamp, John Bindon. 101M UKN. prod/rel: Vic Films, Fenchurch Films

Steaming, 1981, Play
Steaming 1984 d: Joseph Losey. lps: Vanessa Redgrave, Sarah Miles, Diana Dors. 95M UKN. prod/rel: Columbia-Emi-Warner, World Film Services

Up the Junction, London 1963, Novel
Up the Junction 1965 d: Kenneth Loach. lps: Carol White, Geraldine Sherman, Vickery Turner. MTV. 70M UKN. prod/rel: BBC

Up the Junction 1967 d: Peter Collinson. lps: Suzy Kendall, Dennis Waterman, Liz Fraser. 119M UKN. prod/rel: Paramount, British Home Entertainment

DUNNE, DOMINICK (1926–, USA
A Season in Purgatory, Novel
Season in Purgatory, A 1996 d: David Greene. lps: Patrick Dempsey, Sherilyn Fenn, Craig Sheffer. TVM. 240M USA.

The Two Mrs. Grenvilles, Novel
Two Mrs. Grenvilles, The 1987 d: John Erman. lps: Ann-Margret, Claudette Colbert, Stephen Collins. TVM. 200M USA. *Society* prod/rel: Preston Fisher Prod.

DUNNE, JOHN GREGORY (1932–, USA
True Confessions, 1977, Novel
True Confessions 1981 d: Ulu Grosbard. lps: Robert de Niro, Robert Duvall, Charles Durning. 108M USA. prod/rel: United Artists, Chartoff/Winkler

DUNNE, LEE
Goodbye to the Hill, London 1965, Novel
Paddy 1969 d: Daniel Haller. lps: Des Cave, Milo O'Shea, Dearbhla Molloy. 87M UKN/IRL. *Goodbye to the Hill* prod/rel: Dun Laoghaire Productions, 20th Century-Fox

DUNNING, FRANCES
The Night Hostess, New York 1928, Play
Woman Racket, The 1929 d: Robert Ober, Albert Kelley. lps: Tom Moore, Blanche Sweet, Sally Starr. 8r USA. *Lights and Shadows* (UKN) prod/rel: Metro-Goldwyn-Mayer Pictures

DUNNING, PHILIP
Broadway a Play, New York 1927, Play
Broadway 1929 d: Paul Fejos. lps: Glenn Tryon, Evelyn Brent, Merna Kennedy. 9661f USA. prod/rel: Universal Pictures

Broadway 1942 d: William A. Seiter. lps: George Raft, Pat O'Brien, Janet Blair. 91M USA. prod/rel: Universal

Lilly Turner, New York 1932, Play
Lilly Turner 1933 d: William A. Wellman. lps: Ruth Chatterton, George Brent, Frank McHugh. 65M USA. prod/rel: First National Pictures©

The Night Hostess, New York 1928, Play
Woman Racket, The 1929 d: Robert Ober, Albert Kelley. lps: Tom Moore, Blanche Sweet, Sally Starr. 8r USA. *Lights and Shadows* (UKN) prod/rel: Metro-Goldwyn-Mayer Pictures

Page Miss Glory, New York 1934, Play
Page Miss Glory 1935 d: Mervyn Leroy. lps: Marion Davies, Pat O'Brien, Dick Powell. 90M USA. prod/rel: Warner Bros. Productions Corp., Cosmopolitan Production

Remember the Day, Play
Remember the Day 1941 d: Henry King. lps: Claudette Colbert, John Payne, Shepperd Strudwick. 86M USA. prod/rel: 20th Century Fox

DUPE, GILBERT
Le Bateau a Soupe, Novel
Bateau a Soupe, Le 1946 d: Maurice Gleize. lps: Charles Vanel, Lucienne Laurence, Gina Manes. 105M FRN. prod/rel: Agence Generale Cinematographique

La Ferme du Pendu, Novel
Ferme du Pendu, La 1945 d: Jean Dreville. lps: Charles Vanel, Alfred Adam, Guy Decomble. 90M FRN. *La Ferme du Maudit; Hanged Man's Farm* prod/rel: Productions Andre Tranche

Figure de Proue, Novel
Figure de Proue 1947 d: Christian Stengel. lps: Georges Marchal, Pierre Dudan, Antoine Balpetre. 90M FRN. prod/rel: C.G.C., Pathe-Cinema

Rendez-Vous Avec la Chance, Novel
Rendez-Vous Avec la Chance 1949 d: Emile Edwin Reinert. lps: Henri Guisol, Daniele Delorme, Suzanne Flon. 72M FRN. *Le Lit a Deux Places* prod/rel: Simon Barstoff, Silver Films

Le Village Perdu, Novel
Village Perdu, Le 1947 d: Christian Stengel. lps: Alfred Adam, Yves Furet, Gaby Morlay. 95M FRN. prod/rel: Agence Generale Cinematographique

DUPONT, MARCEL
Hantise, Novel
Hantise 1921 d: Jean Kemm. lps: Genevieve Felix, Felix Ford, Gaston Jacquet. 1900m FRN.

DUPORT
Trois Marins Dans un Couvent, Play
Trois Marins Dans un Couvent 1949 d: Emile Couzinet. lps: Frederic Duvalles, Marcel Vallee, Pierre Brebans. 80M FRN. prod/rel: Burgus Films

DUPREZ, FRED
Lend Me Your Wife, Play
Lend Me Your Wife 1935 d: W. P. Kellino. lps: Henry Kendall, Kathleen Kelly, Cyril Smith. 61M UKN. prod/rel: Grafton, MGM

DUPUY-MAZUEL, HENRI
Chrestos, Novel
Aux Portes de Paris 1934 d: Charles Barrois, Jacques de Baroncelli (Uncredited). lps: Josette Day, Gaby Morlay, Armand Bernard. 74M FRN. **Aux Portes de la Ville** prod/rel: Films Artistiques Francais

Echec Au Roy
Echec Au Roy 1943 d: Jean-Paul Paulin. lps: Lucien Baroux, Odette Joyeux, Gabrielle Dorziat. 95M FRN. prod/rel: Jean Clerc, S.U.F.

L' Homme Riche, Paris 1914, Play
Billions 1920 d: Ray C. Smallwood. lps: Alla Nazimova, Charles Bryant, William Irving. 6r USA. prod/rel: the Nazimova Productions, Metro Pictures Corp.©

Jerome Perreau, Novel
Jerome Perreau 1935 d: Abel Gance. lps: Georges Milton, Samson Fainsilber, Tania Fedor. 115M FRN. *The Queen and the Cardinal* (USA); *Jerome Perreau -Heros Des Barricades* prod/rel: Les Productions Parisiennes

Le Joueur d'Echecs, Novel
Joueur d'Echecs, Le 1938 d: Jean Dreville. lps: Conrad Veidt, Francoise Rosay, Micheline Francey. 90M FRN. *The Chess Player* (USA); *The Devil Is an Empress* prod/rel: Societe Des Films Vega

Le Miracle Des Loups, Novel
Miracle Des Loups, Le 1924 d: Raymond Bernard. lps: Vanni Marcoux, Yvonne Sergyl, Charles Dullin. 3000m FRN. *The Miracle of the Wolves* (USA) prod/rel: Societe Des Films Historique

Miracle Des Loups, Le 1930 d: Raymond Bernard. lps: Vanni Marcoux, Yvonne Sergyl, Charles Dullin. F FRN. *The Miracle of the Wolves* prod/rel: Les Films Historiques

Miracle Des Loups, Le 1961 d: Andre Hunebelle. lps: Jean Marais, Rosanna Schiaffino, Jean-Louis Barrault. 130M FRN/ITL. *La Congiura Dei Potenti* (ITL); *The Miracle of the Wolves; Blood on His Sword* (USA) prod/rel: P.A.C., Societe Nouvelle Pathe-Cinema

Tarakanova, Novel
Tarakanova 1930 d: Raymond Bernard. lps: Edith Jehanne, Olaf Fjord, Paule Andral. 3065m FRN. prod/rel: Franco-Film Aubert, Societe Des Films Historiques

DUQUESNE, JACQUES
Maria Vandamme, Novel
Maria Vandamme 1988 d: Jacques Ertaud. lps: Corinne Dacla, Bernard Fresson, Ronny Coutteure. TVM. 330M FRN.

DUQUESNEL, FELIX
Patachon, Paris 1907, Play
Gay Deceiver, The 1926 d: John M. Stahl. lps: Lew Cody, Malcolm McGregor, Marceline Day. 6624f USA. *Toto* prod/rel: Metro-Goldwyn-Mayer Pictures

Su Ultima Noche 1931 d: Chester M. Franklin. lps: Ernesto Vilches, Conchita Montenegro, Maria AlbA. 75M USA. *Toto* prod/rel: Metro-Goldwyn-Mayer Corp., Culver Export Co.

DURA, MICHEL
Amitie, Play
Amicizia 1938 d: Oreste Biancoli. lps: Elsa Merlini, Nino Besozzi, Enrico Viarisio. 73M ITL. *Friendship* (USA) prod/rel: Aurora-Fono Roma, I.C.I.

DURACK, DAME MARY
Kings in Grass Castles, Novel
Kings in Grass Castles 1998 d: John Woods. lps: Stephen Dillane, Essie Davis, Flanagan FionnulA. TVM. 240M ASL/IRL. prod/rel: Barron Entertainment, Seven Network Australia

DURAFOUR, M.
Notre Reve Qui Etes aux Cieux, Novel
Fruits Sauvages, Les 1953 d: Herve Bromberger. lps: Estella Blain, Georges Chamarat, Nadine Basile. 94M FRN. *Wild Fruit* (USA) prod/rel: Agiman, Georges, Filmsonor

DURAN, MICHEL
Bolero, Play
Bolero 1941 d: Jean Boyer. lps: Arletty, Meg Lemonnier, Andre Luguet. 96M FRN. prod/rel: Pathe-Cinema

Liberte Provisoire, Paris 1934, Play
He Stayed for Breakfast 1940 d: Alexander Hall. lps: Loretta Young, Melvyn Douglas, Alan Marshall. 89M USA. prod/rel: Columbia Pictures Corp.©

Les Pittuiti's, Play
Mon Pote le Gitan 1959 d: Francois Gir. lps: Jean Richard, Brigitte Auber, Louis de Funes. 87M FRN. prod/rel: Floralies Films, C.I.C.C.

Trois. Six. Neuf, Play
Trois. Six. Neuf 1936 d: Raymond Rouleau. lps: Rene Lefevre, Renee Saint-Cyr, Meg Lemonnier. 102M FRN. prod/rel: Imperial Film Production

DURANG, CHRISTOPHER
Beyond Therapy, Play
Beyond Therapy 1987 d: Robert Altman. lps: Julie Hagerty, Jeff Goldblum, Glenda Jackson. 94M USA. prod/rel: New World Pictures, Sandcastle 5

DURANT, HAROLD RIGGS
A Man and His Mate, Springfield, MA. 1908, Play
Man and His Mate, A 1915 d: John G. Adolfi. lps: Sam de Grasse, Henry Woodruff, Gladys Brockwell. 4r USA. prod/rel: Reliance Motion Picture Corp., Mutual Film Corp.

DURANT, HAROLD RIGGS
Marcel's Birthday Present, Play
Gift Girl, The 1917 d: Rupert Julian. lps: Louise Lovely, Emory Johnson, Rupert Julian. 5r USA. prod/rel: Bluebird Photoplays, Inc.©

DURANTE, RINA
Tramontana, Short Story
Tramontana, Il 1966 d: Adriano Barbano. lps: Flavio d'Autilia, Giuseppe Mantovano, Brizio Montinaro. 84M ITL. prod/rel: Maria Teresa Giaccari

DURAS, MARGUERITE (1914–1996), INC, Donnadieu, Marguerite
L' Amant, Novel
Amant, L' 1992 d: Jean-Jacques Annaud. lps: Jane March, Tony Leung, Frederique Meininger. 115M FRN/UKN. *The Lover* (UKN) prod/rel: Burrill Productions (London), Giai Phong Film

Un Barrage Contre le Pacifique, 1950, Novel
Barrage Contre le Pacifique 1958 d: Rene Clement. lps: Anthony Perkins, Jo Van Fleet, Silvana Mangano. 104M FRN/USA/ITL. *La Diga Sul Pacifico* (ITL); *This Angry Age* (USA); *The Sea Wall* prod/rel: Columbia, de Laurentiis Cin.Ca

Des Journees Entieres Dans Les Arbres, 1954, Novel
Des Journees Entieres Dans Les Arbres 1976 d: Marguerite Duras. lps: Madeleine Renaud, Jean-Pierre Aumont, Bulle Ogier. 95M FRN. *Entire Days Among the Trees* (UKN); *Days in the Trees* prod/rel: Theatre D'orsay, Duras Films

Dit-Elle Detruire, Paris 1969, Novel
Detruire, Dit-Elle 1969 d: Marguerite Duras. lps: Catherine Sellers, Nicole Hiss, Henri Garcin. 90M FRN. *She Said Destroy; La Chaise Longue* prod/rel: Ancinex, Madeleine Films

Dix Heures Et Demie du Soir En Ete, Paris 1960, Novel
10.30 P.M. Summer 1966 d: Jules Dassin. lps: Peter Finch, Melina Mercouri, Romy Schneider. 85M USA/SPN. prod/rel: Jorilie Productions, Argos Films

Le Marin de Gibraltar, Paris 1952, Novel
Sailor from Gibraltar, The 1967 d: Tony Richardson. lps: Jeanne Moreau, Ian Bannen, Vanessa Redgrave. 91M UKN. prod/rel: Woodfall Films, United Artists

Moderato Cantabile, Paris 1958, Novel
Moderato Cantabile 1960 d: Peter Brook. lps: Jeanne Moreau, Jean-Paul Belmondo, Didier Haudepin. 105M FRN/ITL. *Seven Days. Seven Nights* (UKN); *Storia Di Una Strano Amore* prod/rel: Raoul J. Levy, Iena

La Musica, Play
Musica, La 1966 d: Paul Seban, Marguerite Duras. lps: Delphine Seyrig, Robert Hossein, Julie Dassin. 80M FRN. prod/rel: Films Raoul Ploquin, Artistes Associes

DURBRIDGE, FRANCIS
Radio Play
Paul Temple's Triumph 1950 d: MacLean Rogers. lps: John Bentley, Dinah Sheridan, Jack Livesey. 80M UKN. prod/rel: Nettlefold, Butcher's Film Service

DURHAM, MARILYN
The Man Who Loved Cat Dancing, Novel
Man Who Loved Cat Dancing, The 1973 d: Richard C. Sarafian. lps: Burt Reynolds, Sarah Miles, Lee J. Cobb. 114M USA. prod/rel: MGM

DURHAM, W. HANSON
Aunty's Romance, Play
Aunty's Romance 1912 d: George D. Baker. lps: Florence Turner, Maurice Costello, William SheA. 1000f USA. prod/rel: Vitagraph Co. of America

On Donovan's Division, Story
On Donovan's Division 1912 d: Walter Edwin. lps: Edna Flugrath, Bigelow Cooper, Charles Ogle. 1000f USA. prod/rel: Edison

DURIAN, WOLF
Story
Kai Aus Der Kiste 1989 d: Gunther Meyer. lps: Christoph Zeller, Jurgen Watzke, Klaus-Dieter Klebsch. 93M GDR. *Kai Out of the Box* prod/rel: Defa Studio Fru Spielfilme, Fernsehen Der D.D.R.

DURICKOVA, MARIA
Majka Tarakja, Novel
Majka Tarakja 1979 d: Peter Solan. lps: Anetka Lakatosova, Ivan Mistrik, Hana PastejrikovA. TVM. 70M CZC.

DURING, STELLA
The Temptation of Carlton Earlye, Novel
Temptation of Carlton Earlye, The 1923 d: Wilfred Noy. lps: C. Aubrey Smith, Gertrude McCoy, James Lindsay. 6276f UKN. prod/rel: British Actors, C. Aubrey Smith Theatres

DURKIN, D.
Union Depot, 1929, Play
Union Depot 1932 d: Alfred E. Green. lps: Douglas Fairbanks Jr., Joan Blondell, Guy Kibbee. 65M USA. *Gentleman for a Day* (UKN) prod/rel: First National Pictures©

DURLAM, ARTHUR
State Trooper, Short Story
Young Dynamite 1937 d: Leslie Goodwins. lps: Frankie Darro, Kane Richmond, Carleton Young. 57M USA. *State Trooper* prod/rel: Conn Productions, Ambassador Pictures

DURR, MAX
Die Verschwundene Frau, Novel
Verschwundene Frau, Die 1937 d: E. W. Emo. lps: Lucie Englisch, Paul Kemp, Hans Moser. 85M AUS. prod/rel: Oskar Gluck

DURRANT, THEO
The Marble Forest, 1951, Novel
MacAbre 1958 d: William Castle. lps: William Prince, Jim Backus, Christine White. 73M USA. prod/rel: Allied Artists, Susina Associates

DURRELL, GERALD (1925–, UKN, Durrell, Gerald Malcolm
My Family and Other Animals, Book
  My Family and Other Animals 1987 d: Peter Barber-Fleming. lps: Hannah Gordon, Brian Blessed, Darren Redmayne. TVM. 230M UKN/ASL/USA.

DURRELL, LAWRENCE (1912–1990), UKN, Durrell, Lawrence George
The Alexandria Quartet, 1956-60, Novel
  Justine 1969 d: George Cukor, Joseph Strick (Uncredited). lps: Anouk Aimee, Dirk Bogarde, Robert Forster. 116M USA. prod/rel: Berman-Century Productions
Judith, Novel
  Judith 1966 d: Daniel Mann. lps: Sophia Loren, Peter Finch, Jack Hawkins. 109M USA/UKN/ISR. *Conflict* prod/rel: Cumulus, Paramount

DURRENMATT, FRIEDRICH (1921–1990), SWT
Der Besuch Der Alten Dame, Zurich 1956, Play
  Besuch, Der 1964 d: Bernhard Wicki. lps: Ingrid Bergman, Anthony Quinn, Irina Demick. 101M GRM/ITL/FRN. *La Vendetta Della Signora* (ITL); *La Rancune* (FRN); *The Visit* (USA) prod/rel: Les Films Du Siecle, P.E.C.F. (Paris)
Die Ehe Des Herrn Mississippi, Zurich 1952, Play
  Ehe Des Herrn Mississippi, Die 1961 d: Kurt Hoffmann. lps: O. E. Hasse, Johanna von Koczian, Martin Held. 95M GRM/SWT. *Le Mariage de Monsieur Mississippi*; *Il Matrimonio Del Signore Mississippi* prod/rel: Praesens-Film
Es Geschah Am Hellichten Tag, Story
  Cold Light of Day, The 1995 d: Rudolf Van Den Berg. lps: Richard E. Grant, Lynsey Baxter, Simon Cadell. 96M NTH/UKN. prod/rel: Meteor, Capitol
Grieche Sucht Griechin, 1955, Short Story
  Grieche Sucht Griechin 1966 d: Rolf Thiele. lps: Heinz Ruhmann, Irina Demick, Charles Regnier. 91M GRM. *Greek Man Seeks Greek Woman* prod/rel: Franz Seitz, Nora
Die Panne, 1956, Short Story
  Piu Bella Serata Della Mia Vita, La 1972 d: Ettore ScolA. lps: Alberto Sordi, Michel Simon, Pierre Brasseur. 108M ITL/FRN. *La Plus Belle Soiree de Ma Vie* (FRN); *The Most Wonderful Evening of My Life* prod/rel: Dino de Laurentiis, Inter MA. Co. (Roma)
  Shantata, Court Chalu Aahe 1970 d: Satyadev Dubey. lps: Amol Palekar, Sulabha Deshpande, Arvind Deshpande. 138M IND. *Silence! the Court Is in Session* prod/rel: Satyadev-Govind Prod.
La Promessa, Novel
  Promessa, La 1979 d: Alberto Negrin. lps: Rossano Brazzi, Raymond Pellegrin, MacHa Meryl. MTV. F ITL. prod/rel: Chiara Film Internazionali, Rai-Tv
Die Richter Und Sein Henker, 1950-51, Novel
  Richter Und Sein Henker, Der 1976 d: Maximilian Schell. lps: Jon Voight, Jacqueline Bisset, Martin Ritt. 103M GRM/ITL. *End of the Game* (USA); *Getting Away With Murder*; *The Judge and His Hangman*; *Il Giudice E I Suo Boia* (ITL); *Deception* prod/rel: M.F.G., T.R.a.C.
Romulus Der Grosse, 1956, Play
  Romulus Der Grosse 1965 d: Helmut Kautner. 93M GRM.
Das Versprechen, Zurich 1958, Novel
  Es Geschah Am Hellichten Tag 1958 d: Ladislao VajdA. lps: Heinz Ruhmann, Michel Simon, Gert Frobe. 102M GRM/SWT/SPN. *It Happened in Broad Daylight* (USA); *Assault in Broad Daylight*; *El Cebo* (SPN); *Ca S'est Passe En Plein Jour*; *Das Verbrechen* prod/rel: Praesens-Film (Zurich), Ccc-Filmproduktion (Berlin)
  Versprechen, Das 1983 d: Alberto Negrin. 95M ITL.

DURSO, JOSEPH
My Luke and I, Book
  Love Affair: the Eleanor & Lou Gehrig Story, A 1977 d: Fielder Cook. lps: Blythe Danner, Edward Herrmann, Patricia Neal. TVM. 100M USA. prod/rel: Charles Fries Productions, Stonehenge Productions

DURU
La Mascotte, Opera
  Mascotte, La 1935 d: Leon Mathot. lps: Lucien Baroux, Germaine Roger, Armand Dranem. 100M FRN. prod/rel: Films Mascottes

DUSE, CARLO
Story
  Retroscena 1939 d: Alessandro Blasetti. lps: Filippo Romito, Elisa Cegani, Camillo Pilotto. 100M ITL. prod/rel: Continentalcine, E.N.I.C.

DUSEK, VACLAV
Krehke Vztahy, Novel
  Krehke Vztahy 1979 d: Juraj Herz. lps: Vladimir Kratina, Radim Hlozek, Zora U. KeslerovA. 87M CZC. *Fragile Relationship*; *Tender Relationships* prod/rel: Filmove Studio Barrandov

DUSOE, ROBERT C.
The Devil Thumbs a Ride, Novel
  Devil Thumbs a Ride, The 1947 d: Felix E. Feist. lps: Lawrence Tierney, Ted North, Nan Leslie. 63M USA. prod/rel: RKO

DUSQUESNE, A.
Jusqu'au Dernier, Novel
  Jusqu'au Dernier 1956 d: Pierre Billon. lps: Raymond Pellegrin, Jeanne Moreau, Paul Meurisse. 90M FRN. prod/rel: Films Marceau

D'USSEAU, ARNOLD
Tomorrow the World, New York 1943, Play
  Tomorrow the World 1944 d: Leslie Fenton. lps: Fredric March, Betty Field, Agnes Moorehead. 86M USA. prod/rel: United Artists, Lester Cowan Prods.

DUSSIEUX
Die Frau Im Schrank, Play
  Frau Im Schrank, Die 1927 d: Rudolf Biebrach. lps: Ruth Weyher, Willy Fritsch, Felicitas Malten. 2178m GRM. prod/rel: UFA

DUVAL, GEORGES
Le Coup de Fouet, Play
  Coup de Fouet, Le 1913 d: Georges MoncA. lps: Prince, Charles Lorrain, Pepa Bonafe. 600m FRN. prod/rel: Pathe Freres
Veronique, Opera
  Veronique 1949 d: Robert Vernay. lps: Giselle Pascal, Marina Hotine, Jean Desailly. 100M FRN. prod/rel: Jason, Latino Consortium Cinema

DUVERNET, HENRI
Dans le Gouffre, Story
  Dans le Gouffre 1916 d: Pierre Bressol. lps: Pierre Bressol, Delvil, Amelie de Pouzols. 1230m FRN. prod/rel: Serie D'art Pathe Freres

DUVERNOIS, HENRI
Apres l'Amour, Play
  Apres l'Amour 1924 d: Maurice Champreux. lps: Andre Nox, Blanche Montel, Emile Drain. F FRN. prod/rel: Gaumont
  Apres l'Amour 1931 d: Leonce Perret. lps: Gaby Morlay, Victor Francen, Jacques Varennes. 73M FRN. prod/rel: Pathe-Natan
  Apres l'Amour 1947 d: Maurice Tourneur. lps: Pierre Blanchar, Simone Renant, Fernand Fabre. 90M FRN. prod/rel: Films Modernes
La Dame de Bronze Et le Monsieur de Cristal, Play
  Dame de Bronze Et le Monsieur de Cristal, La 1929 d: Marcel Manchez. lps: Marcel Vallee, Marcelle Barry, Jeanne Berangere. 1700m FRN. prod/rel: Societe Des Films Du Grand Guignol
Faubourg-Montmartre, Novel
  Faubourg-Montmartre 1924 d: Charles Burguet. lps: Gaby Morlay, Camille Bardou, Maurice Schutz. 2400m FRN. prod/rel: Charles Burguet
  Faubourg-Montmartre 1931 d: Raymond Bernard. lps: Charles Vanel, Gaby Morlay, Line Noro. 115M FRN. prod/rel: Pathe-Natan
La Guitare Et le Jazz-Band, Play
  Guitare Et le Jazz-Band, La 1923 d: Gaston Roudes. lps: Violette Trezel, France Dhelia, Jean Devalde. 1725m FRN. prod/rel: Films Sphynx
Jeanne, Play
  Jeanne 1934 d: Georges Marret. lps: Andre Luguet, Gaby Morlay, Helene Perdriere. 85M FRN. prod/rel: Productions Georges Marret, Societe Des Films Gaby Morlay
Maxime, Paris 1929, Novel
  Maxime 1958 d: Henri Verneuil. lps: Charles Boyer, Michele Morgan, Arletty. 124M FRN. prod/rel: Films Raoul Ploquin, Cocinor
La Poule, Novel
  Poule, La 1932 d: Rene Guissart. lps: Armand Dranem, Arlette Marchal, Marguerite Moreno. 69M FRN. prod/rel: Films Paramount
Les Soeurs Hortensias, Novel
  Soeurs Hortensias, Les 1935 d: Rene Guissart. lps: Meg Lemonnier, Therese Dorny, Lucien Baroux. 100M FRN. prod/rel: Flores-Film
Toi C'est Moi, Opera
  Toi C'est Moi 1936 d: Rene Guissart. lps: Jacques Pills, Georges Tabet, Claude May. 90M FRN. prod/rel: Paris-Cine-Films

DUVEYRIER, C.
Michele Perrin, 1834, Play
  Michele Perrin 1913 d: Eleuterio Rodolfi. lps: Ermete Novelli, Gigetta Morano, Alfredo Bertone. 1187m ITL. *Michael Perrine* (USA); *Spy for a Day* prod/rel: S.A. Ambrosio

DWIVEDI, PRABHULAL
Gadano Bel, Play
  Gadano Bel 1950 d: Ratibhai Punatar. lps: Nirupa Roy, Dulari, CharabalA. 123M IND. prod/rel: Ajit Pictures

DWYER, JAMES FRANCIS
My Maryland Maryland, 1920, Short Story
  Bride of the Storm 1926 d: J. Stuart Blackton. lps: Dolores Costello, John Harron, Otto Matieson. 6826f USA. prod/rel: Vitagraph Co. of America, Warner Brothers Pictures
Mr. Leander, Short Story
  Girl in the House-Boat, The 1913 d: Ashley Miller. lps: Harry Gripp, Bessie Learn, Richard Neill. 1000f USA. prod/rel: Edison

DWYER, K. R.
Shattered, Book
  Passagers, Les 1976 d: Serge Leroy. lps: Jean-Louis Trintignant, Bernard Fresson, Richard Constantini. 103M FRN/ITL. *Shattered* (UKN); *L' Homme Qui Nous Suit*; *The Passengers*

DYAR, RALPH E.
A Voice in the Dark, New York 1919, Play
  Voice in the Dark, A 1921 d: Frank Lloyd. lps: Ramsey Wallace, Irene Rich, Alec B. Francis. 4256f USA. *Out of the Dark* prod/rel: Goldwyn Pictures

DYER, ANSON (1876–1962), UKN
The Vicar of Bray, Story
  Vicar of Bray, The 1937 d: Henry Edwards. lps: Stanley Holloway, Margaret Vines, Esmond Knight. 68M UKN. prod/rel: Jh Productions, Associated British Picture Corporation

DYER, BERNARD VICTOR
Port Afrique, Novel
  Port Afrique 1956 d: Rudolph Mate. lps: Pier Angeli, Philip Carey, Dennis Price. 92M UKN. prod/rel: Coronado, Columbia

DYER, CHARLES (1928–, UKN, Dyer, Charles Raymond
Rattle of a Simple Man, London 1962, Play
  Rattle of a Simple Man 1964 d: Muriel Box. lps: Harry H. Corbett, Diane Cilento, Michael Medwin. 96M UKN. prod/rel: Martello, Warner-Pathe
Staircase, London 1966, Play
  Staircase 1969 d: Stanley Donen. lps: Rex Harrison, Richard Burton, Cathleen Nesbitt. 100M USA. prod/rel: Stanley Donen Films, 20th Century Fox

DYER, GEORGE
The Five Fragments, Boston 1932, Novel
  Fog Over Frisco 1934 d: William Dieterle. lps: Bette Davis, Lyle Talbot, Margaret Lindsay. 68M USA. *The Gentleman from San Francisco*; *The Golden Gate*; *Fog Over San Francisco* prod/rel: First National Pictures©
  Spy Ship 1942 d: B. Reeves Eason. lps: Craig Stevens, Irene Mannings, Maris Wrixon. 62M USA. prod/rel: Warner Bros.

DYGAT, STANISLAW
Disneyland, Warsaw 1965, Novel
  Jowita 1967 d: Janusz Morgenstern. lps: Daniel Olbrychski, Barbara Lass, Kalina Jedrusik. 97M PLN. *Yovita* (USA); *Jovita* prod/rel: Syrena Film Unit, Film Polski
Jezioro Bodenskie, 1946, Novel
  Jezioro Bodenskie 1985 d: Janusz Zaorski. lps: Gustaw Holoubek, Krzysztof Pieczynski, Malgorzata PieczynskA. 85M PLN. *Bodensee*
Karnawal, 1968, Novel
  Jezioro Bodenskie 1985 d: Janusz Zaorski. lps: Gustaw Holoubek, Krzysztof Pieczynski, Malgorzata PieczynskA. 85M PLN. *Bodensee*
Pozegnania, Warsaw 1948, Novel
  Pozegnania 1958 d: Wojciech J. Has. lps: Gustaw Holoubek, Tadeusz Janczar, Maria Wachowiak. 101M PLN. *Partings* (USA); *Lydia Ate the Apple*; *Farewells* prod/rel: Syrena Film Unit

DYNEVOR, GERALD
New Eve and Old Adam, Short Story
  New Eve and Old Adam 1967 d: Gerald Dynevor. MTV. 60M UKN. prod/rel: Granada

DYOTT, GEORGE M.
Man Hunting in the Jungle, 1930, Book
  Manhunt in the Jungle 1958 d: Tom McGowan. lps: Robin Hughes, Luis Alvarez, James Wilson. 79M USA. prod/rel: Warner Bros.

E

EAGAN, ALBERTA STEDMAN
They Call It Sin, New York 1933, Novel
   They Call It Sin 1932 d: Thornton Freeland. lps: Loretta Young, David Manners, George Brent. 75M USA. *The Way of Life* (UKN) prod/rel: First National Pictures©

EARECKSON, JONI
Joni, Book
   Joni 1980 d: James F. Collier. lps: Joni Eareckson, Bert Remsen, Katherine de Hetre. 108M USA. prod/rel: World Wide Pictures

EARL, KENNETH
Story
   Big Trees, The 1952 d: Felix E. Feist. lps: Kirk Douglas, Patrice Wymore, Eve Miller. 89M USA. prod/rel: Warner Bros.

EARL, LAURENCE
Escape of the Amethyst, Book
   Yangtse Incident 1957 d: Michael Anderson. lps: Richard Todd, William Hartnell, Akim Tamiroff. 113M UKN. *Battle Hell* (USA); *Escape of the Amethyst* prod/rel: Everest, British Lion

EAST, BEN
Silence of the North, Book
   Silence of the North 1981 d: Allan King. lps: Ellen Burstyn, Tom Skerritt, Gordon Pinsent. 94M CND. *Silence in the North*; *Comes a Time* prod/rel: Universal Films, Universal Productions Canada Inc.

EASTLAKE, WILLIAM (1917–, USA, Eastlake, William Derry
Castle Keep, New York 1965, Novel
   Castle Keep 1969 d: Sydney Pollack. lps: Burt Lancaster, Patrick O'Neal, Jean-Pierre Aumont. 108M USA. prod/rel: Columbia, Filmways

EASTMAN, REBECCA LANE HOOPER
The Big Little Person, New York 1917, Novel
   Big Little Person, The 1919 d: Robert Z. Leonard. lps: Mae Murray, Clarissa Selwynne, Rudolph Valentino. 6r USA. prod/rel: Universal Film Mfg. Co.©

EASTWOOD, JAMES
Devil Girl from Mars, Play
   Devil Girl from Mars 1954 d: David MacDonald. lps: Hugh McDermott, Hazel Court, Patricia Laffan. 76M UKN. prod/rel: Danzigers, British Lion
Mark of the Leopard, Short Story
   Beyond Mombasa 1956 d: George Marshall. lps: Cornel Wilde, Donna Reed, Leo Genn. 90M UKN/USA. prod/rel: Columbia, Hemisphere Films

EATON, W. A.
The Fireman's Wedding, Poem
   Fireman's Wedding, The 1918. lps: Eric Williams. SHT UKN. prod/rel: Eric Williams Speaking Pictures

EBENHACK, ARTHUR
He Stopped at Murder, Story
   Going the Limit 1926 d: Chet Withey. lps: George O'Hara, Sally Long, Brooks Benedict. 4690f USA. prod/rel: R-C Pictures, Film Booking Offices of America

EBERHART, MIGNON G. (1899–, USA, Eberhart, Mignon Good
Dead Yesterday, 1936, Short Story
   Great Hospital Mystery, The 1937 d: James Tinling. lps: Jane Darwell, Sig Ruman, Sally Blane. 60M USA. *Dead Yesterday* prod/rel: Twentieth Century-Fox Film Corp.©
From This Dark Stairway, New York 1931, Novel
   Dark Stairway, The 1938 d: Arthur Woods. lps: Hugh Williams, Chili Bouchier, Garry Marsh. 72M UKN. prod/rel: Warner Bros.
   Murder of Dr. Harrigan, The 1936 d: Frank McDonald. lps: Mary Astor, Kay Linaker, Ricardo Cortez. 67M USA. prod/rel: Warner Bros. Pictures©
Hasty Wedding, Novel
   Three's a Crowd 1945 d: Lesley Selander. lps: Pamela Blake, Charles Gordon, Gertrude Michael. 58M USA. prod/rel: Republic
Murder By an Aristocrat, New York 1932, Novel
   Murder By an Aristocrat 1936 d: Frank McDonald. lps: Lyle Talbot, Marguerite Churchill, William B. Davidson. 62M USA. prod/rel: Warner Bros. Pictures©
Mystery of Hunting's End, New York 1930, Novel
   Mystery House 1938 d: Noel Smith. lps: Dick Purcell, Ann Sheridan, Anne Nagel. 61M USA. *The Mystery of Hunting's End* prod/rel: Warner Bros. Pictures©

The Patient in Room 18, Garden City, N.Y. 1929, Novel
   Patient in Room 18, The 1938 d: Crane Wilbur, Bobby Connolly. lps: Patric Knowles, Ann Sheridan, Eric Stanley. 60M USA. prod/rel: Warner Bros. Pictures©, First National Picture
While the Patient Slept, New York 1930, Novel
   While the Patient Slept 1935 d: Ray Enright. lps: Aline MacMahon, Guy Kibbee, Lyle Talbot. 67M USA. prod/rel: First National Productions Corp., Clue Club Picture
The White Cockatoo, New York 1933, Novel
   White Cockatoo, The 1935 d: Alan Crosland. lps: Jean Muir, John Eldredge, Ruth Donnelly. 72M USA. prod/rel: Warner Bros. Pictures©

EBERLE, JANE
Jennie Heil, 1939, Short Story
   Jennie 1940 d: David Burton. lps: Virginia Gilmore, William Henry, George Montgomery. 75M USA. *Jennie Heil* prod/rel: Twentieth Century-Fox Film Corp.©

EBERMAYER, ERICH
Befreite Hande, Novel
   Befreite Hande 1939 d: Hans Schweikart. lps: Brigitte Horney, Olga Tschechowa, Ewald Balser. 96M GRM. *Freed Hands* (USA) prod/rel: Bavaria, Schorcht
Der Fall Claasen, Novel
   Grune Domino, Der 1935 d: Herbert Selpin. lps: Brigitte Horney, Karl Ludwig Diehl, Theodor Loos. 75M GRM. prod/rel: UFA
Der Falle Claasen, Play
   Domino Vert, Le 1935 d: Henri Decoin, Herbert Selpin. lps: Danielle Darrieux, Jany Holt, Maurice Escande. 90M FRN. prod/rel: U.F.a.
Romanze, Play
   Jahre Vergehen, Die 1944 d: Gunther Rittau. lps: Carl Kuhlmann, Heidemarie Hatheyer, Werner Fuetterer. 80M GRM. *Der Senator* prod/rel: Tobis, Ring

EBERT, WALTER
Novel
   Zarte Haut in Schwarzer Seide 1961 d: Max Pecas. lps: Elke Sommer, Ivan Desny, Danik Patisson. 90M GRM/FRN. *Daniela! De Quoi Tu Te Meles* (FRN); *Daniella By Night* (USA); *Tender Skin in Black Silk* prod/rel: Contact Organisation, P.I.P.
Susanne in Berlin, Novel
   Man Between, The 1953 d: Carol Reed. lps: James Mason, Claire Bloom, Hildegard Knef. 101M UKN. prod/rel: London Films, British Lion Production Assets
Verbrechen Nach Schulschluss, Baden-Baden 1956, Novel
   Verbrechen Nach Schulschluss 1959 d: Alfred Vohrer. lps: Christian Wolff, Peter Van Eyck, Heidi Bruhl. 106M GRM. *The Young Go Wild* (USA); *After School* (UKN); *Crime After School* prod/rel: Ultra Film, Europa
   Verbrechen Nach Schulschluss 1975 d: Alfred Vohrer. lps: Felix Franchi, Evelyne Kraft, Sascha Hehn. 84M GRM. *Crime After School* prod/rel: Tv 13, Terra

EBY, LOIS
The Velvet Fleece, Novel
   Larceny 1948 d: George Sherman. lps: John Payne, Joan Caulfield, Dan DuryeA. 89M USA. prod/rel: Universal

ECHARD, MARGARET
A Man Without Friends, 1940, Novel
   Lightning Strikes Twice 1951 d: King Vidor. lps: Richard Todd, Ruth Roman, Mercedes McCambridge. 91M USA. prod/rel: Warner Bros.

ECHEGARAY, JOSE (1832–1916), SPN, Echegaray Y Eizaguirre, Jose
Play
   A Fuerza de Arrastrarse 1924 d: Jose Buchs. lps: Amalia de Isaura, Jose Romeu, Antonio Martinez. 1700m SPN. *By Dint of Crawling* prod/rel: Film Espanola (Madrid)
El Gran Galeoto, Madrid 1881, Play
   Celebrated Scandal, The 1915 d: James Durkin. lps: Betty Nansen, Edward Jose, Walter Hitchcock. 5r USA. *A Celebrated Scandal* prod/rel: Fox Film Corp., William Fox Photoplays Supreme
   Gran Galeoto, El 1951 d: Rafael Gil. lps: Ana Mariscal, Rafael Duran, Jose Maria Lado. 96M SPN. *The Great Pimp*
   Lovers? 1927 d: John M. Stahl. lps: Ramon Novarro, Alice Terry, Edward Martindel. 5291f USA. *The Great Galeoto* prod/rel: Metro-Goldwyn-Mayer Pictures
   World and His Wife, The 1920 d: Robert G. VignolA. lps: Alma Rubens, Montagu Love, Gaston Glass. 6702f USA. prod/rel: Cosmopolitan Productions, Famous Players-Lasky Corp.

Mancha Que Limpia, Play
   Mancha Que Limpia 1924 d: Jose Buchs. lps: Aurora Redondo, Jose Crespo, Carmen Viance. F SPN. *The Stain That Cleans* prod/rel: Film Espanola, S.A. (Madrid)

ECHEGARAY, MIGUEL
Gigantes Y Cabezudos, Opera
   Gigantes Y Cabezudos 1925 d: Florian Rey. lps: Carmen Viance, Jose Nieto, Marina Torres. 77M SPN. *Giants and Bigheads* prod/rel: Atlantida

ECKERSLEY, ARTHUR
Money for Nothing, Play
   Money for Nothing 1916 d: Maurice Elvey. lps: Guy Newall, Manora Thew, Hayford Hobbs. 2800f UKN. prod/rel: London, Jury
Trouble for Nothing, Play
   Trouble for Nothing 1916 d: Maurice Elvey. lps: Guy Newall, Hayford Hobbs, Jeff Barlow. 2300f UKN. prod/rel: London, Jury

ECKHARDT, FRITZ
Rendez-Vous in Wien, Play
   Rendez-Vous in Wien 1959 d: Helmut Weiss. lps: Josef Meinrad, Hans Holt, Peter Weck. 94M AUS. *Wodka, Wienerin Whisky* prod/rel: Cosmopol

ECO, UMBERTO (1932–, ITL
Il Nome Della Rosa, 1980, Novel
   Name of the Rose, The 1986 d: Jean-Jacques Annaud. lps: Sean Connery, F. Murray Abraham, Christian Slater. 130M ITL/GRM/FRN. *Der Name Der Rose* (GRM); *Le Nom de la Rose* (FRN); *Il Nome Della Rosa* (ITL) prod/rel: Neu Constantin (West Berlin), Cristaldifilm (Rome)

EDEL, EDMUND
Poker, Novel
   Wenn Die Mutter Und Die Tochter. 1928 d: Carl Boese. lps: Trude Hesterberg, Vera Schmiterlow, Camilla von Hollay. 2856m GRM. prod/rel: Carl Boese-Film

EDELMAN, MAURICE
A Call on Kuprin, Novel
   Call on Kuprin, A 1961 d: John Jacobs. lps: Marius Goring, Eric Portman, John Gregson. MTV. UKN. prod/rel: BBC

EDEN, JACK
L' Inconnue, Short Story
   Inconnue, L' 1922 d: Charles Maudru. lps: Paul Guide, Lois Meredith, Monique Chryses. 1900m FRN. prod/rel: Maurice De Marsan

EDEN, ROB
$20 a Week, New York 1931, Novel
   $20 a Week 1935 d: Wesley Ford. lps: James Murray, Pauline Starke, Dorothy Revier. 80M USA. *The Man Maker* prod/rel: Alexander Brothers Studios, State Rights
Dancing Feet, New York 1931, Novel
   Dancing Feet 1936 d: Joseph Santley. lps: Ben Lyon, Joan Marsh, Edward Nugent. 72M USA. prod/rel: Republic Pictures Corp.
Jenifer Hale, Novel
   Jenifer Hale 1937 d: Bernerd Mainwaring. lps: Rene Ray, Ballard Berkeley, John Longden. 66M UKN. prod/rel: Fox British
Second Choice, New York 1932, Novel
   I Demand Payment 1938 d: Clifford Sanforth. lps: Jack La Rue, Betty Burgess, Matty Kemp. 59M USA. prod/rel: Imperial Distributing Corp., Imperial Pictures

EDENS, OLIVE
Heart and Hand, 1927, Short Story
   House Divided, A 1932 d: William Wyler. lps: Walter Huston, Kent Douglas, Helen Chandler. 68M USA. *Heart and Hand*; *The Woman Breaker* prod/rel: Universal Pictures Corp.©

EDGAR, GEORGE
Kent the Fighting Man, Novel
   Kent the Fighting Man 1916 d: A. E. Coleby. lps: Bdr. Billy Wells, Hettie Payne, A. E. Coleby. 5500f UKN. prod/rel: I. B. Davidson, Tiger
The Pride of the Fancy, Novel
   Pride of the Fancy, The 1920 d: Albert Ward. lps: Rex Davis, Daisy Burrell, Tom Reynolds. 6000f UKN. prod/rel: G. B. Samuelson, General

EDGAR, MARRIOTT
The Service Flat, Play
   Here's George 1932 d: Redd Davis. lps: George Clarke, Pat Paterson, Ruth Taylor. 64M UKN. prod/rel: Thomas Charles Arnold, Producers Distributing Corporation

EDGELOW, THOMAS
The Amateur Adventuress, 1918, Short Story
   Amateur Adventuress, The 1919 d: Henry Otto. lps: Emmy Wehlen, Allan Sears, Eugene Pallette. 5r USA. prod/rel: Metro Pictures Corp.©, All-Star Series

Handcuffs and Kisses, 1920, Short Story
Handcuffs Or Kisses 1921 d: George Archainbaud. lps: Elaine Hammerstein, Julia Swayne Gordon, Dorothy Chappell. 6r USA. prod/rel: Selznick Pictures, Select Pictures

It Isn't Being Done This Season, 1918, Short Story
It Isn't Being Done This Season 1921 d: George L. Sargent. lps: Corinne Griffith, Sally Crute, Webster Campbell. 5r USA. prod/rel: Vitagraph Co. of America

Life's Twist, Short Story
Life's Twist 1920 d: W. Christy Cabanne. lps: Bessie Barriscale, Walter McGrail, King Baggot. 5300f USA. prod/rel: B. B. Features, Robertson-Cole Distributing Corp.

Short Story
Mysterious Mrs. M., The 1917 d: Lois Weber. lps: Mary MacLaren, Harrison Ford, Evelyn Selbie. 5r USA. *The Mysterious Mrs. Musslewhite* prod/rel: Bluebird Photoplays, Inc.©

EDGINTON, MAY, Edgington, May
Celle Qui Domine Les Hommes, Story
Celle Qui Domine 1927 d: Carmine Gallone. lps: Leon Mathot, Jose Davert, Soava Gallone. F FRN. prod/rel: Paris International Film (P.I.F)

A Child in Their Midst, Novel
Man of Mayfair 1931 d: Louis Mercanton. lps: Jack Buchanan, Joan Barry, Warwick Ward. 83M UKN. prod/rel: Paramount British, Paramount

The Heart Is Young, 1930, Short Story
False Madonna, The 1931 d: Stuart Walker. lps: Kay Francis, William "Stage" Boyd, Conway Tearle. 72M USA. *The False Idol* (UKN) prod/rel: Paramount Publix Corp.©

The Joy Girl, 1926, Short Story
Joy Girl, The 1927 d: Allan Dwan. lps: Olive Borden, Neil Hamilton, Marie Dressler. 6162f USA. prod/rel: Fox Film Corp.

Judgement, 1924, Short Story
Her Husband's Secret 1925 d: Frank Lloyd. lps: Antonio Moreno, Patsy Ruth Miller, Ruth Clifford. 6151f USA. *Judgment* prod/rel: Frank Lloyd Productions, First National Pictures

The Man Who Dared, Novel
Creation 1922 d: Humberston Wright. lps: Dorothy Fane, Frank Dane, Sir Simeon Stuart. 5000f UKN. prod/rel: Raleigh King

The Prude's Fall, London 1920, Play
Prude's Fall, The 1924 d: Graham Cutts. lps: Jane Novak, Julanne Johnson, Warwick Ward. 5675f UKN. prod/rel: Gainsborough, Woolf & Freedman

Purple and Fine Linen, 1926, Short Story
Adventure in Manhattan 1936 d: Edward Ludwig. lps: Jean Arthur, Joel McCrea, Reginald Owen. 73M USA. *Manhattan Madness* (UKN) prod/rel: Columbia Pictures

Three Hours 1927 d: James Flood. lps: Corinne Griffith, John Bowers, Hobart Bosworth. 5774f USA. *Purple and Fine Linen* prod/rel: Corinne Griffith Productions, First National Pictures

Secrets, London 1922, Play
Secrets 1924 d: Frank Borzage. lps: Norma Talmadge, Eugene O'Brien, Patterson Dial. 8363f USA. prod/rel: Joseph M. Schenck, Associated First National Pictures

Secrets 1933 d: Frank Borzage, Marshall Neilan (Uncredited). lps: Mary Pickford, Leslie Howard, C. Aubrey Smith. 85M USA. prod/rel: United Artists Corp., the Pickford Corp.©

Triumph, New York 1924, Novel
Triumph 1924 d: Cecil B. de Mille. lps: Leatrice Joy, Rod La Rocque, Victor Varconi. 8288f USA. prod/rel: Famous Players-Lasky, Paramount Pictures

World Without End, Story
His Supreme Moment 1925 d: George Fitzmaurice. lps: Blanche Sweet, Ronald Colman, Kathleen Myers. 6500f USA. prod/rel: Samuel Goldwyn Productions, First National Pictures

EDGLEY, LESLIE
Fear No More, New York 1946, Novel
Fear No More 1961 d: Bernard Wiesen. lps: Jacques Bergerac, Mala Powers, John Harding. 80M USA. prod/rel: Scaramouche Productions

EDGU, FERIT
Hakkari'de Bir Mevsim, Novel
Hakkari'de Bir Mevsim 1987 d: Erden Kiral. lps: Genko Erkal, Serif Sezer, Erkan Yucel. 109M TRK/GRM. *A Season in Hakkari* prod/rel: Kentel Film, Data a.S.

EDHOLM, CHARLES
White Slippers, Novel
White Slippers 1924 d: Sinclair Hill. lps: Matheson Lang, Joan Lockton, Gordon Hopkirk. 6180f UKN. *The Port of Lost Souls* prod/rel: Stoll

EDINGTON, A. CHANNING
The Studio Murder Mystery, Chicago 1929, Novel
Studio Murder Mystery, The 1929 d: Frank Tuttle. lps: Doris Hill, Neil Hamilton, Fredric March. 62M USA. prod/rel: Paramount Famous Lasky Corp.

EDINGTON, CARMEN
Studio Murder Mystery, The 1929 d: Frank Tuttle. lps: Doris Hill, Neil Hamilton, Fredric March. 62M USA. prod/rel: Paramount Famous Lasky Corp.

EDMISTON, JAMES
The Fastest Man on Earth, Story
Devil's Hairpin, The 1957 d: Cornel Wilde. lps: Cornel Wilde, Jean Wallace, Arthur Franz. 83M USA. prod/rel: Paramount, Theodore Prods.

EDMOND, C.
L' Aieule, 1863, Play
Avo, L' 1909. 253m ITL. *L' Avo Avvelenatore*; *The Grandfather* (UKN) prod/rel: Cines

EDMONDS, E. V.
The King's Romance, Play
King's Romance, The 1914 d: Ernest G. Batley. lps: Fred Morgan, Ethel Bracewell, Henry Victor. 4074f UKN. *The Revolutionist* (USA); *Revolution* prod/rel: British and Colonial, Kinematograph Trading Co.

EDMONDS, WALTER D. (1903–, USA, Edmonds, Walter Dumaux
Novel
Harness Fever 1976 d: Don Chaffey. lps: Robert Bettles, Tom Farley, Andrew McFarlane. 90M ASL/USA. *Born to Run* (USA) prod/rel: Walt Disney

Drums Along the Mohawk, Boston/New York 1936, Novel
Drums Along the Mohawk 1939 d: John Ford. lps: Claudette Colbert, Henry Fonda, Edna May Oliver. 103M USA. prod/rel: 20th Century-Fox Film Corp.©

The Farmer Takes a Wife, 1934, Play
Farmer Takes a Wife, The 1935 d: Victor Fleming. lps: Janet Gaynor, Henry Fonda, Charles Bickford. 94M USA. prod/rel: Fox Film Corp.©

Farmer Takes a Wife, The 1953 d: Henry Levin. lps: Betty Grable, John Carroll, Dale Robertson. 81M USA. prod/rel: 20th Century-Fox

Red Wheels Rolling, 1940, Novel
Chad Hanna 1940 d: Henry King. lps: Henry Fonda, Dorothy Lamour, Linda Darnell. 88M USA. prod/rel: 20th Century-Fox Film Corp.

Rome Haul, 1929, Novel
Farmer Takes a Wife, The 1935 d: Victor Fleming. lps: Janet Gaynor, Henry Fonda, Charles Bickford. 94M USA. prod/rel: Fox Film Corp.©

Farmer Takes a Wife, The 1953 d: Henry Levin. lps: Betty Grable, John Carroll, Dale Robertson. 81M USA. prod/rel: 20th Century-Fox

EDMUND, JOHN
Story
Big Timber 1921 d: John W. Noble. lps: Richard C. Travers, Ruth Dwyer, William Pike. F CND. *Stranger of the North*; *Clansman of the North* prod/rel: Maritime Motion Picture Co. of Canada

EDOGAWA, RAMPO
Kyofo Nikei Ningen, Short Story
Kyofu Nikei Ningen 1969 d: Teruo Ishii. lps: Teruo Toshida, Minoru Oki, Asao Koike. 99M JPN. *Horror of a Deformed Man*; *Horror of Malformed Men* prod/rel: Toei Co.

Moju, Short Story
Moju 1969 d: Yasuzo MasumurA. lps: Eiji Funakoshi, Mako Midori, Noriko Sengoku. 90M JPN. *The Blind Beast* (USA); *Warehouse* prod/rel: Daiei Motion Picture Co.

EDQVIST, DAGMAR INGEBORG
Fallet Ingegerd Bremssen, 1937, Novel
Fallet Ingegerd Bremssen 1942 d: Anders Henrikson. lps: Sonja Wigert, Anders Henrikson, Dagmar Ebbeson. 87M SWD. *The Ingegerd Bremssen Case* prod/rel: Ab Europa Film

Kamrathustru, 1932, Novel
Livet Gar Vidare 1941 d: Anders Henrikson. lps: Edvin Adolphson, Hasse Ekman, Aino Taube. 84M SWD. *Kamrathustru*; *Life Goes on* prod/rel: Terrafilms Produktions Ab

Musik I Morker, 1937, Novel
Lianbron 1965 d: Sven Nykvist. 87M SWD. *The Vine Bridge*

Musik I Morker 1947 d: Ingmar Bergman. lps: Mai Zetterling, Birger Malmsten, Naima Wifstrand. 90M SWD. *Night Is My Future* (UKN); *Music in Darkness*; *Music in the Dark* prod/rel: Terrafilm

Rymlingen Fast, 1933, Novel
Kvinna Ombord, En 1941 d: Gunnar Skoglund. lps: Edvin Adolphson, Karin Ekelund, Erik Hampe Faustman. 84M SWD. *A Woman on Board* prod/rel: Terrafilms Produktions Ab

EDSCHMID, KASIMIR
Wenn Es Rosen Sind Werden Sie Bluhen, 1950, Novel
Deutsche Revolution, Eine 1981 d: Helmut Herbst. lps: Greger Hansen, Franz Wittich, Marquard Bohm. 97M GRM. *A German Revolution* prod/rel: Cinegrafik, Basis

EDWARDS, ANNE
Haunted Summer, Novel
Haunted Summer 1989 d: Ivan Passer. lps: Philip Anglim, Laura Dern, Alice Krige. 106M USA. prod/rel: Cannon

EDWARDS, GEORGE
Tropic of Desire, Novel
Tropic of Desire 1979 d: Cash Baxter. lps: Matt Collins, Roxanne Gregory, Barbara Baxley. 91M USA. prod/rel: Reel Movies International

EDWARDS, HENRY
The Bargain, Play
Bargain, The 1921 d: Henry Edwards. lps: Henry Edwards, Chrissie White, Rex McDougall. 5800f UKN. prod/rel: Hepworth

Doorsteps, Play
Doorsteps 1916 d: Henry Edwards. lps: Florence Turner, Henry Edwards, Campbell Gullan. 4415f UKN. prod/rel: Turner Films, Hepworth

EDWARDS, JAMES G.
Murder in the Surgery, New York 1935, Novel
Mystery of the White Room 1939 d: Otis Garrett. lps: Bruce Cabot, Helen Mack, Joan Woodbury. 59M USA. *Murder in the Surgery* prod/rel: Crime Club Productions, Universal Pictures Co.

EDWARDS, NORMAN
Wrong Number, Play
Wrong Number 1959 d: Vernon Sewell. lps: Peter Reynolds, Lisa Gastoni, Peter Elliott. 59M UKN. prod/rel: Anglo-Amalgamated, Merton Park

EDWARDS, ROWLAND G.
The Wound Stripe, 1925, Play
Man from Yesterday, The 1932 d: Berthold Viertel. lps: Claudette Colbert, Clive Brook, Charles Boyer. 71M USA. *The Woman of Flame* prod/rel: Paramount Publix Corp.©

EDWARDS, TICKNER
Tansy, Novel
Tansy 1921 d: Cecil M. Hepworth. lps: Alma Taylor, Gerald Ames, James Carew. 5570f UKN. prod/rel: Hepworth

EELS, GEORGE
Hedda and Louella, Book
Malice in Wonderland 1985 d: Gus Trikonis. lps: Elizabeth Taylor, Jane Alexander, Richard Dysart. TVM. 100M USA. *The Rumor Mill* prod/rel: Itc Productions

EFTIMIADES, MARIA
Book
Amy Fisher: My Story 1992 d: Bradford May. lps: Ed Marinaro, Noelle Parker, Boyd Kestner. TVM. 92M USA. *Lethal Lolita - Amy Fisher: My Own Story*; *Lethal Lolita*

EGAN, MICHAEL
The Dominant Sex, London 1934, Play
Dominant Sex, The 1937 d: Herbert Brenon. lps: Phillips Holmes, Diana Churchill, Romney Brent. 74M UKN. prod/rel: British International Pictures, Associated British Picture Corporation

EGE, HENRIK N.
The Silver Spoon, Radio Play
Let's Make a Night of It 1937 d: Graham Cutts. lps: Charles "Buddy" Rogers, June Clyde, Claire Luce. 94M UKN. *Radio Revue of 1937* prod/rel: Associated British Picture Corporation

EGER, RUDOLF
Die Grosse Und Die Kleine Welt, Play
Grosse Und Die Kleine Welt, Die 1921 d: Max Mack. lps: Alfred Abel, Eugen Burg, Hans Albers. 1995m GRM. prod/rel: Deulig-Film

Mir Lond Nod Lugg, Play
Mir Lond Nod Lugg 1940 d: Hermann Haller. lps: Paul Hubschmid, Lisa Della Casa, Max Knapp. 109M SWT. *On Ne Cede Pas* prod/rel: Neue Interna-Film

EGGE, PETER
Kjaerlighet Og Vennskap, 1904, Play
Karlek Och Vanskap 1941 d: Leif Sinding. NRW. *Kjaerlighet Og Vennskap*

EGGLESTON, EDWARD (1837–1902), USA
Hoosier Schoolboy, New York 1883, Novel
Hoosier Schoolboy, The 1937 d: William Nigh. lps: Mickey Rooney, Anne Nagel, Frank Shields. 62M USA. *Yesterday's Hero* (UKN); *Forgotten Hero* prod/rel: Monogram Pictures Corp.©

The Hoosier Schoolmaster, New York 1871, Novel
Hoosier Schoolmaster, The 1914 d: Max Figman. lps: Max Figman, Lolita Roberts. 5r USA. prod/rel: Masterpiece Film Manufacturing Co., Alliance Films Corp.
Hoosier Schoolmaster, The 1924 d: Oliver L. Sellers. lps: Henry Hull, Jane Thomas, Frank Dane. 5556f USA. prod/rel: Whitman Bennett Productions, W. W. Hodkinson Corp.
Hoosier Schoolmaster, The 1935 d: Lewis D. Collins. lps: Norman Foster, Charlotte Henry, Sarah Padden. 75M USA. *The Schoolmaster* (UKN) prod/rel: Monogram Pictures Corp.©, Paul Malver Production

EGLETON, CLIVE
Seven Days to a Killing, Novel
Black Windmill, The 1974 d: Don Siegel. lps: Michael Caine, Joseph O'Conor, Donald Pleasence. 106M UKN. prod/rel: Universal, Zanuck-Brown

EGYED, ZOLTAN
School of Drama, Play
Dramatic School 1938 d: Robert B. Sinclair. lps: Luise Rainer, Paulette Goddard, Alan Marshal. 80M USA. prod/rel: MGM, Loew's, Inc.©

EHLE, JOHN
The Journey of August King, 1971, Novel
Journey of August King, The 1995 d: John Duigan. lps: Jason Patric, Thandie Newton, Larry Drake. 91M USA. prod/rel: Miramax
Winter People, Novel
Winter People 1988 d: Ted Kotcheff. lps: Kurt Russell, Kelly McGillis, Lloyd Bridges. 110M USA. prod/rel: Nelson Entertainment, Castle Rock Entertainment

EHRENBERG, ILJA
Short Story
Dymky 1966 d: Vojtech Jasny. lps: Jana Brejchova, Richard Munch, Vivi Bach. 77M CZC/AUS. *Pfeifen Betten Turteltauben* (AUS); *Pipes*; *Dimky*; *Pfeifen* prod/rel: Filmove Studio Barrandov, Constantin
Die Liebe Der Jeanne Ney, Novel
Liebe Der Jeanne Ney, Die 1927 d: G. W. Pabst. lps: Edith Jehanne, Brigitte Helm, Hertha von Walther. 2643m GRM. *The Love of Jeanne Ney* (USA); *Lusts of the Flesh* (UKN); *The Loves of Jeanne Ney* prod/rel: UFA

EHRLICH, MAX SIMON
First Train to Babylon, New York 1955, Novel
Naked Edge, The 1961 d: Michael Anderson. lps: Gary Cooper, Deborah Kerr, Eric Portman. 99M UKN. prod/rel: Pennebaker, Inc., Baroda Productions
The Reincarnation of Peter Proud, Novel
Reincarnation of Peter Proud, The 1974 d: J. Lee Thompson. lps: Michael Sarrazin, Jennifer O'Neill, Margot Kidder. 104M USA. prod/rel: Bing Crosby
Spin the Glass Web, 1952, Novel
Glass Web, The 1953 d: Jack Arnold. lps: Edward G. Robinson, John Forsythe, Kathleen Hughes. 81M USA. prod/rel: Universal-International

EHRLICHMAN, JOHN
The Company, Book
Washington: Behind Closed Doors 1977 d: Gary Nelson. lps: Cliff Robertson, Jason Robards Jr., Stefanie Powers. TVM. 625M USA. prod/rel: Paramount Tv

EICHELBAUM, SAMUEL
Un Guapo Del 1900, Play
Guapo Del 1900, Un 1960 d: Leopoldo Torre-Nilsson. lps: Arturo Garcia Buhr, Elida Gay Palmer, Alfredo Alcon. 75M ARG. *Tough Guy of 1900* prod/rel: Producciones Angel

EICKE, DORIS
Was macht Papa Denn in Italien?, Novel
Was macht Papa Denn in Italien? 1961 d: Hans D. Schwarze. lps: Willy Fritsch, Jane Tilden, Barbara Frey. 97M GRM. *So What Is Papa Doing in Italy?* prod/rel: Franz Seitz, Constantin

EINSTEIN, CHARLES
The Bloody Spur, 1953, Novel
While the City Sleeps 1956 d: Fritz Lang. lps: Dana Andrews, Ida Lupino, Rhonda Fleming. 100M USA. prod/rel: RKO, Thor
Nowhere to Run, Novel
Nowhere to Run 1978 d: Richard Lang. lps: David Janssen, Stefanie Powers, Allen Garfield. TVM. 100M USA. prod/rel: Mtm Productions

EIS, EGON
Prison Sans Barreaux, Play
Prison Without Bars 1938 d: Brian Desmond Hurst. lps: Corinne Luchaire, Edna Best, Barry K. Barnes. 80M UKN. prod/rel: London Films, United Artists
L' Uomo Dall'Artiglio, Novel
Uomo Dall'Artiglio, L' 1931 d: Nunzio MalasommA. lps: Dria Paola, Elio Steiner, Carlo FontanA. 80M ITL. prod/rel: Cines, Anonima Pittaluga

EIS, OTTO
Prison Sans Barreaux, Play
Prison Without Bars 1938 d: Brian Desmond Hurst. lps: Corinne Luchaire, Edna Best, Barry K. Barnes. 80M UKN. prod/rel: London Films, United Artists
L' Uomo Dall'Artiglio, Novel
Uomo Dall'Artiglio, L' 1931 d: Nunzio MalasommA. lps: Dria Paola, Elio Steiner, Carlo FontanA. 80M ITL. prod/rel: Cines, Anonima Pittaluga

EISEMANN, MICHAEL
Die Katz' Im Sack, Play
Quadrille d'Amour 1934 d: Germain Fried, Richard Eichberg. lps: Pierre Brasseur, Irene de Zilahy, Mady Berry. 95M FRN. prod/rel: Societe Internationale Cinematographique

EISENBERG, DENNIS
Meyer Lansky: Mogul of the Mob, Book
Lansky 1999 d: John McNaughton. lps: Richard Dreyfus, Eric Roberts, Anthony LapagliA. TVM. 120M USA. prod/rel: Hbo Pictures, Frederick Zollo Prods.

EISINGER, JO
The Walks Came Tumbling Down, Novel
Walls Came Tumbling Down, The 1946 d: Lothar Mendes. lps: Lee Bowman, Marguerite Chapman, Edgar Buchanan. 82M USA. prod/rel: Columbia

EISLER
Causa Kaiser, Play
Mariage a Responsabilite Limitee 1933 d: Jean de Limur. lps: Pierre Larquey, Florelle, Jean Wall. 75M FRN. prod/rel: Vandor-Film

EISNER, JACK P.
The Survivor, Book
War and Love 1985 d: Moshe Mizrahi. lps: Sebastian Keneas, Kyra Sedgwick, David Spielberg. 112M USA. *The Children's War*; *Love and War* prod/rel: Cannon Films

EKLUND, ERNST
Quartetto Pazzo, Play
Quartetto Pazzo 1947 d: Guido Salvini. lps: Anna Magnani, Rina Morelli, Gino Cervi. 70M ITL. prod/rel: S.a.F.I.C., Italfilm

EKSTROM, JAN
Morianerna, Stockholm 1964, Novel
Morianerna 1965 d: Arne Mattsson. lps: Anders Henrikson, Eva Dahlbeck, Ella Henriksson. 100M SWD. *The Body) Morianna (I* (USA); *Morianna*; *I the Body*; *Blackamoors* prod/rel: Bison Film, Inge Varson
Trafracken, Novel
Trafracken 1966 d: Lars-Magnus Lindgren. lps: Gunnar Bjornstrand, Essy Persson, Catrin Westerlund. 85M SWD. *The Sadist* (UKN); *The Crowded Coffin*; *The Coffin* prod/rel: Flamingo

EKSTROM, PETER
Ung Sommar, Novel
Ung Sommar 1954 d: Kenne Fant. lps: Edvin Adolphson, Lennart Lindberg, Birgit Lundin. 82M SWD. *Young Summer* prod/rel: Nordisk

EKSTROM, PETER OLOF
Sommerdansen, Novel
Hon Dansade En Sommar 1951 d: Arne Mattsson. lps: Ulla Jacobsson, Folke Sundquist, Edvin Adolphson. 93M SWD. *She Only Danced One Summer*; *One Summer of Happiness*; *Sommardansen* prod/rel: Nordisk, Constantin

EKUNI, KAORI
Rakka Suru Yugata, Novel
Rakka Suru Yugata 1998 d: Naoe Gozu. lps: Tomoyo Harada, Atsuro Watanabe, Miho Kanno. 106M JPN. *Falling Into the Evening* prod/rel: Shochiku Co., Tv Man Union

ELDER, LAUREN
And I Alone Survived, Book
And I Alone Survived 1978 d: William A. Graham. lps: Blair Brown, Vera Miles, David Ackroyd. TVM. 100M USA. prod/rel: NBC, Jerry Leider Prods.

ELDER, ROB
Crash, Book
Crash 1978 d: Barry Shear. lps: William Shatner, Adrienne Barbeau, Brooke Bundy. TVM. 100M USA. *The Crash of Flight 401* prod/rel: ABC, Charles Fries Productions

ELDER, SARAH
Crash 1978 d: Barry Shear. lps: William Shatner, Adrienne Barbeau, Brooke Bundy. TVM. 100M USA. *The Crash of Flight 401* prod/rel: ABC, Charles Fries Productions

ELFMAN, BLOSSOM
The Girls of Huntington House, Novel
Girls of Huntington House, The 1973 d: Alf Kjellin. lps: Shirley Jones, Mercedes McCambridge, Pamela Sue Martin. TVM. 73M USA. prod/rel: Lorimar Productions

ELIN, PELIN
Geratsite, 1911, Novel
Geratsite 1958 d: Anton Marinovich. lps: Georgi Stamatov, Angelina Sarova, Ivan Dimov. 96M BUL. *The Geraks*; *The Gerak Family*
Yan Bibiyan, 1933, Novel
Yan Bibiyan 1984 d: Vassil Apostolov. lps: Michael Donchev, Georgi Kaloyanchev, Nikola Todev. 84M BUL.
Zemya, 1922, Novel
Zemya 1957 d: Zahari Zhandov. lps: Bogomil Simeonov, Ginka Stancheva, Slavka SlavovA. 102M BUL. *Earth*; *Land*; *Zemja*

ELIOT, ARTHUR
The Better 'Ole; Or the Romance of Old Bill, Oxford 1917, Play
Better 'Ole; Or, the Romance of Old Bill, The 1918 d: George Pearson. lps: Charles Rock, Arthur Cleave, Hugh E. Wright. 6600f UKN. *Carry on* prod/rel: Welsh, Pearson
Better 'Ole, The 1926 d: Charles F. Reisner. lps: Sydney Chaplin, Doris Hill, Harold Goodwin. 8469f USA. prod/rel: Warner Brothers Pictures

ELIOT, GEORGE (1819–1880), UKN, Evans, Mary Ann
Adam Bede, 1859, Novel
Adam Bede 1918 d: Maurice Elvey. lps: Bransby Williams, Ivy Close, Malvina Longfellow. 5400f UKN. prod/rel: International Exclusives
Adam Bede 1991 d: Giles Foster. lps: Iain Glen, Patsy Kensit, Susannah Harker. TVM. 102M UKN. prod/rel: BBC Tv, BBC Films
Daniel Deronda, 1876, Novel
Daniel Deronda 1921 d: W. C. Rowden. lps: Reginald Fox, Ann Trevor, Clive Brook. 5600f UKN. prod/rel: Master, Butcher's Film Service
Gwendolin 1914 d: Travers Vale. lps: Alan Hale, Isabel ReA. 2r USA. prod/rel: Biograph Co.
Felix Holt the Radical, 1866, Novel
Felix Holt 1915 d: Travers Vale. lps: Charles Hill Mailes, Jack Drumier, Vola Smith. 2r USA. prod/rel: Biograph Co.
Middlemarch, 1872, Novel
Middlemarch 1994 d: Anthony Page. lps: Juliet Aubrey, Simon Chandler, Ian Driver. MTV. 357M UKN/USA. prod/rel: BBC
The Mill on the Floss, London 1860, Novel
Mill on the Floss, The 1915 d: W. Eugene Moore. lps: Mignon Anderson, Harris Gordon, W. Eugene Moore. 5r USA. prod/rel: Thanhouser Corp., Mutual Film Corp.
Mill on the Floss, The 1937 d: Tim Whelan. lps: Frank Lawton, Victoria Hopper, Fay Compton. 94M UKN. prod/rel: Morgan, National Provincial Film Distributors
Mill on the Floss, The 1997 d: Graham Theakston. lps: Emily Watson, Ifan Meredith, James Frain. 90M UKN. prod/rel: Carnival Films, Uge D.A. Intl.
Mr. Gilfil's Love Story, 1857, Short Story
Mr. Gilfil's Love Story 1920 d: A. V. Bramble. lps: R. Henderson Bland, Mary Odette, Peter Upcher. 5400f UKN. *Love Story of Mr. Gilfil* prod/rel: Ideal
Romola, London 1862, Novel
Romola 1911 d: Mario Caserini. lps: Maria Caserini Gasparini, Amleto Novelli, Fernanda Negri-Pouget. 255m ITL. prod/rel: Cines
Romola 1925 d: Henry King. lps: Lillian Gish, Dorothy Gish, William Powell. 12r USA. prod/rel: Inspiration Pictures, Metro-Goldwyn Distributing Corp.
Silas Marner, London 1861, Novel
Are Children to Blame? 1922 d: Paul Price. lps: Em Gorman, Alex Shannon, Joseph Marquis. 5r USA. **Are the Children to Blame?** prod/rel: Chopin Features, Certified Pictures
Bangaru Papa 1954 d: B. N. Reddi. lps: S. V. Ranga Rao, K. Jaggaiah, JamunA. 183M IND. *Golden Child* prod/rel: Vauhini
Fair Exchange, A 1909 d: D. W. Griffith. lps: Henry B. Walthall, James Kirkwood, MacK Sennett. 995f USA. prod/rel: Biograph Co.
Little Outcast, The 1920 d: Paul Price. lps: Em Gorman, Joseph Marquis, Alex Shannon. 5r USA. *The Waif at the Crossroads* prod/rel: Chopin Features, State Rights

Silas Marner 1911 d: Theodore Marston. lps: Frank Crane, William Bowman, Alphonse Ethier. 1000f USA. prod/rel: Thanhouser

Silas Marner 1913 d: Charles J. Brabin. lps: William West, Gladys Hulette. 2000f USA. prod/rel: Edison

Silas Marner 1916 d: Ernest C. Warde. lps: Frederick Warde, Louise Emerald Bates, Morgan Jones. 7r USA. prod/rel: Thanhouser Film Corp., Mutual Film Corp.

Silas Marner 1985 d: Giles Foster. lps: Ben Kingsley, Jenny Agutter, Patrick Ryecart. TVM. 91M UKN. prod/rel: BBC

Simple Twist of Fate, A 1994 d: Gillies MacKinnon. lps: Steve Martin, Gabriel Byrne, Catherine O'HarA. 106M USA. prod/rel: Buena Vista, Touchstone

ELIOT, GEORGE FIELDING
Federal Bullets, London 1937, Novel
Federal Bullets 1937 d: Karl Brown. lps: Milburn Stone, Zeffie Tilbury, Terry Walker. 61M USA. prod/rel: Monogram Pictures Corp.©

ELIOT, T. S. (1888–1965), USA
Murder in the Cathedral, London 1935, Play
Murder in the Cathedral 1952 d: George Hoellering. lps: Father John Groser, Alexander Gauge, Donald Bisset. 136M UKN. prod/rel: Film Traders
Murder in the Cathedral 1964 d: George R. FoA. lps: Cyril Cusack, Dennis Quilley, John Bennett. MTV. UKN. prod/rel: BBC

ELISEO, DON
Un Embrujo, Novel
Embrujo, Un 1998 d: Carlos CarrerA. lps: Blanca Guerra, Mario Zaragoza, Daniel AcunA. 125M MXC. *Under a Spell* prod/rel: Salamandra Producciones, Tabasco Films

ELIZABETH
Mr. Skeffington, Novel
Mr. Skeffington 1944 d: Vincent Sherman. lps: Bette Davis, Claude Rains, Walter Abel. 146M USA. prod/rel: Warner Bros.

ELKIN, STANLEY (1930–, USA
The Bailbondsman, 1973, Novel
Alex and the Gypsy 1976 d: John Korty. lps: Jack Lemmon, Genevieve Bujold, James Woods. 106M USA. *Love and Other Crimes* prod/rel: 20th Century-Fox

ELKUNCHWAR, MAHESH
Holi, Play
Holi 1983 d: Ketan MehtA. lps: Sanjeev Gandhi, Manoj Pandya, Rahul Ranade. 116M IND. *The Festival of Fire*; *Festival of Colour* prod/rel: Film Unit, Neo Film Associates
Party, Play
Party 1984 d: Govind Nihalani. lps: Vijaya Mehta, Rohini Hattangadi, Manohar Singh. 118M IND. prod/rel: Nfdc

ELLERY, WILLIS P.
Story
Better Days 1927 d: Frank S. Mattison. lps: Dorothy Devore, Mary Carr, Gareth Hughes. 6660f USA. prod/rel: Pacific Pictures, First Division Pictures

ELLI, FRANK
The Riot, New York 1967, Novel
Riot 1969 d: Buzz Kulik. lps: Jim Brown, Gene Hackman, Ben Carruthers. 97M USA. prod/rel: William Castle Enterprises

ELLIN, STANLEY (1916–1986), USA
The Best of Everything, 1952, Short Story
Nothing But the Best 1963 d: Clive Donner. lps: Alan Bates, Denholm Elliott, Harry Andrews. 99M UKN. prod/rel: Domino Productions, Anglo-Amalgamated
The Bind, Novel
Sunburn 1979 d: Richard C. Sarafian. lps: Farrah Fawcett, Charles Grodin, Art Carney. 101M UKN/USA. prod/rel: Paramount, Hemdale
Dreadful Summit, Novel
Big Night, The 1951 d: Joseph Losey. lps: John Drew Barrymore, Preston Foster, Howland Chamberlin. 75M USA. prod/rel: United Artists, Philip A. Waxman Prods.
House of Cards, New York 1967, Novel
House of Cards 1969 d: John Guillermin. lps: George Peppard, Inger Stevens, Orson Welles. 105M USA. prod/rel: Westward Productions
The July Group, Novel
July Group, The 1982 d: George McCowan. lps: Ken Pogue, Nicholas Campbell, Chapelle Jaffe. TVM. 80M CND. prod/rel: Canadian Broadcasting Corp.
The Key to Nicholas Street, New York 1952, Novel
A Double Tour 1959 d: Claude Chabrol. lps: Madeleine Robinson, Antonella Lualdi, Jean-Paul Belmondo. 101M FRN/ITL. *Web of Passion* (UKN); *A Doppia Mandata* (ITL); *Leda* (USA) prod/rel: Paris-Films Production, Panitalia

ELLINGTON, E. A.
Story
Gilda 1946 d: Charles Vidor. lps: Rita Hayworth, Glenn Ford, George MacReady. 110M USA. prod/rel: Columbia

ELLIOTT, FRANCIS PERRY
The Haunted Pajamas, Indianapolis 1911, Novel
Haunted Pajamas, The 1917 d: Fred J. Balshofer. lps: Harold Lockwood, Carmel Myers, Ed Sedgwick. 5r USA. prod/rel: Yorke Film Corp., Metro Pictures Corp.©
Lend Me Your Name!, Chicago 1917, Novel
Lend Me Your Name 1918 d: Fred J. Balshofer. lps: Harold Lockwood, Bessie Eyton, Pauline Curley. 5r USA. prod/rel: Yorke Film Corp., Metro Pictures Corp.©
Love Me for Myself, Novel
Square Deceiver, The 1917 d: Fred J. Balshofer. lps: Harold Lockwood, Pauline Curley, William Clifford. 5r USA. *Love Me for Myself Alone* prod/rel: Yorke Film Corp., Metro Pictures Corp.©
Pals First, New York 1915, Novel
Pals First 1918 d: Edwin Carewe. lps: Harold Lockwood, Rubye de Remer, James Lackaye. 6r USA. prod/rel: Yorke Film Corp., Metro Pictures Corp.©
Pals First 1926 d: Edwin Carewe. lps: Lloyd Hughes, Dolores Del Rio, Alec B. Francis. 6843f USA. prod/rel: Edwin Carewe Productions, First National Pictures

ELLIOTT, GERALD
Nine Days Blunder, Novel
Cross Currents 1935 d: Adrian Brunel. lps: Ian Colin, Marjorie Hume, Evelyn Foster. 66M UKN. prod/rel: British and Dominions, Paramount British

ELLIOTT, JAMES
A Tribute to Mother, Story
Tribute to Mother, A 1915 d: Raymond L. Schrock. lps: John Maurice Sullivan, Mrs. John Maurice Sullivan, Morgan Thorpe. 2r USA. prod/rel: Imp

ELLIOTT, JANICE
The Buttercup Chain, Novel
Buttercup Chain, The 1970 d: Robert Ellis Miller. lps: Hywel Bennett, Leigh Taylor-Young, Jane Asher. 95M UKN. prod/rel: Columbia British
Secret Places, Novel
Secret Places 1985 d: Zelda Barron. lps: Marie-Therese Relin, Tara MacGowran, Claudine Auger. 98M UKN. prod/rel: Rank, Skreba

ELLIOTT, SUMNER LOCKE
Careful, He Might Hear You, 1963, Novel
Sumner Locke Elliott's Careful, He Might Hear You 1983 d: Carl Schultz. lps: Wendy Hughes, Robyn Nevin, Nicholas Gledhill. 110M ASL. *Careful, He Might Hear You* prod/rel: Syme Entertainment Pty. Ltd.©, New South Wales Film Corporation

ELLIS, ALICE THOMAS
Clothes in the Wardrobe, Novel
Clothes in the Wardrobe 1992 d: Waris Hussein. lps: Julie Walters, Joan Plowright, Jeanne Moreau. TVM. 79M UKN. *The Summer House* prod/rel: BBC Films

ELLIS, BRET EASTON
Less Than Zero, Novel
Less Than Zero 1987 d: Marek KanievskA. lps: Andrew McCarthy, Robert Downey Jr., Jami Gertz. 100M USA. prod/rel: 20th Century Fox, Avnet/Kerner

ELLIS, EDITH
My Man, New York 1910, Play
Triumph of the Weak, The 1918 d: Tom Terriss. lps: Alice Joyce, Walter McGrail, Eulalie Jensen. 4776f USA. *The Strength of the Weak* prod/rel: Vitagraph Co. of America©, Blue Ribbon Feature
The Point of View, New York 1912, Play
Point of View, The 1920 d: Alan Crosland. lps: Elaine Hammerstein, Rockliffe Fellowes, Warren Cook. 6r USA. prod/rel: Selznick Pictures Corp.©, Select Pictures Corp.
White Collars, New York 1923, Play
Idle Rich, The 1929 d: William C. de Mille. lps: Conrad Nagel, Bessie Love, Leila Hyams. 7351f USA. prod/rel: Metro-Goldwyn-Mayer Pictures
Rich Man, Poor Girl 1938 d: Reinhold Schunzel. lps: Robert Young, Lew Ayres, Ruth Hussey. 72M USA. *White Collars*; *It's Now Or Never* prod/rel: Metro-Goldwyn-Mayer Corp., Loew's, Inc.©
Women, 1928, Play
Affairs of a Gentleman 1934 d: Edwin L. Marin. lps: Paul Lukas, Leila Hyams, Patricia Ellis. 70M USA. prod/rel: Universal Pictures Corp.

ELLIS, EDWARD
Affairs of a Gentleman 1934 d: Edwin L. Marin. lps: Paul Lukas, Leila Hyams, Patricia Ellis. 70M USA. prod/rel: Universal Pictures Corp.

ELLIS, ELIZABETH
Barbara Winslow - Rebel, New York 1906, Novel
Dangerous Maid, The 1923 d: Victor Heerman. lps: Constance Talmadge, Conway Tearle, Morgan Wallace. 7337f USA. prod/rel: Joseph M. Schenck Productions, Associated First National Pictures

ELLIS, JOHN BRECKENRIDGE
Fran, Indianapolis 1912, Novel
Love Hunger, The 1919 d: William P. S. Earle. lps: Lillian Walker, L. C. Shumway, Herbert Prior. 5r USA. *Fixing It*; *The Lion Girl* prod/rel: Lillian Walker Pictures, Inc., W. W. Hodkinson Corp.
Lahoma, Indianapolis 1913, Novel
Lahoma 1920 d: Edgar Lewis. lps: Peaches Jackson, Louise Burnham, Beatrice Burnham. 7r USA. prod/rel: Edgar Lewis Productions, Inc., Pathe Exchange, Inc.©
Little Fiddler of the Ozarks, Chicago 1913, Novel
Cinderella of the Hills 1921 d: Howard M. Mitchell. lps: Barbara Bedford, Carl Miller, Cecil Van Auker. 4800f USA. prod/rel: Fox Film Corp.
The Picture on the Wall, Kansas City 1920, Novel
Shadow on the Wall, The 1925 d: B. Reeves Eason. lps: Eileen Percy, Creighton Hale, William V. Mong. 5800f USA. prod/rel: Gotham Productions, Lumas Film Corp.
Stork's Nest, New York 1905, Novel
Emmy of Stork's Nest 1915 d: William Nigh. lps: Mary Miles Minter, Niles Welch, R. A. Bresee. 5r USA. *The Stork's Nest* prod/rel: Columbia Pictures Corp., Metro Pictures Corp.©

ELLIS, KENNETH M.
The Trial of Vivienne Ware, New York 1931, Novel
Trial of Vivienne Ware, The 1932 d: William K. Howard. lps: Joan Bennett, Donald Cook, Skeets Gallagher. 56M USA. prod/rel: Fox Film Corp.©, William K. Howard Production

ELLIS, MEL
The Wild Horse Killers, Novel
Wild Horse Hank 1978 d: Eric Till. lps: Linda Blair, Michael Wincott, Al Waxman. 96M CND. *Long Shot*; *Hard Ride Hank*; *Hard Ride to Rantan*; *Hank* prod/rel: Film Consortium of Canada Inc.

ELLIS, SIDNEY R.
Darkest Russia, New York 1894, Play
Darkest Russia 1917 d: Travers Vale. lps: Alice Brady, John Bowers, J. Herbert Frank. 5r USA. prod/rel: World Film Corp.©

ELLIS, WALTER
Almost a Honeymoon, London 1930, Play
Almost a Honeymoon 1930 d: Monty Banks. lps: Clifford Mollison, Dodo Watts, Lamont Dickson. 100M UKN. prod/rel: British International Pictures, Wardour
Almost a Honeymoon 1938 d: Norman Lee. lps: Tommy Trinder, Linden Travers, Edmund Breon. 80M UKN. prod/rel: Welwyn, Pathe
Monsieur de Minuit, Le 1931 d: Harry Lachman. lps: Jean Weber, Josseline Gael, Odette Talazac. 95M FRN. prod/rel: Films Albatros
Bedtime Story, London 1937, Play
Bedtime Story 1938 d: Donovan Pedelty. lps: Jack Livesey, Lesley Wareing, Eliot Makeham. 71M UKN. prod/rel: Admiral, Grand National
Hawleys of the High Street, 1922, Play
Hawleys of High Street 1933 d: Thomas Bentley. lps: Leslie Fuller, Judy Kelly, Francis Lister. 68M UKN. prod/rel: British International Pictures, Wardour
A Little Bit of Fluff, London 1915, Play
Let Me Explain Dear 1932 d: Gene Gerrard, Frank Miller. lps: Gene Gerrard, Viola Lyel, Claude Hulbert. 82M UKN. prod/rel: British International Pictures, Wardour
Little Bit of Fluff, A 1919 d: Kenelm Foss. lps: Ernest Thesiger, Dorothy Minto, Bertie Wright. 5000f UKN. prod/rel: Q Films, Ruffells
Little Bit of Fluff, A 1928 d: Jess Robbins, Wheeler Dryden. lps: Sydney Chaplin, Betty Balfour, Edmund Breon. 7900f UKN. *Skirts* (USA) prod/rel: British International Pictures, Wardour
S.O.S., London 1928, Play
Her Last Affaire 1935 d: Michael Powell. lps: Hugh Williams, Viola Keats, Francis L. Sullivan. 78M UKN. prod/rel: New Ideal, Producers' Distributing Corporation
S.O.S. 1928 d: Leslie Hiscott. lps: Robert Loraine, Bramwell Fletcher, Ursula Jeans. 7251f UKN. prod/rel: Strand Films, Allied Artists

145

ELLISON, HAL
Tomboy, Novel
  Terrain Vague 1960 d: Marcel Carne. lps: Daniele Gaubert, Jean-Louis Bras, Maurice Caffarelli. 103M FRN/ITL. *Gioventu Nuda* (ITL) prod/rel: Gray Films, Films Rive Gauche

ELLISON, HARLAN (1934–, USA, Ellison, Harlan Jay
Story
  Boy and His Dog, A 1975 d: L. Q. Jones. lps: Don Johnson, Susanne Benton, Jason Robards Jr. 87M USA. prod/rel: Lg Jaf

ELLMAN, RICHARD
Oscar Wilde, Biography
  Wilde 1997 d: Brian Gilbert. lps: Stephen Fry, Jude Law, Vanessa Redgrave. 117M UKN. prod/rel: Samuelson Production, Dove International

ELLROY, JAMES (1948–, USA
Blood on the Moon, Novel
  Cop 1987 d: James B. Harris. lps: James Woods, Lesley Ann Warren, Charles Durning. 110M USA. *Blood on the Moon* prod/rel: Atlantic
Brown's Requiem, 1981, Novel
  Brown's Requiem 1998 d: Jason Freeland. lps: Michael Rooker, William Sasso, Kevin Corrigan. 104M USA. prod/rel: J & T Prods., Savvy Lad
L.A. Confidential, Novel
  L.A. Confidential 1997 d: Curtis Hanson. lps: Kevin Spacey, Russell Crowe, Guy Pearce. 136M USA. prod/rel: Arnon Milchan, David L. Wolper

ELLSBERG, EDWARD
Pigboats, New York 1931, Novel
  Hell Below 1932 d: Jack Conway. lps: Robert Montgomery, Walter Huston, Madge Evans. 105M USA. *Pigboats* prod/rel: Metro-Goldwyn-Mayer Corp.©

ELSSCHOT, WILLEM
Het Dwaallicht, 1947, Short Story
  Dwaallicht, Het 1973 d: Frans Buyens. lps: Eva Kant, Romain Deconinck, Dora Van Der Groen. 91M BLG/NTH. *Will-O'-the-Wisp*

ELSTER, KRISTIAN, JR.
Den Hemmelighetsfulde Leilighet, 1928, Short Story
  Hemmelighetsfulle Leiligheten, Den 1948 d: Tancred Ibsen. 75M NRW.

ELSTON, ALLAN VAUGHAN
The Belled Palm, Short Story
  Paradise Isle 1937 d: Arthur G. Collins. lps: Movita, Warren Hull, George Piltz. 73M USA. *Siren of the South Seas* prod/rel: Monogram Pictures Corp.©

ELWEN, EVA
Nun Mary Latimer, Novel
  Mary Latimer, Nun 1920 d: Bert Haldane. lps: Malvina Longfellow, Warwick Ward, Ethel Fisher. 5000f UKN. prod/rel: Famous Pictures

ELY, DAVID
Seconds, New York 1963, Novel
  Seconds 1966 d: John Frankenheimer. lps: Rock Hudson, Salome Jens, John Randolph. 106M USA. prod/rel: Douglas & Lewis Productions, Joel Productions

EMANUELLI, ENRICO
Settimana Nera, Novel
  Violenza Segreta 1963 d: Giorgio Moser. lps: Giorgio Albertazzi, Maryam, Alexandra Stewart. 100M ITL. prod/rel: Film Studio, Globe International Film

EMBLING, JOHN
Tom, Novel
  Fighting Back 1982 d: Michael Caulfield. lps: Lewis Fitz-Gerald, Paul (3) Smith, Kris McQuade. 101M ASL. prod/rel: Samson Productions©, Adams Packer

EMERICK, GEORGE H.
Finnegan's Ball, 1894, Play
  Finnegan's Ball 1927 d: James P. Hogan. lps: Blanche Mehaffey, MacK Swain, Cullen Landis. 6700f USA. prod/rel: Graf Brothers Studio, First Division Pictures

EMERSON, JOHN
Conspiracy, New York 1913, Novel
  Conspiracy 1930 d: W. Christy Cabanne. lps: Bessie Love, Ned Sparks, Hugh Trevor. 69M USA. prod/rel: RKO Productions
The Conspiracy, New York 1912, Play
  Conspiracy, The 1914 d: Allan Dwan. lps: John Emerson, Lois Meredith, Francis Byrne. 4-5r USA. prod/rel: Famous Players Film Co., Paramount Pictures Corp.
The Social Register, New York 1931, Play
  Social Register 1934 d: Marshall Neilan. lps: Colleen Moore, Charles Winninger, Pauline Frederick. 72M USA. prod/rel: Associated Film Productions©, Columbia Pictures Corp.©

The Whole Town's Talking, New York 1923, Play
  Ex-Bad Boy 1931 d: Vin Moore. lps: Robert Armstrong, Jean Arthur, Lola Lane. 67M USA. *His Temporary Affair* (UKN); *The Whole Town's Talking* prod/rel: Universal Pictures Corp.©
  Whole Town's Talking, The 1926 d: Edward Laemmle. lps: Edward Everett Horton, Virginia Lee Corbin, Trixie FriganzA. 6662f USA. prod/rel: Universal Pictures

EMERY, GILBERT
The Hero, New York 1921, Play
  Hero, The 1923 d: Louis J. Gasnier. lps: Gaston Glass, Barbara La Marr, John Sainpolis. 6800f USA. *His Brother's Wife* prod/rel: Preferred Pictures, Al Lichtman Corp.
Tarnish, New York 1923, Play
  Tarnish 1924 d: George Fitzmaurice. lps: May McAvoy, Ronald Colman, Marie Prevost. 6831f USA. prod/rel: Goldwyn Pictures, Associated First National Pictures

EMERY, STEUART M.
The Wild, Wild Child, 1925, Short Story
  Wild, Wild Susan 1925 d: A. Edward Sutherland. lps: Bebe Daniels, Rod La Rocque, Henry Stephenson. 5774f USA. prod/rel: Famous Players-Lasky, Paramount Pictures

EMINESCU, MIHAI (1849–1889), RMN
Fat-Frumos Din Tei, 1875, Verse
  Blanca 1955 d: Mihai Iacob, Constantin Neagu. 29M RMN.

EMMANUELE, LUIGI
Short Story
  Angelo Per Satana, Un 1966 d: Camillo Mastrocinque. lps: Barbara Steele, Anthony Steffen, Claudio GorA. 90M ITL. *An Angel for Satan* (UKN) prod/rel: Discobolo Film
Le Vergini Di Roma, Short Story
  Vergini Di Roma, Le 1960 d: Vittorio Cottafavi, Carlo Ludovico BragagliA. lps: Louis Jourdan, Sylvia Syms, Nicole Courcel. 80M ITL/FRN. *Les Vierges de Rome* (FRN); *Amazons of Rome* (USA); *The Virgins of Rome*; *Warrior Women* prod/rel: Regina Film, Cine Italia Film (Roma)

EMMONS, DELLA GOULD
Sacajawea of the Shoshones, Novel
  Far Horizons, The 1955 d: Rudolph Mate. lps: Fred MacMurray, Charlton Heston, Donna Reed. 108M USA. *Untamed West* prod/rel: Paramount, Pine-Thomas

EMPEY, ARTHUR GUY
Over the Top, New York 1917, Book
  Over the Top 1918 d: Wilfred North. lps: Arthur Guy Empey, Lois Meredith, James Morrison. 9r USA. prod/rel: Vitagraph Co. of America©, Greater Vitagraph, Inc.

ENDE, MICHAEL
Momo, Novel
  Momo 1986 d: Johannes Schaaf. lps: Radost Bokel, Mario Adorf, Armin Mueller-Stahl. 110M GRM/ITL. prod/rel: Rialto, Iduna
Die Unendliche Geschichte: von a Bis Z, 1979, Novel
  Neverending Story II, The 1990 d: George Miller. lps: Jonathan Brandis, Kenny Morrison, Clarissa Burt. 89M GRM. *The Neverending Story Ii: the Next Chapter*; *Die Unendliche Geschichte II -Auf Der Suche Nach Phantasien*
  Neverending Story, The 1984 d: Wolfgang Petersen. lps: Noah Hathaway, Barret Oliver, Tami Stronach. 94M UKN/GRM. *Die Unendliche Geschichte* (GRM) prod/rel: Neue Constantin Filmproduktion, Bavaria Studio

ENDERLING, PAUL
Die Umwege Des Schonen Karl, Novel
  Umwege Des Schonen Karl, Die 1938 d: Carl Froelich. lps: Heinz Ruhmann, Karin Hardt, Sybille Schmitz. 101M GRM. prod/rel: Tonfilmstudio Carl Froelich

ENDFIELD, CY
The Argyle Album, Radio Play
  Argyle Secrets, The 1948 d: Cy Endfield. lps: William Gargan, Marjorie Lord, Ralph Byrd. 63M USA. prod/rel: Film Classsics

ENDICOTT, RUTH BELMORE
Carolyn of the Corners, New York 1918, Novel
  Carolyn of the Corners 1919 d: Robert T. Thornby. lps: Bessie Love, Charles Edler, Charlotte Mineau. 5r USA. prod/rel: Anderson-Brunton Co., Pathe Exchange, Inc.©

ENDO, SHUSAKU (1923–, JPN
Dokkoisho, 1967, Novel
  Nihon No Seishun 1968 d: Masaki Kobayashi. lps: Makoto Fujita, Tomoko Naraoka, Toshio KurosawA. 130M JPN. *Diary of a Tired Man*; *Hymn to a Tired Man*; *The Youth of Japan*; *Nippon No Seishun*; *Japanese Youth* prod/rel: Toho Co.
Watashi Ga Suteta Onna, Novel
  Watashi Ga Suteta Onna 1969 d: Kirio UrayamA. lps: Choichiro Kawarazaki, Toshie Kobayashi, Ruriko AsaokA. 116M JPN. *The Girl I Abandoned* (USA) prod/rel: Nikkatsu Corporation
The Woman I Abandoned, Novel
  Aisuru 1997 d: Kei Kumai. lps: Miki Sakai, Atsuro Watabe, Kyoko KishidA. 113M JPN. *To Love* prod/rel: Nikkatsu Corp.

ENDORE, GUY
Story
  Fear No Evil 1969 d: Paul Wendkos. lps: Louis Jourdan, Carroll O'Connor, Bradford Dillman. TVM. 100M USA. prod/rel: Universal
Methinks the Lady, Novel
  Whirlpool 1950 d: Otto Preminger. lps: Richard Conte, Gene Tierney, Jose Ferrer. 97M USA. prod/rel: 20th Century Fox
The Werewolf of Paris, New York 1933, Novel
  Curse of the Werewolf, The 1961 d: Terence Fisher. lps: Clifford Evans, Oliver Reed, Yvonne Romain. 88M UKN. prod/rel: Hotspur, Hammer

ENGEL, ALEXANDER
Play
  Just a Gigolo 1931 d: Jack Conway. lps: William Haines, Irene Purcell, C. Aubrey Smith. 71M USA. *The Dancing Partner* (UKN); *The Princess and the Dancer* prod/rel: Metro-Goldwyn-Mayer Corp., Metro-Goldwyn-Mayer Dist. Corp.©
Eheringe, Play
  Eheferien 1927 d: Victor Janson. lps: Lilian Harvey, Harry Halm, Ida Perry. 2245m GRM. *Matrimonial Holidays* prod/rel: Richard Eichberg-Film
Der Ewige Jungeling, Play
  Vintage Wine 1935 d: Henry Edwards. lps: Seymour Hicks, Claire Luce, Eva Moore. 80M UKN. prod/rel: Real Art, Gaumont-British

ENGEL, GEORG
Die Herrin Und Ihr Knecht, Novel
  Herrin Und Ihr Knecht, Die 1929 d: Richard Oswald. lps: Henny Porten, Igo Sym, Alexander Wiruboff. 2630m GRM. prod/rel: Henny Porten-Filmproduktion

ENGELHARD, JACK
Indecent Proposal, Novel
  Indecent Proposal 1993 d: Adrian Lyne. lps: Robert Redford, Demi Moore, Woody Harrelson. 117M USA. prod/rel: Paramount

ENGELS, ERICH (1889–, GRM
Freitag Der 13, Play
  Freitag Der 13 1944 d: Erich Engels. lps: Fita Benkhoff, Angelika Hauff, Fritz Kampers. 85M GRM. *Friday the 13th* prod/rel: Terra, Stern

ENGLAND, BARRY
Conduct Unbecoming, Play
  Conduct Unbecoming 1975 d: Michael Anderson. lps: Michael York, Richard Attenborough, Trevor Howard. 107M UKN. prod/rel: British Lion, Crown
Figures in a Landscape, Novel
  Figures in a Landscape 1970 d: Joseph Losey. lps: Robert Shaw, Malcolm McDowell, Henry Woolf. 110M UKN. *The Hunted* prod/rel: 20th Century-Fox, Cinecrest

ENGLAND, GEORGE ALLAN
The Alibi, Boston 1916, Novel
  Alibi, The 1916 d: Paul Scardon. lps: Betty Howe, James Morrison, Paul Scardon. 5r USA. prod/rel: Vitagraph Co. of America©, Blue Ribbon Feature
The Brass Check, 1916, Short Story
  Brass Check, The 1918 d: Will S. Davis. lps: Francis X. Bushman, Beverly Bayne, Augustus Phillips. 7r USA. prod/rel: Metro Pictures Corp.©
Cursed, Boston 1919, Novel
  Devil Within, The 1921 d: Bernard J. Durning. lps: Dustin Farnum, Virginia Valli, Nigel de Brulier. 5997f USA. prod/rel: Fox Film Corp.
The Gift Supreme, New York 1916, Novel
  Gift Supreme, The 1920 d: Oliver L. Sellers. lps: Bernard Durning, Melbourne McDowell, Eugenie Besserer. 6r USA. prod/rel: C. R. Macauley Photoplays, Inc.©, Republic Distributing Corp.

ENGLISH, RICHARD
Story
  Copper Canyon 1950 d: John Farrow. lps: Ray Milland, Hedy Lamarr, MacDonald Carey. 83M USA. prod/rel: Paramount

Short Stories
Ding Dong Williams 1945 d: William Berke. lps: Glenn Vernon, Marcy McGuire, Felix Bressart. 62M USA. *Melody Maker* (UKN) prod/rel: RKO

Story
Follow the Band 1943 d: Jean Yarbrough. lps: Eddie Quillan, Mary Beth Hughes, Leon Errol. 61M USA. *Trombone from Heaven* prod/rel: Universal

ENGSTRAND, STUART
Beyond the Forest, Novel
Beyond the Forest 1949 d: King Vidor. lps: Bette Davis, Joseph Cotten, David Brian. 96M USA. *Rosa Moline* prod/rel: Warner Bros.

ENNA, FRANCO
Tempo Di Massacro, Novel
Omicidio Per Appuntamento 1967 d: Mino Guerrini. lps: Giorgio Ardisson, Ella Karin, Hans von Borsody. 105M ITL/GRM. *Agent 3S3 Setzt Alles Auf Eine Karte* (GRM); *Agent 3S3 Bets It All* prod/rel: Discobolo Film (Roma), Parnass Film (Munich)
L' Ultima Chance, Novel
Ultima Chance, L' 1973 d: Maurizio Lucidi. lps: Fabio Testi, Ursula Andress, Eli Wallach. 105M ITL. *Stateline Motel* (UKN); *The Last Chance* prod/rel: Fra Cin.Ca, Alpherat

ENQUIST, PER OLOV
Play
Hour of the Lynx, The 1990 d: Stuart Burge. lps: Simon Donald, Sylvestra Le Touzel, Eleanor Bron. TVM. 70M UKN. prod/rel: BBC
Magnetisorens Femte Vinter, Novel
Magnetisorens Femte Vinter 1999 d: Morten Henriksen. lps: Ole Lemmeke, Rolf Lassgard, Johanna Sallstrom. 119M DNM/NRW/SWD. *The Magnetist's Fifth Winter* prod/rel: Magic Hour Films (Denmark), Norsk Film (Norway)

ENRIGHT, NICK
Blackrock, Play
Blackrock 1997 d: Steve Vidler. lps: Laurence Breuls, Linda Cropper, Simon Lyndon. 100M ASL. prod/rel: Palm Beach Pictures, Polygram Filmed Entertainment

ENTHOVEN, GABRIEL
Ellen Young, Play
Quest of Life, The 1916 d: Ashley Miller. lps: Maurice, Florence Walton, Robert Brower. 5r USA. prod/rel: Famous Players Film Co., Paramount Pictures Corp.

EPHRON, HENRY
Take Her, She's Mine, New York 1961, Play
Take Her, She's Mine 1963 d: Henry Koster. lps: James Stewart, Sandra Dee, Robert Morley. 98M USA. prod/rel: 20th Century-Fox Film Corporation

EPHRON, NORA
Heartburn, Novel
Heartburn 1986 d: Mike Nichols. lps: Meryl Streep, Jack Nicholson, Jeff Daniels. 108M USA. prod/rel: Paramount

EPHRON, PHOEBE
Take Her, She's Mine, New York 1961, Play
Take Her, She's Mine 1963 d: Henry Koster. lps: James Stewart, Sandra Dee, Robert Morley. 98M USA. prod/rel: 20th Century-Fox Film Corporation

ERASTOV, GEORGE
Sold, 1910, Play
Sold 1915 d: Edwin S. Porter, Hugh Ford. lps: Pauline Frederick, Thomas Holding, Julian L'Estrange. 5r USA. prod/rel: Famous Players Film Co.©, Paramount Pictures Corp.

ERBEN, KAREL JAROMIR
Svatebni Kosile Ze Sbirky Kytice, Poem
Svatebni Kosile 1925 d: Theodor Pistek. lps: Suzanne Marwille, Karel Lamac, Joe Jencik. CZC. *The Wedding Shirt* prod/rel: Josef Kokeisl

ERCHOW, PAVEL
Story
Skazka O Konke-Gorbunke 1961 d: Aleksandr Radunskiy, Zoya TulubyevA. lps: Maya Plisetskaya, Vladimir Vasilyev, Alla ShcherbininA. 82M USS. *The Little Humpbacked Horse* (USA); *Koniok Gorbunok*

ERCKMANN, EMILE
L' Ami Fritz, Novel
Ami Fritz, L' 1933 d: Jacques de Baroncelli. lps: Simone Bourday, Lucien Duboscq, Jacques de Feraudy. 90M FRN. prod/rel: Les Films Artistiques Francais
The Bells, Play
Bells, The 1913 d: Oscar Apfel. lps: E. P. Sullivan, Irving Cummings, Gertrude Robinson. 2r USA. prod/rel: Reliance
Le Juif Polonais, Paris 1869, Play
Bells, The 1918 d: Ernest C. Warde. lps: Frank Keenan, Lois Wilson, Joseph J. Dowling. 5r USA. prod/rel: Anderson-Brunton Co., Pathe Exchange, Inc.©

Bells, The 1926 d: James Young. lps: Lionel Barrymore, Fred Warren, Boris Karloff. 6300f USA. prod/rel: Chadwick Pictures
Bells, The 1931 d: Harcourt Templeman, O. M. Werndorff. lps: Donald Calthrop, Jane Welsh, Edward Sinclair. 75M UKN/GRM. prod/rel: Producers Distributing Corporation, British Sound Films Productions
Juif Polonais, Le 1931 d: Jean Kemm. lps: Harry Baur, Simone Mareuil, Georges La Cressonniere. 95M FRN. prod/rel: Etablissements Jacques Haik
Les Rantzau, Play
Rantzau, Les 1924 d: Gaston Roudes. lps: France Dhelia, Georges Melchior, Maurice Schutz. 1900m FRN. prod/rel: Gaston Roudes, Sphinx

ERDMAN, PAUL (1932–, CND, Erdman, Paul E.)
Silver Bears, Novel
Silver Bears 1977 d: Ivan Passer. lps: Michael Caine, Cybill Shepherd, Louis Jourdan. 113M UKN/USA. prod/rel: Columbia, EMI

ERENBURG, ILJA (1891–1967), RSS
The Communard's Pipe
Trubka Kummunara 1929 d: Konstantin Mardzhanov. lps: N. Chkheidze, Sergei Zabozlaiev, Veriko Andzhaparidze. 65M USS.

ERICHSEN, UWE
Die Katze, Novel
Katze, Die 1987 d: Dominik Graf. lps: Gotz George, Gudrun Landgrebe, Joachim Kemmer. 118M GRM. *Lives of a Cat* prod/rel: Bavaria, ZDF

ERICKSON, PAUL
Shadow of a Man, Play
Shadow of a Man 1955 d: Michael McCarthy. lps: Paul Carpenter, Rona Anderson, Jane Griffiths. 69M UKN. prod/rel: E. J. Fancey, New Realm

ERLANDE, A.
Stella Lucente, Novel
Stella Lucente 1922 d: Raoul d'Auchy. lps: Manuel Camere, Madeleine Lyrisse, Claude Merelle. 1935m FRN. prod/rel: Films D'auchy

ERLICH, JACK
The Gun and the Pulpit, Novel
Gun and the Pulpit, The 1974 d: Daniel Petrie. lps: Marjoe Gortner, Slim Pickens, David Huddleston. TVM. 78M USA. prod/rel: Danny Thomas Productions

ERMOLLI, MARIA
L'ha Fatto Una Signora, Play
L'ha Fatto Una Signora 1938 d: Mario Mattoli. lps: Rosina Anselmi, Michele Abbruzzo, Alida Valli. 75M ITL. prod/rel: I.C.A.R., Generalcine

ERNEST, PAUL
The Old Gang, Story
Kid Dynamite 1943 d: Wallace Fox. lps: Leo Gorcey, Huntz Hall, Bobby Jordan. 73M USA. *Queen of Broadway*; *Little Mobsters* prod/rel: Monogram, Banner Prods.

ERNST, HANS
Im Herbst Verbluhen Die Rosen, Novel
Wetterleuchten Um Maria 1957 d: Luis Trenker. lps: Marianne Hold, Bert Fortell, Harald Maresch. 95M GRM. *Heat Lightning on Maria* prod/rel: Neubach, Constantin

ERSKINE, JOHN
Bachelor of Arts, Indianapolis 1934, Novel
Bachelor of Arts 1934 d: Louis King. lps: Tom Brown, Anita Louise, Arline Judge. 74M USA. prod/rel: Fox Film Corp.
Diane de Poitiers, Book
Diane 1955 d: David Miller. lps: Lana Turner, Pedro Armendariz, Roger Moore. 110M USA. prod/rel: MGM
The Private Life of Helen of Troy, Indianapolis 1925, Novel
Private Life of Helen of Troy, The 1927 d: Alexander KordA. lps: Maria Corda, Lewis Stone, Ricardo Cortez. 7694f USA. *Helen of Troy* prod/rel: First National Pictures
Sincerity, Indianapolis 1929, Novel
Lady Surrenders, A 1930 d: John M. Stahl. lps: Genevieve Tobin, Conrad Nagel, Rose Hobart. 102M USA. *Blind Wives* (UKN) prod/rel: Universal Pictures

ERSKINE, LAURIE YORK
The Confidence Man, New York 1925, Novel
Confidence Man, The 1924 d: Victor Heerman. lps: Thomas Meighan, Virginia Valli, Laurence Wheat. 7304f USA. prod/rel: Famous Players-Lasky, Paramount Pictures
Renfrew of the Royal Mounted, New York 1922, Novel
Renfrew of the Royal Mounted 1937 d: Al Herman. lps: James Newill, Carol Hughes, William Royle. 64M USA. prod/rel: Grand National Films©

Renfrew Rides Again, New York 1927, Novel
Fighting Mad 1939 d: Sam Newfield. lps: James Newill, Sally Blane, Dave O'Brien. 54M USA. *Renfrew of the Royal Mounted in Fighting Mad* prod/rel: Criterion Pictures Corp., Monogram Pictures Corp.©
Renfrew Rides North, New York 1931, Novel
Murder on the Yukon 1940 d: Louis J. Gasnier. lps: James Newill, Polly Ann Young, Dave O'Brien. 58M USA. prod/rel: Criterion Pictures Corp.©, Monogram Pictures Corp.
Renfrew on the Great White Trail 1938 d: Al Herman. lps: James Newill, Terry Walker, Robert Frazer. 59M USA. *On the Great White Trail* (UKN); *Renfrew Rides North*; *Renfrew of the Great White Trail* prod/rel: Criterion Pictures Corp., Grand National Films
Yukon Flight 1940 d: Ralph Staub. lps: James Newill, Louise Stanley, Dave O'Brien. 57M USA. *Renfrew of the Royal Mounted in Yukon Flight* prod/rel: Criterion Pictures Corp.©, Monogram Pictures Corp.
Renfrew Rides the Range, New York 1935, Novel
Crashing Thru 1939 d: Elmer Clifton. lps: James Newill, Jean Carmen, Warren Hull. 65M USA. *Renfrew of the Royal Mounted in Crashin' Thru*; *Renfrew Crashes Through*; *Crashin' Thru* prod/rel: Criterion Pictures Corp.
Renfrew Rides the Sky, New York 1928, Novel
Sky Bandits 1940 d: Ralph Staub. lps: James Newill, Louise Stanley, Dave O'Brien. 56M USA. *Renfrew of the Mounted in Sky Bandits* prod/rel: Criterion Pictures Corp., Monogram Pictures Corp.
Renfrew's Long Trail, Novel
Danger Ahead 1940 d: Ralph Staub. lps: James Newill, Dorothea Kent, Dave O'Brien. 60M USA. prod/rel: Criterion Pictures Corp.

ERSKINE, ROSALIND
Leidenschaftliche Blumchen, Novel
Leidenschaftliche Blumchen 1978 d: Andre Farwagi. lps: Nastassja Kinski, Gerry Sundquist, Kurt Raab. 98M GRM. *Passion Flower Hotel* (USA); *Boarding School*; *Virgin Campus*; *Passionate Little Flowers* prod/rel: Ccc Filmkunst

ERTZ, SUSAN
In the Cool of the Day, New York 1960, Novel
In the Cool of the Day 1963 d: Robert Stevens. lps: Peter Finch, Jane Fonda, Angela Lansbury. 91M UKN/USA. prod/rel: MGM British

ERVINE, ST. JOHN G.
Boyd's Shop, Play
Boyd's Shop 1960 d: Henry Cass. lps: Eileen Crowe, Geoffrey Golden, Aiden O'Kelly. 56M UKN. prod/rel: Rank Film Distributors, Emmett Dalton
The First Mrs. Fraser, London 1929, Play
First Mrs. Fraser, The 1932 d: Sinclair Hill. lps: Henry Ainley, Joan Barry, Dorothy Dix. 84M UKN. prod/rel: Sterling

ESBERN, STIG
Story
Mockery 1927 d: Benjamin Christensen. lps: Lon Chaney, Ricardo Cortez, Barbara Bedford. 5957f USA. *Terror* prod/rel: Metro-Goldwyn-Mayer Pictures

ESCALANTE (HIJO), EDUARDO
Les Barraques, Opera
Barracas 1925 d: Mario Roncoroni. lps: Pepito Alcacer, Enriqueta Roig, Jose Angeles. 64M SPN. *Les Barraques (O Una Tragedia de la Huerta)*; *Les Barraques* prod/rel: Apolo Films (Valencia)

ESCHASSERIAUX, BERNARD
Les Dimanches de Ville d'Avray, Paris 1958, Novel
Dimanches de Ville d'Avray, Les 1962 d: Serge Bourguignon. lps: Hardy Kruger, Patricia Gozzi, Nicole Courcel. 110M FRN. *Sundays and Cybele* (USA); *Cybele*; *Cybele Ou Les Dimanches de Ville-D'avray* prod/rel: Terra Films, Fides

ESCONDA, YVONNE
Six Chevaux Bleus, Novel
Six Chevaux Bleus 1967 d: Philippe JouliA. lps: Yvonne Clech, Henri Cremieux, Patrick Boitot. 90M FRN. *Zossia*

ESMANN, GUSTAV
Den Kaere Familie, 1892, Play
Kara Familjen, Den 1962 d: Erik Balling. lps: Jarl Kulle, Helle Virkner, Gunnar Lauring. 103M SWD/DNM. *Den Kaere Familie*; *Dear Family* prod/rel: Nordisk, Schorcht

ESMOND, H. V., Esmond, Henry V.
Eliza Comes to Stay, London 1913, Play
Dangerous to Men 1920 d: William C. Dowlan. lps: Viola Dana, Milton Sills, Edward Connelly. 5981f USA. *Eliza Comes to Stay* prod/rel: Screen Classics, Inc., Metro Pictures Corp.©

Eliza Comes to Stay 1936 d: Henry Edwards. lps: Betty Balfour, Seymour Hicks, Oscar Asche. 70M UKN. prod/rel: Twickenham, Twickenham Film Distributors

The Law Divine, Novel
Law Divine, The 1920 d: Challis Sanderson, H. B. Parkinson. lps: H. V. Esmond, Eva Moore, Evelyn Brent. 4700f UKN. prod/rel: Master, Butcher's Film Service

Leonie, Play
Sword of Damocles, The 1920 d: George Ridgwell. lps: Jose Collins, H. V. Esmond, Claude Fleming. 4920f UKN. prod/rel: British & Colonial, Butcher's Film Service

One Summer's Day, London 1897, Play
One Summer's Day 1917 d: Frank G. Bayley. lps: Fay Compton, Owen Nares, Sam Livesey. 4000f UKN. prod/rel: British Actors, Int Ex

Under the Greenwood Tree, London 1907, Play
Under the Greenwood Tree 1918 d: Emile Chautard. lps: Elsie Ferguson, Eugene O'Brien, Edmund Burns. 4543f USA. prod/rel: Famous Players-Lasky Corp.©, Artcraft Pictures

When We Were Twenty-One, New York 1900, Play
Truth About Youth, The 1930 d: William A. Seiter. lps: Loretta Young, David Manners, Conway Tearle. 6235f USA. *When We Were 21* prod/rel: First National Pictures

When We Were Twenty-One 1915 d: Edwin S. Porter, Hugh Ford. lps: William Elliott, Charles Waldron, Marie Empress. 5r USA. prod/rel: Famous Players Film Co., Paramount Pictures Corp.

When We Were Twenty-One 1921 d: Henry King. lps: H. B. Warner, Claire Anderson, James Morrison. F USA. prod/rel: Jesse D. Hampton, Pathe Exchange, Inc.

ESPE, WALTER MARIA
Der Fall Grootman, Play
Crime of the Century, The 1933 d: William Beaudine. lps: Jean Hersholt, Stuart Erwin, Wynne Gibson. 75M USA. prod/rel: Paramount Productions, Inc.

Der Schone Florian, Musical Play
Egon, Der Frauenheld 1957 d: Hans Albin. lps: Theo Lingen, Susi Nicoletti, Paul Henckels. 85M GRM. *Egon the Ladykiller* prod/rel: Hoela, Panorama

ESPIAU, MARCEL
Guignol, Play
Prisonnier de Mon Coeur 1931 d: Jean Tarride. lps: Marie Glory, Roland Toutain, Andre Berley. 88M FRN. prod/rel: Verba-Film

ESPINA DE SERNA, CONCHA (1880–1955), SPN
Altar Mayor, 1926, Novel
Altar Mayor 1943 d: Gonzalo Delgras. lps: Maruchi Fresno, Margarita Robles, Maria Dolores PraderA. 107M SPN.

Dulce Nombre, 1921, Novel
Dulce Nombre 1951 d: Enrique Gomez Bascuas. lps: Isabel de Castro, Manuel Monroy, Mercedes Mozart. 84M SPN.

La Esfinge Maragata, 1914, Novel
Esfinge Maragata, La 1948 d: Antonio Obregon. lps: Paquita de Ronda, Luis Pena, Juan de LandA. 85M SPN.

La Nina de Luzmela, 1909, Novel
Nina de Luzmela, La 1949 d: Jose Gascon. lps: Maria Rosa Salgado, Oswaldo Gennazzani, Jose Suarez. 87M SPN. *That Luzmela Girl*

ESQUIER, CH.
Sanatorium Pour Maigrir, Play
Sanatorium Pour Maigrir 1909. lps: M. Gibaro, Simon, Prince. FRN. prod/rel: Pathe Freres

ESQUIVEL, LAURA
Como Agua Para Chocolate, Novel
Como Agua Para Chocolate 1991 d: Alfonso Arau. lps: Marco Leonardi, Lumi Cavazos, Regina Torne. 114M MXC. *Like Water for Chocolate*; *Water for Chocolate* prod/rel: Cinevista, Ncca

ESSEX, HARRY J.
The Electric Man, Story
Man Made Monster 1941 d: George Waggner. lps: Lionel Atwill, Lon Chaney Jr., Anne Nagel. 60M USA. *The Electric Man* (UKN); *The Atomic Monster*; *Mysterious Dr. R.*; *Man-Made Monster* prod/rel: Universal

ESTAUNIE, EDOUARD
Madame Clapain, Novel
Secret de Madame Clapain, Le 1943 d: Andre Berthomieu. lps: Raymond Rouleau, Fernand Charpin, Michele AlfA. 95M FRN. *L' Etrange Madame Clapain* prod/rel: Jason

ESTREMERA, ANTONIO
Don Quintin El Amargao, Opera
Don Quintin El Amargao 1925 d: Manuel NoriegA. lps: Lina Moreno, Consuelo Reyes, Jose Arguelles. 80M SPN. prod/rel: Cartago Films (Madrid)

ESTRIDGE, ROBIN
Permission to Kill, Novel
Permission to Kill 1975 d: Cyril Frankel. lps: Dirk Bogarde, Ava Gardner, Bekim Fehmiu. 97M UKN/AUS. *Vollmacht Zum Mord* (AUS) prod/rel: Warner Bros., Sascha

ETCHERELLI, CLAIRE
Elise Ou la Vraie Vie, Novel
Elise Ou la Vraie Vie 1970 d: Michel Drach. lps: Marie-Jose Nat, Mohamed Chouikh, Bernadette Lafont. 110M FRN/ALG. prod/rel: Port-Royal Films, O.N.I.C.

EUNSON, DALE M.
Dear Evelyn, Play
Guest in the House, A 1944 d: John Brahm, Andre de Toth (Uncredited). lps: Anne Baxter, Ralph Bellamy, Aline MacMahon. 121M USA. prod/rel: United Artists, Hunt Stromberg

Loco, New York 1946, Play
How to Marry a Millionaire 1953 d: Jean Negulesco. lps: Marilyn Monroe, Betty Grable, Lauren Bacall. 95M USA. prod/rel: 20th Century-Fox

EURIPIDES (480bc–405bc), GRC
Alcesti, Play
Sostituzione, La 1971 d: Franco B. Taviani. lps: Adalberto Maria Merli, Maria Carrilho, Piero Anchisi. MTV. 60M ITL. prod/rel: Ager Cin.Ca, Rai-Tv

Bacchae, c495 bc, Play
Baccanti, Le 1961 d: Giorgio Ferroni. lps: Taina Elg, Pierre Brice, Alberto Lupo. 100M ITL/FRN. *Les Bacchantes* (FRN); *The Bacchantes* prod/rel: Vic Film (Roma), Lyre (Paris)

Dionysus in '69 1970 d: Brian Depalma, Robert Fiore. lps: William Finley, William Shephard, Joan MacIntosh. 90M USA.

Electra, 413 bc, Play
Elektra 1962 d: Michael Cacoyannis. lps: Irene Papas, Aleka Katseli, Ioannis Fertis. 113M GRC. *Electra* (USA) prod/rel: Finos

Hippolytus, 428 bc, Play
Phaedra 1962 d: Jules Dassin. lps: Melina Mercouri, Raf Vallone, Anthony Perkins. 116M USA/FRN/GRC.

Iphigenia in Aulis, c407 bc, Play
Ifigenia 1977 d: Michael Cacoyannis. lps: Irene Papas, Tatiana Papamoskou, Kostas Kazakos. 127M GRC. *Iphigenia*

Medea, 431 bc, Play
Dream of Passion, A 1978 d: Jules Dassin. lps: Melina Mercouri, Ellen Burstyn, Andreas Voutsinas. 110M GRC. *Medea*; *Maya and Breuda*

Epistrofi Tis Midias, I 1968 d: Yan Hristian. lps: Marianna Kourakou, Anna Fonsou, Aleka Katseli. 97M GRC. *Medea's Return*

Medea 1970 d: Pier Paolo Pasolini. lps: Maria Callas, Giuseppe Gentile, Massimo Girotti. 118M ITL/GRM/FRN. *Medee* (FRN) prod/rel: San Marco Film (Roma), Rosima Anstalt

The Trojan Women, 415 bc, Play
Trojan Women, The 1971 d: Michael Cacoyannis. lps: Katharine Hepburn, Vanessa Redgrave, Genevieve Bujold. 111M USA/GRC.

EUSTIS, HELEN
The Fool Filler, New York 1954, Novel
Fool Killer, The 1963 d: Servando Gonzalez. lps: Anthony Perkins, Edward Albert, Dana Elcar. 99M USA/MXC. *The Legend of the Fool Killer*; *El Asesino de Tontos* (MXC); *A Violent Journey* prod/rel: Landau Co., Jack J. Dreyfus Jr.

EVANDER, GUNNAR
Mandagarna Med Fanny, Novel
Mandagarna Med Fanny 1977 d: Lars Lennart Forsberg. lps: Tommy Johnson, Ingvar Kjellson, Maria Selbing. 106M SWD. *Robert and Fanny* prod/rel: Svenska Filminstitutet, Svensk Filmindustri

EVANS, DAVID
Boomerang, Play
Boomerang 1934 d: Arthur Maude. lps: Nora Swinburne, Lester Matthews, Millicent Wolf. 82M UKN. prod/rel: Maude Productions, Columbia

You Must Get Married, Novel
You Must Get Married 1936 d: A. Leslie Pearce. lps: Frances Day, Robertson Hare, Neil Hamilton. 68M UKN. prod/rel: City, General Film Distributors

EVANS, E. EYNON
Bless This House, Play
Room in the House 1955 d: Maurice Elvey. lps: Patrick Barr, Hubert Gregg, Marjorie Rhodes. 74M UKN. prod/rel: Act Films, Monarch

The Wishing Well, Play
Happiness of Three Women, The 1954 d: Maurice Elvey. lps: Brenda de Banzie, Petula Clark, Donald Houston. 78M UKN. *Wishing Well* (USA); *The Happiness of 3 Women* prod/rel: Advance, Adelphi

EVANS, EVAN
Montana Rides, Novel
Branded 1950 d: Rudolph Mate. lps: Alan Ladd, Mona Freeman, Charles Bickford. 95M USA. prod/rel: Paramount

EVANS, GEORGE
Confessions from the David Galaxy Affair, Novel
Confessions from the David Galaxy Affair 1979 d: Willy Roe. lps: Alan Lake, Glynn Edwards, Anthony Booth. 96M UKN. *Secrets of a Sexy Game*; *Star Sex*

EVANS, HELENA
A Cigarette - That's All, Story
Cigarette - That's All, A 1915 d: Phillips Smalley. lps: Phillips Smalley, Rupert Julian, Maude George. 2r USA. prod/rel: Gold Seal

EVANS, IDA M.
Limousine Life, 1917, Story
Limousine Life 1918 d: John Francis Dillon. lps: Olive Thomas, Lee Phelps, Joe Bennett. 4830f USA. prod/rel: Triangle Film Corp., Triangle Distributing Corp.

Town Pumps and Gold Leaf, Story
Question of Hats and Gowns, A 1914 d: Ashley Miller. lps: Miriam Nesbitt, Augustus Phillips. 2000f USA. prod/rel: Edison

Virginia, Short Story
Path She Chose, The 1920 d: Phil Rosen. lps: Anne Cornwall, J. Farrell MacDonald, Claire Anderson. 5r USA. *Virginia* prod/rel: Universal Film Mfg. Co.©

The Way of a Maid With a Man, 1918, Short Story
Way of a Man With a Maid, The 1918 d: Donald Crisp. lps: Bryant Washburn, Wanda Hawley, Fred Goodwins. 4418f USA. prod/rel: Famous Players-Lasky Corp.©, Paramount Pictures

EVANS, LARRY
Cassidy, 1913, Short Story
Cassidy 1917 d: Arthur Rosson. lps: Dick Rosson, Frank Currier, Pauline Curley. 5r USA. prod/rel: Triangle Film Corp., Triangle Distributing Corp.

Conahan, Short Story
Silent Lie, The 1917 d: Raoul Walsh. lps: Miriam Cooper, Ralph Lewis, Charles Clary. 5-6r USA. *Camille of the Yukon* prod/rel: Fox Film Corp.©

Judgment of the Hills, Short Story
Judgment of the Hills 1927 d: James Leo Meehan. lps: Virginia Valli, Frankie Darro, Orville Caldwell. 5700f USA. prod/rel: R-C Pictures, Film Booking Offices of America

Once to Every Man, New York 1913, Novel
Fighting Heart, The 1925 d: John Ford. lps: George O'Brien, Billie Dove, J. Farrell MacDonald. 6978f USA. *Once to Every Man* (UKN) prod/rel: Fox Film Corp.

Once to Every Man 1919 d: T. Hayes Hunter. lps: Jack Sherrill, Mabel Withey, Roy Applegate. 6r USA. prod/rel: Frohman Amusement Corp., State Rights

One Clear Call, Short Story
Wife He Bought, The 1918 d: Harry Salter. lps: Carmel Myers, Kenneth Harlan, Howard Crampton. 5r USA. *One Clear Call* prod/rel: Bluebird Photoplays, Inc.©

The Painted Lady, 1912, Short Story
Nada Mas Que Una Mujer 1934 d: Harry Lachman. lps: Berta Singerman, Alfredo Del Diestro, Juan TorenA. 9r USA. *Only a Woman*; *La Llama Blanca*; *La Venda En Los Ojos*

Painted Lady, The 1924 d: Chester Bennett. lps: George O'Brien, Dorothy MacKaill, Harry T. Morey. 6938f USA. prod/rel: Fox Film Corp.

Pursued 1934 d: Louis King. lps: Rosemary Ames, Victor Jory, Russell Hardie. 70M USA. *Wanted* prod/rel: Fox Film Corp.©

When a Man Sees Red 1917 d: Frank Lloyd. lps: William Farnum, Jewel Carmen, Lulu May Bower. 5-7r USA. prod/rel: Fox Film Corp., William Fox©

Someone in the House, New York 1918, Play
Someone in the House 1920 d: John Ince. lps: Edmund Lowe, Vola Vale, Edward Connelly. 6r USA. prod/rel: Metro Pictures Corp.©

Then I'll Come Back to You, New York 1915, Novel
Then I'll Come Back to You 1916 d: George Irving. lps: Alice Brady, Jack Sherrill, Eric Blind. 5r USA. prod/rel: World Film Corp.©, Frohman Amusement Corp.

Winner Take All, New York 1920, Novel
Winner Take All 1924 d: W. S. Van Dyke. lps: Buck Jones, Peggy Shaw, Edward Hearn. 5949f USA. prod/rel: Fox Film Corp.

EVANS, MAX
The Hi-Lo Country, 1961, Novel
Hi-Lo Country, The 1998 d: Stephen Frears. lps: Woody Harrelson, Billy Crudup, Patricia Arquette. 114M USA. prod/rel: Gramercy Pictures, Polygram Filmed Entertainment

The Rounders, New York 1960, Novel
Rounders, The 1964 d: Burt Kennedy. lps: Glenn Ford, Henry Fonda, Sue Ane Langdon. 85M USA. prod/rel: Metro-Goldwyn-Mayer, Inc.

EVANS, NICHOLAS
The Horse Whisperer, Novel
Horse Whisperer, The 1998 d: Robert Redford. lps: Robert Redford, Kristin Scott-Thomas, Sam Neill. 168M USA. prod/rel: Buena Vista, Touchstone Pictures©

EVANS, PETER
Biography
Richest Man in the World: the Story of Aristotle Onassis 1988 d: Waris Hussein. lps: Raul Julia, Jane Seymour, Anthony Quinn. TVM. 200M USA. *Onassis: the Richest Man in the World* prod/rel: the Konigsberg Sanitsky Company, Television Espanola

EVANS, WAINWRIGHT
The Companionate Marriage, New York 1927, Novel
Companionate Marriage, The 1928 d: Erle C. Kenton. lps: Betty Bronson, Alec B. Francis, William Welsh. 6132f USA. *The Jazz Bride* (UKN) prod/rel: C. M. Corp., First National Pictures

The Koudenhoffen Case, New York 1925, Book
One Mile from Heaven 1937 d: Allan Dwan. lps: Claire Trevor, Sally Blane, Douglas Fowley. 68M USA. prod/rel: Twentieth Century-Fox Film Corp.©

EVANS, WILL
Tons of Money, London 1922, Play
J'ai une Idee 1934 d: Roger Richebe. lps: Raimu, Georges Morton, Simone Deguyse. 100M FRN. prod/rel: Societe Parisienne Du Film Parlant
Tons of Money 1924 d: Frank H. Crane. lps: Leslie Henson, Flora Le Breton, Mary Brough. 6400f UKN. prod/rel: Walls & Henson, Stoll
Tons of Money 1931 d: Tom Walls. lps: Ralph Lynn, Yvonne Arnaud, Mary Brough. 97M UKN. prod/rel: British and Dominions, Woolf & Freedman

EVARTS, HAL G.
The Cross Pull, New York 1920, Novel
Born to Fight 1932 d: Walter Mayo. lps: El Brendel, Janet Chandler, Onslow Stevens. F USA. *Cross Pull* prod/rel: Fox Film Corp.
Silent Call, The 1921 d: Larry Trimble. lps: Strongheart, John Bowers, Kathryn McGuire. 6784f USA. prod/rel: H. O. Davis, Associated First National Pictures
Spanish Acres, Boston 1925, Novel
Santa Fe Trail, The 1930 d: Otto Brower, Edwin H. Knopf. lps: Richard Arlen, Rosita Moreno, Eugene Pallette. 5839f USA. *The Law Rides West* (UKN); *Spanish Acres* prod/rel: Paramount-Publix Corp.

EVERETT, HERBERT
All the World's a Stage, Novel
All the World's a Stage 1917 d: Harold Weston. lps: Eve Balfour, Esme Beringer, James Lindsay. 5000f UKN. prod/rel: Hagen & Double

EVERETT, PETER
Negatives, London 1964, Novel
Negatives 1968 d: Peter Medak. lps: Peter McEnery, Diane Cilento, Glenda Jackson. 98M UKN. *Sleep Is Lovely* prod/rel: Kettledrum Productions, Narizzano Productions

EVERS, MYRLIE
For Us the Living, Book
For Us the Living 1982 d: Michael Schultz. lps: Howard E. Rollins Jr., Irene Cara, Margaret Avery. TVM. 90M USA. *For Us the Living: the Medgar Evers Story* prod/rel: Charles Fries, American Playhouse

EVREINOV, NICOLAS
La Comedie du Bonheur, Play
Comedie du Bonheur, La 1940 d: Marcel L'Herbier. lps: Michel Simon, Ramon Novarro, Micheline Presle. 108M FRN. *The Comedy of Happiness* prod/rel: Discina-Scalera

EWER, MONICA
Not for Sale, Novel
Not for Sale 1924 d: W. P. Kellino. lps: Mary Odette, Ian Hunter, Gladys Hamer. 6460f UKN. prod/rel: Stoll
Ring O'Roses, Novel
He Found a Star 1941 d: John Paddy Carstairs. lps: Vic Oliver, Sarah Churchill, Evelyn Dall. 88M UKN. prod/rel: John Corfield, General Film Distributors

EWERS, HANNS HEINZ
Alraune, Novel
Alraune 1928 d: Henrik Galeen. lps: Brigitte Helm, Paul Wegener, Ivan Petrovich. 3346m GRM. *A Daughter of Destiny*; *Unholy Love*; *Mandragore*; *Mandrake* prod/rel: Ama
Alraune 1930 d: Richard Oswald. lps: Brigitte Helm, Albert Bassermann, Agnes Straub. 87M GRM. *Daughter of Evil*

Alraune 1952 d: Arthur M. Rabenalt. lps: Hildegard Knef, Erich von Stroheim, Karlheinz Bohm. 92M GRM. *Mandrake*; *Unnatural*; *Vengeance*; *Mandragore* prod/rel: Carlton, Gloria

Fundvogel, Novel
Fundvogel 1930 d: Wolfgang Hoffmann-Harnisch. lps: Camilla Horn, Franz Lederer, Paul Wegener. 2505m GRM. prod/rel: Excelsior-Film-Produktion

Der Student von Prag, Novel
Student von Prag, Der 1913 d: Stellan Rye. lps: Paul Wegener, John Gottowt, Lyda SalmonovA. 1538m GRM. *Asylum of Horror*; *A Bargain With Satan*; *The Student of Prague* prod/rel: Deutsche Bioscop
Student von Prag, Der 1926 d: Henrik Galeen. lps: Conrad Veidt, Werner Krauss, Agnes Esterhazy. 3173m GRM. *The Man Who Cheated Life* (USA); *The Student of Prague* prod/rel: Sokal-Film
Student von Prag, Der 1935 d: Arthur Robison. lps: Anton Walbrook, Theodor Loos, Dorothea Wieck. 79M GRM. *The Student of Prague* (UKN) prod/rel: Cine-Allianz

EWING, ELYNOR
Wind of the Pampas, Story
Winds of the Pampas 1927 d: Arthur Varney-Serrao. lps: Ralph Cloninger, Harry Holden, Vesey O'Davoren. 5436f USA. prod/rel: Cloninger Productions, Hi-Mark Productions

EXBRAYAT, CHARLES
L' Assassin Est Dans l'Annuaire, Novel
Assassin Est Dans l'Annuaire, L' 1961 d: Leo Joannon. lps: Fernandel, Georges Chamarat, Marie DeA. 98M FRN. prod/rel: S.N.E.G., Marianne Productions
Avanti la Musica, Novel
Cambio Della Guardia, Il 1962 d: Giorgio Bianchi. lps: Fernandel, Gino Cervi, Frank Fernandel. 92M ITL/FRN. *En Avant la Musique* (FRN); *Avanti la Musica!* prod/rel: Apo Film (Roma), Paris Elysees Productions (Paris)
Espion Ou Est-Tu M'entends-Tu?, Novel
Pas de Caviar Pour Tante Olga 1965 d: Jean Becker. lps: Pierre Brasseur, Sophie Daumier, Pierre Vernier. 101M FRN. prod/rel: Films Du Trapeze
La Honte de la Famille, Novel
Honte de la Famille, La 1969 d: Richard Balducci. lps: Michel Galabru, Micheline Dax, Paul Preboist. 90M FRN. prod/rel: Promocinema
Une Ravissante Idiote, Paris 1962, Novel
Ravissante Idiote, Une 1964 d: Edouard Molinaro. lps: Anthony Perkins, Brigitte Bardot, Gregoire Aslan. 110M FRN/ITL. *Un' Adorobile Idiota* (ITL); *A Ravishing Idiot* (USA); *Agent 38-24-36 (the Warm-Blooded Spy)*; *The Ravishing Idiots* prod/rel: Belles Rives Productions, Flora Film

EXLEY, FREDERICK EARL
A Fan's Notes, Novel
Fan's Notes, A 1972 d: Eric Till. lps: Jerry Orbach, Burgess Meredith, Patricia Collins. 100M CND/USA. prod/rel: Coquihala Films Ltd., Warner Bros.

EYMOUCHE, CLAUDE
Vous Interessez-Vous a la Chose?, Novel
Vous Interessez-Vous a la Chose? 1973 d: Jacques Baratier. lps: Nathalie Delon, Muriel Catala, Didier Haudepin. 90M FRN/GRM. *Haben Sie Interesse an Der Sache?* (GRM); *First Time With Feeling* (UKN); *Are You Interested?* prod/rel: Rapid, Francos

EYNIKEL, HILDE
De Definitieve Biografie Damiaan, Biography
Father Damien 1999 d: Paul Cox. lps: David Wenham, Kate Ceberano, Chris Haywood. 109M BLG/NTH. prod/rel: E.R.A. Films (Belgium), Jos Stelling Films (Netherlands)

EYRE, LAURENCE
Martinique, New York 1920, Play
Volcano 1926 d: William K. Howard. lps: Bebe Daniels, Ricardo Cortez, Wallace Beery. 5462f USA. prod/rel: Famous Players-Lasky, Paramount Pictures
Merry Wives of Gotham; Or Two and Sixpence, New York 1924, Play
Lights of Old Broadway 1925 d: Monta Bell. lps: Marion Davies, Conrad Nagel, Frank Currier. 6595f USA. *Little Old New York* (UKN); *Merry Wives of Gotham* prod/rel: Cosmopolitan Productions, Metro-Goldwyn Distributing Corp.

EYSLER, EDMUND
Bruder Straubinger, Opera
Kussen Ist Keine Sund 1950 d: Hubert MarischkA. lps: Elfie Mayerhofer, Curd Jurgens, Gisela Fackeldey. 107M AUS. *Kissing Is No Sin* prod/rel: Aco, Schonbrunn

Schutzenliesel, Opera
Schutzenliesel 1954 d: Rudolf Schundler. lps: Herta Staal, Helmuth Schneider, Susi Nicoletti. 100M GRM. *Sure-Shot Lisa* prod/rel: Central-Europa, Prisma

Der Unsterbliche Lump, Novel
Unsterbliche Lump, Der 1953 d: Arthur M. Rabenalt. lps: Karlheinz Bohm, Ingrid Stenn, Heliane Bei. 105M GRM. *The Undying Bum* prod/rel: Carlton, N.F.

F

FABBRI, DIEGO
La Bugiarda, Milan 1956, Play
Bugiarda, La 1965 d: Luigi Comencini. lps: Catherine Spaak, Enrico Maria Salerno, Marc Michel. 104M ITL/SPN/FRN. *La Mentirosa* (SPN); *Six Days a Week* (USA); *Le Partage de Catherine* (FRN); *La Menteuse* prod/rel: Ultra Film (Roma), Consortium Pathe (Paris)

FABIAN, WARNER
Flaming Youth, New York 1923, Novel
Flaming Youth 1923 d: John Francis Dillon. lps: Colleen Moore, Milton Sills, Elliott Dexter. 8434f USA. prod/rel: Associated First National Pictures
Sailors' Wives, New York 1924, Novel
Sailors' Wives 1928 d: Joseph Henabery. lps: Mary Astor, Lloyd Hughes, Earle Foxe. 5485f USA. prod/rel: First National Pictures
Summer Widowers, New York 1926, Novel
Summer Bachelors 1926 d: Allan Dwan. lps: Madge Bellamy, Allan Forrest, Matt Moore. 6727f USA. prod/rel: Fox Film Corp.
Week-End Girl, New York 1932, Novel
Week Ends Only 1932 d: Alan Crosland. lps: Joan Bennett, Ben Lyon, John Halliday. 70M USA. prod/rel: Fox Film Corp.©

FABRE, DOMINIQUE
Un Beau Monstre, Novel
Bel Mostro, Il 1971 d: Sergio Gobbi. lps: Helmut Berger, Charles Aznavour, Virna Lisi. 115M ITL/FRN. *Un Beau Monstre* (FRN); *A Strange Love Affair* (UKN) prod/rel: Mega Film, Paris-Cannes Productions
Un Meurtre Est un Meurtre, Novel
Meurtre Est un Meurtre, Un 1972 d: Etienne Perier. lps: Jean-Claude Brialy, Stephane Audran, Robert Hossein. 85M FRN/ITL. *La Sedia a Rotelle* (ITL); *A Murder Is a Murder* (UKN); *A Murder Is a Murder. Is a Murder* prod/rel: Tritone Filmindustria, Planfilm

FABRE, EMILE
La Maison d'Argile, Play
Maison d'Argile, La 1918 d: Gaston Ravel. lps: Leon Mathot, Georges Mauloy, Suzanne Munte. 1610m FRN. prod/rel: Optima

FABRET, GEORGES
Vacances, Play
Vacances 1931 d: Robert Boudrioz. lps: Lucien Galas, Florelle, Georges CharliA. 82M FRN. prod/rel: Gaumont-Franco-Film-Aubert

FABRICE, DELPHI
Derniere Aventure du Prince Curacao, Novel
Derniere Aventure du Prince Curacao, La 1912. lps: Robert Hasti, Carmen Deraisy. 360m FRN. prod/rel: Scagl

FABRICUS, JEAN
Insult, Play
Insult 1932 d: Harry Lachman. lps: Elizabeth Allan, John Gielgud, Hugh Williams. 80M UKN. prod/rel: Paramount British, Paramount

FACCHINETTI, VITTORINO
Antonio Di Padova Il Santo Dei Miracoli, Novel
Antonio Di Padova 1931 d: Giulio Antamoro. lps: Carlo Pinzauti, Elio Cosci, Ruggero Barni. 90M ITL. *Antonio Di Padova Il Santo Dei Miracoli* prod/rel: S.a.C.R.a.S.

FACCO DE LAGARDO, UGO
Il Commissario Pepe, Novel
Commissario Pepe, Il 1969 d: Ettore ScolA. lps: Ugo Tognazzi, Silvia Dionisio, Tano CimarosA. 107M ITL. prod/rel: Dean Film, Juppiter Cin.Ca

FADEEV, ALEXANDER (1901–1956), RSS, Fadayev, Aleksandr Aleksandrovich
Molodaya Gvardiya, 1945, Novel
Molodaya Gvardiya 1948 d: Sergei Gerasimov. lps: Sergei Bondarchuk, Vyacheslav Tikhonov, MakarovA. 189M USS. *The Young Guard*; *Molodaja Gvardija*

Les Pas Perdus, Novel
   Pas Perdus, Les 1964 d: Jacques Robin. lps: Michele Morgan, Jean-Louis Trintignant, Catherine Rouvel. 98M FRN. prod/rel: Cinerofa Production

Portes Des Lilas, Novel
   Porte Des Lilas 1957 d: Rene Clair. lps: Pierre Brasseur, Georges Brassens, Henri Vidal. 96M FRN/ITL. *Quartiere Dei Lilla* (ITL); *Gates of Paris* (USA); *Gate of Lilacs* prod/rel: Cinetel, Film Sonor

La Soupe aux Choux, Novel
   Soupe aux Choux, La 1981 d: Jean Girault. lps: Louis de Funes, Jean Carmet, Jacques Villeret. 105M FRN. prod/rel: Films Christian Fechner

Le Triporteur, Novel
   Triporteur, Le 1957 d: Jack Pinoteau. lps: Darry Cowl, Beatrice Altariba, Pierre Mondy. 93M FRN. prod/rel: Films Du Cyclope

Les Vieux de la Vieille, Novel
   Vieux de la Vieille, Les 1960 d: Gilles Grangier. lps: Jean Gabin, Pierre Fresnay, Noel-Noel. 93M FRN/ITL. *Gli Allegri Veterani* (ITL); *Old Guard* prod/rel: Cite Films, Terra Films

FALLON, THOMAS F.
The Last Warning, New York 1922, Play
   House of Fear, The 1939 d: Joe May. lps: William Gargan, Irene Hervey, Dorothy Arnold. 67M USA. prod/rel: Crime Club Productions, Universal Pictures Co.©

   Last Warning, The 1929 d: Paul Leni. lps: Laura La Plante, Montagu Love, Roy d'Arcy. 7980f USA. prod/rel: Universal Pictures

FALLOT, PIERRE
La Patte d'Elephant, Novel
   Empreinte Rouge, L' 1936 d: Maurice de Canonge. lps: Colette Darfeuil, Maurice Lagrenee, Andre Berley. 94M FRN. prod/rel: Unis Films

FANCK, ARNOLD
Die Weisse Holle von Piz Palu, Short Story
   Fohn 1950 d: Rolf Hansen. lps: Hans Albers, Liselotte Pulver, Antje Weisgerber. 107M GRM/SWT. *The White Hell of Pitz Palu* (USA); *Fohn - Sturm in Der Ostwand*; *Drei Menschen Am Piz Palu*; *Sous la Rafale* prod/rel: Rolf Hansen-Film, Harry R. Sokal-Produktion

FANG FANG
Maifu, Novel
   Maifu 1997 d: Huang Jianxin, Yang Yazhou. lps: Feng Gong, Jiang Shan, Teng Rujun. 104M CHN. *Surveillance* prod/rel: XIaoxiang Film Studio, Ginwa Enterprise Group

FANSTEN, JACQUES
C'est Pour la Bonne Cause, Novel
   C'est Pour la Bonne Cause 1997 d: Jacques Fansten. lps: Dominique Blanc, Antoine de Caunes, Loic Freynet. 106M FRN/BLG. *It's for a Good Cause* (USA) prod/rel: Atlantique Prod.

FANTE, JOHN
Novel
   Bandini 1988 d: Dominique Deruddere. lps: Faye Dunaway, Joe Mantegna, Ornella Muti. 100M BLG/USA. *Bandini Wait Until Spring* (USA) prod/rel: Orion Classics

Full of Life, 1952, Book
   Full of Life 1956 d: Richard Quine. lps: Judy Holliday, Richard Conte, Salvatore Baccaloni. 87M USA. *The Lady Is Waiting* prod/rel: Columbia

FARAGO, ALEXANDER
The Girl Who Dared (Scandal in Budapest), 1911, Play
   Top Hat 1935 d: Mark Sandrich. lps: Fred Astaire, Ginger Rogers, Edward Everett Horton. 101M USA. prod/rel: RKO Radio Pictures©

FARAGO, LADISLAS
The Broken Seal, New York 1967, Book
   Tora! Tora! Tora! 1970 d: Kinji Fukasaku. lps: Jason Robards Jr., Shogo Shimada, Koreya SendA. USA/JPN.

Patton: Ordeal and Triumph, New York 1964, Biography
   Patton 1970 d: Franklin J. Schaffner. lps: George C. Scott, Karl Malden, Stephen Young. 171M USA. *Patton: a Salute to a Rebel; Patton: Lust for Glory; Patton: Salute to a Rebel* prod/rel: Twentieth Century-Fox Film Corporation

FARAGO, SANDOR
The Boy the Girl and the Dog, Story
   Marry the Boss's Daughter 1941 d: Thornton Freeland. lps: Brenda Joyce, Bruce Edwards, George Barbier. 60M USA. prod/rel: 20th Century Fox

FARINA, SALVATORE
Capelli Biondi, 1876, Novel
   Capelli Biondi 1919. 1635m ITL. prod/rel: Costantini

FARINACCI, ROBERTO
Redenzione, Play
   Redenzione 1942 d: Marcello Albani. lps: Carlo Tamberlani, Mario Ferrari, Camillo Pilotto. 85M ITL. prod/rel: Marfilm, Artisti Associati

FARJEON, B. J.
Miriam Rozella, Novel
   Miriam Rozella 1924 d: Sidney Morgan. lps: Moyna McGill, Owen Nares, Gertrude McCoy. 7500f UKN. prod/rel: Astra-National

FARJEON, B. L.
Aaron the Jew, Novel
   Just Deception, A 1917 d: A. E. Coleby. lps: Augustus Yorke, Blanche Forsythe, Maud Yates. 5635f UKN. prod/rel: I. B. Davidson, Tiger

FARJEON, J. JEFFERSON
Play
   Haus Nummer 17 1928 d: Geza von Bolvary. lps: Fritz Greiner, Carl de Vogt, Lien Deyers. 2253m GRM. prod/rel: Deutsche Vereins Film Ag

After Dark, 1926, Play
   After Dark 1932 d: Albert Parker. lps: Horace Hodges, Grethe Hansen, Hugh Williams. 45M UKN. prod/rel: Fox British, Fox

The Ghost Camera, Story
   Ghost Camera, The 1933 d: Bernard Vorhaus. lps: Henry Kendall, Ida Lupino, John Mills. 68M UKN. prod/rel: H & S Films, Real Art

The House Opposite, Play
   House Opposite, The 1931 d: Walter Summers. lps: Henry Kendall, Frank Stanmore, Celia Glyn. 67M UKN. prod/rel: British International Pictures, Pathe

Number Seventeen, Play
   Number Seventeen 1928 d: Geza von Bolvary. lps: Guy Newall, Lien Dyers, Carl de Vogt. 6517f UKN. prod/rel: Fellner & Somlo, Woolf & Freedman

   Number Seventeen 1932 d: Alfred Hitchcock. lps: Anne Grey, John Stuart, Donald Calthrop. 64M UKN. prod/rel: British International Pictures, Wardour

FARKAS, KARL
Die Wunderbar, 1930, Play
   Wonder Bar 1934 d: Lloyd Bacon. lps: Al Jolson, Kay Francis, Dolores Del Rio. 84M USA. prod/rel: First National Pictures©

FARLEY, ELLEN
The Folly of Anne, Story
   Folly of Anne, The 1914 d: John B. O'Brien. lps: Lillian Gish, Elmer Clifton, William E. Lawrence. SHT USA. prod/rel: Majestic

FARLEY, WALTER (1920–1989), USA, Farley, Walter Lorimer
The Black Stallion Returns, Novel
   Black Stallion Returns, The 1983 d: Robert DalvA. lps: Kelly Reno, Vincent Spano, Allen Garfield. 93M USA. prod/rel: MGM, United Artists

The Black Stallion, Novel
   Black Stallion, The 1979 d: Carroll Ballard. lps: Mickey Rooney, Kelly Reno, Teri Garr. 118M USA. prod/rel: United Artists

FARNHAM, MATEEL HOWE
Wild Beauty, New York 1930, Novel
   Wayward 1932 d: Edward Sloman. lps: Nancy Carroll, Richard Arlen, Pauline Frederick. 74M USA. prod/rel: Paramount Publix Corp.©

FARNOL, JEFFREY (1878–1952), UKN, Farnol, John Jeffrey
The Amateur Gentleman, London 1913, Novel
   Amateur Gentleman, The 1920 d: Maurice Elvey. lps: Langhorne Burton, Madge Stuart, Cecil Humphreys. 7435f UKN. prod/rel: Stoll

   Amateur Gentleman, The 1926 d: Sidney Olcott. lps: Richard Barthelmess, Dorothy Dunbar, Gardner James. 7790f USA. prod/rel: Inspiration Pictures, First National Pictures

   Amateur Gentleman, The 1936 d: Thornton Freeland. lps: Douglas Fairbanks Jr., Elissa Landi, Gordon Harker. 102M UKN. prod/rel: Criterion, United Artists

The Definite Object, Boston 1917, Novel
   Definite Object, The 1920 d: Edgar J. Camiller. lps: Ann Elliott, Peter Upcher, Lionel Scott. 4200f UKN. prod/rel: Eros Films

   Manhattan 1924 d: R. H. Burnside. lps: Richard Dix, Jacqueline Logan, Gregory Kelly. 6415f USA. prod/rel: Famous Players-Lasky, Paramount Pictures

The Money Moon, Novel
   Money Moon, The 1920 d: Fred Paul. lps: Stella Patrick Campbell, Gordon Craig. UKN. prod/rel: Alliance Film Corp.

FARNUM, DOROTHY
Jenny Lind, Novel
   Jenny Lind 1931 d: Arthur Robison. lps: Grace Moore, Andre Luguet, Francoise Rosay. 92M USA. prod/rel: Metro-Goldwyn-Mayer Corp.

The Man Who Wouldn't Love, Story
   Sinner Or Saint 1923 d: Lawrence C. Windom. lps: Betty Blythe, William P. Carleton, Gypsy O'Brien. 5388f USA. prod/rel: B. B. Productions, Selznick Distributing Corp.

FARRAR, ROBERT
Watch That Man, Novel
   Man Who Knew Too Little, The 1997 d: Jon Amiel. lps: Bill Murray, Peter Gallagher, Joanne Whalley-Kilmer. 94M USA/GRM. prod/rel: Regency Enterprises, Anon Milchan/Polar

FARRELL, BARRY
Pat and Roald, Book
   Patricia Neal Story, The 1981 d: Anthony Harvey, Anthony Page. lps: Glenda Jackson, Dirk Bogarde, Mildred Dunnock. TVM. 100M USA. *An Act of Love*

FARRELL, CLIFF
Outlawed Guns, 1934, Short Story
   Outlawed Guns 1935 d: Ray Taylor. lps: Buck Jones, Ruth Channing, Frank McGlenn Sr. 62M USA. prod/rel: Universal Pictures Corp.©

FARRELL, HENRY
Novel
   Belle Fille Comme Moi, Une 1972 d: Francois Truffaut. lps: Bernadette Lafont, Claude Brasseur, Charles Denner. 98M FRN. *Such a Gorgeous Kid Like Me* (USA); *A Gorgeous Bird Like Me* (UKN) prod/rel: Les Films Du Carrosse

The Hostage, New York 1959, Novel
   Hostage, The 1967 d: Russell S. Doughton Jr. lps: Don O'Kelly, Harry Dean Stanton, John Carradine. 84M USA. prod/rel: Heartland Productions

How Awful About Allan, Novel
   How Awful About Allan 1970 d: Curtis Harrington. lps: Anthony Perkins, Julie Harris, Joan Hackett. TVM. 74M USA. prod/rel: Aaron Spelling Productions

Hush Now, Sweet Charlotte, Short Story
   Hush. Hush, Sweet Charlotte 1964 d: Robert Aldrich. lps: Bette Davis, Olivia de Havilland, Joseph Cotten. 134M USA. *What Ever Happened to Cousin Charlotte?* prod/rel: Associates & Aldrich Co.

What Ever Happened to Baby Jane Hudson?, New York 1960, Novel
   What Ever Happened to Baby Jane? 1962 d: Robert Aldrich. lps: Bette Davis, Joan Crawford, Victor Buono. 132M USA. prod/rel: Associates & Aldrich Co.

   What Ever Happened to Baby Jane? 1991 d: David Greene. lps: Vanessa Redgrave, Lynn Redgrave, John Glover. TVM. 100M USA.

FARRELL, JAMES THOMAS (1904–1979), USA, Farrell, J. T.
Studs Lonigan, 1934, Novel
   Studs Lonigan 1960 d: Irving Lerner. lps: Christopher Knight, Frank Gorshin, Venetia Stevenson. 95M USA. prod/rel: Longridge, United Artists

   Studs Lonigan 1979 d: James Goldstone. lps: Harry Hamlin, Colleen Dewhurst, Brad Dourif. TVM. 300M USA. prod/rel: Lorimar Productions

FARRELL, M. J.
Spring Meeting, London 1938, Play
   Spring Meeting 1941 d: Walter C. Mycroft. lps: Nova Pilbeam, Basil Sydney, Henry Edwards. 93M UKN. *Three Wise Brides* (USA) prod/rel: Associated British Picture Corporation, Pathe

Treasure Hunt, London 1949, Play
   Treasure Hunt 1952 d: John Paddy Carstairs. lps: Jimmy Edwards, Martita Hunt, Naunton Wayne. 79M UKN. prod/rel: Romulus, British Lion

FARRERE, CLAUDE
Novel
   Mann, Der Den Mord Beging, Der 1930 d: Curtis Bernhardt. lps: Conrad Veidt, Trude von Molo, Heinrich George. 92M GRM. *Nachte Am Bosporus; The Man Who Murdered* prod/rel: Terra-Film

La Bataille, Paris 1908, Novel
   Bataille, La 1923 d: Edouard-Emile Violet, Sessue HayakawA. lps: Sessue Hayakawa, Tsuru Aoki, Felix Ford. 2600m FRN. prod/rel: Film d'Art (Vandal Et Delac)

   Bataille, La 1933 d: Nicolas Farkas. lps: Charles Boyer, Annabella, Valery Inkijinoff. 90M UKN. prod/rel: Lianofilm Production

   Battle, The 1934 d: Nicolas Farkas. lps: Charles Boyer, John Loder, Merle Oberon. 85M UKN. *Thunder in the East* (USA); *Hara-Kiri* prod/rel: Lionofilm, Gaumont-British

Danger Line, The 1924 d: Edouard-Emile Violet. lps: Sessue Hayakawa, Tsuru Aoki, Gina Palerme. 5800f USA. *The Battle* prod/rel: R-C Pictures, Film Booking Offices of America

L' Homme Qui Assassina, Paris 1908, Novel
Homme Qui Assassina, L' 1912 d: Henri Andreani. lps: Firmin Gemier, Jean Toulout, Michelle. 1250m FRN. prod/rel: Grands Films Populaires

Homme Qui Assassina, L' 1930 d: Jean Tarride, Curtis Bernhardt. lps: Jean Angelo, Marie Bell, Gabriel Gabrio. 88M FRN. prod/rel: Etablissements Braunberger-Richebe

Right to Love, The 1920 d: George Fitzmaurice. lps: Mae Murray, David Powell, Holmes Herbert. 6661f USA. prod/rel: Famous Players-Lasky Corp.©, George Fitzmaurice Production

Les Hommes Nouveaux, Novel
Hommes Nouveaux, Les 1922 d: Edouard-Emile Violet, E. B. Donatien. lps: E. B. Donatien, Marthe Ferrare, Georges Melchior. 2222m FRN. prod/rel: Dal Films

Hommes Nouveaux, Les 1936 d: Marcel L'Herbier. lps: Harry Baur, Nathalie Paley, Gabriel Signoret. 110M FRN. prod/rel: S.F.P.E.

La Maison Des Hommes Vivants, Novel
Maison Des Hommes Vivants, La 1929 d: Marcel Dumont, Gaston Roudes. lps: Rudolf Klein-Rogge, Simone Vaudry, Michele Verly. 2200m FRN. prod/rel: Astor-Film

Les Petites Alliees, Novel
Petites Alliees, Les 1936 d: Jean Dreville. lps: Constant Remy, Maurice Escande, Madeleine Renaud. 90M FRN. prod/rel: Forrester-Parant

La Veille d'Armes, Paris 1917, Play
Night Watch, The 1928 d: Alexander KordA. lps: Billie Dove, Paul Lukas, Donald Reed. 6676f USA. *His Wife's Affair* prod/rel: First National Pictures

Veille d'Armes 1925 d: Jacques de Baroncelli. lps: Maurice Schutz, Nina Vanna, Annette Benson. 2400m FRN. *In the Night Watch* prod/rel: Films Baroncelli

Veille d'Armes 1935 d: Marcel L'Herbier. lps: Annabella, Rosine Derean, Victor Francen. 120M FRN. *Sacrifice d'Honneur*; *The Vigil* prod/rel: Imperial-Film

Woman from Monte Carlo, The 1932 d: Michael Curtiz. lps: Lil Dagover, Walter Huston, Warren William. 65M USA. *The Captain's Wife*; *The Marked Woman* prod/rel: First National Pictures©

FARRINGTON, FIELDEN
A Little Game, Novel
Little Game, A 1971 d: Paul Wendkos. lps: Diane Baker, Ed Nelson, Howard Duff. TVM. 74M USA. prod/rel: Universal

The Strangers in 7a, Novel
Strangers in 7a, The 1972 d: Paul Wendkos. lps: Andy Griffith, Ida Lupino, Michael Brandon. TVM. 73M USA. prod/rel: Palomar Pictures International

FARRIS, JACK
Ramey, Novel
Greatest Gift, The 1974 d: Boris Sagal. lps: Glenn Ford, Julie Harris, Lance Kerwin. TVM. 100M USA. prod/rel: NBC, Universal

FARRIS, JOHN
The Fury, Novel
Fury, The 1978 d: Brian DepalmA. lps: Kirk Douglas, John Cassavetes, Carrie Snodgress. 118M USA. prod/rel: 20th Century Fox

Harrison High, Novel
Because They're Young 1960 d: Paul Wendkos. lps: Dick Clark, Michael Callan, Tuesday Weld. 102M USA. prod/rel: Columbia, Drexel

FARROW, JOHN
The Registered Woman, Play
Woman of Experience, A 1931 d: Harry J. Brown. lps: Helen Twelvetrees, William Bakewell, Lew Cody. 76M USA. *Registered Woman* (UKN) prod/rel: RKO Pathe Pictures, Charles R. Rogers Production

FARULLI, UGO
Le Signorine Della Villa Accanto, Play
Signorine Della Villa Accanto, Le 1942 d: Gian Paolo Rosmino. lps: Antonio Gandusio, Peppino de Filippo, Marisa Vernati. 88M ITL. prod/rel: Appia Film, Esedra

FASQUELLE, SOLANGE
Le Trio Infernal, Novel
Trio Infernal 1974 d: Francis Girod. lps: Michel Piccoli, Romy Schneider, Mascha GonskA. 103M FRN/ITL/GRM. *Trio Infernale* (ITL); *The Infernal Trio* (USA) prod/rel: Oceania P.I.C., Fox Europa

FASSBINDER, RAINER WERNER (1946–1982), GRM
Schatten Der Engel, Play
Schatten Der Engel 1976 d: Daniel Schmid. lps: Ingrid Caven, Rainer Werner Fassbinder, Klaus Lowitsch. 108M SWT/GRM. *Shadows of Angels* (USA) prod/rel: Albatros, Filmverlag Der Autoren

FASSETT, C. W.
Fate's Alibi, Story
Fate's Alibi 1915 d: Frank Lloyd. lps: Helen Leslie, Marc Robbins, Millard K. Wilson. SHT USA. prod/rel: Laemmle

FAST, HOWARD (1914–, USA, Cunningham, E. V., Ericson, Walter
Fallen Angel, Boston 1952, Novel
Jigsaw 1968 d: James Goldstone. lps: Harry Guardino, Bradford Dillman, Hope Lange. 97M USA. prod/rel: Universal

Mirage 1965 d: Edward Dmytryk. lps: Gregory Peck, Walter Matthau, Diane Baker. 109M USA. prod/rel: Universal Pictures

Freedom Road, 1944, Novel
Freedom Road 1979 d: Jan Kadar. lps: Kris Kristofferson, Muhammad Ali, Ron O'Neal. TVM. 200M USA. prod/rel: NBC, Zev Broun

The Immigrants, Novel
Immigrants, The 1978 d: Alan J. Levi. lps: Stephen macht, Sharon Gless, Aimee Eccles. TVM. 200M USA. prod/rel: Universal, Operation Prime Time

Penelope, New York 1965, Novel
Penelope 1966 d: Arthur Hiller. lps: Natalie Wood, Ian Bannen, Dick Shawn. 98M USA. prod/rel: Euterpe, Inc.

Rachel, 1945, Short Story
Rachel and the Stranger 1948 d: Norman Foster. lps: William Holden, Loretta Young, Robert Mitchum. 93M USA. prod/rel: RKO Radio

Sally, Novel
Face of Fear, The 1971 d: George McCowan. lps: Elizabeth Ashley, Jack Warden, Ricardo Montalban. TVM. 72M USA. prod/rel: Quinn Martin Prods.

Shirley, Novel
What's a Nice Girl Like You.? 1971 d: Jerry Paris. lps: Brenda Vaccaro, Jack Warden, Roddy McDowall. TVM. 74M USA. prod/rel: Universal

Spartacus, 1951, Novel
Spartacus 1960 d: Stanley Kubrick. lps: Kirk Douglas, Laurence Olivier, Jean Simmons. 196M USA. prod/rel: Universal

Sylvia, New York 1960, Novel
Sylvia 1965 d: Gordon Douglas. lps: Carroll Baker, George Maharis, Joanne Dru. 115M USA. prod/rel: Marpol Productions, Paramount Pictures

The Winston Affair, New York 1959, Novel
Man in the Middle 1963 d: Guy Hamilton. lps: Robert Mitchum, France Nuyen, Barry Sullivan. 94M UKN/USA. *The Winston Affair* prod/rel: Belmont Productions, Pennebaker, Inc.

FASTER, OTTO
Prazske Svadlenky, Play
Prazske Svadlenky 1929 d: Premysl Prazsky. lps: Theodor Pistek, Mana Zeniskova, Karel Lamac. 1866m CZC. *Prague Seamstresses* prod/rel: Bratri Deglove, Degl a Spol

FAUCHOIS, RENE
Boudu Sauve Des Eaux, 1919, Play
Boudu Sauve Des Eaux 1932 d: Jean Renoir. lps: Michel Simon, Charles Granval, Marcelle HainiA. 89M FRN. *Boudu Saved from Drowning* (USA) prod/rel: Michel Simon

Down and Out in Beverly Hills 1986 d: Paul Mazursky. lps: Nick Nolte, Richard Dreyfuss, Bette Midler. 103M USA. prod/rel: Touchstone Films, Silver Screen Partners Ii

Prenez Garde a la Peinture, 1932, Play
Christopher Bean 1933 d: Sam Wood. lps: Marie Dressler, Lionel Barrymore, Helen Mack. 90M USA. *The Late Christopher Bean*; *Her Sweetheart* prod/rel: Metro-Goldwyn-Mayer Corp.

Prenez Garde a la Peinture 1932 d: Henri Chomette. lps: Jean Aquistapace, Milly Mathis, Charlotte Clasis. 86M FRN. prod/rel: Films Epoc

Reves d'Amour, 1944, Play
Reves d'Amour 1946 d: Christian Stengel. lps: Pierre Richard-Willm, Annie Ducaux, Mila Parely. 105M FRN. *Dreams of Love* (USA) prod/rel: Pathe Cinema

Le Singe Qui Parle, Paris 1925, Novel
Monkey Talks, The 1927 d: Raoul Walsh. lps: Olive Borden, Jacques Lerner, Don Alvarado. 5500f USA. prod/rel: Fox Film Corp.

FAULEY, WILBUR FINLEY
Jenny Be Good, New York 1919, Novel
Jenny Be Good 1920 d: William D. Taylor. lps: Mary Miles Minter, Jay Belasco, Margaret Shelby. 5980f USA. prod/rel: Realart Pictures Corp.©

The Adventures of a Nice Young Lady Queenie, New York 1921, Novel
Queenie 1921 d: Howard M. Mitchell. lps: Shirley Mason, George O'Hara, Wilson Hummell. 5174f USA. prod/rel: Fox Film Corp.

FAULK, JOHN HENRY
Fear on Trial, Autobiography
Fear on Trial 1975 d: Lamont Johnson. lps: George C. Scott, William Devane, Dorothy Tristan. TVM. 100M USA. prod/rel: Alan Landsburg Productions

FAULKNER, NORBERT
Portrait of a Lady With Red Hair, Story
Lady With Red Hair 1940 d: Curtis Bernhardt. lps: Miriam Hopkins, Claude Rains, Richard Ainley. 81M USA. prod/rel: Warner Bros. Pictures©

FAULKNER, W.
The Leg, Story
Noga 1991 d: Nikita Tjagunov. lps: Ivan Chuzhoj, Pyotr Mamonov, Sherakil Abdulkajsov. 87M RSS. *The Leg* prod/rel: 12a

FAULKNER, WILLIAM (1897–1962), USA
Barn Burning, 1939, Short Story
Barn Burning 1980 d: Peter Werner. lps: Tommy Lee Jones, Diane Kagan, Sean Whittington. MTV. 38M USA. *Barn Burner* prod/rel: Learning in Focus

Long Hot Summer, The 1958 d: Martin Ritt. lps: Paul Newman, Orson Welles, Joanne Woodward. 117M USA. prod/rel: 20th Century-Fox, Jerry Wald Prods.

The Hamlet, 1940, Novel
Long Hot Summer, The 1958 d: Martin Ritt. lps: Paul Newman, Orson Welles, Joanne Woodward. 117M USA. prod/rel: 20th Century-Fox, Jerry Wald Prods.

Intruder in the Dust, 1948, Novel
Intruder in the Dust 1949 d: Clarence Brown. lps: David Brian, Claude Jarman Jr., Juano Hernandez. 87M USA. prod/rel: MGM

Pylon, 1935, Novel
Tarnished Angels, The 1957 d: Douglas Sirk. lps: Rock Hudson, Robert Stack, Dorothy Malone. 93M USA. *Pylon* prod/rel: Universal-International

The Reivers; a Reminiscence, New York 1962, Novel
Reivers, The 1969 d: Mark Rydell. lps: Steve McQueen, Sharon Farrell, Will Geer. 107M USA. *The Yellow Winton Flyer* prod/rel: Duo Productions, Solar Productions

A Rose for Emily, 1930, Short Story
Rose for Emily, A 1983 d: John Carradine. 27M USA.

Sanctuary, New York 1931, Novel
Sanctuary 1961 d: Tony Richardson. lps: Lee Remick, Yves Montand, Bradford Dillman. 90M USA. prod/rel: Darryl F. Zanuck Productions, 20th Century-Fox

Story of Temple Drake, The 1933 d: Stephen Roberts. lps: Miriam Hopkins, Jack La Rue, William Gargan. 72M USA. *The Shame of Temple Drake* prod/rel: Paramount Productions©

The Sound and the Fury, 1929, Novel
Sound and the Fury, The 1959 d: Martin Ritt. lps: Yul Brynner, Joanne Woodward, Margaret Leighton. 115M USA. prod/rel: 20th Century-Fox

The Spotted Horses, 1933, Short Story
Long Hot Summer, The 1958 d: Martin Ritt. lps: Paul Newman, Orson Welles, Joanne Woodward. 117M USA. prod/rel: 20th Century-Fox, Jerry Wald Prods.

Tomorrow, 1940, Short Story
Tomorrow 1972 d: Joseph Anthony. lps: Robert Duvall, Olga Bellin, Sudie Bond. 103M USA. prod/rel: Film Group Productions

Turn About, 1932, Short Story
Today We Live 1932 d: Howard Hawks. lps: Joan Crawford, Gary Cooper, Robert Young. 115M USA. prod/rel: Metro-Goldwyn-Mayer Corp.©

FAUSER, JORG
Der Schneemann, Novel
Schneemann, Der 1984 d: Peter F. Bringmann. lps: Marius Muller-Westernhagen, Polly Eltes, Heinz Wanitschek. 106M GRM. *The Snowman* prod/rel: Bavaria, N.F. Geria Ii

FAVA, GIUSEPPE
Gente Di Rispetto, Novel
Gente Di Rispetto 1975 d: Luigi ZampA. lps: Jennifer O'Neill, James Mason, Franco Nero. 115M ITL. *The Flower in His Mouth* (USA) prod/rel: C.C. Champion, Gold Film

La Violenza, Play
Violenza: Quinto Potere, La 1972 d: Florestano Vancini. lps: Enrico Maria Salerno, Gastone Moschin, Riccardo CuccrollA. 101M ITL. *Sicilian Checkmate*;

Commissione Parlamentare d'Inchiesta Sul Fenomeno Della Mafia in Sicilia prod/rel: Dino de Laurentiis Cin.Ca, Cinema International Corporation

FAVART
Les Trois Sultanes, Play
Trois Sultanes, Les 1911 d: Adrien Caillard. lps: Georges Treville, Berthier, Amelie Dieterle. 300m FRN. prod/rel: Scagl

FAY, WILLIAM
The Disappearance of Dolan, Story
Champ for a Day 1953 d: William A. Seiter. lps: Alex Nicol, Audrey Totter, Charles Winninger. 90M USA. prod/rel: Republic Pictures Corp.

The Man Who Sank the Navy, Short Story
Guy Who Came Back, The 1951 d: Joseph M. Newman. lps: Paul Douglas, Joan Bennett, Linda Darnell. 92M USA. *The Guy Who Sank the Navy* prod/rel: 20th Century-Fox

FAZEKAS, MIHALY
Ludas Matyi, 1815, Verse
Ludas Matyi 1949 d: Laszlo Ranody, Kalman Nadasdy. lps: Imre Soos, Teri Horvath, Gyorgy Solthy. 106M HNG. *The Goose Boy Mattie; The Goose Boy*
Ludas Matyi 1977 d: Attila Dargay. ANM. 76M HNG. *Mattie the Gooseboy; Mattig the Gooseboy; Matt the Gooseboy*

FEARING, KENNETH (1902–1961), USA
The Big Clock, 1946, Novel
Big Clock, The 1948 d: John Farrow. lps: Ray Milland, Maureen O'Sullivan, Charles Laughton. 95M USA. prod/rel: Paramount
No Way Out 1987 d: Roger Donaldson. lps: Gene Hackman, Kevin Costner, Sean Young. 114M USA. *Deceit* prod/rel: Orion

FECHNER, ELLEN
Story
Meine Frau Teresa 1942 d: Arthur M. Rabenalt. lps: Elfie Mayerhofer, Hans Sohnker, Mady Rahl. 85M GRM. *Heute macht Die Ganze Welt Musik Fur Mich; My Wife Teresa* prod/rel: Tobis

FEDDER, CHARLOTTE
Shattered Dreams, Autobiography
Shattered Dreams 1990 d: Robert Iscove. lps: Lindsay Wagner, Michael Nouri, Georgann Johnson. TVM. 100M USA.

FEDERER, HEINRICH
Niklaus von Flue, Leipzig 1928, Book
Niklaus von Flue - Pacem in Terris 1963 d: Michel Dickoff. lps: Raimund Bucher, Maria Emo, Heinz Woester. 131M SWT. *Nicolas de Flue - Paix Sur Terre; Mein Herr Und Mein Gott* prod/rel: Novum Ars Film

FEDERICO, G. A.
La Serva Padrona, Opera
Serva Padrona, La 1934 d: Giorgio Mannini. lps: Bruna Dragoni, Vincenzo Bettoni, Enrica Mayer. 62M ITL. prod/rel: Lirica Film, Caesar Film

FEDERMANN, REINHARD
Romeo Und Julia in Wien, Novel
Nina 1956 d: Rudolf Jugert. lps: Karlheinz Bohm, Anouk Aimee, Peter Carsten. 89M GRM. *Romeo Und Julia in Wien* prod/rel: Corona, Bavaria

FEDIN, KONSTANTIN (1892–, RSS, Fedin, Konstantin Aleksandrovich
Goroda I Gody, 1924, Novel
Goroda I Gody 1930 d: Yevgeni Chervyakov. 94M USS.
Goroda I Gody 1973 d: Alexander Zarkhi. lps: Igor Starygin, Barbara Brylska, Irina PechernikovA. 110M USS/GDR. *Towns and Years; Cities and Times; Cities and Years*

FEI LIWEN
Chuan Chang Zhui Zong, Novel
Chuan Chang Zhui Zong 1959 d: Lin Nong. lps: Ren Yi, Zhang Yuan, Yan Xueqing. 7r CHN. *Searching the Ship Plant* prod/rel: Changchun Film Studio

FEIFER, GEORGE
The Girl from Petrovka, Novel
Girl from Petrovka, The 1974 d: Robert Ellis Miller. lps: Goldie Hawn, Hal Holbrook, Anthony Hopkins. 103M USA. prod/rel: Universal

FEIFFER, JULES
Little Murders, New York 1967, Play
Little Murders 1971 d: Alan Arkin. lps: Elliott Gould, Marcia Rodd, Vincent GardeniA. 110M USA. prod/rel: Brodsky-Gould, 20th Century Fox

FEIJOO, SAMUEL
Juan Quinquin En Pueblo Mocho, 1964, Novel
Aventuras de Juan Quin Quin, Las 1967 d: Julio Garcia EspinosA. lps: Julio Martinez, Erdwin Fernandez, Adelaida Raymat. 110M CUB. *The Adventures of Juan Quin Quin* prod/rel: Humberto Hernandez

FEINER, RUTH
Three Cups of Coffee, Novel
Woman's Angle, The 1952 d: Leslie Arliss. lps: Edward Underdown, Cathy O'Donnell, Lois Maxwell. 86M UKN. prod/rel: Ab-Pathe, Bow Bells

FEINMANN, J. P.
Two to Tango, Novel
Two to Tango 1987 d: Robert McCallum. lps: Nina Hartley, Krista Lane, Tony MontanA. 87M USA. prod/rel: New Horizons Picture Group, Aries

FEINMANN, JOSE PABLO
Ni El Tiro Del Final, Novel
Bitter End, The 1997 d: Juan Jose CampanellA. lps: Denis Leary, Aitana Sanchez-Gijon, Terence Stamp. 119M USA. *Love Walked in* prod/rel: Jempsa Entertainment, Apostle Pictures Productions

FEKETE, GYULA
Az Orvos Halala, 1963, Novel
Orvos Halala, Az 1966 d: Frigyes Mamcserov. lps: Antal Pager, Marii Szemes, Karoly Kovacs. 94M HNG. *Death of a Doctor*

FEKETE, ISTVAN
Vuk, Novel
Vuk 1982 d: Attila Dargay. ANM. 85M HNG/GRM. *Der Fuchs Wuk* (GRM); *The Intrepid Fox* prod/rel: Infafilm, Hungarofilm

FELDSHUH, DAVID
Miss Evers' Boys, Play
Miss Evers' Boys 1997 d: Joseph Sargent. lps: Alfre Woodard, Laurence Fishburne, Craig Sheffer. TVM. 120M USA. prod/rel: Hbo Nyc Prods., Anasazi Prods.

FELIN Y CODINA, JOSE
Maria Del Carmen, Novel
Serenade 1921 d: Raoul Walsh. lps: Miriam Cooper, George Walsh, Rosita Marstini. 6380f USA. prod/rel: R. A. Walsh Productions, Associated First National Pictures

FELISATTI, MASSIMO
La Madama, Novel
Madama, La 1976 d: Duccio Tessari. lps: Tom Skerritt, Carole Andre, Christian de SicA. 94M ITL. prod/rel: Filmes Cin.Ca, Titanus
Violenza a Roma, Novel
..a Tutte le Auto Della Polizia 1975 d: Mario Caiano. lps: Antonio Sabato, Luciana Paluzzi, Enrico Maria Salerno. 100M ITL. prod/rel: Capitol Cin.Ca, Jarama Film

FELIU Y CODINA, JOSE
La Dolores, Opera
Dolores, La 1923 d: Maximiliano Thous. lps: Ana Giner Soler, Leopoldo Pitarch, Jose Latorre. 2575m SPN. prod/rel: Compania Cin.Ca Hispano-Portuguesa, P.A.C.E.

FELLMAR, KARL
Der Mann in Der Wanne, Play
Mann in Der Wanne, Der 1952 d: Franz Antel. lps: Axel von Ambesser, Maria Andergast, Jeanette Schultze. 93M AUS. prod/rel: Neusser

FELLOW, JOHN D.
La Fille de Feu, Novel
Fille de Feu, La 1958 d: Alfred Rode. lps: Claudine Dupuis, Erno Crisa, Yoko Tani. 93M FRN. *Fire in the Flesh* (USA) prod/rel: Alfred Rode, Soc. Francaise Des Films

FELLUAN, VICTOR HUGO
Story
Disonorata Senza Colpa 1954 d: Giorgio W. Chili. lps: Milly Vitale, Alberto Farnese, Cesare Fantoni. 90M ITL. prod/rel: General Film

FELSEN, HENRY GREGOR
Why Rustlers Never Win, Novel
Once Upon a Horse 1958 d: Hal Kanter. lps: Dan Rowan, Dick Martin, Martha Hyer. 85M USA. *Hot Horse* prod/rel: Universal-International

FELTZ, KURT
Die Glucklichste Frau Der Welt, Opera
Bonjour Kathrin 1955 d: Karl Anton. lps: Caterina Valente, Peter Alexander, Silvio Francesco. 96M GRM. *Hello Catherine* prod/rel: Alfred Greven
Saison in Salzburg, Opera
Lascia Cantare Il Cuore 1943 d: Roberto Savarese. lps: Vivi Gioi, Elena Luber, Loris Gizzi. 84M ITL. prod/rel: Fono Roma, Artisti Associati
Saison in Salzburg 1952 d: Ernst MarischkA. lps: Adrian Hoven, Walter Muller, Hans Richter. 105M AUS. prod/rel: Wien
Saison in Salzburg 1961 d: Franz J. Gottlieb. lps: Peter Alexander, Gunther Philipp, Waltraut Haas. 97M AUS. prod/rel: Sascha

..Und Die Musik Spielt Dazu 1943 d: Carl Boese. lps: Vivi Gioi, Maria Andergast, Georg Alexander. 88M GRM. *Saison in Salzburg* prod/rel: Deka, Karp

FELUAN, VICTOR HUGO
I Congiurati Di Belfiore, Play
Giglio Infranto, Il 1956 d: Giorgio W. Chili. lps: Milly Vitale, Helene Remy, Alberto Farnese. 101M ITL. prod/rel: Col Film

FENADY, ANDREW J.
The Man With Bogart's Face, Novel
Man With Bogart's Face, The 1980 d: Robert Day. lps: Robert Sacchi, Michelle Phillips, Olivia Hussey. 106M USA. *Sam Marlowe Private Eye* prod/rel: Twentieth Century Fox

FENAKEL, JUDIT
A Szerelem Hatarai, Novel
Szerelem Hatarai, A 1973 d: Janos Szucs. lps: Andrea Drahota, Tibor Bitskey, Nora Kaldy. 80M HNG. prod/rel: Mafilm

FENELLI, MARIO
Las Huellas, Novel
Orme, Le 1975 d: Luigi Bazzoni. lps: Florinda Bolkan, Peter McEnery, Caterina Boratto. 91M ITL. prod/rel: Cinemarte, Cineriz

FENG DEYING
Ku Cai Hua, Novel
Ku Cai Hua 1965 d: Li Ang. lps: Qu Yun, Yuan XIa, Wang Zhigang. F CHN. *Bitter Cauliflower* prod/rel: August First Film Studio

FENG JICAI
Paoda Shuang Deng, Novel
Paoda Shuang Deng 1993 d: He Ping. lps: Ning Jing, Wu Gang, Zhao XIaorui. 115M CHN/HKG. *Red Firecracker Green Firecracker* prod/rel: XI'an Film Studio, Wen Partners Organization

FENG ZHI
Di Hou Wu Gong Dui, Novel
Di Hou Wu Gong Dui 1995 d: Lei XIanhe, Kang Ning. lps: Wu Jingan, Ru Ping, Dong Ziwu. F CHN. *Armed Troops Behind Enemy Lines (Parts 1 & 2)* prod/rel: Changchun Film Studio

FENN, FREDERICK
Op O' Me Thumb, New York 1905, Play
Suds 1920 d: John Francis Dillon. lps: Mary Pickford, William Austin, Theodore Roberts. 5-6r USA. *The Duchess of Suds; Op O' Me Thumb* prod/rel: Mary Pickford Co.©, United Artists Corp.

FENOGLIO, BEPPE
Una Questione Privata, Novel
Questione Privata, Una 1966 d: Giorgio Trentin. lps: Nino Segurini, Giovanna Lenzi, Valeria Ciangottini. 98M ITL. prod/rel: Langa Cin.Ca

FENOLLOSA, MARY MCNEIL
The Dragon Painter, Boston 1906, Novel
Dragon Painter, The 1919 d: William Worthington. lps: Sessue Hayakawa, Tsuru Aoki, Toyo FujitA. 5r USA. prod/rel: Haworth Pictures Corp.©, Robertson-Dale Co

FENTON, FRANCIS
Paid With Tears, Story
Passion Song, The 1928 d: Harry O. Hoyt. lps: Gertrude Olmstead, Noah Beery, Bill Elliott. 5080f USA. prod/rel: Excellent Pictures, Interstate Pictures

FENWICK, JEAN-NOEL
Les Palmes de M. Schutz, Play
Palmes de M. Schutz, Les 1997 d: Claude Pinoteau. lps: Isabelle Huppert, Philippe Noiret, Charles Berling. 108M FRN. *Pierre and Marie* prod/rel: L. Dilms, France 2 Cinema

FERBER, EDNA (1887–1968), USA
Cimarron, New York 1930, Novel
Cimarron 1931 d: Wesley Ruggles. lps: Richard Dix, Irene Dunne, Estelle Taylor. 124M USA. prod/rel: RKO Radio Pictures, Inc.
Cimarron 1960 d: Anthony Mann, Charles Walters. lps: Glenn Ford, Maria Schell, Anne Baxter. 147M USA. prod/rel: MGM
Classified, Short Story
Classified 1925 d: Alfred Santell. lps: Corinne Griffith, Jack Mulhall, Ward Crane. 6927f USA. prod/rel: Corinne Griffith Productions, First National Pictures
Come and Get It, New York 1935, Novel
Come and Get It! 1936 d: Howard Hawks, William Wyler. lps: Edward Arnold, Joel McCrea, Frances Farmer. 99M USA. *Roaring Timber* prod/rel: Howard Productions, Inc., United Artists
Dinner at Eight, New York 1932, Play
Dinner at Eight 1933 d: George Cukor. lps: Marie Dressler, John Barrymore, Wallace Beery. 113M USA. prod/rel: Metro-Goldwyn-Mayer Corp.

Dinner at Eight 1989 d: Ron Lagomarsino. lps: Lauren Bacall, Charles Durning, Ellen Greene. TVM. 100M USA.

Fanny Herself, New York 1917, Novel
No Woman Knows 1921 d: Tod Browning. lps: Stuart Holmes, Mabel Julienne Scott, Earl Schenck. 7031f USA. prod/rel: Universal Film Mfg. Co.

The Gay Old Dog, 1917, Short Story
Gay Old Dog, The 1919 d: Hobart Henley. lps: John Cumberland, Mary Chambers, Emily Lorraine. 5130f USA. prod/rel: Hobart Henley Productions, Pathe Exchange, Inc.©

Giant, 1952, Novel
Giant 1956 d: George Stevens. lps: Elizabeth Taylor, Rock Hudson, James Dean. 201M USA. prod/rel: Warner Bros., Giant Prods.

Gigolo, New York 1922, Novel
Gigolo 1926 d: William K. Howard. lps: Rod La Rocque, Jobyna Ralston, Louise Dresser. 7295f USA. prod/rel: de Mille Pictures, Producers Distributing Corp.

Glamour, 1932, Short Story
Glamour 1934 d: William Wyler. lps: Paul Lukas, Constance Cummings, Philip Reed. 75M USA. prod/rel: Universal Pictures Corp.©

Ice Palace, 1958, Novel
Ice Palace 1960 d: Vincent Sherman. lps: Richard Burton, Robert Ryan, Carolyn Jones. 124M USA. prod/rel: Warner Bros.

Mother Knows Best, Garden City, N.Y. 1927, Novel
Hard to Get 1929 d: William Beaudine. lps: Dorothy MacKaill, Charles Delaney, James Finlayson. 7328f USA. prod/rel: First National Pictures

Mother Knows Best 1928 d: John G. Blystone. lps: Madge Bellamy, Louise Dresser, Barry Norton. 9r USA. *Does Mother Know Best* prod/rel: Fox Film Corp.

Old Man Minick, 1922, Short Story
Expert, The 1932 d: Archie Mayo. lps: Charles "Chic" Sale, Dickie Moore, Earle Foxe. 69M USA. *Old Man Minick* prod/rel: Warner Bros. Pictures©

No Place to Go 1939 d: Terry O. Morse. lps: Dennis Morgan, Gloria Dickson, Fred Stone. 57M USA. *Not Wanted*; *Old Man Minick* prod/rel: Warner Bros. Pictures©

Welcome Home 1925 d: James Cruze. lps: Luke Cosgrave, Warner Baxter, Lois Wilson. 5909f USA. prod/rel: Famous Players-Lasky, Paramount Pictures

Our Mrs. McChesney, New York 1915, Play
Our Mrs. McChesney 1918 d: Ralph Ince. lps: Ethel Barrymore, Huntley Gordon, Wilfred Lytell. 5r USA. prod/rel: Metro Pictures Corp.©

The Royal Family, New York 1927, Play
Royal Family of Broadway, The 1930 d: George Cukor, Cyril Gardner. lps: Fredric March, Ina Claire, Mary Brian. 82M USA. *Theatre Royal* prod/rel: Paramount Publix Corp.©

Saratoga Trunk, 1941, Novel
Saratoga Trunk 1945 d: Sam Wood. lps: Ingrid Bergman, Gary Cooper, Flora Robson. 135M USA. prod/rel: Warner Bros.

Showboat, New York 1926, Novel
Show Boat 1929 d: Harry Pollard. lps: Laura La Plante, Joseph Schildkraut, Otis Harlan. 12r USA. prod/rel: Universal Pictures

Show Boat 1936 d: James Whale. lps: Irene Dunne, Allan Jones, Charles Winninger. 115M USA. prod/rel: Universal Productions©, James Whale Production

Show Boat 1951 d: George Sidney. lps: Howard Keel, Ava Gardner, Kathryn Grayson. 108M USA. prod/rel: MGM

So Big!, Garden City, N.Y. 1924, Novel
So Big 1924 d: Charles J. Brabin. lps: Colleen Moore, Joseph de Grasse, John Bowers. 8562f USA. prod/rel: First National Pictures

So Big 1932 d: William A. Wellman. lps: Barbara Stanwyck, George Brent, Dickie Moore. 82M USA. prod/rel: Warner Bros. Pictures©

So Big 1953 d: Robert Wise. lps: Jane Wyman, Sterling Hayden, Nancy Olson. 101M USA. prod/rel: Warner Bros.

Stage Door, New York 1936, Play
Stage Door 1937 d: Gregory La CavA. lps: Katharine Hepburn, Ginger Rogers, Adolphe Menjou. 92M USA. prod/rel: RKO Radio Pictures©

FERDINAND, ROGER
L' Amant de Borneo, Play
Amant de Borneo, L' 1942 d: Jean-Pierre Feydeau, Rene Le Henaff. lps: Jean Tissier, Arletty, Pauline Carton. 90M FRN. prod/rel: C.C.F.C.

Chotard Et Cie, Play
Chotard Et Cie 1932 d: Jean Renoir. lps: Fernand Charpin, Jeanne Boitel, Jane Lory. 77M FRN. prod/rel: Films Roger Ferdinand

Les Croulants Se Portent Bien, Play
Croulants Se Portent Bien, Les 1961 d: Jean Boyer. lps: Nadia Gray, Fernand Gravey, Pierre Dux. 90M FRN. prod/rel: Marceau, Cocinor

Un Homme En Or, Play
Homme En Or, Un 1934 d: Jean Dreville. lps: Harry Baur, Pierre Larquey, Suzy Vernon. 78M FRN. *A Man and His Woman* (USA) prod/rel: Films R.F.

Ils Ont Vingt Ans, Play
Ils Ont Vingt Ans 1950 d: Rene Delacroix. lps: Francois Patrice, Jacqueline Gauthier, Andre Versini. 88M FRN. prod/rel: Films F.a.O.F., Fred D'orengiani

Les J 3, Play
J 3, Les 1945 d: Roger Richebe. lps: Gerard Nery, Saturnin Fabre, Giselle Pascal. 85M FRN. prod/rel: Films Roger Richebe

La Pere de Mademoiselle, Play
Pere de Mademoiselle, Le 1953 d: Marcel L'Herbier, Robert-Paul Dagan. lps: Arletty, Andre Luguet, Denise Grey. 100M FRN. *The Father of the Girl* prod/rel: Films F.aO.

Le President Haudecoeur, Play
President Haudecoeur, Le 1939 d: Jean Dreville. lps: Harry Baur, Robert Pizani, Betty Stockfeld. 110M FRN. prod/rel: Films Marcel Pagnol

Touche-a-Tout, Play
Touche-a-Tout 1935 d: Jean Dreville. lps: Fernand Gravey, Suzy Vernon, Colette Darfeuil. 117M FRN. prod/rel: Films R.F.

Une Fille Trois Garcons, Play
Trois Garcons, une Fille 1948 d: Maurice Labro. lps: Jean Marchat, Bernard La Jarrige, Gaby Morlay. 90M FRN. prod/rel: F.a.C.

Trois Pour Cent, Play
Trois Pour Cent 1933 d: Jean Dreville. lps: Gabriel Signoret, Jeanne Boitel, Claire Gerard. 97M FRN. *Le Petit Millionaire* prod/rel: Films R.F.

FERDOWSI
Shahnameh, c1010
Siavosh Dar Takhte Jamshid 1967 d: Ferydoun RahnemA. lps: Minou Farjad, Marva Nabili, Abbas Moayeri. 100M IRN. *Siavacch a Persepolis*; *The King's Book*; *The Book of Kings*; *Siavosh in Persepolis*; *Siavash in Persepolis* prod/rel: Djame Djam, Iran Film

FERGUSON, AUSTIN
Jet Stream, Novel
Mayday at 40,000 Feet 1976 d: Robert Butler. lps: David Janssen, Don Meredith, Christopher George. TVM. 100M USA. *000 Feet! Mayday: 40* prod/rel: Andrew J. Fenady Associates, Warner Bros. Tv

FERGUSON, MARGARET
Sign of the Ram, Book
Sign of the Ram 1948 d: John Sturges. lps: Susan Peters, Alexander Knox, Phyllis Thaxter. 84M USA. prod/rel: Columbia

FERGUSON, W. B.
Crackerjack, Novel
Crackerjack 1938 d: Albert de Courville. lps: Tom Walls, Lilli Palmer, Noel Madison. 79M UKN. *The Man With a Hundred Faces* (USA); *Man With 100 Faces* prod/rel: Gainsborough, General Film Distributors

FERGUSON, WILLIAM BLAIR MORTON
Garrison's Finish, New York 1907, Novel
Garrison's Finish 1914 d: Francis J. Grandon. 3r USA. prod/rel: Selig Polyscope Co.

Garrison's Finish 1923 d: Arthur Rosson. lps: Jack Pickford, Madge Bellamy, Charles A. Stevenson. 7898f USA. prod/rel: Jack Pickford Productions, Allied Producers and Distributors

Zollenstein, New York 1908, Novel
Zollenstein 1917 d: Edgar Jones. lps: Vola Vale, Monroe Salisbury, Daniel Gilfether. 4r USA. prod/rel: Falcon Features, General Film Co.©

FERGUSSON, HARVEY (1890–1971), USA
Hot Saturday, New York 1926, Novel
Hot Saturday 1932 d: William A. Seiter. lps: Nancy Carroll, Cary Grant, Randolph Scott. 73M USA. prod/rel: Paramount Publix Corp.©

Wolf Song, 1927, Short Story
Wolf Song 1929 d: Victor Fleming. lps: Gary Cooper, Lupe Velez, Louis Wolheim. 6769f USA. prod/rel: Paramount Famous Lasky Corp.

FERMAUD, MICHEL
Les Portes Claquent, Play
Portes Claquent, Les 1960 d: Jacques Poitrenaud, Michel Fermaud. lps: Dany Saval, Francoise Dorleac, Maurice Sarfati. 90M FRN. prod/rel: Francos Film

FERNALD, C. B.
The Pursuit of Pamela, London 1913, Play
Pursuit of Pamela, The 1920 d: Harold Shaw. lps: Edna Flugrath, Templar Powell, Douglas Munro. 5241f UKN. prod/rel: London, Jury

FERNANDES, MILLOR
Do Tamanho de Um Defunto, 1957, Play
Ladrao Em Noite de Chuva 1960 d: Armando Couto. 80M BRZ.

FERNANDEZ ARDAVIN, LUIS
Play
Rosa de Madrid 1927 d: Eusebio F. Ardavin. lps: Conchita Dorado, Pedro Larranaga, Carmen Toledo. F SPN. *Rose from Madrid* prod/rel: Producciones Ardavin (Madrid)

El Bandido de la Sierra, Play
Bandido de la Sierra, El 1926 d: Eusebio F. Ardavin. lps: Josefina Diaz de Artigas, Santiago Artigas, Mercedes Prendes. 4500m SPN. *The Bandit of the Mountains* prod/rel: Producciones Ardavin (Madrid)

La Bejarana, Opera
Bejarana, La 1925 d: Eusebio F. Ardavin. lps: Celia Escudero, Jose Nieto, Maria Luz Callejo. 2508m SPN. *The Girl from Bejar* prod/rel: Producciones Ardavin (Madrid)

FERNANDEZ CABALLERO
Gigantes Y Cabezudos, Opera
Gigantes Y Cabezudos 1925 d: Florian Rey. lps: Carmen Viance, Jose Nieto, Marina Torres. 77M SPN. *Giants and Bigheads* prod/rel: Atlantida

FERNANDEZ DE MORATIN, LEANDRO (1760–1828), SPN
El Medico a Palos, Play
Medico a Palos, El 1926 d: Sabino A. Micon. lps: Marina Torres, Erna Becker, Faustino Bretano. SPN. prod/rel: Ediciones Garrido (Madrid)

FERNANDEZ FLOREZ, WENCESLAO (1886–, SPN
El Bosque Animado, 1943, Novel
Fendetestas 1975 d: Antonio F. Simon. 30M SPN.

La Casa de la Lluvia, 1925, Short Story
Casa de la Lluvia, La 1943 d: Antonio Roman. lps: Blanca de Silos, Luis Hurtado, Carmen Viance. 88M SPN. *The House in the Rain*

Fantasmas, 1930, Short Story
Destino Se Disculpa, El 1944 d: Jose Luis Saenz de HerediA. lps: Rafael Duran, Fernando Fernan Gomez, Maria Esperanza Navarro. 109M SPN. *Destiny Says Sorry*

Ha Entrado un Ladron, 1920, Novel
Ha Entrado un Ladron 1948 d: Jose Gascon. lps: Roberto Font, Margaret Genske, Juny Orly. 101M SPN. *A Thief Has Arrived*

El Hombre Que Se Quiso Matar, 1930, Short Story
Hombre Que Se Quiso Matar, El 1941 d: Rafael Gil. lps: Antonio Casal, Rosita Yarza, Xan Das Bolas. 80M SPN. *The Man Who Wanted to Kill Himself*

Hombre Que Se Quiso Matar, El 1970 d: Rafael Gil. lps: Tony Leblanc, Antonio Garisa, Elisa Ramirez. 90M SPN. *The Man Who Wanted to Kill Himself*

Huella de Luz, 1925, Short Story
Huella de Luz 1943 d: Rafael Gil. lps: Isabel de Pomes, Juan Espantaleon, Antonio Casal. 77M SPN. *Traces of Light*

Los Que No Fuimos a la Guerra, 1930, Novel
Los Que No Fuimos a la Guerra 1961 d: Julio Diamante. lps: Laura Valenzuela, Agustin Gonzalez, Pepe Isbert. 94M SPN. *Cuando Estallo la Paz*; *When Peace Broke Out*; *Those of Us Who Didn't Go to War*

Luz de Luna, 1915, Novel
Camarote de Lujo 1957 d: Rafael Gil. lps: Antonio Casal, Maria Mahor, Manolo Moran. 97M SPN. *Luxury Cabin*

El Malvado Carabel, 1931, Novel
Malvado Carabel, El 1934 d: Edgar Neville. lps: Antonita Colome, Antonio Vico, Ana de SiriA. 87M SPN. *The Wicked Carabel*

Malvado Carabel, El 1955 d: Fernando Fernan Gomez. lps: Fernando Fernan Gomez, Maria Luz Galicia, Julia Caba AlbA. 77M SPN. *The Wicked Carabel*

Unos Pasos de Mujer, 1934, Short Story
Pasos de Mujer, Unos 1941 d: Eusebio F. Ardavin. lps: Lina Yegros, Fernando Fernandez de Cordoba, Raul Rodriguez. 81M SPN. *Steps of Women*

Por Que Te Engana Tu Marido?, 1940, Short Story
Por Que Te Engana Tu Marido? 1968 d: Manuel Summers. lps: Alfredo Landa, Laly Soldevila, Esperanza Roy. 92M SPN. *Why Is Your Husband Unfaithful?*; *Why Does Your Husband Cheat on You?*

El Sistema Pelegrin, 1949, Novel
Sistema Pelegrin, El 1951 d: Ignacio F. Iquino. lps: Fernando Fernan Gomez, Isabel de Castro, Sergio OrtA. 96M SPN. *The Pelegrin Method*

Volvoreta, 1917, Novel
  Volvoreta 1976 d: Jose Antonio Nieves Conde. lps: Amparo Munoz, Antonio Mayans, Ramiro Oliveros. 99M SPN.

FERNANDEZ, GEORGE
Vietnam Trilogy, Play
  Cease Fire 1985 d: David Nutter. lps: Don Johnson, Lisa Blount, Robert F. Lyons. 97M USA. *In Country*; *Ceasefire* prod/rel: Cineworld, Double Helix Films

FERNANDEZ SHAW, CARLOS
La Chavala, Opera
  Chavala, La 1925 d: Florian Rey. lps: Elisa Ruiz Romero, Juan de Orduna, Maria Luz Callejo. SPN. *The Girl* prod/rel: Atlantida
La Revoltosa, Opera
  Revoltosa, La 1924 d: Florian Rey. lps: Josefina Tapias, Juan de Orduna, Jose Moncayo. 71M SPN. *The Mischievous One*; *The Riotous Girl* prod/rel: Goya Film (Madrid)

FERNAU, JOACHIM
Komm Nur Mein Liebstes Vogelein., Novel
  Komm Nur, Mein Liebstes Vogelein 1968 d: Rolf Thiele. lps: Maria Brockerhoff, Francesca Farinacci, Tanja Gruber. 95M GRM/ITL. *My Dear Little Bird Come Now*; *Come Along My Dearest* prod/rel: Roxy, Sancro

FERNER, MAX
Der Hunderter Im Westentascher, Play
  Donner, Blitz Und Sonnenschein 1936 d: Erich Engels. lps: Karl Valentin, Liesl Karlstadt, Ilse Petri. 92M GRM. prod/rel: N.F.K., Regina
Der Mude Theodor, Play
  Mude Theodor, Der 1936 d: Veit Harlan. lps: Weiss Ferdl, Erika Glassner, Gertrud Boll. 82M GRM. prod/rel: Majestic, Syndikat-Film
  Service de Nuit 1931 d: Henri Fescourt. lps: Marcel Barencey, Mylo d'Arcylle, Robert Darthez. 75M FRN. *Theodore Est Fatigue*; *Les Nuits de Papa*; *Pour Service de Nuit* prod/rel: Etablissements Jacques Haik, Minerva
Salvator, Play
  Monche, Madchen Und Panduren 1952 d: Ferdinand Dorfler. lps: Joe Stockel, Erich Ponto, Marianne Schonauer. 85M GRM. *Monks Girls and Hungarian Soldiers* prod/rel: Dorfler, Deutsche Cosmopol

FERNIC, P. A.
La Bete aux Sept Manteaux, Novel
  Bete aux Sept Manteaux, La 1936 d: Jean de Limur. lps: Jules Berry, Meg Lemonnier, Jacques Maury. 98M FRN. *L' Homme a la Cagoule Noire* prod/rel: Georges Chevalier

FERNIERE, JEAN-PIERRE
Du Grabuge Chez Les Veuves, Novel
  Du Grabuge Chez Les Veuves 1963 d: Jacques Poitrenaud. lps: Danielle Darrieux, Dany Carrel, Enzo DoriA. 95M FRN/ITL. *Strana Voglia Di Una Vedova* (ITL); *Les Veuves* prod/rel: Marceau-Cocinor, Laetitia Films

FERRANTE, ELENA
L' Amore Molesto, Novel
  Amore Molesto, L' 1995 d: Mario Martone. lps: Anna Bonaiuto, Angela Luce, Carmela Pecoraro. 104M ITL. *Nasty Love*; *Wounded Love* prod/rel: Teatri Uniti, Lucky Red

FERRARI, PAOLO
Amore Senza Stima, Play
  Amore Senza Stima 1914. lps: Giannina Chiantoni, Oreste Calabresi, Ernesto Sabbatini. 800m ITL. *A Wife's Devotion* (UKN) prod/rel: Cines
Cause Ed Effetti, 1871, Play
  Cause Ed Effetti 1917 d: Ugo Gracci. lps: Mercedes Brignone, Ugo Gracci, Ettore Mazzanti. 1508m ITL. prod/rel: Veritas
  Vie Del Cuore, Le 1942 d: Camillo Mastrocinque. lps: Miria Di San Servolo, Sandro Ruffini, Adriano Rimoldi. 83M ITL. prod/rel: Viralba, Cine Tirrenia
Il Duello, 1868
  Duello, Il 1914. lps: Ruggero Ruggeri, Tilde Teldi, Corrado RaccA. 1132m ITL. prod/rel: Cines
Il Ridicolo, 1859, Play
  Ridicolo, Il 1916 d: Eduardo BencivengA. lps: Mario Bonnard, Olga Benetti, Elsa Lazzerini. 1296m ITL. prod/rel: Caesar Film
Il Suicidio, 1875, Play
  Suicidio, Il 1916 d: Alberto Carlo Lolli. lps: Fernando Del Re, Enna Saredo, Guido Trento. 1251m ITL. prod/rel: Meridio Film

FERRAVILLA, EDUARDO
La Class de Asen, 1879, Play
  Class de Asen, La 1914 d: Arnaldo Giacomelli. lps: Eduardo FerravillA. ITL. prod/rel: Comerio

Massinelli in Vacanza, Play
  Massinelli in Vacanza 1914 d: Arnaldo Giacomelli. lps: Eduardo FerravillA. ITL. prod/rel: Luca Comerio

FERREIRA, VERGILIO
Cantico Final, 1959, Novel
  Cantico Final 1976 d: Manuel Guimaraes, Dordio Guimaraes. lps: Rui de Carvalho, Manuela Cardo, Fernando Curado Ribeiro. 106M PRT. *The Last Song*
Manha Submersa, 1954, Novel
  Manha Submersa 1980 d: Lauro Antonio. lps: Eunice Munoz, Jose Severino, Joaquim Manuel Dias. 127M PRT. *Morning Undersea*; *Hidden Dawn* prod/rel: Lauro Antonio

FERRER, DR.
El Rebozo de Soledad, Novel
  Rebozo de Soledad, El 1952 d: Roberto Gavaldon. lps: Pedro Armendariz, Arturo de Cordova, Estelle IndA. 108M MXC. *Soledad*; *The Shawl of Solitude* prod/rel: Mier Y Brooks

FERRIER, PAUL
Josephine Vendue Par Ses Soeurs, Opera
  Josephine Vendue Par Ses Soeurs 1913 d: Georges DenolA. lps: Baron Fils, Louis Blanche, Mado Floreal. 725m FRN. prod/rel: Pathe Freres

FERRIERE, JEAN-PIERRE
Cadavres En Vacances, Novel
  Cadavres En Vacances 1961 d: Jacqueline Audry. lps: Jeanne Valerie, Simone Renant, Michel Bardinet. 100M FRN. *Corpses on Holiday* prod/rel: Createurs Associes
Constance aux Enfers, Paris 1963, Novel
  Constance aux Enfers 1964 d: Francois Villiers, Alfonso Balcazar. lps: Michele Morgan, Dany Saval, Simon Andreu. 90M FRN/SPN. *Un Balcon Sobre El Infierno* (SPN); *Web of Fear* (USA) prod/rel: Luxor Films, Capitole Films

FERRIS, PAUL
The Detective, Novel
  Detective, The 1985 d: Don Leaver. lps: Tom Bell, Mark Eden, Vivienne Ritchie. MTV. 150M UKN. prod/rel: BBC

FERRIS, WALLY
Across 110th Street, Novel
  Across 110th Street 1972 d: Barry Shear. lps: Anthony Quinn, Yaphet Kotto, Anthony FranciosA. 100M USA. prod/rel: United Artists, Film Guarantors

FERROLLI, BEATRICE
Duett Zu Dritt, Play
  Duett Zu Dritt 1977 d: Gerhard JandA. lps: Heinz Marecek, Mascha Gonska, Iris Berben. 89M AUS. *A Duo-Trio* prod/rel: Sascha

FESSIER, MICHAEL
The Boy from Oklahoma, Short Story
  Boy from Oklahoma, The 1954 d: Michael Curtiz. lps: Will Rogers Jr., Nancy Olson, Lon Chaney Jr. 88M USA. prod/rel: Warner Bros.
The Woman They Almost Lynched, 1951, Short Story
  Woman They Almost Lynched, The 1953 d: Allan Dwan. lps: John Lund, Brian Donlevy, Joan Leslie. 90M USA. prod/rel: Republic

FESTA CAMPANILE, PASQUALE (1927-1986), ITL
Conviene Dar Bene l'Amore, Novel
  Conviene Far Bene l'Amore 1975 d: Pasquale Festa Campanile. lps: Luigi Proietti, Agostina Belli, Eleonora Giorgi. 106M ITL. *The Sex machine* (USA) prod/rel: Clesi Cin.Ca, Titanus
Il Ladrone, Novel
  Ladrone, Il 1979 d: Pasquale Festa Campanile. lps: Enrico Montesano, Edwige Fenech, Bernadette Lafont. 112M ITL/FRN. *The Good Thief* (USA); *The Bad Thief*; *Le Larron* (FRN) prod/rel: Italian International Film, Daimo Film (Roma)
La Nonna Sabella, Novel
  Nonna Sabella, La 1957 d: Dino Risi. lps: Tina Pica, Sylva Koscina, Renato Salvatori. 95M ITL. *Oh! Sabella* (UKN); *Grandmother Sabella* prod/rel: Titanus
La Ragazza Di Trieste, Novel
  Ragazza Di Trieste, La 1983 d: Pasquale Festa Campanile. lps: Ben Gazzara, Ornella Muti, Jean-Claude Brialy. 103M ITL. *The Girl from Trieste* prod/rel: Faso

FEUCHTWANGER, LION (1884-1958), GRM
Die Geschwister Oppenheim, 1933, Novel
  Semja Oppenheim 1939 d: Grigori Roshal. lps: Vladimir Balasjov, Josif Toltsjanov, Ada Voitsik. 103M USS. *The Oppenheim Family*; *Semla Oppenheim*; *Semya Oppengeim*

Goya; Oder Der Arge Weg Der Erkenntnis, 1951, Novel
  Goya 1971 d: Konrad Wolf. lps: Donatas Banionis, Fred Duren, Olivera KatarinA. 134M GDR/USS/BUL. *Goya Oder Der Arge Weg Zur Erkenntnis*; *Goya Or the Road to Awareness*; *Gojja Ili Tjazkij Put Poznanija* (USS) prod/rel: Defa, Lenfilm
Jud Suss, 1925, Novel
  Jew Suss 1934 d: Lothar Mendes. lps: Conrad Veidt, Benita Hume, Frank Vosper. 109M UKN. *Power* (USA) prod/rel: Gaumont-British
  Jud Suss 1940 d: Veit Harlan. lps: Werner Krauss, Ferdinand Marian, Kristina Soderbaum. 96M GRM. *Jew Suss*

FEUILLADE, LOUIS
Les Deux Gamines, Novel
  Deux Gamines, Les 1950 d: Maurice de Canonge. lps: Jean-Jacques Delbo, Leo Marjane, Suzy Prim. 93M FRN. prod/rel: Films Artistiques Francais

FEUILLET, OCTAVE (1821-1890), FRN
Dalila, 1857, Novel
  Dalila 1919 d: Guglielmo Braconcini. lps: Anna Lazzarini, Guglielmo Braconcini, Franco Mari. 1396m ITL. prod/rel: Partenope Film
Honneur d'Artiste, Novel
  Honneur d'Artiste 1917 d: Jean Kemm. lps: Henry Krauss, Georges Mauloy, Simone Frevalles. 1580m FRN. prod/rel: Scagl
Julie, 1869
  Giulia Di Trecoeur 1921 d: Camillo de Riso. lps: Vera Vergani, Giorgio Bonaiti, Luigi Maggi. 1772m ITL. prod/rel: Caesar Film
Le Roman d'un Jeune Homme Pauvre, 1858, Novel
  Novela de un Joven Pobre, La 1942 d: Luis Bayon HerrerA. lps: Hugo Del Carril, Armando Bo. 98M ARG. *Story of a Poor Young Man*
  Novela de un Joven Pobre, La 1968 d: Enrique Cahen. lps: Leo Dan, Nini Marshall, Erika Wallner. 110M ARG. *The Story of a Poor Young Man*
  Parisian Romance, A 1932 d: Chester M. Franklin. lps: Lew Cody, Joyce Compton, Marion Shilling. 77M USA. prod/rel: Allied Pictures Corp., Chester M. Franklin Production
  Roman d'un Jeune Homme Pauvre, Le 1913 d: Albert Capellani, Georges DenolA. lps: Gabriel de Gravone, Henri Etievant, Paulette Noizeux. 595m FRN. prod/rel: Scagl
  Roman d'un Jeune Homme Pauvre, Le 1927 d: Gaston Ravel. lps: Suzy Vernon, Wladimir Gaidarow, Maly Delschaft. 2476m FRN/GRM. *Mit Gift Jager* (GRM) prod/rel: Alga-Films, Societe Des Cineromans
  Roman d'un Jeune Homme Pauvre, Le 1935 d: Abel Gance. lps: Pierre Fresnay, Marie Bell, Marcelle Praince. 120M FRN. prod/rel: Productions Maurice Lehmann
  Romance of a Poor Young Man, The 1914. lps: Edward Cecil, Charles Hill Mailes, Marie Newton. 2r USA. prod/rel: Biograph Co.
  Romanzo Di un Giovane Povero, Il 1920 d: Amleto Palermi. lps: Pina Menichelli, Luigi Serventi, Gustavo Salvini. 2357m ITL. prod/rel: Rinascimento Film
  Romanzo Di un Giovane Povero, Il 1943 d: Guido Brignone. lps: Ermete Zacconi, Amedeo Nazzari, Caterina Boratto. 85M ITL. prod/rel: S.a.F.a.
  Romanzo Di un Giovane Povero, Il 1958 d: Marino Girolami, Luis MarquinA. lps: Giancarlo Sojo, Susana Canales, Maria Fiore. 90M ITL/SPN. *Estampas de Ayer* (SPN); *Historia de un Joven Pobre* prod/rel: Theseus Film (Roma), Ria Producciones (Madrid)
  Romanzo Di un Giovane Povero, Il 1974 d: Cesare Canevari. lps: Raffaele Curi, Maria Pia Giancaro, Alessandro Quasimodo. 95M ITL. prod/rel: Andromeda Film
  Ultimo Dei Frontignac, L' 1911 d: Mario Caserini?. lps: Alberto A. Capozzi, Mary Cleo Tarlarini, Luigi Maggi. 1254m ITL. *Il Romanzo Di un Giovane Povero*; *The Last of the Frontignacs* (UKN) prod/rel: S.A. Ambrosio
Un Roman Parisien, Paris 1882, Play
  Parisian Romance, A 1916 d: Frederick A. Thompson. lps: H. Cooper Cliffe, Dorothy Green, Marguerite Skirvin. 5r USA. prod/rel: Fox Film Corp., William Fox©
Le Sphinx, 1874, Novel
  Sfinge, La 1920 d: Roberto Leone Roberti. lps: Francesca Bertini, Mario Parpagnoli, Elena LundA. 1384m ITL. prod/rel: Bertini

FEUSTEL, GUNTER
Die Fliegende Windmuhle, Novel
  Fliegende Windmuhle, Die 1981 d: Gunter Ratz. ANM. 87M GRM. prod/rel: Defa-Studio Fur Trickfilme

FEVAL, PAUL
Les Aventures de Lagardere, Novel
   Aventures de Lagardere, Les 1967 d: Jean-Pierre
   Decourt. lps: Jean Piat, Raymond Gerome, Jacques
   Dufilho. 215M FRN/ITL. *Il Gobbo Di Parigi* (FRN); *Le
   Bossu* prod/rel: Opera, Orff
Le Bossu, 1875, Novel
   Bossu, Le 1914 d: Andre Heuze. lps: Henry Krauss,
   Yvette Andreyor, Georges Terof. 1200m FRN.
   Bossu, Le 1934 d: Rene Sti. lps: Robert Vidalin, Samson
   Fainsilber, Josseline Gael. 128M FRN. prod/rel: Films
   Albatros
   Bossu, Le 1944 d: Jean Delannoy. lps: Pierre Blanchar,
   Paul Bernard, Yvonne Gaudeau. 110M FRN. prod/rel:
   Jason-Regina
   Bossu, Le 1959 d: Andre Hunebelle. lps: Jean Marais,
   Sabina Sesselmann, Bourvil. 115M FRN/ITL. prod/rel:
   P.A.C., Globe International
   Bossu, Le 1997 d: Philippe de BrocA. lps: Daniel
   Auteuil, Fabrice Luchini, Vincent Perez. 128M
   FRN/ITL/GRM. *On Guard!* (UKN) prod/rel: Aliceleo©,
   Tfi Films Prod. (France)©
   Bossu, Ou le Petit Parisien, Le 1925 d: Jean Kemm.
   lps: Gaston Jacquet, Claude France, Marcel Vibert.
   SRL. 7EP FRN. *Le Bossu* prod/rel: Jacques Haik
Les Couteau d'Or, Novel
   Couteau d'Or, Les 1914 d: Jacques Volnys. 1010m
   FRN. prod/rel: Minerva
Les Habits Noirs, Novel
   Habits Noirs, Les 1914 d: Daniel Riche. lps: Henri
   Collen, Germaine Dermoz. 1735m FRN.

FEVAL, PAUL (FILS)
Le Calvaire de Mignon, Novel
   Calvaire de Mignon, Le 1916 d: Marcel Simon. lps:
   Jean Toulout, Georges Treville, Andree Pascal. 1606m
   FRN. prod/rel: Grands Films Populaires
Le Fils de Lagardere, Novel
   Figlio Di Lagardere, Il 1952 d: Fernando Cerchio. lps:
   Rossano Brazzi, Milly Vitale, Gabrielle Dorziat. 85M
   ITL/FRN. *Le Fils de Lagardere* (FRN) prod/rel:
   Venturini Prod. Cin.Ca
   Fils de Lagardere, Le 1913 d: Henri Andreani. lps:
   Louis Ravet, Maxime Lery, Berthe Bovy. 1500m FRN.
   prod/rel: Les Grands Films Populaires

FEYDEAU, GEORGES (1862–1921), FRN
Champignol Malgre Lui, Play
   Champignol Maigre Lui 1933 d: Fred Ellis. lps: Aime
   Simon-Girard, Janine Guise, Lulu Vattier. 96M FRN.
   prod/rel: Hesge
   Champignol Malgre Lui 1913. lps: Madeleine
   Aubrey, Semery, Fernand Rivers. 1050m FRN. prod/rel:
   L. Aubert
La Dame de Chez Maxim, 1898, Play
   Dame de Chez Maxim, La 1950 d: Marcel Aboulker.
   lps: Saturnin Fabre, Arlette Poirier, Marcelle Monthil.
   92M FRN. prod/rel: M.A.I.C., S.N.E.G.
   Dame de Chez Maxim's, La 1912 d: Emile Chautard.
   lps: Renee Sylvaire, Moret, Duquesne. 857m FRN.
   prod/rel: Acad
   Dame de Chez Maxim's, La 1923 d: Amleto Palermi.
   lps: Pina Menichelli, Marcel Levesque, Ugo Gracci.
   2049m ITL. prod/rel: Rinascimento Film
   Dame de Chez Maxim's, La 1932 d: Alexander
   KordA. lps: Florelle, Andre Lefaur, Charlotte Lyses.
   109M FRN. *La Dame de Chez Maxim* prod/rel:
   Productions Korda
   Dame de Chez Maxim's, La 1990 d: Jean-Paul
   Roussillon. lps: Annie Ducaux, Denise Gence, Jean Le
   Poulain. 170M FRN.
   Girl from Maxim's, The 1932 d: Alexander KordA.
   lps: Leslie Henson, Frances Day, George Grossmith.
   82M UKN. prod/rel: United Artists, London Films
Le Dindon, 1896, Play
   Dindon, Le 1913 d: Marcel Simon. lps: Germain, Lucy
   Jousset, Armand Lurville. 1050m FRN. prod/rel: le Film
   d'Art
   Dindon, Le 1951 d: Claude BarmA. lps: Jacques
   Charon, Nadine Alari, Robert Hirsch. 85M FRN.
   prod/rel: Armor-Silver
   Tacchino, Il 1923 d: Mario Bonnard. lps: Marcel
   Levesque, Lia Formia, Mario Bonnard. 2103m ITL.
   prod/rel: Bonnard
Dormez, Je le Veux, Play
   Dormez, Je le Veux 1916 d: Marcel Simon. lps: Boucot,
   Gorby, Madeleine Guitty. 710m FRN. prod/rel:
   Cinedrama
La Duchesse Des Folies-Bergere, Play
   Duchesse Des Folies-Bergere, La 1913 d: Emile
   Chautard. lps: Marcel Simon, Cueille, Alice de Tender.
   945m FRN. prod/rel: Eclair

Un Fil a la Patte, 1899, Play
   Fil a la Patte, Un 1914 d: Henri Pouctal, Marcel
   Simon. lps: Germain, Lucy Jousset, Elie Febvre. 1450m
   FRN. prod/rel: Film d'Art
   Fil a la Patte, Un 1924 d: Robert Saidreau. lps:
   Germain, Armand Bernard, Marcelle Yrven. 1610m
   FRN. prod/rel: Films Diamant
   Fil a la Patte, Un 1933 d: Karl Anton. lps: Robert
   Burnier, Andre Berley, Spinelly. 90M FRN. prod/rel:
   Films Fred Bacos
   Fil a la Patte, Un 1954 d: Guy Lefranc. lps: Suzy
   Delair, Gabrielle Dorziat, Noel-Noel. 86M FRN.
   prod/rel: Cinephonic, Cite Film
L' Hotel du Libre-Echange, Paris 1894, Play
   Aktenskapsbrottaren 1964 d: Hasse Ekman. 93M
   SWD. *The Marriage Wrestler*
   Hotel de Libre Echange, L' 1916 d: Marcel Simon.
   lps: Marcel Simon, Armand Lurville, Jane Faber. 1240m
   FRN. prod/rel: Cinedrama Paz
   Hotel du Libre Echange, L' 1934 d: Marc Allegret.
   lps: Fernandel, Mona Lys, Raymond Cordy. 106M FRN.
   prod/rel: Or-Films
   Hotel Paradiso 1966 d: Peter Glenville. lps: Alec
   Guinness, Gina Lollobrigida, Robert Morley. 99M
   UKN/USA/FRN. *Paradiso -Hotel du Libre-Exchange*
   (FRN) prod/rel: MGM Pictures, Trianon Productions
Leonie Est Est En Avance, Play
   Leonie Est En Avance 1935 d: Jean-Pierre Feydeau.
   lps: Marfa Dhervilly, Germaine Michel, Christiane
   Delyne. 1000m FRN.
   P'tit Vient Vite, Le 1972 d: Louis-Georges Carrier.
   lps: Yvon Deschamps, Denise Filiatrault, Janine Sutto.
   96M CND. prod/rel: Mojack Film Ltee., Cine-Art
Mais N'te Promene Donc Pas Toute Nue!, Play
   Mais N'te Promene Donc Pas Toute Nue! 1936 d:
   Leo Joannon. lps: Sinoel, Jean Tissier, Arletty. 20M
   FRN. prod/rel: Radio-Cinema
Monsieur Chasse, 1896, Play
   Monsieur Chasse 1946 d: Willy Rozier. lps: Frederic
   Duvalles, Noelle Norman, Marguerite Deval. 85M FRN.
   prod/rel: Sport Films
Occupe-Toi d'Amelie, 1911, Play
   Occupati d'Amelia 1925 d: Telemaco Ruggeri. lps:
   Pina Menichelli, Marcel Levesque, Elena LundA. 2174m
   ITL. prod/rel: Rinascimento Film
   Occupe-Toi d'Amelie 1912 d: Emile Chautard. lps:
   Marcel Simon, Geo Leclerc, Alice de Tender. 892m FRN.
   prod/rel: Acad
   Occupe-Toi d'Amelie 1932 d: Richard Weisbach,
   Marguerite Viel. lps: Renee Bartout, Jean Weber,
   Raymond Dandy. 107M FRN. prod/rel: As Film
   Occupe-Toi d'Amelie 1949 d: Claude Autant-LarA.
   lps: Danielle Darrieux, Jean Desailly, Roland Armontel.
   92M FRN/ITL. *Occupati d'Amelia* (ITL); *Keep an Eye on
   Amelia* (UKN); *Oh Amelia* (USA); *Look After Amelia*
   prod/rel: Lux Films
On Purge Bebe, 1910, Play
   On Purge Bebe 1908-15. 550m FRN. prod/rel: le Film
   d'Art
   On Purge Bebe 1931 d: Jean Renoir. lps: Michel
   Simon, Marguerite Pierry, Jacques Louvigny. 62M
   FRN. prod/rel: Etablissements Braunberger-Richebe
La Puce a l'Oreille, Paris 1907, Play
   Flea in Her Ear, A 1968 d: Jacques Charon. lps: Rex
   Harrison, Rosemary Harris, Louis Jourdan. 95M
   USA/FRN. *La Puce a l'Oreille* (FRN) prod/rel: 20th
   Century-Fox Film Corporation
   Puce a l'Oreille, La 1914 d: Marcel Simon. lps:
   Germain, Armand Lurville, Lucy Jousset. 1200m FRN.
   prod/rel: le Film d'Art
FEYDEAU, J. P.
Un Cas Singulier, Play
   Cas Sur Mille, Un 1948 d: Jean-Pierre Feydeau. lps:
   Noelle Norman, Daniel Clerice, Tony Laurent. 22M
   FRN. prod/rel: Les Films Tellus
FEYNMAN, RICHARD
Surely You're Joking Mr. Feynman?, Autobiography
   Infinity 1996 d: Matthew Broderick. lps: Matthew
   Broderick, Patricia Arquette, Peter Riegert. 119M USA.
   prod/rel: First Look Pictures
FIASTRI, IAIA
Amori Miei, Musical Play
   Amori Miei 1978 d: Steno. lps: Monica Vitti, Enrico
   Maria Salerno, Johnny Dorelli. 102M ITL. *My Darlings*;
   My Loves prod/rel: Vides Cin.Ca, Cineriz

FICHELSCHER, W. F.
Das Tanzende Herz, Novel
   Tanzende Herz, Das 1953 d: Wolfgang Liebeneiner.
   lps: Gertrud Kuckelmann, Gunnar Moller, Paul
   Horbiger. 90M GRM. *The Dancing Heart* (USA)
   prod/rel: Capitol, Prisma
FIDLER, KATHLEEN
Flash the Sheepdog, Novel
   Flash the Sheepdog 1967 d: Laurence Henson. lps:
   Earl Younger, Ross Campbell, Alex Allan. 58M UKN.
   prod/rel: Children's Film Foundation, International
   Film Associates
FIECHTER, JEAN-JACQUES
Tire a Part, Novel
   Tire a Part 1996 d: Bernard Rapp. lps: Terence Stamp,
   Daniel Mesguich, Maria de Medeiros. 84M FRN.
   Limited Edition prod/rel: S.F.P. Cinema, Lili Prods.
FIELD, EDWARD SALISBURY
Twin Beds, New York 1914, Play
   Life of the Party, The 1934 d: Ralph Dawson. lps:
   Jerry Verno, Betty Astell, Eric Fawcett. 53M UKN.
   prod/rel: Warner Bros., First National
   Twin Beds 1920 d: Lloyd Ingraham. lps: Carter de
   Haven, Flora Parker de Haven, Helen Raymond. 6r
   USA. prod/rel: Carter de Haven Productions©, First
   National Exhibitors Circuit, Inc.
   Twin Beds 1929 d: Alfred Santell. lps: Jack Mulhall,
   Patsy Ruth Miller, Edythe Chapman. 7266f USA.
   prod/rel: First National Pictures
   Twin Beds 1942 d: Tim Whelan. lps: Joan Bennett,
   George Brent, Mischa Auer. 85M USA. prod/rel: United
   Artists
Wedding Bells, Play
   Wedding Bells 1921 d: Chet Withey. lps: Constance
   Talmadge, Harrison Ford, Emily Chichester. 6000f
   USA. prod/rel: Constance Talmadge Productions,
   Associated First National Pictures
Zander the Great, New York 1923, Play
   Zander the Great 1925 d: George W. Hill. lps: Marion
   Davies, Holbrook Blinn, Harrison Ford. 6844f USA.
   prod/rel: Cosmopolitan Pictures, Metro-Goldwyn
   Distributing Corp.
FIELD, EUGENE
The Dream Ship, Poem
   Dream Ship, The 1914 d: Harry Pollard. lps:
   Margarita Fischer, Harry Pollard, Joseph Harris. SHT
   USA. prod/rel: Beauty
FIELD, JULIAN
Tempermental Lady, 1936, Short Story
   Sitting on the Moon 1936 d: Ralph Staub. lps: Roger
   Pryor, Grace Bradley, Pert Kelton. 66M USA. prod/rel:
   Republic Pictures Corp.©
FIELD, MEDORA
Blood on Her Shoe, 1942, Novel
   Girl Who Dared, The 1944 d: Howard Bretherton. lps:
   Adrian Booth, Peter Cookson, Kirk Alyn. 54M USA.
   prod/rel: Republic
Who Killed Aunt Aggie?, New York 1939, Novel
   Who Killed Aunt Maggie? 1940 d: Arthur Lubin. lps:
   John Hubbard, Wendy Barrie, Edgar Kennedy. 70M
   USA. *Belle of Atlanta* prod/rel: Republic Pictures Corp.©
FIELD, RACHEL
All This and Heaven Too, New York 1938, Novel
   All This, and Heaven Too 1940 d: Anatole Litvak. lps:
   Bette Davis, Charles Boyer, Jeffrey Lynn. 143M USA.
   prod/rel: Warner Bros. Pictures
And Now Tomorrow, Novel
   And Now Tomorrow 1944 d: Irving Pichel. lps: Alan
   Ladd, Loretta Young, Susan Hayward. 84M USA.
   prod/rel: Paramount
The Londonderry Air, Play
   Londonderry Air, The 1938 d: Alex Bryce. lps: Sara
   Allgood, Liam Gaffney, Phyllis Ryan. 47M UKN.
   prod/rel: Fox British
Time Out of Mind, Novel
   Time Out of Mind 1947 d: Robert Siodmak. lps: Robert
   Hutton, Ella Raines, Phyllis Calvert. 88M USA.
   prod/rel: Universal-International
FIELDING, HENRY (1707–1754), UKN
Joseph Andrews, 1742, Novel
   Joseph Andrews 1977 d: Tony Richardson. lps:
   Ann-Margret, Peter Firth, Michael Hordern. 104M
   UKN. prod/rel: United Artists, Woodfall
Tom Jones a Foundling, 1749, Novel
   Bawdy Adventures of Tom Jones, The 1975 d: Cliff
   Owen. lps: Trevor Howard, Nicky Henson,
   Terry-Thomas. 93M UKN. *The Adventures of Tom
   Jones; The Bawdy Tales of Tom Jones* prod/rel:
   Universal, Robert Sadoff

Tom Jones 1917 d: Edwin J. Collins. lps: Langhorne Burton, Miss June, Sybil Arundale. 6700f UKN. prod/rel: Ideal

Tom Jones 1963 d: Tony Richardson. lps: Albert Finney, Susannah York, Hugh Griffith. 129M UKN. prod/rel: Woodfall Film Productions, United Artists

FIELDING, HOWARD
The Inspirations of Harry Larrabee, Short Story
Inspirations of Harry Larrabee, The 1917 d: Bertram Bracken. lps: Margaret Landis, Clifford Gray, Winnifred Greenwood. 4r USA. prod/rel: Balboa Amusement Producing Co., Fortune Photoplay

Mentioned in Confidence, Short Story
Mentioned in Confidence 1917 d: Edgar Jones. lps: R. Henry Grey, Frank Brownlee, Melvin Mayo. 4r USA. prod/rel: Balboa Amusement Producing Co., Fortune Photoplay

FIELDING, JOY
See Jane Run, Book
See Jane Run 1994 d: John Patterson. lps: Joanna Kerns, John Shea, Katy Boyer. TVM. 90M USA. prod/rel: Hearst Entertainment

FIELDS, DOROTHY
Let's Face It, Musical Play
Let's Face It 1943 d: Sidney Lanfield. lps: Bob Hope, Betty Hutton, Zasu Pitts. 76M USA. prod/rel: Paramount

Mexican Hayride, Musical Play
Mexican Hayride 1948 d: Charles T. Barton. lps: Bud Abbott, Lou Costello, Virginia Grey. 77M USA. prod/rel: Universal-International

Something for the Boys, New York 1943, Musical Play
Something for the Boys 1944 d: Lewis Seiler. lps: Carmen Miranda, Michael O'Shea, Vivian Blaine. 87M USA. prod/rel: 20th Century Fox

Sweet Charity, New York 1966, Play
Sweet Charity 1969 d: Bob Fosse. lps: Shirley MacLaine, Sammy Davis Jr., Ricardo Montalban. 152M USA. prod/rel: Universal Pictures

Up in Central Park, New York 1945, Musical Play
Up in Central Park 1948 d: William A. Seiter. lps: Deanna Durbin, Dick Haymes, Vincent Price. 88M USA. prod/rel: Universal-International

FIELDS, HERBERT
Du Barry Was a Lady, New York 1939, Musical Play
Du Barry Was a Lady 1943 d: Roy Del Ruth. lps: Red Skelton, Lucille Ball, Gene Kelly. 101M USA. prod/rel: MGM

Fifty Million Frenchmen, New York 1929, Play
Fifty Million Frenchmen 1931 d: Lloyd Bacon. lps: Ole Olsen, Chic Johnson, Claudia Dell. 68M USA. *50 Million Frenchmen* prod/rel: Warner Bros. Pictures©

Let's Face It, Musical Play
Let's Face It 1943 d: Sidney Lanfield. lps: Bob Hope, Betty Hutton, Zasu Pitts. 76M USA. prod/rel: Paramount

The Melody Man, New York 1924, Musical Play
Melody Man, The 1930 d: R. William Neill. lps: William Collier Jr., Alice Day, John St. Polis. 68M USA. prod/rel: Columbia Pictures

Mexican Hayride, Musical Play
Mexican Hayride 1948 d: Charles T. Barton. lps: Bud Abbott, Lou Costello, Virginia Grey. 77M USA. prod/rel: Universal-International

Panama Hattie, New York 1940, Musical Play
Panama Hattie 1942 d: Norman Z. McLeod, Vincente Minnelli (Uncredited). lps: Ann Sothern, Red Skelton, Rags Ragland. 79M USA. prod/rel: MGM

Present Arms, New York 1928, Musical Play
Leathernecking 1930 d: Eddie Cline. lps: Irene Dunne, Ken Murray, Louise FazendA. 80M USA. *Present Arms* (UKN) prod/rel: RKO Productions

Something for the Boys, New York 1943, Musical Play
Something for the Boys 1944 d: Lewis Seiler. lps: Carmen Miranda, Michael O'Shea, Vivian Blaine. 87M USA. prod/rel: 20th Century Fox

Up in Central Park, New York 1945, Musical Play
Up in Central Park 1948 d: William A. Seiter. lps: Deanna Durbin, Dick Haymes, Vincent Price. 88M USA. prod/rel: Universal-International

FIELDS, JOSEPH
Anniversary Waltz, New York 1954, Play
Happy Anniversary 1959 d: David Miller. lps: David Niven, Mitzi Gaynor, Carl Reiner. 81M USA. prod/rel: United Artists, Fields

The Doughgirls, New York 1942, Play
Doughgirls, The 1944 d: James V. Kern. lps: Ann Sheridan, Alexis Smith, Jack Carson. 102M USA. prod/rel: Warner Bros.

Junior Miss, New York 1941, Play
Junior Miss 1945 d: George Seaton. lps: Peggy Ann Garner, Allyn Joslyn, Stephen Dunne. 94M USA. prod/rel: 20th Century-Fox

FIENBURGH, WILFRED
No Love for Johnnie, London 1959, Novel
No Love for Johnnie 1961 d: Ralph Thomas. lps: Peter Finch, Stanley Holloway, Mary Peach. 111M UKN. prod/rel: Five Star Films, Rank Film Distributors

FIERSTEIN, HARVEY
Torch Song Trilogy, Play
Torch Song Trilogy 1988 d: Paul Bogart. lps: Anne Bancroft, Matthew Broderick, Harvey Fierstein. 117M USA. prod/rel: New Line

FIGDOR, KARL
Das Madchen Aus Frisco, Short Story
Madchen Aus Frisco, Das 1927 d: Wolfgang Neff. lps: Erna Morena, Helga Thomas, Rudolf Klein-Rogge. 2086m GRM. prod/rel: Orplid-Film

FIGUEIREDO, GUILHERME
Historia Para Se Ouvir de Noite, 1964, Novel
Fome de Amor 1968 d: Nelson Pereira Dos Santos. lps: Leila Diniz, Arduino Colasanti, Irene StefaniA. 83M BRZ. *Hungry for Love; Hunger for Love; Fome de Amor. Voce Nunca Tomou Bauho de Sol Inteiramente Nua?; Soif d'Amour* prod/rel: P.C. Herbert Richers, Paulo Porto

FIKER, EDUARD
Paklic, Novel
Paklic 1944 d: Miroslav Cikan. lps: Oldrich Novy, Jirina Steimarova, Jaroslav Marvan. 2463m CZC. *The Skeleton Key* prod/rel: Nationalfilm

FILHO, ODYLO COSTA
A Faca E O Rio, Novel
Joao En Het Mes 1972 d: George Sluizer. lps: Jofre Soares, Ana Maria Miranda, Douglas Santos. 98M NTH/BRZ/BLG. *A Faca E O Rio* (BRZ); *Joao and the Knife; Joao the Knife and the River* prod/rel: Sluizer Films

FINCH, CHRISTOPHER
Rainbow, Book
Rainbow 1978 d: Jackie Cooper. lps: Andrea McArdle, Piper Laurie, Don Murray. TVM. 100M USA. prod/rel: Ten-Four Productions

FINCH, MATTHEW
Dentist in the Chair, London 1955, Novel
Dentist in the Chair 1960 d: Don Chaffey. lps: Bob Monkhouse, Peggy Cummins, Kenneth Connor. 88M UKN. prod/rel: Renown, Briand

FINDLEY, FERGUSON
Waterfront, Novel
Mob, The 1951 d: Robert Parrish. lps: Broderick Crawford, Betty Buehler, Richard Kiley. 87M USA. *Remember That Face* (UKN) prod/rel: Columbia

FINDLEY, TIMOTHY (1930–, CND
The Wars, Novel
Wars, The 1983 d: Robin Philips. lps: Martha Henry, Jackie Burroughs, Brent Carver. 118M CND/GRM. prod/rel: Nielsen-Ferns Intl. Ltd (Toronto), National Film Board (Montreal)

FINEMAN, IRVING
Lovers Must Learn, New York 1932, Novel
Rome Adventure 1962 d: Delmer Daves. lps: Suzanne Pleshette, Troy Donahue, Angie Dickinson. 119M USA. *Lovers Must Learn* (UKN) prod/rel: Warner Bros. Pictures

FINKEL, ABEM
It Might Have Happened, Story
Deceiver, The 1931 d: Louis King. lps: Lloyd Hughes, Dorothy Sebastian, Ian Keith. 68M USA. *Unwanted* prod/rel: Columbia Pictures Corp.

FINKELHOFFE, FRED F.
Brother Rat, New York 1936, Play
About Face 1952 d: Roy Del Ruth. lps: Gordon MacRae, Eddie Bracken, Dick Wesson. 94M USA. prod/rel: Warner Bros.

Brother Rat 1938 d: William Keighley. lps: Priscilla Lane, Wayne Morris, Johnnie "Scat" Davis. 90M USA. prod/rel: Warner Bros. Pictures, Inc.

FINN, JONATHAN
Chalked Out, 1937, Play
You Can't Get Away With Murder 1939 d: Lewis Seiler. lps: Humphrey Bogart, Billy Halop, Gale Page. 78M USA. *Crime Is a Racket; Chalked Out* prod/rel: Warner Bros. Pictures©, First National Picture

FINNEY, CHARLES G.
The Circus of Dr. Lao, New York 1961, Novel
Seven Faces of Dr. Lao, The 1964 d: George Pal. lps: Tony Randall, Barbara Eden, Arthur O'Connell. 100M USA. *7 Faces of Dr. Lao* prod/rel: Galaxy Productions, Scarus, Inc.

FINNEY, JACK (1911–1995), USA, Finney, Walter Braden
Short Story
Five Against the House 1955 d: Phil Karlson. lps: Guy Madison, Kim Novak, Brian Keith. 84M USA. prod/rel: Columbia, Doyle Prods.

Assault on a Queen, New York 1959, Novel
Assault on a Queen 1966 d: Jack Donohue. lps: Frank Sinatra, Anthony Franciosa, Virna Lisi. 106M USA. prod/rel: Seven Arts Productions, Sinatra Enterprises

The Body Snatchers, 1954, Novel
Body Snatchers 1993 d: Abel FerrarA. lps: Terry Kinney, Meg Tilly, Gabrielle Anwar. 88M USA. prod/rel: Warner Bros.©

Invasion of the Body Snatchers 1956 d: Don Siegel. lps: Kevin McCarthy, Dana Wynter, Larry Gates. 80M USA. *They Came from Another World; Sleep No More* prod/rel: Allied Artists

Invasion of the Body Snatchers 1978 d: Philip Kaufman. lps: Donald Sutherland, Brooke Adams, Leonard Limoy. 116M USA. prod/rel: United Artists

Good Neighbor Sam, New York 1963, Novel
Good Neighbor Sam 1964 d: David Swift. lps: Jack Lemmon, Romy Schneider, Dorothy Provine. 130M USA. prod/rel: David Swift Productions

House of Numbers, 1956, Novel
House of Numbers 1957 d: Russell Rouse. lps: Jack Palance, Barbara Lang, Harold J. Stone. 92M USA. prod/rel: MGM

Marion's Wall, Novel
Maxie 1985 d: Paul Aaron. lps: Glenn Close, Mandy Patinkin, Ruth Gordon. 98M USA. *I'll Meet You in Heaven; Free Spirit* prod/rel: Orion, Aurora

FIORI, GIUSEPPE
La Societa Del Malessere, Book
Barbagia 1969 d: Carlo Lizzani. lps: Mario Girotti, Don Backy, Frank Wolff. 101M ITL. *Bandits in Sardinia; La Societa Del Malessere; Barbagia -la Societa Del Malessere* prod/rel: Dino de Laurentiis Cin.Ca, Paramount

FIRNER, IRMA
Kinder Der Liebe, Play
Kinder Der Liebe 1949 d: Walter Firner. lps: Kathe Dorsch, Hans Holt, Gustav Waldau. 93M AUS. *Das Kuckucksei* prod/rel: Forst

FIRNER, WALTER
Kinder Der Liebe, Play
Kinder Der Liebe 1949 d: Walter Firner. lps: Kathe Dorsch, Hans Holt, Gustav Waldau. 93M AUS. *Das Kuckucksei* prod/rel: Forst

FIRTH, TIM
Neville's Island, Play
Neville's Island 1998 d: Terry Johnson. lps: Timothy Spall, Jeff Rawle, David Bamber. TVM. 90M UKN. prod/rel: Primetime Plc©

FISCHER, ARTHUR
Greven Av Gamla Sta'n, Play
Munkbrogreven 1935 d: Edvin Adolphson, Sigurd Wallen. lps: Ingrid Bergman, Waldemar Dahlquist, Sigurd Wallen. 79M SWD. *Count from Munkbro; The Count of the Old Town* prod/rel: Svensk Filmindustri, Ab Fribergs Filmbyra

FISCHER, ERICA
Aimee & Jaguar, Book
Aimee & Jaguar 1999 d: Max Farberbock. lps: Maria Schrader, Juliane Kohler, Heike Makatsch. 127M GRM. prod/rel: Senator Film, Hanno Huth

FISCHER, KARL
Der Funf-Minuten-Vater, Play
Funf-Minuten-Vater, Der 1951 d: J. A. Hubler-KahlA. lps: Karl Fischer, Fritz Eckhardt, Dagny Servaes. 86M AUS. *Die Wirtin Zum Roten Ochsen* prod/rel: Czerny

FISCHER, KURT JOACHIM
Heiratsschwindlerin, Book
Hochstaplerin Der Liebe 1954 d: Hans H. Konig. lps: Hilde Krahl, Hans Nielsen, Viktor Staal. 85M AUS. prod/rel: Helios

FISCHER, LECK
Barnet, 1936, Play
Barnet 1940 d: Benjamin Christensen. lps: Mogens Wieth, Grethe Paaske, Beatrice Bonnesen. 87M DNM. *The Child*

Moderhjertet, 1943, Play
Kris 1946 d: Ingmar Bergman. lps: Dagny Lind, Stig Olin, Ernst Eklund. 93M SWD. *Crisis*

FISCHER, MARIE LOUISE
Frauenstation, Novel
Frauenstation 1975 d: Rolf Thiele. lps: Horst Buchholz, Stephen Boyd, Lillian Muller. 85M GRM. *Women in Hospital* (USA); *Gynecology Section* prod/rel: Cinema 77

Peter Und Sabine, Novel
  Peter Und Sabine 1968 d: August Rieger. lps: Hans-Dieter Schwarze, Maria Sebaldt, Ingeborg Schoner. 96M GRM. *Peter and Sabine; Hot Blood* prod/rel: Lisa, Gloria

FISCHER, PARKER
Stripped for a Million, Short Story
  Stripped for a Million 1919 d: M. de La Parelle. lps: Crane Wilbur, Anita King, J. H. Keller. 4916f USA. prod/rel: Victor Kremer Film Features, State Rights

FISCHER, SIEGFRIED
Greven Av Gamla Sta'n, Play
  Munkbrogreven 1935 d: Edvin Adolphson, Sigurd Wallen. lps: Ingrid Bergman, Waldemar Dahlquist, Sigurd Wallen. 79M SWD. *Count from Munkbro; The Count of the Old Town* prod/rel: Svensk Filmindustri, Ab Fribergs Filmbyra

FISH, ROBERT L. (1912–, USA, Fish, Robert Lloyd, Pike, Robert L.
The Assassination Bureau Ltd, 1963, Novel
  Assassination Bureau, The 1969 d: Basil Dearden. lps: Oliver Reed, Diana Rigg, Telly Savalas. 110M UKN. prod/rel: Heathfield Films, Paramount
Mute Witness, New York 1963, Novel
  Bullitt 1968 d: Peter Yates. lps: Steve McQueen, Jacqueline Bisset, Robert Vaughn. 114M USA. prod/rel: Warner Bros., Seven Arts
Twist of Fate, 1978, Novel
  Twist of Fate 1989 d: Ian Sharp. lps: Ben Cross, Veronica Hamel, Bruce Greenwood. TVM. 200M USA.

FISHER, BOB
The Impossible Years, New York 1965, Play
  Impossible Years, The 1968 d: Michael Gordon. lps: David Niven, Lola Albright, Chad Everett. 99M USA. prod/rel: Marten Productions

FISHER, CARRIE (1956–, USA
Postcards from the Edge, Novel
  Postcards from the Edge 1990 d: Mike Nichols. lps: Meryl Streep, Shirley MacLaine, Dennis Quaid. 101M USA.

FISHER, CLAY
Santa Fe Passage, Short Story
  Santa Fe Passage 1955 d: William Witney. lps: John Payne, Faith Domergue, Rod Cameron. 90M USA. prod/rel: Republic
The Tall Men, 1954, Novel
  Tall Men, The 1955 d: Raoul Walsh. lps: Clark Gable, Robert Ryan, Jane Russell. 122M USA. prod/rel: 20th Century-Fox
Yellowstone Kelly, 1957, Novel
  Yellowstone Kelly 1959 d: Gordon Douglas. lps: Clint Walker, Edd Byrnes, John Russell. 91M USA. prod/rel: Warner Bros.

FISHER, DAVID
The Pack, Novel
  Pack, The 1977 d: Robert Clouse. lps: Joe Don Baker, Hope Alexander-Willis, Richard B. Shull. 99M USA. *Long Hard Night* (UKN); *Killers Who Wore Collars; The Long Dark Night; We've Got a Bone to Pick With You* prod/rel: Fred Weintraub, Paul Heller

FISHER, HARRY CONWAY
The Green Gullabaloo, Short Story
  Adventure Shop, The 1918 d: Kenneth Webb. lps: Corinne Griffith, Walter McGrail, Warren Chandler. 5r USA. prod/rel: Vitagraph Co. of America©, Blue Ribbon Feature

FISHER, IRVING
Prohibition Still at Its Worst, 1928, Novel
  Deliverance 1928 d: Ben K. Blake. 6r USA. prod/rel: Stanley Advertising Co.
Proibition at Its Worst, 1926, Novel
  Deliverance 1928 d: Ben K. Blake. 6r USA. prod/rel: Stanley Advertising Co.

FISHER, MICHAEL
Bethnal Green, Novel
  Place to Go, A 1963 d: Basil Dearden. lps: Rita Tushingham, Mike Sarne, Bernard Lee. 86M UKN. prod/rel: Bryanston, Excalibur

FISHER, STEVE
Story
  Noose for a Gunman 1960 d: Edward L. Cahn. lps: Jim Davis, Lyn Thomas, Ted de CorsiA. 69M USA. prod/rel: Premium, United Artists
The Fastest Gun, Short Story
  Quick Gun, The 1964 d: Sidney Salkow. lps: Audie Murphy, Merry Anders, James Best. 88M USA. *The Fast Gun; The Fastest Gun* prod/rel: Admiral Pictures
The Girl in the Red Bikini, Novel
  September Storm 1960 d: Byron Haskin. lps: Joanne Dru, Mark Stevens, Robert Strauss. 99M USA. prod/rel: Alco

I Wake Up Screaming, Novel
  I Wake Up Screaming 1941 d: H. Bruce Humberstone. lps: Betty Grable, Victor Mature, Carole Landis. 82M USA. *Hot Spot* (UKN) prod/rel: 20th Century Fox
  Vicki 1953 d: Harry Horner. lps: Jeanne Crain, Jean Peters, Elliott Reid. 85M USA. prod/rel: 20th Century-Fox
If You Break My Heart, 1937, Short Story
  Nurse from Brooklyn 1938 d: S. Sylvan Simon. lps: Sally Eilers, Paul Kelly, Larry Blake. 65M USA. prod/rel: Universal Pictures Co.©
Shore Leave, 1938, Short Story
  Navy Secrets 1939 d: Howard Bretherton. lps: Grant Withers, Fay Wray, Craig Reynolds. 60M USA. *Navy Girl* prod/rel: Monogram Pictures Corp.©
Susan, 1952, Play
  Susan Slept Here 1954 d: Frank Tashlin. lps: Dick Powell, Debbie Reynolds, Anne Francis. 98M USA. prod/rel: RKO Radio

FISHER, VARDIS (1895–, USA, Fisher, Alvero Vardis
Mountain Man, 1965, Novel
  Jeremiah Johnson 1972 d: Sydney Pollack. lps: Robert Redford, Will Geer, Stefan Gierasch. 108M USA. *The Saga of Jeremiah Johnson; The Crow Killer* prod/rel: Warner Communications, Joe Wizan

FISKE, HARRISON GREY
The District Attorney, New York 1895, Play
  District Attorney, The 1915 d: Barry O'Neil. lps: A. H. Van Buren, Dorothy Bernard, George Soule Spencer. 5r USA. prod/rel: Lubin Mfg. Co.©, V-L-S-E, Inc.

FITCH, CLYDE
The Bachelor, New York 1909, Play
  Virtuous Vamp, A 1919 d: David Kirkland. lps: Constance Talmadge, Conway Tearle, Harda Belle Daube. 5r USA. prod/rel: John Emerson-Anita Loos Production, Constance Talmadge Film Co.
The Battle of Bunker Hill, Play
  Battle of Bunker Hill, The 1911 d: J. Searle Dawley. lps: Mabel Trunnelle, Charles Ogle, Guy Coombs. 1000f USA. prod/rel: Edison
Beau Brummell, New York 1908, Play
  Beau Brummell 1924 d: Harry Beaumont. lps: John Barrymore, Mary Astor, Willard Louis. 9900f USA. *Beau Brummel* prod/rel: Warner Brothers Pictures
  Beau Brummell 1954 d: Curtis Bernhardt. lps: Stewart Granger, Elizabeth Taylor, Peter Ustinov. 111M UKN/USA. prod/rel: MGM British
Captain Jinks of the Horse Marines, New York 1916, Play
  Captain Jinks of the Horse Marines 1916 d: Fred E. Wright. lps: Richard C. Travers, Ann Murdock, John Junior. 5r USA. prod/rel: Essanay Film Mfg. Co.©, V-L-S-E, Inc.
The City, New York 1909, Play
  City, The 1916 d: Theodore Wharton. lps: Thurlow Bergen, William Riley Hatch, Richard Stewart. 5r USA. prod/rel: F. Ray Comstock Photoplay Co., World Film Corp.©
  City, The 1926 d: R. William Neill. lps: Nancy Nash, Robert Frazer, George Irving. 5508f USA. prod/rel: Fox Film Corp.
The Climbers, New York 1901, Play
  Climbers, The 1915 d: Barry O'Neil. lps: Gladys Hanson, George Soule Spencer, Jack Standing. 5r USA. prod/rel: Lubin Mfg. Co.©, V-L-S-E, Inc.
  Climbers, The 1919 d: Tom Terriss. lps: Corinne Griffith, Percy Marmont, Hugh Huntley. 4644f USA. prod/rel: Vitagraph Co. of America©
  Climbers, The 1927 d: Paul L. Stein. lps: Irene Rich, Clyde Cook, Forrest Stanley. 6631f USA. prod/rel: Warner Brothers Pictures
The Cowboy and the Lady, New York 1899, Play
  Cowboy and the Lady, The 1915 d: Edwin Carewe. lps: S. Miller Kent, Helen Case, Gertrude Short. 5r USA. prod/rel: Rolfe Photoplays, Inc., Metro Pictures Corp.©
  Cowboy and the Lady, The 1922 d: Charles Maigne. lps: Mary Miles Minter, Tom Moore, Viora Daniels. 4918f USA. prod/rel: Famous Players-Lasky, Paramount Pictures
The Frisky Mrs. Johnson, New York 1903, Play
  Frisky Mrs. Johnson, The 1920 d: Eddie Dillon. lps: Billie Burke, Ward Crane, Huntley Gordon. 5586f USA. prod/rel: Famous Players-Lasky Corp.©, Paramount Pictures
The Girl and the Judge, New York 1901, Play
  Girl and the Judge, The 1918 d: John B. O'Brien. lps: Olive Tell, David Powell, Charlotte Granville. 5r USA. prod/rel: Empire All Star Corp., Mutual Film Corp.

The Girl With the Green Eyes, New York 1902, Play
  Girl With the Green Eyes, The 1916 d: Herbert Blache. lps: Katherine Kaelred, Julian L'Estrange, Edith Lyle. 5r USA. *The Girl With Green Eyes* prod/rel: Popular Plays and Players, Inc.©, Pathe Exchange, Inc.
Girls, New York 1908, Play
  Girls 1919 d: Walter Edwards. lps: Marguerite Clark, Harrison Ford, Helene Chadwick. 4459f USA. prod/rel: Famous Players-Lasky Corp.©, Paramount Pictures
Her Great Match, New York 1905, Play
  Her Great Match 1915 d: Rene Plaissetty. lps: Gail Kane, Vernon Steele, Ned Burton. 5r USA. prod/rel: Popular Plays and Players, Metro Pictures Corp.©
Her Own Way, New York 1903, Play
  Her Own Way 1915 d: Herbert Blache. lps: Florence Reed, Robert Barrat, Fraunie Fraunholz. 5r USA. prod/rel: Popular Plays and Players, Inc., Metro Pictures Corp.©
Her Sister, New York 1907, Play
  Her Sister 1917 d: John B. O'Brien. lps: Olive Tell, David Powell, Eileen Dennes. 5r USA. prod/rel: Empire All Star Corp.©, Mutual Film Corp.
Lovers' Lane, Boston 1915, Play
  Lovers' Lane 1924 d: Phil Rosen, William Beaudine (Uncredited). lps: Robert Ellis, Gertrude Olmstead, Crauford Kent. 6400f USA. prod/rel: Warner Brothers Pictures
The Moth and the Flame, New York 1898, Play
  Moth and the Flame, The 1915 d: Sidney Olcott. lps: Stewart Baird, Adele Rey, Edwin Mordant. 4r USA. prod/rel: Famous Players Film Co., Paramount Pictures Corp.
Nathan Hale, New York 1899, Play
  Heart of a Hero, The 1916 d: Emile Chautard. lps: Robert Warwick, Gail Kane, Clara Whipple. 6r USA. *Nathan Hale* prod/rel: World Film Corp.©
The Straight Road, New York 1907, Play
  Straight Road, The 1914 d: Allan Dwan. lps: Gladys Hanson, William Russell, Iva Shepard. 4r USA. prod/rel: Famous Players Film Co., Paramount Pictures Corp.
The Stubbornness of Geraldine, New York 1902, Play
  Stubbornness of Geraldine, The 1915 d: Gaston Mervale. lps: Laura Nelson Hall, Vernon Steele, Marie Empress. 5r USA. prod/rel: Art Film Co., State Rights
The Truth, Cleveland 1906, Play
  Truth, The 1920 d: Lawrence C. Windom. lps: Madge Kennedy, Thomas J. Carrigan, Helen Greene. 5r USA. prod/rel: Goldwyn Pictures Corp.©, Goldwyn Distributing Corp.
The Way of the World, New York 1901, Play
  Way of the World, The 1916 d: Lloyd B. Carleton. lps: Hobart Bosworth, Dorothy Davenport, Emory Johnson. 5r USA. prod/rel: Universal Film Mfg. Co.©, Red Feather Photoplays
The Woman in the Case, New York 1905, Play
  Law and the Woman, The 1922 d: Penrhyn Stanlaws. lps: Betty Compson, William P. Carleton, Cleo Ridgely. 6461f USA. prod/rel: Famous Players-Lasky, Paramount Pictures
  Wiser Sex, The 1932 d: Berthold Viertel. lps: Claudette Colbert, Melvyn Douglas, Lilyan Tashman. 72M USA. *The Weaker Sex* prod/rel: Paramount Publix Corp.©
  Woman in the Case, The 1916 d: Hugh Ford. lps: Pauline Frederick, Alan Hale, Paul Gordon. 5r USA. prod/rel: Famous Players Film Co., Paramount Pictures Corp.

FITCH, GEORGE
At Good Old Siwash, Boston 1911, Novel
  Their Hero 1912. lps: George Lessey, Mr. O'More, Harry Beaumont. 1000f USA. prod/rel: Edison
  Those Were the Days! 1940 d: Theodore Reed. lps: William Holden, Bonita Granville, Ezra Stone. 76M USA. *Good Old School Days* (UKN); *Good Old Siwash; Those Were the Days (at Good Old Siwash); At Good Old Siwash* prod/rel: Paramount Pictures©

FITERE, JEAN-MARIE
Violette Noziere, Novel
  Violette Noziere 1978 d: Claude Chabrol. lps: Isabelle Huppert, Stephane Audran, Jean Carmet. 123M FRN/CND. *Violette* (USA) prod/rel: Filmel (Paris), Fr3 (Paris)

FITTS, MARGARET
Short Story
  King and Four Queens, The 1956 d: Raoul Walsh. lps: Clark Gable, Eleanor Parker, Jo Van Fleet. 86M USA. prod/rel: United Artists, Russ-Field-Gabco

FITZ, HANS
Der Frontgockel, Play
  Frontgockel, Der 1955 d: Ferdinand Dorfler. lps: Peter Pasetti, Beppo Brem, Harald Juhnke. 95M GRM. *Cock of the Walk* prod/rel: Dorfler, UFA

FITZBALL, EDWARD
Maritana, London 1845, Opera
Don Caesar de Bazan 1915 d: Robert G. VignolA. lps: W. Lawson Butt, Alice Hollister, Harry Millarde. 4r USA. prod/rel: Kalem Co., Broadway Favorite Special

FITZGERALD, EDITH
1930, Play
Illicit 1931 d: Archie Mayo. lps: Barbara Stanwyck, James Rennie, Ricardo Cortez. 81M USA. prod/rel: Warner Bros. Pictures©

Compromised, Play
Compromised 1931 d: John G. Adolfi. lps: Rose Hobart, Ben Lyon, Juliette Compton. 65M USA. *We Three* (UKN) prod/rel: First National Pictures, Inc.
Compromising Daphne 1930 d: Thomas Bentley. lps: Jean Colin, Charles Hickman, C. M. Hallard. 86M UKN. *Compromised!* (USA) prod/rel: British International Pictures, Wardour

Many a Slip, New York 1930, Play
Many a Slip 1931 d: Vin Moore. lps: Joan Bennett, Lew Ayres, Slim Summerville. 74M USA. *Babies Won't Tell* prod/rel: Universal Pictures Corp.©

FITZGERALD, EDWARD
The Rubaiyat of Omar Khayyam, London 1899, Book
Lover's Oath, A 1925 d: Ferdinand P. Earle. lps: Ramon Novarro, Kathleen Key, Edwin Stevens. 5896f USA. prod/rel: Ferdinand P. Earle, Astor Pictures

FITZGERALD, F. SCOTT (1896–1940), USA
Babylon Revisited, 1931, Short Story
Last Time I Saw Paris, The 1954 d: Richard Brooks. lps: Van Johnson, Elizabeth Taylor, Donna Reed. 116M USA. prod/rel: MGM

The Beautiful and Damned, New York 1922, Novel
Beautiful and Damned, The 1922 d: William A. Seiter. lps: Marie Prevost, Kenneth Harlan, Harry Myers. 7r USA. prod/rel: Warner Brothers Pictures

Bernice Bobs Her Hair, 1920, Short Story
Bernice Bobs Her Hair 1976 d: Joan Micklin Silver. lps: Shelley Duvall, Veronica Cartwright, Bud Cort. MTV. 45M USA. *Rites of Passage* prod/rel: Learning in Focus

The Great Gatsby, 1925, Novel
Great Gatsby, The 1926 d: Herbert Brenon. lps: Warner Baxter, Lois Wilson, Neil Hamilton. 7296f USA. prod/rel: Famous Players-Lasky, Paramount Pictures
Great Gatsby, The 1949 d: Elliott Nugent. lps: Alan Ladd, Betty Field, MacDonald Carey. 92M USA. prod/rel: Paramount
Great Gatsby, The 1974 d: Jack Clayton. lps: Robert Redford, Sam Waterston, Mia Farrow. 140M USA. prod/rel: Paramount

Grit, Short Story
Grit 1924 d: Frank Tuttle. lps: Glenn Hunter, Helenka Adamowska, Roland Young. 5800f USA. prod/rel: Film Guild, W. W. Hodkinson Corp.

Head and Shoulders, 1920, Short Story
Chorus Girl's Romance, The 1920 d: William C. Dowlan. lps: Viola Dana, Gareth Hughes, Phil Ainsworth. 5-6r USA. *Head and Shoulders* prod/rel: Metro Pictures Corp.©

The Last Tycoon, 1941, Novel
Last Tycoon, The 1976 d: Elia Kazan. lps: Robert de Niro, Tony Curtis, Robert Mitchum. 124M USA. prod/rel: Horizon

Myra Meets His Family, 1920, Short Story
Husband Hunter 1920 d: Howard M. Mitchell. lps: Eileen Percy, Emory Johnson, Jane Miller. 4800f USA. *Myra Meets His Family* prod/rel: Fox Film Corp., William Fox©

Offshore Pirate, 1920, Short Story
Off-Shore Pirate, The 1921 d: Dallas M. Fitzgerald. lps: Viola Dana, Jack Mulhall, Edward Jobson. 6r USA. prod/rel: Metro Pictures

Tender Is the Night, New York 1934, Novel
Tender Is the Night 1962 d: Henry King. lps: Jennifer Jones, Jason Robards Jr., Joan Fontaine. 146M USA. prod/rel: 20th Century-Fox Film Corporation
Tender Is the Night 1985 d: Robert Knights. lps: Peter Strauss, Mary Steenburgen, Edward Asner. MTV. 311M UKN/USA. prod/rel: BBC, Showtime

FITZGIBBON, CONSTANTINE (1919–, USA
When the Kissing Had to Stop, Novel
When the Kissing Had to Stop 1962 d: Bill Hitchcock. lps: Denholm Elliott, Peter Vaughan, Douglas Wilmer. MTV. 156M UKN. prod/rel: Rediffusion

FITZHUGH, LOUISE
Harriet the Spy
Harriet the Spy 1996 d: Bronwen Hughes. lps: Michelle Trachtenberg, Rosie O'Donnell, Vanessa Lee Chester. 101M USA. prod/rel: Paramount Pictures, Rastar Production

FITZPATRICK, SIR PERCY
Jock of the Bushveld, Book
Jock of the Bushveld 1988 d: Gray Hofmeyr. lps: Jonathan Rands, Gordon Mulholland, Jocelyn Broderick. 101M SAF. prod/rel: Toron

FITZSIMMONS, CORTLAND
70,000 Witnesses, New York 1931, Novel
70,000 Witnesses 1932 d: Ralph Murphy. lps: Phillips Holmes, Dorothy Jordan, Charles Ruggles. 72M USA. prod/rel: Charles R. Rogers Productions, Paramount Publix Corp.©

Death on the Diamond: a Baseball Mystery Story, New York 1934, Novel
Death on the Diamond 1934 d: Edward Sedgwick. lps: Robert Young, Madge Evans, Joseph Sawyer. 72M USA. prod/rel: Metro-Goldwyn-Mayer Corp.

The Whispering Window, New York 1936, Novel
Longest Night, The 1936 d: Errol Taggart. lps: Robert Young, Florence Rice, Ted Healy. 50M USA. prod/rel: Metro-Goldwyn-Mayer Corp.©

FITZ-SIMONS, FOSTER
Bright Leaf, 1948, Novel
Bright Leaf 1950 d: Michael Curtiz. lps: Gary Cooper, Lauren Bacall, Patricia Neal. 110M USA. prod/rel: Warner Bros.

FLAGG, FANNIE
Fried Green Tomatoes at the Whistle Stop Cafe, Novel
Fried Green Tomatoes 1991 d: Jon Avnet. lps: Kathy Bates, Jessica Tandy, Mary Stuart Masterson. 130M USA. *Fried Green Tomatoes at the Whistle Stop Cafe* (UKN) prod/rel: Fried Green Tomatoes Productions, Act III

FLAGG, JAMES MONTGOMERY
The Adventures of Kitty Cobb, New York 1912, Book
Adventures of Kitty Cobb, The 1914. lps: Marian Swayne, Howard Missimer, Jack Hopkins. 4r USA. prod/rel: Colonial, Warner's Features

FLANAGAN, RICHARD
The Sound of One Hand Clapping, Novel
Sound of One Hand Clapping, The 1998 d: Richard Flanagan. lps: Kerry Fox, Rosie Flanagan, Kristof Kaczmarek. 93M ASL. prod/rel: Australian Film Finance Corp., Artist Services

FLANIGAN, SARA
Wildflower, Book
Wildflower 1991 d: Diane Keaton. lps: Beau Bridges, Susan Blakely, William McNamarA. TVM. 100M USA. prod/rel: Freed-Laufer Prod., the Polone Company

FLANNAGAN, JIM
The Haunting of Sarah Hardy, Novel
Haunting of Sarah Hardy, The 1989 d: Jerry London. lps: Sela Ward, Michael Woods, Roscoe Born. TVM. 100M USA. prod/rel: Paramount

FLANNAGAN, ROY
The Whipping, New York 1930, Novel
Ready for Love 1934 d: Marion Gering. lps: Richard Arlen, Ida Lupino, Marjorie Rambeau. 65M USA. prod/rel: Paramount Productions©

FLATOW, CURT
Das Fenster Xum Flur, Play
Im Parterre Links 1963 d: Kurt Fruh. lps: Valerie Steinmann, Paul Buhlmann, Bella Neri. 94M SWT. *Rez-de-Chaussee Gauche; Das Fenster Zum Flur; Frau Weiser Und Ihre Kinder* prod/rel: Gloriafilm, Praesens-Film
Das Fenster Zum Flur, Play
Ihr Schonster Tag 1962 d: Paul Verhoeven. lps: Inge Meysel, Rudolf Platte, Sonja Ziemann. 93M GRM. *Her Finest Day* prod/rel: Melodie, Nora

FLAUBERT, GUSTAVE (1821–1880), FRN
Un Cuore Semplice, Novel
Cuore Semplice, Un 1976 d: Giorgio FerrarA. lps: Adriana Asti, Joe Dallesandro, Alida Valli. 105M ITL. *A Simple Heart* prod/rel: Cooperativa Nashira, Ital Noleggio Cin.Co

L' Education Sentimentale, 1869, Novel
Education Sentimentale, L' 1961 d: Alexandre Astruc. lps: Jean-Claude Brialy, Marie-Jose Nat, Dawn Addams. 92M FRN/ITL. *Lessons in Love* (UKN) prod/rel: Societe Francaise de Cinematographie, Globe Film International

Madame Bovary, Paris 1857, Novel
Wife Number Two 1917 d: William Nigh. lps: Valeska Suratt, Eric Mayne, Mathilde Brundage. 5r USA. prod/rel: Fox

Madame Bovary 1933 d: Jean Renoir. lps: Valentine Tessier, Max Dearly, Pierre Renoir. 101M FRN. prod/rel: Nouvelle Societe De Films
Madame Bovary 1937 d: Gerhard Lamprecht. lps: Pola Negri, Ferdinand Marian, Aribert Wascher. 94M GRM.
Madame Bovary 1947 d: Carlos Schlieper. lps: Alberto Bello. 85M ARG.
Madame Bovary 1949 d: Vincente Minnelli. lps: Jennifer Jones, Van Heflin, Louis Jourdan. 115M USA. prod/rel: MGM
Madame Bovary 1975 d: Rodney Bennett. lps: Francesca Annis, Tom Conti, Richard Beale. MTV. 200M UKN.
Madame Bovary 1979 d: Daniele d'AnzA. TVM. F ITL.
Madame Bovary 1991 d: Claude Chabrol. lps: Isabelle Huppert, Jean-Francois Balmer, Christophe Malavoy. 130M FRN. prod/rel: Mk2, Ced
Nackte Bovary, Die 1969 d: Hans Schott-Schobinger. lps: Edwige Fenech, Gerhard Riedmann, Peter Carsten. 96M GRM/ITL. *I Peccati Di Madame Bovary* (ITL); *The Sins of Madame Bovary; Play the Game Or Leave the Bed* (UKN); *Madame Bovary; Naked Lady Bovary* prod/rel: Tritone Filmindustria (Roma), Roger Fritz Filmproduktion (Berlin)
Unholy Love 1932 d: Albert Ray. lps: Joyce Compton, H. B. Warner, Lila Lee. 78M USA. *Deceit* (UKN); *Madame Bovary; Indecent* prod/rel: Allied Pictures Corp., Albert Ray Production

Salammbo, 1862, Novel
Salambo 1911 d: Arturo Ambrosio. lps: Gigetta Morano, Alberto A. Capozzi, Oreste Grandi. 384m ITL. *Salammbo* prod/rel: S.A. Ambrosio
Salambo 1914 d: Domenico Gaido. lps: Suzanne de Labroy, Mario Guaita-Ausonia, Cristina Ruspoli. 1830m ITL. prod/rel: Roma-Photodrama, Pasquali E C.
Salambo 1961 d: Sergio Grieco. lps: Jeanne Valerie, Jacques Sernas, Edmund Purdom. 105M ITL/FRN. *The Loves of Salammbo* (USA); *Salammbo* (FRN) prod/rel: Stella Film (Napoli), Fides (Paris)
Salammbo 1925 d: Pierre Marodon. lps: Jeanne de Balzac, Rolla Norman, Victor VinA. 3500m FRN. *Der Kampf Um Karthago; Salambo* prod/rel: Aubert, Sascha Films (Vienna)

La Tentation de Saint Antoine, 1849
Tentazioni Di Sant'antonio, Le 1911. lps: Alberto A. Capozzi, Fernanda Negri-Pouget, Mary Cleo Tarlarini. 307m ITL. *Conversion of St. Anthony* (USA) prod/rel: S.A. Ambrosio

FLAVIN, MARTIN (1883–1967), USA, Flavin, Martin Archer
Broken Dishes, New York 1929, Play
Calling All Husbands 1940 d: Noel Smith. lps: George Tobias, Lucille Fairbanks, Ernest Truex. 64M USA. *Broken Dishes* prod/rel: Warner Bros. Pictures, Inc.
Love Begins at 20 1936 d: Frank McDonald. lps: Hugh Herbert, Dorothy Vaughan, Patricia Ellis. 58M USA. *All One Night* (UKN) prod/rel: First National Productions Corp., Warner Bros. Pictures©
Too Young to Marry 1931 d: Mervyn Leroy. lps: O. P. Heggie, Emma Dunn, Loretta Young. 57M USA. *Broken Dishes* prod/rel: First National Pictures©

The Criminal Code, New York 1929, Play
Codigo Penal, El 1931 d: Phil Rosen. lps: Barry Norton, Maria Alba, Carlos Villarias. 10r USA.
Convicted 1950 d: Henry Levin. lps: Glenn Ford, Broderick Crawford, Millard Mitchell. 91M USA. prod/rel: Columbia
Criminal Code, The 1931 d: Howard Hawks. lps: Walter Huston, Phillips Holmes, Constance Cummings. 96M USA. prod/rel: Columbia Pictures Corp.
Criminel 1932 d: Jack Forrester. lps: Harry Baur, Jean Servais, Helene Perdiere. 110M FRN. *Le Code Criminel; Criminels* prod/rel: Forrester-Parant Productions
Penitentiary 1938 d: John Brahm. lps: Walter Connolly, John Howard, Jean Parker. 79M USA. prod/rel: Columbia Pictures Corp. of California©

Cross Roads, New York 1929, Play
Age of Consent, The 1932 d: Gregory La CavA. lps: Richard Cromwell, Dorothy Wilson, Eric Linden. 80M USA. *Are These Our Children?* (UKN); *Fraternity House; Crossroads* prod/rel: RKO Radio Pictures, Inc.

FLECKER, JAMES ELROY (1884–1915), UKN
Hassan, London 1922, Play
Lady of the Harem, The 1926 d: Raoul Walsh. lps: Ernest Torrence, William Collier Jr., Greta Nissen. 5717f USA. prod/rel: Famous Players-Lasky, Paramount Pictures

FLEETWOOD, HUGH
The Order of Death, Novel
  Order of Death 1983 d: Roberto FaenzA. lps: Harvey Keitel, John Lydon, Nicole GarciA. 113M ITL. *Cop Killers; Corrupt; Copkiller; L' Assassino Dei Poliziotti* prod/rel: New Line Cinema, Coop Jean Vigo

FLEISCHMAN, ALBERT SIDNEY
Blood Alley, Novel
  Blood Alley 1955 d: William A. Wellman. lps: John Wayne, Lauren Bacall, Paul Fix. 115M USA. prod/rel: Warner Bros., Batjac

By the Great Horn Spoon!, Boston 1963, Novel
  Adventures of Bullwhip Griffin, The 1967 d: James Neilson. lps: Roddy McDowall, Suzanne Pleshette, Karl Malden. 111M USA. prod/rel: Walt Disney Productions, Buena Vista

Counterspy Express, 1954, Novel
  Spy in the Sky 1958 d: W. Lee Wilder. lps: Steve Brodie, Sandra Francis, Andrea Domburg. 74M USA. prod/rel: Allied Artists

Yellowleg, New York 1960, Novel
  Deadly Companions, The 1961 d: Sam Peckinpah. lps: Maureen O'Hara, Brian Keith, Steve Cochran. 90M USA. *Trigger Happy* prod/rel: Carousel

FLEISSER, MARIELUISE (1901–1974), GRM
Pionere in Ingolstadt, 1970, Play
  Pioniere in Ingolstadt 1971 d: R. W. Fassbinder. lps: Hanna Schygulla, Harry Baer, Irm Hermann. 84M GRM. *Recruits in Ingolstadt; Pioneers in Ingolstadt*

FLEMING, BERRY
Colonel Effingham's Raid, Novel
  Colonel Effingham's Raid 1945 d: Irving Pichel. lps: Charles Coburn, Joan Bennett, William Eythe. 70M USA. *Man of the Hour* (UKN) prod/rel: 20th Century-Fox

FLEMING, BRANDON
The Eleventh Commandment, Play
  Eleventh Commandment, The 1924 d: George A. Cooper. lps: Fay Compton, Stewart Rome, Lillian Hall-Davis. 7600f UKN. prod/rel: Gaumont

The Message, Story
  Message, The 1930 d: Sewell Collins. lps: Arthur Wontner, Rosalinde Fuller, Frederick Leister. 28M UKN. prod/rel: Gaumont

The Pillory, Short Story
  Eleventh Commandment, The 1933 d: George Melford, W. Christy Cabanne. lps: Marian Marsh, Lee Moran, Alan Hale. 66M USA. prod/rel: Allied Pictures Corp.©

Tattenham Corner, 1934, Play
  All in 1936 d: Marcel Varnel. lps: Ralph Lynn, Gina Malo, Jack Barty. 71M UKN. prod/rel: Gainsborough, Gaumont-British

FLEMING, CARROLL
The Master Hand, New York 1907, Play
  Master Hand, The 1915 d: Harley Knoles. lps: Nat C. Goodwin, Carroll Fleming, Florence Malone. 5r USA. prod/rel: Premo Feature Film Corp., World Film Corp.©

Sis Hopkins, Buffalo, N.Y. 1899, Play
  Sis Hopkins 1919 d: Clarence Badger. lps: Mabel Normand, John Bowers, Sam de Grasse. 5r USA. prod/rel: Goldwyn Pictures Corp.©, Goldwyn Distributing Corp.
  Sis Hopkins 1941 d: Joseph Santley. lps: Judy Canova, Bob Crosby, Charles Butterworth. 98M USA. prod/rel: Republic

FLEMING, DAVID
Vengeance, Short Story
  Double X 1991 d: Shani S. Grewal. lps: Simon Ward, William Katt, Norman Wisdom. 97M UKN. *Double X: the Name of the Game* prod/rel: Feature Film Company, String of Pearls

FLEMING, IAN (1908–1964), UKN, Fleming, Ian Lancaster
Casino Royale, London 1953, Novel
  Casino Royale 1967 d: John Huston, Ken Hughes. lps: Peter Sellers, Ursula Andress, David Niven. 131M UKN. prod/rel: Columbia, Famous Artists

Chitty Chitty Bang Bang: the Magical Car, London 1964, Novel
  Chitty Chitty Bang Bang 1968 d: Ken Hughes. lps: Dick Van Dyke, Sally Ann Howes, Lionel Jeffries. 145M UKN. prod/rel: United Artists, Warfield-Dfi

Diamonds are Forever, Novel
  Diamonds are Forever 1971 d: Guy Hamilton. lps: Sean Connery, Jill St. John, Charles Gray. 120M UKN. prod/rel: United Artists, Eon

Dr. No, London 1958, Novel
  Dr. No 1962 d: Terence Young. lps: Sean Connery, Ursula Andress, Joseph Wiseman. 105M UKN. prod/rel: Eon Productions, United Artists

For Your Eyes Only, Short Story
  For Your Eyes Only 1981 d: John Glen. lps: Roger Moore, Carole Boquet, Topol. 127M UKN. prod/rel: United Artists, Eon

From Russia With Love, London 1957, Novel
  From Russia With Love 1963 d: Terence Young. lps: Sean Connery, Daniela Bianchi, Pedro Armendariz. 116M UKN. prod/rel: Eon Productions, Danjaq, S.a.

Goldfinger, London 1959, Novel
  Goldfinger 1964 d: Guy Hamilton. lps: Sean Connery, Honor Blackman, Gert Frobe. 109M UKN. prod/rel: Eon Productions, Danjaq, S.a.

Live and Let Die, Novel
  Live and Let Die 1973 d: Guy Hamilton. lps: Roger Moore, Yaphet Kotto, Jane Seymour. 121M UKN. prod/rel: United Artists, Eon

The Man With the Golden Gun, Novel
  Man With the Golden Gun, The 1974 d: Guy Hamilton. lps: Roger Moore, Christopher Lee, Gordon Everett. 125M UKN. prod/rel: United Artists, Eon

Moonraker, Novel
  Moonraker 1979 d: Lewis Gilbert. lps: Roger Moore, Lois Chiles, Michael Lonsdale. 126M UKN. prod/rel: United Artists, Eon

Octopussy, Short Story
  Octopussy 1983 d: John Glen. lps: Roger Moore, Maud Adams, Louis Jourdan. 131M UKN. prod/rel: Eon, Danjac

On Her Majesty's Secret Service, London 1963, Novel
  On Her Majesty's Secret Service 1969 d: Peter Hunt. lps: George Lazenby, Diana Rigg, Telly Savalas. 140M UKN. prod/rel: Eon Productions, Danjaq, S.a.

The Property of a Lady, Short Story
  Octopussy 1983 d: John Glen. lps: Roger Moore, Maud Adams, Louis Jourdan. 131M UKN. prod/rel: Eon, Danjac

Risico, Short Story
  For Your Eyes Only 1981 d: John Glen. lps: Roger Moore, Carole Boquet, Topol. 127M UKN. prod/rel: United Artists, Eon

The Spy Who Loved Me, Novel
  Spy Who Loved Me, The 1977 d: Lewis Gilbert. lps: Roger Moore, Barbara Bach, Curd Jurgens. 125M UKN. prod/rel: United Artists, Eon

Thunderball, London 1961, Novel
  Never Say Never Again 1983 d: Irvin Kershner. lps: Sean Connery, Edward Fox, Max von Sydow. 134M UKN. prod/rel: Warner Bros., Woodcote
  Thunderball 1965 d: Terence Young. lps: Sean Connery, Claudine Auger, Adolfo Celi. 132M UKN. prod/rel: Eon Productions, Danjaq, S.a.

You Only Live Twice, London 1964, Novel
  You Only Live Twice 1967 d: Lewis Gilbert. lps: Sean Connery, Akiko Wakabayashi, Tetsuro TambA. 117M UKN. prod/rel: Eon Productions, Danjaq, S.a.

FLEMING, JOAN (1908–), UKN
The Deeds of Dr. Deadcert, Novel
  Family Doctor 1958 d: Derek Twist. lps: Rick Jason, Marius Goring, Lisa Gastoni. 85M UKN. *Rx Murder* (USA) prod/rel: 20th Century-Fox, Templar

FLEMING, JOHN
The Velvet Fleece, Novel
  Larceny 1948 d: George Sherman. lps: John Payne, Joan Caulfield, Dan DuryeA. 89M USA. prod/rel: Universal

FLEMING-ROBERTS, G. T.
Blackmail With Feathers, Story
  Find the Blackmailer 1943 d: D. Ross Lederman. lps: Jerome Cowan, Faye Emerson, Gene Lockhart. 55M USA. prod/rel: Warner Bros.

FLENDER, HAROLD
Paris Blues, New York 1957, Novel
  Paris Blues 1961 d: Martin Ritt. lps: Paul Newman, Joanne Woodward, Sidney Poitier. 99M USA. prod/rel: Pennebaker, Inc., Diane Productions

FLETCHER, CURLY
The Strawberry Roan, Los Angeles 1931, Poem
  Strawberry Roan 1933 d: Alan James. lps: Ken Maynard, Ruth Hall, Harold Goodwin. 62M USA. *Flying Fury* (UKN); *Red Roan* prod/rel: Ken Maynard Productions, Universal Pictures Corp.©

FLETCHER, GEOFFREY
The London Nobody Knows, Book
  London Nobody Knows, The 1968 d: Norman Cohen. lps: James Mason. DOC. 48M UKN. prod/rel: Norcon, British Lion

FLETCHER, GUY
Mary Was Love, Novel
  Those Who Love 1929 d: Manning Haynes. lps: Blanche Adele, William Freshman, W. Lawson Butt. 87M UKN. *Mary Was Love* prod/rel: British International Pictures, First National-Pathe

FLETCHER, J. S.
The Marriage Lines, Novel
  Marriage Lines, The 1921 d: Wilfred Noy. lps: Barbara Hoffe, Lewis Dayton, Sam Livesey. 5880f UKN. prod/rel: Master Films, Butcher's Film Service

The Root of All Evil, Novel
  Root of All Evil, The 1947 d: Brock Williams. lps: Phyllis Calvert, Michael Rennie, John McCallum. 110M UKN. prod/rel: Gainsborough, General Film Distributors

The Town of Crooked Ways, Novel
  Town of Crooked Ways, The 1920 d: Bert Wynne. lps: Edward O'Neill, Poppy Wyndham, Denis Cowles. 5120f UKN. prod/rel: a.R.T. Films, Stoll

FLETCHER, LUCILLE
80 Dollars to Stamford, Novel
  Hit and Run 1982 d: Charles Braverman. lps: Paul Perri, Claudia Cron, Will Lee. 93M USA. *Revenge Squad; Taxi* prod/rel: Comworld

Blindfold, New York 1960, Novel
  Blindfold 1966 d: Philip Dunne. lps: Rock Hudson, Claudia Cardinale, Guy Stockwell. 102M USA. prod/rel: Universal

Night Watch, Play
  Night Watch 1973 d: Brian G. Hutton. lps: Elizabeth Taylor, Laurence Harvey, Billie Whitelaw. 98M UKN. prod/rel: Avco, Brut

Sorry Wrong Number, Radio Play
  Sorry, Wrong Number 1948 d: Anatole Litvak. lps: Barbara Stanwyck, Burt Lancaster, Ann Richards. 90M USA. prod/rel: Paramount
  Sorry, Wrong Number 1989 d: Tony Wharmby. lps: Loni Anderson, Carl Weintraub, Patrick MacNee. TVM. 100M USA.

FLEXNER, ANNE CRAWFORD
All Souls' Eve, New York 1920, Play
  All Souls' Eve 1921 d: Chester M. Franklin. lps: Mary Miles Minter, Jack Holt, Carmen Phillips. 5778f USA. prod/rel: Realart Pictures

The Blue Pearl, New York 1918, Play
  Blue Pearl, The 1920 d: George Irving. lps: Edith Hallor, Faire Binney, Lumsden Hare. 6r USA. prod/rel: L. Lawrence Weber Photo Dramas, Inc.©, Republic Distributing Corp.

FLINT, EVA KAY
Subway Express, New York 1929, Play
  Subway Express 1931 d: Fred Newmeyer. lps: Jack Holt, Aileen Pringle, Jason Robards. 68M USA. prod/rel: Columbia Pictures Corp.©

The Up and Up, New York 1930, Play
  Reckless Living 1931 d: Cyril Gardner. lps: Ricardo Cortez, Mae Clarke, Norman Foster. 68M USA. *Twenty Grand; The Up and Up* prod/rel: Universal Pictures Corp.©

FLOOD, CYNTHIA
The Californian Aunts, Short Story
  Martha, Ruth and Edie 1988 d: Norma Bailey, Daniele J. SuissA. lps: Jennifer Dale, Margaret Langrick, Andrea Martin. 91M CND. prod/rel: Sunrise

FLORA, FLETCHER
Hildegarde Withers Makes the Scene
  Very Missing Person, A 1972 d: Russ Mayberry. lps: Eve Arden, James Gregory, Julie Newmar. TVM. 73M USA. prod/rel: Universal

FLORIGNY, R.
L' Amour Qui Doute, Novel
  Vol, Le 1925 d: Robert Peguy. lps: Charles Vanel, Denise Legeay, Lucien Dalsace. 1850m FRN. prod/rel: Films Y. Barbaza

FLOURNOY, RICHARD F.
Here Comes the Groom, Provincetown, MA. 1933, Play
  Here Comes the Groom 1934 d: Edward Sedgwick. lps: Jack Haley, Mary Boland, Neil Hamilton. 66M USA. prod/rel: Paramount Productions©

Spook House, Story
  Beware, Spooks! 1939 d: Edward Sedgwick. lps: Joe E. Brown, Mary Carlisle, Clarence Kolb. 68M USA. prod/rel: Columbia Pictures Corp.

FLOWER, NEWMAN
Crucifixion, Novel
  Soul of Guilda Lois, The 1919 d: Frank Wilson. lps: Violet Hopson, Basil Gill, Cameron Carr. 5500f UKN. *A Soul's Crucifixion* prod/rel: Broadwest, Granger

Is God Dead?, Novel
  Answer, The 1916 d: Walter West. lps: Muriel Martin-Harvey, George Foley, Dora Barton. 4604f UKN. prod/rel: Broadwest, Browne

FLUHARTY, VERNON I.
Decision at Sundown, Book
Decision at Sundown 1957 d: Budd Boetticher. lps: Randolph Scott, Karen Steele, Noah Beery Jr. 77M USA. prod/rel: Columbia, Producers Actors Prod.

FLYGARE-CARLEN, EMILIE
Rosen Pa Tistelon, 1842, Novel
Rosen Pa Tistelon 1945 d: Ake Ohberg. 104M SWD. *Rose of Thistle Island*

FLYNN, ERROL
My Wicked, Wicked Ways, Autobiography
My Wicked, Wicked Ways. the Legend of Errol Flynn, The 1985 d: Don Taylor. lps: Duncan Regehr, Barbara Hershey, Lee Purcell. TVM. 100M USA. prod/rel: CBS Entertainment

FLYNN, J. M.
The Action Man, New York 1961, Novel
Soleil Des Voyous, Le 1967 d: Jean Delannoy. lps: Jean Gabin, Robert Stack, Margaret Lee. 100M FRN/ITL. *Il Piu Grande Colpo Del Secolo* (ITL); *Action Man* (USA); *Leather and Nylon* prod/rel: Fida Cinematografica, Films Copernic

FLYNN, THOMAS T.
Story
Man from Laramie, The 1955 d: Anthony Mann. lps: James Stewart, Arthur Kennedy, Donald Crisp. 104M USA. prod/rel: Columbia, William Goetz Prods.

FO, DARIO
Fanfani Rapito, Play
Fanfani Rapito 1975 d: Dimitris Makris. lps: Dimitris Makris. F ITL. *Fanfani Kidnapped*

FODOR, LADISLAUS (1898–, HNG, Fodor, Lazlo
Play
Night Before the Divorce, The 1942 d: Robert Siodmak. lps: Lynn Bari, Mary Beth Hughes, Joseph Allen Jr. 62M USA. prod/rel: 20th Century Fox

Arztliches Geheimnis, Play
Liebe Ohne Illusion 1955 d: Erich Engel. lps: Curd Jurgens, Heidemarie Hatheyer, Sonja Ziemann. 90M GRM. *Love Without Illusions* prod/rel: C.C.C., Prisma

Blondie White, Play
Footsteps in the Dark 1941 d: Lloyd Bacon. lps: Errol Flynn, Brenda Marshall, Ralph Bellamy. 96M USA. prod/rel: Warner Bros.

The Church Mouse, Play
Church Mouse, The 1934 d: Monty Banks. lps: Laura La Plante, Ian Hunter, Edward Chapman. 76M UKN. prod/rel: Warner Bros., First National

Ekszerrablas a Vaci-Uccaban, 1931, Play
Jewel Robbery 1932 d: William Dieterle. lps: William Powell, Kay Francis, Hardie Albright. 70M USA. prod/rel: Warner Bros. Pictures©
Peterville Diamond, The 1942 d: Walter Forde. lps: Anne Crawford, Donald Stewart, Renee Houston. 85M UKN. prod/rel: Warner Bros., First National

Eine Frau Lugt, 1934, Play
Thunder in the Night 1935 d: George Archainbaud. lps: Edmund Lowe, Karen Morley, Polly Ann Young. 69M USA. *A Woman Lies* prod/rel: Fox Film Corp., 20th Century-Fox Film Corp.©

Fraulein Fortuna, Play
Haus Voll Liebe, Ein 1954 d: Hans Schweikart. lps: Gertrud Kuckelmann, Michael Cramer, Erni Mangold. 83M GRM/AUS. *Gluck Ins Haus*; *A House Full of Love* prod/rel: Meteor, Europa

Gioco Pericoloso, Play
Gioco Pericoloso 1942 d: Nunzio MalasommA. lps: Elsa Merlini, Elisa Cegani, Renato Cialente. 85M ITL. prod/rel: Cines, Juventus Film

Hau-Ruck, Play
Gluck Muss Man Haben 1953 d: Axel von Ambesser. lps: Wolfgang Lukschy, Bruni Lobel, Paul Horbiger. 95M AUS. *Drei von Denen Man Spricht* prod/rel: N.W., Lux

Ho-Rukk, Play
Danza Dei Milioni, La 1940 d: Camillo Mastrocinque. lps: Nino Besozzi, Jole Voleri, Miretta Mauri. 70M ITL. *Il Quadrante Della Fortuna* prod/rel: I.C.I.

Isle of Terror, Play
Isle of Missing Men 1942 d: Richard Oswald. lps: John Howard, Gilbert Roland, Helen Gilbert. 67M USA. *Isle of Terror*; *Isle of Fury* prod/rel: Monogram

Der Kuss Vor Dem Spiegel, Vienna 1932, Play
Kiss Before the Mirror, The 1933 d: James Whale. lps: Nancy Carroll, Frank Morgan, Paul Lukas. 66M USA. prod/rel: Universal Pictures Corp.©
Wives Under Suspicion 1938 d: James Whale. lps: Warren William, Gail Patrick, Ralph Morgan. 75M USA. *Suspicion* prod/rel: Universal Pictures Co.©

Lilas Blanc, Play
Cinquieme Empreinte, La 1934 d: Karl Anton. lps: Jean Max, Alice Field, Paulette Dubost. 85M FRN. *Lilas Blanc* prod/rel: Films Fred Bacos, Fox-Film

Matura, Budapest 1935, Play
Girls' Dormitory 1936 d: Irving Cummings. lps: Herbert Marshall, Ruth Chatterton, Simone Simon. 66M USA. prod/rel: Twentieth Century-Fox Film Corp.©

Mature, Play
Very Young Lady, A 1941 d: Harold Schuster. lps: Jane Withers, Nancy Kelly, John Sutton. 80M USA. prod/rel: 20th Century Fox

A Templom Egere, Budapest 1927, Play
Beauty and the Boss 1932 d: Roy Del Ruth. lps: Warren William, Marian Marsh, Charles Butterworth. 75M USA. *Church Mouse* prod/rel: Warner Bros. Pictures, Inc.

The Unguarded Hour, London 1935, Play
Unguarded Hour, The 1936 d: Sam Wood. lps: Loretta Young, Franchot Tone, Lewis Stone. 88M USA. prod/rel: Metro-Goldwyn-Mayer Corp.©

White Lilac, Play
White Lilac 1935 d: Albert Parker. lps: Basil Sydney, Judy Gunn, Claude Dampier. 67M UKN. prod/rel: Fox British

FOELDES, EMRIC
Alias the Doctor, Play
Cas du Docteur Brenner, Le 1932 d: John Daumery. lps: Jean Marchat, Simone Genevois, Jeanne Grumbach. 75M FRN. prod/rel: Warner Bros., First National

FOERSTER, EBERHARD
Seine Majestat Gustav Krause, Play
Seniorchef, Der 1942 d: Peter P. Brauer. lps: Otto Wernicke, Werner Fuetterer, Karin Himboldt. 108M GRM. prod/rel: Terra, D.F.V.

FOGAZZARO, ANTONIO (1842–1911), ITL
Daniele Cortis, 1885, Novel
Daniele Cortis 1947 d: Mario Soldati. lps: Sarah Churchill, Gino Cervi, Vittorio Gassman. 90M ITL. prod/rel: Universalia, Minerva Film

Malombra, 1881, Novel
Malombra 1917 d: Carmine Gallone. lps: Lyda Borelli, Amleto Novelli, Giulia Cassini-Rizzotto. 1705m ITL. prod/rel: Cines
Malombra 1942 d: Mario Soldati. lps: Isa Miranda, Andrea Checchi, Irasema Dilian. 94M ITL. prod/rel: Lux Film
Malombra: le Perversioni Sessuali Di Una Adolescente 1983 d: Bruno Alberto Gaburro. lps: Paola Senatore, Maurice Poli, Gloria Brini. 91M ITL. *Malombra -the Sexual Perversions of an Adolescent*; *Malombra* prod/rel: Film Holiday Production

Piccolo Mondo Antico, 1896, Novel
Piccolo Mondo Antico 1940 d: Mario Soldati. lps: Alida Valli, Massimo Serato, Ada Dondini. 106M ITL. *Little Old-Fashioned World* prod/rel: Artisti Tecnici Associati, Milano, I.C.I.

FOGELSTROM, PER ANDERS
Mina Drommars Stad, Novel
Mina Drommars Stad 1976 d: Ingvar Skogsberg. lps: Eddie Axberg, Britt Louise Tillbom, Kjell-Hugo Grandin. 111M SWD. *City of My Dreams*; *My Dream City* prod/rel: Svensk Filmindustri

FOGLAR, JAROSLAV
Zahada Hlavolamu, Book
Zahada Hlavolamu 1993 d: Petr Kotek. lps: Onrej Hst, David Divis, Martin Vlasak. 110M CZC.

FOLCH I TORRES, JOSEP MARIA
El Cami de la Felicitat, Novel
Cami de la Felicitat ,El 1925 d: Jose G. Barranco. lps: Pilarcita Gil, Carmen Abril, Armando Lucas. SPN. *El Camino de la Felicidad* prod/rel: Magna Films (Barcelona)

FOLDES, EMRIC, Foeldes, Emric
Diploma, Play
Man's Past, A 1927 d: George Melford. lps: Conrad Veidt, Barbara Bedford, Ian Keith. 5916f USA. prod/rel: Universal Pictures

A Kuruzslo, 1927, Play
Alias the Doctor 1932 d: Michael Curtiz. lps: Richard Barthelmess, Marian Marsh, Lucille La Verne. 62M USA. *Environment* prod/rel: First National Pictures, Inc.

FOLDES, YOLANDA
Golden Earrings, Novel
Golden Earrings 1947 d: Mitchell Leisen. lps: Ray Milland, Marlene Dietrich, Murvyn Vye. 95M USA. prod/rel: Paramount

Make You a Good Wife, Novel
My Own True Love 1948 d: Compton Bennett. lps: Phyllis Calvert, Melvyn Douglas, Wanda Hendrix. 84M USA. prod/rel: Paramount

FOLEY, CHARLES
Au Telephone, Play
Au Telephone 1915?. 360m FRN. prod/rel: Eclipse

La Chambre Au Judas, Novel
Chambre Au Judas, La 1912 d: Henri Desfontaines. lps: Claude Garry, Carmen Deraisy, Marie-Ange Feriel. 360m FRN. prod/rel: Eclipse

Deux Femmes, Novel
Etrangere, L' 1917 d: Georges Pallu. lps: Maurice Lehmann, Jean Duval, Andree Pascal. 1725m FRN. prod/rel: Photo Radio

FOLEY, WINIFRED
A Child in the Forest, Book
Abide With Me 1977 d: Moira Armstrong. lps: Cathleen Nesbitt, Ann Francis, Zena Walker. TVM. 70M UKN. prod/rel: BBC

FOLISTER, J.
Un Bouquet de Flirts, Short Story
Bouquet de Flirts, Un 1931 d: Charles de Rochefort. lps: Felix Paquet, Josette Day, Pierre Stephen. 40M FRN. prod/rel: Rheingold Laffite Et Cie

FOLLETT, KEN (1949–, UKN, Follett, Kenneth Martin
Eye of the Needle, Novel
Eye of the Needle 1981 d: Richard Marquand. lps: Donald Sutherland, Stephen MacKenna, Philip Martin Brown. 112M UKN. prod/rel: United Artists, Kings Road

The Key to Rebecca, Novel
Key to Rebecca, The 1985 d: David Hemmings. lps: Cliff Robertson, David Soul, Anthony Quayle. TVM. 200M USA. prod/rel: O.P.T., Castle Combe

FOLLY, CHARLES
Fleur d'Ombre, Novel
All'ombra Di un Trono 1921 d: Carmine Gallone. lps: Soava Gallone, Pietro Schiavazzi, Umberto Casilini. 2215m ITL. prod/rel: Films Gallone

FONSECA, RUBEM
O Caso de F.a., 1969, Short Story
Lucia McCartney, Uma Garota de Programa 1971 d: David Neves. lps: Adriana Pietro, Nelson Dantai, Odete LarA. 72M BRZ.

Lucia McCartney, 1969, Short Story
Lucia McCartney, Uma Garota de Programa 1971 d: David Neves. lps: Adriana Pietro, Nelson Dantai, Odete LarA. 72M BRZ.

FONSON, FRANZ
Le Mariage de Mademoiselle Beulemans, Play
Mariage de Mademoiselle Beulemans, Le 1926 d: Julien Duvivier. lps: Andree Brabant, Gustave Libeau, Jean Dehelly. 1800m FRN. prod/rel: Film d'Art (Vandal Et Delac)
Mariage de Mademoiselle Beulemans, Le 1950 d: Andre Cerf. lps: Christian Alers, Saturnin Fabre, Pierre Larquey. 95M FRN/BLG. prod/rel: Tellus Films
Mariage de Mademoiselle Beulemans, Le 1983 d: Michel Rochat. lps: Ana Guedroitz, Leonil McCormack, Jacques Lippe. TVM. 110M BLG.
Mariage de Mlle Beulemans, Le 1932 d: Jean Choux. lps: Lily Bourget, Charles Mahieu, Pierre Alcover. 102M FRN. prod/rel: Films Reingold-Lafitte Et Cie

FONSON, JEAN-FRANCOIS
La Demoiselle de Magasin, Play
Along Came Ruth 1924 d: Eddie Cline. lps: Viola Dana, Walter Hiers, Tully Marshall. 5000f USA. prod/rel: Metro-Goldwyn Pictures

FONTAINE, LORNE H.
The Scarlet Strain, Novel
Scarlet Shadow, The 1919 d: Robert Z. Leonard. lps: Mae Murray, Martha Mattox, Frank Elliott. 6r USA. *The Scarlet Strain* prod/rel: Universal Film Mfg. Co.©

FONTAINE, ROBERT L.
Happy Time, Novel
Happy Time, The 1952 d: Richard Fleischer. lps: Charles Boyer, Linda Christian, Louis Jourdan. 94M USA. prod/rel: Columbia

FONTANE, THEODOR (1819–1898), GRM
Story
Unterm Birnbaum 1974 d: Ralf Kirsten. lps: Angelica Domrose, Erik S. Klein, Hannjo Hasse. 86M GDR. *Under the Pear Tree* prod/rel: Defa

Effi Briest, 1894-95, Novel
Effi Briest 1970 d: Wolfgang Luderer. lps: Angelica Domrose, Horst Schulze, Dietrich Korner. 125M GDR.
Fontane Effi Briest 1974 d: R. W. Fassbinder. lps: Hanna Schygulla, Wolfgang Schenck, Ulli Lommel. 140M GRM. *Effi Briest* (USA) prod/rel: Tango-Film

Rosen Im Herbst 1955 d: Rudolf Jugert. lps: Ruth Leuwerik, Bernhard Wicki, Carl Raddatz. 107M GRM. *Effi Briest; Roses in Autumn* prod/rel: Divina, Gloria

Schritt Vom Wege, Der 1939 d: Gustaf Grundgens. lps: Marianne Hoppe, Karl Ludwig Diehl, Paul Hartmann. 101M GRM. *The False Step* (USA); *Effie Briest* prod/rel: Terra, Neue Filmkunst

Frau Jenny Treibel, 1892, Novel
Corinna Schmidt 1951 d: Arthur Pohl. lps: Trude Hesterberg, Willi Kleinoschegg. 96M GDR.

Grete Minde, 1879, Novel
Grete Minde - Der Wald Ist Voller Wolfe 1977 d: Heidi Genee. lps: Katerina Jacob, Siemen Ruhaak, Hannelore Elsner. 100M AUS/GRM. *Grete Minde - the Woods are Full of Wolves*; *Grete Minde* prod/rel: Solaris, Bernd Eichinger

Irrungen Wirrungen, 1888, Short Story
Alte Lied, Das 1945 d: Fritz Peter Buch. lps: Winnie Markus, Ernst von Klipstein, Hannes Keppler. 94M GRM. prod/rel: Berlin-Film
Ball Im Metropol 1937 d: Frank Wisbar. 84M GRM.

Mathilde Mohring, 1907, Novel
Ich Glaube an Dich 1945 d: Rolf Hansen. lps: Heidemarie Hatheyer, Viktor Staal, Paul Klinger. 77M GRM. *Mathilde Mohring*; *Mein Herz Gehort Dir*; *My Heart Belongs to You*; *Erlebnisse Einer Grossen Liebe* prod/rel: Berlin, Union

Stine, 1890, Short Story
Alte Lied, Das 1945 d: Fritz Peter Buch. lps: Winnie Markus, Ernst von Klipstein, Hannes Keppler. 94M GRM. prod/rel: Berlin-Film

Unterm Birnbaum, 1885, Short Story
Stumme Gast, Der 1945 d: Harald Braun. lps: Rene Deltgen, Gisela Uhlen, Rudolf Fernau. 105M GRM. *The Silent Guest* prod/rel: UFA, Viktoria

FONTANES
La Fille du Garde-Chasse, Story
Fille du Garde-Chasse, La 1912 d: Alexandre Devarennes. lps: Jean Kemm, Damores, Darcet. 1000m FRN. prod/rel: Odeon Films

FONTANES, ALEXANDRE
Bibi la Puree, Play
Bibi la Puree 1925 d: Maurice Champreux. lps: Georges Biscot, Lise Jaux, Henri-Amedee. F FRN. prod/rel: Gaumont
Bibi la Puree 1934 d: Leo Joannon. lps: Georges Biscot, Berangere, Josette Day. 95M FRN. prod/rel: Roxy Films

FONVEILLE, LLOYD
Story
Cherry 2000 1987 d: Steve de Jarnatt. lps: Melanie Griffith, Ben Johnson, Harry Carey Jr. 98M USA. prod/rel: Orion

FOOT, ALISTAIR
No Sex Please - We're British, Play
No Sex Please - We're British 1973 d: Cliff Owen. lps: Ronnie Corbett, Beryl Reid, Arthur Lowe. 91M UKN. prod/rel: Columbia, Bhp

FOOTE, BRADBURY
High Wall, Play
High Wall 1947 d: Curtis Bernhardt. lps: Robert Taylor, Audrey Totter, Herbert Marshall. 99M USA. prod/rel: MGM

FOOTE, HORTON (1916–, USA
1918, Play
1918 1984 d: Ken Harrison. lps: William Converse-Roberts, Hallie Foote, Matthew Broderick. 94M USA. prod/rel: Cinecom

The Chase, New York 1952, Play
Chase, The 1966 d: Arthur Penn. lps: Marlon Brando, Jane Fonda, Robert Redford. 135M USA. prod/rel: Columbia

The Habitation of Dragons, 1988, Play
Habitation of Dragons, The 1992 d: Michael Lindsay-Hogg. lps: Brad Davis, Lucinda Jenney, Frederic Forrest. TVM. F USA.

The Traveling Lady, 1954, Play
Baby, the Rain Must Fall 1965 d: Robert Mulligan. lps: Lee Remick, Steve McQueen, Don Murray. 100M USA. *Traveling Lady* prod/rel: Park Place Productions, Solar Productions

The Trip to Bountiful, Play
Trip to Bountiful, The 1986 d: Peter Masterson. lps: Geraldine Page, John Heard, Carlin Glynn. 106M USA. prod/rel: Island, Film Dallas

Valentine's Day, Play
On Valentine's Day 1986 d: Ken Harrison. lps: William Converse-Roberts, Hallie Foote, Michael Higgins. TVM. 280M USA. *Story of a Marriage* prod/rel: Angelika Films

FOOTE, JOHN TAINTOR
The Look of Eagles, New York 1916, Novel
Kentucky 1938 d: David Butler. lps: Loretta Young, Richard Greene, Walter Brennan. 96M USA. prod/rel: Twentieth Century-Fox Film Corp.©

The Song of the Dragon, New York 1923, Novel
Convoy 1927 d: Joseph C. Boyle, Lothar Mendes (Uncredited). lps: Lowell Sherman, Dorothy MacKaill, William Collier Jr. 7724f USA. prod/rel: Robert Kane Productions, First National Pictures

Toby's Bow, New York 1919, Play
Toby's Bow 1919 d: Harry Beaumont. lps: Tom Moore, Doris Pawn, MacEy Harlam. 5r USA. prod/rel: Goldwyn Pictures Corp.©, Goldwyn Distributing Corp.

FOOTE, SHELBY
September September, Novel
Memphis 1992 d: Yves Simoneau. lps: Cybill Shepherd, John Laughlin, J. E. Freeman. TVM. 100M USA. prod/rel: Propaganda Films, River Siren Prods.

FOOTNER, HUBERT, Footner, Hulbert
The Huntress, New York 1922, Novel
Huntress, The 1923 d: Lynn Reynolds. lps: Colleen Moore, Lloyd Hughes, Russell Simpson. 6236f USA. prod/rel: Associated First National Pictures

Jack Chanty: a Story of Athabasca, New York 1913, Novel
Jack Chanty 1915 d: Max Figman. lps: Max Figman, Lolita Robertson, Edwin Harvey. 5r USA. prod/rel: Masterpiece Film Mfg. Co., Alliance Films Corp.

A New Girl in Town, 1922, Short Story
Dangerous Blonde, The 1924 d: Robert F. Hill. lps: Laura La Plante, Edward Hearn, Arthur Hoyt. 4919f USA. prod/rel: Universal Pictures

Ramshackle House, New York 1922, Novel
Ramshackle House 1924 d: F. Harmon Weight. lps: Betty Compson, Robert Lowing, John Davidson. 6257f USA. prod/rel: Tilford Cinema Corp., Producers Distributing Corp.

The Sealed Valley, New York 1914, Novel
Sealed Valley 1915 d: Lawrence McGill. lps: Dorothy Donnelly, J. W. Johnston, Rene Ditline. 5r USA. prod/rel: Metro Pictures Corp.©

Shirley Kaye, New York 1916, Play
Shirley Kaye 1917 d: Joseph Kaufman. lps: Clara Kimball Young, Corliss Giles, George Fawcett. 5r USA. prod/rel: C. K. Y. Film Corp.©, Select Pictures Corp.

FORBES, ARCHIBALD
The Fourth Brother, Unpublished, Play
China 1943 d: John Farrow. lps: Loretta Young, Alan Ladd, William Bendix. 79M USA. prod/rel: Paramount

FORBES, C. SCOTT
The Meter Man, London 1964, Play
Penthouse, The 1967 d: Peter Collinson. lps: Suzy Kendall, Terence Morgan, Tony Beckley. 96M UKN. prod/rel: Tahiti Films, Paramount

FORBES, COLIN
Avalanche Express, Novel
Avalanche Express 1979 d: Mark Robson, Monte Hellman (Uncredited). lps: Robert Shaw, Lee Marvin, Linda Evans. 88M USA. prod/rel: 20th Century-Fox Film Corp., Lorimar

FORBES, ESTHER (c1894–, USA
Johnny Tremain, Novel
Johnny Tremain 1957 d: Robert Stevenson. lps: Hal Stalmaster, Luana Patten, Jeff York. 81M USA. prod/rel: Buena Vista

FORBES, JAMES
The Chorus Lady, New York 1906, Play
Chorus Lady, The 1915 d: Frank Reicher. lps: Cleo Ridgely, Marjorie Daw, Mrs. Lewis McCord. 5r USA. prod/rel: Jesse L. Lasky Feature Play Co.©, Paramount Pictures Corp.
Chorus Lady, The 1924 d: Ralph Ince. lps: Margaret Livingston, Alan Roscoe, Virginia Lee Corbin. 6020f USA. prod/rel: Regal Pictures, Producers Distributing Corp.

The Commuters, New York 1910, Play
Commuters, The 1915 d: George Fitzmaurice. lps: Irene Fenwick, Charles Judels, George Le Guere. 4920f USA. *The Commuters* prod/rel: George Kleine©

Precious, New York 1929, Play
Bachelor's Affairs 1932 d: Alfred L. Werker. lps: Adolphe Menjou, Minna Gombell, Rita La Roy. 76M USA. *Precious*; *Fancy Free* prod/rel: Fox Film Corp.

FORBES, JAMES GRANT
The Famous Mrs. Fair, New York 1920, Play
Famous Mrs. Fair, The 1923 d: Fred Niblo. lps: Myrtle Stedman, Huntley Gordon, Marguerite de La Motte. 7775f USA. prod/rel: Louis B. Mayer Productions, Metro Pictures

The Traveling Salesman, New York 1908, Play
Traveling Salesman, The 1916 d: Joseph Kaufman. lps: Frank McIntyre, Doris Kenyon, Harry Northrup. 5r USA. prod/rel: Famous Players Film Co.©, Paramount Pictures Corp.
Traveling Salesman, The 1921 d: Joseph Henabery. lps: Roscoe Arbuckle, Betty Ross Clark, Frank Holland. 4514f USA. prod/rel: Famous Players-Lasky, Paramount Pictures

FORBES, KATHRYN (1909–1966), USA, McLean, Kathryn Anderson
Mamma's Bank Account, Book
I Remember Mama 1948 d: George Stevens. lps: Irene Dunne, Barbara Bel Geddes, Oscar HomolkA. 134M USA. prod/rel: RKO Radio

FORBES, MURRAY
Hollow Triumph, Novel
Hollow Triumph 1948 d: Steve Sekely. lps: Paul Henreid, Joan Bennett, Eduard Franz. 83M USA. *The Scar* (UKN) prod/rel: Eagle-Lion

FORBES, ROSITA
If the Gods Laugh, London 1925, Novel
Fighting Love 1927 d: Nils Chrisander. lps: Jetta Goudal, Victor Varconi, Henry B. Walthall. 7017f USA. **If the Gods Laugh** prod/rel: de Mille Pictures, Producers Distributing Corp.

King's Mate, Novel
White Sheik, The 1928 d: Harley Knoles. lps: Lillian Hall-Davis, Jameson Thomas, Warwick Ward. 8980f UKN. prod/rel: British International Pictures, Wardour

FORD, COREY
Cloak and Dagger, Novel
Cloak and Dagger 1946 d: Fritz Lang. lps: Gary Cooper, Lilli Palmer, Robert AldA. 106M USA. prod/rel: Warner Bros.

Echoes That Old Refrain, 1937, Short Story
Winter Carnival 1939 d: Charles F. Reisner. lps: Richard Carlson, Ann Sheridan, Helen Parrish. 105M USA. prod/rel: Walter Wanger Productions©, United Artists Corp.

FORD, DANIEL
Go Tell the Spartans, Novel
Go Tell the Spartans 1978 d: Ted Post. lps: Burt Lancaster, Craig Wasson, Jonathan Lippe. 114M USA. prod/rel: Sparta, United Artists

FORD, FORD MADOX (1873–1939), UKN, Hueffer, Ford Madox
Romance, 1903, Novel
Road to Romance, The 1927 d: John S. Robertson. lps: Ramon Novarro, Marceline Day, Marc MacDermott. 6544f USA. *Romance* (UKN) prod/rel: Metro-Goldwyn-Mayer Pictures

FORD, HARRIET
The Argyle Case, New York 1912, Play
Argyle Case, The 1917 d: Ralph Ince. lps: Robert Warwick, Elaine Hammerstein, Charles Hines. 5-7r USA. prod/rel: Robert Warwick Film Corp.©, Selznick Pictures
Argyle Case, The 1929 d: Howard Bretherton. lps: Thomas Meighan, H. B. Warner, Lila Lee. 7794f USA. prod/rel: Warner Brothers Pictures

The Case of the Black Parrot, Novel
Case of the Black Parrot, The 1941 d: Noel Smith. lps: William Lundigan, Maris Wrixon, Eddie Foy Jr. 60M USA. prod/rel: Warner Bros.

The Dummy, New York 1914, Play
Dummy, The 1917 d: Francis J. Grandon. lps: Jack Pickford, Frank Losee, Edwin Stanley. 5r USA. prod/rel: Famous Players Film Co.©, Paramount Pictures Corp.
Dummy, The 1929 d: Robert Milton. lps: Ruth Chatterton, Fredric March, John Cromwell. 5357f USA. prod/rel: Paramount Famous Lasky Corp.

The Fourth Estate, New York 1909, Play
Fourth Estate, The 1916 d: Frank Powell. lps: Ruth Blair, Clifford Bruce, Victor Benoit. 5r USA. prod/rel: Fox Film Corp., William Fox©

A Lady in Love, Play
Lady in Love, A 1920 d: Walter Edwards. lps: Ethel Clayton, Harrison Ford, Boyd Irwin. 4607f USA. prod/rel: Famous Players-Lasky Corp.©, Paramount-Artcraft Pictures

Make Your Own Bed, Play
Make Your Own Bed 1944 d: Peter Godfrey. lps: Jack Carson, Jane Wyman, Alan Hale. 82M USA. prod/rel: Warner Bros.

FORD, HARRY CHAPMAN
Anna Ascends, New York 1920, Play
Anna Ascends 1922 d: Victor Fleming. lps: Alice Brady, Robert Ellis, David Powell. 5959f USA. prod/rel: Famous Players-Lasky Corp., Paramount Pictures

Eve's Leaves, New York 1925, Play
  Eve's Leaves 1926 d: Paul Sloane. lps: Leatrice Joy, William Boyd, Robert Edeson. 6754f USA. prod/rel: de Mille Pictures, Producers Distributing Corp.

Two Gates, Story
  Shadow of the Law, The 1926 d: Wallace Worsley. lps: Clara Bow, Forrest Stanley, Stuart Holmes. 4526f USA. prod/rel: Associated Exhibitors

FORD, JESSE HILL
The Liberation of Lord Byron Jones, Boston 1965, Novel
  Liberation of L.B. Jones, The 1970 d: William Wyler. lps: Lee J. Cobb, Anthony Zerbe, Roscoe Lee Browne. 102M USA. *The Liberation of Lord Byron Jones* prod/rel: Liberation Co., Columbia

FORD, JOHN (1586–c1640), UKN
'Tis Pity She's a Whore, 1633, Play
  Addio Fratello Crudele 1971 d: Giuseppe Patroni Griffi. lps: Charlotte Rampling, Oliver Tobias, Fabio Testi. 111M ITL. *'Tis Pity She's a Whore* (USA) prod/rel: Clesi Cin.Ca
  'Tis Pity She's a Whore 1980 d: Roland Joffe. lps: Cherie Lunghi, Tim Pigott-Smith, Colin Douglas. MTV. 120M UKN. prod/rel: BBC

FORD, JULIE ANNE
The Book of Athuan, Radio Play
  Halo for Athuan, A 1985 d: Alan Burke. lps: Gwen Plumb, Ron Haddrick, Fiona Stewart. TVM. F ASL. *The Book of Athuan*; *Athuan* prod/rel: Australian Broadcasting Corp.

FORD, PAUL LEICESTER (1865–1902), USA
The Great K & A Train Robbery, New York 1897, Novel
  Great K & A Train Robbery, The 1926 d: Lewis Seiler. lps: Tom Mix, Dorothy Dwan, William Walling. 4800f USA. prod/rel: Fox Film Corp.
Janice Meredith; a Story of the American Revolution, New York 1899, Novel
  Janice Meredith 1924 d: E. Mason Hopper. lps: Marion Davies, Holbrook Blinn, Harrison Ford. 11r USA. *The Beautiful Rebel* prod/rel: Cosmopolitan Pictures, Metro-Goldwyn Distributing Corp.

FORD, SEWELL
Cherub Divine, New York 1909, Novel
  Money to Burn 1922 d: Rowland V. Lee. lps: William Russell, Sylvia Breamer, Hallam Cooley. 4850f USA. prod/rel: Fox Film Corp.
Tessie and the Little Sap, 1925, Short Story
  Tessie 1925 d: Dallas M. Fitzgerald. lps: May McAvoy, Robert Agnew, Lee Moran. 6221f USA. prod/rel: Arrow Pictures

FORDHAM, PETA
Th Robbers' Tale; the Real Story of the Great Train Robbery, London 1965, Book
  Gentlemen Bitten Zur Kasse, Die 1965 d: John Olden, Claus Peter Witt. lps: Horst Tappert, Hans Cossy, Gunther Neutze. MTV. 104M GRM. *The Great British Train Robbery* (USA); *Der Postzug-Uberfall; Der Grosse Postraub* prod/rel: Norddeutscher Rundfunk, Real Film

FOREMAN, L. L.
Story
  Gambler Wore a Gun, The 1961 d: Edward L. Cahn. lps: Jim Davis, Mark Allen, Addison Richards. 67M USA. prod/rel: Zenith
Adios My Texas, Story
  Lone Gun, The 1954 d: Ray Nazarro. lps: George Montgomery, Dorothy Malone, Frank Faylen. 78M USA. prod/rel: United Artists, World Films
Platt River Gamble, Short Story
  Arrow in the Dust 1954 d: Lesley Selander. lps: Sterling Hayden, Coleen Gray, Keith Larsen. 80M USA. prod/rel: Allied Artists
The Renegade, 1942, Novel
  Savage, The 1952 d: George Marshall. lps: Charlton Heston, Susan Morrow, Peter Hanson. 95M USA. *Warbonnet* prod/rel: Paramount
The Storm Rider, Novel
  Storm Rider, The 1957 d: Edward Bernds. lps: Scott Brady, Mala Powers, Bill Williams. 72M USA. prod/rel: 20th Century Fox, Regal Films

FORES, JOHN
The Springboard, Novel
  Out of the Clouds 1955 d: Basil Dearden, Michael Relph. lps: Anthony Steel, Robert Beatty, David Knight. 88M UKN. prod/rel: Ealing Studios, General Film Distributors

FOREST, LOUIS
The Curious Conduct of Judge Legarde, Washington D.C. 1912, Play
  Curious Conduct of Judge Legarde, The 1915 d: Will S. Davis. lps: Lionel Barrymore, Edna Pendleton, William H. Tooker. 5r USA. prod/rel: Life Photo Film Corp., State Rights

FORESTER, C. S. (1899–1966), UKN, Forester, Cecil Scott
Story
  Commandos Strike at Dawn 1942 d: John Farrow. lps: Paul Muni, Lillian Gish, Robert Coote. 98M USA. prod/rel: Columbia
The African Queen, 1935, Novel
  African Queen, The 1951 d: John Huston. lps: Humphrey Bogart, Katharine Hepburn, Robert Morley. 105M UKN/USA. prod/rel: Romulus, Horizon
  African Queen, The 1976 d: Richard C. Sarafian. lps: Warren Oates, Mariette Hartley, Johnny SekkA. TVM. 50M USA.
Brown on Resolution, 1929, Novel
  Brown on Resolution 1935 d: Walter Forde, Anthony Asquith. lps: Betty Balfour, John Mills, Barry MacKay. 80M UKN. *Born for Glory* (USA); *Forever England; Torpedo Raider* prod/rel: Gaumont-British
  Single-Handed 1953 d: Roy Boulting. lps: Jeffrey Hunter, Michael Rennie, Wendy Hiller. 85M UKN. *Sailor of the King* (USA); *Brown on Resolution; Able Seaman Brown; Sailor of the Sea* prod/rel: 20th Century Productions, 20th Century-Fox
Captain Horatio Hornblower, 1939, Novel
  Captain Horatio Hornblower R.N. 1951 d: Raoul Walsh. lps: Gregory Peck, Virginia Mayo, Robert Beatty. 118M UKN/USA. *Captain Horatio Hornblower* (USA); *Horatio Hornblower* prod/rel: Warner Bros., First National
Eagle Squadron, 1942, Short Story
  Eagle Squadron 1942 d: Arthur Lubin. lps: Robert Stack, Diana Barrymore, John Loder. 109M USA. prod/rel: Universal
The Gun, 1933, Novel
  Pride and the Passion, The 1957 d: Stanley Kramer. lps: Cary Grant, Sophia Loren, Frank SinatrA. 132M USA. prod/rel: United Artists, Stanley Kramer
Payment Deferred, 1926, Novel
  Payment Deferred 1932 d: Lothar Mendes. lps: Charles Laughton, Maureen O'Sullivan, Dorothy Peterson. 80M USA. prod/rel: Metro-Goldwyn-Mayer Corp., Metro-Goldwyn-Mayer Dist. Corp.©
Sink the Bismarck!, Book
  Sink the Bismarck! 1960 d: Lewis Gilbert. lps: Kenneth More, Dana Wynter, Carl Mohner. 98M UKN. prod/rel: 20th Century-Fox

FORESTIER, PATRICK
Hors la Vie, Book
  Hors la Vie 1991 d: Maroun Bagdadi. lps: Hippolyte Girardot, Rafic Ali Ahmad, Hussein Sbeity. 97M FRN/ITL/BLG. prod/rel: Galatee Films, Films a2 (Paris)

FORMAN, HENRY JAMES
The Pony Express, New York 1925, Novel
  Pony Express, The 1925 d: James Cruze. lps: Betty Compson, Ricardo Cortez, Ernest Torrence. 9949f USA. prod/rel: Famous Players-Lasky, Paramount Pictures

FORMAN, JUSTUS MILES
Buchanan's Wife, New York 1906, Novel
  Buchanan's Wife 1918 d: Charles J. Brabin. lps: Virginia Pearson, Marc McDermott, Victor Sutherland. 5r USA. prod/rel: Fox Film Corp., William Fox©
The Carterets, Story
  Face Between, The 1922 d: Bayard Veiller. lps: Bert Lytell, Andree Tourneur, Sylvia Breamer. 4997f USA. *The Phantom Bride* prod/rel: Metro Pictures
The Garden of Lies, New York 1902, Novel
  Garden of Lies, The 1915 d: Augustus Thomas. lps: Jane Cowl, Violet Horner, William Russell. 5r USA. prod/rel: All Star Feature Corp., Universal Film Mfg. Co.©

FORREST, A. J.
Interpol, Book
  Interpol 1957 d: John Gilling. lps: Victor Mature, Anita Ekberg, Trevor Howard. 92M UKN. *Pickup Alley* (USA) prod/rel: Warwick, Columbia

FORREST, DAVID
The Great Dinosaur Robbery, Novel
  One of Our Dinosaurs Is Missing 1975 d: Robert Stevenson. lps: Peter Ustinov, Helen Hayes, Clive Revill. 94M USA. prod/rel: Buena Vista, Walt Disney

FORREST, GEORGE
Song of Norway, New York 1944, Play
  Song of Norway 1970 d: Andrew L. Stone. lps: Toralv Maurstad, Florence Henderson, Christina Schollin. 142M USA. prod/rel: ABC Pictures

FORRESTER, IZOLA
A Cafe in Cairo, 1924, Short Story
  Cafe in Cairo, A 1924 d: Chet Withey. lps: Priscilla Dean, Robert Ellis, Carl Stockdale. 5656f USA. prod/rel: Hunt Stromberg Productions, Producers Distributing Corp.
The Dangerous Inheritance; Or Mystery of the Tittani Rubies, Boston 1920, Novel
  How Women Love 1922 d: Kenneth Webb. lps: Betty Blythe, Gladys Hulette, Julia Swayne Gordon. 5377f USA. prod/rel: B. B. Productions
The Gray Path, 1922, Short Story
  Youth for Sale 1924 d: W. Christy Cabanne. lps: May Allison, Sigrid Holmquist, Richard Bennett. 6000f USA. *Youth to Sell* prod/rel: C. C. Burr Pictures
Restless Wives, Short Story
  Restless Wives 1924 d: Gregory La CavA. lps: Doris Kenyon, James Rennie, Montagu Love. 6317f USA. prod/rel: C. C. Burr Pictures
Salvage, 1924, Short Story
  Wreckage 1925 d: Scott R. Dunlap. lps: May Allison, Holmes Herbert, John Miljan. 6r USA. prod/rel: Banner Productions, Henry Ginsberg Distributing Corp.

FORRESTER, LARRY
A Girl Called Fathom, London 1967, Novel
  Fathom 1967 d: Leslie H. Martinson. lps: Anthony Franciosa, Raquel Welch, Ronald Fraser. 104M UKN. *A Girl Called Fathom* prod/rel: 20th Century-Fox

FORRO, PAUL
Mon Beguin, Novel
  Mon Beguin 1929 d: Hans Behrendt. lps: Marie Glory, Enrico Benfer, Georges Deneubourg. 74M FRN. *Miss Lohengrin*

FORST, E.
The Family Tree
  Fools and Their Money 1919 d: Herbert Blache. lps: Emmy Wehlen, Jack Mulhall, Emmett King. 5r USA. *The Family Trees* prod/rel: Metro Pictures Corp.©

FORSTER, E. M. (1879–1970), UKN, Forster, Edward Morgan
Howards End, 1910, Novel
  Howards End 1992 d: James Ivory. lps: Anthony Hopkins, Vanessa Redgrave, Helena Bonham-Carter. 142M UKN. prod/rel: Mayfair Entertainment, Merchant Ivory Productions
Maurice, 1971, Novel
  Maurice 1987 d: James Ivory. lps: James Wilby, Hugh Grant, Rupert Graves. 140M UKN. prod/rel: Cinecom, Merchant Ivory
A Passage to India, 1924, Novel
  Passage to India, A 1965 d: Waris Hussein. lps: Sybil Thorndike, Zia Mohyeddin, Cyril Cusack. MTV. 110M UKN. prod/rel: BBC
  Passage to India, A 1984 d: David Lean. lps: Judy Davis, James Fox, Peggy Ashcroft. 163M UKN. prod/rel: Emi, Gw Films
A Room With a View, 1908, Novel
  Room With a View, A 1986 d: James Ivory. lps: Maggie Smith, Helena Bonham-Carter, Denholm Elliott. 120M UKN. prod/rel: Merchant-Ivory, Goldcrest
Where Angels Fear to Tread, 1905, Novel
  Where Angels Fear to Tread 1966 d: Naomi Capon. lps: Alec McCowen, Anna Massey, Wendy Hiller. MTV. F UKN. prod/rel: BBC
  Where Angels Fear to Tread 1991 d: Charles Sturridge. lps: Helena Bonham-Carter, Judy Davis, Rupert Graves. 112M UKN. prod/rel: Where Angels Fear to Tread Ltd., Sovereign Pictures

FORSTER, EBERHARD
Frau Nach Mass, Play
  Frau Nach Mass 1940 d: Helmut Kautner. lps: Hans Sohnker, Leny Marenbach, Dorit Kreysler. 94M GRM. prod/rel: Terra

FORSTER, FRIEDRICH (1869–1966), GRM, Forster, Friedrich Wilhelm
Antiquitaten, Play
  Keusche Sunderin, Die 1943 d: Joe Stockel. lps: Joe Stockel, Elise Aulinger, Gabriele Reismuller. 87M GRM. prod/rel: Bavaria, Kristall
Robinson Soll Nicht Sterben, Berlin 1932, Play
  Robinson Soll Nicht Sterben 1957 d: Josef von Baky. lps: Romy Schneider, Horst Buchholz, Erich Ponto. 98M GRM. *The Girl and the Legend* (USA); *Robinson Shall Not Die* prod/rel: N.D.F.

FORSTER, JOHN
Heldentum Nach Ladenschluss, Book
  Heldentum Nach Ladenschluss 1955 d: Franz Seitz. lps: Josef Sieber, Horst Uhse, Charles Regnier. 90M GRM. *Heroism After Shop Hours* prod/rel: Arca, Omega

FORSTER, MARGARET (1938–, UKN
Georgy Girl, London 1965, Novel
Georgy Girl 1966 d: Silvio Narizzano. lps: James Mason, Alan Bates, Lynn Redgrave. 99M UKN. prod/rel: Everglades Productions, Columbia

FORSTER, THOMAS B.
La Chaine Des Peuves, Play
Vingt-Sept Rue de la Paix 1936 d: Richard Pottier. lps: Jules Berry, Renee Saint-Cyr, Suzy Prim. 100M FRN. prod/rel: Milo Film Productions

Prison Sans Barreaux, Play
Prison Sans Barreaux 1937 d: Leonide Moguy. lps: Roger Duchesne, Annie Ducaux, Corinne Luchaire. 98M FRN. *Prison Without Bars* prod/rel: Arnold Pressburger, Cipra

FORSTER-BURGGRAF, FRIEDRICH
Gastspiel in Kopenhagen, Play
Schwedische Nachtigall, Die 1941 d: Peter P. Brauer. lps: Ilse Werner, Carl Ludwig Diehl, Aribert Wascher. 96M GRM. prod/rel: Terra, Kristall

FORSYTH, FREDERICK (1938–, UKN
The Day of the Jackal, 1971, Novel
Day of the Jackal, The 1973 d: Fred Zinnemann. lps: Edward Fox, Terence Alexander, Bernard Archard. 142M UKN/USA/FRN. prod/rel: Universal, Warwick
Jackal, The 1997 d: Michael Caton-Jones. lps: Bruce Willis, Richard Gere, Sidney Poitier. 124M USA. prod/rel: Mutual Film Co, Alphaville

The Dogs of War, Novel
Dogs of War, The 1980 d: John Irvin. lps: Christopher Walken, Tom Berenger, Colin Blakely. 119M UKN. prod/rel: United Artists, Silverwold

The Fourth Protocol, Novel
Fourth Protocol, The 1987 d: John MacKenzie. lps: Michael Caine, Pierce Brosnan, Joanna Cassidy. 117M UKN. prod/rel: Rank, Fourth Protocol Films

The Odessa File, 1972, Novel
Odessa File, The 1974 d: Ronald Neame. lps: Jon Voight, Maximilian Schell, Maria Schell. 129M UKN/GRM. *Die Akte Odessa* (GRM) prod/rel: Columbia, Domino

FORSYTH, JAMES
Old Mick-MacK, Radio Play
End of the Road, The 1954 d: Wolf RillA. lps: Finlay Currie, Duncan Lamont, Naomi Chance. 76M UKN. prod/rel: Group Three, British Lion

FORT, GARRETT
The Prince of Head Waiters, 1927, Short Story
Prince of Headwaiters, The 1927 d: John Francis Dillon. lps: Lewis Stone, Priscilla Bonner, E. J. Ratcliffe. 6400f USA. prod/rel: Sam E. Rork Productions, First National Pictures

FORT, KAREL
Play
Z Ceskych Mlynu 1941 d: Miroslav Cikan. lps: Theodor Pistek, Zorka Janu, Jindrich PlachtA. 2223m CZC. *From the Czech Mills* prod/rel: Slavia-Film, UFA

FORT, MARIO
Widow's Island, Novel
Romance in Flanders, A 1937 d: Maurice Elvey. lps: Paul Cavanagh, Marcelle Chantal, Garry Marsh. 73M UKN. *Lost on the Western Front* (USA); *Widow's Island* prod/rel: Franco-London, British Lion

FORTE, VINCENT
The Trailmakers, Novel
Wild Women 1970 d: Don Taylor. lps: Hugh O'Brian, Anne Francis, Marilyn Maxwell. TVM. 74M USA. prod/rel: Aaron Spelling Productions

FORZANO, GIOVACCHINO (1883–1970), ITL
Le Campane Di San Lucio, 1916, Play
Campane Di San Lucio, Le 1921 d: Guido Brignone. lps: Mercedes Brignone, Alberto Pasquali, Franz SalA. 1667m ITL. prod/rel: Rodolfi Film

I Cento Giorni, Play
Campo Di Maggio 1935 d: Giovacchino Forzano. lps: Corrado Racca, Enzo Biliotti, Emilia Varini. 100M ITL. prod/rel: Consorizio Vis, E.N.I.C.

Un Colpo Di Vento, Play
Colpo Di Vento, Un 1936 d: Charles-Felix Tavano, Jean Dreville. lps: Ermete Zacconi, Dria Paola, Gino Sabbatini. 70M ITL. prod/rel: Forzano Film, E.N.I.C.

Il Conte Di Brechard, Play
Conte Di Brechard, Il 1938 d: Mario Bonnard. lps: Amedeo Nazzari, Luisa Ferida, Camillo Pilotto. 95M ITL. *The Count of Brechard* (USA) prod/rel: E.I.a., Amato Film

Don Buonaparte, Play
Don Buonaparte 1941 d: Flavio CalzavarA. lps: Ermete Zacconi, Osvaldo Valenti, Oretta Fiume. 83M ITL. prod/rel: Pisorno, Viralba

Il Dono Del Mattino, Play
Dono Del Mattino, Il 1932 d: Enrico Guazzoni. lps: Germana Paolieri, Carlo Lombardi, Arturo Falconi. 76M ITL. prod/rel: Caesar Film

Fiordalisi d'Oro, Play
Fiordalisi d'Oro 1936 d: Giovacchino Forzano. lps: Marie Bell, Annibale Ninchi, Fosco Giachetti. 83M ITL. prod/rel: Forzano Film, Cine Tirrenia

Maestro Landi, Play
Maestro Landi 1935 d: Giovacchino Forzano. lps: Odoardo Spadaro, Ugo Ceseri, Pina Cei. 78M ITL. prod/rel: Consorzio Vis, Tirrenia

La Reginetta Delle Rose, 1912, Opera
Reginetta Delle Rose, La 1914 d: Luigi CarambA. lps: Ester Soarez, Ruggero Galli, Sig. CicognA. 1600m ITL. prod/rel: Musical Film

Villafranca, Play
Villafranca 1933 d: Giovacchino Forzano. lps: Corrado Racca, Annibale Betrone, Giulio Donadio. 105M ITL. prod/rel: Forzano Film, Fono Roma

FOSCOLO, UGO (1778–1827), ITL
Le Ultime Lettere Di Jacopo Ortis, 1798, Novel
Jacopo Ortis 1911. 216m ITL. prod/rel: Cines
Ultime Lettere Di Jacopo Ortis 1973 d: Peter Del Monte. lps: Stefano Oppedisano, Ornella Ghezzi, Sergio Tofano. MTV. F ITL. prod/rel: Rai Radiotelisione Italiana
Ultime Lettere Di Jacopo Ortis, Le 1921 d: Lucio d'AmbrA. lps: Renato Piacentini, Nera Badaloni. 1271m ITL. prod/rel: D'ambra Film

FOSS, KENELM
Till Our Ship Comes in, Novel
Till Our Ship Comes in 1919 d: Frank Miller. lps: Kenelm Foss, Barbara Everest, Jack Miller. SHS. UKN. *Married Bliss* prod/rel: Q Film Productions, Ideal

FOSSEY, DIAN
Book
Gorillas in the Mist 1988 d: Michael Apted. lps: Sigourney Weaver, Bryan Brown, Julie Harris. 129M USA. prod/rel: Universal

FOSTER, BENNETT
The Outlaws are in Town, 1949, Short Story
Desperados are in Town, The 1956 d: Kurt Neumann. lps: Robert Arthur, Kathy Nolan, Rhys Williams. 73M USA. *The Desperadoes are in Town* prod/rel: 20th Century-Fox, Regal Films

FOSTER, DAVID S.
The Oval Diamond, 1915, Novel
Oval Diamond, The 1916 d: W. Eugene Moore. lps: Barbara Gilroy, Harris Gordon, Arthur Bauer. 5r USA. prod/rel: Thanhouser Film Corp., Mutual Film Corp.

The Road to London, New York 1914, Novel
Road to London, The 1921 d: Eugene Mullin. lps: Bryant Washburn, Joan Morgan, George Folsey. 4574f UKN/USA. prod/rel: Screenplays Productions, Phillips

FOSTER, GEORGE
A Rift in the Loot, Play
Birds of a Feather 1935 d: John Baxter. lps: George Robey, Horace Hodges, Jack Melford. 69M UKN. prod/rel: Baxter and Barter, Universal

FOSTER, MAXIMILIAN
Poor Man Rich Man, New York 1916, Novel
Rich Man, Poor Man 1918 d: J. Searle Dawley. lps: Marguerite Clark, Richard Barthelmess, George Backus. 5r USA. prod/rel: Famous Players-Lasky Corp., Paramount Pictures

The Silent Partner, 1908, Short Story
Silent Partner, The 1923 d: Charles Maigne. lps: Leatrice Joy, Owen Moore, Robert Edeson. 5866f USA. prod/rel: Famous Players-Lasky, Paramount Pictures

The Trap, New York 1920, Novel
Highest Bidder, The 1921 d: Wallace Worsley. lps: Madge Kennedy, Lionel Atwill, Vernon Steele. 4960f USA. prod/rel: Goldwyn Pictures

FOSTER, MICHAEL
Story
Song for Miss Julie, A 1945 d: William Rowland. lps: Shirley Ross, Barton Hepburn, Jane Farrar. 69M USA. prod/rel: Republic, Pre-Em Pictures, Inc.

FOSTER, THOMAS B.
Das Letzte Rezept, Play
Letzte Rezept, Das 1952 d: Rolf Hansen. lps: Heidemarie Hatheyer, O. W. Fischer, Sybil Werden. 95M GRM. *Desires* (USA); *The Last Prescription* prod/rel: Meteor-Fama, Ring

FOSTER, W. BERT
Hardwick of Hambone, Short Story
Bulldog Pluck 1927 d: Jack Nelson. lps: Bob Custer, Viora Daniels, Bobby Nelson. 5013f USA. prod/rel: Bob Custer Productions

Men in the Raw, Short Story
Men in the Raw 1923 d: George Marshall. lps: Jack Hoxie, Marguerite Clayton, Sid Jordan. 4313f USA. prod/rel: Universal Pictures

FOSTER, WILLIAM
Smoked Glasses, Play
Blind Man's Bluff 1936 d: Albert Parker. lps: Basil Sydney, Enid Stamp-Taylor, Barbara Greene. 72M UKN. prod/rel: Fox British

FOTHERBY, T. F.
Decoy Be Damned, Novel
Shadow of Fear 1963 d: Ernest Morris. lps: Paul Maxwell, Clare Owen, Anita West. 60M UKN. prod/rel: Butcher's Films

FOTHERGILL, JOHN
An Innkeeper's Diary, Book
Fothergill 1981 d: Claude Whatham. lps: Robert Hardy, Lynn Fairleigh, Philip Donaghy. TVM. 75M UKN. prod/rel: BBC

FOUQUE, FRIEDRICH DE LA MOTTE
Undine, 1811, Short Story
Neptune's Daughter 1912 d: W. Christy Cabanne. lps: Martha Russell, Francis X. Bushman, Harry Cashman. 1000f USA. prod/rel: Essanay
Undine 1912 d: Theodore Marston. lps: Florence Labadie, William Russell, James Cruze. 2r USA. prod/rel: Thanhouser
Undine 1916 d: Henry Otto. lps: Ida Schnall, Douglas Gerrard, Edna Maison. 5r USA. *Answer of the Sea* prod/rel: Bluebird Photoplays, Inc., Universal Film Mfg. Co.©
Undine 74 1974 d: Rolf Thiele. lps: Angela von Radloff, Ingo Thouret, Gundy Grand. 84M AUS/GRM. prod/rel: Caro, T.I.T.

FOURNIER, ALAIN (1886–1914), FRN, Alain-Fournier, Fournier, Henri-Alban
Le Grand Meaulnes, 1913, Novel
Grand Meaulnes, Le 1967 d: Jean-Gabriel Albicocco. lps: Brigitte Fossey, Jean Blaise, Juliette Villard. 115M FRN. *The Wanderer* (USA) prod/rel: Madeleine Films, Awa Films

FOURNIER, MARC
Paillasse, Play
Femme du Saltimbanque, La 1910 d: Georges DenolA. lps: Georges Dorival, Georges Treville, Marthe Mellot. 385m FRN. prod/rel: Scagl

FOURNIER, ROGER
Moi Mon Corps Mon Ame Montreal Etc., Novel
Au Revoir, a Lundi 1980 d: Maurice Dugowson. lps: Miou-Miou, Carole Laure, Claude Brasseur. 104M CND/FRN. *See You Monday 'Bye*; *See You Monday* prod/rel: Somerville House Prods. Ltd. (Montreal), Fildebroc (Paris)

FOWLER, BRENDA
The Doormat, New York 1922, Play
Honeymoon Express, The 1926 d: James Flood. lps: Willard Louis, Irene Rich, Holmes Herbert. 6768f USA. prod/rel: Warner Brothers Pictures

FOWLER, GENE (1890–1960), USA, Fowler, Eugene Devlan
Beau James, Book
Beau James 1957 d: Melville Shavelson. lps: Bob Hope, Vera Miles, Paul Douglas. 100M USA. prod/rel: Paramount, Hope Enterprises

The Great Magoo, New York 1932, Play
Shoot the Works 1934 d: Wesley Ruggles. lps: Jack Oakie, Ben Bernie, Dorothy Dell. 82M USA. *Thank Your Stars* (UKN); *The Great Magoo* prod/rel: Paramount Productions©
Some Like It Hot 1939 d: George Archainbaud. lps: Bob Hope, Shirley Ross, Una Merkel. 64M USA. *Rhythm Romance* prod/rel: Paramount Pictures©

Union Depot, 1929, Play
Union Depot 1932 d: Alfred E. Green. lps: Douglas Fairbanks Jr., Joan Blondell, Guy Kibbee. 65M USA. *Gentleman for a Day* (UKN) prod/rel: First National Pictures©

FOWLER, HELEN
The Intruder, 1952, Novel
Strange Intruder 1956 d: Irving Rapper. lps: Edmund Purdom, Ida Lupino, Ann Harding. 77M USA. prod/rel: Allied Artists

FOWLES, JOHN (1926–, UKN
The Collector, London 1963, Novel
Collector, The 1965 d: William Wyler. lps: Samantha Eggar, Terence Stamp, Mona Washbourne. 120M UKN/USA. prod/rel: Columbia

The Ebony Tower, Novel
Ebony Tower, The 1987 d: Robert Knights. lps: Laurence Olivier, Toyah Wilcox, Greta Scacchi. TVM. 120M UKN. prod/rel: Granada Tv

The French Lieutenant's Woman, 1959, Novel
French Lieutenant's Woman, The 1981 d: Karel Reisz. lps: Meryl Streep, Jeremy Irons, Hilton McRae. 127M UKN. prod/rel: Uip, Juniper

The Magus, 1965, Novel
Magus, The 1968 d: Guy Green. lps: Michael Caine, Anthony Quinn, Candice Bergen. 116M UKN. *The God Game* prod/rel: Blazer Films, 20th Century-Fox

FOX, JAMES
White Mischief, Book
White Mischief 1988 d: Michael Radford. lps: Charles Dance, Greta Scacchi, Joss Ackland. 105M UKN. prod/rel: Umbrella

FOX JR., JOHN (1863–1919), USA, Fox, John William
The Heart of the Hills, New York 1913, Novel
Heart O' the Hills 1919 d: Sidney A. Franklin. lps: Mary Pickford, Harold Goodwin, Allan Sears. 6329f USA. prod/rel: Mary Pickford Co.©, First National Exhibitors Circuit

The Kentuckians, New York 1897, Novel
Kentuckians, The 1921 d: Charles Maigne. lps: Monte Blue, Wilfred Lytell, Diana Allen. 5981f USA. prod/rel: Famous Players-Lasky, Paramount Pictures

The Little Shepherd of Kingdom Come, New York 1903, Novel
Little Shepherd of Kingdom Come, The 1920 d: Wallace Worsley. lps: Jack Pickford, Clara Horton, Pauline Starke. 5830f USA. prod/rel: Goldwyn Pictures Corp.©, Goldwyn Distributing Corp.
Little Shepherd of Kingdom Come, The 1928 d: Alfred Santell. lps: Richard Barthelmess, Molly O'Day, Nelson McDowell. 7700f USA. *Kentucky Courage* prod/rel: First National Pictures
Little Shepherd of Kingdom Come, The 1961 d: Andrew V. McLaglen. lps: Jimmie Rodgers, Luana Patten, Chill Wills. 108M USA. prod/rel: Associated Producers, Inc.

A Mountain Europa, New York 1899, Novel
Cumberland Romance, A 1920 d: Charles Maigne. lps: Mary Miles Minter, Monte Blue, John Bowers. 5679f USA. *A Mountain Europa* prod/rel: Realart Pictures Corp.©

The Trail of the Lonesome Pine, New York 1908, Novel
Trail of the Lonesome Pine, The 1914 d: Frank L. Dear. lps: Dixie Compton, Mrs. Stuart Robson, Richard Allen. 5r USA. prod/rel: Broadway Picture Producing Co., State Rights
Trail of the Lonesome Pine, The 1916 d: Cecil B. de Mille. lps: Charlotte Walker, Theodore Roberts, Thomas Meighan. 5r USA. prod/rel: Jesse L. Lasky Feature Play Co.©, Paramount Pictures Corp.
Trail of the Lonesome Pine, The 1923 d: Charles Maigne. lps: Mary Miles Minter, Antonio Moreno, Ernest Torrence. 5695f USA. prod/rel: Famous Players-Lasky
Trail of the Lonesome Pine, The 1936 d: Henry Hathaway. lps: Sylvia Sidney, Henry Fonda, Fred MacMurray. 102M USA. prod/rel: Walter Wanger Productions, Paramount Productions©

FOX, NORMAN A.
The Rawhide Years, 1953, Novel
Rawhide Years, The 1956 d: Rudolph Mate. lps: Tony Curtis, Colleen Miller, Arthur Kennedy. 85M USA. prod/rel: Universal-International

Roughshod, Novel
Gunsmoke 1953 d: Nathan Juran. lps: Audie Murphy, Susan Cabot, Paul Kelly. 79M USA. prod/rel: Universal-International

Tall Man Riding, 1951, Novel
Tall Man Riding 1955 d: Lesley Selander. lps: Randolph Scott, Dorothy Malone, Peggie Castle. 83M USA. prod/rel: Warner Bros.

FOX, PAUL HERVEY
Story
Stars are Singing, The 1953 d: Norman Taurog. lps: Rosemary Clooney, Anna Maria Alberghetti, Lauritz Melchior. 99M USA. prod/rel: Paramount

The Soul Kiss, New York 1908, Play
Soldiers and Women 1930 d: Edward Sloman. lps: Aileen Pringle, Grant Withers, Judith Wood. 69M USA. prod/rel: Columbia Pictures

FOX, PAULA
Desperate Characters, Novel
Desperate Characters 1971 d: Frank D. Gilroy. lps: Shirley MacLaine, Kenneth Mars, Gerald S. O'Loughlin. 88M USA. *Desperate Encounters* prod/rel: Itc, T.D.J.

FOXHALL, GEORGE
McPhee's Sensational Rest, 1917, Short Story
Good-By Girls! 1923 d: Jerome Storm. lps: William Russell, Carmel Myers, Tom Wilson. 4746f USA. *Don't Get Excited* prod/rel: Fox Film Corp.

FOYLE, JAMES
Drugstore Cowboy, Novel
Drugstore Cowboy 1989 d: Gus Van Sant Jr. lps: Matt Dillon, Kelly Lynch, James Remar. 100M USA. prod/rel: Avenue

FRACCAROLI, ARNALDO
Biraghin, Play
Biraghin 1946 d: Carmine Gallone. lps: Lilia Silvi, Andrea Checchi, Lauro Gazzolo. F ITL. prod/rel: Excelsa Film, Minerva Film

Ostrega Che Sbrego!, Play
Figaro E la Sua Gran Giornata 1931 d: Mario Camerini. lps: Gianfranco Giachetti, Leda Gloria, Maurizio d'AncorA. 85M ITL. prod/rel: Cines, Anonima Pittaluga

Quello Che Non T'aspetti, Play
Fabbrica Dell'imprevisto, La 1943 d: Jacopo Comin. lps: Maurizio d'Ancora, Vera Bergman, Oretta Fiume. 75M ITL. *Quello Che Non T'aspetti* prod/rel: Atesia Film, Kino Film

Siamo Tutti Milanesi, 1952, Play
Siamo Tutti Milanesi 1954 d: Mario Landi. lps: Carlo Campanini, Liliana Bonfatti, Ugo Tognazzi. 90M ITL. prod/rel: Royalty Film, Cei-Incom

FRADY, MARSHALL
Wallace, Biography
George Wallace 1997 d: John Frankenheimer, Gary Sinise. lps: Mare Winningham, Clarence Williams III, Joe Don Baker. TVM. 240M USA. prod/rel: Tnt

FRALEY, JOSEPH
Story
Good Guys Wear Black 1978 d: Ted Post. lps: Chuck Norris, Anne Archer, James Franciscus. 95M USA. prod/rel: American Cinema

FRALEY, OSCAR
The Untoucables, New York 1957, Book
Scarface Mob, The 1962 d: Phil Karlson. lps: Robert Stack, Keenan Wynn, Barbara Nichols. 105M USA. *Untouchables: the Scarface Mob* prod/rel: Desilu Productions

FRAME, JANET (1924–, NZL, Frame Clutha, Janet Paterson
An Angel at My Table, 1984, Autobiography
Angel at My Table, An 1990 d: Jane Campion. lps: Kerry Fox, Alexia Keogh, Karen Fergusson. 158M NZL/ASL. prod/rel: Hisbiscus Films Ltd.©, New Zealand Film Commission

Envoy from Mirror City, 1985, Autobiography
Angel at My Table, An 1990 d: Jane Campion. lps: Kerry Fox, Alexia Keogh, Karen Fergusson. 158M NZL/ASL. prod/rel: Hisbiscus Films Ltd.©, New Zealand Film Commission

A State of Siege, 1966, Novel
State of Siege, A 1979 d: Vincent Ward. lps: Anne Flannery, Peggy Walker, John Bullock. 52M NZL.

To the Is-Land, 1982, Autobiography
Angel at My Table, An 1990 d: Jane Campion. lps: Kerry Fox, Alexia Keogh, Karen Fergusson. 158M NZL/ASL. prod/rel: Hisbiscus Films Ltd.©, New Zealand Film Commission

FRANCA JUNIOR, OSWALDO
Um Brasileiro Jorge, 1967, Novel
Jorge, Um Brasileiro 1988 d: Paulo Thiago. lps: Carlos Alberto Ricelli, Dean Stockwell, Gloria Pires. 130M BRZ. *Jorge a Brazilian*

FRANCE, ANATOLE (1844–1924), FRN, Thibault, Jacques Anatole Francois
L'affaire Crainquebille, 1901, Short Story
Crainquebille 1922 d: Jacques Feyder. lps: Maurice de Feraudy, Marguerite Carre, Francoise Rosay. 1800m FRN. *Coster Bill of Paris* (USA) prod/rel: Trarieux, Legrand-Vita Films (Vienne)

L' Affaire Crainquebille, 1901, Short Story
Crainquebille 1933 d: Jacques de Baroncelli. lps: Felicien Tramel, Gaston Modot, Rachel Devirys. 65M FRN. prod/rel: Films Artistiques Francais
Crainquebille 1953 d: Ralph Habib. lps: Yves Deniaud, Pierre Mondy, Christian Fourcade. 87M FRN. prod/rel: Calamy

La Comedie de Celui Qui Epousa une Femme Muette, 1912, Play
Ya Qi 1948 d: Wu Renzhi. 98M CHN. *The Dumb Wife*

Le Crime de Sylvestre Bonnard, Paris 1881, Novel
Chasing Yesterday 1935 d: George Nicholls Jr. lps: O. P. Heggie, Anne Shirley, Etienne Girardot. 80M USA. *Prince Charming; Golden Legends; Crime of Sylvestre Bonnard; Sylvestre Bonnard; Paris in Spring* prod/rel: RKO Radio Pictures, Inc.
Crime de Sylvestre Bonnard, Le 1919. lps: Pierre Frondaie. 1150m FRN. prod/rel: Gaumont
Crime de Sylvestre Bonnard, Le 1929 d: Andre Berthomieu. lps: Emile Matrat, Therese Kolb, Gina Barbieri. 2650m FRN. prod/rel: Etoile Film

Histoire Comique, 1903, Novel
Felicie Nanteuil 1942 d: Marc Allegret. lps: Micheline Presle, Mady Berry, Claude Dauphin. 99M FRN. *Le Plus Grand Amour; Histoire Comique* prod/rel: Imperia

Jocaste
Jocaste 1924 d: Gaston Ravel. lps: Gabriel Signoret, Sandra Milowanoff, Abel Tarride. 2000m FRN. prod/rel: Films De France

Le Lys Rouge, Novel
Lys Rouge, Le 1920 d: Charles Maudru. lps: Jean Dax, Suzanne Delve, Gaston Jacquet. 1980m FRN. prod/rel: Films le Lys Rouge

Les Noces Corinthiennes, Play
Noces Corinthiennes, Les 1908-18. lps: Jeanne Marie-Laurent. FRN.

Thais, Paris 1890, Novel
Thais 1914 d: Arthur Maude, Constance Crawley. lps: Arthur Maude, Constance Crawley, George Gebhardt. 4r USA. prod/rel: Loftus Features, Crawley-Maude Features
Thais 1917 d: Frank H. Crane, Hugo Ballin. lps: Mary Garden, Hamilton Revelle, Crauford Kent. 5r USA. prod/rel: Goldwyn Pictures Corp.©, Goldwyn Distributing Corp.
Thais 1983 d: Ryszard Ber. lps: Dorota Kwiatkowska, Jerzy Kryszak. 104M PLN.

FRANCHEVILLE, ROBERT
Chemin de Ronde, Play
Amori Pericolosi 1964 d: Giulio Questi, Carlo Lizzani. lps: Juliette Mayniel, Frank Wolff, Graziella GranatA. 106M ITL/FRN. prod/rel: Zebra Film, Fulco Film (Roma)

L' Enfant de Ma Soeur, Play
Enfant de Ma Soeur, L' 1932 d: Henry Wulschleger. lps: Bach, Georges Treville, Simone Heliard. 90M FRN. prod/rel: Alex Nalpas

La Porte Close, Novel
Etrange Aventure du Docteur Works, L' 1921 d: Robert Saidreau. lps: Jean Herve, Marthe Ferrare, Yves Martel. 1200m FRN.

FRANCHY, FRANZ
Tre Giorni in Paradiso, Novel
Castelli in Aria 1939 d: Augusto GeninA. lps: Lilian Harvey, Vittorio de Sica, Carla SvevA. 96M ITL/GRM. *Ins Blaue Leben* (GRM); *Tre Giorni in Paradiso* prod/rel: Astra Film, Generalcine

FRANCI, ARTURO
La Duchessa Del Bal Tabarin, 1916, Opera
Duchessa Del Bal Tabarin, La 1917 d: Nino Martinengo. lps: Olga Paradisi, Amerigo Di Giorgio, Edy DarcleA. 1379m ITL. prod/rel: Cyrius Film

FRANCIOSA, MASSIMO
Una Chitarra in Paradiso, Short Story
Toto E Marcellino 1958 d: Antonio Musu. lps: Toto, Pablito Calvo, Memmo Carotenuto. 100M ITL/FRN. prod/rel: Euro International Film

FRANCIS, DICK (1920–, UKN
Dead Cert, Novel
Dead Cert 1974 d: Tony Richardson. lps: Scott Antony, Judi Dench, Michael Williams. TVM. 100M UKN. prod/rel: United Artists, Woodfall

FRANCIS, OWEN
Big, 1934, Short Story
Magnificent Brute, The 1936 d: John G. Blystone. lps: Victor McLaglen, Binnie Barnes, William Hall. 80M USA. *A Fool for Blondes; Big* prod/rel: Universal Productions©

FRANCK, DAN
La Separation, Novel
Separation, La 1994 d: Christian Vincent. lps: Isabelle Huppert, Daniel Auteuil, Jerome Deschamps. 88M FRN. *The Separation* prod/rel: Renn, France 2

FRANCK, JOSEPH MARIA
Dschungel, Play
Vom Schicksal Verweht 1942 d: Nunzio MalasommA. lps: Sybille Schmitz, Albrecht Schoenhals, Rudolf Fernau. 95M GRM. prod/rel: F.D.F.

Vom Schicksal Verweht, Play
Giungla 1942 d: Nunzio MalasommA. lps: Vivi Gioi, Rudolf Fernau, Albrecht Schoenhals. 83M ITL. prod/rel: I.C.I., S.a.F.I.C.

FRANCK, PAUL
The Church Mouse, Play
Church Mouse, The 1934 d: Monty Banks. lps: Laura La Plante, Ian Hunter, Edward Chapman. 76M UKN. prod/rel: Warner Bros., First National

Geschaft Mit Amerika, Play
Due Cuori Felici 1932 d: Baldassarre Negroni. lps: Rina Franchetti, Mimi Aylmer, Vittorio de SicA. 78M ITL. prod/rel: Cines, Anonima Pittaluga

Monsieur, Madame Et Bibi 1932 d: Jean Boyer, Max Neufeld. lps: Marie Glory, Robert Lefevre, Jean Dax. 77M FRN. prod/rel: Pathe-Natan

Yes, Mr. Brown 1932 d: Herbert Wilcox, Jack Buchanan. lps: Jack Buchanan, Elsie Randolph, Margot Grahame. 94M UKN. prod/rel: British and Dominions, Woolf & Freedman

Joe and Josette, Play
Josette 1938 d: Allan Dwan. lps: Don Ameche, Simone Simon, Robert Young. 74M USA. *Jo and Josette* prod/rel: Twentieth Century-Fox Film Corp.©

Palace-Hotel, Play
Femme de Mes Reves, La 1931 d: Jean Bertin. lps: Suzy Vernon, Violaine Barry, Roland Toutain. 77M FRN. prod/rel: Societe Des Films Osso

FRANCKE, CAROLINE
Bombshell, Play
Bombshell 1933 d: Victor Fleming. lps: Jean Harlow, Lee Tracy, Frank Morgan. 97M USA. *Blonde Bombshell* (UKN) prod/rel: Metro-Goldwyn-Mayer Corp.

FRANCKE, PETER
Anderthalb Weidinger, Novel
Gottes Engel Sind Uberball 1948 d: Hans Thimig. lps: Attila Horbiger, Heiki Eis, Lotte Lang. 87M AUS. prod/rel: Unitas

In Hamburg Sind Die Nachte Lang, Novel
In Hamburg Sind Die Nachte Lang 1955 d: Max Michel. lps: Barbara Rutting, Alexander Golling, Erwin Strahl. 100M GRM. *The Nights are Long in Hamburg* prod/rel: Kronen, Rank

FRANCO, JESUS
Los Demonios, Novel
Demons, Les 1973 d: Jesus Franco. lps: Karin Field, Doris Thomas, John Foster. 94M FRN/PRT/SPN. *Os Demonios* (PRT); *Les Demons du Sexe*; *The Demons*; *The Sex Demons*; *Demonios, Los* prod/rel: Comptoir Francais Du Film, Interfilme

FRANCOUX, JEAN
Mahlia la Metisse, Novel
Mahlia la Metisse 1942 d: Walter Kapps. lps: Kathe von Nagy, Jean Servais, Pierre Magnier. 93M FRN. prod/rel: Combel Films

FRANGIAS, ANDREAS
I Kangeloporto, Novel
Kangeloporto, I 1979 d: Dimitris Makris. lps: Phaedon Georgitsis, Vangelis Kazan, Eva Kotamanidou. 102M GRC. *The Door With Bars*; *The Iron Gate*

FRANK, ANNE (1929–1944), GRM
Anne Frank: the Diary of a Young Girl, Book
Diary of Anne Frank, The 1959 d: George Stevens. lps: Millie Perkins, Joseph Schildkraut, Shelley Winters. 171M USA. prod/rel: 20th Century-Fox

FRANK, BERNARD
Fragments d'Epaves, Novel
En Plongee 1926 d: Jacques Robert. lps: Lilian Constantini, Olga Noel, Daniel Mendaille. F FRN. *Fragments d'Epaves* prod/rel: Societe Des Cineromans

FRANK, BRUNO (1887–1945), GRM
Cervantes, Amsterdam 1934, Novel
Avventure E Gli Amori Di Miguel Cervantes, Le 1967 d: Vincent Sherman. lps: Horst Buchholz, Gina Lollobrigida, Jose Ferrer. 135M ITL/FRN/SPN. *Les Aventures Extraordinaires de Cervantes* (FRN); *The Young Rebel* (USA); *Cervantes* (SPN) prod/rel: Prisma Film (Spain), Protor Film (Roma)

Perlenkomodie, 1928, Play
Zweierlei Moral 1930 d: Gerhard Lamprecht. 84M GRM. *Frau Wera's Schwarze Perlen*

Sturm Im Wasserglas, 1930, Play
Blumenfrau von Lindenau, Die 1931 d: Georg Jacoby. lps: Paul Otto, Renate Muller, Harald Paulsen. 92M GRM/AUS. *Sturm Im Wasserglas*

Storm in a Teacup 1937 d: Victor Saville, Ian Dalrymple. lps: Vivien Leigh, Rex Harrison, Sara Allgood. 87M UKN. prod/rel: London Films, Victor Saville Productions

Sturm Im Wasserglas 1960 d: Josef von Baky. lps: Therese Giehse, Ingrid Andree, Hanns Lothar. 97M GRM. *Tempest in a Water Glass* prod/rel: Filmaufbau, Europa

Der Roman Eines Gunstlings Trenck, 1926, Novel
Trenck 1932 d: Ernst Neubach, Heinz Paul. lps: Hans Stuwe, Dorothea Wieck, Olga TschechowA. 100M GRM. *Trenck -Roman Einer Grossen Liebe*; *Trenck Der Roman Eines Gunstlings* prod/rel: Phoebus, Rhein-Main

FRANK, CHRISTOPHER
L' Annee Des Meduses, Novel
Annee Des Meduses, L' 1984 d: Christopher Frank. lps: Valerie Kaprisky, Bernard Giraudeau, Caroline Cellier. 110M FRN. prod/rel: T Films, Fr 3

C'est Daimer, L' Important, Novel
Important, C'est d'Aimer, L' 1974 d: Andrzej Zulawski. lps: Romy Schneider, Fabio Testi, Jacques Dutronc. 128M FRN/ITL/GRM. *The Most Important Thing: Love* (USA); *L' Importante E Amare* (ITL); *Nachtblende* (GRM); *The Inportant Thing Is Too Love*; *Night Filter* prod/rel: Rizzoli Film

FRANK, GEROLD
Beloved Infidel, Book
Beloved Infidel 1959 d: Henry King. lps: Gregory Peck, Deborah Kerr, Eddie Albert. 123M USA. prod/rel: 20th Century-Fox, Jerry Wald

The Boston Strangler, New York 1966, Book
Boston Strangler, The 1968 d: Richard Fleischer. lps: Tony Curtis, Henry Fonda, George Kennedy. 120M USA. prod/rel: 20th Century Fox

I'll Cry Tomorrow, Book
I'll Cry Tomorrow 1955 d: Daniel Mann. lps: Susan Hayward, Richard Conte, Eddie Albert. 117M USA. prod/rel: MGM

FRANK, JOSEF MARIA
Ein Traum Zerbricht, Novel
Zwischen Hamburg Und Haiti 1940 d: Erich Waschneck. lps: Gisela Uhlen, Gustav Knuth, Walter Franck. 85M GRM. prod/rel: Universum, Kristall

FRANK, JULIAN
The Call, Play
Infatuation 1930 d: Sasha Geneen. lps: Godfrey Tearle, Jeanne de Casalis, Jack Raine. 35M UKN. prod/rel: Alpha

FRANK, LEONHARD (1882–1961), GRM
Die Junger Jesu, 1949, Novel
Chronik Eines Mordes 1965 d: Joachim Hasler. lps: Angelica Domrose, Ulrich Thien. 91M GDR. *Chronicle of a Murder*

Karl Und Anna, 1926, Short Story
Desire Me 1947 d: George Cukor (Uncredited), Mervyn Leroy (Uncredited). lps: Greer Garson, Richard Hart, Robert Mitchum. 91M USA. *A Woman of My Own* prod/rel: MGM

Frau Und Der Fremde, Die 1984 d: Rainer Simon. lps: Joachim Latsch, Kathrin Waligura, Peter Zimmermann. 97M GDR. *The Woman and the Stranger*

Heimkehr 1928 d: Joe May. lps: Lars Hanson, Dita Parlo, Gustav Frohlich. 3006m GRM. *Homecoming* prod/rel: Joe May-Film

Die Rauberbande, Novel
Rauberbande, Die 1928 d: Hans Behrendt. lps: Gustl Stark-Gstettenbaur, Martin Herzberg, Paul Horbiger. 2722m GRM. *The Robber Band* prod/rel: Felsom-Film, Deutschen Vereins-Film Ag

FRANK, MARCEL
Tant Qu'il Y Aura Des Femmes, Play
Tant Qu'il Y Aura Des Femmes 1955 d: Edmond T. Greville. lps: Pierre Destailles, Mireille Perrey, Edith Georges. 75M FRN. *Le Congres de Clermont-Ferrand* prod/rel: Films De Venloo

FRANK, MARTIN
F. Est un Salaud, Novel
F. Est un Salaud 1998 d: Marcel Gisler. lps: Frederic Andrau, Vincent Branchet, Urs-Peter Halter. 95M SWT/FRN. *F. Is a Bastard* prod/rel: Vega Film (Switzerland), Arena Films

FRANK, PAT
The Girl Who Almost Got Away, Short Story
Man's Favorite Sport? 1964 d: Howard Hawks. lps: Rock Hudson, Paula Prentiss, Maria Perschy. 120M USA. prod/rel: Laurel Productions, Gibraltar Productions

Hold Back the Night, 1952, Novel
Hold Back the Night 1956 d: Allan Dwan. lps: John Payne, Mona Freeman, Peter Graves. 80M USA. prod/rel: Allied Artists, Hayes Goetz Prods.

FRANK, WALDEMAR
Hochzeitsreise Ohne Mann, Play
Ehe Man Ehemann Wird 1941 d: Alwin Elling. lps: Ewald Balser, Heli Finkenzeller, Maria Paudler. 97M GRM. prod/rel: Astra, Karp

Polterabend, Play
Polterabend 1940 d: Carl Boese. lps: Grethe Weiser, Camilla Horn, Rudi Godden. 88M GRM. prod/rel: Astra, Adler

FRANK, WOLFGANG
Schiff 16, Book
Sotto Dieci Bandiere 1960 d: Duilio Coletti, Silvio Narizzano. lps: Van Heflin, Charles Laughton, Mylene Demongeot. 112M ITL/UKN/USA. *Under Ten Flags* (UKN) prod/rel: Dino de Laurentiis Cin.Ca

FRANKAU, GILBERT (1884–1952), UKN
Christopher Strong: a Romance, New York 1932, Novel
Christopher Strong 1933 d: Dorothy Arzner. lps: Katharine Hepburn, Colin Clive, Billie Burke. 77M USA. *The Great Desire*; *The White Moth* prod/rel: RKO Radio Pictures, Inc.

Gerald Cranston's Lady, New York 1924, Novel
Gerald Cranston's Lady 1924 d: Emmett J. Flynn. lps: James Kirkwood, Alma Rubens, Walter McGrail. 6674f USA. prod/rel: Fox Film Corp.

If I Marry Again, Story
If I Marry Again 1925 d: John Francis Dillon. lps: Doris Kenyon, Lloyd Hughes, Frank Mayo. 7401f USA. prod/rel: First National Pictures

The Love Story of Aliette Brunton, Novel
Love Story of Aliette Brunton, The 1924 d: Maurice Elvey. lps: Isobel Elsom, Henry Victor, James Carew. 7300f UKN. prod/rel: Stoll

FRANKEN, ROSE (1895–, USA
Another Language, New York 1932, Play
Another Language 1933 d: Edward H. Griffith. lps: Helen Hayes, Robert Montgomery, Louise Closser Hale. 79M USA. prod/rel: Metro-Goldwyn-Mayer Corp.

Claudia, Novel
Claudia 1943 d: Edmund Goulding. lps: Dorothy McGuire, Robert Young, Ina Claire. 91M USA. prod/rel: Twentieth Century-Fox

FRANKLIN, EDGAR
Adopted Father, 1916, Short Story
Everybody's Old Man 1936 d: James Flood. lps: Irvin S. Cobb, Rochelle Hudson, Johnny Downs. 84M USA. prod/rel: Twentieth Century-Fox Film Corp.©

Twenty Dollars a Week 1924 d: F. Harmon Weight. lps: George Arliss, Taylor Holmes, Edith Roberts. 5990f USA. *The Man Maker* (UKN); *$20 a Week* prod/rel: Distinctive Pictures, Selznick Distributing Corp.

Working Man, The 1933 d: John G. Adolfi. lps: George Arliss, Bette Davis, Hardie Albright. 77M USA. *The Adopted Father* prod/rel: Warner Bros. Pictures©

Annexing Bill, Short Story
Annexing Bill 1918 d: Albert Parker. lps: Gladys Hulette, Creighton Hale, Margaret Greene. 5r USA. prod/rel: Astra Film Corp., Pathe Exchange, Inc.©

B, 1916, Short Story
Rail Rider, The 1916 d: Maurice Tourneur. lps: House Peters, Zena Keefe, Bertram Marburgh. 5r USA. prod/rel: Paragon Films, Inc., World Film Corp.©

Beware of the Bride, 1920, Short Story
Beware of the Bride 1920 d: Howard M. Mitchell. lps: Eileen Percy, Walter McGrail, Hallam Cooley. 5r USA. prod/rel: Fox Film Corp.©, 20th Century Brand

Don't Ever Marry, 1919, Short Story
Don't Ever Marry 1920 d: Marshall Neilan, Victor Heerman. lps: Matt Moore, Marjorie Daw, Thomas Guise. 6518f USA. prod/rel: Marshall Neilan Productions©, First National Exhibitors Circuit

The Dub, 1916, Short Story
Dub, The 1919 d: James Cruze. lps: Wallace Reid, Nina Byron, Charles Ogle. 4401f USA. prod/rel: Famous Players-Lasky Corp.©, Paramount Pictures

Everything But the Truth, 1919, Short Story
Everything But the Truth 1920 d: Eddie Lyons, Lee Moran. lps: Eddie Lyons, Lee Moran, Beatrice La Plante. 4775f USA. prod/rel: Universal Film Mfg. Co.©

Fixed By George, 1920, Short Story
Fixed By George 1920 d: Eddie Lyons, Lee Moran. lps: Eddie Lyons, Lee Moran, Beatrice La Plante. 4580f USA. prod/rel: Universal Film Mfg. Co.©

Good Looking and Rich, Short Story
Easy Millions 1933 d: Fred Newmeyer. lps: Dorothy Burgess, Skeets Gallagher, Merna Kennedy. 69M USA. *Good Looking and Rich* prod/rel: Freuler Film Associates, Monarch Productions

Lady Barnacle, 1917, Short Story
Lady Barnacle 1917 d: John H. Collins. lps: Viola Dana, Robert Walker, Augustus Phillips. 5r USA. prod/rel: Metro Pictures Corp.©

One Bright Idea, 1918, Short Story
All Night 1918 d: Paul Powell. lps: Carmel Myers, Rudolph Valentino, Charles Dorian. 5r USA. *One Bright Idea* prod/rel: Bluebird Photoplays, Inc.©

Opportunity, 1917, Short Story
Opportunity 1918 d: John H. Collins. lps: Viola Dana, Hale Hamilton, Frank Currier. 5r USA. prod/rel: Metro Pictures Corp.©

Poker Faces, 1923, Short Story
Poker Faces 1926 d: Harry Pollard. lps: Edward Everett Horton, Laura La Plante, George Siegmann. 7808f USA. prod/rel: Universal Pictures

Protecting Prue, 1924, Short Story
My Lady of Whims 1925 d: Dallas M. Fitzgerald. lps: Clara Bow, Donald Keith, Carmelita Geraghty. 7r USA. prod/rel: Dallas M. Fitzgerald Productions, Arrow Pictures

Rescuing Anne, Novel
Anne One Hundred 1933 d: Henry Edwards. lps: Betty Stockfeld, Gyles Isham, Dennis Wyndham. 66M UKN. prod/rel: British and Dominions, Paramount British

Right After Brown, Short Story
Web of Chance, The 1919 d: Alfred E. Green. lps: Peggy Hyland, Harry Ham, Edwin Booth Tilton. 5r USA. prod/rel: Fox Film Corp., William Fox©

Stay Home, 1921, Short Story
I Can Explain 1922 d: George D. Baker. lps: Gareth Hughes, Bartine Burkette, Grace Darmond. 5164f USA. *Stay Home* prod/rel: S-L Pictures, Metro Pictures

Whatever She Wants, 1921, Short Story
Whatever She Wants 1921 d: C. R. Wallace. lps: Eileen Percy, Herbert Fortier, Richard Wayne. 4616f USA. prod/rel: Fox Film Corp.

Where Was I?, 1924, Short Story
Where Was I? 1925 d: William A. Seiter. lps: Reginald Denny, Marion Nixon, Pauline Garon. 6630f USA. prod/rel: Universal Pictures

FRANKLIN, GEORGE CORY
Into the Crimson West, 1930, Short Story
Prairie Schooners 1940 d: Sam Nelson. lps: Bill Elliott, Evelyn Young, Dub Taylor. 58M USA. *Through the Storm* (UKN); *Into the Crimson West* prod/rel: Columbia Pictures Corp.©

FRANKLIN, MILES (1879–1954), ASL, Franklin, Stella Maria Miles
My Brilliant Career, 1901, Novel
My Brilliant Career 1979 d: Gillian Armstrong. lps: Judy Davis, Sam Neill, Wendy Hughes. 101M ASL. prod/rel: New South Wales Film Corp., Guo Film Distributors

FRANSSENS, JEAN PAUL
Broederweelde, Novel
No Trains No Planes 1999 d: Jos Stelling. lps: Dirk Van Dijck, Ten Damme Ellen, Henri Garcin. 113M NTH. prod/rel: Jos Stelling Films, Vpro

De Wisselwachter, Novel
Wisselwachter, de 1986 d: Jos Stelling. lps: Jim Van Der Woude, Stephane Excoffier, Johnny Kraaykamp. 94M NTH. *The Pointsman* prod/rel: Jos Stelling Prod.

FRANZOS, KARL EMIL
Judith Trachtenberg, New York 1891, Novel
Daughter of Her People, A 1932 d: George Roland. lps: Joseph Greenberg, Chaim Shneyer, Morris Dorf. 75M USA. *Yidishe Tochter* prod/rel: Standard Film Co.
Judith Trachtenberg 1920 d: Henrik Galeen. lps: Leontine Kuhnberg, Ernst Deutsch, Leonhard Haskel. 2373m GRM.

FRAPIE, LEON
La Maternelle, Novel
Maternelle, La 1925 d: Gaston Roudes. lps: France Dhelia, Lucien Dalsace, Paul Ollivier. 2350m FRN. *Petite Mere* prod/rel: Grandes Productions Cinematographiques
Maternelle, La 1933 d: Jean Benoit-Levy, Marie Epstein. lps: Madeleine Renaud, Henri Debain, Mady Berry. 100M FRN. *Nursery School* prod/rel: Benoit-Levy, Jean
Maternelle, La 1948 d: Henri Diamant-Berger. lps: Pierre Larquey, Yves Vincent, Marcel Mouloudji. 105M FRN. prod/rel: Gregoire Geftman

FRAPPA, JEAN-JOSE
La Dame de Haut-le-Bois, Novel
Dame de Haut-le-Bois, La 1946 d: Jacques Daroy. lps: Francoise Rosay, Madeleine Rousset, Raymond Loyer. 95M FRN. prod/rel: Rhodia Films

L' Homme Riche, Paris 1914, Play
Billions 1920 d: Ray C. Smallwood. lps: Alla Nazimova, Charles Bryant, William Irving. 6r USA. prod/rel: the Nazimova Productions, Metro Pictures Corp.©

La Princesse aux Clowns, Novel
Princesse aux Clowns, La 1925 d: Andre Hugon. lps: Huguette Duflos, Charles de Rochefort, Guy Favieres. 2700m FRN. prod/rel: Etablissements Louis Aubert

FRASER, CEDRIC D.
M'lord of the White Road, Novel
M'lord of the White Road 1923 d: Arthur Rooke. lps: Victor McLaglen, Marjorie Hume, James Lindsay. 6800f UKN. prod/rel: I. B. Davidson, Granger

FRASER, FERRIN
Fang and Claw, New York 1935, Book
Fang and Claw 1935 d: Frank Buck, Ray Taylor. lps: Frank Buck. DOC. 74M USA. prod/rel: Van Beuren Corp.©, RKO Radio Pictures

FRASER, GEORG
Ein Anstandiger Mensch, Play
Skandal in Der Botschaft 1950 d: Erik Ode. lps: Viktor de Kowa, Jeanette Schultze, Michi TanakA. 95M GRM. *Scandal at the Embassy* prod/rel: Eichberg, N.F.

Joe and Josette, Play
Josette 1938 d: Allan Dwan. lps: Don Ameche, Simone Simon, Robert Young. 74M USA. *Jo and Josette* prod/rel: Twentieth Century-Fox Film Corp.©

FRASER, GEORGE MACDONALD (1925–, UKN
Royal Flash, Novel
Royal Flash 1975 d: Richard Lester. lps: Malcolm McDowell, Alan Bates, Florinda Bolkan. 118M UKN. prod/rel: 20th Century Fox, Two Roads

FRASER, JOHN CRAWFORD
The Ace of Spades, Novel
Ace of Spades, The 1935 d: George Pearson. lps: Michael Hogan, Dorothy Boyd, Richard Cooper. 66M UKN. prod/rel: Real Art, Radio

FRASER, WILLIAM ALEXANDER
Thoroughbreds, New York 1902, Novel
Million Dollar Handicap, The 1925 d: Scott Sidney. lps: Vera Reynolds, Edmund Burns, Ralph Lewis. 6117f USA. *The Pride of the Paddock* prod/rel: Metropolitan Pictures, Producers Distributing Corp.

FRASER-SIMSON, HAROLD
A Southern Maid, London 1920, Musical Play
Southern Maid, A 1933 d: Harry Hughes. lps: Bebe Daniels, Clifford Mollison, Harry Welchman. 85M UKN. prod/rel: British International Pictures, Wardour

FRASER-SMITH, CECILY
A Honeymoon Adventure, Novel
Honeymoon Adventure, A 1931 d: Maurice Elvey. lps: Benita Hume, Harold Huth, Peter Hannen. 67M UKN. *Footsteps in the Night* (USA) prod/rel: Associated Talking Pictures, Radio

FRATELLI QUINTERO
El Genio Alegre, 1906
Anima Allegra 1919 d: Roberto Leone Roberti. lps: Francesca Bertini, Livio Pavanelli, Luigi Cigoli. 1551m ITL. prod/rel: Caesar Film

FRAYN, MICHAEL (1933–, UKN
Noises Off, Play
Noises Off 1992 d: Peter Bogdanovich. lps: Carol Burnett, Michael Caine, Denholm Elliott. 104M USA. prod/rel: Touchstone Pictures, Amblin Entertainment

FRAZEE, STEVE
Death Rides the Trail, Short Story
Wild Heritage 1958 d: Charles Haas. lps: Will Rogers Jr., Maureen O'Sullivan, Rod McKuen. 78M USA. *Death Rides This Trail* prod/rel: Universal-International

Desert Guns, New York 1957, Novel
Gold of the Seven Saints 1961 d: Gordon Douglas. lps: Clint Walker, Roger Moore, Leticia Roman. 88M USA. prod/rel: Warner Bros. Pictures

High Hell, Novel
High Hell 1958 d: Burt Balaban. lps: John Derek, Elaine Stewart, Patrick Allen. 85M UKN. prod/rel: Paramount, Rich & Rich

Many Rivers to Cross, Short Story
Many Rivers to Cross 1954 d: Roy Rowland. lps: Eleanor Parker, Robert Taylor, Victor McLaglen. 92M USA. prod/rel: MGM

My Brother Down There, Story
Running Target 1956 d: Marvin R. Weinstein. lps: Arthur Franz, Doris Dowling, Richard Reeves. 83M USA. *My Brother Down There* prod/rel: United Artists, Canyon Pictures

FRAZER, WILLIAM E.
Hunting the Highway Pirates, 1937, Article
Tip-Off Girls 1938 d: Louis King. lps: Lloyd Nolan, Mary Carlisle, Evelyn Brent. 61M USA. *Highway Racketeers* prod/rel: Paramount Pictures©

FRAZER-SIMPSON, CICELY
The Clock, Novel
Fatal Hour, The 1937 d: George Pearson. lps: Edward Rigby, Moira Reed, Moore Marriott. 66M UKN. prod/rel: British and Dominions, Paramount British

FREDE, RICHARD
The Interns, New York 1960, Novel
Interns, The 1962 d: David Swift. lps: Michael Callan, Cliff Robertson, James MacArthur. 120M USA. prod/rel: Interns Co., Columbia

FREDERICKS, ARNOLD
One Million Francs, New York 1912, Novel
One Million Dollars 1915 d: John W. Noble. lps: William Faversham, Henry Bergman, George Le Guere. 5r USA. prod/rel: Rolfe Photoplays Inc., Metro Pictures Corp.©

FREDERSDORF, H. B.
Ich Zahle Taglich Meine Sorgen, Novel
Ich Zahle Taglich Mein Sorgen 1960 d: Paul Martin. lps: Peter Alexander, Ingeborg Schoner, Gunther Philipp. 93M GRM. *I Count My Woes Daily* prod/rel: Studio, Constantin

FREDRICKSON, OLIVE
Silence of the North, Book
Silence of the North 1981 d: Allan King. lps: Ellen Burstyn, Tom Skerritt, Gordon Pinsent. 94M CND. *Silence in the North*; *Comes a Time* prod/rel: Universal Films, Universal Productions Canada Inc.

FREDRO, ALEXANDER (1793–1876), PLN, Fredro, Aleksander
Zemsta, 1833, Play
Zemsta 1957 d: Antoni Bohdziewicz. lps: Jan Kurnakowicz, Jacek Woszczerowicz. 93M PLN. *Revenge*

FREED, DONALD
Secret Honor, Play
Secret Honor 1984 d: Robert Altman. lps: Philip Baker Hall. 90M USA. *Secret Honor: a Political Myth*; *Lords of Treason*; *Secret Honor: the Last Testament of Richard M. Nixon* prod/rel: Cinecom, Sandcastle 5

FREED, JOSH
Moonwebs, Book
Ticket to Heaven 1981 d: Ralph L. Thomas. lps: Nick Mancuso, Saul Rubinek, Meg Foster. 107M CND. *The Moon Stalkers* prod/rel: Ronald I. Cohen Productions Inc., Stalkers Productions Inc.

FREEDMAN, BENEDICT
Mrs. Mike, Book
Mrs. Mike 1949 d: Louis King. lps: Dick Powell, Evelyn Keyes, J. M. Kerrigan. 99M USA. prod/rel: United Artists

FREEDMAN, DAVID
Anatomy of Ballyhoo: Phantom Fame, New York 1931, Book
Half Naked Truth, The 1932 d: Gregory La CavA. lps: Lupe Velez, Lee Tracy, Eugene Pallette. 77M USA. *Phantom Fame*; *The Half-Naked Truth* prod/rel: RKO Radio Pictures©

Day at the Brokers, 1936, Play
New Faces of 1937 1937 d: Leigh Jason. lps: Joe Penner, Milton Berle, Parkyakarkus. 100M USA. *Young People* prod/rel: RKO Radio Pictures©

Inc. Mendel, New York 1929, Play
Heart of New York, The 1932 d: Mervyn Leroy. lps: George Sidney, Anna Apfel, Aline MacMahon. 74M USA. prod/rel: Warner Bros. Pictures©

FREEDMAN, NANCY
Mrs. Mike, Book
Mrs. Mike 1949 d: Louis King. lps: Dick Powell, Evelyn Keyes, J. M. Kerrigan. 99M USA. prod/rel: United Artists

FREELING, NICOLAS (1927–, UKN
Novel
Van Der Valk Und Das Madchen 1972 d: Peter Zadek. lps: Frank Finlay, Francoise Prevost, Cyd Hayman. TVM. 108M GRM/UKN. *Gun Before Butter* prod/rel: Iduna Film

Love in Amsterdam, Novel
Amsterdam Affair 1968 d: Gerry O'HarA. lps: Wolfgang Kieling, William Marlowe, Catherine Schell. 91M UKN. prod/rel: London Independent Producers, Trio-Group W

FREEMAN, CHARLES
Hand in Glove, 1944, Play
Urge to Kill 1960 d: Vernon Sewell. lps: Patrick Barr, Howard Pays, Ruth Dunning. 58M UKN. prod/rel: Anglo-Amalgamated, Merton Park

FREEMAN, DEVERY
Story
Tell It to the Judge 1949 d: Norman Foster. lps: Rosalind Russell, Robert Cummings, Gig Young. 87M USA. prod/rel: Columbia

Father Sky, Novel
Taps 1981 d: Harold Becker. lps: George C. Scott, Timothy Hutton, Ronny Cox. 122M USA. *T.a.P.S.* prod/rel: 20th Century Fox
Public Pigeon No. 1, 1956, Television Play
Public Pigeon No. 1 1957 d: Norman Z. McLeod. lps: Red Skelton, Vivian Blaine, Janet Blair. 75M USA. prod/rel: Universal-International

FREEMAN, EVERETT
Thousand Dollars a Minute, 1935, Short Story
$1000 a Minute 1935 d: Aubrey Scotto. lps: Roger Pryor, Leila Hyams, George Hayes. 70M USA. prod/rel: Republic Pictures Corp.©

FREEMAN, GILLIAN
Novel
Liberty Man, The 1958 d: Lionel Brett. lps: Richard Pasco, Jane Barrett. MTV. 90M UKN. prod/rel: Granada

FREEMAN, LEA DAVID
Ruby, Play
Lazy River 1934 d: George B. Seitz. lps: Robert Young, Jean Parker, Ted Healy. 75M USA. *Louisiana*; *Ruby*; *Dance Hall Daisy*; *Bride of the Bayou*; *In Old Louisiana* prod/rel: Metro-Goldwyn-Mayer Corp.©

FREEMAN, LEONARD
The All-American, Story
All-American, The 1953 d: Jesse Hibbs. lps: Tony Curtis, Lori Nelson, Richard Long. 83M USA. *The Winning Way* (UKN) prod/rel: Universal-International

FREEMAN, LUCY
Betrayal, Book
Betrayal 1978 d: Paul Wendkos. lps: Lesley Ann Warren, Rip Torn, Richard Masur. TVM. 100M USA. prod/rel: NBC, Emi Television

FREEMAN, MARY E. WILKINS (1852–1930), USA
An Alabaster Box, New York 1917, Novel
Alabaster Box, An 1917 d: Chet Withey. lps: Alice Joyce, Marc McDermott, Harry Ham. 5r USA. prod/rel: Vitagraph Co. of America©, Blue Ribbon Feature
Madelon, New York 1896, Novel
False Evidence 1919 d: Edwin Carewe. lps: Viola Dana, Pat O'Malley, Wheeler Oakman. 5r USA. *Madelon of the Redwoods* prod/rel: Metro Pictures Corp.©

FREEMANTLE, BRIAN
Charlie Muffin, Novel
Charlie Muffin 1979 d: Jack Gold. lps: David Hemmings, Sam Wanamaker, Jennie Linden. TVM. 109M UKN. *A Deadly Game* prod/rel: Euston Films, Thames Tv

FRENCH, ANNE WARNER
The Gay and Festive Claverhouse, Boston 1914, Novel
Gay and Festive Claverhouse 1918? d: Charles J. Brabin. lps: Francis X. Bushman, Beverly Bayne. 5r USA. prod/rel: Metro Pictures Corp.

FRENCH, MARILYN (1929–, USA, Solwoska, Mara
The Women's Room, Novel
Women's Room, The 1980 d: Glenn Jordan. lps: Lee Remick, Colleen Dewhurst, Patty Duke. TVM. 150M USA.

FRENSSEN, GUSTAV
Die Sandgrafin, Novel
Sandgrafin, Die 1927 d: Hans Steinhoff. lps: Christa Tordy, Kathe von Nagy, Jack Trevor. 2782m GRM. prod/rel: Orplid-Film

FRERE, MAUD
La Delice, Novel
Isabelle Devant le Desir 1974 d: Jean-Pierre Berckmans. lps: Anicee Alvina, Jean Rochefort, Mathieu Carriere. 90M FRN/BLG. *Isabelle and Lust*

FREUCHEN, PETER
Die Flucht Ins Weisse Land, 1929, Book
Eskimo 1933 d: W. S. Van Dyke. lps: Mala, Lotus Long, Joseph Sawyer. 120M USA. *Mala the Magnificent* (UKN) prod/rel: Metro-Goldwyn-Mayer Corp.©
Storfanger, 1927, Book
Eskimo 1933 d: W. S. Van Dyke. lps: Mala, Lotus Long, Joseph Sawyer. 120M USA. *Mala the Magnificent* (UKN) prod/rel: Metro-Goldwyn-Mayer Corp.©

FREUD, ESTHER
Hideous Kinky, Novel
Hideous Kinky 1998 d: Gillies MacKinnon. lps: Kate Winslet, Said Taghmaoui, Bella RizA. 97M UKN/FRN. prod/rel: Greenpoint Films (U.K.), Amlf (France)

FREUND, JULIUS
Durchlaucht Radieschen, Play
Durchlaucht Radieschen 1927 d: Richard Eichberg. lps: Xenia Desni, Werner Fuetterer, Hans Junkermann. 2105m GRM. prod/rel: Eichberg-Film

FREUSTIE, JEAN
Le Toubib, Novel
Toubib, Le 1979 d: Pierre Granier-Deferre. lps: Alain Delon, Veronique Jannot, Bernard Giraudeau. 95M FRN. *The Greatest Attack* (UKN); *Prelude to Apocalypse*; *Harmonie*; *The Medic* prod/rel: Adel, Antenne 2

FREY, DARCY
Something's Got to Give, Article
Pushing Tin 1999 d: Mike Newell. lps: John Cusack, Billy Bob Thornton, Cate Blanchett. 124M USA. prod/rel: 20th Century Fox, Fox 2000 Pictures

FRICK, MARLENA
The Homecoming, Short Story
Heureux Qui Comme Ulysse 1970 d: Henri Colpi. lps: Fernandel, Max Amyl, Gilberte Rivet. 91M FRN/ITL. *Ulisse Non Deve Morire* (ITL) prod/rel: Terra Films, Cite Films

FRIDEGARD, JAN
En Natt I Juli, 1933, Novel
Nar Angarna Blommar 1946 d: Erik Faustman. lps: Sigurd Wallen, Dagny Lind, Birger Malmsten. 77M SWD. *When Meadows Bloom* prod/rel: Filmo
Lars Hard Jag, 1935, Novel
Lars Hard 1948 d: Erik Faustman. lps: Torsten Bergstrom, Rut Holm, Ann Mari Uddenberg. 95M SWD. prod/rel: Ab Sandrew-Produktion

FRIED, HARRY
Three Flights Up, Story
Dancing Sweeties 1930 d: Ray Enright. lps: Grant Withers, Sue Carol, Eddie Phillips. 5656f USA. *Three Flights Up* prod/rel: Warner Brothers Pictures

FRIEDMAN, BRUCE JAY (1930–, USA
The Lonely Guy's Book of Life, Novel
Lonely Guy, The 1984 d: Arthur Hiller. lps: Steve Martin, Charles Grodin, Judith Ivey. 93M USA. prod/rel: Universal

FRIEDMAN, CARL
The Shovel and the Loom, Novel
Left Luggage 1998 d: Jeroen Krabbe. lps: Laura Fraser, Isabella Rossellini, Maximilian Schell. 100M NTH/BLG/USA. prod/rel: Left Luggage Bv©, Shooting Star/Flying Dutchman Prods.

FRIEDMAN, DAVID F.
Brand of Shame, Novel
Brand of Shame 1968 d: B. Ron Elliott. lps: Donna Duzzit, Steve Stunning, Bart Black. 74M USA. *The Brand*

FRIEDMAN, JAY
Detroit Abe, Novel
Doctor Detroit 1983 d: Michael Pressman. lps: Dan Aykroyd, Howard Hesseman, T. K. Carter. 89M USA. *Dr. Detroit* prod/rel: Universal

FRIEL, BRIAN (1929–, IRL
Dancing at Lughnasa, 1989, Play
Dancing at Lughnasa 1998 d: Pat O'Connor. lps: Meryl Streep, Michael Gambon, Catherine McCormack. 95M IRL/UKN/USA. prod/rel: Ferndale Films Ltd.©, Capital Films

FRIEND, OSCAR J.
Click of the Triangle T, Chicago 1925, Novel
Phantom Bullet, The 1926 d: Cliff Smith. lps: Hoot Gibson, Eileen Percy, Allan Forrest. 6148f USA. prod/rel: Universal Pictures

FRIES, AVA OSTERN
Troop Beverly Hills
Troop Beverly Hills 1989 d: Jeff Kanew. lps: Shelley Long, Craig T. Nelson, Betty Thomas. 105M USA. *Be Prepared* prod/rel: Columbia

FRIESE, ERNST
Der Mann in Der Wanne, Play
Mann in Der Wanne, Der 1952 d: Franz Antel. lps: Axel von Ambesser, Maria Andergast, Jeanette Schultze. 93M AUS. prod/rel: Neusser

FRIIS, JENS ANDREAS
Fra Finmarken: Skildringer, Kristiania 1881, Novel
Laila 1958 d: Rolf Husberg. lps: Erika Remberg, Joachim Hansen, Birger Malmsten. 100M SWD/GRM. *Laila - Liebe Unter Der Mitternachtssonne* (GRM); *Make Way for Lila* (USA); *Lila* prod/rel: Sandrews, Rhombus Film

FRIML, RUDOLF (1879–1972), CZC, Friml, Charles Rudolf
The Firefly, New York 1912, Operetta
Firefly, The 1937 d: Robert Z. Leonard. lps: Jeanette MacDonald, Allan Jones, Warren William. 131M USA. prod/rel: Metro-Goldwyn-Mayer Corp.©

FRISBY, TERENCE
There's a Girl in My Soup, London 1966, Play
There's a Girl in My Soup 1970 d: Roy Boulting. lps: Peter Sellers, Goldie Hawn, Tony Britton. 96M UKN. prod/rel: Ascot Productions, Charter

FRISCH, MAX (1911–1991), SWT
Blaubart, 1982, Novel
Blaubart 1984 d: Krzysztof Zanussi. lps: Vadim Glowna, Karin Baal, Vera TschechowA. MTV. 92M GRM/SWT. *Bluebeard* prod/rel: Wdr, Drs
Homo Faber, 1957, Novel
Passagier Faber 1990 d: Volker Schlondorff. lps: Sam Shepard, Julie Delpy, Barbara SukowA. 117M GRM. *Voyager* (USA); *Passenger Faber*; *Homo Faber* prod/rel: Bioskop Film (Munich), Action Films (Paris)

FRISON-ROCHE, ROGER (1906–, FRN
Premier de Cordee, Novel
Premier de Cordee 1943 d: Louis Daquin. lps: Andre Le Gall, Lucien Blondeau, Irene Corday. 106M FRN. prod/rel: Wipf, Louis

FRITSCH, GERHARD
Moos Auf Den Steinen, Novel
Moos Auf Den Steinen 1968 d: Georg Lhotzky. lps: Erika Pluhar, Heinz Trixner, Louis Ries. 82M AUS. *Moss on the Stones* prod/rel: West-Film

FRIZ, GIULIANO
La Porta Del Cannone, Novel
Porta Del Cannone, La 1969 d: Leopoldo SavonA. lps: Gianni Garko, Irina Demick, Gianna SerrA. 97M ITL/YGS. prod/rel: Inteuropa Cin.Ca, Prodi Cin.Ca (Roma)

FROEST, FRANK
The Grell Mystery, London 1913, Novel
Grell Mystery, The 1917 d: Paul Scardon. lps: Earle Williams, Miriam Miles, Jean Dumar. 5r USA. prod/rel: Vitagraph Co. of America©, Blue Ribbon Feature
The Maelstrom, New York 1916, Novel
Maelstrom, The 1917 d: Paul Scardon. lps: Earle Williams, Dorothy Kelly, Denton Vane. 5r USA. prod/rel: Vitagraph Co. of America©, Greater Vitagraph (V-L-S-E)

FRONDAIE, PIERRE
L' Appassionnata, Play
Appassionnata, L' 1929 d: Leon Mathot, Andre Liabel. lps: Renee Heribel, Fernand Fabre, Therese Kolb. F FRN. prod/rel: Paris-International-Film
Beatrice Devant le Desir, Novel
Beatrice Devant le Desir 1943 d: Jean de Marguenat. lps: Renee Faure, Fernand Ledoux, Jules Berry. 97M FRN. prod/rel: C.I.M.E.P.
Deux Fois Vingt Ans, Novel
Deux Fois Vingt Ans 1930 d: Charles-Felix Tavano. lps: Paul Ollivier, Germaine Rouer, AnnabellA. 91M FRN. prod/rel: Gaumont-Franco-Film-Aubert
L' Eau du Nil, Novel
Eau du Nil, L' 1928 d: Marcel Vandal. lps: Jean Murat, Lee Parry, Max Maxudian. F FRN. *La Femme la Plus Riche du Monde* prod/rel: Vandal Et Delac
L' Homme a l'Hispano, Novel
Homme a l'Hispano, L' 1926 d: Julien Duvivier. lps: Huguette Duflos, Georges Galli, Madeleine Rodrigue. SRL. 7EP FRN. prod/rel: Film d'Art (Vandal Et Delac)
Homme a l'Hispano, L' 1932 d: Jean Epstein. lps: Jean Murat, Marie Bell, Joan HeldA. 95M FRN. *The Man in the Hispano-Suiza* prod/rel: Vandal Et Delac
L' Homme Qui Assassina, Play
Stamboul 1931 d: Reginald Denham, Dimitri Buchowetzki. lps: Warwick Ward, Rosita Moreno, Margot Grahame. 75M UKN. prod/rel: Paramount British, Paramount
L' Insoumise, Play
Fazil 1928 d: Howard Hawks. lps: Charles Farrell, Greta Nissen, Mae Busch. 7217f USA. prod/rel: Fox Film Corp.
Iris Perdue Et Retrouvee, Novel
Iris Perdue Et Retrouvee 1933 d: Louis J. Gasnier. lps: Pierre Blanchar, Raymonde Allain, Charles Granval. 85M FRN. prod/rel: Films Paramount
La Maison Cernee, Novel
Route Imperiale, La 1935 d: Marcel L'Herbier. lps: Pierre Richard-Willm, Kathe von Nagy, Kissa Kouprine. 98M FRN. prod/rel: Films Union
La Menace, Play
Menace, La 1927 d: Jean Bertin. lps: Leon Bary, Noelle Barrey, Jacqueline Forzane. F FRN. prod/rel: Rene Fernand
Montmartre, Play
Montmartre 1914 d: Rene Leprince. lps: Pierre Frondaie, Jean Toulout, Leontine Massart. FRN. prod/rel: Pathe
Port-Arthur, Novel
Port Arthur 1936 d: Nicolas Farkas. lps: Anton Walbrook, Karin Hardt, Rene Deltgen. 81M GRM/CZC. prod/rel: Slavia-Film

Port-Arthur 1936 d: Nicolas Farkas. lps: Anton Walbrook, Charles Vanel, Danielle Darrieux. 105M FRN/CZC. *I Give My Life* prod/rel: Ste Des Prods. Cinematographiques F.C.L., Slavia-Film

Le Voleur de Femmes, Novel
Ladro Di Donne 1936 d: Abel Gance. lps: Annie Ducaux, Jules Berry, Valentino Bruchi. 87M ITL. prod/rel: Pisorno, Cine Tirrenia
Voleur de Femmes, Le 1936 d: Abel Gance. lps: Annie Ducaux, Jules Berry, Blanchette Brunoy. 90M FRN. prod/rel: Films Union

FROSCHEL, GEORG
Die Geliebte Roswolskys, Novel
Skandal in Baden-Baden 1928 d: Erich Waschneck. lps: Brigitte Helm, Ernst Stahl-Nachbaur, Leo Peukert. 1848m GRM. prod/rel: UFA

Die Letzten Nachte Der Mrs. Orchard, Short Story
Anwalt Des Herzens, Der 1927 d: Wilhelm Thiele. lps: Lil Dagover, Jean Murat, Ernst Stahl-Nachbaur. 2727m GRM. *Die Letzten Nachte Der Mrs. Orchard* prod/rel: Greenbaum-Film, Phoebus-Film Ag

Weib in Flammen, Novel
Weib in Flammen 1928 d: Max Reichmann. lps: Olga Tschechowa, Ferdinand von Alten, Alexei Bondireff. 2568m GRM. prod/rel: Tschechowa-Film

FROST, KELMAN D.
Son of the Sahara, Novel
Son of the Sahara 1967 d: Frederic Goode. lps: Darryl Read, Kit Williams, Ria Mills. SRL. 120M UKN. prod/rel: Children's Film Foundation, Ab-Pathe

FROST, REX
Small Hotel, Play
Small Hotel 1957 d: David MacDonald. lps: Gordon Harker, Marie Lohr, John Loder. 59M UKN. prod/rel: Welwyn, Ab-Pathe

FROST, WALTER
Cape Smoke, 1925, Play
Black Magic 1929 d: George B. Seitz. lps: Josephine Dunn, Earle Foxe, John Holland. 5855f USA. prod/rel: Fox Film Corp.

The Man Between, 1913, Novel
Black Magic 1929 d: George B. Seitz. lps: Josephine Dunn, Earle Foxe, John Holland. 5855f USA. prod/rel: Fox Film Corp.

FROWEIN, EBERHARD
Du Und Ich, Novel
Du Und Ich 1938 d: Wolfgang Liebeneiner. lps: Brigitte Horney, Joachim Gottschalk, Paul Bildt. 107M GRM. prod/rel: Minerva-Tonfilm

Mein Eigenes Propres Geld, Book
Am Seidenen Faden 1938 d: R. A. Stemmle. lps: Willy Fritsch, Kathe von Nagy, Carl Kuhlmann. 90M GRM. prod/rel: UFA

La Ragazza E Il Diamante, Novel
Lisetta 1933 d: Carl Boese. lps: Elsa Merlini, Vittorio de Sica, Renato Cialente. 84M ITL. prod/rel: Italfonosap, Anonima Pittaluga

FROYEZ
Les Yeux Qui Changent, Play
Mains Vengeresses, Les 1911 d: Georges MoncA. lps: Georges Grand, Jeanne Delvair. 405m FRN. prod/rel: Scagl

FRUTOS, LUIS PASCUAL
Maruxa, Opera
Maruxa 1923 d: Henri Vorins. lps: Florian Rey, Jose Aguilera, Asuncion Delgado. SPN. prod/rel: Celta Film (Vigo), Ernesto Gonzalez (Madrid)

FRUTTERO
La Donna Della Domenico, Novel
Donna Della Domenica, La 1976 d: Luigi Comencini. lps: Marcello Mastroianni, Jacqueline Bisset, Jean-Louis Trintignant. 105M ITL/FRN. *La Femme du Dimanche* (FRN); *The Sunday Woman* (USA) prod/rel: Primex Italiana (Roma), Production Fox Europa (Paris)

FRY, ROSALIE K.
Secret of the Ron Mor Skerry, Novel
Secret of Roan Inish, The 1993 d: John Sayles. lps: Mick Lally, Ellen Colgan, John Lynch. F USA/IRL. *The Story of Roan Inish* prod/rel: Jones Entertainment, Skerry Movies Corp.

FRYER, AUSTIN
The Pauper Millionaire, Novel
Pauper Millionaire, The 1922 d: Frank H. Crane. lps: C. M. Hallard, Katherine Blair, John H. Roberts. 4993f UKN. prod/rel: Ideal

FUCHS, DANIEL (1909–, USA
Crazy Over Pigeons, 1939, Short Story
Day the Bookies Wept, The 1939 d: Leslie Goodwins. lps: Joe Penner, Betty Grable, Richard Lane. 64M USA. prod/rel: RKO Radio Pictures, Inc.

Low Company, Novel
Gangster, The 1947 d: Gordon Wiles. lps: Barry Sullivan, Belita, Joan Lorring. 84M USA. prod/rel: Allied Artists

FUENTES, CARLOS (1928–, MXC
Aura, Mexico City 1962, Novel
Strega in Amore, La 1966 d: Damiano Damiani. lps: Richard Johnson, Rosanna Schiaffino, Gian Maria Volonte. 110M ITL. *The Witch in Love* (UKN); *The Witch* (USA); *The Strange Obsession*; *Aura* prod/rel: Arco Film, Cidif

The Old Gringo, 1985, Novel
Old Gringo 1989 d: Luis Puenzo. lps: Jane Fonda, Gregory Peck, Jimmy Smits. 119M USA. prod/rel: Columbia

FUGARD, ATHOL (1932–, SAF
Boesman and Lena, 1969, Play
Boesman and Lena 1973 d: Ross Devenish. lps: Yvonne Bryceland, Sandy Tube, Percy Sieff. 102M SAF.

FUJEROVA, OLGA
Zena Na Rozcesti Z Casopisu Prazanka, Novel
Zena Na Rozcesti 1937 d: Oldrich Kminek. lps: Zita Kabatova, Eduard Kohout, Zdenek Stepanek. 2693m CZC. *Woman at the Crossroads* prod/rel: Elekta

FUKAZAWA, SHICHIRO
Fuefuki-Gawa, 1958-59, Novel
Fuefuki-Gawa 1960 d: Keisuke KinoshitA. lps: Masao OdA. 117M JPN. *The River Fuefuki*

Narayamabushi-Ko, 1956, Short Story
Narayama Bushi-Ko 1958 d: Keisuke KinoshitA. lps: Kinuyo Tanaka, Teiji Takahashi, Yuko Mochizuki. 98M JPN. *Ballad of Narayama* (USA); *Legend of the Narayama*; *The Ballad of the Narayama*; *Song of the Narayama* prod/rel: Shochiku Co.
Narayama Bushi-Ko 1983 d: Shohei ImamurA. lps: Sumiko Sakamoto, Ken Ogata, Takejo Aki. 130M JPN. *The Ballad of Narayama* prod/rel: Toei Co.

Tohoku No Jinmutachi, 1957, Short Story
Tohoku No Zunmutachi 1957 d: Kon IchikawA. lps: Hiroshi Akutagawa, Minoru Chiaki, Haruko Togo. 58M JPN. *The Men of Tohoku*; *Man of the North*; *Tohoku No Jinmutachi* prod/rel: Toho Co.

FUKS, LADISLAV
Pan Theodor Mundstock, 1963, Novel
Kartka Z Podrozy 1983 d: Waldemar Dziki. lps: Wladyslaw Kowalski, Rafal Wieczynski. 81M PLN. *Postcard from a Journey*; *A Postcard from the Trip*; *Card from the Journey*

Pribeh Kriminalniho Rady, 1971, Novel
Wsrod Nocnej Ciszy 1978 d: Tadeusz Chmielewski. lps: Tomasz Zaliwski, Piotr Lysak, Miroslaw Konarowski. 116M PLN. *Quiet Is the Night*; *Cicha Noc*; *Silent Night*; *Amidst the Night's Silence* prod/rel: Zespoly Filmowe

Spalovac Mrtvol, 1967, Novel
Spalovac Mrtvol 1968 d: Juraj Herz. lps: Rudolf Hrusinsky, Vlasta Chramostova, Jana StehnovA. 102M CZC. *The Cremator* (USA); *The Cremator of Corpses*; *Incinerator of Cadavers*; *Carnival of Heretics*

FULDA, LUDWIG
Die Durchgangerin, Play
Durchgangerin, Die 1928 d: Hanns Schwarz. lps: Kathe von Nagy, Vivian Gibson, Hans Brausewetter. 2306m GRM. *Love's Sacrifice* prod/rel: Joe May Produktion, Deutschen Lichtspiel Syndikats

Fraulein Frau, Play
Fraulein Frau 1934 d: Carl Boese. lps: Jenny Jugo, Paul Horbiger, Olga Limburg. 92M GRM. prod/rel: T.K. Tonfilm, Sudwest

The Twin Sister, 1902, Play
Two-Faced Woman 1941 d: George Cukor. lps: Greta Garbo, Melvyn Douglas, Constance Bennett. 94M USA. prod/rel: MGM

Das Verlorene Paradies, Berlin 1890, Play
Lost Paradise, The 1914 d: J. Searle Dawley, Oscar Apfel. lps: H. B. Warner, Catherine Carter, Rita Stanwood. 5r USA. prod/rel: Famous Players Film Co., Paramount Pictures Corp.

FULGA, LAURENTIU
Alexandra Si Infernul, 1966, Novel
Alexandra Si Infernul 1975 d: Iulian Mihu. 101M RMN. *Alexandra and Hell*

FULLER, A. C.
Remote Control, New York 1929, Play
Remote Control 1930 d: Nick Grinde, Malcolm St. Clair. lps: William Haines, Charles King, Mary Doran. 5958f USA. prod/rel: Metro-Goldwyn-Mayer Pictures

FULLER, CHARLES
A Soldier's Play, 1982, Play
Soldier's Story, A 1984 d: Norman Jewison. lps: Howard E. Rollins Jr., Adolph Caesar, Art Evans. 102M USA. prod/rel: Columbia-Delphi

FULLER, JOHN G.
The Ghost of Flight 401, Book
Ghost of Flight 401, The 1978 d: Steven Hilliard Stern. lps: Ernest Borgnine, Gary Lockwood, Kim Basinger. TVM. 100M USA. prod/rel: NBC, Paramount

The Interrupted Journey, Book
Ufo Incident, The 1975 d: Richard A. CollA. lps: James Earl Jones, Estelle Parsons, Barnard Hughes. TVM. 100M USA. *Interrupted Journey* prod/rel: Universal

FULLER, SAMUEL (1912–1997), USA
The Dark Page, 1944, Novel
Scandal Sheet 1952 d: Phil Karlson. lps: Broderick Crawford, John Derek, Donna Reed. 82M USA. *The Dark Page* (UKN) prod/rel: Columbia

FULLER, SARITA
Their Own Desire, Story
Their Own Desire 1929 d: E. Mason Hopper. lps: Norma Shearer, Belle Bennett, Lewis Stone. 5927f USA. prod/rel: Metro-Goldwyn-Mayer Pictures

FULLERTON, ALEXANDER
Lionheart, Novel
Lionheart 1968 d: Michael Forlong. lps: James Forlong, Louise Rush, Ian Jessup. 57M UKN. prod/rel: Children's Film Foundation, Forlong

FULOP-MILLER, RENE
Triumph Over Pain, Book
Great Moment, The 1944 d: Preston Sturges. lps: Joel McCrea, Betty Field, Harry Carey. 83M USA. *Great Without Glory*; *Triumph Over Pain* prod/rel: Paramount

FULTON, MAUDE
Play
Her Secret 1933 d: Warren Millais. lps: Sari Maritza, William Collier Jr., Alan Mowbray. 73M USA. *The Girl from Georgia* (UKN); *Waffles* prod/rel: Helen Mitchell, Ltd., Ideal Pictures Corp.

The Brat, Los Angeles 1916, Play
Brat, The 1919 d: Herbert Blache. lps: Alla Nazimova, Charles Bryant, Amy Veness. 6r USA. prod/rel: the Nazimova Productions, Metro Pictures Corp.©
Brat, The 1931 d: John Ford. lps: Sally O'Neil, Alan Dinehart, Frank Albertson. 67M USA. prod/rel: Fox Film Corp., John Ford Production
Girl from Avenue A, The 1940 d: Otto Brower. lps: Jane Withers, Kent Taylor, Katharine Aldridge. 73M USA. *The Brat* prod/rel: 20th Century-Fox Film Corp.©

The Humming Bird, New York 1923, Play
Humming Bird, The 1924 d: Sidney Olcott. lps: Gloria Swanson, Edmund Burns, William Ricciardi. 7577f USA. prod/rel: Famous Players-Lasky, Paramount Pictures

FUNABASHI, SEIICHI
Yuki Fujin Ezu, Novel
Yuki Fujin Ezu 1950 d: Kenji Mizoguchi. lps: Michiyo Kogure, Yoshiko Kuga, Ken UeharA. 88M JPN. *The Picture of Madame Yuki* (USA); *Portrait of Madame Yuki* (UKN); *Sketch of Madame Yuki* prod/rel: Takimura Productions, Shin Toho Co.

FUNCK-BRENTANO, FRANTZ
L' Affaire du Collier de la Reine, Novel
Affaire du Collier de la Reine, L' 1911 d: Camille de Morlhon. lps: Berthe Bovy, Edmond Duquesne, Auguste Volny. 690m FRN. *La Collier de la Reine* prod/rel: Pathe Freres, Serie D'art Pathe Freres

FUNK, PETER V. K.
My Six Loves, New York 1963, Novel
My Six Loves 1963 d: Gower Champion. lps: Debbie Reynolds, Cliff Robertson, David Janssen. 105M USA. prod/rel: Paramount Pictures

FURBER, DOUGLAS
Me and My Girl, London 1937, Musical Play
Lambeth Walk, The 1939 d: Albert de Courville. lps: Lupino Lane, Sally Gray, Seymour Hicks. 84M UKN. prod/rel: C.a.P.a.D, Pinebrook

Mr. Abdulla, Play
Lucky Girl 1932 d: Gene Gerrard, Frank Miller. lps: Gene Gerrard, Molly Lamont, Gus McNaughton. 75M UKN. prod/rel: British International Pictures, Wardour

That's a Good Girl, London 1928, Musical Play
That's a Good Girl 1933 d: Jack Buchanan. lps: Jack Buchanan, Elsie Randolph, Dorothy Hyson. 83M UKN. prod/rel: British and Dominions, United Artists

Toni, London 1924, Musical Play
Toni 1928 d: Arthur Maude. lps: Jack Buchanan, Dorothy Boyd, W. Lawson Butt. 5548f UKN. prod/rel: British International Pictures, Wardour

FURMANOV, DIMITRIY (1891–1926), RSS
Chapayev, 1923, Novel
Chapayev 1935 d: Sergei Vasiliev, Georgi Vasiliev. lps: Boris Bobochkin, Boris Blinov, Barbara MyasnikovA. 100M USS.

FURNESS, EDITH ELLIS
Mary Jane's Pa, New York 1908, Play
    Mary Jane's Pa 1917 d: William P. S. Earle. lps: Marc McDermott, Eulalie Jensen, Mildred Manning. 5r USA. prod/rel: Vitagraph Co. of America©, Blue Ribbon Feature
    Mary Jane's Pa 1935 d: William Keighley. lps: Guy Kibbee, Aline MacMahon, Tom Brown. 71M USA. *Wanderlust* (UKN) prod/rel: First National Pictures©

FURNISS, GRACE LIVINGSTON
Gretna Green, New York 1903, Play
    Gretna Green 1915 d: Thomas N. Heffron, Hugh Ford. lps: Marguerite Clark, Arthur Hoops, Helen Luttrell. 4r USA. prod/rel: Famous Players Film Co., Paramount Pictures Corp.

The Pride of Jennico, New York 1900, Play
    Pride of Jennico, The 1914 d: J. Searle Dawley. lps: House Peters, Hal Clarendon, Marie Leonhard. 4r USA. prod/rel: Famous Players Film Co., State Rights

FURTHMAN, JULES
Gay Deception, Story
    Pretty Baby 1950 d: Bretaigne Windust. lps: Betsy Drake, Dennis Morgan, Zachary Scott. 92M USA. prod/rel: Warner Bros.

FURTHMANN, JULIUS G.
Short Story
    Camouflage Kiss, A 1918 d: Harry Millarde. lps: June Caprice, Bernard Thornton, Pell Trenton. 5r USA. prod/rel: Fox Film Corp., William Fox©

Bound on the Wheel, Story
    Bound on the Wheel 1915 d: Joseph de Grasse. lps: Lon Chaney, Elsie Jane Wilson, George Berrell. 3r USA. prod/rel: Rex

A Fiery Introduction, Story
    Fiery Introduction, A 1915 d: Charles Giblyn. lps: Cleo Madison, S. J. Bingham, Ray Hanford. 2r USA. prod/rel: Gold Seal

Little Blonde in Black, Story
    Little Blonde in Black 1915 d: Robert Z. Leonard. lps: Ella Hall, Robert Leonard, Harry Carter. 2r USA. prod/rel: Laemmle

Mountain Justice, Story
    Mountain Justice 1915 d: Joseph de Grasse. lps: Arthur Shirley, Lon Chaney, Grace Thompson. 2r USA. prod/rel: Rex

The Sheriff of Long Butte, Story
    Quits 1915 d: Joseph de Grasse. lps: Lon Chaney, Arthur Shirley. SHT USA. prod/rel: Rex

Steady Company, Story
    Steady Company 1915 d: Joseph de Grasse. lps: Pauline Bush, Lon Chaney. SHT USA. prod/rel: Rex

FUSINATO, ARNALDO
Le Due Madri, Poem
    Due Madri, Le 1909. 200m ITL. *The Two Mothers* (USA) prod/rel: S.A. Ambrosio

FUTRELLE, JACQUES (1875–1912), USA
Story
    Painted World, The 1919 d: Ralph Ince. lps: Anita Stewart, E. K. Lincoln, Julia Swayne Gordon. 5r USA. prod/rel: Vitagraph Co. of America©

The Chase of the Golden Plate, Novel
    Man Behind the Mask, The 1936 d: Michael Powell. lps: Hugh Williams, Jane Baxter, Maurice Schwartz. 79M UKN. prod/rel: Joe Rock, MGM

Elusive Isabel, Indianapolis 1909, Novel
    Adventures in Diplomacy 1914. lps: Alec B. Francis, Belle Adair, J. Gunnis Davis. 3r USA. prod/rel: Eclair
    Elusive Isabel 1916 d: Stuart Paton. lps: Florence Lawrence, Sidney Bracey, Harry Millarde. 6r USA. prod/rel: Bluebird Photoplays, Inc.©

The High Hand, Indianapolis 1911, Novel
    High Hand, The 1915 d: William D. Taylor. lps: Carlyle Blackwell, William Brunton, Neva Gerber. 6r USA. prod/rel: Favorite Players Film Co., Alliance Films Corp.

A Model Young Man, Story
    Model Young Man, A 1914 d: James Young. lps: Sidney Drew, Ethel Lloyd. 1000f USA. prod/rel: Vitagraph Co. of America

My Lady's Garter, Chicago 1912, Novel
    My Lady's Garter 1920 d: Maurice Tourneur. lps: Sylvia Breamer, Wyndham Standing, Holmes Herbert. 4823f USA. prod/rel: Maurice Tourneur Productions, Inc., Famous Players-Lasky Corp.©

The Painted World, Story
    Painted World, The 1914 d: Ralph Ince. lps: Julia Swayne Gordon, Anita Stewart, Janice Cummings. 3r USA. prod/rel: Broadway Star, Vitagraph Co. of America

FUTRELLE, MAY PEEL
Secretary of Frivolous Affairs, Indianapolis 1911, Novel
    Secretary of Frivolous Affairs, The 1915 d: Thomas Ricketts. lps: Harold Lockwood, May Allison, Hal Clements. 4r USA. prod/rel: American Film Mfg Co.©, Mutual Film Corp.

FYLES, FRANKLIN
The Girl I Left Behind Me, New York 1893, Play
    Girl I Left Behind Me, The 1915 d: Lloyd B. Carleton. lps: Robert Edeson, Claire Whitney, Stuart Holmes. 5r USA. prod/rel: Box Office Attraction Co., William Fox©

FYOT, PIERRE
Les Remparts du Silence, Book
    Mer de Chine: le Pays Pour Memoire 1990 d: Jacques Perrin. lps: Jane Birkin, Samuel Fuller, Jean-Francois Balmer. TVM. 90M FRN.

G

GABAULT, PAUL
The Richest Girl, New York 1909, Play
    Richest Girl, The 1918 d: Albert Capellani. lps: Ann Murdock, David Powell, Paul Capellani. 5r USA. prod/rel: Empire All Star Corp., Mutual Film Corp.

GABEIRA, FERNANDO
O Que E Isso, Companheiro?, Book
    O Que E Isso, Companheiro? 1997 d: Bruno Barreto. lps: Alan Arkin, Pedro Cardoso, Fernanda Torres. 105M BRZ. *Four Days in September* prod/rel: L.C. Barreto/ Equador Films, Sony Corp. of America

GABLER, NEAL
An Empire of Their Own: How the Jews Invented Hollywood, Book
    Hollywoodism: Jews, Movies, and the American Dream 1998 d: Simcha Jacobovici. DOC. 98M CND. prod/rel: Associated Producers, Halpern/Jacobovici

GABORIAU, EMILE (1835–1873), FRN
L' Affaire Orcival, Novel
    Affaire d'Orcival, L' 1914 d: Gerard Bourgeois. lps: Henry Roussell, Henri Gouget, Jules Mondos. 1035m FRN. prod/rel: Eclair

L' Affaire Rouge, Paris 1866, Novel
    Family Stain, The 1915 d: Will S. Davis. lps: Frederick Perry, Walter Miller, Stephen Grattan. 5-6r USA. prod/rel: Fox Film Corp., William Fox©

La Clique Doree, Paris 1871, Novel
    Evil Women Do, The 1916 d: Rupert Julian. lps: Elsie Jane Wilson, Francelia Billington, Rupert Julian. 5r USA. *The Clique of Gold* prod/rel: Bluebird Photoplays, Inc.©

Le Dossier Nr. 113, Paris 1867, Short Story
    File No. 113 1915. lps: Franklin Ritchie, Louise Vale, William Jefferson. 2r USA. prod/rel: Biograph Co.
    File No. 113 1932 d: Chester M. Franklin. lps: William Collier Jr., June Clyde, Mary Nolan. 63M USA. *File 113* prod/rel: Allied Pictures Corp., State Rights
    Thou Shalt Not Steal 1917 d: William Nigh. lps: Virginia Pearson, Claire Whitney, Eric Mayne. 5r USA. prod/rel: Fox Film Corp., William Fox©

Monsieur Lecoq, Paris 1869, Novel
    Monsieur Lecoq 1914 d: Maurice Tourneur. lps: Georges Treville, Harry Baur, Jules Mondos. 940m FRN. prod/rel: Eclair
    Monsieur Lecoq 1915. lps: William Morris, Alphonse Ethier, Florence Labadie. 4r USA. prod/rel: Thanhouser Film Corp., Mutual Film Corp.

GABRIEL
Une Cause Celebre, Novel
    Cause Celebre, Une 1913. lps: Henry Roussell, Edmond Duquesne, Yvonne Pascal. 929m FRN. prod/rel: Acad

GABRIEL, GILBERT WOLFF
James Lewis I, 1932, Novel
    This Woman Is Mine 1941 d: Frank Lloyd. lps: Franchot Tone, John Carroll, Walter Brennan. 92M USA. *I James Lewis* prod/rel: Universal

GABRIEL, JOHN
Won By a Head, Novel
    Won By a Head 1920 d: Percy Nash. lps: Rex Davis, Frank Tennant, Vera Cornish. 4198f UKN. prod/rel: Sterling, British Exhibitors' Films

GABY, ALEX
Fifty-Two Miles to Terror, 1956, Short Story
    Hot Rods to Hell 1967 d: John Brahm. lps: Dana Andrews, Jeanne Crain, Mimsy Farmer. 92M USA. *52 Miles to Midnight*; *52 Miles to Terror* prod/rel: Four Leaf Productions

GADDA, CARLO EMILIO (1893–1973), ITL
Quer Pasticciaccio Brutto de Via Merulana, Milan 1957, Novel
    Maledetto Imbroglio, Un 1959 d: Pietro Germi. lps: Pietro Germi, Claudia Cardinale, Eleonora Rossi-Drago. 120M ITL. *The Facts of Murder* (USA); *A Cursed Tangle*; *A Sordid Affair* prod/rel: Riama Cin.Ca, Cineriz

GADDIS, PEGGY
Doubling for Lora, Story
    Her Big Night 1926 d: Melville Brown. lps: Laura La Plante, Einar Hansen, Zasu Pitts. 7603f USA. *The Big Night* prod/rel: Universal Pictures

The Part-Time Wife, 1925, Short Story
    Part Time Wife, The 1925 d: Henry McCarty. lps: Alice Calhoun, Robert Ellis, Freeman Wood. 6100f USA. prod/rel: Gotham Productions, Lumas Film Corp.

GADDIS, THOMAS E. (1908–1984), USA, Gaddis, Thomas Eugene
Birdman of Alcatraz: the Story of Robert Stroud, New York 1955, Book
    Birdman of Alcatraz 1962 d: John Frankenheimer. lps: Burt Lancaster, Karl Malden, Thelma Ritter. 148M USA. prod/rel: Norma Productions, United Artists

Killer: a Journal of Murder, Book
    Killer: a Journal of Murder 1995 d: Tim Metcalfe. lps: James Woods, Robert Sean Leonard, Ellen Greene. 92M USA. prod/rel: Spelling Films, Ixtlan

GADKARI, RAM GANESH
Thakicha Lagna, Play
    Thakicha Lagna 1935 d: Vishram Bedekar, Vamanrao N. Bhat. lps: Damuanna Malvankar, Balwantrao Pethe, Shankarrao Majumdar. 152M IND. *Thaki's Marriage*; *Thakiche Lagna*

GAFFNEY, ARCH A.
Ad-Man, 1932, Play
    No Marriage Ties 1933 d: J. Walter Ruben. lps: Richard Dix, Elizabeth Allan, Doris Kenyon. 73M USA. *The Public Be Sold*; *Ad-Man* prod/rel: RKO Radio Pictures©

GAGE, NICHOLAS
Eleni, Book
    Eleni 1985 d: Peter Yates. lps: Kate Nelligan, John Malkovich, Linda Hunt. 117M USA. *Eleni - a Son's Revenge* prod/rel: Warner Bros., CBS Productions

GAILLARD, ROBERT
L' Homme de la Jamaique, Novel
    Homme de la Jamaique, L' 1950 d: Maurice de Canonge. lps: Pierre Brasseur, Georges Tabet, Vera Norman. 120M FRN. prod/rel: U.G.C., Bellair Films

Marie Des Isles, Novel
    Marie Des Isles 1959 d: Georges Combret. lps: Belinda Lee, Magali Noel, Folco Lulli. 100M FRN/ITL. *I Flibustieri Della Martinica* (ITL); *Marie of the Isles* (USA); *The Wild and the Wanton* prod/rel: Radius Productions, Tiber Produzione

GAILLARDET, F.
La Tour de Nesle, 1832, Play
    Tour de Nesle, La 1912 d: Albert Capellani. lps: Henry Krauss, Paul Capellani, Jeanne Delvair. FRN. prod/rel: Scagl
    Tour de Nesle, La 1937 d: Gaston Roudes. lps: Jean Weber, Tania Fedor, Jacques Varennes. 95M FRN. prod/rel: Edmond Ratisbonne
    Tour de Nesle, La 1954 d: Abel Gance. lps: Pierre Brasseur, Silvana Pampanini, Paul Guers. 130M FRN/ITL. *La Torre Del Piacere* (ITL); *The Tower of Lust* (UKN) prod/rel: Fernand Rivers
    Turm Der Verbotenen Liebe, Der 1968 d: Franz Antel. lps: Terry Torday, Jean Piat, Uschi Glas. 92M GRM/ITL/FRN. *Le Dolcezze Del Peccato* (ITL); *The Tower of Forbidden Love*; *Tower of Screaming Virgins* (USA); *She Lost Her You Know What*; *The Sweetness of Sin* prod/rel: Rapid, Films Cin.Ca

GAINES, CHARLES
Pumping Iron II: the Unprecedented Woman, Book
    Pumping Iron II: the Women 1985 d: George Butler. lps: Rachel McLish, Bev Francis. DOC. 107M USA. prod/rel: Bar Belle Productions, White Mountain

Stay Hungry, Novel
    Stay Hungry 1976 d: Bob Rafelson. lps: Jeff Bridges, Sally Field, Arnold Schwarzenegger. 102M USA. prod/rel: Harold Schneider, Bob Rafelson

GAINES, ERNEST J. (1933–, USA
The Autobiography of Miss Jane Pittman, 1971, Novel
  Autobiography of Miss Jane Pittman, The 1974 d: John Korty. lps: Cicely Tyson, Michael Murphy, Richard Dysart. TVM. 110M USA. *Fight for Freedom* prod/rel: Tomorrow Entertainment
A Gathering of Old Men, 1983, Novel
  Gathering of Old Men, A 1987 d: Volker Schlondorff. lps: Richard Widmark, Louis Gossett Jr., Holly Hunter. TVM. 100M USA/GRM. *Ein Aufstand Alter Manner* (GRM); *Murder on the Bayou* prod/rel: Consolidated, Jennie & Co.
The Sky Is Gray, 1966, Short Story
  Sky Is Gray, The 1977 d: Stan Lathan. lps: Olivia Cole, Cleavon Little. MTV. 44M USA. prod/rel: Learning in Focus

GAINES, ROBERT
Final Night, Novel
  Front Page Story 1954 d: Gordon Parry. lps: Jack Hawkins, Elizabeth Allan, Eva Bartok. 99M UKN. *Newspaper Story* prod/rel: Jay Lewis, British Lion

GALA, ANTONIO
Los Buenos Dias Perdidos, 1973, Play
  Buenos Dias Perdidos, Los 1975 d: Rafael Gil. lps: Juan Luis Galiardo, Teresa Rabal, Queta Claver. 105M SPN. *The Good Days Lost*
Turkish Passion, Novel
  Mas Alla Del Jardin 1996 d: Pedro OleA. lps: Conchita Velasco, Fernando Guillen, Manuel BanderA. 91M SPN. *Beyond the Garden* prod/rel: Sogetel, Lola Films

GALACTION, GALA
Moara Lui Califar, 1902, Short Story
  Moara Lui Califar 1984 d: Serban Marinescu. lps: Ion Marinescu, Elena Albu, Petre Tanasievici. 70M RMN. *Califar's Mill*

GALANOS, ALEKOS
Ta Kokkina Phanaria, Play
  Kokkina Phanaria 1962 d: Vassilis Georgiadis. lps: Katerina Helmi, Jenny Karezi, Mary Chronopoulou. 120M GRC. *Red Lanterns* (USA); *Ta Kokkina Farina* prod/rel: Th. A. Damaskinos, V.G. Michaelides

GALANTE, PIERRE
Le Destin S'amuse, Short Story
  Destin S'amuse, Le 1946 d: Emile Edwin Reinert. lps: Dany Robin, Andre Claveau, Robert Murzeau. 85M FRN. *Coup de Maitre* prod/rel: Films Ariane

GALAR (LEO GALETTO)
Il Trattato Scomparso, Play
  Masque Qui Tombe, Le 1933 d: Mario Bonnard. lps: Jean Worms, Tania Fedor, Lucienne Le Marchand. 85M FRN.
  Trattato Scomparso, Il 1933 d: Mario Bonnard. lps: Leda Gloria, Giuditta Rissone, Nini Dinelli. 78M ITL. prod/rel: Cines, Anonima Pittaluga

GALBALLY, FRANK
Juryman, Novel
  Storyville 1992 d: Mark Frost. lps: James Spader, Joanne Whalley-Kilmer, Jason Robards Jr. 113M USA. prod/rel: Twentieth Century-Fox, Spelling/Davis

GALCHRIST, RUPERT
Master of Dragonard Hill, Novel
  Master of Dragonard Hill 1989 d: Gerard Kikoine. lps: Oliver Reed, Eartha Kitt, Herbert Lom. 92M USA. *Dragonard* prod/rel: Cannon

GALDI, DAVIDE
La Sartina Di Montesarno Carmela, Novel
  Carmela, la Sartina Di Montesanto 1916 d: Elvira Notari. lps: Tina Somma, Camillo Talamo, Goffredo d'AndreA. 1285m ITL. prod/rel: Film-Dora
Il Cenciaiuolo Della Sanita, Novel
  Cenciaiuolo Della Sanita, Il 1917 d: Franco Dias. lps: Maria Carli, Oreste Tesorone, Mario GambardellA. 1408m ITL. prod/rel: Dramatica Film

GALDIERI, ROCCO
Aniello 'A Ffede, Novel
  Fatalita 1947 d: Giorgio Bianchi. lps: Massimo Girotti, Amedeo Nazzari, Maria Michi. 95M ITL. prod/rel: Universalcine, Generalcine

GALE, ZONA (1874–1938), USA
Faint Perfume, New York 1923, Novel
  Faint Perfume 1925 d: Louis J. Gasnier. lps: Seena Owen, William Powell, Alyce Mills. 6186f USA. prod/rel: B. P. Schulberg Productions
Miss Lulu Bett, New York 1920, Novel
  Miss Lulu Bett 1921 d: William C. de Mille. lps: Lois Wilson, Milton Sills, Theodore Roberts. 5904f USA. prod/rel: Famous Players-Lasky, Paramount Pictures
The Way, Short Story
  When Strangers Meet 1934 d: W. Christy Cabanne. lps: Richard Cromwell, Sheila Terry, Julie Haydon. 74M USA. prod/rel: Liberty Pictures Corp.©

GALGOCZI, ERZSEBET
Pokhalo, 1972, Novel
  Pokhalo 1974 d: Imre Mihalyfi. 98M HNG. *Cobweb*
Torventen Belul, 1980, Novel
  Egymasra Nezve 1982 d: Karoly Makk. lps: Grazyna Szapolowska, Jadwiga Jankowska-Cieslak, Jozef Kroner. 109M HNG. *Another Day* (USA); *Another Way* prod/rel: Mafilm, Dialog Filmstudio

GALGUT, DAMON
The Quarry, Novel
  Quarry, The 1998 d: Marion Hansel. lps: John Lynch, Jonne Phillips, Oscar Petersen. 114M BLG/FRN/NTH. prod/rel: Man's Film, Tchin Tchin

GALL, ISTVAN
A Menesgazda, Novel
  Menesgazda, A 1978 d: Andras Kovacs. lps: Jozsef Madaras, Karoly Sinka, Ferenc Fabian. 100M HNG. *The Chief of the Horse Farm*; *The Stud-Farm* prod/rel: Mafilm, Objektiv

GALLAGHER, J. P.
The Scarlet Pimpernel of the Vatican, Book
  Scarlet and the Black, The 1982 d: Jerry London. lps: Gregory Peck, Christopher Plummer, John Gielgud. TVM. 155M USA/ITL. prod/rel: CBS, Itc

GALLAGHER, STEVEN
Chimera, 1982, Novel
  Chimera 1991 d: Lawrence Gordon Clark. lps: John Lynch, Christine Kavanagh, Kenneth Cranham. TVM. 240M UKN. prod/rel: Zenith, Anglia Tv

GALLAHER, DONALD
Sh! the Octopus, New York 1928, Play
  Sh! the Octopus 1937 d: William McGann. lps: Hugh Herbert, Allen Jenkins, Marcia Ralston. 60M USA. prod/rel: Warner Bros. Pictures©, First National Picture

GALLAND, VICTORIA
The Golden Gallows, 1921, Short Story
  Golden Gallows, The 1922 d: Paul Scardon. lps: Miss Du Pont, Edwin Stevens, Eve Southern. 4808f USA. prod/rel: Universal Film Mfg. Co.

GALLEGOS, ROMULO (1884–1969), VNZ, Gallegos Freire, Romulo
Dona Barbara, 1929, Novel
  Dona Barbara 1943 d: Fernando de Fuentes. lps: Maria Felix, Maria Elena Marques, Julian Soler. 138M MXC.

GALLET, LOUIS
Patrie, 1869, Play
  Patrie 1914 d: Albert Capellani. lps: Henry Krauss, Paul Capellani, Vera Sergine. 1885m FRN. prod/rel: Scagl
  Patrie 1945 d: Louis Daquin. lps: Pierre Blanchar, Jean Desailly, Lucien Nat. 95M FRN. prod/rel: Filmsonor

GALLEY, FRANCIS
Le Coup de Minuit, Play
  Coup de Minuit, Le 1916 d: Maurice Poggi. lps: Maurice Poggi, Pierre Etchepare, Alice de Tender. 450m FRN. prod/rel: Films Lordier

GALLICO, PAUL (1897–1976), USA, Gallico, Paul William
Story
  Fire in the Sky, A 1978 d: Jerry Jameson. lps: Richard Crenna, Elizabeth Ashley, David Dukes. TVM. 150M USA. prod/rel: NBC, Columbia
Short Story
  Miracle in the Wilderness 1991 d: Kevin Dobson. lps: Kris Kristofferson, Kim Cattrall, John Dennis Johnston. TVM. 110M USA.
Story
  Pride of the Yankees, The 1942 d: Sam Wood. lps: Gary Cooper, Teresa Wright, Babe Ruth. 128M USA. prod/rel: RKO Radio
The Adventure of Joe Smith - American, Story
  Big Operator, The 1959 d: Charles Haas. lps: Mickey Rooney, Steve Cochran, Mamie Van Doren. 91M USA. *Anatomy of a Syndicate* prod/rel: Metro-Goldwyn-Mayer Corp., Albert Zugsmith-Fryman Enterprises
  Joe Smith, American 1942 d: Richard Thorpe. lps: Robert Young, Marsha Hunt, Harvey Stephens. 63M USA. *Highway to Freedom* (UKN) prod/rel: MGM
The Enchanted Hour, Novel
  Next to No Time 1958 d: Henry Cornelius. lps: Kenneth More, Betsy Drake, Harry Green. 93M UKN. prod/rel: British Lion, Montpelier
The Hand of Mary Constable, Novel
  Daughter of the Mind 1969 d: Walter Grauman. lps: Don Murray, Ray Milland, Gene Tierney. TVM. 74M USA. prod/rel: 20th Century-Fox
LudmilA. a Legend of Liechtenstein, London 1955, Short Story
  Kinder Der Berge 1958 d: Georg Tressler. lps: Barbara Rutting, Maximilian Schell, Heinrich Gretler. 99M SWT/LCH. *Les Enfants de la Montagne; Ein Wunderbarer Sommer; Das Gluck Auf Der Alm; Ludmila Die Kuh; A Wonderful Summer* prod/rel: Rialto-Filmproduktion
The Man Who Hated People, Short Story
  Lili 1953 d: Charles Walters. lps: Leslie Caron, Jean-Pierre Aumont, Mel Ferrer. 81M USA. prod/rel: MGM
Matilda, Novel
  Matilda 1978 d: Daniel Mann. lps: Elliott Gould, Robert Mitchum, Harry Guardino. 103M USA. prod/rel: Film Finance Group
Mrs. 'Arris Goes to Paris, Short Story
  Mrs. 'Arris Goes to Paris 1991 d: Anthony Shaw. lps: Angela Lansbury, Diana Rigg, Lothaire Bluteau. TVM. 120M USA. prod/rel: Accent Films, Novo Films
Never Take No for an Answer, Novel
  Peppino E Violetta 1951 d: Maurice Cloche, Ralph Smart. lps: Vittorio Manunta, Denis O'Dea, Frank Coulson. 90M ITL/FRN/UKN. *Peppino Et Violetta* (FRN); *Never Take No for an Answer* (UKN) prod/rel: Film Constellation (Paris), Independent Film Distributors
The Poseidon Adventure, Novel
  Poseidon Adventure, The 1972 d: Ronald Neame. lps: Gene Hackman, Ernest Borgnine, Red Buttons. 117M USA. prod/rel: 20th Century Fox
The Romance of Henry Menafee, Book
  Merry Andrew 1958 d: Michael Kidd. lps: Danny Kaye, Pier Angeli, Salvatore Baccaloni. 103M USA. prod/rel: MGM, Sol C. Siegel Prods.
The Snow Goose
  Snow Goose, The 1971 d: Patrick Garland. lps: Richard Harris, Jenny Agutter. MTV. 50M UKN.
Thomasina - the Cat Who Thought She Was God, New York 1957, Novel
  Three Lives of Thomasina, The 1963 d: Don Chaffey. lps: Patrick McGoohan, Susan Hampshire, Karen Dotrice. 97M UKN/USA. prod/rel: Walt Disney Productions
Tightwad, 1936, Short Story
  Wild Money 1937 d: Louis King. lps: Edward Everett Horton, Louise Campbell, Lynne Overman. 71M USA. prod/rel: Paramount Pictures©
Trial By Terror, 1952, Book
  Assignment - Paris! 1952 d: Robert Parrish, Vincent Sherman (Uncredited). lps: Dana Andrews, Marta Toren, George Sanders. 85M USA. *Assignment Paris* prod/rel: Columbia
'Twas the Night Before Christmas, 1937, Short Story
  No Time to Marry 1938 d: Harry Lachman. lps: Richard Arlen, Mary Astor, Lionel Stander. 63M USA. prod/rel: Columbia Pictures Corp. of California©
Wedding Present, 1935, Short Story
  Wedding Present 1936 d: Richard Wallace. lps: Cary Grant, Joan Bennett, George Bancroft. 80M USA. prod/rel: Paramount Pictures
The Zoo Gang, Novel
  Zoo Gang, The 1973 d: Sidney Hayers, John Hough. lps: Brian Keith, John Mills, Lilli Palmer. MTV. 300M UKN.

GALLICO, PAULINE
Trial By Terror, 1952, Book
  Assignment - Paris! 1952 d: Robert Parrish, Vincent Sherman (Uncredited). lps: Dana Andrews, Marta Toren, George Sanders. 85M USA. *Assignment Paris* prod/rel: Columbia

GALLINA, GIACINTO
Mia Fia, 1878, Play
  Mia Fia 1928 d: Orlando Vassallo. lps: Wanda Tiziani, Gino Viotti, Ugo Gracci. 1911 ITL. prod/rel: Ars Italica Film
El Moroso de la Nona, 1875, Play
  Moroso de la Nona, El 1927 d: Orlando Vassallo. lps: Lia Maris, Raimondo Van Riel, Renato ViscA. 1883m ITL. *Il Moroso Della Nonna* prod/rel: Arturo Gallea

GALLO, MAX
Une Affaire Intime, Novel
  Boulevard Des Assassins 1982 d: Boramy Tioulong. lps: Jean-Louis Trintignant, Victor Lanoux, Stephane Audran. 110M FRN. prod/rel: Les Films de la Drouette
For Those I Loved, Book
  Au Nom de Tous Les Miens 1983 d: Robert Enrico. lps: Brigitte Fossey, Jacques Penot, Michael York. 150M FRN/CND. prod/rel: Producteurs Associes (Paris), T.F.1 Films Production (Paris)
  For Those I Loved 1983 d: Robert Enrico. lps: Brigitte Fossey, Jacques Penot, Michael York. 150M FRN/CND. prod/rel: Producteurs Associes (Paris), T.F.1 Films Production (Paris)

171

GALLON, TOM

Boden's Boy, Novel
Boden's Boy 1923 d: Henry Edwards. lps: Henry Edwards, Chrissie White, Francis Lister. 5600f UKN. prod/rel: Hepworth

The Cruise of the Make-Believes, Boston 1907, Novel
Cruise of the Make-Believes, The 1918 d: George Melford. lps: Lila Lee, Harrison Ford, Raymond Hatton. 4502f USA. prod/rel: Famous Players-Lasky Corp.©, Paramount Pictures

A Dead Man's Love
Fiancee du Disparu, La 1921 d: Charles Maudru. lps: Amy Verity, Marie-Ange Feriel, Gaston Jacquet. 1790m FRN. *L' Amour du Mort* prod/rel: Societe D'editions Cinematographiques

Dicky Monteith, Play
Dicky Monteith 1922 d: Kenelm Foss. lps: Stewart Rome, Joan Morgan, Jack Minster. 5000f UKN. prod/rel: Astra Films

Felix Gets a Month, Play
As He Was Born 1919 d: Wilfred Noy. lps: Stanley Logan, Odette Goimbault, Mary Dibley. 4865f UKN. prod/rel: Butcher's Film Service
Naked Man, The 1923 d: Henry Edwards. lps: Henry Edwards, Chrissie White, James Carew. 6125f UKN. prod/rel: Hepworth, Ideal

The Great Gay Road, Novel
Great Gay Road, The 1920 d: Norman MacDonald. lps: Stewart Rome, Pauline Johnson, John Stuart. 5300f UKN. prod/rel: Broadwest, Walturdaw
Great Gay Road, The 1931 d: Sinclair Hill. lps: Stewart Rome, Frank Stanmore, Kate Cutler. 88M UKN. prod/rel: Stoll, Butcher's Film Service

The Hanging Judge, Story
Hanging Judge, The 1918 d: Henry Edwards. lps: Henry Edwards, Chrissie White, Hamilton Stewart. 5300f UKN. prod/rel: Hepworth, Moss

The Lackey and the Lady, Novel
Lackey and the Lady, The 1919 d: Thomas Bentley. lps: Odette Goimbault, Roy Travers, Leslie Howard. 5000f UKN. prod/rel: British Actors, Phillips

The Man in Motley, Novel
Man in Motley, The 1916 d: Ralph Dewsbury. lps: Fred Morgan, Hayford Hobbs, Winifred Sadler. 4757f UKN. prod/rel: London, Jury

Meg the Lady, Novel
Meg the Lady 1916 d: Maurice Elvey. lps: Elisabeth Risdon, Fred Groves, Eric Stuart. 4740f UKN. prod/rel: London, Diploma

The Princess of Happy Chance, Novel
Princess of Happy Chance, The 1916 d: Maurice Elvey. lps: Elisabeth Risdon, Gerald Ames, Hayford Hobbs. 4885f UKN. prod/rel: London, Jury

A Rogue in Love, Novel
Rogue in Love, A 1916 d: Bannister Merwin. lps: James Reardon. 3800f UKN. prod/rel: London, Jury
Rogue in Love, A 1922 d: Albert Brouett. lps: Frank Stanmore, Ann Trevor, Gregory Scott. 5590f UKN. prod/rel: Diamond Super, Globe

Tatterly - the Story of a Dead Man, New York 1897, Novel
Off the Highway 1925 d: Tom Forman. lps: William V. Mong, Marguerite de La Motte, John Bowers. 7641f USA. prod/rel: Hunt Stromberg Corp., Producers Distributing Corp.
Tatterly 1916 d: H. Lisle Lucoque. lps: Cecil Mannering, Mercy Hatton, Charles Rock. 5400f UKN. prod/rel: Lucoque

The Touch of a Child, Story
Touch of a Child, The 1918 d: Cecil M. Hepworth. lps: Alma Taylor, Henry Edwards, Stewart Rome. 4750f UKN. prod/rel: Hepworth, Moss

The Woman Who Was Nothing, Novel
Woman Who Was Nothing, The 1917 d: Maurice Elvey. lps: Lilian Braithwaite, Madge Titheradge, George Tully. 5390f UKN. prod/rel: Butcher's Film Service

Young Eve and Old Adam, Novel
Young Eve and Old Adam 1920. UKN. prod/rel: Union Photoplays

GALLONE, CARMINE

Marter Der Liebe, Short Story
Marter Der Liebe 1928 d: Carmine Gallone. lps: Olga Tschechowa, Hans Stuwe, Henri Baudin. 2643m GRM. *Love's Crucifixion* prod/rel: Erda-Film

GALOPIN, ARNOULD

L' Homme Au Complet Gris, Novel
Homme Au Complet Gris, L' 1914 d: Henry Houry. lps: Henry Houry. 531m FRN. prod/rel: Eclipse

La Mascotte Des Poilus, Novel
Mascotte Des Poilus, La 1918. lps: Artheme Servaes, Josette Andriot. 1300m FRN. prod/rel: Eclair

The Mystery of Green Park, Novel
Mystery of Green Park, The 1914. 2r USA. prod/rel: Urban-Eclipse

Les Poilus de la 9E, Novel
Poilus de la 9E, Les 1915 d: G. Remond. lps: Gaston Modot, Artheme Servaes, Josette Andriot. 1320m FRN. prod/rel: Eclair

Tao, Novel
Tao 1923 d: Gaston Ravel. lps: Joe Hamman, Mary Harald, Andre Deed. SRL. 10EP FRN. *Le Fantome Noir* prod/rel: Societe Des Cineromans

GALSWORTHY, JOHN (1867–1933), UKN

The Apple Tree, 1918, Short Story
Summer Story, A 1988 d: Piers Haggard. lps: James Wilby, Imogen Stubbs, Kenneth Colley. 95M UKN. prod/rel: Warner, Itc

Escape, London 1926, Play
Escape 1930 d: Basil Dean. lps: Gerald Du Maurier, Edna Best, Gordon Harker. 70M UKN. prod/rel: Associated Talking Pictures, Radio
Escape 1948 d: Joseph L. Mankiewicz. lps: Rex Harrison, Peggy Cummins, William Hartnell. 79M UKN. prod/rel: 20th Century Productions, 20th Century-Fox

The First and the Last, 1918, Short Story
First and the Last, The 1937 d: Basil Dean, Alexander Korda (Uncredited). lps: Vivien Leigh, Leslie Banks, Laurence Olivier. 75M UKN. *21 Days Together* (USA); *21 Days*; *Twenty-One Days* prod/rel: London Films, Denham Films
Letzten Werden Die Ersten Sein, Die 1957 d: Rolf Hansen. lps: O. E. Hasse, Ulla Jacobsson, Maximilian Schell. 90M GRM. *The Last Will Be the First; Thy Last Will Be the First* prod/rel: C.C.C., Constantin
Stranger, The 1924 d: Joseph Henabery. lps: Betty Compson, Richard Dix, Lewis Stone. 6660f USA. prod/rel: Famous Players-Lasky, Paramount Pictures

Justice, London 1910, Play
Justice 1917 d: Maurice Elvey. lps: Gerald Du Maurier, Hilda Moore, Lilian Braithwaite. 5780f UKN. prod/rel: Ideal

Loyalties, London 1922, Play
Loyalties 1933 d: Basil Dean. lps: Basil Rathbone, Heather Thatcher, Miles Mander. 74M UKN. prod/rel: Associated British, Associated Talking Pictures

The Man of Property, 1906, Novel
That Fortsyte Woman 1949 d: Compton Bennett. lps: Errol Flynn, Robert Young, Janet Leigh. 114M USA. *The Fortsyte Saga* (UKN) prod/rel: MGM

Old English, 1924, Play
Old English 1930 d: Alfred E. Green. lps: George Arliss, Leon Janney, Doris Lloyd. 87M USA. prod/rel: Warner Brothers Pictures

Over the River, London 1933, Novel
One More River 1934 d: James Whale. lps: Diana Wynyard, Frank Lawton, Mrs. Patrick Campbell. 90M USA. *Over the River* (UKN) prod/rel: Universal Pictures Corp.©

The Skin Game, London 1920, Play
Skin Game, The 1920 d: B. E. Doxat-Pratt. lps: Edmund Gwenn, Mary Clare, Helen Haye. 6000f UKN/NTH. *Hard Tegen Hard* (NTH); *Hard Against Hard* prod/rel: Granger-Binger Film
Skin Game, The 1931 d: Alfred Hitchcock. lps: Edmund Gwenn, Phyllis Konstam, John Longden. 88M UKN. prod/rel: British International Pictures, Wardour

The White Monkey, London 1924, Novel
White Monkey, The 1925 d: Phil Rosen. lps: Barbara La Marr, Thomas Holding, Henry Victor. 6121f USA. prod/rel: Associated Pictures, First National Pictures

GALVEZ, MANUEL (1882–1962), ARG

La Maestra Normal, Novel
Maestra Normal, La 1997 d: Carlos Orgambide. lps: Carolina Fal, Adrian Yospe, Pepe Soriano. F ARG. *The School Teacher*

La Muerte En Las Calles, 1949, Novel
Muerte En Las Calles, La 1952 d: Leo Fleider. lps: Francisco Lopez Silva, Norma Gimenez, Jorge Rigaud. 80M ARG.

Nacha Regules, 1919, Novel
Nacha Regules 1950 d: Luis Cesar Amadori. lps: Gori Munoz, Diana Maggi. 107M ARG.

GAMBERONI, CARLO

Il Baratro
Baratro, Il 1912 d: Mario Bernardi. lps: Albano Masiero, E. Bagnali, Rolando Boscoli. 650m ITL. prod/rel: Fratelli Roatto

GAMBIER, KENYON

Black One-Eyed Man, a Huge, 1917, Short Story
Love in a Hurry 1919 d: Dell Henderson. lps: Carlyle Blackwell, Evelyn Greeley, George MacQuarrie. 5182f USA. *The Hugh Black One-Eyed Man*; *Allies* prod/rel: World Film Corp.©

GAMBINI, PIER ANTONIO QUARANTOTTI

La Rosa Rossa, Novel
Rosa Rossa, La 1973 d: Franco Giraldi. lps: Giampiero Albertini, Antonio Battistella, Elisa Cegani. MTV. F ITL. *The Red Rose* prod/rel: Cine Edizioni Pubblicita, Rai Radiotelevisione Italiana

GAMBINI, QUARANTOTTI

Les Regates de San Francisco, Story
Regates de San Francisco, Les 1959 d: Claude Autant-LarA. lps: Suzy Delair, Folco Lulli, Daniele Gaubert. 75M FRN/ITL. *Il Risveglio Dell'istinto* (ITL) prod/rel: Iena Production, C.E.I.a.P.

GAMET, KENNETH

Story
Flying Leathernecks 1951 d: Nicholas Ray. lps: John Wayne, Robert Ryan, Don Taylor. 102M USA. prod/rel: RKO Radio, Howard Hughes

GANDERA, FELIX

L'amour, Madame, Play
Amour, Madame, L' 1952 d: Gilles Grangier. lps: Francois Perier, Arletty, Mireille Perrey. 89M FRN. prod/rel: Films Raoul Ploquin, Sirius

Atout-Coeur, Play
Arlette Et l'Amour 1943 d: Robert Vernay. lps: Josette Day, Andre Luguet, Andre Alerme. 104M FRN. *Atout Coeur* prod/rel: S.N.E.G.
Atout-Coeur 1931 d: Henry Roussell. lps: Jean Angelo, Alice Cocea, Marcel Levesque. 95M FRN. prod/rel: Pathe-Nathan

Le Chanteur de Mexico, Opera
Chanteur de Mexico, Le 1956 d: Richard Pottier. lps: Luis Mariano, Bourvil, Annie Cordy. 103M FRN/SPN. *El Cantor de Mejico* (SPN) prod/rel: Benito Perojo, Jason Interprods.

Le Conte Galant
Folle Nuit, La 1932 d: Robert Bibal. lps: Marguerite Deval, Suzanne Bianchetti, Guy Parzy. 84M FRN. *Le Derivatif* prod/rel: Films Leon Poirier

Le Couche de la Mariee, Play
Couche de la Mariee, Le 1933 d: Roger Lion. lps: Jean Weber, Suzanne Rissler, Josette Day. 75M FRN. prod/rel: Europa-Films

Les Deux "Monsieur" de Madame, Play
Deux "Monsieur" de Madame, Les 1933 d: Abel Jacquin, Georges Pallu. lps: Pierre Dac, Jeanne Cheirel, Simone Deguyse. F FRN. prod/rel: Films Reyssier
Deux "Monsieur" de Madame, Les 1951 d: Robert Bibal. lps: Jean Paredes, Jacques Berthier, Arlette Poirier. 90M FRN. prod/rel: Olympic

La Facon de Se Donner, Play
D'amour Et d'Eau Fraiche 1933 d: Felix GanderA. lps: Renee Saint-Cyr, Claude Dauphin, Jean Aquistapace. 84M FRN. *La Facon de Se Donner*; *Passage Cloute* prod/rel: Productions Felix Gandera

La Filleule d'Amerique, Play
Filleule d'Amerique, Une 1920 d: Louis de Carbonnat. lps: Louise Marquet, Madeleine James, Felix Huguenet. F FRN. prod/rel: Aigle Films

Nicole E Sa Vertu, Play
Nicole Et Sa Vertu 1931 d: Rene Hervil. lps: Andre Roanne, Robert Goupil, Alice CoceA. 100M FRN. prod/rel: Etablissements Jacques Haik

Quick, Play
Quick 1932 d: Robert Siodmak. lps: Jules Berry, Lilian Harvey, Pierre Brasseur. 87M FRN. prod/rel: U.F.a., a.C.E.

GANDILLOT, LEON

Les Femmes Collantes, Play
Femmes Collantes, Les 1920 d: Georges MoncA. lps: Prince-Rigadin, Simone Joubert, Lucy Mareil. 1380m FRN. prod/rel: Pathe
Femmes Collantes, Les 1938 d: Pierre Caron. lps: Josseline Gael, Betty Stockfeld, Henri Garat. 95M FRN. prod/rel: Ste Prod. Du Film Les Femmes Collantes

Ferdinand le Noceur, Play
Ferdinand le Noceur 1913 d: Georges MoncA. lps: Prince, Yvonne Maelec, Gabrielle Lange. 680m FRN. prod/rel: Pathe
Ferdinand le Noceur 1935 d: Rene Sti. lps: Fernandel, Paulette Dubost, Pauline Carton. 99M FRN. prod/rel: Gamma Films

La Mariee Recalcitrante, Play
Mariee Recalcitrante, La 1916 d: Georges MoncA. lps: Henri-Amedee Charpentier, Prince, Lucy Mareil. 680m FRN. prod/rel: Pathe Freres

GANEM, CHEKRI
Antar
    Antar 1912. lps: Leon Bernard, Jacques Gretillat, Romuald Joube. 385m FRN. prod/rel: Scagl

GANGHOFER, LUDWIG
Der Besondere, Novel
    Alm an Der Grenze, Die 1951 d: Walter Janssen. lps: Richard Haussler, Inge Egger, Willy Rosner. 93M GRM. *Der Besondere; The Meadow on the Border* prod/rel: Peter Ostermayr, Unitas
Der Edelweisskonig, Novel
    Edelweisskonig, Der 1919 d: Peter Ostermayr. 1462m GRM. *King of the Edelweiss* prod/rel: Munchener Lichtspielkunst
    Edelweisskonig, Der 1938 d: Paul May. lps: Hansi Knoteck, Paul Richter, Gustl Stark-Gstettenbaur. 82M GRM. *King of the Edelweiss* prod/rel: Tonlicht, Kopp
    Edelweisskonig, Der 1957 d: Gustav Ucicky. lps: Attila Horbiger, Rudolf Lenz, Christiane Horbiger-Wessely. 82M GRM. *King of the Edelweiss* prod/rel: Peter Ostermayr
    Edelweisskonig, Der 1975 d: Alfred Vohrer. lps: Robert Hoffmann, Adrian Hoven, Ute Kittelberger. 85M GRM. *Ludwig Ganghofer: Der Edelweisskonig*; *King of the Edelweiss* prod/rel: Ctv 72-Filmkunst
Der Geigenmacher von Mittenwald, Play
    Geigenmacher von Mittenwald, Der 1950 d: Rudolf Schundler. lps: Willy Rosner, Paul Richter, Ingeborg Cornelius. 90M GRM. *The Violin Maker of Mittenwald* prod/rel: Peter Ostermayr
Gewitter Im Mai, Novel
    Gewitter Im Mai 1919 d: Ludwig Beck. 1838m GRM. prod/rel: Munchener Lichtspielkunst
    Gewitter Im Mai 1937 d: Hans Deppe. lps: Viktor Staal, Hansi Knoteck, Anny Seitz. 76M GRM. prod/rel: Universum
    Gewitter Im Mai 1988 d: Xaver Schwarzenberger. lps: Gabriel Barylli, Claudia Messner, Michael Greiling. 96M AUS/GAIM. *Tempest in May*; *May Storms* prod/rel: Induna, M.R.
Der Herrgottsschnitzer von Ammergau, Novel
    Herrgottsschnitzer von Ammergau, Der 1952 d: Harald Reinl. lps: Ingeborg Cornelius, Erich Auer, Willy Rosner. 90M GRM. *The Sculptor of Ammergau* prod/rel: Peter Ostermayr, Kopp
Der Jager von Fall, Novel
    Jager von Fall, Der 1918 d: Ludwig Beck. lps: Thea Steinbrecher, Victor Gehring. 1756m GRM. *The Hunter of Fall* prod/rel: Munchener Kunstfilm Peter Ostermayr
    Jager von Fall, Der 1926 d: Franz Seitz. lps: Wilhelm Dieterle, Grete Reinwald, Fritz Kampers. 2834m GRM. *The Hunter of Fall* prod/rel: Munchener Lichtspelkunst Ag
    Jager von Fall, Der 1936 d: Hans Deppe. lps: Paul Richter, Georgia Holt, Hans Adalbert Schlettow. 87M GRM. *The Hunter of Fall* prod/rel: Tonlicht, UFA
    Jager von Fall, Der 1957 d: Gustav Ucicky. lps: Rudolf Lenz, Traute Wassler, Erwin Strahl. 87M GRM. *The Hunter of Fall* prod/rel: Peter Ostermayr
    Jager von Fall, Der 1974 d: Harald Reinl. lps: Gerlinde Doberl, Alexander Stephan, Siegfried Rauch. 90M GRM. *The Hunter of Fall* prod/rel: Ctv 72, Constantin
Der Klosterjager, Novel
    Klosterjager, Der 1920 d: Franz Osten. 1470m GRM. *The Gamekeeper* prod/rel: Munchener Lichtspielkunst Ag
    Klosterjager, Der 1953 d: Harald Reinl. lps: Erich Auer, Paul Hartmann, Marianne Koch. 80M GRM. *The Cloister's Hunter* prod/rel: Peter Ostermayr, Kopp
Die Martinsklause, Novel
    Martinsklause, Die 1951 d: Richard Haussler. lps: Heinz Engelmann, Willy Rosner, Gisela Fackeldey. 95M GRM. *St. Martin's Pass* prod/rel: Ostermayr, Kopp
Der Ochsenkrieg, Novel
    Ochsenkrieg, Der 1920 d: Franz Osten. lps: Anton Ernst Ruckert, Thea Steinbrecher, Fritz Greiner. 1883m GRM. *The War of Oxen* prod/rel: Munchener Lichtspielkunst Ag
    Ochsenkrieg, Der 1942 d: Hans Deppe. lps: Friedrich Ulmer, Ernst Sattler, Thea Aichbichler. 92M GRM. prod/rel: Universum, Unitas
    Ochsenkrieg, Der 1986 d: Sigi Rothemund. lps: Denise Virieux, Christian Spatzek, Rolf Zacher. 310M GRM/AUS/CZC. prod/rel: Iduna-Film, Mr-Film
Schloss Hubertus, Novel
    Schloss Hubertus 1934 d: Hans Deppe. lps: Hansi Knoteck, Paul Richter, Friedrich Ulmer. 85M GRM. *Hubertus Castle* prod/rel: UFA, Kopp

    Schloss Hubertus 1954 d: Helmut Weiss. lps: Friedrich Domin, Marianne Koch, Lil Dagover. 90M GRM. *Hubertus Castle* prod/rel: Peter Ostermayr, Kopp
    Schloss Hubertus 1973 d: Harald Reinl. lps: Robert Hoffmann, Karlheinz Bohm, Karl Lange. 94M GRM. *Hubertus Castle* prod/rel: C.T.V. 72, Constantin
Das Schweigen Im Walde, Novel
    Schweigen Im Walde, Das 1929 d: William Dieterle. lps: Wilhelm Dieterle, Rina Marsa, Karl Gillmann. 2408m GRM. *Le Silence Dans la Foret; La Nuit de la Saint-Jean* prod/rel: Universal Pictures Corp. Gmbh
    Schweigen Im Walde, Das 1937 d: Hans Deppe. lps: Paul Richter, Hansi Knoteck, Friedrich Ulmer. 78M GRM. prod/rel: Universum, Unitas
    Schweigen Im Walde, Das 1955 d: Helmut Weiss. lps: Rudolf Lenz, Sonja Sutter, Angelika Hauff. 90M GRM. *Forest Silence* prod/rel: Ostermayr, Kopp
    Schweigen Im Walde, Das 1976 d: Alfred Vohrer. lps: Alexander Stephan, Evelyn Opela, Belinda Mayne. 94M GRM. *Forest Silence* prod/rel: Ctv 72, Terra
Die Trutze Auf Trutzberg, Novel
    Schafer Vom Trutzberg, Der 1959 d: Eduard von Borsody. lps: Heidi Bruhl, Hans von Borsody, Franziska Kinz. 95M GRM. *The Shepherd of Trutzberg* prod/rel: Peter Ostermayr, Bavaria
Waldrausch, Novel
    Waldrausch 1939 d: Paul May. lps: Paul Richter, Hansi Knoteck, Erika Dannhoff. 81M GRM. prod/rel: Tonlicht-Film, Kopp
    Waldrausch 1962 d: Paul May. lps: Marianne Hold, Gerhard Riedmann, Ingeborg Schoner. 93M AUS. prod/rel: Sascha, Gloria
    Waldrausch 1977 d: Horst Hachler. lps: Uschi Glas, Alexander Stephan, Siegfried Rauch. 101M GRM. *Forest Rush* prod/rel: Ctv 72, Terra-Filmkunst

GANGOPADHYAY, MANILAL
Swayamsiddha, Novel
    Ardhangi 1955 d: P. Pullaiah. lps: A. Nageshwara Rao, K. Jaggaiah, Savitri. 186M IND. *The Better Half* prod/rel: Ragini Films
    Pennin Perumai 1956 d: P. Pullaiah. lps: Gemini Ganesh, Sivaji Ganesan, Savitri. 186M IND. *Proud of This Girl* prod/rel: Ragini Films

GANGULY, SUNIL
Aranye Dinratri, Novel
    Aranye Dinratri 1969 d: Satyajit Ray. lps: Soumitra Chatterjee, Subhendu Chatterjee, Samit BhanjA. 115M IND. *Days and Nights in the Forest* (USA); *Aranyer Din Raatri* prod/rel: Priya Films
Pratidwandi, Novel
    Pratidwandi 1970 d: Satyajit Ray. lps: Dhritiman Chatterjee, Indira Devi, Debraj Roy. 110M IND. *The Adversary* (UKN); *Siddhartha and the City; The Rival* prod/rel: Priya Films

GANN, ERNEST K. (1910–, USA, Gann, Ernest Kellogg)
The Aviator, Novel
    Aviator, The 1984 d: George Miller. lps: Christopher Reeve, Rosanna Arquette, Jack Warden. 98M YGS/USA. prod/rel: MGM, United Artists
Blaze of Noon, Novel
    Blaze of Noon 1947 d: John Farrow. lps: William Holden, Howard Da Silva, Anne Baxter. 91M USA. prod/rel: Paramount
Fate Is the Hunter, New York 1961, Novel
    Fate Is the Hunter 1964 d: Ralph Nelson. lps: Glenn Ford, Nancy Kwan, Rod Taylor. 106M USA. prod/rel: Arcola Pictures
Fiddler's Green, 1950, Novel
    Raging Tide, The 1951 d: George Sherman. lps: Richard Conte, Shelley Winters, Stephen McNally. 93M USA. prod/rel: Universal-International
The Gremlin's Castle, Short Story
    Last Flight of Noah's Ark, The 1980 d: Charles Jarrott. lps: Elliott Gould, Genevieve Bujold, Ricky Schroder. 98M USA. prod/rel: Walt Disney
The High and the Mighty, 1953, Novel
    High and the Mighty, The 1954 d: William A. Wellman. lps: John Wayne, Claire Trevor, Laraine Day. 147M USA. prod/rel: Warner Bros., Wayne-Fellows Prods.
Island in the Sky, Novel
    Island in the Sky 1953 d: William A. Wellman. lps: John Wayne, Lloyd Nolan, Walter Abel. 109M USA. prod/rel: Warner Bros., Wayne-Fellows
Masada, Novel
    Masada 1980 d: Boris Sagal. lps: Peter O'Toole, Peter Strauss, Barbara CarrerA. TVM. 400M USA. *The Antagonists* (UKN) prod/rel: Amon Milchan Prods., Universal TV

Soldier of Fortune, 1954, Novel
    Soldier of Fortune 1955 d: Edward Dmytryk. lps: Clark Gable, Susan Hayward, Michael Rennie. 96M USA. prod/rel: 20th Century-Fox
Twilight for the Gods, 1956, Novel
    Twilight for the Gods 1958 d: Joseph Pevney. lps: Rock Hudson, Cyd Charisse, Arthur Kennedy. 119M USA. *The Damned* prod/rel: Universal-International

GANNE, LOUIS
Les Saltimbanques, Opera
    Saltimbanques, Les 1930 d: Jaquelux, Robert Land. lps: Kathe von Nagy, Nicolas Koline, Max Hansen. 1965m FRN/GRM/ITL. *I Saltimbanchi* (ITL); *Gaukler* (GRM) prod/rel: Albert Lauzin, Nero-Film

GANNET, LOTTA
Her Decision, Short Story
    Her Decision 1918 d: Jack Conway. lps: Gloria Swanson, J. Barney Sherry, Darrel Foss. 5r USA. prod/rel: Triangle Film Corp., Triangle Distributing Corp.

GANNETT, RUTH STILES
My Father's Dragon, Book
    Elmer No Boken 1999 d: Masami HatA. ANM. 99M JPN. *My Father's Dragon* prod/rel: Shochiku Co., Sony Music Entertainment

GANTHONY, RICHARD
A Message from Mars, London 1899, Play
    Message from Mars, A 1913 d: Wallett Waller. lps: Charles Hawtrey, E. Holman Clark, Crissie Bell. 4000f UKN. prod/rel: United Kingdom Films
    Message from Mars, A 1921 d: Maxwell Karger. lps: Bert Lytell, Raye Dean, Maude Milton. 5187f USA. prod/rel: Metro Pictures

GANTILLON, SIMON
Maya, Play
    Maya 1949 d: Raymond Bernard. lps: Jean-Pierre Grenier, Marcel Dalio, Viviane Romance. 78M FRN. prod/rel: Films Izarra

GANTZER, FRITZ
Kreuz Im Moor, Novel
    Liebe Der Bruder Rott, Die 1929 d: Erich Waschneck. lps: Olga Tschechowa, Jean Dax, Paul Henckels. 2365m GRM. *Irrlichter*; *Will O' the Wisp* prod/rel: Tschechowa-Film

GAO SHIGUO
Guitai, Play
    Guitai 1965 d: Yin Zhi. lps: Da Shichang, Wei Heling, Zhang XIoaling. 8r CHN. *The Counter* prod/rel: Tianma Film Studio

GARAI-ARVAY
Die Dame in Schwarz, Novel
    Dame in Schwarz, Die 1928 d: Franz Osten. lps: Marcella Albani, Liane Haid, Charles Lincoln. 2166m GRM. *The Lady in Black* prod/rel: Peter Ostermayr-Filmprod.
Die Raffinierteste Frau Berlins, Novel
    Raffinierteste Frau Berlins, Die 1927 d: Franz Osten. lps: Mary Johnson, Luigi Serventi, Andre Mattoni. 2372m GRM. *The Cleverest Woman in Berlin* prod/rel: Peter Ostermayr-Film-Prod.

GARCIA ALVAREZ, E.
Alma de Dios, Opera
    Alma de Dios 1923 d: Manuel NoriegA. lps: Elisa Ruiz Romero, Irene Alba, Juan Bonafe. 2167m SPN. prod/rel: Atlantida
El Pobre Valbuena, Opera
    Pobre Valbuena, El 1923 d: Jose Buchs. lps: Antonio Gil, Alfonso Aguilar, Manuel San German. F SPN. *Poor Valbueno* prod/rel: Film Espanola (Madrid)

GARCIA BLASQUEZ, JOSE ANTONIO
Non Ho Trovato Rose Per Mia Madre, Short Story
    No Encontre Rosas Para Mi Madre 1972 d: Francisco Rovira BeletA. lps: Renaud Verley, Susan Hampshire, Gina LollobrigidA. 99M SPN/FRN/ITL. *Roses Rouges Et Piments Verts* (FRN); *Peccato Mortale* (ITL); *I Found No Roses for My Mother; The Lonely Woman* (USA) prod/rel: Hidalgo Andrea Velasco (Madrid), C.P. Cin.Ca (Roma)

GARCIA GUTIERREZ, ANTONIO (1813–1884), SPN
El Trovador, Madrid 1836, Play
    Trovatore, Il 1910 d: Louis J. Gasnier. lps: Francesca Bertini, Gemma Farina, Achille Vitti. 435m ITL/FRN. *Le Trouvere* (FRN); *The Troubadour* (UKN) prod/rel: Pathe Freres, Film d'Arte Italiana
    Trovatore, Il 1914 d: Charles Simone. lps: Jean Thrall, Agnes Mapes, Morgia Litton. 5-6r USA. *Il Trovatore* prod/rel: Centaur Film Co.
    Trovatore, Il 1922 d: Edwin J. Collins. lps: Bertram Burleigh, Lillian Douglas, Cyril Dane. 842f UKN. prod/rel: Master Films, Gaumont

GARIS, ROGER
The Pony Cart, London 1959, Play
Never Take Sweets from a Stranger 1960 d: Cyril Frankel. lps: Gwen Watford, Patrick Allen, Felix Aylmer. 81M UKN. *Never Take Candy from a Stranger* (USA); *The Molester* prod/rel: Hammer Film Productions, Columbia

GARLAND, HAMLIN (1860–1940), USA
Captain of the Grey Horse Troop, London 1902, Novel
Captain of the Gray Horse Troop, The 1917 d: William Wolbert. lps: Antonio Moreno, Edith Storey, Mrs. Bradbury. 5r USA. *The Long Fight* prod/rel: Vitagraph Co. of America©, Greater Vitagraph (V-L-S-E)
Cavanaugh - Forest Ranger; a Romance of the Mountain West, New York 1910, Novel
Cavanaugh of the Forest Rangers 1918 d: William Wolbert. lps: Alfred Whitman, Nell Shipman, Otto Lederer. 5r USA. prod/rel: Vitagraph Co. of America©, Blue Ribbon Feature
Ranger of the Big Pines 1925 d: W. S. Van Dyke. lps: Kenneth Harlan, Helene Costello, Eulalie Jensen. 7032f USA. prod/rel: Vitagraph Co. of America
Hesper: a Novel, New York 1903, Novel
Hesper of the Mountains 1916 d: Wilfred North. lps: Lillian Walker, Donald Hall, Evart Overton. 5r USA. prod/rel: Vitagraph Co. of America©, Blue Ribbon Feature
Money Magic, New York 1907, Novel
Money Magic 1917 d: William Wolbert. lps: William Duncan, Edith Storey, Antonio Moreno. 5r USA. prod/rel: Vitagraph Co. of America©, Blue Ribbon Feature

GARLAND, JUNE
Widows are Dangerous, London 1953, Play
Trouble With Eve 1960 d: Francis Searle. lps: Robert Urquhart, Hy Hazell, Garry Marsh. 64M UKN. *In Trouble With Eve* (USA); *In Walked Eve* prod/rel: Mancunian Film Corp., Butcher's Film Service

GARNEAU, MICHEL
Les Celebrations, Play
Celebrations, Les 1979 d: Yves Simoneau. lps: Leo Munger, Normand Levesque, J. Yves Dussault. 86M CND. prod/rel: Les Films Gamma Inc.

GARNER, HELEN (1942–, ASL
Monkey Grip, Novel
Monkey Grip 1982 d: Ken Cameron. lps: Noni Hazlehurst, Colin Friels, Alice Garner. 102M ASL. prod/rel: Pavilion Films©, Roadshow

GARNER, HUGH
The Sin Sniper, Novel
Stone Cold Dead 1979 d: George Mendeluk. lps: Richard Crenna, Paul Williams, Linda Sorensen. 100M CND. *The Sin Sniper; Point Two Two* prod/rel: Ko-Zak Productions Inc., Dimension

GARNETT, DAVID (1892–1981), UKN, Burke, Leda
The Sailor's Return, Novel
Sailor's Return, The 1977 d: Jack Gold. lps: Tom Bell, Shope Shodeinde, Mick Ford. 108M UKN. prod/rel: Thames Tv, Euston Films

GARNIER, HUGUETTE
Quand Nous Etions Deux, Novel
Quand Nous Etions Deux 1929 d: Leonce Perret. lps: Andre Roanne, Maurice de Canonge, Alice Roberte. F FRN. prod/rel: Gaumont-Franco-Film-Aubert

GARRARD, JAMES
Cold Comfort, Play
Cold Comfort 1989 d: Vic Sarin. lps: Maury Chaykin, Margaret Langrick, Paul Gross. 92M CND. prod/rel: Norstar

GARRETT, ALMEIDA
Frei Luis de Sousa, 1859, Play
Frei Luis de Sousa 1949 d: Antonio Lopes Ribeiro. lps: Tomas de Macedo, Maria Dulce, Raul de Carvalho. 118M PRT. *Friar Luis de Sousa*

GARRETT, LAURIE
The Coming Plague, Book
Coming Plague, The 1997 d: Ned Judge. DOC. 240M USA. prod/rel: Turner Original Productions

GARRETT, WILLIAM
The Man in the Mirror, Novel
Man in the Mirror, The 1936 d: Maurice Elvey. lps: Edward Everett Horton, Genevieve Tobin, Garry Marsh. 82M UKN. prod/rel: Jh Productions, Wardour
The Professional Guest, Novel
Professional Guest, The 1931 d: George King. lps: Gordon Harker, Richard Bird, Garry Marsh. 42M UKN. prod/rel: George King, Fox

The Secret of the Hills, London 1920, Novel
Secret of the Hills, The 1921 d: Chester Bennett. lps: Antonio Moreno, Lillian Hall, Kingsley Benedict. 5r USA. prod/rel: Vitagraph Co. of America

GARRICK, DAVID (1717–1779), UKN
The Country Girl, Play
Country Girl, The 1915. lps: Florence Labadie, Harry Benham, Justus D. Barnes. 2r USA. prod/rel: Thanhouser

GARRICK, JOHN
Le Vautour, Novel
Rapace, Le 1968 d: Jose Giovanni. lps: Lino Ventura, Xavier Marc, Rosa Furman. 110M FRN/ITL/MXC. *Il Rapace* (ITL); *Birds of Prey* prod/rel: P.A.C., Valoria

GARRISON, JIM
Trail of the Assassins, Book
JFK 1991 d: Oliver Stone. lps: Kevin Costner, Sissy Spacek, Kevin Bacon. 189M USA. prod/rel: Warner Bros., le Studio Canal Plus

GARSTIN, CROSBIE
China Seas, New York 1931, Novel
China Seas 1935 d: Tay Garnett. lps: Clark Gable, Jean Harlow, Wallace Beery. 90M USA. prod/rel: Metro-Goldwyn-Mayer Corp.
The Figurehead, Poem
Figurehead, The 1953 d: John Halas, Joy Batchelor. ANM. 8M UKN.

GARTH, CASWELL
Little Tommy Tucker, Play
Out of the Blue 1931 d: Gene Gerrard, John Orton. lps: Gene Gerrard, Jessie Matthews, Kay Hammond. 88M UKN. prod/rel: British International Pictures, Pathe

GARTH, DAVID
Cabin Cruiser, 1936, Short Story
Hideaway Girl 1937 d: George Archainbaud. lps: Martha Raye, Robert Cummings, Shirley Ross. 71M USA. prod/rel: Paramount Pictures©
Four Men and a Prayer, New York 1937, Novel
Four Men and a Prayer 1938 d: John Ford. lps: Loretta Young, Richard Greene, George Sanders. 85M USA. prod/rel: Twentieth Century-Fox Film Corp.©
Let Freedom Swing, 1937, Short Story
There Goes the Groom 1937 d: Joseph Santley. lps: Burgess Meredith, Ann Sothern, Louise Henry. 66M USA. *Don't Forget to Remember* prod/rel: RKO Radio Pictures©
A Love Like That, New York 1937, Novel
Breakfast for Two 1937 d: Alfred Santell. lps: Barbara Stanwyck, Herbert Marshall, Glenda Farrell. 67M USA. *A Love Like That; Here Comes the Groom* prod/rel: RKO Radio Pictures, Inc.

GARVE, ANDREW (1908–, UKN, Bax, Roger, Somers, Paul
Beginner's Luck, Novel
Desperate Man, The 1959 d: Peter Maxwell. lps: Jill Ireland, Conrad Phillips, William Hartnell. 57M UKN. prod/rel: Anglo-Amalgamated, Merton Park
Death and the Sky Above, Novel
Two Letter Alibi 1962 d: Robert Lynn. lps: Peter Williams, Petra Davies, Ursula Howells. 60M UKN. prod/rel: British Lion, Playpont
The Megstone Plot, Novel
Touch of Larceny, A 1959 d: Guy Hamilton. lps: James Mason, Vera Miles, George Sanders. 91M UKN/USA. prod/rel: Paramount, Ivan Foxwell

GARVICE, CHARLES
The Coronet of Shame, 1900, Novel
Kroon Der Schande, de 1918 d: Maurits H. Binger. lps: Willem Van Der Veer, Annie Bos, Adelqui Millar. 1935m NTH. *The Crown of Shame; The Coronet of Shame* (UKN) prod/rel: Filmfabriek-Hollandia
Diana and Destiny, Novel
Diana and Destiny 1916 d: F. Martin Thornton. lps: Evelyn Boucher, Wyndham Guise, Roy Travers. 5000f UKN. prod/rel: Windsor, Gaumont
A Fair Imposter, Novel
Fair Imposter, A 1916 d: Alexander Butler. lps: Madge Titheradge, Gerald McCarthy, Charles Rock. 5000f UKN. prod/rel: G. B. Samuelson, Moss
Just a Girl, Novel
Just a Girl 1916 d: Alexander Butler. lps: Owen Nares, Daisy Burrell, J. Hastings Batson. 6300f UKN. prod/rel: G. B. Samuelson, Moss
Linked By Fate, Novel
Linked By Fate 1919 d: Albert Ward. lps: Isobel Elsom, Malcolm Cherry, Clayton Green. 5000f UKN. prod/rel: G. B. Samuelson, General
Nance, Novel
Nance 1920 d: Albert Ward. lps: Isobel Elsom, James Lindsay, Ivan Samson. 5500f UKN. prod/rel: G. B. Samuelson, General

The Rugged Path, Novel
Rugged Path, The 1918. lps: Marjorie Villis, Hayford Hobbs, Cameron Carr. 5000f UKN. prod/rel: New Agency, Lucoque
The Verdict of the Heart, Novel
Verdict of the Heart, The 1915 d: Wilfred Noy. lps: Harry Welchman, Barbara Hoffe, Frank Royde. 3200f UKN. prod/rel: Clarendon, Moss
With All Her Heart, Novel
With All Her Heart 1920 d: Frank Wilson. lps: Milton Rosmer, Mary Odette, Jack Vincent. 4845f UKN. prod/rel: I. B. Davidson, Ruffells

GARY, ROMAIN (1914–1980), RSS, Kacew, Romain
Clair de Femme, Novel
Clair de Femme 1979 d: Costa-Gavras. lps: Yves Montand, Romy Schneider, Romolo Valli. 105M FRN/GRM/ITL. *Chiaro Di Donna* (ITL); *The Love of a Woman*; *Womanlight* (USA); *Die Liebe Einer Frau* (GRM) prod/rel: Janus, Iduna
The Colors of the Day, 1953, Novel
Man Who Understood Women, The 1959 d: Nunnally Johnson. lps: Henry Fonda, Leslie Caron, Cesare DanovA. 105M USA. prod/rel: 20th Century-Fox, Nunnally Johnson
Dance of Genghis Cohn, Novel
Genghis Cohn 1993 d: Elijah Moshinsky. lps: Robert Lindsay, Antony Sher, Diana Rigg. TVM. 80M UKN.
Lady L, Paris 1963, Novel
Lady L 1965 d: Peter Ustinov. lps: Sophia Loren, Paul Newman, David Niven. 124M USA/ITL/FRN. prod/rel: C.C. Champion, Les Films Concordia
Les Oiseaux Vont Mourir Au Perou, 1962, Short Story
Oiseaux Vont Mourir Au Perou, Les 1968 d: Romain Gary. lps: Jean Seberg, Maurice Ronet, Danielle Darrieux. 95M FRN. *The Birds Come to Die in Peru* (UKN); *Birds in Peru* (USA) prod/rel: Universal Productions France
La Promesse de l'Aube, Paris 1960, Book
Promesse de l'Aube, La 1970 d: Jules Dassin. lps: Melina Mercouri, Assaf Dayan, Didier Haudepin. 102M FRN/USA. *Promise at Dawn* (USA) prod/rel: Avco Embassy Pictures, Nathalie Films
The Roots of Heaven, 1956, Novel
Roots of Heaven, The 1958 d: John Huston. lps: Errol Flynn, Juliette Greco, Trevor Howard. 131M USA. prod/rel: 20th Century-Fox

GARY, ROMAIN
White Dog, Novel
White Dog 1982 d: Samuel Fuller. lps: Kristy McNichol, Paul Winfield, Burl Ives. 90M USA. prod/rel: Paramount Pictures

GARY, ROMAIN (1914–1980), RSS, Kacew, Romain
Your Ticket Is No Longer Valid, Novel
Your Ticket Is No Longer Valid 1980 d: George Kaczender. lps: Richard Harris, George Peppard, Jeanne Moreau. 92M CND. *Finishing Touch; A Slow Descent Into Hell; Au-Dela de Cette Limite Votre Ticket N'est Plus Valable; L' Ultime Passion* prod/rel: Moviecorp V Inc., Rsl Films Ltd.

GASIOROWSKI, WACLAW
Pani Walewska, Book
Conquest 1937 d: Clarence Brown. lps: Greta Garbo, Charles Boyer, Reginald Owen. 115M USA. *Marie Walewska* (UKN); *Madame Waleska* prod/rel: Metro-Goldwyn-Mayer Corp.

GASKELL, JANE
All Neat in Black Stockings, London 1966, Novel
All Neat in Black Stockings 1968 d: Christopher Morahan. lps: Victor Henry, Susan George, Jack Shepherd. 99M UKN. prod/rel: Anglo-Amalgamated, Miron Films

GASKELL, MRS. (1810–1865), UKN, Gaskell, Elizabeth Cleghorn
A Manchester Marriage, Novel
Heartstrings 1923 d: Edwin Greenwood. lps: Gertrude McCoy, Victor McLaglen, Edith Bishop. 5170f UKN. prod/rel: British & Colonial
The Sins of a Father, Novel
Sins of a Father, The 1923 d: Edwin Greenwood. lps: Madge Stuart, Russell Thorndike. 2117f UKN. prod/rel: British & Colonial, Walturdaw

GASKIN, CATHERINE (1929–, ASL
Sara Dane, Novel
Sara Dane 1982 d: Rod Hardy, Gary Conway. lps: Juliet Jordan, Harold Hopkins, Brenton Whittle. MTV. 400M ASL.

GASTE, LOUIS
Une Nuit aux Baleares, Opera
Nuit aux Baleares, Une 1956 d: Paul Mesnier. lps: Georges Guetary, Jean-Marc Thibault, Claude Bessy. 90M FRN. prod/rel: Taurus Films

GEELMUYDEN, HANS
Trine!, 1940, Novel
Trine 1952 d: Toralf Sando. 99M NRW.

GEER, ANDREW
The Sea Chase, 1948, Novel
Sea Chase, The 1955 d: John Farrow. lps: John Wayne, Lana Turner, David Farrar. 117M USA. prod/rel: Warner Bros.

GEFFROY, GUSTAVE
L' Apprentie
Apprentie, L' 1914 d: Emile Chautard. lps: Edmond Duquesne, Henri Gouget, Henri Bosc. 1250m FRN. prod/rel: Acad

GEHRI, ALFRED
Im Sechsten Stock, Play
Im Sechsten Stock 1961 d: John Olden. lps: Sabine Sinjen, Helmut Lohner, Klausjurgen Wussow. 94M GRM. *Im 6 Stock*; *Sixth Floor* prod/rel: Real, Europa
Sixieme Etage, Play
Sixieme Etage 1939 d: Maurice Cloche. lps: Jean Daurand, Janine Darcey, Germaine Sablon. 96M FRN. prod/rel: C.I.C.C.

GEHRIG, ELEANOR
My Luke and I, Book
Love Affair: the Eleanor & Lou Gehrig Story, A 1977 d: Fielder Cook. lps: Blythe Danner, Edward Herrmann, Patricia Neal. TVM. 100M USA. prod/rel: Charles Fries Productions, Stonehenge Productions

GEHRKE, MARTHA MARIA
Morder Ohne Mord, Novel
Luge, Die 1950 d: Gustav Frohlich. lps: Otto Gebuhr, Sybille Schmitz, Cornell Borchers. 84M GRM. *The Lie* prod/rel: Junge Film-Union, N.F.

GEISSLER, HORST WOLFRAM
Der Liebe Augustin, Novel
Liebe Augustin, Der 1940 d: E. W. Emo. lps: Paul Horbiger, Maria Andergast, Michael Bohnen. 95M GRM. *Dear Augustine* prod/rel: Universum, U.F.H.

GEISSLER, JOSEF
Weltrekord Im Seitensprung, Play
Weltrekord Im Seitensprung 1940 d: Georg Zoch. lps: Ludwig Schmitz, Julia Serda, Else Elster. 101M GRM. prod/rel: Deka, Karp

GELBART, LARRY
A Funny Thing Happened on the Way to the Forum, New York 1962, Play
Funny Thing Happened on the Way to the Forum, A 1966 d: Richard Lester. lps: Zero Mostel, Phil Silvers, Jack Gifford. 99M UKN/USA. prod/rel: Quadrangle Films, United Artists

GELBER, JACK (1932–, USA
The Connection, New York 1959, Play
Connection, The 1962 d: Shirley Clarke. lps: Warren Finnerty, Jerome Raphel, James Anderson. 110M USA. prod/rel: Alle/Hogdon

GELINAS, GRATIEN (1909–, CND
Tit-Coq, Play
Tit-Coq 1952 d: Rene Delacroix, Gratien Gelinas. lps: Gratien Gelinas, Fred Barry, Monique Miller. 101M CND. prod/rel: Les Productions Gratien Gelinas Ltd.

GELLER, STEPHEN
She Let Him Continue, New York 1966, Novel
Pretty Poison 1968 d: Noel Black. lps: Tuesday Weld, Anthony Perkins, Beverly Garland. 89M USA. *She Let Him Continue* prod/rel: Lawrence Turman Films, Molino Productions

GELZER, JAY
Broadway Musketeers, 1928, Short Story
Broadway Babies 1929 d: Mervyn Leroy. lps: Alice White, Charles Delaney, Fred Kohler. 8087f USA. *Broadway Daddies* (UKN) prod/rel: First National Pictures
Compromise, New York 1923, Novel
Compromise 1925 d: Alan Crosland. lps: Irene Rich, Clive Brook, Louise FazendA. 6789f USA. prod/rel: Warner Brothers Pictures
The Flower of the Flock, 1921, Short Story
Driven 1923 d: Charles J. Brabin. lps: Emily Fitzroy, Burr McIntosh, Charles Emmett MacK. 5400f USA. prod/rel: Charles J. Brabin, Universal Film Mfg. Co.
Rich People, 1928, Short Story
Rich People 1929 d: Edward H. Griffith. lps: Constance Bennett, Regis Toomey, Robert Ames. 7074f USA. *The Racketeer* prod/rel: Pathe Exchange, Inc.

GEMELLI, ENRICO
Cararbinie, 1892, Play
Carabiniere 1913 d: Ubaldo Maria Del Colle. lps: Alberto A. Capozzi, Ugo Pardi, Teresina Melidoni. 981m ITL. *Carabinie*; *The Italian Gendarme* (USA) prod/rel: Pasquali E C.

GENEE, RICHARD
Nanon, Play
Nanon 1924 d: Hanns Schwarz. lps: Agnes Esterhazy, Harry Liedtke, Hanni Weisse. 2475m GRM. prod/rel: Trianon-Film Ag
Nanon 1938 d: Herbert Maisch. lps: Erna Sack, Johannes Heesters, Otto Gebuhr. 80M GRM. prod/rel: UFA, Paikert

GENET, JEAN (1910–1986), FRN
Le Balcon, 1956, Play
Balcony, The 1963 d: Joseph Strick. lps: Shelley Winters, Peter Falk, Lee Grant. 84M USA. prod/rel: Walter Reade-Sterling, Inc., Allen-Hodgdon Productions
Les Bonnes, 1948, Play
Maids, The 1975 d: Christopher Miles. lps: Glenda Jackson, Susannah York, Vivien Merchant. 95M UKN/CND. prod/rel: Ely Landau, Cinevision
Le Condamne a Mort, 1942, Verse
Possession du Condamne 1967 d: Albert Andre L'Heureux. 14M BLG. *Condemned and Possessed*
Haute Surveillance, Paris 1949, Play
Black Mirror 1981 d: Pierre-Alain Jolivet. lps: Louise Marleau, Lenore Zann, Francoise Dorner. 87M CND/FRN. *Haute Surveillance* (FRN) prod/rel: Mirada Productions Ltd. (Montreal), Prod. Cinematographique Parisienne
Deathwatch 1965 d: Vic Morrow. lps: Leonard Nimoy, Michael Forest, Paul Mazursky. 88M USA.
Querelle de Brest, 1952, Novel
Querelle de Brest 1982 d: R. W. Fassbinder. lps: Brad Davis, Franco Nero, Jeanne Moreau. 105M GRM/FRN. *Querelle - Ein Pakt Mit Dem Teufel*; *Querelle* (UKN) prod/rel: Albatross, Gaumont

GENEVOIX, MAURICE
Raboliot, Novel
Raboliot 1945 d: Jacques Daroy. lps: Julien Bertheau, Lise Delamare, Blanchette Brunoy. 103M FRN. prod/rel: Prisonniers Associes

GENINA, AUGUSTO
L' Anima Del Demi-Monde, Short Story
Nini Verbena 1913 d: Baldassarre Negroni. lps: Francesca Bertini, Emilio Ghione, Alberto Collo. 860m ITL. *The Bondage of Evil* (USA)
Liebeskarneval, Short Story
Liebeskarneval 1928 d: Augusto GeninA. lps: Carmen Boni, Jack Trevor, Hans Junkermann. 2389m GRM. prod/rel: Nero-Film
L' Orizzontale, Novel
Innamorata, L' 1920 d: Gennaro Righelli. lps: Italia Almirante Manzini, Annibale Beltrone, Alberto Collo. 1640m ITL. prod/rel: Fert

GENJI, KEITA
Zuiko-San, Novel
Shin Santo Juyaku: Teishu Kyo Iku No Maki 1961 d: Shue Matsubayashi. lps: Hisaya Morishige, Asami Kuji, Keiju Kobayashi. 90M JPN. *Wanton Journey* prod/rel: Toho Co.

GENTRY, CURT
Helter Skelter, Book
Helter Skelter 1976 d: Tom Gries. lps: Steve Railsback, George Dicenzo, Nancy Wolfe. TVM. 194M USA. *Massacre in Hollywood* prod/rel: Lorimar Productions

GEOFFREY, WALLACE
The Perfect Woman, London 1948, Play
Perfect Woman, The 1949 d: Bernard Knowles. lps: Patricia Roc, Stanley Holloway, Nigel Patrick. 89M UKN. prod/rel: General Film Distributors, Two Cities
The Scotland Yard Mystery, Play
Scotland Yard Mystery, The 1934 d: Thomas Bentley. lps: Gerald Du Maurier, George Curzon, Grete Natzler. 76M UKN. *The Living Dead* (USA) prod/rel: British International Pictures, Wardour

GEOFFREYS, OLIVER W.
The Marionettes, Play
Ransom, The 1916 d: Edmund Lawrence. lps: Julia Dean, Louise Huff, J. Albert Hall. 5r USA. *She Pays* prod/rel: Triumph Film Corp.©, Equitable Motion Pictures Corp.

GEORGE, ELIOT
The Leather Boys, London 1961, Novel
Leather Boys, The 1963 d: Sidney J. Furie. lps: Rita Tushingham, Dudley Sutton, Gladys Henson. 108M UKN. prod/rel: Raymond Stross Productions, Garrick

GEORGE, ERNEST
Down Our Street, Play
Down Our Street 1932 d: Harry Lachman. lps: Nancy Price, Elizabeth Allan, Morris Harvey. 87M UKN. prod/rel: Paramount British, Paramount

GEORGE, GEORGE W.
Backtrack, Story
Fort Dobbs 1958 d: Gordon Douglas. lps: Clint Walker, Virginia Mayo, Brian Keith. 90M USA. prod/rel: Warner Bros.

GEORGE, JEAN CRAIGHEAD (1919–, USA
My Side of the Mountain, New York 1969, Novel
My Side of the Mountain 1969 d: James B. Clark. lps: Teddy Eccles, Theodore Bikel, Tudi Wiggins. 101M USA/CND. prod/rel: Robert B. Radnitz Productions

GEORGE, KATHLEEN G.
Ten Against Caesar, 1952, Story
Gun Fury 1953 d: Raoul Walsh. lps: Rock Hudson, Donna Reed, Philip Carey. 83M USA. prod/rel: Columbia

GEORGE, PETER BRYAN
Red Alert, New York 1958, Novel
Dr. Strangelove 1963 d: Stanley Kubrick. lps: Peter Sellers, George C. Scott, Sterling Hayden. 94M UKN.; *Dr. Strangelove: Or How I Learned to Stop Worrying and Love the Bomb* prod/rel: Hawk Films, Stanley Kubrick

GEORGIUS
Pas de Femmes, Play
Pas de Femmes 1932 d: Mario Bonnard. lps: Jacqueline Jacquet, Georgius, Fernandel. 80M FRN. prod/rel: Prima-Film

GERALD, FLORENCE
The Woman Pays, Play
Woman Pays, The 1915 d: Edgar Jones. lps: Valli Valli, Edward Brennan, Marie Empress. 5r USA. prod/rel: Columbia Pictures Corp., Metro Pictures Corp.©

GERALDY, PAUL
L' Homme de Joie, Play
Homme de Joie, L' 1950 d: Gilles Grangier. lps: Jean-Pierre Aumont, Simone Renant, Jacques Morel. 95M FRN. prod/rel: Ariane
Les Noces d'Argent, Paris 1917, Play
Nest, The 1927 d: William Nigh. lps: Holmes Herbert, Thomas Holding, Pauline Frederick. 7393f USA. prod/rel: Excellent Pictures

GERARD, JAMES W.
My Four Years in Germany, New York 1917, Book
My Four Years in Germany 1918 d: William Nigh. lps: Halbert Brown, Willard Dashiell, Louis Dean. 9-10r USA. prod/rel: My Four Years in Germany, Inc.©, First National Exhibitors Circuit

GERARD, LOUISE
A Son of the Sahara, New York 1922, Novel
Son of the Sahara, A 1924 d: Edwin Carewe. lps: Claire Windsor, Bert Lytell, Walter McGrail. 7603f USA. *The Sultan's Slave* prod/rel: Edwin Carewe Productions, Associated First National Pictures

GERARD, MAURICE
The Secret of the Moor, Novel
Secret of the Moor, The 1919 d: Lewis Willoughby. lps: Gwen Williams, Philip Hewland, Henry Thompson. 5095f UKN. prod/rel: British Lion, Granger

GERARD, ROSEMOND
Un Bon Petit Diable, Paris 1911, Play
Good Little Devil, A 1914 d: Edwin S. Porter, J. Searle Dawley. lps: Mary Pickford, William Norris, Ernest Truex. 5r USA. prod/rel: Famous Players Film Co., State Rights

GERBIDON
The Hotel Mouse, Play
Hotel Mouse, The 1923 d: Fred Paul. lps: Lillian Hall-Davis, Campbell Gullan, Warwick Ward. 6500f UKN. prod/rel: British Super, Jury

GERBIDON, MARCEL
L' Amoureuse Aventure, Play
Amoureuse Aventure, L' 1931 d: Wilhelm Thiele. lps: Marie Glory, Jeanne Boitel, Albert Prejean. 84M FRN. prod/rel: Vandal Et Delac
Un Chien Qui Rapporte, Play
Chien Qui Rapporte, Un 1931 d: Jean Choux. lps: Arletty, Rene Lefevre, Medy. 87M FRN. prod/rel: Superfilm
Coiffeur Pour Dames, Play
Coiffeur Pour Dames 1931 d: Rene Guissart. lps: Fernand Gravey, Mona Goya, Irene Brillant. 80M FRN. *Artist With the Ladies* (USA) prod/rel: Films Paramount
Dicky, Play
Monsieur Breloque a Disparu 1937 d: Robert Peguy. lps: Lucien Baroux, Junie Astorm, Marcel Simon. 95M FRN. prod/rel: B.A.P. Films
Trappola d'Amore 1940 d: Raffaello Matarazzo. lps: Giuseppe Porelli, Carla Candiani, Paolo StoppA. 80M ITL. *Le Prodezze Di Dicky*; *Dicky* prod/rel: Oceano Film, Generalcine

L' Ecole Des Cocottes, Play
Ecole Des Cocottes, L' 1935 d: Piere Colombier. lps: Renee Saint-Cyr, Pauline Carton, Raimu. 106M FRN. prod/rel: Pathe-Natan

Un Fils d'Amerique, Play
Fils d'Amerique, Un 1925 d: Henri Fescourt. lps: Gabriel Gabrio, Marie-Louise Iribe, Alice Tissot. 1750m FRN. prod/rel: Films De France
Fils d'Amerique, Un 1932 d: Carmine Gallone. lps: Annabella, Albert Prejean, Gaston Dubosc. 91M FRN/HNG. *Az Amerikai Flu* (HNG) prod/rel: Societe Des Films Osso

Le Mari Garcon, Play
Mari Garcon, Le 1933 d: Alberto Cavalcanti. lps: Jean Debucourt, Yvonne Garat, Jeanne Cheirel. 85M FRN. *Le Garcon Divorce* prod/rel: Amax-Films

Le Porion, Play
Porion, Le 1921 d: Georges Champavert. lps: Juliette Malherbe, Claude Benedict, Rene Maupre. 1750m FRN. prod/rel: Films Prismos

Un Soir de Reveillon, Opera
Soir de Reveillon, Un 1933 d: Karl Anton. lps: Henri Garat, Meg Lemonnier, Arletty. 85M FRN. prod/rel: Films Paramount

Souris d'Hotel, Play
Souris d'Hotel 1927 d: Adelqui Millar. lps: Ica de Lenkeffy, Arthur Pusey, Suzanne Delmas. 2500m FRN. prod/rel: Albatros

GERBIDOU, MARCEL
The French Doll, New York 1922, Play
French Doll, The 1923 d: Robert Z. Leonard. lps: Mae Murray, Orville Caldwell, Rod La Rocque. 7028f USA. prod/rel: Tiffany Productions, Metro Pictures

GERMAIN, A.
Visages de Femmes, Play
Visages de Femmes 1938 d: Rene Guissart. lps: Pierre Brasseur, Felicien Tramel, Huguette Duflos. 85M FRN. prod/rel: Societe Du Film Fred

GERMAIN, HENRI
Le Baron Mystere, Novel
Baron Mystere, Le 1918 d: Maurice Challiot. lps: Henri Rollan, Albert Bras, Rene Debray. 600m FRN. prod/rel: Natura Film
La Fille du Boche, Novel
Fille du Boche, La 1915 d: Henri Pouctal. lps: Camille Bert, Mevisto, Jeanne Brindeau. 2230m FRN. prod/rel: Film Francais
Le Sorcier, Novel
Sorcier, Le 1919 d: Maurice Challiot. lps: Alcover, Maurice Lagrenee, Jane Ader. 1193m FRN. prod/rel: Natura Films

GERMAIN, JOSE
A l'Ombre Des Tombeaux, Novel
Vestale du Gange, La 1927 d: Andre Hugon. lps: Georges Melchior, Regina Thomas, Bernhard Goetzke. 2900m FRN. *The Temple of Shadows* prod/rel: Hugon-Films
L' Amant de Borneo, Play
Amant de Borneo, L' 1942 d: Jean-Pierre Feydeau, Rene Le Henaff. lps: Jean Tissier, Arletty, Pauline Carton. 90M FRN. prod/rel: C.C.F.C.

GERMAINE, MARY
Wildflower, Story
Wildflower 1914 d: Allan Dwan. lps: Marguerite Clark, Harold Lockwood, James Cooley. 4163f USA. prod/rel: Famous Players Film Co., Paramount Pictures Corp.

GERNET, N. V.
Kata a Krokodyl, Book
Kata a Krokodyl 1965 d: Vera Plivova-SimkovA. lps: Ivetta Hollanerova, Tomas Drbohlav, Barborka ZikovA. 72M CZC. *Kate and the Crocodile; Katia and the Crocodile* prod/rel: Barrandov

GEROULD, KATHARINE FULLERTON
Conquistador, New York 1923, Novel
Romance of the Rio Grande 1929 d: Alfred Santell. lps: Warner Baxter, Mona Maris, Mary Duncan. 8652f USA. *Romance of Rio Grande* prod/rel: Fox Film Corp.
Romance of the Rio Grande 1940 d: Herbert I. Leeds. lps: Cesar Romero, Patricia Morison, Lynne Roberts. 73M USA. prod/rel: Twentieth Century-Fox Film Corp.©
Yankee Senor, The 1926 d: Emmett J. Flynn. lps: Tom Mix, Olive Borden, Tom Kennedy. 4902f USA. prod/rel: Fox Film Corp.

GEROULE, HENRI
L' Ami de Ma Femme, Play
Je Te Confie Ma Femme 1933 d: Rene Guissart. lps: Jean Aquistapace, Jeanne Cheirel, Edith MerA. 75M FRN. prod/rel: Rene Guissart, Yves Mirande

Octave, Play
Octave 1909. lps: Harry Baur, Rouviere, Mary Hett. 200m FRN. prod/rel: Scagl
Vengez-Moi Mon Gendre!. 1916. lps: Prince. 580m FRN. prod/rel: Pathe Freres

GERRARD, PAUL
Dynamite Girl, Novel
Femmes d'Abord, Les 1962 d: Raoul Andre. lps: Eddie Constantine, Bernadette Lafont, Dario Moreno. 103M FRN. *Ladies First* (USA); *Dynamite Girl* prod/rel: Vega, C.C.F.C.

GERRARD, RICHARD H.
Sweet Adeline, 1903, Song
Sweet Adeline 1926 d: Jerome Storm. lps: Charles Ray, Gertrude Olmstead, Jack Clifford. 7r USA. prod/rel: Chadwick Pictures

GERSHE, LEONARD
Butterflies are Free, New York 1969, Play
Butterflies are Free 1972 d: Milton Katselas. lps: Edward Albert, Goldie Hawn, Paul Michael Glaser. 109M USA. prod/rel: Columbia

GERSHWIN, GEORGE (1897–1937), USA
Girl Crazy, New York 1930, Musical Play
Girl Crazy 1932 d: William A. Seiter. lps: Bert Wheeler, Robert Woolsey, Stanley Fields. 75M USA. prod/rel: RKO Radio Pictures©
La la Lucille, New York 1919, Musical Play
La la Lucille 1920 d: Eddie Lyons, Lee Moran. lps: Eddie Lyons, Lee Moran, Anne Cornwall. 5r USA. prod/rel: Universal Film Mfg. Co.©
Lady Be Good, New York 1924, Musical Play
Lady Be Good 1928 d: Richard Wallace. lps: Jack Mulhall, Dorothy MacKaill, John Miljan. 6600f USA. prod/rel: First National Pictures
Song of the Flame, New York 1925, Musical Play
Song of the Flame 1930 d: Alan Crosland. lps: Alexander Gray, Bernice Claire, Noah Beery. 6501f USA. prod/rel: First National Pictures
Tip-Toes, London 1926, Musical Play
Tiptoes 1927 d: Herbert Wilcox. lps: Dorothy Gish, Will Rogers, Nelson Keys. 6286f UKN. *Tip Toes* prod/rel: British National, Paramount

GERSTACKERS, FRIEDRICH
Die Flusspiraten Vom Mississippi, Novel
Flusspiraten Vom Mississippi, Die 1963 d: Jurgen Roland. lps: Brad Harris, Horst Frank, Sabine Sinjen. 102M GRM/FRN/ITL. *The Pirates of the Mississippi* (USA); *Agguato Sul Grande Fiume* (ITL); *Les Pirates du Mississippi* (FRN); *River Pirates of the Mississippi* prod/rel: Rapid, Gianni Fuchs
Regulatoren von Arkansas, Novel
Goldsucher von Arkansas, Die 1964 d: Paul Martin, Alberto Cardone. lps: Mario Adorf, Brad Harris, Horst Frank. 98M GRM/ITL/FRN. *Alla Conquista Dell'arkansas* (ITL); *Massacre at Marble City* (UKN); *Les Chercheurs d'Or de l'Arkansas* (FRN); *Conquerors of Arkansas*; *Goldseekers of Arkansas* prod/rel: Constantin Film, Rapid Film (Munich)

GERSTNER, HERMANN
Die Bruder Grimm, Munich 1952, Biography
Wonderful World of the Brothers Grimm, The 1963 d: Henry Levin, George Pal. lps: Laurence Harvey, Claire Bloom, Karlheinz Bohm. 130M USA. prod/rel: Metro-Goldwyn-Mayer, Inc., Cinerama, Inc.

GEVEL, CLAUDE
L'amour, Madame, Play
Amour, Madame, L' 1952 d: Gilles Grangier. lps: Francois Perier, Arletty, Mireille Perrey. 89M FRN. prod/rel: Films Raoul Ploquin, Sirius
Monsieur, Play
Monsieur 1964 d: Jean-Paul Le Chanois. lps: Jean Gabin, Liselotte Pulver, Mireille Darc. 105M FRN/ITL/GRM. *Intrigo a Parigi* (ITL) prod/rel: Films Copernic, Corona Films

GEVERS, MARIE
Paix Sur Les Champs, Novel
Paix Sur Les Champs 1970 d: Jacques Boigelot. lps: Christian Barbier, Helena Manson, Georges Poujouly. 100M BLG.

GEYER, SIEGFRIED
Kleine Komedie, Play
By Candlelight 1933 d: James Whale. lps: Elissa Landi, Paul Lukas, Nils Asther. 70M USA. prod/rel: Universal Pictures Corp.
Die Sachertorte, Play
Im Prater Bluh'n Wieder Die Baume 1958 d: Hans Wolff. lps: Johanna Matz, Gerhard Riedmann, Nina Sandt. 95M AUS. prod/rel: Paula Wessely

GFELLER, ALEX
Story
E Nachtlang Fuurland 1982 d: Clemens Klopfenstein, Remo Legnazzi. lps: Max Rudlinger, Christine Lauterberg, Adelheid Beyeler. 95M SWT. *Tierra Del Fuego a Whole Night Long* prod/rel: Ombra Isrg

GHEORGHIU, VIRGIL
La Vingt-Cinquieme Heure, Novel
Vingt-Cinquieme Heure, La 1966 d: Henri Verneuil. lps: Anthony Quinn, Virna Lisi, Michael Redgrave. 134M FRN/ITL/YGS. *La Venticinquesima Ora* (ITL); *The 25th Hour* (USA) prod/rel: Les Films Concordia, C.C. Champion

GHERARDI, GHERARDO
Play
Canto Della Vita, Il 1945 d: Carmine Gallone. lps: Alida Valli, Carlo Ninchi, Roberto Bruni. 84M ITL. prod/rel: Excelsa Film
Forse Eri Tu l'Amore 1940 d: Gennaro Righelli. lps: Loretta Vinci, Sandro Ruffini, Gemma d'AlbA. 90M ITL. prod/rel: Mediterranea Film, C.I.N.F.
L' Arcidiavolo, Play
Arcidiavolo, L' 1940 d: Tony Frenguelli. lps: Carlo Ninchi, Germana Paolieri, Mario GallinA. 84M ITL. prod/rel: Fides Film, E.N.I.C.
I Figli Del Marchese Lucera, Play
Figli Del Marchese Lucera, I 1938 d: Amleto Palermi. lps: Armando Falconi, Caterina Boratto, Sergio Tofano. 83M ITL. prod/rel: Scalera Film
Partire, Play
Partire 1938 d: Amleto Palermi. lps: Vittorio de Sica, Maria Denis, Silvana Jachino. 74M ITL. prod/rel: Astra Film, Generalcine
Questi Ragazzi, Play
Questi Ragazzi 1937 d: Mario Mattoli. lps: Vittorio de Sica, Paola Barbara, Giuditta Rissone. 68M ITL. prod/rel: Romulus, Lupa

GHERMAN, YURI
Short Stories
Moi Drug Ivan Lapshin 1986 d: Alexei Gherman. lps: Andrej Boltnev, Nina Ruslanova, Andrei Mironov. 100M USS. *My Friend Ivan Lapshin*; *Moj Droeg Ivan Lapsjin* prod/rel: Lenfilm

GHILAIN, EDDY
Silence Clinique, Novel
Baraka Sur X 13 1965 d: Maurice Cloche, Silvio Siano. lps: Gerard Barray, Sylva Koscina, Jose Suarez. 99M FRN/ITL/SPN. *Agente X77 Ordine Di Uccidere* (ITL); *Operacion Silencio* (SPN); *Agente X77* prod/rel: Capitole Film (Paris), Intercontinental

GHIOTTO, RENATO
Scacco Alla Regina, Novel
Scacco Alla Regina 1969 d: Pasquale Festa Campanile. lps: Rosanna Schiaffino, Haydee Politoff, Romolo Valli. 98M ITL/GRM. *Check to the Queen* prod/rel: Finarco, Filmarte

GHISLANZONI, ANTONIO
Aida, Cairo 1871, Opera
Aida 1953 d: Clemente Fracassi. lps: Sophia Loren, Lois Maxwell, Luciano Della MarrA. 96M ITL. prod/rel: Oscar Film, Cei-Incom.

GHOSH, SUBODH
Story
Ajantrik 1958 d: Ritwik Ghatak. lps: Kali Banerjee, Gyanesh Mukherjee, Shriman Deepak. 120M IND. *The Pathetic Fallacy*; *Ajaantrik*; *Mechanical Man*; *Pathetic Folly*; *The Unmechanical* prod/rel: L.B. Films

GIACCA, FULVIA
Sandok Il MacIste Della Giungla, Novel
Sandok, Il MacIste Della Giungla 1964 d: Umberto Lenzi. lps: Sean Flynn, Alessandra Panaro, Marie Versini. 90M ITL/FRN. *Le Temple de l'Elephant Blanc* (FRN); *Temple of the White Elephants*; *Il Tempio Dell'elefante Bianco*; *Sandok -the Giant of the Jungle* prod/rel: Filmes Cin.Ca (Roma), Capitole Films (Paris)

GIACOMETTI, PAOLO
La Colpa Vendica la Colpa, 1854, Play
Colpa Vendica la Colpa, La 1919 d: Eduardo BencivengA. lps: Amleto Novelli, Enna Saredo, Alberto d'AnversA. 1204m ITL. prod/rel: Caesar Film
La Morte Civile, 1861, Play
Figlia Del Forzato, La 1955 d: Gaetano AmatA. lps: Luisa Rossi, Arnoldo Foa, Adriano Rimoldi. 90M ITL. *La Morte Civile* prod/rel: Eden Film
Morte Civile, La 1910 d: Gerolamo Lo Savio?. lps: Ermete Novelli, Olga Giannini Novelli, Francesca Bertini. 250m ITL/FRN. *La Mort Civile* (FRN) prod/rel: Pathe Freres, Film d'Arte Italiana

Morte Civile, La 1913 d: Ubaldo Maria Del Colle. lps: Adriana Costamagna, Dillo Lombardi, Arturo Garzes. 1200m ITL. prod/rel: Savoia Film

Morte Civile, La 1919 d: Eduardo BencivengA. lps: Amleto Novelli, Enna Saredo, Domenico Cini. 1225m ITL. prod/rel: Caesar Film

Morte Civile, La 1942 d: Ferdinando M. Poggioli. lps: Carlo Ninchi, Dina Sassoli, Renato Cialente. 85M ITL. prod/rel: I.C.A.R., Generalcine

GIACOSA, GIUSEPPE (1847–1906), ITL
La Boheme, Turin 1896, Opera
Addio Mimi! 1947 d: Carmine Gallone. lps: Marta Eggerth, Jan Kiepura, Janis Carter. 90M ITL. *Her Wonderful Lie* (USA); *La Boheme* prod/rel: Cineopera, Ceiad

Boheme, La 1965 d: Franco Zeffirelli. lps: Gianni Raimondi, Rolando Panerai, Gianni Maffeo. 107M SWT/ITL. prod/rel: Cosmotel Produktion (Zurich)

Come le Foglie, 1900, Play
Come le Foglie 1917 d: Gennaro Righelli. lps: Maria Jacobini, Ignazio Lupi, Alberto Collo. 1920m ITL. prod/rel: Tiber Film

Come le Foglie 1934 d: Mario Camerini. lps: Isa Miranda, Mimi Aylmer, Nino Besozzi. 80M ITL. *Like the Leaves* (USA) prod/rel: I.C.I., S.A. Industrie Cinematografiche

Tristi Amori, 1887, Play
Tristi Amori 1917 d: Giuseppe Sterni. lps: Lina Millefleurs, Giuseppe Sterni, Emilio Graziani-Walter. 1505m ITL. prod/rel: Milano Film

Tristi Amori 1943 d: Carmine Gallone. lps: Jules Berry, Gino Cervi, Andrea Checchi. 92M ITL. prod/rel: Cines, Juventus Film

GIAGNI, GIANDOMENICO
La Domenica Della Buona Gente, Radio Play
Domenica Della Buona Gente, La 1954 d: Anton Giulio Majano. lps: Maria Fiore, Sophia Loren, Renato Salvatori. 95M ITL. *Good People's Sunday* prod/rel: Trionfalcine, Siden Film

GIANCANA, ANTOINETTE
Mafia Princess, Book
Mafia Princess 1986 d: Robert Collins. lps: Tony Curtis, Susan Lucci, Kathleen Widdoes. TVM. 100M USA. prod/rel: NBC, Group W

GIANNELLI, RAFFAELLO
La Ragazza Del Palio, Novel
Ragazza Del Palio, La 1957 d: Luigi ZampA. lps: Diana Dors, Vittorio Gassman, Franca Valeri. 102M ITL. *The Girl and the Palio* (USA); *The Love Specialist; The Girl Who Rode in the Palio* prod/rel: Ge-Si Cin.Ca, Olimpo Cin.Ca

GIANNINI, GUGLIELMO
Play
Affare Si Complica, L' 1941 d: Pier Luigi Faraldo. lps: Silvana Jachino, Luisa Garella, Pina Renzi. 78M ITL. prod/rel: Societa Cin.Ca Italiana Anonima

L' Anonima Roylott, Play
Anonima Roylott, L' 1936 d: Raffaello Matarazzo. lps: Giulio Donadio, Romano Calo, Camillo Pilotto. 72M ITL. prod/rel: Fiorda & C., Warner Bros.-First National Italiana

La Donna Perduta, Opera
Donna Perduta, La 1941 d: Domenico M. Gambino. lps: Elli Parvo, Luisella Beghi, Carlo Campanini. 96M ITL. prod/rel: Iris Film

Grattacieli, Play
Grattacieli 1943 d: Guglielmo Giannini. lps: Renato Cialente, Luigi Pavese, Paolo StoppA. 86M ITL. prod/rel: Cines, Juventus Film

GIBBON, LEWIS GRASSIC (1901–1935), UKN, Mitchell, James Leslie
Cloud Howe, Novel
Cloud Howe 1982 d: Tom Cotter. lps: Vivien Heilbron. MTV. 200M UKN. prod/rel: BBC Scotland

Grey Granite, Novel
Grey Granite 1983 d: Tom Cotter. lps: Vivien Heilbron. MTV. 225M UKN. prod/rel: BBC Scotland

Sunset Song, Novel
Sunset Song 1971. lps: Vivien Heilbron, Paul Young, Andrew Keir. MTV. UKN. prod/rel: BBC Scotland

GIBBONS, KAYE
Ellen Foster, Novel
Ellen Foster 1997 d: John Erman. lps: Julie Harris, Jena Malone, Ted Levine. TVM. 120M USA. prod/rel: Hallmark Prods.

GIBBONS, STELLA (1902–), UKN
Cold Comfort Farm, 1933, Novel
Cold Comfort Farm 1968. lps: Alastair Sim, Fay Compton, Sarah Badel. MTV. 150M UKN. prod/rel: BBC

Cold Comfort Farm 1995 d: John Schlesinger. lps: Kate Beckinsale, Sheila Burrell, Eileen Atkins. TVM. 104M UKN. prod/rel: BBC Television, Thames Television

GIBBS, ANTHONY
The Elder Brother, Novel
Elder Brother, The 1937 d: Frederick Hayward. lps: John Stuart, Marjorie Taylor, Basil Langton. 67M UKN. prod/rel: Triangle, Paramount

Young Apollo, Novel
Men of Tomorrow 1932 d: Zoltan Korda, Leontine Sagan. lps: Maurice Braddell, Joan Gardner, Emlyn Williams. 88M UKN. *Young Apollo* prod/rel: Paramount, London Films

GIBBS, ARCHIE
U-Boat Prisoner; the Life of a Texas Sailor, Book
U-Boat Prisoner 1944 d: Lew Landers. lps: Bruce Bennett, Erik Rolf, John Abbott. 65M USA. *Dangerous Mists* (UKN) prod/rel: Columbia

GIBBS, ARTHUR HAMILTON (1884–1964), UKN, Gibbs, A. Hamilton
Chances, Boston 1930, Novel
Chances 1931 d: Allan Dwan. lps: Douglas Fairbanks Jr., Rose Hobart, Anthony Bushell. 72M USA. prod/rel: First National Pictures, Inc.

The Persistent Lovers, Novel
Persistent Lovers, The 1922 d: Guy Newall. lps: Guy Newall, Ivy Duke, A. Bromley Davenport. 6420f UKN. prod/rel: George Clark Productions, Stoll

Soundings, Boston 1925, Novel
Whirlwind of Youth, The 1927 d: Rowland V. Lee. lps: Lois Moran, Vera Voronina, Donald Keith. 5866f USA. prod/rel: Paramount Famous Lasky Corp.

GIBBS, GEORGE
Novel
Voltaire 1933 d: John G. Adolfi. lps: George Arliss, Margaret Lindsay, Doris Kenyon. 72M USA. prod/rel: Warner Bros. Pictures©

The Bolted Door, New York 1910, Novel
Bolted Door, The 1923 d: William Worthington. lps: Frank Mayo, Charles A. Stevenson, Phyllis Haver. 4126f USA. prod/rel: Universal Pictures

The Flaming Sword, New York 1914, Novel
Flaming Sword, The 1915 d: Edwin Middleton. lps: Lionel Barrymore, Jane Grey, Miss Diestel. 5r USA. prod/rel: Rolfe Photoplays Inc., Metro Pictures Corp.©

Paradise Garden, New York 1916, Novel
Paradise Garden 1917 d: Fred J. Balshofer. lps: Harold Lockwood, Vera Sisson, Virginia Rappe. 6-7r USA. prod/rel: Yorke Film Corp., Big Star Production

Sackcloth and Scarlet, London 1924, Novel
Sackcloth and Scarlet 1925 d: Henry King. lps: Alice Terry, Orville Caldwell, Dorothy Sebastian. 6752f USA. prod/rel: Kagor Productions, Paramount Pictures

The Silent Battle, New York 1913, Novel
Silent Battle, The 1916 d: Jack Conway. lps: J. Warren Kerrigan, Lois Wilson, Maude George. 5r USA. prod/rel: Bluebird Photoplays, Inc.©

The Splendid Outcast, New York 1920, Novel
Honor First 1922 d: Jerome Storm. lps: John Gilbert, Renee Adoree, Hardee Kirkland. 5075f USA. prod/rel: Fox Film Corp.

The Yellow Door, New York 1915, Novel
Great Deception, The 1926 d: Howard Higgin. lps: Ben Lyon, Aileen Pringle, Basil Rathbone. 5855f USA. prod/rel: Robert Kane Productions, First National Pictures

The Yellow Dove, New York 1915, Novel
Shadows of Suspicion 1919 d: Edwin Carewe. lps: Harold Lockwood, Naomi Childers, Helen Lindroth. 5r USA. prod/rel: Yorke Film Corp., Metro Pictures Corp.

Youth Triumphant, New York 1921, Novel
Enemies of Children 1923 d: Lillian Ducey, John M. Voshell. lps: Anna Q. Nilsson, George Siegmann, Claire McDowell. 5800f USA. *Youth Triumphant* prod/rel: Fisher Productions, Mammoth Pictures

GIBBS, PHILIP HAMILTON (1877–1962), UKN, Gibbs, Sir Philip
The Crossword Puzzle, Novel
Paradise 1928 d: Denison Clift. lps: Betty Balfour, Joseph Striker, Alexander d'Arcy. 7247f UKN. prod/rel: British International Pictures, Wardour

Darkened Rooms, 1928, Short Story
Darkened Rooms 1929 d: Louis J. Gasnier. lps: Evelyn Brent, Neil Hamilton, Doris Hill. 6066f USA. prod/rel: Paramount Famous Lasky Corp

Fellow Prisoners, 1930, Short Story
Captured! 1933 d: Roy Del Ruth. lps: Leslie Howard, Douglas Fairbanks Jr., Paul Lukas. 72M USA. *Fellow Prisoners* prod/rel: Warner Bros. Pictures, Inc.

Heirs Apparent, London 1923, Novel
High Steppers 1926 d: Edwin Carewe. lps: Lloyd Hughes, Mary Astor, Dolores Del Rio. 6136f USA. prod/rel: Edwin Carewe Productions, First National Pictures

Out of the Ruins, London 1927, Novel
Out of the Ruins 1928 d: John Francis Dillon. lps: Richard Barthelmess, Robert Frazer, Marian Nixon. 6100f USA. prod/rel: First National Pictures

The Reckless Lady, London 1924, Novel
Reckless Lady, The 1926 d: Howard Higgin. lps: Belle Bennett, James Kirkwood, Lois Moran. 7336f USA. prod/rel: First National Pictures

The Street of Adventure, Novel
Street of Adventure, The 1921 d: Kenelm Foss. lps: Lionelle Howard, Margot Drake, H. V. Tollemach. 5000f UKN. prod/rel: Astra Films

GIBEAU, YVES
Allons Z'enfants, Novel
Allons Z'enfants 1980 d: Yves Boisset. lps: Jean-Pierre Aumont, Jean Carmet, Lucas Belvaux. 120M FRN. prod/rel: Sara Films, Antenne 2

La Ligne Droite, Novel
Ligne Droite, La 1961 d: Jacques Gaillard. lps: Daniel Ivernel, Janine Darcey, Jean-Claude Massoulier. 92M FRN. prod/rel: Ajym Films

GIBRAN, KAHLIL
The Broken Wings, New York 1957, Novel
Lal Aghnihat Elmoutakasra 1964 d: Yusuf Malouf. lps: Pierre Bordey, Saladin Nader, Nidal Ash Kar. 90M LBN. *The Broken Wings* (USA)

GIBSON, CHARLES DANA
The Education of Mr. Pipp, New York 1905, Play
Education of Mr. Pipp, The 1914 d: Augustus Thomas. lps: Digby Bell, Edna Brun, Belle Daube. 5r USA. prod/rel: All Star Feature Corp., Alco Film Corp.

GIBSON, GUY (1918–1944), UKN
Enemy Coast Ahead, Book
Dam Busters, The 1955 d: Michael Anderson. lps: Richard Todd, Michael Redgrave, Derek Farr. 125M UKN. prod/rel: Associated British Picture Corporation, Ab-Pathe

GIBSON, IAN
Books
Death in Granada 1997 d: Marcos ZuringaA. lps: Andy Garcia, Esai Morales, Edward James Olmos. 142M SPN/PRC. prod/rel: Enrique Cerezo Pc, Miramar Films

GIBSON, WILLIAM (1914–, USA
Short Story
New Rose Hotel 1998 d: Abel FerrarA. lps: Christopher Walken, Willem Dafoe, Asia Argento. 92M USA. prod/rel: Edward R. Pressman Film Corporation, Quadra Entertainment

The Cobweb, 1954, Novel
Cobweb, The 1955 d: Vincente Minnelli. lps: Richard Widmark, Lauren Bacall, Gloria Grahame. 124M USA. prod/rel: MGM

The Miracle Worker, New York 1959, Play
Miracle Worker, The 1962 d: Arthur Penn. lps: Anne Bancroft, Patty Duke, Victor Jory. 106M USA. prod/rel: Playfilms Productions

Miracle Worker, The 1979 d: Paul Aaron. lps: Patty Duke, Melissa Gilbert, Diana Muldaur. TVM. 100M USA.

Two for the Seesaw, New York 1958, Play
Two for the Seesaw 1962 d: Robert Wise. lps: Shirley MacLaine, Robert Mitchum, Edmon Ryan. 120M USA. prod/rel: Seesaw Pictures, Mirisch Pictures

GIDDY, HORTON
Contraband, Play
Luck of a Sailor, The 1934 d: Robert Milton. lps: Greta Nissen, David Manners, Clifford Mollison. 66M UKN. *Contraband* prod/rel: British International Pictures, Wardour

GIDE, ANDRE (1869–1951), FRN, Gide, Andre Paul Guillaume
La Symphonie Pastorale, 1919, Novel
Denen Kokyogaku 1938 d: Satsuo Yamamoto. 76M JPN. *La Symphonie Pastorale*

Symphonie Pastorale, La 1946 d: Jean Delannoy. lps: Michele Morgan, Pierre Blanchar, Line Noro. 95M FRN. *Pastoral Symphony* prod/rel: Films Gibe

GIELGUD, VAL
Death at Broadcasting House, Novel
Death at Broadcasting House 1934 d: Reginald Denham. lps: Ian Hunter, Austin Trevor, Mary Newland. 71M UKN. prod/rel: Associated British Film Distributors, Phoenix Films

GIEROW, KARL RAGNAR
Av Hjartans Lust, 1944, Novel
  Alt for Kvinden 1964 d: Annelise Reenberg. lps:
  Henrik Bentzon, Heny Nielsen, Thecla Boesen. 99M
  DNM. *Greven Fra Liljenborg* prod/rel: Saga Studio
Av Hjartans Lust, 1944, Play
  Av Hjartans Lust 1960 d: Rolf Husberg. lps: Jarl Kulle,
  Margita Ahlin, Edvin Adolphson. 98M SWD. *To One's
  Heart's Content* prod/rel: Ab Europa Film

GIES, MIEP
Anne Frank Remembered, Book
  Attic: the Hiding of Anne Frank, The 1988 d: John
  Erman. lps: Mary Steenburgen, Paul Scofield, Huub
  Stapel. TVM. 100M USA. prod/rel: Telecom
  Entertainment

GIESY, JOHN U.
The House in the Mist, 1917, Short Story
  Eyes of Mystery, The 1918 d: Tod Browning. lps:
  Edith Storey, Bradley Barker, Harry Northrup. 5r USA.
  prod/rel: Metro Pictures Corp.
The Triple Cross, 1918, Serial Story
  Kaiser's Shadow, The 1918 d: R. William Neill. lps:
  Dorothy Dalton, Thurston Hall, Edward Cecil. 4379f
  USA. *The Kaiser's Shadow Or the Triple Cross* prod/rel:
  Thomas H. Ince Corp.©, Famous Players-Lasky Corp.

GIFFORD, BARRY
59° and Raining; the Story of Perdita Durango,
Novel
  Perdita Durango 1997 d: Alex de La IglesiA. lps: Rosie
  Perez, Javier Bardem, Harley Cross. 126M SPN/MXC.
  prod/rel: Sogetel©, Lola Films (Spain)©
Wild at Heart, Novel
  Wild at Heart 1990 d: David Lynch. lps: Nicolas Cage,
  Laura Dern, Diane Ladd. 127M USA. prod/rel:
  Polygram, Propaganda

GIFFORD, THOMAS
The Glendower Legacy, Novel
  Dirty Tricks 1980 d: Alvin Rakoff. lps: Elliott Gould,
  Kate Jackson, Arthur Hill. 94M CND. *Accroche-Toi.
  J'arrive*; *Spy Games* prod/rel: Filmplan International
  Inc.

GIGNOUX, REGIS
Le Fruit Vert, Play
  Between Us Girls 1942 d: Henry Koster. lps: Diana
  Barrymore, Robert Cummings, Kay Francis. 89M USA.
  Boy Meets Baby; *Love and Kisses*; *What Happened
  Caroline?*; *Caroline* prod/rel: Universal
  Frutto Acerbo 1934 d: Carlo Ludovico BragagliA. lps:
  Lotte Menas, Nino Besozzi, Maria WronskA. 76M ITL.
  prod/rel: Industrice Cin.Che Italiane (I.C.I.)

GIGUERE, REAL
Les Marcheurs de la Nuit, Unpublished, Novel
  Cain 1965 d: Pierre Patry. lps: Real Giguere, Ginette
  Letondal, Yves Letourneau. 76M CND. *Les Marcheurs
  de la Nuit* prod/rel: Cooperatio Inc.

GILBERT, ANTHONY
The Mouse Who Wouldn't Play Ball, Novel
  Candles at Nine 1944 d: John Harlow. lps: Jessie
  Matthews, Beatrix Lehmann, John Stuart. 86M UKN.
  prod/rel: British National, Anglo-American
The Vanishing Corpse, Novel
  They Met in the Dark 1943 d: Carl Lamac. lps: James
  Mason, Joyce Howard, Tom Walls. 104M UKN. prod/rel:
  Independent Producers, Excelsior
The Woman in Red, Novel
  My Name Is Julia Ross 1945 d: Joseph H. Lewis. lps:
  Nina Foch, Dame May Whitty, George MacReady. 65M
  USA. prod/rel: Columbia

GILBERT, EDWIN
Hot Nocturne, Play
  Blues in the Night 1941 d: Anatole Litvak. lps:
  Priscilla Lane, Richard Whorf, Betty Field. 88M USA.
  Hot Nocturne; *New Orleans Blues* prod/rel: Warner
  Bros.

GILBERT, F. S.
Et Puis S'en Vont, Novel
  Cannabis 1969 d: Pierre Koralnik. lps: Curd Jurgens,
  Jane Birkin, Serge Gainsbourg. 100M FRN/GRM/ITL.
  Cannabis - Engel Der Gewalt (GRM); *Cannabis - Angel
  of Violence*; *New York-Parigi Per Una Condanna a
  Morte* (ITL); *Gymkhana* prod/rel: P.E.C., Euro-France
  Films

GILBERT, JEAN
La Chaste Suzanne, Opera
  Chaste Suzanne, La 1937 d: Andre Berthomieu. lps:
  Meg Lemonnier, Raimu, Henri Garat. 90M FRN.
  prod/rel: British Unity Pictures
Die Geliebte Seiner Hoheit, Opera
  Geliebte Seiner Hoheit, Die 1928 d: Jacob Fleck,
  Luise Fleck. lps: Lia Eibenschutz, Vivian Gibson, Paul
  Richter. 2272m GRM. prod/rel: Orplid-Film

Die Leichte Isabell, Opera
  Leichte Isabell, Die 1927 d: Eddy Busch, Arthur
  Wellin. lps: Lee Parry, Gustav Frohlich, Hans
  Wassmann. 2047m GRM. prod/rel: Maxim-Film, Ebner
  & Co.
Prinzessin Olala, Opera
  Prinzessin Olala 1928 d: Robert Land. lps: Carmen
  Boni, Walter Rilla, Georg Alexander. 2922m GRM. *The
  Art of Love* prod/rel: Super-Film

GILBERT, MICHAEL (1912–, UKN
Amateur in Violence, Novel
  Unstoppable Man, The 1960 d: Terry Bishop. lps:
  Cameron Mitchell, Marius Goring, Harry H. Corbett.
  68M UKN. prod/rel: Argo Film Productions,
  Anglo-Amalgamated
Death Has Deep Roots, Novel
  Guilty? 1956 d: Edmond T. Greville. lps: John Justin,
  Barbara Laage, Donald Wolfit. 93M UKN/FRN. *Je
  Plaide Non Coupable* (FRN); *Crime Passionnel* prod/rel:
  Elysee Film, Gibraltar Productions
Death in Captivity, Novel
  Danger Within 1959 d: Don Chaffey. lps: Richard
  Todd, Richard Attenborough, Bernard Lee. 101M UKN.
  Breakout (USA) prod/rel: British Lion, Colin Lesslie

GILBERT, OSCAR-PAUL
Mollenard, Novel
  Mollenard 1937 d: Robert Siodmak. lps: Harry Baur,
  Albert Prejean, Gabrielle Dorziat. 91M FRN. *Capitaine
  Corsaire*; *Capitaine Mollenard*; *Hatred* prod/rel:
  Productions Corniglion-Molinier
Nord Atlantique, Novel
  Nord Atlantique 1939 d: Maurice Cloche. lps: Rene
  Dary, Albert Prejean, Marie DeA. 95M FRN. prod/rel:
  Eclair Journal
Les Pirates du Rail, Novel
  Pirates du Rail, Les 1937 d: Christian-Jaque. lps:
  Charles Vanel, Erich von Stroheim, Simone Renant. F
  FRN. prod/rel: F.R.D.
Shanghai Chambard Et Cie, Novel
  Drame de Shanghai, Le 1938 d: G. W. Pabst. lps:
  Raymond Rouleau, Louis Jouvet, Christiane Mardayn.
  105M FRN. *The Shanghai Drama* prod/rel: Lucia Film

GILBERT, ROBERT
Das Lies Ist Aus, Novel
  Unter Den Tausand Laternen 1952 d: Erich Engel.
  lps: Michel Auclair, Hanna Rucker, Gisela Trowe. 94M
  GRM. *Die Stimme Des Anderen*; *Beneath the Thousand
  Lanterns* prod/rel: Real, Doring

GILBERT, STEPHEN
Ratman's Notebooks, Novel
  Willard 1971 d: Daniel Mann. lps: Bruce Davison,
  Sondra Locke, Elsa Lanchester. 95M USA. prod/rel:
  Cinerama Releasing Corp., Bing Crosby

GILBERT, W. S. (1836–1911), UKN, Gilbert, William
Schwenck
H.M.S. Pinafore, London 1878, Opera
  H.M.S. Pinafore 1950. 70M USA. prod/rel: Hoffberg
Hope, Short Story
  Hope 1919 d: Rex Wilson. lps: Isobel Elsom, Malcolm
  Cherry, Wyndham Guise. 5334f UKN. *Sweethearts*
  (USA) prod/rel: G. B. Samuelson, Granger
The Mikado, London 1885, Opera
  Cool Mikado, The 1963 d: Michael Winner. lps:
  Frankie Howerd, Stubby Kaye, Tommy Cooper. 81M
  UKN. prod/rel: Film Production of Gilbert & Sullivan,
  United Artists
  Fan Fan 1918 d: Chester M. Franklin, Sidney A.
  Franklin. lps: Virginia Lee Corbin, Francis Carpenter,
  Carmen de Rue. 5r USA. *The Mikado* prod/rel: Fox Film
  Corp., William Fox©
  Mikado, The 1939 d: Victor Schertzinger. lps: Kenny
  Baker, Jean Colin, Martyn Green. 91M UKN. prod/rel:
  General Film Distributors, G and S Films
  Mikado, The 1967 d: Stuart Burge. lps: Donald Adams,
  Philip Potter, John Reed. 122M UKN. prod/rel: B.H.E.
  Productions, Eagle
The Pirates of Penzance, London 1880, Opera
  Pirate Movie, The 1982 d: Ken Annakin. lps: Kristy
  McNichol, Christopher Atkins, Ted Hamilton. 105M
  ASL/USA. prod/rel: David Joseph, Joseph Hammond
  Intl. Prods. Pty Ltd.©
  Pirates of Penzance, The 1983 d: Wilford Leach. lps:
  Kevin Kline, Angela Lansbury, Linda Ronstadt. 112M
  UKN. prod/rel: Universal

GILBOORD, MARGARET GIBSON
Making It, Short Story
  Outrageous! 1977 d: Richard Benner. lps: Craig
  Russell, Hollis McLaren, Richert Easley. 96M CND.
  prod/rel: Film Consortium of Canada Inc.

GILBRETH JR., FRANK (1911–, USA, Gilbreth Jr.,
Frank Bunker
Belles on Their Toes, Book
  Belles on Their Toes 1952 d: Henry Levin. lps: Myrna
  Loy, Jeanne Crain, Edward Arnold. 89M USA. prod/rel:
  20th Century-Fox
Cheaper By the Dozen, Book
  Cheaper By the Dozen 1950 d: Walter Lang. lps:
  Clifton Webb, Myrna Loy, Jeanne Crain. 85M USA.
  prod/rel: 20th Century-Fox

GILDEN, K. B.
Hurry Sundown, New York 1964, Novel
  Hurry Sundown 1967 d: Otto Preminger. lps: Michael
  Caine, Jane Fonda, John Phillip Law. 142M USA.
  prod/rel: Sigma Productions

GILFORD, J. B.
Short Story
  Ultima Senora Anderson, La 1970 d: Eugenio
  Martin. lps: Carroll Baker, Michael Craig, Miranda
  CampA. 87M SPN/ITL. *In Fondo Alla Piscina* (ITL);
  The Last Mrs. Anderson; *In the Bottom of the Pool*; *Death
  at the Deep End of the Swimming Pool*; *At the Bottom of
  the Swimming Pool* prod/rel: Tritone Filmindustria
  (Roma), Filmayer Production

GILL, DEREK
The Dove, Book
  Dove, The 1974 d: Charles Jarrott. lps: Timothy
  Bottoms, Deborah Raffin, John McLiam. 105M
  USA/UKN. prod/rel: Paramount
If You Could See What I Hear, Book
  If You Could See What I Hear 1981 d: Eric Till. lps:
  Marc Singer, R. H. Thomson, Sarah Torgov. 103M CND.
  Au-Dela du Regard; *Something Else Again* prod/rel:
  Cypress Grove Films Ltd., Shelter Films Ltd.

GILL, GLAUCIO
Procura-Se Uma Rosa, Play
  Rosa Per Tutti, Una 1967 d: Franco Rossi. lps: Claudia
  Cardinale, Nino Manfredi, Mario Adorf. 110M ITL.
  Every Man's Woman (UKN); *A Rose for Everyone* (USA);
  Everyman's Woman prod/rel: Vides, Columbia-Ceiad

GILL, TOM
The Gay Bandit of the Border, New York 1931, Novel
  Gay Caballero, The 1932 d: Alfred L. Werker. lps:
  George O'Brien, Victor McLaglen, Cecilia Parker. 62M
  USA. *The Gay Bandit* prod/rel: Fox Film Corp.©
Gentleman of the Jungle, 1940, Novel
  Tropic Zone 1953 d: Lewis R. Foster. lps: Ronald
  Reagan, Rhonda Fleming, EstelitA. 94M USA. prod/rel:
  Paramount, Pine-Thomas
In the Mexican Quarter, 1930, Short Story
  Border Cafe 1937 d: Lew Landers. lps: Harry Carey,
  John Beal, ArmidA. 67M USA. *Mexican Quarter*; *In the
  Mexican Quarter* prod/rel: RKO Radio Pictures, Inc.

GILLES, PHILIPPE
Les Trente Millions de Gladiator, Play
  Trente Millions de Gladiator, Les 1914 d: Georges
  MoncA. lps: Prince, Andre Simon, Clo MarrA. 900m
  FRN. prod/rel: Pathe Freres

GILLES, PIERRE
L' Enfant-Roi, Novel
  Enfant Roi, L' 1924 d: Jean Kemm. lps: Andree Lionel,
  Joe Hamman, Louis Sance. SRL. 8EP FRN. prod/rel:
  Societe Des Cineromans

GILLESE, JOHN PATRICK
Kirby's Gander, Toronto 1957, Novel
  Wings of Chance 1959 d: Edward Dew. lps: Jim L.
  Brown, Richard Tretter, Frances Rafferty. 76M CND.
  prod/rel: Tiger Productions Ltd.

GILLETTE, WILLIAM
Held By the Enemy, New York 1886, Play
  Held By the Enemy 1920 d: Donald Crisp. lps: Agnes
  Ayres, Jack Holt, Wanda Hawley. 6r USA. prod/rel:
  Famous Players-Lasky Corp.©, Paramount Pictures
Secret Service, New York 1896, Play
  Secret Service 1919 d: Hugh Ford. lps: Robert
  Warwick, Wanda Hawley, Theodore Roberts. 6r USA.
  prod/rel: Famous   Players-Lasky   Corp.©,
  Paramount-Artcraft Pictures
  Secret Service 1932 d: J. Walter Ruben. lps: Richard
  Dix, Shirley Grey, William Post Jr. 69M USA. prod/rel:
  RKO Radio Pictures©
Sherlock Holmes, Buffalo 1899, Play
  Adventures of Sherlock Holmes, The 1939 d: Alfred
  L. Werker. lps: Basil Rathbone, Nigel Bruce, Ida Lupino.
  85M USA. *Sherlock Holmes* (UKN) prod/rel: Twentieth
  Century-Fox Film Corp.
  Sherlock Holmes 1916 d: Arthur Berthelet. lps:
  William Gilette, Marjorie Kay, Ernest Maupain. 7r USA.
  prod/rel: Essanay Film Mfg. Co.©, V-L-S-E, Inc.
  Sherlock Holmes 1922 d: Albert Parker. lps: John
  Barrymore, Roland Young, Carol Dempster. 8200f USA.
  Moriarty prod/rel: Metro-Goldwyn-Mayer Pictures

Sherlock Holmes 1932 d: William K. Howard. lps: Clive Brook, Ernest Torrence, Miriam Jordan. 68M USA. prod/rel: Fox Film Corp.©

Too Much Johnson, New York 1894, Play
Too Much Johnson 1920 d: Donald Crisp. lps: Bryant Washburn, Lois Wilson, Adele Farrington. 4431f USA. prod/rel: Famous Players-Lasky Corp.©, Paramount-Artcraft Pictures

GILLHAM, BILL
A Place to Hide, Novel
Break Out 1984 d: Frank Godwin. lps: David Jackson, Ian Bartholomew, John Bowler. 63M UKN. *Breakout* prod/rel: Eyeline, Children's Film and Tv Foundation

GILLIAT, SIDNEY
Meet a Body, Play
Green Man, The 1956 d: Robert Day. lps: Alastair Sim, George Cole, Terry-Thomas. 90M UKN. prod/rel: Grenadier, British Lion

GILLIES, JACK
The Gold Inside, London 1960, Play
Cash on Demand 1961 d: Quentin Lawrence. lps: Peter Cushing, Andre Morell, Richard Vernon. 86M UKN. prod/rel: Columbia, Woodpecker

GILLIGAN, EDMUND
The Gaunt Woman, 1943, Novel
Sealed Cargo 1951 d: Alfred L. Werker. lps: Dana Andrews, Claude Rains, Carla BalendA. 90M USA. *The Gaunt Woman* prod/rel: RKO Radio

GILLMORE, RUFUS
The Alster Case, New York 1914, Novel
Alster Case, The 1915 d: J. Charles Haydon. lps: Bryant Washburn, John Cossar, Ruth Stonehouse. 5r USA. prod/rel: Essanay Film Mfg. Co.©, V-L-S-E, Inc.

GILLOIS, ANDRE
125 Rue Montmartre, Novel
125, Rue Montmartre 1959 d: Gilles Grangier. lps: Lino Ventura, Andrea Parisy, Robert Hirsch. 86M FRN. prod/rel: Orex Films

GILMAN, CHARLOTTE PERKINS
The Yellow Wallpaper, Short Story
Yellow Wallpaper, The 1991 d: John Clive. lps: Julia Watson, Stephen Dillane, Carolyn Pickles. TVM. 75M UKN. prod/rel: BBC

GILMAN, DAVID
Ghost in the machine, Play
Bad Manners 1997 d: Jonathan Kaufer. lps: David Strathairn, Bonnie Bedelia, Saul Rubinek. 88M USA. prod/rel: J. Todd Harris/ Stephen Nemeth, Davis Entertainment

GILMAN, MILDRED
Sob Sister, New York 1931, Novel
Sob Sister 1931 d: Alfred Santell. lps: James Dunn, Linda Watkins, Molly O'Day. 71M USA. *The Blonde Reporter* (UKN); *Sob Sisters* prod/rel: Fox Film Corp.©, Alfred Santell Production

GILMAN, PETER
Diamond Head, New York 1960, Novel
Diamond Head 1962 d: Guy Green. lps: Charlton Heston, Yvette Mimieux, James Darren. 107M USA. prod/rel: Jerry Bresler

GILMORE, PAUL
Captain Alvarez, Play
Captain Alvarez 1914 d: Rollin S. Sturgeon. lps: Edith Storey, Myrtle Gonzales, William D. Taylor. 6r USA. prod/rel: Vitagraph Co. of America©, Broadway Star Feature

GILROY, FRANK D.
From Noon Till Three, 1973, Novel
From Noon Till Three 1975 d: Frank D. Gilroy. lps: Charles Bronson, Jill Ireland, Douglas Fowley. 99M USA. prod/rel: United Artists, Francovich-Self

The Last Notch, Television Play
Fastest Gun Alive, The 1956 d: Russell Rouse. lps: Glenn Ford, Jeanne Crain, Broderick Crawford. 92M USA. prod/rel: MGM

The Only Game in Town, New York 1968, Play
Only Game in Town, The 1970 d: George Stevens. lps: Elizabeth Taylor, Warren Beatty, Charles Braswell. 113M USA. prod/rel: 20th Century-Fox Film Corporation, George Stevens Films

The Subject Was Roses, New York 1964, Play
Subject Was Roses, The 1968 d: Ulu Grosbard. lps: Patricia Neal, Jack Albertson, Martin Sheen. 107M USA. prod/rel: Edgar Lansbury Productions

GILTENE, JEAN
Pas de Pitie Pour Les Femmes, Novel
Pas de Pitie Pour Les Femmes 1950 d: Christian Stengel. lps: Michel Auclair, Marcel Herrand, Simone Renant. 95M FRN. prod/rel: Producteurs Associes, Equipe Technique Cinematographique

GILTNER, LEIGH GORDON
The Broadway Bubble, 1920, Short Story
Broadway Bubble, The 1920 d: George L. Sargent. lps: Corinne Griffith, Joe King, Stanley Wamerton. 5r USA. prod/rel: Vitagraph Co. of America©

The Understudy, Short Story
Understudy, The 1917 d: William Bertram. lps: Ethel Ritchie, Neil Hardin, Bruce Smith. 4r USA. prod/rel: Falcon Features, General Film Co.©

GIMINEZ, JOHN
The Addict, Play
Way Out 1966 d: Irvin S. Yeaworth Jr. lps: Frank Rodriguez, James Dunleavy, Sharyn Jiminez. 102M USA. prod/rel: Valley Forge Films

GINSBURY, NORMAN
The First Gentleman, London 1945, Play
First Gentleman, The 1948 d: Alberto Cavalcanti. lps: Jean-Pierre Aumont, Joan Hopkins, Cecil Parker. 111M UKN. *Affairs of a Rogue* (USA) prod/rel: Columbia British

GINTY, E. B.
The Man from Texas, Play
Man from Texas, The 1948 d: Leigh Jason. lps: James Craig, Lynn Bari, Johnny Johnston. 71M USA. prod/rel: Eagle-Lion

GINZBURG, NATALIA (1916–1991), ITL
Caro Michele, 1973, Novel
Caro Michele 1976 d: Mario Monicelli. lps: Mariangela Melato, Delphine Seyrig, Aurore Clement. 110M ITL. *Dear Michael* prod/rel: Documento Film, Cineriz

Ti Ho Sposato Per Allegria, Turin 1966, Novel
Ti Ho Sposato Per Allegria 1967 d: Luciano Salce. lps: Monica Vitti, Giorgio Albertazzi, Maria Grazia BuccellA. 99M ITL. *I Married You for Fun* (USA); *I Married You for Gaiety* prod/rel: Fair Film, Titanus

GIOLI, VINICIO
Casa NovA. Vita Nova, Play
Arrangiatevi! 1959 d: Mauro Bolognini. lps: Toto, Peppino de Filippo, Laura Adani. 105M ITL. prod/rel: Cineriz

GIONO, JEAN (1895–1970), FRN
Story
Mann Mit Den Baumen, Der 1990 d: Werner Kubny. lps: Ferdinand Dux, Anna Ludwig, Franz Bulin. 80M GRM. prod/rel: Kubny Filmproduktion, Wdr

Le Bout de la Route, 1937, Play
Bout de la Route, Le 1948 d: Emile Couzinet. lps: Jose Luccioni, France Descaut, Mona Dol. 85M FRN. prod/rel: Burgus-Films

Le Chant du Monde, 1934, Novel
Chant du Monde, Le 1965 d: Marcel Camus. lps: Hardy Kruger, Marilu Tolo, Charles Vanel. 105M FRN/ITL. *Ossessione Nuda* (ITL); *The World Song* prod/rel: Orphee, Marceau-Cocinor

Les Grands Chemins, Paris 1951, Novel
Grands Chemins, Les 1963 d: Christian Marquand. lps: Robert Hossein, Anouk Aimee, Renato Salvatori. 93M FRN/ITL. *Il Baro* (ITL); *Of Flesh and Blood* (USA) prod/rel: Copernic Films, Films Du Saphrene

Jean le Bleu, 1932, Novel
Femme du Boulanger, La 1938 d: Marcel Pagnol. lps: Raimu, Fernand Charpin, Ginette Leclerc. 130M FRN. *The Baker's Wife* (USA) prod/rel: Films Marcel Pagnol

Jofroi de la Maussan, 1930, Short Story
Jofroi 1933 d: Marcel Pagnol. lps: Vincent Scotto, Henri Poupon, Annie Toinon. 52M FRN. *Ways of Love* (USA) prod/rel: Auteurs Associes

Regain, 1930, Novel
Regain 1937 d: Marcel Pagnol. lps: Fernandel, Orane Demazis, Gabriel Gabrio. 90M FRN. *Harvest* (USA); *Arsule* prod/rel: Films Marcel Pagnol

Un Roi Sans Divertissement, 1947, Novel
Roi Sans Divertissement, Un 1962 d: Francois Leterrier. lps: Claude Giraud, Charles Vanel, Colette Renard. 85M FRN. *La Poursuite*; *The Pursuit* prod/rel: Films Jean Giono

Un de Baumugnes, 1929, Novel
Angele 1934 d: Marcel Pagnol. lps: Fernandel, Orane Demazis, Henri Poupon. 164M FRN. *Heartbeat* prod/rel: Films Marcel Pagnol

GIORDANO, UMBERTO (1867–1948), ITL
Andrea Chenier, Milan 1896, Opera
Andrea Chenier 1955 d: Clemente Fracassi. lps: Antonella Lualdi, Raf Vallone, Michel Auclair. 100M ITL/FRN. *Le Souffle de la Liberte* (FRN); *Andre Chenier* prod/rel: Lux Film (Roma), Lux de France (Paris)

GIOVANNI, JOSE (1923–, FRN
Les Aventuriers, Paris 1960, Novel
Aventuriers, Les 1966 d: Robert Enrico. lps: Lino Ventura, Alain Delon, Joanna Shimkus. 110M FRN/ITL. *I Tre Avventurieri* (ITL); *The Last Adventure* (UKN) prod/rel: S.N.C., Compagnia Generale Finanziaria Cin.Ca

Le Deuxieme Souffle, Novel
Deuxieme Souffle, Le 1966 d: Jean-Pierre Melville. lps: Lino Ventura, Paul Meurisse, Christine Fabrega. 170M FRN. *Second Breath* (UKN); *Second Wind* prod/rel: Les Productions Montaigne

L' Excommunie, Novel
Nomme la Rocca, Un 1962 d: Jean Becker. lps: Jean-Paul Belmondo, Christine Kaufmann, Pierre Vaneck. 106M FRN/ITL. *Quello Che Spara Per Primo* (ITL); *A Man Named Rocca* (USA) prod/rel: Films Du Cyclope, Da Ma Cin.Ca

Le Gitan, Novel
Gitan, Le 1975 d: Jose Giovanni. lps: Alain Delon, Paul Meurisse, Annie Girardot. 102M FRN/ITL. *Lo Zingaro*; *The Gypsy* prod/rel: Mondial Te.Fi.

Le Haut Fer, Paris 1962, Novel
Grandes Gueules, Les 1965 d: Robert Enrico. lps: Bourvil, Lino Ventura, Marie Dubois. 130M FRN/ITL. *Una Vampata di Violenza* (ITL); *The Wise Guys* (USA); *Jailbirds' Vacation* prod/rel: Belles Rives, S.N.C.

Ho, Novel
Ho! 1968 d: Robert Enrico. lps: Jean-Paul Belmondo, Joanna Shimkus, Sydney Chaplin. 107M FRN/ITL. *Ho! Criminal Face*; *Criminal Face*; *Storia Di un Criminale* (ITL) prod/rel: Marceau Cocinor, Filmsonor

La Loi du Survivant, Novel
Loi du Survivant, La 1966 d: Jose Giovanni. lps: Michel Constantin, Alexandra Stewart, Roger Blin. 100M FRN. *Le Desesperado* prod/rel: Stephan Films, S.N.C.

Le Ruffian, Novel
Ruffian, Le 1983 d: Jose Giovanni. lps: Lino Ventura, Bernard Giraudeau, Claudia Cardinale. 108M FRN/CND. *The Ruffian* prod/rel: Corporation Image M & M Ltee. (Montreal), Films Christian Fechner (Paris)

La Scoumoune, Novel
Scoumoune, La 1973 d: Jose Giovanni. lps: Jean-Paul Belmondo, Claudia Cardinale, Michel Constantin. 96M FRN/ITL. *Il Clan Dei Marsigliesi* (ITL); *The Hit Man* (UKN); *Killer Man* (USA); *Lo Scomunicato*; *Mafia Warfare* prod/rel: Lira, Praesidens

Le Trou, Paris 1957, Novel
Classe Tous Risques 1959 d: Claude Sautet. lps: Lino Ventura, Sandra Milo, Jean-Paul Belmondo. 110M FRN/ITL. *Asfalto Che Scottia* (ITL); *The Big Risk* (USA) prod/rel: Mondex Films, Films Odeon

Trou, Le 1960 d: Jacques Becker. lps: Catherine Spaak, Philippe Leroy, Jean Keraudy. 145M FRN/ITL. *Il Buco* (ITL); *The Night Watch* (USA); *The Hole* (UKN) prod/rel: Play-Art, Filmsonor

GIOVANNINI, SANDRO
La Bisarca, Radio Play
Bisarca, La 1950 d: Giorgio C. Simonelli. lps: Peppino de Filippo, Silvana Pampanini, Aroldo Tieri. 90M ITL. prod/rel: C.M. Produzione Film

Giove in Doppiopetto, Play
Giove in Doppiopetto 1955 d: Daniele d'AnzA. lps: Carlo Dapporto, Delia Scala, Lucy d'Albert. 96M ITL. prod/rel: Film Costellazione, Cei-Incom

Un Mandarino Per Teo, Musical Play
Mandarino Per Teo, Un 1960 d: Mario Mattoli. lps: Walter Chiari, Sandra Mondaini, Ave Ninchi. 98M ITL. prod/rel: Film Columbus, Flora Film

Un Paio d'Ali, Musical Play
Come Te Movi, Te Fulmino! 1958 d: Mario Mattoli. lps: Renato Rascel, Giovanna Ralli, Mario Carotenuto. 90M ITL. prod/rel: Riama Film, Cineriz

Rugantino, Play
Rugantino 1973 d: Pasquale Festa Campanile. lps: Adriano Celentano, Claudia Mori, Paolo StoppA. 120M ITL/SPN. *Un Trabajo Tranquilo* (SPN) prod/rel: Filmes Cin.Ca, Clan Film

GIPSON, FRED
Circles Round the Wagon, 1949, Novel
Hound-Dog Man 1959 d: Don Siegel. lps: Fabian, Carol Lynley, Stuart Whitman. 87M USA. *Hound Dog Man* prod/rel: 20th Century-Fox

The Home Place, 1950, Novel
Return of the Texan 1952 d: Delmer Daves. lps: Dale Robertson, Joanne Dru, Walter Brennan. 88M USA. prod/rel: 20th Century-Fox

Old Yeller, Novel
Old Yeller 1957 d: Robert Stevenson. lps: Dorothy McGuire, Fess Parker, Tommy Kirk. 84M USA. prod/rel: Buena Vista, Walt Disney Prods.

Savage Sam, New York 1962, Novel
Savage Sam 1963 d: Norman Tokar. lps: Brian Keith, Tommy Kirk, Kevin Corcoran. 103M USA. prod/rel: Walt Disney Productions, Buena Vista

GIRARD, BERNARD
Stab of Pain, Story
This Woman Is Dangerous 1952 d: Felix E. Feist. lps: Joan Crawford, Dennis Morgan, David Brian. 100M USA. prod/rel: Warner Bros.

GIRAUD, GIOVANNI, ITL
L' Ajo Nell'Imbarazzo, 1807, Play
Ajo Nell'imbarazzo, L' 1911. lps: Fernanda Negri-Pouget. 301m ITL. *Old-Fashioned Education* (UKN) prod/rel: Cines
Ajo Nell'imbarazzo, L' 1963 d: Vasco Ugo Finni. lps: Plinio Clabassi, Cecilia Fusco, Tonino Boyer. F ITL. prod/rel: Cine Lirica Italiana
Ajo Nell'imbarazzo, L' 1963 d: Vasco Ugo Finni. lps: Plinio Clabassi, Cecilia Fusco, Tonino Boyer. F ITL. prod/rel: Cine Lirica Italiana
Nipoti d'America, Le 1921 d: Camillo de Riso. lps: Camillo de Riso, Camillo Talamo, Mary Fleuron. 855m ITL. *Don Camillo E l'Americano*; *Camillo E l'Americano* prod/rel: Caesar Film

GIRAUDOUX, JEAN (1882–1944), FRN
La Folle de Chaillot, Paris 1945, Play
Madwoman of Chaillot, The 1969 d: Bryan Forbes, John Huston. lps: Katharine Hepburn, Charles Boyer, Claude Dauphin. 145M UKN/USA. prod/rel: Commonwealth United Corporation, Warner-Pathe
Siegfried Et le Limousin, 1922, Novel
Zweite Leben, Das 1954 d: Victor Vicas. lps: Michel Auclair, Barbara Rutting, Simone Simon. 90M GRM/FRN. *Double Destin* (FRN); *A Double Life* (USA); *Double Destiny*; *The Second Life* prod/rel: Madeleine Films, Trans Rhein Films

GIRETTE, MARCEL
Johannes Fils de Johannes, Novel
Johannes Fils de Johannes 1918 d: Andre Hugon. lps: Andre Nox, Rene Lorsay, MusidorA. 1115m FRN. prod/rel: Films A. Hugon

GISKES, H. J.
London Calling North Pole, Novel
Londra Chiama Polo Nord 1957 d: Duilio Coletti. lps: Curd Jurgens, Dawn Addams, Dario Michaelis. 100M ITL. *The House of Intrigue* (USA) prod/rel: Excelsa Film, Titanus

GISSING, GEORGE (1857–1903), UKN, Gissing, George Robert
Demos, Novel
Demos 1921 d: Denison Clift. lps: Milton Rosmer, Evelyn Brent, Warwick Ward. 5700f UKN. *Why Men Forget* (USA) prod/rel: Ideal

GITTELSON, CELIA
Saving Grace, Novel
Saving Grace 1986 d: Robert M. Young. lps: Tom Conti, Fernando Rey, Erland Josephson. 112M USA. prod/rel: Columbia, Embassy Film Associates

GITTINS, ANTHONY
An Error of Judgement, Short Story
Case for the Crown, The 1934 d: George A. Cooper. lps: Miles Mander, Meriel Forbes, Whitmore Humphries. 71M UKN. prod/rel: British and Dominions, Paramount British

GIUDICE, LUCIEN
Firmin le Muet de Saint-Pataclet, Novel
Firmin, le Muet de Saint-Pataclet 1938 d: Jacques Severac. lps: Antonin Berval, Colette Darfeuil, Marfa Dhervilly. 85M FRN. prod/rel: Les Produceurs Associes

GIUSTI, RUSSO
L' Eredita Dello Zio Buonanima, Play
Eredita Dello Zio Buonanima, L' 1975 d: Alfonso BresciA. lps: Franco Franchi, Riccardo Garrone, Grazia Di MarzA. 94M ITL. *Porgi l'AltrA. Sberla* prod/rel: Canguro Produzioni Int.Li Cin.Che, Capitol International

GIUSTI-SINOPOLI, GIUSEPPE
La Zolfara, 1895, Play
Zolfara, La 1912 d: Alfredo Robert. lps: Attilio Rapisarda, Mariano Bottino, Cesira Archetti. 800m ITL. prod/rel: Roma Film

GLADKOV, ALEKSANDR
Davnym-Davno, 1942, Play
Gusarskaya Ballada 1962 d: Eldar Ryazanov. lps: Larisa Golubkina, Yuri Yakovlev, Igor Ilinsky. 94M USS. *The Ballad of a Hussar* (USA); *Hussar's Ballad*; *The Hussar Ballad* prod/rel: Mosfilm

GLASER, FR.
Ratten Der Grosstadt, Novel
Ratten Der Grosstadt 1930 d: Wolfgang Neff. lps: Mary Kid, Oscar Marion. 1844m GRM. prod/rel: Filmproduktion Loew & Co.

GLASGOW, ELLEN (1874–1945), USA, Glasgow, Ellen Anderson Gholson
In This Our Life, 1941, Novel
In This Our Life 1942 d: John Huston. lps: Bette Davis, Olivia de Havilland, George Brent. 97M USA. prod/rel: Warner Bros.

GLASPELL, SUSAN (1882–1948), USA
Brook Evans, London 1928, Novel
Right to Love, The 1930 d: Richard Wallace. lps: Ruth Chatterton, Paul Lukas, David Manners. 7120f USA. prod/rel: Paramount-Publix Corp.

GLASS, FRANKCINA
Novel
Marvin and Tige 1982 d: Eric Weston. lps: John Cassavetes, Billy Dee Williams, Denise Nicholas-Hill. 104M USA. *Like Father and Son*; *Like Father Like Son* prod/rel: Major

GLASS, MONTAGUE
Business Before Pleasure, New York 1917, Play
In Hollywood With Potash and Perlmutter 1924 d: Alfred E. Green. lps: Alexander Carr, George Sidney, Vera Gordon. 6685f USA. *So This Is Hollywood* (UKN) prod/rel: Goldwyn Pictures, Associated First National Pictures
Partners Again, New York 1922, Play
Partners Again 1926 d: Henry King. lps: George Sidney, Alexander Carr, Betty Jewel. 5562f USA. prod/rel: Samuel Goldwyn, Inc., United Artists
Potash and Perlmutter, New York 1921, Play
Potash and Perlmutter 1923 d: Clarence Badger. lps: Alexander Carr, Barney Bernard, Vera Gordon. 7636f USA. *Dr. Sunshine* (UKN) prod/rel: Goldwyn Pictures, Associated First National Pictures

GLATZLE, MARY
Muggable Mary, Book
Muggable Mary, Street Cop 1982 d: Sandor Stern. lps: Karen Valentine, John Getz, Anne Desalvo. TVM. 96M USA. *Street Cop*

GLAUSER, FRIEDRICH
Meutre a l'Asile, Zurich 1936, Novel
Matto Regiert 1947 d: Leopold Lindtberg. lps: Heinrich Gretler, Heinz Woester, Elisabeth Muller. 113M SWT. *Meurtre a l'Asile*; *Le Regne de Matto*; *Nel Regno Di Matto*; *Kriminalfall Dr. Borstill* prod/rel: Praesens-Film
Wachtmeister Studer, Zurich 1936, Novel
Wachtmeister Studer 1939 d: Leopold Lindtberg. lps: Heinrich Gretler, Bernhard Danegger, Anne-Marie Blanc. 112M SWT. *Kriminalkommissar Studer*; *Le Brigadier Studer*; *Il Sergente Studer* prod/rel: Praesens-Film

GLAZAROVA, JARMILA
Advent, 1950, Novel
Advent 1956 d: Vladimir Vlcek. lps: Marie Vasova, Gustav Hilmar. 76M CZC. *The Gates of Dawn*
Vlci Jama, 1941, Novel
Vlci Jama 1958 d: Jiri Weiss. lps: Jana Brejchova, Jirina Sejbalova, Miroslav Dolezal. 93M CZC. *Wolf Trap* prod/rel: Filmove Studio Barrandov

GLEASON, JAMES
The Fall Guy, New York 1924, Play
Fall Guy, The 1930 d: A. Leslie Pearce. lps: Jack Mulhall, Mae Clarke, Ned Sparks. 70M USA. *Trust Your Wife* (UKN) prod/rel: RKO Productions
Is Zat So?, New York 1925, Play
Is Zat So? 1927 d: Alfred E. Green. lps: George O'Brien, Edmund Lowe, Kathryn Perry. 6950f USA. prod/rel: Fox Film Corp.
Two Fisted 1935 d: James Cruze. lps: Lee Tracy, Grace Bradley, Kent Taylor. 65M USA. *Two-Fisted*; *Gettin' Smart* prod/rel: Paramount Productions©
Mr. Bones, Musical Play
Mammy 1930 d: Michael Curtiz. lps: Al Jolson, Lois Moran, Louise Dresser. 84M USA. prod/rel: Warner Brothers Pictures
Rain Or Shine, New York 1928, Play
Rain Or Shine 1930 d: Frank CaprA. lps: Joe Cook, Louise Fazenda, Joan Peers. 87M USA. prod/rel: Columbia Pictures
The Shannons of Broadway, New York 1927, Play
Goodbye Broadway 1938 d: Ray McCarey. lps: Alice Brady, Charles Winninger, Tom Brown. 70M USA. *Shannons of Broadway*; *The Thing Is the Play* prod/rel: Universal Pictures Co.©
Shannons of Broadway, The 1929 d: Emmett J. Flynn. lps: James Gleason, Lucille Gleason, Mary Philbin. 6155f USA. prod/rel: Universal Pictures

GLEMSER, BERNARD
Girl on a Wing, Novel
Come Fly With Me 1963 d: Henry Levin. lps: Dolores Hart, Hugh O'Brian, Karlheinz Bohm. 109M UKN/USA. prod/rel: MGM British

GLENNON, GORDON
Garden City, Play
Private Information 1952 d: Fergus McDonnell. lps: Jill Esmond, Jack Watling, Carol Marsh. 65M UKN. prod/rel: Act Films, Monarch

GLICKMAN, WILL
Mrs. Gibbons' Boys, Play
Mrs. Gibbons' Boys 1962 d: Max Varnel. lps: Kathleen Harrison, Lionel Jeffries, Diana Dors. 82M UKN. prod/rel: British Lion, Byron

GLOAG, JULIAN
Our Mother's House, New York 1963, Novel
Our Mother's House 1967 d: Jack Clayton. lps: Dirk Bogarde, Margaret Brooks, Pamela Franklin. 105M UKN/USA. prod/rel: Heron Film Productions, Filmways, Inc.

GLOWACKI, JANUSZ
Polowanie Na Muchy, Short Story
Polowanie Na Muchy 1969 d: Andrzej WajdA. lps: Malgorzata Braunek, Zygmunt Malanowicz, Ewa SkarzankA. 108M PLN. *Hunting Flies* (USA); *Flies Hunting*; *The Fly Hunt* prod/rel: P.R.F. Zespoly Filmowe

GLUCK, SINCLAIR
The Last Trap; a Detective Story, New York 1928, Novel
Dark Hour, The 1936 d: Charles Lamont. lps: Irene Ware, Lloyd Whitlock, Berton Churchill. 71M USA. *The Last Trap* prod/rel: Chesterfield Motion Pictures Corp.

GLUTH, OSKAR
Das Starkere Leben, Novel
Erbe Vom Pruggerhof, Das 1956 d: Hans H. Konig. lps: Heinrich Gretler, Edith Mill, Armin Dahlen. 96M GRM. *The Inheritance of the Prugger Estate* prod/rel: Suddeutsche, Bergland

GLYDER, JOHN
The Compulsory Husband, Novel
Compulsory Husband, The 1930 d: Monty Banks, Harry Lachman. lps: Monty Banks, Gladys Frazin, Clifford Heatherley. 84M UKN. prod/rel: British International Pictures, Wardour
The Compulsory Wife, Play
Compulsory Wife, The 1937 d: Arthur Woods. lps: Henry Kendall, Joyce Kirby, Margaret Yarde. 57M UKN. prod/rel: Warner Bros., First National

GLYN, ELINOR (1864–1943), UKN, Glyn, Elinor Sutherland
Beyond the Rocks, New York 1906, Novel
Beyond the Rocks 1922 d: Sam Wood. lps: Gloria Swanson, Rudolph Valentino, Edythe Chapman. 6740f USA. prod/rel: Famous Players-Lasky Corp., Paramount Pictures
The Career of Katherine Bush, New York 1916, Novel
Career of Katherine Bush, The 1919 d: R. William Neill. lps: Catherine Calvert, John Goldsworthy, Crauford Kent. 4756f USA. *The Career of Catherine Bush* prod/rel: Famous Players-Lasky Corp.©, Paramount-Artcraft Special
His Hour, New York 1910, Novel
His Hour 1924 d: King Vidor. lps: Aileen Pringle, John Gilbert, Emily Fitzroy. 6300f USA. prod/rel: Louis B. Mayer Productions, Metro-Goldwyn Distributing Corp.
It, Novel
It 1927 d: Clarence Badger, Josef von Sternberg. lps: Clara Bow, Antonio Moreno, William Austin. 6452f USA. prod/rel: Famous Players-Lasky, Paramount Pictures
Knowing Men, Novel
Knowing Men 1930 d: Elinor Glyn. lps: Carl Brisson, Elissa Landi, Jeanne de Casalis. 88M UKN. prod/rel: Talkicolor, United Artists
Love's Blindness, New York 1925, Novel
Love's Blindness 1926 d: John Francis Dillon. lps: Pauline Starke, Antonio Moreno, Lilyan Tashman. 6099f USA. prod/rel: Metro-Goldwyn-Mayer Pictures
Man and Maid, Philadelphia 1922, Novel
Man and Maid 1925 d: Victor Schertzinger. lps: Lew Cody, Renee Adoree, Paulette Duval. 5307f USA. prod/rel: Metro-Goldwyn Pictures
The Man and the Moment, New York 1914, Novel
Mad Hour 1928 d: Joseph C. Boyle. lps: Sally O'Neill, Alice White, Donald Reed. 6625f USA. prod/rel: First National Pictures
Man and the Moment, The 1918 d: Arrigo Bocchi. lps: Manora Thew, Hayford Hobbs, Charles Vane. 5850f UKN. prod/rel: Windsor, Walturdaw

One Day; a Sequel to "Three Weeks", New York 1909, Novel

One Day 1916 d: Hal Clarendon. lps: Victor Sutherland, Jeanne Iver, Hal Clarendon. 5r USA. prod/rel: B. S. Moss Motion Picture Corp., Moss Films

One Hour, Novel

One Hour 1917 d: Paul McAllister, Edwin L. Hollywood. lps: Zena Keefe, Alan Hale, D. J. Flannigan. 6r USA. prod/rel: B. S. Moss Motion Picture Corp.©, M. H. Hoffman, Inc.

The Price of Things, Novel

Price of Things, The 1930 d: Elinor Glyn. lps: Elissa Landi, Stewart Rome, Walter Tennyson. 84M UKN. prod/rel: Elinor Glyn, United Artists

The Reason Why, London 1911, Novel

Reason Why, The 1918 d: Robert G. VignolA. lps: Clara Kimball Young, Milton Sills, Florence Billings. 5r USA. prod/rel: C. K. Y. Film Corp.©, Select Pictures Corp.

Soul Mates 1925 d: Jack Conway. lps: Aileen Pringle, Edmund Lowe, Phillips Smalley. 5590f USA. prod/rel: Metro-Goldwyn-Mayer Pictures

Six Days, Philadelphia 1923, Novel

Six Days 1923 d: Charles J. Brabin. lps: Corinne Griffith, Frank Mayo, Myrtle Stedman. 8010f USA. prod/rel: Goldwyn Pictures, Goldwyn-Cosmopolitan Distributing Corp.

Three Weeks, London 1907, Novel

Three Weeks 1915 d: Perry N. Vekroff. lps: Madlaine Traverse, George Pearce, John Webb Dillon. 5r USA. prod/rel: Reliable Feature Film Corp., State Rights

Three Weeks 1924 d: Alan Crosland. lps: Aileen Pringle, Conrad Nagel, John Sainpolis. 7540f USA. *The Romance of a Queen* (UKN) prod/rel: Goldwyn Pictures, Goldwyn-Cosmopolitan Distributing Corp.

The Vicissitudes of Evangeline, New York 1905, Novel

Red Hair 1928 d: Clarence Badger. lps: Clara Bow, Lane Chandler, William Austin. 6331f USA. prod/rel: Paramount Famous Lasky Corp.

GODARD, ALAIN
Coup de Tete, Novel

Coup de Tete 1978 d: Jean-Jacques Annaud. lps: Patrick Dewaere, France Dougnac, Jean Bouise. 90M FRN. *Hothead* prod/rel: Gaumont International, S.F.P.

GODBER, JOHN
Up 'N' Under, 1984, Play

Up 'N' Under 1998 d: John Godber. lps: Gary Olsen, Richard Ridings, Samantha Janus. 99M UKN. prod/rel: Entertainment Film Distributors, Touchdown Film©

GODDARD, CHARLES W.
The Broken Wing, New York 1920, Play

Broken Wing, The 1923 d: Tom Forman. lps: Kenneth Harlan, Miriam Cooper, Walter Long. 6216f USA. prod/rel: B. P. Schulberg Productions, Preferred Pictures

Broken Wing, The 1932 d: Lloyd Corrigan. lps: Lupe Velez, Leo Carrillo, Melvyn Douglas. 74M USA. prod/rel: Paramount Publix Corp.

The Ghost Breaker, New York 1909, Play

Ghost Breaker, The 1914 d: Cecil B. de Mille, Oscar Apfel. lps: H. B. Warner, Theodore Roberts, Rita Stanwood. 5r USA. prod/rel: Jesse L. Lasky Feature Play Co.©, Paramount Pictures Corp.

Ghost Breaker, The 1922 d: Alfred E. Green. lps: Wallace Reid, Lila Lee, Walter Hiers. 5130f USA. prod/rel: Famous Players-Lasky, Paramount Pictures

Ghost Breakers, The 1940 d: George Marshall. lps: Bob Hope, Paulette Goddard, Richard Carlson. 82M USA. prod/rel: Paramount Pictures©

Scared Stiff 1953 d: George Marshall. lps: Dean Martin, Jerry Lewis, Lizabeth Scott. 108M USA. prod/rel: Paramount

The Misleading Lady, New York 1913, Play

Misleading Lady, The 1916 d: Arthur Berthelet. lps: Henry B. Walthall, Edna Mayo, Sidney Ainsworth. 5r USA. prod/rel: Essanay Film Mfg. Co.©, V-L-S-E, Inc.

Misleading Lady, The 1920 d: George Irving, George W. Terwilliger. lps: Bert Lytell, Lucy Cotton, Cyril Chadwick. 6r USA. prod/rel: Metro Pictures Corp.©

Misleading Lady, The 1932 d: Stuart Walker. lps: Claudette Colbert, Edmund Lowe, Stuart Erwin. 75M USA. *Sensation* prod/rel: Paramount Publix Corp.©

GODDARD, ROBERT
Into the Blue, Novel

Into the Blue 1998 d: Jack Gold. lps: John Thaw, Matthew Marsh, Celia Imrie. TVM. 104M UKN. prod/rel: Carlton Tv©, Triumph Proscenium Productions

GODDEN, RUMER (1907–1998), UKN, Dixon, Rumer Haynes
Battle of the Villa Fiorita, London 1963, Novel

Battle of the Villa Fiorita, The 1965 d: Delmer Daves. lps: Maureen O'Hara, Rossano Brazzi, Richard Todd. 111M UKN/USA. *The Affair at the Villa Fiorita* prod/rel: Warner Bros. Pictures, Warner-Pathe

Black Narcissus, Novel

Black Narcissus 1947 d: Michael Powell, Emeric Pressburger. lps: Deborah Kerr, Sabu, David Farrar. 100M UKN. prod/rel: General Film Distributors, the Archers

An Episode of Sparrows, Novel

Innocent Sinners 1958 d: Philip Leacock. lps: Flora Robson, David Kossoff, Barbara Mullen. 95M UKN. prod/rel: Rank, Rank Film Distributors

The Greengage Summer, London 1958, Novel

Greengage Summer, The 1961 d: Lewis Gilbert. lps: Kenneth More, Danielle Darrieux, Susannah York. 99M UKN. *Loss of Innocence* (USA) prod/rel: P.K.L. Pictures, Columbia

In This House of Brede, Novel

In This House of Brede 1975 d: George Schaefer. lps: Diana Rigg, Judi Bowker, Gwen Watford. TVM. 100M UKN/USA. prod/rel: CBS, General Electric Theater

The River, Novel

River, The 1951 d: Jean Renoir. lps: Nora Swinburne, Esmond Knight, Arthur Shields. 99M UKN/FRN/IND. *Le Fleuve* (FRN) prod/rel: Oriental, International

Take Three Tenses, Novel

Enchantment 1948 d: Irving Reis. lps: David Niven, Teresa Wright, Jayne Meadows. 102M USA. prod/rel: RKO Radio

GODEFROY, GEORGES
Le Gentleman de Hong-Kong, Novel

Riviere Des Trois Jonques, La 1956 d: Andre Pergament. lps: Dominique Wilms, Lise Bourdin, Jean Gaven. 92M FRN. *The River of Three Junks* (USA); *Adventure in Indo-China* prod/rel: Jeannic Films, Eole Films

La Riviere Des Trois Jonques, Paris 1956, Novel

Geheimnis Der Drei Dschunken, Das 1965 d: Ernst Hofbauer. lps: Stewart Granger, Rosanna Schiaffino, Harald Juhnke. 89M GRM/ITL. *a-009 Missione Hong Kong* (ITL); *Red Dragon* (USA); *Mission to Hong Kong*; *The Secret of the Three Junks* prod/rel: Arca-Film (Berlin), P.E.A. (Roma)

GODEY, JOHN (1912–, USA
The Taking of Pelham One-Two-Three, Novel

Taking of Pelham One-Two-Three, The 1974 d: Joseph Sargent. lps: Walter Matthau, Robert Shaw, Martin Balsam. 105M USA. prod/rel: Palomar, Palladium

The Three Worlds of Johnny Handsome, Novel

Johnny Handsome 1989 d: Walter Hill. lps: Mickey Rourke, Ellen Barkin, Elizabeth McGovern. 94M USA. prod/rel: Tri-Star

A Thrill a Minute With Jack Albany, New York 1967, Novel

Never a Dull Moment 1968 d: Jerry Paris. lps: Dick Van Dyke, Edward G. Robinson, Dorothy Provine. 100M USA. prod/rel: Walt Disney Productions, Buena Vista

GODFERNAUX, ANDRE
Triplepatte, Play

Triplepatte 1922 d: Raymond Bernard. lps: Henri Debain, Pierre Palau, Edith Jehanne. 1700m FRN. prod/rel: Societe Des Films Tristan Bernard

GODFREY, A. E.
Little Miss Nobody, London 1898, Musical Play

Little Miss Nobody 1923 d: Wilfred Noy. lps: Flora Le Breton, John Stuart, Ben Field. 5750f UKN. prod/rel: Carlton Productions, Butcher's Film Service

GODFREY, PETER
Wanton Murder, Novel

Girl in Black Stockings, The 1957 d: Howard W. Koch. lps: Lex Barker, Anne Bancroft, Mamie Van Doren. 73M USA. prod/rel: United Artists, Bel-Air

GODFREY, PHILIP
The Grange Mystery, Novel

Black Abbot, The 1934 d: George A. Cooper. lps: John Stuart, Judy Kelly, Richard Cooper. 56M UKN. prod/rel: Radio, Real Art

GODWIN, JOHN
Without Mercy, New York 1920, Novel

Without Mercy 1925 d: George Melford. lps: Dorothy Phillips, Rockliffe Fellowes, Vera Reynolds. 7r USA. prod/rel: Metropolitan Pictures, Producers Distributing Corp.

GODWIN, WILLIAM (1756–1836), UKN
Caleb Williams, Novel

Caleb Williams 1983 d: Herbert Wise. lps: Mick Ford, Stephen Rea, Gunther Maria Halmer. MTV. 430M UKN/GRM. prod/rel: Tyne Tees

GOES, ALBRECHT
Unruhige Nacht, Hamburg 1950, Novel

Unruhige Nacht 1958 d: Falk Harnack. lps: Bernhard Wicki, Ulla Jacobsson, Hansjorg Felmy. 102M GRM. *The Restless Night* (USA); *All Night Through*; *Unpeaceful Night* prod/rel: Carlton Film, Real Film

GOETZ, CURT
Dr. Med. Hiob Pratorius, 1934, Play

Dr. Med. Hiob Pratorius 1965 d: Kurt Hoffmann. lps: Heinz Ruhmann, Liselotte Pulver, Fritz Tillmann. 92M GRM. prod/rel: Hans Domnick, Independent

Frauenarzt Dr. Pratorius 1950 d: Curt Goetz, Karl P. Gillmann. lps: Curt Goetz, Valerie von Martens, Erich Ponto. 90M GRM. *Dr. Pratorius -Gynecologist* prod/rel: Domnick, Tischendorf

People Will Talk 1951 d: Joseph L. Mankiewicz. lps: Cary Grant, Finlay Currie, Jeanne Crain. 110M USA. *Doctor Praetorius* prod/rel: 20th Century-Fox

Das Haus in Montevideo, Play

Haus in Montevideo, Das 1951 d: Curt Goetz, Valerie von Maertens. lps: Curt Goetz, Valerie von Martens, Ruth Niehaus. 106M GRM. *The House in Montevideo* prod/rel: Domnick, UFA

Haus in Montevideo, Das 1963 d: Helmut Kautner. lps: Heinz Ruhmann, Ruth Leuwerik, Paul Dahlke. 123M GRM. *The House in Montevideo* prod/rel: Hans Domnick, Constantin

Hokuspokus, Play

Hokuspokus 1930 d: Gustav Ucicky. lps: Willy Fritsch, Gustaf Grundgens, Lilian Harvey. 84M GRM.

Hokuspokus 1953 d: Kurt Hoffmann. lps: Curt Goetz, Valerie von Martens, Hans Nielsen. 90M GRM. prod/rel: Domnick, UFA

Hokuspokus - Oder Wie Lasse Ich Meinen Mann Verschwinden? 1966 d: Kurt Hoffmann. lps: Heinz Ruhmann, Liselotte Pulver, Richard Munch. 100M GRM. *Hokuspokus Or How Can I Get Rid of My Husband?* prod/rel: Hans Domnick, Independent

Temporary Widow, The 1930 d: Gustav Ucicky. lps: Lilian Harvey, Laurence Olivier, Athole Stewart. 84M UKN/GRM. prod/rel: UFA, Wardour

Der Lugner Und Die Nonne, Play

Lugner Und Die Nonne, Der 1967 d: Rolf Thiele, Joseph Czech. lps: Curd Jurgens, Robert Hoffmann, Heidelinde Weis. 99M AUS. *The Liar and the Nun* prod/rel: Durer

GOETZ, E.R.
Fifty Million Frenchmen, New York 1929, Play

Fifty Million Frenchmen 1931 d: Lloyd Bacon. lps: Ole Olsen, Chic Johnson, Claudia Dell. 68M USA. *50 Million Frenchmen* prod/rel: Warner Bros. Pictures©

GOFF, IVAN
Portrait in Black, Play

Portrait in Black 1960 d: Michael Gordon. lps: Lana Turner, Anthony Quinn, Lloyd Nolan. 113M USA. prod/rel: Universal

GOFFIN, ROBERT
A la Belle Sirene, Novel

Increvable, L' 1959 d: Jean Boyer. lps: Darry Cowl, Line Renaud, Francis Blanche. 84M FRN. prod/rel: Films Du Cyclope

GOGOL, NIKOLAY (1809–1852), RSS
Story

Rebel Son, The 1938 d: Adrian Brunel, Alex Granowsky. lps: Harry Baur, Roger Livesey, Anthony Bushell. 80M UKN. *Taras Bulba* prod/rel: Omnia Films, London Films

Diary of a Madman, 1836, Short Story

Dnevnikat Na Edin Lud 1996 d: Marius Kurkinski. BUL. *Diary of a Madman*

Journal d'un Fou, Le 1963 d: Roger Coggio. lps: Roger Coggio, Dorothee Blank, Jean Champion. 114M FRN. prod/rel: Films Marceau-Cocinor

Journal d'un Fou, Le 1987 d: Roger Coggio. lps: Roger Coggio, Fanny Cottencon, Jean-Pierre Darras. 89M FRN.

The Government Inspector, 1836, Play

Ammaldar 1953 d: Keshav Narayan Kale, Madhukar Kulkarni. lps: P. L. Deshpande, G. D. Madgulkar, Keshav Narayan Kale. 118M IND. *Law Enforcer* prod/rel: Mangal Pictures

President Panchatcharam 1959 d: A. Bhimsingh. lps: S. S. Rajendran, S. V. Sahasranamam, T. R. Ramchandran. 162M IND. prod/rel: Savithri Pictures

Igroki, 1842, Play
Gamblers, The 1970 d: Ron Winston. lps: Suzy Kendall, Don Gordon, Pierre Olaf. 93M USA. prod/rel: Sidney Glazier Productions

Kak Possorilis Ivan Ivanovich S Ivanom Nikiforovitchem, 1835, Short Story
Kak Possorilis Ivan Ivanovich S Ivanom Nikiforovitchem 1941 d: Andrei Kustov. 69M USS.
Kak Possorilis Ivan Ivanovich S Ivanom Nikiforovitchem 1959 d: Vladimir Karasov. 69M USS.

Mayskaya Noch, 1831, Short Story
Mayskaya Noch 1940 d: Nikolay Sadkovitch. 69M USS.

Myortvye Dushi, 1842, Novel
Mertviye Dushi 1960 d: Leonid Trauberg. lps: Vladimir Belokurov, Viktor Stanitsin, Boris Livanov. 103M USS. *Dead Souls*; *Mjortvaje Duschy*; *Mertvye Dusi*; *Myortvye Dushi* prod/rel: Mosfilm

Noch Pered Rozhdestvom, 1832, Short Story
Vechera Na Khutore Bliz Dikanki 1961 d: Aleksandr Rou. lps: Aleksandr Khvylya, L. Myznikova, Yu. Tavrov. 60M USS. *A Night Before Christmas* (USA); *Noch Pered Rozhdestvom* prod/rel: Gorky Film Studio

Propavshaya Gramota, 1831, Short Story
Propavshaya Gramota 1972 d: Boris IVchenko. 78M USS.

La Prospettiva, Short Story
Passeggiata, La 1953 d: Renato Rascel. lps: Renato Rascel, Valentina Cortese, Paolo StoppA. F ITL. prod/rel: Film Costellazione, 20th Century-Fox

Revizor, 1836, Play
Delibabok Orszaga 1983 d: Marta Meszaros. 83M HNG. *The Land of Mirages*
Inkognito Iz Peterburga 1977 d: Leonid Gaidai. 91M USS. *The Incognito from St. Petersburg*; *Stranger from St. Petersburg*
Inspector General, The 1949 d: Henry Koster. lps: Danny Kaye, Walter Slezak, Barbara Bates. 102M USA. *Happy Times* prod/rel: Warner Bros.
Revizor 1933 d: Martin Fric. lps: Vlasta Burian, Vaclav Tregl, Jaroslav Marvan. 1973m CZC. *Government Inspector*; *The Inspector General*; *Accountant*; *The Inspector*; *Revisor* prod/rel: Meissner
Revizor 1952 d: Vladimir Petrov. 90M USS. *The Inspector General*; *The Inspecting General*
Revizor 1996 d: Sergei Gazarov. lps: Nikita Mikhalkov, Yevgeny Mironov, Marina NeyolovA. F RSS. *The Inspector General* prod/rel: Nikita & Pyotr Film Company, Most Group
Stadt Steht Kopf, Eine 1932 d: Gustaf Grundgens. lps: Gustaf Grundgens, S. Z. Sakall, Jenny Jugo. 80M GRM.

Shinel, 1842, Short Story
Bespoke Overcoat, The 1955 d: Jack Clayton. lps: Alfie Bass, David Kossoff, Alan Tilvern. 32M UKN. prod/rel: Remus, Independent Film Distributors
Cappotto, Il 1952 d: Alberto LattuadA. lps: Renato Rascel, Giulio Stival, Yvonne Sanson. 100M ITL. *The Overcoat* prod/rel: Faro Film, Titanus
Garam Coat 1955 d: Amar Kumar. lps: Balraj Sahni, Nirupa Roy, Jayant. 129M IND. *The Clerk and the Coat*; *Garm Coat* prod/rel: Cine Co-Op
Shinel 1926 d: Grigori Kozintsev, Leonid Trauberg. lps: Andrei Kostritchkin, Sergei Gerasimov, Antonina YeremeivA. 1921m USS. *The Overcoat* (USA); *The Cloak*; *Sinel*; *Shinjel*
Shinel 1960 d: Alexei Batalov. lps: Rolan Bykov, Yuri Tolubeyev, A. YezhkinA. 78M USS. *The Overcoat* (USA); *The Cloak*; *Shinjel* prod/rel: Lenfilm

Sorochinskaya Jamarka, 1831, Short Story
Sorochinsky Yarmarok 1939 d: Nikolai Ekk. 96M USS. *The Sorochinski Fair*; *Sorochinskaya Yamarka*; *Sorochinsky Jamarka*

Taras Boulba, St. Petersburg 1835, Novel
Taras Bulba 1924 d: Wladimir von Strischewski. lps: J. E. Duvan Torzoff, Helena Makowska, Ossip Runitsch. 3174m GRM. *Die Tochter Des Woiwoden*; *Kosaken-Ende* prod/rel: Emrolieff-Film
Taras Bulba 1962 d: J. Lee Thompson. lps: Yul Brynner, Tony Curtis, Christine Kaufmann. 122M USA. prod/rel: Hecht-Curtleigh Productions, United Artists
Taras Bulba 2 1924 d: Wladimir von Strischewski. lps: J. E. Duvan Torzoff, Helena Makowska, Ossip Runitsch. GRM. *Kosaken-Ende* prod/rel: Ermolieff-Film
Taras Bulba, Il Cosacco 1963 d: Ferdinando Baldi. lps: Vladimir Medar, Lorella de Luca, Fosco Giachetti. 92M ITL. prod/rel: I.a.C., I.D.C.
Tarass Boulba 1936 d: Alexis Granowsky. lps: Harry Baur, Danielle Darrieux, Jean-Pierre Aumont. 105M FRN. prod/rel: G.G. Film

Viy, 1835, Short Story
Maschera Del Demonio, La 1960 d: Mario BavA. lps: Barbara Steele, John Richardson, Andrea Checchi. 88M ITL/GRM. *Die Stunde Wenn Drakula Kommt* (GRM); *Revenge of the Vampire* (UKN); *Black Sunday* (USA); *The Demon's Mask*; *House of Fright* prod/rel: Galatea, Jolly Film
Viy 1967 d: Alexander Ptushko. USS.

Zapiski Sumasshedshego, 1835, Short Story
Sofi 1967 d: Robert Carlisle. lps: Tom Troupe. 96M USA. *Diary of a Madman* prod/rel: Robert Carlisle Productions

Zhenitba, 1841, Play
Zhenitba 1937 d: Erast Garin, Khessia LokshinA. 98M USS. *The Wedding*

GOHRE, FRANK
Schnelles Geld, Novel
Schnelles Geld 1981 d: Raimund Koplin, Renate Stegmuller. lps: Karl Ghirardelli, Agnes Dunneisen, Willy Thomczyk. 95M GRM. *Der Lange Schatten Eines Morgens*; *Fast Money* prod/rel: Koplin, Stegmuller-Produktion

GOJAWICZYNSKA, POLA
Dziewczeta Z Nowolipek, 1935, Novel
Dziewczeta Z Nowolipek 1938 d: Joseph Leytes. lps: Elzbieta Barzczewska, Jadwiga Andrzejewska, Tamara WiszniewskA. 98M PLN. *Girls of Nowolipek*
Dziewczeta Z Nowolipek 1985 d: Barbara Sass. lps: Ewa Kasprzyk, Izabela Drobotowicz-Orkisz, Maria Ciunelis. 94M PLN. *The Girls from Nowolipki Street*; *The Girls of Nowlipki*; *Rajska Jablon*

Rajska Jablon, 1937, Novel
Rajska Jablon 1985 d: Barbara Sass. lps: Izabela Drobotowicz-Orkisz, Ewa Kasprzyk, Marta Klubowicz. 106M PLN. *The Apple-Tree of Paradise*

GOLDBAUM, WENZEL
Hochverrat, Play
Hochverrat 1929 d: Johannes Meyer. lps: Gerda Maurus, Gustav Frohlich, Harry Hardt. 2188m GRM. *High Treason* prod/rel: UFA

GOLDBERG, MARSHALL
The Critical List, Novel
Critical List, The 1978 d: Lou Antonio. lps: Lloyd Bridges, Melinda Dillon, Buddy Ebsen. TVM. 200M USA. *L.A. Medical Center - the Critical List* prod/rel: NBC, Mtm Productions

Skeletons, Novel
Critical List, The 1978 d: Lou Antonio. lps: Lloyd Bridges, Melinda Dillon, Buddy Ebsen. TVM. 200M USA. *L.A. Medical Center - the Critical List* prod/rel: NBC, Mtm Productions

GOLDBERG, VICKI
Biography
Margaret Bourke-White: the True Story 1989 d: Lawrence Schiller. lps: Farrah Fawcett, Frederic Forrest, Mitchell Ryan. TVM. 105M USA.; *Double Exposure: the Story of Margaret Bourke-White*

GOLDEN, JOHN
After Tomorrow, New York 1931, Play
After Tomorrow 1932 d: Frank Borzage. lps: Charles Farrell, Marian Nixon, Minna Gombell. 79M USA. prod/rel: Fox Film Corp.

Eva the Fifth; the Odyssey of a Tom Show, New York 1928, Play
Girl in the Show, The 1929 d: Edgar Selwyn. lps: Bessie Love, Raymond Hackett, Edward Nugent. 81M USA. *Eva the Fifth* prod/rel: Metro-Goldwyn-Mayer Pictures

Salt Water, New York 1929, Play
Her First Mate 1933 d: William Wyler. lps: Slim Summerville, Zasu Pitts, Una Merkel. 70M USA. prod/rel: Universal Pictures Corp.©

Two Worlds, Play
Strange Experiment 1937 d: Albert Parker. lps: Donald Gray, Anne Wemyss, Mary Newcomb. 74M UKN. prod/rel: Fox British

GOLDENBERG, DICK
Family Business, Play
Family Business 1982 d: John Stix. lps: Milton Berle, Richard Greene, Jeffrey Marcus. TVM. 74M USA. prod/rel: South Carolina Educational

GOLDFADEN, ABRAHAM
Der Fanatik Oder Id Tsvey Kuni Lemels, 1880, Play
Shnei Kuni Lemel 1965 d: Israel Becker. lps: Mike Burstein, Germaine Unikovsky, Rina Ganor. 90M ISR. *The Flying Matchmaker* (USA); *Two Kuni Lemel* prod/rel: Flying Matchmaker, Ltd.

GOLDING, LOUIS
Mr. Emmanuel, Novel
Mr. Emmanuel 1944 d: Harold French. lps: Felix Aylmer, Greta Gynt, Walter RillA. 97M UKN. prod/rel: Two Cities, Eagle-Lion

GOLDING, SAMUEL RUSKIN
The Girl Who Came Back, Hoboken 1920, Play
Girl Who Came Back, The 1923 d: Tom Forman. lps: Miriam Cooper, Gaston Glass, Kenneth Harlan. 6100f USA. prod/rel: B. P. Schulberg Productions, Preferred Pictures

GOLDING, WILLIAM (1911-1993), UKN, Golding, William Gerald
Lord of the Flies, London 1954, Novel
Lord of the Flies 1963 d: Peter Brook. lps: James Aubrey, Tom Chapin, Hugh Edwards. 91M UKN. prod/rel: Allen-Hodgdon Productions, Two Arts
Lord of the Flies 1990 d: Harry Hook. lps: Balthazar Getty, Chris Furrh, Danuel Pipoly. 95M USA. prod/rel: Castle Rock Entertainment
Lord of the Flies 1990 d: Vladimir Tulkin. 50M KZK.

GOLDMAN, JAMES
The Lion in Winter, New York 1966, Play
Lion in Winter, The 1968 d: Anthony Harvey. lps: Peter O'Toole, Katharine Hepburn, Jane Merrow. 134M UKN. prod/rel: Haworth Productions, Avco Embassy

GOLDMAN, MAYER C.
The Public Defender, New York 1917, Book
Public Defender, The 1917 d: Burton L. King. lps: Frank Keenan, Alma Hanlon, Robert Edeson. 6r USA. prod/rel: Harry Raver, Inc., State Rights

GOLDMAN, RAYMOND LESLIE
Battling Bunyon Ceases to Be Funny, 1924, Short Story
Battling Bunyon 1925 d: Paul C. Hurst. lps: Wesley Barry, Molly Malone, Frank Campeau. 4900f USA. prod/rel: Crown Productions, Associated Exhibitors

Bing Bang Boom, 1920, Short Story
Bing Bang Boom 1922 d: Fred J. Butler. lps: David Butler, Doris Pawn, Edwin Wallock. 5r USA. prod/rel: Sol Lesser Productions, Western Pictures Exploitation Co.

GOLDMAN, WENDY
Casual Sex?, Play
Casual Sex? 1988 d: Genevieve Robert. lps: Lea Thompson, Victoria Jackson, Stephen Shellen. 88M USA. prod/rel: Universal

GOLDMAN, WILLIAM (1931-, USA
Heat, 1985, Novel
Heat 1987 d: Dick Richards, Jerry Jameson. lps: Burt Reynolds, Karen Young, Peter MacNicol. 103M USA. prod/rel: New Century, Vista

Magic, 1976, Novel
Magic 1978 d: Richard Attenborough. lps: Anthony Hopkins, Ann-Margret, Burgess Meredith. 107M USA.

Marathon Man, 1974, Novel
Marathon Man 1976 d: John Schlesinger. lps: Dustin Hoffman, Laurence Olivier, Roy Scheider. 126M USA. prod/rel: Paramount

No Way to Treat a Lady, New York 1964, Novel
No Way to Treat a Lady 1968 d: Jack Smight. lps: Rod Steiger, Lee Remick, George Segal. 108M USA. prod/rel: Sol C. Siegel Pictures, Paramount

The Princess Bride, Novel
Princess Bride, The 1987 d: Rob Reiner. lps: Peter Falk, Cary Elwes, Mandy Patinkin. 99M USA. prod/rel: 20th Century Fox

Soldier in the Rain, New York 1960, Novel
Soldier in the Rain 1963 d: Ralph Nelson. lps: Jackie Gleason, Steve McQueen, Tuesday Weld. 88M USA. prod/rel: Allied Artist, Cedar Productions

GOLDONI, CARLO (1707-1793), ITL
Le Baruffe Chiozzotte, Play
Paese Senza Pace, Il 1943 d: Leo Menardi. lps: Cesco Baseggio, Isa Pola, Rossano Brazzi. 80M ITL. *Le Baruffe Chiozzotte* prod/rel: I.N.a.C., Cervinia

La Locandiera, 1753, Play
Locandiera, La 1912 d: Alfredo Robert. lps: Alfredo Robert, Ettore Mazzanti. ITL. prod/rel: Milano Films
Locandiera, La 1912 d: Alberto Nepoti. lps: Adriana Costamagna, Emma Vecla, Annibale Durelli. 486m ITL. prod/rel: Savoia Film
Locandiera, La 1929 d: Telemaco Ruggeri. lps: Germina Degli Uberti, Elio Steiner, Lucia Zanussi. 2377m ITL. prod/rel: a.G. Film
Locandiera, La 1944 d: Luigi Chiarini. lps: Luisa Ferida, Armando Falconi, Osvaldo Valenti. 71M ITL. prod/rel: Cines, E.N.I.C.
Locandiera, La 1981 d: Paolo CavarA. lps: Claudia Mori, Adriano Celentano, Paolo Villaggio. 105M ITL. *Mistress of the Inn* prod/rel: Dada, Rai

Madchen Mit Dem Guten Ruf, Das 1938 d: Hans Schweikart. lps: Olga Tschechowa, Attila Horbiger, Josef Eichheim. 79M GRM. *The Girl With the Good Reputation; Mirandolina -Das Madchen Mit Dem Schlecten Ruf*

I Rusteghi, 1761, Play
Badarinii 1960 d: Gheorghe Naghi, Sica Alexandrescu. 90M RMN. *The Boors; Badaranii*

La Serva Amorosa, 1752, Play
Servante Aimante, La 1996 d: Jean Douchet. lps: Catherine Hiegel, Alain Pralon, Claire Vernet. 166M FRN. *The Loving Servant* prod/rel: Sfp Prods., Films De L'estran

GOLDROSEN, JOHN
The Buddy Holly Story, Biography
Buddy Holly Story, The 1978 d: Steve Rash. lps: Gary Busey, Don Stroud, Charles Martin Smith. 113M USA. prod/rel: Columbia

GOLDSMITH, BARBARA
Little GloriA. Happy at Last, Novel
Little GloriA. Happy at Last 1982 d: Waris Hussein. lps: Bette Davis, Angela Lansbury, Glynis Johns. TVM. 200M USA. prod/rel: NBC, Metromedia

GOLDSMITH, CLIFFORD
Play
Father Was a Fullback 1949 d: John M. Stahl. lps: Fred MacMurray, Maureen O'Hara, Rudy Vallee. 84M USA. prod/rel: 20th Century-Fox

What a Life, New York 1938, Play
What a Life 1939 d: Theodore Reed. lps: Jackie Cooper, Betty Field, John Howard. 80M USA. *What a Life!* prod/rel: Paramount Pictures©

GOLDSMITH, L. S.
The Man Who Stole a Dream, Novel
Manhandled 1949 d: Lewis R. Foster. lps: Dorothy Lamour, Sterling Hayden, Dan DuryeA. 97M USA. *Betrayal; A Man Who Stole a Dream* prod/rel: Pine-Thomas, Paramount

GOLDSMITH, MYRON G.
Manila Espionage, Book
I Was an American Spy 1951 d: Lesley Selander. lps: Ann Dvorak, Gene Evans, Douglas Kennedy. 85M USA. prod/rel: Allied Artists

GOLDSMITH, OLIVER (1728–1774), IRL
She Stoops to Conquer, London 1773, Play
She Stoops to Conquer 1910. SHT USA. prod/rel: Thanhouser

She Stoops to Conquer 1914 d: George Loane Tucker. lps: Henry Ainley, Jane Gail, Gregory Scott. 3060f UKN. prod/rel: London, Gaumont

She Stoops to Conquer 1923 d: Edwin Greenwood. lps: Madge Stuart, Walter Tennyson. 2362f UKN. prod/rel: British & Colonial, Walturdaw

The Vicar of Wakefield, 1766, Novel
Vicar of Wakefield, The 1910 d: Theodore Marston. lps: Frank Hart Crane, Mrs. Rosamunde, William Garwood. 1000f USA. prod/rel: Thanhouser

Vicar of Wakefield, The 1912 d: Frank Powell. lps: Florence Barker. 923f UKN. prod/rel: Britannia Films, Pathe

Vicar of Wakefield, The 1913 d: John Douglas. lps: Christine Rayner, Alys Collier. 3000f UKN. prod/rel: Planet Films, Davison Film Sales Agency

Vicar of Wakefield, The 1913 d: Frank Wilson. lps: Violet Hopson, Harry Royston, Warwick Buckland. 3275f UKN. prod/rel: Hepworth, Kinematograph Trading Co.

Vicar of Wakefield, The 1916 d: Fred Paul. lps: John Hare, Laura Cowie, Ben Webster. 6000f UKN. prod/rel: Ideal

Vicar of Wakefield, The 1917 d: Ernest C. Warde. lps: Frederick Warde, Gladys Leslie, Kathryn Adams. 5-6r USA. prod/rel: Thanhouser Film Corp., Pathe Exchange, Inc.

GOLDSMITH, OLIVIA
The First Wives Club, Novel
First Wives Club, The 1996 d: Hugh Wilson. lps: Goldie Hawn, Bette Midler, Diane Keaton. 102M USA. prod/rel: Scott Rudin Production

GOLDSTEIN, MARILYN
Always a Victim
Murder: By Reason of Insanity 1985 d: Anthony Page. lps: Candice Bergen, Jurgen Prochnow, Hector Elizondo. TVM. 100M USA. *My Sweet Victim*

GOLLOMB, JOSEPH
The Female of the Species, Short Story
More Deadly Than the Male 1919 d: Robert G. VignolA. lps: Ethel Clayton, Ed Coxen, Herbert Heyes. 4213f USA. prod/rel: Famous Players-Lasky Corp.©, Paramount-Artcraft Pictures

Hunt the Woman, Short Story
Girl at Bay, A 1919 d: Thomas R. Mills. lps: Corinne Griffith, Walter Miller, Harry Davenport. 5r USA. prod/rel: Vitagraph Co. of America©

GOLON, ANNE (1921–, FRN
Angelique Et le Roi, Novel
Angelique Et le Roi 1965 d: Bernard Borderie. lps: Michele Mercier, Robert Hossein, Jean Rochefort. 104M FRN/ITL/GRM. *Angelica Alla Corte Del Re* (FRN); *Angelique Und Der Konig* (GRM) prod/rel: Francos Filmss, C.I.C.C.

Angelique Et le Sultan, Novel
Angelique Et le Sultan 1968 d: Bernard Borderie. lps: Michele Mercier, Robert Hossein, Jean-Claude Pascal. 105M FRN/GRM/ITL. *Angelica E Il Gran Sultano* (ITL); *Angelique Und Der Sultan* (GRM) prod/rel: C.I.C.C., Gloria Films

Marquise Des Anges Angelique, Novel
Angelique, Marquise Des Anges 1964 d: Bernard Borderie. lps: Michele Mercier, Robert Hossein, Jean Rochefort. 116M FRN/ITL/GRM. *Angelica* (ITL); *Angelique* (UKN) prod/rel: Francos Films, C.I.C.C.

Indomptable Angelique, Novel
Indomptable Angelique 1967 d: Bernard Borderie. lps: Michele Mercier, Robert Hossein, Pasquale Martino. 95M FRN/ITL/GRM. *L' Indomabile Angelica* (ITL); *Unbezahmbare Angelique* (GRM); *Untameable Angelique* prod/rel: C.I.C.C., Cinephonic (Paris)

Marveilleuse Angelique, Novel
Merveilleuse Angelique 1964 d: Bernard Borderie. lps: Michele Mercier, Claude Girard, Jean Rochefort. 105M FRN/ITL/GRM. *La Meravigliosa Angelica* (ITL); *Angelique -the Road to Versailles* (UKN); *Angelique 2.Teil* (GRM) prod/rel: Franco Films, C.I.C.C.

GOLON, SERGE (1903–, FRN
Angelique Et le Roi, Novel
Angelique Et le Roi 1965 d: Bernard Borderie. lps: Michele Mercier, Robert Hossein, Jean Rochefort. 104M FRN/ITL/GRM. *Angelica Alla Corte Del Re* (FRN); *Angelique Und Der Konig* (GRM) prod/rel: Francos Filmss, C.I.C.C.

Angelique Et le Sultan, Novel
Angelique Et le Sultan 1968 d: Bernard Borderie. lps: Michele Mercier, Robert Hossein, Jean-Claude Pascal. 105M FRN/GRM/ITL. *Angelica E Il Gran Sultano* (ITL); *Angelique Und Der Sultan* (GRM) prod/rel: C.I.C.C., Gloria Films

Marquise Des Anges Angelique, Novel
Angelique, Marquise Des Anges 1964 d: Bernard Borderie. lps: Michele Mercier, Robert Hossein, Jean Rochefort. 116M FRN/ITL/GRM. *Angelica* (ITL); *Angelique* (UKN) prod/rel: Francos Films, C.I.C.C.

Indomptable Angelique, Novel
Indomptable Angelique 1967 d: Bernard Borderie. lps: Michele Mercier, Robert Hossein, Pasquale Martino. 95M FRN/ITL/GRM. *L' Indomabile Angelica* (ITL); *Unbezahmbare Angelique* (GRM); *Untameable Angelique* prod/rel: C.I.C.C., Cinephonic (Paris)

Marveilleuse Angelique, Novel
Merveilleuse Angelique 1964 d: Bernard Borderie. lps: Michele Mercier, Claude Girard, Jean Rochefort. 105M FRN/ITL/GRM. *La Meravigliosa Angelica* (ITL); *Angelique -the Road to Versailles* (UKN); *Angelique 2.Teil* (GRM) prod/rel: Franco Films, C.I.C.C.

GOMBERG, SY
When Leo Comes Marching Home, Story
When Willie Comes Marching Home 1950 d: John Ford. lps: Dan Dailey, Corinne Calvet, Colleen Townsend. 86M USA. *Front and Center* prod/rel: 20th Century-Fox

GOMBROWICZ, WITOLD
Die Sonne Angreifen, Novel
Sonne Angreifen, Die 1970 d: Peter Lilienthal. lps: Jess Hahn, Willy Semmelrogge, Ingo Thouret. MTV. 92M GRM. prod/rel: Iduna Film

GOMES, ALFREDO DIAS
O Pagador de Promessas, Sao Paolo 1960, Play
Pagador de Promessas, O 1961 d: Anselmo Duarte. lps: Leonardo Vilar, Gloria Menezes, Dionisio Azevedo. 97M BRZ. *The Keeper of Promises; The Given Word; The Promise* prod/rel: Oswaldo Massaini Productions

GOMEZ DE MIGUEL, EMILIO
El Idiota, Play
Idiota, El 1926 d: Juan Andreu Moragas. lps: Juan Santacana, Maruja Roig. SPN. prod/rel: Ediciones Benito Lopez Ruano (Valencia)

GOMEZ HIDALGO, F.
La Malcasada, Play
Malcasada, La 1926 d: Francisco Gomez Hidalgo. lps: Maria Banquer, Jose Nieto, Jose Calle. 4373m SPN. prod/rel: Latino Films (Madrid)

GOMEZ, LEOPOLD
Bourrasque, Play
Bourrasque 1935 d: Pierre Billon. lps: Pierre Alcover, Germaine Rouer, Jacques Gretillat. 80M FRN. *Moghreb* prod/rel: S.P.A.C.

Cas de Conscience, Play
Cas de Conscience 1939 d: Walter Kapps. lps: Roger Karl, Suzy Prim, Jules Berry. 86M FRN. *Le Creancier* prod/rel: Ste De Production Du Film Cas Conscience

La Rancon, Play
Derniere Chevauchee, La 1946 d: Leon Mathot. lps: Jacques Dumesnil, Mireille Balin, Paulette Dubost. 92M FRN. *Le Caid* prod/rel: Ste Africaine Cinematographique

GOMI, KOSUKE
Yagyu Bugeicho, 1956-59, Novel
Yagyu Bugeicho 1957 d: Hiroshi Inagaki. lps: Toshiro Mifune, Koji Tsuruta, Yoshiko KugA. 106M JPN. *Secret Scrolls (Part I)* (USA); *Yagyu Secret Scrolls; Yagyu Confidential; Ninjitsu; Soryu Hiken* prod/rel: Toho Co.

Yagyu Bugeicho -Soryu Hiken 1958 d: Hiroshi Inagaki. lps: Toshiro Mifune, Koji Tsuruta, Yoshiko KugA. 106M JPN. *Secret Scrolls (Part Ii)* (USA); *Ninjitsu* prod/rel: Toho Co.

GOMIKAWA, JUMPEI
Ningen No Joken Vol. 1 & 2, Kyoto 1958, Novel
Ningen No Joken I 1959 d: Masaki Kobayashi. lps: Tatsuya Nakadai, Michiyo Aratama, So YamamurA. 208M JPN. *No Greater Love* (USA); *The War and a Man; The Human Condition* prod/rel: Ninjin Club, Shochiku Co.

Ningen No Joken Vol. 3 & 4, Novel
Ningen No Joken II 1959 d: Masaki Kobayashi. lps: Tatsuya Nakadai, Michiyo Aratama, Keiji SadA. 181M JPN. *Road to Eternity* (USA); *The Human Condition Part 2* prod/rel: Shochiku Co.

Ningen No Joken Vol. 5 & 6, Novel
Ningen No Joken III 1961 d: Masaki Kobayashi. lps: Tatsuya Nakadai, Michiyo Aratama, Taketoshi Naito. 190M JPN. *A Soldier's Prayer* (USA); *The Human Condition Part 3* prod/rel: Ningen Club, Shochiku Co.

Senso to Ningen, Novel
Senso to Ningen 1970 d: Satsuo Yamamoto. lps: Kei Yamamoto, Hideki Takahashi, Mizuho Suzuki. 198M JPN. *Human Being and War; The Battle of Manchuria; Men and War; Man and War* prod/rel: Nikkatsu Corporation

GONCHAROV, IVAN ALEKSANDROVICH (1812–1891), RSS
Oblomov, 1859, Novel
Neskolko Dnei Iz Zhizni I.I. Oblomov 1980 d: Nikita Mikhalkov. lps: Oleg Tabakov, Yelena Solovei, Andrey Popov. 146M USS. *A Few Days in the Life of I.I. Oblomov; Oblomov* (USA); *Neskolko Dnej Iz Zizni I I Oblomov; Several Days in the Life of I.I. Oblomov*

GONDINET, EDMOND
Voyage d'Agrement, 1881, Play
Viaggio Di Piacere, Un 1922 d: Ermanno Geymonat. lps: Camillo de Riso, Silvana Morello, Umberto Zanuccoli. 1531m ITL. prod/rel: Caesar Film

GONNET, C. A.
Aloha le Chant Des Iles, Novel
Aloha, le Chant Des Iles 1937 d: Leon Mathot. lps: Jean Murat, Daniele Parola, Andre Alerme. 111M FRN. prod/rel: Compagnie Francaise Cinematographique

GONZALEZ MELENDEZ, GABRIEL
Sobrenatural, Novel
Sobrenatural 1996 d: Daniel Gruener. lps: Susana Zabaleta, Alejandro Tommasi, Delia CasanovA. 100M MXC. *Supernatural* prod/rel: Televicine

GOODCHILD, GEORGE
Colorado Jim; Or the Taming of Angela, London 1920, Novel
Colorado Pluck 1921 d: Jules G. Furthman. lps: William Russell, Margaret Livingston, William Buckley. 4700f USA. prod/rel: Fox Film Corp.

Jack O'Lantern, Play
Condemned to Death 1932 d: Walter Forde. lps: Arthur Wontner, Edmund Gwenn, Gordon Harker. 75M UKN. *Jack O'Lantern* prod/rel: Twickenham, Woolf & Freedman

No Exit, London 1936, Play
No Escape 1936 d: Norman Lee. lps: Valerie Hobson, Billy Milton, Robert Cochran. 80M UKN. *No Exit* prod/rel: Welwyn, Pathe

The Splendid Crime, London 1930, Novel
Public Defender 1931 d: J. Walter Ruben. lps: Richard Dix, Shirley Grey, Purnell Pratt. 70M USA. *The Million Dollar Swindle; The Reckoner* prod/rel: RKO Radio Pictures©

Trooper O'Neil, London 1921, Novel
Trooper O'Neill 1922 d: Scott R. Dunlap, C. R. Wallace. lps: Buck Jones, Beatrice Burnham, Francis McDonald. 4862f USA. prod/rel: Fox Film Corp.

GOODE, REGINALD BUTLER
Syncopating Sue, Play
Syncopating Sue 1926 d: Richard Wallace. lps: Corinne Griffith, Tom Moore, Rockliffe Fellowes. 6770f USA. *Broadway Blues; Tin Pan Alley* prod/rel: Corinne Griffith Productions, First National Pictures

GOODE, RUTH
Impresario, Book
Tonight We Sing 1953 d: Mitchell Leisen. lps: David Wayne, Tamara Toumanova, Ezio PinzA. 113M USA. prod/rel: 20th Century-Fox

GOODFELLOW, DOROTHY
The Street of the Flying Dragon, 1920, Short Story
Five Days to Live 1922 d: Norman Dawn. lps: Sessue Hayakawa, Tsuru Aoki, Goro Kino. 5210f USA. *The Street of the Flying Dragon* prod/rel: R-C Pictures

GOODHART, WILLIAM
Generation, New York 1965, Play
Generation 1969 d: George Schaefer. lps: David Janssen, Kim Darby, Carl Reiner. 104M USA. *A Time for Giving* (UKN) prod/rel: Avco Embassy Pictures

GOODHUE, WILLIS MAXWELL
Play
Sin of Nora Moran, The 1933 d: Phil Goldstone. lps: Zita Johann, Paul Cavanagh, Alan Dinehart. 65M USA. *Voice from the Grave; The Woman in the Chair* prod/rel: Majestic Pictures Corp.

Hello Bill, Play
Fixer, The 1915. lps: George Bickel, Harry Watson, Ben Taggart. 4682f USA. *Hello Bill* prod/rel: George Kleine©, Kleine-Edison Feature Service

GOODIN, PEGGY
Clementine, Novel
Mickey 1948 d: Ralph Murphy. lps: Lois Butler, Bill Goodwin, Irene Hervey. 87M USA. prod/rel: Eagle Lion

Take Care of My Little Girl, 1950, Novel
Take Care of My Little Girl 1951 d: Jean Negulesco. lps: Jeanne Crain, Dale Robertson, Mitzi Gaynor. 94M USA. prod/rel: 20th Century-Fox

GOODIS, DAVID
The Burglar, 1953, Novel
Burglar, The 1957 d: Paul Wendkos. lps: Dan Duryea, Jayne Mansfield, Martha Vickers. 90M USA. prod/rel: Columbia
Casse, Le 1971 d: Henri Verneuil. lps: Jean-Paul Belmondo, Omar Sharif, Dyan Cannon. 120M FRN/ITL. *Gli Scassinatori* (ITL); *The Burglars* (USA) prod/rel: Vides Cin.Ca

Dark Passage, 1946, Novel
Dark Passage 1947 d: Delmer Daves. lps: Humphrey Bogart, Lauren Bacall, Bruce Bennett. 106M USA. prod/rel: Warner Bros.

Down There, New York 1956, Novel
Tirez Sur le Pianiste 1960 d: Francois Truffaut. lps: Charles Aznavour, Nicole Berger, Marie Dubois. 80M FRN. *Shoot the Piano Player* (USA); *Shoot the Pianist* (UKN) prod/rel: Films De La Pleiade

Epaves, Novel
Rue Barbare 1983 d: Gilles Behat. lps: Bernard Giraudeau, Christine Boisson, Jean-Pierre Kalfon. 107M FRN. *Street of the Damned; Street of the Lost* prod/rel: Les Films de la Tour, Farena

The Moon in the Gutter, 1954, Novel
Lune Dans le Caniveau, La 1983 d: Jean-Jacques Beineix. lps: Gerard Depardieu, Nastassja Kinski, Victoria Abril. 137M FRN/ITL. *Moon in the Gutter* (UKN) prod/rel: Gaumont, Tfi Films

Nightfall, 1947, Novel
Nightfall 1956 d: Jacques Tourneur. lps: Aldo Ray, Anne Bancroft, Brian Keith. 78M USA. prod/rel: Columbia, Copa Prods.

Of Missing Persons, Novel
Section Des Disparus 1956 d: Pierre Chenal. lps: Maurice Ronet, Nicole Maurey, Ubaldo Martinez. 85M FRN/ARG. prod/rel: C.I.C.C. Guaranteed Pictures

Street of No Return, Novel
Sans Espoir de Retour 1989 d: Samuel Fuller. lps: Keith Carradine, Valentina Vargas, Bill Duke. 92M FRN/PRT. *Street of No Return* (USA) prod/rel: Thunder Films, Fr 3

The Wounded and the Slain, 1959, Novel
Descente aux Enfers 1986 d: Francis Girod. lps: Claude Brasseur, Sophie Marceau, Betsy Blair. 88M FRN. *Descent Into Hell* prod/rel: Partner's, la Cinq

GOODLOE, ABBIE CARTER
Claustrophobia, 1926, Short Story
I Live My Life 1935 d: W. S. Van Dyke. lps: Joan Crawford, Brian Aherne, Frank Morgan. 99M USA. *Glitter; If You Love Me* prod/rel: Metro-Goldwyn-Mayer Corp., A. W. S. Van Dyke Production

GOODMAN, CHARLES A.
I'll Trade You an Elk, Novel
Wacky Zoo of Morgan City, The 1970 d: Marvin J. Chomsky. lps: Joe Flynn, Hal Holbrook, Michael-James Wixted. TVM. 95M USA.

GOODMAN, DANIEL CARSON
The Single Standard, Play
Battle of the Sexes, The 1914 d: D. W. Griffith. lps: Lillian Gish, Owen Moore, Mary Alden. 5r USA. *The Single Standard* prod/rel: Mutual Film Corp., Majestic Motion Picture Co.
Battle of the Sexes, The 1928 d: D. W. Griffith. lps: Jean Hersholt, Phyllis Haver, Belle Bennett. 8180f USA. prod/rel: United Artists, Art Cinema Corp.

Zudora, Story
Zudora 1914 d: Frederick Sullivan, Howell Hansel. lps: James Cruze, Marguerite Snow, Harry Benham. SRL. 40r USA. *Zudora in the Twenty Million Dollar Mystery; The Twenty Million Dollar Mystery* prod/rel: Thanhouser Syndicate

GOODMAN, GEORGE J. W.
The Wheeler Dealers, New York 1959, Novel
Wheeler Dealers, The 1963 d: Arthur Hiller. lps: James Garner, Lee Remick, Phil Harris. 106M USA. *Separate Beds* (UKN) prod/rel: Filmways, Inc., MGM

GOODMAN, JACK
Gay Blades, Story
Gay Blades 1946 d: George Blair. lps: Allan Lane, Jean Rogers, Edward Ashley. 67M USA. *Tournament Tempo* prod/rel: Republic

GOODMAN, JULES ECKERT
Business Before Pleasure, New York 1917, Play
In Hollywood With Potash and Perlmutter 1924 d: Alfred E. Green. lps: Alexander Carr, George Sidney, Vera Gordon. 6685f USA. *So This Is Hollywood* (UKN) prod/rel: Goldwyn Pictures, Associated First National Pictures

Just Outside the Door, New York 1915, Play
Just Outside the Door 1921 d: George Irving. lps: Edith Hallor, Betty Blythe, J. Barney Sherry. 5r USA. prod/rel: Weber Productions, Select Pictures

The Man Who Stood Still, New York 1908, Play
Man Who Stood Still, The 1916 d: Frank H. Crane. lps: Lew Fields, Doris Kenyon, George Trimble. 5r USA. prod/rel: Paragon Films, Inc., World Film Corp.©

Mother, New York 1910, Play
Mother 1914 d: Maurice Tourneur. lps: Emma Dunn, Eddie Baker, Henri Desfontaines. 4r USA. *Some Soul of Goodness* prod/rel: William A. Brady Picture Plays, Inc., World Film Corp.©

Partners Again, New York 1922, Play
Partners Again 1926 d: Henry King. lps: George Sidney, Alexander Carr, Betty Jewel. 5562f USA. prod/rel: Samuel Goldwyn, Inc., United Artists

The Point of View, New York 1912, Play
Love's Crucible 1916 d: Emile Chautard. lps: Frances Nelson, Douglas MacLean, June Elvidge. 5r USA. prod/rel: William A. Brady Picture Plays, Inc., World Film Corp.©

The Silent Voice, New York 1914, Play
Man Who Played God, The 1922 d: F. Harmon Weight. lps: George Arliss, Ann Forrest, Ivan Simpson. 5855f USA. *The Silent Voice* prod/rel: Distinctive Productions, United Artists
Man Who Played God, The 1932 d: John G. Adolfi. lps: George Arliss, Bette Davis, Violet Heming. 83M USA. *The Silent Voice* (UKN) prod/rel: Warner Bros. Pictures©
Silent Voice, The 1915 d: William J. Bowman. lps: Francis X. Bushman, Marguerite Snow, Lester Cuneo. 6r USA. prod/rel: Quality Pictures Corp., Metro Pictures Corp.©
Sincerely Yours 1955 d: Gordon Douglas. lps: Liberace, Joanne Dru, Dorothy Malone. 115M USA. prod/rel: Warner Bros., International Artists Ltd.

The Trap, New York 1915, Play
Trap, The 1919 d: Frank Reicher. lps: Olive Tell, Sidney Mason, Jere Austin. 6r USA. *A Woman's Law* (UKN) prod/rel: Universal Film Mfg. Co.©

GOODRICH, ARTHUR FREDERICK
Gleam O'Dawn, New York 1908, Novel
Gleam O'Dawn 1922 d: John Francis Dillon. lps: John Gilbert, Barbara Bedford, James Farley. 4178f USA. prod/rel: Fox Film Corp.

So This Is London, London 1923, Play
So This Is London 1930 d: John G. Blystone. lps: Will Rogers, Irene Rich, Frank Albertson. 8300f USA. prod/rel: Fox Film Corp.
So This Is London 1939 d: Thornton Freeland. lps: Robertson Hare, Alfred Drayton, George Sanders. 89M UKN. prod/rel: 20th Century Productions, 20th Century-Fox

Yes Or No, New York 1917, Play
Yes Or No 1920 d: R. William Neill. lps: Norma Talmadge, Rockliffe Fellowes, Lowell Sherman. 6r USA. prod/rel: Norma Talmadge Film Co., First National Exhibitors Circuit

GOODRICH, FRANCES
The Diary of Anne Frank, Play
Diary of Anne Frank, The 1980 d: Boris Sagal. lps: Melissa Gilbert, Maximilian Schell, Joan Plowright. TVM. 100M USA. prod/rel: NBC, Twentieth Century Fox
Diary of Anne Frank, The 1987 d: Gareth Davies. lps: Katharine Schlesinger, Emrys James, Elizabeth Bell. TVM. 120M UKN.

Up Pops the Devil, New York 1930, Play
Thanks for the Memory 1938 d: George Archainbaud. lps: Bob Hope, Shirley Ross, Charles Butterworth. 77M USA. prod/rel: Paramount Pictures©
Up Pops the Devil 1931 d: A. Edward Sutherland. lps: Carole Lombard, Norman Foster, Stuart Erwin. 85M USA. prod/rel: Paramount Publix Corp.

GOODRICH, JOHN
Crack-Up, 1936, Short Story
Crack-Up 1936 d: Malcolm St. Clair. lps: Peter Lorre, Brian Donlevy, Helen Wood. 70M USA. prod/rel: Twentieth Century-Fox Film Corp.

GOODRIDGE, HARRY
A Seal Called Andre, Novel
Andre 1994 d: George Miller. lps: Tina Majorino, Chelsea Field, Shane Meier. 95M USA. prod/rel: Kushner-Locke

GOODWIN, DANIEL CARSON
The Green-Eyed Devil, Story
Green-Eyed Devil, The 1914 d: James Kirkwood. lps: Lillian Gish, George Siegmann, Spottiswoode Aitken. 2r USA. prod/rel: Reliance

GOODWIN, JOHN
The Avenger, New York 1926, Novel
Avenger, The 1933 d: Edwin L. Marin. lps: Ralph Forbes, Adrienne Ames, Arthur Vinton. 79M USA. prod/rel: Monogram Pictures Corp.

The House of Marney, Novel
House of Marney, The 1926 d: Cecil M. Hepworth. lps: Alma Taylor, John Longden, James Carew. 6583f UKN. prod/rel: Nettlefold, Allied Artists

The Man With the Brooding Eyes, Story
Brooding Eyes 1926 d: Edward J. Le Saint. lps: Lionel Barrymore, Ruth Clifford, Robert Ellis. 5763f USA. prod/rel: Banner Productions

GORBAZ, ANDRE
La Gourde d'Eau-de-Vie, Short Story
Bourse Et la Vie, La 1928 d: Jean Brocher. 57M SWT. prod/rel: Cinemas Populaires Romands

GORDEAUX, PAUL
Guignol, Play
Prisonnier de Mon Coeur 1931 d: Jean Tarride. lps: Marie Glory, Roland Toutain, Andre Berley. 88M FRN. prod/rel: Verba-Film

GORDIMER, NADINE (1923–, SAF
A World of Strangers, 1958, Novel
Dilemma 1962 d: Henning Carlsen. lps: Ivan Jackson, Zakes Mokae, Evelyn Frank. 92M DNM/SAF. *A World of Strangers* prod/rel: Minerva, Christensen

GORDIN, JACOB
The Kreutzer Sonata, New York 1906, Play
Kreutzer Sonata 1915 d: Herbert Brenon. lps: Nance O'Neil, Theda Bara, William E. Shay. 5r USA. prod/rel: William Fox Vaudeville Co., William Fox©

Mirele Efros, 1898, Play
Mirele Efros 1939 d: Josef Berne. lps: Berta Gersten, Michael Rosenberg, Ruth Elbaum. 90M USA. prod/rel: Credo Pictures, Josef Berne Production

Der Yiddishe Kenigin Lear, 1889, Play
Yiddish King Lear, The 1935 d: Harry Thomashefsky. lps: Maurice Krohner, Fannie Levenstein, Jacob Bergreen. 70M USA. prod/rel: Lear Pictures

GORDON, ALEX
The Cipher, New York 1961, Book
Arabesque 1966 d: Stanley Donen. lps: Gregory Peck, Sophia Loren, Alan Badel. 105M UKN/USA. prod/rel: Universal, Stanley Donen Enterprises

GORDON, ARTHUR
Norman Vincent Peale: Minister to Millions,
Englewood Cliffs NJ. 1958, Biography
One Man's Way 1964 d: Denis Sanders. lps: Don
Murray, Diana Hyland, William Windom. 105M USA.
The Norman Vincent Peale Story prod/rel: Frank Ross
Productions, Columbia

Reprisal!, 1950, Novel
Reprisal! 1956 d: George Sherman. lps: Guy Madison,
Felicia Farr, Kathryn Grant. 74M USA. prod/rel:
Columbia

GORDON, BARBARA
I'm Dancing As Fast As I Can, Book
I'm Dancing As Fast As I Can 1982 d: Jack Hofsiss.
lps: Jill Clayburgh, Nicol Williamson, Dianne Wiest.
107M USA. prod/rel: Paramount

GORDON, CLIFF
Choir Practice, Radio Play
Valley of Song 1953 d: Gilbert Gunn. lps: Mervyn
Johns, Clifford Evans, Maureen Swanson. 74M UKN.
Men are Children Twice (USA); *Choir Practice* prod/rel:
Associated British Picture Corporation, Ab-Pathe

GORDON, DAN
Sleep All Winter, Short Story
Showdown, The 1950 d: Dorrell McGowan, Stuart E.
McGowan. lps: Bill Elliott, Harry Morgan, Walter
Brennan. 86M USA. prod/rel: Republic

GORDON, GORDON
Case File F.B.I., 1953, Novel
Down Three Dark Streets 1954 d: Arnold Laven. lps:
Broderick Crawford, Ruth Roman, Martha Hyer. 85M
USA. prod/rel: United Artists, Edward Small

Make Haste to Live, 1950, Novel
Make Haste to Live 1954 d: William A. Seiter. lps:
Dorothy McGuire, Stephen McNally, Mary Murphy.
90M USA. prod/rel: Republic

Operation Terror, New York 1961, Novel
Experiment in Terror 1962 d: Blake Edwards. lps:
Lee Remick, Stefanie Powers, Glenn Ford. 123M USA.
The Grip of Fear (UKN) prod/rel: Geoffrey-Kate
Productions, Warner Bros.

Undercover Cat, New York 1963, Novel
That Darn Cat! 1965 d: Robert Stevenson. lps: Hayley
Mills, Dean Jones, Dorothy Provine. 116M USA.
prod/rel: Buena Vista

That Darn Cat 1997 d: Bob Spiers. lps: Christina Ricci,
Doug E. Doug, Dean Jones. 89M USA. prod/rel: Robert
Simonds, Walt Disney Pictures

GORDON, HOMER KING
Short Story
Judgement Book, The 1935 d: Charles Hutchison.
lps: Conway Tearle, Bernadene Hayes, Howard Lang.
67M USA. prod/rel: Beaumont Pictures

GORDON, KILBOURNE
Big Game, New York 1920, Play
Big Game 1921 d: Dallas M. Fitzgerald. lps: May
Allison, Forrest Stanley, Edward Cecil. 6r USA.
prod/rel: Metro Pictures

Kongo, New York 1926, Play
Kongo 1932 d: William J. Cowen. lps: Walter Huston,
Lupe Velez, Conrad Nagel. 86M USA. prod/rel:
Metro-Goldwyn-Mayer Corp., Metro-Goldwyn-Mayer
Dist. Corp.©

GORDON, LARRY
The Devil's 8, Novel
Devil's 8, The 1969 d: Burt Topper. lps: Christopher
George, Fabian, Ralph Meeker. 98M USA. *The Devil's
Eight* prod/rel: American International

GORDON, LEON
The Garden of Weeds, New York 1924, Play
Garden of Weeds, The 1924 d: James Cruze. lps: Betty
Compson, Rockliffe Fellowes, Warner Baxter. 6230f
USA. prod/rel: Famous Players-Lasky, Paramount
Pictures

GORDON, LESLIE HOWARD
The House of Unrest, Play
House of Unrest, The 1931 d: Leslie H. Gordon. lps:
Dorothy Boyd, Malcolm Keen, Tom Helmore. 58M
UKN. prod/rel: Associated Picture Productions,
Producers' Distributing Corporation

Little Brother of God, Novel
Little Brother of God 1922 d: F. Martin Thornton.
lps: Victor McLaglen, Valia, Alec Fraser. 6560f UKN.
prod/rel: Stoll

GORDON, MILDRED
Case File F.B.I., 1953, Novel
Down Three Dark Streets 1954 d: Arnold Laven. lps:
Broderick Crawford, Ruth Roman, Martha Hyer. 85M
USA. prod/rel: United Artists, Edward Small

Make Haste to Live, 1950, Novel
Make Haste to Live 1954 d: William A. Seiter. lps:
Dorothy McGuire, Stephen McNally, Mary Murphy.
90M USA. prod/rel: Republic

Operation Terror, New York 1961, Novel
Experiment in Terror 1962 d: Blake Edwards. lps:
Lee Remick, Stefanie Powers, Glenn Ford. 123M USA.
The Grip of Fear (UKN) prod/rel: Geoffrey-Kate
Productions, Warner Bros.

Undercover Cat, New York 1963, Novel
That Darn Cat! 1965 d: Robert Stevenson. lps: Hayley
Mills, Dean Jones, Dorothy Provine. 116M USA.
prod/rel: Buena Vista

That Darn Cat 1997 d: Bob Spiers. lps: Christina Ricci,
Doug E. Doug, Dean Jones. 89M USA. prod/rel: Robert
Simonds, Walt Disney Pictures

GORDON, NEIL
The Shakespeare Murders, Novel
Claydon Treasure Mystery, The 1938 d: Manning
Haynes. lps: John Stuart, Garry Marsh, Evelyn Ankers.
63M UKN. prod/rel: Fox British

Third Clue, The 1934 d: Albert Parker. lps: Basil
Sydney, Molly Lamont, Robert Cochran. 72M UKN.
prod/rel: Fox British

GORDON, RICHARD (1921–, UKN, Ostlere, Gordon
The Captain's Table, Novel
Captain's Table, The 1959 d: Jack Lee. lps: John
Gregson, Peggy Cummins, Donald Sinden. 89M UKN.
prod/rel: Rank Film

Doctor at Large, Novel
Doctor at Large 1957 d: Ralph Thomas. lps: Dirk
Bogarde, Muriel Pavlow, Donald Sinden. 104M UKN.
prod/rel: Rank, Rank Film Distributors

Doctor at Sea, Novel
Doctor at Sea 1955 d: Ralph Thomas. lps: Dirk
Bogarde, Brenda de Banzie, Brigitte Bardot. 93M UKN.
prod/rel: Group Films, Rank Film Distributors

Doctor in Clover, London 1960, Novel
Doctor in Clover 1966 d: Ralph Thomas. lps: Leslie
Phillips, James Robertson Justice, Shirley Anne Field.
101M UKN. *Carnaby M.D.* (USA) prod/rel: Rank, Rank
Film Distributors

Doctor in Love, London 1957, Novel
Doctor in Love 1960 d: Ralph Thomas. lps: Michael
Craig, James Robertson Justice, Virginia Maskell. 98M
UKN. prod/rel: Rank, Rank Film Distributors

Doctor in the House, Novel
Doctor in the House 1954 d: Ralph Thomas. lps: Dirk
Bogarde, Muriel Pavlow, Kenneth More. 91M UKN.
prod/rel: Group Films, General Film Distributors

Doctor on Toast, Novel
Doctor in Trouble 1970 d: Ralph Thomas. lps: Leslie
Phillips, Harry Secombe, Angela Scoular. 90M UKN.
prod/rel: Rank Film Distributors, Welbeck

GORDON, RUTH (1896–1985), USA, Jones, Ruth
Gordon
Over Twenty-One, New York 1944, Play
Over 21 1945 d: Charles Vidor. lps: Irene Dunne,
Alexander Knox, Charles Coburn. 103M USA. prod/rel:
Columbia

Years Ago, Play
Actress, The 1953 d: George Cukor. lps: Spencer Tracy,
Jean Simmons, Teresa Wright. 91M USA. prod/rel:
MGM

GORDON-LENNOX, COSMO
Her Sister, New York 1907, Play
Her Sister 1917 d: John B. O'Brien. lps: Olive Tell,
David Powell, Eileen Dennes. 5r USA. prod/rel: Empire
All Star Corp.©, Mutual Film Corp.

GORE-BROWNE, ROBERT
Cynara, London 1930, Play
Cynara 1932 d: King Vidor. lps: Ronald Colman, Kay
Francis, Phyllis Barry. 80M USA. *I Have Been Faithful*;
Way of a Lancer prod/rel: Howard Productions, Inc.,
United Artists

The Key, London 1933, Play
Key, The 1934 d: Michael Curtiz. lps: William Powell,
Edna Best, Colin Clive. 71M USA. *High Peril*; *Sue of
Fury* prod/rel: Warner Bros. Pictures©

GORES, JOE (1931–, USA
Blind Chess, Novel
Blind Chess 1988 d: Jerry Jameson. lps: Burt
Reynolds, Ossie Davis, Scott Plank. TVM. 90M USA.
prod/rel: Universal

Hammett, Novel
Hammett 1982 d: Wim Wenders. lps: Frederic Forrest,
Peter Boyle, Elisha Cook Jr. 97M USA. prod/rel: Orion,
Warner Bros.

GORKY, MAXIM (1868–1936), RSS, Gorki, Maxim,
Peshkov, Aleksey Maksimovich
Short Story
Kain I Artyom 1930 d: Pavel Petrov-Bytov. lps: Nikolai
Simonov, Emil Gal, Yelena YegorovA. 105M USS. *Cain
and Artem* prod/rel: Sowkino

Chelkash, 1895, Short Story
Chelkash 1957 d: Fyodor Filippov. lps: Andrey Popov,
Viktor Matveyev, Aleksey Boyko. 45M USS.

Dachniki, 1904, Play
Dachniki 1967 d: Boris Babochkin. lps: Nikolai
Annenkov, Rufina Nifontova, Ghenrietta YegorovA.
104M USS. *Summer Residents in the Countryside*;
Summer Residents

Sommergaste 1976 d: Peter Stein. lps: Sabine
Andreas, Edith Clever, Eberhard Feik. 120M GRM.
Summer Guests (UKN) prod/rel: Regina Ziegler,
Constantin

Delo Artamonovykh, 1925, Novel
Delo Artamanovich 1941 d: Grigori Roshal. F USS.
The Artamanov Affair; *Delo Artamonovyh*; *Artamonov
and Sons*; *Delo Artamonovika*

Detstvo, 1913, Autobiography
Detstvo Gorkovo 1938 d: Mark Donskoi. lps: Alexei
Lyarski, Varvara Massalitinova, Y. AlekseyevA. 100M
USS. *The Childhood of Maxim Gorki*; *Gorky's
Childhood*; *Childhood of Gorky*

Foma Gordeyev, St. Petersburg 1899, Novel
Foma Gordeev 1959 d: Mark Donskoi. lps: Sergei
Lukyanov, Georgiy Yepifantsev, Pavel Tarasov. 96M
USS. *The Gordeyev Family* (USA); *Foma Gordeyev*
prod/rel: Gorky Film Studio

The Lower Depths, 1902, Play
Neecha Nagar 1946 d: Chetan Anand. lps: Rafiq
Anwar, Uma Anand, Rafi Peer. 122M IND. *Lowly City*
prod/rel: India Pictures

Malva, 1897, Short Story
Malva 1957 d: Vladimir Braun. lps: Zidra Ritenberg, P.
Oussovnitchenko, A. Ignatyev. 85M USS. prod/rel:
Filmstudio Kiev

Mat, 1906, Novel
Mat 1926 d: V. I. Pudovkin. lps: Nikolai Batalov, Vera
Baranowskaja, Anna ZemtsovA. 90M USS. *Mother*
prod/rel: Mezhrabpom-Russ

Mat 1956 d: Mark Donskoi. lps: Alexei Batalov, Vera
Maretskaya, N. Kolofidine. 104M USS. *Mother*; *1905*

Moi Universiteti, 1921-22, Autobiography
Moi Universiteti 1940 d: Mark Donskoi. lps: N.
Valbert, N. Protnikov, Stepan Kayukov. 98M USS.
University of Life; *My Universities*

Na Dne, Moscow 1902, Play
Bas-Fonds, Les 1936 d: Jean Renoir. lps: Jean Gabin,
Louis Jouvet, Suzy Prim. 95M FRN. *The Lower Depths*;
Underworld prod/rel: Films Albatros

Donzoko 1957 d: Akira KurosawA. lps: Toshiro
Mifune, Isuzu Yamada, Ganjiro NakamurA. 137M JPN.
The Lower Depths (USA); *Donzoku* prod/rel: Toho Co.

Ye Dian 1948 d: Tso Lin. 116M CHN. *Night Lodging*

V Lyudyakh, 1915, Autobiography
V Lyudykah 1939 d: Mark Donskoi. lps: Varvara
Massalitinova, Mikhail Troyanovsky, E. AlexeyevA.
98M USS. *My Apprenticeship*; *Among People*; *Out in the
World*; *V Ljudjah*; *On His Own*

The Vacationers, Play
Letniye Lyudi 1995 d: Sergei Ursulyak. lps: Sergei
Makovetsky, Irina Kupchenko, Svetlana RyabovA. F
RSS. *Summer People* prod/rel: Roskomkino,
East-European Film Company

Vassa Zheleznova, 1910, Play
Vassa 1982 d: Gleb Panfilov. lps: Inna Churikova,
Vadim Medvedev, Nikolai Skorobogatov. 140M USS.

Vassa Zheleznova 1953 d: Leonid Lukov. 95M USS.
The Mistress; *Vassa Zeleznova*

Vragi, 1906, Play
Vragi 1938 d: Alexander Ivanovsky. 80M USS. *The
Enemies*

Yegor Bulychov I Drugiye, 1932, Play
Yegor Bulychov I Drugiye 1971 d: Sergei Soloviev.
lps: Mikhail Ulyanov, Maya Bulgakova, E. VasilyevA.
90M USS. *Yegor Bulychov and Others*; *Egor Bulycov I
Drugie*; *Egor Bulytchev and Others*

GORLING, LARS
491, Stockholm 1962, Novel
491 (Fyrahundranittioett) 1964 d: Vilgot Sjoman.
lps: Lars Lind, Leif Nymark, Stig Tornblom. 105M
SWD. *491* (USA) prod/rel: Svensk Filmindustri

GORMAN, HERBERT
Suzy, New York 1934, Novel
Suzy 1936 d: George Fitzmaurice. lps: Jean Harlow,
Franchot Tone, Cary Grant. 95M USA. prod/rel:
Metro-Goldwyn-Mayer Corp.©

GORMAN, JACK
Corruption, Play
Corruption 1917 d: John Gorman. lps: Helen Martin, Henry Sedley, John J. Dunn. 6r USA. *The Mother and the Law* prod/rel: Super Art Film Corp., State Rights

GORMAN, JOHN
Play
Prince of Broadway, The 1926 d: John Gorman. lps: George Walsh, Alyce Mills, Freeman Wood. 5800f USA. prod/rel: Chadwick Pictures

GORSSE, HENRI
Le Spectre de Monsieur Imberger, Play
Mystere Imberger, Le 1935 d: Jacques Severac. lps: Simone Deguyse, Jean Galland, Gaston Modot. 82M FRN. *Le Spectre de M. Imberger* prod/rel: Compagnie Autonome De Cinematographie

GOS, CHARLES
La Croix du Cervin, Lausanne 1919, Novel
Croix du Cervin, La 1922 d: Marcel Grosnier, Jacques Beranger. lps: Greta Prozor, Clara Brooke, Augustin Currat. 84M SWT. *Sur Les Hautes Cimes (L'ascension du Mont Cervin); Das Kreuz Am Matterhorn* prod/rel: S.a.F., Film-Artes

GOSCINNY
Novel
All'ovest Di Sacramento 1971 d: Federico Chentrens. lps: Robert Hossein, Silvia Monti, Xavier Gelin. 87M ITL/FRN. *La Loi a l'Ouest de Pecos (FRN); Trouble in Sacramento; Judge Roy Bean* prod/rel: Milvia Cin.Ca (Roma), Comacico (Paris)

GOSLING, PAULA
Fair Game, Novel
Cobra 1986 d: George Pan Cosmatos. lps: Sylvester Stallone, Brigitte Nielsen, Reni Santoni. 87M USA. prod/rel: Warner, Cannon

GOSS, CHARLES FREDERICK
The Redemption of David Corson, New York 1900, Novel
Redemption of David Corson, The 1914. lps: William Farnum, Constance Mollineaux, Hal Clarendon. 4r USA. prod/rel: Famous Players Film Co., State Rights

GOTANDA, PHILIP KAN
The Wash, Play
Wash, The 1988 d: Michael Toshiyuki Uno. lps: Mako, Nobu McCarthy, Patty Yasutake. 94M USA. prod/rel: Skouras, Exclusive

GOTO, BEN
Novel
Catastrophe 1999 - Prophecies of Nostradamus 1974 d: Shiro Moritani. lps: Keiju Kobayashi, Tetsuro Tamba, Hiroshi FujiokA. 78M JPN. prod/rel: Toho

GOTTA, SALVATOR
A Bocca Nuda, Novel
Diamanti 1939 d: Corrado d'Errico. lps: Doris Duranti, Lamberto Picasso, Laura Nucci. 70M ITL. prod/rel: Alfa Film, C.I.N.F.
La Damigella Di Bard, Play
Damigella Di Bard, La 1936 d: Mario Mattoli. lps: Emma Gramatica, Luigi Cimara, Mirella Pardi. 75M ITL. prod/rel: I.C.I.
I Giganti Innamorati, Novel
Donna Della Montagna, La 1943 d: Renato Castellani. lps: Marina Berti, Amedeo Nazzari, Maurizio d'AncorA. 93M ITL. *The Woman from the Mountain; L' Ombra Della Montagna* prod/rel: Lux Film
Piccolo Alpino, Novel
Piccolo Alpino 1940 d: Oreste Biancoli. lps: Elio Sannangelo, Mario Ferrari, Filippo Scelzo. 96M ITL. prod/rel: Manderfilm
La Piu Bella Donna Del Mondo, 1919, Novel
Piu Bella Donna Del Mondo, La 1920 d: Luigi Mele. lps: Tilde Teldi, Evelyn Morgan, Lydia de Roberti. 1757m ITL. prod/rel: Latina-Ars
La Signora Di Tutti, Novel
Signora Di Tutti, La 1934 d: Max Ophuls. lps: Isa Miranda, Memo Benassi, Tatiana PavlovA. 95M ITL. prod/rel: Novella Film, Anonima Pittaluga

GOTTHELF, JEREMIAS (1797–1854), SWT, Bitzius, Albert
Oder Die Versohnung Geld Und Geist, Soleure 1843, Novel
Geld Und Geist 1964 d: Franz Schnyder. lps: Margrit Winter, Erwin Kohlund, Peter Arens. 121M SWT. *La Reconciliation; Soldi E Spirito; Menschen Der Berge* prod/rel: Neue Film
Die Kaserei in Der Vehfreude, Berlin 1850, Novel
Kaserei in Der Vehfreude, Die 1958 d: Franz Schnyder. lps: Annemarie Duringer, Franz Matter, Heinrich Gretler. 86M SWT. *Wildwest Im Emmenthal; Oh Diese Weiber; Annelie Vom Berghof; La from de Fefreude; Caseificio Di Vehfreude, Il* prod/rel: Neue Film

Uli Der Pachter, Berlin 1849, Novel
Uli Der Pachter 1955 d: Franz Schnyder. lps: Hannes Schmidhauser, Liselotte Pulver, Emil Hegetschweiler. 115M SWT. ...*Und Ewig Ruft Die Heimat; Uli le Fermier; ..Und Ewig Ruft Die Heimat; Uli Il Mezzadro* prod/rel: Praesens-Film
Wie Anne Babi Jowager Haushaltet Und Wie Es Ihm Mit Dem., Soleure 1843-44, Novel
Anne Babi Jowager 1960 d: Franz Schnyder. lps: Margrit Winter, Annemarie Duringer, Peter Brogle. 206M SWT. *Wie Anne Babi Haushaltet Und Wie Es.* prod/rel: Neue Film
Wie Uli Der Knecht Glucklich Wird, Zurich 1841, Novel
Uli Der Knecht 1954 d: Franz Schnyder. lps: Hannes Schmidthauser, Liselotte Pulver, Heinrich Gretler. 115M SWT. *Uli le Valet de Ferme; Uli Il Servo; Junge Jahre Der Liebe* prod/rel: Gloriafilm

GOTTLIEB, ALEX
Susan, 1952, Play
Susan Slept Here 1954 d: Frank Tashlin. lps: Dick Powell, Debbie Reynolds, Anne Francis. 98M USA. prod/rel: RKO Radio

GOTTLIEB, PAUL
Agency, Novel
Agency 1979 d: George Kaczender. lps: Robert Mitchum, Lee Majors, Valerie Perrine. 94M CND. *Mind Games; Les Espions Dans la Ville; L' Agence de la Peur* prod/rel: Moviecorp III Inc., Rsl Films Ltd.

GOTTWALD, FRITZ
The Command to Love, New York 1927, Play
Boudoir Diplomat, The 1930 d: Malcolm St. Clair. lps: Betty Compson, Ian Keith, Mary Duncan. 68M USA. prod/rel: Universal Pictures
Don Juan Diplomatico 1931 d: George Melford. lps: Miguel Faust Rocha, Lia Tora, Celia Montalvan. 8r USA. *Diplomatico de Salon* prod/rel: Universal Pictures Corp.
Liebe Ist Zollfrei, Play
Liebe Ist Zollfrei 1941 d: E. W. Emo. lps: Hans Moser, Susi Peter, Hans Olden. 96M GRM/AUS. prod/rel: Wien-Film
Das Madchen Im Fenster, Play
Wie Ein Dieb in Der Nacht 1945 d: Hans Thimig. lps: Gusti Huber, Wolf Albach-Retty, Georg Lorenz. 85M AUS. *Der Herzensdieb* prod/rel: Wien

GOTZ, KURT
Die Tote von Beverly Hills, Berlin 1951, Novel
Tote von Beverly Hills, Die 1964 d: Michael Pfleghar. lps: Heidelinde Weis, Klausjurgen Wussow, Horst Frank. 110M GRM. *The Corpse of Beverly Hills (USA); That Girl from Beverly Hills; Lu (UKN); Dead Woman from Beverly Hills* prod/rel: Modern Art, Constantin

GOUDEKET, MAURICE
Pas un Mot a la Reine-Mere, Play
Pas un Mot a la Reine-Mere 1946 d: Maurice Cloche. lps: Suzanne Dehelly, Liliane Bert, Andre Brunot. 85M FRN. prod/rel: C.C.F.C.

GOUDGE, ELIZABETH
Green Dolphin Street, Novel
Green Dolphin Street 1947 d: Victor Saville. lps: Lana Turner, Van Heflin, Richard Hart. 141M USA. prod/rel: MGM

GOULD, AMY KENNEDY
Checkmate, Novel
Checkmate 1935 d: George Pearson. lps: Maurice Evans, Felix Aylmer, Evelyn Foster. 68M UKN. prod/rel: British and Dominions, Paramount British
Wayward Youth, Play
Way of Youth, The 1934 d: Norman Walker. lps: Aileen Marson, Irene Vanbrugh, Sebastian Shaw. 65M UKN. prod/rel: British and Dominions, Paramount British

GOULD, J. HEYWOOD
Cocktail, Book
Cocktail 1988 d: Roger Donaldson. lps: Tom Cruise, Bryan Brown, Elisabeth Shue. 103M USA. prod/rel: Buena Vista, Touchstone

GOULD, JUDITH
Sins, Novel
Sins 1985 d: Douglas Hickox. lps: Joan Collins, Marisa Berenson, Jean-Pierre Aumont. TVM. 420M USA/FRN. *Les Griffes du Destin* (FRN)

GOULD, LOIS
Such Good Friends, Novel
Such Good Friends 1971 d: Otto Preminger. lps: Dyan Cannon, James Coco, Jennifer O'Neill. 102M USA. prod/rel: Sigma

GOULD, NAT
The Chance of a Lifetime, Novel
Chance of a Lifetime, The 1916 d: Bertram Phillips. lps: Queenie Thomas, Austin Camp, Fay Temple. 5250f UKN. prod/rel: Holmfirth, Pathe

A Dead Certainty, Novel
Dead Certainty, A 1920 d: George Dewhurst. lps: Gregory Scott, Poppy Wyndham, Cameron Carr. 4494f UKN. prod/rel: Broadwest, Walturdaw
A Fortune at Stake, Novel
Fortune at Stake, A 1918 d: Walter West. lps: Violet Hopson, Gerald Ames, Edward O'Neill. 6500f UKN. prod/rel: Broadwest, Royal
A Gamble for Love, Novel
Gamble for Love, A 1917 d: Frank Wilson. lps: Violet Hopson, Gerald Ames, James Lindsay. 5609f UKN. prod/rel: Broadwest
A Great Coup, Novel
Great Coup, A 1919 d: George Dewhurst. lps: Stewart Rome, Poppy Wyndham, Gregory Scott. 4400f UKN. prod/rel: Broadwest, Walturdaw
A Rank Outsider, Novel
Rank Outsider, A 1920 d: Richard Garrick. lps: Gwen Stratford, Cameron Stratford, Lewis Dayton. 4236f UKN. prod/rel: Broadwest, Walturdaw
A Turf Conspiracy, Novel
Turf Conspiracy, A 1918 d: Frank Wilson. lps: Violet Hopson, Gerald Ames, Joan Legge. 5600f UKN. prod/rel: Broadwest, Granger

GOULD, SABINE BARING
Bladys of the Stewpony, Novel
Bladys of the Stewpony 1919 d: L. C. MacBean. lps: Marguerite Fox, Arthur Chisholm, Wyndham Guise. 5000f UKN. prod/rel: Ben Priest Films

GOULDING, EDMUND
Dancing Mothers, New York 1924, Play
Dancing Mothers 1926 d: Herbert Brenon. lps: Alice Joyce, Conway Tearle, Clara Bow. 7169f USA. prod/rel: Famous Players-Lasky, Paramount Pictures
Ellen Young, Play
Quest of Life, The 1916 d: Ashley Miller. lps: Maurice, Florence Walton, Robert Brower. 5r USA. prod/rel: Famous Players Film Co., Paramount Pictures Corp.

GOUNOD, CHARLES (1818–1893), FRN, Gounod, Charles Francois
Faust, Paris 1859, Opera
Faust 1909 d: Edwin S. Porter, J. Searle Dawley. 1000f USA. prod/rel: Edison
Faust 1911 d: Cecil M. Hepworth. lps: Hay Plumb, Claire Pridelle, Jack Hulcup. SSF. 15M UKN. prod/rel: Hepworth
Faust 1922 d: Challis Sanderson. lps: Dick Webb, Sylvia Caine, Lawford Davidson. 1152f UKN. prod/rel: Master Films, Gaumont
Faust 1927 d: H. B. Parkinson. lps: Herbert Langley, A. B. Imeson, Margot Lees. 1657f UKN. prod/rel: Song Films
Faust 1936 d: Albert Hopkins. lps: Webster Booth, Anne Ziegler, Dennis Hoey. 43M UKN. *Faust Fantasy* prod/rel: Publicity Picture Productions, National Interest
Faust a Marketka, Paris 1859, Opera
Faust 1913 d: Stanislav HlavsA. lps: Frantisek Krampera, Stanislav Hlavsa, Marie SoukupovA. CZC. prod/rel: Kinofa

GOURDON, PIERRE
Une Idylle Dans la Zone Rouge, Play
Promesses 1935 d: Rene Delacroix. lps: Pierre Mingand, Lucien Galas, Monique Rolland. 77M FRN. prod/rel: Fiat Film

GOW, JAMES
Tomorrow the World, New York 1943, Play
Tomorrow the World 1944 d: Leslie Fenton. lps: Fredric March, Betty Field, Agnes Moorehead. 86M USA. prod/rel: United Artists, Lester Cowan Prods.

GOWAN, MAURICE
Story
Man of the Moment 1955 d: John Paddy Carstairs. lps: Norman Wisdom, Lana Morris, Belinda Lee. 88M UKN. prod/rel: Rank Film Distributors, Group

GOWDY, BARBARA
Short Story
Kissed 1996 d: Lynne Stopkewich. lps: Molly Parker, Peter Outerbridge, Jay Brazeau. 78M CND. prod/rel: Boneyard Film Company©, British Columbia Film

GOWING, SIDNEY
A Daughter in Revolt, Novel
Daughter in Revolt, A 1927 d: Harry Hughes. lps: Mabel Poulton, Edward O'Neill, Patrick Susands. 7300f UKN. prod/rel: Nettlefold, Allied Artists

GOZLAN, LEON
Histoire de 130 Femmes, Novel
Nave Delle Donne Maledette, La 1953 d: Raffaello Matarazzo. lps: Kerima, May Britt, Ettore Manni. 97M ITL. *The Ship of Condemned Women (USA); Le Navire Des Filles Perdues* prod/rel: Excelsa Film, Minerva Film

Le Notti Del Cimitero, Novel
Diabolici, I 1921 d: Augusto GeninA. lps: Edy Darclea, Umberto Casilini, Vasco Creti. 1772m ITL. prod/rel: Photodrama

GOZZI, CARLO (1720–1806), ITL, Gozzi, Count Carlo
Turandot, Play
Turandot, Princesse de Chine 1934 d: Serge Veber, Gerhard Lamprecht. lps: Kathe von Nagy, Pierre Blanchar, Marcel Dalio. 83M FRN. prod/rel: U.F.a., a.C.E.

GRABBE, CHRISTIAN DIETRICH (1801–1836), GRM
Don Juan Und Faust, 1829, Play
Don Juan Et Faust 1922 d: Marcel L'Herbier. lps: Jaque Catelain, Vanni Marcoux, Jacques Lerner. 2000m FRN. prod/rel: Gaumont

GRACE, DICK
The Lost Squadron, New York 1932, Novel
Lost Squadron, The 1932 d: George Archainbaud. lps: Richard Dix, Mary Astor, Erich von Stroheim. 79M USA. prod/rel: RKO Radio Pictures©

GRACQ, JULIEN
Le Roi Cophetua, 1970, Short Story
Rendez-Vous a Bray 1971 d: Andre Delvaux. lps: Anna Karina, Bulle Ogier, Mathieu Carriere. 93M FRN/GRM/BLG. *Rendezvous at Bray* (UKN); *Rendezvous in Bray* prod/rel: Cinevog Films, Parc

GRACZYCK, ED
Come Back to the Five and Dime Jimmy Dean, Jimmy Dean, Play
Come Back to the Five and Dime, Jimmy Dean, Jimmy Dean 1982 d: Robert Altman. lps: Sandy Dennis, Cher, Karen Black. 109M USA. prod/rel: Viacom

GRADE, CHAIM
My Quarrel With Hersh Rasseyner, Autobiography
Quarrel, The 1990 d: Ellis Cohen. lps: R. H. Thomson, Saul Rubinek, Marlee Shapiro. 88M CND.

GRADY, JAMES
Six Days of the Condor, Novel
Three Days of the Condor 1975 d: Sydney Pollack. lps: Robert Redford, Faye Dunaway, Cliff Robertson. 118M USA. prod/rel: Dino de Laurentiis, 20th Century Fox

GRAEME, BRUCE
Blackshirt, Novel
Black Mask 1935 d: Ralph Ince. lps: Wylie Watson, Aileen Marson, Ellis Irving. 67M UKN. prod/rel: Warner Bros., First National

The Disappearance of Roger Tremayne, Novel
Ten Days in Paris 1939 d: Tim Whelan. lps: Rex Harrison, Kaaren Verne, C. V. France. 82M UKN. *Missing Ten Days* (USA); *Spy in the Pantry* prod/rel: Columbia, Irving Asher Productions

The Hate Ship, Novel
Hate Ship, The 1929 d: Norman Walker. lps: Jameson Thomas, Jean Colin, Jack Raine. 83M UKN. prod/rel: British International Pictures, First National-Pathe

Suspense, Novel
Face in the Night 1957 d: Lance Comfort. lps: Griffith Jones, Lisa Gastoni, Vincent Ball. 75M UKN. *Menace in the Night* (USA) prod/rel: Gibraltar, Grand National

The Way Out, Novel
Dial 999 1955 d: Montgomery Tully. lps: Gene Nelson, Mona Freeman, John Bentley. 86M UKN. *The Way Out* (USA) prod/rel: Merton Park, Anglo-Amalgamated

GRAESER, ERDMANN
Lemkes Sel. Witwe, Novel
Lemkes Sel. Witwe 1928 d: Carl Boese. lps: Lissi Arna, Fritz Kampers, Margarete Kupfer. 2484m GRM. *Lemke's Blessed Widow* prod/rel: Carl Boese-Film

GRAEVE, OSCAR
You Just Can't Wait, 1918, Short Story
Home Town Girl, The 1919 d: Robert G. VignolA. lps: Vivian Martin, Ralph Graves, Lee Phelps. 5r USA. *You Just Can't Wait* prod/rel: Famous Players-Lasky Corp.©, Paramount Pictures

GRAF, OSKAR MARIA
Story
Triumph Der Gerechten 1987 d: Josef Bierbichler. lps: Josef Bierbichler, Rudi Klaffenbock, Alfons Scharf. 81M GRM. prod/rel: Bierbichler Filmproduktion

Das Bayrische Dekameron, 1928, Novel
Glocklein Unterm Himmelbett, Das 1970 d: Hans Heinrich. lps: Hansi Kraus, Christine Schubert, Ralf Wolter. 84M GRM. *The Bell Beneath the Fourposter* prod/rel: Franz Seitz, Terra

Bolwieser, 1931, Novel
Bolwieser 1977 d: R. W. Fassbinder. lps: Kurt Raab, Elisabeth Trissenaar, Bernhard Helferich. 200M GRM. prod/rel: Bavaria ZDF, Filmverlag Der Autoren

GRAFF, SIGMUND
Die Vier Musketiere, Play
Vier Musketiere, Die 1935 d: Heinz Paul. lps: Hans Brausewetter, Fritz Kampers, Paul Westermeier. 119M GRM. *The Four Musketeers* (USA) prod/rel: Terra-Film

GRAFTON, EDITH
Investigation, Story
System, The 1953 d: Lewis Seiler. lps: Frank Lovejoy, Joan Weldon, Robert Arthur. 90M USA. prod/rel: Warner Bros.

GRAFTON, SAMUEL
System, The 1953 d: Lewis Seiler. lps: Frank Lovejoy, Joan Weldon, Robert Arthur. 90M USA. prod/rel: Warner Bros.

GRAGNON, ALFRED
L' Attentat de la Maison Rouge, Play
Attentat de la Maison Rouge, L' 1917 d: Gaston Silvestre. lps: Jean Worms, Andre Marnay, Guerard. 1297m FRN. prod/rel: Films Gaston Silvestre

L' Enigmatique Gentleman, Play
Secret de l'Emeralde, Le 1936 d: Maurice de Canonge. lps: Maurice Lagrenee, Colette Broido, Rene Ferte. 84M FRN. *L' Enigmatique Gentleman* prod/rel: Lutece-Film

Grey Contre X, Short Story
Grey Contre X 1939 d: Pierre Maudru, Alfred Gragnon. lps: Maurice Lagrenee, Pierre Stephen, Jeanne Helbling. 85M FRN. *Inspecteur Grey Contre X* prod/rel: Paris-Clichy Films

La Treizieme Enquete de Grey, Play
Treizieme Enquete de Grey, La 1937 d: Pierre Maudru. lps: Maurice Lagrenee, Paule Dagreve, Raymond Cordy. 85M FRN. prod/rel: Films Regent

GRAHAM, CAROLINE
The Killings at Badgers Drift, Novel
Midsomer Murders: the Killings at Badgers Drift 1998 d: Jeremy Silberston. lps: John Nettles, Daniel Casey, Jane Wymark. TVM. 120M UKN. prod/rel: Bentley Prods., a & E Network

GRAHAM, CARROLL
Border Town, New York 1934, Novel
Bordertown 1935 d: Archie Mayo. lps: Paul Muni, Bette Davis, Eugene Pallette. 89M USA. *New Bordertown* prod/rel: Warner Bros. Productions

GRAHAM, GORDON
The Boys, Play
Boys, The 1998 d: Rowan Woods. lps: David Wenham, Toni Collette, Lynette Curran. 85M ASL/UKN. prod/rel: Arenafilm©, Australian Film Commission©

GRAHAM, H.
Little Miss Nobody, London 1898, Musical Play
Little Miss Nobody 1923 d: Wilfred Noy. lps: Flora Le Breton, John Stuart, Ben Field. 5750f UKN. prod/rel: Carlton Productions, Butcher's Film Service

GRAHAM, HARRY
Toni, London 1924, Musical Play
Toni 1928 d: Arthur Maude. lps: Jack Buchanan, Dorothy Boyd, W. Lawson Butt. 5548f UKN. prod/rel: British International Pictures, Wardour

GRAHAM, JAMES
The Wrath of God, Novel
Wrath of God, The 1972 d: Ralph Nelson. lps: Robert Mitchum, Ken Hutchison, Victor Buono. 111M USA. prod/rel: Rainbow, Cinema

GRAHAM, JOHN
Play
Hexenschuss 1987 d: Franz J. Gottlieb. lps: Susanne Uhlen, Helmut Fischer, Herbert Herrmann. 60M GRM. prod/rel: Regina Ziegler Prod., ZDF

Jede Menge Schmidt, Play
Jede Menge Schmidt 1989 d: Franz J. Gottlieb. lps: Helmut Fischer, Anja Schute, Jurgen Thormann. 60M GRM. prod/rel: Regina Ziegler Prod., ZDF

GRAHAM, ROBIN LEE
The Dove, Book
Dove, The 1974 d: Charles Jarrott. lps: Timothy Bottoms, Deborah Raffin, John McLiam. 105M USA/UKN. prod/rel: Paramount

GRAHAM, SHEILAH (1904–1988), UKN
Beloved Infidel, Book
Beloved Infidel 1959 d: Henry King. lps: Gregory Peck, Deborah Kerr, Eddie Albert. 123M USA. prod/rel: 20th Century-Fox, Jerry Wald

GRAHAM, WINIFRED
The Love Story of a Mormon, Novel
Trapped By the Mormons 1922 d: H. B. Parkinson. lps: Evelyn Brent, Lewis Willoughby, Ward McAllister. 6200f UKN. *The Mormon Peril* prod/rel: Master Films, White

GRAHAM, WINSTON (1911–, UKN
Fortune Is a Woman, Novel
Fortune Is a Woman 1957 d: Sidney Gilliat. lps: Jack Hawkins, Arlene Dahl, Dennis Price. 95M UKN. *She Played With Fire* (USA) prod/rel: Columbia, Launder-Gilliat

Marnie, London 1961, Novel
Marnie 1964 d: Alfred Hitchcock. lps: Sean Connery, Tippi Hedren, Diane Baker. 130M USA. prod/rel: Geoffrey Stanley, Inc., Universal

Night Without Stars, Novel
Night Without Stars 1951 d: Anthony Pelissier. lps: David Farrar, Nadia Gray, Maurice Teynac. 86M UKN. prod/rel: Europa, General Film Distributors

Poldark, Novel
Poldark 1996 d: Richard Laxton. lps: Mel Martin, Michael Attwell, Joan Gruffudd. TVM. 102M UKN.

Poldark: Series 1 and 2 1975 d: Paul Annett, Christopher Barry. lps: Robin Ellis, Angharad Rees, Jill Townsend. MTV. 1376M UKN.

The Sleeping Partner, London 1961, Novel
Carnival of Crime 1961 d: George M. Cahan. lps: Jean-Pierre Aumont, Alix Talton, Tonia Carrero. 83M USA. *Sleeping Partners*

The Walking Stick, London 1967, Novel
Walking Stick, The 1970 d: Eric Till. lps: David Hemmings, Samantha Eggar, Emlyn Williams. 101M UKN. prod/rel: Winkast Film Productions, Gershwin

GRAHAME, KENNETH (1859–1932), UKN
The Wind in the Willows, 1908, Novel
Ichabod and Mr. Toad 1949 d: James Algar, Jack Kinney. ANM. 68M USA. *The Adventures of Ichabod and Mr. Toad* prod/rel: RKO Radio, Walt Disney

Wind in the Willows 1949 d: James Algar, Jack Kinney. ANM. 33M USA.

Wind in the Willows, The 1983 d: Brian Cosgrove, Mark Hall. ANM. 78M UKN.

Wind in the Willows, The 1983 d: Arthur Rankin Jr., Jules Bass. ANM. 97M USA.

Wind in the Willows, The 1984 d: Jackie Cockle. ANM. 78M UKN.

Wind in the Willows, The 1996 d: Dave Unwin. ANM. 78M UKN.

Wind in the Willows, The 1996 d: Terry Jones. lps: Steve Coogan, Eric Idle, Terry Jones. 87M UKN. prod/rel: Allied Filmmakers, N.V., Guild

GRAHAME, RONALD
Queen of the Wicked, Play
Queen of the Wicked 1916 d: Albert Ward. lps: Henry Lonsdale, Nina Lynn, Janet Alexander. 5500f UKN. prod/rel: British Empire Films

GRAMANTIERI, TULLO
La Fornarina, Novel
Fornarina, La 1944 d: Enrico Guazzoni. lps: Lida Baarova, Walter Lazzaro, Annaliese Uhlig. 96M ITL. prod/rel: E.I.a., Mediterranea Film

GRAMEGNA, L.
I Dragoni Azzurri, Novel
Pietro Micca 1938 d: Aldo Vergano, Pietro Scharoff. lps: Guido Celano, Renato Cialente, Mino Doro. 90M ITL. prod/rel: Taurinia Film, C.I.N.F.

GRAMMATICUS, SAXO
Book
Prinsen Af Jylland 1994 d: Gabriel Axel. lps: Christian Bale, Gabriel Byrne, Helen Mirren. 107M DNM/FRN/UKN. *Prince of Jutland* prod/rel: Allarts, Ariane

GRANADA, JOSE MARIA
El Nino de Oro, Play
Nino de Oro, El 1925 d: Jose Maria GranadA. lps: Jose Maria Granada, Inocencia Alcubierre, Fernando Fresno. F SPN. prod/rel: Antonio De Portago

GRANCHER, MARCEL-ERIC
Le Charcutier de MacHonville, Novel
Charcutier de MacHonville, Le 1946 d: Vicky Ivernel. lps: Bach, Felix Oudart, Milly Mathis. 95M FRN. prod/rel: Amon Films

Feysse Sur Mer, Novel
Coeur-Sur-Mer 1950 d: Jacques Daniel-Norman. lps: Andre Claveau, Daisy Daix, Pauline Carton. 105M FRN. prod/rel: Roy-Films

GRAND, GORDON
Major Denning's Trust Estate, Story
Sport of Kings 1947 d: Robert Gordon. lps: Paul Campbell, Gloria Henry, Harry Davenport. 68M USA. *Heart Royal* (UKN) prod/rel: Columbia

GRANDES, ALMUDENA
Malena Es un Nombre de Tango, Novel
Malena Es un Nombre de Tango 1996 d: Gerardo Herrero. lps: Ariadna Gil, Marta Belaustegui, Carlos Lopez. 109M SPN/FRN/GRM. *Malena Is a Name from a Tango* prod/rel: Alta, Tornasol

GRANGE, EUGENE
Le Bapteme du Petit Oscar, Play
Bapteme du Petit Oscar, Le 1932 d: Jean Dreville. lps: Rene Donnio, Charles Lorrain, A. Ternet. 1200m FRN.

Les Crochets du Pere Martin, 1858, Play
Gerla Di Papa Martin, La 1909 d: Mario Caserini. 314m ITL. *A Father's Heart* (UKN); *Honour Thy Father* prod/rel: Cines
Gerla Di Papa Martin, La 1914 d: Eleuterio Rodolfi. lps: Ermete Novelli, Gigetta Morano, Umberto Scalpellini. 823m ITL. prod/rel: S.A. Ambrosio
Gerla Di Papa Martin, La 1923 d: Mario Bonnard. lps: Francesco Amodio, Amalia Raspantini, Giuseppe Amato. 1795m ITL. prod/rel: Caesar Film
Gerla Di Papa Martin, La 1940 d: Mario Bonnard. lps: Ruggero Ruggeri, Germana Paolieri, Bella Starace Sainati. 94M ITL. prod/rel: Lux Film

La Voleuse d'Enfants, Play
Voleuse d'Enfants, La 1912 d: Georges DenolA. lps: Georges Saillard, Lucie Brille. 745m FRN. prod/rel: Scagl

GRANGER, ROBERT A.
Ten Against Caesar, 1952, Story
Gun Fury 1953 d: Raoul Walsh. lps: Rock Hudson, Donna Reed, Philip Carey. 83M USA. prod/rel: Columbia

GRANICHSTAEDTEN, BRUNO
Die Konigin, Play
Queen's Affair, The 1934 d: Herbert Wilcox. lps: Anna Neagle, Fernand Gravey, Muriel Aked. 77M UKN. *Runaway Queen* (USA); *The Queen* prod/rel: British and Dominions, United Artists

Der Orlow, Operetta
Diamant Des Zaren, Der 1932 d: Max Neufeld. lps: Liane Haid, Ivan Petrovich, Viktor de KowA. 89M GRM. *Der Orlow* prod/rel: Sokal, Karp
Orlow, Der 1927 d: Jacob Fleck, Luise Fleck. lps: Ivan Petrovich, Vivian Gibson, Evi EvA. 2553m GRM. *Hearts and Diamonds* prod/rel: Hegewald-Film

GRANIER, DOMINIQUE
La Femme Publique, Novel
Femme Publique, La 1984 d: Andrzej Zulawski. lps: Francis Huster, Valerie Kaprisky, Lambert Wilson. 115M FRN. *The Public Woman* prod/rel: Hachette-Fox

GRANT, JAMES EDWARD
Story
Proud Rebel, The 1958 d: Michael Curtiz. lps: Alan Ladd, Olivia de Havilland, David Ladd. 103M USA. prod/rel: Buena Vista, Formosa Prods.

Big Brown Eyes, 1935, Short Story
Big Brown Eyes 1936 d: Raoul Walsh. lps: Joan Bennett, Cary Grant, Walter Pidgeon. 77M USA. prod/rel: Walter Wanger Productions

Full Measure, 1934, Short Story
Great Guy 1936 d: John G. Blystone. lps: James Cagney, Mae Clarke, James Burke. 75M USA. *Pluck of the Irish* (UKN) prod/rel: Grand National Films©, Douglas Maclean Productions

The Green Shadow, New York 1935, Novel
Muss 'Em Up 1936 d: Charles Vidor. lps: Preston Foster, Margaret Callahan, Alan Mowbray. 70M USA. *House of Fate* (UKN); *The Green Shadow*; *Sinister House* prod/rel: RKO Radio Pictures©, Pandro S. Berman Production

Hahsit Babe, 1935, Short Story
Big Brown Eyes 1936 d: Raoul Walsh. lps: Joan Bennett, Cary Grant, Walter Pidgeon. 77M USA. prod/rel: Walter Wanger Productions

Johnny Cave Goes Subtle, 1934, Short Story
Great Guy 1936 d: John G. Blystone. lps: James Cagney, Mae Clarke, James Burke. 75M USA. *Pluck of the Irish* (UKN) prod/rel: Grand National Films©, Douglas Maclean Productions

A Lady Comes to Burkburnett, 1939, Short Story
Boom Town 1940 d: Jack Conway. lps: Clark Gable, Spencer Tracy, Claudette Colbert. 117M USA. prod/rel: Metro-Goldwyn-Mayer Corp.

Larceny on the Right, 1934, Short Story
Great Guy 1936 d: John G. Blystone. lps: James Cagney, Mae Clarke, James Burke. 75M USA. *Pluck of the Irish* (UKN) prod/rel: Grand National Films©, Douglas Maclean Productions

Lefty Farrell, Novel
Two of a Kind 1951 d: Henry Levin. lps: Alexander Knox, Edmond O'Brien, Terry Moore. 75M USA. *Lefty Farrell* prod/rel: Columbia

The Whipsaw, 1934, Short Story
Whipsaw 1935 d: Sam Wood. lps: Myrna Loy, Spencer Tracy, Harvey Stephens. 84M USA. *Unexpected Bride* prod/rel: Metro-Goldwyn-Mayer Corp.©

GRANT, MARIAN
Queen's Local, Play
Hunted Men 1938 d: Louis King. lps: Lloyd Nolan, J. Carrol Naish, Lynne Overman. 65M USA. *Crime Gives Orders* prod/rel: Paramount Pictures©

GRANT, MAXWELL
The Fox Hound, Short Story
International Crime 1938 d: Charles Lamont. lps: Rod La Rocque, Astrid Allwyn, Thomas Jackson. 65M USA. *The Shadow Speaks*; *The Shadow Murder Case* prod/rel: Colony Pictures, Grand National Films©

The Ghost of the Manor, 1933, Short Story
Shadow Strikes, The 1937 d: Lynn Shores. lps: Rod La Rocque, Lynn Anders, James Blakely. 61M USA. *The Shadow*; *Womantrap*; *Mr. Shadow* prod/rel: Colony Pictures, Grand National Films©

GRANT, NEIL
Dusty Ermine, London 1935, Play
Dusty Ermine 1936 d: Bernard Vorhaus. lps: Ronald Squire, Anthony Bushell, Jane Baxter. 84M UKN. *Hideout in the Alps* (USA); *Rendezvous in the Alps* prod/rel: Wardour, Twickenham

The Nelson Touch, London 1931, Play
His Lordship 1936 d: Herbert Mason. lps: George Arliss, Rene Ray, Romilly Lunge. 71M UKN. *Man of Affairs* (USA); *Man of Affaires*; *The Nelson Touch* prod/rel: Gaumont-British

GRANVILLE-BARKER, HARLEY (1877–1946), UKN
Prunella Or Love in a Dutch Garden, London 1904, Play
Prunella 1918 d: Maurice Tourneur. lps: Marguerite Clark, Jules Raucourt, Henry Leone. 4742f USA. prod/rel: Famous Players-Lasky Corp.©, Paramount Pictures

GRASS, GUNTER (1927–, GRM, Grass, Gunter Wilhelm
Die Blechtrommel, 1959, Novel
Blechtrommel, Die 1979 d: Volker Schlondorff. lps: David Bennent, Mario Adorf, Angela Winkler. 142M GRM/FRN. *Le Tambour* (FRN); *The Tin Drum* (UKN) prod/rel: Franz Seitz, Argos

Katz Und Maus, Neuwid Am Rhein 1961, Short Story
Katz Und Maus 1967 d: Hansjurgen Pohland. lps: Lars Brandt, Peter Brandt, Wolfgang Neuss. 88M GRM/PLN. *Kot I Mysz* (PLN); *Cat and Mouse* (USA) prod/rel: Modern Art, Zespol Rytm

GRASSO SR., GIOVANNI
Dodici Anni Dopo, 1917, Play
Mala Pasqua 1919 d: Ignazio Lupi. lps: Giovanni Grasso Sr., Linda Moglia, Tina SommA. 1295m ITL. *Sei Anni Dopo*; *A Te la Mala Pasqua!* prod/rel: Poli Film

GRATIX, F. DAWSON
He and Ski, Novel
Olympic Honeymoon 1936 d: Alf Goulding. lps: Claude Hulbert, Monty Banks, Princess Pearl. 64M UKN. *Honeymoon Merry-Go-Round* prod/rel: Fanfare, Associated Talking Pictures

GRAVES, ROBERT (1895–1985), UKN
Claudius the God, 1934, Novel
I, Claudius 1976 d: Herbert Wise. lps: Derek Jacobi, Sian Phillips, Brian Blessed. MTV. 652M UKN.

I Claudius, 1934, Novel
I, Claudius 1976 d: Herbert Wise. lps: Derek Jacobi, Sian Phillips, Brian Blessed. MTV. 652M UKN.

The Shout, 1929, Short Story
Shout, The 1978 d: Jerzy Skolimowski. lps: Alan Bates, Susannah York, John Hurt. 87M UKN. prod/rel: Rank, Recorded Picture

GRAY, BERKELEY
Daredevil Conquest, Novel
Park Plaza 605 1953 d: Bernard Knowles. lps: Tom Conway, Eva Bartok, Joy Shelton. 75M UKN. *Norman Conquest* (USA) prod/rel: B & a Productions, Eros

GRAY, DAMIEN
The Florentine, Play
Florentine, The 1999 d: Nick Stagliano. lps: Michael Madsen, Chris Penn, Jeremy Davies. 104M USA. prod/rel: Initial Entertainment Group, American Zoetrope

GRAY, DAVID
The Best People, New York 1924, Play
Best People, The 1925 d: Sidney Olcott. lps: Warner Baxter, Esther Ralston, Kathlyn Williams. 5700f USA. prod/rel: Famous Players-Lasky Corp., Paramount Pictures
Fast and Loose 1930 d: Fred Newmeyer. lps: Miriam Hopkins, Carole Lombard, Frank Morgan. 75M USA. *The Best People* prod/rel: Paramount-Publix Corp.

GRAY, GEORGE
The Fighting Parson, Play
Fighting Parson, The 1912 d: Bert Haldane, George Gray. lps: George Gray. 3000f UKN. prod/rel: Barker, Jury

GRAY, MAXWELL
The Last Sentence, London 1893, Novel
Last Sentence, The 1917 d: Ben Turbett. lps: Marc MacDermott, Miriam Nesbitt, Grace Williams. 5r USA. prod/rel: Thomas A. Edison, Inc.©, K-E-S-E Service

The Reproach of Annesley, Novel
Reproach of Annesley, The 1915. lps: Franklin Ritchie, Louise Vale, Herbert Barrington. 3r USA. prod/rel: Biograph Co.

The Silence of Dean Maitland, New York 1886, Novel
Sealed Lips 1915 d: John Ince. lps: William Courtenay, Arthur Ashley, Mary Charleson. 5r USA. *The Silence of Dean Maitland* prod/rel: Equitable Motion Pictures Corp.©, World Film Corp.

GRAY, SIMON (1936–, UKN
Butley, 1971, Play
Butley 1973 d: Harold Pinter. lps: Alan Bates, Jessica Tandy, Richard O'Callaghan. 130M UKN/USA. prod/rel: American Express, Ely Landau

The Common Pursuit, 1984, Play
Common Pursuit 1991 d: Christopher Morahan. lps: James Fleet, Stephen Fry, Stella Gonet. TVM. 85M UKN. prod/rel: BBC Tv, BBC Films for Screen Two

GRAY, THOMAS (1716–1771), UKN
Elegy Written in a Country Churchyard, 1751, Poem
Restless Spirit, The 1913 d: Allan Dwan. lps: J. Warren Kerrigan, Pauline Bush, George Periolat. 3r USA. prod/rel: Victor

GRAY, WILLIAM B.
The Volunteer Organist, New York 1902, Novel
Volunteer Organist, The 1913?. 8r USA. prod/rel: Volunteer Organist Co., State Rights

GRAZIANO, ROCKY (1921–1990), USA, Barbella, Thomas Rocco
1955, Autobiography
Somebody Up There Likes Me 1956 d: Robert Wise. lps: Paul Newman, Pier Angeli, Everett Sloane. 113M USA. prod/rel: MGM

GREDSTED, TORRY
Der Indianerjunge Paw, Cologne 1931, Novel
Paw 1959 d: Astrid Henning-Jensen. lps: Jimmy Sterman, Edvin Adolphson, Ninja Tholstrup. 100M DNM. *The Lure of the Jungle*; *Boy of the World*; *Boy of Two Worlds* (USA) prod/rel: Laterna

GREDY, JEAN-PIERRE
Ami-Ami
Femmes Sont Marrantes, Les 1958 d: Andre Hunebelle. lps: Micheline Presle, Yves Robert, Pierre Dudan. 75M FRN. *Women are Talkative* (USA) prod/rel: P.A.C., U.G.C./ P.A.C.

Le Don d'Adele, Play
Don d'Adele, Le 1950 d: Emile Couzinet. lps: Charles Dechamps, Marguerite Pierry, Marcel Vallee. 93M FRN. prod/rel: Burgus Films

Forty Carats, Play
Forty Carats 1973 d: Milton Katselas. lps: Liv Ullmann, Edward Albert, Gene Kelly. 108M USA. *40 Carats* prod/rel: Frankovich

GREEN, ADOLPH
The Bells are Ringing, Musical Play
Bells are Ringing, The 1960 d: Vincente Minnelli. lps: Judy Holliday, Dean Martin, Fred Clark. 125M USA. prod/rel: Metro-Goldwyn-Mayer Corp.

On the Town, Musical Play
On the Town 1949 d: Gene Kelly, Stanley Donen. lps: Gene Kelly, Frank Sinatra, Jules Munshin. 98M USA. prod/rel: MGM

GREEN, ALAN
Beauty and the Beat, 1936, Short Story
Love on the Run 1936 d: W. S. Van Dyke. lps: Joan Crawford, Clark Gable, Franchot Tone. 80M USA. prod/rel: Metro-Goldwyn-Mayer Corp.©

GREEN, ANNA KATHARINE (1846–1935), USA
The Leavenworth Case, New York 1878, Novel
  Leavenworth Case, The 1923 d: Charles Giblyn. lps: Seena Owen, Martha Mansfield, Wilfred Lytell. 5400f USA. prod/rel: Whitman Bennett Productions

  Leavenworth Case, The 1936 d: Lewis D. Collins. lps: Donald Cook, Norman Foster, Erin O'Brien-Moore. 68M USA. prod/rel: Republic Pictures Corp.©

The Mayor's Wife, Indianapolis 1907, Novel
  His Wife's Husband 1922 d: Kenneth Webb. lps: Betty Blythe, Huntley Gordon, Arthur Edmund Carewe. 6092f USA. prod/rel: Pyramid Pictures, American Releasing Corp.

A Strange Disappearance, Novel
  Strange Disappearance, A 1915 d: George A. Lessey. lps: King Baggot, Jane Gail, Edna Hunter. 3r USA. prod/rel: Imp

GREEN, FREDERICK LAWRENCE (1902–1953), IRL
Odd Man Out, London 1945, Novel
  Lost Man, The 1969 d: Robert Alan Aurthur. lps: Sidney Poitier, Joanna Shimkus, Al Freeman Jr. 113M USA. *How Many Roads* prod/rel: Universal Pictures

  Odd Man Out 1947 d: Carol Reed. lps: James Mason, Robert Newton, Kathleen Ryan. 116M UKN. *Gang War* prod/rel: General Film Distributors, Two Cities

On the Night of the Fire, Novel
  On the Night of the Fire 1939 d: Brian Desmond Hurst. lps: Ralph Richardson, Diana Wynyard, Romney Brent. 94M UKN. *The Fugitive* (USA) prod/rel: General Film Distributors, G & S Films

GREEN, GEORGE DAWES
The Juror, Book
  Juror, The 1996 d: Brian Gibson. lps: Demi Moore, Alec Baldwin, Joseph Gordon-Levitt. 116M USA. prod/rel: Columbia

GREEN, GERALD
His Majesty O'Keefe, 1950, Novel
  His Majesty O'Keefe 1954 d: Byron Haskin. lps: Burt Lancaster, Joan Rice, Andre Morell. 90M UKN/USA. prod/rel: Warner Bros., First National

The Hostage Heart, Novel
  Hostage Heart, The 1977 d: Bernard McEveety. lps: Bradford Dillman, Vic Morrow, Cameron Mitchell. TVM. 100M USA. prod/rel: Andrew J. Fenady Associates

The Last Angry Man, 1956, Novel
  Last Angry Man, The 1959 d: Daniel Mann. lps: Paul Muni, David Wayne, Betsy Palmer. 100M USA. prod/rel: Columbia, Fred Kohlmar Prods.

  Last Angry Man, The 1974 d: Jerrold Freedman. lps: Pat Hingle, Lynn Carlin, Paul JabarA. TVM. 78M USA. prod/rel: Screen Gems, Columbia

GREEN, HANNAH
I Never Promised You a Rose Garden, Novel
  I Never Promised You a Rose Garden 1977 d: Anthony Page. lps: Bibi Andersson, Kathleen Quinlan, Ben PiazzA. 96M USA. prod/rel: Imorh, Fadsin

GREEN, JANET
Matilda Shouted Fire, Play
  Midnight Lace 1960 d: David Miller. lps: Doris Day, Rex Harrison, John Gavin. 108M USA. prod/rel: Universal

Murder Mistaken, London 1952, Play
  Cast a Dark Shadow 1955 d: Lewis Gilbert. lps: Dirk Bogarde, Margaret Lockwood, Kay Walsh. 82M UKN. prod/rel: Frobisher, Eros

GREEN, JULIEN (1900–, FRN
Leviathan, 1929, Novel
  Leviathan 1966 d: Leonard Keigel. lps: Louis Jourdan, Lilli Palmer, Marie Laforet. 98M FRN. *The Footbridge* prod/rel: Films Du Valois

GREEN, PAUL (1894–1981), USA, Green, Paul Eliot
The House of Connelly, New York 1931, Play
  Carolina 1934 d: Henry King. lps: Janet Gaynor, Robert Young, Lionel Barrymore. 83M USA. *The House of Connelly* (UKN) prod/rel: Fox Film Corp.

GREEN, WALTON ATWATER
Corsair, New York 1931, Novel
  Corsair 1931 d: Roland West. lps: Chester Morris, Thelma Todd, Emmett Corrigan. 75M USA. prod/rel: United Artists Corp.

One of the Boston Bullertons, Short Story
  Private Affairs 1940 d: Albert S. Rogell. lps: Nancy Kelly, Robert Cummings, Hugh Herbert. 74M USA. *One of the Boston Bullertons* prod/rel: Universal Pictures Co.©

GREENAN, RUSSELL H.
The Secret Life of Algernon Pendleton, Novel
  Secret Life of Algernon, The 1997 d: Charles Jarrott. lps: John Cullum, Carrie-Anne Moss, Charles Durning. 104M CND. prod/rel: Marano Prods., Phare-Est Prods.

GREENBERG, DAN
Philly, Novel
  Private Lessons 1981 d: Alan Myerson. lps: Sylvia Kristel, Howard Hesseman, Eric Brown. 87M USA. *Philly* prod/rel: Barry & Enright

GREENBERG, JOANNE
In This Sign, Novel
  Love Is Never Silent 1985 d: Joseph Sargent. lps: Mare Winningham, Phyllis Frelich, Ed Waterstreet. TVM. 100M USA. *Shattered Silence* prod/rel: NBC, Teleprictures

GREENBURG, DAN
Kiss My Firm But Pliant Lips, New York 1965, Novel
  Live a Little, Love a Little 1968 d: Norman Taurog. lps: Elvis Presley, Michele Carey, Don Porter. 90M USA. prod/rel: Metro-Goldwyn-Mayer, Inc.

GREENE, BETTE
Summer of My German Soldier, Novel
  Summer of My German Soldier 1978 d: Michael Tuchner. lps: Kristy McNichol, Bruce Davison, Esther Rolle. TVM. 100M USA. prod/rel: Highgate Productions

GREENE, CLAY M.
Forgiven; Or the Jack of Diamonds, New York 1886, Play
  Forgiven; Or, the Jack of Diamonds 1914 d: William Robert Daly. lps: Edwin Forsberg, Caroline French, Hector Dion. 6-7r USA. *The Jack O'Diamonds Forgiven; Or* prod/rel: Stellar Photoplay Co., State Rights

Pawn Ticket No. 210, Play
  Pawn Ticket 210 1922 d: Scott R. Dunlap. lps: Shirley Mason, Irene Hunt, Jake Abraham. 4871f USA. prod/rel: Fox Film Corp.

GREENE, FRANCES NIMMO
The Devil to Pay, New York 1918, Novel
  Devil to Pay, The 1920 d: Ernest C. Warde. lps: Roy Stewart, Robert McKim, Fritzi Brunette. 6r USA. prod/rel: Robert Brunton Productions, Pathe Exchange, Inc.©

One Clear Call, New York 1914, Novel
  One Clear Call 1922 d: John M. Stahl. lps: Milton Sills, Claire Windsor, Henry B. Walthall. 7450f USA. prod/rel: Louis B. Mayer Productions, Associated First National Pictures

GREENE, GRAHAM (1904–1991), UKN, Greene, Henry Graham
Short Story
  Four Dark Hours 1937 d: William Cameron Menzies. lps: John Mills, Rene Ray, Robert Newton. 65M UKN. *The Green Cockatoo; Race Gang* prod/rel: 20th Century Fox, New World

  May We Borrow Your Husband? 1986 d: Bob Mahoney. lps: Dirk Bogarde, Charlotte Attenborough, Simon Shepherd. TVM. 105M UKN.

Across the Bridge, 1947, Short Story
  Across the Bridge 1957 d: Ken Annakin. lps: Rod Steiger, David Knight, Marla Landi. 103M UKN. *Across the Forbidden Bridge to Mexico* prod/rel: Rank Film Distributors, Ipf

The Basement Room, 1935, Short Story
  Fallen Idol, The 1948 d: Carol Reed. lps: Ralph Richardson, Michele Morgan, Sonia Dresdel. 95M UKN. *The Lost Illusion* prod/rel: British Lion, London Films

Brighton Rock, 1938, Novel
  Brighton Rock 1947 d: John Boulting. lps: Richard Attenborough, Hermione Baddeley, William Hartnell. 91M UKN. *Young Scarface* (UKN) prod/rel: Associated British Picture Corporation, Charter Films

The Comedians, New York 1966, Novel
  Comedians, The 1967 d: Peter Glenville. lps: Richard Burton, Elizabeth Taylor, Peter Ustinov. 160M USA/FRN. *Les Comediens* (FRN) prod/rel: MGM, Maximilian

The Confidential Agent, 1939, Novel
  Confidential Agent 1945 d: Herman Shumlin. lps: Charles Boyer, Lauren Bacall, Katina Paxinou. 118M USA. prod/rel: Warner Bros.

Dr. Fischer of Geneva; Or the Bomb Party, 1980, Novel
  Dr. Fischer of Geneva 1983 d: Michael Lindsay-Hogg. lps: James Mason, Alan Bates, Greta Scacchi. TVM. 110M UKN. prod/rel: BBC

The End of the Affair, 1951, Novel
  End of the Affair, The 1955 d: Edward Dmytryk. lps: Deborah Kerr, Van Johnson, John Mills. 105M UKN. prod/rel: Coronado, Columbia

England Made Me, 1935, Novel
  England Made Me 1972 d: Peter Duffell. lps: Peter Finch, Michael York, Hildegard Neil. 100M UKN/USA/YGS. *The Rape of the Third Reich* prod/rel: Atlantic, Hemdale

A Gun for Sale, 1936, Novel
  Short Cut to Hell 1957 d: James Cagney. lps: Robert Ivers, Georgann Johnson, William Bishop. 89M USA. prod/rel: Paramount

  This Gun for Hire 1942 d: Frank Tuttle. lps: Alan Ladd, Veronica Lake, Robert Preston. 80M USA. prod/rel: Paramount

The Heart of the Matter, 1948, Novel
  Heart of the Matter, The 1953 d: George M. O'Ferrall. lps: Trevor Howard, Elizabeth Allan, Maria Schell. 105M UKN. prod/rel: London Films, British Lion Production Assets

  Heart of the Matter, The 1983 d: Marco Leto. lps: Jack Hedley, Erica Rogers, Manfred Seipold. MTV. 260M UKN/GRM. *Il Nocciolo Della Questione* prod/rel: Channel Four, Tele-Munchen

The Honorary Consul, 1973, Novel
  Beyond the Limit 1983 d: John MacKenzie. lps: Michael Caine, Richard Gere, Bob Hoskins. 104M UKN. *The Honorary Consul* prod/rel: World Film Services, Film Writers Co.

The Human Factor, 1978, Novel
  Human Factor, The 1979 d: Otto Preminger. lps: Nicol Williamson, Iman, Derek Jacobi. 115M UKN. prod/rel: Rank, Wheel

The Lieutenant Died Last, 1940, Short Story
  Went the Day Well? 1942 d: Alberto Cavalcanti. lps: Leslie Banks, Elizabeth Allan, Frank Lawton. 92M UKN. *48 Hours* (USA) prod/rel: Ealing Studios, United Artists

Loser Takes All, 1955, Novel
  Loser Takes All 1956 d: Ken Annakin. lps: Glynis Johns, Rossano Brazzi, Robert Morley. 88M UKN. prod/rel: British Lion, Independent Film Producers

  Loser Takes All 1989 d: James Scott. lps: Robert Lindsay, Molly Ringwald, John Gielgud. 87M UKN. *Strike It Rich* (USA); *Money Talks* prod/rel: Miramax, British Screen

The Man Within, 1929, Novel
  Man Within, The 1947 d: Bernard Knowles. lps: Michael Redgrave, Jean Kent, Joan Greenwood. 90M UKN. *The Smugglers* (USA) prod/rel: General Film Distributors, Production Film Service

Ministry of Fear, 1943, Novel
  Ministry of Fear 1944 d: Fritz Lang. lps: Ray Milland, Marjorie Reynolds, Carl Esmond. 85M USA. prod/rel: Paramount

Monsignor Quixote, 1982, Novel
  Monsignor Quixote 1985 d: Rodney Bennett. 135M UKN.

Our Man in Havana, 1958, Novel
  Our Man in Havana 1960 d: Carol Reed. lps: Alec Guinness, Burl Ives, Maureen O'HarA. 111M UKN. prod/rel: Columbia, Kingsmead

The Potting Shed, 1957, Play
  Potting Shed, The 1981 d: David Cunliffe. lps: Celia Johnson, Paul Scofield, Anna Massey. MTV. 50M UKN. prod/rel: Ytv

The Power and the Glory, 1940, Novel
  Fugitive, The 1946 d: John Ford, Emilio Fernandez. lps: Henry Fonda, Dolores Del Rio, J. Carrol Naish. 104M USA/MXC. *El Fugitivo* (MXC) prod/rel: RKO Radio

  Power and the Glory, The 1961 d: Marc Daniels. lps: Laurence Olivier, Julie Harris, George C. Scott. MTV. 98M USA. prod/rel: Talent, Paramount

The Quiet American, 1955, Novel
  Quiet American, The 1958 d: Joseph L. Mankiewicz. lps: Audie Murphy, Michael Redgrave, Claude Dauphin. 122M USA. prod/rel: United Artists, Figaro, Inc.

A Shocking Accident, 1967, Short Story
  Shocking Accident, A 1983 d: James Scott. lps: Rupert Everett, Jenny Seagrove, Barbara Hicks. 25M UKN.

Stamboul Train, London 1932, Novel
  Orient Express 1934 d: Paul Martin. lps: Norman Foster, Heather Angel, Dorothy Burgess. 72M USA. *Stamboul Train* (UKN); *Seven Lives Were Changed* prod/rel: Fox Film Corp.©

The Stranger's Hand, Novel
  Mano Dello Straniero, La 1954 d: Mario Soldati. lps: Alida Valli, Trevor Howard, Eduardo Ciannelli. 98M ITL/UKN. *The Stranger's Hand* (UKN) prod/rel: Independent Film Producers, British Lion

The Tenth Man, Novel
  Tenth Man, The 1988 d: Jack Gold. lps: Anthony Hopkins, Kristin Scott-Thomas, Derek Jacobi. TVM. 100M UKN.

The Third Man, 1950, Novel
  Third Man, The 1949 d: Carol Reed. lps: Joseph Cotten, Alida Valli, Orson Welles. 104M UKN. prod/rel: British Lion Production Assets, London Films

Travels With My Aunt, 1969, Novel
Travels With My Aunt 1972 d: George Cukor. lps: Maggie Smith, Alec McCowen, Louis Gossett Jr. 109M UKN/USA. prod/rel: MGM

GREENE, HAROLD
Hide and Seek, Novel
Hide and Seek 1963 d: Cy Endfield. lps: Ian Carmichael, Janet Munro, Hugh Griffith. 90M UKN. prod/rel: Albion, Spectrum

GREENE, SARAH P. MCLEAN
Cape Cod Folks, Boston 1881, Novel
Women Who Give 1924 d: Reginald Barker. lps: Barbara Bedford, Frank Keenan, Renee Adoree. 7500f USA. *Women Who Wait* prod/rel: Louis B. Mayer Productions, Metro-Goldwyn Distributing Corp.

GREENE, WARD
Death in the Deep South, Harrisburg, PA. 1936, Novel
They Won't Forget 1937 d: Mervyn Leroy. lps: Claude Rains, Gloria Dickson, Otto Kruger. 90M USA. *In the Deep South; The Deep South; Death in the Deep South* prod/rel: Warner Bros. Pictures©, Mervyn Leroy Production
The Lady and the Tramp, 1953, Story
Lady and the Tramp 1955 d: Hamilton Luske, Clyde Geronimi. ANM. 75M USA. prod/rel: Walt Disney Prods., Buena Vista

GREENFIELD, IRVING A.
Tagget, Novel
Tagget 1991 d: Richard T. Heffron. lps: Daniel J. Travanti, Roxanne Hart, William Sadler. TVM. 100M USA. *Tagget: Dragonfire*

GREENWALD, HAROLD
Girl of the Night, Novel
Girl of the Night 1960 d: Joseph Cates. lps: Anne Francis, John Kerr, Lloyd Nolan. 87M USA. prod/rel: Vanguard

GREENWOOD, EDWIN
The Lake of Life, Play
East Meets West 1936 d: Herbert Mason. lps: George Arliss, Lucie Mannheim, Godfrey Tearle. 74M UKN. prod/rel: Gaumont-British

GREENWOOD, ROBERT
Mr. Bunting, Novel
Salute John Citizen 1942 d: Maurice Elvey. lps: Edward Rigby, Stanley Holloway, George Robey. 98M UKN. prod/rel: British National, Anglo-American
Mr. Bunting at War, Novel
Salute John Citizen 1942 d: Maurice Elvey. lps: Edward Rigby, Stanley Holloway, George Robey. 98M UKN. prod/rel: British National, Anglo-American

GREENWOOD, WALTER (1903–1974), UKN
Story
No Limit 1935 d: Monty Banks. lps: George Formby, Florence Desmond, Edward Rigby. 79M UKN. prod/rel: Associated Talking Pictures, Associated British Film Distributors
The Cure for Love, London 1945, Play
Cure for Love, The 1950 d: Robert Donat. lps: Robert Donat, Renee Asherson, Marjorie Rhodes. 98M UKN. prod/rel: London Films, Island Productions
Love on the Dole, Novel
Love on the Dole 1941 d: John Baxter. lps: Deborah Kerr, Clifford Evans, Joyce Howard. 100M UKN. prod/rel: Anglo, British National

GREGOR, ARTHUR
Play
What Price Decency? 1933 d: Arthur Gregor. lps: Dorothy Burgess, Walter Byron, Alan Hale. 67M USA. prod/rel: Equitable Pictures, Majestic Pictures Corp.

GREGOR, MANFRED
Die Brucke, Vienna 1958, Novel
Brucke, Die 1959 d: Bernhard Wicki. lps: Volker Bohnet, Fritz Wepper, Michael Hinz. 100M GRM. *The Bridge* (USA) prod/rel: Fono, D.F.H.
Das Urteil, Vienna 1960, Novel
Stadt Ohne Mitleid 1961 d: Gottfried Reinhardt. lps: E. G. Marshall, Robert Blake, Richard Jaeckel. 112M GRM/SWT/USA. *Ville Sans Pitie* (SWT); *Town Without Pity* (USA); *Shocker* prod/rel: Mirisch Corporation, Gloria-Film

GREGORY, FRANK
Living Dangerously, London 1934, Play
Living Dangerously 1936 d: Herbert Brenon. lps: Otto Kruger, Leonora Corbett, Francis Lister. 72M UKN. prod/rel: British International Pictures, Wardour

GREGORY, JACKSON
Bells of San Juan, New York 1919, Novel
Bells of San Juan 1922 d: Scott R. Dunlap. lps: Buck Jones, Fritzi Brunette, Claude Peyton. 4587f USA. prod/rel: Fox Film Corp.

Desert Valley, New York 1921, Novel
Desert Valley 1926 d: Scott R. Dunlap. lps: Buck Jones, Virginia Brown Faire, Malcolm Waite. 4731f USA. prod/rel: Fox Film Corp.
The Everlasting Whisper, New York 1922, Novel
Everlasting Whisper, The 1925 d: John G. Blystone. lps: Tom Mix, Alice Calhoun, Robert Cain. 5611f USA. prod/rel: Fox Film Corp.
The Joyous Troublemaker, New York 1918, Novel
Joyous Troublemaker, The 1920 d: J. Gordon Edwards. lps: William Farnum, Louise Lovely, Henry J. Hebert. 6r USA. *The Joyous Troublemakers; The Joyous Trouble Maker; The Trouble Makers* prod/rel: Fox Film Corp., William Fox©
Judith of Blue Lake Ranch, New York 1919, Novel
Two Kinds of Women 1922 d: Colin Campbell. lps: Pauline Frederick, Thomas Santschi, Charles Clary. 6000f USA. prod/rel: R-C Pictures
Ladyfingers, New York 1920, Novel
Ladyfingers 1921 d: Bayard Veiller. lps: Bert Lytell, Ora Carew, Frank Elliott. 5304f USA. *Alias Ladyfingers* prod/rel: Metro Pictures
Luck, Short Story
Luck 1923 d: C. C. Burr. lps: Johnny Hines, Robert Edeson, Edmund Breese. 6442f USA. prod/rel: C. C. Burr, Mastodon Films
Man to Man, New York 1920, Novel
Man to Man 1922 d: Stuart Paton. lps: Harry Carey, Lillian Rich, Charles Le Moyne. 5629f USA. prod/rel: Universal Film Mfg. Co.
Mystery at Spanish Hacienda, Novel
Laramie Trail, The 1944 d: John English. lps: Robert Livingston, Smiley Burnette, Linda Brent. 55M USA. prod/rel: Republic
The Outlaw, New York 1914, Novel
Hearts and Spurs 1925 d: W. S. Van Dyke. lps: Buck Jones, Carole Lombard, William B. Davidson. 4600f USA. prod/rel: Fox Film Corp.
The Secret of Black Mountain, Short Story
Secret of Black Mountain, The 1917 d: Otto Hoffman. lps: Vola Vale, Philo McCullough, Charles Dudley. 4r USA. prod/rel: Falcon Features, General Film Co.©
Silver Slippers, 1916, Short Story
Man from Painted Post, The 1917 d: Joseph Henabery. lps: Douglas Fairbanks, Eileen Percy, Frank Campeau. 5r USA. *Fancy Jim Sherwood* prod/rel: Douglas Fairbanks Pictures Corp., Artcraft Pictures Corp.©
Six Feet Four, New York 1918, Novel
Six Feet Four 1919 d: Henry King. lps: William Russell, Vola Vale, Charles K. French. 6r USA. prod/rel: American Film Co.©, Pathe Exchange, Inc.
Under Handicap, New York 1914, Novel
Under Handicap 1917 d: Fred J. Balshofer. lps: Harold Lockwood, Anna Little, William Clifford. 8r USA. prod/rel: Yorke Film Corp., Metro Pictures Corp.©

GREGORY, STEPHEN
The Cormorant, Novel
Cormorant, The 1992 d: Peter Markham. lps: Ralph Fiennes, Helen Schlesinger, Thomas Williams. TVM. 88M UKN. prod/rel: Holmes Associates, BBC Wales

GREIG, MAYSIE
Peggy of Beacon Hill, Boston 1924, Novel
Love Gamble, The 1925 d: Edward J. Le Saint. lps: Lillian Rich, Robert Frazer, Pauline Garon. 6r USA. prod/rel: Banner Productions, Henry Ginsberg Distributing Corp.

GREINER, PETER
Kiez - Aufstieg Und Fall Eines Luden, Play
Kiez - Aufstieg Und Fall Eines Luden 1982 d: Walter Bockmayer, Rolf Buhrmann. lps: Wolf-Dietrich Sprenger, Katja Rupe, Brigitte Janner. 106M GRM. *Kiez* prod/rel: Entenprod., Neue Filmprod.

GREINZ, RUDOLF
Der Tyrann Gordian, Novel
Gordian, Der Tyrann 1937 d: Fred Sauer. lps: Weiss Ferdl, Paul Richter, Michael von Newlinski. 95M GRM. prod/rel: Westeuropaische Film

GRENDEL, FREDERIC
La Ceremonie, Paris 1951, Novel
Ceremony, The 1963 d: Laurence Harvey. lps: Laurence Harvey, Sarah Miles, Robert (3) Walker. 108M USA/SPN. *La Ceremonia* (SPN) prod/rel: United Artists Corp., Magla

GRENET-DANCOURT, E.
Le Voyage de Berluron, 1893
Viaggio Di Berluron, Il 1919 d: Camillo de Riso. lps: Camillo de Riso, Eugenia Cigoli, Achille de Riso. 1182m ITL. prod/rel: Caesar Film

GRENVILLE, KATE
Dreamhouse, Novel
Traps 1993 d: Pauline Chan. lps: Saskia Reeves, Robert Reynolds, Sami Frey. F ASL. prod/rel: J. Mcelroy Holdings

GRESHAM, WILLIAM LINDSAY (1909–1962), USA
Nightmare Alley, Novel
Nightmare Alley 1947 d: Edmund Goulding. lps: Tyrone Power, Joan Blondell, Coleen Gray. 111M USA. prod/rel: 20th Century-Fox

GREVENIUS, HERBERT
Krigsmans Erinran, Goteberg 1946, Play
Krigsmans Erinran 1947 d: Erik Faustman. lps: Elof Ahrle, Birgit Tengroth, Gunnar Bjornstrand. 84M SWD. *A Soldier's Duties* prod/rel: Ab Svensk Filmindustri
Lunchrasten, Goteborg 1949, Play
Cafe Lunchrasten 1954 d: Erik Faustman. lps: Stig Jarrel, Nils Hallberg, Eivor Landstrom. 80M SWD. *The Lunchbreak Cafe* prod/rel: Ab Sandrew-Produktion
Sonja, Stockholm 1927, Play
Sonja 1943 d: Erik Faustman. lps: Bengt Ekerot, Gunn Wallgren, Barbro Fleege. 79M SWD. prod/rel: Terrafilms Produktions Ab

GREW, WILLIAM A.
Nice Women, New York 1929, Play
Nice Women 1932 d: Edwin H. Knopf. lps: Sidney Fox, Frances Dee, Alan Mowbray. 72M USA. prod/rel: Universal Pictures Corp.©
The Sap, New York 1924, Play
Sap, The 1926 d: Erle C. Kenton. lps: Kenneth Harlan, Charles Conklin, Mary McAllister. 5519f USA. prod/rel: Warner Brothers Pictures
Sap, The 1929 d: Archie Mayo. lps: Edward Everett Horton, Alan Hale, Patsy Ruth Miller. 7150f USA. prod/rel: Warner Brothers Pictures

GREX, LEO
Stolen Death, Novel
Inspector Hornleigh on Holiday 1939 d: Walter Forde. lps: Gordon Harker, Alastair Sim, Linden Travers. 87M UKN. *Inspector Hornleigh on Vacation* prod/rel: 20th Century Productions, 20th Century-Fox

GREX, PAUL
Les Gosses Dans Les Ruines, Play
Gosses Dans Les Ruines, Les 1918 d: George Pearson. lps: Georges Colin, Simone Prevost, Emmy Lynn. 780m FRN.
Kiddies in the Ruins, The 1918 d: George Pearson. lps: Emmie Lynn, Hugh E. Wright, Georges Colin. 2600f UKN. prod/rel: Welsh, Pearson

GREY, CLIFFORD
For the Love of Mike, London 1931, Play
For the Love of Mike 1932 d: Monty Banks. lps: Bobby Howes, Constance Shotter, Arthur Riscoe. 86M UKN. prod/rel: British International Pictures, Wardour
Mister Cinders, London 1929, Musical Play
Mister Cinders 1934 d: Friedrich Zelnik. lps: Clifford Mollison, Zelma O'Neal, Kenneth Western. 72M UKN. prod/rel: British International Pictures, Wardour
Sally, New York 1920, Musical Play
Sally 1925 d: Alfred E. Green. lps: Colleen Moore, Lloyd Hughes, Leon Errol. 8636f USA. prod/rel: First National Pictures
Sally 1929 d: John Francis Dillon. lps: Marilyn Miller, Alexander Gray, Joe E. Brown. 9277f USA. prod/rel: First National Pictures

GREY, HARRY
The Hoods, Novel
Once Upon a Time in America 1983 d: Sergio Leone. lps: Robert de Niro, James Woods, Elizabeth McGovern. 227M USA/ITL. *C'era Una Volta in America* prod/rel: Warner Bros.
Portrait of a Mobster, New York 1958, Novel
Portrait of a Mobster 1961 d: Joseph Pevney. lps: Vic Morrow, Leslie Parrish, Peter Breck. 108M USA. prod/rel: Warner Bros. Pictures

GREY, MARTIN
For Those I Loved, Book
Au Nom de Tous Les Miens 1983 d: Robert Enrico. lps: Brigitte Fossey, Jacques Penot, Michael York. 150M FRN/CND. prod/rel: Producteurs Associes (Paris), T.F.1 Films Production (Paris)
For Those I Loved 1983 d: Robert Enrico. lps: Brigitte Fossey, Jacques Penot, Michael York. 150M FRN/CND. prod/rel: Producteurs Associes (Paris), T.F.1 Films Production (Paris)

GREY, ROMER
The Maverick Queen, 1953, Novel
Maverick Queen, The 1956 d: Joseph Kane. lps: Barbara Stanwyck, Barry Sullivan, Scott Brady. 92M USA. prod/rel: Republic

GREY, SCHUYLER E.
Love Your Body, Play
Search for Beauty 1934 d: Erle C. Kenton. lps: Buster Crabbe, Ida Lupino, Robert Armstrong. 77M USA. prod/rel: Paramount Productions©

GREY, UPTON
Yellow Corn, Novel
Cupid in Clover 1929 d: Frank Miller. lps: Betty Siddons, Eric Findon, Herbert Langley. SIL. 6471f UKN. prod/rel: British Screen Productions

GREY, ZANE (1872–1939), USA
Arizona Ames, New York 1932, Novel
Thunder Trail 1937 d: Charles T. Barton. lps: Gilbert Roland, Charles Bickford, Marsha Hunt. 56M USA. *Arizona Ames; Buckaroo* prod/rel: Paramount Pictures©

Avalanche, Novel
Avalanche 1928 d: Otto Brower. lps: Jack Holt, Doris Hill, Olga BaclanovA. 6099f USA. prod/rel: Paramount Famous Lasky Corp.

The Border Legion, New York 1916, Novel
Border Legion, The 1919 d: T. Hayes Hunter. lps: Hobart Bosworth, Blanche Bates, Eugene Strong. 5r USA. prod/rel: Goldwyn Distributing Corp., T. Hayes Hunter & Blanche Bates©

Border Legion, The 1924 d: William K. Howard. lps: Antonio Moreno, Helene Chadwick, Rockliffe Fellowes. 7048f USA. prod/rel: Famous Players-Lasky, Paramount Pictures

Border Legion, The 1930 d: Otto Brower, Edwin H. Knopf. lps: Jack Holt, Richard Arlen, Fay Wray. 80M USA. prod/rel: Paramount-Publix Corp.

Border Legion, The 1940 d: Joseph Kane. lps: Roy Rogers, George Hayes, Carol Hughes. 58M USA. *West of the Badlands* prod/rel: Republic Pictures Corp.

Last Round-Up, The 1934 d: Henry Hathaway. lps: Randolph Scott, Barbara Fritchie, Barton MacLane. 65M USA. *The Border Legion* prod/rel: Paramount Productions©

Born to the West, Story
Born to the West 1926 d: John Waters. lps: Jack Holt, Margaret Morris, Raymond Hatton. 6042f USA. prod/rel: Famous Players-Lasky, Paramount Pictures

The Call of the Canyon, New York 1924, Novel
Call of the Canyon, The 1923 d: Victor Fleming. lps: Richard Dix, Lois Wilson, Marjorie Daw. 6993f USA. prod/rel: Famous Players-Lasky, Paramount Pictures

Canon Walls, 1930, Story
Smoke Lightning 1933 d: David Howard. lps: George O'Brien, Virginia Sale, Douglas Dumbrille. 61M USA. *Canyon Walls* prod/rel: Fox Film Corp.©

Code of the West, New York 1924, Novel
Code of the West 1925 d: William K. Howard. lps: Owen Moore, Constance Bennett, Mabel Ballin. 6777f USA. prod/rel: Famous Players-Lasky, Paramount Pictures

Code of the West 1947 d: William Berke. lps: James Warren, Debra Alden, John Laurenz. 57M USA. prod/rel: RKO

Home on the Range 1935 d: Arthur Jacobson. lps: Randolph Scott, Ann Sheridan, Dean Jagger. 55M USA. *Code of the West* prod/rel: Paramount Productions©

Desert Bound, Story
Drums of the Desert 1927 d: John Waters. lps: Warner Baxter, Marietta Millner, Ford Sterling. 5907f USA. prod/rel: Paramount Famous Lasky Corp.

Desert Gold, New York 1913, Novel
Desert Gold 1919 d: T. Hayes Hunter. lps: E. K. Lincoln, Margery Wilson, Eileen Percy. 5-7r USA. prod/rel: Zane Grey Pictures, Inc., W. W. Hodkinson Corp.

Desert Gold 1926 d: George B. Seitz. lps: Neil Hamilton, Shirley Mason, Robert Frazer. 6900f USA. prod/rel: Famous Players-Lasky, Paramount Pictures

Desert Gold 1936 d: James P. Hogan. lps: Buster Crabbe, Robert Cummings, Marsha Hunt. 58M USA. prod/rel: Paramount Productions, Inc.

The Desert of Wheat, New York 1919, Novel
Riders of the Dawn 1920 d: Jack Conway. lps: Roy Stewart, Claire Adams, Marc Robbins. 6-7r USA. *The Desert of Wheat* prod/rel: Zane Grey Pictures, Inc.©, W. W. Hodkinson Corp.

Drift Fence, New York 1932, Novel
Drift Fence 1936 d: Otho Lovering. lps: Buster Crabbe, Katherine de Mille, Tom Keene. 56M USA. *Texas Desperadoes* prod/rel: Paramount Productions©

Fighting Caravans, New York 1929, Novel
Fighting Caravans 1930 d: David Burton, Otto Brower. lps: Gary Cooper, Lili Damita, Ernest Torrence. 91M USA. *Blazing Arrows* prod/rel: Paramount Publix Corp.©

Wagon Wheels 1934 d: Charles T. Barton. lps: Randolph Scott, Gail Patrick, Billy Lee. 56M USA. *Caravans West; Fighting Caravans* prod/rel: Paramount Productions©

Forlorn River, New York 1927, Novel
Forlorn River 1926 d: John Waters. lps: Jack Holt, Raymond Hatton, Arlette Marchal. 5992f USA. *River of Destiny* prod/rel: Famous Players-Lasky, Paramount Pictures

Forlorn River 1937 d: Charles T. Barton. lps: Buster Crabbe, June Martel, John Patterson. 62M USA. prod/rel: Paramount Pictures©

From Missouri, 1926, Short Story
Life in the Raw 1933 d: Louis King. lps: George O'Brien, Claire Trevor, Warner Richmond. 62M USA. *From Missouri; Arizona Wildcat* prod/rel: Fox Film Corp.©

The Heritage of the Desert, New York 1910, Novel
Heritage of the Desert 1933 d: Henry Hathaway. lps: Randolph Scott, Sally Blaine, Vince Barnett. 59M USA. *When the West Was Young* prod/rel: Paramount Publix Corp.©

Heritage of the Desert 1939 d: Lesley Selander. lps: Donald Woods, Evelyn Venable, Russell Hayden. 74M USA. prod/rel: Paramount Pictures©

Heritage of the Desert, The 1924 d: Irvin V. Willat. lps: Bebe Daniels, Ernest Torrence, Noah Beery. 5785f USA. prod/rel: Famous Players-Lasky, Paramount Pictures

Knights of the Range, New York 1936, Novel
Knights of the Range 1940 d: Lesley Selander. lps: Russell Hayden, Victor Jory, Jean Parker. 70M USA. prod/rel: Harry Sherman Productions, Paramount Pictures©

The Last of the Duanes, 1914, Short Story
Last of the Duanes, The 1919 d: J. Gordon Edwards. lps: William Farnum, Louise Lovely, Frances Raymond. 7r USA. prod/rel: Fox Film Corp., William Fox©

Last of the Duanes, The 1924 d: Lynn Reynolds. lps: Tom Mix, Marian Nixon, Brinsley Shaw. 6942f USA. prod/rel: Fox Film Corp.

Last of the Duanes, The 1930 d: Alfred L. Werker. lps: George O'Brien, Lucile Browne, Myrna Loy. 55M USA. prod/rel: Fox Film Corp.

Last of the Duanes, The 1941 d: James Tinling. lps: George Montgomery, Lynne Roberts, Eve Arden. 57M USA. prod/rel: 20th Century Fox

The Last Trail, New York 1909, Novel
Golden West, The 1932 d: David Howard. lps: George O'Brien, Janet Chandler, Marion Burns. 74M USA. prod/rel: Fox Film Corp.©

Last Trail, The 1921 d: Emmett J. Flynn. lps: Maurice B. Flynn, Eva Novak, Wallace Beery. 6355f USA. prod/rel: Fox Film Corp.

Last Trail, The 1927 d: Lewis Seiler. lps: Tom Mix, Carmelita Geraughty, William B. Davidson. 5190f USA. prod/rel: Fox Film Corp.

Last Trail, The 1933 d: James Tinling. lps: George O'Brien, Claire Trevor, El Brendel. 59M USA. prod/rel: Fox Film Corp.©

The Light of Western Stars, New York 1914, Novel
Light of Western Stars, The 1918 d: Charles Swickard. lps: Dustin Farnum, Winifred Kingston, Bert Apling. 7r USA. prod/rel: Sherman Productions, Inc., United Picture Theatres of America, Inc.

Light of Western Stars, The 1925 d: William K. Howard. lps: Jack Holt, Billie Dove, Noah Beery. 6859f USA. prod/rel: Famous Players-Lasky, Paramount Pictures

Light of Western Stars, The 1930 d: Otto Brower, Edwin H. Knopf. lps: Richard Arlen, Mary Brian, Regis Toomey. 80M USA. *Winning the West* prod/rel: Paramount Famous Lasky Corp.

Light of Western Stars, The 1940 d: Lesley Selander. lps: Russell Hayden, Victor Jory, Jo Ann Sayers. 64M USA. *Border Renegade* prod/rel: Paramount Pictures©

Lightning, Short Story
Lightning 1927 d: James C. McKay. lps: Jobyna Ralston, Margaret Livingston, Robert Frazier. 6049f USA. *The Desert Prince* prod/rel: Tiffany Productions

The Lone Star Ranger, New York 1915, Novel
Lone Star Ranger, The 1919 d: J. Gordon Edwards. lps: William Farnum, Louise Lovely, G. Raymond Nye. 5-6r USA. prod/rel: Fox Film Corp., William Fox©

Lone Star Ranger, The 1923 d: Lambert Hillyer. lps: Tom Mix, Billie Dove, L. C. Shumway. 5259f USA. prod/rel: Fox Film Corp.

Lone Star Ranger, The 1930 d: A. F. Erickson. lps: George O'Brien, Sue Carol, Russell Simpson. 70M USA. prod/rel: Fox Film Corp.

Lone Star Ranger, The 1941 d: James Tinling. lps: John Kimbrough, Sheila Ryan, Jonathan Hale. 58M USA. prod/rel: 20th Century-Fox

The Man of the Forest, New York 1920, Novel
Man of the Forest 1926 d: John Waters. lps: Jack Holt, Georgia Hale, El Brendel. 5187f USA. prod/rel: Famous Players-Lasky, Paramount Pictures

Man of the Forest 1933 d: Henry Hathaway. lps: Randolph Scott, Harry Carey, Verna Hillie. 63M USA. *Challenge of the Frontier* prod/rel: Paramount Productions©

Man of the Forest, The 1921 d: Benjamin B. Hampton. lps: Carl Gantvoort, Claire Adams, Robert McKim. 6800f USA. prod/rel: Zane Grey Pictures, W. W. Hodkinson Corp.

The Maverick Queen, 1953, Novel
Maverick Queen, The 1956 d: Joseph Kane. lps: Barbara Stanwyck, Barry Sullivan, Scott Brady. 92M USA. prod/rel: Republic

The Mysterious Rider, New York 1921, Novel
Mysterious Rider 1921 d: Benjamin B. Hampton. lps: Robert McKim, Claire Adams, Carl Gantvoort. 5500f USA. prod/rel: W. W. Hodkinson Corp., Zane Grey Pictures

Mysterious Rider, The 1927 d: John Waters. lps: Jack Holt, Betty Jewel, Charles Sellon. 5957f USA. prod/rel: Famous Players-Lasky, Paramount Pictures

Mysterious Rider, The 1933 d: Fred Allen. lps: Kent Taylor, Lona Andre, Gail Patrick. 61M USA. *Fighting Phantom* prod/rel: Major Pictures Corp., Paramount Productions©

The Mysterious Stranger, New York 1921, Novel
Mysterious Stranger, The 1938 d: Lesley Selander. lps: Douglas Dumbrille, Sidney Toler, Russell Hayden. 74M USA. *Mark of the Avenger* prod/rel: Paramount Pictures©

Nevada; a Romance of the West, New York 1928, Novel
Nevada 1927 d: John Waters. lps: Gary Cooper, Thelma Todd, William Powell. 6258f USA. prod/rel: Paramount Famous Lasky Corp.

Nevada 1935 d: Charles T. Barton. lps: Buster Crabbe, Kathleen Burke, Monte Blue. 60M USA. prod/rel: Paramount Productions©

Nevada 1944 d: Edward Killy. lps: Robert Mitchum, Anne Jeffreys, Nancy Gates. 62M USA. prod/rel: RKO

Open Range, Story
Open Range 1927 d: Cliff Smith. lps: Betty Bronson, Lane Chandler, Fred Kohler. 5599f USA. prod/rel: Paramount Famous Lasky Corp.

Outlaws of Palouse, Short Story
End of the Trail 1936 d: Erle C. Kenton. lps: Jack Holt, Louise Henry, Douglas Dumbrille. 72M USA. *Revenge!* (UKN); *A Man Without Fear; Outlaws of Palouse; Man of the Trail; Road to Nowhere* prod/rel: Columbia Pictures Corp. of California©

Raiders of the Spanish Peaks, 1931-32, Story
Arizona Raiders, The 1936 d: James P. Hogan. lps: Buster Crabbe, Raymond Hatton, Marsha Hunt. 57M USA. *Bad Men of Arizona* prod/rel: Paramount Pictures, Inc.

The Rainbow Trail, New York 1915, Novel
Rainbow Trail, The 1918 d: Frank Lloyd. lps: William Farnum, Ann Forrest, Mary Mersch. 6r USA. prod/rel: Fox Film Corp., William Fox©

Rainbow Trail, The 1925 d: Lynn Reynolds. lps: Tom Mix, Anne Cornwall, George Bancroft. 5251f USA. prod/rel: Fox Film Corp.

Rainbow Trail, The 1932 d: David Howard. lps: George O'Brien, Cecilia Parker, Roscoe Ates. 62M USA. prod/rel: Fox Film Corp.©

Riders of the Purple Sage, New York 1912, Novel
Riders of the Purple Sage 1918 d: Frank Lloyd. lps: William Farnum, Mary Mersch, William Scott. 6470f USA. prod/rel: Fox Film Corp., Fox Standard Pictures

Riders of the Purple Sage 1925 d: Lynn Reynolds. lps: Tom Mix, Beatrice Burnham, Arthur Morrison. 5578f USA. prod/rel: Fox Film Corp.

Riders of the Purple Sage 1931 d: Hamilton MacFadden. lps: George O'Brien, Marguerite Churchill, Noah Beery. 58M USA. prod/rel: Fox Film Corp.©, Hamilton Macfadden Production

Riders of the Purple Sage 1941 d: James Tinling. lps: George Montgomery, Mary Howard, Robert Barrat. 56M USA. prod/rel: 20th Century-Fox Film Corp.

Riders of the Purple Sage 1996 d: Charles Haid. lps: Ed Harris, Amy Madigan, Henry Thomas. TVM. 120M USA. prod/rel: Tnt

Robbers' Roost, New York 1932, Novel
Robbers' Roost 1933 d: Louis King. lps: George O'Brien, Maureen O'Sullivan, Maude Eburne. 64M USA. prod/rel: Fox Film Corp.©
Robbers' Roost 1955 d: Sidney Salkow. lps: George Montgomery, Richard Boone, Sylvia Findley. 82M USA. prod/rel: United Artists Corp., Goldstein-Jacks Prods.

Stairs of Sand, 1928, Novel
Arizona Mahoney 1936 d: James P. Hogan. lps: Buster Crabbe, June Martel, Robert Cummings. 61M USA. *Arizona Thunderbolt*; *Boots and Saddles* prod/rel: Paramount Pictures, Inc.
Stairs of Sand 1929 d: Otto Brower. lps: Wallace Beery, Jean Arthur, Phillips Holmes. 5020f USA. prod/rel: Paramount Famous Lasky Corp.

Sunset Pass, Novel
Sunset Pass 1929 d: Otto Brower. lps: Jack Holt, Nora Lane, John Loder. 5862f USA. prod/rel: Paramount Famous Lasky Corp.
Sunset Pass 1933 d: Henry Hathaway. lps: Randolph Scott, Tom Keene, Kathleen Burke. 64M USA. prod/rel: Paramount Productions©
Sunset Pass 1946 d: William Berke. lps: James Warren, John Laurenz, Nan Leslie. 59M USA. prod/rel: RKO

Thunder Mountain, New York 1935, Novel
Thunder Mountain 1935 d: David Howard. lps: George O'Brien, Barbara Fritchie, Frances Grant. 60M USA. *Roaring Mountain* prod/rel: Atherton Productions©, Twentieth Century-Fox Film Corp.
Thunder Mountain 1947 d: Lew Landers. lps: Tim Holt, Martha Hyer, Richard Martin. 60M USA. prod/rel: RKO

The Thundering Herd, New York 1925, Novel
Thundering Herd 1933 d: Henry Hathaway. lps: Randolph Scott, Judith Allen, Barton MacLane. 58M USA. *Buffalo Stampede* prod/rel: Paramount Productions©
Thundering Herd, The 1925 d: William K. Howard. lps: Jack Holt, Lois Wilson, Noah Beery. 7187f USA. prod/rel: Famous Players-Lasky, Paramount Pictures

To the Last Man, New York 1922, Novel
To the Last Man 1923 d: Victor Fleming. lps: Richard Dix, Lois Wilson, Noah Beery. 6965f USA. prod/rel: Famous Players-Lasky, Paramount Pictures
To the Last Man 1933 d: Henry Hathaway. lps: Randolph Scott, Esther Ralston, Noah Beery. 70M USA. *Law of Vengeance*

Under the Tonto Rim, New York 1926, Novel
Under the Tonto Rim 1928 d: Herman C. Raymaker. lps: Richard Arlen, Alfred Allen, Mary Brian. 5947f USA. prod/rel: Paramount Famous Lasky Corp.
Under the Tonto Rim 1933 d: Henry Hathaway. lps: Stuart Erwin, Verna Hillie, Raymond Hatton. 59M USA. prod/rel: Paramount Productions©
Under the Tonto Rim 1947 d: Lew Landers. lps: Tim Holt, Nan Leslie, Richard Martin. 61M USA.

The U.P. Trail, New York 1918, Novel
U.P. Trail, The 1920 d: Jack Conway. lps: Kathlyn Williams, Marguerite de La Motte, Roy Stewart. 7r USA. prod/rel: Zane Grey Pictures, Inc., Benjamin B. Hampton Production

The Vanishing American, New York 1925, Novel
Vanishing American, The 1925 d: George B. Seitz. lps: Richard Dix, Lois Wilson, Noah Beery. 9916f USA. *The Vanishing Race* prod/rel: Famous Players-Lasky, Paramount Pictures
Vanishing American, The 1955 d: Joseph Kane. lps: Scott Brady, Audrey Totter, Forrest Tucker. 90M USA. prod/rel: Republic

The Wanderer of the Wasteland, New York 1923, Novel
Wanderer of the Wasteland 1924 d: Irvin V. Willat. lps: Jack Holt, Noah Beery, George Irving. 5775f USA. prod/rel: Famous Players-Lasky, Paramount Pictures
Wanderer of the Wasteland 1945 d: Edward Killy, Wallace A. Grissell. lps: James Warren, Richard Martin, Audrey Long. 67M USA. prod/rel: RKO Radio Pictures
Wanderer of the Wasteland, The 1934 d: Otho Lovering. lps: Dean Jagger, Buster Crabbe, Gail Patrick. 66M USA. prod/rel: Paramount Productions©

The Water Hole, 1927, Serial Story
Water Hole, The 1928 d: F. Richard Jones. lps: Jack Holt, Nancy Carroll, John Boles. 6319f USA. prod/rel: Paramount Famous Lasky Corp.

West of the Pecos, New York 1937, Novel
West of the Pecos 1934 d: Phil Rosen. lps: Richard Dix, Martha Sleeper, Samuel S. Hinds. 70M USA. prod/rel: RKO Radio Pictures©
West of the Pecos 1945 d: Edward Killy. lps: Robert Mitchum, Barbara Hale, Richard Martin. 66M USA. prod/rel: RKO Radio Pictures

Western Union, Novel
Western Union 1941 d: Fritz Lang. lps: Randolph Scott, Robert Young, Dean Jagger. 95M USA. prod/rel: 20th Century-Fox

Wild Horse Mesa, Novel
Wild Horse Mesa 1925 d: George B. Seitz. lps: Jack Holt, Noah Beery, Billie Dove. 7164f USA. prod/rel: Famous Players-Lasky, Paramount Pictures
Wild Horse Mesa 1932 d: Henry Hathaway. lps: Randolph Scott, Sally Blaine, Fred Kohler. 72M USA. prod/rel: Paramount Publix Corp.©

Wildfire, New York 1916, Novel
Red Canyon 1949 d: George Sherman. lps: Howard Duff, Ann Blyth, George Brent. 82M USA. *Black Velvet* prod/rel: Universal-International
When Romance Rides 1922 d: Eliot Howe, Charles O. Rush. lps: Claire Adams, Carl Gantvoort, Jean Hersholt. 5003f USA. prod/rel: Benjamin B. Hampton, Goldwyn Pictures

GRIBBLE, HARRY W.
Old Man Murphy, New York 1931, Play
His Family Tree 1935 d: Charles Vidor. lps: James Barton, William Harrigan, Marjorie Gateson. 69M USA. *Old Man Murphy* prod/rel: RKO Radio Pictures©

Trick for Trick, New York 1932, Play
Trick for Trick 1933 d: Hamilton MacFadden. lps: Ralph Morgan, Victor Jory, Sally Blane. 69M USA. prod/rel: Fox Film Corp.©

GRIBBLE, LEONARD
The Arsenal Stadium Mystery, Novel
Arsenal Stadium Mystery, The 1939 d: Thorold Dickinson. lps: Leslie Banks, Greta Gynt, Ian MacLean. 84M UKN. prod/rel: G & S Films, General Film Distributors

Death By Design, Short Story
Death By Design 1943 d: Geoffrey Faithfull. lps: John Longden, Wally Patch. 18M UKN. prod/rel: Guild Films, Butcher's Film Service

GRIBITZ, FRANZ
Es Fing So Harmlos an, Play
Es Fing So Harmlos an 1944 d: Theo Lingen. lps: Johannes Heesters, Inge List, Christl Mardayn. 89M GRM. prod/rel: Bavaria, Allgemeiner

Herz Modern Mobliert, Play
Herz Modern Mobliert 1940 d: Theo Lingen. lps: Hilde Krahl, Gusti Huber, Gustav Frohlich. 94M GRM. prod/rel: Majestic, Hamburg

Eine Jener Seltenen Frauen, Play
Pikanterie 1951 d: Alfred Braun. lps: Irene von Meyendorff, Curd Jurgens, Susanne von Almassy. 90M GRM. *Spicy Story* prod/rel: Skala, Gerda Tilgner

Liebeskomodie, Play
Liebeskomodie 1942 d: Theo Lingen. lps: Magda Schneider, Lizzi Waldmuller, Johannes Riemann. 88M GRM. prod/rel: Berlin, Sudwest

So Ein Fruchtchen, Play
So Ein Fruchtchen 1942 d: Alfred Stoger. lps: Lucie Englisch, Maria Andergast, Paul Horbiger. 84M GRM. prod/rel: Algefa, Carmi

GRIEBITZ, F.
Das Gluck Wohnt Nebenan, Play
Gluck Wohnt Nebenan, Das 1939 d: Hubert MarischkA. lps: Maria Andergast, Olly Holzmann, Wolf Albach-Retty. 77M GRM/AUS. prod/rel: Algefa

GRIEDER, WALTER
Die Hazy Osterwald Story, Zurich 1961, Book
Musique Est Ma Passion, La 1961 d: Franz J. Gottlieb. lps: Wera Frydtberg, Jean Osterwald, Peer Schmidt. 111M SWT/GRM. *Die Hazy-Osterwald-Story*; *Musik Ist Trumpf* prod/rel: Urania-Film, Constantin-Film

GRIFFI, GIUSEPPE PATRONI (1921–, ITL
Anima Nera, Play
Anima Nera 1962 d: Roberto Rossellini. lps: Vittorio Gassman, Annette Stroyberg, Nadja Tiller. 93M ITL. prod/rel: Documento Film (Roma), le Louvre Film (Paris)

GRIFFIN, ELEANORE
Be It Ever So Humble, Story
Hi, Beautiful! 1944 d: Leslie Goodwins. lps: Martha O'Driscoll, Noah Beery Jr., Hattie McDaniel. 66M USA. *Pass to Romance* (UKN); *Be It Ever So Humble* prod/rel: Universal

Class Prophecy, 1935, Short Story
When Love Is Young 1937 d: Hal Mohr. lps: Virginia Bruce, Kent Taylor, Walter Brennan. 76M USA. *Class Prophecy* prod/rel: Universal Pictures Co.©

Thanks for the Ride, 1936, Short Story
Time Out for Romance 1937 d: Malcolm St. Clair. lps: Claire Trevor, Michael Whalen, Joan Davis. 75M USA. prod/rel: 20th Century-Fox Film Corp.©

GRIFFIN, JOHN HOWARD (1920–, USA
Black Like Me, 1960, Novel
Black Like Me 1964 d: Carl Lerner. lps: James Whitmore, Clifton James, Lenka Peterson. 107M USA. *No Man Walks Alone* prod/rel: Julius Tannenbaum, Hilltop Productions

GRIFFIN, CORINNE
Papa's Delicate Condition, Boston 1952, Biography
Papa's Delicate Condition 1963 d: George Marshall. lps: Jackie Gleason, Glynis Johns, Laurel Goodwin. 98M USA. prod/rel: Amro Productions

GRIFFITH, HUBERT
No Crime of Passion, Play
Betrayal 1932 d: Reginald Fogwell. lps: Stewart Rome, Marjorie Hume, Leslie Perrins. 66M UKN. prod/rel: Fogwell Films, Universal

GRIFFITHS, LINDA
The Darling Family, Play
Darling Family, The 1994 d: Alan Zweig. lps: Linda Griffiths, Alan Williams. 86M CND. prod/rel: Darling Family

GRIFFITHS, TREVOR
Comedians, 1976, Play
Comedians 1979 d: Richard Eyre. lps: Bill Fraser, Jonathan Pryce, David Burke. TVM. 95M UKN. prod/rel: BBC

Country: a Tory Story, 1981, Play
Country 1981 d: Richard Eyre. lps: Leo McKern, Wendy Hiller, James Fox. TVM. 80M UKN. prod/rel: BBC

The Party, 1973, Play
Party, The 1987 d: Sebastian Graham-Jones. lps: Andrew Keir, Jack Shepherd, Kenneth Cranham. TVM. F UKN. prod/rel: BBC Scotland

GRILLPARZER, FRANZ (1791–1872), AUS
Das Kloster von Sendomir, Novel
Kloster von Sendomir, Das 1912. lps: Friedrich Feher. GRM. prod/rel: Deutsche Mutoskop Und Biograph

GRIMALDI, AURELIO
Mery Per Sempere, Novel
Mery Per Sempere 1988 d: Marco Risi. lps: Michele Placido, Claudio Amendola, Francesco Benigno. 106M ITL. *Mery for Ever*; *Forever Mary*; *Mary Forever* prod/rel: Numero Uno International

GRIMALDI, GIANNI
Aragoste Di Sicilia, Play
Prima Notte Del Dr. Danieli, Industriale Col Complesso Del Giocattolo 1970 d: Gianni Grimaldi. lps: Francoise Prevost, Lando Buzzanca, Katia ChristinA. 93M ITL/FRN. *La Prima Notte Del Dottore Danieli*; *La Toubib En Delire*; *Beaucoup de Nuits Pour Rien* prod/rel: Princeps Cin.Ca, Medusa Distribuzione

GRIMBLE, SIR ARTHUR
A Pattern of Islands, Book
Pacific Destiny 1956 d: Wolf RillA. lps: Denholm Elliott, Susan Stephen, Michael Hordern. 97M UKN. prod/rel: James Lawrie, British Lion

GRIMM, JACOB (1785–1863), GRM
Short Story
Bruderchen Und Schwesterchen 1953 d: Walter Oehmichen. lps: Gotz Wolf, Maria Kottmeier, Arnold Marquis. 64M GRM. *Little Brother Little Sister* prod/rel: Schonger, Jugendfilm
Novel
Gevatter Tod 1980 d: Wolfgang Hubner. lps: Dieter Franke, Jan Spitzer, Hannes Fischer. 72M GDR. prod/rel: Fernsehen Der D.D.R.
Short Story
Jorinde Und Joringel 1986 d: Wolfgang Hubner. lps: Susanne Luning, Thomas Stecher, Jutta Wachowiak. 75M GDR. prod/rel: Fersehen Der D.D.R.
Julienka a Slnko Kral 1981 d: Martin Tapak. lps: Stefan Skrucany, Tereza Pokorna, Michal Docolomansky. 84M CZC. prod/rel: Slovensky Film
Treue Johannes, Der 1987 d: Slavo Luther. lps: Vladimir Hajdu, Remi Martin, Maru Valdivieso. 94M GRM/CZC/AUS. prod/rel: Omnia, Slovenska Filmova Tvorba
Aschenputtel, Short Story
Aschenputtel 1955 d: Fritz Genschow. lps: Rita-Maria Nowotny, Renee Stobrawa, Fritz Genschow. 72M GRM. *Cinderella* (USA) prod/rel: Genschow, Hamburg
Aschenputtel 1989 d: Karin Brandauer. lps: Petra Vigna, Claudia Knichel, Roswitha Schreiner. TVM. 90M GRM/FRN/CZC. prod/rel: Omnia, Toro
Die Bremer Stadtmusikanten, Short Story
Bremer Stadtmusikanten, Die 1959 d: Rainer Geis. lps: Paul Tripp, Peter Thom, Max Bossl. 77M GRM. *The Bremen Town Musicians* (USA) prod/rel: Schonger, Jugendfilm

Hansel and Gretel 1954 d: John Paul. ANM. 75M USA. prod/rel: RKO, Michael Meyerberg

Hansel and Gretel 1982 d: James Frawley. lps: Joan Collins, Paul Dooley, Ricky Schroder. MTV. 48M USA.

Hansel and Gretel 1987 d: Len Talan. lps: Cloris Leachman, David Warner, Nicola Stapleton. 82M UKN/ISR. prod/rel: Cannon

Hansel Und Gretel 1954 d: Fritz Genschow. lps: Fritz Genschow, Renee Stobrawa, Rita-Maria Nowotny. 87M GRM. prod/rel: Fritz Genschow, Hamburg

Hansel Und Gretel 1954 d: Walter Janssen. lps: Jurgen Miksch, Maren Inken Bielenberg, Jochen Diestelmann. 54M GRM. *Hansel and Gretel* (USA) prod/rel: Schongerfilm, Jugendfilm

Die Kluge Bauerntochter, 1812, Short Story
Wie Heiratet Man Einen Konig 1968 d: Rainer Simon. lps: Cox Habbema, Eberhard Esche, Sigurd Schulz. 79M GDR. *How to Marry a King*

Konig Drosselbart, 1812, Short Story
Konig Drosselbart 1954 d: Herbert B. Fredersdorf. lps: Gisela Fritsch, Ottakar Runze, Kurt Vespermann. 70M GRM. *King Thrushbeard* prod/rel: Delos, Jugendfilm

Konig Drosselbart 1967 d: Walter Beck. lps: Karin Ugowski, Manfred Krug, Martin Flochinger. 68M GDR. *King Drosselbart; King Thrushbeard*

Kral Drozdi Brada 1984 d: Miroslav Luther. lps: Adriana Tarabkova, Lukas Vaculik, Marian LabudA. 95M CZC/GRM. *Konig Drosselbart* (GRM); *King Thrushbeard* prod/rel: Koliba, Omnia

Rotkappchen, Short Story
Rotkappchen 1953 d: Fritz Genschow. lps: Daniela Maris, Werner Stock, Fritz Genschow. 85M GRM. prod/rel: Genschow, Westfilm

Rotkappchen 1954 d: Walter Janssen. lps: Maren Inken Bielenberg, Peter Lehmann, Michael Beutner. 48M GRM. prod/rel: Schonger, Jugendfilm

Rumpelstilzchen, 1812, Short Story
Rumpelstiltskin 1915 d: Raymond B. West. lps: Clyde Tracy, Elizabeth Burbridge, Kenneth Browne. 4-5r USA. prod/rel: New York Motion Picture Corp.©, Mutual Film Corp.

Rumpelstiltskin 1987 d: David Irving. lps: Amy Irving, Billy Barty, Clive Revill. 85M USA. *Rumplestiltskin* prod/rel: Cannon

Rumpelstilzchen 1955 d: Herbert B. Fredersdorf. lps: Werner Kruger, Liane Croon, Wilhelm Grothe. 79M GRM. *Rumpestiltskin* (USA) prod/rel: Forster Film, Jugendfilm

Schneeweisschen Und Rosenrot, 1812, Short Story
Schneeweisschen Und Rosenrot 1955 d: Erich Kobler. lps: Rosemarie Seehofer, Ursula Herion, Heini Gobel. 62M GRM. *Snow White and Rose Red* (USA) prod/rel: Schonger, Jugendfilm

Schneeweisschen Und Rosenrot 1978 d: Siegfried Hartmann. lps: Julie Juristova, Katrin Martin, Pavel Travnicek. 70M GDR. prod/rel: Veb Defa

Snow White 1916 d: J. Searle Dawley. lps: Marguerite Clark, Creighton Hale, Dorothy Cumming. 6r USA. prod/rel: Famous Players Film Co.©, Paramount Pictures Corp.

Schneewittchen, 1812, Short Story
Little Old Men of the Woods, The 1910. 945f USA. prod/rel: Kalem

O Snehurce 1972 d: Vera Plivova-SimkovA. lps: Vaclav Babka, Frantisek Husak, Marie MoravcovA. 73M CZC. *Snow-White* prod/rel: Filmstudio Barrandov

Schneewittchen 1928 d: Aloys Alfons Zengerling. lps: Hilde Wenzel, M. Arco. 1920m GRM. prod/rel: Marchen-Film-Produktion

Schneewittchen Und Die Sieben Zwerge 1956 d: Erich Kobler. lps: Elke Arendt, Addi Adametz, Erwin Platzer. 77M GRM. *Snow White and the Seven Dwarfs*; *Snow White* prod/rel: Schongerfilm

Schneewittchen Und Die Sieben Zwerge 1961 d: Gottfried Kolditz. lps: Doris Weikow, Marianne Christina Schilling, Wolf-Dieter Panse. 63M GDR. *Snow White and the Seven Dwarfs* prod/rel: Defa

Snow White 1987 d: Michael Berz. lps: Diana Rigg, Nicola Stapleton, Sarah Patterson. 85M USA. *Snow White and the Seven Dwarfs*; *Cannon Movie Tales: Snow White* prod/rel: Cannon

Snow White and the Seven Dwarfs 1937 d: David Hand. ANM. 86M USA. prod/rel: Walt Disney Productions, RKO Radio Pictures©

Snow White and the Seven Dwarfs 1983 d: Peter Medak. lps: Elizabeth McGovern, Vanessa Redgrave, Rex Smith. MTV. 53M USA.

Das Tapfere Schneiderlein, Short Story
Sedem Jednou Ranou 1988 d: Dusan Trancik. lps: Miroslav Noga, Gunter MacK, Amanda Sandrelli. 95M CZC/GRM/FRN. *Das Tapfere Schneiderlein* (GRM); *The Boastful Tailor; Brave Little Tailor* prod/rel: Slovenska Filmova Bratislava, Omnia

Tapfere Schneiderlein, Das 1956 d: Helmut Spiess. lps: Kurt Schmidtchen, Christel Bodenstein, Gisela Kretzschmar. 83M GDR. *The Brave Little Tailor* (USA)

Der Teufel Mit Den Drei Goldenen Haaren, Short Story
Teufel Mit Den Drei Goldenen Haaren, Der 1955 d: Hans F. Wilhelm. lps: Alexander Golling, Peter Schreiber, Hans Cossy. 85M GRM. *The Devil With the Three Golden Hairs* prod/rel: Domo, Karp

Wer Reisst Denn Gleich Vorm Teufel Aus? 1978 d: Egon Schlegel. lps: Hans-Joachim Frank, Katrin Martin, Rolf Ludwig. 94M GDR. *Der Teufel Mit Den 3 Goldenen Haaren* prod/rel: Defa

GRIMSHAW, BEATRICE

My Lady of the Island, Chicago 1916, Novel
Thunder Island 1921 d: Norman Dawn. lps: Edith Roberts, Fred de Silva, Jack O'Brien. 4279f USA. prod/rel: Universal Film Mfg. Co.

GRIN, ALEKSANDR (1880–1932), RSS, Grinevsky, Aleksandr Stepanovich

Dzhessi I Morgiana, 1928, Novel
Morgiana 1972 d: Juraj Herz. lps: Iva Janzurova, Josef Abrham, Petr Cepek. 108M CZC.

Izbavitelj, Short Story
Izbavitelj 1977 d: Krsto Papic. lps: Ivica Vidovic, Mirjana Majurec, Relja Basic. 90M YGS. *The Redeemer; The Rat Saviour* prod/rel: Jadran, Croatia

GRINSTEAD, JESSE EDWARD

The Scourge of the Little C, New York 1925, Novel
Tumbling River 1927 d: Lewis Seiler. lps: Tom Mix, Dorothy Dwan, William Conklin. 4675f USA. *The Scourge of the Little C* prod/rel: Fox Film Corp.

GRIPE, MARIA

Agnes Cecilia, Novel
Agnes Cecilia - En Sallsam Historia 1991 d: Anders Gronros. lps: Gloria Tapia, Ronn Elfors, Stina Ekblad. F SWD. *Agnes Cecilia*

Glasblasarns Barn, 1964, Novel
Glasblasarns Barn 1998 d: Anders Gronros. lps: Stellan Skarsgard, Pernilla August, Thommy Berggren. 110M SWD/NRW/DNM. *The Glassblower's Children* prod/rel: Birkeland Film Co., Nordic Screen Prod.

GRISCOM, LLOYD

Tenth Avenue, New York 1927, Play
Tenth Avenue 1928 d: William C. de Mille. lps: Phyllis Haver, Victor Varconi, Joseph Schildkraut. 6370f USA. *Hell's Kitchen* (UKN) prod/rel: de Mille Studio Productions, Pathe Exchange, Inc.

GRISHAM, JOHN

Story
Gingerbread Man, The 1998 d: Robert Altman. lps: Kenneth Branagh, Embeth Davidtz, Robert Downey Jr. 114M USA. prod/rel: Island Pictures©, Enchanter Entertainment

The Chamber, Novel
Chamber, The 1996 d: James Foley. lps: Chris O'Donnell, Gene Hackman, Faye Dunaway. 113M USA. prod/rel: Davis Entertainment, Brian Glazer

The Client, Novel
Client, The 1994 d: Joel Schumacher. lps: Susan Sarandon, Tommy Lee Jones, Mary-Louise Parker. 121M USA. prod/rel: Warner Bros., Regency

The Firm, Novel
Firm, The 1993 d: Sydney Pollack. lps: Tom Cruise, Jeanne Tripplehorn, Gene Hackman. 154M USA. prod/rel: Paramount

The Pelican Brief, Novel
Pelican Brief, The 1993 d: Alan J. PakulA. lps: Julia Roberts, Denzel Washington, Sam Shepard. 141M USA. prod/rel: Warner Bros.

The Rainmaker, Novel
John Grisham's the Rainmaker 1997 d: Francis Ford CoppolA. lps: Matt Damon, Claire Danes, Jon Voight. 135M USA. *The Rainmaker* prod/rel: Constellation Films, Douglas/Reuther

A Time to Kill, Novel
Time to Kill, A 1996 d: Joel Schumacher. lps: Sandra Bullock, Samuel L. Jackson, Matthew McConaughey. 150M USA. prod/rel: Monarchy, Warner Bros.

GRISOLA, MICHEL

Flic Ou Voyou, Novel
Flic Ou Voyou? 1979 d: Georges Lautner. lps: Jean-Paul Belmondo, Michel Galabru, Maurice Laforet. 107M FRN. prod/rel: Gaumont, Cerito

GROC, LEON

Le Disparu de l'Ascenseur, Novel
Disparu de l'Ascenseur, Le 1931 d: Giulio Del Torre. lps: Jacques Varennes, Jenny Luxeuil, Claude Eller. 81M FRN. prod/rel: Alex Nalpas

GROH, OTTO EMMERICH

Die Fahne, Play
Gouverneur, Der 1939 d: Victor Tourjansky. lps: Brigitte Horney, Willy Birgel, Hannelore Schroth. 99M GRM. prod/rel: Terra, Panorama

Trenck Der Pandur, Play
Trenck Der Pandur 1940 d: Herbert Selpin. lps: Hans Albers, Kathe Dorsch, Sybille Schmitz. 80M GRM. prod/rel: Tobis, Dafa

GRONIN, YVONNE

Karleks Pris, Novel
Rusar I Hans Famn 1996 d: Lennart Hjulstrom. lps: Gunilla Nyroos, Reine Brynolfsson, Anna Bjork. 80M SWD. *Rushing Into His Arms* prod/rel: Gotafilm, Svensk Filmindustri

GROOM, ARTHUR WILLIAM

John of the Fair, London 1950, Novel
John of the Fair 1952 d: Michael McCarthy. lps: John Charlesworth, Arthur Young, Richard George. 62M UKN. prod/rel: Merton Park Studios, Children's Film Foundation

GROPPER, MILTON HERBERT

The Big Fight, New York 1928, Play
Big Fight, The 1930 d: Walter Lang. lps: Lola Lane, Ralph Ince, Guinn (Big Boy) Williams. 5850f USA. prod/rel: James Cruze Productions, Sono Art-World Wide Pictures

Ladies of the Evening, New York 1924, Play
Ladies of Leisure 1930 d: Frank CaprA. lps: Barbara Stanwyck, Ralph Graves, Lowell Sherman. 102M USA. prod/rel: Columbia Pictures

Women of Glamour 1937 d: Gordon Wiles. lps: Virginia Bruce, Melvyn Douglas, Reginald Denny. 72M USA. *Women of Glamour* prod/rel: Columbia Pictures Corp. of California©

New Toys, New York 1924, Play
New Toys 1925 d: John S. Robertson. lps: Richard Barthelmess, Mary Hay, Katherine Wilson. 7250f USA. prod/rel: Inspiration Pictures, First National Pictures

We Americans, New York 1926, Play
We Americans 1928 d: Edward Sloman. lps: George Sidney, Patsy Ruth Miller, George Lewis. 8700f USA. *The Heart of a Nation* (UKN) prod/rel: Universal Pictures

GROS, BRIGITTE

Elle Court, Elle Court, la Banlieue, Novel
Elle Court, Elle Court, la Banlieue 1973 d: Gerard Pires. lps: Marthe Keller, Jacques Higelin, Annie Cordy. 100M FRN/ITL. prod/rel: Films Du Jeudi, Golan

GROSMAN, LADISLAV

Obchod Na Korze, Prague 1965, Novel
Obchod Na Korse 1965 d: Jan Kadar, Elmar Klos. lps: Jozef Kroner, Ida Kaminska, Hana SlivkovA. 128M CZC. *The Shop on the High Street; Shop on Main Street* (USA) prod/rel: Filmove Studio Barrandov

GROSS, CORDELIA BAIRD

It's Hard to Find Mecca, Short Story
This Could be the Night 1957 d: Robert Wise. lps: Jean Simmons, Paul Douglas, Anthony FranciosA. 104M USA. prod/rel: MGM

Protection for a Tough Racket, Short Story
This Could be the Night 1957 d: Robert Wise. lps: Jean Simmons, Paul Douglas, Anthony FranciosA. 104M USA. prod/rel: MGM

GROSS, HEINZ

Toller Hecht Auf Krummer Tour, Bad Worishofen 1959, Novel
Toller Hecht Auf Krummen Touren 1961 d: Akos von Rathony. lps: Christine Kaufmann, Michael Hinz, William Bendix. 97M GRM. *The Phony American* (USA); *It's a Great Life; Toller Hecht Auf Krummer Tour; The Long Way Round* prod/rel: Astra, Filmkunst

GROSS, LAURENCE

Whistling in the Dark, New York 1932, Play
Whistling in the Dark 1932 d: Elliott Nugent. lps: Ernest Truex, Una Merkel, Edward Arnold. 78M USA. *Scared!* (UKN) prod/rel: Metro-Goldwyn-Mayer Corp., Metro-Goldwyn-Mayer Dist. Corp.

Whistling in the Dark 1941 d: S. Sylvan Simon. lps: Red Skelton, Ann Rutherford, Virginia Grey. 77M USA. prod/rel: Metro-Goldwyn-Mayer Corp.

GROSS, LEONARD
The Last Jews in Berlin, Novel
   Forbidden 1986 d: Anthony Page. lps: Jacqueline Bisset, Jurgen Prochnow, Irene Worth. TVM. 114M UKN/GRM/USA. *Versteckt* (GRM); *Hidden* prod/rel: Mark Forstater Productions (London), Clasart Film Und Fernseh Produktions

GROSS, MILTON
High Spirits, Story
   Ghost Catchers 1944 d: Eddie Cline. lps: Ole Olsen, Chic Johnson, Gloria Jean. 68M USA. prod/rel: Universal

GROSS, MRS. ALEXANDER
Break the Walls Down, 1914, Play
   Serving Two Masters 1921. lps: Josephine Earle, Dallas Anderson, Pat Somerset. 4900f USA. prod/rel: Lee-Bradford Corp.

GROSS, YORAM
Save the Lady, Novel
   Save the Lady 1982 d: Leon Thau. lps: Wallas Eaton, John Ewart, Bill Kerr. 76M ASL. prod/rel: Tasmanian Film Corporation©, Young Australia Films

GROSSBACH, ROBERT
Easy and Hard Ways Out, Novel
   Best Defense 1984 d: Willard Huyck. lps: Dudley Moore, Eddie Murphy, Kate Capshaw. 94M USA. *Best Defence* prod/rel: Paramount

GROSSI, TOMMASO (1790–1853), ITL
Marco Visconti, 1834, Novel
   Marco Visconti 1909 d: Mario Caserini. lps: Fernanda Negri-Pouget. 220m ITL. prod/rel: Cines
   Marco Visconti 1911 d: Ugo FalenA. lps: Dillo Lombardi, Gemma de Sanctis, Francesca Bertini. 296m ITL. prod/rel: Film d'Arte Italiana
   Marco Visconti 1925 d: Aldo de Benedetti. lps: Amleto Novelli, Cecyl Tryan, Ruggero Barni. 2524m ITL. prod/rel: Montalbano
   Marco Visconti 1941 d: Mario Bonnard. lps: Carlo Ninchi, Mariella Lotti, Roberto VillA. 108M ITL. prod/rel: S.a.Consorzio Italiano Film, E.N.I.C.

GROSSMAN, BUDD
Libby, Play
   Bachelor Flat 1962 d: Frank Tashlin. lps: Terry-Thomas, Tuesday Weld, Richard Beymer. 92M USA. prod/rel: Jack Cummings Productions

GROSSMAN, DAVID (1954–, ISR
Novel
   Chi'uch Hagdi 1985 d: Shimon Dotan. lps: Rami Danon, Makram Khoury, Tuncel Curtiz. F ISR. *The Smile of the Lamb*; *Hyinch Ha'gdi*; *Hyiuch Hagdi*

GROSSMAN, MRS. ALEXANDER
Break Down the Walls, Play
   Walls of Prejudice 1920 d: Charles Calvert. lps: Josephine Earle, Dallas Anderson, Pat Somerset. 5200f UKN. prod/rel: Gaumont, British Screencraft

GROSSMAN, VASILY (1905–1964), RSS, Grossman, Vasily Semyonovich
In the Town of Berdichev, Novel
   Kommissar 1987 d: Alexander Askoldov. lps: Nonna Mordjukova, Rolan Bykov, Raisa NedashkovskayA. 110M USS. *Komissar* prod/rel: Gorky Studios
V Gorode Berdicheve, 1934, Short Story
   Komissar 1967 d: Alexander Askoldov. lps: Nonna Mordyukova, Rolan Bykov, Raisa NedashkovskayA. 110M USS. *Commissar*; *Komisar* prod/rel: Filmstudio M. Gorki

GROSSMITH, GEORGE (1847–1912), UKN
Diary of a Nobody, 1892, Book
   Diary of a Nobody 1964 d: Ken Russell. lps: Murray Melvin. MTV. 45M UKN. prod/rel: BBC

GROSSMITH, WEEDON (1854–1919), UKN
Diary of a Nobody 1964 d: Ken Russell. lps: Murray Melvin. MTV. 45M UKN. prod/rel: BBC

GROSSO, SONNY
A Question of Honor, Book
   Question of Honor, A 1982 d: Jud Taylor. lps: Ben Gazzara, Paul Sorvino, Robert Vaughn. TVM. 150M USA. prod/rel: CBS, Roger Gimbel

GROTE, HERMANN
Quax Auf Abwegen, Short Story
   Quax in Fahrt 1945 d: Helmut Weiss. lps: Heinz Ruhmann, Hertha Feiler, Karin Himboldt. 92M GRM. *Quax in Africa* prod/rel: Terra, Nordwest
Quax, Der Bruchpilot, Short Story
   Quax, Der Bruchpilot 1941 d: Kurt Hoffmann. lps: Heinz Ruhmann, Lothar Firmans, Karin Himboldt. 91M GRM. prod/rel: Terra, Nordwest

GROTZACH, ROBERT
Dyckerpotts Erben, Play
   Dyckerpotts Erben 1928 d: Hans Behrendt. lps: Lotte Lorring, Georg Alexander, Fred Solm. 2176m GRM. prod/rel: Felsom-Film, Deutsche Vereins-Film Ag

GROULT, BENOIT
Les Vaisseaux du Coeur, Novel
   Salt on Our Skin 1992 d: Andrew Birkin. lps: Greta Scacchi, Vincent d'Onofrio, Anais Jeanneret. 106M GRM/CND/FRN. *Les Vaisseaux du Coeur* prod/rel: Neue Constantin, Torii

GROUSSARD, SERGE
The Blood of Israel, Book
   21 Hours at Munich 1976 d: William A. Graham. lps: William Holden, Shirley Knight, Franco Nero. TVM. 101M USA. *Twenty-One Hours at Munich* prod/rel: Filmways Production, Moonlight
Des Gens Sans Importance, Novel
   Des Gens Sans Importance 1955 d: Henri Verneuil. lps: Jean Gabin, Francoise Arnoul, Pierre Mondy. 101M FRN. *Be Beautiful But Shut Up* (USA) prod/rel: Cocinor, Chaillot Films

GROVE, F. C.
Forget-Me-Not, London 1879, Play
   Forget-Me-Not 1917 d: Emile Chautard. lps: Kitty Gordon, Montagu Love, Alec B. Francis. 5r USA. *Forget-Me-Nots* prod/rel: World Film Corp.©, Peerless

GROVER, LEONARD
Rainy the Lion Killer, Story
   Rainy, the Lion Killer 1914 d: Sidney Drew. lps: Sidney Drew. 2r USA. *Henry Stanley the Lion Killer*; *Stanley the Lion-Killer* prod/rel: Vitagraph Co. of America

GROY, HOMER
Article
   I Shot Jesse James 1949 d: Samuel Fuller. lps: Preston Foster, Barbara Britton, John Ireland. 81M USA. prod/rel: Lippert

GRUBB, DAVID
Night of the Hunter, 1953, Novel
   Night of the Hunter 1991 d: David Greene. lps: Richard Chamberlain, Diana Scarwid, Amy Bebout. TVM. 100M USA.
   Night of the Hunter, The 1955 d: Charles Laughton. lps: Robert Mitchum, Shelley Winters, Lillian Gish. 90M USA. prod/rel: United Artists, Paul Gregory Prods.

GRUBB, DAVIS
Fool's Parade, Novel
   Fools' Parade 1971 d: Andrew V. McLaglen. lps: James Stewart, George Kennedy, Anne Baxter. 98M USA. *Dynamite Man from Glory Jail* (UKN) prod/rel: Stanmore, Columbia Pictures

GRUBER, FRANK
Story
   Texas Rangers, The 1951 d: Phil Karlson. lps: William Bishop, George Montgomery, Gale Storm. 74M USA. prod/rel: Columbia, Edward Small Prods.
Backlash, Novel
   Backlash 1956 d: John Sturges. lps: Richard Widmark, Donna Reed, William Campbell. 84M USA. prod/rel: Universal-International
Bitter Sage, 1954, Novel
   Tension at Table Rock 1956 d: Charles Marquis Warren. lps: Richard Egan, Dorothy Malone, Cameron Mitchell. 93M USA. prod/rel: RKO Radio
Broken Lance, Novel
   Great Missouri Raid, The 1950 d: Gordon Douglas. lps: MacDonald Carey, Wendell Corey, Ward Bond. 85M USA. prod/rel: Paramount
Buffalo Grass, Novel
   Big Land, The 1956 d: Gordon Douglas. lps: Alan Ladd, Virginia Mayo, Edmond O'Brien. 93M USA. *Stampeded* (UKN) prod/rel: Warner Bros.
Dog Show Murder, 1938, Short Story
   Death of a Champion 1939 d: Robert Florey. lps: Lynne Overman, Virginia Dale, Donald O'Connor. 67M USA. *Dog Show Murder* prod/rel: Paramount Pictures, Inc.
The Kansan, Novel
   Kansan, The 1943 d: George Archainbaud. lps: Richard Dix, Jane Wyatt, Victor Jory. 79M USA. *Wagon Wheels* (UKN) prod/rel: United Artists, Paramount-Harry Sherman Action Special
The Lock and the Key, 1948, Novel
   Man in the Vault 1956 d: Andrew V. McLaglen. lps: William Campbell, Karen Sharpe, Anita Ekberg. 73M USA. prod/rel: RKO, Batjac
The Oregon Trail, Novel
   Oregon Trail, The 1945 d: Thomas Carr. lps: Sunset Carson, Peggy Stewart, Frank Jaquet. 55M USA. prod/rel: Republic

Detective Simon Lash, Novel
   Accomplice 1946 d: Walter Colmes. lps: Richard Arlen, Veda Ann Borg, Tom Dugan. 68M USA. prod/rel: P.R.C.
Town Tamer, New York 1958, Novel
   Town Tamer 1965 d: Lesley Selander. lps: Dana Andrews, Lon Chaney, Terry Moore. 89M USA. prod/rel: a.C. Lyles Productions
Twenty Plus Two, New York 1961, Novel
   Twenty Plus Two 1961 d: Joseph M. Newman. lps: David Janssen, Dina Merrill, Jeanne Crain. 102M USA. *It Started in Tokyo* (UKN); *It Happened in Tokyo* prod/rel: Allied Artists

GRUBER, GISI
Die Sieben Kleider Der Katrin, Book
   Sieben Kleider Der Kathrin, Die 1954 d: Hans Deppe. lps: Sonja Ziemann, Grethe Weiser, Georg ThomallA. 105M GRM. *Die 7 Kleider Der Katrin*; *Katrin's Seven Dresses* prod/rel: Hans Deppe

GRUEN, M.
Road House, Novel
   Road House 1948 d: Jean Negulesco. lps: Ida Lupino, Richard Widmark, Cornel Wilde. 95M USA. prod/rel: 20th Century-Fox

GRUN, BERNARD
Balalaika, London 1936, Musical Play
   Balalaika 1939 d: Reinhold Schunzel. lps: Nelson Eddy, Ilona Massey, Charles Ruggles. 102M USA. prod/rel: Metro-Goldwyn-Mayer Corp.

GRUNBAUM, FRITZ
Der Zigeunerprimas, Opera
   Zigeunerprimas, Der 1929 d: Carl Wilhelm. lps: Raimondo Van Riel, Margarete Schlegel, Ernst Verebes. 2351m GRM. prod/rel: Aco-Film

GRUNDER, KARL
S'vreneli Am Thunersee, Berne 1925, Musical Play
   S'vreneli Am Thunersee 1936 d: Paul Schmid. lps: Lotti Geissler, Hans Stump, Max Haufler. 71M SWT. *Vreneli du Lac de Thoune* prod/rel: Paul Schmid-Filmproduktion

GRUNDY, MABEL BARNES
Candytuft - I Mean Veronica, Novel
   Candytuft, I Mean Veronica 1921 d: Frank Richardson. lps: Mary Glynne, Leslie Faber, George Relph. 5000f UKN. prod/rel: Zodiac, Cosmograph
The Mating of Marcus, Novel
   Mating of Marcus, The 1924 d: W. P. Kellino. lps: David Hawthorne, George Bellamy, Molly Johnson. 6000f UKN. prod/rel: Stoll

GRUNDY, SIDNEY
A Bunch of Violets, London 1894, Play
   Bunch of Violets, A 1916 d: Frank Wilson. lps: Chrissie White, Gerald Lawrence, Violet Hopson. 3725f UKN. prod/rel: Hepworth, Ward
A Pair of Spectacles, London 1890, Play
   Pair of Spectacles, A 1916 d: Alexander Butler. lps: John Hare, Peggy Hyland, Booth Conway. 3000f UKN. prod/rel: G. B. Samuelson, Moss
Sowing the Wind, London 1893, Play
   Sowing the Wind 1916 d: Cecil M. Hepworth. lps: Henry Ainley, Alma Taylor, Stewart Rome. 5100f UKN. prod/rel: Hepworth
   Sowing the Wind 1921 d: John M. Stahl. lps: Anita Stewart, James Morrison, Myrtle Stedman. 9r USA. prod/rel: Anita Stewart Productions, Associated First National Pictures

GRUNWALD, ALFRED
Play
   Just a Gigolo 1931 d: Jack Conway. lps: William Haines, Irene Purcell, C. Aubrey Smith. 71M USA. *The Dancing Partner* (UKN); *The Princess and the Dancer* prod/rel: Metro-Goldwyn-Mayer Corp., Metro-Goldwyn-Mayer Dist. Corp.©
Ball Im Savoy, Play
   Ball at the Savoy 1936 d: Victor Hanbury. lps: Conrad Nagel, Marta Labarr, Fred Conyngham. 74M UKN. prod/rel: Stafford Films, Radio
   Ball Im Savoy 1955 d: Paul Martin. lps: Eva-Ingeborg Scholz, Rudolf Prack, Nadja Tiller. 90M GRM. *The Ball at the Savoy* prod/rel: Central, Europa
Eine Frau Die Weiss Was Sie Will, Operetta
   Frau, Die Weiss, Was Sie Will, Eine 1934 d: Victor Janson. lps: Lil Dagover, Anton Edthofer, Maria Beling. 84M GRM/CZC. prod/rel: Meissner, Slavia-Film
   Frau, Die Weiss, Was Sie Will, Eine 1958 d: Arthur M. Rabenalt. lps: Lilli Palmer, Peter Schutte, Maria Sebaldt. 101M GRM. *A Woman Who Knows What She Wants* prod/rel: Bavaria
Zena, Ktera Vi Co Chce 1934 d: Vaclav Binovec. lps: Marketa Krausova, Jiri Steimar, Truda GrosslichtovA. 2446m CZC. *A Woman Who Knows What She Wants* prod/rel: Meissner, Slavia-Film

Hoheit Tanzt Walzer, Operetta
  Hoheit Tanzt Walzer 1935 d: Max Neufeld. lps: Hans Homma, Anna Kallina, Phillis Fehr. 103M AUS/CZC. *Tanacek Panny Marinky* (CZC) prod/rel: Elekta
  Valse Eternelle 1936 d: Max Neufeld. lps: Pierre Brasseur, Jean Servais, Renee Saint-Cyr. 102M FRN/CZC. prod/rel: Elekta

GRZIMEK, DR. BERNHARD
Kein Platz Fur Wilde Tiere, Book
  Kein Platz Fur Wilde Tiere 1956 d: Bernard Grzimek, Michael Grzimek. DOC. 81M GRM. *No Room for Wild Animals* prod/rel: Okapia, Michael Grzimek

GSELL, PAUL
Les Gosses Dans Les Ruines, Play
  Gosses Dans Les Ruines, Les 1918 d: George Pearson. lps: Georges Colin, Simone Prevost, Emmy Lynn. 780m FRN.
  Kiddies in the Ruins, The 1918 d: George Pearson. lps: Emmie Lynn, Hugh E. Wright, Georges Colin. 2600f UKN. prod/rel: Welsh, Pearson

GU HUA
Fu Rong Zhen, 1979, Novel
  Furong Zhen 1985 d: XIe Jin. lps: Liu XIaoqing, Jiang Wen, Zhen Zaishi. 160M CHN. *A Small Town Called Hisbiscus; Furong Garrison; Hisbiscus Town* prod/rel: Shanghai Film Studio
Zhen Nu, Novel
  Zhen Nu 1988 d: Huang Jianzhong. lps: Gu Yan, He Wei, Fu Yiwei. 10r CHN. *Two Virtuous Women* prod/rel: Beijing Film Studio

GU LONG
Novel
  Bian Cheng Lang Zi 1993 d: Frankie Chan. lps: Frankie Chan, Ti Lung, Xu Huanshan. F HKG/CHN/TWN. *The Warrior's Tragedy* prod/rel: Xunqi Film Studio (Hong Kong), Longxiang Film Making Corp. (Taiwan)

GU YU
Forced Bonding Cannot Be Sweet, Novel
  Liang Jia Chun 1951 d: Ju Baiyin, XIu Bingduo. lps: Wang Longji, Qing Yi, Shi Hanwei. 10r CHN. *Two Families' Happiness* prod/rel: Changjiang Film Studio
Overture, Short Story
  Manggao Zhi Ge 1976 d: Chang Yan, Zhang Puren. lps: Yu Ping, Liu Wenzhi, Zhou LinA. 9r CHN. *Song of Mangguo* prod/rel: Changchun Film Studio
Yi Jian Tian, Novel
  Yi Jian Tian 1954 d: Li Enjie. lps: Li Jioufang, Wu Bing, Chen Qiang. 9r CHN. *Proposal* prod/rel: Beijing Film Studio

GUAN HANQING
Dou Er Yuan, c1230, Play
  Dou Er Yuan 1959 d: Zhang XInshi. lps: Wang XIulan, Yan Fengchun, Yang Hushan. 129M CHN. prod/rel: Changchun Film Studio
San Kan Hu Die Meng, c1230, Play
  San Kan Hu Die Meng 1958 d: Cai ZhenyA. 110M CHN.
Wang Jiang Ting, c1230, Play
  Wang Jiang Ting 1958 d: Zhou Feng. 90M CHN.

GUARDATI, TOMMASO
Novelliere
  Come Fu Che Masuccio Salernitano, Fuggendo Con le Brache in Mano, Riusci a Conservalo Sano 1973 d: Silvio Amadio. lps: Romano Bernardi, Giulio Donnini, Giorgio Favretto. 94M ITL. *Masuccio Salernitano* prod/rel: Domizia Cin.Ca, Alexa Cin.Ca

GUARE, JOHN (1938–, USA
Six Degrees of Separation, Play
  Six Degrees of Separation 1994 d: Fred Schepisi. lps: Stockard Channing, Will Smith, Donald Sutherland. 111M USA.

GUARESCHI, GIOVANNI
Story
  Don Camillo Monsignore. Ma Non Troppo 1961 d: Carmine Gallone. lps: Fernandel, Gino Cervi, Gina Rovere. 117M ITL/FRN. *Don Camillo -Monseigneur* (FRN) prod/rel: Cineriz
Short Stories
  Retour de Don Camillo, Le 1953 d: Julien Duvivier. lps: Fernandel, Gino Cervi, Edouard Delmont. 115M FRN/ITL. *Il Ritorno Di Don Camillo* (ITL); *The Return of Don Camillo* prod/rel: Francinex (Paris), Filmsonor
Il Compagno Don Camillo, Novel
  Compagno Don Camillo, Il 1965 d: Luigi Comencini. lps: Fernandel, Gino Cervi, Saro Urzi. 109M ITL/FRN/GRM. *Don Camillo En Russie* (FRN) prod/rel: Rizzoli Film (Roma), Francoriz Production (Paris)

Don Camillo E I Giovani d'Oggi, Novel
  Don Camillo E I Giovani d'Oggi 1972 d: Mario Camerini. lps: Gastone Moschin, Lionel Stander, Carole Andre. 111M ITL. prod/rel: Rizzoli Film (Roma), Francoriz Prod. (Paris)
Il Marito in Collegio, Novel
  Marito in Collegio, Il 1977 d: Maurizio Lucidi. lps: Pino Caruso, Enrico Montesano, Silvia Dionisio. 90M ITL. *School for Husbands* prod/rel: Italian International Film
Le Petit Monde de Don Camillo, Novel
  Petit Monde de Don Camillo, Le 1951 d: Julien Duvivier. lps: Fernandel, Gino Cervi, Sylvie. 96M FRN/ITL. *Il Piccolo Mondo Di Don Camillo* (ITL); *Don Camillo*; *The Little World of Don Camillo* prod/rel: Francinex (Paris), Rizzoli Film (Roma)

GUARINI, GIOVAN BATTISTA (1538–1612), ITL, Guarini, Giambattista
Il Pastor Fido, 1590, Poem
  Pastor Fido, Il 1918 d: Telemaco Ruggeri. lps: Mary Bayma-Riva, Annibale Ninchi, Guido Guiducci. 1321m ITL. prod/rel: Floreal Film

GUARNIERI, GIANFRANCESCO
Gimba: Presidente Dos Valentes, 1959, Play
  Gimba 1962 d: Flavio Rangel. 80M BRZ.

GUASTI, AMERIGO
Centoventi H.P., 1906, Play
  Centoventi H.P. 1915 d: Oreste Gherardini. lps: Yvonne de Fleuriel, Guido Trento, Piero Concialdi. ITL. prod/rel: Napoli Film

GUDMUNSSON, KRISTMAN
Morgen Des Lebens, Novel
  Du Darfst Nicht Langer Schweigen 1955 d: R. A. Stemmle. lps: Heidemarie Hatheyer, Wilhelm Borchert, Werner Hinz. 95M GRM. *You Can No Longer Remain Silent* prod/rel: Alfred Greven

GUEDEL, JOHN
Tornado, Novel
  Tornado 1943 d: William Berke. lps: Chester Morris, Nancy Kelly, William Henry. 83M USA. prod/rel: Paramount, Pine-Thomas

GUENTER, C. H.
Mister Dynamit - Morgen Kusst Euch Der Tod, Novel
  Mister Dynamit - Morgen Kusst Euch Der Tod 1967 d: Franz J. Gottlieb. lps: Lex Barker, Maria Perschy, Brad Harris. 111M AUS/GRM/ITL. *Muori Lentamente. Ta la Godi Di Piu* (ITL); *Die Slowly -You'll Enjoy It More*; *Mr. Dynamite - Death Will Kiss You Tomorrow* prod/rel: Parnass, Teide

GUERIN, MICHELLE
Les Oranges d'Israel, Novel
  Valse a Trois 1974 d: Fernand Rivard. lps: Ian Ireland, Karin Schubert, Paule Belanger. 90M CND. *Valse a 3.*; *Les Oranges d'Israel* prod/rel: Enterprises Audio-Visuelles Media Sept, Victor Lallouz Productions Co. Ltd.

GUERINON
A l'Ombre Des Tombeaux, Novel
  Vestale du Gange, La 1927 d: Andre Hugon. lps: Georges Melchior, Regina Thomas, Bernhard Goetzke. 2900m FRN. *The Temple of Shadows* prod/rel: Hugon-Films

GUERNON, CHARLES
Eyes of Youth, New York 1917, Play
  Eyes of Youth 1919 d: Albert Parker. lps: Clara Kimball Young, Milton Sills, Vincent Serrano. 7r USA. prod/rel: Garson Productions, Equity Pictures Corp.
  Eyes of Youth 1920. lps: Abbie Mitchell. USA. prod/rel: Quality Amusement Co.
  Love of Sunya, The 1927 d: Albert Parker. lps: Gloria Swanson, John Boles, Anders Randolf. 7311f USA. prod/rel: Swanson Producing Corp., United Artists
Titans, New York 1922, Play
  Storm Breaker, The 1925 d: Edward Sloman. lps: House Peters, Ruth Clifford, Nina Romano. 6064f USA. *The Titans* prod/rel: Universal Pictures

GUERRA, TONINO
Short Story
  Frullo Del Passero, Il 1988 d: Gianfranco Mingozzi. lps: Philippe Noiret, Ornella Muti, Nicola Farron. 105M ITL/FRN. *La Fruit de Passion* (FRN); *The Fluttering of a Sparrow*; *Moments of Love*; *La Femme de Mes Amours* prod/rel: Basic Cinemat, Reteitalia

GUERRINI, MINO
I Ventenni Non Sono Deliquneti, Book
  Nuovi Angeli, I 1962 d: Ugo Gregoretti. DOC. 105M ITL. *The New Angels* (USA) prod/rel: Arco Film, Galatea

GUEST, JUDITH (1936–, USA, Guest, Judith Ann
Ordinary People, Novel
  Ordinary People 1980 d: Robert Redford. lps: Donald Sutherland, Mary Tyler Moore, Judd Hirsch. 125M USA. prod/rel: Paramount

GUGGENHEIM, KURT
La Nuit Sans Permission, Zurich 1941, Novel
  Nuit Sans Permission, La 1943 d: Franz Schnyder. lps: Paul Hubschmid, Robert Troesch, Robert Freitag. 84M SWT. *Wilder Urlaub* prod/rel: Praesens-Film

GUGLIELMO, MARCO
Er Piu de Roma, Novel
  Principe Fusto, Il 1960 d: Maurizio ArenA. lps: Maurizio Arena, Lorella de Luca, Cathia Caro. 100M ITL. prod/rel: M.A. Produzione Cin.Ca, Eurocine

GUICHES, GUSTAVE
Les Deux Soldats, Novel
  Deux Soldats, Les 1923 d: Jean Herve. lps: Germaine Rouer, Maurice Escande, Daniel Mendaille. 1800m FRN.

GUIDO, BEATRIZ (1925–1988), ARG
La Caida, Novel
  Caida, La 1959 d: Leopoldo Torre-Nilsson. lps: Elsa Daniel, Lautaro Murua, Duilio Marzio. 86M ARG. *La Meno En la Trampa*; *The Fall* prod/rel: Argentine Sono
Convalecencia, Story
  Piel de Verano 1961 d: Leopoldo Torre-Nilsson. lps: Graciela Borges, Alfredo Alcon, Franca Boni. 100M ARG. *Summer Skin* (USA); *Summerskin* prod/rel: Producciones Angel
La Mano En la Trampa, Buenos Aires 1961, Novel
  Mano En la Trampa, La 1961 d: Leopoldo Torre-Nilsson. lps: Elsa Daniel, Francisco Rabal, Leonardo Favio. 90M ARG/SPN. *The Hand in the Trap* (USA) prod/rel: Producciones Angel, Uninci, S.a.

GUIHAN, FRANCES
A Dangerous Adventure, Story
  Dangerous Adventure, A 1922 d: Sam Warner, Jack L. Warner. lps: Philo McCullough, Grace Darmond, Derelys Perdue. 6500f USA. prod/rel: Warner Brothers Pictures

GUILLEMAUD, MARCEL
La Carotte, Play
  Carotte, La 1914. lps: Charles Lamy, Lucien Cazalis, Catherine Fonteney. 780m FRN. prod/rel: Scagl
Le Million, Paris 1910, Play
  Milione, Il 1920 d: Wladimiro Apolloni. lps: Elsa d'Auro, Fernando Ribacchi, Rinaldo Rinaldi. 1651m ITL. prod/rel: Celio Film
  Million, Le 1931 d: Rene Clair. lps: Rene Lefevre, Annabella, Wanda Greville. 91M FRN. prod/rel: Societe Des Films Sonores Tobis
  Million, The 1915 d: Thomas N. Heffron. lps: Edward Abeles, Ruby Hoffman, William Roselle. 4r USA. prod/rel: Famous Players Savage Co., Famous Players Film Co.

GUILLEN, PASCUAL
La Copla Andaluza, Play
  Copla Andaluza, La 1928 d: Ernesto Gonzalez. lps: Maria Luz Callejo, Javier de Rivera, Jose Montenegro. F SPN. prod/rel: Ernesto Gonzalez (Madrid)

GUILLON, JAN
Tacknamen: Coq Rouge, Novel
  Tacknamen: Coq Rouge 1989 d: Pelle Berglund. lps: Stellan Skarsgard, Lennart Hjulstrom, Krister Henriksson. 90M SWD. *Codename: Coq Rouge* prod/rel: Spice Film, Sandrew Film & Theater

GUILLOT, RENE
Fort de la Solitude, Novel
  Fort de la Solitude 1947 d: Robert Vernay. lps: Paul Bernard, Claudine Dupuis, Alexandre Rignault. 90M FRN. *Poste Sud*; *Ras El Gua* prod/rel: U.G.C., Tamara Films

GUILLOU, JAN
Den Enda Segern, Novel
  Hamilton 1998 d: Harald Zwart. lps: Peter Stormare, Lena Olin, Mark Hamill. 127M SWD. prod/rel: Moviola, Tv4
Ingen Mans Land, Novel
  Hamilton 1998 d: Harald Zwart. lps: Peter Stormare, Lena Olin, Mark Hamill. 127M SWD. prod/rel: Moviola, Tv4

GUIMARAES, BERNARDO
O Seminarista, 1895, Novel
  Seminarista, O 1976 d: Geraldo Santos PereirA. 103M BRZ. *The Seminarist*

GUIMARD, PAUL
Les Choses de la Vie, Paris 1967, Novel
Choses de la Vie, Les 1970 d: Claude Sautet. lps: Michel Piccoli, Romy Schneider, Lea Massari. 89M FRN/ITL/SWT. *L' Amante* (ITL); *The Things of Life* (USA); *These Things Happen* prod/rel: Lira Films, Fida Cinematografica

GUIMERA, ANGEL
La Filla Del Mar, 1900, Play
Hija Del Mar, La 1953 d: Antonio Momplet. lps: Virgilio Teixeira, Isabel de Castro, Manuel LunA. 85M SPN. *Daughter of the Sea*

La Hija Del Mar
Hija Del Mar, La 1928 d: Jose Maria Maristany. lps: Marina Torres. SPN.

Maria Rosa, Spain 1890, Play
Maria Rosa 1916 d: Cecil B. de Mille. lps: Geraldine Farrar, Wallace Reid, Pedro de CordobA. 5r USA. prod/rel: Jesse L. Lasky Feature Play Co.©, Paramount Pictures Corp.
Maria Rosa 1964 d: Armando Moreno. lps: Nuria Espert, Francisco Rabal, Luis DavilA. 121M SPN.

Mosen Janot
Padre Juanico, El 1923. lps: Joaquin Montero, Maria Morera, Rosario CoscollA. F SPN. prod/rel: Canigo Films (Barcelona)

Terra Baixa, Madrid 1896, Play
Feudalismo (Scene Siciliane) 1912 d: Alfredo Robert. lps: Attilio Rapisarda, Cesira Archetti-Vecchioni, Mariano Bottino. 960m ITL. prod/rel: Roma Film
Marta of the Lowlands 1914 d: J. Searle Dawley. lps: Bertha Kalich, Wellington Playter, Hal Clarendon. 5r USA. prod/rel: Famous Players Film Co., Paramount Pictures Corp.

GUINDE, EMILE
Le Matelot 512, Novel
Matelot 512, Le 1984 d: Rene Allio. lps: Jacques Penot, Dominique Sanda, Bruno Cremer. 100M FRN. prod/rel: C.M.C.C., Fr 3

GUIRALDES, RICARDO (1886–1927), ARG
Don Segundo Sombra, 1926, Novel
Don Segundo Sombra 1969 d: Manuel Antin. lps: Juan Carballido, Juan Carlos Gene, Adolfo Guiraldes. 100M ARG.

GUIRAUD, EDMOND
Le Bonheur du Jour, Play
Bonheur du Jour, Le 1927 d: Gaston Ravel. lps: Henry Krauss, Elmire Vautier, Pierre Batcheff. F FRN. prod/rel: Jacques Haik

GUITRY, SACHA (1885–1957), FRN, Guitry, Alexandre Pierre Georges
Story
Vie a Deux, La 1958 d: Clement Duhour, Sacha Guitry (Uncredited). lps: Pierre Brasseur, Pauline Carton, Danielle Darrieux. 108M FRN. *Life Together* prod/rel: Clement Duhour, C.L.M.

Aux Deux Colombes, Play
Aux Deux Colombes 1949 d: Sacha Guitry. lps: Sacha Guitry, Lana Marconi, Marguerite Pierry. 95M FRN. prod/rel: Roy-Films

Beaumarchais, Play
Beaumarchais l'Insolent 1996 d: Edouard Molinaro. lps: Fabrice Luchini, Manuel Blanc, Sandrine Kiberlain. 104M FRN. *Beaumarchais the Scoundrel*; *Beaumarchais* prod/rel: le Studio Canal, Telema

Le Blanc Et le Noir, Play
Blanc Et le Noir, Le 1930 d: Robert Florey, Marc Allegret. lps: Raimu, Andre Alerme, Suzanne Dantes. 107M FRN. prod/rel: Etablissements Braunberger-Richebe

Bonne Chance, Short Story
Lucky Partners 1940 d: Lewis Milestone. lps: Ronald Colman, Ginger Rogers, Jack Carson. 99M USA. prod/rel: RKO Radio Pictures©

Deburau, Play
Deburau 1950 d: Sacha Guitry. lps: Sacha Guitry, Lana Marconi, Henry Laverne. 93M FRN. prod/rel: C.I.C.C.
Lover of Camille, The 1924 d: Harry Beaumont. lps: Monte Blue, Willard Louis, Pat Moore. 7300f USA. prod/rel: Warner Brothers Pictures

Desire, Play
Desire 1937 d: Sacha Guitry. lps: Sacha Guitry, Jacqueline Delubac, Arletty. 106M FRN. prod/rel: Cineas

Faison un Reve, 1917, Play
Sleeping Partners 1930 d: Seymour Hicks. lps: Seymour Hicks, Lyn Harding, Herbert Waring. 87M UKN. prod/rel: Geneen, Paramount

Mon Pere Avait Raison, Play
Mon Pere Avait Raison 1936 d: Sacha Guitry. lps: Sacha Guitry, Jacqueline Delubac, Paul Bernard. 87M FRN. prod/rel: Cineas

Le Nouveau Testament, Play
Nouveau Testament, Le 1936 d: Sacha Guitry, Alexandre Ryder. lps: Sacha Guitry, Jacqueline Delubac, Christian Gerard. 85M FRN. prod/rel: Cineas

Quadrille, Play
Quadrille 1937 d: Sacha Guitry. lps: Sacha Guitry, Gaby Morlay, Jacqueline Delubac. 109M FRN. prod/rel: Emile Natan

Toa, Play
Toa 1949 d: Sacha Guitry. lps: Sacha Guitry, Lana Marconi, Jeanne Fusier-Gir. 85M FRN. prod/rel: Films Minerva

GUITTON, JEAN
Au Diable la Vertu, Play
Au Diable la Vertu 1952 d: Jean Laviron. lps: Julien Carette, Henri Genes, Christian Duvaleix. 90M FRN. prod/rel: Marceau, Arca Films

Un Coup Dur, Play
Coup Dur, Un 1949 d: Jean Loubignac. lps: Georges Cahuzac, Rene Hell, Claude Nicot. 21M FRN. prod/rel: Optimax Films

Le Cure de Saint-Amour, Play
Cure de Saint-Amour, Le 1952 d: Emile Couzinet. lps: Frederic Duvalles, Pierre Larquey, Jeanne Fusier-Gir. 88M FRN. prod/rel: Burgus Films

Et la Police N'en Savait Rien, Play
Martyr de Bougival, Le 1949 d: Jean Loubignac. lps: Bach, Roland Armontel, Jeanne Fusier-Gir. 110M FRN. prod/rel: Optimax Films

Fallait Pas M'ecraser, Play
Maris de Ma Femme, Les 1936 d: Maurice Cammage. lps: Roger Treville, Paul Pauley, Christiane Delyne. 85M FRN. prod/rel: Maurice Cammage

Jim la Houlette, Play
Jim la Houlette 1935 d: Andre Berthomieu. lps: Fernandel, Mireille Perrey, Jacques Varennes. 90M FRN. *Jim la Houlette -Roi Des Voleurs* prod/rel: Gamma
Jim la Houlette Roi Des Voleurs 1926 d: Nicolas Rimsky, Roger Lion. lps: Nicolas Rimsky, Gaby Morlay, Louis Vonelly. 2150m FRN. prod/rel: Films Albatros

Legere Et Court-Vetue, Play
Legere Et Court Vetue 1952 d: Jean Laviron. lps: Jean Paredes, Louis de Funes, Madeleine Lebeau. 88M FRN. prod/rel: Arca Films

Une Nuit aux Baleares, Opera
Nuit aux Baleares, Une 1956 d: Paul Mesnier. lps: Georges Guetary, Jean-Marc Thibault, Claude Bessy. 90M FRN. prod/rel: Taurus Films

La Nuit du 3, Play
Devoyes, Les 1925 d: Henri Vorins. lps: Max Maxudian, Marguerite Madys, Marie Glory. SRL. 5EP FRN. *La Nuit du 3* prod/rel: Grandes Productions Cinematographiques

On a Trouve une Femme Nue, Play
On a Trouve une Femme Nue 1934 d: Leo Joannon. lps: Jean Aquistapace, Mireille Balin, Jeanne Loury. 90M FRN. *On a Perdu une Femme Nue* prod/rel: Metropa Films

Le Plus Heureux Des Hommes, Play
Plus Heureux Des Hommes, Le 1952 d: Yves Ciampi. lps: Fernand Gravey, Maria Mauban, Christiane Barry. 87M FRN. prod/rel: Films Du Cyclope, Indus Films

GULBRANNSSEN, TRYGVE
Novel
Und Ewig Singen Die Walder 1959 d: Paul May. lps: Gert Frobe, Joachim Hansen, Hansjorg Felmy. 105M AUS. *Duel With Death* (USA); *Vengeance in Timber Valley*; *Beyond Sing the Woods* prod/rel: Wiener Mundus

Das Erbe von Bjorndal, Novel
Erbe von Bjorndal, Das 1960 d: Gustav Ucicky. lps: Joachim Hansen, Maj-Britt Nilsson, Hans Nielsen. 96M AUS. *The Heritage of Bjorndal* prod/rel: Wiener Mundus

GULICK, BILL, Gulick, William
Bend of the Snake, 1950, Novel
Bend of the River 1952 d: Anthony Mann. lps: James Stewart, Julie Adams, Arthur Kennedy. 91M USA. *Where the River Bends* (UKN) prod/rel: Universal-International

Hallelujah Train, New York 1963, Novel
Hallelujah Trail, The 1965 d: John Sturges. lps: Burt Lancaster, Lee Remick, Jim Hutton. 167M USA. prod/rel: Kappa Corporation, Mirisch Corporation

Man from Texas, 1950, Serial Story
Road to Denver, The 1955 d: Joseph Kane. lps: John Payne, Mona Freeman, Lee J. Cobb. 90M USA. prod/rel: Republic

GUNJI, JIROMASA
Samurai Nippon, Novel
Samurai 1965 d: Kihachi Okamoto. lps: Toshiro Mifune, Keiju Kobayashi, Michiyo AratamA. 123M JPN. *Samurai Assassin* (USA) prod/rel: Toho Co., Toshiro Mifune Production

GUNN, JAMES
Deadlier Than the Male, Novel
Born to Kill 1947 d: Robert Wise. lps: Claire Trevor, Lawrence Tierney, Walter Slezak. 92M USA. *Lady of Deceit* (UKN) prod/rel: RKO

GUNN, JAMES E.
The Immortals, Story
Immortal, The 1969 d: Joseph Sargent. lps: Christopher George, Barry Sullivan, Ralph Bellamy. TVM. 75M USA. prod/rel: Paramount

GUNN, JEANNIE
We of the Never Never, Autobiography
We of the Never Never 1982 d: Igor Auzins. lps: Angela Punch-McGregor, Arthur Dignam, Tony Barry. 134M ASL. prod/rel: Adams Packer Film Prods.©, Film Corporation of Western Australia©

GUNN, NEIL
Novel
Blood Hunt 1985 d: Peter Barber-Fleming. lps: Iain Glen, Michael Carter, Nigel Stock. TVM. 90M UKN. prod/rel: BBC

The Silver Darlings, Novel
Silver Darlings, The 1947 d: Clarence Elder, Clifford Evans. lps: Clifford Evans, Helen Shingler, Carl Bernard. 84M UKN. prod/rel: Holyrood, Pathe

GUNN, VICTOR
Novel
Wirtshaus von Dartmoor, Das 1964 d: Rudolf Zehetgruber. lps: Heinz Drache, Paul Klinger, Ingmar Zeisberg. 95M GRM. *The Inn on Dartmoor* (USA)

GUNNARSSON, PETUR
Punktur, Komma, Strik Punktur, Novel
Punktur, Punktur, Comma, Strik 1980 d: Thorsteinn Jonsson. lps: Petur Bjorn Jonsson, Hallur Helgason, Kristbjorn Kjield. 89M ICL. *Dot, Comma, Dash Dot* prod/rel: Odin Film Company

GUNTER, ARCHIBALD CLAVERING
Novel
Man of Mystery, The 1917 d: Frederick A. Thompson. lps: E. H. Sothern, Charlotte Ives, Gilda Varesi. 5r USA. prod/rel: Vitagraph Co. of America©, Blue Ribbon Feature

A Florida Enchantment, New York 1891, Novel
Florida Enchantment, A 1914 d: Sidney Drew. lps: Sidney Drew, Edith Storey, Ethel Louise Lloyd. 5r USA. prod/rel: Vitagraph Co. of America©, Broadway Star Feature

The Man Behind the Door, New York 1907, Novel
Man Behind the Door, The 1914 d: Wally Van. lps: Wally Van, Nitra Frazer, Cissy Fitzgerald. 4r USA. prod/rel: Vitagraph Co. of America©, Broadway Star Feature

Mr. Barnes of New York, New York 1887, Novel
Mr. Barnes of New York 1914 d: Maurice Costello, Robert Gaillord. lps: Maurice Costello, Mary Charleson, Charles Kent. 6r USA. prod/rel: Vitagraph Co. of America©, Broadway Star Feature
Mr. Barnes of New York 1922 d: Victor Schertzinger. lps: Tom Moore, Anna Lehr, Naomi Childers. 4804f USA. prod/rel: Goldwyn Pictures

Mr. Potter of Texas, Novel
Mr. Potter of Texas 1922 d: Leopold Wharton. lps: MacLyn Arbuckle, Louiszita Valentine, Corene Uzzell. 4400f USA. prod/rel: San Antonio Pictures, Producers Security Corp.

My Official Wife, Play
My Official Wife 1926 d: Paul L. Stein. lps: Irene Rich, Conway Tearle, Jane Winton. 7846f USA. prod/rel: Warner Brothers Pictures

The Princess of Copper, New York 1900, Novel
Surprises of an Empty Hotel, The 1916 d: Theodore Marston. lps: Charles Richman, C. Jay Williams, Arline Pretty. 4r USA. prod/rel: Vitagraph Co. of America©, Blue Ribbon Feature

GUNTHER, AGNES
Die Heilige Und Ihr Narr, Novel
Heilige Und Ihr Narr, Die 1928 d: William Dieterle. lps: Lien Deyers, Wilhelm Dieterle, Gina Manes. 2834m GRM. *The Saint and Her Fool* (USA); *La Sainte Et le Fou* prod/rel: Deutsche Film-Union Ag
Heilige Und Ihr Narr, Die 1935 d: Hans Deppe. lps: Hansi Knoteck, Hans Stuwe, Lola Chlud. 82M GRM. prod/rel: Tonlicht, Kopp

Heilige Und Ihr Narr, Die 1957 d: Gustav Uciky. lps: Gerhard Riedmann, Gudula Blau, Hertha Feiler. 98M AUS. prod/rel: Sascha

GUNTHER, JOHN
Death Be Not Proud, Book
Death Be Not Proud 1975 d: Donald Wrye. lps: Arthur Hill, Jane Alexander, Robby Benson. TVM. 100M USA. prod/rel: Westfall Productions, Good Housekeeping

GUNTHER, K. H.
Novel
Serenade Fur Zwei Spione 1965 d: Michael Pfleghar, Alberto Cardone. lps: Hellmut Lange, Luciano Stella, Barbara Lass. 87M GRM/ITL. *Sinfonia Per Due Spie* (ITL); *Serenade for Two Spies* (USA) prod/rel: Modern Art Film, Metheus Film

GUO CHENGQING
Da Dao Ji, Novel
Da Dao Ji 1977 d: Tang Huada, Wang XIuwen. lps: Yang Zaibao, Pan Jun, Zhong XInghuo. 12r CHN. *Story of a Knife* prod/rel: Shanghai Film Studio

GUO MINGDAO
Huangjiang Nuxia, Novel
Huangjiang Nuxia (Part 1) 1930 d: Cheng Kengran, Zheng Yisheng. lps: Xu Qinfang, He Zhigang, Zheng Yisheng. 10r CHN. *Heroine of the Wild River (Part 1)*; *Danao Baolinsi; Uproar in the Baolin Temple* prod/rel: Youlian Film Company

GUO XIANHONG
Zheng Tu, Novel
Zheng Tu 1976 d: Yan Bili, Bao Qicheng. lps: Guo Kaiming, Zhang Fa, Wang Suhong. 11r CHN. *The Revolutionary Road* prod/rel: Shanghai Film Studio

GUO YUAN
Shui Shou Zhang de Gus Hi, Novel
Shui Shou Zhang de Gu Shi 1963 d: Qiang Ming. lps: Meng Qingliang, Zhao Mao, Gu Xiaoshuang. 11r CHN. *A Boatswain's Story* prod/rel: Haiyan Film Studio

GUR, MOTA
Story
Azit Hakalba Hatzanchanit 1972 d: Boaz Davidson. lps: Yossi Pollack, Gideon Shemer, Mona Silberstein. F ISR. *Azit the Paratrooper Dog*

GURR, MICHAEL
Emmett Stone, Play
Emmett Stone 1985 d: Elizabeth Alexander. lps: Kevin Miles, Patricia Kennedy, Dinah Shearing. TVM. F ASL. prod/rel: Australian Film Theatre

A Pair of Claws, Play
Departure 1986 d: Brian Kavanagh. lps: Patricia Kennedy, Michael Duffield, June Jago. F ASL. prod/rel: Cineaust

GURT, ELISABETH
Eine Frau Fur Drei Tage, Novel
Frau Fur Drei Tage, Eine 1944 d: Fritz Kirchhoff. lps: Hannelore Schroth, Carl Raddatz, Ursula Herking. 80M GRM. *Eine Frau Fur 3 Tage* prod/rel: UFA, Sudwest

GURUJI, SANE
Shyamchi Aai, Novel
Shyamchi Aai 1953 d: Pralhad Keshav Atre. lps: Vanamala, Madhav Vaze, Baburao Pendharkar. 152M IND. *Shyam's Mother; Mother of Shyam* prod/rel: Atre Pictures

GUSMAN, LOUIS
Tennessee, Short Story
Sotto Voce 1996 d: Mario Levin. lps: Lito Cruz, Patricio Contreras, Norma Pons. 88M ARG. prod/rel: Arkadin Productions, Instituto Nacional De Cinematografica

GUSTAFSON, BOSSE
Kungsleden, Stockholm 1963, Novel
Kungsleden 1964 d: Gunnar Hoglund. lps: Mathias Henrikson, Maude Adelson, Lars Lind. 107M SWD. *Obsession* (USA); *My Love and I* (UKN); *The Royal Track* prod/rel: Nordisk Tonefilm

GUSTL, HANS
Die Schuld Der Gabriele Rottweil, Novel
Schuld Der Gabriele Rottweil, Die 1944 d: Arthur M. Rabenalt. lps: Heidemarie Hatheyer, Friedrich Domin, Siegfried Breuer. 80M GRM. *Regimentsmusik* prod/rel: Bavaria, Ring

GUTCHEON, BETH
Without a Trace, Novel
Without a Trace 1983 d: Stanley Jaffe. lps: Kate Nelligan, Judd Hirsch, David Dukes. 117M USA. prod/rel: 20th Century Fox

GUTH, PAUL
Le Naif aux Quarante Enfants, Novel
Naif aux Quarante Enfants, Le 1957 d: Philippe Agostini. lps: Michel Serrault, Silva Kocsina, Simone Paris. 98M FRN. prod/rel: C.L.M. Regina

GUTHRIE, JOHN
The Seekers, Novel
Seekers, The 1954 d: Ken Annakin. lps: Jack Hawkins, Glynis Johns, Noel Purcell. 90M UKN. *Land of Fury* (USA) prod/rel: General Film Distributors, Fanfare

GUTHRIE JR., A. B. (1901–1991), USA, Guthrie Jr., Alfred Bertram
The Big Sky, 1947, Novel
Big Sky, The 1952 d: Howard Hawks. lps: Kirk Douglas, Elizabeth Threatt, Dewey Martin. 140M USA. prod/rel: RKO Radio, Winchester Pictures Corp.

These Thousand Hills, 1956, Novel
These Thousand Hills 1959 d: Richard Fleischer. lps: Don Murray, Richard Egan, Lee Remick. 96M USA. prod/rel: 20th Century-Fox

The Way West, New York 1949, Novel
Way West, The 1967 d: Andrew V. McLaglen. lps: Kirk Douglas, Robert Mitchum, Richard Widmark. 122M USA. prod/rel: Harold Hecht Corporation, United Artists

GUTHRIE, WOODY
Autobiography
Bound for Glory 1976 d: Hal Ashby. lps: David Carradine, Ronny Cox, Melinda Dillon. 147M USA. prod/rel: United Artists Corp.

GUTIERREZ, EDUARDO
Juan Moreira, 1879, Novel
Juan Moreira 1936 d: Nelo Cosimi. 89M ARG.
Juan Moreira 1948 d: Luis Barth-MogliA. lps: Floren Delbene, Dorita Ferreiro, Nedda Francy. 86M ARG.

GUTMAN, CLAUDE
La Maison Vide, Novel
Maison Vide, La 1991 d: Denys Granier-Deferre. lps: Joachim Lombard, Serge Merlin, Isabelle Carre. TVM. 100M FRN.

GUTMAN, WALTER
The Trip to Chicago
Unstrap Me 1968 d: George Kuchar. lps: Walter Gutman, George Segal, Janine Soderhjelm. 78M USA. prod/rel: Hawk Serpent Productions

GWALTNEY, FRANCIS
The Day the Century Ended, 1955, Novel
Between Heaven and Hell 1956 d: Richard Fleischer. lps: Robert Wagner, Terry Moore, Broderick Crawford. 94M USA. prod/rel: 20th Century-Fox

GWYNNE, PAUL
The Bandolero, New York 1904, Novel
Bandolero, The 1924 d: Tom Terriss. lps: Pedro de Cordoba, Gustav von Seyffertitz, Manuel Granado. 6994f USA. prod/rel: Metro-Goldwyn Pictures

GYP
Le Dernier Pardon, Novel
Dernier Pardon, Le 1913 d: Maurice Tourneur. lps: Henry Roussell, Renee Sylvaire. FRN. prod/rel: Eclair

Le Friquet, 1894, Novel
Friquet 1919 d: Gero Zambuto. lps: Leda Gys, Alberto Nepoti, Adriana Vergani. 1660m ITL. prod/rel: Lombardo Film

Friquet, Le 1912 d: Maurice Tourneur. lps: Gilbert Dalleu, Henry Roussell, Polaire. 1230m FRN. prod/rel: Acad

Le Mariage de Chiffon, 1894, Novel
Mariage de Chiffon, Le 1917 d: Alberto Carlo Lolli. lps: Mary Bayma-Riva, Ubaldo Maria Del Colle, Annibale Ninchi. 1344m ITL. prod/rel: Floreal Film

Mariage de Chiffon, Le 1941 d: Claude Autant-LarA. lps: Odette Joyeux, Suzanne Dantes, Andre Luguet. 103M FRN. prod/rel: Industrie Cinematographique

Soeurette, Novel
Soeurette 1913 d: Maurice Tourneur. lps: Henry Roussell, Polaire, Renee Sylvaire. 595m FRN. prod/rel: Acad

GYURKO, LASZLO
Elektra Szerelmem, 1968, Play
Szerelmem Elektra 1974 d: Miklos Jancso. lps: Mari Torocsik, Jozsef Madaras, Gyorgy Cserhalmi. 80M HNG. *My Love Electra; Elektreia* (UKN); *Electra My Love; Elektra*

H

HAASE, JOHN
Erasmus With Freckles, New York 1963, Novel
Dear Brigitte 1965 d: Henry Koster. lps: James Stewart, Fabian, Glynis Johns. 100M USA. *Erasmus With Freckles* prod/rel: 20th Century Fox

Me and the Arch Kook Petulia, New York 1966, Novel
Petulia 1968 d: Richard Lester. lps: Julie Christie, George C. Scott, Richard Chamberlain. 105M UKN/USA. prod/rel: Petersham Films, Warner-Pathe

HAAVARDSHOLM, ESPEN
At Dere Tor!, Novel
At Dere Tor! 1980 d: Lasse Glomm. lps: Eirik Kvale, Eindride Eidsvold, Ole Moystad. 92M NRW. *Stop It* prod/rel: Marcusfilm

HABBERTON, JOHN
Helen's Babies, Boston 1876, Novel
Helen's Babies 1915. lps: Harry Benham, Lorraine Huling, Helen Badgley. 2r USA. prod/rel: Thanhouser
Helen's Babies 1924 d: William A. Seiter. lps: Baby Peggy Montgomery, Clara Bow, Jeanne Carpenter. 5620f USA. prod/rel: Principal Pictures

HABE, HANS (1911–1977), HNG
Frau Irene Besser, Novel
Frau Irene Besser 1960 d: John Olden. lps: Luise Ullrich, Rudolf Prack, Ellen Schwiers. 93M GRM. prod/rel: Omega, Hubla-Kahla

In Namen Des Teufels, Novel
Im Namen Des Teufels 1962 d: John Paddy Carstairs. lps: Peter Van Eyck, MacDonald Carey, Marianne Koch. 77M GRM/UKN. *The Devil's Agent* (UKN) prod/rel: British Lion, Emmett Dalton

Das Netz, Novel
Netz, Das 1975 d: Manfred Purzer. lps: Mel Ferrer, Heinz Bennent, Klaus Kinski. 108M GRM. *The Net* prod/rel: Roxy-Film

A Thousand Shall Fall, Autobiography
Cross of Lorraine, The 1943 d: Tay Garnett. lps: Jean-Pierre Aumont, Gene Kelly, Cedric Hardwicke. 90M USA. prod/rel: MGM

HABECK, FRITZ
Mein Leben Reich Mir Die Hand, Short Story
Reich Mir Die Hand, Mein Leben 1955 d: Karl Hartl. lps: Johanna Matz, Oskar Werner, Gertrud Kuckelmann. 103M AUS. *The Life and Loves of Mozart* (USA) prod/rel: Cosmopol

HABER, JOYCE
The Users, Novel
Users, The 1978 d: Joseph Hardy. lps: Jaclyn Smith, Tony Curtis, Red Buttons. TVM. 125M USA. prod/rel: Aaron Spelling Productions

HACHFELD, ECKART
Story
Letzte Fussganger, Der 1960 d: Wilhelm Thiele. lps: Heinz Erhardt, Christine Kaufmann, Michael Lenz. 87M GRM. *The Last Pedestrian* prod/rel: D.F.H.

HACKETT, ALBERT (1900–), USA
The Diary of Anne Frank, Play
Diary of Anne Frank, The 1980 d: Boris Sagal. lps: Melissa Gilbert, Maximilian Schell, Joan Plowright. TVM. 100M USA. prod/rel: NBC, Twentieth Century Fox

Diary of Anne Frank, The 1987 d: Gareth Davies. lps: Katharine Schlesinger, Emrys James, Elizabeth Bell. TVM. 120M UKN.

Up Pops the Devil, New York 1930, Play
Thanks for the Memory 1938 d: George Archainbaud. lps: Bob Hope, Shirley Ross, Charles Butterworth. 77M USA. prod/rel: Paramount Pictures©

Up Pops the Devil 1931 d: A. Edward Sutherland. lps: Carole Lombard, Norman Foster, Stuart Erwin. 85M USA. prod/rel: Paramount Publix Corp.

HACKETT, WALTER
77 Park Lane, London 1928, Play
Seventy-Seven, Park Lane 1931 d: Albert de Courville. lps: Dennis Neilson-Terry, Betty Stockfeld, Malcolm Keen. 82M UKN. *77 Park Lane* prod/rel: Famous Players' Guild, United Artists
Soixante-Dix-Sept Rue Chalgrin 1931 d: Albert de Courville. lps: Jean Murat, Suzy Pierson, Leon Bary. 80M FRN. *Du Crepuscule a l'Aube* prod/rel: Famous Players Guild

Afterwards, London 1933, Play
Their Big Moment 1934 d: James Cruze. lps: Zasu Pitts, Slim Summerville, Kay Johnson. 70M USA. *Afterwards* (UKN) prod/rel: RKO Radio Pictures©

The Barton Mystery, London 1916, Play
Barton Mystery, The 1920 d: Harry Roberts. lps: Lyn Harding, Hilda Bayley, Vernon Jones. 6158f UKN. prod/rel: Stoll
Barton Mystery, The 1932 d: Henry Edwards. lps: Ursula Jeans, Ellis Jeffreys, Lyn Harding. 77M UKN. prod/rel: British and Dominions, Paramount

Captain Applejack, New York 1921, Play
Strangers of the Night 1923 d: Fred Niblo. lps: Matt Moore, Enid Bennett, Barbara La Marr. 7792f USA. *Captain Applejack*; *Ambrose Applejohn's Adventure* prod/rel: Louis B. Mayer Productions, Metro Pictures

Espionage, London 1935, Play
Espionage 1937 d: Kurt Neumann. lps: Edmund Lowe, Madge Evans, Paul Lukas. 67M USA. prod/rel: Metro-Goldwyn-Mayer Corp.©

Freedom of the Seas, London 1918, Play
Freedom of the Seas 1934 d: Marcel Varnel. lps: Clifford Mollison, Wendy Barrie, Zelma O'Neal. 74M UKN. prod/rel: British International Pictures, Wardour

The Fugitives, London 1936, Play
Love Under Fire 1937 d: George Marshall. lps: Loretta Young, Don Ameche, Borrah Minevitch. 75M USA. *Fandango*; *Spanish Fandango* prod/rel: Twentieth Century-Fox Film Corp.©

The Gay Adventure, London 1931, Play
Gay Adventure, The 1936 d: Sinclair Hill. lps: Yvonne Arnaud, Barry Jones, Nora Swinburne. 74M UKN. prod/rel: Grosvenor, Pathe

Hyde Park Corner, London 1934, Play
Hyde Park Corner 1935 d: Sinclair Hill. lps: Gordon Harker, Binnie Hale, Gibb McLaughlin. 85M UKN. prod/rel: Grosvenor, Pathe

It Pays to Advertise, New York 1914, Play
Criez-le Sur Les Toits 1932 d: Karl Anton. lps: Simone Hellard, Edith Mera, Paul Pauley. 77M FRN. *Shout It from the House Tops* (USA) prod/rel: Films Paramount

It Pays to Advertise 1919 d: Donald Crisp. lps: Bryant Washburn, Lois Wilson, Walter Hiers. 5r USA. prod/rel: Famous Players-Lasky Corp.©, Paramount-Artcraft Pictures

It Pays to Advertise 1931 d: Frank Tuttle. lps: Carole Lombard, Norman Foster, Eugene Pallette. 66M USA. *Have You Got It?* prod/rel: Paramount Publix Corp.©

Other Men's Wives, Play 1929, Play
Sweethearts and Wives 1930 d: Clarence Badger. lps: Billie Dove, Clive Brook, Sidney Blackmer. 7003f USA. prod/rel: First National Pictures

Road House, London 1932, Play
Road House 1934 d: Maurice Elvey. lps: Violet Loraine, Gordon Harker, Emlyn Williams. 76M UKN. prod/rel: Gaumont-British

Sorry You've Been Troubled, London 1929, Play
One New York Night 1935 d: Jack Conway. lps: Franchot Tone, Una Merkel, Harvey Stephens. 71M USA. *The Trunk Mystery* (UKN); *Order Please*; *Murder in the Hotel Diplomat*; *Mystery in Room 309* prod/rel: Metro-Goldwyn-Mayer Corp.

Sorry You've Been Troubled 1932 d: Jack Raymond. lps: Hugh Wakefield, Elsie Randolph, Betty Stockfeld. 78M UKN. *Life Goes on* prod/rel: British and Dominions, Paramount

Take a Chance, 1931, Play
Take a Chance 1937 d: Sinclair Hill. lps: Claude Hulbert, Binnie Hale, Henry Kendall. 73M UKN. prod/rel: Grosvenor, Associated British Film Distributors

HACKETT, WILLIAM
Le Mystere Barton, Play
Mystere Barton, Le 1948 d: Charles Spaak. lps: Fernand Ledoux, Madeleine Robinson, Francoise Rosay. 88M FRN. prod/rel: Societe Des Films Alkam, Radio Cinema

HACKNEY, ALAN
Private Life, Novel
I'm All Right, Jack 1959 d: John Boulting. lps: Ian Carmichael, Terry-Thomas, Peter Sellers. 105M UKN. prod/rel: British Lion, Charter

Private's Progress, Novel
Private's Progress 1956 d: John Boulting. lps: Dennis Price, Terry-Thomas, Ian Carmichael. 102M UKN. prod/rel: Charter, British Lion

HADDICK, VICTOR
The Luck of the Irish, Novel
Luck of the Irish, The 1935 d: Donovan Pedelty. lps: Richard Hayward, Kay Walsh, Niall MacGinnis. 81M UKN. prod/rel: Rh Films, Paramount

HAEBERLE, HORATIUS
Story
Last Word, The 1979 d: Roy Boulting. lps: Richard Harris, Karen Black, Martin Landau. 105M USA. prod/rel: Sundance, Suncrest Cinema

HAEDRICH, MARCEL
Crack in the Mirror, Novel
Crack in the Mirror 1960 d: Richard Fleischer. lps: Orson Welles, Juliette Greco, Bradford Dillman. 97M USA. prod/rel: 20th Century-Fox, Darryl F. Zanuck

HAENSEL, CARL
Der Kampf Ums Matterhorn, Novel
Berg Ruft, Der 1937 d: Luis Trenker. lps: Luis Trenker, Heidemarie Hatheyer, Herbert Dirmoser. 95M GRM. prod/rel: Luis Trenker, Prisma

Kampf Ums Matterhorn, Der 1928 d: Mario Bonnard, Nunzio MalasommA. lps: Luis Trenker, Marcella Albani, Peter Voss. 2692m GRM/SWT. *Struggle for the Matterhorn*; *Le Drame du Mont Cervin*; *Coute Que Coute*; *La Conquete Dramatique du Mont Cervin* prod/rel: Homfilm, Berg-Und Sportfilmgesellschaft

HAGAN, JAMES
One Sunday Afternoon, New York 1933, Play
One Sunday Afternoon 1933 d: Stephen Roberts. lps: Gary Cooper, Frances Fuller, Fay Wray. 85M USA. prod/rel: Paramount Productions©

One Sunday Afternoon 1948 d: Raoul Walsh. lps: Dennis Morgan, Janis Paige, Don Defore. 90M USA. prod/rel: Warner

Strawberry Blonde, The 1941 d: Raoul Walsh. lps: James Cagney, Olivia de Havilland, Rita Hayworth. 97M USA. prod/rel: Warner Bros.

HAGERUP, KLAUS
Markus Og Diana, Novel
Markus Og Diana 1997 d: Svein Scharffenberg. lps: Robert Reierskog, Herman Bernhoft, Laila Goody. 86M NRW. *Markus and Diana* prod/rel: Northern Lights, Norsk Film

HAGGAR, JAMES
The Maid of Cefn Ydfa, Play
Maid of Cefn Ydfa, The 1914 d: William Haggar Jr. lps: Will Haggar Jr., Jenny Haggar. 3000f UKN. prod/rel: Haggar

HAGGARD, H. RIDER (1856–1925), UKN, Haggard, Henry Rider
Allan Quartermain, 1885, Novel
Allan Quartermain and the Lost City of Gold 1986 d: Gary Nelson, Newt Arnold. lps: Richard Chamberlain, James Earl Jones, Henry SilvA. 111M USA. prod/rel: Cannon

King Solomon's Treasure 1976 d: Alvin Rakoff. lps: David McCallum, John Colicos, Patrick MacNee. 88M CND. prod/rel: Canafox Films Inc.

Dawn, Novel
Dawn 1917 d: H. Lisle Lucoque. lps: Karina, Hubert Carter, Madeleine Seymour. 5500f UKN. prod/rel: Lucoque

Jess, London 1887, Novel
Heart and Soul 1917 d: J. Gordon Edwards. lps: Theda Bara, Harry Hilliard, Claire Whitney. 5r USA. *Jess* prod/rel: Fox Film Corp., William Fox©

Jess 1912. lps: Marguerite Snow, Florence Labadie, James Cruze. 3r USA. prod/rel: Thanhouser

Jess 1914. lps: Edna Mae Wilson, Antrim Short, Gertrude Short. 4r USA. prod/rel: Kennedy Features, Inc.©

King Solomon's Mines, London 1885, Novel
King Solomon's Mines 1937 d: Robert Stevenson. lps: Paul Robeson, Cedric Hardwicke, Roland Young. 80M UKN. prod/rel: Gaumont-British, General Film Distributors

King Solomon's Mines 1950 d: Compton Bennett, Andrew Marton. lps: Deborah Kerr, Stewart Granger, Richard Carlson. 102M USA. prod/rel: MGM

King Solomon's Mines 1984 d: J. Lee Thompson. lps: Richard Chamberlain, Sharon Stone, Herbert Lom. 100M USA. prod/rel: Cannon Productions

Watusi 1959 d: Kurt Neumann. lps: George Montgomery, Taina Elg, David Farrar. 85M USA. *The Quest for King Solomon's Mines*; *Return to King Solomon's Mines* prod/rel: MGM

Mr. Meeson's Will, New York 1888, Novel
Grasp of Greed, The 1916 d: Joseph de Grasse. lps: Louise Lovely, Lon Chaney, Jay Belasco. 5r USA. *Mr. Meeson's Will* (UKN) prod/rel: Bluebird Photoplays, Inc.©

Mr. Meeson's Will 1915 d: Frederick Sullivan. lps: Florence Labadie, Justus D. Barnes, Bert Delaney. 3r USA. prod/rel: Thanhouser

She, London 1886, Novel
She 1908 d: Edwin S. Porter. lps: Florence Auer. 1000f USA. prod/rel: Edison

She 1911 d: Theodore Marston. lps: Marguerite Snow, James Cruze, William C. Cooper. 2r USA. prod/rel: Thanhouser

She 1916 d: Will Barker, H. Lisle Lucoque. lps: Alice Delysia, Henry Victor, Sydney Bland. 5400f UKN. prod/rel: Barker, Lucoque

She 1917 d: Kenean Buel. lps: Valeska Suratt, Ben Taggart, Miriam Fouche. 5r USA. prod/rel: Fox Film Corp., William Fox©

She 1925 d: Leander de CordovA. lps: Betty Blythe, Carlyle Blackwell, Mary Odette. 8250f UKN. prod/rel: Reciprocity Films

She 1935 d: Irving Pichel, Lansing C. Holden. lps: Helen Gahagan, Randolph Scott, Helen Mack. 101M USA. prod/rel: RKO Radio Pictures©

She 1965 d: Robert Day. lps: Ursula Andress, Peter Cushing, Bernard Cribbins. 105M UKN. prod/rel: Hammer Films Productions, Seven Arts Productions

She 1983 d: Avi Nesher. lps: Sandahl Bergman, David Goss, Quin Kessler. 106M ITL/USA. *The Barbarian*

Vengeance of She, The 1968 d: Cliff Owen. lps: John Richardson, Olinka Berova, Edward Judd. 101M UKN. prod/rel: Hammer Film Productions, Seven Arts Productions

Stella Fregelius, Novel
Stella 1921 d: Edwin J. Collins. lps: Molly Adair, Manning Haynes, Charles Vane. 5500f UKN. prod/rel: Master, Butcher's Film Service

HAGGART, DAVID
The Life of David Haggart, 1821, Novel
Sinful Davey 1969 d: John Huston. lps: John Hurt, Pamela Franklin, Nigel Davenport. 95M UKN. *The Sinful Adventures of Davey Haggart* prod/rel: Mirisch-Webb Productions, United Artists

HAGGENMACHER, PETER
Die Venus Vom Tivoli, Aarau 1931, Novel
Venus Vom Tivoli, Die 1953 d: Leonard Steckel. lps: Hilde Krahl, Paul Hubschmid, Heinrich Gretler. 95M SWT. *Zwiespalt Des Herzens*; *La Venus du Tivoli*; *Komodianten Des Lebens* prod/rel: Gloriafilm

HAGUET, ANDRE
Foyer Perdu, Play
Foyer Perdu 1952 d: Jean Loubignac. lps: Gaby Morlay, Guy Rapp, Mary Marquet. 105M FRN. *Tu Es un Imbecile* prod/rel: Optimax Films

Une Jeune Fille Savait, Play
Jeune Fille Savait, Une 1947 d: Maurice Lehmann. lps: Dany Robin, Francoise Christophe, Andre Luguet. 110M FRN. prod/rel: Lehmann

Mon Ami le Cambioleur, Play
Mon Ami le Cambrioleur 1950 d: Henri Lepage. lps: Philippe Lemaire, Francoise Arnoul, Pierre Louis. 85M FRN. prod/rel: C.F.P.C.

HAIGH, ERNEST
Secrets of Scotland Yard, Book
Leaves from My Life 1921 d: Edward R. Gordon. lps: Ernest Haigh, Geoffrey Benstead, Suzanne Morris. SHS. UKN. prod/rel: Master Films, White

HAIGHT, GEORGE
Goodbye Again, New York 1932, Play
Goodbye Again 1933 d: Michael Curtiz. lps: Warren William, Genevieve Tobin, Joan Blondell. 65M USA. prod/rel: First National Pictures©

Honeymoon for Three 1941 d: Lloyd Bacon. lps: Ann Sheridan, George Brent, Charlie Ruggles. 77M USA. prod/rel: Warner Bros.

Sweet Mystery of Life, New York 1935, Play
Gold Diggers of 1937 1936 d: Lloyd Bacon. lps: Dick Powell, Joan Blondell, Glenda Farrell. 100M USA. prod/rel: Warner Bros. Pictures©

HAILEY, ARTHUR (1920–, UKN
Airport, New York 1968, Book
Airport 1970 d: George Seaton, Henry Hathaway (Uncredited). lps: Burt Lancaster, Dean Martin, Van Heflin. 137M USA. prod/rel: Universal, Ross Hunter Productions

The Final Diagnosis, New York 1959, Novel
Young Doctors, The 1961 d: Phil Karlson. lps: Fredric March, Ben Gazzara, Eddie Albert. 103M USA. prod/rel: Drexel Films, Millar/Turman Productions

Flight Into Danger, Television Play
Zero Hour! 1957 d: Hall Bartlett. lps: Dana Andrews, Linda Darnell, Sterling Hayden. 83M USA. prod/rel: Paramount, Carmel Enterprises

Hotel, New York 1965, Novel
Hotel 1967 d: Richard Quine. lps: Rod Taylor, Catherine Spaak, Karl Malden. 124M USA. prod/rel: Warner Bros. Pictures

The Moneychangers, Novel
Moneychangers, The 1976 d: Boris Sagal. lps: Kirk Douglas, Christopher Plummer, Anne Baxter. TVM. 315M USA. *Arthur Hailey's the Moneychangers* prod/rel: Ross Hunter Productions, Paramount Pictures

Runway Zero 8, Novel
Terror in the Sky 1971 d: Bernard L. Kowalski. lps: Doug McClure, Lois Nettleton, Roddy McDowall. TVM. 74M USA. prod/rel: Paramount

Strong Medicine, Novel
Strong Medicine 1986 d: Guy Green. lps: Ben Cross, Patrick Duffy, Douglas Fairbanks Jr. TVM. 200M USA/UKN. prod/rel: Telepictures Prods., Tvs Ltd. Productions

Time Lock, Television Play
Time Lock 1957 d: Gerald Thomas. lps: Robert Beatty, Lee Patterson, Betty McDowall. 73M UKN. prod/rel: Romulus, Beaconsfield

Wheels, Novel
Arthur Hailey's Wheels 1978 d: Jerry London. lps: Rock Hudson, Lee Remick, Blair Brown. TVM. 500M USA. prod/rel: Universal TV

HAINES, WILLIAM WISTER
Command Decision, New York 1947, Play
Command Decision 1948 d: Sam Wood. lps: Clark Gable, Walter Pidgeon, Van Johnson. 112M USA. prod/rel: MGM

Slim, Boston 1934, Novel
Slim 1937 d: Ray Enright. lps: Pat O'Brien, Henry Fonda, Stuart Erwin. 86M USA. prod/rel: Warner Bros. Pictures©

HAIS-TYNECKY, JOSEF
Batalion a Divadelni Hra Batalion, Novel
Batalion 1927 d: Premysl Prazsky. lps: Karel Hasler, Bronislava Livia, Vladimir Pospisil-Born. 2193m CZC. *The Amazing Battalion*; *Battalion* prod/rel: Premysl Prazsky, Julius Schmitt

Batalion 1937 d: Miroslav Cikan. lps: Frantisek Smolik, Helena Busova, Hana VitovA. 2658m CZC. *Battalion* prod/rel: Metropolitan

HAITOV, NIKOLAI
Koziyat Rog, 1967, Play
Kozuu Pos 1972 d: Metodi Andonov. lps: Anton Gorchev, Katya Paskaleva, Kliment Denchev. 103M BUL. *The Goat Horn* (USA); *Kozijat Rog*; *Koziat Rog*; *Koziyat Rog*

Mazhki Vremena, 1967, Short Story
Muzhki Vremena 1977 d: Edward Zahariev. lps: Grigor Vachkov, Marianna Dimitrova, Nikola Todev. 125M BUL. *Manly Times*; *Muzki Vremena*; *A Time for Men*; *Mazhki Vremena*; *Masjki Vremena*

HAJIBEYOV, UZEIR
Arshin Mal Alan, Opera
Arshin Mal Alan 1937 d: Setrag Vartian. lps: Setrag Vartian, Louise Barsamian, Vart Ankin. F USA. *The Vagabond Lover*; *The Peddler Lover* prod/rel: Marana Films, Inc.

HALASZ, NICHOLAS
I Accuse!, Book
I Accuse! 1958 d: Jose Ferrer. lps: Jose Ferrer, Anton Walbrook, Viveca Lindfors. 99M UKN. prod/rel: MGM British

HALBE, MAX (1875–1944), GRM
Jugend, 1893, Play
Jugend 1922 d: Fred Sauer. lps: Grete Reinwald, Fritz Schulz, Heinz Salfner. 2060m GRM. prod/rel: Hermes-Film

Jugend 1938 d: Veit Harlan. lps: Eugen Klopfer, Kristina Soderbaum, Werner Hinz. 94M GRM. *Youth* (USA) prod/rel: Tobis, Kristall

Mutter Erde, 1898, Play
Leben Ruft, Das 1944 d: Arthur M. Rabenalt. lps: Paul Klinger, Sybille Schmitz, Gerhild Weber. 81M GRM. prod/rel: Terra

Der Strom, 1903, Play
Strom, Der 1942 d: Gunther Rittau. lps: Lotte Koch, Hans Sohnker, Malte Jager. 89M GRM. *Wenn du Noch Ein Heim Hast* prod/rel: Terra

HALBERT JR., H. A.
The Fighting Pedagogue, Story
Below the Rio Grande 1923 d: Neal Hart. lps: Neal Hart. 5r USA. prod/rel: William Steiner Productions

HALE, EDWARD EVERETT (1822–1909), USA
The Man Without a Country, Short Story
Man Without a Country, The 1909 d: Bannister Merwin. 1000f USA. prod/rel: Edison

Man Without a Country, The 1917 d: Ernest C. Warde. lps: Florence Labadie, Henry J. Hebert, J. H. Gilmour. 6r USA. prod/rel: Thanhouser Film Corp., Jewel Productions, Inc.©

Man Without a Country, The 1925 d: Rowland V. Lee. lps: Edward Hearn, Pauline Starke, Lucy Beaumont. 10r USA. *As No Man Has Loved* prod/rel: Fox Film Corp.

Man Without a Country, The 1973 d: Delbert Mann. lps: Cliff Robertson, Beau Bridges, Peter Strauss. TVM. 73M USA. prod/rel: Norman Rosemont Entertainment

HALE, HAMILTON
Dear Me Or April Changes, New York 1921, Play
Purple Highway, The 1923 d: Henry Kolker. lps: Madge Kennedy, Monte Blue, Vincent Coleman. 6574f USA. prod/rel: Kenma Corp., Paramount Pictures

HALE, JOHN
The Whistle Blower, Novel
Whistle Blower, The 1987 d: Simon Langton. lps: Michael Caine, Nigel Havers, John Gielgud. 104M UKN. *The She-Wolf* prod/rel: Rank, Portreeve

HALEK, VITEZSLAV
Muzikantska Liduska, Short Story
Musikantska Liduska 1940 d: Martin Fric. lps: Gustav Hilmar, Marie Blazkova, Jirina StepnickovA. 2639m CZC. *The Musician's Liduska*; *The Musician's Girl*; *Liduska of the Stage*; *Liduska and Her Musician* prod/rel: Lloyd

HALES, A. G.
McGlusky the Sea Rover, Novel
McGlusky the Sea Rover 1935 d: Walter Summers. lps: Jack Doyle, Tamara Desni, Henry Mollison. 58M UKN. *Hell's Cargo* (USA) prod/rel: British International Pictures, Wardour

HALEVY, JULIAN
The Young Lovers, New York 1955, Novel
Young Lovers, The 1964 d: Samuel Goldwyn Jr. lps: Peter Fonda, Sharon Hugueny, Nick Adams. 110M USA. *Chance Meeting* prod/rel: Metro-Goldwyn-Mayer, Inc.

HALEVY, LUDOVIC
L' Abbe Constantin, France 1882, Novel
Abbe Constantin, L' 1925 d: Julien Duvivier. lps: Jean Coquelin, Genevieve Cargese, Claude France. 2000m FRN. prod/rel: Film d'Art (Vandal Et Delac)

Abbe Constantin, L' 1933 d: Jean-Paul Paulin. lps: Francoise Rosay, Leon Belieres, Betty Stockfeld. 90M FRN. prod/rel: Films P.A.D., Aster-Film

Bettina Loved a Soldier 1916 d: Rupert Julian. lps: Louise Lovely, Rupert Julian, George Berrell. 5r USA. *L' Abbe Constantin* prod/rel: Bluebird Photoplays, Inc.©

L' Ete de la Saint-Martin, Play
Ete de la Saint-Martin, L' 1920 d: Georges Champavert. lps: Joseph Boulle, Germaine Syrdet, Marthe Lepers. 1735m FRN. prod/rel: Phocea Film

Fanny Lear, Play
Fanny Lear 1919 d: Jean Manoussi, Robert Boudrioz. lps: Gabriel Signoret, Germaine Dermoz, Yvonne Sergyl. 1620m FRN. prod/rel: Film d'Art

Frou-Frou, Paris 1869, Play
Frou Frou 1914. lps: Maude Fealy, Harry Benham, James Cruze. 4r USA. prod/rel: Thanhouser Film Corp., Mutual Film Corp.

Frou-Frou 1918 d: Alfredo de Antoni. lps: Francesca Bertini, Guido Trento, Cia Fornaroli. 2078m ITL. prod/rel: Caesar Film

Frou-Frou 1923 d: Guy Du Fresnay. lps: Gina Palerme, Jules Raucourt, Suzanne TalbA. 1792m FRN. prod/rel: Caesar Film

Hungry Heart, A 1917 d: Emile Chautard. lps: Alice Brady, Edward Langford, George MacQuarrie. 5r USA. *Frou Frou* prod/rel: World Film Corp.©, Peerless

Toy Wife, The 1938 d: Richard Thorpe. lps: Luise Rainer, Melvyn Douglas, Robert Young. 95M USA. *Frou Frou* (UKN); *Mlle. Froufrou* prod/rel: Metro-Goldwyn-Mayer Corp., Loew's, Inc.©

La Goualeuse, Play
Goualeuse, La 1914 d: Georges Monca, Alexandre Devarennes. lps: Henry Bosc, Jean Toulout, Jane Marnac. 1400m FRN. prod/rel: Les Grands Films Populaires

Goualeuse, La 1938 d: Fernand Rivers. lps: Constant Remy, Jean Martinelli, Lys Gauty. 90M FRN. prod/rel: Films Fernand Rivers

Les Petites Cardinald, Novel
Petites Cardinal, Les 1950 d: Gilles Grangier. lps: Saturnin Fabre, Jean Tissier, Denise Grey. 93M FRN. *La Famille Cardinal* prod/rel: Codo-Cinema

Le Reveillon, 1872, Play
So This Is Paris 1926 d: Ernst Lubitsch. lps: Monte Blue, Patsy Ruth Miller, Lilyan Tashman. 6135f USA. prod/rel: Warner Brothers Pictures

Tricoche Et Cacolet, Play
Tricoche Et Cacolet 1938 d: Piere Colombier. lps: Fernandel, Frederic Duvalles, Ginette Leclerc. 107M FRN. prod/rel: Films Modernes, Natan, Emile

La Vie Parisienne, Opera
Vie Parisienne, La 1977 d: Christian-Jaque. lps: Bernard Alane, Jean-Pierre Darras, Martine Sarcey. 105M FRN/GRM/ITL. *Pariser Leben* (GRM); *Parisian Life* prod/rel: Belles Rives, S.F.P.

HALEY, ALEX (1921–1992), USA, Haley, Alexander Palmer
The Autobiography of Malcolm X, Autobiography
Malcolm X 1992 d: Spike Lee. lps: Denzel Washington, Spike Lee, Christopher Plummer. 201M USA. prod/rel: Warner Bros., Largo

Roots, Book
Roots 1977 d: David Greene, Marvin J. Chomsky. lps: Maya Angelou, Ji-Tu Cumbuka, Moses Gunn. TVM. 600M USA. prod/rel: David L. Wolper Productions

Roots: the Next Generations 1978 d: John Erman, Lloyd Richards. lps: Georg Stanford Brown, Olivia de Havilland, Henry FondA. TVM. 700M USA. prod/rel: David L. Wolper Productions

Search, Book
Roots: the Next Generations 1978 d: John Erman, Lloyd Richards. lps: Georg Stanford Brown, Olivia de Havilland, Henry FondA. TVM. 700M USA. prod/rel: David L. Wolper Productions

HALL, ANGUS
Devilday, Novel
Madhouse 1974 d: Jim Clark. lps: Vincent Price, Peter Cushing, Robert Quarry. 92M UKN/USA. *The Revenge of Dr. Death* prod/rel: Aip, Amicus

The Late Boy Wonder, London 1969, Novel
Up in the Cellar 1970 d: Theodore J. Flicker. lps: Wes Stern, Joan Collins, Larry Hagman. 92M USA. *Three in the Cellar* (UKN); *3 in the Cellar*; *Three in a Cellar*; *Hi in the Cellar* prod/rel: American International Productions

HALL, BERT
En l'Air! (in the Air), New York 1918, Book
Romance of the Air, A 1919 d: Harry Revier, Franklin B. Coates. lps: Edith Day, Stuart Holmes, Herbert Standing. 7r USA.

HALL, BLAIR
Silence Sellers, Short Story
Silence Sellers, The 1917 d: Burton L. King. lps: Olga Petrova, Mahlon Hamilton, Violet Reed. 5r USA. prod/rel: Metro Pictures Corp.©

Alias Mrs. Jessop, Short Story
Alias Mrs. Jessop 1917 d: Will S. Davis. lps: Emily Stevens, Howard Hall, Donald Hall. 5r USA. prod/rel: Metro Pictures Corp.©

The Other Thing, 1917, Short Story
Marriage Lie, The 1918 d: Stuart Paton. lps: Carmel Myers, Kenneth Harlan, Harry Carter. 5r USA. prod/rel: Bluebird Photoplays, Inc.©

HALL, CHIPMAN
Lightly, Novel
Bayo 1985 d: Mort Ransen. lps: Ed McNamara, Patricia Phillips, Stephen McGrath. 98M CND. prod/rel: Bayo Film Productions Ltd., Jape Film Services Inc.

HALL, FRANKLYN
Parted Curtains, Short Story
Parted Curtains 1920 d: Bertram Bracken. lps: Henry B. Walthall, Mary Alden, Edward Cecil. 5739f USA. prod/rel: National Film Corp of America, State Rights

HALL, GEORGE EDWARDES
The $50.000 Jewel Theft, Story
$50000 Jewel Theft, The 1915 d: Murdock MacQuarrie. lps: Murdock MacQuarrie, Howard MacK, Arthur Moon. 2r USA. prod/rel: Big U

The Mystery of the Tapestry Room, Story
Mystery of the Tapestry Room, The 1915 d: Murdock MacQuarrie. lps: Murdock MacQuarrie, Marjorie Beardsley, Kingsley Benedict. 3r USA. prod/rel: Big U

One of the Best, London 1895, Play
One of the Best 1927 d: T. Hayes Hunter. lps: Carlyle Blackwell, Walter Butler, Eve Gray. 8271f UKN. prod/rel: Gainsborough, Piccadilly

Tainted Money, Story
Tainted Money 1915 d: Ulysses Davis. lps: Hobart Bosworth, Ed Clark, J. Curtis. 5r USA. prod/rel: Universal Film Mfg. Co., Broadway Universal Feature

Was She a Vampire?, Story
Was She a Vampire? 1915 d: Albert W. Hale. SHT USA. prod/rel: Powers

The Whirlpool, Play
Nobody's Child 1919 d: George Edwardes Hall. lps: Jose Collins, Godfrey Tearle, Ben Webster. 5200f UKN. prod/rel: British & Colonial, Butcher's Film Service

HALL, HEIDI
The Magnificent Rescue, Short Story
Claudine's Return 1998 d: Antonio Tibaldi. lps: Christina Applegate, Stefano Dionisi, Matt Clark. 90M USA. prod/rel: Jazz Pictures

HALL, HERSCHEL S.
Steel Preferred, New York 1920, Novel
    Steel Preferred 1926 d: James P. Hogan. lps: Vera Reynolds, William Boyd, Hobart Bosworth. 6680f USA. *The Enduring Flame* prod/rel: Metropolitan Pictures, Producers Distributing Corp.
Yancona Yillies, 1920, Short Story
    Chickens 1921 d: Jack Nelson. lps: Douglas MacLean, Gladys George, Claire McDowell. 4753f USA. prod/rel: Thomas H. Ince Productions, Paramount Pictures

HALL, HOLWORTHY
The Six Best Cellars, 1919, Short Story
    Six Best Cellars, The 1920 d: Donald Crisp. lps: Bryant Washburn, Wanda Hawley, Clarence Burton. 4822f USA. prod/rel: Famous Players-Lasky Corp.©, Paramount-Artcraft Pictures
The Valiant, 1920, Play
    Man Who Wouldn't Talk, The 1940 d: David Burton. lps: Lloyd Nolan, Jean Rogers, Richard Clarke. 72M USA. prod/rel: Twentieth Century-Fox Film Corp.
    Valiant, The 1929 d: William K. Howard. lps: Paul Muni, Johnny Mack Brown, Edith Yorke. 5537f USA. prod/rel: Fox Film Corp.

HALL, HOWARD
The Natural Law, New York 1915, Play
    Natural Law, The 1917 d: Charles H. France. lps: Marguerite Courtot, Howard Hall, George Larkin. 7r USA. prod/rel: France Films, Inc., State Rights

HALL, JAMES N. (1887–1951), USA, Hall, James Norman
Botany Bay, 1941, Novel
    Botany Bay 1953 d: John Farrow. lps: Alan Ladd, James Mason, Patricia MedinA. 94M USA. prod/rel: Paramount
High Barbaree, 1945, Novel
    High Barbaree 1947 d: Jack Conway. lps: Van Johnson, June Allyson, Thomas Mitchell. 91M USA. prod/rel: MGM
The Hurricane, Boston 1936, Novel
    Hurricane 1979 d: Jan Troell. lps: Jason Robards Jr., Mia Farrow, Dayton Ka'ne. 119M USA. *Forbidden Paradise* prod/rel: Paramount
    Hurricane, The 1937 d: John Ford, Stuart Heisler (Uncredited). lps: Dorothy Lamour, Jon Hall, Mary Astor. 110M USA. prod/rel: United Artists Corp., Samuel Goldwyn, Inc.©
Men Against the Sea, 1934, Novel
    Mutiny on the Bounty 1935 d: Frank Lloyd. lps: Charles Laughton, Clark Gable, Franchot Tone. 132M USA. prod/rel: Metro-Goldwyn-Mayer Corp.©
Men Without Country, 1944, Novel
    Passage to Marseille 1944 d: Michael Curtiz. lps: Humphrey Bogart, Claude Rains, Michele Morgan. 110M USA. *Passage to Marseilles* prod/rel: Warner Bros.
Mutiny on the Bounty, Boston 1932, Novel
    Mutiny on the Bounty 1935 d: Frank Lloyd. lps: Charles Laughton, Clark Gable, Franchot Tone. 132M USA. prod/rel: Metro-Goldwyn-Mayer Corp.©
    Mutiny on the Bounty 1962 d: Lewis Milestone, Carol Reed. lps: Marlon Brando, Trevor Howard, Richard Harris. 185M USA. prod/rel: Arcola Pictures, MGM
No More Gas, 1940, Novel
    Tuttles of Tahiti, The 1942 d: Charles Vidor. lps: Charles Laughton, Jon Hall, Peggy Drake. 91M USA. prod/rel: RKO Radio

HALL, JANE
These Glamour Girls, Short Story
    These Glamour Girls 1939 d: S. Sylvan Simon. lps: Lew Ayres, Lana Turner, Richard Carlson. 78M USA. *Those Glamorous Girls* prod/rel: Metro-Goldwyn-Mayer Corp., Loew's, Inc.©

HALL, JENNI
Ask Agamemnon, London 1964, Novel
    Goodbye Gemini 1970 d: Alan Gibson. lps: Judy Geeson, Martin Potter, Michael Redgrave. 89M UKN. prod/rel: Josef Shaftel Productions, Ciro

HALL, JOHN T.
Queen of the Moulin Rouge, New York 1908, Play
    Queen of the Moulin Rouge 1922 d: Ray C. Smallwood. lps: Martha Mansfield, Joseph Striker, Henry Harmon. 6704f USA. prod/rel: Pyramid Pictures, American Releasing Corp.

HALL, OAKLEY
Downhill Racers, New York 1963, Novel
    Downhill Racer 1969 d: Michael Ritchie. lps: Michael Redford, Gene Hackman, Camilla Sparv. 101M USA. *The Downhill Racers* prod/rel: Wildwood International
Warlock, 1958, Novel
    Warlock 1959 d: Edward Dmytryk. lps: Henry Fonda, Richard Widmark, Anthony Quinn. 122M USA. prod/rel: 20th Century-Fox

HALL, PATRICK
The Harp That Once, Novel
    Reckoning, The 1970 d: Jack Gold. lps: Nicol Williamson, Rachel Roberts, Paul Rogers. 111M UKN. prod/rel: Columbia British, Columbia

HALL, RADCLYFFE (1886–1943), UKN
The Well of Loneliness, London 1928, Novel
    Children of Loneliness 1934 d: Richard C. Kahn. lps: Dr. S. Dana Hubbard, Wallace Morgan, Luana Walters. 68M USA. prod/rel: Jewel Productions, Inc.

HALL, ROGER
Middle Age Spread, Play
    Middle-Age Spread 1979 d: John Reid. lps: Grant Tilly, Donna Akersten, Dorothy McKegg. 94M NZL.

HALL, W. STRANGE
Spinner O' Dreams, Play
    Spinner O' Dreams 1918 d: Wilfred Noy. lps: Basil Gill, Odette Goimbault, James Carew. 5340f UKN. prod/rel: Butcher's Film Service

HALL, WILBUR
Johnny Cucabod, 1920, Short Story
    Broken Doll, A 1921 d: Allan Dwan. lps: Monte Blue, Mary Thurman, Mary Jane Irving. 4594f USA. prod/rel: Allan Dwan Productions, Associated Producers
On the Threshold, Short Story
    On the Threshold 1925 d: Renaud Hoffman. lps: Gladys Hulette, Henry B. Walthall, Robert Gordon. 6r USA. prod/rel: Renaud Hoffman Productions, Producers Distributing Corp.

HALL, WILLIS
The Long and the Short and the Tall, London 1959, Play
    Long and the Short and the Tall, The 1960 d: Leslie Norman. lps: Richard Todd, Laurence Harvey, Richard Harris. 110M UKN. *Jungle Fighters* (USA) prod/rel: Michael Balcon Productions, Warner-Pathe

HALLAIS, HENRI
Par le Bout du Nez, Opera
    Enlevez-Moi 1932 d: Leonce Perret. lps: Roger Treville, Jean Devalde, Jacqueline Francell. 98M FRN. prod/rel: Pathe-Natan

HALLER, HERMANN
Der Vetter Aus Dingsda, Opera
    Vetter Aus Dingsda, Der 1934 d: Georg Zoch. lps: Lien Deyers, Lizzi Holzschuh, Walter von Lennep. 75M GRM. *Cousin from Podunk; Damenwahl* prod/rel: Victor Klein, Dietz
    Vetter Aus Dingsda, Der 1953 d: Karl Anton. lps: Vera Molnar, Gerhard Riedmann, Grethe Weiser. 95M GRM. prod/rel: Central-Europa, Prisma

HALLET, RICHARD MATTHEWS
The Canyon of the Fools, New York 1922, Novel
    Canyon of the Fools 1923 d: Val Paul. lps: Harry Carey, Marguerite Clayton, Frederick Stanton. 5180f USA. prod/rel: R-C Pictures, Film Booking Offices of America

HALLIDAY, BRETT
Story
    Larceny in Her Heart 1946 d: Sam Newfield. lps: Hugh Beaumont, Cheryl Walker, Ralph Dunn. 68M USA. prod/rel: Producers Releasing Corp.
    Three on a Ticket 1947 d: Sam Newfield. lps: Hugh Beaumont, Cheryl Walker, Paul Bryar. 64M USA. prod/rel: P.R.C.
Detective Michael Shayne, Novel
    Blonde for a Day 1946 d: Sam Newfield. lps: Hugh Beaumont, Kathryn Adams, Frank Ferguson. 68M USA. prod/rel: Producers Releasing Corp.
The Private Practice of Michael Shayne, New York 1940, Novel
    Michael Shayne, Private Detective 1940 d: Eugene J. Forde. lps: Lloyd Nolan, Marjorie Weaver, Joan Valerie. 77M USA. *The Private Practice of Michael Shayne* prod/rel: Twentieth Century-Fox Film Corp.
The Uncomplaining Corpse, Novel
    Murder Is My Business 1946 d: Sam Newfield. lps: Hugh Beaumont, Cheryl Walker, Lyle Talbot. 64M USA. prod/rel: Producers Releasing Corp.

HALLIDAY, MICHAEL
Cat and Mouse, Novel
    Cat and Mouse 1958 d: Paul RothA. lps: Lee Patterson, Ann Sears, Victor Maddern. 79M UKN. *The Desperate Men; The Desperate Ones* prod/rel: Eros, Anvil

HALLOWELL, JAMES MOTT
The Spirit of Lafayette, Garden City, N.Y. 1918, Book
    Spirit of Lafayette, The 1919 d: James Vincent. lps: Robert Elliott, Earl Schenck, Robert MacQuarrie. 10r USA. prod/rel: James Vincent Film Corp., State Rights

HALMI, ROBERT
Visit to a Chief's Son, Book
    Visit to a Chief's Son 1974 d: Lamont Johnson. lps: Richard Mulligan, Johnny Sekka, John Phillip Hodgson. 92M USA. prod/rel: United Artists

HALSEY, FORREST
My Man, New York 1910, Play
    Triumph of the Weak, The 1918 d: Tom Terriss. lps: Alice Joyce, Walter McGrail, Eulalie Jensen. 4776f USA. *The Strength of the Weak* prod/rel: Vitagraph Co. of America©, Blue Ribbon Feature
The Stain, Novel
    Stain, The 1914 d: Frank Powell. lps: Edward Jose, Thurlow Bergen, Virginia Pearson. 6r USA. prod/rel: Eclectic
The Wonderful Thing, New York 1920, Play
    Wonderful Thing, The 1921 d: Herbert Brenon. lps: Norma Talmadge, Harrison Ford, Julia Hoyte. 6880f USA. prod/rel: Norma Talmadge Productions, Associated First National Pictures

HALSTEAD, SARGESON V.
The Blind Chute, Story
    Devil Bear, The 1929 d: Louis W. Chaudet. lps: Carroll Nye, Dorothy Dwan, Mitchell Lewis. 6r CND. prod/rel: Thunder Bay Films Ltd.

HAMBLEDON, PHYLLIS
No Difference to Me, Novel
    No Place for Jennifer 1950 d: Henry Cass. lps: Leo Genn, Rosamund John, Beatrice Campbell. 90M UKN. prod/rel: Associated British Picture Corporation, Ab-Pathe

HAMBY, WILLIAM HENRY
The Desert Fiddler, Garden City, N.Y. 1921, Novel
    Percy 1925 d: R. William Neill. lps: Charles Ray, Louise Dresser, Joseph Kilgour. 5980f USA. *Mother's Boy* (UKN) prod/rel: Thomas H. Ince Corp., Pathe Exchange, Inc.

HAMILL, PETE (1935–, USA
Flesh and Blood, Novel
    Flesh and Blood 1979 d: Jud Taylor. lps: Tom Berenger, Mitchell Ryan, Kristin Griffith. TVM. 200M USA. *Flesh & Blood* prod/rel: CBS, Paramount

HAMILTON, CICELY
Diana of Dobson's, London 1908, Play
    Diana of Dobson's 1917. lps: Cecilia Loftus, A. B. Imeson, Rachel de SollA. 5000f UKN. prod/rel: Barker, Ideal

HAMILTON, CLAYTON
Thirty Days, 1915, Play
    Girl Habit, The 1931 d: Eddie Cline. lps: Charles Ruggles, Sue Conroy, Tamara GevA. 77M USA. prod/rel: Paramount Publix Corp.©
    Thirty Days 1922 d: James Cruze. lps: Wallace Reid, Wanda Hawley, Charles Ogle. 4930f USA. prod/rel: Famous Players-Lasky, Paramount Pictures

HAMILTON, COSMO (1872–1942), UKN, Gibbs, Cosmo Hamilton
Another Scandal, Boston 1924, Novel
    Another Scandal 1924 d: Edward H. Griffith. lps: Lois Wilson, Herbert Holmes, Ralph Bunker. 7322f USA. *I Will Repay* prod/rel: Tilford Cinemaa Corp., W. W. Hodkinson Corp.
The Blindness of Virtue, London 1908, Novel
    Blindness of Virtue, The 1915 d: Joseph Byron Totten. lps: Edna Mayo, Bryant Washburn, Thomas McLarnie. 5-6r USA. prod/rel: Essanay Film Mfg. Co.©, General Film Co.
The Door That Has No Key, Novel
    Door That Has No Key, The 1921 d: Frank H. Crane. lps: George Relph, Betty Faire, Evelyn Brent. 5400f UKN. prod/rel: Alliance Film Corp.
Duke's Son, Novel
    Duke's Son 1920 d: Franklyn Dyall. lps: Guy Newall, Ivy Duke, Hugh Buckler. 6000f UKN. *Squandered Lives* (USA) prod/rel: George Clark, Stoll
Eve in Exile, Novel
    Eve in Exile 1919 d: Burton George. lps: Charlotte Walker, Thomas Santschi, Wheeler Oakman. 6800f USA. prod/rel: American Film Co.©, Pathe Exchange, Inc.
Exchange of Wives, New York 1919, Play
    Exchange of Wives, An 1925 d: Hobart Henley. lps: Eleanor Boardman, Lew Cody, Renee Adoree. 6300f USA. prod/rel: Metro-Goldwyn-Mayer Pictures
His Friend and His Wife, Boston 1920, Novel
    Midsummer Madness 1920 d: William C. de Mille. lps: Jack Holt, Conrad Nagel, Lois Wilson. 5908f USA. *His Friend and His Wife* prod/rel: Famous Players-Lasky Corp.©, William de Mille Productions

His Majesty the King, Novel
　Exile, The 1947 d: Max Ophuls. lps: Douglas Fairbanks Jr., Maria Montez, Rita Corday. 92M USA. prod/rel: Universal

Men, Women and Money, 1918, Short Story
　Men, Women and Money 1919 d: George Melford. lps: Ethel Clayton, James Neill, Jane Wolfe. 4335f USA. prod/rel: Famous Players-Lasky Corp., Paramount Pictures

The Miracle of Love, New York 1915, Novel
　Miracle of Love, The 1920 d: Robert Z. Leonard. lps: Lucy Cotton, Jackie Saunders, Wyndham Standing. 7r USA. prod/rel: Cosmopolitan Productions, International Film Service Co.©

Paradise, Boston 1925, Play
　Paradise 1926 d: Irvin V. Willat. lps: Milton Sills, Betty Bronson, Noah Beery. 7090f USA. prod/rel: Ray Rockett Productions, First National Pictures

The Princess of New York, New York 1911, Novel
　Princess of New York, The 1921 d: Donald Crisp. lps: David Powell, Mary Glynne, Ivo Dawson. 6400f USA/UKN. prod/rel: Famous Players-Lasky, Paramount Pictures

The Prodigal Father, 1924, Short Story
　Perfect Gentleman, The 1935 d: Tim Whelan. lps: Frank Morgan, Cicely Courtneidge, Heather Angel. 73M USA. *The Imperfect Lady* (UKN) prod/rel: Metro-Goldwyn-Mayer Corp.©

Reckless Youth, Story
　Reckless Youth 1922 d: Ralph Ince. lps: Elaine Hammerstein, Niles Welch, Myrtle Stedman. 5700f USA. prod/rel: Selznick Pictures, Select Pictures

Restless Souls, Short Story
　Restless Souls 1919 d: William C. Dowlan. lps: Alma Rubens, Jack Conway, Kathryn Adams. 6r USA. prod/rel: Triangle Film Corp., Triangle Distributing Corp.

Restless Youth, Story
　Restless Youth 1928 d: W. Christy Cabanne. lps: Marceline Day, Ralph Forbes, Norman Trevor. 5963f USA. *Wayward Youth* (UKN) prod/rel: Columbia Pictures

The Rustle of Silk, Boston 1922, Novel
　Rustle of Silk, The 1923 d: Herbert Brenon. lps: Betty Compson, Conway Tearle, Cyril Chadwick. 6947f USA. prod/rel: Famous Players-Lasky, Paramount Pictures

The Sins of the Children, Boston 1916, Novel
　Sins of the Children, The 1918 d: John S. Lopez. lps: Alma Hanlon, Stuart Holmes, Estar Banks. 5r USA. prod/rel: Harry Rapf Productions, State Rights

The Three Passions, Novel
　Three Passions, The 1928 d: Rex Ingram. lps: Alice Terry, Ivan Petrovitch, Shayle Gardner. 8500f UKN. *Les Trois Passions* prod/rel: St. George's Productions, Allied Artists

Who Cares? a Story of Adolescence, Boston 1919, Novel
　Who Cares? 1919 d: Walter Edwards. lps: Constance Talmadge, Harrison Ford, Spottiswoode Aitken. 4520f USA. prod/rel: Select Pictures Corp.©
　Who Cares 1925 d: David Kirkland. lps: Dorothy Devore, William Haines, Lloyd Whitlock. 5600f USA. prod/rel: Columbia Pictures

HAMILTON, DONALD (1916–, USA
Serial Story
　Five Steps to Danger 1957 d: Henry S. Kesler. lps: Sterling Hayden, Werner Klemperer, Richard Gaines. 80M USA. prod/rel: United Artists, Grand Prods.

Ambush at Blanco Canyon, Serial Story
　Big Country, The 1958 d: William Wyler. lps: Gregory Peck, Jean Simmons, Carroll Baker. 156M USA. prod/rel: United Artists, Anthony-Worldwide

The Ambushers, New York 1963, Book
　Ambushers, The 1967 d: Henry Levin. lps: Dean Martin, Janice Rule, Senta Berger. 102M USA. prod/rel: Meadway-Claude Productions #3

Death of a Citizen, New York 1960, Novel
　Silencers, The 1966 d: Phil Karlson. lps: Dean Martin, Stella Stevens, Daliah Lavi. 102M USA. prod/rel: Meadway-Claude Productions, Columbia

Murderers' Row, New York 1962, Novel
　Murderers' Row 1966 d: Henry Levin. lps: Dean Martin, Ann-Margret, Karl Malden. 108M USA. prod/rel: Meadway-Claude Productions #2

The Silencers, New York 1961, Novel
　Silencers, The 1966 d: Phil Karlson. lps: Dean Martin, Stella Stevens, Daliah Lavi. 102M USA. prod/rel: Meadway-Claude Productions, Columbia

Smoky Valley, Novel
　Violent Men, The 1954 d: Rudolph Mate. lps: Edward G. Robinson, Glenn Ford, Barbara Stanwyck. 96M USA. *Rough Company* (UKN) prod/rel: Columbia

The Wrecking Crew, Greenwich, Ct. 1963, Novel
　Wrecking Crew, The 1968 d: Phil Karlson. lps: Dean Martin, Elke Sommer, Sharon Tate. 105M USA. *House of Seven Joys* prod/rel: Meadway-Claude Productions

HAMILTON, HALE
The Return of Mary, Play
　Return of Mary, The 1918 d: Wilfred Lucas. lps: May Allison, Clarence Burton, Claire McDowell. 5r USA. prod/rel: Metro Pictures Corp.©

HAMILTON, HAMILTON
The Sporting Duchess, New York 1895, Play
　Sporting Duchess, The 1915 d: Barry O'Neil. lps: Rose Coghlan, Ethel Clayton, George Soule Spencer. 6r USA. prod/rel: Lubin Mfg. Co., Lubin Liberty Bell Feature

HAMILTON, HARRY
Banjo on My Knee, Indianapolis 1936, Novel
　Banjo on My Knee 1936 d: John Cromwell. lps: Barbara Stanwyck, Joel McCrea, Walter Brennan. 95M USA. prod/rel: Twentieth Century-Fox Film Corp.

HAMILTON, HENRY
London 1911, Play
　Hope, The 1920 d: Herbert Blache. lps: Jack Mulhall, Marguerite la Motte, Ruth Stonehouse. 6r USA. prod/rel: Metro Pictures Corp.©

The Best of Luck, London 1916, Play
　Best of Luck, The 1920 d: Ray C. Smallwood. lps: Kathryn Adams, Jack Holt, Lilie Leslie. 5421f USA. prod/rel: Screen Classics, Inc., Metro Pictures Corp.©

The Derby Winner, London 1894, Play
　Derby Winner, The 1915 d: Harold Shaw. lps: Edna Flugrath, Gerald Ames, Mary Dibley. 4900f UKN. prod/rel: London, Jury

The Great Ruby, London 1898, Play
　Great Ruby, The 1915 d: Barry O'Neil. lps: Octavia Handworth, George Soule Spencer, Beatrice Morgan. 5r USA. prod/rel: Lubin Mfg. Co.©, V-L-S-E, Inc.

The Royal Oak, London 1889, Play
　Royal Oak, The 1923 d: Maurice Elvey. lps: Betty Compson, Henry Ainley, Henry Victor. 6170f UKN. prod/rel: Stoll

Sealed Orders, London 1913, Play
　Stolen Orders 1918 d: Harley Knoles, George Kelson. lps: Kitty Gordon, Carlyle Blackwell, Montagu Love. 8r USA. prod/rel: William A. Brady, State Rights

The Sins of Society, London 1907, Play
　Sins of Society, The 1915 d: Oscar Eagle. lps: Robert Warwick, Alec B. Francis, Ralph Delmore. 5r USA. prod/rel: William A. Brady Picture Plays, Inc., World Film Corp.©

The Sporting Duchess, New York 1895, Play
　Sporting Duchess, The 1920 d: George W. Terwilliger. lps: Alice Joyce, Percy Marmont, Gustav von Seyffertitz. 7r USA. prod/rel: Vitagraph Co. of America©

The Whip, London 1909, Play
　Whip, The 1917 d: Maurice Tourneur. lps: Irving Cummings, Alma Hanlon, Paul McAllister. 8r USA. prod/rel: Paragon Films, Inc.©, State Rights
　Whip, The 1928 d: Charles J. Brabin. lps: Dorothy MacKaill, Ralph Forbes, Anna Q. Nilsson. 6056f USA. prod/rel: First National Pictures

The White Heather, London 1897, Play
　White Heather, The 1919 d: Maurice Tourneur. lps: Ralph Graves, Mabel Ballin, Holmes Herbert. 6r USA. prod/rel: Maurice Tourneur Productions©, Famous Players-Lasky Corp.

HAMILTON, JAMES SHELLEY
The Miracle of Hate, Story
　Man Who Fights Alone, The 1924 d: Wallace Worsley. lps: William Farnum, Lois Wilson, Edward Everett Horton. 6337f USA. prod/rel: Famous Players-Lasky, Paramount Pictures

HAMILTON, NANCY
Return Engagement, 1936, Play
　Fools for Scandal 1938 d: Mervyn Leroy. lps: Carole Lombard, Fernand Gravey, Ralph Bellamy. 85M USA. *Food for Scandal* prod/rel: Warner Bros. Pictures©

HAMILTON, PATRICK (1909–1962), UKN
Play
　Nattmara 1965 d: Arne Mattsson. lps: Ulla Jacobsson, Gunnar Hellmstrom, Sven Lindberg. 101M SWD. *Nightmare* prod/rel: Svensk

Gas Light, London 1938, Play
　Gaslight 1940 d: Thorold Dickinson. lps: Anton Walbrook, Diana Wynyard, Frank Pettingell. 88M UKN. *Angel Street* (USA); *A Stranger Case of Murder* prod/rel: British National, Anglo
　Gaslight 1944 d: George Cukor. lps: Charles Boyer, Ingrid Bergman, Joseph Cotten. 114M USA. *The Murder in Thorton Square* (UKN) prod/rel: MGM

Hangover Square, 1941, Novel
　Hangover Square 1945 d: John Brahm. lps: Laird Cregar, Linda Darnell, George Sanders. 78M USA. prod/rel: 20th Century-Fox

Rope, 1929, Play
　Rope 1948 d: Alfred Hitchcock. lps: James Stewart, Farley Granger, John Dall. 80M USA. prod/rel: Warner Bros.

To the Public Danger, 1939, Radio Play
　To the Public Danger 1948 d: Terence Fisher. lps: Dermot Walsh, Susan Shaw, Barry Letts. 44M UKN. prod/rel: Production Facilities, General Film Distributors

Twenty Thousand Streets Under the Sky; a London Trilogy, 1935, Novel
　Bitter Harvest 1963 d: Peter Graham Scott. lps: Janet Munro, John Stride, Alan Badel. 96M UKN. prod/rel: Rank Film Distributors, Independent Artists

HAMILTON, VIRGINIA (1936–, USA
The Planet of Junior Brown, Novel
　Planet of Junior Brown, The 1997 d: Clement Virgo. lps: Martin Villafana, Lynn Whitfield, Rainbow Sun Francks. 91M CND. prod/rel: Film Works, Canadian Broadcasting Corp.

HAMILTON, WALKER
All the Little Animals, Novel
　All the Little Animals 1998 d: Jeremy Thomas. lps: John Hurt, Christian Bale, Daniel Benzali. 112M UKN. prod/rel: Recorded Pictures Co., British Screen

HAMLIN, JOHN HAROLD
Painted Ponies, Short Story
　Painted Ponies 1927 d: B. Reeves Eason. lps: Hoot Gibson, William Dunn, Charles Sellon. 5416f USA. prod/rel: Universal Pictures

HAMLIN, MARY
Hamilton, New York 1917, Play
　Alexander Hamilton 1931 d: John G. Adolfi. lps: George Arliss, Doris Kenyon, Montagu Love. 73M USA. prod/rel: Warner Bros. Pictures

HAMMER JR., EARL
Spencer's Mountain, New York 1961, Novel
　Spencer's Mountain 1963 d: Delmer Daves. lps: Henry Fonda, Maureen O'Hara, James MacArthur. 119M USA. prod/rel: Warner Bros. Pictures

HAMMERSTEIN, ARTHUR
New Toys, New York 1924, Play
　New Toys 1925 d: John S. Robertson. lps: Richard Barthelmess, Mary Hay, Katherine Wilson. 7250f USA. prod/rel: Inspiration Pictures, First National Pictures

HAMMERSTEIN II, OSCAR (1895–1960), USA
Children of Dreams, 1930, Musical Play
　Children of Dreams 1931 d: Alan Crosland. lps: Paul Gregory, Margaret Schilling, Tom PatricolA. 78M USA. prod/rel: Warner Bros. Pictures, Inc.

Flower Drum Song, New York 1958, Musical Play
　Flower Drum Song 1961 d: Henry Koster. lps: Nancy Kwan, James Shigeta, Juanita Hall. 133M USA. prod/rel: Ross Hunter Productions, Fields Productions

Golden Dawn, New York 1927, Musical Play
　Golden Dawn 1930 d: Ray Enright. lps: Walter Woolf, Vivienne Segal, Noah Beery. 7447f USA. prod/rel: Warner Brothers Pictures

The King and I, New York 1951, Musical Play
　King and I, The 1999 d: Richard Rich. ANM. 87M USA. prod/rel: Warner Bros., Morgan Creek

Music in the Air, New York 1932, Operetta
　Music in the Air 1934 d: Joe May. lps: Gloria Swanson, John Boles, Douglass Montgomery. 85M USA. prod/rel: Fox Film Corp.©

New Moon, New York 1928, Musical Play
　New Moon 1931 d: Jack Conway. lps: Lawrence Tibbett, Grace Moore, Adolphe Menjou. 85M USA. prod/rel: Metro-Goldwyn-Mayer Corp., Metro-Goldwyn-Mayer Dist. Corp.©
　New Moon 1940 d: Robert Z. Leonard. lps: Jeanette MacDonald, Nelson Eddy, Mary Boland. 105M USA. *Lover Come Back; Parisian Belle* prod/rel: Metro-Goldwyn-Mayer Corp., Loew's, Inc.©

Rainbow, New York 1928, Play
　Song of the West 1930 d: Ray Enright. lps: John Boles, Vivienne Segal, Joe E. Brown. 7185M USA. prod/rel: Warner Brothers Pictures

Rose-Marie, New York 1924, Operetta
　Rose Marie 1954 d: Mervyn Leroy. lps: Howard Keel, Ann Blyth, Bert Lahr. 115M USA. prod/rel: Metro-Goldwyn-Mayer Corp.
　Rose-Marie 1927 d: Lucien Hubbard. lps: Joan Crawford, James Murray, House Peters. 7745f USA. prod/rel: Metro-Goldwyn-Mayer Corp.

Rose-Marie 1936 d: W. S. Van Dyke. lps: Jeanette MacDonald, Nelson Eddy, James Stewart. 113M USA. *Indian Love Call*; *Rose Marie* prod/rel: Metro-Goldwyn-Mayer Corp.©

The Sound of Music, New York 1959, Musical Play
Sound of Music, The 1965 d: Robert Wise. lps: Julie Andrews, Christopher Plummer, Eleanor Parker. 174M USA. prod/rel: Argyle Enterprises

Sunny, New York 1925, Musical Play
Sunny 1930 d: William A. Seiter. lps: Marilyn Miller, Lawrence Gray, Joe Donahue. 81M USA. prod/rel: First National Pictures
Sunny 1941 d: Herbert Wilcox. lps: Anna Neagle, Ray Bolger, John Carroll. 98M USA. prod/rel: RKO Radio

Sweet Adeline, New York 1929, Musical Play
Sweet Adeline 1935 d: Mervyn Leroy. lps: Irene Dunne, Donald Woods, Hugh Herbert. 95M USA. prod/rel: Warner Bros. Productions Corp., Warner Bros. Pictures©

Very Warm for May, Musical Play
Broadway Rhythm 1943 d: Roy Del Ruth. lps: George Murphy, Ginny Simms, Charles Winninger. 114M USA. *The Broadway Melody of 1944* prod/rel: Metro-Goldwyn-Mayer Corp.

HAMMETT, DASHIELL (1894–1961), USA, Hammett, Samuel Dashiell
The Dain Curse, Novel
Dain Curse, The 1978 d: E. W. Swackhamer. lps: James Coburn, Hector Elizondo, Jason Miller. TVM. 300M USA. *Private Eye* prod/rel: CBS, Martin Poll

The Glass Key, New York 1931, Novel
Glass Key, The 1935 d: Frank Tuttle. lps: George Raft, Claire Dodd, Edward Arnold. 77M USA. prod/rel: Paramount Productions©
Glass Key, The 1942 d: Stuart Heisler. lps: Brian Donlevy, Veronica Lake, Alan Ladd. 85M USA. prod/rel: Paramount

The Maltese Falcon, New York 1930, Novel
Maltese Falcon, The 1931 d: Roy Del Ruth. lps: Bebe Daniels, Ricardo Cortez, Dudley Digges. 80M USA. *Dangerous Female*; *All Women*; *A Woman of the World* prod/rel: Warner Bros. Pictures©
Maltese Falcon, The 1941 d: John Huston. lps: Humphrey Bogart, Mary Astor, Peter Lorre. 100M USA. prod/rel: Warner Bros.
Satan Met a Lady 1936 d: William Dieterle. lps: Bette Davis, Warren William, Alison Skipworth. 75M USA. *Men on Her Mind*; *Hard Luck Dame*; *The Man in the Black Hat*; *The Man With the Black Hat* prod/rel: Warner Bros. Pictures©

Roadhouse Nights, 1929, Novel
Roadhouse Nights 1930 d: Hobart Henley. lps: Helen Morgan, Charles Ruggles, Fred Kohler. 71M USA. *The River Inn* prod/rel: Paramount Famous Lasky Corp.

The Thin Man, New York 1932, Novel
Thin Man, The 1934 d: W. S. Van Dyke. lps: William Powell, Myrna Loy, Maureen O'Sullivan. 91M USA. prod/rel: Metro-Goldwyn-Mayer Corp.©, Cosmopolitan Production

Woman in the Dark, 1933, Short Story
Woman in the Dark 1934 d: Phil Rosen. lps: Ralph Bellamy, Fay Wray, Melvyn Douglas. 70M USA. prod/rel: RKO Radio Pictures©

HAMMOND, EDWARD
Badges, New York 1924, Play
Ghost Talks, The 1929 d: Lewis Seiler. lps: Helen Twelvetrees, Charles Eaton, Stepin Fetchit. 6482f USA. prod/rel: Fox Film Corp.

HAMNER JR., EARL
The Homecoming, Novel
Homecoming: a Christmas Story, The 1971 d: Fielder Cook. lps: Patricia Neal, Richard Thomas, Edgar Bergen. TVM. 100M USA. *The Homecoming* prod/rel: Lorimar Productions

HAMSUN, KNUT (1859–1952), NRW, Hamsun, Knut Pederson
Landstrykere, 1927, Novel
Landstrykere 1988 d: Ola Solum. lps: Helge Jordal, Trond Petter Stamso Munch, Marika Lagercrantz. 138M NRW. *Wayfarers*; *Wanderers*

Last Chapter, Novel
Air Si Pur, Un 1997 d: Yves Angelo. lps: Fabrice Luchini, Andre Dussollier, Jacques Boudet. 114M FRN/PLN/BLG. *Ostatni Rozdzial* (PLN); *An Air So Pure*; *Last Chapter* prod/rel: Les Films Alain Sarde, Heritage Films

Mysterier, 1892, Novel
Mysteries 1977 d: Paul de Lussanets, Fons Rademakers. lps: Sylvia Kristel, Rutger Hauer, Rita Tushingham. 103M NTH.

Pa Gjengrodde Stier, 1949, Novel
Eiszeit, Die 1975 d: Peter Zadek, Tankred Dorst. lps: O. E. Hasse, Ulrich Wildgruber, Hannelore Hoger. 115M GRM/NRW. *Ice Age*; *Istid* prod/rel: Poliphon, Wdr

Pan, Kristiania 1894, Novel
Kort Ar Sommaren 1962 d: Bjarne Henning-Jensen. lps: Jarl Kulle, Bibi Andersson, Claes Gill. 110M SWD. *Short Is the Summer* (USA); *Pan*; *Det Kom En Sommar* prod/rel: Sandrews
Pan 1937 d: Olaf Fjord. lps: Marieluise Claudius, Christian Kayssler, Werner Schott. 93M GRM. *Das Schicksal Des Leutnant Thomas Glahn*
Pan 1995 d: Henning Carlsen. lps: Sofie Grabol, Lasse Kolsrud, Bjorn Sundquist. 115M DNM/NRW/GRM. *Two Green Feathers*

Posledni Radost, Novel
Posledni Radost 1921 d: Vaclav Binovec. lps: Ivan Nikolajevic Bersenev, V. Ch. Vladimirov, Suzanne Marwille. CZC. *The Last Joy* prod/rel: Weteb, Iris-Film

Siste Kapitel, 1923, Novel
Letzte Kapitel, Das 1961 d: Wolfgang Liebeneiner. lps: Hansjorg Felmy, Karin Baal, Helmut Lohner. 109M GRM. *The Last Chapter* prod/rel: Europa

Sult, Kristiania 1890, Novel
Svalt 1966 d: Henning Carlsen. lps: Per Oscarsson, Birgitte Federspiel, Sigrid Horne-Rasmussen. 110M SWD/DNM/NRW. *Sult* (DNM); *Hunger* (USA) prod/rel: Henning Carlsen, ABC-Film

Victoria, 1898, Novel
Victoria 1978 d: Bo Widerberg. lps: Michaela Jolin, Stephan Schwartz, Pia Skagermark. 106M SWD/GRM. prod/rel: Corona, Bo Widerberg
Viktoria 1935 d: Carl Hoffmann. lps: Luise Ullrich, Mathias Wieman, Alfred Abel. 91M GRM. prod/rel: Minerva-Tonfilm

HAN SUYIN (1917–, CHN, Comber, Elizabeth
A Many Splendored Thing, 1952, Book
Love Is a Many-Splendored Thing 1955 d: Henry King. lps: William Holden, Jennifer Jones, Torin Thatcher. 102M USA. *A Many-Splendored Thing* prod/rel: 20th Century-Fox

HAN ZIYUN
Haishang Hua Liezhuang, Novel
Haishang Hua 1998 d: Hou Hsiao-Hsien. lps: Tony Leung Chiu-Wai, Michiko Hada, Carina Liu. 120M TWN/JPN. *Flowers of Shanghai* prod/rel: Shochiku Co., 3H Films

HANDEL, YEHUDIT
Story
Tzlila Chozeret 1982 d: Shimon Dotan. lps: Doron Nesher, Liron Nirgad, Danny MuggiA. F ISR. *Repeat Dive*; *Tzila Khozereth*

HANDKE, PETER (1942–, AUS
Die Angst Des Tormanns Beim Elfmeter, 1970, Novel
Angst Des Tormanns Bien Elfmeter, Die 1971 d: Wim Wenders. lps: Arthur Brauss, Kai Fischer, Erika Pluhar. 101M GRM. *The Goalie's Anxiety at the Penalty Kick* (USA); *The Anxiety of the Goalkeeper at the Penalty Kick*; *The Goalkeeper's Fear of the Penalty* (UKN) prod/rel: P.I.F.D.a., Filmverlag Der Autoren

Der Kurze Brief Zum Langen Abschied, 1972, Novel
Kurze Brief Zum Langen Abschied, Der 1977 d: Herbert Vesely. lps: Thomas Astan, Geraldine Chaplin, Alexander Hey. 97M GRM. *The Short Letter to the Long Goodbye* prod/rel: Intertel, ZDF

Die Linkshandige Frau, 1976, Novel
Linkshandige Frau, Die 1978 d: Peter Handke. lps: Edith Clever, Bruno Ganz, Michael Lonsdale. 119M GRM. *The Left-Handed Woman* (USA)

HANDLEY, DOROTHY CURNOR
Room for Two, Story
Rosie the Riveter 1944 d: Joseph Santley. lps: Jane Frazee, Frank Albertson, Vera Vague. 75M USA. *In Rosie's Room* (UKN) prod/rel: Republic

HANFF, HELENE
84 Charing Cross Road, Book
84 Charing Cross Road 1987 d: David Jones. lps: Anne Bancroft, Anthony Hopkins, Judi Dench. 99M USA. prod/rel: Columbia, Brooksfilm

HANKIN, ST. JOHN
The Cassilis Engagement, Play
Not Quite a Lady 1928 d: Thomas Bentley. lps: Mabel Poulton, Janet Alexander, Barbara Gott. 7258f UKN. prod/rel: British International Pictures, Wardour

HANKINS, ARTHUR PRESTON
The Boss of Camp Four, Novel
Boss of Camp 4, The 1922 d: W. S. Van Dyke. lps: Buck Jones, Fritzi Brunette, G. Raymond Nye. 4235f USA. prod/rel: Fox Film Corp.

HANLEY, CLIFFORD
Love from Everybody, London 1959, Novel
Don't Bother to Knock 1961 d: Cyril Frankel. lps: Richard Todd, Nicole Maurey, Elke Sommer. 89M UKN. *Why Bother to Knock?* (USA) prod/rel: Haileywood Films, Ab-Pathe

HANLEY, GERALD
Gilligan's Last Elephant, Cleveland 1962, Novel
Last Safari, The 1967 d: Henry Hathaway. lps: Kaz Garas, Stewart Granger, Gabriella Licudi. 110M UKN. prod/rel: Paramount Film Service, Paramount

HANLEY, JAMES F. (1901–1985), IRL
Honeymoon Lane, New York 1926, Play
Honeymoon Lane 1931 d: William James Craft. lps: Eddie Dowling, Ray Dooley, June Collyer. 8r USA. prod/rel: a V & D Production, Sono Art Productions

Second Hand Rose, 1921, Song
Second Hand Rose 1922 d: Lloyd Ingraham. lps: Gladys Walton, George B. Williams, Eddie Sutherland. 4433f USA. prod/rel: Universal Film Mfg. Co.

HANLINE, MAURICE
Bridge Built at Night, Story
Steel Against the Sky 1942 d: A. Edward Sutherland. lps: Lloyd Nolan, Alexis Smith, Craig Stevens. 68M USA. *Dangerously They Live* prod/rel: Warner Bros.

HANLON, BROOKE
Delicatessen, 1925, Short Story
It Must Be Love 1926 d: Alfred E. Green. lps: Colleen Moore, Jean Hersholt, Malcolm McGregor. 6848f USA. prod/rel: John Mccormick Productions, First National Pictures

HANLON BROTHERS, THE
Fantasma, New York 1884, Play
Fantasma 1914 d: Charles M. Seay. lps: George Hanlon Jr., William T. Carleton, William Ruge. 5r USA. prod/rel: Thomas A. Edison, Inc., General Film Co.

HANMURA, RYO
Sengoku Jieitai, Novel
Sengoku Jieitai 1980 d: Kosei Saito. lps: Shin-Ichi Chiba, Isao Natsuki, Tsunehiko Watase. 139M JPN. *Time Slip*; *The Slip of the Battlefield*; *Day of the Apocalypse*; *Time Slip of the Battlefield*; *Time Wars* prod/rel: Haruki Kadokawa Films, Toei Co.

HANNAY III, ALLEN
Love and Other Natural Disasters, Book
Tiger's Tale, A 1987 d: Peter Douglas. lps: C. Thomas Howell, Ann-Margret, Charles Durning. 97M USA. prod/rel: Atlantic

HANNINEN, KAARLO
Kivelion Karkurit, 1923, Novel
Muurmannin Pakolaiset 1926 d: Erkki Karu. lps: Gunnar Brygge, Sulo Raikkonen, Heikki Valisalmi. 2250m FNL. *Flyktingarna Fran Murman* prod/rel: Suomi-Filmi

HANSBERRY, LORRAINE (1930–1965), USA, Hansberry, Lorraine Vivien
A Raisin in the Sun, New York 1959, Play
Raisin in the Sun, A 1961 d: Daniel Petrie. lps: Sidney Poitier, Claudia McNeil, Ruby Dee. 128M USA. prod/rel: Paman-Doris Productions, Columbia

HANSEN, MARTIN A.
Lognern, 1950, Novel
Logneren 1970 d: Knud Leif Thomsen. lps: Frits Helmuth, Ann-Mari Max Hansen, Vigga Bro. 107M DNM. *The Liar*

HANSI
Mon Village
Mon Village 1920 d: J.-P. Pinchon. lps: Albert Bras, Gaston Sylver, Cesar. 1345m FRN. prod/rel: Film d'Art (Vandal Et Delac)

HANUS, OTAKAR
Ja Jsem Vinna!, Novel
Andelickarka 1929 d: Oldrich Kminek. lps: Anita Janova, Vaclav Norman, Josef Rovensky. 2009m CZC. *The Abortionist* prod/rel: Oldrich Kminek, Primusfilm

Laska Slecny Very, Novel
Laska Slecny Very 1922 d: Vaclav Binovec. lps: Suzanne Marwille, Vaclav Vydra Ml., V. Ch. Vladimirov. CZC. *The Love of Miss Vera* prod/rel: Weteb, Iris-Film

Pitva, Short Story
Jeji Hrich 1939 d: Oldrich Kminek. lps: Zita Kabatova, Zdenek Stepanek, Ladislav Bohac. 2435m CZC. *Her Sin* prod/rel: Nationalfilm

HAO RAN
Part Three Bright Road, Novel
Jin Guang Da Dao 2 1976 d: Sun Yu. lps: Zhang Guomin, Zhu Decheng, Pu Ke. 11r CHN. *Bright Road (Part Two)* prod/rel: Changchun Film Studio

Jin Guang Da Dao, Novel
  Jin Guang Da Dao 1975 d: Lin Nong, Sun Yu. lps: Zhang Guomin, Zhu Decheng, Wang Fuli. 13r CHN. *Bright Road (Part One)* prod/rel: Changchun Film Studio

HARADA, YASUKO
Banka, Novel
  Banka 1957 d: Heinosuke Gosho. lps: Yoshiko Kuga, Masayuki Mori, Mieko Takamine. 115M JPN. *Elegy of the North; An Elegy* prod/rel: Kabukiza

HARARI, ROBERT
The Golden Goose, Story
  Millionaire for Christy, A 1951 d: George Marshall. lps: Eleanor Parker, Fred MacMurray, Richard Carlson. 91M USA. *No Room for the Groom* prod/rel: 20th Century-Fox

HARBACH, OTTO (1873–1963), USA, Hauerbach, Otto
The Cat and the Fiddle, New York 1931, Musical Play
  Cat and the Fiddle, The 1933 d: William K. Howard. lps: Jeanette MacDonald, Ramon Novarro, Frank Morgan. 88M USA. prod/rel: Metro-Goldwyn-Mayer Corp.

The Desert Song, New York 1926, Musical Play
  Desert Song, The 1929 d: Roy Del Ruth. lps: John Boles, Carlotta King, Louise FazendA. 106M USA. prod/rel: Warner Brothers Pictures
  Desert Song, The 1943 d: Robert Florey. lps: Dennis Morgan, Irene Manning, Bruce Cabot. 96M USA. prod/rel: Warner Bros.
  Desert Song, The 1953 d: H. Bruce Humberstone. lps: Kathryn Grayson, Gordon MacRae, Steve Cochran. 110M USA. prod/rel: Warner Bros.

The Firefly, New York 1912, Operetta
  Firefly, The 1937 d: Robert Z. Leonard. lps: Jeanette MacDonald, Allan Jones, Warren William. 131M USA. prod/rel: Metro-Goldwyn-Mayer Corp.©

The Girl of My Dreams, New York 1911, Musical Play
  Girl of My Dreams, The 1918 d: Louis W. Chaudet. lps: Billie Rhodes, Leo Pierson, Frank MacQuarrie. 6r USA. prod/rel: National Film Corp. of America, Exhibitors Mutual Distributing Corp.

Going Up, New York 1917, Play
  Going Up 1923 d: Lloyd Ingraham. lps: Douglas MacLean, Hallam Cooley, Arthur Stuart Hull. 6000f USA. prod/rel: Douglas Maclean Productions, Associated Exhibitors

Golden Dawn, New York 1927, Musical Play
  Golden Dawn 1930 d: Ray Enright. lps: Walter Woolf, Vivienne Segal, Noah Beery. 7447f USA. prod/rel: Warner Brothers Pictures

Kid Boots, New York 1923, Musical Play
  Kid Boots 1926 d: Frank Tuttle. lps: Eddie Cantor, Clara Bow, Billie Dove. 8565f USA. prod/rel: Famous Players-Lasky, Paramount Pictures

No No Nanette, New York 1925, Musical Play
  No, No Nanette 1930 d: Clarence Badger. lps: Bernice Claire, Alexander Gray, Lucien Littlefield. 9100f USA. prod/rel: First National Pictures
  No, No Nanette 1940 d: Herbert Wilcox. lps: Anna Neagle, Roland Young, Helen Broderick. 96M USA. prod/rel: RKO Radio Pictures©, Suffolk Productions
  Tea for Two 1950 d: David Butler. lps: Doris Day, Gordon MacRae, Gene Nelson. 98M USA. prod/rel: Warner Bros.

Rose-Marie, New York 1924, Operetta
  Rose Marie 1954 d: Mervyn Leroy. lps: Howard Keel, Ann Blyth, Bert Lahr. 115M USA. prod/rel: Metro-Goldwyn-Mayer Corp.
  Rose-Marie 1927 d: Lucien Hubbard. lps: Joan Crawford, James Murray, House Peters. 7745f USA. prod/rel: Metro-Goldwyn-Mayer Corp.
  Rose-Marie 1936 d: W. S. Van Dyke. lps: Jeanette MacDonald, Nelson Eddy, James Stewart. 113M USA. *Indian Love Call; Rose Marie* prod/rel: Metro-Goldwyn-Mayer Corp.©

The Silent Witness, New York 1916, Play
  Silent Witness, The 1917 d: Harry Lambart. lps: Alphie James, Gertrude McCoy, Junius Mathews. 7r USA. prod/rel: Authors Film Co., M. H. Hoffman, Inc.

Song of the Flame, New York 1925, Musical Play
  Song of the Flame 1930 d: Alan Crosland. lps: Alexander Gray, Bernice Claire, Noah Beery. 6501f USA. prod/rel: First National Pictures

Sunny, New York 1925, Musical Play
  Sunny 1930 d: William A. Seiter. lps: Marilyn Miller, Lawrence Gray, Joe Donahue. 81M USA. prod/rel: First National Pictures

HARBACH, OTTO (1873–19631), USA, Hauerbach, Otto
  Sunny 1941 d: Herbert Wilcox. lps: Anna Neagle, Ray Bolger, John Carroll. 98M USA. prod/rel: RKO Radio

HARBACH, OTTO (1873–1963), USA, Hauerbach, Otto
Up in Mabel's Room, New York 1919, Play
  Up in Mabel's Room 1926 d: E. Mason Hopper. lps: Marie Prevost, Harrison Ford, Phyllis Haver. 6345f USA. prod/rel: Christie Film Co., Producers Distributing Corp.
  Up in Mabel's Room 1944 d: Allan Dwan. lps: Marjorie Reynolds, Dennis O'Keefe, Gail Patrick. 76M USA. prod/rel: United Artists

HARBEN, WILLIAM NATHANIEL, Harben, Will N.
The Cottage of Delight, New York 1919, Novel
  Love Never Dies 1921 d: King Vidor. lps: Lloyd Hughes, Madge Bellamy, Joe Bennett. 6751f USA. prod/rel: King W. Vidor Productions, Associated Producers

The Desired Woman, New York 1913, Novel
  Desired Woman, The 1918 d: Paul Scardon. lps: Harry T. Morey, Florence Deshon, Jean Paige. 5r USA. prod/rel: Vitagraph Co. of America©, Blue Ribbon Feature

HARBINSON, W. A.
The City's Edge, Novel
  City's Edge, The 1983 d: Ken Quinnell. lps: Tommy Lewis, Hugo Weaving, Katrina Foster. 86M ASL. *Edge of the City; The Running Man* prod/rel: Oliver Sullivan Productions, Cb

HARBURG, E. Y.
Finian's Rainbow, New York 1947, Play
  Finian's Rainbow 1968 d: Francis Ford CoppolA. lps: Fred Astaire, Petula Clark, Tommy Steele. 145M USA. prod/rel: Warner Bros., Seven Arts, Inc.

HARCOURT, CYRIL
In the Night, London 1919, Play
  In the Night 1921 d: Frank Richardson. lps: C. M. Hallard, Dorothy Fane, Hayford Hobbs. 5000f UKN/NTH. *In Den Nacht* (NTH); *Der Intringer; The Intruder* prod/rel: Granger-Binger Film

A Lady's Name, New York 1916, Play
  Lady's Name, A 1918 d: Walter Edwards. lps: Constance Talmadge, Harrison Ford, Emory Johnson. 5r USA. prod/rel: Select Pictures Corp.©

A Pair of Silk Stockings, New York 1914, Play
  Pair of Silk Stockings, A 1918 d: Walter Edwards. lps: Constance Talmadge, Harrison Ford, Wanda Hawley. 5r USA. prod/rel: Select Pictures Corp.©
  Silk Stockings 1927 d: Wesley Ruggles. lps: Laura La Plante, John Harron, Otis Harlan. 6166f USA. prod/rel: Universal Pictures
  They Just Had to Get Married 1933 d: Edward Ludwig. lps: Slim Summerville, Zasu Pitts, Roland Young. 75M USA. *Happy Dollars; They Had to Get Married* prod/rel: Universal Pictures Corp.©

A Place in the Sun, Play
  Place in the Sun, A 1916 d: Larry Trimble. lps: Reginald Owen, Margaret Blanche, Malcolm Cherry. 4600f UKN. prod/rel: Turner Films, Butcher

HARDELLET, ANDRE
Ils, Novel
  Ils 1970 d: Jean-Daniel Simon. lps: Michel Duchaussoy, Charles Vanel, Alexandra Stewart. 100M FRN. *Them* prod/rel: C.O.F.C.I.

HARDIMAN, JAMES W.
The House Where Evil Dwells, Novel
  House Where Evil Dwells, The 1982 d: Kevin Connor. lps: Edward Albert, Susan George, Doug McClure. 88M USA/JPN. prod/rel: Martin B. Cohen Productions, Toei Co.

HARDING, BERTITA
Magic Fire, 1953, Biography
  Magic Fire 1956 d: William Dieterle. lps: Alan Badel, Yvonne de Carlo, Carlos Thompson. 95M USA. prod/rel: Republic

The Phantom Crown, New York 1934, Play
  Juarez 1939 d: William Dieterle. lps: Paul Muni, Bette Davis, Brian Aherne. 132M USA. *The Phantom Crown; Maximilian and Carlotta* prod/rel: Warner Bros. Pictures©

HARDING, GEORGE
North to Bushman's Rock, London 1965, Novel
  Ride the High Wind 1965 d: David Millin. lps: Darren McGavin, Maria Perschy, Albert Lieven. 77M SAF. prod/rel: Killarney Film Studio

HARDING, HARRY
The Hawk of Rede, Novel
  Hutch Stirs 'Em Up 1923 d: Frank H. Crane. lps: Charles Hutchison, Joan Barry, Malcolm Tod. 5200f UKN. prod/rel: Ideal

HARDING, MRS. D. C. F.
Oranges and Lemons, 1916, Novel
  Wat Eeuwig Blijft 1920 d: Maurits H. Binger, B. E. Doxat-Pratt. lps: Constance Worth, Bruce Gordon, Adelqui Millar. 5650f NTH/UKN. *Fate's Plaything* (UKN); *What Remains Forever* prod/rel: Anglo-Hollandia Film

HARDINGE, H. C. M.
Carnival, London 1920, Play
  Carnival 1921 d: Harley Knoles. lps: Matheson Lang, Hilda Bayley, Ivor Novello. 7400f UKN. prod/rel: Alliance Film Corp.
  Carnival 1931 d: Herbert Wilcox. lps: Matheson Lang, Joseph Schildkraut, Chili Bouchier. 88M UKN. *Venetian Nights* (USA) prod/rel: British and Dominions, Woolf & Freedman

HARDINGE, REX
The Blazing Launch Murder, Novel
  Sexton Blake and the Bearded Doctor 1935 d: George A. Cooper. lps: George Curzon, Henry Oscar, Tony Sympson. 64M UKN. prod/rel: Fox British, MGM

HARDMAN, RIC
Short Story
  Gunman's Walk 1958 d: Phil Karlson. lps: Van Heflin, Tab Hunter, Kathryn Grant. 97M USA. prod/rel: Columbia

HARDT-WARDEN, BRUNO
Married in Hollywood, Vienna 1928, Play
  Married in Hollywood 1929 d: Marcel Silver. lps: J. Harold Murray, Norma Terris, Walter Catlett. 9700f USA. prod/rel: Fox Film Corp.

Tanz Ins Gluck, Opera
  Tanz Ins Gluck 1951 d: Alfred Stoger. lps: Johannes Heesters, Waltraut Haas, Lucie Englisch. 101M AUS. prod/rel: Mundus, UFA

HARDY, JOCELYN
Everything Is Thunder, Novel
  Everything Is Thunder 1936 d: Milton Rosmer. lps: Constance Bennett, Oscar Homolka, Douglass Montgomery. 77M UKN. prod/rel: Gaumont-British

HARDY, JOSEPH LEE
The Key, London 1933, Play
  Key, The 1934 d: Michael Curtiz. lps: William Powell, Edna Best, Colin Clive. 71M USA. *High Peril; Sue of Fury* prod/rel: Warner Bros. Pictures©

HARDY, LINDSAY
The Grand Duke and Mr. Pimm, New York 1959, Novel
  Love Is a Ball 1962 d: David Swift. lps: Glenn Ford, Hope Lange, Ricardo Montalban. 112M USA. *All This and Money Too* (UKN); *The Grand Duke and Mr. Pimm* prod/rel: Gold Medal Enterprises, Oxford Productions

HARDY, RENE (1911–, FRN
Amere Victoire, Novel
  Amere Victoire 1957 d: Nicholas Ray. lps: Richard Burton, Curd Jurgens, Ruth Roman. 103M FRN/UKN. *Bitter Victory* (UKN) prod/rel: Robert Lafont Productions, Transcontinental

HARDY, STUART
Forbidden Valley, Novel
  Sierra 1950 d: Alfred E. Green. lps: Audie Murphy, Wanda Hendrix, Dean Jagger. 83M USA. prod/rel: Universal-International

The Mountains are My Kingdom, New York 1937, Book
  Forbidden Valley 1938 d: Wyndham Gittens. lps: Noah Beery Jr., Frances Robinson, Robert Barrat. 68M USA. *Mountains are My Kingdom* prod/rel: Universal Pictures Corp.©

HARDY, THOMAS (1840–1928), UKN
Far from the Madding Crowd, London 1874, Novel
  Far from the Madding Crowd 1915 d: Larry Trimble. lps: Florence Turner, Henry Edwards, Malcolm Cherry. 4580f UKN. prod/rel: Turner Films, Ideal
  Far from the Madding Crowd 1967 d: John Schlesinger. lps: Julie Christie, Terence Stamp, Peter Finch. 168M UKN. prod/rel: Vic Films, Appia Films

Jude the Obscure, Novel
  Jude 1996 d: Michael Winterbottom. lps: Christopher Eccleston, Kate Winslet, Liam Cunningham. 123M UKN. prod/rel: Revolutions Films, BBC Films

The Loves of Margery, Short Story
  Romantica Avventura, Una 1940 d: Mario Camerini. lps: Assia Noris, Gino Cervi, Leonardo Cortese. 82M ITL. prod/rel: E.N.I.C.

The Mayor of Casterbridge, 1886, Novel
  Mayor of Casterbridge, The 1921 d: Sidney Morgan. lps: Fred Groves, Pauline Peters, Warwick Ward. 5500f UKN. prod/rel: Progress, Butcher's Film Service
  Mayor of Casterbridge, The 1978 d: David Giles. lps: Alan Bates, Anna Massey, Anne Stallybrass. MTV. 350M UKN. prod/rel: BBC, Pickwick

The Melancholy Hussar of the German Legion,
Short Story
Scarlet Tunic, The 1997 d: Stuart St. Paul. lps:
Jean-Marc Barr, Emma Fielding, Simon Callow. 92M
UKN. prod/rel: Scarlet Films©, the Bigger Picture Co.
Trust

Our Exploits at West Poley, 1892-93, Short Story
Our Exploits at West Poley 1987 d: Diarmuid
Lawrence. lps: Charlie Condon, Jonathan Jackson,
Anthony Bate. 63M UKN. *Exploits in West-Poley*.

Secret Cave, The 1953 d: John Durst. lps: David
Coote, Susan Ford, Nicholas Emdett. 62M UKN.
prod/rel: Merton Park, Children's Film Foundation

Tess of the d'Urbervilles, London 1891, Novel
Dulhan Ek Raat Ki 1967 d: D. D. Kashyap. lps: Nutan,
Dharmendra, Rehman. 170M IND. *Bride for a Single
Night; Bride for a Night*
Tess 1980 d: Roman Polanski. lps: Nastassja Kinski,
Peter Firth, Leigh Lawson. 171M UKN/FRN. prod/rel:
Renn-Burrill
Tess of the d'Urbervilles 1913 d: J. Searle Dawley.
lps: Minnie Maddern Fiske, Raymond Bond, David
Torrence. 5r USA. prod/rel: Famous Players Film Co.,
State Rights
Tess of the d'Urbervilles 1924 d: Marshall Neilan.
lps: Blanche Sweet, Conrad Nagel, Stuart Holmes. 7500f
USA. prod/rel: Metro-Goldwyn Pictures
Tess of the d'Urbervilles 1998 d: Ian Sharp. lps:
Justine Waddell, Jason Flemyng, Oliver Milburn. TVM.
120M UKN. prod/rel: London Weekend Television, a &
E Television Network

Under the Greenwood Tree, 1873, Novel
Under the Greenwood Tree 1929 d: Harry Lachman.
lps: Marguerite Allan, John Batten, Nigel Barrie. 100M
UKN. prod/rel: British International Pictures, Wardour

The Woodlanders, 1877, Novel
Woodlanders, The 1997 d: Phil Agland. lps: Emily
Woof, Rufus Sewell, Cal MacAninch. 98M UKN.
prod/rel: Channel Four Television Corp.©, Pathe Prods.
Ltd.©

HARE, DAVID
Licking Hitler, 1978, Play
Licking Hitler 1978 d: David Hare. lps: Kate Nelligan,
Bill Paterson, Brenda Fricker. MTV. 64M UKN.
prod/rel: BBC

Plenty, 1978, Play
Plenty 1985 d: Fred Schepisi. lps: Meryl Streep, John
Gielgud, Andre Maranne. 124M USA. prod/rel: 20th
Century-Fox, RKO

The Secret Rapture, Play
Secret Rapture, The 1993 d: Howard Davies. lps:
Juliet Stevenson, Joanne Whalley-Kilmer, Penelope
Wilton. 96M UKN. prod/rel: Oasis, Greenpoint

HARE, WALTER BENJAMIN
Aaron Slick from Punkin Crick, 1919, Play
Aaron Slick from Punkin Crick 1951 d: Claude
Binyon. lps: Dinah Shore, Alan Young, Robert Merrill.
95M USA. *Marshmallow Moon* (UKN) prod/rel:
Paramount, Perlberg-Seaton

HAREL, ISSER
The House on Garibaldi Street, Book
House on Garibaldi Street, The 1979 d: Peter
Collinson. lps: Topol, Nick Mancuso, Janet Suzman.
TVM. 100M USA. *Eichmann* prod/rel: Charles Fries
Prods.

HARGREAVES, GERALD P.
Atalanta; a Story of Atlantis, London 1949, Play
Atlantis, the Lost Continent 1961 d: George Pal. lps:
Anthony Hall, Joyce Taylor, John Dall. 90M USA.
prod/rel: Galaxy Productions

HARGREAVES, REGINALD
Article
Reunion 1932 d: Ivar Campbell. lps: Stewart Rome,
Antony Holles, Fred Schwartz. 60M UKN. prod/rel:
Sound City, MGM

HARGROVE, MARION
*Girl He Left Behind; Or All Quiet in the Third
Platoon*, Novel
Girl He Left Behind, The 1956 d: David Butler. lps:
Tab Hunter, Natalie Wood, Jessie Royce Landis. 103M
USA. prod/rel: Warner Bros.

HARICH, WALTHER
Die Drei Um Edith, Novel
Drei Um Edith, Die 1929 d: Erich Waschneck. lps:
Camilla Horn, Jack Trevor, Gustav Diessl. 2412m GRM.
prod/rel: National-Film Ag

Ursula Schwebt Voruber, Novel
Verdacht Auf Ursula 1939 d: Karl Heinz Martin. lps:
Luli Hohenberg, Anneliese Uhlig, Viktor Staal. 80M
GRM. prod/rel: Bavaria, Ass

HARKER, HERBERT
Goldenrod, Novel
Goldenrod 1977 d: Harvey Hart. lps: Tony Lo Bianco,
Gloria Carlin, Donald Pleasence. TVM. 100M
CND/USA. prod/rel: Talent Associates Ltd. (New York),
Film Funding Productions (Toronto)

HARKER, L. ALLEN
Marigold, London 1936, Play
Marigold 1938 d: Thomas Bentley. lps: Sophie Stewart,
Patrick Barr, Phyllis Dare. 73M UKN. prod/rel:
Associated British Picture Corporation

HARKINS JR., JAMES W.
The Fire Patrol, Worcester 1891, Play
Fire Patrol, The 1924 d: Hunt Stromberg. lps: Anna Q.
Nilsson, Will Jeffries, Spottiswoode Aitken. 6600f USA.
prod/rel: Hunt Stromberg Productions, Chadwick
Pictures

The Midnight Alarm, Play
Midnight Alarm, The 1923 d: David Smith. lps: Alice
Calhoun, Percy Marmont, Cullen Landis. 7100f USA.
prod/rel: Vitagraph Co. of America

Northern Lights, New York 1895, Play
Northern Lights 1914 d: Edgar Lewis. lps: Iva
Shepard, William H. Tooker, Harry Spingler. 5r USA.
prod/rel: Life Photo Film Corp., State Rights

HARKINS, PHILIP
Blackburn's Headhunters, 1955, Book
Surrender - Hell! 1959 d: John Barnwell. lps: Keith
Andes, Susan Cabot, Paraluman. 85M USA. prod/rel:
Allied Artists, Cory Film Corp.

HARLAN, WALTER
Das Nurnbergisch Ei, Play
Unsterbliche Herz, Das 1939 d: Veit Harlan. lps:
Heinrich George, Kristina Soderbaum, Paul Henckels.
107M GRM. prod/rel: Tobis, N.W.D.F.

HARLING, ROBERT
Steel Magnolias, Play
Steel Magnolias 1989 d: Herbert Ross. lps: Sally Field,
Dolly Parton, Shirley MacLaine. 118M USA. prod/rel:
Tri-Star, Columbia

HARMON, DAVID
Story
Johnny Concho 1956 d: Don McGuire. lps: Frank
Sinatra, Keenan Wynn, William Conrad. 84M USA.
prod/rel: United Artists, Kent

HARPER, BARBARA
Safe Harbour, Short Story
Port of Escape 1956 d: Tony Young. lps: Googie
Withers, John McCallum, Bill Kerr. 76M UKN. prod/rel:
Wellington, Renown

HARPER, DAVID
Skyjacked, Novel
Skyjacked 1972 d: John Guillermin. lps: Charlton
Heston, Yvette Mimieux, James Brolin. 90M USA. *Sky
Terror; Airborne* prod/rel: MGM

HARPER, PATRICIA
My Baby Loves Music, Story
My Gal Loves Music 1944 d: Edward Lilley. lps: Bob
Crosby, Grace McDonald, Alan Mowbray. 61M USA. *My
Baby Loves Music* prod/rel: Universal

HARR, JONATHAN
A Civil Action, Book
Civil Action, A 1998 d: Steven Zaillian. lps: John
Travolta, Robert Duvall, Tony Shalhoub. 115M USA.
prod/rel: Buena Vista, Touchstone Pictures©

HARRER, HEINRICH
Seven Years in Tibet, Book
Seven Years in Tibet 1997 d: Jean-Jacques Annaud.
lps: Brad Pitt, David Thewlis, B. D. Wong. 139M
USA/UKN. prod/rel: Mandalay Entertainment,
Reperage and Vanguard Films

HARRIMAN, KARL
Sadie, New York 1907, Novel
Chasing Rainbows 1919 d: Frank Beal. lps: Gladys
Brockwell, William Scott, Dick Rosson. 4151f USA.
Sadie prod/rel: Fox Film Corp., William Fox©

HARRINGTON, JOSEPH
Dernier Domicile Connu, Novel
Dernier Domicile Connu 1970 d: Jose Giovanni. lps:
Lino Ventura, Marlene Jobert, Michel Constantin.
102M FRN/ITL. *Ultimo Domicilio Conosciuto* (ITL)
prod/rel: Rizzoli Film, Cite Films

HARRIS, ALFRED
Suivez le Veuf, Novel
Pile Ou Face 1980 d: Robert Enrico. lps: Philippe
Noiret, Michel Serrault, Dorothee. 105M FRN. *Heads
Or Tails*

HARRIS, AUGUSTUS
The Derby Winner, London 1894, Play
Derby Winner, The 1915 d: Harold Shaw. lps: Edna
Flugrath, Gerald Ames, Mary Dibley. 4900f UKN.
prod/rel: London, Jury

The Royal Oak, London 1889, Play
Royal Oak, The 1923 d: Maurice Elvey. lps: Betty
Compson, Henry Ainley, Henry Victor. 6170f UKN.
prod/rel: Stoll

The Sporting Duchess, New York 1895, Play
Sporting Duchess, The 1915 d: Barry O'Neil. lps:
Rose Coghlan, Ethel Clayton, George Soule Spencer. 6r
USA. prod/rel: Lubin Mfg. Co., Lubin Liberty Bell
Feature
Sporting Duchess, The 1920 d: George W.
Terwilliger. lps: Alice Joyce, Percy Marmont, Gustav
von Seyffertitz. 7r USA. prod/rel: Vitagraph Co. of
America©

HARRIS, BARBARA S.
Who Is Julia?, Novel
Who Is Julia? 1986 d: Walter Grauman. lps: Mare
Winningham, Jameson Parker, Jeffrey Demunn. TVM.
100M USA. prod/rel: CBS

HARRIS, CHARLES K.
After the Ball, 1892, Song
After the Ball 1914 d: Pierce Kingsley. lps: Herbert
Kelcey, Effie Shannon, Robert Vaughn. 6r USA.
prod/rel: Photo Drama Co.©
After the Ball 1924 d: Dallas M. Fitzgerald. lps: Gaston
Glass, Miriam Cooper, Thomas Guise. 6500f USA.
prod/rel: Renco Film Co., Film Booking Offices of
America

Alway in the Way, 1903, Song
Always in the Way 1915 d: J. Searle Dawley. lps: Mary
Miles Minter, Ethelmary Oakland, Lowell Sherman. 6r
USA. prod/rel: Dyreda Art Film Corp., Metro Pictures
Corp.©

Break the News to Mother, 1897, Song
Break the News to Mother 1919 d: Julius Steger. lps:
Pearl Shepard, Raymond Bloomer, Gertrude Berkeley.
6r USA. prod/rel: International Film Service, Select
Pictures Corp.©

School Bells, New York 1915, Play
Hearts of Men 1915 d: Perry N. Vekroff. lps: Arthur
Donaldson, Beulah Poynter, Frank Longacre. 4r USA.
School Bells prod/rel: Charles K. Harris Feature Film
Co., World Film Corp.©

What Children Will Do, Short Story
Ashamed of Parents 1921 d: Horace G. Plympton. lps:
Charles Eldridge, Jack Lionel Bohn, Edith Stockton. 6r
USA. prod/rel: Warner Brothers Pictures

HARRIS, CORRA
I'd Climb the Highest Mountain, Novel
I'd Climb the Highest Mountain 1951 d: Henry
King. lps: William Lundigan, Susan Hayward, Rory
Calhoun. 88M USA. prod/rel: 20th Century-Fox

Making Her His Wife, New York 1914, Novel
Husbands and Wives 1920 d: Joseph Levering. lps:
Vivian Martin, Hugh Thompson. 5422f USA. prod/rel:
Gaumont Co.©, State Rights

HARRIS, CREDO FITCH
Toby, Boston 1912, Novel
One Dollar Bid 1918 d: Ernest C. Warde. lps: J.
Warren Kerrigan, Lois Wilson, Joseph J. Dowling. 5r
USA. *Toby* prod/rel: Paralta Plays, Inc., W. W.
Hodkinson Corp.

HARRIS, ELMER
Brothers, Story
Forbidden Woman, The 1927 d: Paul L. Stein. lps:
Jetta Goudal, Ivan Lebedeff, Leonid Snegoff. 6568f
USA. prod/rel: de Mille Pictures, Pathe Exchange, Inc.

Johnny Belinda, New York 1940, Play
Johnny Belinda 1948 d: Jean Negulesco. lps: Jane
Wyman, Lew Ayres, Charles Bickford. 103M USA.
prod/rel: Warner Bros.
Johnny Belinda 1967 d: Paul Bogart. lps: Mia Farrow,
Ian Bannen, Barry Sullivan. MTV. 50M USA.
Johnny Belinda 1982 d: Anthony Harvey. lps:
Rosanna Arquette, Richard Thomas, Dennis Quaid.
TVM. 100M USA. prod/rel: Warner Bros.

Pretty Mrs. Smith, New York 1914, Play
Pretty Mrs. Smith 1915 d: Hobart Bosworth. lps:
Fritzie Scheff, Owen Moore, Louis Bennison. 5r USA.
prod/rel: Oliver Morosco Photoplay Co.©, Paramount
Pictures Corp.

Sham, New York 1909, Play
Sham 1921 d: Thomas N. Heffron. lps: Ethel Clayton,
Clyde Fillmore, Walter Hiers. 4188f USA. prod/rel:
Famous Players-Lasky, Paramount Pictures

So Long Letty, New York 1916, Musical Play
  So Long Letty 1920 d: Al Christie. lps: T. Roy Barnes, Colleen Moore, Grace Darmond. 6r USA. prod/rel: Christie Film Co., Robertson-Cole Distributing Corp.©
  So Long Letty 1929 d: Lloyd Bacon. lps: Charlotte Greenwood, Claude Gillingwater, Grant Withers. 5865f USA. prod/rel: Warner Brothers Pictures

Young Sinners, New York 1929, Play
  Young Sinners 1931 d: John G. Blystone. lps: Thomas Meighan, Hardie Albright, Dorothy Jordan. 79M USA. *Wings of Youth* prod/rel: Fox Film Corp.©

HARRIS, FRANK (1856–1931), IRL
My Reminiscences As a Cowboy, Book
  Cowboy 1958 d: Delmer Daves. lps: Glenn Ford, Jack Lemmon, Anna Kashfi. 92M USA. prod/rel: Columbia, Phoenix Pictures

HARRIS, JED
Broadway; a Play, New York 1927, Play
  Broadway 1929 d: Paul Fejos. lps: Glenn Tryon, Evelyn Brent, Merna Kennedy. 9661f USA. prod/rel: Universal Pictures
  Broadway 1942 d: William A. Seiter. lps: George Raft, Pat O'Brien, Janet Blair. 91M USA. prod/rel: Universal

HARRIS, JOHN
The Sea Shall Not Have Them, Novel
  Sea Shall Not Have Them, The 1954 d: Lewis Gilbert. lps: Michael Redgrave, Dirk Bogarde, Anthony Steel. 93M UKN. prod/rel: Eros, Apollo

HARRIS, KENNETH
Junk, 1920, Short Story
  Idle Rich, The 1921 d: Maxwell Karger. lps: Bert Lytell, Virginia Valli, John Davidson. 4848f USA. *Junk* prod/rel: Metro Pictures

HARRIS, KENNETT
Talismans, Play
  Fools for Luck 1917 d: Lawrence C. Windom. lps: Taylor Holmes, Helen Ferguson, Robert Bolder. 5r USA. prod/rel: Essanay Film Mfg. Co.©, Perfection Pictures

HARRIS, MARILYN
The Girl Called Hatter Fox, Book
  Girl Called Hatter Fox, The 1977 d: George Schaefer. lps: Ronny Cox, Conchata Ferrell, John Durren. TVM. 100M USA. prod/rel: CBS, Emi Television

HARRIS, MARK
Bang the Drum Slowly, 1956, Novel
  Bang the Drum Slowly 1973 d: John Hancock. lps: Michael Moriarty, Robert de Niro, Vincent GardeniA. 97M USA. prod/rel: Paramount

HARRIS, RICHARD
Outside Edge, Play
  Outside Edge 1982 d: Kevin Billington. lps: Paul Eddington, Prunella Scales, Maureen Lipman. MTV. 105M UKN. prod/rel: Lwt
Stepping Out, 1984, Play
  Stepping Out 1991 d: Lewis Gilbert. lps: Liza Minnelli, Shelley Winters, Bill Irwin. 110M USA/CND. prod/rel: Paramount

HARRIS, ROBERT
Fatherland, Novel
  Fatherland 1994 d: Christopher Menaul. lps: Rutger Hauer, Miranda Richardson, Jean Marsh. TVM. 120M USA.

HARRIS, THEODOSIA
Martyrs of the Alamo, Novel
  Martyrs of the Alamo, The 1915 d: W. Christy Cabanne. lps: Sam de Grasse, Walter Long, Tom Wilson. 5r USA. prod/rel: Fine Arts Film Co., Triangle Film Corp.©

HARRIS, THOMAS
Black Sunday, Novel
  Black Sunday 1977 d: John Frankenheimer. lps: Robert Shaw, Bruce Dern, Marthe Keller. 143M USA. prod/rel: Paramount
Red Dragon, Novel
  Manhunter 1986 d: Michael Mann. lps: William L. Petersen, Kim Greist, Joan Allen. 119M USA. *Red Dragon* prod/rel: Red Dragon Productions, de Laurentiis Entertainment Group
The Silence of the Lambs, Novel
  Silence of the Lambs, The 1991 d: Jonathan Demme. lps: Jodie Foster, Anthony Hopkins, Scott Glenn. 118M USA. prod/rel: Orion Pictures, Strong Heart/Demme

HARRIS, TIMOTHY
Good Night and Good Bye, Novel
  Street of Dreams 1988 d: William A. Graham. lps: Ben Masters, Morgan Fairchild, John Hillerman. TVM. 100M USA. prod/rel: Phoenix Entertainment Group

HARRIS-BURLAND, JOHN
The White Rook, New York 1918, Novel
  His Wife's Friend 1919 d: Joseph de Grasse. lps: Dorothy Dalton, Warren Cook, Henry Mortimer. 5613f USA. *The White Rook* prod/rel: Thomas H. Ince Productions, Famous Players-Lasky Corp.

HARRISON, C. WILLIAM
Story
  Guns of Fort Petticoat, The 1957 d: George Marshall. lps: Audie Murphy, Kathryn Grant, Hope Emerson. 82M USA. prod/rel: Columbia, Brown-Murphy Pictures

HARRISON, CRAIG
The Quiet Earth, Novel
  Quiet Earth, The 1985 d: Geoff Murphy. lps: Bruno Lawrence, Alison Routledge, Peter Smith. 100M NZL. prod/rel: Cinepro, Pillsbury Films

HARRISON, EDITH OGDEN
The Lady of the Snows, Novel
  Lady of the Snows, The 1915 d: Richard C. Travers, Edna Mayo, Sidney Ainsworth. 3r USA. prod/rel: Essanay

HARRISON, HARRY (1925–, USA
Make Room! Make Room!, 1966, Novel
  Soylent Green 1973 d: Richard Fleischer. lps: Charlton Heston, Leigh Taylor-Young, Edward G. Robinson. 97M USA. prod/rel: MGM

HARRISON, HENRY SYDNOR
Captivating Mary Carstairs, Boston 1910, Novel
  Captivating Mary Carstairs 1915 d: Bruce Mitchell. lps: Norma Talmadge, Allan Forrest, Bruce M. Mitchell. 5-6r USA. prod/rel: National Film Corp.

HARRISON, JIM
Farmer, Novel
  Carried Away 1996 d: Bruno Barreto. lps: Dennis Hopper, Amy Irving, Amy Locane. 108M USA. *Acts of Love* (UKN) prod/rel: Cinetel, Lisa Hansen/ Paul Hertzberg
Revenge, Novel
  Revenge 1990 d: Anthony Scott. lps: Kevin Costner, Anthony Quinn, Madeleine Stowe. 124M USA. prod/rel: Columbia Tristar, Rastar

HARRISON, MAURICE
Death Keeps a Date, Play
  Final Appointment 1954 d: Terence Fisher. lps: John Bentley, Eleanor Summerfield, Hubert Gregg. 61M UKN. prod/rel: Monarch, Act Films

HARRISON, MRS. BURTON
The Unwelcome Mrs. Hatch, New York 1901, Play
  Unwelcome Mrs. Hatch, The 1914 d: Allan Dwan. lps: Henrietta Crosman, Harold Lockwood, Walter Craven. 4r USA. prod/rel: Famous Players Film Co., Paramount Pictures Corp.

HARRISON, SLIM
Deuxieme Bureau Contre Terroristes, Novel
  Deuxieme Bureau Contre Terroristes 1959 d: Jean Stelli. lps: Frank Villard, Dominique Wilms, Nadine Tallier. 86M FRN. prod/rel: Carmina Films

HARRISON, WILLIAM
Burton and Speke, Novel
  Mountains of the Moon 1990 d: Bob Rafelson. lps: Patrick Bergin, Iain Glen, Richard E. Grant. 135M USA. prod/rel: Tri-Star, Indie Productions

HART, DANIEL L.
The Parish Priest, New York 1900, Play
  Parish Priest, The 1920 d: Joseph J. Franz. lps: William Desmond, Tom Ricketts, Carl Miller. 5500f USA. prod/rel: Jesse D. Hampton Productions, State Rights

HART, FRANCES NOYES
The Bellamy Trial, New York 1927, Novel
  Bellamy Trial, The 1928 d: Monta Bell. lps: Leatrice Joy, Betty Bronson, Edward Nugent. 8268f USA. prod/rel: Metro-Goldwyn-Mayer Pictures

HART, LORENZ (1895–1943), USA
Babes in Arms, New York 1937, Musical Play
  Babes in Arms 1939 d: Busby Berkeley. lps: Mickey Rooney, Judy Garland, Charles Winninger. 93M USA. prod/rel: Metro-Goldwyn-Mayer Corp.
The Melody Man, New York 1924, Musical Play
  Melody Man, The 1930 d: R. William Neill. lps: William Collier Jr., Alice Day, John St. Polis. 68M USA. prod/rel: Columbia Pictures
On Your Toes, New York 1936, Musical Play
  On Your Toes 1939 d: Ray Enright. lps: Vera Zorina, Eddie Albert, Frank McHugh. 93M USA. prod/rel: Warner Bros. Pictures©, First National Picture
Present Arms, New York 1928, Musical Play
  Leathernecking 1930 d: Eddie Cline. lps: Irene Dunne, Ken Murray, Louise FazendA. 80M USA. *Present Arms* (UKN) prod/rel: RKO Productions

Spring Is Here, New York 1929, Musical Play
  Spring Is Here 1930 d: John Francis Dillon. lps: Lawrence Gray, Alexander Gray, Bernice Claire. 6386f USA. prod/rel: First National Pictures
Too Many Girls, New York 1939, Musical Play
  Too Many Girls 1940 d: George Abbott. lps: Lucille Ball, Richard Carlson, Eddie Bracken. 85M USA. prod/rel: RKO Radio Pictures©

HART, MAARTEN 'T
De Kroongetuige, Novel
  Kronvittnet 1989 d: Jon Lindstrom. lps: Per Mattson, Marika Lagercrantz, Gosta Ekman. 103M SWD. *Experiment in Murder* prod/rel: Nordisk Tonefilm
Een Vlucht Regenwulpen, Novel
  Vlucht Regenwulpen, Een 1981 d: Ate de Jong. lps: Jeroen Krabbe, Marijke Merckens, Henriette Tol. 96M NTH. *A Flight of Rainbirds* prod/rel: Sigma Films

HART, MARION
The Cellist, Play
  Connecting Rooms 1969 d: Franklin Gollings. lps: Bette Davis, Michael Redgrave, Alexis Kanner. 102M UKN. prod/rel: London Screen, Telstar

HART, MOSS (1904–1961), USA
Act One, New York 1959, Play
  Act One 1963 d: Dore Schary. lps: George Hamilton, Jason Robards Jr., Jack Klugman. 110M USA. prod/rel: Warner, Dore Schary Productions
Christopher Blake, New York 1946, Play
  Decision of Christopher Blake, The 1948 d: Peter Godfrey. lps: Alexis Smith, Robert Douglas, Cecil Kellaway. 75M USA. *Christopher Blake* prod/rel: Warner Bros.
George Washington Slept Here, 1941, Play
  George Washington Slept Here 1942 d: William Keighley. lps: Jack Benny, Ann Sheridan, Charles Coburn. 93M USA. prod/rel: Warner Bros.
Lady in the Dark, New York 1941, Play
  Lady in the Dark 1944 d: Mitchell Leisen. lps: Ginger Rogers, Ray Milland, Warner Baxter. 100M USA. prod/rel: Paramount
The Man Who Came to Dinner, New York 1939, Play
  Man Who Came to Dinner, The 1941 d: William Keighley. lps: Bette Davis, Ann Sheridan, Monty Woolley. 112M USA. prod/rel: Warner Bros.
  Man Who Came to Dinner, The 1972 d: Buzz Kulik. lps: Orson Welles, Lee Remick, Joan Collins. TVM. 74M USA.
Once in a Lifetime, New York 1930, Play
  Once in a Lifetime 1932 d: Russell MacK. lps: Jack Oakie, Sidney Fox, Aline MacMahon. 91M USA. *Merry-Go-Round* prod/rel: Universal Pictures Corp.©
  Once in a Lifetime 1988 d: Robin Midgley. lps: Zoe Wanamaker, Niall Buggy, Kristoffer Tabori. MTV. UKN/USA. prod/rel: BBC, Wnet
Winged Victory, New York 1943, Play
  Winged Victory 1944 d: George Cukor. lps: Lon McCallister, Jeanne Crain, Edmond O'Brien. 130M USA. prod/rel: 20th Century-Fox
You Can't Take It With You, New York 1936, Play
  You Can't Take It With You 1938 d: Frank CaprA. lps: James Stewart, Jean Arthur, Lionel Barrymore. 127M USA. prod/rel: Columbia Pictures Corp. of California©
  You Can't Take It With You 1979 d: Paul Bogart. lps: Jean Stapleton, Art Carney, Barry Bostwick. TVM. 100M USA.

HART, TOM
The Aura and the Kingfisher, Novel
  Innocent, The 1985 d: John MacKenzie. lps: Andrew Hawley, Tom Bell, Kika Markham. 101M UKN. prod/rel: Tvs, Curzon

HART, WILLIAM S. (1870–1946), USA
Pinto Ben, Poem
  Pinto Ben 1915 d: William S. Hart. lps: William S. Hart. 2r USA. prod/rel: Broncho

HARTAU, FRIEDRICH
Die Letzte Nacht, Play
  Letzte Nacht, Die 1949 d: Eugen York. lps: Sybille Schmitz, Karl John, Carl-Heinz Schroth. 93M GRM. *The Last Night* prod/rel: Real, Doring

HARTE, BRET (1836–1902), USA
The Bad Buck of Santa Ynez, Short Story
  Bad Buck of Santa Ynez, The 1915 d: William S. Hart. lps: William S. Hart, Thelma Salter, Fannie Midgley. 2r USA. prod/rel: Kay-Bee
Bradford's Claim, Short Story
  Bradford's Claim 1910 d: Edwin S. Porter. lps: J. Barney Sherry. 730f USA. prod/rel: Edison

Breed O' the North, Short Story
  Breed O' the North 1914 d: Walter Edwards. lps: Walter Edwards, Clara Williams, Harry Keenan. 2r USA. prod/rel: Broncho

Cressy, Boston 1889, Novel
  Fighting Cressy 1919 d: Robert T. Thornby. lps: Blanche Sweet, Russell Simpson, Edward Peil. 5166f USA. prod/rel: Jesse D. Hampton Productions, Pathe Exchange, Inc.©

The Goddess of Sagebrush Gulch, Short Story
  Goddess of Sagebrush Gulch, The 1912 d: D. W. Griffith. lps: Dorothy Bernard, Blanche Sweet, Wilfred Lucas. SHT USA. prod/rel: Biograph Co.

Her Last Letter, Boston 1905, Poem
  Lily of Poverty Flat, The 1915 d: George E. Middleton. lps: Beatriz Michelena, Frederick Lewis, Andrew Robson. 5r USA. prod/rel: California Motion Picture Corp.©, World Film Corp.

Her Letter, Boston 1905, Poem
  Lily of Poverty Flat, The 1915 d: George E. Middleton. lps: Beatriz Michelena, Frederick Lewis, Andrew Robson. 5r USA. prod/rel: California Motion Picture Corp.©, World Film Corp.

His Answer, Boston 1905, Poem
  Lily of Poverty Flat, The 1915 d: George E. Middleton. lps: Beatriz Michelena, Frederick Lewis, Andrew Robson. 5r USA. prod/rel: California Motion Picture Corp.©, World Film Corp.

The Idyll of Red Gulch, Story
  Man from Red Gulch, The 1925 d: Edmund Mortimer. lps: Harry Carey, Harriet Hammond, Frank Campeau. 5437f USA. prod/rel: Hunt Stromberg Productions, Producers Distributing Corp.

In the Aisles of the Wild, Short Story
  In the Aisles of the Wild 1912 d: D. W. Griffith. lps: Henry B. Walthall, Claire McDowell, Lillian Gish. 1000f USA. prod/rel: Biograph Co.

In the Carquinez Woods, London 1883, Novel
  Half-Breed, The 1916 d: Allan Dwan. lps: Douglas Fairbanks, Alma Rubens, Jewel Carmen. 5r USA. *The Carquinez Woods*; *The Halfbreed*; *In the Carquinez Woods* prod/rel: Fine Arts Film Co., Triangle Film Corp.
  Tongues of Flame 1919 d: Colin Campbell. lps: Marie Walcamp, Al Whitman, Alfred Allen. 5r USA. *In the Carquinez Woods* prod/rel: Bluebird Photoplays, Inc.©

John Burns of Gettysburg, Poem
  John Burns of Gettysburg 1913. lps: Kenean Buel, Guy Coombs, Mrs. Courtot. 1000f USA. prod/rel: Kalem

The Judgment of Bolinas Plain, 1893, Short Story
  Dawn of Understanding, The 1918 d: David Smith. lps: Bessie Love, John Gilbert, J. Frank Glendon. 5r USA. prod/rel: Vitagraph Co. of America©, Blue Ribbon Feature

The Last Drop of Water, Short Story
  Last Drop of Water, The 1911 d: D. W. Griffith. lps: Charles West, Joseph Graybill, Jeanie MacPherson. 1057f USA. prod/rel: Biograph Co.

The Luck of Roaring Camp, 1868, Short Story
  Luck of Roaring Camp, The 1910 d: Edwin S. Porter. lps: J. Barney Sherry, Mary Fuller. 490f USA. prod/rel: Edison
  Luck of Roaring Camp, The 1937 d: Irvin V. Willat. lps: Owen Davis Jr., Joan Woodbury, Charles Brokaw. 61M USA. prod/rel: Monogram Pictures Corp.©
  Outcasts of Poker Flat, The 1952 d: Joseph M. Newman. lps: Anne Baxter, Dale Robertson, Miriam Hopkins. 81M USA. prod/rel: 20th Century-Fox

Maruja, Boston 1885, Novel
  Gray Wolf's Ghost, The 1919 d: Park Frame. lps: H. B. Warner, Marin Sais, Edward Peil. 5r USA. *Maruja*; *The Grey Wolf's Ghost* prod/rel: Jesse D. Hampton Productions, Robertson-Cole Distributing Corp.

M'liss: an Idyll of Red Mountain, Boston 1869, Novel
  Girl Who Ran Wild, The 1922 d: Rupert Julian. lps: Gladys Walton, Marc Robbins, Vernon Steele. 4506f USA. prod/rel: Universal Film Mfg. Co.
  M'liss 1915 d: O. A. C. Lund. lps: Barbara Tennant, Howard Estabrook, O. A. C. Lund. 5r USA. prod/rel: Shubert Feature, World Film Corp.©
  M'liss 1918 d: Marshall Neilan. lps: Mary Pickford, Thomas Meighan, Theodore Roberts. 5r USA. prod/rel: Pickford Film Corp., Famous Players-Lasky Corp.©
  M'liss 1936 d: George Nicholls Jr. lps: Anne Shirley, John Beal, Guy Kibbee. 66M USA. prod/rel: RKO Radio Pictures©

Onoko's Vow, Short Story
  Onoko's Vow 1910 d: Edwin S. Porter. lps: Mary Fuller. 1000f USA. *Ononko's Vow* prod/rel: Edison

The Outcasts of Poker Flat, 1868, Short Story
  Outcasts of Poker Flat, The 1919 d: John Ford. lps: Harry Carey, Cullen Landis, Gloria Hope. 5645f USA. prod/rel: Universal Film Mfg. Co.©
  Outcasts of Poker Flat, The 1937 d: W. Christy Cabanne. lps: Preston Foster, Jean Muir, Van Heflin. 72M USA. prod/rel: RKO Radio Pictures©
  Outcasts of Poker Flat, The 1952 d: Joseph M. Newman. lps: Anne Baxter, Dale Robertson, Miriam Hopkins. 81M USA. prod/rel: 20th Century-Fox

A Phyllis of the Sierras, Boston 1888, Novel
  Phyllis of the Sierras, A 1915 d: George E. Middleton. lps: Beatriz Michelena, William Pike, Andrew Robson. 5r USA. *Minty's Triumph* prod/rel: California Motion Picture Corp., World Film Corp.

The Redman and the Child, Short Story
  Redman and the Child, The 1908 d: D. W. Griffith. lps: Charles Inslee, John Tansey, Harry Salter. 857f USA. prod/rel: Biograph Co.

The Saint of Calamity Gulch, Short Story
  Taking a Chance 1928 d: Norman Z. McLeod. lps: Rex Bell, Lola Todd, Richard Carlyle. 4876f USA. prod/rel: Fox Film Corp.

Salomy Jane's Kiss, 1900, Short Story
  Salomy Jane 1914 d: Lucius Henderson, William Nigh. lps: Beatriz Michelena, House Peters, Andrew Robson. 5-6r USA. prod/rel: California Motion Picture Corp.©, Alco Film Corp.
  Salomy Jane 1914 d: Lucius Henderson, William Nigh. lps: Beatriz Michelena, House Peters, Andrew Robson. 5-6r USA. prod/rel: California Motion Picture Corp.©, Alco Film Corp.
  Salomy Jane 1923 d: George Melford. lps: Jacqueline Logan, George Fawcett, Maurice B. Flynn. 6270f USA. *The Law of the Sierras* prod/rel: Famous Players-Lasky, Paramount Pictures
  Wild Girl 1932 d: Raoul Walsh. lps: Charles Farrell, Joan Bennett, Ralph Bellamy. 74M USA. *Salomy Jane* (UKN) prod/rel: Fox Film Corp.©

The Stolen Claim, Short Story
  Stolen Claim, The 1910 d: Edwin S. Porter. lps: J. Barney Sherry. 1000f USA. prod/rel: Edison

Tennessee's Partner, 1869, Short Story
  Flaming Forties, The 1924 d: Tom Forman. lps: Harry Carey, William Norton, Jacqueline Gadsdon. 5770f USA. prod/rel: Stellar Productions, Producers Distributing Corp.
  Golden Princess, The 1925 d: Clarence Badger. lps: Betty Bronson, Neil Hamilton, Rockliffe Fellowes. 8584f USA. prod/rel: Famous Players-Lasky, Paramount Pictures
  Tennessee's Pardner 1916 d: George Melford. lps: Fannie Ward, Jack Dean, Charles Clary. 5r USA. prod/rel: Jesse L. Lasky Feature Play Co.©, Paramount Pictures Corp.
  Tennessee's Partner 1955 d: Allan Dwan. lps: John Payne, Ronald Reagan, Rhonda Fleming. 87M USA. prod/rel: RKO, Filmcrest

Two Men of Sandy Bar, New York 1876, Play
  Two Men of Sandy Bar 1916 d: Lloyd B. Carleton. lps: Hobart Bosworth, Emory Johnson, Gretchen Lederer. 5r USA. prod/rel: Universal Film Mfg. Co.©, Red Feather Photoplays

The White Rose of the Wilds, Short Story
  White Rose of the Wilds, The 1911 d: D. W. Griffith. lps: Blanche Sweet, Wilfred Lucas, MacK Sennett. 1005f USA. prod/rel: Biograph Co.

HARTLEBEN, O. E.
Rosenmontag, Play
  Rosenmontag 1924 d: Rudolf Meinert. lps: Gerd Briese, Helga Thomas, Maria Reisenhofer. 3154m GRM. *Eine Offizierstragodie*; *Rose Monday* prod/rel: Internationale Film Ag
  Rosenmontag 1955 d: Willy Birgel. lps: Ruth Niehaus, Dietmar Schonherr, Elma KarlowA. 97M GRM. *Rose Monday* prod/rel: Mondial, Gloria
Sommerliebe, Novel
  Sommerliebe 1942 d: Erich Engel. lps: Winnie Markus, O. W. Fischer, Siegfried Breuer. 90M GRM. prod/rel: Wien-Film

HARTLEY, L. P. (1895–1972), UKN, Hartley, Leslie Poles
The Go-Between, 1953, Novel
  Go-Between, The 1970 d: Joseph Losey. lps: Julie Christie, Alan Bates, Dominic Guard. 116M UKN. prod/rel: MGM-Emi, World Film Services
The Hireling, 1957, Novel
  Hireling, The 1973 d: Alan Bridges. lps: Robert Shaw, Sarah Miles, Peter Egan. 108M UKN. prod/rel: Columbia, World Film Services

The Island, 1948, Short Story
  Island, The 1977 d: Robert Fuest. 30M USA.

HARTLEY, WILLIAM B.
The Cruel Tower, Novel
  Cruel Tower, The 1956 d: Lew Landers. lps: John Ericson, Mari Blanchard, Charles McGraw. 79M USA. prod/rel: Allied Artists, Lindsley Parsons Prods.

HARTMAN, ROGER
Impulses, 1919, Short Story
  Sporting Chance, A 1919 d: George Melford. lps: Ethel Clayton, Jack Holt, Anna Q. Nilsson. 4135f USA. prod/rel: Famous Players-Lasky Corp., Paramount Pictures

HARTMANN, MICHAEL
Game for Vultures, Novel
  Game for Vultures 1980 d: James Fargo. lps: Richard Harris, Richard Roundtree, Joan Collins. 106M UKN/SWT/SAF. prod/rel: Columbia

HARTMANN, MORITZ
Der Weisse Schleier, Poem
  Weisse Schleier, Der 1912 d: Adolf Gartner. GRM. prod/rel: Deutsche Mutoskop Und Biograph

HARTUNG, ELLINOR
Scheidungsgrund: Liebe, Novel
  Scheidungsgrund: Liebe 1960 d: Cyril Frankel. lps: O. W. Fischer, Dany Robin, Alice Treff. 85M GRM. *Grounds for Divorce: Love* prod/rel: C.C.C., Bavaria

HARTUNG, HUGO
Ferien Mit Piroschka, Novel
  Ferien Mit Piroschka 1965 d: Franz J. Gottlieb. lps: Gotz George, Marie Versini, Dietmar Schonherr. 94M GRM/AUS/HNG. *Vacation With Piroschka* prod/rel: Sascha, Schlaraffia
Ich Denke Oft an Piroschka, Novel
  Ich Denke Oft an Piroschka 1955 d: Kurt Hoffmann. lps: Liselotte Pulver, Gunnar Moller, Gustav Knuth. 96M GRM. *I Often Think of Piroschka* prod/rel: George Witt-Film, Schorcht
Wir Wunderkinder, Novel
  Wir Wunderkinder 1958 d: Kurt Hoffmann. lps: Johanna von Koczian, Hansjorg Felmy, Wera Frydtberg. 108M GRM. *Aren't We Wonderful?*; *We Whiz Kids* prod/rel: Filmaufbau, Constantin

HARVE, PAUL
Alma, Where Do You Live?, Musical Play
  Alma, Where Do You Live? 1917 d: Hal Clarendon. lps: Ruth MacTammany, George Larkin, Jack Newton. 6r USA. prod/rel: Newfields Producing Corp., State Rights

HARVEY, FRANK (1885–, UKN
Cap Forlorn, 1930, Play
  Cap Perdu, Le 1931 d: E. A. Dupont. lps: Marcelle Romee, Harry Baur, Jean Max. 93M FRN. prod/rel: British International Pictures
  Cape Forlorn 1930 d: E. A. Dupont. lps: Fay Compton, Frank Harvey, Ian Hunter. 86M UKN. *Love Storms* (USA); *The Love Storm* prod/rel: British International Pictures, Wardour

HARVEY, FRANK
Elizabeth of Ladymead, 1948, Play
  Elizabeth of Ladymead 1949 d: Herbert Wilcox. lps: Anna Neagle, Hugh Williams, Bernard Lee. 97M UKN. *The Girl He Left Behind* prod/rel: British Lion, Imperadio
Murder Tomorrow?, London 1938, Play
  Murder Tomorrow 1938 d: Donovan Pedelty. lps: Gwenllian Gill, Jack Livesey, Molly Hamley-Clifford. 69M UKN. prod/rel: Crusade, Paramount
Shall We Forgive Her?, London 1894, Play
  Shall We Forgive Her? 1917 d: Arthur Ashley. lps: June Elvidge, Arthur Ashley, John Bowers. 5r USA. prod/rel: World Film Corp.©, Peerless

HARVEY, JACK
The Phantom of 42nd Street, Novel
  Phantom of 42nd Street, The 1945 d: Al Herman. lps: Dave O'Brien, Katharine Aldridge, Alan Mowbray. 58M USA. prod/rel: Producers Releasing Corp.

HARVEY, JONATHAN
Beautiful Thing, Play
  Beautiful Thing 1996 d: Hettie MacDonald. lps: Linda Henry, Glenn Berry, Scott Neal. 91M UKN. prod/rel: Film Four, World

HARVEY JR., FRANK
The Poltergeist, London 1946, Play
  Things Happen at Night 1948 d: Francis Searle. lps: Gordon Harker, Alfred Drayton, Robertson Hare. 79M UKN. prod/rel: Tudor, Alliance
Saloon Bar, London 1939, Play
  Saloon Bar 1940 d: Walter Forde. lps: Gordon Harker, Elizabeth Allan, Mervyn Johns. 76M UKN. prod/rel: Ealing Studios, Associated British Film Distributors

HARVEY, LOLA
The Idol of Moolah, Play
  Kiss Me Sergeant 1930 d: Monty Banks. lps: Leslie
  Fuller, Gladys Cruickshank, Gladys Frazin. 56M UKN.
  prod/rel: British International Pictures, Wardour

HARVEY, W. F.
Story
  Beast With Five Fingers, The 1946 d: Robert Florey.
  lps: Robert Alda, Andrea King, Peter Lorre. 88M USA.
  prod/rel: Warner Bros.

HARVEY, JOHN
Un' Estate Con Sentimento, Novel
  Estate Con Sentimento, Un' 1970 d: Roberto B.
  ScarsellA. lps: Stefania Sandrelli, Robin Philips,
  Anastasia Stevens. 99M ITL. *Within and Without*
  (UKN) prod/rel: Within and Without, Euro
  International Film

HARWOOD, H. M., Harwood, Harold M., Harwood,
  Harold Marsh
Billeted, London 1917, Play
  Misleading Widow, The 1919 d: John S. Robertson.
  lps: Billie Burke, James L. Crane, Frank Mills. 5r USA.
  Billeted prod/rel: Famous Players-Lasky Corp.©,
  Paramount-Artcraft Pictures
Cynara, London 1930, Play
  Cynara 1932 d: King Vidor. lps: Ronald Colman, Kay
  Francis, Phyllis Barry. 80M USA. *I Have Been Faithful*;
  Way of a Lancer prod/rel: Howard Productions, Inc.,
  United Artists
The Man in Possession, London 1930, Play
  Man in Possession, The 1931 d: Sam Wood. lps:
  Robert Montgomery, Reginald Owen, Irene Purcell.
  84M USA. prod/rel: Metro-Goldwyn-Mayer Corp.,
  Metro-Goldwyn-Mayer Dist. Corp.©
  Personal Property 1937 d: W. S. Van Dyke. lps: Jean
  Harlow, Robert Taylor, Una O'Connor. 88M USA. *The
  Man in Possession* (UKN); *Man in Her House* prod/rel:
  Metro-Goldwyn-Mayer Corp.©
The Pelican, London 1924, Play
  "Marriage License?" 1926 d: Frank Borzage. lps:
  Alma Rubens, Walter McGrail, Richard Walling. 7168f
  USA. *The Pelican* prod/rel: Fox Film Corp.
  Sacrifice 1929 d: Victor Peers. lps: Andree Tourneur,
  G. H. Mulcaster, Lewis Dayton. SIL. 6602f UKN.
  prod/rel: British Instructional, Fox
Please Help Emily, London 1916, Play
  Palm Beach Girl, The 1926 d: Erle C. Kenton. lps:
  Bebe Daniels, Lawrence Gray, Josephine Drake. 6918f
  USA. prod/rel: Famous Players-Lasky, Paramount
  Pictures
  Please Help Emily 1917 d: Dell Henderson. lps: Ann
  Murdock, Rex McDougall, Hubert Druce. 5r USA.
  prod/rel: Empire All Star Corp.©, Mutual Film Corp.

HARWOOD, RONALD (1934–, SAF
The Barber of Stamford Hill, Television Play
  Barber of Stamford Hill, The 1962 d: Caspar Wrede.
  lps: John Bennett, Megs Jenkins, Maxwell Shaw. 64M
  UKN. prod/rel: Ben Arbeid, British Lion
The Dresser, Play
  Dresser, The 1983 d: Peter Yates. lps: Albert Finney,
  Tom Courtenay, Edward Fox. 118M UKN. prod/rel:
  Columbia, Goldcrest
Private Potter, 1961, Television Play
  Private Potter 1962 d: Caspar Wrede. lps: Tom
  Courtenay, Mogens Wieth, Ronald Fraser. 89M UKN.
  prod/rel: MGM, Ben Arbeid

HASEK, JAROSLAV (1883–1923), CZC
Novel
  Schweik's New Adventures 1943 d: Carl Lamac. lps:
  Lloyd Pearson, Julien Mitchell, George Carney. 84M
  UKN. *It Started at Midnight* prod/rel: Eden Films,
  Coronel
Story
  Schwejks Flegeljahre 1964 d: Wolfgang Liebeneiner.
  lps: Peter Alexander, Rudolf Prack, Gunther Philipp.
  92M AUS. *The Trials of Private Schwejk* prod/rel:
  Sascha
Osudy Dobreho Vojaka Svejka Za Svetove Valky,
  Prague 1920-23, Novel
  Brave Soldat Schwejk, Der 1960 d: Axel von
  Ambesser. lps: Heinz Ruhmann, Ernst Stankovski,
  Ursula Borsodi. 96M GRM. *The Good Soldier Schweik*
  (USA) prod/rel: Ccc-Filmkunst, Wienfilm
  Dobry Vojak Svejk 1926 d: Carl Lamac. lps: Karel
  Noll, Antonie Nedosinska, Karel Lamac. 2426m CZC.
  Good Soldier Schweik; *The Good Soldier Svejk* prod/rel:
  Gloriafilm
  Dobry Vojak Svejk 1931 d: Martin Fric. lps: Sasa
  Rasilov, Oskar Marion, Jan Richter. 86M CZC. *The
  Good Soldier Schweik* prod/rel: Gloria

Noviye Pokhozdeniya Shveika 1943 d: Sergei
  Yutkevich. lps: Boris Tenin, Sergei Martinson, Faina
  RanevskayA. 72M USS. *The New Adventures of
  Schweik*; *The Good Soldier Schweik*
  Svejk Na Fronte 1926 d: Carl Lamac. lps: Karel Noll,
  Josef Rovensky, Karel Lamac. CZC. *Schweik at the
  Front*; *Svejk at the Front* prod/rel: Gloria Film
  Svejk V Civilu 1927 d: Gustav Machaty. lps: Karel
  Noll, Dina Gralla, Jiri Hron. 2311m CZC/GRM. *Schwejk
  in Zivil* (GRM); *Schweik As a Civilian*; *Svejk As a
  Civilian*; *Schweik in Civilian Life* prod/rel: Elektafilm,
  Hugo-Engel-Film
  Svejk V Ruskem Zajeti 1926 d: Svatopluk Innemann.
  lps: Karel Noll, Ferenc Futurista, Jan W. Speerger. CZC.
  Schweik in Russian Captivity prod/rel: Gloriafilm

HASENCLEVER, WALTER
Ein Besserer Herr, Play
  Besserer Herr, Ein 1928 d: Gustav Ucicky. lps: Rita
  Roberts, Fritz Kampers, Elisabeth Pinajeff. 2419m
  GRM. prod/rel: Munchener Lichtspielkunst Ag

HASFORD, GUSTAV
The Short-Timers, Novel
  Full Metal Jacket 1987 d: Stanley Kubrick. lps:
  Matthew Modine, Adam Baldwin, Vincent d'Onofrio.
  116M UKN. prod/rel: Warner Bros., Natant

HASHIMOTO, SHINOBU
Nihon Chinbotsu, Novel
  Nihon Chinbotsu 1973 d: Shiro Moritani, Andrew
  Meyer. lps: Lorne Greene, Keiju Kobayashi, Rhonda
  Leigh Hopkins. 140M JPN. *Tidal Wave* (USA); *The
  Submersion of Japan*; *Nippon Chinbotsu* prod/rel: Toho
  Co., New World Pictures

HASKIN, LOUISE
The Man at the Gate, Poem
  Man at the Gate, The 1941 d: Norman Walker. lps:
  Wilfred Lawson, Mary Jerrold, William Freshman. 48M
  UKN. *Men of the Sea* prod/rel: Gregory, Hake & Walker,
  General Film Distributors

HASKOVA, LENKA
Obzalovany, Short Story
  Obzalovany 1964 d: Jan Kadar, Elmar Klos. lps:
  Miroslav MacHacek, Vlado Muller, Jiri Menzel. 95M
  CZC. *The Defendant*; *The Accused* prod/rel:
  Czechoslavia Staatsfilm

HASLER, KAREL
Tulak, Poem
  Tulak 1925 d: Josef Kokeisl. lps: Karel Hasler, Bedrich
  Bozdech, Bozena SvobodovA. 221m CZC. *The Tramp*;
  Silnice Bila Prede Mnou; *The White Road Before Me*
  prod/rel: Filmindustrie
U Svateho Mateje, Poem
  U Svateho Mateje, Kdyz Se Slunko Zasmeje 1928
  d: Josef Kokeisl. lps: Josef Rovensky. CZC. *When the
  Sun Comes Out at the House of St. Matej*; *U Sv. Mateje*;
  By St. Matthias prod/rel: Josef Kokeisl
Vdavala Se Jedna Panna, Poem
  Vdavala Se Jedna Panna 1926 d: Josef Kokeisl. lps:
  Mary Jansova, Jara Kohout, Ladislav Desensky. 171m
  CZC. *A Wedding for a Maiden* prod/rel: Filmindustrie

HASSEL, SVEN
Wheels of Terror, Novel
  Wheels of Terror 1987 d: Gordon Hessler. lps: Bruce
  Davison, David Patrick Kelly, David Carradine. 99M
  USA/UKN. *The Misfit Brigade* prod/rel: Trans World

HASSENCAMP, OLIVER
Bekenntnisse Eines Moblierten Herrn, Novel
  Bekenntnisse Eines Moblierten Herrn 1962 d:
  Franz Peter Wirth. lps: Karl Michael Vogler, Maria
  Sebaldt, Cordula Trantow. 103M GRM. *Confessions of a
  Gentleman* prod/rel: N.D.F., Schorcht

HASSLER, JOHN
A Green Journey, Book
  Love She Sought, The 1990 d: Joseph Sargent. lps:
  Angela Lansbury, Denholm Elliott, Robert Prosky.
  TVM. 100M USA. *A Green Journey* (UKN) prod/rel:
  Orion Tv, Andrew J. Fenady Prods.

HASTINGS, BASIL MCDONALD
That Sort, New York 1914, Play
  That Sort 1916 d: Charles J. Brabin. lps: Warda
  Howard, Duncan McRae, Ernest Maupain. 5r USA.
  That Sort of Girl (UKN) prod/rel: Essanay Film Mfg.
  Co.©, V-L-S-E, Inc.

HASTINGS, CHARLOTTE
Bonaventure, London 1949, Play
  Thunder on the Hill 1951 d: Douglas Sirk. lps:
  Claudette Colbert, Ann Blyth, Robert Douglas. 84M
  USA. *Bonaventure* (UKN) prod/rel:
  Universal-International

Uncertain Joy, London 1953, Play
  Scamp, The 1957 d: Wolf RillA. lps: Richard
  Attenborough, Terence Morgan, Colin Petersen. 88M
  UKN. *Strange Affection* (USA) prod/rel: Grand
  National, Lawrie Productions

HASTINGS, HUGH
Seagulls Over Sorrento, London 1949, Play
  Seagulls Over Sorrento 1954 d: John Boulting, Roy
  Boulting. lps: Gene Kelly, John Justin, Bernard Lee.
  92M UKN. *Crest of the Wave* (USA) prod/rel: MGM
  British

HASTINGS, JOHN
The Night of the Party, Play
  Night of the Party, The 1934 d: Michael Powell. lps:
  Leslie Banks, Ian Hunter, Jane Baxter. 62M UKN. *The
  Murder Party* (USA) prod/rel: Gaumont-British

HASTINGS, MICHAEL
Tom & Viv, Play
  Tom & Viv 1994 d: Brian Gilbert. lps: Willem Dafoe,
  Miranda Richardson, Rosemary Harris. 125M UKN.
  Tom and Viv prod/rel: Samuelson, Harvey Kass

HASTINGS, PATRICK
The Blind Goddess, London 1947, Play
  Blind Goddess, The 1948 d: Harold French. lps: Eric
  Portman, Anne Crawford, Hugh Williams. 87M UKN.
  prod/rel: Gainsborough, General Film Distributors
The River, Play
  Notorious Lady, The 1927 d: King Baggot. lps: Lewis
  Stone, Barbara Bedford, Ann Rork. 6040f USA. prod/rel:
  Sam E. Rork Productions, First National Pictures

HASTINGS, PHYLLIS
Rapture in My Rags, London 1964, Novel
  Rapture 1965 d: John Guillermin. lps: Melvyn Douglas,
  Patricia Gozzi, Dean Stockwell. 104M USA/FRN. *La
  Fleur de l'Age* (FRN) prod/rel: Panoramic Productions

HATCH, ERIC
My Man Godfrey, Boston 1935, Novel
  My Man Godfrey 1936 d: Gregory La CavA. lps:
  William Powell, Carole Lombard, Alice Brady. 95M
  USA. prod/rel: Universal Productions©, Gregory la Cava
  Production
  My Man Godfrey 1957 d: Henry Koster. lps: David
  Niven, June Allyson, Jessie Royce Landis. 92M USA.
  prod/rel: Universal-International
Road Show, Novel
  Road Show 1941 d: Hal Roach, Gordon Douglas. lps:
  Adolphe Menjou, Carole Landis, John Hubbard. 87M
  USA. prod/rel: United Artists, Hal Roach
Spendthrift, 1936, Novel
  Spendthrift 1936 d: Raoul Walsh. lps: Henry Fonda,
  Pat Paterson, Mary Brian. 80M USA. prod/rel: Walter
  Wanger Productions, Paramount Productions©
Unexpected Uncle, Novel
  Unexpected Uncle 1941 d: Peter Godfrey. lps: Charles
  Coburn, Anne Shirley, James Craig. 67M USA. prod/rel:
  RKO Radio
The Year of the Horse, New York 1965, Novel
  Horse in the Gray Flannel Suit, The 1968 d:
  Norman Tokar. lps: Dean Jones, Diane Baker, Lloyd
  Bochner. 113M USA. *Year of the Horse* prod/rel: Walt
  Disney Productions, Buena Vista

HATRY, MICHAEL
Denunzianten, Book
  Tatort - Schimanski: Schwarzes Wochenende
  1985 d: Dominik Graf. lps: Gotz George, Eberhard Feik,
  Chiem Van Houweninge. MTV. 95M GRM. *Schwarzes
  Wochenende*

HATTON, FANNY
The Azure Shore, 1923, Short Story
  Rush Hour, The 1927 d: E. Mason Hopper. lps: Marie
  Prevost, Harrison Ford, Seena Owen. 5880f USA.
  prod/rel: de Mille Pictures, Pathe Exchange, Inc.
The Great Lover, New York 1915, Play
  Great Lover, The 1920 d: Frank Lloyd. lps: John
  Sainpolis, Claire Adams, John Davidson. 5202f USA.
  prod/rel: Goldwyn Pictures Corp.©, Frank Lloyd
  Productions
  Great Lover, The 1931 d: Harry Beaumont. lps:
  Adolphe Menjou, Irene Dunne, Neil Hamilton. 79M
  USA. prod/rel: Metro-Goldwyn-Mayer Corp.,
  Metro-Goldwyn-Mayer Dist. Corp.©
The Indestructible Wife, New York 1918, Play
  Indestructible Wife, The 1919 d: Charles Maigne. lps:
  Alice Brady, Saxon Kling, Sue Balfour. 5r USA. prod/rel:
  Select Pictures Corp.©
Lombardi, Ltd., New York 1917, Play
  Lombardi, Ltd. 1919 d: Jack Conway. lps: Bert Lytell,
  Alice Lake, Jean Acker. 6-7r USA. prod/rel: Screen
  Classics, Inc., Metro Pictures Corp.©

Synthetic Sin, New York 1927, Play
Synthetic Sin 1929 d: William A. Seiter. lps: Colleen Moore, Antonio Moreno, Edythe Chapman. 7035f USA. prod/rel: First National Pictures

Upstairs and Down, New York 1916, Play
Upstairs and Down 1919 d: Charles Giblyn. lps: Olive Thomas, Rosemary Theby, Mary Charleson. 5r USA. *Up-Stairs and Down* prod/rel: Selznick Pictures Corp.©, Select Pictures Corp.

The Walk-Offs, New York 1918, Play
Walk-Offs, The 1920 d: Herbert Blache. lps: May Allison, Emory Johnson, Effie Conley. 6r USA. prod/rel: Screen Classics, Inc., Metro Pictures Corp.©

The Waning Sex, 1923, Play
Waning Sex, The 1926 d: Robert Z. Leonard. lps: Norma Shearer, Conrad Nagel, George K. Arthur. 6039f USA. prod/rel: Metro-Goldwyn-Mayer Pictures

With the Tide, 1923, Short Story
South Sea Love 1923 d: David Soloman. lps: Shirley Mason, J. Frank Glendon, Francis McDonald. 4168f USA. *The Broadway Dancer* prod/rel: Fox Film Corp.

HATTON, FREDERIC
The Azure Shore, 1923, Short Story
Rush Hour, The 1927 d: E. Mason Hopper. lps: Marie Prevost, Harrison Ford, Seena Owen. 5880f USA. prod/rel: de Mille Pictures, Pathe Exchange, Inc.

The Great Lover, New York 1915, Play
Great Lover, The 1920 d: Frank Lloyd. lps: John Sainpolis, Claire Adams, John Davidson. 5202f USA. prod/rel: Goldwyn Pictures Corp.©, Frank Lloyd Productions

Great Lover, The 1931 d: Harry Beaumont. lps: Adolphe Menjou, Irene Dunne, Neil Hamilton. 79M USA. prod/rel: Metro-Goldwyn-Mayer Corp., Metro-Goldwyn-Mayer Dist. Corp.©

The Indestructible Wife, New York 1918, Play
Indestructible Wife, The 1919 d: Charles Maigne. lps: Alice Brady, Saxon Kling, Sue Balfour. 5r USA. prod/rel: Select Pictures Corp.©

Lombardi, Ltd., New York 1917, Play
Lombardi, Ltd. 1919 d: Jack Conway. lps: Bert Lytell, Alice Lake, Jean Acker. 6-7r USA. prod/rel: Screen Classics, Inc., Metro Pictures Corp.©

Synthetic Sin, New York 1927, Play
Synthetic Sin 1929 d: William A. Seiter. lps: Colleen Moore, Antonio Moreno, Edythe Chapman. 7035f USA. prod/rel: First National Pictures

Upstairs and Down, New York 1916, Play
Upstairs and Down 1919 d: Charles Giblyn. lps: Olive Thomas, Rosemary Theby, Mary Charleson. 5r USA. *Up-Stairs and Down* prod/rel: Selznick Pictures Corp.©, Select Pictures Corp.

The Walk-Offs, New York 1918, Play
Walk-Offs, The 1920 d: Herbert Blache. lps: May Allison, Emory Johnson, Effie Conley. 6r USA. prod/rel: Screen Classics, Inc., Metro Pictures Corp.©

The Waning Sex, 1923, Play
Waning Sex, The 1926 d: Robert Z. Leonard. lps: Norma Shearer, Conrad Nagel, George K. Arthur. 6039f USA. prod/rel: Metro-Goldwyn-Mayer Pictures

With the Tide, 1923, Short Story
South Sea Love 1923 d: David Soloman. lps: Shirley Mason, J. Frank Glendon, Francis McDonald. 4168f USA. *The Broadway Dancer* prod/rel: Fox Film Corp.

HATTON, JOSEPH
John Needham's Double; a Novel, New York 1885, Novel
John Needham's Double 1916 d: Lois Weber, Phillips Smalley. lps: Tyrone Power Sr., Marie Walcamp, Agnes Emerson. 5r USA. prod/rel: Bluebird Photoplays, Inc.©

HATVANY, LILI
Tonight Or Never, New York 1930, Play
Tonight Or Never 1931 d: Mervyn Leroy. lps: Gloria Swanson, Melvyn Douglas, Ferdinand Gottschalk. 82M USA. prod/rel: United Artists Corp., Feature Productions©

HAUERBACH, OTTO
Madame Sherry, New York 1910, Musical Play
Madame Sherry 1917 d: Ralph Dean. lps: Gertrude McCoy, Frank L. A. O'Connor, Lucy Carter. 5r USA. prod/rel: Authors' Film Co., State Rights

HAUFF, WALTER
Vrazda Primadony, Novel
Osudne Noci 1928 d: Josef Medeotti-Bohac. lps: Jan W. Speerger, Josef Rovensky, Kitty Barling. CZC. *Fateful Nights* prod/rel: Ab, Lloydfilm

HAUFF, WILHELM (1802–1827), GRM
Short Story
Clown and the Kids, The 1968 d: Mende Brown. lps: Emmett Kelly, Burt Stratford, Katie Dunn. 89M USA/BUL. *Svirachut* (BUL); *The Pied Piper*; *The Musician*

Die Geschichte von Dem Kleinen Muck, 1826, Short Story
Geschichte Vom Kleinen Muck, Die 1953 d: Wolfgang Staudte. lps: Thomas Schmidt, Johannes Maus, Friedrich Richter. 100M GDR. *The Story of Little Mook*; *Little Mook*; *Little Muck's Treasure*; *Ein Abenteuer Aus 1000 Nachts*; *Abenteuer Des Kleinen Muck* prod/rel: Defa

Kleine Muck, Der 1944 d: Franz Fiedler. lps: Gustav Waldau, Ernst Martens, Christa Caporrici. 82M GRM. prod/rel: Sonne-Film, Jugendfilm

Der Junge Englander, 1905, Short Story
Junge Englander, Der 1958 d: Gottfried Kolditz. 48M GDR. *Young Englishman*

Das Kalte Herz, 1828, Short Story
Kalte Herz, Das 1923 d: Fred Sauer. lps: Fritz Schulz, Grete Reinwald, Frieda Richard. 1847m GRM. *Der Pakt Mit Dem Satan*; *The Cold Heart* prod/rel: Hermes-Film

Kalte Herz, Das 1930. 2186m GRM. *The Cold Heart* prod/rel: Mercedes-Film

Kalte Herz, Das 1950 d: Paul Verhoeven. lps: Lutz Moik, Hanna Rucker, Paul Bildt. 106M GDR. *The Cold Heart*; *Heart of Stone* prod/rel: Defa

Das Marchen Vom Falschen Prinzen, 1826, Short Story
Labakan 1956 d: Vaclav KrskA. lps: Eduard Cupak, Jana Rybarova, Karel FialA. 75M CZC/BUL.

Das Wirthaus Im Spessart, 1828, Short Story
Wirtshaus Im Spessart, Das 1958 d: Kurt Hoffmann. lps: Liselotte Pulver, Carlos Thompson, Gunther Luders. 100M GRM. *The Spessart Inn* (USA); *The Inn at Spessart* prod/rel: Georg Witt

Der Zwerg Nase, 1827, Short Story
Zwerg Nase 1952 d: Franceq Stefani. lps: Hans Clarin, Ellinor von Wallerstein, Heini Goebel. 80M GRM. *Nose Dwarf* prod/rel: Schonger, Jugendfilm

HAUGEN, TORMOD
Story
Zeppelin 1981 d: Lasse Glomm. lps: Silvia Myhre, Preben Skjonsberg, Vibecke Lundquist. 78M NRW. prod/rel: Marcusfilm

HAUKELID, KNUT
Skis Against the Atom, London 1954, Book
Heroes of Telemark, The 1965 d: Anthony Mann. lps: Kirk Douglas, Richard Harris, Ulla Jacobsson. 131M UKN. *The Unknown Battle* prod/rel: Benton Film Productions, Rank Film Distributors

HAUPTMANN, GERHART (1862–1946), GRM
Barnwarter Thiel, 1888, Short Story
Bahnwarter Thiel 1982 d: Hans-Joachim Kasprzik. 78M GDR.

Der Biberpelz, 1893, Play
Biberpelz, Der 1928 d: Erich Schonfelder. lps: Lucie Hoflich, Ralph Arthur Roberts, Wolfgang von Schwind. 2568m GRM. *The Beaver Coat* prod/rel: Deutsche Film-Union Ag

Biberpelz, Der 1937 d: Jurgen von Alten. lps: Albert Florath, Heinrich George, Ida Wust. 98M GRM. *The Beaver Coat*

Biberpelz, Der 1949 d: Erich Engel. lps: Fita Benkhoff, Werner Hinz, Kathe Haack. 96M GDR. prod/rel: Defa, Union

Dorothea Angermann, 1926, Play
Dorothea Angermann 1959 d: Robert Siodmak. lps: Ruth Leuwerik, Bert Sotlar, Alfred Schieske. 106M GRM. prod/rel: Divina, Gloria

Fuhrmann Henschel, 1898, Play
Fuhrmann Henschel 1956 d: Josef von Baky. lps: Walter Richter, Nadja Tiller, Camilla SpirA. 105M GRM. *Coachman Henschel* prod/rel: Sascha, UFA

Hanneles Himmelfahrt, 1893, Play
Hanneles Himmelfahrt 1934 d: Thea von Harbou. 64M GRM.

Die Jungfern Vom Bischofsberg, 1907, Play
Jungfern Vom Bischofsberg 1943 d: Peter P. Brauer. 97M GRM.

Die Ratten, 1911, Play
Ratten, Die 1921 d: Hanns Kobe. lps: Emil Jannings, Lucie Hoflich, Eugen Klopfer. 1810m GRM. prod/rel: Grete Ly-Film-Ges.

Ratten, Die 1955 d: Robert Siodmak. lps: Maria Schell, Heidemarie Hatheyer, Curd Jurgens. 91M GRM. *The Rats* prod/rel: C.C.C., UFA

Rose Bernd, 1903, Play
Rose Bernd 1919 d: Alfred Halm. lps: Henny Porten, Emil Jannings, Paul Bildt. 1900m GRM. prod/rel: Messter-Film

Rose Bernd 1957 d: Wolfgang Staudte. lps: Maria Schell, Raf Vallone, Kathe Gold. 98M GRM. *The Sins of Rose Bernd* (USA) prod/rel: Bavaria, Schorcht

Vor Sonnenaufgang, 1889, Play
Vor Sonnenaufgang 1976 d: Oswald Dopke. 104M GRM.

Vor Sonnenuntergang, Berlin 1932, Play
Herrscher, Der 1937 d: Veit Harlan. lps: Emil Jannings, Marianne Hoppe, Harald Paulsen. 106M GRM. *The Ruler* (USA) prod/rel: Tobias-Magna

Vor Sonnenuntergang 1956 d: Gottfried Reinhardt. lps: Hans Albers, Annemarie Duringer, Martin Held. 102M GRM. *Before Sundown* prod/rel: Ccc-Filmkunst, Bavaria

Wanda, 1928, Novel
Konigin Der Arena 1952 d: Rolf Meyer. lps: Maria Litto, Hans Sohnker, Grethe Weiser. 82M GRM. *Queen of the Big Top* prod/rel: Corona, UFA

Die Weber, Play
Weber, Die 1927 d: Friedrich Zelnik. lps: Paul Wegener, Dagny Servaes, Wilhelm Dieterle. 2660m GRM. *The Weavers* prod/rel: Friedrich Zelnik

HAUSER, HEINRICH
Brackwasser, Leipzig 1928, Novel
Bis Zum Ende Aller Tage 1961 d: Franz Peter Wirth. lps: Akiko, Helmut Griem, Carl Lange. 107M GRM. *Girl from Hong Kong* (USA); *Until the End of All Time* prod/rel: Nero Film, Neue Deutsche Filmgesellschaft

HAUSER, THOMAS
The Execution of Charles Horman, Book
Missing 1982 d: Costa-Gavras. lps: Jack Lemmon, Sissy Spacek, Melanie Mayron. 122M USA. prod/rel: Universal, Polygram

HAVILAND-TAYLOR, KATHARINE
Failure, 1932, Short Story
Man to Remember, A 1938 d: Garson Kanin. lps: Anne Shirley, Edward Ellis, Lee Bowman. 80M USA. *Country Doctor* prod/rel: RKO Radio Pictures©

One Man's Journey 1933 d: John S. Robertson. lps: Lionel Barrymore, Joel McCrea, Frances Dee. 72M USA. *The Doctor* prod/rel: RKO Radio Pictures©, Pandro S. Berman Production

HAVLICEK, JAROSLAV
Petrolejove Lampy, Novel
Petrolejove Lampy 1972 d: Juraj Herz. lps: Iva Janzurova, Marie Rosulkova, Ota SklenckA. 100M CZC. *Oil Lamps* prod/rel: Filmstudio Barrandov

Skleneny Vrch, Short Story
Barbora Hlavsova 1942 d: Martin Fric. lps: Terezie Brzkova, Frantisek Smolik, Jirina StepnickovA. 2531m CZC. prod/rel: Nationalfilm

HAVREVOLD, FINN
Marens Lille Ugle, 1957, Novel
Ugler I Mosen 1959 d: Ivo Caprino. 94M NRW.

HAWARD, RENE
Gli Eroi, Novel
Eroi, Gli 1973 d: Duccio Tessari. lps: Rod Steiger, Rosanna Schiaffino, Rod Taylor. 105M ITL/FRN/SPN. *Les Enfants de Choeur* (FRN); *The Heroes*; *Los Heroes Millonarios* (SPN) prod/rel: Gerico Sound, Finarco (Roma)

HAWKES, J. KIRBY
The Guilty Generation, 1928, Play
Guilty Generation, The 1931 d: Rowland V. Lee. lps: Leo Carrillo, Constance Cummings, Robert Young. 82M USA. prod/rel: Columbia Pictures Corp.©

HAWKES, JOHN (1925–, USA, Burne Jr., Clendennin
The Blood Oranges, Novel
Blood Oranges, The 1997 d: Philip Haas. lps: Charles Dance, Colin Lane, Sheryl Lee. 93M USA. prod/rel: Kardana Films, Gotham Entertainment Group

HAWKING, STEPHEN (1942–, UKN, Hawking, Stephen William
A Brief History of Time, 1988, Book
Brief History of Time, A 1991 d: Errol Morris. DOC. 84M UKN/USA.

HAWKINS, JIM
Breakout, Book
One in a Million: the Ron Leflore Story 1978 d: William A. Graham. lps: Levar Burton, Madge Sinclair, Paul Benjamin. TVM. 100M USA. prod/rel: Roger Gimbel Productions, Emi Television

HAWKINS, JOHN
Criminal's Mark, Short Story
Crime Wave 1954 d: Andre de Toth. lps: Gene Nelson, Sterling Hayden, Phyllis Kirk. 74M USA. *The City Is Dark* (UKN) prod/rel: Warner Bros.

Floods of Fear, Novel
Floods of Fear 1958 d: Charles Crichton. lps: Howard Keel, Anne Heywood, Cyril Cusack. 84M UKN. prod/rel: Rank, Rank Film Distributors

The Missing Witness, Short Story
Shadow on the Window 1957 d: William Asher. lps: Philip Carey, Betty Garrett, John Drew Barrymore. 73M USA. prod/rel: Columbia

The Saboteurs, Story
Secret Command, The 1944 d: A. Edward Sutherland. lps: Pat O'Brien, Carole Landis, Chester Morris. 82M USA. *By Secret Command*; *Pilebuck* prod/rel: Columbia, Tourneen Prods.

HAWKINS, WARD
Criminal's Mark, Short Story
Crime Wave 1954 d: Andre de Toth. lps: Gene Nelson, Sterling Hayden, Phyllis Kirk. 74M USA. *The City Is Dark* (UKN) prod/rel: Warner Bros.

Floods of Fear, Novel
Floods of Fear 1958 d: Charles Crichton. lps: Howard Keel, Anne Heywood, Cyril Cusack. 84M UKN. prod/rel: Rank, Rank Film Distributors

The Missing Witness, Short Story
Shadow on the Window 1957 d: William Asher. lps: Philip Carey, Betty Garrett, John Drew Barrymore. 73M USA. prod/rel: Columbia

The Saboteurs, Story
Secret Command, The 1944 d: A. Edward Sutherland. lps: Pat O'Brien, Carole Landis, Chester Morris. 82M USA. *By Secret Command*; *Pilebuck* prod/rel: Columbia, Tourneen Prods.

HAWKS, J. G.
The Haters, Story
Grudge, The 1915 d: William S. Hart. lps: William S. Hart, Charles Ray, Margaret Thompson. 2r USA. prod/rel: Broncho

HAWKSWORTH, HENRY
The Five of Me, Book
Five of Me, The 1981 d: Paul Wendkos. lps: David Birney, Dee Wallace Stone, Mitchell Ryan. TVM. 100M USA. prod/rel: CBS, Jack Farren

HAWLEY, CAMERON (1905–1969), USA
Cash McCall, Novel
Cash McCall 1960 d: Joseph Pevney. lps: James Garner, Natalie Wood, Nina Foch. 102M USA. prod/rel: Warner Bros.

Executive Suite, 1952, Novel
Executive Suite 1954 d: Robert Wise. lps: Fredric March, William Holden, June Allyson. 104M USA. prod/rel: MGM

HAWTHORNE, NATHANIEL (1804–1864), USA
Il Fauno Di Marmo, 1860, Novel
Fauno Di Marmo, Il 1920 d: Mario Bonnard. lps: Elena Sangro, Elsa d'Auro, Carlo Gualandri. 1785m ITL. prod/rel: Celio Film

Feathertop, 1852, Short Story
Feather Top 1912. SHT USA. *Feathertop* prod/rel: Eclair
Feathertop 1913. SHT USA. prod/rel: Kinemacolor
Feathertop 1916 d: Henry J. Vernot. lps: Marguerite Courtot, James Levering, Gerald Griffin. 5r USA. prod/rel: Gaumont Co., Mutual Film Corp.

The House of the Seven Gables, Boston 1851, Novel
House of the Seven Gables, The 1940 d: Joe May. lps: George Sanders, Margaret Lindsay, Vincent Price. 89M USA. *The House of the Seven Gables* prod/rel: Universal Pictures Co.
House of the Seven Gables, The 1910 d: J. Searle Dawley. lps: Mary Fuller. 995f USA. prod/rel: Edison
Twice-Told Tales 1963 d: Sidney Salkow. lps: Vincent Price, Sebastian Cabot, Mari Blanchard. 119M USA. *Nathaniel Hawthorne's "Twice-Told Tales"*; *The Corpse Makers*; *Nights of Terror* prod/rel: Admiral Pictures

The New Adam and Eve, Story
New Adam and Eve, The 1915 d: Richard Garrick. lps: Grace Valentine, Charles Richmond, Mathilde Bering. 3r USA. prod/rel: Rialto

Rappaccini's Daughter, 1846, Short Story
Twice-Told Tales 1963 d: Sidney Salkow. lps: Vincent Price, Sebastian Cabot, Mari Blanchard. 119M USA. *Nathaniel Hawthorne's "Twice-Told Tales"*; *The Corpse Makers*; *Nights of Terror* prod/rel: Admiral Pictures

The Scarlet Letter, New York 1850, Novel
Scarlet Letter, The 1911 d: Joseph Smiley, George Loane Tucker. lps: Lucille Younge, King Baggot, Anita Herndon. 1000f USA. prod/rel: Imp
Scarlet Letter, The 1913 d: David Miles. lps: Linda Arvidson, Charles Perley, Murdock MacQuarrie. SHT USA. prod/rel: Kinemacolor
Scarlet Letter, The 1917 d: Carl Harbaugh. lps: Mary Martin, Stuart Holmes, Kittens Reichert. 5r USA. prod/rel: Fox Film Corp., William Fox©
Scarlet Letter, The 1922 d: Challis Sanderson. lps: Sybil Thorndike, Tony Fraser, Dick Webb. 1198f UKN. prod/rel: Master Films, British Exhibitors' Films
Scarlet Letter, The 1926 d: Victor Sjostrom. lps: Lillian Gish, Lars Hanson, Henry B. Walthall. 8229f USA. prod/rel: Metro-Goldwyn-Mayer Pictures

Scarlet Letter, The 1934 d: Robert G. VignolA. lps: Colleen Moore, Hardie Albright, Henry B. Walthall. 70M USA. prod/rel: Larry Darmour Productions, Majestic Producing Corp.©
Scarlet Letter, The 1979 d: Rick Hauser. lps: Meg Foster, Kevin Conway, John Heard. MTV. 300M USA.
Scarlet Letter, The 1995 d: Roland Joffe. lps: Demi Moore, Gary Oldman, Robert Duvall. 135M USA. prod/rel: Buena Vista, Hollywood
Scharlachrote Buchstabe, Der 1973 d: Wim Wenders. lps: Senta Berger, Lou Castel, Hans Christian Blech. 94M GRM/SPN. *La Letra Escarlata* (SPN); *The Scarlet Letter* (USA) prod/rel: P.I.F.D.a., Wdr
Transgressor, The 1913. lps: Louise Glaum, Charles Ray, John Ince. 2r USA. prod/rel: Broncho

Young Goodman Brown, 1846, Short Story
Young Goodman Brown 1972 d: Donald Fox. lps: Mark Bramball, Peter Kilman, Harry Raybould. 20M USA.

HAY, IAN (1876–1952), UKN, Beith, John Hay
Admirals All, London 1934, Play
Admirals All 1935 d: Victor Hanbury. lps: Wynne Gibson, Gordon Harker, Anthony Bushell. 75M UKN. prod/rel: Stafford, Radio

All at Sea, Play
All at Sea 1935 d: Anthony Kimmins. lps: Tyrrell Davis, Googie Withers, James Carew. 60M UKN. prod/rel: Fox British

Getting Together, New York 1918, Musical Play
Common Cause, The 1918 d: J. Stuart Blackton. lps: Herbert Rawlinson, Sylvia Breamer, Huntley Gordon. 7r USA. prod/rel: Blackton Productions, Inc.©, Vitagraph Co. of America

Good Luck, London 1923, Play
Sporting Lover, The 1926 d: Alan Hale. lps: Conway Tearle, Barbara Bedford, Ward Crane. 6642f USA. *Good Luck* prod/rel: Faultless Pictures, First National Pictures

The Happy Ending, London 1922, Play
Happy Ending, The 1925 d: George A. Cooper. lps: Fay Compton, Jack Buchanan, Joan Barry. 8100f UKN. prod/rel: Gaumont
Happy Ending, The 1931 d: Millard Webb. lps: Anne Grey, Benita Hume, George Barraud. 70M UKN. prod/rel: Gaumont

Happy-Go-Lucky, 1913, Novel
Tilly of Bloomsbury 1921 d: Rex Wilson. lps: Edna Best, Tom Reynolds, Campbell Gullan. 5200f UKN. prod/rel: G. B. Samuelson, Moss
Tilly of Bloomsbury 1931 d: Jack Raymond. lps: Sydney Howard, Phyllis Konstam, Richard Bird. 70M UKN. prod/rel: Sterling
Tilly of Bloomsbury 1940 d: Leslie Hiscott. lps: Sydney Howard, Jean Gillie, Henry Oscar. 83M UKN. prod/rel: Hammersmith, RKO Radio

Housemaster, 1936, Novel
Housemaster 1938 d: Herbert Brenon. lps: Otto Kruger, Diana Churchill, Phillips Holmes. 95M UKN. prod/rel: Associated British Picture Corp.

Leave It to Psmith, London 1930, Play
Leave It to Me 1933 d: Monty Banks. lps: Gene Gerrard, Olive Borden, Molly Lamont. 76M UKN. *Help* prod/rel: British International Pictures, Wardour

The Middle Watch, London 1929, Play
Girls at Sea 1958 d: Gilbert Gunn. lps: Guy Rolfe, Ronald Shiner, Alan White. 80M UKN. prod/rel: Associated British Picture Corporation
Middle Watch, The 1930 d: Norman Walker. lps: Owen Nares, Jacqueline Logan, Jack Raine. 112M UKN. prod/rel: British International Pictures, Wardour
Middle Watch, The 1939 d: Thomas Bentley. lps: Jack Buchanan, Greta Gynt, Fred Emney. 87M UKN. prod/rel: Associated British Picture Corporation

The Midshipmaid, London 1931, Play
Midshipmaid, The 1932 d: Albert de Courville. lps: Jessie Matthews, Fred Kerr, Basil Sydney. 84M UKN. *Midshipmaid Gob* (USA) prod/rel: Gaumont, Woolf & Freedman

Off the Record, London 1947, Play
Carry on Admiral 1957 d: Val Guest. lps: David Tomlinson, Peggy Cummins, Brian Reece. 82M UKN. *The Ship Was Loaded* (USA) prod/rel: George Minter, Renown

Orders are Orders, London 1932, Play
Orders are Orders 1954 d: David Paltenghi. lps: Brian Reece, Margot Grahame, Raymond Huntley. 78M UKN. prod/rel: Group 3, British Lion
Orders Is Orders 1933 d: Walter Forde. lps: Charlotte Greenwood, James Gleason, Cyril Maude. 88M UKN. prod/rel: Gaumont British, Ideal

A Present from Margate, London 1933, Play
Widow from Monte Carlo 1936 d: Arthur G. Collins. lps: Dolores Del Rio, Warren William, Louise FazendA. 63M USA. *Meet the Duchess* prod/rel: Warner Bros. Productions Corp., Warner Bros. Pictures©

The Sport of Kings, London 1924, Play
Sport of Kings, The 1931 d: Victor Saville, T. Hayes Hunter. lps: Leslie Henson, Hugh Wakefield, Gordon Harker. 98M UKN. prod/rel: Gainsborough, Ideal

HAY, JACOB
The Sheriff of Fractured Jaw, Short Story
Sheriff of Fractured Jaw, The 1958 d: Raoul Walsh. lps: Kenneth More, Jayne Mansfield, Henry Hull. 110M UKN. prod/rel: 20th Century Fox, Apollo

HAY, JOHN
Jim Bludso of the Prairie Belle, 1871, Poem
Jim Bludso 1912. lps: J. P. McGowan. 1000f USA. prod/rel: Kalem
Jim Bludso 1917 d: Wilfred Lucas, Tod Browning. lps: Wilfred Lucas, Olga Grey, George E. Stone. 5r USA. prod/rel: Fine Arts Film Co., Triangle Distributing Corp.

Little Breeches, 1871, Poem
Jim Bludso 1917 d: Wilfred Lucas, Tod Browning. lps: Wilfred Lucas, Olga Grey, George E. Stone. 5r USA. prod/rel: Fine Arts Film Co., Triangle Distributing Corp.
Little Breeches 1914. 400f USA. prod/rel: Lubin

HAY JR., JAMES
The Man Who Forgot, New York 1915, Novel
Man Who Forgot, The 1917 d: Emile Chautard. lps: Robert Warwick, Doris Kenyon, Gerda Holmes. 5r USA. prod/rel: Paragon Films, Inc., World Film Corp.©

HAYAKAWA, SESSUE (1889–1973), JPN
Shadows, Play
Heart in Pawn, A 1919 d: William Worthington. lps: Sessue Hayakawa, Vola Vale, Tsuru Aoki. 5r USA. *Shadows* prod/rel: Haworth Pictures Corp.©, Robertson-Cole Co.

HAYASAKA, AKIRA
Dautaun Hirozu, Novel
Dauntaun Hirozu 1988 d: Yoji YamadA. lps: Hiroko Yakushimaru, Hashinosuke Nakamura, Toshiro YanagibA. 120M JPN. *Hope and Pain* prod/rel: Shochiku Co.

HAYASHI, FUBO
Tange Sazen, Novel
Tange Sazen 1963 d: Seiichiro UchikawA. lps: Tetsuro Tamba, Haruko Wanibuchi, Michiko SagA. 95M JPN. prod/rel: Shochiku Co.

HAYASHI, FUMIKO
Bangiku, 1948, Short Story
Bangiku 1954 d: Mikio Naruse. lps: Yuko Mochizuki. 117M JPN. *Late Chrysanthemums*

Chairo No Me, 1950, Novel
Tsuma 1953 d: Mikio Naruse. lps: Ken UeharA. 89M JPN. *Wife*

Horoki, Tokyo 1928, Biography
Horoki 1962 d: Mikio Naruse. lps: Hideko Takamine, Kinuyo Tanaka, Daisuke Kato. 124M JPN. *A Recording of Wandering*; *A Wanderer's Notebook*; *Lonely Lane* (USA) prod/rel: Toho Co.

Inazuma, 1935, Novel
Inazuma 1952 d: Mikio Naruse. lps: Chieko Nakakita, Hideko Takamine, Mitsuko MiurA. 93M JPN. *Lightning*
Inazuma 1967 d: Hideo ObA. lps: Chieko Baisho, Yuko Hama, Mihoko Inagaki. 85M JPN. *A Flash of Lightning*

Meshi, 1951, Novel
Meshi 1951 d: Mikio Naruse. lps: Setsuko Hara, Haruko Sugimura, Ken UeharA. 97M JPN. *A Married Life*; *Repast*; *The Rice* prod/rel: Toho Co.

Shirasagi, 1949, Short Story
Bangiku 1954 d: Mikio Naruse. lps: Yuko Mochizuki. 117M JPN. *Late Chrysanthemums*

Suisen, 1949, Short Story
Bangiku 1954 d: Mikio Naruse. lps: Yuko Mochizuki. 117M JPN. *Late Chrysanthemums*

HAYCOX, ERNEST
Apache Trail, Story
Apache Trail 1942 d: Richard Thorpe. lps: Lloyd Nolan, Donna Reed, William Lundigan. 66M USA. prod/rel: Metro-Goldwyn-Mayer Corp.

Bugles in the Afternoon, 1944, Novel
Bugles in the Afternoon 1952 d: Roy Rowland. lps: Ray Milland, Helena Carter, Hugh Marlowe. 85M USA. prod/rel: Warner Bros.

Canyon Passage, 1945, Novel
Canyon Passage 1946 d: Jacques Tourneur. lps: Dana Andrews, Brian Donlevy, Susan Hayward. 99M USA. prod/rel: Universal

The Man in the Saddle, 1938, Novel
Man in the Saddle 1951 d: Andre de Toth. lps: Randolph Scott, Joan Leslie, Ellen Drew. 87M USA. *The Outcast* (UKN) prod/rel: Columbia, Scott-Brown Prods.

Stage Station, Novel
Apache War Smoke 1952 d: Harold F. Kress. lps: Gilbert Roland, Glenda Farrell, Robert Horton. 67M USA. prod/rel: Metro-Goldwyn-Mayer Corp.

Stage to Lordsburg, 1937, Short Story
Stagecoach 1939 d: John Ford. lps: Claire Trevor, John Wayne, Thomas Mitchell. 96M USA. prod/rel: United Artists Corp., Walter Wanger Productions©
Stagecoach 1966 d: Gordon Douglas. lps: Bing Crosby, Alex Cord, Mike Connors. 115M USA. prod/rel: Martin Rackin Productions
Stagecoach 1986 d: Ted Post. lps: Willie Nelson, Kris Kristofferson, Johnny Cash. TVM. 100M USA.

Sundown Jim, 1940, Novel
Sundown Jim 1942 d: James Tinling. lps: John Kimbrough, Virginia Gilmore, Arleen Whelan. 58M USA. prod/rel: 20th Century Fox

Trail Town, 1941, Novel
Abilene Town 1946 d: Edwin L. Marin. lps: Randolph Scott, Ann Dvorak, Rhonda Fleming. 89M USA. *The Homesteaders* prod/rel: United Artists

Trouble Shooter, Garden City, N.Y. 1937, Novel
Union Pacific 1939 d: Cecil B. de Mille. lps: Barbara Stanwyck, Joel McCrea, Akim Tamiroff. 135M USA. prod/rel: Paramount Pictures©

HAYDEN, JOHN
A Sap from Syracuse, Play
Sap from Syracuse, The 1930 d: A. Edward Sutherland. lps: Jack Oakie, Ginger Rogers, Granville Bates. 6108f USA. *The Sap Abroad* (UKN) prod/rel: Paramount-Publix Corp.

HAYDEN, STERLING (1916–1986), USA
Wanderer, Autobiography
Havarist, Der 1983 d: Wolf-Eckart Buhler. lps: Burkhard Driest, Rudiger Vogler, Hannes Wader. 100M GRM. *Captain of a Sinking Ship* prod/rel: Red Harvest, Starfilm

HAYDEN, TOREY
One Child, Book
Untamed Love 1994 d: Paul Aaron. lps: Cathy Lee Crosby, John Getz, Gary Frank. TVM. 93M USA. prod/rel: Cathy Lee Crosby Productions

HAYES, ALFRED (1911–1985), UKN
The Girl on the Via Flaminia, Novel
Acte d'Amour, Un 1953 d: Anatole Litvak. lps: Kirk Douglas, Dany Robin, Barbara Laage. 108M FRN/USA. *Act of Love* (USA); *Quelque Part Dans le Monde* prod/rel: Filmaur, Benagoss

HAYES, BILLY
Midnight Express, Book
Midnight Express 1978 d: Alan Parker. lps: Brad Davis, Randy Quaid, Bo Hopkins. 120M UKN/USA. prod/rel: Columbia, Casablanca

HAYES, DOUGLAS
The Comedy Man, Novel
Comedy Man, The 1963 d: Alvin Rakoff. lps: Kenneth More, Cecil Parker, Dennis Price. 92M UKN. prod/rel: British Lion, Grayfilms

HAYES, HAROLD T. P.
Article
Gorillas in the Mist 1988 d: Michael Apted. lps: Sigourney Weaver, Bryan Brown, Julie Harris. 129M USA. prod/rel: Universal

HAYES, J. MILTON
The Green Eye of the Yellow God, Poem
Green Eye of the Yellow God, The 1913 d: Charles H. France. lps: Charles Ogle, Laura Sawyer. 1000f USA. prod/rel: Edison

HAYES, JOSEPH
Novel
Neunzig Minuten Nach Mitternacht 1962 d: Jurgen Goslar. lps: Christine Kaufmann, Martin Held, Hilde Krahl. 77M GRM. *Terror After Midnight* (USA); *90 Minutes After Midnight* prod/rel: Roxy, Constantin

Bon Voyage, New York 1957, Novel
Bon Voyage! 1962 d: James Neilson. lps: Fred MacMurray, Jane Wyman, Tommy Kirk. 132M USA. prod/rel: Walt Disney

The Desperate Hours, Novel
Desperate Hours 1990 d: Michael Cimino. lps: Mickey Rourke, Anthony Hopkins, Mimi Rogers. 105M USA. prod/rel: 20th Century Fox
Desperate Hours, The 1955 d: William Wyler. lps: Humphrey Bogart, Fredric March, Arthur Kennedy. 112M USA. prod/rel: Paramount

The Third Day, New York 1964, Novel
Third Day, The 1965 d: Jack Smight. lps: George Peppard, Elizabeth Ashley, Roddy McDowall. 119M USA. prod/rel: Warner Bros. Pictures

HAYES, KENT
Broken Promise, Book
Broken Promise 1981 d: Don Taylor. lps: Melissa Michaelson, Chris Sarandon, George Coe. TVM. 100M USA. prod/rel: CBS, Emi

HAYES, MARIJANE
Bon Voyage, New York 1957, Novel
Bon Voyage! 1962 d: James Neilson. lps: Fred MacMurray, Jane Wyman, Tommy Kirk. 132M USA. prod/rel: Walt Disney

HAYES, NELSON
Bahama Passage, Novel
Bahama Passage 1941 d: Edward H. Griffith. lps: Madeleine Carroll, Sterling Hayden, Flora Robson. 83M USA. prod/rel: Paramount

HAYES, NICHOLAS
The Rise of Constable Rafferty, Play
Rafferty's Rise 1918 d: J. M. Kerrigan. lps: Fred O'Donovan, Kathleen Murphy, Brian Magowan. 2535f IRL/UKN. prod/rel: Film Company of Ireland

HAYES, STEVEN
Short Story
Escort West 1958 d: Francis D. Lyon. lps: Victor Mature, Elaine Stewart, Faith Domergue. 75M USA. prod/rel: United Artists, Romina

HAYES, WILLIAM EDWARD
The Black Doll, New York 1936, Novel
Black Doll, The 1937 d: Otis Garrett. lps: Nan Grey, Donald Woods, Edgar Kennedy. 66M USA. prod/rel: Crime Club Productions, Inc.

HAYNES, BRIAN
Spyship, Book
Spyship 1983 d: Michael Custance. lps: Tom Wilkinson, Lesley Nightingale, Peter Eyre. MTV. 330M UKN. prod/rel: BBC Pebble Mill

HAYOSHI, FUMIKO
Ukigumo, 1935, Novel
Ukigumo 1955 d: Mikio Naruse. lps: Hideko Takamine, Masayuki Mori, Isao YamagatA. 123M JPN. *Floating Clouds* prod/rel: Toho Co.

HAYS, JACK
Mr. Lemon of Orange, 1930, Play
Mr. Lemon of Orange 1931 d: John G. Blystone. lps: El Brendel, Fifi d'Orsay, William Collier Sr. 72M USA. prod/rel: Fox Film Corp.©

HAZARD, JOHN W.
Flying Teakettle, 1950, Article
You're in the Navy Now 1951 d: Henry Hathaway. lps: Gary Cooper, Millard Mitchell, Eddie Albert. 93M USA. *U.S.S. Teakettle* prod/rel: 20th Century-Fox

HAZARD, LAWRENCE
Good Company, Play
From Hell to Heaven 1933 d: Erle C. Kenton. lps: Jack Oakie, Carole Lombard, Sidney Blackmer. 70M USA. *A Good Thing*; *Eleven Lives* prod/rel: Paramount Productions©

Man's Castle, 1932, Play
Man's Castle 1933 d: Frank Borzage. lps: Spencer Tracy, Loretta Young, Glenda Farrell. 75M USA. *Hank O'Blue*; *A Man's Castle* prod/rel: Columbia Pictures Corp., Frank Borzage Production

HAZELTINE, HORACE
The Appearance of Evil, Short Story
Appearance of Evil, The 1918 d: Lawrence C. Windom. lps: June Elvidge, Frank Mayo, Douglas Redmond Jr. 4352f USA. prod/rel: World Film Corp.©

The Sable Lorcha, Chicago 1912, Novel
Sable Lorcha, The 1915 d: Lloyd Ingraham. lps: Tully Marshall, Thomas Jefferson, Charles Lee. 5r USA. prod/rel: Fine Arts Film Co., Triangle Film Corp.©

HAZELTON, GEORGE COCHRANE
Mistress Nell, New York 1900, Play
Mistress Nell 1915 d: James Kirkwood. lps: Mary Pickford, Owen Moore, Arthur Hoops. 5r USA. prod/rel: Famous Players Film Co., Paramount Pictures Corp.

The Raven; the Love Story of Edgar Allan Poe, New York 1909, Novel
Raven, The 1915 d: Charles J. Brabin. lps: Henry B. Walthall, Warda Howard, Ernest Maupain. 6r USA. prod/rel: Essanay Film Mfg. Co.©, V-L-S-E, Inc.

HAZZARD, JACK E.
Turn to the Right, New York 1916, Play
Turn to the Right 1922 d: Rex Ingram. lps: Alice Terry, Jack Mulhall, Harry Myers. 7703f USA. prod/rel: Metro Pictures

HE JINGZHI
Bai Mao Nu, Play
Bai Mao Nu 1950 d: Wang Bin, Shui HuA. lps: Tian Hua, Li Baifang, Chen Qiang. 13r CHN. *The White-Haired Girl* prod/rel: Northeast Film Studio

HE QIU
Xin Ju Zhang Dao Lai Zhi, Play
Xin Ju Zhang Dao Lai Xhi Qian 1956 d: Lu Ban. lps: Li Jingbo, Pu Ke, Chen Guangting. 5r CHN. *Before the New Director Arrives* prod/rel: Changchun Film Studio

HE WEI
Fu Shi, Novel
Fu Shi 1957 d: Ren Sun. lps: Che Xuan, He XIaoshu, Zhang Fengxiao. 5r CHN. *The Re-Examination* prod/rel: Changchun Film Studio

HEAD, ANN
Novel
Mr. and Mrs. Bo Jo Jones 1971 d: Robert Day. lps: Desi Arnaz Jr., Christopher Norris, Dan Dailey. TVM. 74M USA. prod/rel: 20th Century-Fox

HEALD, TIM
Deadline, Novel
Bognor: Deadline 1981 d: Carol Wiseman. lps: David Horovitch, Joanna McCallum, Ewan Roberts. MTV. 180M UKN. *Deadline* prod/rel: Thames Television Network

Let Sleeping Dogs Lie, Novel
Bognor: Let Sleeping Dogs Lie 1981 d: Neville Green. lps: David Horovitch, Joanna McCallum, Ewan Roberts. MTV. 180M UKN. *Let Sleeping Dogs Lie* prod/rel: Thames Television Network

Unbecoming Habits, Novel
Bognor: Unbecoming Habits 1981 d: Robert Tronson. lps: David Horovitch, Joanna McCallum, Ewan Roberts. MTV. 180M UKN. *Unbecoming Habits* prod/rel: Thames Television Network

HEALEY, BEN
Waiting for a Tiger, Novel
Taste of Excitement 1969 d: Don Sharp. lps: Eva Renzi, David Buck, Peter Vaughan. 99M UKN. prod/rel: Crispin, Trio-Group W

HEALY, JOHN
The Grass Arena, Novel
Grass Arena, The 1991 d: Gillies MacKinnon. lps: Mark Rylance, Andrew Dicks, Billy Boyle. TVM. 90M UKN. prod/rel: BBC Tv, BBC Films for Screen Two

HEARD, H. F.
A Taste for Honey, New York 1941, Novel
Deadly Bees, The 1967 d: Freddie Francis. lps: Suzanna Leigh, Frank Finlay, Guy Doleman. 123M UKN. prod/rel: Amicus Productions, Paramount

HEARN, LAFCADIO (1850–1904), USA
Yuki-Onna, Short Story
Kaidan Yukijoro 1968 d: Tokuzo TanakA. lps: Shiho Fujimura, Akira Ishihama, MacHiko HasegawA. 80M JPN. *Ghost of Snow-Girl Prostitute*; *Yukionna -Woman of the Snow*; *Yukionna*; *Snow Ghost* prod/rel: Daiei Motion Picture Co.

HEARST, PATRICIA CAMPBELL (1954–, USA, Hearst, Patty
Every Secret Thing, Autobiography
Patty Hearst 1988 d: Paul Schrader. lps: Natasha Richardson, William Forsythe, Ving Rhames. 108M USA/UKN. *Patty Hearst: Her Own Story*; *Patty* prod/rel: Atlantic Entertainment, Zenith

HEARTH, AMY HILL
Having Our Say, 1993, Book
Having Our Say: the Delany Sisters' First 100 Years 1999 d: Lynne Littman. lps: Diahann Carroll, Ruby Dee, Amy Madigan. TVM. 120M USA. prod/rel: Kraft Premiere Movie, Tele Vest

HEATH, A. B.
The Scarlet West, Story
Scarlet West, The 1925 d: John G. Adolfi. lps: Robert Frazer, Clara Bow, Robert Edeson. 8390f USA. prod/rel: Frank J. Carroll Productions, First National Pictures

HEATH, PERCY
Slightly Scarlet, Play
Enigmatique Monsieur Parkes, L' 1930 d: Louis J. Gasnier. lps: Adolphe Menjou, Claudette Colbert, Emile Chautard. 71M USA. prod/rel: Films Paramount, Paramount Famous Lasky Corp.

HEATH, WILLIAM L.
Violent Saturday, 1955, Novel
Violent Saturday 1955 d: Richard Fleischer. lps: Victor Mature, Richard Egan, Stephen McNally. 91M USA. prod/rel: 20th Century-Fox

HEBBEL, CHRISTIAN FRIEDRICH (1813–1863), GRM, Hebbel, Friedrich
Agnes Bernauer, 1852, Play
Jugement de Dieu, Le 1949 d: Raymond Bernard. lps: Pierre Renoir, Jean-Claude Pascal, Andree Debar. 98M FRN. *The Judgment of God* prod/rel: B.U.P.

Mutter Und Kind, 1859, Poem
Mutter Und Kind 1924 d: Carl Froelich. lps: Henny Porten, Friedrich Kayssler, Erna MorenA. 2407m GRM. *Mother and Child* prod/rel: Tofa, N.D.L.S.

Mutter Und Kind 1933 d: Hans Steinhoff. lps: Henny Porten, Peter Voss, Wolfgang Keppler. 89M GRM. *Mother and Child*

Der Rubin, 1851, Play
Verzauberte Prinzessin, Die 1939 d: Aloys Alfons Zengerling. lps: Olaf Bach, Hermann Wagner. 55M GRM.

HEBDEN, MARK
Eye-Witness, Novel
Eyewitness 1970 d: John Hough. lps: Mark Lester, Lionel Jeffries, Susan George. 91M UKN. *Sudden Terror* prod/rel: MGM-Emi, Itc

HEBERT, ANNE (1916–, CND
Kamouraska, Novel
Kamouraska 1973 d: Claude JutrA. lps: Genevieve Bujold, Richard Jordan, Philippe Leotard. 124M CND/FRN. *Kamouraska Power of Passion* prod/rel: Les Prods. Carle-Lamy Ltee. (Montreal), Parc Film (Paris)

HEBERT, JACQUES
L' Affaire Coffin, Book
Affaire Coffin, L' 1980 d: Jean-Claude Labrecque. lps: August Schellenberg, Yvon Dufour, Micheline Lanctot. 106M CND. *The Coffin Affair; Coffin* prod/rel: Les Productions Videofilms Ltee., Les Films Cine Scene Ltee.

HECHLER, KENNETH WILLIAM
Bridge at Remagen, New York 1957, Novel
Bridge at Remagen, The 1969 d: John Guillermin. lps: George Segal, Robert Vaughn, Ben GazzarA. 116M USA. prod/rel: United Artists

HECHT, BEN (1892–1964), USA
Story
Outlaw, The 1943 d: Howard Hughes, Howard Hawks (Uncredited). lps: Jane Russell, Jack Buetel, Thomas Mitchell. 124M USA. prod/rel: United Artists

Actor's Blood, 1936, Short Story
Actors and Sin 1952 d: Ben Hecht. lps: Edward G. Robinson, Eddie Albert, Marsha Hunt. 86M USA. prod/rel: United Artists, Sid Kuller

Caballero of the Law, 1933, Short Story
Crime Without Passion 1934 d: Ben Hecht, Charles MacArthur. lps: Claude Rains, Margo, Whitney Bourne. 80M USA. prod/rel: Hecht-Macarthur, Inc.

Concerning a Woman of Sin, 1945, Short Story
Actors and Sin 1952 d: Ben Hecht. lps: Edward G. Robinson, Eddie Albert, Marsha Hunt. 86M USA. prod/rel: United Artists, Sid Kuller

The Florentine Dagger, New York 1928, Story
Florentine Dagger, The 1935 d: Robert Florey. lps: Donald Woods, C. Aubrey Smith, Henry O'Neill. 69M USA. prod/rel: Warner Bros. Pictures©

The Front Page, New York 1928, Play
Front Page, The 1931 d: Lewis Milestone. lps: Adolphe Menjou, Pat O'Brien, Mary Brian. 103M USA. prod/rel: the Caddo Co.©, Lewis Milestone Productionn

Front Page, The 1974 d: Billy Wilder. lps: Walter Matthau, Jack Lemmon, Carol Burnett. 105M USA. prod/rel: Universal

His Girl Friday 1940 d: Howard Hawks. lps: Cary Grant, Rosalind Russell, Ralph Bellamy. 92M USA. prod/rel: Columbia Pictures Corp.©

Switching Channels 1988 d: Ted Kotcheff. lps: Kathleen Turner, Burt Reynolds, Christopher Reeve. 105M USA. prod/rel: Tri-Star

Gaily Gaily, New York 1963, Novel
Gaily, Gaily 1969 d: Norman Jewison. lps: Beau Bridges, Melina Mercouri, Brian Keith. 107M USA. *Chicago Chicago* (UKN) prod/rel: Mirisch Productions, Cartier Productions

The Great Magoo, New York 1932, Play
Shoot the Works 1934 d: Wesley Ruggles. lps: Jack Oakie, Ben Bernie, Dorothy Dell. 82M USA. *Thank Your Stars* (UKN); *The Great Magoo* prod/rel: Paramount Productions©

Some Like It Hot 1939 d: George Archainbaud. lps: Bob Hope, Shirley Ross, Una Merkel. 64M USA. *Rhythm Romance* prod/rel: Paramount Pictures©

I Hate Actors, 1944, Novel
Je Hais Les Acteurs 1986 d: Gerard Krawczyk. lps: Jean Poiret, Michel Blanc, Bernard Blier. 95M FRN. *I Hate Actors* (USA)

Jumbo, New York 1935, Play
Billy Rose's Jumbo 1962 d: Charles Walters. lps: Doris Day, Stephen Boyd, Jimmy Durante. 124M USA. *Jumbo* prod/rel: Euterpe, Inc., Arwin Productions

Man-Eating Tiger, Allentown, PA. 1927, Play
Spring Tonic 1935 d: Clyde Bruckman. lps: Lew Ayres, Claire Trevor, Jack Haley. 55M USA. *Man-Eating Tiger; Hold That Tiger* prod/rel: Fox Film Corp.©

Miracle in the Rain, 1943, Novel
Miracle in the Rain 1956 d: Rudolph Mate. lps: Jane Wyman, Van Johnson, Peggie Castle. 107M USA. prod/rel: Warner Bros.

Specter of the Rose, 1945, Short Story
Specter of the Rose 1946 d: Ben Hecht. lps: Judith Anderson, Michael Chekhov, Ivan Kirov. 90M USA. *Spectre of the Rose* (UKN) prod/rel: Republic

Twentieth Century, New York 1932, Play
Twentieth Century 1934 d: Howard Hawks. lps: John Barrymore, Carole Lombard, Roscoe Karns. 91M USA. prod/rel: Columbia Pictures Corp.©, Howard Hawks Production

The Unholy Night, Novel
Spectre Vert, Le 1930 d: Jacques Feyder, Lionel Barrymore. lps: Andre Luguet, Jetta Goudal, Pauline Garon. 105M USA/FRN. *The Green Ghost* prod/rel: Metro-Goldwyn-Mayer Pictures

HECKELMAN, CHARLES
Deputy Marshal, Novel
Deputy Marshal 1949 d: William Berke. lps: Jon Hall, Frances Langford, Dick Foran. 72M USA. prod/rel: Lippert

HECKSTALL SMITH, VIOLET
The Unwritten Law, Play
Unwritten Law, The 1929 d: Sinclair Hill. lps: Ion Swinley, Rosalinde Fuller, Robert Bruce. 30M UKN. prod/rel: British Sound Film Productions, British Instructional Film Distributors

HEDBERG, OLLE
Iris Och Lojtnantshjarta, 1934, Novel
Iris Och Lojtnantshjarta 1946 d: Alf Sjoberg. lps: Mai Zetterling, Alf Kjellin, Holger Lowenadler. 86M SWD. *Iris* (UKN); *Iris and the Lieutenant*

Stopp! Tank Pa Nagot Annat, 1939, Novel
Stopp! Tank Pa Nagot Annat 1944 d: Ake Ohberg. lps: Eva Henning, Hasse Ekman, Olof Winnerstrand. 110M SWD. *Stop! Think of Something Else* prod/rel: Ab Europa Film

HEDBERG, TOR
Johan Ulfstjerna, Stockholm 1907, Play
Johan Ulfstjerna 1923 d: John W. Brunius. lps: Ivan Hedqvist, Anna Olin, Einar Hansson. 1493m SWD. *Human Destinies* prod/rel: Ab Svensk Filmindustri

Johan Ulfstjerna 1936 d: Gustaf Edgren. lps: Gosta Ekman, Edith Erastoff, Bjorn Berglund. 79M SWD. prod/rel: Ab Svensk Filmindustri

Nationalmonumenttet, Stockholm 1923, Play
Det Ar Min Modell 1946 d: Gustaf Molander. lps: Maj-Britt Nilsson, Alf Kjellin, Olof Winnerstrand. 104M SWD. *It's My Model* prod/rel: Ab Svensk Filmindustri

HEDGES, PETER
What's Eating Gilbert Grape, Novel
What's Eating Gilbert Grape 1993 d: Lasse Hallstrom. lps: Johnny Depp, Juliette Lewis, Mary Steenburgen. 118M USA. *Gilbert Grape*

HEER, JAKOB CHRISTOPH
An Heiligen Wassern, Stuttgart 1898, Novel
An Heiligen Wassern 1932 d: Erich Waschneck. lps: Eduard von Winterstein, Karin Hardt, Reinhold Bernt. 84M GRM/SWT. *Les Eaux Saintes* (SWT); *Sieg Der Liebe; Sturzende Wasser* prod/rel: Fanal-Filmproduktion, Interna-Tonfilm

An Heiligen Wassern 1961 d: Alfred Weidenmann. lps: Hansjorg Felmy, Cordula Trantow, Gisela von Collande. 100M SWT. *Les Eaux Saintes; Les Eaux Saintes du Valais*; **De l'Eau Au Prix de Leur Sang** prod/rel: Cine Custodia Film

Der Konig Der Bernina, Stuttgart 1900, Novel
Eternal Love 1929 d: Ernst Lubitsch. lps: John Barrymore, Camilla Horn, Victor Varconi. 6515f USA. *King of the Mountains* prod/rel: Feature Productions, United Artists

Konig Der Bernina, Der 1957 d: Alfred Lehner. lps: Helmuth Schneider, Waltraut Haas, Walter Janssen. 93M AUS/SWT. *Le Roi de la Bernina* prod/rel: Urania-Filmproduktion, Zenith-Film

HEFER, HAIM
Story
Gesher Tzar Me'od 1985 d: Nissim Dayan. lps: Aharon Ipale, Salwa Haddad, Makram Khoury. F ISR. *On a Narrow Bridge*

HEGGEN, THOMAS (1919–1949), USA
Mister Roberts, 1946, Novel
Ensign Pulver 1964 d: Joshua Logan. lps: Robert Walker Jr., Burl Ives, Walter Matthau. 104M USA. *Mr. Pulver and the Captain* prod/rel: Warner Bros. Pictures

Mister Roberts 1955 d: John Ford, Mervyn Leroy. lps: Henry Fonda, James Cagney, William Powell. 123M USA. prod/rel: Warner Bros.

HEIBERG, JOHAN LUDVIG
Elverhoj, 1828, Play
Elverhoj 1939 d: Sven Methling. lps: Eva Heramb, Edouard Mielche, Karin Nellemose. 93M DNM.

HEIDISH, MARCY
A Woman Called Moses, Book
Woman Called Moses, A 1978 d: Paul Wendkos. lps: Cicely Tyson, Will Geer, Robert Ooks. TVM. 200M USA. prod/rel: Henry Jaffe Enterprises

HEIJERMANS, HERMAN
Droomkoninkje, 1924, Novel
Die Vom Schicksal Verfolgten 1927 d: Henk Kleinmann. lps: Aud Egede Nissen, Wilhelm Dieterle, Henkie Klein. 1844m GRM/NTH. *Droomkoninkje* (NTH); *Little Dream King*; *Those Pursued By Fate* prod/rel: V.D.Veer/Kleinman Film (Amsterdam), Omnia-Film (Berlin)

In de Jonge Jan, Play
Case of Arson, A 1913 d: A. E. Coleby. lps: Henri de Vries. 4000f UKN. prod/rel: Britannic Film Producing Syndicate, Big A

Op Hoop Van Zegen, 1900, Play
Fahrt Ins Verderben, Die 1924 d: James Bauer. lps: Adele Sandrock, Hans Adalbert Schlettow, Barbara von Annenkoff. 2245m GRM/NTH. *Op Hoop Van Zegen* (NTH); *Hoffnung Auf Segen; The Good Hope; The Voyage to Destruction* prod/rel: Lucifer-Film (Amsterdam), Lucifer-Film Gmbh (Berlin)

Op Hoop Van Zegen 1918 d: Maurits H. Binger. lps: Esther de Boer-Van Rijk, Willem Van Der Veer, Frits Bouwmeester. 1750m NTH. *The Good Hope* prod/rel: Filmfabriek-Hollandia

Op Hoop Van Zegen 1934 d: Alex Benno, Louis Saalborn. lps: Esther de Boer-Van Rijk, Jan Van Ees, Frits Van Dongen. 99M NTH. *The Good Hope*

Op Hoop Van Zegen 1986 d: Guido Pieters. lps: Danny de Munk, Renee Soutendijk, Rijk de Gooyer. 105M NTH. *The Good Hope*

Schakels, 1903, Play
Schakels 1920 d: Maurits H. Binger. lps: Jan Van Dommelen, Paula de Waart, Louis Davids. 1869m NTH. *Links* prod/rel: Filmfabriek-Hollandia

HEIMANN, ERWIN
Hast Noch Der Sohne Ja?, Frauenfeld 1956, Novel
Hast Noch Der Sohne Ja? 1959 d: Lukas Ammann. lps: Renate Steiger, Max Liniger, Schaggi Streuli. 88M SWT. *Patrie Te Reste-T-Il Des Fils?* prod/rel: Neue Terra Film

HEINE, HEINRICH (1797–1856), GRM, Heine, Chaim Harry
The Pilgrimage, Poem
Pilgrimage, The 1912. 1000f USA. prod/rel: Kalem

HEINESEN, WILLIAM
We Must Dance, Short Story
Dansinn 1998 d: Agust Gudmundsson. lps: Palina Jonsdottir, Dofri Hermannsson, Baldur Trausti Hreinsson. 86M ICL. *The Dance* prod/rel: Isfilm, Oxford Film Co.

HEINLEIN, ROBERT A. (1907–1988), USA, Heinlein, Robert Anson
The Puppet Masters, 1951, Novel
Brain Eaters, The 1958 d: Bruno Ve SotA. lps: Joanna Lee, Jody Fair, Edwin Nelson. 60M USA. *The Keepers of the Earth*; *The Keepers* prod/rel: American International

Rocket Ship Galileo, 1947, Novel
Destination Moon 1950 d: Irving Pichel. lps: John Archer, Warner Anderson, Tom Powers. 91M USA. prod/rel: Eagle-Lion Classics, George Pal Prods.

Starship Troopers, Novel
Starship Troopers 1997 d: Paul Verhoeven. lps: Casper Van Dien, Dina Meyer, Denise Richards. 129M USA. prod/rel: Tristar Pictures©, Touchstone Pictures©

HEINRICH, WILLI
Schmetterlinge Weinen Nicht, Novel
Schmetterlinge Weinen Nicht 1970 d: Klaus Uberall. lps: Siegfried Wischnewski, Gaby Fuchs, Lydia Bauer. 88M SWT/GRM. *Butterflies Don't Cry* prod/rel: Peter Schamoni, Constantin

The Willing Flesh, Novel
Cross of Iron 1977 d: Sam Peckinpah. lps: James Coburn, Maximilian Schell, James Mason. 100M UKN/GRM. *Steiner-Das Eiserne Kreuz* (GRM) prod/rel: Emi-Rapid Film, Terra Filmkunst

HELD, L.
Der Vogelhandler, Vienna 1891, Operetta
Vogelhandler, Der 1953 d: Arthur M. Rabenalt. lps: Ilse Werner, Eva Probst, Erni Mangold. 92M GRM. *The Bird Dealer* prod/rel: Berolina, Deutsche Cosmopol
Vogelhandler, Der 1962 d: Geza von CziffrA. lps: Conny Froboess, Peter Weck, Maria Sebaldt. 87M GRM. *The Bird Dealer* prod/rel: Divina, Gloria

HELGE, MATS
Eagle Island, Novel
Eagle Island 1987 d: Mats Helge Olsson. lps: Tom O'Rourke, Summer Lee Thomas, Terry D. Seago. 90M SWD. prod/rel: Zodiac Filmgroup

HELIAS, PIERRE-JAKEZ
Le Cheval d'Orgueil, Book
Cheval d'Orgueil, Le 1980 d: Claude Chabrol. lps: Jacques Dufilho, Bernadette Le Sache, Francois Cluzet. 118M FRN. *The Proud Ones* (UKN); *The Horse of Pride* prod/rel: Production Bela, Tf1

HELLER, ALFRED
Madel in Not, Novel
Amante Segreta, L' 1941 d: Carmine Gallone. lps: Alida Valli, Fosco Giachetti, Vivi Gioi. 101M ITL. prod/rel: Sangraf, I.C.I.

HELLER, EVA
Beim Nachsten Mann Wird Alles Anders, Novel
Beim Nachsten Mann Wird Alles Anders 1988 d: Xaver Schwarzenberger. lps: Antje Schmidt, Volkert Kraeft, Dominic Raacke. 101M GRM. *With the Next Man Everything Will Be Different* prod/rel: Rialto, Tobis

HELLER, FRANK
Die Finanzen Des Grossherzogs, Novel
Finanzen Des Grossherzogs, Die 1924 d: F. W. Murnau. lps: Mady Christians, Harry Liedtke, Alfred Abel. 2483m GRM. *The Finances of the Grand Duke*; *The Grand Duke's Finances*
Finanzen Des Grossherzogs, Die 1934 d: Gustaf Grundgens. lps: Viktor de Kowa, Hilde Weissner, Heinz Ruhmann. 96M GRM. *The Grand Duke's Finances* prod/rel: Tofa

HELLER, FRED
Le Grand Bluff, Play
Grand Bluff, Le 1933 d: Maurice Champreux. lps: Jose Noguero, Florelle, Lolita Benavente. 75M FRN. prod/rel: Gaumont-Franco-Film-Aubert

HELLER, GREGORY K.
Novel
Alphabet City 1984 d: Amos Poe. lps: Vincent Spano, Kate Vernon, Michael Winslow. 98M USA. prod/rel: Atlantic 9000

HELLER, JOSEPH (1923–, USA
Catch 22, New York 1961, Novel
Catch-22 1970 d: Mike Nichols. lps: Alan Arkin, Martin Balsam, Richard Benjamin. 122M USA. prod/rel: Paramount, Filmways

HELLINGER, MARK (1903–1947), USA
Night Court, Play
Night Court 1932 d: W. S. Van Dyke. lps: Phillips Holmes, Walter Huston, Anita Page. 95M USA. *Justice for Sale* (UKN) prod/rel: Metro-Goldwyn-Mayer Corp., Metro-Goldwyn-Mayer Dist. Corp.©

HELLMAN, LILLIAN (1905–1984), USA
Another Part of the Forest, 1947, Play
Another Part of the Forest 1948 d: Michael Gordon. lps: Fredric March, Dan Duryea, Edmond O'Brien. 107M USA. prod/rel: Universal

The Children's Hour, New York 1934, Play
Children's Hour, The 1961 d: William Wyler. lps: Audrey Hepburn, Shirley MacLaine, James Garner. 108M USA. *The Loudest Whisper* (UKN); *Infamous* prod/rel: United Artists
These Three 1936 d: William Wyler. lps: Miriam Hopkins, Merle Oberon, Joel McCreA. 93M USA. prod/rel: United Artists Corp., Samuel Goldwyn, Inc.

The Little Foxes, New York 1939, Play
Little Foxes, The 1941 d: William Wyler. lps: Bette Davis, Herbert Marshall, Teresa Wright. 116M USA. prod/rel: RKO Radio

Pentimento, 1973, Short Story
Julia 1977 d: Fred Zinnemann. lps: Jane Fonda, Vanessa Redgrave, Jason Robards Jr. 124M USA. prod/rel: 20th Century-Fox

The Searching Wind, New York 1944, Play
Searching Wind, The 1946 d: William Dieterle. lps: Robert Young, Ann Richards, Sylvia Sidney. 108M USA. prod/rel: Paramount

Toys in the Attic, New York 1960, Play
Toys in the Attic 1963 d: George Roy Hill. lps: Dean Martin, Geraldine Page, Yvette Mimieux. 90M USA. prod/rel: Mirisch Co., Claude Productions

Watch on the Rhine, New York 1941, Play
Watch on the Rhine 1943 d: Herman Shumlin, Vincent Sherman. lps: Bette Davis, Paul Lukas, Geraldine Fitzgerald. 114M USA. prod/rel: Warner Bros.

HELLMER, KLAUS
Der Engel Mit Dem Flammenschwert, Novel
Engel Mit Dem Flammenschwert, Der 1954 d: Gerhard Lamprecht. lps: Gertrud Kuckelmann, Martin Benrath, Paul Bildt. 105M GRM. *The Angel With the Flaming Sword* prod/rel: Omega, N.F.

Herz Ohne Gnade, Novel
Herz Ohne Gnade 1958 d: Victor Tourjansky. lps: Barbara Rutting, Hansjorg Felmy, Werner Hinz. 95M GRM. *Heart Without Mercy* prod/rel: Real, N.F.

Wie Ein Sturmwind, Novel
Wie Ein Sturmwind 1957 d: Falk Harnack. lps: Lilli Palmer, Willy A. Kleinau, Ivan Desny. 100M GRM. *The Night of the Storm* (UKN); *Tempestuous Love* (USA); *Wie Der Sturmwind*; *Like a Storm Wind* prod/rel: C.C.C., N.F.

HELLSTROM, GUSTAV (1882–1953), SWD
Storm Over Tjuro, 1942, Novel
Storm Over Tjuro 1954 d: Arne Mattsson. lps: Adolf Jahr, Gunnel Brostrom, Siggi Furst. 86M SWD. prod/rel: Sandrew

HELSETH, EDWARD
Un Aller Simple, Novel
Aller Simple, Un 1970 d: Jose Giovanni. lps: Jean-Claude Bouillon, Maurice Garrel, Jean Gaven. 105M FRN/ITL/SPN. *Solo Andata* (ITL); *La Puerta Cerrada* (SPN) prod/rel: Rizzoli Film, Cite Films

HELSETH, HENRY
The Chair for Martin Rome, Novel
Cry of the City 1948 d: Robert Siodmak. lps: Victor Mature, Richard Conte, Fred Clark. 96M USA. *The Chair for Martin Rome*; *The Law and Martin Rome*; *Martin Rome* prod/rel: Twentieth Century-Fox

HELSETH, HENRY EDWARD, Helseth, Henry Story
Outside the Wall 1950 d: Crane Wilbur. lps: Richard Basehart, Marilyn Maxwell, Signe Hasso. 80M USA. prod/rel: Universal-International

HELTAI, EUGENE
Az En Masodik Felesegem, 1907, Novel
Senora Casada Necesita Marido 1935 d: James Tinling. lps: Catalina Barcena, Antonio Moreno, Jose Crespo. 6449f USA. *A Married Woman Needs a Husband*; *Mi Segunda Mujer*; *My Second Wife* prod/rel: Fox Film Corp.©

Az En Masodik Felesegen, 1907, Novel
Lady Escapes, The 1937 d: Eugene J. Forde. lps: Gloria Stuart, Michael Whalen, George Sanders. 63M USA. *My Second Wife*; *Escape from Love*; *Lady in Flight* prod/rel: Twentieth Century-Fox Film Corp.©

HELTAI, JENO
Jaguar, 1914, Novel
Jaguar 1967 d: Janos Domolky. lps: Laszlo Mensaros, Mari Torocsik, Tamas Major. 86M HNG.

Man Steigt Nach, Play
Man Steigt Nach 1928 d: Erno Metzner. lps: Erna Morena, Vivian Gibson, Livio Pavanelli. 1986m GRM. prod/rel: Phonix-Film Ag

HELTON, JACQUELINE
Journal
Sunshine 1973 d: Joseph Sargent. lps: Cristina Raines, Cliff de Young, Robin Bush. TVM. 130M USA. prod/rel: Universal

HELVICK, JAMES
Beat the Devil, 1951, Novel
Beat the Devil 1953 d: John Huston. lps: Humphrey Bogart, Jennifer Jones, Gina LollobrigidA. 100M USA/ITL/UKN. *Il Tesoro Dell'africa* (ITL) prod/rel: Romulus Films, Santana Pictures

HELWIG, PAUL
Flitterwochen, Play
Mein Mann Darf Es Nicht Wissen 1940 d: Paul Heidemann. lps: Mady Rahl, Hans Nielsen, Grethe Weiser. 85M GRM. *Sabine Und Der Zufall* prod/rel: Tobis, Knevels

HELWIG, WERNER
Raubfischer in Hellas, Novel
Raubfischer in Hellas 1959 d: Horst Haechler. lps: Maria Schell, Cliff Robertson, Cameron Mitchell. 105M GRM/USA/YGS. *As the Sea Rages* (USA); *Fish Poachers of the Greek Isles* prod/rel: Tele, Columbia

HELY, ELIZABETH
The Smugglers, Novel
Smugglers, The 1968 d: Alfred Hayes. lps: Shirley Booth, Carol Lynley, Kurt Kasznar. TVM. 100M USA. prod/rel: Universal TV

HELYAR, JOHN
Barbarians at the Gates, Book
Barbarians at the Gate 1993 d: Glenn Jordan. lps: James Garner, Jonathan Pryce, Peter Riegert. TVM. 113M USA. prod/rel: Home Box Office©, Hbo Pictures

HEMING, JACK
The Scoop, Play
Scoop, The 1934 d: MacLean Rogers. lps: Anne Grey, Tom Helmore, Peggy Blythe. 68M UKN. prod/rel: British and Dominions, Paramount British

HEMINGWAY, ERNEST (1898–1961), USA, Hemingway, Ernest Miller
Short Stories
Adventures of a Young Man 1962 d: Martin Ritt. lps: Richard Beymer, Paul Newman, Diane Baker. 145M USA. *Hemingway's Adventures of a Young Man* (UKN) prod/rel: 20th Century-Fox

A Farewell to Arms, New York 1929, Novel
Farewell to Arms, A 1932 d: Frank Borzage. lps: Helen Hayes, Gary Cooper, Adolphe Menjou. 90M USA. prod/rel: Paramount Productions©
Farewell to Arms, A 1957 d: Charles Vidor. lps: Rock Hudson, Jennifer Jones, Vittorio de SicA. 152M USA. prod/rel: 20th Century-Fox, Selznick Co.

For Who the Bell Tolls, 1940, Novel
For Whom the Bell Tolls 1943 d: Sam Wood. lps: Gary Cooper, Ingrid Bergman, Akim Tamiroff. 170M USA. prod/rel: Paramount

Islands in the Stream, 1970, Novel
Islands in the Stream 1977 d: Franklin J. Schaffner. lps: George C. Scott, David Hemmings, Claire Bloom. 105M USA. prod/rel: Connaught

The Killers, New York 1927, Short Story
Killers, The 1946 d: Robert Siodmak. lps: Burt Lancaster, Ava Gardner, Edmond O'Brien. 102M USA. *A Man Afraid* prod/rel: Universal-International
Killers, The 1964 d: Don Siegel. lps: Lee Marvin, Angie Dickinson, John Cassavetes. TVM. 95M USA. *Ernest Hemingway's the Killers*; *Johnny North* prod/rel: Revue Productions

My Old Man, 1923, Short Story
Under My Skin 1950 d: Jean Negulesco. lps: John Garfield, Micheline Presle, Orley Lindgren. 86M USA. *The Big Fall*; *My Old Man* prod/rel: 20th Century-Fox

The Old Man and the Sea, 1952, Novel
Old Man and the Sea, The 1958 d: John Sturges, Henry King (Uncredited). lps: Spencer Tracy, Felipe Pazos, Harry Bellaver. 86M USA. prod/rel: Warner Bros.
Old Man and the Sea, The 1990 d: Jud Taylor. lps: Anthony Quinn, Gary Cole, Patricia Clarkson. TVM. 100M USA. *Ernest Hemingway's the Old Man and the Sea* prod/rel: Stroke Enterprises, Green Pond Prods.
Rojin to Umi 1990 d: John Junkerman. lps: Shigeru Itokazu. 101M JPN. *Uminchu - the Old Man and the East China Sea* prod/rel: Shiglo Ltd.

The Short Happy Life of Francis MacOmber, 1938, Short Story
MacOmber Affair, The 1947 d: Zoltan KordA. lps: Robert Preston, Joan Bennett, Gregory Peck. 90M USA. *Without Honor* prod/rel: United Artists

The Snows of Kilimanjaro, 1938, Short Story
Snows of Kilimanjaro, The 1952 d: Henry King. lps: Gregory Peck, Ava Gardner, Susan Hayward. 117M USA. prod/rel: 20th Century-Fox

Soldier's Home, 1930, Short Story
Soldier's Home 1977 d: Robert Malcolm Young. lps: Richard Backus, Nancy Marchand. MTV. 39M USA. prod/rel: Learning in Focus

The Sun Also Rises, 1926, Novel
Sun Also Rises, The 1957 d: Henry King. lps: Tyrone Power, Ava Gardner, Mel Ferrer. 130M USA. prod/rel: 20th Century-Fox
Sun Also Rises, The 1984 d: James Goldstone. lps: Jane Seymour, Hart Bochner, Robert Carradine. TVM. 200M USA. prod/rel: 20th Century Fox

To Have and Have Not, 1937, Novel
Breaking Point, The 1950 d: Michael Curtiz. lps: John Garfield, Patricia Neal, Phyllis Thaxter. 97M USA. prod/rel: Warner Bros.
Gun Runners, The 1958 d: Don Siegel. lps: Audie Murphy, Eddie Albert, Patricia Owens. 83M USA. prod/rel: United Artists, Seven Arts
To Have and Have Not 1944 d: Howard Hawks. lps: Humphrey Bogart, Lauren Bacall, Hoagy Carmichael. 100M USA. prod/rel: Warner Bros.

HEMINGWAY, JOAN
Rosebud, Novel
Rosebud 1974 d: Otto Preminger. lps: Peter O'Toole, Richard Attenborough, Cliff Gorman. 126M USA. prod/rel: Sigma, United Artists

HEMINGWAY, MAGGIE
The Bridge, Novel
Bridge, The 1990 d: Sydney MacArtney. lps: Saskia Reeves, David O'Hara, Joss Ackland. 102M UKN. prod/rel: Moonlight (Bridge) Ltd., British Screen

HEMMER, JARL
Anna Ringars, 1925, Play
Vaivaisukon Morsian 1944 d: Toivo SarkkA. lps: Ansa Ikonen, Kyllikki Vare. 113M FNL. *The Unhappy Bride*

Den Bla Veckan, 1928, Short Story
Sininen VIIkko 1954 d: Matti KassilA. lps: Gunvor Sandkvist, Matti Oravisto, Toivo MakelA. 79M FNL. *Blue Week; Den Bla Veckan* prod/rel: Suomen Filmiteollisuus

Fattiggubbens Brud, 1926, Short Story
Vaivaisukon Morsian 1944 d: Toivo SarkkA. lps: Ansa Ikonen, Kyllikki Vare. 113M FNL. *The Unhappy Bride*

En Man Och Has Samvete, 1931, Novel
1918 1956 d: Toivo SarkkA. lps: Ake Lindman, Pentti Irjala, Ann Savo. 100M FNL. *1918 - Mies Ja Hanen Omatuntonsa; 1918 - Man and His Conscience* prod/rel: Oy Suomen Filmiteolisuus

HEMMERDE, E. G.
Die Frau Auf Der Folter, Play
Frau Auf Der Folter, Die 1928 d: Robert Wiene. lps: Lili Damita, Wladimir Gaidarow, Johannes Riemann. 2544m GRM. *A Scandal in Paris; The Butterfly on the Wheel* prod/rel: Felsom-Film, Deutsche Vereins-Film Ag

HEMMERDE, EDWARD
A Butterfly on the Wheel, London 1911, Play
Butterfly on the Wheel, A 1915 d: Maurice Tourneur. lps: Holbrook Blinn, Vivian Martin, George Ralph. 5r USA. prod/rel: Shubert Film Corp., World Film Corp.©

HEMON, LOUIS (1880–1913), FRN
Maria Chapdelaine; Recit du Canada Francais, 1916, Novel
Maria Chapdelaine 1934 d: Julien Duvivier. lps: Madeleine Renaud, Jean Gabin, Jean-Pierre Aumont. 75M FRN. prod/rel: Alex Nalpas, Societe Nouvelle De Cinematographique
Maria Chapdelaine 1983 d: Gilles Carle. lps: Carole Laure, Claude Rich, Amulette Garneau. 108M CND/FRN. prod/rel: 1861-8140 Quebec Inc., Astral Bellevue Pathe Inc.
Naked Heart, The 1950 d: Marc Allegret. lps: Michele Morgan, Kieron Moore, Francoise Rosay. 96M UKN/CND/FRN. *Maria Chapdelaine* prod/rel: British Lion, Everest

Monsieur Ripois and Nemesis, 1925, Novel
Knave of Hearts 1954 d: Rene Clement. lps: Gerard Philipe, Valerie Hobson, Joan Greenwood. 103M UKN/FRN. *Lovers Happy Lovers* (USA); *Monsieur Ripois; Lover Boy* prod/rel: Transcontinental Films, Ab-Pathe

HEMPSTEAD, DAVID
Hell and High Water, Novel
Hell and High Water 1954 d: Samuel Fuller. lps: Richard Widmark, Bella Darvi, Victor Francen. 103M USA. prod/rel: 20th Century-Fox

HENDERSON, BRUCE B.
And the Sea Will Tell, Book
And the Sea Will Tell 1991 d: Tommy Lee Wallace. lps: Richard Crenna, Rachel Ward, Hart Bochner. TVM. 200M USA.

HENDERSON, ISAAC
The Mummy and the Humming Bird, New York 1902, Play
Mummy and the Humming Bird, The 1915 d: James Durkin. lps: Charles Cherry, Lillian Tucker, William Sorelle. 5r USA. prod/rel: Famous Players Film Co.©, Charles Frohman Co.

HENDERSON, JESSIE E.
The Mouth of the Dragon, 1923, Short Story
Perfect Flapper, The 1924 d: John Francis Dillon. lps: Colleen Moore, Sydney Chaplin, Phyllis Haver. 7000f USA. prod/rel: Associated First National Pictures

Wanted: a Blemish, 1919, Short Story
Amateur Devil, An 1920 d: Maurice Campbell. lps: Bryant Washburn, Charles Wyngate, Ann May. 4464f USA. *Wanted -a Blemish* prod/rel: Famous Players-Lasky Corp.©, Paramount Pictures

HENDERSON, LAWRENCE
Sitting Target, Novel
Sitting Target 1971 d: Douglas Hickox. lps: Oliver Reed, Jill St. John, Ian McShane. 93M UKN. *Screaming Target* prod/rel: MGM

HENDERSON, RAY (1896–1970), USA, Brost, Raymond
Flying High, New York 1930, Musical Play
Flying High 1931 d: Charles F. Reisner. lps: Bert Lahr, Charlotte Greenwood, Pat O'Brien. 80M USA. *Happy Landing* (UKN) prod/rel: Metro-Goldwyn-Mayer Corp., Metro-Goldwyn-Mayer Dist. Corp.©

Follow Thru, New York 1929, Musical Play
Follow Thru 1930 d: Laurence Schwab, Lloyd Corrigan. lps: Charles "Buddy" Rogers, Nancy Carroll, Zelma O'Neal. 8386f USA. prod/rel: Paramount-Publix Corp.

That Old Gang of Mine, 1923, Song
That Old Gang of Mine 1925 d: May Tully. lps: MacLyn Arbuckle, Brooke Johns, Tommy Brown. 5r USA. prod/rel: Kerman Films

HENDERSON, ZENNA
Pilgrimage, Novel
People, The 1971 d: John Korty. lps: Kim Darby, William Shatner, Diane Varsi. TVM. 74M USA. prod/rel: Metromedia Productions, American Zoetrope

HENDRIE, ERNEST
The Elder Miss Blossom, London 1898, Play
Elder Miss Blossom, The 1918 d: Percy Nash. lps: Isobel Elsom, Owen Nares, C. M. Hallard. 5000f UKN. *Wanted a Wife* (USA) prod/rel: G. B. Samuelson, Sun

HENDRYX, JAMES B.
Flat Gold, Short Story
Mints of Hell, The 1919 d: Park Frame. lps: William Desmond, Vivian Rich, Edward Jobson. 5r USA. prod/rel: Jesse D. Hampton Productions, Robertson-Cole Co.

The Promise; a Tale of the Great Northwest, New York 1915, Novel
Promise, The 1917 d: Fred J. Balshofer. lps: Harold Lockwood, May Allison, Lester Cuneo. 5r USA. prod/rel: Yorke Film Corp.©, Metro Pictures Corp.

Snowdrift, New York 1922, Novel
Snowdrift 1923 d: Scott R. Dunlap. lps: Buck Jones, Irene Rich, G. Raymond Nye. 4617f USA. prod/rel: Fox Film Corp.

The Texan, New York 1918, Novel
Texan, The 1920 d: Lynn Reynolds. lps: Tom Mix, Gloria Hope, Pat Chrisman. 5r USA. prod/rel: Fox Film Corp., William Fox©

HENESTROSA, ANDRES
Antonieta, Novel
Antonieta 1982 d: Carlos SaurA. lps: Isabelle Adjani, Hanna Schygulla, Carlos Bracho. 108M SPN/MXC/FRN. *Antonietta* prod/rel: Gaumont, Fr 3

HENGGE, PAUL
Der Rosengarten, Novel
Rosengarten, Der 1989 d: Fons Rademakers. lps: Liv Ullmann, Maximilian Schell, Peter FondA. 111M GRM/USA. *The Rose Garden* prod/rel: Pathe International

HENLEY, BETH (1952–, USA
Crimes of the Heart, 1982, Play
Crimes of the Heart 1986 d: Bruce Beresford. lps: Diane Keaton, Jessica Lange, Sissy Spacek. 105M USA. prod/rel: de Laurentiis Entertainment Group, Crimes of the Heart Productions

The Miss Firecracker Contest, 1985, Play
Miss Firecracker 1989 d: Thomas Schlamme. lps: Holly Hunter, Mary Steenburgen, Tim Robbins. 102M USA. prod/rel: Corsair Pictures

HENNEQUIN, A. N.
Niniche, 1878, Play
Niniche 1918 d: Camillo de Riso. lps: Tilde Kassay, Camillo de Riso, Gustavo SerenA. 1393m ITL. prod/rel: Caesar Film

HENNEQUIN, MAURICE
Bebe, Play
Bebe 1913 d: Georges MoncA. 585m FRN. prod/rel: Pathe Freres

Compartiment de Dames Seules, Play
Compartiment de Dames Seules 1934 d: Christian-Jaque. lps: Armand Bernard, Pierre Larquey, Alice Tissot. 101M FRN. *Ladies Only* prod/rel: C.D.F.

Coralie Et Cie, 1899, Play
Coralie & C. 1914. lps: Giuseppe Gambardella, Lea Giunchi, Lorenzo Soderini. 1500m ITL. *Madame Coralie E C.* prod/rel: Cines
Coralie Et Cie 1933 d: Alberto Cavalcanti. lps: Josette Day, Jeanne Helbling, Robert Burnier. 90M FRN. prod/rel: Films Jean Dehelly

Le Coup de Fouet, Play
Coup de Fouet, Le 1913 d: Georges MoncA. lps: Prince, Charles Lorrain, Pepa Bonafe. 600m FRN. prod/rel: Pathe Freres

Diane Au Bain, Play
Cercasi Modella 1932 d: E. W. Emo. lps: Elsa Merlini, Gianfranco Giachetti, Nino Besozzi. 80M ITL. prod/rel: Itala, S.a.P.F.

Et Moi J'te Dis Qu'elle T'a Fait de l'Oeil, Play
Et Moi J'te Dis Qu'elle T'a Fait d' l'Oeil 1950 d: Maurice Gleize. lps: Bernard Lancret, Madeleine Lebeau, Frederic Duvalles. 85M FRN. prod/rel: Mondia Films
Et Moi, J'te Dis Qu'elle T'a Fait de l'Oeil 1935 d: Jack Forrester. lps: Colette Darfeuil, Frederic Duvalles, Jules Berry. 80M FRN. *J'te Dis Qu'elle T'a Fait de l'Oeil* prod/rel: Forrester-Parent Productions

Famille Bolero, Play
Famille Bolero 1914 d: Georges MoncA. lps: Prince. 700m FRN. prod/rel: Pathe Freres

La Femme a Papa, Play
Femme a Papa, La 1914 d: Georges MoncA. lps: Prince, Marcelle Praince?. 740m FRN. prod/rel: Pathe Freres

Florette Et Patapon, 1905, Play
Florette E Patapon 1913 d: Mario Caserini. lps: Maria Caserini Gasparini, Gentile Miotti, Camillo de Riso. 2500m ITL. prod/rel: Film Artistica Gloria
Florette E Patapon 1927 d: Amleto Palermi. lps: Ossi Oswalda, Marcel Levesque, Livio Pavanelli. 2080m ITL. prod/rel: Palermi
Florette Et Patapon 1913. 1500m FRN.

La Gueule du Loup, 1904, Play
Gola Del Lupo, La 1923 d: Torello Rolli. lps: Camillo de Riso, Francesco Amodio, Fernanda Negri-Pouget. 1336m ITL. prod/rel: Caesar Film

Les Joies du Foyer, 1894
Gioie Del Focolare, Le 1920 d: Baldassarre Negroni. lps: Diomira Jacobini, Alberto Collo, Ida Carloni-Talli. 1340m ITL. *Le Gioie Della Famiglia* prod/rel: Film d'Arte Italiana

A Kiss in a Taxi, Play
Kiss in a Taxi, A 1927 d: Clarence Badger. lps: Bebe Daniels, Chester Conklin, Douglas Gilmore. 6439f USA. prod/rel: Famous Players-Lasky, Paramount Pictures

Madame la Presidente, Paris C.1898, Play
Madame la Presidente 1916 d: Frank Lloyd. lps: Anna Held, Forrest Stanley, Herbert Standing. 5r USA. *Madame Presidente* prod/rel: Oliver Morosco Photoplay Co.©, Paramount Pictures Corp.

M'amour, 1901, Play
Amor Mio! 1916 d: Eleuterio Rodolfi. lps: Suzanne Armelle, Eleuterio Rodolfi, Armand Pouget. 1343m ITL. prod/rel: Jupiter Film

Le Monsieur de 5 Heures, Play
Monsieur de 5 Heures, Le 1938 d: Pierre Caron. lps: Andre Lefaur, Meg Lemonnier, Armand Bernard. 90M FRN. prod/rel: Films Saca

Noblesse Oblige!, 1910, Play
Noblesse Oblige 1918 d: Marcello Dudovich?. lps: Linda Moglia, Lucy Sangermano, Vasco Creti. 1760m ITL. prod/rel: S.A. Ambrosio

On Ne Roule Pas Antoinette, Play
On Ne Roule Pas Antoinette 1936 d: Paul Madeux, Christian-Jaque (Spv). lps: Armand Bernard, Paul Pauley, Simone Renant. 77M FRN. prod/rel: Henri Ullmann

Le Paradis, Play
Belle de Montparnasse, La 1937 d: Maurice Cammage. lps: Jeanne Aubert, Colette Darfeuil, Frederic Duvalles. 87M FRN. prod/rel: Cinereve
Paradis, Le 1914 d: Gaston Leprieur. lps: Raoul Villot, Charles Reschal, Pierre Etchepare. FRN. prod/rel: Grands Films Populaires, G. Lordier

Passionnement, Opera
Passionnement 1932 d: Rene Guissart, Louis Mercanton (Uncredited). lps: Florelle, Fernand Gravey, Rene Koval. 80M FRN. prod/rel: Films Paramount

Patachon, Paris 1907, Play
Gay Deceiver, The 1926 d: John M. Stahl. lps: Lew Cody, Malcolm McGregor, Marceline Day. 6624f USA. *Toto* prod/rel: Metro-Goldwyn-Mayer Pictures
Su Ultima Noche 1931 d: Chester M. Franklin. lps: Ernesto Vilches, Conchita Montenegro, Maria AlbA. 75M USA. *Toto* prod/rel: Metro-Goldwyn-Mayer Corp., Culver Export Co.

Le Pillole Di Ercole, Play
Pillole Di Ercole, Le 1960 d: Luciano Salce. lps: Nino Manfredi, Sylva Koscina, Vittorio de SicA. 85M ITL. *Hercules' Pills; Le Pillole d'Ercole* prod/rel: Dino de Laurentiis Cin.Ca, Maxima Film

Place aux Femmes!, 1898, Play
Largo Alle Donne! 1924 d: Guido Brignone. lps: Oreste Bilancia, Leonie Laporte, Alberto Collo. 1603m ITL. prod/rel: Alba Film

La Presidente, Play
Presidente, La 1938 d: Fernand Rivers. lps: Elvire Popesco, Henri Garat, Andre Lefaur. 85M FRN. prod/rel: Films Fernand Rivers

La Presidentessa, Play
Presidentessa, La 1952 d: Pietro Germi. lps: Silvana Pampanini, Carlo Dapporto, Ave Ninchi. 87M ITL. *Mademoiselle la Presidente* (FRN); *Mademoiselle Gobette; The Lady President* prod/rel: Excelsa Film, Giuseppe Amato

Presidentessa, La 1976 d: Luciano Salce. lps: Johnny Dorelli, Mariangela Melato, Gianrico Tedeschi. 105M ITL. *The First Lady* prod/rel: Capital Film, Gold Film

La Reine de Biarritz, Play
Reine de Biarritz, La 1934 d: Jean Toulout. lps: Jean Dax, Andre Burgere, Alice Field. 80M FRN. prod/rel: Vega Films

La Sonnette d'Alarme, Play
Sonnette d'Alarme, La 1935 d: Christian-Jaque. lps: Jean Murat, Josette Day, Pierre Stephen. 70M FRN. prod/rel: Productions Sigma

Train de Plaisir, 1884, Play
Treno Doria 1924 d: Luciano DoriA. lps: Elena Sangro, Alberto Collo, Lydia QuarantA. 1926m ITL. prod/rel: Fert

Vingt Jours a l'Ombre, 1907, Play
Venti Giorni All'ombra 1918 d: Gennaro Righelli. lps: Diomira Jacobini, Alberto Collo, Ferdinand Guillaume. 1284m ITL. prod/rel: Tiber

Vous N'avez Rien a Declarer?, Play
Vous N'avez Rien a Declarer? 1916. lps: Marcel Simon, Boucot, Jane Renouardt. 1300m FRN. prod/rel: Cinedrama Paz

Vous N'avez Rien a Declarer? 1936 d: Leo Joannon, Yves Allegret. lps: Raimu, Andre Alerme, Germaine Aussey. 102M FRN. prod/rel: Pierre Braunberger

Vous N'avez Rien a Declarer? 1959 d: Clement Duhour. lps: Darry Cowl, Jean Richard, Madeleine Lebeau. 90M FRN. prod/rel: Films Sirius, C.L.M.

HENNESSEY, KATHERINE
Story
Little Annie Rooney 1925 d: William Beaudine. lps: Mary Pickford, William Haines, Walter James. 8850f USA. prod/rel: Mary Pickford Co., United Artists

HENRICKS, PAUL
Sieben Tage Frist, Novel
Sieben Tage Frist 1969 d: Alfred Vohrer. lps: Joachim Fuchsberger, Karin Hubner, Konrad Georg. 100M GRM. *Seven Days Time* prod/rel: Roxy, Inter

HENRIOT, PAUL
L' Istruttoria, Play
Istruttoria, L' 1914 d: Enrico Guazzoni. lps: Ruggero Ruggeri, Tilde Teldi, Odoardo Bonafini. 735m ITL. *The Judge of Instruction* (UKN)

HENRY, HARRIET
Jackdaw's Strut, New York 1930, Novel
Bought 1931 d: Archie Mayo. lps: Constance Bennett, Richard Bennett, Ben Lyon. 83M USA. prod/rel: Warner Bros. Pictures, Inc.

Lady With a Past, New York 1931, Novel
Lady With a Past 1932 d: Edward H. Griffith. lps: Constance Bennett, Ben Lyon, David Manners. 80M USA. *Reputation* (UKN) prod/rel: RKO Radio Pictures©, Charles R. Rogers Production

HENRY, JOAN
Who Lie in Gaol, Novel
Weak and the Wicked, The 1953 d: J. Lee Thompson. lps: Glynis Johns, John Gregson, Jane Hylton. 88M UKN. *Young and Willing* (USA) prod/rel: Marble Arch, Associated British Picture Corporation

Yield to the Night, Novel
Yield to the Night 1956 d: J. Lee Thompson. lps: Diana Dors, Yvonne Mitchell, Michael Craig. 99M UKN. *Blonde Sinner* (USA) prod/rel: Kenwood, Ab-Pathe

HENRY, MARGUERITE (1902–, USA
Brighty of the Grand Canyon, New York 1953, Novel
Brighty of the Grand Canyon 1967 d: Norman Foster. lps: Joseph Cotten, Pat Conway, Dick Foran. 89M USA. *Brighty* (UKN); *Brighty of Grand Canyon*

Justin Morgan Had a Horse, Novel
Justin Morgan Had a Horse 1972 d: Hollingsworth Morse. lps: Don Murray, Lana Wood, Gary Crosby. TVM. 91M USA.

King of the Wind, Novel
King of the Wind 1989 d: Peter Duffell. lps: Frank Finlay, Jenny Agutter, Nigel Hawthorne. TVM. 102M UKN/USA. prod/rel: Enterprise, Htv International

Misty of Chincoteague, Chicago 1947, Novel
Misty 1961 d: James B. Clark. lps: David Ladd, Arthur O'Connell, Pam Smith. 92M USA. prod/rel: Twentieth Century-Fox Film Corporation

San Domingo the Medicine Hat Stallion, Novel
Peter Lundy and the Medicine Hat Stallion 1977 d: Michael O'Herlihy. lps: Leif Garrett, Milo O'Shea, Bibi Besch. TVM. 100M USA. prod/rel: Ed Friendly Prods.

HENRY, NOELLE
Je Ne Suis Pas une Heroine, Novel
So Little Time 1952 d: Compton Bennett. lps: Marius Goring, Maria Schell, Gabrielle Dorziat. 88M UKN. prod/rel: Ab-Pathe, Mayflower

HENRY, O. (1862–1910), USA, Porter, William Sydney
Afternoon Miracle, An, Short Story
Afternoon Miracle, An 1920 d: David Smith. 2r USA. prod/rel: Vitagraph

All on Account of an Egg, Short Story
All on Account of an Egg 1913. SHT USA. prod/rel: Eclair

Atavism of John Tom Little Bear, The, Short Story
Atavism of John Tom Little Bear, The 1917 d: David Smith. lps: Al Jennings, Dan Duffy, Jake Abraham. 2r USA. prod/rel: Broadway Star, Vitagraph

Badge of Policeman O'Roon, The, Short Story
Badge of Policeman O'Roon, The 1913. 2r USA. prod/rel: Eclair

Badge of Policeman O'Roon, The, The World 1904, Short Story
Doctor Rhythm 1938 d: Frank Tuttle. lps: Bing Crosby, Beatrice Lillie, Mary Carlisle. 80M USA. *The Badge of Policeman O'Roon; Dr. Rhythm* prod/rel: Major Pictures Corp., Emanuel Cohen Production

Blackjack Bargainer, A, Short Story
Splendid Scapegrace, A 1913 d: Charles J. Brabin. lps: Marc MacDermott, Charles Ogle, Bigelow Cooper. 1000f USA. prod/rel: Edison

Blackjack Bargainer, A 1918?. lps: William Wadsworth, Franklyn Hall, Russell Simpson. 3r USA. prod/rel: Edison

Blind Man's Holiday, 1905, Short Story
Blind Man's Holiday 1917 d: Martin Justice. lps: Jean Paige, Carlton King, John Costello. 4r USA. prod/rel: Broadway Star Features Co.©, General Film Co.

Brick Dust Row, 1906, Short Story
Everybody's Girl 1918 d: Tom Terriss. lps: Alice Joyce, Walter McGrail, May Hopkins. 5r USA. prod/rel: Vitagraph Co. of America©, Blue Ribbon Feature

Brief Debut of Tildy, The, Short Story
Brief Debut of Tildy, The 1918 d: George Ridgwell. lps: Alice Terry, Betty Blythe, William SheA. 2r USA. prod/rel: Broadway Star

Buried Treasure, The, Short Story
Buried Treasure, The 1919 d: Kenneth Webb. lps: Edward Earle, Agnes Ayres. 2r USA. prod/rel: Vitagraph

Buyer from Cactus City, The, Short Story
Buyer from Cactus City, The 1918 d: Ashley Miller. lps: William Dunn, Miriam Miles, Denton Vane. 2r USA. prod/rel: Broadway Star

By Injunction, Short Story
By Injunction 1918 d: David Smith. lps: Margaret Gibson, Chet Ryan, W. L. Rodgers. 2r USA. prod/rel: Broadway Star

Caballero's Way, Short Story
Caballero's Way, The 1914. lps: J. W. Johnston, Arthur Dunn, Edna Payne. 3r USA. prod/rel: Eclair

Caballero's Way, 1904, Short Story
Return of the Cisco Kid, The 1939 d: Herbert I. Leeds. lps: Warner Baxter, Lynn Bari, Cesar Romero. 70M USA. prod/rel: Twentieth Century-Fox Film Corp.©

Caballero's Way, Short Story
Border Terror, The 1919 d: Harry Harvey. lps: Yvette Mitchell. 2r USA. prod/rel: Universal

Call Loan, The, Short Story
Call Loan, The 1920 d: David Smith. 2r USA. prod/rel: Vitagraph

Chaparral Christmas Gift, A, Short Story
Mexican's Gratitude, The 1914 d: Richard Ridgely. lps: Bigelow Cooper, Mabel Trunnelle, Richard Tucker. 1000f USA. prod/rel: Edison

Chaparral Prince, A, Short Story
Western Prince Charming, A 1912. lps: Edna Hammond. 1000f USA. prod/rel: Edison

Cherchez la Femme, 1909, Short Story
Find the Woman 1918 d: Tom Terriss. lps: Alice Joyce, Walter McGrail, Arthur Donaldson. 5r USA. prod/rel: Vitagraph Co. of America©, Blue Ribbon Feature

Church With an Overshot Wheel, The, Short Story
Church With an Overshot Wheel, The 1919 d: Joseph Byron Totten. lps: William H. Turner. 2r USA. prod/rel: Vitagraph

Clarion Call, The, Short Story
Clarion Call, The 1918 d: Ashley Miller. lps: Walter McGrail, Bernard Randall, Alice Terry. 2r USA. prod/rel: Broadway Star

Clarion Call, The, 1908, Short Story
O. Henry's Full House (*) 1952 d: Henry Koster, Henry King. lps: Charles Laughton, David Wayne, Marilyn Monroe. 117M USA. *Bagdad on the Subway* prod/rel: 20th Century-Fox

Coming Out of Maggie, The, Short Story
Coming Out of Maggie, The 1917 d: Martin Justice. lps: Nellie Spencer, Carlton King. 2r USA. prod/rel: Broadway Star

Compliments of the Season, Short Story
Compliments of the Season 1918 d: Ashley Miller. lps: Aida Horton. 2r USA. prod/rel: Broadway Star

Cop and the Anthem, The, Short Story
Cop and the Anthem, The 1917 d: Thomas R. Mills. lps: Thomas R. Mills. 2r USA. prod/rel: Broadway Star

Cop and the Anthem, The, 1906, Short Story
A la Belle Etoile 1966 d: Pierre Prevert. lps: Ursula Kubler, Annette Poivre, Raymond Bussieres. 55M FRN.

Day Resurgent, The, Short Story
Day Resurgent, The 1920 d: Joseph Byron Totten. lps: Gypsy O'Brien. 2r USA. prod/rel: Vitagraph

Defeat of the City, The, 1908, Short Story
Defeat of the City, The 1917 d: Thomas R. Mills. lps: J. Frank Glendon, Agnes Ayres, Frank Chapman. 4r USA. prod/rel: Broadway Star Features Co.©, General Film Co.

Departmental Case, A, Short Story
Departmental Case, A 1917 d: Martin Justice. lps: Charles Kent, Carlton King, Mary Cunningham. 2r USA. prod/rel: Broadway Star

Discounters of Money, Short Story
Discounters of Money 1917 d: Martin Justice. lps: Carleton King, Catherine Charleton, Bobby Connelly. 2r USA. prod/rel: Broadway Star

Double-Dyed Deceiver, A, 1905, Short Story
Double Dyed Deceiver, The 1920 d: Alfred E. Green. lps: Jack Pickford, Marie Dunn, James Neill. 5r USA. *A Double-Dyed Deceiver* prod/rel: Goldwyn Pictures Corp.©, Goldwyn Distributing Corp.

Texan, The 1930 d: John Cromwell. lps: Gary Cooper, Fay Wray, Oscar Apfel. 79M USA. *The Big Race* (UKN) prod/rel: Paramount-Publix Corp.

Double-Dyed Deceiver, A, Everybody's Magazine 1905, Short Story
Llano Kid, The 1939 d: Edward D. Venturini. lps: Tito Guizar, Gale Sondergaard, Alan Mowbray. 68M USA. *The Double-Dyed Deceiver* prod/rel: Paramount Pictures©, Harry Sherman Productions

Dream, The, Short Story
Dream, The 1920 d: Joseph Byron Totten. lps: Alice Calhoun, Charles Kent. 2r USA. prod/rel: Vitagraph

Dry Valley Johnson, Short Story
Dry Valley Johnson 1917. 4r USA. prod/rel: Broadway Star, Vitagraph

Duplicity of Hargraves, The, 1902, Short Story
Duplicity of Hargraves, The 1917 d: Thomas R. Mills. lps: Charles Kent, J. Frank Glendon, Myrtis Coney. 4r USA. prod/rel: Broadway Star Features Co., General Film Co.

Enchanted Kiss, The, Short Story
Enchanted Kiss, The 1917 d: David Smith. lps: Chet Ryan, W. L. Rodgers, Charles Wheelock. 2r USA. prod/rel: Broadway Star

Enchanted Profile, The, Short Story
Enchanted Profile, The 1918 d: Martin Justice. lps: Agnes Ayres, Evart Overton, Nellie Parker Spaulding. 2r USA. prod/rel: Broadway Star

Fifth Wheel, The, Short Story
Fifth Wheel, The 1918 d: David Smith. lps: W. L. Rodgers, Lydia Yeamans Titus, Charles Wheelock. 2r USA. prod/rel: Broadway Star

Fortune's Mask, 1904, Short Story
Fortune's Mask 1922 d: Robert Ensminger. lps: Earle Williams, Patsy Ruth Miller, Henry J. Hebert. 5000f USA. prod/rel: Vitagraph Co. of America

Fourth in Salvador, The, Short Story
Fourth in Salvador, The 1918 d: David Smith. lps: Chet Ryan, W. L. Rodgers, Jack Wetherby. 2r USA. prod/rel: Broadway Star, Vitagraph

Friendly Call, The, Short Story
Friendly Call, The 1920 d: Thomas R. Mills. lps: Julia Swayne Gordon, Roy Applegate, Denton Vane. 2r USA. prod/rel: Vitagraph

Furnished Room, The, Short Story
Furnished Room, The 1917 d: Thomas R. Mills. lps: Agnes Ayres, J. Frank Glendon. 2r USA. prod/rel: Broadway Star

Ghost of a Chance, The, Short Story
Ghost of a Chance, The 1919 d: Kenneth Webb. lps: Edward Earle, Agnes Ayres. 2r USA. prod/rel: Vitagraph

Gift of the Magi, The, Short Story
Sacrifice, The 1909 d: D. W. Griffith. lps: Florence Lawrence, MacK Sennett, Arthur Johnson. 438f USA. prod/rel: Biograph Co.
Gift of the Magi, The 1917 d: Brinsley Shaw. lps: William Dunn, Patsy de Forrest, Claire McCormick. 2r USA. prod/rel: Broadway Star, Vitagraph

Gift of the Magi, The, 1906, Short Story
O. Henry's Full House (**) 1952 d: Henry Hathaway, Howard Hawks. lps: Jeanne Crain, Farley Granger. USA.

Gift of the Magi, The, Short Story
Gift of Love, The 1978 d: Don Chaffey. lps: Marie Osmond, Timothy Bottoms, Sondra West. TVM. 100M USA. prod/rel: NBC, Osmond

Girl and the Graft, The, Short Story
Girl and the Graft, The 1918 d: William P. S. Earle. lps: Agnes Ayres, Edward Earle. 2r USA. prod/rel: Broadway Star

Gold That Glittered, The, Short Story
Gold That Glittered, The 1917 d: Thomas R. Mills. lps: Albert Roccardi, Mildred Manning, Frank Brule. 2r USA. prod/rel: Broadway Star

Green Door, The, Short Story
Green Door, The 1917 d: Thomas R. Mills. lps: Mildred Manning, Walter McGrail. 2r USA. prod/rel: Broadway Star

Guardian of the Accolade, The, Short Story
Guardian of the Accolade, The 1919 d: Henry Houry. lps: Agnes Ayres. 2r USA. prod/rel: Vitagraph

Guilty Party, The, Short Story
Guilty Party, The 1917 d: Thomas R. Mills. lps: Frank Brule, Patsy de Forrest, Audrey Barry. 2r USA. prod/rel: Broadway Star

Halberdier of the Little Rheinschloss, The, Short Story
Thirty Days at Hard Labor 1912. lps: Robert Brower, Mary Fuller, Harold M. Shaw. 1000f USA. prod/rel: Edison

Halberdier of the Little Rheinschloss, The, 1907, Short Story
You're Fired 1919 d: James Cruze. lps: Wallace Reid, Wanda Hawley, Henry Woodward. 4183f USA. prod/rel: Famous Players-Lasky Corp.©, Paramount Feature

Hiding of Black Bill, The, Short Story
Hiding of Black Bill, The 1918 d: David Smith. lps: W. L. Rodgers, Chet Ryan. 2r USA. prod/rel: Broadway Star

His Duty, Short Story
His Duty 1909 d: D. W. Griffith, Frank Powell. lps: Frank Powell, Kate Bruce, Owen Moore. 429f USA. prod/rel: Biograph Co.

His Masterpiece, Short Story
His Masterpiece 1909 d: Bannister Merwin. lps: Florence Turner. 545f USA. prod/rel: Edison

Hygeia at the Solito, Short Story
Hygeia at the Solito 1917 d: David Smith. lps: Chet Ryan, W. L. Rodgers, W. M. McPhearson. 2r USA. prod/rel: Broadway Star

Indian Summer of Dry Valley Johnson, The, 1907, Short Story
Indian Summer of Dry Valley Johnson, The 1917 d: Martin Justice. lps: Carlton King, Jean Page, Ann Brody. 4r USA. *Dry Valley Johnson* prod/rel: Broadway Star Features Co., Inc.©, General Film Co.

Jimmy Hayes and Muriel, Short Story
Jimmy Hayes and Muriel 1914 d: Tom Mix. lps: Tom Mix. SHT USA. prod/rel: Selig Polyscope Co.

John Tom Little Bear, Short Story
John Tom Little Bear 1917 d: David Smith. lps: S. E. Jennings. 2r USA. prod/rel: Broadway Star

Last Leaf, The, Short Story
Last Leaf, The 1917 d: Ashley Miller. lps: Mildred Manning, Bernard Siegel, Patsy de Forrest. 2r USA. prod/rel: Broadway Star

Last of the Troubadours, The, Short Story
Last of the Troubadours, The 1917 d: David Smith. lps: S. E. Jennings, Dan Duffy, Nolan Leary. 2r USA. prod/rel: Broadway Star

Law and Order, Short Story
Law and Order 1917 d: David Smith. lps: Chet Ryan, Frances Parks, Dan Duffy. 2r USA. prod/rel: Broadway Star

Little Speck in Garnered Fruit, A, Short Story
Little Speck in Garnered Fruit, A 1917 d: Martin Justice. lps: Carlton King, Nellie Spencer. 2r USA. prod/rel: Broadway Star

Lonesome Road, The, Short Story
Lonesome Road, The 1917 d: David Smith. lps: S. E. Jennings, Chet Ryan, Frances Parks. 2r USA. prod/rel: Broadway Star

Lost on Dress Parade, Short Story
Lost on Dress Parade 1918 d: Martin Justice. lps: Patsy de Forrest, Evart Overton. 2r USA. prod/rel: Broadway Star

Lotus and the Bottle, The, 1902, Short Story
American Live Wire, An 1918 d: Thomas R. Mills. lps: Earle Williams, Grace Darmond, Hal Clements. 5r USA. prod/rel: Vitagraph Co. of America©, Blue Ribbon Feature

Love Philtre of Ikey Schoenstein, The, Short Story
Love Philtre of Ikey Schoenstein, The 1917 d: Thomas R. Mills. lps: Mildred Manning, William Shea, Nellie Anderson. 2r USA. prod/rel: Broadway Star

Madame Bo-Peep of the Ranches, New York 1910, Short Story
Madame Bo-Peep 1917 d: Chet Withey. lps: Seena Owen, Allan Sears, F. A. Turner. 5r USA. *Madam Bo'peep* prod/rel: Fine Arts Film Co., Triangle Film Corp.

Madison Square Arabian Night, A, Short Story
Madison Square Arabian Night, A 1918 d: Ashley Miller. lps: Duncan McRae, Patsy de Forrest, Miriam Miles. 2r USA. prod/rel: Broadway Star

Mammon and the Archer, Short Story
Mammon and the Archer 1918 d: Kenneth Webb. lps: Edward Earle, Agnes Ayres, Herbert Fortier. 2r USA. prod/rel: Broadway Star

Marionettes, The, Short Story
Marionettes, The 1917 d: Thomas R. Mills. lps: J. Frank Glendon, Frank Crane, Mildred Manning. 2r USA. prod/rel: Broadway Star

Marquis and Miss Sally, The, Short Story
Marquis and Miss Sally, The 1918 d: Allen Watt. 2r USA. prod/rel: Broadway Star

Matter of Mean Elevation, A, 1910, Short Story
Changing Woman, The 1918 d: David Smith. lps: Hedda Nova, J. Frank Glendon, Otto Lederer. 4321f USA. prod/rel: Vitagraph Co. of America©, Blue Ribbon Feature

Memento, The, 1908, Short Story
Garter Girl, The 1920 d: Edward H. Griffith. lps: Corinne Griffith, Sally Crute, Earl Metcalfe. 5r USA. *Memento, The* prod/rel: Vitagraph Co. of America©

Moment of Victory, The, Short Story
Moment of Victory, The 1918 d: David Smith. lps: Chet Ryan, Margaret Gibson, W. L. Rodgers. 2r USA. prod/rel: Broadway Star

Municipal Report, A, 1909, Short Story
I Will Repay 1917 d: William P. S. Earle. lps: Corinne Griffith, William Dunn, Mary Maurice. 5r USA. *A Municipal Report* prod/rel: Vitagraph Co. of America©, Greater Vitagraph (V-L-S-E)

Nemesis and the Candy Man, Short Story
Nemesis and the Candy Man 1918 d: Ashley Miller. lps: Edmund Burns, William Dunn, Nina Byron. 2r USA. prod/rel: Broadway Star

Night in New Arabia, A, 1910, Short Story
Night in New Arabia, A 1917 d: Thomas R. Mills. lps: J. Frank Glendon, Patsy de Forrest, Horace Vinton. 4r USA. prod/rel: Broadway Star Features Co.©, General Film Co.

No Story, Short Story
No Story 1917 d: Thomas R. Mills. lps: Thomas R. Mills, Stanley Walpole, Alice Brodier. 2r USA. prod/rel: Broadway Star

One Dollar's Worth, Short Story
One Dollar's Worth 1917 d: David Smith. lps: W. L. Rodgers, Chet Ryan, Jack Pierce. 2r USA. prod/rel: Broadway Star

One Thousand Dollars, 1908, Short Story
One Thousand Dollars 1918 d: Kenneth Webb. lps: Edward Earle, Agnes Ayres, Florence Deshon. 5r USA. prod/rel: Vitagraph Co. of America©, Blue Ribbon Feature

Passing of Black Eagle, The, Short Story
Passing of Black Eagle, The 1920 d: Joe Ryan. lps: Joe Ryan. 2r USA. prod/rel: Vitagraph

Passing of Black Eagle, The, 1909, Short Story
Black Eagle 1948 d: Robert Gordon. lps: William Bishop, Virginia Patton, Gordon Jones. 76M USA. prod/rel: Columbia

Past One at Rooney's, Short Story
Past One at Rooney's 1917 d: Thomas R. Mills. lps: Gordon Gray, Mildred Manning, William Martin. 2r USA. prod/rel: Broadway Star

Philistine in Bohemia, A, Short Story
Philistine in Bohemia, A 1920 d: Edward H. Griffith. lps: Edna Murphy, Rod La Rocque. 2r USA. prod/rel: Vitagraph

Purple Dress, The, Short Story
Purple Dress, The 1918 d: Martin Justice. lps: Evart Overton, Agnes Ayres, Adele de Garde. 2r USA. prod/rel: Broadway Star

Ramble in Aphasia, A, Short Story
Ramble in Aphasia, A 1918 d: Kenneth Webb. lps: Edward Earle, Agnes Ayres. 2r USA. prod/rel: Broadway Star

Ransom of MacK, The, Short Story
Ransom of MacK, The 1920 d: David Smith. 2r USA. prod/rel: Vitagraph

Ransom of Red Chief, 1907, Short Story
O. Henry's Full House (***) 1952 d: Jean Negulesco. USA.

Rathskeller and the Rose, The, Short Story
Rathskeller and the Rose, The 1918 d: George Ridgwell. lps: Adele de Garde, Evart Overton, Arthur Donaldson. 2r USA. prod/rel: Broadway Star

Renaissance at Charleroi, The, 1903, Short Story
Renaissance at Charleroi, The 1917 d: Thomas R. Mills. lps: J. Frank Glendon, Eleanor Lawson, Agnes Ayres. 4r USA. prod/rel: Broadway Star Features Co.©, General Film Co.

Roads We Take, The, Short Story
Roads We Take, The 1920 d: David Smith. lps: William McCall, Jay Morlay. 2r USA. prod/rel: Vitagraph

Rubaiyat of a Scotch High Ball, The, Short Story
Rubaiyat of a Scotch High Ball, The 1918 d: Martin Justice. lps: Edward Earle, Agnes Ayres. 2r USA. prod/rel: Broadway Star

Ruler of Men, A, Short Story
Ruler of Men, A 1920 d: David Smith. 2r USA. prod/rel: Vitagraph

Saving of Young Anderson, The, Short Story
Saving of Young Anderson, The 1914. 2r USA. prod/rel: Reliance

Schools and Schools, Short Story
Schools and Schools 1918 d: Martin Justice. lps: Jean Paige, Charles Hutchison, Frances McHenry. 2r USA. prod/rel: Broadway Star

Service of Love, A, Short Story
Service of Love, A 1917 d: John S. Robertson. lps: Walter McGrail, Mildred Manning. 2r USA. prod/rel: Broadway Star

Shamrock and the Palm, The, Short Story
Pat Clancy's Adventure 1911. lps: Edward O'Connor, Charles M. Seay. 1000f USA. prod/rel: Edison

Shocks of Doom, Short Story
Shocks of Doom 1919 d: Henry Houry. lps: Edward Earle, Agnes Ayres. 2r USA. prod/rel: Vitagraph

Sisters of the Golden Circle, Short Story
Sisters of the Golden Circle 1918 d: Kenneth Webb. lps: Edward Earle, Agnes Ayres, Alice Terry. 2r USA. prod/rel: Broadway Star

Skylight Room, The, 1906, Short Story
Skylight Room, The 1917 d: Martin Justice. lps: Carlton King, Jean Paige, Grace Ashley. 4r USA. prod/rel: Broadway Star Features Co.©, General Film Co.

Song and the Sergeant, The, Short Story
Song and the Sergeant, The 1918 d: George Ridgwell. lps: Alice Terry, Stanley Dunn, Templer Saxe. 2r USA. prod/rel: Broadway Star

Springtime a la Carte, Short Story
Springtime a la Carte 1918 d: Kenneth Webb. lps: Edward Earle, Agnes Ayres. 2r USA. prod/rel: Broadway Star

Stirrup Brother, The, Short Story
Stirrup Brother, The 1914. lps: J. W. Johnston. 2r USA. prod/rel: Eclair

Strictly Business, Short Story
Strictly Business 1917 d: Thomas R. Mills. lps: Doris Kenyon, Alice Terry. 2r USA. prod/rel: Broadway Star

Telemachus, Friend, Short Story
Telemachus, Friend 1920 d: David Smith. lps: Jay Morley. 2r USA. prod/rel: Vitagraph

Thimble, Thimble, Short Story
Thimble, Thimble 1920 d: Edward H. Griffith. lps: Rod La Rocque. 2r USA. prod/rel: Vitagraph

Thing's the Play, The, Short Story
Thing's the Play, The 1918 d: George Ridgwell. lps: Mildred Manning, Jack Crosby, Rex Burnett. 2r USA. prod/rel: Broadway Star

Third Ingredient, The, Short Story
Third Ingredient, The 1917 d: Thomas R. Mills. lps: Mildred Manning, Alice Mann, J. Frank Glendon. 2r USA. prod/rel: Broadway Star

Tobin's Palm, Short Story
Tobin's Palm 1918 d: Kenneth Webb. 2r USA. prod/rel: Broadway Star

Transients in Arcadia, Short Story
Transients in Arcadia 1918 d: Kenneth Webb. lps: Edward Earle, Agnes Ayres. 2r USA. prod/rel: Broadway Star

Transients in Arcadia 1925 d: Daniel Keefe. 2r USA. prod/rel: Fox Film Corp., William Fox©

Trimmed Lamp, The, Short Story
Trimmed Lamp, The 1918 d: George Ridgwell. lps: Mildred Manning, Alice Terry, Elma Peterson. 2r USA. prod/rel: Broadway Star

Trying to Get Arrested, Short Story
Trying to Get Arrested 1909 d: D. W. Griffith. lps: Florence Lawrence, Owen Moore, Arthur Johnson. 344f USA. prod/rel: Biograph Co.

Two Renegades, The, Short Story
Two Renegades, The 1917 d: David Smith. lps: W. L. Rodgers, Chet Ryan. 2r USA. prod/rel: Broadway Star

Unknown Quantity, The, 1910, Short Story
Unknown Quantity, The 1919 d: Thomas R. Mills. lps: Corinne Griffith, Huntley Gordon, Harry Davenport. 5r USA. prod/rel: Vitagraph Co. of America©

Vanity and Some Sables, Short Story
Vanity and Some Sables 1917 d: John S. Robertson. lps: Wallace MacDonald, Mildred Manning, Robert Gaillord. 2r USA. prod/rel: Broadway Star

Venturers, The, Short Story
Venturers, The 1917 d: Thomas R. Mills. lps: Jack Ellis, J. Frank Glendon, Agnes Eyre. 2r USA. prod/rel: Broadway Star

While the Auto Waits, Short Story
While the Auto Waits 1920 d: Joseph Byron Totten. 2r USA. prod/rel: Vitagraph

Whirligig of Life, The, Short Story
Trapper's Five Dollar Bill, The 1911. lps: Edward O'Connor, Rolinda Bainbridge, Robert Brower. 980f USA. prod/rel: Edison

Whirligigs, Short Story
Whirligig of Life, The 1917 d: Floyd France. lps: George O'Donnell, Dick L'Estrange, Rolinda Bainbridge. 2r USA. prod/rel: Edison

Whistling Dick's Christmas Stocking, Short Story
Whistling Dick's Christmas Stocking 1917 d: George Ridgwell. lps: George Cooper, Adele de Garde. 2r USA. prod/rel: Broadway Star

Whistling Dick's Christmas Stocking, 1909, Short Story
Unwilling Hero, An 1921 d: Clarence Badger. lps: Will Rogers, Molly Malone, John Bowers. 4759f USA. *Whistling Dick* prod/rel: Goldwyn Pictures

HENRY, WILL
Frontier Fury, Novel
Pillars of the Sky 1956 d: George Marshall. lps: Jeff Chandler, Dorothy Malone, Ward Bond. 95M USA. *The Tomahawk and the Cross* (UKN) prod/rel: Universal-International

Journey to Shiloh, New York 1960, Novel
Journey to Shiloh 1968 d: William Hale. lps: James Caan, Michael Sarrazin, Brenda Scott. 101M USA. prod/rel: Universal Pictures

MacKenna's Gold, New York 1963, Novel
MacKenna's Gold 1968 d: J. Lee Thompson. lps: Gregory Peck, Omar Sharif, Telly Savalas. 128M USA. *McKenna's Gold* prod/rel: Highroad Productions

The North Star, Novel
Tashunga 1996 d: Nils Gaup. lps: Christopher Lambert, James Caan, Catherine McCormack. 88M NRW/FRN/UKN. *North Star* prod/rel: Federal Films, Afcl Prods.

Who Rides With Wyatt?, New York 1955, Novel
Young Billy Young 1969 d: Burt Kennedy. lps: Robert Mitchum, Robert Walker Jr., David Carradine. 89M USA. *Who Rides With Kane?* prod/rel: Talbot-Youngstein Productions

HENSHEW, THOMAS W.
His Misjudgement, Story
His Misjudgement 1911. lps: Robert Conness. 1000f USA. prod/rel: Edison

HENSTELL, DIANA
Friend, Novel
Deadly Friend 1987 d: Wes Craven. lps: Matthew Laborteaux, Kristy Swanson, Anne Twomey. 87M USA. A.I. prod/rel: Warner Bros., Pan Arts

HENTSCHKE, HEINZ
Ball Der Nationen, Opera
Ball Der Nationen 1954 d: Karl Ritter. lps: Zsa Zsa Gabor, Gustav Frohlich, Paul Henckels. 100M GRM. *International Ball* prod/rel: Buhne Und Film, Panorama

Hochzeitsnacht Im Paradies, Opera
Hochzeitsnacht Im Paradies 1950 d: Geza von Bolvary. lps: Johannes Heesters, Fritz Remond, Claude Farell. 95M GRM. *Wedding Night in Paradise* prod/rel: Meteor, Herzog

Hochzeitsnacht Im Paradies 1962 d: Paul Martin. lps: Marika Rokk, Peter Alexander, Waltraut Haas. 104M AUS. prod/rel: Sascha

Maske in Blau, Opera
Maske in Blau 1942 d: Paul Martin. lps: Klari Tabody, Wolf Albach-Retty, Hans Moser. 94M GRM/HNG. *A Kek Alarc* (HNG); *Mask in Blue* prod/rel: N.F.K., Schorcht

Maske in Blau 1953 d: Georg Jacoby. lps: Marika Rokk, Paul Hubschmid, Wilfried Seyferth. 100M GRM. *Marika; Mask in Blue* prod/rel: Roja, UFA

HENZE, HANS WERNER
Der Junge Lord; Komische Oper in Zwei Akten, Berlin 1965, Opera
Junge Lord, Der 1965 d: Gustav Rudolf Sellner. lps: Edith Mathis, Donald Grobe, Loren Driscoll. 137M GRM. *The Young Lord* (USA) prod/rel: Beta Film, United Film

HENZE, PAUL
Novel
Most Dangerous Man in the World, The 1988 d: Gavin Millar. lps: Martin Shaw, Ian Sears, Tom Radcliffe. TVM. 95M UKN. prod/rel: BBC, Iberoamericana

HERALD, HEINZ
The Burning Bush, Play
Vicious Circle, The 1948 d: W. Lee Wilder. lps: Conrad Nagel, Reinhold Schunzel, Lyle Talbot. 77M USA. *Woman in Brown* (UKN); *The Circle* prod/rel: United Artists

HERANDEZ, JOSE
Martin Fierro, 1872-79, Verse
Martin Fierro 1968 d: Leopoldo Torre-Nilsson. lps: Alfredo Alcon, Lautaro Murua, Graciela Borges. 135M ARG.

HERBERT, A. P. (1890–1971), UKN, Herbert, Alan Patrick
The House By the River, 1921, Novel
House By the River, The 1950 d: Fritz Lang. lps: Louis Hayward, Jane Wyatt, Lee Bowman. 88M USA. prod/rel: Republic, Fidelity Pictures

The Water Gipsies, London 1930, Novel
Water Gipsies, The 1932 d: Maurice Elvey. lps: Ann Todd, Sari Maritza, Ian Hunter. 80M UKN. prod/rel: Associated Talking Pictures, Radio

HERBERT, BOB
No Names. No Packdrill, Play
Rebel 1985 d: Michael Jenkins. lps: Matt Dillon, Debbie Byrne, Bryan Brown. 93M ASL. prod/rel: Village Roadshow Corporation, Philip Emanuel Productions Ltd.©

HERBERT, CARL
Her American Prince, 1906, Play
Her American Prince 1916 d: D. H. Turner. lps: Ormi Hawley, Bradley Barker, Arthur Donaldson. 5r USA. prod/rel: Kinemacolor Co., Mutual Film Corp.

HERBERT, F. HUGH (1897–1957), USA
For Love Or Money, New York 1947, Play
This Happy Feeling 1958 d: Blake Edwards. lps: Debbie Reynolds, Curd Jurgens, John Saxon. 92M USA. *For Love Or Money* prod/rel: Universal-International

Kiss and Tell, New York 1943, Play
Kiss and Tell 1945 d: Richard Wallace. lps: Shirley Temple, Jerome Courtland, Walter Abel. 90M USA. prod/rel: Columbia

The Moon Is Blue, New York 1951, Play
Jungfrau Auf Dem Dach, Die 1954 d: Otto Preminger. lps: Hardy Kruger, Johanna Matz, Johannes Heesters. F GRM.

Moon Is Blue, The 1953 d: Otto Preminger. lps: William Holden, David Niven, Maggie McNamarA. 99M USA. prod/rel: United Artists, Holmby Prods.

Smarty, Philadelphia 1927, Play
Smarty 1934 d: Robert Florey. lps: Warren William, Joan Blondell, Edward Everett Horton. 64M USA. *Hit Me Again* (UKN); *Self-Portrait*; *Mona Lisa* prod/rel: Warner Bros. Pictures©

There You are, New York 1925, Play
There You are! 1926 d: Edward Sedgwick. lps: Conrad Nagel, Edith Roberts, George Fawcett. 5652f USA. prod/rel: Metro-Goldwyn-Mayer Pictures

HERBERT, FRANK (1920–1986), USA, Herbert, Frank Patrick
Dune, 1965, Novel
Dune 1984 d: David Lynch. lps: Francesca Annis, Max von Sydow, Brad Dourif. 140M USA. prod/rel: Universal, Dino de Laurentiis Productions

HERBERT, H. H.
The Ever Open Door, London 1913, Play
Ever-Open Door, The 1920 d: Fred Goodwins. lps: Hayford Hobbs, Daphne Glenne, Margaret Hope. 4850f UKN. prod/rel: Ideal

HERBERT, JAMES
Haunted, Novel
Haunted 1995 d: Lewis Gilbert. lps: Aidan Quinn, Kate Beckinsale, Anthony Andrews. 107M UKN/USA. prod/rel: Entertainment, Double A

The Rats, Novel
Deadly Eyes 1982 d: Robert Clouse. lps: Sam Groom, Sara Botsford, Scatman Crothers. 87M CND. *The Rats; Night Eyes* prod/rel: Golden Harvest Films Ltd., Filmtrust Productions Inc.

The Survivor, Novel
Survivor, The 1980 d: David Hemmings. lps: Robert Powell, Jenny Agutter, Peter Sumner. 99M ASL/UKN. prod/rel: Tuesday Films Production, Pact Productions Pty Ltd.©

HERBERT, JOHN
Fortune and Men's Eyes, Play
Fortune and Men's Eyes 1971 d: Harvey Hart. lps: Wendell Burton, Michael Greer, Zooey Hall. 102M CND. *Aux Yeux du Sort Et Des Humains*; *Des Prisons Et Des Hommes* prod/rel: Cinemex (Canada) Ltd., Metro-Goldwyn-Mayer

HERBERT, MURRAY
The Angel of the Ward, Novel
Angel of the Ward, The 1915 d: Tom Watts. lps: Evelyn Cecil, Arthur Chisholm, Herbert Trumper. 3000f UKN. prod/rel: Barker, Gerrard

HERBERT, VICTOR (1859–1924), IRL
Babes in Toyland, New York 1903, Operetta
Babes in Toyland 1934 d: Charles Rogers, Gus Meins. lps: Stan Laurel, Oliver Hardy, Charlotte Henry. 79M USA. *March of the Wooden Soldiers; Laurel and Hardy in Toyland; March of the Toys; Revenge Is Sweet* prod/rel: Hal Roach Studios, Inc.

Babes in Toyland 1961 d: Jack Donohue. lps: Ray Bolger, Tommy Sands, Annette Funicello. 105M USA. prod/rel: Walt Disney Productions, Buena Vista

Babes in Toyland 1986 d: Clive Donner. lps: Drew Barrymore, Richard Mulligan, Eileen Brennan. TVM. 150M USA. prod/rel: the Finnegan-Pinchuk Company, Orion Tv

The Fortune Teller, New York 1929, Operetta
Buenaventura, La 1934 d: William McGann. lps: Enrico Caruso Jr., Anita Campillo, Luis Alberni. 6907f MXC. prod/rel: First National Pictures, Inc.

Mademoiselle Modiste; a Comic Opera, New York 1905, Musical Play
Kiss Me Again 1931 d: William A. Seiter. lps: Walter Pidgeon, Bernice Clair, Frank McHugh. 76M USA. *Toast of the Legion* (UKN); *Mademoiselle Modiste* prod/rel: First National Pictures©

Mademoiselle Modiste 1926 d: Robert Z. Leonard. lps: Corinne Griffith, Norman Kerry, Willard Louis. 6230f USA. prod/rel: Corinne Griffith Productions, First National Pictures

Naughty Marietta, London 1910, Operetta
Naughty Marietta 1935 d: W. S. Van Dyke. lps: Jeanette MacDonald, Nelson Eddy, Frank Morgan. 106M USA. prod/rel: Metro-Goldwyn-Mayer Corp.©

Old Dutch, New York 1909, Musical Play
Old Dutch 1915 d: Frank H. Crane. lps: Lew Fields, Vivian Martin, Charles Judels. 5r USA. prod/rel: Shubert Film Corp., World Film Corp.©

The Red Mill, New York 1906, Musical Play
Red Mill, The 1926 d: Roscoe Arbuckle. lps: Marion Davies, Owen Moore, Louise FazendA. 6337f USA. prod/rel: Cosmopolitan Productions, Metro-Goldwyn-Mayer Distributing Corp.

HERBURGER, GUNTER
Die Eroberung Der Zitadelle, 1972, Short Story
Eroberung Der Zitadelle, Die 1976 d: Bernhard Wicki. lps: Andras Fricsay, Antonia Reininghaus, Armando BranciA. 151M GRM. *The Conquest of the Citadel; The Capturing of the Citadel* prod/rel: Scorpion, Filmverlag Der Autoren

Hauptlehrer Hofer, 1975, Short Story
Hauptlehrer Hofer 1974 d: Peter Lilienthal. lps: Andre Watt, Sebastian Bleisch, Kim Parnass. 111M GRM. *Schoolmaster Hofer; Lehrer Hofer; Head Teacher Hofer* prod/rel: F.F.a.T., Imbild

HERCULANO, ALEXANDRE
O Bobo, 1884, Novel
Bobo, O 1987 d: Jose Alvaro Morais. lps: Fernando Heitor, Paula Guedes, Luis Lucas. 123M PRT. *The Fool*

HERCZEG, FERENC
A Dolovai Nabob Leanya, 1894, Play
Rakoczy-Marsch 1933 d: Gustav Frohlich. lps: Camilla Horn, Gustav Frohlich, Leopold Kramer. 101M GRM/AUS.; *Rakoszy-Marsch* prod/rel: Markisch, Mondial

A Kek Roka, 1917, Play
Blaufuchs, Der 1938 d: Victor Tourjansky. lps: Zarah Leander, Willy Birgel, Paul Horbiger. 101M GRM. *Blue Fox* (USA) prod/rel: UFA, Europa

Seven Sisters, Play
Seven Sisters 1915 d: Sidney Olcott. lps: Marguerite Clark, Conway Tearle, Lila Barclay. 5r USA. *The Seven Sisters* prod/rel: Famous Players Film Co., Paramount Pictures Corp.

Utolso Tanc, Play
Ultimo Ballo, L' 1941 d: Camillo Mastrocinque. lps: Elsa Merlini, Amedeo Nazzari, Renato Cialente. 90M ITL. prod/rel: Juventus Film

HERCZEG, FRANZ
Die Sieben Tochter Dre Frau Gyurkovics, Novel
Flickorna Gyurkovics 1926 d: Ragnar Hylten-Cavallius. lps: Betty Balfour, Willy Fritsch, Werner Fuetterer. 2360m SWD/GRM. *Die Sieben Tochter Der Frau Gyurkovics* (GRM); *A Sister of Six*; *Gyurkovics Girls* prod/rel: UFA

HERCZEG, GEZA
The Burning Bush, Play
Vicious Circle, The 1948 d: W. Lee Wilder. lps: Conrad Nagel, Reinhold Schunzel, Lyle Talbot. 77M USA. *Woman in Brown* (UKN); *The Circle* prod/rel: United Artists

Die Wunderbar, 1930, Play
Wonder Bar 1934 d: Lloyd Bacon. lps: Al Jolson, Kay Francis, Dolores Del Rio. 84M USA. prod/rel: First National Pictures©

HEREDIA, RAFAEL RAMIREZ
Salon Mexico, Short Story
Salon Mexico 1996 d: Jose Luis Garcia Agraz. lps: Maria Rojo, Edith Gonzalez, Blanca GuerrA. 87M MXC. prod/rel: Televicine

HERENDEEN, FREDERICK
All the King's Horses, New York 1934, Musical Play
All the King's Horses 1935 d: Frank Tuttle. lps: Carl Brisson, Mary Ellis, Edward Everett Horton. 86M USA. *Be Careful Young Lady* prod/rel: Paramount Productions, Inc.

HERGESHEIMER, JOSEPH (1880–1954), USA
The Bright Shawl, New York 1922, Novel
Bright Shawl, The 1923 d: John S. Robertson. lps: Richard Barthelmess, George Beranger, Edward G. Robinson. 7503f USA. prod/rel: Inspiration Pictures, Associated First National Pictures

Goddess of Love Cytherea, New York 1922, Novel
Cytherea 1924 d: George Fitzmaurice. lps: Irene Rich, Lewis Stone, Norman Kerry. 7400f USA. *The Forbidden Way* prod/rel: Madison Productions, Associated First National Pictures

Java Head, New York 1919, Novel
Java Head 1923 d: George Melford. lps: Leatrice Joy, Jacqueline Logan, Frederick Strong. 7865f USA. prod/rel: Famous Players-Lasky, Paramount Pictures
Java Head 1934 d: J. Walter Ruben, Thorold Dickinson. lps: Anna May Wong, Elizabeth Allan, John Loder. 85M UKN. prod/rel: Associated Talking Pictures, Associated British Film Distributors

Tampico, New York 1926, Novel
Woman I Stole, The 1933 d: Irving Cummings. lps: Jack Holt, Fay Wray, Noah Beery. 70M USA. *Tampico* prod/rel: Columbia Pictures Corp.©

Tol'able David, 1919, Short Story
Tol'able David 1921 d: Henry King. lps: Richard Barthelmess, Gladys Hulette, Walter Lewis. 7118f USA. prod/rel: Inspiration Pictures, Associated First National Pictures
Tol'able David 1930 d: John G. Blystone. lps: Richard Cromwell, Noah Beery, Joan Peers. 65M USA. prod/rel: Columbia Pictures

Wild Oranges, New York 1919, Novel
Wild Oranges 1924 d: King Vidor. lps: Virginia Valli, Frank Mayo, Ford Sterling. 6837f USA. prod/rel: Goldwyn Pictures, Goldwyn-Cosmopolitan Distributing Corp.

HERI, HENRIK
King Rene's Daughter, Play
King Rene's Daughter 1913. lps: Maude Fealy, Harry Benham, Mignon Anderson. 3r USA. prod/rel: Thanhouser

HERIAT, PHILIPPE
Les Fruits de l'Ete, Short Story
Fruits de l'Ete, Les 1954 d: Raymond Bernard. lps: Edwige Feuillere, Etchika Choureau, Jeanne Fusier-Gir. 105M FRN/GRM. *Fruits of Summer* (UKN) prod/rel: C.C.F.C., Carlton Films

Les Joies de la Famille, Paris 1960, Play
Rosie! 1968 d: David Lowell Rich. lps: Rosalind Russell, Brian Aherne, Sandra Dee. 98M USA. prod/rel: Ross Hunter Productions, Universal

HERLIHY, JAMES LEO (1927–, USA
All Fall Down, New York 1960, Novel
All Fall Down 1962 d: John Frankenheimer. lps: Warren Beatty, Karl Malden, Angela Lansbury. 111M USA. prod/rel: MGM, John Houseman Production

Blue Denim, New York 1958, Play
Blue Denim 1959 d: Philip Dunne. lps: Carol Lynley, Brandon de Wilde, MacDonald Carey. 89M USA. *Blue Jeans* (UKN) prod/rel: 20th Century-Fox

Midnight Cowboy, New York 1965, Novel
Midnight Cowboy 1969 d: John Schlesinger. lps: Dustin Hoffman, Jon Voight, Sylvia Miles. 113M USA. prod/rel: Jerome Hellman Productions

HERMAN, HENRY
The Silver King, London 1882, Play
Silver King, The 1919 d: George Irving. lps: William Faversham, Barbara Castleton, Nadia Gary. 5r USA. prod/rel: Famous Players-Lasky Corp.©, Paramount-Artcraft Special
Silver King, The 1929 d: T. Hayes Hunter. lps: Percy Marmont, Jean Jay, Chili Bouchier. SIL. 8462f UKN. prod/rel: Welsh-Pearson-Elder, Paramount

The Sword of Fate, Novel
Sword of Fate, The 1921 d: Frances E. Grant. lps: David Hawthorne, Lionel d'Aragon, Dorothy Moody. 5200f UKN. prod/rel: Screen Plays, British Exhibitors' Films

HERMAN, JERRY
Hello, Dolly!, New York 1964, Play
Hello, Dolly! 1969 d: Gene Kelly. lps: Barbra Streisand, Walter Matthau, Michael Crawford. 149M USA. prod/rel: Chenault Productions, 20th Century-Fox

HERMAN, MURIEL
Mary Had a Little., London 1951, Play
Mary Had a Little. 1961 d: Edward Buzzell. lps: Agnes Laurent, Hazel Court, Jack Watling. 84M UKN. prod/rel: Caralan, Dador

HERMANN, K.
Christiane F., Book
Christiane F. Wir Kinder Vom Bahnhof Zoo 1981 d: Ulrich Edel. lps: Nadja Brunckhorst, Thomas Haustein, Jens Kuphal. 138M GRM. *We Children from Bahnhof Zoo* (USA); *Christiane F.* (UKN) prod/rel: Solaris, Maran

HERMANOS ALVAREZ QUINTERO
La Reina Mora, Opera
Reina Mora, La 1922 d: Jose Buchs. lps: Carmen de Cordoba, Consuelo Reyes, Jose Montenegro. 2170m SPN. *The Moorish Queen* prod/rel: Atlantida

HERMANS, WILLEM FREDERIK
De Donkere Kamer Van Damocles, 1958, Novel
Als Twee Druppels Water 1963 d: Fons Rademakers. lps: Lex Schoorel, Mia Goossen, Elise Hoomans. 121M NTH. *Like Two Drops of Water*; *The Spitting Image*; *Dark Room of Damocles*

Paranoia, 1953, Short Story
Paranoia 1967 d: Adriaan Ditvoorst. lps: Kees Van Eijk, Pamela Koevoets, Paul Murk. 102M NTH.

HERMANT, ABEL
La Belle Madame Hebert, 1905, Play
Belle Madame Hebert, La 1921 d: Baldassarre Negroni. lps: Hesperia, Camillo Talamo, Antonietta Zannone. 1359m ITL. prod/rel: Tiber Film

Im Luxuszug, Play
Im Luxuszug 1927 d: Erich Schonfelder. lps: Dina Gralla, Ernst Verebes, Leopold von Ledebur. 2369m GRM. prod/rel: Deutsche Film-Union Ag

Les Noces Venitiennes, Novel
Noces Venitiennes, Les 1958 d: Alberto Cavalcanti. lps: Martine Carol, Philippe Nicaud, Vittorio de SicA. 93M FRN/ITL. prod/rel: Cinetel, Era Cinematografica
Prima Notte, La 1959 d: Alberto Cavalcanti. lps: Martine Carol, Vittorio de Sica, Philippe Nicaud. 92M ITL/FRN. *Les Noces Venitiennes* (FRN); *The First Night* prod/rel: Cinetel (Paris), Era Cinematografica (Roma)

Rue de la Paix, Play
Rue de la Paix 1926 d: Henri Diamant-Berger. lps: Henri Mathot, Andree Lafayette, Suzy Pierson. 2000m FRN. *Sins of Fashion*

Les Transatlantiques, Novel
Transatlantiques, Les 1927 d: Piere Colombier. lps: Aime Simon-Girard, Pepa Bonafe, Marcel Vallee. F FRN. prod/rel: Films Diamant

HERNADI, GYULA
Kialtas, 1967, Short Story
Csend Es Kialtas 1968 d: Miklos Jancso. lps: Zoltan Latinovits, Mari Torocsik, Andras Kozak. 85M HNG. *Silence and Cry* (USA); *Silence and the Cry*

Kialtas Es Kialtas, 1981, Novel
Kialtas Es Kialtas 1988 d: Zsolt Kezdi-Kovacs. lps: Peter Andorai. 86M HNG. *Cry and Cry Again*

Sirokko, Budapest 1969, Novel
Sirokko 1969 d: Miklos Jancso. lps: Jacques Charrier, Marina Vlady, Eva Swann. 82M HNG/FRN. *Winter Wind* (USA); *Sirocco d'Hiver* (FRN); *Teli Sirokko*; *Winter Sirocco*; *Sirocco* prod/rel: Marquise Film, Mafilm Studios

Voros Rekviem, 1975, Short Story
Meg Ker a Nep 1971 d: Miklos Jancso. lps: Lajos Balazsovits, Andras Balint, Gyongyi Buros. 88M HNG. *Red Psalm* (UKN); *And the People Still Ask*; *People Still Ask*; *Red Song*

HERNANDEZ MIR, GUILLERMO
El Patio de Los Naranjos, Novel
Patio de Los Naranjos, El 1926 d: Guillermo Hernandez Mir. lps: Clotilde Romero, Lolita Astolfi, Faustino Bretano. SPN. prod/rel: Pedro Rodriguez Torres

HERNE, JAMES A. (1839–1901), USA, Aherne, James
Hearts of Oak, New York 1880, Play
Hearts of Oak 1914 d: Wray Physioc. lps: Wilbur Hudson, Violet Horner, Em Gorman. 5r USA. prod/rel: Mohawk Film Co.
Hearts of Oak 1924 d: John Ford. lps: Hobart Bosworth, Pauline Starke, Theodore von Eltz. 5336f USA. prod/rel: Fox Film Corp.

Shore Acres, Boston 1892, Play
Shore Acres 1914 d: Jack Pratt. lps: Charles A. Stevenson, William Riley Hatch, Conway Tearle. 5r USA. prod/rel: All Star Feature Corp., Alco Film Corp.
Shore Acres 1920 d: Rex Ingram. lps: Alice Lake, Robert Walker, Edward Connelly. 5985f USA. prod/rel: Screen Classics, Inc., Metro Pictures Corp.©

HERNE, JULIE
The Outsider, New Britain, Ct. 1916, Play
Misfit Wife, The 1920 d: Edmund Mortimer. lps: Alice Lake, Forrest Stanley, William Gettinger. 5650f USA. prod/rel: Metro Pictures Corp.©

The Prude, Story
Dangerous Flirt, The 1924 d: Tod Browning. lps: Evelyn Brent, Edward Earle, Sheldon Lewis. 5297f USA. *A Dangerous Flirtation* (UKN); *The Prude* prod/rel: Gothic Pictures, Film Booking Offices of America

HERRICK, KIMBALL
Night Patrol, 1937, Short Story
Trouble at Midnight 1938 d: Ford Beebe. lps: Noah Beery Jr., Kay Hughes, Larry Blake. 69M USA. *Midnight Raiders* prod/rel: Universal Pictures Co.©

HERRICK, ROBERT (1868–1938), USA
Clark's Field, New York 1914, Novel
Dangerous Money 1924 d: Frank Tuttle. lps: Bebe Daniels, Tom Moore, William Powell. F USA. prod/rel: Famous Players-Lasky, Paramount Pictures

The Healer, New York 1911, Novel
Healer, The 1935 d: Reginald Barker. lps: Ralph Bellamy, Karen Morley, Mickey Rooney. 77M USA. *Little Pal* prod/rel: Monogram Pictures Corp.©

HERRIOT, EDOUARD
Mme Recamier Et Ses Amis, Novel
Madame Recamier 1920 d: Joseph Delmont. lps: Fern Andra, Bernd Aldor, Albert Steinruck. 2218m GRM. prod/rel: Franco Films

HERRIOT, JAMES (1916–1995), UKN, Wight, James Alfred
Books
It Shouldn't Happen to a Vet 1976 d: Eric Till. lps: John Alderton, Colin Blakely, Lisa Harrow. 94M UKN. *All Things Bright and Beautiful* (USA) prod/rel: Emi, Talent Associates

All Creatures Great and Small, Novel
All Creatures Great and Small 1974 d: Claude Whatham. lps: Simon Ward, Anthony Hopkins, Lisa Harrow. 92M UKN. prod/rel: Emi, Venedon

HERRMANN, IGNAT
Artur a Leontyna, Novel
Artur a Leontyna 1940 d: M. J. Krnansky. lps: Jiri Dohnal, Lida Baarova, Frantisek Smolik. 2352m CZC. *Artur and Leontyna* prod/rel: Nationalfilm

Bezdetna, Short Story
Bezdetna 1935 d: M. J. Krnansky. lps: Natasa Gollova, Rudolf Deyl St., Marta MajovA. 2358m CZC. *Childless* prod/rel: Elekta

Kariera Pavla Camrdy, Novel
Kariera Pavla Camrdy 1931 d: M. J. Krnansky. lps: Vladimir Borsky, Adolf Dobrovolny, Helena MonczakovA. 2643m CZC. *Pavel Camrda's Career*; *The Career of Pavel Camrda* prod/rel: Elekta

Otec Kondelik a Zenich Vejvara, Novel
Otec Kondelik a Zenich Vejvara 1937 d: M. J. Krnansky. lps: Theodor Pistek, Antonie Nedosinska, Eva GerovA. 2742m CZC. *Father Kondelik and Bridegroom Vejvara* prod/rel: Korunafilm

Otec Kondelik a Zenich Vejvara I. 1926 d: Karl
Anton. lps: Theodor Pistek, Antonie Nedosinska,
Jarmila VackovA. 2108m CZC. *Father Kondelik and
Bridegroom Vejvara I.*; *Kondelik -Father Vejvara
-Bridegroom* prod/rel: Elekta Journal, Biografia

Otec Kondelik a Zenich Vejvara II. 1926 d: Karl
Anton. lps: Theodor Pistek, Antonie Nedosinska,
Jarmila VackovA. CZC. *Father Kondelik and
Bridegroom Vejvara II* prod/rel: Elekta Journal,
Biografia

Pod Jednou Strechou, Short Story
Pod Jednou Strechou 1938 d: M. J. Krnansky. lps:
Theodor Pistek, Jiri Dohnal, Hana VitovA. 2576m CZC.
Under One Roof; *Safe Home* prod/rel: Reiter

Pribeh Jednoho Dne, Novel
Pribeh Jednoho Dne 1926 d: M. J. Krnansky. lps:
Mary Jansova, Lexa Jarosin, Antonie NedosinskA. CZC.
The Story of One Day prod/rel: Miroslav J. Krnansky,
Biografia

Tchan Kondelik a Zet Vejvara, Novel
Tchan Kondelik a Zet Vejvara 1929 d: Svatopluk
Innemann. lps: Theodor Pistek, Jiri Hron, Antonie
NedosinskA. CZC. *Father-in-Law Kondelik and His
Son-in-Law Vejvara*; *Kondelik - Father-in-Law -
Vejvara - Son-in-Law* prod/rel: Elekta Journal, Vaclav
Pstros

U Snedeneho Kramu, Novel
U Snedeneho Kramu 1933 d: Martin Fric. lps:
Frantisek Smolik, Vlasta Burian, Antonie NedosinskA.
2588m CZC. *The Eaten-Up Shop*; *The Ruined
Shopkeeper*; *The Ransacked Shop*; *The Emptied-Out
Grocer's Shop*; *Eaten Out of House and Home* prod/rel:
Ludvik Kanturek, Moldavia

Vdavky Nanynky Kulichovy, Novel
Vdavky Nanynky Kulichovy 1925 d: M. J. Krnansky.
lps: Vaclav Srb, Antonie Nedosinska, Jarmila VackovA.
1502m CZC. *The Wedding of Nanynka Kulichova*;
Nanynka Kulichova's Marriage prod/rel: Karel Spelina,
Chicago-Film

Vdavky Nanynky Kulichovy 1941 d: Vladimir
Slavinsky. lps: Antonie Nedosinska, Jara Kohout, Hana
VitovA. 2613m CZC. *Nanynka Kulichova's Wedding*
prod/rel: Elekta

HERRNFELD, ANTON
Familientag Im Hause Prellstein, Play
Familientag Im Hause Prellstein 1927 d: Hans
Steinhoff. lps: Anton Herrnfeld, Erika Glassner, S. Z.
Sakall. 2040m GRM. prod/rel: Rex-Film Ag

HERRNFELD, DONATH
Familientag Im Hause Prellstein, Play
Familientag Im Hause Prellstein 1927 d: Hans
Steinhoff. lps: Anton Herrnfeld, Erika Glassner, S. Z.
Sakall. 2040m GRM. prod/rel: Rex-Film Ag

HERRON, STELLA WYNNE
Shoes, 1916, Short Story
Shoes 1916 d: Lois Weber. lps: Mary MacLaren, Harry
Griffith, Mrs. A. E. Witting. 5r USA. prod/rel: Bluebird
Photoplays, Inc.©

HERSCHFIELD, BEN
Bye-Bye Buddy, Story
Bye-Bye Buddy 1929 d: Frank S. Mattison. lps: Agnes
Ayres, Bud Shaw, Fred Shanley. 5700f USA. prod/rel:
Hercules Film Productions, Trinity Pictures

HERSENT
La Ruse, Play
Ruse, La 1921 d: Edouard-Emile Violet. lps: E. B.
Donatien, Marsa Renhardt, Mag Murray. 1455m FRN.
prod/rel: Films Lucifer

HERSEY, JOHN (1914–1993), USA, Hersey, John
Richard
A Bell for Adano, 1944, Novel
Bell for Adano, A 1945 d: Henry King. lps: John
Hodiak, Gene Tierney, William Bendix. 104M USA.
prod/rel: 20th Century-Fox

The War Lover, New York 1959, Novel
War Lover, The 1962 d: Philip Leacock. lps: Steve
McQueen, Robert Wagner, Shirley Anne Field. 105M
UKN/USA. prod/rel: Columbia British

HERTS, BENJAMIN RUSSELL
*Grand Slam; the Rise and Fall of a Bridge
Wizard*, New York 1932, Novel
Grand Slam 1933 d: William Dieterle. lps: Loretta
Young, Paul Lukas, Frank McHugh. 67M USA. prod/rel:
First National Pictures©

HERVE (1825–1892), FRN, Ronger, Florimond
Mam'zelle Nitouche, Paris 1882, Operetta
Diavolo Va in Collegio, Il 1944 d: Jean Boyer. lps:
Lilia Silvi, Leonardo Cortese, Greta GondA. 83M ITL.
Santarellina prod/rel: Excelsa Film, Minerva Film

Mam'zelle Nitouche 1931 d: Marc Allegret. lps: Janie
Marese, Raimu, Andre Alerme. 106M FRN. prod/rel:
Vandor-Film, Ondra-Lamac-Film

Mam'zelle Nitouche 1954 d: Yves Allegret. lps:
Fernandel, Pier Angeli, Jean Debucourt. 90M FRN/ITL.
Santarellina (ITL); *Oh No Mam'zelle* prod/rel:
Paris-Films Production, Panitalia Film

Santarellina 1912 d: Mario Caserini. lps: Gigetta
Morano, Ercole Vaser, Mario Bonnard. 882m ITL.
Ma'mselle Nitouche (UKN); *Mam'selle Nitouche* (USA)
prod/rel: S.A. Ambrosio

Santarellina 1923 d: Eugenio Perego. lps: Leda Gys,
Silvio Orsini, Lorenzo Soderini. 1401m ITL. prod/rel:
Lombardo Film

HERVEY, HARRY
Aunt Emma Paints the Town, Story
So's Your Aunt Emma! 1942 d: Jean Yarbrough. lps:
Zasu Pitts, Roger Pryor, Warren Hymer. 62M USA. *Meet
the Mob*; *Aunt Emma Paints the Town* prod/rel:
Monogran

Lips of Steel, Novel
Prestige 1932 d: Tay Garnett. lps: Ann Harding,
Melvyn Douglas, Adolphe Menjou. 71M USA. prod/rel:
RKO Pathe Pictures©, Charles R. Rogers Production

HERVEY, WILLIAM ADDISON
Aftermath, Play
Aftermath 1914. lps: Virginia Pearson, Owen Moore.
4r USA. prod/rel: Famous Players Film Co., State Rights

HERVIEU, PAUL
La Course du Flambeau, Play
Course du Flambeau, La 1917 d: Charles Burguet.
lps: Leon Mathot, Jacques Robert, Suzanne Delve. 550m
FRN. prod/rel: Optima, Pathe

Le Dedale, Play
Dedale, Le 1912 d: Rene Leprince. lps: Jean Kemm,
Rene Alexandre, Gabrielle Robinne. FRN. prod/rel:
Pathe Freres

Dedale, Le 1917 d: Jean Kemm. lps: Paul Escoffier,
Jean Kemm, Gabrielle Robinne. 1405m FRN. prod/rel:
Scagl

Dedale, Le 1926 d: Gaston Roudes, Marcel Dumont.
lps: Gaston Jacquet, Claude France, Georges Melchior.
F FRN. prod/rel: Astor Film

L' Enigme, Play
Enigme, L' 1918 d: Jean Kemm. lps: Henry Krauss,
Camille Bert, Germaine Dermoz. 1100m FRN. prod/rel:
Scagl

Le Reveil, Play
Reveil, Le 1914. lps: Marie-Louise Derval. FRN.
prod/rel: Scagl

HERZOG, ARTHUR
The Swarm, Novel
Swarm, The 1978 d: Irwin Allen. lps: Michael Caine,
Henry Fonda, Richard Widmark. 116M USA. prod/rel:
Warner Bros.

HERZOG JR., ARTHUR
Mary Had a Little., London 1951, Play
Mary Had a Little 1961 d: Edward Buzzell. lps: Agnes
Laurent, Hazel Court, Jack Watling. 84M UKN.
prod/rel: Caralan, Dador

HERZOG, RUDOLF
Das Fahnlein Der Versprengten, Novel
Alte Kameraden 1934 d: Fred Sauer. lps: Fita
Benkhoff, Eduard Wesener, Ralph Arthur Roberts. 88M
GRM. *Das Fahnlein Der Versprengten* prod/rel: Bavaria

HERZOG, WILHELM
The Dreyfus Case, Play
Dreyfus 1931 d: F. W. Kraemer, Milton Rosmer. lps:
Cedric Hardwicke, Charles Carson, George Merritt.
90M UKN. *The Dreyfus Case* (USA) prod/rel: British
International Pictures, Wardour

HESSE, ERNST
Voruntersuchung, Play
Autour d'une Enquete 1931 d: Henri Chomette,
Robert Siodmak. lps: Annabella, Florelle, Jean Perier.
93M FRN. prod/rel: U.F.a., a.C.E.

Voruntersuchung 1931 d: Robert Siodmak. lps: Albert
Bassermann, Gustav Frolich, Hans Brausewetter. 95M
GRM. *Preliminary Investigation*; *Inquest* prod/rel: UFA

HESSE, HERMANN (1877–1962), GRM
Siddhartha; Eine Indische Dichtung, 1922, Novel
Siddhartha 1972 d: Conrad Rooks. lps: Shashi Kapoor,
Simi Garewal, Romesh SharmA. 95M USA/IND.

Der Steppenwolf, 1927, Novel
Steppenwolf 1974 d: Fred Haines. lps: Max von Sydow,
Dominique Sanda, Carla Romanelli. 106M
USA/SWT/FRN. prod/rel: Produfilm

HETH, EDWARD HARRIS
Any Number Can Play, Novel
Any Number Can Play 1949 d: Mervyn Leroy. lps:
Clark Gable, Alexis Smith, Wendell Corey. 112M USA.
prod/rel: Metro-Goldwyn-Mayer Corp.

HEUBERGER, RICHARD (1850–1914), AUS
Opernball, Vienna 1898, Operetta
Opernball 1939 d: Geza von Bolvary. lps: Marte Harell,
Paul Horbiger, Will Dohm. 107M GRM. *Opera Ball*
(USA) prod/rel: Terra, Herzog

Opernball 1956 d: Ernst MarischkA. lps: Sonja
Ziemann, Adrian Hoven, Hertha Feiler. 107M AUS.
prod/rel: Erma, Herzog

HEUCK, SIGRID
Mondjager, Novel
Mondjager 1989 d: Jens-Peter Behrend. lps: Marie
Bierstedt, Karl Michael Vogler, Agnelo
Temrite-Wadzatse. 90M GRM. prod/rel: Carsten Kruger
Film, S.F.B.

HEUFFER, OLIVER
The Right Honourable, Novel
His Lordship 1932 d: Michael Powell. lps: Jerry Verno,
Janet Megrew, Ben Welden. 79M UKN. prod/rel:
Westminster, United Artists

HEUZE, ANDRE
Le Champion de Ces Dames, Play
Champion de Ces Dames, Le 1937 d: Rene Jayet. lps:
Alice Tissot, Darman, Roger Treville. SHT FRN.

Les Cinq Gentlemen Maudits, Novel
Cinq Gentlemen Maudits, Les 1920 d: Pierre
Regnier, Luitz-Morat. lps: Luitz-Morat, Pierre Regnier,
Andre Luguet. 1855m FRN. *The Five Accursed
Gentlemen*; *Five Doomed Gentlemen* prod/rel: Films
Luitz-Morat

Cinq Gentlemen Maudits, Les 1931 d: Julien
Duvivier. lps: Harry Baur, Rene Lefevre, Rosine Derean.
87M FRN. prod/rel: Vandal Et Delac, Societe Generale
De Cinematographie

En Bordee, Play
En Bordee 1931 d: Henry Wulschleger, Joe Francis.
lps: Bach, Teddy Parent, Suzette Comte. 87M FRN.
prod/rel: Alex Nalpas

Manoeuvres de Nuit, Play
Mam'zelle Spahi 1934 d: Max de Vaucorbeil. lps:
Noel-Noel, Raymond Cordy, Mady Berry. 85M FRN.

La Mariee du Regiment, Play
Mariee du Regiment, La 1935 d: Maurice Cammage.
lps: Pierre Larquey, Suzanne Dehelly, Andre Berley.
90M FRN. prod/rel: Maurice Cammage

HEWERS, HANS H.
Il Ragno, Short Story
Morte Al Lavoro, La 1978 d: Gianni Amelio. lps:
Enrico Pacifici, Elisa Colosimo, Fausta Avelli. MTV. F
ITL. prod/rel: Rai-Tv

HEWLETT, MAURICE (1861–1923), UKN
Open Country, Novel
Open Country 1922 d: Sinclair Hill. lps: Dorinea
Shirley, David Hawthorne, Bertram Burleigh. 4696f
UKN. prod/rel: Stoll

The Spanish Jade, New York 1908, Novel
Spanish Jade, The 1915 d: Wilfred Lucas. lps: Betty
Belairs, Wilfred Lucas, Nigel de Brulier. 6r USA.
prod/rel: Fiction Pictures, Inc., Paramount Pictures
Corp.

Spanish Jade, The 1922 d: John S. Robertson, Tom
Geraghty. lps: David Powell, Evelyn Brent, Marc
McDermott. 6700f UKN/USA. *Spanish Jade* prod/rel:
Famous Players-Lasky, Paramount Pictures

HEYER, GEORGETTE (1902–1974), UKN
Novel
Bezauberndes Arabella 1959 d: Axel von Ambesser.
lps: Johanna von Koczian, Carlos Thompson, Hilde
Hildebrand. 87M GRM. *Enchanting Arabella* prod/rel:
Rhombus, U.F.H.

The Reluctant Widow, Novel
Reluctant Widow, The 1950 d: Bernard Knowles. lps:
Jean Kent, Guy Rolfe, Paul Dupuis. 91M UKN. prod/rel:
General Film Distributors, Two Cities

HEYES, DOUGLAS
The Twelfth of Never, Novel
Lonely Profession, The 1969 d: Douglas Heyes. lps:
Harry Guardino, Dean Jagger, Barbara McNair. TVM.
100M USA. *The Savarona Syndrome* prod/rel:
Universal

HEYLAND, ALEXINE
Annice! Oh, 1918, Short Story
Gold Cure, The 1919 d: John H. Collins. lps: Viola
Dana, John McGowan, William B. Davidson. 5r USA. *Oh
Annice!* prod/rel: Metro Pictures Corp.©

HEYM, STEFAN (1913–, GRM
Hostages, 1942, Novel
Hostages 1943 d: Frank Tuttle. lps: Luise Rainer,
Arturo de Cordova, William Bendix. 88M USA. prod/rel:
Paramount

HEYMANN, C. DAVID
Poor Little Rich Girl, Book
  Poor Little Rich Girl: the Barbara Hutton Story
  1987 d: Charles Jarrott. lps: Farrah Fawcett, Bruce
  Davison, Kevin McCarthy. TVM. 250M USA. *Poor Little
  Rich Girl* prod/rel: Lester Persky Productions, Itc
  Productions

HEYNE, WILHELM
Abwarts, Novel
  Abwarts: Das Duell Uber Der Tiefe 1984 d: Carl
  Schenkel. lps: Renee Soutendijk, Gotz George, Wolfgang
  Kieling. 91M GRM. *Out of Order*; *Der Aufzug*; *Abwarts*;
  Going Down prod/rel: Laura Film, Mutoskop Film

HEYWARD, DUBOSE (1885–1940), USA
Porgy, 1925, Novel
  Porgy and Bess 1959 d: Otto Preminger. lps: Sidney
  Poitier, Dorothy Dandridge, Sammy Davis Jr. 138M
  USA. prod/rel: Columbia, Samuel Goldwyn

HEYWOOD, H.
Un Vol Etrange, Novel
  Vol Etrange, Un 1919 d: Henri Desfontaines. lps:
  Maurice Escande, Louise Colliney, Andree Pascal. FRN.
  prod/rel: Eclipse

HIAASEN, CARL
Strip Tease, Novel
  Striptease 1996 d: Andrew Bergman. lps: Demi Moore,
  Armand Assante, Ving Rhames. 115M USA. prod/rel:
  Lobell, Castle Rock

HIBBERD, JACK
Dimboola, 1974, Play
  Dimboola 1979 d: John Duigan. lps: Bruce Spence,
  Natalie Bate, Max Gillies. 94M ASL. prod/rel: Pram
  Factory Productions©, Guo
A Toast to Melba, Play
  Toast to Melba, A 1980 d: Alan Burke. lps: Robyn
  Nevin, Michael Aitkens, Mervyn Drake. TVM. F ASL.
  prod/rel: Australian Broadcasting Corp.

HICHENS, ROBERT (1864–1950), UKN, Hichens,
Robert Smythe
After the Verdict, Novel
  After the Verdict 1929 d: Henrik Galeen. lps: Olga
  Tschechowa, Warwick Ward, Malcolm Tod. SIL. 9372f
  UKN. prod/rel: Tschechowa, Bifd
Barbary Sheep, London 1907, Novel
  Barbary Sheep 1917 d: Maurice Tourneur. lps: Elsie
  Ferguson, Pedro de Cordoba, Lumsden Hare. 5r USA.
  prod/rel: Artcraft Pictures Corp.©
Bella Donna, London 1909, Novel
  Bella Donna 1915 d: Edwin S. Porter, Hugh Ford. lps:
  Pauline Frederick, Thomas Holding, Julian L'Estrange.
  5r USA. prod/rel: Famous Players Film Co©, Charles
  Frohman Co.
  Bella Donna 1923 d: George Fitzmaurice. lps: Pola
  Negri, Conway Tearle, Conrad Nagel. 7903f USA.
  prod/rel: Famous Players-Lasky Corp., Paramount
  Pictures
  Bella Donna 1934 d: Robert Milton. lps: Conrad Veidt,
  Mary Ellis, Cedric Hardwicke. 91M UKN. prod/rel:
  Twickenham, Gaumont-British
  Temptation 1946 d: Irving Pichel. lps: Merle Oberon,
  George Brent, Charles Korvin. 92M USA. *Bella Donna*
  prod/rel: Universal
The Call of the Blood, Novel
  Appel du Sang, L' 1919 d: Louis Mercanton. lps:
  Charles Le Bargy, Ivor Novello, Phyllis Neilson-Terry.
  2200m FRN. *Call of the Blood* prod/rel: Ste Des Films
  Mercanton
  Call of the Blood 1948 d: John Clements, Ladislao
  VajdA. lps: Kay Hammond, John Clements, John Justin.
  88M UKN/ITL. *Il Richiamo Del Sangue* (ITL) prod/rel:
  Pendennis (London), British Lion
Flames, Novel
  Flames 1917 d: Maurice Elvey. lps: Margaret
  Bannerman, Owen Nares, Edward O'Neill. 5200f UKN.
  prod/rel: Butcher's Film Service
The Fruitful Vine, Novel
  Fruitful Vine, The 1921 d: Maurice Elvey. lps: Basil
  Rathbone, Valia, Robert English. 7100f UKN. prod/rel:
  Stoll
The Garden of Allah, London 1904, Novel
  Garden of Allah, The 1916 d: Colin Campbell. lps:
  Helen Ware, Thomas Santschi, Al W. Filson. 10r USA.
  prod/rel: Selig Polyscope Co.©, State Rights
  Garden of Allah, The 1927 d: Rex Ingram. lps: Alice
  Terry, Ivan Petrovich, Marcel Vibert. 8500f USA.
  prod/rel: Rex Ingram, Metro-Goldwyn-Mayer
  Distributing Corp.
  Garden of Allah, The 1936 d: Richard Boleslawski.
  lps: Marlene Dietrich, Charles Boyer, Tilly Losch. 85M
  USA. prod/rel: United Artists Corp., Selznick
  International Pictures©

Hidden Lives, Play
  Verborgen Leven, Het 1920 d: Maurits H. Binger, B.
  E. Doxat-Pratt. lps: Adelqui Millar, Annie Bos, Renee
  Spiljar. 5000f NTH/UKN. *The Hidden Life* (UKN)
  prod/rel: Anglo-Hollandia Film
The Paradine Case, Novel
  Paradine Case, The 1947 d: Alfred Hitchcock. lps:
  Gregory Peck, Ann Todd, Charles Laughton. 131M
  USA. prod/rel: Selznick Releasing, Vanguard Films
The Slave, Novel
  Slave, The 1918 d: Arrigo Bocchi. lps: Marie de Lisle,
  Hayford Hobbs, Charles Vane. 4707f UKN. prod/rel:
  Windsor, Lift
Snake-Bite, 1919, Short Story
  Lady Who Lied, The 1925 d: Edwin Carewe. lps: Lewis
  Stone, Virginia Valli, Louis Payne. 7111f USA. prod/rel:
  First National Pictures
The Voice from the Minaret, London 1919, Play
  Voice from the Minaret, The 1923 d: Frank Lloyd.
  lps: Norma Talmadge, Eugene O'Brien, Edwin Stevens.
  6685f USA. prod/rel: Norma Talmadge Productions,
  Associated First National Pictures
The Woman With the Fan, Novel
  Woman With the Fan, The 1921 d: Rene Plaissetty.
  lps: Mary Massart, Alec Fraser, Cyril Percival. 4998f
  UKN. prod/rel: Stoll

HICKAM JR., HOMER H.
Rocket Boys, Book
  October Sky 1999 d: Joe Johnston. lps: Jake
  Gyllenhaal, Chris Cooper, Laura Dern. 108M USA.
  prod/rel: Universal Pictures, Charles Gordon

HICKS, EDWIN P.
Capital Offense, Story
  Hot Summer Night 1956 d: David Friedkin. lps: Leslie
  Nielsen, Colleen Miller, Edward Andrews. 86M USA.
  Capital Offense prod/rel: MGM

HICKS, SEYMOUR (1871–1949), UKN, Hicks, Sir
Edward Seymour
Always Tell Your Wife, Play
  Always Tell Your Wife 1923 d: Hugh Croise, Alfred
  Hitchcock. lps: Seymour Hicks, Gertrude McCoy. 2000f
  UKN. prod/rel: Seymour Hicks Productions
Good Luck, London 1923, Play
  Sporting Lover, The 1926 d: Alan Hale. lps: Conway
  Tearle, Barbara Bedford, Ward Crane. 6642f USA. *Good
  Luck* prod/rel: Faultless Pictures, First National
  Pictures
The Matrimonial Bed, New York 1927, Play
  Kisses for Breakfast 1941 d: Lewis Seiler. lps: Dennis
  Morgan, Jane Wyatt, Lee Patrick. 81M USA. *She Stayed
  Kissed* prod/rel: Warner Bros.
  Matrimonial Bed, The 1930 d: Michael Curtiz. lps:
  Frank Fay, Lilyan Tashman, James Gleason. 6242f
  USA. *A Matrimonial Problem* (UKN) prod/rel: Warner
  Brothers Pictures
Money for Nothing, Play
  Vento Di Milioni 1940 d: Dino Falconi. lps: Umberto
  Melnati, Vivi Gioi, Enzo Biliotti. 78M ITL. *Quattrini a
  Palate* prod/rel: Fono-Roma, E.N.I.C.
One of the Best, London 1895, Play
  One of the Best 1927 d: T. Hayes Hunter. lps: Carlyle
  Blackwell, Walter Butler, Eve Gray. 8271f UKN.
  prod/rel: Gainsborough, Piccadilly
Sporting Life, London 1897, Play
  Sporting Life 1918 d: Maurice Tourneur. lps: Ralph
  Graves, Constance Binney, Warner Richmond. 6032f
  USA. prod/rel: Maurice Tourneur Productions, Inc.©,
  State Rights
  Sporting Life 1925 d: Maurice Tourneur. lps: Bert
  Lytell, Marian Nixon, Paulette Duval. 6709f USA.
  prod/rel: Universal Pictures

HIGGINS, AIDAN
Go Down Langrishe, Novel
  Langrishe, Go Down 1978 d: David Jones. lps: Judi
  Dench, Jeremy Irons, Harold Pinter. TVM. 90M UKN.
  prod/rel: BBC

HIGGINS, COLIN
Harold and Maude, Novel
  Harold and Maude 1971 d: Hal Ashby. lps: Ruth
  Gordon, Bud Cort, Vivian Pickles. 92M USA. prod/rel:
  Paramount

HIGGINS, DAVID
His Last Dollar, New York 1904, Play
  His Last Dollar 1914. lps: David Higgins, Betty Gray,
  Hal Clarendon. 4r USA. prod/rel: Famous Players Film
  Co., Paramount Pictures Corp.

HIGGINS, DAVID K.
At Piney Ridge, New York 1897, Play
  At Piney Ridge 1916 d: William Robert Daly. lps: Fritzi
  Brunette, Al W. Filson, Leo Pierson. 5r USA. prod/rel:
  Selig Polyscope Co.©, V-L-S-E, Inc.

HIGGINS, GEORGE V. (1939–, USA
The Friends of Eddie Coyle, Novel
  Friends of Eddie Coyle, The 1973 d: Peter Yates. lps:
  Robert Mitchum, Peter Boyle, Richard Jordan. 103M
  USA. prod/rel: Paul Monash

HIGGINS, JACK (1929–, UKN, Patterson, Harry
The Eagle Has Landed, Novel
  Eagle Has Landed, The 1976 d: John Sturges. lps:
  Michael Caine, Donald Sutherland, Robert Duvall.
  132M UKN. prod/rel: Itc, Associated General
Night of the Fox, Novel
  Night of the Fox 1990 d: Charles Jarrott. lps: George
  Peppard, Deborah Raffin, Michael York. TVM. 200M
  UKN/USA/FRN.
A Prayer for the Dying, Novel
  Prayer for the Dying, A 1987 d: Mike Hodges. lps:
  Mickey Rourke, Alan Bates, Bob Hoskins. 108M UKN.
  prod/rel: Peter Snell, Samuel Goldwyn Co.

HIGHSMITH, PATRICIA (1921–1995), USA
Novel
  Eaux Profondes 1981 d: Michel Deville. lps: Isabelle
  Huppert, Jean-Louis Trintignant, Jean-Luc Moreau.
  107M FRN. prod/rel: Hamster, Gaumont
  Zwei Gesichter Des Januar, Die 1985 d: Wolfgang
  Storch. lps: Yolande Gilot, Charles Brauer, Thomas
  Schucke. 113M GRM. prod/rel: Monaco, Suddeutscher
  Rundfunk
The Blunderer, New York 1954, Novel
  Meurtrier, Le 1962 d: Claude Autant-LarA. lps:
  Marina Vlady, Robert Hossein, Gert Frobe. 107M
  FRN/ITL/GRM. *L' Omicida* (ITL); *Der Morder* (GRM);
  Enough Rope (USA); *The Murderer* prod/rel:
  International Productions, Cocinor
The Cry of the Owl, 1964, Novel
  Cri du L'hibou, Le 1988 d: Claude Chabrol. lps:
  Christophe Malavoy, Mathilda May, Virginie Thevenet.
  108M FRN. *The Cry of the Owl*; *Le Cri du Hibou*
  prod/rel: Italfrance Films, Tf1
  Schrei Der Eule, Der 1987 d: Tom Toelle. lps:
  Matthias Habich, Birgit Doll, Jacques Breuer. TVM.
  133M GRM.
Edith's Diary, 1977, Novel
  Ediths Tagebuch 1983 d: Hans W. Geissendorfer. lps:
  Angela Winkler, Vadim Glowna, Leopold von
  Verschuer. 108M GRM. *Edith's Diary* prod/rel: Hans W.
  Geissendorfer Rpod., Roxy
The Glass Cell, 1964, Novel
  Glaserne Zelle, Die 1978 d: Hans W. Geissendorfer.
  lps: Helmut Griem, Brigitte Fossey, Dieter Laser. 100M
  GRM. *The Glass Cell* (USA) prod/rel: Roxy, Solaris
Ripley's Game, 1974, Novel
  Amerikanische Freund, Der 1977 d: Wim Wenders.
  lps: Bruno Ganz, Dennis Hopper, Gerard Blain. 123M
  GRM. *The American Friend* (USA) prod/rel: Road
  Movies, Wdr
Strangers on a Train, 1950, Novel
  Once You Kiss a Stranger 1969 d: Robert Sparr. lps:
  Paul Burke, Carol Lynley, Martha Hyer. 106M USA.
  The Perfect Set-Up; *Sudden Death*; *You Can't Win Them
  All* prod/rel: Robert Goldstein, Warner Bros.
  Strangers on a Train 1951 d: Alfred Hitchcock. lps:
  Robert Walker, Farley Granger, Ruth Roman. 101M
  USA. prod/rel: Warner Bros.
The Talented Mr. Ripley, New York 1955, Novel
  Plein Soleil 1960 d: Rene Clement. lps: Alain Delon,
  Marie Laforet, Maurice Ronet. 119M FRN/ITL. *In Pieno
  Sole* (ITL); *Purple Noon* (USA); *Blazing Sun* (UKN);
  Lust for Evil prod/rel: Paris Film Productions, Titanus
This Sweet Sickness, 1960, Novel
  Dites-Lui Que Je l'Aime 1977 d: Claude Miller. lps:
  Gerard Depardieu, Miou-Miou, Dominique Laffin.
  107M FRN. *This Sweet Sickness* (UKN) prod/rel:
  Prospectacle, Filmoblic
The Tremor of Forgery, Novel
  Trip Nach Tunis 1993 d: Peter Goedel. lps: David
  Hunt, Karen Sillas, John Seitz. TVM. 97M GRM.

HIGLEY, PHILO
Remember the Day, Play
  Remember the Day 1941 d: Henry King. lps:
  Claudette Colbert, John Payne, Shepperd Strudwick.
  86M USA. prod/rel: 20th Century Fox

HIGUCHI, ICHIYO
Takekurabe, 1896, Novel
  Takekurabe 1955 d: Heinosuke Gosho. lps: Isuzu
  YamadA. 95M JPN. *Growing Up*; *Comparison of
  Heights*; *Daughters of Yoshiwara*

HIJUELOS, OSCAR
The Mambo Kings Play Songs of Love, Novel
  Mambo Kings, The 1992 d: Arne Glimcher. lps:
  Armand Assante, Antonio Banderas, Cathy Moriarty.
  104M USA. prod/rel: Warner Bros., le Studio Canal©

HILL, ALBERT FAY
The North Avenue Irregulars, Novel
  North Avenue Irregulars, The 1979 d: Bruce Bilson. lps: Edward Herrmann, Barbara Harris, Susan Clark. 99M USA. *Hill's Angels* (UKN) prod/rel: Buena Vista, Walt Disney

HILL, GUS
McFadden's Row of Flats, London 1896, Play
  McFadden's Flats 1927 d: Richard Wallace. lps: Charlie Murray, Chester Conklin, Edna Murphy. 7846f USA. prod/rel: Asher-Small-Rogers, First National Pictures
  McFadden's Flats 1935 d: Ralph Murphy. lps: Walter C. Kelly, Richard Cromwell, Jane Darwell. 65M USA. prod/rel: Paramount Productions©

HILL, KATHERINE
The Shuttle Soul, Story
  Dusk to Dawn 1922 d: King Vidor. lps: Florence Vidor, Jack Mulhall, Truman Van Dyke. 5200f USA. prod/rel: Florence Vidor Productions, Associated Exhibitors

HILL, MARION
The Lure of Crooning Water, Novel
  Lure of Crooning Water, The 1920 d: Arthur Rooke. lps: Guy Newall, Ivy Duke, Hugh Buckler. 6323f UKN. prod/rel: George Clark, Stoll

HILL, R. LANCE
The Evil That Men Do, Novel
  Evil That Men Do, The 1983 d: J. Lee Thompson. lps: Charles Bronson, Theresa Saldana, Joseph Maher. 90M USA/MXC. prod/rel: Itc, Capricorn

HILL, REGINALD (1936–, UKN
An Advancement of Learning, London 1972, Novel
  Dalziel and Pascoe: an Advancement of Learning 1996 d: Maurice Phillips. lps: Warren Clarke, Colin Buchanan, Susannah Corbett. TVM. 90M UKN. prod/rel: BBC
An April Shroud, London 1975, Novel
  Dalziel and Pascoe: an Autumn Shroud 1996 d: Richard Standeven. lps: Warren Clarke, Colin Buchanan, Francesca Annis. TVM. 95M UKN. prod/rel: BBC
Bones and Silence, Novel
  Dalziel and Pascoe: Bones and Silence 1998. lps: Warren Clarke, Colin Buchanan, David Royle. TVM. 95M UKN. prod/rel: BBC
Child's Play, London 1987, Novel
  Dalziel and Pascoe: Child's Play 1998 d: David Wheatley. lps: Warren Clarke, Colin Buchanan, David Royle. TVM. 95M UKN. prod/rel: BBC, Portobello Pictures
A Clubbable Woman, London 1970, Novel
  Dalziel and Pascoe: a Clubbable Woman 1996 d: Ross Devenish. lps: Warren Clarke, Colin Buchanan, Susannah Corbett. TVM. 90M UKN. prod/rel: BBC
Deadheads, London 1983, Novel
  Dalziel and Pascoe: Deadheads 1997 d: Edward Bennett. lps: Warren Clarke, Warren Buchanan, Susannah Corbett. TVM. 95M UKN. prod/rel: BBC
Exit Lines, London 1984, Novel
  Dalziel and Pascoe: Exit Lines 1997 d: Ross Devenish. lps: Warren Clarke, Colin Buchanan, Susannah Corbett. TVM. 95M UKN. prod/rel: BBC
A Killing Kindness, London 1980, Novel
  Dalziel and Pascoe: a Killing Kindness 1997 d: Edward Bennett. lps: Warren Clarke, Colin Buchanan, Susannah Corbett. TVM. 95M UKN. prod/rel: BBC
Ruling Passion, London 1973, Novel
  Dalziel and Pascoe: Ruling Passion 1997 d: Gareth Davies. lps: Warren Clarke, Colin Buchanan, Susannah Corbett. TVM. 95M UKN. prod/rel: BBC

HILL, ROBERT
The Beseiged Heart, Play
  Female on the Beach 1955 d: Joseph Pevney. lps: Joan Crawford, Jeff Chandler, Jan Sterling. 97M USA. prod/rel: Universal-International

HILL, S. B.
Burnt in, Novel
  Burnt in 1920 d: Duncan MacRae. lps: Gertrude McCoy, Bertram Burleigh, Sam Livesey. 4994f UKN. prod/rel: British Actors, Phillips

HILL, WELDON
Onionhead, Novel
  Onionhead 1958 d: Norman Taurog. lps: Andy Griffith, Felicia Farr, Walter Matthau. 110M USA. prod/rel: Warner Bros.

HILL, WERNER
Johannisnacht, Novel
  Johannisnacht 1956 d: Harald Reinl. lps: Willy Birgel, Hertha Feiler, Erik Schumann. 97M GRM. *Midsummer Night* prod/rel: Delos, Constantin

HILLER, F. W.
The Accusing Voice, Story
  Accusing Voice, The 1916 d: Harry Davenport. lps: Harry T. Morey, Belle Bruce, Robert Gaillord. 3r USA. prod/rel: Broadway Star, Vitagraph Co. of America

HILLERMAN, TONY (1925–, USA
The Dark Wind, Novel
  Dark Wind, The 1991 d: Errol Morris. lps: Lou Diamond Phillips, Gary Farmer, Fred Ward. 111M USA. prod/rel: Carolco International, North Face Motion Picture Company

HILLIARD, ROBERT
The Avalanche, Philadelphia 1912, Play
  Avalanche, The 1915 d: Will S. Davis. lps: Catherine Countiss, William H. Tooker, Violet Mersereau. 5r USA. prod/rel: Life Photo Film Corp., State Rights

HILLMAN, GORDON MALHERBE
The Great Man Votes, 1931, Short Story
  Great Man Votes, The 1939 d: Garson Kanin. lps: John Barrymore, Peter Holden, Virginia Weidler. 72M USA. prod/rel: RKO Radio Pictures©
Here I Am a Stranger, 1938, Novel
  Here I Am a Stranger 1939 d: Roy Del Ruth. lps: Richard Greene, Richard Dix, Brenda Joyce. 83M USA. prod/rel: Twentieth Century-Fox Film Corp.©

HILTON, JAMES (1900–1954), UKN
Dawn of Reckoning, 1925, Novel
  Rage in Heaven 1941 d: W. S. Van Dyke. lps: Robert Montgomery, Ingrid Bergman, George Sanders. 83M USA. prod/rel: MGM
Goodbye Mr. Chips, 1934, Novel
  Goodbye, Mr. Chips 1939 d: Sam Wood. lps: Robert Donat, Greer Garson, Terry Kilburn. 113M UKN/USA. prod/rel: MGM British
  Goodbye, Mr. Chips 1969 d: Herbert Ross. lps: Peter O'Toole, Petula Clark, Michael Redgrave. 151M UKN. prod/rel: MGM, Keep
  Goodbye, Mr. Chips 1984 d: Gareth Davies. lps: Roy Marsden. MTV. 180M UKN. prod/rel: BBC
Knight Without Armour, 1933, Novel
  Knight Without Armour 1937 d: Jacques Feyder. lps: Marlene Dietrich, Robert Donat, Irene Vanbrugh. 108M UKN/FRN. *Le Chevalier Sans Armure* (FRN) prod/rel: London Films, United Artists
Lost Horizon, New York 1933, Novel
  Lost Horizon 1937 d: Frank CaprA. lps: Ronald Colman, Jane Wyatt, John Howard. 133M USA. *Lost Horizon of Shangri-la* prod/rel: Columbia Pictures Corp. of California©
  Lost Horizon 1973 d: Charles Jarrott. lps: Peter Finch, Liv Ullmann, Sally Kellerman. 143M USA. prod/rel: Columbia
Random Harvest, 1941, Novel
  Random Harvest 1942 d: Mervyn Leroy. lps: Ronald Colman, Greer Garson, Philip Dorn. 126M USA. prod/rel: MGM
So Well Remembered, 1947, Novel
  So Well Remembered 1947 d: Edward Dmytryk. lps: John Mills, Martha Scott, Patricia Roc. 114M UKN. prod/rel: RKO, Alliance
The Story of Dr. Wassell, 1943, Book
  Story of Dr. Wassell, The 1944 d: Cecil B. de Mille. lps: Gary Cooper, Laraine Day, Signe Hasso. 140M USA. prod/rel: Paramount
We are Not Alone, 1937, Novel
  We are Not Alone 1939 d: Edmund Goulding. lps: Paul Muni, Jane Bryan, Flora Robson. 112M USA. prod/rel: Warner Bros.

HIMES, CHESTER (1909–1984), USA, Himes, Chester Bomar
Cotton Comes to Harlem, New York 1965, Novel
  Cotton Comes to Harlem 1970 d: Ossie Davis. lps: Godfrey Cambridge, Raymond St. Jacques, Calvin Lockhart. 97M USA. prod/rel: Formosa
For Love of Imabelle (a Rage in Harlem), 1957, Novel
  Rage in Harlem, A 1991 d: Bill Duke. lps: Forest Whitaker, Gregory Hines, Robin Givens. 115M UKN/USA. prod/rel: Palace Pictures, Miramax Film Corporation
The Heat's on, 1966, Novel
  Come Back, Charleston Blue 1972 d: Mark Warren. lps: Godfrey Cambridge, Raymond St. Jacques, Peter de AndA. 100M USA. prod/rel: Warner Bros., Formosa

HINDJ, ANDREAS
Gioco Pericoloso, Play
  Gioco Pericoloso 1942 d: Nunzio MalasommA. lps: Elsa Merlini, Elisa Cegani, Renato Cialente. 85M ITL. prod/rel: Cines, Juventus Film

HINE, AL
Lord Love a Duck, New York 1961, Novel
  Lord Love a Duck 1966 d: George Axelrod. lps: Roddy McDowall, Tuesday Weld, Lola Albright. 109M USA. prod/rel: Charleston Enterprises

HINES, ALAN
Square Dance, Novel
  Square Dance 1987 d: Daniel Petrie. lps: Winona Ryder, Jason Robards Jr., Jane Alexander. 112M USA. *Home Is Where the Heart Is* prod/rel: NBC Productions, Pacific Arts Pictures

HINES, ARLIN VAN NESS
Her Honor the Mayor, New York 1918, Play
  Her Honor the Mayor 1920 d: Paul Cazeneuve. lps: Eileen Percy, Ramsey Wallace, Charles Force. 5r USA. prod/rel: Fox Film Corp., William Fox©

HINES, BARRY (1939–, UKN
The Gamekeeper, Novel
  Gamekeeper, The 1980 d: Kenneth Loach. lps: Phil Askham, Rita May, Andrew Grubb. TVM. 84M UKN. prod/rel: Atv
A Kestrel for a Knave, London 1968, Novel
  Kes 1969 d: Kenneth Loach. lps: David (3) Bradley, Lynne Perrie, Freddie Fletcher. 113M UKN. prod/rel: Woodfall Films, Kestrel Films

HINES, DAVID
Bondage, Play
  Whore 1991 d: Ken Russell. lps: Theresa Russell, Benjamin Mouton, Antonio Fargas. 85M USA. *Just See It if You Can't Say It* prod/rel: Tri-Mark Pictures

HINRICHS, AUGUST
Das Frohliche Dorf, Play
  Frohliche Dorf, Das 1955 d: Rudolf Schundler. lps: Carl Hinrichs, Hannelore Bollmann, Gerhard Riedmann. 90M GRM. *Krach Um Jolanthe*; *The Happy Village* prod/rel: Berolina, Gloria
Fur Die Katz, Play
  Fur Die Katz 1940 d: Hermann Pfeiffer. lps: Hilde Jansen, Axel Monje, Lina Carstens. 79M GRM. prod/rel: Terra
Krach Um Jolanthe, Play
  Krach Um Jolanthe 1934 d: Carl Froelich. lps: Marianne Hoppe, Olaf Bach, Marieluise Claudius. 99M GRM. prod/rel: Carl Frohlich, Panorama
Wenn Der Hahn Kraht, Play
  Wenn Der Hahn Kraht 1936 d: Carl Froelich. lps: Heinrich George, Hans Brausewetter, Marianne Hoppe. 90M GRM. prod/rel: Carl Froelich, Doring

HINTON, JANE
The Devil Was Sick, Play
  God's Gift to Women 1931 d: Michael Curtiz. lps: Frank Fay, Joan Blondell, Laura La Plante. 72M USA. *Too Many Women* (UKN); *The Devil Was Sick* prod/rel: Warner Bros. Pictures©

HINTON, NIGEL
Buddy's Song, Novel
  Buddy's Song 1991 d: Claude Whatham. lps: Roger Daltrey, Chesney Hawkes, Sharon Duce. 106M UKN. prod/rel: Castle Premier, Buddy

HINTON, S. E. (1948–, USA, Hinton, Susan Eloise
The Outsiders, 1967, Novel
  Outsiders, The 1983 d: Francis Ford CoppolA. lps: Matt Dillon, Ralph MacChio, C. Thomas Howell. 91M USA. prod/rel: Warner Bros.
Rumble Fish, Novel
  Rumble Fish 1983 d: Francis Ford CoppolA. lps: Matt Dillon, Mickey Rourke, Diane Lane. 94M USA. prod/rel: Universal, Zoetrope
Tex, Novel
  Tex 1982 d: Tim Hunter. lps: Matt Dillon, Jim Metzler, Meg Tilly. 103M USA. prod/rel: Buena Vista, Disney
That Was Then - This Is Now, 1971, Novel
  That Was Then. This Is Now 1985 d: Christopher Cain. lps: Emilio Estevez, Craig Sheffer, Kim Delaney. 102M USA. prod/rel: Paramount, That Was Then Joint Venture

HINTZE, NAOMI A.
Aloha Means Goodbye, 1972, Novel
  Aloha Means Goodbye 1974 d: David Lowell Rich. lps: Sally Struthers, Joanna Miles, Henry Darrow. TVM. 100M USA. prod/rel: Universal

HIRABAYASHI, TAIKO
Kanto Mushuku, Novel
  Kanto Mushuku 1963 d: Seijun Suzuki. lps: Akira Kobayashi, Daizaburo Hirata, Chieko MatsubarA. 93M JPN. *Kanto Wanderer* prod/rel: Nikkatsu Corp.

HIRCH, LOUIS A.
Going Up, New York 1917, Play
  Going Up 1923 d: Lloyd Ingraham. lps: Douglas MacLean, Hallam Cooley, Arthur Stuart Hull. 6000f USA. prod/rel: Douglas Maclean Productions, Associated Exhibitors

HIROTSU, KAZUO
Father and Daughter, Novel
Banshun 1949 d: Yasujiro Ozu. lps: Chishu Ryu, Setsuko Hara, Jun Usami. 112M JPN. *Late Spring* prod/rel: Shochiku Co.

HIRSCH, CHARLES-HENRY
Une Belle Garce, Novel
Belle Garce, Une 1930 d: Marco de Gastyne. lps: Gina Manes, Simone Genevois, Gabriel Gabrio. F FRN. prod/rel: Pathe-Nathan

La Chevre aux Pieds d'Or, Novel
Chevre aux Pieds d'Or, La 1925 d: Jacques Robert. lps: Romuald Joube, Lilian Constantini, Gil Clary. F FRN. prod/rel: Jacques Robert

Danseuse Rouge, La 1937 d: Jean-Paul Paulin. lps: Maurice Escande, Jean Worms, Vera Korene. 109M FRN. *La Chevre aux Pieds d'Or* prod/rel: Cinatlantica Films

HIRSCH, HUGO
Toni, London 1924, Musical Play
Toni 1928 d: Arthur Maude. lps: Jack Buchanan, Dorothy Boyd, W. Lawson Butt. 5548f UKN. prod/rel: British International Pictures, Wardour

HIRSCHBERG, ALBERT S.
Fear Strikes Out, Autobiography
Fear Strikes Out 1957 d: Robert Mulligan. lps: Anthony Perkins, Karl Malden, Norma Moore. 100M USA. *The Jim Piersall Story* prod/rel: Paramount

HIRSCHFELD, LUDWIG
Play
Mad Martindales, The 1942 d: Alfred L. Werker. lps: Jane Withers, Marjorie Weaver, Alan Mowbray. 65M USA. *Not for Children* prod/rel: 20th Century-Fox

Geschaft Mit Amerika, Play
Due Cuori Felici 1932 d: Baldassarre Negroni. lps: Rina Franchetti, Mimi Aylmer, Vittorio de SicA. 78M ITL. prod/rel: Cines, Anonima Pittaluga

Monsieur, Madame Et Bibi 1932 d: Jean Boyer, Max Neufeld. lps: Marie Glory, Robert Lefevre, Jean Dax. 77M FRN. prod/rel: Pathe-Natan

Yes, Mr. Brown 1932 d: Herbert Wilcox, Jack Buchanan. lps: Jack Buchanan, Elsie Randolph, Margot Grahame. 94M UKN. prod/rel: British and Dominions, Woolf & Freedman

HIRSCHFIELD, BURT
Aspen, Novel
Aspen 1977 d: Douglas Heyes. lps: Sam Elliott, Perry King, Gene Barry. TVM. 300M USA. *The Innocent and the Damned; The Aspen Murder* prod/rel: Universal, Roy Huggins

HIRSHBEIN, PERETZ
Grine Felder, New York 1918, Play
Greene Felde 1937 d: Edgar G. Ulmer, Jacob Ben-Ami. lps: Michael Goldstein, Helen Beverly, Isidore Cashier. 105M USA. *Green Fields; Grine Felder* prod/rel: Collective Film Producers©

HISAITA, EIJIRO
Joseimatsuri, Novel
Yoru No Onnatachi 1948 d: Kenji Mizoguchi. lps: Kinuyo Tanaka, Sanae Takasugi, Tomie TsunodA. 73M JPN. *Women of the Night* (USA) prod/rel: Shochiku Co.

HITCHCOCK, RAYMOND
Percy, Novel
Percy 1970 d: Ralph Thomas. lps: Hywel Bennett, Denholm Elliott, Elke Sommer. 103M UKN. prod/rel: Anglo-Emi, Welbeck

HITCHENS, DOLORES
Fool's Gold, New York 1958, Novel
Bande a Part 1964 d: Jean-Luc Godard. lps: Anna Karina, Sami Frey, Claude Brasseur. 95M FRN. *Band of Outsiders* (USA); *The Outsiders* (UKN) prod/rel: Anouchka Films, Orsay Films

HJORTSBERG, WILLIAM
Falling Angel, Novel
Angel Heart 1987 d: Alan Parker. lps: Mickey Rourke, Robert de Niro, Lisa Bonet. 113M USA. prod/rel: Tri-Star, Carolco International

HLASKO, MAREK
Nastepny Do Raju, 1958, Short Story
Baza Ludzi Umarlych 1958 d: Czeslaw Petelski. lps: Zygmunt Kestowicz, Emil Karewicz, Teresa IzewskA. 105M PLN. *Damned Roads; The Depot of the Dead* prod/rel: Zrf Studio

Osmy Dzien Tygodnia, 1957, Novel
Osmy Dzien Tygodnia 1958 d: Aleksander Ford. lps: Zbigniew Cybulski, Tadeusz Lomnicki, Sonja Ziemann. 91M PLN/GRM. *The Eighth Day of the Week* (USA); *Der Achte Wochentag* (GRM); *Der Achte Der Woche* prod/rel: C.C.C., Studio Warschau

Petla, 1956, Short Story
Petla 1957 d: Wojciech J. Has. lps: Gustaw Holoubek, Aleksandra Slaska, Stanislaw Milski. 104M PLN. *The Noose* (USA)

HOAG, TAMI
Night Sins, Novel
Night Sins 1997 d: Robert Allan Ackerman. lps: Valerie Bertinelli, Harry Hamlin, Karen Sillas. TVM. 240M USA. prod/rel: Michele Brustin Prods., Scripps Howards Entertainment

HOARE, DOUGLAS
The Double Event, 1917, Play
Double Event, The 1921 d: Kenelm Foss. lps: Mary Odette, Roy Travers, Lionelle Howard. 5000f UKN. prod/rel: Astra Films

Double Event, The 1934 d: Leslie H. Gordon. lps: Jane Baxter, Ruth Taylor, O. B. Clarence. 68M UKN. prod/rel: Triumph, Producers Distributing Corporation

The Officer's Mess, London 1918, Play
Officer's Mess, The 1931 d: Manning Haynes. lps: Richard Cooper, Harold French, Elsa Lanchester. 98M UKN. prod/rel: Harry Rowson, Paramount

Peaches, 1915, Play
Weddings are Wonderful 1938 d: MacLean Rogers. lps: June Clyde, Esmond Knight, Rene Ray. 79M UKN. prod/rel: Canterbury, RKO Radio

HOARE, JOHN
Red Planet, 1933, Play
Red Planet Mars 1952 d: Harry Horner. lps: Peter Graves, Andrea King, Marvin Miller. 87M USA. *Miracle from Mars* prod/rel: United Artists, Melaby Pictures

HOBAN, RUSSELL (1925–, USA
Turtle Diary, Novel
Turtle Diary 1985 d: John Irvin. lps: Glenda Jackson, Ben Kingsley, Michael Gambon. 96M UKN. prod/rel: Rank, United British Artists

HOBART, ALICE TISDALE
The Cup and the Sword, Novel
This Earth Is Mine 1959 d: Henry King. lps: Rock Hudson, Jean Simmons, Claude Rains. 124M USA. prod/rel: Universal-International, Vintage Prods.

Oil for the Lamps of China, New York 1933, Novel
Law of the Tropics 1941 d: Ray Enright. lps: Constance Bennett, Jeffrey Lynn, Regis Toomey. 76M USA. prod/rel: Warner Bros.

Oil for the Lamps of China 1935 d: Mervyn Leroy. lps: Pat O'Brien, Josephine Hutchinson, Jean Muir. 97M USA. prod/rel: First National Productions Corp., Cosmopolitan Production

HOBART, GEORGE V.
Alma - Where Do You Live?, Musical Play
Alma, Where Do You Live? 1917 d: Hal Clarendon. lps: Ruth MacTammany, George Larkin, Jack Newton. 6r USA. prod/rel: Newfields Producing Corp., State Rights

Experience; a Morality Play of Today, New York 1915, Novel
Experience 1921 d: George Fitzmaurice. lps: Richard Barthelmess, John Miltern, Marjorie Daw. 6560f USA. prod/rel: Famous Players-Lasky, Paramount Pictures

Mrs. Black Is Back, New York 1904, Play
Mrs. Black Is Back 1914 d: Thomas N. Heffron. lps: May Irwin, Charles Lane, Elmer Booth. 4r USA. prod/rel: Famous Players Film Co., Paramount Pictures Corp.

Old Dutch, New York 1909, Musical Play
Old Dutch 1915 d: Frank H. Crane. lps: Lew Fields, Vivian Martin, Charles Judels. 5r USA. prod/rel: Shubert Film Corp., World Film Corp.©

Our Mrs. McChesney, New York 1915, Play
Our Mrs. McChesney 1918 d: Ralph Ince. lps: Ethel Barrymore, Huntley Gordon, Wilfred Lytell. 5r USA. prod/rel: Metro Pictures Corp.©

Sonny, New York 1921, Play
Sonny 1922 d: Henry King. lps: Richard Barthelmess, Margaret Seddon, Pauline Garon. 6968f USA. prod/rel: Inspiration Pictures, Associated First National Pictures

Welcome to Our City, New York 1910, Play
Welcome to Our City 1922 d: Robert H. Townley. lps: MacLyn Arbuckle, Bessie Emerick, Fred Dalton. 5100f USA. prod/rel: San Antonio Pictures, Producers Security Corp.

Wildfire, New York 1908, Play
Wildfire 1915 d: Edwin Middleton. lps: Lillian Russell, Lionel Barrymore, Sam J. Ryan. 5r USA. prod/rel: World Film Corp.©, Shubert Feature

Wildfire 1925 d: T. Hayes Hunter. lps: Aileen Pringle, Edna Murphy, Holmes Herbert. 6550f USA. prod/rel: Distinctive Pictures, Vitagraph Co. of America

The Yankee Girl, New York 1910, Play
Yankee Girl, The 1915 d: Phillips Smalley. lps: Blanche Ring, Herbert Standing, Howard Davies. 5r USA. prod/rel: Oliver Morosco Photoplay Co., Paramount Pictures Corp.

HOBART, VERE
Ring Around the Moon, New York 1935, Novel
Ring Around the Moon 1936 d: Charles Lamont. lps: Donald Cook, Barbara Bedford, Erin O'Brien-Moore. 70M USA. prod/rel: Chesterfield Motion Pictures Corp.©

HOBBLE, JOHN L.
Daddies, Play
Daddies 1924 d: William A. Seiter. lps: Mae Marsh, Harry Myers, Claude Gillingwater. 6800f USA. prod/rel: Warner Brothers Pictures

HOBHOUSE, ADAM
Hangover Murders, New York 1935, Novel
Remember Last Night? 1934 d: James Whale. lps: Edward Arnold, Constance Cummings, Sally Eilers. 81M USA. *Hangover Murders* prod/rel: Universal Pictures Corp.©

HOBL, JOSEF
Sumrak Nad Detvou, Play
Matcina Zpoved 1937 d: Karel SpelinA. lps: Raoul Schranil, Andrej Bagar, Ruzena Porubska-HurbanovA. 2278m CZC. *A Mother's Confession; Matkina Spoved* prod/rel: Dafa

HOBSON, LAURA Z.
Consenting Adult, Novel
Consenting Adult 1985 d: Gilbert Cates. lps: Marlo Thomas, Martin Sheen, Barry Tubb. TVM. 100M USA. prod/rel: ABC, Martin Starger

Gentleman's Agreement, Novel
Gentleman's Agreement 1947 d: Elia Kazan. lps: Gregory Peck, Dorothy McGuire, John Garfield. 118M USA. prod/rel: 20th Century-Fox

The Tenth Month, Novel
Tenth Month, The 1979 d: Joan Tewkesbury. lps: Carol Burnett, Keith Michell, Dina Merrill. TVM. 130M USA.

HOCH, EDWARD D.
A Girl Like Cathy, Short Story
It Takes All Kinds 1969 d: Eddie Davis. lps: Robert Lansing, Vera Miles, Barry Sullivan. 97M ASL/USA. *To Catch a Thief It Takes All Kinds* prod/rel: Goldsworthy Productions, Commonwealth United Productions

HOCHHUTH, ROLF
Arztinnen, 1980, Play
Arztinnen 1983 d: Horst Seemann. lps: Judy Winter, Inge Keller, Walther Reyer. 107M GDR/SWD/GRM. *Lady Doctors; Women Doctors* prod/rel: Veb Defa-Studio, Manfred Durniok

Eine Liebe in Deutschland, 1978, Novel
Amour En Allemagne, Un 1983 d: Andrzej WajdA. lps: Hanna Schygulla, Marie-Christine Barrault, Armin Mueller-Stahl. 110M FRN/GRM. *Eine Liebe in Deutschland* (GRM); *A Love in Germany* (USA) prod/rel: Ccc Filmkunst (West Berlin), Gaumont

HOCHNER, A. E.
Looking for Miracles, Novel
Looking for Miracles 1991 d: Kevin Sullivan. lps: Greg Spottiswood, Joe Flaherty, Patricia Gage. TVM. 103M CND.

HOCHWALDER, FRITZ (1911–1986), AUS
Der Fluchtling, 1945, Play
Frau Am Wege, Die 1948 d: Eduard von Borsody. lps: Brigitte Horney, Robert Freytag, Otto Wogerer. 84M AUS. prod/rel: Forst

HOCKENS, SHEILA
Emma and I, Book
Second Sight: a Love Story 1984 d: John Korty. lps: Elizabeth Montgomery, Barry Newman, Nicholas Pryor. TVM. 100M USA.

HOCKING, ANNE
The Wicked Flee, Novel
Surgeon's Knife, The 1957 d: Gordon Parry. lps: Donald Houston, Adrienne Corri, Lyndon Brook. 83M UKN. prod/rel: Grand National, Gibraltar

HOCKING, JOSEPH
All Men are Liars, Novel
All Men are Liars 1919 d: Sidney Morgan. lps: Alice Russon, Bruce (3) Gordon, Jessie Earle. 4800f UKN. prod/rel: Progress, Butcher's Film Service

Prodigal Daughters, New York 1921, Novel
Prodigal Daughters 1923 d: Sam Wood. lps: Gloria Swanson, Ralph Graves, Vera Reynolds. 6216f USA. prod/rel: Famous Players-Lasky, Paramount Pictures

HOCKING, SILAS K.
Dick's Fairy, Novel
Dick's Fairy 1921 d: Bert Wynne. lps: Joan Griffiths, Hargrave Mansell, Albert Brantford. 5000f UKN. prod/rel: Seal, Curry

Her Benny, Novel
Her Benny 1920 d: A. V. Bramble. lps: Sydney Wood, Babs Reynolds, Charles Buckmaster. 5900f UKN. prod/rel: Diamond Super, Granger

The Shadow Between, Novel
Shadow Between, The 1920 d: George Dewhurst. lps: Doris Lloyd, Lewis Dayton, Sir Simeon Stuart. 5000f UKN. prod/rel: Seal, Granger

HODGES, HOLLIS
The Fabricator, Novel
Why Would I Lie? 1980 d: Larry Peerce. lps: Treat Williams, Lisa Eichhorn, Gabriel Swann. 105M USA. *Why Should I Lie?* prod/rel: MGM, United Artists

HODGES, HORACE
Grumpy, New York 1921, Play
Grumpy 1923 d: William C. de Mille. lps: Theodore Roberts, May McAvoy, Conrad Nagel. 5621f USA. prod/rel: Famous Players-Lasky, Paramount Pictures
Grumpy 1930 d: George Cukor, Cyril Gardner. lps: Cyril Maude, Phillips Holmes, Frances Dade. 74M USA. prod/rel: Paramount-Publix Corp.

HODGINS, ERIC
Mr. Blanding Builds His Dream House, Novel
Mr. Blandings Builds His Dream House 1948 d: H. C. Potter. lps: Cary Grant, Myrna Loy, Melvyn Douglas. 94M USA. prod/rel: RKO Radio

HODGSON, W. H. (1875–1918), UKN, Hodgson, William Hope
The Voice of the Night, Short Story
Matango 1963 d: Inoshiro Honda, Eiji TsuburayA. lps: Akiro Kubo, Yoshio Tsuchiya, Hiroshi Koizumi. 89M JPN. *Attack of the Mushroom People* (USA); *Matango -Fungus of Terror* prod/rel: Toho Co.

HODSON, JAMES
Return to the Wood, London 1955, Novel
King and Country 1964 d: Joseph Losey. lps: Dirk Bogarde, Tom Courtenay, Leo McKern. 88M UKN. *Hamp* prod/rel: B.H.E. Productions, Warner-Pathe

HOEG, PETER
Smilla's Sense of Snow, Novel
Smilla's Sense of Snow 1997 d: Bille August. lps: Julia Ormond, Gabriel Byrne, Richard Harris. 121M GRM/DNM/SWD. *Fraulein Smillas Gespur Fur Schnee*; *Smillas Feeling for Snow* prod/rel: Constantin Film Produktion, Smilla Film

HOEL, SIGURD
En Dag I Oktober, 1931, Novel
Egen Ingang 1956 d: Hasse Ekman. lps: Maj-Britt Nilsson, Alf Kjellin, Hasse Ekman. 93M SWD. *Private Entrance* prod/rel: Ab Svensk Filmindustri

Fjorten Dager for Frostnettene, 1935, Novel
For Frostnettene 1966 d: Arnljot Berg. 94M NRW.

Stevnemote Med Glemte Ar, 1954, Novel
Stevnemote Med Glemte Ar 1957 d: Jon Lennart Mjoen. lps: Inger Marie Andersen, Rolf Christensen, Mona Hofland. 90M NRW. *Rendezvous With Forgotten Years*

Syndere I Sommersol, 1928, Novel
Syndere I Sommersol 1934 d: Einer Sissener. 104M NRW. *Sinners I Summertime*

HOEPNER, RUDOLF
Werkmeister Berthold Kramp, Novel
Grosse Preis, Der 1944 d: Karl Anton. lps: Gustav Frohlich, Carola Hohn, Otto Wernicke. 100M GRM. prod/rel: Tobis, Super

HOERL, ARTHUR
Butterfly Mystery, Short Story
Arm of the Law 1932 d: Louis King. lps: Rex Bell, Marceline Day, Lina Basquette. 60M USA. prod/rel: Trojan Pictures, Inc.

They're Off, Story
Speed Classic, The 1928 d: Bruce Mitchell. lps: Rex Lease, Mitchell Lewis, Mildred Harris. 4700f USA. prod/rel: Excellent Pictures, First Division Pictures

Wild Weed, Novel
Wild Weed 1949 d: Sam Newfield. lps: Lila Leeds, Alan Baxter, Lyle Talbot. 90M USA. *The Devil's Weed* (UKN); *She Should'a Said No* prod/rel: Hallmark

HOFFE, MONCKTON
Cristilinda, New York 1926, Novel
Street Angel 1928 d: Frank Borzage. lps: Janet Gaynor, Charles Farrell, Alberto Rabagliati. 9221f USA. prod/rel: Fox Film Corp.

Daybreak, Play
Daybreak 1946 d: Compton Bennett. lps: Ann Todd, Eric Portman, Maxwell Reed. 81M UKN. prod/rel: General Film Distributors, Triton

The Faithful Heart, London 1921, Play
Faithful Heart, The 1922 d: G. B. Samuelson. lps: Owen Nares, Lillian Hall-Davis, Cathleen Nesbitt. 5600f UKN. prod/rel: British Super, Jury
Faithful Heart, The 1932 d: Victor Saville. lps: Herbert Marshall, Edna Best, Anne Grey. 84M UKN. *Faithful Hearts* (USA) prod/rel: Gainsborough, Ideal

Four Days, Play
Four Days 1951 d: John Guillermin. lps: Hugh McDermott, Kathleen Byron, Peter Reynolds. 55M UKN. prod/rel: Vandyke, Grand National

The Lady Eve, Play
Birds and the Bees, The 1956 d: Norman Taurog. lps: George Gobel, David Niven, Mitzi Gaynor. 94M USA. *The Lady Eve* prod/rel: Paramount
Lady Eve, The 1941 d: Preston Sturges. lps: Barbara Stanwyck, Henry Fonda, Charles Coburn. 97M USA. prod/rel: Paramount

The Little Damozel, London 1909, Play
Little Damozel, The 1916 d: Wilfred Noy. lps: Barbara Hoffe, Geoffrey Wilmer, Norah Chaplin. 5050f UKN. prod/rel: British and Dominions
Little Damozel, The 1933 d: Herbert Wilcox. lps: Anna Neagle, James Rennie, Benita Hume. 73M UKN. prod/rel: British and Dominions, Woolf & Freedman

Many Waters (the Unnamed Play), London 1926, Play
Many Waters 1931 d: Milton Rosmer. lps: Lillian Hall-Davis, Arthur Margetson, Elizabeth Allan. 76M UKN. prod/rel: Associated Metropolitan, Pathe

Panthea, London 1913, Play
Panthea 1917 d: Allan Dwan. lps: Norma Talmadge, L. Rogers Lytton, George Fawcett. 5r USA. prod/rel: Norma Talmadge Film Corp.©, Lewis J. Selznick Enterprises, Inc.

The Scent of Sweet Almonds, Play
Pleasure Crazed 1929 d: Donald Gallaher, Charles Klein (Spv). lps: Marguerite Churchill, Kenneth MacKenna, Dorothy Burgess. 5460f USA. *Masquerade* prod/rel: Fox Film Corp.

The Silver Rosary, Short Story
High Seas 1929 d: Denison Clift. lps: Lillian Rich, John Stuart, Randle Ayrton. SIL. 6355f UKN. prod/rel: British International Pictures, First National-Pathe

HOFFENBERG, MASON
Candy, New York 1964, Novel
Candy 1968 d: Christian Marquand, Giancarlo Zagni. lps: Ewa Aulin, Richard Burton, Walter Matthau. 124M USA/FRN/ITL. *Candy E Il Suo Pazzo Mondo* (ITL) prod/rel: Selmur Pictures (Hollywood), Dear Film (Roma)

HOFFER, WILLIAM
Midnight Express, Book
Midnight Express 1978 d: Alan Parker. lps: Brad Davis, Randy Quaid, Bo Hopkins. 120M UKN/USA. prod/rel: Columbia, Casablanca

Not Without My Daughter, Book
Not Without My Daughter 1991 d: Brian Gilbert. lps: Sally Field, Alfred Molina, Sheila Rosenthal. 116M USA. prod/rel: Pathe Entertainment, Inc., Ufland

HOFFMAN, AARON
The Cherry Tree, Play
George Washington Cohen 1928 d: George Archainbaud. lps: George Jessel, Robert Edeson, Corliss Palmer. 5652f USA. prod/rel: Tiffany-Stahl Productions

Friendly Enemies, New York 1923, Play
Friendly Enemies 1925 d: George Melford. lps: Lew Fields, Joe Weber, Virginia Brown Faire. 6288f USA. prod/rel: Belasco Productions, Producers Distributing Corp.
Friendly Enemies 1942 d: Allan Dwan. lps: Charles Winninger, Charlie Ruggles, James Craig. 95M USA. prod/rel: United Artists

Give and Take, New York 1926, Novel
Give and Take 1928 d: William Beaudine. lps: Jean Hersholt, George Sidney, George Lewis. 7098f USA. prod/rel: Universal Pictures

Nothing But Lies, New York 1918, Play
Nothing But Lies 1920 d: Lawrence C. Windom. lps: Taylor Holmes, Justine Johnstone, Jack McGowan. 6r USA. prod/rel: Taylor Holmes Productions, Inc.©, Metro Pictures Corp.

Two Blocks Away, New York 1925, Play
Cohens and the Kellys, The 1926 d: Harry Pollard. lps: Charlie Murray, George Sidney, Vera Gordon. 7774f USA. *Two Blocks Away*; *The Cohens and Kellys* prod/rel: Universal Pictures

Welcome Stranger, New York 1920, Play
Welcome Stranger 1924 d: James Young. lps: Dore Davidson, Florence Vidor, Virginia Brown Faire. 6618f USA. prod/rel: Belasco Productions, Producers Distributing Corp.

HOFFMAN, ALICE
Practical Magic, Novel
Practical Magic 1998 d: Griffin Dunne. lps: Sandra Bullock, Nicole Kidman, Diane Wiest. 105M USA. prod/rel: Warner Bros.© Village Roadshow Films©, Village Roadshow Pictures

HOFFMAN, LAUREN
Bar Girls, Play
Bar Girls 1994 d: Marita Giovanni. lps: Nancy Allison Wolfe, Liza d'Agostino, Camila Griggs. 95M USA. prod/rel: Lavender Hill Mob

HOFFMAN, WILLIAM DAWSON
The Breed of the Border, Story
Breed of the Border, The 1924 d: Harry Garson. lps: Maurice B. Flynn, Dorothy Dwan, Louise Carver. 4930f USA. prod/rel: Harry Garson Productions, Film Booking Offices of America

Gun Gospel, Chicago 1926, Novel
Gun Gospel 1927 d: Harry J. Brown. lps: Ken Maynard, Bob Fleming, Romaine Fielding. 6228f USA. prod/rel: Charles R. Rogers Productions, First National Pictures

HOFFMANN, ERNST THEODOR AMADEUS (1776–1822), GRM, Hoffmann, E. T. a.
Cardillac, Short Story
Liebestraum 1951 d: Paul Martin. lps: Rudolf Forster, Will Quadflieg, Cornell Borchers. 81M GRM. *Dreams of Death* (USA); *Die Todlichen Traume*; *Deadly Dreams* prod/rel: Pontus, N.F.

Die Elixiere Des Teufels, 1815-16, Novel
Elixiere Des Teufels, Die 1973 d: Ralf Kirsten. lps: Benjamin Besson, Jaroslava Schallerova, Andrzej Kopiczynski. 105M GDR/CZC. prod/rel: Defa, Unidoc
Elixiere Des Teufels, Die 1976 d: Manfred Purzer. lps: Dieter Laser, Peter Brogle, Sylvia Manas. 113M GRM. *The Devil's Elixirs* prod/rel: Roxy, Divina

Das Fraulein von Scuderi, 1819, Short Story
Cardillac 1969 d: Edgar Reitz. lps: Hans Christian Blech, Catana Cayetano, Rolf Becker. 97M GRM. prod/rel: Edgar Reitz
Fraulein von Scuderi, Das 1955 d: Eugen York. lps: Henny Porten, Willy A. Kleinau, Anne Vernon. 95M GDR. *Die Schatze Des Teufels* prod/rel: Defa, Pandora
Juwelen 1930 d: Hans Bruckner. 87M AUS.
Liebestraum 1951 d: Paul Martin. lps: Rudolf Forster, Will Quadflieg, Cornell Borchers. 81M GRM. *Dreams of Death* (USA); *Die Todlichen Traume*; *Deadly Dreams* prod/rel: Pontus, N.F.

Nussknacker Und Mausekonig, 1816, Short Story
Imax Nutcracker, The 1997 d: Christine Edzard. lps: Miriam Margolyes, Heathcote Williams, Lotte Johnson. 37M USA. prod/rel: Imax Corp., Sands Films
Nutcracker, The 1986 d: Carroll Ballard. lps: Hugh Bigney, Vanessa Sharp, Patricia Barker. 89M USA. *Nutcracker; the Motion Picture* prod/rel: Atlantic
Nutcracker Fantasy 1979 d: Takeo NakamurA. ANM. 82M JPN. *Nutcracker Fantasies*; *Nutcracker* prod/rel: Sanrio Films

Der Spieler, Short Story
Liebestraum 1951 d: Paul Martin. lps: Rudolf Forster, Will Quadflieg, Cornell Borchers. 81M GRM. *Dreams of Death* (USA); *Die Todlichen Traume*; *Deadly Dreams* prod/rel: Pontus, N.F.

HOFFMANN, HEINRICH
Der Struwwelpeter, Book
Struwwelpeter, Der 1954 d: Fritz Genschow. lps: Renee Stobrawa, Erika Gorner, Fritz Genschow. 78M GRM. prod/rel: Fritz Genschow, Hamburg

HOFFMANN, JOHN
Northern Lights, Play
Northern Lights 1997 d: Linda Yellen. lps: Diane Keaton, Maury Chaykin, Joseph Cross. TVM. 120M USA. prod/rel: Alliance Communications, Prufrock Pictures

HOFFMANN, LEE
The Valdez Horses, Novel
Valdez Il Mezzosangue 1974 d: John Sturges, Duilio Coletti. lps: Charles Bronson, Jill Ireland, Marcel Bozzuffi. 98M ITL/SPN/FRN. *Caballos Salvajes* (SPN); *Chino* (USA); *The Valdez Horses*; *The Wild Horses*; *Valdez the Halfbreed* (UKN) prod/rel: de Laurentiis Inter MA. Co., Coral Producciones Cin.Cas (Madrid)

HOFFMANN-HARNISCH, W.
Fruhlingsmarchen, Musical Play
Fruhlingsmarchen 1934 d: Carl Froelich. lps: Claire Fuchs, Maris Wetra, Ida Wust. 86M GRM. *Verlieb' Dich Nicht in Sizilien* prod/rel: Carl Froelich, Europa

HOFLER, POLLY MARIA
Andre Und Ursula, Novel
Andre Und Ursula 1955 d: Werner Jacobs. lps: Elisabeth Muller, Ivan Desny, Walter Clemens. 80M GRM. *Andre and Ursula* prod/rel: Rotary, D.F.H.

HOFMAN, OTA
Utek, Novel
Utek 1967 d: Stepan Skalsky. lps: Ivan Vyskocil, Roman Skamene, Jaroslav Cmiral. 74M CZC. *Escape* prod/rel: Filmstudio Barrandov

HOGAN, RAY
Story
Hell Bent for Leather 1960 d: George Sherman. lps: Audie Murphy, Felicia Farr, Stephen McNally. 82M USA. prod/rel: Universal

HOGAN, ROBERT J.
Apache Landing, 1951, Novel
Stand at Apache River, The 1953 d: Lee Sholem. lps: Stephen McNally, Julie Adams, Hugh Marlowe. 77M USA. prod/rel: Universal-International

HOHIMER, FRANK
The Home Invaders, Novel
Thief 1981 d: Michael Mann. lps: James Caan, Tuesday Weld, Willie Nelson. 126M USA. *Violent Streets* (UKN) prod/rel: Michael Mann Company, Caan Productions

HOLBERG, LUDVIG (1684–1754), DNM
Erasmus Montanus, 1731, Play
Jorden Er Flad 1976 d: Henrik Stangerup. lps: Fausto Wolff, Wilson Gray, Lucia Mello Kohler. 116M DNM. *The Earth Is Flat*

Jeppe Haa Bjerget, 1722, Play
Jeppe Pass Bjerget 1933 d: Harry Ivarsson, Per Aabel. 80M NRW.

Loffe Som Miljonar 1948 d: Gosta Bernhard. lps: Elof Ahrle, Sture Lagerwall, Irene Soderblom. 89M SWD. *Loffe As a Millionaire* prod/rel: Film Ab Imago, Ab Svea Film

Jeppe Paa Bjerget, 1722, Play
Jeppe Pa Bjerget 1981 d: Kaspar Rostrup. lps: Buster Larsen, Kurt Ravn. 106M DNM. *Jeppe of the Hill; Konge for En Dag*

HOLCROFT, THOMAS (1744–1809), UKN
The Road to Ruin, London 1792, Play
Road to Ruin, The 1913 d: George Gray, Bert Haldane. lps: George Gray, G. Somerset, Harry W. Scaddan. 4000f UKN. prod/rel: Barker, New Era

HOLDEN, ANNE
The Witnesses, Novel
Bedroom Window, The 1987 d: Curtis Hanson. lps: Steve Guttenberg, Elizabeth McGovern, Isabelle Huppert. 112M USA. prod/rel: de Laurentiis

HOLDER, MARYSE
A Winter Tan, Novel
Winter Tan, A 1988 d: Jackie Burroughs, John Frizzell. lps: Jackie Burroughs, Erando Gonzalez, Javier Torres ZarragozA. 91M CND. prod/rel: John B. Frizzell Inc.

HOLDERLIN, FRIEDRICH (1770–1843), GRM
Hyperion; Oder Der Eremit in Griechenland, 1797-99, Novel
Winterreise Im Olympiastadion 1979 d: Klaus Michael Gruber, Ellen Hammer. lps: Willem Menne, Libgart Schwarz, Sabine Andreas. 70M GRM. *Winter Trip in the Olympic Stadium*

Der Tod Des Empedockles, 1826, Play
Tod Des Empedokles, Der 1986 d: Jean-Marie Straub, Daniele Huillet. lps: Andreas von Rauch, Howard Vernon, Vladimir BarattA. 132M GRM/FRN. *Death of Empedocles* (USA); *La Mort d'Empedocle* (FRN); *Wenn Dann Die Grun von Neuem Euch Erglanzt*

HOLDING, ELISABETH SANXAY (1899–1955), USA
The Bride Comes Home, 1935, Short Story
Bride Comes Home, The 1936 d: Wesley Ruggles. lps: Claudette Colbert, Fred MacMurray, Robert Young. 85M USA. prod/rel: Paramount Productions, Inc.

HOLDING, ELISABETH SANXAY (1899–1955)
The Blank Wall, Novel
Reckless Moment, The 1949 d: Max Ophuls. lps: Joan Bennett, James Mason, Geraldine Brooks. 82M USA. *The Blank Wall* prod/rel: Universal

HOLDRIDGE, DESMOND
The End of the River, Novel
End of the River, The 1947 d: Derek Twist. lps: Sabu, Bibi Ferreira, Esmond Knight. 83M UKN. *Blue Days and Green Days* prod/rel: General Film Distributors, the Archers

HOLDSWORTH, MRS. E.
Helen of Four Gates, Novel
Helen of Four Gates 1920 d: Cecil M. Hepworth. lps: Alma Taylor, James Carew, Gerald Ames. 5800f UKN. prod/rel: Hepworth

HOLE, EDWARD V.
Love's a Luxury, Play
Love's a Luxury 1952 d: Francis Searle. lps: Hugh Wakefield, Derek Bond, Michael Medwin. 89M UKN. *The Caretaker's Daughter* (USA) prod/rel: Mancunian, Butcher's Film Service

HOLIDAY, BILLIE (1915–1959), USA, Harris, Eleonora
Lady Sings the Blues, Autobiography
Lady Sings the Blues 1972 d: Sidney J. Furie. lps: Diana Ross, Billy Dee Williams, Richard Pryor. 125M USA. prod/rel: Paramount

HOLLAENDER, FELIX
Der Eid Des Stephan Huller, Novel
Drei Vom Variete 1954 d: Kurt Neumann. lps: Ingrid Andree, Franco Andrei, Erich Schellow. 96M GRM. *Three from the Circus* prod/rel: Standard, D.F.H.

Eid Des Stephan Huller 1, Der 1912 d: Viggo Larsen. lps: Viggo Larsen, Wanda Treumann, Fritz Schroeter. 833m GRM. prod/rel: Vitascope

Varietes 1935 d: Nicolas Farkas. lps: Jean Gabin, Fernand Gravey, AnnabellA. 100M FRN. *Variety* prod/rel: Bavaria-Film, Les Films E.F.

Der Kampf Des Donald Westhof, Novel
Kampf Des Donald Westhof, Der 1927 d: Fritz Wendhausen. lps: Imre Raday, Elizza La Porta, Oscar HomolkA. 3079m GRM. *The Trial of Donald Westhof* prod/rel: UFA

HOLLAND, GEORGE
Once Over Lightly, Play
Don't Tell the Wife 1937 d: W. Christy Cabanne. lps: Guy Kibbee, Una Merkel, Lynne Overman. 63M USA. *Once Over Lightly* prod/rel: RKO Radio Pictures, Inc.

HOLLAND, JAMES G.
Seven Oaks, New York 1875, Novel
Jes' Call Me Jim 1920 d: Clarence Badger. lps: Will Rogers, Irene Rich, Lionel Belmore. 6r USA. prod/rel: Goldwyn Pictures Corp.©, Goldwyn Distributing Corp.

HOLLAND, KATHERINE
Talk About Jacqueline, Novel
Talk About Jacqueline 1942 d: Paul L. Stein. lps: Hugh Williams, Carla Lehmann, Joyce Howard. 84M UKN. prod/rel: Excelsior, MGM

HOLLAND, KATRIN
Man Spricht Uber Jacqueline, Novel
Man Spricht Uber Jacqueline 1937 d: Werner Hochbaum. lps: Wera Engels, Albrecht Schoenhals, Sabine Peters. 83M GRM. *Talk About Jacqueline* prod/rel: Deka-Film

HOLLAND, MARTY
Fallen Angel, Novel
Fallen Angel 1945 d: Otto Preminger. lps: Dana Andrews, Alice Faye, Linda Darnell. 98M USA. prod/rel: 20th Century Fox

HOLLAND, RUPERT SARGENT
The Heart of Sally Temple, New York 1913, Novel
Winning of Sally Temple, The 1917 d: George Melford. lps: Fannie Ward, Jack Dean, Walter Long. 5r USA. prod/rel: Jesse L. Lasky Feature Play Co.©, Paramount Pictures Corp.

HOLLANDER, FELIX
Novel
Variete 1925 d: E. A. Dupont. lps: Emil Jannings, Maly Delschaft, Lya de Putti. 2844m GRM. *Vaudeville* (UKN); *Variety*; *Varietes* prod/rel: UFA

HOLLES, ROBERT
The Siege of Battersea, London 1962, Novel
Guns at Batasi 1964 d: John Guillermin. lps: Richard Attenborough, Flora Robson, John Leyton. 103M UKN. prod/rel: 20th Century-Fox

HOLLISTER, LEN D.
The Life of the Party, Play
Gold Dust Gertie 1931 d: Lloyd Bacon. lps: Ole Olsen, Chic Johnson, Winnie Lightner. 68M USA. *Why Change Your Husband?* (UKN); *Gold Dust Girl; Red Hot Sinners* prod/rel: Warner Bros. Pictures©

HOLLY, EVZEN
Katerina Vzdorovita, Play
Zlata Katerina 1934 d: Vladimir Slavinsky. lps: Antonie Nedosinska, Lida Baarova, Vladimir Borsky. 2949m CZC. *Golden Katherine; Golden Catherine* prod/rel: UFA

Letcova Maminka, Play
Dokud Mas Maminku 1934 d: Jan Svitak. lps: Antonie Nedosinska, Otomar Korbelar, Lida BaarovA. 2561m CZC. *Until You Have Mamma; While You Have a Mother* prod/rel: UFA

HOLM, GUSTAV
Sissy's Brautfahrt, Play
King Steps Out, The 1936 d: Josef von Sternberg. lps: Grace Moore, Franchot Tone, Walter Connolly. 85M USA. *Poor Sister; Cissy* prod/rel: Columbia Pictures Corp. of California©

HOLM, HANS
Ein Madel Wirbelt Durch Die Welt, Novel
Madel Wirbelt Durch Die Welt, Ein 1934 d: Georg Jacoby. lps: Magda Schneider, Harald Paulsen, Hugo Schrader. 75M GRM. prod/rel: Schulz & Wuellner Filmfabrikation

HOLM, JOHN CECIL
Four Cents a Word, Play
Blonde Inspiration 1940 d: Busby Berkeley. lps: John Shelton, Virginia Grey, Albert Dekker. 71M USA. *Fools Rush in; Four Cents a Word* prod/rel: MGM

Gramercy Ghost, Play
Time of Their Lives, The 1946 d: Charles T. Barton. lps: Bud Abbott, Lou Costello, Marjorie Reynolds. 82M USA. *The Ghost Steps Out* prod/rel: Universal

Three Men on a Horse, New York 1935, Play
Three Men on a Horse 1936 d: Mervyn Leroy. lps: Frank McHugh, Sam Levene, Joan Blondell. 88M USA. prod/rel: Warner Bros. Pictures©

HOLM, SIV
Jeg - En Kvinnde, Copenhagen 1961
Jag - En Kvinna (I) 1965 d: Mac Ahlberg. lps: Essy Persson, Jorgen Reenberg, Preben Mahrt. 105M SWD/DNM. *Jeg - En Kvinde* (DNM); *I - a Woman* prod/rel: Novaris Film, Nordisk Films

Jeg - En Kvinne II, Copenhagen 1968, Novel
Jag - En Kvinna (Ii) 1968 d: Mac Ahlberg. lps: Gio Petre, Lars Lunoe, Hjordis Pettersson. 95M SWD/DNM. *Jeg - En Kvinde II* (DNM); *I - a Woman (Ii); Jag - En Kvinna Ii: Aktenskapet; The Voyeur; I - a Woman Part Two: Marriage* prod/rel: Novaris Film, Minerva Film Produktion

HOLM, STIIG
Jeg - En Elsker, Copenhagen 1965, Novel
Jeg - En Elsker 1966 d: Borje Nyberg. lps: Jorgen Ryg, Jessie Flaws, Axel Strobye. 90M DNM/SWD. *Jag -En Alskare* (SWD); *A Lover I* (USA) prod/rel: Novaris Film

HOLMES, JOHN CECIL
Best Foot Forward, Play
Best Foot Forward 1943 d: Edward Buzzell. lps: Lucille Ball, William Gaxton, Virginia Weidler. 95M USA. prod/rel: Metro-Goldwyn-Mayer Corp.

HOLMES, MARJORIE
The Nativity, Novel
Nativity, The 1978 d: Bernard L. Kowalski. lps: Freddie Jones, John Rhys-Davies, Kate O'MarA. TVM. 100M USA. prod/rel: D'angelo-Bullock-Allen Productions, 20th Century-Fox

HOLMES, MARY JANE
Lena Rivers, New York 1856, Novel
Lena Rivers 1910. 1000f USA. prod/rel: Thanhouser
Lena Rivers 1914. lps: Beulah Poynter, Lizzie Conway, Robert Tabor. 5r USA. prod/rel: Cosmos Feature Film Corp.©, State Rights
Lena Rivers 1914. lps: Violet Horner, Harrish Ingraham, Mary Moore. 5r USA. prod/rel: Whitman Features Co.©, Blinkhorn Photoplays Corp.
Lena Rivers 1925 d: Whitman Bennett. lps: Earle Williams, Johnny Walker, Gladys Hulette. 9r USA. prod/rel: Chord Pictures, Arrow Pictures
Lena Rivers 1932 d: Phil Rosen. lps: Charlotte Henry, Beryl Mercer, James Kirkwood. 67M USA. *The Sin of Lena Rivers* prod/rel: Quadruple Film Corp.©, Tiffany Productions

Tempest and Sunshine, New York 1844, Novel
Tempest and Sunshine 1914 d: Frank H. Crane. lps: Alexander Gaden, Dorothy Phillips, Howard Crampton. 2r USA. prod/rel: Imp
Tempest and Sunshine 1916 d: Carleton S. King, Warren Hughes. lps: Evelyn Greeley, Carlton King, Louis B. Foley. 5r USA. prod/rel: Dixie Film Co.©, State Rights

HOLMES, OLIVER WENDELL (1809–1894), USA
Elsie Venner, Novel
Elsie Venner 1914. lps: Arthur Maude, Constance Crawley. 3r USA. prod/rel: Kennedy Features

The Wonderful One-Horse Shay, Poem
Wonderful One-Horse Shay, The 1912. lps: Mrs. George B. Walters, Ethel Clayton. 1000f USA. prod/rel: Lubin

HOLROYD, MICHAEL
Lytton Strachey, Book
Carrington 1995 d: Christopher Hampton. lps: Emma Thompson, Jonathan Pryce, Steven Waddington. 122M UKN/FRN. prod/rel: Polygram, Freeway

HOLROYD, RONALD
Don't Panic Chaps, Radio Play
Don't Panic Chaps! 1959 d: George Pollock. lps: Dennis Price, George Cole, Thorley Walters. 85M UKN. prod/rel: Columbia, Hammer

HOLT, FELIX
The Gabriel Horn, Novel
Kentuckian, The 1955 d: Burt Lancaster. lps: Burt Lancaster, Dianne Foster, Diana Lynn. 104M USA. prod/rel: United Artists, Hecht-Lancaster

HOLT, HENRY
Night Mail, Novel
Spider, The 1939 d: Maurice Elvey. lps: Diana Churchill, Derrick de Marney, Jean Gillie. 81M UKN. prod/rel: Admiral Films, General Film Distributors

HOLTBY, WINIFRED (1898–1935), UKN
South Riding, 1935, Novel
South Riding 1938 d: Victor Saville. lps: Ralph Richardson, Edna Best, Edmund Gwenn. 91M UKN. prod/rel: London Films, United Artists

HOLTZ-BAUMERT, GERHARD
Erscheinen Pflicht, Novel
Erscheinen Pflicht 1983 d: Helmut DziubA. lps: Vivian Hanjohr, Lissy Tempelhof, Peter Sodann. 75M GDR. *Attendance Compulsory* prod/rel: Defa

HOLZ, ARNO (1863–1929), GRM
Traumulus, 1904, Play
Traumulus 1936 d: Carl Froelich. lps: Carl Froelich, Emil Jannings, Harald Paulsen. 100M GRM. prod/rel: Carl Froelich, National

HOLZER, HANS
Murder in Amityville, Book
Amityville Ii: the Possession 1982 d: Damiano Damiani. lps: James Olson, Burt Young, Rutanya AldA. 104M USA. prod/rel: Orion

HOLZNER, MICHAEL
Das Ende Vom Angang, Novel
Ende Vom Anfang, Das 1981 d: Helmut Christian Gorlitz. lps: Michael Fass, Michael Schaaf, Gaston Frecot. 95M GRM. *The End of the Beginning* prod/rel: Ottokar Runze Filmprod., Starlight

HOME, WILLIAM DOUGLAS (1912–1992), UKN
L' Anatra All'arancia, Play
Anatra All'arancia, L' 1975 d: Luciano Salce. lps: Monica Vitti, Ugo Tognazzi, Barbara Bouchet. 102M ITL. *Duck in Orange Sauce* (USA); *Duck a la Orange* prod/rel: Capital Film, Cineriz

The Chiltern Hundreds, London 1947, Play
Chiltern Hundreds, The 1949 d: John Paddy Carstairs. lps: Cecil Parker, A. E. Matthews, David Tomlinson. 84M UKN. *The Amazing Mr. Beecham* (USA) prod/rel: General Film Distributors, Two Cities

The Dame of Sark, Play
Dame of Sark, The 1976 d: Alvin Rakoff. lps: Celia Johnson, Tony Britton. MTV. UKN. prod/rel: Anglia Tv

Now Barabbas., London 1947, Play
Now Barabbas Was a Robber. 1949 d: Gordon Parry. lps: Richard Greene, Cedric Hardwicke, Kathleen Harrison. 87M UKN. prod/rel: Warner Bros., Anatole de Grunwald

The Reluctant Debutante, London 1956, Play
Reluctant Debutante, The 1958 d: Vincente Minnelli. lps: Rex Harrison, Kay Kendall, John Saxon. 94M USA. prod/rel: MGM, Avon Prods.

HOMER (750bc–, GRC
Iliad, Verse
Guerra Di Troia, La 1961 d: Giorgio Ferroni. lps: Steve Reeves, John Drew Barrymore, Juliette Mayniel. 115M ITL/FRN. *La Guerre de Troie* (FRN); *The Trojan Horse* (USA); *The Wooden Horse of Troy* (UKN); *The Trojan War* prod/rel: Europa Cin.Ca (Roma), Les Films Modernes

Helen of Troy 1955 d: Robert Wise. lps: Rossana Podesta, Jacques Sernas, Cedric Hardwicke. 118M USA. prod/rel: Warner Bros.

The Odyssey, Verse
Odissea, L' 1911 d: Francesco Bertolini, Adolfo Padovan. lps: Giuseppe de Liguoro, Eugenia Tettoni, Ubaldo Maria Del Colle. 925m ITL. *Homero's Odyssey* (USA); *Odyssey* prod/rel: Milano Films

Odyssey, The 1997 d: Andrei Konchalovsky. lps: Armand Assante, Greta Scacchi, Geraldine Chaplin. TVM. 240M USA. prod/rel: Hallmark Entertainment Productions, American Zoetrope

Ulisse 1954 d: Mario Camerini. lps: Kirk Douglas, Silvana Mangano, Anthony Quinn. 104M ITL/USA. *Ulysses* (USA); *Odyssee* prod/rel: Carlo Ponti, Dino de Laurentiis

HOMMA, YOHEI
Novel
Kazoku Geemu 1983 d: Yoshimitsu MoritA. lps: Yusaku Matsuda, Juzo Itami, Saori Yuki. 107M JPN. *The Family Game* (USA); *Kazoku Game*; *Kazoku Gaimu* prod/rel: Art Theatre Guild, New Century Producers

HOOD, BASIL
Sweet and Twenty, London 1901, Play
Sweet and Twenty 1919 d: Sidney Morgan. lps: Margaret Blanche, Langhorne Burton, George Keene. 4800f UKN. prod/rel: Progress, Butcher's Film Service

HOOD, THOMAS (1799–1845), UKN
The Dream of Eugene Aram, Poem
Dream of Eugene Aram, The 1923 d: Edwin Greenwood. lps: Russell Thorndike, Olive Sloane, Wallace Bosco. 1908f UKN. prod/rel: British & Colonial, Walturdaw

The Song of the Shirt, 1843, Poem
Song of the Shirt, The 1908 d: D. W. Griffith. lps: Florence Lawrence, Linda Arvidson, Harry Salter. 638f USA. prod/rel: Biograph Co.

HOOKE, NINA WARNER
Darkness I Leave You, Novel
Gypsy and the Gentleman, The 1958 d: Joseph Losey. lps: Melina Mercouri, Keith Michell, Flora Robson. 107M UKN. prod/rel: Rank, Rank Film Distributors

Deadly Record, Novel
Deadly Record 1959 d: Lawrence Huntington. lps: Lee Patterson, Barbara Shelley, Jane Hylton. 58M UKN. prod/rel: Anglo-Amalgamated, Independent Artists

HOOKER, RICHARD
Mash, New York 1968, Novel
M*a*s*h 1970 d: Robert Altman. lps: Donald Sutherland, Elliott Gould, Tom Skerritt. 116M USA. *Mash* prod/rel: Aspen Productions

HOOVER, J. EDGAR (1895–1972), USA, Hoover, John Edgar
The Crime of the Century, Story
Walk East on Beacon 1952 d: Alfred L. Werker. lps: George Murphy, Finlay Currie, Virginia Gilmore. 98M USA. *Crime of the Century* (UKN) prod/rel: Columbia, Rd-Dr Corp.

Persons in Hiding, Boston 1938, Book
Parole Fixer 1940 d: Robert Florey. lps: William Henry, Robert Paige, Gertrude Michael. 68M USA. prod/rel: Paramount Pictures©

Persons in Hiding 1939 d: Louis King. lps: Patricia Morison, Lynne Overman, Helen Twelvetrees. 69M USA. prod/rel: Paramount Pictures©

Queen of the Mob 1940 d: James P. Hogan. lps: Blanche Yurka, Ralph Bellamy, Robert Ryan. 61M USA. *The Woman from Hell* prod/rel: Paramount Pictures©

Undercover Doctor 1939 d: Louis King. lps: Lloyd Nolan, Heather Angel, J. Carrol Naish. 67M USA. *Federal Offense*; *Persons in Hiding*; *Criminal Doctor*; *Parole Fixer* prod/rel: Paramount Pictures©

HOOVER, PUTNAM
The Ace and the Queen, Story
Flying Fool 1925 d: Frank S. Mattison. lps: Gaston Glass, Dick Grace, Wanda Hawley. 4870f USA. prod/rel: Sunset Productions, Aywon Film Corp.

HOPE, ANTHONY (1863–1933), UKN, Hawkins, Anthony Hope
Captain Dieppe, New York 1900, Novel
Adventure in Hearts, An 1920 d: James Cruze. lps: Robert Warwick, Helene Chadwick, Juan de La Cruz. 5r USA. *Captain Dieppe* (UKN) prod/rel: Famous Players-Lasky Corp.©, Paramount-Artcraft Pictures

The Indiscretion of the Duchess, New York 1894, Novel
Naughty Duchess, The 1928 d: Tom Terriss. lps: Eve Southern, H. B. Warner, Duncan Renaldo. 5271f USA. prod/rel: Tiffany-Stahl Productions

Phroso, Novel
Phroso 1921 d: Louis Mercanton. lps: Paul Capellani, Malvina Longfellow, Jeanne Desclos. 2242m FRN. prod/rel: Films Louis Mercanton

The Prisoner of Zenda, London 1894, Novel
Prisoner of Zenda, The 1913 d: Edwin S. Porter, Hugh Ford. lps: James K. Hackett, Beatrice Beckly, Minna Gale Haines. 4r USA. prod/rel: Famous Players Film Co., State Rights

Prisoner of Zenda, The 1915 d: George Loane Tucker. lps: Henry Ainley, Jane Gail, Gerald Ames. 5500f UKN. prod/rel: London, Jury

Prisoner of Zenda, The 1922 d: Rex Ingram. lps: Lewis Stone, Alice Terry, Robert Edeson. 10r USA. prod/rel: Metro-Goldwyn-Mayer Pictures

Prisoner of Zenda, The 1937 d: John Cromwell, W. S. Van Dyke (Uncredited). lps: Ronald Colman, Madeleine Carroll, Douglas Fairbanks Jr. 101M USA. prod/rel: United Artists Corp., Selznick International Pictures©

Prisoner of Zenda, The 1952 d: Richard Thorpe. lps: Stewart Granger, Deborah Kerr, James Mason. 111M USA. prod/rel: MGM

Prisoner of Zenda, The 1979 d: Richard Quine. lps: Peter Sellers, Lynne Frederick, Lionel Jeffries. 109M USA. prod/rel: Universal

Rupert of Hentzau, 1898, Novel
Rupert of Hentzau 1915 d: George Loane Tucker. lps: Henry Ainley, Jane Gail, Gerald Ames. 5500f UKN. prod/rel: London, Jury

Rupert of Hentzau 1923 d: Victor Heerman. lps: Elaine Hammerstein, Bert Lytell, Lew Cody. 9646f USA. prod/rel: Selznick Pictures

Simon Dale, Novel
English Nell 1900. lps: Marie Tempest, Ben Webster, H. B. Warner. UKN. prod/rel: Mutoscope & Biograph

Sophy of Kravonia, London 1905, Novel
Sophy of Kravonia; Or, the Virgin of Paris 1920 d: Gerard Fontaine. lps: Diana Kareni, Walter Gordon, Philip Ashley. 6r USA. *The Virgin of Paris*; *Sophie of Kravonia* prod/rel: Allied Artists, State Rights

HOPE, EDWARD
Serial Story
Down Among the Sheltering Palms 1953 d: Edmund Goulding. lps: William Lundigan, Gloria de Haven, Mitzi Gaynor. 87M USA. prod/rel: 20th Century-Fox

Calm Yourself!, Indianapolis 1934, Novel
Calm Yourself 1935 d: George B. Seitz. lps: Robert Young, Madge Evans, Betty Furness. 71M USA. prod/rel: Metro-Goldwyn-Mayer Corp.

Marry the Girl, 1935, Short Story
Marry the Girl 1937 d: William McGann. lps: Hugh Herbert, Mary Boland, Carol Hughes. 68M USA. prod/rel: Warner Bros. Pictures©, Mervyn Leroy Production

She Loves Me Not, Indianapolis 1933, Novel
How to Be Very, Very Popular 1955 d: Nunnally Johnson. lps: Betty Grable, Sheree North, Charles Coburn. 89M USA. prod/rel: 20th Century-Fox

She Loves Me Not 1934 d: Elliott Nugent. lps: Bing Crosby, Miriam Hopkins, Kitty Carlisle. 85M USA. prod/rel: Paramount Productions©

True to the Army 1942 d: Albert S. Rogell. lps: Allan Jones, Ann Miller, Judy CanovA. 76M USA.

HOPE, GRAHAM
Misconduct, Play
Taxi to Paradise 1933 d: Adrian Brunel. lps: Binnie Barnes, Garry Marsh, Henry Wilcoxon. 45M UKN. prod/rel: George Smith Films, Fox

HOPE, LAURENCE
The Garden of Karma, Poem
Indian Love Lyrics, The 1923 d: Sinclair Hill. lps: Catherine Calvert, Owen Nares, Malvina Longfellow. 6920f UKN. prod/rel: Stoll

HOPKINS, ARTHUR (1878–1950), USA, Hopkins, Arthur Melanchton
Burlesque, New York 1927, Play
Dance of Life, The 1929 d: John Cromwell, A. Edward Sutherland. lps: Hal Skelly, Nancy Carroll, Dorothy Revier. 13r USA. *Burlesque* prod/rel: Paramount Famous Lasky Corp.

Swing High, Swing Low 1937 d: Mitchell Leisen. lps: Carole Lombard, Fred MacMurray, Charles Butterworth. 95M USA. *Morning Noon and Night* prod/rel: Paramount Pictures©

When My Baby Smiles at Me 1948 d: Walter Lang. lps: Betty Grable, Dan Dailey, Jack Oakie. 98M USA. *Burlesque* prod/rel: 20th Century-Fox

HOPKINS, JOHN
This Story of Yours, 1969, Play
Offence, The 1973 d: Sidney Lumet. lps: Sean Connery, Trevor Howard, Vivien Merchant. 112M UKN. *Something Like the Truth* prod/rel: United Artists, Tantallon

HOPKINS, NEJE
Creation's Tears, Short Story
Woman There Was, A 1919 d: J. Gordon Edwards. lps: Theda Bara, Robert Elliott, William B. Davidson. 5r USA. prod/rel: Fox Film Corp., William Fox©

HOPKINS, SEWARD W.
Fate in the Balance, Novel
Gray Towers Mystery, The 1919 d: John W. Noble. lps: Gladys Leslie, Frank Morgan, Warner Richmond. 5r USA. *The Grey Towers Mystery*; *Fate in the Balance* prod/rel: Vitagraph Co. of America©

HOPPER, JAMES
Father and Son, 1924, Short Story
Win That Girl 1928 d: David Butler. lps: David Rollins, Sue Carol, Tom Elliott. 5337f USA. prod/rel: Fox Film Corp.

HOPWOOD, AVERY
Play
Mustergatte, Der 1937 d: Wolfgang Liebeneiner. lps: Heinz Ruhmann, Leny Marenbach, Hans Sohnker. 95M GRM. *Model Husband* (USA) prod/rel: Omega, N.F.

The Bat, New York 1926, Play
Bat, The 1926 d: Roland West. lps: George Beranger, Charles W. Herzinger, Emily Fitzroy. 8219f USA. prod/rel: Feature Productions, United Artists
Bat Whispers, The 1930 d: Roland West. lps: Chester Morris, Una Merkel, Chance E. Ward. 70M USA. prod/rel: United Artists Corp., Art Cinema Corp.

The Best People, New York 1924, Play
Best People, The 1925 d: Sidney Olcott. lps: Warner Baxter, Esther Ralston, Kathlyn Williams. 5700f USA. prod/rel: Famous Players-Lasky Corp., Paramount Pictures
Fast and Loose 1930 d: Fred Newmeyer. lps: Miriam Hopkins, Carole Lombard, Frank Morgan. 75M USA. *The Best People* prod/rel: Paramount-Publix Corp.

Clothes, New York 1906, Play
Clothes 1914 d: Francis Powers. lps: Charlotte Ives, House Peters, Edward MacKay. 4r USA. prod/rel: Famous Players Film Co., State Rights
Clothes 1920 d: Fred Sittenham. lps: Olive Tell, Crauford Kent, Cyril Chadwick. 5r USA. prod/rel: Metro Pictures Corp.©

Fair and Warmer, New York 1915, Play
Fair and Warmer 1919 d: Henry Otto. lps: May Allison, Pell Trenton, Eugene Pallette. 6r USA. prod/rel: Screen Classics, Inc., Metro Pictures Corp.©
Mustergatte, Der 1959 d: Karl Suter. lps: Walter Roderer, Sylvia Frank, Hannes Schmidthauser. 97M SWT. *Le Mari Modele*; *So Ein Mustergatte* prod/rel: Urania-Filmproduktion

Getting Gertie's Garter, New York 1921, Play
Getting Gertie's Garter 1927 d: E. Mason Hopper. lps: Marie Prevost, Charles Ray, Harry Myers. 6859f USA. prod/rel: Metropolitan Pictures Corp. of Calif., Producers Distributing Corp.
Getting Gertie's Garter 1945 d: Allan Dwan. lps: Dennis O'Keefe, Marie McDonald, Barry Sullivan. 72M USA. prod/rel: United Artists, Edward Small
Night of the Garter 1933 d: Jack Raymond. lps: Sydney Howard, Winifred Shotter, Elsie Randolph. 86M UKN. prod/rel: British and Dominions, United Artists

The Girl in the Limousine, New York 1919, Play
Girl in the Limousine, The 1924 d: Larry Semon. lps: Larry Semon, Claire Adams, Charlie Murray. 5630f USA. prod/rel: Chadwick Pictures, Associated First National Pictures

The Gold Diggers of Broadway, New York 1919, Play
Gold Diggers of 1933 1933 d: Mervyn Leroy. lps: Joan Blondell, Ruby Keeler, Aline MacMahon. 96M USA. *High Life* prod/rel: Warner Bros. Pictures©
Gold Diggers of Broadway 1929 d: Roy Del Ruth. lps: Nancy Welford, Conway Tearle, Winnie Lightner. 98M USA. prod/rel: Warner Brothers Pictures
Gold Diggers, The 1923 d: Harry Beaumont. lps: Hope Hampton, Wyndham Standing, Louise FazendA. 5600f USA. prod/rel: Warner Brothers Pictures
Painting the Clouds With Sunshine 1951 d: David Butler. lps: Dennis Morgan, Virginia Mayo, Gene Nelson. 87M USA. *Gold Diggers in Las Vegas* prod/rel: Warner Bros.

Judy Forgot, New York 1910, Play
Judy Forgot 1915 d: T. Hayes Hunter. lps: Marie Cahill, Sam Hardy. 5r USA. prod/rel: Universal Film Mfg. Co.©, Broadway Universal Feature

Ladies' Night in a Turkish Bath, Play
Ladies' Night in a Turkish Bath 1928 d: Eddie Cline. lps: Dorothy MacKaill, Jack Mulhall, Sylvia Ashton. 6592f USA. *Ladies' Night* (UKN) prod/rel: Asher-Small-Rogers, First National Pictures

The Little Clown, Play
Little Clown, The 1921 d: Thomas N. Heffron. lps: Mary Miles Minter, Jack Mulhall, Winter Hall. 5031f USA. prod/rel: Realart Pictures

Little Miss Bluebeard, Play
Marions-Nous 1931 d: Louis Mercanton. lps: Fernand Gravey, Pierre Etchepare, Alice CoceA. 94M FRN. *Sa Nuit de Noces* prod/rel: Films Paramount

Nobody's Widow, New York 1910, Play
Nobody's Widow 1927 d: Donald Crisp. lps: Leatrice Joy, Charles Ray, Phyllis Haver. 6421f USA. prod/rel: de Mille Pictures, Producers Distributing Corp.

Our Little Wife, New York 1916, Play
Mia Moglie Si Diverte 1939 d: Paul Verhoeven. lps: Kathe von Nagy, Albert Matterstock, Paul Kemp. 88M ITL. prod/rel: Itala Film, E.N.I.C.

Our Little Wife 1918 d: Eddie Dillon. lps: Madge Kennedy, George Forth, William B. Davidson. 6r USA. prod/rel: Goldwyn Pictures Corp.©, Goldwyn Distributing Corp.

Sadie Love, New York 1915, Play
Sadie Love 1919 d: John S. Robertson. lps: Billie Burke, James L. Crane, Ida Waterman. 4426f USA. *Twin Souls* prod/rel: Famous Players-Lasky Corp.©, Paramount-Artcraft Pictures

This Woman - This Man, New York 1909, Play
Guilty of Love 1920 d: Harley Knoles. lps: Dorothy Dalton, Edward Langford, Julia Hurley. 4989f USA. *This Woman -This Man* prod/rel: Famous Players-Lasky Corp.©, Paramount-Artcraft Pictures

Why Men Leave Home, New York 1922, Play
Why Men Leave Home 1924 d: John M. Stahl. lps: Lewis Stone, Helene Chadwick, Mary Carr. 8002f USA. prod/rel: Louis B. Mayer Productions, Associated First National Pictures

HORA, JIRI
Bartova Pomsta, Play
Soud Bozi 1938 d: Jiri Slavicek. lps: Frantisek Kreuzmann, Svetla Svozilova, Vera GabrielovA. 2429m CZC. *The Court of God* prod/rel: Lucernafilm

HORAN, EDWARD A.
All the King's Horses, New York 1934, Musical Play
All the King's Horses 1935 d: Frank Tuttle. lps: Carl Brisson, Mary Ellis, Edward Everett Horton. 86M USA. *Be Careful Young Lady* prod/rel: Paramount Productions, Inc.

HOREJSI, JINDRICH
Provdam Svou Zenu, Play
Provdam Svou Zenu 1941 d: Miroslav Cikan. lps: Vlasta Burian, Svetla Svozilova, Jaroslav Marvan. 2316m CZC. *I'll Give My Wife in Marriage* prod/rel: Slavia-Film, Tobis

HORELOVE, ELISKY
Stesti Ma Imeno Jonas, Novel
Stesti Ma Imeno Jonas 1986 d: Libuse KoutnA. lps: Katrin Babinska, Jaroslava Obermaierova, Jiri Krampol. 60M CZC. prod/rel: Cine Aktuel, Ceskoslovenka Tv

HORGAN, PAUL (1903–1995), USA
A Distant Trumpet, New York 1960, Novel
Distant Trumpet, A 1964 d: Raoul Walsh. lps: Troy Donahue, Suzanne Pleshette, Diane McBain. 117M USA. prod/rel: Warner Bros.

HORIE, KENICHI
Taiheiyo Hitoribotchi, Book
Taiheiyo Hitoribotchi 1963 d: Kon IchikawA. lps: Yujiro Ishihara, Masayuki Mori, Kinuyo TanakA. 104M JPN. *Alone on the Pacific* (USA); *Alone in the Pacific*; *My Enemy the Sea*; *Taiheiyo Hitori Bochi*; *The Enemy the Sea* prod/rel:

HORLER, SIDNEY
The Ball of Fortune, Novel
Ball of Fortune, The 1926 d: Hugh Croise. lps: Billy Meredith, James Knight, Mabel Poulton. 6500f UKN. prod/rel: Mercury Film Service
The Honourable Member for Outside Left, Short Story
Honourable Member for Outside Left, The 1925 d: Sinclair Hill. lps: Eric Bransby Williams. 2050f UKN. prod/rel: Stoll
The House of Secrets, London 1926, Novel
House of Secrets, The 1929 d: Edmund Lawrence. lps: Joseph Striker, Marcia Manning, Elmer Grandin. 6400f USA. prod/rel: Chesterfield Motion Picture Corp.
House of Secrets, The 1936 d: Roland Reed. lps: Muriel Evans, Sidney Blackmer, Noel Madison. 70M USA. prod/rel: Chesterfield Motion Picture Corp.©
Romeo and Julia, Novel
Two's Company 1936 d: Tim Whelan. lps: Ned Sparks, Gordon Harker, Mary Brian. 74M UKN. prod/rel: British and Dominions, Soskin Films

HORMAN, ARTHUR T.
The Big Frame, Story
Undertow 1949 d: William Castle. lps: Scott Brady, John Russell, Dorothy Hart. 71M USA. *The Big Frame* prod/rel: Universal-International

HORMANN, SHERRY
Tiger Lowe Panther, Novel
Tiger, Lowe, Panther 1989 d: Dominik Graf. lps: Natja Brunckhorst, Martina Gedeck, Sabine Kaack. TVM. 97M GRM.

HORN, ALFRED ALOYSIUS
Trader Horn, New York 1927, Book
Trader Horn 1931 d: W. S. Van Dyke. lps: Harry Carey, Edwina Booth, Duncan Renaldo. 123M USA. prod/rel: Metro-Goldwyn-Mayer Corp., Metro-Goldwyn-Mayer Dist. Corp.©

HORN, ANDREW
The Big Blue, Short Story
Big Blue, The 1987 d: Andrew Horn. lps: David Brisbin, Taunie Vernon, Sheila McLaughlin. 100M USA/GRM. prod/rel: Angelika

HORN, HOLLOWAY
Eyes of Fate, Story
Eyes of Fate 1933 d: Ivar Campbell. lps: Allan Jeayes, Valerie Hobson, Terence de Marney. 59M UKN. prod/rel: Sound City, Universal

HORN, TOM
Life of Tom Horn Government Scout and Interpreter, Autobiography
Tom Horn 1979 d: William Wiard. lps: Steve McQueen, Linda Evans, Richard Farnsworth. 98M USA. *Horn* prod/rel: Warner Bros.

HORNBLOW, ARTHUR
By Right of Conquest, New York 1909, Novel
Isle of Conquest, The 1919 d: Edward Jose. lps: Norma Talmadge, Natalie Talmadge, Wyndham Standing. 5-6r USA. *The Broken Barrier*; *By Right of Conquest*; *The Call of Nature* prod/rel: Norma Talmadge Film Co., Select Pictures Corp.©
The Mask, New York 1913, Novel
Mask, The 1921 d: Bertram Bracken. lps: Jack Holt, Hedda Nova, Mickey Moore. 7r USA. prod/rel: Col. William N. Selig, Export & Import Film Co.
The Profligate, Novel
Profligate, The 1915. lps: E. H. Calvert, Ruth Stonehouse, Bryant Washburn. 3r USA. prod/rel: Essanay

HORNBURG, MICHAEL
Bongwater, Novel
Bongwater 1998 d: Richard Sears. lps: Luke Wilson, Alicia Witt, Amy Locane. 98M USA. prod/rel: Alliance Independent Films

HORNBY, NICK
Fever Pitch, Book
Fever Pitch 1996 d: David Evans. lps: Colin Firth, Ruth Gemmell, Neil Pearson. 102M UKN. prod/rel: Film Four Distributors, Channel Four Films

HORNE, KENNETH (1900–, UKN
Fools Rush in, London 1946, Play
Fools Rush in 1949 d: John Paddy Carstairs. lps: Sally Ann Howes, Guy Rolfe, Nora Swinburne. 82M UKN. prod/rel: General Film Distributors, Pinewood
Jane Steps Out, 1934, Play
Jane Steps Out 1938 d: Paul L. Stein. lps: Jean Muir, Diana Churchill, Peter Murray Hill. 71M UKN. prod/rel: Associated British Picture Corporation
A Lady Mislaid, 1948, Play
Lady Mislaid, A 1958 d: David MacDonald. lps: Phyllis Calvert, Alan White, Thorley Walters. 59M UKN. prod/rel: Ab-Pathe, Welwyn

HORNEZ, ANDRE
Baratin, Opera
Baratin 1957 d: Jean Stelli. lps: Roger Nicolas, Ginette Baudin, Anne-Marie Carrieres. 85M FRN. prod/rel: Films Hergi/ Raymond Horvilleur

HORNIMAN, ROY
Play
Education of Elizabeth, The 1921 d: Eddie Dillon. lps: Billie Burke, Lumsden Hare, Edith Sharpe. 4705f USA. prod/rel: Famous Players-Lasky, Paramount Pictures
Bellamy the Magnificent, London 1904, Novel
Bedtime Story, A 1933 d: Norman Taurog. lps: Maurice Chevalier, Helen Twelvetrees, Baby Leroy. 87M USA. *A Way to Love* prod/rel: Paramount Productions, Inc.
Gentleman of Paris, A 1927 d: Harry d'Abbadie d'Arrast. lps: Adolphe Menjou, Shirley O'Hara, Arlette Marchal. 5927f USA. prod/rel: Paramount Famous Lasky Corp.
Israel Rank, Novel
Kind Hearts and Coronets 1949 d: Robert Hamer. lps: Dennis Price, Valerie Hobson, Joan Greenwood. 106M UKN. prod/rel: Ealing Studios, General Film Distributors
A Non-Conformist Parson, Novel
Non-Conformist Parson, A 1919 d: A. V. Bramble. lps: Gwen Williams, George Keene, Constance Worth. 6500f UKN. *Heart and Soul* prod/rel: British Lion, Moss

HORNUNG, E. W. (1866–1921), UKN, Hornung, Ernest William
Story
Return of Raffles, The 1932 d: Mansfield Markham. lps: George Barraud, Camilla Horn, Claud Allister. 71M UKN. prod/rel: Markham, Williams & Pritchard

The Amateur Cracksman, London 1899, Novel
Raffles 1930 d: Harry d'Abbadie d'Arrast (Uncredited), George Fitzmaurice. lps: Ronald Colman, Kay Francis, Bramwell Fletcher. 80M USA. prod/rel: Samuel Goldwyn, Inc., United Artists

Raffles 1940 d: Sam Wood. lps: David Niven, Olivia de Havilland, Dudley Digges. 72M USA. *Colonel Rowan of Scotland Yard* prod/rel: United Artists Corp., Howard Productions

Raffles, the Amateur Cracksman 1917 d: George Irving. lps: John Barrymore, Frederick Perry, H. Cooper Cliffe. 7r USA. prod/rel: Hyclass Producing Co.©, L. Lawrence Weber Photo Dramas, Inc.

Raffles, the Amateur Cracksman 1925 d: King Baggot. lps: House Peters, Miss Du Pont, Hedda Hopper. 5557f USA. prod/rel: Universal Pictures

Dead Men Tell No Tales, New York 1899, Novel
Dead Men Tell No Tales 1920 d: Tom Terriss. lps: Catherine Calvert, Percy Marmont, Holmes Herbert. 6154f USA. prod/rel: Vitagraph Co. of America©, Tom Terriss Production

Mr. Justice Raffles, 1909, Novel
Mr. Justice Raffles 1921 d: Gerald Ames, Gaston Quiribet. lps: Gerald Ames, Eileen Dennes, James Carew. 5810f UKN. prod/rel: Hepworth

The Shadow of the Rope, New York 1902, Novel
Out of the Shadow 1919 d: Emile Chautard. lps: Pauline Frederick, Wyndham Standing, Ronald Byram. 4102f USA. *The Shadow of a Rope* prod/rel: Famous Players-Lasky Corp.©, Paramount Pictures

Stingaree, New York 1905, Novel
Stingaree 1915 d: James W. Horne. lps: True Boardman, William Brunton, Janet Rambeau. SRL. 24r USA. prod/rel: Kalem

Stingaree 1916. ASL.

Stingaree 1934 d: William A. Wellman. lps: Richard Dix, Irene Dunne, Mary Boland. 76M USA. prod/rel: RKO Radio Pictures©

Stingaree Stories, Story
At the Sign of the Kangaroo 1917 d: Paul C. Hurst. lps: True Boardman, Paul Hurst, Barney Furey. 2r USA. prod/rel: Kalem

HOROWITZ, ANTHONY
The Falcon's Malteser, Novel
Just Ask for Diamond 1988 d: Stephen Bayley. lps: Peter Eyre, Susannah York, Rene Ruiz. 94M UKN. *The Falcon's Malteser; Diamond's Edge* (USA) prod/rel: Zenith, Red Rooster

HOROWITZ, STEVEN
Calling Dr. Horowitz, Book
Bad Medicine 1985 d: Harvey Miller. lps: Steve Guttenberg, Alan Arkin, Julie Hagerty. 96M USA. prod/rel: 20th Century Fox, Lantana

HORST, J.
Der Herr Kanzleirat, Play
Herr Kanzleirat, Der 1948 d: Hubert MarischkA. lps: Hans Moser, Egon von Jordan, Hedy Fassler. 105M AUS. prod/rel: Donau

HORSTER, HANS ULRICH, Rhein, Eduard
Ein Herz Spielt Falsch, Novel
Herz Spielt Falsch, Ein 1953 d: Rudolf Jugert. lps: O. W. Fischer, Ruth Leuwerik, Gertrud Kuckelmann. 110M GRM. *The Heart Plays Differently* prod/rel: Georg Witt, Bavaria

Der Rote Rausch, Novel
Rote Rausch, Der 1962 d: Wolfgang Schleif. lps: Klaus Kinski, Brigitte Grothum, Sieghardt Rupp. 88M GRM. *Red Rage* prod/rel: Rex, Nora

Ein Student Ging Vorbei, Novel
Student Ging Vorbei, Ein 1960 d: Werner Klinger. lps: Luise Ullrich, Paul Dahlke, Eva Bartok. 93M GRM. *A Student Just Went Past* prod/rel: Hubler-Kahla, N.F.

HORSTER, HANS ULRICH
Suchkind 312, Novel
Suchkind 312 1955 d: Gustav Machaty. lps: Inge Egger, Paul Klinger, Ingrid Simon. 100M GRM. *Lost Child No. 312* prod/rel: Unicorn, N.F.

Die Toteninsel, Novel
Toteninsel, Die 1955 d: Victor Tourjansky. lps: Willy Birgel, Inge Egger, Folke Sundquist. 100M GRM. *Island of the Dead* prod/rel: Unicorn, N.F.

HORTON, ROBERT J.
A Man of Action, Short Story
Rip Roarin' Roberts 1924 d: Richard Thorpe. lps: Buddy Roosevelt, Brenda Lane, Joe Rickson. 4660f USA. prod/rel: Approved Pictures, Weiss Brothers Artclass Pictures

Walloping Wallace 1924 d: Richard Thorpe. lps: Buddy Roosevelt, Violet La Plante, Lew Meehan. 4830f USA. *Range Riders of the Great Wild West* prod/rel: Approved Pictures, Weiss Brothers Artclass Pictures

HORUK, SOL
Impresario, Book
Tonight We Sing 1953 d: Mitchell Leisen. lps: David Wayne, Tamara Toumanova, Ezio PinzA. 113M USA. prod/rel: 20th Century-Fox

HOSCHNA, K.
The Girl of My Dreams, New York 1911, Musical Play
Girl of My Dreams, The 1918 d: Louis W. Chaudet. lps: Billie Rhodes, Leo Pierson, Frank MacQuarrie. 6r USA. prod/rel: National Film Corp. of America, Exhibitors Mutual Distributing Corp.

HOSCHNA, KARL
Madame Sherry, New York 1910, Musical Play
Madame Sherry 1917 d: Ralph Dean. lps: Gertrude McCoy, Frank L. A. O'Connor, Lucy Carter. 5r USA. prod/rel: Authors' Film Co., State Rights

HOSKIN, E.
The World's Best Girl, Novel
Romance of a Movie Star, The 1920 d: Richard Garrick. lps: Violet Hopson, Stewart Rome, Gregory Scott. UKN. prod/rel: Broadwest, Walturdaw

HOSKINS, PERCY
Burn the Evidence, Short Story
Burnt Evidence 1954 d: Daniel Birt. lps: Jane Hylton, Duncan Lamont, Donald Gray. 61M UKN. prod/rel: Act Films, Monarch

Dangerous Cargo, Short Story
Dangerous Cargo 1954 d: John Harlow. lps: Susan Stephen, Jack Watling, Karel Stepanek. 61M UKN. prod/rel: Act Films, Monarch

Gunman, Short Story
Blue Parrot, The 1953 d: John Harlow. lps: Dermot Walsh, Jacqueline Hill, Ballard Berkeley. 69M UKN. prod/rel: Act Films, Monarch

HOSLER, EMIL
Was Frauen Traumen, Novel
One Exciting Adventure 1934 d: Ernst L. Frank. lps: Binnie Barnes, Neil Hamilton, Paul Cavanagh. 73M USA. *What Ladies Dream*; *Escapade* prod/rel: Universal Pictures Co.©

HOSTOVSKY, EGON
Le Vertige de Minuit, Novel
Espions, Les 1957 d: Henri-Georges Clouzot. lps: Curd Jurgens, O. E. Hasse, Vera Clouzot. 125M FRN/ITL. prod/rel: Vera Films, Filmsonor

Ztraceny Stin, Novel
Vyderac 1937 d: Ladislav Brom. lps: Vitezslav Bocek, Adina Mandlova, Bedrich Vrbsky. 2447m CZC. *Blackmailer* prod/rel: Reiter

HOSTRUP, JENS CHRISTIAN
Gjenboerne, 1844, Play
Genboerne 1939 d: Arne Weel. lps: Sigurd Langberg, Karen Marie Lowert, Carl Alstrup. 100M DNM. prod/rel: ASA Film

HOTCHNER, A. E.
Novel
Man Who Lived at the Ritz, The 1988 d: Desmond Davis. lps: Perry King, Leslie Caron, Cherie Lunghi. TVM. 200M UKN/USA/FRN. *The Man Who Stayed at the Ritz*

HOUGH, EMERSON (1857–1923), USA
The Broken Coin, Story
Broken Coin, The 1915 d: Francis Ford, Grace Cunard. lps: Francis Ford, Eddie Polo, Normand MacDonald. SRL. 44r USA. prod/rel: Universal Film Mfg. Co.

The Broken Gate, New York 1917, Novel
Broken Gate, The 1920 d: Paul Scardon. lps: Bessie Barriscale, Joseph Kilgour, Marguerite de La Motte. 6300f USA. prod/rel: J. L. Frothingham Productions, W. W. Hodkinson Corp.

Broken Gate, The 1927 d: James C. McKay. lps: Dorothy Phillips, William Collier Jr., Jean Arthur. 5600f USA. prod/rel: Tiffany Productions

One Hour of Love 1927 d: Robert Florey. lps: Jacqueline Logan, Robert Fraser, Montagu Love. 6500f USA. prod/rel: Tiffany Productions

The Campbells are Coming, Short Story
Campbells are Coming, The 1915 d: Francis Ford, Grace Cunard. lps: Francis Ford, Grace Cunard, Mr. Denecke. 4r USA. prod/rel: Universal Film Mfg. Co.©, Broadway Universal Feature

The Covered Wagon, New York 1922, Novel
Covered Wagon, The 1923 d: James Cruze. lps: Lois Wilson, J. Warren Kerrigan, Ernest Torrence. 9407f USA. prod/rel: Famous Players-Lasky, Paramount Pictures

The Man Next Door, New York 1917, Novel
Man Next Door, The 1923 d: Victor Schertzinger. lps: David Smith, David Torrence, Frank Sheridan, James Morrison. 6945f USA. prod/rel: Vitagraph Co. of America

North of 36, New York 1923, Novel
Conquering Horde, The 1931 d: Edward Sloman. lps: Richard Arlen, Fay Wray, George MendozA. 75M USA. *Stampede* prod/rel: Paramount Publix Corp.

North of 36 1924 d: Irvin V. Willat. lps: Jack Holt, Ernest Torrence, Lois Wilson. 7908f USA. prod/rel: Famous Players-Lasky, Paramount Pictures

The Sagebrusher, New York 1919, Novel
Sagebrusher, The 1920 d: Edward Sloman. lps: Roy Stewart, Marguerite de La Motte, Noah Beery. 7r USA. *Out of the Dark* prod/rel: the Great Authors Pictures, Inc.©, W. W. Hodkinson Corp.

Ship of Souls, New York 1925, Novel
Ship of Souls 1925 d: Charles Miller. lps: Bert Lytell, Lillian Rich, Gertrude Astor. 6r USA. prod/rel: Encore Pictures, Associated Exhibitors

HOUGH, RICHARD
Captain Bligh and Mr. Christian, Book
Mutiny on the Bounty 1983 d: Roger Donaldson. lps: Mel Gibson, Anthony Hopkins, Laurence Olivier. 132M USA/UKN. *The Saga of H.M.S. Bounty*; *The Bounty* prod/rel: Dino de Laurentiis

HOUGH, STANLEY L.
MacE, Short Story
Bandolero! 1968 d: Andrew V. McLaglen. lps: James Stewart, Dean Martin, Raquel Welch. 106M USA. prod/rel: Twentieth Century-Fox Film Corp.

HOUGH, W.
The Time the Place and the Girl, New York 1907, Musical Play
Time, the Place and the Girl, The 1929 d: Howard Bretherton. lps: Grant Withers, Betty Compson, Gertrude Olmstead. 6339f USA. prod/rel: Warner Brothers Pictures

HOUGHTON, STANLEY (1881–1913), UKN, Houghton, William Stanley
Hindle Wakes, London 1912, Play
Hindle Wakes 1918 d: Maurice Elvey. lps: Norman McKinnel, Colette O'Neil, Hayford Hobbs. 5250f UKN. prod/rel: Diamond, Super

Hindle Wakes 1927 d: Maurice Elvey. lps: Estelle Brody, John Stuart, Norman McKinnel. 8800f UKN. *Fanny Hawthorne* (USA) prod/rel: Gaumont

Hindle Wakes 1931 d: Victor Saville. lps: Sybil Thorndike, John Stuart, Norman McKinnel. 79M UKN. prod/rel: Gaumont

Hindle Wakes 1952 d: Arthur Crabtree. lps: Lisa Daniely, Leslie Dwyer, Brian Worth. 82M UKN. *Holiday Week* (USA) prod/rel: Monarch

HOUGRON, JEAN (1923–, FRN
Je Reviendrai a Kandara, Novel
Je Reviendrai a Kandara 1956 d: Victor Vicas. lps: Daniel Gelin, Bella Darvi, Francois Perier. 102M FRN. prod/rel: Jad Films

Mort En Fraude, Novel
Mort En Fraude 1956 d: Marcel Camus. lps: Daniel Gelin, Anne Mechard, Lucien Callamand. 105M FRN. *Fugitive in Saigon* (USA) prod/rel: Intermondia

HOUSEHOLD, GEOFFREY (1900–1988), UKN, Household, Geoffrey Edward West
Brandy for the Parson, Novel
Brandy for the Parson 1952 d: John Eldridge. lps: James Donald, Kenneth More, Jean Lodge. 78M UKN. prod/rel: Group Three, Associated British Film Distributors

Dance of the Dwarfs, Novel
Jungle Heat 1984 d: Gus Trikonis. lps: Peter Fonda, Deborah Raffin, John Amos. 93M USA. *Dance of the Dwarfs* prod/rel: Dove Inc., Panache

Rogue Male, 1939, Novel
Man Hunt 1941 d: Fritz Lang. lps: Walter Pidgeon, Joan Bennett, George Sanders. 95M USA. prod/rel: 20th Century Fox

Rogue Male 1976 d: Clive Donner. lps: Peter O'Toole, Alastair Sim, John Standing. TVM. 96M UKN. prod/rel: BBC, 20th Century Fox

A Rough Shoot, Novel
Rough Shoot 1952 d: Robert Parrish. lps: Joel McCrea, Evelyn Keyes, Herbert Lom. 86M UKN. *Shoot First* (USA) prod/rel: Raymond Stross, United Artists

Watcher in the Shadows, Novel
Deadly Harvest 1972 d: Michael O'Herlihy. lps: Richard Boone, Patty Duke, Michael Constantine. TVM. 73M USA. prod/rel: CBS, Inc.

HOUSEMAN, LAURENCE (1865–1959), UKN
Consider Your Verdict, Radio Play
Consider Your Verdict 1938 d: Roy Boulting. lps: Marius Goring, Manning Whiley, George Carney. 37M UKN. prod/rel: Charter, Anglo

Victoria Regina, London 1937, Play
Victoria the Great 1937 d: Herbert Wilcox. lps: Anna Neagle, Anton Walbrook, Walter RillA. 112M UKN. prod/rel: Imperator, Radio

HOUSMAN, L.
Prunella; Or Love in a Dutch Garden, London 1904, Play
Prunella 1918 d: Maurice Tourneur. lps: Marguerite Clark, Jules Raucourt, Henry Leone. 4742f USA. prod/rel: Famous Players-Lasky Corp.©, Paramount Pictures

HOUSTON, JEANNE WAKATSUKI
Farewell to Manzanar, Book
Farewell to Manzanar 1976 d: John Korty. lps: Yuki Shumoda, Nobu McCarthy, Akemi KikimurA. TVM. 105M USA. prod/rel: Universal, Korty Films, Inc.

HOUSTON, NORMAN
The Love Bandit, 1921, Play
Love Bandit, The 1924 d: Dell Henderson. lps: Doris Kenyon, Victor Sutherland, Jules Cowles. 5800f USA. prod/rel: Charles E. Blaney Productions, Vitagraph Co. of America

Man Bait, Story
Man Bait 1926 d: Donald Crisp. lps: Marie Prevost, Kenneth Thomson, Douglas Fairbanks Jr. 5947f USA. prod/rel: Metropolitan Pictures Corp. of Calif., Producers Distributing Corp.

HOUSTON, ROBERT
Monday Tuesday Wednesday, Novel
Killing Affair, A 1988 d: David Saperstein. lps: Peter Weller, Kathy Baker, John Glover. 100M USA. *My Sister's Keeper; Sister's Keeper* prod/rel: Hemdale

HOUSUM, ROBERT
The Gipsy Trail, New York 1917, Play
Gypsy Trail, The 1918 d: Walter Edwards. lps: Bryant Washburn, Wanda Hawley, Casson Ferguson. 5r USA. *The Gipsy Trail* prod/rel: Paramount Pictures, Famous Players-Lasky Corp.©

A Very Good Young Man, New York 1918, Play
Very Good Young Man, A 1919 d: Donald Crisp. lps: Bryant Washburn, Helene Chadwick, Julia Faye. 4350f USA. prod/rel: Famous Players-Lasky Corp.©, Paramount Pictures

HOUTS, MARSHALL
Who Killed Sir Harry Oakes?, Book
Eureka 1982 d: Nicolas Roeg. lps: Gene Hackman, Theresa Russell, Rutger Hauer. 129M USA/UKN. prod/rel: MGM, United Artists

HOVICK, LOUISE
Doll Face, Play
Doll Face 1945 d: Lewis Seiler. lps: Vivian Blaine, Dennis O'Keefe, Perry Como. 81M USA. *Come Back to Me* (UKN) prod/rel: 20th Century Fox

HOWARD, BRONSON (1842–1908), USA
Aristocracy, New York 1892, Play
Aristocracy 1914 d: Thomas N. Heffron. lps: Tyrone Power Sr., Marguerite Skirvin, Edna Mayo. 4r USA. prod/rel: Famous Players Film Co., Paramount Pictures Corp.

The Banker's Daughter, New York 1878, Play
Banker's Daughter, The 1914 d: Edward M. Roskam, William F. Haddock. lps: Katherine La Salle, David Wall, William H. Tooker. 5r USA. prod/rel: Life Photo Film Corp.©, State Rights

The Henrietta, New York 1887, Play
Saphead, The 1920 d: Herbert Blache. lps: Buster Keaton, Carol Holloway, William H. Crane. 6650f USA. prod/rel: Metro Pictures Corp.©

One of Our Girls, New York 1885, Play
One of Our Girls 1914 d: Thomas N. Heffron. lps: Hazel Dawn, Hal Clarendon, William Roselle. 4r USA. prod/rel: Famous Players Film Co., State Rights

Shenandoah, Play
Shenandoah 1913 d: Kenean Buel. lps: Robert Vignola, Henry Hallam, Alice Hollister. 3000f USA. prod/rel: Kalem

The Young Mrs. Winthrop, New York 1882, Play
Young Mrs. Winthrop 1915 d: Richard Ridgely. lps: Mrs. Wallace Erskine, Robert Conness, Mabel Trunnelle. 2r USA. prod/rel: Edison
Young Mrs. Winthrop 1920 d: Walter Edwards. lps: Ethel Clayton, Harrison Ford, Helen Dunbar. 4707f USA. prod/rel: Famous Players-Lasky Corp.©, Paramount-Artcraft Pictures

HOWARD, CLARK
Short Story
Last of the Good Guys, The 1978 d: Theodore J. Flicker. lps: Robert Culp, Dennis Dugan, Richard NaritA. TVM. 100M USA. prod/rel: Columbia Pictures

The Arm, Novel
Big Town, The 1987 d: Ben Bolt. lps: Matt Dillon, Diane Lane, Tommy Lee Jones. 110M USA. *The Arm* prod/rel: Columbia

HOWARD, CLIFFORD
Blossom, Short Story
Locked Lips 1920 d: William C. Dowlan. lps: Tsuru Aoki, Stanhope Wheatcroft, Magda Lane. 5r USA. prod/rel: Universal Film Mfg. Co.©

The Closing Chapter, Story
Closing Chapter, The 1915 d: Murdock MacQuarrie. lps: Murdock MacQuarrie, Adele Farrington. 3r USA. prod/rel: Big U

HOWARD, ELIZABETH JANE (1923–, UKN
Story
Mr. Wrong 1986 d: Gaylene Preston. lps: Heather Bolton, David Letch, Gary Stalker. 89M NZL. *Dark of the Night* (USA) prod/rel: New Zealand Film Commission, Barclays

After Julius, Novel
After Julius 1979 d: John Glenister. lps: Faith Brook, Petra Markham, Paul Copley. MTV. UKN. prod/rel: Yorkshire Tv

Getting It Right, Novel
Getting It Right 1989 d: Randall Kleiser. lps: Jesse Birdsall, Helena Bonham-Carter, Peter Cook. 102M UKN/USA. prod/rel: Mceg

Something in Disguise, Novel
Something in Disguise 1982 d: Moira Armstrong. lps: Anton Rodgers, Elizabeth Garvie, Richard Vernon. MTV. 312M UKN. prod/rel: Thames Tv

HOWARD, ERIC
Pards in Paradise, Short Story
Gunfire 1935 d: Harry L. Fraser. lps: Rex Bell, Ruth Mix, Buzz Barton. 56M USA. prod/rel: Resolute Productions, State Rights

HOWARD, GEORGE BRONSON (1884–1922), USA
Birds of Prey; Being Pages from the Book of Broadway, New York 1918, Novel
Birds of Prey 1927 d: William James Craft. lps: Priscilla Dean, Hugh Allan, Gustav von Seyffertitz. 6008f USA. prod/rel: Columbia Pictures

The Black Book, New York 1920, Novel
Man from Headquarters, The 1928 d: Duke Worne. lps: Cornelius Keefe, Edith Roberts, Charles West. 5946f USA. prod/rel: Trem Carr Productions

Devil's Chaplain, New York 1922, Novel
Devil's Chaplain 1929 d: Duke Worne. lps: Cornelius Keefe, Virginia Brown Faire, Josef Swickard. 5451f USA. prod/rel: Trem Carr Productions, Rayart Pictures

God's Man, New York 1915, Novel
God's Man 1917 d: George Irving. lps: H. B. Warner, Kate Lester, Albert Tavernier. 9r USA. prod/rel: Frohman Amusement Corp., State Rights

The Higher Law, Story
Higher Law, The 1914 d: Charles Giblyn. lps: Murdock MacQuarrie, Pauline Bush, Lon Chaney. 2r USA. prod/rel: Bison

The Oubliette, Story
Oubliette, The 1914 d: Charles Giblyn. lps: Murdock MacQuarrie, Pauline Bush, Doc Crane. 3r USA. prod/rel: Bison

A Romance of New York Yesterday and Today, New York 1911, Novel
Enemy to Society, An 1915 d: Edgar Jones. lps: Hamilton Revelle, Lois Meredith, H. Cooper Cliffe. 5r USA. prod/rel: Columbia Pictures Corp., Metro Pictures Corp.©

Snobs, New York 1911, Play
Snobs 1915 d: Oscar Apfel. lps: Victor Moore, Anita King, Constance Johnson. 5r USA. prod/rel: Jesse L. Lasky Feature Play Co.©, Paramount Pictures Corp.

HOWARD, HARTLEY
Department K, London 1964, Novel
Assignment K 1967 d: Val Guest. lps: Stephen Boyd, Camilla Sparv, Leo McKern. 97M UKN. *Department K* prod/rel: Gildor Films, Mazurka Productions

HOWARD, JENNIFER
The Wager, Short Story
Gentleman's Agreement 1935 d: George Pearson. lps: Frederick Peisley, Vivien Leigh, Antony Holles. 71M UKN. prod/rel: British and Dominions, Paramount British

HOWARD, JOSEPH
The Time the Place and the Girl, New York 1907, Musical Play
Time, the Place and the Girl, The 1929 d: Howard Bretherton. lps: Grant Withers, Betty Compson, Gertrude Olmstead. 6339f USA. prod/rel: Warner Brothers Pictures

HOWARD, KEBLE
The Fast Lady, Short Story
Fast Lady, The 1962 d: Ken Annakin. lps: James Robertson Justice, Leslie Phillips, Stanley Baxter. 95M UKN. prod/rel: Rank Film Distributors, Independent Artists

The God in the Garden, Novel
God in the Garden, The 1921 d: Edwin J. Collins. lps: Edith Craig, Arthur Pusey, Mabel Poulton. 5510f UKN. prod/rel: Master, Butcher's Film Service

King of the Castle, Play
King of the Castle 1925 d: Henry Edwards. lps: Marjorie Hume, Brian Aherne, Dawson Millward. 6950f UKN. prod/rel: Stoll

Lord Babs, London 1928, Play
Lord Babs 1932 d: Walter Forde. lps: Bobby Howes, Jean Colin, Pat Paterson. 65M UKN. prod/rel: Gainsborough, Ideal

Miss Charity, Novel
Miss Charity 1921 d: Edwin J. Collins. lps: Margery Meadows, Dick Webb, Joan Lockton. 5000f UKN. prod/rel: Master, Butcher's Film Service

HOWARD, LEIGH
Blind Date, Novel
Blind Date 1959 d: Joseph Losey. lps: Hardy Kruger, Stanley Baker, Micheline Presle. 95M UKN. *Chance Meeting* (USA) prod/rel: Rank Film Distributors, Independent Artists

HOWARD, PAUL
Chains of Bondage, Novel
Chains of Bondage 1916 d: A. E. Coleby. lps: Basil Gill, Evelyn Millard, Arthur Rooke. 4000f UKN. prod/rel: I. B. Davidson, Tiger

HOWARD, PETER
Decision at Midnight, Novel
Decision at Midnight 1963 d: Lewis Allen. lps: Martin Landau, Nora Swinburne, Walter Fitzgerald. 93M USA. prod/rel: R.a.M.

Give a Dog a Bone, Play
Give a Dog a Bone 1967 d: Henry Cass. lps: Ronnie Stevens, Peter Davies, Ivor Danvers. 77M UKN. prod/rel: Westminster, Moral Rearmament

Happy Deathday, Play
Happy Deathday 1969 d: Henry Cass. lps: Cyril Luckham, Harry Baird, Clement McCallin. 89M UKN. prod/rel: Moral Rearmament, Westminster

The Hurricane, London 1960, Novel
Voice of the Hurricane 1964 d: George Fraser. lps: Muriel Smith, Phyllis Konstam, Reginald Owen. 80M USA. *The Hurricane* prod/rel: Ram Productions, Moral Re-Armament

Mr. Brown Comes Down the Hill, Play
Mr. Brown Comes Down the Hill 1966 d: Henry Cass. lps: Eric Flynn, Mark Heath, Lillias Walker. 88M UKN. prod/rel: Moral Rearmament, Westminster

Pay the Piper, Novel
Intimate Stranger, The 1956 d: Joseph Losey. lps: Richard Basehart, Mary Murphy, Constance Cummings. 95M UKN. *The Guilty Secret* (USA); *Finger of Guilt* prod/rel: Anglo-Guild, Anglo-Amalgamated

HOWARD, SIDNEY COE (1891–1939), USA, Howard, Sidney
Half Gods, New York 1929, Play
Free Love 1931 d: Hobart Henley. lps: Conrad Nagel, Genevieve Tobin, Monroe Owsley. 70M USA. *Blind Wives; The Modern Wife* prod/rel: Universal Pictures Corp.©

Lucky Sam McCarver, New York 1925, Play
We're All Gamblers 1927 d: James Cruze. lps: Thomas Meighan, Marietta Millner, Cullen Landis. 5935f USA. prod/rel: Paramount Famous Lasky Corp.

Ned McCobb's Daughter, Play
Ned McCobb's Daughter 1929 d: William J. Cowen. lps: Irene Rich, Theodore Roberts, Robert Armstrong. 6015f USA. prod/rel: Pathe Exchange, Inc.

Ode to Liberty, Washington, D.C. 1934, Play
He Stayed for Breakfast 1940 d: Alexander Hall. lps: Loretta Young, Melvyn Douglas, Alan Marshall. 89M USA. prod/rel: Columbia Pictures Corp.©

The Silver Cord, New York 1926, Play
Silver Cord, The 1933 d: John Cromwell. lps: Irene Dunne, Joel McCrea, Laura Hope Crews. 76M USA. prod/rel: RKO Radio Pictures©, Pandro S. Berman Production

They Knew What They Wanted, New York 1924, Play
Lady to Love, A 1929 d: Victor Sjostrom. lps: Vilma Banky, Edward G. Robinson, Robert Ames. 8142f USA. *Sunkissed* prod/rel: Metro-Goldwyn-Mayer Pictures
Secret Hour, The 1928 d: Rowland V. Lee. lps: Pola Negri, Jean Hersholt, Kenneth Thomson. 7194f USA. *Beggars of Love* prod/rel: Paramount Famous Lasky Corp.

They Knew What They Wanted 1940 d: Garson Kanin. lps: Carole Lombard, Charles Laughton, William Gargan. 96M USA. prod/rel: RKO Radio Pictures©
Yellow Jack, New York 1934, Play
Yellow Jack 1938 d: George B. Seitz. lps: Robert Montgomery, Virginia Bruce, Lewis Stone. 83M USA. prod/rel: Metro-Goldwyn-Mayer Corp., Loew's, Inc.©

HOWARD, WALTER
The Lifeguardsman, Play
Lifeguardsman, The 1916 d: Frank G. Bayley. lps: Annie Saker, Alfred Paumier, Leslie Carter. 4279f UKN. prod/rel: British Actors, Int-Ex
The Prince and the Beggarmaid, London 1908, Play
Prince and the Beggar Maid, The 1921 d: A. V. Bramble. lps: Henry Ainley, Kathleen Vaughan, Harvey Braban. 4960f UKN. prod/rel: Ideal
The Story of the Rosary, London 1913, Play
Story of the Rosary, The 1920 d: Percy Nash. lps: Malvina Longfellow, Dick Webb, Charles Vane. 5000f UKN. prod/rel: Master Films, British Exhibitors' Films
Two Little Drummer Boys, Play
Two Little Drummer Boys 1928 d: G. B. Samuelson. lps: Wee Georgie Wood, Alma Taylor, Paul Cavanagh. 7500f UKN. prod/rel: Samuelson, Victoria

HOWARTH, DAVID
Novel
Ni Liv 1957 d: Arne Skouen. lps: Jack Fjeldstad, Henny Moan, Alf Malland. 80M NRW. *We Die Alone; Nine Lives* prod/rel: Interessentskapet Ni Liv, W. Munter Rolfsen

HOWATCH, SUSAN (1940–, UKN
Penmaric, Novel
Penmaric 1979 d: Tina Wakerell, Derek Martinus. lps: Ralph Bates, Paul Darrow, June Ellis. MTV. 619M UKN.

HOWE, GEORGE LOCKE
Call It Treason, 1949, Book
Decision Before Dawn 1951 d: Anatole Litvak. lps: Richard Basehart, Gary Merrill, Oskar Werner. 119M USA. prod/rel: 20th Century-Fox

HOWE, JULIA WARD (1819–1910), USA
The Battle Hymn of the Republic, Short Story
Battle Hymn of the Republic, The 1911 d: Larry Trimble. lps: Ralph Ince, Julia Swayne Gordon, Edith Storey. SHT USA. prod/rel: Vitagraph Co. of America

HOWE, TINA
Painting Churches, Play
Portrait, The 1993 d: Arthur Penn. lps: Gregory Peck, Lauren Bacall, Cecilia Peck. TVM. 85M USA.

HOWELL, DOROTHY
The Black Sheep, Story
Guilty? 1930 d: George B. Seitz. lps: Virginia Valli, John Holland, John St. Polis. 67M USA. prod/rel: Columbia Pictures
The Lightning Express, Story
Rich Men's Sons 1927 d: Ralph Graves. lps: Ralph Graves, Shirley Mason, Robert Cain. 5854f USA. prod/rel: Columbia Pictures
The Lost House, Story
Kid Sister, The 1927 d: Ralph Graves. lps: Marguerite de La Motte, Ann Christy, Malcolm McGregor. 5477f USA. *Her Sister's Honour* prod/rel: Columbia Pictures
The Spice of Life, Story
Quitter, The 1929 d: Joseph Henabery. lps: Ben Lyon, Dorothy Revier, Fred Kohler. 5671f USA. prod/rel: Columbia Pictures

HOWKER, JANNI
The Nature of the Beast, Novel
Nature of the Beast, The 1988 d: Franco Rosso. lps: Lynton Dearden, Paul Simpson, Tony Melody. 96M UKN. prod/rel: Rosso Productions, Film Four International

HOWSON, ALBERT S.
A Dog of the Regiment, Story
Dog of the Regiment, A 1927 d: D. Ross Lederman. lps: Rin-Tin-Tin, Dorothy Gulliver, Tom Gallery. 5003f USA. prod/rel: Warner Brothers Pictures

HOYLAND, JOHN
The Ivy Garland, Novel
Out of the Darkness 1985 d: John Krish. lps: Gary Halliday, Michael Flowers, Emma Ingham. 68M UKN. prod/rel: Rank, Children's Film & Television Foundation

HOYT, CHARLES HALE
A Black Sheep and How It Came to Washington, New York 1896, Musical Play
Black Sheep, A 1915 d: Thomas N. Heffron. lps: Otis Harlan, James Bradbury, Grace Darmond. 5r USA. prod/rel: Selig Polyscope Co.©, Selig Red Seal Play
A Bunch of Keys, 1882, Play
Bunch of Keys, A 1915 d: Richard Foster Baker. lps: Johnny Slavin, William Burress, June Keith. 5r USA. prod/rel: Essanay Film Mfg. Co.©, V-L-S-E, Inc.

A Midnight Bell, Play
Midnight Bell, A 1913 d: Charles H. France. lps: Clara Dale, Theodore Gamble, Thomas Commerford. 2000f USA. prod/rel: Selig
Midnight Bell, A 1921 d: Charles Ray. lps: Charles Ray, Donald MacDonald, Van Dyke Brooke. 6140f USA. prod/rel: Charles Ray Productions, Associated First National Pictures
A Texas Steer, 1890, Play
Texas Steer, A 1915 d: Giles R. Warren. lps: Tyrone Power Sr., Grace Darmond, Frances Bayless. 5r USA. prod/rel: Selig Polyscope Co.©, Red Seal Play of Quality
Texas Steer, A 1927 d: Richard Wallace. lps: Will Rogers, Louise Fazenda, Sam Hardy. 7418f USA. prod/rel: Sam E. Rork Productions, First National Pictures
A Trip to Chinatown, Short Story
Trip to Chinatown, A 1926 d: Robert Kerr, George Marshall (Spv). lps: Margaret Livingston, Earle Foxe, J. Farrell MacDonald. 5594f USA. prod/rel: Fox Film Corp.

HOYT, HARRY O.
The Five of Spades, Story
Avenging Rider, The 1943 d: Sam Nelson. lps: Tim Holt, Cliff Edwards, Ann Summers. 55M USA. prod/rel: RKO
Triple Trouble, Short Story
Adorable Deceiver, The 1926 d: Phil Rosen. lps: Alberta Vaughn, Daniel Makarenko, Harland Tucker. 4879f USA. prod/rel: R-C Pictures, Film Booking Offices of America

HOYT, VANCE JOSEPH
Malibu, Boston 1931, Novel
Sequoia 1934 d: Chester M. Franklin. lps: Jean Parker, Russell Hardie, Samuel S. Hinds. 79M USA. *Malibu* prod/rel: Monogram Pictures Corp.©

HRABAL, BOHUMIL (1914–, CZC
Story
Intimni Osvetleni 1965 d: Ivan Passer. lps: Vera Kresadlova, Zdenek Bezusek, Karel Blazek. 72M CZC. *Intimate Lightning* (UKN) prod/rel: Filmove Studio Barrandov
Slavnosti Snezenek 1983 d: Jiri Menzel. lps: Rudolf Hrusinsky, Jaromir Hanzlik, Jiri Schmitzer. 95M CZC. *Snowdrop Festival* (USA); *The Snowdrop Festivities* prod/rel: Filmove Studio Barrandov
Ostre Sledovane Vlaky, Prague 1965, Novel
Ostre Sledovane Vlaky 1966 d: Jiri Menzel. lps: Vlastimil Brodsky, Vaclav Neckar, Jitka BendovA. 101M CZC. *Closely Observed Trains* (UKN); *Well Guarded Trains; On the Lookout for Trains; A Difficult Love; Special Priority Trains* prod/rel: Filmove Studio Barrandov
Postriziny, 1976, Short Story
Postriziny 1980 d: Jiri Menzel. lps: Jiri Schmitzer, Magda Vasaryova, Rudolfy Hrusinsky. 98M CZC. *Cutting It Short* (UKN); *Short Cut* (USA); *Clippings; Cuttings*

HU KE
Huai Shu Zhuang, Play
Huai Shu Zhuang 1962 d: Wang Ping. lps: Hu Peng, Kong Rui, Ge Zhenbang. 11r CHN. *Huaishu Village; Locust Tree Village* prod/rel: August First Film Studio

HU WANCHUN
Jia Ting Wen Ti, Novel
Jia Ting Wen Ti 1964 d: Fu Chaowu. lps: Zhang Fa, Zhang Liang, Zhao Lian. 10r CHN. *Family Matters* prod/rel: Tianma Film Studio

HU ZHENG
Feng Shui Chang Liu, Novel
Feng Shui Chang Liu 1963 d: Sha Meng. lps: Gao Baocheng, Wang Zhigang, Zhang Ping. 11r CHN. *The Feng River Flows Far* prod/rel: Beijing Film Studio

HUANG HUIZHONG
Tu Tan Yu Qiao Niu, Novel
Tu Tan Yu Qiao Niu 1994 d: Lei XIanhe, Li Jun. lps: Lu Liang, Li Ting, Li Yongtian. 9r CHN. *Bald-Cop and Girl Student* prod/rel: Changchun Film Studio

HUBALEK, CLAUS
Der Hauptmann Und Sein Held, Novel
Hauptmann Und Sein Held, Der 1955 d: Max Nosseck. lps: Jo Herbst, Ingeborg Schoner, Ernst Schroder. 85M GRM. *The Captain and His Hero* prod/rel: C.C.C., Defir

HUBBARD, ELBERT
A Message to Garcia, 1899, Essay
Message to Garcia, A 1916 d: Richard Ridgely. lps: Mabel Trunnelle, Robert Conness, Herbert Prior. 4691f USA. prod/rel: Thomas A. Edison, Inc.©, K-E-S-E Service
Message to Garcia, A 1936 d: George Marshall. lps: Wallace Beery, Barbara Stanwyck, John Boles. 85M USA. prod/rel: Twentieth Century-Fox Film Corp.©

HUBBARD, GEORGE
Short Story
Gauntlet, The 1920 d: Edwin L. Hollywood. lps: Harry T. Morey, Louiszita Valentine, Frank Hagney. 4629f USA. *The Gauntlet of Greed* prod/rel: Vitagraph Co. of America©
Where the Heat Lies, 1922, Short Story
Love Gambler, The 1922 d: Joseph J. Franz. lps: John Gilbert, Carmel Myers, Bruce (4) Gordon. 4682f USA. prod/rel: Fox Film Corp.
Without Compromise, New York 1922, Novel
Without Compromise 1922 d: Emmett J. Flynn. lps: William Farnum, Lois Wilson, Robert McKim. 5173f USA. prod/rel: Fox Film Corp.

HUBBARD, PHILIP
East Is East, Play
East Is East 1916 d: Henry Edwards. lps: Florence Turner, Henry Edwards, Ruth MacKay. 4895f UKN. prod/rel: Turner Films, Butcher

HUBBELL, RAYMOND
Sonny, New York 1921, Play
Sonny 1922 d: Henry King. lps: Richard Barthelmess, Margaret Seddon, Pauline Garon. 6968f USA. prod/rel: Inspiration Pictures, Associated First National Pictures

HUBER, HELMUTH
Story
Begegnung in Salzburg 1964 d: Max Friedmann. lps: Curd Jurgens, Nadia Gray, Viktor de KowA. 100M GRM/FRN. *Encounter in Salzburg* prod/rel: Bamberger, Paris-Inter

HUBERT, HENRI
Le Gars du Milieu, Play
Nuit de Folies, Une 1934 d: Maurice Cammage. lps: Fernandel, Jacques Varennes, Marcelle Parysis. 90M FRN. prod/rel: Fortuna-Film-Production

HUBLER, RICHARD G.
I've Got Mine, 1946, Novel
Beachhead 1954 d: Stuart Heisler. lps: Tony Curtis, Frank Lovejoy, Mary Murphy. 89M USA. prod/rel: United Artists, Aubrey Schenck

HUCH, RICARDA (1864–1947), GRM
Der Fall Deruga, 1917, Novel
Fall Deruga, Der 1938 d: Fritz Peter Buch. lps: Willy Birgel, Geraldine Katt, Dagny Servaes. 106M GRM. prod/rel: Universum, Schorcht
..Und Nichts Als Die Wahrheit 1958 d: Franz Peter Wirth. lps: O. W. Fischer, Marianne Koch, Ingrid Andree. 96M GRM. *..and Nothing But the Truth*
Der Letzte Sommer, 1902, Novel
Letzte Sommer, Der 1954 d: Harald Braun. lps: Hardy Kruger, Mathias Wieman, Liselotte Pulver. 110M GRM. *The Last Summer* prod/rel: N.D.F., Bavaria

HUCKABY, ELIZABETH
Book
Crisis at Central High 1981 d: Lamont Johnson. lps: Joanne Woodward, Charles Durning, Henderson Forsythe. TVM. 125M USA. prod/rel: CBS, Time-Life

HUDSON, W. H. (1841–1922), ARG, Hudson, William Henry
Green Mansions, 1904, Novel
Green Mansions 1959 d: Mel Ferrer. lps: Audrey Hepburn, Anthony Perkins, Lee J. Cobb. 104M USA. prod/rel: MGM

HUFFAKER, CLAIR (1927–1990), USA
Badman, New York 1957, Novel
War Wagon, The 1967 d: Burt Kennedy. lps: John Wayne, Kirk Douglas, Howard Keel. 101M USA. prod/rel: Batjac Productions, Universal
Flaming Star, Novel
Flaming Star 1960 d: Don Siegel. lps: Elvis Presley, Barbara Eden, Steve Forrest. 101M USA. prod/rel: 20th Century Fox
Guns of Rio Conchos, Greenwich CT. 1964, Novel
Rio Conchos 1964 d: Gordon Douglas. lps: Stuart Whitman, Richard Boone, Anthony FranciosA. 107M USA. prod/rel: 20th Century-Fox Film Corporation
Nobody Loves a Drunken Indian, New York 1967, Novel
Flap 1969 d: Carol Reed. lps: Anthony Quinn, Claude Akins, Tony Bill. 106M USA. *The Last Warrior* (UKN); *Nobody Loves Flapping Eagle; Nobody Loves a Drunken Indian* prod/rel: Warner Bros. Pictures
Posse from Hell, New York 1958, Novel
Posse from Hell 1961 d: Herbert Coleman. lps: Audie Murphy, Zohra Lampert, John Saxon. 89M USA. prod/rel: Universal Pictures
Seven Ways from Sundown, Novel
Seven Ways from Sundown 1960 d: Harry Keller. lps: Audie Murphy, Barry Sullivan, Venetia Stevenson. 86M USA. prod/rel: Universal

HUFFINGTON, ARIANNA STASSINOPOULOS
Picasso: Creator and Destroyer, Book
   Surviving Picasso 1996 d: James Ivory. lps: Anthony Hopkins, Natascha McElhone, Julianne Moore. 123M USA/UKN. prod/rel: Wolper, Merchant Ivory

HUGGINS, ROSS
Appointment With Fear, Novel
   State Secret 1950 d: Sidney Gilliat. lps: Douglas Fairbanks Jr., Glynis Johns, Jack Hawkins. 104M UKN. *The Great Manhunt* prod/rel: British Lion Production Assets, London Films

HUGGINS, ROY
Story
   3,000 Mile Chase, The 1977 d: Russ Mayberry. lps: Glenn Ford, Cliff de Young, Blair Brown. TVM. 100M USA. *The Three-Thousand Mile Chase* prod/rel: Public Arts Prods., Universal TV
Appointment With Fear, Story
   Good Humor Man, The 1950 d: Lloyd Bacon. lps: Jack Carson, Lola Albright, George Reeves. 79M USA. prod/rel: Columbia
Double Take, Story
   I Love Trouble 1947 d: S. Sylvan Simon. lps: Franchot Tone, Janet Blair, Janis Carter. 94M USA. prod/rel: Columbia, Cornell Prods.
Too Late for Tears, 1947, Serial Story
   Too Late for Tears 1949 d: Byron Haskin. lps: Lizabeth Scott, Don Defore, Dan DuryeA. 99M USA. *Killer Bait* prod/rel: United Artists, Streamline Pictures

HUGHES, DAVID
The Pork Butcher, Novel
   Souvenir 1988 d: Geoffrey Reeve. lps: Christopher Plummer, Catherine Hicks, Christopher Cazenove. 93M UKN. *The Pork Butcher* prod/rel: Curzon, Fancy Free

HUGHES, DOROTHY B.
The Fallen Sparrow, Novel
   Fallen Sparrow, The 1943 d: Richard Wallace. lps: John Garfield, Maureen O'Hara, Walter Slezak. 94M USA. prod/rel: RKO Radio
The Hanged Man, Novel
   Hanged Man, The 1965 d: Don Siegel. lps: Edmond O'Brien, Vera Miles, Robert Culp. TVM. 87M USA. prod/rel: Universal
In a Lonely Place, Novel
   In a Lonely Place 1950 d: Nicholas Ray. lps: Humphrey Bogart, Gloria Grahame, Frank Lovejoy. 94M USA. *Behind This Mask* prod/rel: Columbia, Santana Pictures
Ride the Pink Horse, Novel
   Ride the Pink Horse 1947 d: Robert Montgomery. lps: Robert Montgomery, Wanda Hendrix, Thomas Gomez. 101M USA. prod/rel: Universal-International

HUGHES, HATCHER (1881–1945), USA
Hell-Bent Fer Heaven, New York 1924, Play
   Hell-Bent Fer Heaven 1926 d: J. Stuart Blackton. lps: Patsy Ruth Miller, John Harron, Gayne Whitman. 6578f USA. *The Hypocrite*; *Hell-Bent for Heaven* prod/rel: Warner Brothers Pictures

HUGHES, KEN
High Wray, Novel
   House Across the Lake, The 1954 d: Ken Hughes. lps: Alex Nicol, Hillary Brooke, Sidney James. 69M UKN. *Heatwave* (USA) prod/rel: Hammer, Ab-Pathe
Sammy, 1958, Television Play
   Small World of Sammy Lee, The 1963 d: Ken Hughes. lps: Anthony Newley, Robert Stephens, Wilfrid Brambell. 107M UKN. prod/rel: Bryanston, Seven Arts Productions

HUGHES, LANGSTON (1902–1967), USA, Hughes, James Langston
Thank You M'am, 1963, Short Story
   Thank You, M'am 1976 d: Andrew Sugerman. 12M USA.

HUGHES, LLEWELLYN
Chap Called Barwell, 1929, Short Story
   Sky Hawk, The 1929 d: John G. Blystone. lps: Helen Chandler, John Garrick, Gilbert Emery. 6888f USA. prod/rel: Fox Film Corp.
Heartbreak, 1931, Short Story
   Heartbreak 1931 d: Alfred L. Werker. lps: Charles Farrell, Madge Evans, Paul Cavanagh. 59M USA. *Love and War* prod/rel: Fox Film Corp.

HUGHES, RICHARD (1900–1977), UKN
A High Wind in Jamaica, London 1929, Novel
   High Wind in Jamaica, A 1965 d: Alexander MacKendrick. lps: Anthony Quinn, James Coburn, Dennis Price. 103M UKN. prod/rel: 20th Century-Fox

HUGHES, RUPERT
All for a Girl, New York 1908, Play
   All for a Girl 1915 d: Roy Applegate. lps: Renee Kelly, Roy Applegate, Frank de Vernon. 5r USA. *All for the Love of a Girl* prod/rel: Mirograph Corp., State Rights

The Bridge, New York 1909, Play
   Bigger Man, The 1915 d: John W. Noble. lps: Henry Kolker, Elsie Balfour, Orlando Daly. 5r USA. *The Better Man*; *The Bridge Or the Bigger Man* prod/rel: Rolfe Photoplays, Inc., Metro Pictures Corp.
Canavan the Man Who Had His Way, 1909, Short Story
   Danger Signal, The 1915 d: Walter Edwin. lps: Arthur Hoops, Ruby Hoffman, John Davidson. 5r USA. *Canavan - the Man Who Had His Way* prod/rel: George Kleine, Klein-Edison Feature Service
   Hold Your Horses 1921 d: E. Mason Hopper. lps: Tom Moore, Sylvia Ashton, Naomi Childers. 5r USA. prod/rel: Goldwyn Pictures
   It Had to Happen 1936 d: Roy Del Ruth. lps: George Raft, Rosalind Russell, Leo Carrillo. 79M USA. prod/rel: Twentieth Century-Fox Film Corp.
The Cup of Fury, New York 1919, Novel
   Cup of Fury, The 1920 d: T. Hayes Hunter. lps: Helene Chadwick, Rockliffe Fellowes, Frank Leigh. 6-7r USA. prod/rel: Eminent Authors Pictures, Inc., Goldwyn Distributing Corp.
Don't You Care!, 1914, Short Story
   Don't 1925 d: Alf Goulding. lps: Sally O'Neil, John Patrick, Bert Roach. 5529f USA. *The Rebellious Girl* prod/rel: Metro-Goldwyn-Mayer Pictures
Empty Pockets, New York 1915, Novel
   Empty Pockets 1918 d: Herbert Brenon. lps: Ketty Galanta, Barbara Castleton, Bert Lytell. 6r USA. prod/rel: Herbert Brenon Film Corp., First National Exhibitors Circuit
Excuse Me, New York 1911, Play
   Excuse Me 1915 d: Henry W. Savage. lps: George F. Marion, Robert Fischer, Harrison Ford. 5r USA. prod/rel: Henry W. Savage, Inc., Pathe Exchange, Inc.
   Excuse Me 1924 d: Alf Goulding. lps: Norma Shearer, Conrad Nagel, Renee Adoree. 5747f USA. prod/rel: Metro-Goldwyn Pictures
From the Ground Up, 1921, Short Story
   From the Ground Up 1921 d: E. Mason Hopper. lps: Tom Moore, Helene Chadwick, De Witt Jennings. 4532f USA. prod/rel: Goldwyn Pictures
The Girl on the Barge, 1927, Short Story
   Girl on the Barge, The 1929 d: Edward Sloman. lps: Jean Hersholt, Sally O'Neill, Malcolm McGregor. 7510f USA. prod/rel: Universal Pictures
Kidnapt, 1933, Short Story
   Miss Fane's Baby Is Stolen 1934 d: Alexander Hall. lps: Dorothea Wieck, Alice Brady, William Frawley. 70M USA. *Kidnapped* (UKN) prod/rel: Paramount Productions
Ladies' Man, New York 1930, Novel
   Ladies' Man 1931 d: Lothar Mendes. lps: William Powell, Kay Francis, Carole Lombard. 76M USA. prod/rel: Paramount Publix Corp.
Miss 318 and Mr. 37, Story
   Out of the Ruins 1915 d: Ashley Miller. lps: Mabel Trunnelle, Pat O'Malley, Nellie Grant. 3r USA. prod/rel: Edison
The Mobilization of Johanna, 1917, Short Story
   Johanna Enlists 1918 d: William D. Taylor. lps: Mary Pickford, Emory Johnson, Anne Schaefer. 4388f USA. *Mobilizing of Johanna* prod/rel: Pickford Film Corp., Famous Players-Lasky Corp.
Nina of the Theatre, Story
   Nina of the Theatre 1914 d: George Melford. lps: Alice Joyce, Tom Moore, Jere Austin. 2r USA. prod/rel: Kalem
No One Man, New York 1931, Novel
   No One Man 1932 d: Lloyd Corrigan. lps: Carole Lombard, Ricardo Cortez, Paul Lukas. 73M USA. prod/rel: Paramount Publix Corp.
Obscurity, Story
   Breach of Promise 1932 d: Paul L. Stein. lps: Chester Morris, Mae Clarke, Mary Doran. 67M USA. prod/rel: World Wide Pictures, Inc.
The Old Nest, 1911, Short Story
   Old Nest, The 1921 d: Reginald Barker. lps: T. D. Crittenden, Mary Alden, Nick Cogley. 8021f USA. prod/rel: Goldwyn Pictures
Patent Leather Kid, 1927, Short Story
   Patent Leather Kid, The 1927 d: Alfred Santell. lps: Richard Barthelmess, Molly O'Day, Lawford Davidson. 12r USA. prod/rel: First National Pictures
The President's Mystery Sotyr, 1935, Novel
   President's Mystery, The 1936 d: Phil Rosen. lps: Henry Wilcoxon, Betty Furness, Evelyn Brent. 81M USA. *One for All* (UKN) prod/rel: Republic Pictures Corp.
She Goes to War, Short Story
   She Goes to War 1929 d: Henry King. lps: Eleanor Boardman, John Holland, Edmund Burns. 9500f USA. prod/rel: Inspiration Pictures, United Artists

Souls for Sale, New York 1922, Novel
   Souls for Sale 1923 d: Rupert Hughes. lps: Eleanor Boardman, Mae Busch, Barbara La Marr. 7864f USA. prod/rel: Goldwyn Pictures
The Thirteenth Commandment, New York 1916, Novel
   Thirteenth Commandment, The 1920 d: Robert G. VignolA. lps: Ethel Clayton, Charles Meredith, Monte Blue. 5r USA. *Impulses* prod/rel: Famous Players-Lasky Corp., Paramount-Artcraft Pictures
True As Steel, 1923, Short Story
   True As Steel 1924 d: Rupert Hughes. lps: Aileen Pringle, Huntley Gordon, Cleo Madison. 7r USA. prod/rel: Goldwyn Pictures, Metro-Goldwyn Distributing Corp.
Two Women, New York 1910, Play
   Ghosts of Yesterday, The 1918 d: Charles Miller. lps: Norma Talmadge, Eugene O'Brien, Stuart Holmes. 6r USA. *Two Women* prod/rel: Norma Talmadge Film Corp., Select Pictures Corp.
The Unpardonable Sin, New York 1918, Novel
   Unpardonable Sin, The 1919 d: Marshall Neilan. lps: Blanche Sweet, Matt Moore, Wallace Beery. 9r USA. prod/rel: Harry Garson
We Can't Have Everything, New York 1917, Novel
   We Can't Have Everything 1918 d: Cecil B. de Mille. lps: Kathlyn Williams, Elliott Dexter, Wanda Hawley. 6r USA. prod/rel: Famous Players-Lasky Corp., Cecil B. de Mille Production
What Will People Say?, New York 1914, Novel
   What Will People Say? 1915 d: Alice Blache. lps: Olga Petrova, Fraunie Fraunholz, Fritz de Lint. 5r USA. prod/rel: Popular Play and Players, Inc., Metro Pictures Corp.

HUGHES, THOMAS (1822–1896), UKN
Tom Brown's Schooldays, London 1857, Novel
   Tom Brown's Schooldays 1916 d: Rex Wilson. lps: Joyce Templeton, Jack Coleman, Jack Hobbs. 5700f UKN. prod/rel: Windsor, Int Ex
   Tom Brown's Schooldays 1940 d: Robert Stevenson. lps: Cedric Hardwicke, Freddie Bartholomew, Gale Storm. 86M USA. *Adventures at Rugby* prod/rel: RKO Radio Pictures, the Play's the Thing Productions
   Tom Brown's Schooldays 1951 d: Gordon Parry. lps: John Howard Davies, Robert Newton, Diana Wynyard. 96M UKN. prod/rel: Talisman, Renown

HUGO, VICTOR (1802–1885), FRN, Hugo, Victor Marie
Le Crucifix, Poem
   Crucifix, Le 1909 d: Louis Feuillade. 78m FRN. prod/rel: Gaumont
Ernani, 1830
   Ernani 1911 d: Louis J. Gasnier. lps: Francesca Bertini. 305m ITL. *Hernani* (UKN) prod/rel: la Milanese
La Gioconda, Play
   Tiranno Di Padova, Il 1947 d: Max Neufeld. lps: Clara Calamai, Elsa de Giorgi, Carlo Lombardi. F ITL. *Tyrant of Padua Angelo* prod/rel: Scalera Film
Hernani, Play
   Hernani 1910 d: Albert Capellani. lps: Paul Capellani, Henry Krauss, Jeanne Delvair. FRN. prod/rel: Scagl
L' Homme Qui Rit, 1869, Novel
   Man Who Laughs, The 1927 d: Paul Leni. lps: Conrad Veidt, Mary Philbin, Olga BaclanovA. 10r USA. prod/rel: Universal Pictures
   Uomo Che Ride, L' 1966 d: Sergio Corbucci. lps: Jean Sorel, Lisa Gastoni, Edmund Purdom. 105M ITL/FRN. *L' Homme Qui Rit* (FRN); *The Man With the Golden Mask*; *The Man Who Laughs* (USA) prod/rel: Sanson Film (Roma), Cipra (Paris)
Lucrece Borgia, Paris 1833, Play
   Eternal Sin, The 1917 d: Herbert Brenon. lps: Florence Reed, William E. Shay, Stephen Grattan. 6r USA. *Lucretia Borgia*; *The Queen Mother* prod/rel: Herbert Brenon Film Corp., Lewis J. Selznick Enterprises, Inc.
   Lucrece Borgia 1935 d: Abel Gance. lps: Edwige Feuillere, Gabriel Gabrio, Josette Day. 95M FRN. *Lucretia Borgia* prod/rel: Henri E. Ullmann
   Lucrecia Borgia 1947 d: Luis Bayon HerrerA. 90M ARG.
   Lucrezia Borgia 1940 d: Hans Hinrich. lps: Isa Pola, Friedrich Benfer, Carlo Ninchi. 76M ITL. prod/rel: Scalera Film
   Lucrezia Borgia, l'Amante Del Diavolo 1968 d: Osvaldo Civirani. lps: Olinka Berova, Lou Castel, Leon Askin. 102M ITL/AUS. *Lucrezia Borgia -Die Tochter Des Papstes* (AUS); *Lucrezia*; *Lucrezia Borgia -the Devil's Lover* prod/rel: Denwer Film (Roma), Vienna Film

Notti Di Lucrezia Borgia, Le 1959 d: Sergio Grieco. lps: Belinda Lee, Michele Mercier, Jacques Sernas. 110M ITL/FRN. *Les Nuits de Lucrece Borgia* (FRN); *Nights of Temptation* (UKN); *The Nights of Lucretia Borgia* (USA) prod/rel: Musa Cin.Ca (Napoli), Fides (Paris)

Marie Tudor, Play
Marie Tudor 1913 d: Albert Capellani. lps: Romuald Joube, Leon Bernard, Jeanne Delvair. 1600m FRN. prod/rel: Scagl

Marion Delorme, 1831, Play
Marion Delorme 1912 d: Albert Capellani. lps: Paul Capellani, Nelly Cormon, Henry Krauss. FRN. prod/rel: Pathe Freres
Marion Delorme 1918 d: Henry Krauss. lps: Nelly Cormon, Pierre Renoir, Pierre Alcover. 1500m FRN. prod/rel: Scagl

Les Miserables, Paris 1862, Novel
Bishop's Candlesticks, The 1913 d: Herbert Brenon. lps: Frank Smith, William E. Shay. 2r USA. prod/rel: Imp
Bouassa, El 1944 d: Kamel Salim. 120M EGY. *Les Miserables*; *Al- Bu'asa*
Ezai Padum Padu 1950 d: K. Ramnoth. lps: Chittor V. Nagaiah, Serukalathur Sama, Jawar Seetaraman. 198M IND. *Ezhai Padum Padi*; *Plight of the Poor*; *Les Miserables*; *Beedala Patlu* prod/rel: Pakshiraja Studios
Fantine; Or, a Mother's Love 1909 d: Van Dyke Brooke. lps: Mary Maurice. 997f USA. *A Mother's Love* prod/rel: Vitagraph Co. of America
Galley Slave, The 1909 d: J. Stuart Blackton (Spv). lps: Maurice Costello, William Humphrey, Charles Kent. 885f USA. prod/rel: Vitagraph Co. of America
Gavrosh 1937 d: Tatyana Lukashevich. 75M USS.
Jan Barujan 1931 d: Tomu UchidA. 163M JPN. *Jean Valjean*
Jean Valjean 1909. 990f USA. prod/rel: Vitagraph
Les Miserables 1918 d: Frank Lloyd. lps: William Farnum, Hardee Kirkland, Jewel Carmen. 9-10r USA. prod/rel: Fox Film Corp., William Fox©
Les Miserables 1922. lps: Lyn Harding. 1195f UKN. prod/rel: Master Films, British Exhibitors' Films
Les Miserables 1935 d: Richard Boleslawski. lps: Fredric March, Charles Laughton, Cedric Hardwicke. 108M USA. *Les Miserables* prod/rel: United Artists Corp, 20th Century Pictures©
Les Miserables 1952 d: Lewis Milestone. lps: Michael Rennie, Robert Newton, Debra Paget. 105M USA. prod/rel: 20th Century-Fox
Les Miserables 1978 d: Glenn Jordan. lps: Richard Jordan, Anthony Perkins, Cyril Cusack. TVM. 142M UKN/USA. prod/rel: CBS, Itc Entertainment
Les Miserables 1998 d: Bille August. lps: Liam Neeson, Geoffrey Rush, Uma Thurman. 134M USA. prod/rel: Sony Pictures Entertainment, Columbia Pictures
Miserabili, I 1947 d: Riccardo FredA. lps: Gino Cervi, Valentina Cortese, Hans Hinrich. 140M ITL. *Les Miserables* (USA) prod/rel: Lux Film
Miserables, Les 19— d: Marcel Bluwal. lps: Georges Geret, Nicole Jaket, Francois Marthouset. TVM. 245M FRN.
Miserables, Les 1912 d: Albert Capellani. lps: Marie Ventura, Mistinguett, Henry Krauss. 3450m FRN. prod/rel: Scagl
Miserables, Les 1925 d: Henri Fescourt. lps: Gabriel Gabrio, Sandra Milowanoff, Andree Rolane. 3500m FRN. prod/rel: Films De France, Societe Des Cineromans
Miserables, Les 1933 d: Raymond Bernard. lps: Harry Baur, Charles Vanel, Florelle. 266M FRN. prod/rel: Pathe-Natan
Miserables, Les 1957 d: Jean-Paul Le Chanois. lps: Jean Gabin, Daniele Delorme, Bernard Blier. 217M FRN/GRM/ITL. prod/rel: Serena Film, Soc. Pathe-Cinema
Miserables, Les 1982 d: Robert Hossein. lps: Lino Ventura, Michel Bouquet, Jean Carmet. 187M FRN. prod/rel: G.E.F., S.F.P.C.
Miserables, Les 1995 d: Claude Lelouch. lps: Jean-Paul Belmondo, Michel Boujenah, Alessandra Martines. 177M FRN. *Les Miserables du Vingtieme Siecle*; *Les Miserables du XXe Siecle* prod/rel: Films 13, Tf1
Miserables, Los 1943 d: Fernando A. Rivero. lps: Domingo Soler, Andres Soler, David SilvA. 103M MXC. *Les Miserables*
New Life, A 1909. 1000f USA. prod/rel: Edison
Ordeal, The 1909. 950f USA. prod/rel: Edison

Price of a Soul, The 1909 d: Edwin S. Porter. 560f USA. prod/rel: Edison
Re Mizeraburu 1950 d: Daisuke Ito, Masahiro Makino. 112M JPN. *Les Miserables*

Notre-Dame de Paris, Paris 1831, Novel
Nanbanji No Semushi-Otoko 1957 d: Torajiro Saito. lps: Achako Hanabishi, Naritoshi Hayashi, Shunji Sakai. 78M JPN. *Return to Manhood* prod/rel: Daiei Motion Picture Co.
Darling of Paris, The 1917 d: J. Gordon Edwards. lps: Theda Bara, Glenn White, Walter Law. 5r USA. prod/rel: Fox Film Corp., William Fox©
Esmeralda 1922 d: Edwin J. Collins. lps: Sybil Thorndike, Booth Conway, Arthur Kingsley. 1100f UKN. prod/rel: Master Films, British Exhibitors' Films
Hunchback of Notre Dame, The 1923 d: Wallace Worsley. lps: Lon Chaney, Ernest Torrence, Patsy Ruth Miller. 12r USA. prod/rel: Universal Pictures
Hunchback of Notre Dame, The 1939 d: William Dieterle. lps: Charles Laughton, Cedric Hardwicke, Thomas Mitchell. 117M USA. prod/rel: RKO Radio Pictures©
Hunchback of Notre Dame, The 1977 d: Alan Cooke. lps: Kenneth Haigh, Warren Clarke, Michelle Newell. TVM. 100M UKN. prod/rel: BBC
Hunchback of Notre Dame, The 1982 d: Michael Tuchner. lps: Anthony Hopkins, Derek Jacobi, Lesley-Anne Down. TVM. 150M UKN. *Hunchback* prod/rel: CBS, Columbia
Hunchback of Notre Dame, The 1996 d: Gary Trousdale, Kirk Wise. ANM. 86M USA. prod/rel: Walt Disney Pictures
Hunchback of Notre Dame, The 1997 d: Peter Medak. lps: Mandy Patinkin, Richard Harris, Salma Hayek. TVM. 96M CND/USA.
Notre Dame de Paris 1911 d: Albert Capellani. lps: Stacia Napierkowska, Henry Krauss, Claude Garry. 810m FRN. *The Hunchback of Notre Dame* (USA) prod/rel: Scagl, Serie D'art Pathe Freres
Notre Dame de Paris 1957 d: Jean Delannoy. lps: Gina Lollobrigida, Anthony Quinn, Robert Hirsch. 100M FRN/ITL. *Hunchback of Notre Dame*; *Notre-Dame de Paris* prod/rel: Panitalia, Paris Films Prods.

Les Pauvres Gens, 1859, Verse
Pauvres Gens, Les 1937 d: Antoine Mourre. lps: Pierre Alcover, Claude Roy, Marcelle Brou. 29M FRN.

Quatrevingt-Treize, 1874, Novel
Marchese Di Lantenac, La 1911. 151m ITL. *The Marquis of Lantenac* (UKN) prod/rel: S.A. Ambrosio

Le Roi S'amuse, 1832, Play
Duke's Jester, Or a Fool's Revenge, The 1909 d: J. Stuart Blackton (Spv). lps: Maurice Costello, William Humphrey. 945f USA. *A Fool's Revenge* prod/rel: Vitagraph Co. of America
Fool's Revenge, A 1909 d: D. W. Griffith. lps: Marion Leonard, Owen Moore, Florence Lawrence. 1000f USA. prod/rel: Biograph Co.
Re Si Diverte, Il 1941 d: Mario Bonnard. lps: Michel Simon, Maria Mercader, Paola BarbarA. 92M ITL. *The King's Jester* (USA); *Rigoletto* prod/rel: Scalera Film
Rigoletto 1922 d: George Wynn. lps: Wyn Richmond, Clive Brook, A. B. Imeson. 1124f UKN. prod/rel: Master Films, Gaumont
Rigoletto 1927 d: H. B. Parkinson. lps: Herbert Langley, Karina, A. B. Imeson. 1669f UKN. prod/rel: Song Films
Roi S'amuse, Le 1909 d: Albert Capellani. lps: Silvain, Paul Capellani, Marcelle Geniat. 350m FRN. prod/rel: Scagl

Ruy Blas, 1838, Play
Adventurer, The 1920 d: J. Gordon Edwards. lps: William Farnum, Estelle Taylor, Paul Cazeneuve. 6r USA. prod/rel: Fox Film Corp., William Fox©
Ruy Blas 1909 d: J. Stuart Blackton (Spv). lps: William Humphrey, Maurice Costello, Julia Arthur. 900f USA. prod/rel: Vitagraph Co. of America
Ruy Blas 1914 d: Lucius Henderson. lps: William Garwood. 3r USA. prod/rel: Majestic
Ruy Blas 1916. lps: Marquet, Albert Lambert, Gervais. 1900m FRN. prod/rel: Phoebus Film
Ruy Blas 1947 d: Pierre Billon. lps: Danielle Darrieux, Jean Marais, Marcel Herrand. 93M FRN/ITL. prod/rel: Andre Paulve, Georges Legrand
Ruy-Blas 1912. lps: Gustavo Serena, Francesca Bertini. 800m ITL. prod/rel: Film d'Arte Italiana

Les Travailleurs de la Mer, 1866, Novel
Sea Devils 1953 d: Raoul Walsh. lps: Yvonne de Carlo, Rock Hudson, Maxwell Reed. 90M UKN. prod/rel: Coronado, RKO-Radio
Toilers of the Sea 1923 d: R. William Neill. lps: Lucy Fox, Holmes Herbert, Horace Tesseron. 5128f USA/ITL. prod/rel: Community International Corp., Selznick Distributing Corp.
Toilers of the Sea 1936 d: Selwyn Jepson, Ted Fox. lps: Cyril McLaglen, Mary Lawson, Ian Colin. 83M UKN. prod/rel: L. C. Beaumont, Columbia
Travailleurs de la Mer, Les 1918 d: Andre Antoine. lps: Romuald Joube, Marc Gerard, Andree Brabant. 2160m FRN. prod/rel: Scagl

HUGON, ANDRE
Le Heros de la Marne, Novel
Heros de la Marne, Le 1938 d: Andre Hugon. lps: Raimu, Bernard Lancret, Germaine Dermoz. 93M FRN. *Heros de la Marne Jean Lefrancois*; *Heroes of the Marne* (USA) prod/rel: Productions Andre Hugon

HUGOT, GEORGES
Les Tribulations d'une Marraine, Play
Tribulations d'une Marraine, Les 1916. lps: Polin, Le Petit Abelard, Paule Morly. 630m FRN. prod/rel: Franco Film

HUIE, WILLIAM BRADFORD (1910–1986), USA
The Americanization of Emily, New York 1959, Novel
Americanization of Emily, The 1964 d: Arthur Hiller. lps: James Garner, Julie Andrews, Melvyn Douglas. 115M USA. *Emily* prod/rel: Filmways, Inc.
The Execution of Private Slovik, Book
Execution of Private Slovik, The 1974 d: Lamont Johnson. lps: Martin Sheen, Mariclare Costello, Ned Beatty. TVM. 120M USA. prod/rel: Universal, Levinson-Link
The Klansman, Novel
Klansman, The 1974 d: Terence Young. lps: Lee Marvin, Richard Burton, Cameron Mitchell. 90M USA. *The Burning Cross*; *Kkk* prod/rel: Paramount
The Revolt of Mamie Stover, 1951, Novel
Revolt of Mamie Stover, The 1956 d: Raoul Walsh. lps: Jane Russell, Richard Egan, Joan Leslie. 93M USA. prod/rel: 20th Century-Fox
Torture Execution of a Hero Marine, 1958, Story
Outsider, The 1961 d: Delbert Mann. lps: Tony Curtis, James Franciscus, Bruce Bennett. 108M USA. *The Sixth Man* prod/rel: Universal Pictures
Wild River, Novel
Wild River 1960 d: Elia Kazan. lps: Lee Remick, Montgomery Clift, Jo Van Fleet. 115M USA. *The Woman and the Wild River* prod/rel: 20th Century Fox

HULBERT, JACK (1892–1978), UKN
Under Your Hat, London 1938, Play
Under Your Hat 1940 d: Maurice Elvey. lps: Jack Hulbert, Cicely Courtneidge, Austin Trevor. 79M UKN. prod/rel: Grand National, British Lion

HULL, ALEXANDER
Shep of the Painted Hills, 1930, Novel
Painted Hills, The 1951 d: Harold F. Kress. lps: Paul Kelly, Bruce Cowling, Gary Gray. 69M USA. *Shep of the Painted Hills* prod/rel: MGM

HULL, EDITH MAUDE
The Desert Healer, Boston 1923, Novel
Old Loves and New 1926 d: Maurice Tourneur. lps: Lewis Stone, Barbara Bedford, Walter Pidgeon. 7423f USA. *The Desert Healer* prod/rel: Sam E. Rork Productions, First National Pictures
The Shadow of the East, Boston 1921, Novel
Shadow of the East, The 1924 d: George Archainbaud. lps: Frank Mayo, Mildred Harris, Norman Kerry. 5874f USA. *Shadow of the Desert* prod/rel: Fox Film Corp.
The Sheik, London 1919, Novel
Sheik, The 1921 d: George Melford. lps: Agnes Ayres, Rudolph Valentino, Adolphe Menjou. 6579f USA. prod/rel: Famous Players-Lasky, Paramount Pictures
The Sons of the Sheik, Novel
Son of the Sheik, The 1926 d: George Fitzmaurice. lps: Rudolph Valentino, Vilma Banky, George Fawcett. 6685f USA. prod/rel: Feature Productions, United Artists

HULL, GEORGE CHARLES
Breathes There the Man, 1917, Short Story
Light of Victory, The 1919 d: William Wolbert. lps: Monroe Salisbury, Betty Compson, Bob Edmond. 5r USA. *The Island of Adventure*; *The Renegade* prod/rel: Bluebird Photoplays, Inc.©, Universal Film Mfg. Co.
The Sea Flower, Short Story
Sea Flower, The 1918 d: Colin Campbell. lps: Juanita Hansen, Alfred Whitman, Fred Huntley. 5r USA. prod/rel: Bluebird Photoplays, Inc.©

HULL, HENRY
East Side - West Side, Play
East Side - West Side 1923 d: Irving Cummings. lps: Kenneth Harlan, Eileen Percy, Maxine Elliott Hicks. 6r USA. prod/rel: Principal Pictures

HULME, KATHRYN C. (1900–1981), USA, Hulme, Kathryn Cavarly
The Nun's Story, Book
Nun's Story, The 1959 d: Fred Zinnemann. lps: Audrey Hepburn, Peter Finch, Edith Evans. 150M USA. prod/rel: Warner Bros.

HULSE, JERRY
Judy, Book
Family of Strangers 1993 d: Sheldon Larry. lps: Melissa Gilbert, Patty Duke, Martha Gibson. TVM. 90M USA/CND.

HUME, CYRIL
Wife of the Centaur, 1923, Novel
Wife of the Centaur 1924 d: King Vidor. lps: Eleanor Boardman, John Gilbert, Aileen Pringle. 6586f USA. prod/rel: Metro-Goldwyn Pictures

HUME, DAVID
Crime Unlimited, Novel
Crime Unlimited 1935 d: Ralph Ince. lps: Esmond Knight, Lilli Palmer, Cecil Parker. 72M UKN. prod/rel: Warner Bros., First National
Too Dangerous to Live 1939 d: Leslie Norman, Anthony Hankey. lps: Sebastian Shaw, Greta Gynt, Reginald Tate. 74M UKN. prod/rel: Warner Bros., First National
They Called Him Death, Novel
This Man Is Dangerous 1941 d: Lawrence Huntington. lps: James Mason, Mary Clare, Margaret Vyner. 82M UKN. *The Patient Vanishes* prod/rel: Rialto, Pathe

HUME, DORIS
Dark Purpose, New York 1960, Novel
Intrigo, L' 1964 d: Vittorio Sala, George Marshall. lps: Shirley Jones, Rossano Brazzi, George Sanders. 97M ITL/FRN. *Dark Purpose* (USA) prod/rel: Galatea (Roma), Lyre Productions (Paris)
The Sin of Susan Slade, New York 1961, Novel
Susan Slade 1961 d: Delmer Daves. lps: Troy Donahue, Connie Stevens, Dorothy McGuire. 116M USA. prod/rel: Warner Bros. Pictures

HUME, FERGUS
The Mystery of a Hansom Cab, Novel
Mystery of a Hansom Cab, The 1915 d: Harold Weston. lps: Milton Rosmer, Fay Temple, A. V. Bramble. 5500f UKN. prod/rel: British & Colonial, Ideal
The Other Man, 1920, Novel
Other Person, The 1921 d: B. E. Doxat-Pratt, Maurits H. Binger. lps: Zoe Palmer, Adelqui Millar, Arthur Pusey. 5319f UKN/NTH. *Onder Spiritistischen Dwang*; *Under Spiritualistic Coercion*; **De Andere Persoon** prod/rel: Granger-Binger Film
The Top Dog, Novel
Top Dog, The 1918 d: Arrigo Bocchi. lps: Kenelm Foss, Odette Goimbault, Hayford Hobbs. 6250f UKN. prod/rel: Windsor, Walturdaw

HUMMERT, FRANK
Manhattan Merry-Go-Round, Musical Play
Manhattan Merry-Go-Round 1937 d: Charles F. Reisner. lps: Phil Regan, Ann Dvorak, Leo Carrillo. 82M USA. *Manhattan Music Box* (UKN) prod/rel: Republic Pictures Corp.©

HUMPHREY, WILLIAM (1924–, USA
Home from the Hill, 1958, Novel
Home from the Hill 1960 d: Vincente Minnelli. lps: Robert Mitchum, Luana Patten, George Peppard. 148M USA. prod/rel: MGM

HUMPHREYS, JOSEPHINE
Rich in Love, Novel
Rich in Love 1992 d: Bruce Beresford. lps: Albert Finney, Jill Clayburgh, Kathryn Erbe. 105M USA. prod/rel: MGM, Upi

HUMPHRIES, JOSEPH
The Ragged Earl, New York 1899, Play
Ragged Earl, The 1914 d: Lloyd B. Carleton. lps: Andrew Mack, William Conklin, Edward Peil. 5r USA. prod/rel: Popular Plays and Players, Inc.©, Alco Film Corp.

HUNGER, ANNA
Story
Pearl of the South Pacific 1955 d: Allan Dwan. lps: Virginia Mayo, Dennis Morgan, David Farrar. 86M USA. prod/rel: RKO, Film Crest Prods.

HUNGERFORD, MARGARET WOLFE (1855?–1897), IRL, Duchess, The
Molly Bawn, 1878, Novel
Molly Bawn 1916 d: Cecil M. Hepworth. lps: Alma Taylor, Stewart Rome, Violet Hopson. 4510f UKN. prod/rel: Hepworth

HUNOLD, GUNTHER
Book
Schulmadchen-Report 1. Teil - Was Eltern Nicht Fur Moglich Halten 1970 d: Ernst Hofbauer. lps: Gunther Kieslich, Friedrich von Thun, Helga Kruck. 92M GRM. *Was Eltern Nicht Fur Moglich Halten* prod/rel: Rapid, Constantin

HUNT, ROBERT B.
Man Or Mouse, Story
There's One Born Every Minute 1942 d: Harold Young. lps: Hugh Herbert, Peggy Moran, Tom Brown. 60M USA. *Man Or Mouse* prod/rel: Universal

HUNTER, EVAN (1926–, USA, McBain, Ed
Blackboard Jungle, 1954, Novel
Blackboard Jungle, The 1955 d: Richard Brooks. lps: Glenn Ford, Anne Francis, Louis Calhern. 101M USA. prod/rel: Metro-Goldwyn-Mayer Corp.
Blood Relatives, 1975, Novel
Liens de Sang, Les 1978 d: Claude Chabrol. lps: Donald Sutherland, Aude Landry, Lisa Langlois. 94M FRN/CND. *Blood Relatives* (USA) prod/rel: Cinevideo Inc. (Montreal), Filmel (Paris)
Buddwing, New York 1964, Novel
Mister Buddwing 1965 d: Delbert Mann. lps: James Garner, Jean Simmons, Suzanne Pleshette. 100M USA. *Woman Without a Face* (UKN) prod/rel: Ddd Productions, Cherokee Productions
The Chisholms, Novel
Chisholms, The 1978 d: Mel Stuart. lps: Robert Preston, Rosemary Harris, Ben Murphy. TVM. 300M USA. prod/rel: CBS, Alan Landsburg Productions
Cop Hater, 1958, Novel
Cop Hater 1958 d: William Berke. lps: Robert Loggia, Gerald S. O'Loughlin, Ellen Parker. 75M USA. prod/rel: United Artists, Barbizon Prods.
Every Little Crook and Nanny, 1972, Novel
Every Little Crook and Nanny 1972 d: Cy Howard. lps: Lynn Redgrave, Victor Mature, Paul Sand. 92M USA.
Fuzz, 1968, Novel
Fuzz 1972 d: Richard A. CollA. lps: Burt Reynolds, Jack Weston, Tom Skerritt. 92M USA. prod/rel: Filmways
A Horses Head, 1967, Novel
Cri du Cormoran, le Soir, Au-Dessus Des Jonges, Le 1970 d: Michel Audiard. lps: Michel Serrault, Paul Meurisse, Maurice Biraud. 85M FRN. *Le Paume* prod/rel: Gaumont International
Killer's Wedge, 1959, Novel
Soupe aux Poulets, La 1963 d: Philippe Agostini. lps: Jean Servais, Claude Brasseur, Gerard Blain. 90M FRN. prod/rel: Maintenon Films, France Vedettes Films
King's Ransom, 1959, Novel
Tengoku to Jigoku 1963 d: Akira KurosawA. lps: Toshiro Mifune, Tatsuya Nakadai, Kyoko KagawA. 143M JPN. *High and Low* (USA); *Heaven and Hell*; *The Ransom* prod/rel: Kurosawa Fimls, Toho Co.
Lady Lady I Did It!, 1961, Novel
Kofuku 1981 d: Kon IchikawA. lps: Toshiyuki Nagashima, Yutaka Mizutani, Rie NakaharA. 106M JPN. *Lonely Hearts* (USA); *Happiness* prod/rel: for Life Records
Last Summer, New York 1968, Novel
Last Summer 1969 d: Frank Perry. lps: Barbara Hershey, Richard Thomas, Bruce Davison. 97M USA. prod/rel: Alsid Productions, Francis Productions
Lightning, Novel
Ed McBain's 87th Precinct 1995 d: Bruce Paltrow. lps: Randy Quaid, Alex McArthur, Ving Rhames. TVM. 90M USA. prod/rel: Diana Kerew Productions, Hearst
A Matter of Conviction, New York 1959, Novel
Young Savages, The 1961 d: John Frankenheimer. lps: Burt Lancaster, Dina Merrill, Shelley Winters. 103M USA. *A Matter of Conviction* prod/rel: Contemporary Productions, United Artists
The Mugger, 1956, Novel
Mugger, The 1958 d: William Berke. lps: Kent Smith, Nan Martin, James Franciscus. 74M USA. prod/rel: United Artists, Barbizon
The Pusher, 1956, Novel
Pusher, The 1959 d: Gene Milford. lps: Cathy Carlyle, Felice Orlandi, Douglas Fletcher Rodgers. 82M USA.
Strangers When We Meet, 1958, Novel
Strangers When We Meet 1960 d: Richard Quine. lps: Kirk Douglas, Kim Novak, Ernie Kovacs. 117M USA. prod/rel: Columbia

Ten Plus One, 1963, Novel
Sans Mobile Apparent 1971 d: Philippe Labro. lps: Jean-Louis Trintignant, Dominique Sanda, Sacha Distel. 102M FRN/ITL. *Senza Movente* (ITL); *Without Apparent Motive* (USA) prod/rel: Jacques Strauss-President Films, Cinetel
Walk Proud, 102M, Novel
Walk Proud 1979 d: Robert Collins. lps: Robby Benson, Sarah Holcomb, Henry Darrow. 102M USA. *Gang* prod/rel: Universal

HUNTER, HALL
Bengal Tiger, 1952, Novel
Bengal Brigade 1954 d: Laslo Benedek. lps: Rock Hudson, Arlene Dahl, Ursula Thiess. 87M USA. *Bengal Rifles* (UKN) prod/rel: Universal-International

HUNTER, HORACE
Under Suspicion, Play
Under Suspicion 1919 d: Walter West. lps: Horace Hunter, Hilda Bayley, Jack Jarman. 5000f UKN. prod/rel: Broadwest, Moss

HUNTER, IAN MCLELLAN
Story
Roman Holiday 1987 d: Noel Nosseck. lps: Catherine Oxenberg, Tom Conti, Ed Begley Jr. TVM. 100M USA. prod/rel: Jerry Ludwig Enterprises, Paramount Tv

HUNTER, JACK D.
The Blue Max, New York 1964, Novel
Blue Max, The 1966 d: John Guillermin. lps: George Peppard, James Mason, Ursula Andress. 156M UKN/USA. prod/rel: 20th Century-Fox

HUNTER, JOHN A.
African Bush Adventures, Book
Killers of Kilimanjaro 1959 d: Richard Thorpe. lps: Robert Taylor, Anthony Newley, Anne Aubrey. 91M UKN. *Adamson of Africa* prod/rel: Columbia, Warwick

HUNTER, KRISTIN
The Landlord, New York 1966, Novel
Landlord, The 1970 d: Hal Ashby. lps: Beau Bridges, Pearl Bailey, Diana Sands. 114M USA. prod/rel: Mirisch Productions, Cartier Productions

HUNTER, RUSSELL
The Changeling, Story
Changeling, The 1980 d: Peter Medak. lps: George C. Scott, Trish Van Devere, Melvyn Douglas. 107M CND. *L' Enfant du Diable* prod/rel: Chessman Park Productions Ltd., Tiberius Film Productions Ltd.

HUNYADY, SANDOR
Bakaruhaban, 1935, Short Story
Bakaruhaban 1957 d: Imre Feher. lps: Ivan Darvas, Margit Bara, Sandor Pecsi. 92M HNG. *A Sunday Romance*
Girl Downstairs, The 1938 d: Norman Taurog. lps: Franchot Tone, Franciska Gaal, Rita Johnson. 77M USA. *The Awakening of Katrina*; *Katherine the Last* prod/rel: Metro-Goldwyn-Mayer Corp., Loew's, Inc.©
Bors Istvan, Play
Scarpe Grosse 1940 d: Dino Falconi. lps: Amedeo Nazzari, Lilia Silvi, Elena Altieri. 83M ITL. prod/rel: Fonoroma, E.N.I.C.
Il Capitano Degli Ussari, Play
Capitano Degli Ussari, Il 1941 d: Sandor Szlatinay. lps: Clara Tabody, Enrico Viarisio, Carlo Romano. 68M ITL. prod/rel: Nuova Film, I.C.I.
Fekete Szaru Csereszyne, 1931, Play
Storm at Daybreak 1932 d: Richard Boleslawski. lps: Kay Francis, Nils Asther, Jean Parker. 82M USA. *Strange Rhapsody* prod/rel: Metro-Goldwyn-Mayer Corp.©
A Voroslampas Haz, 1937, Novel
Erkolcsos Ejszaka, Egy 1977 d: Karoly Makk. lps: Iren Psota, Margit Makay, Gyorgy Cserhalmi. 103M HNG. *A Very Moral Night* prod/rel: Dialog Filmstudio

HUO DA
Hong Chen, Novel
Hong Chen 1994 d: Gu Rong. lps: Xu Songzi, Tao Zeru, Xu Lei. 12r CHN. *An Unwelcome Lady* prod/rel: Beijing Film Studio

HURLBUT, GLADYS
By Your Leave, Wells, Emma B. C., Play
By Your Leave 1934 d: Lloyd Corrigan. lps: Frank Morgan, Genevieve Tobin, Neil Hamilton. 82M USA. prod/rel: RKO Radio Pictures, Inc.
Higher and Higher, Musical Play
Higher and Higher 1943 d: Tim Whelan. lps: Michele Morgan, Jack Haley, Frank SinatrA. 90M USA. prod/rel: RKO

HURLBUT, WILLIAM, Hurlbut, William J.
Body and Soul, Play
Body and Soul 1915 d: George Irving. lps: Florence Rockwell, Kenneth Hunter, Robert Whitworth. 5r USA. prod/rel: Frohman Amusement Corp., World Film Corp.©

The Fighting Hope, New York 1908, Play
Fighting Hope, The 1915 d: George Melford. lps: Laura Hope Crews, George Gebhardt, Gerald Ward. 5r USA. prod/rel: Jesse L. Lasky Feature Play Co.©, Paramount Pictures Corp.

Hail and Farewell, New York 1923, Play
Heart of a Siren 1925 d: Phil Rosen. lps: Barbara La Marr, Conway Tearle, Harry T. Morey. 6700f USA. *Heart of a Temptress* prod/rel: Associated Pictures, First National Pictures

Lilies of the Field, New York 1921, Play
Lilies of the Field 1924 d: John Francis Dillon. lps: Corinne Griffith, Conway Tearle, Alma Bennett. 8510f USA. prod/rel: Corinne Griffith Productions, Associated First National Pictures
Lilies of the Field 1930 d: Alexander KordA. lps: Corinne Griffith, Ralph Forbes, John Loder. 5979f USA. prod/rel: First National Pictures

New York, New York 1910, Play
New York 1916 d: George Fitzmaurice. lps: Florence Reed, Fania Marinoff, John Miltern. 5r USA. prod/rel: Pathe Exchange, Inc., Gold Rooster Plays

Romance and Arabella, New York 1917, Play
Romance and Arabella 1919 d: Walter Edwards. lps: Constance Talmadge, Harrison Ford, Gertrude Claire. 5r USA. prod/rel: Select Pictures Corp.

Saturday to Monday, New York 1917, Play
Experimental Marriage 1919 d: Robert G. VignolA. lps: Constance Talmadge, Harrison Ford, Walter Hiers. 5r USA. *Saturday to Monday* prod/rel: Select Pictures Corp.©

The Strange Woman, New York 1913, Play
Strange Woman, The 1918 d: Edward J. Le Saint. lps: Gladys Brockwell, William Scott, Charles Clary. 6r USA. prod/rel: Fox Film Corp., William Fox©

Trimmed in Scarlet, New York 1920, Play
Trimmed in Scarlet 1923 d: Jack Conway. lps: Kathlyn Williams, Roy Stewart, Lucille Rickson. 4765f USA. prod/rel: Universal Pictures

HURN, PHILIP
Soft Shoulders, Story
Wild Company 1930 d: Leo McCarey. lps: H. B. Warner, Frank Albertson, Sharon Lynn. 73M USA. *Roadhouse* prod/rel: Fox Film Corp.

HURST, FANNIE (1889–1968), USA
Back Pay, Short Story
Back Pay 1922 d: Frank Borzage. lps: Seena Owen, Matt Moore, Barney Sherry. 6460f USA. prod/rel: Cosmopolitan Productions, Paramount Pictures
Back Pay 1930 d: William A. Seiter. lps: Corinne Griffith, Grant Withers, Montagu Love. 5672f USA. prod/rel: First National Pictures

Back Street, New York 1931, Novel
Back Street 1932 d: John M. Stahl. lps: Irene Dunne, John Boles, June Clyde. 89M USA. prod/rel: Universal Pictures Corp., John M. Stahl Production
Back Street 1941 d: Robert Stevenson. lps: Charles Boyer, Margaret Sullavan, Richard Carlson. 89M USA. prod/rel: Universal
Back Street 1961 d: David Miller. lps: Susan Hayward, John Gavin, Vera Miles. 107M USA. prod/rel: Ross Hunter Productions, Carrollton, Inc.

Five and Ten, New York 1929, Novel
Five and Ten 1931 d: Robert Z. Leonard, Jack Conway (Uncredited). lps: Irene Rich, Marion Davies, Leslie Howard. 88M USA. *Daughter of Luxury* (UKN) prod/rel: Metro-Goldwyn-Mayer Corp.©

Give the Little Girl a Hand, 1929, Short Story
Painted Angel, The 1929 d: Millard Webb. lps: Billie Dove, Edmund Lowe, George MacFarlane. 6470f USA. *The Broadway Hostess* prod/rel: First National Pictures

Golden Fleece, 1917, Short Story
Her Great Chance 1918 d: Charles Maigne. lps: Alice Brady, David Powell, Nellie Parker Spaulding. 5r USA. prod/rel: Select Pictures Corp.

The Good Provider, 1914, Short Story
Good Provider, The 1922 d: Frank Borzage. lps: Vera Gordon, Dore Davidson, Miriam BattistA. 7753f USA. prod/rel: Cosmopolitan Productions, Paramount Pictures

Humoresque, 1919, Short Story
Humoresque 1920 d: Frank Borzage. lps: Vera Gordon, Dore Davidson, Alma Rubens. 5987f USA. prod/rel: Cosmopolitan Productions, International Film Service Co.©

Humoresque 1946 d: Jean Negulesco. lps: Joan Crawford, John Garfield, Oscar Levant. 125M USA. prod/rel: Warner Bros.

Imitation of Life, New York 1933, Novel
Imitation of Life 1934 d: John M. Stahl. lps: Claudette Colbert, Warren William, Ned Sparks. 116M USA. prod/rel: Universal Pictures Corp.©
Imitation of Life 1959 d: Douglas Sirk. lps: Lana Turner, John Gavin, Sandra Dee. 124M USA. prod/rel: Universal-International

Just Around the Corner, 1914, Short Story
Just Around the Corner 1921 d: Frances Marion. lps: Margaret Seddon, Lewis Sargent, Sigrid Holmquist. 6173f USA. prod/rel: Cosmopolitan Productions, Paramount Pictures

Lummox, New York 1923, Novel
Lummox 1930 d: Herbert Brenon. lps: Winifred Westover, Dorothy Janis, Lydia Yeamans Titus. 7533f USA. prod/rel: Feature Productions, United Artists

Mannequin, New York 1926, Novel
Mannequin 1926 d: James Cruze. lps: Alice Joyce, Warner Baxter, Dolores Costello. 6981f USA. prod/rel: Famous Players-Lasky, Paramount Pictures

The Nth Commandment, 1916, Short Story
Nth Commandment, The 1923 d: Frank Borzage. lps: Colleen Moore, James Morrison, Eddie Phillips. 7339f USA. *The Higher Law* (UKN) prod/rel: Cosmopolitan Productions, Paramount Pictures

Oats for the Woman, 1917, Short Story
Day She Paid, The 1919 d: Rex Ingram. lps: Francelia Billington, Charles Clary, Harry Van Meter. 5r USA. *Oats and the Woman* prod/rel: Universal Film Mfg. Co.©

Roulette, 1922, Short Story
Wheel of Chance 1928 d: Alfred Santell. lps: Richard Barthelmess, Bodil Rosing, Warner Oland. 6895f USA. *Roulette* prod/rel: First National Pictures

Sister Act, 1937, Short Story
Four Daughters 1938 d: Michael Curtiz. lps: Claude Rains, Rosemary Lane, Lola Lane. 90M USA. *Sister Act*; *Because of a Man* prod/rel: Warner Bros. Pictures©, First National Picture
Four Wives 1939 d: Michael Curtiz. lps: Claude Rains, Eddie Albert, Priscilla Lane. 110M USA. *Family Reunion*; *Family Affair*; *American Family*; *Sister Act* prod/rel: Warner Bros. Pictures©
Young at Heart 1954 d: Gordon Douglas. lps: Doris Day, Frank Sinatra, Gig Young. 117M USA. prod/rel: Warner Bros., Arwin Prods.

Stardust, New York 1919, Novel
Stardust 1921 d: Hobart Henley. lps: Hope Hampton, Edna Ross, Thomas Maguire. 5800f USA. prod/rel: Hobart Henley Productions, Associated First National Pictures

The Untamed Lady, Story
Untamed Lady, The 1926 d: Frank Tuttle. lps: Gloria Swanson, Lawrence Gray, Joseph Smiley. 6132f USA. prod/rel: Famous Players-Lasky, Paramount Pictures

HURST, HAWTHORNE
Goldie Gets Along, New York 1931, Novel
Goldie Gets Along 1933 d: Malcolm St. Clair. lps: Lili Damita, Charles Morton, Sam Hardy. 68M USA. *Beautifully Trimmed*; *Goldie* prod/rel: King Motion Pictures©, J. G. Bachmann Production

HURST, VIDA
Blind Date, New York 1931, Novel
Blind Date 1934 d: R. William Neill. lps: Ann Sothern, Neil Hamilton, Paul Kelly. 75M USA. *Her Sacrifice* (UKN) prod/rel: Columbia Pictures Corp.

Honeymoon Limited, New York 1932, Novel
Honeymoon Limited 1935 d: Arthur Lubin. lps: Neil Hamilton, Irene Hervey, Lloyd Hughes. 74M USA. prod/rel: Monogram Pictures Corp.©, Mrs. Wallace Reid Production

Tango, New York 1935, Novel
Tango 1936 d: Phil Rosen. lps: Marian Nixon, Chick Chandler, Warren Hymer. 70M USA. prod/rel: Invincible Pictures Corp.©, Chesterfield Motion Pictures Corp.

HURST, WILLIAM O. H.
Novel
In the Hands of the Law 1917. lps: Lois Meredith. 5r USA. prod/rel: Balboa Amusement Producing Co., B. S. Moss Motion Pictures Corp.

HUSSEIN, ABDULLAH
Return Journey, Novel
Brothers in Trouble 1995 d: Udayan Prasad. lps: Om Puri, Angeline Ball, Pavan MalhotrA. TVM. 104M UKN. prod/rel: Renegade Films, BBC Films

HUSSON, ALBERT
Les Cuisine de Anges, Play
We're No Angels 1955 d: Michael Curtiz. lps: Humphrey Bogart, Aldo Ray, Peter Ustinov. 106M USA. prod/rel: Paramount

Le Cuisine Des Anges, Play
We're No Angels 1989 d: Neil Jordan. lps: Robert de Niro, Sean Penn, Demi Moore. 100M USA. prod/rel: Paramount

HUTCHINSON, A. S. M. (1879–, UKN, Hutchinson, Arthur Stuart-Menteth
The Happy Warrior, London 1912, Novel
Happy Warrior, The 1917 d: F. Martin Thornton. lps: James Knight, Evelyn Boucher, Joan Legge. 3468f UKN. prod/rel: Harma
Happy Warrior, The 1925 d: J. Stuart Blackton. lps: Malcolm McGregor, Alice Calhoun, Mary Alden. 7865f USA. prod/rel: Vitagraph Co. of America

If Winter Comes, Boston 1921, Novel
If Winter Comes 1923 d: Harry Millarde. lps: Percy Marmont, Arthur Metcalfe, Sidney Herbert. 12r USA. prod/rel: Fox Film Corp.
If Winter Comes 1947 d: Victor Saville. lps: Walter Pidgeon, Deborah Kerr, Janet Leigh. 97M USA. prod/rel: MGM

Once Aboard the Lugger, Novel
Once Aboard the Lugger 1920 d: Gerald Ames, Gaston Quiribet. lps: E. Holman Clark, Eileen Dennes, Evan Thomas. 5250f UKN. prod/rel: Hepworth, Imperial

One Increasing Purpose, Boston 1925, Novel
One Increasing Purpose 1927 d: Harry Beaumont. lps: Edmund Lowe, Lila Lee, Holmes Herbert. 7677f USA. prod/rel: Fox Film Corp.

This Freedom, Novel
This Freedom 1923 d: Denison Clift. lps: Fay Compton, Clive Brook, John Stuart. 7220f UKN. prod/rel: Ideal

HUTCHINSON, E. M.
Over the Hills to the Poorhouse, Novel
Over the Hills to the Poorhouse 1908 d: Wallace McCutcheon. lps: Florence Auer, Robert Vignola, Wallace McCutcheon. 790f USA. prod/rel: Biograph Co.

HUTCHINSON, ERNEST
The Right to Strike, London 1920, Play
Right to Strike, The 1923 d: Fred Paul. lps: Lillian Hall-Davis, Fred Paul, Campbell Gullan. 6170f UKN. prod/rel: British Super, Jury

HUTCHISON, BRUCE
Park Avenue Logger, 1935, Short Story
Park Avenue Logger 1937 d: David Howard. lps: George O'Brien, Beatrice Roberts, Willard Robertson. 65M USA. *Millionaire Playboy* (UKN); *Tall Timber* prod/rel: George A. Hirliman Prouctions, RKO Radio Pictures©

HUTH, ANGELA (1938–, UKN
The Land Girls, Novel
Land Girls, The 1998 d: David Leland. lps: Catherine McCormack, Rachel Weisz, Anna Friel. 110M UKN/FRN. prod/rel: Intermedia Landgirls Ltd.©, Intermedia Films

Virginia Fly Is Drowning, Novel
Virginia Fly Is Drowning 1982 d: Mark Cullingham. lps: Anna Massey. MTV. 60M UKN. prod/rel: BBC

HUTH, JOCHEN
Story
Jacqueline 1959 d: Wolfgang Liebeneiner. lps: Johanna von Koczian, Walther Reyer, Gotz George. 104M GRM. prod/rel: U.F.H.

Ultimo, Play
Leben Kann So Schon Sein, Das 1938 d: Rolf Hansen. lps: Ilse Werner, Rudi Godden, Gustav Waldau. 83M GRM. *Eine Frau Furs Leben*; *Life Can Be So Beautiful*; *Ultimo* prod/rel: UFA, Dietz

Die Vier Gesellen, Play
Vier Gesellen, Die 1938 d: Carl Froelich. lps: Ingrid Bergman, Sabine Peters, Carsta Lock. 96M GRM. *Die 4 Gesellen*; *Ja Ja Die Liebe* prod/rel: Froelich-Studio, Herzog

HUTSON, SANDY
The Class of Miss MacMichael, Novel
Class of Miss MacMichael, The 1978 d: Silvio Narizzano. lps: Glenda Jackson, Oliver Reed, Michael Murphy. 100M UKN. prod/rel: Brut, Kettledrum

HUTSON, SHAUN
Slugs, Novel
Slugs, the Movie 1988 d: Piquer Simon. lps: Michael Garfield, Santiago Alvarez, Philip McHale. 92M USA/SPN. *Muerte Viscosa Slugs* (SPN); *Slugs*; *Muerte Viscosa* prod/rel: Dister Prod.

235

HUTTLOVA, JAROMIRA
Ideal Septimy, Novel
Ideal Septimy 1938 d: Vaclav Kubasek. lps: Jindrich Plachta, Zdenka Baldova, Jiri Dohnal. 2334m CZC. *Septima's Ideal*; *High School Dream* prod/rel: Nationalfilm

HUTTON, MICHAEL CLAYTON
The Happy Family, Play
Happy Family, The 1952 d: Muriel Box. lps: Stanley Holloway, Kathleen Harrison, Naunton Wayne. 86M UKN. *Mr. Lord Says No* (USA); *Live and Let Live* prod/rel: London Independent, Apex

HUXLEY, ALDOUS (1894–1963), UKN, Huxley, Aldous Leonard
Short Story
Piccolo Archimede, Il 1979 d: Gianni Amelio. lps: John Steiner, Laura Betti, Aldo Salvi. MTV. 83M ITL. prod/rel: Rai Radiotelevisione Italiana
Brave New World, 1932, Novel
Brave New World 1980 d: Burt Brinckerhoff. lps: Keir Dullea, Bud Cort, Julie Cobb. TVM. 150M USA. prod/rel: NBC, Universal
Brave New World 1998 d: Leslie Libman, Larry Williams. lps: Peter Gallagher, Leonard Nimoy, Tim Guinee. TVM. 120M USA. prod/rel: Michael Joyce Prods., Dan Wigutow Prods.
The Gioconda Smile, 1922, Short Story
Woman's Vengeance, A 1947 d: Zoltan KordA. lps: Charles Boyer, Ann Blyth, Jessica Tandy. 96M USA. *Mortal Coils* prod/rel: Universal-International
Young Archimedes, 1924, Novel
Prelude to Fame 1950 d: Fergus McDonnell. lps: Guy Rolfe, Kathleen Ryan, Kathleen Byron. 88M UKN. prod/rel: General Film Distributors, Two Cities

HUXLEY, ELSPETH (1907–, UKN, Huxley, Elspeth Josceline Grant
The Flame Trees of Thika, Novel
Flame Trees of Thika, The 1981 d: Roy Ward Baker. lps: Hayley Mills, David Robb, Holly Aird. TVM. 350M UKN. prod/rel: Thames Tv, Euston

HYAMS, EDWARD
Sylvester, Novel
You Know What Sailors are 1954 d: Ken Annakin. lps: Akim Tamiroff, Donald Sinden, Sarah Lawson. 89M UKN. prod/rel: Group Films, General Film Distributors

HYAMS, JOE
Bogie, Biography
Bogie 1980 d: Vincent Sherman. lps: Kevin O'Connor, Kathryn Harrold, Ann Wedgeworth. TVM. 100M USA. *Bogie: the Last Hero* prod/rel: CBS, Charles Fries Prods.

HYDE, JANE
The Place at the Coast, Novel
Place at the Coast, The 1987 d: George Ogilvie. lps: John Hargreaves, Tushka Bergen, Aileen Britton. 93M ASL. prod/rel: New South Wales Film Corp.©, Daedalus II Films Pty Ltd.©

HYDE, KENNETH
The Rossiters, Play
Rossiter Case, The 1951 d: Francis Searle. lps: Helen Shingler, Clement McCallin, Sheila Burrell. 75M UKN. prod/rel: Hammer, Exclusive

HYDE, MONTGOMERY
The Trials of Oscar Wilde, Book
Trials of Oscar Wilde, The 1960 d: Ken Hughes. lps: Peter Finch, Yvonne Mitchell, James Mason. 123M UKN. *The Man With the Green Carnation* (USA); *The Green Carnation* prod/rel: Eros, Viceroy

HYMAN, MAC
No Time for Sergeants, Novel
No Time for Sergeants 1958 d: Mervyn Leroy. lps: Andy Griffith, Myron McCormick, Nick Adams. 114M USA. prod/rel: Warner Bros.

HYMER, JOHN B.
Alias the Deacon, New York 1925, Play
Alias the Deacon 1928 d: Edward Sloman. lps: Jean Hersholt, June Marlowe, Ralph Graves. 6869f USA. prod/rel: Universal Pictures
Half a Sinner 1934 d: Kurt Neumann. lps: Sally Blane, Joel McCrea, Berton Churchill. 73M USA. *Alias the Deacon* prod/rel: Universal Pictures Corp.©
Aloma of the South Seas, New York 1925, Play
Aloma of the South Seas 1926 d: Maurice Tourneur. lps: Gilda Gray, Percy Marmont, Warner Baxter. 8514f USA. prod/rel: Famous Players-Lasky Corp., Paramount Pictures
Aloma of the South Seas 1941 d: Alfred Santell. lps: Dorothy Lamour, Jon Hall, Lynne Overman. 77M USA. prod/rel: Paramount
Crime, New York 1927, Play
Law of the Underworld 1938 d: Lew Landers. lps: Chester Morris, Anne Shirley, Richard Bond. 61M USA. *Crime*; *See No Evil* prod/rel: RKO Radio Pictures©

The Deacon, New York 1925, Play
Alias the Deacon 1940 d: W. Christy Cabanne. lps: Bob "Bazooka" Burns, Mischa Auer, Peggy Moran. 74M USA. prod/rel: Universal Pictures Co.
East Is West, Play
East Is West 1922 d: Sidney A. Franklin. lps: Constance Talmadge, Edmund Burns, E. Alyn Warren. 7737f USA. prod/rel: Constance Talmadge Productions, Associated First National Pictures
East Is West 1930 d: Monta Bell. lps: Lupe Velez, Lew Ayres, Edward G. Robinson. 75M USA. prod/rel: Universal Pictures
Fast Life, New York 1928, Play
Fast Life 1929 d: John Francis Dillon. lps: Douglas Fairbanks Jr., Loretta Young, William Holden. 7541f USA. prod/rel: First National Pictures
The Hurdy-Gurdy Man, 1922, Play
Love, Live and Laugh 1929 d: William K. Howard. lps: George Jessel, Lila Lee, David Rollins. 8090f USA. prod/rel: Fox Film Corp.
In the Shadow, Novel
In the Shadow 1915 d: Harry Handworth. lps: Harry Handworth, Marie Boyd, William A. Williams. 5r USA. *In the Shadows* prod/rel: Excelsior Feature Film Co., Alliance Films Corp.
The Lost Game, Short Story
Law of the Underworld 1938 d: Lew Landers. lps: Chester Morris, Anne Shirley, Richard Bond. 61M USA. *Crime*; *See No Evil* prod/rel: RKO Radio Pictures©
The Path Forbidden, Novel
Path Forbidden, The 1914 d: Harry Handworth. lps: Octavia Handworth, Gordon Demain, William A. Williams. 5r USA. prod/rel: Excelsior Feature Film Co.©, Alliance Films Corp.
Scarlet Pages, New York 1929, Play
Scarlet Pages 1930 d: Ray Enright. lps: Elsie Ferguson, John Halliday, Marion Nixon. 5906f USA. prod/rel: First National Pictures

HYND, ALAN
Betrayal from the East, Novel
Betrayal from the East 1945 d: William Berke. lps: Lee Tracy, Nancy Kelly, Richard Loo. 82M USA. prod/rel: RKO Radio

HYNES, GERTRUDE
Keeping It Dark, Story
Keeping It Dark 1915 d: Horace Davey. lps: Billie Rhodes, Harry Rattenberry, Ray Gallagher. SHT USA. prod/rel: Nestor

I

IBRAILEANU, GARABET
AdelA. Fragment Din Jurnalul Lui Emil Codrescu, 1933, Novel
Adela 1985 d: Mircea Veroiu. lps: Stefan Sileanu, Florina Luican, Marina Procopie. 82M RMN.

IBSEN, HENRIK (1828–1906), NRW, Ibsen, Henrik Johan
Et Dukkehjem, Copenhagen 1879, Play
Casa de Munecas 1943 d: Ernesto ArancibiA. lps: Orestes Caviglia, Delia Garces, Jorge Rigaud. 95M ARG. *The Dollhouse*
Casa Di Bambola 1919 d: Febo Mari. lps: Febo Mari, Nietta Mordeglia, Oreste Grandi. 1539m ITL. prod/rel: Mari Film
Doll's House, A 1917 d: Joseph de Grasse. lps: Dorothy Phillips, William Stowell, Lon Chaney. 5r USA. prod/rel: Bluebird Photoplays, Inc.©
Doll's House, A 1918 d: Maurice Tourneur. lps: Elsie Ferguson, Holmes Herbert, Alex Shannon. 4576f USA. prod/rel: Famous Players-Lasky Corp.©, Artcraft Pictures
Doll's House, A 1922 d: Charles Bryant. lps: Alan Hale, Alla Nazimova, Nigel de Brulier. 6650f USA. prod/rel: Nazimova Productions, United Artists
Doll's House, A 1961 d: Robert Tronson. lps: Paul Rogers, Zena Walker, Kenneth Griffith. MTV. UKN. prod/rel: Rediffusion
Doll's House, A 1972 d: Joseph Losey. lps: Jane Fonda, Jane Warner, Trevor Howard. 106M UKN/FRN. *Maison de Poupee* (FRN) prod/rel: World Film Services, Les Films de la Boetie
Doll's House, A 1973 d: Patrick Garland. lps: Claire Bloom, Anthony Hopkins, Ralph Richardson. 105M UKN. prod/rel: Elkins, Freeward

Doll's House, A 1992 d: David Thacker. lps: Juliet Stevenson, Trevor Eve, David Calder. TVM. 135M UKN.
Nora 1944 d: Harald Braun. lps: Luise Ullrich, Viktor Staal, Gustav Diessl. 102M GRM. *A Doll's House* prod/rel: UFA, Astor
En Folkefiende, 1882, Play
Enemy of the People, An 1978 d: George Schaefer. lps: Steve McQueen, Bibi Andersson, Charles Durning. 106M USA.
Ganashatru 1989 d: Satyajit Ray. lps: Soumitra Chatterjee, Dhritiman Chatterjee, Ruma Guha-ThakurtA. 100M IND. *An Enemy of the People* (UKN); *Ganasatru* prod/rel: Nfdc
Volksfeind, Ein 1937 d: Hans Steinhoff. lps: Heinrich George, Herbert Hubner, Franziska Kinz. 101M GRM. prod/rel: F.D.F.
Fru Inger Til Ostraad, 1857, Play
Fru Inger Tol Ostrat 1975 d: Sverre Udnaes. lps: Ingrid Vardund, Ulf Palme, Keve Hjelm. 97M NRW. *Lady Inger of Ostrat*
Fruen Frahavet, 1888, Play
Donna Del Mare, La 1922 d: Nino Valentini. lps: Renee Pelar, Roberto Villani, Ines Fogazzari. 1747m ITL. prod/rel: Milano Film
Gengangere, 1881, Play
Ghosts 1915 d: George Nicholls. lps: Henry B. Walthall, Mary Alden, Nigel de Brulier. 5r USA. *The Curse*; *The Wreck* prod/rel: Majestic Motion Picture Co., Mutual Film Corp.
Spettri, Gli 1918 d: A. G. CaldierA. lps: Ermete Zacconi, Ines Cristina Zacconi, Gioacchino Grassi. 1461m ITL. *La Regina Di Marechiaro* prod/rel: Milano Films
Hedda Gabler, 1890, Play
Hedda 1975 d: Trevor Nunn. lps: Glenda Jackson, Peter Eyre, Timothy West. 102M UKN. prod/rel: Brut
Hedda Gabler 1917 d: Frank Powell. lps: Nance O'Neil, Aubrey Beattie, Lillian Paige. 5r USA. prod/rel: Frank Powell Producing Corp., Mutual Film Corp.
Hedda Gabler 1920 d: Gero Zambuto. lps: Italia Almirante Manzini, Ettore Piergiovanni, Oreste BilanciA. 2893m ITL. prod/rel: Itala Film
Hedda Gabler 1924 d: Franz Eckstein. lps: Asta Nielsen, Paul Morgan, Albert Steinruck. 2577m GRM.
Hedda Gabler 1972 d: Waris Hussein. lps: Janet Suzman, Ian McKellen, Tom Bell. MTV. UKN. prod/rel: BBC
Hedda Gabler 1979 d: Jan Decorte. lps: Jan Pauwels, Rita Wouters, Cara Van Wersch. 110M BLG.
John Gabriel Borkman, 1896, Play
John Gabriel Borkman 1958 d: Christopher Morahan. lps: Laurence Olivier, Maxine Audley, George Relph. MTV. 78M UKN. prod/rel: Atv
The Lady from the Sea, 1888, Play
Lady from the Sea, The 1911 d: Theodore Marston. lps: Marguerite Snow, William Russell, William Garwood. SHT USA. prod/rel: Thanhouser
Lille Eyolf, 1894, Play
Jazeero 1989 d: Govind Nihalani. 144M IND. *Little Eyolf*; *Jazeerey*
Peer Gynt, Copenhagen 1867, Play
Peer Gynt 1915 d: Oscar Apfel. lps: Cyril Maude, Myrtle Stedman, Fanny Stockbridge. 5r USA. prod/rel: Oliver Morosco Photoplay Co.©, Paramount Pictures Corp.
Peer Gynt 1934 d: Fritz Wendhausen. lps: Hans Albers, Marieluise Claudius, Lucie Hoflich. 113M GRM. prod/rel: Bavaria, Europa
Peer Gynt 1941 d: David Bradley. lps: Charlton Heston, Betty Hanisee, Mrs. Herbert Hyde. 85M USA. prod/rel: Willow Corporation, Brandon
Samfundets Stotter, Odense 1877, Play
Dharmaveer 1937 d: Winayak. lps: Ratnaprabha, Winayak, Baburao Pendharkar. 157M IND. *The Godman*; *Dharamveer* prod/rel: Huns Pictures
Pillars of Society, The 1911. SHT USA. prod/rel: Thanhouser
Pillars of Society 1916 d: Raoul Walsh. lps: Henry B. Walthall, Mary Alden, Juanita Archer. 5r USA. prod/rel: Fine Arts Film Co., Triangle Film Corp.
Pillars of Society 1920 d: Rex Wilson. lps: Ellen Terry, Norman McKinnel, Mary Rorke. 5000f UKN. prod/rel: R.W. Syndicate, Moss
Stutzen Der Gesellschaft 1935 d: Douglas Sirk. lps: Heinrich George, Maria Krahn, Horst Teetzmann. 80M GRM. *Pillars of Society* (UKN) prod/rel: Robert Neppach

Vildanden, 1884, Play
Vildanden 1963 d: Tancred Ibsen. lps: Henki Kolstad, Wenche Foss, Lars Nordrum. 105M NRW. *The Wild Duck*

Wild Duck, The 1983 d: Henri Safran. lps: Liv Ullmann, Jeremy Irons, Lucinda Jones. 92M ASL. prod/rel: Phillip Emanuel, Film Bancor of Australia

Wildente, Die 1976 d: Hans W. Geissendorfer. lps: Bruno Ganz, Peter Kern, Anne Bennent. 105M AUS/GRM. *The Wild Duck*

IBUSE, MASUJI (1898–1993), JPN
Kuroi Ame, 1965-66, Novel
Kuroi Ame 1988 d: Shohei ImamurA. lps: Yoshiko Tanaka, Kazuo Kitamura, Etsuko IchiharA. 123M JPN. *Black Rain* (USA) prod/rel: Imamura Productions, Hayashibara Group
Okomasan, 1941, Novel
Hideko No Shasho-San 1941 d: Mikio Naruse. 70M JPN. *Hideko the Bus Conductor*

ICHISE, TAKA
Story
American Yakuza 1994 d: Frank Cappello. lps: Viggo Mortensen, Ryo Ishbashi, Michael Nouri. 91M USA/JPN. prod/rel: First Look, Ozla

IDE, LEONARD
Concealment, 1930, Play
Secret Bride 1934 d: William Dieterle. lps: Barbara Stanwyck, Warren William, Glenda Farrell. 65M USA. *Concealment* (UKN); *His Secret Bride* prod/rel: Warner Bros. Production Corp., Warner Bros. Pictures©

IDELL, ALBERT E.
Centennial Summer, Novel
Centennial Summer 1946 d: Otto Preminger. lps: Jeanne Crain, Cornel Wilde, Linda Darnell. 102M USA. prod/rel: Twentieth Century-Fox

IDRIS, YOUSSEF
Al- Haram, Novel
Haram, Al- 1964 d: Henry Barakat. lps: Fatin Hamama, Abdallah Gheth, Zaki Rustum. 105M EGY. *Le Peche; El Haram* prod/rel: Mounir Rafla

IHARA, SAIKAKU (1642–1693), JPN
Koshoku Ichidai Onna, 1686, Novel
Saikaku Ichidai Onna 1952 d: Kenji Mizoguchi. lps: Kinuyo Tanaka, Matsura Tsuke, Ichiro Sugai. 143M JPN. *The Life of Oharu* (USA); *Life of a Woman By Saikaku; Oharu; Koshoku Ichidai Onna* prod/rel: Shintoho Co., Koi Productions
The Sensualist, Novel
Sensualist, The 1992 d: Yukio Abe. ANM. 54M JPN. prod/rel: Ren Usami, Tsuemasa Hatano

IIZAWA, TADASHI
Gurama-to No Yuwaku, Play
Gurama-to No Yuwaku 1959 d: Yuzo KawashimA. lps: Hisaya Morishige, Frankie Sakai, Kokinji KatsurA. 104M JPN. *Temptation in Glamour Island* prod/rel: Tokyo Eiga Co.

IKEDA, RIYOKO
Berusaiyu No Bara, Novel
Berusaiyu No Bara 1978 d: Jacques Demy. lps: Catriona MacColl, Barry Stokes, Christine Bohm. 124M JPN/FRN. *The Rose of Versailles; Lady Oscar; Lady'o; Versailles No Bara* prod/rel: Killy Music Corporation, Shiseido Co.

IKUSHIMA, HARUO
Short Story
Moeru Tairiku 1968 d: Shogoro NishimurA. lps: Tetsuya Watari, Chieko Matsubara, Miyoko AkazA. 90M JPN. *Blazing Continent* prod/rel: Nikkatsu Corp.

ILARI, NINO
I Vaschi Della Bujosa, Novel
Delitto Di Castel Giubileo, Il 1918 d: Nino Martinengo. lps: Nino Martinengo, Bice Zacchi, Nadya Milar. 1585m ITL. *I Vaschi Della Bujosa* prod/rel: Bob-Film

ILES, FRANCIS (1893–1970), UKN
Before the Fact, Novel
Suspicion 1941 d: Alfred Hitchcock. lps: Cary Grant, Joan Fontaine, Cedric Hardwicke. 99M USA. *Before the Fact* prod/rel: RKO Radio
Malice Aforethought, Novel
Malice Aforethought 1979 d: Cyril Coke. lps: Hywel Bennett, Judy Parfitt, Cheryl Campbell. MTV. 200M UKN. prod/rel: BBC

ILF, ILYA (1897–1937), RSS, Ilf, Ilya Arnoldovich
Dvenadtsat Stulyev, Moscow 1928, Novel
Doce Sillas, Los 1962 d: Tomas Gutierrez AleA. lps: Enrique Santiesteban, Reynaldo Miravalles, Rene Sanchez. 90M CUB. *The Twelve Chairs*
Dreizehn Stuhle 1938 d: E. W. Emo. lps: Heinz Ruhmann, Hans Moser, Annie Rosar. 87M GRM. *13 Stuhle* prod/rel: Emo-Film

Dvanact Kresel 1933 d: Martin Fric, Michael Waszynski. lps: Vlasta Burian, Adolf Dymsza, Zula PogorzelskA. 1838m CZC/PLN. *Dwanascie Krzesel* (PLN); *Twelve Armchairs* prod/rel: Terra, Rex-Film Varsava
Dvinatsat Stulyev 1971 d: Leonid Gaidai. lps: Leonid Gaidai, Archil Gomiashvili, Sergey Filippov. F USS. *The Twelve Chairs; Dvenadtstat Stulyev; Dvenadcat Stulev*
Gluck Liegt Auf Der Strasse, Das 1957 d: Franz Antel. lps: Walter Giller, Georg Thomalla, Doris Kirchner. 93M GRM. *13 Stuhle; Thirteen Chairs* prod/rel: Rhombus, UFA
It's in the Bag 1945 d: Richard Wallace. lps: Fred Allen, Jack Benny, William Bendix. 87M USA. *The Fifth Chair* (UKN) prod/rel: United Artists
Keep Your Seats Please 1936 d: Monty Banks. lps: George Formby, Florence Desmond, Gus McNaughton. 82M UKN. prod/rel: Associated Talking Pictures, Associated British Film Distributors
Twelve Chairs, The 1970 d: Mel Brooks. lps: Mel Brooks, Ron Moody, Frank LangellA. 94M USA. prod/rel: Twelve Chairs Co.
Una Su Tredici 1969 d: Nicolas Gessner, Luciano Lucignani. lps: Vittorio Gassman, Sharon Tate, Orson Welles. 100M ITL/FRN. *12 + 1* (FRN); *Twelve Plus One* (USA); *Lucky 13; 13 Chairs; Una Su 13* prod/rel: Compagnia Cin.Ca Finanziaria (Roma), Comptoir Francais Prod. Cin.Que (Paris)
Zolotoy Telyonok, 1931, Novel
Mechty Idiota 1993 d: Vasily Pichul. lps: Sergej Krylov, Andrej Smirnov, Alika SmekhovA. 90M RSS/FRN. *Dreams of an Idiot* prod/rel: Ttl, Salome
Zolotoy Telyonok 1968 d: Mikhail Schweitzer. lps: Sergey Yursky, Leonid Kuravlyov, Zinovij Gerdt. 174M USS. *The Golden Calf; Zolotoj Telenok*

ILG, PAUL
Le Batard, Zurich 1913, Novel
Batard, Le 1941 d: Edmund Heuberger. lps: Leopold Biberti, Petra Marin, Robi Rapp. 87M SWT. *Trois Dans la Ville; Das Menschlein Matthias; Piccolo Matthias Il* prod/rel: Gotthard-Film

ILHAN, ATTILA
Novel
Sokaktaki Adam 1995 d: Biket Ilhan. F TRK. *The Man in the Street*

ILLES, EUGEN
Was She to Blame?; Or Souls That Meet in the Dark, Book
Was She to Blame? Or, Souls That Meet in the Dark 1915. 5r USA. *Was She to Blame?* prod/rel: Linick & Melchior, Elm Features

ILLICA, LUIGI (1857–1919), ITL
Andrea Chenier, Milan 1896, Opera
Andrea Chenier 1955 d: Clemente Fracassi. lps: Antonella Lualdi, Raf Vallone, Michel Auclair. 100M ITL/FRN. *Le Souffle de la Liberte* (FRN); *Andre Chenier* prod/rel: Lux Film (Roma), Lux de France (Paris)
La Boheme, Turin 1896, Opera
Addio Mimi! 1947 d: Carmine Gallone. lps: Marta Eggerth, Jan Kiepura, Janis Carter. 90M ITL. *Her Wonderful Lie* (USA); *La Boheme* prod/rel: Cineopera, Ceiad
Boheme, La 1965 d: Franco Zeffirelli. lps: Gianni Raimondi, Rolando Panerai, Gianni Maffeo. 107M SWT/ITL. prod/rel: Cosmotel Produktion (Zurich)

ILLIG, WERNER
Story
Lied Der Wuste, Das 1939 d: Paul Martin. lps: Zarah Leander, Herbert Wilk, Gustav Knuth. 86M GRM. *Desert Song* (USA) prod/rel: UFA

ILLYES, GYULA
A Kulonc, Play
Kulonc, A 1980 d: Laszlo Vamos. lps: Imre Sinkovits, Istvan Faraday, Peter Kertesz. TVM. 123M HNG.

IM CHUL-WOO
Gesom E Kako Shipta, Novel
Gesom E Kako Shipta 1993 d: Park Gwang-Su. lps: Ahn Song-Ki, Moon Sung-Kuen, Shim Hae-Jin. 102M SKR. *To the Starry Island* prod/rel: Park Gwang-Su, Samsung Nices

IMPEKOVEN, TONI
Diener Lassen Bitten, Play
Diener Lassen Bitten 1936 d: Hans H. Zerlett. lps: Hans Sohnker, Fita Benkhoff, Joe Stockel. 91M GRM. prod/rel: Euphono, Panorama
Das Ekel, Play
Ekel, Das 1939 d: Hans Deppe. lps: Hans Moser, Josefine Dora, Kurt Meisel. 80M GRM. prod/rel: Tobis

Das Kleine Hofkonzert, Play
Chanson du Souvenir, La 1936 d: Serge de Poligny, Douglas Sirk. lps: Max Michel, Pierre Magnier, Marta Eggerth. 95M FRN. *Concert a la Cour; Song of Remembrance* prod/rel: U.F.a., a.C.E.
Hofkonzert, Das 1936 d: Douglas Sirk. lps: Marta Eggerth, Johannes Heesters, Otto Tressler. 85M GRM. prod/rel: UFA
Kleine Hofkonzert, Das 1945 d: Paul Verhoeven. lps: Elfie Mayerhofer, Erich Ponto, Hans Nielsen. 70M GRM. *A Little Courtly Concert* prod/rel: Tobis, Atlantic

INAMDAR, V. M.
Shapa, Novel
Mukhti 1970 d: N. Lakshminarayan. lps: Kalpana, Rajasekhar, Udaya Kumar. 145M IND. *Deliverance; Mukti* prod/rel: Navodaya Chitra

INGALLS, RACHEL
The End of Tragedy, Novel
Dead on the Money 1991 d: Mark Cullingham. lps: Corbin Bernsen, John Glover, Amanda Pays. TVM. 100M USA. prod/rel: Turner Pictures©, Perfect Circle Corp.

INGE, WILLIAM (1913–1973), USA
Bus Stop, New York 1955, Play
Bus Stop 1956 d: Joshua Logan. lps: Marilyn Monroe, Don Murray, Arthur O'Connell. 96M USA. *The Wrong Kind of Girl* prod/rel: 20th Century-Fox Film Corp.
Come Back Little Sheba, New York 1950, Play
Come Back, Little Sheba 1952 d: Daniel Mann. lps: Shirley Booth, Burt Lancaster, Terry Moore. 99M USA. prod/rel: Paramount, Wallis-Hazen, Inc.
Come Back, Little Sheba 1977 d: Silvio Narizzano. lps: Laurence Olivier, Joanne Woodward, Carrie Fisher. TVM. 100M UKN. prod/rel: Granada Tv
The Dark at the Top of the Stairs, New York 1957, Play
Dark at the Top of the Stairs, The 1960 d: Delbert Mann. lps: Robert Preston, Dorothy McGuire, Eve Arden. 123M USA. prod/rel: Warner Bros.
Good Luck Miss Wyckoff, 1970, Novel
Good Luck, Miss Wyckoff 1979 d: Marvin J. Chomsky. lps: Anne Heywood, Donald Pleasence, Robert Vaughn. 105M USA. *The Sin; The Shaming; Secret Yearnings*
A Loss of Roses, New York 1959, Play
Stripper, The 1963 d: Franklin J. Schaffner. lps: Joanne Woodward, Richard Beymer, Claire Trevor. 95M USA. *Woman of Summer* (UKN); *Celebration; A Woman in July* prod/rel: Jerry Wald Productions
Picnic, New York 1953, Play
Picnic 1955 d: Joshua Logan. lps: William Holden, Kim Novak, Rosalind Russell. 115M USA. prod/rel: Columbia

INGHAM, TRAVIS
Biddy, 1933, Short Story
Most Precious Thing in Life 1934 d: Lambert Hillyer. lps: Jean Arthur, Donald Cook, Richard Cromwell. 68M USA. prod/rel: Columbia Pictures Corp.©

INGLETON, E. M.
The Flash of an Emerald, Short Story
Flash of an Emerald, The 1915 d: Albert Capellani. lps: Robert Warwick, Dorothy Fairchild, Jean Stewart. 5r USA. prod/rel: World Film Corp.©, Shubert Feature

INGLIN, MEINRAD
Der Schwarze Tanner, Short Story
Schwarze Tanner, Der 1986 d: Xavier Koller. lps: Otto machtlinger, Renate Steiger, Liliana Heimberg. 107M SWT. prod/rel: Catpics, S.R.F.

INGLINS, MEINRAD
Das Gefrorene Herz, Short Story
Gefrorene Herz, Das 1979 d: Xavier Koller. lps: Sigfrit Steiner, Emilia Krakowska, Paul Buhlmann. MTV. 108M SWT. *The Frozen Heart* prod/rel: Cine Group Zurich

INGOLDSBY, THOMAS
The Little Vulgar Boy, Poem
Little Vulgar Boy, The 1913 d: Wilfred Noy. 1000f UKN. prod/rel: Clarendon

INGRAM, ELEANOR M.
An Amazing Adventure, Story
Amazing Adventure, The 1917 d: Burton George. lps: Roberta Wilson, Charles Perley, Miss Gillette. 2r USA. prod/rel: Rex
The House of the Little Shoes, Novel
Little Shoes, The 1917 d: Arthur Berthelet. lps: Henry B. Walthall, Mary Charleson, Patrick Calhoun. 5r USA. prod/rel: Essanay Film Mfg. Co.©, K-E-S-E Service

The Unafraid, Philadelphia 1913, Novel
Unafraid, The 1915 d: Cecil B. de Mille. lps: Rita Jolivet, House Peters, Page Peters. 4r USA. prod/rel: Jesse L. Lasky Feature Play Co.©, Paramount Pictures Corp.

INGSTER, BORIS
The Karate Killers, Novel
Karate Killers, The 1967 d: Barry Shear. lps: Robert Vaughn, David McCallum, Joan Crawford. 92M USA. prod/rel: Arena, MGM

INNAURATO, ALBERT
Gemini, Play
Happy Birthday, Gemini 1980 d: Richard Benner. lps: Madeline Kahn, Rita Moreno, Robert Viharo. 107M USA. prod/rel: United Artists

INNES, HAMMOND (1913–, UKN, Hammond-Innes, Ralph
Campbell's Kingdom, Novel
Campbell's Kingdom 1957 d: Ralph Thomas. lps: Dirk Bogarde, Stanley Baker, Michael Craig. 100M UKN. prod/rel: Rank, Rank Film Distributors
Levkas Man, Novel
Levkas Man 1980 d: Carl Schultz. lps: Robert Coleby, Marius Goring, Kenneth Cope. 300M UKN/GRM/ASL. prod/rel: Portman, Studio Hamburg
The Lonely Skier, Novel
Snowbound 1948 d: David MacDonald. lps: Robert Newton, Dennis Price, Herbert Lom. 85M UKN. prod/rel: RKO Radio, Gainsborough
The White South, Novel
Hell Below Zero 1954 d: Mark Robson. lps: Alan Ladd, Joan Tetzel, Basil Sydney. 90M UKN. prod/rel: Warwick, Columbia
The Wreck of the Mary Deare, 1956, Novel
Wreck of the Mary Deare, The 1959 d: Michael Anderson. lps: Gary Cooper, Charlton Heston, Michael Redgrave. 105M USA/UKN. prod/rel: MGM, Julian Blaustein Prods.

INNES, MICHAEL (1906–, UKN, Stewart, J. I. M.
Christmas at Candleshoe, Novel
Candleshoe 1977 d: Norman Tokar. lps: David Niven, Jodie Foster, Helen Hayes. 101M USA/UKN. prod/rel: Walt Disney Productions

INOUE, YASUSHI (1907–1991), JPN
Furin Kazan, Tokyo 1955, Novel
Furin Kazan 1969 d: Hiroshi Inagaki. lps: Toshiro Mifune, Kinnosuke Nakamura, Yoshiko SakumA. 166M JPN. *Under the Banner of Samurai* (USA); *Samurai Banners* prod/rel: Mifune Productions, Toho Co.
Hongakubo Ibun, Novel
Sen No Rikyu - Hongakubo Ibun 1989 d: Kei Kumai. lps: Toshiro Mifune, Eiji Okuda, Kinnosuke YorozuyA. 107M JPN. *Death of a Tea Master* prod/rel: the Seiyu Ltd.
Kaseki, 1967, Novel
Kaseki 1975 d: Masaki Kobayashi. lps: Shin Saburi, Hisashi Igawa, Mayumi OgawA. 209M JPN. *Fossils* prod/rel: Haiyuza Film Production Co., Yonki-No-Kai
Koya, Novel
Koya 1993 d: Tetsutaro Murano. lps: Yoko Natori, Daisuke Ryu, Satoshi SadanagA. 100M JPN. *Koya: Memorial Notes of Choken* prod/rel: Tetsu Productions

INSUA, ALBERTO
La Mujer El Torero Y El Toro, 1926, Novel
Mujer, El Torero Y El Toro, La 1950 d: Fernando Butragueno. lps: Mario Cabre, Jacqueline Plesis, Curro Caro. 95M SPN.
El Negro Que Tenia El Alma Blanca, 1922, Novel
Negro Que Tenia El Alma Blanca, El 1926 d: Benito Perojo. lps: Raymond de Sarka, Conchita Piquer, Valentin ParerA. 83M SPN/FRN. *La Fatalite du Destin* (FRN); *Le Danseur de Jazz*; *Ame Blanche Peau Noire*; *The Black Man With a White Soul* prod/rel: Goya Films (Madrid)
El Negro Que Tenia El Alma Blanca, 1922, Novel
Negro Que Tenia El Alma Blanca, El 1933 d: Benito Perojo. lps: Antonita Colome, Angelillo, Marino Barreto. 83M SPN. *The Black Man With the White Soul*
Negro Que Tenia El Alma Blanca, El 1951 d: Hugo Del Carril. lps: Maria Rosa Salgado, Antonio Casal, Maria Asquerino. 94M ARG/SPN.
Los Vencedores de la Muerte, Novel
Vencedores de la Muerte, Los 1927 d: Antonio Calvache. lps: Juan de Orduna, Africa Llamas, Manuel Gonzalez. SPN. prod/rel: Film Numancia (Madrid)

INVERNIZIO, CAROLINA
Il Bacio Di Una Morta, 1903, Novel
Bacio Di Una Morta, Il 1917 d: Enrico Vidali. lps: Maria Gandini, Enrico Vidali, Lina de ChiesA. 1565m ITL. prod/rel: Italica Film

Bacio Di Una Morta, Il 1949 d: Guido Brignone. lps: Virginia Belmont, Gianna Maria Canale, Peter Trent. 90M ITL. *A Dead Woman's Kiss* (USA) prod/rel: Flora Film, Variety Film
Bacio Di Una Morta, Il 1974 d: Carlo Infascelli. lps: Silvia Dionisio, Orso Maria Guerrini, Peter Lee Lawrence. 95M ITL. prod/rel: Infafilm, Jumbo
Bacio, Il 1974 d: Mario Lanfranchi. lps: Maurizio Bonuglia, Eleonora Giorgi, Antonio Pierfederici. 105M ITL. prod/rel: Intervision S.P.a., Euro International Film
La Figlia Del Mendicante, Novel
Figlia Del Mendicante, La 1950 d: Carlo Campogalliani. lps: Paola Barbara, Jole Fierro, Franco Pesce. 90M ITL. prod/rel: Excelsior Film
La Mano Della Morta, Novel
Mano Della Morta, La 1949 d: Carlo Campogalliani. lps: Maria Martin, Adriano Rimoldi, Carlo Ninchi. 90M ITL. prod/rel: Icet
L' Orfana Del Ghetto, Novel
Orfana Del Ghetto, L' 1955 d: Carlo Campogalliani. lps: Franca Marzi, Luisella Boni, Renato Baldini. 89M ITL. prod/rel: Ambra Film
Piccoli Martiri, Novel
Piccolo Martiri 1917 d: Enrico Vidali. lps: Maria Gandini, Enrico Vidali, Francois-Paul Donadio. 1324m ITL. *L' Eroismo Di Ketty* prod/rel: Italica
Raffaella O I Misteri Del Vecchio Mercato, Novel
Nano Rosso, Il 1917 d: Elvira Notari. lps: Mario Alki, Mariu Gleck, Mademoiselle Noris. 1544m ITL. *La Fata Di Borgo Loreto* prod/rel: Films-Dora
La Regina Del Mercato, Novel
Regina Del Mercato, La 1921 d: Giovanni PezzingA. lps: Ruy Vismara, Eugenia Tettoni, Nino Novelli. 1023m ITL. prod/rel: Italica Film
Rina l'Angelo Delle Alpe, 1877, Novel
Angelo Delle Alpi, L' 1957 d: Carlo Campogalliani. lps: Luisella Boni, Alberto Farnese, Gino Sinimberghi. 2552m ITL. prod/rel: Prora Film
Rina, l'Angelo Delle Alpi 1917 d: Enrico Vidali. lps: Maria Gandini, Lina de Chiesa, Enrico Vidali. 1892m ITL. prod/rel: Italica
Satanella, 1897, Novel
Satanella 1919 d: Joseph Guarino, A. G. CaldierA. lps: La Perlowa, Guglielmo Bocchialini. 3717m ITL. prod/rel: Italica Film
La Sepolta Viva, 1900, Novel
Sepolta Viva, La 1916 d: Enrico Vidali. lps: Maria Gandini, Angelo Ferrari, Lina de ChiesA. 1355m ITL. prod/rel: Italica Film
La Trovatella Di Milano, Novel
Trovatella Di Milano, La 1956 d: Giorgio Capitani. lps: Massimo Serato, Otello Toso, Franca Marzi. F ITL. prod/rel: Filmex (Torino)
La Vendetta Di Una Pazza, Novel
Vendetta Di Una Pazza, La 1952 d: Pino Mercanti. lps: Lida Baarova, Otello Toso, Mino Doro. 85M ITL. prod/rel: Romana Film, Siden Film

IONESCO, EUGENE (1912–1994), RMN
Le Nouveau Locataire, 1958, Play
New Tenant, The 1964 d: George Brandt. 30M UKN.
Le Rhinoceros, 1959, Play
Nashorner, Die 1963 d: Jan LenicA. ANM. 11M PLN/GRM. *Rhinoceros* (USA); *Rhinoceroses*
Rhinoceros 1973 d: Tom O'Horgan. lps: Zero Mostel, Gene Wilder, Karen Black. 101M USA.

IRVINE, LUCY
Castaway, Book
Castaway 1987 d: Nicolas Roeg. lps: Oliver Reed, Amanda Donohue, Tony Rickards. 117M UKN. prod/rel: Cannon, United British Artists

IRVING, CLIFFORD
Trial, Book
Trial: the Price of Passion 1992 d: Paul Wendkos. lps: Peter Strauss, Beverly d'Angelo, Ned Beatty. TVM. 180M USA. prod/rel: Sokolow, Tri-Star Tv

IRVING, HARRY R.
Bohunk, Play
Black Fury 1935 d: Michael Curtiz. lps: Paul Muni, Karen Morley, William Gargan. 95M USA. *Black Hell* prod/rel: First National Productions Corp.

IRVING, JOHN (1942–, USA, Irving, John Winslow
The Hotel New Hampshire, 1981, Novel
Hotel New Hampshire, The 1983 d: Tony Richardson. lps: Rob Lowe, Jodie Foster, Matthew Modine. 108M USA/CND. *L' Hotel New Hampshire* prod/rel: Woodfall America Ltd. (Los Angeles), Filmline Productions Inc. (Montreal)

A Prayer for Owen Meany, Novel
Simon Birch 1998 d: Mark Steven Johnson. lps: Ian Michael Smith, Joseph Mazzello, Ashley Judd. 113M USA. prod/rel: Buena Vista, Hollywood Pictures
The World According to Garp, 1978, Novel
World According to Garp, The 1982 d: George Roy Hill. lps: Robin Williams, Mary Beth Hurt, Glenn Close. 136M USA. prod/rel: Warner Bros.

IRVING, WASHINGTON (1783–1859), USA, Knickerbocker, Dietrich
Astoria, Novel
John Colter's Escape 1912. lps: Herbert Rawlinson, Bessie Eyton. SHT USA. prod/rel: Selig Polyscope Co.
Father Knickerbocker's History of New York, 1809, Book
Knickerbocker Holiday 1944 d: Harry J. Brown. lps: Nelson Eddy, Charles Coburn, Constance Dowling. 85M USA. prod/rel: United Artists
The Legend of Sleepy Hollow, 1820, Short Story
Ichabod and Mr. Toad 1949 d: James Algar, Jack Kinney. ANM. 68M USA. *The Adventures of Ichabod and Mr. Toad* prod/rel: RKO Radio, Walt Disney
Legend of Sleepy Hollow 1908. 825f USA. prod/rel: Kalem
Legend of Sleepy Hollow, The 1949 d: Clyde Geronimi. ANM. 75M USA. prod/rel: RKO, Walt Disney
Legend of Sleepy Hollow, The 1980 d: Henning Schellerup. lps: Jeff Goldblum, Paul Sand, John Sylvester White. TVM. 97M USA. prod/rel: Slick Sun Classic Productions
Rip Van Winkle, 1820, Short Story
Rip Van Winkle 1903 d: Alf Collins. lps: Alf Collins, William Carrington. 450f UKN. prod/rel: Gaumont
Rip Van Winkle 1908 d: Otis Turner. lps: Hobart Bosworth, Betty Harte. 1000f USA. prod/rel: Selig Polyscope Co.
Rip Van Winkle 1910 d: Theodore Marston. lps: Frank Crane, Alphonse Ethier. 1000f USA. prod/rel: Thanhouser
Rip Van Winkle 1912 d: Charles Kent. lps: Robert McWade, Rose Tapley, Helene Costello. 2000f USA. prod/rel: Vitagraph Co. of America
Rip Van Winkle 1912. 2r USA. prod/rel: Union Features
Rip Van Winkle 1912. 2r USA. prod/rel: Reliance
Rip Van Winkle 1914 d: Stuart Kinder. lps: Fred Storey, Ella Brandon, Martin Stuart. 3000f UKN. *Forgotten* prod/rel: Climax
Rip Van Winkle 1914. lps: Thomas Jefferson, Clairette Claire, H. B. Blackmore. 5r USA. prod/rel: B. A. Rolfe Photoplays, Alco Film Corp.
Rip Van Winkle 1921 d: Ward Lascelle. lps: Thomas Jefferson, Milla Davenport, Daisy Robinson. 6700f USA. prod/rel: Ward Lascelle Productions, W. W. Hodkinson Corp.
The Spectre Bridegroom, Story
Spectre Bridegroom, The 1913. lps: Alec B. Francis. 2r USA. prod/rel: Eclair

IRWIN, EDWARD
The Bargain, Play
Bargain, The 1921 d: Henry Edwards. lps: Henry Edwards, Chrissie White, Rex McDougall. 5800f UKN. prod/rel: Hepworth

IRWIN, THEODORE D.
Collusion, New York 1932, Novel
Unknown Blonde 1934 d: Hobart Henley. lps: Edward Arnold, Dorothy Revier, Walter Catlett. 67M USA. *The Man Who Pawned His Soul* (UKN); *Broken Lives* prod/rel: Majestic Pictures Corp.

IRWIN, VIOLET
Human Desire, Boston 1913, Novel
Human Desire 1919 d: Wilfred North. lps: Anita Stewart, Conway Tearle, Eulalie Jensen. 6r USA. prod/rel: Louis B. Mayer Productions, Anita Stewart Productions

IRWIN, WALLACE (1875–1959), USA, Irwin, Wallace Admah
American Beauty, 1927, Short Story
American Beauty 1927 d: Richard Wallace. lps: Billie Dove, Lloyd Hughes, Walter McGrail. 6333f USA. *The Beautiful Fraud* (UKN) prod/rel: First National Pictures
Blooming Angel, New York 1919, Novel
Blooming Angel, The 1920 d: Victor Schertzinger. lps: Madge Kennedy, Pat O'Malley, Margery Wilson. 4392f USA. prod/rel: Goldwyn Pictures Corp.©, Goldwyn Distributing Corp.
Free, 1918, Short Story
Uplifters, The 1919 d: Herbert Blache. lps: May Allison, Pell Trenton, Alfred Hollingsworth. 5r USA. *Free* prod/rel: Metro Pictures Corp.©

Gentleman's Agreement, 1914, Short Story
Gentleman's Agreement, A 1918 d: David Smith. lps: Alfred Whitman, Nell Shipman, Juan de La Cruz. 4266f USA. prod/rel: Vitagraph Co. of America©, Blue Ribbon Feature

Hashimura Togo, New York 1914, Novel
Hashimura Togo 1917 d: William C. de Mille. lps: Sessue Hayakawa, Margaret Loomis, Tom Forman. 5r USA. prod/rel: Jesse L. Lasky Feature Play Co.©, Paramount Pictures Corp.

Lew Taylor's Wives, New York 1923, Novel
Lew Tyler's Wives 1926 d: Harley Knoles. lps: Frank Mayo, Ruth Clifford, Hedda Hopper. 6757f USA. prod/rel: Preferred Pictures

North Shore, Boston 1932, Novel
Woman in Red, The 1935 d: Robert Florey. lps: Barbara Stanwyck, Gene Raymond, Genevieve Tobin. 68M USA. *North Shore* prod/rel: First National Productions Corp., First National Pictures©

Sophie Semenoff, 1920, Short Story
Making the Grade 1921 d: Fred J. Butler. lps: David Butler, Helen Ferguson, William Walling. 4735f USA. *Sophie Semenoff* prod/rel: David Butler Productions

Tomorrow's Bread, 1924, Short Story
Golden Bed, The 1925 d: Cecil B. de Mille. lps: Lillian Rich, Vera Reynolds, Henry B. Walthall. 8584f USA. prod/rel: Famous Players-Lasky, Paramount Pictures

Trimmed With Red, New York 1920, Novel
Help Yourself 1920 d: Hugo Ballin. lps: Madge Kennedy, E. J. Radcliffe, Mrs. David Landau. 5-7r USA. *Trimmed With Red* prod/rel: Goldwyn Pictures Corp.©, Goldwyn Distributing Corp.

Venus in the East, New York 1918, Novel
Venus in the East 1919 d: Donald Crisp. lps: Bryant Washburn, Anna Q. Nilsson, Margery Wilson. 4347f USA. prod/rel: Famous Players-Lasky Corp.©, Paramount Pictures

IRWIN, WILL
Beating Back, 1913, Story
Beating Back 1914 d: Carroll Fleming. lps: Al Jennings, Madeline Fairbanks, Frank Jennings. 5r USA. prod/rel: Thanhouser Film Corp.©, Mutual Film Corp.

The Exalted Flapper, 1925, Short Story
Exalted Flapper, The 1929 d: James Tinling. lps: Sue Carol, Barry Norton, Irene Rich. 5806f USA. prod/rel: Fox Film Corp.

ISAACS, SUSAN
Compromising Positions, Novel
Compromising Positions 1985 d: Frank Perry. lps: Susan Sarandon, Raul Julia, Edward Herrmann. 98M USA. prod/rel: Paramount

ISABEKOV, DULAT
The Ordinary Life
Namis 1996 d: Ulzhan KoldauovA. lps: Shynar Askarova, Bayan Alim-Akyn, T. Jamankulov. 74M KZK. *The Honor* prod/rel: bcd

ISAKOVIC, ANTONIJE
Paprat I Vatra, Belgrade 1962, Novel
Tri 1965 d: Aleksandar Petrovic. lps: Slobodan Perovic, Velimir Zivojinovic, Ali Raner. 79M YGS. *Three; Trio* prod/rel: Avala Film

ISAKSSON, ULLA
Paradistorg, Novel
Paradistorg 1977 d: Gunnel Lindblom. lps: Birgitta Valberg, Agneta Ekmanner, Margareta Bystrom. 113M SWD. *Summer Paradise* (USA); *Paradise Square; Paradise Place* prod/rel: Ingmar Bergman Cinematograph, Svenska Filminstitutet

De Tva Saliga, Novel
Tva Saliga, de 1985 d: Ingmar Bergman. lps: Harriet Andersson, Per Myrberg, Christina Schollin. 81M SWD. prod/rel: Svt 2, ZDF

Det Vangila Vardiga, Story
Nara Livet 1958 d: Ingmar Bergman. lps: Ingrid Thulin, Bibi Andersson, Eva Dahlbeck. 83M SWD. *So Close to Life; Brink of Life* (USA) prod/rel: Nordisk Tonefilm

ISHAM, FREDERIC STEWART
Aladdin from Broadway, New York 1913, Novel
Aladdin from Broadway 1917 d: William Wolbert. lps: Antonio Moreno, Edith Storey, William Duncan. 5r USA. prod/rel: Vitagraph Co. of America©, Blue Ribbon Feature

Black Friday, Indianapolis 1904, Novel
Black Friday 1916 d: Lloyd B. Carleton. lps: Dorothy Davenport, Emory Johnson, Richard Morris. 5r USA. prod/rel: Universal Film Mfg. Co.©, Red Feather Photoplays

Half a Chance, Indianapolis 1909, Novel
Half a Chance 1913 d: Oscar Apfel. lps: George Siegmann, Irene Howley, Rosanna Logan. 3r USA. prod/rel: Reliance
Half a Chance 1920 d: Robert T. Thornby. lps: Mahlon Hamilton, Lillian Rich, Mary McAllister. 6-7r USA. prod/rel: Jesse D. Hampton Productions, Pathe Exchange, Inc.©

A Man and His Money, Indianapolis 1912, Novel
Man and His Money, A 1919 d: Harry Beaumont. lps: Tom Moore, Seena Owen, Sidney Ainsworth. 5r USA. prod/rel: Goldwyn Pictures Corp.©, Goldwyn Distributing Corp.

Nothing But the Truth, Indianapolis 1914, Novel
Nothing But the Truth 1920 d: David Kirkland. lps: Taylor Holmes, Elsie MacKaye, Ned Sparks. 6r USA. prod/rel: Taylor Holmes Productions, Inc.©, Metro Pictures Corp.
Nothing But the Truth 1929 d: Victor Schertzinger. lps: Richard Dix, Berton Churchill, Louis John Bartels. 7256f USA. prod/rel: Paramount Famous Lasky Corp.
Nothing But the Truth 1941 d: Elliott Nugent. lps: Bob Hope, Paulette Goddard, Edward Arnold. 90M USA. prod/rel: Paramount

The Nut-Cracker, Indianapolis 1920, Novel
Nutcracker, The 1926 d: Lloyd Ingraham. lps: Edward Everett Horton, Mae Busch, Harry Myers. 5782f USA. *You Can't Fool Your Wife* prod/rel: Samuel S. Hutchinson Productions, Associated Exhibitors

The Social Buccaneer, Indianapolis 1910, Novel
Social Buccaneer, The 1916 d: Jack Conway. lps: J. Warren Kerrigan, Louise Lovely, Maude George. 5r USA. *Social Buccaneers* prod/rel: Bluebird Photoplays, Inc.©

Three Live Ghosts, New York 1918, Novel
Three Live Ghosts 1922 d: George Fitzmaurice. lps: Norman Kerry, Anna Q. Nilsson, Edmund Goulding. 6600f USA/UKN. prod/rel: Famous Players-Lasky, Paramount Pictures
Three Live Ghosts 1929 d: Thornton Freeland. lps: Beryl Mercer, Hilda Vaughn, Harry Stubbs. 7486f USA. prod/rel: Joseph M. Schenck Productions, United Artists
Three Live Ghosts 1935 d: H. Bruce Humberstone. lps: Beryl Mercer, Richard Arlen, Claud Allister. 70M USA. prod/rel: Metro-Goldwyn-Mayer Corp.©

ISHERWOOD, CHRISTOPHER (1904–1986), UKN
The Berlin Stories, 1945, Book
Cabaret 1972 d: Bob Fosse. lps: Liza Minnelli, Michael York, Helmut Griem. 124M USA. prod/rel: Allied Artists
I Am a Camera 1955 d: Henry Cornelius. lps: Julie Harris, Laurence Harvey, Shelley Winters. 99M UKN. prod/rel: Romulus, Remus

ISHIGURO, KAZUO (1954–, JPN
The Remains of the Day, Novel
Remains of the Day, The 1993 d: James Ivory. lps: Anthony Hopkins, Emma Thompson, James Fox. 134M UKN/USA. prod/rel: Columbia, Merchant Ivory

ISHIHARA, SHINTARO
Aoi Satsujinsha, 1966, Novel
Fukushu No Uta Ga Kikoeru 1968 d: Yoshihisa Sadanaga, Shigeyuki Yamane. lps: Yoshio Harada, Ryohei Uchida, Arisa Ohtori. 90M JPN. *Song of Vengeance*

Chosen, Tokyo 1960, Novel
Ai to Honoho to 1961 d: Eizo SugawA. lps: Tatsuya Mihashi, Yoko Tsukasa, Yumi ShirakawA. 99M JPN. *Challenge to Live* prod/rel: Toho Co.

Kaseki No Mori, 1970, Novel
Kaseki No Mori 1973 d: Masahiro ShinodA. lps: Kenichi Hagiwara, Sayoko Ninomiya, Masako Yagi. 118M JPN. *The Petrified Forest*

Kawaita Hana, 1958, Short Story
Kawaita Hana 1964 d: Masahiro ShinodA. lps: Ryo Ikebe, Mariko Kaga, Takashi FujikA. 98M JPN. *Pale Flower*

Shokei No Heya, 1956, Short Story
Shokei No Heya 1956 d: Kon IchikawA. lps: Hiroshi Kawaguchi, Keizo Kawasaki, Ayako Wakao. 95M JPN. *Punishment Room* prod/rel: Daiei Motion Picture Co.

Wakai Kemono, Novel
Wakai Kemono 1958 d: Shintaro IshiharA. lps: Akira Kubo, Reiko Dan, Seizaburo Kawazu. 99M JPN. *The Young Beast* prod/rel: Toho Co.

ISHIKAWA, TATSUZO
Aoiro Kakumei, 1952-53, Novel
Aoiro Kakumei 1953 d: Kon IchikawA. lps: Koreya Senda, Asami Kuji, Rentaro Mikuni. 108M JPN. *The Blue Revolution* prod/rel: Toho Co.

Mitasareta Seikatsu, Novel
Mitasareta Seikatsu 1962 d: Susumu Hani. lps: Ineko Arima, Koshiro Harada, Ai George. 107M JPN. *A Full Life* (USA) prod/rel: Shochiku

ISHIKAWA, YOSHIMI
Sutoroberi Road, Novel
Sutoroberi Road 1991 d: Koreyoshi KuraharA. lps: Ken Matsudaira, Pat Morita, Mako. 117M JPN. *Strawberry Road* prod/rel: Tokyo Hoei Television Co.

ISHIZAKA, YOJIRO
Hi No Ataru Sakamichi, 1958, Novel
Hi No Ataru Sakamichi 1958 d: Tomotaka TasakA. 105M JPN. *Street in the Sun*

Ishinaka-Sensei Gyojuki, 1948-49, Novel
Ishinaka Sensei Gyojoki 1950 d: Mikio Naruse. 96M JPN. *Conduct Report of Professor Ishinaka; Conduct Report on Professor Ishinawa*

Kiri No Naka No Shojo, 1955, Short Story
Kuchizuke III: Onna Doshi 1955 d: Mikio Naruse, Masanori Kakei. 115M JPN. *The Kiss Part III: Women's Ways; The First Kiss*

Kuchizuke, 1954, Short Story
Kuchizuke III: Onna Doshi 1955 d: Mikio Naruse, Masanori Kakei. 115M JPN. *The Kiss Part III: Women's Ways; The First Kiss*

Magokoro, 1939, Short Story
Magokoro 1939 d: Mikio Naruse. 80M JPN. *Sincerity*

Onna Doshi, 1955, Short Story
Kuchizuke III: Onna Doshi 1955 d: Hideo Suzuki. JPN.

Suzukake No Sanpomichi, Play
Suzukake No Sanpomichi 1959 d: Hiromichi HorikawA. lps: Yoko Tsukasa, Keiko Tsushima, Kyoko AoyamA. 71M JPN. *The Path Under the Plane-Trees; The Path Under the Platanes* prod/rel: Toho Co.

Wakai Hito, 1933-36, Novel
Wakai Hito 1937 d: Shiro ToyodA. 81M JPN. *Young People*
Wakai Hito 1952 d: Kon IchikawA. lps: Ryo Ikebe, Kumoko Shimazaki, Asami Hisaji. 113M JPN. *Young Generation; Young People* prod/rel: Toho Co.

ISLAND, BERT F.
Kommissar X: Drei Gelbe Katzen, Novel
Kommissar X: Drei Gelbe Katzen 1966 d: Rudolf Zehetgruber. lps: Luciano Stella, Brad Harris, Ann Smyrner. 95M AUS/ITL/FRN. prod/rel: Danubia, Danny

Kommissar X: Drei Goldene Schlangen, Novel
Kommissar X: Drei Goldene Schlangen 1968 d: Roberto Mauri. lps: Luciano Stella, Brad Harris, Loni Heuser. 88M GRM/ITL. *Commissioner X - Three Golden Snakes* prod/rel: Terra, Parnass

Kommissar X: Drei Grune Hunde, Novel
Kommissar X: Drei Grune Hunde 1967 d: Rudolf Zehetgruber, Gianfranco Parolini. lps: Luciano Stella, Brad Harris, Olinka BerovA. 93M GRM/FRN/ITL. *Commissaire X Traque Les Chiens Verts* (FRN); *Commissioner X -Three Green Dogs; Strategic Command Chiama Jo Walker* (ITL) prod/rel: Cinescolo (Milano), Parnass Film (Munich)

Kommissar X: in Den Klauen Des Goldenen Drachen, Novel
Kommissar X: in Den Klauen Des Goldenen Drachen 1966 d: Gianfranco Parolini. lps: Luciano Stella, Brad Harris, Barbara Frey. 96M AUS/ITL/GRM. prod/rel: Parnass, Avala

Kommissar X: Jagd Auf Unbekannt, Novel
Kommissar X: Jagd Auf Unbekannt 1965 d: Rudolf Zehetgruber, Gianfranco Parolini. lps: Luciano Stella, Brad Harris, Maria Perschy. 92M GRM/ITL/YGS. *Dodici Donne d'Oro* (ITL); *Kiss Kiss Kill Kill* (UKN); *Kommissar X - Hunter of the Unknown; Commissioner X - Unknown Prey* prod/rel: Metheus Film (Roma), Parnass Film (Munich)

ISRAEL, CHARLES
The Mark, New York 1958, Novel
Mark, The 1961 d: Guy Green. lps: Maria Schell, Stuart Whitman, Rod Steiger. 127M UKN. prod/rel: Raymond Stross Productions, 20th Century-Fox

ISTRATI, PANAIT
Les Chardons du Baragan, 1928, Novel
Ciulinii Baraganului 1957 d: Louis Daquin, Gheorghe Vitanidis. lps: Ruxandra Ionescu, Ana Vladescu, Florin Piersic. 113M FRN/RMN. *Les Chardons du Baragan* (FRN); *The Thistles of Baragan; The Thistles of the Baragan; Baragan Thistles*

Codin, 1926, Novel
Codine 1962 d: Henri Colpi. lps: Alexandru Virgil Platon, Razvan Petresco, Francoise Brion. 98M FRN/RMN. prod/rel: Como Films, Les Films Tamara

ITARD, JEAN
Memoire Et Rapport Sur Victor de l'Aveyron, Paris 1801-07
  Enfant Sauvage, L' 1970 d: Francois Truffaut. lps: Francois Truffaut, Jean-Pierre Cargol, Jean Daste. 90M FRN. *The Wild Child* (USA); *The Wild Boy* (UKN) prod/rel: Films Du Carrosse, Les Productions Artistes Associes

ITO, SACHIO
Nogiku No Haka, 1906, Novel
  Nogiku No Gotoki Kimi Nariki 1955 d: Keisuke KinoshitA. 92M JPN. *She Was Like a Wild Chrysanthemum*; *You are Like a Daisy*; *You Were Like a Wild Chrysanthemum*

ITSUKI, HIROSUKI
Saraba Mosukuwa Gurentai, Tokyo 1967, Short Story
  Saraba Mosukuwa Gurentai 1968 d: Hiromichi HorikawA. lps: Yuzo Kayama, Toshiko Morita, Shigeru KoyamA. 97M JPN. *Goodbye Moscow* prod/rel: Toho Co.

IVANOV, VSEVOLOD (1895–1963), RSS, Ivanov Vsevolod Vyacheslavovich
Bronepoezd No.14-69, 1922, Play
  Tommy 1931 d: Yakov Protazanov. 63M USS. *Siberian Patrol*; *Sibirsky Patrol*

IVANS, Van Schevichaven, Jakob
De Man Op Den Achtergrond, 1918, Novel
  Man Op Den Achtergrond, de 1923 d: Ernest Winar. lps: Eduard Ijdo, Adolphe Engers, Paula de Waart. 2405m NTH/GRM. *Der Mann Im Hintergrund* (GRM); *The Man in the Background* prod/rel: Ofo Film (Hague), Filmindustrie Und Handels-a.G. (Berlin)

IVASIUC, ALEXANDRU
Apa, 1973, Novel
  Trei Zile Si Trei Nopti 1976 d: Dinu Tanase. 113M RMN. *Three Days and Three Nights*

IVERS, AXEL
Parkstrasse 13, Play
  Parkstrasse 13 1939 d: Jurgen von Alten. lps: Olga Tschechowa, Hilde Hildebrand, Iwan Petrovich. 82M GRM. *Verhor Um Mitternacht* prod/rel: Astra, Adler

IVERS, JULIA CRAWFORD
Fatherhood, Story
  Fatherhood 1915 d: Hobart Bosworth. lps: Hobart Bosworth, Joseph Flores, Hart Hoxie. 4r USA. prod/rel: Universal Film Mfg. Co.©

IWASHITA, SHUNSAKU
Muhomatsu No Issho, Novel
  Muhomatsu No Issho 1958 d: Hiroshi Inagaki. lps: Toshiro Mifune, Hideko Takamine, Hiroshi AkutagawA. 104M JPN. *The Rickshaw Man* (UKN) prod/rel: Toho Co.

IWASZKIEWICZ, JAROSLAW
Brzezina, 1933, Short Story
  Brzezina 1971 d: Andrzej WajdA. lps: Daniel Olbrychski, Emilia Krakowska, Olgierd Lukaszewicz. MTV. 99M PLN. *The Birch Wood* (USA); *Birchwood*

Kochankowie Z Marony, 1961, Short Story
  Kochankowie Z Marony 1966 d: Jerzy Zarzycki. lps: Barbara Horawianka, Andrzej Antkowiak. 102M PLN. *The Lovers of Marona*

Kosciot W Skaryszewie, 1967, Short Story
  Rys 1981 d: Stanislaw Rozewicz. lps: Jerzy Radziwilowicz, Franciszek Pieczka, Piotr Bajor. 84M PLN. *The Smile of the Evil Eye*; *Lynx*

Matka Joanna Od Aniolow, 1946, Short Story
  Matka Joanna Od Aniolow 1961 d: Jerzy Kawalerowicz. lps: Lucyna Winnicka, Mieczyslaw Voit, Anna CiepielewskA. 125M PLN. *The Devil and the Nun* (UKN); *Joan of the Angels*; *Mother Joan of the Angels*; *Mother Joan and Angels* prod/rel: Zespol Realizatorow Filmowych Kadr

Panny Z Wilko, 1933, Short Story
  Panny Z Wilko 1979 d: Andrzej WajdA. lps: Daniel Olbrychski, Anna Seniuk, Christine Pascal. 116M PLN/FRN. *Les Demoiselles de Wilko* (FRN); *The Maids of Wilko* (USA); *The Girls from Wilko*; *The Young Ladies of Wilko*; *The Young Girls of Wilko* (UKN) prod/rel: Prf Zespoly Filmowe, Filmgruppe X

Roza, 1936, Short Story
  Ubranie Prawie Nowe 1963 d: Wlodzimierz Haupe. lps: Lucyna Winnicka, Hanna Skarzanka, Ryszarda Hanin. 95M PLN. *A Hand-Me-Down Suit*; *The Suit Almost New*; *New Clothes*; *The Almost-New Suit*

Slawa I Chwala, Novel
  Slawa I Chwala 1997 d: Kazimierz Kuc. lps: Joanna Szczepkowska, Teresa Budzisz-Krzyzanowska, Anna Radwan. F PLN. *Fame and Glory* prod/rel: Open, Tvp

IWERING, TOMMY
Novel
  Sweet Revenge 1987 d: Terence Young. lps: David Carradine, Lauren Hutton, George Segal. 87M USA/ITL. *Marathon* (ITL); *Run for Your Life* prod/rel: Rai, Fremantle

IYER, G. V.
Bedara Kannappa, Play
  Bedara Kannappa 1954 d: H. L. N. SimhA. lps: Rajkumar, G. V. Iyer, Pandharibai. 155M IND. prod/rel: Gubbi Karnataka Films

IZHAR, S.
Story
  Khirbet Hiza'a 1978 d: Ram Loevy. lps: Dalik Volonitz, Shraga Harpaz, Gidi Gov. TVM. F ISR. prod/rel: Israel Television

IZUMI, KYOKA
Baishoku Kamonanban, 1920, Novel
  Orizuru Osen 1934 d: Kenji Mizoguchi. lps: Isuzu Yamada, Daijiro Natsukawa, Mitsusaburo Ramon. 100M JPN. *The Downfall of Osen* (USA); *The Downfall* (UKN); *Paper Cranes from Osen* prod/rel: Daiichi Eiga Co.

Kagero-Za, Novel
  Kagero-Za 1981 d: Seijun Suzuki. lps: Katsuo Nakamura, Mariko Koga, Yusaku MatsudA. 139M JPN. *Theatre Troupe Kagero*; *Theatre of Shimmering Light*; *Heat-Haze Theatre* prod/rel: Cinema Placet

Koya Hijiri, Tokyo 1901, Novel
  Byakuya No Yojo 1958 d: Eisuke TakizawA. lps: Yumeji Tsukioka, Ryoji Hayama, Tadashi Kobayashi. 88M JPN. *The Temptress and the Monk* (USA); *Death By Witchcraft*; *The Temptress*; *The Enchantress* prod/rel: Nikkatsu Corporation

Nihonbashi, 1914, Novel
  Nihonbashi 1956 d: Kon IchikawA. lps: Chikage Awashima, Fujiko Yamamoto, Ayako Wakao. 112M JPN. *Bridge of Japan* prod/rel: Daiei Motion Picture Co.

Shirasagi, 1909, Novel
  Shirasagi 1958 d: Teinosuke KinugasA. lps: Fujiko Yamamoto. 97M JPN. *The White Heron*; *Snowy Heron*

Taki No Shiraito, Novel
  Taki No Shiraito 1933 d: Kenji Mizoguchi. lps: Tokihiko Okada, Takako Irie, Suzuko Taki. 110M JPN. *The Water Magician* (UKN); *White Threads of the Waterfall*; *White Threads of the Cascades* prod/rel: Irie Productions

Uta Andon, 1910, Novel
  Uta Andon 1943 d: Mikio Naruse. 93M JPN. *Song of the Lantern*; *The Song Lantern*
  Uta Andon 1960 d: Teinosuke KinugasA. 114M JPN. *The Lantern*; *The Old Lantern*

Yashagaike, 1913, Play
  Yasha-Ga-Ike 1979 d: Masahiro ShinodA. lps: Tsutomu Yamazaki, Go Kato, Koji NanbarA. 123M JPN. *The Yasha Pond*; *Demon Pond* (USA); *Yashagaike* prod/rel: Shochiku Co.

J

JACCARD, CIELA
I.O.U.'S of Death, Story
  Senor Jim 1936 d: Jacques Jaccard. lps: Conway Tearle, Barbara Bedford, Alberta Dugan. 61M USA. *Murder in the Dark* (UKN) prod/rel: Beaumont Pictures, State Rights

JACKSON, CHARLES REGINALD (1903–1968), USA
The Lost Weekend, 1944, Novel
  Lost Weekend, The 1945 d: Billy Wilder. lps: Ray Milland, Jane Wyman, Phillip Terry. 101M USA. prod/rel: Paramount

JACKSON, CHARLES TENNEY
Captain Sazarac, Indianapolis 1922, Novel
  Eagle of the Sea, The 1926 d: Frank Lloyd. lps: Florence Vidor, Ricardo Cortez, Sam de Grasse. 7250f USA. *The Sea Eagle* prod/rel: Famous Players-Lasky, Paramount Pictures

The Day of Souls, Indianapolis 1910, Novel
  Show, The 1926 d: Tod Browning. lps: John Gilbert, Renee Adoree, Lionel Barrymore. 6309f USA. prod/rel: Metro-Goldwyn-Mayer Pictures

The Golden Fetter, Short Story
  Golden Fetter, The 1917 d: Edward J. Le Saint. lps: Wallace Reid, Anita King, Tully Marshall. 5r USA. prod/rel: Jesse L. Lasky Feature Play Co.©, Paramount Pictures Corp.

The Midlanders, Indianapolis 1912, Novel
  Midlanders, The 1920 d: Ida May Park, Joseph de Grasse. lps: Bessie Love, Truman Van Dyke, Frances Raymond. 6r USA. prod/rel: Andrew J. Callaghan Productions©, Federated Film Exchanges of America, Inc

JACKSON, FELIX
Story
  Bundle of Joy 1957 d: Norman Taurog. lps: Debbie Reynolds, Eddie Fisher, Adolphe Menjou. 98M USA. prod/rel: RKO

JACKSON, FREDERICK (1886–1953), USA
Novel
  Precious Packet, The 1916 d: Donald MacKenzie. lps: Ralph Kellard, Lois Meredith, W. Tabor Wetmore. 5r USA. prod/rel: Pathe Exchange, Inc.©, Gold Rooster Plays

Story
  Sensations of 1945 1944 d: Andrew L. Stone. lps: Eleanor Powell, Dennis O'Keefe, C. Aubrey Smith. 87M USA. *Sensations* prod/rel: United Artists

Annie for Spite, 1916, Short Story
  Annie-for-Spite 1917 d: James Kirkwood. lps: Mary Miles Minter, George Fisher, Eugenie Forde. 5r USA. *Sally Shows the Way* prod/rel: American Film Co.©, Mutual Film Corp.

Beauty to Let, Short Story
  Money Isn't Everything 1918 d: Edward Sloman. lps: Margarita Fischer, Jack Mower, Morris Foster. 5r USA. prod/rel: American Film Co.©, Pathe Exchange, Inc.

The Bishop Misbehaves, New York 1935, Play
  Bishop Misbehaves, The 1935 d: E. A. Dupont. lps: Edmund Gwenn, Maureen O'Sullivan, Norman Foster. 86M USA. *The Bishop's Misadventures* (UKN) prod/rel: Metro-Goldwyn-Mayer Corp.

Black Marriage, Story
  Her Man O' War 1926 d: Frank Urson. lps: Jetta Goudal, William Boyd, Jimmie Adams. 6106f USA. prod/rel: de Mille Pictures, Producers Distributing Corp.

A Full House, New York 1915, Play
  Full House, A 1920 d: James Cruze. lps: Bryant Washburn, Lois Wilson, Guy Milham. 4200f USA. prod/rel: Famous Players-Lasky Corp.©, Paramount-Artcraft Pictures

The Gray Parasol, 1918, Short Story
  Grey Parasol, The 1918 d: Lawrence C. Windom. lps: Wellington Cross, Claire Anderson, Joe Bennett. 5r USA. *The Gray Parasol* prod/rel: Triangle Film Corp., Triangle Distributing Corp.

Her First Affaire, London 1930, Play
  Her First Affaire 1932 d: Allan Dwan. lps: Ida Lupino, George Curzon, Diana Napier. 72M UKN. prod/rel: St. George's Productions, Sterling

Her Martyrdom, Story
  Her Martyrdom 1915. lps: Arthur Johnson, Lottie Briscoe, Howard Mitchell. 3r USA. prod/rel: Lubin

Her Past, London 1929, Play
  My Sin 1931 d: George Abbott. lps: Tallulah Bankhead, Fredric March, Harry Davenport. 79M USA. *Her Past* prod/rel: Paramount Publix Corp.

High Speed, 1918, Short Story
  High Speed 1924 d: Herbert Blache. lps: Herbert Rawlinson, Carmelita Geraghty, Bert Roach. 4927f USA. prod/rel: Universal Pictures

The Hole in the Wall, New York 1920, Play
  Hole in the Wall, The 1921 d: Maxwell Karger. lps: Alice Lake, Allan Forrest, Frank Brownlee. 6100f USA. prod/rel: Metro Pictures

  Hole in the Wall, The 1929 d: Robert Florey. lps: Claudette Colbert, Edward G. Robinson, David Newell. 73M USA. prod/rel: Paramount Famous Lasky Corp.

The Iron Woman, 1932, Play
  That's My Uncle 1935 d: George Pearson. lps: Mark Daly, Richard Cooper, Betty Astell. 58M UKN. *The Iron Woman* prod/rel: Twickenham, Universal

Jack of Diamonds, Story
  Ladies Beware 1927 d: Charles Giblyn. lps: George O'Hara, Nola Luxford, Florence Wix. 4900f USA. prod/rel: R-C Pictures Film, Film Booking Offices of America

La la Lucille, New York 1919, Musical Play
  La la Lucille 1920 d: Eddie Lyons, Lee Moran. lps: Eddie Lyons, Lee Moran, Anne Cornwall. 5r USA. prod/rel: Universal Film Mfg. Co.©

Morocco Box, 1923, Short Story
  Love Letters 1924 d: David Soloman. lps: Shirley Mason, Gordon Edwards, Alma Francis. 4749f USA. prod/rel: Fox Film Corp.

The Naughty Wife, New York 1917, Play
Let's Elope 1919 d: John S. Robertson. lps: Marguerite Clark, Gaston Glass, Frank Mills. 5r USA. *The Naughty Wife; Losing Eloise; A Honeymoon for Three; Three Is a Crowd* prod/rel: Famous Players-Lasky Corp.©, Paramount Pictures

One a Minute, Play
One a Minute 1921 d: Jack Nelson. lps: Douglas MacLean, Marian de Beck, Victor Potel. 4510f USA. prod/rel: Thomas H. Ince Productions, Paramount Pictures

School for Husbands, 1932, Play
School for Husbands 1937 d: Andrew Marton. lps: Diana Churchill, June Clyde, Rex Harrison. 71M UKN. prod/rel: Wainwright, General Film Distributors

Stop Flirting, London 1923, Play
Stop Flirting 1925 d: Scott Sidney. lps: John T. Murray, Wanda Hawley, Hallam Cooley. 5161f USA. prod/rel: Christie Film Co., Producers Distributing Corp.

The Widow's Might, 1931, Play
Widow's Might, The 1935 d: Cyril Gardner. lps: Laura La Plante, Yvonne Arnaud, Garry Marsh. 77M UKN. *Widows Might* prod/rel: Warner Bros., First National

JACKSON, HELEN HUNT (1830–1885), USA, Jackson, Helen Maria Fiske Hunt
Ramona, Boston 1884, Novel
Ramona 1910 d: D. W. Griffith. lps: Mary Pickford, Henry B. Walthall, Frank Grandin. 995f USA. prod/rel: Biograph Co.
Ramona 1916 d: Donald Crisp. lps: Adda Gleason, Monroe Salisbury, Richard Sterling. 12r USA. prod/rel: Clune Film Producing Co., State Rights
Ramona 1928 d: Edwin Carewe. lps: Dolores Del Rio, Warner Baxter, Roland Drew. 7650f USA. prod/rel: Inspiration Pictures, United Artists
Ramona 1936 d: Henry King. lps: Loretta Young, Don Ameche, Kent Taylor. 84M USA. prod/rel: Twentieth Century-Fox Film Corp.©

JACKSON, JOSEPH
The Champ, Story
Be Yourself! 1930 d: Thornton Freeland. lps: Fanny Brice, Robert Armstrong, Harry Green. 77M USA. *The Champ* prod/rel: United Artists

JACKSON, SHIRLEY (1919–1965), USA
The Bird's Nest, 1954, Novel
Lizzie 1957 d: Hugo Haas. lps: Eleanor Parker, Richard Boone, Joan Blondell. 81M USA. prod/rel: MGM, Bryna Prods.

The Bus, Short Story
Hosszu Alkony 1997 d: Attila Janisch. lps: Mari Torocsik, Denes Ujlaki, Imre CsujA. 68M HNG. *Long Twilight* prod/rel: Mtv-Fms Studio, Budapest Film Studio

The Haunting of Hill House, New York 1959, Novel
Haunting, The 1963 d: Robert Wise. lps: Julie Harris, Claire Bloom, Richard Johnson. 112M UKN. prod/rel: Argyle Enterprises, MGM

JACKSON, STANLEY
The Man Who Wouldn't Talk, Novel
Man Who Wouldn't Talk, The 1958 d: Herbert Wilcox. lps: Anna Neagle, Anthony Quayle, Katherine Kath. 97M UKN. prod/rel: Everest, British Lion

JACKSON VEYAN, JOSE
Los Granujas, Play
Granujas, Los 1924 d: Fernando Delgado, Manuel NoriegA. lps: Alfredo Hurtado, Elisa Ruiz Romero, Clotilde Romero. 42M SPN. *The Rogues* prod/rel: Ediciones Maricampo (Madrid)

Los Guapos, Play
Guapos O Gente Brava, Los 1923 d: Manuel NoriegA. lps: Eugenia Zuffoli, Manuel Rusell, Javier de RiverA. 2205m SPN. prod/rel: Atlantida

JACOBI, CARL
The Riddle: Woman, Play
Riddle: Woman, The 1920 d: Edward Jose. lps: Geraldine Farrar, Montagu Love, William T. Carleton. 5785f USA. prod/rel: Associated Exhibitors, Inc., Pathe Exchange, Inc.©

JACOBI, WILHELM
Der Doppelmensch, Play
Himmel Auf Erden, Der 1927 d: Alfred Schirokauer. lps: Reinhold Schunzel, Charlotte Ander, Adele Sandrock. 2676m GRM. prod/rel: Reinhold Schunzel Film-Prod.

JACOBS, CLAIRE R.
There Was a Little Boy, Book
There Was a Little Boy 1993 d: Mimi Leder. lps: Cybill Shepherd, John Heard, Scott Bairstow. TVM. 120M USA.

JACOBS, JACK
Man of Fire, Television Play
Man on Fire 1957 d: Ranald MacDougall. lps: Bing Crosby, Inger Stevens, Mary Fickett. 95M USA. prod/rel: MGM

JACOBS, JIM
Grease, Musical Play
Grease 1978 d: Randall Kleiser. lps: John Travolta, Olivia Newton-John, Stockard Channing. 111M USA. prod/rel: Paramount

JACOBS, T. C. H.
Traitor Spy, Novel
Traitor Spy 1939 d: Walter Summers. lps: Bruce Cabot, Marta Labarr, Tamara Desni. 75M UKN. *The Torso Murder Mystery* (USA) prod/rel: Rialto, Pathe

JACOBS, W. W. (1863–1943), UKN, Jacobs, William Wymark
Beauty and the Barge, London 1904, Play
Beauty and the Barge 1914 d: Harold Shaw. lps: Cyril Maude, Lillian Logan, Gregory Scott. 1242f UKN. prod/rel: London, Fenning

Beauty and the Barge 1937 d: Henry Edwards. lps: Gordon Harker, Judy Gunn, Jack Hawkins. 71M UKN. prod/rel: Twickenham, Wardour

The Bosun's Mate, Short Story
Boatswain's Mate, The 1924 d: Manning Haynes. lps: Florence Turner, Victor McLaglen, Johnny Butt. 1900f UKN. prod/rel: Artistic

Bosun's Mate, The 1914 d: Harold Shaw. lps: W. H. Berry, Mary Brough, Wyndham Guise. 1130f UKN. prod/rel: London, Fenning

Bosun's Mate, The 1953 d: Richard Warren. lps: Cameron Hall, Barbara Mullen, Edwin Richfield. 30M UKN. prod/rel: Anvil, General Film Distributors

The Bravo, Short Story
Bravo, The 1928 d: Geoffrey H. Malins. lps: Frank Stanmore. 2000f UKN. prod/rel: Welsh-Pearson

Captains All, Short Story
Constable's Move, The 1923 d: Manning Haynes. lps: Charles Ashton, Johnny Butt. 1900f UKN. prod/rel: Artistic

The Changeling, Short Story
Changeling, The 1928 d: Geoffrey H. Malins. lps: Frank Stanmore, James Reardon, Annie Esmond. 2000f UKN. prod/rel: Welsh-Pearson

Deep Waters, Short Story
Convert, The 1923 d: Manning Haynes. lps: Johnny Butt, Robert Vallis, Cynthia Murtagh. 1900f UKN. prod/rel: Artistic

Dixon's Return, Short Story
Dixon's Return 1924 d: Manning Haynes. lps: Moore Marriott, Leal Douglas, Tom Coventry. 1800f UKN. prod/rel: Artistic

Double Dealing, Short Story
Double Dealing 1928 d: Geoffrey H. Malins. lps: Pat Aherne, Dodo Watts, Philip Hewland. 2000f UKN. prod/rel: Welsh-Pearson

The Head of the Family, Short Story
Head of the Family, The 1922 d: Manning Haynes. lps: Johnny Butt, Cynthia Murtagh, Charles Ashton. 5500f UKN. prod/rel: Artistic

Her Uncle, Short Story
Her Uncle 1915 d: George Loane Tucker. lps: Charles Rock, Edward Silwood, Judd Green. 1350f UKN. prod/rel: London, Jury

His Lordship, Short Story
His Lordship 1915 d: George Loane Tucker. lps: Frank Stanmore, Judd Green, Mary Brough. 2065f UKN. prod/rel: London, Jury

In Borrowed Plumes, Short Story
In Borrowed Plumes 1928 d: Geoffrey H. Malins. lps: Charles Paton, Harry Terry, Bobby Kerrigan. 2000f UKN. prod/rel: Welsh-Pearson

The Interruption, Novel
Footsteps in the Fog 1955 d: Arthur Lubin. lps: Stewart Granger, Jean Simmons, Bill Travers. 90M UKN. prod/rel: Film Locations, Columbia

Lawyer Quince, Short Story
Lawyer Quince 1914 d: Harold Shaw. lps: Charles Rock, Lillian Logan, Gregory Scott. 1078f UKN. prod/rel: London, Fenning

Lawyer Quince 1924 d: Manning Haynes. lps: Moore Marriott, Cynthia Murtagh, Charles Ashton. 2200f UKN. prod/rel: Artistic

Light Freights, Short Story
Odd Freak, An 1916 d: George Loane Tucker. lps: Frank Stanmore, Judd Green. 1360f UKN. prod/rel: London, Jury

Odd Freak, An 1923 d: Manning Haynes. lps: Johnny Butt, Gladys Hamer, Moore Marriott. 1900f UKN. prod/rel: Artistic

A Marked Man, Short Story
Marked Man, A 1916 d: Frank Miller. lps: Frank Stanmore, Judd Green, James Reardon. 1795f UKN. prod/rel: London, Jury

A Master of Craft, Short Story
Master of Craft, A 1922 d: Thomas Bentley. lps: Fred Groves, Mercy Hatton, Judd Green. 4937f UKN. prod/rel: Ideal

Mixed Relations, Short Story
Mixed Relations 1916 d: George Loane Tucker. lps: Frank Stanmore. 1828f UKN. prod/rel: London, Jury

The Money Box, 1931, Short Story
Our Relations 1936 d: Harry Lachman. lps: Stan Laurel, Oliver Hardy, Sidney Toler. 74M USA. *The Money Box* prod/rel: Hal Roach Studios, Metro-Goldwyn-Mayer Corp.©

The Monkey's Paw, 1902, Short Story
Espiritismo 1961 d: Benito Alazraki. lps: Nora Veyran, Jose Luis Jimenez, Jorge Mondragon. 90M MXC. *Spiritism* (USA) prod/rel: Cinematografica Caldreron

Monkey's Paw, The 1915 d: Sidney Northcote. lps: John Lawson. 2800f UKN. prod/rel: Magnet

Monkey's Paw, The 1923 d: Manning Haynes. lps: Moore Marriott, Marie Ault, Charles Ashton. 5700f UKN. prod/rel: Artistic

Monkey's Paw, The 1933 d: Wesley Ruggles. lps: C. Aubrey Smith, Ivan Simpson, Louise Carter. 56M USA. prod/rel: RKO Radio Pictures©

Monkey's Paw, The 1948 d: Norman Lee. lps: Milton Rosmer, Megs Jenkins, Joan Seton. 64M UKN. prod/rel: Kay Films, Butcher's Film Service

Odd Charges, Short Story
Odd Charges 1916 d: Frank Miller. lps: Frank Stanmore, James Reardon, Kenelm Foss. 2300f UKN. prod/rel: London, Jury

Passion Island, Novel
Passion Island 1927 d: Manning Haynes. lps: Lillian Oldland, Moore Marriott, Randle Ayrton. 7500f UKN. prod/rel: Fnp Manufacturing Co., Fnp

The Persecution of Bob Pretty, Short Story
Persecution of Bob Pretty, The 1916 d: Frank Miller. lps: Frank Stanmore, Vivian Gibson, James Reardon. 1100f UKN. prod/rel: London, Jury

Peter's Pence, Short Story
Oh Dear Uncle! 1939 d: Richard Llewellyn. lps: Frank O'Brian, Syd Crossley, Scott Harold. 22M UKN. prod/rel: Sun Films, Renown

Sam's Boy, Novel
Sam's Boy 1922 d: Manning Haynes. lps: Johnny Butt, Tom Coventry, Bobbie Rudd. 4300f UKN. prod/rel: Artistic

The Skipper of the Osprey, Short Story
Skipper of the Osprey 1933 d: Norman Walker. lps: Renee Gadd, Ian Hunter, D. A. Clarke-Smith. 29M UKN. prod/rel: Associated Talking Pictures, Associated British Film Distributors

Skipper of the Osprey, The 1916 d: Frank Miller. lps: Hayford Hobbs, Renee Wakefield, Frank Stanmore. 1320f UKN. prod/rel: London, Jury

The Skipper's Wooing, Novel
Skipper's Wooing, The 1922 d: Manning Haynes. lps: Gordon Hopkirk, Cynthia Murtagh, Johnny Butt. 5200f UKN. prod/rel: Artistic

The Third String, Short Story
Third String, The 1914 d: George Loane Tucker. lps: Jane Gail, Frank Stanmore, George Bellamy. 1990f UKN. prod/rel: London, Fenning

Third String, The 1932 d: George Pearson. lps: Sandy Powell, Kay Hammond, Mark Daly. 65M UKN. prod/rel: Welsh-Pearson, Gaumont

Two of a Trade, Short Story
Two of a Trade 1928 d: Geoffrey H. Malins. lps: Charles Paton, James Reardon, Fred Rains. 2000f UKN. prod/rel: Welsh-Pearson

A Will and a Way, Novel
Will and a Way, A 1922 d: Manning Haynes. lps: Ernest Hendrie, Pollie Emery, Johnny Butt. 3570f UKN. prod/rel: Artistic

JACOBSEN, JORGEN-FRANZ
Barbara, 1939, Novel
Barbara 1961 d: Frank Wisbar. lps: Harriet Andersson, Helmut Griem, Maria Sebaldt. 96M GRM. prod/rel: U.F.H.

Barbara 1998 d: Nils Malmros. lps: Anneke von Der Lippe, Lars Simonsen, Helene Egelund. 144M DNM/SWD/NRW. prod/rel: Per Holst Film (Copenhagen), Svensk Filmindustri (Stockholm)

JACOBSEN, NORMAN
The Price of Applause, Short Story
Price of Applause, The 1918 d: Thomas N. Heffron. lps: Jack Livingston, Claire Anderson, Joe King. 5r USA. prod/rel: Triangle Film Corp., Triangle Distributing Corp.

JACOBSON, EGON
Article
M 1931 d: Fritz Lang. lps: Peter Lorre, Ellen Widmann, Inge Landgut. 118M GRM. *M - Eine Stadt Sucht Einen Morder; Morder Unter Uns*
M 1951 d: Joseph Losey. lps: David Wayne, Howard Da Silva, Luther Adler. 88M USA. prod/rel: Columbia, Superior Pictures

JACOBSON, LEOPOLD
Married in Hollywood, Vienna 1928, Play
Married in Hollywood 1929 d: Marcel Silver. lps: J. Harold Murray, Norma Terris, Walter Catlett. 9700f USA. prod/rel: Fox Film Corp.
Ein Waltzertraum, Leipzig 1907, Opera
Smiling Lieutenant, The 1931 d: Ernst Lubitsch. lps: Maurice Chevalier, Claudette Colbert, Miriam Hopkins. 88M USA. prod/rel: Paramount Publix Corp.©, Ernst Lubitsch Production

JACOBY, HANS
Der Unmoralische Herr Thomas Traumer, Short Story
Mann, Der Nicht Nein Sagen Konnte, Der 1958 d: Kurt Fruh, Hans Mehringer (Uncredited). lps: Heinz Ruhmann, Hannelore Schroth, Siegfried Lowitz. 93M SWT/DNM/GRM. *Manden Der Ikki Kunne Sige Nej* (DNM); *L' Homme Qui Ne Savait Pas Dire Non* prod/rel: Pen-Filmproduktion (Locarno), Rialto-Film (Copenhagen)

JACOBY, WILHELM
Pension Scholler, Play
Pension Scholler 1930 d: Georg Jacoby. lps: Paul Henckels, Fritz Kampers, Viktor de KowA. F GRM.
Pension Scholler 1952 d: Georg Jacoby. lps: Ludwig Schmitz, Fita Benkhoff, Rudolf Platte. 90M GRM. *Scholler's Inn* prod/rel: Magna, Deutsche London
Pension Scholler 1960 d: Georg Jacoby. lps: Theo Lingen, Christa Williams, Rudolf Vogel. 93M GRM. prod/rel: Real, Europa

JACOT, MICHEL
Le Cri du Papillon, Novel
Posledni Motyl 1989 d: Karel KachynA. lps: Tom Courtenay, Brigitte Fossey, Freddie Jones. TVM. 110M CZC/FRN/UKN. *Le Cri du Papillon* (FRN); *The Last Butterfly; Le Dernier Papillon* prod/rel: Filmexport, Filmove Studio Barrandov

JACQUES, NORBERT (1880–1954), GRM
Dr. Mabuse, Novel
Dr. Mabuse, Der Spieler 1921 d: Fritz Lang. lps: Rudolf Klein-Rogge, Bernhard Goetzke, Alfred Abel. 3496m GRM. prod/rel: Uco-Film
Testament Des Dr. Mabuse, Das 1933 d: Fritz Lang. lps: Rudolf Klein-Rogge, Gustav Diesl, Rudolf Schundler. 120M GRM. *The Testament of Dr. Mabuse* (USA); *Crimes of Dr. Mabuse* (UKN); *The Last Will of Dr. Mabuse*
Testament Des Dr. Mabuse, Das 1962 d: Werner Klinger. lps: Gert Frobe, Helmut Schmid, Charles Regnier. 88M GRM. *The Terror of Dr. Mabuse* (USA); *Terror of the Mad Doctor; The Last Will of Dr. Mabuse; The Testament of Dr. Mabuse*
Todesstrahlen Des Dr. Mabuse, Die 1964 d: Hugo Fregonese. lps: Peter Van Eyck, O. E. Hasse, Yvonne Furneaux. 91M GRM/FRN/ITL. *Les Rayons Mortels du Docteur Mabuse* (FRN); *Secrets of Dr. Mabuse* (USA); *I Raggi Mortali Del Dr. Mabuse* (ITL); *The Mirror Death Ray of Dr. Mabuse; Death Rays of Dr. Mabuse* prod/rel: C.C.C. Filmkunst (Berlin), Cineproduzioni Associate (Roma)
Unsichtbaren Krallen Des Dr. Mabuse, Die 1962 d: Harald Reinl. lps: Lex Barker, Karin Dor, Siegfried Lowitz. 89M GRM. *The Invisible Dr. Mabuse* (USA); *The Invisible Horror; The Invisible Claws of Dr. Mabuse*
Plusch Und Plumowsky, Novel
Frauenhaus von Rio, Das 1927 d: Hans Steinhoff. lps: Suzy Vernon, Vivian Gibson, Ernst Deutsch. 2683m GRM. *Plusch Und Plumowski* prod/rel: George Jacoby-Film

JACUSSO, NINO
Story
Zeit Der Stille 1986 d: Thorsten Nater. lps: Irina Hoppe, Pavel Sacher, Wolfgang Starck. 82M GRM. prod/rel: Thorsten-Nater-Filmprod.

JAEGER, HENRY
Das Freudenhaus, Novel
Freudenhaus, Das 1971 d: Alfred Weidenmann. lps: Karin Jacobsen, Herbert Fleischmann, Gisela Peltzer. 92M GRM. *House of Ill Repute* prod/rel: Studio-Film, Inter
Gluck Auf Kumpel Oder Der Grosse Beschiss, Novel
Tot Auf Halde 1995 d: Theodor KotullA. lps: Susanne Schulten, Peter Striebeck, Jane Arikin. TVM. 95M GRM.
Verdammt Zur Sunde, Novel
Verdammt Zur Sunde 1964 d: Alfred Weidenmann. lps: Martin Held, Tilla Durieux, Else Knott. 104M GRM. *Die Festung; Damned to Sin* prod/rel: Eichberg, Team

JAENICKE, KATHE
Primel macht Ihr Haus Verruckt, Novel
Primel macht Ihr Haus Verruckt 1979 d: Monica Teuber. lps: Sharon Brauner, Phillip Mann, Walter Wollner. 87M GRM. *Primel Drives the Family Crazy* prod/rel: Cine-Tele Team, Bronx

JAFFE, RONA (1932–, USA
The Best of Everything, Novel
Best of Everything, The 1959 d: Jean Negulesco. lps: Hope Lange, Suzy Parker, Martha Hyer. 121M USA. prod/rel: 20th Century-Fox
Mazes & Monsters, Novel
Rona Jaffe's Mazes & Monsters 1982 d: Steven Hilliard Stern. lps: Tom Hanks, Wendy Crewson, David Wallace. TVM. 100M USA/CND. *Mazes and Monsters*

JAGDFELD, G. B.
Kata a Krokodyl, Book
Kata a Krokodyl 1965 d: Vera Plivova-SimkovA. lps: Ivetta Hollanerova, Tomas Drbohlav, Barborka ZikovA. 72M CZC. *Kate and the Crocodile; Katia and the Crocodile* prod/rel: Barrandov

JAKES, JOHN (1932–, USA
The Bastard, Novel
Bastard, The 1978 d: Lee H. Katzin. lps: Andrew Stevens, Tom Bosley, Kim Cattrall. TVM. 200M USA. *The Kent Chronicles* prod/rel: Universal TV, Operation Prime Time
Love and War, Novel
North and South 1985 d: Richard T. Heffron. lps: Patrick Swayze, James Read, Lesley-Anne Down. TVM. 521M USA.
North and South: Book 2 1986 d: Kevin Connor. lps: Patrick Swayze, James Read, Lesley-Anne Down. TVM. 554M USA.
The Rebels, Novel
Rebels, The 1979 d: Russ Mayberry. lps: Andrew Stevens, Don Johnson, Doug McClure. TVM. 200M USA. prod/rel: Universal, Operation Prime Time

JAKOBSTETTER, FRITZ
Jennys Bummel, Berlin 1926, Play
Stranded in Paris 1926 d: Arthur Rosson. lps: Bebe Daniels, James Hall, Ford Sterling. 6106f USA. *You Never Can Tell* prod/rel: Famous Players-Lasky, Paramount Pictures

JAMES, EDGAR
Justice, New York 1915, Play
Not Guilty 1915 d: Joseph A. Golden. lps: Cyril Scott, Catherine Proctor, Ada Boshell. 5r USA. *Justice* prod/rel: Triumph Film Corp.©, Equitable Motion Pictures Corp.
The Master of the House, New York 1912, Play
Master of the House, The 1915 d: Joseph A. Golden. lps: Julius Steger, Austin Webb, Grace Reals. 5r USA. prod/rel: Triumph Film Corp., Equitable Motion Pictures Corp.

JAMES, FREDERICK H.
La Baccarat, Play
His Daughter Pays 1918 d: Paolo TrincherA. lps: Gertrude McCoy, Charles Graham, Pauline Curley. 7r USA. prod/rel: Piedmont Pictures Corp.©, State Rights

JAMES, GERTRUDE DE S. WENTWORTH
The Devil's Profession, Novel
Devil's Profession, The 1915 d: F. C. S. Tudor. lps: Rohan Clensy, Alesia Leon, Sidney Strong. 3300f UKN. prod/rel: Arrow, Yorkshire Cinematograph Co.
The Scarlet Kiss, Novel
Scarlet Kiss, The 1920 d: Fred Goodwins. lps: Marjorie Hume, Cyril Raymond, Maud Cressall. 5000f UKN. prod/rel: Martin's Photoplays, Faulkner

JAMES, HENRY (1843–1916), USA
Novel
Diario Di un Uomo Di Cinquant'anni 1980 d: Andrea Frazzi, Antonio Frazzi. lps: Giulio Brogi, Gianfranco de Grassi, Elisabetta Pozzi. MTV. F ITL.

The Altar of the Dead, 1895, Short Story
Chambre Verte, La 1978 d: Francois Truffaut. lps: Francois Truffaut, Nathalie Baye, Jean Daste. 94M FRN. *The Green Room* (USA) prod/rel: Les Films Du Carrosse, Artistes Associes
The Aspern Papers, 1888, Short Story
Aspern 1981 d: Eduardo de Gregorio. lps: Alida Valli, Bulle Ogier, Jean Sorel. 96M PRT/FRN. *Les Papiers d'Aspern* (FRN)
Lost Moment, The 1947 d: Martin Gabel. lps: Susan Hayward, Agnes Moorehead, Robert Cummings. 89M USA. prod/rel: Universal-International
The Beast in the Jungle, 1903, Short Story
Chambre Verte, La 1978 d: Francois Truffaut. lps: Francois Truffaut, Nathalie Baye, Jean Daste. 94M FRN. *The Green Room* (USA) prod/rel: Les Films Du Carrosse, Artistes Associes
The Bench of Desolation, 1910, Short Story
De Gray -le Banc de Desolation 1973 d: Claude Chabrol. MTV. 52M FRN. *Le Banc de la Desolation; The Bench of Desolation*
The Bostonians, 1886, Novel
Bostonians, The 1984 d: James Ivory. lps: Christopher Reeve, Vanessa Redgrave, Madeleine Potter. 122M UKN. prod/rel: Merchant Ivory, Rediffusion
Daisy Miller, 1877, Short Story
Daisy Miller 1974 d: Peter Bogdanovich. lps: Cybill Shepherd, Barry Brown, Cloris Leachman. 92M USA. prod/rel: Copa de Oro
The Europeans, 1878, Novel
Europeans, The 1979 d: James Ivory. lps: Lee Remick, Robin Ellis, Wesley Addy. 90M UKN. prod/rel: Merchant Ivory, National
The Jolly Corner, 1908, Short Story
Jolly Corner, The 1977 d: Arthur Barron. lps: Fritz Weaver, Salome Jens. MTV. 41M USA. prod/rel: Learning in Focus
Portrait of a Lady, 1881, Novel
Portrait of a Lady 1967 d: James Cellan Jones. lps: Richard Chamberlain, Suzanne Neve, Edward Fox. MTV. 240M UKN/USA.
Portrait of a Lady 1996 d: Jane Campion. lps: Nicole Kidman, John Malkovich, Barbara Hershey. 144M UKN/USA. prod/rel: Polygram Film Productions B.V., Propaganda Films
The Pupil, Short Story
Eleve, L' 1996 d: Olivier Schatzky. lps: Vincent Cassel, Caspar Salmon, Caroline Cellier. 92M FRN. *The Pupil* prod/rel: Ocelot
The Turn of the Screw, New York 1898, Short Story
Innocents, The 1961 d: Jack Clayton. lps: Deborah Kerr, Michael Redgrave, Peter Wyngarde. 99M UKN. prod/rel: 20th Century-Fox, Achilles Film Productions
Turn of the Screw 1974 d: Dan Curtis. lps: Lynn Redgrave, Jasper Jacob, Eva Griffith. TVM. 146M USA/UKN. prod/rel: Dan Curtis Productions
Turn of the Screw, The 1989 d: Graeme Clifford. lps: Amy Irving, David Hemmings, Balthazar Getty. MTV. 55M USA.
Turn of the Screw, The 1992 d: Rusty Lemorande. lps: Patsy Kensit, Stephane Audran, Julian Sands. 95M UKN/FRN. prod/rel: Electric Pictures, Michael White
Turn of the Screw, The 1995 d: Tom McLoughlin. lps: Valerie Bertinelli, Aled Roberts, Florence Heath. 88M USA. *The Haunting of Helen Walker*
Washington Square, 1881, Novel
Heiress, The 1949 d: William Wyler. lps: Olivia de Havilland, Ralph Richardson, Miriam Hopkins. 115M USA. prod/rel: Paramount
Washington Square 1997 d: Agnieszka Holland. lps: Jennifer Jason Leigh, Albert Finney, Ben Chaplin. 115M USA. prod/rel: Hollywood Pictures©, Caravan Pictures
What Maisie Knew, 1897, Novel
What Maisie Knew 1976 d: Babette Mangolte. 55M USA.
The Wings of the Dove, 1902, Novel
Wings of the Dove, The 1997 d: Iain Softley. lps: Helena Bonham-Carter, Linus Roache, Alison Elliott. 102M UKN/USA. prod/rel: Renaissance Dove©, Miramax Films©
Wings of the Dove, The 1997 d: John Gorrie. lps: Elizabeth Spriggs, Betsy Blair, John Castle. MTV. UKN. prod/rel: BBC

JAMES, J. RANDOLPH
Nearer! Nearer!, Novel
Red Pearls 1930 d: Walter Forde. lps: Lillian Rich, Frank Perfitt, Arthur Pusey. SIL. 6536f UKN. prod/rel: Nettlefold, Butcher's Film Service

JAMES, LIONEL
The Reverse of the Medal, Short Story
   Reverse of the Medal, The 1923 d: George A. Cooper. lps: Clive Brook, John Stuart, Olaf Hytten. 1945f UKN. prod/rel: Quality Plays, Gaumont

JAMES, M. R. (1862–1936), UKN, James, Montague Rhodes
Short Story
   Ash Tree, The 1975 d: Lawrence Gordon Clark. lps: Edward Petheridge, Lucy Griffiths, Lalla Ward. MTV. UKN. prod/rel: BBC
Casting the Runes, 1911, Short Story
   Casting the Runes 1979 d: Lawrence Gordon Clark. lps: Edward Petheridge, Christopher Good, Jan Francis. MTV. UKN. prod/rel: Yorkshire Tv
   Night of the Demon 1957 d: Jacques Tourneur. lps: Dana Andrews, Peggy Cummins, Niall MacGinnis. 82M UKN. *Curse of the Demon* (USA); *Haunted* prod/rel: Columbia, Sabre

JAMES, P. D. (1920–, UKN, White, Phyllis Dorothy James
The Black Tower, Novel
   Dalgliesh: the Black Tower 1987 d: Ronald Wilson. lps: Roy Marsden, Pauline Collins, Martin Jarvis. MTV. 300M UKN. *The Black Tower*
Cover Her Face, Novel
   Dalgliesh: Cover Her Face 1985 d: John Davies. lps: Roy Marsden, Phyllis Calvert, Bill Fraser. MTV. 294M UKN. *Cover Her Face*
Death of an Expert Witness, Novel
   Dalgliesh: Death of an Expert Witness 1983 d: Herbert Wise. lps: Roy Marsden, Barry Foster, Geoffrey Palmer. MTV. 300M UKN. *Death of an Expert Witness*
Devices and Desires, Novel
   Dalgliesh: Devices and Desires 1990 d: John Davies. lps: Roy Marsden, Betty Marsden, Susannah York. MTV. 296M UKN. *Devices and Desires*
Shroud for a Nightingale, Novel
   Dalgliesh: Shroud for a Nightingale 1984 d: John Gorrie. lps: Roy Marsden, Joss Ackland, Sheila Allen. MTV. 250M UKN. *Shroud for a Nightingale*
A Taste for Death, Novel
   Dalgliesh: a Taste for Death 1988 d: John Davies. lps: Roy Marsden, Simon Ward, Wendy Hiller. MTV. 292M UKN. *A Taste for Death*
A Unsuitable Job for a Woman, Novel
   Unsuitable Job for a Woman, An 1981 d: Christopher Petit. lps: Pippa Guard, Billie Whitelaw, Paul Freeman. 94M UKN. prod/rel: Goldcrest, Nffc

JAMES, RIAN
Crooner, New York 1932, Novel
   Crooner 1932 d: Lloyd Bacon. lps: David Manners, Ann Dvorak, Ken Murray. 69M USA. prod/rel: First National Pictures, Inc.
Hat-Check Girl, New York 1932, Novel
   Hat Check Girl 1932 d: Sidney Lanfield. lps: Sally Eilers, Ben Lyon, Ginger Rogers. 65M USA. *Embassy Girl* (UKN) prod/rel: Fox Film Corp.©
Love Is a Racket, New York 1931, Novel
   Love Is a Racket 1932 d: William A. Wellman. lps: Douglas Fairbanks Jr., Ann Dvorak, Frances Dee. 74M USA. *Such Things Happen* prod/rel: First National Pictures©
The White Parade, New York 1934, Novel
   White Parade, The 1934 d: Irving Cummings. lps: John Boles, Loretta Young, Jane Darwell. 83M USA. *Young Ladies in White* prod/rel: Fox Film Corp.©

JAMES, WILL
Lone Cowboy, New York 1930, Autobiography
   Lone Cowboy, The 1933 d: Paul Sloane. lps: Jackie Cooper, Lila Lee, Barton MacLane. 75M USA. *He's My Pal*; *Pardners* prod/rel: Paramount Productions©
Sand, Novel
   Will James' Sand 1949 d: Louis King. lps: Mark Stevens, Coleen Gray, Rory Calhoun. 78M USA. *Sand* (UKN) prod/rel: 20ᵗʰ Century Fox
Smoky the Cowhorse, New York 1926, Novel
   Smoky 1933 d: Eugene J. Forde. lps: Victor Jory, Irene Bentley, Hank Mann. 69M USA. prod/rel: Fox Film Corp.©
   Smoky 1946 d: Louis King. lps: Fred MacMurray, Anne Baxter, Bruce Cabot. 87M USA. prod/rel: 20ᵗʰ Century Fox
   Smoky 1966 d: George Sherman. lps: Fess Parker, Diana Hyland, Katy Jurado. 103M USA. prod/rel: Arcola Pictures, 20ᵗʰ Century-Fox

JANEWAY, ELIZABETH
Daisy Kenyon, Novel
   Daisy Kenyon 1947 d: Otto Preminger. lps: Joan Crawford, Henry Fonda, Dana Andrews. 99M USA. prod/rel: 20ᵗʰ Century Fox

JANNEY, RICHARD
The Miracle of the Bells, Novel
   Miracle of the Bells, The 1948 d: Irving Pichel. lps: Alida Valli, Fred MacMurray, Frank SinatrA. 120M USA. prod/rel: RKO Radio

JANNEY, SAM
Loose Ankles, New York 1926, Play
   Ladies at Play 1926 d: Alfred E. Green. lps: Doris Kenyon, Lloyd Hughes, Louise FazendA. 6119f USA. *A Desperate Woman* prod/rel: First National Pictures
   Loose Ankles 1930 d: Ted Wilde. lps: Loretta Young, Douglas Fairbanks Jr., Louise FazendA. 6190f USA. prod/rel: First National Pictures

JANOWITZ, TAMA
Short Stories
   Slaves of New York 1989 d: James Ivory. lps: Bernadette Peters, Adam Coleman Howard, Chris Sarandon. 125M USA. prod/rel: Tri-Star

JANSON, KRISTOFER
Liv, 1866, Short Story
   Liv 1934 d: Rasmus Breistein. 92M NRW.

JANTSCH, KARL
Story
   Schicksal in Ketten 1946 d: Eduard Hoesch. lps: Maria Andergast, Rudolf Prack, Hans Holt. 81M AUS. *Der Weite Weg* prod/rel: Donau, Deutsche Commerz

JANUSSE, LILLY
Novel
   Batticuore 1939 d: Mario Camerini. lps: Assia Noris, John Lodge, Luigi Almirante. 87M ITL. prod/rel: Era, Generalcine

JAOUI, AGNES
Un Air de Famille, Play
   Air de Famille, Un 1996 d: Cedric Klapisch. lps: Jean-Pierre Bacri, Agnes Jaoui, Jean-Pierre Darroussin. 107M FRN. prod/rel: Telema©, le Studio Canal©©

JAPRISOT, SEBASTIEN
Adieu l'Ami, Novel
   Adieu l'Ami 1968 d: Jean Herman. lps: Alain Delon, Charles Bronson, Olga Georges-Picot. 115M FRN/ITL. *Due Sporche Carogne* (ITL); *Farewell Friend* (USA); *Honor Among Thieves*; *So Long Friend*; *Code, The* prod/rel: Greenwich Films Production, Medusa Distribuzione
Compartiment Tueurs, Paris 1962, Novel
   Compartiment Tueurs 1965 d: Costa-Gavras. lps: Simone Signoret, Yves Montand, Pierre Mondy. 95M FRN. *The Sleeping Car Murders* prod/rel: P.E.C.F., Marianne Productions
La Dame Dans l'Auto Avec Des Lunettes Et un Fusil, Paris 1966, Novel
   Dame Dans l'Auto Avec Des Lunettes Et un Fusil, La 1970 d: Anatole Litvak. lps: Samantha Eggar, Oliver Reed, John McEnery. 110M FRN/UKN. *The Lady in the Car With Glasses and a Gun* (UKN) prod/rel: Lira Films, Columbia Films
L' Ete Meurtrier, Novel
   Ete Meurtrier, Un 1983 d: Jean Becker. lps: Isabelle Adjani, Alain Souchon, Suzanne Flon. 133M FRN. *One Deadly Summer* (USA) prod/rel: Snc, Capac

JARA CARRILLO, PEDRO
La Yegua Lucera, Poem
   Jaca Lucera, La 1926 d: Luis Baleriola, Pedro Jara Carrillo. lps: Conchita Perez Jimenez, Pepita Mateos, Antonio Pellicer. SPN. prod/rel: Luis Baleriola

JARAY, HANS
Play
   Pan Na Roztrhani 1934 d: Miroslav Cikan. lps: Frantisek Smolik, Ljuba Hermanova, Vaclav Tregl. 2424m CZC. *Very Busy Gentlemen*; *Man in Demand on All Sides* prod/rel: Meissner
..Heute Abend Bei Mir, Play
   ..Heute Abend Bei Mir 1934 d: Carl Boese. lps: Jenny Jugo, Paul Horbiger, Theo Lingen. 91M GRM. prod/rel: Klagemann-Film

JARDIEL PONCELA, ENRIQUE (1901–1952), SPN
Un Adulterio Decente, 1935, Play
   Adulterio Casi Decente, Un 1969 d: Rafael Gil. lps: Carmen Sevilla, Fernando Fernan Gomez, Manolo Gomez Bur. 89M SPN. *Un Adulterio Decente*; *A Near-Honest Adultery*
Angelina; O El Honor de un Brigadier, Madrid 1934, Play
   Angelina O El Honor de un Brigadier 1935 d: Louis King. lps: Rosita Diaz, Jose Crespo, Enrique de Rosas. 8r USA. *Little Angel*; *Angelina* prod/rel: Fox Film Corp.
Blanca Por Fuera Y Rosa Por Dentro, 1943, Play
   Blanca Por Fuera, Rosa Por Dentro 1971 d: Pedro LazagA. lps: Jose Luis Lopez Vazquez, Esperanza Roy, Jose Rubio. 109M SPN. *Pink Inside White Outside*

Las Cinco Advertencias de Satanas, 1938, Play
   Cinco Advertencias de Satanas, Las 1938 d: Isidro Socias. lps: Felix de Pomes, Pastora Pena, Julio PenA. 89M SPN. *Las 5 Advertencias de Satanas*; *Satan's Five Warnings*
   Cinco Advertencias de Satanas, Las 1969 d: Jose Luis Merino. lps: Arturo Fernandez, Cristina Galbo, Americo CoimbrA. 100M SPN/PRT. *Os 5 Avisos de Satanas* (PRT); *Satan's Five Warnings*; *Las 5 Advertencias de Satanas*
Eloisa Esta Debajo de un Almendro, 1943, Play
   Eloisa Esta Debajo de un Almendro 1943 d: Rafael Gil. lps: Amparo Rivelles, Rafael Duran, Alberto RomeA. 109M SPN. *Eloisa Is Under an Almond Tree*
Es Peligroso Asomarse Al Exterior, 1944, Play
   Es Peligroso Asomarse Al Exterior 1945 d: Alejandro Ulloa, Arthur Duarte. lps: Ana Maria Campoy, Alejandro Ulloa, Erico FragA. 86M SPN/PRT. *E Perigoso Debrucar-Se* (PRT); *It's Dangerous to Lean Out of the Window*
Los Ladrones Somos Gente Honrada, 1941, Play
   Ladrones Somos Gente Honrada, Los 1942 d: Ignacio F. Iquino. lps: Amparo Rivelles, Manuel Luna, Mercedes Vecino. 99M SPN. *We Thieves are Honest People*; *Thieves are Honourable People*
   Ladrones Somos Gente Honrada, Los 1956 d: Pedro L. Ramirez. lps: Jose Luis Ozores, Pepe Isbert, Encarnita Fuentes. 89M SPN. *Thieves are Honorable People*
Armando Y Su Padre Margarita, 1931, Play
   Margarita, Armando Y Su Padre 1939 d: Francisco MujicA. 90M ARG.
Un Marido de Ida Y Vuelta, 1939, Play
   Marido de Ida Y Vuelta, Un 1957 d: Luis LuciA. lps: Emma Penella, Fernando Fernan Gomez, Fernando Rey. 96M SPN. *The Dead Husband Returns*
Tu Y Yo Somos Tres, 1946, Play
   Tu Y Yo Somos Tres 1961 d: Rafael Gil. lps: Analia Gade, Alberto de Mendoza, Jose Rubio. 89M SPN/ARG. *You and Me are Three*
Usted Tiene Ojos de Mujer Fatal, 1926, Play
   Usted Tiene Ojos de Mujer Fatal 1962 d: Jose Maria ElorrietA. lps: Manolo Gomez Bur, Susana Campos, Virgilio TeixeirA. 87M SPN.

JARDIN, ALEXANDRE
Le Zebre, Novel
   Zebre, Le 1992 d: Jean Poiret. lps: Caroline Cellier, Thierry Lhermitte, Christian PereirA. 90M FRN.

JARNO, GEORG
Die Forsterchristl, Opera
   Forsterchristl, Die 1926 d: Friedrich Zelnik. lps: Lya Mara, Harry Liedtke, Wilhelm Dieterle. 2623m GRM. *Flower of the Forest*; *The Forester's Daughter* prod/rel: Sudfilm
   Forsterchristl, Die 1931 d: Friedrich Zelnik. lps: Paul Horbiger, Paul Richter, Adele Sandrock. 80M GRM. *The Forester's Daughter*
   Forsterchristl, Die 1952 d: Arthur M. Rabenalt. lps: Johanna Matz, Angelika Hauff, Kathe von Nagy. 104M GRM. *The Forester's Daughter* prod/rel: Carlton, Panorama
   Forsterchristl, Die 1962 d: Franz J. Gottlieb. lps: Sabine Sinjen, Peter Weck, Sieghardt Rupp. 104M GRM. *The Forester's Daughter* prod/rel: Carlton, Constantin

JAROS, PETER
Tisicrocna Vcela, Novel
   Tisicrocna Vcela 1983 d: Juraj Jakubisko. lps: Stefan Kvietik, Jozef Kroner, Ivana ValesovA. 150M CZC/GRM/AUS. *Die Tausendjahrige Biene* (GRM); *The Bee Millenium*; *The Thousand-Year-Old Bee*; *The Millenial Bee* prod/rel: Slovensky Film, Janus

JARRETT, DANIEL
Salt Water, New York 1929, Play
   Her First Mate 1933 d: William Wyler. lps: Slim Summerville, Zasu Pitts, Una Merkel. 70M USA. prod/rel: Universal Pictures Corp.©

JARRY, ALFRED (1873–1907), FRN, Jarry, Alfred-Henry
Parpaillon; Ou a la Recherche de l'Homme a la Pompe d'Ursus
   Parpaillon 1992 d: Luc Moullet. lps: Remy Martin, Catherine Michaud, Frank Getreau. TVM. 85M FRN.
Ubu Roi, 1896, Play
   Kral Ubu 1996 d: F. A. Brabec. lps: Marian Labuda, Lucie Bila, Boleslav PolivkA. 86M CZC. *King Ubu* prod/rel: Czech Tv
   Ubu Et la Grande Gidouille 1979 d: Jan LenicA. ANM. 80M FRN. *Ubu and the Great Gidouille*

JASMIN, CLAUDE
Le Corde Au Cou, Novel
    Corde Au Cou, La 1964 d: Pierre Patry. lps: Jean Duceppe, Guy Godin, Andree Lachapelle. 105M CND. *Rope Around the Neck* (USA) prod/rel: Cooperatio Inc.

Delivrez-Nous du Mal, Novel
    Delivrez-Nous du Mal 1965 d: Jean-Claude Lord. lps: Yvon Deschamps, Guy Godin, Catherine Begin. 81M CND. prod/rel: Cooperatio Inc.

La Sabliere, Novel
    Mario 1984 d: Jean Beaudin. lps: Xavier Norman-Petermann, Francis Reddy, Nathalie Chalifour. 97M CND. *Mario S'en Va-T-En Guerre* prod/rel: Office National Du Film, Cinema International Canada

JAUBERT, JEAN-PIERRE
Novel
    Nach Langer Zeit 1993 d: Robert Mazoyer. lps: Maria Schell, Jacques Godin, Stephane Bierry. TVM. 360M GRM/FRN/CND.

JAUSION, JEAN
Un Homme Marche Dans la Ville, Novel
    Homme Marche Dans la Ville, Un 1949 d: Marcello Pagliero. lps: Jean-Pierre Kerien, Coco Aslan, Ginette Leclerc. 95M FRN. prod/rel: Sacha Gordine

JAY, HARRIET
Alone in London, London 1885, Play
    Alone in London 1915 d: Larry Trimble. lps: Florence Turner, Henry Edwards, Edward Lingard. 4525f UKN. prod/rel: Turner Films, Ideal

JAY, MONICA
Geraldine; for the Love of a Transvestite, Book
    Just Like a Woman 1992 d: Chris Monger. lps: Julie Walters, Adrian Pasdar, Paul Freeman. TVM. 106M UKN. prod/rel: Rank, Zenith Productions

JAYAKANTHAN
Kai Vilangu
    Kaval Daivam 1969 d: K. Vijayan. lps: S. V. Subbaiah, Sivaji Ganesan, Nagesh. 145M IND. *The Guardian Deity* prod/rel: Ambal Prod.

Sila Neragalil Sila Manithargal
    Sila Nerangalil Sila Manithargal 1975 d: A. Bhimsingh. lps: Laxmi, Srikanth, Y. G. Parthasarathy. 130M IND. *Sometimes Some People*; *Some People Sometimes* prod/rel: a.B.S. Prod.

JAYNE, MITCHELL F.
Old Fish Hawk, Novel
    Fish Hawk 1980 d: Donald Shebib. lps: Will Sampson, Charlie Fields, Geoffrey Bowes. 95M CND. prod/rel: the Fish Hawk Company Inc., Jon Slan Productions Inc.

JAYNES, CLARE
Instruct My Sorrows, Novel
    My Reputation 1946 d: Curtis Bernhardt. lps: Barbara Stanwyck, George Brent, Lucile Watson. 96M USA. prod/rel: Warner Bros.

JEAN, ALBERT
Le Vinaigre Des Quatre Voleurs, Novel
    Cavalier de Croix-Mort, Le 1947 d: Lucien Gasnier-Raymond. lps: Madeleine Robinson, Yves Vincent, Frank Villard. 90M FRN. *Une Aventure de Vidocq* prod/rel: Simoun Films

JEAN, RAYMOND
La Letrice, Novel
    Lectrice, La 1988 d: Michel Deville. lps: Miou-Miou, Christian Ruche, Sylvie Laporte. 98M FRN. prod/rel: Elefilm, Aaa

JEAN-CHARLES
La Foire aux Cancres, Book
    Foire aux Cancres, La 1963 d: Louis Daquin. lps: Jean Poiret, Sophie Desmarets, Dominique Paturel. 88M FRN. prod/rel: Les Films Raoul Ploquin

JEANNE, RENE
Duel, Novel
    Duel 1927 d: Jacques de Baroncelli. lps: Gabriel Gabrio, Mady Christian, Andree Standard. 2000m FRN. prod/rel: Societe Des Cineromans, Films De France

JEANS, RONALD
Peace and Quiet, Play
    Peace and Quiet 1929 d: Sinclair Hill. lps: Ralph Lynn, Winifred Shotter. 12M UKN. prod/rel: British Sound Film Productions

Young Wives' Tale, London 1949, Play
    Young Wives' Tale 1951 d: Henry Cass. lps: Joan Greenwood, Nigel Patrick, Derek Farr. 79M UKN. prod/rel: Associated British Picture Corporation, Ab-Pathe

JEFFERSON, JOSEPH
The Shadows of a Great City, New York 1884, Play
    Shadows of a Great City 1913 d: Frank Wilson. lps: Alec Worcester, Chrissie White, Harry Royston. 3700f UKN. prod/rel: Hepworth

    Shadows of a Great City, The 1915. lps: Adelaide Thurston, Thomas Jefferson. 5r USA. prod/rel: Popular Plays and Players, Inc.©, Metro Pictures Corp.

JEFFERSON, L. V.
The Final Gold, Story
    Finest Gold, The 1915 d: Murdock MacQuarrie. lps: Murdock MacQuarrie, Arthur Moon, Hale Buckham. SHT USA. prod/rel: Big U

Horse Sense, Story
    Set-Up, The 1926 d: Cliff Smith. lps: Art Acord, Alta Allen, Albert Schaeffer. 4600f USA. prod/rel: Universal Pictures

Nothing Ever Happens Right, Story
    Nothing Ever Happens Right 1915 d: Roy McCray. lps: Ernest Shields, Queenie Rossen. SHT USA. prod/rel: Joker

The Phantom Fortune, Story
    Phantom Fortune, The 1915 d: Henry Otto. lps: Hobart Henley, O. C. Jackson, Kathleen Wilmarth. 3r USA. prod/rel: Gold Seal

The Redeeming Sin, Story
    Redeeming Sin, The 1925 d: J. Stuart Blackton. lps: Alla Nazimova, Lou Tellegen, Carl Miller. 6227f USA. prod/rel: Vitagraph Co. of America

The Struggle, Story
    Struggle, The 1915 d: Joseph de Grasse. lps: Pauline Bush, William Clifford. SHT USA. prod/rel: Rex

The Supreme Test, Short Story
    Supreme Test, The 1915 d: Edward J. Le Saint. lps: Henrietta Crosman, Wyndham Standing, Adele Farrington. 5r USA. prod/rel: Universal Film Mfg. Co.©, Broadway Universal Feature

The Winning Wallop, Story
    Winning Wallop, The 1926 d: Charles Hutchison. lps: William Fairbanks, Shirley Palmer, Charles K. French. 5000f USA. prod/rel: Gotham Productions, Lumas Film Corp.

JEFFREY, BETTY
White Coolies, Diary
    Paradise Road 1997 d: Bruce Beresford. lps: Glenn Close, Pauline Collins, Cate Blanchett. 122M ASL/USA. prod/rel: Village Roadshow Pictures, Twentieth Century Fox Film Corp.

JEGERLEHNER, JOHANNES
Petronella, 1912, Novel
    Petronella 1927 d: Hanns Schwarz. lps: Maly Delschaft, Wilhelm Dieterle, Oscar HomolkA. 3116m GRM/SWT. *Das Geheimnis Der Berge*; *Die Glocke von St. Marein* prod/rel: Helvetia-Film, Glarus

JEHOSCHUA, ABRAHAM B.
Story
    Schweigen Des Dichters, Das 1986 d: Peter Lilienthal. lps: Jakov Lind, Len Ramras, Daniel Kedem. 102M GRM. *The Silence of the Poet* prod/rel: Edgar Reitz Film, Wdr

JEKELY, ZOLTAN
A 272. Tagy Leirasa, 1975, Verse
    Kard, A 1976 d: Janos Domolky. lps: Hedi Temessy, Peter Hauman, Mari Szemes. 80M HNG. *En Vagyok a Falu Rossza Egyedul*; *The Sword*

JELINCK, HENRIETTE
La Marche du Fou, Novel
    Etes-Vous Fiancee a un Marin Grec Ou a un Pilote de Ligne? 1970 d: Jean Aurel. lps: Jean Yanne, Francoise Fabian, Francis Blanche. 105M FRN/ITL. *Il Cammino Del Folle* (ITL) prod/rel: Copro Film, Films De La Pleiade

JELLICOE, ANN
The Knack, London 1962, Play
    Knack. and How to Get It, The 1965 d: Richard Lester. lps: Rita Tushingham, Ray Brooks, Michael Crawford. 84M UKN. *The Knack* prod/rel: Woodfall Film Productions, United Artists

JELLINEK, OSKAR
The Peasant Judge, 1933, Novel
    Thy Neighbor's Wife 1953 d: Hugo Haas. lps: Cleo Moore, Hugo Haas, Ken Carlton. 79M USA. prod/rel: 20ᵗʰ Century-Fox, Hugo Haas Prods.

JENBACH, B.
Die Czardasfurstin, Vienna 1915, Operetta
    Czardasfurstin, Die 1927 d: Hanns Schwarz. lps: Liane Haid, Oscar Marion, Imre Raday. 2596m GRM. prod/rel: Ostermayr-Film

    Czardasfurstin, Die 1934 d: Georg Jacoby. lps: Marta Eggerth, Hans Sohnker, Paul Horbiger. 85M GRM. *Die Csardasfurstin* prod/rel: UFA

    Czardasfurstin, Die 1951 d: Georg Jacoby. lps: Marika Rokk, Johannes Heesters, Franz Schafheitlin. 94M GRM. *The Czardas Princess*; *Die Csardasfurstin* prod/rel: Deutsche Styria, UFA

JENKINS, DAN
Semi-Tough, Book
    Semi-Tough 1977 d: Michael Ritchie. lps: Burt Reynolds, Kris Kristofferson, Jill Clayburgh. 108M USA. prod/rel: United Artists

JENKINS, GEOFFREY
Dirty Games, Novel
    Dirty Games 1989 d: Gray Hofmeyr. lps: Valentina Vargas, Jan-Michael Vincent, Ronald France. 96M USA/SAF. prod/rel: August Entertainment, Overseas Film

A Twist of Sand, London 1959, Novel
    Twist of Sand, A 1967 d: Don Chaffey. lps: Richard Johnson, Honor Blackman, Jeremy Kemp. 91M UKN/SAF. *The Ghost of Wolfpack* prod/rel: Christina Films, United Artists

JENKINS, HARRY
Die Frau Und Der Smaragd, Play
    Coup de Feu a l'Aube 1932 d: Serge de Poligny. lps: Jean Galland, Roger Karl, Annie Ducaux. 80M FRN. *La Femme Et le Diamant* prod/rel: U.F.a., a.C.E.

JENKINS, HERBERT
Short Stories
    Bindle 1926 d: H. B. Parkinson. lps: Tom Reynolds, Annie Esmond, Charles Garry. SHS. UKN. prod/rel: H. B. Parkinson

Patricia Brent - Spinster, Novel
    Patricia Brent, Spinster 1919 d: Geoffrey H. Malins. lps: Ena Beaumont, Lawrence Leyton, Victor Robson. 5480f UKN. prod/rel: Garrick Films

The Temperance Fete, Story
    Temperance Fete, The 1931 d: Graham Cutts. lps: George Robey, Sydney Fairbrother, Connie Ediss. 45M UKN. prod/rel: Fogwell Films, MGM

JENKINS, WILL F.
The Purple Hieroglyph, 1920, Short Story
    Murder Will Out 1930 d: Clarence Badger. lps: Jack Mulhall, Lila Lee, Noah Beery. 6200f USA. prod/rel: First National Pictures

    Purple Cipher, The 1920 d: Chester Bennett. lps: Earle Williams, Vola Vale, Ernest Shields. 5r USA. *The Purple Hieroglyph* prod/rel: Vitagraph Co. of America©

JENKS, G. E.
Haunting Winds, Story
    Haunting Winds 1915 d: Carl M. Le Viness. lps: Sydney Ayres, Doris Pawn, Frank MacQuarrie. SHT USA. prod/rel: Powers

The Weird Nemesis, Story
    Weird Nemesis, The 1915 d: Jacques Jaccard. lps: Hazel Buckham, Allan Forrest, Helen Leslie. 2r USA. prod/rel: Victor

JENNE, ANTONIN
Kacka Vomacena, Novel
    Pani Kacka Zasahuje. 1939 d: Karel SpelinA. lps: Betty Kysilkova, Eman Fiala, Hana VitovA. 2470m CZC. *Mrs. Kacka Intervenes.* prod/rel: Dafa

JENNINGS, AL J.
Beating Back, 1913, Story
    Beating Back 1914 d: Carroll Fleming. lps: Al Jennings, Madeline Fairbanks, Frank Jennings. 5r USA. prod/rel: Thanhouser Film Corp.©, Mutual Film Corp.

JENNINGS, DEAN
The San Quentin Story, 1950, Book
    Steel Cage, The 1954 d: Walter Doniger. lps: Paul Kelly, Maureen O'Sullivan, Walter Slezak. 80M USA. prod/rel: United Artists, Phoenix Films

We Only Kill Each Other, Book
    Bugsy 1991 d: Barry Levinson. lps: Warren Beatty, Annette Bening, Harvey Keitel. 136M USA. prod/rel: Columbia Tristar, Mulholland Productions

JENNINGS, GERTRUDE E.
The Young Person in Pink, London 1920, Play
Girl Who Forgot, The 1939 d: Adrian Brunel. lps: Elizabeth Allan, Ralph Michael, Enid Stamp-Taylor. 79M UKN. *The Young Person in Pink* prod/rel: Daniel Birt, Butcher's Film Service

JENNINGS, WILLIAM DALE
The Cowboys, Novel
Cowboys, The 1972 d: Mark Rydell. lps: John Wayne, Roscoe Lee Browne, Bruce Dern. 135M USA. prod/rel: Warner Bros.

JENSEN, ANDREW
The Trial of Chaplain Jensen, Book
Trial of Chaplain Jensen, The 1975 d: Robert Day. lps: James Franciscus, Charles Durning, Joanna Miles. TVM. 78M USA. prod/rel: 20th Century-Fox, Monash/Pressman Production

JENSEN, AXEL
Line, Oslo 1959, Novel
Line 1961 d: Nils Reinhardt Christensen. lps: Margaret Robsahm, Toralv Maurstad, Henki Kolstad. 90M NRW. *The Passionate Demons* (USA) prod/rel: Concord Film Production, Norsk Film

JENSEN, ERIK AALBAEK
Gertrud, 1956, Novel
Ekko Af Et Skud 1970 d: Erik Frohn Nielsen. lps: Ole Ishoy, Brigitte Kolerus, Ove Rud. 99M DNM. *Echo of a Shot*
Kridtstregen, 1976, Novel
Forraederne 1984 d: Ole Roos. lps: Hans Chr. Aegidius, Allan Olsen, Sanne Salomonsen. 114M DNM. *The Traitor; The Traitors*

JENSEN, JOHANNES VILHELM (1873–1950), DNM
Gudrun, Copenhagen 1936, Novel
Gudrun 1963 d: Anker Sorensen. lps: Laila Andersson, Jorgen Buckhoj, Poul Reichhardt. 95M DNM. *A Woman! Suddenly* (USA) prod/rel: Morten Schyberg Productions
De Naaede Forgen, 1925, Short Story
Naede Fargen, de 1948 d: Carl T. Dreyer. 12M DNM. *They Caught the Ferry*; **De Naaede Faergen**

JENSEN, OSKAR
Der Schweigende Mund, Novel
Es Geht Um Mein Leben 1936 d: Richard Eichberg. lps: Karl Ludwig Diehl, Kitty Jantzen, Theo Lingen. 86M GRM. prod/rel: Eichberg, Herzog

JENSEN, WILHELM
Story
Gradiva 1970 d: Giorgio Albertazzi. lps: Laura Antonelli, Peter Chatel, Giorgio Albertazzi. 95M ITL. prod/rel: Fulco Film

JEPSON, EDGAR
Ann Annington, Indianapolis 1918, Novel
Her Winning Way 1921 d: Joseph Henabery. lps: Mary Miles Minter, Gaston Glass, Carrie Clark Ward. 4715f USA. prod/rel: Realart Pictures, Paramount Pictures
The Loudwater Mystery, Novel
Loudwater Mystery, The 1921 d: Norman MacDonald. lps: Gregory Scott, Pauline Peters, Clive Brook. 7108f UKN. prod/rel: Broadwest, Walturdaw
Pollyooly, Indianapolis 1912, Novel
Polly Redhead 1917 d: Jack Conway. lps: Ella Hall, Gertrude Astor, Gretchen Lederer. 5r USA. prod/rel: Bluebird Photoplays, Inc.©

JEPSON, SELWYN
Lady Noggs - Peeress, Novel
Lady Noggs - Peeress 1920 d: Sidney Morgan. lps: Joan Morgan, George Bellamy, Yvonne Duquette. 5000f UKN. prod/rel: Progress, Butcher's Film Service
Man Running, Novel
Stage Fright 1950 d: Alfred Hitchcock. lps: Jane Wyman, Marlene Dietrich, Michael Wilding. 111M UKN/USA. prod/rel: Warner Bros., First National
The Qualified Adventurer, Novel
Qualified Adventurer, The 1925 d: Sinclair Hill. lps: Matheson Lang, Genevieve Townsend, Fred Raynham. 6850f UKN. prod/rel: Stoll

JEROME, JEROME K. (1859–1927), UKN, Jerome, Jerome Klapka
All Roads Lead to Calvary, Novel
All Roads Lead to Calvary 1921 d: Kenelm Foss. lps: Minna Grey, Bertram Burleigh, Mary Odette. 5000f UKN. prod/rel: Astra Films
Miss Hobbs, New York 1899, Play
Miss Hobbs 1920 d: Donald Crisp. lps: Wanda Hawley, Harrison Ford, Helen Jerome Eddy. 4471f USA. prod/rel: Realart Pictures Corp.©
The New Lady Bantock, 1909, Play
Strictly Confidential 1919 d: Clarence Badger. lps: Madge Kennedy, John Bowers, Robert Bolder. 4774f USA. prod/rel: Goldwyn Pictures Corp.©, Goldwyn Distributing Corp.

The Passing of the Third Floor Back, London 1908, Play
Passing of the Third Floor Back, The 1918 d: Herbert Brenon. lps: Johnston Forbes-Robertson, Augusta Haviland, Molly Pearson. USA.
Passing of the Third Floor Back, The 1935 d: Berthold Viertel. lps: Conrad Veidt, Anna Lee, Rene Ray. 90M UKN. prod/rel: Gaumont-British
Three Men in a Boat (to Say Nothing of the Dog), London 1889, Novel
Drei Mann in Einem Boot 1961 d: Helmut Weiss. lps: Hans-Joachim Kuhlenkampff, Heinz Erhardt, Walter Giller. 93M AUS. *Three Men in a Boat* prod/rel: Kurt Ulrich, Wiener Mundus
Hanging a Picture 1915. lps: Eric Williams. UKN. prod/rel: Eric Williams Speaking Pictures
Three Men in a Boat 1920 d: Challis Sanderson. lps: Lionelle Howard, Manning Haynes, Johnny Butt. 5000f UKN. prod/rel: Artistic
Three Men in a Boat 1933 d: Graham Cutts. lps: William Austin, Edmund Breon, Billy Milton. 60M UKN. prod/rel: Associated Talking Pictures, Associated British Film Distributors
Three Men in a Boat 1956 d: Ken Annakin. lps: Laurence Harvey, Jimmy Edwards, David Tomlinson. 94M UKN. prod/rel: Romulus, Remus
Three Men in a Boat 1975 d: Stephen Frears. lps: Tim Curry, Michael Palin, Stephen Moore. TVM. 65M UKN. prod/rel: BBC

JERROLD, DOUGLAS
Black-Eyed Susan, London 1829, Play
Black-Eyed Susan 1908. 880f UKN. prod/rel: Gaumont
Black-Eyed Susan 1914 d: Maurice Elvey. lps: Elisabeth Risdon, Fred Groves, A. V. Bramble. 2864f UKN. *The Battling British* (USA); *In the Days of Trafalgar* prod/rel: British and Colonial, Kinematograph Trading Co.

JERSCHKE, OSKAR
Traumulus, 1904, Play
Traumulus 1936 d: Carl Froelich. lps: Carl Froelich, Emil Jannings, Harald Paulsen. 100M GRM. prod/rel: Carl Froelich, National

JERSILD, P. C.
Barnens O, Novel
Barnens O 1981 d: Kay Pollak. lps: Tomas Fryk, Anita Ekstrom, Ingvar Hirdwall. 110M SWD. *Children's Island* prod/rel: Svenska Filminstitut, Treklovern Hb

JERUSALEM, ELSE
Der Heilige Skarabaus, Novel
Rothausgasse, Die 1928 d: Richard Oswald. lps: Gustav Frohlich, Camilla von Hollay, Lotte Stein. 2237m GRM. prod/rel: Richard Oswald-Film-Prod.

JESSE, F. TENNYSON (18——1958), UKN, Jesse, Fryniwyd Tennyson
Billeted, London 1917, Play
Misleading Widow, The 1919 d: John S. Robertson. lps: Billie Burke, James L. Crane, Frank Mills. 5r USA. *Billeted* prod/rel: Famous Players-Lasky Corp.©, Paramount-Artcraft Pictures
The Pelican, London 1924, Play
"Marriage License?" 1926 d: Frank Borzage. lps: Alma Rubens, Walter McGrail, Richard Walling. 7168f USA. *The Pelican* prod/rel: Fox Film Corp.
Sacrifice 1929 d: Victor Peers. lps: Andree Tourneur, G. H. Mulcaster, Lewis Dayton. SIL. 6602f UKN. prod/rel: British Instructional, Fox
Quarantine, New York 1924, Play
Lovers in Quarantine 1925 d: Frank Tuttle. lps: Bebe Daniels, Harrison Ford, Alfred Lunt. 6570f USA. prod/rel: Famous Players-Lasky, Paramount Pictures

JESSEL, GEORGE
Story
You're My Everything 1949 d: Walter Lang. lps: Anne Baxter, Dan Dailey, Shari Robinson. 94M USA. prod/rel: 20th Century-Fox

JESSEL, JOHN
The Adaptive Ultimate, 1941, Short Story
She-Devil, The 1957 d: Kurt Neumann. lps: Mari Blanchard, Jack Kelly, Albert Dekker. 77M USA. *She Devil* prod/rel: 20th Century-Fox

JESSEL, LEON
Schwarzwaldmadel, Opera
Schwarzwaldmadel 1920 d: Arthur Wellin. lps: Uschi Elleot, Ria Jende, Gustav Charle. 1910m GRM. prod/rel: Luna-Film
Schwarzwaldmadel 1929 d: Victor Janson. lps: Liane Haid, Fred Louis Lerch, Walter Janssen. 2653m GRM. prod/rel: Merkur-Film
Schwarzwaldmadel 1933 d: Georg Zoch. lps: Hans Sohnker, Maria Berling, Walter Janssen. 96M GRM.

Schwarzwaldmadel 1950 d: Hans Deppe. lps: Sonja Ziemann, Rudolf Prack, Fritz Kampers. 100M GRM. *Black Forest Girl* prod/rel: Berolina, UFA

JESSUP, RICHARD (1925–1982), USA
Chuka, Greenwich, Ct. 1961, Novel
Chuka 1967 d: Gordon Douglas. lps: Rod Taylor, John Mills, Ernest Borgnine. 105M USA. prod/rel: Paramount
The Cincinnati Kid, Boston 1963, Novel
Cincinnati Kid, The 1965 d: Norman Jewison. lps: Edward G. Robinson, Steve McQueen, Joan Blondell. 113M USA. prod/rel: MGM, Filmways
The Cunning and the Haunted, 1954, Novel
Young Don't Cry, The 1957 d: Alfred L. Werker. lps: Sal Mineo, James Whitmore, J. Carrol Naish. 89M USA. prod/rel: Columbia, Philip A. Waxman Pictures
The Deadly Duo, New York 1960, Novel
Deadly Duo 1962 d: Reginald Le Borg. lps: Craig Hill, Marcia Henderson, Robert Lowery. 70M USA.

JEW, JONATHAN
Schneeschuhbanditen, Novel
Schneeschuhbanditen 1928 d: Uwe Jens Krafft. lps: Aud Egede Nissen, Paul Richter, Uwe Jens Krafft. 2298m GRM. prod/rel: Terra-Film

JHABVALA, RUTH PRAWER (1927–, GRM
Heat and Dust, 1975, Novel
Heat and Dust 1982 d: James Ivory. lps: Christopher Cazenove, Greta Scacchi, Julian Glover. 130M UKN. prod/rel: Merchant Ivory
The Householder, London 1960, Novel
Gharbar 1963 d: James Ivory. lps: Shashi Kapoor, Leela Naidu, Durga Khote. 101M IND/USA. *The Householder* (USA) prod/rel: Merchant-Ivory Productions

JI XUEXU
Xiao Bai Qi de Feng Bo, Novel
Xiao Bai Qi de Feng Bo 1956 d: Gao Heng. lps: Jiang Tianlu, Li Wei, Wu Yin. 6r CHN. *The Little White Flag Dispute* prod/rel: Shanghai Film Studio

JIA PINGAO
Ye Shan, Novel
Ye Shan 1985 d: Yan Xueshu. lps: Du Yuan, Yue Hong, XIn Ming. 100M CHN. *In the Wild Mountains*; *Wild Mountains* prod/rel: XI'an Film Studio

JILEK, LADISLAV
Pro Kamarada, Radio Play
Pro Kamarada 1940 d: Miroslav Cikan. lps: Theodor Pistek, Ladislav Bohac, Jaroslav VojtA. 2184m CZC. *For My Fellow; For a Friend* prod/rel: Nationalfilm

JILEMNICKY, PETR
Skareda Dedina, Novel
Skareda Dedina 1975 d: Karel KachynA. lps: Vilem Pfeifer, Maria MacKovicova, Karel Chromik. 80M CZC. *The Ugly Village* prod/rel: Filmstudio Barrandov

JIMENEZ, JUAN RAMON (1881–1958), SPN
Platero Y Yo, 1914, Autobiography
Platero Y Yo 1968 d: Alfredo Castellon. lps: Maria Cuadra, Simon Martin, Roberto Camardiel. 95M SPN. *The Silversmith and I; Platero and I*

JIN YONG
Bi Xue Jian, Novel
Bi Xue Jian 1993 d: Zhang Haijing. lps: Wu Ma, Huang Jingyan, Chen Long. 9r CHN/HKG. *The Sword Stained With Royal Blood* prod/rel: Pearl River Film Company, Shengyi XI'an Film Corp. Ltd.
Dong XIe XI Du, Novel
Dung Che Sai Duk 1993 d: Wong Kar-Wai. lps: Brigitte Lin Ching Hsia, Carina Liu, Maggie Cheung. 95M HKG/CHN. *Dong XIe XI Du* (CHN); *Dungche Saiduk; Ashes of Time* prod/rel: Zedong Film Production Co., Beijing Film Studio

JIN ZHENGJIA
Outside the Soccer Field, Play
Qiu Mi 1963 d: Xu Changlin. lps: Tie Niu, Sun Jinglu, Chen Xu. 9r CHN. *Soccer Fans* prod/rel: Tianma Film Studio

JIRASEK, ALOIS
Story
Ztracenci 1957 d: Milos Makovec. lps: Gustav Valach, Alena Vranova, Stanislav Fiser. 82M CZC. *Three Men Missing*
Filosofska Historie, Novel
Filosofska Historie 1937 d: Otakar VavrA. lps: Jan Pivec, Ladislav Bohac, Vladimir Hlavaty. 2523m CZC. *A Philosophical Story; Philosophical History* prod/rel: Moldavia
Jan Rohac, 1922, Play
Jan Rohac Z Dube 1947 d: Vladimir Borsky. lps: Otomar Korbelar, Ladislav Bohac. 85M CZC. *Warriors of Faith; Jan Rohac of Duba*

Lucerna, Play
Lucerna 1925 d: Carl Lamac. lps: Theodor Pistek, Anny Ondra, Karel Lamac. 1574m CZC. *The Lantern* prod/rel: Poja Film, American
Lucerna 1938 d: Carl Lamac. lps: Otomar Korbelar, Jarmila Berankova, Jarmila KsirovA. 2319m CZC. *The Lantern* prod/rel: Terra

Psohlavci, Novel
Psohlavci 1931 d: Svatopluk Innemann. lps: Bedrich Karen, Marie Grossova, Radola Rensky. 2961m CZC. *The Dog-Heads* prod/rel: Ab, Oceanfilm

Vojnarka, Play
Vojnarka 1936 d: Vladimir Borsky. lps: Jirina Stepnickova, Karel Pecian, Vaclav Vydra St. 2893m CZC. prod/rel: Terra

JOAQUIN, NICK
Play
Portrait of the Artist As Filipino 1965 d: Lamberto V. AvellanA. lps: Daisy Avellana, Naty Crame-Rogers, Sarah Joaquin. 107M PHL. prod/rel: Diadem

JOB, THOMAS
Uncle Henry, Play
Strange Affair of Uncle Harry, The 1945 d: Robert Siodmak. lps: George Sanders, Geraldine Fitzgerald, Ella Raines. 82M USA. *The Zero Murder Case; Uncle Harry* prod/rel: Universal

JOFFE, ALEX
Adieu Cherie, Short Story
Adieu Cherie 1945 d: Raymond Bernard. lps: Danielle Darrieux, Gabrielle Dorziat, Louis Salou. 115M FRN. prod/rel: Osso Roitfeld

JOHANNSEN, ERNST
Vier von Der Infanterie, Novel
Westfront 1918 1930 d: G. W. Pabst. lps: Fritz Kampers, Gustav Diessl, Hans Joachim Moebis. 97M GRM. *Vier von Der Infanterie; Four from the Infantry; Comrades of 1918* prod/rel: Nero-Film, Neue Filmkunst

JOHNS, FLORENCE
Miss Benton R.N., 1930, Play
Registered Nurse 1934 d: Robert Florey. lps: Bebe Daniels, Lyle Talbot, John Halliday. 64M USA. prod/rel: First National Pictures©

JOHNS, JOHN
The Return of Casey Jones, 1933, Short Story
Return of Casey Jones, The 1933 d: John P. McCarthy. lps: Charles Starrett, Ruth Hall, Robert Elliott. 67M USA. *Train 2419* (UKN) prod/rel: Monogram Pictures Corp.©

JOHNSON, ADRIEN
Fama, Play
Fior Di Levante 1925 d: Roberto Leone Roberti. lps: Francesca Bertini, Giorgio Bonaiti, Augusto Mastripietri. 1746m ITL. *Amore Di Donna* prod/rel: Bertini

JOHNSON, DOROTHY M.
The Hanging Tree, 1957, Novel
Hanging Tree, The 1959 d: Delmer Daves. lps: Gary Cooper, Maria Schell, Karl Malden. 106M USA. prod/rel: Warner Bros.

A Man Called Horse, 1950, Short Story
Man Called Horse, A 1970 d: Elliot Silverstein. lps: Richard Harris, Judith Anderson, Jean Gascon. 114M USA. prod/rel: Sandy Howard Productions

The Man Who Shot Liberty Valance, New York 1953, Short Story
Man Who Shot Liberty Valance, The 1962 d: John Ford. lps: John Wayne, James Stewart, Vera Miles. 123M USA. prod/rel: Paramount Pictures, John Ford Productions

JOHNSON, E. RICHARD
Mongo's Back in Town, Novel
Mongo's Back in Town 1971 d: Marvin J. Chomsky. lps: Joe Don Baker, Sally Field, Telly Savalas. TVM. 73M USA. *Steel Wreath* prod/rel: Bob Banner Associates

JOHNSON, EMILIE
Blind Hearts, Story
Blind Hearts 1921 d: Rowland V. Lee. lps: Hobart Bosworth, Wade Boteler, Irene Blackwell. 5488f USA. prod/rel: Hobart Bosworth Productions, Associated Producers

The Fourth Commandment, Story
Fourth Commandment, The 1927 d: Emory Johnson. lps: Henry Victor, June Marlowe, Belle Bennett. 7560f USA. prod/rel: Universal Pictures

JOHNSON, EYVIND (1900–1976), SWD
Romanen Om Olof, Stockholm 1945, Novel
Har Har du Ditt Liv 1966 d: Jan Troell. lps: Eddie Axberg, Ulla Sjoblom, Gunnar Bjornstrand. 167M SWD. *Here's Your Life* (USA); *Here Is Your Life* prod/rel: Svensk Filmindustri

JOHNSON, GEORGE M.
Short Story
Shadow Ranch 1930 d: Louis King. lps: Buck Jones, Marguerite de La Motte, Kate Price. 5766f USA. prod/rel: Columbia Pictures

Cowboy Stan Willis, Story
Terror of Bar X, The 1927 d: Scott Pembroke. lps: Bob Custer, Ruby Blaine, William Rhine. 4982f USA. prod/rel: Bob Custer Productions, Film Booking Offices of America

JOHNSON, GLADYS E.
Two-Bit Seats, 1917, Short Story
Two-Bit Seats 1917 d: Lawrence C. Windom. lps: Taylor Holmes, Marguerite Clayton, Sidney Ainsworth. 5r USA. prod/rel: Essanay Film Mfg. Co., Perfection Pictures

JOHNSON, JAMES WELDON (1871–1938), USA
Go Down Death - a Funeral Sermon, 1927, Poem
Go Down, Death! 1944 d: Spencer Williams. lps: Myra Hemmings, Samuel H. James, Spencer Williams. 54M USA. prod/rel: Sack Amusement, Harlemwood

JOHNSON, JULIAN
Hari Kari, New York 1913, Play
Who's Your Servant? 1920. lps: Lois Wilson, Yukio Aoyama, Andrew Robson. 4950f USA. prod/rel: Robertson-Cole Distributing Corp.

JOHNSON, LAURENCE E.
It's a Wise Child, New York 1929, Play
It's a Wise Child 1931 d: Robert Z. Leonard. lps: Marion Davies, Lester Vail, Ben Alexander. 75M USA. prod/rel: Metro-Goldwyn-Mayer Corp., Metro-Goldwyn-Mayer Dist. Corp.©

JOHNSON, LAURIE
Lock Up Your Daughters, London 1959, Play
Lock Up Your Daughters! 1969 d: Peter Coe. lps: Christopher Plummer, Susannah York, Glynis Johns. 103M UKN. prod/rel: Domino Productions, Columbia

JOHNSON, LOUANNE
My Posse Don't Do Homework, Book
Dangerous Minds 1995 d: John N. Smith. lps: Michelle Pfeiffer, George Dzundza, Courtney B. Vance. 99M USA. prod/rel: Buena Vista, Hollywood

JOHNSON, MARION PAGE
G.I. Honeymoon, Play
G.I. Honeymoon 1945 d: Phil Karlson. lps: Gale Storm, Peter Cookson, Arline Judge. 70M USA. prod/rel: Monogram

JOHNSON, MERLE
The Divine Gift, Story
Who are My Parents? 1922 d: J. Searle Dawley. lps: L. Rogers Lytton, Peggy Shaw, Florence Billings. 8361f USA. *A Little Child Shall Lead Them* prod/rel: Fox Film Corp.

JOHNSON, NORA
The World of Henry Orient, Boston 1958, Novel
World of Henry Orient, The 1964 d: George Roy Hill. lps: Peter Sellers, Tippy Walker, Merrie Spaeth. 106M USA. prod/rel: Pan Arts Co., United Artists

JOHNSON, NUNNALLY
Rough House Rosie, 1926, Short Story
Rough House Rosie 1927 d: Frank Strayer. lps: Clara Bow, Reed Howes, Arthur Housman. 5952f USA. *Rough-House Rosie* prod/rel: Paramount Famous Lasky Corp.

JOHNSON, OSA
I Married Adventure, New York 1940, Book
I Married Adventure 1940. CMP. 78M USA. prod/rel: Osa Johnson, Inc., Columbia Pictures Corp.©

JOHNSON, OWEN
Children of Divorce, Boston 1927, Novel
Children of Divorce 1927 d: Frank Lloyd, Josef von Sternberg (Uncredited). lps: Clara Bow, Esther Ralston, Gary Cooper. 6871f USA. prod/rel: Famous Players-Lasky, Paramount Pictures

Lawrenceville School Stories, Short Stories
Happy Years, The 1950 d: William A. Wellman. lps: Dean Stockwell, Darryl Hickman, Scotty Beckett. 110M USA. *Adventures of Young Dink Stover; Your Only Young Twice* prod/rel: MGM

The Salamander, New York 1913, Novel
Salamander, The 1915 d: Arthur Donaldson. lps: Ruth Findlay, Iva Shepard, John Sainpolis. 5r USA. prod/rel: B. S. Moss Motion Picture Corp., State Rights

The Varmint, New York 1910, Novel
Varmint, The 1917 d: William D. Taylor. lps: Jack Pickford, Louise Huff, Theodore Roberts. 5r USA. prod/rel: Oliver Morosco Photoplay Co.©, Paramount Pictures Corp.

Virtuous Wives, Boston 1917, Novel
Virtuous Wives 1918 d: George Loane Tucker. lps: Anita Stewart, Conway Tearle, Hedda Hopper. 6r USA. prod/rel: Anita Stewart Productions, Inc.©, First National Exhibitors Circuit

The Woman Gives, Boston 1916, Novel
Woman Gives, The 1920 d: R. William Neill. lps: Norma Talmadge, Edmund Lowe, John Halliday. 5923f USA. prod/rel: Norma Talmadge Film Co., First National Exhibitors Circuit

JOHNSON, PAMELA HANSFORD (1912–1981), UKN
The Trojan Brothers, Novel
Trojan Brothers, The 1946 d: MacLean Rogers. lps: Patricia Burke, David Farrar, Barbara Mullen. 86M UKN. *Murder in the Footlights* prod/rel: British National, Anglo-American

JOHNSON, RAY
Book
Dangerous Company 1982 d: Lamont Johnson. lps: Beau Bridges, Carlos Brown, Karen Carlson. TVM. 100M USA. prod/rel: NBC, Lorimar

JOHNSON, RICHARD
Story
Hennessy 1975 d: Don Sharp. lps: Rod Steiger, Lee Remick, Richard Johnson. 104M UKN. *The Fifth of November* prod/rel: American International Pictures, Marseilles

Getting Even, Manuscript
Kind of Hush, A 1998 d: Brian Stirner. lps: Harley Smith, Marcella Plunkett, Ben Roberts. 96M UKN. prod/rel: Capitol Films, British Screen

JOHNSON, ROBERT LEE
The Town in Hell's Backyard, Story
Devil's Trail, The 1942 d: Lambert Hillyer. lps: Bill Elliott, Tex Ritter, Eileen O'Hearn. 61M USA. *Rogues' Gallery* (UKN) prod/rel: Columbia

JOHNSON, STANLEY
The Commissioner, Novel
Commissioner, The 1998 d: George Sluizer. lps: John Hurt, Rosana Pastor, Alice Krige. 111M GRM/UKN/BLG. prod/rel: Metropolis Filmproduktion (Berlin), New Era Vision (London)

JOHNSON, TERRY
Insignificance, 1982, Play
Insignificance 1985 d: Nicolas Roeg. lps: Theresa Russell, Tony Curtis, Michael Emil. 109M UKN. prod/rel: Zenith Productions, Recorded Picture Company

JOHNSON, VELDA
A Howling in the Woods, Novel
Howling in the Woods, A 1971 d: Daniel Petrie. lps: Barbara Eden, Larry Hagman, John Rubinstein. TVM. 100M USA. prod/rel: Universal

JOHNSTON, AGNES CHRISTINE
Sky Life, 1929, Short Story
Under 18 1931 d: Archie Mayo. lps: Marian Marsh, Warren William, Regis Toomey. 81M USA. *Under Eighteen* prod/rel: Warner Bros. Pictures©

JOHNSTON, ALVA
Article
End of the Road 1944 d: George Blair. lps: Edward Norris, John Abbott, June Storey. 61M USA. prod/rel: Republic

JOHNSTON, ANNIE FELLOWS
The Little Colonel, New York 1895, Novel
Little Colonel, The 1935 d: David Butler. lps: Shirley Temple, Lionel Barrymore, Evelyn Venable. 80M USA. prod/rel: Fox Film Corp.©

JOHNSTON, CALVIN
Clay of Ca'lina, 1923, Short Story
Dancing Cheat, The 1924 d: Irving Cummings. lps: Herbert Rawlinson, Alice Lake, Robert Walker. 4727f USA. prod/rel: Universal Pictures

Pedigree, Story
Devil's Trademark, The 1928 d: James Leo Meehan. lps: Belle Bennett, William V. Mong, Marian Douglas. 5984f USA. prod/rel: Fbo Pictures

Temple Dusk, 1920, Short Story
Without Limit 1921 d: George D. Baker. lps: Anna Q. Nilsson, Robert Frazer, Frank Currier. 7r USA. *The Temple of Dusk* prod/rel: S-L Pictures, Metro Pictures

JOHNSTON, JENNIFER (1930–, IRL
How Many Miles to Babylon?
How Many Miles to Babylon? 1982 d: Moira Armstrong. lps: Sian Phillips, Barry Foster, Alan MacNaughton. TVM. 115M UKN. prod/rel: BBC

The Old Jest, 1979, Novel
Dawning, The 1988 d: Robert Knights. lps: Anthony Hopkins, Jean Simmons, Rebecca Pidgeon. 94M UKN. prod/rel: Enterprise, Tvs

The Railway Station Man, Novel
Railway Station Man, The 1993 d: Michael Whyte. lps: Julie Christie, Donald Sutherland, John Lynch. TVM. 90M UKN/USA.

Shadows on Our Skin, Novel
Shadows on Our Skin 1980 d: Jim O'Brien. lps: MacRea Clarke, May Friel, Joe McPartland. TVM. F UKN. prod/rel: BBC

JOHNSTON, MARY
Audrey, Boston 1902, Novel
Audrey 1916 d: Robert G. VignolA. lps: Pauline Frederick, Charles Waldron, Margarete Christians. 5r USA. prod/rel: Famous Players Film Co.©, Paramount Pictures Corp.

Pioneers of the Old South, New Haven 1918, Book
Jamestown 1923 d: Edwin L. Hollywood. lps: Dolores Cassinelli, Robert Gaillord, Harry Kendall. 4r USA. prod/rel: Chronicles of America Pictures, Yale University Press

To Have and to Hold, Boston 1900, Novel
To Have and to Hold 1916 d: George Melford. lps: Mae Murray, Wallace Reid, Tom Forman. 5r USA. prod/rel: Jesse L. Lasky Feature Play Co.©, Paramount Pictures Corp.

To Have and to Hold 1922 d: George Fitzmaurice. lps: Betty Compson, Bert Lytell, Theodore Kosloff. 7518f USA. prod/rel: Famous Players-Lasky, Paramount Pictures

JOHNSTON, WILLIAM ANDREW
The House of Whispers, Boston 1918, Novel
House of Whispers, The 1920 d: Ernest C. Warde. lps: J. Warren Kerrigan, Joseph J. Dowling, Fritzi Brunette. 5r USA. prod/rel: Robert Brunton Productions, W. W. Hodkinson Corp.

Limpy: the Boy Who Felt Neglected, Boston 1917, Novel
When a Feller Needs a Friend 1932 d: Harry Pollard. lps: Jackie Cooper, Charles "Chic" Sale, Ralph Graves. 76M USA. *When a Fellow Needs a Friend* (UKN); *Limpy* prod/rel: Metro-Goldwyn-Mayer Corp., Cosmopolitan Production

JOHNSTONE, CALDER
The Honor of Kenneth McGrath, Story
Honor of Kenneth McGrath, The 1915 d: Sydney Ayres. lps: Sydney Ayres, Doris Pawn, Val Paul. SHT USA. prod/rel: Powers

The Tinker of Stubbinville, Story
Tinker of Stubbinville, The 1915 d: Murdock MacQuarrie. lps: Murdock MacQuarrie. SHT USA. prod/rel: Big U

JOHNSTONE, WILLIAM B.
Take It from Me, Play
Take It from Me 1926 d: William A. Seiter. lps: Reginald Denny, Blanche Mehaffey, Ben Hendricks Jr. 6649f USA. prod/rel: Universal Pictures

JOKAI, MOR (1825–1904), HNG
Story
Szaffi 1986 d: Attila Dargay. ANM. 70M HNG/GRM/CND. *Jonas Und Der Verschwundene Schatz* (GRM) prod/rel: Infafilm, Panonia Struio

Az Aranyember, 1872, Novel
Aranyember 1917 d: Alexander KordA. lps: Oszkar Beregi, Lili Berky, Gabor Rajnay. HNG. *The Man With the Golden Touch*; *Golden Man*

Aranyember, Az 1962 d: Viktor Gertler. lps: Andras Csorba, Ilona Beres, Erno Szabo. 116M HNG. *The Man With the Golden Touch* prod/rel: Hunnia Filmagyar

Fekete Gyemantok, 1870, Novel
Fekete Gyemantok 1976 d: Zoltan Varkonyi. lps: Peter Huszti, Szilvia Sunoyovszky, Peter Hauman. 166M HNG. *Black Diamond*; *Black Diamonds*

Karpathy Zoltan, 1854, Novel
Karpathy Zoltan 1966 d: Zoltan Varkonyi. lps: Ferenc Bessenyei, Zoltan Latinovits, Eva Ruttkai. 87M HNG. *Last Nabob Part Ii: Zoltan Karpathy*; *Zoltan Karpathy*; *The Last of the Nabobs*

A Koszivu Ember Fiai, 1869, Novel
Kosziu Ember Fiai, A 1964 d: Zoltan Varkonyi. lps: Zoltan Varkonyi, Maria Sulyok, Odon Bitskey. 174M HNG. *Men and Banners*

Egy Magyar Nabob, Budapest 1853, Novel
Hungarian Nabob, The 1915 d: Travers Vale. lps: Charles Hill Mailes, Franklin Ritchie, Louise Vale. 4r USA. prod/rel: Biograph Co., General Film Co.

Magyar Nabob. Kapathy Zoltan, Egy 1966 d: Zoltan Varkonyi. lps: Ferenc Bessenyei, Zoltan Latinovits, Eva Ruttkai. 104M HNG. *The Last of the Nabobs*; *A Hungarian Nabob*; *The Last Nabob Part I*; *Egy Magyar Nabob*

Nevtelen Var, 1877, Novel
Nevtelen Var 1982 d: Eva Zsurzs. lps: Gyula Buss. 121M HNG. *The Nameless Castle*

Rab Raby, 1879, Novel
Rab Raby 1965 d: Gyorgy Hintsch. lps: Samu Balazs, Gyula Buss, Adam Szirtes. 106M HNG. *Captive Raby*

Souboj S Bohem, Short Story
Souboj S Bohem 1921 d: Boris Orlicky. lps: Hugo Svoboda, Bronislava Livia, Natasa CygankovA. CZC. *Duel With God* prod/rel: Ab, American

Szegeny Gazdagok, 1860, Novel
Szegeny Gazdagok 1959 d: Frigyes Ban. lps: Gyula Benko, Marianne Krencsey, Margit BarA. 102M HNG. *Fatia Negra*; *Poor Rich*

JOLLEY, ELIZABETH (1923–, UKN
The Last Crop, 1983, Short Story
Last Crop, The 1990 d: Susan Clayton. lps: Kerry Walker, Noah Taylor, Sarah Hooper. TVM. 60M ASL. prod/rel: Film Australia, Australian Film Commission

The Well, Novel
Well, The 1997 d: Samantha Lang. lps: Pamela Rabe, Miranda Otto, Paul Chubb. 102M ASL. prod/rel: Southern Star Xanadu, Nsw Film & Tv Office

JOLLY, CYRILL
The Vengeance of Private Pooley, Novel
Schwur Des Soldaten Pooley, Der 1962 d: Kurt Jung-Alsen. lps: Garfield Morgan, John Rees, Cecile Chevreux. 80M GRM/UKN. *The Story of Private Pooley* (UKN); *The Survivor* (USA) prod/rel: Deutscher Fernsehfunk Ost, Contemporary

JONAS, GEORGE
Vengeance, Book
Sword of Gideon, The 1986 d: Michael Anderson. lps: Steven Bauer, Robert Joy, Leslie Hope. 203M UKN/CND. *The Eleventh Commandment*; *The Munchen Strike* prod/rel: Alliance Entertainment, Les Films Ariane

JONES, ARTHUR EDMUND
The Hypocrites, Story
Hypocrites, The 1915 d: Lois Weber. lps: Myrtle Stedman, Courtenay Foote, Herbert Standing. 4r USA. prod/rel: Bosworth, Inc.©, Paramount Pictures Corp.

JONES, COMMANDER HERBERT A.
Mystery Ship, Short Story
Suicide Fleet 1931 d: Albert S. Rogell. lps: William Boyd, Robert Armstrong, James Gleason. 87M USA. *Mystery Ship* prod/rel: RKO Pathe Pictures, Charles R. Rogers Production

JONES, CONSTANCE
Peabody's Mermaid, Novel
Mr. Peabody and the Mermaid 1948 d: Irving Pichel. lps: William Powell, Ann Blyth, Irene Hervey. 89M USA. prod/rel: Universal

There Was a Little Man, Novel
Luck of the Irish, The 1948 d: Henry Koster. lps: Tyrone Power, Anne Baxter, Cecil Kellaway. 99M USA. *That Shamrock Touch*; *The Shamrock Touch*; *The Fear of Little Men*; *Leave It to the Irish* prod/rel: 20th Century-Fox

JONES, D. F.
Colossus, London 1966, Novel
Forbin Project, The 1969 d: Joseph Sargent. lps: Eric Braeden, Susan Clark, Gordon Pinsent. 100M USA. *Colossus the Forbin Project*; *Colossus 1980*; *The Day the World Changed Hands* prod/rel: Universal Pictures

JONES, DOUGLAS C.
The Court Martial of General George Armstrong Custer, Book
Court Martial of General George Armstrong Custer, The 1978 d: Glenn Jordan. lps: James Olson, Brian Keith, Ken Howard. TVM. 93M USA. prod/rel: Norman Rosemont

JONES, DYLAN
Thicker Than Water, Novel
Thicker Than Water 1994 d: Marc Evans. lps: Theresa Russell, Jonathan Pryce, Catherine Neilson. TVM. 115M UKN. prod/rel: BBC, a & E

JONES, ELWYN
The Ripper File, Book
Murder By Decree 1979 d: Bob Clark. lps: Christopher Plummer, James Mason, Donald Sutherland. 124M UKN/CND. *Sherlock Holmes: Murder By Decree* (USA); *Meurtre Par Decret*; *Sherlock Holmes and Saucy Jack* prod/rel: Highlight Theatrical Prod. Corp. Ltd., Ambassador Films Ltd. (Toronto)

JONES, GUY
Peabody's Mermaid, Novel
Mr. Peabody and the Mermaid 1948 d: Irving Pichel. lps: William Powell, Ann Blyth, Irene Hervey. 89M USA. prod/rel: Universal

There Was a Little Man, Novel
Luck of the Irish, The 1948 d: Henry Koster. lps: Tyrone Power, Anne Baxter, Cecil Kellaway. 99M USA. *That Shamrock Touch*; *The Shamrock Touch*; *The Fear of Little Men*; *Leave It to the Irish* prod/rel: 20th Century-Fox

JONES, HENRY ARTHUR (1851–1929), UKN
Chance the Idol, London 1902, Play
Spielerin, Die 1927 d: Graham Cutts. lps: Agnes Esterhazy, Harry Liedtke, Elza Temary. 2250m GRM. *Chance the Idol* prod/rel: H. R. Sokal-Film

The Dancing Girl, London 1891, Play
Dancing Girl, The 1915 d: Allan Dwan. lps: Florence Reed, Fuller Mellish, Lorraine Huling. 5r USA. prod/rel: Famous Players Film Co., Paramount Pictures Corp.

The Evangelist, New York 1907, Play
Evangelist, The 1915 d: Barry O'Neil. lps: Gladys Hanson, George Soule Spencer, Edith Ritchie. 4r USA. prod/rel: Lubin Mfg. Co.©, Lubin Unit Program

Hoodman Blind, London 1885, Play
Hoodman Blind 1913 d: James Gordon. lps: Betty Harte, Herbert Barrington, Mrs. Guy Standing. 5r USA. prod/rel: Pilot Films Corp., State Rights

Hoodman Blind 1923 d: John Ford. lps: David Butler, Gladys Hulette, Regina Connelly. 5434f USA. prod/rel: Fox Film Corp.

Man of Sorrow, A 1916 d: Oscar Apfel. lps: William Farnum, Dorothy Bernard, Dorothea Wolbert. 6r USA. *Hoodman Blind* prod/rel: Fox Film Corp., William Fox©

The Hypocrites, 1906, Play
Hypocrites, The 1916 d: George Loane Tucker. lps: Elisabeth Risdon, Charles Rock, Cyril Raymond. 5600f UKN. *The Morals of Weybury* prod/rel: London, Jury

Hypocrites, The 1923 d: Charles Giblyn. lps: Wyndham Standing, Mary Odette, Lillian Douglas. 4500f UKN/NTH. *Farizeeers* (NTH); *The Pharisees*; **De Hypocrieten** prod/rel: Granger-Binger Film

James the Fogey, Play
Call of Youth, The 1920 d: Hugh Ford. lps: Mary Glynne, Ben Webster, Jack Hobbs. 3871f UKN/USA. prod/rel: Famous Players-Lasky British Producers, Paramount Pictures

Judah, London 1890, Play
Cheater, The 1920 d: Henry Otto. lps: May Allison, King Baggot, Frank Currier. 6r USA. *Judah* prod/rel: Screen Classics, Inc., Metro Pictures Corp.©

The Lie, New York 1914, Play
Lie, The 1918 d: J. Searle Dawley. lps: Elsie Ferguson, David Powell, Betty Howe. 5r USA. prod/rel: Famous Players-Lasky Corp.©, Artcraft Pictures

The Lifted Veil, Play
Beyond 1921 d: William D. Taylor. lps: Ethel Clayton, Charles Meredith, Earl Schenck. 5248f USA. prod/rel: Famous Players-Lasky Corp., Paramount Pictures

Lydia Gilmore, New York 1912, Play
Lydia Gilmore 1916 d: Edwin S. Porter, Hugh Ford. lps: Pauline Frederick, Vincent Serrano, Thomas Holding. 5r USA. prod/rel: Famous Players Film Co.©, Paramount Pictures Corp.

The Masqueraders, London 1894, Play
Masqueraders, The 1915 d: James Kirkwood. lps: Hazel Dawn, Elliott Dexter, Frank Losee. 5r USA. prod/rel: Famous Players Film Co., Paramount Pictures Corp.

Michael and His Lost Angel, London 1896, Play
Whispering Devils 1920 d: Harry Garson. lps: Conway Tearle, Rosemary Theby, Sam Southern. 6r USA. *Michael and His Lost Angel* prod/rel: Harry Garson Productions, Equity Pictures Corp.

The Middleman, London 1889, Play
Middleman, The 1915 d: George Loane Tucker. lps: Albert Chevalier, Jane Gail, Gerald Ames. 4900f UKN. prod/rel: London, Jury

Mrs. Dane's Defence, London 1900, Play
Mrs. Dane's Defence 1933 d: A. V. Bramble. lps: Joan Barry, Basil Gill, Francis James. 67M UKN. prod/rel: National Talkies, Paramount

Mrs. Dane's Defense 1918 d: Hugh Ford. lps: Pauline Frederick, Frank Losee, Leslie Austen. 5r USA. prod/rel: Famous Players Film Co.©, Paramount Pictures Corp.

The Physician, London 1897, Play
Physician, The 1928 d: Georg Jacoby. lps: Miles Mander, Elga Brink, Ian Hunter. 8260f UKN. prod/rel: Gaumont

Saints and Sinners, London 1884, Play
Saints and Sinners 1916 d: James Kirkwood. lps: Peggy Hyland, Albert Tavernier, Estar Banks. 5r USA. prod/rel: Famous Players Film Co.©, Paramount Pictures Corp.

The Silver King, London 1882, Play
  Silver King, The 1919 d: George Irving. lps: William Faversham, Barbara Castleton, Nadia Gary. 5r USA. prod/rel: Famous Players-Lasky Corp.©, Paramount-Artcraft Special
  Silver King, The 1929 d: T. Hayes Hunter. lps: Percy Marmont, Jean Jay, Chili Bouchier. SIL. 8462f UKN. prod/rel: Welsh-Pearson-Elder, Paramount

We Can't Be As Bad As That, New York 1910, Play
  Society Exile, A 1919 d: George Fitzmaurice. lps: Elsie Ferguson, William P. Carleton, Warburton Gamble. 6r USA. prod/rel: Famous Players-Lasky Corp.©, Artcraft Pictures

JONES, JAMES (1921-1977), USA
From Here to Eternity, 1951, Novel
  From Here to Eternity 1953 d: Fred Zinnemann. lps: Deborah Kerr, Burt Lancaster, Montgomery Clift. 118M USA. prod/rel: Columbia
  From Here to Eternity 1978 d: Buzz Kulik. lps: Natalie Wood, William Devane, Steve Railsback. TVM. 300M USA. prod/rel: NBC, Columbia Pictuers
Some Came Running, 1957, Novel
  Some Came Running 1958 d: Vincente Minnelli. lps: Frank Sinatra, Dean Martin, Shirley MacLaine. 136M USA. prod/rel: MGM
The Thin Red Line, New York 1962, Novel
  Thin Red Line, The 1964 d: Andrew Marton. lps: Keir Dullea, Jack Warden, James Philbrook. 99M USA. prod/rel: Security Pictures, Allied Artists
  Thin Red Line, The 1998 d: Terrence Malick. lps: Sean Penn, Adrien Brody, Jim Caviezel. 170M USA. prod/rel: 20th Century Fox Film Corp.©, Fox 2000 Pictures

JONES, JOANNA
Nurse Is a Neighbour, London 1958, Novel
  Nurse on Wheels 1963 d: Gerald Thomas. lps: Juliet Mills, Ronald Lewis, Joan Sims. 86M UKN. prod/rel: Gregory, Hake & Walker, Anglo-Amalgamated

JONES, KAYLIE
A Soldier's Daughter Never Cries, Novel
  Soldier's Daughter Never Cries, A 1998 d: James Ivory. lps: Kris Kristofferson, Barbara Hershey, Leelee Sobieski. 127M UKN. prod/rel: Merchant Ivory Productions©, Capitol Films

JONES, LEROI (1934-, USA
Dutchman, New York 1964, Play
  Dutchman 1967 d: Anthony Harvey. lps: Shirley Knight, Al Freeman Jr., Robert Calvert. 56M UKN. prod/rel: Gene Persson Enterprises, Dutchman Film Co.
Slave, 1964, Play
  Fable, A 1971 d: Al Freeman Jr. lps: Al Freeman Jr., Hildy Brooks, James Patterson. 80M USA.

JONES, MADISON
An Exile, New York 1967, Novel
  I Walk the Line 1970 d: John Frankenheimer. lps: Gregory Peck, Tuesday Weld, Estelle Parsons. 98M USA. *An Exile* prod/rel: John Frankenheimer Productions, Edward Lewis Productions

JONES, MARC EDMUND
In the Firelight, Poem
  In the Firelight 1913 d: Thomas Ricketts. lps: Ed Coxen, Charlotte Burton, William Bertram. 2000f USA. prod/rel: American

Lucky Damage, Story
  Skin Deep 1922 d: Lambert Hillyer. lps: Milton Sills, Florence Vidor, Marcia Manon. 6303f USA. prod/rel: Thomas H. Ince Corp., Associated First National Pictures
  Skin Deep 1929 d: Ray Enright. lps: Monte Blue, Davey Lee, Betty Compson. 5964f USA. prod/rel: Warner Brothers Pictures

JONES, MARJORIE
Some Fixer, Story
  Some Fixer 1915 d: Al Christie. lps: Corinne Lessler, Eddie Lyons, Lee Moran. SHT USA. prod/rel: Nestor

JONES, MERVYN
John and Mary, London 1966, Novel
  John and Mary 1969 d: Peter Yates. lps: Dustin Hoffman, Mia Farrow, Michael Tolan. 92M USA. prod/rel: Debrod Productions

JONES, PETER
Marian, Play
  Marilyn 1953 d: Wolf RillA. lps: Maxwell Reed, Sandra Dorne, Leslie Dwyer. 70M UKN. *Roadhouse Girl*; *Marion* prod/rel: Nettlefold, Butcher's Film Service

JONES, RAYMOND F.
This Island Earth, 1952, Novel
  This Island Earth 1955 d: Joseph M. Newman, Jack Arnold. lps: Jeff Morrow, Faith Domergue, Rex Reason. 87M USA. *War of the Planets* prod/rel: Universal-International

JONES, ROBERT PAGE
The Heisters, New York 1964, Novel
  Homme de Marrakech, L' 1966 d: Jacques Deray. lps: George Hamilton, Claudine Auger, Alberto de MendozA. 95M FRN/ITL/SPN. *Los Saqueadores Del Domingo* (SPN); *L' Uomo Di Casablanca* (ITL); *El Hombre de Marrakech*; *That Man George* (USA); *Our Man in Marrakesh* prod/rel: Europazur, Producciones Benito Perojo

JONES, S.
Poppy Comes to Town, New York 1923, Musical Play
  Poppy 1936 d: A. Edward Sutherland, Stuart Heisler (Uncredited). lps: W. C. Fields, Rochelle Hudson, Richard Cromwell. 73M USA. prod/rel: Paramount Productions©

JONES, TERRY
Secrets, Play
  Consuming Passions 1988 d: Giles Foster. lps: Vanessa Redgrave, Jonathan Pryce, Tyler Butterworth. 90M UKN/USA. prod/rel: Samuel Goldwyn, Euston Films

JONSON, BEN (1573-1637), UKN
Volpone, 1607, Play
  Volpone 1940 d: Maurice Tourneur. lps: Harry Baur, Louis Jouvet, Fernand Ledoux. 94M FRN. prod/rel: Ile De France-Films

JONSSON, REIDAR
Mitt Liv Som Hund, Autobiography
  Mitt Liv Som Hund 1985 d: Lasse Hallstrom. lps: Anton Glanzelius, Tomas von Bromssen, Anki Liden. 101M SWD. *My Life As a Dog* (UKN) prod/rel: Svenski Filmindustri, Film-Teknik
Swedish Heroes, Book
  Svenska Hjaltar 1997 d: Daniel Bergman. lps: Niclas Olund, Cajsa-Lisa Ejemyr, Kent-Arne Dahlgren. 106M SWD. *Swedish Heroes* prod/rel: Svensk Filmindustri, Tv4

JOPE-SLADE, CHRISTINE
Britannia of Billingsgate, London 1931, Play
  Britannia of Billingsgate 1933 d: Sinclair Hill. lps: Violet Loraine, Gordon Harker, Kay Hammond. 99M UKN. prod/rel: Gaumont-British, Ideal

JOPPOLO, BENJAMIN
I Carabinieri, Paris 1958, Play
  Carabiniers, Les 1962 d: Jean-Luc Godard. lps: Marino Mase, Albert Juross, Genevieve GaleA. 80M FRN/ITL. *The Riflemen* (USA); *The Soldiers* prod/rel: Rome-Paris Films, Marceauc Cocinor

JORDAN, ANNE
Kitchen Privileges, 1935, Short Story
  Luckiest Girl in the World, The 1936 d: Edward Buzzell. lps: Jane Wyatt, Louis Hayward, Nat Pendleton. 75M USA. prod/rel: Universal Pictures Corp.©

JORDAN, ELIZABETH
Black Butterflies, New York 1927, Novel
  Black Butterflies 1928 d: James W. Horne. lps: Jobyna Ralston, Olga Busch, Robert Frazer. 6220f USA. *Buttlerflies* (UKN) prod/rel: Quality Distributing Corp.
The Girl in the Mirror, New York 1919, Novel
  Girl in Number 29, The 1920 d: John Ford. lps: Frank Mayo, Elinor Fair, Claire Anderson. 4775f USA. *The Girl in the Mirror* prod/rel: Universal Film Mfg. Co.©

JORDAN, KATE
A City Sparrow, 1917, Serial Story
  City Sparrow, A 1920 d: Sam Wood. lps: Ethel Clayton, Walter Hiers, Clyde Fillmore. 4618f USA. prod/rel: Famous Players-Lasky Corp.©, Paramount Pictures
Creeping Tides, Boston 1913, Novel
  Tides of Fate, The 1917 d: Marshall Farnum. lps: Alexandra Carlisle, Frank Holland, William Sheer. 5r USA. *Creeping Tides* prod/rel: Equitable Motion Pictures Corp., World Film Corp.©
The Next Corner, Boston 1921, Novel
  Next Corner, The 1924 d: Sam Wood. lps: Conway Tearle, Lon Chaney, Dorothy MacKaill. 7081f USA. prod/rel: Famous Players-Lasky, Paramount Pictures
  Nuit d'Espagne 1931 d: Henri de La Falaise. lps: Geymond Vital, Jeanne Helbling, Rose Dionne. F USA. prod/rel: RKO-Radio Pictures
  Transgression 1931 d: Herbert Brenon. lps: Kay Francis, Paul Cavanagh, Ricardo Cortez. 72M USA. *The Next Corner*; *Around the Corner* prod/rel: RKO Radio Pictures©, Herbert Brenon's Production
Orchestra D-2, 1915, Short Story
  Castles in the Air 1919 d: George D. Baker. lps: May Allison, Ben Wilson, Clarence Burton. 5r USA. *Orchestra D-2* prod/rel: Metro Pictures Corp.©
Secret Strings, New York 1914, Play
  Secret Strings 1918 d: John Ince. lps: Olive Tell, Hugh Thompson, William J. Kelly. 5r USA., Metro Pictures Corp.©

The Spirit of the Road, Story
  In Search of a Thrill 1923 d: Oscar Apfel. lps: Viola Dana, Warner Baxter, Mabel Van Buren. 5500f USA. prod/rel: Metro Pictures
Time, the Comedian, New York 1905, Novel
  Time, the Comedian 1925 d: Robert Z. Leonard. lps: Mae Busch, Lew Cody, Gertrude Olmstead. 4757f USA. prod/rel: Metro-Goldwyn-Mayer Pictures

JORDON, ELIZABETH
Daddy and I, New York 1935, Novel
  Make Way for a Lady 1936 d: David Burton. lps: Herbert Marshall, Anne Shirley, Gertrude Michael. 65M USA. *Daddy and I* prod/rel: RKO Radio Pictures©

JORGENSEN, CHRISTINE
Christine Jorgensen: a Personal Autobiography, New York 1967, Autobiography
  Christine Jorgensen Story, The 1970 d: Irving Rapper. lps: John Hansen, Quinn Redeker, John W. Himes. 89M USA. *Christine* prod/rel: United Artists

JOSE, EDWARD
God's Prodigal, Novel
  God's Prodigal 1923 d: Bert Wynne, Edward Jose. lps: Gerald Ames, Flora Le Breton, Frank Stanmore. 5000f UKN. prod/rel: International Artists

JOSEPH, M. K.
A Soldier's Tale, Novel
  Soldier's Tale, A 1988 d: Larry Parr. lps: Gabriel Byrne, Marianne Basler, Judge Reinhold. 94M NZL. prod/rel: Atlantic

JOSEPH, MICHAEL
Account Rendered, Play
  Account Rendered 1932 d: Leslie H. Gordon. lps: Cecil Ramage, Reginald Bach, Marilyn Mawm. 35M UKN. prod/rel: Producers Distributing Corporation

JOSEPHSON, MATTHEW
Robber Barons, New York 1934, Book
  Toast of New York, The 1937 d: Rowland V. Lee. lps: Edward Arnold, Cary Grant, Frances Farmer. 109M USA. *The Robber Barons* prod/rel: RKO Radio Pictures©
Zola and His Time, New York 1928, Book
  Life of Emile Zola, The 1937 d: William Dieterle. lps: Paul Muni, Gale Sondergaard, Joseph Schildkraut. 123M USA. *I Accuse* (UKN) prod/rel: Warner Bros. Pictures©

JOSEPHSON, RAGNAR
Kanske En Diktare, 1932, Play
  Farliga Vagar 1942 d: Anders Henrikson. 86M SWD. *Dangerous Roads*; *Flyktingar*
  Kanske En Diktare 1933 d: Lorens Marmstedt. 78M SWD. *A Poet Maybe*

JOSEPHUS, FLAVIUS
The Jewish Antiquities, 93-94 A.D., Book
  Salome 1918 d: J. Gordon Edwards. lps: Theda Bara, G. Raymond Nye, Alan Roscoe. 8r USA. prod/rel: Fox Film Corp., William Fox©

JOSHI, C. V.
Lagna Pahave Karun, Short Story
  Lagna Pahava Karun 1940 d: Winayak. lps: Damuanna Malvankar, V. Jog, Shakuntala Bhome. 150M IND. *Get Married and See* prod/rel: Navyug Chitrapat

JOSHI, V. B.
Prithvi Vallabh, Novel
  Prithvi Vallabh 1924 d: Manilal Joshi. lps: Parshwanath Yeshwant Altekar, Wagle Sandow, Begum FatmA. 7456f IND. *The Lord of Love and Power* prod/rel: Ashoka Pictures

JOSIPOVICI
Le Livre de Goha le Simple, Novel
  Goha 1958 d: Jacques Baratier. lps: Omar Sharif, Zina Bouzaiane, Lauro Gazzolo. 83M FRN/TNS. prod/rel: U.G.C., Films Franco-Africains

JOSSELIN, JEAN-FRANCOIS
Quelques Jours Avec Moi, Novel
  Quelques Jours Avec Moi 1987 d: Claude Sautet. lps: Daniel Auteuil, Sandrine Bonnaire, Jean-Pierre Marielle. 131M FRN. prod/rel: Sara Films, Cinea

JOSSELYN, TALBERT
Smugglers' Cove, Short Story
  Smugglers' Cove 1948 d: William Beaudine. lps: Leo Gorcey, Huntz Hall, Gabriel Dell. 66M USA. prod/rel: Monogram

JOSSELYN, TALBOT
Navy Bound, 1935, Short Story
  Navy Bound 1951 d: Paul Landres. lps: Tom Neal, Wendy Waldron, Regis Toomey. 61M USA. prod/rel: Monogram

JOUDRY-STEELE, PATRICIA
Teach Me How to Cry, Play
  Restless Years, The 1958 d: Helmut Kautner. lps: John Saxon, Sandra Dee, Luana Patten. 86M USA. *The Wonderful Years* (UKN) prod/rel: Universal-International

JOUGLET, RENE
Le Jardinier d'Argenteuil, Novel
  Jardinier d'Argenteuil, Le 1966 d: Jean-Paul Le Chanois. lps: Jean Gabin, Liselotte Pulver, Curd Jurgens. 90M FRN/GRM. *Gauner Und Die Nacht von Nizza Bluten* (GRM); *Blossoms Crooks and a Night in Nice* prod/rel: Films Copernic-Gafer, Films Vertrieb

JOULLOT
Court-Circuit, Play
  Court-Circuit 1929 d: Maurice Champreux. lps: Gabriel Vierge, Charpentier, Laure Savidge. 1800m FRN.

JOURDA, DANIEL
Au Dela Des Lois Humaines
  Au-Dela Des Lois Humaines 1920 d: Gaston Roudes, Marcel Dumont. lps: Rachel Devirys, Germaine Sablon, Georges Saillard. F FRN. prod/rel: Gallo Films
Crime Et Redemption, Play
  Dette, La 1920 d: Gaston Roudes. lps: Pierre Magnier, Gina Relly, Helene Darly. 1675m FRN. prod/rel: Gallo Films
Le Doute, Play
  Doute, Le 1920 d: Gaston Roudes. lps: Louise Colliney, Jacques de Feraudy, Rachel Devirys. F FRN. prod/rel: Gallo Film

JOUVE, PIERRE-JEAN (1887–1976), FRN
Paulina 1880, 1925, Novel
  Paulina 1880 1972 d: Jean-Louis Bertucelli. lps: Eliana de Santis, Olga Karlatos, Maximilian Schell. 110M FRN/GRM. prod/rel: Albina, Artistes Associes

JOVANOVIC, DUSAN
The Liberation of Skopje, Play
  Liberation of Skopje, The 1981 d: William Fitzwater. lps: Sasa Stanojevic, Perica Martinovic, Inge Apelt. TVM. F ASL. prod/rel: Ferryman Television

JOVER Y VALENTI
Los Ninos Del Hospicio, Play
  Ninos Del Hospicio, Los 1926 d: Jose Fernandez. lps: Amparo Ferrer, Carlitos Beraza Melo, Jose Hernandez. SPN. prod/rel: Cinematografica Fer-Vall-Duch (Valencia)

JOYCE, HAROLD
Murder on Sunset Boulevard, Short Story
  Sunset Strip Case, The 1938 d: Louis J. Gasnier. lps: Sally Rand, Reed Hadley, Sugar Kane. 62M USA. *High Explosive* (UKN); *The Sunset Murder Case*; *Murder on Sunset Boulevard*; *Murder on Sunset Blvd* prod/rel: Grand National Pictures©

JOYCE, JAMES (1882–1941), IRL
Dubliners, 1914, Short Story
  Dead, The 1987 d: John Huston. lps: Donal McCann, Anjelica Huston, Rachel Dowling. 82M USA/UKN/GRM. *The Dead -Die Toten* (GRM) prod/rel: Vestron, Zenith
Finnegan's Wake, 1939, Novel
  Passages from "Finnegan's Wake" 1967 d: Mary Ellen Bute. lps: Martin J. Kelly, Jane Reilly, Peter Haskell. 97M USA. *Passages from James Joyce's "Finnegan's Wake"*; *Finnegan's Wake* prod/rel: Expanding Cinema, Evergreen Films
A Portrait of the Artist As a Young Man, 1916, Novel
  Portrait of the Artist As a Young Man 1977 d: Joseph Strick. lps: Bosco Hogan, T. P. McKenna, John Gielgud. 98M UKN. prod/rel: Howard Mahler Films
Ulysses, 1922, Novel
  Ulysses 1967 d: Joseph Strick. lps: Milo O'Shea, Barbara Jefford, Maurice Roeves. 140M UKN/USA. *James Joyce's Ulysses* prod/rel: Ulysses Film Production, British Lion

JOYEUX, ODETTE
La Mariee Est Trop Belle, Novel
  Mariee Est Trop Belle, La 1956 d: Pierre Gaspard-Huit. lps: Brigitte Bardot, Louis Jourdan, Micheline Presle. 95M FRN. *The Bride Is Much Too Beautiful* (USA); *The Bride Is Too Beautiful* (UKN); *La Mariee Etait Trop Belle* prod/rel: S.N. Pathe Cinema, Christine Gouze-Renal

JUDD, HARRISON
Shadow of a Doubt, Novel
  Temoin, Le 1977 d: Jean-Pierre Mocky. lps: Alberto Sordi, Philippe Noiret, Roland Dubillard. 110M FRN/ITL. *Il Testimone* (ITL); *The Witness* (UKN) prod/rel: Produzioni Atlas Consorziate (Roma), Belstar Productions

JUDD, NAOMI (1946–, USA, Judd, Diana Ellen
Love Can Build a Bridge, Autobiography
  Naomi & Wynonna: Love Can Build a Bridge 1995 d: Bobby Roth. lps: Kathleen York, Viveka Davis, Bruce Greenwood. TVM. 240M USA. prod/rel: Avnet/ Korner

JUDGE, JAMES P.
Square Crooks, New York 1926, Play
  Baby, Take a Bow 1934 d: Harry Lachman. lps: Shirley Temple, James Dunn, Claire Trevor. 73M USA. *Always Honest*; *Going Straight* prod/rel: Fox Film Corp.
  Square Crooks 1928 d: Lewis Seiler. lps: Robert Armstrong, Johnny Mack Brown, Dorothy Dwan. 5397f USA. prod/rel: Fox Film Corp.

JUDSON, JEANNE
The Call of Life, New York 1919, Novel
  Beckoning Roads 1920 d: Howard Hickman. lps: Bessie Barriscale, Niles Welch, George Periolat. 5033f USA. prod/rel: B. B. Features, Robertson-Cole Distributing Corp.

JUDSON, WILLIAM
Cold River, Novel
  Cold River 1981 d: Fred G. Sullivan. lps: Suzanne Weber, Pat Petersen, Richard Jaeckel. 94M USA. prod/rel: Cold River Pictures

JUHN, KURT
Novel
  Prvni Polibeni 1935 d: Vladimir Slavinsky. lps: Jiri Plachy, Marketa Krausova, Hana BelskA. 2439m CZC. *The First Kiss* prod/rel: Julius Schmitt, Ab

JULLIAN, MARCEL
Rocca: Mortels Rendez-Vous, Novel
  Rocca: Mortels Rendez-Vous 1994 d: Paul Planchon. lps: Raymond Pellegrin, Jan Rouiller, Henri Guybet. TVM. 91M FRN.

JUN, OTTO
Prosim Pane Profesore!, Novel
  Prosim Pane Profesore! 1940 d: Karel Hasler. lps: Theodor Pistek, Jiri Vondrovic, R. A. StrejkA. 2128m CZC. *Please Sir!* prod/rel: Zdar (Vladimir Posusta)

JUN QING
Changing Heaven, Novel
  Min Bing de Er Zi 1958 d: Huang Can. lps: Jia Naiguang, Zhou Shengguan, Huang Ling. 8r CHN. *Son of the Militia* prod/rel: Changchun Film Studio
Li Ming de He Bian, Novel
  Li Ming de He Bian 1958 d: Chen Ge. lps: Sun Yu, Zhang Yang, Wang JianhuA. 9r CHN. *The Riverbank at Dawn* prod/rel: Changchun Film Studio

JUNGMEYER, JACK
When the Daltons Rode, New York 1931, Book
  When the Daltons Rode 1940 d: George Marshall. lps: Randolph Scott, Kay Francis, Brian Donlevy. 80M USA. prod/rel: Universal Pictures Co.©

JUNICHI, WATANABE
Shitsurakuen, Novel
  Shitsurakuen 1997 d: Yoshimitsu MoritA. lps: Koji Yakusho, Hitomi Kuroki, Akira Terao. 119M JPN. *Lost Paradise* prod/rel: Ace Pictures, Kadokawa Shoten

JUNIOR, F. K.
Poetic License, Story
  Poetic License 1922 d: George A. Cooper. lps: Shayle Gardner, Winifred McCarthy, Ivo Dawson. 2300f UKN. prod/rel: Quality Plays, Walturdaw
The Thief, Story
  Thief, The 1922 d: George A. Cooper. lps: Malcolm Tod, Mildred Evelyn, Harry J. Worth. 1355f UKN. prod/rel: Quality Plays, Walturdaw

JUNKIN, HARRY W.
A Public Figure, Television Play
  Slander 1956 d: Roy Rowland. lps: Van Johnson, Ann Blyth, Steve Cochran. 81M USA. prod/rel: MGM

JUSTER, NORMAN
The Phantom Tollbooth, New York 1961, Novel
  Phantom Tollbooth, The 1969 d: David Monahan, Charles M. Jones. lps: Butch Patrick. ANM. 90M USA. prod/rel: Metro-Goldwyn-Mayer, Inc.

JUUL, OLE
Det Tossede Paradis, Copenhagen 1953, Novel
  Tossede Paradis, Det 1962 d: Gabriel Axel. lps: Dirch Passer, Hans W. Petersen, Ove Sprogoe. 104M DNM. *Crazy Paradise*

K

KACAN, METIN
Novel
  Agir Roman 1997 d: Mustafa Altioklar. lps: Mujde Ar, Okan Bayulgen, Mustafa Ugurlu. 118M TRK/HNG/FRN. *Cholera Street* prod/rel: Belge Film, Ozen Film

KADAR, LASZLO
Magdat Kicsapja, Play
  MaddalenA. Zero in Condotta 1940 d: Vittorio de SicA. lps: Vittorio de Sica, Vera Bergman, Carla Del Poggio. 78M ITL. prod/rel: Artisti Associati

KADELBURG, GUSTAV
Der Weg Zur Holle, Play
  Tolle Lola, Die 1927 d: Richard Eichberg. lps: Lilian Harvey, Harry Halm, Hans Junkermann. 1985m GRM. *La Terrible Lola* prod/rel: Richard Eichberg-Film
  Tolle Lola, Die 1954 d: Hans Deppe. lps: Herta Staal, Wolf Albach-Retty, Grethe Weiser. 95M GRM. *Neat Lola* prod/rel: Hans Deppe-Film, N.F.

KADEN-BANDROWSKI, JULIUSZ
Czarne Skrzydla, 1928-29, Novel
  Czarne Skrzydla 1962 d: Ewa Petelska, Czeslaw Petelski. lps: Beata Tyszkiewicz, Kazimierz Opalinski, Czeslaw Wollejko. 104M PLN. *Black Wings*

KADES, HANS
Der Erfolgreiche, Novel
  Grosse Versuchung, Die 1952 d: Rolf Hansen. lps: Dieter Borsche, Ruth Leuwerik, Harald Holberg. 95M GRM. *The Great Temptation* prod/rel: Rotary, D.F.H.
San Salvatore, Novel
  San Salvatore 1956 d: Werner Jacobs. lps: Dieter Borsche, Will Quadflieg, Antje Weisgerber. 100M GRM. prod/rel: Rotary, Bavaria

KADISON, ELLIS
Story
  Don't Give Up the Ship 1959 d: Norman Taurog. lps: Jerry Lewis, Dina Merrill, Diana Spencer. 89M USA. prod/rel: Paramount, Hal B. Wallis

KAEMPFERT, WALDEMAR
The Diminishing Draft, 1918, Short Story
  Amour de Poche, Un 1957 d: Pierre Kast. lps: Jean Marais, Genevieve Page, Agnes Laurent. 88M FRN. *Nude in His Pocket* (USA); *Girl in His Pocket*; *A Pocket Love* prod/rel: S.N.E.Gaumont, Madeleine Films

KAFFKA, MARGIT
Hangyaboly, 1917, Novel
  Hangyaboly 1971 d: Zoltan Fabri. lps: Gyorgyi Andai, Jaroslava Schallerova, Mari Torocsik. 104M HNG. *Ant's Nest*

KAFKA, FRANZ (1883–1924), CZC
Amerika, 1927, Novel
  Klassenverhaltnisse 1984 d: Jean-Marie Straub, Daniele Huillet. lps: Christian Heinisch, Reinald Schnell, Mario Adorf. TVM. 127M GRM/FRN. *Rapports de Classes* (FRN); *Class Relations*; *Class Conditions*; *Class Relationships* prod/rel: Janus Film Und Fernsehen, Hessischen Rundfunk (Frankfurt)
Ein Brudermord, 1919, Short Story
  Brudermord, Ein 1981 d: Brothers Quay. ANM. 5M UKN. prod/rel: Atelier Koninck, Greater London Arts Association
Ein Hungerkunstler, 1924, Short Story
  Hunger Artist, The 1976 d: Fred Smith. 10M USA.
In Der Strafkolonie, 1919, Short Story
  Colonia Penal, La 1971 d: Raul Ruiz. lps: Monica Echeverria, Luis Alarcon, Anibal ReynA. 72M CHL. *Penal Camp*; *The Penal Colony* prod/rel: Alcaman
Der Prozess, Berlin 1925, Novel
  Prozess, Der 1962 d: Orson Welles. lps: Anthony Perkins, Jeanne Moreau, Romy Schneider. 118M GRM/ITL/FRN. *Il Processo* (ITL); *Le Proces* (FRN); *The Trial* (USA) prod/rel: Paris Europa Production, Hisa-Film
  Trial, The 1992 d: David Jones. lps: Kyle MacLachlan, Anthony Hopkins, Jason Robards Jr. 120M UKN. prod/rel: BBC, Europanda
Das Schloss, Munich 1926, Novel
  Linna 1986 d: Jaakko PakkasvirtA. 99M FNL. *The Castle*
  Schloss, Das 1968 d: Rudolf Noelte. lps: Maximilian Schell, Cordula Trantow, Trudik Daniel. 93M GRM/SWT. *The Castle* (USA) prod/rel: Noelte, Alfa
Der Verschollene, Short Story
  Klassenverhaltnisse 1984 d: Jean-Marie Straub, Daniele Huillet. lps: Christian Heinisch, Reinald Schnell, Mario Adorf. TVM. 127M GRM/FRN. *Rapports*

de Classes (FRN); *Class Relations*; *Class Conditions*; *Class Relationships* prod/rel: Janus Film Und Fernsehen, Hessischen Rundfunk (Frankfurt)

Die Verwandlung, 1912, Short Story
Forvandlingen 1975 d: Ivo Dvorak. lps: Ernst Gunther, Gunn Wallgren, Peter Schildt. 88M SWD. *Metamorphosis* (USA)

KAFKA, HANS
Carrefour, Short Story
Dead Man's Shoes 1939 d: Thomas Bentley. lps: Leslie Banks, Wilfred Lawson, Judy Kelly. 70M UKN. prod/rel: Associated British Picture Corporation

KAGAMI, JIRO
Novel
Nusumareta Koi 1951 d: Kon IchikawA. lps: Asami Kuji, Masayuki Mori, Yuji KawakitA. 89M JPN. *Stolen Love* prod/rel: Shintoho Co.

KAGEYAMA, HIDEKO
Warawa No Hanshogai, Autobiography
Waga Koi Wa Moenu 1949 d: Kenji Mizoguchi. lps: Kinuyo Tanaka, Ichiro Sugai, Mitsuko Mito. 84M JPN. *My Love Has Been Burning* (UKN); *Flame of My Love* (USA); *My Love Burns* prod/rel: Shochiku Co.

KAHLER, HUGH MACNAIR
Fool's First, 120, Short Story
Fools First 1922 d: Marshall Neilan. lps: Richard Dix, Claire Windsor, Claude Gillingwater. 5773f USA. prod/rel: Marshall Neilan Productions, Associated First National Pictures

Once a Peddler, 1921, Short Story
Little Giant, The 1926 d: William Nigh. lps: Glenn Hunter, Edna Murphy, David Higgins. 6850f USA. prod/rel: Universal Pictures

The Six Best Cellars, 1919, Short Story
Six Best Cellars, The 1920 d: Donald Crisp. lps: Bryant Washburn, Wanda Hawley, Clarence Burton. 4822f USA. prod/rel: Famous Players-Lasky Corp.©, Paramount-Artcraft Pictures

KAHN, EDGAR
Spatzen in Gottes Hand, Play
Gluck Aus Ohio 1951 d: Heinz Paul. lps: Hermann Brix, Edith Prager, Loni Heuser. 85M GRM. *Spatzen in Gottes Hand*; *Good Fortune from Ohio* prod/rel: Merkur, Danubia

KAHN JR., E. J.
The Gentle Wolfhound, Story
Three Stripes in the Sun 1955 d: Richard Murphy. lps: Aldo Ray, Mitsuko Kimura, Philip Carey. 93M USA. *The Gentle Sergeant* (UKN) prod/rel: Fred Kohlmer, Columbia Pictures Corporation

KAISER, GEORG (1878–1945), GRM
Der Brand Im Opernhaus, 1919, Play
Brand in Der Oper 1930 d: Carl Froelich. lps: Gustaf Grundgens, Gustav Frolich, Alexa Engstrom. 104M GRM. *Fire in the Opera House*; *Barcarole*; *The Love Duet*

Der Mutige Seefahrer, 1926, Play
Ghost Comes Home, The 1940 d: Wilhelm Thiele. lps: Frank Morgan, Billie Burke, Ann Rutherford. 79M USA. *The Ghost Man*; *Hooray I'm Alive* prod/rel: Metro-Goldwyn-Mayer Corp., Loew's, Inc.©

Hurrah! Ich Lebe! 1928 d: Wilhelm Thiele. lps: Nicolas Koline, Nathalie Lissenko, Betty Astor. 2583m GRM. *Hurrah! I'm Alive!*; *Die Falsche Wittwe* prod/rel: UFA

Mutige Seefahrer, The 1935 d: Hans Deppe. lps: Paul Kemp, Lucie Englisch, Maria Krahn. 88M GRM.

Zwei Krawatten, 1930, Play
Zwei Krawatten 1930 d: Felix Basch, Richard Weichart. 89M GRM. *Two Neckties* (USA)

KAKODKAR, CHANDRAKANT
Nilambiri, Novel
Do Raaste 1969 d: Raj KhoslA. lps: Rajesh Khanna, Mumtaz, Balraj Sahni. 165M IND. *Two Roads* prod/rel: Raj Khosla Films

KALEB, VJEKOSLAV
Divota Prasine, 1954, Novel
Divota Prasine 1976 d: Milan Ljubic. lps: Ljubisa Samardzic, Silvo Bozic, Joze Zupan. 90M YGS. *Cudoviti Prah*; *The Glorious Dust*

KALER, JAMES OTIS
Toby Tyler; Or Ten Weeks With a Circus, New York 1881, Novel
Circus Days 1923 d: Eddie Cline. lps: Jackie Coogan, Barbara Tennant, Russell Simpson. 6183f USA. prod/rel: Sol Lesser, Associated First National Pictures

Toby Tyler 1960 d: Charles T. Barton. lps: Kevin Corcoran, Henry Calvin, Gene Sheldon. 96M USA. *Toby Tyler Or Ten Weeks With a Circus* prod/rel: Walt Disney

KALEY, JAY J.
Deuces Wild, Story
Saddle Aces 1935 d: Harry L. Fraser. lps: Rex Bell, Ruth Mix, Buzz Barton. 56M USA. prod/rel: Resolute Productions, Resolute Pictures Corp.

KALFON, PIERRE
Ernesto Guevara, une Legende du Siecle Che, Book
El Che 1997 d: Maurice Dugowson. DOC. 96M FRN/SPN. prod/rel: Cineteve (France), Ilgedo Komunikazioa (Spain)

KALKUS, ALBERT
Die Junggesellenfalle, Play
Junggesellenfalle 1953 d: Fritz Bottger. lps: Oskar Sima, Rudolf Platte, Rudolf Carl. 90M GRM. *Ich Mocht' Gern Dein Herz Klopfen Hor'n*; *The Bachelor Trap* prod/rel: Merkur, Union

KALLIFATIDES, THEODOR
Karleken, Novel
Karleken 1980 d: Theodor Kallifatides. lps: Per Ragnar, Lena Olin, Anna Godenius. 74M SWD. *Love* prod/rel: Svenska Filminstitutet

KALMAN, EMMERICH (1882–1953), HNG
Die Czardasfurstin, Vienna 1915, Operetta
Czardasfurstin, Die 1927 d: Hanns Schwarz. lps: Liane Haid, Oscar Marion, Imre Raday. 2596m GRM. prod/rel: Ostermayr-Film

Czardasfurstin, Die 1934 d: Georg Jacoby. lps: Marta Eggerth, Hans Sohnker, Paul Horbiger. 85M GRM. *Die Csardasfurstin* prod/rel: UFA

Czardasfurstin, Die 1951 d: Georg Jacoby. lps: Marika Rokk, Johannes Heesters, Franz Schafheitlin. 94M GRM. *The Czardas Princess*; *Die Csardasfurstin* prod/rel: Deutsche Styria, UFA

Princesse Czardas 1934 d: Andre Beucler, Georg Jacoby. lps: Meg Lemonnier, Jacques Pills, Lyne Clevers. 85M FRN. *Serenade* prod/rel: U.F.a., a.C.E.

Golden Dawn, New York 1927, Musical Play
Golden Dawn 1930 d: Ray Enright. lps: Walter Woolf, Vivienne Segal, Noah Beery. 7447f USA. prod/rel: Warner Brothers Pictures

Grafin Maritza, Vienna 1924, Operetta
Grafin Mariza 1925 d: Hans Steinhoff. lps: Vivian Gibson, Harry Liedtke, Colette Brettel. 2324m GRM. *Countess Mariza* prod/rel: Terra-Film Ag

Grafin Mariza 1932 d: Richard Oswald. lps: Dorothea Wieck, Hubert Marischka, Charlotte Ander. 113M GRM. *Countess Mariza* prod/rel: Roto, Sud-Film

Grafin Mariza 1958 d: Rudolf Schundler. lps: Christine Gorner, Rudolf Schock, Renate Ewert. 110M GRM. *Countess Mariza* prod/rel: Carlton, Constantin

Die Zirkusprinzessin, 1926, Operetta
Zirkusprinzessin, Die 1928 d: Victor Janson. lps: Harry Liedtke, Marianne Winkelstern, Hilda Rosch. 2829m GRM. prod/rel: Aafa-Film Ag

KALMAR, BERT
Animal Crackers, New York 1928, Musical Play
Animal Crackers 1930 d: Victor Heerman. lps: Groucho Marx, Harpo Marx, Chico Marx. 97M USA. prod/rel: Paramount-Publix Corp.

The Life of Marilyn Miller, Book
Look for the Silver Lining 1949 d: David Butler. lps: June Haver, Ray Bolger, Gordon MacRae. 100M USA. *Silver Lining* prod/rel: Warner Bros.

The Ramblers, New York 1926, Musical Play
Cuckoos, The 1930 d: Paul Sloane. lps: Bert Wheeler, Robert Woolsey, June Clyde. 90M USA. *Radio Revels* prod/rel: RKO Productions

Top Speed, New York 1929, Musical Play
Top Speed 1930 d: Mervyn Leroy. lps: Joe E. Brown, Bernice Claire, Jack Whiting. 70M USA. prod/rel: First National Pictures

KALMON, H.
The Lunatic, Play
What a Mother-in-Law! 1934 d: Harry S. Brown. lps: Ludwig Satz, Claire Adams, George Tobias. 65M USA. *Oy Di Shviger!* prod/rel: Quality Film Corp.

KALMONOWITZ, H.
Ewige Naranim, Play
Eternal Fools 1930 d: Sidney M. Goldin. lps: Yudel Dubinsky, Jehuda Bleich, Bella Gudinsky. 6120f USA. *Ewige Naranim* prod/rel: Judea Films

KALTOFEN, GUDRUN
Das Zaubermannchen, Play
Zaubermannchen, Das 1960 d: Christoph Engel. lps: Karl-Heinz Rothin, Karin Lesch, Nikolaus ParylA. 75M GDR. *Rumpelstilzchen*; *The Wizard* prod/rel: Defa

KALUCHEV, EMIL
Short Story
Kamionat 1980 d: Hristo Hristov. lps: Djoko Rosic, Stefan Dimitrov, Vesselin Vulkov. 107M BUL. *The Lorry*; *The Truck* prod/rel: Bulgarische Kinematografie

KAM YUNG
Shu Jian En Chou Lu, Novel
Shu Jian En Chou Lu 1987 d: Hsu An-HuA. lps: Da Shichang, Zhang Duofu, Liu JiA. 180M HKG/CHN. *The Romance of Book & Sword*; *The Book and the Sword*

KAMARE, STEPHAN
Nuit de Mai, Play
Nuit de Mai 1934 d: Henri Chomette, Gustav Ucicky. lps: Fernand Gravey, Kathe von Nagy, Lucien Baroux. 80M FRN. prod/rel: U.F.a., a.C.E.

KAMBHAR, CHANDRASEKHAR
Rushya Shringa, Play
Rushya Shringa 1976 d: V. R. K. Prasad. lps: Rathna, Suresh Heblikar, Sundarshree. 112M IND. *The Fertility God* prod/rel: Young Cinema

KAMINSKY, STUART
Frequence Meurtre, Novel
Frequence Meurtre 1988 d: Elisabeth Rappeneau. lps: Catherine Deneuve, Andre Dussollier, Martin Lamotte. 103M FRN. prod/rel: Productions de la Gueville, Capac

KAMLESHWAR
Aandhi, Novel
Aandhi 1975 d: Gulzar. lps: Suchitra Sen, Sanjeev Kumar, Om Shivpuri. 133M IND. *The Storm* prod/rel: Filmyug, Om Prakash

KAMPENDOCK, GUSTAV
Story
Das War Mein Leben 1944 d: Paul Martin. lps: Carl Raddatz, Hansi Knoteck, Leny Marenbach. 106M GRM. *That Was My Life* prod/rel: Berlin, Emka

KANDEL, ABEN
City for Conquest, New York 1936, Novel
City for Conquest 1940 d: Anatole Litvak. lps: James Cagney, Ann Sheridan, Frank Craven. 103M USA. prod/rel: Warner Bros. Pictures, Inc.

Hot Money, New York 1931, Play
Bluffeur, Le 1932 d: Andre Luguet, Henry Blanke. lps: Andre Luguet, Jeannette Ferney, Emile Chautard. 80M USA. prod/rel: Warner Bros., First National

High Pressure 1931 d: Mervyn Leroy. lps: William Powell, Evelyn Brent, George Sidney. 74M USA. prod/rel: Warner Bros. Pictures©, the Vitaphone Corp.

Hot Money 1936 d: William McGann. lps: Ross Alexander, Beverly Roberts, Joseph Cawthorn. 69M USA. *There's Millions in It* prod/rel: Warner Bros. Pictures©

KANE, JOEL
The Tin Badge, Story
Tin Star, The 1957 d: Anthony Mann. lps: Henry Fonda, Anthony Perkins, Betsy Palmer. 93M USA. prod/rel: Paramount, Perlsea Co.

KANE, MICHAEL
Your Uncle William, Short Story
Successful Failure 1934 d: Arthur Lubin. lps: William Collier Sr., Lucille Gleason, Russell Hopton. 62M USA. prod/rel: Monogram Pictures Corp.©, George Yohalem Production

KANE, PETER
La Violenza E Il Furore, Novel
Autostop 1977 d: Pasquale Festa Campanile. lps: Franco Nero, Corinne Clery, David Hess. 102M ITL. *Autostop Rosso Sangue*; *Death Drive*; *Hitch-Hike* prod/rel: Explorer Film International, Medusa Distribuzione

KANG QU
Plant in Spring - Harvest in Fall, Novel
Ta Ai Shang le Gu XIang 1958 d: Huang Shu, Zhang Qi. lps: Lin Ruwei, Sun Heting, Meng Zhaobo. 10r CHN. *She Loves Her Hometown* prod/rel: Changchun Film Studio

KANGA, FIRDAUS
Trying to Grow, Novel
Sixth Happiness 1997 d: Waris Hussein. lps: Firdaus Kanga, Souad Faress, Khodus WadiA. 98M UKN. prod/rel: BBC Films©, British Film Institute©

KANIN, FAY
Goodbye My Fancy, New York 1949, Play
Goodbye, My Fancy 1951 d: Vincent Sherman. lps: Joan Crawford, Robert Young, Frank Lovejoy. 107M USA. prod/rel: Warner Bros.

KANIN, GARSON
Born Yesterday, New York 1946, Play
Born Yesterday 1950 d: George Cukor. lps: Judy Holliday, William Holden, Broderick Crawford. 103M USA. prod/rel: Columbia

Born Yesterday 1993 d: Luis Mandoki. lps: Melanie Griffith, John Goodman, Don Johnson. 100M USA. prod/rel: Warner Bros., Hollywood

Do Re Mi, Short Story
Girl Can't Help It, The 1956 d: Frank Tashlin. lps: Tom Ewell, Jayne Mansfield, Edmond O'Brien. 99M USA. prod/rel: 20th Century-Fox

The Live Wire, New York 1950, Play
Right Approach, The 1961 d: David Butler. lps: Frankie Vaughan, Martha Hyer, Juliet Prowse. 92M USA. prod/rel: Twentieth Century-Fox Film Corporation

Where It's at, Play
Where It's at 1969 d: Garson Kanin. lps: David Janssen, Robert Drivas, Rosemary Forsyth. 106M USA. prod/rel: Frank Ross-T.F.T., United Artists

KANIUK, YORAM
Himmo Melech Yerushalayam, Novel
Himmo, Melech Yerushalayam 1987 d: Amos Guttman. lps: Alona Kimchi, Dov Navon, Amiram Gavriel. 77M ISR. *Himmo King of Jerusalem* prod/rel: U.D.I.

Susetz, Book
Susetz 1977 d: Yaki YoshA. lps: Shmuel Kraus, Gedalia Besser, Arik Lavie. 90M ISR. *Rockinghorse*

KANNAN, B.
Jatikal, Play
Vedham Pudithu 1987 d: BharathirajA. lps: Satyaraj, Sarita, RajA. 144M IND. *The New Vidas*; *Vedham Puthithu*; *Vedam Puthithu* prod/rel: Janani Art Creations

KANT, HERMANN
Der Aufenthalt, Novel
Aufenthalt, Der 1983 d: Frank Beyer. lps: Sylvester Groth, Klaus Piontek, Fred Duren. 101M GDR. *Turning Point*; *The Stay* prod/rel: Defa, Unidoc

KANTOF, ALBERT
Gli Eroi, Novel
Eroi, Gli 1973 d: Duccio Tessari. lps: Rod Steiger, Rosanna Schiaffino, Rod Taylor. 105M ITL/FRN/SPN. *Les Enfants de Choeur* (FRN); *The Heroes*; *Los Heroes Millonarios* (SPN) prod/rel: Gerico Sound, Finarco (Roma)

KANTOR, LEONARD
Dead Pigeon, New York 1953, Play
Tight Spot 1955 d: Phil Karlson. lps: Ginger Rogers, Edward G. Robinson, Lorne Greene. 97M USA. prod/rel: Columbia

KANTOR, MACKINLAY (1904–, USA
1935, Short Story
Mountain Music 1937 d: Robert Florey. lps: Martha Raye, Bob "Bazooka" Burns, John Howard. 76M USA. prod/rel: Paramount Pictures©

Arouse and Beware, New York 1936, Novel
Man from Dakota, The 1940 d: Leslie Fenton. lps: Wallace Beery, John Howard, Dolores Del Rio. 75M USA. *Arouse and Beware* (UKN) prod/rel: Metro-Goldwyn-Mayer Corp., Loew's, Inc.©

Gentle Annie, 1942, Novel
Gentle Annie 1944 d: Andrew Marton. lps: James Craig, Donna Reed, Marjorie Main. 80M USA. prod/rel: MGM

Glory for Me, 1945, Novel
Best Years of Our Lives, The 1946 d: William Wyler. lps: Fredric March, Myrna Loy, Teresa Wright. 172M USA. *Glory for Me* prod/rel: RKO Radio

God and My Country, Cleveland 1954, Novel
Follow Me, Boys 1966 d: Norman Tokar. lps: Fred MacMurray, Vera Miles, Lillian Gish. 132M USA. prod/rel: Walt Disney Productions, Buena Vista

Gun Crazy, 1940, Short Story
Deadly Is the Female 1949 d: Joseph H. Lewis. lps: John Dall, Peggy Cummins, Berry Kroeger. 87M USA. *Gun Crazy* prod/rel: United Artists

Happy Land, 1943, Novel
Happy Land 1943 d: Irving Pichel. lps: Don Ameche, Frances Dee, Harry Carey. 75M USA. prod/rel: 20th Century-Fox

The Romance of Rosy Ridge, 1937, Novel
Romance of Rosy Ridge, The 1947 d: Roy Rowland. lps: Van Johnson, Thomas Mitchell, Janet Leigh. 105M USA. *The Missouri Story* prod/rel: MGM

The Voice of Bugle Ann, New York 1935, Novel
Voice of Bugle Ann, The 1936 d: Richard Thorpe. lps: Lionel Barrymore, Maureen O'Sullivan, Eric Linden. 72M USA. prod/rel: Metro-Goldwyn-Mayer Corp.©

Wicked Water, Novel
Outlaw Territory 1953 d: John Ireland, Lee Garmes. lps: Joanne Dru, MacDonald Carey, John Ireland. 79M USA. *Hannah Lee* prod/rel: Realart

KAPLAN, DE WITTE
Mothers of Men, New York 1919, Novel
Mothers of Men 1920 d: Edward Jose. lps: Claire Whitney, Lumsden Hare, Gaston Glass. 6494f USA. prod/rel: Film Specials, Inc.©, Edward Jose Productions

KAPLAN, LOUISE J.
Female Perversions; the Temptations of Emma Bovary, Book
Female Perversions 1996 d: Susan Streitfeld. lps: Tilda Swinton, Amy Madigan, Karen Sillas. 116M USA/GRM. prod/rel: Map Films, Inc., Transatlantic Entertainment

KAPLAN, MARC
Story
Fastbreak 1979 d: Jack Smight. lps: Gabe Kaplan, Harold Sylvester, Michael Warren. 97M USA. *Fast Break* prod/rel: Kings Road, Columbia

KAPLAN, MINDY
Devotion, Novel
Devotion 1995 d: Mindy Kaplan. lps: Jan Derbyshire, Cindy Girling, Kate TwA. 123M USA. prod/rel: Northern Arts, Dancing Arrow Prods.

KAPLICKY, VACLAV
Kladivo Na Carodejnice, Novel
Kladivo Na Carodejnice 1969 d: Otakar VavrA. lps: Vladimir Smeral, Elo Romancik, Lola SkrbkovA. 105M CZC. *A Hammer Against Witches*; *Hammer for the Witches*; *Witchhammer* prod/rel: Filmstudio Barrandov

KAPPUS, FRANTZ KAVER
Die Frau Des Kunstlers, Novel
Voleurs de Gloire, Les 1926 d: Pierre Marodon. lps: Henri Baudin, Ernst Verebes, Lotte Neumann. 2500m FRN. prod/rel: Hermes Film

KARANTH, SHIVRAMA
Chomana Dudi, 1933, Novel
Chomana Dudi 1975 d: B. V. Karanth. lps: M. V. Vasudeva Rao, Padma Kumtha, Jayaran. 140M IND. *Chomana's Drum*; *Chomana Dhudi* prod/rel: Praja Films

KARAS, ROMUALD
Blizna, Short Story
Blizna 1976 d: Krzysztof Kieslowski. lps: Franciszek Pieczka, Mariusz Dmochowski, Jerzy Stuhr. 103M PLN. *A Scar* prod/rel: P.R.F. Zespoly Filmowe, Gruppe Tor

KARASLAVOV, GEORGI
Selkor, 1933, Novel
Selcor 1975 d: Atanas Traikov. lps: Anton Gorchev, Grigor Vachkov, Stoycho Mazgalov. 87M BUL. *The Village Correspondent*; *Selkor*; *The Provincial Correspondent*

Snakha, 1942, Novel
Snaha 1954 d: Anton Marinovich, Krastyo Mirski. lps: Peter Dimitrov, Margarita Duparinova, Vera KovachevA. 116M BUL. *Daughter-in-Law*; *Snakha*

Tango, 1948, Novel
Tango 1969 d: Vassil Mirchev. lps: Nevena Kokanova, Peter Penkov, Boris Arabov. 78M BUL.

Tatul, 1938, Novel
Tatul 1972 d: Atanas Traikov. lps: Elena Stefanova, Meglena Karalambova, Ivan Nalbantov. 98M BUL. *Thorn-Apple*

KARAVELOV, LYUBEN
Balgari Ot Staro Vreme, 1867, Novel
Bulgari Ot Staro Vreme 1945 d: Dimiter Minkov. lps: Stoyan Buchvarov, Elena Hranova, Petko Atanassov. 71M BUL. *Bulgarians of Ancient Times*; *Balgari Ot Staro Vreme*

KARGE, MANFRED
Conquest of the South Pole, Play
Conquest of the South Pole 1989 d: Gillies MacKinnon. lps: Stevan Rimkus, Leonard O'Malley, Gordon Cameron. 95M UKN. prod/rel: Jam Jar Films, Channel 4

KARIG, WALTER
Zotz!, New York 1947, Novel
Zotz! 1962 d: William Castle. lps: Tom Poston, Julia Meade, Jim Backus. 87M USA. prod/rel: William Castle Pictures

KARINTHY, FERENC
Budapesti Tavasz, 1953, Novel
Budapesti Tavasz 1955 d: Felix Mariassy. lps: Miklos Gabor, Tibor Molnar, Zsuzsa Gordon. 98M HNG. *Springtime in Budapest*; *Spring in Budapest*

Hazszentelo, 1977, Short Story
Gyertek El a Nevnapomra 1984 d: Zoltan Fabri. lps: Ildiko Piros, Istvan Bujtor, Ferenc Kallai. 121M HNG. *The House-Warming*

Szerelem Ifusag, 1957, Short Story
Bolond Aprilis 1957 d: Zoltan Fabri. lps: Laszlo Mensaros, Marianne Krencsey, Maria Sulyok. 84M HNG. *April Clouds*; *Summer Clouds*

KARINTHY, FRIGYES
Popp Und Mingel, 1937, Novel
Popp Und Mingel 1975 d: Ula Stockl. lps: Lisa Kreuzer, Paul Heuhaus, Patrick Kreuzer. 53M GRM.

Kerem! Tanar Ur, 1916, Short Story
Tanar Ur, Kerem! 1956 d: Frigyes Mamcserov. lps: Istvan Horesnyi, Istvan Taub, Elemer Frank. 70M HNG. *Professor Please.*

Utazas a Koponyam Korul, 1937, Novel
Utazas a Koponyam Korul 1970 d: Gyorgy Revesz. lps: Zoltan Latinovits, Eva Ruttkai, Mari Torocsik. 84M HNG. *Journey Inside My Brain*; *A Journey Round My Skull*; *Journey Around My Skull*; *A Trip Around My Cranium*

KARMEL, ALEX
Mary Ann, New York 1958, Novel
Something Wild 1961 d: Jack Garfein. lps: Carroll Baker, Ralph Meeker, Mildred Dunnock. 112M USA. prod/rel: Prometheus Enterprises, United Artists

KARNO, FRED (1866–1941), UKN, Westcott, Frederick John
The Bailiff, Sketch
Bailiffs, The 1932 d: Frank Cadman. lps: Bud Flanagan, Chesney Allen, Florence Harwood. 24M UKN. prod/rel: Associated Talking Pictures, Ideal

Jailbirds, Sketch
Jailbirds 1939 d: Oswald Mitchell. lps: Albert Burdon, Shaun Glenville, Charles Farrell. 74M UKN. *Jail Birds* prod/rel: Butcher's Film Service

Mumming Birds, Sketch
My Old Duchess 1933 d: Lupino Lane. lps: George Lacy, Betty Ann Davies, Dennis Hoey. 65M UKN. *Oh What a Duchess!*; *The Mummers* prod/rel: British International Pictures, Pathe

When We are Married, Sketch
Don't Rush Me! 1936 d: Norman Lee. lps: Robb Wilton, Muriel Aked, Haver & Lee. 72M UKN. prod/rel: Fred Karno Films, Producers Distributing Corporation

KARSNER, DAVID
Red Meat, Novel
I Loved a Woman 1933 d: Alfred E. Green. lps: Edward G. Robinson, Kay Francis, Genevieve Tobin. 91M USA. *Red Meat* prod/rel: First National Pictures©, the Vitaphone Corp.

Silver Dollar, New York 1932, Book
Silver Dollar 1932 d: Alfred E. Green. lps: Edward G. Robinson, Bebe Daniels, Aline MacMahon. 84M USA. prod/rel: First National Pictures©

KASAHARA, RYOZO
Story
Blind Fury 1989 d: Phil Noyce. lps: Rutger Hauer, Terry O'Quinn, Brandon Call. 86M USA. prod/rel: Columbia, Tri-Star

KASCHNITZ, MARIE-LUISE
Angyalfold, 1929, Novel
Angyalok Foldje 1962 d: Gyorgy Revesz. lps: Klari Tolnay, Zoltan Maklary, Franciska Gyori. 94M HNG. *The Land of Angels* prod/rel: Hunnia

KASHMIRI, AGA HASHR
Yahudi Ki Ladki, 1915, Play
Yahudi 1958 d: Bimal Roy. lps: Sohrab Modi, Dilip Kumar, Meena Kumari. 161M IND. *The Jew* prod/rel: Bombay Films

KASSAK, FRED
Bonne Vie Et Meurtres, Novel
Elle Boit Pas, Elle Fume Pas, Elle Drague Pas, Mais. Elle Cause! 1969 d: Michel Audiard. lps: Bernard Blier, Mireille Darc, Annie Girardot. 80M FRN. prod/rel: Gaumont International

Carambolages, Novel
Carambolages 1963 d: Marcel Bluwal. lps: Jean-Claude Brialy, Louis de Funes, Sophie Daumier. 95M FRN. prod/rel: S.N.E.G., Trianon Production

Une Chambre Et un Meurtre
Assassin Connait la Musique, L' 1963 d: Pierre Chenal. lps: Maria Schell, Paul Meurisse, Sylvie Breal. 82M FRN. *Une Chaumiere Et un Meurtre* prod/rel: Hoche Production, General Productions

On N'enterre Pas le Dimanche, Novel
On N'enterre Pas le Dimanche 1959 d: Michel Drach. lps: Philippe Mory, Christina Bendz, Hella Petri. 95M FRN. *We Don't Bury on Sundays*; *No Burials on Sunday* prod/rel: Port Royal Films

KASTANAKES, THRASOS
Ho Chatze Manouel: Mysthistorema, Athens 1956, Novel
Chiens Dans la Nuit, Les 1965 d: Willy Rozier. lps: Maria Xenia, Georges Riviere, Claude Cerval. 95M FRN/GRC. *The Girl Can't Stop* (USA) prod/rel: Les Films Marceau, Cocinor

KASTLE, HERBERT
Cross-Country, Novel
Cross Country 1983 d: Paul Lynch. lps: Richard Beymer, Nina Axelrod, Michael Ironside. 104M CND. prod/rel: Filmline Productions Inc., New World-Mutual

KASTNER, ERICH
Das Doppelte Lottchen, Vienna 1949, Novel
  Doppelte Lottchen, Das 1950 d: Josef von Baky. lps: Jutta Gunther, Isa Gunther, Antje Weisgerber. 105M GRM. *Lisa and Lottie; Two Times Lotte* prod/rel: Carlton, Alcron
  Parent Trap, The 1961 d: David Swift. lps: Hayley Mills, Maureen O'Hara, Brian Keith. 124M USA. *Petticoats and Bluejeans* prod/rel: Walt Disney Productions
  Parent Trap, The 1998 d: Nancy Meyers. lps: Lindsay Lohan, Dennis Quaid, Natasha Richardson. 127M USA. prod/rel: Buena Vista, Walt Disney Pictures
  Twice Upon a Time 1953 d: Emeric Pressburger. lps: Hugh Williams, Elizabeth Allan, Jack Hawkins. 75M UKN. prod/rel: London Films, British Lion Production Assets
Drei Manner Im Schnee, Zurich 1934, Novel
  Drei Manner Im Schnee 1955 d: Kurt Hoffmann. lps: Paul Dahlke, Claus Biedersteadt, Gunther Luders. 94M AUS. prod/rel: Ring
  Drei Manner Im Schnee 1973 d: Alfred Vohrer. lps: Klaus Schwarzkopf, Roberto Blanco, Thomas Fritsch. 92M GRM. *Three Men in the Snow* prod/rel: Roxy, Constantin
  Paradise for Three 1938 d: Edward Buzzell. lps: Frank Morgan, Robert Young, Mary Astor. 75M USA. *Romance for Three* (UKN); *Three Men in the Snow* prod/rel: Metro-Goldwyn-Mayer Corp., Loew's, Inc.©
  Stackars Miljonarer 1936 d: Tancred Ibsen, Ragnar Arvedson. lps: Adolf Jahr, Ernst Eklund, Tollie Zellman. 99M SWD. *Poor Millionaires* prod/rel: Ab Irefilm, Ab Anglofilm
Emil Und Die Detektive, Berlin 1928, Novel
  Emil and the Detectives 1935 d: Milton Rosmer. lps: George Hayes, Mary Glynne, John Williams. 70M UKN. *Emil* (USA) prod/rel: J. G. & R. B. Wainwright, Gaumont-British
  Emil and the Detectives 1964 d: Peter Tewkesbury. lps: Walter Slezak, Heinz Schubert, Peter Ehrlich. 100M USA/GRM. prod/rel: Walt Disney Productions
  Emil Und Die Detektive 1931 d: Gerhard Lamprecht. lps: Rolf Wenkhaus, Fritz Rasp, Olga Engl. 73M GRM. *Emil and the Detectives* (USA), UFA
  Emil Und Die Detektive 1955 d: R. A. Stemmle. lps: Peter Finkbeiner, Kurt Meisel, Margarete Haagen. 90M GRM. *Emil and the Detectives* prod/rel: Berolina, UFA
Fabian. Die Geschichte Eines Moralisten, 1931, Novel
  Fabian 1980 d: Wolfgang Gremm. lps: Hans-Peter Hallwachs, Hermann Lause, Silvia Janisch. 117M GRM. prod/rel: Regina Ziegler, United Artists
Das Fliegende Klassenzimmer, 1933, Novel
  Fliegende Klassenzimmer, Das 1954 d: Kurt Hoffmann. lps: Paul Dahlke, Paul Klinger, Herbert Hubner. 90M GRM. *The Flying Classroom* (USA) prod/rel: Carlton, N.F.
  Fliegende Klassenzimmer, Das 1973 d: Werner Jacobs. lps: Heinz Reincke, Joachim Fuchsberger, Diana Korner. 92M GRM. *The Flying Classroom* prod/rel: Franz Seitz, Terra
Georg Und Die Zwischenfalle, 1938, Novel
  Kleine Grenzverkehr 1943 d: Hans Deppe. lps: Willy Fritsch, Hertha Feiler, Hilde Sessak. 82M GRM. *Small Border Traffic* prod/rel: UFA, D.F.V.
  Salzburger Geschichten 1957 d: Kurt Hoffmann. lps: Marianne Koch, Paul Hubschmid, Peter Mosbacher. 90M GRM. *Salzburg Stories* prod/rel: Georg Witt, Constantin
Die Konferenz Der Tiere, 1930, Short Story
  Konferenz Der Tiere, Die 1969 d: Curt LindA. ANM. 92M GRM. prod/rel: Linda, Gloria
Liebe Will Gelernt Sein, Play
  Liebe Will Gelernt Sein 1963 d: Kurt Hoffmann. lps: Martin Held, Barbara Rutting, Gotz George. 93M GRM. *You Have to Learn to Love* prod/rel: Independent, Constantin
Punktchen Und Anton, 1930, Novel
  Punktchen Und Anton 1953 d: Thomas Engel, Erich Engel. lps: Sabine Eggerth, Peter Feldt, Klaus Kaap. 90M AUS/GRM. *Spot and Tony* prod/rel: Rhombus Ringfilm, UFA
  Punktchen Und Anton 1999 d: Caroline Link. lps: Elea Geissler, Max Felder, Juliane Kohler. 110M GRM. *Annaluise and Anton* prod/rel: Bavaria Film, Lunaris Film & Tv
Tri Muzi Ve Snehu, Novel
  Tri Muzi Ve Snehu 1936 d: Vladimir Slavinsky. lps: Hugo Haas, Jindrich Plachta, Vladimir Borsky. 2877m CZC. *Three Men in the Snow* prod/rel: Metropolitan

Die Verschwundene Miniatur, 1935, Novel
  Verschwundene Miniatur, Die 1954 d: Carl-Heinz Schroth. lps: Paola Loew, Ralph Lothar, Paul Westermeier. 87M GRM. *The Missing Miniature* prod/rel: Carlton, Europa

KATA, ELIZABETH
Be Ready With Bells and Drums, New York 1961, Novel
  Patch of Blue, A 1965 d: Guy Green. lps: Sidney Poitier, Shelley Winters, Elizabeth Hartman. 105M USA. prod/rel: Pandro S. Berman Productions

KATAEV, VALENTIN (1897–1986), RSS, Katayev, Valentin Petrovich
Beleyet Parus Odinokiy, 1936, Novel
  Byeleyet Parus Odinoky 1937 d: Vladimir Legoshin. 92M USS. *The Lone White Sail; Lonely White Sail*
Khutorok V Stepi, 1956, Novel
  Khutorok V Stepi 1971 d: Boris Buneyev. 94M USS. *The Cottage in the Steppe; The Small Farm in the Steppe*
Za Vlast Sovetov, 1949, Novel
  Za Vlast Sovetov 1956 d: Boris Buneyev. 99M USS. *For Soviet Power*

KATAYORI, TOSHISHIDE
Novel
  Buwana Toshi No Uta 1965 d: Susumu Hani. lps: Kiyoshi Atsumi, Tsutomu Shimomoto, Hamisi Salehe. 115M JPN. *Bwana Toshi* (USA); *The Song of Bwana Toshi* prod/rel: Toho Co., Hani Productions

KATCHA, VAHE
Short Story
  Repas Des Fauves, Le 1964 d: Christian-Jaque. lps: Claude Rich, Francis Blanche, Antonella Lualdi. 97M FRN/ITL/SPN. *La Cena de Los Cobardes* (SPN); *Il Pasto Delle Belve* (ITL) prod/rel: Terra Films, Films Borderie
Galia, Novel
  Galia 1966 d: Georges Lautner. lps: Mireille Darc, Venantino Venantini, Francoise Prevost. 110M FRN/ITL. *And My Lovers I; I and My Love; Galia Ou Duel a Fleur de Peau; A Fleur de Peau* prod/rel: Speva Films, Cine-Alliance
L' Hamecon, Paris 1957, Novel
  Hook, The 1962 d: George Seaton. lps: Kirk Douglas, Robert (3) Walker, Nick Adams. 98M USA. prod/rel: Perlberg-Seaton Productions, MGM
La Mort d'un Juif, Novel
  Sabra 1970 d: Denys de La Patelliere. lps: Akim Tamiroff, Assaf Dayan, Jean Claudio. 98M FRN/ITL/ISR. *Death of a Jew* (USA); *Shalom; Mort d'un Juif; Moto Shel Yehudi* (ISR) prod/rel: Films Copernic, Fono Roma

KATCHER, LEO
Story
  Eddy Duchin Story, The 1956 d: George Sidney. lps: Tyrone Power, Kim Novak, Victoria Shaw. 123M USA. *The Duchin Story* prod/rel: Columbia
The Big Bankroll; the Life and Times of Arnold Rothstein, New York 1959, Biography
  King of the Roaring Twenties - the Story of Arnold Rothstein 1961 d: Joseph M. Newman. lps: Jack Carson, David Janssen, Dianne Foster. 106M USA. *The Big Bankroll* (UKN) prod/rel: Allied Artists
The Hard Man, 1957, Novel
  Hard Man, The 1957 d: George Sherman. lps: Guy Madison, Valerie French, Lorne Greene. 80M USA. prod/rel: Columbia, Romson Prods.
Party Girl, Novel
  Party Girl 1958 d: Nicholas Ray. lps: Robert Taylor, Cyd Charisse, Lee J. Cobb. 99M USA. prod/rel: MGM, Euterpe Prod.

KATO, DAISUKE
Autobiography
  Minami No Shima Ni Yuki Ga Fura 1961 d: Seiji Hisamatsu. lps: Daisuke Kato, Hisaya Morishige, Tatsuya Mihashi. 103M JPN. *Snow in the South Seas* (USA) prod/rel: Toho Co.

KATSCHER, ROBERT
Die Wunderbar, 1930, Play
  Wonder Bar 1934 d: Lloyd Bacon. lps: Al Jolson, Kay Francis, Dolores Del Rio. 84M USA. prod/rel: First National Pictures©

KATSCHER, RUDOLF
L' Uomo Dall'Artiglio, Novel
  Uomo Dall'Artiglio, L' 1931 d: Nunzio MalasommA. lps: Dria Paola, Elio Steiner, Carlo FontanA. 80M ITL. prod/rel: Cines, Anonima Pittaluga

KATZ, ROBERT
Il Caso Moro, Novel
  Caso Moro, Il 1986 d: Giuseppe FerrarA. lps: Gian Maria Volonte, Margarita Lozano, Mattia SbragiA. 110M ITL. *The Moro Affair* prod/rel: Yarno

Cassandra Crossing, Novel
  Cassandra Crossing, The 1977 d: George Pan Cosmatos. lps: Sophia Loren, Richard Harris, Burt Lancaster. 129M UKN/GRM/ITL. prod/rel: Compagnia Cin.Ca Champion (Roma), Internationale Cine Productions (Munich)
Morte a Roma, Book
  Rappresaglia 1973 d: George Pan Cosmatos. lps: Richard Burton, Marcello Mastroianni, Leo McKern. 107M ITL/FRN. *S.S. Represailles* (FRN); *Death in Rome; Massacre in Rome* (UKN) prod/rel: Compagnia Cin.Ca Champion (Roma), Les Films Concordia

KATZENBACH, JOHN
In the Heat of Summer, Novel
  Mean Season, The 1985 d: Philip Borsos. lps: Kurt Russell, Mariel Hemingway, Richard Jordan. 103M USA. prod/rel: Orion, Turman-Foster Company
Just Cause, Novel
  Just Cause 1995 d: Arne Glimcher. lps: Sean Connery, Laurence Fishburne, Kate Capshaw. 102M USA. prod/rel: Lee Rich Productions

KAUFFMAN, REGINALD WRIGHT
Money to Burn, New York 1924, Novel
  Money to Burn 1926 d: Walter Lang. lps: Malcolm McGregor, Dorothy Devore, Eric Mayne. 5900f USA. prod/rel: Gotham Productions, Lumas Film Corp.
Our Undisciplined Daughters, Short Story
  School for Girls 1934 d: William Nigh. lps: Helen Foster, Sidney Fox, Paul Kelly. 73M USA. prod/rel: Liberty Pictures Corp.©
The Spider's Web, New York 1913, Novel
  Midnight Life 1928 d: Scott R. Dunlap. lps: Francis X. Bushman, Gertrude Olmstead, Eddie Buzzell. 4863f USA. *Midnight* (UKN) prod/rel: Gotham Productions, Lumas Film Corp.

KAUFMAN, BARRY NEIL
Son Rise: a Miracle of Love, Book
  Son Rise: a Miracle of Love 1979 d: Glenn Jordan. lps: James Farentino, Kathryn Harrold, Stephen Elliott. TVM. 100M USA. *Son-Rise: a Miracle of Love; Miracle of Love* prod/rel: Rothman-Wohl Production, Filmways

KAUFMAN, BEL (1926–1977), USA
Up the Down Staircase, Englewood Cliffs 1965, Novel
  Up the Down Staircase 1967 d: Robert Mulligan. lps: Sandy Dennis, Patrick Bedford, Eileen Heckart. 123M USA. prod/rel: Park Place Productions, Warner Bros.

KAUFMAN, EDWARD A.
The Secret Mating, Short Story
  Soul Mates 1916 d: William Russell, John Prescott. lps: William Russell, Charlotte Burton, Leona Hutton. 5r USA. *The Secret Mating* prod/rel: American Film Co., Mutual Film Corp.

KAUFMAN, GEORGE S. (1889–1961), USA, Kaufman, George Simon
Animal Crackers, New York 1928, Musical Play
  Animal Crackers 1930 d: Victor Heerman. lps: Groucho Marx, Harpo Marx, Chico Marx. 97M USA. prod/rel: Paramount-Publix Corp.
The Band Wagon, New York 1931, Play
  Dancing in the Dark 1949 d: Irving Reis. lps: William Powell, Betsy Drake, Mark Stevens. 92M USA. prod/rel: 20th Century Fox
Beggar on Horseback, New York 1924, Play
  Beggar on Horseback 1925 d: James Cruze. lps: Edward Everett Horton, Esther Ralston, Erwin Connelly. 7197f USA. prod/rel: Famous Players-Lasky Corp., Paramount Pictures
The Butter and Egg Man, New York 1925, Play
  Angel from Texas, An 1940 d: Ray Enright. lps: Eddie Albert, Wayne Morris, Rosemary Lane. 69M USA. prod/rel: Warner Bros. Pictures, Inc.
  Butter and Egg Man, The 1928 d: Richard Wallace. lps: Jack Mulhall, Greta Nissen, Sam Hardy. 6300f USA. *Actress and Angel* (UKN) prod/rel: First National Pictures
  Dance Charlie Dance 1937 d: Frank McDonald. lps: Stuart Erwin, Jean Muir, Glenda Farrell. 65M USA. prod/rel: Warner Bros. Pictures, Inc.
  Hello Sweetheart 1935 d: Monty Banks. lps: Claude Hulbert, Gregory Ratoff, Jane Carr. 70M UKN. prod/rel: Warner Bros., First National
  Tenderfoot, The 1932 d: Ray Enright. lps: Joe E. Brown, Ginger Rogers, Lew Cody. 73M USA. prod/rel: First National Pictures©
  Three Sailors and a Girl 1953 d: Roy Del Ruth. lps: Jane Powell, Gordon MacRae, Gene Nelson. 95M USA. prod/rel: Warner Bros.

The Cocoanuts, New York 1925, Musical Play
Cocoanuts, The 1929 d: Robert Florey, Joseph Santley. lps: Groucho Marx, Harpo Marx, Chico Marx. 96M USA. prod/rel: Paramount Famous Lasky Corp.

The Dark Tower, New York 1933, Play
Dark Tower, The 1943 d: John Harlow. lps: Ben Lyon, Anne Crawford, David Farrar. 93M UKN. prod/rel: Warner Bros., First National
Man With Two Faces, The 1934 d: Archie Mayo. lps: Edward G. Robinson, Mary Astor, Ricardo Cortez. 72M USA. *The Mysterious Mr. Chautard; The Dark Tower; The Strange Case of Mr. Chautard; Dark Victory* prod/rel: First National Pictures©

Dinner at Eight, New York 1932, Play
Dinner at Eight 1933 d: George Cukor. lps: Marie Dressler, John Barrymore, Wallace Beery. 113M USA. prod/rel: Metro-Goldwyn-Mayer Corp.
Dinner at Eight 1989 d: Ron Lagomarsino. lps: Lauren Bacall, Charles Durning, Ellen Greene. TVM. 100M USA.

Dulcy, New York 1921, Play
Dulcy 1923 d: Sidney A. Franklin. lps: Constance Talmadge, Claude Gillingwater, Jack Mulhall. 6859f USA. prod/rel: Constance Talmadge Film Co., Associated First National Pictures
Dulcy 1940 d: S. Sylvan Simon. lps: Ann Sothern, Ian Hunter, Roland Young. 67M USA. prod/rel: Metro-Goldwyn-Mayer Corp.©
Not So Dumb 1930 d: King Vidor. lps: Marion Davies, Elliott Nugent, Raymond Hackett. 7650f USA. *Rosalie* (UKN); *Dulcy* prod/rel: Metro-Goldwyn-Mayer Pictures

First Lady, New York 1935, Play
First Lady 1937 d: Stanley Logan. lps: Kay Francis, Anita Louise, Verree Teasdale. 82M USA. prod/rel: Warner Bros. Pictures©

George Washington Slept Here, 1941, Play
George Washington Slept Here 1942 d: William Keighley. lps: Jack Benny, Ann Sheridan, Charles Coburn. 93M USA. prod/rel: Warner Bros.

The Good Fellow, New York 1926, Play
Good Fellows, The 1943 d: Jo Graham. lps: Cecil Kellaway, Mabel Paige, Helen Walker. 70M USA. prod/rel: Paramount

June Moon, New York 1929, Play
Blonde Trouble 1937 d: George Archainbaud. lps: Johnny Downs, Eleanore Whitney, Lynne Overman. 67M USA. prod/rel: Paramount Pictures, Inc.
June Moon 1931 d: A. Edward Sutherland. lps: Jack Oakie, Frances Dee, Wynne Gibson. 73M USA. *Night Life* prod/rel: Paramount Publix Corp.

The Man Who Came to Dinner, New York 1939, Play
Man Who Came to Dinner, The 1941 d: William Keighley. lps: Bette Davis, Ann Sheridan, Monty Woolley. 112M USA. prod/rel: Warner Bros.
Man Who Came to Dinner, The 1972 d: Buzz Kulik. lps: Orson Welles, Lee Remick, Joan Collins. TVM. 74M USA.

Once in a Lifetime, New York 1930, Play
Once in a Lifetime 1932 d: Russell MacK. lps: Jack Oakie, Sidney Fox, Aline MacMahon. 91M USA. *Merry-Go-Round* prod/rel: Universal Pictures Corp.©
Once in a Lifetime 1988 d: Robin Midgley. lps: Zoe Wanamaker, Niall Buggy, Kristoffer Tabori. MTV. UKN/USA. prod/rel: BBC, Wnet

The Royal Family, New York 1927, Play
Royal Family of Broadway, The 1930 d: George Cukor, Cyril Gardner. lps: Fredric March, Ina Claire, Mary Brian. 82M USA. *Theatre Royal* prod/rel: Paramount Publix Corp.©

The Sold Gold Cadillac, New York 1953, Play
Solid Gold Cadillac, The 1956 d: Richard Quine. lps: Judy Holliday, Paul Douglas, Fred Clark. 99M USA. prod/rel: Columbia

Someone in the House, New York 1918, Play
Someone in the House 1920 d: John Ince. lps: Edmund Lowe, Vola Vale, Edward Connelly. 6r USA. prod/rel: Metro Pictures Corp.©

Stage Door, New York 1936, Play
Stage Door 1937 d: Gregory La CavA. lps: Katharine Hepburn, Ginger Rogers, Adolphe Menjou. 92M USA. prod/rel: RKO Radio Pictures©

To the Ladies!, New York 1922, Play
Elmer and Elsie 1934 d: Gilbert Pratt. lps: George Bancroft, Frances Fuller, Roscoe Karns. 65M USA. *Ladies First* prod/rel: Paramount Productions©
To the Ladies 1923 d: James Cruze. lps: Edward Everett Horton, Theodore Roberts, Helen Jerome Eddy. 6268f USA. prod/rel: Famous Players-Lasky, Paramount Pictures

You Can't Take It With You, New York 1936, Play
You Can't Take It With You 1938 d: Frank CaprA. lps: James Stewart, Jean Arthur, Lionel Barrymore. 127M USA. prod/rel: Columbia Pictures Corp. of California©
You Can't Take It With You 1979 d: Paul Bogart. lps: Jean Stapleton, Art Carney, Barry Bostwick. TVM. 100M USA.

KAUFMAN, PHILIP
Story
Raiders of the Lost Ark 1981 d: Steven Spielberg. lps: Harrison Ford, Karen Allen, Paul Freeman. 115M USA. prod/rel: Paramount

KAUFMAN, SUE
Diary of a Mad Housewife, New York 1967, Novel
Diary of a Mad Housewife 1970 d: Frank Perry. lps: Richard Benjamin, Frank Langella, Carrie Snodgress. 103M USA. prod/rel: Frank Perry Films

KAUFMANN, REGINALD WRIGHT
The House of Bondage, New York 1910, Play
House of Bondage, The 1913 d: Raymond B. West. lps: Anna Little, Mrs. Joe Knight, Charles Ray. 3r USA. prod/rel: Kb
The House of Bondage, New York 1910, Novel
House of Bondage, The 1914 d: Pierce Kingsley. lps: Lottie Pickford, Armand Cortes, Sue Willis. 6r USA. prod/rel: Photo Drama Motion Picture Co.©

KAUFMANN, WILL
Der Schone Florian, Musical Play
Egon, Der Frauenheld 1957 d: Hans Albin. lps: Theo Lingen, Susi Nicoletti, Paul Henckels. 85M GRM. *Egon the Ladykiller* prod/rel: Hoela, Panorama

KAUS, GINA
Play
Night Before the Divorce, The 1942 d: Robert Siodmak. lps: Lynn Bari, Mary Beth Hughes, Joseph Allen Jr. 62M USA. prod/rel: 20th Century Fox
Dark Angel, Novel
Her Sister's Secret 1946 d: Edgar G. Ulmer. lps: Nancy Coleman, Margaret Lindsay, Philip Reed. 86M USA. prod/rel: P.R.C.
Isle of Terror, Play
Isle of Missing Men 1942 d: Richard Oswald. lps: John Howard, Gilbert Roland, Helen Gilbert. 67M USA. *Isle of Terror; Isle of Fury* prod/rel: Monogram
Rock Bottom, Story
Three Secrets 1950 d: Robert Wise. lps: Eleanor Parker, Patricia Neal, Ruth Roman. 98M USA. prod/rel: Warner Bros., United States Pictures
Les Soeurs Kleh, Novel
Conflit 1938 d: Leonide Moguy. lps: Claude Dauphin, Armand Bernard, Corinne Luchaire. 94M FRN. *Les Soeurs Garnier; The Affair Lafont* prod/rel: C.I.P.R.a., Arnold Pressburger
Teufel in Seide, Gutersloh 1956, Novel
Teufel in Seide 1956 d: Rolf Hansen. lps: Lilli Palmer, Curd Jurgens, Winnie Markus. 105M GRM. *Devil in Silk* (USA) prod/rel: Fono-Film, D.F.H.
Die Uberfahrt, New York 1932, Novel
Luxury Liner 1933 d: Lothar Mendes. lps: George Brent, Zita Johann, Frank Morgan. 72M USA. prod/rel: Paramount Productions©

KAUTSKY, RUDOLF
Deti V Notesu, Play
Baron Prasil 1940 d: Martin Fric. lps: Vlasta Burian, Meda Valentova, Zorka Janu. 2658m CZC. *Baron Munchausen* (USA); *Baron Munchhausen; Munchhausen* prod/rel: Slavia-Film, UFA

KAVANAGH, H. T.
Short Stories
Darby O'Gill and the Little People 1959 d: Robert Stevenson. lps: Janet Munro, Sean Connery, Kieron Moore. 90M USA/UKN. prod/rel: Buena Vista, Walt Disney Prods.

KAVANAGH, P. J.
Scarf Jack, Novel
Scarf Jack 1981 d: Chris McMaster. lps: Roy Boyd, Keith Jayne, Jo Kendall. MTV. 150M UKN. prod/rel: Southern Tv

KAVANAUGH, KATHARINE
Adam's Evening, Play
His Exciting Night 1938 d: Gus Meins. lps: Charles Ruggles, Richard Lane, Stepin Fetchit. 61M USA. *Adam's Evening* prod/rel: Universal Pictures Co.©
Let's Get Together, Hollywood 1935, Play
Every Saturday Night 1936 d: James Tinling. lps: June Lang, Thomas Beck, Jed Prouty. 62M USA. prod/rel: Twentieth Century-Fox Film Corp.©

KAWABATA, YASUNARI (1899–1972), JPN
Asakusa No Shimai, 1932, Short Story
Otome-Gokoro Sannin Shimai 1935 d: Mikio Naruse. lps: Chikako Hosokawa, Masako Tsutsumi, Ryuko Umezono. 75M JPN. *Three Sisters With Maiden Hearts*
Hi Mo Tsuki Mo, Tokyo 1953, Novel
Hi Mo Tsuki Mo 1969 d: Noboru NakamurA. lps: Shima Iwashita, Masayuki Mori, Yoshiko KugA. 98M JPN. *Through Days and Months* (USA) prod/rel: Shochiku Co.
Izu No Odoriko, 1925, Short Story
Izu No Odoriko 1933 d: Heinosuke Gosho. 93M JPN. *Dancing Girls of Izu; The Izu Dancer; Dancer of Izu*
Izu No Odoriko 1960 d: Yoshiro Kawazu. 88M JPN. *Dancing Girls of Izu; Dancing Girl*
Izu No Odoriko 1967 d: Hideo Onchi. lps: Toshio Kurosawa, Yoko Naito, Tatsuyoshi EharA. 85M JPN. *Izu Dancer*
Koto, Tokyo 1962, Novel
Koto 1963 d: Noboru NakamurA. lps: Shima Iwashita, Seiji Miyaguchi, Teruo YoshidA. 107M JPN. *Twin Sisters of Kyoto* (USA); *The Old Capital* prod/rel: Shochiku Co.
Koto 1980 d: Kon IchikawA. lps: Momoe Yamaguchi, Tomokazu Miura, Keiko Kishi. 125M JPN. *Ancient City; The Ancient City of Koto* prod/rel: Horikaku Production Co.
Maihime, 1951, Short Story
Maihime 1951 d: Mikio Naruse. 85M JPN. *Dancing Princess; The Dancer; Dancing Girl*
Mizumi, 1954, Short Story
Onna No Misumi 1966 d: Yoshishige YoshidA. lps: Mariko Okada, Shinsuke Ashida, Shigeru Tsuyuguchi. F JPN. *Women of the Lake; The Lake; Onna No Mizuumi* prod/rel: Gendai Eiga
Nemureru Bijo, 1960, Short Story
Nemureru Bijo 1968 d: Kozaburo YoshimurA. lps: Takahiro Tamura, Yoshiko Kayama, Kitsuko MatsuokA. 95M JPN. *The House of the Sleeping Virgins* (USA); *Sleeping Beauty; The House of Sleeping Virgins* prod/rel: Kindai Eiga Kyokai Co.
Senbazuru, Tokyo 1958, Novel
Senbazuru 1969 d: Yasuzo MasumurA. lps: Mikijiro Hira, Ayako Wakao, Eiko AzusA. 97M JPN. *Thousand Cranes* (USA); *Sembazuru* prod/rel: Daiei Motion Picture Co.
Utsukushisa to Kanshim' to, 1961-64, Novel
Utsukushisa to Kanashimi to 1965 d: Masahiro ShinodA. lps: Mariko Kaga, Kaoru YachigusA. 106M JPN. *With Beauty and Sorrow*
Yama-No Oto, 1954, Novel
Yama No Oto 1954 d: Mikio Naruse. lps: So Yamamura, Setsuko Hara, Yoko Sugi. 94M JPN. *Sounds from the Mountains; The Echo; Sounds of the Mountain; Sound of the Mountain*
Yukiguni, 1947, Novel
Yukiguni 1957 d: Shiro ToyodA. lps: Keiko Kishi, Ryo Ikebe, Kaoru YachigusA. 134M JPN. *Snow Country* prod/rel: Toho Co.
Yukiguni 1965 d: Hideo ObA. lps: Shima Iwashita, Isao Kimura, Mariko KagA. 115M JPN. *Snow Country* (USA); *Love in the Snow* prod/rel: Shochiku Co.

KAWAGUCHI, MATSUTARO
Gion Bayashi, Novel
Gion Bayashi 1953 d: Kenji Mizoguchi. lps: Michiyo Kogure, Ayako Wakao, Seizaburo Kawazu. 87M JPN. *Gion Music Festival* (UKN); *Gion Festival Music; A Geisha* (USA); *Gion Music* prod/rel: Daiei Motion Picture Co.
Mermaid, Novel
Suna No Kaori 1968 d: Katsumi Iwauchi. lps: Mie Hama, Jin Nakayama, Megumi Matsuoto. 90M JPN. *The Night of the Seagull* (USA) prod/rel: Toho Co.
Nichiren, Novel
Nichiren 1978 d: Noboru NakamurA. lps: Kinnosuke Yorozuya, Katsuo Nakamura, Keiko MatsusakA. 143M JPN. *The Priest Nichiren* prod/rel: Nagata Productions

KAWATA, TAKESHI
Kuraishisu Nijugoju Nen, Novel
Solar Crisis 1992 d: Richard C. Sarafian. lps: Tim Matheson, Charlton Heston, Peter Boyle. 111M USA/JPN. *Kuraishisu Nijugoju Nen* (JPN); *Starfire; Crisis 2050* prod/rel: Gakken, Nhk

KAWATAKE, MOKUAMI
Play
Buraikan 1970 d: Masahiro ShinodA. lps: Tatsuya Nakadai, Suisen Ichikawa, Shima IwashitA. 105M JPN. *The Scandalous Adventures of Buraikan* (USA); *Outlaws* prod/rel: Ninjin Club, Toho Co.

KAWAUCHI, KOHAN
Novel
　Gekko Kamen 1981 d: Yukihiro SawadA. lps: Daisuke Kuwabara, Etsuko Shiomi, Takuya FujiokA. 108M JPN. *The Moon Mask Rider* prod/rel: Nippon Herald Films

KAWAUCHI, YASUNORI
Tokyo Nagare Mono, Novel
　Tokyo Nagare Mono 1966 d: Seijun Suzuki. lps: Tetsuya Watari, Chieko Matsubara, Hideaki Nitani. 83M JPN. *Tokyo Drifter; The Man from Tokyo* prod/rel: Nikkatsu Corporation

KAY, JULIANE
Vagabunden, Play
　Vagabunden Der Liebe 1950 d: Rolf Hansen. lps: Paula Wessely, Attila Horbiger, Elfe Gerhart. 108M AUS. prod/rel: Ofa, Bavaria

KAYE, BENJAMIN M.
She Couldn't Say No, New York 1926, Play
　She Couldn't Say No 1940 d: William Clemens. lps: Roger Pryor, Eve Arden, Cliff Edwards. 64M USA. prod/rel: Warner Bros. Pictures©

KAYE, M. M. (1909–, IND, Kaye, Mary Margaret Mollie, Hamilton, Mollie
The Far Pavilions, Novel
　Far Pavilions, The 1983 d: Peter Duffell. lps: Ben Cross, Amy Irving, Omar Sharif. TVM. 288M UKN. prod/rel: Hbo, Channel Four

KAYE, NOWELL
The Presumption of Stanley Hay M.P., Novel
　Presumption of Stanley Hay, M.P., The 1925 d: Sinclair Hill. lps: David Hawthorne, Betty Faire, Fred Raynham. 4275f UKN. prod/rel: Stoll

KAYE-SMITH, SHEILA (1887–1956), UKN
Joanna Godden, Novel
　Loves of Joanna Godden, The 1947 d: Charles Frend, Robert Hamer. lps: Googie Withers, Jean Kent, John McCallum. 89M UKN. prod/rel: Ealing Studios, General Film Distributors

KAZAKEVICH, EMMANUIL
Vesna Na Odere, 1950, Novel
　Vesna Na Oderye 1968 d: Leon Saakov. lps: Anatoli Kuznetsov, Anatoli Grachov, Lyudmila ChursinA. 102M USS. *Spring on the Oder*

KAZAN, ELIA (1909–, TRK, Kazanjoglous, Elia
America America, New York 1962, Book
　America, America 1963 d: Elia Kazan. lps: Stathis Giallelis, Frank Wolff, Harry Davis. 174M USA. *The Anatolian Smile* prod/rel: Warner Bros., Athena Enterprises

The Arrangement, New York 1967, Novel
　Arrangement, The 1969 d: Elia Kazan. lps: Kirk Douglas, Faye Dunaway, Deborah Kerr. 127M USA. prod/rel: Athena Enterprises, Warner Bros.

KAZANTZAKIS, NIKOS (1883–1957), GRC
O Christos Xanastavronetai, 1948, Novel
　Celui Qui Doit Mourir 1956 d: Jules Dassin. lps: Jean Servais, Carl Mohner, Gregoire Aslan. 126M FRN/ITL. *Colui Che Deve Morire* (ITL); *He Who Must Die* (USA); *Les Feux de la Sarakina* prod/rel: Prima Films, Indus Films

O Teleftaios Peirasmos, 1955, Novel
　Last Temptation of Christ, The 1988 d: Martin Scorsese. lps: Willem Dafoe, Harvey Keitel, Barbara Hershey. 164M USA/CND. prod/rel: Universal

Vios Kai Politeia Tou Alexi Zobra, 1946, Novel
　Zorba the Greek 1964 d: Michael Cacoyannis. lps: Anthony Quinn, Alan Bates, Irene Papas. 146M USA/GRC. *Zormba* (GRC); *Alexis Zorbas* prod/rel: Twentieth Century-Fox Film Corporation, Rockley

KE FU
Two Marriages, Play
　Huan le Ren Jian 1959 d: Wu Tian. lps: Guo Yiwen, Guo Zhenqing, Bai Dezhang. 11r CHN. *Changed Lives* prod/rel: Changchun Film Studio

KEABLE, ROBERT (1887–1927), UKN
Recompense, London 1924, Novel
　Recompense 1925 d: Harry Beaumont. lps: Marie Prevost, Monte Blue, John Roche. 7379f USA. prod/rel: Warner Brothers Pictures

KEANE, CHRISTOPHER
The Hunter, Book
　Hunter, The 1979 d: Buzz Kulik. lps: Steve McQueen, Eli Wallach, Kathryn Harrold. 98M USA. prod/rel: Paramount

KEANE, DAY
La Bete a l'Affut, Novel
　Bete a l'Affut, La 1959 d: Pierre Chenal. lps: Francoise Arnoul, Henri Vidal, Michel Piccoli. 95M FRN/ITL. prod/rel: Films Du Trident, Hoche Productions

KEANE, JOHN B.
The Field, 1966, Play
　Field, The 1990 d: Jim Sheridan. lps: Richard Harris, Sean Bean, Frances Tomelty. 113M UKN/IRL. prod/rel: Granada

KEANE, MOLLY (1904–, IRL, Keane, Mary Nesta
Time After Time, Novel
　Time After Time 1985 d: Bill Hays. lps: John Gielgud, Googie Withers, Helen Cherry. TVM. 103M UKN. prod/rel: BBC

KEARNEY, PATRICK
A Man's Man, New York 1925, Novel
　Man's Man, A 1929 d: James Cruze. lps: William Haines, Josephine Dunn, Sam Hardy. 6683f USA. prod/rel: Metro-Goldwyn-Mayer Pictures

Old Man Murphy, New York 1931, Play
　His Family Tree 1935 d: Charles Vidor. lps: James Barton, William Harrigan, Marjorie Gateson. 69M USA. *Old Man Murphy* prod/rel: RKO Radio Pictures©

KEATING, H. R. F. (1926–, UKN
The Perfect Murder, Novel
　Perfect Murder, The 1988 d: Zafar Hai. lps: Naseeruddin Shah, Stellan Skarsgard, Madhur Jaffrey. 90M IND/UKN. prod/rel: Enterprise, Merchant Ivory

KEATING, WILLIAM J.
The Man Who Rocked the Boat, 1956, Novel
　Slaughter on Tenth Avenue 1957 d: Arnold Laven. lps: Richard Egan, Jan Sterling, Dan DuryeA. 103M USA. prod/rel: Universal-International

KEEFE, FREDERICK L.
The Interpreter, 1945, Short Story
　Before Winter Comes 1969 d: J. Lee Thompson. lps: David Niven, Topol, Anna KarinA. 108M UKN. *The Interpreter* prod/rel: Windward Films, Columbia

KEELER, HARRY STEPHEN
The Twelve Coins of Confucius, Short Story
　Mysterious Mr. Wong, The 1935 d: William Nigh. lps: Bela Lugosi, Wallace Ford, Arline Judge. 60M USA. prod/rel: Monogram Pictures Corp.©, George Yohalem Production

KEEN, HERBERT
The Broken Melody, London 1892, Play
　Broken Melody, The 1929 d: Fred Paul. lps: Georges Galli, Audree Sayre, Enid Stamp-Taylor. SIL. 6414f UKN. prod/rel: Welsh-Pearson-Elder, Paramount

KEENE, CAROLYN (1892–1982), USA, Adams, Harriet Strateyer
The Hidden Staircase, New York 1930, Novel
　Nancy Drew and the Hidden Staircase 1939 d: William Clemens. lps: Bonita Granville, Frankie Thomas, John Litel. 78M USA. prod/rel: Warner Bros. Pictures©

The Password to Larkspur Lane, New York 1933, Novel
　Nancy Drew -Detective 1938 d: William Clemens. lps: Bonita Granville, John Litel, James Stephenson. 60M USA. *Passport to Larkspur Lane* prod/rel: Warner Bros. Pictures©

KEENE, DAY
Le Canard En Fer-Blanc, Novel
　Canard En Fer Blanc, Le 1967 d: Jacques Poitrenaud. lps: Roger Hanin, Corinne Marchand, Lila KedrovA. 105M FRN/SPN. *Mercenarios Del Aire* (SPN); *The Old Tin Can* prod/rel: Progefi Santos Alcocer

Chautauqua, New York 1960, Novel
　Trouble With Girls, The 1969 d: Peter Tewkesbury. lps: Elvis Presley, Marlyn Mason, Nicole Jaffe. 97M USA. *Chautauqua* prod/rel: Metro-Goldwyn-Mayer, Inc.

Dark Witness, Novel
　Cause Toujours, Mon Lapin! 1961 d: Guy Lefranc. lps: Eddie Constantine, Francois Chaumette, Renee CosimA. 89M FRN. prod/rel: Jacques Roitfeld, Belmont Films

Joy House, New York 1954, Novel
　Felins, Les 1964 d: Rene Clement. lps: Alain Delon, Jane Fonda, Lola Albright. 110M FRN. *The Love Cage* (UKN); *The Joy House* (USA); *Ni Saints Ni Saufs*; *Le Crime Et Ses Plaisirs* prod/rel: C.I.P.R.a., Cite Films

Murder on Side
　Meutre En Douce 1990 d: Patrick Dromgoole. lps: Jacques Weber, Jacques Spiesser, Sandrine Dumas. TVM. 85M FRN/CND/SWT.

KEENE, TOM
Spyship, Book
　Spyship 1983 d: Michael Custance. lps: Tom Wilkinson, Lesley Nightingale, Peter Eyre. MTV. 330M UKN. prod/rel: BBC Pebble Mill

KEIR, URSULA
The Vintage, 1953, Novel
　Vintage, The 1957 d: Jeffrey Hayden. lps: Pier Angeli, Mel Ferrer, John Kerr. 92M USA. *Harvest Thunder; The Purple Harvest* prod/rel: MGM

KEITH, AGNES NEWTON
Three Came Home, 1947, Autobiography
　Three Came Home 1950 d: Jean Negulesco. lps: Claudette Colbert, Patric Knowles, Florence Desmond. 106M USA. prod/rel: 20th Century-Fox

KEKULE, DAGMAR
Kraftprobe, Novel
　Kraftprobe 1982 d: Heidi Genee. lps: Kristin Genee, Kai Taschner, Hannelore Hoger. 84M GRM. *Test of Strength* prod/rel: Telefilm Saar, B.R.

KELIHER, EVAN
Rebel High, Novel
　Rebel High 1987 d: Harry Jakobs. lps: Wayne Flemming, Ralph Millman, Ken Robinson. 82M USA. prod/rel: Manson International

KELLAND, CLARENCE BUDINGTON (1881–1964), USA
Short Story
　Scattergood Baines 1941 d: W. Christy Cabanne. lps: Guy Kibbee, Carol Hughes, John Archer. 69M USA. prod/rel: RKO, Pyramid Pictures

Story
　Scattergood Meets Broadway 1941 d: W. Christy Cabanne. lps: Guy Kibbee, William Henry, Frank Jenks. 68M USA. prod/rel: RKO, Pyramid Pictures

Short Story
　Scattergood Pulls the Strings 1941 d: W. Christy Cabanne. lps: Guy Kibbee, Susan Peters, James Corner. 69M USA. prod/rel: RKO, Pyramid Pictures
　Scattergood Rides High 1942 d: W. Christy Cabanne. lps: Guy Kibbee, Dorothy Moore, Charles Lind. 63M USA. prod/rel: RKO, Pyramid Pictures
　Scattergood Survives a Murder 1942 d: W. Christy Cabanne. lps: Guy Kibbee, John Archer, Margaret Hayes. 66M USA. prod/rel: RKO, Pyramid Pictures

Arizona, New York 1939, Novel
　Arizona 1940 d: Wesley Ruggles. lps: Jean Arthur, William Holden, Warren William. 127M USA. prod/rel: Columbia Pictures Corp.

Backbone, 1922, Short Story
　Backbone 1923 d: Edward Sloman. lps: Edith Roberts, Alfred Lunt, William B. MacK. 6821f USA. prod/rel: Distinctive Pictures, Goldwyn Distributing Corp.

The Cat's-Paw, New York 1934, Novel
　Cat's Paw, The 1934 d: Sam Taylor. lps: Harold Lloyd, Una Merkel, George Barbier. 101M USA. prod/rel: Harold Lloyd Corp., Twentieth Century-Fox

Conflict, Novel
　Conflict, The 1921 d: Stuart Paton. lps: Priscilla Dean, Edward Connelly, Hector V. Sarno. 6205f USA. prod/rel: Universal Film Mfg. Co.

Contraband, New York 1923, Novel
　Contraband 1925 d: Alan Crosland. lps: Lois Wilson, Noah Beery, Raymond Hatton. 6773f USA. prod/rel: Famous Players-Lasky, Paramount Pictures

Dance Magic, New York 1927, Novel
　Dance Magic 1927 d: Victor Hugo Halperin. lps: Pauline Starke, Ben Lyon, Louis John Bartels. 6588f USA. prod/rel: Robert Kane Productions, First National Pictures

Dreamland, New York 1935, Novel
　Strike Me Pink 1936 d: Norman Taurog. lps: Eddie Cantor, Ethel Merman, Sally Eilers. 100M USA. *Dreamland; Shoot the Chutes* prod/rel: Samuel Goldwyn, Inc., United Artists Corp.

Efficiency Edgar's Courtship, 1916, Short Story
　Efficiency Edgar's Courtship 1917 d: Lawrence C. Windom. lps: Taylor Holmes, Virginia Valli, Ernest Maupain. 5r USA. prod/rel: Essanay Film Mfg. Co.©, K-E-S-E Service

Face the Facts, 1936, Short Story
　Mr. Boggs Steps Out 1938 d: Gordon Wiles. lps: Stuart Erwin, Helen Chandler, Harry Tyler. 68M USA. *Face the Facts; Mr. Boggs Buys a Barrel* prod/rel: Grand National Films©

For Beauty's Sake, Short Story
　For Beauty's Sake 1941 d: Shepard Traube. lps: Ned Sparks, Marjorie Weaver, Ted North. 62M USA. prod/rel: 20th Century Fox

The Great Crooner, New York 1933, Novel
　Mr. Dodd Takes the Air 1937 d: Alfred E. Green. lps: Kenny Baker, Jane Wyman, Gertrude Michael. 85M USA. prod/rel: Warner Bros. Pictures©, Mervyn Leroy Production

Hearts and Fists, 1924, Short Story
Hearts and Fists 1926 d: Lloyd Ingraham. lps: John Bowers, Marguerite de La Motte, Alan Hale. 5438f USA. prod/rel: H. C. Weaver Productions

The Hidden Spring, New York 1915, Novel
Hidden Spring, The 1917 d: E. Mason Hopper. lps: Harold Lockwood, Lester Cuneo, Vera Sisson. 5r USA. *The Secret Spring* prod/rel: Yorke Film Corp., Metro Pictures Corp.©

Knots and Windshakes, 1920, Short Story
French Heels 1922 d: Edwin L. Hollywood. lps: Irene Castle, Ward Crane, Charles Gerrard. 6700f USA. prod/rel: Holtre Productions, W. W. Hodkinson Corp.

Miracle, New York 1925, Novel
Woman's Faith, A 1925 d: Edward Laemmle. lps: Alma Rubens, Percy Marmont, Jean Hersholt. 6023f USA. *Miracle* prod/rel: Universal Pictures

Opera Hat, 1935, Short Story
Mr. Deeds Goes to Town 1936 d: Frank Capra. lps: Gary Cooper, Jean Arthur, George Bancroft. 118M USA. *A Gentleman Goes to Town*; *Opera Hat* prod/rel: Columbia Pictures Corp. of California©

Silver Spoon, Serial Story
Highways By Night 1942 d: Peter Godfrey. lps: Richard Carlson, Jane Randolph, Jane Darwell. 63M USA. prod/rel: RKO Radio

The Source, New York 1918, Novel
Source, The 1918 d: George Melford. lps: Wallace Reid, Anna Little, Theodore Roberts. 4637f USA. prod/rel: Famous Players-Lasky Corp.©, Paramount Pictures

Speak Easily, New York 1932, Novel
Speak Easily 1932 d: Edward Sedgwick. lps: Buster Keaton, Jimmy Durante, Ruth Selwyn. 82M USA. prod/rel: Metro-Goldwyn-Mayer Corp., Buster Keaton Production

Stand-in, 1937, Story
Stand-in 1937 d: Tay Garnett. lps: Leslie Howard, Humphrey Bogart, Joan Blondell. 91M USA. prod/rel: United Artists Corp.©, Walter Wanger Productions

The Steadfast Heart, New York 1924, Novel
Steadfast Heart, The 1923 d: Sheridan Hall. lps: Marguerite Courtot, Miriam Battista, Joseph Striker. 7012f USA. prod/rel: Distinctive Pictures, Goldwyn-Cosmopolitan Distributing Corp.

Sudden Jim, New York 1917, Novel
Sudden Jim 1917 d: Victor Schertzinger. lps: Charles Ray, Sylvia Breamer, Joseph J. Dowling. 5r USA. prod/rel: Triangle Film Corp., Triangle Distributing Corp.

Thirty-Day Princess, 1933, Story
Thirty Day Princess 1934 d: Marion Gering. lps: Sylvia Sidney, Cary Grant, Edward Arnold. 75M USA. *Thirty-Day Princess*; *30 Day Princess* prod/rel: Paramount Productions©, B. P. Schulberg Production

Valley of the Sun, Story
Valley of the Sun 1942 d: George Marshall. lps: Lucille Ball, James Craig, Cedric Hardwicke. 84M USA. prod/rel: RKO

You Never Can Tell, Story
Investment, The 1914 d: Lloyd B. Carleton. SHT USA. prod/rel: Lubin

KELLEHER, ED
Stand-Ins, Play
Stand-Ins 1997 d: Harvey Keith. lps: Daphne Zuniga, Costas Mandylor, Missy Crider. 88M USA. prod/rel: Overseas Filmgroup, Tetragrammation Films

KELLER, GOTTFRIED (1819–1890), SWT
Story
Merette 1982 d: Jean-Jacques Lagrange. lps: Jean Bouise, Anne Bos, Isabelle Sadoyan. MTV. 97M SWT. prod/rel: Television Suisse Romande, Antenne 2

Das Fahnlein Der Sieben Aufrechten, Liepzig 1861, Short Story
Hermin Und Die Sieben Aufrechten 1935 d: Frank Wisbar. lps: Heinrich George, Karin Hardt, Albert Lieven. 111M GRM/SWT. *Das Fahnlein Der Sieben Aufrechten*; *Le Fanion Des Sept Braves*

Kleider machen Leute, 1873, Short Story
Kleider machen Leute 1940 d: Helmut Kautner. lps: Heinz Ruhmann, Hertha Feiler, Aribert Wascher. 107M GRM. *Clothes Make the Man*; *Clothes Make People* prod/rel: Terra, a.K.a.

Der Landvogt von Griefensee, 1877, Short Story
Landvogt von Greifensee, Der 1979 d: Wilfried Bolliger. lps: Christian Quadflieg, Adelheid Arndt, Laura Trotter. 100M SWT. *The Bailiff of Greifensee*; *Le Bailli de Greifensee*

Die Missbrauchten Liebesbriefe, Stuttgart 1865, Short Story
Missbrauchten Liebesbriefe, Die 1940 d: Leopold Lindtberg. lps: Paul Hubschmid, Anne-Marie Blanc, Heinrich Gretler. 95M SWT. *Lettres d'Amour*; *Le Lettere d'Amore Smarrite*; *Les Lettres d'Amour Mal Employees* prod/rel: Praesens-Film

Missbrauchten Liebesbriefe, Die 1969 d: Hans D. Schwarze. 91M GRM. *The Abused Love Letters*

Regine, 1872, Short Story
Regine 1934 d: Erich Waschneck. lps: Luise Ullrich, Anton Walbrook, Olga Tschechowa. 95M GRM.

Regine 1956 d: Harald Braun. lps: Johanna Matz, Erik Schumann, Horst Buchholz. 107M GRM.

Romeo Und Julia Auf Dem Dorfe, Braunschweig 1865, Short Story
Espoirs 1940 d: Willy Rozier. lps: Constant Remy, Pierre Larquey, Jacqueline Roman. 92M FRN. *Le Champ Maudit* prod/rel: Sport-Films

Jugendliebe 1944 d: Eduard von Borsody. lps: Rose Marten, John Pauls-Harding, Willy Rosner. 79M GRM. *Wenn Die Kornblumen Bluhen Ubers Jahr*

Romeo Und Julia Auf Dem Dorfe 1941 d: Hans Trommer, Valerien Schmidely. lps: Margrit Winter, Erwin Kohlund, Johannes Steiner. 103M SWT. *Romeo Et Juliette Au Village*; *Romeo E Giulietta Al Villaggio*; *Der Schwarze Geiger* prod/rel: Pro Film Genossenschaft

Romeo Und Julia Auf Dem Dorfe 1983 d: Siegfried Kuhn. lps: Grit Stephan, Thomas Wetzel, Hilmar Baumann. 92M GDR.

Ursula, Novel
Ursula 1978 d: Egon Gunther. lps: Suzanne Stoll, Jorg Reichlin, Matthias Habich. MTV. 115M GDR/SWT. prod/rel: Tv D.R.S., Cine-Groupe

KELLER, HENRI
La Course a la Vertu, Play
Course a la Vertu, La 1936 d: Maurice Gleize. lps: Colette Darfeuil, Alice Tissot, Andre Berley. 82M FRN. prod/rel: Max Lerel

KELLER, PAUL
Die Drei Ringe, Short Story
Kinderseelen Klagen Euch an 1927 d: Curtis Bernhardt. lps: Claire Rommer, Fritz Rasp, Harry Hardt. 2478m GRM. prod/rel: Leo-Film Ag

Ferien Vom Ich, 1916, Novel
Ferien Vom Ich 1934 d: Hans Deppe. lps: Hermann Speelmans, Paul Henckels, Carola Hohn. 95M GRM. *Vacation from Yourself*

Ferien Vom Ich 1952 d: Hans Deppe. lps: Rudolf Prack, Marianne Hold, Werner Fuetterer. 105M GRM. *Vacation from Yourself* prod/rel: Hd-Film, Gloria

Ferien Vom Ich 1963 d: Hans Grimm. lps: Walther Reyer, Hans Holt, Genevieve Cluny. 90M GRM. *Vacation from Yourself* prod/rel: Franz Seitz, Constantin

Der Sohn Der Hagar, Novel
Sohn Der Hagar, Der 1926 d: Fritz Wendhausen. lps: Mady Christians, Werner Fuetterer, Lia Eibenschutz. 2693m GRM. *Out of the Mist* prod/rel: Deutsche Vereins-Film Ag

Sohn Ohne Heimat 1955 d: Hans Deppe. lps: Werner Krauss, Elisabeth Flickenschildt, Paul Bosinger. 99M GRM. *Son Without a Home* prod/rel: H.D., Constantin

Waldwinter, Novel
Waldwinter 1936 d: Fritz Peter Buch. lps: Hansi Knoteck, Viktor Staal, Hans Zesch-Ballot. 92M GRM. *Forest Winter* prod/rel: UFA

Waldwinter 1956 d: Wolfgang Liebeneiner. lps: Claus Holm, Sabine Bethmann, Rudolf Forster. 97M GRM. *Forest Winter* prod/rel: Apollo, D.F.H.

KELLERMAN, JONATHAN
When the Bough Breaks, Novel
When the Bough Breaks 1986 d: Waris Hussein. lps: Ted Danson, Richard Masur, Rachel Ticotin. TVM. 100M USA. prod/rel: T.D.F. Prod., Taft Entertainment

KELLERMANN, BERNHARD
Les Aventures de Schwedenklees, Novel
Nuit de Decembre 1939 d: Curtis Bernhardt. lps: Pierre Blanchar, Renee Saint-Cyr, Gilbert Gil. 82M FRN. *Heure Exquise* prod/rel: Metzger Et Woog

Das Meer, Novel
Meer, Das 1927 d: Peter Paul Felner. lps: Heinrich George, Olga Tschechowa, Simone Vaudry. 2579m GRM. prod/rel: Fefi, Peter Paul Felner-Film

Der Tunnel, Novel
Tunnel, Der 1933 d: Curtis Bernhardt. lps: Paul Hartmann, Olly von Flint, Gustaf Grundgens. 83M GRM. *The Tunnel* prod/rel: Vandor-Bavaria, Filmkunst

Tunnel, Le 1933 d: Curtis Bernhardt. lps: Jean Gabin, Madeleine Renaud, Edmond Van Daele. 73M FRN. prod/rel: Vandor-Film

Tunnel, The 1935 d: Maurice Elvey. lps: Richard Dix, Leslie Banks, Madge Evans. 94M UKN. *Transatlantic Tunnel* (USA) prod/rel: Gaumont-British

KELLEY, ETHEL MAY
Turn About Eleanor, Indianapolis 1917, Novel
Deciding Kiss, The 1918 d: Tod Browning. lps: Edith Roberts, Winnifred Greenwood, Hallam Cooley. 5r USA. prod/rel: Bluebird Photoplays, Inc.©

KELLEY, JUDITH
Marriage Is a Private Affair, Novel
Marriage Is a Private Affair 1944 d: Robert Z. Leonard. lps: Lana Turner, John Hodiak, James Craig. 117M USA. prod/rel: MGM

KELLINO, PAMELA
Del Palma, 1948, Novel
Lady Possessed 1952 d: William Spier, Roy Kellino. lps: James Mason, June Havoc, Stephen Dunne. 87M USA. prod/rel: Republic

KELLOGG, MARJORIE
Tell Me That You Love Me Junie Moon, New York 1968, Novel
Tell Me That You Love Me, Junie Moon 1970 d: Otto Preminger. lps: Liza Minnelli, Ken Howard, Robert Moore. 113M USA. prod/rel: Sigma Productions

KELLOGG, VIRGINIA
Story
Screaming Eagles 1956 d: Charles Haas. lps: Tom Tryon, Jan Merlin, Alvy Moore. 81M USA. prod/rel: Allied Artists

White Heat, Story
White Heat 1949 d: Raoul Walsh. lps: James Cagney, Virginia Mayo, Edmond O'Brien. 114M USA. prod/rel: Warner Bros.

KELLY, ANTHONY PAUL
Three Faces East, New York 1918, Play
British Intelligence 1940 d: Terry O. Morse. lps: Boris Karloff, Margaret Lindsay, Maris Wrixon. 62M USA. *Enemy Agent* (UKN) prod/rel: Warner Bros. Pictures, Inc.

Three Faces East 1926 d: Rupert Julian. lps: Jetta Goudal, Robert Ames, Henry B. Walthall. 7419f USA. prod/rel: Cinema Corp. of America, Producers Distributing Corp.

Three Faces East 1930 d: Roy Del Ruth. lps: Constance Bennett, Erich von Stroheim, Anthony Bushell. 71M USA. prod/rel: Warner Brothers Pictures

KELLY, ELEANOR MERCEIN
Kildares of Storm, New York 1916, Novel
Kildare of Storm 1918 d: Harry L. Franklin. lps: Emily Stevens, King Baggot, Crauford Kent. 5r USA. *Kildares of Storm* prod/rel: Metro Pictures Corp.©

KELLY, FLORENCE FINCH
With Hoops of Steel, Indianapolis 1900, Novel
With Hoops of Steel 1918 d: Eliot Howe. lps: Henry B. Walthall, Mary Charleson, William de Vaull. 5999f USA. prod/rel: Paralta Plays, Inc., W. W. Hodkinson Corp.

KELLY, GEORGE EDWARD (1887–1974), USA, Kelly, George
Craig's Wife, New York 1925, Play
Craig's Wife 1928 d: William C. de Mille. lps: Irene Rich, Warner Baxter, Virginia Bradford. 6670f USA. prod/rel: Pathe Exchange, Inc.

Craig's Wife 1936 d: Dorothy Arzner. lps: Rosalind Russell, John Boles, Billie Burke. 85M USA. prod/rel: Columbia Pictures Corp.

Harriet Craig 1950 d: Vincent Sherman. lps: Joan Crawford, Wendell Corey, Lucile Watson. 94M USA. prod/rel: Columbia

The Show-Off, New York 1924, Play
Men are Like That 1930 d: Frank Tuttle. lps: Hal Skelly, Doris Hill, Charles Sellon. 5467f USA. *The Show-Off*; *The Virtuous Wife* prod/rel: Paramount Famous Lasky Corp.

Show Off, The 1926 d: Malcolm St. Clair. lps: Ford Sterling, Lois Wilson, Louise Brooks. 6196f USA. *The Show-Off* prod/rel: Famous Players-Lasky, Paramount Pictures

Show-Off, The 1934 d: Charles F. Reisner. lps: Spencer Tracy, Madge Evans, Lois Wilson. 80M USA. prod/rel: Metro-Goldwyn-Mayer Corp.©

Show-Off, The 1946 d: Harry Beaumont. lps: Red Skelton, Marilyn Maxwell, Marjorie Main. 84M USA. prod/rel: MGM

The Torchbearers, New York 1922, Play
Doubting Thomas 1935 d: David Butler. lps: Will Rogers, Billie Burke, Alison Skipworth. 78M USA. *The Torch Bearers* prod/rel: Fox Film Corp.

Too Busy to Work 1939 d: Otto Brower. lps: Jed Prouty, Spring Byington, Kenneth Howell. 64M USA. *The Little Theater* prod/rel: Twentieth Century-Fox Film Corp.©

KELLY, MYRA
Little Aliens, New York 1910, Novel
  Little Miss Smiles 1922 d: John Ford. lps: Shirley Mason, Gaston Glass, George B. Williams. 4484f USA. prod/rel: Fox Film Corp.

KELLY, PAUL
Coplan Prend Des Risques, Novel
  Coplan Prend Des Risques 1963 d: Maurice Labro. lps: Dominique Paturel, Virna Lisi, Jacques Balutin. 105M FRN/ITL/BLG. *Agente Coplan: Missione Spionaggio* (ITL); *The Spy I Love* (USA) prod/rel: Cinephonic, Da-Ma Cinematografica

KELLY, T. HOWARD
His Buddy's Wife, Story
  His Buddy's Wife 1925 d: Tom Terriss. lps: Glenn Hunter, Edna Murphy, Gordon Begg. 5226f USA. *His Pal's Wife* prod/rel: Associated Exhibitors
Lover's Island, Short Story
  Lover's Island 1925 d: Henri Diamant-Berger. lps: Hope Hampton, James Kirkwood, Louis Wolheim. 4624f USA. prod/rel: Encore Pictures, Associated Exhibitors

KELMAN, JUDITH
Somebody's Waiting, Novel
  With Harmful Intent 1993 d: Richard Friedman. lps: Joan Van Ark, Christopher Noth, Rick Springfield. TVM. 88M USA.

KEMAL, ORHAN
Bereketli Topraklar Uzerinde, Novel
  Bereketli Topraklar Uzerinde 1980 d: Erden Kiral. lps: Yaman Okay, Erkan Yucel, Nur Surer. 130M TRK. *On Fertile Lands* prod/rel: Doga, Polar

KEMAL, YASHAR
Memed My Hawk, Novel
  Memed 1983 d: Peter Ustinov. lps: Peter Ustinov, Herbert Lom, Dennis Quilley. 110M UKN/YGS. *Mehmed My Hawk*; *The Lion and the Hawk* prod/rel: Fuad Kavur, Peter Ustinov Productions
Yer Demir Got Bakir, Novel
  Yer Demir, Gok Bakir 1987 d: Zulfu Livaneli. lps: Rutkay Aziz, Yavuzer Cetinkaya, MacIde Tanir. 98M TRK/GRM. *Eisenerde - Kupferhimmel* (GRM); *Copper Sky Iron Earth* prod/rel: Road-Movies, Interfilm

KEMBER, PAUL
Not Quite Jerusalem, 1982, Play
  Not Quite Jerusalem 1984 d: Lewis Gilbert. lps: Joanna Pacula, Sam Robards, Todd Graff. 114M UKN. *Not Quite Paradise* (USA) prod/rel: Rank, Acorn Pictures

KEMELMAN, HARRY (1908–, USA
Friday the Rabbi Slept Late, Novel
  Lanigan's Rabbi 1976 d: Lou Antonio. lps: Art Carney, Stuart Margolin, Janis Paige. TVM. 100M USA. *Friday the Rabbi Slept Late* prod/rel: Universal

KEMP, MATTY
Story
  French Line, The 1953 d: Lloyd Bacon. lps: Jane Russell, Gilbert Roland, Arthur Hunnicutt. 102M USA. prod/rel: RKO, Howard Hughes

KEMPINSKI, TOM
Duet for One, 1981, Play
  Duet for One 1986 d: Andrei Konchalovsky. lps: Julie Andrews, Alan Bates, Max von Sydow. 107M UKN. prod/rel: Cannon
Separation, Play
  Separation 1990 d: Barry Davis. lps: David Suchet, Rosanna Arquette. TVM. 80M UKN/USA. prod/rel: BBC Tv, Mark Forstater Productions

KEMPLEY, WALTER
L' Ordinateur Des Pompes Funebres, Novel
  Ordinateur Des Pompes Funebres, L' 1976 d: Gerard Pires. lps: Jean-Louis Trintignant, Mireille Darc, Bernadette Lafont. 85M FRN/ITL. *Caccia Al Montone* (ITL) prod/rel: P.A.C., Lira

KEMPNER-HOCHSTADT, MAX
Play
  Vetter Aus Dingsda, Der 1953 d: Karl Anton. lps: Vera Molnar, Gerhard Riedmann, Grethe Weiser. 95M GRM. prod/rel: Central-Europa, Prisma

KEMPOWSKI, WALTER
Novel
  Herzlich Willkommen 1989 d: Hark Bohm. lps: Uwe Bohm, David Bohm, Hark Bohm. TVM. 123M GRM. *Crossing Borders* prod/rel: Hamburger Kinokompanie, ZDF

KEMPSTER, AQUILA
Salvage, New York 1906, Novel
  Lucky Carson 1921 d: Wilfred North. lps: Earle Williams, Earl Schenck, Betty Ross Clark. 5r USA. prod/rel: Vitagraph Co. of America

KENDALL, DAVID
Lazaro, Book
  Where the River Runs Black 1986 d: Christopher Cain. lps: Charles Durning, Alessandro Rabelo, Marcelo Rabelo. 100M USA. *Lazaro* prod/rel: MGM, Ipi

KENDRICK, BAYNARD H.
Bright Victory, Novel
  Bright Victory 1951 d: Mark Robson. lps: Arthur Kennedy, Peggy Dow, Julie Adams. 97M USA. *Lights Out* (UKN) prod/rel: Universal-International
Eyes in the Night, Novel
  Eyes in the Night 1942 d: Fred Zinnemann. lps: Ann Harding, Edward Arnold, Donna Reed. 80M USA. prod/rel: MGM
The Last Express, New York 1937, Novel
  Last Express, The 1938 d: Otis Garrett. lps: Kent Taylor, Dorothea Kent, Don Brodie. 63M USA. prod/rel: Crime Club Productions, Universal Pictures Co.©

KENEALLY, THOMAS (1935–, ASL
The Chant of Jimmie Blacksmith, 1972, Novel
  Chant of Jimmie Blacksmith, The 1978 d: Fred Schepisi. lps: Tommy Lewis, Freddy Reynolds, Ray Barrett. 125M ASL. prod/rel: Film House, Australian Film Commission
Gossip from the Forest, Novel
  Gossip from the Forest 1979 d: Brian Gibson. lps: Michael Jayston, John Shrapnel, Hugh Burden. TVM. 90M UKN. *Gossip from the Front* prod/rel: Granada

KENEDI, ALEXANDER
The Boy the Girl and the Dog, Story
  Marry the Boss's Daughter 1941 d: Thornton Freeland. lps: Brenda Joyce, Bruce Edwards, George Barbier. 60M USA. prod/rel: 20th Century Fox

KENNAWAY, J.
Dollar Bottom and Taylor's Finest Hour, Book
  Chariots of Fire 1981 d: Hugh Hudson. lps: Ben Cross, Ian Charleson, Nigel Havers. 123M UKN. prod/rel: Twentieth Century Fox, Allied Stars

KENNAWAY, JAMES
Household Ghosts, Novel
  Country Dance 1969 d: J. Lee Thompson. lps: Peter O'Toole, Susannah York, Michael Craig. 112M UKN/USA. *Brotherly Love* (USA); *The Same Skin* prod/rel: MGM-Emi, Windward-Keep
Tunes of Glory, 1956, Novel
  Tunes of Glory 1960 d: Ronald Neame. lps: Alec Guinness, John Mills, Dennis Price. 107M UKN. prod/rel: United Artists, Knightsbridge
Violent Playground, Novel
  Violent Playground 1958 d: Basil Dearden. lps: Stanley Baker, Peter Cushing, Anne Heywood. 108M UKN. prod/rel: Rank, Rank Film Distributors

KENNEDY, ADAM
The Domino Principle, Novel
  Domino Principle, The 1977 d: Stanley Kramer. lps: Gene Hackman, Candice Bergen, Richard Widmark. 100M USA/UKN/MXC. *The Domino Killings* (UKN); *El Domino Principe* (MXC) prod/rel: Itc, Associated General

KENNEDY, ALFRED C.
After the Rain, 1931, Play
  Painted Woman, The 1932 d: John G. Blystone. lps: Spencer Tracy, Peggy Shannon, William "Stage" Boyd. 73M USA. *After the Rain*; *Trade Winds*; *Water-Front*; *Tropical Lady* prod/rel: Fox Film Corp.©

KENNEDY, BART
A Sailor Tramp, Novel
  Sailor Tramp, A 1922 d: F. Martin Thornton. lps: Victor McLaglen, Pauline Johnson, Hugh E. Wright. 5593f UKN. prod/rel: Welsh-Pearson, Jury

KENNEDY, BURT
Backtrack, Story
  Fort Dobbs 1958 d: Gordon Douglas. lps: Clint Walker, Virginia Mayo, Brian Keith. 90M USA. prod/rel: Warner Bros.

KENNEDY, CHARLES RYAN
The Servant in the House, New York 1908, Play
  Servant in the House, The 1915. lps: Tyrone Power Sr. SHT USA. prod/rel: Selig Polyscope Co.
  Servant in the House, The 1920 d: Jack Conway. lps: Jean Hersholt, Jack Curtis, Edward Peil. 8-9r USA. prod/rel: Triangle Film Corp., Film Booking Office, Inc.

KENNEDY, JAY RICHARD
The Chairman, Novel
  Chairman, The 1969 d: J. Lee Thompson. lps: Gregory Peck, Anne Heywood, Arthur Hill. 104M USA/UKN. *The Most Dangerous Man in the World* (UKN) prod/rel: 20th Century-Fox, Apjac

KENNEDY, LUDOVIC
The Airman and the Carpenter, Book
  Crime of the Century 1996 d: Mark Rydell. lps: Stephen Rea, Isabella Rossellini, J. T. Walsh. TVM. 120M USA. prod/rel: Astoria Productions, Hbo Pictures
Ten Rillington Place, Book
  10, Rillington Place 1971 d: Richard Fleischer. lps: Richard Attenborough, Judy Geeson, John Hurt. 111M UKN. *The Strangler of Rillington Place*; *Ten Rillington Place* prod/rel: Columbia, Genesis

KENNEDY, MARGARET (1896–1967), UKN
The Constant Nymph, 1924, Novel
  Constant Nymph, The 1928 d: Adrian Brunel, Basil Dean. lps: Ivor Novello, Mabel Poulton, Frances Doble. 11r UKN. prod/rel: Gainsborough, Woolf & Freedman
  Constant Nymph, The 1933 d: Basil Dean. lps: Victoria Hopper, Brian Aherne, Leonora Corbett. 98M UKN. prod/rel: Gaumont-British
  Constant Nymph, The 1943 d: Edmund Goulding. lps: Charles Boyer, Joan Fontaine, Alexis Smith. 112M USA. prod/rel: Warner Bros.
Escape Me Never, London 1933, Play
  Escape Me Never 1935 d: Paul Czinner. lps: Elisabeth Bergner, Hugh Sinclair, Griffith Jones. 95M UKN. prod/rel: British and Dominions, United Artists
  Escape Me Never 1947 d: Peter Godfrey. lps: Errol Flynn, Ida Lupino, Eleanor Parker. 104M USA. prod/rel: Warner Bros.
The Midas Touch, Novel
  Midas Touch, The 1939 d: David MacDonald. lps: Barry K. Barnes, Judy Kelly, Frank Cellier. 68M UKN. prod/rel: Warner Bros., First National

KENNEDY, WILLIAM (1928–, USA, Kennedy, William Joseph
Ironweed, Novel
  Ironweed 1987 d: Hector Babenco. lps: Jack Nicholson, Meryl Streep, Tom Waits. 135M USA. prod/rel: Tri-Star

KENNEDY, WILLIAM P.
Toy Soldiers, Novel
  Toy Soldiers 1991 d: Daniel Petrie Jr. lps: Sean Astin, Wil Wheaton, Keith Coogan. 112M USA. prod/rel: Tristar Pictures, Island World Inc.

KENNERLY, DAVID HUME
Shooter, Book
  Shooter 1988 d: Gary Nelson. lps: Jeffrey Nordling, Alan Ruck, Noble Willingham. TVM. 100M USA. prod/rel: Paramount Pictures

KENNETT, JOHN
Peril for the Guy, Novel
  Peril for the Guy 1956 d: James Hill. lps: Christopher Warbey, Frazer Hines, Ali Alleney. 55M UKN. prod/rel: World Wide, Children's Film Foundation

KENNINGTON, ALAN
The Night Has Eyes, Novel
  Night Has Eyes, The 1942 d: Leslie Arliss. lps: James Mason, Wilfred Lawson, Mary Clare. 79M UKN. *Terror House* (USA) prod/rel: Associated British Picture Corporation, Pathe
She Died Young, Novel
  You Can't Escape 1956 d: Wilfred Eades. lps: Noelle Middleton, Guy Rolfe, Robert Urquhart. 77M UKN. prod/rel: Forth Films, Ab-Pathe

KENNY, MARY
And They Shall Walk, Autobiography
  Sister Kenny 1946 d: Dudley Nichols. lps: Rosalind Russell, Alexander Knox, Dean Jagger. 116M USA. prod/rel: RKO Radio

KENNY, PAUL
Novel
  Coplan: Coup Durs 1989 d: Gilles Behat. lps: Philippe Caroit, Pierre Dux, Daniel Olbrychski. TVM. 105M FRN/GRM/SWT. *Coplan: Entfuhrung Nach Berlin* (GRM); *Coups Durs*
  Coplan: le Vampire Des Caraibes 1989 d: Yvan Butler. lps: Philippe Caroit, Patricia Millardet, France ZobdA. 90M FRN/GRM/SWT. *Coplan: Der Vampir Der Karibik* (GRM); *Le Vampire Des Caraibes*
  Coplan: Retour aux Sources 1989 d: Philippe Toledano. lps: Philippe Caroit, Patachou, Pierre Dux. TVM. 90M FRN/GRM/SWT. *Coplan: Rache in Caracas* (GRM)
  Moresque Obiettivo Allucinante 1967 d: Riccardo FredA. lps: Lang Jeffries, Sabine Sun, Robert Party. 90M ITL/SPN/FRN. *Coplan Ouvre le Feu a Mexico* (FRN); *Entre Las Redes* (SPN); *Between the Nets* prod/rel: Balcazar, C.F.F.P.
Action Immediate, Novel
  Action Immediate 1956 d: Maurice Labro. lps: Henri Vidal, Barbara Laage, Jacques Dacqmine. 100M FRN. *To Catch a Spy* (USA) prod/rel: S.F.C., Cinephonic

Coplan Paie le Cercueil, Novel
Coplan Sauve Sa Peau 1967 d: Yves Boisset. lps: Claudio Brook, Margaret Lee, Jean Servais. 108M FRN/ITL. *Horror: l'Assassino Ha le Ore Contate* (ITL); *Coplan Saves His Skin* (USA); *Devil's Garden*; *Les Jardins du Diable* prod/rel: Comptoir Francais Du Film Production, Cine-Socolo

Coplan Tente Sa Chance, Novel
Coplan, Agent Secret Fx18 1964 d: Maurice Cloche. lps: Ken Clark, Jany Clair, Cristina Gajoni. 97M FRN/ITL/SPN. *Uccidete Agente Segreto 777-Stop* (ITL) prod/rel: C.F.P.P., Producciones Cin.Cas Centro

Stoppez Coplan, Novel
Coplan Fx18 Casse Tout 1965 d: Riccardo FredA. lps: Richard Wyler, Robert Manuel, Jany Clair. 95M FRN/ITL. *Agente 777 Missione Supergame* (ITL); *The Exterminators* (USA); *Fx-18 Superspy*; *Fermati Coplan* prod/rel: C.F.F.P., Camera Films

KENRICK, TONY
Faraday's Flowers, Novel
Shanghai Surprise, The 1986 d: Jim Goddard. lps: Sean Penn, Madonna, Paul Freeman. 97M UKN/USA. prod/rel: Handmade, Vista Organisation

Two for the Price of One, Novel
Nobody's Perfekt 1981 d: Peter Bonerz. lps: Gabe Kaplan, Alex Karras, Robert Klein. 96M USA. prod/rel: Columbia

KENT, GEORGE
Cockleshell Heroes, Book
Cockleshell Heroes 1955 d: Jose Ferrer. lps: Jose Ferrer, Trevor Howard, Dora Bryan. 98M UKN. prod/rel: Warwick, Columbia

KENT, ROBERT E.
Story
Bad Men of Missouri 1941 d: Ray Enright. lps: Dennis Morgan, Jane Wyman, Wayne Morris. 74M USA. prod/rel: Warner Bros.

Night Freight, Story
Truck Busters 1943 d: B. Reeves Eason. lps: Richard Travis, Virginia Christine, Don Costello. 58M USA. prod/rel: Warner Bros.

Timber, Story
King of the Lumberjacks 1940 d: William Clemens. lps: John Payne, Gloria Dickson, Stanley Fields. 58M USA. *Timber* prod/rel: Warner Bros. Pictures©

KENTON, ERLE C.
Bridge, Story
Name the Woman 1928 d: Erle C. Kenton. lps: Anita Stewart, Huntley Gordon, Gaston Glass. 5544f USA. prod/rel: Columbia Pictures

KENWARD, ALAN R.
Proof Thro' the Night, Play
Cry Havoc 1943 d: Richard Thorpe. lps: Margaret Sullavan, Ann Sothern, Joan Blondell. 97M USA. prod/rel: MGM

KENYON, CHARLES
The Claim, New York 1917, Play
Claim, The 1918 d: Frank Reicher. lps: Edith Storey, Wheeler Oakman, Mignon Anderson. 5r USA. prod/rel: Metro Pictures Corp.©

Husband and Wife, New York 1915, Play
Husband and Wife 1916 d: Barry O'Neil. lps: Ethel Clayton, Holbrook Blinn, Gerda Holmes. 5r USA. prod/rel: World Film Corp.©, Peerless

The Kindling, New York 1911, Play
Kindling, The 1915 d: Cecil B. de Mille. lps: Charlotte Walker, Thomas Meighan, Raymond Hatton. 4-5r USA. prod/rel: Jesse L. Lasky Feature Play Co.©, Paramount Pictures Corp.

KEON, MICHAEL
The Durian Tree, New York 1960, Novel
Seventh Dawn, The 1964 d: Lewis Gilbert. lps: William Holden, Susannah York, Capucine. 123M UKN/USA. *Wherever Love Takes Me*; *The Third Road*; *The 7th Dawn* prod/rel: Holdean Productions, United Artists

KEOWN, ERIC
Sir Tristram Goes West, Story
Ghost Goes West, The 1935 d: Rene Clair. lps: Robert Donat, Jean Parker, Eugene Pallette. 90M UKN. *Le Fantome a Vendre* (FRN); *The Laying of the Glourie Ghost* prod/rel: London Films, United Artists

KEOWN, TIM
Bad As I Wanna Be, Book
Bad As I Wanna Be: the Dennis Rodman Story 1998 d: Jean de Segonzac. lps: Dwayne Adway, John Terry, Dee Wallace Stone. TVM. 120M USA. prod/rel: Mandalay Television, Mandalay Sports Entertainment

KERCKHOFF, SUSANNE
Tochter Aus Gutem Hause, Novel
Ihr Erstes Erlebnis 1939 d: Josef von Baky. lps: Ilse Werner, Johannes Riemann, Volker von Collande. 89M GRM. *Her First Experience* (USA) prod/rel: Universum, a.K.a.

KEREMEN, FRANZOS
Das Schiff Der Verlorenen Menschen, Novel
Schiff Der Verlorenen Menschen, Das 1929 d: Maurice Tourneur. lps: Marlene Dietrich, Fritz Kortner, Robin Irvine. 2659m GRM. *Le Navire Des Hommes Perdus*; *The Ship of Lost Men* prod/rel: Max Glass-Film-Produktion

KERKER, GUSTAV
The Belle of New York, New York 1897, Musical Play
Belle of New York, The 1919 d: Julius Steger. lps: Marion Davies, Raymond Bloomer, L. Rogers Lytton. 5r USA. prod/rel: Marion Davies Film Corp.©, Select Pictures Corp.

Belle of New York, The 1951 d: Charles Walters. lps: Fred Astaire, Vera-Ellen, Marjorie Main. 82M USA. prod/rel: Metro-Goldwyn-Mayer Corp.

KERMORVAN, YVES
Le Garde du Corps, Novel
Garde du Corps, Le 1983 d: Francois Leterrier. lps: Jane Birkin, Gerard Jugnot, Sami Frey. 100M FRN. prod/rel: Uranium, Ugc

KERN, ERICH
Menschen Im Netz, Munich 1957, Book
Menschen Im Netz 1959 d: Franz Peter Wirth. lps: Hansjorg Felmy, Johanna von Koczian, Hannes Messemer. 100M GRM. *Unwilling Agent* (USA); *People in the Net*; *People Trapped* prod/rel: Filmaufbau, I.F.C.

KERN, JEROME (1885–1945), USA, Kern, Jerome David
The Cat and the Fiddle, New York 1931, Musical Play
Cat and the Fiddle, The 1933 d: William K. Howard. lps: Jeanette MacDonald, Ramon Novarro, Frank Morgan. 88M USA. prod/rel: Metro-Goldwyn-Mayer Corp.

Music in the Air, New York 1932, Operetta
Music in the Air 1934 d: Joe May. lps: Gloria Swanson, John Boles, Douglass Montgomery. 85M USA. prod/rel: Fox Film Corp.©

Oh Boy!, New York 1917, Musical Play
Oh, Boy! 1919 d: Albert Capellani. lps: June Caprice, Creighton Hale, Zena Keefe. 6r USA. prod/rel: Albert Capellani Productions, Inc., Pathe Exchange, Inc.©

Oh Lady Lady!, New York 1918, Musical Play
Oh, Lady! Lady! 1920 d: Maurice Campbell. lps: Bebe Daniels, Harrison Ford, Walter Hiers. 4212f USA. *Oh Lady Lady* prod/rel: Realart Pictures Corp.©

Sunny, New York 1925, Musical Play
Sunny 1930 d: William A. Seiter. lps: Marilyn Miller, Lawrence Gray, Joe Donahue. 81M USA. prod/rel: First National Pictures

Sunny 1941 d: Herbert Wilcox. lps: Anna Neagle, Ray Bolger, John Carroll. 98M USA. prod/rel: RKO Radio

Sweet Adeline, New York 1929, Musical Play
Sweet Adeline 1935 d: Mervyn Leroy. lps: Irene Dunne, Donald Woods, Hugh Herbert. 95M USA. prod/rel: Warner Bros. Productions Corp., Warner Bros. Pictures©

Very Warm for May, Musical Play
Broadway Rhythm 1943 d: Roy Del Ruth. lps: George Murphy, Ginny Simms, Charles Winninger. 114M USA. *The Broadway Melody of 1944* prod/rel: Metro-Goldwyn-Mayer Corp.

KERN, WILL
Hellcab, Play
Chicago Cab 1998 d: Mary Cybulski, John Tintori. lps: Paul Dillon, Michael Ironside, Laurie Metcalf. 95M USA. *Hellcab* prod/rel: Gft Entertainment, Child's Will

KERNMAYR, HANS GUSTL
Erzherzog Johanns Grosse Liebe, Novel
Erzherzog Johanns Grosse Liebe 1950 d: Hans Schott-Schobinger. lps: O. W. Fischer, Marte Harell, Franz Pfaudler. 97M AUS. prod/rel: Patria, Panorama

Der Glaserne Berg, Novel
Unternehmen Edelweiss 1954 d: Heinz Paul. lps: Joachim Mock, Albert Hehn, Alice Graf. 90M GRM. *Operation Edelweiss* prod/rel: Heinz Paul, D.F.H.

Jede Nacht in Einem Anderen Bett, Play
Jede Nacht in Einem Andern Bett 1957 d: Paul Verhoeven. lps: Gerhard Riedmann, Waltraut Haas, Elma KarlowA. 108M GRM. *Every Night a Different Bed* prod/rel: Delos, Prisma

Weil du Arm Bist Musst du Fruher Sterben, Novel
Weil du Arm Bist, Musst du Fruher Sterben 1956 d: Paul May. lps: Bernhard Wicki, Hanna Rucker, Ilse Steppat. 98M GRM. *Because You are Poor You Die Sooner* prod/rel: Divina, Gloria

KEROUAC, JACK (1922–1969), USA
The Subterraneans, 1958, Novel
Subterraneans, The 1960 d: Ranald MacDougall. lps: Leslie Caron, George Peppard, Janice Rule. 89M USA. prod/rel: Arthur Freed, MGM

KEROUL, HENRI
Une Nuit de Noces, Play
Nuit de Noces 1935 d: Georges Monca, Maurice Keroul. lps: Armand Bernard, Florelle, Claude May. 90M FRN. prod/rel: Films Eclat, Hausmann-Films

Nuit de Noces 1949 d: Rene Jayet. lps: Martine Carol, Mona Goya, Jean Paredes. 85M FRN. *Une Nuit de Noces*; *Wedding Night* prod/rel: Paral Films

Nuit de Noces, Une 1920 d: Marcel Simon. lps: Fernand Rivers, Yvonne Chazel, Annette Grange. 1500m FRN. prod/rel: Pathe

KEROUL, MAURICE
La Toison d'Or, Play
Toison d'Or, La 1916. lps: Cesar, Alice de Tender. 860m FRN. prod/rel: Eclair

KERR, GEOFFREY
Cottage to Let, London 1940, Play
Cottage to Let 1941 d: Anthony Asquith. lps: Leslie Banks, Alastair Sim, John Mills. 90M UKN. *Bombsight Stolen* (USA) prod/rel: Gainsborough, General Film Distributors

KERR, JEAN (1923–, USA, Collins, Jean
The King of Hearts, New York 1954, Play
That Certain Feeling 1956 d: Norman Panama, Melvin Frank. lps: Bob Hope, Eva Marie Saint, George Sanders. 103M USA. prod/rel: Paramount, P & F Prods.

Mary Mary, New York 1961, Play
Mary, Mary 1963 d: Mervyn Leroy. lps: Debbie Reynolds, Barry Nelson, Diane McBain. 126M USA. prod/rel: Warner Bros. Pictures

Please Don't Eat the Daisies, Play
Please Don't Eat the Daisies 1960 d: Charles Walters. lps: Doris Day, David Niven, Janis Paige. 111M USA. prod/rel: MGM

KERR, MICHAEL
Virtuoso, Book
Virtuoso 1989 d: Tony Smith. lps: Alfred Molina, Alison Steadman, John Heard. TVM. 103M UKN. prod/rel: BBC

KERR, SOPHIE
Beauty's Worth, 1920, Short Story
Beauty's Worth 1922 d: Robert G. VignolA. lps: Marion Davies, Forrest Stanley, June Elvidge. 6751f USA. prod/rel: Cosmopolitan Productions, Paramount Pictures

The Blue Envelope, Garden City, N.Y. 1917, Novel
Blue Envelope Mystery, The 1916 d: Wilfred North. lps: Lillian Walker, John Drew Bennett, Bob Hay. 5r USA. prod/rel: Vitagraph Co. of America©, Greate Vitagraph (V-L-S-E, Inc)

Kayo! Oke!, 1930, Short Story
People Will Talk 1935 d: Alfred Santell. lps: Mary Boland, Charles Ruggles, Leila Hyams. 68M USA. prod/rel: Paramount Productions©

Relative Values, 1923, Short Story
Young Ideas 1924 d: Robert F. Hill. lps: Laura La Plante, T. Roy Barnes, Lucille Ricksen. 4095f USA. *Relativity* prod/rel: Universal Pictures

The See-Saw; a Story of Today, New York 1919, Novel
Invisible Bond, The 1920 d: Charles Maigne. lps: Irene Castle, Huntley Gordon, Claire Adams. 4986f USA. *The See-Saw*; *Should a Wife Forgive?* prod/rel: Famous Players-Lasky Corp.©, Paramount-Artcraft Pictures

Sitting on the World, 1920, Short Story
Fickle Women 1920 d: Fred J. Butler, Hugh McClung. lps: David Butler, Eugenie Besserer, Harry Todd. 4837f USA. *Sitting on the World* prod/rel: D. N. Schwab Productions, Inc., State Rights

Sweetie Peach, Short Story
House That Jazz Built, The 1921 d: Penrhyn Stanlaws. lps: Wanda Hawley, Forrest Stanley, Gladys George. 5225f USA. prod/rel: Realart Pictures

Worldly Goods, 1924, Short Story
Worldly Goods 1924 d: Paul Bern. lps: Agnes Ayres, Pat O'Malley, Victor Varconi. 6055f USA. prod/rel: Famous Players-Lasky, Paramount Pictures

KERRUISH, JESSIE DOUGLAS
A Romance of Old Bagdad, Novel
Romance of Old Bagdad, A 1922 d: Kenelm Foss. lps: Matheson Lang, Manora Thew, Henry Victor. 6300f UKN. prod/rel: Astra Films

The Undying Monster, Novel
Undying Monster, The 1942 d: John Brahm. lps: James Ellison, Heather Angel, John Howard. 60M USA. *The Hammond Mystery* (UKN) prod/rel: 20th Century-Fox

KERSH, GERALD
Night and the City, 1938, Novel
Night and the City 1950 d: Jules Dassin. lps: Richard Widmark, Gene Tierney, Googie Withers. 101M UKN/USA. prod/rel: 20th Century Productions, 20th Century-Fox
Night and the City 1992 d: Irwin Winkler. lps: Robert de Niro, Jessica Lange, Cliff Gorman. 104M USA.

KERTESZ, AKOS
Makra, 1971, Novel
Makra 1974 d: Tamas Renyi. lps: Mari Csomos. 104M HNG.

Sikator, 1965, Novel
Sikator 1966 d: Tamas Renyi. lps: Mari Torocsik, Gabor Koncz, Istvan Degi. 89M HNG. *Deadlock*

KERY, JEAN
Huit Hommes Dans un Chateau, Novel
Huit Hommes Dans la Chateau 1942 d: Richard Pottier. lps: Rene Dary, Louis Salou, Jacqueline Gauthier. 93M FRN. prod/rel: Sirius

KESEY, KEN (1935–, USA, Kesey, Ken Elton)
One Flew Over the Cuckoo's Nest, 1962, Novel
One Flew Over the Cuckoo's Nest 1975 d: Milos Forman. lps: Jack Nicholson, Louise Fletcher, William Redfield. 134M USA. prod/rel: United Artists, Fantasy Films

Sometimes a Great Notion, 1966, Novel
Sometimes a Great Notion 1971 d: Paul Newman. lps: Paul Newman, Henry Fonda, Michael Sarrazin. 113M USA. *Never Give an Inch* (UKN) prod/rel: Universal

KESSEL, JOSEPH
Les Amants du Tage, 1954, Novel
Amants du Tage, Les 1955 d: Henri Verneuil. lps: Francoise Arnoul, Daniel Gelin, Trevor Howard. 123M FRN. *Lover's Net* (USA); *The Lovers of Lisbon* (UKN); *Port of Shame* prod/rel: E.G.C., Hoche Production

L' Armee Des Ombres, 1943, Novel
Armee Des Ombres, L' 1969 d: Jean-Pierre Melville. lps: Lino Ventura, Simone Signoret, Jean-Pierre Cassel. 143M FRN/ITL. *L' Armata Degli Eroi* (ITL); *The Army in the Shadows* (UKN); *Army of the Shadows*; *Shadow Army* prod/rel: Films Corona, Fono Roma

Le Bataillon du Ciel, 1947, Novel
Bataillon du Ciel, Le 1945 d: Alexander Esway. lps: Pierre Blanchar, Janine Crispin, Rene Lefevre. 100M FRN. prod/rel: Pathe-Cinema

Les Bateliers de la Volga, Novel
Bateliers de la Volga, Les 1936 d: Wladimir von Strischewski. lps: Pierre Blanchar, Vera Korene, Charles Vanel. 91M FRN. prod/rel: Milo-Films

Belle de Jour, 1928, Novel
Belle de Jour 1967 d: Luis Bunuel. lps: Catherine Deneuve, Jean Sorel, Pierre Clementi. 102M FRN/ITL. *Bella Di Giorno* (ITL) prod/rel: Paris-Films Production, Five Film

Les Cavaliers, 1967, Novel
Horsemen, The 1971 d: John Frankenheimer. lps: Omar Sharif, Leigh Taylor-Young, Jack Palance. 109M USA. prod/rel: Columbia

Le Coup de Grace, 1931, Novel
Sirocco 1951 d: Curtis Bernhardt. lps: Humphrey Bogart, Marta Toren, Lee J. Cobb. 98M USA. prod/rel: Columbia, Santana Pictures

L' Equipage, Paris 1923, Novel
Equipage, L' 1927 d: Maurice Tourneur. lps: Georges Charlia, Claire de Lorez, Jean Dax. F FRN. *The Last Flight* (USA); *The Crew* (UKN) prod/rel: Lutece Films
Equipage, L' 1935 d: Anatole Litvak. lps: Annabella, Suzanne Despres, Charles Vanel. 111M FRN. prod/rel: Pathe-Natan
Woman I Love, The 1937 d: Anatole Litvak. lps: Paul Muni, Louis Hayward, Miriam Hopkins. 88M USA. *The Woman Between* (UKN); *Escadrille* prod/rel: RKO Radio Pictures©

Fortune Carree, Novel
Fortune Carree 1954 d: Bernard Borderie. lps: Pedro Armendariz, Folco Lulli, Paul Meurisse. 130M FRN/ITL. *Il Diavolo Del Deserto Shaitan* (ITL); *Conqueror of the Desert* (USA) prod/rel: C.I.C.C., S.N. Pathe-Cinema

Le Lion, Paris 1958, Novel
Lion, The 1962 d: Jack Cardiff. lps: William Holden, Trevor Howard, Capucine. 96M UKN/USA. prod/rel: 20th Century-Fox

Nuits de Princes, 1927, Novel
Ab Mitternacht 1938 d: Carl Hoffmann. lps: Gina Falckenberg, Peter Voss, Rene Deltgen. 78M GRM.
Nuits de Princes 1929 d: Marcel L'Herbier. lps: Gina Manes, Jaque Catelain, Nestor Ariany. 80M FRN. *Nuits de Tziganes* prod/rel: Sequana Films
Nuits de Princes 1937 d: Wladimir von Strischewski. lps: Jean Murat, Kathe von Nagy, Marina Shubert. 102M FRN. prod/rel: Productions J.N. Ermolieff

La Passante du San-Souci, Novel
Passante du Sans-Souci, La 1982 d: Jacques Rouffio. lps: Romy Schneider, Michel Piccoli, Wendelin Werner. 115M FRN/GRM. *Die Spaziergangerin von Sans-Souci* (GRM); *La Passante*; *The Strolling Woman* prod/rel: Ccc Filmkunst, Elephant

KESSELMAN, WENDY
Angelita, Novel
Dos Mundos de Angelita, Los 1982 d: Jeanne Morrison. lps: Marien Perez Riera, Rosalba Rolon, Angel Domenech Soto. 100M USA. *The Two Worlds of Angelita* prod/rel: First Run Features

I Love You I Love You Not, Play
I Love You, I Love You Not 1997 d: Billy Hopkins. lps: Jeanne Moreau, Claire Danes, Jude Law. 92M FRN/GRM/USA. prod/rel: Polar Entertainment, Die Hauskunst & Rimb

My Sister in This House, Play
Sister My Sister 1994 d: Nancy Meckler. lps: Julie Walters, Joely Richardson, Jodhi May. 102M UKN. prod/rel: Arrow, Film Four

KESSELRING, JOSEPH
Maker of Men Aggie Appleby, 1932, Play
Aggie Appleby, Maker of Men 1933 d: Mark Sandrich. lps: Wynne Gibson, Charles Farrell, William Gargan. 73M USA. *Cupid in the Rough* (UKN) prod/rel: RKO Radio Pictures, Inc.

Arsenic and Old Lace, New York 1941, Play
Arsenic and Old Lace 1944 d: Frank CaprA. lps: Cary Grant, Priscilla Lane, Raymond Massey. 118M USA. prod/rel: Warner Bros.
Arsenic and Old Lace 1969 d: Robert Scheerer. lps: Helen Hayes, Lillian Gish, Robert Crane. TVM. 74M USA.

KESSLER, LYLE
Orphans, Play
Orphans 1988 d: Alan J. PakulA. lps: Albert Finney, Matthew Modine, Kevin Anderson. 115M USA. prod/rel: Lorimar

KESSON, JESSIE
Another Place Another Time, Novel
Another Time, Another Place 1983 d: Michael Radford. lps: Phyllis Logan, Giovanni Mauriello, Denise Coffey. 102M UKN. prod/rel: Cinegate, Umbrella

The White Bird Passes, Autobiography
White Bird Passes, The 1980 d: Michael Radford. lps: Isobel Black. MTV. F UKN. prod/rel: BBC Scotland

KESTER, PAUL
Beverly's Balance, New York 1915, Play
Food for Scandal 1920 d: James Cruze. lps: Wanda Hawley, Harrison Ford, Ethel Grey Terry. 4648f USA. prod/rel: Realart Pictures Corp.©

Gone to the Dogs, Story
Gypsy Trail, The 1915 d: Harry Handworth. lps: Antonio Moreno, Frankie Mann, Donald Hall. 2r USA. *Gone to the Dogs* prod/rel: Vitagraph Co. of America

KESTER, VAUGHAN
The Just and the Unjust, Indianapolis 1912, Novel
Hell's 400 1926 d: John Griffith Wray. lps: Margaret Livingston, Harrison Ford, Henry Kolker. 5582f USA. *Just and Unjust* prod/rel: Fox Film Corp.

The Manager of the B and A, New York 1901, Novel
Manager of the B. & A., The 1916 d: J. P. McGowan. lps: Helen Holmes, Leo Maloney, Paul Hurst. 5r USA. *The Man from Medicine Hat* prod/rel: Signal Film Corp., Mutual Film Corp.

The Prodigal Judge, Indianapolis 1911, Novel
Prodigal Judge, The 1922 d: Edward Jose. lps: Jean Paige, MacLyn Arbuckle, Ernest Torrence. 7803f USA. prod/rel: Vitagraph Co. of America

KETRON, LARRY
Fresh Horses, Play
Fresh Horses 1988 d: David Anspaugh. lps: Molly Ringwald, Andrew McCarthy, Patti d'Arbanville. 105M USA. prod/rel: Columbia

The Trading Post, Play
Only Thrill, The 1997 d: Peter Masterson. lps: Diane Keaton, Sam Shepard, Diane Lane. 103M USA. *Tennessee Valley* prod/rel: Moonstone, Prestige

KETTENBACH, HANS WERNER
Im Jahr Der Schildkrote, Novel
Im Jahr Der Schildkrote 1988 d: Ute Wieland. lps: Heinz Bennent, Karina Fallenstein, Anke Tegtmeyer. 97M GRM. *The Year of the Turtle* prod/rel: Geissendorfer Film, Wdr

Minnie, Novel
Tennessee Waltz 1989 d: Nicolas Gessner. lps: Julian Sands, Stacey Dash, Ned Beatty. 99M SWT/USA. *Tennessee Nights* prod/rel: Nelson

KETZEK, FRANTISEK
Bila Vrana, Opera
Bila Vrana 1938 d: Vladimir Slavinsky. lps: Jindrich Plachta, Adina Mandlova, Frantisek Kristof-Vesely. 3094m CZC. *White Crow* prod/rel: Elekta

KEUN, IRMGARD
Das Kunstseidene Madchen, Novel
Kunstseidene Madchen, Das 1960 d: Julien Duvivier. lps: Giulietta Masina, Agnes Fink, Gustav Knuth. 105M GRM/FRN/ITL. *La Grande Vie* (FRN); *Rayon Lady*; *La Gran Vita* (ITL) prod/rel: Kurt Ulrich, D.F.H.

Nach Mitternacht, Novel
Nach Mitternacht 1981 d: Wolfgang Gremm. lps: Desiree Nosbusch, Wolfgang Jorg, Nicole Heesters. 110M GRM. *After Midnight* prod/rel: Regina Ziegler, Paramount

KEY, FRANCIS SCOTT
From Tyranny to Liberty, Short Story
From Tyranny to Liberty 1910 d: J. Searle Dawley. lps: Marc McDermott, George Lessey, Mary Fuller. 975f USA. prod/rel: Edison

KEY, MRS. E. J.
A Daughter of Love, Novel
Daughter of Love, A 1925 d: Walter West. lps: Violet Hopson, John Stuart, Jameson Thomas. 5050f UKN. prod/rel: Stoll

KEYES, CLAY
Charing Cross Road, Radio Play
Charing Cross Road 1935 d: Albert de Courville. lps: John Mills, June Clyde, Derek Oldham. 72M UKN. prod/rel: British Lion

KEYES, DANIEL (1927–, USA)
Flowers for Algernon, New York 1966, Novel
Charly 1968 d: Ralph Nelson. lps: Cliff Robertson, Claire Bloom, Leon Janney. 106M USA. prod/rel: Selmur, Robertson Associates

KEYES, GLADYS
Charing Cross Road, Radio Play
Charing Cross Road 1935 d: Albert de Courville. lps: John Mills, June Clyde, Derek Oldham. 72M UKN. prod/rel: British Lion

KHAJURIA, NARENDRA
Pyasi Dharti, Play
Gallan Hoyian Beetiyan 1966 d: Kumar Kuldip. lps: Ram Kumar Abrol, Jitender Sharma, Kaberi. 117M IND. *Gallon Hoyian Beetiyan* prod/rel: Tawi Films

KHANOLKAR, C. T.
Kalaya Tasmeya, Play
Ankahee 1984 d: Amol Palekar. lps: Amol Palekar, Deepti Naval, Shriram Lagoo. 135M IND. *The Unexpected*; *The Unspoken* prod/rel: Suchimisha

Kondura, 1966, Novel
Kondura 1977 d: Shyam Benegal. lps: Vanisree, Smita Patil, Satyadev Dubey. 137M IND. *The Sage from the Sea*; *Anugharam*; *The Boon* prod/rel: Raviraj Int.

KHONKAI, KAMARN
Kru Ban Nok, Novel
Kru Ban Nok 1978 d: Surasri Phatum. lps: Piya Trakulrat, Vasana Siddhivej, Somochart Prachatai. 133M THL. *Rural Teachers* prod/rel: Duangkamol Entertainments

KICKHAM, CHARLES
The Homes of Tipperary, Play
Knocknagow 1918 d: Fred O'Donovan. lps: Fred O'Donovan, Kathleen Murphy, Brian Magowan. 7910f IRL/UKN. prod/rel: Film Company of Ireland
Willy Reilly and His Colleen 1918 d: Fred O'Donovan. lps: Brian Magowan, Kathleen Murphy. 5000f IRL/UKN. prod/rel: Film Company of Ireland

KIDDER, EDWARD E.
Peaceful Valley, New York 1893, Play
Peaceful Valley 1920 d: Jerome Storm. lps: Charles Ray, Lydia Knott, Harry Myers. 6r USA. prod/rel: Charles Ray Productions, Inc., Associated First National Pictures, Inc.

A Poor Relation, 1911, Play
Poor Relation, A 1921 d: Clarence Badger. lps: Will Rogers, Sylvia Breamer, Wallace MacDonald. 4609f USA. prod/rel: Goldwyn Pictures

Shannon of the Sixth, New York 1898, Play
Shannon of the Sixth 1914 d: George Melford. lps: Douglas Gerrard, Edward Clisbee, Paul Hurst. 5r USA. prod/rel: Kalem Co., General Film Co.

KIELLAND, ALEXANDER (1849–1907), NRW, Kielland, Alexander Lange
Jacob, 1891, Novel
Jacobs Stege 1942 d: Gustaf Molander. lps: Sture Lagerwall, Birgit Tengroth, Hjordis Petterson. 104M SWD. *Jacob's Ladder* prod/rel: Ab Svensk Filmindustri
Torres Snortevold 1940 d: Tancred Ibsen. 102M NRW. *Jacob*
Sankt Hans Fest, 1887, Short Story
Sankt Hans Fest 1947 d: Toralf Sando. 88M NRW.

KIELLAND, AXEL
Herren Og Hans Tjenere, 1955, Play
Herren Og Hans Tjenere 1959 d: Arne Skouen. lps: Wenche Foss. 84M NRW. *The Master and His Servants; A God and His Servants*

KIENZLE, WILLIAM X. (1928–, USA, Kienzle, William X., Boyle, Mark
The Rosary Murders, Novel
Rosary Murders, The 1987 d: Fred Walton. lps: Donald Sutherland, Charles Durning, Belinda Bauer. 105M USA. prod/rel: New Line

KIERKEGAARD, OLE LUND
Story
Gummi Tarzan 1982 d: Soren Kragh-Jacobsen. lps: Alex Svanbjerg, Otto Brandenburg, Peter Schroeder. 98M DNM. *Rubber Tarzan; Pudding Tarzan* prod/rel: Metronome, Atlas

KIHN, HANS ALFRED
Die Erbschleicher, Play
Erbschleicher, Die 1937 d: Hans Deppe. lps: Josef Eichheim, Fritz Kampers, Oskar SimA. 86M GRM. *Meiseken* prod/rel: F.D.F., Globus
Meiseken, Play
Kleinstadtsunder 1927 d: Bruno Rahn. lps: Asta Nielsen, Hermann Picha, Maria Paudler. 2555m GRM. *Small Town Sinners* (USA) prod/rel: Rahn-Film-Prod.
Wirtin an Der Lahn, Die 1955 d: J. A. Hubler-KahlA. lps: Dorit Kreysler, Oskar Sima, Hanita HallA. 97M GRM. *The Inn on the Lahn* prod/rel: Neubach, Atlantic

KIKUCHI, HIDEYUKI
Novel
Wicked City 1993 d: Yoshiaki Kawajiri. ANM. 81M JPN. prod/rel: Hideyuki Kikuchi, Tokuma Shoten

KIKUCHI, KAN
Green Pearl, Novel
San Zimei 1934 d: Li Pingqian. lps: Hudie, Yan Yuexian, Lin Li. 9r CHN. *Three Sisters* prod/rel: Mingxing Film Company
Kafuku, 1936-37, Novel
Kafuku 1937 d: Mikio Naruse. 180M JPN. *Learn from Experience*
Kesa's Husband, Play
Jigokumon 1953 d: Teinosuke KinugasA. lps: Kazuo Hasegawa, MacHiko Kyo, Isao YamagatA. 89M JPN. *Gate of Hell* (USA); *Hell's Gate* prod/rel: Daiei Motion Picture Co.
Toki No Ujigami, 1924, Play
Toki No Ujigami 1932 d: Kenji Mizoguchi. 60M JPN. *Man of the Moment* (USA); *The Man of the Right Moment; Timely Mediator*

KIKUTA, KAZUO
Shizukanaru Ketto, Play
Shizukanaru Ketto 1949 d: Akira KurosawA. lps: Toshiro Mifune, Takashi Shimura, Miki Sanjo. 95M JPN. *The Silent Duel; The Quiet Duel; The Quiet Fight* prod/rel: Daiei Motion Picture Co.

KILBOURNE, FANNY
The Girl Who Was the Life of the Party, 1923, Short Story
Girls Men Forget 1924 d: Maurice Campbell. lps: Johnny Walker, Patsy Ruth Miller, Alan Hale. 5116f USA. prod/rel: Principal Pictures
Sunny Goes Home, Short Story
Major and the Minor, The 1942 d: Billy Wilder. lps: Ginger Rogers, Ray Milland, Diana Lynn. 100M USA. prod/rel: Paramount
You're Never Too Young 1955 d: Norman Taurog. lps: Dean Martin, Jerry Lewis, Diana Lynn. 102M USA. prod/rel: Paramount, York Pictures

KILDARE, OWEN FRAWLEY
My Mamie Rose; the Story of My Regeneration, New York 1903, Book
Fools' Highway 1924 d: Irving Cummings. lps: Mary Philbin, Pat O'Malley, William Collier Jr. 6800f USA. prod/rel: Universal Pictures
Regeneration 1915 d: Raoul Walsh. lps: Rockliffe Fellowes, Anna Q. Nilsson, William Sheer. 5r USA. prod/rel: Fox Film Corp., William Fox©

KILPATRICK, FLORENCE
Virginia's Husband, Play
Virginia's Husband 1928 d: Harry Hughes. lps: Mabel Poulton, Lillian Oldland, Pat Aherne. 6300f UKN. prod/rel: Nettlefold, Butcher's Film Service
Virginia's Husband 1934 d: MacLean Rogers. lps: Dorothy Boyd, Reginald Gardiner, Enid Stamp-Taylor. 71M UKN. prod/rel: George Smith, Fox
Wilcat Hetty, Play
Hellcat, The 1928 d: Harry Hughes. lps: Mabel Poulton, Eric Bransby Williams, John Hamilton. 6559f UKN. *Wild Cat Hetty* prod/rel: Nettlefold, Butcher's Film Service

KIM SONG DONG
Mandala, Novel
Mandala 1981 d: Im Kwon-Taek. lps: Jon Moo Song, Ahn Song-Ki, Pang Hi. 112M SKR. *Two Monks* prod/rel: Hwa Chun Trading Company

KIM YU-JUNG
Deng-Byod, Novel
Deng-Byod 1984 d: Hah Myong-Jung. lps: Hah Myong-Jung, Cho Yong-Won, Lee Heh-Young. 100M KOR. prod/rel: Hwa Chun Trading Company

KIMBLE, LAWRENCE
Death on a Side Street, Story
One-Way Street 1950 d: Hugo Fregonese. lps: James Mason, Dan Duryea, Marta Toren. 79M USA. *Death on a Side Street; The Deep End* prod/rel: Universal-International

KIMBROUGH, EMILY
Our Hearts Were Young and Gay, Book
Our Hearts Were Young and Gay 1944 d: Lewis Allen. lps: Gail Russell, Diana Lynn, Charlie Ruggles. 81M USA. prod/rel: Paramount

KIMMICH, MAX W.
Nacht Ohne Abschied, Short Story
Nacht Ohne Abschied 1943 d: Erich Waschneck. lps: Anna Dammann, Karl Ludwig Diehl, Hans Sohnker. 78M GRM. prod/rel: UFA
Unter Falsche Flagge, Novel
Madame Spy 1934 d: Karl Freund. lps: Fay Wray, Nils Asther, Edward Arnold. 70M USA. prod/rel: Universal Pictures Corp.©
Unter Falscher Flagge 1932 d: Johannes Meyer. lps: Charlotte Susa, Gustav Frohlich. F GRM. prod/rel: Tobis Films, Universal

KIMMINS, ANTHONY (1901–1964), UKN
The Amorous Prawn, London 1959, Play
Amorous Prawn, The 1962 d: Anthony Kimmins. lps: Ian Carmichael, Joan Greenwood, Cecil Parker. 89M UKN. *The Playgirl and the Minister* (USA); *The Amorous Mr. Prawn* prod/rel: Covent Garden Film, British Lion
Night Club Queen, 1933, Play
Night Club Queen 1934 d: Bernard Vorhaus. lps: Mary Clare, Lewis Casson, Jane Carr. 87M UKN. prod/rel: Real Art, Universal
While Parents Sleep, London 1932, Play
While Parents Sleep 1935 d: Adrian Brunel. lps: Jean Gillie, Ellis Jeffreys, Enid Stamp-Taylor. 72M UKN. prod/rel: Transatlantic, British and Dominions

KIMURA, SOJU
Netsudeichi, Novel
Netsudeichi 1950 d: Kon IchikawA. lps: Susumu Fujita, Harue Tone, Yuji Hori. 90M JPN. *The Hot Marshland; Heat and Mud* prod/rel: Shintoho Co.

KINCH, MARTIN
Me, Play
Me 1976 d: John Palmer. lps: Brenda Donohue, Chapelle Jaffe, Stephen Markle. 82M CND. prod/rel: World Leisure Corporation Ltd., Muddy York Motion Pictures Ltd.

KIND, JOHANN F.
Der Freischutz, Berlin 1821, Opera
Freischutz, Der 1968 d: Joachim Hess. lps: Tom Krause, Toni Blankenheim, Arlene Saunders. MTV. 127M GRM. *The Free-Shooter; The Marksman* prod/rel: Polyphon Film & Tv Productions

KING, BASIL
The City of Comrades, New York 1919, Novel
City of Comrades, The 1919 d: Harry Beaumont. lps: Tom Moore, Seena Owen, Otto Hoffman. 5r USA. prod/rel: Goldwyn Pictures Corp.©, Goldwyn Distributing Corp.
The Ghost's Story, Story
Earthbound 1940 d: Irving Pichel. lps: Warner Baxter, Andrea Leeds, Lynn Bari. 67M USA. prod/rel: Twentieth Century-Fox Film Corp.©

In the Garden of Charity, New York 1903, Novel
Tides of Passion 1925 d: J. Stuart Blackton. lps: Mae Marsh, Ben Hendricks, Laska Winter. 6279f USA. prod/rel: Vitagraph Co. of America
The Inner Shrine, New York 1909, Novel
Inner Shrine, The 1917 d: Frank Reicher. lps: Margaret Illington, Hobart Bosworth, Elliott Dexter. 5r USA. prod/rel: Jesse L. Lasky Feature Play Co.©, Paramount Pictures Corp.
Let Not Man Put Asunder, New York 1901, Novel
Let Not Man Put Asunder 1924 d: J. Stuart Blackton. lps: Pauline Frederick, Lou Tellegen, Leslie Austen. 9r USA. prod/rel: Vitagraph Co. of America
The Lifted Veil, New York 1917, Novel
Lifted Veil, The 1917 d: George D. Baker. lps: Ethel Barrymore, William B. Davidson, Charles K. French. 5r USA. prod/rel: Metro Pictures Corp.©
The Spreading Dawn, 1916, Short Story
Spreading Dawn, The 1916 d: Larry Trimble. lps: Jane Cowl, Orme Caldara, Harry Springer. 5r USA. prod/rel: Goldwyn Pictures Corp.©, Goldwyn Distributing Corp.
The Street Called Straight, 1912, Short Story
Street Called Straight, The 1920 d: Wallace Worsley. lps: Milton Sills, Naomi Childers, Charles Clary. 5r USA. prod/rel: Eminent Authors Pictures, Inc., Goldwyn Distributing Corp.
The Wild Olive, New York 1910, Novel
Wild Olive, The 1915 d: Oscar Apfel. lps: Myrtle Stedman, Forrest Stanley, Mary Ruby. 5r USA. prod/rel: Oliver Morosco Photoplay Co.©, Bosworth, Inc.

KING, BRADLEY
Her Reputation, Indianapolis 1923, Novel
Her Reputation 1923 d: John Griffith Wray. lps: May McAvoy, Lloyd Hughes, James Corrigan. 6566f USA. prod/rel: Thomas H. Ince Corp., Associated First National Pictures

KING, CAPT. JOHN
A Woman's Past, Play
Woman's Past, A 1915 d: Frank Powell. lps: Nance O'Neil, Alfred Hickman, Clifford Bruce. 5r USA. prod/rel: Fox Film Corp., William Fox©

KING, FRANK
The Ghoul, Novel
Ghoul, The 1933 d: T. Hayes Hunter. lps: Boris Karloff, Cedric Hardwicke, Ernest Thesiger. 79M UKN. prod/rel: Gaumont British, Woolf & Freedman
The Ghoul, London 1928, Novel
What a Carve Up! 1961 d: Pat Jackson. lps: Sidney James, Kenneth Connor, Shirley Eaton. 88M UKN. *No Place Like Homicide* (USA) prod/rel: New World Pictures, Regal Films International
This Is Mary's Chair, Play
Death of an Angel 1952 d: Charles Saunders. lps: Jane Baxter, Patrick Barr, Julie Somers. 64M UKN. prod/rel: Hammer, Lesser

KING, GEN. CHARLES
A Daughter of the Sioux; a Tale of the Indian Frontier, New York 1903, Novel
Daughter of the Sioux, A 1925 d: Ben Wilson. lps: Ben Wilson, Neva Gerber, Robert Walker. 4700f USA. prod/rel: Davis Distributing Division
Fort Frayne, Philadelphia 1901, Novel
Fort Frayne 1926 d: Ben Wilson. lps: Ben Wilson, Neva Gerber, Ruth Royce. 5r USA. prod/rel: Davis Distributing Division
Tonio Son of the Sierras; a Story of the Apache Wars, New York 1906, Novel
Tonio, Son Ot the Sierras 1925 d: Ben Wilson. lps: Ben Wilson, Neva Gerber, Chief Yowlachie. 5r USA. prod/rel: Davis Distributing Division
Under Fire, Philadelphia 1895, Novel
Under Fire 1926 d: Clifford S. Elfelt. lps: Bill Patton, Jean Arthur, Cathleen Calhoun. 5r USA. prod/rel: Clifford S. Elfelt Productions, Davis Distributing Division
Warrior Gap; a Story of the Sioux Outbreak of '68, New York 1897, Novel
Warrior Gap 1925 d: Alvin J. Neitz. lps: Ben Wilson, Neva Gerber, Robert Walker. 4900f USA. prod/rel: Davis Distributing Division, Vital Exchanges

KING, GEORGE S.
The Last Slaver, New York 1933, Novel
Slave Ship 1937 d: Tay Garnett. lps: Warner Baxter, Wallace Beery, Elizabeth Allan. 92M USA. *The Last Slaver* prod/rel: Twentieth Century-Fox Film Corp.©

KING, HAROLD
Paradigm Red
Red Alert 1977 d: William Hale. lps: William Devane, Michael Brandon, Adrienne Barbeau. TVM. 100M USA. prod/rel: Jozak Productions, Paramount Pictures

KING, HUGH
The Big Rainbow, Story
   Underwater! 1955 d: John Sturges. lps: Richard Egan, Jane Russell, Gilbert Roland. 99M USA. prod/rel: RKO Radio, Howard Hughes

KING, JOE
Liquid Dynamite, Story
   Liquid Dynamite 1915 d: Cleo Madison. lps: Mr. Abbott, Cleo Madison, Tom Chatterton. SHT USA. prod/rel: Rex

KING, LARRY L.
The Best Little Whorehouse in Texas, Play
   Best Little Whorehouse in Texas, The 1982 d: Colin Higgins. lps: Burt Reynolds, Dolly Parton, Dom Deluise. 114M USA. prod/rel: Universal, RKO

KING, PHILIP (1904–1979), UKN
On Monday Next, London 1949, Play
   Curtain Up 1952 d: Ralph Smart. lps: Robert Morley, Margaret Rutherford, Kay Kendall. 82M UKN. *On Monday Next* prod/rel: General Film Distributors, Constellation
Sailor Beware, London 1955, Play
   Sailor Beware! 1956 d: Gordon Parry. lps: Peggy Mount, Shirley Eaton, Ronald Lewis. 80M UKN. *Panic in the Parlor* (USA) prod/rel: Romulus, Remus
See How They Run, London 1945, Play
   See How They Run 1955 d: Leslie Arliss. lps: Ronald Shiner, Greta Gynt, James Hayter. 84M UKN. prod/rel: Winwell, British Lion
Serious Charge, London 1955, Play
   Serious Charge 1959 d: Terence Young. lps: Anthony Quayle, Sarah Churchill, Andrew Ray. 99M UKN. *Immoral Charge* (USA); *A Touch of Hell* prod/rel: Alva Films, Eros
Watch It Sailor!, London 1960, Play
   Watch It Sailor! 1961 d: Wolf RillA. lps: Dennis Price, Marjorie Rhodes, Irene Handl. 81M UKN. prod/rel: Columbia, Cormorant

KING, RALEIGH
Jix, Novel
   Ringing the Changes 1929 d: Leslie Hiscott. lps: Henry Edwards, Margot Landa, James Fenton. SIL. 6915f UKN. prod/rel: Strand Films, Argosy

KING, RUFUS
The Case of the Constant God, 1936, Short Story
   Love Letters of a Star 1936 d: Lewis R. Foster, Milton Carruth. lps: Henry Hunter, Polly Rowles, C. Henry Gordon. 66M USA. *The Case of the Constant God* prod/rel: Universal Productions©
Invitation to a Murder, Play
   Hidden Hand, The 1942 d: Ben Stoloff. lps: Craig Stevens, Elisabeth Fraser, Julie Bishop. 68M USA. prod/rel: Warner Bros.
Murder at the Vanities, New York 1933, Play
   Murder at the Vanities 1934 d: Mitchell Leisen. lps: Jack Oakie, Kitty Carlisle, Carl Brisson. 89M USA. prod/rel: Paramount Productions©
Murder By the Clock, New York 1929, Novel
   Murder By the Clock 1931 d: Edward Sloman. lps: William "Stage" Boyd, Lilyan Tashman, Irving Pichel. 76M USA. prod/rel: Paramount Publix Corp.©
Museum Piece No. 13, Story
   Secret Beyond the Door 1947 d: Fritz Lang. lps: Michael Redgrave, Joan Bennett, Anne Revere. 99M USA. prod/rel: Universal, Walter Wanger
North Star; a Dog Story of the Canadian Northwest, New York 1925, Novel
   North Star 1925 d: Paul Powell. lps: Virginia Lee Corbin, Stuart Holmes, Ken Maynard. 4715f USA. prod/rel: Howard Estabrook Productions, Associated Exhibitors
The Victoria Docks at Eight, Novel
   White Tie and Tails 1946 d: Charles T. Barton. lps: Dan Duryea, William Bendix, Ella Raines. 81M USA. prod/rel: Universal

KING, SHERWOOD
If I Die Before I Wake, Novel
   Lady from Shanghai, The 1948 d: Orson Welles. lps: Rita Hayworth, Orson Welles, Everett Sloane. 87M USA. prod/rel: Columbia

KING, STEPHEN (1947–, USA, King, Stephen Edwin Short Story
   Creepshow 2 1987 d: Michael Gornick. lps: Lois Chiles, George Kennedy, Dorothy Lamour. 90M USA. prod/rel: New World
Apt Pupil, Novel
   Apt Pupil 1998 d: Bryan Singer. lps: Ian McKellen, Brad Renfro, Bruce Davison. 111M USA. prod/rel: Sony Pictures Entertainment, Tristar Pictures

The Body, Short Story
   Stand By Me 1986 d: Rob Reiner. lps: Wil Wheaton, River Phoenix, Corey Feldman. 89M USA. *The Body* prod/rel: Columbia, Act III Productions
Carrie, 1974, Novel
   Carrie 1976 d: Brian DepalmA. lps: Sissy Spacek, Piper Laurie, Amy Irving. 97M USA. prod/rel: United Artists Corp., Red Bank
Cat from Hell, Story
   Tales from the Darkside: the Movie 1990 d: John Harrison. lps: Deborah Harry, Matthew Lawrence, Christian Slater. 93M USA. prod/rel: Paramount
Children of the Corn, Short Story
   Children of the Corn Ii: the Final Sacrifice 1992 d: David F. Price. lps: Terence Knox, Paul Scherrer, Ryan Bollman. 89M USA. *Children of the Corn: Deadly Harvest* prod/rel: Fifth Avenue Entertainment
Christine, 1983, Novel
   Christine 1983 d: John Carpenter. lps: Keith Gordon, Keith Stockwell, Alexandra Paul. 116M USA. prod/rel: Columbia
Cujo, 1981, Novel
   Cujo 1984 d: Lewis Teague. lps: Dee Wallace Stone, Danny Pintauro, Daniel Hugh Kelly. 91M USA. prod/rel: Warner Bros., Taft Entertainment Corp.
Cycle of the Werewolf, Novel
   Silver Bullet 1985 d: Daniel Attias. lps: Gary Busey, Corey Haim, Megan Follows. 95M USA. *Stephen King's Silver Bullet* prod/rel: Paramount, Dino de Laurentiis
The Dead Zone, Novel
   Dead Zone, The 1983 d: David Cronenberg. lps: Christopher Walken, Martin Sheen, Brooke Adams. 103M USA. prod/rel: Paramount, Dead Zone Prod.
Firestarter, 1980, Novel
   Firestarter 1984 d: Mark L. Lester. lps: David Keith, Drew Barrymore, Freddie Jones. 116M USA. prod/rel: Universal-International
The General, Short Story
   Cat's Eye 1985 d: Lewis Teague. lps: Drew Barrymore, James Woods, Alan King. 94M USA. *Stephen King's Cat's Eye* prod/rel: MGM, United Artists
Graveyard Shift, Short Story
   Stephen King's Graveyard Shift 1990 d: Ralph S. Singleton. lps: David Andrews, Kelly Wolf, Stephen macht. 87M USA. *Graveyard Shift* prod/rel: Graveyard, Inc.
It, 1986, Novel
   It 1990 d: Tommy Lee Wallace. lps: Harry Anderson, Dennis Christopher, Tim Curry. TVM. 192M USA. *Stephen King's It* prod/rel: Green-Epstein Prods.
The Lawnmower Man, Short Story
   Lawnmower Man, The 1992 d: Brett Leonard. lps: Jeff Fahey, Pierce Brosnan, Jenny Wright. 108M UKN/USA. prod/rel: Allied Vision (London), Lane Pringle (Los Angeles)
The Ledge, Short Story
   Cat's Eye 1985 d: Lewis Teague. lps: Drew Barrymore, James Woods, Alan King. 94M USA. *Stephen King's Cat's Eye* prod/rel: MGM, United Artists
Misery, Novel
   Misery 1990 d: Rob Reiner. lps: James Caan, Kathy Bates, Richard Farnsworth. 107M USA. prod/rel: Castle Rock Entertainment, Nelson Entertainment
Needful Things, Novel
   Needful Things 1994 d: Fraser C. Heston. lps: Max von Sydow, Ed Harris, Bonnie BedeliA. 120M USA. prod/rel: Castle Rock, New Line
The Night Flier, Story
   Stephen King's the Night Flyer 1997 d: Mark PaviA. lps: Miguel Ferrer, Julie Entwisle, Dan Monahan. 97M USA. prod/rel: New Amsterdam Entertainment, Stardust Intl.
Night Shift, 1978, Short Story
   Children of the Corn 1984 d: Fritz Kiersch. lps: Peter Horton, Linda Hamilton, R. G. Armstrong. 93M USA. prod/rel: New World
Pet Sematary, Novel
   Pet Sematary 1989 d: Mary Lambert. lps: Dale Midkiff, Fred Gwynne, Denise Crosby. 102M USA. prod/rel: Paramount
Quitters Inc., Short Story
   Cat's Eye 1985 d: Lewis Teague. lps: Drew Barrymore, James Woods, Alan King. 94M USA. *Stephen King's Cat's Eye* prod/rel: MGM, United Artists
The Running Man, Novel
   Running Man, The 1987 d: Paul Michael Glaser. lps: Arnold Schwarzenegger, Maria Conchita Alonso, Yaphet Kotto. 100M USA. prod/rel: Tri-Star, Braveworld

Salem's Lot, 1974, Novel
   Salem's Lot 1979 d: Tobe Hooper. lps: David Soul, James Mason, Lance Kerwin. TVM. 200M USA. *Salem's Lot: the Movie* prod/rel: Warner Bros. Tv, Serendipity Productions
The Shining, 1976, Novel
   Shining, The 1980 d: Stanley Kubrick. lps: Jack Nicholson, Shelley Duvall, Danny Lloyd. 119M UKN. prod/rel: Warner Bros.
Sometimes They Come Back, Short Story
   Stephen King's Sometimes They Come Back 1991 d: Tom McLoughlin. lps: Tim Matheson, Brooke Adams, Robert Hy Gorman. TVM. 100M USA. *Sometimes They Come Back*
The Stand, 1978, Novel
   Stephen King's the Stand 1994 d: Mick Garris. lps: Gary Sinise, Molly Ringwald, Ossie Davis. TVM. 345M USA.
Thinner, 1984, Novel
   Stephen King's Thinner 1996 d: Tom Holland. lps: Robert John Burke, Joe Mantegna, Michael Constantine. 92M USA. prod/rel: Spelling Films Inc., Richard P. Rubinstein Production
The Tommyknockers, Novel
   Tommyknockers, The 1993 d: John Power. lps: Jimmy Smits, Marg Helgenberger, Robert Carradine. TVM. 114M USA. *Stephen King's the Tommyknockers*

KING-HALL, MAGDALEN
The Life and Death of the Wicked Lady Skelton, Novel
   Wicked Lady, The 1945 d: Leslie Arliss. lps: Margaret Lockwood, James Mason, Patricia Roc. 104M UKN. prod/rel: Gainsborough, Eagle-Lion
   Wicked Lady, The 1983 d: Michael Winner. lps: Faye Dunaway, Alan Bates, John Gielgud. 98M UKN. prod/rel: Columbia, Cannon

KING-HALL, STEPHEN
Admirals All, London 1934, Play
   Admirals All 1935 d: Victor Hanbury. lps: Wynne Gibson, Gordon Harker, Anthony Bushell. 75M UKN. prod/rel: Stafford, Radio
Bunga-Bunga, Novel
   Tropical Trouble 1936 d: Harry Hughes. lps: Douglass Montgomery, Betty Ann Davies, Alfred Drayton. 70M UKN. prod/rel: City, General Film Distributors
The Middle Watch, London 1929, Play
   Girls at Sea 1958 d: Gilbert Gunn. lps: Guy Rolfe, Ronald Shiner, Alan White. 80M UKN. prod/rel: Associated British Picture Corporation
   Middle Watch, The 1930 d: Norman Walker. lps: Owen Nares, Jacqueline Logan, Jack Raine. 112M UKN. prod/rel: British International Pictures, Wardour
   Middle Watch, The 1939 d: Thomas Bentley. lps: Jack Buchanan, Greta Gynt, Fred Emney. 87M UKN. prod/rel: Associated British Picture Corporation
The Midshipmaid, London 1931, Play
   Midshipmaid, The 1932 d: Albert de Courville. lps: Jessie Matthews, Fred Kerr, Basil Sydney. 84M UKN. *Midshipmaid Gob* (USA) prod/rel: Gaumont, Woolf & Freedman
Off the Record, London 1947, Play
   Carry on Admiral 1957 d: Val Guest. lps: David Tomlinson, Peggy Cummins, Brian Reece. 82M UKN. *The Ship Was Loaded* (USA) prod/rel: George Minter, Renown

KINGMAN, LAWRENCE
His Majesty O'Keefe, 1950, Novel
   His Majesty O'Keefe 1954 d: Byron Haskin. lps: Burt Lancaster, Joan Rice, Andre Morell. 90M UKN/USA. prod/rel: Warner Bros., First National

KINGSLEY, CHARLES (1819–1875), UKN
The Sands of Dee, Poem
   Sands of Dee, The 1912 d: D. W. Griffith. lps: Mae Marsh, Claire McDowell, Charles Hill Mailes. SHT USA. prod/rel: Biograph Co.
The Three Fishers, Poem
   Unchanging Sea, The 1910 d: D. W. Griffith. lps: Linda Arvidson, Arthur Johnson, Gladys Egan. 952f USA. prod/rel: Biograph Co.
The Water Babies, 1863, Novel
   Water Babies; Or, the Little Chimney Sweep, The 1907 d: Percy Stow. 955f UKN. prod/rel: Clarendon
   Water Babies, The 1979 d: Lionel Jeffries. lps: James Mason, Billie Whitelaw, Joan Greenwood. 95M UKN/PLN. *Dzieci Wodne* (PLN); *Slip Slide Adventures* prod/rel: Ariadne, Studio Miniatur Filmowych
Westward Ho!, 1855, Novel
   Westward Ho! 1919 d: Percy Nash. lps: Renee Kelly, Charles Quartermaine, Eric Harrison. 6000f UKN. prod/rel: Master Films, British Exhibitors' Films

KINGSLEY, FLORENCE MORSE
Short Story
Sloth 1917 d: Theodore Marston. lps: Charlotte Walker, Jack Meredith, D. J. Flannigan. 5r USA. prod/rel: Mcclure Pictures, Inc., Triangle Distributing Corp.

An Alabaster Box, New York 1917, Novel
Alabaster Box, An 1917 d: Chet Withey. lps: Alice Joyce, Marc McDermott, Harry Ham. 5r USA. prod/rel: Vitagraph Co. of America©, Blue Ribbon Feature

Hurrying Fate and Geraldine, New York 1913, Novel
Cupid Forecloses 1919 d: David Smith. lps: Bessie Love, Wallace MacDonald, Frank Hayes. 5r USA. *Cupid's Understudy* prod/rel: Vitagraph Co. of America©

To the Highest Bidder, New York 1911, Novel
To the Highest Bidder 1918 d: Tom Terriss. lps: Alice Joyce, Percy Standing, Walter McGrail. 4755f USA. prod/rel: Vitagraph Co. of America©, Blue Ribbon Feature

KINGSLEY, MICHAEL
Shadow Over Alveron, Novel
Shadow Over Elveron 1968 d: James Goldstone. lps: James Franciscus, Leslie Nielsen, Shirley Knight. TVM. 100M USA. prod/rel: Universal

KINGSLEY, PIERCE
Deserted at the Altar, 1922, Play
Deserted at the Altar 1922 d: William K. Howard, Albert Kelley. lps: Tully Marshall, Bessie Love, William Scott. 6850f USA. prod/rel: Phil Goldstone Productions

Silver Threads Among the Gold, Story
Silver Threads Among the Gold 1911 d: Edwin S. Porter. lps: Mabel Trunnelle, Robert Brower, Ben Wilson. 500f USA. prod/rel: Edison

Tracy the Outlaw, Play
Tracy the Outlaw 1928 d: Otis B. Thayer. lps: Jack Hoey, Rose Chadwick, Dave Marrell. 6400f USA. prod/rel: Foto Art Productions, New-Cal Film Corp.

KINGSLEY, SIDNEY
Dead End, New York 1936, Play
Dead End 1937 d: William Wyler. lps: Sylvia Sidney, Joel McCrea, Humphrey Bogart. 95M USA. prod/rel: Samuel Goldwyn, Inc., United Artists

Detective Story, New York 1949, Play
Detective Story 1951 d: William Wyler. lps: Kirk Douglas, Eleanor Parker, William Bendix. 103M USA. prod/rel: Paramount

Homecoming, Book
Homecoming 1948 d: Mervyn Leroy. lps: Clark Gable, Lana Turner, Anne Baxter. 113M USA. prod/rel: MGM

Men in White, New York 1933, Play
Men in White 1934 d: Richard Boleslawski. lps: Clark Gable, Myrna Loy, Jean Hersholt. 80M USA. prod/rel: Metro-Goldwyn-Mayer Corp.©
Men in White 1960 d: Don Richardson. lps: Richard Basehart. MTV. USA. prod/rel: CBS

KING-SMITH, DICK
The Sheep-Pig, Novel
Babe 1995 d: Chris Noonan. lps: James Cromwell, Magda Szubanski, Zoe Burton. 94M ASL. *Babe the Gallant Pig* prod/rel: Universal, Kennedy-Miller

KINGSTON, JEROME
Sinners All, Novel
Help Yourself 1932 d: John Daumery. lps: Benita Hume, Martin Walker, D. A. Clarke-Smith. 74M UKN. prod/rel: Warner Bros.-First National, Warner Bros.
Soir Des Rois, Le 1932 d: John Daumery. lps: Jacques Maury, Pierre Juvenet, Simone Mareuil. 74M FRN. *Soyez Les Bienvenus* prod/rel: Warner Bros., First National

KINKEAD, CLEVES
Common Clay, Boston 1915, Play
Common Clay 1919 d: George Fitzmaurice. lps: Fannie Ward, William E. Lawrence, Fred Goodwins. 7r USA. prod/rel: Astra Film Corp., Pathe Exchange, Inc.©
Common Clay 1930 d: Victor Fleming. lps: Constance Bennett, Lew Ayres, Tully Marshall. 7961f USA. prod/rel: Fox Film Corp.
Private Number 1936 d: Roy Del Ruth. lps: Robert Taylor, Loretta Young, Patsy Kelly. 79M USA. *Secret Interlude* (UKN); *Confessions of a Servant Girl* prod/rel: Twentieth Century-Fox Film Corp.©

KINSELLA, FRANK
Bred in the Bone, Story
Bred in the Bone 1915 d: Paul Powell. lps: Dorothy Gish, George Beranger, Margery Wilson. 4r USA. prod/rel: Reliance Motion Picture Corp., Mutual Film Corp.

KINSELLA, W. P.
Shoeless Joe, Book
Field of Dreams 1989 d: Phil Alden Robinson. lps: Kevin Costner, Amy Madigan, Gaby Hoffman. 106M USA. *Shoeless Joe* prod/rel: Universal

KIOSTEROD, ERLAND
Hotel St. Pauli, Novel
Hotel St. Pauli 1988 d: Petter Vennerod, Svend Wam. lps: Amanda Ooms, Oyvin Berven, John Ege. 108M NRW. prod/rel: Mefistofilm

KIPLING, RUDYARD (1865–1936), UKN
Captains Courageous, London 1897, Novel
Captains Courageous 1937 d: Victor Fleming. lps: Spencer Tracy, Freddie Bartholomew, Melvyn Douglas. 118M USA. prod/rel: Metro-Goldwyn-Mayer Corp.
Captains Courageous 1977 d: Harvey Hart. lps: Karl Malden, Jonathan Kahn, Johnny Doran. TVM. 100M USA. prod/rel: Norman Rosemont Productions

The City of Terrible Night, Short Story
City of Terrible Night, The 1915 d: George A. Lessey. lps: King Baggot. 2r USA. prod/rel: Imp

A Fool There Was, Poem
Fool, The 1913 d: George Pearson. lps: Godfrey Tearle, Mary Malone, James Carew. 3343f UKN. prod/rel: Big Ben Films, Union

Gunga Din, 1890, Poem
Gunga Din 1939 d: George Stevens. lps: Cary Grant, Victor McLaglen, Douglas Fairbanks Jr. 119M USA. prod/rel: RKO Radio Pictures©

His Apologies, 1932, Poem
His Apologies 1935 d: Widgey R. Newman. lps: Moore Marriott, Violet Hopson. 18M UKN. prod/rel: Westanmor, Famous

The Jungle Book
Bestia Umana, La 1916 d: Leopoldo Carlucci. lps: Dora White, Angelo Vianello, Elda Bruni-De Negri. 1500m ITL.

Kim, 1901, Novel
Kim 1950 d: Victor Saville. lps: Errol Flynn, Dean Stockwell, Paul Lukas. 113M USA. prod/rel: MGM
Kim 1984 d: John Davies. lps: Peter O'Toole, Bryan Brown, John Rhys-Davies. TVM. 150M USA/UKN. prod/rel: CBS, London Films

The King's Ankus, 1895, Short Story
Rudyard Kipling's Jungle Book 1942 d: Zoltan KordA. lps: Sabu, Joseph Calleia, John Qualen. 109M USA. *The Jungle Book* (UKN) prod/rel: United Artists

The Light That Failed, New York 1890, Novel
Light That Failed, The 1916 d: Edward Jose. lps: Robert Edeson, Jose Collins, Lillian Tucker. 5r USA. prod/rel: Feature Film Corp., Pathe Exchange, Inc.©
Light That Failed, The 1923 d: George Melford. lps: Jacqueline Logan, Percy Marmont, David Torrence. 7013f USA. prod/rel: Famous Players-Lasky, Paramount Pictures
Light That Failed, The 1939 d: William A. Wellman. lps: Ronald Colman, Walter Huston, Ida Lupino. 97M USA. prod/rel: Paramount Pictures©, William Wellman Production
Luce Che Si Spegne, La 1915 d: Umberto Paradisi. lps: Nello Carotenuto, Mario Cimarra, Laura Darville. ITL. prod/rel: Pasquali E C.
Lumiere Qui S'eteint, La 1917 d: Louis J. Gasnier. lps: Leon Mathot. FRN. prod/rel: Pathe Freres

The Man Who Would Be King, 1888, Short Story
Man Who Would Be King, The 1975 d: John Huston. lps: Sean Connery, Michael Caine, Christopher Plummer. 128M USA. prod/rel: Royal Service Company

Naulahka; a Story of West and East, London 1892, Novel
Naulahka, The 1918 d: George Fitzmaurice. lps: Antonio Moreno, Doraldina, Helene Chadwick. 6r USA. prod/rel: Astra Film Corp., Pathe Exchange, Inc.©

Rikki-Tikki-Tavi, Novel
Rikki-Tikki-Tavi 1975 d: Alexander Zguridi. lps: Margarita Terechova, Alexei Batalov, Igor Alekseyev. 70M USS. *Riky-Tiky-Tavy* prod/rel: Zentrnaucfilm

The Second Jungle Book, Book
Rudyard Kipling's the Second Jungle Book: Mowgli and Baloo 1997 d: Duncan McLachlan. lps: James Williams, Bill Campbell, Roddy McDowall. 88M USA. prod/rel: Raju Patel, Tristar Pictures

Soldiers Three, 1888, Short Story
Soldiers Three 1911 d: George D. Baker. lps: John Bunny, William Shea, Sidney Bracey. SHT USA. prod/rel: Vitagraph Co. of America
Soldiers Three 1951 d: Tay Garnett. lps: Stewart Granger, Walter Pidgeon, David Niven. 92M USA. prod/rel: MGM

Toomai of the Elephants, 1894, Short Story
Elephant Boy 1937 d: Robert Flaherty, Zoltan KordA. lps: Sabu, Walter Hudd, Allan Jeayes. 80M UKN. prod/rel: London Films, United Artists

The Vampire, New York 1897, Poem
Fool There Was, A 1915 d: Frank Powell. lps: Theda Bara, Edward Jose, Runa Hodges. 6r USA. *The Vampire* prod/rel: William Fox Vaudeville Co., Box Office Attraction Co.
Vampire of the Desert, The 1913. lps: Helen Gardner, Flora Finch, Tefft Johnson. 2000f USA. prod/rel: Vitagraph Co. of America
Vampire, The 1910. 1000f USA. prod/rel: Selig Polyscope Co.

Wee Willie Winkie, 1888, Short Story
Wee Willie Winkie 1937 d: John Ford. lps: Shirley Temple, Victor McLaglen, June Lang. 105M USA. prod/rel: Twentieth Century-Fox Film Corp.©

Without Benefit of Clergy, New York 1899, Novel
Without Benefit of Clergy 1921 d: James Young. lps: Virginia Brown Faire, Thomas Holding, Evelyn Selbie. 5200f USA. prod/rel: Robert Brunton Productions, Pathe Exchange, Inc.

KIRK, JEREMY
The Build-Up Boys, New York 1951, Novel
Madison Avenue 1962 d: H. Bruce Humberstone. lps: Dana Andrews, Eleanor Parker, Jeanne Crain. 94M USA. prod/rel: Twentieth Century-Fox Film Corporation

KIRK, RALPH G.
Malloy Campeador, 1921, Short Story
Scrapper, The 1922 d: Hobart Henley. lps: Herbert Rawlinson, Gertrude Olmstead, Welsh. 4491f USA. prod/rel: Universal Film Mfg. Co.

United States Flavor, 1914, Short Story
Men of Steel 1926 d: George Archainbaud. lps: Milton Sills, Doris Kenyon, May Allison. 9143f USA. prod/rel: First National Pictures

KIRKBRIDE, RONALD DE LEVINGTON
A Girl Named Tamiko, New York 1959, Novel
Girl Named Tamiko, A 1962 d: John Sturges. lps: Laurence Harvey, France Nuyen, Martha Hyer. 110M USA. prod/rel: Hal Wallis Productions, Paramount

KIRKEGAARD, OLE LUND
Short Story
Otto Er Et Naesehorn 1982 d: Rumle Hammerich. lps: Kristjan Markersen, Erik Petersen, Axel Strobye. 87M DNM. *Otto the Rhino; Otto Is a Rhino* prod/rel: Metronome, Danish Film Institute

Hodja Fra Pjort, Novel
Hodja Fra Pjort 1986 d: Brita WielopolskA. lps: David Bertelsen, Zuhal Ozdemir, Lars Junggren. 76M DNM. *Hodja from Pjort* prod/rel: Metronome, Danske Filminstitutet

KIRKLAND, WINNIFRED A.
Luella's Love Story, Story
Luella's Love Story 1913 d: L. Rogers Lytton, James Young. lps: Julia Swayne Gordon, Tefft Johnson, Mary Maurice. 1000f USA. prod/rel: Vitagraph Co. of America

KIRKPATRICK, JOHN ALEXANDER
Ada Beats the Drum, New York 1930, Play
Mama Steps Out 1937 d: George B. Seitz. lps: Alice Brady, Betty Furness, Ivan Lebedeff. 71M USA. *Burnt Fingers* prod/rel: Metro-Goldwyn-Mayer Corp.©

The Book of Charm, New York 1925, Play
Boy Friend, The 1926 d: Monta Bell. lps: Marceline Day, John Harron, George K. Arthur. 5584f USA. prod/rel: Metro-Goldwyn-Mayer Pictures

KIRKWOOD, JAMES
A Chorus Line, Play
Chorus Line, A 1985 d: Richard Attenborough. lps: Michael Douglas, Terrence Mann, Alyson Reed. 118M USA. prod/rel: Columbia, Embassy Film Associates

Some Kind of Hero, Novel
Some Kind of Hero 1982 d: Michael Pressman. lps: Richard Pryor, Margot Kidder, Ray Sharkey. 97M USA. prod/rel: Paramount

KIRST, HANS HELLMUT
08/15, Novel
08/15 I 1954 d: Paul May. lps: Joachim Fuchsberger, Eva-Ingeborg Scholz, Paul Bosinger. 95M GRM. *Null-Acht-Fuffzehn* prod/rel: Divina, Gloria

08/15 - II. Teil, Novel
08/15 II 1955 d: Paul May. lps: Hans Christian Blech, O. E. Hasse, Joachim Fuchsberger. 110M GRM. prod/rel: Divina, Gloria

08/15 - in Der Heimat, Novel
08/15 in Der Heimat 1955 d: Paul May. lps: O. E. Hasse, Gustav Knuth, Hans Christian Blech. 96M GRM. *08/15 Back Home* prod/rel: Divina, Gloria

Fabrik Der Offiziere, Novel
Fabrik Der Offiziere 1960 d: Frank Wisbar. lps: Carl Lange, Helmut Griem, Erik Schumann. 96M GRM. *The Officer Factory* prod/rel: D.F.H.
Fabrik Der Offiziere 1988 d: Wolf Vollmar. lps: Manfred Zapatka, Karl-Heinz Diess, Thomas Holzmann. 119M GRM/CZC. *The 20th of July* prod/rel: Mondara-Film, Filmove Studio Barrandov

Die Nacht Der Generale, Munich 1962, Novel
Night of the Generals, The 1966 d: Anatole Litvak. lps: Peter O'Toole, Omar Sharif, Tom Courtenay. 147M UKN/FRN. *La Nuit Des Generaux* (FRN) prod/rel: Horizon Pictures, Filmsonor

KIRSTEIN, LINCOLN
Lay This Laurel, Book
Glory 1989 d: Edward Zwick. lps: Matthew Broderick, Denzel Washington, Cary Elwes. 122M USA. prod/rel: Tri-Star

KISCH, EGON ERWIN
Nanebevstoupeni Tonky Sibenice, Short Story
Tonka Sibenice 1930 d: Karl Anton. lps: Ita Rina, Vera Baranovskaja, Josef Rovensky. 2312m CZC. *Tonka -Tart of the Gallows Mob; Tonka of the Gallows* prod/rel: Karl Anton, Elekta

Pasak Holek, Novel
Pasak Holek 1929 d: Hans Tintner. lps: Werner Fuetterer, Josef Rovensky, Bozena SvobodovA. 1652m CZC. *The Pimp* prod/rel: Ab, la Tricolore

KISHIDA, KUNIO
Izumi, 1939, Novel
Izumi 1956 d: Masaki Kobayashi. lps: Keiji SadA. 129M JPN. *The Fountainhead; The Fountain; The Spring*

Shu-U, 1926, Play
Shuu 1956 d: Mikio Naruse. 91M JPN. *Sudden Rain; Shu-U*

Zenma, 1951, Novel
Zenma 1951 d: Keisuke KinoshitA. 108M JPN. *The Good Fairy; Zemma; The Good Demon*

KISHON, EPHRAIM
Der Blaumilchkanal, Novel
Blaumilchkanal, Der 1969 d: Ephraim Kishon. lps: Bomba Zur, Nissim Azikri, Shraga Friedman. 90M GRM/ISR. *Canal of Blue Milk* prod/rel: Sender Freies Berlin, Canal

KISTEMAECKERS, HENRI
La Blessure, 1900, Play
Blessure, La 1922 d: Roberto Leone Roberti. lps: Francesca Bertini, Giorgio Bonaiti, Mary Fleuron. 1745m ITL. *La Ferita* prod/rel: Francesca Bertini

L' Embuscade, Play
Embuscade, L' 1939 d: Fernand Rivers. lps: Georges Rollin, Jules Berry, Valentine Tessier. 90M FRN. prod/rel: Films Fernand Rivers

La Flambee, 1911, Play
Fiammata, La 1922 d: Carmine Gallone. lps: Soava Gallone, Andrea Habay, Alfredo Martinelli. 1576m ITL. *The Turning Point* (UKN) prod/rel: Caesar Film
Fiammata, La 1952 d: Alessandro Blasetti. lps: Amedeo Nazzari, Eleonora Rossi-Drago, Elisa Cegani. 100M ITL. *Pride Love and Suspicion* prod/rel: Cines, Excelsa Film
Flambee, La 1934 d: Jean de Marguenat. lps: Constant Remy, Jacques Gretillat, Suzanne Rissler. 82M FRN. prod/rel: Europa-Films

L' Instinct, Play
Instinct, L' 1916 d: Henri Pouctal. lps: Raphael Duflos, Jean Marie de L'isle, Huguette Duflos. 1545m FRN. prod/rel: Eclectic
Instinct, L' 1929 d: Leon Mathot, Andre Liabel. lps: Madeleine Carroll, Leon Mathot, Irene Brillant. F FRN. prod/rel: Paris International Films

Le Marchand de Bonheur, Play
Marchand de Bonheur, Le 1918 d: Georges-Andre Lacroix. lps: Leon Mathot, Marc Gerard, Suzy Prim. FRN. prod/rel: le Film d'Art
Marchand de Bonheur, Le 1927 d: Joseph Guarino. lps: Georges Melchior, Rita Jolivet, Genevieve Gargese. 2200m FRN. prod/rel: Monat-Film

Marthe, Play
Marthe 1919 d: Gaston Roudes. lps: Pierre Magnier, Paulette Duval, Berthe Jalabert. 1625m FRN. prod/rel: Gallo Film

La Nuit Est a Nous, Play
Nuit Est a Nous, La 1929 d: Henry Roussell, Carl Froelich. lps: Henry Roussell, Marie Bell, Mary Costes. F FRN. *The Night Is Ours* prod/rel: Films P.J. De Venloo, Carl Froelich Film
Nuit Est a Nous, La 1953 d: Jean Stelli. lps: Jean Danet, Simone Renant, Jean Debucourt. 90M FRN. prod/rel: Henri Ullman, C.N.C.

L' Occident, Paris 1913, Play
Eye for Eye 1918 d: Albert Capellani. lps: Alla Nazimova, Charles Bryant, Donald Gallagher. 7r USA. prod/rel: Nazimova Productions, Metro Pictures Corp.©
Occident, L' 1928 d: Henri Fescourt. lps: Claudia Victrix, Jaque Catelain, Lucien Dalsace. 2000m FRN. prod/rel: Societe Des Cineromans, Films De France
Occident, L' 1937 d: Henri Fescourt. lps: Charles Vanel, Rama Tahe, Helene Robert. 100M FRN. prod/rel: Productions Claude Dolbert

Plein aux As, Short Story
Plein aux As 1933 d: Jacques Houssin. lps: Felicien Tramel, Romain Bouquet, Charlotte Clasis. 100M FRN. prod/rel: Equateur Film

Le Roi Des Palaces, Play
King of the Ritz 1932 d: Carmine Gallone. lps: Stanley Lupino, Betty Stockfeld, Hugh Wakefield. 81M UKN. prod/rel: Gainsborough, British Lion
Roi Des Palaces ,le 1932 d: Carmine Gallone. lps: Jules Berry, Betty Stockfeld, Simone Simon. 84M FRN. prod/rel: Societe Des Films Osso

Un Soir Au Front, Play
Soir Au Front, Un 1931 d: Alexandre Ryder. lps: Jeanne Boitel, Pierre Richard-Willm, Jean Debucourt. 84M FRN. prod/rel: Societe Des Films Osso

Woman of Bronze, Play
Woman of Bronze, The 1923 d: King Vidor. lps: Clara Kimball Young, John Bowers, Kathryn McGuire. 5643f USA. prod/rel: Samuel Zierler Photoplay Corp., Metro Pictures

KITAMURA, KOMATSU
Tokyo No Gassho, Novel
Tokyo No Gassho 1931 d: Yasujiro Ozu. lps: Tokihiko Okada, Rieko Yagume, Hideo SagawarA. 91M JPN. *The Chorus of Tokyo; Tokyo Chorus* prod/rel: Shochiku Co.

KIVI, ALEKSIS
Kihlaus, 1866, Play
Kihlaus 1922 d: Teuvo Puro. lps: Iisakki Lattu, Annie Mork, Martti TuukkA. 1150m FNL. *The Betrothal; Forlovningen* prod/rel: Suomi-Filmi
Kihlaus 1955 d: Erik Blomberg. lps: Hannes Hayrinen, Heimo Lepisto, Mirjami Kuosomanen. 78M FNL. *The Betrothal; Forlvningen* prod/rel: Kansan Elokuva

Nummisuutarit, 1864, Play
Nummisuutarit 1923 d: Erkki Karu. lps: Axel Slangus, Adolf Lindfors, Alarik Korhonen. 2100m FNL. *The Village Shoemakers; Sockenskomakarne* prod/rel: Suomi-Filmi
Nummisuutarit 1938 d: Wilho Ilmari. lps: Unto Salminen, Aku Korhonen, Suri Angerkoski. 117M FNL. *The Village Shoemakers; Sockenskomakarna* prod/rel: Suomen Filmiteollisuus
Nummisuutarit 1957 d: Valentin VaalA. lps: Martti Kuningas, Lauri Leino, Alice Lylyl. 93M FNL. *The Village Shoemakers; Sockenskomakarna* prod/rel: Suomi-Filmi

Seitseman Veljesta, 1870, Novel
Seitseman Veljesta 1939 d: Wilho Ilmari. lps: Edvin Laine, Eino Kaipainen, Kaarlo Kyto. 108M FNL. *Seven Brothers; Sju Broder* prod/rel: Suomen Filmiteollisuus

KJELGAARD, JAMES ARTHUR
Big Red, New York 1945, Novel
Big Red 1962 d: Norman Tokar. lps: Walter Pidgeon, Gilles Payant, Janette Bertrand. 89M USA. prod/rel: Walt Disney Productions, Buena Vista

KLABAN, HELEN
Hey I'm Alive!, Book
Hey, I'm Alive! 1975 d: Lawrence Schiller. lps: Edward Asner, Sally Struthers, Milton Selzer. TVM. 78M USA. prod/rel: Charles Fries Productions, Worldvision

KLANE, ROBERT
Fire Sale, Novel
Fire Sale 1977 d: Alan Arkin. lps: Alan Arkin, Rob Reiner, Vincent GardeniA. 87M USA. prod/rel: Marvin Worth

Where's Poppa?, Novel
Where's Poppa? 1970 d: Carl Reiner. lps: George Segal, Ruth Gordon, Trish Van Devere. 84M USA. *Going Ape* prod/rel: Where's Poppa Co., United Artists

KLAUSEN, GINA
Confessions of a Kept Woman, Novel
Let's Get Married 1960 d: Peter Graham Scott. lps: Anthony Newley, Anne Aubrey, Bernie Winters. 91M UKN. prod/rel: Eros, Viceroy

KLAUSNER, MARGOT
Story
Eshet Hagibor 1963 d: Peter Frye. lps: Batya Lancet, Gideon Shemer, Shmuel Omani. F ISR. *The Hero's Wife*

KLAVAN, ANDREW
True Crime, Novel
True Crime 1999 d: Clint Eastwood. lps: Clint Eastwood, Isaiah Washington, Denis Leary. 127M USA. prod/rel: Warner Bros., Zanuck Co.

KLECANDA, JAN
Adjunkt Vrba, Novel
Adjunkt Vrba 1929 d: M. J. Krnansky. lps: Karel Lamac, Karel Hasler, Jarmila LhotovA. 1000m CZC. *Vrba the Clerk* prod/rel: Fortunafilm, Rudolf Vancura

Pater Vojtech, Novel
Pater Vojtech 1928 d: Martin Fric. lps: Josef Rovensky, Karel Lamac, L. H. StrunA. 2336m CZC. *Father Vojtech* prod/rel: Bratri Deglove, Degl a Spol
Pater Vojtech 1936 d: Martin Fric. lps: Rolf Wanka, L. H. Struna, Jaroslav Marvan. 2803m CZC. *Father Vojtech* prod/rel: Ab

Sest Musketyru, Novel
Sest Musketyru 1925 d: Premysl Prazsky. lps: Karel Lamac, Eman Fiala, Jiri Hojer. 1554m CZC. *The Six Musketeers* prod/rel: Lloydfilm

Stary Hrich, Novel
Stary Hrich 1929 d: M. J. Krnansky. lps: Josef Rovensky, Melita Jelenska, Jarmila LhotovA. 2592m CZC. *The Sin of the Past* prod/rel: Jan Kyzour

KLEE, ERNST
Der Zappler, Novel
Zappler, Der 1982 d: Wolfram Deutschmann. lps: Karsten Kunitz, Nicolaj Niemann, Andreas Peter. 72M GRM. *The Twitcher* prod/rel: C & H, Sungen-Gruttgen

KLEIMAN, DENA
A Deadly Silence, Book
Deadly Silence, A 1989 d: John Patterson. lps: Mike Farrell, Heather Fairchild, Bruce Weitz. TVM. 100M USA. prod/rel: Robert Greenwald Productions

KLEIN, ALAN
What a Crazy World, Play
What a Crazy World 1963 d: Michael Carreras. lps: Joe Brown, Susan Maugham, Marty Wilde. 88M UKN. prod/rel: Capricorn, Warner-Pathe

KLEIN, ALEXANDER
The Counterfeit Traitor, New York 1958, Novel
Counterfeit Traitor, The 1962 d: George Seaton. lps: William Holden, Lilli Palmer, Hugh Griffith. 140M USA. prod/rel: Paramount, Perlberg-Seaton

KLEIN, CHARLES
The Auctioneer, New York 1913, Play
Auctioneer, The 1927 d: Alfred E. Green. lps: George Sidney, Marion Nixon, Gareth Hughes. 5500f USA. prod/rel: Fox Film Corp.

The Daughters of Men, New York 1906, Play
Daughters of Men, The 1914 d: George W. Terwilliger. lps: George Soule Spencer, Ethel Clayton, Percy Winter. 5r USA. prod/rel: Lubin Mfg. Co.©, General Film Co.

The District Attorney, New York 1895, Play
District Attorney, The 1915 d: Barry O'Neil. lps: A. H. Van Buren, Dorothy Bernard, George Soule Spencer. 5r USA. prod/rel: Lubin Mfg. Co.©, V-L-S-E, Inc.

The Gamblers, New York 1910, Play
Gamblers, The 1914 d: George W. Terwilliger. lps: Gaston Bell, George Soule Spencer, Ethel Clayton. 5r USA. prod/rel: Lubin Mfg. Co.©, General Film Co.
Gamblers, The 1919 d: Paul Scardon. lps: Harry T. Morey, Agnes Ayres, Charles Kent. 6r USA. prod/rel: Vitagraph Co. of America©
Gamblers, The 1929 d: Michael Curtiz. lps: H. B. Warner, Lois Wilson, Jason Robards. 6611f USA. prod/rel: Warner Brothers Pictures

Heartease, New York 1897, Play
Heartsease 1919 d: Harry Beaumont. lps: Tom Moore, Helene Chadwick, Larry Steers. 4950f USA. prod/rel: Goldwyn Pictures Corp.©, Goldwyn Distributing Corp.

The Lion and the Mouse, New York 1905, Play
Lion and the Mouse, The 1914 d: Barry O'Neil. lps: Ethel Clayton, Gaston Bell, Richard Morris. 6r USA. prod/rel: Lubin Mfg. Co.©, General Film Co.
Lion and the Mouse, The 1919 d: Tom Terriss. lps: Alice Joyce, Conrad Nagel, Anders Randolf. 5874f USA. prod/rel: Vitagraph Co. of America©

Maggie Pepper, New York 1911, Play
Maggie Pepper 1919 d: Chet Withey. lps: Ethel Clayton, Elliott Dexter, Winnifred Greenwood. 4426f USA. prod/rel: Famous Players-Lasky Corp.©, Paramount Pictures

The Music Master, Novel
Music Master, The 1927 d: Allan Dwan. lps: Alec B. Francis, Lois Moran, Neil Hamilton. 7754f USA. prod/rel: Fox Film Corp.

The Third Degree, New York 1909, Play
Third Degree, The 1914 d: Barry O'Neil. lps: Bernard Siegel, Gaston Bell, George Soule Spencer. 5r USA. prod/rel: Lubin Mfg. Co.©, General Film Co.

Third Degree, The 1919 d: Tom Terriss. lps: Alice Joyce, Gladden James, Anders Randolf. 6-7r USA. prod/rel: Vitagraph Co. of America©

Third Degree, The 1926 d: Michael Curtiz. lps: Dolores Costello, Louise Dresser, Rockliffe Fellowes. 7647f USA. prod/rel: Warner Brothers Pictures

KLEIN, EDUARD
Severino, Novel
Severino 1977 d: Claus Dobberke. lps: Gojko Mitic, Violeta Andrei, Mircea Anghelescu. 80M GDR. prod/rel: Defa

KLEIN, ERNEST
At the End of the World, Play
At the End of the World 1921 d: Penrhyn Stanlaws. lps: Betty Compson, Milton Sills, Mitchell Lewis. 5729f USA. prod/rel: Famous Players-Lasky Corp., Paramount Pictures

KLEIN, ERNST
Die Dame Mit Dem Tigerfell, Novel
Dame Mit Dem Tigerfell, Die 1927 d: Willi Wolff. lps: Ellen Richter, Mary Kid, Georg Alexander. 2436m GRM. prod/rel: Ellen Richter-Film

Kampfer, Novel
Liebesreigen 1927 d: Rudolf Walther-Fein. lps: Claire Rommer, Marcella Albani, Wilhelm Dieterle. 2450m GRM. prod/rel: Aafa-Film Ag

Madame Circe, Novel
Schonste Frau von Paris, Die 1928 d: Jacob Fleck, Luise Fleck. lps: Elga Brink, Werner Fuetterer, Warwick Ward. 2162m GRM. prod/rel: Orplid-Film

Muz Bez Srdce, Novel
Mann Ohne Herz, Der 1923 d: Franz W. Koebner, Josef Hornak. lps: Lotte Neumann, Karel Lamac, Luigi Serventi. 2291m GRM/CZC. *Muz Bez Srdce*; *Man Without a Heart* prod/rel: Moldavia

Nuttchen, Novel
Eva in Seide 1928 d: Carl Boese. lps: Lissi Arna, Walter Rilla, Margarete Kupfer. 3006m GRM. prod/rel: Carl Boese-Film

Trust Der Diebe, Novel
Trust Der Diebe 1929 d: Erich Schonfelder. lps: Agnes Esterhazy, Paul Otto, Eva von Berne. 2290m GRM. prod/rel: Nero-Film Ag

KLEIN, JOE
Primary Colors, Novel
Primary Colors 1998 d: Mike Nichols. lps: John Travolta, Emma Thompson, Billy Bob Thornton. 143M USA. prod/rel: Universal Pictures, Mutual Film Co.

KLEIN, JOHN
T-Bone 'N Weasel, Novel
T-Bone 'N Weasel 1992 d: Lewis Teague. lps: Gregory Hines, Christopher Lloyd, Ned Beatty. 93M USA.

KLEIN, NORMA
Novel
Mom, the Wolfman and Me 1980 d: Edmond Levy. lps: Patty Duke, David Birney, Keenan Wynn. TVM. 104M USA. prod/rel: Timelife

KLEINE, DOROTHEA
In Namen Der Unschuld, Novel
In Namen Der Unschuld 1997 d: Andreas Kleinert. lps: Barbara Sukowa, Matthias Habich, Udo Samel. 104M GRM. *In the Name of the Innocent* prod/rel: Tele-Munchen Film, Ferehproduktion-Rtl 2

KLEPPER, JOCHEN
Der Kahn Der Frohlichen Leute, Novel
Kahn Der Frohlichen Leute, Der 1950 d: Hans Heinrich. lps: Petra Peters, Fritz Wagner, Paul Esser. 89M GRM. prod/rel: Defa

KLICPERA, IVAN
Jindra - Hrabenka Ostrovinova, Novel
Jindra 1919 d: Oldrich Kminek. lps: Nina Lausmanova, Karel Schleichert, Oldrich Kminek. CZC. prod/rel: Tcheco, la Tricolore

Jindra, Hrabenka Ostrovinova 1924 d: Vaclav Kubasek. lps: Mary Jansova, Gitta d'Amaro, Frantisek Havel. 1786m CZC. *Jindra -Countess of Ostrovin* prod/rel: Pronax-Film, Biografia

Jindra, Hrabenka Ostrovinova 1933 d: Carl Lamac. lps: Jarmila Lhotova, Theodor Pistek, Ruzena SlemrovA. 2319m CZC. *Jindra -the Countess Ostrovin* prod/rel: Lloyd

KLIER, HEINRICH
Bergwind, Novel
Bergwind 1964 d: Eduard von Borsody. lps: Alwy Becker, Hans von Borsody, Wolf Albach-Retty. 88M AUS. *Nur Der Himmel Uber Uns* prod/rel: Benesch

KLIMA, IVAN
En Karleks Sommar, Novel
Karleks Sommar, En 1979 d: Mats Arehn. lps: Gosta Ekman, Maria Andersson, Anita Ekstrom. 101M SWD. *A Summer's Love* prod/rel: Nordisk Tonefilm, Svensk Filmindustri

KLINER, HARRY
The Faceless Man, 1966, Play
Counterfeit Killer, The 1968 d: Joseph Leytes, Stuart Rosenberg. lps: Jack Lord, Shirley Knight, Jack Weston. 95M USA. *Crackshot*; *The Faceless Man* prod/rel: Universal

KLINGTON, MIRIAM
Il Tempio Del Sacrificio, Novel
Tempio Del Sacrificio, Il 1920 d: Luigi Mele. lps: Celio Bucchi, Antonietta Calderari, Raoul Cini. 1520m ITL. prod/rel: Latina-Ars

KLITGAARD, MOGENS
Elly Petersen, 1941, Novel
Elly Petersen 1944 d: Alice O'Fredericks, Jon Iversen. 104M DNM.

KLOEPPFFER, WALTHER
Fogg Bringt Ein Madchen Mit, Novel
Drei Vater Um Anna 1939 d: Carl Boese. lps: Ilse Werner, Hans Stuwe, Theodor Danegger. 87M GRM. *Three Fathers for Anna* (USA) prod/rel: UFA

KLOREN, GEORG
Spione Am Werk, Novel
On Secret Service 1933 d: Arthur Woods. lps: Greta Nissen, Carl Ludwig Diehl, Don Alvarado. 91M UKN. *Secret Agent* (USA); *Spy 77* prod/rel: British International Pictures, Wardour

KLORER, JOHN D.
Gay Deception, Story
Pretty Baby 1950 d: Bretaigne Windust. lps: Betsy Drake, Dennis Morgan, Zachary Scott. 92M USA. prod/rel: Warner Bros.

Southwest Pass, Story
Seven Miles from Alcatraz 1942 d: Edward Dmytryk. lps: James Craig, Bonita Granville, Frank Jenks. 62M USA. prod/rel: RKO Radio

KLOSTERMANN, KAREL
Mlhy Na Blatech, Novel
Mlhy Na Blatech 1943 d: Frantisek Cap. lps: Zdenek Stepanek, Marie Blazkova, Vladimir Salac. 2512m CZC. *Mist Over the Swamps*; *Mist in the Moorland* prod/rel: Lucernafilm

Pozdni Laska, Novel
Pozdni Laska 1935 d: Vaclav Kubasek. lps: Jan W. Speerger, Jirina Steimarova, Stanislav Neumann. 2698m CZC. *Belated Love* prod/rel: Fortunafilm, Ringler

Ze Sveta Lesnich Samot, Novel
Ze Sveta Lesnich Samot 1933 d: M. J. Krnansky. lps: J. O. Martin, Marlis Ginalska, Alexander Trebovsky. 1903m CZC. *From the World of Wood Cottages*; *For Forest Loneliness*; *From the World of Forest Solitude* prod/rel: Beda Heller

KLOTZ, CLAUDE
Dracua Pere Et Fils, Novel
Dracula Pere Et Fils 1976 d: Edouard Molinaro. lps: Christopher Lee, Bernard Menez, Marie-Helene Breillat. 96M FRN. *Dracula and Son* (USA) prod/rel: Gaumont International, Produktion 2000

KLUGE, ALEXANDER
Anita G, 1962, Short Story
Abschied von Gestern 1966 d: Alexander Kluge. lps: Alexandra Kluge, Hans Korte, Eva Marie Neinecke. 88M GRM. *Yesterday Girl* (USA) prod/rel: Kairos Film, Independent

KLUGE, KURT
Die Zaubergeige, 1940, Novel
Zaubergeige, Die 1944 d: Herbert Maisch. lps: Will Quadflieg, Gisela Uhlen, Eugen Klopfer. 100M GRM. prod/rel: Berlin, Astor

KLUGE, P. F.
Eddie and the Cruisers, Novel
Eddie and the Cruisers 1984 d: Martin Davidson. lps: Tom Berenger, Michael Pare, Joe Pantoliano. 92M USA. prod/rel: Embassy Pictures, Aurora

KLUGER, JEFFREY
Lost Moon, Book
Apollo 13 1995 d: Ron Howard. lps: Tom Hanks, Bill Paxton, Kevin Bacon. 140M USA. prod/rel: Imagine

KLURFELD, HERMAN
Walter Winchell: His Life and Times, Book
Winchell 1998 d: Paul Mazursky. lps: Stanley Tucci, Glenne Headly, Paul Giamatti. TV1. 105M USA. prod/rel: Fried Films, Hbo Pictures

KNAPP, GEORGE L.
La Terribula, Short Story
Lost Souls 1916. USA. prod/rel: Roland West Film Corp.©

La Terribula, 1915, Short Story
Woman's Honor, A 1916 d: Roland West. lps: Jose Collins, Arthur Donaldson, Mrs. Cecil Raleigh. 5r USA. prod/rel: Fox Film Corp., William Fox©

KNAPP, PENELOPE
Marcene, Novel
Broken Butterfly, The 1919 d: Maurice Tourneur. lps: Lew Cody, Mary Alden, Pauline Starke. 5r USA. prod/rel: Maurice Tourneur Productions, Robertson-Cole Distributing Corp.

KNEALE, NIGEL (1922–, UKN
The Creature, Television Play
Abominable Snowman, The 1957 d: Val Guest. lps: Forrest Tucker, Peter Cushing, Maureen Connell. 91M UKN. *The Abominable Snowman of the Himalayas* (USA) prod/rel: Warner Bros., Hammer

KNEBEL, FLETCHER
The Enemy Within, Novel
Enemy Within, The 1994 d: Jonathan Darby. lps: Forest Whitaker, Jason Robards Jr., Sam Waterston. TVM. 100M USA. prod/rel: Vincent Picture Productions, Home Box Office

Seven Days in May, New York 1962, Novel
Seven Days in May 1964 d: John Frankenheimer. lps: Burt Lancaster, Kirk Douglas, Ava Gardner. 120M USA. prod/rel: Seven Arts Productions, Joel Productions

Vanished, Novel
Vanished 1971 d: Buzz Kulik. lps: Richard Widmark, Skye Aubrey, Tom Bosley. TVM. 200M USA. prod/rel: Universal

KNECHTL-OSTENBURG, FRITZ
Abenteuer in Budapest, Novel
Sonnenschein un Wolkenbruch 1955 d: Rudolf Nussgruber. lps: Susi Nicoletti, Jester Naefe, Loni Heuser. 88M AUS. prod/rel: Wien

KNEPLER, PAUL
The Dubarry, Opera
I Give My Heart 1935 d: Marcel Varnel. lps: Gitta Alpar, Patrick Waddington, Owen Nares. 91M UKN. *The Loves of Madame Dubarry* (USA); *The Dubarry* prod/rel: British International Pictures, Wardour

KNIBBS, HENRY HERBERT
Overland Red, Boston 1914, Novel
Overland Red 1920 d: Lynn Reynolds. lps: Harry Carey, Vola Vale, Charles Le Moyne. 6r USA. prod/rel: Universal Film Mfg. Co.©

Sunset Trail, The 1924 d: Ernst Laemmle. lps: William Desmond, Gareth Hughes, Lucille Hutton. 4920f USA. prod/rel: Universal Pictures

The Ridin' Kid from Powder River, Story
Mounted Stranger, The 1930 d: Arthur Rosson. lps: Hoot Gibson, Louise Lorraine, Francis Ford. 65M USA. prod/rel: Universal Pictures

Ridin' Kid from Powder River, The 1924 d: Edward Sedgwick. lps: Hoot Gibson, Gladys Hulette, Gertrude Astor. 5727f USA. *The Saddle Hawk* prod/rel: Universal Pictures

Sundown Slim, Boston 1915, Novel
Burning Trail, The 1925 d: Arthur Rosson. lps: William Desmond, Albert J. Smith, Mary McIvor. 4783f USA. prod/rel: Universal Pictures

Sundown Slim 1920 d: Val Paul. lps: Harry Carey, Otto Meyers, Ed Jones. 5r USA. prod/rel: Universal Film Mfg. Co.©

Unbroken Promise, The 1919 d: Frank Powell. lps: Jane Miller, Sidney Mason, Billy Human. 5r USA. prod/rel: Sunset Pictures Corp., Triangle Distributing Corp.

KNIGHT, ERIC (1897–1943), UKN
Lassie Come Home, 1940, Novel
Gypsy Colt 1953 d: Andrew Marton. lps: Donna Corcoran, Ward Bond, Frances Dee. 72M USA. prod/rel: MGM

Lassie Come Home 1943 d: Fred M. Wilcox. lps: Roddy McDowall, Donald Crisp, Dame May Whitty. 88M USA. prod/rel: MGM

KNIGHT, HARRY ADAM
Beyond Bedlam, Novel
Beyond Bedlam 1993 d: Vadim Jean. lps: Craig Fairbrass, Elizabeth Hurley, Keith Allen. 89M UKN. prod/rel: Feature Film, Metrodome

Carnosaur, Novel
Carnosaur 1993 d: Adam Simon. lps: Diane Ladd, Raphael Sbarge, Jennifer Runyon. 89M USA. prod/rel: New Horizons

KNIGHT, P.
Getting Together, New York 1918, Musical Play
Common Cause, The 1918 d: J. Stuart Blackton. lps: Herbert Rawlinson, Sylvia Breamer, Huntley Gordon. 7r USA. prod/rel: Blackton Productions, Inc.©, Vitagraph Co. of America

KNITTEL, JOHN
El Hakim, Novel
El Hakim 1957 d: Rolf Thiele. lps: O. W. Fischer, Robert Graf, Elisabeth Muller. 110M GRM. *El Hakim* prod/rel: Roxy, N.F.

Therese Etienne, 1927, Novel
Therese Etienne 1957 d: Denys de La Patelliere. lps: Francoise Arnoul, Pierre Vaneck, James Robertson Justice. 92M FRN/ITL/SWT. *Teresa Etienne* (ITL) prod/rel: Cite-Films (Paris), Monica Film (Roma)

Via Mala, Novel
Via Mala 1944 d: Josef von Baky. lps: Karin Hardt, Viktor Staal, Carl Wery. 108M GRM. *Die Strasse Des Bosen* prod/rel: UFA, Atlantic
Via Mala 1961 d: Paul May. lps: Gert Frobe, Joachim Hansen, Christine Kaufmann. 93M GRM. prod/rel: C.C.C., Gloria
Via Mala 1985 d: Tom Toelle. lps: Mario Adorf, Maruschka Detmers, Milena Vukotic. MTV. 275M GRM/FRN/AUS. prod/rel: Iduna, Mr-Film

Der Weg Durch Die Nacht, Novel
Weg Durch Die Nacht, Der 1929 d: Robert Dinesen. lps: Kathe von Nagy, Imre Raday, Margarethe Schon. GRM. prod/rel: Maxim-Film

KNITTELL, JOHN
Hidden Lives, Play
Verborgen Leven, Het 1920 d: Maurits H. Binger, B. E. Doxat-Pratt. lps: Adelqui Millar, Annie Bos, Renee Spiljar. 5000f NTH/UKN. *The Hidden Life* (UKN) prod/rel: Anglo-Hollandia Film

KNOBLOCK, EDWARD (1874–1945), UKN
Appearances, Play
Appearances 1921 d: Donald Crisp. lps: David Powell, Mary Glynne, Langhorne Burton. 5374f USA/UKN. prod/rel: Famous Players-Lasky British Producers, Paramount Pictures

Conchita, Play
Love Comes Along 1930 d: Rupert Julian. lps: Bebe Daniels, Lloyd Hughes, Montagu Love. 78M USA. prod/rel: RKO Productions

The Faun; Or Thereby Hangs a Tale, New York 1911, Play
Marriage Maker, The 1923 d: William C. de Mille. lps: Agnes Ayres, Jack Holt, Charles de Roche. 6295f USA. *The Faun; Spring Magic* prod/rel: Famous Players-Lasky, Paramount Pictures

The Headmaster, London 1913, Play
Headmaster, The 1921 d: Kenelm Foss. lps: Cyril Maude, Margot Drake, Miles Malleson. 5500f UKN. prod/rel: Astra Films

Kismet, London 1911, Play
Kismet 1914 d: Leedham Bantock. lps: Oscar Asche, Lily Brayton, Herbert Grimwood. 4000f UKN. prod/rel: Zenith
Kismet 1920 d: Louis J. Gasnier. lps: Otis Skinner, Rosemary Theby, Elinor Fair. 5r USA. prod/rel: Waldorf Film Corp., Robertson-Cole Distributing Corp.©
Kismet 1930 d: John Francis Dillon. lps: Otis Skinner, Loretta Young, David Manners. 90M USA. prod/rel: First National Pictures
Kismet 1931 d: William Dieterle. lps: Gustav Frohlich, Dita Parlo, Vladimir Sokoloff. F USA. prod/rel: First National Pictures
Kismet 1944 d: William Dieterle. lps: Marlene Dietrich, Edward Arnold, Ronald Colman. 100M USA. *Oriental Dreams* prod/rel: MGM
Kismet 1955 d: Vincente Minnelli, Stanley Donen (Uncredited). lps: Howard Keel, Ann Blyth, Dolores Gray. 113M USA. prod/rel: MGM

The Lullaby, New York 1923, Play
Sin of Madelon Claudet, The 1931 d: Edgar Selwyn. lps: Helen Hayes, Lewis Stone, Neil Hamilton. 74M USA. *The Lullaby* (UKN); *Lullaby* prod/rel: Metro-Goldwyn-Mayer Corp., Metro-Goldwyn-Mayer Dist. Corp.©

Milestones, London 1912, Play
Milestones 1916 d: Thomas Bentley. lps: Isobel Elsom, Owen Nares, Campbell Gullan. 8640f UKN. prod/rel: G. B. Samuelson, Moss
Milestones 1920 d: Paul Scardon. lps: Lewis Stone, Alice Hollister, Gertrude Robinson. 5782f USA. prod/rel: Goldwyn Pictures Corp.©, Goldwyn Distributing Corp.

Mumsie, Play
Mumsie 1927 d: Herbert Wilcox. lps: Pauline Frederick, Nelson Keys, Herbert Marshall. 6858f UKN. prod/rel: Herbert Wilcox, Woolf & Freedman

My Lady's Dress, London 1914, Play
Blind Wives 1920 d: Charles J. Brabin. lps: Marc MacDermott, Estelle Taylor, Harry Sothern. 9r USA. *My Lady's Dress* prod/rel: Fox Film Corp., William Fox©
My Lady's Dress 1917 d: Alexander Butler. lps: Gladys Cooper, Malcolm Cherry, Andre Beaulieu. 8516f UKN. prod/rel: G. B. Samuelson, Moss

The Shulamite, London 1906, Play
Shulamite, The 1915 d: George Loane Tucker. lps: Norman McKinnel, Manora Thew, Gerald Ames. 4805f UKN. prod/rel: London, Jury
Under the Lash 1921 d: Sam Wood. lps: Gloria Swanson, Mahlon Hamilton, Russell Simpson. 5675f USA. *The Shulamite* (UKN) prod/rel: Famous Players-Lasky, Paramount Pictures

Speakeasy, Story
Speakeasy 1929 d: Ben Stoloff. lps: Lola Lane, Paul Page, Sharon Lynn. 5775f USA. prod/rel: Fox Film Corp.

KNOTT, FREDERICK
Dial M for Murder, New York 1952, Play
Dial M for Murder 1954 d: Alfred Hitchcock. lps: Ray Milland, Grace Kelly, Robert Cummings. 105M USA. prod/rel: Warner Bros.
Dial M for Murder 1981 d: Boris Sagal. lps: Angie Dickinson, Christopher Plummer, Anthony Quayle. TVM. 100M USA. prod/rel: NBC, Time-Life
Perfect Murder, A 1998 d: Andrew Davis. lps: Michael Douglas, Gwyneth Paltrow, Viggo Mortensen. 105M USA. prod/rel: Warner Bros.©, Kopelson Entertainment

Mr. Fox of Venice, London 1959, Play
Honey Pot, The 1967 d: Joseph L. Mankiewicz. lps: Rex Harrison, Susan Hayward, Cliff Robertson. 150M UKN/USA/ITL. *It Comes Up Murder; Anyone for Venice?* prod/rel: Famous Artists Productions, United Artists

Wait Until Dark, New York 1966, Play
Wait Until Dark 1967 d: Terence Young. lps: Audrey Hepburn, Alan Arkin, Richard CrennA. 108M USA. prod/rel: Warner Bros., Seven Arts, Inc.

KNOWLES, JAMES SHERIDAN (1784–1862), UKN
Virginius, 1820, Play
Virginius 1909 d: J. Stuart Blackton. lps: Maurice Costello, Earle Williams. 955f USA. prod/rel: Vitagraph Co. of America
Virginius 1912 d: Hal Reid. lps: Hal Reid. 2r USA. prod/rel: Reliance

KNUDSEN, JAKOB
Den Gamle Praest, 1899, Novel
Gamle Praest, Den 1939 d: Jon Iversen. lps: Svend Aggerholm, Mette Bjerre, Rasmus Christiansen. 86M DNM. *The Old Clergyman* prod/rel: Palladium

KOBAL, JOHN
Rita Hayworth, Book
Rita Hayworth: the Love Goddess 1983 d: James Goldstone. lps: Lynda Carter, Michael Lerner, John Considine. TVM. 100M USA.

KOBAYASHI, TAKIJI (1903–1933), JPN
Kani-Kosen, 1929, Novel
Kanikosen 1953 d: So YamamurA. lps: So Yamamura, Masayuki Mori, Akitake Kono. 112M JPN. *Crab-Canning Ship; Crab-Canning Boat* prod/rel: Gendai Productions

KOBELL, FRANZ
Short Story
Seltsame Geschichte Des Brandner Kasper, Die 1949 d: Josef von Baky. lps: Paul Horbiger, Viktor Staal, Ursula Lingen. 100M GRM. *The Strange Story of Brandner Kasper; Das Tor Zum Paradies; The Gate to Paradise* prod/rel: Bavaria

KOBER, ARTHUR (1900–, PLN
Having Wonderful Time, New York 1937, Play
Having Wonderful Time 1938 d: Alfred Santell. lps: Ginger Rogers, Douglas Fairbanks Jr., Peggy Conklin. 71M USA. prod/rel: RKO Radio Pictures©

KOBHIO, BASSEK BA
Sango Malo - le Maitre du Canton, Novel
Sango Malo 1990 d: Bassek Ba Kobhio. lps: Jerome Bolo, Marcel Mvondo II, Edwige Ntongon. 93M CMR/BRK. *Chronique d'une Saison Paysanne; Le Maitre du Canton; The Master of the District* prod/rel: Les Films Terre Africain, Camerou Radio and Tv

KOBO, ABE (1924–1993), JPN
Moetsukita Chizu, 1967, Novel
Moetsukita Chizu 1968 d: Hiroshi TeshigaharA. lps: Shintaro Katsu, Etsuko Ichihara, Osamu OhharA. 118M JPN. *The Ruined Map* (USA); *The Man Without a Map; The Burned Map* prod/rel: Katsu Production

Suna No Onna, Tokyo 1952, Novel
Suna No Onna 1964 d: Hiroshi TeshigaharA. lps: Eiji Okada, Kyoko Kishida, Koji Mitsui. 123M JPN. *Woman in the Dunes* (USA); *Woman of the Dunes; Woman in the Sand; Sand-Woman* prod/rel: Teshigahara Productions

KOBO, ADE
Otoshiana, 1972, Play
Kashi to Kodomo 1962 d: Hiroshi TeshigaharA. lps: Hisashi Igawa, K. MiyaharA. 97M JPN. *The Pitfall* (USA); *Cheap Sweet and a Kid; Otoshi Ana* prod/rel: Teshigahara Productions

Tanin No Kao, 1964, Novel
Tanin No Kao 1966 d: Hiroshi TeshigaharA. lps: Tatsuya Nakadai, MacHiko Kyo, Kyoko KishidA. 124M JPN. *The Face of Another* (USA); *I Have a Stranger's Face* prod/rel: Teshigahara Production Picture

KOBR, JAN
Okovy, Novel
Okovy 1925 d: Vaclav Kubasek. lps: Jan W. Speerger, Marie Cerna, Frantisek Havel. CZC. *Fetters* prod/rel: Pronax-Film, Biografia

KOCH, C. J.
The Year of Living Dangerously, 1978, Novel
Year of Living Dangerously, The 1983 d: Peter Weir. lps: Mel Gibson, Sigourney Weaver, Linda Hunt. 117M ASL/USA. prod/rel: Metro-Goldwyn-Mayer, Mcelroy and Mcelroy

KOCH, CHRISTOPHER
Boys in the Island, Novel
Boys in the Island 1988 d: Geoffrey Bennett. lps: Yves Stenning, James Fox, Jane Stephens. F ASL.

KOCH, HENNY
Il Birichino Di Papa, Novel
Birichino Di Papa, Il 1943 d: Raffaello Matarazzo. lps: Chiaretta Gelli, Armando Falconi, Dina Galli. 80M ITL. prod/rel: Lux Film

KOCH, JIRIJ
Sehnsucht, Novel
Sehnsucht 1989 d: Jurgen Brauer. lps: Ulrike Krumbiegel, Ulrich Muhe, Thomas Buchel. 97M GDR. prod/rel: Defa-Studio Fur Spielfilme, Gruppe Johannisthal

KOCH, MAE
The Silent Plea, Story
Silent Plea, The 1915 d: Lionel Belmore. lps: Edith Storey, Harry T. Morey, Donald Hall. 3r USA. prod/rel: Broadway Star, Vitagraph Co. of America

KODA, AYA
Novel
Ototo 1960 d: Kon IchikawA. lps: Keiko Kishi, Hiroshi Kawaguchi, Kinuyo TanakA. 98M JPN. *Younger Brother; Her Brother* prod/rel: Daiei Motion Picture Co.

KOENIG, LAIRD
Attention Les Enfants Regardent 1977 d: Serge Leroy. lps: Alain Delon, Sophie Renoir, Richard Constantini. 102M FRN. *Careful the Children are Watching* prod/rel: Adel

The Little Girl Who Lives Down the Lane, Novel
Little Girl Who Lives Down the Lane, The 1977 d: Nicolas Gessner. lps: Jodie Foster, Martin Sheen, Alexis Smith. 94M CND/FRN. *La Petit Fille Au Bout du Chemin* (FRN) prod/rel: Carnelian Productions (Montreal), Intercontinental Leisure Ind. (Montreal)

The Neighbour, Novel
Killing 'Em Softly 1982 d: Max Fischer. lps: George Segal, Irene Cara, Clark Johnson. 81M CND. *The Man in 5a; The Neighbour; The Man Next Door; Killing' Em Softly* prod/rel: Neighbour Films Inc., Les Productions Claude Leger Inc.

Soleil Rouge, Novel
Soleil Rouge 1971 d: Terence Young. lps: Charles Bronson, Toshiro Mifune, Alain Delon. 107M FRN/ITL/SPN. *Sole Rosso* (ITL); *Red Sun* (UKN) prod/rel: Oceania P.I.C., Corona

KOEPPEN, WOLFGANG
Das Treibhaus, Novel
Treibhaus, Das 1987 d: Peter Goedel. lps: Christian Doermer, Laila Florentine Freer, Jorg Hube. 99M GRM. prod/rel: Peter Goedel Filmproduktion, Wdr

KOFOLD, J.
Behind the Green Lights, New York 1933, Book
Behind the Green Lights 1935 d: W. Christy Cabanne. lps: Norman Foster, Judith Allen, Sidney Blackmer. 70M USA. prod/rel: Mascot Pictures Corp.

KOHLER-RECHNITZ, INKA
Story
Zehn Kleine Negerlein 1954 d: Rolf von Sydow. lps: Thomas Ngambi, Harry Mambo, Josefine Bachert. 77M GRM. *Ten Little Negroes* prod/rel: Delos, Jugendfilm

KOHN, ROSE SIMON
Pillar to Post, New York 1943, Play
  Pillow to Post 1945 d: Vincent Sherman. lps: Ida Lupino, Sydney Greenstreet, William Prince. 92M USA. prod/rel: Warner Bros.

KOHNER, FREDERICK
Story
  Liebe, Tanz Und 1000 Schlager 1955 d: Paul Martin. lps: Caterina Valente, Peter Alexander, Rudolf Platte. 105M GRM. *Love Dancing and a Thousand Hits* prod/rel: C.C.C., Gloria
The Birds and the Bees, Play
  Three Daring Daughters 1947 d: Fred M. Wilcox. lps: Jeanette MacDonald, Jose Iturbi, Jane Powell. 115M USA. *The Birds and the Bees* prod/rel: MGM
Gidget, 1957, Novel
  Gidget 1959 d: Paul Wendkos. lps: Sandra Dee, James Darren, Cliff Robertson. 95M USA. prod/rel: Columbia
Gidget Goes to New York, Novel
  Gidget Grows Up 1970 d: James Sheldon. lps: Karen Valentine, Edward Mulhare, Paul Peterson. TVM. 74M USA. prod/rel: Columbia Pictures Tv, Screen Gems

KOHOUT, JARA
Lojzicka, Opera
  Lojzicka 1936 d: Miroslav Cikan. lps: Jarmila Berankova, Jara Kohout, Bozena SvobodovA. 2608m CZC. prod/rel: Gloria

KOIZUMI, YAKUMO
Kwaidan, Novel
  Kwaidan 1964 d: Masaki Kobayashi. lps: Michiyo Aratama, Misako Watanabe, Rentaro Mikuni. 164M JPN. *Weird Tales*; *Kaidan*; *Ghost Stories* prod/rel: Ninjin Club, Bungei

KOKKO, YRJO
Pessi Ja Illusia, Novel
  Pessi Ja Illusia 1983 d: Heikki Partanen. lps: Sami Kangas, Annu Marttila, Jorma Uotinen. 76M FNL. *Pessi and Illusia*; *Pessi and Illusion* prod/rel: Partanen & Rautoma Films

KOLAR, SLAVKO
Svoga Tela Gospodar, 1942, Play
  Svoga Tjela Gospodar 1957 d: Fedor Hanzekovic. lps: Marija Kohn, Mladen Serment, Julije Perlaki. 109M YGS. *My Own Master*; *Svoga Tela Gospodar*; *Master of One's Own Body*

KOLAR, STANISLAV
Princ Z Ulice, Novel
  Evas Tochter 1928 d: Carl Lamac. lps: Anny Ondra, Wolfgang Zilzer, Karel Lamac. 2488m GRM/CZC. *Dcery Eviny*; *Princ Z Ulice*; *Das Paradies von Heute*; *Eve's Daughters*; *Prince from the Street* prod/rel: Bratri Deglove, H. R. Sokal Film

KOLB, ANNETTE
Die Schaukel, Novel
  Schaukel, Die 1983 d: Percy Adlon. lps: Anja Jaenicke, Lena Stolze, Rolf Illig. 133M GRM. *The Swing* (USA) prod/rel: Pelemele Film, Roxy-Film

KOLB, JEAN
Le Concierge Revient de Suite, Play
  Concierge Revient de Suite, Le 1937 d: Fernand Rivers. lps: Jean Kolb, Andre Simeon, C. P. Cousin. SHT FRN.

KOLB, KEN
The Couch Trip, Novel
  Couch Trip, The 1988 d: Michael Ritchie. lps: Dan Aykroyd, Walter Matthau, Charles Grodin. 97M USA. prod/rel: Orion
Getting Straight, Philadelphia 1967, Novel
  Getting Straight 1970 d: Richard Rush. lps: Elliott Gould, Candice Bergen, Robert F. Lyons. 126M USA. prod/rel: the Organization, Columbia

KOLDINSKY, ALOIS
Hrabenka Z Podskali, Play
  Hrabenka Z Podskali 1925 d: Carl Lamac. lps: Theodor Pistek, Anny Ondra, Vladimir Majer. CZC. *The Countess from Podskali* prod/rel: Bratri Deglove, Elpe

KOLITZ, ZVI
Story
  Hagiva 1955 d: Thorold Dickinson. lps: Michael Wagner, Edward Mulhare, Haya Harareet. 102M ISR. *Hill 24 Doesn't Answer* (UKN); *Giva 24 Aina Onah* prod/rel: Sikor Film

KOLL, KILIAN
Urlaub Auf Ehrenwort, Novel
  Urlaub Auf Ehrenwort 1937 d: Karl Ritter. lps: Ingeborg Theek, Rolf Moebius, Fritz Kampers. 87M GRM. *Furlough on Word of Honor* (USA); *Leave on Word of Honor*
  Urlaub Auf Ehrenwort 1955 d: Wolfgang Liebeneiner. lps: Claus Biederstaedt, Eva-Ingeborg Scholz, Reinhard Kolldehoff. 100M GRM. prod/rel: Algefa, Bavaria

KOLLE, OSWALD
Das Wunder Der Liebe, Bielefeld 1969, Book
  Oswalt Kolle: Das Wunder Der Liebe -Sexualitat in Der Ehe 1968 d: Franz J. Gottlieb. lps: Biggi Freyer, Wilfried Gossler, Katarina Haertel. 82M GRM. *The Miracle of Love* (USA); *The Wonder of Love* (UKN); *Oswalt Kolle: the Wonder of Love -Sexuality in Marriage* prod/rel: Arca-Winston Films

KOLLNER, H. F.
Viva la Musica, Novel
  Leichte Muse 1941 d: Arthur M. Rabenalt. lps: Willy Fritsch, Adelheid Seeck, Willi Rose. 104M GRM. *Was Eine Frau Im Fruhling Traumt* prod/rel: Terra, Prisma

KOLLO, WALTER (1878-1940), GRM
Die Tolle Komtess, Operetta
  Tolle Komtess, Die 1928 d: Richard Lowenbein. lps: Dina Gralla, Werner Fuetterer, Ralph Arthur Roberts. 2349m GRM. *The Crazy Countess* prod/rel: Richard Eichberg-Film

KOLLO, WILLI
Meine Freundin Barbara, Play
  Meine Freundin Barbara 1937 d: Fritz Kirchhoff. lps: Grethe Weiser, Paul Hoffmann, Franz Zimmermann. 81M GRM. *My Friend Barbara* prod/rel: Fanal-Film

KOLOZSVARI, GRANDPIERRE EMIL
A Csillagszemu, 1953, Novel
  Csillagszemu, A 1977 d: Miklos Markos. lps: Iren Bordan, Jozsef Madaras, Agi Szirtes. 97M HNG. *Starry-Eye*

KOMATSU, SAKYO
Fukkatsu No Hi, Novel
  Fukkatsu No Hi 1979 d: Kinji Fukasaku. lps: Shin-Ichi Chiba, Chuck Connors, Glenn Ford. 155M JPN. *The Day of Resurrection*; *Virus* (USA); *Resurrection Day* prod/rel: Haruki Kadokawa Films, Tokyo Broadcasting System
Sayonara Jiyupeta, Novel
  Sayonara Jiyupeta 1983 d: Koji Hashimoto. lps: Tomokazu Miura, Diana Dangley, Miyuki Ono. 130M JPN. *Bye, Jupiter Bye* prod/rel: Toho Co., Kabushiki-Kaisha Io
Shuto Shoshitsu, Book
  Shuto Shoshitsu 1987 d: Toshio MasudA. lps: Tsunehiko Watase, Yuko Naotari, Shinji YamashitA. 120M JPN. *Tokyo Blackout* prod/rel: Daiei Co., Kansai Telecasting

KOMATSUZAKI, SHIGERU
Kaitei Gunkan / Kaitei Okoku, Novel
  Kaitei Gunkan 1963 d: Inoshiro HondA. lps: Tadao Takashima, Yoko Fujiyama, Yu Fujiki. 96M JPN. *The Flying Supersub Atoragon*; *Atragon the Flying Sub*; *Atragon* (USA); *Atoragon*; *Underwater Warship* prod/rel: Toho Co.

KOMROFF, MANUEL
The $1000 Bill, 1935, Short Story
  Small Town Boy 1937 d: Glenn Tryon. lps: Stuart Erwin, Joyce Compton, Erville Alderson. 61M USA. *The Thousand Dollar Bill*; *$1000 Bill* prod/rel: Grand National Films©, Zion Myers Production
The Magic Bow, Novel
  Magic Bow, The 1946 d: Bernard Knowles. lps: Stewart Granger, Phyllis Calvert, Jean Kent. 106M UKN. prod/rel: General Film Distributors, Gainsborough

KON, TOKO
Akutaro, Novel
  Akutaro 1963 d: Seijun Suzuki. lps: Ken Yamanouchi, Masako Zumi, Midori Ashiro. 95M JPN. *The Bastard*; *The Young Rebel*; *The Incorrigible One* prod/rel: Nikkatsu Corp.
Kawachi Karumen, Novel
  Kawachi Karumen 1966 d: Seijun Suzuki. lps: Yumiko Nogawa, Ruriko Ito, Chikako Miyagi. 89M JPN. *Carmen from Kawachi* prod/rel: Nikkatsu Corp.
O-Gin Sama, Tokyo 1927, Short Story
  Oghin-Sama 1960 d: Kinuyo TanakA. lps: Ineko Arima, Ganjiro Nakamura, Mieko Takamine. 102M JPN. *Love Under the Crucifix* (USA); *Ogin Sama*; *O-Gin Sama* prod/rel: Shochiku Co.
Tento Gekijo, 1957, Novel
  Nusumareta Yokujo 1958 d: Shohei ImamurA. lps: Osamu Takizawa, Kin Sugai, Shinichi YanagawA. 92M JPN. *The Stolen Desire*

KONG JIESHENG
Jue XIang, Novel
  Jue XIang 1985 d: Zhang Zeming. lps: Kong XIanzhu, Chen Rui, Feng Diqing. 100M CHN. *Swan Song*; *Favorite Piece of Music* prod/rel: Pearl River Film Studio

KONG JUE
Xin Er Nu Ying XIong Zhuan, Novel
  Xin Er Nu Ying XIong Zhuan 1951 d: Shi Dongshan, Lu Ban. lps: Jin XIng, Yao XIangli, Yan Zhenhe. 14r CHN. *New Heroes and Heroines* prod/rel: Beijing Film Studio

KONG SHANGREN
Peach Flower Legend, Play
  Tao Hua Shan 1963 d: Sun Jing. lps: Wang Danfeng, Feng Ji, Yu Junfang. 12r CHN. *Peach Flower Fan* prod/rel: XI'an Film Studio
Tao Hua Shan, c1690, Play
  Li XIangjun 1940 d: Wu Cun. 98M CHN.

KONIG, JOEL
David, Book
  David 1979 d: Peter Lilienthal. lps: Mario Fischel, Valtr Taub, Irene Vrkljan. 127M GRM. prod/rel: von Vietinghoff, Project

KONIGSFELD
Jan Derriksens Dienstjahr, Novel
  Dame Und Ihr Chauffeur, Die 1928 d: Manfred NoA. lps: Charlotte Ander, Elisabeth Pinajeff, Fritz Kampers. 2849m GRM. *The Lady and the Chauffeur* prod/rel: Noa-Film

KONING
La Fille de Madame Angot, Brussels 1872, Operetta
  Fille de Madame Angot, La 1935 d: Jean Bernard-Derosne. lps: Andre Bauge, Jean Aquistapace, MoniquellA. 85M FRN. prod/rel: Ste Francaise De Prod. Cinematographique

KONINGSBERGER, HANS
The Revolutionary, New York 1967, Novel
  Revolutionary, The 1970 d: Paul Williams. lps: Jon Voight, Jennifer Salt, Seymour Cassel. 101M UKN/USA. prod/rel: Pressman-Williams Enterprises, United Artists
A Walk With Love and Death, New York 1961, Novel
  Walk With Love and Death, A 1969 d: John Huston. lps: Anjelica Huston, Assaf Dayan, Anthony Higgins. 90M USA. prod/rel: 20th Century-Fox Film Corporation

KONOPNICKA, MARIA
O Krasnoludkach I O Sierotce Marysi, 1896, Short Story
  Marysia I Krasnoludki 1961 d: Jerzy Szeski, Konrad Paradowski. lps: Malgosia Piekarska, Wojciech Siemion, Izabella OlszewskA. 79M PLN. *Orphan Mary and the Dwarfs*; *Mary and the Goblins*

KONOPNICKI, GUY
Pas de Kaddish Pour Sylberstein, Novel
  K 1997 d: Alexandre Arcady. lps: Patrick Bruel, Isabella Ferrari, Marthe Keller. 135M FRN. prod/rel: New Light Films, Tf1 Films

KONRAD, EDMOND
Kde Se Zebra, Play
  Svet Kde Se Zebra 1938 d: Miroslav Cikan. lps: Hugo Haas, Marie Glazrova, Ladislav Bohac. 2266m CZC. *The World Where One Goes Begging*; *The Beggar Life*; *The World of Beggars* prod/rel: Lucernafilm
Kvocna, Short Story
  Kvocna 1937 d: Hugo Haas. lps: Ruzena Naskova, Svetla Svozilova, Jirina SejbalovA. 2367m CZC. *Mother-Hen* prod/rel: Lucernafilm

KONSALIK, H. G.
Strafbataillon 999, Novel
  Strafbataillon 999 1960 d: Harald Philipp. lps: Werner Peters, Heinz Weiss, Sonja Ziemann. 109M GRM. *Punishment Battalion* (USA); *March to the Gallows* prod/rel: Willy Zeyn, Constantin

KONSALIK, HEINZ G.
Novel
  Liebe Ist Starker Als Der Tod 1988 d: Juraj Herz. lps: Gigi Proietti, Eleonore Klarwein, Helen VitA. TVM. 90M GRM.
Liebesnachte in Der Taiga, Novel
  Liebesnachte in Der Taiga 1967 d: Harald Philipp. lps: Thomas Hunter, Marie Versini, Stanislav Ledinek. 105M GRM. *Love-Nights in the Taiga*; *Code Name Is Kill*; *Nights of Love in the Taiga*; *Escape from Taiga* prod/rel: Franz Seitz
Ein Toter Taucher Nimmt Kein Gold, Novel
  Toter Taucher Nimmt Kein Gold, Ein 1975 d: Harald Reinl. lps: Horst Janson, Hans Hass Jr., Marius Weyers. 95M GRM. *No Gold for a Dead Diver* (UKN); *Dead Divers Get No Gold* prod/rel: Rapid, Terra

Und Die Nacht Kennt Kein Erbarmen, Novel
  Listen to My Story 1974 d: Jurgen Goslar. lps: Sandra Prinzloo, Wolfgang Kieling, Marius Weyers. 91M SAF/GRM. *..Und Die Nacht Kennt Kein Erbarmen* (GRM); *Entmundigt* prod/rel: Centaurus

Wer Stirbt Schon Gerne Unter Palmen?, Novel
  Wer Stirbt Schon Gerne Unter Palmen? 1974 d: Alfred Vohrer. lps: Thomas Hunter, Hannes Messemer, Maria Gudy. 84M GRM. *Nobody Likes to Die Under Palms* prod/rel: Tv 13, Terra

KONSTANTIN, KAREL
Ryba Na Suchu, Play
  Ryba Na Suchu 1942 d: Vladimir Slavinsky. lps: Vlasta Burian, Marie Strosova-Steimarova, Vitezslav VejrazkA. 2430m CZC. *Fish Out of Water* prod/rel: Lucernafilm

KONVITZ, JEFFREY
The Sentinel, Novel
  Sentinel, The 1977 d: Michael Winner. lps: Cristina Raines, Martin Balsam, Chris Sarandon. 105M USA. prod/rel: Universal

KONWICKI, TADEUSZ (1926–, PLN
Kronika Wypadkow Milosnych, Autobiography
  Kronika Wypadkow Milosnych 1985 d: Andrzej WajdA. lps: Piotr Wawrzynczak, Paulina Mlynarska, Tadeusz Konwicki. 125M PLN. *A Chronicle of Amorous Incidents*; *Chronicle of a Love Affair*; *The Love Affairs Chronicle*; *Chronicle of Love Affairs* prod/rel: Zespoly Filmowe, Gruppe Perspektywa
La Petite Apocalypse, Novel
  Petite Apocalypse, La 1992 d: Costa-Gavras. lps: Jiri Menzel, Andre Dussollier, Pierre Arditi. 110M FRN/ITL/PLN.

KOONTZ, DEAN R. (1945–, USA, Koontz, Dean Ray
Demon Seed, Novel
  Demon Seed 1977 d: Donald Cammell. lps: Julie Christie, Fritz Weaver, Gerrit Graham. 94M USA. *Proteus Generation* prod/rel: MGM, United Artists
Face of Fear, Novel
  Face of Fear 1990 d: Farhad Mann. lps: Lee Horsley, Pam Dawber, Kevin Conroy. TVM. 89M USA. prod/rel: Papazian Hirsch, the Lee Rich Company
Hideaway, Novel
  Hideaway 1995 d: Brett Leonard. lps: Jeff Goldblum, Christine Lahti, Alicia Silverstone. 103M USA. prod/rel: S/Q
Intensity, Novel
  Intensity 1997 d: Yves Simoneau. lps: John C. McGinley, Molly Parker, Tori Paul. TVM. 240M USA. prod/rel: Mandalay Entertainment, Tristar Television
Mr. Murder, Novel
  Dean Koontz's Mr. Murder 1999 d: Dick Lowry. lps: Stephen Baldwin, Julie Warner, Bill Smitrovich. TVM. 240M USA. prod/rel: Patchett Kaufmann Entertainment, Elephant Walk Entertainment
Phantoms, Novel
  Phantoms 1998 d: Joe Chappelle. lps: Peter O'Toole, Rose McGowan, Joanna Going. 95M USA. prod/rel: Dimension Films, Neo Motion Pictures
Twilight, Novel
  Servants of Twilight 1991 d: Jeffrey Obrow. lps: Bruce Greenwood, Belinda Bauer, Grace Zabriskie. TVM. 96M USA. *Dean R. Koontz's Servants of Twilight*
Watchers, Novel
  Watchers 1988 d: Jon Hess. lps: Corey Haim, Michael Ironside, Barbara Williams. 92M CND/USA. prod/rel: Guild, Concorde
Watchers Reborn, Novel
  Watchers Reborn 1998 d: John Carl Buechler. lps: Mark Hamill, Stephen macht, Lou Rawls. F USA.
Whispers, Novel
  Whispers 1990 d: Douglas Jackson. lps: Victoria Tennant, Chris Sarandon, Jean Leclerc. 96M CND.

KOPIT, ARTHUR (1937–, USA, Kopit, Arthur Lee
Indians, 1969, Play
  Buffalo Bill and the Indians Or Sitting Bull's History Lesson 1976 d: Robert Altman. lps: Paul Newman, Burt Lancaster, Joel Grey. 123M USA. *Buffalo Bill* prod/rel: United Artists
Oh Dad, Poor Dad, Mamma's Hung You in the Closet and I'm Feeling So Sad, 1960, Play
  Oh Dad, Poor Dad, Mama's Hung You in the Closet and I'm Feeling So Sad 1967 d: Richard Quine, Alexander MacKendrick. lps: Rosalind Russell, Robert Morse, Barbara Harris. 86M USA. prod/rel: Seven Arts Productions, Ray Stark

KOPTA, JOSEF
Hldac C. 47, Novel
  Hldac C. 47 1937 d: Josef Rovensky. lps: Jaroslav Prucha, Marie Glazrova, Karel Vesely. 1943m CZC. *Watchman No.47* prod/rel: Elekta

Treti Rota, Novel
  Treti Rota 1931 d: Svatopluk Innemann. lps: Otomar Korbelar, Vladimir Hlavaty, Alexander Trebovsky. 2957m CZC. *The Third Squad*; *The Third Company* prod/rel: Vladimir Kabelik, Ludvik Kanturek

KOPTA, JOSEPH
Watchman 47, Novel
  Pickup 1951 d: Hugo Haas, Edgar E. Walden. lps: Hugo Haas, Beverly Michaels, Allan Nixon. 76M USA. prod/rel: Columbia, Forum Prods.

KORDA, MICHAEL (1933–, UKN
Queenie, Novel
  Queenie 1987 d: Larry Peerce. lps: Mia Sara, Kirk Douglas, Martin Balsam. TVM. 245M USA. prod/rel: von Zemeck-Samuels Productions, Highgate Pictures

KOREF, ELMIRA
Die Kleine Passion, Play
  Wetterleuchten Am Dachstein 1952 d: Anton Kutter. lps: Gisela Fackeldey, Marianne Koch, Jutta Bornemann. 107M GRM/AUS. *Die Herrin Vom Salzerhof* prod/rel: Suddeutsche

KORHERR, HELMUT
Jesus von Ottakring, Play
  Jesus von Ottakring 1976 d: Wilhelm Pellert. lps: Rudolf Prack, Hilde Sochor, Peter Hey. 94M AUS. *Jesus of Ottakring*; *Die Neider Nicht Gezahlt* prod/rel: Gruppe Borobya

KORNIYCHUK, ALEKSANDER (1905–, RSS, Korneichuk, Alexander Evdokimovich
Bogdan Khmelnytsky, 1939, Play
  Bogdan Khmelnitsky 1941 d: Igor Savchenko. 114M USS. *Bohdan Khmelnytsky*
Front, 1942, Play
  Front 1943 d: Georgi Vasiliev, Sergei Vasiliev. 116M USS. *The Front*
Partizany V Stepnakh Ukrayiny, 1941, Play
  Partizani V Stepyakh Ukrainy 1943 d: Igor Savchenko. 78M USS. *Partisans in the Plains of Ukraine*; *The Partisans in the Ukrainian Steppes*; *Partizany V Stepyakh Ukrayiny*
Stranitsa Dnevnika, 1965, Play
  A Tepyer Sudi. 1967 d: Vladimir Dovgan. lps: Irina Vavilova, Georgi Zhzhonov, Boris Livanov. 92M USS. *And Now Pass Judgement.*
V Stepyakh Ukrayiny, 1941, Play
  V Stepjah Ukrainy 1952 d: Timofey Levchuk. 108M USS. *In the Ukrainian Steppes*; *V Stepyakh Ukrayiny*

KOROLENKO, VLADIMIR GALAKTIONOVICH (1853–1921), RSS
Slepoy Musykant, Moscow 1888, Novel
  Slepoy Muzykant 1961 d: Tatyana Lukashevich. lps: Boris Livanov, Vasili Livanov, Marina StrizhenovA. 78M USS. *Sound of Life* (USA) prod/rel: Mosfilm

KORTOOMS, TOON
Help! de Dokter Verzuipt!, Novel
  Help, de Dokter Verzuipt! 1974 d: Nikolai Van Der Heyde. lps: Jules Croiset, Martine Bijl, Piet Bambergen. 94M NTH. *Help -the Doctor's Drowning!*; *Help! the Doctor Is Drowning* prod/rel: Fuga, Maggan

KOSINSKI, JERZY (1933–1991), PLN, Kosinski, Jerzy Nikodem
Being There, 1970, Novel
  Being There 1979 d: Hal Ashby. lps: Peter Sellers, Shirley MacLaine, Jack Warden. 130M USA. prod/rel: Lorimar, North Star

KOSOTOROV, ALEKSANDER
Mecta Ljubvi, 1911, Play
  Sogno d'Amore 1922 d: Gennaro Righelli. lps: Italia Almirante Manzini, Andrea Habay, Oreste BilanciA. 1694m ITL. prod/rel: Fert

KOSTOV, STEFAN
Golemanov, 1928, Play
  Golemanov 1958 d: Kiril Ilinchev. lps: Nikola Popov, Andrei Chaprazov, Penka IkonomovA. 85M BUL.

KOSZTOLANYI, DEZSO
Aranysarkany, 1925, Novel
  Aranysarkany 1966 d: Laszlo Ranody. lps: Laszlo Mensaros. 93M HNG. *The Golden Kite*; *The Golden Cage*
Edes Anna, 1926, Novel
  Edes Anna 1958 d: Zoltan Fabri. lps: Mari Torocsik, Maria Mezey, Karoly Kovacs. 87M HNG. *Anna*; *Schuldig?*
Furdes, 1943, Short Story
  Szines Tintakrol Almodom 1980 d: Laszlo Ranody. lps: Mari Torocsik, Karoly Kovacs, Adam Kosztolanyi. 91M HNG. *I Dream About Colours*; *Colours* prod/rel: Hungarian Filmproduction

Kinai Kancso, 1943, Short Story
  Szines Tintakrol Almodom 1980 d: Laszlo Ranody. lps: Mari Torocsik, Karoly Kovacs, Adam Kosztolanyi. 91M HNG. *I Dream About Colours*; *Colours* prod/rel: Hungarian Filmproduction
A Kulcs, 1943, Short Story
  Szines Tintakrol Almodom 1980 d: Laszlo Ranody. lps: Mari Torocsik, Karoly Kovacs, Adam Kosztolanyi. 91M HNG. *I Dream About Colours*; *Colours* prod/rel: Hungarian Filmproduction
Pacsirta, 1924, Novel
  Pacsirta 1964 d: Laszlo Ranody. lps: Zoltan Latinovits, Klari Tolnay, Mari Torocsik. 106M HNG. *Skylark*; *The Lark*

KOTHAWALA, JERBANU
Emerald of the East, Novel
  Emerald of the East 1928 d: Jean de Kuharski. lps: Joshua Kean, Mary Odette, Jean de Kuharski. 5600f UKN. *Das Herz Des Maharadscha* prod/rel: British Pacific, British International Pictures

KOTLOWITZ, ALEX
There are No Children Here, Book
  There are No Children Here 1993 d: Anita W. Addison. lps: Oprah Winfrey, Keith David, Mark Lane. TVM. 90M USA.

KOTLYAREVSKY, IWAN
Natalka Poltavka, 1818, Opera
  Natalka Poltavka 1937 d: Edgar G. Ulmer, Vasile Avramenko. lps: Thalia Sabanieeva, Dimitri Creona, Olena DibrovA. 86M USA. prod/rel: Avramenko Film Productions©, Kinotrade

KOTSYUBINSKIY, MIHHAYLO MIKHAYLOVICH
Tine Zabutykh Predkiv, 1911, Novel
  Tine Zabutykh Predkiv 1965 d: Sergei Paradjanov. lps: Ivan Nikolaichuk, Larisa Kadochnikova, Tatyana BestayevA. 100M USS. *Shadows of Forgotten Ancestors* (USA); *Tini Zabytych Predkiv*; *Shadows of Our Forgotten Ancestors*; *Teni Zabytykh Predkov*; *In the Shadow of the Past* prod/rel: Dovzhenko Film Studio

KOTZWINKLE, WILLIAM
Jack in the Box, Novel
  Book of Love 1990 d: Robert Shaye. lps: Chris Young, Keith Coogan, Aeryk Egan. 87M USA. prod/rel: New Line Cinema

KOVACEVIC, DUSAN
Urnebesna Tragedija, Play
  Urnebesna Tragedija 1995 d: Goran Markovic. lps: Danilo-Bata Stojkovic, Lazar Ristovski, Milena Dravic. 95M BUL/FRN. *The Tragic Burlesque*; *Tragedy Burlesque* prod/rel: Dari Films, la Sept Cinema (France)

KOVELOFF, HILDE
Prison Sans Barreaux, Play
  Prison Without Bars 1938 d: Brian Desmond Hurst. lps: Corinne Luchaire, Edna Best, Barry K. Barnes. 80M UKN. prod/rel: London Films, United Artists

KOVIC, RON
Born on the Fourth of July, Book
  Born on the Fourth of July 1989 d: Oliver Stone. lps: Tom Cruise, Willem Dafoe, Raymond J. Barry. 144M USA. prod/rel: Universal, Ixtlan

KOWALSKI, FRANK
Ten Second Jailbreak, Novel
  Breakout 1975 d: Tom Gries. lps: Charles Bronson, Jill Ireland, John Huston. 96M USA/SPN/FRN. prod/rel: Columbia, Persky-Bright

KOZIK, CHRISTA
Moritz in Der Litfassaule, Book
  Moritz in Der Litfassaule 1983 d: Rolf Losansky. lps: Dirk Muller, Dieter Mann, Walfriede Schmitt. 88M GDR. *Moritz in the Advertising Pillar*; *Maurice from the Advertising Pillar* prod/rel: Defa-Studio Fur Spielfilme, Gruppe Johannisthal

KOZU, KAZUO
Hebisume to Hakuhatsuki, Short Story
  Hebimusume to Hakuhatsuki 1968 d: Noriaki YuasA. lps: Yachie Matsui, Mayumi Takahashi, Yoshio KitaharA. 82M JPN. *The Snake Girl and the Silver-Haired Witch* prod/rel: Daiei Motion Picture Co.

KRAATZ, CURT
Der Hochtourist, Play
  Hochtourist, Der 1931 d: Alfred Zeisler. lps: Otto Wallburg, Maria Solveg, Erika Glassner. 86M GRM. prod/rel: UFA, Sudwest
  Hochtourist, Der 1942 d: Adolf Schlissleder. lps: Joe Stockel, Trude Hesterberg, Alice Treff. 84M GRM. prod/rel: Bavaria
  Hochtourist, Der 1961 d: Ulrich Erfurth. lps: Willy Millowitsch, Claude Farell, Helen VitA. 88M GRM. *High Season Tourist* prod/rel: U.F.H.

KRAATZ, KURT
Polnische Wirtschaft, Play
  Polnische Wirtschaft 1928 d: E. W. Emo. lps: Hans
  Brausewetter, Iwa Wanja, Siegfried Arno. 2135m GRM.
  prod/rel: Strauss-Film

KRABBE, TIM
The Golden Egg, Novel
  Vanishing, The 1993 d: George Sluizer. lps: Jeff
  Bridges, Kiefer Sutherland, Nancy Travis. 110M USA.
  prod/rel: 20th Century Fox

KRACKARDT, H.
Ich Heirate Herrn Direktor, Novel
  Ich Heirate Herrn Direktor 1960 d: Wolfgang
  Liebeneiner. lps: Heidelinde Weis, Gerhard Riedmann,
  Hans Sohnker. 97M AUS. prod/rel: Ofa

KRAG, VILHELM
Baldevins Bryllup, Oslo 1900, Play
  Baldevins Brollop 1938 d: Gideon Wahlberg, Emil A.
  Lingheim. lps: Edvard Persson, Arthur Fischer, Bullan
  Weijden. 105M SWD. *Baldwin's Wedding* (USA);
  Baldevin's Wedding prod/rel: Olle Ekman, Ab Europa
  Film

KRALY, HANS
Kohlheisels Tochter, Novel
  Ja, Ja, Die Liebe in Tirol 1955 d: Geza von Bolvary.
  lps: Gerhard Riedmann, Hans Moser, Doris Kirchner.
  104M GRM. *Oh That Tyrolean Love* prod/rel: Berolina,
  Constantin

KRAMAREVSKIY, L.
Cholpon - Utrennyaya Zvezda, 1944, Ballet
  Cholpon - Utrennyaya Zvezda 1960 d: Roman
  Tikhomirov. lps: Reina Chokoyeva, Uran Sarbagishev,
  Nikolay Tugelov. 75M USS. *Morning Star* (USA);
  Cholpon prod/rel: Lenfilm, Frunze Film Studio

KRAMM, JOSEPH (1908–, USA
The Shrike, New York 1952, Play
  Shrike, The 1955 d: Jose Ferrer. lps: Jose Ferrer, June
  Allyson, Joy Page. 88M USA. prod/rel:
  Universal-International

KRAMP, WILLY
Story
  Lamm, Das 1964 d: Wolfgang Staudte. lps: Ronald
  Dehne, Elke Aberle, Dieter Kirchlechner. 87M GRM.
  The Lamb prod/rel: Fono

KRANTZ, JUDITH (1928–, USA
Daisy, Novel
  Princess Daisy 1983 d: Waris Hussein. lps: Merete Van
  Kamp, Lindsay Wagner, Paul Michael Glaser. TVM.
  200M USA.

Scruples, Novel
  Scruples 1980 d: Alan J. Levi. lps: Lindsay Wagner,
  Barry Bostwick, Marie-France Pisier. TVM. 300M USA.
  prod/rel: Lou-Step Prods., Warner Bros. Tv

KRASNA, NORMAN
Dear Ruth, New York 1944, Play
  Dear Ruth 1947 d: William D. Russell. lps: Mona
  Freeman, Joan Caulfield, William Holden. 95M USA.
  prod/rel: Paramount

John Loves Mary, New York 1947, Play
  John Loves Mary 1949 d: David Butler. lps: Ronald
  Reagan, Jack Carson, Edward Arnold. 96M USA.
  prod/rel: Warner Bros.

Kind Sir, New York 1953, Play
  Indiscreet 1958 d: Stanley Donen. lps: Cary Grant,
  Ingrid Bergman, Cecil Parker. 100M UKN/USA.
  prod/rel: Warner Bros., Grandon Prods.

Small Miracle, New York 1934, Play
  Four Hours to Kill! 1935 d: Mitchell Leisen. lps:
  Richard Barthelmess, Joe Morrison, Helen Mack. 74M
  USA. *Small Miracle*; *Night Drama* prod/rel: Paramount
  Productions©

Sunday in New York, New York 1961, Play
  Sunday in New York 1963 d: Peter Tewkesbury. lps:
  Jane Fonda, Cliff Robertson, Rod Taylor. 105M USA.
  prod/rel: Seven Arts Productions

Who Was That Lady?, Play
  Who Was That Lady? 1960 d: George Sidney. lps: Tony
  Curtis, Janet Leigh, Dean Martin. 114M USA. prod/rel:
  Columbia

KRASZEWSKI, JOSZEF IGNACY
Hrabina Cosel, 1874, Novel
  Hrabina Cosel 1968 d: Jerzy Antczak. lps: Daniel
  Olbrychski, Jadwiga Baranska, Mariusz Dmochowski.
  153M PLN. *Countess Cosel* (UKN)

KRAUSSE, KAY
Invitation to Murder, 1937, Short Story
  Private Detective 1939 d: Noel Smith. lps: Jane
  Wyman, Dick Foran, Gloria Dickson. 57M USA. *Lady
  Dick*; *The Lady Detective* prod/rel: Warner Bros.
  Pictures©

KRAUSSER, HELMUT
Fette Welt, Novel
  Fette Welt 1998 d: Jan Schutte. lps: Jurgen Vogel, Julia
  Filiminow, Stefan Dietrich. 90M GRM. *Fat World*
  prod/rel: Polygram Filmed Entertainment, Senator
  Filmproduktion

KREIDER, J. BASIL
Bubbles, Short Story
  Bubbles 1920 d: Wayne MacK. lps: Jack Connolly,
  Mary Anderson, Jack Mower. 4570f USA. prod/rel:
  Super Art, State Rights

KREITSEK, HOWARD B.
Ten Second Jailbreak, Novel
  Breakout 1975 d: Tom Gries. lps: Charles Bronson, Jill
  Ireland, John Huston. 96M USA/SPN/FRN. prod/rel:
  Columbia, Persky-Bright

KREKER, ERWIN
Hochzeitsreise Ohne Mann, Play
  Ehe Man Ehemann Wird 1941 d: Alwin Elling. lps:
  Ewald Balser, Heli Finkenzeller, Maria Paudler. 97M
  GRM. prod/rel: Astra, Karp

KREMER, THEODORE
Bertha the Sewing machine Girl, Play
  Bertha, the Sewing machine Girl 1926 d: Irving
  Cummings. lps: Madge Bellamy, Allan Simpson, Sally
  Phipps. 5245f USA. prod/rel: Fox Film Corp.

KRENOVSKY, MILOS
Divoch, Novel
  Divoch 1936 d: Jan Svitak. lps: Rolf Wanka, Theodor
  Pistek, Nancy RubensovA. 2529m CZC. *Wild Girl*
  prod/rel: Meteor, Meissner

  Wildfang, Der 1936 d: Jan Svitak. lps: Rolf Wanka,
  Roszi Czikos, Fritz Imhoff. 2067m GRM/CZC. *Rote
  Rosen - Blaue Adria*; *Divoch* prod/rel: Metropolitan,
  Meteor

Vandiny Trampoty, Novel
  Vandiny Trampoty 1938 d: Miroslav Cikan. lps: Vera
  Ferbasova, Theodor Pistek, Jiri Dohnal. 2238m CZC.
  Vanda's Troubles prod/rel: Moldavia

KRESSING, HARRY
The Cook, New York 1965, Novel
  Something for Everyone 1970 d: Harold Prince. lps:
  Michael York, Angela Lansbury, Anthony Higgins.
  113M USA. *Black Flowers for the Bride*; *The Cook*
  prod/rel: Media Productions

KREUTZER, GUIDO
Es Flustert Die Nacht., Short Story
  Es Flustert Die Nacht. 1929 d: Victor Janson. lps: Lil
  Dagover, Hans Stuwe, Alexander Murski. 2600m GRM.
  prod/rel: Aafa-Film Ag

Das Grune Monokel, Novel
  Grune Monokel, Das 1929 d: Rudolf Meinert. lps:
  Ralph Cancy, Betty Bird, Suzy Vernon. 2017m GRM.
  prod/rel: Deutsches Lichtspiel-Syndikat

Schminke, Novel
  Da Halt Die Welt Den Atem an 1927 d: Felix Basch.
  lps: Marcella Albani, Werner Krauss, Alfons Fryland.
  2455m GRM/FRN. *Maquillage* (FRN) prod/rel: Lothar
  Stark Gmbh

KRIEZA, MIROSLAV
Cvrcak Pod Vodopadom, 1937, Short Story
  Put U Raj 1971 d: Mario Fanelli. lps: Boris Buzancic,
  Ljuba Tadic, Zvonimir Strmac. 90M YGS. *Way to
  Paradise*

Vucjak, 1925, Play
  Horvatov Izbor 1985 d: Eduard Galic. lps: Rade
  Serbedzija, Milena Dravic, Mira Furlan. 113M YGS.
  Horvat's Choice

KRISHNAMURTHY, KU. SA.
Andaman Kaithi, Play
  Andaman Kaithi 1952 d: V. Krishnan. lps: K.
  Sarangapani, T. S. Baliah, M. G. Ramachandran. 190M
  IND. *The Prisoner of the Andamans* prod/rel:
  Radhakrishna Films

KRISHNARAO, A. N.
Jeevana Nataka, Play
  Jeevana Nataka 1942 d: Wahab Kashmiri. lps: Gubbi
  Veeranna, D. Kemparaj Urs, Shanta Hublikar. 160M
  IND. prod/rel: Gubbi Films

KRISTENSEN, TOM
Haervaerk, 1930, Novel
  Haervaerk 1977 d: Ole Roos. lps: Ole Ernst, Jesper
  Christensen, Kirsten Peuliche. 133M DNM. *Havoc*

KRITZ, HUGO MARIA
Story
  Frau Am Dunklen Fenster, Eine 1960 d: Franz Peter
  Wirth. lps: Marianne Koch, Christiane Nielsen, Robert
  Graf. 97M GRM. *The Woman at the Dark Window*
  prod/rel: Real, Europa

Schweigende Mund, Der 1951 d: Karl Hartl. lps:
  Oscar Homolka, Gisela Uhlen, Curd Jurgens. 97M AUS.
  prod/rel: Excelsior, UFA

Die Abenteuer Des Herrn von Barabas, Novel
  Wer Bist du Den Ich Liebe? 1949 d: Geza von
  Bolvary. lps: Jester Naefe, Adrian Hoven, Ivan
  Petrovich. 100M GRM. *Who Is This Person I Love?*
  prod/rel: Merkur, UFA

Gestandnis Unter Vier Augen, Novel
  Gestandnis Unter Vier Augen 1954 d: Andre Michel.
  lps: Hildegard Knef, Carl Raddatz, Ivan Desny. 90M
  GRM. *Confession With One Listener* prod/rel: D.L.F.,
  D.F.H.

Golowin Geht Durch Die Stadt, Novel
  Golowin Geht Durch Die Stadt 1940 d: R. A.
  Stemmle. lps: Carl Raddatz, Anneliese Uhlig, Roma
  Bahn. 83M GRM. prod/rel: Bavaria, Regina

Die Grosse Und Die Kleine Welt, Novel
  Grosse Und Die Kleine Welt, Die 1936 d: Johannes
  Riemann. lps: Viktor de Kowa, Heinrich George, Adele
  Sandrock. 98M GRM. prod/rel: Bavaria

Die Heimliche Grafin, Novel
  Heimliche Grafin, Die 1942 d: Geza von Bolvary. lps:
  Marte Harell, Wolf Albach-Retty, Paul Horbiger. 96M
  GRM/HNG. prod/rel: Wien, Schorcht

Man Rede Mir Nicht von Liebe, Novel
  Man Rede Mir Nicht von Liebe 1943 d: Erich Engel.
  lps: Heidemarie Hatheyer, Mathias Wieman, Friedrich
  Domin. 92M GRM. prod/rel: Bavaria

KRIZOVA, MARIE
Novel
  Vzdusne Torpedo 48 1936 d: Miroslav Cikan. lps:
  Otomar Korbelar, Antonin Novotny, Raoul Schranil.
  2561m CZC. *Air Torpedo*; *Pripad Plukovnika Svarce*
  prod/rel: Lloyd

Velke Pokuseni, Novel
  V Pokuseni 1938 d: Miroslav Cikan. lps: Jiri Dohnal,
  Ladislav Bohac, Marie GlazrovA. 2201m CZC. *In
  Temptation* prod/rel: la Tricolore

KROETZ, FRANZ XAVER (1946–, GRM
Wildwechsel, 1968, Play
  Wildwechsel 1972 d: R. W. Fassbinder. lps: Jorg von
  Liebenfels, Ruth Drexel, Eva Mattes. 102M GRM. *Wild
  Game* (UKN); *Jail Bait* (USA); *Game Pass* prod/rel:
  Inter Tel, Atlas

KROG, HELGE
Pa Solsiden, 1927, Play
  Pa Solsiden 1956 d: Edith Carlmar. 81M NRW.

KROHNKE, ERIC
Short Story
  Night Hair Child 1971 d: James Kelly, Andrea
  Bianchi. lps: Mark Lester, Britt Ekland, Hardy Kruger.
  95M UKN/ITL/SPN. *La Tua Presenza Nuda* (ITL);
  Child of the Night; *Night Child*; *What the Peeper Saw*
  (USA); *Diabolica Malicia* (SPN) prod/rel: Cemo Film
  (Roma), Corona Filmproduktion (Munich)

KROLL, HARRY HARRISON
The Cabin in the Cotton, New York 1931, Novel
  Cabin in the Cotton 1932 d: Michael Curtiz, William
  Keighley. lps: Richard Barthelmess, Dorothy Jordan,
  Bette Davis. 78M USA. prod/rel: First National
  Pictures, Inc.

KRONBAUER, RUDOLF JAROSLAV
Rina, Novel
  Rina 1926 d: J. S. Kolar. lps: Jarmila Kronbauerova,
  Vaclav Norman, Theodor Pistek. 2898m CZC. *Tri Lasky
  Riny Sezimove*; *The Three Loves of Rina Sezimova*
  prod/rel: Reiter, Elekta

KROTKOW, JURI
Short Story
  Red Monarch 1982 d: Jack Gold. lps: Colin Blakely,
  David Suchet, Carroll Baker. TVM. 100M UKN.
  prod/rel: Enigma, Goldcrest

KRPATA, KAREL
Mistr Ostreho Mece, Play
  Pocestne Pani Pardubicke 1944 d: Martin Fric. lps:
  Frantisek Smolik, Jirina Stepnikova, Eman FialA.
  2653m CZC. *The Respectable Ladies of Pardubicke*; *The
  Honorable Ladies of Pardubice*; *The Virtuous Dames of
  Pardubice*; *Respectable Women of Pardubice, The*
  prod/rel: Nationalfilm

KRSKA, VACLAV
Odchazeti S Podzimem, Novel
  Ohnive Leto 1939 d: Frantisek Cap, Vaclav KrskA. lps:
  Vaclav Sova, Otylie Beniskova, Lida BaarovA. 2509m
  CZC. *Fiery Summer* prod/rel: Lucernafilm

KRUCZKOWSKI, LEON
Germans, Novel
  Jubileusz 1995 d: Zbigniew Kaminski. lps: Beata
  Tyszkiewicz, Katarzyna Figura, Edward ZentarA. F
  PLN/USA. *Jubilee* prod/rel: Rubikon (Usa), Figaro
  (Poland)

Pierwszy Dzien Wolnosci, Play
Pierwszy Dzien Wolnosci 1964 d: Aleksander Ford. lps: Tadeusz Lomnicki, Beata Tyszkiewicz, Tadeusz Fijewski. 90M PLN. *The First Day of Freedom* prod/rel: Film Polski

KRUDY, GYULA
Szindbad Iffusaga, 1911, Novel
Szindbad 1971 d: Zoltan Huszarik. lps: Zoltan Latinovits, Margit Dayka, Eva Ruttkai. 98M HNG. *Sinbad*; *Sindbad*

Szindbad Utazasai, 1912, Novel
Szindbad 1971 d: Zoltan Huszarik. lps: Zoltan Latinovits, Margit Dayka, Eva Ruttkai. 98M HNG. *Sinbad*; *Sindbad*

KRUMGOLD, JOSEPH (1908–1980), USA, Krumgold, Joseph Quincy
..and Now Miguel, New York 1953, Novel
..and Now Miguel 1966 d: James B. Clark. lps: Pat Cardi, Michael Ansara, Guy Stockwell. 95M USA. prod/rel: Robert B. Radnitz Productions

KRUSCHEL, KARL-HEINZ
Sabine Wulff, Novel
Sabine Wulff 1978 d: Erwin StrankA. lps: Karin Duwel, Manfred Ernst, Jurgen Heinrich. 92M GDR. prod/rel: Defa, Gruppe Berlin

KRUSE, JOHN
Hell Drivers, Short Story
Hell Drivers 1957 d: Cy Endfield. lps: Stanley Baker, Herbert Lom, Peggy Cummins. 108M UKN. prod/rel: Rank, Aqua

KU LUNG
Chueh-Tai Shuang Chiao, Novel
Chueh-Tai Shuang Chiao 1979 d: Ch'u Yuan. lps: Alexander Fu Sheng, Jimmy Wang Yu, Wen Hsueh-Erh. 77M HKG. *The Brave Archer* prod/rel: Shaw Brothers

KUBATOVA, MARIE
Story
Kapitan Korda 1979 d: Josef PinkavA. lps: Michal Vavrusa, Vladimir Brabec, Milena DvorskA. 86M CZC. *Captain Korda* prod/rel: Kratky, Vyrobni Skupina

Chlapi Prece Neplacou, Novel
Chlapi Prece Neplacou 1980 d: Josef PinkavA. lps: Ladislav Frej, Jaroslava Tvrznikova, Vera TichankovA. 84M CZC. *Men Never Cry* prod/rel: Studio Gottwaldov

KUBIN, ALFRED
Die Andere Seite, 1908, Novel
Traumstadt 1973 d: Johannes Schaaf. lps: Per Oscarsson, Rosemarie Fendel, Eva-Maria Meineke. 124M GRM. *City of Dreams*; *Dreamtown*; *Dream City* prod/rel: Independent, Maran

KUBOVY, ANTONIN
Jan Vyrava, Play
Jan Vyrava 1937 d: Vladimir Borsky. lps: Zdenek Stepanek, Stanislav Strnad, Ladislav Brom. 2279m CZC. prod/rel: Projektor

KUCERA, EDUARD
Jarka a Vera, Novel
Jarka a Vera 1938 d: Vaclav Binovec. lps: Ladislav Pesek, Eva Gerova, Frantisek Kreuzmann. 2377m CZC. *Jarka and Vera* prod/rel: Lucernafilm

KUCHLER-SILBERMAN, LENA
My Hundred Children, Book
Lena: My Hundred Children 1988 d: Edwin Sherin. lps: Linda Lavin, Leonore Harris, Cynthia Wilde. TVM. 100M USA. *Lena: My 100 Children* prod/rel: Robert Greenwald, Hungarofilm

KUHLMEY, JOCHEN
Neigungsehe, Play
Neigungsehe 1944 d: Carl Froelich. lps: Henny Porten, Paul Westermeier, Kathe Dyckhoff. 94M GRM. prod/rel: UFA, Turck

KUHNE, DAVID
Novel
Gritos En la Noche 1961 d: Jesus Franco. lps: Howard Vernon, Conrado San Martin, Diana Lorys. 95M SPN/FRN. *The Awful Dr. Orloff* (USA); *L' Horrible Dr. Orloff* (FRN); *The Demon Doctor* (UKN); *Cries in the Night*; *El Doctor Demonio* prod/rel: Hispamer Films

KUHNERT, ARTHUR A.
Kleiner Fisch Im Grossen Netz, Story
Lockende Gefahr 1950 d: Eugen York. lps: Angelika Hauff, Walter Richter, Adi Lodel. 76M GRM. *Der Totschlager*; *Dangerous Temptation* prod/rel: Real, Doring

KUKLA, KAREL LADISLAV
Bahno Prahy, Short Story
Bahno Prahy 1927 d: M. J. Krnansky. lps: Bronislava Livia, L. H. Struna, Jan SvobodA. CZC. *The Bog of Prague*; *The Mire of Prague* prod/rel: Fiserfilm, Filmove Zavody

Zlocin V Lorete, Novel
Loretanske Zvonky 1929 d: M. J. Krnansky. lps: Alois Charvat, Milka Balek-Brodska, Anita JanovA. CZC. *The Bells of the Loretto Church* prod/rel: Miroslav J. Krnansky

KULB, KARL GEORG
Die Glucklichste Ehe Der Welt, Play
Man Spielt Nicht Mit Der Liebe 1949 d: Hans Deppe. lps: Lil Dagover, Bruni Lobel, Paul Klinger. 90M GRM. *You Don't Play Around With Love* prod/rel: C.C.C., Schorcht

Sensation in Budapest, Play
Sensation Im Savoy 1950 d: Eduard von Borsody. lps: Sybille Schmitz, Paul Klinger, Karl Schonbock. 80M GRM. *Sensation at the Savoy Hotel* prod/rel: Allegro, Danubia

KUMMER, CLARE
Good Gracious Annabelle, New York 1916, Play
Annabelle's Affairs 1931 d: Alfred L. Werker. lps: Victor McLaglen, Jeanette MacDonald, Roland Young. 75M USA. *Good Gracious Annabelle*; *Two Can Play*; *The Affairs of Annabelle* prod/rel: Fox Film Corp.
Good Gracious, Annabelle 1919 d: George Melford. lps: Billie Burke, Herbert Rawlinson, Gilbert Douglas. 4246f USA. *Good Gracious Annabelle!* prod/rel: Famous Players-Lasky Corp.©, Paramount Pictures

Her Master's Voice, New York 1933, Play
Her Master's Voice 1936 d: Joseph Santley. lps: Edward Everett Horton, Peggy Conklin, Laura Hope Crews. 75M USA. prod/rel: Walter Wanger Productions, Paramount Productions©

The Rescuing Angel, New York 1917, Play
Rescuing Angel, The 1919 d: Walter Edwards. lps: Shirley Mason, Forrest Stanley, Arthur Edmund Carewe. 5r USA. prod/rel: Famous Players-Lasky Corp.©, Paramount Pictures

A Successful Calamity, New York 1917, Play
Successful Calamity, A 1932 d: John G. Adolfi. lps: George Arliss, Mary Astor, Evelyn Knapp. 73M USA. prod/rel: Warner Bros. Pictures©

KUMMER, FREDERIC ARNOLD
The Brute, New York 1912, Novel
Brute, The 1914 d: Thomas N. Heffron. lps: Malcolm Williams, House Peters, Helen Hilton. 4r USA. prod/rel: Famous Players Film Co., State Rights

A Close Call, Short Story
Yellow Pawn, The 1916 d: George Melford. lps: Cleo Ridgely, Wallace Reid, William Conklin. 5r USA. prod/rel: Jesse L. Lasky Feature Play Co.©, Paramount Pictures Corp.

The Green God, New York 1911, Novel
Green God, The 1918 d: Paul Scardon. lps: Harry T. Morey, Betty Blythe, Arthur Donaldson. 5r USA. prod/rel: Vitagraph Co. of America©, Blue Ribbon Feature

The Ivory Snuff Box, New York 1912, Novel
Ivory Snuff Box, The 1915 d: Maurice Tourneur. lps: Holbrook Blinn, Alma Belwin, Norman Trevor. 5r USA. prod/rel: William A. Brady Picture Plays, Inc., World Film Corp.©

Love's Greatest Mistake, New York 1927, Novel
Love's Greatest Mistake 1927 d: A. Edward Sutherland. lps: Evelyn Brent, William Powell, James Hall. 6007f USA. prod/rel: Famous Players-Lasky, Paramount Pictures

Mr. Buttles, Short Story
Mr. Buttles 1915 d: Joseph Byron Totten. lps: Harry Dunkinson, Richard C. Travers, Edna Mayo. 3r USA. prod/rel: Essanay

The Other Woman, 1910, Play
Other Woman, The 1918 d: Albert Parker. lps: Peggy Hyland, Milton Sills, Anna Lehr. 5r USA. prod/rel: Astra Film Corp., Pathe Exchange, Inc.©

The Painted Woman, New York 1913, Play
Slave Market, The 1917 d: Hugh Ford. lps: Pauline Frederick, Thomas Meighan, Albert Hart. 5r USA. prod/rel: Famous Players Film Co.©, Paramount Pictures Corp.

Plaster Saints, New York 1922, Novel
Spitfire, The 1924 d: W. Christy Cabanne. lps: Betty Blythe, Lowell Sherman, Elliott Dexter. 6109f USA. prod/rel: Murray W. Garsson Productions, Associated Exhibitors

A Song of Sixpence, New York 1913, Novel
Song of Sixpence, A 1917 d: Ralph Dean. lps: Marie Wayne, Robert Conness, Margaret Townsend. 5r USA. *A Woman's Way* prod/rel: Van Dyke Film Production Co., Art Dramas, Inc.

The Town Scandal, Story
Town Scandal, The 1923 d: King Baggot. lps: Gladys Walton, Edward Hearn, Edward McWade. 4704f USA. *The Chicken That Came Home to Roost*; *The Chicken* prod/rel: Universal Pictures

KUNCEWICZOWA, MARIA
Cudzoziemka, 1935, Novel
Cudzoziemka 1986 d: Ryszard Ber. 105M PLN.

KUNDERA, MILAN (1929–, CZC
Truchlivy Buh Ja, 1963, Short Story
Ja, Truchlivy Buh 1969 d: Antonin Kachlik. lps: Milos Kopecky, Hana Lelitova, Pavel Landovsky. 85M CZC. *I the Doleful God*; *I the Sad God*

Nikdo Se Nebude Smat, 1963, Short Story
Nikdo Se Nebude Smat 1965 d: Hynek Bocan. lps: Jan Kacer, Jiri Menzel, Stepanka RehakovA. 95M CZC. *Nobody Shall be Laughing*; *No Laughing Matter*; *Nobody Gets the Last Laugh*; *Nobody Will Laugh* prod/rel: Filmove Studio Barrandov

Wesnesitelna Lehkost Byti, 1985, Novel
Unbearable Lightness of Being, The 1987 d: Philip Kaufman. lps: Daniel Day-Lewis, Juliette Binoche, Lena Olin. 172M USA. prod/rel: Orion

Zert, 1967, Novel
Zert 1968 d: Jaromil Jires. lps: Josef Somr, Jana Ditetova, Ludek Munzar. 80M CZC. *The Joke* prod/rel: Studio Barrandov

KUNEN, JAMES SIMON
The Strawberry Statement: Notes of a College Revolutionary, New York 1969, Novel
Strawberry Statement, The 1970 d: Stuart Hagmann. lps: Bruce Davison, Kim Darby, Bud Cort. 110M USA. prod/rel: Metro-Goldwyn-Mayer, Inc.

KUNHARDT JR., PHILIP
My Father's House, Novel
My Father's House 1975 d: Alex Segal. lps: Cliff Robertson, Robert Preston, Eileen Brennan. TVM. 100M USA. prod/rel: Filmways

KUNIEDA, KANJI
Story
Utamaro O Meguru Gonin No Onna 1946 d: Kenji Mizoguchi. lps: Minosuke Bando, Kinuyo Tanaka, Hiroko Kowasaki. 93M JPN. *Utamaro and His Five Women* (USA); *Five Women Around Utamaro* prod/rel: Shochiku Co.

KUNJUKUTTAN, MADAMPU
Ashwathama, Novel
Ashwathama 1979 d: K. R. Mohanan. lps: Madampu Kunjukuttan, Vidhubala, Ravi Menon. 121M IND. *The Wandering Soul*; *Aswathama* prod/rel: Mohan Mohammed Pictures

KUNNEKE, EDUARD
Gluckliche Reise, Opera
Gluckliche Reise 1933 d: Alfred Abel. lps: Paul Henckels, Adele Sandrock, Magda Schneider. 78M GRM. *Happy Voyage*
Gluckliche Reise 1954 d: Thomas Engel. lps: Paul Hubschmid, Inge Egger, Paul Klinger. 87M GRM. *Happy Voyage* prod/rel: Capitol, Prisma

Der Vetter Aus Dingsda, Opera
Vetter Aus Dingsda, Der 1934 d: Georg Zoch. lps: Lien Deyers, Lizzi Holzschuh, Walter von Lennep. 75M GRM. *Cousin from Podunk*; *Damenwahl* prod/rel: Victor Klein, Dietz
Vetter Aus Dingsda, Der 1953 d: Karl Anton. lps: Vera Molnar, Gerhard Riedmann, Grethe Weiser. 95M GRM. prod/rel: Central-Europa, Prisma

KUNZE, REINER
Die Wunderbaren Jahre, Novel
Wunderbaren Jahre, Die 1979 d: Reiner Kunze. lps: Gabi Marr, Martin May, Dietrich Mattausch. 104M GRM. *The Wonderful Years* prod/rel: Franz Seitz, Caro

KUO CHENG
Short Stories
Guodao Fengbi 1997 d: Ho Ping. lps: Annie Shizuka Inoh, Chang Shih, To Tzong-HuA. 122M TWN. *Wolves Cry Under the Moon* prod/rel: Scholar Films

KUPRIN, ALEKSANDER IVANOVICH (1870–1938), RSS
Short Story
Poedinok 1957 d: Vladimir Petrov. lps: I. Pusyryov, Irina Skobtseva, Andrey Popov. 104M USS. *The Duel* prod/rel: Mosfilm

Granatovyy Braslet, 1911, Short Story
Granatovyy Braslet 1965 d: Abram Room. lps: Ariadna Shengelaya, Igor Ozerov, Oleg Basilashvili. 90M USS. *The Garnet Bracelet* (USA) prod/rel: Mosfilm

Oleissa, 1898, Short Story
Haxan 1955 d: Andre Michel. lps: Maurice Ronet, Marina Vlady, Nicole Courcel. 97M SWD/FRN. *La Sorciere* (FRN); *Blonde Witch*; *The Sorceress*; *Das Madchen Aus Dem Wald*; *Blonde Hexe, Die* prod/rel: Films Metzger Et Woog, Iena

Poyedinok, 1905, Short Story
Surocka 1982 d: Josif Heifitz. 98M USS. *Shurochka*

Yama, Novel
Gion No Shimai 1936 d: Kenji Mizoguchi. lps: Isuzu Yamada, Yoko Umemura, Eitaro Shindo. 69M JPN. *Sisters of the Gion* (USA) prod/rel: Daiichi Film Co.

KUREISHI, HANIF
My Son the Fanatic, Short Story
My Son the Fanatic 1997 d: Udayan Prasad. lps: Om Puri, Rachel Griffiths, Stellan Skarsgard. 87M UKN. prod/rel: Zephyr Films, BBC Films

KURNITZ, HARRY
Story
Hatari! 1962 d: Howard Hawks. lps: John Wayne, Hardy Kruger, Elsa Martinelli. 159M USA. prod/rel: Paramount

Once More With Feeling, Play
Once More, With Feeling 1960 d: Stanley Donen. lps: Yul Brynner, Kay Kendall, Gregory Ratoff. 92M USA. prod/rel: Columbia, Stanley Donen

KUROIWA, RUIKA
Flower in the Wilderness, Novel
Konggu Lan 1925 d: Zhang Shichuan. lps: Zhang Zhiyun, Yang Naimei, Zhu Fei. 11r CHN. *Orchid in the Empty Valley* prod/rel: Mingxing Film Company

KURYS, DIANE
Coup de Foudre, Book
Coup de Foudre 1983 d: Diane Kurys. lps: Guy Marchand, Jean-Pierre Bacri, Miou-Miou. 110M FRN. *At First Sight* (UKN); *Entre Nous* (USA); *Between Us* prod/rel: Partners Productions, Alexandre Films

KURZ, P.
Martin Luther His Life and Times, Book
Martin Luther, His Life and Time 1924. 6-8r USA. prod/rel: Lutheran Film Division

KUSELL, DANIEL
The Gingham Girl, New York 1922, Musical Play
Gingham Girl, The 1927 d: David Kirkland. lps: Lois Wilson, George K. Arthur, Charles Crockett. 6257f USA. prod/rel: R-C Pictures, Film Booking Offices of America

The Party's Over, New York 1933, Play
Party's Over, The 1934 d: Walter Lang. lps: Stuart Erwin, Ann Sothern, Arline Judge. 68M USA. prod/rel: Columbia Pictures Corp.©

KUTLU, AYLA
Novel
Sen de Gitme 1997 d: Tunc Basaran. lps: Isik Yenersu, Olivia Bonamy, Fikret Hakan. 107M TRK. *Please Don't Go* prod/rel: Magnum Film

KVAPIL, JAROSLAV
Bludicka, Play
Ty Petrinske Strane 1922 d: Thea CervenkovA. lps: Rudolf Myzet, Anci Jelinkova, Jan W. Speerger. CZC. *The Petrin Hillside*; *Bludicka*; *Will-O'-the-Wisp* prod/rel: Filmovy Ustav, la Tricolore

Oblaka, Play
Skrivanci Pisen 1933 d: Svatopluk Innemann. lps: Jarmila Novotna, Adolf Horalek, Hermina FordovA. 2206m CZC. *Song of the Lark*; *The Lark's Song* prod/rel: Elekta

KYNE, PETER B. (1880–1957), USA, Kyne, Peter Bernard
Story
Ride, Kelly, Ride 1941 d: Norman Foster. lps: Eugene Pallette, Marvin Stephens, Rita Quigley. 59M USA. prod/rel: 20th Century Fox

Short Story
Wild Horse 1930 d: Richard Thorpe, Sidney Algier. lps: Hoot Gibson, Alberta Vaughn, Stepin Fetchit. 77M USA. *Silver Devil* (UKN) prod/rel: Allied Pictures Corp.

All for Love, 1928, Short Story
Local Bad Man, The 1932 d: Otto Brower. lps: Hoot Gibson, Sally Blaine, Edward Peil. 59M USA. *Looting Looters* prod/rel: Allied Pictures Corp.

Valley of Wanted Men 1935 d: Alan James. lps: Frankie Darro, Grant Withers, Dru Layron. 62M USA. *Wanted Men* (UKN); *All for Love* prod/rel: Conn Pictures Corp.

Back to Yellow Jacket, Short Story
Back to Yellow Jacket 1922 d: Ben Wilson. lps: Roy Stewart, Kathleen Kirkham, Earl Metcalfe. 5901f USA. prod/rel: Ben Wilson Productions, Arrow Film Corp.

The Big Bonanza, Novel
Big Bonanza, The 1944 d: George Archainbaud. lps: Richard Arlen, Robert Livingston, Jane Frazee. 68M USA. prod/rel: Republic

Blue Blood and the Pirates, 1912, Short Story
Breed of the Sea 1926 d: Ralph Ince. lps: Ralph Ince, Margaret Livingston, Pat Harmon. 5408f USA. prod/rel: R-C Pictures, Film Booking Offices of America

Bread Upon the Waters, 1923, Short Story
Hero on Horseback, A 1927 d: Del Andrews. lps: Hoot Gibson, Ethlyne Clair, Edwards Davis. 5551f USA. prod/rel: Universal Pictures

Brothers Under Their Skins, 1921, Short Story
Brothers Under the Skin 1922 d: E. Mason Hopper. lps: Pat O'Malley, Helene Chadwick, Mae Busch. 4983f USA. prod/rel: Goldwyn Pictures

Cappy Ricks, New York 1915, Novel
Cappy Ricks 1921 d: Tom Forman. lps: Thomas Meighan, Charles Abbe, Agnes Ayres. 5962f USA. prod/rel: Famous Players-Lasky, Paramount Pictures

Cappy Ricks Comes Back, New York 1934, Short Story
Cappy Ricks Returns 1935 d: MacK V. Wright. lps: Robert McWade, Florine McKinney, Lois Wilson. 67M USA. prod/rel: Republic Pictures Corp., Trem Carr Production

Cornflower Cassie's Concert, 1924, Short Story
Beauty and the Bad Man 1925 d: William Worthington. lps: Mabel Ballin, Forrest Stanley, Russell Simpson. 5794f USA. prod/rel: Peninsula Studios

Dog Meat, Story
Blue Blood 1951 d: Lew Landers. lps: Bill Williams, Jane Nigh, Arthur Shields. 72M USA. prod/rel: Monogram

The Enchanted Hill, New York 1924, Novel
Enchanted Hill, The 1926 d: Irvin V. Willat. lps: Jack Holt, Florence Vidor, Noah Beery. 6326f USA. prod/rel: Famous Players-Lasky, Paramount Pictures

A Film Star's Holiday, Short Story
Pride of the Legion, The 1932 d: Ford Beebe. lps: Victor Jory, Rin-Tin-Tin Jr., Barbara Kent. 70M USA. *The Big Pay-Off* (UKN) prod/rel: Mascot Pictures Corp., State Rights

The Go-Getter, Short Story
Go Getter, The 1937 d: Busby Berkeley. lps: George Brent, Anita Louise, Charles Winninger. 92M USA. *The Go-Getter* prod/rel: Warner Bros. Pictures©

Go-Getter, The 1923 d: Edward H. Griffith. lps: T. Roy Barnes, Seena Owen, William Norris. 7771f USA. prod/rel: Cosmopolitan Productions, Paramount Pictures

The Great Mono Miracle, Novel
Face in the Fog, A 1936 d: Robert F. Hill. lps: June Collyer, Lloyd Hughes, Jack Mulhall. 51M USA. prod/rel: Victory Pictures Corp.©, State Rights

The Harbor Bar, 1914, Short Story
Loving Lies 1924 d: W. S. Van Dyke. lps: Evelyn Brent, Monte Blue, Joan Lowell. 6526f USA. prod/rel: Associated Authors, Allied Producers and Distributors

Humanizing Mr. Winsby, 1915, Short Story
Making a Man 1922 d: Joseph Henabery. lps: Jack Holt, J. P. Lockney, Eva Novak. 5594f USA. prod/rel: Famous Players-Lasky, Paramount Pictures

It Happened While He Fished, Short Story
It Happened While He Fished 1915 d: Horace Davey. lps: John Francis Dillon, Neal Burns, Billie Rhodes. SHT USA. prod/rel: Nestor

Jim the Conqueror, Short Story
Jim the Conqueror 1927 d: George B. Seitz. lps: William Boyd, Elinor Fair, Walter Long. 5324f USA. prod/rel: Metropolitan Pictures Corp. of Calif., Producers Distributing Corp.

The Joy of Living, 1914, Story
Black Gold 1936 d: Russell Hopton. lps: Frankie Darro, Leroy Mason, Gloria SheA. 58M USA. prod/rel: Conn Pictures Corp.

The Just Judge, Short Story
Self-Defense 1932 d: Phil Rosen. lps: Pauline Frederick, Claire Windsor, Theodore von Eltz. 70M USA. *My Mother*; *Self Defense* prod/rel: Monogram Pictures Corp.

Kindred of the Dust, New York 1920, Novel
Kindred of the Dust 1922 d: Raoul Walsh. lps: Miriam Cooper, Ralph Graves, Lionel Belmore. 7439f USA. prod/rel: R. A. Walsh Co., Associated First National Pictures

The Land Just Over Yonder, 1915, Short Story
Land Just Over Yonder, The 1916 d: Julius Frankenburg. lps: George Chesebro, Arthur Millett, George Best. 6r USA. prod/rel: Dudley Motion Picture Mfg. Co., State Rights

The Last Assignment, 1913, Short Story
Fighting Coward 1935 d: Dan Milner. lps: Ray Walker, Joan Woodbury, William Farnum. 70M USA. *The Last Assignment*; *Wanted Men* prod/rel: Victory Pictures Corp.©, State Rights

Light in Darkness, 1916, Short Story
Light in Darkness 1917 d: Alan Crosland. lps: Shirley Mason, Frank Morgan, William H. Tooker. 5087f USA. prod/rel: Thomas A. Edison, Inc.©, K-E-S-E Service

The Long Chance, New York 1914, Novel
Long Chance, The 1915 d: Edward J. Le Saint. lps: Frank Keenan, Fred Church, Harry Blaising. 6r USA. prod/rel: Universal Film Mfg. Co.©, Broadway Universal Feature

Long Chance, The 1922 d: Jack Conway. lps: Henry B. Walthall, Marjorie Daw, Ralph Graves. 4331f USA. prod/rel: Universal Film Mfg. Co.

The Man in Hobbles, 1913, Short Story
Man in Hobbles, The 1928 d: George Archainbaud. lps: John Harron, Lila Lee, Lucien Littlefield. 5967f USA. prod/rel: Tiffany-Stahl Productions

A Man's Man, 1917, Serial Story
Man's Man, A 1917 d: Oscar Apfel. lps: J. Warren Kerrigan, Lois Wilson, Kenneth Harlan. 7r USA. prod/rel: Paralta Plays, Inc., W. W. Hodkinson Corp.

Man's Man, A 1923 d: Oscar Apfel. lps: J. Warren Kerrigan, Lois Wilson, Kenneth Harlan. 5r USA. prod/rel: Film Booking Offices of America

A Motion to Adjourn, 1914, Short Story
Headline Crasher 1937 d: Leslie Goodwins. lps: Frankie Darro, Kane Richmond, Jack Ingram. 58M USA. prod/rel: Conn Pictures Corp.

Motion to Adjourn, A 1921 d: Roy Clements. lps: Harry Rattenberry, Roy Stewart, Sidney d'Albrook. 6r USA. prod/rel: Ben Wilson Productions, Arrow Film Corp.

Never the Twain Shall Meet, New York 1923, Novel
Never the Twain Shall Meet 1925 d: Maurice Tourneur. lps: Anita Stewart, Bert Lytell, Huntley Gordon. 8143f USA. prod/rel: Metro-Goldwyn-Mayer Distributing Corp., Cosmopolitan Corp.

Never the Twain Shall Meet 1931 d: W. S. Van Dyke. lps: Leslie Howard, Conchita Montenegro, C. Aubrey Smith. 80M USA. prod/rel: Metro-Goldwyn-Mayer Corp., Metro-Goldwyn-Mayer Dist. Corp.©

The New Freedom, Short Story
Men of Action 1935 d: Alan James. lps: Frankie Darro, Leroy Mason, Barbara Worth. 61M USA. *Born to Fight* prod/rel: Conn Pictures Corp.

Young Dynamite 1937 d: Leslie Goodwins. lps: Frankie Darro, Kane Richmond, Carleton Young. 57M USA. *State Trooper* prod/rel: Conn Productions, Ambassador Pictures

The New Pardner, Short Story
Hot Off the Press 1935 d: Al Herman. lps: Jack La Rue, Virginia Pine, Monte Blue. 57M USA. prod/rel: Victory Pictures Corp.©, State Rights

Non Shenanigans, Story
More Pay - Less Work 1926 d: Albert Ray. lps: Albert Gran, Mary Brian, E. J. Ratcliffe. 6027f USA. prod/rel: Fox Film Corp.

Oh Promise Me, 1926, Short Story
Buckaroo Kid, The 1926 d: Lynn Reynolds. lps: Hoot Gibson, Ethel Shannon, Burr McIntosh. 6167f USA. prod/rel: Universal Pictures

Flaming Guns 1932 d: Arthur Rosson. lps: Tom Mix, Ruth Hall, William Farnum. 57M USA. *Rough Riding Romeo* (UKN) prod/rel: Universal Pictures Corp.©

On Irish Hill, Short Story
Kelly of the Secret Service 1936 d: Robert F. Hill. lps: Jack Mulhall, Lloyd Hughes, Fuzzy Knight. 69M USA. prod/rel: Victory Pictures Corp., State Rights

One Day's Work, Short Story
Rio Grande Romance 1936 d: Robert F. Hill. lps: Edward Nugent, Maxine Doyle, Fuzzy Knight. 60M USA. *Framed* (UKN); *Put on the Spot* prod/rel: Victory Pictures Corp.©, State Rights

One Eighth Apache, Short Story
Danger Ahead 1935 d: Al Herman. lps: Lawrence Gray, Eddie Phillips, Fuzzy Knight. 65M USA. prod/rel: Victory Pictures Corp.

One Eighth Apache 1922 d: Ben Wilson. lps: Roy Stewart, Kathleen Kirkham, Wilbur McGaugh. 5634f USA. prod/rel: Berwilla Film Corp., Arrow Film Corp.

One Touch of Nature, 1913, Short Story
One Touch of Nature 1917 d: Edward H. Griffith. lps: John Drew Bennett, Edward Lawrence, Viola Cain. 5r USA. prod/rel: Thomas A. Edison, Inc.©, K-E-S-E Service

Pals in Paradise, Story
Pals in Paradise 1926 d: George B. Seitz. lps: Marguerite de La Motte, John Bowers, Rudolf Schildkraut. 6696f USA. prod/rel: Metropolitan Pictures Corp. of Calif., Producers Distributing Corp.

The Parson of Panamint, 1915, Short Story
  Parson of Panamint, The 1916 d: William D. Taylor. lps: Dustin Farnum, Winifred Kingston, Pomeroy Cannon. 5r USA. prod/rel: Pallas Pictures, Paramount Pictures Corp.
  Parson of Panamint, The 1941 d: William McGann. lps: Charles Ruggles, Ellen Drew, Phillip Terry. 84M USA. prod/rel: Paramount
  While Satan Sleeps 1922 d: Joseph Henabery. lps: Jack Holt, Wade Boteler, Mabel Van Buren. 6069f USA. prod/rel: Famous Players-Lasky, Paramount Pictures

The Pride of Palomar, New York 1921, Novel
  Pride of Palomar, The 1922 d: Frank Borzage. lps: Forrest Stanley, Marjorie Daw, Tote Du Crow. 7494f USA. prod/rel: Cosmopolitan Corp., Paramount Pictures

Renunciation, Story
  Judge Not; Or, the Woman of Mona Diggings 1915 d: Robert Z. Leonard. lps: Harry Carey, Harry Carter, Marc Robbins. 6r USA. *Renunciation* prod/rel: Universal Film Mfg. Co.©, Broadway Universal Feature

Rustling for Cupid, 1926, Short Story
  Rustling for Cupid 1926 d: Irving Cummings. lps: George O'Brien, Anita Stewart, Russell Simpson. 4835f USA. prod/rel: Fox Film Corp.

Salt of the Earth, 1917, Short Story
  Salt of the Earth 1917 d: Saul Harrison. lps: Russell Simpson, William Wadsworth, Peggy Adams. 5r USA. prod/rel: Thomas A. Edison, Inc.©, Perfection Pictures

The Sheriff of Cinnabar, Story
  Red Courage 1921 d: B. Reeves Eason. lps: Hoot Gibson, Joel Day, Molly Malone. 4481f USA. prod/rel: Universal Film Mfg. Co.

Shipmates, Short Story
  Taming the Wild 1936 d: Robert F. Hill. lps: Rod La Rocque, Maxine Doyle, Barbara Pepper. 55M USA. *Madcap* (UKN) prod/rel: Victory Pictures Corp.©, State Rights

The Ten Dollar Raise, 1909, Short Story
  $10 Raise 1935 d: George Marshall. lps: Edward Everett Horton, Karen Morley, Alan Dinehart. 70M USA. *Mr. Faintheart* (UKN); *Ten Dollar Raise* prod/rel: Fox Film Corp.©
  Ten Dollar Raise, The 1921 d: Edward Sloman. lps: William V. Mong, Marguerite de La Motte, Pat O'Malley. 5726f USA. prod/rel: J. L. Frothingham, Associated Producers

Thoroughbreds, 1925, Short Story
  Golden Strain, The 1925 d: Victor Schertzinger. lps: Hobart Bosworth, Kenneth Harlan, Madge Bellamy. 5989f USA. prod/rel: Fox Film Corp.

Three Godfathers, New York 1913, Novel
  Godchild, The 1974 d: John Badham. lps: Jack Palance, Jack Warden, Keith Carradine. TVM. 78M USA. prod/rel: MGM, Mor
  Hell's Heroes 1930 d: William Wyler. lps: Charles Bickford, Raymond Hatton, Fred Kohler. 65M USA. prod/rel: Universal Pictures
  Marked Men 1920 d: John Ford. lps: Harry Carey, J. Farrell MacDonald, Joe Harris. 5-6r USA. prod/rel: Universal Film Mfg. Co.©
  Three Godfathers 1936 d: Richard Boleslawski. lps: Chester Morris, Lewis Stone, Walter Brennan. 85M USA. *Miracle in the Sand* prod/rel: Metro-Goldwyn-Mayer Corp.©
  Three Godfathers 1948 d: John Ford. lps: John Wayne, Pedro Armendariz, Harry Carey Jr. 106M USA. prod/rel: Metro-Goldwyn-Mayer Corp.
  Three Godfathers, The 1916 d: Edward J. Le Saint. lps: Stella Razetto, Harry Carey, George Berrell. 6r USA. prod/rel: Bluebird Photoplays, Inc.©
  Tres Hombres Malos 1948 d: Raul de AndA. lps: Raul de Anda, Luis Aguilar, Carlos Lopez MoctezumA. 95M MXC.

Tide of Empire, New York 1928, Novel
  Tide of Empire 1929 d: Allan Dwan. lps: Renee Adoree, Tom Keene, George Fawcett. 6552f USA. prod/rel: Cosmopolitan Productions, Metro-Goldwyn-Mayer Distributing Corp.

Tidy Toreador, 1927, Short Story
  Galloping Fury 1927 d: B. Reeves Eason. lps: Hoot Gibson, Otis Harlan, Sally Rand. 5503f USA. prod/rel: Universal Pictures

The Tie That Binds, Story
  Tie That Binds, The 1923 d: Joseph Levering. lps: Walter Miller, Barbara Bedford, Raymond Hatton. 7r USA. prod/rel: Jacob Wilk, Warner Brothers Pictures

To Him Who Dares, 1911, Short Story
  Born to Fight 1936 d: Charles Hutchison. lps: Frankie Darro, Kane Richmond, Eddie Phillips. 69M USA. prod/rel: Conn Pictures Corp.

The Understanding Heart, New York 1926, Novel
  Understanding Heart, The 1927 d: Jack Conway. lps: Joan Crawford, Rockliffe Fellowes, Francis X. Bushman Jr. 6657f USA. prod/rel: Cosmopolitan Productions, Metro-Goldwyn-Mayer Distributing Corp.

The Valley of the Giants, Garden City, N.Y. 1918, Novel
  Valley of the Giants 1938 d: William Keighley. lps: Wayne Morris, Claire Trevor, Charles Bickford. 79M USA. prod/rel: Warner Bros. Pictures©
  Valley of the Giants, The 1919 d: James Cruze. lps: Wallace Reid, Grace Darmond, William Brunton. 4625f USA. *In the Valley of the Giants* prod/rel: Famous Players-Lasky Corp.©, Paramount Pictures
  Valley of the Giants, The 1927 d: Charles J. Brabin. lps: Milton Sills, Doris Kenyon, Arthur Stone. 6600f USA. prod/rel: First National Pictures

What the River Foretold, Story
  What the River Foretold 1915 d: William Franey, Joseph J. Franz. lps: Sherman Bainbridge, Edythe Sterling, Jack Holt. 3r USA. prod/rel: Bison

Without Orders, 1936, Short Story
  Without Orders 1936 d: Lew Landers. lps: Robert Armstrong, Sally Eilers, Vinton Haworth. 64M USA. prod/rel: RKO Radio Pictures©

KYZLINKOVA, MARIE
Z Lasky, Novel
  Z Lasky 1928 d: Vladimir Slavinsky. lps: Marie Grossova, Mana Zeniskova, Jan W. Speerger. 2141m CZC. *With Love; For Love* prod/rel: Gloriafilm

L

LA BERN, ARTHUR (1909–, UKN
Goodbye Piccadilly, Farewell Leicester Square, Novel
  Frenzy 1972 d: Alfred Hitchcock. lps: Alec McCowen, Barry Foster, Anna Massey. 118M UKN/USA. prod/rel: Universal, Alfred Hitchcock

It Always Rains on Sundays, Novel
  It Always Rains on Sundays 1947 d: Robert Hamer. lps: Googie Withers, Jack Warner, John McCallum. 92M UKN. prod/rel: Ealing Studios, General Film Distributors

Night Darkens the Street, Novel
  Good Time Girl 1948 d: David MacDonald. lps: Jean Kent, Dennis Price, Flora Robson. 93M UKN. prod/rel: General Film Distributors, Triton

Paper Orchid, Novel
  Paper Orchid 1949 d: Roy Ward Baker. lps: Hugh Williams, Hy Hazell, Sidney James. 86M UKN. prod/rel: Ganesh, Columbia

LA COSSITT, HENRY
The Mob, 1928, Short Story
  Homicide Squad, The 1931 d: Edward L. Cahn, George Melford. lps: Leo Carrillo, Noah Beery, Mary Brian. 70M USA. *Lost Men* (UKN) prod/rel: Universal Pictures Corp.©

LA FARGE, OLIVER (1901–1963), USA, la Farge, Oliver Hazzard Perry
Laughing Boy, Boston 1929, Novel
  Laughing Boy 1934 d: W. S. Van Dyke. lps: Ramon Novarro, Lupe Velez, Chief Thunderbird. 80M USA. prod/rel: Metro-Goldwyn-Mayer Corp.©

LA FAYETTE, MARIE-MADELEINE (1643–1693), FRN, De la Fayette, Comtesse
La Princesse de Cleves, 1678, Novel
  Princesse de Cleves, La 1960 d: Jean Delannoy. lps: Marina Vlady, Jean Marais, Lea Padovani. 110M FRN/ITL. *La Principessa Di Cleves* (ITL) prod/rel: Cinetel, Silver Films

LA FONTAINE, GEORGE
Flashpoint, Book
  Flashpoint 1984 d: William Tannen. lps: Kris Kristofferson, Treat Williams, Rip Torn. TVM. 94M USA. *Border Patrol* prod/rel: Tri-Star, Home Box Office

Two-Minute Warning, Novel
  Two-Minute Warning 1976 d: Larry Peerce. lps: Charlton Heston, John Cassavetes, Martin Balsam. 116M USA. prod/rel: Filmways

LA MURE, PIERRE
Moulin Rouge, Novel
  Moulin Rouge 1952 d: John Huston. lps: Jose Ferrer, Colette Marchand, Zsa Zsa Gabor. 120M UKN/USA. prod/rel: Romulus, Moulin

LA PLANTE, LYNDA
Bella Mafia, Novel
  Bella Mafia - Parts I & II 1997 d: David Greene. lps: Vanessa Redgrave, Dennis Farina, Nastassja Kinski. TVM. 240M USA. prod/rel: Konigsberg Co.

LA ROSA, ENZO
Colpi Di Timone, Play
  Colpi Di Timone 1942 d: Gennaro Righelli. lps: Dina Sassoli, Elena Altieri, Amelia Chellini. 95M ITL. prod/rel: Lux Film

Martin Toccaferro, Play
  Martin Toccaferro 1954 d: Leonardo de Mitri. lps: Peppino de Filippo, Titina di Filippo, Wanda Osiris. 100M ITL. prod/rel: Amore Film

LA ROSA, LINDA
Le Coeur En Fuite, Novel
  Alexandra 1991 d: Denis Amar. lps: Anne Roussel, Andrea Occhipinti, Matthias Habich. TVM. 200M ITL/FRN/GRM. *Princesse Alexandra*

LAAR, CLEMENS
Meines Vaters Pferde, Novel
  Meines Vaters Pferde 1954 d: Gerhard Lamprecht. lps: Eva Bartok, Curd Jurgens, Reinhold Schunzel. 110M GRM. *The Horses of My Father* prod/rel: Carlton, N.F.

LABARRIERE, DOMINIQUE
Le Feu Sous la Peau, Novel
  Feu Sous la Peau, Le 1985 d: Gerard Kikoine. lps: Kevin Bernhardt, Eva Czemerys, Michel Jacob. 93M FRN. prod/rel: Eurogroup Film, Multimedia

LABICHE, EUGENE (1815–1888), FRN, Labiche, Eugene Marin
L' Affaire de la Rue de Lourcine, 1857, Play
  Affaire de la Rue de Lourcine, L' 1932 d: Marcel Dumont. lps: Victor Vina, Jeanne Bayle, Juliette Zahn. 45M FRN. prod/rel: Compagnie Parisienne Cinematographique

La Cagnotte, 1864, Play
  Trois Jours de Bringue a Paris 1953 d: Emile Couzinet. lps: Lucien Baroux, Milly Mathis, Catherine Cheiney. 84M FRN. prod/rel: Burgus Films

Un Chapeau de Paille d'Italie, 1847, Play
  Cappello Di Paglia Di Firenze 1918 d: Enrico Vidali. lps: Joe Dollway, Bualo. 1243m ITL. prod/rel: Italica Film
  Chapeau de Paille d'Italie, Un 1927 d: Rene Clair. lps: Albert Prejean, Marise Maia, Olga TschechowA. 90M FRN. *The Italian Straw Hat; The Horse Ate the Hat* prod/rel: Films Albatros
  Chapeau de Paille d'Italie, Un 1940 d: Maurice Cammage. lps: Fernandel, Jacqueline Laurent, Josseline Gael. 85M FRN. prod/rel: Prodiex
  Florentiner Hut, Der 1939 d: Wolfgang Liebeneiner. lps: Heinz Ruhmann, Herti Kirchner, Christl Mardayn. 91M GRM. *The Leghorn Hat* (USA) prod/rel: Terra
  Slameny Klobouk 1972 d: Oldrich Lipsky. 88M CZC. *The Straw Hat*

Les Deux Timides, 1860, Play
  Deux Timides, Les 1928 d: Rene Clair. lps: Maurice de Feraudy, Pierre Batcheff, Vera Flory. 95M FRN. *The Two Timid Ones* prod/rel: Albatros, Sequana
  Jeunes Timides 1941 d: Yves Allegret. lps: Pierre Brasseur, Claude Dauphin, Jacqueline Laurent. 83M FRN. *Les Deux Timides* prod/rel: Imperia

Edgar Et Sa Bonne, Play
  Edgar Et Sa Bonne 1914. lps: Jacques de Feraudy, Cesar. 570m FRN. prod/rel: Eclair

La Fille Bien Gardee, Play
  Fille Bien Gardee, La 1923 d: Louis Feuillade. lps: Alice Tissot, Rene Poyen, Rene Donnio. 1880m FRN. prod/rel: Gaumont

Der Kernpunkt, Play
  Guten Tag, Schwiegermama 1928 d: Johannes Brandt. lps: Evi Eva, Albert Paulig. 1005m GRM. prod/rel: J. Rosenfeld Film-Prod.

Maman Sabouleux, Play
  Ma Tante Dictateur 1939 d: Rene Pujol. lps: Christian Gerard, Gaby Wagner, Marguerite Moreno. 95M FRN. *Monsieur Nicolas -Nourrice* prod/rel: Giffra

La Poudre aux Yeux, 1861, Play
  Huan Tian XI Di 1949 d: Zheng XIaoqiu. 90M CHN. *Hilarity*

Si Jamais Je Te Pince., Play
  Si Jamais Je Te Pince 1917 d: Georges MoncA. lps: Prince, Saturnin Fabre, Simone Joubert. 750m FRN. prod/rel: Pathe Freres

Les Trente Millions de Gladiator, Play
  Trente Millions de Gladiator, Les 1914 d: Georges MoncA. lps: Prince, Andre Simon, Clo MarrA. 900m FRN. prod/rel: Pathe Freres

Le Voyage de Monsieur Perrichon, 1860, Play
Viaggio Del Signor Perrichon, Il 1944 d: Paolo MoffA. lps: Antonio Gandusio, Adriano Rimoldi, Paola Borboni. 78M ITL. prod/rel: a.C.I., Europa
Voyage de Monsieur Perrichon, Le 1934 d: Jean Tarride. lps: Leon Belieres, Jeanne Cheirel, Andre Roanne. 90M FRN. prod/rel: Ceres-Film

LABORDE, JEAN
Les Assassins de l'Ordre, Novel
Assassins de l'Ordre, Les 1970 d: Marcel Carne. lps: Jacques Brel, Catherine Rouvel, Paola PitagorA. 110M FRN/ITL. *Inchiesta Su un Delitto Della Polizia* (ITL); *La Force Et le Droit* prod/rel: West Film, Belles Rives
Les Bonnes Causes, Paris 1960, Novel
Bonnes Causes, Les 1963 d: Christian-Jaque. lps: Marina Vlady, Bourvil, Virna Lisi. 120M FRN/ITL. *Il Delitto du Pre* (ITL); *Don't Tempt the Devil* (USA) prod/rel: Mediterranee Ciema, Flora Film
Caline Olivia, Novel
Da Berlino l'Apocalisse 1967 d: Mario Maffei. lps: Roger Hanin, Margaret Lee, Claude Dauphin. 100M ITL/FRN/GRM. *Heisses Pflaster Fur Spione* (GRM); *Le Tigre Sort Sans Sa Mere* (FRN); *The Spy Pit* prod/rel: European Incorporation (Roma), Transister Film (Paris)
La Second Verite, Novel
Seconde Verite, La 1965 d: Christian-Jaque. lps: Robert Hossein, Michele Mercier, Bernard Tiphaine. 95M FRN/ITL. *Amante Infedele* (ITL); *Un Homme a Part Entiere*; *Pour un Si Doux Regard* prod/rel: Agnes Delahaie, Valoria Films

LABRIC, ROGER
L' Avion de Minuit, Novel
Avion de Minuit, L' 1938 d: Dimitri Kirsanoff. lps: Jules Berry, Andre Luguet, Colette Darfeuil. 91M FRN. prod/rel: Amical Films

LABRO, PHILIPPE
L' Etudiant Etranger, Book
Foreign Student, The 1994 d: Eva Sereny. lps: Robin Givens, Marco Hofschneider, Rick Johnson. 91M USA/FRN. *L' Etudiant Etranger* (FRN)

LABRY, MICHEL
Les Sextuples de Locmaria, Novel
Ne Jouez Pas Avec Les Martians 1967 d: Henri Lanoe. lps: Jean Rochefort, Macha Meril, Andre Vallardy. 85M FRN. *Comme Mars En Careme*; *Regular As Clockwork*; *Mars En Careme*; *Don't Play With Martians*; *Don't Mess With the Martians* prod/rel: Fildebroc, Productions Artistes Associes

LACABA, JOSE F.
The Hostage, Article
Bayan Ko -Kapit Sa Patalim 1984 d: Lino BrockA. lps: Phillip Salvador, Gina Alajar, Claudia Zobel. 108M PHL/FRN. *Bayan Ko: My Own Country* prod/rel: Malaya Films (Manila), Stephan Films (Paris)
The Strike, Article
Bayan Ko -Kapit Sa Patalim 1984 d: Lino BrockA. lps: Phillip Salvador, Gina Alajar, Claudia Zobel. 108M PHL/FRN. *Bayan Ko: My Own Country* prod/rel: Malaya Films (Manila), Stephan Films (Paris)

LACEY, FRANKLIN
The Music Man, New York 1957, Musical Play
Music Man, The 1962 d: Morton Da CostA. lps: Robert Preston, Shirley Jones, Buddy Hackett. 151M USA. prod/rel: Warner Bros. Pictures

LACEY, FRANKLYN
Story
Rain for a Dusty Summer 1971 d: Arthur Lubin. lps: Ernest Borgnine, Aldo Sambrell, Humberto Almazan. USA/SPN. *Miguel Pro* (SPN); *Guns of the Revolution* prod/rel: Do-Bar

LACKAYE JR., WILLIAM
Miss Benton R.N., 1930, Play
Registered Nurse 1934 d: Robert Florey. lps: Bebe Daniels, Lyle Talbot, John Halliday. 64M USA. prod/rel: First National Pictures©

LACOUR, JOSE-ANDRE
L' Annee du Bac, Play
Annee du Bac, L' 1963 d: Maurice Delbez, Jose-Andre Lacour. lps: Jean Desailly, Simone Valere, Paul Amiot. 102M FRN. prod/rel: Bertho Films, Carlton Film Export
Le Mort En Ce Jardin, Paris 1954, Novel
Mort En Ce Jardin, La 1956 d: Luis Bunuel. lps: Simone Signoret, Georges Marchal, Michel Piccoli. 145M FRN/MXC. *La Muerte En Este Jardin* (MXC); *Death in the Garden*; *Gina* (USA); *Evil Eden*; *Evil of Eden* prod/rel: Dismage, Producciones Tepayac

LACY, ERNEST
The Ragged Earl, New York 1899, Play
Ragged Earl, The 1914 d: Lloyd B. Carleton. lps: Andrew Mack, William Conklin, Edward Peil. 5r USA. prod/rel: Popular Plays and Players, Inc.©, Alco Film Corp.

LADA, JOSEF
Short Stories
Princezne Julince, O 1987 d: Antonin Kachlik. lps: Lucie Tomkova, Petr Mikula, Jindrich BonaventurA. 91M CZC. *O Zatoulane Princezne*; *The Lost Princess* prod/rel: Filmove Studio Barrandov

LADY GREGORY
1921, Play
Rising of the Moon, The 1957. lps: Maureenel Cusack, Frank Lawton, Edward Lexy. UKN/IRL.

LAFAURIE, CHARLES
Le Collier de Chanvre, Novel
Collier de Chanvre, Le 1940 d: Leon Mathot. lps: Andre Luguet, Jacqueline Delubac, Georges Grey. 90M FRN. *Le Mystere du Bois Belleau* prod/rel: C.F.C., Vega
Parce Que Je T'aime, Play
Parce Que Je T'aime 1929 d: H. C. Grantham-Hayes. lps: Nicolas Rimsky, Diana Hart, Elsa Tamary. F FRN. prod/rel: Integral Films

LAFERRIERE, DANY
Comment Faire l'Amour Avec un Negro Sans Se Fatiguer, Novel
Comment Faire l'Amour Avec un Negre Sans Se Fatiguer 1988 d: Jacques W. Benoit. lps: Isaach de Bankole, Maka Kotto, Antoine Durand. 98M CND/FRN. *How to Make Love to a Negro Without Getting Tired* prod/rel: Aska, Molecule

LAFFAN, KEVIN
It's a 2'6" Above the Ground World, Play
It's a 2'6" Above the Ground World 1972 d: Ralph Thomas. lps: Hywel Bennett, Nanette Newman, Russell Lewis. 96M UKN. *The Love Ban*; *Anyone for Sex* prod/rel: British Lion, Welbeck

LAFFITE, PAUL
Rothschild, Short Story
Rothchild 1933 d: Marco de Gastyne. lps: Harry Baur, Alfred Pasquali, Claudie Cleves. 97M FRN. prod/rel: E.R. Escalmel

LAFFREDO, GAETANO
Le Vergini Di Roma, Short Story
Vergini Di Roma, Le 1960 d: Vittorio Cottafavi, Carlo Ludovico BragagliA. lps: Louis Jourdan, Sylvia Syms, Nicole Courcel. 80M ITL/FRN. *Les Vierges de Rome* (FRN); *Amazons of Rome* (USA); *The Virgins of Rome*; *Warrior Women* prod/rel: Regina Film, Cine Italia Film (Roma)

LAFITTE, PAUL
Rothschild, Short Story
Guv'nor, The 1935 d: Milton Rosmer. lps: George Arliss, Gene Gerrard, Viola Keats. 88M UKN. *Mr. Hobo* (USA) prod/rel: Gaumont-British

LAFORET DIAZ, CARMEN (1921–, SPN
Nada, 1945, Novel
Graciela 1956 d: Leopoldo Torre-Nilsson. lps: Ernesto Bianco, Susana Campos, Elsa Daniel. 87M ARG.
Nada 1947 d: Edgar Neville. lps: Conchita Montes, Tomas Blanco, Mary Delgado. 120M SPN. *Nothing*

LAGERKVIST, PAR (1891–1974), SWD
Barabbas, 1950, Novel
Barabba 1961 d: Richard Fleischer. lps: Anthony Quinn, Silvana Mangano, Arthur Kennedy. 150M ITL. *Barabbas* (USA) prod/rel: Columbia, Dino de Laurentiis Cin.Ca
Barabbas 1953 d: Alf Sjoberg. lps: Ulf Palme, Inge Waern, Olof Widgren. 111M SWD. prod/rel: Ab Sandrew

LAGERLOF, SELMA (1858–1940), SWD, Lagerlof, Selma Ottiliana Lovisa
Charlotte Lowenskold, 1925, Novel
Charlotte Lowenskold 1979 d: Jackie Soderman. lps: Ingrid Janbell, Lars Green, Gunnel Brostrom. MTV. 124M SWD. prod/rel: Sandrews, Sveriges Television
Dunungen, 1894, Short Story
Dunungen 1919 d: Ivan Hedqvist. lps: Ivan Hedqvist, Renee Bjorling, Jenny Tschernichin-Larsson. 2698m SWD. *The Downy Girl* (USA); *The Quest of Happiness* prod/rel: Ab Svenska Biografteatern
Dunungen 1941 d: Weyler Hildebrand. lps: Karin Nordgren, Adolf Jahr, Hilda Borgstrom. 90M SWD. *Downy Girl* prod/rel: Ab Svensk Filmindustri
Gosta Berlings Saga, Novel
Gosta Berlings Saga 1924 d: Mauritz Stiller. lps: Lars Hanson, Greta Garbo, Ellen Cederstrom. 165M SWD. *The Atonement of Gosta Berling* (UKN); *The Legend of Gosta Berling*; *The Saga of Gosta Berling*; *The Story of Gosta Berling* prod/rel: Svensk Filmindustri

Herr Arnes Pengar, 1903, Novel
Herr Arnes Pennigar 1954 d: Gustaf Molander. lps: Ulla Jacobsson, Ulf Palme, Bibi Andersson. 86M SWD. *Sir Arne's Treasure*
Jerusalem, Novel
Jerusalem 1996 d: Bille August. lps: Maria Bonnevie, Ulf Friberg, Pernilla August. 171M SWD. prod/rel: Svt Drama, Svensk Filmindustri
Kejsarn Av Portugallien, Stockholm 1914, Novel
Kejsarn Av Portugallien 1944 d: Gustaf Molander. lps: Victor Sjostrom, Gunn Wallgren, Karl-Arne Holmsten. 109M SWD. *The Emperor of Portugal* prod/rel: Ab Svensk Filmindustri
Kejsarn Av Portugallien 1992 d: Lars Molin. lps: Ingvar Hirdwall, Gunilla Nyroos, Inga Landgre. TVM. 170M SWD.
Tower of Lies, The 1925 d: Victor Sjostrom. lps: Norma Shearer, Lon Chaney, Ian Keith. 6849f USA. prod/rel: Metro-Goldwyn-Mayer Pictures
Korkarlen, 1912, Novel
Charrette Fantome, La 1939 d: Julien Duvivier. lps: Pierre Fresnay, Marie Bell, Louis Jouvet. 90M FRN. *The Phantom Wagon* (USA); *Le Charretier de la Mort* prod/rel: Transcontinental Films, Columbia Pictures
Korkarlen 1921 d: Victor Sjostrom. lps: Victor Sjostrom, Hilda Borgstrom, Tore Svennberg. 60M SWD. *The Stroke of Midnight* (USA); *Thy Soul Shall Bear Witness*; *The Grey Cart*; *The Phantom Horse*; *Clay* prod/rel: Svensk Filmindustri
Korkarlen 1958 d: Arne Mattsson. lps: George Fant, Ulla Jacobsson, Anita Bjork. 110M SWD. *The Phantom Carriage*; *The Phantom Chariot* prod/rel: Ab Nordisk
Lowenskolda Ringen, 1925, Novel
Charlotte Lowenskold 1930 d: Gustaf Molander. lps: Stina Berg, Selma Lagerlof. 93M SWD. *Charlotte Lowenskjold*
Nils Holgerssons Underbara Resa, 1906-07, Novel
Nils Holgerssons Underbara Resa 1962 d: Kenne Fant. lps: Sven Lundberg, Max von Sydow, Annika Tretow. 95M SWD. *The Wonderful Adventures of Nils*; *The Marvelous Journey of Nils Holgersson* prod/rel: Ab Svensk Filmindustri, Nordisk Tonefilm
Zakoldovanny Malchik 1956. ANM. 48M USS. prod/rel: Soyuzmultfilm
Tosen Fran Stormyrtorpet, Stockholm 1908, Short Story
Husmandstosen 1952 d: Alice O'Fredericks. lps: Jorn Jeppesen, Svend Methling, Jacob Nielsen. 103M DNM. prod/rel: Asa
Madchen Vom Moorhof, Das 1935 d: Douglas Sirk. lps: Friedrich Kayssler, Theodor Loos, Eduard von Winterstein. 82M GRM.
Madchen Vom Moorhof, Das 1958 d: Gustav Ucicky. lps: Maria Emo, Claus Holm, Wolfgang Lukschy. 87M GRM. *The Girl of the Moors* (USA); *The Girl from the Moor Estate* prod/rel: Real Film
Suotorpan Tytto 1940 d: Toivo SarkkA. lps: Regina Linnanheimo, Tauno Palo, Yrjo Tuominen. 71M FNL. *Tosen Fran Stormyrtorpet* prod/rel: Suomen Filmiteollisuus
Tosen Fran Stormyrtorpet 1918 d: Victor Sjostrom. lps: Lars Hanson, Greta Almroth, Georg Blomstedt. 1749m SWD. *Girl from Stormy Croft* (UKN); *The Woman He Chose* (UKN); *A Girl from the Marsh Croft*; *The Lass from the Stormy Croft*; *Girl from the Stormy Croft, A*
Tosen Fran Stormyrtorpet 1947 d: Gustaf Edgren. lps: Margareta Fahlen, Alf Kjellin, Ingrid Borthen. 91M SWD. *A Girl from the Marsh Croft*

LAHR, JOHN (1941–, USA
Prick Up Your Ears, Biography
Prick Up Your Ears 1987 d: Stephen Frears. lps: Gary Oldman, Alfred Molina, Vanessa Redgrave. 111M UKN. prod/rel: Zenith, Civilhand

LAINE, PASCAL
La Dentelliere, Novel
Dentelliere, La 1977 d: Claude GorettA. lps: Isabelle Huppert, Yves Beneyton, Florence Giorgetti. 110M SWT/FRN/GRM. *Die Spitzenklopplerin* (GRM); *The Lacemaker* (USA) prod/rel: Citel, Action
Tendres Cousins, Novel
Tendres Cousines 1980 d: David Hamilton. lps: Anja Shute, Thierry Tevini, Jean Rougerie. 90M FRN/GRM. *Zartliche Cousinen* (GRM); *Cousins in Love* prod/rel: Tv 13, Planet

LAINSCEK, FERI
Novel
Halgato 1995 d: Andrej Mlakar. lps: Vlado Kreslin, Joze Kramberger, Mirjam Korbar. 105M SLO.

LAIT, JACK
Chicago Confidential, Book
  Chicago Confidential 1957 d: Sidney Salkow. lps: Brian Keith, Beverly Garland, Dick Foran. 73M USA. prod/rel: United Artists
Girl Without a Room, Short Story
  Girl Without a Room 1933 d: Ralph Murphy. lps: Marguerite Churchill, Charles Farrell, Charles Ruggles. 75M USA. *No Bed of Her Own*; *She Made Her Bed* prod/rel: Charles R. Rogers Productions, Paramount Productions©
The Great Air Mail Robbery, Story
  Sky Raider, The 1925 d: T. Hayes Hunter. lps: Capt. Charles Nungesser, Jacqueline Logan, Gladys Walton. 6638f USA. prod/rel: Encore Pictures, Associated Exhibitors
Help Wanted, New York 1914, Play
  Help Wanted 1915 d: Hobart Bosworth. lps: Lois Meredith, Hobart Bosworth, Owen Moore. 5r USA. prod/rel: Oliver Morosco Photoplay Co.©, Bosworth, Inc.
I Can't Go Home, Short Story
  Girl Without a Room 1933 d: Ralph Murphy. lps: Marguerite Churchill, Charles Farrell, Charles Ruggles. 75M USA. *No Bed of Her Own*; *She Made Her Bed* prod/rel: Charles R. Rogers Productions, Paramount Productions©
New York Confidential, 1948, Book
  New York Confidential 1955 d: Russell Rouse. lps: Richard Conte, Broderick Crawford, Marilyn Maxwell. 87M USA. prod/rel: Warner Bros., Green-Rouse Prods.
One of Us, New York 1918, Play
  Love Burglar, The 1919 d: James Cruze. lps: Wallace Reid, Anna Q. Nilsson, Raymond Hatton. 4467f USA. prod/rel: Famous Players-Lasky Corp.©, Paramount Pictures
Put on the Spot, New York 1930, Novel
  Bad Company 1931 d: Tay Garnett. lps: Ricardo Cortez, Helen Twelvetrees, John Garrick. 75M USA. *The Gangster's Wife*; *The Mad Marriage* prod/rel: RKO Radio Pictures, Inc.

LAJTAI, LOUIS
Blajackor, Opera
  Blajackor 1945 d: Rolf Husberg. lps: Nils Poppe, Annalisa Ericson, Karl-Arne Holmsten. 105M SWD. *Blue-Jackets* prod/rel: Wive

LAKE, JAMES
Snowball, Novel
  Snowball 1960 d: Pat Jackson. lps: Gordon Jackson, Kenneth Griffith, Zena Walker. 69M UKN. prod/rel: Rank Film Distributors, Independent Artists

LAKE, STUART N.
Story
  Winchester '73 1950 d: Anthony Mann. lps: James Stewart, Shelley Winters, Dan DuryeA. 92M USA. prod/rel: Universal-International
  Winchester '73 1967 d: Herschel Daugherty. lps: Tom Tryon, John Saxon, Dan DuryeA. TVM. 100M USA. prod/rel: Universal
The Westerner, Story
  Westerner, The 1940 d: William Wyler. lps: Gary Cooper, Walter Brennan, Fred Stone. 100M USA. prod/rel: United Artists Corp., Samuel Goldwyn, Inc.
Wyatt Earp - Frontier Marshal, New York 1931, Book
  Frontier Marshal 1934 d: Lewis Seiler. lps: George O'Brien, Irene Bentley, George E. Stone. 66M USA. prod/rel: Fox Film Corp.©
  Frontier Marshal 1939 d: Allan Dwan. lps: Randolph Scott, Nancy Kelly, Cesar Romero. 72M USA. *Frontier Marshal; the Saga of Tombstone Arizona*; *Frontier Marshal Wyatt Earp* prod/rel: Twentieth Century-Fox Film Corp.©
  My Darling Clementine 1946 d: John Ford. lps: Henry Fonda, Linda Darnell, Victor Mature. 97M USA. prod/rel: 20th Century-Fox
  Powder River 1953 d: Louis King. lps: Rory Calhoun, Cameron Mitchell, Penny Edwards. 78M USA. prod/rel: 20th Century-Fox

LALIC, MIHAILO
Hajka, 1960, Novel
  Hajka 1977 d: Zivojin Pavlovic. lps: Rade Serbedzija, Pavle Vuisic, Boro Begovic. 93M YGS. *Witch Hunt; The Manhunt; Pursuit; The Chase*
Lelejska Gora, 1957, Novel
  Lelejska Gora 1968 d: Zdravko Velimirovic. lps: Slobodan Dimitrijevic, Milivoje Zivanovic, Anka Zupanc. 95M YGS. *Mountain of Lament; Mountain of Horror; Moaning Mountain; Mount Lelej*
Svadba, 1962, Novel
  Svadba 1973 d: Radomir Saranovic. lps: Dragomir Bojanic, Vladimir Popovic, Mihailo Janketic. 92M YGS/USS. *The Wedding*

LALLIER, BERNARD-PAUL
Le Saut de l'Ange, Novel
  Saut de l'Ange, Le 1971 d: Yves Boisset. lps: Jean Yanne, Sterling Hayden, Senta Berger. 93M FRN/ITL. *Da Parte Degli Amici Firmato Mafia* (ITL); *Cobra* (UKN); *Angel's Leap*; *Code Name: Cobra* prod/rel: International Apollo Film

LAMARTINE, ALPHONSE
Genevieve; Memoire d'une Servante, Novel
  Chi E Senza Peccato. 1953 d: Raffaello Matarazzo. lps: Amedeo Nazzari, Yvonne Sanson, Francoise Rosay. 100M ITL. prod/rel: Titanus, Labor Film

LAMB, ARTHUR J.
The Mansion of Aching Hearts, 1902, Song
  Mansion of Aching Hearts, The 1925 d: James P. Hogan. lps: Ethel Clayton, Barbara Bedford, Priscilla Bonner. 6147f USA. prod/rel: B. P. Schulberg Productions

LAMB, MAX
Emporia, New York 1961, Novel
  Waco 1966 d: R. G. Springsteen. lps: Howard Keel, Jane Russell, Brian Donlevy. 85M USA. prod/rel: A. C. Lyles Productions

LAMBERT, B.
Guilt, Short Story
  Martha, Ruth and Edie 1988 d: Deepa Mehta Saltzman. CND.

LAMBERT, BETTY
Jennie's Story, Play
  Heart of the Sun 1998 d: Francis Damberger. lps: Christianne Hirt, Shaun Johnston, Michael Riley. 94M CND. prod/rel: Dancing Stones Film, Makara Pictures

LAMBERT, CHARLES
The Wolves of Kromer, Play
  Wolves of Kromer, The 1998 d: Will Gould. lps: Lee Williams, James Layton, Rita Davies. 82M UKN. prod/rel: Discodog, Charles Lambert

LAMBERT, DEREK
Touch the Lion's Paw, Novel
  Rough Cut 1980 d: Don Siegel. lps: Burt Reynolds, David Niven, Lesley-Anne Down. 112M USA/UKN. *Roughcut* prod/rel: Paramount, David Merrick

LAMBERT, GAVIN
Inside Daisy Clover, New York 1963, Novel
  Inside Daisy Clover 1965 d: Robert Mulligan. lps: Natalie Wood, Christopher Plummer, Robert Redford. 128M USA. prod/rel: Park Place Productions

LAMBERT, KATHE
Haus Des Lebens, Novel
  Haus Des Lebens 1952 d: Karl Hartl. lps: Gustav Frohlich, Cornell Borchers, Hansi Knoteck. 104M GRM. *House of Life* prod/rel: Helios, Bavaria

LAMBERT, RAE
Once Upon a Forest, Short Story
  Once Upon a Forest 1992 d: Charles Grosvenor. ANM. 71M USA.

LAMBERT, REITA
The Widow's Might, 1931, Story
  Careless Lady 1932 d: Kenneth MacKennA. lps: Joan Bennett, John Boles, Minna Gombell. 68M USA. *Widow's Might*; *When Girls Leave Home* prod/rel: Fox Film Corp.

LAMBERT, RITA
Clipped Wings, 1928, Short Story
  Hello Sister 1930 d: Walter Lang. lps: Olive Borden, Lloyd Hughes, George Fawcett. 6200f USA. *Clipped Wings* (UKN) prod/rel: James Cruze, Inc., Sono Art-World Wide Pictures

LAMBESC, MICHEL
Cher Voyou, Novel
  Homme a la Buick, L' 1967 d: Gilles Grangier. lps: Fernandel, Danielle Darrieux, Jean-Pierre Marielle. 96M FRN. prod/rel: Films Copernic, Gafer Productions
La Horse, Novel
  Horse, La 1969 d: Pierre Granier-Deferre. lps: Jean Gabin, Daniele Ajoret, Pierre Dux. 90M FRN/ITL/GRM. *Il Clan Degli Uomini Violenti* (ITL); *Der Erbarmungslose* (GRM); *Man Without Mercy* prod/rel: P.A.C., S.N.C.

LAMBIN, PIERRE
Minuit Quai de Bercy, Novel
  Minuit Quai de Bercy 1952 d: Christian Stengel. lps: Madeleine Robinson, Philippe Lemaire, Lysiane Rey. 95M FRN. *La Maison du Crime* prod/rel: Equipe Technique De Prod. Cinematograph.

LAMONT, FRANCES
An Adventure, Book
  Miss Morrison's Ghosts 1981 d: John Bruce. lps: Wendy Hiller, Hannah Gordon, Bosco Hogan. TVM. 100M UKN. prod/rel: Anglia Tv

L'AMOUR, LOUIS (1908–1988), USA, Burns, Tex
Story
  Kid Rodelo 1966 d: Richard Carlson. lps: Don Murray, Broderick Crawford, Richard Carlson. 91M USA/SPN. prod/rel: Trident, Fenix
  Stranger on Horseback 1955 d: Jacques Tourneur. lps: Joel McCrea, Miroslava, Kevin McCarthy. 66M USA. prod/rel: United Artists, Leonard Goldstein
The Broken Gun, Novel
  Cancel My Reservation 1972 d: Paul Bogart. lps: Bob Hope, Eva Marie Saint, Ralph Bellamy. 87M USA. prod/rel: Naho Enterprises
The Burning Hills, Novel
  Burning Hills, The 1956 d: Stuart Heisler. lps: Tab Hunter, Natalie Wood, Skip Homeier. 94M USA. prod/rel: Warner Bros.
Catlow, Novel
  Catlow 1971 d: Sam Wanamaker. lps: Yul Brynner, Richard Crenna, Leonard Nimoy. 101M UKN/USA. prod/rel: Gold Star Films, Euan Lloyd
The Daybreakers, Novel
  Sacketts, The 1979 d: Robert Totten. lps: Sam Elliott, Tom Selleck, Jeff Osterhage. TVM. 200M USA. *The Daybreakers; Louis l'Amour's the Sacketts* prod/rel: Douglas Netter/M. B. Scott Productions, Shalako Enterprises
The Gift of Cochise, Short Story
  Hondo 1953 d: John Farrow. lps: John Wayne, Geraldine Page, Ward Bond. 84M USA. prod/rel: Warner Bros., Wayne-Fellows
Guns of the Timberland, Novel
  Guns of the Timberland 1960 d: Robert D. Webb. lps: Alan Ladd, Jeanne Crain, Gilbert Roland. 91M USA. prod/rel: Warner Bros.
Kilkenny, Novel
  Blackjack Ketchum, Desperado 1956 d: Earl Bellamy. lps: Howard Duff, Victor Jory, Maggie Mahoney. 76M USA. prod/rel: Columbia, Clover Productions
The Last Stand at Papago Wells, Novel
  Apache Territory 1958 d: Ray Nazarro. lps: Rory Calhoun, Barbara Bates, John Dehner. 75M USA. prod/rel: Columbia, Rorvic
The Man Called Noon, Novel
  Man Called Noon, The 1973 d: Peter Collinson. lps: Richard Crenna, Stephen Boyd, Rosanna Schiaffino. 95M USA/SPN/ITL. *Lo Chiamavano Mezzogiorno* (ITL); *Le Pistolero Cherche Son Nom*; *Un Hombre Llamado Noon* (SPN) prod/rel: Frontier Film Ltd (London), Finarco (Roma)
Plunder, Story
  Tall Stranger, The 1957 d: Thomas Carr. lps: Joel McCrea, Virginia Mayo, Barry Kelley. 81M USA. prod/rel: Universal-International
The Quick and the Dead, Novel
  Quick and the Dead, The 1987 d: Robert Day. lps: Tom Conti, Kate Capshaw, Sam Elliott. TVM. 93M USA. prod/rel: Hbo Pictures
Sackett, Novel
  Sacketts, The 1979 d: Robert Totten. lps: Sam Elliott, Tom Selleck, Jeff Osterhage. TVM. 200M USA. *The Daybreakers; Louis l'Amour's the Sacketts* prod/rel: Douglas Netter/M. B. Scott Productions, Shalako Enterprises
Shalako, New York 1962, Novel
  Shalako! 1968 d: Edward Dmytryk. lps: Sean Connery, Brigitte Bardot, Stephen Boyd. 113M UKN/GRM. prod/rel: Kingston Films, Palomar Pictures International
Taggart, New York 1959, Novel
  Taggart 1964 d: R. G. Springsteen. lps: Tony Young, Dan Duryea, Dick Foran. 85M USA. prod/rel: Gordon Kay & Associates
Utah Blaine, Novel
  Utah Blaine 1957 d: Fred F. Sears. lps: Rory Calhoun, Susan Cummings, Angela Stevens. 75M USA. prod/rel: Columbia, Clover Prods.

LAMPEL, PETER MARTIN
Giftgas Uber Berlin, Play
  Giftgas 1929 d: Michael Dubson. lps: Lissi Arna, Vera Baranowskaja, Hans Stuwe. 2447m GRM. prod/rel: Filmproduktion Loew Und Co.
Revolte Im Erziehungshaus, Play
  Revolte Im Erziehungshaus 1929 d: Georg Asagaroff. lps: Renate Muller, Oscar Homolka, Ilse Stobrawa. 2477m GRM. *Revolt in the Reformatory* prod/rel: Grohnert-Film-Produktion

LAMPELL, MILLARD
The Hero, 1949, Book
  Saturday's Hero 1951 d: David Miller. lps: John Derek, Donna Reed, Sidney Blackmer. 109M USA. *Idols in the Dust* (UKN); *The Hero* prod/rel: Columbia

LANGFORD, FRANCES
Article
  Purple Heart Diary 1951 d: Richard Quine. lps: Frances Langford, Judd Holdren, Ben Lessey. 73M USA. *No Time for Tears* (UKN) prod/rel: Columbia

LANGFUS, ANNA
Saute Barbara, Novel
  Pour un Sourire 1969 d: Francois Dupont-Midy. lps: Marina Vlady, Bruno Cremer, Philippe Clay. 95M FRN. prod/rel: Alpha

LANGHAM, JAMES R.
Sing a Song of Homicide, Story
  Night in New Orleans, A 1942 d: William Clemens. lps: Preston Foster, Patricia Morison, Albert Dekker. 75M USA. *The Morning After* prod/rel: Paramount

LANGLEY, ADRIA LOCKE
A Lion Is in the Streets, 1945, Novel
  Lion Is in the Streets, A 1953 d: Raoul Walsh. lps: James Cagney, Barbara Hale, Anne Francis. 88M USA. prod/rel: Warner Bros., Cagney Prods.

LANGLEY, NOEL
Edward, My Son, London 1947, Play
  Edward, My Son 1948 d: George Cukor. lps: Spencer Tracy, Deborah Kerr, Ian Hunter. 112M UKN/USA. prod/rel: MGM British
Little Lambs Eat Ivy, London 1948, Play
  Father's Doing Fine 1952 d: Henry Cass. lps: Richard Attenborough, Heather Thatcher, Noel Purcell. 83M UKN. prod/rel: Marble Arch, Ab-Pathe
Queer Cargo, London 1934, Play
  Queer Cargo 1938 d: Harold Schuster. lps: John Lodge, Judy Kelly, Keneth Kent. 62M UKN. *Pirates of the Seven Seas* prod/rel: Associated British Picture Corporation

LANGNER, LAWRENCE (1890–1962), UKN
The Pursuit of Happiness, New York 1933, Play
  Pursuit of Happiness, The 1934 d: Alexander Hall. lps: Francis Lederer, Joan Bennett, Charles Ruggles. 85M USA. prod/rel: Paramount Productions©

LANHAM, EDWIN
Story
  Senator Was Indiscreet, The 1947 d: George S. Kaufman. lps: William Powell, Ella Raines, Arleen Whelan. 81M USA. *Mr. Ashton Was Indiscreet* (UKN) prod/rel: Universal
Serial Story
  It Shouldn't Happen to a Dog 1946 d: Herbert I. Leeds. lps: Allyn Joslyn, Carole Landis, Margo Woode. 70M USA. *It Couldn't Happen to a Dog* prod/rel: 20th Century-Fox

LANNER, JOSEPH
Das Hauschen in Grinzing, Opera
  Gluck von Grinzing, Das 1933 d: Otto Kanturek. lps: Ivan Petrovich, Gretl Theimer, Marion Taal. 80M AUS/CZC. *Das Hauschen in Grinzing* prod/rel: Oka (Otto Kanturek), Emco
  V Tom Domecku Pod Emauzy 1933 d: Otto Kanturek. lps: Antonin Novotny, Theodor Pistek, Adina MandlovA. 2046m CZC. *In the Little House Under Emauzy*; *In the Little House Below Emauzy* prod/rel: Oka (Otto Kanturek), Emco

LANOYE, TOM
Alles Moet Weg, Novel
  Alles Moet Weg 1997 d: Jan Verheyen. lps: Stany Crets, Peter Van Den Begin, Bart de Pauw. 106M BLG. *Everything Must Go* prod/rel: Favourite Films, Phantom Films

LANSBERG, OLLE
Kare John, Stockholm 1959, Novel
  Kare John 1964 d: Lars-Magnus Lindgren. lps: Jarl Kulle, Christina Schollin, Helena Nilsson. 111M SWD. *Dear John* (USA) prod/rel: Ab Svensk

LANSBURGH, LARRY
Story
  Littlest Outlaw, The 1955 d: Roberto Gavaldon. lps: Pedro Armendariz, Joseph Calleia, Rodolfo AcostA. 75M USA. prod/rel: Buena Vista, Walt Disney Prods.

LANSFORD, WILLIAM DOUGLAS
Pancho Villa, Los Angeles 1965, Novel
  Villa Rides 1968 d: Buzz Kulik. lps: Yul Brynner, Robert Mitchum, Maria Grazia BuccellA. 125M USA. prod/rel: Paramount Pictures

LANTZ, LOUIS
Story
  River of No Return 1954 d: Otto Preminger. lps: Robert Mitchum, Marilyn Monroe, Rory Calhoun. 91M USA. prod/rel: 20th Century-Fox

LANZA, CESARE
Nene, Novel
  Nene 1977 d: Salvatore Samperi. lps: Leonora Fani, Tino Schirinzi, Paola Senatore. 100M ITL. prod/rel: San Francisco Film, Columbia-Ceiad

LANZMANN, JACQUES
Le Rat d'Amerique, Novel
  Rat d'Amerique, Le 1962 d: Jean-Gabriel Albicocco. lps: Charles Aznavour, Marie Laforet, Franco Fabrizi. 95M FRN/ITL. *Il Sentiero Dei Disperati* (ITL) prod/rel: Franco-London Films, Madeleine Films

LAPAIRE, LEO
Die Ewige Maske, Zurich 1934, Novel
  Ewige Maske, Die 1935 d: Werner Hochbaum. lps: Peter Petersen, Mathias Wieman, Olga TschechowA. 85M AUS/SWT. *The Eternal Mask* (USA); *L' Autre Qui Est En Nous*; *Cas de Conscience*; *Das Doppelleben Des Rd. Dumartin* prod/rel: Progress-Film

LAPIERRE, DOMINIQUE
City of Joy, Novel
  City of Joy 1992 d: Roland Joffe. lps: Patrick Swayze, Pauline Collins, Om Puri. 134M UKN/FRN. prod/rel: Lightmotive Ltd. (London), Pricel (Paris)
Is Paris Burning?, New York 1965, Novel
  Paris Brule-T-Il? 1966 d: Rene Clement. lps: Jean-Paul Belmondo, Charles Boyer, Leslie Caron. 175M FRN. *Is Paris Burning?* (UKN) prod/rel: Transcontinental Films, Marianne Productions

LAPIERRE, HENRI
Le Mort du Lac, Novel
  Dis-Moi Qui Tuer? 1965 d: Etienne Perier. lps: Michele Morgan, Paul Hubschmid, Daniel Ollier. 90M FRN. prod/rel: Films Number One, Trianon Prod.

LAPORTE, GILBERT
Monsieur Bon Appetit, Novel
  Peau de l'Ours, La 1957 d: Claude Boissol. lps: Jean Richard, Nicole Courcel, Jacques Simonet. 79M FRN. prod/rel: Elpinor Films, Gaumont

LAPPIN, PETER
General Mickey, New Rochelle 1952, Novel
  Green Tree, The 1965 d: Joseph Roland, Ruth Zimmerman. lps: Robert Gho, Natale Peretti, Patrizia Terreno. 75M USA/ITL. *Albero Verde* (ITL) prod/rel: Rol Film Co.

LARDNER, RING (1885–1933), USA, Lardner, Ringgold Wilmer
Alibi Ike, 1915, Short Story
  Alibi Ike 1935 d: Ray Enright. lps: Joe E. Brown, Olivia de Havilland, William Frawley. 73M USA. prod/rel: Warner Bros. Productions Corp.
The Big Town, 1938, Novel
  So This Is New York 1948 d: Richard Fleischer. lps: Henry Morgan, Rudy Vallee, Bill Goodwin. 79M USA. prod/rel: United Artists
Champion, 1929, Short Story
  Champion 1949 d: Mark Robson. lps: Kirk Douglas, Marilyn Maxwell, Ruth Roman. 99M USA. prod/rel: United Artists
Elmer the Great, New York 1928, Play
  Cowboy Quarterback, The 1939 d: Noel Smith. lps: Bert Wheeler, Gloria Dickson, Marie Wilson. 56M USA. *Lighthorse Harry* prod/rel: Warner Bros. Pictures, Inc.
  Elmer the Great 1933 d: Mervyn Leroy. lps: Joe E. Brown, Patricia Ellis, Claire Dodd. 70M USA. prod/rel: First National Pictures©
  Fast Company 1929 d: A. Edward Sutherland. lps: Evelyn Brent, Jack Oakie, Skeets Gallagher. 6863f USA. prod/rel: Paramount Famous Lasky Corp.
The Golden Honeymoon, 1929, Short Story
  Golden Honeymoon, The 1977 d: Noel Black. lps: Teresa Wright, James Whitmore. MTV. 52M USA. prod/rel: Learning in Focus
June Moon, New York 1929, Play
  Blonde Trouble 1937 d: George Archainbaud. lps: Johnny Downs, Eleanore Whitney, Lynne Overman. 67M USA. prod/rel: Paramount Pictures, Inc.
  June Moon 1931 d: A. Edward Sutherland. lps: Jack Oakie, Frances Dee, Wynne Gibson. 73M USA. *Night Life* prod/rel: Paramount Publix Corp.

L'ARENTINO, PIETRO
Capricciosi Ragionamenti, Short Story
  Notti Peccaminose de Pietro l'Aretino 1972 d: Manlio Scarpelli. lps: Giuseppe Alotta, Belinda Bron, Franco Ferrini. 98M ITL. prod/rel: Cineproduzioni Peg
Lettere, Short Story
  Notti Peccaminose de Pietro l'Aretino 1972 d: Manlio Scarpelli. lps: Giuseppe Alotta, Belinda Bron, Franco Ferrini. 98M ITL. prod/rel: Cineproduzioni Peg
Piacevoli Ragionamenti, Short Story
  Notti Peccaminose de Pietro l'Aretino 1972 d: Manlio Scarpelli. lps: Giuseppe Alotta, Belinda Bron, Franco Ferrini. 98M ITL. prod/rel: Cineproduzioni Peg

I Ragionamenti, Book
  Giochi Proibiti Dell'aretino Pietro, I 1972 d: Piero Regnoli. lps: Femi Benussi, Shirley Corrigan, Rosemarie Lindt. 94M ITL. *Tales of Erotica* (UKN) prod/rel: Parf Cin.Ca, Florida

L'ARETINO, PIETRO (1492–1556), ITL
Ragionamenti Amorosi, Story
  Bella Antonia Prima Monica E Poi Dimonia 1972 d: Mariano Laurenti. lps: Edwige Fenech, Piero Focaccia, Riccardo Garrone. 83M ITL. *Naughty Nun* (UKN) prod/rel: Flora Film, National Cinematografica

LARKIN JR., JOHN
Society Girl, New York 1931, Play
  Society Girl 1932 d: Sidney Lanfield. lps: James Dunn, Peggy Shannon, Spencer Tracy. 74M USA. prod/rel: Fox Film Corp.©

LARNER, JEREMY (1937–, USA
Drive He Said, 1964, Novel
  Drive, He Said 1972 d: Jack Nicholson. lps: William Tepper, Karen Black, Michael MargottA. 90M USA.

LARRIC, J.
Der Optimist, Play
  Optimist, Der 1938 d: E. W. Emo. lps: Viktor de Kowa, Gusti Huber, Henny Porten. 80M AUS. prod/rel: Emo-Film

L'ARRONGE, ADOLPHE
Mein Leopold, Play
  Mein Leopold 1913 d: Heinrich Bolten-Baeckers. lps: Richard Georg, Leo Peukert, Paula Levermann. 1793m GRM. prod/rel: Deutsche Gaumont
  Mein Leopold 1924 d: Heinrich Bolten-Baeckers. lps: Arthur Kraussneck, Walter Slezak, Georg Alexander. 2218m GRM. prod/rel: B.B. Film-Fabrikation Heinrich Bolten
  Mein Leopold 1931 d: Hans Steinhoff. lps: Max Adalbert, Lucie Englisch, Gustav Frohlich. F GRM.
  Mein Leopold 1955 d: Geza von Bolvary. lps: Karlheinz Bohm, Karl Ludwig Diehl, Paul Horbiger. 90M GRM. *Ein Herz Bleibt Allein*; *My Leopold* prod/rel: Berolina, Melodie

LARROUY, MAURICE
Coups de Roulis, Novel
  Coups de Roulis 1931 d: Jean de La Cour. lps: Max Dearly, Edith Manet, Lucienne Herval. 115M FRN. prod/rel: Etablissements Jacques Haik
Le Revolte, Novel
  Revolte, Le 1938 d: Leon Mathot, Robert Bibal. lps: Rene Dary, Katia Lova, Pierre Renoir. 105M FRN. prod/rel: C.I.C.C.
Sirenes Et Tritons; le Roman du Sous-Marin, Paris 1927, Novel
  Devil and the Deep 1932 d: Marion Gering. lps: Tallulah Bankhead, Gary Cooper, Charles Laughton. 78M USA. prod/rel: Paramount Publix Corp.

LARSEN, GUNNAR
To Mistenkelige Personer, 1933, Novel
  To Mistenkelige Personer 1950 d: Tancred Ibsen. 101M NRW.

LARSEN, JENS PEDAR
En Loppe Kan Ogsa Go, Novel
  En Loppe Kan Ogsa Go 1997 d: Stellan Olsson. lps: Christina Brix Christensen, Niels Hausgaard, Erik Clausen. 95M DNM. *Don't They? Fleas Bark Too* prod/rel: ASA Film, Danish Film Institute

LARSEN, RICHARD W.
The Deliberate Stranger, Novel
  Deliberate Stranger, The 1985 d: Marvin J. Chomsky. lps: Mark Harmon, Frederic Forrest, George Grizzard. TVM. 200M USA. prod/rel: NBC

LARTEGUY, JEAN
Les Centurions, Paris 1960, Novel
  Lost Command 1966 d: Mark Robson. lps: Anthony Quinn, Alain Delon, George Segal. 130M USA. *Not for Honor and Glory*; *The Centurions* prod/rel: Red Lion Productions, Columbia

LASDUN, JAMES
Story
  Beseiged 1998 d: Bernardo Bertolucci. lps: Thandie Newton, David Thewlis, Claudio SantamariA. 94M ITL. *L'Assedio* prod/rel: Fiction S.R.L. Roma©, Navert Film

LASH, JOSEPH P. (1909–1987), USA
Eleanor and Franklin, Book
  Eleanor and Franklin 1976 d: Daniel Petrie. lps: Jane Alexander, Edward Herrmann, Rosemary Murphy. TVM. 208M USA. prod/rel: ABC, Talent Associates
  Eleanor and Franklin: the White House Years 1977 d: Daniel Petrie. lps: Jane Alexander, Edward Herrmann, Priscilla Pointer. TVM. 150M USA. prod/rel: ABC, Talent Associates Ltd.

Helen and Teacher, Book
Helen Keller. the Miracle Continues 1983 d: Alan Gibson. lps: Blythe Danner, Mare Winningham, Perry King. TVM. 104M UKN/USA. prod/rel: Opt, Tcf

LASKI, MARGHANITA (1915–, UKN
Little Boy Lost, 1949, Novel
Little Boy Lost 1953 d: George Seaton. lps: Bing Crosby, Claude Dauphin, Gabrielle Dorziat. 95M USA. prod/rel: Paramount, Perlberg-Seaton

The Victorian Chaise-Longue, Short Story
Victorian Chaise-Longue, The 1962 d: James MacTaggart. lps: Frances White. MTV. 40M UKN. prod/rel: BBC

LASKY JR., JESSE
Bridge Built at Night, Story
Steel Against the Sky 1942 d: A. Edward Sutherland. lps: Lloyd Nolan, Alexis Smith, Craig Stevens. 68M USA. *Dangerously They Live* prod/rel: Warner Bros.

Private Beach, Beverly Hills 1934, Play
Music Is Magic 1935 d: George Marshall. lps: Alice Faye, Ray Walker, Bebe Daniels. 67M USA. *Private Beach*; *Ball of Fire* prod/rel: Fox Film Corp., Twentieth Century-Fox Film Corp.©

LASSEAUX, MARCEL
Famine Club, Play
Ange de la Nuit, L' 1942 d: Andre Berthomieu. lps: Jean-Louis Barrault, Michele Alfa, Henri Vidal. 95M FRN. *Angel of the Dark* (UKN) prod/rel: Pathe-Cinema

LASZLO, ALADAR
The Girl Who Dared (Scandal in Budapest), 1911, Play
Top Hat 1935 d: Mark Sandrich. lps: Fred Astaire, Ginger Rogers, Edward Everett Horton. 101M USA. prod/rel: RKO Radio Pictures©

LASZLO, MIKLOS
Parfumerie, Play
You've Got Mail 1998 d: Nora Ephron. lps: Tom Hanks, Meg Ryan, Parker Posey. 119M USA. prod/rel: Warner Bros.©, Lauren Shuler Donner

LASZLO, NIKOLAUS
Illatszertar, 1936, Play
In the Good Old Summertime 1949 d: Robert Z. Leonard. lps: Judy Garland, Van Johnson, S. Z. Sakall. 102M USA. prod/rel: MGM

Shop Around the Corner, The 1939 d: Ernst Lubitsch. lps: Margaret Sullavan, James Stewart, Frank Morgan. 100M USA. prod/rel: Metro-Goldwyn-Mayer Corp., Loew's, Inc.©

LATEUR, FRANK, Streuvels, Stijn
De Vlaschaard, 1908, Novel
Vlaschaard, de 1983 d: Jan Gruyaert. lps: Vic Moeremans, Dora Van Der Groen, Rene Van Sambeek. 90M BLG/NTH. *Le Champ de Lin*; *The Flaxfield* (USA) prod/rel: Jan von Raemdonck

Wenn Die Sonne Wieder Scheint 1943 d: Boleslav Barlog. lps: Paul Wegener, Maria Koppenhofer, Paul Klinger. 87M GRM. *Der Flachsacker* prod/rel: Terra, Sudwest

LATHAM, AARON
Article
Perfect 1985 d: James Bridges. lps: John Travolta, Jamie Lee Curtis, Jann Wenner. 120M USA. prod/rel: Columbia-Delphi III Productions

LATHROP, LOTTIE BLAIR
Under Southern Skies, New York 1901, Play
Under Southern Skies 1915 d: Lucius Henderson. lps: Mary Fuller, Charles Ogle, Clara Beyers. 5r USA. prod/rel: Universal Film Mfg. Co.©, Broadway Universal Feature

LATIMER, JONATHAN (1906–, USA
The Dead Don't Care, New York 1938, Novel
Last Warning, The 1938 d: Albert S. Rogell. lps: Preston Foster, Kay Linaker, Frank Jenks. 63M USA. *The Dead Don't Care* prod/rel: Crime Club Productions, Universal Pictures Co.©

Headed for a Hearse, New York 1935, Novel
Westland Case, The 1937 d: W. Christy Cabanne. lps: Preston Foster, Carol Hughes, Barbara Pepper. 62M USA. prod/rel: Crime Club Productions, Universal Pictures Co.©

The Lady in the Morgue, New York 1936, Novel
Lady in the Morgue, The 1938 d: Otis Garrett. lps: Preston Foster, Patricia Ellis, Frank Jenks. 70M USA. *The Case of the Missing Blonde* (UKN); *Corpse in the Morgue* prod/rel: Crime Club Productions, Universal Pictures Co.©

LAUFS, CARL
Une Idee Folle, Play
Idee Folle, Une 1932 d: Max de Vaucorbeil. lps: Lucien Baroux, Arielle, Marc Dantzer. 95M FRN. *Une Idee de Genie* prod/rel: Via Film

Pension Scholler, Play
Pension Scholler 1930 d: Georg Jacoby. lps: Paul Henckels, Fritz Kampers, Viktor de KowA. F GRM.

Pension Scholler 1952 d: Georg Jacoby. lps: Ludwig Schmitz, Fita Benkhoff, Rudolf Platte. 90M GRM. *Scholler's Inn* prod/rel: Magna, Deutsche London

Pension Scholler 1960 d: Georg Jacoby. lps: Theo Lingen, Christa Williams, Rudolf Vogel. 93M GRM. prod/rel: Real, Europa

Ein Toller Einfall, Play
Toller Einfall, Ein 1932 d: Kurt Gerron. lps: Willy Fritsch, Dorothea Wieck, Rozsi Barsony. 86M GRM. prod/rel: UFA

LAUGHLIN, CLARA E.
The Penny Philanthropist; a Story That Could Be True, New York 1912, Novel
Penny Philanthropist, The 1917 d: Guy W. McConnell. lps: Ralph Morgan, Peggy O'Neill, Frank Weed. 7r USA. prod/rel: Wholesome Films Corp., State Rights

LAUMANN, E. M.
La Douleur, Novel
Douleur, La 1925 d: Gaston Roudes. lps: Constant Remy, France Dhelia, Lucien Dalsace. 2300m FRN. prod/rel: Grandes Productions Cinematographiques

LAUMER, KEITH
The Monitors, New York 1966, Novel
Monitors, The 1969 d: Jack SheA. lps: Guy Stockwell, Susan Oliver, Avery Schreiber. 92M USA. prod/rel: Wilding, Inc., Second City Productions

LAUNDER, FRANK
Meet a Body, Play
Green Man, The 1956 d: Robert Day. lps: Alastair Sim, George Cole, Terry-Thomas. 90M UKN. prod/rel: Grenadier, British Lion

LAUREN, S. K.
Distant Fields, London 1937, Play
Married and in Love 1940 d: John Farrow. lps: Helen Vinson, Alan Marshal, Barbara Read. 59M USA. *Distant Fields* prod/rel: RKO Radio Pictures©

Men Must Fight, New York 1932, Play
Men Must Fight 1932 d: Edgar Selwyn. lps: Diana Wynyard, Phillips Holmes, Ruth Selwyn. 73M USA. *What Women Give* prod/rel: Metro-Goldwyn-Mayer Corp., Metro-Goldwyn-Mayer Dist. Corp.©

Storks Don't Bring Babies, Story
My Blue Heaven 1950 d: Henry Koster. lps: Betty Grable, Dan Dailey, David Wayne. 96M USA. prod/rel: 20th Century-Fox

Those We Love, New York 1930, Play
Those We Love 1932 d: Robert Florey. lps: Kenneth MacKenna, Mary Astor, Lilyan Tashman. 77M USA. prod/rel: K.B.S. Film Corp., World Wide Pictures©

LAURENCE, MARGARET (1926–1987), CND, Laurence, Jean Margaret Wemyss
A Jest of God, New York 1966, Novel
Rachel, Rachel 1968 d: Paul Newman. lps: Joanne Woodward, Estelle Parsons, James Olson. 101M USA. *Now I Lay Me Down*; *A Jest of God* prod/rel: Kayos Productions, Warner Bros.

LAURENT, JACQUES
Quai de Grenelle, Novel
Quai de Grenelle 1950 d: Emile Edwin Reinert. lps: Henri Vidal, Maria Mauban, Francoise Arnoul. 96M FRN. *La Mort a Boire*; *Danger Is a Woman*; *Snake of Death* (UKN) prod/rel: Metzger Et Woog

LAURENTS, ARTHUR
Gypsy, New York 1959, Play
Gypsy 1962 d: Mervyn Leroy. lps: Natalie Wood, Rosalind Russell, Karl Malden. 149M USA. prod/rel: Warner Bros. Pictures

Home of the Brave, New York 1945, Play
Home of the Brave 1949 d: Mark Robson. lps: Douglas Dick, Steve Brodie, Jeff Corey. 85M USA. prod/rel: United Artists, Screen Plays Corp.

The Time of the Cuckoo, New York 1952, Play
Summertime 1955 d: David Lean. lps: Katharine Hepburn, Rossano Brazzi, Isa MirandA. 99M USA/UKN. *Summer Madness* (UKN) prod/rel: London Films, Lopert Films

The Turning Point, 1977, Novel
Turning Point, The 1977 d: Herbert Ross. lps: Shirley MacLaine, Anne Bancroft, Mikhail Baryshnikov. 119M USA. prod/rel: Hera, 20th Century Fox

The Way We Were, 1972, Novel
Way We Were, The 1973 d: Sydney Pollack. lps: Barbra Streisand, Robert Redford, Bradford Dillman. 118M USA. prod/rel: Rastar

West Side Story, New York 1957, Play
West Side Story 1961 d: Robert Wise, Jerome Robbins. lps: Natalie Wood, Richard Beymer, Russ Tamblyn. 155M USA. prod/rel: Mirisch Pictures, Seven Arts Productions

LAUREY, JOY
Joy, Novel
Joy 1983 d: Serge Bergon. lps: Claudia Udy, Gerard-Antoine Huart, Agnes Torrent. 90M FRN/CND. prod/rel: Atc 3000 (Paris), Moviecorp Ix Inc. (Montreal)

LAURIE JR, JOE
Union Depot, 1929, Play
Union Depot 1932 d: Alfred E. Green. lps: Douglas Fairbanks Jr., Joan Blondell, Guy Kibbee. 65M USA. *Gentleman for a Day* (UKN) prod/rel: First National Pictures©

LAURITZEN, JONREED
The Rose and the Flame, Novel
Kiss of Fire 1955 d: Joseph M. Newman. lps: Jack Palance, Barbara Rush, Rex Reason. 87M USA. prod/rel: Universal-International

LAUTENSACK, HEINRICH
Die Pfarrhauskomedie, Play
Pfarrhauskomodie, Die 1971 d: Veit Relin. lps: Maria Schell, Veit Relin, Hugo Lindinger. 83M GRM. *Parsonage Comedy* prod/rel: Schell-Relin, Lisa

LAUWICK, HERVE
Retour de Flamme, Novel
Retour de Flamme 1942 d: Henri Fescourt. lps: Renee Saint-Cyr, Denise Grey, Roger Pigaut. 105M FRN. prod/rel: General Films

LAVALLEE, DAVID
Event 1000, Novel
Gray Lady Down 1978 d: David Greene. lps: Charlton Heston, David Carradine, Stacy Keach. 111M USA. *Grey Lady Down* prod/rel: Universal

LAVEDAN, HENRI
Catherine, 1898, Play
Caterina 1921 d: Mario Caserini. lps: Vera Vergani, Nerio Bernardi, Nella SerravezzA. 1630m ITL. prod/rel: Cines

Le Duel, 1905, Play
Duel, Le 1939 d: Pierre Fresnay. lps: Raimu, Raymond Rouleau, Yvonne Printemps. 84M FRN. prod/rel: C.I.C.C.

LAVERY, EMMETT
La Premiere Legion, New York 1934, Play
First Legion, The 1951 d: Douglas Sirk. lps: Charles Boyer, William Demarest, Lyle Bettger. 86M USA. prod/rel: United Artists, Sedif

LAVIN, NORA
The Hop Dog, Novel
Adventure in the Hopfields 1954 d: John Guillermin. lps: Mandy Miller, Mona Washbourne, Hilda Fenemore. 60M UKN. prod/rel: Vandyke, Children's Film Foundation

LAWES, LEWIS E.
Chalked Out, 1937, Play
You Can't Get Away With Murder 1939 d: Lewis Seiler. lps: Humphrey Bogart, Billy Halop, Gale Page. 78M USA. *Crime Is a Racket*; *Chalked Out* prod/rel: Warner Bros. Pictures©, First National Picture

Invisible Stripes, New York 1938, Novel
Invisible Stripes 1939 d: Lloyd Bacon. lps: George Raft, Jane Bryan, William Holden. 81M USA. prod/rel: Warner Bros. Pictures©, First National Picture

Twenty Thousand Years in Sing Sing, Garden City, N.Y. 1932, Book
20,000 Years in Sing Sing 1933 d: Michael Curtiz. lps: Spencer Tracy, Bette Davis, Arthur Byron. 81M USA. prod/rel: First National Pictures©

Castle on the Hudson 1940 d: Anatole Litvak. lps: John Garfield, Pat O'Brien, Ann Sheridan. 78M USA. *Years Without Days* (UKN); *City of Lost Men* prod/rel: Warner Bros. Pictures, Inc.

LAWLER, RAY (1922–, ASL, Lawler, Raymond Evenor
The Summer of the Seventeenth Doll, Melbourne 1954, Play
Summer of the 17th Doll 1959 d: Leslie Norman. lps: Ernest Borgnine, Anne Baxter, John Mills. 94M UKN/ASL. *Season of Passion* (USA) prod/rel: Hecht-Hill-Lancaster Pty.

LAWLOR, CHARLES B.
Sidewalks of New York, Song
Sidewalks of New York 1923 d: Lester Park. lps: Hanna Lee, Bernard Siegel, King Bradley. 6r USA. prod/rel: Lester Park

LAWRENCE, D. H. (1885–1930), UKN, Lawrence, David Herbert
Novel
Boy in the Bush, The 1984 d: Rob Stewart. lps: Kenneth Branagh, Steve Bisley, Lou Brown. TVM. 188M ASL/UKN. prod/rel: Portman Productions, ABC

The Blind Man, Short Story
Blind Man, The 1967 d: Claude Whatham. MTV. 60M UKN. prod/rel: Granada

The Blue Moccasins, Short Story
Blue Moccasins, The 1967 d: Desmond Davis. MTV. 60M UKN. prod/rel: Granada

The Captain's Doll, 1923, Short Story
Captain's Doll, The 1983 d: Claude Whatham. lps: Jeremy Irons, Gila von Weitershausen, Jane Lapotaire. MTV. 110M UKN. prod/rel: BBC, Primetime

Daughters of the Vicar, Short Story
Daughters of the Vicar 1967 d: Gerald Dynevor. MTV. 60M UKN. prod/rel: Granada

The Fox, 1922, Short Story
Fox, The 1968 d: Mark Rydell. lps: Sandy Dennis, Keir Dullea, Anne Heywood. 110M USA. prod/rel: Raymond Stross, Motion Pictures International

Jimmy and the Desperate Woman, Short Story
Jimmy and the Desperate Woman 1967 d: Gerald Dynevor. MTV. 60M UKN. prod/rel: Granada

Kangaroo, 1923, Novel
Kangaroo 1986 d: Tim Burstall. lps: Colin Friels, Judy Davis, John Walton. 108M ASL. prod/rel: Naked Country Productions©, Ross Dimsey

Lady Chatterley's Lover, 1928, Novel
Amant de Lady Chatterley, L' 1955 d: Marc Allegret. lps: Danielle Darrieux, Leo Genn, Erno CrisA. 101M FRN. *Lady Chatterley's Lover* (UKN) prod/rel: Regie Du Film, Orsay Films
Lady Chatterley 1992 d: Ken Russell. lps: Joely Richardson, Sean Bean, James Wilby. TVM. F UKN. prod/rel: Global Arts, BBC
Lady Chatterley's Lover 1981 d: Just Jaeckin. lps: Sylvia Kristel, Nicholas Clay, Shane Briant. 105M UKN/FRN. *L' Amant de Lady Chatterley* (FRN) prod/rel: Cannon, Producteur Associes

Mother and Daughter, Short Story
Mother and Daughter 1967 d: Richard Everitt. MTV. 60M UKN. prod/rel: Granada

The Rainbow, 1915, Novel
Rainbow, The 1989 d: Ken Russell. lps: Sammi Davis, Paul McGann, Amanda Donohue. 113M UKN. prod/rel: Vestron Pictures

The Rocking Horse Winner, 1932, Short Story
Rocking Horse Winner, The 1949 d: Anthony Pelissier. lps: John Mills, Valerie Hobson, John Howard Davies. 90M UKN. prod/rel: General Film Distributors, Two Cities
Rocking Horse Winner, The 1977 d: Peter Medak. 30M UKN.
Rocking Horse Winner, The 1983 d: Robert Bierman. lps: Eleanor David, Charles Keating, Charles Hathorn. 33M UKN.

Samson and Delilah, Short Story
Samson and Delilah 1967 d: Peter Plummer. MTV. 60M UKN. prod/rel: Granada

Sons and Lovers, 1913, Novel
Sons and Lovers 1960 d: Jack Cardiff. lps: Trevor Howard, Dean Stockwell, Wendy Hiller. 100M UKN. prod/rel: 20th Century-Fox

Strike Pay and Her Turn, Short Story
Strike Pay and Her Turn 1967 d: Richard Everitt. MTV. 60M UKN. prod/rel: Granada

Tickets Please and Monkey Nuts, Short Story
Tickets Please and Monkey Nuts 1967 d: Claude Whatham. MTV. 60M UKN. prod/rel: Granada

The Trespasser, 1912, Novel
Trespasser, The 1982 d: Colin Gregg. lps: Alan Bates, Pauline Moran, Dinah Stabb. TVM. 90M UKN. prod/rel: Polytel, London Weekend Television

Two Blue Birds and in Love, Short Story
Two Blue Birds and in Love 1967 d: Desmond Davis. MTV. 60M UKN. prod/rel: Granada

The Virgin and the Gypsy, London 1930, Novel
Virgin and the Gypsy, The 1970 d: Christopher Miles. lps: Joanna Shimkus, Franco Nero, Honor Blackman. 95M UKN. prod/rel: Kenwood Productions, London Screenplays

The White Stocking, Short Story
White Stocking, The 1967 d: Claude Whatham. MTV. 60M UKN. prod/rel: Granada

The Widowing of Mrs. Holroyd, Play
Widowing of Mrs. Holroyd, The 1961 d: Claude Whatham. MTV. UKN. prod/rel: Granada

Women in Love, 1920, Novel
Women in Love 1969 d: Ken Russell. lps: Alan Bates, Oliver Reed, Glenda Jackson. 129M UKN. prod/rel: Brandywine Productions, United Artists

LAWRENCE, HENRY LIONEL
The Children of Light, London 1960, Novel
Damned, The 1962 d: Joseph Losey. lps: MacDonald Carey, Shirley Anne Field, Viveca Lindfors. 96M UKN. *These are the Damned* (USA); *On the Brink* prod/rel: Hammer Film Productions, Swallow Productions

LAWRENCE, JEROME
First Monday in October, Play
First Monday in October 1981 d: Ronald Neame. lps: Walter Matthau, Jill Clayburgh, Barnard Hughes. 95M USA. prod/rel: Paramount

Inherit the Wind, New York 1955, Play
Inherit the Wind 1960 d: Stanley Kramer. lps: Spencer Tracy, Fredric March, Gene Kelly. 127M USA. prod/rel: Lomitas, United Artists
Inherit the Wind 1988 d: David Greene. lps: Kirk Douglas, Jason Robards Jr., Jean Simmons. TVM. 100M USA. prod/rel: Vincent Pictures Productions, MGM Television
Inherit the Wind 1999 d: Daniel Petrie. lps: Jack Lemmon, George C. Scott, Piper Laurie. TVM. 127M USA. prod/rel: MGM Television, Showtime Network

LAWRENCE, JOSEPHINE (1897–1978), USA
Years are So Long, New York 1934, Novel
Make Way for Tomorrow 1937 d: Leo McCarey. lps: Victor Moore, Beulah Bondi, Fay Bainter. 92M USA. *The Years are So Long*; *When the Wind Blows* prod/rel: Paramount Pictures©

LAWRENCE, MARGERY
Madonna of the Seven Moons, Novel
Madonna of the Seven Moons 1944 d: Arthur Crabtree. lps: Phyllis Calvert, Stewart Granger, Patricia Roc. 110M UKN. prod/rel: Gainsborough Pictures, Eagle-Lion

A Woman Who Needed Killing, 1927, Short Story
Dangerous Woman, A 1929 d: Rowland V. Lee. lps: Olga Baclanova, Clive Brook, Neil Hamilton. 6643f USA. *The Woman Who Needed Killing* prod/rel: Paramount Famous Lasky Corp.

LAWRENCE, MARJORIE
Interrupted Melody, Autobiography
Interrupted Melody 1955 d: Curtis Bernhardt. lps: Eleanor Parker, Glenn Ford, Roger Moore. 106M USA. prod/rel: MGM

LAWRENCE, REGINALD
Men Must Fight, New York 1932, Play
Men Must Fight 1932 d: Edgar Selwyn. lps: Diana Wynyard, Phillips Holmes, Ruth Selwyn. 73M USA. *What Women Give* prod/rel: Metro-Goldwyn-Mayer Corp., Metro-Goldwyn-Mayer Dist. Corp.©

LAWRENCE, T. E. (1888–1935), UKN, Lawrence, Thomas Edward
Seven Pillars of Wisdom, 1926, Book
Lawrence of Arabia 1962 d: David Lean. lps: Peter O'Toole, Alec Guinness, Anthony Quinn. 222M UKN/USA. prod/rel: Columbia, Horizon

LAWRENCE, VINCENT
Among the Married, New York 1929, Play
Men Call It Love 1931 d: Edgar Selwyn. lps: Adolphe Menjou, Leila Hyams, Mary Duncan. 72M USA. *Among the Married* prod/rel: Metro-Goldwyn-Mayer Corp., Metro-Goldwyn-Mayer Dist. Corp.©

In Love With Love, New York 1923, Play
Crazy That Way 1930 d: Hamilton MacFadden. lps: Kenneth MacKenna, Joan Bennett, Regis Toomey. 5800f USA. prod/rel: Fox Film Corp.
In Love With Love 1924 d: Rowland V. Lee. lps: Marguerite de La Motte, Allan Forrest, Harold Goodwin. 5677f USA. prod/rel: Fox Film Corp.

Sour Grapes, New York 1926, Play
Let's Try Again 1934 d: Worthington Miner. lps: Clive Brook, Diana Wynyard, Helen Vinson. 67M USA. *The Marriage Symphony* (UKN); *Sour Grapes* prod/rel: RKO Radio Pictures©

Spring Fever, New York 1925, Musical Play
Love in the Rough 1930 d: Charles F. Reisner. lps: Robert Montgomery, Dorothy Jordan, Benny Rubin. 7785f USA. *Like Kelly Can* prod/rel: Metro-Goldwyn-Mayer Pictures
Spring Fever 1927 d: Edward Sedgwick. lps: William Haines, Joan Crawford, George K. Arthur. 6705f USA. prod/rel: Metro-Goldwyn-Mayer Pictures

LAWRENCE, WOOD
Mizpah; Or Love's Sacrifice, Play
Mizpah; Or, Love's Sacrifice 1915 d: Stuart Kinder. lps: Kahli Ru. 4000f UKN. prod/rel: Magnet

LAWSHE, ER
Patsy, c1914, Play
Patsy 1921 d: John McDermott. lps: Zasu Pitts, John MacFarlane, Tom Gallery. 5500f USA. prod/rel: Fred Swanton, Truart Film Corp.

LAWSON, CAPTAIN WILBUR
The Wonderful Adventure, Play
Wonderful Adventure, The 1915 d: Frederick A. Thompson. lps: William Farnum, Dorothy Green, Mary G. Martin. 5r USA. prod/rel: Fox Film Corp., William Fox©

LAWSON, JOHN
Humanity, Play
Humanity; Or, Only a Jew 1913 d: John Lawson, Bert Haldane. lps: John Lawson, Lucille Sidney, Charles Stafford. 3000f UKN. prod/rel: Barker, Magnet

LAWSON, JOHN HOWARD
Success Story, New York 1932, Play
Success at Any Price 1934 d: J. Walter Ruben. lps: Douglas Fairbanks Jr., Genevieve Tobin, Frank Morgan. 77M USA. *Success Story* prod/rel: RKO Radio Pictures©

LAWSON, JONELL
Roses are for the Rich, Novel
Roses are for the Rich 1987 d: Michael Miller. lps: Lisa Hartman, Bruce Dern, Joe Penny. TVM. 200M USA. prod/rel: Phoenix Entertainment Group

LAWSON, THOMAS WILLIAM
Friday the Thirteenth, New York 1907, Novel
Friday the Thirteenth 1916 d: Emile Chautard. lps: Robert Warwick, Gerda Holmes, Clarence Harvey. 5r USA. *Friday the 13th* prod/rel: World Film Corp.©, Peerless

LAWTON, HARRY
Willie Boy; a Desert Manhunt, Balboa Island, CA. 1960, Novel
Tell Them Willie Boy Is Here 1969 d: Abraham Polonsky. lps: Robert Redford, Katharine Ross, Robert Blake. 98M USA. *Willie Boy* prod/rel: Universal Pictures

LAXNESS, HALLDOR (1902–, ICL, Gudjonsson, Halldor
Fuglinn I Fjorunni, 1931-32, Novel
Salka Valka 1954 d: Arne Mattsson. lps: Birgitta Pettersson, Gunnel Brostrom, Folke Sundquist. 131M SWD/ICL.

LAXNESS, HALLDOR (1902–, ICL
Kristnihald Undir Jokli, Novel
Kristnihald Undir Jokli 1989 d: Gudny Halldorsdottir. lps: Sigurdur Sigurjonsson, Margret Helga Johannsdottir, Bladvin Halldorsson. 81M ICL/GRM. *Am Gletscher* (GRM); *Beneath the Glacier*

LAXNESS, HALLDOR (1902–, ICL, Gudjonsson, Halldor
Pu Vinvidur Hreini, 1931-32, Novel
Salka Valka 1954 d: Arne Mattsson. lps: Birgitta Pettersson, Gunnel Brostrom, Folke Sundquist. 131M SWD/ICL.

LAY, ANDRE
Les Hommes de Las Vegas, Paris 1969, Novel
Las Vegas, 500 Millones 1968 d: Antonio Isasi. lps: Gary Lockwood, Elke Sommer, Lee J. Cobb. 129M SPN/FRN/GRM. *An Einem Freitag in Las Vegas* (GRM); *Les Hommes de Las Vegas* (FRN); *Radiografia d'un Colpo d'Oro* (ITL); *They Came to Rob Las Vegas* (USA); *On a Friday in Las Vegas* prod/rel: Isasi Producciones Cin.Cas (Madrid), Capitole Films (Paris)

Ma Mort a Des Yeux Bleus, Novel
Mourir d'Amour 1960 d: Dany Fog. lps: Paul Guers, Nadia Gray, Elga Andersen. 90M FRN. *La Mort a Les Yeux Bleus* prod/rel: Films Univers

La Mort a Les Yeux Bleus, Novel
Mort a Les Yeux Bleus, La 1960 d: Dany Fog. lps: Paul Guers, Elga Andersen, Nadia Gray. 80M FRN. prod/rel: Films Univers

L' Oraison du Plus Fort, Novel
Etrangers, Les 1968 d: Jean-Pierre Desagnat. lps: Senta Berger, Michel Constantin, Julian Mateos. 100M FRN/ITL/GRM. *Quelli Che Sanno Uccidere* (ITL); *Geier Konnen Warten* (GRM); *Que Esperen Los Cuervos* (SPN); *Vultures Can Wait* prod/rel: P.A.C., S.N.C.

LAY JR., BEIRNE
Story
Above and Beyond 1952 d: Norman Panama, Melvin Frank. lps: Robert Taylor, Eleanor Parker, James Whitmore. 122M USA. prod/rel: MGM

Twelve O'Clock High, Novel
Twelve O'Clock High 1949 d: Henry King. lps: Gregory Peck, Hugh Marlowe, Gary Merrill. 132M USA. prod/rel: 20th Century-Fox

LAZARUS, ERNA
The Bride Said No, Story
I'm Nobody's Sweetheart Now 1940 d: Arthur Lubin. lps: Dennis O'Keefe, Constance Moore, Helen Parrish. 64M USA. prod/rel: Universal Pictures Co.©

LAZARUS, MILTON
Song of Norway, New York 1944, Play
Song of Norway 1970 d: Andrew L. Stone. lps: Toralv Maurstad, Florence Henderson, Christina Schollin. 142M USA. prod/rel: ABC Pictures

Whatever Goes Up, New York 1935, Play
Sudden Money 1939 d: Nick Grinde. lps: Charles Ruggles, Marjorie Rambeau, Billy Lee. 60M USA. *Sweepstakes Millionaire* prod/rel: Paramount Pictures©

LAZZARINO, ALEX
Broken Promise, Book
Broken Promise 1981 d: Don Taylor. lps: Melissa Michaelson, Chris Sarandon, George Coe. TVM. 100M USA. prod/rel: CBS, Emi

LE BARON, WILLIAM
I Love You, New York 1919, Play
Lovin' the Ladies 1930 d: Melville Brown. lps: Richard Dix, Lois Wilson, Allen Kearns. 68M USA. *Roughneck Lover* prod/rel: RKO Productions

Nobody's Money, New York 1921, Play
Nobody's Money 1923 d: Wallace Worsley. lps: Jack Holt, Wanda Hawley, Harry Depp. 5584f USA. prod/rel: Famous Players-Lasky, Paramount Pictures

Something to Brag About, New York 1925, Play
Baby-Face Harrington 1935 d: Raoul Walsh. lps: Charles Butterworth, Una Merkel, Harvey Stephens. 61M USA. *Baby Face* prod/rel: Metro-Goldwyn-Mayer Corp.

The Very Idea, New York 1917, Play
Very Idea, The 1920 d: Lawrence C. Windom. lps: Taylor Holmes, Virginia Valli, Betty Ross Clark. 6r USA. prod/rel: Taylor Holmes Productions, Inc.©, Metro Pictures Corp.

LE BRANDT, JOSEPH
On the Stroke of Twelve, 1898, Play
On the Stroke of Twelve 1927 d: Charles J. Hunt. lps: David Torrence, June Marlowe, Danny O'SheA. 5970f USA. prod/rel: Trem Carr Productions, Rayart Pictures

LE BRAZ, ANATOLE
Le Gardien du Feu, Short Story
Gardien du Feu, Le 1924 d: Gaston Ravel. lps: Rene Navarre, Marie-Louise Iribe, Alice Tissot. 2000m FRN. prod/rel: Films De France

LE BRETON, AUGUSTE
Brigade Anti-Gangs, Novel
Brigade Anti-Gangs 1966 d: Bernard Borderie. lps: Robert Hossein, Raymond Pellegrin, Gabriele Tinti. 115M FRN/ITL. *Pattuglia Anti-Gang* (ITL); *Brigade Antigang* prod/rel: Franco Films, C.I.C.C.

Le Clan Des Siciliens, Paris 1967, Novel
Clan Des Siciliens, Le 1969 d: Henri Verneuil. lps: Jean Gabin, Alain Delon, Irina Demick. 124M FRN. *The Sicilian Clan* (UKN) prod/rel: Fox Europa, Les Films Du Siecle

Du Rififi a Paname, Paris 1965, Novel
Du Rififi a Panama 1966 d: Denys de La Patelliere. lps: Jean Gabin, Gert Frobe, George Raft. 100M FRN/ITL/GRM. *Rififi Internazionale* (ITL); *Rififi in Paris* (UKN); *The Upper Hand* (USA) prod/rel: Copernic Films, Fida Cinematografica

Du Rififi Chez Les Femmes, Paris 1957, Novel
Du Rififi Chez Les Femmes 1959 d: Alex Joffe. lps: Nadja Tiller, Robert Hossein, Silvia Monfort. 110M FRN/ITL. *Rififi Fra le Donne* (ITL); *Riff Raff Girls* (USA); *Rififi for Girls*; *Rififi and the Women* (UKN) prod/rel: Productions De L'etoile, Dismage

Du Rififi Chez Les Hommes, Novel
Du Rififi Chez Les Hommes 1955 d: Jules Dassin. lps: Jean Servais, Carl Mohner, Robert Manuel. 116M FRN. *Rififi* (USA) prod/rel: Indus Films, S.N. Pathe-Cinema

La Loi Des Rues, Novel
Loi Des Rues, La 1956 d: Ralph Habib. lps: Raymond Pellegrin, Silvana Pampanini, Fernand Ledoux. 110M FRN. *Law of the Streets* (USA) prod/rel: Transcontinental Film, Paul Graetz

Rafles Sur la Ville, Novel
Rafles Sur la Ville 1957 d: Pierre Chenal. lps: Charles Vanel, Bella Darvi, Danik Patisson. 86M FRN. *Sinners of Paris* (USA); *Trap for a Killer* prod/rel: Metzger Et Voog

Razzia Sur la Chnouf, Novel
Razzia Sur la Chnouf 1955 d: Henri Decoin. lps: Jean Gabin, Lino Ventura, Albert Remy. 105M FRN. *Razzia* (USA); *Chnouf -to Take It Is Deadly*; *Chnouf* (UKN) prod/rel: Jad Films, S.N.E.G.

Le Rouge Est Mis, Novel
Rouge Est Mis, Le 1957 d: Gilles Grangier. lps: Jean Gabin, Annie Girardot, Paul Frankeur. 85M FRN. *Speaking of Murder* (USA) prod/rel: Gaumont, Cite Films

LE BRETON, JOHN
A Sister to Assist 'Er, Play
Sister to Assist 'Er, A 1922 d: George Dewhurst. lps: Mary Brough, Pollie Emery, Muriel Aked. 5200f UKN. prod/rel: Baron Films, Gaumont
Sister to Assist 'Er, A 1927 d: George Dewhurst. lps: Mary Brough, Pollie Emery, Humberston Wright. 6000f UKN. prod/rel: Gaumont
Sister to Assist 'Er, A 1930 d: George Dewhurst. lps: Barbara Gott, Pollie Emery, Donald Stuart. 64M UKN. prod/rel: E. A. Thompson, Gaumont
Sister to Assist 'Er, A 1938 d: Widgey R. Newman, George Dewhurst. lps: Muriel George, Pollie Emery, Charles Paton. 72M UKN. prod/rel: Associated Industries, Columbia
Sister to Assist 'Er, A 1948 d: George Dewhurst. lps: Muriel Aked, Muriel George, Michael Howard. 60M UKN. prod/rel: Bruton, Trytel

LE CARRE, JOHN (1931–, UKN, Cornwell, David John Moore
Call for the Dead, London 1961, Novel
Deadly Affair, The 1966 d: Sidney Lumet. lps: James Mason, Simone Signoret, Maximilian Schell. 107M UKN. prod/rel: Columbia, Sidney Lumet

The Little Drummer Girl, 1983, Novel
Little Drummer Girl, The 1985 d: George Roy Hill. lps: Diane Keaton, Klaus Kinski, Yorgo Voyagis. 130M USA. prod/rel: Warner Bros., Pan Arts

The Looking Glass War, London 1965, Novel
Looking Glass War, The 1969 d: Frank R. Pierson. lps: Christopher Jones, Pia Degermark, Ralph Richardson. 107M UKN. prod/rel: Frankovich Productions, Columbia

A Murder of Quality, Novel
Murder of Quality, A 1991 d: Gavin Millar. lps: Denholm Elliott, Joss Ackland, Glenda Jackson. TVM. 102M USA. prod/rel: Portobello Films, Thames Television

A Perfect Spy, Novel
Perfect Spy, A 1988 d: Peter Smith. lps: Alec Guinness, Peggy Ashcroft, Sarah Badel. TVM. 376M UKN. prod/rel: BBC

The Russia House, 1989, Novel
Russia House, The 1990 d: Fred Schepisi. lps: Sean Connery, Michelle Pfeiffer, Roy Scheider. 123M USA/UKN. prod/rel: Pathe Entertainment

Smiley's People, Novel
Smiley's People 1982 d: Simon Langton. lps: Alec Guinness, Curd Jurgens, Eileen Atkins. MTV. 300M UKN/USA. prod/rel: BBC

The Spy Who Came in from the Cold, London 1963, Novel
Spy Who Came in from the Cold, The 1965 d: Martin Ritt. lps: Richard Burton, Claire Bloom, Oskar Werner. 112M UKN. prod/rel: Salem Films, Paramount

Tinker Tailor Soldier Spy, Novel
Tinker, Tailor, Soldier, Spy 1979 d: John Irvin. lps: Joss Ackland, Michael Aldridge, Ian Bannen. TVM. 350M UKN. prod/rel: BBC, Paramount

LE CHUNG-JOON
Chukje, Novel
Chukje 1997 d: Im Kwon-Taek. lps: Ahn Sung-Kee, Oh Jung-Hae, Han Eun-Jin. 106M SKR. *Festival* prod/rel: Taehung Pictures

LE CLEZIO, JEAN-MARIE
Mondo, Novel
Mondo 1997 d: Tony Gatlif. lps: Ovidiu Balan, Pierrette Fesch, Philippe Petit. 95M FRN. prod/rel: Kg Prods., Canal Plus

LE FANU, SHERIDAN (1814–1873), IRL, le Fanu, Joseph Sheridan
Carmilla, London 1872, Short Story
Cripta E l'Incubo, La 1964 d: Camillo Mastrocinque. lps: Christopher Lee, Jose Campos, Nela Conjiu. 82M ITL/SPN. *La Maldicion de Los Karnstein* (SPN); *Terror in the Crypt* (USA); *Crypt of Horror* (UKN); *The Crypt and the Nightmare*; *Curse of the Karnstein, The* prod/rel: Mec Cin.Ca (Roma), Hispamer Film (Madrid)
Et Mourir de Plaisir 1960 d: Roger Vadim. lps: Mel Ferrer, Elsa Martinelli, Annette Stroyberg. 100M FRN/ITL. *Il Sangue E la Rosa* (ITL); *Blood and Roses* (USA); *And Die of Pleasure*; *Le Sang Et la Rose*; *Du Sang Et Des Roses* prod/rel: Films E.G.E., Documento Film
Lust for a Vampire 1970 d: Jimmy Sangster. lps: Ralph Bates, Barbara Jefford, Suzanna Leigh. 95M UKN. *To Love a Vampire* prod/rel: MGM-Emi, Hammer

Novia Ensangrentada, La 1972 d: Vicente ArandA. lps: Simon Andreu, Maribel Martin, Alexandra Bastedo. 101M SPN. *The Blood-Spattered Bride* (USA); *Bloody Fiancee*; *The Bloody Bride*; *The Blood Splattered Bride*; *Till Death Do Us Part*
Vampire Lovers, The 1970 d: Roy Ward Baker. lps: Ingrid Pitt, Peter Cushing, George Cole. 91M UKN. prod/rel: Hammer Film Productions, American International Pictures
Vampyr 1931 d: Carl T. Dreyer. lps: Julian West, Rena Mandel, Jan Hieronimko. 75M FRN/GRM. *Vampyr Ou l'Etrange Aventure de David Gray* (FRN); *Der Traum Des Allan Gray*; *The Strange Adventure of David Gray* (UKN); *Adventures of David Gray*; *Castle of Doom* prod/rel: Carl Theodor Dreyer, le Baron De Gunzburg

Room in the Dragon Volant, 1872, Short Story
Vampyr 1931 d: Carl T. Dreyer. lps: Julian West, Rena Mandel, Jan Hieronimko. 75M FRN/GRM. *Vampyr Ou l'Etrange Aventure de David Gray* (FRN); *Der Traum Des Allan Gray*; *The Strange Adventure of David Gray* (UKN); *Adventures of David Gray*; *Castle of Doom* prod/rel: Carl Theodor Dreyer, le Baron De Gunzburg

Shamus O'Brien, Poem
Shamus O'Brien 1912 d: Otis Turner. lps: King Baggot, Vivian Prescott, William Robert Daly. 2000f USA. prod/rel: Imp

Uncle Silas, 1864, Novel
Uncle Silas 1947 d: Charles H. Frank. lps: Jean Simmons, Katina Paxinou, Derrick de Marney. 103M UKN. *The Inheritance* (USA) prod/rel: General Film Distributors, Two Cities

LE FAURE, GEORGES
La Conscience de Peones, Short Story
Conscience de Peones, La 1917. lps: Edouard-Emile Violet, Fred ZorillA. 740m FRN. prod/rel: Acad

La Double Existence de Lord Samsey, Novel
Double Existence de Lord Samsey, La 1924 d: Georges Monca, Maurice Keroul. lps: Genevieve Felix, Fernand Herrmann, Maxime Desjardins. 2000m FRN. prod/rel: Grandes Productions Cinematographiques

La Grande Epreuve, Novel
Grande Epreuve, La 1927 d: Alexandre Ryder, A. Duges. lps: Maxime Desjardins, Michele Verly, Berthe Jalabert. F FRN. prod/rel: Jacques Haik

L' Homme Bleu, Novel
Homme Bleu, L' 1919 d: Jean Manoussi. lps: Gabriel Signoret, Pierre Magnier, Georges Treville. 1650m FRN. prod/rel: Film d'Art

The Soul of Bronze, Story
Soul of Bronze, The 1921. lps: Harry Houdini. F USA. prod/rel: Houdini Picture Corp.

LE FRANCOIS, W. S.
Gung Ho, Book
Gung Ho 1985 d: Ron Howard. lps: Michael Keaton, Gedde Watanabe, George Wendt. 111M USA. prod/rel: Paramount

LE GALLIENNE, RICHARD (1866–1947), UKN Book
Chain Invisible, The 1916 d: Frank Powell. lps: Bruce McRae, Gerda Holmes, Alfred Hickman. 5r USA. *The Invisible Chain* prod/rel: Equitable Motion Pictures Corp.©

LE HALLIER, JEAN
Un Certain Monsieur, Novel
Certain Monsieur, Un 1949 d: Yves Ciampi. lps: Rene Dary, Pierre Destailles, Helene Perdriere. 90M FRN. prod/rel: Eclectique Film

LE MAY, ALAN
Along Came Jones, Novel
Along Came Jones 1945 d: Stuart Heisler. lps: Gary Cooper, Loretta Young, Dan DuryeA. 90M USA. prod/rel: United Artists Corp., Cinema Artists Corp.

The Unforgiven, Novel
Unforgiven, The 1960 d: John Huston. lps: Burt Lancaster, Audrey Hepburn, Audie Murphy. 125M USA. prod/rel: United Artists

LE NOIR, PHILIP
The Man Who Wouldn't Take Off His Hat, 1922, Short Story
Devil's Bowl, The 1923 d: Neal Hart. lps: Catherine Bennett, W. J. Allen, Fonda Holt. 5r USA. *In the Devil's Bowl* prod/rel: William Steiner Productions

LE QUEUX, WILLIAM
The Invasion of 1910, Novel
Raid of 1915, The 1914 d: Fred W. Durrant. lps: Leo Lilley, Diana Shaw, Mr. Dunn. 2268f UKN. **If England Were Invaded** prod/rel: Gaumont

Sadounah, Novel
Sadounah 1915 d: Louis Mercanton. lps: Jean Peyriere, Paul Guide, Regina Badet. 1840m FRN. prod/rel: Eclipse

The Sons of Satan, Novel
Sons of Satan, The 1915 d: George Loane Tucker. lps: Gerald Ames, Blanche Bryan, Hayford Hobbs. 4730f UKN. prod/rel: London, Jury

LE SUEUR, DANIEL
Madame l'Ambassadrice, Novel
Madame l'Ambassadrice 1921 d: Ermanno Geymonat. lps: Yvonne de Fleuriel, Cav. Roberto Villani, Rita d'Harcourt. 1316m ITL. prod/rel: S.A. Ambrosio

LE VINO, ALBERT SHELBY
Husbands Preferred, Story
Truthful Sex, The 1926 d: Richard Thomas. lps: Mae Busch, Huntley Gordon, Ian Keith. 5831f USA. *When We are Married* prod/rel: Columbia Pictures

LEA, FANNY HEASLIP
The Four Marys, New York 1937, Novel
Man-Proof 1937 d: Richard Thorpe. lps: Myrna Loy, Franchot Tone, Rosalind Russell. 74M USA. *The Four Marys* prod/rel: Metro-Goldwyn-Mayer Corp.©

The Peacock Screen, 1911, Short Story
Cheaters 1934 d: Phil Rosen. lps: William Boyd, June Collyer, Dorothy MacKaill. 68M USA. prod/rel: Liberty Pictures Corp.

With This Ring, New York 1925, Novel
With This Ring 1925 d: Fred Windermere. lps: Alyce Mills, Forrest Stanley, Lou Tellegen. 5333f USA. prod/rel: B. P. Schulberg Productions

LEA, TIMOTHY
Confessions from the Pop Scene, Novel
Confessions of a Pop Performer 1975 d: Norman Cohen. lps: Robin Askwith, Anthony Booth, Bill Maynard. 91M UKN. prod/rel: Columbia-Warner, Swiftdown

Confessions of a Driving Instructor, Novel
Confessions of a Driving Instructor 1976 d: Norman Cohen. lps: Robin Askwith, Anthony Booth, Sheila White. 90M UKN. prod/rel: Columbia-Warner, Swiftdown

LEA, TOM
The Brave Bulls, Novel
Brave Bulls, The 1951 d: Robert Rossen. lps: Mel Ferrer, Miroslava, Anthony Quinn. 108M USA. prod/rel: Columbia

The Wonderful Country, 1952, Novel
Wonderful Country, The 1959 d: Robert Parrish. lps: Robert Mitchum, Pedro Armendariz, Julie London. 98M USA. prod/rel: United Artists, D.R.M. Prods.

LEAKE, GRACE SOTHCOTE
The House of Refuge, New York 1932, Novel
Bondage 1933 d: Alfred Santell. lps: Dorothy Jordan, Alexander Kirkland, Isabel Jewell. 65M USA. *The House of Refuge* prod/rel: Fox Film Corp.

LEAR, PETER
Goldengirl, Novel
Goldengirl 1979 d: Joseph Sargent. lps: Susan Anton, James Coburn, Curd Jurgens. TVM. 104M USA. *Golden Girl* prod/rel: NBC, Viacom

LEASOR, JAMES (1923–, UKN
Boarding Party, Novel
Sea Wolves, The 1980 d: Andrew V. McLaglen. lps: Gregory Peck, Roger Moore, David Niven. 120M UKN/USA/SWT. prod/rel: Richmond-Lorimar-Varius

The One That Got Away, Book
One That Got Away, The 1957 d: Roy Ward Baker. lps: Hardy Kruger, Colin Gordon, Michael Goodliffe. 111M UKN. prod/rel: Rank, Rank Film Distributors

Passport to Oblivion, London 1964, Novel
Where the Spies are 1966 d: Val Guest. lps: David Niven, Francoise Dorleac, Cyril Cusack. 113M UKN/USA. *Passport to Oblivion; One Spy Too Many* prod/rel: MGM, Val Guest

LEAVITT, DAVID
The Lost Language of Cranes, Novel
Lost Language of Cranes, The 1991 d: Nigel Finch. lps: Brian Cox, Eileen Atkins, Angus MacFadyen. TVM. 90M UKN. prod/rel: BBC Tv, BBC Films for Screen Two

LEBL, JULIUS
Provdam Svou Zenu, Play
Provdam Svou Zenu 1941 d: Miroslav Cikan. lps: Vlasta Burian, Svetla Svozilova, Jaroslav Marvan. 2316m CZC. *I'll Give My Wife in Marriage* prod/rel: Slavia-Film, Tobis

LEBLANC, ALAIN
Un Pont Entre Deux Rives, Novel
Pont Entre Deux Rives, Un 1999 d: Gerard Depardieu, Frederic Auburtin. lps: Carole Bouquet, Gerard Depardieu, Charles Berling. 88M FRN. *A Bridge Between Two Shores* prod/rel: D.D. Prods., Tf1 Film Prods.

LEBLANC, MAURICE
813, Short Stories
"813" 1920 d: Scott Sidney. lps: Wedgewood Nowell, Kathryn Adams, Laura La Plante. 6r USA. *Eight-Thirteen* prod/rel: Christie Film Co., Robertson-Cole Distributing Corp.

L' Agence Barnett, Novel
Arsene Lupin, Detective 1937 d: Henri Diamant-Berger. lps: Jules Berry, Gabriel Signoret, Suzy Prim. 98M FRN.

Arsene Lupin, Paris 1907, Novel
Arsene Lupin 1916 d: George Loane Tucker. lps: Gerald Ames, Manora Thew, Kenelm Foss. 6400f UKN. prod/rel: London, Jury
Arsene Lupin 1917 d: Paul Scardon. lps: Earle Williams, Ethel Grey Terry, Brinsley Shaw. 5r USA. prod/rel: Vitagraph Co. of America©, Greater Vitagraph (V-L-S-E, Inc.)
Arsene Lupin 1932 d: Jack Conway. lps: John Barrymore, Lionel Barrymore, Karen Morley. 84M USA. prod/rel: Metro-Goldwyn-Mayer Corp.

LEBOW, BARBARA
A Shayna Maidel, Play
Miss Rose White 1992 d: Joseph Sargent. lps: Kyra Sedgwick, Amanda Plummer, Maximilian Schell. TVM. 100M USA. prod/rel: Lorimar, Inc.©, Marian Rees Associates

LEBRETON
Une Petite Femme En Or, Play
Petite Femme En Or, Une 1933 d: Andre Pellenc. lps: Anthony Gildes, Fernand Rene, Marcel Carpentier. SHT FRN.

LEBRUN, MICHEL
A Malin Et Demi, Novel
Lionceaux, Les 1959 d: Jacques Bourdon. lps: Jean Sorel, Anna Gaylor, Roland Rodier. 88M FRN. *The Playful Kind* prod/rel: Estela Films, Cocinor

Cette Nuit-la, Novel
Cette Nuit-la 1958 d: Maurice Cazeneuve. lps: Mylene Demongeot, Jean Servais, Maurice Ronet. 100M FRN. *Night Heat* (UKN); *Un Silence de Mort* prod/rel: Soprofilm

Dans Mon Joli Pavillon, Novel
Durs a Cuire, Les 1964 d: Jack Pinoteau. lps: Roger Pierre, Jean Poiret, Stephane Audran. 83M FRN. prod/rel: Cimatel, S.N. Pathe-Cinema

Portrait-Robot, Novel
Portrait Robot 1960 d: Paul Paviot. lps: Maurice Ronet, Andrea Parisi, Jacques Riberolles. 78M FRN. *Portrait Robot Ou Echec a l'Assassin; L' Echec d'un Assassin* prod/rel: Pavox Films, Cinetel

Un Soleil de Plomb, Novel
Homme de Mykonos, L' 1965 d: Rene Gainville. lps: Gabriele Tinti, Anne Vernon, Veronique Vendel. 90M FRN/ITL/BLG. prod/rel: Comptoir Francais de Production de Films, Cine Italia

La Tete du Client, Novel
Tete du Client, La 1964 d: Jacques Poitrenaud. lps: Jean Poiret, Michel Serrault, Sophie Desmarets. 96M FRN/SPN. *Las Noches de Monsieur Max* (SPN) prod/rel: Societe Francaise de Cinematographie, France Cinema Productions

La Veuve, Paris 1958, Novel
Corde Raide, La 1959 d: Jean-Charles Dudrumet. lps: Annie Girardot, Francois Perier, Gerard Buhr. 79M FRN. *Lovers on a Tightrope* (USA) prod/rel: Panda Films

LECAS, GERARD
L' Ennemi Public No. 2, Novel
Ennemi Public No. 2, L' 1983 d: Edouard Niermans. lps: Jean-Francois Stevenin, Jean-Pierre Sentier, Florent Pagny. TVM. 90M FRN/LXM/SWT. prod/rel: TF 1, Hamster Prod.

LECCISOTTI, TOMMASO
Montecassino, Book
Montecassino 1946 d: Arturo Gemmiti. lps: Alberto Carlo Lolli, Ubaldo Lay, Gilberto Severi. F ITL. *Montecassino Nel Cerchio Di Fuoco* prod/rel: Pastor Film, Scalera Film

LECLERQ, A.
Jalouse, Play
Etes-Vous Jalouse? 1937 d: Henri Chomette. lps: Suzy Prim, Gabrielle Dorziat, Andre Luguet. 100M FRN. prod/rel: F.R.D.

LECOCQ, CHARLES (1832–1918), FRN
La Fille de Madame Angot, Brussels 1872, Operetta
Fille de Madame Angot, La 1935 d: Jean Bernard-Derosne. lps: Andre Bauge, Jean Aquistapace, MoniquellA. 85M FRN. prod/rel: Ste Francaise De Prod. Cinematographique

LEDDA, GAVINO
L'educazione Di un Pastore Padre Padrone, Novel
Padre Padrone 1977 d: Paolo Taviani, Vittorio Taviani. lps: Omero Antonutti, Saverio Marconi, Marcella Michelangeli. 111M ITL. *Father Master* (USA) prod/rel: Cinema S.R.L., Rai-Tv

LEDERER, COM. W. J.
The Skipper Surprised His Wife, Article
Skipper Surprised His Wife, The 1950 d: Elliott Nugent. lps: Robert Walker, Joan Leslie, Edward Arnold. 85M USA. prod/rel: MGM

LEDERER, EMMANUEL
Are You a Mason?, New York 1901, Play
Are You a Mason? 1915 d: Thomas N. Heffron. lps: John Barrymore, Alfred Hickman, Charles Dixon. 5r USA. *The Joiner* prod/rel: Famous Players Film Co., Paramount Pictures Corp.
Are You a Mason? 1934 d: Henry Edwards. lps: Sonnie Hale, Robertson Hare, Davy Burnaby. 85M UKN. prod/rel: Real Art, Universal

LEDERER, WILLIAM J. (1912–, USA, Lederer, William Julius
The Ugly American, New York 1958, Novel
Ugly American, The 1963 d: George Englund. lps: Marlon Brando, Eiji Okada, Sandra Church. 120M USA. *The Quiet American* prod/rel: Universal Pictures

LEDUC, VIOLETTE (1907–1972), FRN
Therese Et Isabelle, Paris 1966, Novel
Therese and Isabelle 1969 d: Radley H. Metzger. lps: Essy Persson, Anna Gael, Simone Paris. 118M USA/GRM/FRN. *Therese Und Isabell* (GRM); *Therese Et Isabelle* prod/rel: Amsterdam Film Corp., Berolina Films

LEE, BERT
Black Hand George, Play
Black Hand Gang, The 1930 d: Monty Banks. lps: Wee Georgie Wood, Dolly Harmer, Violet Young. 63M UKN. prod/rel: British International Pictures, Wardour

Please Teacher, London 1935, Play
Please Teacher 1937 d: Stafford Dickens. lps: Bobby Howes, Rene Ray, Wylie Watson. 76M UKN. prod/rel: Associated British Picture Corporation, Wardour

LEE BIHUA
Yanzhi Kou, Novel
Yanzhi Kou 1987 d: Guan Jinpeng. lps: Mei Yanfang, Leslie Cheung, Zhu Baoyi. 96M HKG. *Rouge* prod/rel: Goldest Harvest, Golden Way

LEE, EDNA
All That Heaven Allows, Novel
All That Heaven Allows 1956 d: Douglas Sirk. lps: Jane Wyman, Rock Hudson, Agnes Moorehead. 89M USA. prod/rel: Universal-International

Queen Bee, 1949, Novel
Queen Bee 1955 d: Ranald MacDougall. lps: Joan Crawford, Barry Sullivan, Betsy Palmer. 95M USA. prod/rel: Columbia

LEE, GYPSY ROSE (1913–1970), USA, Hovick, Louise
The G-String Murders, Novel
Lady of Burlesque 1943 d: William A. Wellman. lps: Barbara Stanwyck, Michael O'Shea, J. Edward Bromberg. 91M USA. *Striptease Lady* (UKN); *The G-String Murders* prod/rel: United Artists, Hunt Stromberg

LEE, HARPER (1926–, USA, Lee, Nelle Harper
To Kill a Mockingbird, Philadelphia 1960, Novel
To Kill a Mockingbird 1962 d: Robert Mulligan. lps: Gregory Peck, Mary Badham, Philip Alford. 129M USA. prod/rel: Pakula-Mulligan Productions, Brentwood Productions

LEE, HARRY
All That Heaven Allows, Novel
All That Heaven Allows 1956 d: Douglas Sirk. lps: Jane Wyman, Rock Hudson, Agnes Moorehead. 89M USA. prod/rel: Universal-International

LEE, JAMES
Career, New York 1957, Play
Career 1960 d: Joseph Anthony. lps: Anthony Franciosa, Dean Martin, Shirley MacLaine. 105M USA. prod/rel: Paramount, Hal B. Wallis

LEE, JENNETTE BARBOUR PERRY
Simeon Tetlow's Shadow, New York 1909, Novel
Ruler of the Road 1918 d: Ernest C. Warde. lps: Frank Keenan, Kathryn Lean, Thomas Jackson. 5r USA. prod/rel: Pathe Exchange, Inc.©

LEE, LAUREL
Walking Through the Fire, Book
Walking Through the Fire 1979 d: Robert Day. lps: Bess Armstrong, Tom Mason, Richard Masur. TVM. 100M USA. prod/rel: CBS, Time-Life Television

LEE, LAURIE (1914–1997), UKN
Cider With Rosie, 1959, Autobiography
Cider With Rosie 1971 d: Claude Whatham. lps: Rosemary Leach, Peter Chandler. TVM. 95M UKN. prod/rel: BBC

Laurie Lee's Cider With Rosie 1998 d: Charles Beeson. lps: Juliet Stevenson, Robert Lang, Angela Pleasence. 100M UKN. *Cider With Rosie* prod/rel: Carlton Television©, Turning Point Productions

LEE, LEONARD
Sweet Poison, Novel
Along Came a Spider 1969 d: Lee H. Katzin. lps: Suzanne Pleshette, Ed Nelson, Andrew Prine. TVM. 74M USA. prod/rel: Twentieth Century-Fox Tv

LEE, NORMAN
Josser K.C., Play
Josser, K.C. 1929 d: Hugh Croise. lps: Ernie LotingA. 19M UKN. prod/rel: British Sound Film Productions, Bifd

LEE, ROBERT E.
First Monday in October, Play
First Monday in October 1981 d: Ronald Neame. lps: Walter Matthau, Jill Clayburgh, Barnard Hughes. 95M USA. prod/rel: Paramount

Inherit the Wind, New York 1955, Play
Inherit the Wind 1960 d: Stanley Kramer. lps: Spencer Tracy, Fredric March, Gene Kelly. 127M USA. prod/rel: Lomitas, United Artists

Inherit the Wind 1988 d: David Greene. lps: Kirk Douglas, Jason Robards Jr., Jean Simmons. TVM. 100M USA. prod/rel: Vincent Pictures Productions, MGM Television

Inherit the Wind 1999 d: Daniel Petrie. lps: Jack Lemmon, George C. Scott, Piper Laurie. TVM. 127M USA. prod/rel: MGM Television, Showtime Network

LEE, ROBERT MASON
Death and Deliverance, Book
Ordeal in the Arctic 1993 d: Mark Sobel. lps: Richard Chamberlain, Catherine Mary Stewart, Melanie Mayron. TVM. 89M CND/USA. prod/rel: Citadel, Alliance

LEES, HANNAH
Death in the Doll's House, 1943, Short Story
Shadow on the Wall 1949 d: Pat Jackson. lps: Ann Sothern, Zachary Scott, Nancy Davis. 84M USA. *Death in the Doll's House* prod/rel: MGM

LEES, RICHARD
Right of Way, Play
Right of Way 1983 d: George Schaefer. lps: Bette Davis, James Stewart, Melinda Dillon. TVM. 106M USA. prod/rel: Hbo, Schaefer-Karpf Productions

LEFEVRE, RENE
Les Musiciens du Ciel, Novel
Musiciens du Ciel, Les 1939 d: Georges Lacombe. lps: Rene Lefevre, Michel Simon, Michele Morgan. 98M FRN. prod/rel: Regina

Rue Des Prairies, Novel
Rue Des Prairies 1959 d: Denys de La Patelliere. lps: Jean Gabin, Marie-Jose Nat, Claude Brasseur. 87M FRN/ITL. *Mio Figlio* (ITL); *Rue de Paris* (USA); *Streets of Paris* prod/rel: Films Ariane, Filmsonor

LEFLORE, RON
Breakout, Book
One in a Million: the Ron Leflore Story 1978 d: William A. Graham. lps: Levar Burton, Madge Sinclair, Paul Benjamin. TVM. 100M USA. prod/rel: Roger Gimbel Productions, Emi Television

LEFRANCQ, GERMAINE
Vingt-Cinq Ans de Bonheur, Play
Vingt-Cinq Ans de Bonheur 1943 d: Rene Jayet. lps: Jean Tissier, Denise Grey, Annie France. 80M FRN. prod/rel: Continental-Films

LEGAY, PIET
Commando 44, Novel
Commando Suicida 1968 d: Camillo Bazzoni. lps: Aldo Ray, Tano Cimarosa, Ugo Fangareggi. 100M ITL/SPN. *Comando Suicida* (SPN); *Suicide Commandos* (USA); *Suicide Commando*; *Comandos* prod/rel: Cine Realizzazioni Ermanno Donati, Estela Film (Madrid)

LEGER, JACK-ALAIN
Mon Premier Amour, Novel
Mon Premier Amour 1978 d: Elie Chouraqui. lps: Anouk Aimee, Richard Berry, Gabriele Ferzetti. 125M FRN. prod/rel: Gaumont, Fr 3

Monsignor, Novel
Monsignor 1983 d: Frank Perry. lps: Christopher Reeve, Genevieve Bujold, Fernando Rey. 122M USA. prod/rel: 20th Century Fox

LEGER, KAREL
Loupeznici Na Chlumu, Short Story
Loupeznici Na Chlumu 1926 d: Milos Hajsky. lps: Karel MacHek, Ludvik Veverka, L. H. StrunA. CZC. *The Highwaymen of Chlum* prod/rel: Fortuna Film

LEGOUVE, ERNEST
Adrienne Lecouvreur, Paris 1849, Play
Adriana Lecouvreur 1919 d: Ugo FalenA. lps: Bianca Stagno-Bellincioni, Enrico Roma, Marion May. 2196m ITL. prod/rel: Tespi Film

Adrienne Lecouvreur 1913 d: Louis Mercanton, Henri Desfontaines. lps: Sarah Bernhardt, Max Maxudian, Lou Tellegen. 857m FRN. *An Actress's Romance Adrienne Lecouvreur; Or* prod/rel: Urban Trading

Dream of Love 1928 d: Fred Niblo. lps: Nils Asther, Joan Crawford, Aileen Pringle. 5764f USA. *Adrienne Lecouvreur* prod/rel: Metro-Goldwyn-Mayer Pictures

La Bataille de Dames; Ou un Duel En Amour, Paris 1851, Novel
Devil-May-Care 1929 d: Sidney A. Franklin. lps: Ramon Novarro, Dorothy Jordan, Marion Harris. 8782f USA. *Battle of the Ladies; Devil May Care* prod/rel: Metro-Goldwyn-Mayer Pictures

Les Doigts de Fee, 1858, Play
Dita Di Fata 1921 d: Nino Giannini. lps: Myriel, Arturo Stinga, Alfredo Martinelli. 1565m ITL. prod/rel: Photodrama

LEGRAND, ANDRE
L' Ile Sans Amour, Novel
Ile Sans Amour, L' 1919 d: Andre Liabel. lps: Jean Legrand, Renee Sylvaire, Elmire Vautier. 1330m FRN. prod/rel: Films Andre Legrand, Vita-Film

LEGUIN, URSULA K.
The Lathe of Heaven, Novel
Lathe of Heaven, The 1980 d: David Loxton, Fred Barzyk. lps: Kevin Conway, Bruce Davison, Margaret Avery. TVM. 105M USA.

LEGUINA, JOAQUIN
Tu Nombre Envenena Mis Suenos, Novel
Tu Nombre Envenena Mis Suenos 1996 d: Pilar Miro. lps: Emma Suarez, Carmelo Gomez, Angel de Andres Lopez. 121M SPN. *Your Name Poisons My Dreams* prod/rel: Sogetel, Central De Producciones Audiovisuales

LEHAR, FRANZ (1870–1948), HNG
Clo-Clo, Operetta
Dreams Come True 1936 d: Reginald Denham. lps: Frances Day, Nelson Keys, Hugh Wakefield. 78M UKN. prod/rel: London and Continental, Reunion

Eva, Operetta
Eva 1935 d: Johannes Riemann. lps: Magda Schneider, Heinz Ruhmann, Hans Sohnker. 96M AUS. *Das Fabriksmadel Eva* prod/rel: Atlantis

Das Furstenkind, Vienna 1909, Operetta
Furstenkind, Das 1927 d: Jacob Fleck, Luise Fleck. lps: Vivian Gibson, Harry Liedtke, Evi EvA. 2460m GRM. prod/rel: Hegewald-Film

Gipsy Love, London 1912, Operetta
Rogue Song, The 1929 d: Lionel Barrymore. lps: Lawrence Tibbett, Catherine Dale Owen, Nance O'Neil. 115M USA. prod/rel: Metro-Goldwyn-Mayer Pictures

Der Graf von Luxembourg, Vienna 1909, Operetta
Count of Luxembourg, The 1926 d: Arthur Gregor. lps: George Walsh, Helen Lee Worthing, Michael Dark. 6400f USA. prod/rel: Chadwick Pictures

Graf von Luxemburg, Der 1957 d: Werner Jacobs. lps: Gerhard Riedmann, Renate Holm, Germaine Damar. 90M GRM. *The Count of Luxembourg* prod/rel: C.C.C., Constantin

Das Land Des Lachelns, Berlin 1929, Operetta
Land Des Lachelns, Das 1930 d: Max Reichmann. lps: Richard Tauber, Mary Losseff, Bruno Kastner. 94M GRM. *Land of Smiles*

Land Des Lachelns, Das 1952 d: Hans Deppe. lps: Marta Eggerth, Jan Kiepura, Walter Muller. 107M GRM. *Land of Smiles* (USA); *The Smiling Land* prod/rel: Berolina, Herzog

Die Lustige Witwe, Vienna 1905, Operetta
Merry Widow, The 1934 d: Ernst Lubitsch. lps: Maurice Chevalier, Jeanette MacDonald, Edward Everett Horton. 110M USA. *The Lady Dances* prod/rel: Metro-Goldwyn-Mayer Corp.©

Merry Widow, The 1952 d: Curtis Bernhardt. lps: Lana Turner, Fernando Lamas, Una Merkel. 105M USA. prod/rel: MGM

Le Tzarewitch, Berlin 1927, Operetta
Son Altesse Imperiale 1933 d: Jean Bernard-Derosne, Victor Janson. lps: Jorge Rigaud, Marie Glory, Germaine Aussey. F FRN. *Le Tzarewitch* prod/rel: U.F.a., a.C.E.

Wo Die Lerche Singt, Operetta
Wo Die Lerche Singt 1936 d: Carl Lamac. lps: Marta Eggerth, Hans Sohnker, Lucie Englisch. 97M GRM/HNG/SWT. *Pacsirta* (HNG); *L' Alouette* prod/rel: Film-Aktiengesellschaft Berna

Wo Die Lerche Singt 1956 d: Hans Wolff. lps: Doris Kirchner, Renate Holm, Lutz Landers. 97M AUS. prod/rel: Paula Wessely

Der Zarewitsch, Berlin 1927, Operetta
Zarewitsch, Der 1933 d: Victor Janson. lps: Marta Eggerth, Hans Sohnker, Ery Bos. F GRM.

Zarewitsch, Der 1954 d: Arthur M. Rabenalt. lps: Luis Mariano, Sonja Ziemann, Ivan Petrovich. 100M GRM/FRN. *Le Tzarevitch* (FRN); *The Little Czar* prod/rel: Films Roger Richebe, Ccc-Filmkunst

LEHMAN, ERNEST
Tell Me About It Tomorrow, Novel
Sweet Smell of Success, The 1957 d: Alexander MacKendrick. lps: Burt Lancaster, Tony Curtis, Susan Harrison. 93M USA. prod/rel: United Artists, Norma-Curtleigh Prods.

LEHMAN, MILTON
Article
Killer That Stalked New York, The 1950 d: Earl McEvoy. lps: Evelyn Keyes, Charles Korvin, Lola Albright. 79M USA. *The Frightened City* (UKN) prod/rel: Columbia

LEHMAN, PAUL EVAN
Idaho, New York 1933, Novel
Idaho Kid, The 1936 d: Robert F. Hill. lps: Rex Bell, Marion Shilling, David Sharpe. 60M USA. prod/rel: Colony Pictures, State Rights

LEHMAN, ZIEGFRIED
Story
Adamah 1947 d: Helmar Lerski. F ISR. *Tomorrow Is a Wonderful Day; Adama; Earth* prod/rel: Forum Film Ltd.

LEHMANN, ARTHUR-HEINZ
Zwei Himmlische Dickschadel, Novel
Zwei Himmlische Dickschadel 1974 d: Werner Jacobs. lps: Klaus Lowitsch, Reiner Schone, Franziska Oehme. 95M GRM. *Two Heavenly Blockheads* prod/rel: Ctv 72, Constantin

LEHMANN, ROSAMUND (1901–1990), UKN, Lehmann, Rosamund Nina
The Weather in the Streets, 1936, Novel
Weather in the Streets, The 1984 d: Gavin Millar. lps: Michael York, Joanna Lumley, Lisa Eichhorn. MTV. 125M UKN. prod/rel: BBC

LEHRER, JAMES
Viva Max!, New York 1966, Novel
Viva Max! 1969 d: Jerry Paris. lps: Peter Ustinov, Pamela Tiffin, Jonathan Winters. 96M USA. prod/rel: Mark Carliner Productions

LEIBER, FRITZ (1910–, USA, Lathrop, Francis
Conjure Wife, Story
Night of the Eagle 1962 d: Sidney Hayers. lps: Peter Wyngarde, Janet Blair, Margaret Johnston. 87M UKN. *Witch, Burn Burn* (USA); *Conjure Wife* prod/rel: Anglo-Amalgamated, Independent Artists

Weird Woman 1944 d: Reginald Le Borg. lps: Lon Chaney Jr., Anne Gwynne, Evelyn Ankers. 64M USA. prod/rel: Universal

LEIDMANN, EVA
Ein Madchen Geht an Land, Novel
Madchen Geht an Land, Ein 1938 d: Werner Hochbaum. lps: Elisabeth Flickenschildt, Maria Paudler, Roma Bahn. 89M GRM. *A Girl Goes on Shore* prod/rel: UFA

Das Madchen Irene, Play
Madchen Irene, Das 1936 d: Reinhold Schunzel. lps: Lil Dagover, Sabine Peters, Geraldine Katt. 101M GRM. prod/rel: UFA, Jugendfilm

LEIGH, JAMES
Making It, Novel
Making It 1971 d: John Erman. lps: Kristoffer Tabori, Marlyn Mason, Bob Balaban. 97M USA. prod/rel: Alfran

LEIGHTON, LEE
Lawman, Novel
Star in the Dust 1956 d: Charles Haas. lps: John Agar, Mamie Van Doren, Richard Boone. 80M USA. prod/rel: Universal-International

LEIGHTON, ROBERT
Convict 99, Play
Convict 99 1909 d: Arthur Gilbert. lps: Frank Beresford. 1060f UKN. prod/rel: Gaumont

Convict 99 1919 d: G. B. Samuelson. lps: C. M. Hallard, Daisy Burrell, Wee Georgie Wood. 6075f UKN. prod/rel: G. B. Samuelson, Granger

LEIGHTON, WILLIAM R.
The Ableminded Lady, Short Story
  Ableminded Lady, The 1922 d: Oliver L. Sellers, Don Gamble. lps: Henry B. Walthall, Elinor Fair, Helen Raymond. 4800f USA. prod/rel: Pacific Film Co.

LEIMBACH, MARTY
Dying Young, Novel
  Dying Young 1991 d: Joel Schumacher. lps: Julia Roberts, Campbell Scott, Vincent d'Onofrio. 111M USA. prod/rel: 20th Century Fox, Fogwood Films

LEINERT, MEINRAD
Funfmadelhaus, Novel
  Funfmaderlhaus 1943 d: Sigfrit Steiner. lps: Emil Gyr, Rico Senn, Madeleine Koebel. 90M SWT. *Der Doppelte Matthias Und Seine Tochter* prod/rel: Gotthard, Atlantic

LEINSTER, COLIN
The Heritage of Michael Flaherty, Novel
  Outsider, The 1979 d: Tony Luraschi. lps: Craig Wasson, Patricia Quinn, Sterling Hayden. 128M NTH/USA. prod/rel: Paramount

LEINSTER, MURRAY
Monster from the Earth's End, Greenwich CT. 1959, Novel
  Navy Vs. the Night Monsters, The 1966 d: Michael Hoey. lps: Mamie Van Doren, Anthony Eisley, Pamela Mason. 87M USA. *Monsters of the Night* (UKN); *The Night Crawlers* prod/rel: Standard Club of California Productions
The Owner of the Aztec, 1926, Short Story
  Good As Gold 1927 d: Scott R. Dunlap. lps: Buck Jones, Frances Lee, Carl Miller. 4545f USA. prod/rel: Fox Film Corp.
The Waiting Asteroid, New York 1961, Novel
  Terronauts, The 1967 d: Montgomery Tully. lps: Simon Oates, Zena Marshall, Charles Hawtrey. 75M UKN. *The Terrornauts* (USA) prod/rel: Amicus Productions, Anglo-Embassy

LEIPZIGER, LEO
Die Ballhaus-Anna, Novel
  Ballhaus-Anna, Die 1911 d: Walter Schmidthassler. lps: Olivia Veit. 950m GRM. prod/rel: Vitascope

LEITER, KARL HANS
Fraulein Casanova, Novel
  Fraulein Casanova 1953 d: E. W. Emo. lps: Gertrud Kuckelmann, Angelika Hauff, Loni Heuser. 90M AUS. prod/rel: Mundus

LEITZBACH, ADELINE
Success, New York 1918, Play
  Success 1923 d: Ralph Ince. lps: Brandon Tynan, Naomi Childers, Mary Astor. 6800f USA. prod/rel: Murray W. Garsson, Metro Pictures

LEKEUX, MARTIAL
Passeurs d'Hommes, Novel
  Passeurs d'Hommes 1937 d: Rene Jayet. lps: Constant Remy, Paul Azais, Junie Astor. 96M FRN. prod/rel: Sobel Film

LELAND, DAVID
Made in Britain, Play
  Made in Britain 1982 d: Alan Clarke. lps: Tim Roth, Terry Richards, Bill Stewart. MTV. 76M UKN. prod/rel: Central

LELLI, RENATO
Sulle Strade Di Notte, Play
  Colpevoli, I 1957 d: Turi Vasile. lps: Isa Miranda, Carlo Ninchi, Vittorio de SicA. 85M ITL/FRN. *Responsabilite Limitee?* (FRN) prod/rel: Colosseum Film, Italia Film (Roma)

LEM, STANISLAW (1921–, PLN
Astronauci, Warsaw 1951, Novel
  Schweigende Stern, Der 1960 d: Kurt Maetzig. lps: Lucyna Winnicka, Yoko Tani, Oldrich Lukes. 130M GDR/PLN. *First Spaceship on Venus* (USA); *Milczaca Gwiazda* (PLN); *The Silent Planet*; *The Silent Planet*; *Spaceship to Venus* prod/rel: Defa, Iluzjon Film Unit
Solaris, 1961, Novel
  Solyaris 1972 d: Andrei Tarkovsky. lps: Natalya Bondarchuk, Donatas Banionis, Juri Jarvet. 165M USS. *Solaris; Soljaris*
Szpital Przemienienia, 1975, Novel
  Szpital Przemienienia 1978 d: Edward Zebrowski. lps: Jerzy Binczycki, Henryk Bista, Ewa DalkowskA. 90M PLN. *The Hospital of Transfiguration*; *Transfiguration Hospital* prod/rel: Prf Zespoly Filmowe, Filmgruppe Tor
Test Pilota Pirxa, Short Story
  Test Pilota Pirxa 1978 d: Marek Piestrak. lps: Sergei Desnytsky, Boleslaw Abart, Wladimir Iwaszow. 95M PLN/USS. *Doznaniye Pilota Pikrsa* (USS); *The Test of Pilot Pirx*; *Test Pilot Pirx*; *Pirx Test-Flight* prod/rel: Zespoly Filmowe, Taliifilm

LEMAIRE, JOHAN
Mooi Juultje Van Volendam, 1920, Play
  Mooi Juultje Van Voldendam 1924 d: Alex Benno. lps: Annie Bos, Jan Kiveron, August Van Der Hoeck. 2000m NTH/BLG. *Het Schone Meisje Van Volendam* (BLG); *La Belle de Volendam*; *Beautiful Julie of Volendam*; *The Beautiful Girl of Volendam*; *The Beauty of Volendam* prod/rel: Alex Benno, Actueel Film

LEMAITRE, CLAUDE
Il Buon Samaritano, Novel
  Buon Samaritano, Il 1919 d: Eleuterio Rodolfi. lps: Mercedes Brignone, Domenico Serra, Margherita Donadoni. 1453m ITL. prod/rel: Rodolfi Film

LEMAY, ALAN
Ghost Mountain, Story
  Rocky Mountain 1950 d: William Keighley. lps: Errol Flynn, Patrice Wymore, Scott Forbes. 83M USA. prod/rel: Warner Bros.
The Searchers, 1954, Novel
  Searchers, The 1956 d: John Ford. lps: John Wayne, Jeffrey Hunter, Vera Miles. 119M USA. prod/rel: Warner Bros., C. V. Whitney Pictures
Thunder in the Dust, 1934, Novel
  Sundowners, The 1950 d: George Templeton. lps: Robert Sterling, John Drew Barrymore, Robert Preston. 83M USA. *Thunder in the Dust* (UKN) prod/rel: Eagle-Lion, Nuys Theatre Corp.

LEMELIN, ROGER
Le Crime d'Ovide Plouffe, Novel
  Crime d'Ovide Plouffe, Le 1984 d: Denys Arcand. lps: Gabriel Arcand, Anne Letourneau, Jean Carmet. 107M CND/FRN. *The Crime of Ovide Plouffe*; *Murder in the Family*; *Les Plouffe II* prod/rel: Cine Plouffe II Inc., International Cinema Corp.
Les Plouffe, Novel
  Plouffe, Les 1981 d: Gilles Carle. lps: Emile Genest, Juliette Huot, Anne Letourneau. 227M CND. *Il Etait une Fois Des Gens Heureux: Les Plouffe*; *The Plouffe Family* prod/rel: Cine London Inc., International Cinema Corp.

LEMMER, G.J.
Behind the Green Lights, New York 1933, Book
  Behind the Green Lights 1935 d: W. Christy Cabanne. lps: Norman Foster, Judith Allen, Sidney Blackmer. 70M USA. prod/rel: Mascot Pictures Corp.

LEMOINE, G.
Une Femme Qui Se Jette Par la Fenetre, 1847
  Moglie Che Si Getto Dalla Finestra, La 1920 d: Gian Bistolfi. lps: Rosetta d'Aprile, Mira Terribili, Umberto Zanuccoli. ITL.

LEMONNIER, CAMILLE (1844–1913), BLG
Le Mort, 1882, Novel
  Mort, Le 1936 d: E. G. de Meyst. 67M BLG/FRN.

LENERO, VICENTE
Los Albaniles, Play
  Albaniles, Los 1976 d: Jorge Fons. lps: Ignacio Lopez Tarso, Jaime Fernandez, David SilvA. 113M MXC. *The Bricklayers* prod/rel: Conacine, Marco Polo

LENGEL, WILLIAM CHARLES
The Song of His Soul, 1916, Short Story
  Tin Pan Alley 1920 d: Frank Beal. lps: Albert Ray, Elinor Fair, George Hernandez. 5r USA. prod/rel: Fox Film Corp., William Fox©
Words and Music By., 1919, Story
  Words and Music By. 1919 d: Scott R. Dunlap. lps: Albert Ray, Elinor Fair, Robert Bolder. 5r USA. *Words and Music* prod/rel: Fox Film Corp., Excel Picture

LENGYEL, JOZSEF
Oldas Es Kotes, 1964, Short Story
  Oldas Es Kotes 1963 d: Miklos Jancso. lps: Zoltan Latinovits, Miklos Szakats, Andor Ajtay. 100M HNG. *Cantata* (UKN); *Loosening and Tightening* prod/rel: Budapest Filmstudios

LENGYEL, MELCHIOR
Antonia, Play
  Temptation 1934 d: Max Neufeld. lps: Frances Day, Stewart Rome, Anthony Hankey. 77M UKN. prod/rel: Milofilm, Gaumont-British
The Czarina, Play
  Catherine the Great 1934 d: Paul Czinner. lps: Elisabeth Bergner, Douglas Fairbanks Jr., Flora Robson. 96M UKN. *The Rise of Catherine the Great* prod/rel: United Artists, London Films
Gypsy Melody, Short Story
  Caravane 1934 d: Erik Charell. lps: Charles Boyer, Annabella, Pierre Brasseur. 99M USA. prod/rel: Fox Film Corp.
Taifun, Budapest 1909, Play
  Ciclone, Il 1916 d: Eugenio Perego. lps: Amedeo Chiantoni, Alfonsina Pieri, Ruggero Lupi. 1394m ITL. *Taifun* prod/rel: Cinema-Drama

Die Tanzerin, Novel
  Beruhmte Frau, Die 1927 d: Robert Wiene. lps: Lili Damita, Fred Solm, Warwick Ward. 2559m GRM. *The Dancer of Barcelona* prod/rel: F.P.G. Film-Prod.

LENGYEL, MENYHERT
Angyal, Vienna 1932, Play
  Angel 1937 d: Ernst Lubitsch. lps: Marlene Dietrich, Herbert Marshall, Melvyn Douglas. 90M USA. prod/rel: Paramount Pictures, Inc.
A Carno Szinmu; Harom Felvonasban, Budapest 1913, Play
  Forbidden Paradise 1924 d: Ernst Lubitsch. lps: Pola Negri, Rod La Rocque, Adolphe Menjou. 7543f USA. prod/rel: Famous Players-Lasky, Paramount Pictures
  Royal Scandal, A 1945 d: Otto Preminger, Ernst Lubitsch. lps: Tallulah Bankhead, William Eythe, Anne Baxter. 94M USA. *Czarina* (UKN) prod/rel: 20th Century-Fox
Taifun, Budapest 1909, Play
  Typhoon, The 1914 d: Reginald Barker. lps: Sessue Hayakawa, Tsuru Aoki, Charles K. French. 5r USA. prod/rel: New York Motion Picture Corp.©, Paramount Pictures Corp.

LENIHAN, WINIFRED
Blind Mice, New York 1930, Play
  Working Girls 1931 d: Dorothy Arzner. lps: Charles "Buddy" Rogers, Frances Dee, Paul Lukas. 77M USA. prod/rel: Paramount Publix Corp.©

LENIN
Un' Alba
  Alba, Un' 1920 d: Eugenio FontanA. lps: Nada de Wincy, Egea, Guido Guiducci. 1203m ITL. *Un' Alba Di Lenin* prod/rel: Politica Film

LENNART, ISOBEL
Funny Girl, New York 1964, Musical Play
  Funny Girl 1968 d: William Wyler. lps: Barbra Streisand, Omar Sharif, Kay Medford. 155M USA. prod/rel: Rastar Productions, Columbia

LENNOX, COSMO GORDON
The Puppet Man, Novel
  Puppet Man, The 1921 d: Frank H. Crane. lps: Hugh Miller, Molly Adair, Hilda Anthony. 5818f UKN. *Puppets of Fate* prod/rel: British & Colonial, Film Booking Offices

LENNOX, MICHAEL
Story
  Forteresse, La 1947 d: Fedor Ozep. lps: Paul Dupuis, Nicole Germain, Jacques Auger. 99M CND. prod/rel: Quebec Productions Corp., Eagle Lion
  Whispering City 1947 d: Fedor Ozep. lps: Mary Anderson, Paul Lukas, Helmut Dantine. 91M CND. *Crime City*; *The Stronghold* prod/rel: Quebec Productions Corp., Eagle Lion

LENOIR, MICHEL
Reproduction Interdite, Novel
  Reproduction Interdite 1956 d: Gilles Grangier. lps: Michel Auclair, Paul Frankeur, Annie Girardot. 90M FRN. *The Schemer* (USA); *Meutre a Montmartre* prod/rel: Orex Films, Lucien Viard

LENORMAND, HENRI-RENE (1882–1951), FRN
Le Simoun, 1921, Play
  Simoun, Le 1933 d: Firmin Gemier. lps: Firmin Gemier, Esther Kiss, Max Maxudian. 70M FRN. prod/rel: Cinedrame

LENSKY, BORIS
Play
  Zijn Viool 1914 d: Louis H. Chrispijn, Maurits H. Binger. lps: Boris Lensky, Mientje Kling, Jan Holtrop. 875m NTH. *De Stradivarius*; *His Violin*; *The Stradivarius*; *A Broken Melody* (UKN) prod/rel: Filmfabriek-Hollandia

LENYEL, WILLIAM C.
Shattered Glass, Play
  24 Hours 1931 d: Marion Gering. lps: Clive Brook, Miriam Hopkins, Regis Toomey. 68M USA. *The Hours Between* (UKN); *Twenty-Four Hours* prod/rel: Paramount Publix Corp.©

LENZ, LEO
Ehe in Dosen, Play
  Ehe in Dosen 1939 d: Johannes Meyer. lps: Leny Marenbach, Johannes Riemann, Ralph Arthur Roberts. 96M GRM. prod/rel: Cine-Allianz, Bavaria
Polterabend, Play
  Polterabend 1940 d: Carl Boese. lps: Grethe Weiser, Camilla Horn, Rudi Godden. 88M GRM. prod/rel: Astra, Adler

LENZ, SIEGFRIED (1926–, GRM
Deutschstunde, 1968, Novel
  Deutschstunde 1971 d: Peter Beauvais. 220M GRM. *German Lesson*

Das Feuerschiff, 1960, Short Story
 Feuerschiff, Das 1963 d: Ladislao VajdA. lps: James Robertson Justice, Michael Hinz, Dieter Borsche. 84M GRM. *The Lightship; The Fire Boat* prod/rel: Fono, Columbia-Bavaria
Das Feuerschiff, 1960, Novel
 Lightship, The 1985 d: Jerzy Skolimowski. lps: Klaus Maria Brandauer, Robert Duvall, Tom Bower. 89M USA. prod/rel: CBS, Warner
Der Mann Im Strom, 1957, Novel
 Mann Im Strom, Der 1958 d: Eugen York. lps: Hans Albers, Gina Albert, Helmut Schmid. 95M GRM. *Man in the Current* prod/rel: C.C.C., Europa
Zeit de Schuldlosen, 1962, Play
 Zeit Der Schuldlosen, Die 1964 d: Thomas Fantl. lps: Erik Schumann, Peter Pasetti, Wolfgang Kieling. 95M GRM. *The Time of the Innocent* prod/rel: Peter Carsten, Columbia-Bavaria

LENZI, UMBERTO
Forte Madras, Novel
 Tre Sergenti Del Bengala, I 1965 d: Umberto Lenzi. lps: Richard Harrison, Ugo Sasso, Nazzareno ZamperlA. 95M ITL/SPN. *Los Tres Invencibles Sargentos* (SPN); *Tres Sargentos Bengalies; Adventures of the Bengal Lancers* prod/rel: Fono Roma, Filmes (Roma)

LEON, HENNIE
Story
 Longest Hundred Miles, The 1967 d: Don Weis. lps: Doug McClure, Katharine Ross, Ricardo Montalban. TVM. 100M USA. *Escape from Bataan* prod/rel: Universal TV

LEON, VIKTOR
Der Fidele Bauer, Opera
 Fidele Bauer, Der 1927 d: Franz Seitz. lps: Werner Krauss, Carmen Boni, Andre Nox. 2506m GRM. prod/rel: Fery-Film
 Fidele Bauer, Der 1951 d: Georg MarischkA. lps: Paul Horbiger, Heinrich Gretler, Rudolf Carl. 105M AUS. prod/rel: Berna, Donau
Das Furstenkind, Opera
 Furstenkind, Das 1927 d: Jacob Fleck, Luise Fleck. lps: Vivian Gibson, Harry Liedtke, Evi EvA. 2460m GRM. prod/rel: Hegewald-Film
Die Geschiedene Frau, Opera
 Geschiedene Frau, Die 1926 d: Victor Janson. lps: Mady Christians, Marcella Albani, Walter RillA. 2541m GRM. prod/rel: Aafa-Film
 Geschiedene Frau, Die 1953 d: Georg Jacoby. lps: Marika Rokk, Johannes Heesters, Hans Leibelt. 100M GRM. *The Divorced Woman* prod/rel: Cine-Allianz, Gloria
Die Lustige Witwe, Vienna 1905, Operetta
 Merry Widow, The 1925 d: Erich von Stroheim. lps: Mae Murray, John Gilbert, Roy d'Arcy. 10r USA. prod/rel: Metro-Goldwyn-Mayer Pictures
 Merry Widow, The 1934 d: Ernst Lubitsch. lps: Maurice Chevalier, Jeanette MacDonald, Edward Everett Horton. 110M USA. *The Lady Dances* prod/rel: Metro-Goldwyn-Mayer Corp.©
 Merry Widow, The 1952 d: Curtis Bernhardt. lps: Lana Turner, Fernando Lamas, Una Merkel. 105M USA. prod/rel: MGM
La Veuve Joyeuse, Book
 Veuve Joyeuse, La 1934 d: Ernst Lubitsch. lps: Maurice Chevalier, Jeanette MacDonald, Daniele ParolA. 105M USA. prod/rel: Metro-Goldwyn-Mayer

LEON Y ROMAN, RICARDO
El Amor de Los Amores, 1912, Novel
 Amor de Los Amores, El 1960 d: Juan de OrdunA. lps: Arturo de Cordova, Emma Penella, Jorge Mistral. 114M SPN/MXC. *The Greatest Love*

LEONARD, DAVID
Victims of Persecution, Play
 Victims of Persecution 1933 d: Bud Pollard. lps: Mitchell Harris, Betty Hamilton, Judah Bleich. 60M USA. prod/rel: Bud Pollard Productions, William Goldberg Productions

LEONARD, ELMORE (1925–, USA, Leonard Jr., Elmore John
52 Pickup, Novel
 52 Pick-Up 1987 d: John Frankenheimer. lps: Roy Scheider, Ann-Margret, Vanity. 114M USA. *Fifty-Two Pick-Up* prod/rel: Cannon Films
 Ambassador, The 1984 d: J. Lee Thompson. lps: Robert Mitchum, Ellen Burstyn, Rock Hudson. 95M USA. *The Peacemaker* prod/rel: Cannon Productions, Northbrook Films
Big Bounce, New York 1969, Novel
 Big Bounce, The 1969 d: Alex March. lps: Ryan O'Neal, Leigh Taylor-Young, James Daly. 102M USA. prod/rel: Greenway Productions, Warner Bros.

The Captives, Story
 Tall 'T', The 1957 d: Budd Boetticher. lps: Randolph Scott, Richard Boone, Maureen O'Sullivan. 78M USA. prod/rel: Columbia
Cat Chaser, Novel
 Cat Chaser 1989 d: Abel FerrarA. lps: Kelly McGillis, Peter Weller, Frederic Forrest. 98M USA. prod/rel: Vestron
Glitz, Novel
 Glitz 1989 d: Sandor Stern. lps: Jimmy Smits, Markie Post, John Diehl. TVM. 100M USA. prod/rel: Lorimar Telepictures
Hombre, London 1961, Novel
 Hombre 1967 d: Martin Ritt. lps: Paul Newman, Fredric March, Diane Cilento. 111M USA. prod/rel: Hombre Productions, 20th Century-Fox
Last Stand at Saber River, Novel
 Last Stand at Saber River 1997 d: Dick Lowry. lps: Tom Selleck, Suzy Amis, Rachel Duncan. TVM. 120M USA. prod/rel: Brandman Productions
The Law at Randado, Novel
 Border Shootout 1990 d: C. J. McIntyre. lps: Cody Glenn, Jeff Kaake, Glenn Ford. 110M USA. *Law at Randado* prod/rel: Turner, Phoenix
The Moonshine War, New York 1969, Novel
 Moonshine War, The 1970 d: Richard Quine. lps: Patrick McGoohan, Richard Widmark, Alan AldA. 100M USA. prod/rel: Filmways, Inc.
Out of Sight, Novel
 Out of Sight 1998 d: Steven Soderbergh. lps: George Clooney, Jennifer Lopez, Ving Rhames. 123M USA. prod/rel: Universal Pictures, Jersey Films
Rum Punch, Novel
 Jackie Brown 1997 d: Quentin Tarantino. lps: Pam Grier, Samuel L. Jackson, Robert Forster. 155M USA. prod/rel: a Band Apart, Miramax Films
Stick, Novel
 Stick 1985 d: Burt Reynolds. lps: Burt Reynolds, Candice Bergen, George Segal. 109M USA. prod/rel: Universal
Touch, Novel
 Touch 1997 d: Paul Schrader. lps: Bridget Fonda, Christopher Walken, Skeet Ulrich. 96M USA/FRN. prod/rel: Lila Cazes, Lumiere International
Valdez Is Coming, Novel
 Valdez Is Coming 1971 d: Edwin Sherin. lps: Burt Lancaster, Susan Clark, Jon Cypher. 90M USA. prod/rel: Norlan, Ira Steiner

LEONARD, HERBERT
The Girl of My Heart, Play
 Girl of My Heart, The 1915 d: Leedham Bantock. lps: Herbert Leonard, Mary Linley, J. Graeme Campbell. 4500f UKN. prod/rel: British Empire

LEONARD, HUGH (1926–, IRL, Byrne, John Keyes
The Big Birthday, Play
 Broth of a Boy 1959 d: George Pollock. lps: Barry Fitzgerald, Tony Wright, June Thorburn. 77M UKN. prod/rel: British Lion, Emmett Dalton
Home Before Night, Novel
 Da 1988 d: Matt Clark. lps: Barnard Hughes, Martin Sheen, Karl Hayden. 102M USA. prod/rel: Filmdallas Pictures

LEONCAVALLO, RUGGERO (1857–1919), ITL
Der Bajazzo, Opera
 Lache Bajazzo 1943 d: Leopold Hainisch. lps: Monika Burg, Paul Horbiger, Beniamino Gigli. 87M GRM. prod/rel: Tobis, Sudwest
I Pagliacci, Milan 1892, Opera
 Pagliacci 1931 d: Joe W. Coffman. lps: Fernando Bertini, Alba Novella, Mario Valle. 80M USA. prod/rel: Audio Cinema, Leo Brecher
 Pagliacci 1936 d: Karl Grune. lps: Richard Tauber, Steffi Duna, Diana Napier. 92M UKN. *A Clown Must Laugh* (USA) prod/rel: Trafalgar, United Artists
 Pagliacci 1982 d: Franco Zeffirelli. lps: Teresa Stratas, Placido Domingo, Juan Pons. 70M ITL.
 Pagliacci, I 1915 d: Francesco Bertolini. lps: Achille Vitti, Annibale Ninchi, Bianca Virginia Camagni. 1200m ITL. prod/rel: Mediolanum Film
 Pagliacci, I 1923 d: G. B. Samuelson, Walter Summers. lps: Lillian Hall-Davis, Adelqui Millar, Campbell Gullan. 6000f UKN. prod/rel: Napoleon
 Pagliacci, I 1943 d: Giuseppe Fatigati. lps: Alida Valli, Paul Horbiger, Beniamino Gigli. 72M ITL/GRM. prod/rel: Itala Film, I.C.I.
 Pagliacci, I 1949 d: Mario CostA. lps: Gina Lollobrigida, Tito Gobbi, Afro Poli. 90M ITL. *Love of a Clown (Pagliacci)* (USA); *Amore Tragico* prod/rel: Itala Film, Artisti Associati

 Pagliacci, I 1970 d: Herbert von Karajan. lps: Jon Vickers, Raina Corsi-Kabaiwanska, Peter Glossop. 79M GRM/AUS/SWT. prod/rel: Cosmotel, Zweiten Deutschen Fernsehen

LEONNEC
Le Taxi 313 X 7, Short Story
 Taxi 313 X 7, Le 1923 d: Piere Colombier. lps: Saint-Granier, Marguerite Madys, Gine Avril. 1275m FRN. prod/rel: Gaumont

LEONOV, LEONID MAKSIMOVICH (1899–1994), RSS
Nashestviye, 1942, Play
 Nashestviye 1945 d: Abram Room, Oleg Zhakov. 100M USS. *Invasion*
Russkiy Les, 1953, Novel
 Russkij Les 1964 d: Vladimir Petrov. 171M USS. *The Russian Forest; Russkiy Les*

LEOPOLD, KEITH
When We Ran, Novel
 Run, Chrissie, Run 1984 d: Chris Langman. lps: Carmen Duncan, Michael Aitkens, Shane Briant. 95M ASL. *Moving Targets* (USA); *Reunion* prod/rel: South Australian Film Corp.

LEPAGE, ROBERT
Les Sept Branches de la Riviere Ota, Play
 No 1998 d: Robert Lepage. lps: Anne-Marie Cadieux, Alexis Martin, Marie Brassard. 85M CND. prod/rel: Alliance, in Extremis Images Inc.©

LEPERE, NAAR
Never Pass This Way Again, Book
 Passport to Terror 1989 d: Lou Antonio. lps: Lee Remick, Norma Aleandro, Roy Thinnes. TVM. 96M USA. *Dark Holiday* prod/rel: Orion

LEPRINCE DE BEAUMONT, MARIE
La Belle Et la Bete, 1785-89, Short Story
 Belle Et la Bete, La 1945 d: Rene Clement, Jean Cocteau. lps: Jean Marais, Josette Day, Marcel Andre. 100M FRN. *Beauty and the Beast* (USA)
 Panna a Netvor 1978 d: Juraj Herz. lps: Zdena Studenkova, Vlastimil Harapes, Zuzana KocurikovA. 90M CZC. *Beauty and the Beast* (USA); *The Maiden and the Beast* prod/rel: Filmove Studio Barrandov

LEPRINCE, G.
Les Francs-MacOns, Play
 Francs-MacOns 1914. lps: Rene Grehan, Vandenne. 835m FRN. prod/rel: Mondial Film
 Rien Que Des Mensonges 1932 d: Karl Anton. lps: Robert Burnier, Marguerite Moreno, Jackie Monnier. 84M FRN. *Trois Points C'est Tout; Francs-MacOns; Le Cercle Vicieux* prod/rel: Films Paramount

LERBS, KARL
Manuel Erkennt Seine macht, Novel
 Jonny Rettet Nebrador 1953 d: Rudolf Jugert. lps: Hans Albers, Margot Hielscher, Trude Hesterberg. 95M GRM. *Johnny Saves Nebrador* prod/rel: Meteor, N.F.

LERCH, HANSRUEDI
Karl Dallebach, Biography
 Dallebach Karl 1970 d: Kurt Fruh. lps: Walo Luond, Lukas Ammann, Annemarie Duringer. 113M SWT. prod/rel: Stella, Atlantic

L'ERMITE, PIERRE
Comment J'ai Tue Mon Enfant, Novel
 Comment J'ai Tue Mon Enfant 1925 d: Alexandre Ryder. lps: Jacqueline Forzane, Sylvia Grey, Max de Rieux. 2334m FRN.
La Femme aux Yeux Fermes, Novel
 Femme aux Yeux Fermes, La 1925 d: Alexandre Ryder. lps: Maryse Maia, Jean Lorette, Mme. de Rodde. 2000m FRN. prod/rel: Iris Films
La Grande Amie, Novel
 Grande Amie, La 1926 d: Max de Rieux. lps: Aime Simon-Girard, Eliane de Creus, Jose Davert. 3200m FRN. prod/rel: Ste Cinematogrphique Rene Fernand

LERMONTOV, MIKHAIL (1814–1841), RSS, Lermontov Mikhail Yuryevich
Ashik Kerib, 1837, Short Story
 Ashik Kerib 1988 d: Sergei Paradjanov, Dodo Abachidze. lps: Yuri Mgoyan, Sofico Tchiaoureli, Levan Natroshvili. 78M USS. *The Hoary Legends of the Caucasus; Asug Qaribi; The Lovelorn Minstrel; Asik Kerib* prod/rel: Georgia Film Studio
Demon, 1841, Poem
 Demon 1911 d: Giovanni Vitrotti, F. Kortfus. lps: M. Tamarov, Cemesnova-Moridgi, Navatzi. 425m ITL/USS. *Il Demone; The Demon* (UKN) prod/rel: S.A. Ambrosio /Timan-Rejngradt
Geroi Nashego Vremeni, 1840, Novel
 Bela 1967 d: Stanislav Rostotsky. lps: Vladimir Ivashov, Silvia Berova, Alexey Chernov. 114M USS. *Geroi Nashego Vremeni Part 2* prod/rel: Zentrales Filmstudio

Knjazhna Mary 1955 d: Isider Annensky. 101M USS. *The Princess Mary*

Maxim Maximych Taman 1967 d: Stanislav Rostotsky. lps: Vladimir Ivashov, Alexey Chernov, Alexander Orlov. 103M USS. *Geroi Nashego Vremeni Part 1*

Maskarad, 1836, Play
Maskarad 1941 d: Sergei Gerasimov. lps: Sergei Gerasimov. 110M USS. *Masquerade*

Vadim, 1832-34, Novel
Giorno Del Furore, Il 1973 d: Antonio CalendA. lps: Oliver Reed, Claudia Cardinale, John McEnery. 118M ITL/UKN. *Fury* (UKN); *One Russian Summer* (USA); *Un Uomo* prod/rel: Dama Film (Roma), Lowndes Production (London)

LERNER, ALAN JAY (1918–1986), USA
Brigadoon, New York 1947, Play
Brigadoon 1954 d: Vincente Minnelli. lps: Gene Kelly, Van Johnson, Cyd Charisse. 108M USA. prod/rel: Metro-Goldwyn-Mayer Corp.

On a Clear Day You Can See Forever, New York 1965, Play
On a Clear Day You Can See Forever 1970 d: Vincente Minnelli. lps: Barbra Streisand, Yves Montand, Bob Newhart. 130M USA. prod/rel: Paramount Pictures

Paint Your Wagon, New York 1951, Musical Play
Paint Your Wagon 1969 d: Joshua Logan. lps: Clint Eastwood, Lee Marvin, Jean Seberg. 166M USA. prod/rel: Alan Jay Lerner Productions, Paramount

LERNER, MARY
The Living Child, Story
Breaking Point, The 1921 d: Paul Scardon. lps: Bessie Barriscale, Walter McGrail, Ethel Grey Terry. 5788f USA. prod/rel: J. L. Frothingham Productions, W. W. Hodkinson Corp.

LERNET-HOLENIA, ALEXANDER
A la Guerre Comme a la Guerre, Novel
A la Guerre Comme a la Guerre 1971 d: Bernard Borderie. lps: Leonard Whiting, Curd Jurgens, Marianne Comtell. 90M FRN/ITL/GRM. *Le Eccitanti Guerre Di Adeleine* (ITL); *How Do I Get to Be a Hero?*; *Wie Bitte Werde Ich Ein Held?* (GRM) prod/rel: Sancrosiap, Terza

An Klingenden Ufern, Novel
An Klingenden Ufern 1948 d: Hans Unterkircher. lps: Marianne Schonauer, Curd Jurgens, Cacilia Kahr. 89M AUS. prod/rel: Violantha

Ich War Jack Mortimer, Novel
Gefahrliches Abenteuer 1953 d: Emile Edwin Reinert. lps: Gustav Frohlich, Cornell Borchers, Francis Lederer. 89M AUS. *Abenteuer in Wien* prod/rel: Pabst & Kiba, Herzog

Ich War Jack Mortimer 1935 d: Carl Froelich. lps: Anton Walbrook, Eugen Klopfer, Sybille Schmitz. 85M GRM. prod/rel: Carl Froelich-Filmproduktion

Stolen Identity 1953 d: Gunther V. Fritsch. lps: Francis Lederer, Donald Buka, Joan Camden. 81M USA/AUS. prod/rel: Helen Ainsworth

Maresi, Novel
Maresi 1948 d: Hans Thimig. lps: Attila Horbiger, Maria Schell, Siegfried Breuer. 86M AUS. *Der Angeklagte Hat Das Wort* prod/rel: Unitas

Die Standarte, Novel
Standarte, Die 1977 d: Ottokar Runze. lps: Simon Ward, Siegfried Rauch, Viktor Staal. 120M AUS/GRM/SPN. *The Standard*; *Battleflag* (UKN) prod/rel: Ottokar Runze, Norddeutsche Filmproduktion

LEROUX, GASTON (1868–1927), FRN
Novel
Fantasma, Il 1915. lps: Eugenia Tettoni. 900m ITL. prod/rel: Savoia Film

Alsace, Play
Alsace 1916 d: Henri Pouctal. lps: Dieudonne, Barbier, Camille Bardou. 1650m FRN. prod/rel: le Film d'Art

Balaoo, Paris 1912, Novel
Balaoo Ou Des Pas Au Plafond 1912 d: Victorin Jasset. lps: Lucien Bataille, Camille Bardou, Henri Gouget. 652m FRN. *Balaoo* (USA) prod/rel: Eclair

Il Y a Des Pieds Au Plafond 1912 d: Abel Gance. lps: Jean Toulout, Mathilde Thizeau. FRN. prod/rel: le Film Francais

Wizard, The 1927 d: Richard Rosson. lps: Edmund Lowe, Leila Hyams, Gustav von Seyffertitz. 5629f USA. prod/rel: Fox Film Corp.

Cheri-Bibi, Novel
Cheri-Bibi 1914 d: Charles Krauss. lps: Charles Keppens, Georges Paulais, Marise Dauvray. 1330m FRN. prod/rel: Eclair

Cheri-Bibi Et Cecily, Paris 1916, Novel
Cheri-Bibi 1931 d: Carlos Borcosque. lps: Ernesto Vilches, Maria F. Ladron de Guevara, Maria Tubau. 80M USA.

Phantom of Paris, The 1931 d: John S. Robertson. lps: John Gilbert, Leila Hyams, Lewis Stone. 74M USA. *Cheri-Bibi* prod/rel: Metro-Goldwyn-Mayer Corp., Metro-Goldwyn-Mayer Dist. Corp.©

Le Fantome de l'Opera, Paris 1910, Novel
Fantasma Dell'opera, Il 1998 d: Dario Argento. lps: Julian Sands, Asia Argento, Andrea Di Stefano. 103M ITL. *The Phantom of the Opera* prod/rel: Medusa Film, Rete Italia

Phantom of the Opera, The 1925 d: Rupert Julian, Edward Sedgwick. lps: Lon Chaney, Mary Philbin, Norman Kerry. 8464f USA. prod/rel: Universal Pictures

Phantom of the Opera, The 1929 d: Rupert Julian, Ernst Laemmle. lps: Lon Chaney, Mary Philbin, Norman Kerry. 75M USA. prod/rel: Universal

Phantom of the Opera, The 1943 d: Arthur Lubin. lps: Nelson Eddy, Susanna Foster, Claude Rains. 92M USA. prod/rel: Universal

Phantom of the Opera, The 1962 d: Terence Fisher. lps: Herbert Lom, Heather Sears, Thorley Walters. 84M UKN. prod/rel: Hammer Film Productions, Universal-International

Phantom of the Opera, The 1982 d: Robert Markowitz. lps: Maximilian Schell, Jane Seymour, Michael York. TVM. 100M USA. prod/rel: Robert Halmi Inc.

Phantom of the Opera, The 1987. ANM. 60M USA. prod/rel: Aiden Grennell

Phantom of the Opera, The 1989 d: Dwight H. Little. lps: Robert Englund, Jill Schoelen, Alex Hyde-White. 90M USA. prod/rel: 21St Century, Breton Film

Phantom of the Opera, The 1990 d: Tony Richardson. lps: Burt Lancaster, Charles Dance, Teri Polo. TVM. 200M UKN/USA. prod/rel: Saban-Scherick Prods.

L' Homme Qui Revient de Loin, Novel
Homme Qui Revient de Loin, L' 1917 d: Rene Navarre. lps: Rene Navarre, Andre Marnay, Alice Beylat. 1500m FRN. prod/rel: Films R. Navarre

Homme Qui Revient de Loin, L' 1949 d: Jean Castanier. lps: Paul Bernard, Daniel Lecourtois, AnnabellA. 95M FRN. *The Man Who Returned from Afar* prod/rel: L.P.C.

Le Lys, Play
Lily, The 1926 d: Victor Schertzinger. lps: Belle Bennett, Ian Keith, Reata Hoyt. 6268f USA. prod/rel: Fox Film Corp.

Mister Flow, Novel
Mister Flow 1936 d: Robert Siodmak. lps: Louis Jouvet, Fernand Gravey, Edwige Feuillere. 100M FRN. *Les Amants Traques*; *Compliments of Mr. Flow* prod/rel: Vondas Films

Le Mystere de la Chambre Jaune, Paris 1908, Novel
Mystere de la Chambre Jaune, Le 1913 d: Emile Chautard. lps: Marcel Simon, Laurence Duluc, Jean Garat. 905m FRN. *The Mystery of the Yellow Room* prod/rel: Acad

Mystere de la Chambre Jaune, Le 1930 d: Marcel L'Herbier. lps: Roland Toutain, Leon Belieres, Huguette Duflos. 108M FRN. *The Mystery of the Yellow Room* prod/rel: Societe Des Films Osso

Mystere de la Chambre Jaune, Le 1948 d: Henri Aisner. lps: Serge Reggiani, Pierre Renoir, Marcel Herrand. 90M FRN. *The Mystery of the Yellow Room* prod/rel: Alcina

Mystery of the Yellow Room, The 1919 d: Emile Chautard. lps: William Walcott, Edmund Elton, George Cowl. 6r USA. prod/rel: Mayflower Photoplay Corp.©, Emile Chautard Pictures Corp.

La Nouvelle Aurore, 1918, Novel
Cheri-Bibi 1954 d: Marcello Pagliero. lps: Lea Padovani, Jean Richard, Arnoldo FoA. 84M FRN/ITL. *Il Forzato Della Guiana* (ITL) prod/rel: U.G.C., Memnon Films

Le Parfum de la Dame En Noir, Novel
Parfum de la Dame En Noir, Le 1914 d: Maurice Tourneur. lps: Maurice de Feraudy, Jean Garat, Fernande Van Doren. 1220m FRN. *Rouletabille II -la Derniere Incarnation de Larsan* prod/rel: Eclair, Acad

Parfum de la Dame En Noir, Le 1930 d: Marcel L'Herbier. lps: Roland Toutain, Huguette, Wera Engels. 109M FRN. *The Perfume of the Lady in Black* prod/rel: Societe Des Films Osso

Parfum de la Dame En Noir, Le 1949 d: Louis Daquin. lps: Helene Perdriere, Serge Reggiani, Lucien Nat. 100M FRN. prod/rel: Alcina

Rouletabille Aviateur, Novel
Rouletabille Aviateur 1932 d: Steve Sekely. lps: Roland Toutain, Leon Belieres, Lisette Lanvin. 82M FRN. prod/rel: Societe Des Films Osso

Rouletabille Chez Les Bohemiens, Novel
Rouletabille Chez Les Bohemiens 1922 d: Henri Fescourt. lps: Romuald Joube, Suzanne Talba, Edith Jehanne. SRL. 8430m FRN. prod/rel: Societe Des Cineromans

LEROY, SERGE
La Traque, Novel
Traque, La 1975 d: Serge Leroy. lps: Mimsy Farmer, Jean-Pierre Marielle, Philippe Leotard. 95M FRN/ITL. *Il Sapore Della Paura* (ITL) prod/rel: P.I.C.

LESAGE, ALAIN-RENE (1668–1747), FRN
Le Diable Boiteaux, 1707, Novel
Diavolo Zoppo, Il 1910 d: Luigi Maggi. lps: Ernesto Vaser, Gigetta Morano, Ercole Vaser. 236M ITL. *The Devil on Two Sticks* (USA) prod/rel: S.A. Ambrosio

Gil Blas, 1715-35, Novel
Aventures de Gil Blas de Santillane, Les 1955 d: Rene Jolivet, Ricardo Munoz Suay. lps: Georges Marchal, Barbara Laage, Susana Canales. 95M FRN/SPN. *Adventures of Gil Blas* (USA); *Gil Blas de Santillane*; *Una Aventura de Gil Blas* (SPN) prod/rel: Vascos Films Producciones, Benito Perojo

LESKOV, NIKOLAY SEMYONOVICH (1831–1895), RSS
Story
Crack in the Ice, A 1964 d: Ronald Eyre. lps: Bill Fraser, James Maxwell, Derek Newark. MTV. UKN. prod/rel: BBC

Crack in the Ice, A 1985 d: Anthony Garner. MTV. UKN. prod/rel: BBC

Kotin and Platonida, 1867, Short Story
Coilin and Platonida 1976 d: James Scott. lps: Marion Joyce, Sean Ban Bolustrom, Bairbre MacDonnchA. 85M UKN.

Ledi Makbet Mtenskogo Uezda, 1864, Short Story
Katerina Ismaylova 1966 d: Mikhail Shapiro. lps: Galina Vishnevskaja, Alexandr Sokolov, Nikolay Boyarski. 149M USS. *Lady MacBeth of Mtsensk* (UKN); *Katerina Ismailova*; *Katerina Izmaylova*; *Katerina Izmailova* prod/rel: Lenfilm

Sibirska Ledi Magbet 1962 d: Andrzej WajdA. lps: Olivera Markovic, Ljuba Tadic, Miodrag Lazarevic. 95M YGS/PLN. *Powiatowa Lady Makbet* (PLN); *Fury Is a Woman* (USA); *Siberian Lady MacBeth*; *Serbian Lady MacBeth*; *Lady MacBeth of Mtsensk* prod/rel: Avala

Pavlin, 1874, Novel
Tragodie Einer Leidenschaft 1949 d: Kurt Meisel. lps: Joana Maria Gorvin, Hermine Korner, Carl Kuhlmann. 89M GRM. *A Tragedy of Passion* prod/rel: Witt, Bavaria

Tupeinyi Khudozhnik, 1883, Short Story
Drama Iz Starinnoi Zhizni 1971 d: Ilya Averbach. 90M USS. *A Drama of Former Times*; *Drama from Olden Times*; *A Dramatic Tale of Yore*

LESLEY-MANVILLE, BETTY
Raising Daisy Rothschild, Book
Last Giraffe, The 1979 d: Jack Couffer. lps: Susan Anspach, Simon Ward, Gordon Jackson. TVM. 100M USA. *Raising Daisy Rothschild* prod/rel: Westfall Production

LESLEY-MANVILLE, JOCK
Raising Daisy Rothschild, Book
Last Giraffe, The 1979 d: Jack Couffer. lps: Susan Anspach, Simon Ward, Gordon Jackson. TVM. 100M USA. *Raising Daisy Rothschild* prod/rel: Westfall Production

LESLIE, DAVID STUART
In My Solitude, Novel
Two Left Feet 1963 d: Roy Ward Baker. lps: Michael Crawford, Nyree Dawn Porter, Julia Foster. 93M UKN. prod/rel: British Lion, Roy Baker

Two Gentlemen Sharing, London 1963, Novel
Two Gentlemen Sharing 1970 d: Ted Kotcheff. lps: Robin Philips, Judy Geeson, Hal Frederick. 105M UKN. prod/rel: Epstein-Kulick Productions

LESLIE, ROBERT FRANKLIN
The Bears and I, Novel
Bears and I, The 1974 d: Bernard McEveety. lps: Patrick Wayne, Chief Dan George, Andrew Duggan. 89M USA. prod/rel: Buena Vista, Walt Disney

LESOU, PIERRE
Le Doulos, Paris 1957, Novel
Doulos, Le 1962 d: Jean-Pierre Melville. lps: Jean-Paul Belmondo, Serge Reggiani, Jean Desailly. 108M FRN/ITL. *Lo Spione* (ITL); *Doulos -the Finger Man* (USA); *The Fingerman* prod/rel: Rome-Paris Films, C.C. Champion

Main Pleine, Novel
Lucky Jo 1964 d: Michel Deville. lps: Eddie Constantine, Pierre Brasseur, Georges Wilson. 95M FRN. prod/rel: Jacques Roitfeld, Ele-Films

LESSING, BRUNO, Block, Rudolph Edgar
Aschenbroedel, Story
Aschenbroedel 1916 d: Ben Wilson. lps: Ben Wilson, Dorothy Phillips, Joseph Girard. 2r USA. *The Marriage Broker* prod/rel: Victor

A Daughter of Israel, Novel
Faith of Her Fathers, The 1915 d: Charles Giblyn. lps: Cleo Madison, Murdock MacQuarrie, Joe King. 3r USA. prod/rel: Gold Seal

An Interruption, Short Story
Hunchback's Romance, The 1915 d: Sidney M. Goldin. lps: Rebecca Gernstein. 2r USA. prod/rel: Imp

The Song of Songs, Story
When the Call Came 1915 d: Sidney M. Goldin, De Villiers. lps: Edith Roberts, Otto Kruger, John Sharkey. 2r USA. prod/rel: Imp

LESSING, DORIS (1919–, UKN, Lessing, Doris May
The Grass Is Singing, 1950, Novel
Grass Is Singing, The 1981 d: Michael Raeburn. lps: Karen Black, John Thaw, John Kani. 104M UKN/SWD. *Killing Heat* (USA); *Graset Sjunger* prod/rel: Satori

Memoirs of a Survivor, 1974, Novel
Memoirs of a Survivor 1981 d: David Gladwell. lps: Julie Christie, Christopher Guard, Leonie Mellinger. 117M UKN. prod/rel: Emi, Memorial

LESSING, GOTTHOLD EPHRAIM (1729–1781), GRM
Emilia Galotti, 1772, Play
Emilia Galotti 1913 d: Friedrich Feher. lps: Friedrich Feher, Kurt Stieler. GRM. prod/rel: Deutsche Mutoskop Und Biograph
Emilia Galotti 1958 d: Martin Hellberg. lps: Karin Hubner, Gerhard Bienert, Maly Delschaft. 97M GDR. prod/rel: Defa
Emilia Galotti 1968 d: Franz Peter Wirth. 110M GRM.

Minna von Barnheim; Oder Das Soldatengluck, Hamburg 1767, Play
Fraulein von Barnhelm, Das 1940 d: Hans Schweikart. lps: Kathe Gold, Ewald Balser, Fita Benkhoff. 98M GRM. prod/rel: Bavaria
Heldinnen 1960 d: Dietrich Haugk. lps: Marianne Koch, Johanna von Koczian, Paul Hubschmid. 100M GRM. *Heroines* prod/rel: H.R. Sokal Film, U.F.H.
Minna von Barnheim 1966 d: Ludwig Cremer. 105M GRM.
Minna von Barnheim 1976 d: Franz Peter Wirth. 114M GRM.
Minna von Barnhelm 1962 d: Martin Hellberg. 107M GDR.

Nathan Der Weise, 1779, Play
Nathan Der Weise 1967 d: Franz Peter Wirth. 160M GRM.

LESTER, ELLIOTT
The Medicine Man, Play
Medicine Man, The 1930 d: Scott Pembroke. lps: Jack Benny, Betty Bronson, E. Alyn Warren. 7839f USA. prod/rel: Tiffany Productions

The Mud Turtle, New York 1925, Play
City Girl 1930 d: F. W. Murnau, A. F. Erickson. lps: David Torrence, Edith Yorke, Dawn O'Day. 77M USA. *Our Daily Bread* prod/rel: Fox Film Corp.

Two Seconds, New York 1931, Play
Two Seconds 1932 d: Mervyn Leroy. lps: Edward G. Robinson, Vivienne Osborne, Preston Foster. 70M USA. prod/rel: First National Pictures©

LESTIENNE, VALDEMAR
L' Amant de Poche, Novel
Amant de Poche, L' 1977 d: Bernard Queysanne. lps: Mimsy Farmer, Paul Sellier, Andrea Ferreol. 90M FRN. *Lover Boy* (UKN) prod/rel: Generale de Films, Gaumont

LESTOQ, W. H.
Jane, London 1890, Play
Jane 1915 d: Frank Lloyd. lps: Charlotte Greenwood, Sydney Grant, Forrest Stanley. 5r USA. prod/rel: Oliver Morosco Photoplay Co.©, Paramount Pictures Corp.

LESTRINGUEZ, PIERRE
Cartouche - Roi de Paris, Play
Cartouche, Roi de Paris 1948 d: Guillaume Radot. lps: Roger Pigaut, Jean Davy, Renee Devillers. 80M FRN. prod/rel: Guillaume Radot, Midi Cinema

LESUER, DANIEL
Justice de Femme!, Novel
Justice de Femme! 1917 d: Diana Karenne. lps: Diana Karenne, Alberto A. Capozzi, Mario MecchiA. 1815m ITL. prod/rel: Karenne Film

LETANG, LOUIS
La Divine, Novel
Demon de la Haine, Le 1921 d: Leonce Perret. lps: Eugene Breon, Marcya Capri, Lucy Fox. 2075m FRN/USA. *The Money Maniac; A Race for Millions* prod/rel: Films Leonce Perret, Pathe Exchange, Inc.

Rolande Immolee, Paris 1914, Novel
Demon de la Haine, Le 1921 d: Leonce Perret. lps: Eugene Breon, Marcya Capri, Lucy Fox. 2075m FRN/USA. *The Money Maniac; A Race for Millions* prod/rel: Films Leonce Perret, Pathe Exchange, Inc.

LETESSIER, DOROTHEE
Le Voyage a Paimpol, Novel
Voyage a Paimpol, Le 1985 d: John Berry. lps: Myriam Boyer, Michel Boujenah, Michele Brousse. 90M FRN.

LETRAZ
Chauffeur Antoinette, Play
Love Contract, The 1932 d: Herbert Selpin. lps: Winifred Shotter, Owen Nares, Sunday Wilshin. 80M UKN. prod/rel: British and Dominions, Woolf & Freedman

LETTE, KATHY
Puberty Blues, Novel
Puberty Blues 1982 d: Bruce Beresford. lps: Nell Schofield, Jad Capelja, Geoff Rhoe. 87M ASL. prod/rel: Limelight Productions Pty Ltd.©, Australian Film Commission

LEUTHEGE, E. B.
Der Frauendiplomat, Play
How's Chances 1934 d: Anthony Kimmins. lps: Harold French, Tamara Desni, Davy Burnaby. 73M UKN. *The Diplomatic Lover* prod/rel: Sound City, Fox

LEUWEN
Le Postillon de Lonjumeau, Paris 1836, Opera
Postillon von Lonjumeau, Der 1935 d: Carl Lamac. lps: Alfred Neugebauer, Thekla Ahrens, Leo Slezak. 95M AUS/USA. *Der Konig Lachelt - Paris Lacht; Le Postillon de Lonjumeau; Postillon Im Hochzeitsrock* prod/rel: Thekla-Film, Atlantis-Film

LEV, YIGAEL
Story
Simpatya Bishviel Kelev 1981 d: Sam Firstenberg. lps: Pesach Guttmark, Shmuel Atzmon, Haim Shinar. SHT ISR. *For the Sake of a Dog*

LEVEL, MAURICE
L' Epouvante, Paris 1908, Novel
A Minuit, le 7 1936 d: Maurice de Canonge. lps: Paul Bernard, Raymond Cordy, Colette Broido. 98M FRN. prod/rel: Societe Des Films D'aventures, Lutece-Film
Derniere Heure, Edition Speciale 1949 d: Maurice de Canonge. lps: Paul Meurisse, Odette Joyeux, Pierre Dac. 90M FRN. prod/rel: Sirius, Bellair Films
Roadhouse Murder, The 1932 d: J. Walter Ruben. lps: Eric Linden, Dorothy Jordan, Purnell Pratt. 73M USA. prod/rel: RKO Radio Pictures©

Lady Harrington, Novel
Lady Harrington 1926 d: Fred Leroy Granville, H. C. Grantham-Hayes. lps: Claude France, Warwick Ward, Maurice de Feraudy. SRL. FRN. prod/rel: Argus Film

The Letters, Story
Letters, The 1922 d: George A. Cooper. lps: Hugh Miller, Madge Stuart. 1362f UKN. prod/rel: Quality Plays, Walturdaw

LEVEN, JEREMY
Creator, Novel
Creator 1985 d: Ivan Passer. lps: Peter O'Toole, Mariel Hemingway, Vincent Spano. 107M USA. prod/rel: Universal

LEVENKRON, STEPHEN
The Best Little Girl in the World, Novel
Best Little Girl in the World, The 1981 d: Sam O'Steen. lps: Jennifer Jason Leigh, Charles Durning, Eva Marie Saint. TVM. 100M USA. prod/rel: Metromedia, Aaron Spelling

LEVENQ, EDMOND
La Croix Sur le Rocher, Novel
Croix Sur le Rocher, La 1927 d: Edmond Levenq, Jean Rosne. lps: Helene Hallier, Maurice de La Mea, Georges Saacke. 2200m FRN. prod/rel: Etoile-Film

LEVENSON, LEW
Shattered Glass, Play
24 Hours 1931 d: Marion Gering. lps: Clive Brook, Miriam Hopkins, Regis Toomey. 68M USA. *The Hours Between* (UKN); *Twenty-Four Hours* prod/rel: Paramount Publix Corp.©

LEVER, LADY ARTHUR
Brown Sugar, London 1920, Play
Brown Sugar 1922 d: Fred Paul. lps: Owen Nares, Lillian Hall-Davis, Eric Lewis. 5600f UKN. prod/rel: British Super, Jury
Brown Sugar 1931 d: Leslie Hiscott. lps: Constance Carpenter, Francis Lister, Allan Aynesworth. 70M UKN. prod/rel: Twickenham, Warner Bros.

LEVERAGE, HENRY
The Twinkler, Short Story
Twinkler, The 1916 d: Edward Sloman. lps: William Russell, Charlotte Burton, Clarence Burton. 5r USA. prod/rel: American Film Co., Mutual Film Corp.

Whispering Wires, New York 1918, Novel
Whispering Wires 1926 d: Albert Ray. lps: Anita Stewart, Edmund Burns, Charles Clary. 5906f USA. prod/rel: Fox Film Corp.

LEVI, CARLO (1902–, ITL
Cristo Ei E Fermato a Eboli, 1945, Novel
Cristo Si E Fermato a Eboli 1979 d: Francesco Rosi. lps: Gian Maria Volonte, Irene Papas, Paolo Bonicelli. 151M ITL/FRN. *Christ Stopped at Eboli* (USA); *Eboli; Le Christ S'est Arrete a Eboli* (FRN) prod/rel: Vides Cin.Ca, Fides Cin.Ca

LEVI, PAOLO
Ritratto Di Provincia in Rosso, Novel
Al Piacere Di Rivederla 1976 d: Marco Leto. lps: Ugo Tognazzi, Franco Graziosi, Francoise Fabian. 102M ITL/FRN. *Portrait de Province En Rouge* (FRN) prod/rel: Plexus Film (Roma), P.E.C.F. (Paris)

LEVI, PRIMO (1919–1987), ITL
La Tregua, Book
Tregua, La 1997 d: Francesco Rosi. lps: John Turturro, Massimo Ghini, Rade SerbedzijA. 126M ITL/FRN/GRM. *The Truce* prod/rel: 3 Emme Cinematografica (Roma), T & C Films Ag (Zurich)

LEVIN, EDWINA
The Devil's Riddle, 1919, Story
Devil's Riddle, The 1920 d: Frank Beal. lps: Gladys Brockwell, William Scott, Richard Cummings. 5r USA. prod/rel: Fox Film Corp., William Fox©

False Colors, Story
Reputation 1921 d: Stuart Paton. lps: Priscilla Dean, May Giraci, Harry Van Meter. 7153f USA. *False Colors* prod/rel: Universal Film Mfg. Co.

Happiness a la Mode, 1919, Short Story
Happiness a la Mode 1919 d: Walter Edwards. lps: Constance Talmadge, Harrison Ford, Betty Schade. 5r USA. prod/rel: Select Pictures Corp.©

LEVIN, IRA (1929–, USA
The Boys from Brazil, Novel
Boys from Brazil, The 1978 d: Franklin J. Schaffner. lps: Gregory Peck, Laurence Olivier, James Mason. 123M USA/UKN. prod/rel: Itc, Producer Circle

Critic's Choice, New York 1960, Play
Critic's Choice 1963 d: Don Weis. lps: Bob Hope, Lucille Ball, Marilyn Maxwell. 100M USA. prod/rel: Warner Bros., Frank P. Rosenberg

Deathtrap, Play
Deathtrap 1982 d: Sidney Lumet. lps: Michael Caine, Christopher Reeve, Dyan Cannon. 116M USA. prod/rel: Warner

Dr. Cook's Garden, Play
Dr. Cook's Garden 1970 d: Ted Post. lps: Bing Crosby, Frank Converse, Blythe Danner. TVM. 74M USA. prod/rel: Paramount

A Kiss Before Dying, 1953, Novel
Kiss Before Dying, A 1956 d: Gerd Oswald. lps: Robert Wagner, Jeffrey Hunter, Virginia Leith. 94M USA. prod/rel: United Artists, Crown
Kiss Before Dying, A 1991 d: James Dearden. lps: Matt Dillon, Sean Young, Max von Sydow. 95M USA. prod/rel: Universal, Initial Film

Rosemary's Baby, New York 1967, Novel
Rosemary's Baby 1968 d: Roman Polanski. lps: Mia Farrow, John Cassavetes, Ruth Gordon. 136M USA. prod/rel: William Castle Enterprises

Sliver, Novel
Sliver 1993 d: Phil Noyce. lps: Sharon Stone, William Baldwin, Tom Berenger. 108M USA. prod/rel: Paramount

The Stepford Wives, Novel
Stepford Wives, The 1975 d: Bryan Forbes. lps: Katharine Ross, Peter Masterson, Paula Prentiss. 115M USA. prod/rel: Palomar Pictures

LEVIN, MEYER (1905–, USA
Compulsion, 1956, Novel
Compulsion 1959 d: Richard Fleischer. lps: Orson Welles, Diane Varsi, Dean Stockwell. 105M USA. prod/rel: 20th Century-Fox

My Father's House, 1947, Novel
Beit Avi 1947 d: Herbert Kline. lps: Ronnie Cohen, Irene Broza, Yitzhak Danziger. F ISR. *My Father's House*

LEVINSON, RICHARD (1934–1987), USA, Levinson, Richard Leighton
Prescription: Murder, Play
  Prescription: Murder 1967 d: Richard Irving. lps: Peter Falk, Gene Barry, Katherine Justice. TVM. 100M USA. prod/rel: Universal

That Certain Summer, Play
  That Certain Summer 1972 d: Lamont Johnson. lps: Hal Holbrook, Martin Sheen, Joe Don Baker. TVM. 73M USA. prod/rel: Universal

LEVITHAN, NADAV
Story
  Sipur Intimi 1981 d: Nadav Levithan. lps: Chava Alberstein, Alex Peleg, Shmuel Shiloh. 85M ISR. *An Intimate Story* prod/rel: Le'an Films

LEVY, BENN W. (1900–, UKN, Levy, Benn Wolfe
Ever Green, London 1930, Play
  Evergreen 1934 d: Victor Saville. lps: Jessie Matthews, Sonnie Hale, Betty Balfour. 91M UKN. prod/rel: Gaumont-British

Springtime for Henry, New York 1931, Play
  Springtime for Henry 1934 d: Frank Tuttle. lps: Otto Kruger, Nancy Carroll, Heather Angel. 73M USA. *Forbidden Lips* prod/rel: Fox Film Corp.©, Jesse L. Lasky Production

LEVY, EDWARD
The Beast Within, Novel
  Beast Within, The 1982 d: Philippe MorA. lps: Ronny Cox, Bibi Besch, Paul Clemens. 98M USA. prod/rel: MGM, United Artists

LEVY, JOSE G.
A Daughter of England, Play
  Daughter of England, A 1915 d: Leedham Bantock. lps: Marga Rubia Levy, Frank Randall, Frank Dane. 3500f UKN. prod/rel: British Empire

Madame la Presidente, Paris C.1898, Play
  Madame la Presidente 1916 d: Frank Lloyd. lps: Anna Held, Forrest Stanley, Herbert Standing. 5r USA. *Madame Presidente* prod/rel: Oliver Morosco Photoplay Co.©, Paramount Pictures Corp.

Le Zebre, Play
  Glad Eye, The 1920 d: Kenelm Foss. lps: James Reardon, Dorothy Minto, Hayford Hobbs. 6000f UKN. prod/rel: Reardon British Films, IFT

  Glad Eye, The 1927 d: Maurice Elvey, Victor Saville. lps: Estelle Brody, Hal Sherman, John Stuart. 7700f UKN. prod/rel: Gaumont

LEVY, MELVIN
A House in the Country, New York 1937, Play
  Hideaway 1937 d: Richard Rosson. lps: Fred Stone, J. Carrol Naish, Emma Dunn. 60M USA. *A House in the Country* prod/rel: RKO Radio Pictures©

LEVY, STEVEN
The Unicorn's Secret, Book
  Hunt for the Unicorn Killer, The 1999 d: William A. Graham. lps: Kevin Anderson, Tom Skerritt, Naomi Watts. TVM. 240M USA. prod/rel: Dan Wigutow Prods., Regency Television

LEWANDOWSKI, DAN
Worth Winning, Novel
  Worth Winning 1989 d: Will MacKenzie. lps: Mark Harmon, Madeleine Stowe, Lesley Ann Warren. 102M USA. *Three Beds for a Bachelor* prod/rel: 20th Century Fox

LEWIN, ELSA
I Anna, Novel
  Solo Fur Klarinette 1998 d: Nico Hofmann. lps: Gotz George, Corinna Harfouch, Tim Bergmann. 95M GRM. *Solo for Clarinet* prod/rel: Regina Ziegler, Prosieben

LEWIS, ALFRED HENRY
The Tenderfoot, Short Story
  Tenderfoot, The 1917 d: William Duncan. lps: William Duncan, Carol Holloway, Florence Dye. 5r USA. prod/rel: Vitagraph Co. of America©, Blue Ribbon Feature

Wolfville: Episodes of Cowboy Life, New York 1897, Book
  Dead Shot Baker 1917 d: William Duncan. lps: William Duncan, Carol Holloway, J. W. Ryan. 5r USA. *Dead-Shot Baker* prod/rel: Vitagraph Co. of America©, Greater Vitagraph (V-L-S-E)

LEWIS, ARTHUR H.
Lament for the Molly Maguires, New York 1964, Novel
  Molly Maguires, The 1970 d: Martin Ritt. lps: Richard Harris, Sean Connery, Samantha Eggar. 125M USA. prod/rel: Tamm Productions, Paramount

LEWIS, C. S. (1898–1963), UKN, Lewis, Clive Staples
Novel
  Chronicles of Narnia: Prince Caspian, The 1989 d: Marilyn Fox. lps: Sophie Wilcox, Sophie Cook, Jonathan Scott. MTV. 57M UKN. prod/rel: BBC

  Chronicles of Narnia: the Silver Chair, The 1990 d: Alex Kirby. lps: David Thwaites, Camilla Power, Warwick Davies. MTV. 158M UKN. prod/rel: BBC

  Chronicles of Narnia: the Voyage of the Dawn Treader, The 1989 d: Alex Kirby. lps: Sophie Wilcox, Sophie Cook, Jonathan Scott. MTV. 109M UKN.

The Lion the Witch and the Wardrobe, 1950, Novel
  Chronicles of Narnia: the Lion, the Witch and the Wardrobe, The 1989 d: Marilyn Fox. lps: Richard Dempsey, Sophie Cook, Jonathan Scott. MTV. 163M UKN. prod/rel: BBC

  Lion, the Witch and the Wardrobe, The 1972. lps: Elizabeth Crowther, Zuleika Robson, Paul Waller. SRL. UKN. prod/rel: Patricia Lonsdale (P)

  Lion, the Witch and the Wardrobe, The 1978 d: Bill Melendez. ANM. 100M USA/UKN. prod/rel: Bill Melendez Prod.

LEWIS, EDWIN
Relations are Best Apart, Play
  What Every Woman Wants 1954 d: Maurice Elvey. lps: William Sylvester, Elsy Albiin, Brenda de Banzie. 88M UKN. prod/rel: Advance, Adelphi

LEWIS, ERNEST
Beth the Sheepdog, Novel
  Loyal Heart 1946 d: Oswald Mitchell. lps: Percy Marmont, Harry Welchman, Patricia Marmont. 80M UKN. prod/rel: British National, Strand

LEWIS, ETHELREDA
Trader Horn, New York 1927, Book
  Trader Horn 1931 d: W. S. Van Dyke. lps: Harry Carey, Edwina Booth, Duncan Renaldo. 123M USA. prod/rel: Metro-Goldwyn-Mayer Corp., Metro-Goldwyn-Mayer Dist. Corp.©

LEWIS, EUGENE B.
Hell's Neck, Story
  Fight for Love, A 1919 d: John Ford. lps: Harry Carey, Neva Gerber, Joe Harris. 5615f USA. prod/rel: Universal Film Mfg. Co.©

LEWIS, GENE
Bob Goes to a Party, Story
  I'll Remember April 1945 d: Harold Young. lps: Gloria Jean, Kirby Grant, Milburn Stone. 63M USA. prod/rel: Universal

LEWIS, HELEN PROTHERO
As God Made Her, 1919, Novel
  Zooals Ik Ben. 1920 d: Maurits H. Binger, B. E. Doxat-Pratt. lps: Mary Odette, Henry Victor, Adelqui Millar. 6000f NTH. *As God Made Her; Just As I Am* prod/rel: Anglo-Hollandia

Love and a Whirlwind, Novel
  Love and a Whirlwind 1922 d: Duncan MacRae, Harold Shaw. lps: Clive Brook, Marjorie Hume, Reginald Fox. 6858f UKN. prod/rel: Alliance, Cosmograph

The Silver Bridge, Novel
  Silver Bridge, The 1920 d: Dallas Cairns. lps: Dallas Cairns, Betty Farquhar, Madeleine Meredith. 5000f UKN. prod/rel: Cairns Torquay Films

LEWIS, HERBERT CLYDE
Story
  Free for All 1949 d: Charles T. Barton. lps: Robert Cumming, Ann Blyth, Percy Kilbride. 83M USA. prod/rel: Universal-International

LEWIS, HILDA
The Day Is Ours, Novel
  Mandy 1952 d: Alexander MacKendrick. lps: Phyllis Calvert, Jack Hawkins, Terence Morgan. 93M UKN. *Crash of Silence* (USA); *The Story of Mandy* prod/rel: Ealing Studios, General Film Distributors

LEWIS, LEOPOLD
The Bells, London 1871, Play
  Bells, The 1923 d: Edwin Greenwood. lps: Russell Thorndike, Arthur Walcott, Daisy Agnew. 2100f UKN. prod/rel: British & Colonial, Walturdaw

LEWIS, M. G.
The Monk, Novel
  Monk, The 1990 d: Francisco Lara Polop. lps: Paul McGann, Sophie Ward, Isla Blair. 106M UKN/SPN. *El Fraile* (SPN); *Seduction of a Priest*; *Final Temptation* prod/rel: Celtic Films (London), Mediterraneo Cine-Tv (Madrid)

LEWIS, MARY E.
The Making of Maddalena; Or the Compromise, Play
  Making of Maddalena, The 1916 d: Frank Lloyd. lps: Edna Goodrich, Forrest Stanley, Howard Davies. 5r USA. prod/rel: Oliver Morosco Photoplay Co.©, Paramount Pictures Corp.

LEWIS, MATTHEW GREGORY (1775–1818), UKN
Le Moine, Novel
  Moine, Le 1972 d: Ado Kyrou. lps: Franco Nero, Nathalie Delon, Nicol Williamson. 90M FRN/ITL/GRM. *Il Monaco* (ITL); *The Monk* prod/rel: Tritone Filmindustria, Maya

LEWIS, MYRA
Book
  Great Balls of Fire 1989 d: Jim McBride. lps: Dennis Quaid, Winona Ryder, Alec Baldwin. 102M USA. prod/rel: Orion, Adam Fields Prods.

LEWIS, OSCAR (1914–1970), USA
The Children of Sanchez, Novel
  Children of Sanchez, The 1978 d: Hall Bartlett. lps: Anthony Quinn, Dolores Del Rio, Melanie Farrar. 117M USA/MXC. *Los Hijos de Sanchez* (MXC) prod/rel: Hall Bartlett, Carmel Enterprises

LEWIS, RAY
Novel
  Loyalty 1918 d: Jack Pratt. lps: Betty Brice, Murdock MacQuarrie, Jean Hathaway. 6r USA. prod/rel: Bernstein Film Productions, State Rights

LEWIS, ROBERT
Dead Reckoning, Play
  Dead Reckoning 1990 d: Robert Lewis. lps: Cliff Robertson, Susan Blakely, Rick Springfield. TVM. 100M USA. prod/rel: Houston Lady Productions, Mca Television Entertainment

LEWIS, SAMUEL G.
The Making of Maddalena; Or the Compromise, Play
  Making of Maddalena, The 1916 d: Frank Lloyd. lps: Edna Goodrich, Forrest Stanley, Howard Davies. 5r USA. prod/rel: Oliver Morosco Photoplay Co.©, Paramount Pictures Corp.

LEWIS, SINCLAIR (1885–1951), USA, Lewis, Harry Sinclair
Ann Vickers, New York 1933, Novel
  Ann Vickers 1933 d: John Cromwell. lps: Irene Dunne, Walter Huston, Bruce Cabot. 75M USA. prod/rel: RKO Radio

Babbitt, New York 1922, Novel
  Babbitt 1924 d: Harry Beaumont. lps: Willard Louis, Mary Alden, Carmel Myers. 7914f USA. prod/rel: Warner Brothers Pictures

  Babbitt 1934 d: William Keighley. lps: Guy Kibbee, Aline MacMahon, Claire Dodd. 75M USA. prod/rel: First National Productions Corp.

Cass Timberlane, 1945, Novel
  Cass Timberlane 1947 d: George Sidney. lps: Spencer Tracy, Lana Turner, Zachary Scott. 120M USA. prod/rel: MGM

Dodsworth, New York 1929, Novel
  Dodsworth 1936 d: William Wyler. lps: Walter Huston, Ruth Chatterton, Paul Lukas. 101M USA. prod/rel: Samuel Goldwyn, Inc., United Artists

Elmer Gantry, 1927, Novel
  Elmer Gantry 1960 d: Richard Brooks. lps: Burt Lancaster, Jean Simmons, Arthur Kennedy. 145M USA. prod/rel: United Artists

Free Air, New York 1919, Novel
  Free Air 1922 d: Edward H. Griffith. lps: Tom Douglas, Marjorie Seaman, George Pauncefort. 5600f USA. prod/rel: Outlook Photoplays, W. W. Hodkinson Corp.

The Ghost Patrol, Short Story
  Ghost Patrol, The 1923 d: Nat Ross. lps: Ralph Graves, Bessie Love, George Nichols. 4228f USA. prod/rel: Universal Pictures

Let's Play King, 1931, Short Story
  Majestat Auf Abwegen 1958 d: R. A. Stemmle. lps: Fita Benkhoff, Chariklia Baxevanos, Agnes Fink. 92M GRM. *His Majesty on the Wrong Path*

  Newly Rich 1931 d: Norman Taurog. lps: Mitzi Green, Jackie Searl, Edna May Oliver. 77M USA. *Forbidden Adventure* (UKN); *Let's Play King* prod/rel: Paramount Publix Corp.©

Main Street; the Story of Carol Kennicott, New York 1920, Novel
  I Married a Doctor 1936 d: Archie Mayo. lps: Josephine Hutchinson, Pat O'Brien, Ross Alexander. 87M USA. *Main Street* prod/rel: Warner Bros. Pictures©, First National Picture

  Main Street 1923 d: Harry Beaumont. lps: Florence Vidor, Monte Blue, Harry Myers. 8943f USA. prod/rel: Warner Brothers Pictures

Mantrap, New York 1926, Novel
  Mantrap 1926 d: Victor Fleming. lps: Ernest Torrence, Clara Bow, Percy Marmont. 6077f USA. prod/rel: Famous Players-Lasky, Paramount Pictures

  Untamed 1940 d: George Archainbaud. lps: Ray Milland, Patricia Morison, Akim Tamiroff. 83M USA. prod/rel: Paramount Pictures

Martin Arrowsmith, 1925, Novel
Arrowsmith 1931 d: John Ford. lps: Ronald Colman, Helen Hayes, Richard Bennett. 108M USA. prod/rel: United Artists

LEWIS, STEPHEN
Sparrers Can't Sing, Stratford 1960, Play
Sparrows Can't Sing 1963 d: Joan Littlewood. lps: James Booth, Barbara Windsor, Roy Kinnear. 94M UKN. prod/rel: Carthage Productions, Elstree

LEWIS, TED (1940–, UKN
Jack's Return Home, Novel
Get Carter 1970 d: Mike Hodges. lps: Michael Caine, Britt Ekland, John Osborne. 112M UKN. prod/rel: MGM British, Emg-Emi

LEY, WILLY
Conquest of Space, 1949, Book
Conquest of Space 1955 d: Byron Haskin. lps: Walter Brooke, Eric Fleming, Mickey Shaughnessy. 80M USA. prod/rel: Paramount, George Pal

LEYCESTER, LAURA
The Five Wishes, Play
Five Wishes, The 1916 d: Wilfred Noy?. 1035f UKN. prod/rel: Clarendon

The Rising Generation, London 1923, Play
Rising Generation, The 1928 d: Harley Knoles, George Dewhurst. lps: Alice Joyce, Jameson Thomas, Robin Irvine. 7200f UKN. prod/rel: Westminster Pictures, Williams & Pritchard

LHANDE, PIERRE
Le Christ Dans la Banlieue, Book
Notre-Dame de la Mouise 1941 d: Robert Peguy, Rene Delacroix. lps: Odette Joyeux, Odette Barancey, Edouard Delmont. 90M CND/FRN. prod/rel: Fiatfilm (Paris), France Film (Montreal)

Mirentxu, Novel
Mayorazgo de Basterretxe, El 1928 d: Mauro AzconA. lps: Eduardo Morata, Margarita Arregui, Orlando VillafrancA. 1450m SPN. *The Basterretxe Estate* prod/rel: Estudios Azkona (Baracaldo)

Mon Petit Pretre, Novel
Mains Liees, Les 1955 d: Roland-Jean Quignon, Aloysius Vachet. lps: Paul Vandenberghe, Nadine Alari, Catherine Erard. 110M FRN. prod/rel: Raymond Desbonnets

L'HERBIER, MARCEL (1888–1979), FRN
L' Ange de Minuit
Bouclette 1918 d: Louis Mercanton, Rene Hervil. lps: Signoret, Harry Pilcer, Max Maxudian. 2300m FRN. *L' Ange de Minuit* prod/rel: Eclipse

L'HOTE, JEAN
Un Dimanche Au Champ d'Honneur, Paris 1958, Novel
Gans von Sedan, Die 1959 d: Helmut Kautner. lps: Hardy Kruger, Jean Richard, Dany Carrel. 90M GRM/FRN. *Sans Tambour Ni Trompette* (FRN); *The Goose of Sedan* prod/rel: C.a.P.A.C., UFA

Sans Tambour, Ni Trompette 1949 d: Roger Blanc. lps: Gaby Morlay, Jean Gabriello, Jules Berry. 89M FRN. *La Fleur Au Fusil* prod/rel: Generale Films

LI BIHUA, Lee, Lillian
Ba Wang Bie Ji, Novel
Ba Wang Bie Ji 1993 d: Chen Kaige. lps: Leslie Cheung, Zhang Fengyi, Gong Li. 156M HKG/CHN. *Farewell My Concubine* (UKN); *Farewell to My Concubine* prod/rel: Tomson (Hk) Film Corp. Ltd., China Film Co-Production Corp.

LI FEIGAN, Ba Jin
Han Ye, 1944, Novel
Han Ye 1984 d: Qiu Wen. 105M CHN.

Jia, 1933, Novel
Jia 1941 d: Bu Wancang, Hsu Hsin-Fu. 197M CHN. *Family*

Jia 1957 d: Chen XIhe, Ye Ming. lps: Wei Heling, Sun Daolin, Zhang Ruifang. 128M CHN. *Family* prod/rel: Shanghai Film Studio

Tuan Yuan, 1956, Short Story
Yingxiong Ernu 1964 d: Wu Zhaodi. lps: Tian Fang, Zhou Wenbing, Liu Shangxian. 117M CHN. *The Heroic Son and Daughter; Heroic Sons and Daughters* prod/rel: Changchun Film Studio

LI LI
Love the Man, Not His Position, Story
Ru Chi Duo Qing 1956 d: Fang Ying. lps: Ye Linlang, Song Xuejuan, Qin Han. 7r CHN. *Such Affection* prod/rel: Changchun Film Studio

LI RUQIN
Island Militia Women, Novel
Hai XIa 1975 d: Qian Jiang, Chen Huaiai. lps: Wu Haiyan, Cai Ming, Zhao Lian. 12r CHN. prod/rel: Beijing Film Studio

LI XIAO
Men Gum (Gang Law), Novel
Yao a Yao Yao Dao Waipo Qiao 1995 d: Zhang Yimou. lps: Gong Li, Li Baotian, Li Xuejian. 108M HKG/FRN/CHN. *Shanghai Triad* prod/rel: Shanghai Film Studio, Alpha Films

LI XINTIAN
Shan Shan de Hong XIng, Novel
Shan Shan de Hong XIng 1974 d: Li Jun, Li Ang. lps: Zhu XInyun, Bo Guanjun, Gao Baocheng. 11r CHN. *A Sparkling Red Star* prod/rel: August First Film Studio

LI YANG
A Hero Returns Home, Novel
Sheng Li Chong Feng 1951 d: Tang XIaodan. lps: Feng Ji, Su Yi, Ling Yun. 10r CHN. *Reunited in Victory* prod/rel: Shanghai Film Studio

LI YINRU
Yehou Chunfeng Dou Gu Cheng, Novel
Yehuo Chunfeng Dou Gu Cheng 1963 d: Yan Jizhou. lps: Wang XIaotang, Wang XIngang, Chen Lizhong. 11r CHN.; *Struggle in an Ancient City With Wild Fire and Spring Wind* prod/rel: August First Film Studio

LI YIQING
Uncle Shangang, Novel
Bei Gao Shan Gang Ye 1994 d: Fan Yuan. lps: Li Rentang, Yang Hua, Dong Danjun. 11r CHN. *The Accused Uncle Shangang* prod/rel: Emei Film Studio

LI ZHUN
Bu Neng Zou Nie Tiao Lu, Novel
Bu Neng Zou Nei Tiao Lu 1954 d: Ying Yunwei. lps: Wei Heling, Lan Gu, Zhao Shuyin. 6r CHN. *That's Not the Way to Go* prod/rel: Shanghai Film Studio

The Indigenous Specialist, Play
Cong Ming de Ren 1958 d: Xu Tao. lps: Wun XIying, Zhang Yunxiang, Fan Lai. 10r CHN. *An Intelligent Person* prod/rel: Haiyan Film Studio

Snow and Ice Melt, Novel
Bing Jian Qian Jin 1958 d: Yan Gong. lps: Li Mengrao, Guo Shutian, He XIaoshu. 8r CHN. *Moving Forward Shoulder to Shoulder* prod/rel: Changchun Film Studio

The Story of Li Shuangshuang, Novel
Li Shuangshuang 1962 d: Lu Ren. lps: Zhang Ruifang, Zhong XInghuo, Zhang Wenrong. 11r CHN. prod/rel: Haiyan Film Studio

LIAN, TORUN
Bare Skyer Beveger Stjernene, Novel
Bare Skyer Beveger Stjernene 1998 d: Torun Lian. lps: Thea Sofie Rusten, Jan Tore Kristoffersen, Anneke von Der Lippe. 95M NRW. *Only Clouds Move the Stars* prod/rel: Sf Norge, Kilmkameratene

LIANG BIN
Hongqi Pu, 1958, Novel
Hongqi Pu 1960 d: Ling Zhifeng. lps: Cui Wei, Chen Fan, Cai Songling. 147M CHN. *Song of the Red Flag* prod/rel: Beijing Film Studio, Tianjing Film Studio

LIANG FENGYI
Wo Yao Huo XIa Chu, Novel
Wo Yao Huo XIa Chu 1995 d: Raymond Lee. lps: Zhang Aijia, Yuan Yongyi, Zhou Huajian. F CHN/HKG. *I Want to Live* prod/rel: Beijing Film Studio, Dongfang Film & Tv Company

LIANG MAN
Our Recollections of Youth, Novel
Shang Yi Dang 1992 d: He Qun, Liu Baolin. lps: Ge You, Ju Xue, Geng Ge. 9r CHN. *To Be Taken in* prod/rel: Fujian Film Studio

LIBBEY, LAURA JEAN
When Love Grows Cold, Story
When Love Grows Cold 1925 d: Harry O. Hoyt. lps: Natacha Rambova, Clive Brook, Sam Hardy. 6500f USA. prod/rel: R-C Pictures, Film Booking Offices of America

LIBERATI, FRANCO
L' Inferno, Play
Inferno, L' 1914. 800m ITL. prod/rel: Roma Film

LIBIN, Z.
Broken Hearts, Story
Broken Hearts 1926 d: Maurice Schwartz. lps: Maurice Schwartz, Lila Lee, Wolf Goldfaden. 8200f USA. *Souls in Exile* (UKN); *Di Tsebrokhene Hertser* prod/rel: Jaffe Art Films

LIBIN, ZALMEN
Di Gebrokhene Hertser Oder Libe un Flikht, New York 1903, Play
Unfortunate Bride, The 1932 d: Henry Lynn. lps: Maurice Schwartz, Lila Lee, Wolf Goldfaden. F USA. *Di Umgliklikhe Kale* prod/rel: Lynn Productions

LICHTENBERG, WILHELM
Wem Gott Ein Amt Gibt, Play
Winzig Simuliert, de 1942 d: Rudolf Bernhard. lps: Rudolf Bernhard, Elsie Attenhofer, Hans Fehrmann. 94M SWT. *Winzig Simule; Der Pechvogel; Der Simulant* prod/rel: Probst-Film

Der Zobelpelz, Novel
Grosstadtnacht 1950 d: Hans Wolff. lps: Inge Konradi, Wolf Albach-Retty, Hedwig Bleibtreu. 95M AUS. prod/rel: Helios

LICHTENBERGER, ANTON
Le Petit Roi, Novel
Petit Roi, Le 1933 d: Julien Duvivier. lps: Robert Lynen, Arlette Marchal, Jean Toulout. 90M FRN. prod/rel: Vandal Et Delac

LIDELL, H.
Jerry's Mother-in-Law, Play
Jerry's Mother-in-Law 1913 d: James Young. lps: Sidney Drew, Clara Kimball Young, Kate Price. 2000f USA. prod/rel: Vitagraph Co. of America

LIDZ, FRANZ
Unstrung Heroes, Book
Unstrung Heroes 1995 d: Diane Keaton. lps: Andie MacDowell, John Turturro, Michael Richards. 94M USA.

LIEBE, HAPSBURG
The Little Good
Circumstantial Evidence 1912 d: Otis B. Thayer. lps: William Duncan, Lester Cuneo, Myrtle Stedman. 1000f USA. prod/rel: Selig Polyscope Co.

Trimmed and Burning, 1921, Short Story
Trimmed 1922 d: Harry Pollard. lps: Hoot Gibson, Patsy Ruth Miller, Alfred Hollingsworth. 4583f USA. prod/rel: Universal Film Mfg. Co.

LIEBER, JOEL
Move!, New York 1968, Novel
Move 1970 d: Stuart Rosenberg. lps: Elliott Gould, Paula Prentiss, Genevieve Waite. 90M USA. prod/rel: Pandro S. Berman Productions

LIEBERMAN, HERBERT
Crawlspace, Novel
Crawlspace 1971 d: John Newland, Buzz Kulik. lps: Arthur Kennedy, Teresa Wright, Tom Happer. TVM. 73M USA. prod/rel: Titus Productions

LIEBERMAN-LIVNE, TZVI
Story
Me'al Hachuravot 1936 d: Natan Axelrod, Alfred Wolf. lps: Yehuda Gabai, Danya Levine, Kelman Konstantiel. F ISR. *Over the Ruins; Me'al Hekhoravot*
Oded Hanoded 1932 d: Haim Halachmi. lps: Shimon Finkel, Shimon Pevsner, Shifra Ashman. 70M ISR. *Oded the Wanderer* prod/rel: Film Erets-Israeli, Chaim Halachmi & Partners

LIEBERSON, GODDARD
Three for Bedroom C, 1947, Novel
Three for Bedroom C 1952 d: Milton Bren. lps: Gloria Swanson, Fred Clark, James Warren. 74M USA. prod/rel: Warner Bros., Brenco Pictures

LIEBLER, THEODORE
Success, New York 1918, Play
Success 1923 d: Ralph Ince. lps: Brandon Tynan, Naomi Childers, Mary Astor. 6800f USA. prod/rel: Murray W. Garsson, Metro Pictures

LIECK, WALTER
Annelie, Play
Annelie, Die Geschichte Eines Lebens 1941 d: Josef von Baky. lps: Luise Ullrich, Werner Krauss, Karl Ludwig Diehl. 92M GRM. *Die Geschichte Eines Lebens; Annelie* prod/rel: UFA, Prisma

LIEF, J. O.
Two for Tonight, Play
Two for Tonight 1935 d: Frank Tuttle. lps: Bing Crosby, Joan Bennett, Mary Boland. 61M USA. prod/rel: Paramount Productions©

LIEF, MAX
Two for Tonight 1935 d: Frank Tuttle. lps: Bing Crosby, Joan Bennett, Mary Boland. 61M USA. prod/rel: Paramount Productions©

LIEFERANT, HENRY
Doctors' Wives, New York 1930, Novel
Doctors' Wives 1931 d: Frank Borzage. lps: Warner Baxter, Joan Bennett, Cecilia Loftus. 82M USA. prod/rel: Fox Film Corp.

LIEFERANT, SYLVIA
Doctors' Wives 1931 d: Frank Borzage. lps: Warner Baxter, Joan Bennett, Cecilia Loftus. 82M USA. prod/rel: Fox Film Corp.

LIENERT, MEINRAD
Der Doppelte Matthias Und Seine Tochter, Berlin 1929, Novel
  Doppelte Matthias Und Seine Tochter, Der 1941 d: Sigfrit Steiner, Emile Edwin Reinert. lps: Emil Gyr, Madeleine Koebel, Sylva Denzler. 106M SWT. *Le Double Matthias Et Ses Filles* prod/rel: Gotthard-Film

LIETZ, HANS-GEORG
Story
  Weite Strassen - Stille Liebe 1969 d: Hermann Zschoche. lps: Manfred Krug, Jutta Hoffmann, Jaecki Schwarz. 75M GDR. *Wide Roads - Quiet Love* prod/rel: Defa

LIGABUE, LUCIANO
Fuori E Dentro Il Borgo, Short Stories
  Radio Freccia 1998 d: Luciano Ligabue. lps: Stefano Accorsi, Luciano Federico, Alessio ModicA. 112M ITL. prod/rel: Fandango, Medusa Film

LIGGERT, WALTER W.
When Terror Stalked Behind, 1930, Story
  Wild North, The 1952 d: Andrew Marton. lps: Stewart Granger, Wendell Corey, Cyd Charisse. 97M USA. *The Big North* prod/rel: MGM

LIGHTNER, FRANCES
Puppets, Play
  Puppets 1926 d: George Archainbaud. lps: Milton Sills, Gertrude Olmstead, Francis McDonald. 7486f USA. prod/rel: Al Rockett Productions, First National Pictures

LIGHTON, WILLIAM RHEEM
Billy Fortune and the Hard Proposition, Englewood Cliffs, Nj.1912, Novel
  Water, Water, Everywhere 1920 d: Clarence Badger. lps: Will Rogers, Irene Rich, Rowland Lee. 4207f USA. prod/rel: Goldwyn Pictures Corp.©, Goldwyn Distributing Corp.

LIITOJA, HILLAR
The Last Supper, Play
  Last Supper, The 1995 d: Cynthia Roberts. lps: Ken McDougall, Jack Nicholsen, Daniel MacIvor. 96M CND. prod/rel: Greg Klymkiw Production

LILAR, SUZANNE
La Confession Anonyme, Novel
  Benvenuta 1983 d: Andre Delvaux. lps: Vittorio Gassman, Fanny Ardant, Francoise Fabian. 105M BLG/FRN/ITL. prod/rel: la Nouvelle Imageries, Ugc

LILJENCRANTZ, OTTILIA ADELINA
The Thrall of Leif the Lucky; a Story of Viking Days, Chicago 1902, Novel
  Viking, The 1929 d: R. William Neill. lps: Donald Crisp, Pauline Starke, Leroy Mason. 8394f USA. prod/rel: Metro-Goldwyn-Mayer Pictures

LILLEY, EDWARD CLARK
Ladies' Day, Play
  Ladies' Day 1943 d: Leslie Goodwins. lps: Lupe Velez, Eddie Albert, Patsy Kelly. 62M USA. prod/rel: RKO Radio

LILLIBRIDGE, WILLIAM OTIS
Ben Blair: the Story of a Plainsman, Chicago 1905, Novel
  Ben Blair 1916 d: William D. Taylor. lps: Dustin Farnum, Winifred Kingston, Herbert Standing. 5r USA. prod/rel: Pallas Pictures, Paramount Pictures Corp.
Where the Trail Divides, New York 1907, Novel
  Where the Trail Divides 1914 d: James Neill. lps: Robert Edeson, Winifred Kingston, Theodore Roberts. 5r USA. prod/rel: Jesse L. Lasky Feature Play Co.©, Paramount Pictures Corp.

LILLO, GEORGE (1693–1739), UKN
George Barnwell, London 1731, Play
  George Barnwell the London Apprentice 1913 d: Hay Plumb. lps: Alec Worcester, Flora Morris. 2500f UKN. *In the Toils of the Temptress* (USA) prod/rel: Hepworth

LIN HAIYIN
Cheng Nan Jiu Shi, Novel
  Cheng Nan Jiu Shi 1982 d: Wu Yi-Gong. lps: Shen Ji, Zheng Zhenyao, Hong Rong. 88M CHN. *My Memories of Old Beijing*; *Chengnan Jiushi* prod/rel: Shanghai Film Studio

LIN QINNAN
Jiaotou Lan'e, Novel
  Chezhong Dao 1920 d: Ren Pengnian. lps: Ding Yuanyi, Bao Guirong, Zhang Shengwu. 6000f CHN. *Robbery En Route*; *The Thief in the Car* prod/rel: Commercial Press Motion Picture Section

LINARES, MARIA-LUISA
L' Autre Femme, Novel
  Autre Femme, L' 1963 d: Francois Villiers. lps: Annie Girardot, Francisco Rabal, Richard Johnson. 85M FRN/ITL/SPN. *La Otra Mujer* (SPN); *Quelle Terrible Notte* (ITL) prod/rel: Films Caravelle, Orsay Films

C'est la Faute d'Adam, Novel
  C'est la Faute d'Adam 1957 d: Jacqueline Audry. lps: Dany Robin, Jacques Sernas, Gaby SylviA. 96M FRN. *It's All Adam's Fault*; *It's Adam's Fault* prod/rel: Sonofilms, Socipex
Chaque Jour a Son Secret, Novel
  Chaque Jour a Son Secret 1958 d: Claude Boissol. lps: Daniele Delorme, Jean Marais, Francoise Fabian. 83M FRN. prod/rel: Socipex, Gray Films
Un Mari a Prix Fixe, Novel
  Mari a Prix Fixe, Un 1965 d: Claude de Givray. lps: Anna Karina, Roger Hanin, Gabrielle Dorziat. 80M FRN. prod/rel: Progefi, Lux

LINARES RIVAS, MANUEL
La Mala Ley, Play
  Mala Ley, La 1924 d: Manuel NoriegA. lps: Hortensia Gelabert, Emilio Thuiller, Fernando Diaz de MendozA. SPN. prod/rel: Ediciones Maricampo (Madrid)

LINCKE, PAUL
Frau Luna, Opera
  Frau Luna 1941 d: Theo Lingen. lps: Lizzi Waldmuller, Fita Benkhoff, Irene von Meyendorff. 96M GRM. prod/rel: Majestic, Kristall

LINCOLN, JOSEPH C., Lincoln, Joseph Crosby
Cap'n Eri; a Story of the Coast, New York 1904, Novel
  Captain Eri 1915 d: George A. Lessey. lps: George Bunny, Martha Knapp, William Mandeville. 5r USA. *Cap'n Eri* prod/rel: Eastern Film Corp.
Cy Whittaker's Place, New York 1908, Novel
  Cy Whittaker's Ward 1917 d: Ben Turbett. lps: Shirley Mason, William Wadsworth, William Burton. 4599f USA. prod/rel: Thomas A. Edison, Inc.©, Perfection Pictures
Doctor Nye of North Ostable, New York 1923, Novel
  Idle Tongues 1924 d: Lambert Hillyer. lps: Percy Marmont, Doris Kenyon, Claude Gillingwater. 5447f USA. *Doctor Nye* prod/rel: Thomas H. Ince Corp., First National Pictures
Mary-'Gusta, New York 1916, Novel
  Petticoat Pilot, A 1918 d: Rollin S. Sturgeon. lps: Vivian Martin, Theodore Roberts, James Neill. 4575f USA. *Mary 'Gusta* prod/rel: Famous Players-Lasky Corp., Pallas Pictures
Partners of the Tide, New York 1905, Novel
  Partners of the Tide 1915 d: George A. Lessey. SHT USA. prod/rel: Eastern Film Corp.
  Partners of the Tide 1921 d: L. V. Jefferson. lps: Jack Perrin, Marion Faducha, Gordon Mullen. 6500f USA. prod/rel: Irvin V. Willat Productions, W. W. Hodkinson Corp.
The Postmaster, Novel
  Tea and Toast 1913 d: C. Jay Williams, Charles H. France. lps: William Wadsworth, Alice Washburn, Gertrude McCoy. 600f USA. prod/rel: Edison
The Rise of Roscoe Paine, New York 1912, Novel
  No Trespassing 1922 d: Edwin L. Hollywood. lps: Irene Castle, Howard Truesdell, Emily Fitzroy. 6900f USA. *The Rise of Roscoe Payne* prod/rel: Holtre Productions, W. W. Hodkinson Corp.
Rugged Water, London 1924, Novel
  Rugged Water 1925 d: Irvin V. Willat. lps: Lois Wilson, Wallace Beery, Warner Baxter. 6015f USA. prod/rel: Famous Players-Lasky, Paramount Pictures

LINCOLN, NATALIE SUMNER
The Man Inside, New York 1914, Novel
  Man Inside, The 1916 d: John G. Adolfi. lps: Edwin Stevens, Tina Marshall, Charles Burbridge. 5r USA. prod/rel: Universal Film Mfg. Co.©, Broadway Universal Feature

LINCOLN, VICTORIA (1904–1981), USA, Lincoln, Victoria Endicott
February Hill, New York 1934, Novel
  Primrose Path 1940 d: Gregory La CavA. lps: Ginger Rogers, Joel McCrea, Marjorie Rambeau. 93M USA. prod/rel: RKO Radio Pictures©, Gregory la Cava Production

LINDAU, CARL
Schutzenliesel, Opera
  Schutzenliesel 1954 d: Rudolf Schundler. lps: Herta Staal, Helmuth Schneider, Susi Nicoletti. 100M GRM. *Sure-Shot Liesel* prod/rel: Central-Europa, Prisma

LINDAU, PAUL
Der Andere, 1893, Play
  Andere, Der 1913 d: Max Mack. lps: Albert Bassermann, Emerich Hanus, Rely Ridon. 1766m GRM. *The Other* prod/rel: Vitascope
  Andere, Der 1930 d: Robert Wiene. lps: Fritz Kortner, Kathe von Nagy, Heinrich George. 104M GRM. *The Man Within* (USA); *The Other*; *Dr. Hallers* prod/rel: Terra-Film

Caso Haller, Il 1933 d: Alessandro Blasetti. lps: Marta Abba, Memo Benassi, Camillo Pilotto. 76M ITL. *Il Caso Del Giudice Haller*; *Il Giudice Haller* prod/rel: Cines, Anonima Pittaluga
  Procureur Hallers, Le 1930 d: Robert Wiene. lps: Colette Darfeuil, Suzanne Delmas, Jean Max. F FRN. prod/rel: Films Albatros

LINDBERGH, CHARLES A. (1902–1974), USA, Lindbergh, Charles Augustus
The Spirit of St. Louis, 1953, Book
  Spirit of St. Louis, The 1957 d: Billy Wilder. lps: James Stewart, Murray Hamilton, Patricia Smith. 135M USA. prod/rel: Warner Bros., Leland Hayward Prods.

LINDEN, CHRISTA
Die Starkere, Novel
  Starkere, Die 1953 d: Wolfgang Liebeneiner. lps: Gertrud Kuckelmann, Hans Sohnker, Antje Weisgerber. 90M GRM. *The Stronger Party* prod/rel: Capitol, Prisma

LINDER, MARK
The Squealer, New York 1928, Play
  Squealer, The 1930 d: Harry J. Brown. lps: Jack Holt, Dorothy Revier, Davey Lee. 67M USA. prod/rel: Columbia Pictures

LINDGREN, ASTRID (1907–, SWD
Story
  Alla Vi Barn I Bullerbyn 1960 d: Olle Hellbom. lps: Kaj Andersson, Jan Erik Husbom, Thomas Johansson. 76M SWD. *All We Children from Bullerbyn* prod/rel: Artfilm-Production
  Alla Vi Barn I Bullerbyn 1986 d: Lasse Hallstrom. lps: Linda Bergstrom, Crispin Dickson Wendenius, Henrik Larsson. 91M SWD. *The Children of Bullerby Village* prod/rel: Svensk Filmindustri
  Luffaren Och Rasmus 1955 d: Rolf Husberg. lps: Eskil Dalenius, Ake Gronberg, Ake Sridell. 83M SWD. *Rasmus and the Tramp* prod/rel: Ab Sandrew-Bauman, Olle Nordemar
  Madicken Pa Junibacken 1979 d: Goran Graffman. lps: Jonna Liljendahl, Liv Alsterlund, Monica Nordquist. 104M SWD. *Mischievous Meg*; *Madicken*; *Du Ar Inte Klok Madicken* prod/rel: Svensk Filmindustri, Artfilm
  Mer Om Oss Barn I Bullerbyn 1988 d: Lasse Hallstrom. lps: Linda Bergstrom, Crispin Dickson Wendenius, Henrik Larsson. 89M SWD. *More About the Children of Bullerby Villlage* prod/rel: Svensk Filmindustri
  New Adventures of Pippi Longstocking, The 1988 d: Ken Annakin. lps: Tami Erin, David Seaman Jr., Cory Crow. 100M USA/SWD. prod/rel: Columbia, Svensk Filmindustri
  Rasmus Paa Luffen 1982 d: Olle Hellbom. lps: Erik Lindgren, Allan Edwall, Amy Storm. 105M SWD. prod/rel: Svensk Filmindustri
  Varldens Basta Karlsson 1974 d: Olle Hellbom. lps: Lars Soderdahl, Mats Wickstrom, Stig Ossian Ericsson. 100M SWD. prod/rel: Sf-Film
Broderna Lejonhjarta, Novel
  Broderna Lejonhjarta 1977 d: Olle Hellbom. lps: Staffan Gotestam, Lars Soderdahl, Allan Edwall. 108M SWD. *The Brothers Lionheart* prod/rel: Svensk Filmindustri
Kalle Blomkvist, Novel
  Kalle Blomkvist - Masterdetektiven Lever Farligt 1997 d: Goran Carmback. lps: Malte Forsberg, Josefin Arling, Totte Steneby. 86M SWD. *The Master Detective Lives Dangerously* prod/rel: Svensk Filmindustri
Masterdetektiven Och Rasmus, Novel
  Masterdetektiven Och Rasmus 1953 d: Rolf Husberg. lps: Eskil Dalenius, Lars-Erik Lundberg, Peter Adam. 88M SWD. *Master Detective and Rasmus* prod/rel: Art-Film
Mio, Min Mio!, Novel
  Mio, Min Mio! 1987 d: Vladimir Grammatikov. lps: Nicholas Pickard, Christian Bale, Timothy Bottoms. 99M USS/NRW. *Mio in the Land of Faraway*; *Mio Moj Mio*; *Mio My Mio!* prod/rel: Nordisk Tonefilm, Norway Film Development
Pippi Langstrump, 1945, Novel
  Pippi Langstrump 1949 d: Per Gunwall. lps: Viveca Serlachius, Benkt-Ake Benktsson, Tord Gahnmark. 82M SWD. *Pippi Long Stocking* prod/rel: Ab Sandrew
  Pippi Langstrump 1969 d: Olle Hellbom. lps: Inger Nilsson, Par Sundberg, Maria Persson. 100M SWD/GRM. *Pippi Longstocking* (USA); *Pippi Langstrumpf* prod/rel: Beta, Kb Nord Art
  Pippi Longstocking 1997 d: Clive A. Smith. ANM. 75M CND/GRM/SWD. prod/rel: Nelvana Ltd. (Canada), Tfc Trickomany Gmbh (Germany)

Ronja de Roversdochter, Novel
Ronja Rovardotter 1984 d: Tage Danielsson. lps: Hanna Zetterberg, Dan Hafstrom, Borje Ahlstedt. 124M NRW/SWD. *Ronja Roverdatter* (SWD); *The Robber's Daughter Ronja* prod/rel: Ab Svensk Filmindustri, Ab Svenska Ord

LINDNER, ROBERT MITCHELL
Destiny's Tot, New York 1955, Short Story
Pressure Point 1962 d: Hubert Cornfield. lps: Sidney Poitier, Bobby Darin, Peter Falk. 91M USA. *Point Blank* prod/rel: Larcas Productions

LINDO, FRANK
Home Sweet Home, Play
Home 1915 d: Maurice Elvey. lps: Elisabeth Risdon, Fred Groves, A. V. Bramble. 4000f UKN. prod/rel: British & Colonial, Ashley

LINDOP, AUDREY ERSKINE
I Start Counting, Novel
I Start Counting 1969 d: David Greene. lps: Jenny Agutter, Bryan Marshall, Clare Sutcliffe. 105M UKN. prod/rel: United Artists, Triumvirate
I Thank a Fool, London 1958, Novel
I Thank a Fool 1962 d: Robert Stevens. lps: Susan Hayward, Peter Finch, Diane Cilento. 100M UKN/USA. prod/rel: Eaton Productions, MGM British
The Singer Not the Song, London 1953, Novel
Singer Not the Song, The 1961 d: Roy Ward Baker. lps: Dirk Bogarde, John Mills, Mylene Demongeot. 132M UKN. prod/rel: Rank Organisation, Rank Film Distributors
The Tall Headlines, Novel
Tall Headlines, The 1952 d: Terence Young. lps: Mai Zetterling, Michael Denison, Flora Robson. 100M UKN. *The Frightened Bride* prod/rel: Grand National, Raymond Stross

LINDSAY, HOWARD (1889–1968), USA
Call Me Madam, New York 1950, Musical Play
Call Me Madam 1953 d: Walter Lang. lps: Ethel Merman, Donald O'Connor, Vera-Ellen. 117M USA. prod/rel: 20th Century-Fox
Life With Father, Play
Life With Father 1947 d: Michael Curtiz. lps: Irene Dunne, William Powell, Elizabeth Taylor. 118M USA. prod/rel: Warner Bros.
Oh Promise Me, New York 1930, Play
Love, Honor and Oh, Baby! 1933 d: Edward Buzzell. lps: Slim Summerville, Zasu Pitts, George Barbier. 63M USA. prod/rel: Universal Pictures Corp.©
Remains to Be Seen, New York 1951, Play
Remains to Be Seen 1953 d: Don Weis. lps: June Allyson, Van Johnson, Louis Calhern. 89M USA. prod/rel: MGM
A Slight Case of Murder, New York 1935, Play
Slight Case of Murder, A 1938 d: Lloyd Bacon. lps: Edward G. Robinson, Jane Bryan, Allen Jenkins. 85M USA. prod/rel: Warner Bros. Pictures©, First National Picture
Stop, You're Killing Me 1952 d: Roy Del Ruth. lps: Broderick Crawford, Claire Trevor, Virginia Gibson. 86M USA. prod/rel: Warner Bros.
State of the Union, New York 1945, Play
State of the Union 1948 d: Frank CaprA. lps: Spencer Tracy, Katharine Hepburn, Angela Lansbury. 124M USA. *The World and His Wife* (UKN) prod/rel: MGM
Tall Story, New York 1959, Play
Tall Story 1960 d: Joshua Logan. lps: Anthony Perkins, Jane Fonda, Ray Walston. 91M USA. prod/rel: Warner Bros.
Tommy, New York 1928, Play
She's My Weakness 1930 d: Melville Brown. lps: Arthur Lake, Sue Carol, Lucien Littlefield. 73M USA. prod/rel: RKO Productions
Your Uncle Dudley, New York 1929, Play
Too Busy to Work 1939 d: Otto Brower. lps: Jed Prouty, Spring Byington, Kenneth Howell. 64M USA. *The Little Theater* prod/rel: Twentieth Century-Fox Film Corp.©
Your Uncle Dudley 1935 d: Eugene J. Forde. lps: Edward Everett Horton, Lois Wilson, John McGuire. 70M USA. prod/rel: Twentieth Century-Fox Film Corp.©

LINDSAY, JACK
All on the Never-Never, Novel
Live Now - Pay Later 1962 d: Jay Lewis. lps: Ian Hendry, June Ritchie, John Gregson. 104M UKN. prod/rel: Regal Films International, Woodlands

LINDSAY, JOAN
Picnic at Hanging Rock, 1967, Novel
Picnic at Hanging Rock 1975 d: Peter Weir. lps: Rachel Roberts, Dominic Guard, Helen Morse. 110M ASL. prod/rel: Picnic Productions, Australia Film Corporation

LINDSAY, NORMAN (1879–1969), ASL, Lindsay, Alfred William Norman
Age of Consent, New York 1938, Novel
Age of Consent 1969 d: Michael Powell. lps: James Mason, Helen Mirren, Jack MacGowran. 98M ASL. prod/rel: Nautilus Productions
The Cautious Amorist, Novel
Our Girl Friday 1953 d: Noel Langley. lps: Joan Collins, George Cole, Kenneth More. 87M UKN. *Adventures of Sadie* (USA) prod/rel: Renown

LINDSEY, BENJAMIN B.
The Companionate Marriage, New York 1927, Novel
Companionate Marriage, The 1928 d: Erle C. Kenton. lps: Betty Bronson, Alec B. Francis, William Welsh. 6132f USA. *The Jazz Bride* (UKN) prod/rel: C. M. Corp., First National Pictures

LINDSEY, BENJAMIN B.
The Koudenhoffen Case, New York 1925, Book
One Mile from Heaven 1937 d: Allan Dwan. lps: Claire Trevor, Sally Blane, Douglas Fowley. 68M USA. prod/rel: Twentieth Century-Fox Film Corp.©

LINDSEY, ROBERT
The Falcon and the Snowman, Book
Falcon and the Snowman, The 1984 d: John Schlesinger. lps: Timothy Hutton, Sean Penn, David Suchet. 131M USA. prod/rel: Orion, Hemdale

LINFORD, DEE
The Bull of the West, Novel
Bull of the West, The 1971 d: Paul Stanley, Jerry Hopper. lps: Charles Bronson, Lee J. Cobb, George Kennedy. MTV. 100M USA. prod/rel: Universal
Man Without a Star, New York 1952, Novel
Man Called Gannon, A 1969 d: James Goldstone. lps: Anthony Franciosa, Judi West, Michael Sarrazin. 105M USA. prod/rel: Universal Pictures
Man Without a Star 1955 d: King Vidor. lps: Kirk Douglas, Jeanne Crain, Claire Trevor. 89M USA. prod/rel: Universal-International

LINGEN, THEO
Johann, Play
Johann 1943 d: R. A. Stemmle. lps: Theo Lingen, Fita Benkhoff, Irene von Meyendorff. 74M GRM. prod/rel: Bavaria, Bejohr

LINK, WILLIAM
Prescription: Murder, Play
Prescription: Murder 1967 d: Richard Irving. lps: Peter Falk, Gene Barry, Katherine Justice. TVM. 100M USA. prod/rel: Universal
That Certain Summer, Play
That Certain Summer 1972 d: Lamont Johnson. lps: Hal Holbrook, Martin Sheen, Joe Don Baker. TVM. 73M USA. prod/rel: Universal

LINKE, JOHANNES
Der Ewige Quell, Novel
Ewige Quell, Der 1939 d: Fritz Kirchhoff. lps: Eugen Klopfer, Bernhard Minetti, Lina Carstens. 85M GRM. prod/rel: Bavaria

LINKLATER, ERIC (1899–1974), UKN
Laxdale Hall, 1951, Novel
Laxdale Hall 1952 d: John Eldridge. lps: Ronald Squire, Kathleen Ryan, Raymond Huntley. 77M UKN. *Scotch on the Rocks* (USA) prod/rel: Group Three, Associated British Film Distributors
Poet's Pub, 1929, Novel
Poet's Pub 1949 d: Frederick Wilson. lps: Derek Bond, Rona Anderson, James Robertson Justice. 79M UKN. prod/rel: General Film Distributors, Aquila Films
Private Angelo, 1946, Novel
Private Angelo 1949 d: Peter Ustinov, Michael Anderson. lps: Godfrey Tearle, Maria Denis, Peter Ustinov. 106M UKN. prod/rel: Pilgrim Pictures, Associated British-Pathe

LINNA, VAINO
Musta Rakkaus, 1948, Novel
Musta Rakkaus 1957 d: Edvin Laine. lps: Eeva-Kaarina Volanen, Jussi Jurkka, Edvin Laine. 101M FNL. *Black Love*; *Mork Karlek* prod/rel: Suomen Filmiteollisuus
Taalla Pohjantahden Alla, 1962, Novel
Akseli Ja Elina Pohjantahden 1970 d: Edvin Laine. lps: Aarno Sulkanen, Ulla Eklund, Anja PohjolA. F FNL. *Akseli and Elina Under the North Sea*; *Akseli Ja Elina*; *Akseli and Elina*
Taalla Pohjantahden Alla 1968 d: Edvin Laine. lps: Aarno Sulkanen, Risto Taulo, Titta Karakorpi. 186M FNL. *Here Beneath the North Star*; *Here Under the North Star*
Tuntematon Sotilas, 1954, Novel
Tuntematon Sotilas 1955 d: Edvin Laine. lps: Kosti Klemlae, Jussi Jurkka, Matti Ranin. 132M FNL. *The Unknown Soldier* prod/rel: Oy Suomen Filmiteollisus
Tuntematon Sotilas 1985 d: Rauni Mollberg. lps: Paavo Liski, Risto Tuorila, Pirkka-Pekka Petelius. 195M FNL. *The Unknown Soldier*

LINNANKOSKI, JOHANNES
Maitotytto Hilja, 1913, Short Story
Hilja, Maitotytto 1953 d: Toivo SarkkA. lps: Ann Savo, Tauno Palo, Saulo HaarlA. 87M FNL. *Hilja the Milkmaid*
Laulu Tulipunaisesta Kukasta, 1905, Novel
Laulu Tulipunaisesta Kukasta 1938 d: Teuvo Tulio. lps: Kille Oksanen, Rakel Linnanheimo, Mirjami Kuosmanen. 110M FNL. *The Song of the Scarlet Flower*; *Sangen Om Den Eldroda Blomman*; *The Song of the Blood-Red Flower* prod/rel: Teuvo Tulio
Laulu Tulipunaisesta Kukasta 1971 d: Mikko Niskanen. lps: Pertti Melasniemi, Marjukka Arasola, Aune Hurme-Virtanen. 99M FNL. *The Song of the Scarlet Flower*; *Song of the Blood-Red Flower*; *Sangen Om Den Eldroda Blomman* prod/rel: Ac-Tuotanto
Sangen Om Den Eldroda Blomman 1918 d: Mauritz Stiller. lps: Lars Hanson, Axel Hultman, Louise Fahlman. 2704m SWD. *Song of the Scarlet Flower*; *The Flame of Life*; *Across the Rapids* prod/rel: Ab Svenska Biografteatern
Sangen Om Den Eldroda Blomman 1934 d: Per-Axel Branner. lps: Edvin Adolphson, Inga Tidblad, Birgit Tengroth. 96M SWD. *Song of the Scarlet Flower* prod/rel: Ab Wive, Warner Bros-First National Film Ab
Sangen Om Den Eldroda Blomman 1956 d: Gustaf Molander. lps: Ulla Jacobsson, Jarl Kulle, Anita Bjork. 104M SWD. *The Song of the Scarlet Flower* prod/rel: Ab Svensk Filmindustri

LINQUIST, DONALD
Berlin Tunnel 21, Novel
Berlin Tunnel 21 1981 d: Richard Michaels. lps: Richard Thomas, Horst Buchholz, Jose Ferrer. TVM. 150M USA. prod/rel: CBS, Filmways

LINTON, HARRY B.
My Wife's Family, London 1931, Play
My Wife's Family 1931 d: Monty Banks. lps: Gene Gerrard, Muriel Angelus, Jimmy Godden. 80M UKN. prod/rel: British International Pictures, Wardour
My Wife's Family 1941 d: Walter C. Mycroft. lps: Charles Clapham, John Warwick, Patricia Roc. 82M UKN. prod/rel: Associated British Picture Corporation, Pathe
My Wife's Family 1956 d: Gilbert Gunn. lps: Ronald Shiner, Ted Ray, Greta Gynt. 76M UKN. prod/rel: Forth Films, Ab-Pathe

LINTZ, GERTRUDE DAVIES
Animals are My Hobby, Book
Buddy 1997 d: Caroline Thompson. lps: Rene Russo, Robbie Coltrane, Alan Cumming. 84M USA. prod/rel: Jim Henson Pictures, American Zoetrope

LION, LEON M.
The Chinese Puzzle, London 1918, Play
Chinese Puzzle, The 1919 d: Fred Goodwins. lps: Leon M. Lion, Lilian Braithwaite, Milton Rosmer. 5000f UKN. prod/rel: Ideal
Chinese Puzzle, The 1932 d: Guy Newall. lps: Leon M. Lion, Lilian Braithwaite, Elizabeth Allan. 81M UKN. prod/rel: Twickenham, Woolf & Freedman
The Cobweb, Play
Cobweb, The 1917 d: Cecil M. Hepworth. lps: Henry Edwards, Alma Taylor, Stewart Rome. 5700f UKN. prod/rel: Hepworth, Harma
Strangling Threads 1923 d: Cecil M. Hepworth. lps: Alma Taylor, Campbell Gullan, James Carew. 6648f UKN. prod/rel: Hepworth, Ideal
Dicky Monteith, Play
Dicky Monteith 1922 d: Kenelm Foss. lps: Stewart Rome, Joan Morgan, Jack Minster. 5000f UKN. prod/rel: Astra Films
Felix Gets a Month, Play
As He Was Born 1919 d: Wilfred Noy. lps: Stanley Logan, Odette Goimbault, Mary Dibley. 4865f UKN. prod/rel: Butcher's Film Service
Naked Man, The 1923 d: Henry Edwards. lps: Henry Edwards, Chrissie White, James Carew. 6125f UKN. prod/rel: Hepworth, Ideal
Spinner O' Dreams, Play
Spinner O' Dreams 1918 d: Wilfred Noy. lps: Basil Gill, Odette Goimbault, James Carew. 5340f UKN. prod/rel: Butcher's Film Service

LIPA, VACLAV
Nepocestna Zena, Novel
Nepocestna Zena 1930 d: Oldrich Kminek. lps: Josef Rovensky, Anita Janova, Karel Tresnak. 1961m CZC. *The Dishonorable Woman* prod/rel: Oldrich Kminek, Primusfilm

LIPMAN, WILLIAM
Yonder Grow the Daisies, New York 1929, Novel
  Double Cross Roads 1930 d: Alfred L. Werker. lps: Robert Ames, Lila Lee, Edythe Chapman. 5800f USA. prod/rel: Fox Film Corp.

LIPPINCOTT, DAVID
The Voice of Armageddon, Novel
  Armaguedon 1977 d: Alain JessuA. lps: Alain Delon, Jean Yanne, Renato Salvatori. 95M FRN/ITL. *Quel Giorno Il Mondo Tremera* (ITL); *Armageddon* (USA) prod/rel: Filmes, Lira Films

LIPPINCOTT, NORMAN
Murder at Glen Athol, Garden City, N.Y. 1935, Novel
  Murder at Glen Athol 1936 d: Frank Strayer. lps: Iris Adrian, Irene Ware, John Miljan. 68M USA. *The Criminal Within* (UKN) prod/rel: Invincible Pictures Corp.©, Chesterfield Motion Pictures Corp.

LIPPL, ALOIS JOHANNES
Der Engel Mit Dem Saitenspiel, Novel
  Engel Mit Dem Saitenspiel, Der 1944 d: Heinz Ruhmann. lps: Hertha Feiler, Hans Sohnker, Hans Nielsen. 101M GRM. prod/rel: Terra, Bejohr
Die Pfingstorgel, Play
  Pfingstorgel, Die 1938 d: Franz Seitz. lps: Maria Andergast, Gustav Waldau, Hilde Sessak. 87M GRM. prod/rel: Diana, Donau

LIPPMAN, JULIE MATHILDE
Burkeses Amy, New York 1915, Novel
  Hoodlum, The 1919 d: Sidney A. Franklin. lps: Mary Pickford, Kenneth Harlan, Ralph Lewis. 6462f USA. *The Ragamuffin* (UKN) prod/rel: Mary Pickford Co.©, First National Exhibitors Circuit©

LIPPOLD, EVA
Books
  Verlobte, Die 1980 d: Gunther Rucker, Gunter Reisch. lps: Jutta Wachowiak, Regimantas Adomaitis, Slavka BudinovA. 105M GDR. *The Fiancee* (USA) prod/rel: Defa, Fernsehen Der Ddr

LIPPSCHUTZ, ARTHUR
Der Doppelmensch, Play
  Himmel Auf Erden, Der 1927 d: Alfred Schirokauer. lps: Reinhold Schunzel, Charlotte Ander, Adele Sandrock. 2676m GRM. prod/rel: Reinhold Schunzel Film-Prod.

LIPSCHUTZ
Gretchen, Play
  Sechs Madchen Suchen Nacht Quartier 1928 d: Hans Behrendt. lps: Jenny Jugo, Truus Van Aalten, Ellen Muller. 2663m GRM. prod/rel: Felsom-Film, Defa

LIPSCOMB, W. P.
Clive of India, London 1934, Play
  Clive of India 1935 d: Richard Boleslawski. lps: Ronald Colman, Loretta Young, Colin Clive. 93M USA. prod/rel: 20th Century Pictures, Inc., United Artists
The Safe, Play
  Safe, The 1932. lps: Angela Baddeley, Michael Hogan. 20M UKN. prod/rel: Sound City, MGM

LIPSKY, ELEAZAR
Short Story
  Ready for the People 1964 d: Buzz Kulik. lps: Simon Oakland, Everett Sloane, Anne Helm. 54M USA. prod/rel: Warner Bros. Pictures
Kiss of Death, Novel
  Fiend Who Walked the West, The 1958 d: Gordon Douglas. lps: Hugh O'Brian, Robert Evans, Dolores Michaels. 103M USA. *The Hell Bent Kid* prod/rel: 20th Century-Fox
  Kiss of Death 1947 d: Henry Hathaway. lps: Victor Mature, Brian Donlevy, Coleen Gray. 98M USA. prod/rel: 20th Century-Fox
The People Against O'Hara, 1950, Novel
  People Against O'Hara, The 1951 d: John Sturges. lps: Spencer Tracy, Pat O'Brien, Diana Lynn. 102M USA. prod/rel: MGM

LISHMAN, BILL
Mother Goose, Autobiography
  Fly Away Home 1996 d: Carroll Ballard. lps: Jeff Daniels, Anna Paquin, Dana Delany. 107M USA. prod/rel: Columbia Pictures Industries, Sandollar Production

LISLE, DAVID
The Impossible Mrs. Bellew, New York 1916, Novel
  Impossible Mrs. Bellew, The 1922 d: Sam Wood. lps: Gloria Swanson, Robert Cain, Conrad Nagel. 7155f USA. prod/rel: Famous Players-Lasky, Paramount Pictures

LISPECTOR, CLARICE (1925–1977), UKR
O Corpo, 1974, Short Story
  Corpo, O 1989 d: Jose Antonio GarciA. lps: Antonio Fagundes, Marieta Severo, Claudia Jimenez. 78M BRZ. *The Body* prod/rel: Embrafilme, Olympus

A Hora Da Estrela, 1977, Novel
  Hora Da Estrela, A 1985 d: Suzana Amaral. lps: Marcelia Cartaxo, Jose Dumont, Tamara Taxman. 96M BRZ. *The Hour of the Star* prod/rel: Raiz Producoes Cinematograficas
Perto Do Coracao Selvagem, 1943, Novel
  Perto Do Coracao Selvagem 1966 d: Mauricio Rittner. BRZ.

LIST, JULIE AUTUMN
The Day the Loving Stopped, Book
  Day the Loving Stopped, The 1981 d: Daniel Mann. lps: Dennis Weaver, Valerie Harper, Dominique Dunne. TVM. 104M USA. prod/rel: ABC, Paul Monash

LIST, SHELLEY
Nobody Makes Me Cry, Novel
  Between Friends 1983 d: Lou Antonio. lps: Elizabeth Taylor, Carol Burnett, Barbara Bush. TVM. 100M USA/CND. *Nobody Makes Me Cry* (CND); *Intimate Strangers* prod/rel: Hbo, Robert Cooper Film III Inc. (Toronto)

LITTELL, ROBERT (1939–, USA
The Amateur, Novel
  Amateur, The 1982 d: Charles Jarrott. lps: John Savage, Christopher Plummer, Marthe Keller. 112M CND. *L' Homme de Prague* prod/rel: Balkan Film Productions Ltd., Tiberius Film Corp.

LITTLETON, SCOTT
Inside Story, Story
  Night Editor 1946 d: Henry Levin. lps: William Gargan, Janis Carter, Jeff Donnell. 68M USA. *The Trespasser* (UKN) prod/rel: Columbia

LITTLEWOOD, JOAN
Oh! What a Lovely War, 1965, Play
  Oh! What a Lovely War 1969 d: Richard Attenborough. lps: Dirk Bogarde, Phyllis Calvert, Jean-Pierre Cassel. 144M UKN. *War and Peace Season* prod/rel: Accord Films, Paramount

LITVAK, ANATOLE
Le Tueur, Story
  Meet Me at Dawn 1947 d: Thornton Freeland. lps: William Eythe, Hazel Court, Margaret Rutherford. 99M UKN. *The Gay Duellist* (USA) prod/rel: Excelsior, 20th Century-Fox

LITVINOVA, RENATA
To Possess and to Belong, Novel
  Strana Gluchich 1998 d: Valeri Todorovsky. lps: Chulpan Khamatova, Dina Korzun, Maxim Sukhanov. 119M RSS. *The Land of the Deaf* prod/rel: Gorky Filmstudio, Studio Grashdane-Racoon Film

LIU BAIYU
Six a.M., Novel
  He Ping Bao Wei Zhe 1950 d: Shi Lan. lps: Ge Zhenbang, Liu Jia, Wang Shui. 6r CHN. *Guardian of Peace* prod/rel: Beijing Film Studio

LIU CANGLANG
Hong Qi Ge, Novel
  Hong Qi Ge 1950 d: Wu Zuguang. lps: Lu En, Yue Shen, Zhang Wei. 10r CHN. *Song of the Red Flag* prod/rel: Northeast Film Studio

LIU DAWEI
The Best News, Story
  Shui Ku Shang de Ge Sheng 1958 d: Yu Yanfu. lps: Pu Ke, Zhang Guilan, Li Yalin. 7r CHN. *Song Over the Reservoir* prod/rel: Changchun Film Studio

LIU LIU
Brave Hero, Novel
  Lie Huo Jin Gang 1991 d: He Qun, Jiang Hao. lps: Shen Junyi, Li Qiang, Zhao XIaorui. 18r CHN. *Steel Meets Fire* prod/rel: Pearl River Film Studio, Nanyang Art and Culture Co. of Hainan
Marvelous Hero, Novel
  Lie Huo Jin Gang 1991 d: He Qun, Jiang Hao. lps: Shen Junyi, Li Qiang, Zhao XIaorui. 18r CHN. *Steel Meets Fire* prod/rel: Pearl River Film Studio, Nanyang Art and Culture Co. of Hainan

LIU PENGDE
The Bridge, Novel
  Liang Jia Ren 1963 d: Yuan Naicheng. lps: Fang Hua, Wang Jianhua, Chen Xuejie. 8r CHN. *Two Families* prod/rel: Changchun Film Studio

LIU SHAOTANG
Gua Peng Nu Jie, Novel
  Gua Peng Nu Jie 1985 d: Wang Yi. lps: Lin Quan, Zhang Jiumei, Xu Dongfang. 10r CHN. *Woman Melon Garden Guard* prod/rel: Pearl River Film Studio

LIU XINGLONG
Feng Huang Qing, Novel
  Feng Huang Qing 1993 d: He Qun. lps: Li Baotian, Wang Xueqin, Ju Xue. 9r CHN. *Country Teachers* prod/rel: Tianjin Film Studio, XIaoxiang Film Studio

LIU ZHEN
Sister Chun, Novel
  Mama Yao Wo Chu Jia 1956 d: Huang Shu. lps: Bo Ruitong, Jiangyan, Liu Shilong. 8r CHN. *Mother Wants Me to Marry* prod/rel: Changchun Film Studio
Xiao Huo Ban, Novel
  Xiao Huo Ban 1956 d: Ge XIn. lps: Cai Yuanyuan, Zhao Yurong, Guo Yuntai. 8r CHN. *Little Playmates* prod/rel: Shanghai Film Studio

LIU ZHIXIA
Fei Hu Dui, Novel
  Fei Hu Dui 1995 d: Wang Jixing. lps: Liu Wei, Li Xuejian, Li Qiang. F CHN. *Flying Tiger Brigade* prod/rel: Emei Film Studio
Tie Dao You Ji Dui, Novel
  Tie Dao You Ji Dui 1956 d: Zhao Ming. lps: Cao Huiqu, Qin Yi, Feng Ji. 9r CHN. *Guerrillas on the Railway* prod/rel: Shanghai Film Studio

LIU ZONGDAI
Jing Hun Tao Hua Dang, Novel
  Jing Hun Tao Hua Dang 1994 d: Zeng Jianfeng. lps: Wang Luyao, Wen Haitao, Yang Chiyu. 9r CHN. *Peach Blossom Party* prod/rel: XIaoxiang Film Studio

LIVINGS, HENRY
Eh?, London 1964, Play
  Work Is a Four Letter Word 1967 d: Peter Hall. lps: David Warner, Cilla Black, Elizabeth Spriggs. 93M UKN. prod/rel: Cavalcade Films, Universal Pictures, Ltd.

LIVINGSTON, FLORENCE BINGHAM
The Custard Cup, New York 1921, Novel
  Custard Cup, The 1923 d: Herbert Brenon. lps: Mary Carr, Myrta Bonillas, Miriam BattistA. 6166f USA. prod/rel: Fox Film Corp.

LIVINGSTON, HAZEL
Rosemary, 1926, Novel
  Secret Studio, The 1927 d: Victor Schertzinger. lps: Olive Borden, Clifford Holland, Noreen Phillips. 5870f USA. prod/rel: Fox Film Corp.

LIVINGSTON, MAE
Thanks God - I'll Take It from Here, Novel
  Without Reservations 1946 d: Mervyn Leroy. lps: Claudette Colbert, John Wayne, Don Defore. 107M USA. prod/rel: RKO Radio

LIVINGSTONE, FRANCES
The Vavasour Ball, Story
  Vavasour Ball, The 1914 d: Van Dyke Brooke. lps: Van Dyke Brooke, Leo Delaney, Norma Talmadge. 2000f USA. prod/rel: Vitagraph Co. of America

LJUNGQUIST, WALTER
Nycklar Till Okant Rum, 1950, Novel
  Vita Katten, Den 1950 d: Hasse Ekman. lps: Alf Kjellin, Eva Henning, Sture Lagerwall. 92M SWD. *The White Cat* prod/rel: Hasse Ekmanfilm, Ab Sandrew-Ateljeerna
Ombye Av Tag, 1933, Novel
  Ombye Av Tag 1943 d: Hasse Ekman. lps: Sonja Wigert, Hasse Ekman, Georg Rydeberg. 92M SWD. *Unexpected Meeting*; *Changing Trains* prod/rel: Terrafilms Produktions Ab
Vandring Med Manen, 1941, Novel
  Vandring Med Manen 1945 d: Hasse Ekman. lps: Eva Henning, Alf Kjellin, Stig Jarrel. 105M SWD. *Wandering With the Moon* prod/rel: Ab Svensk Filmindustri

LLEWELLYN, FEWLASS (1886–1941), UKN
The Coal King, Play
  Coal King, The 1915 d: Percy Nash. lps: Douglas Cox, May Lynn, Frank Tennant. 3600f UKN. prod/rel: Neptune, Kinematograph Trading Co.

LLEWELLYN, RICHARD (1906–1983), UKN, Lloyd, Richard David Vivian Llewellyn
How Green Was My Valley, 1939, Novel
  How Green Was My Valley 1941 d: John Ford. lps: Walter Pidgeon, Maureen O'Hara, Donald Crisp. 118M USA. prod/rel: 20th Century-Fox
  How Green Was My Valley 1976 d: Ronald Wilson. lps: Stanley Baker, Sian Phillips, Nerys Hughes. MTV. 300M USA.
None But the Lonely Heart, 1943, Novel
  None But the Lonely Heart 1944 d: Clifford Odets. lps: Cary Grant, Ethel Barrymore, Barry Fitzgerald. 113M USA. prod/rel: RKO Radio
Noose, London 1947, Play
  Noose 1948 d: Edmond T. Greville. lps: Carole Landis, Derek Farr, Joseph CalleiA. 95M UKN. *The Silk Noose* (USA) prod/rel: Pathe, Edward Dryhurst
Poison Pen, London 1937, Play
  Poison Pen 1939 d: Paul L. Stein. lps: Flora Robson, Robert Newton, Ann Todd. 79M UKN. prod/rel: Associated British Picture Corporation

LLEWELLYN-RHYS, JOHN
The World Owes Me a Living, Novel
  World Owes Me a Living, The 1945 d: Vernon Sewell. lps: David Farrar, Judy Campbell, Sonia Dresdel. 91M UKN. prod/rel: British National, Anglo-American

LLOSA, MARIO VARGAS
La Ciudad Y Los Perros, Novel
  Ciudad Y Los Perros, La 1985 d: Francisco Lombardi. lps: Pablo Serra, Gustavo Bueno, Juan Manuel OchoA. 144M PRU. *The City and the Dogs* (UKN) prod/rel: Inca Films

LLOYD, A. R.
With Father's Help, Story
  With Father's Help 1915 d: Al Christie. lps: John Francis Dillon, Billie Rhodes. SHT USA. prod/rel: Nestor

LLOYD, JOHN
The Invaders, Novel
  Invaders, The 1913 d: George Melford. lps: Paul Hurst, Jane Wolfe, Marin Sais. 2000f USA. prod/rel: Kalem
The Ripper File, Book
  Murder By Decree 1979 d: Bob Clark. lps: Christopher Plummer, James Mason, Donald Sutherland. 124M UKN/CND. *Sherlock Holmes: Murder By Decree* (USA); *Meurtre Par Decret*; *Sherlock Holmes and Saucy Jack* prod/rel: Highlight Theatrical Prod. Corp. Ltd., Ambassador Films Ltd. (Toronto)

LO SCHIAVO, G. G.
Piccola Pretura, Novel
  In Nome Della Legge 1949 d: Pietro Germi. lps: Massimo Girotti, Charles Vanel, Jone Salinas. 100M ITL. *In the Name of the Law* (UKN); *Mafia* prod/rel: Lux Film

LOBATO, MONTEIRO
O Comprador de Fazendas, 1918, Short Story
  Comprador de Fazendas, O 1951 d: Alberto Pieralisi. 89M BRZ. *The Farm Buyer*
  Comprador de Fazendas, O 1974 d: Alberto Pieralisi. 87M BRZ.
O Saci, 1921, Short Story
  Saci, O 1952 d: Rodolfo Nanni. 65M BRZ.
O Sitio Do Picapau Amarelo, 1939, Short Story
  Picapau Amarelo, O 1974 d: Geraldo Sarno. 85M BRZ.

LOCHER, OTTO
Novel
  Brot Und Steine 1979 d: Mark M. Rissi. lps: Liselotte Pulver, Henryk Rhyn, Beatrice Kessler. 99M SWT/BLG. *Bread and Stones*; *Pain Et Pierres* prod/rel: Logos-Film

LOCKE, CHARLES O.
The Hell-Bent Kid, 1957, Book
  From Hell to Texas 1958 d: Henry Hathaway. lps: Don Murray, Diane Varsi, Chill Wills. 100M USA. *Manhunt* (UKN); *The Hell-Bent Kid* prod/rel: 20th Century-Fox

LOCKE, D. R.
Hannah Jane, Poem
  Senator's Lady, The 1914. lps: Edna Maison, Bert Hadley. SHT USA. prod/rel: Powers

LOCKE, EDWARD, Locke, Edward J.
The Case of Becky, New York 1912, Play
  Case of Becky, The 1915 d: Frank Reicher. lps: Blanche Sweet, Theodore Roberts, James Neill. 5r USA. prod/rel: Jesse L. Lasky Feature Play Co.©, Paramount Pictures Corp.
  Case of Becky, The 1921 d: Chester M. Franklin. lps: Constance Binney, Glenn Hunter, Frank McCormack. 5498f USA. prod/rel: Realart Pictures, Paramount Pictures
The Climax, London 1910, Play
  Climax, The 1930 d: Renaud Hoffman. lps: Jean Hersholt, Kathryn Crawford, Leroy Mason. 65M USA. prod/rel: Universal Pictures
  Climax, The 1944 d: George Waggner. lps: Susanna Foster, Turhan Bey, Boris Karloff. 86M USA. prod/rel: Universal
The Revolt, New York 1915, Novel
  Revolt, The 1916 d: Barry O'Neil. lps: Frances Nelson, Arthur Ashley, Clara Whipple. 5r USA. prod/rel: World Film Corp.©, Peerless

LOCKE, RAYMOND FRIDAY
Streets Paved With Gold, Novel
  Rope of Flesh 1965 d: Russ Meyer. lps: Hal Hopper, Antoinette Cristiani, John Furlong. 92M USA. *Mudhoney!*; *Mud Honey*; *Rope*

LOCKE, WILLIAM J. (1863–1930), UKN, Locke, William John, Locke, W. J.
The Beloved Vagabond, London 1906, Novel
  Beloved Vagabond, The 1915 d: Edward Jose. lps: Edwin Arden, Kathryn Brown-Decker, Bliss Milford. 6r USA. prod/rel: Pathe Exchange, Inc.©

  Beloved Vagabond, The 1923 d: Fred Leroy Granville. lps: Carlyle Blackwell, Madge Stuart, Phyllis Titmuss. 10r UKN. prod/rel: Astra-National
  Beloved Vagabond, The 1936 d: Curtis Bernhardt. lps: Maurice Chevalier, Betty Stockfeld, Margaret Lockwood. 78M UKN. prod/rel: Associated British Film Distributors, Toeplitz Productions
  Vagabond Bien-Aime, Le 1936 d: Curtis Bernhardt. lps: Maurice Chevalier, Betty Stockfeld, Made Siame. 105M FRN. *Vagabond Par Amour* prod/rel: Toeplitz Productions
Derelicts, Novel
  Derelicts 1917 d: Sidney Morgan. lps: Violet Graham, Sydney Vautier, Julian Royce. 5000f UKN. prod/rel: Unity-Super, Olympic
The Fortunate Youth, New York 1914, Novel
  Fortunate Youth, The 1916 d: Joseph Smiley. lps: Wilmuth Merkyl, William Cohill, John Smiley. 5r USA. prod/rel: Ocean Film Corp., State Rights
The Glory of Clementina, New York 1911, Novel
  Glory of Clementina, The 1915 d: Ashley Miller. lps: Miriam Nesbitt, Marc MacDermott, Bigelow Cooper. 2r USA. prod/rel: R-C Pictures
  Glory of Clementina, The 1922 d: Emile Chautard. lps: Pauline Frederick, Edward Martindel, George Cowl. 5700f USA. prod/rel: R-C Pictures
Idols, London 1899, Novel
  Idols 1916 d: Webster Cullison. lps: Katherine Kaelred, Arnold Daly. USA. prod/rel: Equitable Motion Pictures Corp.©, World Film Corp.
  Oath, The 1921 d: Raoul Walsh. lps: Miriam Cooper, Robert Fischer, Conway Tearle. 7806f USA. prod/rel: Mayflower Photoplay Corp., Associated First National Pictures
Jaffery, New York 1915, Novel
  Jaffery 1916 d: George Irving. lps: C. Aubrey Smith, Eleanor Woodruff, Paul Doucet. 6r USA. prod/rel: the Frohman Amusement Corp., International Film Serive, Inc.©
The Joyous Adventures of Aristiede Pujol, Novel
  Joyous Adventures of Aristide Pujol, The 1920 d: Frank Miller. lps: Kenelm Foss, Pauline Peters, Barbara Everest. 5000f UKN. prod/rel: Foss, Phillips
The Morals of Marcus Ordeyne, London 1905, Novel
  Morals 1921 d: William D. Taylor. lps: May McAvoy, William P. Carleton, Marion Skinner. 5152f USA. *The Morals of Marcus* prod/rel: Realart Pictures, Paramount Pictures
  Morals of Marcus, The 1915 d: Edwin S. Porter, Hugh Ford. lps: Marie Doro, Eugene Ormonde, Julian L'Estrange. 5r USA. prod/rel: Famous Players Film Co., Paramount Pictures Corp.
  Morals of Marcus, The 1935 d: Miles Mander. lps: Lupe Velez, Ian Hunter, Adrianne Allen. 76M UKN. prod/rel: Real Art, Gaumont-British
The Mountebank, London 1921, Novel
  Side Show of Life, The 1924 d: Herbert Brenon. lps: Ernest Torrence, Anna Q. Nilsson, Louise Lagrange. 7511f USA. *The Sideshow of Life* prod/rel: Famous Players-Lasky, Paramount Pictures
An Old World Romance, 1909, Novel
  Song of the Soul, The 1920 d: John W. Noble. lps: Vivian Martin, Fritz Leiber, Charles Graham. 5r USA. prod/rel: Messmore Kendall©, Kendall-Chambers Corp.
The Shorn Lamb, 1930, Novel
  Strangers in Love 1932 d: Lothar Mendes. lps: Kay Francis, Fredric March, Stuart Erwin. 70M USA. *The Black Robe*; *Intimate* prod/rel: Paramount Publix Corp.©
Simon the Jester, New York 1909, Novel
  Simon the Jester 1925 d: George Melford. lps: Eugene O'Brien, Lillian Rich, Edmund Burns. 6168f USA. prod/rel: Metropolitan Pictures Corp. of Calif., Producers Distributing Corp.
  Simon, the Jester 1915 d: Edward Jose. lps: Edwin Arden, Irene Warfield, Alma Tell. 5r USA. prod/rel: Pathe Exchange, Inc., Gold Roosterplays
Stella Maris, New York 1913, Novel
  Stella Maris 1918 d: Marshall Neilan. lps: Mary Pickford, Conway Tearle, Marcia Manon. 6r USA. prod/rel: Pickford Film Corp., Famous Players-Lasky Corp.
  Stella Maris 1925 d: Charles J. Brabin. lps: Mary Philbin, Elliott Dexter, Gladys Brockwell. 5786f USA. prod/rel: Universal Pictures
The Tale of Triona, London 1912, Novel
  Fool's Awakening, A 1924 d: Harold Shaw. lps: Harrison Ford, Enid Bennett, Alec B. Francis. 5760f USA. prod/rel: Metro Pictures

The Usurper, Novel
  Usurper, The 1919 d: Duncan MacRae. lps: Gertrude McCoy, Cecil Ward, Stephen Ewart. 4782f UKN. prod/rel: British Actors, Phillips
Viviette, 1910, Novel
  Viviette 1918 d: Walter Edwards. lps: Vivian Martin, Eugene Pallette, Harrison Ford. 4374f USA. prod/rel: Famous Players-Lasky Corp.©, Paramount Pictures
Where Love Is, New York 1903, Novel
  Where Love Is 1917. lps: Ann Murdock, Henry Stanford, Shirley Mason. 5r USA. prod/rel: Thomas A. Edison, Inc., Mutual Film Corp.©
The White Dove, New York 1899, Novel
  White Dove, The 1920 d: Henry King. lps: H. B. Warner, James O. Burrows, Claire Adams. 5-6r USA. *Judge Not Thy Wife* prod/rel: Jesse D. Hampton Productions, Robertson-Cole Distributing Corp.
The Wonderful Year, Novel
  Wonderful Year, The 1921 d: Kenelm Foss. lps: Mary Odette, Lionelle Howard, Randle Ayrton. 6000f UKN. prod/rel: Astra Films

LOCKHART, CAROLINE
The Dude Wrangler, Garden City, N.Y. 1921, Novel
  Dude Wrangler, The 1930 d: Richard Thorpe. lps: Tom Keene, Lina Basquette, Francis X. Bushman. 60M USA. *Feminine Touch* (UKN) prod/rel: Sono-Art Productions
The Fighting Shepherdess, Boston 1919, Novel
  Fighting Shepherdess, The 1920 d: Edward Jose. lps: Anita Stewart, Wallace MacDonald, Noah Beery. 5r USA. prod/rel: Louis B. Mayer Productions, Anita Stewart Productions, Inc.
The Man from the Bitter Roots, New York 1915, Novel
  Man from Bitter Roots, The 1916 d: Oscar Apfel. lps: William Farnum, Betty Schade, Betty Harte. 5r USA. prod/rel: Fox Film Corp., William Fox©

LOCKHART, R. H. BRUCE (1887–1970), UKN, Lockhart, Sir Robert Hamilton
British Agent, London 1932, Novel
  British Agent 1934 d: Michael Curtiz. lps: Kay Francis, Leslie Howard, William Gargan. 81M USA. prod/rel: First National Productions Corp.

LOCKHART, ROBIN BRUCE
Ace of Spies, Book
  Reilly: Ace of Spies 1983 d: Jim Goddard. lps: Sam Neill, Leo McKern, Norman Rodway. MTV. 600M UKN. *Reilly: the Ace of Spies*

LOCKRIDGE, ROSS (1914–1948), USA
Raintree County, 1948, Novel
  Raintree County, The 1957 d: Edward Dmytryk. lps: Elizabeth Taylor, Montgomery Clift, Eva Marie Saint. 168M USA. prod/rel: MGM

LOCKWOOD, CHARLES A.
Hellcats of the Sea, 1955, Book
  Hellcats of the Navy 1957 d: Nathan Juran. lps: Ronald Reagan, Nancy Davis, Arthur Franz. 81M USA. prod/rel: Columbia, Morningside

LODER, KURT
I Tina, Autobiography
  What's Love Got to Do With It 1993 d: Brian Gibson. lps: Angela Bassett, Laurence Fishburne, Vanessa Bell Calloway. 118M USA.

LODOLI, MARCO
Snack Bar Budapest, Novel
  Snack Bar Budapest 1988 d: Tinto Brass. lps: Giancarlo Giannini, Raffaella Baracchi, Philippe Leotard. 102M ITL. prod/rel: San Francisco, Metro

LODOVICO, CESARE VICO
Ruota, Play
  Tutta la Vita in Una Notte 1939 d: Corrado d'Errico. lps: Luisa Ferida, Camillo Pilotto, Germana Paolieri. 70M ITL. prod/rel: Imperator Film, E.I.a.

LOEB, H. W.
Victoria Himmeldonnerwetter, Novel
  Kaiserin von China, Die 1953 d: Steve Sekely. lps: Grethe Weiser, Nadja Tiller, Joachim Brennecke. 85M GRM. *The Empress of China* prod/rel: C.C.C., Prisma

LOEB, LEE
Blossoms for Effie, Short Story
  Affairs of Geraldine, The 1946 d: George Blair. lps: Jane Withers, Jimmy Lydon, Raymond Walburn. 68M USA. prod/rel: Republic Pictures Corp.

LOEWE, FREDERICK
Paint Your Wagon, New York 1951, Musical Play
  Paint Your Wagon 1969 d: Joshua Logan. lps: Clint Eastwood, Lee Marvin, Jean Seberg. 166M USA. prod/rel: Alan Jay Lerner Productions, Paramount

LOFTING, HUGH (1886–1947), UKN, Lofting, Hugh
John
Short Stories
Doctor Dolittle 1967 d: Richard Fleischer. lps: Rex
Harrison, Samantha Eggar, Anthony Newley. 152M
USA. prod/rel: Apjac
Doctor Dolittle 1998 d: Betty Thomas. lps: Eddie
Murphy, Ossie Davis, Oliver Platt. 85M USA. *Dr.
Dolittle* prod/rel: 20th Century Fox©, Davis
Entertainment Co.

LOFTS, NORAH (1904–1983), UKN
Chinese Finale, London 1935, Short Story
Seven Women 1965 d: John Ford. lps: Anne Bancroft,
Sue Lyon, Margaret Leighton. 93M USA. prod/rel: John
Ford Productions, Bernard Smith Productions
Jassy, Novel
Jassy 1947 d: Bernard Knowles. lps: Margaret
Lockwood, Patricia Roc, Dennis Price. 102M UKN.
prod/rel: General Film Distributors, Gainsborough

LOGALTON, H. G.
The Fast Pace, Story
Spider Webs 1927 d: Wilfred Noy. lps: Niles Welch,
Alice Lake, J. Barney Sherry. 5900f USA. prod/rel:
Artlee Pictures

LOGAN, GWENDOLYN
East Is East, Play
East Is East 1916 d: Henry Edwards. lps: Florence
Turner, Henry Edwards, Ruth MacKay. 4895f UKN.
prod/rel: Turner Films, Butcher
Sayonara, Short Story
Tokio Siren, A 1920 d: Norman Dawn. lps: Tsuru Aoki,
Jack Livingston, Goro Kino. 5r USA. prod/rel: Universal
Film Mfg. Co.©

LOGAN, JOSHUA
Higher and Higher, Musical Play
Higher and Higher 1943 d: Tim Whelan. lps: Michele
Morgan, Jack Haley, Frank SinatrA. 90M USA. prod/rel:
RKO

LOGGAN, MICHAEL
Carre de Dames Pour un As, Novel
Carre de Dames Pour un As 1966 d: Jacques
Poitrenaud. lps: Roger Hanin, Sylva Koscina, Catherine
Allegret. 90M FRN/SPN/ITL. *Layton. Bambole E Karate*
(ITL); *Carre de Dames Pour Leyton; Demasiadas
Mujeres Para Layton* (SPN) prod/rel: Ste Francaise De
Cinematographie, Agata Films

LOGUE, CHARLES A.
The Grappler, Story
Hard Fists 1927 d: William Wyler. lps: Art Acord,
Louise Lorraine, Lee Holmes. 4387f USA. prod/rel:
Universal Pictures

LOHMEYER, WALTER GOTTFRIED
Alimente, Short Story
Alimente 1929 d: Carl Boese. lps: Anita Dorris,
Gerhard Dammann, Kurt Vespermann. 2064m GRM.
prod/rel: Eisbar-Film

LOHNER-BEDA, FRITZ
Ball Im Savoy, Play
Ball at Savoy 1936 d: Victor Hanbury. lps: Conrad
Nagel, Marta Labarr, Fred Conyngham. 74M UKN.
prod/rel: Stafford Films, Radio
Ball Im Savoy 1955 d: Paul Martin. lps: Eva-Ingeborg
Scholz, Rudolf Prack, Nadja Tiller. 90M GRM. *The Ball
at the Savoy* prod/rel: Central, Europa

LO-JOHANSSON, IVAR
Bara En Mor, 1939, Novel
Bara En Mor 1949 d: Alf Sjoberg. lps: Eva Dahlbeck,
Ragnar Falck, Ulf Palme. 99M SWD. *Only a Mother*
(USA)
Kungsgatan, 1935, Novel
Kungsgatan 1943 d: Gosta Cederlund. lps: Barbro
Kollberg, Sture Lagerwall, Marianne Lowgren. 96M
SWD. *King's Street* prod/rel: Imago

LOMAX, FAWCETT
The Wrong Woman, Play
Wrong Woman, The 1915 d: Richard Ridgely. lps:
Mabel Trunnelle, Gladys Hulette, Augustus Phillips. 3r
USA. prod/rel: Edison

LOMAX, JOHN
L' Enlevement, Story
Enlevement, L' 1912. 255m FRN. prod/rel: Pathe
Freres

LOMBARD, CARL
The Disappearance of Rory Brophy, Novel
Disappearance of Finbar, The 1996 d: Susan
Clayton. lps: Jonathan Rhys-Myers, Luke Griffin,
Fanny Risberg. 102M UKN/IRL/SWD. prod/rel: First
City Features (U.K.)©, Samson Films (Ireland)©

LONDON, ARTUR
L' Aveu; Dans l'Engrenage du Proces de Prague,
Paris 1968, Novel
Aveu, L' 1970 d: Costa-Gavras. lps: Yves Montand,
Simone Signoret, Gabriele Ferzetti. 138M FRN/ITL. *La
Confessione* (ITL); *The Confession* prod/rel: Corona,
Selenia Cin.Ca

LONDON, CHARMIAN
The Book of Jack London, Biography
Jack London 1942 d: Alfred Santell. lps: Michael
O'Shea, Susan Hayward, Osa Massen. 94M USA.
Adventures of Jack London; The Life of Jack London
prod/rel: United Artists, Samuel Bronston

LONDON, JACK (1876–1916), USA, London, John
Griffith
Story
Kit Und Co - Lockruf Des Goldes 1974 d: Konrad
Petzold. lps: Dean Reed, Rolf Hoppe, Renate Blume.
87M GDR. *Kit and Co* prod/rel: Defa
Po Zakonu 1926 d: Lev Kuleshov. lps: Vladimir Vogel,
Sergei Komarov, Alexandra KhokhlovA. 1700m USS.
*The Unexpected; By the Law; Expiation; Dura Lex; Po
Zakonoe* prod/rel: Goskino
The Abysmal Brute, New York 1913, Novel
Abysmal Brute, The 1923 d: Hobart Henley. lps:
Reginald Denny, Mabel Julienne Scott, Charles K.
French. 7373f USA. prod/rel: Universal Pictures
Conflict 1936 d: David Howard. lps: John Wayne, Jean
Rogers, Tommy Bupp. 61M USA. *The Abysmal Brute;
The Showdown* prod/rel: Universal Productions, Inc.
Adventure, London 1911, Novel
Adventure 1925 d: Victor Fleming. lps: Tom Moore,
Pauline Starke, Wallace Beery. 6602f USA. prod/rel:
Famous Players-Lasky Corp., Paramount Pictures
The Assassination Bureau Ltd, 1963, Novel
Assassination Bureau, The 1969 d: Basil Dearden.
lps: Oliver Reed, Diana Rigg, Telly Savalas. 110M UKN.
prod/rel: Heathfield Films, Paramount
Brown Wolf, 1906, Short Story
Brown Wolf 1971 d: George Kaczender. 25M CND.
Burning Daylight, New York 1910, Novel
Burning Daylight 1920 d: Edward Sloman. lps:
Mitchell Lewis, Helen Ferguson, William V. Mong. 6r
USA. prod/rel: C. E. Shurtleff, Inc., Metro Pictures
Corp.©
Burning Daylight 1928 d: Charles J. Brabin. lps:
Milton Sills, Doris Kenyon, Arthur Stone. 6500f USA.
prod/rel: First National Pictures
**Burning Daylight: the Adventures of "Burning
Daylight" in Alaska** 1914 d: Hobart Bosworth. lps:
Hobart Bosworth, Rhea Haines, Elmer Clifton. 5r USA.
prod/rel: Bosworth, Inc.©, Paramount Pictures Corp.
**Burning Daylight: the Adventures of "Burning
Daylight" in Civilization** 1914 d: Hobart Bosworth.
lps: Hobart Bosworth, Myrtle Stedman. 5r USA.
prod/rel: Bosworth, Inc.©, Paramount Pictures Corp.
Call of the Wild, New York 1903, Novel
Call of the Wild 1972 d: Ken Annakin. lps: Charlton
Heston, Michele Mercier, Raimund Harmstorf. 105M
UKN/GRM/ITL. *Il Richiamo Della Foresta* (ITL); *Ruf
Der Wildnis* (GRM); *L'Appel de la Foret* (FRN) prod/rel:
C.C.C. Filmkunst (Berlin), Massfilm (London)
Call of the Wild 1976 d: Jerry Jameson. lps: John Beck,
Bernard Fresson, John McLiam. TVM. 100M USA.
prod/rel: Charles Fries Productions, NBC
Call of the Wild, The 1908 d: D. W. Griffith. lps:
Florence Lawrence, Charles Gorman, MacK Sennett.
988f USA. prod/rel: Biograph Co.
Call of the Wild, The 1923 d: Fred Jackman. lps: Jack
Mulhall, Walter Long, Sidney d'Albrook. 6725f USA.
prod/rel: Hal Roach Studios
Call of the Wild, The 1935 d: William A. Wellman. lps:
Clark Gable, Jack Oakie, Loretta Young. 91M USA.
prod/rel: 20th Century Pictures, Inc., United Artists
Richiamo Della Foresta, Il 1992 d: Alan Smithee. lps:
Ricky Schroder, Gordon Tootoosis, Duncan Fraser.
TVM. 120M ITL/CND. *Call of the Wild*
Cry of the Black Wolves, Novel
Schrei Der Schwarzen Wolfe, Der 1972 d: Harald
Reinl. lps: Ron Ely, Raimund Harmstorf, Gila von
Weitershausen. 110M GRM. *Cry of the Black Wolves*
prod/rel: Lisa, Constantin
Demetrios Contos, 1905, Short Story
Devil's Skipper, The 1928 d: John G. Adolfi. lps: Belle
Bennett, Montagu Love, Gino Corrado. 5510f USA.
prod/rel: Tiffany-Stahl Productions
Flush of Gold, 1910, Short Story
Alaska 1944 d: George Archainbaud. lps: Kent Taylor,
Margaret Lindsay, John Carradine. 76M USA. prod/rel:
Monogram

Gold Raiders of the North, Novel
North to the Klondike 1942 d: Erle C. Kenton. lps:
Broderick Crawford, Andy Devine, Lon Chaney Jr. 58M
USA. prod/rel: Universal
The Iron Heel
Zheleznaya Pyata Oligarkhij 1998 d: Alexander
Bashirov. lps: Alexander Bashior, Rita Margo, Elena
YudanovA. 70M RSS. *The Iron Heel of the Oligarchy*
prod/rel: Deboshir Film
John Barleycorn, New York 1913, Novel
John Barleycorn 1914 d: Hobart Bosworth, J. Charles
Haydon. lps: Elmer Clifton, Matty Roubert, Viola Barry.
6r USA. prod/rel: Bosworth, Inc.©, State Rights
Just Meat, Short Story
For Love of Gold 1908 d: D. W. Griffith. lps: Harry
Salter, Charles Gorman, Charles Inslee. 548f USA.
prod/rel: Biograph Co.
Klondike Fever, Book
Jack London's Klondike Fever 1979 d: Peter Carter.
lps: Rod Steiger, Angie Dickinson, Jeff East. 118M CND.
Klondike Fever; Jack London Story prod/rel: Cfi
Investments Inc., Klondike Fever Film Productions Ltd.
Martin Eden, 1906, Novel
Adventures of Martin Eden, The 1942 d: Sidney
Salkow. lps: Glenn Ford, Claire Trevor, Evelyn Keyes.
87M USA. *Martin Eden* prod/rel: Columbia
Martin Eden 1914 d: Hobart Bosworth. lps: Hobart
Bosworth, Myrtle Stedman, Herbert Rawlinson. 6r
USA. prod/rel: Bosworth, Inc., State Rights
Martin Eden 1979 d: Giacomo Battiato. lps:
Christopher Connelly, Delia Boccardo, Capucine. TVM.
240M ITL.
The Mexican, 1913, Short Story
Fighter, The 1952 d: Herbert Kline. lps: Richard
Conte, Vanessa Brown, Lee J. Cobb. 78M USA. prod/rel:
United Artists, Gh Productions
Meksikanets 1957 d: Vladimir Kaplunovsky. lps:
Tatiana SamoilovA. 82M USS. *The Mexican* (USA)
Mexicano, El 1944 d: Agustin P. Delgado. lps: David
Silva, Lupita Gallardo, Miguel Inclan. 78M MXC.
Morganson's Finish, Short Story
Morganson's Finish 1926 d: Fred Windermere. lps:
Anita Stewart, Johnny Walker, Mahlon Hamilton.
6500f USA. prod/rel: Tiffany Productions
The Mutiny of the Elsinore, New York 1914, Novel
Mutines de l'Elseneur, Les 1936 d: Pierre Chenal.
lps: Winna Winfried, Jean Murat, Andre Berley. 90M
FRN. prod/rel: General Production, Transuniversal
Films
Mutiny of the Elsinore, The 1920 d: Edward Sloman.
lps: Mitchell Lewis, Helen Ferguson, Noah Beery. 5950f
USA. *The Mutiny* prod/rel: C. E. Shurtleff, Inc., Metro
Pictures Corp.©
Mutiny of the Elsinore, The 1937 d: Roy Lockwood.
lps: Paul Lukas, Lyn Harding, Kathleen Kelly. 79M
UKN. prod/rel: Argyle British, Associated British
Picture Corporation
An Odyssey of the North, 1900, Short Story
Odyssey of the North, An 1914 d: Hobart Bosworth.
lps: Hobart Bosworth, Rhea Haines, Gordon Sackville.
6r USA. prod/rel: Bosworth, Inc.©, Paramount Pictures
Corp.
A Raid on the Oyster Pirates, 1905, Short Story
Tropical Nights 1928 d: Elmer Clifton. lps: Patsy Ruth
Miller, Malcolm McGregor, Ray Hallor. 5449f USA.
prod/rel: Tiffany-Stahl Productions
The Sea Wolf, New York 1904, Novel
Barricade 1950 d: Peter Godfrey. lps: Dane Clark,
Ruth Roman, Raymond Massey. 75M USA. prod/rel:
Warner Bros.
Lupo Dei Mari, Il 1975 d: Giuseppe Vari. lps: Chuck
Connors, Giuseppe Pambieri, Barbara Bach. 100M ITL.
Wolf Larsen (USA); *Legend of the Sea Wolf; Wolf of the
Seven Seas; Larsen -Wolf of the Seven Seas* prod/rel:
Cinetirrena, National Cin.Ca
Sea Wolf, The 1913 d: Hobart Bosworth. lps: Hobart
Bosworth, Viola Barry, Herbert Rawlinson. 7r USA.
prod/rel: Bosworth, Inc.©, State Rights
Sea Wolf, The 1920 d: George Melford. lps: Noah
Beery, Mabel Julienne Scott, Tom Forman. 6797f USA.
prod/rel: Famous Players-Lasky Corp.©,
Paramount-Artcraft Pictures
Sea Wolf, The 1926 d: Ralph Ince. lps: Ralph Ince,
Claire Adams, Theodore von Eltz. 6763f USA. prod/rel:
Ralph W. Ince Corp., Producers Distributing Corp.
Sea Wolf, The 1930 d: Alfred Santell. lps: Milton Sills,
Jane Keith, Raymond Hackett. 8000f USA. prod/rel: Fox
Film Corp.
Sea Wolf, The 1941 d: Michael Curtiz. lps: Edward G.
Robinson, John Garfield, Ida Lupino. 100M USA.
prod/rel: Warner Bros.

Sea Wolf, The 1993 d: Michael Anderson. lps: Charles Bronson, Christopher Reeve, Catherine Mary Stewart. 89M USA. prod/rel: Bob Banner, Primedia

Seewolf, Der 1971 d: Wolfgang Staudte. lps: Raimund Harmstorf, Edward Meeks, Beatrice Cardon. MTV. 96M GRM/RMN. *Lupul Marilor* (RMN); *The Sea Wolf* prod/rel: Tele, Constantin

Wolf Larsen 1958 d: Harmon Jones. lps: Barry Sullivan, Peter Graves, Gita Hall. 83M USA. prod/rel: Allied Artists, Linsley Parsons

The Siege of the Lancashire Queen, 1905, Short Story
Prowlers of the Sea 1928 d: John G. Adolfi. lps: Carmel Myers, Ricardo Cortez, George Fawcett. 5160f USA. *Sea Prowlers* prod/rel: Tiffany-Stahl Productions

Smoke Bellew, New York 1912, Novel
Chechako, The 1914? d: Hobart Bosworth. lps: Jack Conway, Myrtle Stedman, Joe Ray. 5r USA. prod/rel: Bosworth, Inc., Paramount Pictures Corp.
Smoke Bellew 1929 d: Scott R. Dunlap. lps: Conway Tearle, Barbara Bedford, Mark Hamilton. 6605f USA. prod/rel: Big 4 Productions, First Division Distributors

Son of the Wolf, 1900, Short Story
Son of the Wolf, The 1922 d: Norman Dawn. lps: Wheeler Oakman, Edith Roberts, Sam Allen. 4970f USA. prod/rel: R-C Pictures

The Star Rover, New York 1915, Novel
Star Rover, The 1920 d: Edward Sloman. lps: Courtenay Foote, Thelma Percy, Pomeroy Cannon. 6r USA. prod/rel: C. E. Shurtleff, Inc., Metro Pictures Corp.©

The Story of Jees Uck, 1904, Short Story
Mohican's Daughter, The 1922 d: Stanner E. V. Taylor. lps: Nancy Deaver, Hazel Washburn, Saxon Kling. 4697f USA. prod/rel: P. T. B. Inc., American Releasing Corp.

That Spot, 1910, Short Story
Sign of the Wolf 1941 d: Howard Bretherton. lps: Michael Whalen, Grace Bradley, Darryl Hickman. 69M USA. prod/rel: Monogram

A Thousand Deaths, 1899, Short Story
Torture Ship 1939 d: Victor Hugo Halperin. lps: Lyle Talbot, Julie Bishop, Irving Pichel. 62M USA. prod/rel: Producers Distributing Corp.

To Build a Fire, 1910, Short Story
To Build a Fire 1970 d: David Cobham. lps: Ian Hogg. 56M UKN.
To Build a Fire 1975 d: Robert Stitzel. 15M USA.

Two Men of the Desert, Short Story
Two Men of the Desert 1913 d: D. W. Griffith. lps: Harry Carey, Donald Crisp, Blanche Sweet. SHT USA. prod/rel: Biograph Co.

Valley of the Moon, New York 1913, Novel
Valley of the Moon, The 1914 d: Hobart Bosworth. lps: Jack Conway, Myrtle Stedman, Hobart Bosworth. 6r USA. prod/rel: Bosworth, Inc., State Rights

White and Yellow, 1905, Short Story
Haunted Ship, The 1927 d: Forrest Sheldon. lps: Dorothy Sebastian, Montagu Love, Thomas Santschi. 4752f USA. prod/rel: Tiffany-Stahl Productions

White Fang, New York 1905, Novel
Belisch Klyk 1946 d: Alexander Zguridi. lps: O. Shaow, E. Ismailova, L. Swerdein. 81M USS. *White Fang; Belyi Klyk*
White Fang 1925 d: Larry Trimble. lps: Theodore von Eltz, Ruth Dwyer, Matthew Betz. 5800f USA. prod/rel: R-C Pictures, Film Booking Offices of America
White Fang 1936 d: David Butler. lps: Michael Whalen, Jean Muir, Slim Summerville. 70M USA. prod/rel: Twentieth Century-Fox Film Corp.©
White Fang 1990 d: Randall Kleiser. lps: Klaus Maria Brandauer, Ethan Hawke, Seymour Cassel. 109M USA. prod/rel: Hybrid Productions, Walt Disney
Zanna Bianca 1973 d: Lucio Fulci. lps: Franco Nero, Fernando Rey, Raimund Harmstorf. 101M ITL/FRN/SPN. *Croc-Blanc* (FRN); *White Fang* (UKN); *Colmillo Blanco* (SPN); *Die Teufelsschlucht Der Wilden Wolfe* (GRM); *Devil's Canyon of the Wild Wolves* prod/rel: Oceania P.I.C. (Roma), Incine Compagnia Industrial Cin.Ca

White Silence, 1900, Short Story
Romance of the Redwoods 1939 d: Charles Vidor. lps: Charles Bickford, Jean Parker, Al Bridge. 67M USA. *Power to Burn* prod/rel: Columbia Pictures Corp. of California©

Yellow Handkerchief, Short Story
Stormy Waters 1928 d: Edgar Lewis. lps: Eve Southern, Malcolm McGregor, Roy Stewart. 5735f USA. *The Captain of the Hurricane* prod/rel: Tiffany-Stahl Productions

LONDON, LOUIS S.
Schizo
All Woman 1967 d: Frank Warren. lps: Robert Alda, Rebecca Sand, William Redfield. 83M USA. *All Girl*; *Schizo* prod/rel: Three Stories High Co., Franklin Prods.

LONG, AMELIA REYNOLDS
The Thought Monster, Short Story
Fiend Without a Face 1958 d: Arthur Crabtree. lps: Marshall Thompson, Kim Parker, Kynaston Reeves. 74M UKN. prod/rel: Eros, Mlc Producers Associates

LONG, GABRIELLE MARGARET VERE (1886–1952), UKN, Shearing, Joseph, Bowen, Marjorie
Airing in a Closed Carriage, Novel
Mark of Cain, The 1948 d: Brian Desmond Hurst. lps: Eric Portman, Sally Gray, Patrick Holt. 88M UKN. prod/rel: General Film Distributors, Two Cities

Blanche Fury, Novel
Blanche Fury 1948 d: Marc Allegret. lps: Stewart Granger, Valerie Hobson, Walter Fitzgerald. 95M UKN. prod/rel: General Film Distributors, Cineguild

Mistress Nell Gwynne, Novel
Nell Gwynne 1926 d: Herbert Wilcox. lps: Dorothy Gish, Randle Ayrton, Juliette Compton. 7760f UKN. *Nell Gwyn* (USA) prod/rel: W.M. Productions, British National

LONG, JAMES O.
Killer: a Journal of Murder, Book
Killer: a Journal of Murder 1995 d: Tim Metcalfe. lps: James Woods, Robert Sean Leonard, Ellen Greene. 92M USA. prod/rel: Spelling Films, Ixtlan

LONG, JEFF
Outlaw, Book
Manhunt for Claude Dallas 1986 d: Jerry London. lps: Matt Salinger, Claude Akins, Lois Nettleton. TVM. 93M USA.

LONG, JOHN LUTHER
The Fox-Woman, Philadelphia 1900, Novel
Fox Woman, The 1915 d: Lloyd Ingraham. lps: Teddy Sampson, Seena Owen, Elmer Clifton. 4r USA. prod/rel: the Majestic Motion Picture Co., Majestic Masterpiece

Madame Butterfly, New York 1898, Novel
Madama Butterfly 1955 d: Carmine Gallone. lps: Kaoru Yachigusa, Michiko Tanaka, Nicola Filacuridi. 114M ITL/JPN. *Madame Butterfly* (UKN) prod/rel: Rizzoli Film, Produzione Gallone (Roma)
Madame Butterfly 1915 d: Sidney Olcott. lps: Mary Pickford, Marshall Neilan, Olive West. 5r USA. prod/rel: Famous Players Film Co.©, Paramount Pictures Corp.
Madame Butterfly 1932 d: Marion Gering. lps: Sylvia Sidney, Cary Grant, Charlie Ruggles. 88M USA. prod/rel: Paramount Productions©
Madame Butterfly 1995 d: Frederic Mitterand. lps: Ying Huang, Richard Troxell, Ning Liang. 135M FRN/JPN/GRM. prod/rel: Erato Films, Ideale Audience

LONG, SUMNER ARTHUR
Story
Lassie's Great Adventure 1963 d: William Beaudine. lps: Jon Provost, June Lockhart, Hugh Reilly. MTV. 103M USA. *Lassie's Greatest Adventure* (UKN); *The Journey*; *Lassie* prod/rel: Wrather

Never Too Late, New York 1962, Play
Never Too Late 1965 d: Bud Yorkin. lps: Paul Ford, Connie Stevens, Maureen O'Sullivan. 105M USA. prod/rel: Tandem Enterprises, Warner Bros.

LONGDEN, DERIC
Diana's Story, Book
Wide Eyed and Legless 1993 d: Richard Loncraine. lps: Julie Walters, Jim Broadbent, Thora Hird. TVM. 90M UKN.

Lost for Words, Book
Lost for Words 1998 d: Alan J. W. Bell. lps: Thora Hird, Pete Postlethwaite, Penny Downie. 90M UKN. prod/rel: Yorkshire Television©, Bard Entertainments
Wide Eyed and Legless 1993 d: Richard Loncraine. lps: Julie Walters, Jim Broadbent, Thora Hird. TVM. 90M UKN.

LONGEN, EMIL ARTUR
Der K. Und K. Feldmarschall, Play
C. A. K. Polni Marsalek 1930 d: Carl Lamac. lps: Vlasta Burian, Theodor Pistek, Helena MonczakovA. 2520m CZC. *His Majesty's Field Marshal*; *Imperial and Royal Field Marshal* prod/rel: Elekta
Falsche Feldmarschall, Der 1930 d: Carl Lamac. lps: Vlasta Burian, Alexander Roda-Roda, Harry Frank. 2341m GRM/CZC. *Der K. Und K. Feldmarschall*; *The Field Marshal* prod/rel: Elekta, Ondra-Lamac-Film
Monsieur le Marechal 1931 d: Carl Lamac. lps: Fernand-Rene, Helene Robert, Anthony Gildes. 80M FRN/CZC. *Feld Marechal* prod/rel: Standard

Kasta Pro Sebe, Play
Adjutant Seiner Hoheit, Der 1933 d: Martin Fric. lps: Vlasta Burian, Werner Futterer, Gretl Theimer. 2282m GRM/CZC. prod/rel: Meissner
Pobocnik Jeho Vysosti 1933 d: Martin Fric. lps: Vlasta Burian, Suzanne Marwille, Nora Stallich. 2202m CZC. *His Highness's Adjutant*; *Assistant to His Highness* prod/rel: Meissner

Uz Me Vezou, Play
Anton Spelec, Ostrostrelec 1932 d: Martin Fric. lps: Vlasta Burian, Ruzena Slemrova, Jaroslav Marvan. 2323m CZC. *The Thrower Anton Spelec*; *Anton Spelec -Sharp-Shooter* prod/rel: Meissner

V Tlame Velryby, Play
Nezlobte Dedecka 1934 d: Carl Lamac. lps: Vlasta Burian, Cenek Slegl, Adina MandlovA. 2136m CZC. *Don't Make Grandpa Angry* prod/rel: Meissner

LONGFELLOW, HENRY WADSWORTH (1807–1882), USA
The Blind Girl of Castle Guille, Poem
Blind Girl of Castle Guille, The 1913. SHT USA. prod/rel: Patheplay

The Children's Hour, Poem
Children's Hour, The 1913. lps: Madeline Fairbanks, Marion Fairbanks, Helen Badgley. SHT USA. prod/rel: Thanhouser

The Courtship of Miles Standish, 1858, Poem
Courtship of Miles Standish, The 1910 d: Otis Turner. lps: Hobart Bosworth, Betty Harte, Robert Leonard. 1000f USA. prod/rel: Selig Polyscope Co.
Courtship of Miles Standish, The 1923 d: Frederick Sullivan. lps: Charles Ray, Enid Bennett, E. Alyn Warren. 9r USA. prod/rel: Charles Ray Productions, Associated Exhibitors

Evangeline, 1847, Poem
Evangeline 1911. 1000f USA. prod/rel: Selig Polyscope Co.
Evangeline 1913 d: E. P. Sullivan, William H. Cavanaugh. lps: Laura Lyman, John F. Carleton, E. P. Sullivan. 5r CND. prod/rel: Canadian Bioscope Company Ltd.
Evangeline 1919 d: Raoul Walsh. lps: Miriam Cooper, Alan Roscoe, Spottiswoode Aitken. 5200f USA. prod/rel: Fox Film Corp., William Fox©
Evangeline 1929 d: Edwin Carewe. lps: Dolores Del Rio, Roland Drew, Alec B. Francis. 8268f USA. prod/rel: Edwin Carewe Productions, Feature Productions

The Flaming Forge, Poem
Flaming Forge, The 1913 d: Lanier Bartlett. lps: Wheeler Oakman. SHT USA. prod/rel: Selig Polyscope Co.

His Mother's Birthday, Poem
His Mother's Birthday 1913. lps: William E. Shay. SHT USA. prod/rel: Imp

King Robert of Sicily, Poem
King Robert of Sicily 1913. 2000f USA. prod/rel: Essanay

The Legend Beautiful, Poem
Vision Beautiful, The 1912. lps: Hobart Bosworth. 1000f USA. prod/rel: Selig Polyscope Co.

The Midnight Ride of Paul Revere, Poem
Midnight Ride of Paul Revere, The 1914 d: Charles J. Brabin. lps: Augustus Phillips, Carlton King, Harry Linson. 2r USA. prod/rel: Edison

The Song of Hiawatha, Boston 1855, Poem
Death of Minnehaha, The 1910. SHT USA. prod/rel: Imp
Hiawatha 1903 d: Joe Rosenthal. 800f UKN/CND. *Hiawatha the Messiah of the Ojibway* prod/rel: Urban Trading Co.
Hiawatha 1909 d: William V. Ranous. lps: Gladys Hulette. 985f USA. prod/rel: Imp
Hiawatha 1913. lps: Soon-Goot. 4r USA. *Hiawatha: the Indian Passion Play* prod/rel: F. E. Moore©, State Rights
Hiawatha 1952 d: Kurt Neumann. lps: Vince Edwards, Yvette Dugay, Keith Larsen. 80M USA. prod/rel: Allied Artists

The Spanish Student, Poem
Southern Love 1924 d: Herbert Wilcox. lps: Betty Blythe, Herbert Langley, Randle Ayrton. 7800f UKN. *A Woman's Secret* (USA) prod/rel: Graham-Wilcox

The Village Blacksmith, 1841, Poem
Village Blacksmith, The 1905 d: Percy Stow. lps: Roy Byford. 340f UKN. prod/rel: Clarendon, Gaumont
Village Blacksmith, The 1908 d: A. E. Coleby. lps: George Roberts. 220f UKN. prod/rel: Cricks & Martin
Village Blacksmith, The 1913. lps: Harry Myers, Bartley McCullum, Mrs. George B. Walters. 1000f USA. prod/rel: Lubin
Village Blacksmith, The 1913. SHT USA. prod/rel: Powers

Village Blacksmith, The 1917 d: A. E. Coleby, Arthur Rooke. lps: Janet Alexander, A. E. Coleby, Arthur Rooke. 3970f UKN. prod/rel: I. B. Davidson, Tiger

Village Blacksmith, The 1922 d: John Ford. lps: William Walling, Virginia True Boardman, Virginia Valli. 7540f USA. prod/rel: Fox Film Corp.

The Wreck of the Hesperus, 1841, Poem
Wreck of the Hesperus, The 1926 d: Frank Tilley. lps: Jean Colin, Darby Foster, Alexander Butler. 2000f UKN. prod/rel: British Projects, Bsc

Wreck of the Hesperus, The 1927 d: Elmer Clifton. lps: Sam de Grasse, Virginia Bradford, Francis Ford. 6447f USA. prod/rel: de Mille Pictures, Pathe Exchange, Inc.

Wreck of the Hesperus, The 1948 d: John Hoffman. lps: Willard Parker, Edgar Buchanan, Patricia Barry. 70M USA. prod/rel: Columbia

LONGONI, ANGELO
Naja, Play
Naja 1998 d: Angelo Longoni. lps: Enrico Lo Verso, Stefano Accorsi, Francesco Siciliano. 100M ITL. *The Draft* prod/rel: Cecchi Gor Tiger Cin.Ca

Uomini Senza Donne, Play
Uomini Senza Donne 1996 d: Angelo Longoni. lps: Alessandro Gassman, Gianmarco Tognazzi, Alessandra Acciai. 100M ITL. *Men Without Women* prod/rel: Thunder Film, Cecchi Gori Group Tigre Cinematografica

LONGSTREET, STEPHEN
The Gay Sisters, Novel
Gay Sisters, The 1942 d: Irving Rapper. lps: Barbara Stanwyck, George Brent, Geraldine Fitzgerald. 108M USA. prod/rel: Warner Bros.

Paper Door, Short Story
Secret Door, The 1962 d: Gilbert L. Kay. lps: Robert Hutton, Sandra Dorne, Peter Illing. 71M UKN/USA. *Now It Can Be Told* prod/rel: Dorton Productions, Fifeshire Productions

Silver River, Novel
Silver River 1948 d: Raoul Walsh. lps: Errol Flynn, Ann Sheridan, Thomas Mitchell. 110M USA. prod/rel: Warner Bros.

Stallion Road, Novel
Stallion Road 1947 d: James V. Kern, Raoul Walsh (Uncredited). lps: Zachary Scott, Ronald Reagan, Alexis Smith. 97M USA. prod/rel: Warner Bros.

Wild Harvest, New York 1960, Novel
Wild Harvest 1961 d: Jerry A. Baerwitz. lps: Dolores Faith, Dean Fredericks, Susan Kelly. 80M USA. prod/rel: Hollywood Artists Productions

LONGUS
Daphnis and Chloe, c200, Novel
Dhafnis Ke Hloi 66 1967 d: Mika Zaharopoulou. lps: Telis Zotos, Elisabeth Wiener, Dominique Paturel. 80M GRC. *Daphnis and Chloe 66*

Mikres Aphrodites 1962 d: Nikos Koundouros. lps: Takis Emmanuel, Eleni Prokopiou, Vangelis Ioannides. 98M GRC. *Young Aphrodites* (UKN); *Petites Aphrodites*

LONGWORTH, CLARA
Play With Souls, New York 1922, Novel
Playing With Souls 1925 d: Ralph Ince. lps: Jacqueline Logan, Mary Astor, Belle Bennett. 5831f USA. prod/rel: Thomas H. Ince Corp., First National Pictures

LONGYEAR, BARRY
Enemy Mine, Story
Enemy Mine 1985 d: Wolfgang Petersen. lps: Dennis Quaid, Louis Gossett Jr., Brion James. 108M USA/GRM. *Enemy Mine -Geliebter Feind* prod/rel: 20th Century Fox, Kings Road Entertainment

LONN, OYSTEIN
Thranes Metode, Short Story
Thranes Metode 1999 d: Unni Straume. lps: Bjorn Sundquist, Petronella Barker, Nils O. Oftebro. 82M NRW. *Thrane's Method* prod/rel: Speranza Films, Unni Straume Filmproduksjon

LONNROT, ELIAS (1802–1884), FNL
Kalevala, 1835, Verse
Sampo 1959 d: Alexander Ptushko, Gregg Sebelious. lps: Urho Somersalmi, A. Orochko, I. Voronov. 99M USS/FNL. *The Day the Earth Froze* (USA); *The Magic Sampo*

LONS, HERMANN
Dahinten in Der Heide, Books
Dahinten in Der Heide 1936 d: Carl Boese. lps: Hilde Weissner, Hans Stuwe, Hermann Speelmans. 105M GRM. *Back in the Country* (USA) prod/rel: Aco, Adler

Das Zweite Gesicht, Novel
Rot Ist Die Liebe 1957 d: Karl Hartl. lps: Cornell Borchers, Dieter Borsche, Barbara Rutting. 90M GRM. *Love Is Red* prod/rel: Bavaria

LONSDALE, FREDERICK (1881–1954), UKN, Leonard, Frederick
Aren't We All?, London 1923, Play
Aren't We All? 1932 d: Harry Lachman. lps: Gertrude Lawrence, Hugh Wakefield, Owen Nares. 80M UKN. prod/rel: Paramount British, Paramount

Kiss in the Dark, A 1925 d: Frank Tuttle. lps: Adolphe Menjou, Aileen Pringle, Lillian Rich. 5767f USA. prod/rel: Famous Players-Lasky, Paramount Pictures

Canaries Sometimes Sing, Play
Canaries Sometimes Sing 1930 d: Tom Walls. lps: Tom Walls, Yvonne Arnaud, Cathleen Nesbitt. 80M UKN. prod/rel: British and Dominions, Woolf & Freedman

The Devil to Pay, Play
Cattivo Soggetto, Un 1933 d: Carlo Ludovico BragagliA. lps: Vittorio de Sica, Irina Lucacevich, Giuditta Rissone. 63M ITL. *La Tragedia Della Cerniera*; *Venere Bruna*; *Papa Paga* prod/rel: Za-Bum, Artisti Associati

The Fake, London 1924, Play
Fake, The 1927 d: Georg Jacoby. lps: Henry Edwards, Elga Brink, Juliette Compton. 8500f UKN. prod/rel: Neo-Art Productions, Williams & Pritchard Films

The High Road, London 1927, Play
Lady of Scandal, The 1930 d: Sidney A. Franklin. lps: Ruth Chatterton, Basil Rathbone, Ralph Forbes. 6858f USA. *The High Road* (UKN) prod/rel: Metro-Goldwyn-Mayer Pictures

The Last of Mrs. Cheyney, London 1925, Play
Frau Cheneys Ende 1961 d: Franz J. Wild. lps: Lilli Palmer, Carlos Thompson, Martin Held. 93M GRM/SWT. *Mrs. Cheney's Demise*; *Frau Cheyneys Ende* prod/rel: Roxy, Europa

Last of Mrs. Cheyney, The 1929 d: Sidney A. Franklin, Dorothy Arzner (Uncredited). lps: Norma Shearer, Basil Rathbone, George Barraud. 94M USA. prod/rel: Metro-Goldwyn-Mayer Pictures

Last of Mrs. Cheyney, The 1937 d: Richard Boleslawski, George Fitzmaurice. lps: Joan Crawford, William Powell, Robert Montgomery. 98M USA. prod/rel: Metro-Goldwyn-Mayer Corp.©

Law and the Lady, The 1951 d: Edwin H. Knopf. lps: Greer Garson, Michael Wilding, Fernando Lamas. 105M USA. *The Law and Lady Loverly* prod/rel: MGM

The Maid of the Mountains, London 1917, Musical Play
Maid of the Mountains, The 1932 d: Lupino Lane. lps: Nancy Brown, Harry Welchman, Betty Stockfeld. 80M UKN. prod/rel: British International Pictures, Wardour

Never Come Back, London 1932, Play
Just Smith 1933 d: Tom Walls. lps: Tom Walls, Carol Goodner, Anne Grey. 76M UKN. *Never Come Back*; *Leave It to Smith* (USA) prod/rel: Gaumont-British, Woolf & Freedman

On Approval, London 1927, Play
On Approval 1930 d: Tom Walls. lps: Tom Walls, Yvonne Arnaud, Winifred Shotter. 98M UKN. prod/rel: British and Dominions, Woolf & Freedman

On Approval 1944 d: Clive Brook. lps: Clive Brook, Beatrice Lillie, Googie Withers. 80M UKN. prod/rel: General Film Distributors, Independent Producers

Spring Cleaning, New York 1923, Play
Fast Set, The 1924 d: William C. de Mille. lps: Betty Compson, Adolphe Menjou, Elliott Dexter. 6754f USA. prod/rel: Famous Players-Lasky, Paramount Pictures

Women Who Play 1932 d: Arthur Rosson. lps: Mary Newcomb, Benita Hume, George Barraud. 78M UKN. *Spring Cleaning* prod/rel: Paramount British, Paramount

LOOMIS, CHARLES B.
Up from the Depths, Play
Up from the Depths 1915 d: Paul Powell. lps: Courtenay Foote, Gladys Brockwell, Thomas Jefferson. 4r USA. prod/rel: Reliance Motion Picture Corp., Mutual Film Corp.

LOOMIS, FREDERIC M.
Article
Paid in Full 1950 d: William Dieterle. lps: Robert Cummings, Diana Lynn, Lizabeth Scott. 105M USA. *Bitter Victory* prod/rel: Paramount

LOOS, ANITA (1893–1981), USA
But Gentlemen Marry Brunettes, 1928, Novel
Gentlemen Marry Brunettes 1955 d: Richard Sale. lps: Jane Russell, Jeanne Crain, Alan Young. 97M USA. prod/rel: United Artists, Russ-Field Corp.

Gentlemen Prefer Blondes, New York 1925, Novel
Gentlemen Prefer Blondes 1928 d: Malcolm St. Clair. lps: Ruth Taylor, Alice White, Ford Sterling. 6871f USA. prod/rel: Paramount Famous Lasky Corp.

Gentlemen Prefer Blondes 1953 d: Howard Hawks. lps: Marilyn Monroe, Jane Russell, Charles Coburn. 91M USA. prod/rel: 20th Century-Fox

The Social Register, New York 1931, Play
Social Register 1934 d: Marshall Neilan. lps: Colleen Moore, Charles Winninger, Pauline Frederick. 72M USA. prod/rel: Associated Film Productions©, Columbia Pictures Corp.©

A Ten-Cent Adventure, Story
Ten-Cent Adventure, A 1915 d: Sidney A. Franklin, Chester M. Franklin. lps: George E. Stone, Carmen de Rue, Richard Cummings. SHT USA. prod/rel: Majestic

The Whole Town's Talking, New York 1923, Play
Ex-Bad Boy 1931 d: Vin Moore. lps: Robert Armstrong, Jean Arthur, Lola Lane. 67M USA. *His Temporary Affair* (UKN); *The Whole Town's Talking* prod/rel: Universal Pictures Corp.©

Whole Town's Talking, The 1926 d: Edward Laemmle. lps: Edward Everett Horton, Virginia Lee Corbin, Trixie FriganzA. 6662f USA. prod/rel: Universal Pictures

LOPE DE VEGA Y CARPIO, FELIX
El Perro Del Hortelano, Play
Perro Del Hortelano, El 1996 d: Pilar Miro. lps: Emma Suarez, Carmelo Gomez, Fernando Conde. 107M SPN. *The Dog in the Manger* prod/rel: Lola Films, Enrique Cerezo Prods.

LOPES, MOACIR C.
Novel
Ostra E O Vento, O 1997 d: Walter Lima Jr. lps: Leandra Leal, Lima Duarte, Fernando Torres. 118M BRZ. *The Oyster and the Wind* prod/rel: Ravina Producoes E Comunicacoes, Riofilme

LOPEZ DE SAA, LEOPOLDO
Por un Milagro de Amor, Poem
Por un Milagro de Amor 1928 d: Luis R. Alonso. lps: Josefina Tapias, Fernando Diaz de Mendoza, Manuel Montenegro. SPN. *Golondrinas Y Gaviotas* prod/rel: Ediciones Alonso (Madrid)

LOPEZ, FRANCIS
Cinq Millions Comptant, Opera
Cinq Millions Comptant 1956 d: Andre Berthomieu. lps: Ded Rysel, Darry Cowl, Jane SourzA. 90M FRN. prod/rel: Mars, Lyrica

LOPEZ NUNEZ, JUAN
El Nino de Las Monjas, Novel
Nino de Las Monjas, El 1925 d: Antonio Calvache. lps: Eugenia Zuffoli, Maruja Lopetegui, Eladio Amoros. SPN. prod/rel: Regia Films (Madrid)

LOPEZ PAEZ, JORGE
Story
Dona Herlinda Y Su Hijo 1986 d: Jaime Humberto Hermosillo. lps: Guadalupe Del Toro, Marco Antonio Trevino, Arturo MezA. 95M MXC. *Dona Herlinda and Her Son* (USA) prod/rel: Clasa Films Mundiales

LOPEZ PINILLOS, JOSE
El Caudal de Los Hijos, Madrid 1921, Play
Hijos Mandan, Los 1939 d: Gabriel SoriA. lps: Blanca de Castejon, Fernando Soler, Arturo de CordovA. 77M USA. *The Son Commands* prod/rel: Cobian Productions, Twentieth Century-Fox Film Corp.

LOPEZ RIENDA, RAFAEL
Aguilas de Acero, Novel
Aguilas de Acero 1927 d: Florian Rey. lps: Pedro Larranaga, Elita Panquer, Ricardo Nunez. 37M SPN. *Los Misterios de Tanger*; *Steel Eagles*; *The Mysteries of Tangier* prod/rel: Ediciones Lopez Rienda (Madrid)

Juan Leon Legionario, Novel
Heroes de la Legion, Las 1927 d: Rafael Lopez RiendA. lps: Pablo Rossi, Carmen Sanchez, Manuel Chavarri. F SPN. prod/rel: Ediciones Lopez Rienda (Madrid)

LOPEZ RUBIO, JOSE
Una Madeja de Lana Azul Celeste, 1952, Play
Madeja de Lana Azul Celeste, Una 1964 d: Jose Luis Madrid. lps: Marisa de Leza, Luis Davila, Lucia Prado. 68M SPN.

La Otra Orilla, 1955, Play
Otra Orilla, La 1966 d: Jose Luis Madrid. lps: Marisa de Leza, Luis Davila, Jose Maria Seoane. 96M SPN. *From the Other Side*; *The Other Shore*

Un Trono Para Cristy, 1957, Play
Trono Para Cristy 1959 d: Luis Cesar Amadori. lps: Christine Kaufmann, Dieter Borsche, Zully Moreno. 89M SPN/GRM. *Eine Thron Fur Christine* (GRM); *A Throne for Christine* prod/rel: Germania, Procusa

LOPEZ, SABATINO
La Buona Figliola, 1909, Play
Buona Figliola, La 1920 d: Mario Caserini. lps: Vera Vergani, Nerio Bernardi, Nella SerravezzA. 1906m ITL. prod/rel: Cines

LOPEZ SILVA, J.
La Chavala, Opera
  Chavala, La 1925 d: Florian Rey. lps: Elisa Ruiz Romero, Juan de Orduna, Maria Luz Callejo. SPN. *The Girl* prod/rel: Atlantida

La Revoltosa, Opera
  Revoltosa, La 1924 d: Florian Rey. lps: Josefina Tapias, Juan de Orduna, Jose Moncayo. 71M SPN. *The Mischievous One; The Riotous Girl* prod/rel: Goya Film (Madrid)

LOPEZ TORREGROSA, T.
Los Chicos de la Escuela, Opera
  Chicos de la Escuela, Los 1925 d: Florian Rey. lps: Isabel Alemany, Maria Luz Callejo, Manuel San German. 59M SPN. *The Schoolboys* prod/rel: Atlantida

LORAINE, PHILIP
Day of the Arrow, New York 1964, Novel
  Eye of the Devil 1966 d: J. Lee Thompson. lps: Deborah Kerr, David Niven, Donald Pleasence. 90M USA/UKN. *13* prod/rel: Filmways, Inc., MGM

LORD, ARLINE
The Majo, Short Story
  Romance of Seville, A 1929 d: Norman Walker. lps: Alexander d'Arcy, Marguerite Allan, Randle Ayrton. SIL. 5610f UKN. prod/rel: British International Pictures, First National-Pathe

LORD, GABRIELLE
Fortress, Novel
  Fortress 1985 d: Arch Nicholson. lps: Rachel Ward, Sean Garlick, Rebecca Rigg. 89M ASL/USA. prod/rel: Hbo Premiere Films, Crawford Prods.©

LORD, ROBERT
Come Back to Aaron, Story
  Matinee Idol, The 1928 d: Frank CaprA. lps: Bessie Love, Johnny Walker, Lionel Belmore. 5925f USA. prod/rel: Columbia Pictures

LORD, WALTER (1917–, USA
A Night to Remember, Book
  Night to Remember, A 1958 d: Roy Ward Baker. lps: Kenneth More, David McCallum, Jill Dixon. 123M UKN. prod/rel: Rank, Rank Film Distributors

LORENZ
Intermezzo Am Abend, Play
  Alles Fur Gloria 1941 d: Carl Boese. lps: Laura Solari, Johannes Riemann, Lizzi Waldmuller. 94M GRM. prod/rel: Deka, Karp

LORENZ, HANZ
Ratsel Um Beate, Play
  Ratsel Um Beate 1938 d: Johannes Meyer. lps: Lil Dagover, Albrecht Schoenhals, Kathe Haack. 85M GRM. prod/rel: Cine-Allianz, Schorcht

LORENZ, LOVIS H.
Zu Neuen Ufern, Novel
  Zu Neuen Ufern 1937 d: Douglas Sirk. lps: Zarah Leander, Willy Birgel, Viktor Staal. 105M GRM. *Life Begins Anew* (USA); *To New Shores* (UKN); *Paramatta; Bagne de Femmes* prod/rel: Universum, Kristall

LORENZINI, PAOLO
I Due Sergenti, Novel
  Due Sergenti, I 1936 d: Enrico Guazzoni. lps: Gino Cervi, Evi Maltagliati, Mino Doro. 93M ITL. prod/rel: Manderfilm

LORENZ-LAMBRECHT, HEINZ
Umwege Zur Heimat, Novel
  Cavalerie Legere 1935 d: Roger Vitrac, Werner Hochbaum. lps: Gabriel Gabrio, Constant Remy, Mona GoyA. 96M FRN. prod/rel: Fabrikation Deutscher Filme, a.CE.
  Leichte Kavallerie 1935 d: Werner Hochbaum. lps: Marika Rokk, Heinz von Cleve, Fritz Kampers. 88M GRM. prod/rel: F.D.F., Deutsche Commerz

LORIGA, RAY
La Pistola de Mi Hermano, Novel
  Pistola de Mi Hermano, La 1997 d: Ray LorigA. lps: Daniel Gonzalez, Nico Bidasolo, Andres Gertrudix. 85M SPN. *My Brother's Gun* prod/rel: P.C., Tve

LORIMER, GEORGE HORACE
Jack Spurlock - Prodigal, New York 1908, Novel
  Jack Spurlock, Prodigal 1918 d: Carl Harbaugh. lps: George Walsh, Ruth Taylor, Dan Mason. 6r USA. *In Onion There Is Strength* prod/rel: Fox Film Corp., William Fox©
  Self-Made Man, A 1922 d: Rowland V. Lee. lps: William Russell, Renee Adoree, Mathilde Brundage. 4920f USA. prod/rel: Fox Film Corp.

LORIMER, GRAEME
Feature for June, Play
  June Bride 1948 d: Bretaigne Windust. lps: Robert Montgomery, Bette Davis, Fay Bainter. 97M USA. prod/rel: Warner Bros.

LORIMER, NORMA
On Desert Altars, New York 1915, Novel
  Woman! Woman! 1919 d: Kenean Buel. lps: Evelyn Nesbit, Clifford Bruce, Gareth Hughes. 5r USA. prod/rel: Fox Film Corp., Standard Picture

The Shadow of Egypt, Novel
  Shadow of Egypt, The 1924 d: Sidney Morgan. lps: Carlyle Blackwell, Alma Taylor, Milton Rosmer. 7700f UKN. *The Shadow of the Mosque* prod/rel: Astra-National

There Was a King in Egypt, New York 1918, Novel
  Lure of Egypt, The 1921 d: Howard Hickman. lps: Robert McKim, Claire Adams, Joseph J. Dowling. 6r USA. prod/rel: Federal Photoplays of California, Pathe Exchange

LORIMER, WRIGHT
The Shepherd King, New York 1904, Play
  Shepherd King, The 1923 d: J. Gordon Edwards. lps: Violet Mersereau, Edy Darclea, Virginia Lucchetti. 8500f USA. prod/rel: Fox Film Corp.

LORIOT, NOELLE
Docteur Francoise Gailland, Novel
  Docteur Francoise Gailland 1975 d: Jean-Louis Bertucelli. lps: Annie Girardot, Francois Perier, Jean-Pierre Cassel. 100M FRN. *No Time for Breakfast* (USA); *Dr. Francoise; Un Cri; Just a Woman* prod/rel: Action, Filmedis

LORRAIN, FRANCOISE
La Colonne de Cendres, Novel
  Hoa-Binh 1970 d: Raoul Coutard. lps: Phi Lan, Zuan Ha, Le Quynh. 90M FRN. *Peace; Colonne de Cendres* prod/rel: Madeleine Films, Parc Films

LORRAINE, PHILIP
Break in the Circle, Novel
  Break in the Circle 1955 d: Val Guest. lps: Forrest Tucker, Eva Bartok, Marius Goring. 92M UKN. prod/rel: Hammer, Concanen Recordings

LORRE, PETER (1904–1964), HNG
Der Verlorene, Novel
  Verlorene, Der 1951 d: Peter Lorre. lps: Peter Lorre, Karl John, Renate Mannhardt. 98M GRM. *The Lost One* (UKN); *The Lost Man* prod/rel: Arnold Pressburger Filmproduktion

LORTZ, RICHARD
Voices, Play
  Voices 1973 d: Kevin Billington. lps: David Hemmings, Gayle Hunnicutt, Lynn Farleigh. 91M UKN. *House of Voices* prod/rel: Hemdale, Warden

LORTZING, ALBERT
Zar Und Zimmermann, Leipzig 1837, Opera
  Zar Und Zimmermann 1970 d: Joachim Hess. lps: Raymond Wolansky, Peter Haage, Hans Sotin. MTV. 137M GRM. prod/rel: Polyphon Film & Tv Productions

LOTHAR
Gefahrdete Madchen, Novel
  Gefahrdete Madchen 1927 d: Heinz Schall. lps: Nina Vanna, Margarete Kupfer, Harry Hardt. 2286m GRM. prod/rel: Koop-Film-Co.

LOTHAR, ERNST
The Clairvoyant, Novel
  Clairvoyant, The 1935 d: Maurice Elvey. lps: Claude Rains, Fay Wray, Jane Baxter. 80M UKN. *The Evil Mind* prod/rel: Gainsborough, Gaumont-British

Der Engel Mit Der Posaune, Novel
  Angel With the Trumpet, The 1950 d: Anthony Bushell. lps: Eileen Herlie, Norman Wooland, Basil Sydney. 98M UKN. *Angel With a Trumpet* prod/rel: British Lion Production Assets, London Films
  Engel Mit Der Posaune, Der 1948 d: Karl Hartl, Anthony Bushell. lps: Paula Wessely, Attila Horbiger, Hedwig Bleibtreu. 137M AUS/UKN. *The Angel With the Trumpet* (UKN) prod/rel: Vindobona, Bavaria

Little Friend, Novel
  Little Friend 1934 d: Berthold Viertel. lps: Matheson Lang, Nova Pilbeam, Lydia Sherwood. 85M UKN. prod/rel: Gaumont-British

The Mills of God, Novel
  Act of Murder, An 1948 d: Michael Gordon. lps: Fredric March, Florence Eldridge, Edmond O'Brien. 91M USA. *Live Today for Tomorrow; I Stand Accused; Case Against Calvin Cooke* prod/rel: Universal International

LOTHAR, RUDOLPH
The Command to Love, New York 1927, Play
  Boudoir Diplomat, The 1930 d: Malcolm St. Clair. lps: Betty Compson, Ian Keith, Mary Duncan. 68M USA. prod/rel: Universal Pictures
  Don Juan Diplomatico 1931 d: George Melford. lps: Miguel Faust Rocha, Lia Tora, Celia Montalvan. 8r USA. *Diplomatico de Salon* prod/rel: Universal Pictures Corp.

The Critical Year, Story
  For Wives Only 1926 d: Victor Heerman. lps: Marie Prevost, Victor Varconi, Charles Gerrard. 5800f USA. prod/rel: Metropolitan Pictures Corp. of Calif., Producers Distributing Corp.

Folies-Bergere, Play
  Folies-Bergere 1935 d: Marcel Achard. lps: Maurice Chevalier, Nathalie Paley, Sim VivA. 75M FRN. prod/rel: 20th Century-Fox

Die Frau Mit Der Maske, Berlin 1922, Novel
  Masked Dancer, The 1924 d: Burton L. King. lps: Lowell Sherman, Helene Chadwick, Leslie Austen. 4987f USA. prod/rel: Eastern Productions

Konig Harlekin, Munich 1904, Play
  Magic Flame, The 1927 d: Henry King. lps: Ronald Colman, Vilma Banky, Agostino Borgato. 8308f USA. prod/rel: Samuel Goldwyn, Inc., United Artists

The Red Cat, New York 1934, Play
  Folies Bergere de Paris 1935 d: Roy Del Ruth. lps: Maurice Chevalier, Merle Oberon, Ann Sothern. 85M USA. *The Man from the Folies Bergere* (UKN); *Folies Bergere; Folies-Bergere* prod/rel: 20th Century Pictures©, Darryl Zanuck Production
  On the Riviera 1951 d: Walter Lang. lps: Danny Kaye, Gene Tierney, Corinne Calvet. 90M USA. prod/rel: 20th Century-Fox
  That Night in Rio 1941 d: Irving Cummings. lps: Alice Faye, Don Ameche, Carmen MirandA. 90M USA. *Road to Rio* prod/rel: 20th Century-Fox

Return of a Stranger, Play
  Return of a Stranger 1937 d: Victor Hanbury. lps: Griffith Jones, Ellis Jeffreys, Athole Stewart. 70M UKN. *The Face Behind the Scar* (USA); *Return of the Stranger* prod/rel: Premier, Stafford

LOTI, PIERRE (1850–1923), FRN, Viaud, Louis Marie Julien
Madame Chrysantheme, 1888, Novel
  Premiere Der Butterfly 1939 d: Carmine Gallone. lps: Maria Cebotari, Fosco Giachetti, Lucie Englisch. 95M GRM.
  Sogno Di Butterfly, Il 1939 d: Carmine Gallone. lps: Maria Cebotari, Fosco Giachetti, Germana Paolieri. 100M ITL. *The Dream of Butterfly* prod/rel: Grandi Film Storici, I.C.I.

Pecheur d'Islande, 1886, Novel
  Pecheur d'Islande 1915 d: Henri Pouctal. lps: Romuald Joube, Camille Bert, Andree Lyonel. FRN. prod/rel: le Film d'Art
  Pecheur d'Islande 1924 d: Jacques de Baroncelli. lps: Charles Vanel, Sandra Milowanoff, Roger San JuanA. 2700m FRN. prod/rel: Films Baroncelli
  Pecheur d'Islande 1933 d: Pierre Guerlais. lps: Thomy Bourdelle, Marguerite Weintenberger, Yvette Guilbert. 75M FRN. prod/rel: Productions Pierre Guerlais
  Pecheur d'Islande 1959 d: Pierre Schoendoerffer. lps: Jean-Claude Pascal, Juliette Mayniel, Charles Vanel. 87M FRN. prod/rel: Georges De Beauregard

Ramuntcho, 1896, Novel
  Mariage de Ramuntcho, Le 1946 d: Max de Vaucorbeil. lps: Andre Dassary, Gaby Sylvia, Mona Dol. 80M FRN. prod/rel: Films De France
  Ramuntcho 1919 d: Jacques de Baroncelli. lps: Yvonne Anny, Rene Lorsay, Jacques Roussel. 920m FRN. prod/rel: Film d'Art
  Ramuntcho 1937 d: Rene Barberis. lps: Madeleine Ozeray, Line Noro, Paul Cambo. 90M FRN. prod/rel: F.I.C.
  Ramuntcho 1958 d: Pierre Schoendoerffer. lps: Francois Guerin, Mijanou Bardot, Roger Hanin. 90M FRN. prod/rel: Georges De Beauregard

Le Roman d'un Spahi, 1881, Novel
  Roman d'un Spahi, Le 1914 d: Henri Pouctal. lps: Lucien Callamand, Pierre Magnier, Emilienne Dux. 1555m FRN. prod/rel: Film d'Art
  Roman d'un Spahi, Le 1936 d: Michel Bernheim. lps: Jorge Rigaud, Mireille Balin, Antonin Berval. 82M FRN. prod/rel: Productions Claude Dolbert

LOTINGA, ERNIE (1876–1951), UKN, Lotinga, Ernest
K.C. Josser, Play
  Josser, K.C. 1929 d: Hugh Croise. lps: Ernie LotingA. 19M UKN. prod/rel: British Sound Film Productions, Bifd

The Orderly Room, Play
  Orderly Room, The 1928 d: Hugh Croise. lps: Ernie LotingA. SND. 17M UKN. prod/rel: de Forest Phonofilms

The Police Force, Play
  Doing His Duty 1929 d: Hugh Croise. lps: Ernie LotingA. 13M UKN. prod/rel: British Sound Film Productions, Bifd

P.C. Josser 1931 d: Milton Rosmer. lps: Ernie Lotinga, Jack Frost, Maisie Darrell. 90M UKN. *Josser P.C.* prod/rel: Gainsborough, Woolf & Freedman

LOTT, MILTON
The Last Hunt, Novel
  Last Hunt, The 1955 d: Richard Brooks. lps: Robert Taylor, Stewart Granger, Debra Paget. 108M USA. prod/rel: MGM

LOUDEN, THOMAS
The Champion, New York 1921, Play
  World's Champion, The 1922 d: Phil Rosen. lps: Wallace Reid, Lois Wilson, Lionel Belmore. 5030f USA. prod/rel: Famous Players-Lasky, Paramount Pictures

LOUREIRO, JOSE
Who Killed Pixote?, Book
  Quem Matou Pixote? 1996 d: Jose Joffily. lps: Cassiano Carneiro, Luciana Rigueira, Joana Fomm. 120M BRZ. *Who Killed Pixote?* prod/rel: Coeves Films

LOUVET DE COUVRAY
Les Aventures du Chevalier de Faublas, Novel
  Aventures du Chevalier de Faublas, Les 1913 d: Henri Pouctal. FRN. prod/rel: Film d'Art

LOUYS, PIERRE (1870–1925), FRN, Louis, Pierre
Aphrodite, Novel
  Aphrodite 1982 d: Robert Fuest. lps: Valerie Kaprisky, Horst Buchholz, Catherine Jourdan. 95M FRN/SWT. prod/rel: Films de la Tour, Carlton Film

Les Aventures du Roi Pausole, 1901, Novel
  Aventures du Roi Pausole, Les 1933 d: Alexis Granowsky. lps: Josette Day, Edwige Feuillere, Andre Berley. 75M FRN. prod/rel: Algra, Societe Des Films Sonores Tobis

Bilitis, Novel
  Bilitis 1977 d: David Hamilton. lps: Patti d'Arbanville, Mona Kristensen, Bernard Giraudeau. 93M FRN. prod/rel: Films 21, Mars Int.

La Femme Et le Pantin, Paris 1898, Novel
  Cet Obscur Objet du Desir 1977 d: Luis Bunuel. lps: Fernando Rey, Carole Bouquet, Angela MolinA. 103M FRN/SPN. *That Obscure Object of Desire* (USA)
  Devil Is a Woman, The 1935 d: Josef von Sternberg. lps: Marlene Dietrich, Lionel Atwill, Cesar Romero. 83M USA. *Caprice Espagnole*; *Carnival in Spain* prod/rel: Paramount Productions, Inc.
  Femme Et le Pantin, La 1929 d: Jacques de Baroncelli. lps: Conchita Montenegro, Andree Canti, Raymond Destac. 2250m FRN. prod/rel: Societe Des Cineromans, Films De France
  Femme Et le Pantin, La 1958 d: Julien Duvivier. lps: Brigitte Bardot, Antonio Vilar, Espanita Cortez. 100M FRN/ITL. *A Woman Like Satan* (USA); *Femmina* (ITL); *The Female* prod/rel: Christine Gouze-Renal, Societe Nouvelle Pathe-Cinema
  Woman and the Puppet, The 1920 d: Reginald Barker. lps: Geraldine Farrar, Lou Tellegen, Dorothy Cumming. 6095f USA. prod/rel: Goldwyn Pictures Corp.©, Goldwyn Distributing Corp.

LOUYS, YVES
Short Story
  Mob 39 1940 d: Arthur Porchet. lps: Jim Gerald, Jean Nello, Pauline Carton. 77M SWT. *Granzbsetzig 39*; *Sous le Casque!*; *Mobilisation 39*; *D'rossliwirtin Eusere Soldate-Muetter* prod/rel: D.F.G. Geneve

LOUZEIRO, JOSE
Infancia Dos Mortos, 1977, Novel
  Pixote, a Lei Do Mais Fraco 1981 d: Hector Babenco. lps: Fernando Ramos Da Silva, Jorge Juliao, Gilberta MourA. 125M BRZ. *Pixote: la Ley Del Mas Debil* (UKN); *The Law of the Weaker Pixote*; *Pixote* prod/rel: Embrafilme

O Passageiro Da Agonia Lucio Flavio, 1975, Novel
  Lucio Flavio, O Passageiro Da Agonia 1978 d: Hector Babenco. lps: Reginaldo Farias, Ana Maria Magalhaes, Milton Candido. 118M BRZ. *Lucio Flavio* (UKN)

LOVE, EDMUND G.
Short Story
  Destination Gobi 1953 d: Robert Wise. lps: Richard Widmark, Don Taylor, Max Showalter. 89M USA. *Gobi Outpost*; *Sixty Saddles for Gobi* prod/rel: 20th Century-Fox

LOVECRAFT, H. P. (1890–1937), USA, Lovecraft, Howard Phillips
The Colour Out of Space, 1927, Short Story
  Monster of Terror 1965 d: Daniel Haller. lps: Boris Karloff, Nick Adams, Freda Jackson. 81M UKN. *Monster, Die Die* (USA); *House at the End of the World* prod/rel: Anglo-Amalgamated, Aip

The Dunwich Horror, 1933, Short Story
  Dunwich Horror, The 1970 d: Daniel Haller. lps: Dean Stockwell, Ed Begley, Lloyd Bochner. 90M USA. *Dunwich* prod/rel: American International Pictures

Herbert West: the Re-Animator, Story
  Re-Animator 1985 d: Stuart Gordon. lps: Jeffrey Combs, Bruce Abbott, Barbara Crampton. 84M USA. prod/rel: Empire Pictures, Re-Animator Productions

The Shuttered Room, 1959, Short Story
  Shuttered Room, The 1967 d: David Greene. lps: Gig Young, Carol Lynley, Oliver Reed. 99M UKN. prod/rel: Seven Arts Productions, Troy-Schenck Pictures

The Statement of Randolph Carter, Short Story
  Unnameable II, The 1992 d: Jean-Paul Ouellette. lps: John Rhys-Davies, Mark Kinsey Stephenson, Julie Strain. 95M USA. *The Unnameable Returns* prod/rel: Yankee Classic, Am East
  Unnameable, The 1988 d: Jean-Paul Ouellette. lps: Charles (4) King, Mark Kinsey Stephenson, Alexandra Durrell. 87M USA. prod/rel: Yankee Classic

The Strange Case of Charles Dexter Ward
  Resurrected, The 1991 d: Dan O'Bannon. lps: Chris Sarandon, Jane Sibett, John Terry. 105M USA. prod/rel: Scotti Bros.

The Unnameable, Short Story
  Unnameable 2, The 1992 d: Jean-Paul Ouellette. lps: John Rhys-Davies, Mark Kinsey Stephenson, Julie Strain. 95M USA. *The Unnameable Returns* prod/rel: Yankee Classic, Am East
  Unnameable, The 1988 d: Jean-Paul Ouellette. lps: Charles (4) King, Mark Kinsey Stephenson, Alexandra Durrell. 87M USA. prod/rel: Yankee Classic

LOVELL, JIM
Lost Moon, Book
  Apollo 13 1995 d: Ron Howard. lps: Tom Hanks, Bill Paxton, Kevin Bacon. 140M USA. prod/rel: Imagine

LOVELL, MARC
Apple Pie in the Sky, Novel
  Trouble With Spies, The 1984 d: Burt Kennedy. lps: Donald Sutherland, Ned Beatty, Ruth Gordon. 91M USA. prod/rel: Deg-Hbo

LOVEN, KARL
Gipfelkreuz, Novel
  Gesetz Ohne Gnade 1951 d: Harald Reinl. lps: Karl Loven, Harriet Gessner, Rudolf Schatzberg. 88M GRM/AUS. *Das Gipfelkreuz*; *Law Without Mercy* prod/rel: Aafa, Jugend

LOVER, SAMUEL (1797–1868), IRL
Handy Andy, Novel
  Handy Andy 1921 d: Bert Wynne. lps: Peter Coleman, Kathleen Vaughan, Warwick Ward. 5000f UKN. prod/rel: Ideal

Rory O'More, 1839, Novel
  Rory O'More 1911 d: Sidney Olcott. lps: Jack J. Clark, Gene Gauthier, Robert VignolA. 1000f USA. *Rory O'Moore* prod/rel: Kalem

LOVINESCU, HORIA
Citadela Sfarimata, 1955, Play
  Citadela Sfarimata 1957 d: Marc Maurette. lps: Ion Fintesteanu, Gyorgy Kovacs. 107M RMN/FRN. *The Crumbling Citadel*

Febre, 1963, Play
  Poveste Sentimentala 1961 d: Iulian Mihu. lps: Irina Petrusca, Victor Rebengiuc, Emil BottA. 94M RMN. *A Sentimental Story*

Moartea Unui Artist, 1965, Play
  Moartea Unui Artist 1991 d: Horea Popescu. 113M RMN.

Surorile Boga, 1959, Play
  Surorile 1984 d: Iulian Mihu. 119M RMN. *The Sisters*

LOVRAK, MARTE
Druzba Pere Kvrzice, Novel
  Druzba Pere Kvrzice 1971 d: Vladimir Tadej. lps: Mladen Vasari, Adem Cejvan, Boris Dvornik. 85M YGS. *Little Peter's Diary* prod/rel: Croatia-Film

LOWDER, DENNIS
Bellman and True, Novel
  Bellman and True 1988 d: Richard Loncraine. lps: Bernard Hill, Kieran O'Brien, Richard Hope. 121M UKN. prod/rel: Handmade Films, Euston Films

LOWELL, JOAN
The Cradle of the Deep, New York 1920, Novel
  Adventure Girl 1934 d: Herman C. Raymaker. lps: Joan Lowell, William Sawyer, Otto Siegler. 76M USA. *Joan Lowell Adventure Girl* prod/rel: the Van Beuren Corp.

LOWENSTEIN, WENDY
Dead Men Don't Dig Coal, Book
  Strikebound 1984 d: Richard Lowenstein. lps: Chris Haywood, Carol Burns, Hugh Keays-Byrne. 101M ASL. *Sunbeam Shaft* prod/rel: Trm Productions Pty Ltd.©, Film Victoria

LOWINGER, GRETL
Der Keusche Adam, Play
  Keusche Adam, Der 1950 d: Karl Sztollar, Paul Lowinger. lps: Paul Lowinger, Gustav Waldau, Gretl Lowinger. 97M AUS. prod/rel: Helios, Constantin

Valentins Sundenfall, Play
  Valentins Sundenfall 1951 d: Paul Lowinger, August Rieger. lps: Josef Egger, Sepp Rist, Paul Lowinger. 90M AUS. prod/rel: Schonbrunn

LOWINGER, PAUL
Der Keusche Adam, Play
  Keusche Adam, Der 1950 d: Karl Sztollar, Paul Lowinger. lps: Paul Lowinger, Gustav Waldau, Gretl Lowinger. 97M AUS. prod/rel: Helios, Constantin

LOWNDES, MRS. BELLOC (1868–1947), UKN, Lowndes, Marie Adelaide
Chink in the Armour, Novel
  House of Peril, The 1922 d: Kenelm Foss. lps: Fay Compton, Roy Travers, A. B. Imeson. 5000f UKN. prod/rel: Astra Films

Ivy, Novel
  Ivy 1947 d: Sam Wood. lps: Joan Fontaine, Patric Knowles, Herbert Marshall. 99M USA. prod/rel: Universal

Letty Lynton, New York 1931, Novel
  Letty Lynton 1932 d: Clarence Brown. lps: Joan Crawford, Robert Montgomery, Nils Asther. 84M USA. prod/rel: Metro-Goldwyn-Mayer Corp., Metro-Goldwyn-Mayer Dist. Corp.©

The Lodger, London 1913, Novel
  Lodger: a Story of the London Fog, The 1926 d: Alfred Hitchcock. lps: Ivor Novello, June, Malcolm Keen. 7500f UKN. *The Case of Jonathan Drew* (USA); *The Lodger* prod/rel: Gainsborough, Woolf & Freedman
  Lodger, The 1932 d: Maurice Elvey. lps: Ivor Novello, Elizabeth Allan, A. W. Baskcomb. 85M UKN. *The Phantom Fiend* (USA) prod/rel: Twickenham, Woolf & Freedman
  Lodger, The 1944 d: John Brahm. lps: Laird Cregar, Merle Oberon, George Sanders. 84M USA. prod/rel: 20th Century-Fox
  Man in the Attic 1954 d: Hugo Fregonese. lps: Jack Palance, Constance Smith, Byron Palmer. 81M USA. prod/rel: 20th Century-Fox, Panoramic

Shameful Behavior?, New York 1910, Short Story
  Shameful Behavior? 1926 d: Albert Kelley. lps: Edith Roberts, Richard Tucker, Martha Mattox. 5218f USA. prod/rel: Preferred Pictures

LOWRY, MALCOLM (1909–1957), UKN, Lowry, Clarence Malcolm Boden
Under the Volcano, Novel
  Under the Volcano 1984 d: John Huston. lps: Albert Finney, Jacqueline Bisset, Anthony Andrews. 112M USA. prod/rel: Universal

LOWRY, ROBERT (1919–, USA
Where Is My Wandering Boy Tonight?, 1877, Song
  Where Is My Wandering Boy Tonight? 1922 d: James P. Hogan, Millard Webb. lps: Cullen Landis, Carl Stockdale, Virginia True Boardman. 7r USA. prod/rel: B. F. Zeidman Productions, Equity Pictures

LOYSON, P. H.
Ames Ennemies, 1907, Novel
  Anime Nemiche 1917. lps: Maria Jacobini, Bianca QuarantA. 810m ITL. prod/rel: Alba Film

LU MEI
Hong Qi Ge, Novel
  Hong Qi Ge 1950 d: Wu Zuguang. lps: Lu En, Yue Shen, Zhang Wei. 10r CHN. *Song of the Red Flag* prod/rel: Northeast Film Studio

LU SHI
Double Bell Watch, Novel
  Guo Qing Shi Dian Zhong 1956 d: Wu Tian. lps: Yin Zhiming, Zhao Lian, Zhao Zhiyue. 10r CHN. *10:00 on the National Holiday* prod/rel: Changchun Film Studio

LU TIEREN
Number One Killer in Shanghai, Novel
  Dong Fang Di Yi Chi Ke 1993 d: Zhao Wenxin. lps: Shen Junyi, XIa Jing, Wang Zhifei. 9r CHN. *Number One Killer in the East* prod/rel: Guangxi Film Studio

LU XIN
Zhu Jian, Story
  Zhu Jian 1994 d: Zhang Huaxun. lps: Gao Fa, Ma Jingwu, Ruan Xun. 9r CHN. *Casting Swords* prod/rel: Beijing Film Studio

LU XUN (1881–1936), CHN, Lu Hsun, Chou Shu-Jen
A Q Zheng Zhuan, Story
  A Q Zhengzhuan 1981 d: Ling Fan. lps: Yan Shunkai, Li Wei, Wang SuyA. 12r CHN. *The True Story of a Q* prod/rel: Shanghai Film Studio
Yao, Story
  Yao 1981 d: Lu Shaolian. lps: Liang Yin, Chen Qi, Qu Yun. 9r CHN. *Medicine* prod/rel: Changchun Film Studio

LU ZHENG
Battling the Enemy at His Headquarters, Novel
  Bao Mi Ju de Qiang Sheng 1979 d: Chang Yan. lps: Chen Shaoze, XIang Mei, Ni ZhenghuA. 12r CHN. *Gunfire at the Secret Bureau* prod/rel: Changchun Film Studio

LU ZHUGUO
Zhan Huo Zhong de Qing Chun, Novel
  Zhan Huo Zhong de Qing Chun 1959 d: Wang Yan. lps: Wang Suya, Pang Xueqing, Lin Nong. 10r CHN. *Youth in the Flames of War* prod/rel: Changchun Film Studio

LUBOMYRSKYJ, STEPHEN
Zorstoki Svitanki, Novel
  Zorstoki Svitanki 1966 d: John Krasnozony. lps: Mike Nosovenko, Vera Nosovenko, John Krasnozony. 182M CND. *Cruel Dawn* prod/rel: Oshawa Ukrainian Film Club, Wasik Films

LUC, JEAN-BERNARD
Le Complexe de Philemon, Play
  Relaxe-Toi, Cherie 1964 d: Jean Boyer. lps: Fernandel, Sandra Milo, Jean-Pierre Marielle. 85M FRN/ITL. *Pazza, Pazza Ho Una Moglie Pazza* (ITL); *Le Complexe de Philemon*; *Le Defoule* prod/rel: Films Corona, Ceres Films
Hibernatus, Novel
  Hibernatus 1969 d: Edouard Molinaro. lps: Louis de Funes, Claude Gensac, Olivier de Funes. 90M FRN/ITL. *Louis de Funes E Il Nonno Surgelato* (ITL) prod/rel: Gaumont International, Rizzoli Films

LUCA DE TENA, JUAN IGNACIO
La Condesa Maria, Play
  Condesa Maria, La 1927 d: Benito Perojo, Alexandre KamenkA. lps: Sandra Milowanoff, Andree Standard, Jose Nieto. 2400m SPN/FRN. *La Comtesse Marie* (FRN); *Countess Maria* prod/rel: Albatros (Paris), Julisar (Madrid)

LUCAS, CLEO
I Jerry Take Thee Joan, New York 1911, Novel
  Merrily We Go to Hell 1932 d: Dorothy Arzner. lps: Fredric March, Sylvia Sidney, Adrianne Allen. 88M USA. *Merrily We Go to ..* (UKN); *Jerry and Joan* prod/rel: Paramount Publix Corp.©

LUCAS, GEORGE
Story
  Raiders of the Lost Ark 1981 d: Steven Spielberg. lps: Harrison Ford, Karen Allen, Paul Freeman. 115M USA. prod/rel: Paramount
  Willow 1988 d: Ron Howard. lps: Val Kilmer, Joanne Whalley-Kilmer, Warwick Davis. 125M USA. prod/rel: MGM, United Artists

LUCAS, IB
The Silhouette, Novel
  I Wonder Who's Kissing You Now 1999 d: Henning Carlsen. lps: Tommy Kenter, Marika Lagercrantz, Morten Grunwald. 96M DNM. prod/rel: Buena Vista (Denmark), Dagmar Film Productions

LUCAS, PIERRE
Police Des Moeurs, Novel
  Police Des Moeurs 1987 d: Jean Rougeron. lps: Yves Jouffroy, Henri Poirier, Laurence Savin. 85M FRN. *Les Filles de Saint Tropez*; *Saint Tropez Vice* prod/rel: Maillot Films

LUCE, ANNA
Retaggio Di Sangue, Novel
  Retaggio Di Sangue 1956 d: Max Calandri. lps: Roberto Mauri, Anna Di Lorenzo, Ettore SerrA. 2180m ITL. prod/rel: Scaligera Film, Filmar

LUCE, CLARE BOOTHE (1903–1987), USA
Come to the Stable, Story
  Come to the Stable 1949 d: Henry Koster. lps: Loretta Young, Celeste Holm, Hugh Marlowe. 95M USA. prod/rel: 20th Century-Fox
The Women, New York 1936, Play
  Opposite Sex, The 1956 d: David Miller. lps: June Allyson, Joan Collins, Dolores Gray. 117M USA. prod/rel: Metro-Goldwyn-Mayer Corp.
  Women, The 1939 d: George Cukor. lps: Joan Crawford, Norma Shearer, Rosalind Russell. 133M USA. prod/rel: Metro-Goldwyn-Mayer Corp., Loew's, Inc.©

LUCENTE, ERNESTO
Successo a Paganigua, Story
  Segreto Inviolabile, Il 1939 d: Julio Fleischner. lps: Tony d'Algy, Maria Mercader, Jose Nieto. 82M ITL/SPN. *Su Mayor Aventura* (SPN) prod/rel: Nembo Film

LUCENTINI
La Donna Della Domenico, Novel
  Donna Della Domenica, La 1976 d: Luigi Comencini. lps: Marcello Mastroianni, Jacqueline Bisset, Jean-Louis Trintignant. 105M ITL/FRN. *La Femme Du Dimanche* (FRN); *The Sunday Woman* (USA) prod/rel: Primex Italiana (Roma), Production Fox Europa (Paris)

LUCHAIRE, JULIEN
Altitude 3200, Play
  Altitude 3200 1938 d: Jean Benoit-Levy, Marie Epstein. lps: Jean-Louis Barrault, Fabien Loris, Charles Dorat. 91M FRN. *Youth in Revolt* (USA); *Le Grand Reve*; *Nous Les Jeunes* prod/rel: Transcontinental Film

LUCIANI, MARIO
Il Mondo Vuole Cosi, Play
  Mondo Vuole Cosi, Il 1946 d: Giorgio Bianchi. lps: Clara Calamai, Vittorio de Sica, Massimo Serato. 88M ITL. prod/rel: Aura Film, Excelsa

LUCIO, CELSO
Los Aparecidos, Opera
  Aparecidos, Los 1927 d: Jose Buchs. lps: Amelia Munoz, Jose Maria Jimeno, Jose Montenegro. F SPN. *The Ghosts* prod/rel: Ediciones Forns-Buchs (Madrid)

LUDDECKE, JORG
Morituri, Bayreuth 1963, Novel
  Morituri 1965 d: Bernhard Wicki. lps: Marlon Brando, Trevor Howard, Yul Brynner. 128M USA. *Code Name Morituri Saboteur*; *The Saboteur* prod/rel: Arcola-Colony Productions

LUDERS, GUSTAV
The Prince of Pilsen, New York 1902, Musical Play
  Prince of Pilsen, The 1926 d: Paul Powell. lps: George Sidney, Anita Stewart, Allan Forrest. 6600f USA. prod/rel: Belasco Productions, Producers Distributing Corp.

LUDLOW, PATRICK
Faces, Play
  Faces 1934 d: Sidney Morgan. lps: Anna Lee, Harold French, Walter Sondes. 68M UKN. prod/rel: British and Dominions, Paramount British

LUDLUM, ROBERT (1927–, USA
The Holcroft Covenant, Novel
  Holcroft Covenant, The 1985 d: John Frankenheimer. lps: Michael Caine, Anthony Andrews, Victoria Tennant. 112M UKN/USA. prod/rel: Thorn-Emi, Holcroft Films
The Osterman Weekend, Novel
  Osterman Weekend, The 1983 d: Sam Peckinpah. lps: Burt Lancaster, John Hurt, Rutger Hauer. 102M USA. prod/rel: 20th Century Fox
The Rhinemann Exchange, Novel
  Rhinemann Exchange, The 1977 d: Burt Kennedy. lps: Stephen Collins, Lauren Hutton, Claude Akins. TVM. 250M USA. prod/rel: Universal

LUDWIG, OTTO (1813–1865), GRM
Der Erbforster, 1853, Play
  Erbforster, Der 1944 d: Alois J. Lippl. lps: Eugen Klopfer, Otto Gebuhr, Hansi Wendler. 80M GRM. prod/rel: Tobis, Atlantic
Zwischen Himmel Und Erde, 1856, Novel
  Zwischen Himmel Und Erde 1942 d: Harald Braun. lps: Werner Krauss, Wolfgang Lukschy, Gisela Uhlen. 101M GRM. prod/rel: UFA, Filmkunst
  Zwischen Himmel Und Holle 1934 d: Franz Seitz. 92M GRM. *Liebe Lasst Sich Nicht Erzwingen*; *Zwischen Himmel Und Erde*

LUGUET, ANDRE
La Patronne, Play
  Patronne, La 1949 d: Robert Dhery. lps: Andre Luguet, Andre Gabriello, Annie Ducaux. 87M FRN. prod/rel: Fides, U.G.C.

LUKEZIC, JOYCE
False Arrest, Book
  False Arrest 1991 d: B. W. L. Norton. lps: Donna Mills, Steven Bauer, Lane Smith. TVM. 182M USA. prod/rel: Leonard Hill Films©, Ron Gilbert Associates

LUMLEY, RALPH R.
In the Soup, London 1900, Play
  In the Soup 1936 d: Henry Edwards. lps: Ralph Lynn, Judy Gunn, Morton Selten. 72M UKN. prod/rel: Twickenham, Twickenham Film Distributors

LUND, DORIS
Eric, Book
  Eric 1975 d: James Goldstone. lps: Patricia Neal, Claude Akins, Sian Barbara Allen. TVM. 100M USA. prod/rel: Lorimar Productions

LUNDELL, ULF
Jack, Novel
  Jack 1977 d: Jan Halldoff. lps: Goran Stangertz, Kjell Bergquist, Orjan Ramberg. 120M SWD. *What the Hell Jack!* prod/rel: Stockholm Film, Europa Film

LUNDKVIST, NILS ARTUR
Hasthandlarens Flickor, 1935, Short Story
  Hasthandlarens Flickor 1954 d: Egil Holmsen. lps: Barbro Larsson, Margaretha Lowler, George Fant. 87M SWD. *Time of Desire* (USA)
Komedi I Hagerskog, 1959, Novel
  Komedi I Hagerskog 1968 d: Torgny Anderberg. lps: Anita Bjork, Monica Nordquist, Ulf Brunnberg. 100M SWD. *Comedy at Hagerskog*; *Odd Lovers* prod/rel: Omega
Vindingevals, 1956, Novel
  Vindingevals 1968 d: Ake Falck. lps: Diana Kjaer, Tina Hedstrom, Hans Ernback. 99M SWD. *Waltz of Sex* (UKN); *Vindinge Waltz* prod/rel: Minerva

LUNEL, ERNEST
La Chambre de la Bonne, Play
  Chambre de la Bonne, La 1918. lps: Avelot, Geo Lastry, Calve. 275m FRN. prod/rel: Pathe Freres

LUO GUANGBING
Red Rock, Novel
  Lie Huozhong Yongsheng 1965 d: Shui HuA. lps: Zhao Dan, Yu Lan, Li Jian. 15r CHN. *Living Forever in Burning Flames*; *Red Crag* prod/rel: Beijing Film Studio

LUO GUANZHONG
San Guo Yanyi, 1522, Novel
  Diao Chan 1938 d: Bu Wancang. 90M CHN.
Shuihu Zhuan, c1500, Novel
  Lin Chong 1958 d: Su Shi, Wu Yonggang. lps: Su Shi, Zhang Yi, Lin Bing. 9r CHN. prod/rel: Jiangnan Film Studio
  Wu Song 1963 d: Ying Yunwei, Yu Zhongying. 109M CHN.
  Wu Song and Pan Jinlian 1938 d: Wu Cun. lps: Jin Yan, Liu Qiong. 90M CHN.
  Ye Zhu Lin 1965 d: Wu Cun. 109M CHN.
  Yingxiong Bense 1993 d: Chen Huiyi. lps: Liang Jiahui, Wang Zuxian, Xu Jingjiang. 10r CHN/HKG. *Blood of the Leopard*; *True Colors of a Hero* prod/rel: Pearl River Film Studio, Hong Kong Entertainment Film Co.

LUPICA, MIKE
Power, Murder Money, Novel
  Money, Power, Murder 1989 d: Lee Philips. lps: Kevin Dobson, Blythe Danner, Josef Sommer. 91M USA. prod/rel: Skids Productions, CBS Entertainment

LUPINO, STANLEY
Hold My Hand, London 1931, Musical Play
  Hold My Hand 1938 d: Thornton Freeland. lps: Stanley Lupino, Fred Emney, Barbara Blair. 76M UKN. prod/rel: Associated British Picture Corporation
Love Lies, Musical Play
  Love Lies 1931 d: Lupino Lane. lps: Stanley Lupino, Dorothy Boyd, Jack Hobbs. 70M UKN. prod/rel: British International Pictures, Wardour
The Love Race, London 1930, Musical Play
  Love Race, The 1931 d: Lupino Lane, Pat Morton. lps: Stanley Lupino, Jack Hobbs, Dorothy Boyd. 83M UKN. prod/rel: British International Pictures, Pathe
Over She Goes, 1936, Play
  Over She Goes 1937 d: Graham Cutts. lps: Stanley Lupino, Laddie Cliff, Claire Luce. 74M UKN. prod/rel: Associated British Pictures Corp.
Sporting Love, London 1934, Musical Play
  Sporting Love 1936 d: J. Elder Wills. lps: Stanley Lupino, Laddie Cliff, Eda Peel. 70M UKN. prod/rel: Hammer, British Lion

LURIE, ALISON (1926–, USA
The War Between the Tates, Novel
  War Between the Tates, The 1977 d: Lee Philips. lps: Elizabeth Ashley, Richard Crenna, Ann Wedgeworth. TVM. 100M USA. prod/rel: Talent Associates Ltd.

LUSSU, EMILIO
Un Anno Sull'altopiano, Novel
  Uomini Contro 1970 d: Francesco Rosi. lps: Mark Frechette, Alain Cuny, Gian Maria Volonte. 101M ITL/YGS. *Ljudi Protiv* (YGS); *Just Another War*; *Many Wars Ago*; *Un Anno Sull'altipiano* prod/rel: Prima Cin.Ca (Roma), Dubrava Film (Zagreb)

LUSTGARTEN, EDGAR (1907–1979), UKN
Game for Three Losers, Novel
  Game for Three Losers 1965 d: Gerry O'HarA. lps:
  Michael Gough, Mark Eden, Toby Robins. 55M UKN.
  prod/rel: Anglo-Amalgamated, Merton Park

LUSTIG, ARNOST
Noc a Nadeje, Prague 1957, Novel
  Transport Z Raje 1962 d: Zbynek Brynych. lps:
  Zdenek Stepanek, Cestmir Randa, Ilja Prachar. 100M
  CZC. *Transport from Paradise* (USA) prod/rel:
  Barrandov Film Studio
Tma Ne Ma Stin, Prague 1958, Short Story
  Demanty Noci 1964 d: Jan Nemec. lps: Ladislav
  Jansky, Antonin Kumbera, Ilse BischofovA. 75M CZC.
  Diamonds of the Night (USA) prod/rel: Ceskoslovensky
  Film

LUTHER, BARBARA
Moon Walk, 1962, Short Story
  Ticklish Affair, A 1963 d: George Sidney. lps: Shirley
  Jones, Gig Young, Red Buttons. 88M USA. *Moon Walk*
  prod/rel: Enterpe, Inc.

LUTHER, MARK LEE
The Crucible, New York 1907, Novel
  Crucible, The 1914 d: Edwin S. Porter, Hugh Ford. lps:
  Marguerite Clark, Harold Lockwood, Justine Johnston.
  4-5r USA. prod/rel: Famous Players Film Co.,
  Paramount Pictures Corp.
The Hope Chest, Boston 1918, Novel
  Hope Chest, The 1918 d: Elmer Clifton. lps: Dorothy
  Gish, Richard Barthelmess, George Fawcett. 4686f
  USA. prod/rel: New Art Film Co., Famous
  Players-Lasky Corp.©

LUTHGE, BOBBY E.
Darf Man? Darf Man Nicht?, Play
  Nachte Am Nil 1949 d: Arthur M. Rabenalt. lps: Sonja
  Ziemann, Wolfgang Lukschy, Ina Caroll. 102M GRM.
  Nights on the Nile prod/rel: Cordial, Herzog
Drei Tage Mittelarrest, Play
  Drei Tage Mittelarrest 1955 d: Georg Jacoby. lps:
  Ernst Waldow, Grethe Weiser, Erwin Strahl. 95M GRM.
  *Three Days Solitary Confinement; Three Days in the
  Guardhouse* prod/rel: Standard, D.F.H.

LUTTWAK, EDWARD N.
Coup d'Etat, Novel
  Power Play 1978 d: Martyn Burke. lps: Peter O'Toole,
  David Hemmings, Donald Pleasence. 115M CND/UKN.
  *State of Shock; Coup d'Etat; Operation Overthrow; Le
  Jeu de la Puissance* prod/rel: Magnum Intl. Prods.
  (Coup) (Toronto), Cowry Film Productions Ltd.
  (London)

LUTZ, GRACE LIVINGSTON HILL
The Best Man, 1913, Novel
  Best Man, The 1914 d: Charles J. Brabin. lps: Marc
  MacDermott, Gertrude McCoy, Mrs. William Bechtel. 2r
  USA. prod/rel: Edison
  Best Man, The 1919 d: Thomas N. Heffron. lps: J.
  Warren Kerrigan, Lois Wilson, Alfred Whitman. 5r
  USA. prod/rel: Jesse D. Hampton Productions, W. W.
  Hodkinson Corp.
The Enchanted Barn, Philadelphia 1918, Novel
  Enchanted Barn, The 1919 d: David Smith. lps:
  Bessie Love, J. Frank Glendon, Joseph Singleton. 5r
  USA. prod/rel: Vitagraph Co. of America©, Blue Ribbon
  Feature

LUTZ, JOHN
The Ex, Novel
  Ex, The 1996 d: Mark L. Lester. lps: Yancy Butler, Suzy
  Amis, Nick Mancuso. 87M CND. prod/rel: Ex and on
  Productions©, American World Pictures
Swf Seeks Same, Novel
  Single White Female 1992 d: Barbet Schroeder. lps:
  Bridget Fonda, Jennifer Jason Leigh, Steven Weber.
  108M USA. prod/rel: Columbia Pictures

LUTZ, JOSEEPH MARIA
Der Brandner Kaspar Schaut Ins Paradies, Play
  Seltsame Geschichte Des Brandner Kasper, Die
  1949 d: Josef von Baky. lps: Paul Horbiger, Viktor Staal,
  Ursula Lingen. 100M GRM. *The Strange Story of
  Brandner Kasper; Das Tor Zum Paradies; The Gate to
  Paradise* prod/rel: Bavaria

LUTZKENDORF, FELIX
Liebesbriefe, Play
  Liebesbriefe 1943 d: Hans H. Zerlett. lps: Kathe
  Haack, Hermann Thimig, Suse Graf. 100M GRM.
  prod/rel: UFA

LUU SON MINH
Duyen Nghiep, Short Story
  Duyen Nghiep 1998 d: Nguyen Vu Chau. lps: Tung
  Thuy, Minh Hoa, Nguyen Trung Hieu. 86M VTN. *Fated
  Vocation* prod/rel: Viet Nam Feature Film

LUXEL, CLAUDE
Entre Onze Heures Et Minuit, Novel
  Entre Onze Heures Et Minuit 1948 d: Henri Decoin.
  lps: Louis Jouvet, Madeleine Robinson, Robert Arnoux.
  92M FRN. *Between Eleven and Midnight* (USA); *Odeon
  36.72* prod/rel: Roitfeld, Francinex

LYALL, GAVIN (1932–, UKN
  Novel
  Secret Servant, The 1984. lps: Charles Dance, Dan
  O'Herlihy. MTV. 150M UKN. prod/rel: BBC

LYLE JR., EUGENE P.
Blaze Derringer, New York 1910, Novel
  American Pluck 1925 d: Richard Stanton. lps: George
  Walsh, Wanda Hawley, Sidney de Grey. 5900f USA.
  Pluck prod/rel: Chadwick Pictures
  Americano, The 1917 d: John Emerson. lps: Douglas
  Fairbanks, Alma Rubens, Spottiswoode Aitken. 5r USA.
  prod/rel: Triangle Distributing Corp., Fine Arts Film
  Co.
D'artagnan of Kansas, 1912, Short Story
  Modern Musketeer, A 1917 d: Allan Dwan. lps:
  Douglas Fairbanks, Marjorie Daw, Kathleen Kirkham.
  5r USA. prod/rel: Douglas Fairbanks Pictures Corp.,
  Artcraft Pictures Corp.©
The Ringtailed Galliwampus, 1922, Short Story
  Try and Get It 1924 d: Cullen Tate. lps: Bryant
  Washburn, Billie Dove, Edward Everett Horton. 5707f
  USA. prod/rel: Samuel V. Grand, Producers
  Distributing Corp.

LYMINGTON, JOHN
Night of the Big Heat, Novel
  Night of the Big Heat 1967 d: Terence Fisher. lps:
  Christopher Lee, Peter Cushing, Patrick Allen. 94M
  UKN. *Island of the Burning Damned* (USA); *Island of
  the Burning Doomed* prod/rel: Planet Films

LYNCH, BENITO (1885?–1951), ARG
Los Caranchos de la Florida, 1916, Novel
  Caranchos de la Florida, Los 1938 d: Alberto de
  ZavaliA. lps: Amelia Bence. 78M ARG.
El Ingles de Los Guesos, 1924, Novel
  Ingles de Los Guesos, El 1940 d: Carlos Hugo
  Christensen. lps: Arturo Garcia Buhr, Anita Jordan,
  Pedro MarateA. 79M ARG.

LYNDE, FRANCIS
The Real Man, New Ork 1915, Novel
  Bucking the Line 1921 d: Carl Harbaugh. lps: Maurice
  B. Flynn, Molly Malone, Norman Selby. 4544f USA.
  prod/rel: Fox Film Corp.
Stranded in Arcady, New York 1917, Novel
  Stranded in Arcady 1917 d: Frank H. Crane. lps:
  Irene Castle, Elliott Dexter, Pell Trenton. 5r USA.
  prod/rel: Astra Film Corp., Pathe Exchange, Inc.©

LYNDON, BARRE
The Amazing Dr. Clitterhouse, New York 1937, Play
  Amazing Doctor Clitterhouse, The 1938 d: Anatole
  Litvak. lps: Edward G. Robinson, Claire Trevor,
  Humphrey Bogart. 87M USA. prod/rel: Warner Bros.
  Pictures
The Man in Half Moon Street, London 1939, Play
  Man in Half Moon Street, The 1944 d: Ralph
  Murphy. lps: Nils Asther, Helen Walker, Reinhold
  Schunzel. 92M USA. prod/rel: Paramount
  Man Who Could Cheat Death, The 1959 d: Terence
  Fisher. lps: Anton Diffring, Hazel Court, Christopher
  Lee. 83M UKN. *The Man in Rue Noir* prod/rel: Hammer,
  Cadogan
Sundown, Short Story
  Sundown 1941 d: Henry Hathaway. lps: Gene Tierney,
  Bruce Cabot, George Sanders. 90M USA. prod/rel:
  United Artists, Walter Wanger
They Came By Night, London 1937, Play
  They Came By Night 1940 d: Harry Lachman. lps:
  Will Fyffe, Phyllis Calvert, Anthony Hulme. 72M
  UKN/USA. prod/rel: 20th Century Productions, 20th
  Century-Fox

LYNN, LORETTA
  Autobiography
  Coal Miner's Daughter, The 1980 d: Michael Apted.
  lps: Sissy Spacek, Tommy Lee Jones, Beverly d'Angelo.
  125M USA. *Nashville Lady* prod/rel: Universal

LYNN, MARGARET
The Other Man, Novel
  Other Man, The 1970 d: Richard A. CollA. lps: Roy
  Thinnes, Arthur Hill, Joan Hackett. TVM. 100M USA.
  prod/rel: Universal

LYON, ARTHUR
Castles Burning, Novel
  Slow Burn 1986 d: Matthew Chapman. lps: Eric
  Roberts, Beverly d'Angelo, Dennis Lipscomb. TVM.
  88M USA. prod/rel: Castles Burning, Mca Pay Tv

LYON, DANA
The Frightened Child, 1948, Novel
  House on Telegraph Hill 1951 d: Robert Wise. lps:
  Richard Basehart, Valentina Cortese, William
  Lundigan. 93M USA. prod/rel: 20th Century-Fox

LYON, EARLE
Stagecoach to Fury, Novel
  Stagecoach to Fury 1956 d: William F. Claxton. lps:
  Forrest Tucker, Mari Blanchard, Wallace Ford. 76M
  USA. prod/rel: 20th Century-Fox, Regal Films

LYONS, A. NEIL
London Pride, London 1916, Play
  London Pride 1920 d: Harold Shaw. lps: Edna
  Flugrath, Fred Groves, O. B. Clarence. 5200f UKN.
  prod/rel: London, Jury

LYONS, IVAN
Who Is Killing the Great Chefs of Europe?, Novel
  Who Is Killing the Great Chefs of Europe? 1978 d:
  Ted Kotcheff. lps: George Segal, Jacqueline Bisset,
  Robert Morley. 112M USA/GRM. *Die Schlemmer-Orgie*
  (GRM); *Too Many Chefs* (UKN) prod/rel: Warner Bros.

LYONS, NAN
Who Is Killing the Great Chefs of Europe? 1978 d:
  Ted Kotcheff. lps: George Segal, Jacqueline Bisset,
  Robert Morley. 112M USA/GRM. *Die Schlemmer-Orgie*
  (GRM); *Too Many Chefs* (UKN) prod/rel: Warner Bros.

LYTTKENS, ALICE
Ich Komme Nicht Zum Abendessen, Novel
  Frau Am Scheidewege, Die 1938 d: Josef von Baky.
  lps: Magda Schneider, Karin Hardt, Ewald Balser. 95M
  GRM/HNG. *Asszony a Valaszuton* (HNG); *Das
  Schicksal Einer Arztin* prod/rel: Hunnia

LYTTKENS, YNGVE
Yngsjomordet, Stockholm 1951, Novel
  Yngsjomordet 1966 d: Arne Mattsson. lps: Gunnel
  Lindblom, Gosta Ekman Jr., Christina Schollin. 120M
  SWD. *Woman of Darkness* (USA) prod/rel: Svensk
  Filmindustri

LYTTON, BART
Hangman's Village, Story
  Hitler's Madman 1943 d: Douglas Sirk. lps: Patricia
  Morison, John Carradine, Alan Curtis. 84M USA.
  Hitler's Hangman prod/rel: MGM

LYTTON, EDWARD GEORGE BULWER
  (1803–1873), UKN, Bulwer-Lytton, Edward George
The Christian Martyrs, Novel
  Christian Martyrs, The 1909 d: Otis Turner. lps:
  Hobart Bosworth, Betty Harte, Robert Leonard. 950f
  USA. prod/rel: Selig Polyscope Co.
Damon and Pythias, Novel
  Damon and Pythias 1908 d: Otis Turner. lps: Hobart
  Bosworth, Betty Harte, Otis Turner. SHT USA.
  prod/rel: Selig Polyscope Co.
  Damon and Pythias 1914 d: Otis Turner. lps: Cleo
  Madison, Anna Little, William Worthington. 5-6r USA.
  prod/rel: Universal Film Mfg. Co.
Ernest Maltravers, Novel
  End of the Road, The 1913 d: William Robert Daly. 2r
  USA. prod/rel: Gem
  Ernest Maltravers 1914 d: Travers Vale. lps: Alan
  Hale, Louise Vale, Jack Drumier. 2r USA. prod/rel:
  Biograph Co.
  Ernest Maltravers 1920 d: Jack Denton. lps: Cowley
  Wright, Lillian Hall-Davis, Hubert Gordon Hopkirk.
  5000f UKN. prod/rel: Ideal
Eugene Aram, London 1832, Novel
  Eugene Aram 1914 d: Edwin J. Collins. lps: Jack Leigh,
  Mary Manners, John Sargent. 4300f UKN. prod/rel:
  Cricks
  Eugene Aram 1915 d: Richard Ridgely. lps: Marc
  MacDermott, Mabel Trunnelle, Edward Earle. 4r USA.
  prod/rel: Thomas A. Edison, Inc.©, General Film Co.
  Eugene Aram 1924 d: Arthur Rooke. lps: Arthur
  Wontner, Barbara Hoffe, Mary Odette. 8000f UKN.
  prod/rel: I. B. Davidson, Granger
*The Haunted and the Haunters; Or the House and
  the Brain*, 1849, Short Story
  Night Comes Too Soon 1948 d: Denis Kavanagh. lps:
  Valentine Dyall, Anne Howard, Alec Faversham. 52M
  UKN. *The Ghost of Rashmon Hall* prod/rel: Federated,
  British Animated
Justinian and Theodora, Novel
  Justinian and Theodora 1911 d: Otis Turner. lps:
  Hobart Bosworth, Betty Harte, Bebe Daniels. 1000f
  USA. prod/rel: Selig Polyscope Co.
The Lady of Lyons, London 1838, Play
  In the Name of Love 1925 d: Howard Higgin. lps:
  Ricardo Cortez, Greta Nissen, Wallace Beery. 5862f
  USA. prod/rel: Famous Players-Lasky, Paramount
  Pictures

Lady of Lyons, The 1913 d: Leon Bary. lps: Cecil Mannering. 3900f UKN. prod/rel: Hepworth, Co-Operative

The Last Days of Pompeii, 1834, Novel
Derniers Jours de Pompei, Les 1908. 380m FRN. prod/rel: Raleigh Et Robert

Derniers Jours de Pompei, Les 1948 d: Marcel L'Herbier, Paolo MoffA. lps: Micheline Presle, Georges Marchal, Marcel Herrand. 110M FRN/ITL. *Gli Ultimi Giorni Di Pompei* (ITL); *The Last Days of Pompeii*; *Sins of Pompei* prod/rel: Salvo D'angelo Films, Universalia

Jone O Gli Ultimi Giorni Di Pompei 1913 d: Enrico Vidali, Ubaldo Maria Del Colle. lps: Suzanne de Labroy, Cristina Ruspoli, Luigi Mele. 2500m ITL. *Last Days of Pompeii* (UKN) prod/rel: Pasquali E C.

Last Days of Pompeii, The 1935 d: Ernest B. Schoedsack. lps: Preston Foster, Basil Rathbone, Dorothy Wilson. 96M USA. prod/rel: RKO Radio Pictures©, Merian C. Cooper Production

Letzten Tage von Pompei, Die 1959 d: Mario Bonnard, Sergio Leone. lps: Steve Reeves, Christine Kaufmann, Barbara Carroll. 97M GRM/ITL/SPN. *Gli Ultimi Giorni Di Pompei* (ITL); *The Last Days of Pompeii*; *Los Ultimos Dias de Pompeya* (SPN) prod/rel: Cineproduzioni Associate (Roma), Procusa Film (Madrid)

Ultimi Giorni Di Pompei, Gli 1908 d: Luigi Maggi. lps: Umberto Mozzato, Lydia de Roberti, Luigi Maggi. 366m ITL. *Jone; The Last Days of Pompei* (USA); *The Last Days of Pompeii* (UKN) prod/rel: S.A. Ambrosio

Ultimi Giorni Di Pompei, Gli 1913 d: Eleuterio Rodolfi. lps: Fernanda Negri-Pouget, Eugenia Tettoni Florio, Ubaldo Stefani. 1958m ITL. *Last Days of Pompeii* (UKN) prod/rel: S.A. Ambrosio

Ultimi Giorni Di Pompei, Gli 1926 d: Amleto Palermi, Carmine Gallone. lps: Rina de Liguoro, Maria Corda, Victor Varconi. 3683m ITL. prod/rel: S.A. Grandi Film

Money, London 1840, Play
Money 1915 d: A. C. Marston, Lawrence Marston. lps: Thornton Cole, George Robinson, A. C. Marston. 2r USA. prod/rel: Biograph Co.

Money 1921 d: Duncan MacRae. lps: Henry Ainley, Faith Bevan, Margot Drake. 4500f UKN. prod/rel: Ideal

Night and Morning, Novel
Night and Morning 1915 d: Wilfred Noy. lps: Dorothy Bellew. 2995f UKN. prod/rel: Clarendon, Westminster

Paul Clifford, Novel
King's Highway, The 1927 d: Sinclair Hill. lps: Matheson Lang, Joan Lockton, James Carew. 7900f UKN. prod/rel: Stoll

Richelieu; Or the Conspiracy, London 1839, Play
Cardinal Richelieu 1936 d: Rowland V. Lee. lps: George Arliss, Maureen O'Sullivan, Edward Arnold. 82M USA. prod/rel: 20th Century Pictures, Inc., United Artists

Cardinal Richelieu's Ward 1914. lps: James Cruze, Florence Labadie, Morris Foster. 4-6r USA. prod/rel: Thanhouser Film Corp., Thanhouser "Big" Productions

Cardinal's Edict, The 1911. 1000f USA. prod/rel: Edison

Richelieu 1914 d: Allan Dwan. lps: Murdock MacQuarrie, Pauline Bush, William C. Dowlan. 4r USA. prod/rel: Universal Film Mfg. Co.©

Richelieu Or the Conspiracy 1909 d: J. Stuart Blackton. lps: Maurice Costello, William Humphrey, James Young. SHT USA.

Rienzi, 1835, Novel
Cola Di Rienzi 1910 d: Mario Caserini. lps: Amleto Novelli, Fernanda Negri-Pouget. 310m ITL. *Rienzi* (UKN) prod/rel: Cines

The Roman, Novel
Roman, The 1910 d: Otis Turner. lps: Hobart Bosworth, Betty Harte, Robert Leonard. 1000f USA. prod/rel: Selig Polyscope Co.

M

MA FENG
Novel
Tai Yang Gang Gang Chu Shan 1960 d: Wang Yi. lps: Ren Yi, Liang Yin, XIa Peijie. 8r CHN. *The Sun Just Came Over the Mountains* prod/rel: Changchun Film Studio

---

Jie Hun, Novel
Jie Hun 1953 d: Yan Gong. lps: Zhang XIqi, Chen Qiang, Di Li. 8r CHN. *Getting Married* prod/rel: Northeast Film Studio

Lu Liang Ying XIong, Novel
Lu Liang Ying XIong 1950 d: Lu Ban, Yi Ling. lps: Li Baiwan, Guo Yuntai, Fu Ke. 10r CHN. *Heroes of Luliang* prod/rel: Beijing Film Studio

Sannian Zao Zhidao, Novel
Sannian Zao Zhidao 1958 d: Wang Yan. lps: Chen Qiang, Ma Shida, Wang Chunying. 9r CHN. *Knew That Three Years Ago* prod/rel: Changchun Film Studio

MAAS, PETER
Marie: a True Story, Book
Marie 1986 d: Roger Donaldson. lps: Sissy Spacek, Jeff Daniels, Keith SzarabajkA. 111M USA. *Marie: a True Story* prod/rel: MGM, United Artists

La Mela Marcia, Novel
Cosa Nostra 1972 d: Terence Young. lps: Charles Bronson, Lino Ventura, Mario Pilar. 127M FRN/ITL. *Joe Valachi: a Segreti Di Cosa Nostra*; *The Valachi Papers* (UKN); *Joe Valachi* (ITL); *Carteggio Valachi* prod/rel: de Laurentiis Int. Manu. Co. (Roma), Euro France Films (Paris)

Serpico, Book
Serpico 1973 d: Sidney Lumet. lps: Al Pacino, John Randolph, Jack Kehoe. 130M USA/ITL. prod/rel: de Laurentiis Intermaco, Artists Entertainment Complex

Serpico: the Deadly Game 1976 d: Robert Collins. lps: David Birney, Allen Garfield, Burt Young. TVM. 100M USA. *The Deadly Game* prod/rel: Dino de Laurentiis Prods., Paramount Tv

MABIE, LOUISE KENNEDY
Wings of Pride, New York 1913, Novel
Wings of Pride 1920 d: B. A. Rolfe, John B. O'Brien. lps: Olive Tell, Denton Vane, Raye Dean. 6r USA. prod/rel: Jans Pictures, Inc., State Rights

MAC ORLAN, PIERRE
La Bandera, 1931, Novel
Bandera, La 1935 d: Julien Duvivier. lps: Jean Gabin, Annabella, Robert Le Vigan. 100M FRN. *Escape from Yesterday* (UKN); *La Grande Releve* prod/rel: Societe Nouvelle De Cinematographie

Marguerite de la Nuit, 1925, Short Story
Marguerite de la Nuit 1955 d: Claude Autant-LarA. lps: Pierre Palau, Michele Morgan, Yves Montand. 128M FRN/ITL. *Margherita Della Notte* (ITL); *Marguerite of the Night* prod/rel: S.N.E.G., Gaumont Actualites

Le Quai Des Brumes, 1927, Novel
Quai Des Brumes 1938 d: Marcel Carne. lps: Jean Gabin, Michele Morgan, Michel Simon. 91M FRN. *Port of Shadows* (USA) prod/rel: Gregoire Rabinovitch, Cine-Alliance

La Tradition de Minuit, 1930, Novel
Tradition de Minuit, La 1939 d: Roger Richebe. lps: Marcel Dalio, Pierre Larquey, Viviane Romance. 105M FRN. prod/rel: Societe Des Films Roger Richebe

MACANNA, FERDIA
The Last of the High Kings, Novel
Last of the High Kings, The 1996 d: David Keating. lps: Catherine O'Hara, Jared Leto, Christina Ricci. 104M IRL/UKN/DNM. prod/rel: Parallel Film Productions, Northolme Entertainment

MACARDLE, DONALD
Thursday's Child, Novel
Thursday's Child 1943 d: Rodney Ackland. lps: Sally Ann Howes, Wilfred Lawson, Kathleen O'Regan. 81M UKN. prod/rel: Associated British Picture Corporation, Pathe

MACARDLE, DOROTHY
Uneasy Freehold, Novel
Uninvited, The 1944 d: Lewis Allen. lps: Ruth Hussey, Ray Milland, Donald Crisp. 98M USA. prod/rel: Paramount

MACARTHUR, CHARLES (1895–1956), USA
The Front Page, New York 1928, Play
Front Page, The 1931 d: Lewis Milestone. lps: Adolphe Menjou, Pat O'Brien, Mary Brian. 103M USA. prod/rel: the Caddo Co.©, Lewis Milestone Productionn

Front Page, The 1974 d: Billy Wilder. lps: Walter Matthau, Jack Lemmon, Carol Burnett. 105M USA. prod/rel: Universal

His Girl Friday 1940 d: Howard Hawks. lps: Cary Grant, Rosalind Russell, Ralph Bellamy. 92M USA. prod/rel: Columbia Pictures Corp.©

Switching Channels 1988 d: Ted Kotcheff. lps: Kathleen Turner, Burt Reynolds, Christopher Reeve. 105M USA. prod/rel: Tri-Star

---

Jumbo, New York 1935, Play
Billy Rose's Jumbo 1962 d: Charles Walters. lps: Doris Day, Stephen Boyd, Jimmy Durante. 124M USA. *Jumbo* prod/rel: Euterpe, Inc., Arwin Productions

My Lulu Belle, 1925, Play
Lulu Belle 1948 d: Leslie Fenton. lps: Dorothy Lamour, George Montgomery, Albert Dekker. 87M USA. prod/rel: Columbia

Twentieth Century, New York 1932, Play
Twentieth Century 1934 d: Howard Hawks. lps: John Barrymore, Carole Lombard, Roscoe Karns. 91M USA. prod/rel: Columbia Pictures Corp.©, Howard Hawks Production

MACARTHUR, JAMES
Beside the Bonnie Brier Bush, London 1895, Play
Beside the Bonnie Brier Bush 1921 d: Donald Crisp. lps: Donald Crisp, Mary Glynne, Langhorne Burton. 4662f UKN/USA. *The Bonnie Brier Bush* (USA); *The Bonnie Briar Bush* prod/rel: Famous Players-Lasky British Producers, Paramount Pictures

MACAULAY, PAULINE
The Astrakhan Coat, Play
Taste of Hemlock, A 1988 d: Geoffrey Darwin. lps: Randy Harrington, Eric Tynan Young, Reed Armstrong. 90M USA. prod/rel: International Artists

MACAULEY, CHARLES R.
Humanity, Short Story
Whom the Gods Would Destroy 1919 d: Frank Borzage. lps: Jack Mulhall, Pauline Starke, Kathryn Adams. 7r USA. *Whom the Gods Destroy*; *Humanity* prod/rel: C. R. Macauley Photoplays, First National Exhibitors Circuit

MACAULEY, RICHARD
All Is Confusion, 1934, Short Story
Riding on Air 1937 d: Edward Sedgwick. lps: Joe E. Brown, Guy Kibbee, Florence Rice. 70M USA. *All Is Confusion*; *Sky High* prod/rel: David L. Loew Productions, Edward Sedgwick Production

The Good Die Young, Novel
Good Die Young, The 1954 d: Lewis Gilbert. lps: Laurence Harvey, Gloria Grahame, Richard Basehart. 98M UKN. prod/rel: Remus, Independent Film Distributors

Ready, Willing and Able, Short Story
Ready, Willing and Able 1937 d: Ray Enright. lps: Ruby Keeler, Lee Dixon, Allen Jenkins. 93M USA. prod/rel: Warner Bros. Pictures©

Special Arrangements, 1935, Short Story
Melody for Two 1937 d: Louis King. lps: James Melton, Patricia Ellis, Marie Wilson. 60M USA. *King of Swing*; *Special Arrangements* prod/rel: Warner Bros. Pictures©

Women are Bum Newspapermen, 1934, Short Story
Front Page Woman 1935 d: Michael Curtiz. lps: Bette Davis, George Brent, Winifred Shaw. 82M USA. *Women are Born Newspapermen* prod/rel: Warner Bros. Productions Corp., Warner Bros. Pictures©

MACBETH, R. G.
Policing the Plains, Novel
Policing the Plains 1927 d: A. D. Kean. lps: Dorothy Fowler, Jack Downing, Donald Hayes. 8r CND. prod/rel: Canadian Historic Features Ltd.

MACCLURE, VICTOR
Death on the Set, Novel
Death on the Set 1935 d: Leslie Hiscott. lps: Henry Kendall, Eve Gray, Jeanne Stuart. 73M UKN. *Murder on the Set* prod/rel: Twickenham, Universal

MACCRACKEN, MARY
A Circle of Children, Book
Circle of Children, A 1977 d: Don Taylor. lps: Jane Alexander, Rachel Roberts, David Ogden Stiers. TVM. 100M USA. prod/rel: 20th Century-Fox Tv, Edgar J. Scherick Associates

Lovey, a Very Special Child, Book
Lovey: a Circle of Children, Part II 1978 d: Jud Taylor. lps: Jane Alexander, Ronny Cox, Kris McKeon. TVM. 100M USA. prod/rel: Time-Life Television

MACCURDY, JAMES KYRTLE
A Little Girl in a Big City, 1909, Play
Little Girl in a Big City, A 1925 d: Burton L. King. lps: Gladys Walton, Niles Welch, Mary Thurman. 6r USA. prod/rel: Lumas Film Corp.

MACDERMOT, GALT
Hair, Musical Play
Hair 1979 d: Milos Forman. lps: John Savage, Treat Williams, Beverly d'Angelo. 121M USA. prod/rel: United Artists

MACDERMOTT, WESLEY C.
A Girl of Yesterday, Story
Girl of Yesterday, A 1915 d: Allan Dwan. lps: Mary Pickford, Gertrude Norman, Frances Marion. 5r USA. prod/rel: Famous Players Film Co., Paramount Pictures Corp.

MACDONALD, BETTY
The Egg and I, Novel
Egg and I, The 1947 d: Chester Erskine. lps: Claudette Colbert, Fred MacMurray, Marjorie Main. 108M USA. prod/rel: Universal

MACDONALD, GEORGE (1824–1905), UKN
The Princess and the Goblin, Novel
Hercegno Es a Kobold, A 1991 d: Jozsef Gemes. ANM. 82M HNG/UKN. *The Princess and the Goblin* (UKN) prod/rel: Siriol, Pannonia

MACDONALD, JOHN D. (1916–1986), USA, MacDonald, John Dann
Condiminium, Novel
Condominium 1979 d: Sidney Hayers. lps: Dan Haggerty, Steve Forrest, Ralph Bellamy. TVM. 195M USA. *Condominium: When the Hurricane Struck* (UKN) prod/rel: Opt, Universal

Darker Than Amber, Greenwich, Ct. 1966, Novel
Darker Than Amber 1970 d: Robert Clouse. lps: Rod Taylor, Suzy Kendall, Theodore Bikel. 97M USA. prod/rel: Major Pictures

The Executioners, New York 1958, Novel
Cape Fear 1961 d: J. Lee Thompson. lps: Gregory Peck, Robert Mitchum, Polly Bergen. 105M USA. prod/rel: Universal

Cape Fear 1991 d: Martin Scorsese. lps: Robert de Niro, Nick Nolte, Jessica Lange. 128M USA. prod/rel: Universal, Amblin

A Flash of Green, Novel
Flash of Green, A 1984 d: Victor Nunez. lps: Ed Harris, Blair Brown, Richard Jordan. 131M USA. prod/rel: Spetrafilm

MACDONALD, JOHN D.
The Girl, the Gold Watch and Everything, Novel
Girl, the Gold Watch & Everything, The 1980 d: William Wiard. lps: Robert Hays, Pam Dawber, Jill Ireland. TVM. 104M USA. prod/rel: Operation Prime Time, Fellows-Keegan

MACDONALD, JOHN D. (1916–1986), USA, MacDonald, John Dann
Kona Coast, Short Story
Kona Coast 1968 d: Lamont Johnson. lps: Richard Boone, Vera Miles, Joan Blondell. 93M USA. prod/rel: Pioneer Productions

Taint of the Tiger, 1958, Short Story
Man-Trap 1961 d: Edmond O'Brien. lps: Jeffrey Hunter, David Janssen, Stella Stevens. 93M USA. *Deadlock; Restless* prod/rel: Tiger Production, Paramount

MACDONALD, MRS. BARRY
What Should a Woman Do to Promote Youth and Happiness, Novel
What Should a Woman Do to Promote Youth and Happiness? 1915?. 5r USA. prod/rel: Barry Macdonald Film Co.

MACDONALD, PHILIP
Circle of Danger, Novel
Circle of Danger 1951 d: Jacques Tourneur. lps: Ray Milland, Patricia Roc, Marius Goring. 86M UKN. *White Heather* prod/rel: Coronado, RKO Radio

Escape, Novel
Nightmare 1942 d: Tim Whelan. lps: Diana Barrymore, Brian Donlevy, Gavin Muir. 81M USA. prod/rel: Universal

A Gentleman's Gentleman, Play
Gentleman's Gentleman, A 1939 d: R. William Neill. lps: Eric Blore, Marie Lohr, Peter Coke. 70M UKN. prod/rel: Warner Bros., First National

The List of Adrian Messenger, New York 1959, Novel
List of Adrian Messenger, The 1963 d: John Huston. lps: George C. Scott, Dana Wynter, Clive Brook. 98M USA. prod/rel: Joel Productions, Universal Pictures

Menace, New York 1933, Novel
Menace 1934 d: Ralph Murphy. lps: Gertrude Michael, Paul Cavanagh, Henrietta Crosman. 58M USA. prod/rel: Paramount Productions©

The Nursemaid Who Disappeared, Novel
Nursemaid Who Disappeared, The 1939 d: Arthur Woods. lps: Arthur Margetson, Peter Coke, Lesley Brook. 86M UKN. prod/rel: Warner Bros., First National

Patrol, New York 1928, Novel
Lost Patrol, The 1929 d: Walter Summers. lps: Cyril McLaglen, Sam Wilkinson, Terence Collier. SIL. 7250f UKN. prod/rel: British Instructional, Fox

Lost Patrol, The 1934 d: John Ford. lps: Victor McLaglen, Boris Karloff, Wallace Ford. 74M USA. *Patrol* prod/rel: RKO Radio Pictures©, John Ford Production

The Rasp, Novel
Rasp, The 1931 d: Michael Powell. lps: Claude Horton, Phyllis Loring, C. M. Hallard. 44M UKN. prod/rel: Film Engineering, Fox

Rynox, Novel
Rynox 1931 d: Michael Powell. lps: Stewart Rome, Dorothy Boyd, John Longden. 47M UKN. prod/rel: Film Engineering, Ideal

Who Killed John Savage? 1937 d: Maurice Elvey. lps: Nicholas Hannen, Barry MacKay, Edward Chapman. 69M UKN. prod/rel: Warner Bros., First National

Warrant for X, 1938, Novel
Twenty Three Paces to Baker Street 1956 d: Henry Hathaway. lps: Van Johnson, Vera Miles, Cecil Parker. 103M USA. *23 Paces to Baker Street* prod/rel: 20th Century-Fox

X V Rex, London 1933, Novel
Hour of 13, The 1952 d: Harold French. lps: Peter Lawford, Dawn Addams, Roland Culver. 78M UKN/USA. *The Hour of Thirteen* prod/rel: MGM British

Mystery of Mr. X, The 1934 d: Edgar Selwyn. lps: Robert Montgomery, Elizabeth Allan, Lewis Stone. 84M USA. *The Mystery of the Dead Police* prod/rel: Metro-Goldwyn-Mayer Corp.©

MACDONALD, ROSS (1915–1983), USA, Millar, Kenneth
Blue City, Novel
Blue City 1986 d: Michelle Manning. lps: Judd Nelson, Ally Sheedy, David Caruso. 83M USA. prod/rel: Paramount

The Drowning Pool, Novel
Drowning Pool, The 1975 d: Stuart Rosenberg. lps: Paul Newman, Joanne Woodward, Anthony FranciosA. 108M USA. prod/rel: Coleytown, First Artists

The Moving Target, New York 1949, Novel
Harper 1966 d: Jack Smight. lps: Paul Newman, Lauren Bacall, Julie Harris. 121M USA. *The Moving Target* (UKN) prod/rel: Warner Bros. Pictures

The Three Roads, Novel
Double Negative 1980 d: George Bloomfield. lps: Michael Sarrazin, Susan Clark, Anthony Perkins. 96M CND. *Deadly Companion* prod/rel: Quadrant Films Ltd., Udo Communications Inc.

The Underground Man, Novel
Underground Man, The 1974 d: Paul Wendkos. lps: Peter Graves, Jo Ann Pflug, Jack Klugman. TVM. 100M USA. *Archer* prod/rel: Paramount

MACDONALD, SHARMAN
The Winter Guest, Play
Winter Guest, The 1997 d: Alan Rickman. lps: Phyllida Law, Emma Thompson, Gary Hollywood. 106M UKN/USA. prod/rel: Capitol Films, Pressman/Lipper Prods.©

MACDONALD, WALLACE
Story
Sea Riders, The 1922 d: Edward H. Griffith. lps: Edward Phillips, Betty Bouton, Charles Eldridge. 6r CND. *Sea Raiders* prod/rel: Maritime Motion Picture Co. of Canada

MACDONALD, WILLIAM COLT
Along the Navajo Trail, Novel
Along the Navajo Trail 1945 d: Frank McDonald. lps: Roy Rogers, George Hayes, Dale Evans. 66M USA. prod/rel: Republic

Ghost-Town Gold, New York 1935, Novel
Ghost-Town Gold 1936 d: Joseph Kane. lps: Robert Livingston, Ray Corrigan, Max Terhune. 57M USA. prod/rel: Republic Pictures Corp.©

Law of the Forty-Fives, New York 1933, Novel
Law of 45'S, The 1935 d: John P. McCarthy. lps: Guinn (Big Boy) Williams, Molly O'Day, Al St. John. 57M USA. *Mysterious Mr. Sheffield* (UKN); *The Law of the 45'S* prod/rel: Beacon Productions, State Rights

Powdersmoke Range, New York 1934, Novel
Powdersmoke Range 1935 d: Wallace Fox. lps: Harry Carey, Hoot Gibson, Bob Steele. 71M USA. prod/rel: RKO Radio Pictures©

Riders of the Whistling Skull, New York 1934, Novel
Riders of the Whistling Skull, The 1937 d: MacK V. Wright. lps: Robert Livingston, Ray Corrigan, Max Terhune. 55M USA. *The Golden Trail* (UKN) prod/rel: Republic Pictures Corp.©

MACDONNELL, GORDON
Jump for Glory, Novel
Jump for Glory 1937 d: Raoul Walsh. lps: Douglas Fairbanks Jr., Valerie Hobson, Alan Hale. 89M UKN. *When Thief Meets Thief* (USA) prod/rel: Criterion, United Artists

To Catch a Thief, Play
To Catch a Thief 1936 d: MacLean Rogers. lps: John Garrick, Mary Lawson, H. F. Maltby. 66M UKN. prod/rel: GS Enterprises, Radio

MACDONNELL, MARGARET
To Catch a Thief 1936 d: MacLean Rogers. lps: John Garrick, Mary Lawson, H. F. Maltby. 66M UKN. prod/rel: GS Enterprises, Radio

MACDONOUGH, GLEN
Babes in Toyland, New York 1903, Operetta
Babes in Toyland 1934 d: Charles Rogers, Gus Meins. lps: Stan Laurel, Oliver Hardy, Charlotte Henry. 79M USA. *March of the Wooden Soldiers; Laurel and Hardy in Toyland; March of the Toys; Revenge Is Sweet* prod/rel: Hal Roach Studios, Inc.

Babes in Toyland 1961 d: Jack Donohue. lps: Ray Bolger, Tommy Sands, Annette Funicello. 105M USA. prod/rel: Walt Disney Productions, Buena Vista

Babes in Toyland 1986 d: Clive Donner. lps: Drew Barrymore, Richard Mulligan, Eileen Brennan. TVM. 150M USA. prod/rel: the Finnegan-Pinchuk Company, Orion Tv

MACDOUGALL, ROGER
Escapade, London 1953, Play
Escapade 1955 d: Philip Leacock. lps: John Mills, Yvonne Mitchell, Alastair Sim. 87M UKN. prod/rel: Pinnacle, Eros

The Gentle Gunman, Play
Gentle Gunman, The 1952 d: Basil Dearden, Michael Relph. lps: John Mills, Dirk Bogarde, Robert Beatty. 86M UKN. prod/rel: Ealing Studios, General Film Distributors

A Son to Dorothy, London 1950, Play
To Dorothy, a Son 1954 d: Muriel Box. lps: Shelley Winters, Peggy Cummins, John Gregson. 84M UKN. *Cash on Delivery* (USA); *That's My Baby!* prod/rel: Welbeck, Independent Film Distributors

MACFARLANE, PETER CLARK
Held to Answer, Boston 1916, Novel
Held to Answer 1923 d: Harold Shaw. lps: House Peters, Grace Carlyle, John Sainpolis. 5601f USA. prod/rel: Metro Pictures

Tongues of Flame, New York 1924, Novel
Tongues of Flame 1924 d: Joseph Henabery. lps: Thomas Meighan, Bessie Love, Eileen Percy. 6763f USA. prod/rel: Famous Players-Lasky, Paramount Pictures

The Side-Show Girl, 1918, Short Story
Molly of the Follies 1919 d: Edward Sloman. lps: Margarita Fischer, Jack Mower, Lule Warrenton. 5r USA. prod/rel: American Film Co.©, American "Flying a" Picture

MACGERR, PAT
Bonnes a Tuer, Novel
Bonnes a Tuer 1954 d: Henri Decoin. lps: Danielle Darrieux, Michel Auclair, Corinne Calvet. 90M FRN/ITL. *Quattro Donne Nella Notte* (ITL); *One Step to Eternity* (USA) prod/rel: Films E.G.E., C.F.C.

MACGILL, PATRICK
Suspense, Play
Suspense 1930 d: Walter Summers. lps: Mickey Brantford, Cyril McLaglen, Jack Raine. 81M UKN. prod/rel: British International Pictures, Wardour

MACGOWAN, ALICE
Judith of the Cumberlands, New York 1908, Novel
Judith of the Cumberlands 1916 d: J. P. McGowan. lps: Helen Holmes, Leo Maloney, Paul Hurst. 5r USA. *The Moonshine Menace* prod/rel: Signal Film Corp., Mutual Film Corp.

MACGOWAN, MRS. GRACE
The Power and the Glory, New York 1910, Novel
Power and the Glory, The 1918 d: Lawrence C. Windom. lps: June Elvidge, Frank Mayo, Ricca Allen. 5r USA. prod/rel: World Film Corp.©

MACGRATH, HAROLD
The Beautiful Bullet, 1927, Short Story
Danger Street 1928 d: Ralph Ince. lps: Warner Baxter, Martha Sleeper, Duke Martin. 5621f USA. prod/rel: Fbo Pictures

Bitter Apples, 1925, Short Story
Bitter Apples 1927 d: Harry O. Hoyt. lps: Monte Blue, Myrna Loy, Paul Ellis. 5463f USA. prod/rel: Warner Brothers Pictures

The Carpet from Bagdad, Indianapolis 1911, Novel
Carpet from Bagdad, The 1915 d: Colin Campbell. lps: Kathlyn Williams, Charles Clary, Wheeler Oakman. 5r USA. prod/rel: Selig Polyscope Co.©, Selig Red Seal Plays

Drums of Jeopardy, New York 1920, Novel
Drums of Jeopardy 1931 d: George B. Seitz. lps: Lloyd Hughes, Warner Oland, June Collyer. 65M USA. *Mark of Terror* prod/rel: Tiffany Productions©

Drums of Jeopardy, The 1923 d: Eddie Dillon. lps: Elaine Hammerstein, Jack Mulhall, Wallace Beery. 6529f USA. prod/rel: Hoffman Productions, Truart Film Corp.

Girl in His House, New York 1918, Novel
Girl in His House, The 1918 d: Thomas R. Mills. lps: Earle Williams, Grace Darmond, Jake Abraham. 4256f USA. prod/rel: Vitagraph Co. of America©, Blue Ribbon Feature

The Goose Girl, New York 1909, Novel
Goose Girl, The 1915 d: Frederick A. Thompson. lps: Marguerite Clark, Monroe Salisbury, Sydney Deane. 4996f USA. prod/rel: Jesse L. Lasky Feature Play Co.©, Paramount Pictures Corp.

Half a Rogue, Indianapolis 1906, Novel
Half a Rogue 1916 d: Henry Otto. lps: King Baggot, Edna Hunter, Clara Beyers. 5r USA. prod/rel: Universal Film Mfg. Co.©, Red Feather Photoplays

Hearts and Masks, Indianapolis 1905, Novel
Hearts and Masks 1914 d: Colin Campbell. lps: Kathlyn Williams, Wheeler Oakman. 3r USA. prod/rel: Selig Polyscope Co.

Hearts and Masks 1921 d: William A. Seiter. lps: Elinor Field, Francis McDonald, Lloyd Bacon. 5200f USA. prod/rel: Federated Productions, Film Booking Offices of America

The Luck of the Irish, New York 1917, Novel
Luck of the Irish, The 1920 d: Allan Dwan. lps: James Kirkwood, Anna Q. Nilsson, Harry Northrup. 7r USA. prod/rel: Mayflower Photoplay Corp.©, Allan Dwan Productions

The Lure of the Mask, Indianapolis 1908, Novel
Lure of the Mask, The 1915 d: Thomas Ricketts. lps: Harold Lockwood, Elsie Jane Wilson, Irving Cummings. 4r USA. prod/rel: American Film Mfg. Co.©, Mutual Film Corp.

The Man on the Box, Indianapolis 1904, Novel
Man on the Box, The 1914 d: Cecil B. de Mille, Oscar Apfel. lps: Max Figman, Lolita Robertson, C. F. Le None. 5r USA. prod/rel: Jesse L. Lasky Feature Play Co.©, State Rights

Man on the Box, The 1925 d: Charles F. Reisner. lps: Sydney Chaplin, David Butler, Alice Calhoun. 7481f USA. prod/rel: Warner Brothers Pictures

The Million Dollar Mystery, Story
Million Dollar Mystery, The 1914 d: Howell Hansel. lps: Florence Labadie, Sidney Bracey, Marguerite Snow. SRL. 46r USA. prod/rel: Thanhouser Film Corp., State Rights

Parrot and Company, Indianapolis 1913, Novel
Not Guilty 1921 d: Sidney A. Franklin. lps: Sylvia Breamer, Richard Dix, Molly Malone. 6170f USA. *Parrot and Co.* prod/rel: Whitman Bennett Productions, Associated First National Pictures

Pidgin Island, Indianapolis 1914, Novel
Pidgin Island 1916 d: Fred J. Balshofer. lps: Harold Lockwood, May Allison, Pomeroy Cannon. 5r USA. prod/rel: Yorke Film Corp.©, Metro Pictures Corp.

The Place of Honeymoons, Indianapolis 1912, Novel
Place of Honeymoons, The 1920 d: Kenean Buel. lps: Montagu Love, Emily Stevens, Frankie Mann. 5r USA. prod/rel: Atlas Film Corp., Pioneer Film Corp.©

The Puppet Crown, Indianapolis 1901, Novel
Puppet Crown, The 1915 d: George Melford. lps: Ina Claire, Carlyle Blackwell, Cleo Ridgely. 5r USA. prod/rel: Jesse L. Lasky Feature Play Co.©, Paramount Pictures Corp.

The Ragged Edge, New York 1922, Novel
Ragged Edge, The 1923 d: F. Harmon Weight. lps: Alfred Lunt, Mimi Palmieri, Charles Fang. 6800f USA. prod/rel: Distinctive Pictures, Goldwyn-Cosmopolitan Distributing Corp.

The Splendid Hazard, New York 1910, Novel
Splendid Hazard, A 1920 d: Arthur Rosson, Allan Dwan. lps: Henry B. Walthall, Rosemary Theby, Norman Kerry. 5r USA. prod/rel: Allan Dwan Productions, Mayflower Photoplay Corp.©

The Voice in the Fog, Indianapolis 1915, Novel
Voice in the Fog, The 1915 d: Frank Reicher. lps: Donald Brian, Ernest Joy, Florence Smith. 5r USA. prod/rel: Jesse L. Lasky Feature Play Co.©, Paramount Pictures Corp.

The Wrong Coat, Story
Pleasures of the Rich 1926 d: Louis J. Gasnier. lps: Helene Chadwick, Mary Carr, Marcin Asher. 6471f USA. prod/rel: Tiffany Productions, Renown Pictures

The Yellow Typhoon, New York 1919, Novel
Yellow Typhoon, The 1920 d: Edward Jose. lps: Anita Stewart, Ward Crane, Donald MacDonald. 6347f USA. *The Yellow Taifun* prod/rel: Anita Stewart Productions, Inc.©, Associated First National Pictures

You Can't Always Tell, Short Story
Right to the Heart 1942 d: Eugene J. Forde. lps: Brenda Joyce, Joseph Allen Jr., Cobina Wright Jr. 74M USA. *You Can't Always Tell* prod/rel: 20th Century Fox

You Can't Always Tell, 1925, Short Story
Womanpower 1926 d: Harry Beaumont. lps: Ralph Graves, Kathryn Perry, Margaret Livingston. 6240f USA. prod/rel: Fox Film Corp.

MACHA, KAREL HYNEK (1810–1836), CZC
Cikani, Short Story
Cikani 1921 d: Karl Anton. lps: Hugo Svoboda, Olga Augustova, Theodor Pistek. 2173m CZC. *The Gipsies; Gypsy* prod/rel: Ab, la Tricolore

MACHADO, ANIBAL
O Iniciado Do Vento, 1959, Short Story
Menino E O Vento, O 1967 d: Carlos Hugo Christensen. lps: Enio Goncalves, Luiz Fernando Ianelli, Wilma Henriques. 104M BRZ. *The Boy and the Wind*

A Garota Tati, 1959, Short Story
Tati, a Garota 1973 d: Bruno Barreto. lps: Hugo Carvana, Dina Sfat, Marcelo Carvalho. 100M BRZ.

MACHADO, ARIBAL
Viagem Aos Seios de Duilia, 1959, Short Story
Viagem Aos Seios de Duilia 1963 d: Carlos Hugo Christensen. lps: Artur Semedo. 104M BRZ.

MACHADO, MARIA CLARA
A Bruxinha Que Era Boa, 1957, Play
Danca Das Bruxas, A 1970 d: Francisco Dreux. 100M BRZ.

O Cavalinho Azul, 1960, Play
Cavalinho Azul, O 1985 d: Eduardo Escorel. 82M BRZ.

O Fantasminha Pluft, 1957, Play
Pluft, O Fantasminha 1962 d: Romain Lesage. 95M BRZ.

MACHADO Y RUIZ, ANTONIO (1875–1939), SPN
La Duquesa de Benameji, 1932, Play
Duquesa de Benameji, La 1949 d: Luis LuciA. lps: Amparo Rivelles, Jorge Mistral, Manuel LunA. 103M SPN. *La Reina de Sierra Morena; Duchess of Benameji; Queen of Sierra Morena*

Lola Se Va a Los Puertos, 1929, Play
Lola Se Va a Los Puertos, La 1947 d: Juan de OrdunA. lps: Juanita Reina, Manuel Luna, Ricardo Acero. 120M SPN. *Lola Goes Abroad*

La Tierra de Alvar Gonzalez, 1939, Verse
Laguna Negra, La 1952 d: Arturo Ruiz-Castillo. lps: Maruchi Fresno, Tomas Blanco, Maria Jesus Valdes. 100M SPN. *The Black Lake; The Black Lagoon*

MACHADO Y RUIZ, MANUEL (1874–1947), SPN
La Duquesa de Benameji, 1932, Play
Duquesa de Benameji, La 1949 d: Luis LuciA. lps: Amparo Rivelles, Jorge Mistral, Manuel LunA. 103M SPN. *La Reina de Sierra Morena; Duchess of Benameji; Queen of Sierra Morena*

Lola Se Va a Los Puertos, 1929, Play
Lola Se Va a Los Puertos, La 1947 d: Juan de OrdunA. lps: Juanita Reina, Manuel Luna, Ricardo Acero. 120M SPN. *Lola Goes Abroad*

MACHAR, JOSEF SVATOPLUK
Magdalena, Novel
Magdalena 1920 d: Vladimir Majer. lps: Ferry Majerova, Jaroslav Vojta, Karel Lamac. 2021m CZC. prod/rel: Lloydfilm

MACHARD, ALFRED
Cerny Muz, Novel
Gehetzte Menschen 1932 d: Friedrich Feher. lps: Eugen Klopfer, Jan Feher-Weiss, Camilla SpirA. 2621m GRM/CZC. *Steckbrief Z 48; Le Loup Garon; Hunted People* prod/rel: Panfilm Emco-Film

Stvani Lide 1933 d: Friedrich Feher, Jan Svitak. lps: Josef Rovensky, Jan Feher-Weiss, Magda SonjA. 1800m CZC/GRM. *Outcasts; Hunted People* prod/rel: Pan Film (Jan Schmitt)

Coquecigrole, Novel
Coquecigrole 1931 d: Andre Berthomieu. lps: Danielle Darrieux, Max Dearly, Armand Bour. 96M FRN. prod/rel: Etablissements Jacque Haik

La Femme d'une Nuit, Novel
Femme d'une Nuit, La 1930 d: Marcel L'Herbier. lps: Francesca Bertini, Jean Murat, Boris de Fas. 88M FRN. prod/rel: Etablissements Braunberger-Richebe

La Guerre Des Momes, Novel
Trois Kk, Les 1918 d: Jacques de Baroncelli. 390m FRN. *Trois K* prod/rel: Lumina

L' Homme Sans Coeur, Novel
Homme Sans Coeur, L' 1936 d: Leo Joannon. lps: Pierre Renoir, Marie Glory, Lucienne Le Marchand. 88M FRN. prod/rel: France-Europe-Films

Le Loup-Garou, Novel
Loup-Garou, Le 1923 d: Jacques Roullet, Pierre Bressol. lps: Pierre Bressol, Madeleine Guitty, Jeanne Delvair. SRL. 3450m FRN. *The Werewolf* prod/rel: Films C.P.

La Marmaille, Novel
Marmaille, La 1935 d: Bernard-Deschamps. lps: Pierre Larquey, Florelle, Paul Azais. 90M FRN. prod/rel: General-Film

Popaul Et Virginie, Novel
Popaul Et Virginie 1919 d: Adrien Caillard. lps: Maurice Touze, La Petite Cretot, Mme. Ninove. 1300m FRN. prod/rel: Scagl

Poucette; Ou le Plus Jeune Detective du Monde, Novel
Poucette Ou le Plus Jeune Detective du Monde 1919 d: Adrien Caillard. lps: Maurice Touze, Simone Genevois, Paul Duc. 2500m FRN. prod/rel: Visio Films

Printemps Sexuel, Story
Domani E Troppo Tardi 1950 d: Leonide Moguy. lps: Vittorio de Sica, Lois Maxwell, Gabrielle Dorziat. 100M ITL. *Tomorrow Is Too Late* (UKN) prod/rel: Novella Film, Rizzoli Film

Qu'as-Tu Fait de Mon Coeur?, Novel
Quand Minuit Sonnera 1936 d: Leo Joannon. lps: Pierre Renoir, Marie Bell, Roger Karl. 80M FRN. prod/rel: France-Europe-Films

Salto Mortale, Novel
Salto Mortale 1931 d: E. A. Dupont. lps: Daniel Mendaille, Gina Manes, Leon Roger-Maxime. 89M FRN. prod/rel: Etablissements Braunberger-Richebe

Trique - Gamin de Paris, Novel
Trique, Gamin de Paris 1960 d: Marco de Gastyne. lps: Gil Vidal, Claudine Maugey, Jacqueline Danno. 90M FRN. *Les Fugitives* prod/rel: Lux C.C.F., Nat Films

MACHARG, WILLIAM BRIGGS
The Blind Man's Eyes, Boston 1916, Novel
Blind Man's Eyes 1919 d: John Ince. lps: Bert Lytell, Naomi Childers, Frank Currier. 5r USA. prod/rel: Metro Pictures Corp.©

The Price of a Party, Short Story
Price of a Party, The 1924 d: Charles Giblyn. lps: Hope Hampton, Harrison Ford, Arthur Edmund Carewe. 5456f USA. prod/rel: Howard Estabrook Productions, Associated Exhibitors

Wine, 1922, Short Story
Wine 1924 d: Louis J. Gasnier. lps: Clara Bow, Forrest Stanley, Huntley Gordon. 6220f USA. prod/rel: Universal Pictures

MACHIAVELLI, NICCOLO (1469–1527), ITL
La Mandragola, 1514, Play
Mandragola, La 1965 d: Alberto LattuadA. lps: Rosanna Schiaffino, Philippe Leroy, Jean-Claude Brialy. 103M ITL/FRN. *La Mandragore* (FRN); *Mandragola -the Love Root; The Mandrake; The Love Root* prod/rel: Arco Film (Roma), C.C.F. Lux (Paris)

MACHIN, ALFRED
Novel
Cuor Di Vagabondo 1936 d: Jean Epstein. lps: Ermete Zacconi, Madeleine Renaud, Fosco Giachetti. 71M ITL. *Per le Strade Del Mondo* prod/rel: Forzano Film, E.N.I.C.

MACHUGH, AUGUSTIN
The Meanest Man in the World, New York 1920, Play
Meanest Man in the World, The 1943 d: Sidney Lanfield. lps: Jack Benny, Priscilla Lane, Eddie "Rochester" Anderson. 57M USA. prod/rel: 20th Century-Fox

Officer 666, New York 1912, Play
Officer 666 1914 d: Frank Powell. lps: Howard Estabrook, Sydney Seaward, Dan Moyles. 4766f USA. prod/rel: George Kleine©, George Kleine Attractions

Officer 666 1920 d: Harry Beaumont. lps: Tom Moore, Jean Calhoun, Jerome Patrick. 5r USA. prod/rel: Goldwyn Pictures Corp.©, Goldwyn Distributing Corp.

MACILWRAITH, BILL
The Anniversary, London 1966, Play
Anniversary, The 1967 d: Roy Ward Baker, Alvin Rakoff. lps: Bette Davis, Sheila Hancock, Jack Hedley. 95M UKN. prod/rel: Hammer Film Prods., Seven Arts Prods.

MACINNES, COLIN (1914–1976), UKN
Absolute Beginners, Novel
Absolute Beginners 1985 d: Julien Temple. lps: David Bowie, James Fox, Lionel Blair. 108M UKN. prod/rel: Virgin, Goldcrest

MACINNES, HELEN (1907–1985), UKN
Above Suspicion, Novel
Above Suspicion 1943 d: Richard Thorpe. lps: Joan Crawford, Fred MacMurray, Conrad Veidt. 90M USA. prod/rel: MGM

Assignment in Brittany, Novel
Assignment in Brittany 1943 d: Jack Conway. lps: Jean-Pierre Aumont, Susan Peters, Richard Whorf. 96M USA. prod/rel: MGM

The Salburg Connection, Novel
Salzburg Connection, The 1972 d: Lee H. Katzin. lps: Barry Newman, Anna Karina, Karen Jensen. 94M USA. prod/rel: 20th Century-Fox

The Venetian Affair, New York 1963, Novel
Venetian Affair, The 1966 d: Jerry Thorpe. lps: Robert Vaughn, Elke Sommer, Felicia Farr. 92M USA. prod/rel: Jerry Thorpe Productions, MGM

MACK, CHARLES E.
Two Black Crows in the A. E. F. the, Indianapolis 1928, Novel
Anybody's War 1930 d: Richard Wallace. lps: George Moran, Charles E. MacK, Joan Peers. 8120f USA. *Two Black Crows in the a.EF.* prod/rel: Paramount-Publix Corp.

MACK, WILLARD
Blind Youth, New York 1917, Play
Blind Youth 1920 d: Edward Sloman, Alfred E. Green. lps: Walter McGrail, Leatrice Joy, Ora Carew. 6r USA. prod/rel: National Pictures, National Pictures Theatres, Inc.©

The Common Sin, Story
Common Sin, The 1920 d: Burton L. King. lps: Grace Darling, Rod La Rocque, Anders Randolf. 6r USA. prod/rel: Burton King Productions, Hallmark Pictures Corp.

The Dove, New York 1925, Play
Dove, The 1927 d: Roland West. lps: Norma Talmadge, Noah Beery, Gilbert Roland. 9100f USA. prod/rel: Norma Talmadge Productions, United Artists
Girl and the Gambler, The 1939 d: Lew Landers. lps: Leo Carrillo, Tim Holt, Steffi DunA. 62M USA. *The Dove* prod/rel: RKO Radio Pictures©
Girl of the Rio 1932 d: Herbert Brenon. lps: Dolores Del Rio, Norman Foster, Leo Carrillo. 69M USA. *The Dove* (UKN) prod/rel: RKO Radio Pictures©, Herbert Brenon Production

The Drag-Net, Play
Drag-Net, The 1936 d: Vin Moore. lps: Rod La Rocque, Marian Nixon, Betty Compson. 64M USA. *The Dragnet* prod/rel: Burroughs-Tarzan Pictures, A. W. N. Selig

The Dream Girl, Play
Aladdin's Other Lamp 1917 d: John H. Collins. lps: Viola Dana, Robert Walker, Augustus Phillips. 5r USA. prod/rel: Rolfe Photoplays, Inc., Metro Pictures Corp.©

A Gutter Magdalen, Short Story
Gutter Magdalene, The 1916 d: George Melford. lps: Fannie Ward, Jean Dean, Charles West. 5r USA. prod/rel: Jesse L. Lasky Feature Play Co.©, Paramount Pictures Corp.

Kick in, New York 1914, Play
Kick in 1917 d: George Fitzmaurice. lps: William Courtenay, Robert Clugston, Mollie King. 5r USA. prod/rel: Astra Film Corp., Pathe Exchange, Inc.©
Kick in 1922 d: George Fitzmaurice. lps: Betty Compson, Bert Lytell, May McAvoy. 7074f USA. prod/rel: Famous Players-Lasky, Paramount Pictures
Kick in 1931 d: Richard Wallace. lps: Clara Bow, Regis Toomey, Wynne Gibson. 75M USA. prod/rel: Paramount Publix Corp.©

The Noose, New York 1926, Play
I'd Give My Life 1936 d: Edwin L. Marin. lps: Guy Standing, Tom Brown, Frances Drake. 82M USA. *The Noose* prod/rel: Paramount Pictures©
Noose, The 1928 d: John Francis Dillon. lps: Richard Barthelmess, Montagu Love, Robert Emmett O'Connor. 7331f USA. *The Governor's Wife* prod/rel: First National Pictures

Spring 3100, New York 1928, Play
Jealousy 1934 d: R. William Neill. lps: Nancy Carroll, George Murphy, Donald Cook. 68M USA. *Spring Three Thousand One Hundred*; *Spring 3100* prod/rel: Columbia Pictures Corp. of California©

Tiger Rose, New York 1917, Play
Tiger Rose 1923 d: Sidney A. Franklin. lps: Lenore Ulric, Forrest Stanley, Joseph J. Dowling. 7400f USA. prod/rel: Warner Brothers Pictures
Tiger Rose 1929 d: George Fitzmaurice. lps: Monte Blue, Lupe Velez, H. B. Warner. 5509f USA. prod/rel: Warner Brothers Pictures

Your Friend and Mine, Play
Your Friend and Mine 1923 d: Clarence Badger. lps: Enid Bennett, Huntley Gordon, Willard Mack. 5750f USA. prod/rel: S-L Pictures, Metro Pictures

MACKAY, W. GAYER
The King's Outcast, Play
King's Outcast, The 1915 d: Ralph Dewsbury. lps: Gerald Ames, Blanche Bryan, Charles Rock. 3500f UKN. *His Vindication* (USA) prod/rel: London, Jury

MACKAYE, DOROTHY
Ladies They Talk About, Play
Ladies They Talk About 1933 d: William Keighley, Howard Bretherton. lps: Barbara Stanwyck, Preston Foster, Lyle Talbot. 69M USA. prod/rel: Warner Bros. Pictures©

Lady Gangster, Play
Lady Gangster 1942 d: Robert Florey. lps: Faye Emerson, Julie Bishop, Frank Wilcox. 62M USA. prod/rel: Warner Bros.

MACKAYE, PERCY (1875–1956), USA, MacKaye, Percy Wallace
The Scarecrow; Or the Glass of Truth, New York 1908, Novel
Puritan Passions 1923 d: Frank Tuttle. lps: Glenn Hunter, Mary Astor, Osgood Perkins. 6859f USA. *The Scarecrow* prod/rel: Film Guild, W. W. Hodkinson Corp.

MACKAYE, STEELE
Hazel Kirke, New York 1880, Play
Hazel Kirke 1912 d: Oscar Apfel. lps: Mabel Trunnelle, Herbert Prior, E. P. Sullivan. SHT USA. prod/rel: Majestic
Hazel Kirke 1916 d: Leopold Wharton, Theodore Wharton. lps: Pearl White, Bruce McRae, William Riley Hatch. 5r USA. prod/rel: Wharton, Inc., Pathe Exchange, Inc.

In Spite of All, Play
In Spite of All 1915 d: Ashley Miller. lps: Robert Conness, Robert Brower, Mrs. Wallace Erskine. 3r USA. prod/rel: Edison

MACKEN, WALTER
Home Is the Hero, New York 1954, Play
Home Is the Hero 1959 d: Fielder Cook. lps: Arthur Kennedy, Walter MacKen, Eileen Crowe. 83M UKN. *Sins of the Father* prod/rel: Emmett Dalton Productions, British Lion

MACKENZIE, COMPTON (1883–1972), UKN
Carnival, London 1912, Novel
Ballet Girl, The 1916 d: George Irving. lps: Alice Brady, Holbrook Blinn, Robert Frazer. 5r USA. prod/rel: William A. Brady Picture Plays, Inc., World Film Corp.©
Carnival 1946 d: Stanley Haynes. lps: Sally Gray, Michael Wilding, Stanley Holloway. 93M UKN. prod/rel: General Film Distributors, Two Cities
Dance Pretty Lady 1932 d: Anthony Asquith. lps: Ann Casson, Carl Harbord, Michael Hogan. 64M UKN. *Carnival* prod/rel: British Instructional, Wardour

The Early Life and Adventures of Sylvia Scarlett, New York 1918, Novel
Sylvia Scarlett 1936 d: George Cukor. lps: Katharine Hepburn, Cary Grant, Brian Aherne. 94M USA. prod/rel: RKO Radio Pictures©

Rockets Galore, 1957, Novel
Rockets Galore 1958 d: Michael Relph. lps: Jeannie Carson, Donald Sinden, Roland Culver. 94M UKN. *Mad Little Island* (USA) prod/rel: Rank, Rank Film Distributors

Sinister Street, 1914, Novel
Sinister Street 1922 d: George A. Beranger. lps: John Stuart, Amy Verity, Maudie Dunham. 4495f UKN. prod/rel: Ideal

Whisky Galore!, 1947, Novel
Whisky Galore! 1948 d: Alexander MacKendrick. lps: Basil Radford, Joan Greenwood, James Robertson Justice. 82M UKN. *Tight Little Island* (USA); *Liquid Treasure* prod/rel: Ealing Studios, General Film Distributors

MACKENZIE, DONALD
The Scent of Danger, Boston 1958, Novel
Moment of Danger 1960 d: Laslo Benedek. lps: Trevor Howard, Dorothy Dandridge, Edmund Purdom. 96M UKN. *Malaga* (USA); *The Takers* prod/rel: Cavalcade Films, Douglas Fairbanks Ltd.

Nowhere to Go, Novel
Nowhere to Go 1958 d: Seth Holt. lps: George Nader, Maggie Smith, Bernard Lee. 97M UKN/USA. prod/rel: MGM, Ealing Films

MACKEY, W. GAYER
Mr. Wake's Patient, Play
Dr. Wake's Patient 1916 d: Fred Paul. lps: Phyllis Dare, Gerald McCarthy, James Lindsay. 4300f UKN. prod/rel: G. B. Samuelson, Moss

MACKIE, PHILIP
The Whole Truth, Television Play
Whole Truth, The 1958 d: John Guillermin. lps: Stewart Granger, Donna Reed, George Sanders. 85M UKN. prod/rel: Columbia, Valiant

MACKINNON, ALLAN
The Judge Sees the Light, Short Story
Circumstantial Evidence 1952 d: Daniel Birt. lps: Rona Anderson, Patrick Holt, John Arnatt. 61M UKN. prod/rel: Act Films, Monarch

MACKLE, BARBARA JANE
83 Hours 'Til Dawn, Book
83 Hours 'Til Dawn 1990 d: Donald Wrye. lps: Peter Strauss, Robert Urich, Paul Winfield. TVM. 100M USA. prod/rel: Consolidated Prods., Consolidated Entertainment©

MACKLIN, ROBERT
Juryman, Novel
Storyville 1992 d: Mark Frost. lps: James Spader, Joanne Whalley-Kilmer, Jason Robards Jr. 113M USA. prod/rel: Twentieth Century-Fox, Spelling/Davis

MACLACHLAN, PATRICIA
Plain and Tall Sarah, Novel
Sarah, Plain and Tall 1991 d: Glenn Jordan. lps: Glenn Close, Christopher Walken, Lexi Randall. TVM. 100M USA. *Skylark*

MACLANE, MARY
I Mary MacLane, New York 1917, Autobiography
Men Who Have Made Love to Me 1918 d: Arthur Berthelet. lps: Mary MacLane, Ralph Graves, R. Paul Harvey. 7r USA. prod/rel: Essanay Film Mfg. Co.©, George K. Spoor Ultra Picture

MACLAVERTY, BERNARD
Cal, Novel
Cal 1984 d: Pat O'Connor. lps: Helen Mirren, John Lynch, Donal McCann. 102M UKN. prod/rel: Warner, Goldcrest

Lamb, Novel
Lamb 1986 d: Colin Gregg. lps: Liam Neeson, Hugh O'Conor, Ian Bannen. 110M UKN. prod/rel: Cannonfour, Flickers

MACLEAN, ALISTAIR (1922–1987), UKN
Bear Island, 1971, Novel
Bear Island 1979 d: Don Sharp. lps: Donald Sutherland, Vanessa Redgrave, Richard Widmark. 118M UKN/CND. *Le Secret de la Banquise* prod/rel: Columbia Pictures Corp. (Los Angeles), Bear Island Films (U.K.) Ltd.

Breakheart Pass, 1974, Novel
Breakheart Pass 1976 d: Tom Gries. lps: Charles Bronson, Ben Johnson, Richard CrennA. 95M USA. prod/rel: United Artists Corp., Elliott Kastner

Caravan to Vaccares, 1970, Novel
Caravan to Vaccares 1974 d: Geoffrey Reeve. lps: Charlotte Rampling, David Birney, Michael Lonsdale. 98M UKN/FRN. *Le Passager* (FRN) prod/rel: Bryanston, Crowndale

Death Train, Novel
Death Train 1992 d: David S. Jackson. lps: Pierce Brosnan, Patrick Stewart, Alexandra Paul. TVM. 95M USA/UKN/CRT. *Alistair MacLean's Death Train*; *Detonator*

Fear Is the Key, 1961, Novel
Fear Is the Key 1972 d: Michael Tuchner. lps: Barry Newman, Suzy Kendall, John Vernon. 108M UKN. prod/rel: Emi, Klk

Force Ten from Navarone, 1968, Novel
Force 10 from Navarone 1978 d: Guy Hamilton. lps: Robert Shaw, Edward Fox, Harrison Ford. 117M UKN/USA. *Force Ten from Navarone* prod/rel: Columbia, Aip

The Guns of Navarone, London 1957, Novel
Guns of Navarone, The 1961 d: J. Lee Thompson. lps: Gregory Peck, David Niven, Anthony Quinn. 157M UKN/USA. prod/rel: Open Road Films, Columbia

Ice Station Zebra, London 1963, Novel
Ice Station Zebra 1968 d: John Sturges. lps: Rock Hudson, Ernest Borgnine, Patrick McGoohan. 152M USA. prod/rel: Filmways, Inc.

Night Watch, Novel
Alistair MacLean's Night Watch 1995 d: David S. Jackson. lps: Pierce Brosnan, Alexandra Paul, William Devane. TVM. 120M UKN/USA. *Night Watch* prod/rel: British Lion, Jadran

Puppet on a Chain, 1969, Novel
Puppet on a Chain 1970 d: Geoffrey Reeve, Don Sharp. lps: Sven-Bertil Taube, Barbara Parkins, Alexander Knox. 98M UKN. prod/rel: Scotia-Barber, Big City

River of Death, Novel
  River of Death 1988 d: Steve Carver. lps: Michael Dudikoff, Donald Pleasence, Herbert Lom. 111M USA. *River for Death* prod/rel: Cannon

The Secret Ways, New York 1959, Novel
  Secret Ways, The 1961 d: Phil Karlson. lps: Richard Widmark, Sonja Ziemann, Senta Berger. 112M USA. prod/rel: Heath Productions, Universal

When Eight Bells Toll, 1966, Novel
  When Eight Bells Toll 1971 d: Etienne Perier. lps: Anthony Hopkins, Robert Morley, Nathalie Delon. 94M UKN.

Where Eagles Dare, London 1966, Novel
  Where Eagles Dare 1968 d: Brian G. Hutton, Yakima Canutt. lps: Richard Burton, Clint Eastwood, Mary Ure. 158M UKN/USA. prod/rel: Winkast Film Productions, MGM

MACLENNAN, HUGH (1907–1990), CND
Two Solitudes, Novel
  Two Solitudes 1978 d: Lionel Chetwynd. lps: Jean-Pierre Aumont, Stacy Keach, Gloria Carlin. 117M CND. *Deux Solitudes* prod/rel: Two Solitudes Film Corp., New World-Mutual

MACLEOD, ROBERT
The Appaloosa, Connecticut 1963, Book
  Appaloosa, The 1966 d: Sidney J. Furie. lps: Marlon Brando, John Saxon, Anjanette Comer. 98M USA. *Southwest to Sonora* (UKN) prod/rel: Universal

The Californio, Greenwich CT. 1967, Book
  100 Rifles 1969 d: Tom Gries. lps: Jim Brown, Raquel Welch, Burt Reynolds. 110M USA/SPN. *Los Cien Rifles* (SPN) prod/rel: Marvin Schwartz Productions

MACLEOD, WENDY
The House of Yes, Play
  House of Yes, The 1997 d: Mark Waters. lps: Parker Posey, Josh Hamilton, Tori Spelling. 90M USA. prod/rel: Bandera Entertainment

MACPHERSON, JEAN DU ROCHER
Evidence, New York 1914, Play
  Evidence 1929 d: John G. Adolfi. lps: Pauline Frederick, William Courtenay, Conway Tearle. 7152f USA. prod/rel: Warner Brothers Pictures

MACPHERSON, JEAN DU ROCHER
Evidence 1915 d: Edwin August. lps: Edwin August, Lillian Tucker, Haidee Wright. 5r USA. prod/rel: F. Ray Comstock Film Corp., World Film Corp.©

MACPHERSON, L. DU ROCHER
Washington Melodrama, Play
  Washington Melodrama 1941 d: S. Sylvan Simon. lps: Kent Taylor, Dan Dailey, Ann Rutherford. 80M USA. prod/rel: MGM

MACRAE, ARTHUR
Traveller's Joy, London 1948, Play
  Traveller's Joy 1949 d: Ralph Thomas. lps: John McCallum, Googie Withers, Yolande Donlan. 78M UKN. prod/rel: Gainsborough, General Film Distributors

Under Your Hat, London 1938, Play
  Under Your Hat 1940 d: Maurice Elvey. lps: Jack Hulbert, Cicely Courtneidge, Austin Trevor. 79M UKN. prod/rel: Grand National, British Lion

MACRI, GIUSEPPE
"Fiat Voluntas Dei", Play
  "Fiat Voluntas Dei" 1935 d: Amleto Palermi. lps: Angelo Musco, Maria Denis, Sarah Ferrati. 75M ITL. prod/rel: Artisti Associati

MACROLAN, PIERRE
L' Antre de Misericorde, Novel
  Antre de Misericorde, L' 1976 d: Bernard d'Albrigeon. lps: Pascal Sellier, Roger Jacquet, Paul Leperson. 90M FRN. prod/rel: Television Francais

MACTETA, GRIGORIJ
Pomsta More, Short Story
  Pomsta More 1921 d: Vladimir Pospisil-Born. lps: Mary Jansova, Vladimir Pospisil-Born, Robert Ford. CZC. *The Revenge of the Sea* prod/rel: Bohemian-Rival, Patriafilm

MACY, DORA
Air Hostess, 1933, Short Story
  Air Hostess 1933 d: Albert S. Rogell. lps: Evalyn Knapp, James Murray, Arthur Pierson. 67M USA. prod/rel: Columbia Pictures Corp.

Ex-Mistress, New York 1930, Novel
  My Past 1931 d: Roy Del Ruth. lps: Lewis Stone, Ben Lyon, Bebe Daniels. 74M USA. *Ex-Mistress* (UKN) prod/rel: Warner Bros. Pictures©

Night Nurse, New York 1930, Novel
  Night Nurse 1931 d: William A. Wellman. lps: Barbara Stanwyck, Ben Lyon, Joan Blondell. 72M USA. prod/rel: Warner Bros. Pictures©

MADACH, IMRE
Az Ember Tragediaja, 1863, Verse
  Angyali Udvozlet 1985 d: Andras Jeles. lps: Peter Bocsor, Julia Mero, Eszter Gyalog. 100M HNG. *Angelic Greeting*; *The Annunciation*

MADDEN, EDWARD
The Mills of the Gods, Poem
  Devil's Toy, The 1916 d: Harley Knoles. lps: Edwin Stevens, Adele Blood, Montagu Love. 5r USA. prod/rel: Premo Film Corp., Equitable Motion Pictures Corp.©

MADDUX, RACHEL
The Orchard Children, Book
  Who'll Save Our Children? 1978 d: George Schaefer. lps: Shirley Jones, Len Cariou, Cassie Yates. TVM. 100M USA. *Who Will Save Our Children?* prod/rel: Time-Life Television

A Walk in the Spring Rain, New York 1966, Novel
  Walk in the Spring Rain, A 1970 d: Guy Green. lps: Ingrid Bergman, Anthony Quinn, Fritz Weaver. 98M USA. prod/rel: Pingree Productions, Columbia

MADIS, ALEX
Chipee, Play
  Chipee 1937 d: Roger Goupillieres. lps: Victor Boucher, Nita Raya, Andree Guize. 84M FRN. *Coup de Foudre* prod/rel: C.G.F.

Chou-Chou Poids-Plume, Play
  Chouchou Poids Plume 1932 d: Robert Bibal. lps: Geo Laby, Colette Broido, Wanda Greville. 87M FRN. prod/rel: Films Leon Poirier

  Chou-Chou Poids-Plume 1925 d: Gaston Ravel. lps: Andre Roanne, Olga Day, Andre Lefaur. F FRN.

Couchette No.3, Opera
  Surprises du Sleeping, Les 1933 d: Karl Anton. lps: Claude Dauphin, Florelle, Jacques Louvigny. 92M FRN. *Couchette No.3* prod/rel: S.a.P.E.C.

Matricule 33, Play
  Matricule 33 1933 d: Karl Anton. lps: Edwige Feuillere, Andre Luguet, Abel Tarride. 91M FRN. prod/rel: S.a.P.E.C.

MADISON, MARTHA
Subway Express, New York 1929, Play
  Subway Express 1931 d: Fred Newmeyer. lps: Jack Holt, Aileen Pringle, Jason Robards. 68M USA. prod/rel: Columbia Pictures Corp.©

The Up and Up, New York 1930, Play
  Reckless Living 1931 d: Cyril Gardner. lps: Ricardo Cortez, Mae Clarke, Norman Foster. 68M USA. *Twenty Grand*; *The Up and Up* prod/rel: Universal Pictures Corp.©

MADROUSSE, LUCIE DELORME
Histoire de Six Petites Filles, Novel
  Istitutrice Di Sei Bambine, L' 1920 d: Mario Bonnard. lps: Elsa d'Auro, Fernando Ribacchi, Paola Boetzky. 1343m ITL. prod/rel: Celio Film

MAEL, PIERRE
Loin Des Yeux Pres du Coeur, Novel
  Loin Des Yeux, Pres du Coeur 1915 d: Louis Le Forestier. lps: Aime Simon-Gerard, Yvonne Sergyl. 1055m FRN. prod/rel: Scagl

MAETERLINCK, MAURICE (1862–1949), BLG
The Burgomaster of Stilemonde, London 1919, Play
  Burgomaster of Stilemonde, The 1928 d: George J. Banfield. lps: John Martin-Harvey, Fern Andra, Robert Andrews. 7934f UKN. prod/rel: British Filmcraft, Woolf & Freedman

Monna Vanna, 1902, Play
  Monna Vanna 1916 d: Mario Caserini. lps: Madeleine Celiat, Hamilton Revelle, Francois-Paul Donadio. 852m ITL. prod/rel: S.A. Ambrosio

Mort de Tintagiles, 1894, Play
  Death of Tintagiles, The 1977 d: Malcolm Edwards. 37M UKN.

L' Oiseau Bleu, Moscow 1908, Play
  Blue Bird, The 1910. lps: Pauline Gilmer, Olive Walter, Margaret Murray. 1380f UKN. prod/rel: Gaumont

  Blue Bird, The 1940 d: Walter Lang. lps: Shirley Temple, Spring Byington, Nigel Bruce. 88M USA. prod/rel: 20th Century-Fox

  Bluebird, The 1918 d: Maurice Tourneur. lps: Robin MacDougall, Tula Belle, Edwin E. Reed. 6r USA. *The Blue Bird* prod/rel: Famous Players-Lasky Corp.©, Artcraft Picture

  Sinyaya Ptitsa 1975 d: George Cukor. lps: Elizabeth Taylor, Jane Fonda, Ava Gardner. 99M USS/USA. *The Blue Bird* (USA) prod/rel: Twentieth Century-Fox

Pelleas Et Melisande, 1892, Play
  Pelleas and Melisande 1913 d: Mr. MacDonald. lps: Constance Crawley, Arthur Maude. 3r USA. prod/rel: Bison

  Pelleas Et Melisande 1973 d: Joseph Benedek. lps: Philippe Morand, Sophie Barjac, Pierre Bianco. MTV. 104M BLG.

MAGE, JACQUES
Story
  Nackte Und Der Satan, Die 1959 d: Victor Trivas. lps: Horst Frank, Michel Simon, Paul Dahlke. 97M GRM. *The Head* (USA); *A Head for the Devil*; *The Screaming Head*; *The Naked and Satan*; *Satan and the Naked Woman* prod/rel: Rapid, Prisma

MAGEE, DOUG
Slow Coming Dark, Book
  Somebody Has to Shoot the Picture 1990 d: Frank R. Pierson. lps: Roy Scheider, Bonnie Bedelia, Robert Carradine. TVM. 105M USA.

MAGGIORA, GINO
Brogliaccio d'Amore, Novel
  Brogliaccio d'Amore 1976 d: Decio SillA. lps: Enrico Maria Salerno, Senta Berger, Paolo Carlini. 100M ITL. prod/rel: Dunamis Cin.Ca, Maxi Cin.Ca

MAGHERINI, GRAZIELLA
La Sindrome Di Stendhal, Novel
  Sindrome Di Stendhal, La 1996 d: Dario Argento. lps: Asia Argento, Thomas Kretschmann, Marco Leonardi. 119M ITL. *The Stendhal Syndrome* prod/rel: Medusa Film

MAGLIN, RUDOLF BOLO
Gilberte de Courgenay, Zurich 1939, Novel
  Gilberte de Courgenay 1941 d: Franz Schnyder. lps: Anne-Marie Blanc, Helene Dalmet, Heinrich Gretler. 115M SWT. prod/rel: Praesens-Film

MAGNAN, PIERRE
La Maison Assassinee, Novel
  Maison Assassinee, La 1989 d: Georges Lautner. lps: Patrick Bruel, Sophie Brochet, Agnes Blanchot. 110M FRN. *The Murdered House*

MAGNANI, LUIGI
Novel
  Neveu de Beethoven, Le 1985 d: Paul Morrissey. lps: Wolfgang Reichmann, Dietmar Prinz, Jane Birkin. 103M FRN/AUS/GRM. *Beethoven's Nephew* (USA); *Beethoven* prod/rel: C.B.L., Orfilm

MAGNIER, CLAUDE
Monsieur Masure, Paris 1956, Play
  Reveille-Toi, Cherie 1960 d: Claude Magnier. lps: Daniel Gelin, Francois Perier, Genevieve Cluny. 92M FRN. *Bonne Nuit Monsieur Masure* prod/rel: Panda Films

  Where Were You When the Lights Went Out? 1968 d: Hy Averback. lps: Doris Day, Patrick O'Neal, Terry-Thomas. 94M USA. prod/rel: Metro-Goldwyn-Mayer, Inc.

Oscar, Play
  Oscar 1967 d: Edouard Molinaro. lps: Louis de Funes, Claude Rich, Claude Gensac. 85M FRN. prod/rel: Gaumont International

  Oscar 1991 d: John Landis. lps: Sylvester Stallone, Ornella Muti, Don Ameche. 109M USA. prod/rel: Buena Vista, Touchstone Pictures

MAGOG, H. G.
L' Enfant Des Halles, Novel
  Enfant Des Halles, L' 1924 d: Rene Leprince. lps: Gabriel Signoret, Suzanne Bianchetti, Monique Chryses. SRL. 7900m FRN. prod/rel: Societe Des Cineromans

MAGORIAN, MICHELLE
Goodnight Mister Tom, Novel
  Goodnight Mister Tom 1998 d: Jack Gold. lps: John Thaw, Nick Robinson, Annabelle Apsion. TVM. 120M UKN. prod/rel: Carlton Television©

MAGRUDER, MARY LANIER
Courage, Short Story
  Satan and the Woman 1928 d: Burton L. King. lps: Claire Windsor, Cornelius Keefe, Vera Lewis. 6400f USA. prod/rel: Excellent Pictures

MAGYIVANYI, ZOLTAN
Short Story
  Sette Peccati, I 1942 d: Ladislao Kish. lps: Maria Denis, Massimo Serato, Irasema Dilian. 85M ITL. prod/rel: Sabaudia Film, a.C.I.

MAHALIN, PAUL
Mademoiselle Montecristo, Novel
  Mademoiselle Montecristo 1918 d: Camillo de Riso. lps: Tilde Kassay, Guido Trento, Olga Benetti. SRL. 4314m ITL. *Mademoiselle Di Montecristo* prod/rel: Caesar Film

MAHAN, PATTE WHEAT
Three for a Wedding, New York 1965, Novel
  Doctor, You've Got to Be Kidding 1967 d: Peter Tewkesbury. lps: George Hamilton, Sandra Dee, Celeste Holm. 94M USA. *Three for a Wedding*; *This Way Out Please* prod/rel: Trident Productions, MGM

MAHAPATRA, BASANT
Shesha Shrabana, Play
  Sesha Shrabana 1976 d: Prashanta NandA. lps: Prashanta Nanda, Maheshweta, Mohammed Mohsin. 129M IND. *The Last Monsoon*; *Shesha Sravana* prod/rel: Shri Jagannath Films

MAHEN, JIRI
Janosik, Play
  Janosik 1935 d: Martin Fric. lps: Palo Bielik, Zlata Hajdukova, Andrej Bagar. 2266m CZC. prod/rel: Lloyd

MAHER, MARTIN
Bringing Up the Brass, 1951, Book
  Long Gray Line, The 1955 d: John Ford. lps: Tyrone Power, Maureen O'Hara, Robert Francis. 138M USA. prod/rel: Columbia, Rotha Prods.

MAHFUZ, NAJIB (1911–, EGY, Mahfouz, Naguib
Qasr Al-Shauq, 1957, Novel
  Qasr Ash-Shawq 19— d: Hassan Al Imam. 130M EGY. *Le Palais Des Passions*; *Qasr Al-Shauq*; *Kasr El Shawk*

MAHMOODY, BETTY
Not Without My Daughter, Book
  Not Without My Daughter 1991 d: Brian Gilbert. lps: Sally Field, Alfred Molina, Sheila Rosenthal. 116M USA. prod/rel: Pathe Entertainment, Inc., Ufland

MAHNER, JOHN C.
Devil Girl from Mars, Play
  Devil Girl from Mars 1954 d: David MacDonald. lps: Hugh McDermott, Hazel Court, Patricia Laffan. 76M UKN. prod/rel: Danzigers, British Lion

MAHONEY, BARBARA
Passionate Man, a Sensitive, Novel
  Sensitive, Passionate Man, A 1977 d: John Newland. lps: Angie Dickinson, David Janssen, Mariclare Costello. TVM. 100M USA. prod/rel: Factor-Newland Productions

MAHR, RUDI
Und Keiner Schamte Sich, Novel
  ..Und Keiner Schamte Sich 1960 d: Hans Schott-Schobinger. lps: Gustav Frohlich, Margret Aust, Barbara Frey. 103M GRM. *And Nobody Was Ashamed*; *And No One Was Ashamed* prod/rel: Iso, Adria

MAIBAUM, RICHARD
Sweet Mystery of Life, New York 1935, Play
  Gold Diggers of 1937 1936 d: Lloyd Bacon. lps: Dick Powell, Joan Blondell, Glenda Farrell. 100M USA. prod/rel: Warner Bros. Pictures©

MAIDEN, CECIL
Show Flat, Play
  Show Flat 1936 d: Bernerd Mainwaring. lps: Eileen Munro, Anthony Hankey, Clifford Heatherley. 70M UKN. prod/rel: British and Dominions, Paramount British

MAIER, WILLIAM
Pleasure Island, 1949, Novel
  Girls of Pleasure Island, The 1953 d: F. Hugh Herbert, Alvin Ganzer. lps: Leo Genn, Audrey Dalton, Don Taylor. 95M USA. prod/rel: Paramount

MAILER, NORMAN (1923–, USA
An American Dream, New York 1965, Novel
  American Dream, An 1966 d: Robert Gist. lps: Stuart Whitman, Barry Sullivan, Janet Leigh. 107M USA. *See You in Hell Darling* (UKN) prod/rel: Warner Bros.
The Executioner's Song, 1979, Book
  Executioner's Song -the Gary Gilmore Story, The 1982 d: Lawrence Schiller. lps: Tommy Lee Jones, Christine Lahti, Rosanna Arquette. TVM. 200M USA. *The Executioner's Song* prod/rel: NBC, Film Communications
The Naked and the Dead, 1948, Novel
  Naked and the Dead, The 1958 d: Raoul Walsh. lps: Aldo Ray, Cliff Robertson, Raymond Massey. 131M USA. prod/rel: Warner Bros.
Tough Guys Don't Dance, 1984, Novel
  Tough Guys Don't Dance 1987 d: Norman Mailer. lps: Ryan O'Neal, Isabella Rossellini, Debra Sandlund. 108M USA. prod/rel: Cannon

MAILLARD, A.
Les Deux Sergents, 1823, Play
  Due Sergenti, I 1909. 269m ITL. *The Two Sergeants* (UKN) prod/rel: Itala Film
  Due Sergenti, I 1913 d: Ubaldo Maria Del Colle. lps: Alberto A. Capozzi, Ugo Pardi, Orlando Ricci. 1800m ITL. *The Two Sergeants* (USA); *I Due Sergenti Al Cordone Sanitario Di Porto Vandre* prod/rel: Pasquali E C.

MAILLET, ANTONINE (1929–, CND
Gapi Et Sullivan, Play
  Gapi 1982 d: Paul Blouin. lps: Gilles Pelletier, Guy Provost. 100M CND. prod/rel: Radio-Canada

MAIN, IAN
Subway in the Sky, London 1957, Play
  Subway in the Sky 1959 d: Muriel Box. lps: Van Johnson, Hildegard Knef, Albert Lieven. 86M UKN. prod/rel: Britannia, Orbit

MAINE, CHARLES ERIC
Escapement, Novel
  Escapement 1957 d: Montgomery Tully. lps: Rod Cameron, Mary Murphy, Meredith Edwards. 76M UKN. *The Electronic Monster* (USA); *The Dream machine*; *Zex the Electronic Fiend*; *Zex* prod/rel: Anglo-Amalgamated, Anglo-Guild
The Mind of Mr. Soames, London 1961, Novel
  Mind of Mr. Soames, The 1969 d: Alan Cooke. lps: Terence Stamp, Robert Vaughn, Nigel Davenport. 98M UKN. prod/rel: Amicus Productions, Columbia
Spaceways, Radio Play
  Spaceways 1953 d: Terence Fisher. lps: Howard Duff, Eva Bartok, Alan Wheatley. 76M UKN. prod/rel: Wh Productions, Hammer
Timeslip, Television Play
  Timeslip 1955 d: Ken Hughes. lps: Gene Nelson, Faith Domergue, Joseph Tomelty. 93M UKN. *The Atomic Man* (USA) prod/rel: Anglo-Guild, Anglo-Amalgamated

MAINWARING, DANIEL (1902–1977), USA, Homes, Geoffrey
Build My Gallows High, Novel
  Against All Odds 1984 d: Taylor Hackford. lps: Jeff Bridges, Rachel Ward, James Woods. 128M USA. prod/rel: Columbia
  Out of the Past 1947 d: Jacques Tourneur. lps: Robert Mitchum, Kirk Douglas, Jane Greer. 97M USA. *Build My Gallows High* (UKN) prod/rel: RKO Radio
Forty Whacks, Novel
  Crime By Night 1944 d: William Clemens. lps: Jane Wyman, Faye Emerson, Charles Lang. 72M USA. prod/rel: Warner Bros.
No Hands on the Clock, Novel
  No Hands on the Clock 1941 d: Frank McDonald. lps: Chester Morris, Jean Parker, Rose Hobart. 76M USA. prod/rel: Paramount
Redwood Highway, Story
  Hot Cargo 1946 d: Lew Landers. lps: William Gargan, Jean Rogers, Philip Reed. 57M USA. prod/rel: Paramount, Pine-Thomas

MAIR, FRANCOIS
Le Poilu de la Victoire, Play
  Poilu de la Victoire, Le 1915 d: Roger Lion?. lps: Pierre Etchepare, Polin. 460m FRN. prod/rel: Franco-Film

MAIR, JOHN
Never Come Back, Novel
  Tiger By the Tail 1955 d: John Gilling. lps: Larry Parks, Constance Smith, Lisa Daniely. 85M UKN. *Cross Up* (USA) prod/rel: Tempean, Eros

MAIROCK, ANDRE
Der Jager Vom Roteck, Novel
  Jager Vom Roteck, Der 1955 d: Hermann Kugelstadt. lps: Michael Cramer, Doris Kirchner, Oskar SimA. 88M GRM. *The Hunter of Roteck* prod/rel: Panorama

MAITRA, RABINDRANATH
Manmoyee Girls' School, Play
  Manmoyee Girls' School 1935 d: Jyotish Bannerji. lps: Tulsi Chakraborty, Radharani, Jahar Ganguly. 152M IND. prod/rel: Radha Films
  Manmoyee Girls' School 1958 d: Hemchandra Chunder. lps: Dhiraj Bhattachayra, Bhanu Bannerjee, Jahar Ganguly. F IND.

MAJAKOVSKIJ, VLADIMIR
Il Bagno, Play
  Bagno, Il 1972 d: Ugo Gregoretti. lps: Gigio Morra, Toni Bertelli, Italo Spinelli. 90M ITL. prod/rel: Unitelefilm

MAJANO, ANTON GIULIO
La Barriera, Novel
  Pieta Per Chi Cade 1954 d: Mario CostA. lps: Amedeo Nazzari, Antonella Lualdi, Nadia Gray. 90M ITL. prod/rel: Rizzoli Film, Royal Film
Uragano Ai Tropici, Novel
  Uragano Ai Tropici 1939 d: Gino Talamo, Pier Luigi Faraldo. lps: Fosco Giachetti, Rubi Dalma, Mino Doro. 2088m ITL. prod/rel: Ponzano Film, Europa Film

MAJEROVA, MARIE
Panenstvi, Novel
  Panenstvi 1937 d: Otakar VavrA. lps: Lida Baarova, Jaroslava Skorkovska, Frantisek Kreuzmann. 2355m CZC. *Virginity*; *Innocence*; *Maidenhood* prod/rel: Lucernafilm
Sirena, 1935, Novel
  Sirena 1947 d: Karel Stekly. lps: Marie Vasova, Ladislav Bohac. 83M CZC. *The Strike*

MAJERUS, JANET
Grandpa and Frank, Novel
  Home to Stay 1978 d: Delbert Mann. lps: Henry Fonda, Michael McGuire, Frances Hyland. TVM. 100M USA/CND. prod/rel: Time-Life Films Inc. Prods. (New York), D.W. Reid Film Corp. (Toronto)

MAJOCCHI, ANDREA
Fra Bisturi E Forbici, Novel
  Disperato Addio 1956 d: Lionello de Felice. lps: Massimo Girotti, Lise Bourdin, Andrea Checchi. 85M ITL. prod/rel: Cin.Ca Mambretti
Vita Di Chirurgo, Novel
  Disperato Addio 1956 d: Lionello de Felice. lps: Massimo Girotti, Lise Bourdin, Andrea Checchi. 85M ITL. prod/rel: Cin.Ca Mambretti

MAJOR, CHARLES
Sweet Alyssum; a Story of the Indiana Oilfields, 1911, Short Story
  Sweet Alyssum 1915 d: Colin Campbell. lps: Tyrone Power Sr., Kathlyn Williams, Edith Johnson. 5r USA. prod/rel: Selig Polyscope Co.©, Red Seal Play
When Knighthood Was in Flower, Indianapolis 1898, Novel
  Dorothy Vernon of Haddon Hall 1924 d: Marshall Neilan. lps: Mary Pickford, Anders Randolf, Marc MacDermott. 9351f USA. prod/rel: Mary Pickford Productions, United Artists
  Sword and the Rose, The 1953 d: Ken Annakin. lps: Richard Todd, Glynis Johns, James Robertson Justice. 91M UKN/USA. *When Knighthood Was in Flower* prod/rel: Walt Disney British Prods., RKO-Radio
  When Knighthood Was in Flower 1922 d: Robert G. VignolA. lps: Marion Davies, Forrest Stanley, Lyn Harding. 12r USA. prod/rel: Cosmopolitan Pictures, Paramount Pictures
Yolanda, New York 1905, Novel
  Yolanda 1924 d: Robert G. VignolA. lps: Marion Davies, Lyn Harding, Holbrook Blinn. 11r USA. prod/rel: Cosmopolitan Pictures, Metro-Goldwyn Distributing Corp.

MAJUMDAR, KAMAL KUMAR
Antarjali Jatra, 1960, Novel
  Antarjali Jatra 1988 d: Gautam Ghose. lps: Promode Ganguly, Shatrughan Sinha, Shampa Ghosh. 140M IND. *Last Rites*; *The Voyage Beyond*; *Mahayatra*; *The Journey*; *Antaryali Yatra* prod/rel: Nfdc

MAKIN, W. J.
The Doctor's Secret, 1938, Short Story
  Return of Dr. X, The 1939 d: Vincent Sherman. lps: Humphrey Bogart, Rosemary Lane, Dennis Morgan. 60M USA. prod/rel: Warner Bros. Pictures©
Murder at Covent Garden, Novel
  Murder at Covent Garden 1932 d: Leslie Hiscott, Michael Barringer. lps: Dennis Neilson-Terry, Anne Grey, Walter Fitzgerald. 68M UKN. prod/rel: Twickenham, Woolf & Freedman
Overcoat Sam, Short Story
  Overcoat Sam 1937 d: Wallace Orton. lps: George Mozart, Vera Sherbourne, Frederick Peisley. 43M UKN. prod/rel: Uk Films, MGM

MAKIS, JEAN
La Griffe, Short Story
  Legions d'Honneur 1938 d: Maurice Gleize. lps: Marie Bell, Milly Mathis, Charles Vanel. 96M FRN. prod/rel: Films De France

MAKOUL, RUDY
Story
  Geisha Boy, The 1958 d: Frank Tashlin. lps: Jerry Lewis, Marie McDonald, Sessue HayakawA. 98M USA. prod/rel: Paramount, York Pictures

MALA QINFU
Cao Yuan Shang de Ren Men, Novel
  Cao Yuan Shang de Ren Men 1953 d: Xu Tao. lps: Wu Rina, Enhesheng, Zhao Lu. 10r CHN. *People of the Grasslands* prod/rel: Northeast Film Studio

MALAMUD, BERNARD (1914–1986), USA
The Angel Levine, 1955, Short Story
  Angel Levine, The 1970 d: Jan Kadar. lps: Harry Belafonte, Zero Mostel, Ida KaminskA. 105M USA. prod/rel: Belafonte Enterprises

The Assistant, 1957, Novel
Assistant, The 1997 d: Daniel Petrie. lps: Gil Bellows, Kate Greenhouse, Armin Mueller-Stahl. 106M CND/UKN. prod/rel: Handmade, Paragon Entertainment Corp.

The Fixer, 1966, Novel
Fixer, The 1968 d: John Frankenheimer. lps: Alan Bates, Dirk Bogarde, Georgia Brown. 132M USA. prod/rel: MGM

The Last Mohican, Novel
Vestito Per un Saggio, Un 1979 d: Giuliana Berlinguer. lps: Gastone Moschin, Flavio Bucci, Elsa Vazzoler. MTV. F ITL. prod/rel: Rai Radiotelevisione Italiana

The Natural, 1952, Novel
Natural, The 1984 d: Barry Levinson. lps: Robert Redford, Robert Duvall, Glenn Close. 134M USA. prod/rel: Tri-Star

MALAPARTE, CURZIO (1898–1957), ITL, Suckert, Curzio Malaparte
Il Cristo Proibito, Novel
Cristo Proibito, Il 1951 d: Curzio Malaparte. lps: Raf Vallone, Elena Varzi, Alain Cuny. 100M ITL. *Strange Deception*; *Forbidden Christ* (UKN) prod/rel: Excelsa Film, Minerva Film

La Pelle, Novel
Pelle, La 1981 d: Liliana Cavani. lps: Marcello Mastroianni, Burt Lancaster, Claudia Cardinale. 131M ITL/FRN. *La Peau* (FRN); *The Skin* prod/rel: Opera, Gaumont

MALCOLM, CHARLES HORACE
Bachelor Brides, 1925, Play
Bachelor Brides 1926 d: William K. Howard. lps: Rod La Rocque, Eulalie Jensen, Elinor Fair. 6612f USA. *Bachelor's Brides* prod/rel: de Mille Pictures, Producers Distributing Corp.

MALCOLM X (1925–1965), USA, Little, Malcolm, El-Shabazz, El-Hajj Malik
The Autobiography of Malcolm X, Autobiography
Malcolm X 1992 d: Spike Lee. lps: Denzel Washington, Spike Lee, Christopher Plummer. 201M USA. prod/rel: Warner Bros., Largo

MALDAGNE, PIERRE
Sans Pitie, Novel
Sans Pitie 1916. FRN.

MALET, LEO
120 Rue de la Gare, Novel
120, Rue de la Gare 1945 d: Jacques Daniel-Norman. lps: Rene Dary, Sophie Desmarets, Jean Paredes. 90M FRN. prod/rel: Sirius

Enigme aux Folies Bergere, Novel
Enigme aux Folies Bergere 1959 d: Jean Mitry. lps: Bella Darvi, Frank Villard, Yvonne Menard. 82M FRN. prod/rel: Gimeno Phillips Films

L' Homme Au Sang Bleu, Novel
Nestor Burma: l'Homme Aus Sang Bleu 1994 d: Alain Schwarzstein. lps: Guy Marchand, Anny Romand, Catherine Alcover. TVM. 100M FRN. *L' Homme Au Sang Bleu*

Nestor Burma - Detective de Choc, Novel
Nestor Burma Detective de Choc 1981 d: Jean-Luc Miesch. lps: Michel Serrault, Jane Birkin, Guy Marchand. 100M FRN. *Schlock Detective Nestor Burma* (UKN) prod/rel: Zenith, Fr 3

Nestor Burma Dans l'Ile, Novel
Nestor Burma Dans l'Ile 1994 d: Jean-Paul Mudry. lps: Guy Marchand, Pierre Tornade, Geraldine Cotte. TVM. 90M FRN/SWT.

Nestor Burma Et le Monstre, Novel
Nestor Burma Et le Monstre 1994 d: Alain Schwarzstein. lps: Guy Marchand, Pierre Tornade, Geraldine Cotte. TVM. 90M FRN/SWT.

MALET, LUCAS
The Wages of Sin, Novel
Wages of Sin, The 1918 d: Arrigo Bocchi. lps: Kenelm Foss, Odette Goimbault, Mary Marsh Allen. 5190f UKN. prod/rel: Windsor, Walturdaw

MALEWSKA, MATHILDE
Meine Schone Mama, Novel
Meine Schone Mama 1958 d: Paul Martin. lps: Barbara von Nady, Paul Hubschmid, Nadia Gray. 89M GRM/AUS. *My Pretty Mama* prod/rel: Bavaria, Cosmopol

MALININ, GRISHA
Novel
Maria Montecristo 1950 d: Luis Cesar Amadori. lps: Zully Moreno, Arturo de Cordova, Carlos Lopez MoctezumA. 97M MXC. prod/rel: Filmadora Mexicana

MALKIN, PETER Z.
Eichmann in My Hands, Book
Man Who Captured Eichmann, The 1996 d: William A. Graham. lps: Robert Duvall, Arliss Howard, Jeffrey Tambor. TVM. 120M USA. prod/rel: Stan Margulies Co., Butchers Run Films

MALLESON, MILES
Conflict, London 1925, Play
Woman Between, The 1931 d: Miles Mander. lps: Owen Nares, Adrianne Allen, David Hawthorne. 89M UKN. *The Woman Decides* (USA); *Conflict* prod/rel: British International Pictures, Wardour

A Night in Montmartre, 1926, Play
Night in Montmartre, A 1931 d: Leslie Hiscott. lps: Horace Hodges, Franklin Dyall, Hugh Williams. 70M UKN. prod/rel: Gaumont

MALLET, ROBERT
L' Equipage Au Complet, Paris 1957, Play
Valiant, The 1962 d: Roy Ward Baker, Giorgio Capitani. lps: John Mills, Ettore Manni, Roberto Risso. 90M UKN/ITL. *L' Affondamento Della Valiant* (ITL) prod/rel: B.H.P. Films Ltd. (London), Euro International Film (Roma)

MALLET-JORIS, FRANCOISE (1930–, BLG, Mallet, Francoise
La Chambre Rouge, 1955, Novel
Chambre Rouge, La 1973 d: Jean-Pierre Berckmans. lps: Maurice Ronet, Sharon Gurney, Francoise Brion. 100M BLG/FRN.

Les Poubelles, 1956, Short Story
Travail, C'est la Liberte, Le 1959 d: Louis Grospierre. lps: Raymond Devos, Judith Magre, Jany Clair. 87M FRN. prod/rel: C.F.P.C.

Le Rempart Des Beguines, 1951, Novel
Rempart Des Beguines, Le 1972 d: Guy Casaril. lps: Anicee Alvina, Nicole Courcel, Venantino Venantini. 91M FRN/ITL. *Gli Amori Impossibili* (ITL); *The Beguines* (UKN) prod/rel: Paris Film, Anteo

MALLOCH, G. R.
Mostly Fools, Play
Devil's Maze, The 1929 d: V. Gareth Gundrey. lps: Renee Clama, Trilby Clark, Ian Fleming. 82M UKN. prod/rel: Gaumont-British

MALLOCK, F. WYNDHAM
Important People, Play
Important People 1934 d: Adrian Brunel. lps: Stewart Rome, Dorothy Boyd, Jack Raine. 48M UKN. prod/rel: GS Enterprises, MGM

MALLORY, JAY
Sweet Aloes, London 1934, Play
Give Me Your Heart 1936 d: Archie Mayo. lps: Kay Francis, George Brent, Roland Young. 88M USA. *Sweet Aloes* (UKN); *I Give My Heart*; *I Gave My Heart* prod/rel: Warner Bros. Pictures©, Cosmopolitan Production

MALMAR, MACINTOCH
Story
Victim, The 1972 d: Herschel Daugherty. lps: Elizabeth Montgomery, Eileen Heckart, Sue Ane Langdon. TVM. 73M USA. *Out of Contention* prod/rel: Universal

MALORY, SIR THOMAS (c1408–1471), UKN
Le Morte d'Arthur, 1485, Verse
Excalibur 1981 d: John Boorman. lps: Nigel Terry, Helen Mirren, Nicholas Clay. 140M UKN/USA. *Merlin and the Knights of King Arthur*; *Knights* prod/rel: Orion, Warner

Knights of the Round Table 1953 d: Richard Thorpe. lps: Robert Taylor, Ava Gardner, Mel Ferrer. 115M UKN/USA. prod/rel: MGM British

Lancelot and Guinevere 1962 d: Cornel Wilde. lps: Cornel Wilde, Jean Wallace, Brian Aherne. 117M UKN. *Sword of Lancelot* (USA) prod/rel: Emblem Productions, Universal-International

MALOT, HECTOR
Romain Kalbris, Novel
Romain Kalbris 1911 d: Georges DenolA. lps: Landrin, Gregoire, Eugenie Nau. 250m FRN. prod/rel: Scagl
Romain Kalbris 1923 d: Georges MoncA. lps: Armand Numes, Catherine Fonteney, Jacqueline Passo. 1650m FRN. prod/rel: Scagl

Sans Famille, Novel
Ritorno Al Nido 1944 d: Giorgio Ferroni. lps: Luciano de Ambrosiis, Erminio Spalla, Bianca DoriA. 78M ITL. prod/rel: Scalera Film
Sans Famille 1913 d: Georges MoncA. lps: Maria Fromet, Georges Treville, Lerand. 2180m FRN. prod/rel: Scagl
Sans Famille 1925 d: Georges Monca, Maurice Keroul. lps: Henri Baudin, Denise Lorys, Leslie Shaw. SRL. 6EP FRN. *No Relations* prod/rel: Argus Films

Sans Famille 1934 d: Marc Allegret. lps: Robert Lynen, Berangere, Vanni Marcoux. 114M FRN. prod/rel: Pierre Braunberger
Sans Famille 1957 d: Andre Michel. lps: Gino Cervi, Pierre Brasseur, Bernard Blier. 100M FRN/ITL. *Senza Famiglia* (ITL); *The Adventures of Remi* prod/rel: Societe De Prods. Cinemato. Europeennes, Francinex
Senza Famiglia 1945 d: Giorgio Ferroni. lps: Luciano de Ambrosiis, Erminio Spalla, Luciano Zambon. 82M ITL. prod/rel: Scalera Film

MALPASS, ERIC
Als Mutter Streikte, Novel
Als Mutter Streikte 1973 d: Eberhard Schroeder. lps: Peter Hall, Johanna Matz, Gila von Weitershausen. 90M GRM. *When Mother Went on Strike* prod/rel: Seitz, Terra-Filmkunst

Morgens Um 7 Ist Die Welt Noch in Ordnung, Novel
Morgens Um 7 Ist Die Welt Noch in Ordung 1968 d: Kurt Hoffmann. lps: Archibald Eser, Gerlinde Locker, Peter Arens. 98M GRM. *At 7 in the Morning All Is Still Well in the World*; *The World Is Still in Order at Seven in the Morning* prod/rel: Independent, Constantin

Wenn Suss Das Mondlicht Auf Den Hugeln Schlaft, Novel
Wenn Suss Das Mondlicht Auf Hugeln Schlaft 1969 d: Wolfgang Liebeneiner. lps: Werner Hinz, Luitgard Im, Werner Bruhns. 97M GRM. *When the Moonlight Sleeps Upon the Hills* prod/rel: Independent, Constantin

MALRAUX, A. L.
Greetings from Hong Kong
Razzia Sur le Plaisir 1976 d: Marius Lesoeur, Jesus Franco. lps: Florentina Fuga, Evelyne Deher, Evelyne Scott. 87M FRN. *Les Filles Dans une Cage Doree*; *Une Cage Doree*

MALRAUX, ANDRE (1901–1976), FRN, Malraux, Georges Andre
L' Espoir, 1937, Novel
Espoir 1939 d: Andre Malraux. lps: Andres Mejuto, Nicolas Rodriguez, Jose Maria Lado. 80M FRN/SPN. *Sierra de Teruel* (SPN); *Man's Hope* (UKN); *Days of Hope* prod/rel: Productions Corniglion-Molinier

MALTBY, H. F.
Bees and Honey, 1928, Play
His Lordship Regrets 1938 d: MacLean Rogers. lps: Claude Hulbert, Winifred Shotter, Gina Malo. 78M UKN. prod/rel: Canterbury, RKO Radio

Fifty-Fifty, London 1932, Play
Just My Luck 1933 d: Jack Raymond. lps: Ralph Lynn, Winifred Shotter, Davy Burnaby. 77M UKN. prod/rel: British and Dominions, Woolf & Freedman

For the Love of Mike, London 1931, Play
For the Love of Mike 1932 d: Monty Banks. lps: Bobby Howes, Constance Shotter, Arthur Riscoe. 86M UKN. prod/rel: British International Pictures, Wardour

Fraud, Play
Howard Case, The 1936 d: Frank Richardson. lps: Jack Livesey, Olive Melville, Arthur Seaton. 62M UKN. prod/rel: Sovereign, Universal

The Laughter of Fools, 1909, Play
Laughter of Fools, The 1933 d: Adrian Brunel. lps: Pat Paterson, Derrick de Marney, Helen Ferrers. 47M UKN. prod/rel: George Smith, Fox

Profit - and the Loss, Play
Profit and the Loss 1917 d: A. V. Bramble, Eliot Stannard. lps: James Carew, Randle Ayrton, Margaret Halstan. 5300f UKN. prod/rel: Ideal

The Right Age to Marry, 1925, Play
Right Age to Marry, The 1935 d: MacLean Rogers. lps: Frank Pettingell, Joyce Bland, Tom Helmore. 69M UKN. prod/rel: GS Enterprises, Radio

The Rotters, Play
Rotters, The 1921 d: A. V. Bramble. lps: Joe Nightingale, Sydney Fairbrother, Sydney Paxton. 5000f UKN. prod/rel: Ideal

A Temporary Gentleman, London 1919, Play
Temporary Gentleman, A 1920 d: Fred W. Durrant. lps: Owen Nares, Madge Titheradge, Tom Reynolds. 6000f UKN. prod/rel: G. B. Samuelson, Granger

The Youngest of Three, 1905, Play
Over the Garden Wall 1934 d: John Daumery. lps: Bobby Howes, Marian Marsh, Margaret Bannerman. 68M UKN. prod/rel: British International Pictures, Wardour

MALTZ, ALBERT (1908–, USA
Merry-Go-Round, New York 1932, Play
Afraid to Talk 1932 d: Edward L. Cahn. lps: Eric Linden, Sidney Fox, Tully Marshall. 76M USA. *Merry-Go-Round* prod/rel: Universal Pictures Corp.

MAMANI, ABDOULAYE
Sarraounia, Book
  Sarraounia 1986 d: Abid Med Hondo. lps: Ai Keita,
  Lynn Watts, Jean-Roger Milo. 120M BRK. prod/rel: Les
  Films Soleil

MAMET, DAVID (1947–, USA
American Buffalo, 1975, Play
  American Buffalo 1996 d: Michael Corrente. lps:
  Dustin Hoffman, Dennis Franz, Sean Nelson. 87M
  USA/UKN. prod/rel: Sam Goldwyn Co., Capitol Films
Sexual Perversity in Chicago, 1978, Play
  About Last Night 1986 d: Edward Zwick. lps: Rob
  Lowe, Demi Moore, James Belushi. 113M USA. *Sexual
  Perversity in Chicago* prod/rel: Tri-Star-Delphi IV and V

MAMMERI, MOULOUD
La Colline Oubliee, Novel
  Colline Oubliee, La 1997 d: Abderrahmane
  Bouguermouh. lps: Djamila Amzal, Mohand Chabane,
  Samira Abtout. 107M ALG/FRN. *The Forgotten Hill*
  prod/rel: Caaic (Algeria), Im Products Films (France)

MAMOULIAN, ROUBEN
The Devil's Hornpipe, Unproduced, Play
  Never Steal Anything Small 1959 d: Charles
  Lederer. lps: James Cagney, Shirley Jones, Roger Smith.
  115M USA. prod/rel: Universal-International

MANAS, ALFREDO
La Historia de Los Tarantos, Play
  Tarantos, Los 1963 d: Francisco Rovira BeletA. lps:
  Carmen Amaya, Sara Lezana, Daniel Martin. 92M SPN.
  prod/rel: Tecisa

MANAS, JOSE ANGEL
Paginas de Una Historia: Mensaka, Novel
  Paginas de Una Historia: Mensaka 1998 d: Salvador
  Garcia Ruiz. lps: Gustavo Salmeron, Tristan Ulloa,
  Adria Collado. 105M SPN. *Mensaka* prod/rel: Alta
  Films, Tornasol Films

MANCHETTE, JEAN-PATRICK
Folle a Tuer, Novel
  Folle a Tuer 1975 d: Yves Boisset. lps: Marlene Jobert,
  Tomas Milian, Michael Lonsdale. 97M FRN/ITL. *Una
  Donna Da Uccidere* (ITL) prod/rel: Lira Artistiche
  Internazionali
Nada!, Novel
  Nada! 1973 d: Claude Chabrol. lps: Fabio Testi,
  Mariangela Melato, Maurice Garrel. 134M FRN/ITL.
  Sterminate "Gruppo Zero" (ITL); *The Nada Gang*
  (USA) prod/rel: Italian International Film, Verona
  Produzione
Polar, Novel
  Polar 1984 d: Jacques Bral. lps: Jean-Francois Balmer,
  Sandra Montaigu, Pierre Santini. 97M FRN. prod/rel:
  G.I.E., Les Films Noirs
La Position du Tireur Couche, Novel
  Choc, Le 1982 d: Robin Davis. lps: Alain Delon,
  Catherine Deneuve, Philippe Leotard. 105M FRN.
  prod/rel: Sara Films, T. Films
Pour la Peau d'un Flic, Novel
  Pour la Peau d'un Flic 1981 d: Alain Delon. lps: Alain
  Delon, Anne Parillaud, Michel Auclair. 105M FRN.
  Three Men to Kill prod/rel: Adel, Jugendfilm
Trois Hommes a Abattre, Novel
  Trois Hommes a Abattre 1980 d: Jacques Deray. lps:
  Alain Delon, Dalila Di Lazzaro, Pierre Dux. 97M FRN.
  Three Men to Destroy prod/rel: Adel, Antenne 2

MANCINI, FLAVIANO C.
Gens Nova, Play
  Gens Nova 1920 d: Luigi Maggi. lps: Narciso Maffeis,
  Maria Roasio, Giovanni CimarA. 1175m ITL. prod/rel:
  S.A. Ambrosio

MANCINI, GAETANO CAMPANILE
La Signorina Di Bergerac, Short Story
  Ultimo Dei Bergerac, L' 1934 d: Gennaro Righelli.
  lps: Arturo Falconi, Ketty Maya, Livio Pavanelli. 71M
  ITL. prod/rel: Faro Film, Anonima Pittaluga

MANDARA, LUCIO
Er Piu de Roma, Novel
  Principe Fusto, Il 1960 d: Maurizio ArenA. lps:
  Maurizio Arena, Lorella de Luca, Cathia Caro. 100M
  ITL. prod/rel: M.A. Produzione Cin.Ca, Eurocine

MANDEL, FRANK
The Desert Song, New York 1926, Musical Play
  Desert Song, The 1929 d: Roy Del Ruth. lps: John
  Boles, Carlotta King, Louise FazendA. 106M USA.
  prod/rel: Warner Brothers Pictures

  Desert Song, The 1943 d: Robert Florey. lps: Dennis
  Morgan, Irene Manning, Bruce Cabot. 96M USA.
  prod/rel: Warner Bros.

  Desert Song, The 1953 d: H. Bruce Humberstone. lps:
  Kathryn Grayson, Gordon MacRae, Steve Cochran.
  110M USA. prod/rel: Warner Bros.

Good News, New York 1927, Musical Play
  Good News 1930 d: Nick Grinde, Edgar J. MacGregor.
  lps: Mary Lawlor, Stanley Smith, Bessie Love. 8100f
  USA. prod/rel: Metro-Goldwyn-Mayer Pictures

  Good News 1947 d: Charles Walters. lps: June Allyson,
  Peter Lawford, Patricia Marshall. 95M USA. prod/rel:
  MGM

My Lady Friends, New York 1919, Play
  My Lady Friends 1921 d: Lloyd Ingraham. lps: Carter
  de Haven, Flora Parker de Haven, Thomas Lingham.
  5650f USA. prod/rel: Carter de Haven Productions,
  Associated First National Pictures

No No Nanette, New York 1925, Musical Play
  No, No Nanette 1930 d: Clarence Badger. lps: Bernice
  Claire, Alexander Gray, Lucien Littlefield. 9100f USA.
  prod/rel: First National Pictures

  No, No Nanette 1940 d: Herbert Wilcox. lps: Anna
  Neagle, Roland Young, Helen Broderick. 96M USA.
  prod/rel: RKO Radio Pictures©, Suffolk Productions

  Tea for Two 1950 d: David Butler. lps: Doris Day,
  Gordon MacRae, Gene Nelson. 98M USA. prod/rel:
  Warner Bros.

MANDELSTAMM, VALENTIN
L' Affaire du Grand-Theatre, Novel
  Affaire du Grand Theatre, L' 1916 d: Henri Pouctal.
  lps: Henry Roussell, Max Barbier, Jean Garat. 1365m
  FRN. prod/rel: Film d'Art
L' Empire du Diamant, Paris 1914, Novel
  Empire du Diamant, L' 1922 d: Leonce Perret. lps:
  Leon Mathot, Fernand Mailly, Lucy Fox. 1800m FRN.
  prod/rel: Films Leonce Perret

  Empire of Diamonds, The 1920 d: Leonce Perret. lps:
  Robert Elliott, Lucy Fox, Henry Gsell. 6r USA. *L'
  Empire du Diamant* prod/rel: Leonce Perret
  Productions, Pathe Exchange, Inc.©
Jim Blackwood Jockey, Novel
  Jim Blackwood Jockey 1909 d: Georges MoncA. lps:
  Villa, Henri Etievant, Amelie Dieterle. 185m FRN.
  prod/rel: Scagl
La Vol Supreme, Short Story
  Vol Supreme, Le 1917 d: Rene Plaissetty. lps: Jean
  Croue, Fred Zorilla, Gabrielle Robinne. 1525m FRN.
  prod/rel: Scagl

MANDER, MILES
Those Common People, Play
  First Born, The 1928 d: Miles Mander. lps: Miles
  Mander, Madeleine Carroll, John Loder. 7786f UKN.
  prod/rel: Mander Productions Syndicate, Gainsborough

MANDLEY, PERCY G.
Eight Bells, New York 1933, Play
  Eight Bells 1935 d: R. William Neill. lps: Ann Sothern,
  Ralph Bellamy, John Buckler. 69M USA. prod/rel:
  Columbia Pictures Corp.©

MANDY, IVAN
Borika Vendegei, 1965, Short Story
  Lanyarcok Tukorben 1973 d: Robert Ban. lps: Erika
  Bodnar, Marta Egri, Ilona Kallai. 91M HNG. *Parallel
  Faces*
Ciklon, 1966, Short Story
  Ketten Haltak Meg 1964 d: Gyorgy Palasthy, Antal
  Forgacs. lps: Gyorgy Banffy, Zsuzsa Banki, Laszlo
  Markus. 77M HNG. *Two Have Died*
Csutak Es a Szurke Lo, 1959, Novel
  Csutak Es a Szurke Lo 1960 d: Zoltan Varkonyi. lps:
  Gabor Veres, Ferenc Kiss, Anna Baro. 78M HNG.
  Csutak and the Grey Horse
A Locsolokocsi, 1965, Novel
  Locsolokocsi, A 1974 d: Zsolt Kezdi-Kovacs. lps: Peter
  Lengyel, Erika Maretics, Andras Markus. 89M HNG.
  The Orange Watering Truck
A Palya Szelen, 1963, Novel
  Regi Idok Focija 1973 d: Pal Sandor. lps: Dezso Garas,
  Gizi Peter, Tamas Major. 85M HNG. *Football of the
  Good Old Days*
Regi Idok Mozija, 1967, Short Story
  Regi Idok Focija 1973 d: Pal Sandor. lps: Dezso Garas,
  Gizi Peter, Tamas Major. 85M HNG. *Football of the
  Good Old Days*

MANHOFF, BILL
The Owl and the Pussycat, New York 1964, Play
  Owl and the Pussycat, The 1970 d: Herbert Ross. lps:
  George Segal, Barbra Streisand, Robert Klein. 96M
  USA. prod/rel: Rastar Productions

MANIATES, BELLE K., Maniates, Belle Kanaris
Amarilly of Clothes-Line Alley, Boston 1915, Novel
  Amarilly of Clothes-Line Alley 1918 d: Marshall
  Neilan. lps: Mary Pickford, Norman Kerry, Herbert
  Standing. 5r USA. prod/rel: Mary Pickford Film Corp.,
  Famous Players-Lasky Corp.©

The Littlest Scrub Lady, Short Story
  Mirandy Smiles 1918 d: William C. de Mille. lps:
  Vivian Martin, Douglas MacLean, Lewis Willoughby.
  4570f USA. prod/rel: Famous Players-Lasky Corp.©,
  Paramount Pictures
Penny of Top Hill Trail, Novel
  Penny of Top Hill Trail 1921 d: Arthur Berthelet. lps:
  Sam Lauder, Bessie Love, Wheeler Oakman. 5000f USA.
  prod/rel: Andrew J. Callaghan, Federated Film
  Exchange

MANKELL, HENNING
Comedia Infantil, Novel
  Comedia Infantil 1998 d: Solveig Nordlund. lps:
  Sergio Titos, Joao Manja, Joaquina Odete. 92M
  SWD/MZM/PRT. prod/rel: Torromfilm, Prole Filme

MANKIEWICZ, DON M.
Trial, 1955, Novel
  Trial 1955 d: Mark Robson. lps: Glenn Ford, Dorothy
  McGuire, Arthur Kennedy. 105M USA. prod/rel: MGM

MANKIEWICZ, HERMAN J.
The Good Fellow, New York 1926, Play
  Good Fellows, The 1943 d: Jo Graham. lps: Cecil
  Kellaway, Mabel Paige, Helen Walker. 70M USA.
  prod/rel: Paramount
The Wild Man of Borneo, New York 1927, Play
  Wild Man of Borneo, The 1941 d: Robert B. Sinclair.
  lps: Frank Morgan, Mary Howard, Billie Burke. 78M
  USA. prod/rel: MGM

MANKOWITZ, WOLF (1924–1998), UKN, Mankowitz,
Cyril Wolf
Expresso Bongo, London 1958, Musical Play
  Expresso Bongo 1959 d: Val Guest. lps: Laurence
  Harvey, Sylvia Syms, Yolande Donlan. 111M UKN.
  prod/rel: Conquest, Britannia
A Kid for Two Farthings, Novel
  Kid for Two Farthings, A 1955 d: Carol Reed. lps:
  Celia Johnson, Diana Dors, David Kossoff. 96M UKN.
  prod/rel: Big Ben Films, London Films
Make Me an Offer, Novel
  Make Me an Offer 1954 d: Cyril Frankel. lps: Peter
  Finch, Adrienne Corri, Rosalie Crutchley. 88M UKN.
  prod/rel: Group Three, British Lion

MANLEY, WILLIAM FORD
Wild Waves, New York 1932, Play
  Big Broadcast, The 1932 d: Frank Tuttle. lps: Bing
  Crosby, Kate Smith, George Burns. 80M USA. prod/rel:
  Paramount Publix Corp.

MANN, ABBY (1927–, USA
Judgment at Nuremberg, 1959, Play
  Judgment at Nuremberg 1961 d: Stanley Kramer.
  lps: Spencer Tracy, Burt Lancaster, Richard Widmark.
  183M USA. prod/rel: Roxlom Films

MANN, ALFRED THEODOR
Herr Meister Und Frau Meisterin, Short Story
  Herr Meister Und Frau Meisterin 1928 d: Alfred
  Theodor Mann. lps: Maly Delschaft, Carl de Vogt, Hans
  Albers. 2413m GRM. prod/rel: Naxos-Film

MANN, E. B., Mann, Edward Beverly
The Death Whistler, Story
  Range Warfare 1935 d: S. Roy Luby. lps: Reb Russell,
  Lucille Lund, Wally Wales. 60M USA. *Vengeance*
  prod/rel: Willis Kent Productions, State Rights
Stampede, New York 1934, Novel
  Stampede 1949 d: Lesley Selander. lps: Rod Cameron,
  Johnny Mack Brown, Gale Storm. 78M USA. prod/rel:
  Allied Artists

  Stormy Trails 1936 d: Sam Newfield. lps: Rex Bell, Bob
  Hodges, Lois Wilde. 60M USA. prod/rel: Colony
  Pictures, Grand National Films

MANN, HEINRICH (1871–1950), GRM
Empfang Bei Der Welt, 1956, Novel
  Belcanto Oder Darf Eine Nutte Schluchzen? 1977
  d: Robert Van Ackeren. lps: Nikolaus Dutsch, Romy
  Haag, Udo Kier. 94M GRM. *Belcanto* prod/rel: Lit.
  Colloquium, Robert Van Ackeren
Professor Unrat, 1905, Novel
  Blaue Engel, Der 1930 d: Josef von Sternberg. lps:
  Emil Jannings, Marlene Dietrich, Kurt Gerron. 107M
  GRM. *The Blue Angel* prod/rel: UFA, Atlas

  Blue Angel, The 1959 d: Edward Dmytryk. lps: Curd
  Jurgens, May Britt, Theodore Bikel. 108M USA.
  prod/rel: 20th Century-Fox
Der Untertan, 1914-18, Novel
  Untertan, Der 1951 d: Wolfgang Staudte. lps: Werner
  Peters, Erich Nadler, Gertrud Bergmann. 97M GDR.
  The Kaiser's Lackey; *The Underdog*; *The Submissive*
  prod/rel: Defa

MANN, KLAUS
Flucht in Den Norden, 1934, Novel
Flucht in Den Norden 1986 d: Ingemo Engstrom. lps: Katharina Thalbach, Jukka-Pekka Palo, Lena Olin. 126M GRM/FNL. *Pako Pohjoiseen* (FNL) prod/rel: Theuring-Engstrom, Jorn Donner Prod.

Mephisto, 1936, Novel
Mephisto 1981 d: Istvan Szabo. lps: Klaus Maria Brandauer, Krystyna Janda, Ildiko Bansagi. 144M AUS/HNG/GRM. prod/rel: Mafilm, Manfred Durniok

MANN, PEGGY
There are Two Kinds of Terrible, Novel
Two Kinds of Love 1983 d: Jack Bender. lps: Lindsay Wagner, Ricky Schroder, Peter Weller. TVM. 100M USA. prod/rel: CBS Entertainment

MANN, RICHARD
A Room Without a Door, Novel
Iguana Dalla Lingua Di Fuoco, L' 1971 d: Riccardo FredA. lps: Luigi Pistilli, Dagmar Lassander, Anton Diffring. 90M ITL/FRN/GRM. prod/rel: Oceania Produzioni Internazionali (Roma), Les Films Corona (Nanterre)

MANN, RODERICK
Foreign Body, Novel
Foreign Body 1987 d: Ronald Neame. lps: Victor Banerjee, Trevor Howard, Warren Mitchell. 111M UKN. prod/rel: Rank, Orion (U.K.)

MANN, THOMAS (1875–1955), GRM
Bekenntnisse Des Hochstaplers Felix Krull, 1922, Novel
Bekenntnisse Des Hochstaplers Felix Krull 1957 d: Kurt Hoffmann. lps: Horst Buchholz, Liselotte Pulver, Ingrid Andree. 107M GRM. *Confessions of Felix Krull* (USA); *Confessions of the Con-Man Felix Krull* prod/rel: Filmaufbau, Europa
Bekenntnisse Des Hochstaplers Felix Krull 1981 d: Bernhard Sinkel. lps: John Moulder-Brown, Oliver Wehe, Klaus Schwarzkopf. MTV. 300M GRM. *Confessions of the Con-Man Felix Krull* prod/rel: ZDF, Orf

Buddenbrooks, Berlin 1901, Novel
Buddenbrooks, Die 1923 d: Gerhard Lamprecht. lps: Peter Esser, Mady Christians, Alfred Abel. 2383m GRM.
Buddenbrooks, Die 1959 d: Alfred Weidenmann. lps: Liselotte Pulver, Nadja Tiller, Hansjorg Felmy. 219M GRM. prod/rel: Filmaufbau, Europa

Doktor Faustus, 1947, Novel
Doktor Faustus 1981 d: Franz Seitz. lps: Jon Finch, Andre Heller, Hanns Zischler. 137M GRM. *Doctor Faustus* prod/rel: Franz Seitz-Film, Iduna

Ein Gluck, 1904, Short Story
Walsungenblut 1964 d: Rolf Thiele. lps: Rudolf Forster, Gerd Baltus, Elena Nathanail. 86M GRM. *Blood of the Walsungs* prod/rel: Franz Seitz, Columbia-Bavaria

The Holy Sinner, Short Story
Crede-Mi 1997 d: Bia Lessa, Dany Roland. 66M BRZ. prod/rel: Bl Producoes Artisticas, Riofilme

Konigsliche Hoheit, 1909, Novel
Konigliche Hoheit 1953 d: Harald Braun. lps: Dieter Borsche, Ruth Leuwerik, Rudolf Fernau. 90M GRM. *Royal Highness* prod/rel: Filmaufbau, Bavaria

Lotte in Weimar, 1939, Novel
Lotte in Weimar 1975 d: Egon Gunther. lps: Martin Hellberg, Rolf Ludwig, Jutta Hoffmann. 119M GDR. prod/rel: Defa

Der Tod in Venedig, 1912, Short Story
Morte a Venezia 1971 d: Luchino Visconti. lps: Dirk Bogarde, Bjorn Andersen, Silvana Mangano. 128M ITL/FRN. *Mort a Venise* (FRN); *Death in Venice* (UKN) prod/rel: Alfa Cin.Ca, Dear International

Tonio Kroger, Berlin 1903, Short Story
Tonio Kroger 1964 d: Rolf Thiele. lps: Jean-Claude Brialy, Nadja Tiller, Werner Hinz. 90M GRM/FRN. prod/rel: Mondex Films, Procinex

Unordnung Und Fruhes Leid, 1925, Short Story
Unordnung Und Fruhes Leid 1975 d: Franz Seitz. lps: Martin Held, Ruth Leuwerik, Sabine von Maydell. 86M GRM. *Disorder and Early Sorrow* prod/rel: Franz Seitz, G.G.B.

Walsungenblut, 1921, Short Story
Walsungenblut 1964 d: Rolf Thiele. lps: Rudolf Forster, Gerd Baltus, Elena Nathanail. 86M GRM. *Blood of the Walsungs* prod/rel: Franz Seitz, Columbia-Bavaria

Der Zauberberg, 1924, Novel
Zauberberg, Der 1981 d: Hans W. Geissendorfer. lps: Christoph Eichhorn, Rod Steiger, Marie-France Pisier. 153M GRM/FRN/ITL. *The Magic Mountain* prod/rel: Franz Seitz Filmproduktion, ZDF

MANNERS, J. HARTLEY
Getting Together, New York 1918, Musical Play
Common Cause, The 1918 d: J. Stuart Blackton. lps: Herbert Rawlinson, Sylvia Breamer, Huntley Gordon. 7r USA. prod/rel: Blackton Productions, Inc.©, Vitagraph Co. of America

Happiness, 1914, Play
Happiness 1924 d: King Vidor. lps: Laurette Taylor, Pat O'Malley, Hedda Hopper. 7745f USA. prod/rel: Metro Pictures

The House Next Door, New York 1914, Play
House Next Door, The 1914 d: Barry O'Neil. lps: Gaston Bell, George Soule Spencer, Ethel Clayton. 5r USA. prod/rel: Lubin Mfg. Co.©, General Film Co.

Peg O' My Heart, New York 1912, Play
Peg O' My Heart 1919 d: William C. de Mille. lps: Wanda Hawley, Thomas Meighan, Theodore Roberts. 5r USA. prod/rel: Famous Players-Lasky Corp.
Peg O' My Heart 1922 d: King Vidor. lps: Laurette Taylor, Mahlon Hamilton, Russell Simpson. 7900f USA. prod/rel: Metro Pictures
Peg O' My Heart 1933 d: Robert Z. Leonard. lps: Marion Davies, Onslow Stevens, J. Farrell MacDonald. 86M USA. prod/rel: Metro-Goldwyn-Mayer Corp.©

MANNHEIMER, ALBERT
The Birds and the Bees, Play
Three Daring Daughters 1947 d: Fred M. Wilcox. lps: Jeanette MacDonald, Jose Iturbi, Jane Powell. 115M USA. *The Birds and the Bees* prod/rel: MGM

MANNHEIMER, W. A.
Mr. Romeo, New York 1927, Play
Chicken a la King 1928 d: Henry Lehrman. lps: Nancy Carroll, George Meeker, Arthur Stone. 6417f USA. *The Gay Deceiver* prod/rel: Fox Film Corp.

MANNIN, ETHEL (1900–1978), UKN
Dancing Boy, Novel
Beloved Imposter 1936 d: Victor Hanbury. lps: Rene Ray, Fred Conyngham, Germaine Aussey. 86M UKN. *Beloved Impostor* prod/rel: Stafford, Radio

MANNING, BRUCE
The Ninth Guest, New Orleans 1930, Novel
Ninth Guest, The 1934 d: R. William Neill. lps: Donald Cook, Genevieve Tobin, Hardie Albright. 69M USA. prod/rel: Columbia Pictures Corp.©

Party Wire, New York 1934, Novel
Party Wire 1935 d: Erle C. Kenton. lps: Victor Jory, Jean Arthur, Charley Grapewin. 70M USA. prod/rel: Columbia Pictures Corp.©

MANNING, OLIVIA (1908–1980), UKN
Fortunes of War, Novel
Fortunes of War 1987 d: James Cellan Jones. lps: Kenneth Branagh, Emma Thompson, Ronald Pickup. MTV. 350M UKN. prod/rel: BBC

MANNIX, DANIEL P.
African Bush Adventures, Book
Killers of Kilimanjaro 1959 d: Richard Thorpe. lps: Robert Taylor, Anthony Newley, Anne Aubrey. 91M UKN. *Adamson of Africa* prod/rel: Columbia, Warwick

The Fox and the Hound, Novel
Fox and the Hound, The 1981 d: Art Stevens, Ted Berman. ANM. 83M USA. prod/rel: Disney, Buena Vista

The Healer, Book
Shadow of Fear 1979 d: Noel Nosseck. lps: Ike Eisenmann, John Anderson, Peter Haskell. TVM. 95M USA.

MANNOCK, P. L.
Constant Hot Water, Short Story
Constant Hot Water 1923 d: George A. Cooper. lps: Gladys Jennings, John Stuart, Lawford Davidson. 2157f UKN. prod/rel: Quality Plays, Gaumont

MANOIR, GEORGES
Monsieur de Falindor, Play
Monsieur de Falindor 1946 d: Rene Le Henaff. lps: Pierre Jourdan, Jacqueline Dor, Marcelle Duval. 75M FRN. prod/rel: Berton Et Cie, Andre Hugon

MANOUSSI, JEAN
Le Chevalier Au Masques, Play
Purple Mask, The 1955 d: H. Bruce Humberstone. lps: Tony Curtis, Colleen Miller, Dan O'Herlihy. 82M USA. prod/rel: Universal-International

MANOV, EMIL
Pleneno Yato, 1947, Novel
Pleneno Yato 1962 d: Dutcho Mundrov. lps: Peter Slabakov, Kiril Kovachev, Dimiter Buynozov. 90M BUL. *Captured Squadron*

MANSE, JEAN
Ignace, Opera
Ignace 1937 d: Piere Colombier. lps: Fernandel, Alice Tissot, Saturnin Fabre. 102M FRN. prod/rel: Ayres D'aguiar

MANTEGAZZA, PAOLO
Un Giorno a Madera, 1876, Novel
Giorno a Madera, Un 1924 d: Mario Gargiulo. lps: Tina Xeo, Livio Pavanelli, Carlo Reiter. 1525m ITL. prod/rel: Lombardo, Flegrea Film

MANTELLO, H. H.
Heiratsschwindlerin, Book
Hochstaplerin Der Liebe 1954 d: Hans H. Konig. lps: Hilde Krahl, Hans Nielsen, Viktor Staal. 85M AUS. prod/rel: Helios

MANTLEY, JOHN
The 27th Day, Novel
27th Day, The 1957 d: William Asher. lps: Gene Barry, Valerie French, George Voskovec. 75M USA. *The Twenty-Seventh Day* prod/rel: Columbia, Romson Prods.

The Snow Birch, 1958, Novel
Woman Obsessed 1959 d: Henry Hathaway. lps: Susan Hayward, Stephen Boyd, Barbara Nichols. 103M USA. prod/rel: 20th Century-Fox

MANTON, JO
Sister Dora, Book
Sister Dora 1977 d: Marc Miller. lps: Dorothy Tutin, Bernard Archard, Peter Cellier. MTV. UKN. prod/rel: Yorkshire Tv

MANVILLE, ANITA
Story
Tumulto de Paixoes 1958 d: Zygmunt Sulistrowski. lps: John Sutton, Richard Olizar, Gina Albert. 92M BRZ/GRM. *Tom Dooley - Held Der Grunen Holle*; *Ruf Der Wildnis*; *Tom Dooley - Hero of the Green Hell* prod/rel: Alfa, Sulistrowski

MANZARI, NICOLA
I Morti Non Pagano Tasse, Play
Morti Non Pagano Tasse, I 1953 d: Sergio Grieco. lps: Tino Scotti, Titina de Filippo, Franca Marzi. 85M ITL. prod/rel: Domino Film

Tutto Per la Donna, Play
Tutto Per la Donna 1940 d: Mario Soldati. lps: Junie Astor, Antonio Centa, Miretta Mauri. 71M ITL. prod/rel: Urbe Cinem, I.C.I.

MANZI, ALBERTO
Orzowei, Novel
Orzowei 1975 d: Yves Allegret. lps: Stanley Baker, Doris Kunstmann, Peter Marshall. 105M GRM/ITL. *La Figlia Della Savana Orzowei* (ITL) prod/rel: Oniro (Roma), R.M. Produktion (Munchen)

MANZI, HOMERO
Pampa Barbara
Pampa Salvaje 1966 d: Hugo Fregonese. lps: Robert Taylor, Marc Lawrence, Ron Randell. 112M SPN/USA/ARG. *Savage Pampas* (USA) prod/rel: Samuel Bronston Productions, Dasa Films

MANZONI, ALESSANDRO (1785–1873), ITL
La Colonna Infame, Novel
Colonna Infame, La 1973 d: Nelo Risi. lps: Helmut Berger, Vittorio Caprioli, Francisco Rabal. 105M ITL. prod/rel: Filmes, I.N.C.

I Promessi Sposi, 1827, Novel
Innominato, L' 1909 d: Mario Caserini. lps: Fernanda Negri-Pouget. 258m ITL. prod/rel: Cines
Promessi Sposi, I 1908 d: Mario Morais. 235m ITL. prod/rel: L. Comerio E C.
Promessi Sposi, I 1911 d: Ugo FalenA. ITL. prod/rel: Film d'Arte Italiana
Promessi Sposi, I 1913 d: Ubaldo Maria Del Colle, Ernesto Maria Pasquali. lps: Cristina Ruspoli, Giovanni Ciusa, Giovanni Enrico Vidali. 2000m ITL. *The Betrothed* (USA) prod/rel: Pasquali E C.
Promessi Sposi, I 1913 d: Eleuterio Rodolfi. lps: Gigetta Morano, Mario Voller Buzzi, Ersilia Scalpellini. 1800m ITL. *The Betrothed* (USA) prod/rel: S.A. Ambrosio
Promessi Sposi, I 1922 d: Mario Bonnard. lps: Emilia Vidali, Domenico Serra, Nini Dinelli. 3816m ITL. prod/rel: Bonnard Film
Promessi Sposi, I 1941 d: Mario Camerini. lps: Gino Cervi, Dina Sassoli, Ruggero Ruggeri. 112M ITL. *The Spirit and the Flesh* (USA) prod/rel: Lux Film
Promessi Sposi, I 1964 d: Mario Maffei. lps: Gil Vidal, Maria Silva, Carlo Campanani. 100M ITL/SPN. *Promesa Sagrada* (SPN) prod/rel: Cineproduzioni Emo Bistolfi (Roma), Copercines (Madrid)

MAO DUN (1896–1981), CHN, Mao Tun, Shen Yen-Ping
Chun Can, Short Story
Chuncan 1933 d: Cheng Bugao. lps: XIao Ying, Yan Yuexian, Gong Jianong. 10r CHN. *Spring Silkworms* prod/rel: Mingxing Film Company

Zi Ye, Novel
Zi Ye 1981 d: Sang Hu, Fu Jinggong. lps: Li Rentang, Qiao Qi, Cheng XIaoying. 139M CHN. *Midnight*; *Zhi Ye* prod/rel: Shanghai Film Studio

MAPES, VICTOR
The Boomerang, New York 1915, Play
Love Doctor, The 1929 d: Melville Brown. lps: Richard Dix, June Collyer, Morgan Farley. 5503f USA. prod/rel: Paramount Famous Lasky Corp.
The Curious Conduct of Judge Legarde, Washington D.C. 1912, Play
Curious Conduct of Judge Legarde, The 1915 d: Will S. Davis. lps: Lionel Barrymore, Edna Pendleton, William H. Tooker. 5r USA. prod/rel: Life Photo Film Corp., State Rights
The Hottentot, New York 1920, Play
Going Places 1939 d: Ray Enright. lps: Dick Powell, Anita Louise, Allen Jenkins. 84M USA. prod/rel: Warner Bros. Pictures©
Hottentot, The 1922 d: James W. Horne, Del Andrews. lps: Douglas MacLean, Madge Bellamy, Lilie Leslie. 5953f USA. prod/rel: Thomas H. Ince Productions, Associated First National Pictures
Hottentot, The 1929 d: Roy Del Ruth. lps: Edward Everett Horton, Patsy Ruth Miller, Douglas Gerrard. 77M USA. prod/rel: Warner Brother Pictures
The Kangaroos, New York 1926, Play
High Flyers 1937 d: Eddie Cline. lps: Bert Wheeler, Robert Woolsey, Lupe Velez. 70M USA. *The Kangaroos* prod/rel: RKO Radio Pictures©
The New Henrietta, New York 1913, Play
Saphead, The 1920 d: Herbert Blache. lps: Buster Keaton, Carol Holloway, William H. Crane. 6650f USA. prod/rel: Metro Pictures Corp.©

MAQUET, AUGUSTE
La Maison du Baigneur, Play
Maison du Baigneur, La 1914 d: Adrien Caillard, Georges MoncA. lps: Gabriel de Gravone, Leon Bernard, Renee Methivier. 1790m FRN. prod/rel: Scagl

MARAINI, DACIA
Diario Di Una Telefonista, Short Story
Certo, Certissimo, Anzi. Probabile 1969 d: Marcello Fondato. lps: Claudia Cardinale, Catherine Spaak, John Phillip Law. 120M ITL. prod/rel: Clesi Cin.Ca, Euro International Film
Donna in Guerra, Novel
Io Sono Mia 1978 d: Sofia ScandurrA. lps: Stefania Sandrelli, Maria Schneider, Michele Placido. 100M ITL/GRM/SPN. *Liebe Ist Etwas Zartliches* (GRM); *Yo Soy Mia* (SPN); *Love Is Something Tender* prod/rel: Clesi Cin.Ca, Spirale '76 (Roma)
L' Eta Del Malessere, Turin 1963, Novel
Eta Del Malessere, L' 1968 d: Giuliano Biagetti. lps: Haydee Politoff, Jean Sorel, Eleonora Rossi-Drago. 115M ITL. *Love Problems* (USA); *The Age of Uneasiness* prod/rel: Salaria Film, Cormons Film
The Long Life of Marianna Ucria, Novel
Marianna Ucria 1997 d: Roberto FaenzA. lps: Emmanuelle Laborit, Eva Grieco, Roberto HerlitzkA. 108M ITL/FRN. prod/rel: Cgg Tiger Cinematografica (Italy), Arturus Prods. (France)
Memorie Di Una Ladra, Novel
Teresa la Ladra 1973 d: Carlo Di PalmA. lps: Monica Vitti, Stefano Satta Flores, Isa Danieli. 125M ITL. *Teresa the Thief* (UKN) prod/rel: Euro International Film

MARAINI, FOSCO
L' Isola Delle Pescatrici, Bari 1960, Novel
Violated Paradise 1963 d: Marion Gering, Robert de Leonardis. lps: Kazuko Mine. 68M ITL/JPN. *The Diving Girls' Island*; *Diving Girls of Japan*; *Scintillating Sin*; *Sea Nymphs* prod/rel: Marion Gering

MARASCO, ROBERT
Burnt Offerings, Novel
Burnt Offerings 1976 d: Dan Curtis. lps: Karen Black, Oliver Reed, Burgess Meredith. 115M USA. prod/rel: United Artists Corp., Pea-Dan Curtis
Child's Play, Play
Child's Play 1972 d: Sidney Lumet. lps: James Mason, Robert Preston, Beau Bridges. 100M USA. prod/rel: Paramount

MARAUN, FRANK
Die Dame Mit Dem Schwarzen Herzen, Short Story
Ihr Dunkler Punkt 1928 d: Johannes Guter. lps: Lilian Harvey, Willy Fritsch, Hermann Speelmans. 2621m GRM. prod/rel: UFA

MARBURGH, BERTRAM
Marrying Money, New York 1914, Play
Marrying Money 1915 d: James Young. lps: Clara Kimball Young, Chester Barnett, William Jefferson. 5r USA. *Marriage a la Carte* prod/rel: World Film Corp.©, Shubert Feature

MARCATO
Il Commissario Di Torino, Novel
Uomo Una Citta, Un 1974 d: Romolo Guerrieri. lps: Enrico Maria Salerno, Francoise Fabian, Luciano Salce. 115M ITL. prod/rel: Goriz Film, Cineriz

MARCEAU, FELICIEN
La Bonne Soupe, 1958, Play
Bonne Soupe, La 1964 d: Robert Thomas. lps: Annie Girardot, Marie Ball, Gerard Blain. 98M FRN/ITL. *La Pappa Reale* (ITL); *Careless Love* prod/rel: Belstar Productions, Les Films Du Siecle
Le Corps de Mon Ennemi, Novel
Corps de Mon Ennemi, Le 1976 d: Henri Verneuil. lps: Jean-Paul Belmondo, Marie-France Pisier, Bernard Blier. 121M FRN. prod/rel: Cerito
L' Oeuf, 1957, Play
Oeuf, L' 1971 d: Jean Herman. lps: Guy Bedos, Marie Dubois, Bernadette Lafont. 90M FRN. *The Egg*
La Race Des Seigneurs, Novel
Race Des Seigneurs, La 1974 d: Pierre Granier-Deferre. lps: Alain Delon, Sydne Rome, Jeanne Moreau. 92M FRN/ITL. *L' Arrivista* (ITL) prod/rel: Jupiter Generale Cin.Ca, la Boetie

MARCELLINI, ROMOLO
Una Moneta Spezzata, Short Story
F.B.I. Operazione Baalbeck 1964 d: Marcello Giannini. lps: Rossana Podesta, Jacques Sernas, George Sanders. 95M ITL/FRN/LBN. *La Moneta Spezzata*; *Un Aereo Per Baalbeck* prod/rel: F.I.C.I.T. (Roma), Coliseum Film

MARCH, ANTHONY
Quit for the Next, New York 1945, Novel
Once Before I Die 1965 d: John Derek. lps: John Derek, Ursula Andress, Richard Jaeckel. 96M USA/PHL. *No Toys for Christmas* prod/rel: F.8 Productions

MARCH, JOSEPH MONCURE
The Set-Up, 1928, Poem
Set-Up, The 1949 d: Robert Wise. lps: Robert Ryan, Audrey Totter, George Tobias. 72M USA.
The Wild Party, 1928, Verse
Wild Party, The 1975 d: James Ivory. lps: James Coco, Raquel Welch, Perry King. 91M USA.

MARCH, TIMOTHY
Let's Do It Again, Novel
Let's Do It Again 1976 d: Sidney Poitier. lps: Sidney Poitier, Bill Cosby, Jimmy Walker. 113M USA. prod/rel: Verdon, First Artists

MARCH, WILLIAM (1893–1954), USA, Campbell, William Edward March
The Bad Seed, Play
Bad Seed, The 1956 d: Mervyn Leroy. lps: Nancy Kelly, Patty McCormack, Henry Jones. 129M USA. prod/rel: Warner Bros.
Bad Seed, The 1985 d: Paul Wendkos. lps: Blair Brown, Lynn Redgrave, David Carradine. TVM. 100M USA. prod/rel: ABC, Warner

MARCHAL, FRANK
Nathalie Agent Secret, Novel
Nathalie Agent Secret 1959 d: Henri Decoin. lps: Martine Carol, Felix Marten, Andre Versini. 92M FRN/ITL. *Atomic Agent* (USA) prod/rel: S.F.C., Sirius
Nathalie Princesse, Novel
Nathalie 1957 d: Christian-Jaque. lps: Martine Carol, Mischa Auer, Michel Piccoli. 95M FRN/ITL. *The Foxiest Girl in Paris* (USA) prod/rel: Societe Francaise De Cinematografie

MARCHAND, LEOPOLD
Balthazar, Play
Balthazar 1937 d: Piere Colombier. lps: Jules Berry, Andre Alerme, Daniele ParolA. 90M FRN. prod/rel: Heraut Films
Cartouche - Roi de Paris, Play
Cartouche, Roi de Paris 1948 d: Guillaume Radot. lps: Roger Pigaut, Jean Davy, Renee Devillers. 80M FRN. prod/rel: Guillaume Radot, Midi Cinema
Ces Messieurs de la Sante, Play
Ces Messieurs de la Sante 1933 d: Piere Colombier. lps: Edwige Feuillere, Pauline Carton, Raimu. 115M FRN. prod/rel: Pathe-Nathan
Durand Bijoutier, Play
Durand Bijoutier 1938 d: Jean Stelli. lps: Jacques Baumer, Blanche Montel, Monique Rolland. 87M FRN. prod/rel: Productions F. Campaux
Le Mage du Carlton, Play
Fakir du Grand Hotel, Le 1933 d: Pierre Billon. lps: Armand Bernard, Paulette Dubost, Annie Ducaux. 100M FRN. prod/rel: Dana-Film
Mon Gosse de Pere, Play
Mon Gosse de Pere 1930 d: Jean de Limur. lps: Adolphe Menjou, Roger Treville, Alice CoceA. F FRN. prod/rel: Pathe-Natan

Mon Gosse de Pere 1952 d: Leon Mathot. lps: Maurice Teynac, Siren Adjemova, Jacques Francois. 88M FRN. prod/rel: Joelle Films
Nous Ne Sommes Plus Des Enfants, Play
Nous Ne Sommes Plus Des Enfants 1934 d: Augusto GeninA. lps: Claude Dauphin, Jean Wall, Gaby Morlay. 80M FRN. prod/rel: Films Gaby Morlay, Eureka Films
Poule Sur un Mur, Play
Poule Sur un Mur, Une 1936 d: Maurice Gleize. lps: Jules Berry, Pierre Larquey, Christiane Delyne. 90M FRN. prod/rel: Productions Henry Doru
Le Tailleur Au Chateau, Paris 1924, Play
Love Me Tonight 1932 d: Rouben Mamoulian. lps: Maurice Chevalier, Jeanette MacDonald, Charlie Ruggles. 104M USA. prod/rel: Paramount Publix Corp.©, Rouben Mamoulian Production
Le Valet Maitre, Play
Valet Maitre, Le 1941 d: Paul Mesnier. lps: Elvire Popesco, Marguerite Deval, Henri Garat. 90M FRN. prod/rel: S.P.C.

MARCHANT, WILLIAM
The Desk Set, New York 1955, Play
Desk Set, The 1957 d: Walter Lang. lps: Spencer Tracy, Katharine Hepburn, Gig Young. 103M USA. *His Other Woman* (UKN) prod/rel: 20th Century-Fox

MARCHES, LEO
Une Petite Femme Dans le Train, Play
Jsem Devce S Certem V Tele 1933 d: Karl Anton. lps: Frantisek Smolik, Lida Baarova, Ludvik VeverkA. 2611m CZC. *I Am a Girl With the Devil in My Body*; *The Devil in Me* prod/rel: Ab

MARCHESE, PIPPO
I Don, Play
Re Di Denari 1936 d: Enrico Guazzoni. lps: Angelo Musco, Rosina Anselmi, Nerio Bernardi. 86M ITL. *Re Di Danari* prod/rel: Capitani Film

MARCHESI, MARCELLO
Valentina, Play
Buongiorno Primo Amore! 1957 d: Marino Girolami. lps: Claudio Villa, Maurizio Arena, Fulvia Franco. 90M ITL/SPN. *Valentina* (SPN) prod/rel: Produzioni D.S. (Roma), Union Film (Madrid)
Za-Bum, Musical Play
Circo Equestre Za-Bum 1944 d: Mario Mattoli. lps: Alida Valli, Aldo Fabrizi, Roldano Lupi. 85M ITL. prod/rel: Produzione Associata, Titanus

MARCIN, MAX
Are You My Wife?, New York 1910, Novel
Here Comes the Bride 1919 d: John S. Robertson. lps: John Barrymore, Faire Binney, Frank Losee. 4436f USA. prod/rel: Famous Players-Lasky Corp.©, Paramount Pictures
Badges, New York 1924, Play
Ghost Talks, The 1929 d: Lewis Seiler. lps: Helen Twelvetrees, Charles Eaton, Stepin Fetchit. 6482f USA. prod/rel: Fox Film Corp.
The Big Fight, New York 1928, Play
Big Fight, The 1930 d: Walter Lang. lps: Lola Lane, Ralph Ince, Guinn (Big Boy) Williams. 5850f USA. prod/rel: James Cruze Productions, Sono Art-World Wide Pictures
Cheating Cheaters, New York 1916, Play
Cheating Cheaters 1919 d: Allan Dwan. lps: Clara Kimball Young, Anna Q. Nilsson, Jack Holt. 5r USA. prod/rel: C.K.Y. Film Corp.©, Select Pictures Corp.
Cheating Cheaters 1927 d: Edward Laemmle. lps: Betty Compson, Kenneth Harlan, Sylvia Ashton. 5623f USA. *The Law's the Law*
Cheating Cheaters 1934 d: Richard Thorpe. lps: Fay Wray, Cesar Romero, Hugh O'Connell. 70M USA. prod/rel: Universal Pictures Corp.
Eyes of Youth, New York 1917, Play
Eyes of Youth 1919 d: Albert Parker. lps: Clara Kimball Young, Milton Sills, Vincent Serrano. 7r USA. prod/rel: Garson Productions, Equity Pictures Corp.
Eyes of Youth 1920. lps: Abbie Mitchell. USA. prod/rel: Quality Amusement Co.
Love of Sunya, The 1927 d: Albert Parker. lps: Gloria Swanson, John Boles, Anders Randolf. 7311f USA. prod/rel: Swanson Producing Corp., United Artists
Here Comes the Bride, New York 1917, Play
Here Comes the Bride 1919 d: John S. Robertson. lps: John Barrymore, Faire Binney, Frank Losee. 4436f USA. prod/rel: Famous Players-Lasky Corp.©, Paramount Pictures
The House of Glass, New York 1915, Play
House of Glass, The 1918 d: Emile Chautard. lps: Clara Kimball Young, Pell Trenton, Corliss Giles. 5r USA. prod/rel: C. K. Y. Film Corp.©, Select Pictures Corp.

Lure of Jade, The 1921 d: Colin Campbell. lps: Pauline Frederick, Thomas Holding, Arthur Rankin. 5935f USA. prod/rel: Robertson-Cole Co., R-C Pictures

Seltsame Vergangenheit Der Thea Carter, Die 1929 d: Josef Levigard. lps: June Marlowe, Olaf Fonss, Hermann Vallentin. 2188m GRM. prod/rel: Universal Pictures Corp.

The Humbug, New York 1929, Play
Love Captive, The 1934 d: Max Marcin. lps: Nils Asther, Gloria Stuart, Paul Kelly. 63M USA. *The Humbug*; *Dangerous to Women* prod/rel: Universal Pictures Corp.©

The Nightcap, New York 1921, Play
Secrets of the Night 1925 d: Herbert Blache. lps: James Kirkwood, Madge Bellamy, Tom Ricketts. 6700f USA. *The Nightcap* prod/rel: Universal Pictures

Obey the Law, Play
Obey the Law 1926 d: Alfred Raboch. lps: Bert Lytell, Edna Murphy, Hedda Hopper. 5626f USA. prod/rel: Columbia Pictures

See My Lawyer, New York 1915, Play
See My Lawyer 1921 d: Al Christie. lps: T. Roy Barnes, Grace Darmond, Lloyd Whitlock. 6r USA. prod/rel: Christie Film Co., Robertson-Cole Distributing Corp.

Silence, New York 1924, Play
Silence 1926 d: Rupert Julian. lps: Vera Reynolds, H. B. Warner, Raymond Hatton. 7518f USA. prod/rel: de Mille Pictures, Producers Distributing Corp.
Silence 1931 d: Louis J. Gasnier, Max Marcin. lps: Clive Brook, Marjorie Rambeau, Peggy Shannon. 60M USA. prod/rel: Paramount Publix Corp.©

The Substitute Prisoner, New York 1911, Play
Blind Love 1920 d: Oliver D. Bailey. lps: Lucy Cotton, George Le Guere, Thurlow Bergen. 6r USA. prod/rel: Gerald F. Bacon Productions, State Rights

The Woman in Room 13, New York 1919, Play
Woman in Room 13, The 1920 d: Frank Lloyd. lps: Pauline Frederick, Charles Clary, John Bowers. 5r USA. prod/rel: Goldwyn Pictures Corp.©, Goldwyn Distributing Corp.
Woman in Room 13, The 1932 d: Henry King. lps: Elissa Landi, Ralph Bellamy, Neil Hamilton. 69M USA. prod/rel: Fox Film Corp.©

MARC-MICHEL
Un Chapeau de Paille d'Italie, 1847, Play
Cappello Di Paglia Di Firenze 1918 d: Enrico Vidali. lps: Joe Dollway, Bualo. 1243m ITL. prod/rel: Italica Film
Chapeau de Paille d'Italie, Un 1927 d: Rene Clair. lps: Albert Prejean, Marise Maia, Olga TschechowA. 90M FRN. *The Italian Straw Hat*; *The Horse Ate the Hat* prod/rel: Films Albatros
Chapeau de Paille d'Italie, Un 1940 d: Maurice Cammage. lps: Fernandel, Jacqueline Laurent, Josseline Gael. 85M FRN. prod/rel: Prodiex
Florentiner Hut, Der 1939 d: Wolfgang Liebeneiner. lps: Heinz Ruhmann, Herti Kirchner, Christl Mardayn. 91M GRM. *The Leghorn Hat* (USA) prod/rel: Terra
Slameny Klobouk 1972 d: Oldrich Lipsky. 88M CZC. *The Straw Hat*

Les Deux Timides, 1860, Play
Deux Timides, Les 1928 d: Rene Clair. lps: Maurice de Feraudy, Pierre Batcheff, Vera Flory. 95M FRN. *The Two Timid Ones* prod/rel: Albatros, Sequana
Jeunes Timides 1941 d: Yves Allegret. lps: Pierre Brasseur, Claude Dauphin, Jacqueline Laurent. 83M FRN. *Les Deux Timides* prod/rel: Imperia

La Fille Bien Gardee, Play
Fille Bien Gardee, La 1923 d: Louis Feuillade. lps: Alice Tissot, Rene Poyen, Rene Donnio. 1880m FRN. prod/rel: Gaumont

Maman Sabouleux, Play
Ma Tante Dictateur 1939 d: Rene Pujol. lps: Christian Gerard, Gaby Wagner, Marguerite Moreno. 95M FRN. *Monsieur Nicolas -Nourrice* prod/rel: Giffra

La Poudre aux Yeux, 1861, Play
Huan Tian XI Di 1949 d: Zheng XIaoqiu. 90M CHN. *Hilarity*

Si Jamais Je Te Pince., Play
Si Jamais Je Te Pince 1917 d: Georges MoncA. lps: Prince, Saturnin Fabre, Simone Joubert. 750m FRN. prod/rel: Pathe Freres

MARC'O
Play
Idoles, Les 1968 d: Marc'o. lps: Bulle Ogier, Valerie Lagrange, Jean-Pierre Kalfon. 105M FRN. prod/rel: International Thanos Films

MARCOS, PLINIO
Navalha Na Carne, 1968, Play
Navalha Na Carne, A 1970 d: Braz Chediak. 90M BRZ.

Quebradas Da Vida, 1973, Short Story
Barra Pesada 1977 d: Reginaldo FariA. lps: Katia d'Angelo, Ivan Candido. 95M BRZ. *Heavy Trouble*

MARCOSSON, ISAAC FREDERICK
The World Struggle for Oil, 1924, Article
World Struggle for Oil, The 1924 d: Hank E. Butler. DOC. 6321f USA. prod/rel: United States Bureau of Mines, Sinclair Consolidated Oil Corp.

MARCUS, ALAN
The Marauders, Novel
Marauders, The 1955 d: Gerald Mayer. lps: Dan Duryea, Jeff Richards, Keenan Wynn. 81M USA. prod/rel: MGM

MARCUS, FRANK
The Killing of Sister George, Bristol 1965, Play
Killing of Sister George, The 1968 d: Robert Aldrich. lps: Beryl Reid, Susannah York, Coral Browne. 138M USA. prod/rel: Associates & Aldrich Co., Palomar

MARCUS, LAWRENCE B., Marcus, Larry
Short Story
Paula 1952 d: Rudolph Mate. lps: Loretta Young, Kent Smith, Alexander Knox. 80M USA. *The Silent Voice* (UKN) prod/rel: Columbia

Cause for Alarm, Radio Play
Cause for Alarm 1950 d: Tay Garnett. lps: Loretta Young, Barry Sullivan, Bruce Cowling. 73M USA. prod/rel: MGM

The Gentle Web, Story
Unguarded Moment, The 1956 d: Harry Keller. lps: Esther Williams, George Nader, Edward Andrews. 95M USA. prod/rel: Universal-International

No Escape, Novel
Dark City 1950 d: William Dieterle. lps: Dean Jagger, Lizabeth Scott, Viveca Lindfors. 98M USA. prod/rel: Paramount

MARDIGANIAN, AURORA
Ravished Armenia, New York 1918, Book
Auction of Souls 1919 d: Oscar Apfel. lps: Aurora Mardiganian, Anna Q. Nilsson, Eugenie Besserer. 7820f USA. *Ravished Armenia*; *Armenia Crucified* prod/rel: Selig Studios, First National Exhibitors Circuit

MARDRUS, LUCIE DELARUE
L' Ex-Voto, Novel
Diable Au Coeur, Le 1927 d: Marcel L'Herbier. lps: Betty Balfour, Jaque Catelain, Roger Karl. 90M FRN. *Little Devil-May-Care* prod/rel: Cinegraphic, Gaumont British

MARENCO, LEOPOLDO
Giorgio Gandi, 1861, Play
Giorgio Gandi 1916 d: Emilio Graziani-Walter. lps: Myriam, Ugo Gracci, Giulio Donadio. 881m ITL. prod/rel: Regina Film

MARES, JOLANTEH
Novel
Three Women 1924 d: Ernst Lubitsch. lps: May McAvoy, Pauline Frederick, Marie Prevost. 8200f USA. prod/rel: Warner Brothers Pictures

MARET, GEORGES
La Goualeuse, Play
Goualeuse, La 1914 d: Georges Monca, Alexandre Devarennes. lps: Henry Bosc, Jean Toulout, Jane Marnac. 1400m FRN. prod/rel: Les Grands Films Populaires
Goualeuse, La 1938 d: Fernand Rivers. lps: Constant Remy, Jean Martinelli, Lys Gauty. 90M FRN. prod/rel: Films Fernand Rivers

MARET, JACQUES
Men Without a Past, Play
Station Six Sahara 1962 d: Seth Holt. lps: Carroll Baker, Ian Bannen, Denholm Elliott. 101M UKN/GRM. *Endstation Dreizehn Sahara* (GRM); *Destination 13 Sahara* prod/rel: Ccc-Filmkunst, Ccc Films

MARGERIT, ROBERT
Mont-Dragon, Novel
Mont-Dragon 1971 d: Jean Valere. lps: Jacques Brel, Carole Andre, Francoise Prevost. 90M BLG/FRN. prod/rel: Alcinter, Ste D'expansion Du Spectacle

MARGOLIN, PHILIP M.
The Last Innocent Man, Novel
Last Innocent Man, The 1987 d: Roger Spottiswoode. lps: Ed Harris, Roxanne Hart, David Suchet. TVM. 109M USA. prod/rel: Hbo Pictures, Maurice Singer Prod.

MARGOLIS, HERBERT
Radio Play
Pier 23 1951 d: William Berke. lps: Hugh Beaumont, Ann Savage, Edward Brophy. 58M USA. prod/rel: Lippert, Spartan Prods.

Danger Zone, Radio Play
Danger Zone 1951 d: William Berke. lps: Hugh Beaumont, Edward Brophy, Richard Travis. 56M USA. prod/rel: Lippert, Spartan

MARGONI, PATTERSON
Big-Hearted Jim, 1926, Short Story
Brotherly Love 1928 d: Charles F. Reisner. lps: Karl Dane, George K. Arthur, Jean Arthur. 6053f USA. prod/rel: Metro-Goldwyn-Mayer Pictures

MARGUERITTE, PAUL
Les Frontieres du Coeur, Novel
Frontieres du Coeur, Les 1914 d: Bernard-Deschamps. lps: Marcel Vibert, Cecile Guyon. 1010m FRN.

MARGUERITTE, VICTOR
Frontieres du Coeur, Les 1914 d: Bernard-Deschamps. lps: Marcel Vibert, Cecile Guyon. 1010m FRN.

La Garconne, 1922, Novel
Garconne, La 1924 d: Armand Du Plessis. lps: France Dhelia, Gaston Jacquet, Maggy Derval. 2400m FRN. prod/rel: Armand Du Plessy
Garconne, La 1936 d: Jean de Limur. lps: Marie Bell, Arletty, Henri Rollan. 95M FRN. prod/rel: Franco-London-Film
Garconne, La 1957 d: Jacqueline Audry. lps: Andree Debar, Jean Danet, Fernand Gravey. 93M FRN. *Bachelor Girl* prod/rel: Elysee Films

L' Imprevu, Play
Imprevu, L' 1916 d: Leonce Perret. lps: Henry Roussell, Paul Guide, Marcelle Geniat. 1200m FRN. prod/rel: Gaumont

MARI, ISA
Roma - Via Delle Mantellate, Roma 1953
Nella Citta l'Inferno 1958 d: Renato Castellani. lps: Anna Magnani, Giulietta Masina, Myriam Bru. 110M ITL/FRN. *L' Enfer Dans la Ville* (FRN); *Wild Women and the Wild* (USA); *Hell in Town*; *Caged* (UKN) prod/rel: Francinex (Paris), Riama Film (Roma)

MARIA, JAROSLAV
Werther, Novel
Werther 1926 d: Milos Hajsky. lps: Milos Hajsky, Marta Mayrova, Ela PoznerovA. CZC. *Utrpeni Mlade Lasky*; *The Torment of Young Love* prod/rel: Milos Hajsky, Fortuna Film

MARIANI, VITTORIO
Il Ritorno Di Un'anima, Novel
Ritorno d'Anima 1917 d: Mario Ceccatelli. lps: Eugenia Tettoni, Emilio Pettini. 894m ITL. prod/rel: Italo-Egiziana Film

MARIAS, JAVIER
All Souls, Novel
Robert Ryland's Last Journey 1996 d: Gracia QuerejetA. lps: Ben Cross, William Franklyn, Cathy Underwood. 103M SPN. prod/rel: Alta Films

MARIBEAU
Die Frau Im Schrank, Play
Frau Im Schrank, Die 1927 d: Rudolf Biebrach. lps: Ruth Weyher, Willy Fritsch, Felicitas Malten. 2178m GRM. prod/rel: UFA

MARIEL, PIERRE
L' Orphelin du Cirque, Novel
Orphelin du Cirque, L' 1926 d: Georges Lannes. lps: Andre Nox, Suzy Vernon, Berthe Jalabert. SRL. 3000m FRN. prod/rel: Weil Et Lauzin

MARIEMY, ELISABETH
Les Vacances de Xavier, Book
Vacances de Xavier, Les 1933 d: R. P. Danion. lps: Jacques Doizy. SHT FRN. *Croise Veux-Tu*; *La Grande Angoisse* prod/rel: Edition Bonne Presse

MARINKOVIC, RANKO
Kiklop, 1966, Novel
Kiklop 1982 d: Antun Vrdoljak. lps: Frano Lasic, Ljuba Tadic, Rade SerbedzijA. 137M YGS. *The Cyclops*

MARION, FRANCES
The Fisher-Girl, Story
Daughter of the Sea, A 1915 d: Charles M. Seay. lps: Muriel Ostriche, William H. Tooker, Clara Whipple. 5r USA. *The Fisher Girl* prod/rel: Equitable Motion Pictures Corp.©, World Film Corp.

MARION JR., GEORGE
Peachie, Story
Beautiful Liar, The 1921 d: Wallace Worsley. lps: Katherine MacDonald, Charles Meredith, Joseph J. Dowling. 5236f USA. prod/rel: Preferred Pictures, Associated First National Pictures

Too Many Girls, New York 1939, Musical Play
Too Many Girls 1940 d: George Abbott. lps: Lucille Ball, Richard Carlson, Eddie Bracken. 85M USA. prod/rel: RKO Radio Pictures©

MARIS, JANIS
Il Sorriso Della Pithia
　Trombata, La 1979 d: Sergio Bergonzelli. lps: Karin Well, Larry Daniels, Tina Carol. 90M ITL. *Quattro Ladroni a Caccia Di Milioni* prod/rel: Soulis Georgiades

MARISCHKA, ERNST (1893-1963), GRM
Story
　Song to Remember, A 1945 d: Charles Vidor. lps: Cornel Wilde, Merle Oberon, Paul Muni. 113M USA. *The Love of Madame Sand; The Song That Lived Forever* prod/rel: Columbia

Die Konigin, Play
　Queen's Affair, The 1934 d: Herbert Wilcox. lps: Anna Neagle, Fernand Gravey, Muriel Aked. 77M UKN. *Runaway Queen* (USA); *The Queen* prod/rel: British and Dominions, United Artists

Der Orlow, Operetta
　Diamant Des Zaren, Der 1932 d: Max Neufeld. lps: Liane Haid, Ivan Petrovich, Viktor de KowA. 89M GRM. *Der Orlow* prod/rel: Sokal, Karp
　Orlow, Der 1927 d: Jacob Fleck, Luise Fleck. lps: Ivan Petrovich, Vivian Gibson, Evi EvA. 2553m GRM. *Hearts and Diamonds* prod/rel: Hegewald-Film

Walzerkreig, Play
　Waltzes from Vienna 1933 d: Alfred Hitchcock. lps: Jessie Matthews, Edmund Gwenn, Fay Compton. 81M UKN. *Strauss' Great Waltz* (USA) prod/rel: Tom Arnold, Gaumont-British

MARIVALE, G. C.
Die Kronzeugin, Play
　Kronzeugin, Die 1937 d: Georg Jacoby. lps: Ivan Petrovich, Sybille Schmitz, Sabine Peters. 84M GRM. prod/rel: F.D.F.

MARK, TED
The Man from O.R.G.Y., New York 1965, Novel
　Man from O.R.G.Y., The 1970 d: James A. Hill. lps: Robert Walker Jr., Steve Rossi, Slappy White. 92M USA. *The Real Gone Girls* prod/rel: United Hemisphere Productions, Delta Films International

MARKEN, WOLFGANG
Karl Der Grosse, Novel
　Ganzer Kerl, Ein 1935 d: Carl Boese. lps: Hermann Speelmans, Lien Deyers, Joe Stockel. 92M GRM. *Karl Raumt Auf* prod/rel: Bavaria, Dietz

MARKEY, GENE
Blinky, 1923, Short Story
　Blinky 1923 d: Edward Sedgwick. lps: Hoot Gibson, Esther Ralston, Mathilde Brundage. 5807f USA. prod/rel: Universal Pictures
　Range Courage 1927 d: Ernst Laemmle. lps: Fred Humes, Gloria Grey, Dick Winslow. 4388f USA. prod/rel: Universal Pictures

The Gay Nineties, Story
　Florodora Girl, The 1930 d: Harry Beaumont. lps: Marion Davies, Lawrence Gray, Walter Catlett. 79M USA. *The Gay Nineties* (UKN) prod/rel: Metro-Goldwyn-Mayer Pictures

The Great Companions, Novel
　Meet Me at the Fair 1952 d: Douglas Sirk. lps: Dan Dailey, Diana Lynn, Hugh O'Brian. 87M USA. prod/rel: Universal-International

His Majesty's Pyjamas, Novel
　Love in Exile 1936 d: Alfred L. Werker. lps: Clive Brook, Helen Vinson, Mary Carlisle. 78M UKN. prod/rel: Capitol, General Film Distributors

Stepping High, Garden City, N.Y. 1929, Novel
　Syncopation 1929 d: Bert Glennon. lps: Barbara Bennett, Bobby Watson, Ian Hunter. 7626f USA. prod/rel: RKO Productions

MARKFIELD, WALLACE
To an Early Grave, New York 1964, Novel
　Bye Bye Braverman 1968 d: Sidney Lumet. lps: George Segal, Jack Warden, Joseph Wiseman. 94M USA. prod/rel: Warner Bros., Sidney Lumet

MARKING, YAY
The Crucible
　Cry Freedom 1959 d: Lamberto V. AvellanA. lps: Pancho Magalona, Rosa Rosal, Johnny Reyes. 93M PHL.

MARKO, ZEKIAL
Scratch a Thief, New York 1961, Novel
　Once a Thief 1965 d: Ralph Nelson. lps: Alain Delon, Jack Palance, Ann-Margret. 106M USA/FRN. *Les Tueurs de San Francisco* (FRN) prod/rel: Cipra, Ralph Nelson

MARKS, LEO
Cloudburst, Play
　Cloudburst 1951 d: Francis Searle. lps: Robert Preston, Elizabeth Sellars, Colin Tapley. 92M UKN. prod/rel: Exclusive, Hammer

The Girl Who Couldn't Quite, London 1947, Play
　Girl Who Couldn't Quite, The 1950 d: Norman Lee. lps: Bill Owen, Elizabeth Henson, Iris Hoey. 85M UKN. prod/rel: John Argyle, Monarch

MARKS, PERCY
The Plastic Age, New York 1924, Novel
　Plastic Age, The 1925 d: Wesley Ruggles. lps: Donald Keith, Clara Bow, Mary Alden. 6488f USA. prod/rel: B. P. Schulberg Productions
　Red Lips 1928 d: Melville Brown. lps: Marion Nixon, Charles "Buddy" Rogers, Stanley Taylor. 6947f USA. *Cream of the Earth* (UKN); *The Plastic Age* prod/rel: Universal Pictures

MARKSON, BEN
Play
　Is My Face Red? 1932 d: William A. Seiter. lps: Ricardo Cortez, Helen Twelvetrees, Jill Esmond. 66M USA. prod/rel: RKO Radio Pictures©

MARKSON, DAVID
The Ballad of Dingus Magee, Indianapolis 1965, Novel
　Dirty Dingus Magee 1970 d: Burt Kennedy. lps: Frank Sinatra, George Kennedy, Anne Jackson. 91M USA. prod/rel: Metro-Goldwyn-Mayer

MARKSTEIN, GEORGE (1928-, USA
Espion Leve-Toi, Novel
　Espion, Leve-Toi 1981 d: Yves Boisset. lps: Lino Ventura, Krystyna Janda, Michel Piccoli. 99M FRN. prod/rel: Cathala, TF 1

The Tiptoe Boys, Novel
　Who Dares Wins 1982 d: Ian Sharp. lps: Lewis Collins, Judy Davis, Richard Widmark. 125M UKN. *The Final Option* (USA) prod/rel: Rank, Richmond Light Horse

MARKUS, STEFAN
Helena, 1921, Short Story
　Flucht Ins Paradies, Die 1923 d: Charles Erik Schneider. lps: Jules Strassman, Marga Marfels, Josef Roemer. 1730m GRM/SWT. *Le Lac de la Liberte* (SWT); *Das Paradies Am See* prod/rel: Weser-Film, Gotthard-Film

Das Verlorene Paradies, 1921, Short Story
　Flucht Ins Paradies, Die 1923 d: Charles Erik Schneider. lps: Jules Strassmann, Marga Marfels, Josef Roemer. 1730m GRM/SWT. *Le Lac de la Liberte* (SWT); *Das Paradies Am See* prod/rel: Weser-Film, Gotthard-Film

MARLOT, R.
Il Faut Vivre Dangereusement, Novel
　Il Faut Vivre Dangereusement 1975 d: Claude Makovski. lps: Annie Girardot, Claude Brasseur, Sydne Rome. 100M FRN. prod/rel: Les Films de la Chouette, O.R.T.F.

MARLOW, BRIAN
The Brown Derby, 1925, Play
　Brown Derby, The 1926 d: Charles Hines. lps: Johnny Hines, Diana Kane, Ruth Dwyer. 6700f USA. prod/rel: C. C. Burr Pictures

MARLOWE, CHARLES
When Knights Were Bold, London 1907, Play
　Cavaliere Del Silenzio, Il 1916 d: Oreste Visalli. lps: Jeanne Nolly, Giulio Del Torre, Claudia Zambuto. 1180m ITL. prod/rel: Aquila Film
　When Knights Were Bold 1916 d: Maurice Elvey. lps: James Welch, Janet Ross, Gerald Ames. 4800f UKN. prod/rel: London, Jury
　When Knights Were Bold 1929 d: Tim Whelan. lps: Nelson Keys, Miriam Seegar, Eric Bransby Williams. SIL. 7213f UKN. prod/rel: British & Dominions, Woolf & Freedman
　When Knights Were Bold 1936 d: Jack Raymond. lps: Jack Buchanan, Fay Wray, Garry Marsh. 75M UKN. prod/rel: Capitol, General Film Distributors

MARLOWE, CHRISTOPHER (1564-1593), UKN
Doctor Faustus, 1594, Play
　Doctor Faustus 1967 d: Nevill Coghill, Richard Burton. lps: Richard Burton, Elizabeth Taylor, Andreas Teuber. 93M UKN/ITL. prod/rel: Columbia, Oxford University

Edward II, 1594, Play
　Edward II 1991 d: Derek Jarman. lps: Steven Waddington, Kevin Collins, Andrew Tiernan. 91M UKN. prod/rel: Edward II Ltd., Working Title

MARLOWE, DEREK (1938-, UKN
A Dandy in Aspic, London 1966, Novel
　Dandy in Aspic, A 1968 d: Anthony Mann, Laurence Harvey. lps: Laurence Harvey, Tom Courtenay, Mia Farrow. 107M UKN/USA. prod/rel: Columbia British, Columbia

Echoes of Celandine, Novel
　Disappearance, The 1977 d: Stuart Cooper. lps: Donald Sutherland, Francine Racette, Christopher Plummer. 102M UKN/CND. prod/rel: Trofar Ltd. (London), Tiberius Film Productions Ltd. (Toronto)

MARLOWE, HUGH
A Candle for the Dead, Novel
　Violent Enemy, The 1969 d: Don Sharp. lps: Tom Bell, Susan Hampshire, Ed Begley. 94M UKN. *Came the Hero* prod/rel: Monarch, Trio Films

MARMOL, JOSE PEDRO CRISTOLOGO
Amalia, 1851, Novel
　Amalia 1936 d: Luis Barth-MogliA. lps: Floren Delbene, Herminia Franco, Miguel Gomez Bao. 104M ARG.

MARMUR, JACLAND
No Home of His Own, Short Story
　Return from the Sea 1954 d: Lesley Selander. lps: Neville Brand, Jan Sterling, Lloyd Corrigan. 80M USA. prod/rel: Allied Artists

MARONE, PUBLIO VIRGILIO
Eneide
　Didone Abbandonata 1910 d: Luigi Maggi. lps: Alberto A. Capozzi, Mirra Principi, Giuseppe Gray. 319m ITL. *Dido Forsaken By Aeneas* (UKN) prod/rel: S.A. Ambrosio

MAROT, GASTON
Les Aventures de Thomas Plumepatte, Play
　Aventures de Thomas Plumepatte, Les 1916?. lps: Robert Maire, Robert Bogar, Leo Courtois. 1280m FRN.

MAROTTA, GIUSEPPE
L' Oro Di Napoli, Book
　Oro Di Napoli, L' 1954 d: Vittorio de SicA. lps: Toto, Eduardo de Filippo, Lianella Carell. 107M ITL. *L' Or de Naples* (FRN); *Every Day's a Holiday* (UKN); *Gold of Naples* (USA) prod/rel: Dino de Laurentiis, Carlo Ponti

MARQUAND, JOHN PHILLIPS (1893-1960), USA
B.F.'S Daughter, 1946, Novel
　B.F.'S Daughter 1948 d: Robert Z. Leonard. lps: Barbara Stanwyck, Van Heflin, Charles Coburn. 108M USA. *Polly Fulton* (UKN) prod/rel: MGM

The Girl and Mr. Moto, 1936, Short Story
　Think Fast, Mr. Moto 1937 d: Norman Foster. lps: Peter Lorre, Virginia Field, Thomas Beck. 70M USA. prod/rel: Twentieth Century-Fox Film Corp.©

Esquire H.M. Pulman, 1941, Novel
　H.M. Pulman Esq. 1941 d: King Vidor. lps: Hedy Lamarr, Robert Young, Ruth Hussey. 120M USA. prod/rel: MGM

The Late George Apley, 1937, Novel
　Late George Apley, The 1947 d: Joseph L. Mankiewicz. lps: Ronald Colman, Peggy Cummins, Vanessa Brown. 98M USA. prod/rel: 20th Century-Fox

Melville Goodwin U.S.A., 1951, Novel
　Top Secret Affair 1956 d: H. C. Potter. lps: Susan Hayward, Kirk Douglas, Paul Stewart. 100M USA. *Their Secret Affair* (UKN) prod/rel: Warner Bros.

Only a Few of Us Left, 1922, Short Story
　High Speed Lee 1923 d: Dudley Murphy. lps: Reed Howes. 4816f USA. prod/rel: Atlantice Features, Arrow Film Corp.

The Right That Failed, Short Story
　Right That Failed, The 1922 d: Bayard Veiller. lps: Bert Lytell, Virginia Valli, De Witt Jennings. 5r USA. *Keep Off the Grass* prod/rel: Metro Pictures

Stopover Tokyo, 1957, Novel
　Stopover Tokyo 1957 d: Richard L. Breen. lps: Robert Wagner, Joan Collins, Edmond O'Brien. 100M USA. prod/rel: Walter Reisch, 20th Century-Fox

Thank You Mr. Moto, Boston 1936, Novel
　Thank You, Mr. Moto 1937 d: Norman Foster. lps: Peter Lorre, Thomas Beck, Pauline Frederick. 68M USA. prod/rel: Twentieth Century-Fox Film Corp.©

MARQUET
Jeanne la Maudite, Play
　Jeanne la Maudite 1913 d: Georges DenolA. lps: Jacquinet, Mosnier, Rachel Behrendt. 935m FRN. prod/rel: Scagl

MARQUETTE, DORIS
The Garden of Weeds, New York 1924, Play
　Garden of Weeds, The 1924 d: James Cruze. lps: Betty Compson, Rockliffe Fellowes, Warner Baxter. 6230f USA. prod/rel: Famous Players-Lasky, Paramount Pictures

MARQUINA, EDUARDO (1879-1946), SPN
Dona Maria la Brava, 1909, Play
　Dona Maria la Brava 1947 d: Luis MarquinA. lps: Tina Gasco, Asuncion Sancho, Luis Hurtado. 109M SPN. *Dona Maria the Brave*

MARQUIS, DON (1878–1937), USA
The Cruise of the Jasper B, New York 1916, Novel
  Cruise of the Jasper B, The 1926 d: James W. Horne.
  lps: Rod La Rocque, Mildred Harris, Jack Ackroyd.
  5780f USA. prod/rel: de Mille Pictures, Producers
  Distributing Corp.
The Old Soak, New York 1922, Play
  Good Old Soak, The 1937 d: J. Walter Ruben. lps:
  Wallace Beery, Una Merkel, Eric Linden. 76M USA. *The
  Old Soak* prod/rel: Metro-Goldwyn-Mayer Corp.©
  Old Soak, The 1926 d: Edward Sloman. lps: Jean
  Hersholt, George Lewis, June Marlowe. 7445f USA.
  prod/rel: Universal Pictures

MARQUIS, RENE
Pour Maman, Short Story
  Pour Maman 1910 d: Emile Chautard. lps: Marcelle
  Barry, Maria Fromet, La Petite Schifner. 218m FRN.
  prod/rel: Acad

MARRADEN, BEATRICE
Ships That Pass in the Night, Novel
  Ships That Pass in the Night 1921 d: Percy Nash. lps:
  Filippi Dowson, Francis Roberts, Daisy Markham. 5400f
  UKN. prod/rel: Screen Plays, British Exhibitors' Films

MARRAZZO, GIUSEPPE
Il Camorrista, Novel
  Camorrista, Il 1986 d: Giuseppe Tornatore. lps: Ben
  Gazzara, Laura Del Sol, Leo GullottA. 146M ITL. *The
  Camorra Member; The Professor; The Camorra Man*
  prod/rel: Titanus Produzione, Rete Italia

MARRIOTT, ANTHONY
No Sex Please - We're British, Play
  No Sex Please - We're British 1973 d: Cliff Owen. lps:
  Ronnie Corbett, Beryl Reid, Arthur Lowe. 91M UKN.
  prod/rel: Columbia, Bhp

MARRIOTT, CRITTENDEN
The Isle of Dead Ships, Philadelphia 1909, Novel
  Isle of Lost Ships, The 1923 d: Maurice Tourneur. lps:
  Anna Q. Nilsson, Milton Sills, Frank Campeau. 7425f
  USA. prod/rel: Maurice Tourneur Productions
  Isle of Lost Ships, The 1929 d: Irvin V. Willat. lps:
  Jason Robards, Virginia Valli, Clarissa Selwynne. 7576f
  USA. prod/rel: First National Pictures

MARRS, JIM
Crossfire, Book
  JFK 1991 d: Oliver Stone. lps: Kevin Costner, Sissy
  Spacek, Kevin Bacon. 189M USA. prod/rel: Warner
  Bros., le Studio Canal Plus

MARRYAT, FREDERICK (1792–1848), UKN
The Little Savage, 1848-49, Novel
  Little Savage, The 1959 d: Byron Haskin. lps: Pedro
  Armendariz, Christiane Martel, Rodolfo Hoyos Jr. 72M
  USA. prod/rel: 20th Century-Fox, Associated Producers
Mr. Midshipman Easy, 1836, Novel
  Midshipman Easy 1915 d: Maurice Elvey. lps:
  Elisabeth Risdon, Fred Groves, A. V. Bramble. 2700f
  UKN. prod/rel: British and Colonial, Ideal
  Midshipman Easy 1935 d: Carol Reed. lps: Hughie
  Green, Margaret Lockwood, Harry Tate. 77M UKN.
  Men of the Sea (USA) prod/rel: Associated Talking
  Pictures, Associated British Film Distributors

MARS, ANTONY
Le Fils a Papa, Play
  Fils a Papa, Le 1913 d: Georges MoncA. lps: Prince,
  Gabrielle Lange, Pepa Bonafe. 680m FRN. prod/rel:
  Pathe Freres
Madame l'Admirale, Play
  Ammiraglia, L' 1914 d: Nino OxiliA. lps: Dina Galli,
  Sig. Orsini, Stanislao Ciarli. 650m ITL. prod/rel: Cines
Le Mari Sans Femme, Play
  Mariti Allegri, I 1914 d: Camillo de Riso. lps: Camillo
  de Riso, Lydia Quaranta, Letizia QuarantA. ITL.
  prod/rel: Film Artistica Gloria
Les Surprises du Divorce, 1888, Play
  Sorprese Del Divorzio, Le 1923 d: Guido Brignone.
  lps: Lia Miari, Leonie Laporte, Alberto Collo. 1774m
  ITL. prod/rel: Alba Film
  Sorprese Del Divorzio, Le 1939 d: Guido Brignone.
  lps: Armando Falconi, Filippo Scelzo, Sergio Tofano.
  84M ITL. prod/rel: Scalera Film
  Surprises du Divorce, Les 1912 d: Georges MoncA.
  lps: Prince, Leon Bernard, Suzanne Demay. 710m FRN.
  prod/rel: Scagl
  Surprises du Divorce, Les 1933 d: Jean Kemm. lps:
  Mauricet, Nadine Picard, Maximilienne. 87M FRN.
  prod/rel: Alex Nalpas
Les Vingt-Huit Jours de Clairette, Opera
  Vingt-Huit Jours de Clairette, Les 1933 d: Andre
  Hugon. lps: Mireille, Janine Guise, Armand Bernard.
  98M FRN. prod/rel: Hugon-Films,
  Gaumont-Franco-Film-Aubert

Le Voyage de Corbillon, Play
  Voyage de Corbillon, Le 1914 d: Georges DenolA. lps:
  Prince, Andre Simon, Clo MarrA. 890m FRN. prod/rel:
  Scagl

MARSE, JUAN (1933–, SPN
Libertad Provisional, 1976, Short Story
  Libertad Provisional 1976 d: Roberto Bodegas. lps:
  Conchita Velasco, Patxi Andion, Montserrat Salvador.
  98M SPN. *Provisional Freedom*
La Muchacha de Las Brages de Oro, 1978, Novel
  Muchacha de Las Bragas de Oro, La 1979 d: Vicente
  ArandA. lps: Victoria Abril, Lautaro Murua, Hilda VerA.
  115M SPN/VNZ. *The Girl in the Golden Knickers; The
  Girl in the Golden Panties; The Girlw With the Golden
  Panties*
Si Te Dican Que Cai, 1973, Novel
  Si Te Dicen Que Cai 1988 d: Vicente ArandA. lps:
  Victoria Abril, Jorge Sanz, Antonio Banderas. 115M
  SPN. *Don't Tell Them I Fell; No Les Digas Que Cai; If
  They Tell You That I Fell; Aventis*

MARSH, RICHARD
The Beetle, Novel
  Beetle, The 1919 d: Alexander Butler. lps: Maudie
  Dunham, Hebden Foster, Fred Morgan. 5600f UKN.
  prod/rel: Barker, Urban
In Full Cry, Novel
  In Full Cry 1921 d: Einar J. Bruun. lps: Gregory Scott,
  Pauline Peters, Cecil Mannering. 5700f UKN. prod/rel:
  Broadwest, Walturdaw
Nelly, Novel
  Nelly 1915. 1150f UKN. prod/rel: Britannia, Pathe

MARSH, RONALD
Irene, Novel
  Once a Sinner 1950 d: Lewis Gilbert. lps: Pat
  Kirkwood, Jack Watling, Joy Shelton. 80M UKN.
  prod/rel: John Argyle, Butcher's Film Service

MARSHALL, ALAN
Hammers Over the Anvil, Book
  Hammers Over the Anvil 1991 d: Ann Turner. lps:
  Charlotte Rampling, Russell Crowe, Alexander
  Outhred. F ASL.
I'm Jumping Over Puddles Again, Autobiography
  Uz Zase Skacu Pres Kaluze 1970 d: Karel KachynA.
  lps: Vladimir Dlouhy, Karel Hlusicka, Zdenka
  HadrbolcovA. 90M CZC. *I'm Jumping Over Puddles
  Again* (UKN); *Jumping Over Puddles Again; Jumping
  the Puddles Again* prod/rel: Filmstudio Barrandov

MARSHALL, ANTHONY
Swordsman of Siena, Novel
  Mercenaire, Le 1962 d: Etienne Perier, Baccio
  Bandini. lps: Stewart Granger, Sylva Koscina, Christine
  Kaufmann. 100M FRN/ITL. *La Congiura Dei Dieci*
  (ITL); *Swordsman of Siena* (USA); *Il Mercenario; Lo
  Spadaccino Di Siena* prod/rel: Cipra, Jacques Bar
  (Paris)

MARSHALL, ARMINA
The Pursuit of Happiness, New York 1933, Play
  Pursuit of Happiness, The 1934 d: Alexander Hall.
  lps: Francis Lederer, Joan Bennett, Charles Ruggles.
  85M USA. prod/rel: Paramount Productions©

MARSHALL, BRUCE
Novel
  Wunder Des Malachias, Das 1961 d: Bernhard Wicki.
  lps: Horst Bollmann, Richard Munch, Christiane
  Nielsen. 122M GRM. *Father Malachy's Miracle* (USA);
  *The Miracle of Malachias; Malachias; The Miracle of
  Father Malachias* prod/rel: D.F.H., U.F.H.
Vespers in Vienna, Novel
  Red Danube, The 1949 d: George Sidney. lps: Walter
  Pidgeon, Ethel Barrymore, Peter Lawford. 119M USA.
  prod/rel: MGM

MARSHALL, CATHERINE (1914–1983), USA
A Man Called Peter, Biography
  Man Called Peter, A 1955 d: Henry Koster. lps:
  Richard Todd, Jean Peters, Marjorie Rambeau. 119M
  USA. prod/rel: 20th Century-Fox

MARSHALL, EDISON
The Far Call, 1928, Short Story
  Far Call, The 1929 d: Allan Dwan. lps: Charles Morton,
  Leila Hyams, Arthur Stone. 5313f USA. prod/rel: Fox
  Film Corp.
The Isle of Retribution, Boston 1923, Novel
  Isle of Retribution, The 1926 d: James P. Hogan. lps:
  Lillian Rich, Robert Frazer, Victor McLaglen. 6388f
  USA. prod/rel: R-C Pictures, Film Booking Offices of
  America
The Skyline of Spruce, Boston 1922, Novel
  Shadows of the North 1923 d: Robert F. Hill. lps:
  William Desmond, Virginia Brown Faire, Fred Kohler.
  4943f USA. *The Skyline of Spruce* prod/rel: Universal
  Pictures

The Snowshoe Trail, Boston 1921, Novel
  Snowshoe Trail, The 1922 d: Chester Bennett. lps:
  Jane Novak, Roy Stewart, Lloyd Whitlock. 5382f USA.
  prod/rel: Chester Bennett Productions, Film Booking
  Offices of America
Son of Fury, Novel
  Son of Fury 1942 d: John Cromwell. lps: Tyrone
  Power, Gene Tierney, George Sanders. 98M USA. *Son of
  Fury - the Story of Benjamin Blake* prod/rel: 20th
  Century-Fox
  Treasure of the Golden Condor 1953 d: Delmer
  Daves. lps: Cornel Wilde, Constance Smith, Finlay
  Currie. 93M USA. *Condor's Nest* prod/rel: 20th
  Century-Fox
The Strength of the Pines, Boston 1921, Novel
  Strength of the Pines 1922 d: Edgar Lewis. lps:
  William Russell, Irene Rich, Lule Warrenton. 4382f
  USA. prod/rel: Fox Film Corp.
The Viking, 1951, Novel
  Vikings, The 1958 d: Richard Fleischer. lps: Kirk
  Douglas, Tony Curtis, Ernest Borgnine. 114M USA.
  prod/rel: United Artists, Bryna Prods.
Yankee Pasha: the Adventures of Jason Starbuck,
1941, Novel
  Yankee Pasha 1954 d: Joseph Pevney. lps: Jeff
  Chandler, Rhonda Fleming, Mamie Van Doren. 84M
  USA. prod/rel: Universal-International

MARSHALL, GEORGE
And the Best Man Won, Short Story
  And the Best Man Won 1915 d: Horace Davey. lps:
  Billie Rhodes, Ray Gallagher, Neal Burns. SHT USA.
  prod/rel: Nestor

MARSHALL, JAMES LESLIE
Santa Fe; the Railroad That Built an Empire,
1945, Book
  Santa Fe 1951 d: Irving Pichel. lps: Randolph Scott,
  Janis Carter, Jerome Courtland. 89M USA. prod/rel:
  Columbia, Producers Actors

MARSHALL, JAMES VANCE
A River Ran Out of Eden, Novel
  Golden Seal, The 1983 d: Frank ZunigA. lps: Steve
  Railsback, Michael Beck, Penelope Milord. 94M USA.
  prod/rel: Samuel Goldwyn Company, New Realm
Walkabout, Novel
  Walkabout 1971 d: Nicolas Roeg. lps: Jenny Agutter,
  Lucien John, David Gumpilil. 100M ASL. prod/rel: Max
  L. Raab, Si Litvinoff

MARSHALL, PETER
The Raging Moon, Novel
  Raging Moon, The 1970 d: Bryan Forbes. lps: Malcolm
  McDowell, Nanette Newman, Georgia Brown. 111M
  UKN. *Long Ago Tomorrow* (USA) prod/rel: MGM-Emi,
  Emi

MARSHALL, ROBERT
The Second in Command, London 1900, Play
  Second in Command, The 1915 d: William J.
  Bowman. lps: Francis X. Bushman, Marguerite Snow,
  William Clifford. 5r USA. prod/rel: Quality Pictures
  Corp., Metro Pictures Corp.©
The Unforseen, London 1902, Play
  Unforseen, The 1917 d: John B. O'Brien. lps: Olive
  Tell, David Powell, Lionel Adams. 5-6r USA. prod/rel:
  Empire All Star Corp.©, Mutual Film Corp.

MARSHALL, ROSAMUND
The Bixby Girls, Novel
  All the Fine Young Cannibals 1960 d: Michael
  Anderson. lps: Robert Wagner, Natalie Wood, Susan
  Kohner. 112M USA. prod/rel: MGM
Kitty, Novel
  Kitty 1945 d: Mitchell Leisen. lps: Ray Milland,
  Paulette Goddard, Patric Knowles. 103M USA. prod/rel:
  Paramount

MARSTON, LAWRENCE
An Innocent Sinner, Play
  Innocent Sinner, An 1915 d: Kenean Buel. lps:
  Katherine La Salle. 3r USA. prod/rel: Kalem

MARTENS, G. M.
Les Gueux Au Paradis, Play
  Gueux Au Paradis, Les 1945 d: Rene Le Henaff. lps:
  Raimu, Fernandel, Armand Bernard. 85M FRN. *Hoboes
  in Paradise* (USA) prod/rel: C.P.L.F., Gaumont

MARTET, JEAN
Chasse a l'Homme, Novel
  Maria du Bout du Monde 1950 d: Jean Stelli. lps:
  Denise Cardi, Paul Meurisse, Jacques Berthier. 90M
  FRN. prod/rel: Codo-Cinema
Le Colonel Durand, Novel
  Colonel Durand, Le 1948 d: Rene Chanas. lps: Paul
  Meurisse, Michele Martin, Louis Seigner. 110M FRN.
  prod/rel: Acteurs Et Techniciens Francais

Goubbiah, Novel
Goubbiah Mon Amour 1956 d: Robert Darene. lps: Jean Marais, Delia Scala, KerimA. 95M FRN/ITL. *Fuga Nel Sole* (ITL); *Goubbiah*; *Mon Amour*; *Kiss of Fire* (UKN) prod/rel: Consortium Du Film, Italie Produzione

Monseigneur, Novel
Monseigneur 1949 d: Roger Richebe. lps: Bernard Blier, Fernand Ledoux, Nadia Gray. 96M FRN. prod/rel: Films Richebe

MARTIN, A. E.
The Outsiders, Novel
Glass Cage, The 1955 d: Montgomery Tully. lps: John Ireland, Honor Blackman, Geoffrey Keen. 59M UKN. *The Glass Tomb* (USA) prod/rel: Hammer, Exclusive

MARTIN, AL
Make Way for Love, Story
Reckless Age 1944 d: Felix E. Feist. lps: Gloria Jean, Henry Stephenson, Kathleen Howard. 63M USA. prod/rel: Universal

MARTIN, CHARLES
I'll Be Seeing You, Novel
I'll Be Seeing You 1944 d: William Dieterle, George Cukor (Uncredited). lps: Ginger Rogers, Joseph Cotten, Shirley Temple. 85M USA. *Double Furlough* prod/rel: RKO Radio

Terror at Black Falls, Novel
Terror at Black Falls 1962 d: Richard C. Sarafian. lps: House Peters Jr., John Alonzo, Sandra Knight. 76M USA. prod/rel: Beckman

MARTIN, CHARLES M.
Left Handed Law, New York 1936, Novel
Left-Handed Law 1937 d: Lesley Selander. lps: Buck Jones, Noel Francis, Frank Larue. 68M USA. *Left Handed Law* prod/rel: Universal Pictures Co.©

MARTIN, DAVID
Clowning Around Encore, Novel
Clowning Around Encore 1992 d: George Whaley. lps: Clayton Williamson, Frederique Fouche, Ernie Dingo. TVM. F ASL. prod/rel: Barron Films

Clowning Sim, Novel
Clowning Around 1991 d: George Whaley. lps: Clayton Williamson, Jean-Michel Dagory, Ernie Dingo. TVM. F ASL. *Clowning Sim* prod/rel: Barron Films

MARTIN, DON
Confession, Play
Confession 1955 d: Ken Hughes. lps: Sydney Chaplin, Audrey Dalton, John Bentley. 90M UKN. *The Deadliest Sin* (USA) prod/rel: Anglo Guild, Anglo-Amalgamated

Hell's Highway, Story
Violent Road 1958 d: Howard W. Koch. lps: Brian Keith, Dick Foran, Efrem Zimbalist Jr. 86M USA. *Hell's Highway*; *The Steel Jungle* prod/rel: Warner Bros., Lakeside Pictures

MARTIN, DOUGLAS D.
The Tombstone Epitaph, Albuquerque 1951, Novel
Hour of the Gun 1967 d: John Sturges. lps: James Garner, Jason Robards Jr., Robert Ryan. 101M USA. *The Law and Tombstone* prod/rel: Mirisch Corporation, Kappa Corporation

MARTIN, E. LEBRETON
Boys of the Otter Patrol, Novel
Boys of the Otter Patrol 1918 d: Percy Nash. lps: Alfred Harding, Dorothy Mason, Edward Dryhurst Roberts. 5000f UKN. prod/rel: Transatlantic

MARTIN, EDOUARD
Le Voyage de Monsieur Perrichon, 1860, Play
Viaggio Del Signor Perrichon, Il 1944 d: Paolo MoffA. lps: Antonio Gandusio, Adriano Rimoldi, Paola Borboni. 78M ITL. prod/rel: a.C.I., Europa
Voyage de Monsieur Perrichon, Le 1934 d: Jean Tarride. lps: Leon Belieres, Jeanne Cheirel, Andre Roanne. 90M FRN. prod/rel: Ceres-Film

MARTIN, ERNEST
The Coal King, Play
Coal King, The 1915 d: Percy Nash. lps: Douglas Cox, May Lynn, Frank Tennant. 3600f UKN. prod/rel: Neptune, Kinematograph Trading Co.

MARTIN GAITE, CARMEN
Las Ataduras, 1960, Short Story
Emilia, Parada Y Fonda 1976 d: Angelino Fons. lps: Ana Belen, Maria Luisa San Jose, Francisco Rabal. 103M SPN. *Emily. Halt and Inn*; *EmiliA. Roadside Motel*

MARTIN, GEORGE R. R.
Nightflyers, Novel
Nightflyers 1987 d: Robert Collector. lps: Catherine Mary Stewart, Michael Praed, John Standing. 89M USA. prod/rel: Vista, New Century

MARTIN, GEORGE VICTOR
Our Vines Have Tender Grapes, Novel
Our Vines Have Tender Grapes 1945 d: Roy Rowland. lps: Edward G. Robinson, Margaret O'Brien, Agnes Moorehead. 103M USA. *For Our Vines Have Tender Grapes* prod/rel: MGM

MARTIN, GILLIAN
Between Two Women, Novel
Between Two Women 1986 d: Jon Avnet. lps: Farrah Fawcett, Colleen Dewhurst, Michael Nouri. TVM. 100M USA. prod/rel: Jon Avnet Company

MARTIN, HANSJORG
Kein Schnaps Fur Tamara, Novel
Tamara 1968 d: Hansjurgen Pohland. lps: Petrus Schloemp, Barbara Rutting, Hansi Linder. 95M GRM. prod/rel: Modern Art

MARTIN, HELEN R.
Barnabetta, New York 1914, Novel
Erstwhile Susan 1919 d: John S. Robertson. lps: Constance Binney, Jere Austin, Alfred Hickman. 5380f USA. prod/rel: Realart Pictures Corp.©

MARTIN, HELEN REIMENSNYDER
The Parasite, Philadelphia 1913, Novel
Parasite, The 1925 d: Louis J. Gasnier. lps: Owen Moore, Madge Bellamy, Bryant Washburn. 5140f USA. prod/rel: B. P. Schulberg Productions

The Snob; the Story of a Marriage, New York 1924, Novel
Snob, The 1924 d: Monta Bell. lps: John Gilbert, Norma Shearer, Conrad Nagel. 6495f USA. prod/rel: Metro-Goldwyn-Mayer Pictures

MARTIN, JOHN BARTLOW
Smashing the Bookie Gang Marauders, Novel
Scene of the Crime 1949 d: Roy Rowland. lps: Van Johnson, Arlene Dahl, Gloria de Haven. 95M USA. prod/rel: MGM

MARTIN, MARIE BUXTON
Within the Rock, New York 1925, Novel
Within the Rock 1935 d: Albert Ray. lps: Lon Chaney Jr., Lila Lee, Edmund Breese. 62M USA. *Woman of Destiny* (UKN); *The Marriage Bargain* prod/rel: Showmen's Productions©, State Rights

MARTIN, NELL
Lord Byron of Broadway, New York 1928, Novel
Lord Byron of Broadway 1930 d: William Nigh, Harry Beaumont. lps: Charles Kaley, Ethelind Terry, Marion Shilling. 7200f USA. *What Price Melody?* (UKN) prod/rel: Metro-Goldwyn-Mayer Pictures

MARTIN, PETE
I Posed As a Communist for the F.B.I., Book
I Was a Communist for the F.B.I. 1951 d: Gordon Douglas. lps: Frank Lovejoy, Dorothy Hart, Philip Carey. 83M USA. prod/rel: Warner Bros.

MARTIN, RAIMUND
Junger Wein, Play
Herzensfreud - Herzenslied 1940 d: Hubert MarischkA. lps: Magda Schneider, Paul Klinger, Carola Hohn. 98M GRM. prod/rel: Algefa, Kopp

MARTIN RECUERDA, JOSE
Las Salvajes En Puente San Gil, 1963, Play
Salvajes En Puente San Gil, Las 1967 d: Antoni Ribas. lps: Adolfo Marsillach, Elena Maria Tejeiro, Maria SilvA. 90M SPN. *The Wild Ones of San Gil Bridge*; *Savages of St. Gil's Bridge*; *The Wild Women in Puente San Gil*; *The Wild Girls at Puente San Gil*

MARTIN, TOWNSEND
A Most Immoral Lady, New York 1928, Play
Most Immoral Lady, A 1929 d: John Griffith Wray. lps: Leatrice Joy, Walter Pidgeon, Sidney Blackmer. 7145f USA. prod/rel: First National Pictures

MARTIN, TROY KENNEDY
The Italian Job, Novel
Italian Job, The 1969 d: Peter Collinson. lps: Michael Caine, Noel Coward, Benny Hill. 100M UKN. *The Mastermind* prod/rel: Paramount, Oakhurst

MARTIN, VALERIE
Mary Reilly, Novel
Mary Reilly 1996 d: Stephen Frears. lps: Julia Roberts, John Malkovich, George Cole. 108M USA. prod/rel: Tristar

MARTIN, W. THORNTON
The Gravy Game, 1933, Short Story
Band Plays on, The 1934 d: Russell MacK. lps: Robert Young, Stuart Erwin, Preston Foster. 89M USA. *Back Field*; *Kid from College* prod/rel: Metro-Goldwyn-Mayer Corp.

MARTIN, WYNDHAM
The Man from the Desert, Short Story
Desert Driven 1923 d: Val Paul. lps: Harry Carey, Marguerite Clayton, George Waggner. 5840f USA. prod/rel: R-C Pictures, Film Booking Offices of America

The Mysterious Mr. Garland, London 1922, Novel
Star Reporter, The 1921 d: Duke Worne. lps: Billie Rhodes, Truman Van Dyke, William Horne. 5622f USA. prod/rel: Berwilla Film Corp., Arrow Film Corp.

MARTIN-CROSS, J. H.
Under the Frozen Falls, Novel
Under the Frozen Falls 1948 d: Darrell Catling. lps: Harold Warrender, Jacques Brown, Ivan Brandt. 44M UKN. prod/rel: Gb Instructional, General Film Distributors

MARTINDALE, MAY
Gamblers All, London 1915, Play
Gamblers All 1919 d: Dave Aylott. lps: Madge Titheradge, Owen Nares, Ruby Miller. 5500f UKN. prod/rel: G. B. Samuelson, Granger

MARTINEZ REVERTE, JORGE
Galvez En Euskadi, Novel
Como Levantar 1000 Kilos 1991 d: Antonio Hernandez. lps: Antonio Valero, Ana Duato, Patrick Bauchau. 96M SPN. *Como Levantar Mil Kilos*

MARTINEZ RUIZ, JOSE (1873–1967), SPN, Azorin
La Guerrilla, 1936, Play
Guerrilla, La 1972 d: Rafael Gil. lps: Francisco Rabal, Jacques Destoop, La PochA. 94M SPN/FRN. *The Guerilla*

MARTINEZ SIERRA, GREGORIO (1881–1947), SPN
El Amor Brujo, 1915, Play
Amor Brujo, El 1967 d: Francisco Rovira BeletA. lps: Antonio Gades, Rafael de Cordoba, Nuria Torray. 102M SPN. *Sorcerer's Love*; *Witch Love*; *Evil Love*; *Bewitched Love*

Cancion de Cuna, Madrid 1911, Play
Cancion de Cuna 1941 d: Gregorio Martinez SierrA. lps: Miguel Gomez Bao, Maria Duval. F ARG. *Cradle Song*
Cancion de Cuna 1961 d: Jose Maria ElorrietA. lps: Lina Rosales, Soledad Miranda, Jaime Avellan. 93M SPN. *Cradle Song*
Cradle Song 1933 d: Mitchell Leisen, Mina Moise. lps: Dorothea Wieck, Evelyn Venable, Kent Taylor. 78M USA. prod/rel: Paramount Productions, Inc.

Julieta Compra un Hijo, Madrid 1927, Play
Julieta Compra un Hijo 1935 d: Louis King. lps: Catalina Barcena, Gilbert Roland, Luana Alcaniz. 74M USA. *Juliet Buys a Baby*; *Juliet Buys a Son* prod/rel: Fox Film Corp.©

Mama, Spain 1913, Play
Mama 1931 d: Gregorio Martinez Sierra, Benito Perojo. lps: Catalina Barcena, Rafael Rivelles, Maria Luz Callejo. 80M USA. prod/rel: Fox Film Corp.©

Mujer, Barcelona 1925, Play
Yo, Tu Y Ella 1933 d: John Reinhardt. lps: Catalina Barcena, Gilbert Roland, Rosita Moreno. 8r USA. *I. Thou. and She*; *Io. Tu. Y. Ella* prod/rel: Fox Film Corp.

Primavera En Otono, Madrid 1911, Play
Primavera En Otono 1932 d: Eugene J. Forde. lps: Catalina Barcena, Antonio Moreno, Mimi AgugliA. 75M USA. prod/rel: Fox Film Corp.

Sueno de Una Noche de Agosto, Madrid 1918, Play
Viuda Romantica, Una 1933 d: Louis King. lps: Catalina Barcena, Gilbert Roland, Mona Maris. 73M USA. *The Romantic Widow* prod/rel: Fox Film Corp.

Tu Eres la Paz, 1906, Novel
Tu Eres la Paz 1942 d: Gregorio Martinez SierrA. lps: Alicia Barrie, Floren Delbene. 74M ARG.

MARTINI, FAUSTO MARIA
Cortile, Sketch
Cortile 1931 d: Carlo Campogalliani. lps: Ettore Petrolini, Dria Paola, Augusto Contardi. 25M ITL. prod/rel: Cines

Il Fiore Sotto Gli Occhi, Play
Fiore Sotto Gli Occhi, Il 1944 d: Guido Brignone. lps: Mariella Lotti, Claudio Gora, Luigi CimarA. 88M ITL. prod/rel: Generalcine, I.C.A.R.

MARTINI, MARIO
Viento Negro, Novel
Viento Negro 1964 d: Servando Gonzalez. lps: Jose Elias Moreno, David Reynoso, Enrique Lizalde. 105M MXC. *Black Wind* prod/rel: S.T.P.C.

MARTINO, LUCIANO
Ai Galli Piacciono le Stelle, Play
Ragazzi Dei Parioli, I 1959 d: Sergio Corbucci. lps: Raf Mattioli, Alessandra Panaro, Enio Girolami. 102M ITL. prod/rel: Ajace Produzione Cin.Che

MARTINSON, HARRY (1904–1978), SWD, Martinson, Harry Edmund
Vagen Till Klockrike, 1948, Novel
Vagen Till Klockrike 1953 d: Gunnar Skoglund. 102M SWD. *Road to Klockrike*

MARTOGLIO, NINO
L' Aria Del Continente, Play
  Aria Del Continente, L' 1935 d: Gennaro Righelli. lps: Angelo Musco, Leda Gloria, Rosina Anselmi. 84M ITL. *Continental Atmosphere* (USA) prod/rel: Capitani Film

Il Divo, Play
  Troppo Tardi T'ho Conosciuta 1940 d: Emanuele Caracciolo. lps: Alfredo de Sanctis, Christl School, Franco Lo Giudice. 78M ITL. prod/rel: Anonima Cin.Ca Impero, Cinef

Il Marchese Di Ruvolito, Play
  Marchese Di Ruvolito, Il 1939 d: Raffaello Matarazzo. lps: Eduardo de Filippo, Peppino de Filippo, Rosina Anselmi. 93M ITL. prod/rel: Irpinia Cin.Ca, Generalcine

O Pallio, 1906, Play
  Capitan Blanco, Il 1914 d: Nino Martoglio, Roberto Danesi. lps: Giovanni Grasso, Virginia Balistrieri, Toto MajoranA. 1300m ITL. prod/rel: Morgana Film

San Giuvanni Decullatu, 1908, Play
  San Giovanni Decollato 1917 d: Telemaco Ruggeri. lps: Angelo Musco, Lea Pasquali, Turi Pandolfini. 1670m ITL. prod/rel: Cinemadrama
  San Giovanni Decollato 1940 d: Amleto Palermi. lps: Toto, Titina de Filippo, Silvana Jachino. 87M ITL. prod/rel: Capitani Film, E.N.I.C.

Sua Eccellenza Di Falconmarzano, Play
  Sempre Piu Difficile 1943 d: Renato Angiolillo, Piero Ballerini. lps: Germana Paolieri, Nerio Bernardi, Adriano Rimoldi. 86M ITL. prod/rel: Incine, Scalera Film

MARTON, GEORGE
Catch Me a Spy, Novel
  Catch Me a Spy 1971 d: Dick Clement. lps: Kirk Douglas, Marlene Jobert, Trevor Howard. 94M UKN/USA/FRN. *Les Doigts Croises* (FRN); *To Catch a Spy* (USA); *Keep Your Fingers Crossed* prod/rel: Rank, Ludgate

Play Dirty, Novel
  Play Dirty 1968 d: Andre de Toth. lps: Michael Caine, Nigel Davenport, Nigel Green. 117M UKN. *Written on the Sand* prod/rel: United Artists, Lowndes

MARTOS, FRANZ
Alexandra, Play
  Princess Charming 1934 d: Maurice Elvey. lps: Evelyn Laye, Yvonne Arnaud, George Grossmith. 78M UKN. *The Escape of Princess Charming* prod/rel: Gainsborough, Gaumont-British

Sybil, Play
  Duchess of Buffalo, The 1926 d: Sidney A. Franklin. lps: Constance Talmadge, Tullio Carminati, Edward Martindel. 6940f USA. *Sybil* prod/rel: Constance Talmadge Productions, First National Pictures

MARTYN, WYNDHAM
All the World to Nothing, Boston 1912, Novel
  All the World to Nothing 1919 d: Henry King. lps: William Russell, Winifred Westover, Morris Foster. 6r USA. prod/rel: William Russell Productions, American Film Co.©

One Week-End, New York 1919, Novel
  Number 99 1920 d: Ernest C. Warde. lps: J. Warren Kerrigan, Fritzi Brunette, Emmett King. 4409f USA. *No.99* prod/rel: Robert Brunton Productions, W. W. Hodkinson Corp.

MARUYAMA, MICHIRO
Anatahan, Short Story
  Anatahan 1954 d: Josef von Sternberg. lps: Akemi Negishi, Tadashi Suganuma, Kisaburo SawamurA. 92M USA/JPN. *The Saga of Anatahan* prod/rel: Daiwa Productions-Towa, Pathe Contemporary

MARVEL, HOLT
Radio Play
  Goodnight Vienna 1932 d: Herbert Wilcox. lps: Jack Buchanan, Anna Neagle, Gina Malo. 76M UKN. *Magic Night* (USA) prod/rel: British and Dominions, Woolf & Freedman

Invitation to the Waltz, Radio Play
  Invitation to the Waltz 1935 d: Paul Merzbach. lps: Lilian Harvey, Carl Esmond, Harold Warrender. 77M UKN. prod/rel: British International Pictures, Wardour

MARX, ARTHUR
The Impossible Years, New York 1965, Play
  Impossible Years, The 1968 d: Michael Gordon. lps: David Niven, Lola Albright, Chad Everett. 99M USA. prod/rel: Marten Productions

MARY, JULES
Les Dernieres Cartouches, Novel
  Dernieres Cartouches, Les 1912. FRN. prod/rel: Films Jules Tallandier

En Detresse, Novel
  En Detresse 1918 d: Henri Pouctal. lps: Louis Delaunay, Jacques Normand, Margo WarnA. 1170m FRN. prod/rel: Film d'Art

La Fille Sauvage, Novel
  Fille Sauvage, La 1922 d: Henri Etievant. lps: Nathalie Lissenko, Romuald Joube, Irene Wells. SRL. 12EP FRN. prod/rel: Ermolieff

Le Grand-Pere, Play
  Grand-Pere, Le 1911 d: Georges DenolA. lps: Mosnier, Roger Monteaux, Berangere. 270m FRN. prod/rel: Scagl

La Maison du Mystere, Novel
  Maison du Mystere, La 1922 d: Alexander Volkov. lps: Ivan Mosjoukine, Helene Darly, Charles Vanel. SRL. 9630m FRN. prod/rel: Films Albatros

La Pocharde, Novel
  Pocharde, La 1921 d: Henri Etievant. lps: Jacqueline Forzane, Norville, Alexandre Volkoff. SRL. 12EP FRN. prod/rel: Ermolieff Film
  Pocharde, La 1936 d: Jean Kemm, Jean-Louis Bouquet. lps: Jean Debucourt, Bernard Lancret, Germaine Rouer. 87M FRN. prod/rel: Films Artistiques Francais
  Pocharde, La 1952 d: Georges Combret. lps: Pierre Brasseur, Monique Melinand, Alfred Adam. 92M FRN. prod/rel: Radius Production

Le Revanche de Roger la Honte, Novel
  Revanche de Roger-la-Honte, La 1946 d: Andre Cayatte. lps: Lucien Coedel, Maria Casares, Paulette Dubost. 90M FRN. prod/rel: Gray Films

Roger Larocque, Novel
  Victima Del Odio 1921 d: Jose Buchs. lps: Florian Rey, Carmen Otero, Angel Arribas. 1252m SPN. *Victim of Hate*; *Victima de la Calumnia* prod/rel: Atlantida (Madrid)

Roger-la-Honte, Novel
  Roger la Honte 1913 d: Adrien Caillard. lps: Paul Capellani, Georges Treville, Andree Pascal. 2150m FRN. prod/rel: Scagl
  Roger la Honte 1932 d: Gaston Roudes. lps: Constant Remy, Germaine Rouer, Samson Fainsilber. 95M FRN. prod/rel: Compagnie Cinematographique Continentale
  Roger la Honte 1966 d: Riccardo FredA. lps: Georges Geret, Irene Papas, Anne Vernon. 105M FRN/ITL. *Trappola Per l'Assassino* (ITL); *Trap for the Assassin* (USA) prod/rel: C.F.F.P., Produzione Mancori
  Roger-la-Honte 1922 d: Jacques de Baroncelli. lps: Gabriel Signoret, Rita Jolivet, Louise Sylvie. 2800m FRN. prod/rel: Film d'Art (Vandal Et Delac)
  Roger-la-Honte 1945 d: Andre Cayatte. lps: Lucien Coedel, Maria Casares, Paul Bernard. 100M FRN. prod/rel: Gray-Films

The Shadow of Roger Laroque, Novel
  Man of Shame, The 1915 d: Harry Myers. lps: Wilton Lackaye, Evelyn Dubois, Harry Myers. 5r USA. prod/rel: Universal Film Mfg. Co.©, Broadway Universal Feature

MAS, A.
El Punao de Rosas, Opera
  Punao de Rosas, El 1923 d: Rafael Salvador. lps: Angeles Ortiz, Pedro Fernandez Cuenca, Jose OrtegA. SPN. prod/rel: Rafael Salvador Films (Madrid)

MASCAGNI, PIETRO (1863–1945), ITL
Amica, Monte Carlo 1905, Opera
  Amica 1916 d: Enrico Guazzoni. lps: Leda Gys, Amleto Novelli, Nella MontagnA. 1212m ITL. prod/rel: Cines

MASCHWITZ, ERIC
Short Story
  Little Red Monkey 1953 d: Ken Hughes. lps: Richard Conte, Rona Anderson, Russell Napier. 74M UKN. *The Case of the Red Monkey* (USA) prod/rel: Anglo-Amalgamated, Merton Park

Balalaika, London 1936, Musical Play
  Balalaika 1939 d: Reinhold Schunzel. lps: Nelson Eddy, Ilona Massey, Charles Ruggles. 102M USA. prod/rel: Metro-Goldwyn-Mayer Corp.

Croquette, Novel
  Croquette 1927 d: Louis Mercanton. lps: Nicolas Koline, Betty Balfour, Rachel Devirys. F FRN. *Monkeynuts*; *Une Histoirs de Cirque*; *La Mome du Cirque* prod/rel: Louis Mercanton

Invitation to the Waltz, Radio Play
  Invitation to the Waltz 1935 d: Paul Merzbach. lps: Lilian Harvey, Carl Esmond, Harold Warrender. 77M UKN. prod/rel: British International Pictures, Wardour

MASEFIELD, JOHN (1878–1967), UKN
The Box of Delights, Novel
  Box of Delights, The 1984 d: Renny Rye. lps: Patrick Troughton, Devin Stanfield, Robert Stephens. TVM. 166M UKN. prod/rel: BBC

MASENZA, CLAUDIO
Le Faremo Tanto Male, Play
  Faremo Tanto Male, Le 1998 d: Pino Quartullo. lps: Stefania Sandrelli, Pino Quartullo, Ricky Memphis. 102M ITL. *We'll Really Hurt You* prod/rel: Italian Intl. Film, Blu Film

MASON, A. E. W. (1865–1948), UKN, Mason, Alfred Edward Woodley
At the Villa Rose, 1910, Novel
  At the Villa Rose 1920 d: Maurice Elvey. lps: Manora Thew, Langhorne Burton, Teddy Arundell. 7038f UKN. prod/rel: Stoll
  At the Villa Rose 1929 d: Leslie Hiscott. lps: Norah Baring, Austin Trevor, Richard Cooper. 100M UKN. *Mystery at the Villa Rose* (USA) prod/rel: Twickenham, Warner Bros.
  At the Villa Rose 1939 d: Walter Summers. lps: Keneth Kent, Judy Kelly, Walter RillA. 74M UKN. *House of Mystery* (USA); *The Human Ghost* prod/rel: Associated British Picture Corporation
  Mystere de la Villa Rose, Le 1929 d: Louis Mercanton, Rene Hervil. lps: Leon Mathot, Simone Vaudry, Louis Baron Fils. F FRN. *The Mystery of the Villa Rose* prod/rel: Etablissements Jacques Haik

The Broken Road, Novel
  Broken Road, The 1921 d: Rene Plaissetty. lps: Harry Ham, Mary Massart, Tony Fraser. 5224f UKN. prod/rel: Stoll

Colonel Smith, London 1909, Play
  Green Stockings 1916 d: Wilfred North. lps: Lillian Walker, Frank Currier, Louise Beaudet. 5r USA. prod/rel: Vitagraph Co. of America©, Blue Ribbon Feature

The Drum, 1937, Novel
  Drum, The 1938 d: Zoltan KordA. lps: Sabu, Raymond Massey, Valerie Hobson. 104M UKN. *Drums* (USA) prod/rel: United Artists, London Films

Fire Over England, 1936, Novel
  Fire Over England 1937 d: William K. Howard. lps: Laurence Olivier, Flora Robson, Leslie Banks. 92M UKN. prod/rel: Mayflower, Pendennis

The Four Feathers, London 1902, Novel
  Four Feathers 1915 d: J. Searle Dawley. lps: Howard Estabrook, Irene Warfield, Arthur Ewers. 5r USA. prod/rel: Dyreda Art Film Corp., Metro Pictures Corp.©
  Four Feathers, The 1929 d: Merian C. Cooper, Ernest B. Schoedsack. lps: Richard Arlen, Fay Wray, Clive Brook. 7472f USA. prod/rel: Paramount Famous Lasky Corp.
  Four Feathers, The 1921 d: Rene Plaissetty. lps: Harry Ham, Mary Massart, Cyril Percival. 6290f UKN. prod/rel: Stoll
  Four Feathers, The 1939 d: Zoltan KordA. lps: John Clements, Ralph Richardson, C. Aubrey Smith. 130M UKN. prod/rel: London Films, United Artists
  Four Feathers, The 1978 d: Don Sharp. lps: Beau Bridges, Robert Powell, Simon Ward. TVM. 100M UKN/USA. prod/rel: NBC, Trident Films Ltd.
  Storm Over the Nile 1955 d: Zoltan Korda, Terence Young. lps: Anthony Steel, Laurence Harvey, James Robertson Justice. 107M UKN. *The Four Feathers* prod/rel: London Films, Big Ben

Green Stockings, 1909, Play
  Flirting Widow, The 1930 d: William A. Seiter. lps: Dorothy MacKaill, Basil Rathbone, Leila Hyams. 70M USA. *Green Stockings* prod/rel: First National Pictures
  Her Imaginary Lover 1933 d: George King. lps: Laura La Plante, Percy Marmont, Lady Tree. 65M UKN. prod/rel: Warner Bros., First National

The House of the Arrow, London 1924, Novel
  House of the Arrow, The 1930 d: Leslie Hiscott. lps: Dennis Neilson-Terry, Benita Hume, Richard Cooper. 76M UKN. prod/rel: Twickenham, Warner Bros.
  House of the Arrow, The 1940 d: Harold French. lps: Keneth Kent, Diana Churchill, Belle Chrystal. 66M UKN. *Castle of Crimes* (USA) prod/rel: Associated British Picture Corporation
  House of the Arrow, The 1953 d: Michael Anderson. lps: Oscar Homolka, Yvonne Furneaux, Robert Urquhart. 73M UKN. prod/rel: Associated British Picture Corporation, Ab-Pathe
  Maison de la Fleche, La 1930 d: Henri Fescourt. lps: Leon Mathot, Alice Field, AnnabellA. 82M FRN. prod/rel: Etablissements Jacques Haik

Man and His Kingdom, Novel
  Man and His Kingdom 1922 d: Maurice Elvey. lps: Valia, Harvey Braban, Bertram Burleigh. 5438f UKN. prod/rel: Stoll

Miranda of the Balcony, Novel
Slaves of Destiny 1924 d: Maurice Elvey. lps: Matheson Lang, Valia, Henry Victor. 5150f UKN. *Miranda of the Balcony* prod/rel: Stoll

A Present from Margate, London 1933, Play
Widow from Monte Carlo 1936 d: Arthur G. Collins. lps: Dolores Del Rio, Warren William, Louise FazendA. 63M USA. *Meet the Duchess* prod/rel: Warner Bros. Productions Corp., Warner Bros. Pictures©

The Princess Clementina, Novel
Princess Clementina 1911 d: Will Barker. lps: H. B. Irving, Alice Young, Dorothea Baird. 1800f UKN. prod/rel: Barker

A Romance of Wastdale, Novel
Romance of Wastdale, A 1921 d: Maurice Elvey. lps: Milton Rosmer, Valia Venitskaya, Fred Raynham. 6060f UKN. prod/rel: Stoll

Running Water, Novel
Running Water 1922 d: Maurice Elvey. lps: Madge Stuart, Lawford Davidson, Julian Royce. 6075f UKN. prod/rel: Stoll

The Truants, Novel
Truants, The 1922 d: Sinclair Hill. lps: Joan Morgan, Philip Simmonds, Lawford Davidson. 5550f UKN. prod/rel: Stoll

The Winding Stair, New York 1923, Novel
Winding Stair, The 1925 d: John Griffith Wray. lps: Alma Rubens, Edmund Lowe, Warner Oland. 6r USA. prod/rel: Fox Film Corp.

The Witness for the Defence, London 1911, Play
Witness for the Defense, The 1919 d: George Fitzmaurice. lps: Elsie Ferguson, Vernon Steele, Warner Oland. 5r USA. prod/rel: Famous Players-Lasky Corp.©, Paramount-Artcraft Special

MASON, BASIL

The Ghosts of Mr. Pim, Play
Easy Money 1934 d: Redd Davis. lps: Mary Newland, Gerald Rawlinson, George Carney. 73M UKN. prod/rel: British and Dominions, Paramount British

Sign Please, Short Story
Brides to Be 1934 d: Reginald Denham. lps: Betty Stockfeld, Constance Shotter, Ronald Ward. 68M UKN. prod/rel: British and Dominions, Paramount British

MASON, BRUCE

The End of the Golden Weather, Play
End of the Golden Weather, The 1992 d: Ian Mune. lps: Stephen Fulford, Stephen Papps, Paul Gittins. 103M NZL. prod/rel: New Zealand Film Commission, South Pacific Pictures

MASON, EDITH HUNTINGTON

The Real Agatha, Novel
Real Agatha, The 1914 d: Richard C. Travers. lps: Oscar G. Briggs, Ruth Stonehouse, Helen Dunbar. 2r USA. prod/rel: Essanay

MASON, FRANK VAN WYCK (1901–1978), USA, Coffin, Geoffrey, Weaver, Ward

International Team, 1935, Short Story
Spy Ring, The 1938 d: Joseph H. Lewis. lps: William Hall, Jane Wyman, Jane Carleton. 65M USA. *International Spy* prod/rel: Universal Pictures Co.

MASON, GRACE SARTWELL

Clarissa and the Post Road, 1923, Short Story
Man Crazy 1927 d: John Francis Dillon. lps: Dorothy MacKaill, Jack Mulhall, Edythe Chapman. 5542f USA. prod/rel: Charles R. Rogers Productions, First National Pictures

Our Miss Keane, 1923, Short Story
Honeymoon in Bali 1939 d: Edward H. Griffith. lps: Fred MacMurray, Madeleine Carroll, Allan Jones. 95M USA. *Husbands Or Lovers* (UKN); *Husbands and Lovers*; *My Love for Yours*; **Are Husbands Necessary?** prod/rel: Paramount Pictures©

The Shadow of Rosalie Byrnes, New York 1919, Novel
Shadow of Rosalie Byrnes, The 1920 d: George Archainbaud. lps: Elaine Hammerstein, Edward Langford, Anita Booth. 5420f USA. *Rosalie Byrnes* prod/rel: Selznick Pictures Corp.©, Select Pictures Corp.

MASON, HOWARD

Photo Finish, London 1954, Novel
Follow That Horse! 1960 d: Alan Bromly. lps: David Tomlinson, Cecil Parker, Richard Wattis. 79M UKN. prod/rel: Cavalcade Films, Warner-Pathe

MASON, RICHARD

The Shadow and the Peak, Novel
Passionate Summer 1958 d: Rudolph Cartier. lps: Virginia McKenna, Bill Travers, Yvonne Mitchell. 104M UKN. *Storm in Jamaica* prod/rel: Briar, Rank Film Distributors

The Wind Cannot Read, Novel
Wind Cannot Read, The 1958 d: Ralph Thomas. lps: Dirk Bogarde, Yoko Tani, John Fraser. 115M UKN. prod/rel: Rank, Rank Film Distributors

The World of Suzie Wong, Novel
World of Suzie Wong, The 1960 d: Richard Quine. lps: William Holden, Nancy Kwan, Sylvia Syms. 126M UKN/USA. prod/rel: Paramount British

MASON, ROBERT

Weapon, Novel
Solo 1996 d: Norberto BarbA. lps: Mario Van Peebles, Barry Corbin, Bill Sadler. 94M USA. prod/rel: John Flock, Orpheus Films

MASS, VLADIMIR

Cheryomushki Moskva, Moscow 1959, Opera
Cheryomushki 1963 d: Herbert Rappaport. lps: Olga Zabotkina, Vladimir Vasilyev, M. KhotuntsevA. 92M USS. *Song Over Moscow* (USA); *Wild Cherry Trees*; *Cheremushki* prod/rel: Lenfilm

MASSARD, ARMAND

Alcide Pepie, Play
Alcide Pepie 1934 d: Rene Jayet. lps: Alice Tissot, Emile Seylis, Marcel Le Marchand. 26M FRN. prod/rel: Pathe Consortium Cinema

MASSIE, CHRIS

Corridor of Mirrors, Novel
Corridor of Mirrors 1948 d: Terence Young. lps: Eric Portman, Edana Romney, Barbara Mullen. 105M UKN. prod/rel: Apollo Films, General Film Distributors

Pity My Simplicity, Novel
Love Letters 1945 d: William Dieterle. lps: Jennifer Jones, Joseph Cotten, Ann Richards. 101M USA. prod/rel: Paramount

MASSIE, ROBERT K.

Nicholas and Alexandria, Book
Nicholas and Alexandra 1971 d: Franklin J. Schaffner. lps: Michael Jayston, Janet Suzman, Roderic Noble. 189M UKN. prod/rel: Columbia, Horizon

Peter the Great, Book
Peter the Great 1985 d: Marvin J. Chomsky, Lawrence Schiller. lps: Maximilian Schell, Ursula Andress, Omar Sharif. TVM. 366M USA.

MASSIERA, LEOPOLD

Du Sang Sous le Chapiteau, Novel
Du Sang Sous le Chapiteau 1956 d: Georges Peclet. lps: Achille Zavatta, Ginette Leclerc, Serge Davin. 85M FRN. prod/rel: Societe Francaise De Production

MASSON, RENE

Les Gamins du Roi de Sicile, Novel
Jeux Dangereux 1958 d: Pierre Chenal. lps: Pascale Audret, Jean Servais, Joel Flateau. 95M FRN/ITL. *Dangerous Games* (USA) prod/rel: Metzger Et Woog, Zodiaque Production

Pantalaskas, Novel
Pantalaskas 1959 d: Paul Paviot. lps: Julien Carette, Carl Studer, Hubert Deschamps. 90M FRN. prod/rel: Pavox Films, Alter Films

MASSON-FORESTIER

Attaque Nocturne, Play
Attaque Nocturne 1931 d: Marc Allegret. lps: Fernandel, Madeleine Guitty, Emile Saint-Ober. 25M FRN. prod/rel: Braunberger-Richebe

MASTERS, E. LANNING

The Primrose Path, Story
Primrose Path, The 1925 d: Harry O. Hoyt. lps: Wallace MacDonald, Clara Bow, Arline Pretty. 6r USA. prod/rel: Arrow Pictures

MASTERS, JOHN (1914–1983), IND

Bhowani Junction, 1954, Novel
Bhowani Junction 1956 d: George Cukor. lps: Ava Gardner, Stewart Granger, Bill Travers. 109M UKN/USA. prod/rel: Metro-Goldwyn-Mayer British

The Deceivers, Novel
Deceivers, The 1988 d: Nicholas Meyer. lps: Pierce Brosnan, Shashi Kapoor, Saeed Jaffrey. 112M UKN/IND. prod/rel: Merchant-Ivory, Michael White

MASTERSON, PETER

The Best Little Whorehouse in Texas, Play
Best Little Whorehouse in Texas, The 1982 d: Colin Higgins. lps: Burt Reynolds, Dolly Parton, Dom Deluise. 114M USA. prod/rel: Universal, RKO

MASTERSON, WHIT

711 - Officer Needs Help, New York 1965, Novel
Warning Shot 1967 d: Buzz Kulik. lps: David Janssen, Ed Begley, Keenan Wynn. 100M USA. prod/rel: Bob Banner Associates

All Throught the Night, 1955, Novel
Cry in the Night, A 1956 d: Frank Tuttle. lps: Edmond O'Brien, Brian Donlevy, Natalie Wood. 75M USA. prod/rel: Warner Bros., Jaguar Prods.

Badge of Evil, 1955, Novel
Touch of Evil 1958 d: Orson Welles. lps: Orson Welles, Charlton Heston, Janet Leigh. 95M USA. prod/rel: Universal-International

The Death of Me Yet, Novel
Death of Me Yet, The 1971 d: John Llewellyn Moxey. lps: Doug McClure, Darren McGavin, Rosemary Forsyth. TVM. 74M USA. prod/rel: Aaron Spelling Productions

Evil Go Evil Come, New York 1961, Novel
Yellow Canary, The 1963 d: Buzz Kulik. lps: Pat Boone, Barbara Eden, Steve Forrest. 93M USA. *Evil Go Evil Come* prod/rel: Cooga Mooga Film Productions

MASTERTON, GRAHAM

The Manitou, Novel
Manitou, The 1978 d: William Girdler. lps: Susan Strasberg, Tony Curtis, Michael AnsarA. 105M USA. prod/rel: William Girdler Films

MASTORAKIS, NICO (1941–, GRC

The Greek Tycoon, Novel
Greek Tycoon, The 1978 d: J. Lee Thompson. lps: Anthony Quinn, Jacqueline Bisset, Raf Vallone. 107M USA. prod/rel: Universal

MASTRIANI, FRANCESCO

Il Barcaiolo Di Amalfi, Novel
Barcaiolo Di Amalfi, Il 1958 d: Mino Roli. lps: Franca Marzi, Mario Vitale, Guido Celano. F ITL. *Il Barcaiolo d'Amalfi* prod/rel: Siro Film, Regionale

La Cieca Di Sorrento, 1826, Novel
Cieca Di Sorrento, La 1916 d: Gustavo SerenA. lps: Gustavo Serena, Olga Benetti, Lea Giunchi. 1544m ITL. prod/rel: Caesar Film

Cieca Di Sorrento, La 1934 d: Nunzio MalasommA. lps: Dria Paola, Corrado Racca, Anna Magnani. 68M ITL. prod/rel: Manenti Film

Cieca Di Sorrento, La 1952 d: Giacomo Gentilomo. lps: Antonella Lualdi, Paul Campbell, Enzo Biliotti. 93M ITL. prod/rel: Astoria Film

Prigionieri Delle Tenebre 1953 d: Enrico BombA. lps: Milly Vitale, Folco Lulli, Eduardo Ciannelli. 88M ITL. prod/rel: Bomba & C.

Francesco Lannois, 1851, Novel
Mio Cadavere, Il 1917 d: Anton Giulio Bragaglia, Riccardo Cassano (Uncredited). lps: Ida Querio, Mario Parpagnoli, Nello Carotenuto. 1380m ITL. prod/rel: Novissima Film

Medea Di Portamedina, 1882, Novel
Medea Di Portamedina 1919 d: Elvira Notari. lps: Mary Cavaliere, Umberto Mucci, Isabella Zanchi. 1444m ITL. prod/rel: Films Dora

Le Ombre, 1883, Play
Ombre, Le 1918 d: Oreste Gherardini. lps: Federico Stella, Tina Somma, Rita AlmanovA. 1690m ITL. prod/rel: Saneff

La Sepolta Viva, Novel
Sepolta Viva, La 1949 d: Guido Brignone. lps: Milly Vitale, Evi Maltagliati, Paul Muller. 95M ITL. *Buried Alive* prod/rel: Flora Film, Variety Film

MASTRONARDI, LUCIO

Il Maestro Di Vigevano, Novel
Maestro Di Vigevano, Il 1963 d: Elio Petri. lps: Alberto Sordi, Claire Bloom, Vito de Taranto. 100M ITL. *The School Teacher from Vigevano* prod/rel: Dino de Laurentiis Cin.Ca

MASTROSIMONE, WILLIAM

Extremities, Play
Extremities 1986 d: Robert M. Young. lps: Farrah Fawcett, James Russo, Diana Scarwid. 89M USA. prod/rel: Atlantic Releasing Corporation

Nanawatai, Play
Beast, The 1988 d: Kevin Reynolds. lps: George Dzundza, Jason Patric, Steven Bauer. 109M USA. *The Beast of War* prod/rel: Columbia

MATA, PEDRO

Novel
Herzen Ohne Ziel 1928 d: Gustav Ucicky, Benito Perojo. lps: Hanna Ralph, Livio Pavanelli, Betty Bird. 1888m GRM/SPN. *Corazones Sin Rumbo* (SPN); *Hearts Without Destination* prod/rel: Julio Cesar (Madrid), Phoebus Films (Munich)

MATALON, RONIT

Book
Sipur Shematchil Belevaya Shel Nachash 1993 d: Dina Zvi-Riklis. lps: Moshe IVgi, Rita Shukrun, Levana Finkelstein. 85M ISR. *Sipor Sh'matchil Be'halvayah Shel Nachash*; *Dreams of Innocence*

MATAVULJ, SIMO

Bakonja Fra Brne, 1892, Novel
Bakonja Fra Brne 1951 d: Fedor Hanzekovic. lps: Milan Ajvaz, Misa Mirkovic, Mira StupicA. 104M YGS.

MATHER, ANN
Leopard in the Snow, Novel
 Leopard in the Snow 1977 d: Gerry O'HarA. lps: Keir Dullea, Susan Penhaligon, Kenneth More. 94M UKN/CND. prod/rel: Seastone Productions Ltd. (London), Leopard in the Snow Ltd. (Toronto)

MATHER, BERKELEY
Information Received, Novel
 Information Received 1961 d: Robert Lynn. lps: Sabina Sesselmann, William Sylvester, Hermione Baddeley. 77M UKN. prod/rel: United Co-Production, Rank Film Distributors

MATHERS, HELEN
Cherry Ripe, Novel
 Cherry Ripe 1921 d: Kenelm Foss. lps: Mary Odette, Lionelle Howard, Roy Travers. 5000f UKN. prod/rel: Astra Films
Comin' Thro' the Rye, Novel
 Comin' Thro' the Rye 1916 d: Cecil M. Hepworth. lps: Alma Taylor, Stewart Rome, Margaret Blanche. 5600f UKN. prod/rel: Hepworth, Harma
 Comin' Thro' the Rye 1923 d: Cecil M. Hepworth. lps: Alma Taylor, Shayle Gardner, Eileen Dennes. 7900f UKN. prod/rel: Hepworth Picture Plays

MATHESON, C. M.
The Feather, Novel
 Feather, The 1929 d: Leslie Hiscott. lps: Jameson Thomas, Vera Flory, Randle Ayrton. 90M UKN. prod/rel: Strand Films, United Artists

MATHESON, RICHARD (1926–, USA
The Beardless Warriors, Boston 1960, Novel
 Young Warriors, The 1967 d: John Peyser. lps: James Drury, Steve Carlson, Jonathan Daly. 93M USA. *The Beardless Warriors*; *Eagle Warriors* prod/rel: Universal Pictures
Bid Time Return, Novel
 Somewhere in Time 1980 d: Jeannot Szwarc. lps: Christopher Reeve, Jane Seymour, Christopher Plummer. 104M USA. prod/rel: Universal
Duel, Short Story
 Duel 1971 d: Steven Spielberg. lps: Dennis Weaver, Jacqueline Scott, Eddie Firestone. TVM. 90M USA. prod/rel: Universal
Dying Room Only, Short Story
 Dying Room Only 1973 d: Philip Leacock. lps: Cloris Leachman, Ross Martin, Ned Beatty. TVM. 73M USA. prod/rel: Lorimar
Hell House, Novel
 Legend of Hell House, The 1973 d: John Hough. lps: Clive Revill, Pamela Franklin, Roddy McDowall. 94M UKN/USA. prod/rel: 20th Century Fox, Academy
I Am Legend, New York 1954, Novel
 Omega Man, The 1971 d: Boris Sagal. lps: Charlton Heston, Anthony Zerbe, Rosalind Cash. 98M USA. *I Am Legend* prod/rel: Warner Bros.
 Ultimo Uomo Della Terra, L' 1964 d: Ubaldo Ragona, Sidney Salkow. lps: Vincent Price, Franca Bettoja, Emma Danieli. 86M ITL/USA. *The Last Man on Earth* (USA); *The Night Creatures*; *Vento Di Morte*; *Wind of Death*; *Vento Di Montagna* prod/rel: la Regina Cin.Ca, Associated Producers, Inc.
Julie, Short Story
 Trilogy of Terror 1975 d: Dan Curtis. lps: Karen Black, Robert Burton, John Karlen. TVM. 78M USA. prod/rel: ABC Circle Films
Millicent and Therese, Short Story
 Trilogy of Terror 1975 d: Dan Curtis. lps: Karen Black, Robert Burton, John Karlen. TVM. 78M USA. prod/rel: ABC Circle Films
Prey, Short Story
 Trilogy of Terror 1975 d: Dan Curtis. lps: Karen Black, Robert Burton, John Karlen. TVM. 78M USA. prod/rel: ABC Circle Films
Ride the Nightmare, Novel
 Cold Sweat 1971 d: Terence Young. lps: Charles Bronson, Liv Ullmann, James Mason. 94M UKN/FRN/ITL. *De la Part Des Copains* (FRN); *L' Uomo Dalle Due Ombre* (ITL) prod/rel: Fair Film (Roma), Corona
The Shrinking Man, Novel
 Incredible Shrinking Man, The 1957 d: Jack Arnold. lps: Grant Williams, Randy Stuart, April Kent. 81M USA. prod/rel: Universal-International
 Incredible Shrinking Woman, The 1981 d: Joel Schumacher. lps: Lily Tomlin, Charles Grodin, Ned Beatty. 89M USA. prod/rel: Universal
Someone Is Bleeding, Novel
 Seins de Glace, Les 1974 d: Georges Lautner. lps: Alain Delon, Mireille Darc, Claude Brasseur. 120M FRN/ITL. *Esecutore Oltre la Legge* (ITL); *Someone Is Bleeding* (UKN); *Icy Breasts* (USA) prod/rel: Capitolina Produzioni Cin.Che (Roma), Lira

The Stranger Within, Short Story
 Stranger Within, The 1974 d: Lee Philips. lps: Barbara Eden, Nehemiah Persoff, George Grizzard. TVM. 78M USA. *Trespass* prod/rel: Lorimar Productions
What Dreams May Come, Novel
 What Dreams May Come 1998 d: Vincent Ward. lps: Robin Williams, Cuba Gooding Jr., Annabella SciorrA. 113M USA/NZL. prod/rel: Polygram Films, Polygram Filmed Entertainment©

MATHEWS, FRANCES AYMAR
Where Did Lottie Go?, Short Story
 Thirteenth Girl, The 1915 d: Theodore Marston. lps: Arline Pretty, Julia Swayne Gordon, Lillian Burns. 3r USA. prod/rel: Broadway Star, Vitagraph Co. of America

MATHIES, PAUL
Matura-Reise, Berne 1942, Novel
 Leben Beginnt, Das 1942 d: Sigfrit Steiner. lps: Anne-Marie Blanc, Margrit Winter, Blanchette Aubrey. 88M SWT. *Maturareise*; *Jeunes Filles Aujourd'hui* prod/rel: Gloria, Zurich

MATHIESSEN, PETER
At Play in the Fields of the Lord, Novel
 At Play in the Fields of the Lord 1991 d: Hector Babenco. lps: Tom Berenger, Aidan Quinn, Kathy Bates. 187M USA/BRZ. *Brincando Nos Campos Do Senhor* (BRZ); *Jugando En Los Campos de Senor* prod/rel: Saul Zaentz Company

MATSCHER, HANS
Spiel Auf Der Tenne, Novel
 Spiel Auf Der Tenne 1937 d: Georg Jacoby. lps: Heli Finkenzeller, Richard Haussler, Joe Stockel. 84M GRM. prod/rel: Euphono

MATSCHNERS, HANS
Jungfrauenkrieg, Novel
 Jungfrauenkrieg 1957 d: Hermann Kugelstadt. lps: Oskar Sima, Heinrich Gretler, Lucie Englisch. 92M AUS. prod/rel: Ofa, Schonbrunn

MATSUURA, TAKEO
Rabu Reta, Novel
 Rabu Reta 1959 d: Seijun Suzuki. lps: Kyosuke MaChida, Frank Nagai, Hisako TsukubA. 40M JPN. *Love Letter* prod/rel: Nikkatsu Corporation

MATTHEWS, ADELAIDE
The First Mrs. Chiverick, Play
 Scrambled Wives 1921 d: Edward H. Griffith. lps: Marguerite Clark, Leon P. Gendron, Ralph Bunker. 6460f USA. prod/rel: Marguerite Clark Productions, Associated First National Pictures
Just Married, Play
 Just Married 1928 d: Frank Strayer. lps: James Hall, Ruth Taylor, Harrison Ford. 6039f USA. prod/rel: Paramount Famous Lasky Corp.
The Teaser, New York 1921, Play
 Teaser, The 1925 d: William A. Seiter. lps: Laura La Plante, Pat O'Malley, Hedda Hopper. 6800f USA. prod/rel: Universal Pictures

MATTHIAS, PAUL
Matura-Reise, Berne 1942, Novel
 Jeunes Filles d'Aujourd'hui 1942 d: Sigfrit Steiner, Jacques Feyder. lps: Anne-Marie Blanc, Blanche Aubry, Marion Cherbuliez. 101M SWT. *Matura-Reise*; *Jeunes Filles Sans Uniforme*; *Gita Premio Ne Ticino*; *Das Leben Beginnt* prod/rel: Gloriafilm

MATTHIESSEN, PETER (1927–, USA
Travelin' Man, 1957, Short Story
 Young One, The 1960 d: Luis Bunuel. lps: Zachary Scott, Key Meersman, Bernie Hamilton. 96M MXC. *Island of Shame* (UKN); *La Joven*; *La Jeune Fille* prod/rel: Producciones Olmeca

MATTSON, OLLE
Briggen Tre Liljor, Book
 Briggen Tre Liljor 1961 d: Hans Abramson. lps: Siggi Furst, Eddie Axberg, Annika Lindkog. 87M SWD. *The Brig "Three Lilies"* prod/rel: Ab Svensk Filmindustri

MATTSSON, GUNNAR
Prinsessan, Stockholm 1960, Novel
 Prinsessan 1966 d: Ake Falck. lps: Grynet Molvig, Lars Passgard, Monica Nielsen. 104M SWD. *A Time in the Sun* (USA); *The Princess* prod/rel: Europa Film

MAUCH, THOMAS
Wallers Letzter Gang, Novel
 Wallers Letzter Gang 1988 d: Christian Wagner. lps: Rolf Illig, Herbert Knaup, Sibylle CanonicA. 100M GRM. *Waller's Last Run* prod/rel: Christian Wagner Filmproduktion, B.R.

MAUDRU, PIERRE
Le Talion, Play
 Talion, Le 1921 d: Charles Maudru. lps: Gaston Jacquet, Yane Exiane, Georges Lannes. 1620m FRN. prod/rel: le Lys Rouge (Maurice De Marsan)

MAUGHAM, ROBIN (1916–1981), UKN, Maugham, Lord Robert Cecil Romer
Line on Ginger, 1949, Novel
 Intruder, The 1953 d: Guy Hamilton. lps: Jack Hawkins, George Cole, Dennis Price. 84M UKN. prod/rel: British Lion, Ivan Foxwell
The Rough and the Smooth, London 1951, Novel
 Rough and the Smooth, The 1959 d: Robert Siodmak. lps: Nadja Tiller, Tony Britton, William Bendix. 99M UKN. *Portrait of a Sinner* (USA) prod/rel: Renown, George Minter
The Servant, London 1948, Novel
 Servant, The 1963 d: Joseph Losey. lps: Dirk Bogarde, Sarah Miles, Wendy Craig. 115M UKN. prod/rel: Springbok Films, Elstree
The Slaves of Timbuktu, Book
 Schiave Esistono Ancora, Le 1964 d: Roberto Malenotti, Folco Quilici. DOC. 100M ITL/FRN. *Les Esclaves Existent Toujours* (FRN); *Slave Trade in the World Today* (USA) prod/rel: Ge.Si. Cinematografica, C.I.S.A. (Roma)

MAUGHAM, W. SOMERSET (1874–1965), UKN
The Alien Corn, 1940, Short Story
 Quartet 1948 d: Arthur Crabtree, Ralph Smart. lps: Dirk Bogarde, Francoise Rosay, Raymond Lovell. UKN.
The Ant & the Grasshopper, 1936, Short Story
 Encore 1951 d: Harold French, Pat Jackson. lps: Nigel Patrick, Roland Culver, Alison Leggatt. 86M UKN. prod/rel: General Film Distributors, Two Cities
The Beachcomber, 1931, Short Story
 Vessel of Wrath 1938 d: Erich Pommer. lps: Charles Laughton, Elsa Lanchester, Robert Newton. 93M UKN. *The Beachcomber* (USA) prod/rel: Mayflower, Associated British Picture Corporation
Caesar's Wife, London 1919, Play
 Another Dawn 1937 d: William Dieterle. lps: Kay Francis, Errol Flynn, Ian Hunter. 73M USA. *Caesar's Wife* prod/rel: Warner Bros. Pictures, Inc.
 Infatuation 1925 d: Irving Cummings. lps: Corinne Griffith, Percy Marmont, Malcolm McGregor. 5794f USA. prod/rel: Corinne Griffith Productions, First National Pictures
Christmas Holiday, 1939, Novel
 Christmas Holiday 1944 d: Robert Siodmak. lps: Deanna Durbin, Gene Kelly, Richard Whorf. 92M USA. prod/rel: Universal
The Circle, London 1921, Play
 Circle, The 1925 d: Frank Borzage. lps: Eleanor Boardman, Malcolm McGregor, Alec B. Francis. 5511f USA. prod/rel: Metro-Goldwyn-Mayer Pictures
 Strictly Unconventional 1930 d: David Burton. lps: Catherine Dale Owen, Paul Cavanagh, Tyrrell Davis. 60M USA. *The Circle* prod/rel: Metro-Goldwyn-Mayer Pictures
Colonel's Lady, 1947, Short Story
 Quartet 1948 d: Ken Annakin, Harold French. lps: Cecil Parker, Nora Swinburne, Linden Travers. 120M UKN. *Somerset Maugham's Quartet* prod/rel: General Film Distributors, Gainsborough
The Constant Wife, New York 1926, Play
 Charming Sinners 1929 d: Robert Milton, Dorothy Arzner. lps: Ruth Chatterton, Clive Brook, Mary Nolan. 66M USA. *The Constant Wife* (UKN) prod/rel: Paramount Famous Lasky Corp.
 Finden Sie, Dass Constanze Sich Richtig Verhalt? 1962 d: Tom Pevsner. lps: Lilli Palmer, Peter Van Eyck, Carlos Thompson. 81M GRM. *The Constant Wife*; *Is Constance Acting Right?* prod/rel: Peter Goldbaum, Europa
East of Suez, London 1922, Play
 East of Suez 1925 d: Raoul Walsh. lps: Pola Negri, Edmund Lowe, Rockliffe Fellowes. 6716f USA. prod/rel: Famous Players-Lasky, Paramount Pictures
The Explorer, London 1909, Novel
 Explorer, The 1915 d: George Melford. lps: Lou Tellegen, James Neill, Dorothy Davenport. 5r USA. prod/rel: Jesse L. Lasky Feature Play Co.©, Paramount Pictures Corp.
The Facts of Life, 1940, Short Story
 Quartet 1948 d: Arthur Crabtree, Ralph Smart. lps: Dirk Bogarde, Francoise Rosay, Raymond Lovell. UKN.
Gigolo and Gigolette, 1940, Short Story
 Encore 1951 d: Anthony Pelissier. lps: Terence Morgan, David Hutcheson, Charles Goldner. UKN.
The Hairless Mexican, 1928, Short Story
 Secret Agent, The 1936 d: Alfred Hitchcock. lps: Madeleine Carroll, Peter Lorre, Robert Young. 85M UKN. prod/rel: Gaumont British
The Hour Before the Dawn, 1942, Novel
 Hour Before the Dawn, The 1944 d: Frank Tuttle. lps: Franchot Tone, Veronica Lake, Binnie Barnes. 75M USA. prod/rel: Paramount

Jack Straw, New York 1908, Play
Jack Straw 1920 d: William C. de Mille. lps: Robert Warwick, Carroll McComas, Sylvia Ashton. 4707f USA. prod/rel: Famous Players-Lasky Corp.©, Paramount-Artcraft Pictures

The Kite, 1931, Short Story
Quartet 1948 d: Ken Annakin, Harold French. lps: Cecil Parker, Nora Swinburne, Linden Travers. 120M UKN. *Somerset Maugham's Quartet* prod/rel: General Film Distributors, Gainsborough

Lady Frederick, London 1907, Play
Divorcee, The 1919 d: Herbert Blache. lps: Ethel Barrymore, Holmes Herbert, E. J. Radcliffe. 5r USA. *Lady Frederick* prod/rel: Metro Pictures Corp.©

The Land of Promise, London 1913, Play
Canadian, The 1926 d: William Beaudine. lps: Thomas Meighan, Mona Palma, Wyndham Standing. 7753f USA. prod/rel: Famous Players-Lasky, Paramount Pictures
Land of Promise, The 1917 d: Joseph Kaufman. lps: Billie Burke, Thomas Meighan, Helen Tracy. 5r USA. prod/rel: Famous Players Film Co.©, Paramount Pictures Corp.

The Letter, 1925, Short Story
Donna Bianca, La 1931 d: Jack Salvatori. lps: Matilde Casagrande, Carlo Lombardi, Lamberto Picasso. 60M FRN. prod/rel: Paramount
Letter, The 1929 d: Monta Bell, Jean de Limur. lps: Jeanne Eagels, O. P. Heggie, Reginald Owen. 61M USA. prod/rel: Paramount Famous Lasky Corp.
Letter, The 1940 d: William Wyler. lps: Bette Davis, Herbert Marshall, James Stephenson. 95M USA. prod/rel: Warner Bros. Pictures©
Letter, The 1982 d: John Erman. lps: Lee Remick, Ronald Pickup, Jack Thompson. TVM. 100M USA. prod/rel: Hajero Productions
Lettre, La 1930 d: Louis Mercanton. lps: Marcelle Romee, Gabriel Gabrio, Paul Capellani. 7r FRN. prod/rel: Films Paramount, Paramount-Publix Copr.
Unfaithful, The 1947 d: Vincent Sherman. lps: Ann Sheridan, Zachary Scott, Lew Ayres. 109M USA. prod/rel: Warner Bros.
Weib Im Dschungel 1930 d: Dimitri Buchowetzki. lps: Charlotte Ander, Ernst Stahl-Nachbaur, Erich Ponto. 61M FRN.

The Magician, London 1908, Novel
Magician, The 1926 d: Rex Ingram. lps: Alice Terry, Paul Wegener, Ivan Petrovich. 6960f USA. prod/rel: Metro-Goldwyn-Mayer Pictures

The Moon and Sixpence, 1919, Novel
Moon and Sixpence, The 1942 d: Albert Lewin. lps: George Sanders, Herbert Marshall, Doris Dudley. 89M USA. prod/rel: United Artists

Mr. Knowall, 1947, Short Story
Trio 1950 d: Ken Annakin, Harold French. lps: James Hayter, Kathleen Harrison, Felix Aylmer. 91M UKN. prod/rel: General Film Distributors, Gainsborough

The Narrow Corner, London 1932, Novel
Isle of Fury 1936 d: Frank McDonald. lps: Humphrey Bogart, Margaret Lindsay, Donald Woods. 60M USA. *Three in Eden* prod/rel: Warner Bros. Pictures©
Narrow Corner, The 1933 d: Alfred E. Green. lps: Douglas Fairbanks Jr., Patricia Ellis, Ralph Bellamy. 71M USA. prod/rel: Warner Bros. Pictures©

Of Human Bondage, London 1915, Novel
Of Human Bondage 1934 d: John Cromwell. lps: Leslie Howard, Bette Davis, Frances Dee. 83M USA. prod/rel: RKO Radio Pictures©, Pandro S. Berman Production
Of Human Bondage 1946 d: Edmund Goulding. lps: Eleanor Parker, Paul Henreid, Alexis Smith. 105M USA. prod/rel: Warner Bros.
Of Human Bondage 1964 d: Ken Hughes, Henry Hathaway (Uncredited). lps: Kim Novak, Laurence Harvey, Robert Morley. 99M UKN/USA. prod/rel: Seven Arts Productions, MGM

Our Betters, New York 1917, Play
Our Betters 1933 d: George Cukor. lps: Constance Bennett, Gilbert Roland, Charles Starrett. 80M USA. prod/rel: RKO Radio Pictures©

The Painted Veil, New York 1925, Novel
Painted Veil, The 1934 d: Richard Boleslawski, W. S. Van Dyke (Uncredited). lps: Greta Garbo, Herbert Marshall, George Brent. 84M USA. prod/rel: Metro-Goldwyn-Mayer Corp.©
Seventh Sin, The 1957 d: Ronald Neame, Vincente Minnelli (Uncredited). lps: Eleanor Parker, Bill Travers, George Sanders. 93M USA. prod/rel: Metro-Goldwyn-Mayer Corp.

Rain, 1921, Short Story
Miss Sadie Thompson 1953 d: Curtis Bernhardt. lps: Rita Hayworth, Jose Ferrer, Aldo Ray. 91M USA. prod/rel: Columbia, Beckwith Corp.
Rain 1932 d: Lewis Milestone. lps: Joan Crawford, Walter Huston, William Gargan. 93M USA. prod/rel: United Artists Corp., Feature Productions©
Sadie 1980 d: Robert C. Chinn. lps: Chris Cassidy, Jerome Deeds, Gary DanA. 88M USA.
Sadie Thompson 1928 d: Raoul Walsh. lps: Gloria Swanson, Lionel Barrymore, Raoul Walsh. 8600f USA. prod/rel: Gloria Swanson Productions, United Artists

The Razor's Edge, 1944, Novel
Razor's Edge, The 1946 d: Edmund Goulding. lps: Tyrone Power, Gene Tierney, John Payne. 146M USA. prod/rel: 20th Century-Fox
Razor's Edge, The 1984 d: John Byrum. lps: Bill Murray, Theresa Russell, Catherine Hicks. 130M USA. prod/rel: Columbia

The Sacred Flame, New York 1928, Play
Heilige Flamme, Die 1931 d: Berthold Viertel, William Dieterle. lps: Gustav Frohlich, Dita Parlo, Hans Heinrich von Twardowski. 86M GRM.
Llama Sagrada, La 1931 d: William McGann. lps: Elvira Morla, Martin Garralaga, Luana Alcaniz. 7r USA. *Amor Contra Amor* prod/rel: Warner Bros. Pictures©
Right to Live, The 1935 d: William Keighley. lps: Josephine Hutchinson, George Brent, Colin Clive. 73M USA. *The Sacred Flame* (UKN); *The Future Belongs to You* prod/rel: Warner Bros. Productions Corp., Warner Bros. Pictures©
Sacred Flame, The 1929 d: Archie Mayo. lps: Pauline Frederick, Conrad Nagel, William Courtenay. 6051f USA. prod/rel: Warner Brothers Pictures

Sanatorium, 1947, Short Story
Trio 1950 d: Ken Annakin, Harold French. lps: James Hayter, Kathleen Harrison, Felix Aylmer. 91M UKN. prod/rel: General Film Distributors, Gainsborough

Smith, London 1909, Play
Smith 1917 d: Maurice Elvey. lps: Elisabeth Risdon, Fred Groves, Manora Thew. 3440f UKN. prod/rel: London, Jury

The Tenth Man, 1913, Play
Tenth Man, The 1936 d: Brian Desmond Hurst. lps: John Lodge, Antoinette Cellier, Aileen Marson. 68M UKN. prod/rel: British International Pictures, Wardour

Theatre, 1941, Play
Julia, du Bist Zauberhaft 1962 d: Alfred Weidenmann. lps: Lilli Palmer, Jean Sorel, Jeanne Valerie. 97M AUS/FRN. *Adorable Julia* (FRN); *Adorable Julie*; *The Seduction of Julia* prod/rel: Productions de L'etoile, Wiener Mundus

Too Many Husbands, Atlantic City, N.J. 1919, Play
Three for the Show 1955 d: H. C. Potter. lps: Betty Grable, Jack Lemmon, Gower Champion. 93M USA. prod/rel: Columbia
Too Many Husbands 1940 d: Wesley Ruggles. lps: Jean Arthur, Fred MacMurray, Melvyn Douglas. 84M USA. *My Two Husbands* (UKN) prod/rel: Columbia Pictures Corp.©

Triton, 1928, Short Story
Secret Agent, The 1936 d: Alfred Hitchcock. lps: Madeleine Carroll, Peter Lorre, Robert Young. 85M UKN. prod/rel: Gaumont British

The Verger, 1947, Short Story
Trio 1950 d: Ken Annakin, Harold French. lps: James Hayter, Kathleen Harrison, Felix Aylmer. 91M UKN. prod/rel: General Film Distributors, Gainsborough

Vessel of Wrath, 1931, Short Story
Beachcomber, The 1954 d: Muriel Box. lps: Robert Newton, Glynis Johns, Donald Sinden. 90M UKN. prod/rel: General Film Distributors, London Independent

Winter Cruise, 1947, Short Story
Encore 1951 d: Harold French, Pat Jackson. lps: Nigel Patrick, Roland Culver, Alison Leggatt. 86M UKN. prod/rel: General Film Distributors, Two Cities

MAULDIN, BILL

Willie and Joe, 1945, Book
Up Front 1951 d: Alexander Hall. lps: David Wayne, Tom Ewell, Marina Berti. 92M USA. prod/rel: Universal-International

MAULE, ESSON

The Fiery Cross, Novel
Flame in the Heather 1935 d: Donovan Pedelty. lps: Gwenllian Gill, Barry Clifton, Bruce Seton. 66M UKN. prod/rel: Crusade, Paramount

MAULE, HAMILTON
Story
Banning 1967 d: Ron Winston. lps: Robert Wagner, Guy Stockwell, James Farentino. 102M USA. prod/rel: Universal Pictures

Paddy, Novel
Footsteps 1972 d: Paul Wendkos. lps: Richard Crenna, Joanna Pettet, Forrest Tucker. TVM. 73M USA. *Footsteps: Nice Guys Finish Last*; *Nice Guys Finish Last* prod/rel: Metromedia Productions

MAUPIN, ARMISTEAD (1944–, USA
Novel
Tales of the City 1993 d: Alastair Reid. lps: Olympia Dukakis, Donald Moffat, Chloe Webb. MTV. 305M USA. *Armistead Maupin's Tales of the City*

More Tales of the City, Novel
Armistead Maupin's More Tales of the City 1998 d: Pierre Gang. lps: Laura Linney, Olympia Dukakis, Colin Ferguson. TVM. 300M USA/CND. prod/rel: Prods. la Fete, Working Title Television

MAUPREY, ANDRE
Le Cavalier Lafleur, Opera
Cavalier Lafleur, Le 1934 d: Pierre-Jean Ducis. lps: Fernandel, Christiane Delyne, Jacques Louvigny. 85M FRN. prod/rel: Gamma Film

MAURA, H.
Julieta Compra un Hijo, Madrid 1927, Play
Julieta Compra un Hijo 1935 d: Louis King. lps: Catalina Barcena, Gilbert Roland, Luana Alcaniz. 74M USA. *Juliet Buys a Baby*; *Juliet Buys a Son* prod/rel: Fox Film Corp.©

MAURETTE, MARCELLE
Anastasia, Play
Anastasia 1956 d: Anatole Litvak. lps: Yul Brynner, Ingrid Bergman, Helen Hayes. 105M UKN/USA. prod/rel: 20th Century-Fox
Anastasia 1997 d: Don Bluth, Gary Goldman. ANM. 94M USA. prod/rel: Fox Family Films, Twentieth Century Fox Film Corp.©

MAUREY, MAX
Le Pharmacien, Play
Cliente Pas Serieuse, Une 1934 d: Rene Gaveau. lps: Henriette Lafont, Georges Bever, Raymond Rognoni. 950m FRN. *Le Pharmicien* prod/rel: Les Films Artistiques Francais

Rosalie, Play
Rosalie 1929 d: Maurice Champreux, Robert Beaudoin. lps: Madame Hermann, Fernand Hermann, Madeleine Guitty. SHT FRN. prod/rel: Gaumont

La Savelli, Play
Fanatisme 1934 d: Gaston Ravel, Tony Lekain. lps: Pola Negri, Andree Lafayette, Jean Yonnel. 80M FRN. *La Savelli* prod/rel: Via Film

MAURIAC, FRANCOIS (1885–1970), FRN
Les Anges Noirs, 1936, Novel
Anges Noirs, Les 1937 d: Willy Rozier. lps: Germaine Dermoz, Suzy Prim, Fernand Charpin. 95M FRN. prod/rel: Burdiga-Film

Le Noeud de Viperes, Novel
Noeud de Viperes, Le 1990 d: Jacques TreboutA. lps: Pierre Dux, Suzanne Flon, Michel Peyrelon. TVM. 100M FRN.

Therese Desqueyroux, Paris 1927, Novel
Therese Desqueyroux 1962 d: Georges Franju. lps: Emmanuelle Riva, Philippe Noiret, Sami Frey. 109M FRN. *Therese* (UKN) prod/rel: Filmel

MAURICE, MARTIN
Amour Terre Inconnue, Novel
Come, Quando, Perche 1968 d: Antonio Pietrangeli, Valerio Zurlini. lps: Daniele Gaubert, Philippe Leroy, Horst Buchholz. 102M ITL. *How When Why?*; *When and With Whom How*; *Come Quando Con Chi?* prod/rel: Documento Film, Columbia

MAURIERE, GABRIEL
Peau de Peche, Novel
Peau de Peche 1926 d: Jean Benoit-Levy, Marie Epstein. lps: Denise Lorys, Maurice Touze, Simone Mareuil. F FRN. *Peau-de-Peche*

MAUROIS, ANDRE (1885–1967), FRN, Herzog, Ernile
Climats, 1928, Novel
Climats 1962 d: Stellio Lorenzi. lps: Marina Vlady, Emmanuelle Riva, Jean-Pierre Marielle. 143M FRN. *Climates of Love* (UKN) prod/rel: Filmel

Edouard VII Et Son Temps, 1933, Novel
Entente Cordiale 1939 d: Marcel L'Herbier. lps: Victor Francen, Pierre Richard-Willm, Gaby Morlay. 110M FRN. prod/rel: Flora-Film, Arcadia Films

Schule Fur Ehegluck, Book
Schule Fur Ehegluck 1954 d: Toni Schelkopf, Rainer Geis. lps: Liselotte Pulver, Paul Hubschmid, Wolf Albach-Retty. 100M GRM. *The Institute for Marital Happiness* prod/rel: Oska, Union

Thanatos Palace Hotel, 1951, Short Story
  Sursis Pour un Vivant 1958 d: Victor Merenda, Ottorino Franco Bertolini. lps: Dawn Addams, Henri Vidal, Lino VenturA. 88M FRN/ITL. *Pensione Edelweiss* (ITL); *Le Mystere de la Pension Edelweiss* prod/rel: C.C.C., Mediterranee Cinema (Paris)

MAURY, ALFRED
Tomorrow's Harvest, Play
  Till We Meet Again 1944 d: Frank Borzage. lps: Ray Milland, Barbara Britton, Lucile Watson. 88M USA. prod/rel: Paramount

MAXFIELD, HARRY S.
Legacy of a Spy, New York 1958, Novel
  Double Man, The 1967 d: Franklin J. Schaffner. lps: Yul Brynner, Britt Ekland, Clive Revill. 105M UKN. *Legacy of a Spy* prod/rel: Albion Film Corporation, Warner-Pathe

MAXIM, HUDSON
Defenceless America, New York 1915, Book
  Battle Cry of Peace, The 1915 d: J. Stuart Blackton, Wilfred North. lps: Charles Richman, L. Rogers Lytton, Charles Kent. 9r USA. *A Call to Arms Against War*; *An American Home*; *The Battle Cry of War* prod/rel: Vitagraph Co. of America©, Blue Ribbon Feature

MAXWELL, GAVIN
Ring of Bright Water, London 1960, Novel
  Ring of Bright Water 1969 d: Jack Couffer. lps: Bill Travers, Virginia McKenna, Peter Jeffrey. 107M UKN. prod/rel: Brightwater Film, Palomar Pictures International

MAXWELL, WILLIAM BABINGTON, Maxwell, W. B.
The Devil's Garden, Indianapolis 1913, Novel
  Devil's Garden, The 1920 d: Kenneth Webb. lps: Lionel Barrymore, May McAvoy, Doris Rankin. 6r USA. prod/rel: Whitman Bennett Productions©, First National Exhibitors Circuit

Honor in Pawn, Novel
  Honour in Pawn 1916 d: Harold Weston. lps: Manora Thew, Julian Royce, George Bellamy. 4800f UKN. prod/rel: Broadwest

A Little More, London 1921, Novel
  Gilded Highway, The 1926 d: J. Stuart Blackton. lps: Dorothy Devore, John Harron, MacLyn Arbuckle. 6927f USA. prod/rel: Warner Brothers Pictures

Mrs. Thompson, New York 1911, Novel
  Just a Mother 1923. lps: Burtram Gurleigh, Isabel Elson. 5r USA. prod/rel: Norca Pictures
  Mrs. Thompson 1919 d: Rex Wilson. lps: Minna Grey, C. M. Hallard, Isobel Elsom. 5000f UKN. prod/rel: G. B. Samuelson, General

The Ragged Messenger, London 1904, Novel
  Madonna of the Streets 1924 d: Edwin Carewe. lps: Alla Nazimova, Milton Sills, Claude Gillingwater. 7507f USA. prod/rel: Edwin Carewe Productions, First National Pictures
  Madonna of the Streets 1930 d: John S. Robertson. lps: Evelyn Brent, Robert Ames, Ivan Linow. 72M USA. prod/rel: Columbia Pictures
  Ragged Messenger, The 1917 d: Frank Wilson. lps: Violet Hopson, Gerald Ames, Basil Gill. 5025f UKN. prod/rel: Broadwest

MAY, KARL FRIEDRICH (1842–1912), May, Karl
Novel
  Viva Gringo 1966 d: Georg MarischkA. lps: Guy Madison, Geula Nuni, Rik BattagliA. 90M ITL/SPN/GRM. *El Ultimo Rey de Los Incas* (SPN); *The Last King of the Incas*; *Das Vermachtnis Des Inka* (GRM); *Zavetat Na Inkata* (BUL); *The Legend of the Incas* prod/rel: P.E.A. (Roma), Franz Marischka Prod. (Munich)

Durchs Wilde Kurdistan, Novel
  Durchs Wilde Kurdistan 1965 d: Franz J. Gottlieb. lps: Lex Barker, Marie Versini, Ralf Wolter. 103M GRM/SPN. *Salvaje Kurdistan* (SPN); *Wild Kurdistan* (UKN) prod/rel: C.C.C., Balcazar

Im Reiche Des Silbernen Lowen, Novel
  Im Reiche Des Silbernen Lowen 1965 d: Franz J. Gottlieb, Jose Antonio de La LomA. lps: Lex Barker, Dieter Borsche, Marie Versini. 95M GRM/SPN. *El Ataque de Los Kurdos* (SPN); *In the Realm of the Silver Lion* prod/rel: C.C.C., Balcazar

Der Lowe von Babylon, Novel
  Ruinas de Babilonia, Las 1959 d: Ramon Torrado, Johannes Kai. lps: Georg Thomalla, Helmuth Schneider, Theo Lingen. 99M SPN/GRM. *Der Lowe von Babylon* (GRM); *En Las Ruinas de Babilonia*; *The Ruins of Babylon*; *The Lion of Babylon* prod/rel: D.C.F., Aquila

Old Shatterhand, Novel
  Old Shatterhand 1964 d: Hugo Fregonese. lps: Lex Barker, Pierre Brice, Daliah Lavi. 122M GRM/FRN/ITL. *La Battaglia Di Fort Apache* (ITL); *Les*

Cavaliers Rouges (FRN); *Apaches' Last Battle*; *Shatterhand* (USA); *Old Seterhand* prod/rel: C.C.C., Criterion

Old Surehand, Freiberg Im Breisgau 1894, Novel
  Old Surehand I 1965 d: Alfred Vohrer. lps: Stewart Granger, Larry Pennell, Pierre Brice. 93M GRM/YGS. *Lavirint Smrti* (YGS); *Flaming Frontier* (UKN) prod/rel: Rialto Film, Jadran Film

Der Olprinz, Stuttgart 1893, Novel
  Olprinz, Der 1965 d: Harald Philipp. lps: Stewart Granger, Pierre Brice, Macha Meril. 90M GRM/YGS. *Rampage at Apache Wells* (USA); *Kralj Petroleja* (YGS); *Der Olprinz*; *The Oil Prince* prod/rel: Rialto Film, Jadran Film

Die Pyramide Des Sonnengottes, Novel
  Pyramide Des Sonnengottes, Die 1965 d: Robert Siodmak. lps: Lex Barker, Michele Girardon, Gerard Barry. 98M GRM/FRN/ITL. *Pyramid of the Sun God* prod/rel: C.C.C., Franco-London

Der Schatz Der Azteken, Novel
  Schatz Der Azteken, Der 1965 d: Robert Siodmak. lps: Lex Barker, Gerard Barray, Michele Girardon. 99M GRM/FRN/ITL. *Les Mercenaires du Rio Grande* (FRN); *Treasure of the Aztecs*; *I Violenti Di Rio Bravo* (ITL) prod/rel: C.C.C., Franco-London

Der Schatz Im Silbersee, Stuttgart 1890, Novel
  Schatz Im Silbersee, Der 1962 d: Harald Reinl. lps: Lex Barker, Gotz George, Herbert Lom. 111M GRM/FRN/YGS. *Le Tresor du Lac d'Argent* (FRN); *Blago U Srebrnom Jezeru* (YGS); *Treasure of Silver Lake* (USA) prod/rel: S.N.C., Rialto Film

Der Schut, Novel
  Schut, Der 1964 d: Robert Siodmak. lps: Lex Barker, Ralf Wolter, Marie Versini. 118M GRM/ITL/FRN. *Una Carabina Per Schut* (ITL); *The Yellow Devil*; *The Shoot* (USA) prod/rel: C.C.C., Criterion

Unter Geiern, Radebeul-Ober. 1914, Novel
  Unter Geiern 1964 d: Alfred Vohrer. lps: Stewart Granger, Pierre Brice, Elke Sommer. 102M GRM/ITL/YGS. *La Dove Scende Il Sole* (ITL); *Medju Jastrebovima* (YGS); *Frontier Hellcat* (USA); *Among Vultures*; *Parmi Les Vautours* (FRN) prod/rel: Rialto Film, Atlantis Film

Winnetou Der Rote Gentleman, Freiberg 1893, Novel
  Winnetou I 1963 d: Harald Reinl. lps: Lex Barker, Pierre Brice, Mario Adorf. 101M GRM/ITL/YGS. *La Valle Dei Lunghi Coltelli* (ITL); *Vinetu* (YGS); *La Revolte Des Indiens Apaches* (FRN); *Apache Gold* (USA); *Winnetou the Warrior* prod/rel: Film Preben Philipsen, Rialto
  Winnetou II 1964 d: Harald Reinl. lps: Lex Barker, Pierre Brice, Anthony Steel. 94M GRM/FRN/ITL. *Le Tresor Des Montagnes Bleues* (FRN); *Giorni Di Fuoco* (ITL); *Vinetu II* (YGS); *Winnetou: Last of the Renegades*; *Last of the Renegades* (USA) prod/rel: Rialto-Film Preben Philipsen, S.N.C.
  Winnetou III 1965 d: Harald Reinl. lps: Lex Barker, Pierre Brice, Rik BattagliA. 92M GRM/YGS. *Vinetu III* (YGS); *The Desperado Trail* (UKN); *Winnetou: the Desperado Trail*

MAY, MARGERY LAND
The Bleeders, 1919, Short Story
  Beauty Market, The 1920 d: Colin Campbell. lps: Katherine MacDonald, Roy Stewart, Kathleen Kirkham. 6r USA. prod/rel: Katherine Macdonald Pictures Corp., Attractions Distributing Corp.©

Such As Sit in Judgement, London 1923, Novel
  Those Who Judge 1924 d: Burton L. King. lps: Patsy Ruth Miller, Lou Tellegen, Mary Thurman. 5700f USA. prod/rel: Banner Productions

MAYAMA, SEIKA
Genroku Chushingura, Play
  Genroku Chushingura Part I 1941 d: Kenji Mizoguchi. lps: Chojuro Kawarazaki, Yoshizaburo Arashi, Utaemon IchikawA. 112M JPN. *The Loyal 47 of the Genroku Era* (UKN); *The Loyal 47* (USA); *The 47 Ronin* prod/rel: Koa Production, Shochiku Co.

MAYER, EDWIN JUSTUS
The Firebrand, New York 1924, Play
  Affairs of Cellini, The 1934 d: Gregory La CavA. lps: Constance Bennett, Fredric March, Frank Morgan. 90M USA. *The Firebrand* prod/rel: 20th Century Pictures, Inc., United Artists

MAYER, HY
His Priceless Treasure, Story
  His Priceless Treasure 1913 d: Allen Curtis. SHT USA. prod/rel: Imp

MAYERL, BILLY
Sporting Love, London 1934, Musical Play
  Sporting Love 1936 d: J. Elder Wills. lps: Stanley Lupino, Laddie Cliff, Eda Peel. 70M UKN. prod/rel: Hammer, British Lion

MAYHEW, HENRY
Books
  Fool, The 1990 d: Christine Edzard. lps: Derek Jacobi, Cyril Cusack, Ruth Mitchell. 137M UKN. prod/rel: Hobo, Sands Films

MAYLE, PETER
Toujours Provence, Book
  Year in Provence, A 1989 d: David Tucker. lps: John Thaw, Lindsay Duncan, Bernard Spiegel. TVM. 360M UKN.

A Year in Provence, Book
  Year in Provence, A 1989 d: David Tucker. lps: John Thaw, Lindsay Duncan, Bernard Spiegel. TVM. 360M UKN.

MAYNARD, JOYCE
To Die for, Novel
  To Die for 1995 d: Gus Van Sant Jr. lps: Nicole Kidman, Matt Dillon, Joaquin Phoenix. 103M USA.

MAYNARD, NAN
This Is My Street, Novel
  This Is My Street 1963 d: Sidney Hayers. lps: Ian Hendry, June Ritchie, Avice Landone. 94M UKN. prod/rel: Anglo-Amalgamated, Adder

MAYNE, G. E. R.
A Garret in Bohemia, Novel
  Garret in Bohemia, A 1915 d: Harold Shaw. lps: Edna Flugrath, Ben Webster, Christine Rayner. 2795f UKN. prod/rel: London, Jury

The Heart of Sister Ann, Novel
  Heart of Sister Ann, The 1915 d: Harold Shaw. lps: Edna Flugrath, Hayford Hobbs, Guy Newall. 3945f UKN. prod/rel: London, Jury

MAYO, ELEANOR R.
Turn Home, 1945, Novel
  Tarnished 1950 d: Harry Keller. lps: Byron Barr, Barbara Fuller, Don Beddoe. 60M USA. prod/rel: Republic

MAYO, JOHN
Hammerhead, London 1964, Novel
  Hammerhead 1968 d: David Miller. lps: Vince Edwards, Judy Geeson, Peter Vaughan. 99M UKN. prod/rel: Irving Allen Ltd., Columbia

MAYO, MARGARET
Baby Mine, New York 1910, Play
  Baby Mine 1917 d: John S. Robertson, Hugo Ballin. lps: Madge Kennedy, Frank Morgan, Kathryn Adams. 6r USA. prod/rel: Goldwyn Pictures Corp.©, Goldwyn Distributing Corp.
  Baby Mine 1927 d: Robert Z. Leonard. lps: Karl Dane, George K. Arthur, Charlotte Greenwood. 5139f USA. prod/rel: Metro-Goldwyn-Mayer Pictures

Behind the Scenes, Play
  Behind the Scenes 1914 d: James Kirkwood. lps: Mary Pickford, Russell Bassett, James Kirkwood. 5r USA. prod/rel: Famous Players Film Co., Paramount Pictures Corp.

Polly of the Circus, New York 1907, Play
  Polly of the Circus 1917 d: Charles Horan, Edwin L. Hollywood. lps: Mae Marsh, Vernon Steele, Wellington Playter. 8r USA. prod/rel: Goldwyn Pictures Corp.©, Goldwyn Distributing Corp.
  Polly of the Circus 1932 d: Alfred Santell. lps: Clark Gable, Marion Davies, Raymond Hatton. 72M USA. prod/rel: Metro-Goldwyn-Mayer Corp., Metro-Goldwyn-Mayer Dist. Corp.©

Poor Boob, Play
  Poor Boob, The 1919 d: Donald Crisp. lps: Bryant Washburn, Wanda Hawley, Dick Rosson. 4307f USA. prod/rel: Famous Players-Lasky Corp.©, Paramount Pictures Corp.

Twin Beds, New York 1914, Play
  Life of the Party, The 1934 d: Ralph Dawson. lps: Jerry Verno, Betty Astell, Eric Fawcett. 53M UKN. prod/rel: Warner Bros., First National
  Twin Beds 1920 d: Lloyd Ingraham. lps: Carter de Haven, Flora Parker de Haven, Helen Raymond. 6r USA. prod/rel: Carter de Haven Productions©, First National Exhibitors Circuit, Inc.
  Twin Beds 1929 d: Alfred Santell. lps: Jack Mulhall, Patsy Ruth Miller, Edythe Chapman. 7266f USA. prod/rel: First National Pictures
  Twin Beds 1942 d: Tim Whelan. lps: Joan Bennett, George Brent, Mischa Auer. 85M USA. prod/rel: United Artists

MAYRARGUE, LUCIEN
Neufe de Trefle, Novel
  Neuf de Trefle 1937 d: Lucien Mayrargues. lps: Albert Prejean, Frederic Duvalles, Alice Field. 87M FRN. prod/rel: Spectacles Du Film

MAYSE, ARTHUR
The Desperate Search, Novel
Desperate Search 1952 d: Joseph H. Lewis. lps: Howard Keel, Jane Greer, Patricia MedinA. 73M USA. prod/rel: MGM

MAZEAUD, EMILE
Dardamelle, Play
Carnaval 1953 d: Henri Verneuil. lps: Fernandel, Jacqueline Pagnol, Saturnin Fabre. 92M FRN. *Dardamelle* prod/rel: Ste Nouvelle Des Films M. Pagnol

MAZZUCCHELLI, MARIO
La Monaca Di Monza, Milan 1961, Novel
Monaca Di Monza, La 1968 d: Eriprando Visconti. lps: Anne Heywood, Antonio Sabato, Hardy Kruger. 102M ITL. *The Awful Story of the Nun of Monza* (UKN); *The Lady of Monza* (USA); *Una Storia Lombarda; The Nun of Monza* prod/rel: Clesi Cinematografica, Finanziaria San Marco

MAZZUCCHI, GINO
Story
Mille Di Garibaldi, I 1933 d: Alessandro Blasetti. lps: Aida Bellia, Giuseppe Gulino, Gianfranco Giachetti. 90M ITL. *La Sposa Garibaldina Gesuzza; 1860; Garibaldi* prod/rel: Cines, Anonima Pittaluga

MCALLISTER, PAUL
The Stolen Voice, Story
Stolen Voice, The 1915. lps: Robert Warwick, Frances Nelson. 5r USA. prod/rel: William A. Brady Picture Plays, Inc., World Film Corp.©

MCARTHUR, WILSON
Yellow Stockings, Novel
Yellow Stockings 1928 d: Theodor Komisarjevsky. lps: Percy Marmont, Marjorie Mars, Georges Galli. 7836f UKN. prod/rel: Welsh-Pearson-Elder, Famous-Lasky

MCBAIN, ALASTAIR
Cloak and Dagger, Novel
Cloak and Dagger 1946 d: Fritz Lang. lps: Gary Cooper, Lilli Palmer, Robert AldA. 106M USA. prod/rel: Warner Bros.

MCBRIDE, CHRIS
Bwana, Novel
White Lions, The 1979 d: Mel Stuart. lps: Michael York, Glynnis O'Connor, Donald Moffat. 96M USA. *Bwana* prod/rel: Alan Landsburg Prod.

MCCABE, PATRICK
The Butcher Boy, 1992, Novel
Butcher Boy, The 1997 d: Neil Jordan. lps: Eamonn Owens, Alan Boyle, Stephen ReA. 110M USA. prod/rel: Geffen Pictures©, Butcher Boy Film

MCCALL, ANTHONY
Holocaust, Novel
To Kill the King 1974 d: George McCowan. lps: Patrick O'Neal, Susan Tyrrell, Barry Morse. 86M CND. *Trigger* prod/rel: Franiposy Film Co. Ltd., Creative Entertainment Corp.

MCCALL, CHERYL
Streets of the Lost, Article
Streetwise 1984 d: Martin Bell, Mary Ellen Mark. DOC. 91M USA. prod/rel: Angelika Films, Bear Creek

MCCALL JR., MARY
Fraternity, Short Story
On the Sunny Side 1942 d: Harold Schuster. lps: Roddy McDowall, Jane Darwell, Stanley Clements. 69M USA. prod/rel: 20th Century-Fox

The Goldfish Bowl, Boston 1932, Novel
It's Tough to Be Famous 1932 d: Alfred E. Green. lps: Douglas Fairbanks Jr., Mary Brian, Walter Catlett. 79M USA. *Tough to Be Famous* prod/rel: First National Pictures©

Revolt, Novel
Scarlet Dawn 1932 d: William Dieterle. lps: Douglas Fairbanks Jr., Nancy Carroll, Lilyan Tashman. 60M USA. *Revolt* prod/rel: Warner Bros. Pictures©

MCCALL, SIDNEY
The Breath of God, Boston 1905, Novel
Breath of the Gods, The 1920 d: Rollin S. Sturgeon. lps: Tsuru Aoki, Stanhope Wheatcroft, Arthur Edmund Carewe. 6225f USA. prod/rel: Universal Film Mfg. Co.©

Red Horse Hill, Boston 1909, Novel
Eternal Mother, The 1917 d: Frank Reicher. lps: Ethel Barrymore, Frank Mills, J. W. Johnston. 5r USA. *Red Horse Hill* prod/rel: Metro Pictures Corp.©

MCCANLEY, SUE
Other Halves, Novel
Other Halves 1985 d: John Laing. lps: Lisa Harrow, Mark Pilisi, Fraser Stephen-Smith. 102M NZL. prod/rel: Oringham, Galatea

MCCAREY, RAY
The Romantic Mr. Hinklin, Story
You Can't Fool Your Wife 1940 d: Ray McCarey. lps: Lucille Ball, James Ellison, Robert Coote. 68M USA. *The Romantic Mr. Hinklin* prod/rel: RKO Radio Pictures©

MCCARRY, CHARLES (1929–, USA
The Better Angels, Novel
Wrong Is Right 1982 d: Richard Brooks. lps: Sean Connery, George Grizzard, Robert Conrad. 118M USA. *The Man With the Deadly Lens* (UKN) prod/rel: Columbia

MCCARTEN, ANTHONY
Via Satellite, Play
Via Satellite 1998 d: Anthony McCarten. lps: Danielle Cormack, Tim Balme, Rima Te WiatA. 89M NZL. prod/rel: Portman, New Zealand Film Commission

MCCARTHY, J. P.
Kid Boots, New York 1923, Musical Play
Kid Boots 1926 d: Frank Tuttle. lps: Eddie Cantor, Clara Bow, Billie Dove. 8565f USA. prod/rel: Famous Players-Lasky, Paramount Pictures

MCCARTHY, JUSTIN HUNTLY
If I Were King, London 1901, Novel
Beloved Rogue, The 1927 d: Alan Crosland. lps: John Barrymore, Conrad Veidt, Marceline Day. 9264f USA. *The Ragged Lover* prod/rel: Feature Productions, United Artists
If I Were King 1920 d: J. Gordon Edwards. lps: William Farnum, Betty Ross Clark, Fritz Leiber. 8r USA. prod/rel: Fox Film Corp., William Fox©
If I Were King 1938 d: Frank Lloyd. lps: Ronald Colman, Frances Dee, Basil Rathbone. 101M USA. prod/rel: Paramount Pictures©
Vagabond King, The 1930 d: Ludwig Berger. lps: Dennis King, Jeanette MacDonald, O. P. Heggie. 9413f USA. prod/rel: Paramount Famous Lasky Corp.
Vagabond King, The 1956 d: Michael Curtiz. lps: Oreste, Kathryn Grayson, Rita Moreno. 88M USA. prod/rel: Paramount

MCCARTHY, MARY (1912–1989), USA, McCarthy, Mary Therese
Story
Petty Girl, The 1950 d: Henry Levin. lps: Robert Cummings, Joan Caulfield, Elsa Lanchester. 87M USA. *Girl of the Year* (UKN) prod/rel: Columbia

The Group, New York 1963, Novel
Group, The 1966 d: Sidney Lumet. lps: Candice Bergen, Joan Hackett, Joanna Pettet. 150M USA. prod/rel: Famous Artists Productions, Famartists Productions

MCCARTY-BAKER, AMY
The Florentine, Play
Florentine, The 1999 d: Nick Stagliano. lps: Michael Madsen, Chris Penn, Jeremy Davies. 104M USA. prod/rel: Initial Entertainment Group, American Zoetrope

MCCAULEY, STEPHEN
The Object of My Affection, Novel
Object of My Affection, The 1998 d: Nicholas Hytner. lps: Jennifer Aniston, Paul Rudd, Alan AldA. 112M USA. prod/rel: 20th Century Fox©, Laurence Mark

MCCLOSKEY, LAWRENCE
Beth, Short Story
Fortune's Child 1919 d: Joseph Gleason. lps: Gladys Leslie, Kempton Greene, Stanley Walpole. 5r USA. prod/rel: Vitagraph Co. of America©, Blue Ribbon Photodrama

The Hidden Path, Story
Discarded Woman, The 1920 d: Burton L. King. lps: Grace Darling, James Cooley, Rod La Rocque. 6r USA. *The Hidden Path* prod/rel: Burton King Productions, Hallmark Pictures Corp.©

The Upheaval, Short Story
Upheaval, The 1916 d: Charles Horan. lps: Lionel Barrymore, Marguerite Skirvin, Franklyn HannA. 5r USA. prod/rel: Rolfe Photoplays Inc.©, Metro Pictures Corp.

MCCONNELL, GUY M.
Peaks of Gold, Story
Tropical Love 1921 d: Ralph Ince. lps: Ruth Clifford, F. A. Turner, Reginald Denny. 5r USA. prod/rel: Playgoers Pictures, Porto Rico Photoplays

MCCORMICK, LANGDON
The Life of an Actress, 1907, Play
Life of an Actress 1927 d: Jack Nelson. lps: Barbara Bedford, Bert Sprotte, Lydia Knott. 6400f USA. *Romance of an Actress* prod/rel: Chadwick Pictures

Shipwrecked, New York 1924, Play
Shipwrecked 1926 d: Joseph Henabery. lps: Seena Owen, Joseph Schildkraut, Matthew Betz. 5865f USA. prod/rel: Metropolitan Pictures Corp. of Calif., Producers Distributing Corp.

The Storm, New York 1919, Play
Storm, The 1922 d: Reginald Barker. lps: Matt Moore, House Peters, Josef Swickard. 7400f USA. prod/rel: Universal Film Mfg. Co.
Storm, The 1930 d: William Wyler. lps: Lupe Velez, Paul Cavanagh, William "Stage" Boyd. 80M USA. prod/rel: Universal Pictures

The Torrent, Story
Torrent, The 1924 d: A. P. Younger, William Doner. lps: William Fairbanks, Ora Carew, Frank Elliott. 6r USA. prod/rel: Phil Goldstone Productions, Truart Film Corp.

MCCOY, HORACE
Kiss Tomorrow Goodbye, 1948, Novel
Kiss Tomorrow Goodbye 1950 d: Gordon Douglas. lps: James Cagney, Barbara Payton, Helena Carter. 102M USA. prod/rel: Warner Bros.

No Pockets in a Shroud, Novel
Linceul N'a Pas de Poches, Un 1975 d: Jean-Pierre Mocky. lps: Michel Serrault, Sylvia Kristel, Jean Carmet. 135M FRN.

Scalpel, 1952, Novel
Bad for Each Other 1953 d: Irving Rapper. lps: Charlton Heston, Lizabeth Scott, Dianne Foster. 83M USA. *Scalpel* prod/rel: Columbia

Storm in the City, Story
Turning Point, The 1952 d: William Dieterle. lps: Edmond O'Brien, William Holden, Alexis Smith. 85M USA. *This Is Dynamite* prod/rel: Paramount

They Shoot Horses, Don't They?, New York 1935, Novel
They Shoot Horses, Don't They? 1969 d: Sydney Pollack. lps: Jane Fonda, Red Buttons, Michael Sarrazin. 129M USA. prod/rel: Palomar Pictures International, Cinerama Releasing Corp.

MCCOY, WILLIAM M.
Little Red Decides, 1917, Short Story
Little Red Decides 1918 d: Jack Conway. lps: Barbara Connolly, Goro Kino, Frederick Vroom. 5r USA. prod/rel: Triangle Film Corp., Triangle Distributing Corp.

MCCRACKEN, ESTHER
No Medals, London 1944, Play
Weaker Sex, The 1948 d: Roy Ward Baker. lps: Ursula Jeans, Cecil Parker, Joan Hopkins. 84M UKN. *No Medals for Martha; The Housewives' Story* prod/rel: Two Cities, General Film Distributors

Quiet Wedding, London 1938, Play
Happy Is the Bride 1958 d: Roy Boulting. lps: Ian Carmichael, Janette Scott, Cecil Parker. 84M UKN. prod/rel: British Lion, Panther Productions
Quiet Wedding 1941 d: Anthony Asquith. lps: Margaret Lockwood, Derek Farr, Marjorie Fielding. 80M UKN. prod/rel: Paramount, Conqueror

Quiet Weekend, London 1941, Play
Quiet Weekend 1946 d: Harold French. lps: Derek Farr, Barbara White, Frank Cellier. 93M UKN. prod/rel: Associated British Picture Corporation, Pathe

MCCRAE, JOHN
In Flanders Fields, Poem
Armistice 1929 d: Victor Saville. 15M UKN. prod/rel: Gainsborough, Woolf & Freedman
Memories 1929 d: R. E. Jeffrey. lps: Jameson Thomas, John Stuart, John Longden. 10M UKN. prod/rel: British International Pictures, Wardour

MCCREARY, LEW
The Minus Man, 1990, Novel
Minus Man, The 1999 d: Hampton Fancher. lps: Owen Wilson, Brian Cox, Mercedes Ruehl. 115M USA. prod/rel: Tsg Pictures, Shooting Gallery

MCCULLERS, CARSON (1917–1967), USA, McCullers, Carson Smith
The Ballad of the Sad Cafe, 1951, Short Story
Ballad of the Sad Cafe, The 1991 d: Simon Callow. lps: Vanessa Redgrave, Keith Carradine, Rod Steiger. 101M USA/UKN. prod/rel: Merchant-Ivory, Film Four

The Heart Is a Lonely Hunter, Boston 1940, Novel
Heart Is a Lonely Hunter, The 1968 d: Robert Ellis Miller. lps: Alan Arkin, Laurinda Barrett, Stacy Keach. 124M USA. prod/rel: Warner Bros, Seven Arts, Inc.

The Member of the Wedding, 1946, Novel
Member of the Wedding, The 1952 d: Fred Zinnemann. lps: Julie Harris, Ethel Waters, Brandon de Wilde. 91M USA. prod/rel: Columbia, Stanley Kramer Prods.

Reflections in a Golden Eye, Boston 1941, Novel
Reflections in a Golden Eye 1967 d: John Huston. lps: Marlon Brando, Elizabeth Taylor, Brian Keith. 109M USA. prod/rel: Warner Bros., Seven Arts International, Ltd.

MCCULLEY, JOHNSTON (1883–1958), USA, Brien, Raley, Drayne, George
The Broken Dollar, 1927, Short Story
Black Jack 1927 d: Orville O. Dull. lps: Buck Jones, Barbara Bennett, Theodore Lorch. 4777f USA. prod/rel: Fox Film Corp.

The Brute Breaker, 1918, Novel
Brute Breaker, The 1919 d: Lynn Reynolds. lps: Frank Mayo, Kathryn Adams, Harry Northrup. 5785f USA. prod/rel: Universal Film Mfg. Co.©

Ice Flood, The 1926 d: George B. Seitz. lps: Kenneth Harlan, Viola Dana, Frank Hagney. 5747f USA. prod/rel: Universal Pictures

Captain Fly-By-Night, Novel
Captain Fly-By-Night 1922 d: William K. Howard. lps: Johnny Walker, Francis McDonald, Shannon Day. 4940f USA. prod/rel: R-C Pictures, Film Booking Offices of America

The Curse of Capistrano, 1919, Novel
Mark of Zorro, The 1920 d: Fred Niblo. lps: Douglas Fairbanks, Marguerite de La Motte, Noah Beery. 8r USA. *The Curse of Capistrano* prod/rel: Douglas Fairbanks Pictures Corp.©, United Artists Corp.

Mark of Zorro, The 1940 d: Rouben Mamoulian. lps: Tyrone Power, Linda Darnell, Basil Rathbone. 93M USA. *The Californian* prod/rel: 20th Century-Fox Film Corp.©

Mark of Zorro, The 1974 d: Don McDougall. lps: Frank Langella, Ricardo Montalban, Gilbert Roland. TVM. 78M USA. prod/rel: 20th Century-Fox

Don Peon, Novel
California Conquest 1952 d: Lew Landers. lps: Cornel Wilde, Teresa Wright, Lisa Ferraday. 79M USA. prod/rel: Columbia, Esskay Pictures

King of Cactusville, 1923, Short Story
Outlaw Deputy, The 1935 d: Otto Brower. lps: Tim McCoy, Nora Lane, Bud Osborne. 56M USA. *Outlaw Law* prod/rel: Puritan Pictures Corp., State Rights

Little Erolinda, 1916, Short Story
Kiss, The 1921 d: Jack Conway. lps: George Periolat, William E. Lawrence, J. P. Lockney. 4488f USA. prod/rel: Universal Film Mfg. Co.

Unclaimed Goods, 1917, Short Story
Unclaimed Goods 1918 d: Rollin S. Sturgeon. lps: Vivian Martin, Harrison Ford, Casson Ferguson. 5r USA. prod/rel: Famous Players-Lasky Corp.©, Paramount Pictures

A White Man's Chance, Short Story
White Man's Chance, A 1919 d: Ernest C. Warde. lps: J. Warren Kerrigan, Lillian Walker, Joseph J. Dowling. 5r USA. prod/rel: Kerrigan Productions Co., Robert Brunton Productions

MCCULLOUGH, COLLEEN (1937–, ASL
An Indecent Obsession, Novel
Indecent Obsession, An 1985 d: Lex Marinos. lps: Wendy Hughes, Gary Sweet, Richard Moir. 106M ASL. prod/rel: Pbl Productions Pty. Ltd.©, Hoyts/Michael Edgley International

The Thorn Birds, Novel
Thorn Birds, The 1982 d: Daryl Duke. lps: Richard Chamberlain, Rachel Ward, Jean Simmons. TVM. 456M USA. prod/rel: David L. Wolper-Stan Margulies Prods., Edward Lewis Prods.

Tim, Novel
Tim 1979 d: Michael Pate. lps: Piper Laurie, Mel Gibson, Alwyn Kurts. 109M ASL. prod/rel: Pisces Productions Pty. Ltd.©, Australian Film Commission

MCCUNN, RUTHANNE LUM
Thousand Pieces of Gold, Novel
1,000 Pieces of Gold 1991 d: Nancy Kelly. lps: Rosalind Chao, Chris Cooper, Michael Paul Chan. 105M USA. *Thousand Pieces of Gold*

MCCUTCHEON, GEORGE BARR (1866–1928), USA
Beverly of Graustark, New York 1904, Novel
Beverly of Graustark 1914. lps: Linda Arvidson, Clara T. Bracey, Charles Perley. 3r USA. prod/rel: Klaw & Erlanger

Beverly of Graustark 1926 d: Sidney A. Franklin. lps: Marion Davies, Antonio Moreno, Creighton Hale. 6977f USA. prod/rel: Metro-Goldwyn-Mayer Distributing Corp.

Black Is White, New York 1914, Novel
Black Is White 1920 d: Charles Giblyn. lps: Dorothy Dalton, Claire Mersereau, Lillian Lawrence. 5562f USA. prod/rel: Thomas H. Ince Productions, Famous Players-Lasky Corp.

Brewster's Millions, New York 1902, Novel
Brewster's Millions 1914 d: Oscar Apfel, Cecil B. de Mille. lps: Edward Abeles, Joseph Singleton, Sydney Deane. 5r USA. prod/rel: Jesse L. Lasky Feature Play Co., State Rights

Brewster's Millions 1921 d: Joseph Henabery. lps: Roscoe Arbuckle, Betty Ross Clark, Fred Huntley. 5502f USA. prod/rel: Famous Players-Lasky, Paramount Pictures

Brewster's Millions 1935 d: Thornton Freeland. lps: Jack Buchanan, Lili Damita, Nancy O'Neil. 84M UKN. prod/rel: British and Dominions, United Artists

Brewster's Millions 1945 d: Allan Dwan. lps: Dennis O'Keefe, Helen Walker, Eddie "Rochester" Anderson. 79M USA. prod/rel: United Artists

Brewster's Millions 1985 d: Walter Hill. lps: Richard Pryor, John Candy, Lonette McKee. 102M USA. prod/rel: Universal

Miss Brewster's Millions 1926 d: Clarence Badger. lps: Bebe Daniels, Warner Baxter, Ford Sterling. 6457f USA. prod/rel: Famous Players-Lasky, Paramount Pictures

Three on a Spree 1961 d: Sidney J. Furie. lps: Jack Watling, Carole Lesley, John Slater. 91M UKN. *Brewster's Millions* prod/rel: Caralan Productions, Dador

The Butterfly Man, New York 1910, Novel
Butterfly Man, The 1920 d: Ida May Park. lps: Lew Cody, Louise Lovely, Rosemary Theby. 6r USA. prod/rel: L. J. Gasnier Productions, Robertson-Cole Distributing Corp.

Castle Craneycrow, Chicago 1902, Novel
Prisoner, The 1923 d: Jack Conway. lps: Herbert Rawlinson, Eileen Percy, George Cowl. 4795f USA. prod/rel: Universal Pictures

The City of Masks, New York 1918, Novel
City of Masks, The 1920 d: Thomas N. Heffron. lps: Robert Warwick, Lois Wilson, Theodore Kosloff. 4708f USA. prod/rel: Famous Players-Lasky Corp.©, Paramount-Artcraft Pictures

Cowardice Court, New York 1906, Novel
Cowardice Court 1919 d: William C. Dowlan. lps: Peggy Hyland, Jack Livingston, Arthur Hoyt. 5r USA. prod/rel: Fox Film Corp., William Fox©

A Fool and His Money, New York 1913, Novel
Fool and His Money, A 1920 d: Robert Ellis. lps: Eugene O'Brien, Rubye de Remer, Arthur Housman. 5-6r USA. prod/rel: Selznick Pictures Corp.©, Select Pictures Corp.

Fool and His Money, A 1925 d: Erle C. Kenton. lps: Madge Bellamy, William Haines, Stuart Holmes. 5801f USA. prod/rel: Columbia Pictures

Graustark, New York 1901, Novel
Graustark 1915 d: Fred E. Wright. lps: Francis X. Bushman, Beverly Bayne, Thomas Commerford. 6r USA. prod/rel: Essanay Film Mfg. Co.©, V-L-S-E, Inc.

Graustark 1925 d: Dimitri Buchowetzki. lps: Norma Talmadge, Eugene O'Brien, Marc MacDermott. 5900f USA. prod/rel: Joseph M. Schenck Productions, First National Pictures

Green Fancy, New York 1917, Novel
Mystery Girl, The 1918 d: William C. de Mille. lps: Ethel Clayton, Henry Woodward, Clarence Burton. 4395f USA. prod/rel: Famous Players-Lasky Corp.©, Paramount Pictures

The Hollow of Her Hand, New York 1912, Novel
In the Hollow of Her Hand 1918 d: Charles Maigne. lps: Alice Brady, Percy Marmont, Myrtle Stedman. 5r USA. *The Hollow of Her Hand* prod/rel: Select Pictures Corp.©

Husband of Edith, New York 1908, Novel
Fast Worker, The 1924 d: William A. Seiter. lps: Reginald Denny, Laura La Plante, Ethel Grey Terry. 6896f USA. *The Lightning Lover* prod/rel: Universal Pictures

The Man from Brodney's, New York 1908, Novel
Man from Brodney's, The 1923 d: David Smith. lps: J. Warren Kerrigan, Alice Calhoun, Wanda Hawley. 7100f USA. prod/rel: Vitagraph Co. of America

Nedra, New York 1905, Novel
Nedra 1915 d: Edward Jose. lps: George Probert, Fania Marinoff, Margaret Greene. 5r USA. prod/rel: Pathe Exchange, Inc., Gold Rooster Plays

The Prince of Graustark, New York 1914, Novel
Prince of Graustark, The 1916 d: Fred E. Wright. lps: Bryant Washburn, Marguerite Clayton, Ernest Maupain. 5r USA. prod/rel: Essanay Film Mfg. Co.©, K-E-S-E Service

The Rose in the Ring, New York 1910, Novel
Circus Man, The 1914 d: Oscar Apfel. lps: Theodore Roberts, Florence Dagmar, Jode Mullally. 5r USA. *The Ringmaster* prod/rel: Jesse L. Lasky Feature Play Co.©, Paramount Pictures Corp.

Sherry, New York 1919, Novel
Sherry 1920 d: Edgar Lewis. lps: Pat O'Malley, Lillian Hall, Harry Spingler. 7r USA. prod/rel: Edgar Lewis Productions, Inc., Pathe Exchange, Inc.©

Truxton King; a Story of Graustark, New York 1909, Novel
Truxton King 1923 d: Jerome Storm. lps: John Gilbert, Ruth Clifford, Frank Leigh. 5613f USA. *Truxtonia* (UKN) prod/rel: Fox Film Corp.

What's-His-Name, New York 1911, Novel
What's His Name 1914 d: Cecil B. de Mille. lps: Max Figman, Lolita Robertson, Sydney Deane. 5r USA. prod/rel: Jesse L. Lasky Feature Play Co.©, Paramount Pictures Corp.

MCCUTCHEON, HUGH
To Dusty Death, Novel
Pit of Darkness 1961 d: Lance Comfort. lps: William Franklyn, Moira Redmond, Bruno Barnabe. 76M UKN. prod/rel: Butcher's Films

MCDERMOTT, JOHN
Rivets, Play
Fast Workers 1933 d: Tod Browning. lps: John Gilbert, Robert Armstrong, Mae Clarke. 68M USA. *Rivets* (UKN) prod/rel: Metro-Goldwyn-Mayer Corp., Tod Browning's Production

MCDONALD, ANNE
Annie's Coming Out, Book
Annie's Coming Out 1984 d: Gil Brealey. lps: Angela Punch-McGregor, Drew Forsythe, Tina Arhondis. 96M ASL. *A Test of Love* (USA) prod/rel: Film Australia©, Australian Film Commission©

MCDONALD, GREGORY
The Brave, Novel
Brave, The 1997 d: Johnny Depp. lps: Johnny Depp, Marlon Brando, Marshall Bell. 123M USA. prod/rel: Acappella Pictures

Fletch, Novel
Fletch 1985 d: Michael Ritchie. lps: Chevy Chase, Joe Don Baker, Dana Wheeler Nicholson. 99M USA. prod/rel: Universal

MCDONALD, IAN
The Hummingbird Tree, Novel
Hummingbird Tree, The 1992 d: Noella Smith. lps: Patrick Bergin, Susan Wooldridge, Tom Beasley. TVM. 81M UKN.

MCDONALD, RONALD
Gambier's Advocate, London 1914, Novel
Gambier's Advocate 1915 d: James Kirkwood. lps: Hazel Dawn, James Kirkwood, Fuller Mellish. 5r USA. *Clarissa* prod/rel: Famous Players Film Co., Paramount Pictures Corp.

MCDONELL, GORDON
Uncle Charlie, Story
Shadow of a Doubt 1943 d: Alfred Hitchcock. lps: Teresa Wright, Joseph Cotten, MacDonald Carey. 108M USA. prod/rel: Universal

Shadow of a Doubt 1991 d: Karen Arthur. lps: Mark Harmon, Margaret Welsh, Norman Skaggs. TVM. 100M USA.

Step Down to Terror 1958 d: Harry Keller. lps: Charles Drake, Colleen Miller, Rod Taylor. 76M USA. *The Silent Stranger* (UKN) prod/rel: Universal-International

MCDONOUGH, JAMES R.
Platoon Leader, Book
Platoon Leader 1988 d: Aaron Norris. lps: Michael Dudikoff, Robert F. Lyons, Michael de Lorenzo. 100M USA. prod/rel: Cannon

MCENROE, ROBERT C.
The Silver Whistle, New York 1948, Play
Mr. Belvedere Rings the Bell 1951 d: Henry Koster. lps: Clifton Webb, Joanne Dru, Hugh Marlowe. 88M USA. prod/rel: 20th Century-Fox

MCEVOY, CHARLES
The Likes of Her, London 1923, Play
Sally in Our Alley 1931 d: Maurice Elvey. lps: Gracie Fields, Ian Hunter, Florence Desmond. 77M UKN. prod/rel: Associated Talking Pictures, Radio

The Man in the Attic, Play
Man in the Attic, The 1915 d: Ralph Dewsbury. lps: Blanche Bryan, Charles Rock, Philip Hewland. 3478f UKN. prod/rel: London, Jury

The Third Generation, Novel
Third Generation 1915 d: Harold Shaw. lps: Edna Flugrath, Sydney Vautier, Charles Rock. 4650f UKN. prod/rel: London, Jury

Village Wedding, Play
Man in the Shadows, The 1915 d: Charles McEvoy. 3000f UKN. prod/rel: Charles Mcevoy, Yorkshire Cinematograph Co.

MCEVOY, JOSEPH PATRICK
Are You Listening?, Boston 1932, Novel
Are You Listening? 1932 d: Harry Beaumont. lps: William Haines, Madge Evans, Anita Page. 76M USA. prod/rel: Metro-Goldwyn-Mayer Corp.

The Comic Supplement (of American Life), Washington D.C. 1925, Play
It's a Gift 1934 d: Norman Z. McLeod. lps: W. C. Fields, Baby Leroy, Kathleen Howard. 73M USA. *Back Porch* prod/rel: Paramount Productions©

Hollywood Girl, New York 1929, Novel
Masque d'Hollywood, Le 1931 d: John Daumery, Clarence Badger. lps: Geymond Vital, Suzy Vernon, Rolla Norman. 90M USA. prod/rel: Warner Bros., First National

Show Girl in Hollywood 1930 d: Mervyn Leroy. lps: Alice White, Jack Mulhall, Blanche Sweet. 80M USA. prod/rel: First National Pictures

It's the Old Army Game, Story
It's the Old Army Game 1926 d: A. Edward Sutherland. lps: W. C. Fields, Louise Brooks, Blanche Ring. 6889f USA. prod/rel: Famous Players-Lasky, Paramount Pictures

The Potters, Chicago 1923, Novel
Potters, The 1927 d: Fred Newmeyer. lps: W. C. Fields, Mary Alden, Ivy Harris. 6680f USA. prod/rel: Famous Players-Lasky, Paramount Pictures

Show Girl, New York 1928, Novel
Show Girl 1928 d: Alfred Santell. lps: Alice White, Donald Reed, Lee Moran. 6252f USA. prod/rel: First National Pictures

MCEWAN, IAN (1948–, UKN
Story
Schmetterlinge 1987 d: Wolfgang Becker. lps: Bertram von Boxberg, Lena Boehncke, Dieter Oberholz. 57M GRM. prod/rel: Deutsche Film Und Fernsehakademie

The Cement Garden, Novel
Cement Garden, The 1992 d: Andrew Birkin. lps: Andrew Robertson, Charlotte Gainsbourg, Alice Coulthard. 105M UKN/GRM/FRN. prod/rel: Metro Tartan, Constantin

The Comfort of Strangers, 1981, Novel
Comfort of Strangers, The 1991 d: Paul Schrader. lps: Christopher Walken, Natasha Richardson, Rupert Everett. 105M USA/ITL. *Cortesie Per Gli Ospiti* (ITL) prod/rel: Rank, Erre

First Love, Last Rites, Short Story
First Love, Last Rites 1997 d: Jesse Peretz. lps: Natasha Gregson Wagner, Giovanni Ribisi, Eli Marienthal. 101M USA. prod/rel: Forensic, Toast Films

The Imitation Game, 1981, Play
Imitation Game, The 1980 d: Richard Eyre. lps: Harriet Walter, Lorna Charles, Simon Chandler. TVM. 90M UKN. prod/rel: BBC

The Innocent, Novel
Innocent, The 1993 d: John Schlesinger. lps: Anthony Hopkins, Isabella Rossellini, Campbell Scott. 119M UKN/GRM. ..*Und Der Himmel Steht Still* (GRM) prod/rel: Island Lakeheart, Sievernich

MCFADDEN, CYRA
Serial, Novel
Serial 1980 d: Bill Persky. lps: Tuesday Weld, Sally Kellerman, Bill MacY. 91M USA. prod/rel: Paramount

MCFADDEN, ELIZABETH A.
Double Door, New York 1933, Play
Double Door 1934 d: Charles Vidor. lps: Mary Morris, Kent Taylor, Anne Revere. 75M USA. prod/rel: Paramount Productions

MCGAHAN, ANDREW
Praise, Novel
Praise 1998 d: John Curran. lps: Peter Fenton, Sacha Holder, Marta Dusseldorp. 97M ASL. prod/rel: Emcee Film

MCGAHERN, JOHN (1934–, IRL
Wheels, 1970, Short Story
Wheels 1976 d: Cathal Black. 18M IRL.

MCGIBNEY, DONALD
Two Arabian Knights, Short Story
Two Arabian Knights 1927 d: Lewis Milestone. lps: William Boyd, Mary Astor, Louis Wolheim. 8250f USA. prod/rel: Caddo Co., United Artists

When the Desert Calls, 1920, Short Story
When the Desert Calls 1922 d: Ray C. Smallwood. lps: Violet Heming, Robert Frazer, Sheldon Lewis. 6159f USA. prod/rel: Pyramid Pictures, American Releasing Corp.

MCGILL, ANGUS
Yea Yea Yea, Novel
Press for Time 1966 d: Robert Asher. lps: Norman Wisdom, Derek Bond, Angela Browne. 102M UKN. prod/rel: Rank Film Distributors, Ivy

MCGILL, MARCUS
Hide and I'll Find You, Novel
It's a Bet 1935 d: Alexander Esway. lps: Gene Gerrard, Helen Chandler, Judy Kelly. 69M UKN. *A Safe Bet* prod/rel: British International Pictures, Wardour

MCGINLEY, PATRICK
Goosefoot, Novel
Fantasist, The 1986 d: Robin Hardy. lps: Christopher Cazenove, Timothy Bottoms, John Kavanagh. 98M UKN/IRL. prod/rel: New Irish Film Productions, Itc Entertainment

MCGINNESS, JOE
Fatal Vision, Book
Fatal Vision 1984 d: David Greene. lps: Karl Malden, Eva Marie Saint, Gary Cole. TVM. 200M USA. prod/rel: NBC

MCGIVERN, WILLIAM P. (1924–1982), USA, McGivern, William Peter
The Big Heat, Serial Story
Big Heat, The 1953 d: Fritz Lang. lps: Glenn Ford, Gloria Grahame, Jocelyn Brando. 89M USA. prod/rel: Columbia

The Caper of the Golden Bulls, New York 1966, Novel
Caper of the Golden Bulls, The 1966 d: Russell Rouse. lps: Stephen Boyd, Giovanna Ralli, Yvette Mimieux. 105M USA. *Carnival of Thieves* (UKN) prod/rel: Embassy

Un Choix d'Assassins, Novel
Choix d'Assassins, Un 1967 d: Philippe Fourastie. lps: Bernard Noel, Duda Cavalcanti, Guido Alberti. 100M FRN/ITL. prod/rel: Rome-Paris-Films, Sepic

The Darkest Hour, Serial Story
Hell on Frisco Bay 1955 d: Frank Tuttle. lps: Alan Ladd, Edward G. Robinson, Joanne Dru. 98M USA. *The Darkest Hour* prod/rel: Warner Bros., Jaguar

Night of the Juggler, Novel
Night of the Juggler 1980 d: Robert Butler, Sidney J. Furie (Uncredited). lps: James Brolin, Cliff Gorman, Richard Castellano. 101M USA. prod/rel: Columbia

Odds Against Tomorrow, 1957, Novel
Odds Against Tomorrow 1959 d: Robert Wise. lps: Robert Ryan, Harry Belafonte, Shelley Winters. 96M USA. prod/rel: United Artists, Harbel

Rogue Cop, 1954, Novel
Rogue Cop 1954 d: Roy Rowland. lps: Robert Taylor, Janet Leigh, George Raft. 92M USA. *Kelvaney* prod/rel: MGM

Shield for Murder, 1951, Novel
Shield for Murder 1954 d: Edmond O'Brien, Howard W. Koch. lps: Edmond O'Brien, Marla English, John Agar. 80M USA. prod/rel: United Artists, Camden Prods.

MCGLINN, R. E.
Play
Test, The 1916 d: George Fitzmaurice. lps: Jane Grey, Lumsden Hare, Claude Fleming. 5r USA. prod/rel: Astra Film Corp., Pathe Exchange, Inc.©

MCGOUGH, ROGER
After the Merrymaking, 1971, Verse
Plod 1972 d: Michael Cort. lps: The Scaffold. 30M UKN.

MCGOVERN, JAMES
Erika, 1956, Novel
Fraulein 1958 d: Henry Koster. lps: Mel Ferrer, Dana Wynter, Dolores Michaels. 100M USA. prod/rel: 20th Century-Fox

MCGOWAN, JOHN
Girl Crazy, New York 1930, Musical Play
Girl Crazy 1932 d: William A. Seiter. lps: Bert Wheeler, Robert Woolsey, Stanley Fields. 75M USA. prod/rel: RKO Radio Pictures©

Girl Crazy 1943 d: Norman Taurog. lps: Mickey Rooney, Judy Garland, Gil Stratton. 99M USA. *When the Girls Meet the Boys* prod/rel: MGM

When the Boys Meet the Girls 1965 d: Alvin Ganzer. lps: Herman & His Hermits, Liberace, Harve Presnell. 102M USA. *Girl Crazy* prod/rel: Four Leaf Productions

Heads Up, New York 1929, Musical Play
Heads Up 1930 d: Victor Schertzinger. lps: Charles "Buddy" Rogers, Victor Moore, Helen Kane. 6785f USA. prod/rel: Paramount-Publix Corp.

Hold Everything, New York 1928, Musical Play
Hold Everything 1930 d: Roy Del Ruth. lps: Joe E. Brown, Winnie Lightner, Georges Carpentier. 7513f USA. prod/rel: Warner Brothers Pictures

Tenth Avenue, New York 1927, Play
Tenth Avenue 1928 d: William C. de Mille. lps: Phyllis Haver, Victor Varconi, Joseph Schildkraut. 6370f USA. *Hell's Kitchen* (UKN) prod/rel: de Mille Studio Productions, Pathe Exchange, Inc.

MCGOWAN, JOHN WESLEY
Excess Baggage, New York 1927, Play
Excess Baggage 1928 d: James Cruze. lps: William Haines, Josephine Dunn, Neely Edwards. 7182f USA. prod/rel: Metro-Goldwyn-Mayer Pictures

MCGOWAN, ROBERT
After the Play, Story
After the Play 1916 d: William Worthington. lps: Herbert Rawlinson, Edna Maison, Herbert Barrington. 1r USA. prod/rel: Victor

In Search of a Wife, Story
In Search of a Wife 1915 d: William Worthington. lps: Herbert Rawlinson, Agnes Vernon, Marjorie Beardsley. 2r USA. prod/rel: Gold Seal

MCGRADY, MIKE
The Motel Tapes, Novel
Talking Walls 1984 d: Stephen F. VeronA. lps: Stephen Shellen, Sybil Danning, Marie Laurin. 85M USA. *Motel Vacancy* prod/rel: New World

MCGRATH, JOHN
The Cheviot, the Stag and the Black, Black Oil, 1974, Play
Cheviot, the Stag and the Black, Black Oil, The 1974 d: John MacKenzie. lps: John Bett, David MacLennan, Dolina MacLennan. MTV. 90M UKN. prod/rel: BBC

Events While Guarding the Bofors Gun, 1966, Play
Bofors Gun, The 1968 d: Jack Gold. lps: Nicol Williamson, Ian Holm, David Warner. 106M UKN. prod/rel: Rank Film Distributors, Everglades

MCGRATH, PATRICK
The Grotesque, Book
Grotesque, The 1995 d: John-Paul Davidson. lps: Alan Bates, Sting, Theresa Russell. 97M UKN. *Gentlemen Don't Eat Poets* (USA) prod/rel: Starlight, XIngu Films

MCGREEVEY, JOHN
Prescription: Murder, Book
Murder in Texas 1981 d: William Hale. lps: Katharine Ross, Sam Elliott, Farrah Fawcett. TVM. 200M USA.

MCGREGOR, ELIZABETH
Little White Lies, Book
Little White Lies 1998 d: Philip Saville. lps: Tara Fitzgerald, Martin Wenner, Cherie Lunghi. TVM. 120M UKN. prod/rel: BBC, the Drama House

MCGROARTY, JOHN STEVEN
California: Its History and Romance (Chapter 8), Book
Argonauts of California - 1849, The 1916 d: Henry Kabierske. lps: Grant Churchill, Gertrude Kaby, Dorothy Barrett. 10r USA. *The Argonauts* prod/rel: Monrovia Feature Film Co., State Rights

MCGUANE, THOMAS (1939–, USA, McGuane, Thomas Francis
Keep the Change, Novel
Keep the Change 1992 d: Andrew Tennant. lps: William L. Petersen, Lolita Davidovich, Rachel Ticotin. 95M USA.

Ninety-Two in the Shade, 1973, Novel
92° in the Shade 1975 d: Thomas McGuane. lps: Peter Fonda, Warren Oates, Elizabeth Ashley. 93M USA. *Ninety-Two in the Shade* prod/rel: Elliott Kastner

The Sporting Club, 1968, Novel
Sporting Club, The 1971 d: Larry Peerce. lps: Robert Fields, Nicolas Coster, Maggie Blye. 105M USA.

MCGUINNESS, JAMES K.
Pearls and Emeralds, Story
Cocktail Hour 1933 d: Victor Schertzinger. lps: Randolph Scott, Bebe Daniels, Jessie Ralph. 74M USA. prod/rel: Columbia Pictures Corp.

MCGUIRE, DON
Bad Time at Hondo, Story
Bad Day at Black Rock 1955 d: John Sturges. lps: Spencer Tracy, Robert Ryan, Anne Francis. 81M USA. prod/rel: Metro-Goldwyn-Mayer Corp.

Damon and Pythias, Story
Delicate Delinquent, The 1957 d: Don McGuire. lps: Jerry Lewis, Darren McGavin, Martha Hyer. 100M USA. prod/rel: Paramount, York Pictures

MCGUIRE, JAMES P.
Article
Call Northside 777 1948 d: Henry Hathaway. lps: James Stewart, Richard Conte, Kasia Orzazewski. 111M USA. *Calling Northside 777* prod/rel: 20th Century-Fox

MCGUIRE, WILLIAM ANTHONY
The Cost of Living, Cincinnati, Oh. 1913, Play
  Money Means Nothing 1934 d: W. Christy Cabanne. lps: Wallace Ford, Gloria Shea, Edgar Kennedy. 70M USA. prod/rel: Monogram Pictures Corp.©

If I Was Rich, New York 1926, Play
  Let's Be Ritzy 1934 d: Edward Ludwig. lps: Lew Ayres, Patricia Ellis, Isabel Jewell. 72M USA. *Millionaire for a Day* (UKN); **If I Was Rich** prod/rel: Universal Pictures Corp.©

Kid Boots, New York 1923, Musical Play
  Kid Boots 1926 d: Frank Tuttle. lps: Eddie Cantor, Clara Bow, Billie Dove. 8565f USA. prod/rel: Famous Players-Lasky, Paramount Pictures

Rosalie, 1928, Musical Play
  Rosalie 1937 d: W. S. Van Dyke. lps: Eleanor Powell, Nelson Eddy, Frank Morgan. 122M USA. prod/rel: Metro-Goldwyn-Mayer Corp.©, William Anthony Mcguire Production

Six-Cylinder Love, New York 1921, Play
  Honeymoon's Over, The 1939 d: Eugene J. Forde. lps: Stuart Erwin, Marjorie Weaver, Patric Knowles. 70M USA. *Six Cylinder Love*; *The Simple Life* prod/rel: Twentieth Century-Fox Film Corp.©
  Six Cylinder Love 1923 d: Elmer Clifton. lps: Ernest Truex, Florence Eldridge, Donald Meek. 6659f USA. prod/rel: Fox Film Corp.
  Six Cylinder Love 1931 d: Thornton Freeland. lps: Spencer Tracy, Edward Everett Horton, Sidney Fox. 71M USA. *The Minute Man*; *Riding for a Fall* prod/rel: Fox Film Corp.©, Thornton Freeland Production

Tin Gods, 1923, Play
  Tin Gods 1926 d: Allan Dwan. lps: Thomas Meighan, Renee Adoree, Aileen Pringle. 8568f USA. prod/rel: Famous Players-Lasky, Paramount Pictures

Twelve Miles Out, New York 1925, Play
  Twelve Miles Out 1927 d: Jack Conway. lps: John Gilbert, Ernest Torrence, Joan Crawford. 7899f USA. prod/rel: Metro-Goldwyn-Mayer Pictures

MCHUGH, MARTIN
A Minute's Wait, Play
  Rising of the Moon, The 1957 d: John Ford. lps: Noel Purcell, Cyril Cusack, John Cowley. 81M UKN/IRL. prod/rel: Four Provinces, Warner Bros.

MCHUGH, VINCENT
I Am Thinking of My Darling, New York 1943, Novel
  What's So Bad About Feeling Good? 1968 d: George Seaton. lps: George Peppard, Mary Tyler Moore, Dom Deluise. 94M USA. prod/rel: Universal Pictures

MCILVANE, JANE S.
It Happens Every Thursday, Novel
  It Happens Every Thursday 1953 d: Joseph Pevney. lps: John Forsythe, Loretta Young, Frank McHugh. 80M USA. prod/rel: Universal-International

MCILVANNEY, WILLIAM
The Big Man, Novel
  Big Man, The 1990 d: David Leland. lps: Liam Neeson, Joanne Whalley-Kilmer, Ian Bannen. 111M UKN. *The Big Man: Crossing the Line* prod/rel: Palace, Miramax

MCINERNEY, JAY
Big City Bright Lights, Novel
  Bright Lights, Big City 1988 d: James Bridges. lps: Michael J. Fox, Kiefer Sutherland, Frances Sternhagen. 107M USA. prod/rel: United Artists

MCINTYRE, HEATHER
Treble Trouble, Play
  Home and Away 1956 d: Vernon Sewell. lps: Jack Warner, Kathleen Harrison, Lana Morris. 81M UKN. prod/rel: Conquest, Guest

MCINTYRE, JOHN THOMAS
Investigator Ashton-Kirk, Philadelphia 1910, Book
  Affair of Three Nations, An 1915 d: Arnold Daly, Ashley Miller. lps: Arnold Daly, Sheldon Lewis, William Harrigan. 5r USA. prod/rel: Pathe Exchange, Inc., Gold Rooster Plays

House of Fear, 1910, Short Story
  House of Fear, The 1915 d: Arnold Daly, Ashley Miller. lps: Arnold Daly, Sheldon Lewis, Ina Hammer. 5r USA. prod/rel: Pathe Exchange, Inc., Gold Rooster Plays

The Menace of the Mute, 1910, Short Story
  Menace of the Mute, The 1915 d: Ashley Miller, Arnold Daly. lps: Arnold Daly, Sheldon Lewis, Louise Rutter. 5r USA. prod/rel: Pathe Exchange, Inc., Gold Rooster Plays

MCKAY, CLAUDE (1889-1948), JMC
Banjo, Novel
  Big Fella 1937 d: J. Elder Wills. lps: Paul Robeson, Elisabeth Welch, Roy Emerton. 73M UKN. prod/rel: British Lion, Fortune Films

MCKELWAY, ST. CLAIR
Old Eight Eighty, Article
  Mister 880 1950 d: Edmund Goulding. lps: Edmund Gwenn, Burt Lancaster, Dorothy McGuire. 90M USA. prod/rel: 20th Century-Fox

MCKENNA, MARTHE CNOCKHAERT
I Was a Spy, Book
  I Was a Spy 1933 d: Victor Saville. lps: Madeleine Carroll, Conrad Veidt, Herbert Marshall. 89M UKN. prod/rel: Gaumont-British, Woolf & Freedman

Lancer Spy, London 1937, Novel
  Lancer Spy 1937 d: Gregory Ratoff. lps: Dolores Del Rio, George Sanders, Peter Lorre. 84M USA. *Life of a Lancer Spy* prod/rel: Twentieth Century-Fox Film Corp.©

MCKENNA, RICHARD
The Sand Pebbles, New York 1962, Novel
  Sand Pebbles, The 1966 d: Robert Wise. lps: Steve McQueen, Richard Attenborough, Richard CrennA. 188M USA. prod/rel: Argyle Enterprises, Solar Productions

MCKENNA, STEPHEN (1888-1956), UKN
Sonia, Novel
  Sonia 1921 d: Denison Clift. lps: Evelyn Brent, Clive Brook, Cyril Raymond. 6060f UKN. prod/rel: Ideal

MCKENNEY, RUTH
Short Stories
  Margie 1946 d: Henry King. lps: Jeanne Crain, Alan Young, Glenn Langan. 94M USA. prod/rel: 20th Century-Fox

MCKERN, LEO (1920-, ASL, McKern, Reginald
London Story, Radio Play
  Chain of Events 1958 d: Gerald Thomas. lps: Dermot Walsh, Susan Shaw, Lisa Gastoni. 62M UKN. prod/rel: Beaconsfield, British Lion

MCKIE, RONALD
The Mango Tree, Novel
  Mango Tree, The 1977 d: Kevin Dobson. lps: Christopher Pate, Geraldine Fitzgerald, Robert Helpmann. 93M ASL. prod/rel: Pisces, Satori

MCKINNEY, RUTH
My Sister Eileen, Book
  My Sister Eileen 1942 d: Alexander Hall. lps: Rosalind Russell, Brian Aherne, Janet Blair. 96M USA. prod/rel: Columbia
  My Sister Eileen 1955 d: Richard Quine. lps: Betty Garrett, Janet Leigh, Jack Lemmon. 108M USA. prod/rel: Columbia

MCLAREN, JACK
Isle of Escape; a Story of the South Seas, London 1926, Novel
  Isle of Escape 1930 d: Howard Bretherton. lps: Monte Blue, Myrna Loy, Betty Compson. 4914f USA. prod/rel: Warner Brothers Pictures

MCLAUGHLIN, ROBERT H.
The Eternal Magdalene, New York 1915, Play
  Eternal Magdalene, The 1919 d: Arthur Hopkins. lps: Marguerite Marsh, Maxine Elliott, Charles Dalton. 5r USA. prod/rel: Goldwyn Pictures Corp.©, Goldwyn Distributing Corp.

The House Without Children, Cleveland 1917, Play
  House Without Children, The 1919 d: Samuel Brodsky. lps: Richard C. Travers, Gretchen Hartman, George Fox. 6-7r USA. prod/rel: Argus Enterprises, Inc., Film Market, Inc.

MCLAURIN, KATE L.
The Eyes of Julia Deep, Short Story
  Eyes of Julia Deep, The 1918 d: Lloyd Ingraham. lps: Mary Miles Minter, Allan Forrest, Alice Wilson. 5r USA. prod/rel: American Film Co.©, Pathe Exchange, Inc.

The Six-Fifty, New York 1921, Play
  Six-Fifty, The 1923 d: Nat Ross. lps: Renee Adoree, Orville Caldwell, Bert Woodruff. 5100f USA. prod/rel: Universal Pictures

MCLAVERTY, MICHAEL
The Schooner, 1978, Short Story
  Schooner, The 1983 d: Bill Miskelly. 53M IRL.

MCLEISH, ARCHIBALD
Epistle to Be Left in the Earth, 1930, Verse
  Epistle to Be Left in the Earth 1973 d: John Saxton. 20M CND.

MCLEISH, ROBERT
The Gorbals Story, Play
  Gorbals Story, The 1950 d: David MacKane. lps: Howard Connell, Betty Henderson, Russell Hunter. 74M UKN. prod/rel: Eros, New World

MCLELLAN, C. M. S., McLellan, Charles Morton Stuart
Leah Kleschna, New York 1904, Play
  Girl Who Came Back, The 1918 d: Robert G. VignolA. lps: Ethel Clayton, Elliott Dexter, Theodore Roberts. 5r USA. *The Woman Who Came Back* prod/rel: Famous Players-Lasky Corp.©, Paramount Pictures
  Leah Kleschna 1913 d: J. Searle Dawley. lps: Carlotta Nillson, House Peters, Hal Clarendon. 4r USA. prod/rel: Famous Players Film Co., State Rights

Leah Kleschna, New York 1920, Play
  Moral Sinner, The 1924 d: Ralph Ince. lps: Dorothy Dalton, James Rennie, Alphonse Ethier. 5437f USA. prod/rel: Famous Players-Lasky, Paramount Pictures

MCLENDON, JAMES
Eddie MacOn's Run, Novel
  Eddie MacOn's Run 1983 d: Jeff Kanew. lps: Kirk Douglas, John Schneider, Lee Purcell. 95M USA. prod/rel: Universal

MCLEOD, GOAN
The Ronin, Novel
  Samourai, Le 1967 d: Jean-Pierre Melville. lps: Alain Delon, Francois Perier, Nathalie Delon. 105M FRN/ITL. *Frank Costello Faccia d'Angelo* (ITL); *The Godson* (USA); *The Samurai* prod/rel: Filmel, Eugene Lepicier

MCMAHON, THOMAS PATRICK
The Issue of the Bishop's Blood, Novel
  Abduction of Saint Anne, The 1975 d: Harry Falk. lps: Robert Wagner, E. G. Marshall, Kathleen Quinlan. TVM. 78M USA. *They've Kidnapped Anne Benedict* prod/rel: Quinn Martin Productions

MCMILLAN, TERRY
How Stella Got Her Groove Back, Novel
  How Stella Got Her Groove Back 1998 d: Kevin Rodney Sullivan. lps: Angela Bassett, Taye Diggs, Regina King. 124M USA. prod/rel: 20th Century Fox©, Deborah Schindler

Waiting to Exhale, Novel
  Waiting to Exhale 1995 d: Forest Whitaker. lps: Whitney Houston, Angela Bassett, Loretta Devine. 121M USA. prod/rel: Twentieth Century-Fox

MCMURTRY, LARRY (1936-, USA, McMurtry, Larry Jeff
The Evening Star, Novel
  Evening Star, The 1996 d: Robert Harling. lps: Shirley MacLaine, Bill Paxton, Juliette Lewis. 128M USA. prod/rel: Rysher Entertainment Inc., Paramount Pictures

Pass By Horseman, New York 1961, Novel
  Hud 1963 d: Martin Ritt. lps: Paul Newman, Melvyn Douglas, Patricia Neal. 112M USA. prod/rel: Salem Productions, Dover Productions

The Last Picture Show, 1966, Novel
  Last Picture Show, The 1971 d: Peter Bogdanovich. lps: Timothy Bottoms, Jeff Bridges, Cybill Shepherd. 118M USA. prod/rel: B.B.S.

Leaving Cheyenne, 1963, Novel
  Lovin' Molly 1973 d: Sidney Lumet. lps: Anthony Perkins, Beau Bridges, Blythe Danner. 98M USA. *Gid and Johnny Molly* prod/rel: Movielab

Lonesome Dove, Novel
  Lonesome Dove 1988 d: Simon Wincer. lps: Robert Duvall, Tommy Lee Jones, Robert Urich. TVM. 480M USA.

Terms of Endearment, 1975, Novel
  Terms of Endearment 1983 d: James L. Brooks. lps: Shirley MacLaine, Jack Nicholson, Debra Winger. 132M USA. prod/rel: Paramount

Texasville, 1990, Novel
  Texasville 1990 d: Peter Bogdanovich. lps: Jeff Bridges, Cybill Shepherd, Annie Potts. 123M USA.

MCNAB, ANDY
Bravo Two Zero, Book
  Bravo Two Zero 1998 d: Tom Clegg. lps: Sean Bean, Jamie Bartlett, Kevin Collins. TVM. 120M UKN. prod/rel: BBC, Distant Horizon

MCNALLY, JOHN
The Green Eye, Play
  Jealousy 1931 d: G. B. Samuelson. lps: Mary Newland, Malcolm Keen, Harold French. 56M UKN. prod/rel: Majestic, New Era

The Paper Chase, Play
  Wickham Mystery, The 1931 d: G. B. Samuelson. lps: Eve Gray, John Longden, Lester Matthews. 84M UKN. prod/rel: Samuelson, United Artists

MCNALLY, TERRENCE (1939-, USA
Frankie and Johnny in the Clair de Lune, 1987, Play
  Frankie & Johnny 1991 d: Garry Marshall. lps: Al Pacino, Michelle Pfeiffer, Hector Elizondo. 118M USA. *Frankie and Johnny* prod/rel: Paramount

Love! Valour! Compassion!, Play
  Love! Valour! Compassion! 1997 d: Joe Mantello. lps: Jason Alexander, Randy Becker, Stephen Bogardus. 110M USA. prod/rel: Doug Chapin, Barry Krost

MCNAMARA, RACHEL
Lark's Gate, Novel
   Tell Your Children 1922 d: Donald Crisp. lps: Doris
   Eaton, Walter Tennyson, Margaret Halstan. 5532f
   UKN. prod/rel: International Artists, Gaumont

MCNAMARA, SEAN
Spam, Story
   Scrapple 1998 d: Christopher Hanson. lps: Geoffrey
   Hanson, Ryan Massey, Buck Simmonds. 91M USA.
   prod/rel: Sweetwater

MCNAMARA, WALTER
Shams, Story
   Shams of Society 1921 d: Thomas B. Walsh. lps:
   Barbara Castleton, Montagu Love, MacEy Harlam.
   6250f USA. prod/rel: Walsh-Fielding Productions, R-C
   Pictures

MCNAMEE, EOIN
Resurrection Man, Novel
   Resurrection Man 1997 d: Marc Evans. lps: Stuart
   Townsend, Geraldine O'Rawe, James Nesbitt. 102M
   UKN. prod/rel: Polygram Filmed Entertainment,
   Revolution Films

MCNAUGHTON, SARAH
The Fortune of Christina McNab, Novel
   Fortune of Christina McNab, The 1921 d: W. P.
   Kellino. lps: Nora Swinburne, David Hawthorne,
   Francis Lister. 6200f UKN. *Christina McNab* prod/rel:
   Gaumont, Westminster

MCNEIL, JANET
Child in the House, Novel
   Child in the House 1956 d: Cy Endfield, Charles de La
   Tour. lps: Phyllis Calvert, Eric Portman, Stanley Baker.
   88M UKN. prod/rel: Eros, Golden Era

MCNEILE, H. C. ("SAPPER")
The Black Gang, Novel
   Return of Bulldog Drummond, The 1934 d: Walter
   Summers. lps: Ralph Richardson, Ann Todd, Joyce
   Kennedy. 71M UKN. prod/rel: British International
   Pictures, Wardour

Bulldog Drummond, 1920, Novel
   Bulldog Drummond 1923 d: Oscar Apfel. lps: Carlyle
   Blackwell, Evelyn Greeley, Dorothy Fane. 5000f
   UKN/NTH. **De Bloedhond Van Het Geheimzinnige
   Sanatorium**; *Het Geheimzinnige Sanatorium*; *The
   Bulldog of the Mysterious Sanatorium*; *The Mysterious
   Sanatorium* prod/rel: Granger-Binger Film,
   Astra-National

   Bulldog Drummond 1929 d: F. Richard Jones. lps:
   Ronald Colman, Joan Bennett, Lilyan Tashman. 90M
   USA. prod/rel: Samuel Goldwyn, United Artists

Bulldog Drummond and the Oriental Mind, 1937,
Short Story
   Bulldog Drummond's Bride 1939 d: James P. Hogan.
   lps: John Howard, Heather Angel, H. B. Warner. 55M
   USA. *Mr. and Mrs. Bulldog Drummond* prod/rel:
   Paramount Pictures, Inc.

Bulldog Drummond at Bay, Novel
   Bulldog Drummond at Bay 1937 d: Norman Lee. lps:
   John Lodge, Dorothy MacKaill, Victor Jory. 78M UKN.
   prod/rel: British International Pictures, Associated
   British Pictures Corporation

Bulldog Drummond Strikes Back, New York 1933,
Novel
   Bulldog Drummond Strikes Back 1934 d: Roy Del
   Ruth. lps: Ronald Colman, Loretta Young, C. Aubrey
   Smith. 83M USA. prod/rel: 20th Century Pictures, Inc.

Challenge, New York 1937, Novel
   Bulldog Drummond in Africa 1938 d: Louis King.
   lps: John Howard, Heather Angel, H. B. Warner. 60M
   USA. prod/rel: Paramount Pictures, Inc.

Debt of Honour, Short Story
   Debt of Honour 1936 d: Norman Walker. lps: Leslie
   Banks, Will Fyffe, Geraldine Fitzgerald. 83M UKN. *The
   Man Who Could Not Forget* prod/rel: British National,
   General Film Distributors

The Female of the Species, London 1928, Novel
   Bulldog Drummond Comes Back 1937 d: Louis
   King. lps: John Barrymore, John Howard, Louise
   Campbell. 60M USA. prod/rel: Paramount Pictures, Inc.

The Final Count, London 1926, Novel
   Arrest Bulldog Drummond 1939 d: James P. Hogan.
   lps: John Howard, Heather Angel, H. B. Warner. 57M
   USA. *Scotland Yard Vs. Bulldog Drummond* prod/rel:
   Paramount Pictures, Inc.

The Hopeless Case, Short Story
   Poppies of Flanders 1927 d: Arthur Maude. lps:
   Jameson Thomas, Eve Gray, Malcolm Tod. 8750f UKN.
   Poppies in Flanders prod/rel: British International
   Pictures, Wardour

The Impassive Footman, Play
   Impassive Footman, The 1932 d: Basil Dean. lps:
   Owen Nares, Betty Stockfeld, Allan Jeayes. 70M UKN.
   Woman in Chains (USA); *Woman in Bondage* prod/rel:
   Associated Talking Pictures, Radio

The Return of Bulldog Drummond, London 1932,
Novel
   Bulldog Drummond's Revenge 1937 d: Louis King.
   lps: John Barrymore, John Howard, Louise Campbell.
   60M USA. prod/rel: Paramount Pictures, Inc.

Temple Tower, Garden City, N.Y. 1929, Novel
   Bulldog Drummond's Secret Police 1939 d: James
   P. Hogan. lps: John Howard, Heather Angel, H. B.
   Warner. 56M USA. prod/rel: Paramount Pictures, Inc.

   Temple Tower 1930 d: Donald Gallaher. lps: Kenneth
   MacKenna, Marceline Day, Henry B. Walthall. 5200f
   USA. prod/rel: Fox Film Corp.

The Third Round, London 1924, Novel
   Bulldog Drummond's Peril 1938 d: James P. Hogan.
   lps: John Barrymore, John Howard, Louise Campbell.
   68M USA. *Bulldog Drummond Interferes* prod/rel:
   Paramount Pictures, Inc.

   Bulldog Drummond's Third Round 1925 d: Sidney
   Morgan. lps: Jack Buchanan, Betty Faire, Juliette
   Compton. 7300f UKN. *The Third Round* prod/rel:
   Astra-National

Three of a Kind, Novel
   Love on the Spot 1932 d: Graham Cutts. lps:
   Rosemary Ames, Richard Dolman, Aubrey Mather. 64M
   UKN. prod/rel: Associated Talking Pictures, Radio

MCNEILL, ELIZABETH
9½ Weeks, Novel
   9½ Weeks 1984 d: Adrian Lyne. lps: Mickey Rourke,
   Kim Basinger, Margaret Whitton. 116M USA. *Nine and
   a Half Weeks* prod/rel: MGM, United Artists

MCNUTT, PATTERSON
Pigs, New York 1924, Play
   Midnight Kiss, The 1926 d: Irving Cummings. lps:
   Richard Walling, Janet Gaynor, George Irving. 5025f
   USA. *Pigs* prod/rel: Fox Film Corp.

MCNUTT, WILLIAM SLAVENS
Burglar Proof, 1920, Novel
   Burglar Proof 1920 d: Maurice Campbell. lps: Bryant
   Washburn, Lois Wilson, Grace Morse. 5r USA.
   Burglar-Proof prod/rel: Famous Players-Lasky Corp.©,
   Paramount Pictures

His Good Name, 1922, Short Story
   Trifling With Honor 1923 d: Harry Pollard. lps:
   Rockliffe Fellowes, Fritzi Ridgeway, Buddy Messinger.
   7785f USA. *Your Good Name*; *His Good Name* prod/rel:
   Universal Pictures

Leander Clicks, 1928, Short Story
   Hot Tip 1935 d: Ray McCarey, William Sistrom. lps:
   James Gleason, Zasu Pitts, Margaret Callahan. 69M
   USA. *Leander Clicks* prod/rel: RKO Radio Pictures©

MCPARTLAND, JOHN
The Kingdom of Johnny Cool, New York 1959, Novel
   Johnny Cool 1963 d: William Asher. lps: Henry Silva,
   Elizabeth Montgomery, Richard Anderson. 102M USA.
   prod/rel: Chrislaw Productions

No Down Payment, 1957, Novel
   No Down Payment 1957 d: Martin Ritt. lps: Joanne
   Woodward, Sheree North, Tony Randall. 102M USA.
   prod/rel: 20th Century-Fox

MCPHEE, JOHN (1931–, USA, McPhee, John Angus
Ruidoso, Story
   Casey's Shadow 1977 d: Martin Ritt. lps: Walter
   Matthau, Alexis Smith, Robert Webber. 116M USA.
   prod/rel: Columbia

MCPHERSON, SCOTT
Marvin's Room, Play
   Marvin's Room 1996 d: Jerry Zaks. lps: Meryl Streep,
   Leonardo Dicaprio, Diane Keaton. 98M USA. prod/rel:
   Scott Rudin, Tribeca

MCSHANE, MARK
The Passing of Evil, London 1961, Novel
   Grasshopper, The 1970 d: Jerry Paris. lps: Jacqueline
   Bisset, Jim Brown, Joseph Cotten. 95M USA. *The
   Passing of Evil*; *Angel* prod/rel: National General
   Pictures

Seance on a Wet Afternoon, 1964, Novel
   Seance on a Wet Afternoon 1964 d: Bryan Forbes.
   lps: Kim Stanley, Richard Attenborough, Nanette
   Newman. 116M UKN. prod/rel: Beaver Films, Allied
   Film Makers

MCSHERRY, MARY
Good Boy, Short Story
   Scandal at Scourie 1953 d: Jean Negulesco. lps: Greer
   Garson, Walter Pidgeon, Donna Corcoran. 90M USA.
   prod/rel: MGM

MCSWIGAN, MARIE
Snow Treasure, New York 1942, Novel
   Snow Treasure 1968 d: Irving Jacoby. lps: James
   Franciscus, Ilona Rodgers, Paul Austad. 95M USA.
   prod/rel: Sagittarius Productions

MCVEIGH, SUE
Grand Central Murder, Novel
   Grand Central Murder 1942 d: S. Sylvan Simon. lps:
   Van Heflin, Patricia Dane, Cecilia Parker. 73M USA.
   prod/rel: MGM

MCVICAR, JOHN
McVicar By Himself, Autobiography
   McVicar 1980 d: Tom Clegg. lps: Roger Daltrey, Adam
   Faith, Cheryl Campbell. 120M UKN. prod/rel: the Who
   Films, Brent-Walker

MEAD, SHEPHERD
*How to Succeed in Business Without Really
Trying*, New York 1952, Novel
   **How to Succeed in Business Without Really
   Trying** 1967 d: David Swift. lps: Robert Morse, Michele
   Lee, Rudy Vallee. 121M USA. prod/rel: Mirisch
   Corporation, United Artists

MEADE, MARION
Stealing Heaven, Novel
   Stealing Heaven 1988 d: Clive Donner. lps: Kim
   Thomson, Derek de Lint, Denholm Elliott. 116M
   UKN/YGS. prod/rel: Rank, Amy International

MEADOW, HERB
Calico Pony, Novel
   Count Three and Pray 1955 d: George Sherman. lps:
   Van Heflin, Joanne Woodward, Philip Carey. 102M
   USA. *The Calico Pony* prod/rel: Columbia, Copa Prods.

MEANEY, DONALD
The Toll of Youth, Story
   Toll of Youth, The 1915 d: Frank Lloyd. lps: Millard K.
   Wilson, Helen Leslie, Marc Robbins. SHT USA. prod/rel:
   Laemmle

MEANEY, LOTTIE M.
Pay-Day, New York 1916, Play
   Pay Day 1918 d: Sidney Drew, Mrs. Sidney Drew. lps:
   Sidney Drew, Mrs. Sidney Drew, Florence Short. 5r
   USA. prod/rel: Metro Pictures Corp.©, Screen Classics,
   Inc.

A Stitch in Time, New York 1918, Play
   Stitch in Time, A 1919 d: Ralph Ince. lps: Gladys
   Leslie, Eugene Strong, Agnes Ayres. 5r USA. prod/rel:
   Vitagraph Co. of America©

MEANO, CESARE
La Nascita Di Salome, Play
   Nascita Di Salome, La 1940 d: Jean Choux. lps:
   Conchita Montenegro, Armando Falconi, Fernando
   Freyre de Andrade. 2164m ITL/SPN/FRN. *El
   Nacimiento de Salome* (SPN); *La Naissance de Salome*
   (FRN) prod/rel: Stella S.a., I.C.I.

MEARS, MARY
The Forbidden Thing, 1920, Short Story
   Forbidden Thing, The 1920 d: Allan Dwan. lps:
   James Kirkwood, Helen Jerome Eddy, Marcia Manon.
   6r USA. prod/rel: Allan Dwan Productions, Associated
   Producers, Inc.

MEARSON, LLOYD
Lillian Day, Play
   Our Wife 1941 d: John M. Stahl. lps: Melvyn Douglas,
   Ruth Hussey, Ellen Drew. 95M USA. prod/rel: Columbia

MECCOLI, DOMENICO
La Barriera, Novel
   Pieta Per Chi Cade 1954 d: Mario CostA. lps: Amedeo
   Nazzari, Antonella Lualdi, Nadia Gray. 90M ITL.
   prod/rel: Rizzoli Film, Royal Film

MECHTOLD, MARY RIDER
The Mountain Girl, Story
   Mountain Girl, The 1915 d: James Kirkwood. lps:
   Dorothy Gish, Ralph Lewis, W. E. Lawrenson. 2r USA.
   prod/rel: Majestic

The Mountain Rat, Story
   Mountain Rat, The 1914 d: James Kirkwood. lps:
   Dorothy Gish, Henry B. Walthall, Irene Hunt. 4r USA.
   prod/rel: Reliance Motion Picture Cor., Mutual Film
   Corp.

The Official Introducer, Story
   Indiscretion 1915 d: Edgar Jones. lps: Louise Huff,
   Edgar Jones, Josephine Longworth. SHT USA. prod/rel:
   Lubin

MECKEL, CHRISTOPH
Bockshorn, 1973, Novel
   Bockshorn 1983 d: Frank Beyer. lps: Jeff Dominiak,
   Bert Loper, Djoko Rosic. 105M GDR. *Taken for a Ride*;
   The Intimidation prod/rel: Defa

MEDAL, CAMILLE
Et l'On Revient Toujours, Short Story
   Et l'On Revient Toujours 1917 d: Fernand Rivers.
   lps: Fernand Rivers, Paul Duc, Cecile Guyon. 790m
   FRN. prod/rel: Pathe Consortium

MEDCRAFT, RUSSELL G.
Cradle Snatchers, New York 1925, Play
   Cradle Snatchers, The 1927 d: Howard Hawks. lps:
   Louise Fazenda, J. Farrell MacDonald, Ethel Wales.
   6281f USA. prod/rel: Fox Film Corp.
   Why Leave Home? 1929 d: Raymond Cannon. lps: Sue
   Carol, Nick Stuart, Dixie Lee. 6388f USA. prod/rel: Fox
   Film Corp.

MEDEK, RUDOLF
Plukovnik Svec, Play
   Plukovnik Svec 1929 d: Svatopluk Innemann. lps:
   Bedrich Karen, Otto Zahradka, Fred Bulin. 3433m CZC.
   Colonel Svec prod/rel: Oceanfilm

MEDIN, HANS
Der Grune Kaiser, Novel
   Grune Kaiser, Der 1939 d: Paul Mundorf. lps: Gustav
   Diessl, Carola Hohn, Rene Deltgen. 90M GRM. prod/rel:
   UFA, Jugend

MEDOFF, MARK
Children of a Lesser God, 1980, Play
   Children of a Lesser God 1986 d: Randa Haines. lps:
   William Hurt, Marlee Matlin, Piper Laurie. 119M USA.
   prod/rel: Paramount

MEEHAN, JOHN
Barnum Was Right, New York 1923, Play
   Barnum Was Right 1929 d: Del Lord. lps: Glenn
   Tryon, Merna Kennedy, Otis Harlan. 5140f USA.
   prod/rel: Universal Pictures
Bless You Sister, New York 1927, Play
   Miracle Woman 1931 d: Frank CaprA. lps: Barbara
   Stanwyck, David Manners, Sam Hardy. 90M USA.
   prod/rel: Columbia Pictures Corp.©
The Lady Lies, New York 1928, Play
   Lady Lies, The 1929 d: Hobart Henley. lps: Walter
   Huston, Claudette Colbert, Charles Ruggles. 75M USA.
   prod/rel: Paramount Famous Lasky Corp.
   Perche No? 1930 d: Amleto Palermi. lps: Maria
   Jacobini, Livio Pavanelli, Oreste BilanciA. F FRN.
   prod/rel: Paramount

MEGAHY, LYNDON
Taffin, Novel
   Taffin 1988 d: Francis Megahy. lps: Pierce Brosnan,
   Alison Doody, Ray McAnally. 96M UKN/IRL. *Taffin: a
   Different Kind of Hero* prod/rel: Vestron

MEGED, AHARON
Play
   Chamesh Chamesh 1980 d: Shmuel Imberman. lps:
   Liron Nirgad, Dalik Volonitz, Zaharira Harifai. F ISR.
   5:5; Five and Five Musical; Five Five
   I Like Mike 1962 d: Peter Frye. lps: Batya Lancet, Ze'ev
   Berlinski, Gideon Zinger. F ISR.

MEGRUE, ROI COOPER
It Pays to Advertise, New York 1914, Play
   Criez-le Sur Les Toits 1932 d: Karl Anton. lps:
   Simone Hellard, Edith Mera, Paul Pauley. 77M FRN.
   Shout It from the House Tops (USA) prod/rel: Films
   Paramount
   It Pays to Advertise 1919 d: Donald Crisp. lps: Bryant
   Washburn, Lois Wilson, Walter Hiers. 5r USA. prod/rel:
   Famous Players-Lasky Corp.©, Paramount-Artcraft
   Pictures
   It Pays to Advertise 1931 d: Frank Tuttle. lps: Carole
   Lombard, Norman Foster, Eugene Pallette. 66M USA.
   Have You Got It? prod/rel: Paramount Publix Corp.©
Seven Chances, 1924, Play
   Seven Chances 1925 d: Buster Keaton. lps: Buster
   Keaton, T. Roy Barnes, Snitz Edwards. 5113f USA.
   prod/rel: Buster Keaton Productions, Metro-Goldwyn
   Distributing Corp.
Under Cover, New York 1914, Play
   Under Cover 1916 d: Robert G. VignolA. lps: Hazel
   Dawn, Owen Moore, Frank Losee. 5r USA. *Her First
   Consignment* prod/rel: Famous Players Film Co.©,
   Paramount Pictures Corp.
Under Sentence, New York 1916, Play
   Fighting Odds 1917 d: Allan Dwan. lps: Maxine
   Elliott, Henry Clive, Charles Dalton. 6r USA. prod/rel:
   Goldwyn Pictures Corp.©, Goldwyn Distributing Corp.

MEHERIN, ELENORE
Chickie, New York 1925, Novel
   Chickie 1925 d: John Francis Dillon. lps: Dorothy
   MacKaill, John Bowers, Hobart Bosworth. 7600f USA.
   prod/rel: First National Pictures

Sandy, Story
   Sandy 1926 d: Harry Beaumont. lps: Madge Bellamy,
   Leslie Fenton, Harrison Ford. 7850f USA. prod/rel: Fox
   Film Corp.

MEHTA, JAGJIVAN
Sonbaini Chundadi, Play
   Sonbaini Chundadi 1976 d: Girish Manukant. lps:
   Dilip Patel, Ranjitraj, Sohil Virani. 152M IND. prod/rel:
   R.J. Films

MEILHAC, HENRI (1832–1897), FRN
L' Ete de la Saint-Martin, Play
   Ete de la Saint-Martin, L' 1920 d: Georges
   Champavert. lps: Joseph Boulle, Germaine Syrdet,
   Marthe Lepers. 1735m FRN. prod/rel: Phocea Film
Fanny Lear, Play
   Fanny Lear 1919 d: Jean Manoussi, Robert Boudrioz.
   lps: Gabriel Signoret, Germaine Dermoz, Yvonne
   Sergyl. 1620m FRN. prod/rel: Film d'Art
Die Fledermaus, Vienna 1874, Operetta
   Chauve-Souris, La 1931 d: Pierre Billon, Carl Lamac.
   lps: Anny Ondra, Ivan Petrovitch, Mauricet. 80M FRN.
   prod/rel: Vandor-Film, Ondra-Lamac-Film
   Fledermaus, Die 1923 d: Max Mack. lps: Eva May, Lya
   de Putti, Harry Liedtke. 2093m GRM.
   Fledermaus, Die 1931 d: Carl Lamac. lps: Anny
   Ondra, Georg Alexander, Oskar SimA. 96M GRM.
   Fledermaus, Die 1937 d: Paul Verhoeven. lps: Georg
   Alexander, Hans Sohnker, Lida BaarovA. 95M GRM.
   Fledermaus, Die 1945 d: Geza von Bolvary. lps:
   Johannes Heesters, Marte Harell, Hans Brausewetter.
   100M GRM. *The Bat* (USA) prod/rel: Terra, Lloyd
   Fledermaus, Die 1955 d: E. W. Fiedler. lps: Jarmila
   Ksirowa, Sonja Schoner, Erich Arnold. 86M GDR.
   Rauschende Melodien prod/rel: Defa
   Fledermaus, Die 1962 d: Geza von CziffrA. lps: Peter
   Alexander, Marianne Koch, Marika Rokk. 107M AUS.
   prod/rel: Sascha-Film
   Fledermaus, Die 1966 d: Annelise Meineche. lps: Poul
   Reichhardt, Lily Broberg, Holger Jjul-Hansen. 98M
   DNM. *Flegermusen*
   Oh Rosalinda! 1955 d: Michael Powell, Emeric
   Pressburger. lps: Michael Redgrave, Ludmilla Tcherina,
   Anton Walbrook. 101M UKN/GRM. *Fledermaus '55*
   prod/rel: Powell & Pressburger, Ab-Pathe
   Waltz Time 1933 d: Wilhelm Thiele. lps: Evelyn Laye,
   Fritz Schultz, Gina Malo. 82M UKN. prod/rel:
   Gaumont-British, Woolf & Freedman
Frou-Frou, Paris 1869, Play
   Frou Frou 1914. lps: Maude Fealy, Harry Benham,
   James Cruze. 4r USA. prod/rel: Thanhouser Film Corp.,
   Mutual Film Corp.
   Frou-Frou 1918 d: Alfredo de Antoni. lps: Francesca
   Bertini, Guido Trento, Cia Fornaroli. 2078m ITL.
   prod/rel: Caesar Film
   Frou-Frou 1923 d: Guy Du Fresnay. lps: Gina Palerme,
   Jules Raucourt, Suzanne TalbA. 1792m FRN.
   Hungry Heart, A 1917 d: Emile Chautard. lps: Alice
   Brady, Edward Langford, George MacQuarrie. 5r USA.
   Frou Frou prod/rel: World Film Corp.©, Peerless
   Toy Wife, The 1938 d: Richard Thorpe. lps: Luise
   Rainer, Melvyn Douglas, Robert Young. 95M USA. *Frou
   Frou* (UKN); *Mlle.* prod/rel:
   Metro-Goldwyn-Mayer Corp., Loew's, Inc.©
Mam'zelle Nitouche, Paris 1882, Operetta
   Diavolo Va in Collegio, Il 1944 d: Jean Boyer. lps:
   Lilia Silvi, Leonardo Cortese, Greta GondA. 83M ITL.
   Santarellina prod/rel: Excelsa Film, Minerva Film
   Mam'zelle Nitouche 1931 d: Marc Allegret. lps: Janie
   Marese, Raimu, Andre Alerme. 106M FRN. prod/rel:
   Vandor-Film, Ondra-Lamac-Film
   Mam'zelle Nitouche 1954 d: Yves Allegret. lps:
   Fernandel, Pier Angeli, Jean Debucourt. 90M FRN/ITL.
   Santarellina (ITL); *Oh No Mam'zelle* prod/rel:
   Paris-Films Production, Panitalia Film
   Santarellina 1912 d: Mario Caserini. lps: Gigetta
   Morano, Ercole Vaser, Mario Bonnard. 882m ITL.
   Ma'mselle Nitouche (UKN); *Mam'selle Nitouche* (USA)
   prod/rel: S.A. Ambrosio
   Santarellina 1923 d: Eugenio Perego. lps: Leda Gys,
   Silvio Orsini, Lorenzo Soderini. 1401m ITL. prod/rel:
   Lombardo Film
Le Reveillon, 1872, Play
   So This Is Paris 1926 d: Ernst Lubitsch. lps: Monte
   Blue, Patsy Ruth Miller, Lilyan Tashman. 6135f USA.
   prod/rel: Warner Brothers Pictures
Tricoche Et Cacolet, Play
   Tricoche Et Cacolet 1938 d: Piere Colombier. lps:
   Fernandel, Frederic Duvalles, Ginette Leclerc. 107M
   FRN. prod/rel: Films Modernes, Natan, Emile

La Vie Parisienne, Operetta
   Vie Parisienne, La 1977 d: Christian-Jaque. lps:
   Bernard Alane, Jean-Pierre Darras, Martine Sarcey.
   105M FRN. *Pariser Leben* (GRM); *Parisian
   Life* prod/rel: Belles Rives, S.F.P.

MEINEL, VALERIO
Porque Claudia Lessin Vai Morrer, 1978, Novel
   Caso Claudio, O 1979 d: Miguel Borges. lps: Roberto
   Bonfim. 90M BRZ. *The Claudia Case*

MEISEL, WILL
Konigin Einer Nacht, Opera
   Konigin Einer Nacht 1951 d: Kurt Hoffmann. lps: Ilse
   Werner, Hans Holt, Georg ThomallA. 95M GRM. *Queen
   for a Night* prod/rel: Echo, Allianz

MELCHIOR, IB
Article
   When Hell Broke Loose 1958 d: Kenneth L. Crane.
   lps: Charles Bronson, Violet Rensing, Richard Jaeckel.
   78M USA. prod/rel: Paramount, Dolworth Prods.
Seed of Destruction, Story
   Live Fast, Die Young 1958 d: Paul Henreid. lps: Mary
   Murphy, Norma Eberhardt, Mike Connors. 82M USA.
   prod/rel: Universal-International, B.R.K., Inc.

MELDAL-JOHNSON, TREVOR
Always, Book
   Deja Vu 1984 d: Anthony Richmond. lps: Jaclyn Smith,
   Shelley Winters, Nigel Terry. 94M UKN. *Always*
   prod/rel: London Cannon Films, Dixons Films

MELESVILLE
Michele Perrin, 1834, Play
   Michele Perrin 1913 d: Eleuterio Rodolfi. lps: Ermete
   Novelli, Gigetta Morano, Alfredo Bertone. 1187m ITL.
   Michael Perrine (USA); *Spy for a Day* prod/rel: S.A.
   Ambrosio
Sullivan
   Comediante, El 1931 d: Ernesto Vilches, Leonard
   Fields. lps: Ernesto Vilches, Angelita Benitez, Jose
   Soriano VioscA. 72M USA. prod/rel: John H. Auer
   Productions, Ltd.

MELFORD, AUSTIN
Oh Daddy!, London 1930, Play
   Oh Daddy! 1935 d: Graham Cutts, Austin Melford. lps:
   Leslie Henson, Frances Day, Robertson Hare. 77M
   UKN. prod/rel: Gainsborough, Gaumont-British

MELFORD, MARK
Flying from Justice, London 1891, Play
   Flying from Justice 1913 d: Arthur Charrington. lps:
   Mark Melford, Nell Emerald, H. Agar Lyons. 2000f
   UKN. prod/rel: Brightonia, Popular
   Flying from Justice 1915 d: Percy Nash. lps: Gregory
   Scott, Joan Ritz, Douglas Payne. 4010f UKN. prod/rel:
   Neptune
Turned Up, London 1886, Play
   Who's Your Father? 1935 d: Henry W. George. lps:
   Lupino Lane, Peter Haddon, Nita Harvey. 63M UKN.
   prod/rel: St. George's Pictures, Lupino Lane

MELISEK, KAREL
Podej Stesti Ruku, Opera
   Rozkosny Pribeh 1936 d: Vladimir Slavinsky. lps:
   Vera Ferbasova, Zita Kabatova, Frantisek
   Kristof-Vesely. 3040m CZC. *Delightful Story* prod/rel:
   Slavia-Film

MELLWIG, FOLKE
Ryttare I Blatt, Novel
   Ryttare I Blatt 1959 d: Arne Mattsson. lps: Karl-Arne
   Holmsten, Annalisa Ericson, Nils Hallberg. 111M SWD.
   Rider in Blue prod/rel: Sandrew

MELVILLE, ALAN
Castle in the Air, London 1949, Play
   Castle in the Air 1952 d: Henry Cass. lps: David
   Tomlinson, Helen Cherry, Margaret Rutherford. 90M
   UKN. prod/rel: Hallmark, Ab-Pathe
Simon and Laura, London 1954, Play
   Simon and Laura 1955 d: Muriel Box. lps: Peter
   Finch, Kay Kendall, Muriel Pavlow. 91M UKN. prod/rel:
   Rank Film Distributors, Group Films
A Weekend at Thrackley, Play
   Hot Ice 1952 d: Kenneth Hume. lps: John Justin,
   Barbara Murray, Ivor Barnard. 65M UKN. prod/rel:
   Present Day, Swh Piccadilly

MELVILLE, HERMAN (1819–1891), USA
Bartleby, 1853, Short Story
   Bartleby 1970 d: Anthony Friedmann. lps: Paul
   Scofield, John McEnery, Thorley Walters. 79M UKN.
   prod/rel: British Lion, Pantheon
Benito Cereno, 1855, Short Story
   Benito Cereno 1968 d: Serge Roullet. lps: Ruy Guerra,
   Georges Selmark, Tamour Diop. 80M FRN/ITL/BRZ.
   prod/rel: Films Niepce, Films 13

Billy Budd, 1924, Novel
  Billy Budd 1962 d: Peter Ustinov. lps: Robert Ryan, Peter Ustinov, Melvyn Douglas. 125M UKN. prod/rel: Anglo-Allied Pictures, Rank Film Distributors

The Encantades, 1854, Short Story
  Iles Enchantees, Les 1964 d: Carlos Vilardebo. lps: Pierre Vaneck, Pierre Clementi, Amalia Rodrigues. 98M FRN/PRT. *As Ilhas Encantadas* (PRT); *The Enchanted Isles* prod/rel: Films Number One, Antonio Da Cunha Telles

The Lightning-Rod Man, 1854, Short Story
  Lightning-Rod Man, The 1975 d: John de Chancie. 16M USA.

Moby Dick Or the Whale, New York 1851, Novel
  Damon Des Meeres 1931 d: Michael Curtiz, Lloyd Bacon. lps: Wilhelm Dieterle, Lissi Arna, Anton Pointner. F USA/USA. *Moby Dick* prod/rel: Warner Bros. Pictures, Inc.
  Moby Dick 1930 d: Lloyd Bacon. lps: John Barrymore, Joan Bennett, Lloyd Hughes. 70M USA. prod/rel: Warner Brothers Pictures
  Moby Dick 1954 d: Albert McCleery. lps: Victor Jory, Hugh O'Brian. MTV. F USA.
  Moby Dick 1956 d: John Huston. lps: Gregory Peck, Richard Basehart, Leo Genn. 115M UKN/USA. prod/rel: Moulin, Warner Bros.
  Moby Dick 1998 d: Franc Roddam. lps: Patrick Stewart, Henry Thomas, Ted Levine. TVM. 240M USA/ASL/UKN. prod/rel: Whale/Nine Network Australian Prods., United Kingdom-Australia Co Prods.
  Sea Beast, The 1926 d: Millard Webb. lps: John Barrymore, Dolores Costello, George O'HaraR. 10r USA. prod/rel: Warner Brothers Pictures

Omoo, 1851, Novel
  Omoo Omoo 1949 d: Leon Leonard. lps: Ron Randell, Devera Burton, Pedro de CordobA. 58M USA. *The Shark God* (UKN); *The Shark God Oomo Omoo* prod/rel: Lippert, Esla

Typee, 1846, Novel
  Enchanted Island 1958 d: Allan Dwan. lps: Dana Andrews, Jane Powell, Don Dubbins. 94M USA. prod/rel: Warner Bros., RKO

MELVILLE, WALTER
The Beggar Girl's Wedding, Play
  Beggar Girl's Wedding, The 1915 d: Leedham Bantock. lps: Henry Lonsdale, Edith Bracewell, Lauderdale Maitland. 4500f UKN. prod/rel: British Empire

The Female Swindler, Play
  Female Swindler, The 1916 d: Albert Ward. lps: Henry Lonsdale, Alice Belmore, Arthur Poole. 5500f UKN. prod/rel: British Empire

The Girl Who Took the Wrong Turning, London 1906, Play
  Girl Who Took the Wrong Turning, The 1915 d: Leedham Bantock. lps: Henry Lonsdale, Alice Belmore, Nina Lynn. 5000f UKN. prod/rel: British Empire

The Girl Who Wrecked His Home, Play
  Girl Who Wrecked His Home, The 1916 d: Albert Ward. lps: Henry Lonsdale, Alice Belmore, Arthur Poole. 5000f UKN. prod/rel: British Empire Films

The Shopsoiled Girl, Play
  Shopsoiled Girl, The 1915 d: Leedham Bantock. lps: Henry Lonsdale, Alice Belmore, Nina Lynn. 4050f UKN. prod/rel: British Empire

A World of Sin, Play
  World of Sin, A 1915. 4400f UKN. prod/rel: British Empire

MELVYN, GLENN
The Love Match, London 1953, Play
  Love Match, The 1955 d: David Paltenghi. lps: Arthur Askey, Thora Hird, Glenn Melvyn. 85M UKN. prod/rel: British Lion, Group 3

MEMMI, ALBERT (1920–, TNS
Natziv Hamelach, Book
  Natziv Hamelach 1979 d: Haim Shiran. lps: Doron Zvi, Yoseph Shiloah, Rita Shukrun. 105M ISR. *Pillar of Salt* prod/rel: Israel Education Television

MENANDER (342bc–292bc), GRC, Menandros
Dyscolus, 316 bc, Play
  Parthenos, O 1967 d: Dimis Dadiras. lps: Alkis Yanakas, Sapfo Notara, Gisela Dali. 90M GRC. *The Virgin*

MENCHELL, IVAN
The Cemetery Club, Play
  Cemetery Club, The 1993 d: Bill Duke. lps: Ellen Burstyn, Olympia Dukakis, Diane Ladd. 107M USA. *Looking for a Live One* prod/rel: Buena Vista, Touchstone

MENDELSSOHN, PETER
Douloureuse Arcadie, Novel
  Marianne de Ma Jeunesse 1954 d: Julien Duvivier. lps: Marianne Hold, Isabelle Pia, Horst Buchholz. 105M FRN/GRM. *Marianne of My Youth* (USA); *Marianne* (GRM) prod/rel: Filmsonor, Regina

MENDES, CATULLE (1841–1909), FRN
Grande-Maguet, 1888, Novel
  Grande Maguet, La 1947 d: Roger Richebe. lps: Madeleine Robinson, Jean Davy, Marcel Peres. 95M FRN. prod/rel: Films Roger Richebe

MENZEL, GERHARD
Au Bout du Monde, Novel
  Au Bout du Monde 1933 d: Henri Chomette, Gustav Ucicky. lps: Kathe von Nagy, Line Noro, Pierre Blanchar. 80M FRN. *Les Fugitifs* prod/rel: U.F.a., a.C.E.

MENZIES, ARCHIE
Under Your Hat, London 1938, Play
  Under Your Hat 1940 d: Maurice Elvey. lps: Jack Hulbert, Cicely Courtneidge, Austin Trevor. 79M UKN. prod/rel: Grand National, British Lion

MERAY, TIBOR
Catch Me a Spy, Novel
  Catch Me a Spy 1971 d: Dick Clement. lps: Kirk Douglas, Marlene Jobert, Trevor Howard. 94M UKN/USA/FRN. *Les Doigts Croises* (FRN); *To Catch a Spy* (USA); *Keep Your Fingers Crossed* prod/rel: Rank, Ludgate

MERCEIN, ELEANOR
Basquerie, New York 1927, Book
  Mi Ultimo Amor 1931 d: Lewis Seiler. lps: Jose Mojica, Ana Maria Custodio, Mimi AgugliA. 9r USA.
  Their Mad Moment 1931 d: Hamilton MacFadden, Chandler Sprague. lps: Warner Baxter, Dorothy MacKaill, Zasu Pitts. 55M USA. prod/rel: Fox Film Corp.©

MERCER, CHARLES E.
Rachel Cade, New York 1956, Novel
  Rachel Cade 1961 d: Gordon Douglas. lps: Angie Dickinson, Peter Finch, Roger Moore. 123M USA. *The Sins of Rachel Cade* prod/rel: Warner Bros. Pictures

MERCER, DAVID (1928–1980), UKN
In Two Minds, 1967, Play
  Family Life 1971 d: Kenneth Loach. lps: Sandy Ratcliff, Bill Dean, Grace Cave. 108M UKN. *Wednesday's Child* (USA) prod/rel: Emi, Kestrel

A Suitable Case for Treatment, 1966, Television Play
  Morgan - a Suitable Case for Treatment 1966 d: Karel Reisz. lps: Vanessa Redgrave, David Warner, Robert Stephens. 97M UKN. *Morgan!* (USA); *A Suitable Case for Treatment* prod/rel: Quintra Productions, British Lion

MERCIER, A.
L' Aventure Amoureuse, Novel
  Proie du Vent, La 1926 d: Rene Clair. lps: Sandra Milowanoff, Charles Vanel, Jean Murat. 2200m FRN. *The Prey of the Wind* prod/rel: Films Albatros

MERE, CHARLES
La Femme Masquee, Paris 1923, Play
  Masked Woman, The 1927 d: Silvano Balboni. lps: Anna Q. Nilsson, Holbrook Blinn, Einar Hansen. 5434f USA. prod/rel: First National Pictures

La Flamme, Play
  Flamme, La 1925 d: Rene Hervil. lps: Germaine Rouer, Charles Vanel, Colette Darfeuil. SRL. 2800m FRN. prod/rel: Film d'Art (Vandal Et Delac)
  Flamme, La 1936 d: Andre Berthomieu. lps: Gabriel Signoret, Line Noro, Colette Darfeuil. 85M FRN. prod/rel: S.N.C.

Un Homme du Nord, Play
  Fortune de Marseille 1951 d: Henri Lepage, Pierre Mere. lps: Henri Vilbert, Madeleine Lebeau, Pierre Louis. 98M FRN. *Toucas de Marseille* prod/rel: C.F.P.C.

Le Prince Jean, Play
  Prince Jean, Le 1928 d: Rene Hervil. lps: Renee Heribel, Lucien Dalsace, Paul Guide. 2250m FRN. prod/rel: Societe Des Cineromans, Films De France
  Prince Jean, Le 1934 d: Jean de Marguenat. lps: Pierre Richard-Willm, Arnaudy, Nathalie Paley. 95M FRN. prod/rel: Fox Film

La Tentation, Play
  Tentation, La 1929 d: Rene Barberis, Rene Leprince. lps: Claudia Victrix, Lucien Dalsace, Fernand Mailly. F FRN. prod/rel: Societe Des Cineromans, Films De France
  Tentation, La 1936 d: Pierre Caron. lps: Antonin Berval, Marie Bell, Arlette Dubreuil. 97M FRN. prod/rel: Productions Claude Dolbert

Les Trois Masques, Play
  Trois Masques, Les 1921 d: Henry Krauss. lps: Henry Krauss, Henri Rollan, Gine Avril. 1800m FRN. prod/rel: Scagl
  Trois Masques, Les 1929 d: Andre Hugon. lps: Jean Toulout, Francois Rozet, Renee Heribel. F FRN. prod/rel: Pathe-Natan

Le Vertige, Play
  Vertige, Le 1926 d: Marcel L'Herbier. lps: Emmy Lynn, Jaque Catelain, Roger Karl. 91M FRN. prod/rel: Cinegraphic
  Vertige, Le 1935 d: Paul Schiller. lps: Andre Burgere, Jean Toulout, Alice Field. 80M FRN. prod/rel: Fox-Film

MEREDITH, GEORGE (1828–1909), UKN
Diana of the Crossways, Novel
  Diana of the Crossways 1922 d: Denison Clift. lps: Fay Compton, Henry Victor, J. R. Tozer. 4960f UKN. prod/rel: Ideal

MEREDITH, OWEN (1831–1891), UKN, Bulwer-Lytton, Edward Robert Lytton
Lucile, Poem
  Lucile 1912 d: Theodore Marston. lps: Marguerite Snow, James Cruze, Florence Labadie. 3r USA. prod/rel: Thanhouser

MEREDYTH, BESS
The Southerner, Story
  Modern Prodigal, The 1910 d: D. W. Griffith. lps: Guy Hedlund, George Nicholls, Kate Bruce. 992f USA. prod/rel: Biograph Co.

MERGENDAHL, CHARLES
The Bramble Bush, Novel
  Bramble Bush, The 1960 d: Daniel Petrie. lps: Richard Burton, Barbara Rush, Jack Carson. 105M USA. prod/rel: Warner Bros.

MERIMEE, PROSPER (1803–1870), FRN
Short Story
  Venere d'Ille, La 1979 d: Mario Bava, Lamberto BavA. lps: Daria Nicolodi, Adriana Innocenti, Diana de Curtis. MTV. F ITL. prod/rel: Pont Royal Film Tv

Carmen, Paris 1846, Novel
  Andalusische Nachte 1938 d: Herbert Maisch. lps: Imperio Argentina, Friedrich Benfer, Erwin Biegel. 94M GRM/SPN. *Nights in Andalusia* (USA) prod/rel: Tonfilm, Studio Carl Froelich
  Carmen 1909 d: Gerolamo Lo Savio. lps: Vittoria Lepanto, Dante Cappelli, Alberto Nepoti. 285m ITL. prod/rel: Film d'Arte Italiana
  Carmen 1910 d: Andre Calmettes. lps: Max Dearly, Regina Badet. FRN. prod/rel: Film d'Art
  Carmen 1913 d: Theodore Marston. lps: Marguerite Snow, William Garwood, William Russell. 3r USA. prod/rel: Thanhouser
  Carmen 1915 d: Cecil B. de Mille. lps: Geraldine Farrar, Wallace Reid, Pedro de CordobA. 5r USA. prod/rel: Jesse L. Lasky Feature Play Co.©, Paramount Pictures Corp.
  Carmen 1915 d: Raoul Walsh. lps: Theda Bara, Einar Linden, Carl Harbaugh. 5r USA. prod/rel: Fox Film Corp.©, William Fox©
  Carmen 1916 d: Augusto Turchi, Giovanni DoriA. lps: Margherita Carmen Sylva, Andrea Habay, Suzanne Arduini. ITL. prod/rel: Cines
  Carmen 1922 d: George Wynn. lps: Patrick Fitzgerald, Ward McAllister, Maresco Marescini. 1061f UKN. prod/rel: Master Films, Gaumont
  Carmen 1926 d: Jacques Feyder, Francoise Rosay. lps: Louis Lerch, Gaston Modot, Raquel Meller. 3000m FRN. prod/rel: Films Albatros
  Carmen 1927 d: H. B. Parkinson. lps: Herbert Langley, Zeda PaschA. 1657f UKN. prod/rel: Song Films
  Carmen 1943 d: Luis Cesar Amadori. 96M ARG.
  Carmen 1943 d: Christian-Jaque. lps: Viviane Romance, Jean Marais, Adriano Rimoldi. 124M FRN/ITL. prod/rel: Discina, Scalera
  Carmen 1967 d: Herbert von Karajan. lps: Grace Bumbry, Jon Vickers, Mirella Freni. 167M SWT.
  Carmen 1983 d: Carlos SaurA. lps: Antonio Gades, Laura Del Sol, Paco de LuciA. 98M SPN. prod/rel: Emiliano Piedra
  Carmen 1983 d: Francesco Rosi. lps: Julia Migenes, Placido Domingo, Ruggero Raimondi. 152M ITL/FRN. *Bizet's Carmen* prod/rel: Gaumont, Production Marcel Dassault (Paris)
  Carmen Di Trastevere 1962 d: Carmine Gallone. lps: Giovanna Ralli, Jacques Charrier, Lino VenturA. 105M ITL/FRN. *Carmen 63* (FRN) prod/rel: Globe International Film, Carmine Gallone (Roma)
  Carmen Jones 1954 d: Otto Preminger. lps: Harry Belafonte, Dorothy Dandridge, Pearl Bailey. 107M USA. prod/rel: 20th Century-Fox

Carmen, la de Ronda 1959 d: Tulio Demicheli. lps: Sara Montiel, Jorge Mistral, Maurice Ronet. 98M SPN. *The Devil Made a Woman* (USA); *A Girl Against Napoleon* prod/rel: Benito Perojo

Carmen Proibita 1953 d: Giuseppe Maria Scotese, Alejandro PerlA. lps: Ana Esmeralda, Fausto Tozzi, Mariella Lotti. 92M ITL/SPN. *Siempre Carmen* (SPN) prod/rel: Italo-Iberica Film (Roma), Suevia Film (Madrid)

Charlie Chaplin's Burlesque on Carmen 1916 d: Charles Chaplin. lps: Charles Chaplin, Edna Purviance, John Rand. 4r USA. *Carmen*; *Burlesque on Carmen* prod/rel: Essanay Film Mfg. Co.©, V-L-S-E, Inc.

Gypsy Blood 1931 d: Cecil Lewis. lps: Marguerite Namara, Tom Burke, Lance Fairfax. 79M UKN. *Carmen* (USA); *Gipsy Blood* prod/rel: British International Pictures, Wardour

Loves of Carmen, The 1927 d: Raoul Walsh. lps: Dolores Del Rio, Victor McLaglen, Don Alvarado. 8538f USA. prod/rel: Fox Film Corp.

Loves of Carmen, The 1948 d: Charles Vidor. lps: Rita Hayworth, Glenn Ford, Ron Randell. 99M USA. prod/rel: Columbia

Tragedie de Carmen, La 1983 d: Peter Brook. lps: Helene Delavault, Howard Hensel, Agnes Host. 85M FRN/UKN/GRM. *The Tragedy of Carmen* (UKN) prod/rel: Alby-Film, Antenne 2

Uomo, l'Orgoglio, la Vendetta, L' 1967 d: Luigi Bazzoni. lps: Franco Nero, Tina Aumont, Alberto Dell'acquA. 99M ITL/GRM. *Mit Django Kam Der Tod* (GRM); *Pride and Vengeance Man*; *Der Mann Der Stolze Die Rache*; *His Pride and Vengeance Man*; *Pride and Vengeance* prod/rel: Regal Film, Fono Roma (Roma)

Le Carrosse du Saint-Sacrement, 1829, Play
Carrosse d'Or, Le 1952 d: Jean Renoir. lps: Anna Magnani, Duncan Lamont, Paul Campbell. 101M FRN/ITL. *La Carrozza d'Oro* (ITL); *The Golden Carriage*; *The Golden Coach* prod/rel: Panaria Films, Hoche Productions (Paris)

Colomba, 1841, Novel
Colomba 1915 d: Travers Vale. lps: Gretchen Hartman, Joseph McDermott, Edward Cecil. 2r USA.

Colomba 1920 d: Jean Herve. lps: Victor Vina, Mirella Marcovici, Marthe Laverne. F FRN.

Colomba 1933 d: Jacques Severac. lps: Josette Day, Jean Angelo, Gaston Modot. 80M FRN. prod/rel: Compagnie Autonome Cinematographique

Colomba 1947 d: Emile Couzinet. lps: Catherine Damet, Jose Luccioni, Edward Stirling. 94M FRN. prod/rel: Burgus Films

Vendetta 1950 d: Mel Ferrer, Stuart Heisler (Uncredited). lps: Faith Domergue, George Dolenz, Donald BukA. 84M USA. prod/rel: RKO Radio, Hughes Prods.

Lokis, 1869, Short Story
Lokis 1969 d: Janusz Majewski. lps: Jozef Duriasz, Edmund Fetting, Gustaw Lutkiewicz. 105M PLN. *The Bear* (USA) prod/rel: Polski-Film, T.O.R.

Tamango, 1829, Short Story
Tamango 1957 d: John Berry. lps: Dorothy Dandridge, Curd Jurgens, Jean Servais. 98M FRN/ITL. prod/rel: Films Du Cyclope, Daina Cinematografica

MERIVALE, BERNARD
Blondie White, Play
Footsteps in the Dark 1941 d: Lloyd Bacon. lps: Errol Flynn, Brenda Marshall, Ralph Bellamy. 96M USA. prod/rel: Warner Bros.

The Flying Fool, London 1929, Play
Flying Fool, The 1931 d: Walter Summers. lps: Henry Kendall, Benita Hume, Wallace Geoffrey. 76M UKN. prod/rel: British International Pictures, Wardour

Tattenham Corner, 1934, Play
All in 1936 d: Marcel Varnel. lps: Ralph Lynn, Gina Malo, Jack Barty. 71M UKN. prod/rel: Gainsborough, Gaumont-British

The Wrecker, London 1927, Play
Seven Sinners 1936 d: Albert de Courville. lps: Edmund Lowe, Constance Cummings, Thomy Bourdelle. 70M UKN. *Doomed Cargo* (USA); *The Wrecker* prod/rel: Gaumont-British

Wrecker, The 1928 d: Geza von Bolvary. lps: Carlyle Blackwell, Benita Hume, Joseph Striker. 6670f UKN. prod/rel: Gainsborough, Woolf & Freedman

MERIVALE, HERMAN
Forget-Me-Not, London 1879, Play
Forget-Me-Not 1917 d: Emile Chautard. lps: Kitty Gordon, Montagu Love, Alec B. Francis. 5r USA. *Forget-Me-Nots* prod/rel: World Film Corp.©, Peerless

MERLE, ROBERT
Aus Einem Deutschen Leben, Novel
Aus Einem Deutschen Leben 1978 d: Theodor KotullA. lps: Gotz George, Kai Taschner, Elisabeth Schwarz. TVM. 145M GRM. *From a German Life*; *Death Is My Trade*; *Scenes from a German Life* prod/rel: Iduna, Wdr

The Day of the Dolphin, Novel
Day of the Dolphin, The 1973 d: Mike Nichols. lps: George C. Scott, Trish Van Devere, Paul Sorvino. 120M USA. prod/rel: Avco Embassy

Malevil, Novel
Malevil 1981 d: Christian de Chalonge. lps: Michel Serrault, Jacques Dutronc, Jacques Villeret. 120M FRN/GRM. prod/rel: N.E.F. Diffusion, Les Films Gibe Telecip

Week-End a Zuydcoote, Novel
Week-End a Zuydcoote 1964 d: Henri Verneuil. lps: Jean-Paul Belmondo, Catherine Spaak, Georges Geret. 120M FRN/ITL. *Weekend at Dunkirk* (USA) prod/rel: Paris-Films Production, Interopa Film

MERLIN, E. S.
The Brown Derby, 1925, Play
Brown Derby, The 1926 d: Charles Hines. lps: Johnny Hines, Diana Kane, Ruth Dwyer. 6700f USA. prod/rel: C. C. Burr Pictures

MERLINOVA, LIDA
Zlaty Clovek, Novel
Zlaty Clovek 1939 d: Vladimir Slavinsky. lps: Otomar Korbelar, Hana Vitova, Zita KabatovA. 2818m CZC. *The Golden Man* prod/rel: Slavia-Film

MERRICK, HOPE
Mary Girl, Play
Mary Girl 1917 d: Maurice Elvey. lps: Norman McKinnel, Jessie Winter, Margaret Bannerman. 4730f UKN. prod/rel: Butcher

MERRICK, LEONARD
Story
Tragedy of a Comic Song, The 1921 d: Maurice Elvey. lps: Valia, Robert Vallis, Teddy Arundell. 1050f UKN. prod/rel: Stoll

Conrad in Quest of His Youth, London 1903, Novel
Conrad in Quest of His Youth 1920 d: William C. de Mille. lps: Thomas Meighan, Kathlyn Williams, Mabel Van Buren. 5926f USA. prod/rel: Famous Players-Lasky Corp.©, Paramount Pictures

The House of Lynch, London 1907, Novel
School for Wives 1925 d: Victor Hugo Halperin. lps: Conway Tearle, Sigrid Holmquist, Peggy Kelly. 6782f USA. prod/rel: Victory Pictures, Vitagraph Co. of America

The Imposter, New York 1910, Play
Darling of the Rich, The 1922 d: John G. Adolfi. lps: Betty Blythe, Gladys Leslie, Jane Jennings. 6144f USA. prod/rel: B. B. Productions

Daughter of Luxury, A 1922 d: Paul Powell. lps: Agnes Ayres, Tom Gallery, Edith Yorke. 4538f USA. prod/rel: Famous Players-Lasky, Paramount Pictures

Impostor, The 1918 d: Dell Henderson. lps: Ann Murdock, David Powell, Lionel Adams. 5r USA. *The Imposter* prod/rel: Empire All Star Corp.©, Mutual Film Corp.

Laurels and the Lady, 1908, Short Story
Fool's Paradise 1921 d: Cecil B. de Mille. lps: Dorothy Dalton, Mildred Harris, Conrad Nagel. 8681f USA. prod/rel: Famous Players-Lasky, Paramount Pictures

Magnificent Lie, The 1931 d: Berthold Viertel. lps: Ruth Chatterton, Ralph Bellamy, Charles Boyer. 79M USA. prod/rel: Paramount Publix Corp.©

The Worldlings, New York 1900, Novel
Thief in Paradise, A 1925 d: George Fitzmaurice. lps: Doris Kenyon, Ronald Colman, Aileen Pringle. 7355f USA. prod/rel: George Fitzmaurice Productions, First National Pictures

Worldlings, The 1920 d: Eric Harrison. lps: Basil Gill, Ivy Close, Margaret Halstan. 6000f UKN. prod/rel: General Attractions, Globe

MERRILL BOB
Funny Girl, New York 1964, Musical Play
Funny Girl 1968 d: William Wyler. lps: Barbra Streisand, Omar Sharif, Kay Medford. 155M USA. prod/rel: Rastar Productions, Columbia

MERRIMAN, HENRY SETON
The Sowers, New York 1895, Novel
Sowers, The 1916 d: William C. de Mille. lps: Blanche Sweet, Thomas Meighan, Mabel Van Buren. 5r USA. prod/rel: Jesse L. Lasky Feature Play Co.©, Paramount Pictures Corp.

MERRITT, ABRAHAM (1884–1943), USA
7 Footprints to Satan, New York 1928, Novel
Seven Footprints to Satan 1929 d: Benjamin Christensen. lps: Thelma Todd, Creighton Hale, Sheldon Lewis. 5405f USA. prod/rel: First National Pictures

Witch, Burn! Burn, New York 1933, Novel
Devil-Doll, The 1936 d: Tod Browning. lps: Lionel Barrymore, Maureen O'Sullivan, Frank Lawton. 79M USA. *The Witch of Timbuktu*; *The Devil Doll*; *The Witch of Timbuktoo* prod/rel: Metro-Goldwyn-Mayer Corp.

MERSEREAU, JOHN
The Checkered Flag, Boston 1925, Novel
Checkered Flag, The 1926 d: John G. Adolfi. lps: Elaine Hammerstein, Wallace MacDonald, Lionel Belmore. 6071f USA. prod/rel: Banner Productions

The Whispering Canyon, New York 1926, Novel
Whispering Canyon 1926 d: Tom Forman. lps: Jane Novak, Robert Ellis, Lee Shumway. 5652f USA. prod/rel: Banner Productions, Ginsberg-Kann Distributing Corp.

MERSON, BILLY
Serentata, Sketch
Billy's Spanish Love Spasm 1915 d: W. P. Kellino. lps: Billy Merson, Teddie Gerrard, Blanche BellA. 3000f UKN. prod/rel: Homeland, Globe

MERWIN, SAMUEL
Anthony the Absolute, New York 1914, Novel
Door Between, The 1917 d: Rupert Julian. lps: Ruth Clifford, Monroe Salisbury, George A. McDaniel. 5r USA. prod/rel: Bluebird Photoplays, Inc.©

Comrade John, New York 1907, Novel
Comrade John 1915 d: T. Hayes Hunter. lps: William Elliott, Ruth Roland, Lew Cody. 5r USA. prod/rel: Balboa Amusement Producing Co., Pathe Exchange, Inc.

Dinner at Eight, 1912, Short Story
Crooked Streets 1920 d: Paul Powell. lps: Ethel Clayton, Jack Holt, Clyde Fillmore. 4750f USA. *All in the Night* prod/rel: Famous Players-Lasky Corp.©, Paramount-Artcraft Pictures

The Honey Bee, New York 1901, Novel
Honey Bee, The 1920 d: Rupert Julian. lps: Thomas Holding, Nigel Barrie, Marguerita SylvA. 6r USA. prod/rel: American Film Co., Pathe Exchange, Inc.

The Passionate Pilgrim, Indianapolis 1919, Novel
Passionate Pilgrim, The 1921 d: Robert G. VignolA. lps: Matt Moore, Mary Newcomb, Julia Swayne Gordon. 7r USA. prod/rel: Cosmopolitan Productions, Paramount Pictures

The Trufflers, Indianapolis 1916, Novel
Trufflers, The 1917 d: Fred E. Wright. lps: Nell Craig, Sidney Ainsworth, Ernest Maupain. 5r USA. prod/rel: Essanay Film Mfg. Co.©, K-E-S-E Service

MERY
Le Venus d'Arles, Short Story
Venus d'Arles, La 1917 d: Georges DenolA. lps: Armand Tallier, Andre Lefaur, Andree Divonne. 1185m FRN. prod/rel: Scagl

MESSENGER, MAURICE
Murder in the Stalls, Play
Not Wanted on Voyage 1936 d: Emile Edwin Reinert. lps: Bebe Daniels, Ben Lyon, Tom Helmore. 72M UKN. *Treachery on the High Seas* (USA); *Murder in the Stalls* prod/rel: Dela Films, British Lion

MESSITER, IAN
Mr. Drake's Duck, Radio Play
Mr. Drake's Duck 1951 d: Val Guest. lps: Douglas Fairbanks Jr., Yolande Donlan, A. E. Matthews. 85M UKN. *Mrs. Drake's Duck* prod/rel: Angel Productions, Eros

MESZOLY, MIKLOS
Magasiskola, 1967, Short Story
Magasiskola 1970 d: Istvan Gaal. lps: Ivan Andonov, Gyorgy Banffy, Judit Meszleri. 90M HNG. *The Falcon* (USA); *The Falcons* prod/rel:

Pannon Toredek, Novel
Pannon Toredek 1998 d: Andras Solyom. lps: Erika Marozsan, Sandor Almasi, Viktor Nagy. 81M HNG. *Hungarian Fragment* prod/rel: 2. Media Box, Hbo

METALIOUS, GRACE (1924–1964), USA, Metalious, Grace de Repentigny
Peyton Place, 1956, Novel
Peyton Place 1957 d: Mark Robson. lps: Lana Turner, Hope Lange, Lee Philips. 157M USA. prod/rel: 20th Century-Fox

Return to Peyton Place, New York 1959, Novel
Return to Peyton Place 1961 d: Jose Ferrer. lps: Carol Lynley, Jeff Chandler, Eleanor Parker. 123M USA. prod/rel: Jerry Wald Productions, Associated Producers, Inc.

METCALFE, STEPHEN
Strange Snow, Play
Jacknife 1988 d: David Jones. lps: Robert de Niro, Ed Harris, Kathy Baker. 102M USA. prod/rel: Vestron, Kings Road Entertainment

METENIER, OSCAR
Derniere Aventure du Prince Curacao, Novel
Derniere Aventure du Prince Curacao, La 1912. lps: Robert Hasti, Carmen Deraisy. 360m FRN. prod/rel: Scagl

Le Prince Curacao, Novel
Son Altesse 1922 d: Henri Desfontaines. lps: Jean Devalde, Marguerite Madys, Blanche Montel. 1550m FRN. prod/rel: Gaumont - Serie Pax

METZ, VITTORIO
Valentina, Play
Buongiorno Primo Amore! 1957 d: Marino Girolami. lps: Claudio Villa, Maurizio Arena, Fulvia Franco. 90M ITL/SPN. *Valentina* (SPN) prod/rel: Produzioni D.S. (Roma), Union Film (Madrid)

MEWSHAW, MICHAEL
Year of the Gun, Novel
Year of the Gun 1991 d: John Frankenheimer. lps: Andrew McCarthy, Valeria Golino, Sharon Stone. 111M USA. prod/rel: Yog Productions, Initial Films

MEY, LEV ALEKSANDROVICH
Tsarskaya Nevesta, 1849, Play
Tsarskaya Nevesta 1965 d: Vladimir Gorikker. lps: Raisa Nedashkovskaya, Natalya Rudnaya, Otar Koberidze. 95M USS. *The Tsar's Bride* (USA) prod/rel: Riga Film Studio

MEYER, CONRAD FERDINAND (1825–1898), SWT
Gustav Adolfs Page, 1882, Short Story
Gustav Adolfs Page 1960 d: Rolf Hansen. lps: Liselotte Pulver, Curd Jurgens, Ellen Schwiers. 93M AUS/GRM. prod/rel: Goldbaum, Mundus

Die Richterin, 1885, Short Story
Violanta 1978 d: Daniel Schmid. lps: Lucia Bose, Lou Castel, Maria Schneider. 100M SWT. prod/rel: Condor, Artcofilm

Der Schuss von Der Kanzel, Zurich 1877, Short Story
Schuss von Der Kanzel, Der 1942 d: Leopold Lindtberg. lps: Adolf Manz, Irene Naef, Fred Tanner. 104M SWT. *Le Coup de Feu Dans l'Eglise* prod/rel: Praesens-Film

MEYER, KLAUS
Weisse Wolke Carolin, Novel
Weisse Wolke Carolin 1984 d: Rolf Losansky. lps: Andreas Roll, Constanze Berndt, Ute Schorn. 85M GDR. *Little White Cloud Caroline*; *White Cloud Caroline* prod/rel: Defa G, Gruppe Babelsberg

MEYER, NICHOLAS
The Seven-Per-Cent Solution, Novel
Seven-Per-Cent Solution, The 1976 d: Herbert Ross. lps: Nicol Williamson, Robert Duvall, Alan Arkin. 113M USA. prod/rel: Universal

MEYER, ROLF
Das Bad Auf Der Tenne, Story
Bad Auf Der Tenne, Das 1943 d: Volker von Collande. lps: Heli Finkenzeller, Will Dohm, Richard Haussler. 82M GRM. *The Village Bathtub* prod/rel: Tobis, Super

Bad Auf Der Tenne, Das 1956 d: Paul Martin. lps: Sonja Ziemann, Paul Klinger, Nadja Tiller. 88M GRM. *The Village Bathtub* prod/rel: C.C.C., Bavaria

MEYER-FORSTER, WILHELM
Alt Heidelberg, New York 1902, Play
Student Prince in Old Heidelberg, The 1927 d: Ernst Lubitsch. lps: Ramon Novarro, Norma Shearer, Jean Hersholt. 9435f USA. *The Student Prince* (UKN); *Old Heidelberg* prod/rel: Metro-Goldwyn-Mayer Pictures

Karl Heinrich, 1899, Novel
Alt-Heidelberg 1959 d: Ernst MarischkA. lps: Christian Wolff, Gert Frobe, Sabine Sinjen. 105M GRM. *Old Heidelberg* prod/rel: C.C.C., Kurt Ulrich

Old Heidelberg 1915 d: John Emerson. lps: Wallace Reid, Dorothy Gish, Raymond Wells. 5r USA. *In Old Heidelberg* prod/rel: Fine Arts Film Co., Triangle Film Corp.©

Student Prince, The 1954 d: Richard Thorpe. lps: Edmund Purdom, Ann Blyth, John Ericson. 107M USA. prod/rel: MGM

MEYERS, HENRY
Little Miss Bluebeard, Play
Marions-Nous 1931 d: Louis Mercanton. lps: Fernand Gravey, Pierre Etchepare, Alice CoceA. 94M FRN. *Sa Nuit de Noces* prod/rel: Films Paramounts

MEYERS, PATRICK
K 2, Play
K-2 1991 d: Franc Roddam. lps: Michael Biehn, Matt Craven, Raymond J. Barry. 111M USA. *K2* prod/rel: Trans Pacific Films, Majestic Films International

MEYERS, ROBERT
Like Normal People, Book
Like Normal People 1979 d: Harvey Hart. lps: Shaun Cassidy, Linda Purl, Hope Lange. TVM. 100M USA. prod/rel: Christiana Prods., 20th Century-Fox Tv

MEYJES, WALTER
Ecce Homo, Play
Westminster Passion Play - Behold the Man, The 1951 d: Walter RillA. lps: Charles P. Carr. 75M UKN. prod/rel: Film Reports, Companions of the Cross

MEYNELL, LAURENCE
The Breaking Point, London 1957, Novel
Breaking Point, The 1961 d: Lance Comfort. lps: Peter Reynolds, Dermot Walsh, Joanna Dunham. 59M UKN. *The Great Armored Car Swindle* (USA) prod/rel: Butcher's Films

The Creaking Chair, Novel
Street of Shadows 1953 d: Richard Vernon. lps: Cesar Romero, Kay Kendall, Edward Underdown. 84M UKN. *Shadow Man* (USA) prod/rel: Merton Park, William Nassour

The House in Marsh Road, Novel
House in Marsh Road, The 1960 d: Montgomery Tully. lps: Tony Wright, Patricia Dainton, Sandra Dorne. 70M UKN. *Invisible Creature* (USA); *The House on Marsh Road* prod/rel: Grand National, Eternal

One Step from Murder, Novel
Price of Silence, The 1960 d: Montgomery Tully. lps: Gordon Jackson, June Thorburn, Maya Koumani. 73M UKN. prod/rel: Grand National, Eternal

Third Time Unlucky, Novel
Crown V Stevens 1936 d: Michael Powell. lps: Beatrix Thomson, Patric Knowles, Reginald Purdell. 66M UKN. *Third Time Unlucky* prod/rel: Warner Bros., First National

MEYRINK, GUSTAV
Der Golem, 1915, Novel
Golem 1979 d: Piotr Szulkin. lps: Krystyna Janda, Marek Walczewski, Krzysztof Majchrzak. 94M PLN.

Golem, Le 1935 d: Julien Duvivier. lps: Harry Baur, Roger Karl, Germaine Aussey. 100M FRN/CZC. *The Legend of Prague* (UKN); *The Man of Stone*; *The Golem* (USA); *Golem* (CZC) prod/rel: Ab

MI SHATELUOFU
Lenin and the Second Generation, Play
Yi Ge Ming de Ming Yi 1960 d: Li Enjie, Shi Daqian. lps: Zhou Zheng, Yu Shizhi, Tan Kun. 16r CHN. *For the Sake of the Revolution* prod/rel: Beijing Film Studio

MICHAEL, FRIEDRICH
Der Blaue Strohhut, Play
Blaue Strohhut, Der 1949 d: Victor Tourjansky. lps: Margot Hielscher, Karl Schonbock, Gisela Schmidting. 88M GRM. *The Blue Straw Hat* prod/rel: Georg Witt, Schorcht

MICHAEL, JUDITH
Deceptions, Novel
Deceptions 1985 d: Robert Chenault, Melville Shavelson. lps: Stefanie Powers, Barry Bostwick, Jeremy Brett. TVM. 200M USA. prod/rel: NBC, Columbia

MICHAELIS, KARIN (1872–1950), DNM
Das Gefahrliche Alter, Novel
Gefahrliche Alter, Das 1927 d: Eugen Illes. lps: Asta Nielsen, Walter Rilla, Maria Paudler. 2598m GRM. prod/rel: Illes-Film

Die Heilige Luge, 1915, Play
Star for a Night 1936 d: Lewis Seiler. lps: Claire Trevor, Jane Darwell, Evelyn Venable. 76M USA. *The Holy Lie* prod/rel: Twentieth Century-Fox Film Corp.©

MICHAELIS, SOPHUS
Revolutionshochzeit, Play
Revolutionshochzeit 1928 d: Anders W. Sandberg. lps: Diomira Jacobini, Gosta Ekman, Karina Bell. 2975m GRM/DNM. *Revolutionsbryllup* (DNM) prod/rel: Terra-Film

MICHAELS, BARBARA (1927–, USA, Mertz, Barbara Louise Gross, Peters, Elizabeth
Come Home Ammie, Novel
House That Would Not Die, The 1970 d: John Llewellyn Moxey. lps: Barbara Stanwyck, Richard Egan, Michael Anderson Jr. TVM. 74M USA. *The House That Wouldn't Die*; *Come Home Ammie* prod/rel: Aaron Spelling Productions

MICHAELS, GEORGE
African Fury, Book
Skabenga 1953 d: George Michael. lps: George Michael. 60M SAF. *Skabenka*; *African Fury* prod/rel: Allied Artists

MICHAELS, LEONARD
Men's Club, Novel
Men's Club, The 1986 d: Peter Medak. lps: David Dukes, Richard Jordan, Harvey Keitel. 100M USA. prod/rel: Atlantic, Howard Gottfried Productions

MICHAELS, PAT
Article
True Story of Lynn Stuart, The 1958 d: Lewis Seiler. lps: Betsy Palmer, Jack Lord, Barry Atwater. 78M USA. *The Other Life of Lynn Stuart* prod/rel: Columbia

MICHEAUX, OSCAR (1884–1951), USA
The Conquest, Short Story
Exile, The 1931 d: Oscar Micheaux. lps: Eunice Brooks, Charles Moore, Stanley Morrell. 93M USA. prod/rel: Micheaux Film Corp., Oscar Micheaux©

The Homesteader, Sioux City 1917, Novel
Homesteader, The 1919 d: Oscar Micheaux, Jerry Mills. lps: Evelyn Preer, Charles D. Lucas, Iris Hall. 7r USA. prod/rel: Micheaux Book and Film Co., Western Book Supply

House of Mystery, Novel
Broken Violin, The 1927 d: Oscar Micheaux. lps: J. Homer Tutt, Ardella Dabney, Alice B. Russell. 7r USA. prod/rel: Micheaux Film Corp.

MICHEL, GEORGES
Les Montparnos, Paris 1924, Book
Montparnasse 19 1957 d: Jacques Becker. lps: Gerard Philipe, Anouk Aimee, Lilli Palmer. 120M FRN/ITL. *Montparnasse* (ITL); *The Lovers of Montparnasse* (UKN); *Modigliani of Montparnasse* (USA) prod/rel: Astra Cinematografica, Franco-London Film

MICHELET, JAN
Orions Belte, Novel
Orions Belte 1984 d: Ola Solum. lps: Helge Jordal, Sverre Anker Ousdal, Hans Ola Sorlie. 103M NRW. *Orion's Belt* prod/rel: Filmeffekt, Orionfilm

MICHELET, JULES
Story
Kanashimi No Belladonna 1973 d: Eiichi Yamamoto. ANM. 102M JPN. *Belladonna* prod/rel: Nippon Herald Films

MICHELSON, MIRIAM
In the Bishop's Carriage, Indianapolis 1904, Novel
In the Bishop's Carriage 1913 d: Edwin S. Porter, J. Searle Dawley. lps: Mary Pickford, House Peters, David Wall. 4r USA. prod/rel: Famous Players Film Co., State Rights

In the Bishop's Garden, Indianapolis 1904, Novel
She Couldn't Help It 1920 d: Maurice Campbell. lps: Bebe Daniels, Emory Johnson, Wade Boteler. 4423f USA. *In the Bishop's Garden* prod/rel: Realart Pictures Corp.©

Michael Thwaite's Wife, New York 1909, Novel
Better Half, The 1918 d: John S. Robertson. lps: Alice Brady, David Powell, Crauford Kent. 5073f USA. prod/rel: Select Pictures Corp.©

MICHENER, JAMES A. (1907–, USA, Michener, James Albert
The Bridges at Toko-Ri, 1953, Novel
Bridges at Toko-Ri, The 1954 d: Mark Robson. lps: William Holden, Grace Kelly, Fredric March. 103M USA. prod/rel: Paramount

Caravans, 1963, Novel
Caravans 1978 d: James Fargo. lps: Anthony Quinn, Jennifer O'Neill, Michael Sarrazin. 127M USA/IRN. prod/rel: Universal

Centennial, Novel
Centennial 1978 d: Virgil W. Vogel, Paul Krasny. lps: David Janssen, Richard Chamberlain, Robert Conrad. TVM. 1315M USA. prod/rel: NBC, Universal

Dynasty, Novel
James Michener's Dynasty 1976 d: Lee Philips. lps: Sarah Miles, Stacy Keach, Harris Yulin. TVM. 100M USA. *Dynasty* prod/rel: David Paradine Television

The Forgotten Heroes of Korea, Short Story
Men of the Fighting Lady 1954 d: Andrew Marton. lps: Van Johnson, Walter Pidgeon, Louis Calhern. 80M USA. prod/rel: MGM

Hawaii, New York 1959, Novel
Hawaii 1966 d: George Roy Hill. lps: Max von Sydow, Julie Andrews, Richard Harris. 189M USA. prod/rel: Mirisch Corporation, United Artists

Hawaiians, The 1970 d: Tom Gries. lps: Charlton Heston, Geraldine Chaplin, John Phillip Law. 134M USA. *Master of the Islands* (UKN) prod/rel: Mirisch Productions, United Artists

Mr. Morgan, 1951, Short Story
Return to Paradise 1953 d: Mark Robson. lps: Gary Cooper, Roberta Haynes, Barry Jones. 100M USA. prod/rel: United Artists, Aspen Pictures

Sayonara, 1954, Novel
Sayonara 1957 d: Joshua Logan. lps: Marlon Brando, Patricia Owens, Martha Scott. 147M USA. prod/rel: Goetz Pictures, Inc., Pennebaker, Inc.

Tales of the South Pacific, 1947, Short Story
South Pacific 1958 d: Joshua Logan. lps: Mitzi Gaynor, Rossano Brazzi, John Kerr. 171M USA. prod/rel: Magna Theatre Corp., South Pacific Enterprises

Until They Sail, 1951, Short Story
Until They Sail 1957 d: Robert Wise. lps: Jean Simmons, Joan Fontaine, Paul Newman. 95M USA. prod/rel: MGM

MICHIE, GRACE SANDERSON
Pagan Passions, Story
Pagan Passions 1924 d: Colin Campbell. lps: Wyndham Standing, June Elvidge, Barbara Bedford. 5600f USA. prod/rel: Rellimeo Film Syndicate, Selznick Distributing Corp.

MICOLAYSEN, BRUCE
The Perilous Passage, Novel
Passage, The 1979 d: J. Lee Thompson. lps: James Mason, Anthony Quinn, Malcolm McDowell. 98M UKN. prod/rel: Hemdale, Passage

MIDDLEMASS, ROBERT M.
The Valiant, 1920, Play
Man Who Wouldn't Talk, The 1940 d: David Burton. lps: Lloyd Nolan, Jean Rogers, Richard Clarke. 72M USA. prod/rel: Twentieth Century-Fox Film Corp.
Valiant, The 1929 d: William K. Howard. lps: Paul Muni, Johnny Mack Brown, Edith Yorke. 5537f USA. prod/rel: Fox Film Corp.

MIDDLETON, EDGAR C.
Captivation, Play
Captivation 1931 d: John Harvel. lps: Conway Tearle, Betty Stockfeld, Violet Vanbrugh. 76M UKN. prod/rel: John Harvel Productions, Woolf & Freedman

Potiphar's Wife, London 1927, Play
Potiphar's Wife 1931 d: Maurice Elvey. lps: Nora Swinburne, Laurence Olivier, Norman McKinnel. 78M UKN. Her Strange Desire (USA) prod/rel: British International Pictures, First National-Pathe

Tin Gods, Play
Tin Gods 1932 d: F. W. Kraemer. lps: Frank Cellier, Dorothy Bartlam, Peter Evan Thomas. 52M UKN. prod/rel: British International Pictures, Pathe

MIDDLETON, GEORGE
Adam and Eva, New York 1923, Play
Adam and Eva 1923 d: Robert G. VignolA. lps: Marion Davies, T. Roy Barnes, Tom Lewis. 7153f USA. prod/rel: Paramount, Cosmopolitan Productions

The Big Pond, New York 1928, Play
Big Pond, The 1930 d: Hobart Henley. lps: Maurice Chevalier, Claudette Colbert, George Barbier. 75M USA. prod/rel: Paramount-Publix Corp.
Grande Mare, La 1930 d: Jacques Bataille-Henri, Hobart Henley. lps: Maurice Chevalier, Claudette Colbert, Henry Mortimer. 78M USA. prod/rel: Films Paramount, Paramount-Publix Corp.

The Bride, New York 1924, Play
Danger Girl, The 1926 d: Eddie Dillon. lps: Priscilla Dean, John Bowers, Gustav von Seyffertitz. 5660f USA. prod/rel: Metropolitan Pictures, Producers Distributing Corp.

The Cave Girl, New York 1920, Play
Cave Girl, The 1921 d: Joseph J. Franz. lps: Teddie Gerard, Charles Meredith, Wilton Taylor. 4405f USA. prod/rel: Inspiration Pictures, Associated First National Pictures

Her Strange Wedding, Short Story
Her Strange Wedding 1917 d: George Melford. lps: Fannie Ward, Jack Dean, Tom Forman. 5r USA. prod/rel: Jesse L. Lasky Feature Play Co.©, Paramount Pictures Corp.

Polly With a Past, New York 1917, Play
Polly With a Past 1920 d: Leander de CordovA. lps: Ina Claire, Ralph Graves, Marie Wainwright. 6r USA. prod/rel: Metro Pictures Corp.©

The Siren's Song, Play
Siren's Song, The 1915 d: George W. Lederer. lps: Charles Trowbridge, Mlle. Diane, Adolph Link. 5r USA. The Song of the Siren; The Sinner prod/rel: Shubert Film Corp., World Film Corp.©

MIDDLETON, THOMAS (1580–1627), UKN
The Changeling, Play
Middleton's Changeling 1997 d: Marcus Thompson. lps: Ian Dury, Amanda Ray-King, Colm O Maonlai. 96M UKN. prod/rel: High Time Pictures Ltd.©, United Independent Pictures

MIEHE, ULF
Novel
Output 1974 d: Michael Fengler. lps: Lou Castel, Katja Rupe, Bernd Herberger. 96M GRM. prod/rel: P.I.F.D.a., Filmverlag Der Autoren

MIGHELS, PHILIP VERRILL
Bruvver Jim's Baby, New York 1904, Novel
"If Only" Jim 1921 d: Jacques Jaccard. lps: Harry Carey, Carol Halloway, Ruth Royce. 4635f USA. prod/rel: Universal Film Mfg. Co.

MIHAILOVIC, DRAGOSLAV
Lilika, 1967, Short Story
Lilika 1971 d: Branko PlesA. lps: Dragana Kalaba, Branko Plesa, Tamara Miletic. 100M YGS.
Petrijin Venac, 1975, Novel
Petrijin Venac 1980 d: Srdjan Karanovic. lps: Mirjana Karanovic, Dragan Maksimovic, Marko Nikolic. 98M YGS. Petrija's Wreath; Petria's Wreath

MIHURA SANTOS, MIGUEL (1905–, SPN
Carlota, 1958, Play
Carlota 1959 d: Enrique Cahen. lps: Ana Mariscal, Jorge Rigaud, Juanjo Menendez. 100M SPN.
La Decente, 1969, Play
Decente, La 1970 d: Jose Luis Saenz de HerediA. lps: Conchita Velasco, Alfredo Landa, Jose Luis Lopez Vazquez. 98M SPN. The Decent Woman
Las Entretenidas, 1963, Play
Panteras Se Comen a Los Ricos, Las 1969 d: Ramon Fernandez. lps: Fernando Fernan Gomez, Patty Shepard, Manolo Gomez Bur. 83M SPN. Panthers Eat Rich Men; The Panthers Eat the Rich
Maribel Y la Extrana Familia, 1960, Play
Maribel Y la Extrana Familia 1960 d: Jose Maria Forque. lps: Silvia Pinal, Adolfo Marsillach, Julia Caba AlbA. 110M SPN. Maribel and the Estranged Family; Maribel and the Strange Family
Melocoton En Almibar, 1959, Play
Melocoton En Almibar 1960 d: Antonio Del Amo. lps: Marga Lopez, Jose Guardiola, Maria Mahor. 88M SPN. Peaches in Syrup
Sublime Decision!, 1960, Play
Solo Para Hombres 1960 d: Fernando Fernan Gomez. lps: Analia Gade, Fernando Fernan Gomez, Elvira QuintillA. 90M SPN. For Men Only

MIKETTA, HUBERT
Morgengrauen, Play
Morgengrauen 1954 d: Victor Tourjansky. lps: Alexander Kerst, Hans Stuwe, Elisabeth Muller. 100M GRM. At Daybreak prod/rel: Ariston, N.F.

MIKKELSEN, EJNAR
Norden for Lov Og Ret; En Alaska-Historie, Copenhagen 1920, Novel
Frozen Justice 1929 d: Allan Dwan. lps: Lenore Ulric, Robert Frazer, Louis Wolheim. 7170f USA. prod/rel: Fox Film Corp.

MIKKELSEN, LAILA
Liten Ida, Novel
Liten Ida 1981 d: Laila Mikkelsen. lps: Sunniva Lindekleiv, Howard Halvorsen, Lise Fjeldstad. 88M NRW/SWD. Growing Up; Little Ida prod/rel: Svenska Filminstitutet, Norsk Film

MIKRO
Die Ruiter in Die Nag, Bloemfontein 1936, Novel
Ruiter in Die Nag, Die 1963 d: Jan Perold. lps: Annette de Villiers, Johan Van Heerden, Brian O'Shaughnessy. 103M SAF. The Rider in the Night (USA) prod/rel: Suidafrikaanse Rolprentproduksies, Killarney Film Studio

MIKSZATH, KALMAN
Akli Miklos Es. Kir. Udv. Mulattato Tortenete, 1903, Novel
Akli Miklos 1986 d: Gyorgy Revesz. lps: Istvan Hirtling. 90M HNG. Miklos Akli
A Beszelo Kontos, 1889, Novel
Beszelo Kontos, A 1969 d: Tamas Fejer. lps: Istvan Iglodi, Antal Pager, Anna Detre. 97M HNG. The Talking Caftan
Beszterce Ostroma, 1896, Novel
Beszterce Ostroma 1948 d: Marton Keleti. lps: Klari Tolnay, Andor Ajtay, Ida Turai. 98M HNG. The Siege of Beszterce
A Fekete Varos, 1911, Novel
Fekete Varos, A 1971 d: Eva Zsurzs. lps: Antal Pager, Ferenc Bessenyei, Tibor Bitskey. 186M HNG. The Black Town; A Town in Mourning prod/rel: Magyar Telvizio

Kisertet Lublon, 1896, Novel
Kisertet Lublon 1976 d: Robert Ban. lps: Gyorgy Cserhalmi, Iren Bordan, Dezso Garas. 100M HNG. The Phantom on Horseback; The Haunted City prod/rel: Budapest Studio
Kulonos Hazassag, 1901, Novel
Kulonos Hazassag 1951 d: Marton Keleti. lps: Gyula Benko, Miklos Gabor, Lajos Rajczy. 111M HNG. Strange Marriage
A Noszty Fiu Esete Toth Marival, 1908, Novel
Ihr Leibhusar 1937 d: Hubert MarischkA. lps: Magda Schneider, Lucie Englisch, Erika von Thellmann. 85M GRM/AUS/HNG. Oberleutnant Franzl prod/rel: Hunnia-Pictura, Ring
Noszty Fiu Esete Toth Marival, A 1960 d: Viktor Gertler. lps: Tivadar Uray, Karoly Mecs, Marianne Krencsey. 102M HNG. Affair Between the Noszty Boy and Man Toth; Love and Money
A Szelistyei Asszonyok, 1901, Novel
Mit Csinalt Felseged 3-Tol 5-Ig? 1964 d: Karoly Makk. lps: Iren Psota, Ivan Darvas, Eva Papp. 87M HNG. Where Was You Majesty Between 3 and 5?; His Majesty's Dates prod/rel: Mafilm
Szent Peter Esernyoje, 1895, Novel
Szent Peter Esernyoje 1958 d: Frigyes Ban. lps: Karol MacHata, Sandor Pecsi, Mari Torocsik. 93M HNG/CZC. Dazdnik Svateho Petra; St. Peter's Umbrella

MILANESI, GUIDO
Sancta Maria, Novel
Prigionieri Del Male 1956 d: Mario CostA. lps: Francisco Rabal, May Britt, Vera Carmi. 90M ITL/SPN. Revelacion (SPN) prod/rel: Athena Cin.Ca, R.K.O.
Sancta Maria 1941 d: Edgar Neville, Pier Luigi Faraldo. lps: Conchita Montes, Amedeo Nazzari, Armando Falconi. 76M ITL/SPN. La Muchacha de Moscu prod/rel: Fonoroma, E.I.a.

MILANI, MILENA
La Ragazza Di Nome Giulio, Novel
Ragazza Di Nome Giulio, La 1970 d: Tonino Valerii. lps: Silvia Dionisio, Gianni MacChia, Esmerelda Ruspoli. 110M ITL. A Girl Called Jules (UKN); A Girl Named Julius; Model Love prod/rel: Julia Film, P.A.C.

MILANI, MINO
Fantasma d'Amore, Novel
Fantasma d'Amore 1981 d: Dino Risi. lps: Marcello Mastroianni, Romy Schneider, Eva-Maria Meineke. 97M ITL/FRN/GRM. Fantome d'Amour (FRN); Ghost of Love prod/rel: Roxy, Dean

MILANKOV, MOMCILO
Neznanka, 1964, Short Story
Budenje Pacova 1967 d: Zivojin Pavlovic. lps: Slobodan Perovic, Dusica Zegarac, Severin Bijelic. 86M YGS. The Rats Wake Up; The Rats Awake; Budjenje Pacova prod/rel: F.R.Z.

MILES, BERNARD
Lock Up Your Daughters, London 1959, Play
Lock Up Your Daughters! 1969 d: Peter Coe. lps: Christopher Plummer, Susannah York, Glynis Johns. 103M UKN. prod/rel: Domino Productions, Columbia

MILES, CARLTON
Ladies They Talk About, Play
Ladies They Talk About 1933 d: William Keighley, Howard Bretherton. lps: Barbara Stanwyck, Preston Foster, Lyle Talbot. 69M USA. prod/rel: Warner Bros. Pictures©

Lady Gangster, Play
Lady Gangster 1942 d: Robert Florey. lps: Faye Emerson, Julie Bishop, Frank Wilcox. 62M USA. prod/rel: Warner Bros.

MILES, RICHARD
That Cold Day in the Park, New York 1965, Novel
That Cold Day in the Park 1969 d: Robert Altman. lps: Sandy Dennis, Michael Burns, Susanne Benton. 115M USA/CND. prod/rel: Factor-Altman-Mirell Films

MILES, WILLIAM
Among Those Present, Play
Headleys at Home, The 1938 d: Chris Beute. lps: Evelyn Venable, Grant Mitchell, Vince Barnett. 69M USA. Among Those Present (UKN) prod/rel: Standard Pictures Productions©

MILHAUD, ALBERT
Famille Bolero, Play
Famille Bolero 1914 d: Georges MoncA. lps: Prince. 700m FRN. prod/rel: Pathe Freres
La Femme a Papa, Play
Femme a Papa, La 1914 d: Georges MoncA. lps: Prince, Marcelle Praince?. 740m FRN. prod/rel: Pathe Freres

Mam'zelle Nitouche, Paris 1882, Operetta
Diavolo Va in Collegio, Il 1944 d: Jean Boyer. lps: Lilia Silvi, Leonardo Cortese, Greta GondA. 83M ITL. *Santarellina* prod/rel: Excelsa Film, Minerva Film
Mam'zelle Nitouche 1931 d: Marc Allegret. lps: Janie Marese, Raimu, Andre Alerme. 106M FRN. prod/rel: Vandor-Film, Ondra-Lamac-Film
Mam'zelle Nitouche 1954 d: Yves Allegret. lps: Fernandel, Pier Angeli, Jean Debucourt. 90M FRN/ITL. *Santarellina* (ITL); *Oh No Mam'zelle* prod/rel: Paris-Films Production, Panitalia Film
Santarellina 1912 d: Mario Caserini. lps: Gigetta Morano, Ercole Vaser, Mario Bonnard. 882m ITL. *Ma'mselle Nitouche* (UKN); *Mam'selle Nitouche* (USA) prod/rel: S.A. Ambrosio
Santarellina 1923 d: Eugenio Perego. lps: Leda Gys, Silvio Orsini, Lorenzo Soderini. 1401m ITL. prod/rel: Lombardo Film
Niniche, 1878, Play
Niniche 1918 d: Camillo de Riso. lps: Tilde Kassay, Camillo de Riso, Gustavo SerenA. 1393m ITL. prod/rel: Caesar Film

MILLAR, ADELQUI (1891-1956), CHL
Carnaval Tragique, Play
Laughter and Tears 1921 d: B. E. Doxat-Pratt. lps: Evelyn Brent, Adelqui Millar, Dorothy Fane. 5947f UKN/NTH. *Een Lach En Een Traan* (NTH); *A Laugh and a Tear*; **De Schilder En Zijn Pierrette**; *The Artist and His Pierrette*; *Love in Tears* prod/rel: Granger-Binger Film

MILLAR, RONALD (1919-, UKN
Frieda, London 1946, Play
Frieda 1947 d: Basil Dearden. lps: David Farrar, Glynis Johns, Mai Zetterling. 98M UKN. prod/rel: Ealing Studios, General Film Distributors

MILLARD, JOHN
Member of the Jury, Novel
Member of the Jury 1937 d: Bernerd Mainwaring. lps: Ellis Irving, Marjorie Hume, Franklyn Bellamy. 61M UKN. prod/rel: Fox British

MILLARD, JOSEPH
The Gods Hate Kansas, 1941, Short Story
They Came from Beyond Space 1967 d: Freddie Francis. lps: Robert Hutton, Jennifer Jayne, Zia Mohyeddin. 85M UKN. prod/rel: Amicus Productions, Anglo Embassy

MILLARD, OSCAR
Story
Frogmen, The 1951 d: Lloyd Bacon. lps: Richard Widmark, Dana Andrews, Gary Merrill. 96M USA. prod/rel: 20th Century-Fox
Uncensored, Novel
Uncensored 1942 d: Anthony Asquith. lps: Eric Portman, Phyllis Calvert, Griffith Jones. 108M UKN. *We Shall Rise Again* prod/rel: General Film Distributors, Gainsborough

MILLAU, FERNAND
La Maison du Printemps, Play
Maison du Printemps, La 1949 d: Jacques Daroy. lps: Pierre Dudan, Claudine Dupuis, Liliane Maigne. 94M FRN. prod/rel: Protis Films

MILLER, ALICE D. G.
The Fourteenth Lover, Story
Fourteenth Lover, The 1922 d: Harry Beaumont. lps: Viola Dana, Jack Mulhall, Theodore von Eltz. 5180f USA. prod/rel: Metro Pictures

MILLER, ALICE DUER (1874-1942), USA, Bartram, Clara
Are Parents People?, 1924, Short Story
Are Parents People? 1925 d: Malcolm St. Clair. lps: Betty Bronson, Florence Vidor, Adolphe Menjou. 6586f USA. prod/rel: Famous Players-Lasky Corp., Paramount Pictures
Big Executive, 1933, Short Story
Big Executive 1933 d: Erle C. Kenton. lps: Ricardo Cortez, Elizabeth Young, Richard Bennett. 72M USA. prod/rel: Paramount Productions, Inc.
Calderon's Prisoner, New York 1903, Novel
Something Different 1920 d: R. William Neill. lps: Constance Binney, Lucy Fox, Ward Crane. 4756f USA. prod/rel: Realart Pictures Corp.©
The Charm School, 1919, Short Story
Charm School, The 1921 d: James Cruze. lps: Wallace Reid, Lila Lee, Adele Farrington. 4743f USA. prod/rel: Famous Players-Lasky, Paramount Pictures
Collegiate 1936 d: Ralph Murphy. lps: Jack Oakie, Frances Langford, Joe Penner. 80M USA. *The Charm School* (UKN) prod/rel: Paramount Productions, Inc.
Someone to Love 1928 d: F. Richard Jones. lps: Charles "Buddy" Rogers, Mary Brian, William Austin. 6323f USA. prod/rel: Paramount Famous Lasky Corp.

Come Out of the Kitchen!, New York 1916, Novel
Cherie 1930 d: Louis Mercanton. lps: Mona Goya, Saint-Granier, Janine Guise. F FRN. prod/rel: Films Paramount
Come Out of the Kitchen 1919 d: John S. Robertson. lps: Marguerite Clark, Eugene O'Brien, Frances Kaye. 5r USA. *Come Out of Kitchen* prod/rel: Famous Players-Lasky Corp.©, Paramount Pictures
Come Out of the Pantry 1935 d: Jack Raymond. lps: Jack Buchanan, Fay Wray, James Carew. 71M UKN. prod/rel: British and Dominions, United Artists
Honey 1930 d: Wesley Ruggles. lps: Nancy Carroll, Stanley Smith, Skeets Gallagher. 6701f USA. *Come Out of the Kitchen* prod/rel: Paramount Famous Lasky Corp.
Spring in Park Lane 1948 d: Herbert Wilcox. lps: Anna Neagle, Michael Wilding, Tom Walls. 92M UKN. prod/rel: Imperadio, British Lion
Gowns By Roberta, New York 1933, Novel
Lovely to Look at 1952 d: Mervyn Leroy, Vincente Minnelli (Uncredited). lps: Howard Keel, Kathryn Grayson, Red Skelton. 105M USA. prod/rel: MGM
Roberta 1935 d: William A. Seiter. lps: Irene Dunne, Fred Astaire, Ginger Rogers. 106M USA. prod/rel: RKO Radio Pictures©, Pandro S. Berman Production
Her First Elopement, New York 1915, Novel
Her First Elopement 1920 d: Sam Wood. lps: Wanda Hawley, Jerome Patrick, Nell Craig. 5r USA. prod/rel: Realart Pictures Corp.©, Star Production
Ladies Must Live, New York 1917, Novel
Ladies Must Live 1921 d: George Loane Tucker. lps: Robert Ellis, Mahlon Hamilton, Betty Compson. 7482f USA. prod/rel: Mayflower Photoplay Corp., Paramount Pictures
Less Than Kin, New York 1909, Novel
Less Than Kin 1918 d: Donald Crisp. lps: Wallace Reid, Anna Little, Raymond Hatton. 5r USA. prod/rel: Famous Players-Lasky Corp.©, Paramount Pictures
Manslaughter, New York 1921, Novel
Manslaughter 1922 d: Cecil B. de Mille. lps: Thomas Meighan, Leatrice Joy, Lois Wilson. 9061f USA. prod/rel: Famous Players-Lasky, Paramount Pictures
Manslaughter 1930 d: George Abbott. lps: Claudette Colbert, Fredric March, Emma Dunn. 7954f USA. prod/rel: Paramount-Publix Corp.
Requisitoire, Le 1930 d: Dimitri Buchowetzki. lps: Fernand Fabre, Gaston Jacquet, Marcelle Chantal. 84M FRN. *Homicide* prod/rel: Films Paramount
The Princess and the Plumber, 1929, Short Story
Princess and the Plumber, The 1930 d: Alexander KordA. lps: Charles Farrell, Maureen O'Sullivan, H. B. Warner. 6480f USA. prod/rel: Fox Film Corp.
The White Cliffs, Poem
White Cliffs of Dover, The 1944 d: Clarence Brown. lps: Irene Dunne, Alan Marshall, Roddy McDowall. 126M USA. prod/rel: MGM

MILLER, ALLEN C.
The Terror, New York 1931, Play
Doctor X 1932 d: Michael Curtiz. lps: Lionel Atwill, Preston Foster, Fay Wray. 80M USA. prod/rel: First National Pictures, Inc., Warner Bros.

MILLER, ARTHUR (1915-, USA
All My Sons, New York 1947, Play
All My Sons 1948 d: Irving Reis. lps: Edward G. Robinson, Burt Lancaster, Mady Christians. 94M USA. prod/rel: Universal
All My Sons 1986 d: John Power. lps: Aidan Quinn, James Whitmore, Michael Learned. 110M USA.
The Crucible, 1953, Play
Crucible, The 1996 d: Nicholas Hytner. lps: Daniel Day-Lewis, Winona Ryder, Paul Scofield. 123M USA. prod/rel: David V. Picker Production
Sorcieres de Salem, Les 1957 d: Raymond Rouleau. lps: Yves Montand, Simone Signoret, Mylene Demongeot. 145M FRN/GDR. *Die Hexen von Salem* (GDR); *The Crucible* (USA); *The Witches of Salem* prod/rel: C.I.C.C., Films Borderie
Death of a Salesman, New York 1949, Play
Death of a Salesman 1951 d: Laslo Benedek. lps: Fredric March, Mildred Dunnock, Kevin McCarthy. 115M USA. prod/rel: Columbia, Stanley Kramer Co.
Death of a Salesman 1985 d: Volker Schlondorff. lps: Dustin Hoffman, Kate Reid, John Malkovich. TVM. 150M USA/GRM. *Tod Eines Handlungsreisenden* (GRM) prod/rel: CBS, Roxbury and Punch Prods.
Most Pereyti Nelieya 1960 d: Teodor Vulfovich, Nikita Kurikhin. 97M USS. *The Bridge Cannot Be Crossed*; *Death of a Salesman*; *No Crossing the Bridge*
The Golden Years, Play
Golden Years, The 1992 d: Paul Bryers. lps: Ronald Pickup, Robert Powell, Cathy Tyson. TVM. 100M UKN. prod/rel: Brook Productions

The Misfits, 1961, Short Story
Misfits, The 1961 d: John Huston. lps: Clark Gable, Marilyn Monroe, Montgomery Clift. 124M USA. prod/rel: United Artists
Some Kind of Love Story, Play
Everybody Wins 1990 d: Karel Reisz. lps: Debra Winger, Nick Nolte, Will Patton. 97M UKN/USA. prod/rel: Recorded Picture Company
A View from the Bridge, New York 1955, Play
Vu du Pont 1962 d: Sidney Lumet. lps: Raf Vallone, Maureen Stapleton, Jean Sorel. 117M FRN/ITL. *Uno Sguardo Dal Ponte* (ITL); *A View from the Bridge* (USA) prod/rel: Transcontinental Films, Produzione Intercontinentali

MILLER, ARTHUR (2)
Marry the Girl, London 1930, Play
Marry the Girl 1935 d: MacLean Rogers. lps: Sonnie Hale, Winifred Shotter, Hugh Wakefield. 69M UKN. prod/rel: British Lion
Their Night Out, Play
Their Night Out 1933 d: Harry Hughes. lps: Claude Hulbert, Renee Houston, Gus McNaughton. 74M UKN. *His Night Out* prod/rel: British International Pictures, Wardour

MILLER, CHRIS
Multiplicity, Short Story
Multiplicity 1996 d: Harold Ramis. lps: Michael Keaton, Andie MacDowell, Harris Yulin. 117M USA. prod/rel: Trevor Albert Production

MILLER, E. V.
A Daughter of England, Play
Daughter of England, A 1915 d: Leedham Bantock. lps: Marga Rubia Levy, Frank Randall, Frank Dane. 3500f UKN. prod/rel: British Empire

MILLER, GRANT HINDEN
The Dream Monger, Novel
Starlight Hotel 1987 d: Sam Pillsbury. lps: Peter Phelps, Greer Robson, Marshall Napier. 93M NZL. prod/rel: Recorded Releasing, Challenge Film Corp.

MILLER, HENRY (1891-1980), USA, Miller, Henry Valentine
Quiet Days in Clichy, Paris 1956, Novel
Jours Tranquilles a Clichy 1989 d: Claude Chabrol. lps: Andrew McCarthy, Nigel Havers, Barbara de Rossi. 121M FRN/GRM/ITL. *Stille Tage in Clichy* (GRM); *Quiet Days in Clichy*; *Giorni Felici a Clichy* (ITL) prod/rel: Italfrance, Direkt
Stille Dage I Clichy 1970 d: Jens Jorgen Thorsen. lps: Louise White, Ulla Lemvigh-Muller, Avi Sagild. 95M DNM. *Quiet Days in Clichy* (USA); *Not So Quiet Days* prod/rel: S.B.A. Film, Dansk-Svensk Film
Tropic of Cancer, Paris 1934, Novel
Tropic of Cancer 1970 d: Joseph Strick. lps: Rip Torn, James Callahan, Ellen Burstyn. 88M USA. prod/rel: Tropic Film Corporation, Paramount

MILLER, HENRY RUSSELL
The Ambition of Mark Truitt, Indianapolis 1913, Novel
Fruits of Desire, The 1916 d: Oscar Eagle. lps: Robert Warwick, Alec B. Francis, Robert W. Cummings. 5r USA. *The Ambition of Mark Truitt* prod/rel: William A. Brady Picture Plays, Inc., World Film Corp.©
Fruits of Passion 1919 d: George Ridgwell. lps: Alice Mann, Frances Mann, Emil J. de Varney. 5r USA. prod/rel: Mcclure Productions, Triangle Distributing Corp.
The House of Toys, Indianapolis 1914, Novel
House of Toys, The 1920 d: George L. Cox. lps: Seena Owen, Paul Trenton, Helen Jerome Eddy. 6r USA. prod/rel: American Film Co.©, Pathe Exchange, Inc.

MILLER, HERMAN
Coogan's Bluff, Novel
Coogan's Bluff 1968 d: Don Siegel. lps: Clint Eastwood, Lee J. Cobb, Susan Clark. 100M USA. prod/rel: Universal

MILLER, IRENE
The Striped Stocking Gang, Novel
Striped Stocking Gang, The 1915 d: Fred W. Durrant. lps: Margaret Belona, Miriam Ferris. 3527f UKN. *Mrs. Cassell's Profession* prod/rel: Barker, Neptune

MILLER, J. P.
The People Next Door, 1968, Play
People Next Door, The 1970 d: David Greene. lps: Eli Wallach, Julie Harris, Deborah Winters. 93M USA. prod/rel: Avco Embassy Pictures, the People Next Door Co.
The Rabbit Trap, 1955, Television Play
Rabbit Trap, The 1959 d: Philip Leacock. lps: Ernest Borgnine, David Brian, Bethel Leslie. 76M USA. prod/rel: United Artists, Canon Prods.

MILLER, JASON
That Championship Season, Play
    That Championship Season 1982 d: Jason Miller.
    lps: Bruce Dern, Stacy Keach, Robert Mitchum. 108M
    USA. *The Championship Season* prod/rel: Cannon

MILLER, JOSEPHINE
Out of the Night, Short Story
    Footlights and Shadows 1920 d: John W. Noble. lps:
    Olive Thomas, Alex Onslow, Ivo Dawson. 4453f USA.
    Out of the Night prod/rel: Selznick Pictures Corp.©,
    Select Pictures Corp.

MILLER, MARY ASHE
The Man Who Married His Own Wife, 1922, Short
Story
    Man Who Married His Own Wife, The 1922 d: Stuart
    Paton. lps: Frank Mayo, Sylvia Breamer, Marie Crisp.
    4313f USA. prod/rel: Universal Film Mfg. Co.

MILLER, MAX
I Cover the Waterfront, New York 1932, Book
    I Cover the Waterfront 1933 d: James Cruze. lps: Ben
    Lyon, Claudette Colbert, Ernest Torrence. 75M USA.
    Frisco Waterfront prod/rel: United Artists Corp.©,
    Reliance Pictures
    Secret of Deep Harbor 1961 d: Edward L. Cahn. lps:
    Ron Foster, Barry Kelley, Merry Anders. 70M USA.
    prod/rel: Harvard Film Corporation

MILLER, ST. AUBIN
The Golden Chance, Play
    Golden Chance, The 1913 d: Percy Nash. 1100f UKN.
    prod/rel: London Films, Cosmopolitan

MILLER, SUE
Family Pictures, Novel
    Family Pictures 1992 d: Philip Saville. lps: Anjelica
    Huston, Sam Neill, Kyra Sedgwick. TVM. 172M USA.
The Good Mother, Novel
    Good Mother, The 1988 d: Leonard Nimoy. lps: Diane
    Keaton, Liam Neeson, Jason Robards Jr. 103M USA.
    The Price of Passion prod/rel: Buena Vista, Touchstone
    Pictures
Inventing the Abbotts
    Inventing the Abbotts 1997 d: Pat O'Connor. lps:
    Joaquin Phoenix, Billy Crudup, Liv Tyler. 110M USA.
    prod/rel: 20th Century-Fox, Imagine Entertainment

MILLER, WADE
Guilty Bystander, 1947, Novel
    Guilty Bystander 1950 d: Joseph Lerner. lps: Zachary
    Scott, Faye Emerson, Mary Boland. 92M USA. prod/rel:
    Film Classics, Laurel Films
Kitten With a Whip, Greenwich CT. 1964, Novel
    Kitten With a Whip 1964 d: Douglas Heyes. lps:
    Ann-Margret, John Forsythe, Patricia Barry. 83M USA.
    prod/rel: Universal Pictures
The Man Hunter, Novel
    Man Hunter, The 1969 d: Don Taylor. lps: Sandra Dee,
    Roy Thinnes, Albert Salmi. TVM. 100M USA. *The
    Manhunter* prod/rel: Universal

MILLER, WARREN (1921–1966), USA
The Cool World, Boston 1959, Novel
    Cool World, The 1964 d: Shirley Clarke. lps: Hampton
    Clanton, Yolanda Rodriguez, Carl Lee. 125M USA.
    Echoes of the Jungle; *Harlem Story* prod/rel: Fred
    Wiseman
The Way We Live Now, Boston 1958, Novel
    Way We Live Now, The 1970 d: Barry Brown. lps:
    Nicholas Pryor, Joanna Miles, Lois Smith. 110M USA.
    prod/rel: East Coker Co.

MILLER, WINSTON
The Barbarians, Story
    Tripoli 1950 d: Will Price. lps: John Payne, Maureen
    O'Hara, Howard Da SilvA. 95M USA. *First Marines*
    prod/rel: Paramount, Pine-Thomas

MILLHAUSER, BERTRAM
Sucker, New York 1933, Play
    Life of Jimmy Dolan, The 1933 d: Archie Mayo. lps:
    Douglas Fairbanks Jr., Loretta Young, Guy Kibbee. 89M
    USA. *The Kid's Last Fight* (UKN); *Sucker* prod/rel:
    Warner Bros. Pictures©
    They Made Me a Criminal 1939 d: Busby Berkeley.
    lps: John Garfield, Claude Rains, Gloria Dickson. 92M
    USA. prod/rel: Warner Bros. Pictures©

MILLHOLLAND, RAY
Island Doctor, 1939, Short Story
    Girl from God's Country, The 1940 d: Sidney
    Salkow. lps: Chester Morris, Jane Wyatt, Charles
    Bickford. 75M USA. prod/rel: Republic Pictures Corp.©
The Splinter Fleet of the Otranto Barrage,
Indianapolis 1936, Book
    Submarine Patrol 1938 d: John Ford. lps: Richard
    Greene, Nancy Kelly, Preston Foster. 95M USA. *The
    Splinter Fleet*; *Suicide Fleet*; *Wooden Anchors* prod/rel:
    Twentieth Century-Fox Film Corp.©

MILLIGAN, SPIKE (1918–, UKN
The Bed Sitting Room, 1963, Play
    Bed Sitting Room, The 1969 d: Richard Lester. lps:
    Ralph Richardson, Rita Tushingham, Michael Hordern.
    91M UKN. prod/rel: Oscar Lewenstein Productions,
    United Artists

MILLIN, SARAH (1889–1968), SAF, Millin, Sarah
Gertrude
Rhodes, Book
    Rhodes of Africa 1936 d: Berthold Viertel. lps: Walter
    Huston, Oscar Homolka, Basil Sydney. 91M UKN/SAF.
    Rhodes (USA); *Rhodes the Empire Builder* prod/rel:
    Gaumont-British

MILLOCKER, KARL (1842–1899), AUS
Die Dubarry, Operetta
    Dubarry, Die 1951 d: Georg Wildhagen. lps: Sari
    Barabas, Mathieu Ahlersmeyer, Willy Fritsch. 99M
    GRM. prod/rel: Standard, Fama
Gasparone, Operetta
    Gasparone 1937 d: Georg Jacoby. lps: Marika Rokk,
    Johannes Heesters, Heinz Schorlemmer. 92M GRM.
    prod/rel: UFA, Kristall

MILLS, CLIFFORD
The Luck of the Navy, London 1918, Play
    Luck of the Navy 1938 d: Norman Lee. lps: Geoffrey
    Toone, Judy Kelly, Keneth Kent. 72M UKN. *North Sea
    Patrol* (USA) prod/rel: Associated British Picture
    Corporation, Pathe
    Luck of the Navy, The 1927 d: Fred Paul. lps: Evelyn
    Laye, Henry Victor, Hayford Hobbs. 8300f UKN.
    prod/rel: Graham-Wilcox Productions
Where the Rainbow Ends, London 1911, Play
    Where the Rainbow Ends 1921 d: H. Lisle Lucoque.
    lps: Babs Farren, B. Cave Chinn, Muriel Pointer. 5000f
    UKN. prod/rel: British Photoplay Productions, Pioneer

MILLS, HUGH
As You are, Play
    Turned Out Nice Again 1941 d: Marcel Varnel. lps:
    George Formby, Peggy Bryan, Edward Chapman. 81M
    UKN. prod/rel: Associated Talking Pictures, Ealing
    Studios
Prudence and the Pill, London 1965, Novel
    Prudence and the Pill 1968 d: Fielder Cook, Ronald
    Neame. lps: Deborah Kerr, David Niven, Robert Coote.
    92M UKN/USA. prod/rel: Prudence Films, 20th
    Century-Fox

MILLS, JAMES
Panic in Needle Park, Novel
    Panic in Needle Park 1971 d: Jerry Schatzberg. lps:
    Al Pacino, Kitty Winn, Alan Vint. 110M USA. prod/rel:
    Gadd Productions, Didion-Dunne
Report to the Commissioner, Novel
    Report to the Commissioner 1975 d: Milton
    Katselas. lps: Michael Moriarty, Yaphet Kotto, Susan
    Blakely. 112M USA. *Operation Undercover* (UKN)
    prod/rel: United Artists

MILLS, MERVYN
The Long Haul, Novel
    Long Haul, The 1957 d: Ken Hughes. lps: Victor
    Mature, Diana Dors, Patrick Allen. 100M UKN.
    prod/rel: Marksman, Columbia

MILLS, PIERRE
L' Angoisse, Play
    House of Mystery 1961 d: Vernon Sewell. lps: Jane
    Hylton, Peter Dyneley, Nanette Newman. 56M UKN.
    The Unseen prod/rel: Anglo-Amalgamated, Independent
    Artists
    Latin Quarter 1945 d: Vernon Sewell. lps: Derrick de
    Marney, Frederick Valk, Joan Greenwood. 80M UKN.
    Frenzy (USA) prod/rel: British National,
    Anglo-American
    Medium, The 1934 d: Vernon Sewell. lps: Nancy
    O'Neil, Shayle Gardner, Barbara Gott. 38M UKN.
    prod/rel: Film Tests, MGM

MILNE, A. A. (1882–1956), UKN, Milne, Alan Alexander
The Dover Road, New York 1921, Play
    Little Adventuress, The 1927 d: William C. de Mille.
    lps: Vera Reynolds, Phyllis Haver, Robert Ober. 6200f
    USA. *The Dover Road* prod/rel: de Mille Pictures,
    Producers Distributing Corp.
    Where Sinners Meet 1934 d: J. Walter Ruben. lps:
    Clive Brook, Diana Wynyard, Reginald Owen. 72M USA.
    The Dover Road (UKN) prod/rel: RKO Radio Pictures©
Four Days' Wonder, New York 1933, Novel
    Four Days' Wonder 1936 d: Sidney Salkow. lps:
    Jeanne Dante, Kenneth Howell, Martha Sleeper. 62M
    USA. prod/rel: Universal Pictures Corp.©
The Fourth Wall, London 1928, Play
    Birds of Prey 1930 d: Basil Dean. lps: Robert Loraine,
    Warwick Ward, Frank Lawton. 98M UKN. *The Perfect
    Alibi* (USA) prod/rel: Associated Talking Pictures, Radio

The King's Breakfast, Poem
    King's Breakfast, The 1963 d: Wendy Toye. lps:
    Maurice Denham, Mischa Auer, Reginald Beckwith.
    28M UKN. prod/rel: Francis-Montagu
Michael and Mary, London 1930, Play
    Michael and Mary 1931 d: Victor Saville. lps: Herbert
    Marshall, Edna Best, Elizabeth Allan. 85M UKN.
    prod/rel: Gaumont, Ideal
Mr. Pim Passes By, London 1920, Play
    Mr. Pim Passes By 1921 d: Albert Ward. lps: Peggy
    Hyland, Campbell Gullan, Maudie Dunham. 6077f
    UKN. prod/rel: G. B. Samuelson, General

MILO, PORDES
Tanzanwaltz, Berlin 1912, Play
    Lonely Wives 1931 d: Russell MacK. lps: Edward
    Everett Horton, Esther Ralston, Laura Laplante. 87M
    USA. prod/rel: Pathe Exchange©, RKO Radio Pictures

MILTON, JOHN (1608–1674), UKN
Paradise Lost, 1667
    Satana 1912 d: Luigi Maggi. lps: Mario Bonnard, Rina
    Albry, Vitale de Stefano. 1960m ITL. *Il Dramma
    Dell'umanita*; *Satan* (UKN) prod/rel: S.A. Ambrosio

MILTON, PAUL R.
Love Your Body, Play
    Search for Beauty 1934 d: Erle C. Kenton. lps: Buster
    Crabbe, Ida Lupino, Robert Armstrong. 77M USA.
    prod/rel: Paramount Productions©

MILWARD, JO
The Guilty Generation, 1928, Play
    Guilty Generation, The 1931 d: Rowland V. Lee. lps:
    Leo Carrillo, Constance Cummings, Robert Young. 82M
    USA. prod/rel: Columbia Pictures Corp.©

MINANA, FEDERICO
Barca VellA. Dolora Del Mar Azul, Poem
    Tierra Valenciana 1926 d: Mario Roncoroni. lps:
    Carmen Viance, Rafael Hurtado, Joaquin MorA. SPN.
    Rosa de Levante; *Flor de Valencia* prod/rel: Prod. Cin.Ca
    Espanola Levantina Films

MINCHIN, DEVON
The Money Movers, Book
    Money Movers, The 1979 d: Bruce Beresford. lps:
    Terence Donovan, Ed Devereaux, Tony Bonner. 94M
    ASL. prod/rel: South Australian Film Corp.©, Roadshow

MINNEY, R. J.
Carve Her Name With Pride, Book
    Carve Her Name With Pride 1958 d: Lewis Gilbert.
    lps: Virginia McKenna, Paul Scofield, Jack Warner.
    119M UKN. prod/rel: Rank Film Distributors, Keyboard
Clive of India, London 1934, Play
    Clive of India 1935 d: Richard Boleslawski. lps: Ronald
    Colman, Loretta Young, Colin Clive. 93M USA. prod/rel:
    20th Century Pictures, Inc., United Artists
Nothing to Lose, Novel
    Time, Gentlemen, Please 1952 d: Lewis Gilbert. lps:
    Eddie Byrne, Raymond Lovell, Hermione Baddeley.
    83M UKN. *Nothing to Lose* prod/rel: Group 3,
    Associated British Film Distributors

MIQUEL, ANDRE
Layla, Novel
    Layla Ma Raison 1989 d: Taieb Louhichi. lps: Safy
    Boutella, Anca Nicola, Abderrahmane Al-Rachi. 90M
    TNS. *Layla*

MIRANDA, FERNANDO
Barca VellA. Dolora Del Mar Azul, Poem
    Tierra Valenciana 1926 d: Mario Roncoroni. lps:
    Carmen Viance, Rafael Hurtado, Joaquin MorA. SPN.
    Rosa de Levante; *Flor de Valencia* prod/rel: Prod. Cin.Ca
    Espanola Levantina Films

MIRANDE, YVES (1875–1957), FRN
Play
    Mr. What's-His-Name 1935 d: Ralph Ince. lps:
    Seymour Hicks, Olive Blakeney, Enid Stamp-Taylor.
    67M UKN. prod/rel: Warner Bros., First National
L' Ami de Ma Femme, Play
    Je Te Confie Ma Femme 1933 d: Rene Guissart. lps:
    Jean Aquistapace, Jeanne Cheirel, Edith MerA. 75M
    FRN. prod/rel: Rene Guissart, Yves Mirande
L' Arpete, Play
    Arpete, L' 1928 d: E. B. Donatien. lps: Lucienne
    Legrand, Raymond Guerin-Catelain, Louis Ravet.
    2500m FRN. prod/rel: Franco-Film
    It Happened in Paris 1935 d: Robert Wyler, Carol
    Reed. lps: John Loder, Nancy Burne, Edward H.
    Robbins. 68M UKN. prod/rel: Wyndham, Associated
    British Film Distributors
Le Chasseur de Chez Maxim's, Play
    Chasseur de Chez Maxim's, Le 1927 d: Roger Lion,
    Nicolas Rimsky. lps: Nicolas Rimsky, Simone Vaudry,
    Eric Barclay. F FRN. prod/rel: Films Albatros

327

Chasseur de Chez Maxim's, Le 1932 d: Karl Anton. lps: Robert Burnier, Mireille Perrey, Felicien Tramel. 65M FRN. prod/rel: Films Paramount

Chasseur de Chez Maxim's, Le 1939 d: Maurice Cammage. lps: Bach, Genevieve Callix, Roger Treville. 95M FRN. prod/rel: Films Stella Productions

Chasseur de Chez Maxim's, Le 1953 d: Henri Diamant-Berger. lps: Pauline Carton, Yves Deniaud, Raymond Bussieres. 96M FRN. prod/rel: Actor Film, Film d'Art

Embrassez-Moi, Play
Embrassez-Moi 1928 d: Robert Peguy, Max de Rieux. lps: Prince-Rigadin, Suzanne Bianchetti, Jacques ArnnA. F FRN. prod/rel: Alex Nalpas

Embrassez-Moi 1932 d: Leon Mathot. lps: Georges Milton, Tania Fedor, Jeanne Helbling. 89M FRN. prod/rel: Gaumont-Franco-Film-Aubert

La Famille Cucuroux, Play
Famille Cucuroux, La 1953 d: Emile Couzinet. lps: Jean Tissier, Jeanne Fusier-Gir, Nathalie Nattier. 82M FRN. prod/rel: Burgus Films

L' Homme En Habit, Paris 1922, Play
Evening Clothes 1927 d: Luther Reed. lps: Adolphe Menjou, Virginia Valli, Noah Beery. 6287f USA. prod/rel: Famous Players-Lasky, Paramount Pictures

Homme En Habit, Un 1931 d: Rene Guissart, Robert Bossis. lps: Fernand Gravey, Pierre Etchepare, DianA. 88M FRN. prod/rel: Films Paramount

Un Homme Heureux, Play
Pour Vivre Heureux 1932 d: Claudio de La Torre. lps: Noel-Noel, Suzet Mais, Pierre Etchepare. 80M FRN. prod/rel: Films Paramount

The Matrimonial Bed, New York 1927, Play
Kisses for Breakfast 1941 d: Lewis Seiler. lps: Dennis Morgan, Jane Wyatt, Lee Patrick. 81M USA. *She Stayed Kissed* prod/rel: Warner Bros.

Matrimonial Bed, The 1930 d: Michael Curtiz. lps: Frank Fay, Lilyan Tashman, James Gleason. 6242f USA. *A Matrimonial Problem* (UKN) prod/rel: Warner Brothers Pictures

La Merveilleuse Journee, Play
Merveilleuse Journee, La 1928 d: Rene Barberis. lps: Dolly Davis, Andre Roanne, Renee Veller. 2100m FRN. prod/rel: Societe Des Cineromans, Films De France

Merveilleuse Journee, La 1932 d: Robert Wyler, Yves Mirande. lps: Florelle, Milly Mathis, Frederic Duvalles. 87M FRN. prod/rel: Pathe-Natan

Octave, Play
Octave 1909. lps: Harry Baur, Rouviere, Mary Hett. 200m FRN. prod/rel: Scagl

Vengez-Moi Mon Gendre!. 1916. lps: Prince. 580m FRN. prod/rel: Pathe Freres

Pas un Mot a la Reine-Mere, Play
Pas un Mot a la Reine-Mere 1946 d: Maurice Cloche. lps: Suzanne Dehelly, Liliane Bert, Andre Brunot. 85M FRN. prod/rel: C.C.F.C.

Un Petit Trou Pas Cher, Play
Petit Trou Pas Cher, Un 1934 d: Pierre-Jean Ducis. lps: Jules Berry, Albert Malbert, Suzy Prim. 45M FRN. prod/rel: Alliance Cinematographique Europeenne, Pierre-Jean Ducis

Une Petite Femme Dans le Lit, Play
Mon Coeur Balance 1932 d: Rene Guissart. lps: Marie Glory, Marguerite Moreno, Noel-Noel. 77M FRN. *My Heart Wavers; My Heart Hesitates* prod/rel: Films Paramount

Trois Jeunes Filles Nues, Opera
Trois Jeunes Filles Nues 1928 d: Robert Boudrioz. lps: Nicolas Rimsky, Rene Ferte, Jeanne Helbling. 2500m FRN. prod/rel: Integral Films

Un Trou Dans le Mur, Play
Trou Dans le Mur, Un 1931 d: Rene Barberis. lps: Jean Murat, Leon Belieres, Dolly Davis. F FRN. prod/rel: Films Paramount

Trou Dans le Mur, Un 1949 d: Emile Couzinet. lps: Andre Alerme, Marguerite Pierry, Jacqueline Dor. 103M FRN. prod/rel: Burgus Films

Water Nymph, Play
Man of the Moment 1935 d: Monty Banks. lps: Douglas Fairbanks Jr., Laura La Plante, Claude Hulbert. 81M UKN. *Water Nymph* prod/rel: Warner Bros., First National

MIRBEAU, OCTAVE
Les Affaires Sont Les Affaires, Paris 1903, Play
Affaires Sont Les Affaires, Les 1942 d: Jean Dreville. lps: Charles Vanel, Jacques Baumer, Renee Devillers. 82M FRN. prod/rel: Moulins D'or

Business Is Business 1915 d: Otis Turner. lps: Nat C. Goodwin, Mr. Nelson, Maude George. 6r USA. prod/rel: Universal Film Mfg. Co.©

Le Jardin Des Supplices, Paris 1899, Novel
Jardin Des Supplices, Le 1976 d: Christian Gion. lps: Roger Van Hool, Jacqueline Kerry, Tony Taffin. 93M FRN. prod/rel: Alexia, Stephan

Le Journal d'une Femme de Chambre, Paris 1900, Novel
Diary of a Chambermaid 1946 d: Jean Renoir. lps: Paulette Goddard, Burgess Meredith, Francis Lederer. 87M USA. *Le Journal d'une Femme de Chambre* (FRN) prod/rel: United Artists

Journal d'une Femme de Chambre, Le 1963 d: Luis Bunuel. lps: Jeanne Moreau, Michel Piccoli, Georges Geret. 98M FRN/ITL. *Il Diario Di Una Cameriera* (ITL); *Diary of a Chambermaid* (USA) prod/rel: Cine-Alliance, Speva Films

MIROVSKY, VACLAV
Na Ty Louce Zeleny, Opera
Na Ty Louce Zeleny 1936 d: Carl Lamac. lps: Carl Lamac, Helena Busova, Jara Kohout. 2391m CZC. *On the Green Meadow* prod/rel: Elekta

Parizanka, Opera
Slecna Matinka 1938 d: Vladimir Slavinsky. lps: Vera Ferbasova, Stanislav Strnad, Theodor Pistek. 2832m CZC. *Miss Mother* prod/rel: Lucernafilm

Ulicnice, Opera
Ulicnice 1936 d: Vladimir Slavinsky. lps: Vera Ferbasova, Frantisek Sasek, Frantisek Kristof-Vesely. 2931m CZC. *Minx* prod/rel: Slavia-Film

MISASI, NICOLA
La Badia Di Montenero, Novel
Badia Di Montenero, La 1921 d: Renato Bulla Del Torchio. lps: Sari de Wayditsch, Livio Pavanelli, Dillo Lombardi. 1567m ITL. prod/rel: Velia Film

Il Tenente Giorgio, Novel
Tenente Giorgio, Il 1952 d: Raffaello Matarazzo. lps: Massimo Girotti, Milly Vitale, Gualtiero Tumiati. 85M ITL. prod/rel: Flora Film, Variety Film

MISCHKE, FRITZ
Rosen Bluh'n Auf Dem Heidegrab, Short Story
Rosen Bluh'n Auf Dem Heidegrab 1929 d: Curt Blachnitzky. lps: Betty Astor, Hanni Reinwald, Alfons Fryland. 2203m GRM. prod/rel: Trianon-Film

MISENHEIMER, MIKE
Framed, Novel
Framed 1975 d: Phil Karlson. lps: Joe Don Baker, Connie Van Dyke, Gabriel Dell. 101M USA. prod/rel: Briskin

MISHEV, GEORGI
Matriarkhat, 1967, Novel
Matriarhat 1977 d: Lyudmil Kirkov. lps: Katya Paskaleva, Nevena Kokanova, Emilia RadevA. 103M BUL. *Matriarchate; Matriarchy; Matriarkhat*

MISHIMA, YUKIO (1925–1970), JPN, Hiraoka, Kimitake
Ai No Kawaki, Tokyo 1950, Novel
Ai No Kawaki 1967 d: Koreyoshi KuraharA. lps: Nobuo Nakamura, Ruriko Asaoka, Akira Yamauchi. 98M JPN. *Longing for Love; The Thirst for Love* prod/rel: Nikkatsu Corporation

L' Ecole de la Chair, Novel
Ecole de la Chair, L' 1998 d: Benoit Jacquot. lps: Isabelle Huppert, Vincent Martinez, Vincent Lindon. 102M FRN. *The School of Flesh* prod/rel: Orsans Productions, V.M.P.

Gogo No Eiko, 1963, Novel
Sailor Who Fell from Grace With the Sea, The 1976 d: Lewis John Carlino. lps: Sarah Miles, Kris Kristofferson, Jonathan Kahn. 105M UKN. prod/rel: Avco, Sailor Company

Homba, 1969, Novel
Mishima: a Life in Four Chapters 1985 d: Paul Schrader. lps: Ken Ogata, Kenji Sawada, Yasosuke Bando. 120M USA/JPN. *Mishima* prod/rel: Zoetrope Studios, Filmlink International (Tokyo)

Kinkaku-Ji, 1956, Novel
Enjo 1958 d: Kon IchikawA. lps: Raizo Ichikawa, Tatsuya Nakadai, Ganjiro NakamurA. 102M JPN. *Conflagration* (USA); *Flame of Torment* (UKN) prod/rel: Daiei Motion Picture Co.

Mishima: a Life in Four Chapters 1985 d: Paul Schrader. lps: Ken Ogata, Kenji Sawada, Yasosuke Bando. 120M USA/JPN. *Mishima* prod/rel: Zoetrope Studios, Filmlink International (Tokyo)

Kurobana No Yakata, Play
Kurobara No Yakata 1969 d: Kinji Fukasaku. lps: Akihiro Maruyama, Eitaro Ozawa, Masakazu TamurA. 90M JPN. *Black Rose* (USA); *The Black Rose Inn* prod/rel: Shochiku Co.

Kuroktokage, 1962, Play
Kurotokage 1968 d: Kinji Fukasaku. lps: Akihiro Maruyama, Isao Kimura, Junya Usami. 86M JPN. *Black Lizard* (USA) prod/rel: Shochiku Co.

Kyoko No Ie, 1959, Novel
Mishima: a Life in Four Chapters 1985 d: Paul Schrader. lps: Ken Ogata, Kenji Sawada, Yasosuke Bando. 120M USA/JPN. *Mishima* prod/rel: Zoetrope Studios, Filmlink International (Tokyo)

Nikutai No Gakko, Tokyo 1964, Novel
Nikutai No Gakko 1965 d: Ryo KinoshitA. lps: Kyoko Kishida, Tsutomu Yamazaki, Yuki NakagawA. 95M JPN. *School of Love* (USA); *School of Sex; School for Sex* prod/rel: Toho Co.

Shiosai, 1954, Novel
Shiosai 1954 d: Senkichi Taniguchi. lps: Akira Kubo, Kyoko Aoyama, Yoichi TachikawA. 94M JPN. *The Sound of Waves; Surf* prod/rel: Toho Co.

MISTRAL, FREDERIC (1830–1914), FRN
Mireille, Poem
Mireille 1909 d: Henri Cain. lps: Frederic Mistral, Roger Karl, Jaegger. 165m FRN. prod/rel: Film d'Art

Mireille 1922 d: Ernest Servaes. lps: Joe Hamman, Angele Pornot, Carlo BerthosA. 3000m FRN. prod/rel: Servaes Film

Mireille 1933 d: Rene Gaveau, Ernest Servaes. lps: Mireille Lurie, Jean Brunil, Marcel Boudouresque. 75M FRN. prod/rel: Saint-Jacques, Camille, Ste Chantereine D'etudes Cinegraphiques

MISTRY, ROHINTON
Such a Long Journey, Novel
Such a Long Journey 1998 d: Sturla Gunnarsson. lps: Roshan Seth, Soni Razdan, Om Puri. 112M CND/UKN. prod/rel: Red Sky, Film Works

MITANI, KOKI
Radio No Jikan, Play
Radio No Jikan 1998 d: Koki Mitani. lps: Toshiaki Karasawa, Kyoka Suzuki, Masahiko NishimurA. 103M JPN. *Welcome Back Mr. McDonald* prod/rel: Fuji Television Network, Toho Co.

MITCHARD, JACQUELYN
The Deep End of the Ocean, 1996, Novel
Deep End of the Ocean, The 1999 d: Ulu Grosbard. lps: Michelle Pfeiffer, Treat Williams, Whoopi Goldberg. 105M USA. prod/rel: Sony Pictures Entertainment, Columbia Pictures

MITCHELL, ADRIAN (1932–, UKN
Man Friday, 1974, Play
Man Friday 1975 d: Jack Gold. lps: Peter O'Toole, Richard Roundtree, Peter Cellier. 108M UKN/MXC. prod/rel: Avco-Embassy, Itc

MITCHELL, BASIL
The Perfect Woman, London 1948, Play
Perfect Woman, The 1949 d: Bernard Knowles. lps: Patricia Roc, Stanley Holloway, Nigel Patrick. 89M UKN. prod/rel: General Film Distributors, Two Cities

MITCHELL, DAVID
The Light on Synanon, Book
Attack on Fear 1984 d: Mel Damski. lps: Paul Michael Glaser, Linda Kelsey, Kevin Conway. TVM. 100M USA. prod/rel: Viacom, Tomorrow Entertainment

MITCHELL, DODSON
Cornered, New York 1920, Play
Cornered 1924 d: William Beaudine. lps: Marie Prevost, Rockliffe Fellowes, Raymond Hatton. 6500f USA. prod/rel: Warner Brothers Pictures

Road to Paradise 1930 d: William Beaudine. lps: Loretta Young, Jack Mulhall, George Barraud. 6935f USA. *At Bay* prod/rel: First National Pictures

MITCHELL, EDMUND
The Lone Star Rush, London 1902, Novel
Lone Star Rush, The 1915 d: Edmund Mitchell. lps: Robert Fraser, Charles Arling, Rupert Julian. 5r USA. *The Gold Lure* prod/rel: Climax Co.©, Alliance Films Corp.

Only a Nigger, London 1901, Novel
Man Beneath, The 1919 d: William Worthington. lps: Sessue Hayakawa, Helen Jerome Eddy, Pauline Curley. 5r USA. prod/rel: Haworth Pictures Corp., Robertson-Cole Co.

MITCHELL, FRANCES MARIAN
Joan of Rainbow Springs, Boston 1911, Novel
Girl of My Heart, The 1920 d: Edward J. Le Saint. lps: Shirley Mason, Raymond McKee, Martha Mattox. 4340f USA. *Joan of Rainbow Springs* prod/rel: Fox Film Corp., William Fox©

MITCHELL, GEORGE
Compartiment de Dames Seules, Play
Compartiment de Dames Seules 1934 d: Christian-Jaque. lps: Armand Bernard, Pierre Larquey, Alice Tissot. 101M FRN. *Ladies Only* prod/rel: C.D.F.

MITCHELL, J. A.
The Pines of Lory, Novel
　　Pines of Lory, The 1914 d: Ashley Miller. lps: Marc McDermott, Miriam Nesbitt, Bessie Learn. 2r USA. prod/rel: Edison

MITCHELL, JAMES
A Magnum for Schneider, Novel
　　Callan 1974 d: Don Sharp. lps: Edward Woodward, Eric Porter, Carl Mohner. 106M UKN. *This Is Callan; The Neutralizer* prod/rel: Emi, Magnum

MITCHELL, JOHN AMES
Amos Judd, New York 1895, Novel
　　Young Rajah, The 1922 d: Phil Rosen. lps: Rudolph Valentino, Wanda Hawley, Pat Moore. 7705f USA. prod/rel: Famous Players-Lasky, Paramount Pictures

MITCHELL, JULIAN (1935–, UKN
Another Country, 1982, Play
　　Another Country 1984 d: Marek KanievskA. lps: Rupert Everett, Colin Firth, Michael Jenn. 90M UKN. prod/rel: 20th Century Fox, Virgin

MITCHELL, MARGARET (1900–1949), USA
Gone With the Wind, New York 1936, Novel
　　Gone With the Wind 1939 d: Victor Fleming, Sam Wood (Uncredited). lps: Clark Gable, Vivien Leigh, Leslie Howard. 222M USA. prod/rel: Selznick International Pictures©, Metro-Goldwyn-Mayer Corp.

MITCHELL, MARY
Warning to Wantons, Novel
　　Warning to Wantons 1949 d: Donald B. Wilson. lps: Harold Warrender, Anne Vernon, David Tomlinson. 104M UKN. prod/rel: Aquila, General Film Distributors

MITCHELL, NORMA
Cradle Snatchers, New York 1925, Play
　　Cradle Snatchers, The 1927 d: Howard Hawks. lps: Louise Fazenda, J. Farrell MacDonald, Ethel Wales. 6281f USA. prod/rel: Fox Film Corp.
　　Why Leave Home? 1929 d: Raymond Cannon. lps: Sue Carol, Nick Stuart, Dixie Lee. 6388f USA. prod/rel: Fox Film Corp.

MITCHELL, PAIGE
Act of Love, Novel
　　Act of Love 1980 d: Jud Taylor. lps: Ron Howard, Robert Foxworth, Mickey Rourke. TVM. 104M USA. prod/rel: NBC, Paramount

MITCHELL, RUTH COMFORT
Dashing, Story
　　Six Shootin' Romance, A 1926 d: Cliff Smith. lps: Jack Hoxie, Olive Hasbrouck, William Steele. 4837f USA. prod/rel: Universal Pictures
Into Her Kingdom, 1925, Short Story
　　Into Her Kingdom 1926 d: Svend Gade. lps: Corinne Griffith, Einar Hanson, Claude Gillingwater. 6447f USA. prod/rel: Corinne Griffith Productions, First National Pictures

MITCHELL, THOMAS
Bachelor Father, Play
　　Casanova Brown 1944 d: Sam Wood. lps: Gary Cooper, Teresa Wright, Frank Morgan. 99M USA. prod/rel: International, Christie

MITCHELL, W. O. (1914–, CND, Mitchell, William Ormond
Who Has Seen the Wind, Novel
　　Who Has Seen the Wind 1977 d: Allan King. lps: Brian Painchaud, Douglas Junor, Gordon Pinsent. 103M CND. *Mais Qui a Vu le Vent* prod/rel: Souris River Films Ltd., Allan King Associates Ltd.

MITCHUM, ROBERT (1917–1997), USA
Story
　　Thunder Road 1958 d: Arthur Ripley. lps: Robert Mitchum, Gene Barry, Jacques Aubuchon. 92M USA. prod/rel: United Artists, Drm Prods.

MITFORD, NANCY (1904–1973), UKN
Novel
　　Love in a Cold Climate 1980 d: Donald McWhinnie. lps: Judi Dench, Vivian Pickles, Michael Aldridge. MTV. 350M UKN. prod/rel: Thames
The Blessing, 1951, Novel
　　Count Your Blessings 1959 d: Jean Negulesco. lps: Deborah Kerr, Rossano Brazzi, Maurice Chevalier. 102M USA. prod/rel: MGM

MITRA, BIMAL
Saheb Bibi Golam, 1952, Novel
　　Sahib Bibi Aur Ghulam 1962 d: Abrar Alvi. lps: Meena Kumari, Guru Dutt, Waheeda Rehman. 152M IND. *King Queen Or Knave; Master Mistress Servant; King Queen Knave; Queen and Slave King* prod/rel: Guru Dutt Films

MITRA, MANOJ
Bancharamer Bagan, Play
　　Bancharamer Bagan 1980 d: Tapan SinhA. lps: Manoj Mitra, Nirmal Kumar, Dipankar Dey. 133M IND. *Garden of Bancharam*

MITRA, NAREDRANATH
Mahanagar, 1949, Short Story
　　Mahanagar 1963 d: Satyajit Ray. lps: Madhabi Mukherjee, Anil Chatterjee, Haradhan Banerjee. 133M IND. *The Big City* (UKN) prod/rel: R.D.B. & Co.

MITRA, PREMENDRA (1904–, IND
Janaiko Kapuruser Kahini
　　Kapurush 1965 d: Satyajit Ray. lps: Soumitra Chatterjee, Madhabi Mukherjee, Haradhan Bannerjee. 74M IND. *The Coward* prod/rel: R.D.B.

MITTELFUNKT, HILLEL
Bouba, Play
　　Bouba 1987 d: Ze'ev Revach. lps: Ze'ev Revach, Hani Nachmias, Eli Denkner. F ISR. *Boubah; On the Fringe*

MIYAMOTO, TERU
Doro No Kawa, Novel
　　Doro No Kawa 1981 d: Kohei Oguri. lps: Nobutaka Asahara, Takahiro Tamura, Yumiko FujitA. 105M JPN. *Muddy River* (UKN); *Mud River* prod/rel: Kimura Productions
Hotarugawa, Novel
　　Hotarugawa 1987 d: Eizo SugawA. lps: Yukiyo Toake, Takayuki Sakazume, Rentaro Mikuni. 114M JPN. *River of Fireflies* prod/rel: Kinema Tokyo, Nichiei

MIYOSHI
Kanadehon Chushingura, 1748, Play
　　Chushingura 1962 d: Hiroshi Inagaki. lps: Koshiro Matsumoto, Yuzo Kayama, Chusha IchikawA. 204M JPN. *The Loyal Forty-Seven Ronin; The Faithful 47; The 47 Ronin; 47 Samurai* prod/rel: Toho Co.

MIZNER, WILSON
The Deep Purple, Chicago 1910, Play
　　Deep Purple, The 1915 d: James Young. lps: Clara Kimball Young, Milton Sills, Edward M. Kimball. 5r USA. prod/rel: World Film Corp.©
　　Deep Purple, The 1920 d: Raoul Walsh. lps: Miriam Cooper, Helen Ware, Vincent Serrano. 6661f USA. prod/rel: Mayflower Photoplay Corp.©, Realart Pictures Corp.
The Greyhound, New York 1912, Play
　　Greyhound, The 1914 d: Lawrence McGill. lps: Catherine Carter, Elita Proctor Otis, Anna Laughlin. 5r USA. prod/rel: Life Photo Film Corp.©, State Rights

MIZUNO, HAJIME
Buttsuke Honban, Book
　　Buttsuke Honban 1958 d: Kozo Saeki. lps: Frankie Sakai, Keiko Awaji, Tatsuya Nakadai. 98M JPN. *Go and Get It* prod/rel: Tokyo Eiga Co.

MNACKO, LADISLAV
Story
　　Jak Chutna Smrt 1996 d: Milan Cieslar. lps: Juraj Kukura, Miluse Splechtova, Oto Sramek. F CZE. prod/rel: Happy Celluloid Ltd.
Smrt' Sa Vola Engelchen, 1959, Novel
　　Smrt Si Rika Engelchen 1963 d: Jan Kadar, Elmar Klos. lps: Jan Kacer, Vlado Muller, Eva PolakovA. 134M CZC. *Death Calls Itself Engelchen; Death Is Called Engelchen*

MNISZKOWNA, HELENA
Tredowata, Novel
　　Tredowata 1976 d: Jerzy Hoffman. lps: Irena Malkiewicz, Mariusz Dmochowski, Anna DymnA. 100M PLN. *Leper* prod/rel: Zespoly Filmowe Silesia

MO, TIMOTHY
Sour Sweet, 1982, Novel
　　Sour Sweet 1989 d: Mike Newell. lps: Chang Ai-Chia, Danny An-Ning Dun, Soon-Teck Oh. 110M UKN. *Soursweet* prod/rel: Film Four International, First Film

MO YAN
Hong Gao Liang, 1985, Novel
　　Hong Gaoliang 1987 d: Zhang Yimou. lps: Gong Li, Jiang Wen, Liu Ji. 91M CHN. *Red Sorghum* (USA) prod/rel: XI'an Film Studio

MOBERG, VILHELM (1898–1973), SWD, Moberg, Carl Arthur Vilhelm
Ankeman Jarl, 1940, Play
　　Ankeman Jarl 1945 d: Sigurd Wallen. lps: Sigurd Wallen, Dagmar Ebbesen, Arthur Fischer. 97M SWD. *Jarl the Widower* prod/rel: Ab Europa Film
Domaren, 1957, Play
　　Domaren 1960 d: Alf Sjoberg. lps: Ingrid Thulin, Gunnar Hellstrom, Per Myrberg. 109M SWD. *The Judge*
Invandrarna, 1952, Novel
　　Invandrarna 1970 d: Jan Troell. lps: Max von Sydow, Liv Ullmann, Eddie Axberg. 198M SWD. *The New Land* (USA); *Unto a New Land; Nybyggarna; The Settlers; Unto a Good Land*
　　Utvandrarna 1970 d: Jan Troell. lps: Max von Sydow, Liv Ullmann, Eddie Axberg. 191M SWD. *The Emigrants* (UKN) prod/rel: Ab Svensk

Kassabrit, Stockholm 1925, Play
　　Karlek Och Kassabrist 1932 d: Gustaf Molander. lps: Sigurd Wallen, Tutta Rolf, Edvin Adolphson. 72M SWD. *Love and Deficit* prod/rel: Film Ab Minerva, Ab Svensk Filmindustri
Mans Kvinna, 1933, Novel
　　Mans Kvinna 1945 d: Gunnar Skoglund. lps: Edvin Adolphson, Birgit Tengroth, Holger Lowenadler. 88M SWD. *Woman for Men* prod/rel: Ab Svensk Filmindustri
Nybyggarna, 1956, Novel
　　Invandrarna 1970 d: Jan Troell. lps: Max von Sydow, Liv Ullmann, Eddie Axberg. 198M SWD. *The New Land* (USA); *Unto a New Land; Nybyggarna; The Settlers; Unto a Good Land*
Rid I Natt!, 1941, Novel
　　Rid I Natt! 1942 d: Gustaf Molander. lps: Lars Hanson, Oscar Ljung, Erik Berglund. 106M SWD. *Ride Tonight!* (UKN)
Sankt Sedebetyg, 1935, Novel
　　Glad Dig I Din Ungdom 1939 d: Per Lindberg. lps: Birgit Tengroth, Peter Hoglund, Carl Strom. 88M SWD. *Rejoice While You are Young* prod/rel: Ab Svensk Filmindustri
Sista Brevet Till Sverige, 1959, Novel
　　Invandrarna 1970 d: Jan Troell. lps: Max von Sydow, Liv Ullmann, Eddie Axberg. 198M SWD. *The New Land* (USA); *Unto a New Land; Nybyggarna; The Settlers; Unto a Good Land*
Utvandrarna, 1949, Novel
　　Utvandrarna 1970 d: Jan Troell. lps: Max von Sydow, Liv Ullmann, Eddie Axberg. 191M SWD. *The Emigrants* (UKN) prod/rel: Ab Svensk

MODIANO, PATRICK
Une Jeunesse, Novel
　　Jeunesse, Une 1983 d: Moshe Mizrahi. lps: Ariane Larteguy, Patrick Norbert, Jacques Dutronc. 100M FRN. *Youth* prod/rel: G.P.F.I., Films de L'alma
Villa Triste, Novel
　　Parfum d'Yvonne, Le 1994 d: Patrice Leconte. lps: Jean-Pierre Marielle, Hippolyte Girardot, Sandra Majani. 89M FRN. prod/rel: Lambart, Zoulou

MOFFAT, EDWARD STEWART
Hearts Steadfast, New York 1915, Novel
　　Revenge 1918 d: Tod Browning. lps: Edith Storey, Wheeler Oakman, Alberta Ballard. 5r USA. prod/rel: Metro Pictures Corp.©

MOFFATT, GRAHAM
Bunty Pulls the Strings, London 1911, Play
　　Bunty Pulls the Strings 1921 d: Reginald Barker. lps: Leatrice Joy, Russell Simpson, Raymond Hatton. 7r USA. prod/rel: Goldwyn Pictures
Till the Bells Ring, Glasgow 1908, Play
　　Till the Bells Ring 1933 d: Graham Moffatt. lps: Graham Moffatt, Margaret Moffatt, Winifred Moffatt. 46M UKN. prod/rel: British Sound Film Productions, Bayley

MOFFETT, CLEVELAND
The Battle, New York 1908, Play
　　Money Master, The 1915 d: George Fitzmaurice. lps: Frank Sheridan, Paul McAllister, Calvin Thomas. 5r USA. prod/rel: George Kleine, Kleine-Edison Feature Service
The Girl of Gold, 1920, Short Story
　　Girl of Gold, The 1925 d: John Ince. lps: Florence Vidor, Malcolm McGregor, Alan Roscoe. 4969f USA. prod/rel: Regal Pictures, Producers Distributing Corp.
Through the Wall, New York 1909, Play
　　Through the Wall 1916 d: Rollin S. Sturgeon. lps: Nell Shipman, William Duncan, George Holt. 6r USA. prod/rel: Vitagraph Co. of America©, Blue Ribbon Feature

MOFFITT, JOHN C.
The Roaring Girl, Los Angeles 1937, Play
　　Exclusive 1937 d: Alexander Hall. lps: Fred MacMurray, Frances Farmer, Charles Ruggles. 85M USA. *Things Began to Happen* prod/rel: Paramount Pictures

MOHR, MAX
Der Kampfer, Play
　　Ramper, Der Tiermensch 1927 d: Max Reichmann. lps: Paul Wegener, Mary Johnson, Kurt Gerron. 3115m GRM. *The Strange Case of Captain Ramper* (USA); *Ramper the Beastman* prod/rel: Deutsche Film-Union Ag

MOHR, MICHAEL
Soldatensender Calais, Novel
　　Soldatensender Calais 1960 d: Paul May. lps: Hans Reiser, Gert Frobe, Klausjurgen Wussow. 103M GRM. *Headquarters State Secret* (USA); *Army Radio Calais* prod/rel: Bavaria

MOINOT, PIERRE
La Chasse Royale, Novel
  Chasse Royale, La 1969 d: Francois Leterrier. lps: Sami Frey, Claude Brasseur, Jean Champion. 87M FRN/CZC. *Kralovska Polovacka* (CZC); *The Royal Hunting* prod/rel: Como Films, Ceskoslovensky Film

MOISEIWITCH, MAURICE
The Sleeping Tiger, Novel
  Sleeping Tiger, The 1954 d: Joseph Losey. lps: Dirk Bogarde, Alexis Smith, Alexander Knox. 89M UKN. prod/rel: Insignia, Anglo-Amalgamated

MOL, ALBERT
Wat Zien Ik, Novel
  Wat Zien Ik 1971 d: Paul Verhoeven. lps: Ronald Bierman, Sylvia de Leur, Piet Romer. 93M NTH. *Any Special Way* (UKN); *Business Is Business*; *Fun Life of an Amsterdam Streetwalker*; *Memoirs of a Streetwalker* prod/rel: Rob Houwer

MOLBECH, CHRISTIAN
Opad, Play
  Ame d'Artiste 1924 d: Germaine Dulac. lps: Mabel Poulton, Yvette Andreyor, Nicolas Koline. 2250m FRN. *Heart of an Actress*; *Reve Et Realite* prod/rel: Cine-France-Film 1924 (Consortium Westi)

MOLDOVA, GYORGY
Malom a Pokolban, 1968, Novel
  Malom a Pokolban 1987 d: Gyula Maar. lps: Dezso Garas. 100M HNG. *Mills of Hell*

MOLE, FRANCO
The Room of Words, Play
  Room of Words, The 1989 d: Joe d'Amato. lps: Martine Brochard, Linda Carol, David Brandon. 97M ITL. prod/rel: Wind Film

MOLIERE (1622–1673), FRN, Poquelin, Jean Baptiste
L'Avare, 1668, Play
  Avare, L' 1979 d: Louis de Funes, Jean Girault. lps: Louis de Funes, Frank David, Claire Dupray. 125M FRN. prod/rel: Films Christian Fechner
Le Bourgeois Gentilhomme, 1670, Play
  Bourgeois Gentilhomme, Le 1958 d: Jean Meyer. lps: Louis Seigner, Andree de Chauveron, Michele Grellier. 97M FRN. *The Would-Be Gentleman* (USA) prod/rel: L.P.C., Films J.R.D.
Don Juan, 1665, Play
  Don Juan 1908 d: Albert Capellani, Floury. lps: Paul Capellani, Henri Desfontaines. 1082f FRN. prod/rel: Pathe Freres
  Don Juan 1998 d: Jacques Weber. lps: Jacques Weber, Michel Boujenah, Emmanuelle Beart. 104M FRN/SPN/GRM. prod/rel: Blue Dahlia Prod., Tornasol Films (Spain)
Les Femmes Savantes, 1673, Play
  Femmes Savantes, Les 1965 d: Jean Meyer. 100M FRN.
Les Fourberies de Scapin, 1671, Play
  Fourberies de Scapin, Les 1980 d: Roger Coggio. lps: Roger Coggio, Michel Galabru, Jean-Pierre Darras. 107M FRN.
Ou le Mari George Dandin, 1669, Play
  Dandin Gyorgy 1955 d: Zoltan Varkonyi. lps: Sandor Pecsi, Agi Meszaros, Tivadar Uray. 87M HNG. *Georges Dandin*; *Dandin Gyorgy*; *Vagy a Megcsufolt Ferj*
Le Malade Imaginaire, 1673, Play
  Eingebildete Kranke, Der 1952 d: Hans H. Konig. lps: Joe Stockel, Oskar Sima, Inge Egger. 96M GRM. *The Hypochondriac* prod/rel: Konigfilm, Herzog
  Malade Imaginaire, Le 1934 d: Jaquelux, Marc MerendA. lps: Robert Pizani, Nane Germon, Ginette Gaubert. 51M FRN. prod/rel: Pellegrin
  Malade Imaginaire, Le 1966 d: Jean Pignol. lps: Louis Seigner, Georges Chamarat, Jean-Paul Roussillon. 80M FRN.
  Malade Imaginaire, Le 1990 d: Jean-Laurent Cochet. lps: Jacques Charon, Georges Descrieres, Jacques Eyser. TVM. 110M FRN.
  Malade Imaginaire, Le 1990 d: Jacques Deschamps. lps: Jean Dautremay, Christine Murillo, Nelly Borgeaud. TVM. 85M FRN.
  Malato Immaginario, Il 1979 d: Tonino Cervi. lps: Alberto Sordi, Laura Antonelli, Giuliana de Sio. 107M ITL. prod/rel: Mars Prod. Cin.Ca, C.I.C.
Le Medecin Malgre Lui, 1666, Play
  Medecin Malgre Lui, Le 1910 d: Emile Chautard. lps: Maurice de Feraudy. 320m FRN. prod/rel: Acad
  Medecin Malgre Lui, Le 1934 d: Pierre Weill. lps: Alexandre Mathillon, Helene Perdriere, Raymond Menage. 1250m FRN. prod/rel: Raymond Rognoni
  Medico Per Forza, Il 1931 d: Carlo Campogalliani. lps: Ettore Petrolini, Tilde Mercandalli, Letizia QuarantA. 55M ITL. prod/rel: Cines, Anonima Pittaluga

Le Misanthrope, 1666, Play
  Misanthrope, Le 1966 d: Louis-Georges Carrier. lps: Guy Provost, Albert Millaire, Andree Lachappelle. 95M CND. prod/rel: Onyx Films Inc., Les Productions Guy Provost Inc.
Monsieur de Pourceaugnac, 1670, Play
  Monsieur de Pourceaugnac 1932 d: Gaston Ravel, Tony Lekain. lps: Armand Bernard, Josseline Gael, Jaque Catelain. 84M FRN. prod/rel: Star Film
Less Precieuses Ridicules, 1660, Play
  Precieuses Ridicules, Les 1934 d: Leonce Perret. lps: Marcelle Gabarre, Henri Echourin, Pierre Dux. 46M FRN. prod/rel: Levy-Strauss
Tartuffe, 1669, Play
  Tartuff 1925 d: F. W. Murnau. lps: Emil Jannings, Lil Dagover, Werner Krauss. 1876m GRM. *Tartuffe* (UKN); *Tartuffe the Hypocrite*; *Herr Tartuff* prod/rel: UFA
  Tartuffe 1908-18. lps: Emile Matrat, Clement, Jeanne Provost. FRN. prod/rel: le Film d'Art
  Tartuffe 1963 d: Jean Meyer. 98M FRN.
  Tartuffe de Moliere, Le 1984 d: Jacques Lasalle, Gerard Depardieu. lps: Gerard Depardieu, Francois Perier, Elisabeth Depardieu. 140M FRN.

MOLIN, PELLE
Karnfolk, 1897, Short Story
  Adalens Poesi 1948 d: Ivar Johansson. lps: Adolf Jahr, Wilma Malmlof, Nine-Christine Jonsson. 94M SWD. prod/rel: Ab Sandrew-Produktion, Ab Sandrew-Bauman Film
Karnfolkunnel, 1897, Short Story
  Adalens Poesi 1928 d: Theodor Berthels. lps: Jessie Wessel, Einar Axelsson, Eric Laurent. 1760m SWD. *Poetry of Adalen* prod/rel: Industri & Reklamfilm, Maja Engelbrektson

MOLL, ELICK
Night Without Sleep, 1950, Novel
  Night Without Sleep 1952 d: Roy Ward Baker. lps: Gary Merrill, Linda Darnell, Hildegard Knef. 77M USA. prod/rel: 20th Century-Fox

MOLLER, ALFRED
Ratsel Um Beate, Play
  Ratsel Um Beate 1938 d: Johannes Meyer. lps: Lil Dagover, Albrecht Schoenhals, Kathe Haack. 85M GRM. prod/rel: Cine-Allianz, Schorcht

MOLLER, T. J.
Fire
  Captives, The 1970 d: Carl Borch. lps: Brigit Kroyer, Karl Hansen, Orla Nsu. F DNM.

MOLNAR, FERENC (1878–1952), HNG
Delila, 1937, Play
  Blonde Fever 1944 d: Richard Whorf. lps: Philip Dorn, Mary Astor, Felix Bressart. 69M USA. *Autumn Fever* prod/rel: Metro-Goldwyn-Mayer Corp.
Egy - Ketto - Harom, Budapest 1929, Play
  One, Two, Three 1961 d: Billy Wilder. lps: James Cagney, Horst Buchholz, Pamela Tiffin. 115M USA. prod/rel: Mirish Co., Pyramid Productions, a.G.
Fashions for Men, Play
  Fine Clothes 1925 d: John M. Stahl. lps: Lewis Stone, Percy Marmont, Alma Rubens. 6971f USA. *Fashion for Men* prod/rel: Louis B. Mayer Productions, First National Pictures
A Hattyu, Budapest 1921, Play
  One Romantic Night 1930 d: Paul L. Stein. lps: Lillian Gish, Rod La Rocque, Conrad Nagel. 71M USA. *The Swan* prod/rel: United Artists
  Swan, The 1925 d: Dimitri Buchowetzki. lps: Frances Howard, Adolphe Menjou, Ricardo Cortez. 5889f USA. prod/rel: Famous Players-Lasky, Paramount Pictures
  Swan, The 1956 d: Charles Vidor. lps: Grace Kelly, Alec Guinness, Louis Jourdan. 112M USA. prod/rel: MGM
Az Ismeretien Lany, Budapest 1934, Play
  Bride Wore Red, The 1937 d: Dorothy Arzner. lps: Joan Crawford, Franchot Tone, Robert Young. 103M USA. *Once There Was a Lady* prod/rel: Metro-Goldwyn-Mayer Corp.
A Jo Tunder, Budapest 1931, Play
  Good Fairy, The 1935 d: William Wyler. lps: Margaret Sullavan, Herbert Marshall, Frank Morgan. 98M USA. prod/rel: Universal Pictures Corp.[C], William Wyler Production
  Good Fairy, The 1956 d: George Schaefer. lps: Julie Harris, Walter Slezak, Cyril Ritchard. MTV. USA. prod/rel: Hallmark Hall of Fame
  I'll Be Yours 1947 d: William A. Seiter. lps: Deanna Durbin, William Bendix, Adolphe Menjou. 93M USA. prod/rel: Universal-International
Liliom, 1910, Play
  Carousel 1956 d: Henry King. lps: Gordon MacCrae, Shirley Jones, Cameron Mitchell. 128M USA. prod/rel: 20th Century-Fox

  Liliom 1930 d: Frank Borzage. lps: Charles Farrell, Rose Hobart, Estelle Taylor. 94M USA. prod/rel: Fox Film Corp.
  Liliom 1934 d: Fritz Lang. lps: Charles Boyer, Madeleine Ozeray, Pierre Alcover. 120M FRN. prod/rel: Fox Europa
  Trip to Paradise, A 1921 d: Maxwell Karger. lps: Bert Lytell, Virginia Valli, Brinsley Shaw. 5800f USA. prod/rel: Metro Pictures
Nagy Szerelem, 1935, Play
  Double Wedding 1937 d: Richard Thorpe. lps: William Powell, Myrna Loy, Florence Rice. 87M USA. *Three's Company* prod/rel: MGM
Olympia, Budapest 1928, Play
  Breath of Scandal, A 1960 d: Michael Curtiz. lps: Sophia Loren, John Gavin, Maurice Chevalier. 98M USA/ITL/AUS. *Olympia* (ITL) prod/rel: Paramount, Titanus
  His Glorious Night 1929 d: Lionel Barrymore. lps: John Gilbert, Catherine Dale Owen, Nance O'Neil. 7173f USA. *Breath of Scandal* prod/rel: Metro-Goldwyn-Mayer Pictures
  Olimpia 1930 d: Miguel de ZarragA. lps: Jose Crespo, Maria Alba, Elvira MoriA. 9r USA. prod/rel: Metro-Goldwyn-Mayer Pictures
  Olympia 1930 d: Jacques Feyder, Lionel Barrymore. lps: Nora Gregor, Theo Shall, Julia SerdA. 7173f USA. prod/rel: Metro-Goldwyn-Mayer Pictures
  Si l'Empereur Savait Ca 1930 d: Jacques Feyder. lps: Andre Luguet, Francoise Rosay, Tania Fedor. 86M FRN/USA. *Olympia* prod/rel: Metro-Goldwyn-Mayer
Az Ordog; Vigjatek Harom Felvonasban, Budapest 1908, Play
  Devil, The 1915 d: Thomas H. Ince, Reginald Barker. lps: Edward Connelly, Bessie Barriscale, Arthur Maude. 4600f USA. prod/rel: New York Motion Picture Corp.[C], Mutual Film Corp.
  Devil, The 1921 d: James Young. lps: George Arliss, Sylvia Breamer, Lucy Cotton. 5682f USA. prod/rel: Associated Exhibitors, Pathe Exchange, Inc.
  Duivel in Amsterdam, de 1919 d: Theo Frenkel Sr. lps: Eduard Verkade, Louis Bouwmeester, Margie Morris. 2300m NTH. *The Devil in Amsterdam* prod/rel: Amsterdam Film Cie
A Pal-Utcai Fiuk, 1907, Novel
  No Greater Glory 1934 d: Frank Borzage. lps: George Breakston, Jimmy Butler, Jackie Searl. 78M USA. *The Paul Street Boys*; *Men of Tomorrow*; *No Cannons Roar* prod/rel: Columbia Pictures Corp.[C]
  Pal Utcai Fiuk, A 1968 d: Zoltan Fabri. lps: Anthony Kemp, William Burleigh, John Moulder-Brown. 105M HNG/USA. *The Boys of Paul Street* (USA) prod/rel: 20th Century Fox, Hungaro Film
Prisoners, Play
  Prisoners 1929 d: William A. Seiter. lps: Corinne Griffith, Ian Keith, Otto Matiesen. 7857f USA. prod/rel: Walter Morosco Productions, First National Pictures
A Testor, Budapest 1910, Play
  Chocolate Soldier, The 1941 d: Roy Del Ruth. lps: Nelson Eddy, Rise Stevens, Nigel Bruce. 102M USA. prod/rel: MGM
  Guardsman, The 1931 d: Sidney A. Franklin. lps: Alfred Lunt, Lynn Fontanne, Roland Young. 83M USA. *Son of Russia* prod/rel: Metro-Goldwyn-Mayer Corp., Metro-Goldwyn-Mayer Dist. Corp.[C]
  Lily in Love 1985 d: Karoly Makk. lps: Christopher Plummer, Maggie Smith, Adolph Green. 103M USA/HNG. *Jatszani Kell* (HNG); *Double Play*; *Fitz and Lily*; *Playing for Keeps*; *Players* prod/rel: New Line

MOM, ARTURO S.
Un Seguro Sobre la Dicha, 1927, Short Story
  Cock O' the Walk 1930 d: R. William Neill, Walter Lang. lps: Joseph Schildkraut, Myrna Loy, Philip Sleeman. 7200f USA.

MONAGHAN, JAY
Last of the Badmen, Novel
  Bad Men of Tombstone, The 1949 d: Kurt Neumann. lps: Barry Sullivan, Broderick Crawford, Marjorie Reynolds. 75M USA. prod/rel: Allied Artists

MONARI, FRANCA
Brogliaccio d'Amore, Novel
  Brogliaccio d'Amore 1976 d: Decio SillA. lps: Enrico Maria Salerno, Senta Berger, Paolo Carlini. 100M ITL. prod/rel: Dunamis Cin.Ca, Maxi Cin.Ca

MONASH, PAUL
The Singing Idol, Television Play
  Sing, Boy, Sing 1957 d: Henry Ephron. lps: Tommy Sands, Lili Gentle, Edmond O'Brien. 91M USA. *The Singin' Idol* prod/rel: 20th Century-Fox

MONDAINI, GIACI
Buoni Per un Giorno, 1934, Short Story
   Daro un Milione 1935 d: Mario Camerini. lps: Vittorio de Sica, Assia Noris, Luigi Almirante. 76M ITL. *I'll Give a Million* prod/rel: Novella Film, E.I.a.

MONELLI, PAOLO
Le Scarpe Al Sole, Diary
   Scarpe Al Sole, Le 1935 d: Marco Elter. lps: Camillo Pilotto, Cesco Baseggio, Carlo Lodovici. 90M ITL. prod/rel: I.C.I., Artisti Associati

MONJARDIN
Souris Blonde, Opera
   Blanc Comme Neige 1931 d: Francisco Elias, Camille Lemoine. lps: Moussia, Betty Stockfeld, Roland Toutain. 91M FRN. *La Souris Blonde*; *White As Snow* prod/rel: Orphea-Film

MONKS JR., JOHN
Brother Rat, New York 1936, Play
   About Face 1952 d: Roy Del Ruth. lps: Gordon MacRae, Eddie Bracken, Dick Wesson. 94M USA. prod/rel: Warner Bros.
   Brother Rat 1938 d: William Keighley. lps: Priscilla Lane, Wayne Morris, Johnnie "Scat" Davis. 90M USA. prod/rel: Warner Bros. Pictures, Inc.

MONNIER, A.
L' Affaire de la Rue de Lourcine, 1857, Play
   Affaire de la Rue de Lourcine, L' 1932 d: Marcel Dumont. lps: Victor Vina, Jeanne Bayle, Juliette Zahn. 45M FRN. prod/rel: Compagnie Parisienne Cinematographique

MONNIER, THYDE
Le Pain Des Pauvres, Novel
   Vertigine d'Amore 1951 d: Luigi Capuano. lps: Charles Vanel, Elli Parvo, Folco Lulli. F ITL. *Le Pain Des Pauvres* (FRN) prod/rel: I.C.I., Pathe Cinema

MONROE, ROBERT
No Blade Too Sharp, Radio Play
   Crooked Way, The 1949 d: Robert Florey. lps: John Payne, Sonny Tufts, Ellen Drew. 90M USA. prod/rel: Benedict Bogeaus, United Artists

MONSARRAT, NICHOLAS (1910–1979), UKN
The Cruel Sea, 1951, Novel
   Cruel Sea, The 1953 d: Charles Frend. lps: Jack Hawkins, Donald Sinden, Denholm Elliott. 126M UKN. prod/rel: Ealing Studios, General Film Distributors
The Ship That Died of Shame, 1952, Novel
   Ship That Died of Shame, The 1955 d: Basil Dearden, Michael Relph. lps: Richard Attenborough, George Baker, Bill Owen. 95M UKN. *Pt Raiders* (USA) prod/rel: Ealing Studios, General Film Distributors
Something to Hide, 1966, Novel
   Something to Hide 1971 d: Alastair Reid. lps: Peter Finch, Shelley Winters, Colin Blakely. 100M UKN. *Shattered* prod/rel: Avton
The Story of Esther Costello, 1953, Novel
   Story of Esther Costello, The 1957 d: David Miller. lps: Joan Crawford, Rossano Brazzi, Heather Sears. 104M UKN. *The Golden Virgin* (USA) prod/rel: Valiant, Romulus

MONTAGU, ASHLEY
The Elephant Man: a Study in Human Dignity, Book
   Elephant Man, The 1980 d: David Lynch. lps: John Hurt, Anthony Hopkins, John Gielgud. 125M UKN. prod/rel: Emi, Brooksfilm

MONTAGU, EWEN
The Man Who Never Was, Book
   Man Who Never Was, The 1956 d: Ronald Neame. lps: Clifton Webb, Gloria Grahame, Robert Flemyng. 103M UKN. prod/rel: Sumar, 20th Century-Fox

MONTAGU, NELL ST. JOHN
The Hallmark of Cain, Short Story
   All Living Things 1939 d: Andrew Buchanan. lps: Catherine Lacey, Michael Gainsborough, J. Fisher White. 22M UKN. prod/rel: Gb Instructional, Exclusive
   All Living Things 1955 d: Victor M. Gover. lps: Patrick Barr, Kit Terrington. 30M UKN. prod/rel: Pioneer Exclusives, Famous

MONTAGUE, CHARLES EDWARD (1867–1928), UKN, Montague, C. E.
Judith, Short Story
   True Heaven 1929 d: James Tinling. lps: George O'Brien, Lois Moran, Phillips Smalley. 5531f USA. *False Colors* prod/rel: Fox Film Corp.

MONTAGUE, JOHN
The Narrow Path, New York 1909, Play
   Narrow Path, The 1918 d: George Fitzmaurice. lps: Fannie Ward, William E. Lawrence, Irene Aldwyn. 5r USA. prod/rel: Astra Film Corp., Pathe Exchange, Inc.©

MONTAGUE, MARGARET PRESCOTT
In Calvert's Valley, New York 1908, Novel
   Calvert's Valley 1922 d: John Francis Dillon. lps: John Gilbert, Sylvia Breamer, Philo McCullough. 4416f USA. *Calvert's Folly* (UKN) prod/rel: Fox Film Corp.
Linda, Boston 1912, Novel
   Linda 1929 d: Dorothy Reid. lps: Warner Baxter, Helen Foster, Noah Beery. 7r USA. prod/rel: Mrs. Wallace Reid Productions, Willis Kent Productions
The Sowing of Alderson Cree, New York 1907, Novel
   Seeds of Vengeance 1920 d: Oliver L. Sellers. lps: Bernard Durning, Gloria Hope, Eugenie Besserer. 5r USA. *The Sowing of Alderson Cree* prod/rel: C. R. Macauley Photoplays, Inc.©, Select Pictures Corp.
Uncle Sam of Freedom Ridge, New York 1920, Novel
   Uncle Sam of Freedom Ridge 1920 d: George A. Beranger. lps: George MacQuarrie, William D. Corbett, Paul Kelly. 7r USA. *Uncle Sam of the Freedom Ridge* prod/rel: Harry Levey Productions, State Rights

MONTANELLI, INDRO
Story
   Generale Della Rovere, Il 1959 d: Roberto Rossellini. lps: Vittorio de Sica, Hannes Messemer, Vittorio Caprioli. 133M ITL/FRN. *Le General Della Rovere* (FRN) prod/rel: Zebra Film (Roma), S.N.E. Gaumont (Paris)
I Sogni Muoiono All'alba, Play
   Sogni Muoiono All'alba, I 1961 d: Indro Montanelli, Mario Craveri. lps: Lea Massari, Ivo Garrani, Aroldo Tieri. 92M ITL. *Dreams Die at Dawn* prod/rel: Rire Cin.Ca, Cineriz

MONTAYNE, C. S.
Her Night of Nights, 1921, Short Story
   Her Night of Nights 1922 d: Hobart Henley. lps: Marie Prevost, Edward Hearn, Hallam Cooley. 4500f USA. prod/rel: Universal Film Mfg. Co.

MONTAYNE, HAROLD B.
Sisters of Jezebel, 1924, Short Story
   Wings of Youth 1925 d: Emmett J. Flynn. lps: Ethel Clayton, Madge Bellamy, Charles Farrell. 5340f USA. prod/rel: Fox Film Corp.

MONTAZEL, J.
Je N'aime Que Toi, Play
   Je N'aime Que Toi 1949 d: Pierre Montazel. lps: Luis Mariano, Martine Carol, Annette Poivre. 93M FRN. *C'est Toi Que J'aime* prod/rel: Films Gloria

MONTEGUT, MAURICE
Le Geste, Novel
   Geste, Le 1916 d: Georges DenolA. lps: Henri Bosc, Jean Ayme, Vera Sergine. 1310m FRN. prod/rel: Scagl

MONTEIL, ZADOC
Sa Majeste Arsene, Short Story
   Nuits de Pigalle 1958 d: Georges Jaffe. lps: Danielle Godet, Roland Armontel, Yves Deniaud. 82M FRN. prod/rel: Joelle Productions, Films J.C. Carlus

MONTEILHET, HUBERT (1928–, FRN
Le Retour Des Cendres, Paris 1961, Novel
   Return from the Ashes 1965 d: J. Lee Thompson. lps: Maximilian Schell, Samantha Eggar, Ingrid Thulin. 104M UKN/USA. prod/rel: Mirisch Corporation, Orchard Productions

MONTELLO, JOSUE
O Monstro, 1966, Short Story
   Monstro de Santa Tereza, O 1980 d: William Cobbett. lps: Luiz Armando Queiroz, Isolda Cresta, Maria RitA. 90M BRZ. *The Monster of Santa Tereza*
Outra Tarde, Uma Tarde, 1968, Story
   Tarde Outra Tarde, Uma 1975 d: William Cobbett. 85M BRZ. *O Amor Aos 40*

MONTFOREZ, GEORGES
Les Enfants du Marais, Novel
   Enfants du Marais, Les 1999 d: Jean Becker. lps: Jacques Villeret, Jacques Gamblin, Andre Dussollier. 115M FRN. *Children of the Marshland* prod/rel: Films Christian Fechner, U.G.C.F.

MONTFORT, YVAN
Coupable?, Novel
   Coupable? 1950 d: Yvan Noe. lps: Andre Le Gall, Junie Astor, Raymond Pellegrin. 83M FRN. prod/rel: Films Alkam

MONTGOMERY, ED
Article
   I Want to Live! 1958 d: Robert Wise. lps: Susan Hayward, Simon Oakland, Virginia Vincent. 115M USA. prod/rel: United Artists, Figaro, Inc.

MONTGOMERY, EDWARD POOR
Double Harness, London 1933, Play
   Double Harness 1933 d: John Cromwell. lps: Ann Harding, William Powell, Lucile Browne. 74M USA. prod/rel: RKO Radio Pictures

MONTGOMERY, FLORENCE
Incompreso, Novel
   Incompreso 1966 d: Luigi Comencini. lps: Anthony Quayle, John Sharp, Stefano Colagrande. 105M ITL. *Vita Col Figlio*; *Misunderstood* prod/rel: Rizzoli Film, Istituto Nazionale Luce
Misunderstood, Novel
   Misunderstood 1983 d: Jerry Schatzberg. lps: Gene Hackman, Henry Thomas, Rip Torn. 101M USA. prod/rel: MGM, United Artists

MONTGOMERY, JAMES
The Aviator, New York 1910, Play
   Aviateur, L' 1931 d: William A. Seiter. lps: Jeanne Helbling, Douglas Fairbanks Jr., Geymond Vital. 70M USA. prod/rel: Warner Bros., First National
   Going Wild 1930 d: William A. Seiter. lps: Joe E. Brown, Laura Lee, Walter Pidgeon. 67M USA. prod/rel: First National Pictures
   Youth's Desire 1920. lps: Joe Bennett, Doris Baker. 4880f USA. *An Ace in the Hole* prod/rel: Alkire Productions, State Rights
Nothing But the Truth, Play
   Rien Que la Verite 1931 d: Rene Guissart. lps: Saint-Granier, Meg Lemonnier, Janine Voisin. 70M FRN. prod/rel: Films Paramount
Ready Money, New York 1912, Play
   Ready Money 1914 d: Oscar Apfel. lps: Edward Abeles, Theodore Roberts, James Neill. 5r USA. prod/rel: Jesse L. Lasky Feature Play Co.©, Paramount Pictures Corp.
   Riding High 1943 d: George Marshall. lps: Dorothy Lamour, Dick Powell, Victor Moore. 89M USA. *Melody Inn* (UKN) prod/rel: Paramount

MONTGOMERY, JAMES H.
Irene, New York 1919, Musical Play
   Irene 1926 d: Alfred E. Green. lps: Colleen Moore, Lloyd Hughes, George K. Arthur. 8400f USA. prod/rel: First National Pictures
   Irene 1940 d: Herbert Wilcox. lps: Anna Neagle, Ray Milland, Roland Young. 104M USA. prod/rel: RKO Radio Pictures©, Imperado Pictures

MONTGOMERY, L. M. (1874–1942), CND, Montgomery, Lucy Maud
Anne of Green Gables, Boston 1908, Novel
   Anne of Green Gables 1919 d: William D. Taylor. lps: Mary Miles Minter, Paul Kelly, George Stewart. 6r USA. prod/rel: Realart Pictures, Inc.©
   Anne of Green Gables 1934 d: George Nicholls Jr. lps: Anne Shirley, Tom Brown, O. P. Heggie. 79M USA. prod/rel: RKO Radio
   Anne of Green Gables 1985 d: Kevin Sullivan. lps: Megan Follows, Colleen Dewhurst, Patricia Hamilton. TVM. 195M CND.
Anne of Windy Willows, New York 1936, Novel
   Anne of Windy Poplars 1940 d: Jack Hively. lps: Anne Shirley, James Ellison, Henry Travers. 88M USA. *Anne of Windy Willows* (UKN) prod/rel: RKO Radio Pictures, Inc.

MONTHO, GASTON
Dede la Musique, Novel
   Dede la Musique 1939 d: Andre Berthomieu. lps: Albert Prejean, Aimos, Line Noro. 84M FRN. *Dede de Montmartre* prod/rel: Cie Internationale Cinematographique
Le Souffle du Desir, Novel
   Souffle du Desir, Le 1957 d: Henri Lepage. lps: Jacques Castelot, Danielle Godet, Beatrice Arnac. 78M FRN. prod/rel: Cinextension, Gamma Film

MONTI, MARIO
I Briganti Italiani, Novel
   Briganti Italiani, I 1961 d: Mario Camerini. lps: Ernest Borgnine, Bernard Blier, Vittorio Gassman. 108M ITL/FRN. *Les Guerilleros* (FRN); *Seduction of the South* (USA) prod/rel: Fair Film (Roma), Orsay Film (Paris)

MOODY, LAURENCE
The Ruthless Ones, Novel
   What Became of Jack and Jill? 1971 d: Bill Bain. lps: Vanessa Howard, Mona Washbourne, Paul Nicholas. 93M UKN. *Romeo and Juliet - 1971* prod/rel: Palomar Pictures International, Amicus

MOODY, RICK
The Ice Storm, 1994, Novel
   Ice Storm, The 1997 d: Ang Lee. lps: Kevin Kline, Joan Allen, Henry Czerny. 113M USA. prod/rel: Good Machine, Fox Searchlight

MOODY, WILLIAM VAUGHN (1869–1910), USA
The Faith Healer, New York 1910, Play
   Faith Healer, The 1921 d: George Melford. lps: Milton Sills, Ann Forrest, Fontaine La Rue. 6346f USA. *Goodheart* prod/rel: Famous Players-Lasky, Paramount Pictures

The Great Divide, New York 1906, Play
  Great Divide, The 1916 d: Edgar Lewis. lps: House
Peters, Ethel Clayton, Marie Sterling. 5r USA. prod/rel:
Lubin Mfg. Co.©, V-L-S-E, Inc.
  Great Divide, The 1924 d: Reginald Barker. lps: Alice
Terry, Conway Tearle, Wallace Beery. 7811f USA.
prod/rel: Metro-Goldwyn Pictures
  Great Divide, The 1929 d: Reginald Barker. lps:
Dorothy MacKaill, Ian Keith, Lucien Littlefield. 6722f
USA. prod/rel: First National Pictures
  Woman Hungry 1931 d: Clarence Badger. lps: Lila Lee,
Sidney Blackmer, Raymond Hatton. 68M USA. *The
Challenge* (UKN); *Under Western Skies* prod/rel: First
National Pictures©

MOON, LORNA
Dark Star, Indianapolis 1929, Novel
  Fruta Amarga, La 1931 d: Arthur Gregor. lps: Virginia
Fabregas, Juan de Landa, Maria Luz Callejo. 67M USA.
Estrella Negra prod/rel: Metro-Goldwyn-Mayer Corp.
  Min and Bill 1930 d: George W. Hill. lps: Marie
Dressler, Wallace Beery, Dorothy Jordan. 69M USA.
Dark Star prod/rel: Metro-Goldwyn-Mayer Pictures

MOONEY, MARTIN
Inc. Crime, Novel
  Crime Incorporated 1945 d: Lew Landers. lps: Leo
Carrillo, Tom Neal, Martha Tilton. 76M USA. *Crime
Inc.* prod/rel: P.R.C.

MOONEY, MICHAEL M.
The Hindenburg, Book
  Hindenburg, The 1975 d: Robert Wise. lps: George C.
Scott, Anne Bancroft, William Atherton. 125M USA.
prod/rel: Filmmakers Group

MOORCOCK, MICHAEL (1939–, UKN
The Final Programme, Novel
  Final Programme, The 1973 d: Robert Fuest. lps: Jon
Finch, Jenny Runacre, Sterling Hayden. 89M UKN.
Last Days of Man on Earth prod/rel: Goodtime, Gladiole

MOORE, ALICE M.
A Lively Affair, Story
  Lively Affair, A 1912 d: James Young. lps: Clara
Kimball Young, Leo Delaney, Kate Price. 650f USA.
prod/rel: Vitagraph Co. of America

MOORE, BRIAN (1921–, IRL
Black Robe, 1985, Novel
  Black Robe, The 1991 d: Bruce Beresford. lps:
Lothaire Bluteau, August Schellenberg, Aden Young.
101M CND/ASL. prod/rel: Australian Film Finance
Corp.©, Alliance Communications (Toronto)©
Catholics, Novel
  Catholics 1973 d: Jack Gold. lps: Trevor Howard,
Martin Sheen, Raf Vallone. TVM. 73M USA/UKN. *The
Conflict* prod/rel: CBS, Harlech Tv
Cold Heaven, 1983, Novel
  Cold Heaven 1992 d: Nicolas Roeg. lps: Theresa
Russell, Mark Harmon, James Russo. 105M USA.
prod/rel: Hemdale
The Lonely Passion of Judith Hearne, 1955, Novel
  Lonely Passion of Judith Hearne, The 1987 d: Jack
Clayton. lps: Maggie Smith, Bob Hoskins, Wendy Hiller.
120M UKN. prod/rel: Handmade
The Luck of Ginger Coffey, Boston 1960, Novel
  Luck of Ginger Coffey, The 1959 d: Harvey Hart.
MTV. CND.
  Luck of Ginger Coffey, The 1964 d: Irvin Kershner.
lps: Robert Shaw, Mary Ure, Liam Redmond. 100M
CND/USA. prod/rel: Roth-Kershner Prods. (New York),
Crawley Films Ltd. (Ottawa)

MOORE, CARLYLE
Stop Thief, New York 1912, Play
  Stop Thief! 1915 d: George Fitzmaurice. lps: Mary
Ryan, Harry Mestayer, Harold Howard. 4890f USA.
prod/rel: George Kleine©
  Stop Thief 1920 d: Harry Beaumont. lps: Tom Moore,
Hazel Daly, Irene Rich. 5-6r USA. prod/rel: Goldwyn
Pictures Corp.©, Goldwyn Distributing Corp.
The Unknown Purple, New York 1918, Play
  Unknown Purple, The 1923 d: Roland West. lps:
Henry B. Walthall, Alice Lake, Stuart Holmes. 7r USA.
prod/rel: Carlos Productions, Truart Film Corp.

MOORE, CARROLL
Send Me No Flowers, New York 1960, Play
  Send Me No Flowers 1964 d: Norman Jewison. lps:
Rock Hudson, Doris Day, Tony Randall. 100M USA.
prod/rel: Martin Melcher Productions

MOORE, DAN TYLER
The Terrible Game, Novel
  Gymkata 1985 d: Robert Clouse. lps: Kurt Thomas,
Tetchie Agbayani, Richard Norton. 90M USA. prod/rel:
MGM, United Artists

MOORE, FREDERICK
At Dawn, Short Story
  At Dawn 1914 d: Donald Crisp. lps: Wallace Reid,
George Siegmann, Billie West. SHT USA. prod/rel:
Majestic

MOORE, GEORGE (1852–1933), IRL
Esther Waters, 1894, Novel
  Esther Waters 1948 d: Ian Dalrymple, Peter Proud.
lps: Kathleen Ryan, Dirk Bogarde, Cyril Cusack. 109M
UKN. *The Sin of Esther Waters* prod/rel: General Film
Distributors, Wessex

MOORE, GRACE
You're Only Human Once, 1944, Autobiography
  So This Is Love 1953 d: Gordon Douglas. lps: Kathryn
Grayson, Merv Griffin, Joan Weldon. 101M USA. *The
Grace Moore Story* (UKN) prod/rel: Warner Bros.

MOORE, HARRY T.
The Priest of Love, Book
  Priest of Love 1980 d: Christopher Miles. lps: Ian
McKellen, Janet Suzman, Ava Gardner. 125M UKN.
prod/rel: Ronceval, Milesian

MOORE, KATHARINE LESLIE
The Peacock Feather, London 1913, Novel
  Pennies from Heaven 1936 d: Norman Z. McLeod.
lps: Bing Crosby, Madge Evans, Edith Fellows. 83M
USA. prod/rel: Columbia Pictures Corp. of California©,
Major Pictures Corp.

MOORE, OLGA
Quintuplets to You, 1936, Short Story
  You Can't Beat Love 1937 d: W. Christy Cabanne. lps:
Preston Foster, Joan Fontaine, Herbert Mundin. 62M
USA. prod/rel: RKO Radio Pictures©

MOORE, OWEN
Beware of Widows, Play
  Beware of Widows 1927 d: Wesley Ruggles. lps: Laura
La Plante, Bryant Washburn, Paulette Duval. 5777f
USA. prod/rel: Universal Pictures

MOORE, ROBIN
The French Connection, Book
  French Connection, The 1971 d: William Friedkin.
lps: Gene Hackman, Fernando Rey, Roy Scheider. 104M
USA. prod/rel: 20th Century-Fox
The Green Berets, New York 1965, Novel
  Green Berets, The 1968 d: John Wayne, Ray Kellogg.
lps: John Wayne, David Janssen, Jim Hutton. 141M
USA. prod/rel: Batjac Productions, Warner Bros.

MOORE, T. STURGE
A Florentine Tragedy, Play
  Florentine Tragedy, The 1913. lps: Constance
Crawley, Arthur Maude, Edith Bostwick. SHT USA.
prod/rel: Warner's Features

MOORE, THOMAS (1779–1852), IRL
1823, Poem
  Amori Degli Angeli, Gli 1910 d: Giuseppe de Liguoro.
218m ITL. *The Loves of the Angels* (UKN) prod/rel:
Milano Films
Believe Me if All Those Endearing Young Charms,
1807, Poem
  Believe Me, if All Those Endearing Young Charms
1912. lps: Laura Sawyer, Ben Wilson, Bessie Learn.
1000f USA. prod/rel: Edison
  Hidden Charms 1920 d: Samuel Brodsky. lps: Daniel
Kelly, Mrs. Charles Willard, Florence Dixon. 5r USA.
prod/rel: Argus Motion Picture Co., State Rights
Lalla Rooks, 1917, Poem
  Profeta Velato, Il 1912. 861m ITL. *The Veiled Prophet*
(USA) prod/rel: S.A. Ambrosio
You Remember Ellen, Poem
  You Remember Ellen 1912 d: Sidney Olcott. lps: Gene
Gaunthier, Jack J. Clark, Mr. Hollister. 1000f USA.
prod/rel: Kalem

MOOREHEAD, ALAN (1910–1983), ASL, Moorehead,
Alan McCrae
Rage of the Vulture, 1948, Novel
  Thunder in the East 1953 d: Charles Vidor. lps: Alan
Ladd, Deborah Kerr, Charles Boyer. 98M USA. prod/rel:
Paramount

MOORHOUSE, FRANK
Short Stories
  Coca-Cola Kid, The 1985 d: Dusan Makavejev. lps:
Eric Roberts, Greta Scacchi, Bill Kerr. 98M ASL.
prod/rel: Grand Bay Films Intl. Pty Ltd.©, Cinema
Enterprises
The Everlasting Secret Family & Other Secrets,
Book
  Everlasting Secret Family, The 1987 d: Michael
Thornhill. lps: Arthur Dignam, Mark Lee, Heather
Mitchell. 94M ASL. prod/rel: Hemdale Film
Corporation, International Film Management Ltd.©

MORA, FERENC
Enek a Buzamezokrol, 1927, Novel
  Enek a Buzamezokrol 1947 d: Istvan Szots. lps: Alice
Szellay, Janos Gorbe, Jozsef Bihary. 84M HNG. *Song of
the Cornfields*
Hannibal Foltamasztasa, 1949, Novel
  Hannibal Tanar Ur 1956 d: Zoltan Fabri. lps: Erno
Szabo, Noemi Apor, Emmi Buttykay. 92M HNG.
Professor Hannibal prod/rel: Hunnia Studios
Kincskereso Kiskodmon, 1918, Novel
  Kincskereso Kis Kodmon 1973 d: Mihaly Szemes. lps:
Gabor Szucs, Maria Medgyesi, Peter Haumann. 98M
HNG. *The Magic Jacket*

MORAIS, MARIO
L' Avvocato Difensore, Play
  Avvocato Difensore, L' 1934 d: Gero Zambuto. lps:
Gero Zambuto, Letizia Bonini, Osvaldo Genazzani.
2338m ITL. *The Attorney for the Defense* (USA) prod/rel:
Manenti Film

MORAN, DERRY
I Live With Me Dad, Short Story
  I Live With Me Dad 1987 d: Paul Moloney. lps: Peter
Hehir, Haydon Samuels, Dennis Miller. 90M ASL.
prod/rel: Crawford Productions

MORAND, PAUL (1888–1976), FRN
Short Stories
  Open All Night 1924 d: Paul Bern. lps: Viola Dana,
Jetta Goudal, Adolphe Menjou. 5671f USA. *One
Parisian Knight* (UKN) prod/rel: Famous
Players-Lasky, Paramount Pictures
L' Europe Galante, Short Story
  Glace a Trois Faces, La 1927 d: Jean Epstein. lps:
Rene Ferte, Olga Day, Raymond Guerin-Catelain.
1200m FRN. *The Glass With Three Faces*; *The
Three-Way Mirror*; *Mirror With Three Faces* prod/rel:
Films Jean Epstein
Hecate, Novel
  Hecate 1982 d: Daniel Schmid. lps: Bernard Giraudeau,
Lauren Hutton, Jean Bouise. 108M SWT/FRN.
Maitresse de la Nuit Hecate prod/rel: T & C, S.S.R.
L' Homme Presse, Novel
  Homme Presse, L' 1976 d: Edouard Molinaro. lps:
Alain Delon, Mireille Darc, Michel Duchaussoy. 90M
FRN/ITL. *L' Ultimo Giorno d'Amore* (ITL); *The
Hurried Man* (UKN); *Man in a Hurry* (USA) prod/rel:
Irrigazione Cin.Ca, Adel
La Mort du Cygne, Story
  Mort du Cynge, La 1937 d: Jean Benoit-Levy, Marie
Epstein. lps: Jean Perier, Yvette Chauvire, Mia
SlavenskA. 100M FRN. *Ballerina* (USA); *The Death of a
Swan* prod/rel: Cinatlantica Films
  Unfinished Dance, The 1947 d: Henry Koster. lps:
Margaret O'Brien, Cyd Charisse, Karin Booth. 101M
USA. prod/rel: MGM

MORANTE, ELSA (1916–1985), ITL
L' Isola Di Arturo, 1957, Novel
  Isola Di Arturo, L' 1962 d: Damiano Damiani. lps:
Reginald Kernan, Key Meersman, Vanni de Maigret.
94M ITL. *Arturo's Island* (USA) prod/rel: Compagnia
Cin.Ca Champion, Titanus
La Storia, 1974, Novel
  Storia, La 1986 d: Luigi Comencini. lps: Claudia
Cardinale, Francisco Rabal, Andrea SpadA. 153M ITL.
History

MORAVEK, JAN
Skalni Plemeno, Novel
  Skalni Plemeno 1944 d: Ladislav Brom. lps: Otomar
Korbelar, Jaroslav Vojta, Terezie BrzkovA. 2240m CZC.
The Rockpeople; *Sturdy As a Rock* prod/rel:
Nationalfilm

MORAVIA, ALBERTO (1907–1990), ITL, Pincherle,
Alberto
Short Story
  Faccia Da Mascalzone 1955 d: Raffaele Andreassi,
Lance Comfort. lps: Valentina Cortese, Marina Berti,
Lee Patterson. F ITL. prod/rel: Ardita Film
  Ich Und Er 1988 d: Doris Dorrie. lps: Griffin Dunne,
Ellen Greene, Steve Marcus. 88M GRM/USA. *Me and
Him* (USA) prod/rel: Neue Constantin
Agostino, 1944, Novel
  Agostino 1962 d: Mauro Bolognini. lps: Ingrid Thulin,
Paolo Colombo, John Saxon. 102M ITL. *La Perdita
Dell'innocenza* prod/rel: Baltea Film, de Laurentiis
L' Amore Coniugale, 1949, Novel
  Amore Coniugale, L' 1970 d: Dacia Maraini. lps:
Tomas Milian, Macha Meril, Lidia Biondi. 102M ITL.
prod/rel: I Film Dell'orso, Delta Film
Appuntamento Al Mare, 1962, Short Story
  Ore Nude, Le 1964 d: Marco Vicario. lps: Rossana
Podesta, Keir Dullea, Philippe Leroy. 90M ITL. *The
Naked Hours* prod/rel: Atlantica Cin.Ca

La Cintura, Novel
Cintura, La 1988 d: Giuliana GambA. lps: James Russo, Eleonora Brigliadori, Giuliana CalandrA. 92M ITL. prod/rel: Reteitalia, Metrofilm

La Ciociara, Milan 1957, Novel
Ciociara, La 1961 d: Vittorio de SicA. lps: Sophia Loren, Eleonora Braun, Raf Vallone. 110M ITL/FRN. *Two Women* (USA) prod/rel: Compagnia Cin.Ca Champion (Roma), Les Films Marceau (Paris)

Il Conformista, 1951, Novel
Conformista, Il 1970 d: Bernardo Bertolucci. lps: Jean-Louis Trintignant, Stefania Sandrelli, Gastone Moschin. 108M ITL/FRN/GRM. *Le Conformiste* (FRN); *The Conformist* (UKN); *Der Grosse Irrtum* (GRM) prod/rel: Mars Films (Roma), Marianne Productions (Paris)

Delitto Al Circolo Del Tennis, 1952, Short Story
Delitto Al Circolo Del Tennis 1969 d: Franco Rossetti. lps: Anna Gael, Roberto Bisacco, Angela McDonald. 91M ITL/YGS. *The Rage Within* (UKN); *La Rabbia Dentro* prod/rel: Daiano Film, Leone Film (Roma)

Il Disprezzo, Milan 1954, Novel
Mepris, Le 1963 d: Jean-Luc Godard. lps: Brigitte Bardot, Jack Palance, Michel Piccoli. 103M FRN/ITL. *Il Disprezzo* (ITL); *Contempt* (USA) prod/rel: Films Concordia, Rome-Paris Films

La Disubbidienza, Novel
Desobeissance, La 1981 d: Aldo Lado. lps: Mario Adorf, Stefania Sandrelli, Teresa Ann Savoy. 110M FRN/ITL. *La Disubbidienza* (ITL) prod/rel: Nickelodeon, Pantheon

Donna Invisibile, 1970, Short Story
Donna Invisibile, La 1969 d: Paolo SpinolA. lps: Giovanna Ralli, Silvano Tranquilli, Carla GravinA. 92M ITL. prod/rel: Clesi Cin.Ca, San Marco

Faccia Di Mascalzone, 1954, Short Story
Peccato Che Sia Una Canaglia 1955 d: Alessandro Blasetti. lps: Sophia Loren, Vittorio de Sica, Marcello Mastroianni. 100M ITL. *Too Bad She's Bad* (UKN) prod/rel: Documento Film

Gli Indifferenti, Milan 1929, Novel
Indifferenti, Gli 1964 d: Francesco Maselli. lps: Rod Steiger, Claudia Cardinale, Shelley Winters. 115M ITL/FRN. *Les Deux Rivales* (FRN); *Time of Indifference* (USA); *Time for Indifference*; *Desirs Pervers* prod/rel: Vides Cin.Ca, Lux Film

Io E Lui, Short Story
Io E Lui 1973 d: Luciano Salce. lps: Lando Buzzanca, Gabriella Giorgelli, Bulle Ogier. 108M ITL. prod/rel: de Laurentiis Inter MA. Co. (Roma), Columbia (Paris)

Ladri in Chiesa, 1954, Short Story
Risate Di Gioia 1960 d: Mario Monicelli. lps: Anna Magnani, Toto, Ben GazzarA. 106M ITL. *The Passionate Thief* (USA) prod/rel: Titanus

La Marcia Indietro, Short Story
Ragazza Piuttosta Complicata, Una 1968 d: Damiano Damiani. lps: Catherine Spaak, Jean Sorel, Florinda Bolkan. 112M ITL. *A Complicated Girl* (UKN); *Quite a Complicated Girl* prod/rel: Filmena, Fono Roma

La Noia, Milan 1960, Novel
Ennui, L' 1998 d: Cedric Kahn. lps: Charles Berling, Sophie Guillemin, Arielle Dombasle. 120M FRN. *Ennui* prod/rel: Gemini Films, Ima Films

Noia, La 1964 d: Damiano Damiani. lps: Bette Davis, Horst Buchholz, Catherine Spaak. 118M ITL/FRN. *L'erotisme, L' Ennui Et Sa Diversion* (FRN); *The Empty Canvas* (USA) prod/rel: Compagnia Cin.Ca Champion (Roma), Les Films Concordia (Paris)

Gli Ordini Sono Ordini, 1970, Short Story
Ordini Sono Ordini, Gli 1972 d: Franco Giraldi. lps: Monica Vitti, Claudine Auger, Orazio Orlando. 100M ITL. prod/rel: Dean Film, Titanus

La Provinciale, 1952, Novel
Provinciale, La 1953 d: Mario Soldati. lps: Gina Lollobrigida, Gabriele Ferzetti, Franco Interlenghi. 102M ITL. *The Wayward Wife* (UKN) prod/rel: Elektra Compagnia Cin.Ca, Titanus

Racconti Romani, Milan 1954, Short Stories
Giornata Balorda, La 1960 d: Mauro Bolognini. lps: Jean Sorel, Lea Massari, Jeanne Valerie. 102M ITL/FRN. *Ca S'est Passe a Rome* (FRN); *From a Roman Balcony* (USA); *Love Is a Day's Work*; *A Crazy Day*; *A Day of Sin* (UKN) prod/rel: Produzione Intercontinentali, Euro International Film (Roma)

Racconti Romani 1955 d: Gianni Franciolini. lps: Vittorio de Sica, Toto, Silvana Pampanini. 110M ITL. prod/rel: Industrie Cin.Che Sociali, Diana Cin.Ca

Risate Di Gioia, 1954, Short Story
Risate Di Gioia 1960 d: Mario Monicelli. lps: Anna Magnani, Toto, Ben GazzarA. 106M ITL. *The Passionate Thief* (USA) prod/rel: Titanus

La Romana, 1947, Novel
Romana, La 1954 d: Luigi ZampA. lps: Gina Lollobrigida, Daniel Gelin, Franco Fabrizi. 93M ITL/FRN. *La Belle Romaine* (FRN); *Woman of Rome* (USA) prod/rel: Carlo Ponti, Dino de Laurentiis

Romana, La 1988 d: Giuseppe Patroni Griffi. lps: Francesca Dellera, Tony Lo Bianco, Gina LollobrigidA. TVM. 200M ITL.

Troppa Rica, Short Story
Ieri, Oggi, Domani 1963 d: Vittorio de SicA. lps: Sophia Loren, Marcello Mastroianni, Carlo Giuffre. 119M ITL/FRN. *Yesterday Today and Tomorrow* (USA); *Oggi E Domani Ieri*; *Aujourd'hui Et Demain Hier* (FRN) prod/rel: Compagnia Cin.Ca Champion (Roma), Les Films Concordia (Paris)

Un Vieil Imbecile
Bel Age, Le 1958 d: Pierre Kast. lps: Jean-Claude Brialy, Jacques Doniol-Valcroze, Francoise Prevost. 102M FRN. *Love Is When You Make It*; *The Good Age* prod/rel: Films D'aujourd'hui, Films Du Centaire

La Villa Del Venerdi, Novel
Villa Del Venerdi, La 1992 d: Mauro Bolognini. lps: Julian Sands, Joanna Pacula, Tcheky Karyo. 94M ITL. *The Friday Villa*; *In Excess* (UKN) prod/rel: Pac

MORAY, HELGA
Untamed, 1950, Novel
Untamed 1955 d: Henry King. lps: Tyrone Power, Susan Hayward, Richard Egan. 111M USA. prod/rel: 20th Century-Fox

MORBELLI, RICCARDO
I Quattro Moschettieri, Radio Play
Quattro Moschettieri, I 1936 d: Carlo Campogalliani. ANM. 70M ITL. prod/rel: Miniatura Film

MORCH, DEA TRIER
Vinterborn, 1976, Novel
Vinterborn 1978 d: Astrid Henning-Jensen. lps: Ann-Mari Max Hansen, Helle Hertz, Lone Kellermann. 100M DNM. *Winter Children*; *Winter-Born*; *Winterchildren*; *Vinterbjorn* prod/rel: Panorama, Danske Filminstitut

MORE, JULIAN
Expresso Bongo, London 1958, Musical Play
Expresso Bongo 1959 d: Val Guest. lps: Laurence Harvey, Sylvia Syms, Yolande Donlan. 111M UKN. prod/rel: Conquest, Britannia

MOREAU, EMILE
Madame Sans-Gene, Paris 1893, Play
Madame Sans-Gene 1911 d: Andre Calmettes, Henri Desfontaines. lps: Mme. Rejane, Edmond Duquesne, Dorival. FRN. prod/rel: Film d'Art

Madame Sans-Gene 1925 d: Leonce Perret. lps: Gloria Swanson, Emile Drain, Charles de Rochefort. 9994f USA. prod/rel: Famous Players-Lasky, Paramount Pictures

Madame Sans-Gene 1941 d: Roger Richebe. lps: Arletty, Albert Dieudonne, Aime Clariond. 100M FRN. prod/rel: Roger Richebe

Madame Sans-Gene 1961 d: Christian-Jaque. lps: Sophia Loren, Robert Hossein, Julien Bertheau. 118M FRN/ITL/SPN. *Madame* (UKN) prod/rel: Cine-Alliance (Paris), Ge.Si. Cin.Ca

La Reine Elisabeth, Play
Amours de la Reine Elisabeth, Les 1912 d: Henri Desfontaines, Louis Mercanton. lps: Sarah Bernhardt, Lou Tellegen, Georges Charmeroy. 1100m FRN. *Queen Bess -Her Love Story*; *La Reine Elisabeth*; *Elisabeth Reine d'Angleterre*; *Queen Elisabeth* prod/rel: Urban Trading

MOREAU, LOUIS-MATHURIN
L' Affaire du Courrier de Lyon, Play
Affaire du Courrier de Lyon, L' 1937 d: Maurice Lehmann, Claude Autant-LarA. lps: Dita Parlo, Pierre Blanchar, Sylvia Bataille. 102M FRN. *The Courier of Lyon* (USA); *L' Affaire Lesurques*; *Le Courrier de Lyon* prod/rel: Productions Maurice Lehmann

Assassinio Del Corriere Di Leone, L' 1916 d: Gabriel Moreau. lps: Cav. Mario Casaleggio, Gabriel Moreau, Liliane de Rosny. 1340m ITL. prod/rel: Subalpina Film

MOREHOUSE, WARD
Gentlemen of the Press, Story
Gentlemen of the Press 1929 d: Millard Webb. lps: Walter Huston, Katherine Francis, Charles Ruggles. 7176f USA. prod/rel: Paramount Famous Lasky Corp.

New York Town, 1932, Play
Big City Blues 1932 d: Mervyn Leroy. lps: Joan Blondell, Eric Linden, Inez Courtney. 68M USA. prod/rel: Warner Bros. Pictures, Inc.

MOREL, MICHELINE
La Vie Normale, Novel
Vie Normal, La 1966 d: Andre Charpak. lps: Monique Lejeune, Victor Lanoux, Denise Gence. 75M FRN. prod/rel: Jeune Cinema Theatre De France

MORELL, PARKER
Diamond Jim, New York 1934, Book
Diamond Jim 1935 d: A. Edward Sutherland. lps: Edward Arnold, Jean Arthur, Binnie Barnes. 93M USA. prod/rel: Universal Pictures Corp.

MORELLO, VINCENZO
La Flotta Degli Emigranti, 1907, Play
Flotta Degli Emigranti, La 1917 d: Leopoldo Carlucci. lps: Achille Majeroni, Mercedes Brignone, Ugo Gracci. 1695m ITL. prod/rel: de Rosa

Il Malefico Anello, 1909, Play
Malefico Anello, Il 1916 d: Ugo FalenA. lps: Bianca Bellincioni-Stagno, Luigi Serventi, Eric Oulton. 1635m ITL. prod/rel: Tespi Film

MORENO, MARVEL
Oriana, Novel
Oriana 1986 d: Fina Torres. lps: Doris Wells, Claudia Venturini, Hanna Caminos. 83M VNZ/FRN/VNZ. *Oriane* prod/rel: Pandora, Arion

MORESBY-WHITE, GEORGE
No Smoking, Television Play
No Smoking 1955 d: Henry Cass. lps: Reg Dixon, Belinda Lee, Lionel Jeffries. 72M UKN. prod/rel: Tempean, Eros

MORETTI, UGO
Doppia Morte Al Governo Vecchio, Novel
Doppia Delitto 1977 d: Steno. lps: Marcello Mastroianni, Ursula Andress, Peter Ustinov. 108M ITL/FRN. *Enquete a l'Italienne* (FRN); *Double Murder*; *Doppia Morte Al Governo Vecchio* prod/rel: Primex Italiana (Roma), P.E.C.F. (Paris)

Gente Al Babuino, Florence 1957, Novel
Via Margutta 1960 d: Mario Camerini. lps: Antonella Lualdi, Gerard Blain, Franco Fabrizi. 105M ITL/FRN. *La Rue Des Amours Faciles* (FRN); *Run With the Devil* (USA) prod/rel: Documento Film (Roma), le Louvre Films (Paris)

Natale in Casa d'Appuntamento, Novel
Natale in Casa d'Appuntamento 1976 d: Armando Nannuzzi. lps: Ernest Borgnine, Francoise Fabian, Corinne Clery. 115M ITL. *Christmas Time in a Brothel*; *Christmas at the Brothel*; *Love By Appointment*; *Holiday Hookers*; *Amore Per Appuntamento* prod/rel: Leone International Film, Intercinema

Nuda Ogni Sera, Novel
Gioventu Di Notte 1962 d: Mario Sequi. lps: Tod Windsor, Cristina Gajoni, Sami Frey. 100M ITL/FRN. *Jeunesse de Nuit* (FRN); *La Ghenga E Nuda Ogni Sera* prod/rel: Cinecompar (Roma), Lux Compagnie de France

MOREWOOD, AITKEN
Mrs. Campbell Buena Sera
Buona Sera, Mrs. Campbell 1969 d: Melvin Frank. lps: Gina Lollobrigida, Shelley Winters, Phil Silvers. 113M USA. prod/rel: Connaught

MOREY, WALT
Gentle Ben, New York 1965, Novel
Gentle Giant 1967 d: James Neilson. lps: Dennis Weaver, Vera Miles, Ralph Meeker. 93M USA. prod/rel: Ivan Tors Films

Kavik the Wolf Dog, Novel
Courage of Kavik the Wolf Dog, The 1980 d: Peter Carter. lps: Ronny Cox, John Ireland, Linda Sorensen. TVM. 98M CND. *Kavik the Wolf Dog*; *Les Inseparables* prod/rel: Jon Slan Productions Inc.

MORGAN, AINSWORTH
Man of Two Worlds; the Novel of a Stranger, New York 1933, Novel
Man of Two Worlds 1934 d: J. Walter Ruben. lps: Francis Lederer, Elissa Landi, Henry Stephenson. 92M USA. prod/rel: RKO Radio Pictures©, Pandro S. Berman Production

MORGAN, AL
The Great Man, 1955, Novel
Great Man, The 1956 d: Jose Ferrer. lps: Jose Ferrer, Dean Jagger, Keenan Wynn. 92M USA. prod/rel: Universal-International

MORGAN, BEATRICE BURTON
The Little Yellow House, Garden City, N.Y. 1928, Novel
Little Yellow House, The 1928 d: James Leo Meehan. lps: Orville Caldwell, Martha Sleeper, Lucy Beaumont. 7r USA. prod/rel: Fbo Pictures

MORGAN, BYRON
The Air Mail, Novel
  Air Mail, The 1925 d: Irvin V. Willat. lps: Warner Baxter, Billie Dove, Mary Brian. 6976f USA. prod/rel: Famous Players-Lasky Corp., Paramount Pictures
The Bear-Trap, 1919, Short Story
  Excuse My Dust 1920 d: Sam Wood. lps: Wallace Reid, Anna Little, Theodore Roberts. 4330f USA. *The Bear Trap* prod/rel: Famous Players-Lasky Corp.©, Paramount-Artcraft Pictures
The Hell Diggers, 1920, Short Story
  Hell Diggers, The 1921 d: Frank Urson. lps: Wallace Reid, Lois Wilson, Alexander Broun. 4277f USA. *The Gold Dredgers* prod/rel: Famous Players-Lasky, Paramount Pictures
The Hippopotamus Parade, 1919, Short Story
  What's Your Hurry? 1920 d: Sam Wood. lps: Wallace Reid, Lois Wilson, Charles Ogle. 5040f USA. *The Hippopotamus Parade*; *Too Much Speed* prod/rel: Famous Players-Lasky Corp.©, Paramount Pictures
Junkpile Sweepstakes, 1918, Short Story
  Roaring Road, The 1919 d: James Cruze. lps: Wallace Reid, Anna Little, Theodore Roberts. 4309f USA. prod/rel: Famous Players-Lasky Corp.©, Paramount Pictures
The Man from Make Believe, Short Story
  Broadway Cowboy, A 1920 d: Joseph J. Franz. lps: William Desmond, Betty Francisco, Thomas Delmar. 4510f USA. *The Man from Make Believe* prod/rel: Jesse D. Hampton Productions, Pathe Exchange, Inc.©
Man Power, Story
  Man Power 1927 d: Clarence Badger. lps: Richard Dix, Mary Brian, Philip Strange. 5617f USA. *Manpower*; *Dynamite* prod/rel: Paramount Famous Lasky Corp.
The Roaring Road, 1918, Short Story
  Roaring Road, The 1919 d: James Cruze. lps: Wallace Reid, Anna Little, Theodore Roberts. 4309f USA. prod/rel: Famous Players-Lasky Corp.©, Paramount Pictures
Too Much Speed, 1921, Short Story
  Too Much Speed 1921 d: Frank Urson. lps: Wallace Reid, Agnes Ayres, Theodore Roberts. 4629f USA. prod/rel: Famous Players-Lasky, Paramount Pictures
Undertaker's Handicap, 1918, Short Story
  Roaring Road, The 1919 d: James Cruze. lps: Wallace Reid, Anna Little, Theodore Roberts. 4309f USA. prod/rel: Famous Players-Lasky Corp.©, Paramount Pictures

MORGAN, CHARLES (1894–1958), UKN
The Fountain, 1932, Novel
  Fountain, The 1934 d: John Cromwell. lps: Ann Harding, Brian Aherne, Paul Lukas. 85M USA. *Breaking the News* prod/rel: RKO Radio Pictures©
The River Line, 1949, Novel
  Kennwort: Reiher 1964 d: Rudolf Jugert. lps: Peter Van Eyck, Marie Versini, Walter RillA. 95M GRM. *Password: Heron* prod/rel: Seitz, Filmaufbau

MORGAN, GUY
Albert R.N., Play
  Albert R.N. 1953 d: Lewis Gilbert. lps: Anthony Steel, Jack Warner, Robert Beatty. 88M UKN. *Break to Freedom* (USA); *Spare Man* prod/rel: Dial Films, Eros

MORGAN, HOWARD E.
Snow Dust, Story
  Mystery Valley 1928 d: J. P. McGowan. lps: Buddy Roosevelt, Carol Lane, Tom Bay. 4538f USA. prod/rel: Trem Carr Productions, Rayart Pictures

MORGAN, JEFFERSON
Why Have They Taken Our Children?, Book
  Vanished Without a Trace 1993 d: Vern Gillum. lps: Karl Malden, Tim Ransom, Travis Fine. TVM. 89M USA.

MORGAN, JOAN
This Was a Woman, London 1944, Play
  This Was a Woman 1948 d: Tim Whelan. lps: Sonia Dresdel, Barbara White, Walter Fitzgerald. 104M UKN. prod/rel: Excelsior, 20th Century-Fox

MORGAN, KAY SUMMERSBY
Past Forgetting, Autobiography
  Ike: the War Years 1978 d: Melville Shavelson, Boris Sagal. lps: Robert Duvall, Lee Remick, Dana Andrews. TVM. 300M USA. *Ike* prod/rel: ABC Circle Films

MORGAN, LEOTA
Cheating Wives, Story
  Empty Cradle, The 1923 d: Burton L. King. lps: Mary Alden, Harry T. Morey, Mickey Bennett. 6984f USA. prod/rel: State Pictures, Truart Film Corp.
The Streets of New York, Play
  Streets of New York, The 1922 d: Burton L. King. lps: Anders Randolf, Leslie King, Barbara Castleton. 6541f USA. prod/rel: State Pictures, Arrow Film Corp.

MORGAN, SIDNEY
Emergency House, Story
  Plaything of Broadway, The 1921 d: John Francis Dillon. lps: Justine Johnstone, Crauford Kent, MacEy Harlam. 5360f USA. prod/rel: Realart Pictures
Somebody's Darling, Novel
  Somebody's Darling 1925 d: George A. Cooper. lps: Betty Balfour, Rex O'Malley, Fred Raynham. 8800f UKN. prod/rel: Gaumont

MORGAN-WITTS, MAX
The Day the Bubble Burst, Book
  Day the Bubble Burst, The 1982 d: Joseph Hardy. lps: Richard Crenna, Robert Vaughn, Blanche Baker. TVM. 150M USA. prod/rel: CBS, Twentieth Century Fox
The Day the World Ended, Novel
  When Time Ran Out. 1980 d: James Goldstone. lps: Paul Newman, Jacqueline Bisset, William Holden. 121M USA. *The Day the World Ended* prod/rel: Warner
Enola Gay, Book
  Enola Gay: the Men, the Mission, the Atomic Bomb 1980 d: David Lowell Rich. lps: Patrick Duffy, Billy Crystal, Kim Darby. TVM. 150M USA. *Enola Gay* (UKN) prod/rel: NBC, the Production Company
Voyage of the Damned, Book
  Voyage of the Damned 1976 d: Stuart Rosenberg. lps: Faye Dunaway, Oskar Werner, Max von Sydow. 158M UKN/SPN. prod/rel: Itc, Associated General

MORHEI, LOUIS
Radio Play
  Pier 23 1951 d: William Berke. lps: Hugh Beaumont, Ann Savage, Edward Brophy. 58M USA. prod/rel: Lippert, Spartan Prods.

MORHEIM, LOUIS
Danger Zone, Radio Play
  Danger Zone 1951 d: William Berke. lps: Hugh Beaumont, Edward Brophy, Richard Travis. 56M USA. prod/rel: Lippert, Spartan

MORI, OGAI
Gan, 1913, Novel
  Gan 1953 d: Shiro ToyodA. lps: Hideko Takamine, Hiroshi Akutagawa, Eijiro Tono. 104M JPN. *The Mistress* (USA); *Wild Geese* prod/rel: Daiei Motion Picture Co.

MORICZ, ZSIGMOND
Arvacska, 1941, Novel
  Arvacska 1976 d: Laszlo Ranody. lps: Zsuzsa Czinkoczi, Anna Nagy, Sandor Hovath. 92M HNG. *No Man's Daughter*
Egi Madar, 1935, Short Story
  Egi Madar 1957 d: Imre Feher. lps: Adam Szirtes, Ildiko Szabo, Ferenc Kiss. 101M HNG. *A Bird of Heaven*
Legy Jo Mindhalalig, 1921, Novel
  Legy Jo Mindhalalig 1960 d: Laszlo Ranody. lps: Ferenc Bessenyei, Mari Torocsik. 90M HNG. *Be Good Until Death*; *Be Good Forever*; *Be Faithful Unto Death*
Nem Elhetek Muzsikaszo Nelkul, 1916, Novel
  Nem Elhetek Muzsikaszo Nelkul 1979 d: Ferenc Sik. lps: Sandor Oszter, Agnes Szirtes, Klari Tolnay. 88M HNG. *The Music's the Thing*; *I Can't Live Without Music*
Rokonok, 1930, Novel
  Rokonok 1954 d: Felix Mariassy. lps: Klari Tolnay, Laszlo Ungvary, Gyula Gozon. 100M PLN. *Relatives*
Uri Muri, 1928, Play
  Uri Muri 1949 d: Frigyes Ban. lps: Sandor Deak, Agi Meszaros, Sandor TompA. 99M HNG. *Gentry Skylarking*

MORIER, JAMES (1780–1849), UKN, Morier, James Justinian
Adventures of Hajji Baba, 1954, Novel
  Adventures of Hajji Baba, The 1954 d: Don Weis. lps: John Derek, Elaine Stewart, Rosemarie Bowe. 94M USA. prod/rel: 20th Century-Fox, Walter Wanger

MORIKE, EDUARD (1804–1875), GRM
Mozart Auf Der Reise Nach Prag, 1855, Short Story
  Kleine Nachtmusik, Eine 1939 d: Leopold Hainisch. lps: Hannes Stelzer, Kurt Meisel, Annie Rosar. 94M GRM. prod/rel: Tobis, Deick

MORIMURA, SEIICHI
Ningen No Shomei, Novel
  Ningen No Shomei 1977 d: Junya Sato. lps: Mariko Okada, Toshiro Mifune, Yusaku MatsudA. 106M JPN. *Witness of Mankind*; *Proof of the Man*

MORIN, LUDOVIC
Sans Fortune, Story
  Sans Fortune 1922 d: Geo Kessler. lps: Jacques de Feraudy, Paul Jorge, Germaine Sablon. 1460m FRN.

MORITZ, HENRY
The Goslings, Play
  Shantytown 1943 d: Joseph Santley. lps: Mary Lee, John Archer, Marjorie Lord. 65M USA. prod/rel: Republic

MORIYAMA, KEI
Hisshoka, Novel
  Hisshoka 1945 d: Kenji Mizoguchi, Tomotaka TasakA. lps: Shochiku All-Stars. F JPN. *Song of Victory*; *Hissyo Ka*; *Victory Song*

MORLAND, NIGEL
Mrs. Pym of Scotland Yard, Novel
  Mrs. Pym of Scotland Yard 1939 d: Fred Elles. lps: Mary Clare, Edward Lexy, Nigel Patrick. 65M UKN. prod/rel: Hurley Productions, Grand National

MORLEY, CHRISTOPHER (1890–1957), USA, Morley, Christopher Darlington
Kitty Foyle, New York 1939, Novel
  Kitty Foyle 1940 d: Sam Wood. lps: Ginger Rogers, Dennis Morgan, James Craig. 107M USA. prod/rel: RKO Radio Pictures©

MORLEY, ROBERT (1908–1992), UKN
Edward My Son, London 1947, Play
  Edward, My Son 1948 d: George Cukor. lps: Spencer Tracy, Deborah Kerr, Ian Hunter. 112M UKN/USA. prod/rel: MGM British
Goodness How Sad, London 1938, Play
  Return to Yesterday 1940 d: Robert Stevenson. lps: Clive Brook, Anna Lee, Dame May Whitty. 68M UKN. prod/rel: Ealing Studios, C.a.P.A.D.

MORNIN, DANIEL
All Our Fault, Novel
  Nothing Personal 1995 d: Thaddeus O'Sullivan. lps: John Lynch, Ian Hart, James Frain. 86M UKN/IRL. *All Our Fault* prod/rel: Little Bird, Channel 4 Films

MORONVAL, ROLAND
Story
  Suivez-Moi, Jeune Homme! 1958 d: Guy Lefranc. lps: Dany Robin, Daniel Gelin, Michel Galabru. 88M FRN. prod/rel: Societe Nouvelle Pathe-Cinema

MOROSCO, OLIVER
Half Breed, Play
  Half Breed, The 1922 d: Charles A. Taylor. lps: Wheeler Oakman, Ann May, Mary Anderson. 5484f USA. prod/rel: Oliver Morosco Productions, Associated First National Pictures
Pretty Mrs. Smith, New York 1914, Play
  Pretty Mrs. Smith 1915 d: Hobart Bosworth. lps: Fritzie Scheff, Owen Moore, Louis Bennison. 5r USA. prod/rel: Oliver Morosco Photoplay Co.©, Paramount Pictures Corp.
So Long Letty, New York 1916, Musical Play
  So Long Letty 1920 d: Al Christie. lps: T. Roy Barnes, Colleen Moore, Grace Darmond. 6r USA. prod/rel: Christie Film Co., Robertson-Cole Distributing Corp.
  So Long Letty 1929 d: Lloyd Bacon. lps: Charlotte Greenwood, Claude Gillingwater, Grant Withers. 5865f USA. prod/rel: Warner Brothers Pictures

MOROSO, JOHN A.
The Gossamer Web, Story
  Luring Lips 1921 d: King Baggot. lps: Darrel Foss, Ramsey Wallace, William Welsh. 4263f USA. prod/rel: Universal Film Mfg. Co.
Hell's Kitchen, Story
  For the Love of Mike 1927 d: Frank CaprA. lps: Claudette Colbert, Ben Lyon, George Sidney. 6588f USA. prod/rel: Robert Kane Productions, First National Pictures
In the Spring, 1918, Short Story
  Hand at the Window, The 1918 d: Raymond Wells. lps: Margery Wilson, Joe King, Francis McDonald. 5r USA. *The Fingerprint* prod/rel: Triangle Film Corp., Triangle Distributing Corp.
Page Tim O'Brien, 1922, Short Story
  Love in the Dark 1922 d: Harry Beaumont. lps: Viola Dana, Cullen Landis, Arline Pretty. 5900f USA. *Page Tim O'Brien* prod/rel: Metro Pictures
The People Against Nancy Preston, New York 1921, Novel
  Dice of Destiny 1920 d: Henry King. lps: H. B. Warner, Lillian Rich, Rosemary Theby. 5r USA. *Going Straight* prod/rel: Jesse D. Hampton Productions, Pathe Exchange, Inc.©
  People Vs. Nancy Preston, The 1925 d: Tom Forman. lps: Marguerite de La Motte, John Bowers, Frankie Darro. 7r USA. prod/rel: Hunt Stromberg Productions, Producers Distributing Corp.
The Quarry, Boston 1913, Novel
  City of Silent Men 1921 d: Tom Forman. lps: Thomas Meighan, Lois Wilson, Kate Bruce. 6326f USA. prod/rel: Famous Players-Lasky, Paramount Pictures

Shadow of the Law 1930 d: Louis J. Gasnier, Max Marcin. lps: William Powell, Marion Shilling, Natalie Moorhead. 6392f USA. prod/rel: Paramount-Publix Corp.

The Shoes That Danced, 1917, Short Story
Shoes That Danced, The 1918 d: Frank Borzage. lps: Pauline Starke, Wallace MacDonald, Dick Rosson. 5r USA. prod/rel: Triangle Film Corp., Triangle Distributing Corp.

The Stumbling Herd, New York 1923, Novel
Rose of the Tenements 1926 d: Phil Rosen. lps: Shirley Mason, John Harron, Evelyn Selbie. 6678f USA. prod/rel: R-C Pictures, Film Booking Offices of America

Vengeance Is Mine, Novel
Vengeance Is Mine 1918 d: Frank H. Crane. lps: Irene Castle, Frank Sheridan, Elliott Dexter. 5r USA. prod/rel: Astra Film Corp., Pathe Exchange, Inc.

MOROT, RENE
La Mort Des Pirates, Novel
Mort Des Pirates, La 1918. lps: Fleury, Delvil, Lucien Walter. SRL. 8000m FRN. prod/rel: Phocea Films

MORPURGO, MICHAEL
Friend Or Foe, Novel
Friend Or Foe 1982 d: John Krish. lps: Mark Luxford, John Holmes, Stacy Keach. 70M UKN. prod/rel: Children's Film Foundation

Why the Whales Came, Novel
When the Whales Came 1989 d: Clive Rees. lps: Paul Scofield, Helen Pearce, Max Rennie. 97M UKN. *Why the Whales Came* prod/rel: Fox, Golden Swan

MORRELL, DAVID (1943–, CND
Brotherhood of the Rose, Novel
Brotherhood of the Rose 1989 d: Marvin J. Chomsky. lps: Peter Strauss, Robert Mitchum, Connie SelleccA. TVM. 200M USA. prod/rel: NBC

First Blood, Novel
First Blood 1982 d: Ted Kotcheff. lps: Sylvester Stallone, Richard Crenna, Brian Dennehy. 93M USA. prod/rel: Orion

MORRIESON, RONALD HUGH
Came a Hot Friday, Novel
Came a Hot Friday 1985 d: Ian Mune. lps: Billy T. James, Peter Bland, Phillip Gordon. 105M NZL. prod/rel: Shaker Run Productions

Pallet on the Floor, Novel
Pallet on the Floor 1984 d: Lynton Butler. lps: Bruce Spence, Peter McCauley, Jillian O'Brien. 90M NZL.

The Scarecrow, Novel
Scarecrow, The 1981 d: Sam Pillsbury. lps: John Carradine, Tracy Mann, Jonathan Smith. 97M NZL. prod/rel: New Zealand National Film Unit, Oasis

MORRIS
Novel
All'ovest Di Sacramento 1971 d: Federico Chentrens. lps: Robert Hossein, Silvia Monti, Xavier Gelin. 87M ITL/FRN. *La Loi a l'Ouest de Pecos* (FRN); *Trouble in Sacramento*; *Judge Roy Bean* prod/rel: Milvia Cin.Ca (Roma), Comacico (Paris)

MORRIS, COLIN
Reluctant Heroes, London 1950, Play
Reluctant Heroes 1951 d: Jack Raymond. lps: Ronald Shiner, Derek Farr, Christine Norden. 80M UKN. prod/rel: Byron, Associated British Film Distributors

MORRIS, DONALD R.
Warm Bodies, New York 1957, Novel
All Hands on Deck 1961 d: Norman Taurog. lps: Pat Boone, Barbara Eden, Buddy Hackett. 98M USA. prod/rel: Twentieth Century-Fox

MORRIS, EDWIN BATEMAN
The Narrow Street, Philadelphia 1924, Novel
Narrow Street, The 1924 d: William Beaudine. lps: Matt Moore, Dorothy Devore, David Butler. 6700f USA. prod/rel: Warner Brothers Pictures

Wide Open 1930 d: Archie Mayo. lps: Edward Everett Horton, Patsy Ruth Miller, Louise FazendA. 6341f USA. prod/rel: Warner Brothers Pictures

MORRIS, GORDON
Jack in the Pulpit, New York 1925, Play
Jack O' Hearts 1926 d: David M. Hartford. lps: Cullen Landis, Gladys Hulette, Bert Cummings. 5881f USA. prod/rel: David Hartford Productions, American Cinema Association

MORRIS, GOUVERNEUR (1752–1816), USA
Behind the Door, 1918, Short Story
Behind the Door 1920 d: Irvin V. Willat. lps: Hobart Bosworth, Jane Novak, Wallace Beery. 7r USA. prod/rel: Thomas H. Ince Productions, Famous Players-Lasky Corp.

The Better Wife, Short Story
Anybody's Woman 1930 d: Dorothy Arzner. lps: Ruth Chatterton, Clive Brook, Paul Lukas. 7243f USA. prod/rel: Paramount-Publix Corp.

The Lucky Serum, Story
Morals for Men 1925 d: Bernard Hyman. lps: Conway Tearle, Agnes Ayres, Alyce Mills. 7443f USA. prod/rel: Tiffany Productions

The Penalty, New York 1913, Novel
Penalty, The 1920 d: Wallace Worsley. lps: Lon Chaney, Claire Adams, Kenneth Harlan. 7r USA. prod/rel: Eminent Authors Pictures, Inc., Goldwyn Distributing Corp.

The Right to Live, Story
That Model from Paris 1926 d: Louis J. Gasnier, Robert Florey (Uncredited). lps: Marceline Day, Bert Lytell, Eileen Percy. 6200f USA. *Model from Paris* prod/rel: Tiffany Productions

The Senator's Brother, Story
Senator's Brother, The 1914 d: William Humphrey. lps: Leah Baird, William Humphrey, Anders Randolf. 2r USA. prod/rel: Vitagraph Co. of America

Tiger Island, New York 1934, Novel
East of Java 1935 d: George Melford. lps: Charles Bickford, Elizabeth Young, Frank Albertson. 72M USA. *Java Seas* (UKN) prod/rel: Universal Productions©, Paul Kohner Production

When My Ship Comes in, New York 1915, Novel
When My Ship Comes in 1919 d: Robert T. Thornby. lps: Jane Grey, William J. Kelly, Nigel Barrie. 5r USA. prod/rel: A. H. Jacobs Photoplays, Inc., International Film Service, Inc.

The Wild Goose, 1919, Short Story
Wild Goose, The 1921 d: Albert Capellani. lps: Mary MacLaren, Holmes Herbert, Dorothy Bernard. 6497f USA. prod/rel: Cosmopolitan Productions, Famous Players-Lasky

Yellow Men and Gold, New York 1911, Novel
Yellow Men and Gold 1922 d: Irvin V. Willat. lps: Richard Dix, Helene Chadwick, Henry A. Barrows. 5224f USA. prod/rel: Goldwyn Pictures

You Can't Get Away With It, 1913, Short Story
Fallen Angel, The 1918 d: Robert T. Thornby. lps: Jewel Carmen, L. C. Shumway, Charles Clary. 5r USA. *You Can't Get Away With It; Paying the Piper* prod/rel: Fox Film Corp., William Fox©

You Can't Get Away With It 1923 d: Rowland V. Lee. lps: Percy Marmont, Malcolm McGregor, Betty Bouton. 6152f USA. *The Road to Nowhere* prod/rel: Fox Film Corp.

MORRIS, I. N.
The Usurper, New York 1904, Play
Usurper, The 1919 d: James Young. lps: Earle Williams, Louise Lovely, Bob Russell. 5r USA. prod/rel: Vitagraph Co. of America©

MORRIS, MARY MCGARRY
A Dangerous Woman, Novel
Dangerous Woman, A 1993 d: Stephen Gyllenhaal. lps: Debra Winger, Barbara Hershey, Gabriel Byrne. 102M USA. prod/rel: Amblin, Island World

MORRIS, RAMSAY
The Ninety and Nine, New York 1902, Play
Ninety and Nine, The 1916 d: Ralph Ince. lps: Lucille Lee Stewart, William Courtenay, Josephine Lovett. 5r USA. prod/rel: Vitagraph Co. of America©, Blue Ribbon Feature

Ninety and Nine, The 1922 d: David Smith. lps: Warner Baxter, Colleen Moore, Lloyd Whitlock. 6800f USA. prod/rel: Vitagraph Co. of America

MORRIS, RICHARD
Flame of the Timberline, Story
Take Me to Town 1953 d: Douglas Sirk. lps: Ann Sheridan, Sterling Hayden, Philip Reed. 81M USA. prod/rel: Universal-International

The Unsinkable Molly Brown, New York 1960, Musical Play
Unsinkable Molly Brown, The 1964 d: Charles Walters. lps: Debbie Reynolds, Harve Presnell, Ed Begley. 128M USA. prod/rel: Marten Productions

MORRIS, WILLIAM
Mrs. Temple's Telegram, New York 1905, Play
Mrs. Temple's Telegram 1920 d: James Cruze. lps: Bryant Washburn, Wanda Hawley, Carmen Phillips. 4318f USA. prod/rel: Famous Players-Lasky Corp.©, Paramount-Artcraft Pictures

MORRIS-DUMOULIN, GILLES-MAURICE
Des Femmes Disparaissent, Paris 1958, Novel
Des Femmes Disparaissent 1959 d: Edouard Molinaro. lps: Robert Hossein, Magali Noel, Estella Blain. 85M FRN. *The Road to Shame* (USA); *Girls Disappear* (UKN) prod/rel: Sirius, Productions Jacques Roitfeld

MORRISON, ANNE
Pigs, New York 1924, Play
Midnight Kiss, The 1926 d: Irving Cummings. lps: Richard Walling, Janet Gaynor, George Irving. 5025f USA. *Pigs* prod/rel: Fox Film Corp.

MORRISON, ELIZABETH
An Adventure, Book
Miss Morrison's Ghosts 1981 d: John Bruce. lps: Wendy Hiller, Hannah Gordon, Bosco Hogan. TVM. 100M UKN. prod/rel: Anglia Tv

MORRISON, EMMELINE
The Sins Ye Do, Novel
Sins Ye Do, The 1924 d: Fred Leroy Granville. lps: Joan Lockton, Henry Victor, Eileen Dennes. 6340f UKN. prod/rel: Stoll

MORRISON, MARGARET
The Reverse Be My Lot, Novel
Reverse Be My Lot, The 1938 d: Raymond Stross. lps: Ian Fleming, Marjorie Corbett, Mickey Brantford. 68M UKN. prod/rel: Rock Productions, Columbia

MORRISON, TONI (1931–, USA, Wofford, Chloe Anthony)
Beloved, 1987, Novel
Beloved 1998 d: Jonathan Demme. lps: Oprah Winfrey, Danny Glover, Thandie Newton. 172M USA. prod/rel: Buena Vista, Touchstone Pictures©

MORROS, BORIS
Ten Years a Counterspy, Book
Man on a String 1960 d: Andre de Toth. lps: Ernest Borgnine, Kerwin Mathews, Colleen Dewhurst. 92M USA. *Confessions of a Counterspy* (UKN); *Ten Years a Counterspy* prod/rel: Columbia, Rd-Dr

MORROW, HONORE
Benefits Forgot, New York 1917, Novel
Of Human Hearts 1938 d: Clarence Brown. lps: Walter Huston, James Stewart, Gene Reynolds. 105M USA. *Benefits Forgot* prod/rel: Metro-Goldwyn-Mayer Corp., Loew's, Inc.©

The Heart of the Desert, New York 1913, Novel
Red, Red Heart, The 1918 d: Wilfred Lucas. lps: Monroe Salisbury, Ruth Clifford, Val Paul. 5r USA. prod/rel: Bluebird Photoplays, Inc.©

Seven Alone, Novel
Seven Alone 1974 d: Earl Bellamy. lps: Dewey Martin, Aldo Ray, Anne Collings. 97M USA. prod/rel: Doty-Dayton

MORSE, CARLETON E.
I Love a Mystery, Novel
I Love a Mystery 1945 d: Henry Levin. lps: Jim Bannon, Nina Foch, George MacReady. 69M USA. prod/rel: Columbia

MORSE, H. BREWSTER
Portrait of a Lady With Red Hair, Story
Lady With Red Hair 1940 d: Curtis Bernhardt. lps: Miriam Hopkins, Claude Rains, Richard Ainley. 81M USA. prod/rel: Warner Bros. Pictures©

MORSELLI, GUIDO
Un Dramma Borghese, Novel
Dramma Borghese, Un 1979 d: Florestano Vancini. lps: Franco Nero, Dalila Di Lazzaro, Lara Wendel. 104M ITL. prod/rel: a.M.A. Film, U.T.I.

MORTIER
Train de Plaisir, 1884, Play
Treno Doria 1924 d: Luciano DoriA. lps: Elena Sangro, Alberto Collo, Lydia QuarantA. 1926m ITL. prod/rel: Fert

MORTIMER, JOHN (1923–, UKN, Mortimer, John Clifford)
The Dock Brief, London 1958, Play
Dock Brief, The 1962 d: James Hill. lps: Peter Sellers, Richard Attenborough, Beryl Reid. 88M UKN. *Trial and Error* (USA); *A Case for the Jury* prod/rel: Anatole de Grunwald, Ltd., MGM

Lunch Hour, London 1961, Play
Lunch Hour 1962 d: James Hill. lps: Shirley Anne Field, Robert Stephens, Kay Walsh. 64M UKN. prod/rel: Bryanston, Eyeline

Voyage Around My Father, 1971, Play
Voyage Around My Father, A 1982 d: Alvin Rakoff. lps: Laurence Olivier, Alan Bates, Elizabeth Sellars. MTV. 90M UKN. prod/rel: BBC

MORTIMER, LEE
Chicago Confidential, Book
Chicago Confidential 1957 d: Sidney Salkow. lps: Brian Keith, Beverly Garland, Dick Foran. 73M USA. prod/rel: United Artists

New York Confidential, 1948, Book
New York Confidential 1955 d: Russell Rouse. lps: Richard Conte, Broderick Crawford, Marilyn Maxwell. 87M USA. prod/rel: Warner Bros., Green-Rouse Prods.

MORTIMER, LILLIAN
No Mother to Guide Her, Play
   No Mother to Guide Her 1923 d: Charles Horan. lps: Genevieve Tobin, John Webb Dillon, Lolita Robertson. 6650f USA. prod/rel: Fox Film Corp.

MORTIMER, PENELOPE (1918–, UKN, Dimont, Penelope
The Pumpkin Eater, London 1962, Novel
   Pumpkin Eater, The 1964 d: Jack Clayton. lps: Anne Bancroft, Peter Finch, James Mason. 118M UKN. prod/rel: Romulus Films, Columbia

MORTON, ANDREW
Her True Story Diana, Book
   Diana, Her True Story 1993 d: Kevin Connor. lps: Serena Scott Thomas, David Threlfall, Anne Stallybrass. TVM. 240M USA/GRM/FRN.

MORTON, C. S.
Miss Raffles, Story
   Miss Raffles 1914 d: Theodore Marston. lps: Dorothy Kelly, James Morrison. SHT USA. prod/rel: Vitagraph Co. of America

MORTON, EDWARD
San Toy, London 1899, Play
   San Toy 1900. lps: Marie Tempest, Hayden Coffin, Huntley Wright. UKN. prod/rel: Mutoscope & Biograph

MORTON, GUY
The Black Robe, Novel
   Secrets of Chinatown 1934 d: Fred Newmeyer. lps: Nick Stuart, Lucille Browne, Raymond Lawrence. 54M CND. *The Black Robe* prod/rel: Commonwealth Productions Ltd., Northern Films Ltd.
Rangy Pete, Boston 1922, Novel
   Texas Trail, The 1925 d: Scott R. Dunlap. lps: Harry Carey, Ethel Shannon, Charles K. French. 4720f USA. prod/rel: Hunt Stromberg Corp., Producers Distributing Corp.

MORTON, HUGH
The Belle of New York, New York 1897, Musical Play
   Belle of New York, The 1919 d: Julius Steger. lps: Marion Davies, Raymond Bloomer, L. Rogers Lytton. 5r USA. prod/rel: Marion Davies Film Corp.©, Select Pictures Corp.
   Belle of New York, The 1951 d: Charles Walters. lps: Fred Astaire, Vera-Ellen, Marjorie Main. 82M USA. prod/rel: Metro-Goldwyn-Mayer Corp.

MORTON, MARTHA
A Bachelor's Romance, Chicago 1896, Play
   Bachelor's Romance, The 1915. lps: John Emerson, Lorraine Huling, Maggie Halloway Fisher. 4r USA. prod/rel: Famous Players Film Co., Paramount Pictures Corp.
Her Lord and Master, New York 1912, Play
   Her Lord and Master 1921 d: Edward Jose. lps: Alice Joyce, Holmes Herbert, Walter McEwen. 6r USA. prod/rel: Vitagraph Co. of America

MORTON, MICHAEL
Caleb West, New York 1900, Play
   Deep Waters 1920 d: Maurice Tourneur. lps: John Gilbert, Rudolph Christians, Barbara Bedford. 5035f USA. *Master Diver Caleb West* prod/rel: Maurice Tourneur Productions, Inc., Famous Players-Lasky Corp.©
Children of Chance, Novel
   White Shadow, The 1924 d: Graham Cutts. lps: Betty Compson, Clive Brook, Henry Victor. 5047f UKN. *White Shadows* (USA) prod/rel: Balcon, Freedman & Saville, Woolf & Freedman
The Guilty One, New York 1914, Play
   Guilty One, The 1924 d: Joseph Henabery. lps: Agnes Ayres, Edmund Burns, Stanley Taylor. 5365f USA. prod/rel: Famous Players-Lasky, Paramount Pictures
The Imposter, New York 1910, Play
   Darling of the Rich, The 1922 d: John G. Adolfi. lps: Betty Blythe, Gladys Leslie, Jane Jennings. 6144f USA. prod/rel: B. B. Productions
   Daughter of Luxury, A 1922 d: Paul Powell. lps: Agnes Ayres, Tom Gallery, Edith Yorke. 4538f USA. prod/rel: Famous Players-Lasky, Paramount Pictures
   Impostor, The 1918 d: Dell Henderson. lps: Ann Murdock, David Powell, Lionel Adams. 5r USA. *The Imposter* prod/rel: Empire All Star Corp.©, Mutual Film Corp.
My Wife, New York 1907, Play
   My Wife 1918 d: Dell Henderson. lps: Ann Murdock, Rex McDougall, Jules Raucourt. 5r USA. prod/rel: Empire All-Star Corp., Mutual Film Corp.
On With the Dance, New York 1917, Play
   On With the Dance 1920 d: George Fitzmaurice. lps: Mae Murray, David Powell, Alma Tell. 6483f USA. prod/rel: Famous Players-Lasky Corp.©, Paramount-Artcraft Pictures

The Richest Girl, New York 1909, Play
   Richest Girl, The 1918 d: Albert Capellani. lps: Ann Murdock, David Powell, Paul Capellani. 5r USA. prod/rel: Empire All Star Corp., Mutual Film Corp.
The Runaway, New York 1911, Play
   Runaway, The 1917 d: Dell Henderson. lps: Julia Sanderson, Norman Trevor, Ada St. Claire. 5-6r USA. prod/rel: Empire All Star Corp.©, Mutual Film Corp.
Woman to Woman, London 1921, Play
   Woman to Woman 1923 d: Graham Cutts. lps: Betty Compson, Clive Brook, Josephine Earle. 7455f UKN. prod/rel: Balcon, Freedman & Saville, Woolf & Freedman
   Woman to Woman 1929 d: Victor Saville. lps: Betty Compson, Juliette Compton, George Barraud. 90M UKN. prod/rel: Gainsborough, Burlington
   Woman to Woman 1946 d: MacLean Rogers. lps: Douglass Montgomery, Joyce Howard, Adele Dixon. 99M UKN. prod/rel: British National, Anglo-American
The Yellow Ticket, New York 1914, Play
   Yellow Ticket, The 1918 d: William Parke. lps: Fannie Ward, Milton Sills, Warner Oland. 4970f USA. prod/rel: Astra Film Corp., Pathe Exchange, Inc.©
   Yellow Ticket, The 1931 d: Raoul Walsh. lps: Elissa Landi, Laurence Olivier, Lionel Barrymore. 88M USA. *The Yellow Passport* (UKN) prod/rel: Fox Film Corp.©

MORTON, VICTORIA
The Whirlpool, New York 1916, Novel
   Whirlpool, The 1918 d: Alan Crosland. lps: Alice Brady, Holmes Herbert, J. H. Gilmour. 5r USA. prod/rel: Select Pictures Corp.©

MORTON, WILLIAM
Feet of Clay, Story
   Feet of Clay 1917 d: Harry Harvey. lps: Barney Furey, R. Henry Grey, Margaret Landis. 4r USA. prod/rel: Falcon Features, General Film Co.©

MORUM, WILLIAM
Alive and Kicking, Play
   Alive and Kicking 1958 d: Cyril Frankel. lps: Sybil Thorndike, Kathleen Harrison, Estelle Winwood. 94M UKN. prod/rel: Diador, Ab-Pathe
The Late Edwina Black, London 1949, Play
   Late Edwina Black, The 1951 d: Maurice Elvey. lps: David Farrar, Geraldine Fitzgerald, Roland Culver. 78M UKN. *Obsessed* (USA) prod/rel: Independent Film Distributors, Elvey-Gartside

MOSA, SOBRI
Story
   Haditha Al Nasf Metr 1983 d: Samir ZikrA. lps: Abdul Fatah Al Mozaeen, Gyana Ide, Ali Assed. 100M SYR. *The Half Meter Incident*; *Hadisat an-Nusf Meter* prod/rel: Nationale Filmorganisation

MOSCARIELLO, M.
Il Custode, Play
   Toto Cerca Casa 1949 d: Steno, Mario Monicelli. lps: Toto, Alda Mangini, Aroldo Tieri. 90M ITL. *Toto Wants a Home* prod/rel: Artisti Tecnica Associati

MOSCO, MAISIE
The Happy Family, London 1966, Play
   Mumsy, Nanny, Sonny and Girly 1969 d: Freddie Francis. lps: Michael Bryant, Ursula Howells, Pat Heywood. 102M UKN. *Girly* prod/rel: Fitzroy, Francis Films

MOSCOW, ALVIN
Every Secret Thing, Autobiography
   Patty Hearst 1988 d: Paul Schrader. lps: Natasha Richardson, William Forsythe, Ving Rhames. 108M USA/UKN. *Patty Hearst: Her Own Story*; *Patty* prod/rel: Atlantic Entertainment, Zenith

MOSELEY, LEONARD
They Can't Hang Me, Novel
   They Can't Hang Me 1955 d: Val Guest. lps: Terence Morgan, Yolande Donlan, Andre Morell. 75M UKN. prod/rel: Vandyke, Independent Film Distributors

MOSES, BARR
The Clean Gun, Short Story
   Clean Gun, The 1917 d: Harry Harvey. lps: Stanley J. Preston, Edward Jobson, Kathleen Kirkham. 4r USA. prod/rel: Falcon Features, General Film Co.©

MOSHER, HOWARD FRANK
A Stranger in the Kingdom, Novel
   Stranger in the Kingdom, A 1998 d: Jay Craven. lps: David Lansbury, Ernie Hudson, Martin Sheen. 112M USA. prod/rel: Whiskeyjack Pictures, Kingdom Come Pictures
Where the Rivers Flow North, Novel
   Where the Rivers Flow North 1993 d: Jay Craven. lps: Rip Torn, Tantoo Cardinal, Bill Raymond. 106M USA. prod/rel: Caledonia Pictures

MOSKIEWICZ, HELENE
Inside the Gestapo
   Woman at War, A 1990 d: Edward Bennett. lps: Martha Plimpton, Eric Stoltz, Jack Shepherd. TVM. 180M UKN.

MOSLEY, LEONARD OSWALD
The Cat and the Mice, London 1958, Novel
   Foxhole in Cairo 1960 d: John Llewellyn Moxey. lps: James Robertson Justice, Adrian Hoven, Gloria Mestre. 80M UKN. prod/rel: Omnia Films, Britannia

MOSLEY, NICHOLAS (1923–, UKN
Accident, London 1965, Novel
   Accident 1967 d: Joseph Losey. lps: Dirk Bogarde, Stanley Baker, Jacqueline Sassard. 105M UKN. prod/rel: London Independent Producers, Royal Avenue Chelsea
Impossible Object, 1968, Novel
   Questo Impossibile Oggetto 1973 d: John Frankenheimer. lps: Alan Bates, Dominique Sanda, Lea Massari. 110M ITL/FRN. *The Story of a Love Story* (USA); *L' Impossible Objet* (FRN); *Impossible Object* prod/rel: Euro International Film

MOSLEY, WALTER
Always Outgunned Always Outnumbered, Book
   Always Outnumbered 1998 d: Michael Apted. lps: Laurence Fishburne, Bill Cobbs, Natalie Cole. TVM. 120M USA. prod/rel: Palomar Pictures
Devil in a Blue Dress, Novel
   Devil in a Blue Dress 1995 d: Carl Franklin. lps: Denzel Washington, Tom Sizemore, Jennifer Beals. 102M USA. prod/rel: Tri-Star, Clinica Estetico

MOSS, GEOFFREY
Isn't Life Wonderful!, 1924, Short Story
   Isn't Life Wonderful 1924 d: D. W. Griffith. lps: Carol Dempster, Neil Hamilton, Erville Alderson. 8600f USA. prod/rel: United Artists
Sweet Pepper, Novel
   Lockendes Gift 1928 d: Fred Sauer. lps: Eve Gray, Paul Richter, Margit Manstad. 2268m GRM. prod/rel: Orplid-Film

MOSS, PAUL FINDER
Hot Air, Story
   My Dream Is Yours 1949 d: Michael Curtiz. lps: Jack Carson, Doris Day, Lee Bowman. 101M USA. prod/rel: Warner Bros.
   Twenty Million Sweethearts 1934 d: Ray Enright. lps: Dick Powell, Ginger Rogers, Pat O'Brien. 89M USA. *Hot Air*; *Rhythm in the Air*; *On the Air* prod/rel: First National Pictures©

MOSS, W. STANLEY
Ill Met By Moonlight, Book
   Ill Met By Moonlight 1956 d: Michael Powell, Emeric Pressburger. lps: Dirk Bogarde, Marius Goring, David Oxley. 104M UKN. *Night Ambush* (USA) prod/rel: Vega, Rank Film Distributors

MOSSENSOHN, YIGAL
Play
   Eldorado 1963 d: Menahem Golan. lps: Topol, Gila Almagor, Tikvah Mor. F ISR. *El Dorado*
Story
   Kazablan 1974 d: Menahem Golan. lps: Yehoram Gaon, Arieh Elias, Efrat Lavie. 115M ISR.©
Casablan, Tel Aviv 1958, Play
   Casablan 1964 d: Larry Frisch. lps: Nikos Kourkoulos, Maria Xenia, Lykourgos Kallergis. 63M GRC/ISR. prod/rel: Anzervos Corporation

MOTLEY, WILLARD (1912–1965), USA
Knock on Any Door, 1947, Novel
   Knock on Any Door 1949 d: Nicholas Ray. lps: Humphrey Bogart, John Derek, George MacReady. 100M USA. prod/rel: Columbia
Let No Man Write My Epitaph, 1958, Novel
   Let No Man Write My Epitaph 1960 d: Philip Leacock. lps: Burl Ives, Shelley Winters, James Darren. 106M USA. *Reach for Tomorrow* prod/rel: Boris D. Kaplan, Columbia

MOTTL, JAROSLAV
Podej Stesti Ruku, Opera
   Rozkosny Pribeh 1936 d: Vladimir Slavinsky. lps: Vera Ferbasova, Zita Kabatova, Frantisek Kristof-Vesely. 3040m CZC. *Delightful Story* prod/rel: Slavia-Film

MOTTRAM, R. H. (1883–1971), UKN, Mottram, Ralph Hale
The Spanish Farm, Short Story
   Roses of Picardy 1927 d: Maurice Elvey. lps: Lillian Hall-Davis, John Stuart, Humberston Wright. 8500f UKN. prod/rel: Gaumont
The Spanish Farm Trilogy, Novel
   Spanish Farm Trilogy, The 1968. lps: Caroline Mortimer, Cavan Kendall, Jack Woolgar. MTV. 240M UKN. prod/rel: BBC

MOUEZY-EON, ANDRE
L' Amour a l'Americaine, Play
Amour a l'Americaine, L' 1931 d: Claude Heymann, Paul Fejos. lps: Andre Luguet, Julien Carette, Spinelly. 96M FRN. prod/rel: Etablissements Braunberger-Richebe

Bibi la Puree, Play
Bibi la Puree 1925 d: Maurice Champreux. lps: Georges Biscot, Lise Jaux, Henri-Amedee. F FRN. prod/rel: Gaumont
Bibi la Puree 1934 d: Leo Joannon. lps: Georges Biscot, Berangere, Josette Day. 95M FRN. prod/rel: Roxy Films

Le Conte Galant
Folle Nuit, La 1932 d: Robert Bibal. lps: Marguerite Deval, Suzanne Bianchetti, Guy Parzy. 84M FRN. *Le Derivatif* prod/rel: Films Leon Poirier

Les Degourdis de la 11E, Play
Degourdis de la 11E, Les 1937 d: Christian-Jaque. lps: Fernandel, Pauline Carton, Andre Lefaur. 91M FRN. prod/rel: Productions Maurice Lehmann

Les Deux "Monsieur" de Madame, Play
Deux "Monsieur" de Madame, Les 1933 d: Abel Jacquin, Georges Pallu. lps: Pierre Dac, Jeanne Cheirel, Simone Deguyse. F FRN. prod/rel: Films Reyssier
Deux "Monsieur" de Madame, Les 1951 d: Robert Bibal. lps: Jean Paredes, Jacques Berthier, Arlette Poirier. 90M FRN. prod/rel: Olympic

L' Enfant de Ma Soeur, Play
Enfant de Ma Soeur, L' 1932 d: Henry Wulschleger. lps: Bach, Georges Treville, Simone Heliard. 90M FRN. prod/rel: Alex Nalpas

La Filleule d'Amerique, Play
Filleule d'Amerique, Une 1920 d: Louis de Carbonnat. lps: Louise Marquet, Madeleine James, Felix Huguenet. F FRN. prod/rel: Aigle Films

L' Heritier du Bal Tabarin, Play
Heritier du Bal Tabarin, L' 1933 d: Jean Kemm. lps: Frederic Duvalles, Charlotte Lyses, Germaine Michel. 85M FRN. prod/rel: Alex Nalpas

Mam'zelle Culot, Opera
Tampon du Capiston, Le 1930 d: Jean Toulout, Joe Francis. lps: Bach, Helene Hallier, Henry Laverne. F FRN. prod/rel: Alex Nalpas

The Matrimonial Bed, New York 1927, Play
Kisses for Breakfast 1941 d: Lewis Seiler. lps: Dennis Morgan, Jane Wyatt, Lee Patrick. 81M USA. *She Stayed Kissed* prod/rel: Warner Bros.
Matrimonial Bed, The 1930 d: Michael Curtiz. lps: Frank Fay, Lilyan Tashman, James Gleason. 6242f USA. *A Matrimonial Problem* (UKN) prod/rel: Warner Brothers Pictures

Le Plus Beau Gosse de France, Play
Plus Beau Gosse de France, Le 1937 d: Rene Pujol. lps: Georges Biscot, Bernard Lancret, Josseline Gael. 75M FRN. *Le Mari de la Reine*

Sacree Jeunesse, Play
Sacree Jeunesse 1958 d: Andre Berthomieu. lps: Gaby Morlay, Andre Luguet, Jacques Morel. 90M FRN. prod/rel: Films Fernand Rivers

Sidonie Panache, Opera
Sidonie Panache 1934 d: Henry Wulschleger. lps: Bach, Alexandre Mihalesco, Florelle. 120M FRN/ALG. prod/rel: Alex Nalpas, Cie Francaise Cinematographique Lux

Six Cent Mille Francs Par Mois, Play
Six Cent Mille Francs Par Mois 1933 d: Leo Joannon. lps: Germaine Michel, Georges Biscot, Pierre de Guingand. 75M FRN. prod/rel: Norma-Film

Le Tampon du Capiston, Play
Tampon du Capiston, Le 1950 d: Maurice Labro. lps: Rellys, Frederic Duvalles, Pauline Carton. 95M FRN. prod/rel: Pantheon Production

Tire-Au-Flanc!, Paris 1904, Play
Tire-Au Flanc 1912. lps: Armand Morins, Coquet, Andree Coquet. 410m FRN.
Tire Au Flanc 1928 d: Jean Renoir. lps: Georges Pomies, Michel Simon, Fridette Fatton. 2000m FRN. *Tire-Au-Flanc* prod/rel: Neo Films, Pierre Braunberger
Tire Au Flanc 1933 d: Henry Wulschleger. lps: Bach, Felix Oudart, Germaine Lix. 103M FRN. prod/rel: Pierre Braunberger, Alex Nalpas
Tire-Au-Flanc 1961 d: Francois Truffaut, Claude de Givray. lps: Christian de Tiliere, Ricet Barrier, Jacques Balutin. 87M FRN. *The Army Game* (USA); *The Sad Sack*; *Tire Au Flanc 62* prod/rel: S.E.D.I.F., Films Du Carrosse

Tout Pour Rien, Play
Tout Pour Rien 1933 d: Rene Pujol. lps: Frederic Duvalles, Andre Alerme, Jacqueline Francell. 95M FRN. *Le Petit Carambouilleur* prod/rel: Pathe-Natan

MOUILLOT, FREDERICK
What the Butler Saw, London 1905, Play
What the Butler Saw 1924 d: George Dewhurst. lps: Irene Rich, Pauline Garon, Guy Newall. 5855f UKN. prod/rel: Dewhurst, Gaumont

MOUREAU, EMILE
Le Courrier de Lyon, London 1877, Play
Midnight Stage, The 1919 d: Ernest C. Warde. lps: Frank Keenan, Mignon Anderson, Charles Gunn. 5r USA. prod/rel: Anderson-Brunton Co., Pathe Exchange, Inc.©

MOURY, ALAIN
L' Affaire d'une Nuit, Novel
Affaire d'une Nuit, L' 1960 d: Henri Verneuil. lps: Pascale Petit, Roger Hanin, Pierre Mondy. 95M FRN. *It Happened All Night* (USA) prod/rel: Progefi

MOWAT, FARLEY (1921–, CND, Mowat, Farley McGill)
Curse of the Viking Grave, Novel
Curse of the Viking Grave 1992 d: Michael Scott. lps: Nicholas Shields, Gordon Tootoosis, Cedric Smith. 97M CND.

Never Cry Wolf, Book
Never Cry Wolf 1983 d: Carroll Ballard. lps: Charles Martin Smith, Brian Dennehy, Zachary Ittimangnaq. 105M USA. prod/rel: Buena Vista

A Whale for the Killing, Novel
Whale for the Killing, A 1980 d: Richard T. Heffron. lps: Richard Widmark, Peter Strauss, Dee Wallace Stone. TVM. 150M USA/CND. prod/rel: Hugh Hefner Playboy, Beowulf

MOWERY, WILLIAM BYRON
Heart of the North, New York 1930, Novel
Heart of the North 1938 d: Lewis Seiler. lps: Dick Foran, Gloria Dickson, Patric Knowles. 85M USA. prod/rel: Warner Bros. Pictures©, First National Picture

MOYZISCH, L. C.
Operation Cicero, 1950, Novel
Five Fingers 1952 d: Joseph L. Mankiewicz. lps: James Mason, Danielle Darrieux, Michael Rennie. 108M USA. *Fingers* prod/rel: 20th Century-Fox

MOZART, WOLFGANG AMADEUS (1756–1791), AUS
Cosi Fan Tutte, Vienna 1790, Opera
Cosi Fan Tutte 1970 d: Vaclav Kaslik. lps: Gundula Janowitz, Christa Ludwig, Olivera Miljakovic. 159M AUS/GRM.
Cosi Fan Tutte 1991 d: Tinto Brass. lps: Claudia Koll, Franco Branciaroli, Paolo LanzA. 105M ITL. *Thus Do They All*

Don Giovanni, Prague 1787, Opera
Don Giovanni 1955 d: Paul Czinner, Alfred Travers. lps: Cesare Siepi, Otto Edelmann, Elizabeth Grummer. 170M UKN. *Don Juan* prod/rel: Harmony, Maxwell
Don Juan 1922 d: Edwin J. Collins. lps: Pauline Peters, J. R. Tozer, Lillian Douglas. 1000f UKN. prod/rel: Master Films, Gaumont

MRSTIK, VILEM
Pohadka Maje, Novel
Pohadka Maje 1940 d: Otakar VavrA. lps: Natasa Gollova, Jaroslav Vojta, Leopolda DostalovA. 2509m CZC. *The May Story*; *Fable of May*; *Romance*; *May Fairy Tale*; *Fairy Tale of May* prod/rel: Elekta

MRSTIKOVE, ALOIS
Marysa, Play
Marysa 1935 d: Josef Rovensky. lps: Jirina Stepnickova, Frantisek Kovarik, Hermina VojtovA. 2839m CZC. prod/rel: Monopol

MRSTIKOVE, VILEM
Marysa, Play
Marysa 1935 d: Josef Rovensky. lps: Jirina Stepnickova, Frantisek Kovarik, Hermina VojtovA. 2839m CZC. prod/rel: Monopol

MTWA, PERCY
Bopha!, Play
Bopha! 1993 d: Morgan Freeman. lps: Danny Glover, Alfre Woodard, Malcolm McDowell. 113M USA.

MUHLEN-SCHULTE, GEORG
Die Buschhexe, Novel
Dschungel Ruft, Der 1936 d: Harry Piel. lps: Harry Piel, Ursula Grabley, Gerda Maurus. 105M GRM. prod/rel: Ariel, Probster & Zellmann

Holle Ahoi, Novel
Grosse Fall, Der 1945 d: Karl Anton. lps: Gustav Frohlich, Hilde Sessak, Lotte Koch. 89M GRM. *Ihr Grosser Fall*; *Ein Toller Fall*; *The Big Fall* prod/rel: Tobis, Ring

Rittmeister Styx, Novel
Sache Mit Styx, Die 1942 d: Karl Anton. lps: Viktor de Kowa, Margit Symo, Will Dohm. 98M GRM. *Wer Die Heimat Liebt* prod/rel: Tobis, Stern

Der Unmogliche Herr Pitt, Novel
Unmogliche Herr Pitt, Der 1938 d: Harry Piel. lps: Harry Piel, Hilde Weissner, Willi Schur. 92M GRM. *Die Nacht Der 1000 Sensationen* prod/rel: Ariel, Terra

MUIR, AUGUSTUS
Ocean Gold, 1938, Short Story
Phantom Submarine 1940 d: Charles T. Barton. lps: Anita Louise, Bruce Bennett, Oscar O'SheA. 70M USA. *Ocean Gold* prod/rel: Columbia Pictures Corp.©

MUKHAMEDZHANOV, KALTAI
Voskhozhdeniye Na Fudziyamu, 1978, Play
Voshozdenie Na Fudzijamu 1988 d: Bolotbek Shamshiev. 129M USS. *Climbing Mount Fuji*; *The Ascent of Fujiyama*; *Voskohzhdeniye Na Fudziyama*; *The Ascent of Mount Fuji*

MUKHERJEE, PRABHAT KUMAR
Ratnadeep, Novel
Ratnadeep 1951 d: Debaki Bose. lps: A. Gupta, Manju Dey, Molina Devi. F IND. *Jewelled Lamp* prod/rel: Chitramaya
Ratnadeep 1952 d: Debaki Bose. lps: A. Gupta, Manju Dey, Molina Devi. F IND. *Jewelled Lamp* prod/rel: Chitramaya
Ratnadeepam 1953 d: Debaki Bose. lps: A. Gupta, Manju Dey, Molina Devi. F IND. *Jewelled Lamp* prod/rel: Chitramaya

MUKKA, TIMO K
Maa on Syntinen Laulu, 1964, Novel
Maa on Syntinen Laulau 1973 d: Rauni Mollberg. lps: Maritta VIItamaki, Pauli Jauhojarvi, Aimo Saukko. 113M FNL. *The Earth Is a Sinful Song* (USA); *Earth Is Our Sinful Song*; *The Land Is a Sinful Song* prod/rel: Rauni Mollberg, Jorn Donner

MULBERRY, VINCENT
L' Isla Del Diablo, Novel
Isla Del Diablo, La 1995 d: Piquer Simon. lps: Cris Huerta, Eduardo MacGregor, Ruben Galves. 94M SPN. *Devil's Island* prod/rel: Sommi, Videokine

MULFORD, CLARENCE E.
Bar-20 Three, Chicago 1921, Novel
Three on the Trail 1936 d: Howard Bretherton. lps: William Boyd, James Ellison, Onslow Stevens. 67M USA. prod/rel: Harry Sherman Productions, Paramount Productions©

Black Buttes, New York 1923, Novel
Hopalong Rides Again 1937 d: Lesley Selander. lps: William Boyd, George Hayes, Russell Hayden. 65M USA. *Cassidy Bar Twenty* prod/rel: Harry Sherman Productions, Paramount Pictures©

Bring Me His Ears, 1922, Short Story
Borderland 1937 d: Nate Watt. lps: William Boyd, James Ellison, George Hayes. 82M USA. prod/rel: Harry Sherman Productions, Inc.

Ranchman Buck Peters, Chicago 1912, Novel
Bar 20 Justice 1938 d: Lesley Selander. lps: William Boyd, George Hayes, Russell Hayden. 65M USA. *Deputy Sheriff* prod/rel: Harry Sherman Productions, Inc.

Cottonwood Gulch, 1924, Short Story
North of the Rio Grande 1937 d: Nate Watt. lps: William Boyd, George Hayes, Morris Ankrum. 72M USA. *North of Rio Grande* prod/rel: Harry Sherman Productions, Paramount Pictures©

The Heart of Arizona, Novel
Heart of Arizona 1938 d: Lesley Selander. lps: William Boyd, George Hayes, Russell Hayden. 68M USA. *Gunsmoke* prod/rel: Harry Sherman Productions, Paramount Pictures©

Hopalong Cassidy, Chicago 1912, Novel
Hopalong Cassidy 1935 d: Howard Bretherton. lps: William Boyd, James Ellison, Paula Stone. 63M USA. *Hopalong Cassidy Enters*; *Hop-a-Long Cassidy*; *Hop-Along Cassidy* prod/rel: Harry Sherman Productions, Paramount Productions©

Hopalong Cassidy's Protege, New York 1926, Novel
Call of the Prairie 1936 d: Howard Bretherton. lps: William Boyd, James Ellison, Muriel Evans. 65M USA. prod/rel: Harry Sherman Productions, Inc.

The Man from Bar-20; a Story of the Cow Country, Chicago 1918, Novel
Partners of the Plains 1938 d: Lesley Selander. lps: William Boyd, Harvey Clark, Russell Hayden. 70M USA. *Men Must Fight* prod/rel: Harry Sherman Productions, Paramount Productions©

Me An' Shorty, New York 1929, Novel
Cassidy of Bar 20 1938 d: Lesley Selander. lps: William Boyd, Frank Darien, Russell Hayden. 60M USA. *Cassidy of the Bar 20* prod/rel: Harry Sherman Productions, Inc.

The Orphan, New York 1908, Novel
Deadwood Coach, The 1924 d: Lynn Reynolds. lps: Tom Mix, George Bancroft, De Witt Jennings. 6346f USA. prod/rel: Fox Film Corp.

Orphan, The 1920 d: J. Gordon Edwards. lps: William Farnum, Louise Lovely, Henry J. Hebert. 5696f USA. prod/rel: Fox Film Corp., William Fox©

The Round-Up, New York 1933, Novel
Hills of Old Wyoming 1937 d: Nate Watt. lps: William Boyd, George Hayes, Morris Ankrum. 78M USA. prod/rel: Harry Sherman Productions, Paramount Pictures©

Rustler's Valley, New York 1924, Novel
Rustler's Valley 1937 d: Nate Watt. lps: William Boyd, George Hayes, Russell Hayden. 60M USA. prod/rel: Harry Sherman Productions, Paramount Pictures©

Tex, Chicago 1922, Novel
Texas Trail 1937 d: David Selman. lps: William Boyd, George Hayes, Russell Hayden. 62M USA. prod/rel: Harry Sherman Productions, Paramount Pictures©

Trail Dust, New York 1934, Novel
Trail Dust 1936 d: Nate Watt. lps: William Boyd, James Ellison, George Hayes. 77M USA. prod/rel: Harry Sherman Productions, Paramount Pictures©

Tumbleweed Mesquite Jenkins, New York 1932, Novel
Heart of the West 1936 d: Howard Bretherton. lps: William Boyd, James Ellison, George Hayes. 63M USA. prod/rel: Harry Sherman Productions, Paramount Productions©

MULHOLLAND, CLARA
Kathleen Mavourneen, Novel
Kathleen Mavourneen 1937 d: Norman Lee. lps: Sally O'Neil, Tom Burke, Sara Allgood. 77M UKN. *Kathleen* (USA) prod/rel: Welwyn, Argyle-British

MULISCH, HARRY
De Aanslag, 1982, Novel
Aanslag, de 1986 d: Fons Rademakers. lps: Derek de Lint, Marc Van Uchelen, Monique Van de Ven. 155M NTH. *The Assault* (USA) prod/rel: Cannon (Netherlands)

Twee Vrouwen, 1975, Novel
Twee Vrouwen 1978 d: George Sluizer, Jurrien Rood. lps: Bibi Andersson, Anthony Perkins, Sandra Dumas. 115M NTH. *Twice a Woman; Second Touch* prod/rel: William Howard Prod., M.G.S.

MULLALLY, DON
The Desert Flower, New York 1924, Play
Desert Flower, The 1925 d: Irving Cummings. lps: Colleen Moore, Lloyd Hughes, Kate Price. 6383f USA. prod/rel: First National Pictures

MULLEN, CHRIS
A Very British Coup, Novel
Very British Coup, A 1988 d: Mick Jackson. lps: Ray McAnally, Marjorie Yates, Geoffrey Beevers. MTV. 155M UKN.

MULLER, HANS
Le Createur, Play
Vivre 1928 d: Robert Boudrioz. lps: Bernhard Goetzke, Elmire Vautier, Adolphe Cande. 3055m FRN/GRM. *Der Schopfer Zwischen Liebe Und Pflicht* (GRM) prod/rel: Phenix-Films, Studios Reunis

Frischer Wind Aus Kanada, Play
Frischer Wind Aus Kanada 1935 d: Heinz Kenter, Erich Holder. lps: Dorit Kreysler, Max Gulstorff, Harald Paulsen. 87M GRM. prod/rel: UFA

Der Schopfer, Play
Schopfer, Der 1928 d: Robert Boudrioz. lps: Bernhard Goetzke. 3055m GRM. *Zwischen Liebe un Pflicht* prod/rel: Phonix-Film Ag

MULLER, ROBERT
Die Welt in Jenem Sommer, Novel
Welt in Jenem Sommer, Die 1979 d: Ilse Hofmann. lps: Jan-Claudius Schwarzbauer, Hermann Lause, Katrin Schaake. 105M GRM. *The World That Summer* prod/rel: Wdr, B.a.G.

MULLER-SCHLOSSER, HANS
Schneider Wibbel, Play
Schneider Wibbel 1920 d: Manfred NoA. lps: Hermann Picha, Margarete Kupfer, Gustav Trautschold. 1775m GRM. prod/rel: Eiko-Film
Schneider Wibbel 1939 d: Viktor de KowA. lps: Erich Ponto, Fita Benkhoff, Irene von Meyendorff. 85M GRM. prod/rel: Majestic, Schonger
Sonntagskind, Das 1956 d: Kurt Meisel. lps: Heinz Ruhmann, Hannelore Bollmann, Walter Giller. 96M GRM. *Sunday Child* prod/rel: Berolina, UFA

MULVIHILL, WILLIAM
Sands of the Kalahari, New York 1960, Novel
Sands of the Kalahari 1965 d: Cy Endfield. lps: Stanley Baker, Stuart Whitman, Susannah York. 119M UKN/SAF. prod/rel: Pendennis Pictures, Paramount-Embassy

MUMFORD, ETHEL WATTS
Story
Dollar for Dollar 1920 d: Frank Keenan. lps: Frank Keenan, Kathleen Kirkham, Katherine Van Buren. 4652f USA. prod/rel: Frank Keenan Productions, Pathe Exchange, Inc.©

Divorce Coupons, Story
Divorce Coupons 1922 d: Webster Campbell. lps: Corinne Griffith, Holmes Herbert, Mona LisA. 5249f USA. prod/rel: Vitagraph Co. of America

Everything Money Can Buy, 1924, Short Story
After Business Hours 1925 d: Malcolm St. Clair. lps: Elaine Hammerstein, Lou Tellegen, Phyllis Haver. 5600f USA. prod/rel: Columbia Pictures

The Manifestations of Henry Ort, Story
Straight Is the Way 1921 d: Robert G. VignolA. lps: Matt Moore, Mabel Bert, Gladys Leslie. 5-6r USA. prod/rel: Cosmopolitan Productions, Paramount Pictures

MUMFORD, LEWIS (1895–1990), USA
The Culture of Cities, Book
City, The 1939 d: Willard Van Dyke, Ralph Steiner. DOC. 45M USA. prod/rel: American Documentary Film, Inc., Civic Films

MUNDY, TALBOT
Her Reputation, Indianapolis 1923, Novel
Her Reputation 1923 d: John Griffith Wray. lps: May McAvoy, Lloyd Hughes, James Corrigan. 6566f USA. prod/rel: Thomas H. Ince Corp., Associated First National Pictures

King - of the Khyber Rifles, New York 1916, Novel
Black Watch, The 1929 d: John Ford. lps: Victor McLaglen, Myrna Loy, David Rollins. 8487f USA. *King of the Khyber Rifles* (UKN) prod/rel: Fox Film Corp.
King of the Khyber Rifles 1953 d: Henry King. lps: Tyrone Power, Terry Moore, Michael Rennie. 100M USA. prod/rel: 20th Century-Fox

MUNI, BELLA
It Might Have Happened, Story
Deceiver, The 1931 d: Louis King. lps: Lloyd Hughes, Dorothy Sebastian, Ian Keith. 68M USA. *Unwanted* prod/rel: Columbia Pictures Corp.

MUNIZ, LAURO CESAR
O Santo Milagroso, 1967, Play
Santo Milagroso, O 1965 d: Carlos CoimbrA. lps: Dionisio Azevedo, Leonardo Vilar, Vanja Orico. 105M BRZ.

MUNK, KAJ
Havet Og Menneskene, 1948, Play
Havet Og Menneskene 1970 d: Sigfred Aagaard. lps: Jenne Ostergaard, Hans Roy, Aase Lykke. 102M DNM.

Kaerlighed, 1948, Play
Karlek 1952 d: Gustaf Molander. 107M SWD. *Love*

Ordet, 1932, Play
Ordet 1943 d: Gustaf Molander. lps: Victor Sjostrom, Holger Lowenadler, Rune Lindstrom. 108M SWD. *The Word*
Ordet 1954 d: Carl T. Dreyer. lps: Henrik Malberg, Emil Hass Christensen, Birgitte Federspiel. 125M DNM. *The Word* prod/rel: Palladium

MUNKCASI, MIKLOS
Dogkeselyu, Novel
Dogkeselyu 1982 d: Ferenc Andras. lps: Gyorgy Cserhalmi, Hedi Temessy, Zita Perczel. 113M HNG. *The Vulture* prod/rel: Mafilm, Studio Dialog

MUNOZ MOLINA, ANTONIO
Beltenebros, Novel
Beltenebros 1991 d: Pilar Miro. lps: Terence Stamp, Patsy Kensit, Jose Luis Gomez. 114M SPN. *Prince of Shadows* (UKN); *Prince of Darkness* prod/rel: Metro, Iberoamerican

MUNOZ SECA, PEDRO
Los Cuatro Robinsones, Play
Cuatro Robinsones, Los 1926 d: Reinhardt Blothner. lps: Guillermo Munoz Custodio, Ricardo Vargas, Jose Arguelles. SPN. prod/rel: Omnia Film (Madrid)

MUNRO, ALICE (1931–, CND
How I Met My Husband, Short Story
Martha, Ruth and Edie 1988 d: Norma Bailey, Daniele J. SuissA. lps: Jennifer Dale, Margaret Langrick, Andrea Martin. 91M CND. *Sunrise*

MUNRO, C. E.
Adam and Eve, Play
Queen's Evidence 1919 d: James McKay. lps: Godfrey Tearle, Unity More, Janet Alexander. 5000f UKN. prod/rel: British & Colonial, Moss

MUNRO, GEORGE
Murder Gang, London 1935, Play
Sensation 1937 d: Brian Desmond Hurst. lps: John Lodge, Diana Churchill, Francis Lister. 67M UKN. prod/rel: British International Pictures, Associated British Picture Corporation

MUNRO, ROBERT (1902–1959), UKN, Hale, Sonnie
A French Mistress, London 1959, Play
French Mistress, A 1960 d: Roy Boulting. lps: Cecil Parker, James Robertson Justice, Ian Bannen. 98M UKN. prod/rel: British Lion, Charter

MUNSHI, K. M.
Prithvi Vallabh, 1920, Novel
Prithvi Vallabh 1943 d: Sohrab Modi. lps: Sohrab Modi, Durga Khote, Sankatha Prasad. 121M IND. prod/rel: Minerva Movietone

MUNSON, AUDREY
Short Story
Heedless Moths 1921 d: Robert Z. Leonard. lps: Holmes Herbert, Hedda Hopper, Ward Crane. 6r USA. prod/rel: Perry Plays, Equity Pictures

MUNTHE, AXEL (1857–1949), SWD
The Story of San Michele, Book
Axel Munthe, Der Arzt von San Michele 1962 d: Rudolf Jugert, Giorgio Capitani. lps: O. W. Fischer, Rosanna Schiaffino, Valentina Cortese. 134M GRM/ITL/FRN. *Donne Senza Paradiso* (ITL); *La Storia Di San Michele*; *Le Livre de San Michele* (FRN); *The Doctor of San Michele* prod/rel: C.C.C., Cine Italia

MUNZER, KARL
Der Ladenprinz, Novel
Ladenprinz, Der 1928 d: Erich Schonfelder. lps: Ralph Arthur Roberts, Betty Bird, Harry Halm. 2198m GRM. prod/rel: Deutsche Film-Union Ag

MURA
Novel
Cantate Con Me! 1940 d: Guido Brignone. lps: Giuseppe Lugo, Rubi Dalma, Laura Nucci. 83M ITL. *Lasciatemi Cantare!* prod/rel: S.a.F.a., E.N.I.C.

MURAIL, ELVIRE
Escalier C, Novel
Escalier C 1984 d: Jean-Charles TacchellA. lps: Robin Renucci, Jean-Pierre Bacri, Catherine Leprince. 102M FRN. *Staircase C* prod/rel: Films 7, Fr3 Films

MURAMATSU, SHOFU
Jokyo, Novel
Jokyo 1960 d: Kon Ichikawa, Kozaburo YoshimurA. lps: Fujiko Yamamoto, Eiji Funakoshi, Ayako Wakao. 103M JPN. *A Woman's Testament; Code of Women; Jokei; Women's Scroll* prod/rel: Daiei Motion Picture Co.

MURASAKI, SHIKIBU (c978–c1031), JPN
Genji Monogatari, c1001-1005, Novel
Genji Monogatari 1951 d: Kozaburo YoshimurA. lps: Kazuo Hasegawa, Michiyo Kogure, MacHiko Kyo. 124M JPN. *A Tale from Genji; A Tale of Genji*

MURATA, KIYOKO
Nabe-No-Kaka, Novel
Hachigatsu-No-Kyoshikyoku 1991 d: Akira KurosawA. lps: Sachiko Murase, Richard Gere, Hisashi IgawA. 98M JPN/FRN/UKN. *Rhapsodie En Aout* (FRN); *Rhapsody in August* prod/rel: Kurosawa Films, Shochiku Co.

MURCIELAGO VELAZQUEZ, JESUS
Novel
Tlayucan 1961 d: Luis AlcorizA. lps: Andres Soler, Julio Aldama, Jorge Martinez de Hoyos. 105M MXC. *The Pearl of Tlayucan* (USA); *The Pearls of St. Lucia* prod/rel: Producciones Matouk

MURDOCH, IRIS (1919–, IRL, Murdoch, Jean Iris
The Bell, Novel
Bell, The 1982 d: Barry Davis. lps: Ian Holm, Tessa Peake-Jones. MTV. 200M UKN. prod/rel: BBC

A Severed Head, 1961, Novel
Severed Head, A 1970 d: Dick Clement. lps: Lee Remick, Richard Attenborough, Ian Holm. 98M UKN. prod/rel: Columbia, Winkast

MURDOCK, FRANK
Davy Crockett, 1872, Play
Davy Crockett 1916 d: William D. Taylor. lps: Dustin Farnum, Winifred Kingston, Harry de Vere. 5r USA. prod/rel: Pallas Pictures, Paramount Pictures Corp.

MURER, FREDI M.
Hohenfeuer, Novel
Hohenfeuer 1985 d: Fredi M. Murer. lps: Thomas Nock, Johanna Lier, Dorothea Moritz. 118M SWT. *Alpine Fire* prod/rel: Srg, Wdr

MURFIN, JANE
Daybreak, New York 1917, Play
   Daybreak 1918 d: Albert Capellani. lps: Emily Stevens, Julien L'Estrange, Augustus Phillips. 5r USA. prod/rel: Metro Pictures Corp.©

Information Please, New York 1918, Play
   Temperamental Wife, A 1919 d: David Kirkland. lps: Constance Talmadge, Wyndham Standing, Ben Hendricks. 6221f USA. prod/rel: Constance Talmadge Film Co., John Emerson-Anita Loos Production

Lilac Time, New York 1917, Play
   Lilac Time 1928 d: George Fitzmaurice. lps: Colleen Moore, Gary Cooper, Burr McIntosh. 9108f USA. *Love Never Dies* (UKN) prod/rel: First National Pictures

Smilin' Through, New York 1919, Play
   Smilin' Through 1922 d: Sidney A. Franklin. lps: Norma Talmadge, Wyndham Standing, Harrison Ford. 8000f USA. *Smiling Through* prod/rel: Norma Talmadge Productions, Associated First National Pictures
   Smilin' Through 1932 d: Sidney A. Franklin. lps: Norma Shearer, Fredric March, Leslie Howard. 100M USA. prod/rel: Metro-Goldwyn-Mayer Corp., Metro-Goldwyn-Mayer Dist. Corp.©
   Smilin' Through 1941 d: Frank Borzage. lps: Jeanette MacDonald, Gene Raymond, Brian Aherne. 100M USA. prod/rel: MGM

MURGER, HENRI (1822–1861), FRN
La Vie de Boheme, Paris 1848, Play
   Boheme, La 1911. lps: Orlando Ricci. 361m ITL. prod/rel: Cines
   Boheme, La 1917 d: Amleto Palermi. lps: Leda Gys, Luigi Serventi, Bianca Lorenzoni. 1858m ITL. prod/rel: Cosmopoli Film
   Boheme, La 1926 d: King Vidor. lps: Lillian Gish, John Gilbert, Renee Adoree. 8781f USA. prod/rel: Metro-Goldwyn-Mayer Pictures
   Boheme, La 1987 d: Luigi Comencini. lps: Barbara Hendricks, Jose Carreras, Luca Canonici. 102M ITL/FRN.
   Francine 1911 d: Oreste Gherardini. lps: Anny Furlaj, Amleto Novelli. 257m ITL. prod/rel: Cines
   Mimi 1935 d: Paul L. Stein. lps: Douglas Fairbanks Jr., Gertrude Lawrence, Diana Napier. 94M UKN. *La Boheme* prod/rel: British International Pictures, Wardour
   Vida Bohemia, La 1938 d: Josef Berne. lps: Rosita Diaz, Gilbert Roland, Miguel Ligero. 77M USA. *Tragedias de la Vida Bohemia* prod/rel: Cantabria Films, Columbia Pictures Corp.
   Vie de Boheme, La 1916 d: Albert Capellani. lps: Alice Brady, Paul Capellani, Leslie Stowe. 5r USA. *La Boheme*; *Mimi*; *The Bohemians* prod/rel: Paragon Films, Inc., World Film Corp.©
   Vie de Boheme, La 1942 d: Marcel L'Herbier. lps: Maria Denis, Louis Jourdan, Andre Roussin. 120M FRN/ITL. *La Boheme* (ITL) prod/rel: Scalera Film, Invicta

MUROLO, ERNESTO
Addio Mia Bella Napoli!, 1910, Play
   Addio, Mia Bella Napoli! 1946 d: Mario Bonnard. lps: Vera Carmi, Fosco Giachetti, Clelia MataniA. F ITL. prod/rel: Ideal Film, Regionale

MURPHY, AUDIE (1924–1971), USA
To Hell and Back, Autobiography
   To Hell and Back 1955 d: Jesse Hibbs. lps: Audie Murphy, Marshall Thompson, Charles Drake. 106M USA. prod/rel: Universal-International

MURPHY, DENNIS
The Sergeant, New York 1958, Novel
   Sergeant, The 1968 d: John Flynn. lps: Rod Steiger, John Phillip Law, Ludmila Mikael. 108M USA. prod/rel: Warner Bros., Seven Arts, Inc.

MURPHY, G. C. T.
Little Meg and I, Poem
   Little Meg and I 1914. lps: J. Warren Kerrigan, Vera Sisson. SHT USA. prod/rel: Victor

MURPHY, JIM
I Will Kill You, Novel
   Straniero a Sacramento, Uno 1965 d: Sergio Bergonzelli. lps: Mickey Hargitay, Barbara Frey, Luciano Benetti. 102M ITL. *A Stranger in Sacramento* prod/rel: Film D'equipe

MURPHY, JOE
The Kerry Gow, Play
   Kerry Gow, The 1912 d: Sidney Olcott. lps: E. O'Sullivan, Jack J. Clark, Alice Hollister. 3000f USA. prod/rel: Kalem

MURPHY, RALPH
Sh! the Octopus, New York 1928, Play
   Sh! the Octopus 1937 d: William McGann. lps: Hugh Herbert, Allen Jenkins, Marcia Ralston. 60M USA. prod/rel: Warner Bros. Pictures©, First National Picture

MURPHY, RAY LIVINGSTON
Story
   Private's Affair, A 1959 d: Raoul Walsh. lps: Gary Crosby, Barry Coe, Sal Mineo. 93M USA. prod/rel: 20th Century-Fox

MURPHY, ROBERT
Run Cougar Run, Novel
   Run, Cougar, Run 1972 d: Jerome Courtland. lps: Stuart Whitman, Frank Aletter, Lonny Chapman. 75M USA. prod/rel: Walt Disney

MURPHY, WARREN
Novel
   Remo Williams: the Adventure Begins 1985 d: Guy Hamilton. lps: Fred Ward, Joel Grey, Wilford Brimley. 99M USA. *Remo Williams .Unarmed and Dangerous*; *Remo: Unarmed and Dangerous*; *Remo Williams: the Adventure Continues* prod/rel: Orion Pictures

MURPHY, WILL C.
Why Women Sin, New York 1903, Play
   Why Women Sin 1920 d: Burton L. King. lps: Anna Luther, Claire Whitney, E. J. Radcliffe. 6r USA. *Neglected Wives* prod/rel: Wistaria Productions, Inc., Burton King Production

MURRAY, DAVID CHRISTIE
Aunt Rachel, Novel
   Aunt Rachel 1920 d: Albert Ward. lps: Isobel Elsom, Haidee Wright, James Lindsay. 5500f UKN. prod/rel: G. B. Samuelson, Granger

In His Grip, Novel
   In His Grip 1921 d: Charles Calvert. lps: Cecil Morton York, David Hawthorne, Netta Westcott. 5945f UKN. prod/rel: Gaumont, British Screencraft

The Penniless Millionaire, Novel
   Penniless Millionaire, The 1921 d: Einar J. Bruun. lps: Stewart Rome, Fabienne Fabreges, Gregory Scott. 4900f UKN. prod/rel: Broadwest, Walturdaw

MURRAY, DOUGLAS
The Impostor, Play
   Impostor, The 1915 d: Albert Capellani. lps: Jose Collins, Alec B. Francis, Leslie Stowe. 5r USA. *The Impostors* prod/rel: William A. Brady Picture Plays, Inc., World Film Corp.©

The Man from Toronto, London 1918, Play
   Man from Toronto, The 1933 d: Sinclair Hill. lps: Jessie Matthews, Ian Hunter, Fred Kerr. 77M UKN. prod/rel: Gainsborough, Ideal

Perkins, New York 1918, Play
   Lessons in Love 1921 d: Chet Withey. lps: Constance Talmadge, Flora Finch, James Harrison. 5923f USA. prod/rel: Constance Talmadge Productions, Associated First National Pictures

MURRAY, JACK
Otages, Novel
   Marche Ou Creve 1960 d: Georges Lautner. lps: Jacques Chabassol, Juliette Mayniel, Henri Cogan. 100M FRN/BLG. prod/rel: Inter Production, Compagnie Lyonnaise De Cinema

MURRAY, JOHN
Room Service, Play
   Step Lively 1944 d: Tim Whelan. lps: Frank Sinatra, George Murphy, Adolphe Menjou. 88M USA. prod/rel: RKO

MURRAY, MAX
The Neat Little Corpse, Novel
   Jamaica Run 1953 d: Lewis R. Foster. lps: Ray Milland, Arlene Dahl, Wendell Corey. 92M USA. *Jamaica* prod/rel: Paramount, Pine-Thomas

MURRAY, WILLIAM
The Sweet Ride, New York 1967, Novel
   Sweet Ride, The 1968 d: Harvey Hart. lps: Jacqueline Bisset, Michael Sarrazin, Warren Stevens. 110M USA. prod/rel: 20th Century-Fox Film Corporation

MUS, ANTONI
La Senora, Novel
   Senora, La 1987 d: Jordi CadenA. lps: Silvia Tortosa, Hermann Bonnin, Luis Merlo. 94M SPN. *The Lady*; *La Senyora* prod/rel: Virginia

MUSIL, ROBERT (1880–1942), AUS
Die Schwarmer, 1921, Play
   Schwarmer, Die 1984 d: Hans Neuenfels. lps: Hermann Treusch, Elisabeth Trissenaar, Sabine Sinjen. 116M GRM. prod/rel: Regina Ziegler Filmprod., Wdr

Die Verwirrungen Des Zoglings Torless, Berlin 1906, Novel
   Junge Torless, Der 1966 d: Volker Schlondorff. lps: Mathieu Carriere, Bernd Tischer, Marian Seidowsky. 87M GRM/FRN. *Les Desarrois de l'Eleve Torless* (FRN); *Young Torless* (USA) prod/rel: Franz Seitz Filmproduktion, Nouvelles Editions De Films

MUSMANNO, JUDGE M. A.
Jan Volkanik, Short Story
   Black Fury 1935 d: Michael Curtiz. lps: Paul Muni, Karen Morley, William Gargan. 95M USA. *Black Hell* prod/rel: First National Productions Corp.

MUSMANO, M. A.
Ten Days to Die, Novel
   Letzte Akt, Der 1955 d: G. W. Pabst. lps: Albin Skoda, Oskar Werner, Lotte Tobisch. 113M AUS. *The Last Ten Days* (USA); *The Last Ten Days of Hitler*; *Ten Days to Die*; *The Last Act*; *The Last Ten Days of Adolf Hitler* prod/rel: Cosmopol

MUSSOLINI, BENITO
Villafranca, Play
   Villafranca 1933 d: Giovacchino Forzano. lps: Corrado Racca, Annibale Betrone, Giulio Donadio. 105M ITL. prod/rel: Forzano Film, Fono Roma

MUTIS, ALVARO (1923–, CLM
Ilona Llega Con la Lluva, Novel
   Ilona Llega Con la Lluva 1996 d: Sergio CabrerA. lps: Margarita Rosa de Francisco, Humberto Dorado, Imanol Arias. 135M ITL/SPN. *Ilona Comes With the Rain*; *Llona Llega Con la Lluvia* prod/rel: Fotoemme, Emme

MUZZY, BERTHA SINCLAIR
The Range Dwellers, New York 1906, Novel
   Taming of the West, The 1925 d: Arthur Rosson. lps: Hoot Gibson, Marceline Day, Morgan Brown. 5304f USA. prod/rel: Universal Pictures

MYCHO, ANDRE
Une Vie de Chien, Novel
   Vie de Chien, Une 1941 d: Maurice Cammage. lps: Fernandel, Josseline Gael, Therese Dorny. 84M FRN. *Le Mari Quadrupede*; *Pension de Famille*; *Medor* prod/rel: Optimax Films

MYERS, ELIZABETH
Mrs. Christopher, Novel
   Blackmailed 1951 d: Marc Allegret. lps: Mai Zetterling, Dirk Bogarde, Fay Compton. 85M UKN. *The Blackmailer*; *Mrs. Christopher* prod/rel: General Film Distributors, Harold Huth Films

MYGATT, GERALD
Two Can Play, 1922, Short Story
   Two Can Play 1926 d: Nat Ross. lps: George Fawcett, Allan Forrest, Clara Bow. 5465f USA. *The Love Test* (UKN) prod/rel: Encore Pictures, Associated Exhibitors

MYKLE, AGNAR
Story
   Sangen Om Den Rode Rubin 1970 d: Annelise Meineche. lps: Ole Soltoft, Ghita Norby, Lotte Horne. 106M DNM. *The Song of the Red Ruby* (UKN); *Den Rode Rubin* prod/rel: Palladium

MYLANDER, MAUREEN
Gesundheit: Good Health Is a Laughing Matter, 1993, Book
   Patch Adams 1998 d: Tom Shadyac. lps: Robin Williams, Daniel London, Monica Potter. 115M USA. prod/rel: Universal City Studios©, Blue Wolf

MYRER, ANTON (1922–, USA
The Big War, Novel
   In Love and War 1958 d: Philip Dunne. lps: Robert Wagner, Dana Wynter, Jeffrey Hunter. 111M USA. prod/rel: 20th Century-Fox, Jerry Wald

Once an Eagle, Novel
   Once an Eagle 1976 d: E. W. Swackhamer, Richard Michaels. lps: Sam Elliott, Cliff Potts, Darleen Carr. MTV. 450M USA. prod/rel: Universal

MYRIVILIS, STRATIS (1882–, GRC
Our Lady the Siren, Book
   Lydia 1964 d: Diederik d'Ailly. lps: Gordon Pinsent, Anna Hagan, Benentino CostA. 85M CND. prod/rel: Libra Film Productions

MYTON, FRED KENNEDY
Angel-Face Molly, Story
   Heart Bandit, The 1924 d: Oscar Apfel. lps: Viola Dana, Milton Sills, Gertrude Claire. 4900f USA. prod/rel: Metro Pictures

N

NABL, FRANZ
Die Augen, Short Story
  Verzauberte Tag, Der 1944 d: Peter Pewas. lps: Winnie Markus, Hans Stuwe, Ernst Waldow. 99M GRM. prod/rel: Terra, Super

Der Fund, Novel
  Am Abend Nach Der Oper 1944 d: Arthur M. Rabenalt. lps: Gusti Huber, Siegfried Breuer, Erich Ponto. 96M GRM. prod/rel: Terra, Kristall

Das Grab Des Lebendigen, 1917, Novel
  Ortliebschen Frauen, Die 1980 d: Luc Bondy. lps: Libgart Schwarz, Edith Heerdegen, Elisabeth Stepanek. TVM. 113M GRM. *The Ortlieb Women; Josephine; The Ortlieb Family Women* prod/rel: Solaris, von Vietinghoff

NABOKOV, VLADIMIR (1899–1977), RSS
Kamera Obscura, 1932, Novel
  Laughter in the Dark 1969 d: Tony Richardson. lps: Nicol Williamson, Anna Karina, Jean-Claude Drouot. 104M UKN/FRN/ITL. *Chambre Obscure, La* (FRN) prod/rel: Woodfall Films, Winkast Film Productions

Korol, Dama, Valet, 1928, Novel
  Herzbube 1972 d: Jerzy Skolimowski. lps: David Niven, John Moulder-Brown, Gina Lollobrigida. 92M GRM/USA. *King, Queen, Knave* (USA); *Sex, Love, Murder* prod/rel: Maran, Wolper

Lolita, Paris 1955, Novel
  Lolita 1962 d: Stanley Kubrick. lps: James Mason, Shelley Winters, Sue Lyon. 153M UKN/USA. prod/rel: Seven Arts Productions, a.A. Productions
  Lolita 1997 d: Adrian Lyne. lps: Jeremy Irons, Melanie Griffith, Frank Langella. 137M USA/FRN. prod/rel: Pathe, Alphatex, S.a.©

Maschenka, Novel
  Maschenka 1987 d: John Goldschmidt. lps: Cary Elwes, Irina Brook, Freddie Jones. TVM. 103M UKN/GRM/FNL. prod/rel: Clasart, Jorn Donner

Otchayanie, 1937, Novel
  Eine Reise in Lichts 1978 d: R. W. Fassbinder. lps: Dirk Bogarde, Andrea Ferreol, Volker Spengler. 119M GRM. *Despair* (UKN) prod/rel: Nf Geria II, W.D.R.

NADAUD, MARCEL
Chignole, Novel
  Chignole 1917 d: Rene Plaissetty. lps: Kitty Hott, Urban, Armand Numes. 1800m FRN. *Grand Envolee, La* prod/rel: Scagl

Chignole
  Grande Envolee, La 1927 d: Rene Plaissetty. lps: Rosine Maurel, Urban, Andrew Brunelle. 2300m FRN.

Mimi Trottin, Novel
  Mimi-Trottin 1921 d: Henri Andreani. lps: Louise Lagrange, Henri Rollan, Lea Piron. 1965m FRN. prod/rel: Scagl

Ziska, la Danseuse Espionne, Novel
  Ziska, la Danseuse Espionne 1922 d: Henri Andreani. lps: Gaston Jacquet, Lucien Dalsace, Blanche Derval. 4500m FRN. prod/rel: Silex-Film

NADDLETON JR., THOMAS D.
Army Brat, Novel
  Little Mr. Jim 1946 d: Fred Zinnemann. lps: Butch Jenkins, James Craig, Frances Gifford. 92M USA. *Army Brat* prod/rel: MGM

NADERER, HANS
Hinter Klostermauern, Play
  Hinter Klostermauern 1952 d: Harald Reinl. lps: Olga Tschechowa, Frits Van Dongen, Katharina Mayberg. 95M GRM. *Behind Monastery Walls* prod/rel: Delta, Venus

Der Lachende Dritte, Play
  Lachende Dritte, Der 1936 d: Georg Zoch. lps: Lucie Englisch, Josef Eichheim, Sepp Rist. 91M GRM. prod/rel: ABC-Film

NAGAHARA, HIDEKAZU
Sogeki, Play
  Sogeki 1968 d: Hiromichi Horikawa. lps: Yuzo Kayama, Ruriko Asaoka, Masayuki Mori. 87M JPN. *Sun Above, Death Below* (USA) prod/rel: Toho Co.

NAGAI, KAFU (1879–1959), JPN
Bokuto Kidan, Tokyo 1952, Novel
  Bokuto Kidan 1960 d: Shiro Toyoda. lps: Hiroshi Akutagawa, Fujiko Yamamoto, Masao Oda. 150M JPN. *Twilight Story, The* (USA); *A Strange Story of East of the River Sumida* prod/rel: Tokyo Eiga Co.

Odoriko, 1944, Novel
  Odoriko 1957 d: Hiroshi Shimizu. lps: MaChiko Kyo. 96M JPN. *Dancing Girl; Chorus Girl*

Ratai, Tokyo 1954, Novel
  Ratai 1962 d: Masashige Narusawa. lps: Michiko Saga, Ichiro Sugai, Kumeko Urabe. 98M JPN. *Body, The* (USA) prod/rel: Shochiku Co.

NAGATA, HIDEO
Kurumen Yukinu, Play
  Joyu Sumako No Koi 1947 d: Kenji Mizoguchi. lps: Kinuyo Tanaka, So Yamamura, Kikue Mori. 96M JPN. *Loves of Sumako the Actress, The* (USA); *The Loves of Actress Sumako; The Love of Sumako the Actress* prod/rel: Shochiku Co.

NAGATSUKA, TAKASHI
Tsuchi, 1910, Novel
  Tsuchi 1939 d: Tomu Uchida. lps: Isamu Kogugi, Akiko Kazami, Donguriboya. 92M JPN. *Earth, The* prod/rel: Nikkatsu Corp.

NAGEL, JAMES
Hemingway in Love and War, Book
  In Love and War 1996 d: Richard Attenborough. lps: Sandra Bullock, Chris O'Donnell, MacKenzie Astin. 115M USA. prod/rel: New Line, Dimitri Villar Productions

NAGLE, WILLIAM
The Odd Angry Shot, Novel
  Odd Angry Shot, The 1979 d: Tom Jeffrey. lps: Graham Kennedy, John Hargreaves, John Jarratt. 92M ASL. prod/rel: Samson Productions Pty Ltd.©, Guo

NAGY, LAJOS
Razzia, 1929, Short Story
  Razzia 1958 d: Laszlo Nadasy. lps: Adam Szirtes, Janos Gorbe, Elma Bull A. 100M HNG. *Raid*

NAJAC
Bebe, Play
  Bebe 1913 d: Georges Monca. 585m FRN. prod/rel: Pathe Freres

NAKAGAMI, KENJI
Jukyusai No Chizu, Novel
  Jukyusai No Chizu 1979 d: Mitsuo Yanagimachi. lps: Yuji Honma, Keizo Kanie, Hideko Okiyama. 105M JPN. *A Map for 19 Years Old; A Nineteen Year Old's Plan; 19-Sai No Chizu; Jukusai No Chizu* prod/rel: Gunro Prod.

NAKAHARA, FUMIO
Ikinai, Novel
  Ikinai 1998 d: Hiroshi Shimizu. lps: Dankan, Nanako Okouchi, Toshinori Omi. 100M JPN. prod/rel: Office Kitano, Bandai Visual

NAKAJIMA, GENTARO
Uchujin Tokyo Ni Arawaru, Novel
  Uchujin Tokyo Ni Arawaru 1956 d: Koji Shima. lps: Toyomi Karita, Keizo Kawasaki, Isao Yamagata. 87M JPN. *The Cosmic Man Appears in Tokyo; Mysterious Satellite* (USA); *Warning from Space; Unknown Satellite Over Tokyo; Space Men Appear in Tokyo* prod/rel: Daiei Motion Picture Co.

NAKAMURA, ITOKO
Story
  Ai No Borei 1977 d: Nagisa Oshima. lps: Katsuko Yoshiyuki, Tatsuya Fuji, Takahiro Tamur A. 106M JPN/FRN. *Empire Des Passions, L'* (FRN); *Empire of Passion* (UKN); *Phantom Love* (USA); *The Phantom of Love* prod/rel: Oshima Productions, Argos Films, S.a.

NAKANO, MINORU
Tsuma No Bara No Yoni, Play
  Tsuma Yo Bara No Yoni 1935 d: Mikio Naruse. lps: Sachiko Chiba, Yuriko Hanabusa, Tomoko Ito. 74M JPN. *Wife Be Like a Rose; Futarizuma; The Quest; Two Wives; Kimiko* prod/rel: P.C.L.

NAKAZATO, KAIZAN
Daibosatsu Toge, Tokyo 1940, Short Story
  Daibosatsu Toge 1966 d: Kihachi Okamoto. lps: Tatsuya Nakadai, Toshiro Mifune, Yuzo Kayam A. 122M JPN. *The Sword of Doom* (USA) prod/rel: Takarazuka Film Co., Toho Co.

NALKOWSKA, ZOFIA
Granica, 1936, Novel
  Granica 1938 d: Joseph Leytes. 87M PLN.
  Granica 1977 d: Jan Rybkowski. lps: Krystyna Janda, Andrzej Seweryn. 93M PLN. *The Limit; The Boundary*

Romans Teresy Hennert, 1927, Novel
  Romans Teresy Hennert 1978 d: Ignacy Gogolewski. lps: Barbara Brylska, Jozef Duriasz. 86M PLN. *The Romance of Teresa Hennert; Teresa Hennert's Romance; Teresa Hennert's Love Affair*

NAMIKI, GOHEI III
Kanjincho, 1840, Play
  Tora No Oo Fuma Otokotachi 1945 d: Akira Kurosawa. lps: Denjiro Okichi, Susumu Fujita, Kenichi Enomoto. 60M JPN. *The Men Who Tread on the Tiger's Tail; Walkers on the Tiger's Tail; They Who Step on the Tiger's Tail; Walk on Tigers' Tails* prod/rel: Toho Co.

NAMIKI, SENRYU
Kanadehon Chushingura, 1748, Play
  Chushingura 1962 d: Hiroshi Inagaki. lps: Koshiro Matsumoto, Yuzo Kayama, Chusha Ichikawa. 204M JPN. *The Loyal Forty-Seven Ronin; The Faithful 47; 47 the Ronin; 47 Samurai* prod/rel: Toho Co.

NAMORA, FERNANDO
Domingo a Tarde, 1961, Novel
  Domingo a Tarde 1965 d: Antonio de Macedo. lps: Rui de Carvalho, Isabel Ruth, Isabel de Castro. 90M PRT. *Sunday in the Afternoon; Sunday Afternoon; A Summer Afternoon*

A Noite E a Madrugada, 1950, Novel
  Noite E a Madrugada, A 1983 d: Artur Ramos. lps: Antonio Assuncao, Helena Felix, Jose Vian A. 108M PRT.

Retalhos Da Vida de Um Medico, 1949, Short Story
  Retalhos Da Vida de Um Medico 1962 d: Jorge Brum Do Canto. lps: Jorge de Sousa Costa, Irene Cruz, Costa Ferreir A. 93M PRT. *Fragments from the Life of a Physician; The Country Doctor*

NANCE, JOHN J.
Pandora's Clock, Novel
  Pandora's Clock 1996 d: Eric Laneuville. lps: Richard Dean Anderson, Daphne Zuniga, Jane Leeves. TVM. 240M USA. *Doomsday Virus* prod/rel: Citadel Entertainment

NANCEY, NICOLAS
L'heritier du Bal Tabarin, Play
  Heritier du Bal Tabarin, L' 1933 d: Jean Kemm. lps: Frederic Duvalles, Charlotte Lyses, Germaine Michel. 85M FRN. prod/rel: Alex Nalpas

Theodore Et Cie, 1909, Play
  Mare Di Guai, Un 1940 d: Carlo Ludovico Bragaglia. lps: Umberto Melnati, Junie Astor, Luigi Almirante. 76M ITL. prod/rel: Atlas Film, I.C.I.
  Teodoro E Socio 1925 d: Mario Bonnard. lps: Mario Bonnard, Marcel Levesque, Alexiane. 2076m ITL. prod/rel: Bonnard
  Theodore Et Cie 1933 d: Piere Colombier. lps: Raimu, Albert Prejean, Alice Field. 97M FRN. prod/rel: Pathe-Natan

Le Truc du Bresilien, Play
  Truc du Bresilien, Le 1932 d: Alberto Cavalcanti. lps: Robert Arnoux, Colette Darfeuil, Yvonne Garat. 87M FRN. prod/rel: Films Tenax

Le Zebre, Play
  Glad Eye, The 1920 d: Kenelm Foss. lps: James Reardon, Dorothy Minto, Hayford Hobbs. 6000f UKN. prod/rel: Reardon British Films, IFT

Zebre, Le, Play
  Glad Eye, The 1927 d: Maurice Elvey, Victor Saville. lps: Estelle Brody, Hal Sherman, John Stuart. 7700f UKN. prod/rel: Gaumont

NANJO, NORIO
Shikonmado, Story
  Dai Tatsumaki 1964 d: Hiroshi Inagaki. lps: Toshiro Mifune, Somegoro Ichikawa, Yuriko Hoshi. 107M JPN. *Whirlwind* prod/rel: Toho Co, Takarazuka Eiga

NANKIVEL, FRED
Uncle Mun and the Minister, Story
  Uncle Mun and the Minister 1912. lps: Edna Flugrath, Harry Beaumont, William Wadsworth. 1000f USA. prod/rel: Edison

NAPOLITANO, G. G.
La Mariposa, Short Story
  Tam Tam Mayumbe 1955 d: Gian Gaspare Napolitano, Folco Quilici. lps: Pedro Armendariz, Charles Vanel, Kerim A. 95M ITL/FRN. *Missionnaire, Le* (FRN); *Native Drums* (USA); *Tom Toms of Mayumba* (UKN) prod/rel: Documento Film (Roma), Franco London Film (Paris)

NARAYAN, R. K. (1906–, IND, Narayan, Rasipuram Krishnaswami
The Financial Expert, 1952, Novel
  Banker Margayya 1983 d: T. S. Nagabharana. lps: Lokesh, Jayanthi, Master Manjunath. 145M IND. *Margayya the Banker* prod/rel: Komal Prod.

The Guide, New York 1957, Novel
  Guide, The 1965 d: Tad Danielewski, Vijay Anand. lps: Dev Anand, Waheeda Rehman, Kishore Sahu. 179M USA/IND. *Survival* prod/rel: Stratton International, Navketan

Mr. Sampat, 1949, Novel
  Mr. Sampat 1952 d: S. S. Vasan. lps: Motilal, Padmini, Kanhaiyalal. 165M IND. prod/rel: Gemini

Swamy and Friends, 1935, Novel
  Swami 1987 d: Shankar Nag. lps: Manjunath, Raghuram, Rohit Srinath. SRL. IND. *Swamy; Malgudi Days*

NARCEJAC, THOMAS
A Coeur Perdu, Paris 1959, Novel
Meurtre En 45 Tours 1960 d: Etienne Perier. lps: Danielle Darrieux, Michel Auclair, Jean Servais. 110M FRN. *Murder at 45 R.P.M.* prod/rel: Cite Films

Celle Qui N'etait Plus, Novel
Diaboliques, Les 1954 d: Henri-Georges Clouzot. lps: Simone Signoret, Vera Clouzot, Paul Meurisse. 110M FRN. *The Fiends* (UKN); *Diabolique* (USA) prod/rel: Filmsonor
Reflections of Murder 1974 d: John Badham. lps: Tuesday Weld, Sam Waterston, Joan Hackett. TVM. 100M USA. prod/rel: ABC Circle Films
Diabolique 1996 d: Jeremiah Chechik. lps: Sharon Stone, Isabelle Adjani, Chazz Palminteri. 107M USA. prod/rel: Morgan Creek Productions

D'entre Les Morts, 1954, Novel
Vertigo 1958 d: Alfred Hitchcock. lps: James Stewart, Kim Novak, Barbara Bel Geddes. 128M USA. prod/rel: Paramount, Alfred Hitchcock Prods.

Les Louves, Novel
Louves, Les 1956 d: Luis Saslavsky. lps: Francois Perier, Micheline Presle, Jeanne Moreau. 101M FRN. *She-Wolves, The* (UKN); *Demoniaque*; *Demoniac*; *Las Lobas* prod/rel: Zodiaque Films
Letters to an Unknown Lover 1985 d: Peter Duffell. lps: Cherie Lunghi, Yves Beneyton, Ralph Bates. TVM. 100M UKN/FRN. *Louves, Les* (FRN) prod/rel: Portman Prods., Channel Four

Les Magiciennes, Novel
Magiciennes, Les 1960 d: Serge Friedman. lps: Jacques Riberolles, Alice Kessler, Ellen Kessler. 97M FRN. *Double Deception* (USA); *Frantic*; *The Magicians* prod/rel: Speva Films, Intertele Films

Maldonne, Novel
Maldonne 1968 d: Sergio Gobbi. lps: Pierre Vaneck, Elsa Martinelli, Robert Hossein. 98M ITL/FRN. prod/rel: Paris Cannes Production, Mega Films

Malefices, Paris 1961, Novel
Malefices 1961 d: Henri Decoin. lps: Juliette Greco, Jean-Marc Bory, Liselotte Pulver. 104M FRN. *Where the Truth Lies* (USA); *Evil Spell*; *Sorcery*; *Evil Spirits* prod/rel: Marianne Productions, S.N.E.G.
Malefices 1990 d: Carlo RolA. lps: Pierre Malet, Iris Berben, Susanne Lothar. TVM. 90M FRN.

Terminus, Novel
Ruckfahrt in Den Tod 199- d: Hans-Jurgen Togel. lps: Peter Bongartz, Wolfgang Wahl, Iris Berben. TVM. 90M GRM.

Les Victimes, Novel
Victimes, Les 1996 d: Patrick Grandperret. lps: Vincent Lindon, Jacques Dutronc, Karin Viard. 95M FRN. *Victims* prod/rel: Gaumont International

Les Visages de l'Ombre, Paris 1953, Novel
Faces in the Dark 1960 d: David Eady. lps: John Gregson, Mai Zetterling, John Ireland. 85M UKN. prod/rel: Pennington-Eady Productions, Rank Film Distributors

NARIZZANO, SILVIO (1927-, CND
The Butler's Night Off, Story
Butler's Night Off, The 1950 d: Roger Racine. lps: Peter Sturgess, Eric Workman, Paul Colbert. 74M CND. prod/rel: Mount-Royal Films

NASH, ALDEN
And Let Who Will Be Clever, Hollywood 1934, Play
We're Rich Again 1934 d: William A. Seiter. lps: Edna May Oliver, Billie Burke, Marian Nixon. 75M USA. *Arabella* prod/rel: RKO Radio Pictures©

NASH, N. RICHARD (1913-, USA, Nusbaum, Nathan Richard
The Rainmaker, 1955, Television Play
Rainmaker, The 1956 d: Joseph Anthony. lps: Burt Lancaster, Katharine Hepburn, Wendell Corey. 121M USA. prod/rel: Paramount, Wallis-Hazen

NASH, OGDEN (1902-1971), USA, Nash, Ogden Frederick
One Touch of Venus, 1944, Musical Play
One Touch of Venus 1948 d: William A. Seiter. lps: Robert Walker, Ava Gardner, Dick Haymes. 81M USA. prod/rel: Universal

NASON, LEONARD
Rodney, 1933, Short Story
Keep 'Em Rolling 1934 d: George Archainbaud. lps: Walter Huston, Frances Dee, Minna Gombell. 72M USA. *Rodney* prod/rel: RKO Radio Pictures©

NASSAR, RADUAN
Um Copo de Colera, Book
Copo de Colera, Um 1999 d: Aluizio Abranches. lps: Alexandre Borges, Julia Lemmertz, Linneu Dias. 72M BRZ. *A Fit of Rage* prod/rel: Ravina Filmes, Ravina Producoes & Communicacoes

NATANSON, JACQUES
Coeur Bube, Play
Anschluss Um Mitternacht 1929 d: Mario Bonnard. lps: Marcella Albani, Ralph Arthur Roberts, Curt Bois. 2260m GRM. prod/rel: Maxim-Film

Le Greluchon Delicat, Play
Greluchon Delicat, Le 1934 d: Jean Choux. lps: Harry Baur, Alice Cocea, Paul Bernard. 90M FRN. *Le Valet de Coeur* prod/rel: Les Films R.P.

NATHAN, ROBERT (1894-1985), USA
Poems
White Cliffs of Dover, The 1944 d: Clarence Brown. lps: Irene Dunne, Alan Marshall, Roddy McDowall. 126M USA. prod/rel: MGM

The Bishop's Wife, 1928, Novel
Bishop's Wife, The 1947 d: Henry Koster. lps: David Niven, Cary Grant, Loretta Young. 110M USA. *Cary and the Bishop's Wife* prod/rel: RKO Radio

The Enchanted Voyage, 1936, Novel
Wake Up and Dream 1946 d: Lloyd Bacon. lps: John Payne, June Haver, Charlotte Greenwood. 93M USA. *Enchanted Voyage*; *Give Me the Simple Life* prod/rel: 20th Century-Fox

One More Spring, New York 1933, Novel
One More Spring 1935 d: Henry King. lps: Janet Gaynor, Warner Baxter, Walter Woolf King. 87M USA. prod/rel: Fox Film Corp.©

Portrait of Jennie, 1940, Novel
Portrait of Jennie 1948 d: William Dieterle. lps: Jennifer Jones, Joseph Cotten, Ethel Barrymore. 86M USA. *Jennie* (UKN); *Tidal Wave* prod/rel: Selznick Releasing

NATHAN, TOBIE
Sarako Bo, Novel
Saraka Bo 1977 d: Denis Amar. lps: Richard Bohringer, Yvan Attal, Sotigui Kouyate. 89M FRN. prod/rel: Aliceleo, M6 Films

NATHANSON, E. M.
The Dirty Dozen, New York 1965, Novel
Dirty Dozen, The 1967 d: Robert Aldrich. lps: Lee Marvin, Ernest Borgnine, Charles Bronson. 149M UKN/USA. prod/rel: M.K.H. Productions, Metro-Goldwyn-Mayer

NATHENSEN, HENRI
Mendel Philipsen and Son, Novel
Sofie 1992 d: Liv Ullmann. lps: Karen-Lise Mynster, Ghita Norby, Erland Josephson. 152M DNM/NRW/SWD. prod/rel: Nordisk, Svensk Filmindustri

NATOLI, LUIGI
I Beati Paoli, Novel
Cavalieri Dalle Maschera Nera, I 1948 d: Pino Mercanti. lps: Otello Toso, Lea Padovani, Mario Ferrari. 115M ITL. *I Beati Paoli* prod/rel: Org. Filmistica Siciliana

NATSUME, SOSEKI (1867-1916), JPN
Gubijinso, 1908, Novel
Gubijinso 1935 d: Kenji Mizoguchi. lps: Daijiro Natsukawa, Ichiro Tsukida, Chikyoku OkurA. 72M JPN. *The Field Poppy* (UKN); *Poppies* (USA); *Poppy*; *Red Poppy* prod/rel: Daiichi Film Co.

Kokoro, 1914, Novel
Kokoro 1954 d: Kon IchikawA. lps: Masayuki Mori, Michiyo Aratama, Tatsuya Mihashi. 120M JPN. *The Heart* prod/rel: Nikkatsu Corp.

Wagahai Wa Neko de Aru, 1905, Novel
Wagahai Wa Neko de Aru 1936 d: Kajiro Yamamoto. 116M JPN. *I Am a Cat*

Wagahai Wa Neko de Aru, Novel
Wagahai Wa Neko Dearu 1974 d: Kon IchikawA. lps: Tatsuya Nakadai, Kuriko Namino, Juzo Itami. 116M JPN. *I Am a Cat* prod/rel: Geiensha Co.

NATTEFORD, J. F.
The Bar-T Mystery, Story
That Wild West 1924 d: Alvin J. Neitz. lps: William Fairbanks, Dorothy Revier, Jack Richardson. 5r USA. prod/rel: Phil Goldstone Productions

NAUGHTON, BILL
Alfie, London 1963, Play
Alfie 1966 d: Lewis Gilbert. lps: Michael Caine, Shelley Winters, Millicent Martin. 114M UKN. prod/rel: Paramount, Sheldrake Films

All in Good Time, London 1963, Play
Family Way, The 1966 d: Roy Boulting. lps: Hayley Mills, John Mills, Hywel Bennett. 114M UKN. *All in Good Time* prod/rel: Jambox, British Lion

Spring and Port Wine, London 1964, Play
Spring and Port Wine 1970 d: Peter Hammond. lps: James Mason, Susan George, Diana Coupland. 101M UKN. prod/rel: Memorial Enterprises, Warner-Pathe

NAUGHTON, EDMUND
McCabe, Novel
McCabe and Mrs. Miller 1971 d: Robert Altman. lps: Warren Beatty, Julie Christie, Rene Auberjonois. 121M USA. *The Presbyterian Church Wager, The* prod/rel: David Foster, Mitchell Brower

NAVARRO, LEANDRO
Los Hijos de la Noche, Play
Figli Della Notte, I 1939 d: Benito Perojo, Aldo Vergano. lps: Estrellita Castro, Miguel Ligero, Julio PenA. 85M ITL/SPN. *Hijos de la Noche, Los* (SPN); *Children of the Night* prod/rel: Imperator, Ulargui

NAVARRO VILLOSLADA, FRANCISCO
Amaya: O, Los Vascos En El Siglo VIIi, 1879, Novel
Amaya 1952 d: Luis MarquinA. lps: Julio Pena, Susana Canales, Jose Bodalo. 110M SPN.

NAYLOR, GLORIA (1950-, USA
The Women of Brewster Place, Book
Women of Brewster Place, The 1989 d: Donna Deitch. lps: Oprah Winfrey, Mary Alice, Olivia Cole. TVM. 200M USA.

NAYLOR, PHYLLIS REYNOLDS
Shiloh, Novel
Shiloh 1996 d: Dale Rosenbloom. lps: Michael Moriarty, Rod Steiger, Blake Heron. 87M USA. prod/rel: Carl Borack, Utopia Pictures
Shiloh 2: Shiloh Season 1999 d: Sandy Tung. lps: Michael Moriarty, Scott Wilson, Zachary Browne. 96M USA. prod/rel: Dale Rosenbloom, Carl Borack

NDEBELE, NJABULO S.
Fools, Novel
Fools 1997 d: Ramadan Suleman. lps: Patrick Shai, Dambisa Kente, Hlomla DandalA. 91M FRN/SAF/MZM. prod/rel: Jba Prod. / Peripherie Prod. (France), Natives at Large (South Africa)

NEAGU, FANUS
Dincolo de Nisipuri, 1962, Short Story
Dincolo de Nisipuri 1973 d: Radu GabreA. lps: Dan Nutu, George Constantin, Mircea Albulescu. 104M RMN. *Beyond the Sands*

Lisca, 1960, Short Story
Lisca 1984 d: Ioan Carmazan. 99M RMN.

NEAL
Theodore Est Fatigue, Play
Service de Nuit 1931 d: Henri Fescourt. lps: Marcel Barencey, Mylo d'Arcylle, Robert Darthez. 75M FRN. *Theodore Est Fatigue*; *Les Nuits de Papa*; *Pour Service de Nuit* prod/rel: Etablissements Jacques Haik, Minerva

NEAL, MAX
Der Hochtourist, Play
Hochtourist, Der 1931 d: Alfred Zeisler. lps: Otto Wallburg, Maria Solveg, Erika Glassner. 86M GRM. prod/rel: UFA, Sudwest
Hochtourist, Der 1942 d: Adolf Schlissleder. lps: Joe Stockel, Trude Hesterberg, Alice Treff. 84M GRM. prod/rel: Bavaria

Der Hochtourist,, Play
Hochtourist, Der 1961 d: Ulrich Erfurth. lps: Willy Millowitsch, Claude Farell, Helen VitA. 88M GRM. *High Season Tourist* prod/rel: U.F.H.

Der Hunderter Im Westentascher, Play
Donner, Blitz Und Sonnenschein 1936 d: Erich Engels. lps: Karl Valentin, Liesl Karlstadt, Ilse Petri. 92M GRM. prod/rel: N.F.K., Regina

Der Mude Theodor, Novel
Mude Theodor, Der 1936 d: Veit Harlan. lps: Weiss Ferdl, Erika Glassner, Gertrud Boll. 82M GRM. prod/rel: Majestic, Syndikat-Film

Der Scheinheilige Florian, Play
Scheinheilige Florian, Der 1941 d: Joe Stockel. lps: Joe Stockel, Erna Fentsch, Josef Eichheim. 93M GRM. prod/rel: Bavaria, Nordwest

Das Sundige Dorf, Play
Sundige Dorf, Das 1940 d: Joe Stockel. lps: Joe Stockel, Elise Aulinger, Thomas Reyer. 94M GRM. prod/rel: Bavaria
Sundige Dorf, Das 1954 d: Ferdinand Dorfler. lps: Gunther Luders, Beppo Brehm, Karl Peukert. 89M GRM. *Sinful Village* prod/rel: Dorfler, D.F.H.
Sundige Dorf, Das 1966 d: Werner Jacobs. lps: Hans-Jurgen Baumler, Hannelore Auer, Michl Lang. 94M GRM. *Sinful Village* prod/rel: Music House, Nora

NEALE, RALPH
Wayward Youth, Play
Way of Youth, The 1934 d: Norman Walker. lps: Aileen Marson, Irene Vanbrugh, Sebastian Shaw. 65M UKN. prod/rel: British and Dominions, Paramount British

341

NEBEL, FREDERICK
The Bribe, Short Story
  Bribe, The 1948 d: Robert Z. Leonard. lps: Robert Taylor, Ava Gardner, John Hodiak. 98M USA. prod/rel: MGM

NEBEL, FREDERICK, Nebel, Louis Frederick
Fifty Roads to Town, Boston 1936, Novel
  Fifty Roads to Town 1937 d: Norman Taurog. lps: Don Ameche, Ann Sothern, Slim Summerville. 80M USA. *50 Roads Back* prod/rel: Twentieth Century-Fox Film Corp.©

NEBEL, FREDERICK
No Hard Feelings, Story
  Shot in the Dark, A 1941 d: William McGann. lps: William Lundigan, Regis Toomey, Nan Wynn. 57M USA. prod/rel: Warner Bros.

NEBEL, FREDERICK, Nebel, Louis Frederick
Sleepers East, Boston 1933, Novel
  Sleepers East 1934 d: Kenneth MacKennA. lps: Wynne Gibson, Preston Foster, Mona Barrie. 69M USA. prod/rel: Fox Film Corp.©
  Sleepers West 1941 d: Eugene J. Forde. lps: Lloyd Nolan, Lynn Bari, Mary Beth Hughes. 74M USA. prod/rel: 20th Century Fox

NEBHUT, ERNST
Die Schone Lugnerin, Opera
  Schone Lugnerin, Die 1959 d: Axel von Ambesser. lps: Romy Schneider, Jean-Claude Pascal, Helmut Lohner. 98M GRM/FRN. *La Belle Et l'Empereur* (FRN); *Beautiful Liar, The* prod/rel: Real Film, Regina

Teufel Stellt Mr. Darcy Ein Bein, Play
  Damonische Liebe 1951 d: Kurt Meisel. lps: Paul Horbiger, Margot Hielscher, Kurt Meisel. 86M GRM. *Demonic Love* prod/rel: H.M.K., N.F.

NEDBAL, OSKAR
Polska Krev, Opera
  Polenblut 1934 d: Carl Lamac. lps: Anny Ondra, Hans Moser, Ivan Petrovich. F GRM/CZC. *Polish Blood* (USA) prod/rel: Ondra-Lamac Film, Elekta
  Polska Krev 1934 d: Carl Lamac. lps: Anny Ondra, Theodor Pistek, Stefan HozA. 2375m CZC. *Polish Blood* prod/rel: Elekta, Wolframfilm

NEDELCOVICI, BUJOR
Zile de Nisip, 1979, Novel
  Faleze de Nisip 1983 d: Dan PitA. lps: Oana Pellea, Carmen Galin, Valentin Iritescu. 102M RMN. *Sand Cliffs; Cliffs of Sand*

NEELAKANTAN, P.
Nam Iruvar, Play
  Nam Iruvar 1947 d: A. V. Meiyappan. lps: T. R. Mahalingam, B. R. Panthulu, T. R. Ramchandran. 153M IND. *We Two* prod/rel: Avm

NEELY, RICHARD
The Damned Innocents, Novel
  Innocents aux Mains Sales, Les 1975 d: Claude Chabrol. lps: Romy Schneider, Rod Steiger, Paolo Giusti. 125M FRN/GRM/ITL. *Unschuldigen Mit Den Schmutzigen Handen, Die* (GRM); *Innocents With Dirty Hands; Dirty Hands* (USA); *Gli Innocenti Dalle Mani Sporche* (ITL) prod/rel: Juppiter Generale Cin.Ca

Plastic Nightmare, The, Novel
  Shattered 1990 d: Wolfgang Petersen. lps: Tom Berenger, Bob Hoskins, Greta Scacchi. 98M USA/GRM. *Tod Im Spiegel* (GRM); *Plastic Nightmare; Troubles* prod/rel: Capella Films, Davis Entertainment

NEELY, WILLIAM
Stand on It, Novel
  Stroker Ace 1983 d: Hal Needham. lps: Burt Reynolds, Ned Beatty, Jim Nabors. 96M USA. prod/rel: Universal, Warner

NEERA
Crevalcore, 1907, Novel
  Crevalcore 1917 d: Romolo Bacchini. lps: Italia Almirante Manzini, Gigi Armandis, Giulietta de Riso. 1415m ITL. prod/rel: Armenia Film

Il Marito Dell'Amica, 1885, Novel
  Marito Dell'amica, Il 1919 d: Ugo de Simone. lps: Mercedes Brignone, Guido Trento, Mary Hamilton Monteverde. 1191m ITL. prod/rel: Gladiator Film

NEFF, JAMES
Mobbed Up, Book
  Power Play 1992 d: Alastair Reid. lps: Brian Dennehy, Jeff Daniels, Maria Conchita Alonso. 106M USA. *Teamster Boss: the Jackie Presser Story*

NEIDER, CHARLES
The Authentic Death of Hendry Jones, New York 1956, Novel
  One-Eyed Jacks 1961 d: Marlon Brando. lps: Marlon Brando, Karl Malden, Pina Pellicer. 141M USA. prod/rel: Pennebaker, Inc., Paramount

NEIDERMAN, ANDREW
The Devil's Advocate, Novel
  Devil's Advocate, The 1997 d: Taylor Hackford. lps: Keanu Reeves, Al Pacino, Charlize Theron. 144M USA. prod/rel: Warner Bros.©, Regency Enterprises

NEIDHARDT, AUGUST
Schwarzwaldmadel, Opera
  Schwarzwaldmadel 1920 d: Arthur Wellin. lps: Uschi Elleot, Ria Jende, Gustav Charle. 1910m GRM. prod/rel: Luna-Film
  Schwarzwaldmadel 1929 d: Victor Janson. lps: Liane Haid, Fred Louis Lerch, Walter Janssen. 2653m GRM. prod/rel: Merkur-Film
  Schwarzwaldmadel 1933 d: Georg Zoch. lps: Hans Sohnker, Maria Berling, Walter Janssen. 96M GRM.
  Schwarzwaldmadel 1950 d: Hans Deppe. lps: Sonja Ziemann, Rudolf Prack, Fritz Kampers. 100M GRM. *Black Forest Girl* prod/rel: Berolina, UFA

NEIDIG, WILLIAM J.
The Fire Flingers, New York 1919, Novel
  Fire Flingers, The 1919 d: Rupert Julian. lps: Rupert Julian, Jane Novak, E. Alyn Warren. 5776f USA. prod/rel: Universal Film Mfg. Co.©, Special Attraction

The Snob, 1918, Short Story
  Snob, The 1921 d: Sam Wood. lps: Wanda Hawley, Edwin Stevens, Walter Hiers. 4015f USA. *You Can't Figure Women* prod/rel: Realart Pictures

Tracked to Earth, Short Story
  Tracked to Earth 1922 d: William Worthington. lps: Frank Mayo, Virginia Valli, Harold Goodwin. 4477f USA. prod/rel: Universal Film Mfg. Co.

NEILSON, FRANCIS
A Butterfly on the Wheel, London 1911, Play
  Butterfly on the Wheel, A 1915 d: Maurice Tourneur. lps: Holbrook Blinn, Vivian Martin, George Ralph. 5r USA. prod/rel: Shubert Film Corp., World Film Corp.©
  Frau Auf Der Folter, Die 1928 d: Robert Wiene. lps: Lili Damita, Wladimir Gaidarow, Johannes Riemann. 2544m GRM. *Scandal in Paris, A; The Butterfly on the Wheel* prod/rel: Felsom-Film, Deutsche Vereins-Film Ag

NEILSON, HELEN
Murder By Proxy, Novel
  Murder By Proxy 1955 d: Terence Fisher. lps: Dane Clark, Belinda Lee, Betty Ann Davies. 87M UKN. *Blackout* (USA) prod/rel: Hammer, Exclusive

NEIMARK, PAUL
She Lives, Novel
  She Lives! 1973 d: Stuart Hagmann. lps: Desi Arnaz Jr., Season Hubley, Anthony Zerbe. TVM. 73M USA. prod/rel: ABC Circle Films

NEITZ, ALVIN J.
The Eyes Win, Story
  Loco Luck 1927 d: Cliff Smith. lps: Art Acord, Fay Wray, Aggie Herring. 4827f USA. prod/rel: Universal Pictures

NELKEN, DINAH
Ich an Dich, Novel
  Frau Wie Du, Eine 1939 d: Victor Tourjansky. lps: Brigitte Horney, Joachim Gottschalk, Hans Brausewetter. 89M GRM. prod/rel: Bavaria, Kristall

Ich an Mich, Novel
  Tagebuch Einer Verliebten 1953 d: Josef von Baky. lps: Maria Schell, O. W. Fischer, Franco Andrey. 90M GRM. *Diary of a Married Woman; Diary of a Mistress* prod/rel: Magna, Deutsche London

NELSON, ANNE
Murder Under Two Flags, Book
  Show of Force 1989 d: Bruno Barreto. lps: Amy Irving, Andy Garcia, Lou Diamond Phillips. 93M USA. *Bajo Otra Bandera* prod/rel: Paramount

NELSON, BLAKE
Girl, Novel
  Girl 1998 d: Jonathan Kahn. lps: Dominique Swain, Sean Patrick Flanery, Summer Phoenix. 94M USA. prod/rel: Kushner-Locke, Hsx Films

NELSON, J.
Remote Control, New York 1929, Play
  Remote Control 1930 d: Nick Grinde, Malcolm St. Clair. lps: William Haines, Charles King, Mary Doran. 5958f USA. prod/rel: Metro-Goldwyn-Mayer Pictures

NELSON, RAY
Eight O'Clock in the Morning, Story
  They Live 1988 d: John Carpenter. lps: Roddy Piper, Keith David, Meg Foster. 97M USA. prod/rel: Universal

NELSON, SIDNEY
Death Keeps a Date, Play
  Final Appointment 1954 d: Terence Fisher. lps: John Bentley, Eleanor Summerfield, Hubert Gregg. 61M UKN. prod/rel: Monarch, Act Films

NELSON, TOM BLAKE
Eye of God, Play
  Eye of God 1997 d: Tom Blake Nelson. lps: Martha Plimpton, Kevin Anderson, Hal Holbrook. 84M USA. prod/rel: Minnow Pictures, Cyclone Film

NEMCOVA, BOZENA (1820–1962), CZC
Babicka, 1846, Novel
  Babicka 1921 d: Thea CervenkovA. lps: Ludmila Innemannova, A. Alesova, Ruzena MaturovA. 1041m CZC. *Grandmother* prod/rel: Filmovy Ustav, Iris-Film
  Babicka 1940 d: Frantisek Cap. lps: Terezie Brzkova, Svetla Svozilova, Karel Tresnak. 2589m CZC. *The Granny; Grandmother* prod/rel: Lucernafilm
  Viktorka 1935 d: Jan Kyzour. lps: Jarmila Berankova, Ladislav Brom, Jan W. Speerger. UNF. CZC. prod/rel: Jan Kyzour

Pohorska Vesnice, Novel
  Pohorska Vesnice 1928 d: M. J. Krnansky. lps: Fred Bulin, Ivan Frank Kubista, Bozena SvobodovA. 1974m CZC. *The Mountain Village* prod/rel: Fiserfilm

Princ Bajaja, Short Story
  Princ Bajaja 1950 d: Jiri TrnkA. ANM. 80M CZC. *Prince Bayaya; Bayaya; Bajaja*
  Princ Bajaja 1971 d: Antonin Kachlik. lps: Ivan Paluch, Magda Vasaryova, Fero Velecky. 90M CZC. *Prince Bajaja* prod/rel: Filmstudio Barrandov

NEMETH, LASZLO
Iszony, 1947, Novel
  Iszony 1965 d: Gyorgy Hintsch. lps: Andrea Drahota, Gyula Benko, Ferenc Kallai. 113M HNG. *Abhorrence*

NEMIROVSKY, IRENE
Le Bal, Short Story
  Bal, Le 1931 d: Wilhelm Thiele. lps: Germaine Dermoz, Danielle Darrieux, Andre Lefaur. 73M FRN. prod/rel: Vandal Et Delac

David Golder, Novel
  David Golder 1930 d: Julien Duvivier. lps: Harry Baur, Jean Coquelin, Gaston Jacquet. 86M FRN. prod/rel: Vandal Et Delac
  My Daughter Joy 1950 d: Gregory Ratoff. lps: Edward G. Robinson, Richard Greene, Peggy Cummins. 81M UKN. *Operation X* (USA) prod/rel: London Films, British Lion Production Assets

NENADIC, DOBRILO
Dorotej, 1977, Novel
  Dorotej 1981 d: Zdravko Velimirovic. lps: Gojko Santic, Gorica Popovic, Velimir Zivojinovic. 97M YGS.

NEPEAN, EDITH
Gwyneth of the Welsh Hills, Novel
  Gwyneth of the Welsh Hills 1921 d: F. Martin Thornton. lps: Madge Stuart, Eille Norwood, Lewis Gilbert. 6470f UKN. prod/rel: Stoll

NEPOTY, LUCIEN
Les Petits, Play
  Petits, Les 1925 d: Gaston Roudes, Marcel Dumont. lps: Lucien Dalsace, France Dhelia, Jean Dehelly. 2250m FRN. prod/rel: Films Roudes

Petits, Les, Play
  Loi du Printemps, La 1942 d: Jacques Daniel-Norman. lps: Georges Rollin, Pierre Renoir, Huguette Duflos. 100M FRN. prod/rel: Camille Tramichel

La Veille d'Armes, Paris 1917, Play
  Veille d'Armes 1925 d: Jacques de Baroncelli. lps: Maurice Schutz, Nina Vanna, Annette Benson. 2400m FRN. *In the Night Watch* prod/rel: Films Baroncelli
  Woman from Monte Carlo, The 1932 d: Michael Curtiz. lps: Lil Dagover, Walter Huston, Warren William. 65M USA. *The Captain's Wife; The Marked Woman* prod/rel: First National Pictures©
  Veille d'Armes 1935 d: Marcel L'Herbier. lps: Annabella, Rosine Derean, Victor Francen. 120M FRN. *Sacrifice d'Honneur; The Vigil* prod/rel: Imperial-Film

La Vielle d'Armes, Paris 1917, Play
  Night Watch, The 1928 d: Alexander KordA. lps: Billie Dove, Paul Lukas, Donald Reed. 6676f USA. *His Wife's Affair* prod/rel: First National Pictures

NERON, CLAUDE
La Grande Marrade, Novel
  Vincent, Francois, Paul. Et Les Autres 1974 d: Claude Sautet. lps: Yves Montand, Michel Piccoli, Serge Reggiani. 118M FRN/ITL. *Vincent, Francois, Paul and the Others* (USA); *Tre Amici, le Moglie E (Affettuosamente) le Altre* (ITL) prod/rel: President Film (Roma)

Max Et Les Ferrailleurs, Novel
  Max Et Les Ferrailleurs 1970 d: Claude Sautet. lps: Michel Piccoli, Romy Schneider, Bernard Fresson. 125M FRN/ITL. *Il Commissario Pellissier* (ITL); *Max* prod/rel: Fida Cin.Ca, Lira Films

NERUDA, JAN (1834–1891), CZC
Figurky, Short Story
Vzhuru Nohama 1938 d: Jiri Slavicek. lps: Vaclav Tregl, Hana Vitova, Vladimir Borsky. 2302m CZC. *Upside Down* prod/rel: Terra

Kam S Nim?, Story
Kam S Nim? 1922 d: Vaclav Wasserman. lps: Vojtech Zahorik, Hana Jencikova, Josef Brabec. 570m CZC. *Where to Put It?; What to Do With It?* prod/rel: Filmovy Ustav, Record-Film

Trhani, Novel
Trhani 1936 d: Vaclav Wasserman. lps: L. H. Struna, Eman Fiala, Jan Richter. 2152m CZC. *The Ragamuffins; Ragged Men; Quarrymen* prod/rel: Favoritfilm, Lepka

NESBIT, E. (1858–1924), UKN, Nesbit, Edith, Bland, Mrs. Hubert
A Ballad of Splendid Silence, Poem
Ballad of Splendid Silence, A 1913. lps: Eric Williams. UKN. prod/rel: Eric Williams Speaking Pictures, Barker

Five Children and It, 1902, Novel
Five Children and It 198- d: Marilyn Fox. lps: Simon Godwin, Nicole Mowat, Charlie Richards. MTV. 139M UKN.

Railway Children, The, 1906, Novel
Railway Children, The 1970 d: Lionel Jeffries. lps: Dinah Sheridan, Bernard Cribbins, William Mervyn. 108M UKN. prod/rel: MGM-Emi, Emi

NESBIT, W. D.
The Girl of My Dreams, New York 1911, Musical Play
Girl of My Dreams, The 1918 d: Louis W. Chaudet. lps: Billie Rhodes, Leo Pierson, Frank MacQuarrie. 6r USA. prod/rel: National Film Corp. of America, Exhibitors Mutual Distributing Corp.

NESBITT, ROBERT
The Glorious Days, London 1953, Musical Play
Lilacs in the Spring 1954 d: Herbert Wilcox. lps: Anna Neagle, Errol Flynn, David Farrar. 94M UKN. *Let's Make Up* (USA) prod/rel: Everest, Wilcox-Neagle

NESS, ELIOT
The Untouchables, New York 1957, Book
Scarface Mob, The 1962 d: Phil Karlson. lps: Robert Stack, Keenan Wynn, Barbara Nichols. MTV. 105M USA. *Untouchables: the Scarface Mob* prod/rel: Desilu Productions

NESSI, EMILIO
Palla Di Neve, Novel
Palla Di Neve 1996 d: Maurizio Nichetti. lps: Paolo Villaggio, Alessandro Haber, Fabiano Vagnarelli. 93M ITL. *Snowball* prod/rel: Italian International Film, Eurolux Produzione

NESTER, MARCUS P.
Das Leise Gift, Book
Leise Gift, Das 1984 d: Erwin Keusch. lps: Peter Sattmann, Peter Bongartz, Gunter Lamprecht. TVM. 105M GRM.

NESTROY, JOHANN (1801–1862), AUS
Der Bose Geist Lumpazivagabundus, 1835, Play
Lumpazivagabundus 1937 d: Geza von Bolvary. lps: Paul Horbiger, Hans Holt, Hilde Krahl. 85M AUS. *Lumpaci Vagabundus; Lumpaci the Vagabond; Lumpacivagabundus* prod/rel: Styria, Commerz

Lumpazivagabundus 1956 d: Franz Antel. lps: Paul Horbiger, Gunther Philipp, Waltraut Haas. 100M GRM. prod/rel: Rhombus, UFA

Einen Jux Will Er Sich machen, 1844, Play
Einmaleins Der Liebe, Das 1935 d: Carl Hoffmann. lps: Luise Ullrich, Paul Horbiger, Lee Parry. 95M GRM. prod/rel: Minerva-Tonfilm

Einmal Keine Sorgen Haben 1953 d: Georg MarischkA. lps: Walter Muller, Hans Moser, Nadja Tiller. 90M GRM/AUS. *Einen Jux Will Er Sich machen; Just Once to Be Without a Care* prod/rel: Carlton, N.F.

Einen Jux Will Er Sich machen, 1944, Play
Einen Jux Will Er Sich machen 1957 d: Alfred Stoger. lps: Josef Meinrad, Inge Konradi, Ferdinand Maierhofer. 88M AUS.

Der Farber Und Sein Zwillingsbruder, 1890, Play
Wenn Poldi Ins Manover Zieht 1956 d: Hans Quest. lps: Gunther Philipp, Joachim Fuchsberger, Richard Romanowsky. 92M AUS. *Manoverzwilling*

Hinuber - Herbuer, 1844, Play
Gluck Im Winkel 1937 d: Alfred Stoger. 22M GRM. *Happiness Is a Small Corner*

Jux Will Er Sich machen, Play
Jux Will Er Sich machen, Einen 1928 d: Johannes Brandt. lps: Hilde Elsner, Walter Slezak. 968m GRM. prod/rel: I. Rosenfeld Film-Prod.

Der Zerrissene, 1845, Play
Goldene Fessel, Die 1944 d: Hans Thimig. lps: Hans Holt, Hermann Thimig, Attila Horbiger. 92M GRM. prod/rel: Wien, Allgemeiner

NESVADBA, JOSEF
Upir Z Feratu, Short Story
Upir Z Feratu 1982 d: Juraj Herz. lps: Jiri Menzel, Dagmar Veskrnova, Petr Cepek. 97M CZC. *Ferat Vampire; A Vampire from Ferat* prod/rel: Filmstudio Barrandov

NETHERSOLE, OLGA
The Writing on the Wall, New York 1909, Play
Writing on the Wall, The 1916 d: Tefft Johnson. lps: Joseph Kilgour, Virginia Pearson, Robert Gaillord. 5r USA. prod/rel: Vitagraph Co. of America©, Blue Ribbon Feature

NETTER, LEOPOLD
Bartholdi Et Son Vigneron, Play
Liberte 1937 d: Jean Kemm. lps: Maurice Escande, Germaine Rouer, Marcelle Samson. 100M FRN. *La Grande Passion* prod/rel: Films Artistiques Francais

NEUBACH, ERNEST
On Demande un Assassin, Play
On Demande un Assassin 1949 d: Ernst Neubach. lps: Fernandel, Noelle Norman, Felix Oudart. 90M FRN. prod/rel: P.E.N. Films, Cinema Productions

NEUBACH, ERNST
Ich Weiss, Wofur Ich Lebe, Novel
Ich Weiss, Wofur Ich Lebe 1955 d: Paul Verhoeven. lps: Luise Ullrich, Michael Ande, Knut Mahlke. 100M GRM. *I Know What I'm Living for* prod/rel: Neubach, Gloria

Der Mann, Der Seinen Morder Sucht, Play
Man Lebt Nur Einmal 1952 d: Ernst Neubach. lps: Theo Lingen, Paul Horbiger, Rudolf Platte. 75M GRM. *You Only Live Once* prod/rel: C.C.C., Atlantik

Die Prinzessin von St. Wolfgang, Ss
Prinzessin von St. Wolfgang, Die 1957 d: Harald Reinl. lps: Marianne Hold, Gerhard Riedmann, Annie Rosar. 93M GRM. *The Princess of St. Wolfgang* prod/rel: Neubach, Constantin

Sperrbezirk, Novel
Sperrbezirk 1966 d: Will Tremper. lps: Harald Leipnitz, Suzanne Roquette, Guido Baumann. 94M GRM. *Red-Light District* prod/rel: Universum, Gloria

NEUBAUER, VILEM
Filosofka Maja, Novel
Filosofka Maja 1928 d: Oldrich Kminek. lps: Anita Janova, Alois Charvat, Antonie NedosinskA. 2210m CZC. *Maja the Student of Philosophy* prod/rel: Interfilm

Hanka a Jindra, Novel
Hanka a Jindra 1929 d: Oldrich Kminek. lps: Jirina Sejbalova, Vaclav Norman, Antonie NedosinskA. CZC. *Hanka and Jindra* prod/rel: Elektafilm

Osada Mladych Snu, Novel
Osada Mladych Snu 1931 d: Oldrich Kminek. lps: Jiri Steimar, Bozena Svobodova, Asa VasatkovA. 2618m CZC. *Summer Camp of Young Dreams, The* prod/rel: Starfilm

Sextanka, Novel
Sextanka 1927 d: Josef Medeotti-Bohac. lps: Anita Janova, Jan W. Speerger, Josef Rovensky. 2105m CZC. *Pupil of the Sixth Grade* prod/rel: Karel Spelina, Jan Kyzour

Sextanka 1936 d: Svatopluk Innemann. lps: Hana Vitova, Rolf Wanka, Jaroslav Marvan. 2521m CZC. *Sweet Sixteen* prod/rel: Meissner, Metropolitan

Sextanerin, Die 1936 d: Svatopluk Innemann. lps: Ellen Schwanneke, Rolf Wanka, Hella Pitt. 2309m GRM/CZC. *Erste Liebe; First Love; Arme Kleine Inge* prod/rel: Meissner, Metropolitan

NEUERT, HANS
Almenrausch Und Edelweiss, Play
Almenrausch Und Edelweiss 1928 d: Franz Seitz. lps: Charlotte Susa, Leo Peukert, Walter Slezak. 2022m GRM. prod/rel: Munchener Lichtspielkunst Ag

Der Geigenmacher von Mittenwald, Play
Geigenmacher von Mittenwald, Der 1950 d: Rudolf Schundler. lps: Willy Rosner, Paul Richter, Ingeborg Cornelius. 90M GRM. *The Violin Maker of Mittenwald* prod/rel: Peter Ostermayr

NEUFELD, JOHN
Lisa, Bright and Dark, Novel
Lisa, Bright and Dark 1973 d: Jeannot Szwarc. lps: Anne Baxter, John Forsythe, Kay Lenz. TVM. 73M USA. prod/rel: Bob Banner Associates

NEUFELD, MAX
Story
Strassenserenade 1953 d: Georg Jacoby. lps: Vico Torriani, Sybil Werden, Ellinor Jensen. 87M GRM. *Street Serenade* prod/rel: Neue Emelka, Zeyn

NEUHAUS, PAUL
Schweinefleisch in Dosen, Play
Schuld Allein Ist Der Wein 1949 d: Fritz Kirchhoff. lps: Ernst Waldow, Olga Limburg, Inge Stoldt. 92M GRM. *It's All the Wine's Fault* prod/rel: Pontus, Hamburg

NEUMAN, E. JACK
When Rabbit Howls, Book
Voices Within: the Lives of Truddi Chase 1990 d: Lamont Johnson. lps: Shelley Long, Tom Conti, John Rubinstein. TVM. 200M USA. *Voices Within; Shattered*

NEUMANN, ALFRED
Abel, Play
K - Das Haus Des Schweigens 1951 d: Hans Hinrich. lps: Francoise Rosay, Ernst Deutsch, Jochen Blume. 103M GRM. *Jahre Des Schweigens; Years of Silence* prod/rel: Internationale Filmkunst

Der Patriot, Stuttgart 1927, Play
Patriot, The 1928 d: Ernst Lubitsch. lps: Emil Jannings, Florence Vidor, Lewis Stone. 12r USA. prod/rel: Paramount Famous Lasky Corp.

Der Patriot, 1925, Short Story
Patriote, Le 1938 d: Maurice Tourneur. lps: Harry Baur, Pierre Renoir, Josette Day. 105M FRN. *The Mad Emperor* (USA) prod/rel: Ste Des Prods. Cinematographiques F.C.L.

La Tragedie Imperiale, Novel
Tragedie Imperiale, La 1937 d: Marcel L'Herbier. lps: Harry Baur, Jean Worms, Marcelle Chantal. 116M FRN. *Rasputin* (USA); *Diable de Siberie, Le; Raspoutine; Le Fin Des Romanoff* prod/rel: Productions Max Glass

Viele Heissen Kain., Novel
K - Das Haus Des Schweigens 1951 d: Hans Hinrich. lps: Francoise Rosay, Ernst Deutsch, Jochen Blume. 103M GRM. *Jahre Des Schweigens; Years of Silence* prod/rel: Internationale Filmkunst

Viele Heissen Kain, 1950, Short Story
Haus Des Schweigens, Das 1951 d: Hans Heinrich. 101M GRM. *Jahre Des Schweigens*

NEUMANN, BEDA
I Lost My Heart in Heidelberg, Play
Student's Romance, The 1935 d: Otto Kanturek. lps: Grete Natzler, Patric Knowles, Carol Goodner. 78M UKN. *I Lost My Heart in Heidelberg; Old Heidelberg* prod/rel: British International Pictures, Wardour

NEUMANN, ERNST
Student's Romance, The 1935 d: Otto Kanturek. lps: Grete Natzler, Patric Knowles, Carol Goodner. 78M UKN. *I Lost My Heart in Heidelberg; Old Heidelberg* prod/rel: British International Pictures, Wardour

NEUMANN, ROBERT
Abdul the Damned, Novel
Abdul the Damned 1935 d: Karl Grune. lps: Fritz Kortner, Nils Asther, Adrienne Ames. 111M UKN. prod/rel: British International Pictures, Capitol

Der Favorit Der Konigin, Frankfurt Am Main 1953, Novel
Herrscher Ohne Krone 1957 d: Harald Braun. lps: O. W. Fischer, Horst Buchholz, Odile Versois. 104M GRM. *King in Shadow* (USA); *Ruler Without a Crown* prod/rel: Bavaria Filmkunst

NEUTSCH, ERIK
Spur Der Steine, Novel
Spur Der Steine 1966 d: Frank Beyer. lps: Manfred Krug, Krystyna Stypulkowska, Eberhard Esche. 150M GDR. *Traces of the Stones; Tracks of Stones; Spur Eines Steinem* prod/rel: Defa-Studio Fur Spielfilme, Gruppe Heinrich Greif

NEVE, DORIAN
All Mine, Play
Is Divorce a Failure? 1923 d: Wallace Worsley. lps: Leah Baird, Richard Tucker, Walter McGrail. 5448f USA. *When Civilization Failed* prod/rel: Arthur Beck, Associated Exhibitors

NEVEUX, GEORGES (1900–, RSS
Juliette Ou la Cle Des Songes, 1930, Play
Juliette Ou la Cle Des Songes 1951 d: Marcel Carne. lps: Gerard Philipe, Jean-Roger Caussimon, Suzanne Cloutier. 106M FRN. *Juliet Or the Key of Dreams* (USA) prod/rel: Sacha Gordine

NEVILLE, EDGAR
Frente de Madrid, Short Story
Carmen Fra I Rossi 1939 d: Edgar Neville. lps: Fosco Giachetti, Conchita Montes, Juan de LandA. 96M ITL/SPN. *Frente de Madrid* (SPN); *Carmen Among the Reds; Madrid Front* prod/rel: Bassoli Film, I.C.I.

NEVILLE, FRANK
L'apprenti Salaud, Novel
Apprenti Salaud, L' 1977 d: Michel Deville. lps: Robert Lamoureux, Christine Dejoux, Claude Pieplu. 100M FRN. prod/rel: Elefilm, S.F.P.

NEVILLE, MARGOT
The Island of Despair, Novel
Island of Despair, The 1926 d: Henry Edwards. lps: Matheson Lang, Marjorie Hume, Gordon Hopkirk. 6360f UKN. prod/rel: Stoll

Safety First, Novel
Safety First 1926 d: Fred Paul. lps: Brian Aherne, Queenie Thomas, Mary Brough. 6348f UKN. prod/rel: Stoll

Crazy People 1934 d: Leslie Hiscott. lps: Henry Kendall, Nancy O'Neil, Kenneth Kove. 67M UKN. prod/rel: British Lion, MGM

NEVINS, FRANK J.
A Yankee Dared, 1933, Novel
Rock Island Trail 1950 d: Joseph Kane. lps: Forrest Tucker, Adele Mara, Adrian Booth. 90M USA. *Transcontinent Express* (UKN) prod/rel: Republic

NEWALL, GUY
Money for Nothing, Play
Money for Nothing 1916 d: Maurice Elvey. lps: Guy Newall, Manora Thew, Hayford Hobbs. 2800f UKN. prod/rel: London, Jury

Trouble for Nothing, Play
Trouble for Nothing 1916 d: Maurice Elvey. lps: Guy Newall, Hayford Hobbs, Jeff Barlow. 2300f UKN. prod/rel: London, Jury

NEWELL, MAUDE WOODRUFF
Her Unknown Knight, 1921, Short Story
Impulse 1922 d: Norval MacGregor. lps: Neva Gerber, Jack Dougherty, Goldie Madden. 4505f USA. prod/rel: Berwilla Film Corp., Arrow Film Corp.

NEWFIELD, JACK
Don King: Only in America, Book
Don King: Only in America 1997 d: John Herzfeld. lps: Ving Rhames, Vondie Curtis-Hall, Jeremy Piven. TVM. 120M USA. prod/rel: Thomas Carter Co., Hbo Pictures

NEWHOUSE, EDWARD
Short Storys
I Want You 1951 d: Mark Robson. lps: Dana Andrews, Dorothy McGuire, Farley Granger. 102M USA. prod/rel: RKO Radio, Sam Goldwyn

Come Another Day, Story
Shadow in the Sky 1951 d: Fred M. Wilcox. lps: Ralph Meeker, Nancy Davis, James Whitmore. 78M USA. *Rain, Rain, Go Away* prod/rel: MGM

NEWLEY, ANTHONY (1931–1999), UKN
Stop the World - I Want to Get Off, London 1961, Play
Stop the World - I Want to Get Off 1966 d: Philip Saville. lps: Tony Tanner, Millicent Martin, Leila Croft. 100M UKN. prod/rel: Warner Bros. Pictures, Warner-Pathe

NEWMAN, ANDREA (1938–, UKN
Three Into Two Won't Go, London 1967, Novel
Three Into Two Won't Go 1969 d: Peter Hall. lps: Rod Steiger, Claire Bloom, Judy Geeson. 94M UKN. *3 Into 2 Won't Go* prod/rel: Universal, Rank Film Distributors

NEWMAN, BERNARD
They Saved London, Book
Battle of the V 1 1958 d: Vernon Sewell. lps: Michael Rennie, Patricia Medina, Milly Vitale. 85M UKN. *Unseen Heroes* (USA); *Missiles from Hell*; *V 1* prod/rel: Criterion, Eros

NEWMAN, FRANK
Barbara, New York 1968, Novel
Barbara 1970 d: Walter Burns. lps: Jack Rader, Nancy Boyle, Robert McLane. 91M USA. prod/rel: Druidstone-Hottento Production Corp.

NEWMAN, G. F.
The Take, Novel
Take, The 1974 d: Robert Hartford-Davis. lps: Billy Dee Williams, Eddie Albert, Frankie Avalon. 92M USA. prod/rel: World Film Services

NEWMAN, GREATREX
Mister Cinders, London 1929, Musical Play
Mister Cinders 1934 d: Friedrich Zelnik. lps: Clifford Mollison, Zelma O'Neal, Kenneth Western. 72M UKN. prod/rel: British International Pictures, Wardour

NEWMAN, PETER
Yesterday's Enemy, Television Play
Yesterday's Enemy 1959 d: Val Guest. lps: Stanley Baker, Guy Rolfe, Leo McKern. 95M UKN. prod/rel: Columbia, Hammer

NEWMAN, RICHARD
Johnny March, Story
Identity Unknown 1945 d: Walter Colmes. lps: Richard Arlen, Cheryl Walker, Roger Pryor. 71M USA. prod/rel: Republic

NEWSKY, PIERRE
Die Danischeffs, Play
Leibeigenen, Die 1927 d: Richard Eichberg. lps: Heinrich George, Mona Maris, Maria Reisenhofer. 2295m GRM. *Bondage*; *Siervos* prod/rel: Richard Eichberg-Film

NEWSOM, J. D.
Sowing Glory, 1933, Short Story
Trouble in Morocco 1937 d: Ernest B. Schoedsack. lps: Jack Holt, Mae Clarke, Harold Huber. 62M USA. prod/rel: Columbia Pictures Corp. of California©, Larry Darmour Productions

NEWTE, HORACE W. C.
Sparrows, 1909, Novel
Vogelvrij 1916 d: Maurits H. Binger. lps: Annie Bos, Lola Cornero, Pierre Perin. 1435m NTH/UKN. *Sparrows* (UKN); *Gelik de Vogelen Des Hemels*; *Like the Birds of Heaven*; *Outlawed* prod/rel: Filmfabriek-Hollandia

NEWTON, DOUGLAS
Love's Option, Novel
Love's Option 1928 d: George Pearson. lps: Dorothy Boyd, Pat Aherne, James Carew. 5890f UKN. *A Girl of Today* prod/rel: Welsh-Pearson-Elder, Paramount

Men of Steel, Novel
Men of Steel 1932 d: George King. lps: John Stuart, Benita Hume, Franklin Dyall. 71M UKN. prod/rel: Langham, United Artists

Sookey, Novel
Self-Made Lady 1932 d: George King. lps: Heather Angel, Henry Wilcoxon, Amy Veness. 76M UKN. prod/rel: George King Films, United Artists

NEWTON, EDDIE
Casey Jones, Song
Casey Jones 1927 d: Charles J. Hunt. lps: Ralph Lewis, Kate Price, Al St. John. 6673f USA. prod/rel: Trem Carr Productions, Rayart Pictures

NEWTON, W. DOUGLAS
The Brute, New York 1924, Novel
Brute, The 1927 d: Irving Cummings. lps: Monte Blue, Leila Hyams, Clyde Cook. 6901f USA. prod/rel: Warner Brothers Pictures

NEWTON-BUNGEY, E.
The Fordington Twins, Novel
Fordington Twins, The 1920 d: W. P. Kellino. lps: The Terry Twins, Dallas Anderson, Mary Brough. 6570f UKN. prod/rel: Gaumont, Westminster

NEXO, MARTIN ANDERSEN (1869–1954), DNM
Ditte Menneskebarn, 1917-21, Novel
Ditte Menneskebarn 1946 d: Bjarne Henning-Jensen. lps: Tove Maes, Karen Poulsen, Rasmus Ottesen. 105M DNM. *Ditte: Child of Man* prod/rel: Nordisk

Lotterisvenken, 1919, Short Story
Lotterieschwede, Der 1958 d: Joachim Kunert. lps: Erwin Geschonneck, Sonja Sutter, Harry Hindemith. 71M GDR. *The Lottery Swede*

Pelle Erobreren, 1906-10, Novel
Pelle Erobreren 1987 d: Bille August. lps: Max von Sydow, Pelle Hvenegaard, Erik Paske. 157M DNM/SWD. *Pelle the Conqueror* (USA) prod/rel: Danish Film Institute, Swedish Film Institute

NEZVAL, VITEZSLAV (1900–1958), CZC
Valerie a Tyden Divu, 1945, Short Story
Valerie a Tyden Divu 1970 d: Jaromil Jires. lps: Jaroslava Schallerova, Helena Anyzkova, Petr KoprivA. 85M CZC. *Valerie and Her Week of Wonders* (UKN); *Valerie and a Week of Wonders*; *Valerie and the Week of Miracles*

NI KANG
Liu Zhi Qin Mo, Novel
Liu Zhi Qin Mo 1993 d: Wu Mianqin. lps: Lin Qingzia, Yuan Biao, Liu Jialing. 10r CHN/HKG. *Deadly Melody* prod/rel: Shanghai Film Studio, Huangpai Corp. Ltd.

NIALL, IAN
No Resting Place, Novel
No Resting Place 1951 d: Paul RothA. lps: Michael Gough, Eithne Dunne, Noel Purcell. 77M UKN. prod/rel: Colin Lesslie, Associated British Film Distributors

A Tiger Walks, London 1960, Novel
Tiger Walks, A 1964 d: Norman Tokar. lps: Brian Keith, Vera Miles, Pamela Franklin. 91M USA. prod/rel: Walt Disney Productions, Buena Vista

NIBLO, ALFRED
I Congiurati Di Belfiore, Play
Giglio Infranto, Il 1956 d: Giorgio W. Chili. lps: Milly Vitale, Helene Remy, Alberto Farnese. 101M ITL. prod/rel: Col Film

NIBLO JR., FRED
Mother's Boys, Story
Three Sons O' Guns 1941 d: Ben Stoloff. lps: Wayne Morris, Marjorie Rambeau, Irene Rich. 64M USA. prod/rel: Warner Bros.

NICCODEMI, DARIO
L'aigrette, 1912, Play
Aigrette, L' 1917 d: Baldassarre Negroni. lps: Hesperia, Tullio Carminati, Andrea Habay. 2224m ITL. prod/rel: Tiber Film

Fior d'Amore, Play
Fior d'Amore 1921 d: Mario Caserini. lps: Vera Vergani, Mina d'Orvella, Nerio Bernardi. 1545m ITL. prod/rel: U.C.I., Cines

La Maestrina, 1917, Play
Maestrina, La 1919 d: Eleuterio Rodolfi. lps: Mercedes Brignone, Domenico Serra, Giuseppe Brignone. 1455m ITL. prod/rel: Rodolfi Film

Maestrina, La 1933 d: Guido Brignone. lps: Andreina Pagnani, Renato Cialente, Egisto Olivieri. 60M ITL. *The Little School Mistress* prod/rel: G.A.I., Anonima Pittaluga

La Maestrina, Play
Maestrina, La 1942 d: Giorgio Bianchi. lps: Maria Denis, Nino Besozzi, Virgilio Riento. 83M ITL. prod/rel: Nembo Film, Artisti Associati

La Nemica, 1916, Play
Nemica, La 1917 d: Ivo Illuminati. lps: Linda Pini, Memo Benassi, Luigi Duse. 1360m ITL. prod/rel: Silentium Film

Nemica, La 1952 d: Giorgio Bianchi. lps: Elisa Cegani, Frank Latimore, Cosetta Greco. F ITL. prod/rel: Athena Cin.Ca, Rank Film

L'ombra, 1915, Play
Ombra, L' 1917 d: Mario Caserini. lps: Vittoria Lepanto, Luciano Molinari, Berta Nelson. 1335m ITL. prod/rel: Teatro-Lombardo Film

Ombra, L' 1955 d: Giorgio Bianchi. lps: Marta Toren, Pierre Cressoy, Gianna Maria Canale. 104M ITL. prod/rel: Edo Film, Diana Cin.Ca

Ombra, L' 1923 d: Mario Almirante. lps: Italia Almirante Manzini, Alberto Collo, Liliana ArdeA. 1955m ITL. prod/rel: Alba Film

Le Refuge, 1909, Play
Rifugio, Il 1918 d: Giulio Antamoro. lps: Leda Gys, Enrico Roma, Mary Bayma-RivA. 1395m ITL. prod/rel: Lombardo Film

Scampolo, 1915, Play
Scampolo 1917 d: Giuseppe Sterni. lps: Margot Pellegrinetti, Giuseppe Sterni, Luigi Duse. 1775m ITL. prod/rel: Silentium Film

Madchen Der Strasse, Das 1928 d: Augusto GeninA. lps: Carmen Boni, Livio Pavanelli, Hans Junkermann. 2652m GRM. *Scampolo*; *Das Madchen von Der Strass* prod/rel: Nero-Film

Scampolo, Ein Kind Der Strasse 1932 d: Hans Steinhoff. lps: Dolly Haas, Karl Ludwig Diehl, Oskar SimA. 86M AUS/GRM. *Um Einen Groschen Liebe* prod/rel: Lothar Stark-Film

Peu d'Amour, Un 1933 d: Hans Steinhoff. lps: Marcel Andre, Charles Dechamps, Madeleine Ozeray. 65M FRN. *Scampolo*

Scampolo 1941 d: Nunzio MalasommA. lps: Lilia Silvi, Amedeo Nazzari, Carlo Romano. 78M ITL. prod/rel: Excelsa, Itala Film

Scampolo '53 1954 d: Giorgio Bianchi. lps: Maria Fiore, Henri Vidal, Cosetta Greco. 90M ITL/FRN. *Les Femmes Menent le Jeu* (FRN) prod/rel: Peg Produzione Film (Roma), Cite Film (Paris)

Scampolo 1958 d: Alfred Weidenmann. lps: Romy Schneider, Paul Hubschmid, Georg ThomallA. 109M GRM. *Das Madchen Scampolo*

Suzeraine, 1906, Play
Sovranetta 1923 d: Enrico Roma, Mario Gargiulo. lps: Fleurette Du Lac, Enrico RomA. 1122m ITL. prod/rel: Flegrea Film

La Volata, 1918, Play
Volata, La 1919 d: Gaston Ravel. lps: Vera Vergani, Romano Calo, Enta Troubetzkoy. 1721m ITL. prod/rel: Cines

NICHOLLS, BRON
Mullaway, Novel
Mull 1988 d: Don McLennan. lps: Nadine Garner, Bill Hunter, Sue Jones. 90M ASL. *Mullaway* prod/rel: International Film Management Ltd.©, Ukiyo Films

NICHOLLS, HARRY
Jane, London 1890, Play
Jane 1915 d: Frank Lloyd. lps: Charlotte Greenwood, Sydney Grant, Forrest Stanley. 5r USA. prod/rel: Oliver Morosco Photoplay Co.©, Paramount Pictures Corp.

NICHOLS, ANNE
Abie's Irish Rose, New York 1924, Play
    Abie's Irish Rose 1929 d: Victor Fleming. lps: Charles "Buddy" Rogers, Nancy Carroll, Jean Hersholt. 12r USA. prod/rel: Paramount Famous Lasky Corp.
    Abie's Irish Rose 1946 d: A. Edward Sutherland. lps: Joanne Dru, Richard Norris, Michael Chekhov. 96M USA. prod/rel: United Artists, Bing Crosby Productions
The Gilded Cage, New York 1921, Play
    Her Gilded Cage 1922 d: Sam Wood. lps: Gloria Swanson, David Powell, Harrison Ford. 6338f USA. prod/rel: Famous Players-Lasky, Paramount Pictures
Just Married, Play
    Just Married 1928 d: Frank Strayer. lps: James Hall, Ruth Taylor, Harrison Ford. 6039f USA. prod/rel: Paramount Famous Lasky Corp.
Linger Longer Letty, New York 1919, Play
    Give Me a Sailor 1938 d: Elliott Nugent. lps: Martha Raye, Bob Hope, Betty Grable. 80M USA. prod/rel: Paramount Pictures©

NICHOLS, BEVERLY
Evensong, Novel
    Evensong 1934 d: Victor Saville. lps: Evelyn Laye, Fritz Kortner, Alice DelysiA. 84M UKN. prod/rel: Gaumont-British

NICHOLS, GEORGE A.
Sis Hopkins, Buffalo, N.Y. 1899, Play
    Sis Hopkins 1919 d: Clarence Badger. lps: Mabel Normand, John Bowers, Sam de Grasse. 5r USA. prod/rel: Goldwyn Pictures Corp.©, Goldwyn Distributing Corp.
    Sis Hopkins 1941 d: Joseph Santley. lps: Judy Canova, Bob Crosby, Charles Butterworth. 98M USA. prod/rel: Republic

NICHOLS, JOHN
The Milagro Beanfield War, Novel
    Milagro Beanfield War, The 1987 d: Robert Redford. lps: Ruben Blades, Richard Bradford, Sonia BragA. 117M USA. prod/rel: Universal
The Wizard of Loneliness, Novel
    Wizard of Loneliness, The 1988 d: Jenny Bowen. lps: Lukas Haas, Lea Thompson, John Randolph. 11OM USA. prod/rel: Skouras Pictures, Virgin Vision

NICHOLS, JOHN TREADWELL
The Sterile Cuckoo, New York 1965, Novel
    Sterile Cuckoo, The 1969 d: Alan J. PakulA. lps: Liza Minnelli, Wendell Burton, Tim McIntire. 107M USA. *Pookie* (UKN) prod/rel: Boardwalk Productions

NICHOLS, PETER (1927–, UKN
A Day in the Death of Joe Egg, 1967, Play
    Day in the Death of Joe Egg, A 1972 d: Peter Medak. lps: Alan Bates, Janet Suzman, Peter Bowles. 106M UKN. *Joe Egg* prod/rel: Columbia, Domino
The National Health; Or, Nurse Norton's Affair, 1970, Play
    National Health, The 1973 d: Jack Gold. lps: Lynn Redgrave, Eleanor Bron, Sheila Scott-Wilkinson. 97M UKN. *The National Health, Or Nurse Norton's Affair* (USA) prod/rel: Columbia
Privates on Parade, 1977, Play
    Privates on Parade 1983 d: Michael Blakemore. lps: John Cleese, Dennis Quilley, Michael Elphick. 112M UKN. prod/rel: Handmade Films

NICHOLSON, C. H.
To Be a Lady, Story
    To Be a Lady 1934 d: George King. lps: Chili Bouchier, Bruce Lister, Vera Bogetti. 68M UKN. prod/rel: British and Dominions, Paramount British

NICHOLSON, KENYON
The Barker; a Play of Carnival Life, New York 1917, Play
    Barker, The 1928 d: George Fitzmaurice. lps: Milton Sills, Douglas Fairbanks Jr., George Cooper. 7870f USA. prod/rel: First National Pictures
    Diamond Horseshoe 1945 d: George Seaton. lps: Betty Grable, Dick Haymes, Phil Silvers. 106M USA. *Billy Rose's Diamond Horseshoe* prod/rel: 20th Century Fox
    Hoop-la 1933 d: Frank Lloyd. lps: Clara Bow, Preston Foster, Richard Cromwell. 85M USA. *Hoopla* prod/rel: Fox Film Corp.©
Blindspot, Play
    Waterfront 1939 d: Terry O. Morse. lps: Dennis Morgan, Gloria Dickson, Marie Wilson. 60M USA. prod/rel: Warner Bros. Pictures©
Eva the Fifth; the Odyssey of a Tom Show, New York 1928, Play
    Girl in the Show, The 1929 d: Edgar Selwyn. lps: Bessie Love, Raymond Hackett, Edward Nugent. 81M USA. *Eva the Fifth* prod/rel: Metro-Goldwyn-Mayer Pictures

Sailor Beware, New York 1933, Play
    Lady Be Careful 1936 d: Theodore Reed. lps: Lew Ayres, Mary Carlisle, Buster Crabbe. 72M USA. prod/rel: Paramount Pictures©
    Fleet's in, The 1942 d: Victor Schertzinger, Hal Walker (Uncredited). lps: Dorothy Lamour, William Holden, Eddie Bracken. 93M USA. prod/rel: Paramount
    Sailor Beware 1951 d: Hal Walker. lps: Dean Martin, Jerry Lewis, Corinne Calvet. 108M USA. prod/rel: Paramount, Wallis-Hazen
Swing Your Lady, New York 1936, Play
    Swing Your Lady 1938 d: Ray Enright. lps: Humphrey Bogart, Frank McHugh, Louise FazendA. 79M USA. prod/rel: Warner Bros. Pictures©
Torch Song, New York 1930, Play
    Laughing Sinners 1931 d: Harry Beaumont. lps: Joan Crawford, Clark Gable, Neil Hamilton. 72M USA. *The Torch Song*; *Complete Surrender* prod/rel: Metro-Goldwyn-Mayer Corp., Metro-Goldwyn-Mayer Dist. Corp.©
Two Weeks Off, New York 1927, Novel
    Two Weeks Off 1929 d: William Beaudine. lps: Dorothy MacKaill, Jack Mulhall, Gertrude Astor. 8081f USA. prod/rel: First National Pictures

NICHOLSON, MEREDITH
Broken Barriers, New York 1922, Novel
    Broken Barriers 1924 d: Reginald Barker. lps: James Kirkwood, Norma Shearer, Adolphe Menjou. 5717f USA. prod/rel: Metro-Goldwyn Pictures
The Hopper, 1916, Short Story
    Hopper, The 1918 d: Thomas N. Heffron. lps: Irene Hunt, William V. Mong, Thomas KuriharA. 4727f USA. prod/rel: Triangle Film Corp., Triangle Distributing Corp.
The House of a Thousand Candles, New York 1905, Novel
    House of a Thousand Candles, The 1915 d: Thomas N. Heffron. lps: Grace Darmond, Harry Mestayer, George Backus. 5r USA. prod/rel: Selig Polyscope Co.©, Red Seal Play
    Haunting Shadows 1920 d: Henry King. lps: H. B. Warner, Margaret Livingston, Charles Hill Mailes. 5r USA. *House of a Thousand Candles, The* prod/rel: Jesse D. Hampton Productions, Robertson-Cole Distributing Corp.
House of a Thousand Candles, The, New York 1905, Novel
    House of a Thousand Candles, The 1936 d: Arthur Lubin. lps: Phillips Holmes, Mae Clarke, Irving Pichel. 71M USA. prod/rel: Republic Pictures Corp.©
Lords of High Decision, New York 1909, Novel
    Lords of High Decision, The 1916 d: John Harvey. lps: Cyril Scott, Joseph Girard, William Welsh. 5r USA. prod/rel: Universal Film Mfg. Co.©, Red Feather Photoplays
The Port of Missing Men, Indianapolis 1907, Novel
    Port of Missing Men, The 1914 d: Francis Powers. lps: Arnold Daly, Minna Gale Haines, Mortimer Martini. 5r USA. prod/rel: Famous Players Film Co., State Rights

NICHOLSON, MICHAEL
Natasha's Story, Book
    Welcome to Sarajevo 1997 d: Michael Winterbottom. lps: Stephen Dillane, Woody Harrelson, Marisa Tomei. 101M UKN/USA. prod/rel: Channel Four Films, Miramax Films

NICHOLSON, NIGEL
Portrait of a Marriage, Book
    Portrait of a Marriage 1990 d: Stephen Whittaker. lps: Janet McTeer, David Haig, Cathryn Harrison. TVM. 200M UKN/USA/NZL. prod/rel: BBC, Wgbh Boston

NICHOLSON, VIVIAN
Spend, Spend, Spend, Book
    Spend, Spend, Spend 1977 d: John Goldschmidt. lps: Susan Littler, John Duttine, Helen Beck. MTV. 90M UKN. prod/rel: BBC

NICHOLSON, WILLIAM
Shadowlands, Play
    Shadowlands 1993 d: Richard Attenborough. lps: Anthony Hopkins, Debra Winger, John Wood. 131M UKN. prod/rel: Uip, Showlands

NICKLAUS, THELMA
Tamahine, London 1957, Novel
    Tamahine 1963 d: Philip Leacock. lps: Nancy Kwan, John Fraser, Dennis Price. 95M UKN. prod/rel: Associated British Picture Corporation, Warner-Pathe

NICKLISCH, HANS
Story
    Liebe Verboten - Heiraten Erlaubt 1959 d: Kurt Meisel. lps: Ingeborg Schoner, Peter Weck, Elma KarlowA. 93M GRM. *Love Forbidden - Marriage Permitted* prod/rel: Rhombus, U.F.H.

Riviera-Story 1961 d: Wolfgang Becker. lps: Ulla Jacobsson, Wolfgang Preiss, Hartmut Reck. 86M GRM. prod/rel: Cine International, Deutsche Cinevox
Ohne Mutter Geht Es Nicht, Novel
    Ohne Mutter Geht Es Nicht 1958 d: Erik Ode. lps: Ewald Balser, Adelheid Seeck, Heidi Bruhl. 100M GRM. *Nothing Works Without Mom* prod/rel: C.C.C., Bavaria

NICODEMI, ALDO
L'albo, Il Giorno, la Notte, Play
    Alba, Il Giorno, la Notte, L' 1955 d: Fernando Trebitsch. lps: Anita Todesco, Giuliano Falcier. 90M ITL. prod/rel: Regionale

NICOL, DERWENT
Short Stories
    Adventures of Mr. Pusher Long, The 1921 d: Kenneth Graeme. lps: Kenneth Graeme. SHS. UKN. prod/rel: Kenneth Graeme Film Syndicate, Anchor
Short Story
    Great Hunger Duel, The 1922 d: Kenneth Graeme. lps: Kenneth Graeme, Sydney N. Folker, Clive Tristi. 2000f UKN. prod/rel: Kenneth Graeme Film Syndicate, Anchor
    Hypnotic Portrait, The 1922 d: Kenneth Graeme. lps: Kenneth Graeme. 2000f UKN. prod/rel: Kenneth Graeme Film Syndicate, Anchor
    War at Wallaroo Mansions, The 1922 d: Kenneth Graeme. lps: Kenneth Graeme. 2000f UKN. prod/rel: Kenneth Graeme Film Syndicate, Anchor

NICOLARDI, EDUARDO
Voce 'E Notte, Song
    Voce 'E Notte 1919 d: Oreste Gherardini. lps: Tina Somma, Rita Almanova, Mario GambardellA. 1440m ITL. *Canto Nella Notte* prod/rel: Flegrea Film

NICOLE
Les Lions Sont Laches, Novel
    Lions Sont Laches, Les 1961 d: Henri Verneuil. lps: Danielle Darrieux, Jean-Claude Brialy, Michele Morgan. 98M FRN/ITL. *Leoni Scatterrati, I* (ITL); *The Lions are Loose* (USA) prod/rel: Franco-London Film, Vides Film

NICOLSON, ROBERT
Mrs. Ross, London 1961, Novel
    Whisperers, The 1966 d: Bryan Forbes. lps: Edith Evans, Eric Portman, Avis Bunnage. 106M UKN. prod/rel: Seven Pines Productions, United Artists

NIELSEN, LENNART
Krosor 500
    Ride Hard, Ride Wild 1970 d: Elov Peterssons. lps: Brigit Kroyer, Halger Strobye, Dahl Kullenberg. 70M DNM. prod/rel: Bt Kobenhavn

NIGGLI, JOSEFINA
A Mexican Village, 1945, Novel
    Sombrero 1952 d: Norman Foster. lps: Ricardo Montalban, Pier Angeli, Vittorio Gassman. 103M USA. prod/rel: MGM

NIJINSKY, ROMOLA
Nijinsky, Book
    Nijinsky 1980 d: Herbert Ross. lps: Alan Bates, George de La Pena, Alan Badel. 125M USA/UKN. prod/rel: Paramount

NIJINSKY, VASLAV
The Diary of Vaslav Nijinsky, Book
    Nijinsky 1980 d: Herbert Ross. lps: Alan Bates, George de La Pena, Alan Badel. 125M USA/UKN. prod/rel: Paramount

NIKOLAEVA, GALINA
Zhatva, 1950, Novel
    Vozvrashchenie Vassiliya Bortnikova 1953 d: V. I. Pudovkin. lps: Vsevolod Sanayev, S. Loukianov, Inna MakarovA. 110M USS. *The Return of Vassili Bortnikov*; *Vassili Bortnikov's Return*; *The Harvest*

NIKOLAJEVIC, ALEXANDR
Na Rusnem Miste, Play
    Vykrik Do Sibirske Noci 1935 d: V. Ch. Vladimirov. lps: Arno Velecky, V. Ch. Vladimirov, Theodor Pistek. 2422m CZC. *Cry in the Siberian Night* prod/rel: Dafa
Na Vojkom Meste, Play
    Vykrik Do Sibirske Noci 1935 d: V. Ch. Vladimirov. lps: Arno Velecky, V. Ch. Vladimirov, Theodor Pistek. 2422m CZC. *Cry in the Siberian Night* prod/rel: Dafa

NILAND, DARCY
The Shiralee, Novel
    Shiralee, The 1957 d: Leslie Norman. lps: Peter Finch, Elizabeth Sellars, Dana Wilson. 100M UKN/ASL. prod/rel: Ealing Films, MGM
    Shiralee, The 1987 d: George Ogilvie. lps: Bryan Brown, Rebecca Smart, Noni Hazlehurst. TVM. 190M ASL.

NILES, BLAIR
Condemned to Devil's Island, New York 1928, Novel
  Condemned 1929 d: Wesley Ruggles. lps: Ronald Colman, Ann Harding, Dudley Digges. 86M USA. *Condemned to Devil's Island* (UKN) prod/rel: Samuel Goldwyn, Inc., United Artists

NILIN, PAVEL
Chelovek Idyot V Goru, 1936, Novel
  Bolshaya Zhizn (I Seriya) 1940 d: Leonid Lukov. lps: Boris Andreyev, I. Peltser, Pyotr Aleinikov. 97M USS. *A Great Life; Bolsaja Zizn*
  Bolshaya Zhizn (Ii Seriya) 1946 d: Leonid Lukov. lps: Boris Andreyev, Piotr Aleinikov, I. Peltser. 91M USS. *A Great Life -Sequel*
Vpervye Zamuzhem, 1978, Short Story
  Vpervye Zamuzem 1979 d: Josif Heifitz. 99M USS. *Married for the First Time*

NILSEN, ROBERT
The Devil Executor, Novel
  Da Istambul Ordine Di Uccidere 1965 d: Carlo Ferrero. lps: Christopher Logan, Nino Fuscagni, Geraldine Pearsall. 88M ITL. *From Istanbul - Orders to Kill* prod/rel: Sigma Cin.Ca, Selecta

NILSSON PIRATEN, FRITIOF
Bock I Ortagard, 1933, Novel
  Bock I Ortagard 1958 d: Gosta Folke. lps: Edvin Adolphson, Irma Christenson, Gunnel Brostrom. 101M SWD. *A Square Peg in a Round Hole; A Goat in the Garden* prod/rel: Ab Svensk Filmindustri
Bockhandlaren Som Slutade Bada, 1937, Novel
  Bokhandlaren Som Slutade Bara 1969 d: Jarl Kulle. lps: Allan Edwall, Jarl Kulle, Margaretha Krook. 97M SWD. *The Bookseller Who Gave Up Bathing*
Bombi Bitt Och Jag, 1932, Novel
  Bombi Bitt Och Jag 1936 d: Gosta Rodin. lps: Sture Lagerwall, Frank Sundstrom, Harriet Bosse. 76M SWD. *Bombi Bitt and I* prod/rel: Triangelfilm, Svensk Talfilms Distributionsbyra Ab

NIMIER, ROGER (1925–1962), FRN
Histoire d'un Amour, Paris 1953, Novel
  Grandes Personnes, Les 1961 d: Jean Valere. lps: Jean Seberg, Maurice Ronet, Micheline Presle. 96M FRN/ITL. *Desideri Proibiti* (ITL); *A Taste of Love* (UKN); *Time Out for Love* (USA) prod/rel: Films Pomereu, International Productions

NIN, ANAIS (1903–1977), FRN
Henry and June: from the Unexpurgated Diary, 1986, Book
  Henry and June 1990 d: Philip Kaufman. lps: Fred Ward, Uma Thurman, Maria de Medeiros. 136M USA. *Henry & June* prod/rel: Universal Pictures

NISAL, SHANTA
Beghar, Novel
  Umbartha 1982 d: Jabbar Patel. lps: Smita Patil, Girish Karnad, Daya Dongre. 151M IND. *Threshold; Subah; The Dawn* prod/rel: Sujatha Chitra

NISHIGUCHI, KATSUMI
Gionmatsuri, Tokyo 1968, Short Story
  Gion Matsuri 1968 d: Daisuke Ito, Tetsuya Yamanouchi. lps: Kinnosuke Nakamura, Toshiro Mifune, Shima IwashitA. 168M JPN. *The Day the Sun Rose* (USA); *Gion Festival; Festival of Gion* prod/rel: Nihon Eiga Fukko Kyokai

NITEBERG, BJORN
Novel
  Utboropproret 1997 d: Svein Andersen. lps: Rikoll Johnsen, Mari Falkensten, Turid Balke. F NRW. *The Revolt of the Lost Children* prod/rel: Vision Media

NIVOIX, PAUL
Le Bouillant Achille, Play
  Emile l'Africain 1947 d: Robert Vernay. lps: Fernandel, Noelle Norman, Alexandre Rignault. 85M FRN. prod/rel: Latino Consortium Cinema
Direct Au Coeur, Play
  Direct Au Coeur 1932 d: Roger Lion, Arnaudy. lps: Arnaudy, Gustave Libeau, Suzanne Rissler. 104M FRN. prod/rel: Europa-Films
La Maison d'En Face, Play
  Maison d'En Face, La 1936 d: Christian-Jaque. lps: Elvire Popesco, Andre Lefaur, Pierre Stephen. 95M FRN. *The House Across the Street* (USA) prod/rel: F.E.F.

NIWA, FUMIO
Bara Gassen, 1937, Novel
  Bara-Gassen 1950 d: Mikio Naruse. 105M JPN. *The Battle of Roses*
Ikari No MacHi, 1949, Novel
  Ikari No MacHi 1950 d: Mikio Naruse. 105M JPN. *Town of Anger; The Angry Street*

NIZKOVSKY, RUDOLF
Na Svatem Kopecku, Opera
  Na Svatem Kopecku 1934 d: Miroslav Cikan. lps: Jaroslav Vojta, Marie Grossova, Jirina SteimarovA. 2364m CZC. *On Holy Hill* prod/rel: Lepka

NIZZA, ANGELO
I Quattro Moschettieri, Radio Play
  Quattro Moschettieri, I 1936 d: Carlo Campogalliani. ANM. 70M ITL. prod/rel: Miniatura Film

NOACK, BARBARA
Italienreise - Liebe Inbegriffen, Novel
  Italienreise - Liebe Inbegriffen 1958 d: Wolfgang Becker. lps: Paul Hubschmid, Susanne Cramer, Hannelore Schroth. 96M GRM. *Voyage to Italy - Complete With Love* prod/rel: C.C.C., UFA
Die Zurcher Verlobung, Novel
  Zurcher Verlobung, Die 1957 d: Helmut Kautner. lps: Liselotte Pulver, Paul Hubschmid, Bernhard Wicki. 107M GRM. *The Affairs of Julie* (USA); *The Zurich Engagement* prod/rel: Real, Europa

NOACK, HANS-GEORG
Rolltreppe Abwarts, Novel
  Rolltreppe Abwarts 1987 d: Martin Ruffert. lps: Paul Muller-Bruhl, Martin Gerke, Fabian Wagner. 72M GRM. prod/rel: Film-Ag Des Rhein-Seig-Gym. St. Augustin

NOBLE, HOLLISTER
The Golden Anchor, Novel
  Mutiny 1952 d: Edward Dmytryk. lps: Mark Stevens, Angela Lansbury, Patric Knowles. 77M USA. prod/rel: United Artists, King Bros. Prods.
Woman With a Sword, 1948, Book
  Drums in the Deep South 1951 d: William Cameron Menzies. lps: James Craig, Barbara Payton, Guy Madison. 87M USA. prod/rel: RKO Radio

NOBLE, JANET
Away Alone, Play
  Gold in the Streets 1997 d: Elizabeth Gill. lps: Karl Geary, James Belushi, Ian Hart. 94M UKN/IRL. prod/rel: Ferndale Films, Rank Film Distributors

NOBLE, W.
Blue Denim, New York 1958, Play
  Blue Denim 1959 d: Philip Dunne. lps: Carol Lynley, Brandon de Wilde, MacDonald Carey. 89M USA. *Blue Jeans* (UKN) prod/rel: 20th Century-Fox

NODIER, CHARLES
La Legende de Soeur Beatrice
  Legende de Soeur Beatrix, La 1923 d: Jacques de Baroncelli. lps: Sandra Milowanoff, Eric Barclay, Suzanne Bianchetti. 1760m FRN. prod/rel: Films Baroncelli

NOE, YVAN
Un Ami Viendra Ce Soir, Play
  Ami Viendra Ce Soir, Un 1945 d: Raymond Bernard. lps: Michel Simon, Madeleine Sologne, Paul Bernard. 125M FRN. *A Friend Will Come Tonight* (USA) prod/rel: Francinex
L'as, Play
  Ceux du Ciel 1940 d: Yvan Noe. lps: Pierre Renoir, Jean Galland, Aimos. 86M FRN. prod/rel: Fana Films
Dominque, Play
  Dominique 1950 d: Yvan Noe. lps: Michel Barbey, Pierrette Caillol, Roger Monteaux. 88M FRN. prod/rel: Paris Nice Productions
Une Mort Sans Importance, Play
  Mort Sans Importance, Une 1947 d: Yvan Noe. lps: Jean Tissier, Suzy Carrier, Marcelle Geniat. 80M FRN. prod/rel: G. Legrand
Ne Raccrochez Pas, Novel
  Cave Est Piege, Le 1963 d: Victor MerendA. lps: Dany Carrel, Dario Moreno, Christian Mery. 90M FRN. *Chasse a l'Homme* prod/rel: Socino, Eurocine
Teddy and Partner, Play
  Ame de Clown 1933 d: Marc Didier, Yvan Noe. lps: Pierre Fresnay, Pierrette Caillol, Alfred Pasquali. 90M FRN. prod/rel: Compagnie Francaise Cinematographique
Les Vacances Finissent Demain, Novel
  Vacances Finissent Demain, Les 1953 d: Yvan Noe. lps: Suzy Carrier, Pierrette Caillol, Michel Barbey. 97M FRN. prod/rel: Marius Lesoeur

NOEL, JOSEPH
Whispering Sage, New York 1922, Novel
  Whispering Sage 1927 d: Scott R. Dunlap. lps: Buck Jones, Natalie Joyce, Emile Chautard. 4783f USA. prod/rel: Fox Film Corp.

NOEL, STERLING
House of Secrets, Novel
  House of Secrets 1957 d: Guy Green. lps: Michael Craig, Julia Arnall, Brenda de Banzie. 97M UKN. *Triple Deception* (USA) prod/rel: Rank, Rank Film Distributors

NOGAMI, YAEKO (1885–1985), JPN
MacHiko, 1928, Novel
  Hana Hiraku 1948 d: Kon IchikawA. lps: Hideko Takamine, Ken Uehara, Hideko MimurA. 85M JPN. *A Flower Blooms* prod/rel: Shintoho Co.
Rikyu, Novel
  Rikyu 1989 d: Hiroshi TeshigaharA. lps: Rentaro Mikuni, Tsutomu Yamazaki, Yoshiko MitA. 135M JPN. prod/rel: Teshigahara Production, Inc., Shochiku Co.

NOGLY, HANS
Unternehmen Schlafsack, Novel
  Unternehmen Schlafsack 1955 d: Arthur M. Rabenalt. lps: Paul Klinger, Eva-Ingeborg Scholz, Kurt Meisel. 95M GRM. *Operation Sleeping Bag* prod/rel: Real, Rank
Wenn Beide Schuldig Werden, Novel
  Wenn Beide Schuldig Werden 1962 d: Hermann Leitner. lps: Nadia Gray, Ellen Schwiers, Hanns Lothar. 92M AUS. prod/rel: Schonbrunn

NOHAIN, JEAN
Le Bal Des Pompiers, Play
  Bal Des Pompiers, Le 1948 d: Andre Berthomieu. lps: Claude Dauphin, Paulette Dubost, Pierre Louis. 95M FRN. prod/rel: M.A.I.C.
Paris-Paris
  Voyage-Surprise 1946 d: Pierre Prevert. lps: Martine Carol, Rene Bourbon, Sinoel. 85M FRN. *Voyage Surprise* prod/rel: Cooperative Generale Du Cinema, Synops
Plume Au Vent, Opera
  Plume Au Vent 1952 d: Louis Cuny, Ramon Torrado. lps: Carmen Sevilla, Georges Guetary, Jose Luis Ozores. 97M FRN/SPN. *Pluma Al Viento* (SPN) prod/rel: Celia Films, Cocinor

NOLAN, FREDERICK
The Algonquin Project, Novel
  Brass Target 1978 d: John Hough. lps: George Kennedy, John Cassavetes, Sophia Loren. 111M USA. prod/rel: Metro-Goldwyn-Mayer Corp.

NOLAN, WILLIAM F.
Logan's Run, Novel
  Logan's Run 1976 d: Michael Anderson. lps: Michael York, Jenny Agutter, Peter Ustinov. 119M USA. prod/rel: MGM
  Logan's Run 1977 d: Robert Day. lps: Gregory Harrison, Heather Menzies, Donald Moffat. TVM. 70M USA.

NOLL, DIETER
Die Abenteuer Des Werner Holt, Novel
  Abenteuer Des Werner Holt, Die 1963 d: Joachim Kunert. lps: Klaus-Peter Thiele, Manfred Karge, Arno Wyzniewski. 168M GDR. *The Adventures of Werner Holt* (UKN) prod/rel: Defa

NOLL, INGRID
Die Apothekerin, Novel
  Apothekerin, Die 1998 d: Rainer Kaufmann. lps: Katja Riemann, Jurgen Vogel, Richy Muller. 103M GRM. *The Pharmacist* prod/rel: Senator Film Produktion

NOMA, HIROSHI
Shinku Chitai, 1952, Novel
  Shinku Chitai 1952 d: Satsuo Yamamoto. lps: Isao Kimura, Takashi Kanda, Yoshi Kato. 129M JPN. *Vacuum Zone* prod/rel: Shinsei Film Co.

NOON, JEFF
Woundings, Play
  Woundings 1998 d: Roberta Hanley. lps: Julie Cox, Sammi Davis, Twiggy. 102M UKN. prod/rel: Muse Prods., Cinequanon Pictures

NORD, PIERRE
La Bigorne, Caporal de France, Novel
  Bigorne, Caporal de France, La 1957 d: Robert Darene. lps: Francois Perier, Rossana Podesta, Robert Hirsch. 87M FRN. prod/rel: Lux-Films, E.D.I.C.
Double Crime Sur la Ligne Maginot, Novel
  Double Crime Sur la Ligne Maginot 1937 d: Felix GanderA. lps: Victor Francen, Jacques Baumer, Vera Korene. 101M FRN. *Crime in the Maginot Line* (USA) prod/rel: Felix Gandera
Peloton d'Execution, Novel
  Peloton d'Execution 1945 d: Andre Berthomieu. lps: Yvonne Gaudeau, Pierre Renoir, Lucien Coedel. 93M FRN. *Resistance* (USA) prod/rel: Cine Selection
Le Serpent, Novel
  Serpent, Le 1973 d: Henri Verneuil. lps: Yul Brynner, Henry Fonda, Dirk Bogarde. 122M FRN/ITL/GRM. *Serpente, Il* (ITL); *The Serpent* (UKN); *Night Flight from Moscow* (USA); *Der Schlange* (GRM) prod/rel: Euro International Film, Rialto

Terre d'Angoisse, Novel
Deuxieme Bureau Contre Kommandantur 1939 d: Rene Jayet, Robert Bibal. lps: Gabriel Gabrio, Leon Mathot, Junie Astor. 85M FRN. *Terre d'Angoisse* prod/rel: Productions Claude Dolbert

La Vierge du Rhin, Novel
Vierge du Rhin, La 1953 d: Gilles Grangier. lps: Jean Gabin, Elina Labourdette, Albert Dinan. 82M FRN. prod/rel: Vega Films

NORDEN, ERIC
Stagecoach to Fury, Novel
Stagecoach to Fury 1956 d: William F. Claxton. lps: Forrest Tucker, Mari Blanchard, Wallace Ford. 76M USA. prod/rel: 20th Century-Fox, Regal Films

NORDEN, PETER
Dm-Killer, Novel
Dm-Killer 1964 d: Rolf Thiele. lps: Curd Jurgens, Walter Giller, Daliah Lavi. 104M AUS. prod/rel: Wiener Stadthalle

Zwei Girls Vom Roten Stern, Novel
Zwei Girls Vom Roten Stern 1966 d: Sammy Drechsel. lps: Curd Jurgens, Lilli Palmer, Kurt Meisel. 92M GRM/AUS/FRN. *An Affair of State* (USA); *Duel la Vodka* (FRN); *Two Girls from the Red Star* prod/rel: Team, Chronos

NORDH, BERNHARD
Ingen Mans Kvinna, Novel
Ingen Mans Kvinna 1953 d: Lars-Eric Kjellgren. lps: Birger Malmsten, Ann-Marie Gyllenspetz, Alf Kjellin. 95M SWD. *No Man's Woman* prod/rel: Ab Svensk

NORDHOFF, CHARLES (1887–1947), USA
Botany Bay, 1941, Novel
Botany Bay 1953 d: John Farrow. lps: Alan Ladd, James Mason, Patricia MedinA. 94M USA. prod/rel: Paramount

High Barbaree, 1945, Novel
High Barbaree 1947 d: Jack Conway. lps: Van Johnson, June Allyson, Thomas Mitchell. 91M USA. prod/rel: MGM

The Hurricane, Boston 1936, Novel
Hurricane, The 1937 d: John Ford, Stuart Heisler (Uncredited). lps: Dorothy Lamour, Jon Hall, Mary Astor. 110M USA. prod/rel: United Artists Corp., Samuel Goldwyn, Inc.©

Hurricane 1979 d: Jan Troell. lps: Jason Robards Jr., Mia Farrow, Dayton Ka'ne. 119M USA. *Forbidden Paradise* prod/rel: Paramount

Men Against the Sea, 1934, Novel
Mutiny on the Bounty 1935 d: Frank Lloyd. lps: Charles Laughton, Clark Gable, Franchot Tone. 132M USA. prod/rel: Metro-Goldwyn-Mayer Corp.©

Men Without Country, 1944, Novel
Passage to Marseille 1944 d: Michael Curtiz. lps: Humphrey Bogart, Claude Rains, Michele Morgan. 110M USA. *Passage to Marseilles* prod/rel: Warner Bros.

Mutiny on the Bounty, Boston 1932, Novel
Mutiny on the Bounty 1962 d: Lewis Milestone, Carol Reed. lps: Marlon Brando, Trevor Howard, Richard Harris. 185M USA. prod/rel: Arcola Pictures, MGM

Mutiny on the Bounty 1935 d: Frank Lloyd. lps: Charles Laughton, Clark Gable, Franchot Tone. 132M USA. prod/rel: Metro-Goldwyn-Mayer Corp.©

No More Gas, 1940, Novel
Tuttles of Tahiti, The 1942 d: Charles Vidor. lps: Charles Laughton, Jon Hall, Peggy Drake. 91M USA. prod/rel: RKO Radio

NORDHS, BERNHARD
Starkare an Lagen, Novel
Starkare an Lagen 1951 d: Arnold Sjostrand, Bengt Logardt. lps: Bengt Logardt, Margareta Fehlen, Eric Laurent. 88M SWD. *Stronger Than the Law* prod/rel: Sandrew-Baumann

NORDSTROM, FRANCES
The Ruined Lady, New York 1920, Play
One Woman to Another 1927 d: Frank Tuttle. lps: Florence Vidor, Theodore von Eltz, Marie Shotwell. 4022f USA. prod/rel: Paramount Famous Lasky Corp.

NORELS, KAREL
Aan Dood Water, Novel
Laatste Dagen Van Een Eiland, de 1938 d: Ernest Winar. lps: Max Croiset, Jules Verstraete, Aaf Bouber. 80M NTH.

NORMAN, JOHN
Novel
Outlaw 1987 d: John Bud Cardos. lps: Urbano Barbarini, Jack Palance, Rebecca Ferrati. 89M ITL. *Outlaw of Gor* prod/rel: Cannon

Tarnsman of Gor, Novel
Gor 1987 d: Fritz Kiersch. lps: Urbano Barbarini, Oliver Reed, Rebecca Ferratti. 95M ITL/USA. prod/rel: Cannon

NORMAN, MARSHA (1947–, USA
Getting Out, Play
Getting Out 1993 d: John Korty. lps: Rebecca de Mornay, Rob Knepper, Carol Mitchell-Leon. TVM. 94M USA.

'Night, Mother, Play
'Night, Mother 1986 d: Tom Moore. lps: Sissy Spacek, Anne Bancroft, Ed Berke. 96M USA. *Night, Mother* prod/rel: Universal

NORMAND, ROGER
Gueule d'Ange, Play
Gueule d'Ange 1955 d: Marcel Blistene. lps: Maurice Ronet, Viviane Romance, Genevieve Kervine. 100M FRN. *Pleasures and Vices* (USA) prod/rel: Lutetia

NORO, FRED
Un Certain Code, Novel
Ennemis, Les 1961 d: Edouard Molinaro. lps: Roger Hanin, Claude Brasseur, Pascale Audret. 92M FRN. *A Touch of Treason* (USA) prod/rel: Belles Rives, Sirius

NORRIS, CHARLES GILMAN
Brass: a Novel of Marriage, New York 1921, Novel
Brass 1923 d: Sidney A. Franklin. lps: Monte Blue, Marie Prevost, Harry Myers. 8400f USA. prod/rel: Warner Brothers Pictures

Bread, New York 1923, Novel
Bread 1924 d: Victor Schertzinger. lps: Mae Busch, Robert Frazer, Pat O'Malley. 6500f USA. prod/rel: Metro-Goldwyn Pictures

Seed: a Novel of Birth Control, New York 1930, Novel
Seed 1931 d: John M. Stahl. lps: John Boles, Genevieve Tobin, Lois Wilson. 96M USA. prod/rel: Universal Pictures Corp.©

NORRIS, FRANK (1870–1902), USA, Norris, Benjamin Franklin
McTeague; a Story of San Francisco, New York 1899, Novel
Desert Gold 1914 d: Scott Sidney. lps: Charles Ray, Clara Williams, Frank Borzage. 2r USA. *After the Storm*

Greed 1924 d: Erich von Stroheim. lps: Gibson Gowland, Zasu Pitts, Jean Hersholt. 10r USA. prod/rel: Metro-Goldwyn Pictures

Life's Whirlpool 1916 d: Barry O'Neil. lps: Holbrook Blinn, Fania Marinoff, Walter D. Greene. 5r USA. prod/rel: William A. Brady Production, World Film Corp.

Moran of the Lady Letty, New York 1898, Novel
Moran of the Lady Letty 1922 d: George Melford. lps: Dorothy Dalton, Rudolph Valentino, Charles Brinley. 6360f USA. prod/rel: Famous Players-Lasky, Paramount Pictures

The Octopus, 1901, Novel
Octopus, The 1915 d: Thomas Santschi. lps: Thomas Santschi, Lillian Hayward, Leo Pierson. 3r USA. prod/rel: Selig

The Pit, New York 1903, Novel
Corner in Wheat, A 1909 d: D. W. Griffith. lps: Frank Powell, W. Chrystie Miller, Kate Bruce. 953f USA. prod/rel: Biograph Co.

Pit, The 1915 d: Maurice Tourneur. lps: Wilton Lackaye, Gail Kane, Milton Sills. 5r USA. prod/rel: William A. Brady Picture Plays, Inc., World Film Corp.©

NORRIS, KATHLEEN (1880–1960), USA, Norris, Kathleen Thompson
Beauty's Daughter, New York 1935, Novel
Navy Wife 1935 d: Allan Dwan. lps: Claire Trevor, Ralph Bellamy, Jane Darwell. 72M USA. *Beauty's Daughter* prod/rel: Twentieth Century-Fox Film Corp.©

The Callahans and the Murphys, Garden City, N.Y. 1924, Novel
Callahans and the Murphys, The 1927 d: George W. Hill. lps: Marie Dressler, Polly Moran, Sally O'Neil. 6126f USA. prod/rel: Metro-Goldwyn-Mayer Pictures

Christine of the Hungry Heart, 1924, Short Story
Christine of the Hungry Heart 1924 d: George Archainbaud. lps: Florence Vidor, Clive Brook, Ian Keith. 7500f USA. prod/rel: Thomas H. Ince Corp., First National Pictures

Harriet and the Piper, New York 1920, Novel
Harriet and the Piper 1920 d: Bertram Bracken. lps: Anita Stewart, Charles Richman, Ward Crane. 5954f USA. prod/rel: Louis B. Mayer Productions, Anita Stewart Productions©

The Heart of Rachael, Garden City N.Y. 1916, Novel
Heart of Rachael, The 1918 d: Howard Hickman. lps: Bessie Barriscale, Herschal Mayall, Ella Hall. 5r USA. prod/rel: Bessie Barriscale Productions, Paralta Plays, Inc.

Josselyn's Wife, New York 1918, Novel
Josselyn's Wife 1919 d: Howard Hickman. lps: Bessie Barriscale, Nigel Barrie, Kathleen Kirkham. 5r USA. prod/rel: B. B. Features, Inc., Robertson-Cole Co.

Josselyn's Wife 1926 d: Richard Thorpe. lps: Pauline Frederick, Holmes Herbert, Josephine Kaliz. 5800f USA. prod/rel: Tiffany Productions

The Luck of Geraldine Laird, 1919, Novel
Luck of Geraldine Laird, The 1920 d: Edward Sloman. lps: Bessie Barriscale, Niles Welch, Boyd Irwin. 5000f USA. *Woman and Wife* prod/rel: B. B. Features, Robertson-Cole Distributing Corp.

Lucretia Lombard, New York 1922, Novel
Lucretia Lombard 1923 d: Jack Conway. lps: Irene Rich, Monte Blue, Marc MacDermott. 7500f USA. *Flaming Passion* prod/rel: Warner Brothers Pictures

Manhattan Love Song, New York 1934, Novel
Change of Heart 1934 d: John G. Blystone. lps: Janet Gaynor, Charles Farrell, Ginger Rogers. 76M USA. *Manhattan Love Song; The World Is Ours* prod/rel: Fox Film Corp.

Mother, New York 1911, Novel
Mother 1927 d: James Leo Meehan. lps: Belle Bennett, Crauford Kent, William Bakewell. 6885f USA. *The Woman Sees It Through* prod/rel: R-C Pictures, Film Booking Offices of America

My Best Girl, New York 1927, Novel
My Best Girl 1927 d: Sam Taylor. lps: Mary Pickford, Charles "Buddy" Rogers, Sunshine Hart. 7460f USA. prod/rel: Mary Pickford Corp., United Artists

Passion Flower, 1929, Short Story
Passion Flower 1930 d: William C. de Mille. lps: Kay Francis, Kay Johnson, Charles Bickford. 7171f USA. prod/rel: Metro-Goldwyn-Mayer Pictures

Poor, Dear Margaret Kirby, 1913, Short Story
Poor, Dear Margaret Kirby 1921 d: William P. S. Earle. lps: Elaine Hammerstein, William B. Donaldson, Ellen Cassidy. 4581f USA. prod/rel: Selznick Pictures

Rose of the World, New York 1926, Novel
Rose of the World 1925 d: Harry Beaumont. lps: Patsy Ruth Miller, Allan Forrest, Pauline Garon. 7506f USA. prod/rel: Warner Brothers Pictures

Second Hand Wife, New York 1932, Novel
Second Hand Wife 1933 d: Hamilton MacFadden. lps: Sally Eilers, Helen Vinson, Ralph Bellamy. 64M USA. *The Illegal Divorce* (UKN) prod/rel: Fox Film Corp.©

Walls of Gold, New York 1933, Novel
Walls of Gold 1933 d: Kenneth MacKennA. lps: Sally Eilers, Norman Foster, Ralph Morgan. 74M USA. prod/rel: Fox Film Corp.©

NORTH, CARRINGTON
Among Those Present, Play
Headleys at Home, The 1938 d: Chris Beute. lps: Evelyn Venable, Grant Mitchell, Vince Barnett. 69M USA. *Among Those Present* (UKN) prod/rel: Standard Pictures Productions©

NORTH, CLYDE
Remote Control, New York 1929, Play
Remote Control 1930 d: Nick Grinde, Malcolm St. Clair. lps: William Haines, Charles King, Mary Doran. 5958f USA. prod/rel: Metro-Goldwyn-Mayer Pictures

NORTH, STERLING (1906–1974), USA
Midnight and Jeremiah, Novel
So Dear to My Heart 1948 d: Harold Schuster, Hamilton Luske. lps: Burl Ives, Beulah Bondi, Harry Carey. 84M USA. prod/rel: RKO, Walt Disney

Rascal, a Memoir of a Better Era, New York 1963, Novel
Rascal 1969 d: Norman Tokar. lps: Steve Forrest, Bill Mumy, Pamela Toll. 85M USA. prod/rel: Walt Disney Productions

NORTON, ANDRE (1912–, USA, Norton, Alice Mary
The Beastmaster, Novel
Beastmaster 2: Through the Portal of Time 1991 d: Sylvio Tabet. lps: Marc Singer, Kari Wuhrer, Sarah Douglas. 107M USA. prod/rel: Republic, Films 21

NORTON, FREDERICK
Chu Chin Chow, London 1916, Musical Play
Chu Chin Chow 1934 d: Walter Forde. lps: George Robey, Fritz Kortner, Anna May Wong. 102M UKN. prod/rel: Gaumont-British, Gainsborough

Chu Chin Chow 1923 d: Herbert Wilcox. lps: Betty Blythe, Herbert Langley, Randle Ayrton. 13r UKN. prod/rel: Graham-Wilcox

NORTON, MARY
Bonfires and Broomsticks, Short Story
Bedknobs and Broomsticks 1971 d: Robert Stevenson. lps: Angela Lansbury, David Tomlinson, Roddy McDowall. 117M USA. prod/rel: Buena Vista, Walt Disney

The Borrowers, Novel
Borrowers, The 1973 d: Walter C. Miller. lps: Eddie Albert, Tammy Grimes, Judith Anderson. TVM. 73M USA. prod/rel: 20th Century-Fox Tv, Walt Defaria Prods.

The Borrowers, Nove L
Borrowers, The 1997 d: Peter Hewitt. lps: John Goodman, Jim Broadbent, Mark Williams. 87M UKN. prod/rel: Polygram Filmed Entertainment, Working Title

Magic Bed-Knob, The, Short Story
Bedknobs and Broomsticks 1971 d: Robert Stevenson. lps: Angela Lansbury, David Tomlinson, Roddy McDowall. 117M USA. prod/rel: Buena Vista, Walt Disney

NORTON, ROY
The Greater Hate, Story
Love and Hatred 1911. lps: Reeva Greenwood, Charles Ogle, Yale Benner. 1000f USA. prod/rel: Edison

The Masterful Hireling, Story
Masterful Hireling, The 1915. lps: Ivan Christy, Charles Hill Mailes, Mary MalatestA. SHT USA. prod/rel: Biograph Co.

The Mediator, New York 1913, Novel
Mediator, The 1916 d: Otis Turner. lps: George Walsh, Juanita Hansen, James Marcus. 5r USA. prod/rel: Fox Film Corp., William Fox©

Mixed Faces, New York 1921, Novel
Mixed Faces, I 1922 d: Rowland V. Lee. lps: William Russell, Renee Adoree, De Witt Jennings. 4505f USA. prod/rel: Fox Film Corp.

The Plunderer, New York 1912, Novel
Plunderer, The 1915 d: Edgar Lewis. lps: William Farnum, Harry Spingler, William J. Gross. 5r USA. prod/rel: Fox Film Corp., William Fox©
Plunderer, The 1924 d: George Archainbaud. lps: Frank Mayo, Evelyn Brent, Thomas Santschi. 5812f USA. prod/rel: Fox Film Corp.

NORTVEDT, REIDUN
Sundays, Novel
Sondagsengler 1996 d: Berit Nesheim. lps: Marie Theisen, Bjorn Sundquist, Hildegunn Riise. 103M NRW. *The Other Side of Sunday* prod/rel: Norwegian Film Institute, Nrk Drama

NOSTLINGER, CHRISTINE
Konrad Aus Der Konservenbuchse, Novel
Konrad Aus Der Konservenbuchse 1982 d: Claudia Schroder. lps: Violetta Ferrari, Heinz Schubert, Daniel Thorbecke. 80M GRM. *Canned Conrad* prod/rel: Ottokar Runze, Atlas

Wir Pfeifen Auf Den Gurkenkonig, Novel
Wir Pfeifen Auf Den Gurkenkonig 1974 d: Hark Bohm. lps: Sonja Sutter, Karl Michael Vogler, Thomas Blass. 96M GRM. *Down With the King* prod/rel: S.R., S.D.R.

NOTARI, UMBERTO
I Trei Ladri, 1907, Novel
Tre Ladri, I 1954 d: Lionello de Felice. lps: Toto, Jean-Claude Pascal, Simone Simon. 110M ITL/FRN. *Les Trois Voleurs* (FRN) prod/rel: Rizzoli Film (Roma), Francinex

Treno Di Lusso, Novel
Treno Di Lusso 1917 d: Mario Bonnard. lps: Leda Gys, Mario Bonnard, La Troupe Dei Faraboni. 1655m ITL. *L'avventuriera Del Bal Tabarin*; *L'avventuriera Del Circo* prod/rel: General-Megale Film

NOTHOMB, AMELIE
Hygiene de l'Assassin, Novel
Hygiene de l'Assassin 1999 d: Francois Ruggieri. lps: Jean Yanne, Barbara Schulz, Sophie Broustal. 69M FRN. prod/rel: Mfd, Tsf

NOTI, KARL
Drei Tage Mittelarrest, Play
Drei Tage Mittelarrest 1955 d: Georg Jacoby. lps: Ernst Waldow, Grethe Weiser, Erwin Strahl. 95M GRM. *Three Days Solitary Confinement*; *Three Days in the Guardhouse* prod/rel: Standard, D.F.H.

Servus Peter, Play
Czardas Der Herzen 1951 d: Alexander von SlatinA. lps: Wolf Albach-Retty, Hannelore Bollmann, Edith Prager. 90M GRM. *Csardas of the Hearts* prod/rel: Oska, Rena

NOURISSIER, FRANCOIS
Le Corps de Diane, Novel
Telo Diana 1969 d: Jean-Louis Richard. lps: Jeanne Moreau, Charles Denner, Elisabeth Wiener. 96M CZC/FRN. *Le Corps de Diane* (FRN); *The Body of Diana* prod/rel: Renn Productions, Carla Films

NOVAK, KAREL
Medvedi a Tanecnice, Novel
Nocni Motyl 1941 d: Frantisek Cap. lps: Hana Vitova, Svatopluk Benes, Gustav Nezval. 2410m CZC. *The Night Moth*; *Nocturnal Butterfly* prod/rel: Lucernafilm

NOVAK, LADISLAV
Pereje (Pepa), Play
Pereje 1940 d: Karel SpelinA. lps: Elena Tanasco, Svatopluk Benes, Vaclav Tregl. 2357m CZC. *The Rapids* prod/rel: Dafa

NOVARESE, VITTORIO NINO
Furia, Novel
Furia 1946 d: Goffredo Alessandrini. lps: Isa Pola, Adriana Benetti, Gino Cervi. 104M ITL. prod/rel: a.G.I.C., Fabio Franchini
Wild Is the Wind 1957 d: George Cukor. lps: Anna Magnani, Anthony Quinn, Anthony FranciosA. 114M USA. prod/rel: Paramount

NOVELLI
Il Commissario Di Torino, Novel
Uomo Una Citta, Un 1974 d: Romolo Guerrieri. lps: Enrico Maria Salerno, Francoise Fabian, Luciano Salce. 115M ITL. prod/rel: Goriz Film, Cineriz

NOVELLI, AUGUSTO
Acqua Cheta, Play
Acqua Cheta 1933 d: Gero Zambuto. lps: Gianfranco Giachetti, Andreina Pagnani, Germana Paolieri. 72M ITL. prod/rel: Manenti Film, Caesar Film

L'amore Sui Tetti, 1890, Play
Amore Sui Tetti, L' 1915 d: Eleuterio Rodolfi. lps: Eleuterio Rodolfi, Gigetta Morano. 215m ITL. prod/rel: S.A. Ambrosio

Il Coraggio, Play
Nini Falpala 1933 d: Amleto Palermi. lps: Dina Galli, Renzo Ricci, Hilda Springher. 84M ITL. *Falpala* prod/rel: Manenti Film

NOVELLI, ENRICO
Fiorenza Mia!, 1912, Play
Fiorenza Mia! 1915 d: Enrico Novelli. lps: Ermete Novelli, Fiora d'Altena, Alfredo Bracci. ITL.

NOVELLO, IVOR (1893–1951), UKN, Davies, Ivor
The Dancing Years, London 1939, Play
Dancing Years, The 1950 d: Harold French. lps: Dennis Price, Gisele Preville, Patricia Dainton. 97M UKN. prod/rel: Associated British Picture Corporation, Ab-Pathe

Downhill, London 1926, Play
Downhill 1927 d: Alfred Hitchcock. lps: Ivor Novello, Isabel Jeans, Ian Hunter. 7600f UKN. *When Boys Leave Home* (USA) prod/rel: Gainsborough, Woolf & Freedman

Glamorous Night, London 1935, Musical Play
Glamorous Night 1937 d: Brian Desmond Hurst. lps: Mary Ellis, Otto Kruger, Victor Jory. 81M UKN. prod/rel: British International Pictures, Associated British Picture Corporation

I Lived With You, London 1932, Play
I Lived With You 1933 d: Maurice Elvey. lps: Ivor Novello, Ursula Jeans, Ida Lupino. 100M UKN. prod/rel: Twickenham, Woolf & Freedman

King's Rhapsody, London 1949, Musical Play
King's Rhapsody 1955 d: Herbert Wilcox. lps: Anna Neagle, Errol Flynn, Patrice Wymore. 93M UKN. prod/rel: Everest, British Lion

The Rat, London 1924, Play
Rat, The 1925 d: Graham Cutts. lps: Ivor Novello, Mae Marsh, Isabel Jeans. 7323f UKN. prod/rel: Gainsborough, Woolf & Freedman
Rat, The 1937 d: Jack Raymond. lps: Ruth Chatterton, Anton Walbrook, Rene Ray. 72M UKN. prod/rel: Imperator, Radio

Symphony in Two Flats, London 1929, Play
Symphony in Two Flats 1930 d: V. Gareth Gundrey. lps: Ivor Novello, Benita Hume, Cyril Ritchard. 86M UKN. prod/rel: Gainsborough, Gaumont

The Truth Game, London 1928, Play
But the Flesh Is Weak 1932 d: Jack Conway. lps: Robert Montgomery, Heather Thatcher, C. Aubrey Smith. 82M USA. *The Truth Game*; *Mister and Mistress*; *A Family Affair* prod/rel: Metro-Goldwyn-Mayer Corp.

Truth Game, The, London 1928, Play
Free and Easy 1941 d: George Sidney. lps: Robert Cummings, Ruth Hussey, Reginald Owen. 56M USA. prod/rel: MGM

NOVOTNY, JOACHIM
Verdammt, Ich Bin Erwachsen, Novel
..Verdammt, Ich Bin Erwachsen. 1974 d: Rolf Losansky. lps: Ralf Schlosser, Frank Wuttig, Lilo Josefowitz. 100M GDR. *Hell! I'm Mature* prod/rel: Defa

NOWAKOWSKI, MAREK
Story
Prognoza Pogody 1982 d: Antoni Krauze. lps: Halina Buyno-Loza, Zofia Cegielkowa, Barbara ChojeckA. 86M PLN. *Weather Forecast* prod/rel: Film Polski, Gruppe Tor

NOYES, ALFRED (1880–1958), UKN
The Highwayman, 1907, Verse
Highwayman, The 1951 d: Lesley Selander. lps: Philip Friend, Wanda Hendrix, Charles Coburn. 82M USA. prod/rel: Allied Artists

The Highwayman, Poem
Lady and the Bandit, The 1951 d: Ralph Murphy. lps: Louis Hayward, Patricia Medina, Suzanne Dalbert. 79M USA. *Dick Turpin's Ride* (UKN) prod/rel: Columbia

NOZIERE, FERNAND
Cette Vieille Canaille, Play
Cette Vieille Canaille 1933 d: Anatole Litvak. lps: Harry Baur, Alice Field, Pierre Blanchar. 99M FRN. prod/rel: Cipar-Films
Quella Vecchia Canaglia 1934 d: Carlo Ludovico BragagliA. lps: Ruggero Ruggeri, Carmen Boni, Mino Doro. 82M ITL. prod/rel: G.A.I., Amato Film

La Comedie du Bonheur, Play
Ecco la Felicita! 1940 d: Marcel L'Herbier. lps: Michel Simon, Ramon Novarro, Micheline Presle. 102M ITL. *La Commedia Della Felicita* prod/rel: Scalera Film

NUCHTERN, HANS
Verwirrung Um Inge, Novel
Irene in Noten 1953 d: E. W. Emo. lps: Bruni Lobel, Walter Giller, Helli Servi. 92M AUS/YGS. *Irena V Stisci* (YGS); *Wirbel Um Irene* prod/rel: Helios

NUGENT, ELLIOTT (1899–1980), USA
Father's Day, Story
Richest Man in the World, The 1930 d: Sam Wood. lps: Louis Mann, Robert Montgomery, Elliott Nugent. 7775f USA. *Sins of the Children*; *Father's Day* prod/rel: Cosmopolitan Productions, Metro-Goldwyn-Mayer Distributing Corp.

Kempy, New York 1922, Play
Wise Girls 1929 d: E. Mason Hopper. lps: Elliott Nugent, Norma Lee, Roland Young. 8818f USA. *Kempy* prod/rel: Metro-Goldwyn-Mayer Pictures

The Male Animal, New York 1940, Play
Male Animal, The 1942 d: Elliott Nugent. lps: Henry Fonda, Olivia de Havilland, Jack Carson. 101M USA. prod/rel: Warner Bros.
She's Working Her Way Through College 1952 d: H. Bruce Humberstone. lps: Virginia Mayo, Ronald Reagan, Gene Nelson. 101M USA. prod/rel: Warner Bros.

The Poor Nut, New York 1925, Play
Poor Nut, The 1927 d: Richard Wallace. lps: Jack Mulhall, Charlie Murray, Jean Arthur. 6897f USA. prod/rel: Jess Smith Productions, First National Pictures
Local Boy Makes Good 1931 d: Mervyn Leroy. lps: Joe E. Brown, Dorothy Lee, Ruth Hall. 69M USA. *The Poor Nut* prod/rel: First National Pictures©
Athlete Incomplet, L' 1932 d: Claude Autant-LarA. lps: Douglas Fairbanks Jr., Jeannette Ferney, Barbara Leonard. 93M FRN. *L'athlete Maigre Lui*; *Olympic 13 Gagnant*; *Love Is a Racket* prod/rel: Warner Bros., First National

NUGENT, J. C.
Father's Day, Story
Richest Man in the World, The 1930 d: Sam Wood. lps: Louis Mann, Robert Montgomery, Elliott Nugent. 7775f USA. *Sins of the Children*; *Father's Day* prod/rel: Cosmopolitan Productions, Metro-Goldwyn-Mayer Distributing Corp.

Kempy, New York 1922, Play
Wise Girls 1929 d: E. Mason Hopper. lps: Elliott Nugent, Norma Lee, Roland Young. 8818f USA. *Kempy* prod/rel: Metro-Goldwyn-Mayer Pictures

Nightstick, New York 1927, Play
Alibi 1929 d: Roland West. lps: Chester Morris, Harry Stubbs, Mae Busch. 90M USA. *The Perfect Alibi* (UKN); *Nightstick* prod/rel: Feature Productions, United Artists

The Poor Nut, New York 1925, Play
Poor Nut, The 1927 d: Richard Wallace. lps: Jack Mulhall, Charlie Murray, Jean Arthur. 6897f USA. prod/rel: Jess Smith Productions, First National Pictures
Local Boy Makes Good 1931 d: Mervyn Leroy. lps: Joe E. Brown, Dorothy Lee, Ruth Hall. 69M USA. *The Poor Nut* prod/rel: First National Pictures©
Athlete Incomplet, L' 1932 d: Claude Autant-LarA. lps: Douglas Fairbanks Jr., Jeannette Ferney, Barbara Leonard. 93M FRN. *L'athlete Maigre Lui*; *Olympic 13 Gagnant*; *Love Is a Racket* prod/rel: Warner Bros., First National

NUGENT, MAUDE
Sweet Rosie O'Grady, 1896, Song
  Sweet Rosie O'Grady 1926 d: Frank Strayer. lps: Shirley Mason, Cullen Landis, E. Alyn Warren. 6108f USA. prod/rel: Columbia Pictures

NUITTER, CHARLES-LOUIS
Une Tasse de the, 1860
  Tazza Di the, Una 1923 d: Toddi. lps: Diomira Jacobini, Giuseppe Pierozzi, Clara Zambonelli. 745m ITL. prod/rel: Selecta-Toddi

NUS
Les Pauvres de Paris, Play
  Pauvres de Paris, Les 1913 d: Georges DenolA. lps: Jules Mondos, Louis Ravet, Gina Barbieri. 1095m FRN. prod/rel: Scagl

NUSIC, BRANISLAV
Gospoda Ministarka, 1929, Play
  Gospoda Ministarka 1958 d: Zorz Skrigin. lps: Marica Popovic, Jovan Gec, Severin Bijelic. 90M YGS.
Sumnjivo Lice, 1887, Play
  Sumnjivo Lice 1954 d: Soja Jovanovic, Predrag Dinulovic. lps: Mihajlo Paskaljevic, Rade Markovic, Mihajlo Viktorovic. 80M YGS. *A Suspicious Character*

NYITRAY, EMIL
Story
  Millionaire Pirate, The 1919 d: Rupert Julian. lps: Monroe Salisbury, Ruth Clifford, Clyde Fillmore. 5r USA. prod/rel: Bluebird Photoplays, Inc.©
My Lady Friends, New York 1919, Play
  My Lady Friends 1921 d: Lloyd Ingraham. lps: Carter de Haven, Flora Parker de Haven, Thomas Lingham. 5650f USA. prod/rel: Carter de Haven Productions, Associated First National Pictures
What's Your Wife Doing?, New York 1923, Play
  Reckless Romance 1924 d: Scott Sidney. lps: T. Roy Barnes, Harry Myers, Wanda Hawley. 5530f USA. prod/rel: Christie Film Co., Producers Distributing Corp.

O

OAKLEY, BARRY
A Salute to the Great MacArthy, 1970, Novel
  Great MacArthy, The 1975 d: David Baker. lps: John Jarratt, Judy Morris, Kate Fitzpatrick. 98M ASL. *A Salute to the Great MacArthy; The Great McCarthy*

OATES, JOYCE CAROL (1938–, USA
Short Stories
  Getting to Know You 1999 d: Lisanne Skyler. lps: Heather Matarazzo, Zach Braff, Michael Weston. 96M USA. prod/rel: Showdowcatcher Entertainment, Search Party
Foxfire, Novel
  Foxfire 1996 d: Annette Haywood-Carter. lps: Hedy Burress, Angelina Jolie, Jenny Lewis. 100M USA. prod/rel: Rysher Entertainment
Where are You Going, Where Have You Been?, 1967, Short Story
  Smooth Talk 1985 d: Joyce ChoprA. lps: Treat Williams, Laura Dern, Mary Kay Place. 92M USA. prod/rel: Spectrafilm, Nepenthe Productions

OBER, ROBERT
Play
  Fighting Lady, The 1935 d: Carlos Borcosque. lps: Peggy Shannon, Jack Mulhall, Marion Lessing. 50M USA. prod/rel: Fanchon Royer Pictures©

OBERG, F. C.
Das Geschenk Des Inders, Novel
  Geschenk Des Inders 1913 d: Louis Ralph. lps: Louis Ralph, Baptista Schreiber, Adele Reuter-Eichberg. GRM. prod/rel: Karl Werner

OBOLER, ARCH (1909–1987), USA
Alter Ego, Radio Play
  Bewitched 1945 d: Arch Oboler. lps: Edmund Gwenn, Phyllis Thaxter, Stephen McNally. 65M USA. *Alter Ego* prod/rel: Metro-Goldwyn-Mayer Corp.
Mrs. Kinsley's Report, Play
  1 + 1 (Exploring the Kinsey Reports) 1961 d: Arch Oboler. lps: Leo G. Carroll, Kate Reid, Hilda Brawner. 114M CND. *The Kinsey Report* (UKN) prod/rel: Fluorite Ltd.
Strange Holiday, Radio Play
  Strange Holiday 1945 d: Arch Oboler. lps: Claude Rains, Bobbie Stebbins, Barbara Bates. 62M USA. *The Day After Tomorrow* (UKN) prod/rel: Producers Releasing Corp.

O'BRIEN, EDNA (1931–, IRL
The Country Girls, 1960, Novel
  Country Girls, The 1984 d: Desmond Davis. lps: Sam Neill, Maeve Germaine, Jill Doyle. 107M UKN/IRL. prod/rel: Channel Four, London Film
The Lonely Girl, London 1962, Novel
  Girl With Green Eyes 1964 d: Desmond Davis. lps: Peter Finch, Rita Tushingham, Lynn Redgrave. 91M UKN. *The Girl With the Green Eyes; Once Upon a Summer* prod/rel: Woodfall Film Productions, United Artists
A Woman By the Seaside, Short Story
  I Was Happy Here 1965 d: Desmond Davis. lps: Sarah Miles, Cyril Cusack, Julian Glover. 91M UKN. *Time Lost and Time Remembered* (USA); *Passage of Love* prod/rel: Partisan Film Productions, Rank Film Distributors

O'BRIEN, FREDERICK
White Shadows in the South Seas, New York 1919, Novel
  White Shadows in the South Seas 1928 d: W. S. Van Dyke, Robert Flaherty. lps: Monte Blue, Raquel Torres, Robert Anderson. 7968f USA. *Southern Skies* prod/rel: Metro-Goldwyn-Mayer Distributing Corp., Cosmopolitan Productions

O'BRIEN, KATE
Mary Lavelle, Novel
  Talk of Angels 1998 d: Nick Hamm. lps: Polly Walker, Vincent Perez, Franco Nero. 96M USA. prod/rel: Miramax Films, Polaris Pictures Ltd.
That Lady, Novel
  That Lady 1955 d: Terence Young. lps: Olivia de Havilland, Gilbert Roland, Paul Scofield. 100M UKN. prod/rel: Atlanta, 20th Century-Fox

O'BRIEN, LIAM
The Remarkable Mr. Pennypacker, New York 1953, Play
  Remarkable Mr. Pennypacker, The 1959 d: Henry Levin. lps: Clifton Webb, Dorothy McGuire, Charles Coburn. 87M USA. prod/rel: 20th Century-Fox

O'BRIEN, RICHARD
The Rocky Horror Show, Play
  Rocky Horror Picture Show, The 1975 d: Jim Sharman. lps: Tim Curry, Susan Sarandon, Barry Bostwick. 100M USA/UKN. prod/rel: 20th Century Fox

O'BRIEN, ROBERT C.
Mrs. Frisby and the Rats of N.I.M.H., Novel
  Secret of Nimh, The 1982 d: Don Bluth. ANM. 83M USA. *The Secret of N.I.M.H.* prod/rel: MGM, United Artists

O'BRIEN, TIM
Sweetheart of the Song Tra Bong, Short Story
  Soldier's Sweetheart, A 1998 d: Thomas Michael Donnelly. lps: Kiefer Sutherland, Georgina Cates, Skeet Ulrich. 112M USA. prod/rel: Paramount, Showtime Networks

O'BRIEN, WILLIS
Story
  Beast of Hollow Mountain, The 1956 d: Ismael Rodriguez, Edward Nassour. lps: Guy Madison, Patricia Medina, Eduardo NoriegA. 79M USA/MXC. *El Monstruo de la Montana Hueca* (MXC); *La Bestia de la Montana* prod/rel: United Artists Corp., Nassour-Peliculas Rodriguez

O'BRINE, MANNING
Passport to Treason, Novel
  Passport to Treason 1956 d: Robert S. Baker. lps: Rod Cameron, Lois Maxwell, Clifford Evans. 80M UKN. prod/rel: Mid-Century, Eros

OBSTFELDER, SIGBJORN
Korset, 1896, Novel
  Evige Eva, Den 1953 d: Rolf Randall. 77M NRW.

O'CALLAGHAN, SEAN
The Slave Trade, London 1961, Book
  Schiave Esistono Ancora, Le 1964 d: Roberto Malenotti, Folco Quilici. DOC. 100M ITL/FRN. *Les Esclaves Existent Toujours* (FRN); *Slave Trade in the World Today* (USA) prod/rel: Ge.Si. Cinematografica, C.I.S.A. (Roma)

O'CASEY, SEAN (1884–1964), IRL
Bedtime Story, 1951, Play
  Pension Pro Svobodne Pany 1967 d: Jiri Krejcik. lps: Iva Janzurova, Josef Abrham, Jiri Hrzan. 90M CZC. *Boarding House for Single Gentlemen; Boarding House for Bachelors; Boarding House for Gentlemen*
Juno and the Peacock, London 1925, Play
  Juno and the Paycock 1929 d: Alfred Hitchcock. lps: Sara Allgood, Edward Chapman, Sydney Morgan. 99M UKN. *The Shame of Mary Boyle* (USA) prod/rel: British International Pictures, Wardour

Mirror in My House, 1956, Autob
  Young Cassidy 1965 d: Jack Cardiff, John Ford (Uncredited). lps: Rod Taylor, Maggie Smith, Julie Christie. 110M UKN/USA. prod/rel: Sextant Films, MGM
The Plough and the Stars, Dublin 1926, Play
  Plough and the Stars, The 1936 d: John Ford. lps: Barbara Stanwyck, Preston Foster, Barry Fitzgerald. 78M USA. prod/rel: RKO Radio Pictures©

O'CONNELL, THOMAS EDWARD
Interem, Radio Play
  Face Behind the Mask, The 1941 d: Robert Florey. lps: Peter Lorre, Evelyn Keyes, Don Beddoe. 69M USA. *Behind the Mask* (UKN) prod/rel: Columbia

O'CONNER, ELIZABETH
The Irishman, Novel
  Irishman, The 1978 d: Donald Crombie. lps: Michael Craig, Robyn Nevin, Simon Burke. 108M ASL. prod/rel: Forest Home Films©, South Australian Film Corp.

O'CONNOR, EDWIN (1918–1968), USA, O'Connor, Edwin Greene
The Last Hurrah, 1956, Novel
  Last Hurrah, The 1958 d: John Ford. lps: Spencer Tracy, Jeffrey Hunter, Dianne Foster. 121M USA. prod/rel: Columbia
  Last Hurrah, The 1978 d: Vincent Sherman. lps: Carroll O'Connor, Leslie Ackerman, John Anderson. TVM. 100M USA. prod/rel: O'connor, Becker Productions

O'CONNOR, FLANNERY (1925–1964), USA, O'Connor, Mary Flannery
A Circle in the Fire, 1955, Short Story
  Circle in the Fire, A 1975 d: Victor Nunez. 50M USA.
Comforts of Home, 1955, Short Story
  Comforts of Home 1974 d: Jerome Shore. 40M USA.
The Displaced Person, 1955, Short Story
  Displaced Person, The 1977 d: Glenn Jordan. lps: Irene Worth, John Houseman. MTV. 56M USA. prod/rel: Learning in Focus
Good Country People, 1955, Short Story
  Good Country People 1955 d: Flannery O'Connor. 32M USA.
The River, 1955, Short Story
  River, The 1978 d: Barbara Noble. 29M USA.
Wise Blood, 1955, Novel
  Wise Blood 1979 d: John Huston. lps: Brad Dourif, Dan Shor, Amy Wright. 108M USA/GRM. *Die Weisheit Des Blutes* (GRM) prod/rel: New Line Cinema

O'CONNOR, FRANK (1903–1966), IRL, O'Donovan, Michael
Guests of the Nation, 1931, Short Story
  Guests of the Nation 1936 d: Denis Johnston. 50M IRL.
The Majesty of the Law, Play
  Rising of the Moon, The 1957 d: John Ford. lps: Noel Purcell, Cyril Cusack, John Cowley. 81M UKN/IRL. prod/rel: Four Provinces, Warner Bros.

O'CONNOR, MARY
A Kentucky Romance, Story
  Romance of Sunshine Alley 1914 d: Charles Miller. lps: Mildred Harris, Jerome Storm. SHT USA. prod/rel: Broncho
The Little Savior, Short Story
  Souls Triumphant 1917 d: Jack O'Brien. lps: Lillian Gish, Wilfred Lucas, Louise Hamilton. 5r USA. prod/rel: Fine Arts Film Co., Triangle Distributing Corp.
The Little Turncoat, Story
  Little Turncoat, The 1913 d: Fred J. Balshofer. lps: Anna Little, Harold Lockwood. 2r USA. prod/rel: Kb

O'DELL, SCOTT
Island of the Blue Dolphins, Boston 1960, Novel
  Island of the Blue Dolphins 1964 d: James B. Clark. lps: Celia Kaye, Larry Domasin, George Kennedy. 93M USA. prod/rel: Robert B. Radnitz Productions, Universal

ODETS, CLIFFORD (1906–1963), USA
The Big Knife, New York 1949, Play
  Big Knife, The 1955 d: Robert Aldrich. lps: Jack Palance, Ida Lupino, Wendell Corey. 111M USA. prod/rel: United Artists Corp., Aldrich and Associates
Clash By Night, New York 1941, Play
  Clash By Night 1952 d: Fritz Lang. lps: Paul Douglas, Barbara Stanwyck, Robert Ryan. 105M USA. prod/rel: RKO Radio
The Country Girl, New York 1950, Play
  Country Girl, The 1954 d: George Seaton. lps: Bing Crosby, Grace Kelly, William Holden. 104M USA. prod/rel: Paramount
  Country Girl, The 1974 d: Paul Bogart. lps: Jason Robards Jr., Shirley Knight, George Grizzard. TVM. 74M USA.

Golden Boy, New York 1937, Play
Golden Boy 1939 d: Rouben Mamoulian. lps: Barbara Stanwyck, Adolphe Menjou, William Holden. 101M USA. prod/rel: Columbia Pictures Corp.©, Rouben Mamoulian Production

ODIER, DANIEL
Les Annees Lumiere, Novel
Light Years Away 1981 d: Alain Tanner. lps: Trevor Howard, Mick Ford, Bernice Stegers. 105M IRL/FRN/SWT. *Annees Lumiere, Les* (FRN) prod/rel: Slotinit, S.S.R.

ODLUM, JEROME
Dust Be My Destiny, Novel
Dust Be My Destiny 1939 d: Lewis Seiler. lps: John Garfield, Priscilla Lane, Alan Hale. 88M USA. prod/rel: Warner Bros. Pictures©, First National
Story
I Was Framed 1942 d: D. Ross Lederman. lps: Tod Andrews, Julie Bishop, Regis Toomey. 61M USA. prod/rel: Warner Bros.
Each Dawn I Die, Indianapolis 1938, Novel
Each Dawn I Die 1939 d: William Keighley. lps: James Cagney, George Raft, George Bancroft. 92M USA. prod/rel: Warner Bros. Pictures©, First National
The Morgue Is Always Open, Novel
Scream in the Dark, A 1943 d: George Sherman. lps: Robert Lowery, Marie McDonald, Edward Brophy. 53M USA. prod/rel: Republic

O'DONNELL, J.
A Sap from Syracuse, Play
Sap from Syracuse, The 1930 d: A. Edward Sutherland. lps: Jack Oakie, Ginger Rogers, Granville Bates. 6108f USA. *The Sap Abroad* (UKN) prod/rel: Paramount-Publix Corp.

O'DONNELL, JAMES
The Bunker, Book
Bunker, The 1981 d: George Schaefer. lps: Anthony Hopkins, Piper Laurie, Richard Jordan. TVM. 150M USA. *Adolf Hitler: the Bunker* prod/rel: Time-Life, Sfp

O'DONNELL, KENNETH
Johnny, We Hardly Knew Ye, 1972, Book
Johnny, We Hardly Knew Ye 1977 d: Gilbert Cates. lps: Paul Rudd, William Prince, Burgess Meredith. TVM. 100M USA. prod/rel: Talent Associates Ltd., Jamel Productions

OE, KENZABURO (1935–, JPN
Shiiku, 1958, Short Story
Shiiku 1961 d: Nagisa OshimA. lps: Rentaro Mikuni, Sadako Sawamura, Masako NakamurA. 105M JPN. *The Catch; Breeding*

OEMLER, MARIE CONWAY
Slippy McGee: Sometimes Known As the Butterfly Man, Novel
Slippy McGee 1948 d: Albert Kelley. lps: Dale Evans, Donald Barry, Tom Brown. 65M USA. *Slippery McGee* prod/rel: Republic

OESTERREICHER, RUDOLF
Konto X, Play
Duchacek to Zaridi 1938 d: Carl Lamac. lps: Vlasta Burian, Ladislav Hemmer, Milada GampeovA. 2446m CZC. *Duchacek Will Fix It* prod/rel: Metropolitan

O'FAOLAIN, SEAN (1900–1991), IRL, Whelan, Sean
The Woman Who Married Clark Gable, 1948, Short Story
Woman Who Married Clark Gable, The 1986 d: Thaddeus O'Sullivan. lps: Bob Hoskins, Brenda Fricker, Peter Caffrey. 29M IRL/UKN. prod/rel: Brook Films (Dublin), Set 2 (London)

OFFEN, NEIL
Calling Dr. Horowitz, Book
Bad Medicine 1985 d: Harvey Miller. lps: Steve Guttenberg, Alan Arkin, Julie Hagerty. 96M USA. prod/rel: 20th Century Fox, Lantana

O'FLAHERTY, LIAM (1896–1984), IRL
The Informer, London 1925, Novel
Informer, The 1929 d: Arthur Robison. lps: Lya de Putti, Lars Hansen, Warwick Ward. 83M UKN. prod/rel: British International Pictures, Wardour
Informer, The 1935 d: John Ford. lps: Victor McLaglen, Heather Angel, Preston Foster. 97M USA. prod/rel: RKO Radio Pictures©
Uptight 1968 d: Jules Dassin. lps: Raymond St. Jacques, Ruby Dee, Frank SilverA. 104M USA. *Betrayal* prod/rel: Marlukin Productions
Mr. Gilhooley, 1926, Novel
Derniere Jeunesse 1939 d: Jeff Musso. lps: Jacqueline Delubac, Alice Tissot, Raimu. 88M FRN/ITL. *Ultima Giovinezza* (ITL); *La Fin d'une Vie* prod/rel: Scalera Film

The Puritan, 1931, Novel
Puritain, Le 1937 d: Jeff Musso. lps: Jean-Louis Barrault, Pierre Fresnay, Viviane Romance. 97M FRN. *Puritan, The* prod/rel: Films Derby

OGAI, MORI
Chuo Koron, 1915, Short Story
Sansho Dayu 1954 d: Kenji Mizoguchi. lps: Kinuyo Tanaka, Yoshiaki Hanayagi, Kyoko KagawA. 130M JPN. *Sansho the Bailiff* (USA); *Superintendent Sansho, The; The Bailiff; Sansho Daiyu* prod/rel: Daiei Motion Picture Co., Kyoto Studio

OGASAWARA, MOTO
Buttsuke Honban, Book
Buttsuke Honban 1958 d: Kozo Saeki. lps: Frankie Sakai, Keiko Awaji, Tatsuya Nakadai. 98M JPN. *Go and Get It* prod/rel: Tokyo Eiga Co.

OGBURN JR., CHARLTON
The Marauders, New York 1959, Novel
Merrill's Marauders 1962 d: Samuel Fuller. lps: Jeff Chandler, Ty Hardin, Peter Brown. 98M USA. *Marauders, The* prod/rel: United States Productions

OGDEN, DENIS
The Peaceful Inn, Play
Halfway House, The 1944 d: Basil Dearden. lps: Francoise Rosay, Tom Walls, Mervyn Johns. 95M UKN. *The Ghostly Inn* prod/rel: Ealing Studios

OGDEN, GEORGE WASHINGTON
The Bondboy, Chicago 1922, Novel
Bond Boy, The 1922 d: Henry King. lps: Richard Barthelmess, Charles Hill Mailes, Ned Sparks. 6902f USA. prod/rel: Inspiration Pictures, Associated First National Pictures
The Duke of Chimney Butte, Chicago 1920, Novel
Duke of Chimney Butte, The 1921 d: Frank Borzage. lps: Fred Stone, Vola Vale, Josie Sedgwick. 4600f USA. prod/rel: Fred Stone Productions, R-C Pictures
The Rustler of Wind River, Chicago 1917, Novel
Winner Takes All 1918 d: Elmer Clifton. lps: Monroe Salisbury, Betty Schade, Alfred Allen. 5r USA. *The Rustler of Wind River; The Rustling of Wind River* prod/rel: Bluebird Photoplays, Inc.©
The Trail Rider, New York 1924, Novel
Trail Rider, The 1925 d: W. S. Van Dyke. lps: Buck Jones, Nancy Deaver, Lucy Fox. 4752f USA. prod/rel: Fox Film Corp.

OGDON, BRENDA
Virtuoso, Book
Virtuoso 1989 d: Tony Smith. lps: Alfred Molina, Alison Steadman, John Heard. TVM. 103M UKN. prod/rel: BBC

OGLIVIE, ELIZABETH
High Tide at Noon, Novel
High Tide at Noon 1957 d: Philip Leacock. lps: Betta St. John, William Sylvester, Michael Craig. 109M UKN. prod/rel: Rank, Rank Film Distributors

O'GRADY, ROHAN
Let's Kill Uncle, New York 1963, Novel
Let's Kill Uncle 1966 d: William Castle. lps: Nigel Green, Mary Badham, Pat Cardi. 92M USA/UKN. prod/rel: Universal Pictures

O'HANLON, JAMES
Over My Dead Body, Novel
Over My Dead Body 1942 d: Malcolm St. Clair. lps: Milton Berle, Mary Beth Hughes, Reginald Denny. 68M USA. prod/rel: 20th Century-Fox

O'HARA, JOHN (1905–1970), USA, O'Hara, John Henry
Play
Liebling, Ich Muss Dich Erschiessen 1962 d: Jurgen Goslar. lps: Marianne Koch, Walter Giller, Hans Nielsen. 81M GRM. *Darling, I Am Going to Have to Shoot You* prod/rel: Arca, Winston
Butterfield 8, 1935, Novel
Butterfield 8 1960 d: Daniel Mann. lps: Elizabeth Taylor, Laurence Harvey, Eddie Fisher. 108M USA. prod/rel: MGM
The Doctor's Son, Book
Turning Point of Jim Malloy, The 1975 d: Frank D. Gilroy. lps: John Savage, Biff McGuire, Peggy McKay. TVM. 78M USA. *Gibbsville: the Turning Point of Jim Malloy; John O'Hara's Gibbsville* prod/rel: Columbia Pictures
From the Terrace, 1958, Novel
From the Terrace 1960 d: Mark Robson. lps: Paul Newman, Joanne Woodward, Myrna Loy. 144M USA. prod/rel: 20th Century-Fox
Pal Joey, 1939, Short Story
Pal Joey 1957 d: George Sidney. lps: Frank Sinatra, Rita Hayworth, Kim Novak. 111M USA. prod/rel: Columbia, Essex-George Sidney Prod.

A Rage to Live, New York 1949, Novel
Rage to Live, A 1965 d: Walter Grauman. lps: Suzanne Pleshette, Bradford Dillman, Ben GazzarA. 101M USA. prod/rel: Mirisch Corporation, Rage Productions
Ten North Frederick, 1955, Novel
Ten North Frederick 1958 d: Philip Dunne. lps: Gary Cooper, Diane Varsi, Suzy Parker. 102M USA. prod/rel: 20th Century-Fox

O'HARA, MARY (1885–1980), USA, Alsop, Mary O'Hara, Sture-Vasa, Mary
Green Grass of Wyoming, Novel
Green Grass of Wyoming 1948 d: Louis King. lps: Peggy Cummins, Charles Coburn, Robert Arthur. 88M USA. prod/rel: 20th Century-Fox
My Friend Flicka, 1941, Novel
My Friend Flicka 1943 d: Harold Schuster. lps: Roddy McDowall, Preston Foster, Rita Johnson. 89M USA. prod/rel: 20th Century-Fox
Thunderhead, Son of Flicka, Novel
Thunderhead, Son of Flicka 1945 d: Louis King. lps: Roddy McDowall, Preston Foster, Rita Johnson. 78M USA. *Thunderhead* prod/rel: 20th Century-Fox

O'HIGGINS, HARVEY J.
The Argyle Case, New York 1912, Play
Argyle Case, The 1917 d: Ralph Ince. lps: Robert Warwick, Elaine Hammerstein, Charles Hines. 5-7r USA. prod/rel: Robert Warwick Film Corp.©, Selznick Pictures
Argyle Case, The 1929 d: Howard Bretherton. lps: Thomas Meighan, H. B. Warner, Lila Lee. 7794f USA. prod/rel: Warner Brothers Pictures
The Dummy, New York 1914, Play
Dummy, The 1917 d: Francis J. Grandon. lps: Jack Pickford, Frank Losee, Edwin Stanley. 5r USA. prod/rel: Famous Players Film Co.©, Paramount Pictures Corp.
Dummy, The 1929 d: Robert Milton. lps: Ruth Chatterton, Fredric March, John Cromwell. 5357f USA. prod/rel: Paramount Famous Lasky Corp.
Make Your Own Bed, Play
Make Your Own Bed 1944 d: Peter Godfrey. lps: Jack Carson, Jane Wyman, Alan Hale. 82M USA. prod/rel: Warner Bros.

OHNET, GEORGES
L'ame de Pierre, Novel
Ame de Pierre, L' 1928 d: Gaston Roudes. lps: Georges Lannes, Gilbert Dany, Jacqueline Forzane. F FRN. prod/rel: Gaston Roudes
La Comtesse Sarah, 1887, Novel
Comtesse Sarah, La 1912 d: Henri Pouctal. lps: Emile Dehelly, Adolphe Cande, Suzanne Revonne. FRN. prod/rel: Film d'Art
Contessa Sara, La 1919 d: Roberto Leone Roberti. lps: Francesca Bertini, Ugo Piperno, Sandro Salvini. 1541m ITL. prod/rel: Bertini
La Dame En Gris, 1886, Novel
Dame En Gris, La 1919 d: Gian Paolo Rosmino. lps: Helena Makowska, Guido Trento, Gian Paolo Rosmino. 3381m ITL. prod/rel: Gladiator
Les Dames de Croix-Mort, Novel
Dames de Croix-Mort, Les 1916 d: Maurice Mariaud. lps: Leon Mathot, Jeanne Marie-Laurent, Yvonne Sergyl. 1475m FRN. prod/rel: le Film d'Art
Dette de Haine, Novel
Dette de Haine 1915 d: Henri Pouctal. lps: Gilbert Dalleu, Jean Marie de L'isle, Juliette Clarens. 1360m FRN. prod/rel: le Film d'Art
Le Docteur Rameau, Paris 1889, Novel
Dr. Rameau 1915 d: Will S. Davis. lps: Frederick Perry, Jean Southern, Dorothy Bernard. 5r USA. *Infidelity* prod/rel: Fox Film Corp., William Fox©
My Friend, the Devil 1922 d: Harry Millarde. lps: Charles Richman, Ben Grauer, William H. Tooker. 9555f USA. prod/rel: Fox Film Corp.
Le Droit de l'Enfant, Novel
Droit de l'Enfant, Le 1914 d: Henri Pouctal. lps: Huguette Duflos, Raphael Duflos. 1365m FRN. prod/rel: le Film d'Art
Droit de l'Enfant, Le 1948 d: Jacques Daroy. lps: Jean Chevrier, Michel Jourdan, Renee Devillers. 95M FRN. prod/rel: Societe Mediterraneenne De Production
Le Due Rivali, Novel
Lisa Fleuron 1920 d: Roberto Leone Roberti. lps: Francesca Bertini, Mina d'Orvella, Sandro Salvini. 1638m ITL. prod/rel: Bertini
La Fin d'un Joueur, Novel
Fin d'un Joueur, La 1911 d: Andre Calmettes, Henri Etievant. lps: Philippe Garnier, Henri Pouctal, Suzanne Revonne. 230m FRN. prod/rel: le Film d'Art
Gerval, le Maitre de Forges, 1581, Verse
Gerval, le Maitre de Forges 1912. lps: Edmond Duquesne, Louis Gauthier, Mevisto. 565m FRN. prod/rel: Eclair

La Grande Marniere, 1888, Novel
Grande Marniere, La 1913 d: Henri Pouctal. lps: Rolla Norman, Gilbert Dalleu, Nelly Cormon. 1075m FRN. prod/rel: le Film d'Art
Grande Marniera, La 1920 d: Gero Zambuto. lps: Marise Dauvray, Alberto Nepoti, Gero Zambuto. 1441m ITL. prod/rel: Lombardo Film
Grande Marniere, La 1943 d: Jean de Marguenat. lps: Fernand Ledoux, Micheline Francey, Ginette Leclerc. 92M FRN. prod/rel: Les Moulins D'or

Le Maitre de Forges, Paris 1882, Novel
Maitre de Forges, Le 1913 d: Henri Pouctal. lps: Philippe Garnier, Jeanne Hading, Pierre Magnier. FRN. prod/rel: le Film d'Art

Maitre de Forges, Le, Paris 1882, Novel
American Methods 1917 d: Frank Lloyd. lps: William Farnum, Jewel Carmen, Florence Vidor. 5r USA. prod/rel: Fox Film Corp., William Fox©

Le Maitre de Forges, Paris 1882, Novel
Padrone Delle Ferriere, Il 1919 d: Eugenio Perego. lps: Pina Menichelli, Amleto Novelli, Luigi Serventi. 1670m ITL. prod/rel: Itala Film
Maitre de Forges, Le 1933 d: Fernand Rivers, Abel Gance. lps: Henri Rollan, Gaby Morlay, Paule Andral. 98M FRN. prod/rel: Directeurs Francais Associes
Maitre de Forges, Le 1947 d: Fernand Rivers. lps: Jean Chevrier, Helene Perdriere, Jeanne Provost. 90M FRN. prod/rel: Films Fernand Rivers
Padrone Delle Ferriere, Il 1959 d: Anton Giulio Majano. lps: Antonio Vilar, Virna Lisi, Wandisa GuidA. 110M ITL/SPN. *Felipe Derblay* (SPN) prod/rel: Flora Film, Da.MA. Cin.Ca (Roma)

Le Maitre Des Forges, Paris 1882, Novel
Iron Master, The 1914 d: Travers Vale. lps: George Morgan, Viola Smith, Louise Vale. 2r USA. prod/rel: Biograph Co.
Iron Master, The 1933 d: Chester M. Franklin. lps: Reginald Denny, Lila Lee, J. Farrell MacDonald. 69M USA. prod/rel: Allied Pictures Corp.©

Nemrod Et Cie, Novel
Nemrod Et Cie 1916 d: Maurice Mariaud. lps: Leon Mathot, Lebrey, Denise Grey. 1170m FRN. prod/rel: Eclectric Films

Le Roi de Paris, Novel
Roi de Paris, Le 1923 d: Charles Maudru, Maurice de Marsan. lps: Jean Dax, Suzanne Munte, Germaine Vallier. SRL. 4EP FRN.
Roi de Paris, Le 1930 d: Leo Mittler, Maurice de Marsan. lps: Ivan Petrovitch, Suzanne Bianchetti, Gabriel Gabrio. F FRN. prod/rel: Exclusivites Jean De Merly, Greenbaum-Film

Serge Panine, Novel
Serge Panine 1913 d: Henri Pouctal. lps: Romuald Joube, Pierre Magnier, Nelly Cormon. 625m FRN. prod/rel: Film d'Art
Serge Panine 1915 d: Wray Physioc. lps: Laura Lavarnie, William J. Butler, Irma Dawkins. 3r USA. prod/rel: Biograph Co.
Serge Panine 1922 d: Charles Maudru, Maurice de Marsan. lps: Albert de Kersten, Violette Jyl, Suzanne Munte. 2000m FRN/AUS. prod/rel: Sascha-Film, Maurice De Marsan
Serge Panine 1938 d: Charles Mere, Paul Schiller. lps: Francoise Rosay, Youcca Troubetzkoy, Andree Guize. 91M FRN. prod/rel: Productions Francaises Cinematographique

The Soul of Pierre, Novel
Soul of Pierre, The 1915 d: Travers Vale. lps: Franklin Ritchie, Clairette Claire, Vola Smith. 3r USA. prod/rel: Biograph Co.

Volonte, Novel
Volonte 1916 d: Henri Pouctal. lps: Leon Mathot, Paul Amiot, Huguette Duflos. 1520m FRN. prod/rel: le Film d'Art

OHORN
Die Bruder von St. Bernhard, Play
Hinter Klostermauern 1928 d: Franz Seitz. lps: Anita Dorris, Betty Bird, Dene Morel. 2224m GRM. prod/rel: Munchener Lichtspielkunst Ag

OHTA, KYOKO
Story
Yoru No Henrin 1964 d: Noboru NakamurA. lps: Miyuki Kuwano, Mikijiro Hira, Keisuke Sonoi. 105M JPN. *The Beautiful People* (UKN); *The Shape of Night* prod/rel: Shochiku

OKA, SHOHEI
Musashino Fujin, 1951, Novel
Musashino Fujin 1951 d: Kenji Mizoguchi. lps: Kinuyo Tanaka, Masayuki Mori, Akihiko KatayamA. 92M JPN. *The Lady from Musahino* (UKN); *Lady Musashino* (USA); *Madama Musashino*; *Woman of Musashino*; *The Lady of Musashino* prod/rel: Toho Co.

OKADA, SABURO
Mieko, Serial
Naniwa Ereji 1936 d: Kenji Mizoguchi. lps: Isuzu Yamada, Benkei Shiganoya, Eitaro Shindo. 90M JPN. *Naniwa Elegy* (UKN); *Osaka Elegy* (USA); *Naniwa Hika* prod/rel: Daiichi Film Co.

OKAMI, JOJIRO
Space Moons, Short Story
Uchu Daikaiju Dogora 1964 d: Inoshiro HondA. lps: Yosuke Natsuki, Elizabeth Keyt, Nobuo NakamurA. 81M JPN. *Dagora the Space Monster* (USA); *Uchudai Dogora*; *Dogora*; *Space Monster Dogora*; *Dagora* prod/rel: Toho Co.

OKAMOTO, KIDO
Shuzenji Monogatari, Play
Shuzenji Monogatari 1955 d: Noboru NakamurA. lps: Teiji Takahashi, Chikage Awashima, Minosuke Bando. 105M JPN. *The Mask of Destiny* (USA); *The Mask and Destiny* prod/rel: Shochiku Co.

OKONKOWSKI, GEORG
Polnische Wirtschaft, Play
Polnische Wirtschaft 1928 d: E. W. Emo. lps: Hans Brausewetter, Iwa Wanja, Siegfried Arno. 2135m GRM. prod/rel: Strauss-Film

OKONOWSKI, GEORG
Play
Girl in the Taxi, The 1937 d: Andre Berthomieu. lps: Frances Day, Henri Garat, Lawrence Grossmith. 72M UKN. prod/rel: Associated British Film Distributors, British Unity

OKUDA, KIKUMARU
Yusha Nomi, Novel
None But the Brave 1965 d: Frank SinatrA. lps: Frank Sinatra, Clint Walker, Tommy Sands. 105M USA/JPN. *Yusha Nomi* (JPN) prod/rel: Tokyo Eiga Co., Toho Co

OLCOTT, RITA
Song in His Heart, Book
My Wild Irish Rose 1947 d: David Butler. lps: Dennis Morgan, Arlene Dahl, Andrea King. 101M USA. prod/rel: Warner Bros.

OLDFIELD, PETER
Der Gestohlene Geheimvertrag, Novel
Geheimnis von Genf, Das 1927 d: Willy Reiber. lps: Christa Tordy, Alfred Abel, Ernst Reicher. 2396m GRM. prod/rel: Munchener Lichtspielkunst Ag

OLESHA, YURY KARLOVICH (1899–1960), RSS
Tri Tolstyaka, 1928, Short Story
Tri Tolstyaka 1967 d: Alexei Batalov, Iosif Shapiro. lps: Rolan Bykov, Lina Braknite, Petya Artemiev. 114M USS. *The Three Fat Men*

OLIVARI, CARLOS
The Gay Senorita, Story
You Were Never Lovelier 1942 d: William A. Seiter. lps: Fred Astaire, Rita Hayworth, Adolphe Menjou. 97M USA. prod/rel: Columbia

OLIVARI, CARLOS A.
Romance in High C, Story
Romance on the High Seas 1948 d: Michael Curtiz. lps: Jack Carson, Doris Day, Janis Paige. 99M USA. *It's Magic* (UKN) prod/rel: Warner Bros.

OLIVE, FRANK
The Blacksmith's Story, Poem
Blacksmith's Story, The 1913 d: Travers Vale. lps: George Morgan, Kenneth Davenport, Mrs. Travers Vale. 1000f USA. prod/rel: Pilot

OLIVEIRA, CARLOS
Uma Abelha Na Chuva, 1953, Novel
Abelha Na Chuva, Uma 1971 d: Fernando Lopes. lps: Laura Soveral, Joao Guedes, Zita Duarte. 75M PRT. *A Bee in the Rain*; *A Spider in the Rain*; *Uma Avelha Na Chuva* prod/rel: Media

OLIVIER, CLAUDE
Tendre Poulet, Novel
Tendre Poulet 1978 d: Philippe de BrocA. lps: Annie Girardot, Philippe Noiret, Catherine Alric. 105M FRN. *Dear Detective* (USA); *Dear Inspector* prod/rel: Ariane, Mondex

OLIVIER, STUART
The Bride, New York 1924, Play
Danger Girl, The 1926 d: Eddie Dillon. lps: Priscilla Dean, John Bowers, Gustav von Seyffertitz. 5660f USA. prod/rel: Metropolitan Pictures, Producers Distributing Corp.

OLIVIERI, RICCARDO
Veronica Cybo
Veronica Cyba 1910 d: Mario Caserini. 256m ITL. *Veronica Cjbo*; *Veronica Cibo*; *Veronica* (UKN) prod/rel: Cines

OLLIVANT, ALFRED (1874–1927), UKN
Boy Woodburn, Novel
Boy Woodburn 1922 d: Guy Newall. lps: Guy Newall, Ivy Duke, A. Bromley Davenport. 7300f UKN. prod/rel: George Clark Productions, Stoll

Bob, Son of Battle, New York 1898, Novel
Owd Bob 1924 d: Henry Edwards. lps: J. Fisher White, Ralph Forbes, James Carew. 6300f UKN. prod/rel: Atlantic Union, Novello-Atlas
Owd Bob 1938 d: Robert Stevenson. lps: Will Fyffe, John Loder, Margaret Lockwood. 78M UKN. *To the Victor* prod/rel: General Film Distributors, Gainsborough
Thunder in the Valley 1947 d: Louis King. lps: Edmund Gwenn, Lon McCallister, Peggy Ann Garner. 103M USA. *Bob, Son of Battle* (UKN) prod/rel: Twentieth Century-Fox

OLLIVIER, ERIC
Les Godelureaux, Novel
Godelureaux, Les 1960 d: Claude Chabrol. lps: Jean-Claude Brialy, Bernadette Lafont, Charles Belmont. 100M FRN/ITL. *Parigi Di Notte* (ITL) prod/rel: International Productions, Cocinor

OLMSTEAD, HARRY F.
Trigger Fingers, Short Story
Outlaws of the Prairie 1937 d: Sam Nelson. lps: Charles Starrett, Donald Grayson, Iris Meredith. 58M USA. *The Singing Rangers* prod/rel: Columbia Pictures Corp. of California©

War Along the Stage Trails, Story
Stagecoach War 1940 d: Lesley Selander. lps: William Boyd, Russell Hayden, Julie Carter. 63M USA. *War Along the Stage Trail*; *Hold Your Horses* prod/rel: Harry Sherman Productions, Paramount Pictures©

OLSEN, ROLF
Der Januck, Short Story
Dorf Unterm Himmel, Das 1953 d: Richard Haussler. lps: Inge Egger, Renate Mannhardt, Heinrich Gretler. 92M GRM. *The Village Near the Sky* prod/rel: Interlux, Union

OLSEN, THEODORE V.
Arrow in the Sun, New York 1969, Novel
Soldier Blue 1970 d: Ralph Nelson. lps: Candice Bergen, Peter Strauss, Donald Pleasence. 112M USA. prod/rel: Katzka-Berne Productions, Avco Embassy

The Stalking Moon, New York 1965, Novel
Stalking Moon, The 1969 d: Robert Mulligan. lps: Gregory Peck, Eva Marie Saint, Robert Forster. 109M USA. *The Elite Killer* prod/rel: Pakula-Mulligan Productions, Stalking Moon Co.

OLSEN, TILLIE (1913–, USA
Tell Me a Riddle, Novel
Tell Me a Riddle 1980 d: Lee Grant. lps: Melvyn Douglas, Lila Kedrova, Brooke Adams. 90M USA. prod/rel: Filmways

OLSHAN, JOSEPH
Clara's Heart, Novel
Clara's Heart 1988 d: Robert Mulligan. lps: Whoopi Goldberg, Michael Ontkean, Kathleen Quinlan. 108M USA. prod/rel: Warner Bros.

OLUJIC, GROZDANA
Glasam Za Ljubav, 1953, Novel
Glasam Za Ljubav 1965 d: Toma Janic. lps: Bosko Toskic, Slobodanka Markovic, Bane Miladinovic. 89M YGS.

Izlet U Nebo, 1958, Novel
Cudna Devojka 1961 d: Jovan Zivanovic. lps: Spela Rozin, Voja Miric, Zoran Radmilovic. 100M YGS. *The Strange Girl*

OMESSA, HENRI
Le Candidat Lauriston, Novel
Vendetta, La 1961 d: Jean-A. Cherasse. lps: Francis Blanche, Louis de Funes, Rosy Varte. 85M FRN/ITL. *Bandito Si. Ma d'Onore* (ITL) prod/rel: le Trident, S.I.F.E.C.

OMRE, ARTHUR
Flukten, 1936, Novel
Ukjent Mann 1951 d: Astrid Henning-Jensen, Bjarne Henning-Jensen. 104M NRW. *Unknown Man*; *The Stranger*

Smuglere, 1935, Novel
Smuglere 1968 d: Rolf Clemens. lps: Baard Owe, Elsa Lystad, Arne Aas. 104M NRW. *The Smugglers*

ONDAATJE, MICHAEL (1943–, SLN, Ondaatje, Philip Michael
The English Patient, Novel
English Patient, The 1996 d: Anthony MinghellA. lps: Ralph Fiennes, Juliette Binoche, Willem Dafoe. 162M USA. prod/rel: Tiger Moth Productions, Miramax Films

O'NEAL, GEORGE
Mother Lode, New York 1934, Play
Yellow Dust 1936 d: Wallace Fox. lps: Richard Dix, Leila Hyams, Moroni Olsen. 69M USA. *Mother Lode* prod/rel: RKO Radio Pictures©

O'NEIL, TERRY
Bio
Fighting Back 1980 d: Robert Lieberman. lps: Robert Urich, Art Carney, Bonnie BedeliA. TVM. 100M USA. prod/rel: ABC, Mtm

O'NEILL, EUGENE (1885–1953), USA, O'Neill, Eugene Gladstone
Ah Wilderness!, New York 1933, Play
Ah, Wilderness! 1935 d: Clarence Brown. lps: Wallace Beery, Lionel Barrymore, Aline MacMahon. 101M USA. prod/rel: Metro-Goldwyn-Mayer Corp.
Summer Holiday 1948 d: Rouben Mamoulian. lps: Mickey Rooney, Gloria de Haven, Walter Huston. 92M USA. prod/rel: MGM
Anna Christie, New York 1922, Play
Anna Christie 1923 d: John Griffith Wray. lps: Blanche Sweet, William Russell, George F. Marion. 7631f USA. prod/rel: Thomas H. Ince Corp., Associated First National Pictures
Anna Christie 1929 d: Clarence Brown. lps: Greta Garbo, Charles Bickford, George F. Marion. 86M USA. prod/rel: Metro-Goldwyn-Mayer Pictures
Anna Christie 1930 d: Jacques Feyder. lps: Greta Garbo, Hans Junkermann, Salka Viertel. 10r USA. prod/rel: Metro-Goldwyn-Mayer Pictures
Desire Under the Elms, New York 1924, Play
Desire Under the Elms 1958 d: Delbert Mann. lps: Sophia Loren, Anthony Perkins, Burl Ives. 114M USA. prod/rel: Paramount, Don Hartman Prods.
The Emperor Jones, New York 1920, Play
Emperor Jones, The 1933 d: Dudley Murphy. lps: Paul Robeson, Dudley Digges, Frank Wilson. 80M USA. prod/rel: John Krimsky and Gifford Cochran Inc.©, United Artists Corp.
Emperor Jones, The, New York 1920, Play
Emperor Jones, The 1958 d: Ted Kotcheff. lps: Kenneth Spencer, Harry H. Corbett, Constance Smith. MTV. UKN. prod/rel: ABC
The Hairy Ape, 1922, Play
Hairy Ape, The 1944 d: Alfred Santell. lps: Susan Hayward, William Bendix, John Loder. 90M USA. prod/rel: United Artists
The Iceman Cometh, 1946, Play
Iceman Cometh, The 1973 d: John Frankenheimer. lps: Lee Marvin, Fredric March, Robert Ryan. 101M USA.
Long Day's Journey Into Night, New York 1956, Play
Long Day's Journey Into Night 1962 d: Sidney Lumet. lps: Katharine Hepburn, Ralph Richardson, Jason Robards Jr. 180M USA. prod/rel: Landau Productions
Long Day's Journey Into Night 1996 d: David Wellington. lps: William Hutt, Martha Henry, Tom McCamus. 174M CND. prod/rel: Rhombus Media
Mourning Becomes Electra, New York 1931, Play
Mourning Becomes Electra 1947 d: Dudley Nichols. lps: Rosalind Russell, Michael Redgrave, Raymond Massey. 173M USA. prod/rel: RKO Radio
Recklessness, Boston 1914, Play
Constant Woman, The 1933 d: Victor Schertzinger. lps: Conrad Nagel, Leila Hyams, Claire Windsor. 76M USA. *Auction in Souls*; *Hell in a Circus* prod/rel: K.B.S. Productions, Inc.
S.S. Glencairn, 1919, Plays
Long Voyage Home, The 1940 d: John Ford. lps: John Wayne, Thomas Mitchell, Ian Hunter. 105M USA. prod/rel: United Artists Corp., Argosy Corp.
Strange Interlude, New York 1928, Play
Strange Interlude 1932 d: Robert Z. Leonard. lps: Norma Shearer, Clark Gable, May Robson. 112M USA. *Strange Interval* (UKN) prod/rel: Metro-Goldwyn-Mayer Corp., Metro-Goldwyn-Mayer Dist. Corp.©

O'NEILL, PERRY
Story
Pals 1925 d: John P. McCarthy. lps: Louise Lorraine, Art Acord, Leon Kent. 4613f USA. prod/rel: Truart Film Corp.

ONETTI, JUAN CARLOS (1909–, URG
Per Questa Notte, Novel
Per Questa Notte 1977 d: Carlo Di Carlo. lps: Paolo Bonacelli, Adalberto Maria Merli, Olga Karlatos. 100M ITL. *This Is the Night* prod/rel: P.B. Cin.Ca, Ital Noleggio Cin.Ca

ONGARO, ALBERTO
La Partita, Novel
Partita, La 1991 d: Carlo VanzinA. lps: Matthew Modine, Jennifer Beals, Faye Dunaway. 108M ITL. *The Match*; *The Gamble*

ONSTOTT, KYLE (1887–1978), USA
Drum, Novel
Drum 1976 d: Steve Carver. lps: Ken Norton, Lillian Hayman, Brenda Sykes. 100M USA. prod/rel: Dino de Laurentiis
Mandingo, Novel
Mandingo 1975 d: Richard Fleischer. lps: James Mason, Susan George, Perry King. 123M USA. prod/rel: Dino de Laurentiis

OOKA, SHOHEI
Nobi, Tokyo 1952, Novel
Nobi 1959 d: Kon IchikawA. lps: Eiji Funakoshi, Osamu Takizawa, Mickey Curtis. 104M JPN. *Fires on the Plain* (UKN) prod/rel: Daiei Motion Picture Co.

OPATOSHU, JOSEPH
Romance of a Horsethief, Novel
Romance of a Horsethief 1972 d: Abraham Polonsky, Fedor Hanzekovic. lps: Yul Brynner, Eli Wallach, Jane Birkin. 101M USA/FRN/YGS. *Le Roman d'un Voleur de Chevaux* (FRN); *Running Bear*; *Il Romanzo Di un Ladro Di Cavallo* (ITL); *Romansa Konjokradice* (YGS) prod/rel: Jadran Film (Zagreb), International Film Company (Roma)

OPPENHEIM, E. PHILLIPS (1866–1946), UKN, Oppenheim, Edward Phillips
Novel
Master of Merripit, The 1915 d: Wilfred Noy. lps: Dorothy Bellew. 3445f UKN. prod/rel: Clarendon, Renters
The Amazing Partnership, 1914, Novel
Amazing Partnership, The 1921 d: George Ridgwell. lps: Milton Rosmer, Gladys Mason, Arthur Walcott. 5153f UKN. prod/rel: Stoll
The Amazing Quest of Mr. Ernest Bliss, London 1919, Novel
Amazing Quest of Mr. Ernest Bliss, The 1920 d: Henry Edwards. lps: Henry Edwards, Chrissie White, Gerald Ames. SRL. 3450m UKN. prod/rel: Hepworth, Imperial
Amazing Quest of Ernest Bliss, The 1936 d: Alfred Zeisler. lps: Cary Grant, Mary Brian, Henry Kendall. 80M UKN. *Romance and Riches* (USA); *The Amazing Quest*; *Riches and Romance*; *Amazing Adventure* prod/rel: Garrett-Klement Pictures, United Artists
Anna the Adventuress, 1904, Novel
Anna the Adventuress 1920 d: Cecil M. Hepworth. lps: Alma Taylor, James Carew, Gerald Ames. 6280f UKN. prod/rel: Hepworth, National
The Black Box, Boston 1915, Novel
Black Box, The 1915 d: Otis Turner. lps: Herbert Rawlinson, Anna Little, William Worthington. SRL. 30r USA. prod/rel: Universal Film Mfg. Co.
The Cinema Murder (the Other Romilly), Boston 1917, Novel
Cinema Murder, The 1920 d: George D. Baker. lps: Marion Davies, Nigel Barrie, Anders Randolf. 5354f USA. prod/rel: Cosmopolitan Productions, International Film Service Co, Inc.+
The Conspirators, London 1907, Novel
Conspirators, The 1924 d: Sinclair Hill. lps: Betty Faire, David Hawthorne, Moore Marriott. 4700f UKN. *The Barnet Murder Case* prod/rel: Stoll
The Court of St. Simon, Boston 1912, Novel
Silent Master, The 1917 d: Leonce Perret. lps: Robert Warwick, Anna Little, Anna Q. Nilsson. 6-7r USA. *The Court of St. Simon* prod/rel: Selznick Pictures, Lewis J. Selznick Enterprises
The Double Life of Mr. Alfred Burton, 1914, Novel
Double Life of Mr. Alfred Burton, The 1919 d: Arthur Rooke. lps: Kenelm Foss, Ivy Duke, Elaine Madison. 5000f UKN. prod/rel: Lucky Cat, Ideal
The Ex-Duke, London 1927, Novel
Prince of Tempters, The 1926 d: Lothar Mendes. lps: Lois Moran, Ben Lyon, Lya de Putti. 7780f USA. prod/rel: Robert Kane Productions, First National Pictures
Expiation, London 1887, Novel
Expiation 1922 d: Sinclair Hill. lps: Ivy Close, Fred Raynham, Lionelle Howard. 6246f UKN. prod/rel: Stoll

False Evidence, 1896, Novel
False Evidence 1922 d: Harold Shaw. lps: Edna Flugrath, Cecil Humphreys, E. Holman Clark. 6050f UKN. prod/rel: Stoll
The Game of Liberty, 1915, Novel
Game of Liberty, The 1916 d: George Loane Tucker. lps: Gerald Ames, Douglas Munro, Laura Cowie. 5725f UKN. *Under Suspicion* (USA) prod/rel: London, Jury
Gangster's Glory, Boston 1931, Novel
Midnight Club 1933 d: Alexander Hall, George Somnes. lps: Clive Brook, George Raft, Helen Vinson. 64M USA. *E. Phillips Oppenheim's Midnight Club* prod/rel: Paramount Productions©
The Golden Web, Boston 1910, Novel
Golden Web, The 1920 d: Geoffrey H. Malins. lps: Milton Rosmer, Ena Beaumont, Victor Robson. 5000f UKN. prod/rel: Garrick, Anchor
Golden Web, The 1926 d: Walter Lang. lps: Lillian Rich, Huntley Gordon, Jay Hunt. 6224f USA. prod/rel: Gotham Productions, Lumas Film Corp.
The Great Impersonation, Boston 1920, Novel
Great Impersonation, The 1921 d: George Melford. lps: James Kirkwood, Ann Forrest, Winter Hall. 6658f USA. prod/rel: Famous Players-Lasky, Paramount Pictures
Great Impersonation, The 1935 d: Alan Crosland. lps: Edmund Lowe, Valerie Hobson, Vera Eangles. 81M USA. prod/rel: Universal Productions©, Edmund Grainger Production
Great Impersonation, The 1942 d: John Rawlins. lps: Ralph Bellamy, Evelyn Ankers, Aubrey Mather. 71M USA. prod/rel: Universal
The Great Prince Shan, London 1922, Novel
Great Prince Shan, The 1924 d: A. E. Coleby. lps: Sessue Hayakawa, Ivy Duke, ValiA. 6450f UKN. prod/rel: Stoll
The Hillman, London 1917, Novel
In the Balance 1917 d: Paul Scardon. lps: Earle Williams, Grace Darmond, Miriam Miles. 5r USA. *The Hillman* prod/rel: Vitagraph Co. of America©, Blue Ribbon Feature
The Illustrious Prince, Boston 1910, Novel
Illustrious Prince, The 1919 d: William Worthington. lps: Sessue Hayakawa, Mabel Ballin, Harry Lonsdale. 5r USA. prod/rel: Haworth Pictures Corp.©, Robertson-Cole Distributing Corp.
The Inevitable Millionaires, London 1923, Novel
Millionaires 1926 d: Herman C. Raymaker. lps: George Sidney, Louise Fazenda, Vera Gordon. 6903f USA. prod/rel: Warner Brothers Pictures
Jeanne of the Marshes, Boston 1908, Novel
Behind Masks 1921 d: Frank Reicher. lps: Dorothy Dalton, Frederick Vogeding, William P. Carleton. 4147f USA. *Jeanne of the Marshes* (UKN) prod/rel: Famous Players-Lasky Corp., Paramount Pictures Corp.
The Lion and the Lamb, New York 1930, Novel
Lion and the Lamb, The 1931 d: George B. Seitz. lps: Walter Byron, Carmel Myers, Raymond Hatton. 80M USA. prod/rel: Columbia Pictures Corp.©
The Long Arm of Mannister, Boston 1908, Novel
Long Arm of Mannister, The 1919 d: Bertram Bracken. lps: Henry B. Walthall, Helene Chadwick, Olive Ann Alcorn. 6-7r USA. prod/rel: National Film Corp. of America, Pioneer Feature Film Corp.©
A Lost Leader, London 1906, Novel
Lost Leader, A 1922 d: George Ridgwell. lps: Robert English, Dorothy Fane, Lily Iris. 5800f UKN. prod/rel: Stoll
The Master Mummer, London 1905, Novel
Master Mummer, The 1915 d: Walter Edwin. lps: Mary Fuller. 3r USA. prod/rel: Edison
A Master of Men, 1901, Novel
Master of Men, A 1917 d: Wilfred Noy. lps: Malcolm Keen, Dorothy Bellew, Marie Hemingway. 5040f UKN. prod/rel: Harma Photoplays
The Missioner, London 1908, Novel
Missioner, The 1922 d: George Ridgwell. lps: Cyril Percival, Pauline Peters, Olaf Hytten. 6160f UKN. prod/rel: Stoll
Monte-Carlo, Novel
Monte-Carlo 1925 d: Louis Mercanton. lps: Carlyle Blackwell, Betty Balfour, Louis Allibert. 3250m FRN. prod/rel: Phocea
Mr. Grex of Monte Carlo, Boston 1915, Novel
Mr. Grex of Monte Carlo 1915 d: Frank Reicher. lps: Theodore Roberts, Carlyle Blackwell, Dorothy Davenport. 5r USA. prod/rel: Jesse L. Lasky Feature Play Co.©, Paramount Pictures Corp.

Mr. Wingrave, Millionaire (the Malefactor), London 1904, Novel
Test of Honor, The 1919 d: John S. Robertson. lps: John Barrymore, Constance Binney, Marcia Manon. 4684f USA. *The Malefactor* prod/rel: Famous Players-Lasky Corp.©, Paramount Pictures

The Mystery of Mr. Bernard Brown, 1896, Novel
Mystery of Mr. Bernard Brown, The 1921 d: Sinclair Hill. lps: Ruby Miller, Pardoe Woodman, Clifford Heatherley. 5558f UKN. prod/rel: Stoll
Mistero Dei Bernardo Brown, Il 1922 d: Ermanno Geymonat. lps: Vittorio Pieri, Henriette Bonard, Alfredo Martinelli. 1713m ITL. prod/rel: Photo-Drama

The Mystery Road, Boston 1923, Novel
Mystery Road, The 1921 d: Paul Powell. lps: David Powell, Mary Glynne, Ruby Miller. 6800f USA/UKN. prod/rel: Famous Players-Lasky British Producers, Paramount

Number of Deaths, Short Story
Monte Carlo Nights 1934 d: William Nigh. lps: Mary Brian, John Darrow, Kate Campbell. 62M USA. *Numbers of Monte Carlo* prod/rel: Monogram Pictures Corp.©, Paul Malvern Production

Passers-By, Boston 1910, Novel
Pilgrims of the Night 1921 d: Edward Sloman. lps: Lewis Stone, Rubye de Remer, William V. Mong. 5772f USA. prod/rel: J. L. Frothingham, Associated Producers

The Passionate Quest, Boston 1924, Novel
Passionate Quest, The 1926 d: J. Stuart Blackton. lps: May McAvoy, Gardner James, Willard Louis. 6671f USA. prod/rel: Warner Brothers Pictures

A Sleeping Memory (the Great Awakening), New York 1902, Novel
Sleeping Memory, A 1917 d: George D. Baker. lps: Emily Stevens, Frank Mills, Mario Majeroni. 7r USA. prod/rel: Metro Pictures Corp.©

Strange Boarders of Paradise Crescent, London 1935, Novel
Strange Boarders 1938 d: Herbert Mason. lps: Tom Walls, Renee Saint-Cyr, Leon M. Lion. 79M UKN. prod/rel: General Film Distributors, Gainsborough

The Tempting of Tavarnake, Boston 1911, Novel
Sisters of Eve 1928 d: Scott Pembroke. lps: Anita Stewart, Betty Blythe, Creighton Hale. 5553f USA. *Avarice* (UKN) prod/rel: Trem Carr Productions, Rayart Pictures

The Tragedy of Charlecot Mansions, 1914, Short Story
Floor Above, The 1914 d: James Kirkwood. lps: Henry B. Walthall, Dorothy Gish, Earle Foxe. 4r USA. prod/rel: Reliance Motion Picture Co., Mutual Film Corp.

Twice Wed, Novel
Dangerous Lies 1921 d: Paul Powell. lps: David Powell, Mary Glynne, Minna Gray. 6600f USA/UKN. prod/rel: Famous Players-Lasky British Producers, Paramount Pictures

The World's Great Snare, London 1896, Novel
World's Great Snare, The 1916 d: Joseph Kaufman. lps: Pauline Frederick, Irving Cummings, Ferdinand Tidmarsh. 5r USA. prod/rel: Famous Players Film Co.©, Paramount Pictures Corp.

OPPENHEIM, JAMES (1882–1932), USA
Billie, Short Story
Billie 1912. lps: Margaret Shelby, Marc McDermott, Walter Edwin. 1000f USA. prod/rel: Edison

Idle Wives, New York 1914, Novel
Idle Wives 1916 d: Lois Weber, Phillips Smalley. lps: Lois Weber, Phillips Smalley, Mary MacLaren. 7r USA. prod/rel: Universal Film Mfg. Co.©, State Rights

Nerves and the Man, Story
Nerves and the Man 1912. lps: Marc McDermott, Miriam Nesbitt. 1000f USA. prod/rel: Edison

The Stoning, Story
Stoning, The 1915 d: Charles J. Brabin. lps: Viola Dana, Robert Conness, Helen Strickland. 3r USA. prod/rel: Edison

ORANO, MARCELLO
Guardafui, Novel
Pirati Del Golfo, I 1940 d: Romolo Marcellini. lps: Andrea Checchi, Giovanni Grasso, Osvaldo Valenti. UNF. ITL. prod/rel: E.N.I.C.

Marrabo, Ss
Sentinelle Di Bronzo 1937 d: Romolo Marcellini. lps: Fosco Giachetti, Giovanni Grasso, Doris Duranti. 83M ITL. prod/rel: Fono Roma

ORBOK, ATTILA
Der Komet, Budapest 1922, Play
Thin Ice 1937 d: Sidney Lanfield. lps: Sonja Henie, Tyrone Power, Arthur Treacher. 78M USA. *Lovely to Look at* (UKN) prod/rel: Twentieth Century-Fox Film Corp.

A Tuenemeny, Budapest 1922, Play
My Lips Betray 1933 d: John G. Blystone. lps: Lilian Harvey, John Boles, El Brendel. 79M USA. *His Majesty's Car* prod/rel: Fox Film Corp.©

ORCUTT, WILLIAM DANA
The Moth, New York 1912, Novel
Moth, The 1917 d: Edward Jose. lps: Norma Talmadge, Eugene O'Brien, Hassard Short. 6r USA. prod/rel: Norma Talmadge Film Corp.©, Select Picture Corp.

ORCZY, BARONESS (1865–1947), HNG, Orczy, Emmuska, Orczy, Emma Magdalena Rosalia Maria
The Affair at the Novelty Theatre, Short Story
Affair at the Novelty Theatre, The 1924 d: Hugh Croise. lps: Rolf Leslie, Renee Wakefield, Charles Vane. 2200f UKN. prod/rel: Stoll

Beau Brocade, Novel
Beau Brocade 1916 d: Thomas Bentley. lps: Mercy Hatton, Charles Rock, Austin Leigh. 5400f UKN. prod/rel: Lucoque

The Brighton Mystery, Short Story
Brighton Mystery, The 1924 d: Hugh Croise. lps: Rolf Leslie, Renee Wakefield. 2200f UKN. prod/rel: Stoll

The Celestial City, Novel
Celestial City, The 1929 d: John Orton. lps: Norah Baring, Cecil Fearnley, Lewis Dayton. SIL. 8768f UKN. prod/rel: British Instructional, Jmg

The Elusive Pimpernel, 1908, Novel
Elusive Pimpernel, The 1919 d: Maurice Elvey. lps: Cecil Humphreys, Marie Blanche, Norman Page. 5143f UKN. prod/rel: Stoll

The Emperor's Candlesticks, London 1899, Novel
Emperor's Candlesticks, The 1937 d: George Fitzmaurice. lps: William Powell, Luise Rainer, Robert Young. 92M USA. prod/rel: Metro-Goldwyn-Mayer Corp.©

The Hocussing of Cigarette, Short Story
Hocussing of Cigarette, The 1924 d: Hugh Croise. lps: Rolf Leslie, Renee Wakefield, Roy Travers. 2150f UKN. prod/rel: Stoll

I Will Repay, Novel
I Will Repay 1923 d: Henry Kolker. lps: Holmes Herbert, Flora Le Breton, Pedro de CordobA. 6600f UKN. *Swords and the Woman* (USA) prod/rel: Ideal

The Kensington Mystery, Short Story
Kensington Mystery, The 1924 d: Hugh Croise. lps: Rolf Leslie, Renee Wakefield, Reginald Fox. 2150f UKN. *The Affair of Dartmoor Terrace* prod/rel: Stoll

The Laughing Cavalier, Novel
Laughing Cavalier, The 1917 d: A. V. Bramble, Eliot Stannard. lps: A. V. Bramble, Mercy Hatton, George Bellamy. 5509f UKN. prod/rel: Dreadnought, Jury

Leatherface; a Tale of Old Flanders, New York 1916, Novel
Two Lovers 1928 d: Fred Niblo. lps: Ronald Colman, Vilma Banky, Noah Beery. 8817f USA. *The Passionate Adventure* prod/rel: Samuel Goldwyn, Inc., United Artists

A Moorland Tragedy, Story
Moorland Tragedy, A 1933 d: M. A. Wetherell. lps: Haddon Mason, Barbara Coombes, Moore Marriott. 38M UKN. prod/rel: Gem Productions, Equity British

The Mystery of Brudenell Court, Short Story
Mystery of Brudenell Court, The 1924 d: Hugh Croise. lps: Rolf Leslie, Renee Wakefield, John Hamilton. 1831f UKN. prod/rel: Stoll

The Mystery of Dogstooth Cliff, Short Story
Mystery of Dogstooth Cliff, The 1924 d: Hugh Croise. lps: Rolf Leslie, Renee Wakefield. 1940f UKN. prod/rel: Stoll

The Mystery of the Khaki Tunic, Short Story
Mystery of the Khaki Tunic, The 1924 d: Hugh Croise. lps: Rolf Leslie, Renee Wakefield. 2280f UKN. prod/rel: Stoll

The Northern Mystery, Short Story
Northern Mystery, The 1924 d: Hugh Croise. lps: Rolf Leslie, Renee Wakefield. 2075f UKN. prod/rel: Stoll

The Regent's Park Mystery, Short Story
Regent's Park Mystery, The 1924 d: Hugh Croise. lps: Rolf Leslie, Renee Wakefield. 1930f UKN. prod/rel: Stoll

The Return of the Scarlet Pimpernel, Novel
Return of the Scarlet Pimpernel, The 1937 d: Hanns Schwarz. lps: Barry K. Barnes, Sophie Stewart, Margaretta Scott. 94M UKN. prod/rel: London Films, United Artists

The Scarlet Pimpernel, 1905, Novel
Scarlet Pimpernel, The 1917 d: Richard Stanton. lps: Dustin Farnum, Winifred Kingston, William Burress. 5r USA. prod/rel: Fox Film Corp., William Fox©
Scarlet Pimpernel, The 1935 d: Harold Young. lps: Leslie Howard, Merle Oberon, Raymond Massey. 98M UKN. prod/rel: London Films, United Artists

Elusive Pimpernel, The 1950 d: Michael Powell, Emeric Pressburger. lps: David Niven, Margaret Leighton, Jack Hawkins. 109M UKN. *Fighting Pimpernel, The* (USA); *The Scarlet Pimpernel* prod/rel: British Lion Production Assets, London Films
Scarlet Pimpernel, The 1982 d: Clive Donner. lps: Anthony Andrews, Jane Seymour, Ian McKellen. TVM. 150M USA/UKN. prod/rel: London Films

Spy of Napoleon, Novel
Spy of Napoleon 1936 d: Maurice Elvey. lps: Richard Barthelmess, Dolly Haas, Frank Vosper. 101M UKN. prod/rel: Jh Productions, Wardour

The Tragedy of Barnsdale Manor, Short Story
Tragedy of Barnsdale Manor, The 1924 d: Hugh Croise. lps: Rolf Leslie, Renee Wakefield, Cecil Mannering. 2200f UKN. prod/rel: Stoll

The Tremarne Case, Short Story
Tremarne Case, The 1924 d: Hugh Croise. lps: Rolf Leslie, Renee Wakefield. 1900f UKN. prod/rel: Stoll

The Triumph of the Scarlet Pimpernel, Novel
Triumph of the Scarlet Pimpernel, The 1928 d: T. Hayes Hunter. lps: Matheson Lang, Juliette Compton, Nelson Keys. 7946f UKN. *The Scarlet Daredevil* (USA) prod/rel: British & Dominions, Woolf & Freedman

The York Mystery, Short Story
York Mystery, The 1924 d: Hugh Croise. lps: Rolf Leslie, Renee Wakefield, Dallas Cairns. 2150f UKN. prod/rel: Stoll

ORD, ROBERT
The King's Outcast, Play
King's Outcast, The 1915 d: Ralph Dewsbury. lps: Gerald Ames, Blanche Bryan, Charles Rock. 3500f UKN. *His Vindication* (USA) prod/rel: London, Jury

Mr. Wake's Patient, Play
Dr. Wake's Patient 1916 d: Fred Paul. lps: Phyllis Dare, Gerald McCarthy, James Lindsay. 4300f UKN. prod/rel: G. B. Samuelson, Moss

ORDONNEAU, MAURICE
L'auberge du Tohu-Bohu,, Play
Auberge du Tohu-Bohu, L' 1912 d: Georges DenolA. lps: Milo, Landrin, Louis Blanche. 370m FRN. prod/rel: Scagl

Les Saltimbanques, Opera
Saltimbanques, Les 1930 d: Jaquelux, Robert Land. lps: Kathe von Nagy, Nicolas Koline, Max Hansen. 1965m FRN/GRM/ITL. *Saltimbanchi, I* (ITL); *Gaukler* (GRM) prod/rel: Albert Lauzin, Nero-Film

Le Voyage de Berluron, 1893
Viaggio Di Berluron, Il 1919 d: Camillo de Riso. lps: Camillo de Riso, Eugenia Cigoli, Achille de Riso. 1182m ITL. prod/rel: Caesar Film

O'REILLY, BERNARD
Cullenbenbong, Novel
Sons of Matthew 1949 d: Charles Chauvel. lps: Michael Pate, Wendy Gibb, John O'Malley. 90M ASL. *The Rugged O'Riordans* (USA) prod/rel: Universal

Green Mountains, Novel
Sons of Matthew 1949 d: Charles Chauvel. lps: Michael Pate, Wendy Gibb, John O'Malley. 90M ASL. *The Rugged O'Riordans* (USA) prod/rel: Universal

ORIOLO, JOSEPH
Casper the Friendly Ghost, Story
Casper 1995 d: Brad Silberling. lps: Christina Ricci, Bill Pullman, Cathy Moriarty. 100M USA. prod/rel: Amblin, Harvey

ORKENY, ISTVAN
MacSkajatek, 1963, Novel
MacSkajatek 1974 d: Karoly Makk. lps: Elma Bulla, Margit DaykA. 123M HNG. *Catsplay* (USA); *Cat's Game*
Katzenspiel 1983 d: Istvan Szabo. lps: Maria Becker, Joana Maria Gorvin, Jane Tilden. MTV. 83M GRM. *Catsplay*; *Cat's Play* prod/rel: Telefilm Saar, Saarlandischer Rundfunk

Rekviem, 1957-58, Short Story
Requiem 1981 d: Zoltan Fabri. lps: Edit Frajt, Lajos Balazsovits, Laszlo Galffi. 93M HNG.

Totek, 1964, Novel
Isten Hozta, Ornagy Ur! 1969 d: Zoltan Fabri. lps: Zoltan Latinovits, Imre Sinkovits, Marta Fonay. 106M HNG. *The Toth Family*; *The Tot Family* prod/rel: Mafilm Studio 1

ORKOW, MORGAN
Shadow of Their Wings, Story
Wings for the Eagle 1942 d: Lloyd Bacon. lps: Ann Sheridan, Dennis Morgan, Jack Carson. 85M USA. *Shadow of Their Wings* prod/rel: Warner Bros.

ORLEV, URI
The Island on Bird Street, Book
   Island on Bird Street, The 1997 d: Soren Kragh-Jacobsen. lps: Patrick Bergin, Jordan Kiziuk, Jack Warden. 107M DNM/UKN/GRM. *Huset I Fuglegaden* (DNM) prod/rel: M & M. Prods., April Prods.

ORLOG, H.
Listen Lester, Play
   Listen Lester 1924 d: William A. Seiter. lps: Louise Fazenda, Harry Myers, Eva Novak. 6242f USA. prod/rel: Sacramento Pictures, Principal Pictures

ORNITZ, SAMUEL (1890–1957), USA
Tong War, Story
   Chinatown Nights 1929 d: William A. Wellman. lps: Wallace Beery, Florence Vidor, Warner Oland. 7481f USA. *Tong War* prod/rel: Paramount Famous Lasky Corp.

O'ROURKE, FRANK
The Bravados, Novel
   Bravados, The 1958 d: Henry King. lps: Gregory Peck, Joan Collins, Stephen Boyd. 99M USA. prod/rel: 20th Century-Fox
The Great Bank Robbery, New York 1969, Novel
   Great Bank Robbery, The 1969 d: Hy Averback. lps: Clint Walker, Zero Mostel, Kim Novak. 98M USA. prod/rel: Warner Bros., Seven Arts, Inc.
A Mule for the Marquesa, New York 1964, Novel
   Professionals, The 1966 d: Richard Brooks. lps: Burt Lancaster, Lee Marvin, Robert Ryan. 117M USA. prod/rel: Pax Enterprises

ORR, CLIFFORD
The Dartmouth Murders, New York 1929, Novel
   Shot in the Dark, A 1935 d: Charles Lamont. lps: Charles Starrett, Edward Van Sloan, Marion Shilling. 69M USA. prod/rel: Chesterfield Motion Pictures Corp.©

ORR, MARY
Wallflower, New York 1944, Play
   Wallflower 1948 d: Frederick de CordovA. lps: Joyce Reynolds, Janis Paige, Robert Hutton. 77M USA. prod/rel: Warner Bros.

ORTH, MARION
A Midnight Romance, Short Story
   Midnight Romance, A 1919 d: Lois Weber. lps: Anita Stewart, Jack Holt, Edwin Booth Tilton. 5771f USA. prod/rel: Anita Stewart Productions, First National Exhibitors Circuit, Inc.

ORTIZ, DOMINGO SILAS
Modesta, Short Story
   Modesta 1956 d: Benji Doniger. 35M PRC. prod/rel: Film Unit Div. of Community Education

ORTON, JOE (1933–1967), UKN, Orton, John Kingsley
Entertaining Mr. Sloane, London 1964, Play
   Entertaining Mr. Sloane 1970 d: Douglas Hickox. lps: Beryl Reid, Harry Andrews, Peter McEnery. 94M UKN/AUS. prod/rel: Canterbury Films, Warner-Pathe
Loot, 1967, Play
   Loot 1970 d: Silvio Narizzano. lps: Richard Attenborough, Lee Remick, Hywel Bennett. 101M UKN. *Loot. Give Me Money, Honey!* prod/rel: British Lion, Performing Arts

ORUM, POUL
Kun Sandheden, 1974, Novel
   Kun Sandheden 1975 d: Henning Ornbak. lps: Frits Helmuth, Ghita Norby, Preben Neergaard. 97M DNM. *Nothing But the Truth*

ORVAL, CLAUDE
Le Grand Caid, Novel
   Caid, Le 1960 d: Bernard Borderie. lps: Fernandel, Barbara Laage, Georges Wilson. 92M FRN. prod/rel: C.I.C.C.
Nadia, la Femme Traquee, Short Story
   Nadia, la Femme Traquee 1939 d: Claude Orval. lps: Mireille Perrey, Pierre Renoir, Roger Duchesne. 86M FRN. *A l'Ombre du Deuxieme Bureau; L'ombre du Deuxieme Bureau; Nadia, la Lutte Secrete* prod/rel: Normandie Films
Les Nuits de Montmartre, Novel
   Nuits de Montmartre, Les 1955 d: Pierre Franchi. lps: Jean-Marc Thibault, Genevieve Kervine, Louis Seigner. 94M FRN. prod/rel: Filmonde

ORWELL, GEORGE (1903–1950), UKN, Blair, Eric Arthur
Animal Farm, 1945, Novel
   Animal Farm 1955 d: John Halas, Joy Batchelor. ANM. 75M UKN. prod/rel: Ab-Pathe, Halas and Batchelor
Keep the Aspidistra Flying, 1936, Novel
   Keep the Aspidistra Flying 1997 d: Robert Bierman. lps: Richard E. Grant, Helena Bonham-Carter, Julian Wadham. 100M UKN. prod/rel: Uba/Sentinel Films, Bonaparte Films

Nineteen Eighty-Four, 1949, Novel
   Nineteen Eighty-Four 1954 d: Rudolph Cartier. lps: Peter Cushing, Andre Morell, Yvonne Mitchell. MTV. 105M UKN. *1984* prod/rel: BBC
   1984 1956 d: Michael Anderson. lps: Edmond O'Brien, Jan Sterling, Michael Redgrave. 90M UKN. prod/rel: Holiday, Ab-Pathe
   1984 1984 d: Michael Radford. lps: John Hurt, Suzanna Hamilton, Richard Burton. 123M UKN. prod/rel: Umbrella, Rosenblum

ORZESZKOWA, ELIZA
Cham, 1888, Novel
   Cham 1931 d: Jan Nowina-Przybylski. 94M PLN. *Yokels*
Nad Niemnem, 1888, Novel
   Nad Niemnem 1986 d: Zbigniew Kuzminski, Zbigniew Kaminski. lps: Iwona Pawluk, Adam Marjanski, Marta LipinskA. 177M PLN. *On the Niemen River; The River Niemen*

OSARAGI, JIRO
Munakata Shimai, 1949, Novel
   Munakata Shimai 1950 d: Yasujiro Ozu. lps: So Yamamura, Kinuyo Tanaka, Hideko Takamine. 112M JPN. *The Munakata Sisters; Munekata Shimai* prod/rel: Shintoho Co.
Nadare, 1937, Novel
   Nadare 1937 d: Mikio Naruse. 70M JPN. *Avalanche*
Yurei-Sen, Novel
   Yureisen 1957 d: Teiji MatsudA. lps: Kinnosuke Nakamura, Ryutaro Otomo, Ryunosuke TsukigatA. F JPN. *Ghost Ship* prod/rel: Toei Co.

OSBORN JR., JOHN JAY
The Paper Chase, Novel
   Paper Chase, The 1973 d: James Bridges. lps: Timothy Bottoms, John Houseman, Lindsay Wagner. 111M USA. prod/rel: 20th Century Fox

OSBORN, PAUL
The Vinegar Tree, New York 1930, Play
   Should Ladies Behave? 1933 d: Harry Beaumont. lps: Alice Brady, Lionel Barrymore, Conway Tearle. 89M USA. *The Vinegar Tree* prod/rel: Metro-Goldwyn-Mayer Corp.©

OSBORNE, CHARLES
The Face in the Moonlight, New York 1892, Play
   Face in the Moonlight, The 1915 d: Albert Capellani. lps: Robert Warwick, Stella Archer, H. Cooper Cliffe. 5r USA. prod/rel: William A. Brady Picture Plays, Inc., World Film Corp.©

OSBORNE, HAMILTON
The Boomerang, Story
   Boomerang, The 1913 d: Thomas H. Ince. lps: Charles Ray, Louise Glaum, Gertrude Claire. 3r USA. prod/rel: Kb
The Seal of Silence, Story
   Seal of Silence, The 1913 d: Thomas H. Ince. lps: J. Barney Sherry, Rhea Mitchell, Robert Edeson. 2r USA. prod/rel: Kb

OSBORNE, HUBERT
Shore Leave, New York 1922, Play
   Shore Leave 1925 d: John S. Robertson. lps: Richard Barthelmess, Dorothy MacKaill, Ted McNamarA. 6856f USA. prod/rel: Inspiration Pictures, First National Pictures
   Hit the Deck 1930 d: Luther Reed. lps: Jack Oakie, Polly Walker, Roger Gray. 9327f USA. prod/rel: RKO Productions
   Follow the Fleet 1936 d: Mark Sandrich. lps: Fred Astaire, Ginger Rogers, Randolph Scott. 110M USA. prod/rel: RKO Radio Pictures©, Pandro S. Berman Production
   Hit the Deck 1955 d: Roy Rowland. lps: Jane Powell, Tony Martin, Debbie Reynolds. 112M USA. prod/rel: MGM
Two Worlds, Play
   Strange Experiment 1937 d: Albert Parker. lps: Donald Gray, Anne Wemyss, Mary Newcomb. 74M UKN. prod/rel: Fox British

OSBORNE, JOHN (1929–1994), UKN, Osborne, John James
The Entertainer, London 1957, Play
   Entertainer, The 1960 d: Tony Richardson. lps: Laurence Olivier, Brenda de Banzie, Roger Livesey. 96M UKN. prod/rel: Bryanston, Woodfall-Holly
   Entertainer, The 1976 d: Donald Wrye. lps: Jack Lemmon, Ray Bolger, Sada Thompson. TVM. 100M USA. prod/rel: Rso Productions
Inadmissable Evidence, London 1964, Play
   Inadmissable Evidence 1968 d: Anthony Page. lps: Nicol Williamson, Eleanor Fazan, Jill Bennett. 96M UKN. prod/rel: Woodfall Films, Paramount

Look Back in Anger, London 1956, Play
   Look Back in Anger 1959 d: Tony Richardson. lps: Richard Burton, Claire Bloom, Mary Ure. 101M UKN. prod/rel: Ab-Pathe, Woodfall
   Look Back in Anger 1989 d: David Jones. lps: Kenneth Branagh, Emma Thompson, Gerard Horan. TVM. 115M UKN.
Luther, 1961, Play
   Luther 1974 d: Guy Green. lps: Stacy Keach, Patrick Magee, Hugh Griffith. 112M UKN/USA/CND. prod/rel: American Express, Ely Laudau

OSBORNE, WILLIAM HAMILTON
Adrienne Gascoyne, 1915, Short Story
   Hearts Or Diamonds? 1918 d: Henry King. lps: William Russell, Charlotte Burton, Howard Davies. 5r USA. *Hearts and Diamonds; Adrienne Gascoyne* prod/rel: William Russell Productions, Mutual Film Corp.
The Boomerang, New York 1912, Novel
   Boomerang, The 1919 d: Bertram Bracken. lps: Henry B. Walthall, Melbourne MacDowell, Helen Jerome Eddy. 7r USA. prod/rel: National Film Corp., State Rights
Catspaw, New York 1911, Novel
   Catspaw, The 1916 d: George A. Wright. lps: Miriam Nesbitt, Marc McDermott, William Wadsworth. 5r USA. prod/rel: Thomas A. Edison, Inc.©, Kleine-Edison Feature Service
Neal of the Navy, Story
   Neal of the Navy 1915 d: William M. Harvey, William Bertram. lps: Lillian Lorraine, William Courtleigh Jr., William Conklin. SRL. 28r USA. prod/rel: Panama Films, Pathe Exchange Co.
The Red Mouse: a Mystery Romance, New York 1909, Novel
   Half Million Bribe, The 1916 d: Edgar Jones. lps: Hamilton Revelle, Marguerite Snow, John Smiley. 5r USA. prod/rel: Columbia Pictures Corp.©, Metro Pictures Corp.
The Running Fight, New York 1910, Novel
   Running Fight, The 1915 d: James Durkin. lps: Violet Heming, Robert W. Cummings, Thurlow Bergen. 5-6r USA. prod/rel: Pre-Eminent Films, Ltd.©, Paramount Pictures Corp.
The Troop Train, 1918, Story
   Love and the Law 1919 d: Edgar Lewis. lps: Glenn White, Arnold Storrer, Josephine Hill. 6r USA. *The Troop Train* prod/rel: Edgar Lewis Productions, William L. Sherry Service

OSBOURNE, LLOYD (1868–1947), UKN
East Is East, 1920, Short Story
   Where Lights are Low 1921 d: Colin Campbell. lps: Sessue Hayakawa, Togo Yamamoto, Goro Kino. 6r USA. *When Lights are Low* prod/rel: Hayakawa Feature Play Co., R-C Pictures
The Ebb Tide; a Trio and Quartette, 1894, Novel
   Ebb Tide 1915 d: Colin Campbell. lps: Kathlyn Williams, Wheeler Oakman, Harry Lonsdale. 3r USA. prod/rel: Selig Polyscope Co.
   Ebb Tide 1922 d: George Melford. lps: Lila Lee, James Kirkwood, Raymond Hatton. 7336f USA. prod/rel: Famous Players-Lasky, Paramount Pictures
   Ebb Tide 1937 d: James P. Hogan. lps: Frances Farmer, Ray Milland, Oscar HomolkA. 94M USA. prod/rel: Paramount Pictures©, Lucien Hubbard Production
   Adventure Island 1947 d: Sam Newfield. lps: Rory Calhoun, Rhonda Fleming, Paul Kelly. 67M USA. prod/rel: Paramount
Infatuation, Indianapolis 1909, Novel
   Infatuation 1915 d: Harry Pollard. lps: Margarita Fischer, Lucille Ward, Joseph Singleton. 4r USA. prod/rel: American Film Co.©, Mutual Film Corp.
The Man Who, 1921, Short Story
   Man Who, The 1921 d: Maxwell Karger. lps: Bert Lytell, Lucy Cotton, Virginia Valli. 6r USA. prod/rel: Metro Pictures
The Wrecker, 1892, Novel
   Tainata Na Apolonia 1984 d: Ivo Toman. lps: David Vejrazka, Jan Pichocinski, Olga ShoberovA. 95M BUL/CZC. *Vrak* (CZC); *Apollonia's Secret; The Wreck; The Derelict*
The Wrong Box, London 1889, Novel
   Wrong Box, The 1966 d: Bryan Forbes. lps: John Mills, Ralph Richardson, Michael Caine. 110M UKN. prod/rel: Salamander Film Productions, Columbia

O'SHAUGHNESSY, EDITH LOUISE
The Viennese Medley, New York 1924, Novel
   Greater Glory, The 1926 d: Curt Rehfeld. lps: Conway Tearle, Anna Q. Nilsson, May Allison. 9710f USA. *The Viennese Melody* prod/rel: First National Pictures

OSHIKAWA, SHUNRO
Kaitei Gunkan / Kaitei Okoku, Novel
  Kaitei Gunkan 1963 d: Inoshiro HondA. lps: Tadao Takashima, Yoko Fujiyama, Yu Fujiki. 96M JPN. *Atoragon, the Flying Supersub; Atragon the Flying Sub; Atragon* (USA); *Atoragon; Underwater Warship* prod/rel: Toho Co.

OSMOND, MARIAN
Chinese Bungalow, The, Novel
  Chinese Bungalow, The 1926 d: Sinclair Hill. lps: Matheson Lang, Genevieve Townsend, Juliette Compton. 6600f UKN. prod/rel: Stoll
The Chinese Bungalow, Novel
  Chinese Bungalow, The 1930 d: J. B. Williams, Arthur W. Barnes. lps: Matheson Lang, Jill Esmond Moore, Anna Neagle. 74M UKN. prod/rel: Neo-Art, Williams and Pritchard
  Chinese Bungalow, The 1940 d: George King. lps: Paul Lukas, Jane Baxter, Robert Douglas. 72M UKN. *The Chinese Den* (USA) prod/rel: Pennant, British Lion

OSMUN, LEIGHTON GRAVES
The Clutch of Circumstance, New York 1914, Novel
  Clutch of Circumstance, The 1918 d: Henry Houry. lps: Corinne Griffith, Robert Gaillord, David Herblin. 4127f USA. prod/rel: Vitagraph Co. of America©, Blue Ribbon Feature
East Side - West Side, Play
  East Side - West Side 1923 d: Irving Cummings. lps: Kenneth Harlan, Eileen Percy, Maxine Elliott Hicks. 6r USA. prod/rel: Principal Pictures
The Fortune Teller, New York 1919, Play
  Fortune Teller, The 1920 d: Albert Capellani. lps: Marjorie Rambeau, Frederick Burton, Escamillo Fernandez. 7r USA. prod/rel: Albert Capellani Productions, Robertson-Cole Distributing Corp.

OSSOWSKI, LEONIE
Die Grosse Flatter, Novel
  Grosse Flatter, Die 1979 d: Marianne Ludcke. lps: Jochen Schroeder, Hans-Jurgen Muller, Adriane RimschA. 282M GRM. *The Big Flutter* prod/rel: Regina Ziegler Filmprod., Wdr
Stern Ohne Himmel, Novel
  Stern Ohne Himmel 1981 d: Ottokar Runze. lps: Manfred Gliewe, Andreas Mameder, Hieronymus Blosser. 85M GRM. *Star Without Sky; A Star Without a Sky* prod/rel: Ottokar Runze Produktion, Nobis

OSTENSO, MARTHA
Ruf Der Wildganse, Novel
  Ruf Der Wildganse, Der 1961 d: Hans Heinrich. lps: Ewald Balser, Brigitte Horney, Heidemarie Hatheyer. 91M AUS. prod/rel: Wiener Mundus
Wild Geese, New York 1925, Novel
  Wild Geese 1927 d: Phil Stone. lps: Belle Bennett, Russell Simpson, Eve Southern. 6448f USA. prod/rel: Tiffany-Stahl Productions

OSTERGREN, KLAS
Short Story
  Veranda for En Tenor 1998 d: Lisa Ohlin. lps: Johan Kjellgren, Krister Henriksson, Lena B. Erikson. 95M SWD. *Waiting for a Tenor* prod/rel: Svensk Filmindustri, Migma Film

OSTERREICHER
Der Herr Ohne Wohnung, Play
  Herr Ohne Wohnung, Der 1934 d: E. W. Emo. lps: Paul Horbiger, Adele Sandrock, Hermann Thimig. 89M AUS. prod/rel: Projektograph
Der Herr Ohne Wornung, Play
  Who's Your Lady Friend? 1937 d: Carol Reed. lps: Frances Day, Vic Oliver, Betty Stockfeld. 73M UKN. prod/rel: Dorian, Associated British

OSTERREICHER, RUDOLF
Der Garten Eden, Berlin 1926, Play
  Garden of Eden, The 1928 d: Lewis Milestone. lps: Corinne Griffith, Louise Dresser, Lowell Sherman. 7300f USA. prod/rel: Feature Productions, United Artists
Die Sachertorte, Play
  Im Prater Bluh'n Wieder Die Baume 1958 d: Hans Wolff. lps: Johanna Matz, Gerhard Riedmann, Nina Sandt. 95M AUS. prod/rel: Paula Wessely
Das Zweite Leben, 1927, Play
  Three Sinners 1928 d: Rowland V. Lee. lps: Pola Negri, Warner Baxter, Paul Lukas. 7092f USA. prod/rel: Paramount Famous Lasky Corp.
  Once a Lady 1931 d: Guthrie McClintic. lps: Ruth Chatterton, Ivor Novello, Jill Esmond. 80M USA. prod/rel: Paramount Publix Corp.©

OSTRANDER, ISABEL
The Island of Intrigue, New York 1918, Novel
  Island of Intrigue, The 1919 d: Henry Otto. lps: May Allison, Jack Mower, Frederick Vroom. 4300f USA. prod/rel: Metro Pictures Corp.©

Suspense, New York 1918, Novel
  Suspense 1919 d: Frank Reicher. lps: Mollie King, Howard Truesdell, Izeth Munro. 6r USA. *Suspence* prod/rel: Screencraft Pictures, Inc., Frank Reicher Production

OSTROVSKY, ALEXANDER (1823–1886), RSS, Ostrovsky, Aleksandr Nikolayevich
Beshennye Dengi, 1870, Play
  Besenye Dengi 1981 d: Yevgeni Matveyev. 86M USS. *Easy Money; Beshenye Dengi*
Bespridannitsa, 1878, Play
  Bespridannitsa 1936 d: Yakov Protazanov. 80M USS. *Without Dowry; Without a Dowry*
  Zestokij Romans 1984 d: Eldar Ryazanov. lps: Nikita Mikhalkov, Larisa Goeseeva, Alisa Friendlich. 140M USS. *Ruthless Romance; Zhestoki Romans; Zhestokij Romans; Cruel Romance; Dowerless Bride*
Bez Vini Vinovatiye, 1884, Play
  Bez Vini Vinovatiye 1945 d: Vladimir Petrov. 100M USS. *Guilty Though Innocent; Bez Viny Vinovatye; Guilty Though Guiltless; Innocent Though Guilty*
Dokhodnoe Mesto, 1857, Play
  Vankansya 1981 d: Margarita Mikaelyan. 77M USS.
Goriachee Serdtse, 1869, Play
  Goriachee Serdtse 1953 d: Gennadi Kazansky. 179M USS.
Groza, 1859, Play
  Groza 1934 d: Vladimir Petrov. 85M USS. *The Thunderstorm; The Storm*
Kak Zakalyalas Stal, 1932-34, Novel
  Kak Zakalyalas Stal 1942 d: Mark Donskoi. lps: V. Perist-Petrenko, Daniel Sagal, I. FedotovA. 92M USS. *How the Steel Was Tempered; Heroes are Made; Kak Zakaljalas Stal*
  Pavel Korchagin 1957 d: Alexander Alov, Vladimir Naumov. lps: Vassilli Lanovoi. 95M USS. *Pavel Korcagin*
Les, 1871, Play
  Les 1953 d: Vladimir Vengerov, S. Timoshenko. 169M USS. *The Forest*
  Les 1980 d: Vladimir Motyl. 121M USS. *Forest*
Na Boikom Meste, 1865, Play
  Na Boikom Meste 1955 d: Vladimir Sukhobokov, Elena Skatchko. 101M USS.
Na Vsyakogo Mudretsa Dovolno Prostoty, 1868, Play
  Na Vsyakogo Mudretsa Dovolno Prostoty 1952 d: A. Dormenko. 178M USS.
Poslednaya Zhertva, 1878, Play
  Poslednaja Shertwa 1975 d: Petr Todorovsky. lps: Margarita Wolodina, Oleg Strishenov, Mikhail Gluzskij. 99M USS. *The Last Sacrifice; Poslednjaja Zertva; Poslednaya Zhertva* prod/rel: Mosfilm
Pravda Khorosho, a Schaste Luchshe, 1877, Play
  Pravda Khorosho, a Schaste Luchshe 1951 d: Sergei Alexeyev. 149M USS.
Prazdnichnyy Son - Do Obeda, St. Petersburg 1857, Play
  Zhenitba Balzaminova 1965 d: Konstantin Voinov. lps: Georgi Vitsin, Lyudmila Shagalova, Lidia SmirnovA. 90M USS. *The Marriage of Balzaminov* (USA); *Balzaminov's Marriage* prod/rel: Mosfilm
Puchina, 1866, Play
  Puchina 1958 d: Antonin Dawson, Yu. Muzykant. 99M USS.
Snegurochka, 1873, Play
  Snegurotchka 1969 d: Pavel Kadochnikov. lps: Pavel Kadochnikov, Evguenia Filonova, Evgueni Jarikov. 92M USS. *Snow Beauty*
Talanty I Poklonniki, 1882, Play
  Talanty I Poklonniki 1955 d: Andrey Apsolon, Boris Dmokhovski. 89M USS.
  Talanty I Poklonniki 1973 d: Isider Annensky. 90M USS.
Volki I Ovsty, 1875, Play
  Volki I Ovsky 1952 d: Vladimir Sukhobokov. 181M USS.

OSWALDA, OSSI
Der Vierzehnte Am Tisch, Story
  Ctrnacty U Stolu 1943 d: Oldrich Novy, Antonin ZelenkA. lps: Karel Hoger, Ludvik Veverka, Helena FriedlovA. 2413m CZC. *The Fourteenth at the Table* prod/rel: Lucernafilm

OTCENASEK, JAN
Obcan Brych, 1955, Novel
  Obcan Brych 1958 d: Otakar VavrA. lps: Karel Hoger, Vlasta Fialova, Zdenek Stepanek. 102M CZC. *Citizen Brych*

Romeo, Julie a Tma, Prague 1960, Novel
  Romeo, Julie a Tma 1960 d: Jiri Weiss. lps: Ivan Mistrik, Dana Smutna, Jirina SejbalovA. 96M CZC. *Sweet Light in a Dark Room* (USA); *Romeo, Juliet and the Darkness; Romeo, Juliet and Darkness; Sweet Light in the Dark Window* prod/rel: Barrandov Film Studio

OTIS, JAMES
Toby Tyler; Or, Ten Weeks With a Circus, New York 1881, Novel
  Circus Days 1923 d: Eddie Cline. lps: Jackie Coogan, Barbara Tennant, Russell Simpson. 6183f USA. prod/rel: Sol Lesser, Associated First National Pictures

OTOMO, KATSUHIRO
Akira, Novel
  Akira 1988 d: Katsuhiro Otomo. ANM. 124M JPN. prod/rel: Akira Committee Co.

OTT, ESTRID
De Pokkers Unger, Play
  Pokkers Unger, de 1947 d: Astrid Henning-Jensen, Bjarne Henning-Jensen. lps: Henry Nielsen, Preben Neergaard, Tove Maas. 90M DNM. *Those Blasted Kids* prod/rel: Nordisk

OTT, WOLFGANG
Haie Und Kleine Fische, Novel
  Haie Und Kleine Fische 1957 d: Frank Wisbar. lps: Hansjorg Felmy, Sabine Bethmann, Wolfgang Preiss. 120M GRM. *U Boat 55; Sharks and Little Fish* prod/rel: Zeyn, Severin

OTTUM, ROBERT K.
Stand on It, Novel
  Stroker Ace 1983 d: Hal Needham. lps: Burt Reynolds, Ned Beatty, Jim Nabors. 96M USA. prod/rel: Universal, Warner

OUDART, GEORGES
La Meilleure Maitresse, Novel
  Meilleure Maitresse, La 1929 d: Rene Hervil. lps: Sandra Milowanoff, Felicien Tramel, Hubert Daix. 1963m FRN. prod/rel: Film d'Art (Vandal Et Delac)
  Femme Ideale, La 1933 d: Andre Berthomieu. lps: Marie Glory, Arlette Marchal, Rene Lefevre. 98M FRN. *The Ideal Woman* (USA) prod/rel: Films De France

OUGHTON, FREDERICK
Breakout, Book
  Breakout 1959 d: Peter Graham Scott. lps: Lee Patterson, Hazel Court, Terence Alexander. 62M UKN. prod/rel: Anglo-Amalgamated, Independent Artists

OUIDA (1839–1908), UKN, De La Ramee, Marie Louise
Bebee; Or Two Little Wooden Shoes, Philadelphia 1874, Novel
  Little Dutch Girl, The 1915 d: Emile Chautard. lps: Vivian Martin, John Bowers, Chester Barnett. 5r USA. prod/rel: Shubert Film Co., World Film Corp.©
Bebee; Or Two Little Wooden Shoes, Novel
  Two Little Wooden Shoes 1920 d: Sidney Morgan. lps: Joan Morgan, Langhorne Burton, J. Denton-Thompson. 5325f UKN. prod/rel: Progress, Butcher's Film Service
A Dog of Flanders, New York 1872, Novel
  Dog of Flanders, The 1914. lps: Marguerite Snow, Mignon Anderson, James Cruze. 2r USA. prod/rel: Thanhouser
  Boy of Flanders, A 1924 d: Victor Schertzinger. lps: Jackie Coogan, Nigel de Brulier, Lionel Belmore. 7018f USA. prod/rel: Jackie Coogan Productions, Metro-Goldwyn-Mayer Distributing Corp.
  Dog of Flanders, A 1935 d: Edward Sloman. lps: Frankie Thomas, Helen Parrish, Richard Quine. 72M USA. *Boy of Flanders, A* prod/rel: RKO Radio Pictures, Inc.
  Dog of Flanders, A 1959 d: James B. Clark. lps: David Ladd, Donald Crisp, Theodore Bikel. 97M USA. prod/rel: 20th Century-Fox
In Maremma, Novel
  In Maremma 1924 d: Salvatore Aversano. lps: Rina de Liguoro, Adolfo Trouche, Carlo Benetti. 2272m ITL. *Maremma* prod/rel: Trouche
Moths, London 1880, Novel
  Her Greatest Love 1917 d: J. Gordon Edwards. lps: Theda Bara, Harry Hilliard, Glenn White. 5r USA. prod/rel: Fox Film Corp., William Fox©
  Moths 1913 d: W. Christy Cabanne. lps: Maude Fealy, William Russell, Harry Benham. 4r USA. prod/rel: Thanhouser Film Corp., Mutual Film Corp.
  Moths 1922. lps: Cameron Carr. 1129f UKN. prod/rel: Master Films, British Exhibitors' Films
Strathmore; Or, Wrought By His Own Hand, Philadelphia 1866, Play
  Flames of Desire 1924 d: Denison Clift. lps: Wyndham Standing, Diana Miller, Richard Thorpe. 5439f USA. prod/rel: Fox Film Corp.

Strathmore: Or, Wrought By His Own Hand, Philadelphia 1866, Novel
  Strathmore 1915 d: Francis J. Grandon. lps: Charles Clary, Elmer Clifton, Francelia Billington. 4r USA. prod/rel: Reliance Motion Picture Corp., Mutual Film Corp.

Under Two Flags, London 1867, Novel
  Under Two Flags 1912 d: Theodore Marston. lps: Katherine Horn, Florence Labadie, William Garwood. 2r USA. prod/rel: Thanhouser
  Under Two Flags 1912 d: George Nicholls. lps: Vivian Preston, Herschal Mayall. 2r USA. prod/rel: Gem
  Under Two Flags 1915 d: Travers Vale. lps: Louise Vale, Franklin Ritchie, Herbert Barrington. 3r USA. prod/rel: Biograph Co.
  Under Two Flags 1916 d: J. Gordon Edwards. lps: Theda Bara, Herbert Heyes, Stuart Holmes. 6r USA. prod/rel: Fox Film Corp.©
  Under Two Flags 1922 d: Tod Browning. lps: Priscilla Dean, James Kirkwood, John Davidson. 7407f USA. prod/rel: Universal Film Mfg. Co.
  Under Two Flags 1936 d: Frank Lloyd. lps: Ronald Colman, Claudette Colbert, Victor McLaglen. 111M USA. prod/rel: Twentieth Century-Fox Film Corp.©

OURMANZOFF
Le Crime de Vera Mirzewa, Play
  Fall Des Staatsanwalts M.., Der 1928 d: Rudolf Meinert, Giulio Antamoro. lps: Maria Jacobini, Jean Angelo, Warwick Ward. 3694m GRM/FRN/ITL. *The Strange Case of District Attorney M.; Wera Mirzewa; Le Crime de Vera Mirzewa* (FRN); *Vera Mirzewa* prod/rel: Phenix-Films (Paris), Noya Films (Rome)

OURSLER, FULTON (1893–1952), USA, Oursler, Charles Fulton
The Great Jasper, New York 1930, Novel
  Great Jasper, The 1933 d: J. Walter Ruben. lps: Richard Dix, Florence Eldridge, Edna May Oliver. 85M USA. prod/rel: RKO Radio Pictures©

The Greatest Story Ever Told, New York 1949, Book
  Greatest Story Ever Told, The 1965 d: George Stevens. lps: Max von Sydow, Dorothy McGuire, Robert LoggiA. 221M USA. *Jesus* prod/rel: George Stevens Productions, United Artists

The Spider, New York 1927, Play
  Spider, The 1931 d: William Cameron Menzies, Kenneth MacKennA. lps: Edmund Lowe, Lois Moran, Howard Phillips. 65M USA. *The Midnight Cruise* prod/rel: Fox Film Corp.©

Stepchild of the Moon, New York 1926, Novel
  Second Wife 1930 d: Russell MacK. lps: Conrad Nagel, Lila Lee, Hugh Huntley. 68M USA. prod/rel: RKO Productions
  Second Wife 1936 d: Edward Killy. lps: Walter Abel, Gertrude Michael, Erik Rhodes. 59M USA. *The Marriage Business; Second Marriage* prod/rel: RKO Radio Pictures©

OUYANG YUQIAN
Peach Flower Fan, Play
  Tao Hua Shan 1963 d: Sun Jing. lps: Wang Danfeng, Feng Ji, Yu Junfang. 12r CHN. *Peach Flower Fan* prod/rel: XI'an Film Studio

OVERHOLSER, WAYNE D.
Cast a Long Shadow, Novel
  Cast a Long Shadow 1959 d: Thomas Carr. lps: Audie Murphy, Terry Moore, John Dehner. 82M USA. prod/rel: United Artists, Mirisch

OVERLAND, ARNULF (1889–, NRW
Venner, 1917, Play
  Venner 1960 d: Tancred Ibsen. lps: Eva Bergh, Harald Heide-Steen Jr., Thor Hjort-Jenssen. 91M NRW. *Friends* prod/rel: Nordsjofilm

OVERSEAS PRESS CLUB
As We See Russia, 1948, Book
  Guilty of Treason 1949 d: Felix E. Feist. lps: Paul Kelly, Charles Bickford, Bonita Granville. 86M USA. *Treason* (UKN) prod/rel: Eagle Lion, Freedom Productions

OVERTON, JOHN
My Lady April, Novel
  Gipsy Cavalier, A 1922 d: J. Stuart Blackton. lps: Georges Carpentier, Flora Le Breton, Rex McDougall. 6752f UKN. prod/rel: International Artists, Gaumont

OVERWEG, ROBERT
Ein Falscher Fuffziger, Play
  Falscher Fuffziger, Ein 1935 d: Carl Boese. lps: Lucie Englisch, Georg Alexander, Theo Lingen. 82M GRM. prod/rel: Schulz & Wuellner, Adler

OVESEN, HANS
Krigernes Born, Novel
  Krigernes Born 1979 d: Ernst Johansen. lps: Janik Lesniak, Soren Hindborg, Lars Frohling. 87M DNM. *Warrior Children* prod/rel: Panorama

OVID (43bc–17ad), ITL, Publius Ovidius Naso
Metamorphoses, c2-8, Verse
  Metamorphoses 1978 d: Takashi. ANM. 87M JPN/USA. *Winds of Change*

OWEN, COLLINSON
Zero, Novel
  Zero 1928 d: Jack Raymond. lps: Stewart Rome, Fay Compton, Jeanne de Casalis. 8159f UKN. prod/rel: Film Manufacturing Co., First National-Pathe

OWEN, FRANK
The Eddie Chapman Story, London 1953, Biography
  Triple Cross 1966 d: Terence Young. lps: Christopher Plummer, Yul Brynner, Romy Schneider. 140M UKN/FRN. *La Fantastique Histoire Vraie d'Eddie Chapman* (FRN) prod/rel: Cineurop, Anglo-Amalgamated

OWEN, GUY (1925–1981), USA
Ballad of the Flim-Flam Man, New York 1965, Novel
  Flim-Flam Man, The 1967 d: Irvin Kershner. lps: George C. Scott, Sue Lyon, Michael Sarrazin. 104M USA. *One Born Every Minute* (UKN) prod/rel: Lawrence Turman, Inc.

OWEN, HAROLD
Mr. Wu, London 1913, Play
  Mr. Wu 1919 d: Maurice Elvey. lps: Matheson Lang, Lillah McCarthy, Meggie Albanesi. 5170f UKN. prod/rel: Stoll
  Mr. Wu 1927 d: William Nigh. lps: Lon Chaney, Louise Dresser, Renee Adoree. 7603f USA. prod/rel: Metro-Goldwyn-Mayer Pictures
  Wu Li Chang 1930 d: Nick Grinde. lps: Ernesto Vilches, Jose Crespo, Angelita Benitez. 7r USA. prod/rel: Metro-Goldwyn-Mayer Pictures
  Mister Wu 1920. lps: Amedeo Chiantoni, Alfonsina Pieri, Marcello GiordA. 1203m ITL. prod/rel: Sayta

OWEN, HARRISON
The Happy Husband, London 1927, Play
  Uneasy Virtue 1931 d: Norman Walker. lps: Fay Compton, Edmund Breon, Francis Lister. 83M UKN. prod/rel: British International Pictures, Wardour

The Mount Marunga Mystery, Story
  Blue Mountains Mystery, The 1922 d: Raymond Longford, Lottie Lyell. lps: John Faulkner, Marjorie Osborne, Bernice Ware. 5r ASL. *The Blue Mountain Mystery*

OWEN, JEAN Z.
Mrs. Hoyle and the Hotel Royalston, Novel
  According to Mrs. Hoyle 1951 d: Jean Yarbrough. lps: Spring Byington, Anthony Caruso, Brett King. 60M USA. prod/rel: Monogram

OWEN, RONALD T.
The Payoff, Novel
  Payoff 1991 d: Stuart Cooper. lps: Keith Carradine, Harry Dean Stanton, Kim Greist. 120M USA. *Pay Off* prod/rel: Viacom Pictures, Aurora

OWEN, W. ARMITAGE
Lights Out at Eleven, Play
  Save a Little Sunshine 1938 d: Norman Lee. lps: Dave Willis, Pat Kirkwood, Tommy Trinder. 75M UKN. prod/rel: Welwyn, Pathe

OWENS, ROCHELLE
Futz, New York 1967, Play
  Futz 1969 d: Tom O'Horgan. lps: John Bakos, Victor Lipari, Jerry Owen Cunliffe. 92M USA. prod/rel: Guvnor Productions

OXENHAM, JOHN
Hearts in Exile, New York 1904, Novel
  Hearts in Exile 1915 d: James Young. lps: Clara Kimball Young, Clarissa Selwynne, Vernon Steele. 4-5r USA. *Hearts Afire* prod/rel: World Film Corp.©, Shubert Feature
  Hearts in Exile 1929 d: Michael Curtiz. lps: Dolores Costello, Grant Withers, James Kirkwood. 7877f USA. prod/rel: Warner Brothers Pictures

A Maid of the Silver Sea, Novel
  Maid of the Silver Sea, A 1922 d: Guy Newall. lps: Ivy Duke, Guy Newall, A. Bromley Davenport. 5000f UKN. prod/rel: George Clark Productions, Stoll

OXFORD, BUCKLEIGH FRITZ
Thicker Than Water, Story
  Other Kind of Love, The 1924 d: Duke Worne. lps: William Fairbanks, Dorothy Revier, Edith Yorke. 4800f USA. prod/rel: Phil Goldstone Productions

OXFORD, JOHN BARTON
The Man-Tamer, 1918, Short Story
  Man Tamer, The 1921 d: Harry B. Harris. lps: Gladys Walton, Rex de Rosselli, William Welsh. 4516f USA. prod/rel: Universal Film Mfg. Co.

The Road to Thursday, Story
  Hour of Freedom, An 1915 d: Arthur Johnson. lps: Arthur Johnson, Lottie Briscoe. SHT USA. prod/rel: Lubin

Virtue Its Own Reward, Short Story
  Virtue Its Own Reward 1914 d: Joseph de Grasse. lps: Pauline Bush, Lon Chaney, Gertrude Bambrick. 2r USA. prod/rel: Rex

OXILIA, NINO
Addio Giovinezza, 1911, Play
  Addio Giovinezza! 1913 d: Sandro Camasio. lps: Alessandro Bernard, Lydia Quaranta, Amerigo Manzini. 1012m ITL. prod/rel: Itala Film
  Addio Giovinezza 1918 d: Augusto GeninA. lps: Maria Jacobini, Lido Manetti, Helena MakowskA. 2038m ITL. prod/rel: Itala Film
  Addio Giovinezza 1927 d: Augusto GeninA. lps: Carmen Boni, Walter Slezak, Elena Sangro. 2352m ITL. prod/rel: S.A. Pittaluga
  Addio, Giovinezza! 1940 d: Ferdinando M. Poggioli. lps: Maria Denis, Adriano Rimoldi, Carlo Campanini. 88M ITL. prod/rel: I.C.I., S.a.F.I.C.

La Zingara, 1909, Play
  Zingara, La 1912 d: Sandro Camasio. lps: Adriana Costamagna, Maria Jacobini, Wanda Hejmann. 620m ITL. prod/rel: Savoia Film

OXLADE, BOYD
Death in Brunswick, Novel
  Death in Brunswick 1991 d: John Ruane. lps: Sam Neill, Zoe Carides, John Clarke. 109M ASL. prod/rel: Meridian Films Pty Ltd.©, Australian Film Finance Corp.©

OYA, SOICHI
Nippon No Ichiban Nagai Hi, Tokyo 1965, Short Story
  Nihon No Ichiban Nagai Hi 1967 d: Kihachi Okamoto. lps: Seiji Miyaguchi, Toshiro Mifune, Chishu Ryu. 158M JPN. *The Emperor and a General* (USA); *Nippon No Ichiban Nagai Hi* prod/rel: Toho Co.

OYABU, HARUHIKO
Tantei Jimusho 2-3: Kutabare Akutodomo, Novel
  Tantei Jimusho 2-3: Kutabare Akutodomo 1963 d: Seijun Suzuki. lps: Jo Shishido, Reiko Masamori, Kawachi. 89M JPN. *Detective Bureau 2-3: Go to Hell, Bastards!* prod/rel: Nikkatsu Corp.

Yaju No Seishun, Novel
  Yaju No Seishun 1963 d: Seijun Suzuki. lps: Jo Shishido, Ichiro Kijima, Misako Watanabe. 91M JPN. *The Brute; Youth of the Beast* prod/rel: Nikkatsu Corporation

OYEN, HENRY
Gaston Olaf, New York 1917, Novel
  Avenging Trail, The 1918 d: Francis Ford. lps: Harold Lockwood, Sally Crute, Joseph Dailey. 5r USA. prod/rel: Metro Pictures Corp.©, Yorke Film Corp.

The Man Trail, New York 1915, Novel
  Man Trail, The 1915 d: E. H. Calvert. lps: Richard C. Travers, June Keith, Ernest Maupain. 6r USA. prod/rel: Essanay Film Mfg. Co.©

The Snow-Burner, Story
  Snow-Burner, The 1915 d: E. H. Calvert. lps: Richard C. Travers, E. H. Calvert, Lillian Drew. 3r USA. prod/rel: Essanay

OZ, AMOS (1939–, ISR, Klausner, Amos
Book
  Kufsa Shechora 1993 d: Ye'ud Levanon. lps: Ami Traub, Bruria Albek, Matti Seri. F ISR. *Black Box*

Michael Sheli, 1968, Novel
  Michael Sheli 1975 d: Dan Wolman. lps: Oded Kotler, Efrat Lavie, Moti Mozrachi. 90M ISR. *My Michael*

OZAKI, KOYO (1868–1903), JPN, Ozaki, Tokutaro
Konjiki Yasha, Novel
  Konjiki Yasha 1954 d: Koji ShimA. lps: Jun Negami, Fujiko Yamamoto, Kenji SugawarA. 94M JPN. *Golden Demon* (USA); *Demon of Gold* prod/rel: Daiei Motion Picture Co.

356

P

PAASILINNA, ARTO
Hirtettyjen Kettujen Metsa, 1983, Novel
Hirtettyjen Kettujen Metsa 1986 d: Jouko Suikkari. lps: Aarno Sulkanen, Markku Toikka, Veikko Uusimaki. 99M FNL. *Forest of Hanging Foxes* prod/rel: Studio Artesis
Ulvova Myllari, 1981, Novel
Ulvova Myllari 1983 d: Jaakko PakkasvirtA. lps: Vesa-Matti Loiri, Eija Ahvo, Yrjo Jarvinen. 100M FNL. *The Howling Miller; Olvova Myllari*

PACCINO, DARIO
Il Diario Di un Provacatore, Novel
Uomo Della Guerra Possibile, L' 1979 d: Romeo Costantini. lps: Paulo Cesar Pereio, Adriana Falco. 90M ITL. *Una Notte Di Pioggia* prod/rel: Cooperativa Coala

PACKARD, FRANK L., Packard, Frank Lucius
The Beloved Traitor, New York 1915, Novel
Beloved Traitor, The 1918 d: William Worthington. lps: Mae Marsh, E. K. Lincoln, George Fawcett. 5r USA. prod/rel: Goldwyn Pictures Corp.©
Greater Love Hath No Man, New York 1913, Novel
Greater Love Hath No Man 1915 d: Herbert Blache. lps: Emmett Corrigan, Mary Martin, Thomas A. Curran. 5r USA. prod/rel: Popular Plays & Players, Inc., Metro Pictures Corp.©
The Iron Rider, 1916, Short Story
Smiles are Trumps 1922 d: George Marshall. lps: Maurice B. Flynn, Ora Carew, Myles McCarthy. 4049f USA. prod/rel: Fox Film Corp.
The Miracle Man, New York 1914, Novel
Miracle Man, The 1919 d: George Loane Tucker. lps: Thomas Meighan, Betty Compson, Lon Chaney. 8r USA. prod/rel: Mayflower Photoplay Corp.©, Famous Players-Lasky Corp.
Pawned, New York 1921, Novel
Pawned 1922 d: Irvin V. Willat. lps: Tom Moore, Edith Roberts, Charles Gerrard. 4973f USA. prod/rel: Select Pictures, Selznick Distributing Corp.
The Sin That Was His, New York 1917, Novel
Sin That Was His, The 1920 d: Hobart Henley. lps: William Faversham, Lucy Cotton, Pedro de CordobA. 6r USA. prod/rel: Selznick Pictures Corp.©, Select Pictures Corp.
The White Moll, New York 1920, Novel
White Moll, The 1920 d: Harry Millarde. lps: Pearl White, Richard C. Travers, J. Thornton Baston. 5-8r USA. prod/rel: Fox Film Corp., William Fox©
The Wrecking Boss, 1919, Short Story
Crash, The 1928 d: Eddie Cline. lps: Milton Sills, Thelma Todd, Wade Boteler. 6225f USA. *Wrecking Boss, The* prod/rel: First National Pictures

PACKER, JOY
Nor the Moon By Night, Novel
Nor the Moon By Night 1958 d: Ken Annakin. lps: Belinda Lee, Michael Craig, Patrick McGoohan. 92M UKN/SAF. *Elephant Gun* (USA) prod/rel: Rank Film Distributors, Independent Film Producers

PADILLA, JOSE
El Relicario, Song
Relicario, El 1926 d: Miguel Contreras Torres. lps: Miguel Contreras Torres, Sally Rand, Judy King. 7r SPN. *El Relicario de Joseito; La Novela de un Torero* prod/rel: Miguel Contreras Torres

PAGANO, JO
The Condemned, Novel
Sound of Fury, The 1950 d: Cy Endfield. lps: Frank Lovejoy, Kathleen Ryan, Richard Carlson. 92M USA. *Try and Get Me* prod/rel: United Artists, Robert Stillman

PAGE, ALAIN
Tchao Pantin, Novel
Tchao Pantin 1983 d: Claude Berri. lps: Coluche, Agnes Soral, Richard AnconinA. 100M FRN. prod/rel: Renn

PAGE, ELIZABETH
The Tree of Liberty, New York 1939, Novel
Howards of Virginia, The 1940 d: Frank Lloyd. lps: Cary Grant, Martha Scott, Cedric Hardwicke. 122M USA. *The Tree of Liberty* (UKN) prod/rel: Columbia Pictures Corp.©, Frank Lloyd Pictures

PAGE, GERTRUDE
Edge O' Beyond, Novel
Edge O'Beyond 1919 d: Fred W. Durrant. lps: Ruby Miller, Owen Nares, Isobel Elsom. 6000f UKN. prod/rel: G. B. Samuelson, General

Love in the Wilderness, Novel
Love in the Wilderness 1920 d: Alexander Butler. lps: Madge Titheradge, C. M. Hallard, Campbell Gullan. 6000f UKN. prod/rel: G. B. Samuelson, General

Paddy the Next Best Thing, London 1916, Novel
Paddy the Next Best Thing 1923 d: Graham Cutts. lps: Mae Marsh, Darby Foster, Lillian Douglas. 7200f UKN. prod/rel: Graham-Wilcox
Paddy the Next Best Thing 1933 d: Harry Lachman. lps: Janet Gaynor, Warner Baxter, Walter Connolly. 76M USA. prod/rel: Fox Film Corp.©

PAGE, MANN
Lights Out, New York 1922, Play
Lights Out 1923 d: Alfred Santell. lps: Ruth Stonehouse, Walter McGrail, Marie Astaire. 6938f USA. prod/rel: R-C Pictures, Film Booking Offices of America
Crashing Hollywood 1938 d: Lew Landers. lps: Lee Tracy, Paul Guilfoyle, Joan Woodbury. 61M USA. *Lights Out* prod/rel: RKO Radio Pictures, Inc.

PAGE, MARCO
Fast Company, New York 1938, Novel
Fast Company 1938 d: Edward Buzzell. lps: Melvyn Douglas, Florence Rice, Claire Dodd. 75M USA. *The Rare Book Murder* prod/rel: Metro-Goldwyn-Mayer Corp., Loew's, Inc.©

PAGE, SATCHEL
Maybe I'll Pitch Forever, Autobiography
Don't Look Back: the Story of Leroy "Satchel" Page 1981 d: Richard A. CollA. lps: Louis Gossett Jr., Cleavon Little, Ossie Davis. TVM. 98M USA. *Don't Look Back* (UKN) prod/rel: ABC, Tba Productions

PAGE, THOMAS
The Hephaestus Plague, Novel
Bug 1975 d: Jeannot Szwarc. lps: Bradford Dillman, Joanna Miles, Richard Gilliland. 101M USA. *The Hephaestus Plague* prod/rel: Paramount, William Castle

PAGE, THOMAS NELSON (1853–1922), USA
A Captured Santa Claus, Book
Within the Enemy's Lines 1913 d: Charles M. Seay. lps: Augustus Phillips, May Abbey. 2000f USA. prod/rel: Edison
The Outcast, Short Story
Outcast, The 1915 d: John B. O'Brien. lps: Mae Marsh, Robert Harron, Mary Alden. 4r USA. prod/rel: Majestic Motion Picture Co., Mutual Film Corp.

PAGE, TIM
Page After Page, Novel
Frankie's House 1991 d: Peter Fisk. lps: Iain Glen, Kevin Dillon, Steven Vidler. TVM. 108M ASL/UKN/USA. *Frankie's War* prod/rel: Anglia Films, Initial Films & Tv

PAGNOL, MARCEL (1895–1974), FRN
Cesar, 1937, Play
Cesar 1936 d: Marcel Pagnol. lps: Raimu, Pierre Fresnay, Fernand Charpin. 168M FRN. prod/rel: Films Marcel Pagnol
Direct Au Coeur, Play
Direct Au Coeur 1932 d: Roger Lion, Arnaudy. lps: Arnaudy, Gustave Libeau, Suzanne Rissler. 104M FRN. prod/rel: Europa-Films
L'eau Des Collines, Vol. 1: Jean de Florette, 1963, Novel
Jean de Florette 1985 d: Claude Berri. lps: Yves Montand, Gerard Depardieu, Daniel Auteuil. 120M FRN/ITL. prod/rel: Renn Productions, Films a2
L'eau Des Collines, Vol. 2: Manon Des Sources, 1963, Novel
Manon Des Sources 1985 d: Claude Berri. lps: Yves Montand, Daniel Auteuil, Emmanuelle Beart. 114M FRN/ITL/SWT. *Jean de Florette 2E Partie; Manon of the Spring* prod/rel: Renn Productions, Antenne 2 Tv France
Fanny, Paris 1931, Play
Fanny 1932 d: Marc Allegret. lps: Raimu, Fernand Charpin, Pierre Fresnay. 140M FRN. prod/rel: Les Films Marcel Pagnol, Etablissements Braunberger-Richebe
Fanny 1933 d: Mario Almirante. lps: Dria Paola, Alfredo de Sanctis, Lamberto Picasso. 93M ITL. prod/rel: Cines, Anonima Pittaluga
Fanny 1961 d: Joshua Logan. lps: Leslie Caron, Horst Buchholz, Maurice Chevalier. 133M USA. prod/rel: Mansfield Productions, Warner Bros.
Port of Seven Seas 1938 d: James Whale. lps: Wallace Beery, Frank Morgan, Maureen O'Sullivan. 81M USA. *Madelon; Fanny; Life on the Waterfront; Man of the Waterfront* prod/rel: Metro-Goldwyn-Mayer Corp., Loew's, Inc.©

Schwarze Walfisch, Der 1934 d: Fritz Wendhausen. lps: Emil Jannings, Angela Salloker, Max Gulstorff. 100M GRM. *Zum Schwarzen Walfisch* prod/rel: Riton, Super
Marius, Paris 1931, Play
Langtan Till Havet 1931 d: John W. Brunius. lps: Edvin Adolphson, Inga Tidblad, Carl Barcklind. 112M SWD. *Longing for the Sea*
Zum Goldenen Anker 1931 d: Alexander KordA. lps: Ursula Grabley, Jacob Tiedtke, Lucie Hoflich. F GRM.
Marius 1931 d: Alexander Korda, Marcel Pagnol. lps: Raimu, Pierre Fresnay, Orane Demaziz. 130M FRN. prod/rel: Films Marcel Pagnol
Port of Seven Seas 1938 d: James Whale. lps: Wallace Beery, Frank Morgan, Maureen O'Sullivan. 81M USA. *Madelon; Fanny; Life on the Waterfront; Man of the Waterfront* prod/rel: Metro-Goldwyn-Mayer Corp., Loew's, Inc.©
Souvenirs d'Enfance, 1957, Autobiography
Gloire de Mon Pere, Le 1989 d: Yves Robert. lps: Philippe Caubere, Nathalie Roussel, Didier Pain. 111M FRN. *My Father's Glory* (UKN) prod/rel: Gaumont International Production, Producton de la Gueville
Chateau de Ma Mere, La 1990 d: Yves Robert. lps: Philippe Caubere, Nathalie Roussell, Julien CaimacA. 98M FRN. *My Mother's Castle* (UKN) prod/rel: Gaumont International, Productions de la Gueville
Topaze, Paris 1928, Play
Jin Yin Shi Jie 1939 d: Li Pingqian. 100M CHN. *Gold and Silver World*
Mr. Topaze 1961 d: Peter Sellers. lps: Peter Sellers, Nadia Gray, Herbert Lom. 97M UKN. *I Like Money* (USA) prod/rel: Anatole de Grunwald, 20th Century-Fox
Topaze 1932 d: Louis J. Gasnier. lps: Louis Jouvet, Edwige Feuillere, Simone Heliard. 103M FRN. prod/rel: Films Paramount
Topaze 1933 d: Harry d'Abbadie d'Arrast. lps: John Barrymore, Myrna Loy, Albert Conti. 80M USA. prod/rel: RKO Radio Pictures©
Topaze 1936 d: Marcel Pagnol. lps: Arnaudy, Sylvia Bataille, Andre Pollack. 110M FRN. prod/rel: Films Marcel Pagnol
Topaze 1950 d: Marcel Pagnol. lps: Fernandel, Jacques Morel, Helene Perdriere. 135M FRN. prod/rel: Films Marcel Pagnol

PAHLEN, HENRY
Schwarzer Nerz Auf Zarter Haut, Novel
Schwarzer Nerz Auf Zarter Haut 1969 d: Erwin C. Dietrich. lps: Erwin Strahl, Herbert Fux, Tamara Baroni. 87M GRM/SWT. *Black Mink on Tender Skin* prod/rel: Urania, Avis

PAI, KENNETH
Blossom Bridge, Novel
Hua Qiao Rong Ji 1998 d: Yang XIe. lps: Carol Cheng, Kevin Lin, Ku Pao-Ming. 112M HKG/SRK. *My Rice Noodle Soup* prod/rel: Welling Asia

PAILLERON, EDOUARD (1834–1899), FRN
Le Monde Ou l'On s'ennuie, Play
Monde Ou l'On S'ennuie, Le 1934 d: Jean de Marguenat. lps: Andre Luguet, Josseline Gael, Wanda Greville. 89M FRN. prod/rel: S.a.P.E.C.

PAILLOT, FORTUNE
Les Epoux Scandaleux, Novel
Epoux Scandaleux, Les 1935 d: Georges Lacombe. lps: Suzy Vernon, Jeanne Aubert, Rene Lefevre. 90M FRN. *Jean Et Loulou; Epousez Ma Femme* prod/rel: Fina Film Production

PAIN, BARRY
The Octave of Claudius, London 1897, Novel
Blind Bargain, A 1922 d: Wallace Worsley. lps: Lon Chaney, Raymond McKee, Virginia True Boardman. 4473f USA. *The Octave of Claudius* prod/rel: Goldwyn Pictures

PAINE, LAURAN
Lawman, 1955, Novel
Quiet Gun, The 1957 d: William F. Claxton. lps: Forrest Tucker, Mara Corday, Lee Van Cleef. 77M USA. prod/rel: 20th Century-Fox, Regal Films

PAINE, RALPH D.
The Wall Between, New York 1914, Novel
Wall Between, The 1916 d: John W. Noble. lps: Francis X. Bushman, Beverly Bayne, John Davidson. 5r USA. prod/rel: Quality Pictures Corp.©, Metro Pictures Corp.

PAINTER, HAL W.
Mark I Love You, Book
Mark I Love You 1980 d: Gunnar Hellstrom. lps: Kevin Dobson, James Whitmore, Cassie Yates. TVM. 104M USA.

PAIRAULT, SUZANNE
Le Sang Des Bou Okba, Novel
 Soif Des Hommes, La 1949 d: Serge de Poligny. lps: Georges Marchal, Dany Robin, Andree Clement. 105M FRN. prod/rel: L.P.C.

PAIVA, MARCELO RUBENS
Feliz Ano Velho, 1982, Novel
 Feliz Ano Velho 1988 d: Roberto Gervitz. lps: Marcos Breda, Malu Mader, Eva WilmA. 105M BRZ. *Happy Old Year*

PAL, NIRANJAN
His Honour the Judge, Novel
 Gentleman of Paris, A 1931 d: Sinclair Hill. lps: Arthur Wontner, Wanda Greville, Hugh Williams. 76M UKN. prod/rel: Stoll, Gaumont

Prapancha Pash, Short Story
 Prapancha Pash 1929 d: Franz Osten. lps: Seeta Devi, Himansu Rai, Charu Roy. 2523m IND/GRM. *A Throw of Dice*; *Schicksalswurfel*; *Throw of the Dice* prod/rel: British Instructional Film, Himansu Rai Film

Shiraz, Play
 Shiraz 1928 d: Franz Osten. lps: Charu Chandra Roy, Himansu Rai, Seeta Devi. 2561m GRM/IND. *Das Grabmal Einer Groszen Liebe* prod/rel: British Instructional Films, UFA

PALACIO VALDES, ARMANDO (1853–1938), SPN
La Aldea Perdida, 1903, Novel
 Aguas Bajan Negras, Las 1948 d: Jose Luis Saenz de HerediA. lps: Adriano Rimoldi, Charito Granados, Tomas Blanco. 100M SPN. *Waters Run Deep*; *The River Flows Back*

La Fe, 1892, Novel
 Fe, La 1947 d: Rafael Gil. lps: Amparo Rivelles, Rafael Duran, Guillermo Marin. 108M SPN. *Faith*

La Hermana San Sulpicio, 1889, Novel
 Hermana San Sulpicio, La 1927 d: Florian Rey. lps: Imperio Argentina, Ricardo Nunez, Erna Becker. 90M SPN. *La Hermana de San Sulpicio*; *Sister Saint Sulpice* prod/rel: Perseo Films (Madrid)

 Hermana San Sulpicio, La 1934 d: Florian Rey. lps: Imperio Argentina, Miguel Ligero, Salvador Soler. 94M SPN. *Sister Saint Sulpice*

 Hermana San Sulpicio, La 1952 d: Luis LuciA. lps: Carmen Sevilla, Jorge Mistral, Manuel LunA. 88M SPN. *Sister Saint Sulpice*

 Novicia Rebelde, La 1971 d: Luis LuciA. lps: Rocio Durcal, Guillermo Murray, Isabel Garces. 91M SPN. *The Rebel Nun*

Jose, Novel
 Jose 1925 d: Manuel NoriegA. lps: Javier de Rivera, Enriqueta Soler, Carmen Rico. F SPN. prod/rel: Cartago Film (Madrid)

Santa Rogelia, 1926, Novel
 Peccato Di Rogelia Sanchez, Il 1939 d: Carlo Borghesio, Edgar Neville. lps: Germaine Montero, Juan de Landa, Rafael Rivelles. 83M ITL/SPN. *Santa Rogelia*; *The Sin of Rogelia Sanchez*; *Saint Rogela*; *Donna Di Spagna* prod/rel: S.a.F.I.C., E.N.I.C.

 Rogelia 1962 d: Rafael Gil. lps: Pina Pellicer, Arturo Fernandez, Fernando Rey. 98M SPN.

El Senorito Octavio, 1881, Novel
 Senorito Octavio, El 1950 d: Jeronimo MihurA. lps: Conrado San Martin, Tomas Blanco, Elena Espejo. 95M SPN. *The Young Master Octavio*

Sinfonia Pastoral, 1931, Novel
 Bajo El Cielo de Asturias 1950 d: Gonzalo Delgras. lps: Isabel de Castro, Alfonso Estela, Luis Perez de Leon. 90M SPN.

PALADINI, FABRIZIO
Bangkwang, Book
 Vacanza All'inferno, Una 1997 d: Tonino Valerii. lps: Marco Leonardi, F. Murray Abraham, Giancarlo Giannini. 104M ITL. *Vacation in Hell* prod/rel: Metropolis Film

PALAZZESCHI, ALDO (1885–1974), ITL
Sorelle Materassi, 1934, Novel
 Sorelle Materassi 1943 d: Ferdinando M. Poggioli. lps: Pietro Bigerna, Paola Borboni, Margherita Nicosia Bossi. 72M ITL. *The Materassi Sisters* prod/rel: Cines, Universalcine

PALEY, FRANK
Rumble on the Docks, 1953, Novel
 Rumble on the Docks 1956 d: Fred F. Sears. lps: James Darren, Laurie Carroll, Michael Granger. 82M USA. prod/rel: Columbia, Clover Prods.

PALEY, GRACE (1922–, USA, Paley, Grace Goodside
Story
 Enormous Changes at the Last Minute 1983 d: Mirra Bank, Ellen Hovde. lps: Maria Tucci, Lynn Milgrim, Ellen Barkin. 115M USA. *Trumps*; *Enormous Changes* prod/rel: ABC, Ordinary Lives Inc.

PALGI, YOEL
A Great Wind Cometh, Book
 Hanna's War 1988 d: Menahem Golan. lps: Ellen Burstyn, Maruschka Detmers, Anthony Andrews. 148M USA/ISR. *Hannah Senesh* (ISR); *Innocent Heroes* prod/rel: Cannon

PALIN, MICHAEL (1943–, UKN
Secrets, Play
 Consuming Passions 1988 d: Giles Foster. lps: Vanessa Redgrave, Jonathan Pryce, Tyler Butterworth. 90M UKN/USA. prod/rel: Samuel Goldwyn, Euston Films

PALIT, DIBYENDU
Ghar Bari, Novel
 Andhi Gali 1984 d: Buddhadeb DasguptA. lps: Kulbhushan Kharbanda, Deepti Naval, M. K. RainA. 152M IND. *Blind Alley*; *Andhi Galli*; *Dead End* prod/rel: K.B.S. Films

PALLI, ENZO GICCA
Un Viaggio Di Piacere, Novel
 Quattro Notti Con Alba 1962 d: Luigi Filippo d'Amico. lps: Chelo Alonso, Peter Baldwin, Ettore Manni. 95M ITL. *Desert War* (USA); *Accadde Ad El Alamein*; *Polvere Di Eroi* prod/rel: Apo Film, Globe International Film

PALMER, FREDERICK
Invisible Wounds, New York 1925, Novel
 New Commandment, The 1925 d: Howard Higgin. lps: Blanche Sweet, Ben Lyon, Holbrook Blinn. 6980f USA. prod/rel: First National Pictures

PALMER, MICHAEL
Extreme Measures, Novel
 Extreme Measures 1996 d: Michael Apted. lps: Hugh Grant, Gene Hackman, Sarah Jessica Parker. 118M UKN/USA. prod/rel: Simian Films, Castle Rock

PALMER, MINNIE
My Sweetheart, Play
 My Sweetheart 1918 d: Meyrick Milton. lps: Margaret Blanche, Concordia Merrill, Randle Ayrton. 4435f UKN. prod/rel: Ideal

PALMER, STUART
Hildegarde Withers Makes the Scene
 Very Missing Person, A 1972 d: Russ Mayberry. lps: Eve Arden, James Gregory, Julie Newmar. TVM. 73M USA. prod/rel: Universal

Murder on the Blackboard, New York 1932, Novel
 Murder on the Blackboard 1934 d: George Archainbaud. lps: Edna May Oliver, James Gleason, Bruce Cabot. 80M USA. prod/rel: RKO Radio Pictures©

The Penguin Pool Murder, New York 1931, Novel
 Penguin Pool Murder 1932 d: George Archainbaud. lps: Edna May Oliver, James Gleason, Mae Clarke. 75M USA. *The Penguin Pool Mystery* (UKN) prod/rel: RKO Radio Pictures©

The Puzzle of the Red Stallion, New York 1936, Novel
 Murder on a Bridle Path 1936 d: Edward Killy, William Hamilton. lps: James Gleason, Helen Broderick, Louise Latimer. 66M USA. *The Puzzle of the Briar Pipe* prod/rel: RKO Radio Pictures©

The Riddle of the Dangling Pearl, 1933, Short Story
 Plot Thickens, The 1936 d: Ben Holmes. lps: James Gleason, Zasu Pitts, Oscar Apfel. 69M USA. *The Swinging Pearl Mystery* (UKN); *The Riddle of the Dangling Pearl* prod/rel: RKO Radio Pictures©

The Riddle of the Forty Naughty Girls, 1934, Short Story
 Forty Naughty Girls 1937 d: Eddie Cline. lps: James Gleason, Zasu Pitts, Marjorie Lord. 68M USA. *The Riddle of the 40 Naughty Girls*; *40 Naughty Girls* prod/rel: RKO Radio Pictures©

PALMER, SUSAN
The Puzzle of the Pepper Tree, New York 1933, Novel
 Murder on a Honeymoon 1935 d: Lloyd Corrigan. lps: Edna May Oliver, James Gleason, Lola Lane. 74M USA. *The Puzzle of the Pepper Tree* prod/rel: RKO Radio Pictures©

PALMINTERI, CHAZZ (1952–, USA, Palminteri, Calogero
A Bronx Tale, Play
 Bronx Tale, A 1993 d: Robert de Niro. lps: Robert de Niro, Chazz Palminteri, Lillo Brancato. 121M USA. prod/rel: Price, Tribeca

PALOTAI, BORIS
Nappali Sotetseg, Novel
 Nappali Sotetseg 1963 d: Zoltan Fabri. lps: Lajos Basti, Erika Szegedi, Ilona Beres. 106M HNG. *Darkness By Daylight*; *Darkness in Daytime*; *Dunkel Bei Tageslicht* prod/rel: Hunnia

PAMMAN
Chattakari, Novel
 Julie 1975 d: K. S. Sethumadhavan. lps: Laxmi, Om Prakash, Utpal Dutt. 145M IND. prod/rel: Vijaya

PAN, Beresford, Leslie
Big Happiness, London 1917, Novel
 Big Happiness 1920 d: Colin Campbell. lps: Dustin Farnum, Kathryn Adams, Fred MalatestA. 6416f USA. prod/rel: Dustin Farnum Productions, Robertson-Cole Distributing Corp.

The Furnace, London 1920, Novel
 Furnace, The 1920 d: William D. Taylor. lps: Agnes Ayres, Milton Sills, Jerome Patrick. 7r USA. *Breach of Promise, Or the Furnace* prod/rel: Realart Pictures Corp.©, William D. Taylor Productions

The Glory of Love, London 1919, Novel
 While Paris Sleeps 1923 d: Maurice Tourneur. lps: Lon Chaney, Mildred Manning, John Gilbert. 4850f USA. *The Glory of Love* prod/rel: Maurice Tourneur Productions, W. W. Hodkinson Corp.

White Heat, London 1926, Novel
 White Heat 1926 d: Thomas Bentley. lps: Juliette Compton, Wyndham Standing, Vesta SylvA. 7200f UKN. prod/rel: Graham-Wilcox

PANCHOLI, MANUBHAI
Zer to Pidhan Jani Jani, Novel
 Zer to Pidhan Jani Jani 1972 d: Upendra Trivedi. lps: Anupama, Upendra Trivedi, Arvind Trivedi. 127M IND. prod/rel: Rangbhoomi Prod.

PANDELEEV, L.
Novel
 Biao 1949 d: Zuo Lin. lps: Zhao Qiansun, Chen Zhi, Sheng Yang. 11r CHN. *An Orphan of the Streets*; *The Watch* prod/rel: Wenhua Film Company

PANDURO, LEIF
Rend Mig I Traditionerne, 1958, Novel
 Rend Mig I Tradionerne 1979 d: Edward Fleming. lps: Henrik Kofoed, Bodil Kjer, Niels Hinrichsen. 106M DNM. *Traditions, Up Yours!*

De Uanstaendige, 1960, Novel
 Uanstaendige, de 1983 d: Edward Fleming. lps: Lars Bom, Nonny Sand, Thomas Alling. 92M DNM. *The Improper Ones*

Den Ubetaeksomme Elsker, 1973, Novel
 Ubetaeksomme Elsker, Den 1983 d: Claus Ploug. lps: Dick Kayso, Karen-Lise Mynster, Pia Vieth. 100M DNM. *The Imprudent Lover*; *The Impudent Lover*

PANFYOROV, FYODOR
Bruski, 1928-37, Novel
 V Poiskach Radosti 1939 d: Grigori Roshal, Vera StroyevA. 114M USS. *In Search of Happiness*; *Searching for Joy*; *V Poiskakh Radosti*

PANICKER, KAVALAM NARAYANA
Marattam, Play
 Marattam 1989 d: G. Aravindan. lps: Sadanandan Krishnamurthy, Urmila Unni, Keshavan. 90M IND. *Masquerade* (UKN); *Marratom*; *Faces and Masks* prod/rel: Doordarshan

PANIGRAHI, BHAGBATI CHARAN
Mrigaya, Short Story
 Mrigaya 1976 d: Mrinal Sen. lps: Mithun Chakraborty, Mamata Shankar, Robert Wright. 130M IND. *The Royal Hunt*; *Deer Hunt*; *Mrigayaa*; *Marigaya* prod/rel: Udaya Bhaskar

PANIGRAHI, KALINDI CHARAN
Matir Manisha, 1930, Novel
 Matir Manisha 1966 d: Mrinal Sen. lps: Prashanta Nanda, Sujata, Ram ManyA. 113M IND. *Man of the Soil*; *Two Brothers*; *Matira Manisha* prod/rel: Chhayaloke Prod.

PANITZ, EBERHARD
Short Story
 Dritte, Der 1972 d: Egon Gunther. lps: Jutta Hoffmann, Rolf Ludwig, Armin Mueller-Stahl. 111M GDR. *The Third One*; *The Third* prod/rel: Defa, Nobis

PANIZZA, OSKAR
Story
 Liebeskonzil, Das 1981 d: Werner Schroeter. lps: Antonio Salines, Magdalena Montezuma, Kurt Raab. 95M GRM. *Le Concile d'Amour*; *Concilio d'Amore*; *The Love Synod* prod/rel: Saskia, Trio

PANOVA, VERA FYODOROVNA (1905–, RSS
Sentimentalnyi Roman, 1958, Novel
 Sentimentalnyi Roman 1976 d: Igor Maslennikov. 90M USS. *A Sentimental Story*; *Sentimental Romance*

Seryozha, Leningrad 1955, Novel
 Serezha 1960 d: Georgi Daneliya, Igor Talankin. lps: Irina Skobtseva, Sergei Bondarchuk, Borya Barkhatov. 80M USS. *A Summer to Remember* (USA); *The Splendid Days*; *Seryozha (the Splendid Days)*; *Seryozha*; *Sereza* prod/rel: Mosfilm

PANTING, J. HARWOOD
The Unwritten Play, Story
  Unwritten Play, The 1914 d: Theodore Marston. lps: James Morrison, Dorothy Kelly, George Cooper. SHT USA. prod/rel: Vitagraph Co. of America

PANWALKAR, S. D.
Ardh Satya, Short Story
  Ardh Satya 1983 d: Govind Nihalani. lps: Om Puri, Smita Patil, Amrish Puri. 130M IND. *Half-Truth* prod/rel: Neo Film Associates

PANZINI, ALFREDO
Il Padrone Sono Me, 1925, Novel
  Padrone Sono Me, Il 1956 d: Franco Brusati. lps: Myriam Bru, Andreina Pagnani, Paolo StoppA. 100M ITL. *C'est Moi le Maitre* (FRN) prod/rel: Rizzoli Film, Dear Film

PAOLIERI, FERDINANDO
I Fuggiaschi, Novel
  Mercante Di Schiave, Il 1942 d: Duilio Coletti. lps: Annette Bach, Enzo Fiermonte, Elena Zareschi. 83M ITL. *Merchant of Slaves* (USA) prod/rel: Colosseum, I.C.I.

Maestro Landi, Play
  Maestro Landi 1935 d: Giovacchino Forzano. lps: Odoardo Spadaro, Ugo Ceseri, Pina Cei. 78M ITL. prod/rel: Consorzio Vis, Tirrenia

PAOLINELLI, BRUNO
Vita Nuova, Play
  Donne Proibite 1953 d: Giuseppe Amato. lps: Linda Darnell, Valentina Cortese, Lea Padovani. 94M ITL. *Angels of Darkness* (USA); *Forbidden Women* prod/rel: G. Amato

PAPADIAMANTIS, ALEXANDROS
Ta Rodina Akroyialia, Novel
  Ta Rodina Akroyialia 1998 d: Efthimios Hatzis. lps: Stefanos Iatridis, Anna-Maria Papaharalambous, Dimitris Poulikakos. 101M GRC. *Shores of Twilight* prod/rel: Greek Film Centre, Cinergon Prods.

PAPASHVILY, GEORGE
Anything Can Happen, Book
  Anything Can Happen 1952 d: George Seaton. lps: Jose Ferrer, Kim Hunter, Kurt Kasznar. 107M USA. prod/rel: Paramount, Perlberg-Seaton

PAPASHVILY, HELEN
Anything Can Happen 1952 d: George Seaton. lps: Jose Ferrer, Kim Hunter, Kurt Kasznar. 107M USA. prod/rel: Paramount, Perlberg-Seaton

PARADIS, MARJORIE BARTHOLOMEW
It Happened One Day, New York 1932, Novel
  This Side of Heaven 1932 d: William K. Howard. lps: Tom Brown, Mary Carlisle, Lionel Barrymore. 78M USA. *It Happened One Day*; *Big Day, A*; *The Family Scandal* prod/rel: Metro-Goldwyn-Mayer Corp.©, William K. Howard Production

PARAL, V.
Ss
  Soukroma Vichrice 1967 d: Hynek Bocan. lps: Pavel Landovsky, Josef Somr, Daniela KolarovA. 99M CZC. *Private Windstorm* (UKN); *Private Hurricane; A Personal Tempest; A Private Gale* prod/rel: Filmstudio Barrandov

PARAMORE, E.
Ringside, New York 1928, Play
  Night Parade 1929 d: Malcolm St. Clair. lps: Hugh Trevor, Lloyd Ingraham, Dorothy Gulliver. 74M USA. *Sporting Life* (UKN) prod/rel: RKO Productions

PARAPPURAM
Aranazhikaneram, Novel
  Aranazhikaneram 1970 d: K. S. Sethumadhavan. lps: Kottarakkara Sridharan Nair, Sathyan, Prem Nazir. 168M IND. *Just Half an Hour; Ara Nazhika Neram* prod/rel: Manjilas

PARAZ, ALBERT
L'arche de Noe, Novel
  Arche de Noe, L' 1946 d: Henry-Jacques. lps: Pierre Brasseur, Georges Rollin, Claude Larue. 95M FRN. *Noah's Ark* (USA) prod/rel: Jack Cohen, P.I.C.

PARCA, GABRIELLA
Le Italiane Si Confessano, Book
  Italiane E l'Amore, Le 1961 d: Florestano Vancini, Carlo Musso. lps: Mariella Zanetti, Jose Greci, Renza Volpi. 107M ITL. *Latin Lovers* (USA); *Italian Women and Love* prod/rel: Magic Film (Roma), Consortium Pathe (Paris)

PARDINI, VINCENZO
Jodo Cartamigli, Novel
  Mio West, Il 1998 d: Giovanni Veronesi. lps: Leonardo Pieraccioni, Harvey Keitel, David Bowie. 95M ITL. *My West* prod/rel: Cecchi Gori Distribuzione, Cecchi Gori Group

PARDO BAZAN, EMILIA (1852–1921), SPN, Pardon Bazan de Quiroga, Emilia
El Indulto, 1885, Short Story
  Indulto, El 1960 d: Jose Luis Saenz de HerediA. lps: Pedro Armendariz, Conchita Velasco, Manuel Monroy. 105M SPN. *The Pardon*

La Sirena Negra, 1908, Novel
  Sirena Negra, La 1947 d: Carlos Serrano de OsmA. lps: Fernando Fernan Gomez, Isabel de Pomes, Ana FarrA. 77M SPN. *The Black Mermaid*

Un Viaje de Novios, 1881, Novel
  Viaje de Novios, Un 1947 d: Gonzalo Delgras. lps: Josita Hernan, Rafael Duran, Isabel de Pomes. 94M SPN.

PAREDES, AMERIGO
With His Pistol in His Hands, Novel
  Ballad of Gregorio Cortez, The 1982 d: Robert M. Young. lps: Edward James Olmos, James Gammon, Tom Bower. TVM. 105M USA. *Gregorio Cortez* (UKN) prod/rel: Embassy Picture, Esperanza

PARETSKY, SARA
Indemnity, Novel
  V.I. Warshawski 1991 d: Jeff Kanew. lps: Kathleen Turner, Jay O. Sanders, Charles Durning. 89M USA. prod/rel: Hollywood Pictures, Silver Screen Partners IV

PARGITER, EDITH (1913–, UKN
The Assize of the Dying, Novel
  Spaniard's Curse, The 1958 d: Ralph Kemplen. lps: Tony Wright, Lee Patterson, Michael Hordern. 80M UKN. prod/rel: Wentworth, Independent Film Distributors

PARIS, REINE-MARIE
Camille Claudel, Book
  Camille Claudel 1988 d: Bruno Nuytten. lps: Isabelle Adjani, Gerard Depardieu, Laurent Grevill. 173M FRN. *Camille Claudel -Violence and Passion* prod/rel: Films Christian Fechner, Lilith Films

PARISE, GOFFREDO
L'assoluto Nationale, Book
  Assoluto Naturale, L' 1969 d: Mauro Bolognini. lps: Laurence Harvey, Sylva Koscina, Isa MirandA. 90M ITL. *She and He* (UKN); *He and She* prod/rel: Tirrenia Studios, Cineriz

Il Fidanzamento, Novel
  Fidanzamento, Il 1975 d: Gianni Grimaldi. lps: Lando Buzzanca, Martine Brochard, Anna Proclemer. 100M ITL. prod/rel: Italian International Film

PARK, LIEUT. MARVIN
A Foxhole Flicka, Story
  Gallant Bess 1946 d: Andrew Marton. lps: Marshall Thompson, George Tobias, Jim Davis. 98M USA. *Star from Heaven* prod/rel: MGM

PARK, RICHARD
The Ghost Belonged to Me, Novel
  Child of Glass 1978 d: John Erman. lps: Steve Shaw, Katy Kurtzman, Barbara Barrie. TVM. 93M USA. prod/rel: Walt Disney

PARK, RUTH
Playing Beatie Bow, Novel
  Playing Beatie Bow 1986 d: Donald Crombie. lps: Imogen Annesley, Peter Phelps, Mouche Phillips. 93M ASL. *Time Games* prod/rel: Safc Productions Ltd.©, Australian Film Commission

PARKER, DOROTHY (1893–1967), USA, Parker, Dorothy Rothschild
Horsie, 1933, Short Story
  Queen for a Day 1951 d: Arthur Lubin. lps: Phyllis Avery, Darren McGavin, Rudy Lee. 107M USA. *Horsie* prod/rel: United Artists, Stillman

PARKER, GILBERT (1862–1932), CND, Parker, Sir Gilbert
The Going of the White Swan, Story
  Priest and the Man, The 1913 d: J. Searle Dawley. lps: Charles Sutton, Laura Sawyer, James Gordon. 1000f USA. prod/rel: Edison

  Going of the White Swan, The 1914 d: Colin Campbell. lps: Bessie Eyton, Wheeler Oakman, Frank Clark. 2r USA. prod/rel: Selig Polyscope Co.

Jordan Is a Hard Road, Novel
  Jordan Is a Hard Road 1915 d: Allan Dwan. lps: Dorothy Gish, Owen Moore, Frank Campeau. 5r USA. prod/rel: Fine Arts Film Co., Triangle Film Corp.©

The Judgement House, London 1913, Novel
  Judgement House, The 1917 d: J. Stuart Blackton. lps: Conway Tearle, Violet Heming, Wilfred Lucas. 6r USA. *The Judgment House* prod/rel: J. Stuart Blackton Productions, Paramount Pictures Corp.

The Lane That Had No Turning, 1900, Short Story
  Lane That Had No Turning, The 1922 d: Victor Fleming. lps: Agnes Ayres, Theodore Kosloff, Mahlon Hamilton. 4892f USA. prod/rel: Famous Players-Lasky, Paramount Pictures

Lane That Had No Turning, The, 1900, Short Story
  Rightful Heir, The 1913 d: J. Searle Dawley. lps: Charles Sutton, Laura Sawyer, Ben Wilson. 1000f USA. prod/rel: Edison

The Lodge in the Wilderness, 1909, Short Story
  Lodge in the Wilderness, The 1926 d: Henry McCarty. lps: Anita Stewart, Edmund Burns, Duane Thompson. 5119f USA. prod/rel: Tiffany Productions

The Money Master, New York 1915, Novel
  Wise Fool, A 1921 d: George Melford. lps: James Kirkwood, Alice Hollister, Ann Forrest. 7r USA. *The Money Master* prod/rel: Famous Players-Lasky, Paramount Pictures

Pierre and His People, London 1892, Novel
  Pierre of the Plains 1914 d: Lawrence McGill. lps: Edgar Selwyn, William Conklin, Joseph Rieder. 5r USA. prod/rel: All Star Feature Corp.

The Right of Way, London 1901, Novel
  Right of Way, The 1915 d: John W. Noble. lps: William Faversham, Jane Grey, Edward Brennan. 5r USA. prod/rel: Rolfe Photoplays Inc., Metro Pictures Corp.©

  Right of Way, The 1920 d: John Francis Dillon. lps: Bert Lytell, Gibson Gowland, Leatrice Joy. 6340f USA. prod/rel: Screen Classics, Inc., Metro Pictures Corp.©

  Right of Way, The 1931 d: Frank Lloyd. lps: Conrad Nagel, Loretta Young, Fred Kohler. 75M USA. prod/rel: First National Pictures©

  Superior Law, The 1913. lps: J. W. Johnston, Barbara Tennant. 3r USA. prod/rel: Eclair

The Seats of the Mighty, New York 1894, Novel
  Seats of the Mighty, The 1914 d: T. Hayes Hunter. lps: Lionel Barrymore, Millicent Evans, Lois Meredith. 7r USA. prod/rel: Colonial Motion Picture Corp.©, World Film Corp.

She of the Triple Chevron, 1892, Short Story
  Over the Border 1922 d: Penrhyn Stanlaws. lps: Betty Compson, Tom Moore, J. Farrell MacDonald. 6837f USA. prod/rel: Famous Players-Lasky

  Heart of the Wilds 1918 d: Marshall Neilan. lps: Elsie Ferguson, Thomas Meighan, Joseph Smiley. 4380f USA. prod/rel: Famous Players-Lasky Corp.©, Artcraft Pictures

The Translation of a Savage, Novel
  Translation of a Savage, The 1913 d: Walter Edwin. lps: Mary Fuller, Richard Tucker, Gertrude McCoy. 1000f USA. prod/rel: Edison

Translation of a Savage, The, New York 1893, Novel
  Behold My Wife! 1920 d: George Melford. lps: Mabel Julienne Scott, Milton Sills, Winter Hall. 6556f USA. *Translation of a Savage, The* prod/rel: Famous Players-Lasky Corp.©, Paramount Pictures

The Translation of a Savage, New York 1893, Novel
  Behold My Wife! 1935 d: Mitchell Leisen. lps: Sylvia Sidney, Gene Raymond, Juliette Compton. 79M USA. prod/rel: Paramount Productions, Inc.

Wild Youth, Philadelphia 1919, Novel
  Wild Youth 1918 d: George Melford. lps: Louise Huff, Theodore Roberts, Jack Mulhall. 5r USA. prod/rel: Famous Players-Lasky Corp.©, J. Stuart Blackton Production

World for Sale, The, New York 1916, Novel
  World for Sale, The 1918 d: J. Stuart Blackton. lps: Conway Tearle, Anna Little, Norbert Wicki. 5r USA. prod/rel: Blackton Productions, Inc., Paramount Pictures Corp.

You Never Know Your Luck, London 1914, Novel
  You Never Know Your Luck 1919 d: Frank Powell. lps: House Peters, Claire Whitney, Bertram Marburgh. 5r USA. prod/rel: Sunset Pictures Corp., World Film Corp.©

PARKER III, CHAUNCEY G.
The Visitor, Novel
  Of Unknown Origin 1983 d: George Pan Cosmatos. lps: Peter Weller, Jennifer Dale, Lawrence Dane. 91M USA/CND. *The Visitor* prod/rel: of Unknown Origin Film Corp. (Montreal), Les Prods. Mutuelles Ltee. (Montreal)

PARKER, KENNETH
Three Were Renegades, Novel
  Tumbleweed 1953 d: Nathan Juran. lps: Audie Murphy, Lori Nelson, Chill Wills. 80M USA. prod/rel: Universal-International

PARKER, LARRY
We Let Our Son Die, Book
  Promised a Miracle 1988 d: Stephen Gyllenhaal. lps: Rosanna Arquette, Judge Reinhold, Tom Bower. TVM. 100M USA.

PARKER, LEON
Heroes of the Street, Play
  Heroes of the Street 1922 d: William Beaudine. lps: Wesley Barry, Marie Prevost, Jack Mulhall. 6r USA. prod/rel: Warner Brothers Pictures

PARKER, LOTTIE BLAIR
Annie Laurie, Chicago 1897, Play
Way Down East 1920 d: D. W. Griffith. lps: Lillian Gish, Richard Barthelmess, Lowell Sherman. 13r USA. prod/rel: United Artists Corp., D. W. Griffith, Inc.©

Way Down East 1935 d: Henry King. lps: Rochelle Hudson, Henry Fonda, Russell Simpson. 85M USA. prod/rel: Fox Film Corp., Twentieth Century-Fox Film Corp.©

PARKER, LOUIS N. (1852–1944), UKN, Parker, Louis Napoleon
Beauty and the Barge, London 1904, Play
Beauty and the Barge 1914 d: Harold Shaw. lps: Cyril Maude, Lillian Logan, Gregory Scott. 1242f UKN. prod/rel: London, Fenning

Beauty and the Barge 1937 d: Henry Edwards. lps: Gordon Harker, Judy Gunn, Jack Hawkins. 71M UKN. prod/rel: Twickenham, Wardour

The Cardinal, Montreal 1901, Play
Cardinal, The 1936 d: Sinclair Hill. lps: Matheson Lang, June Duprez, Eric Portman. 75M UKN. prod/rel: Grosvenor, Pathe

Abito Nero Da Sposa, L' 1945 d: Luigi ZampA. lps: Fosco Giachetti, Jacqueline Laurent, Carlo Tamberlani. 88M ITL. prod/rel: Vi.VA. Film, Produttori Associati

Disraeli, New York 1911, Play
Disraeli 1916 d: Percy Nash, Charles Calvert. lps: Dennis Eadie, Mary Jerrold, Cyril Raymond. 6500f UKN. prod/rel: Nb Films

Disraeli 1921 d: Henry Kolker. lps: George Arliss, Florence Arliss, Margaret Dale. 6800f USA. prod/rel: Distinctive Productions, United Artists

Disraeli 1929 d: Alfred E. Green. lps: George Arliss, Joan Bennett, Florence Arliss. 89M USA. prod/rel: Warner Brothers Pictures

Drake, London 1912, Play
Drake of England 1935 d: Arthur Woods. lps: Matheson Lang, Athene Seyler, Jane Baxter. 104M UKN. *Drake the Pirate* (USA); *Elizabeth of England* prod/rel: British International Pictures, Wardour

The Great Day, London 1919, Play
Great Day, The 1920 d: Hugh Ford. lps: Arthur Bourchier, Mary Palfrey, Bertram Burleigh. 3700f UKN/USA. prod/rel: Famous Players-Lasky British Producers, Paramount Pictures

Rosemary, London 1896, Play
Rosemary 1915 d: William J. Bowman, Fred J. Balshofer. lps: Marguerite Snow, Paul Gilmore, Virginia Kraft. 5r USA. prod/rel: Quality Pictures Corp., Metro Pictures Corp.©

PARKER, NORTON S.
My Lord of the Double B, Story
Lady from Hell, The 1926 d: Stuart Paton. lps: Roy Stewart, Blanche Sweet, Ralph Lewis. 5337f USA. *The Interrupted Wedding* prod/rel: Stuart Paton Productions, Associated Exhibitors

Seance Mystery, Novel
Sinister Hands 1932 d: Armand Schaefer. lps: Jack Mulhall, Phyllis Barrington, Crauford Kent. 66M USA. prod/rel: Willis Kent Productions, State Rights

PARKER, PHYLLIS
Flight Into Freedom, Story
Steel Fist, The 1952 d: Wesley E. Barry. lps: Roddy McDowall, Kristine Miller, Harry Lauter. 73M USA. prod/rel: Monogram, William F. Broidy

PARKER, ROBERT B.
Poodle Springs, Novel
Poodle Springs 1998 d: Bob Rafelson. lps: James Caan, Dina Meyer, David Keith. TVM. 95M USA. prod/rel: Universal TV Entertainment/Mca, Mirag

PARKER, T. JEFFERSON
Laguna Heat, Novel
Laguna Heat 1987 d: Simon Langton. lps: Harry Hamlin, Jason Robards Jr., Rip Torn. TVM. 115M USA. prod/rel: Jay Weston Prod., Home Box Office

PARKHILL, FORBES
Blazing Guns, 1934, Short Story
Blazing Guns 1935 d: Ray Heinz. lps: Reb Russell, Marion Shilling, Lafe McKee. 58M USA. prod/rel: Willis Kent Productions

PARKIN, FRANK
Krippendorff's Tribe, Book
Krippendorf's Tribe 1998 d: Todd Holland. lps: Richard Dreyfuss, Jenna Elfman, Natasha Lyonne. 94M USA. prod/rel: Touchstone Pictures, Mora-Brezner-Steinberg-Tenenbaum

PARKS, GORDON
The Learning Tree, New York 1963, Novel
Learning Tree, The 1969 d: Gordon Parks. lps: Kyle Johnson, Alexander Clarke, Estelle Evans. 107M USA. *Learn, Baby, Learn* prod/rel: Winger Enterprises

PARKS, LILLIAN ROGERS (1897–, USA
My Thirty Years Backstairs at the White House, Autob
Backstairs at the White House 1979 d: Michael O'Herlihy. lps: Olivia Cole, Leslie Uggams, Louis Gossett Jr. TVM. 450M USA. prod/rel: NBC, Paramount

PARMA, MARCO
Sotto Il Vestito Niente, Novel
Sotto Il Vestito Niente 1985 d: Carlo VanzinA. lps: Tom Schanley, Renee Simonsen, Donald Pleasence. 100M ITL. *Nothing Underneath* (UKN); *Nothing Under the Dress*; *Into the Darkness* prod/rel: Faso

PARR, E. F.
The Escape, Play
Escape, The 1926 d: Edwin Greenwood. lps: Bertram Burleigh, Gladys Jennings. 1610f UKN. prod/rel: Gaumont

The Woman Juror, Play
Woman Juror, The 1926 d: Milton Rosmer. lps: Gladys Jennings, John Stuart, Frank Vosper. 1900f UKN. prod/rel: Gaumont

PARR, LOUISA
Adam and Eve, Play
Queen's Evidence 1919 d: James McKay. lps: Godfrey Tearle, Unity More, Janet Alexander. 5000f UKN. prod/rel: British & Colonial, Moss

PARRISH, ANNE
All Kneeling, 1928, Novel
Born to Be Bad 1950 d: Nicholas Ray. lps: Joan Fontaine, Robert Ryan, Zachary Scott. 94M USA. prod/rel: RKO Radio

PARRISH, RANDALL
Bob Hampton of Placer, Chicago 1910, Novel
Bob Hampton of Placer 1921 d: Marshall Neilan. lps: James Kirkwood, Wesley Barry, Marjorie Daw. 7268f USA. *Custer's Last Stand* prod/rel: Marshall Neilan Productions, Associated First National Pictures

Keith of the Border, Chicago 1910, Novel
Keith of the Border 1918 d: Cliff Smith. lps: Roy Stewart, Josie Sedgwick, Norbert Cills. 5r USA. prod/rel: Triangle Film Corp., Triangle Distributing Corp.

PARROTT, KATHERINE URSULA
Ex-Wife, New York 1929
Divorcee, The 1930 d: Robert Z. Leonard. lps: Norma Shearer, Chester Morris, Conrad Nagel. 83M USA. prod/rel: Metro-Goldwyn-Mayer Pictures

PARROTT, URSULA
Story
There's Always Tomorrow 1956 d: Douglas Sirk. lps: Barbara Stanwyck, Fred MacMurray, Joan Bennett. 84M USA. prod/rel: Universal-International

Brilliant Marriage, Novel
Brilliant Marriage 1936 d: Phil Rosen. lps: Joan Marsh, Holmes Herbert, Barbara Bedford. 65M USA. prod/rel: Invincible Pictures Corp.

A Gentleman's Fate, 1931, Short Story
Gentleman's Fate 1931 d: Mervyn Leroy. lps: John Gilbert, Louis Wolheim, Anita Page. 93M USA. prod/rel: Metro-Goldwyn-Mayer Corp., Metro-Goldwyn-Mayer Dist. Corp.©

Love Affair, 1930, Short Story
Love Affair 1932 d: Thornton Freeland. lps: Dorothy MacKaill, Humphrey Bogart, Jack Kennedy. 68M USA. prod/rel: Columbia Pictures Corp.©

Next Time We Live, New York 1935, Novel
Next Time We Love 1936 d: Edward H. Griffith. lps: Margaret Sullavan, James Stewart, Ray Milland. 87M USA. *Next Time We Live* (UKN) prod/rel: Universal Productions©

Strangers May Kiss, New York 1930, Novel
Strangers May Kiss 1931 d: George Fitzmaurice. lps: Norma Shearer, Robert Montgomery, Neil Hamilton. 85M USA. prod/rel: Metro-Goldwyn-Mayer Corp., Metro-Goldwyn-Mayer Dist. Corp.©

PARRY, BERNARD
The Purse Strings, Play
Purse Strings 1933 d: Henry Edwards. lps: Chili Bouchier, Gyles Isham, G. H. Mulcaster. 69M UKN. prod/rel: British and Dominions, Paramount

PARRY, EDWARD F.
What the Butler Saw, London 1905, Play
What the Butler Saw 1924 d: George Dewhurst. lps: Irene Rich, Pauline Garon, Guy Newall. 5855f UKN. prod/rel: Dewhurst, Gaumont

PARSONNET, MARION
Remember Tomorrow, Story
Dangerously They Live 1942 d: Robert Florey. lps: John Garfield, Nancy Coleman, Raymond Massey. 77M USA. *Remember Tomorrow* prod/rel: Warner Bros.

PARSONS, AGNES
Jewels of Desire, Story
Jewels of Desire 1927 d: Paul Powell. lps: Priscilla Dean, John Bowers, Walter Long. 5427f USA. prod/rel: Metropolitan Pictures Corp. of Calif.

PARSONS, HUBERT
The Dancers, New York 1923, Novel
Dancers, The 1925 d: Emmett J. Flynn. lps: George O'Brien, Alma Rubens, Madge Bellamy. 6583f USA. prod/rel: Fox Film Corp.

Dancers, The 1930 d: Chandler Sprague. lps: Lois Moran, Phillips Holmes, Walter Byron. 7500f USA. prod/rel: Fox Film Corp.

PARSONS, J. PALMER
White Gold, New York 1925, Play
White Gold 1927 d: William K. Howard. lps: Jetta Goudal, Kenneth Thomson, George Bancroft. 6108f USA. prod/rel: de Mille Pictures, Producers Distributing Corp.

PARSONS, NICK
Dead Heart, Play
Dead Heart 1996 d: Nick Parsons. lps: Bryan Brown, Ernie Dingo, Angie Milliken. 103M ASL. prod/rel: Dead Heart Productions

PARTURIER, FRANCOIS
L'amant de Cinq Jours, Novel
Amant de Cinq Jours, L' 1960 d: Philippe de BrocA. lps: Jean Seberg, Jean-Pierre Cassel, Micheline Presle. 95M FRN/ITL. *L'amante Di Cinque Giorni* (ITL); *The Five Day Lover* (USA); *Infidelity* (UKN) prod/rel: Films Ariane, Filmsonor

PASCAL, ERNEST
The Age for Love, New York 1930, Novel
Age for Love, The 1931 d: Frank Lloyd. lps: Billie Dove, Charles Starrett, Adrian Morris. 81M USA. *Age of Love* prod/rel: the Caddo Co., United Artists

The Charlatan, New York 1922, Play
Charlatan, The 1929 d: George Melford. lps: Holmes Herbert, Margaret Livingston, Rockliffe Fellowes. 6097f USA. prod/rel: Universal Pictures

The Dark Swan, New York 1924, Novel
Wedding Rings 1929 d: William Beaudine. lps: H. B. Warner, Lois Wilson, Olive Borden. 6621f USA. *The Dark Swan* prod/rel: First National Pictures

Egypt, Story
Sensation Seekers 1927 d: Lois Weber. lps: Billie Dove, Huntley Gordon, Raymond Bloomer. 7015f USA. prod/rel: Universal Pictures

Hell's Highroad, New York 1925, Novel
Hell's Highroad 1925 d: Rupert Julian. lps: Leatrice Joy, Edmund Burns, Robert Edeson. 6084f USA. prod/rel: Cinema Corp. of America, Producers Distributing Corp.

The Marriage Bed, New York 1927, Novel
Husband's Holiday 1931 d: Robert Milton. lps: Clive Brook, Charles Ruggles, Vivienne Osborne. 70M USA. prod/rel: Paramount Publix Corp.©

The Savage, Story
Savage, The 1926 d: Fred Newmeyer. lps: Ben Lyon, May McAvoy, Tom Maguire. 6275f USA. prod/rel: First National Pictures

PASCOLI, GIOVANNI (1855–1912), ITL
Cavalla Storna, Poem
Cavallina Storna, La 1953 d: Giulio Morelli. lps: Gino Cervi, Franca Marzi, Cesare DanovA. 90M ITL. prod/rel: S.C.I.a.C., Zeus Film

Nido Di Farlotti, Poem
Cavallina Storna, La 1953 d: Giulio Morelli. lps: Gino Cervi, Franca Marzi, Cesare DanovA. 90M ITL. prod/rel: S.C.I.a.C., Zeus Film

Un Ricordo, Poem
Cavallina Storna, La 1953 d: Giulio Morelli. lps: Gino Cervi, Franca Marzi, Cesare DanovA. 90M ITL. prod/rel: S.C.I.a.C., Zeus Film

PASCUTO, GIOVANNI
Strana la Vita, Novel
Strana la Vita 1988 d: Giuseppe Bertolucci. lps: Diego Abatantuono, Monica Guerritore, Domiziana Giordano. 94M ITL. *Life Is Strange* prod/rel: a.M.A. Film, Dania

PASINETTI, PIER MARIA
Rosso Veneziano, Novel
Rosso Veneziano 1975 d: Marco Leto. lps: Raoul Grassilli, Gastone Moschin, Marina Dolfin. MTV. F ITL. prod/rel: Rai Radiotelevisione Italiana

PASKANDI, GEZA
Weiskopf Ur, Hany Ora?, 1968, Short Story
Hany Az Ora, Vekker Ur? 1985 d: Peter Bacso. lps: Tamas Jordan, Ferenc Kallai, Gyorgy Melis. 109M HNG. *What's the Time, Mr. Clock?* prod/rel: Mafilm Objektiv Studio

PASKOV, VIKTOR
Balada Za Georg Henig, 1987, Novel
  Ti, Koito Si Na Nebeto 1990 d: Docho Bodzhakov. 102M BUL. *Thou, Which Art in Heaven*

PASO, ANTONIO
El Orgullo de Albacete, Play
  Orgullo de Albacete, El 1928 d: Luis R. Alonso. lps: Jose Montenegro, Soledad Franco Rodriguez, Alfonso Orozco Romero. SPN. prod/rel: Producciones Hornemann (Madrid)

PASO, MANUEL
La Meraviglia Di Damasco, Musical Play
  Accadde a Damasco E Febbre 1943 d: Primo Zeglio. lps: Paola Barbara, Germana Paolieri, Miguel Liguero. 90M ITL/SPN. *Sucedio En Damasco* (SPN); *La Meraviglia Di Damasco*; *Accadde a Damasco*; *Febbre*; *Fiebre* prod/rel: U.F.I.S.A., E.I.a.
Rosario la Cortijera, Opera
  Rosario la Cortijera 1923 d: Jose Buchs. lps: Elisa Ruiz Romero, Miguel Cuchet, Manuel San German. 2200m SPN. *Rosario, the Girl of the Farm* prod/rel: Films Espanola (Madrid)
Curro Vargas, Opera
  Curro Vargas 1923 d: Jose Buchs. lps: Ricardo Galache, Angelina Breton, Maria Comendador. 3200m SPN. prod/rel: Film Espanola (Madrid)

PASOLINI, PIER PAOLO (1922–1974), ITL
Ragazza Di Vita, 1955, Novel
  Notte Brava, La 1959 d: Mauro Bolognini. lps: Mylene Demongeot, Rosanna Schiaffino, Antonella Lualdi. 105M ITL/FRN. *Garcons, Les* (FRN); *Bad Girls Don't Cry*; *Night Heat* (UKN); *On Any Street*; *The Night Out* prod/rel: Ajace Compagnia Cin.Ca (Roma), Franco London Film (Paris)
Teorema, Milan 1968, Novel
  Teorema 1968 d: Pier Paolo Pasolini. lps: Terence Stamp, Massimo Girotti, Silvana Mangano. 100M ITL. *Theorem* (UKN) prod/rel: Aetos Film, Euro International Film
Una Vita Violenta, 1959, Novel
  Vita Violenta, Una 1962 d: Paolo Heusch, Brunello Rondi. lps: Franco Citti, Serena Vergano, Enrico Maria Salerno. 115M ITL/FRN. *A Violent Life* prod/rel: Zebra Film (Roma), Aera Film (Paris)

PASSENDORF, HANS
Bux, Novel
  Make Up 1937 d: Alfred Zeisler. lps: Nils Asther, June Clyde, Judy Kelly. 70M UKN. prod/rel: Standard International, Associated British Film Distributors

PASSEUR, STEVE (1899–, FRN
Le Pavillon Brule, Play
  Pavillon Brule, Le 1941 d: Jacques de Baroncelli. lps: Michele Alfa, Elina Labourdette, Pierre Renoir. 90M FRN. prod/rel: Synops
Suzanne
  Suzanne 1932 d: Raymond Rouleau, Leo Joannon. lps: Yolande Laffon, Raymond Rouleau, Jean Max. 80M FRN. prod/rel: Productions Georges Marret

PASSILINNA, ARTO
Janiksen Vuosi, 1975, Novel
  Janiksen Vuosi 1977 d: Risto JarvA. lps: Antti Litja, Rita Polster, Martti Kuningas. 129M FNL. *The Year of the Hare*

PASTERNAK, ANNA
Princess in Love, Book
  Princess in Love 1996 d: David Greene. lps: Julie Cox, Christopher Villiers, Christopher Bowen. 95M UKN.

PASTERNAK, BORIS (1890–1960), RSS, Pasternak, Bors Leonidovich
Doktor Zhivago, 1957, Novel
  Doctor Zhivago 1965 d: David Lean. lps: Omar Sharif, Julie Christie, Rod Steiger. 197M USA. *Dr. Zhivago* prod/rel: Carlo Ponti, MGM

PASTONCHI, FRANCESCO
Gli Emigranti, Novel
  Emigranti, Gli 1915 d: Gino ZaccariA. lps: Alberto A. Capozzi, Nilde Bruno, Cesare Zocchi. 1400m ITL. prod/rel: S.A. Ambrosio

PASTUSZEK, ANDRZEJ
Story
  Indeks 1977 d: Janusz Kijowski. lps: Krzysztof Zaleski, Ewa Zukowska, Justyna KulczyckA. 100M PLN. *Index* prod/rel: Film Polski, Zespoly Filmove Pryzmat

PATE, MICHAEL (1920–, ASL
The Steel Monster, Short Story
  Most Dangerous Man Alive, The 1961 d: Allan Dwan. lps: Ron Randell, Debra Paget, Elaine Stewart. 82M USA. *The Steel Monster* prod/rel: Trans-Global Films

PATERNOSTER, SYDNEY
In the Hands of the Spoilers, Novel
  In the Hands of the Spoilers 1916 d: Leon Bary. 4000f UKN. prod/rel: Barker, Neptune

PATERSON, ANDREW BARTON (1864–1941), ASL
The Man from Snowy River, 1895, Poem
  Man from Snowy River, The 1920 d: Beaumont Smith, John Wells. lps: Tal Ordell, Cyril MacKay, John Cosgrove. F ASL.
  Man from Snowy River, The 1982 d: George Miller. lps: Kirk Douglas, Jack Thompson, Tom Burlinson. 106M ASL. prod/rel: Cambridge Films, Michael Edgely International

PATERSON, NEIL
And Delilah, Short Story
  Woman for Joe, The 1955 d: George M. O'Ferrall. lps: Diane Cilento, George Baker, David Kossoff. 91M UKN. prod/rel: Rank Film Distributors, Group
International Incident, Story
  Man on a Tightrope 1953 d: Elia Kazan. lps: Fredric March, Terry Moore, Gloria Grahame. 105M USA. prod/rel: 20th Century-Fox

PATERSON, RICHARD NORTH
Degree of Guilt, Novel
  Degree of Guilt 1995 d: Mike Robe. lps: David James Elliott, Daphne Zuniga, Sharon Lawrence. TVM. 130M USA.

PATON, ALAN (1903–1988), SAF, Paton, Alan Stewart
Cry, the Beloved Country, 1948, Novel
  Cry, the Beloved Country 1952 d: Zoltan KordA. lps: Canada Lee, Charles Carson, Sidney Poitier. 103M UKN/SAF. *African Fury* (USA) prod/rel: London Films, British Lion Production Assets
  Lost in the Stars 1974 d: Daniel Mann. lps: Brock Peters, Melba Moore, Raymond St. Jacques. 114M USA. prod/rel: American Film Theatre
  Cry, the Beloved Country 1995 d: Darrell Roodt. lps: James Earl Jones, Richard Harris, Vusi Kunene. 111M USA. prod/rel: Distant Horizon Productions, Videovision Entertainment

PATON, RAYMOND
The Blackguard, Novel
  Blackguard, The 1925 d: Graham Cutts. lps: June Novak, Walter Rilla, Frank Stanmore. 9200f UKN. prod/rel: UFA, Gainsborough

PATRICK, JOHN (1905–, USA
The Hasty Heart, London 1945, Play
  Hasty Heart, The 1949 d: Vincent Sherman. lps: Ronald Reagan, Patricia Neal, Richard Todd. 107M UKN/USA. prod/rel: Associated British-Pathe, Associated British Picture Corporation
  Hasty Heart, The 1983 d: Martin Speer. lps: Gregory Harrison, Cheryl Ladd, Perry King. TVM. 135M USA.
Love Lies Bleeding, Story
  Strange Love of Martha Ivers, The 1946 d: Lewis Milestone. lps: Barbara Stanwyck, Van Heflin, Kirk Douglas. 117M USA. *Strange Love*; *Love Lies Bleeding* prod/rel: Paramount

PATRNY, JAN
Muzi Nestarnou, Play
  Muzi Nestarnou 1942 d: Vladimir Slavinsky. lps: Zita Kabatova, Frantisek Roland, Jana RomanovA. 2752m CZC. *Men Don't Age* prod/rel: Lucernafilm

PATRONI GRIFFI, GIUSEPPE (1921–, ITL
D'amore Si Muore, Play
  D'amore Si Muore 1972 d: Carlo Carunchio. lps: Silvana Mangano, Lino Capolicchio, Stefania Casini. 95M ITL. prod/rel: Clesi Cin.Ca, Euro International Film
Metti, Una Sera a Cena, Play
  Metti, Una Sera a Cena 1969 d: Giuseppe Patroni Griffi. lps: Jean-Louis Trintignant, Lino Capolicchio, Tony Musante. 125M ITL. *One Night at Dinner* (USA); *The Love Circle* (UKN); *Let's Say One Night for Dinner*; *Imagine One Evening for Dinner* prod/rel: Red Film, San Marco Cin.Ca

PATTANAYAK, KUMAR
Amada Bata, Novel
  Amada Bata 1964 d: Amar Ganguly. lps: Geeta, Jharana Das, Lakhmi. 144M IND. *The Untrodden Road*

PATTEN, LEWIS B.
Back Trail, Novel
  Red Sundown 1956 d: Jack Arnold. lps: Rory Calhoun, Martha Hyer, Dean Jagger. 82M USA. prod/rel: Universal-International
Death of a Gunfighter, New York 1968, Novel
  Death of a Gunfighter 1969 d: Robert Totten, Don Siegel. lps: Richard Widmark, Lena Horne, John Saxon. 94M USA. *Patch*; *The Last Gunfighter* prod/rel: Universal

PATTERSON, JAMES
Kiss the Girls, Novel
  Kiss the Girls 1997 d: Gary Fleder. lps: Morgan Freeman, Ashley Judd, Cary Elwes. 120M USA. prod/rel: Rysher Entertainment, Paramount Pictures©

PATTERSON, JOSEPH MEDILL
Dope, New York 1909, Play
  Dope 1914 d: Herman Lieb. lps: Laura Nelson Hall, Ernest Truex, William H. Tooker. 6r USA. prod/rel: Direct-from-Broadway Feature Film Co., State Rights
The Fourth Estate, New York 1909, Play
  Fourth Estate, The 1916 d: Frank Powell. lps: Ruth Blair, Clifford Bruce, Victor Benoit. 5r USA. prod/rel: Fox Film Corp., William Fox©
A Little Brother of the Rich, New York 1908, Novel
  Little Brother of the Rich, A 1915 d: Hobart Bosworth, Otis Turner. lps: Hobart Bosworth, Jane Novak, J. Edwin Brown. 5r USA. prod/rel: Universal Film Mfg. Co.©
  Little Brother of the Rich, A 1919 d: Lynn Reynolds. lps: Frank Mayo, Kathryn Adams, J. Barney Sherry. 6r USA. prod/rel: Universal Film Mfg. Co.©

PATTERSON, NORMA
Have You Come for Me, Novel
  You Live and Learn 1937 d: Arthur Woods. lps: Glenda Farrell, Claude Hulbert, Glen Alyn. 80M UKN. prod/rel: Warner Bros., First National

PATTI, ERCOLE
Un Amore a Roma, Novel
  Amore a Roma, Un 1960 d: Dino Risi. lps: Mylene Demongeot, Peter Baldwin, Elsa Martinelli. 113M ITL/FRN/GRM. *Inassouvie, L'* (FRN); *Love in Rome*; *Liebesnachte in Rom* (GRM); *Roman Nights of Love* prod/rel: Fair Film, Cie Incom (Roma)
Un Bellissimo Novembre, Novel
  Bellissimo Novembre, Un 1968 d: Mauro Bolognini. lps: Gina Lollobrigida, Paolo Turco, Gabriele Ferzetti. 91M ITL/FRN. *Un Merveilleux Automne* (FRN); *A Wonderful November*; *That Splendid November* (USA) prod/rel: Adelphia Compagnia Cin.Ca (Roma), Les Artistes Associes (Paris)
La Cugina, Novel
  Cugina, La 1974 d: Aldo Lado. lps: Massimo Ranieri, Dayle Haddon, Stefania Casini. 95M ITL. prod/rel: Cinegay, Unidis
Giovannino, Novel
  Giovannino 1976 d: Paolo Nuzzi. lps: Christian de Sica, Tina Aumont, Delia Boccardo. 110M ITL. prod/rel: Euro International Films
Graziella, Novel
  Seduzione, La 1973 d: Fernando Di Leo. lps: Lisa Gastoni, Maurice Ronet, Ornella Muti. 95M ITL. *Seduction* prod/rel: Cineproduzioni Daunia 70, Alpherat
Quartieri Alti, Novel
  Quartieri Alti 1944 d: Mario Soldati. lps: Adriana Benetti, Nerio Bernardi, Enzo Biliotti. 82M ITL. prod/rel: Industrie Cin.Che Italiane

PATTON, FRANCES GRAY
Good Morning, Miss Dove, 1954, Novel
  Good Morning, Miss Dove 1955 d: Henry Koster. lps: Jennifer Jones, Robert Stack, Kipp Hamilton. 107M USA. prod/rel: 20th Century-Fox

PATULLO, GEORGE
The Better Man, Story
  Better Man, The 1915. 2r USA. prod/rel: Majestic
Dry Check Charlie, Story
  Gasoline Gus 1921 d: James Cruze. lps: Roscoe Arbuckle, Lila Lee, Charles Ogle. 5r USA. prod/rel: Famous Players-Lasky, Paramount Pictures
Frenchy, Story
  Frenchy 1914. lps: Vester Pegg, Francelia Billington, Fred Burns. 2r USA. prod/rel: Majestic
The Higher Law, Story
  Mysterious Shot, The 1914 d: Donald Crisp, James Kirkwood. lps: Henry B. Walthall, Jack Pickford, Dorothy Gish. 2r USA. prod/rel: Reliance
The Ledger of Life, 1922, Short Story
  Private Affairs 1925 d: Renaud Hoffman. lps: Gladys Hulette, Robert Agnew, Mildred Harris. 6132f USA. prod/rel: Renaud Hoffman Productions, Producers Distributing Corp.
The Summons, 1914, Short Story
  First Degree, The 1923 d: Edward Sedgwick. lps: Frank Mayo, Sylvia Breamer, Philo McCullough. 4395f USA. prod/rel: Universal Pictures

PAUL, ADOLF
Lola Montez, Story
  Palace of Pleasure, The 1926 d: Emmett J. Flynn. lps: Edmund Lowe, Betty Compson, Henry Kolker. 5467f USA. prod/rel: Fox Film Corp.

PAUL, BARBARA
Kill Free, Novel
  Murder on Demand 1991 d: Alan Metzger. lps: Patrick Duffy, William Devane, Chelsea Field. TVM. 91M USA. *Murder By Demand*; *Murder C.O.D.*

PAUL, I.
Mr. Romeo, New York 1927, Play
  Chicken a la King 1928 d: Henry Lehrman. lps: Nancy Carroll, George Meeker, Arthur Stone. 6417f USA. *The Gay Deceiver* prod/rel: Fox Film Corp.

PAULDING, FREDERICK
Trooper Billy, Play
  Trooper Billy 1913. 2000f USA. prod/rel: Kalem

PAULL, H. M.
The New Clown, London 1902, Play
  New Clown, The 1916 d: Fred Paul. lps: James Welch, Manora Thew, Richard Lindsay. 4500f UKN. prod/rel: Ideal

PAULON, FLAVIO
Short Story
  Carica Delle Patate, La 1979 d: Walter Santesso. lps: Tommaso Polgar, Walter Magara, Luigi d'EcclesiA. 90M ITL. prod/rel: Juventute Cin.Ca, Lumicon

PAULSEN, MARGIT
Liten Ida, Novel
  Liten Ida 1981 d: Laila Mikkelsen. lps: Sunniva Lindekleiv, Howard Halvorsen, Lise Fjeldstad. 88M NRW/SWD. *Growing Up*; *Little Ida* prod/rel: Svenska Filminstitutet, Norsk Film

PAULTON, EDWARD A.
Her Temporary Husband, New York 1922, Play
  Her Temporary Husband 1923 d: John McDermott. lps: Owen Moore, Sydney Chaplin, Sylvia Breamer. 6723f USA. prod/rel: Associated First National Pictures
Money By Wire, Play
  Get Off My Foot 1935 d: William Beaudine. lps: Max Miller, Jane Carr, Chili Bouchier. 82M UKN. prod/rel: Warner Bros., First National
Niobe, London 1892, Play
  Niobe 1915 d: Hugh Ford, Edwin S. Porter. lps: Hazel Dawn, Charles Abbe, Maude Odell. 5r USA. prod/rel: Famous Players Film Co., Paramount Pictures Corp.

PAULTON, ERNEST
A Welcome Wife, Play
  Let's Love and Laugh 1931 d: Richard Eichberg. lps: Gene Gerrard, Muriel Angelus, George Gee. 85M UKN. *Bridegroom for Two* (USA); *The Bridegroom's Widow* prod/rel: British International Pictures, Wardour

PAULTON, HARRY
Niobe, London 1892, Play
  Niobe 1915 d: Hugh Ford, Edwin S. Porter. lps: Hazel Dawn, Charles Abbe, Maude Odell. 5r USA. prod/rel: Famous Players Film Co., Paramount Pictures Corp.

PAUWELS, FRANCOIS
Rechter Thomas, Novel
  Rechter Thomas 1953 d: Walter Smith. lps: Ton Van Duinhoven, Piet Bron, Rini Van Slingelandt. 103M NTH.

PAVEL, OTA
Smrt Krasnych Srncu, Novel
  Smrt Krasnych Srncu 1987 d: Karel KachynA. lps: Karel Hermanek, Marta Vancurova, Rudolf Hrusinsky. 97M CZC. *Forbidden Dreams*; *Death of Beautiful Roe-Deers* prod/rel: Filmove Studio Barrandov

PAVESE, CESARE (1908–1950), ITL
Dialoghi Con Leuco, 1947, Short Story
  Dalla Nube Alla Resistenza 1979 d: Jean-Marie Straub, Daniele Huillet. lps: Olimpia Carlisi, Guido Lombardi, Gino Felici. TVM. 103M ITL/GRM/FRN. *From the Cloud to the Resistance* (UKN); *Von Der Wolke Zum Widerstand*; *Della Nuba Alla Resistenza* prod/rel: Rai-Radiotelevisione Italia (Roma), Ina (Paris)
La Luna E I Falo, 1950, Short Story
  Dalla Nube Alla Resistenza 1979 d: Jean-Marie Straub, Daniele Huillet. lps: Olimpia Carlisi, Guido Lombardi, Gino Felici. TVM. 103M ITL/GRM/FRN. *From the Cloud to the Resistance* (UKN); *Von Der Wolke Zum Widerstand*; *Della Nuba Alla Resistenza* prod/rel: Rai-Radiotelevisione Italia (Roma), Ina (Paris)
Tra Donne Sole, Turin 1949, Short Story
  Amiche, Le 1955 d: Michelangelo Antonioni. lps: Eleonora Rossi-Drago, Gabriele Ferzetti, Franco Fabrizi. 104M ITL. *The Girl Friends* (USA) prod/rel: Trionfalcine, Titanus

PAVLIDIS, L.
Novel
  Ergostasio, to 1981 d: Tasos Psarras. lps: Vassilis Kolovos, Vana Fitsori, Dimitra Hatoupi. 101M GRC. *The Factory* prod/rel: Greek Film Centre, Tassos Psarras

PAVLOVIC, ZIVOJIN
Zadah Tela, 1982, Novel
  Zadah Tela 1983 d: Zivojin Pavlovic. lps: Dusan Janicijevic, Rade Serbedzija, Metka Franko Ferrari. 98M YGS. *Body Scent*; *Body Smell*

PAXTON, GUY
Love's a Luxury, Play
  Love's a Luxury 1952 d: Francis Searle. lps: Hugh Wakefield, Derek Bond, Michael Medwin. 89M UKN. *The Caretaker's Daughter* (USA) prod/rel: Mancunian, Butcher's Film Service

PAYNE, JOHN HOWARD (1791–1852), USA
Home, Sweet Home, 1823, Song
  Home, Sweet Home 1914 d: D. W. Griffith. lps: Henry B. Walthall, Lillian Gish, Dorothy Gish. 6r USA. prod/rel: Majestic Motion Picture Co., Reliance Motion Picture Co.

PAYNE, LAURENCE
The Nose on My Face, London 1961, Novel
  Girl in the Headlines 1963 d: Michael Truman. lps: Ian Hendry, Ronald Fraser, Margaret Johnston. 93M UKN. *The Model Murder Case* (USA); *The Nose on My Face* prod/rel: Viewfinder Films, Bryanston

PAYNE, STEPHEN
Tracks, 1928, Short Story
  Swifty 1935 d: Alan James. lps: Hoot Gibson, June Gale, George Hayes. 62M USA. prod/rel: Wafilms, State Rights

PAYNE, WILL J.
Black Sheep, Short Story
  Family Closet, The 1921 d: John B. O'Brien. lps: Holmes Herbert, Alice Mann, Kempton Greene. 6r USA. prod/rel: Ore-Col Film Corp., Playgoers Pictures

PAYNTER, ERNEST
Maskee, 1926, Short Story
  Shipmates 1931 d: Harry Pollard. lps: Robert Montgomery, Dorothy Jordan, Ernest Torrence. 73M USA. prod/rel: Metro-Goldwyn-Mayer Corp., Metro-Goldwyn-Mayer Dist. Corp.©

PAYSAN, CATHERINE
Je M'appelle Jerico, Paris 1964, Novel
  Ce Sacre Grand-Pere 1968 d: Jacques Poitrenaud. lps: Michel Simon, Marie Dubois, Yves Lefebvre. 95M FRN. *The Marriage Came Tumbling Down* (USA) prod/rel: Champs Elysees Productions, Isabelle Films

PAYSON, WILLIAM FARQUHAR
Barry Gordon, New York 1908, Novel
  Cheated Hearts 1921 d: Hobart Henley. lps: Herbert Rawlinson, Warner Baxter, Marjorie Daw. 4415f USA. prod/rel: Universal Film Mfg. Co.

PAZ, OCTAVIO (1914–, MXC
Sor Juana: Her Life and World (the Traps of Faith), Book
  Yo, la Peor de Todas 1990 d: Maria Luisa Bemberg. lps: Assumpta Serna, Dominique Sanda, Hector Alterio. 105M ARG. *I, the Worst of Them All* prod/rel: Gea Cinematografica, Assai Communications

PAZ, SENAL
El Lobo, El Bosque Y El Hombre Nuevo, Novel
  Fresa Y Chocolate 1993 d: Tomas Gutierrez Alea, Juan Carlos Tabio. lps: Jorge Perugorria, Vladimir Cruz, Mirta IbarrA. 111M CUB. *Strawberry and Chocolate* prod/rel: ICAIC, IMC

PEACH, L. DU GARDE
The Great Mr. Handel, Radio Play
  Great Mr. Handel, The 1942 d: Norman Walker. lps: Wilfred Lawson, Elizabeth Allan, Malcolm Keen. 103M UKN. prod/rel: General Film Distributors, Gregory, Hake & Walker
The Path of Glory, Radio Play
  Path of Glory, The 1934 d: Dallas Bower. lps: Maurice Evans, Valerie Hobson, Felix Aylmer. 68M UKN. prod/rel: Triumph, Producers Distributing Corporation

PEACOCK, WALTER
A Night in Montmartre, 1926, Play
  Night in Montmartre, A 1931 d: Leslie Hiscott. lps: Horace Hodges, Franklin Dyall, Hugh Williams. 70M UKN. prod/rel: Gaumont

PEACOCKE, CAPT. LESLIE T.
Neptune's Bride, Short Story
  Neptune's Bride 1920 d: Leslie T. Peacocke. lps: Roxy Armstrong, Lucille Best, Anita Meredith. 6r USA. prod/rel: Ormsby Film Corp., Western Pictures Exploitation Co.

PEAKE, ELMORE ELLIOTT
An Altar on Little Thunder, 1912, Short Story
  His Divorced Wife 1919 d: Douglas Gerrard. lps: Monroe Salisbury, Charles West, Charles Le Moyne. 5-6r USA. prod/rel: Universal Film Mfg. Co.©

PEAN, PIERRE
Les Chapellieres, Novel
  Olympe de Nos Amours 1989 d: Serge Moati. lps: Marie-France Pisier, Pascale Rocard, Gerard Klein. TVM. 80M FRN.

PEARCE, DONALD
Cool Hand Luke, New York 1965, Novel
  Cool Hand Luke 1967 d: Stuart Rosenberg. lps: Paul Newman, George Kennedy, J. D. Cannon. 127M USA. prod/rel: Warner Bros., Jalem

PEARCE, MICHAEL
Into the West, Short Story
  Into the West 1992 d: Mike Newell. lps: Gabriel Byrne, Ellen Barkin, Ciaran Fitzgerald. 102M IRL.

PEARDON, RYNE DOUGLAS
Simple Simon, Novel
  Mercury Rising 1998 d: Harold Becker. lps: Bruce Willis, Alec Baldwin, Miko Hughes. 112M USA. prod/rel: Universal Pictures, Imagine Entertainment

PEARL, ALAN
The Painted Flapper, Novel
  Painted Flapper, The 1924 d: John Gorman. lps: James Kirkwood, Pauline Garon, Crauford Kent. 6000f USA. prod/rel: Chadwick Pictures

PEARSON, A. Y.
The Police Patrol, Story
  Police Patrol, The 1925 d: Burton L. King. lps: James Kirkwood, Edna Murphy, Edmund Breese. 6r USA. prod/rel: Gotham Productions, Lumas Film Corp.

PEARSON, DREW (1897–1969), USA
Washington Merry-Go-Round, New York 1931, Book
  Washington Merry-Go-Round 1932 d: James Cruze. lps: Lee Tracy, Constance Cummings, Walter Connolly. 78M USA. *Invisible Power* (UKN) prod/rel: Columbia Pictures Corp.©

PEARSON, GEORGE
Squibs, Play
  Squibs 1935 d: Henry Edwards. lps: Betty Balfour, Gordon Harker, Stanley Holloway. 77M UKN. prod/rel: Twickenham, Gaumont-British

PEARSON, HESKETH
The Cage, Story
  Cage, The 1914 d: George Loane Tucker. lps: Lillian Logan, Gerald Ames, Charles Rock. 2010f UKN. prod/rel: London

PEARSON, HUMPHREY
On With the Show, Play
  On With the Show 1929 d: Alan Crosland. lps: Betty Compson, Louise Fazenda, Sally O'Neil. 98M USA. prod/rel: Warner Brothers Pictures

PEARSON, MICHAEL
The Sealed Train, Book
  Zug, Der 1989 d: Damiano Damiani. lps: Ben Kingsley, Dominique Sanda, Leslie Caron. 208M AUS/GRM/ITL. *Il Treno Di Lenin* (ITL); *Lenin, the Sealed Train*; *The Sealed Train*; *The Train*

PEARSON, WILLIAM
A Fever in the Blood, New York 1959, Novel
  Fever in the Blood, A 1961 d: Vincent Sherman. lps: Efrem Zimbalist Jr., Angie Dickinson, Jack Kelly. 117M USA. prod/rel: Warner Bros. Pictures

PEAT, HAROLD REGINALD
Private Peat, Indianpolis 1917, Book
  Private Peat 1918 d: Edward Jose. lps: Harold R. Peat, Miriam Fouche, William Sorelle. 4827f USA. prod/rel: Famous Players-Lasky Corp.©, Paramount-Artcraft Special

PEATTIE, ELIA W.
Thunder, Ss
  Thunder Mountain 1925 d: Victor Schertzinger. lps: Madge Bellamy, Leslie Fenton, Alec B. Francis. 7537f USA. prod/rel: Fox Film Corp.

PECHEREL, JACQUES
Boulevard du Rhum, Novel
  Boulevard du Rhum 1971 d: Robert Enrico. lps: Brigitte Bardot, Lino Ventura, Bill Travers. 135M FRN/ITL/SPN. *La Via Del Rhum* (ITL); *Winner Takes All*; *Rum Runner* prod/rel: Rizzoli Film, S.N.E.G.

PECK, GEORGE WILBUR (1840–1916), USA
Peck's Bad Boy and His Pa, Story
  Peck's Bad Boy 1921 d: Sam Wood. lps: Jackie Coogan, Wheeler Oakman, Doris May. 5000f USA. prod/rel: Irving M. Lesser, Associated First National Pictures

PECK, KIM
Story
  Little Darlings 1980 d: Ronald F. Maxwell. lps: Kristy McNichol, Tatum O'Neal, Armand Assante. 95M USA. prod/rel: Paramount

PECK, RICHARD
Are You in the House Alone?, Novel
Are You in the House Alone? 1978 d: Walter Grauman. lps: Kathleen Beller, Blythe Danner, Tony Bill. TVM. 100M USA. prod/rel: CBS, Stonehenge

Don't Look and It Won't Hurt, Novel
Gas Food Lodgings 1991 d: Allison Anders. lps: Brooke Adams, Ione Skye, Fairuza Balk. 101M USA. prod/rel: Mainline, Cineville Partners

Father Figure, Book
Father Figure 1980 d: Jerry London. lps: Hal Linden, Timothy Hutton, Jeremy Licht. TVM. 95M USA. prod/rel: CBS, Time-Life

PECKA, KAREL
Passage, Novel
Passage 1997 d: Juraj Herz. lps: Jacek Borkowski, Malgorzata Kozuchowska, Zora JandovA. 102M CZC/FRN/BLG. prod/rel: Etamp Film Prods. (Prague), Les Films De La Cassine

PEDLAR, MARGARET
House of Dreams Come True, Novel
House of Dreams 1933 d: Tony Frenguelli. lps: Lester Matthews, Jean Adrienne, Margot Grahame. UKN. prod/rel: Danubia

Splendid Folly, Novel
Splendid Folly 1919 d: Arrigo Bocchi. lps: Manora Thew, Hayford Hobbs, Evelyn Harding. 5000f UKN. prod/rel: Windsor, Walturdaw

PEDROSE, LAWRENCE WILLIAM
On the Wings of the Storm, 1926, Short Story
Wings of the Storm 1926 d: John G. Blystone. lps: Thunder A Dog, Virginia Brown Faire, Reed Howes. 5374f USA. prod/rel: Fox Film Corp.

PEER, A
The Hard Way, Novel
Hard Way, The 1916 d: Walter West. lps: Muriel Martin Harvey, J. R. Tozer, Thomas H. MacDonald. 4800f UKN. prod/rel: Broadwest, Walturdaw

PEIL, PAUL LESLIE
Tucson, Novel
Gunsmoke in Tucson 1958 d: Thomas Carr. lps: Mark Stevens, Forrest Tucker, Gale Robbins. 80M USA. prod/rel: Allied Artists

PEISSON, EDOUARD
Le Garcon Sauvage, Novel
Garcon Sauvage, Le 1951 d: Jean Delannoy. lps: Madeleine Robinson, Frank Villard, Pierre-Michel Beck. 112M FRN. *Savage Triangle* (USA); *Wild Boy*; *Marie Tout Court* prod/rel: Films Gibe

Hans le Marin, Novel
Hans le Marin 1948 d: Francois Villiers. lps: Jean-Pierre Aumont, Maria Montez, Lilli Palmer. 95M FRN. *The Wicked City* (USA) prod/rel: Safia

PEIXOTO, JULIO AFRANIO
Bugrinha, 1922, Novel
Diamante Bruto 1977 d: Orlando SennA. lps: Gilda FerreirA. 90M BRZ. *Rough Diamond*

Maria Bonita, 1914, Novel
Maria Bonita 1936 d: Julien Mandel. 76M BRZ.

PEKIC, BORISLAV
Defence and the Last Days, Novel
Djavolji Raj - Ono Ljeto Bijelih Ruza 1989 d: Rajko Grlic. lps: Tom Conti, Susan George, Rod Steiger. 99M YGS/UKN. *That Summer of White Roses* (UKN); *Davolji Raj*; *White Roses* prod/rel: Amy International, Jadran

PELEGRI, JEAN
Les Oliviers de la Justice, Paris 1959, Novel
Oliviers de la Justice, Les 1962 d: James Blue. lps: Pierre Prothon, Jean Pelegri, Marie Decaitre. 90M FRN. *The Olive Trees of Justice* (USA) prod/rel: Ste Algerienne De Prod. Des Stud. Africa

PELLERIN, M.
Le Tresor de Keriolet, Novel
Tresor de Keriolet, Le 1920 d: Felix Leonnec. lps: Georges Carpentier, Suzy Netmo, Jannick Leonnec. SRL. 5951m FRN.

PELLERT, WILHELM
Jesus von Ottakring, Play
Jesus von Ottakring 1976 d: Wilhelm Pellert. lps: Rudolf Prack, Hilde Sochor, Peter Hey. 94M AUS. *Jesus of Ottakring*; *Die Neider Nicht Gezahlt* prod/rel: Gruppe Borobya

PELLETIER JR,. LOUIS
Howdy Stranger, New York 1937, Play
Cowboy from Brooklyn 1938 d: Lloyd Bacon. lps: Dick Powell, Pat O'Brien, Priscilla Lane. 80M USA. *Romance and Rhythm* (UKN); *Dude Rancher*; *Howdy Stranger*; *The Brooklyn Cowboy* prod/rel: Warner Bros. Pictures, Inc.

PELLEY, WILLIAM DUDLEY
Courtin' Calamity, Story
Courtin' Wildcats 1929 d: Jerome Storm. lps: Hoot Gibson, Eugenia Gilbert, Pete Morrison. 5118f USA. prod/rel: Universal Pictures

Drag, Boston 1925, Play
Drag 1929 d: Frank Lloyd. lps: Richard Barthelmess, Lucien Littlefield, Katherine Claire Ward. 7642f USA. *Parasites* (UKN) prod/rel: First National Pictures

The Fog, Boston 1921, Novel
Fog, The 1923 d: Paul Powell. lps: Mildred Harris, Louise Fazenda, Louise Dresser. 6737f USA. prod/rel: Max Graf Productions, Metro Pictures

The Light in the Dark, Story
Light in the Dark, The 1922 d: Clarence Brown. lps: Hope Hampton, E. K. Lincoln, Lon Chaney. 7500f USA. prod/rel: Hope Hampton Productions, Associated First National Pictures

One-Thing-at-a-Time O'Day, 1917, Short Story
One-Thing-at-a-Time O'Day 1919 d: John Ince. lps: Bert Lytell, Eileen Percy, Joseph Kilgour. 5r USA. prod/rel: Metro Pictures Corp.©

The Stolen Lady, Story
Come Across 1929 d: Ray Taylor. lps: Lina Basquette, Reed Howes, Flora Finch. 5330f USA. prod/rel: Universal Pictures

The Sunset Derby, 1926, Short Story
Sunset Derby, The 1927 d: Albert S. Rogell. lps: Mary Astor, William Collier Jr., Ralph Lewis. 6r USA. prod/rel: First National Pictures

Torment, Story
Torment 1924 d: Maurice Tourneur. lps: Owen Moore, Bessie Love, Jean Hersholt. 5442f USA. prod/rel: Maurice Tourneur Productions, Associated First National Pictures

PELLICO, SILVIO
Le Mie Prigioni, 1832, Novel
Silvio Pellico 1915 d: Livio Pavanelli. lps: Raffaello Mariani, Evelina Paoli, Gioacchino Grassi. 1500m ITL. *Il Martire Dello Spielberg*; *Le Mie Prigioni*; *Silvio Pellico Il Martire Dello Spielberg* prod/rel: Alba Film

PEMAN, JOSE-MARIA (1898–, SPN
Les Trois Etc. du Colonel, Play
Trois Etc. du Colonel, Les 1960 d: Claude Boissol. lps: Anita Ekberg, Vittorio de Sica, Georgia Moll. 100M FRN/ITL/SPN. *Le Tre Eccetera Del Colonello* (ITL); *Three Etc's and the Colonel* (USA); *Los Tres Etceteras Del Coronel* (SPN) prod/rel: Talma Films, Vertix Film

PEMBERTON, MAX
Behind the Curtain, Novel
In Search of a Husband 1915 d: Wilfred Noy. lps: Barbara Hoffe, Murray Carrington, Frank Hilton. 3000f UKN. prod/rel: Clarendon, bct

PEMBERTON-BILLING, NOEL
High Treason, Play
High Treason 1929 d: Maurice Elvey. lps: Jameson Thomas, Benita Hume, Basil Gill. 90M UKN. prod/rel: Gaumont-British

PENDER, M. T.
O'Neil of the Glen, Play
O'Neil of the Glen 1916 d: J. M. Kerrigan. lps: J. M. Kerrigan, Nora Clancy, Fred O'Donovan. 2572f IRL/UKN. prod/rel: Film Co. of Ireland, Davison Film Sales Agency

PENDEXTER, HUGH
A Daughter of the Wolf, 1919, Short Story
Daughter of the Wolf, A 1919 d: Irvin V. Willat. lps: Lila Lee, Elliott Dexter, Clarence Geldart. 4506f USA. prod/rel: Famous Players-Lasky Corp.©, Paramount Pictures

Wolf Law, 1921, Short Story
Wolf Law 1922 d: Stuart Paton. lps: Frank Mayo, Sylvia Breamer, Thomas Guise. 4463f USA. prod/rel: Universal Film Mfg. Co.

PENDSE, SHRIPAD NARAYAN
Garambica Bapu, 1952, Novel
Garambica Bapu 1980 d: Baba Mazgonkar. 119M IND. *Garambicha Bapu*

PENELLA, MANUEL
El Gato Montes, Opera
Tiger Love 1924 d: George Melford. lps: Antonio Moreno, Estelle Taylor, G. Raymond Nye. 5325f USA. prod/rel: Famous Players-Lasky, Paramount Pictures

PENN, LYLE
The Picture Show Man, Novel
Picture Show Man, The 1977 d: John Power. lps: Rod Taylor, John Meillon, Patrick Cargill. 99M ASL. *The Travelling Picture Show Man* prod/rel: Limelight

PENROSE, V.
The Bloody Countess, Novel
Countess Dracula 1970 d: Peter Sasdy. lps: Ingrid Pitt, Nigel Green, Sandor Eles. 93M UKN. prod/rel: Rank Film Distributors, Hammer

PENTECOST, HUGH
If I Should Die, Artic
Appointment With a Shadow 1958 d: Richard Carlson. lps: George Nader, Joanna Moore, Brian Keith. 72M USA. *The Big Story* (UKN) prod/rel: Universal-International

PENZOLDT, ERNST
Korporal Mombour, 1941, Short Story
Es Kommt Ein Tag 1950 d: Rudolf Jugert. lps: Dieter Borsche, Maria Schell, Lil Dagover. 90M GRM. *There Will Come a Day* prod/rel: Filmaufbau, Bavaria

PEPLE, EDWARD, Peple, Edward H., Peple, Edward Henry
The Bachelor Daddy, Short Story
Bachelor Daddy, The 1922 d: Alfred E. Green. lps: Thomas Meighan, Leatrice Joy, Maude Wayne. 6229f USA. prod/rel: Famous Players-Lasky Corp., Paramount Pictures

The Littlest Colonel, New York 1911, Play
Littlest Rebel, The 1935 d: David Butler. lps: Shirley Temple, John Boles, Jack Holt. 73M USA. prod/rel: Twentieth Century-Fox Film Corp.©

The Littlest Rebel, New York 1911, Play
Littlest Rebel, The 1914 d: Edgar Lewis. lps: Mimi Yvonne, E. K. Lincoln, Frederick Fleck. 6r USA. prod/rel: Photoplay Productions Co., State Rights

The Love Route, New York 1906, Play
Love Route, The 1915 d: Allan Dwan. lps: Harold Lockwood, Winifred Kingston, Donald Crisp. 4r USA. prod/rel: Famous Players Film Co., Paramount Pictures Corp.

A Pair of Sixes, New York 1914, Play
Pair of Sixes, A 1918 d: Lawrence C. Windom. lps: Taylor Holmes, Robert Conness, Alice Mann. 6r USA. prod/rel: Essanay Film Mfg. Co.©, George K. Spoor Ultra Feature

Pair of Sixes, A, New York 1914, Play
Queen High 1930 d: Fred Newmeyer. lps: Stanley Smith, Ginger Rogers, Charles Ruggles. 7905f USA. prod/rel: Paramount-Publix Corp.

A Pair of Sixes, New York 1914, Play
On Again -Off Again 1937 d: Eddie Cline. lps: Bert Wheeler, Robert Woolsey, Marjorie Lord. 68M USA. *Easy Going* prod/rel: RKO Radio Pictures©

The Prince Chap, New York 1905, Play
Prince Chap, The 1916 d: Marshall Neilan. lps: Marshall Neilan, Mary Charleson, Bessie Eyton. 5r USA. prod/rel: Selig Polyscope Co.©, V-L-S-E, Inc.

Prince Chap, The 1920 d: William C. de Mille. lps: Thomas Meighan, Lila Lee, Kathlyn Williams. 6r USA. prod/rel: Famous Players-Lasky Corp.©, Paramount-Artcraft Pictures

Beloved Bachelor, The 1931 d: Lloyd Corrigan. lps: Paul Lukas, Dorothy Jordan, Charles Ruggles. 74M USA. *Prince Chap* prod/rel: Paramount Publix Corp.

Richard the Brazen, New York 1906, Novel
Richard the Brazen 1917 d: Perry N. Vekroff. lps: Harry T. Morey, Alice Joyce, William Frederic. 5r USA. prod/rel: Vitagraph Co. of America©, Blue Ribbon Feature

The Silver Girl, New York 1907, Play
Silver Girl, The 1919 d: Frank Keenan, Eliot Howe. lps: Frank Keenan, Kathryn Adams, George Hernandez. 5r USA. prod/rel: Anderson Brunton Co., Frank Keenan Photoplay

The Spitfire, New York 1910, Play
Spitfire, The 1914 d: Edwin S. Porter, Frederick A. Thompson. lps: Carlyle Blackwell, Violet Mersereau, Redfield Clark. 4r USA. prod/rel: Famous Players Film Co., Paramount Pictures Corp.

PERCIVAL, DAVID
Girlfriend, Play
Girl Stroke Boy 1971 d: Bob Kellett. lps: Joan Greenwood, Michael Hordern, Clive Francis. 88M UKN. *Girl/Boy* prod/rel: Hemdale, Virgin

PERCIVAL, W.
Someone in the House, New York 1918, Play
Someone in the House 1920 d: John Ince. lps: Edmund Lowe, Vola Vale, Edward Connelly. 6r USA. prod/rel: Metro Pictures Corp.

PERCY, EDWARD (1891–, UKN, Smith, Edward Percy
If Four Walls Told, London 1922, Play
If Four Walls Told 1922 d: Fred Paul. lps: Lillian Hall-Davis, Fred Paul, Campbell Gullan. 6050f UKN. prod/rel: British Super, Jury

Ladies in Retirement, London 1939, Play
Ladies in Retirement 1941 d: Charles Vidor. lps: Louis Hayward, Ida Lupino, Evelyn Keyes. 92M USA. prod/rel: Columbia
Mad Room, The 1969 d: Bernard Girard. lps: Stella Stevens, Shelley Winters, Skip Ward. 93M USA. prod/rel: Norman Maurer Productions

The Shop at Sly Corner, London 1945, Play
Shop at Sly Corner, The 1947 d: George King. lps: Oscar Homolka, Derek Farr, Muriel Pavlow. 92M UKN. *The Code of Scotland Yard* (USA) prod/rel: Pennant Pictures, London Films

Trunk Crime, Play
Trunk Crime 1939 d: Roy Boulting. lps: Manning Whiley, Barbara Everest, Michael Drake. 51M UKN. *Design for Murder* (USA) prod/rel: Charter, Anglo

PERCYVAL, THOMAS WIGNEY
Grumpy, New York 1921, Play
Grumpy 1923 d: William C. de Mille. lps: Theodore Roberts, May McAvoy, Conrad Nagel. 5621f USA. prod/rel: Famous Players-Lasky, Paramount Pictures
Grumpy 1930 d: George Cukor, Cyril Gardner. lps: Cyril Maude, Phillips Holmes, Frances Dade. 74M USA. prod/rel: Paramount-Publix Corp.
Cascarrabias 1930. lps: Ernesto Vilches, Carmen Guerrero, Della MaganA. F USA. prod/rel: Paramount-Publix Corp.

PEREIRA, MIGUEL ANGEL
Los Humilides, Novel
Ultima Siembra, La 1991 d: Miguel PereirA. lps: Patricio Contreras, Leonor Manso, Alberto Benegas. 91M ARG/UKN. *The Last Sowing*; *The Last Harvest* (UKN) prod/rel: Arena, Jorge Estrada Mora

PEREL, SALOMON
Memoirs
Europa, Europa 1991 d: Agnieszka Holland. lps: Marco Hofschneider, Rene Hofschneider, Julie Delpy. 115M GRM/FRN. *Hitlerjunge Salomon*; *The Lion's Den* prod/rel: Les Films Du Losange (Paris), Filmkunst (Berlin)

PERELMAN, LAURA
All Good Americans, New York 1933, Play
Paris Interlude 1934 d: Edwin L. Marin. lps: Robert Young, Una Merkel, Madge Evans. 73M USA. *All Good Americans* prod/rel: Metro-Goldwyn-Mayer Corp.©
The Night Before Christmas, 1942, Novel
Larceny Inc. 1942 d: Lloyd Bacon. lps: Edward G. Robinson, Jane Wyman, Broderick Crawford. 95M USA. prod/rel: Warner Bros.

PERELMAN, S. J. (1904-1979), USA, Perelman, Sidney Joseph
All Good Americans, New York 1933, Play
Paris Interlude 1934 d: Edwin L. Marin. lps: Robert Young, Una Merkel, Madge Evans. 73M USA. *All Good Americans* prod/rel: Metro-Goldwyn-Mayer Corp.©
The Night Before Christmas, 1942, Novel
Larceny Inc. 1942 d: Lloyd Bacon. lps: Edward G. Robinson, Jane Wyman, Broderick Crawford. 95M USA. prod/rel: Warner Bros.
One Touch of Venus, 1944, Musical Play
One Touch of Venus 1948 d: William A. Seiter. lps: Robert Walker, Ava Gardner, Dick Haymes. 81M USA. prod/rel: Universal

PEREZ DE LA MOTA, ANDRES
Venganza Islena
Venganza Islena 1923 d: Manuel NoriegA. lps: Elisa Ruiz Romero, Felipe Reyes, Francisco OrtegA. 3496m SPN. prod/rel: Atlantida (Madrid)

PEREZ DE ROSAS, J.
La Femme Revee
Femme Revee, La 1929 d: Jean Durand. lps: Arlette Marchal, Alice Roberte, Charles Vanel. 2680m FRN. prod/rel: Franco-Film

PEREZ DE SAAVEDRA, ANGELO
Don Alvaro O la Fuerzo Del Sino, 1835, Play
Forza Del Destino, La 1911. lps: Achille Vitti, Ignazio Mascalchi, Paolo Cantinelli. 415m ITL. prod/rel: Film d'Arte Italiana
Forza Del Destino, La 1950 d: Carmine Gallone. lps: Nelly Corradi, Gino Sinimberghi, Giulio Neri. 87M ITL. *The Force of Destiny* prod/rel: Produzioni Gallone, Union Film

PEREZ ESCRICH, ENRIQUE
El Cura de Aldea, Novel
Cura de Aldea, El 1926 d: Florian Rey. lps: Elisa Ruiz Romero, Marina Torres, Rafael Perez Chaves. 63M SPN. *The Village Priest* prod/rel: Atlantida
El Manuscrito de Una Madre, Story
Manuscrito de Una Madre, El 1928 d: Reinhardt Blothner. lps: Emilio Arne. SPN.

PEREZ GALDOS, BENITO (1843-1920), SPN
El Abuelo, 1897, Novel
Duda, La 1972 d: Rafael Gil. lps: Fernando Rey, Analia Gade, Jose Maria EspinosA. 104M SPN. *The Doubt*
El Abuelo, Novel
Abuelo, El 1998 d: Jose Luis Garci. lps: Fernando Fernan-Gomez, Rafael Alonso, Cayetana Guillen-Cuervo. 147M SPN. *The Grandfather* prod/rel: Nickel Odeon Dos, Rtve
Dona Perfecta, Madrid 1876, Novel
Beauty in Chains 1918 d: Elsie Jane Wilson. lps: Ella Hall, Emory Johnson, Ruby Lafayette. 5r USA. *Dona Perfecta* prod/rel: Universal Film Mfg. Co.©
Fortunata Y Jacinta, 1887, Novel
Fortunata Y Jacinta 1969 d: Angelino Fons. lps: Emma Penella, Liana Orfei, Maximo Valverde. 132M SPN. *Fortunata and Jacinta*
La Loca de la Casa, Play
Loca de la Casa, La 1926 d: Luis R. Alonso. lps: Carmen Viance, Ana de Siria, Manuel San German. SPN. prod/rel: Producciones Hornemann (Madrid)
Marianela, 1878, Novel
Marianela 1940 d: Benito Perojo. lps: Mari Carrillo, Maria Mercader, Julio PenA. 83M SPN.
Marianela 1972 d: Angelino Fons. lps: Rocio Durcal, Pierre Orcel, Jose Suarez. 111M SPN/FRN.
Nazarin, Madrid 1895, Novel
Nazarin 1958 d: Luis Bunuel. lps: Francisco Rabal, Marga Lopez, Rita MacEdo. 94M MXC. prod/rel: Producciones Barbachano Ponce
Tormento, 1884, Novel
Tormento 1974 d: Pedro OleA. lps: Ana Belen, Francisco Rabal, Javier EscrivA. 85M SPN. *Torment*; *Anguish*; *Torture*
Tristana, Madrid 1892, Novel
Tristana 1970 d: Luis Bunuel. lps: Catherine Deneuve, Fernando Rey, Franco Nero. 105M SPN/ITL/FRN. prod/rel: Selenia Cin.Ca, Epoca Films

PEREZ LUGIN, ALEJANDRO
La Casa de la Troya, Madrid 1915, Novel
In Gay Madrid 1930 d: Robert Z. Leonard. lps: Ramon Novarro, Dorothy Jordan, Lottice Howell. 7654f USA. *The House of Troy* prod/rel: Metro-Goldwyn-Mayer Pictures
La Casa de Troya, Novel
Casa de la Troya, La 1924 d: Alejandro Perez Lugin, Manuel NoriegA. lps: Carmen Viance, Luis Pena Sanchez, Juan de OrdunA. 123M SPN. *La Casa de Troya* prod/rel: Troya Film
Currito de la Cruz, Novel
Currito de la Cruz 1925 d: Fernando Delgado, Alejandro Perez Lugin. lps: Elisa Ruiz Romero, Jesus Tordesillas, Antonio Calvache. 5000m SPN. prod/rel: Troya Film (Madrid)

PEREZ-REVERTE, ARTURO
Territorio Comanche, Novel
Territorio Comanche 1997 d: Gerardo Herrero. lps: Imanol Arias, Carmelo Gomez, Cecilia Dopazo. 94M SPN/GRM/FRN. *Comanche Territory* prod/rel: Tornasol Films (Madrid), Road Movies (Berlin)

PERGAUD, LOUIS
La Guerre Des Boutons, Paris 1912, Novel
Guerre Des Gosses, La 1936 d: Jacques Daroy, Eugene Deslaw. lps: Jean Murat, Saturnin Fabre, Claude May. 87M FRN. *Generals Without Buttons* (USA); *La Guerre Des Boutons*; *Nous, Les Gosses* prod/rel: Forrester-Parant Productions, Productions Georges Legrand
Guerre Des Boutons, La 1961 d: Yves Robert. lps: Martin Lartigue, Jean Richard, Yvette Etievant. 90M FRN. *War of the Buttons* (USA) prod/rel: Productions De La Gueville
War of the Buttons, The 1994 d: John Roberts. lps: Liam Cunningham, Gregg Fitzgerald, Colm Meaney. 90M UKN/FRN/IRL. prod/rel: Warner Bros., Enigma

PERGOLESI, GIOVANNI BATTISTA (1710-1736), ITL
La Serva Padrona, Napoli 1733, Opera
Serva Padrona, La 1934 d: Giorgio Mannini. lps: Bruna Dragoni, Vincenzo Bettoni, Enrica Mayer. 62M ITL. prod/rel: Lirica Film, Caesar Film

PERKINS, GRACE
Mike, 1933, Short Story
Torch Singer 1933 d: Alexander Hall, George Somnes. lps: Claudette Colbert, Ricardo Cortez, David Manners. 72M USA. *Broadway Singer* (UKN) prod/rel: Paramount Productions©
No More Orchids, New York 1932, Novel
No More Orchids 1933 d: Walter Lang. lps: Carole Lombard, Lyle Talbot, Walter Connolly. 74M USA. prod/rel: Columbia Pictures Corp.©

Personal Maid, New York 1931, Novel
Personal Maid 1931 d: Lothar Mendes, Monta Bell. lps: Nancy Carroll, Pat O'Brien, Gene Raymond. 77M USA. prod/rel: Paramount Publix Corp.©

PERKINS, KENNETH
The Beloved Brute, New York 1923, Novel
Beloved Brute, The 1924 d: J. Stuart Blackton. lps: Marguerite de La Motte, Victor McLaglen, William Russell. 6719f USA. prod/rel: Vitagraph Co. of America
Better Than a Rodeo, Story
Trail of Courage, The 1928 d: Wallace Fox. lps: Bob Steele, Marjorie Bonner, Thomas Lingham. 4758f USA. prod/rel: Fbo Pictures
Bow Tamely to Me, Story
Escape to Burma 1955 d: Allan Dwan. lps: Barbara Stanwyck, Robert Ryan, David Farrar. 87M USA. prod/rel: RKO, Filmcrest
The Canyon of Light, Novel
Canyon of Light, The 1926 d: Ben Stoloff. lps: Tom Mix, Dorothy Dwan, Carl Miller. 5399f USA. prod/rel: Fox Film Corp.
Desert Voices, 1937, Novel
Desert Pursuit 1952 d: George Blair. lps: Wayne Morris, Virginia Grey, George Tobias. 71M USA. prod/rel: Monogram
The Devil's Saddle, 1926, Short Story
Devil's Saddle, The 1927 d: Albert S. Rogell. lps: Ken Maynard, Kathleen Collins, Francis Ford. 5488f USA. prod/rel: Charles R. Rogers Productions, First National Pictures
The Gun Fanner, New York 1922, Novel
Romance Land 1923 d: Edward Sedgwick. lps: Tom Mix, Barbara Bedford, Frank Brownlee. 4500f USA. prod/rel: Fox Film Corp.
Ride Him Cowboy, New York 1923, Novel
Unknown Cavalier, The 1926 d: Albert S. Rogell. lps: Ken Maynard, Kathleen Collins, David Torrence. 6595f USA. prod/rel: Charles R. Rogers Productions, First National Pictures
Ride Him, Cowboy 1932 d: Fred Allen. lps: John Wayne, Ruth Hall, Henry B. Walthall. 61M USA. *The Hawk* (UKN) prod/rel: Warner Bros. Pictures, Vitagraph, Inc.©
Riding Solo, Short Story
Riding Shotgun 1954 d: Andre de Toth. lps: Randolph Scott, Wayne Morris, Joan Weldon. 75M USA. prod/rel: Warner Bros.
Three Were Thoroughbreds, Story
Relentless 1948 d: George Sherman. lps: Robert Young, Marguerite Chapman, Willard Parker. 93M USA. *Three Were Thoroughbreds* prod/rel: Columbia

PERKONIG, J. F.
Und Ewig Knallen Die Rauber, Novel
..Und Ewig Knallen Die Rauber 1962 d: Franz Antel. lps: Helmut Lohner, Paul Horbiger, Georg ThomallA. 103M AUS. prod/rel: Neue Delta, Art

PEROCHON, ERNEST
Nene, Novel
Nene 1923 d: Jacques de Baroncelli. lps: Edmond Van Daele, Sandra Milowanoff, Francois Viguier. F FRN. prod/rel: Baroncelli Films

PEROUTKA, VLADIMIR
Nevideli Jste Bobika?, Novel
Nevideli Jste Bobika? 1944 d: Vladimir Slavinsky. lps: Zdenka Baldova, Jarmila Smejkalova, Meda ValentovA. 2401m CZC. *Have You Seen Bobik?* prod/rel: Lucernafilm

PERRAULT, CHARLES (1628-1703), FRN
Barbe-Bleue, 1697, Short Story
Barbe-Bleue 1951 d: Christian-Jaque. lps: Cecile Aubrey, Pierre Brasseur, Jacques Sernas. 99M FRN/GRM. *Blaubart* (GRM); *Bluebeard* (USA) prod/rel: Alcina, P.-E. Decharme
Bluebeard 1909 d: J. Searle Dawley. lps: Charles Ogle, Mary Fuller. 400f USA.
La Belle Au Bois Dormant, 1697, Short Story
Hier Et Aujourd'hui 1918 d: Bernard-Deschamps. lps: Henry Houry, Max Charlier, Lilian Greuze. 1050m FRN. prod/rel: Scagl
La Belle Au Bois Dormant, 1697, Ss
Sleeping Beauty 1959 d: Clyde Geronimi. ANM. 75M USA. prod/rel: Buena Vista, Walt Disney Prods.
La Belle Au Bois Dormant, 1697, Short Story
Sleeping Beauty 1983 d: Jeremy Paul Kagan. lps: Beverly d'Angelo, Christopher Reeve, Bernadette Peters. MTV. USA.
Sleeping Beauty 1987 d: David Irving. lps: Morgan Fairchild, Tahnee Welch, Sylvia Miles. 83M USA/ISR. *Cannon Movie Tales: Sleeping Beauty* prod/rel: Cannon

PETEANI, MARIA
Der Page Vom Dalmasse-Hotel, Novel
Page Vom Dalmasse-Hotel, Der 1933 d: Victor Janson. lps: Dolly Haas, Harry Liedtke, Hans Junkermann. 91M GRM. prod/rel: Schulz & Wuellner Filmfabrikation
Page Vom Palast-Hotel, Der 1957 d: Thomas Engel. lps: Erika Remberg, Rudolf Prack, Mady Rahl. 95M AUS. prod/rel: Donau, N.F.

PETER, RENE
La Grande Vedette, Play
Grande Vedette, La 1917 d: Edouard-Emile Violet. lps: Mangin, Fred Zorilla, Rachel Devirys. 1120m FRN. prod/rel: Acad
Naughty Cinderella, New York 1925, Play
Good and Naughty 1926 d: Malcolm St. Clair. lps: Pola Negri, Tom Moore, Ford Sterling. 5503f USA. prod/rel: Famous Players-Lasky, Paramount Pictures
Pouche Cinderella, Paris 1923, Play
This Is the Night 1932 d: Frank Tuttle. lps: Lili Damita, Charles Ruggles, Roland Young. 80M USA. *He Met a French Girl; Pouche; Temporary Fiancee* prod/rel: Paramount Publix Corp.

PETERS, ELLIS (1913–, UKN, Pargeter, Edith Mary Story
Cadfael: Monks Hood 1994 d: Graham Theakston. lps: Derek Jacobi, Sean Pertwee, Peter Copley. MTV. 75M UKN.
Leper of St. Giles, Novel
Cadfael: the Leper of St. Giles 1994 d: Graham Theakston. lps: Derek Jacobi, Sean Pertwee, Peter Copley. MTV. 75M UKN.
One Corpse Too Many, Novel
Cadfael: One Corpse Too Many 1993 d: Graham Theakston. lps: Derek Jacobi, Sean Pertwee, Michael Culver. MTV. 75M UKN.
The Sanctuary Sparrow, Novel
Cadfael: the Sanctuary Sparrow 1994 d: Graham Theakston. lps: Derek Jacobi, Sean Pertwee, Roy Barraclough. MTV. 75M UKN.

PETERS, STEPHEN
The Park Is Mine, Novel
Park Is Mine, The 1985 d: Steven Hilliard Stern. lps: Tommy Lee Jones, Helen Shaver, Yaphet Kotto. TVM. 101M CND. prod/rel: Hbo, Astral Film Enterprises Inc. (Montreal)

PETERSEN, LEIF
Alting Og Et Postnus, 1969, Play
Det Er Nat Med Fru Knudsen 1971 d: Henning Ornbak. lps: Tove Maes, Birger Jensen, Ole Ernst. 89M DNM. *It's All Up With Auntie; Mrs. Knudsen, Down and Out*

PETERSON, JON
Novel
Here Come the Littles 1985 d: Bernard Deyries. ANM. 73M LXM. *Here Comes the Littles*

PETERSON, LOUIS S.
Take a Giant Step, 1954, Play
Take a Giant Step 1959 d: Philip Leacock. lps: Johnny Nash, Estelle Hemsley, Ruby Dee. 99M USA. prod/rel: United Artists, Sheila Prods.

PETERSON, MARGARET
Dust of Desire, New York 1922, Novel
Song of Love, The 1923 d: Chester M. Franklin, Frances Marion. lps: Norma Talmadge, Joseph Schildkraut, Arthur Edmund Carewe. 8000f USA. *Dust of Desire* prod/rel: Norma Talmadge Productions, Associated First National Pictures

PETERSON, RALPH
The Square Ring, Play
Square Ring, The 1953 d: Basil Dearden, Michael Relph. lps: Jack Warner, Robert Beatty, Maxwell Reed. 83M UKN. prod/rel: Ealing Studios, General Film Distributors

PETIEVICH, GERALD
Money Men, Novel
Boiling Point 1993 d: James B. Harris. lps: Wesley Snipes, Dennis Hopper, Lolita Davidovich. 92M USA. prod/rel: Warner Bros., Hexagon
To Live and Die in L.a., Novel
To Live and Die in L.a. 1985 d: William Friedkin. lps: William L. Petersen, Willem Dafoe, John Pankow. 116M USA. prod/rel: MGM, United Artists

PETIT DE MURAT, ULISES
Pampa Barbara
Pampa Salvaje 1966 d: Hugo Fregonese. lps: Robert Taylor, Marc Lawrence, Ron Randell. 112M SPN/USA/ARG. *Savage Pampas* (USA) prod/rel: Samuel Bronston Productions, Dasa Films

PETOFI, SANDOR
Janos Vitez, 1845, Verse
Janos Vitez 1973 d: Marcell Jankovics. ANM. 81M HNG. *Johnnie Corncob; Childe John* prod/rel: Pannonia Film

PETRAKIS, HARRY MARK
A Dream of Kings, New York 1966, Novel
Dream of Kings, A 1969 d: Daniel Mann. lps: Anthony Quinn, Irene Papas, Inger Stevens. 110M USA. prod/rel: National General Productions

PETRESCU, CAMIL
Jocul Ielelor, 1947, Play
Cei Care Platesc Cu Viata 1989 d: Serban Marinescu. 98M RMN. *Those Who Pay With Their Lives*
Mitica Popescu, 1928, Play
Mitica Popescu 1984 d: Manole Marcus. lps: Remus Margineau, Mihaela Caracas, Mircea JidA. 91M RMN.
Ultima Noapte de Dragoste, Intiia Noapte de Razbol, 1930, Novel
Intre Oglinzi Paralele 1978 d: Mircea Veroiu. 100M RMN. *Between Opposite Mirrors; Between Parallel Mirrors; Between Facing Mirrors*
Ultima Noapte de Dragoste 1979 d: Sergiu Nicolaescu. lps: Sergiu Nicolaescu. 91M RMN. *The Last Night of Love*

PETRESCU, CEZAR
Calea Victoriei, 1932, Novel
Calea Victoriei Sau Cheia Visurilor 1966 d: Marius Teodorescu. lps: George Calboreanu. 104M RMN. *Victory Boulevard, Or the Key of Dreams*
Fram, Ursul Polar, 1932, Novel
Saltimbancii 1981 d: Elisabeta Bostan. lps: Carmen Galin, Octavian Cotescu, Gina Patrichi. 110M RMN/USS. *Etot Grustnyj Veselyj Cirk* (USS); *Circus Performers; The Clowns; The Jugglers*
Un Saltimbanc la Polul Nord 1982 d: Elisabeta Bostan. 96M RMN/USS. *Klouny Na Severnom Poljuse* (USS); *Circus Performers at the North Pole*
Intunecare, 1927-28, Novel
Intunecare 1985 d: Alexandru Tatos. 99M RMN. *Gathering Clouds*
Omul Din Vis, 1926, Short Story
Glissando 1985 d: Mircea Daneliuc. lps: Ion Fiscuteanu, Stefan Iordache, Tora Vasilescu. 167M RMN.

PETRICCIONE, DIEGO
'O Quatto 'E Maggio, Play
Non Mi Muovo! 1943 d: Giorgio C. Simonelli. lps: Eduardo de Filippo, Peppino de Filippo, Titina de Filippo. 75M ITL. prod/rel: Cines, Juventus

PETRIE, AL
Tom Dollar, Novel
Tom Dollar 1967 d: Marcello Ciorciolini. lps: Maurice Poli, Georgia Moll, Erika Blanc. 90M ITL/FRN. prod/rel: Tigielle 33 (Roma), Les Films Jacques Leitienne

PETRINI, WANDA
Short Story
Sette Nani Alla Riscossa, I 1952 d: Paolo William TamburellA. lps: Rossana Podesta, Roberto Risso, Georges Marchal. 103M ITL. *The Seven Dwarfs to the Rescue* (USA) prod/rel: P.W.T. Produzione Film

PETRONIUS ARBITER
Satyricon, c50-66 A.D., Novel
Satyricon 1968 d: Gian Luigi Polidoro. lps: Tina Aumont, Don Backy, Franco Fabrizi. 110M ITL. prod/rel: Arco Film, Cineriz
Satyricon, c50-66 A.D., Manus
Fellini-Satyricon 1969 d: Federico Fellini. lps: Martin Potter, Hiram Keller, Salvo Randone. 136M ITL/FRN. *Satyricon* prod/rel: P.E.a., Les Productions Artistes Associes

PETROV, EVGENY (1902–1942), RSS, Katayev, Yevgeni Petrovich
Dvenadtsat Stulyev, Moscow 1928, Novel
Dvanact Kresel 1933 d: Martin Fric, Michael Waszynski. lps: Vlasta Burian, Adolf Dymsza, Zula PogorzelskA. 1838m CZC/PLN. *Dwanascie Krzesel* (PLN); *Twelve Armchairs* prod/rel: Terra, Rex-Film Varsava
Keep Your Seats Please 1936 d: Monty Banks. lps: George Formby, Florence Desmond, Gus McNaughton. 82M UKN. prod/rel: Associated Talking Pictures, Associated British Film Distributors
Dreizehn Stuhle 1938 d: E. W. Emo. lps: Heinz Ruhmann, Hans Moser, Annie Rosar. 87M GRM. *13 Stuhle* prod/rel: Emo-Film
It's in the Bag 1945 d: Richard Wallace. lps: Fred Allen, Jack Benny, William Bendix. 87M USA. *The Fifth Chair* (UKN) prod/rel: United Artists

Gluck Liegt Auf Der Strasse, Das 1957 d: Franz Antel. lps: Walter Giller, Georg Thomalla, Doris Kirchner. 93M GRM. *13 Stuhle; Thirteen Chairs* prod/rel: Rhombus, UFA
Doce Sillas, Los 1962 d: Tomas Gutierrez AleA. lps: Enrique Santiesteban, Reynaldo Miravalles, Rene Sanchez. 90M CUB. *The Twelve Chairs*
Una Su Tredici 1969 d: Nicolas Gessner, Luciano Lucignani. lps: Vittorio Gassman, Sharon Tate, Orson Welles. 100M ITL/FRN. *12 + 1* (FRN); *Twelve Plus One* (USA); *Lucky 13; 13 Chairs; Una Su 13* prod/rel: Compagnia Cin.Ca Finanziaria (Roma), Comptoir Francais Prod. Cin.Que (Paris)
Twelve Chairs, The 1970 d: Mel Brooks. lps: Mel Brooks, Ron Moody, Frank LangellA. 94M USA. prod/rel: Twelve Chairs Co.
Dvinatsat Stulyev 1971 d: Leonid Gaidai. lps: Leonid Gaidai, Archil Gomiashvili, Sergey Filippov. F USS. *The Twelve Chairs; Dvenadtstat Stulyev; Dvenadcat Stulev*
Zolotoy Telyonok, 1931, Novel
Mechty Idiota 1993 d: Vasily Pichul. lps: Sergej Krylov, Andrej Smirnov, Alika SmekhovA. 90M RSS/FRN. *Dreams of an Idiot* prod/rel: Ttl, Salome
Zolotoy Telyonok 1968 d: Mikhail Schweitzer. lps: Sergey Yursky, Leonid Kuravlyov, Zinovij Gerdt. 174M USS. *The Golden Calf; Zolotoj Telenok*

PETTIT, ETHEL
The Rich are Always With Us, New York 1931, Novel
Rich are Always With Us, The 1932 d: Alfred E. Green. lps: Ruth Chatterton, Adrienne Dore, George Brent. 75M USA. prod/rel: First National Pictures©

PETTIT, WILLIAM H.
Nine Girls, Play
Nine Girls 1944 d: Leigh Jason. lps: Ann Harding, Evelyn Keyes, Jinx Falkenburg. 78M USA. prod/rel: Columbia

PETTITT, HENRY
The Harbour Lights, London 1885, Play
Harbour Lights, The 1914 d: Percy Nash. lps: Gerald Lawrence, Mercy Hatton, Daisy Cordell. 3275f UKN. prod/rel: Neptune, Globe
Harbour Lights, The 1923 d: Tom Terriss. lps: Tom Moore, Isobel Elsom, Gerald McCarthy. 5877f UKN. prod/rel: Ideal
In the Ranks, London 1883, Play
In the Ranks 1914 d: Percy Nash. lps: Gregory Scott, Daisy Cordell, James Lindsay. 3945f UKN. prod/rel: Neptune, Jury
Master and Man, London 1889, Play
Master and Man 1915 d: Percy Nash. lps: Gregory Scott, Joan Ritz, Douglas Payne. 3612f UKN. prod/rel: Neptune, Walturdaw

PETTUS, MAUDE
A Gentle Ill Wind, 1916, Short Story
Edge of the Law, The 1917 d: Louis W. Chaudet. lps: Ruth Stonehouse, Lloyd Whitlock, Lydia Yeamans Titus. 5r USA. prod/rel: Universal Film Mfg. Co.©, Butterfly Picture

PEVERELLI, LUCIANA
Story
Principessa Del Sogno, La 1942 d: Roberto Savarese, Maria Teresa Ricci. lps: Irasema Dilian, Antonio Centa, Maria Melato. 85M ITL. prod/rel: Fono-Roma, Artisti Associati
Il Bacio Dell'Aurora, Novel
Francois Il Contrabbandiere 1954 d: Gianfranco Parolini. lps: Doris Duranti, Roberto Mauri, Vira Silenti. F ITL. *Il Bacio Dell'aurora* prod/rel: Marte Film
Violette Nei Capelli, Novel
Violette Nei Capelli 1942 d: Carlo Ludovico BragagliA. lps: Lilia Silvi, Irasema Dilian, Carla Del Poggio. 85M ITL. prod/rel: Fono Roma, Lux Film

PEVSNER, STELLA
A Smart Kid Like You, Novel
Me & Dad's New Wife 1976 d: Larry Elikann. lps: Kristy McNichol, Lance Kerwin, Leif Garrett. TVM. 50M USA.

PEYDRO, V.
Carceleras, Opera
Carceleras 1922 d: Jose Buchs. lps: Elisa Ruiz Romero, Jose Romeu, Jose Montenegro. 2170m SPN. *Convicts' Song* prod/rel: Atlantida

PEYNET, RAYMOND
Il Giro Del Mondo Degli Innamorati Di Peynet, Book
Giro Del Mondo Degli Innamorati Di Peynet, Il 1974 d: Cesare Perfetto. ANM. 88M ITL. *Two Lovers Around the World* prod/rel: N.O.C., I.N.C.

PEYRE MANDARGUES, ANDRE
Violentata Sulla Sabbia, Novel
  Violentata Sulla Sabbia 1971 d: Renzo Cerrato. lps: Carole Andre, Angelo Infanti, Kiki Caron. 86M ITL/FRN. prod/rel: Milvia Cin.Ca (Roma), Comacico (Paris)

PEYRE, JOSEPH
L'escadron Blanc, Novel
  Squadrone Bianco 1936 d: Augusto GeninA. lps: Fulvia Lanzi, Francesca Dalpe, Fosco Giachetti. 96M ITL. *The White Squadron* prod/rel: Roma Film
Sang Et Lumiere, Novel
  Sang Et Lumiere 1954 d: Georges Rouquier, Ricardo Munoz Suay. lps: Daniel Gelin, Zsa Zsa Gabor, Henri Vilbert. 100M FRN/SPN. *Love in a Hot Climate* (USA); *Beauty and the Bullfighter*; *Sangre Y Luces* (SPN) prod/rel: Cite Films, Cocinor

PEYREFITTE, ROGER (1907–, FRN
Les Amities Particulieres, Paris 1945, Novel
  Amities Particulieres, Les 1964 d: Jean Delannoy. lps: Francis Lacombrade, Didier Haudepin, Lucien Nat. 102M FRN. *This Special Friendship* (USA) prod/rel: Pro Ge Fi, C.C.F.
La Maitresse de Piano, 1949, Short Story
  Ritratto Di Borghesia in Nero 1978 d: Tonino Cervi. lps: Ornella Muti, Senta Berger, Capucine. 105M ITL. *Nest of Vipers* (UKN); *Portrait of a Bourgeois in Black* prod/rel: Mars Film Produzione, C.I.C.

PEYTON, K. M.
Novel
  Flambards 1980 d: Lawrence Gordon Clark, Michael Ferguson. lps: Christine McKenna, Edward Judd, Steven Grives. MTV. 676M UKN.
A Pattern of Roses, Novel
  Pattern of Roses, A 1983 d: Lawrence Gordon Clark. lps: Stuart MacKenzie, Jo Searby, Suzanna Hamilton. 75M UKN/GRM. *Es Geschah Am See* (GRM)

PEYTON, KATHLEEN
The Right Hand Man, Novel
  Right Hand Man, The 1986 d: Di Drew. lps: Rupert Everett, Hugo Weaving, Catherine McClements. 97M ASL. *The Right-Hand Man* prod/rel: Uaa (Australasia) Ltd.©, Yarraman Film Production

PEZET, WASHINGTON
Marrying Money, New York 1914, Play
  Marrying Money 1915 d: James Young. lps: Clara Kimball Young, Chester Barnett, William Jefferson. 5r USA. *Marriage a la Carte* prod/rel: World Film Corp.©, Shubert Feature

PEZZANA, ELISA
La Casa Maledetta, Play
  Crimine a Due 1965 d: Romano FerrarA. lps: John Drew Barrymore, Luisa Rivelli, Lisa Gastoni. 90M ITL. *La Casa Sulla Fungaia* prod/rel: Eco Film, Italo American Film

PFALZGRAF, FLORENCE LEIGHTON
Heaven's Gate, 1934, Short Story
  Our Little Girl 1935 d: John S. Robertson. lps: Shirley Temple, Rosemary Ames, Joel McCreA. 65M USA. *Heaven's Gate* prod/rel: Fox Film Corp.©

PHADKE, N. S.
Jeevan Yatra, Novel
  Jeevan Yatra 1946 d: Winayak. lps: Nayantara, Pratima Devi, Lata Mangeshkar. 134M IND. *The Journey of Life* prod/rel: Rajkamal Kalamandir

PHELAN, JIM
Tenapenny People, Novel
  Night Journey 1938 d: Oswald Mitchell. lps: Geoffrey Toone, Patricia Hilliard, Alf Goddard. 76M UKN. prod/rel: British National, Butcher's Film Service

PHELPS, ELIZABETH STUART
The Madonna of the Tubs, Story
  Pull for the Shore, Sailor 1911. lps: Laura Sawyer, James Gordon, Edna May Weick. 1000f USA. prod/rel: Edison

PHELPS, PAULINE
The Girl from Out Yonder, Baltimore 1914, Play
  Out Yonder 1920 d: Ralph Ince. lps: Olive Thomas, Huntley Gordon, Mary Coverdale. 5-6r USA. prod/rel: Selznick Pictures Corp.©, Select Pictures Corp.

PHILBRICK, RODMAN
Freak the Mighty, Novel
  Mighty, The 1998 d: Peter Chelsom. lps: Sharon Stone, Elden Henson, Kieran Culkin. 100M USA. prod/rel: Miramax Film Corp.©, Scholastic/Simon Fields

PHILIP, ALEXANDER
The Crimson West, Novel
  Crimson Paradise, The 1933 d: Robert F. Hill. lps: Nick Stuart, Lucille Browne, Kathleen Dunsmuir. 68M CND. *Fighting Playboy* (USA) prod/rel: Commonwealth Productions Ltd.

PHILIPP, ADOLF
The Corner Grocery, New York 1894, Play
  Corner Grocer, The 1917 d: George Cowl. lps: Lew Fields, Madge Evans, Lillian Cook. 5r USA. *The Corner Grocery* prod/rel: World Film Corp.©, Peerless

PHILIPPE, CHARLES L.
Bubu Di Montparnasse, Novel
  Bubu 1971 d: Mauro Bolognini. lps: Massimo Ranieri, Ottavia Piccolo, Antonio Falsi. 115M ITL. *Bubu Di Montparnasse* prod/rel: B.R.C. Produzioni, Euro International Film

PHILIPPI, ERIC
Story
  Secret of the Blue Room 1933 d: Kurt Neumann. lps: Lionel Atwill, Gloria Stuart, Paul Lukas. 66M USA. *Secrets of the Blue Room* prod/rel: Universal Pictures Corp.©
  Missing Guest, The 1938 d: John Rawlins. lps: Paul Kelly, Constance Moore, William Lundigan. 68M USA. prod/rel: Universal Pictures Co.©
  Murder in the Blue Room 1944 d: Leslie Goodwins. lps: Anne Gwynne, Donald Cook, John Litel. 61M USA. prod/rel: Universal

PHILIPPI, FELIX
Das Erbe, Play
  Erbe, Das 1913. GRM. prod/rel: Deutsche Mutoskop Und Biograph

PHILIPS, FRANCIS CHARLES
As in a Looking Glass, New York 1887, Novel
  As in a Looking Glass 1916 d: Frank H. Crane. lps: Kitty Gordon, F. Lumsden Hare, Frank Goldsmith. 5r USA. prod/rel: World Film Corp.©

PHILLIPS, AUSTIN
The Acid Test, Short Story
  Acid Test, The 1924 d: Sinclair Hill. lps: Eric Bransby Williams, Betty Faire, Eric Hardin. 1798f UKN. prod/rel: Stoll
One Colombo Night, Novel
  One Colombo Night 1926 d: Henry Edwards. lps: Godfrey Tearle, Marjorie Hume, Nora Swinburne. 4475f UKN. *A Colombo Night* prod/rel: Stoll

PHILLIPS, CLAIRE
Manila Espionage, Book
  I Was an American Spy 1951 d: Lesley Selander. lps: Ann Dvorak, Gene Evans, Douglas Kennedy. 85M USA. prod/rel: Allied Artists

PHILLIPS, DAVID GRAHAM (1867–1911), USA, Graham, John
Novel
  Don't Change Your Husband 1919 d: Cecil B. de Mille. lps: Elliott Dexter, Gloria Swanson, Lew Cody. 5r USA. prod/rel: Famous Players-Lasky Corp.©, Artcraft Pictures
The Cost, Indianapolis 1904, Novel
  Cost, The 1920 d: Harley Knoles. lps: Violet Heming, Ralph Kellard, Edward Arnold. 6r USA. prod/rel: Famous Players-Lasky Corp.©, Paramount-Artcraft Pictures
Garlan & Co., Story
  Souls for Sables 1925 d: James C. McKay. lps: Claire Windsor, Eugene O'Brien, Claire Adams. 6500f USA. prod/rel: Tiffany Productions
The Grain of Dust, New York 1911, Novel
  Grain of Dust, A 1915 d: Lloyd B. Carleton. lps: Robert Edeson, Claire Whitney, Byron Douglas. SHT USA. prod/rel: Box Office Attractions
  Grain of Dust, The 1918 d: Harry Revier. lps: Lillian Walker, Ramsey Wallace, Ralph Delmore. 6r USA. *Grain of Dust, A* prod/rel: Ogden Pictures Corp., State Rights
  Grain of Dust, The 1928 d: George Archainbaud. lps: Ricardo Cortez, Claire Windsor, Alma Bennett. 6126f USA. prod/rel: Tiffany-Stahl Productions
The Hungry Heart, New York 1909, Novel
  Hungry Heart, The 1917 d: Robert G. VignolA. lps: Pauline Frederick, Robert Cain, Howard Hall. 5r USA. prod/rel: Famous Players Film Co.©, Paramount Pictures Corp.
Old Wives for New, New York 1908, Novel
  Old Wives for New 1918 d: Cecil B. de Mille. lps: Elliott Dexter, Florence Vidor, Sylvia Ashton. 6r USA. prod/rel: Famous Players-Lasky Corp.©, Artcraft Pictures
The Price She Paid, New York 1912, Novel
  Price She Paid, The 1917 d: Charles Giblyn. lps: Clara Kimball Young, David Powell, Alan Hale. 7r USA. prod/rel: Clara Kimball Young Film Corp.©, Lewis J. Selznick Enterprises
  Price She Paid, The 1924 d: Henry McRae. lps: Alma Rubens, Frank Mayo, Eugenie Besserer. 5957f USA. prod/rel: Columbia Pictures, C. B. C. Film Sales

Susan Lennox, Her Fall and Rise, New York 1917, Novel
  Susan Lenox (Her Fall and Rise) 1931 d: Robert Z. Leonard. lps: Greta Garbo, Clark Gable, Jean Hersholt. 75M USA. *Rise of Helga, The* (UKN); *Susan Lenox*; *Suzanne Lenox*; *Rising to Fame* prod/rel: Metro-Goldwyn-Mayer Corp., Metro-Goldwyn-Mayer Dist. Corp.©

PHILLIPS, GORDON
I'm an Explosive, Novel
  I'm an Explosive 1933 d: Adrian Brunel. lps: William Hartnell, Gladys Jennings, Eliot Makeham. 50M UKN. prod/rel: George Smith Productions, Fox

PHILLIPS, HENRY ALBERT
The Princess from the Poorhouse, Short Story
  Royal Pauper, The 1917 d: Ben Turbett. lps: Francine Larrimore, Herbert Prior, Charles Sutton. 5211f USA. *The Princess from the Poorhouse* prod/rel: Thomas A. Edison, Inc., K-E-S-E Service

PHILLIPS, HENRY WALLACE
Red Saunders Stories, 1902-06, Short Stories
  By Proxy 1918 d: Cliff Smith. lps: Roy Stewart, Maude Wayne, Walter Perry. 5r USA. prod/rel: Triangle Film Corp., Triangle Distributing Corp.
Red-Haired Cupid, 1901, Short Story
  Red-Haired Cupid, The 1918 d: Cliff Smith. lps: Roy Stewart, Charles Dorian, Peggy Pearce. 5r USA. *The Red-Headed Cupid* prod/rel: Triangle Film Corp., Triangle Distributing Corp.

PHILLIPS, MICKEY
Pick Up Sticks, Novel
  Cherry Picker, The 1973 d: Peter Curran. lps: Lulu, Bob Sherman, Spike Milligan. 92M UKN. prod/rel: Fox-Rank, Elsinore

PHILLIPS, MIKE
Blood Rights, Novel
  Blood Rights 1990 d: Lesley Manning. lps: Brian Bovell, Maggie Steed, Struan Rodger. TVM. 165M UKN. prod/rel: BBC

PHILLIPS, WATTS
The Dead Heart, London 1859, Play
  Dead Heart, The 1914 d: Hay Plumb. lps: Alice de Winton, Lionelle Howard, Harry Gilbey. 3225f UKN. prod/rel: Hepworth, Walturdaw

PHILPOTTS, ADELAIDE
Yellow Sands, London 1926, Play
  Yellow Sands 1938 d: Herbert Brenon. lps: Marie Tempest, Belle Chrystal, Wilfred Lawson. 68M UKN. prod/rel: Associated British Picture Corporation

PHILPOTTS, EDEN (1862–1960), UKN
The American Prisoner, Play
  American Prisoner, The 1929 d: Thomas Bentley. lps: Carl Brisson, Madeleine Carroll, Cecil Barry. 75M UKN. prod/rel: British International Pictures, Wardour
The Farmer's Wife, London 1924, Play
  Farmer's Wife, The 1928 d: Alfred Hitchcock. lps: Jameson Thomas, Lillian Hall-Davis, Gordon Harker. 8875f UKN. prod/rel: British International Pictures, Wardour
  Farmer's Wife, The 1941 d: Norman Lee, Leslie Arliss. lps: Basil Sydney, Wilfred Lawson, Nora Swinburne. 82M UKN. prod/rel: Associated British Picture Corporation, Pathe
The Forest on the Hill, Novel
  Forest on the Hill, The 1919 d: Cecil M. Hepworth. lps: Alma Taylor, James Carew, Gerald Ames. 6298f UKN. prod/rel: Hepworth, Butcher's Film Service
The Haven, Novel
  Night Hawk, The 1921 d: John Gliddon. lps: Henri de Vries, Malvina Longfellow, Sydney Seaward. 5000f UKN. prod/rel: International Artists, Anchor
The Mother of Dartmoor, Novel
  Mother of Dartmoor, The 1916 d: George Loane Tucker. lps: Elisabeth Risdon, Bertram Burleigh, Enid Bell. 5500f UKN. prod/rel: London, Jury
The Mother, Novel
  Mother's Influence, A 1916 d: George Loane Tucker. lps: Elisabeth Risdon, Bertram Burleigh, Enid Bell. 2500f UKN. prod/rel: London, Jury
The Secret Woman, Novel
  Secret Woman, The 1918 d: A. E. Coleby. lps: Maud Yates, Janet Alexander, Henry Victor. 6297f UKN. prod/rel: I. B. Davidson, Tiger
Widecombe Fair, Novel
  Widecombe Fair 1928 d: Norman Walker. lps: William Freshman, Marguerite Allan, Wyndham Standing. 6418f UKN. *Widdicombe Fair* prod/rel: British International Pictures, Wardour
Yellow Sands, London 1926, Play
  Yellow Sands 1938 d: Herbert Brenon. lps: Marie Tempest, Belle Chrystal, Wilfred Lawson. 68M UKN. prod/rel: Associated British Picture Corporation

PIANTADOSI, AL
I Didn't Raise My Boy to Be a Soldier, 1915, Song
   I'm Glad My Boy Grew Up to Be a Soldier 1915 d: Frank Beal. lps: Harry Mestayer, Eugenie Besserer, Harry de Vere. 4r USA. *I Didn't Raise My Boy to Be a Soldier* prod/rel: Selig Polyscope Co.©

PIASEKI, SERGIUSZ
L'amante Dell'Orsa Maggiore, Novel
   Amante Dell'orsa Maggiore, L' 1971 d: Valentino Orsini. lps: Giuliano Gemma, Senta Berger, Bruno Cremer. 113M ITL/GRM/FRN. *Der Geliebte de Grossen Barin* (GRM); *Smugglers*; *The Lover of the Great Bear*; *The Bear Lady's Lover* prod/rel: Sancrosiap, Terza Film (Roma)

PIATTI, BRUNO
La Parmigiana, Novel
   Parmigiana, La 1963 d: Antonio Pietrangeli. lps: Catherine Spaak, Nino Manfredi, Didi Perego. 131M ITL. *The Girl from Parma* prod/rel: Documento Film, de Laurentiis

PIAVE, FRANCESCO M. (1810–1876), ITL
Rigoletto, Venice 1851, Opera
   Rigoletto 1947 d: Carmine Gallone. lps: Tito Gobbi, Maria Fillipeschi, Lina Pagliughi. F ITL. prod/rel: Excelsa Film, Minerva Film
   Rigoletto E la Sua Tragedia 1956 d: Flavio CalzavarA. lps: Aldo Silvani, Janet Vidor, Gerard Landry. 85M ITL. *Rigoletto* prod/rel: Diva Film
La Traviata, Venice 1853, Opera
   Traviata, La 1922 d: Challis Sanderson. lps: Thelma Murray, Clive Brook. 1274f UKN. prod/rel: Master Films, Gaumont
   Traviata, La 1927 d: H. B. Parkinson. lps: Anthony Ireland, Peggy Carlisle, Booth Conway. 1605f UKN. prod/rel: Song Films
   Traviata, La 1967 d: Mario Lanfranchi. lps: Anna Moffo, Gino Bechi, Franco Bonisolli. 90M ITL. prod/rel: B.L. Vision, I.C.I.T
   Traviata, La 1982 d: Franco Zeffirelli. lps: Teresa Stratas, Placido Domingo, Cornell MacNeil. 112M ITL. prod/rel: Accent, Rai

PICARD, ANDRE
L'homme En Habit, Paris 1922, Play
   Homme En Habit, Un 1931 d: Rene Guissart, Robert Bossis. lps: Fernand Gravey, Pierre Etchepare, DianA. 88M FRN. prod/rel: Films Paramount
   Evening Clothes 1927 d: Luther Reed. lps: Adolphe Menjou, Virginia Valli, Noah Beery. 6287f USA. prod/rel: Famous Players-Lasky, Paramount Pictures
Kiki, Paris 1920, Play
   Kiki 1926 d: Clarence Brown. lps: Norma Talmadge, Ronald Colman, Gertrude Astor. 8279f USA. prod/rel: Norma Talmadge Productions, First National Pictures
   Kiki 1931 d: Sam Taylor. lps: Mary Pickford, Reginald Denny, Margaret Livingston. 96M USA. prod/rel: United Artists Corp, Feature Productions©
   Kiki 1932 d: Carl Lamac. lps: Anny Ondra, Hermann Thimig, Berthe Ostyn. F GRM.
   Kiki 1932 d: Pierre Billon, Carl Lamac. lps: Anny Ondra, Daniele Bregis, Pierre Richard-Willm. 85M FRN. prod/rel: Ondra-Lamac-Film
   Kiki 1934 d: Raffaello Matarazzo. lps: Lotte Menas, Nino Besozzi, Arturo Falconi. 67M ITL. prod/rel: Industrie Cin.Che Italiana
Mon Homme, Paris 1921, Play
   Shadows of Paris 1924 d: Herbert Brenon. lps: Pola Negri, Charles de Roche, Huntley Gordon. 6549f USA. prod/rel: Famous Players-Lasky, Paramount Pictures

PICKETT, GEORGE
The Silent House, London 1927, Play
   Silent House, The 1929 d: Walter Forde. lps: Mabel Poulton, Gibb McLaughlin, Arthur Pusey. SIL. 9376f UKN. prod/rel: Nettlefold, Butcher's Film Service

PIDGIN, CHARLES FELTON
Quincy Adams Sawyer and Mason's Corner Folks, Boston 1900, Novel
   Quincy Adams Sawyer 1922 d: Clarence Badger. lps: John Bowers, Blanche Sweet, Lon Chaney. 7895f USA. prod/rel: Sawyer-Lubin Productions, Metro Pictures

PIELMEIER, JOHN
Agnes of God, Play
   Agnes of God 1985 d: Norman Jewison. lps: Jane Fonda, Meg Tilly, Anne Bancroft. 98M CND/USA. prod/rel: Columbia-Delphi IV Productions, Albion Films Ltd. (Toronto)

PIERAZZI, RINA MARIA
Inutile Attesa, Novel
   Inutile Attesa 1919 d: Vittorio Tettoni. lps: Lucy Di San Germano, Eugenia Tettoni, Erminia Farnese. 1360m ITL. *Duchessa Di Montefiore, La* prod/rel: Audax Film

PIERCE, FRANK RICHARDSON
The Miracle Baby, 1921, Short Story
   Miracle Baby, The 1923 d: Val Paul. lps: Harry Carey, Margaret Landis, Charles J. L. Mayne. 6336f USA. prod/rel: R-C Pictures, Film Booking Offices of America
   Renegades of the West 1932 d: Casey Robinson. lps: Tom Keene, Betty Furness, Roscoe Ates. 75M USA. prod/rel: RKO Radio Pictures

PIEREGHIN, MARIO
La Guerriera Nera, Short Story
   Putiferio Va Alla Guerra 1968 d: Roberto Gavioli. ANM. 91M ITL. *The Magic Bird* (USA); *Putiferio Goes to War*; *La Piu Piccola Guerra Del Mondo* prod/rel: Gamma Film, Rizzoli Film

PIERSALL, JIMMY
Fear Strikes Out, Autobiography
   Fear Strikes Out 1957 d: Robert Mulligan. lps: Anthony Perkins, Karl Malden, Norma Moore. 100M USA. *The Jim Piersall Story* prod/rel: Paramount

PIERSON, LOUISE RANDALL
Roughly Speaking, Book
   Roughly Speaking 1945 d: Michael Curtiz. lps: Rosalind Russell, Jack Carson, Robert Hutton. 117M USA. prod/rel: Warner Bros.

PIERSON, RANDELL
The Queen of Mean, Book
   Leona Helmsley: the Queen of Mean 1990 d: Richard Michaels. lps: Suzanne Pleshette, Lloyd Bridges, Joe Regalbuto. TVM. 100M USA. *The Queen of Mean*

PIETRAVALLE, LINA
Immacolata, Short Story
   Nozze Di Sangue 1941 d: Goffredo Alessandrini. lps: Fosco Giachetti, Luisa Ferida, Beatrice Mancini. 85M ITL. prod/rel: Sovrania Film, Titanus

PIETRI, GIUSEPPE
La Donna Perduta, Opera
   Donna Perduta, La 1941 d: Domenico M. Gambino. lps: Elli Parvo, Luisella Beghi, Carlo Campanini. 96M ITL. prod/rel: Iris Film

PIEYRE DE MANDIARGUES, ANDRE (1909–, FRN
Ceremonie d'Amour, Novel
   Ceremonie d'Amour 1988 d: Walerian Borowczyk. lps: Marianna Pierro, Mathieu Carriere, Josy Bernard. 104M FRN. prod/rel: Sara Films, Sofica
Vanina, Novel
   Lis de Mer, Le 1970 d: Jacqueline Audry. lps: Carole Andre, Kiki Caron, Angelo Infanti. F FRN. *The Sea Lily* prod/rel: Comacico, le Terrier

PIGOTT, W.
Ace High, Story
   Ace High 1919 d: George Holt. lps: Pete Morrison, Hoot Gibson. 2r USA. prod/rel: Universal Film Mfg. Co.

PILCHER, ROSAMUNDE
Novel
   Rosamunde Pilcher: Karussell Des Lebens 1994 d: Rolf von Sydow. lps: Christiane Horbiger, Barbara Wussow, Jacques Breuer. TVM. 90M GRM. *Karussell Des Lebens*
September, Novel
   September 1994 d: Colin Bucksey. lps: Michael York, Jacqueline Bisset, Mariel Hemingway. MTV. 200M UKN/GRM. prod/rel: Portman Hannibal Productions©, Portman Entertainment
The Shell Seekers, Novel
   Shell Seekers, The 1989 d: Waris Hussein. lps: Angela Lansbury, Sam Wanamaker, Christopher Bowen. TVM. 100M USA/UKN.

PILCHOWSKY, ROBERT
Constanze, Novel
   Geliebte Corinna 1956 d: Eduard von Borsody. lps: Elisabeth Muller, Hans Sohnker, Hannelore Schroth. 100M GRM. *Beloved Corinna* prod/rel: Arca, N.F.
Daddy Und Do, Novel
   Leben Fur Do, Ein 1954 d: Gustav Ucicky. lps: Hans Sohnker, Paola Loew, Charles Regnier. 90M GRM. *A Life for Do* prod/rel: Capitol, Prisma

PILEGGI, NICHOLAS
Wiseguy, Novel
   Goodfellas 1990 d: Martin Scorsese. lps: Robert de Niro, Ray Liotta, Joe Pesci. 146M USA. prod/rel: Warner Bros.

PILHES, RENE-VICTOR
L'imprecateur, Novel
   Imprecateur, L' 1976 d: Jean-Louis Bertucelli. lps: Jean Yanne, Michel Piccoli, Jean-Pierre Marielle. 100M FRN/SWT. *The Accuser* prod/rel: Action, Citel

PILLAI, C. MADHAVAN
Gnanambika, Novel
   Gnanambika 1940 d: S. Nottani. lps: Sebastian Bhagavathar, C. K. Rajam, Aleppey Vincent. 190M IND. *Jnanambika*; *Raga Leela* prod/rel: Shyamala Pictures

PILLAI, C. V. RAMAN
Martanda Varma, 1891, Novel
   Marthanda Varma 1931 d: P. V. Rao. lps: K. Aandy, Menon. A. V. P., V. Naik. 3629m IND. *Martanda Varma* prod/rel: Shri Rajeshwari Films

PILLAI, THAKAZHY SHIVASHANKAR (1912–, MLY, Pillai, Thakashi Sivasankaran
Randidangazhi, Novel
   Randidangazhi 1958 d: P. Subramanyam. lps: Kumari, P. J. Anthony, T. S. Muthiah. 174M IND. *Two Measures of Paddy* prod/rel: Neela Prod.

PILLAU, HORST
Das Fenster Xum Flur, Play
   Im Parterre Links 1963 d: Kurt Fruh. lps: Valerie Steinmann, Paul Buhlmann, Bella Neri. 94M SWT. *Rez-de-Chaussee Gauche*; *Das Fenster Zum Flur*; *Frau Weiser Und Ihre Kinder* prod/rel: Gloriafilm, Praesens-Film

PILNYAK, BORIS (1894–1941), RSS, Vogau, Boris Andreyevich
Povest Nepogashenoi Luny, 1926, Short Story
   Povest Nepogashenoi Luny 1991 d: Yevgeny Tsymbal. 84M RSS. *A Tale of the Unextinguished Moon*

PILOTTO, LIBERO
L'onorevole Campodarsego, 1889, Play
   Onorevole Campodarsego, L' 1915 d: Camillo de Riso. lps: Camillo de Riso, Lola Visconti-Brignone, Carlo Benetti. ITL. prod/rel: Caesar Film

PINCHON, EDGCUMB
Viva Villa, New York 1933, Book
   Viva Villa! 1934 d: Jack Conway, Howard Hawks (Uncredited). lps: Wallace Beery, Leo Carrillo, Fay Wray. 115M USA. prod/rel: Metro-Goldwyn-Mayer Corp.©

PINEL, PHILIPPE F.
Don Cesar de Bazan, 1844, Play
   Rosita 1923 d: Ernst Lubitsch. lps: Mary Pickford, Holbrook Blinn, Irene Rich. 8800f USA. prod/rel: Mary Pickford Co., United Artists
   Spanish Dancer, The 1923 d: Herbert Brenon. lps: Pola Negri, Antonio Moreno, Wallace Beery. 8434f USA. prod/rel: Famous Players-Lasky, Paramount Pictures
   Don Cesare Di Bazan 1942 d: Riccardo FredA. lps: Gino Cervi, Anneliese Uhlig, Enrico Glori. 76M ITL. *La Lamadel Giustiziere* prod/rel: Elica, Artisti Associati

PINELLI, TULLIO
I Padri Etruschi, 1941, Play
   Adultera, L' 1946 d: Duilio Coletti. lps: Clara Calamai, Roldano Lupi, Carlo Ninchi. F ITL. *The Adulteress* prod/rel: Grandi Film Internazionali, Artisti Associati

PINERO, ARTHUR WING (1855–1934), UKN
The Amazons, London 1893, Play
   Amazons, The 1917 d: Joseph Kaufman. lps: Marguerite Clark, Adolphe Menjou, Elsie Lawson. 5r USA. prod/rel: Famous Players Film Co.©, Paramount Pictures Corp.
Dandy Dick, London 1887, Play
   Dandy Dick 1935 d: William Beaudine. lps: Will Hay, Nancy Burne, Esmond Knight. 72M UKN. prod/rel: British International Pictures, Wardour
The Enchanted Cottage, London 1922, Play
   Enchanted Cottage, The 1924 d: John S. Robertson. lps: Richard Barthelmess, May McAvoy, Ida Waterman. 7120f USA. prod/rel: Inspiration Pictures
   Enchanted Cottage, The 1945 d: John Cromwell. lps: Robert Young, Dorothy McGuire, Herbert Marshall. 92M USA. prod/rel: RKO Radio
The Gay Lord Quex, London 1899, Play
   Gay Lord Quex, The 1917 d: Maurice Elvey. lps: Ben Webster, Irene Vanbrugh, Lilian Braithwaite. 5670f UKN. prod/rel: Ideal
   Gay Lord Quex, The 1919 d: Harry Beaumont. lps: Tom Moore, Gloria Hope, Naomi Childers. 5r USA. prod/rel: Goldwyn Pictures Corp.©, Goldwyn Distributing Corp.
His House in Order, London 1906, Play
   His House in Order 1928 d: Randle Ayrton. lps: Tallulah Bankhead, Ian Hunter, David Hawthorne. 7666f UKN. prod/rel: QTS, Ideal
Iris, London 1901, Play
   Iris 1915 d: Cecil M. Hepworth. lps: Henry Ainley, Alma Taylor, Stewart Rome. 5500f UKN. prod/rel: Hepworth, Ideal
   Slave of Vanity, A 1920 d: Henry Otto. lps: Pauline Frederick, Nigel Barrie, Willard Louis. 6r USA. *Iris* prod/rel: Robertson-Cole Studios, Inc., Robertson-Cole Distributing Corp.©

Letty, London 1903, Play
Loves of Letty, The 1920 d: Frank Lloyd. lps: Pauline Frederick, John Bowers, W. Lawson Butt. 5r USA. prod/rel: Goldwyn Pictures Corp.©, Goldwyn Distributing Corp.

The Magistrate, London 1885, Play
Magistrate, The 1921 d: Bannister Merwin. lps: Tom Reynolds, Maudie Dunham, Ethel Warwick. 5400f UKN. prod/rel: Samuelson, General

Those Were the Days 1934 d: Thomas Bentley. lps: Will Hay, Iris Hoey, Angela Baddeley. 80M UKN. *The Magistrate* prod/rel: British International Pictures, Wardour

Mid-Channel, New York 1910, Play
Mid-Channel 1920 d: Harry Garson. lps: Clara Kimball Young, J. Frank Glendon, Edward M. Kimball. 6r USA. prod/rel: Garson Studios, Inc., Equity Pictures Corp.

The "Mind-the-Paint" Girl, London 1912, Play
Mind the Paint Girl 1919 d: Wilfred North. lps: Anita Stewart, Conway Tearle, Victor Steele. 5r USA. *The Mind-the-Paint Girl* prod/rel: Vitagraph Co. of America, Anita Stewart Productions, Inc.

The Profligate, London 1889, Play
Profligate, The 1917 d: Meyrick Milton. lps: Ben Webster, Dorothy Bellew, Langhorne Burton. 4000f UKN. prod/rel: Milton, Walturdaw

Truth About Husbands, The 1920 d: Kenneth Webb. lps: Anna Lehr, Holmes Herbert, Elizabeth Garrison. 5r USA. prod/rel: Whitman Bennett Productions, Associated First National Pictures

The Second Mrs. Tanqueray, London 1893, Play
Second Mrs. Tanqueray, The 1914. lps: Constance Crawley, Arthur Maude. 2r USA. prod/rel: Warner's Features

Second Mrs. Tanqueray, The 1916 d: Fred Paul. lps: George Alexander, Hilda Moore, Norman Forbes. 6000f UKN. prod/rel: Ideal

Second Mrs. Tanqueray, The, London 1893, Play
Seconda Moglie, La 1922 d: Amleto Palermi. lps: Pina Menichelli, Livio Pavanelli, Orietta Claudi. 2946m ITL. prod/rel: Rinascimento Film

The Second Mrs. Tanqueray, London 1893, Play
Second Mrs. Tanqueray, The 1952 d: Dallas Bower. lps: Pamela Brown, Hugh Sinclair, Ronald Ward. 76M UKN. prod/rel: Vandyke, Associated British Film Distributors

Sweet Lavender, London 1888, Play
Sweet Lavender 1915 d: Cecil M. Hepworth. lps: Henry Ainley, Chrissie White, Alma Taylor. 5000f UKN. prod/rel: Hepworth, Lift

Sweet Lavender 1920 d: Paul Powell. lps: Mary Miles Minter, Harold Goodwin, Milton Sills. 5r USA. prod/rel: Realart Pictures Corp.©

Trelawney of the Wells, London 1898, Play
Trelawney of the Wells 1916 d: Cecil M. Hepworth. lps: Alma Taylor, Stewart Rome, Violet Hopson. 4875f UKN. prod/rel: Hepworth, Butcher

Trelawney of the Wells, New York 1898, Play
Actress, The 1928 d: Sidney A. Franklin. lps: Norma Shearer, Owen Moore, Gwen Lee. 6998f USA. *Trelawney of the Wells* prod/rel: Metro-Goldwyn-Mayer Pictures

PINKERTON, KATHERINE
Spring Fever, Story
Nancy from Nowhere 1922 d: Chester M. Franklin. lps: Bebe Daniels, Eddie Sutherland, Vera Lewis. 5167f USA. prod/rel: Realart Pictures, Paramount Pictures

PINKERTON, ROBERT E.
The Test of Donald Norton, Chicago 1924, Novel
Test of Donald Norton, The 1926 d: B. Reeves Eason. lps: George Walsh, Tyrone Power Sr., Robert Graves. 6600f USA. prod/rel: Chadwick Pictures

PINSENT, GORDON (1933–, CND
John and the Missus, Novel
John and the Missus 1986 d: Gordon Pinsent. lps: Gordon Pinsent, Jackie Burroughs, Randy Follet. 100M CND.

PINSKI, DAVID
Yankel de Schmid, New York 1909, Play
Yankel Der Schmidt 1938 d: Edgar G. Ulmer. lps: Moishe Oysher, Miriam Riselle, Florence Weiss. 116M USA. *The Singing Blacksmith*; *Jacob the Blacksmith* prod/rel: Collective Film Producers, Yankel the Blacksmith, Inc.

PINTER, HAROLD (1930–, UKN
Betrayal, 1978, Play
Betrayal 1983 d: David Jones. lps: Jeremy Irons, Ben Kingsley, Patricia Hodge. 95M UKN. prod/rel: Horizon, Sam Spiegel

The Birthday Party, London 1958, Play
Birthday Party, The 1970 d: William Friedkin. lps: Robert Shaw, Patrick Magee, Dandy Nichols. 124M UKN. prod/rel: Palomar Pictures International, Amerbroco

The Caretaker, London 1960, Play
Caretaker, The 1963 d: Clive Donner. lps: Alan Bates, Donald Pleasence, Robert Shaw. 105M UKN. *The Guest* (USA) prod/rel: Caretaker Films, British Lion

The Dumb Waiter, 1960, Play
Dumb Waiter, The 1989 d: Robert Altman. lps: John Travolta, Tom Conti. 58M USA. prod/rel: Sandcastle 5

Basements 1987 d: Robert Altman. lps: John Travolta, Tom Conti, Linda Hunt. TVM. 104M USA/UKN. prod/rel: Sandcastle 5, ABC

The Homecoming, 1965, Play
Homecoming, The 1973 d: Peter Hall. lps: Cyril Cusack, Ian Holm, Michael Jayston. 114M UKN/USA. prod/rel: American Express, Ely Landau

The Room, Play
Room, The 1987 d: Robert Altman. lps: Linda Hunt, Annie Lennox, Julian Sands. 49M USA. prod/rel: Sandcastle 5

Basements 1987 d: Robert Altman. lps: John Travolta, Tom Conti, Linda Hunt. TVM. 104M USA/UKN. prod/rel: Sandcastle 5, ABC

PINTO, MERCEDES
El, Novel
El 1952 d: Luis Bunuel. lps: Delia Garces, Luis Beristain, Arturo de CordovA. 100M MXC. *El: This Strange Passion* (USA); *This Strange Passion*; *He* prod/rel: Danciger

PIOVENE, GUIDO
Lettere Di Una Novizia, Verona 1941, Novel
Lettere Di Una Novizia 1960 d: Alberto LattuadA. lps: Pascale Petit, Jean-Paul Belmondo, Massimo Girotti. 102M ITL/FRN. *La Novice* (FRN); *Letter from a Novice*; *Rita* (USA); *The Novice* prod/rel: Les Films Modernes, Les Films Agiman (Paris)

PIPER, ANNE
Jack Und Jenny, Novel
Jack Und Jenny 1963 d: Victor Vicas. lps: Senta Berger, Brett Halsey, Marion Michael. 86M GRM. *Jack and Jenny* prod/rel: Arca-Winston, Nora

Marry at Leisure, New York 1959, Novel
Nice Girl Like Me, A 1969 d: Desmond Davis. lps: Barbara Ferris, Harry Andrews, Gladys Cooper. 91M UKN. prod/rel: Partisan Film Productions, Anglo Embassy Productions

Yes, Giorgio, Novel
Yes, Giorgio 1982 d: Franklin J. Schaffner. lps: Luciano Pavarotti, Kathryn Harrold, Eddie Albert. 110M USA. prod/rel: MGM, United Artists

PIPER, EVELYN
Bunny Lake Is Missing, New York 1957, Novel
Bunny Lake Is Missing 1965 d: Otto Preminger. lps: Laurence Olivier, Carol Lynley, Keir DulleA. 107M UKN. prod/rel: Columbia, Wheel

The Nanny, New York 1964, Novel
Nanny, The 1965 d: Seth Holt. lps: Bette Davis, Wendy Craig, Jill Bennett. 93M UKN. prod/rel: Seven Arts Productions, Hammer Film Productions

PIPOLO (1933–, ITL, Moccia, Giuseppe
Zio Adolfo, in Arte Fuhrer, Novel
Zio Adolfo in Arte Fuhrer 1978 d: Castellano, Pipolo. lps: Adriano Celentano, Claudio Bigagli, Francoise Bastien. 96M ITL. *Adolfo Hitler Alias Il Mio Zio* prod/rel: Dania Film, Medusa Distribuzione

PIRANDELLO, LUIGI (1867–1936), ITL
Ss
Lume Dell'altra Casa, Il 1920 d: Ugo Gracci. lps: Margot Pellegrinetti, Ugo Gracci, Felice Matellio. 1056m ITL. prod/rel: Silentium Film

Short Story
Manu 1987 d: Alfredo Giannetti. lps: Ana Marie Nascimento Silva, Ray Lovelock, Daniel Ceccaldi. TVM. 85M FRN/ITL.

Novel
Tu Ridi 1998 d: Paolo Taviani, Vittorio Taviani. lps: Antonio Albanese, Sabrina Ferilli, Luca Zingaretti. 102M ITL. *You're Laughing* prod/rel: Filmtre, Dania Film

L'altro Figlio, 1905, Short Story
Xaos 1984 d: Paolo Taviani, Vittorio Taviani. lps: Margarita Lozano, Claudio Bigagli, Massimo Bonetti. 188M ITL. *Kaos* prod/rel: Rai 1, Marin Karmitz

Come Prima, Meglio Di Prima, 1921, Play
This Love of Ours 1945 d: William Dieterle. lps: Merle Oberon, Charles Korvin, Claude Rains. 90M USA. *As It Was Before* prod/rel: Universal

Never Say Goodbye 1956 d: Jerry Hopper, Douglas Sirk (Uncredited). lps: Rock Hudson, Cornell Borchers, George Sanders. 96M USA. prod/rel: Universal-International

Come Tu Mi Vuoi, Milan 1930, Play
As You Desire Me 1932 d: George Fitzmaurice. lps: Greta Garbo, Melvyn Douglas, Erich von Stroheim. 71M USA. prod/rel: Metro-Goldwyn-Mayer Corp.

Enrico IV, 1922, Play
Enrico IV 1944 d: Giorgio PastinA. lps: Osvaldo Valenti, Clara Calamai, Luigi Pavese. 88M ITL. prod/rel: Cines, E.N.I.C.

Enrico IV 1984 d: Marco Bellocchio. lps: Marcello Mastroianni, Claudia Cardinale, Luciano Bartoli. 130M ITL. *Henry IV* prod/rel: Odyssia, Rai

Feu Mathias Pascal, 1904, Novel
Feu Mathias Pascal 1925 d: Marcel L'Herbier. lps: Ivan Mosjoukine, Marcelle Pradot, Michel Simon. 3300m FRN. *Late Matthew Pascal, The*; *Living Dead Man, The* (USA) prod/rel: Cinegraphic, Albatros

Fu Mattia Pascal, Il, 1904, Novel
Homme de Nulle Part, L' 1936 d: Pierre Chenal. lps: Isa Miranda, Pierre Blanchar, Catherine Fonteney. 98M FRN. *Late Mathias Pascal, The* (USA); *Man from Nowhere, The*

Il Fu Mattia Pascal, Novel
Fu Mattia Pascal, Il 1937 d: Pierre Chenal. lps: Pierre Blanchar, Isa Miranda, Irma GramaticA. 93M ITL. prod/rel: Ala, Colosseum Film

Giuoca, Pietro!, Story
Acciaio 1933 d: Walter Ruttmann. lps: Isa Pola, Piero Pastore, Vittorio Bellaccini. 65M ITL/GRM. *Arbeit macht Frei* (GRM); *Steel* prod/rel: Cines, Anonima Pittaluga

Il Gorgo, 1913, Short Story
Wir 1983 d: Henryk Jacek Schoen. lps: Marek Herbik, Marzena Trybala, Ewa DalkowskA. MTV. 76M PLN. *A Whirl*

In Silenzio, Short Story
Canzone Dell'amore, La 1930 d: Gennaro Righelli. lps: Dria Paola, Isa Pola, Mercedes Brignone. 94M ITL. *Silenzio* prod/rel: Cines, S.A. Stefano Pittaluga

In Silenzio, 1905, Short Story
Derniere Berceuse, La 1930 d: Jean Cassagne, Gennaro Righelli. lps: Dolly Davis, Jean Angelo, Grazia Del Rio. F FRN. *Chanson de l'Amour, La*; *Silence* prod/rel: Vandal Et Delac

Wir 1983 d: Henryk Jacek Schoen. lps: Marek Herbik, Marzena Trybala, Ewa DalkowskA. MTV. 76M PLN. *A Whirl*

In Silenzio 1988 d: Luigi Filippo d'Amico. lps: Malto Gazzola, Jerome Bellavista, Karine Verlier. 102M ITL.

Liola, Rome 1916, Play
Liola 1964 d: Alessandro Blasetti. lps: Ugo Tognazzi, Giovanna Ralli, Pierre Brasseur. 100M ITL/FRN. *Coq du Village, Le* (FRN); *Very Handy Man, A* (USA) prod/rel: Napoleon Film, Franco London Film (Paris)

Lumie Di Sicilia, Short Story
Crollo, Il 1920 d: Mario Gargiulo. lps: Tina Xeo, Alberto Francis. 1529m ITL. *Sono Lo Sposo Di Teresina*; *Lumie Di Sicilia* prod/rel: Flegrea Film

Ma Non E Una Cosa Seria, 1910, Short Story
Ma Non E Una Cosa Seria 1936 d: Mario Camerini. lps: Vittorio de Sica, Elisa Cegani, Assia Noris. 78M ITL. *But It's Nothing Serious* prod/rel: Colombo Film S.a., E.N.I.C.

Male Di Luna, 1925, Short Story
Xaos 1984 d: Paolo Taviani, Vittorio Taviani. lps: Margarita Lozano, Claudio Bigagli, Massimo Bonetti. 188M ITL. *Kaos* prod/rel: Rai 1, Marin Karmitz

Pensaci, Giacomino!, 1910, Short Story
Pensaci, Giacomino! 1936 d: Gennaro Righelli. lps: Angelo Musco, Dria Paola, Amelia Chellini. 75M ITL. prod/rel: Capitani Film, I.C.A.R.

Requiem Aeternam Dona Eis, Domine!, 1913, Short Story
Terra Di Nessuno 1939 d: Mario Baffico. lps: Mario Ferrari, Nelly Corradi, Laura Solari. 94M ITL. *Nobody's Land* (USA) prod/rel: Roma Film, Generalcine

Xaos 1984 d: Paolo Taviani, Vittorio Taviani. lps: Margarita Lozano, Claudio Bigagli, Massimo Bonetti. 188M ITL. *Kaos* prod/rel: Rai 1, Marin Karmitz

Lo Scaldino, Ss
Scaldino, Lo 1920 d: Augusto GeninA. lps: Kally Sambucini, Franz Sala, Alfonso Cassini. 1590m ITL. prod/rel: U.C.I., Itala Film

Sei Personaggi in Cerca d'Autore, Play
Six Characters in Search of an Author 1992 d: Bill Bryden. lps: Brian Cox, John Hurt, Susan Fleetwood. TVM. 95M UKN.

Tutto Per Bene, 1906, Short Story
  Todo Sea Para Bien 1957 d: Carlos Rinaldi. lps: Susana Campos, Francisco Petrone, Inda LedesmA. 78M ARG. *All for the Best*

L'uomo, la Bestia, la Virtu, Play
  Uomo, la Bestia, la Virtu, L' 1953 d: Steno. lps: Toto, Viviane Romance, Orson Welles. F ITL. *L'uomo, la Bestia E la Vertu*; *Man, Beast and Virtue* prod/rel: Rosa Film, Paramount

I Vecchi E I Giovani, 1909, Novel
  Vecchi E I Giovani, I 1978 d: Marco Leto. lps: Alain Cuny, Gabriele Ferzetti, Glauco Mauri. MTV. 116M ITL. prod/rel: Filmalpha, Rai Radiotelevisione Italiana

Vestire Gli Ignudi, 1937, Play
  Vestire Gli Ignudi 1954 d: Marcello Pagliero. lps: Eleonora Rossi-Drago, Gabriele Ferzetti, Pierre Brasseur. 104M ITL/FRN. *Vetir Ceux Qui Sont Nus* (FRN) prod/rel: Cin.Ca Grandi Film, Eva Film (Roma)

Il Viaggio, 1910, Short Story
  Viaggio, Il 1921 d: Gennaro Righelli. lps: Maria Jacobini, Carlo Benetti, Alfonso Cassini. 1742m ITL. prod/rel: Fert
  Viaggio, Il 1974 d: Vittorio de SicA. lps: Sophia Loren, Richard Burton, Ian Bannen. 95M ITL/FRN. *The Journey* (UKN); *The Voyage* (USA); *Le Voyage* (FRN) prod/rel: Compagnia Cin.Ca Champion (Roma), Capac Film (Paris)

PIRRO, UGO
Celluloide, Novel
  Celluloide 1996 d: Carlo Lizzani. lps: Massimo Ghini, Giancarlo Giannini, Anna Falchi. 115M ITL. *Celluloid* prod/rel: Dean Film, Istituto Luce

Jovanka E le Altre, Novel
  Jovanka E le Altre 1960 d: Martin Ritt. lps: Silvana Mangano, Vera Miles, Barbara Bel Geddes. 115M ITL/USA. *Five Branded Women* (USA); *Jovanka and the Others* prod/rel: Paramount, Dino de Laurentiis Cin.Ca

Le Soldatesse, Novel
  Soldatesse, Le 1965 d: Valerio Zurlini. lps: Anna Karina, Marie Laforet, Lea Massari. 120M ITL/FRN/GRM. *Des Filles Pour l'Armee* (FRN); *The Camp Followers* (USA) prod/rel: Zebra Film (Roma), Omnia Deutsch (Munich)

PISKOR, KAREL
Svatek Veritelu, Play
  Svatek Veritelu 1939 d: Gina Hasler. lps: Jaroslav Marvan, Jindrich Plachta, Raoul Schranil. 2453m CZC. *Creditors' Day* prod/rel: Lucernafilm

PISTONE, JOSEPH D.
Donnie Brasco: My Undercover Life in the Mafia, Book
  Donnie Brasco 1997 d: Mike Newell. lps: Al Pacino, Johnny Depp, Michael Madsen. 126M USA. prod/rel: Baltimore Pictures, Mark Johnson

PITKIN, WALTER B.
Life Begins at 40, New York 1932, Novel
  Life Begins at 40 1935 d: George Marshall. lps: Will Rogers, Rochelle Hudson, Richard Cromwell. 85M USA. *Life Begins at Forty* prod/rel: Fox Film Corp.©

PITOL, SERGIO
La Vida Conyugal, Novel
  Vida Conyugal, La 1992 d: Carlos CarrerA. lps: Alonso Echanove, Socorro Bonilla, Patricio Castillo. 100M MXC. *Married Life*

PITT, GEORGE DIBDIN
Sweeney Todd; Or the Fiend of Fleet Street, London 1847, Play
  Sweeney Todd 1928 d: Walter West. lps: Moore Marriott, Zoe Palmer, Charles Ashton. 6500f UKN. prod/rel: QTS Productions, Ideal

PITTONI, LEROS
Un Amore Cosi Fragile Cosi Violento, Novel
  Amore Cosi Fragile Cosi Violento, Un 1973 d: Leros Pittoni. lps: Fabio Testi, Paola Pitagora, Maria BaxA. 97M ITL. prod/rel: Roas Produzioni, Interfilm

Tante Sbarre, Novel
  Istruttoria E Chiusa, Dimentichi, L' 1971 d: Damiano Damiani. lps: Franco Nero, Riccardo Cucciolla, Georges Wilson. 106M ITL. *Tante Sbarre* prod/rel: Fair Film, Interfilm

PITTORRU, FABIO
Violenza a Roma, Novel
  ..a Tutte le Auto Della Polizia 1975 d: Mario Caiano. lps: Antonio Sabato, Luciana Paluzzi, Enrico Maria Salerno. 100M ITL. prod/rel: Capitol Cin.Ca, Jarama Film

PITTORU, FABIO
La Madama, Novel
  Madama, La 1976 d: Duccio Tessari. lps: Tom Skerritt, Carole Andre, Christian de SicA. 94M ITL. prod/rel: Filmes Cin.Ca, Titanus

PIXLEY, FRANK
The Prince of Pilsen, New York 1902, Musical Play
  Prince of Pilsen, The 1926 d: Paul Powell. lps: George Sidney, Anita Stewart, Allan Forrest. 6600f USA. prod/rel: Belasco Productions, Producers Distributing Corp.

PLAIN, BELVA (1919–, USA
Evergreen, Novel
  Evergreen 1984 d: Fielder Cook. lps: Lesley Ann Warren, Armand Assante, Ian McShane. TVM. 285M USA. prod/rel: NBC, Edgar J. Scherick

PLANQUETTE, ROBERT (1848–1903), FRN
Les Cloches de Corneville, Paris 1877, Operetta
  Cloches de Corneville, Les 1917 d: Thomas Bentley. lps: Elsie Craven, Moya Mannering, M. R. Morand. 6000f UKN. prod/rel: British Actors, Int Ex

PLANS, JUAN JOSE
Quien Puede Matar a un Nino?, Novel
  Quien Puede Matar a un Nino? 1975 d: Narciso Ibanez Serrador. lps: Lewis Fiander, Prunella Ransome, Antonio Iranzo. 111M SPN. *Island of the Damned* (USA); *Would You Kill a Child?*; *Who Can Kill a Child?*; *Island of Death*; *Death Is Child's Play* prod/rel: Penta

PLASKOVITIS, DIMITRIS
The Dam, Novel
  Fragma, to 1982 d: Dimitris Makris. lps: Nikos Kourkoulos, Daniela Moretti, Danis Katranidis. 115M GRC. *The Dam* prod/rel: Greek Film Centre, Dimitris Makris

PLATH, SYLVIA (1932–1963), USA
The Bell Jar, 1963, Novel
  Bell Jar, The 1979 d: Larry Peerce. lps: Marilyn Hassett, Julie Harris, Anne Jackson. 112M USA. prod/rel: Peerce-Goldston, Avco

PLATO (427bc–348bc), GRC, Platone
I Dialoghi, Dialogues
  Processo E Morte Di Socrate 1940 d: Corrado d'Errico. lps: Ermete Zacconi, Rossano Brazzi, Filippo Scelzo. 105M ITL. *I Dialoghi Di Platone* prod/rel: Scalera Film

PLATT, AGNES
Whispering Gables, Short Story
  Whispering Gables 1927 d: Edwin Greenwood. lps: Gladys Jennings, Reginald Bach, Frances Cuyler. 2100f UKN. prod/rel: Gaumont

PLEIJEL, AGNETA
Nagra Sommarkvallar Pa Jorden, Play
  Nagra Sommarkvallar Pa Jorden 1987 d: Gunnel Lindblom. lps: Sif Ruud, Margareta Bystrom, Per Mattson. 104M SWD. *Summer Nights on the Planet Earth*; *Sommarkvallar Pa Jorden* prod/rel: Spice, Svenska Filminstitutet

PLENZDORF, ULRICH
Die Neuen Leiden Des Jungen W., 1972, Play
  Neuen Leiden Des Jungen W., Die 1975 d: Eberhard Itzenplitz. lps: Klaus Hoffmann, Leonie Thelen, Hans-Werner Bussinger. 112M GRM. *The Sufferings of Young W.* prod/rel: Artus, Sudwestfunk

PLEVAS, J. V.
Maly Bobes Ve Meste, Book
  Maly Bobes Ve Meste 1962 d: Jan Valasek. lps: Jirka Lukes, Dana Medricka, Radovan Lukavsky. 79M CZC. *Little Bobes in the City* prod/rel: Filmstudio Barrandov

PLIMPTON, GEORGE (1927–, USA
Paper Lion, New York 1966, Biography
  Paper Lion 1968 d: Alex March. lps: Alan Alda, Lauren Hutton, David Doyle. 105M USA. prod/rel: Stuart Millar Productions

PLISNIER, CHARLES
Mariages, 1936, Novel
  Mariages 1977 d: Teff Erhat. lps: Chantal Noble, Jean-Pierre Dauzun, Jean-Marie Deblin. MTV. 240M BLG.

Meurtres, Novel
  Meurtres 1950 d: Richard Pottier. lps: Fernandel, Raymond Souplex, Jacques Varennes. 120M FRN. *Three Sinners* (USA) prod/rel: Cine Films, Fides

PLUDRA, BENNO
Story
  Herz Des Piraten, Das 1987 d: Jurgen Brauer. lps: Franziska Alberg, Johanna Schall, Gojko Mitic. 86M GDR. *The Pirate's Heart*; *Heart of the Pirate* prod/rel: Defa, Gruppe Johannisthal

POATE, ERNEST M.
A Trade Secret, 1915, Novel
  Trade Secret, A 1915 d: William F. Haddock. lps: Frederic de Belleville, Betty Marshall. 5r USA. prod/rel: Gotham Film Co., State Rights

POCOCK, ROGER S.
A Man in the Open, Indianapolis 1912, Novel
  Man in the Open, A 1919 d: Ernest C. Warde. lps: Dustin Farnum, Irene Rich, Herschal Mayall. 6r USA. prod/rel: United Picture Theatres of America, Inc.

PODHAJSKY, ALOIS
Ein Leben Fur Die Lipizzaner, Munich 1960, Book
  Miracle of the White Stallions, The 1962 d: Arthur Hiller. lps: Robert Taylor, Lilli Palmer, Curd Jurgens. 117M USA. *The Flight of the White Stallions* (UKN) prod/rel: Walt Disney Productions

POE, EDGAR ALLAN (1809–1949), USA
Short Story
  Sinbad of the Seven Seas 1986 d: Enzo G. Castellari. lps: Lou Ferrigno, John Steiner, Leo GullottA. 93M ITL/USA. *Sindbad of the Seven Seas*; *Sinbad* prod/rel: Cannon

Annabel Lee, Short Story
  Annabel Lee 1921 d: William J. Scully. lps: Jack O'Brien, Lorraine Harding, Florida Kingsley. 4800f USA. prod/rel: Joe Mitchell Chopple, Joan Film Sales

Annabel Lee, 1849, Poem
  Avenging Conscience Or Thou Shalt Not Kill, The 1914 d: D. W. Griffith. lps: Henry B. Walthall, Blanche Sweet, Spottiswoode Aitken. 7-8r USA. *Murderer's Conscience, The* prod/rel: Majestic Motion Picture Co., State Rights

The Bells, Poem
  Bells, The 1913 d: George A. Lessey. lps: Augustus Phillips, May Abbey, Robert Brower. 1000f USA. prod/rel: Edison

The Black Cat, 1843, Short Story
  Black Cat, The 1934 d: Edgar G. Ulmer. lps: Boris Karloff, Bela Lugosi, Julie Bishop. 70M USA. *House of Doom* (UKN); *The Vanishing Body* prod/rel: Universal Pictures Corp.
  Black Cat, The 1941 d: Albert S. Rogell. lps: Basil Rathbone, Hugh Herbert, Broderick Crawford. 70M USA. prod/rel: Universal
  Black Cat, The 1966 d: Harold Hoffman. lps: Robert Frost, Robyn Baker, Sadie French. 73M USA. prod/rel: Falcon International
  Apokal 1971 d: Paul Anczykowski. lps: Heinrich Clasing, Christof Nel, Dorit Amann. 86M GRM. prod/rel: Anczy, Atlantis
  Gatto Nero, Il 1981 d: Lucio Fulci. lps: Patrick Magee, Mimsy Farmer, David Warbeck. 91M ITL. *The Black Cat* (USA); *Il Gatto Di Park Lane* prod/rel: Selenia
  Tales of Terror 1962 d: Roger Corman. lps: Vincent Price, Peter Lorre, Basil Rathbone. 90M USA. *Poe's Tales of Terror* prod/rel: American International
  Unheimliche Geschichten 1932 d: Richard Oswald. lps: Paul Wegener, Maria Koppenhofer, Blandine Ebinger. 89M GRM. *Tales of the Uncanny* prod/rel: Roto, Dietz

The Cask of Amontillado, 1846, Short Story
  Sealed Room 1909 d: D. W. Griffith. lps: Henry B. Walthall, Arthur Johnson, Marion Leonard. 779f USA. prod/rel: Biograph Co.
  Obras Maestras Del Terror 1960 d: Enrique Carreras. lps: Narciso Ibanez Menta, Carlos Estrada, Inez Moreno. 115M ARG. *Master of Horror* (USA); *Masterworks of Terror* prod/rel: Gates-Torres Productions, Vicente Marco Productions

City in the Sea, 1831, Poem
  City Under the Sea, The 1965 d: Jacques Tourneur. lps: Vincent Price, David Tomlinson, Tab Hunter. 84M UKN/USA. *War-Gods of the Deep* (USA); *City in the Sea*; *Warlords of the Deep* prod/rel: Bruton Film Productions, American International Pictures

The Conqueror Worm, Short Story
  Tides of Time, The 1915 d: Joseph Levering. lps: Mary Nash, Harmon MacGregor, Morse Coupal. 3r USA. prod/rel: Knickerbocker Star

Danse MacAbre, Short Story
  Danza MacAbra 1964 d: Antonio Margheriti, Sergio Corbucci. lps: Barbara Steele, Georges Riviere, Margaret Robsahm. 90M ITL/FRN. *Edgar Allan Poe's Castle of Blood*; *La Lunga Notte Del Terrore*; *Coffin of Terror*; *Terrore*; *Castle of Blood* (USA) prod/rel: Vulsinia Film, Globe International Film

A Descent Into the Maelstrom, 1841, Poem
  City Under the Sea, The 1965 d: Jacques Tourneur. lps: Vincent Price, David Tomlinson, Tab Hunter. 84M UKN/USA. *War-Gods of the Deep* (USA); *City in the Sea*; *Warlords of the Deep* prod/rel: Bruton Film Productions, American International Pictures

The Facts in the Case of M. Valdemar, 1845, Short Story
  Tales of Terror 1962 d: Roger Corman. lps: Vincent Price, Peter Lorre, Basil Rathbone. 90M USA. *Poe's Tales of Terror* prod/rel: American International

POIROT-DELPECH, BERTRAND
Le Grand Dadais, Novel
  Grand Dadais, Le 1967 d: Pierre Granier-Deferre. lps: Jacques Perrin, Eva Renzi, Daniele Gaubert. 95M FRN/GRM. *Die Zeit Der Kirschen Ist Vorbei* (GRM); *Virgin Youth*; *The Big Softie*; *Cherry Time Is Past* prod/rel: Films De La Licorne, C.I.C.C.

POITIER, SIDNEY (1924–, USA
Story
  For Love of Ivy 1968 d: Daniel Mann. lps: Sidney Poitier, Abbey Lincoln, Beau Bridges. 102M USA. prod/rel: Palomar

POLACCI, ALFREDO
Short Story
  Trovatella Di Pompei, La 1958 d: Giacomo Gentilomo. lps: Massimo Girotti, Alessandra Panaro, Carlo Giustini. 84M ITL. prod/rel: Aeffe Cin.Ca

POLACEK, KAREL
Dum Na Predmesti, Novel
  Dum Na Predmesti 1933 d: Miroslav Cikan. lps: Hugo Haas, Antonie Nedosinska, Hana VitovA. 2545m CZC. *A House in the Suburbs; The Suburban House* prod/rel: Frantisek Lepka, Josef Hasler
Muzi V Offsidu, Novel
  Muzi V Offsidu 1931 d: Svatopluk Innemann. lps: Hugo Haas, Jozka Vanerova, Felix Kuhne. 2645m CZC. *Men Off-Side; Men in the Offside; The Men in Offside* prod/rel: Ab, Paramount

POLACH, BOHUMIR
Na Ruzich Ustlano, Opera
  Na Ruzich Ustlano 1934 d: Miroslav Cikan. lps: Jindrich Plachta, Antonie Nedosinska, Maria TauberovA. 2730m CZC. *Bed of Roses* prod/rel: Lloyd

POLACZEK, W.
Der Herr Kanzleirat, Play
  Herr Kanzleirat, Der 1948 d: Hubert MarischkA. lps: Hans Moser, Egon von Jordan, Hedy Fassler. 105M AUS. prod/rel: Donau

POLAND, JOSEPH FRANKLIN
An Amateur Widow, Story
  Amateur Widow, An 1919 d: Oscar Apfel. lps: Zena Keefe, Hugh Dillman, Jack Drumier. 5r USA. *Relations* prod/rel: World Film Corp.©

POLEVOY, BORIS NIKOLAEVICH
Doktor Vyera, 1966, Novel
  Doktor Vyera 1968 d: Damir Vyatich-Berezhnykh. lps: Irina Tarkovskaya, Ninel Myshkova, Georgi Zhzhonov. 89M USS. *Doctor Vera*
Na Dikom Beregye, 1962, Novel
  Na Dikom Beregye 1967 d: Anatoli Granik. lps: Boris Andreyev, Vsevolod Safonov, Yelizaveta AkulichevA. 79M USS. *On the Wild Shore; The Wild Shore*

POLGAR, ALFRED
Der Defraudanten, 1931, Play
  Bei Pichler Stimmt Die Kasse Nicht 1961 d: Hans Quest. lps: Theo Lingen, Georg Thomalla, Karin Dor. 98M GRM. *Pichler's Books are Not in Order* prod/rel: Real, Europa

POLIMER, RICHARD K.
No Power on Earth, Short Story
  Big Guy, The 1940 d: Arthur Lubin. lps: Victor McLaglen, Jackie Cooper, Ona Munson. 78M USA. *No Power on Earth* prod/rel: Universal Pictures Co.
  Behind the High Wall 1956 d: Abner Biberman. lps: Tom Tully, Sylvia Sidney, Betty Lynn. 85M USA. prod/rel: Universal-International

POLLARD, E. C.
Collision, Play
  Collision 1932 d: G. B. Samuelson. lps: Sunday Wilshin, Gerald Rawlinson, Wendy Barrie. 88M UKN. prod/rel: Samuelson, United Artists

POLLINI, FRANCIS
Pretty Maids All in a Row, Novel
  Pretty Maids All in a Row 1971 d: Roger Vadim. lps: Rock Hudson, Angie Dickinson, Telly Savalas. 91M USA. prod/rel: Gene Roddenberry, MGM

POLLOCK, ALICE LEAL
The Co-Respondent, New York 1916, Play
  Co-Respondent, The 1917 d: Ralph Ince. lps: Elaine Hammerstein, Wilfred Lucas, George Anderson. 5-6r USA. prod/rel: Advanced Motion Pictures, Jewel Productions, Inc.©
  Whispered Name, The 1924 d: King Baggot. lps: Ruth Clifford, Charles Clary, William E. Lawrence. 5196f USA. *Blackmail; The Co-Respondent* prod/rel: Universal Pictures

POLLOCK, CHANNING (1880–1946), USA
The Beauty Shop, New York 1914, Play
  Beauty Shop, The 1922 d: Eddie Dillon. lps: Raymond Hitchcock, Billy Van, James J. Corbett. 6536f USA. prod/rel: Cosmopolitan Productions, Paramount Pictures
Clothes, New York 1906, Play
  Clothes 1914 d: Francis Powers. lps: Charlotte Ives, House Peters, Edward MacKay. 4r USA. prod/rel: Famous Players Film Co., State Rights
  Clothes 1920 d: Fred Sittenham. lps: Olive Tell, Crauford Kent, Cyril Chadwick. 5r USA. prod/rel: Metro Pictures Corp.©
The Crowded Hour, New York 1918, Play
  Crowded Hour, The 1925 d: E. Mason Hopper. lps: Bebe Daniels, Kenneth Harlan, T. Roy Barnes. 6558f USA. prod/rel: Famous Players-Lasky, Paramount Pictures
The Enemy, New York 1925, Play
  Enemy, The 1927 d: Fred Niblo. lps: Lillian Gish, Ralph Forbes, Ralph Emerson. 8189f USA. prod/rel: Metro-Goldwyn-Mayer Pictures
The Fool, New York 1922, Play
  Fool, The 1925 d: Harry Millarde. lps: Edmund Lowe, Raymond Bloomer, Henry Sedley. 9453f USA. prod/rel: Fox Film Corp.
The Little Gray Lady, New York 1906, Play
  Little Gray Lady, The 1914 d: Francis Powers. lps: Jane Grey, Hal Clarendon, Jane Fearnley. 4-5r USA. prod/rel: Famous Players Film Co., State Rights
My Best Girl, New York 1912, Musical Play
  My Best Girl 1915. lps: Max Figman, Lois Meredith, Lawrence Peyton. 5r USA. prod/rel: Rolfe Photoplays, Inc., Metro Pictures Corp.©
A Perfect Lady, New York 1914, Play
  Perfect Lady, A 1918 d: Clarence Badger. lps: Madge Kennedy, Jere Austin, Rod La Rocque. 5r USA. prod/rel: Goldwyn Pictures Corp.©, Goldwyn Distributing Corp.
The Red Widow, New York 1911, Musical Play
  Red Widow, The 1916 d: James Durkin. lps: John Barrymore, Flora Zabelle, John Hendricks. 5r USA. prod/rel: Famous Players Film Co.©, Paramount Pictures Corp.

POLLOCK, CHANNING
Roads of Destiny, New York 1918, Novel
  Roads of Destiny 1921 d: Frank Lloyd. lps: Pauline Frederick, John Bowers, Richard Tucker. 4955f USA. prod/rel: Goldwyn Pictures

POLLOCK, CHANNING (1880–1946), USA
The Secret Orchard, New York 1907, Play
  Secret Orchard, The 1915 d: Frank Reicher. lps: Blanche Sweet, Cleo Ridgely, Gertrude Kellar. 5r USA. prod/rel: Jesse L. Lasky Feature Play Co.©, Paramount Pictures Corp.
The Sign on the Door, New York 1924, Play
  Sign on the Door, The 1921 d: Herbert Brenon. lps: Norma Talmadge, Charles Richman, Lew Cody. 7100f USA. prod/rel: Norma Talmadge Productions, Associated First National Pictures
  Locked Door, The 1929 d: George Fitzmaurice. lps: Rod La Rocque, Barbara Stanwyck, William Boyd. 6844f USA. prod/rel: Feature Productions, United Artists
The Street of Illusion, Story
  Street of Illusion, The 1928 d: Erle C. Kenton. lps: Virginia Valli, Ian Keith, Harry Myers. 5988f USA. prod/rel: Columbia Pictures
Such a Little Queen, New York 1909, Play
  Such a Little Queen 1914 d: Edwin S. Porter, Hugh Ford. lps: Mary Pickford, Carlyle Blackwell, Harold Lockwood. 5r USA. prod/rel: Famous Players Film Co., Paramount Pictures Corp.
  Such a Little Queen 1921 d: George Fawcett. lps: Constance Binney, Vincent Coleman, J. H. Gilmour. 4942f USA. prod/rel: Realart Pictures
Synthetic Gentleman, New York 1934, Novel
  Midnight Intruder 1937 d: Arthur Lubin. lps: Louis Hayward, Barbara Read, J. C. Nugent. 66M USA. prod/rel: Universal Pictures Co.©

POLLOCK, ROBERT
Loophole, Novel
  Loophole 1981 d: John Quested. lps: Albert Finney, Martin Sheen, Susannah York. 105M UKN. prod/rel: Brent Walker

POMERANCE, BERNARD
The Elephant Man, Play
  Elephant Man, The 1981 d: Jack Hofsiss. lps: Philip Anglim, Kevin Conway, Penny Fuller. TVM. 100M USA. prod/rel: ABC, Marble Arch

POMERANTZ, EDWARD
Into It, Novel
  Caught 1996 d: Robert M. Young. lps: Edward James Olmos, Maria Conchita Alonso, Arie Verveen. 116M USA. prod/rel: Cinehaus, Duart

POMMEROL, JEAN
Un Fruit . Et Puis un Autre Fruit, Novel
  Desir, Le 1928 d: Albert Durec. lps: Olaf Fjord, Roger Karl, Mary SertA. F FRN. prod/rel: Alex Nalpas

PONCHIELLI, AMILCARE (1834–1886), ITL
La Gioconda, Milan 1876, Opera
  Gioconda, La 1953 d: Giacinto Solito. lps: Alba Arnova, Paolo Carlini, Virginia Loy. F ITL. prod/rel: Org. Cin.Ca Internazionale

PONIATOWSKA, ELENA
Gaby, Book
  Gaby 1987 d: Luis Mandoki. lps: Norma Aleandro, Rachel Levin, Liv Ullmann. 114M MXC/USA/USA. *Gaby, a True Story; Gaby, Una Historia Verdadera* prod/rel: Tri-Star
De Noche Vienes, Esmeralda, Short Story
  De Noche Vienes, Esmeralda 1997 d: Jaime Humberto Hermosillo. lps: Maria Rojo, Claudio Obregon, Martha Navarro. 106M MXC. *Esmeralda Comes By Night* prod/rel: IMCine, Resoncia

PONICSAN, DARRYL
Cinderella Liberty, Novel
  Cinderella Liberty 1973 d: Mark Rydell. lps: James Caan, Marsha Mason, Eli Wallach. 117M USA. prod/rel: Sanford
The Last Detail, Novel
  Last Detail, The 1973 d: Hal Ashby. lps: Jack Nicholson, Otis Young, Randy Quaid. 103M USA. prod/rel: Acrobat, Bright-Persky Associates

PONSON DU TERRAIL, PIERRE-ALEXIS
Les Aventures de Rocambole
  Rocambole 1919 d: Giuseppe ZaccariA. lps: Luigi Maggi, Margot Pellegrinetti, Rina Maggi. 6761m ITL. prod/rel: A. de Rosa
Le Feuilleton
  Rocambole 1932 d: Gabriel RoscA. lps: Rolla Norman, Jim Gerald, Gil Clary. 91M FRN. prod/rel: Stella Film
Le Forgeron de la Cour Dieu, 1869, Novel
  Fabbro Del Convento, Il 1922 d: Vincenzo C. Denizot. lps: Paolo Ravigli, Valentina Frascaroli, G. M. de Vivo. SRL. 8156m ITL. prod/rel: Milano Film
  Fabbro Del Convento, Il 1949 d: Max Calandri. lps: Vera Bergmann, Guido Celano, Claudio GorA. 88M ITL. *Rivolta Dei Cosacchi, La* prod/rel: Gennaro Proto
Rocambole, Novel
  Rocambole 1947 d: Jacques de Baroncelli. lps: Pierre Brasseur, Lucien Nat, Sophie Desmarets. 200M FRN/ITL. prod/rel: Andre Paulve (Paris), Scalera Film (Roma)

PONTHIER, FRANCOIS
Manganese, Novel
  Ambitieuse, L' 1958 d: Yves Allegret. lps: Edmond O'Brien, Richard Basehart, Andrea Parisy. 95M FRN/ITL/ASL. *Climbers, The* (USA); *The Restless and the Damned; The Dispossessed* (UKN); *Les Ambitieux* prod/rel: Silver Films, Films Chrysaor

PONTIGGIA, GIUSEPPE
Facciamo Paradiso, Novel
  Facciamo Paradiso 1995 d: Mario Monicelli. lps: Margherita Buy, Lello Arena, Aurore Clement. 108M ITL. *Looking for Paradise; Let's Make Paradise* prod/rel: Clemi Cinematografica

PONZILLO, PASQUALE
O Schiaffo, Play
  Peggio Offesa, 'A 1924 d: Goffredo d'AndreA. lps: Miquel Di Giacomo, Anna Pastore, Francesco Amodio. 1228m ITL. prod/rel: Partenope Film

POOLE, RICHARD
The Peacemaker, 1954, Novel
  Peacemaker, The 1956 d: Ted Post. lps: James Mitchell, Rosemarie Bowe, Jan Merlin. 82M USA. prod/rel: United Artists, Hal R. Makelim Prods.

POOLE, VICTORIA
Thursday's Child, Book
  Thursday's Child 1982 d: David Lowell Rich. lps: Gena Rowlands, Don Murray, Jessica Walter. TVM. 100M USA.

POPESCU, DUMITRU RADU
Caruta Cu Mere, 1962, Short Story
  Caruta Cu Mere 1983 d: George CorneA. 102M RMN.
Duios Anastasia Trecea, 1967, Short Story
  Duios Anastasia Trecea 1979 d: Alexandru Tatos. 97M RMN. *Gently Passed Anastasia; Anastasia Passing Gently; Anastasia Passed By; Gently Was Anastasia Passing*

Padurea, 1962, Short Story
  Un Suris in Plina Vara 1963 d: Geo Saizescu. lps: Sebastian Papaiani, Dem Radulescu. 100M RMN. *A Midsummer Day's Smile*

POPKIN, ZELDA
A Death of Innocence, Novel
  Death of Innocence, A 1971 d: Paul Wendkos. lps: Shelley Winters, Arthur Kennedy, Tisha Sterling. TVM. 73M USA. prod/rel: Mark Carliner Productions

POPOVICI, TITUS
Moartea Lui Ipu, 1970, Short Story
  Moartea Lui Ipu 1972 d: Sergiu Nicolaescu. lps: Amza Pellea, Christian Sofron, Ion Besoiu. 100M RMN. *Atunci I-Am Condamnat Pe Toti la Moarte; Ipu's Death; Then We Condemned Them All to Death*
Setea, 1958, Novel
  Setea 1960 d: Mircea Dragan. lps: Stefan Ciobotarasu, Amza PelleA. 120M RMN. *Thirst*
Strainul, 1955, Novel
  Strainul 1964 d: Mihai Iacob. lps: Irina PetruscA. 106M RMN. *The Stranger*

POPPLEWELL, JACK
Blind Alley, 1953, Play
  Tread Softly Stranger 1958 d: Gordon Parry. lps: Diana Dors, George Baker, Terence Morgan. 90M UKN. prod/rel: Renown, Alderdale
Dead on Nine, Play
  Desilu Playhouse: Dead on Nine 1958-59 d: William F. Claxton. lps: Louis Hayward, Signe Hasso, Maxwell Reed. MTV. 50M USA. *Dead on Nine* prod/rel: CBS, Desilu

PORATH, BEN
Story
  A Chi Tocca..Tocca! 1978 d: Gianfranco Baldanello, Menahem Golan. lps: Fabio Testi, Janet Agren, Assaf Dayan. 120M ITL/GRM/ISR. *Agenten Kennen Keine Tranen* (GRM); *Die Uranium-Verschworung; Kesher Hauranium; Yellowcake Operazione Urano; The Uranium Conspiracy* prod/rel: Dunamis Cin.Ca (Milano), Regina Films (Munich)

PORTER, COLE
Anything Goes, New York 1934, Musical Play
  Anything Goes 1936 d: Lewis Milestone. lps: Bing Crosby, Ethel Merman, Charles Ruggles. 92M USA. *Tops Is the Limit* prod/rel: Paramount Productions, Inc.
  Anything Goes 1956 d: Robert Lewis. lps: Bing Crosby, Donald O'Connor, Zizi Jeanmaire. 106M USA. prod/rel: Paramount
Du Barry Was a Lady, New York 1939, Mplay
  Du Barry Was a Lady 1943 d: Roy Del Ruth. lps: Red Skelton, Lucille Ball, Gene Kelly. 101M USA. prod/rel: MGM
Fifty Million Frenchmen, New York 1929, Play
  Fifty Million Frenchmen 1931 d: Lloyd Bacon. lps: Ole Olsen, Chic Johnson, Claudia Dell. 68M USA. *50 Million Frenchmen* prod/rel: Warner Bros. Pictures©
Let's Face It, Musical Play
  Let's Face It 1943 d: Sidney Lanfield. lps: Bob Hope, Betty Hutton, Zasu Pitts. 76M USA. prod/rel: Paramount
Mexican Hayride, Musical Play
  Mexican Hayride 1948 d: Charles T. Barton. lps: Bud Abbott, Lou Costello, Virginia Grey. 77M USA. prod/rel: Universal-International
Panama Hattie, New York 1940, Musical Play
  Panama Hattie 1942 d: Norman Z. McLeod, Vincente Minnelli (Uncredited). lps: Ann Sothern, Red Skelton, Rags Ragland. 79M USA. prod/rel: MGM
Something for the Boys, New York 1943, Musical Play
  Something for the Boys 1944 d: Lewis Seiler. lps: Carmen Miranda, Michael O'Shea, Vivian Blaine. 87M USA. prod/rel: 20th Century Fox

PORTER, ELEANOR H. (1868–1920), USA, Porter, Eleanor Hodgman
Dawn, New York 1919, Novel
  Dawn 1919 d: J. Stuart Blackton. lps: Sylvia Breamer, Robert Gordon, Harry Davenport. 5537f USA. prod/rel: J. Stuart Blackton Feature Pictures, Inc, Pathe Exchange, Inc.©
Pollyanna, Boston 1913, Novel
  Pollyanna 1920 d: Paul Powell. lps: Mary Pickford, William Courtleigh Jr., Helen Jerome Eddy. 6r USA. prod/rel: Mary Pickford Co.©, United Artists Corp.
  Pollyanna 1960 d: David Swift. lps: Hayley Mills, Jane Wyman, Richard Egan. 134M USA.
  Pollyanna 1973 d: June Wyndham-Davis. lps: Elizabeth Archard, Elaine Stritch, Ray McAnally. MTV. 154M UKN.

PORTER, KATHERINE ANNE (1894–1980), USA
Short Story
  Noon Wine 1985 d: Michael Fields. lps: Fred Ward, Lise Hilboldt, Stellan Skarsgard. TVM. 81M USA. prod/rel: Noon Wine Company, Merchant Ivory Prods.
The Jilting of Granny Weatherall, 1930, Short Story
  Jilting of Granny Weatherall, The 1977 d: Randa Haines. lps: Geraldine Fitzgerald, Lois Smith. MTV. 55M USA. prod/rel: Learning in Focus
Ship of Fools, Boston 1962, Novel
  Ship of Fools 1965 d: Stanley Kramer. lps: Simone Signoret, Oskar Werner, Vivien Leigh. 149M USA. prod/rel: Columbia Pictures

PORTER, ROSE ALBERT
Chrysalis, New York 1932, Play
  All of Me 1934 d: James Flood. lps: Fredric March, Miriam Hopkins, George Raft. 75M USA. *Chrysalis* prod/rel: Paramount Productions, Inc.

PORTER, WILLIAM
Fourteen Hours from Chi, Short Storytor
  Hideout 1949 d: Philip Ford. lps: Lloyd Bridges, Adrian Booth, Ray Collins. 61M USA. prod/rel: Republic

PORTIS, CHARLES (1933–, USA
Norwood, New York 1966, Novel
  Norwood 1970 d: Jack Haley Jr. lps: Glen Campbell, Kim Darby, Joe Namath. 95M USA. prod/rel: Paramount Pictures
True Grit, New York 1968, Novel
  True Grit 1969 d: Henry Hathaway. lps: John Wayne, Kim Darby, Glen Campbell. 128M USA. prod/rel: Paramount Pictures

POSFORD, GEORGE
Radio Play
  Goodnight Vienna 1932 d: Herbert Wilcox. lps: Jack Buchanan, Anna Neagle, Gina Malo. 76M UKN. *Magic Night* (USA) prod/rel: British and Dominions, Woolf & Freedman
Balalaika, London 1936, Musical Play
  Balalaika 1939 d: Reinhold Schunzel. lps: Nelson Eddy, Ilona Massey, Charles Ruggles. 102M USA. prod/rel: Metro-Goldwyn-Mayer Corp.
Invitation to the Waltz, Radio Play
  Invitation to the Waltz 1935 d: Paul Merzbach. lps: Lilian Harvey, Carl Esmond, Harold Warrender. 77M UKN. prod/rel: British International Pictures, Wardour

POSMYSZ-PIASECKA, ZOFIA
Pasazerka, Novel
  Pasazerka 1963 d: Andrzej Munk, Witold Lesiewicz. lps: Jerzy Skolimowski, Aleksandra Slaska, Anna CiepielewskA. 62M PLN. *Passenger* (UKN); *La Passagere; Die Passagierin; Voyageurs* prod/rel: Kamera Film Unit

POSSENDORF, HANS
Sensationsprozess Casilla, Novel
  Sensationsprozess Cassilla 1939 d: Eduard von Borsody. lps: Heinrich George, Jutta Freybe, Albert Hehn. 109M GRM. prod/rel: UFA, Donau

POSSENDORFF, HANS
Le Clown Bux, Novel
  Clown Bux, Le 1935 d: Jacques Natanson. lps: Henri Rollan, Pierre Larquey, Suzy Vernon. 90M FRN. prod/rel: Acta-Films
Klettermaxe, Novel
  Klettermaxe 1927 d: Willy Reiber. lps: Dorothea Wieck, Corry Bell, Ruth Weyher. 2433m GRM. prod/rel: Munchener Lichtspielkunst Ag
  Klettermaxe 1952 d: Kurt Hoffmann. lps: Albert Lieven, Liselotte Pulver, Charlotte Bufford. 85M GRM. *Climber, The* prod/rel: Standard-Porta, N.W.D.F.
L'usuraio, Play
  Usuraio, L' 1943 d: Harry Hasso. lps: Maria de Tasnady, Rafael Calvo, Luis Hurtado. 80M ITL. prod/rel: Bassoli, S.a.C.C.I.

POST, HENRY
Artic
  Red Light Sting, The 1984 d: Rod Holcomb. lps: Farrah Fawcett, Beau Bridges, Harold Gould. TVM. 100M USA. *The Red-Light Sting* prod/rel: Universal

POST, JACQUES
Leer Om Leer, Novel
  Leer Om Leer 1983 d: Juul Claes. lps: Marc Leemans, Mike Verdrengh, machteld Ramoudt. TVM. 63M BLG.

POST, VAN ZO
Diana Ardway, Philadelphia 1913, Novel
  Satan Junior 1919 d: Herbert Blache, John H. Collins. lps: Viola Dana, Milton Sills, Lloyd Hughes. 5r USA. *Diana Ardway* prod/rel: Metro Picture Corp.©

POST, W. H.
Never Say Die, New York 1912, Play
  Never Say Die 1924 d: George J. Crone. lps: Douglas MacLean, Lillian Rich, Helen Ferguson. 5891f USA. prod/rel: Douglas Maclean Productions, Associated Exhibitors
  Never Say Die 1939 d: Elliott Nugent. lps: Martha Raye, Bob Hope, Andy Devine. 80M USA. prod/rel: Paramount Pictures

POSTELNICU, IOANA
Intoarcerea Vlasinilor, 1979, Novel
  Intoarcerea Vlasinilor 1983 d: Mircea Dragan. 108M RMN. *Vlashins' Return*
Plecarea Vlasinilor, 1964, Novel
  Plecarea Vlasinilor 1982 d: Mircea Dragan. 112M RMN. *Vlashins' Leaving*

POTHIER, CHARLES
La Pouponniere, Opera
  Pouponniere, La 1932 d: Jean Boyer. lps: Robert Arnoux, Rene Koval, Germaine Roger. 80M FRN. prod/rel: Films Paramount

POTOCKI, JAN
Le Manuscrit Trouve a Saragosse, 1815, Novel
  Rekopis Znaleziony W Saragossie 1965 d: Wojciech J. Has. lps: Zbigniew Cybulski, Gustaw Holoubek, Barbara KrafftownA. 180M PLN. *The Saragossa Manuscript* (USA); *Adventures of a Nobleman; Manuscript Found in Saragossa; A Diary Found in Saragossa* prod/rel: Kamera Film Unit

POTOK, CHAIM (1929–, USA
The Chosen, Novel
  Chosen, The 1981 d: Jeremy Paul Kagan. lps: Maximilian Schell, Rod Steiger, Robby Benson. 108M USA. prod/rel: the Chosen Film Company, 20th Century-Fox Int. Classics

POTTER, BEATRIX (1866–1943), UKN
Short Stories
  Tales of Beatrix Potter 1971 d: Reginald Mills. lps: Frederick Ashton, Alexander Grant, Michael Coleman. 90M UKN. *Peter Rabbit and Tales of Beatrix Potter* (USA) prod/rel: Emi
The Tailor of Gloucester, Story
  Tailor of Gloucester, The 1990 d: John Michael Philips. lps: Ian Holm, Thora Hird, Benjamin Luxon. 45M UKN.

POTTER, DAVID
Diane of Star Hollow, Story
  Diane of Star Hollow 1921 d: Oliver L. Sellers. lps: Bernard Durning, Evelyn Greeley, George Majeroni. 6r USA. prod/rel: C. R. Macauley Photo Plays, Producers Security Corp.

POTTER, DENNIS (1935–1994), UKN
Brimstone and Treacle, 1978, Play
  Brimstone & Treacle 1981 d: Richard Loncraine. lps: Sting, Denholm Elliott, Joan Plowright. 83M UKN. prod/rel: Namara, Alan E. Salke
Pennies from Heaven, 1981, Play
  Pennies from Heaven 1981 d: Herbert Ross. lps: Steve Martin, Bernadette Peters, Christopher Walken. 108M USA. prod/rel: MGM, United Artists
Sufficient Carbohydrate, Play
  Visitors 1987 d: Piers Haggard. lps: Michael Brandon, John Standing, Nicola Pagett. TVM. 95M UKN. prod/rel: BBC
Ticket to Ride, Novel
  Secret Friends 1991 d: Dennis Potter. lps: Alan Bates, Gina Bellman, Frances Barber. 97M UKN. prod/rel: Feature Film Co., Film Four International

POTTER, GEORGE
The Tiger's Cub, London 1915, Play
  Tiger's Cub, The 1920 d: Charles Giblyn. lps: Pearl White, Thomas J. Carrigan, J. Thornton Baston. 6r USA. *The Tiger Cub* prod/rel: Fox Film Corp., William Fox©

POTTER, H. C.
What's a Fixer for?, New Haven, Ct. 1928, Play
  Fixer Dugan 1939 d: Lew Landers. lps: Lee Tracy, Virginia Weidler, Peggy Shannon. 68M USA. *Double Daring* (UKN); *What's a Fixer for?* prod/rel: RKO Radio Pictures©

POTTER, JAMES BROWN
'Ostler Joe, Short Story
  'Ostler Joe 1908 d: Wallace McCutcheon. lps: D. W. Griffith, Eddie Dillon. 877f USA. prod/rel: Biograph Co.

POTTER, JENNIFER
Strange Days, Novel
  Flight to Berlin 1983 d: Christopher Petit. lps: Tusse Silberg, Paul Freeman, Lisa Kreuzer. 90M UKN/GRM. *Fluchtpunkt Berlin* (GRM) prod/rel: British Film Institute, Road Movies

POTTER, PAUL M.
Agnes, Play
Woman's Experience, A 1918 d: Perry N. Vekroff. lps: Mary Boland, Sam Hardy, Lawrence McGill. 6r USA. prod/rel: Bacon-Backer Film Corp., Independent Sales Corp.©

The Conquerors, New York 1898, Play
War of Wars; Or, the Franco-German Invasion, The 1914 d: Will S. Davis. lps: Edith Hallor, Stuart Holmes, Miss Mayo. 6r USA. *Franco-German Invasion, The; The Conquerors; War of Wars, The* prod/rel: Ramo Films, Inc.©, State Rights
Test of Womanhood, The 1917. lps: Stuart Holmes. 5r USA. prod/rel: Joseph R. Miles, State Rights

The Girl from Rector's, New York 1909, Play
Girl from Rector's, The 1917. lps: Ruth MacTammany, Lillian Concord. 5r USA. prod/rel: Mutual Film Corp., Mutual Star Productions

The Money Habit, Novel
Money Habit, The 1924 d: Walter Niebuhr. lps: Clive Brook, Annette Benson, Nina VannA. 6400f UKN. prod/rel: Commonwealth, Granger

Queen of the Moulin Rouge, New York 1908, Play
Queen of the Moulin Rouge 1922 d: Ray C. Smallwood. lps: Martha Mansfield, Joseph Striker, Henry Harmon. 6704f USA. prod/rel: Pyramid Pictures, American Releasing Corp.

POTTER, STEPHEN (1900–1969), UKN
Gamesmanship / Oneupmanship / Lifemanship, Books
School for Scoundrels Or How to Win Without Actually Cheating 1960 d: Robert Hamer. lps: Ian Carmichael, Terry-Thomas, Janette Scott. 94M UKN. *School for Scoundrels* prod/rel: Guardsman, Wpd

POTTS, RALPH B.
Come Now the Lawyers, Novel
Specialist, The 1975 d: Howard Avedis. lps: Ahna Capri, John Anderson, Adam West. 93M USA. prod/rel: Crown International

POUL, FRANTISEK
Short Story
Kralovna Stribrnych Hor 1939 d: Karel SpelinA. lps: Vilem Pfeiffer, Ella Nollova, Vera KratochvilovA. F CZC. *Queen of the Silver Mountains* prod/rel: Dafa

POULBOT, M.
Les Gosses Dans Les Ruines, Play
Kiddies in the Ruins, The 1918 d: George Pearson. lps: Emmie Lynn, Hugh E. Wright, Georges Colin. 2600f UKN. prod/rel: Welsh, Pearson
Gosses Dans Les Ruines, Les 1918 d: George Pearson. lps: Georges Colin, Simone Prevost, Emmy Lynn. 780m FRN.

POULGY, PAUL
La Fin de Monte-Carlo, Novel
Fin de Monte-Carlo, Le 1926 d: Mario Nalpas, Henri Etievant. lps: Jean Angelo, Francesca Bertini, Jeanne Marie-Laurent. F FRN. prod/rel: Centrale Cine. Et Intl. Standard Film

POULSEN, KNUD
Dyden Gar Amok, Novel
Dyden Gar Amok 1967 d: Sven Methling. lps: John Han-Petersen, Birgitte Federspiel, Axel Strobye. 95M DNM. *Virtue Runs Wild* prod/rel: Saga, Topas

POULTNEY, C. B.
A Wife Or Two, Play
Wife Or Two, A 1936 d: MacLean Rogers. lps: Henry Kendall, Nancy Burne, Betty Astell. 63M UKN. prod/rel: British Lion

POUPLIER, ERIK
Sommar Och Syndare, Novel
Sommar Och Syndare 1960 d: Arne Mattsson. lps: Elsa Prawitz, Karl Arne Holsten, Yvonne Lombard. 84M SWD/DNM. *Summer and Sinners* prod/rel: Lorens Marmstedt

POWELL, DAWN (1897–1965), USA
Story of a Country Boy, New York 1934, Novel
Man of Iron 1935 d: William McGann. lps: Barton MacLane, Dorothy Peterson, Mary Astor. 62M USA. prod/rel: First National Productions Corp., Warner Bros. Pictures©

Walking Down Broadway, Play
Hello, Sister! 1933 d: Erich von Stroheim, Alfred L. Werker. lps: James Dunn, Boots Mallory, Zasu Pitts. 63M USA. *Clipped Wings* (UKN) prod/rel: Fox Film Corp.©

POWELL, JONATHAN
Champion'story, Book
Champions 1983 d: John Irvin. lps: John Hurt, Edward Woodward, Jan Francis. 115M UKN. prod/rel: Embassy, Archerwest

POWELL, LESTER
Return from Darkness, Story
Black Widow 1951 d: Vernon Sewell. lps: Christine Norden, Robert Ayres, Anthony Forwood. 62M UKN. prod/rel: Exclusive, Hammer

POWELL, MICHAEL (1905–1990), UKN
Graf Spee, Book
Battle of the River Plate 1956 d: Michael Powell, Emeric Pressburger. lps: John Gregson, Anthony Quayle, Peter Finch. 119M UKN. *Pursuit of the Graf Spree* (USA) prod/rel: Rank Film Distributors, Arcturus

POWELL, RICHARD
The Philadelphian, 1956, Novel
Young Philadelphians, The 1959 d: Vincent Sherman. lps: Paul Newman, Barbara Rush, Alexis Smith. 136M USA. *The City Jungle* (UKN) prod/rel: Warner Bros.

Pioneer, Go Home!, New York 1959, Novel
Follow That Dream 1962 d: Gordon Douglas. lps: Elvis Presley, Arthur O'Connell, Anne Helm. 110M USA. *Pioneer, Go Home!*; *What a Wonderful Life* prod/rel: Mirisch Co., Universal

POWER, M. S.
The Stalker's Apprentice, Novel
Stalker's Apprentice, The 1998 d: Marcus D. F. White. lps: James Bolam, Peter Davison, Paula Wilcox. TVM. F UKN. prod/rel: Flextech Tv

POWERS, ART
Framed, Novel
Framed 1975 d: Phil Karlson. lps: Joe Don Baker, Connie Van Dyke, Gabriel Dell. 101M USA. prod/rel: Briskin

POWERS, DAVID F.
Johnny, We Hardly Knew Ye, 1972, Book
Johnny, We Hardly Knew Ye 1977 d: Gilbert Cates. lps: Paul Rudd, William Prince, Burgess Meredith. TVM. 100M USA. prod/rel: Talent Associates Ltd., Jamel Productions

POWERS, FRANCIS
The First Born, New York 1897, Play
First Born, The 1921 d: Colin Campbell. lps: Sessue Hayakawa, Helen Jerome Eddy, Sonny Boy Warde. 5-6r USA. prod/rel: Hayakawa Feature Play Co., Robertson-Cole Distributing Corp.

POWERS, GARY FRANCIS
Operation Overflight, Book
Francis Gary Powers:the True Story of the U-2 Spy Incident 1976 d: Delbert Mann. lps: Lee Majors, Noah Beery Jr., Nehemiah Persoff. TVM. 100M USA. prod/rel: Charles Fries Productions, NBC

POWERS, JOHN
The Last of the Knucklemen, Play
Last of the Knucklemen, The 1979 d: Tim Burstall. lps: Gerard Kennedy, Mike Preston, Michael Duffield. 93M ASL. prod/rel: Hexagon©, Victorian Film Corporation

POWERS, JOHN R.
John Robert Powers, Book
Powers Girl, The 1942 d: Norman Z. McLeod. lps: George Murphy, Anne Shirley, Dennis Day. 93M USA. *Hello! Beautiful* (UKN) prod/rel: United Artists

POWYS, STEPHEN
Three Blind Mice, London 1938, Play
Three Blind Mice 1938 d: William A. Seiter. lps: Loretta Young, Joel McCrea, David Niven. 75M USA. prod/rel: Twentieth Century-Fox Film Corp.©
Moon Over Miami 1941 d: Walter Lang. lps: Betty Grable, Don Ameche, Robert Cummings. 91M USA. *Miami* prod/rel: 20th Century-Fox Film Corp.
Three Little Girls in Blue 1946 d: H. Bruce Humberstone. lps: June Haver, Vivian Blaine, George Montgomery. 90M USA. prod/rel: 20th Century-Fox Film Corp.

POYNTER, BEULAH
Her Spendid Folly, Novel
Her Splendid Folly 1933 d: William A. O'Connor. lps: Lillian Bond, Lloyd Whitlock, Theodore von Eltz. 60M USA. *Splendid Folly* prod/rel: Progressive Pictures Corp.

The Little Girl That He Forgot, Play
Little Girl That He Forgot, The 1914. lps: Beulah Poynter. 5r USA. prod/rel: Cosmos Feature Film Corp.©, State Rights

The Marrying of Emmy, 1919, Short Story
Miracle of Money, The 1920 d: Hobart Henley. lps: Margaret Seddon, Bess Gearhart Morrison, David Briggs. 4515f USA. prod/rel: Hobart Henley Productions, Pathe Exchange, Inc.

PRADELS, OCTAVE
Lorsqu'une Femme Veut, Play
Lorsqu'une Femme Veut 1918 d: Georges MoncA. lps: Jean Worms, Simone Frevalles. 1415m FRN. prod/rel: Scagl

Misericorde, Short Story
Misericorde 1917 d: Camille de Morlhon. lps: Gabriel Signoret, Maurice Varny, Marise Dauvray. 1425m FRN. prod/rel: Films Valetta

PRAGA, MARCO
L'amico, 1886, Play
Amico, L' 1921 d: Mario Bonnard. lps: Mario Bonnard, Vittoria Lepanto, Camillo Apolloni. 1456m ITL. prod/rel: Bonnard Film

La Biondina, 1893, Novel
Biondina, La 1923 d: Amleto Palermi. lps: Pina Menichelli, Livio Pavanelli, Gemma de Ferrari. 1674m ITL. prod/rel: Rinascimento Film

Biondina, La, 1893, Novel
Ultimo Incontro 1952 d: Gianni Franciolini. lps: Alida Valli, Amedeo Nazzari, Jean-Pierre Aumont. 88M ITL. *Derniere Rencontre* (FRN) prod/rel: Dino de Laurentiis, Carlo Ponti

La Crisi, 1904, Play
Crisi, La 1922 d: Augusto GeninA. lps: Edy Darclea, Ettore Piergiovanni, Giorgio Bonaiti. 1699m ITL. prod/rel: Cines

L'ondina, 1903, Play
Ondina, L' 1917 d: A. Albertoni. lps: Bianca Virginia Camagni, Uberto Palmarini, Enrico Piacentini. 1566m ITL. prod/rel: Comerio Film

Le Vergini, 1889, Play
Tre Sorelle, Le 1918 d: Giuseppe Sterni. lps: Alba Primavera, Giuseppe Sterni. 1185m ITL. *Le Vergini* prod/rel: Silentium Film

PRANGE, GORDON W.
Tora! Tora! Tora!, New York 1969, Book
Tora! Tora! Tora! 1970 d: Richard Fleischer, Toshio MasudA. lps: Martin Balsam, So Yamamura, Joseph Cotten. 143M USA/JPN. prod/rel: Elmo Williams, Richard Fleischer

PRASKINS, LEONARD
The Charlatan, New York 1922, Play
Charlatan, The 1929 d: George Melford. lps: Holmes Herbert, Margaret Livingston, Rockliffe Fellowes. 6097f USA. prod/rel: Universal Pictures

The Maverick, Short Story
Three Violent People 1956 d: Rudolph Mate. lps: Charlton Heston, Anne Baxter, Gilbert Roland. 100M USA. prod/rel: Paramount

PRATESI, MARIO
L'eredita, Florence 1889, Novel
Viaccia, La 1961 d: Mauro Bolognini. lps: Jean-Paul Belmondo, Claudia Cardinale, Pietro Germi. 106M ITL/FRN. *The Love Makers*; *The Bad Road* prod/rel: Titanus, Arco Film

PRATOLINI, VASCO (1913–, ITL
La Costanza Della Ragione, 1963, Novel
Costanza Della Ragione, La 1964 d: Pasquale Festa Campanile. lps: Sami Frey, Catherine Deneuve, Enrico Maria Salerno. 120M ITL/FRN. *Avec Amour Et Avec Rage* (FRN) prod/rel: Franca Film (Roma), Ste. Novelle de Cie. (Paris)

Cronaca Familiare, Florence 1947, Novel
Cronaca Familiare 1962 d: Valerio Zurlini. lps: Marcello Mastroianni, Jacques Perrin, Salvo Randone. 122M ITL. *Family Diary* (USA); *Family History* prod/rel: Titanus

Cronache Di Poveri Amanti, 1947, Novel
Cronache Di Poveri Amanti 1954 d: Carlo Lizzani. lps: Anna Maria Ferrero, Cosetta Greco, Antonella Lualdi. 115M ITL. *True Stories of Poor Lovers*; *Chronicle of Poor Lovers*; *Stories of Poor Lovers* prod/rel: Cooperativa Spettatori Prod. Cin., Minerva Film

La Domenica Della Buona Gente, Radio Play
Domenica Della Buona Gente, La 1954 d: Anton Giulio Majano. lps: Maria Fiore, Sophia Loren, Renato Salvatori. 95M ITL. *Good People's Sunday* prod/rel: Trionfalcine, Siden Film

Un Eroe Del Nostro Tempo, Novel
Eroe Del Nostro Tempo, Un 1960 d: Sergio CapognA. lps: Marina Berti, Massimo Tonna, Margherita Autuori. 112M ITL. *Camicia Nera* prod/rel: Giuliana Scappino

Metello, 1955, Novel
Metello 1970 d: Mauro Bolognini. lps: Massimo Ranieri, Lucia Bose, Frank Wolff. 112M ITL. prod/rel: Documento Film, Titanus

Le Ragazze Di Sanfrediano, 1949, Novel
Ragazze Di San Frediano, Le 1955 d: Valerio Zurlini. lps: Antonio Cifariello, Corinne Calvet, Marcella Mariani. 114M ITL. *The Girls of San Frediano* prod/rel: Lux Film

Vanda, Short Story
Diario Di un Italiano 1973 d: Sergio CapognA. lps: Donatello, Mara Venier, Pier Paolo Capponi. 95M ITL. prod/rel: Faser Film, Jumbo Cin.Ca

PRATT, THEODORE
The Barefoot Mailman, Novel
Barefoot Mailman, The 1951 d: Earl McEvoy. lps: Robert Cummings, Jerome Courtland, Terry Moore. 83M USA. prod/rel: Columbia

Jook Girl, Novel
Juke Girl 1942 d: Curtis Bernhardt. lps: Ann Sheridan, Ronald Reagan, Richard Whorf. 90M USA. prod/rel: Warner Bros.

Mercy Island, Novel
Mercy Island 1941 d: William Morgan. lps: Ray Middleton, Gloria Dickson, Otto Kruger. 72M USA. prod/rel: Republic

Mr. Limpet, New York 1942, Novel
Incredible Mr. Limpet, The 1964 d: Arthur Lubin. lps: Don Knotts, Carole Cook, Andrew Duggan. 102M USA. *Be Careful How You Wish; Henry Limpet; Mr. Limpet* prod/rel: Warner Bros. Pictures

Mr. Winkle Goes to War, Novel
Mr. Winkle Goes to War 1944 d: Alfred E. Green. lps: Edward G. Robinson, Ruth Warrick, Ted Donaldson. 80M USA. *Arms and the Woman* (UKN) prod/rel: Columbia

PRAXY, RAOUL
Dollars, Play
Jeunes Filles a Marier 1935 d: Jean Vallee. lps: Jules Berry, Josseline Gael, Maurice Escande. 82M FRN. *Huit Jeunes Filles a Marier* prod/rel: Paris-Color-Films

Jeff
Apres Vous, Duchesse 1954 d: Robert de Nesle. lps: Jacqueline Pierreux, Jean Paredes, Jacques Morel. 80M FRN. prod/rel: Comptoir Francais De Prods. Cinematogr.

Par le Bout du Nez, Opera
Enlevez-Moi 1932 d: Leonce Perret. lps: Roger Treville, Jean Devalde, Jacqueline Francell. 98M FRN. prod/rel: Pathe-Natan

PRAZY, RAOUL
Un Tour de Cochon, Play
Tour de Cochon, Un 1934 d: Joseph Tzipine. lps: Romain Bouquet, Mona Goya, Alice Tissot. 85M FRN. prod/rel: Prodis

PREBBLE, JOHN
Bats With Baby Faces, Novel
Sky West and Crooked 1965 d: John Mills. lps: Hayley Mills, Ian McShane, Laurence Naismith. 102M UKN. *Gypsy Girl* (USA); *Bats With Baby Faces* prod/rel: Rank Film Distributors, John Mills

My Great-Aunt Appearing Day, Story
White Feather 1955 d: Robert D. Webb. lps: Robert Wagner, Jeffrey Hunter, Hugh O'Brian. 102M USA. prod/rel: 20th Century-Fox, Panoramic Prods.

PREDA, MARIN
Albastra Zare a Mortii, 1948, Short Story
Portile Albastre Ale Orasului 1973 d: Mircea Muresan. lps: Romeo Pop, Dan Nusu, Ion Caramitru. 98M RMN. *The Blue Gates of the City; At the Blue Gates of the Town*

Desfasurarea, 1952, Short Story
De Sfasurarea 1954 d: Paul Calinescu. lps: Stefan Ciobotarasu, Liviu Ciulei. 73M RMN. *In a Village*

Intinirea Din Paminturi, 1948, Short Story
Intinirea Din Paminturi 1983 d: Dumitru Dinulescu. 27M RMN.

Intrusul, 1968, Novel
Imposibila Iubire 1984 d: Constantin Vaeni. lps: Amza PelleA. 166M RMN. *Impossible Love*

Marele Singuratic, 1972, Novel
Marele Singuratic 1976 d: Iulian Mihu. 108M RMN. *Great Solitary, The*

Morometii, 1955, Novel
Morometii 1988 d: Stere GuleA. lps: Teodora Mares, Florin Zamfirescu, Mitica Popescu. 109M RMN.

PREEDY, GEORGE
General Crack, London 1928, Novel
General Crack 1929 d: Alan Crosland. lps: John Barrymore, Philippe de Lacy, Lowell Sherman. 9809f USA. prod/rel: Warner Brothers Pictures

PREISSOVA, GABRIELA
Jeji Pastorkyna, Play
Jeji Pastorkyna 1929 d: Rudolf Mestak. lps: Gabriela Horvatova, Thilde Ondra, Vaclav Norman. 2545m CZC. *Her Stepdaughter* prod/rel: Republicfilm

Jeji Pastorkyne 1938 d: Miroslav Cikan. lps: Marie Ptakova, Leopolda Dostalova, Marie GlazrovA. 2203m CZC. *Her Stepdaughter* prod/rel: Lloyd

PREJEAN, SISTER HELEN
Dead Man Walking, Book
Dead Man Walking 1995 d: Tim Robbins. lps: Susan Sarandon, Sean Penn, Robert Prosky. 122M USA. prod/rel: Working Title, Havoc

PREMCHAND
Bazaar-E-Husn, 1919, Novel
Seva Sadan 1938 d: K. Subrahmanyam. lps: M. S. Subbulakshmi, F. G. Natesa Iyer, Mrs. Jayalakshmi. 210M IND. *Seva Sadanam* prod/rel: Chandraprabha Cinetone

Godan, 1936, Novel
Godan 1962 d: Trilok Jetley. lps: Raaj Kumar, Kamini Kaushal, ShashikalA. 110M IND. *Godaan; Do Daan*

Sadgati, 1931, Short Story
Sadgati 1981 d: Satyajit Ray. lps: Om Puri, Mohan Agashe, Smita Patil. TVM. 52M IND. *Deliverance* prod/rel: Doordarshan

Satranj Ke Khilari, 1935, Short Story
Shatranj Ke Khiladi 1977 d: Satyajit Ray. lps: Sanjeev Kumar, Saeed Jaffrey, Richard Attenborough. 128M IND. *The Chess Players* (USA); *Shatranj Ke Khilari* prod/rel: Devki Chitra

PREMCHAND, MUNSHI
Do Bailon Ki Katha, 1936, Ss
Heera Moti 1959 d: Krishan ChoprA. lps: Nirupa Roy, Balraj Sahni. 131M IND. *Diamonds and Pearls; Hira Moti*

Do Bailon Ki Katha, 1936, Short Story
Oka Oorie Katha 1977 d: Mrinal Sen. lps: M. V. Vasudeva Rao, Mamata Shankar, G. Narayana Rao. 116M IND. *Story of a Village; The Outsiders; A Village Story* prod/rel: Chandrodaya Art

Gaban, 1930, Novel
Gaban 1966 d: Krishan Chopra, Hrishikesh Mukherjee. lps: Sunil Dutt, Sadhana, Zeb Rehman. 169M IND. prod/rel: B.I. Prod.

PRENTOUT, RICHARD
Le Sentier, Avignon 1959, Novel
Arretez Les Tambours 1961 d: Georges Lautner. lps: Bernard Blier, Lucille Saint-Simon, Lutz Gabor. 108M FRN. *Women and War* (USA); *Women in War* prod/rel: Films De La Bourdonnaye, Compagnie Lyonnaise De Cinema

PRESES, PETER
Der Bockerer, Play
Bockerer, Der 1981 d: Franz Antel. lps: Karl Merkatz, Ida Krottendorf, Alfred Bohm. 104M AUS/GRM. *The Obstinate Man; The Fusspot; Herr Bockerer* prod/rel: T.I.T., Neue Delta

Man Ist Nur Zweim Jung, Play
Man Ist Nur Zweimal Jung 1958 d: Helmut Weiss. lps: Wolf Albach-Retty, Winnie Markus, Heidi Bruhl. 96M AUS. prod/rel: Mundus, Excelsior

PRESNELL, FRANK G.
Send Another Coffin, New York 1939, Novel
Slightly Honorable 1939 d: Tay Garnett. lps: Pat O'Brien, Edward Arnold, Broderick Crawford. 83M USA. *Send Another Coffin; Send in Another Coffin* prod/rel: Walter Wanger Productions©, Tay Garnett Production

PRESNELL, ROBERT
Story
Meet John Doe 1941 d: Frank CaprA. lps: Gary Cooper, Barbara Stanwyck, Edward Arnold. 132M USA. *John Doe, Dynamite* (UKN) prod/rel: Warner Bros.

PRESSBURGER, EMERIC (1885–1951), HNG
Killing a Mouse on Sunday, London 1961, Novel
Behold a Pale Horse 1964 d: Fred Zinnemann. lps: Anthony Peck, Anthony Quinn, Omar Sharif. 118M USA/FRN. *Et Vient le Jour de Vengeance* (FRN) prod/rel: Highland-Brentwood Productions

PRESSLER, MIRJAM
Novemberkatzen, Novel
Novemberkatzen 1985 d: Sigrun Koeppe. lps: Angela Hunger, Ursela Monn, Katharina Brauren. 100M GRM. *November Cats* prod/rel: Quadriga, Tornesch

PRESTON, DOUGLAS
The Relic, Novel
Relic, The 1997 d: Peter Hyams. lps: Penelope Ann Miller, Tom Sizemore, Linda Hunt. 110M USA. prod/rel: Pacific Western, Paramount Pictures Corporation

PRESTON, HUGH
Head Office, Novel
Head Office 1936 d: Melville Brown. lps: Owen Nares, Nancy O'Neil, Arthur Margetson. 90M UKN. prod/rel: Warner Bros., First National

PRESTON, JOHN F.
Rogues of the Turf, Play
Rogues of the Turf 1923 d: Wilfred Noy. lps: Fred Groves, Olive Sloane, James Lindsay. 5899f UKN. prod/rel: Carlton, Butcher's Film Service

PRETI, LUIGI
L'ebreo Fascista, Novel
Ebreo Fascista, L' 1980 d: Franco Mole. lps: Ray Lovelock, Martine Brochard, Silvia Dionisio. 102M ITL. *Lunga Notte, La* prod/rel: Dionysio Cin.Ca

Giovinezza, Giovinezza, Novel
Giovinezza, Giovinezza 1969 d: Franco Rossi. lps: Alain Noury, Roberto Lande, Leonard Mann. 108M ITL. *Youth March* (USA); *Youth, Youth* prod/rel: Daniel Film, Titanus

PRETRE, MARCEL G.
La Chair a Poissons, Novel
Dans l'Eau Qui Fait Des Bulles 1961 d: Maurice Delbez. lps: Louis de Funes, Pierre Dudan, Marthe Mercadier. 90M FRN. *Le Garde-Champetre Mene l'Enquete* prod/rel: Kerfrance

La Revanche Des Mediocres, Novel
Etrange Monsieur Steve, L' 1957 d: Raymond Bailly. lps: Jeanne Moreau, Philippe Lemaire, Armand Mestral. 90M FRN. *Mr. Steve* (USA); *Plus Mort Que Vif* prod/rel: Pierre Chicherio, Pecefilms

PREUSSLER, OTFRIED
Book
Carodejuv Ucen 1977 d: Karel Zeman. ANM. 75M CZC/GRM. *Krabat* (GRM); *Krabat Carodejuv Ucen*; *Magician's Apprentice, The; Carode Juv Ucen* prod/rel: Ceskoslovensky, Bavaria

Neues Vom Rauber Hotzenplotz, Book
Neues Vom Rauber Hotzenplotz 1978 d: Gustav Ehmck. lps: Peter Kern, Barbara Valentin, Carsta Lock. 103M GRM. *The New Adventures of the Robber Hotzenplotz* prod/rel: Ehmck-Film, Jugendfilm

Der Rauber Hotzenplotz, Book
Rauber Hotzenplotz, Der 1973 d: Gustav Ehmck. lps: Gert Frobe, Lina Carstens, Rainer Basedow. 114M GRM. *The Robber Hotzenplotz* prod/rel: Ehmck-Film, Jugendfilm

PREUSSLER, OTTFRIED
Mala Carodejnice, Novel
Mala Carodejnice 1983 d: Zdenek SmetanA. ANM. 91M CZC/GRM. *Wie Die Kleine Hexe Zaubern Lernte* (GRM) prod/rel: Studio Kratky Film Prag

PREVOST D'EXILES, ANTOINE-FRANCOIS (1697–1763), FRN, Prevost, L'Abbe
L'histoire du Chevalier Des Grieux Et de Manon Lescaut, La Haye 1731, Novel
Manon Lescaut 1908. 263m ITL. prod/rel: Itala Film

Manon Lescaut 1912 d: Albert Capellani. lps: Leon Bernard, Matrat, Berangere. 890m FRN. prod/rel: Film d'Art

Manon Lescaut 1914 d: Herbert Hall Winslow. lps: Lina Cavalieri, Lucien Muratore, Dorothy Arthur. 6r USA. prod/rel: Playgoers Film Co.

Manon Lescaut 1918 d: Mario Gargiulo. lps: Tina Xeo, Raffaello Mariani, Giuseppe GiuffridA. 1337m ITL. prod/rel: Flegrea Film

Manon Lescaut 1919 d: Friedrich Zelnik. lps: Lya Mara, Fred Selva-Goebel, Ferdinand Bonn. 1835m GRM. *Das Hohe Lied Der Liebe*

Manon Lescaut 1926 d: Arthur Robison. lps: Lya de Putti, Wladimir Gaidarow, Eduard Rothauser. 2645m GRM.

Manon Lescaut 1940 d: Carmine Gallone. lps: Alida Valli, Vittorio de Sica, Dino Di LucA. 92M ITL. prod/rel: Grandi Film Storici, I.C.I.

Manon 1948 d: Henri-Georges Clouzot. lps: Cecile Aubrey, Serge Reggiani, Michel Auclair. 90M FRN. prod/rel: Alcina

Amori Di Manon Lescaut, Gli 1955 d: Mario CostA. lps: Myriam Bru, Franco Interlenghi, Roger Pigaut. 97M ITL/FRN. *Les Amours de Manon Lescaut* (FRN) prod/rel: Rizzoli Film, Royal Film (Roma)

Manon 70 1968 d: Jean Aurel. lps: Catherine Deneuve, Sami Frey, Jean-Claude Brialy. 110M FRN/GRM/ITL. *Hemmungslose Manon* (GRM); *Manon, Woman Without Scruples; Manon '70; Perverse Moon* prod/rel: Films Corona, Transinter Films

PREVOST D'EXILES, ANTOINE-FRANCOIS
When a Man Loves 1927 d: Alan Crosland. lps: John Barrymore, Dolores Costello, Warner Oland. 10r USA. *His Lady* prod/rel: Warner Brothers Pictures

PREVOST, JEAN
Les Freres Bouquinquant, Novel
Freres Bouquinquant, Les 1947 d: Louis Daquin. lps: Albert Prejean, Roger Pigaut, Madeleine Robinson. 99M FRN. prod/rel: Films Alkam

PREVOST, MARCEL

Les Demi-Vierges, 1895, Novel
Romanzo Di Maud, Il 1917 d: Diana Karenne. lps: Diana Karenne, Alberto A. Capozzi, Francesco Cacace. 1339m ITL. *Demi-Vierges, Les* prod/rel: S.A. Ambrosio

Les Demi- Vierges, 1895, Novel
Demi-Vierges, Les 1924 d: Armand Du Plessis. lps: Germaine Fontanes, Gabriel de Gravone, Gaston Jacquet. SRL. 6EP FRN. prod/rel: First-Films

Les Demi-Vierges, 1895, Novel
Demi-Vierges, Les 1936 d: Pierre Caron. lps: Marie Bell, Madeleine Renaud, Daniel Lecourtois. 89M FRN. prod/rel: Productions Claude Dolbert

Marie Des Angoisses, Novel
Marie Des Angoisses 1935 d: Michel Bernheim. lps: Francoise Rosay, Pierre Dux, Henri Rollan. 82M FRN. prod/rel: Productions Claude Dolbert

Pierre Et Therese, 1909, Novel
Piero E Teresa 1920 d: Mario Caserini. lps: Bianca Stagno-Bellincioni, Alberto A. Capozzi, Ida Carloni-Talli. 1809m ITL. prod/rel: Cines

PRICE, EVADNE

The Emancipation of Ambrose, Play
Wolf's Clothing 1936 d: Andrew Marton. lps: Claude Hulbert, Gordon Harker, George Graves. 80M UKN. prod/rel: Richard Wainwright, Universal

The Haunted Light, 1928, Play
Phantom Light, The 1935 d: Michael Powell. lps: Binnie Hale, Gordon Harker, Ian Hunter. 75M UKN. prod/rel: Gaumont British, Gainsborough

Once a Crook, Play
Once a Crook 1941 d: Herbert Mason. lps: Gordon Harker, Sydney Howard, Frank Pettingell. 81M UKN. prod/rel: 20th Century Productions, 20th Century-Fox

Red for Danger, Play
Blondes for Danger 1938 d: Jack Raymond. lps: Gordon Harker, Enid Stamp-Taylor, Ivan Brandt. 69M UKN. prod/rel: British Lion, Herbert Wilcox

Wanted on Voyage, Novel
Not Wanted on Voyage 1957 d: MacLean Rogers. lps: Ronald Shiner, Brian Rix, Griffith Jones. 82M UKN. prod/rel: Renown, Byron-Ronald Shiner

PRICE, JAMES

Cronache Del 1787-1790 a Botany Bay, in Australia, Book
Giustiziere Dei Mari, Il 1962 d: Domenico PaolellA. lps: Richard Harrison, Michele Mercier, Roldano Lupi. 88M ITL/FRN. *Boucanier Des Iles, Le* (FRN); *The Executioner on the Seas*; *The Executioner on the High Seas*; *Avenger of the Seven Seas* (USA) prod/rel: Documento Film (Roma), le Louvre Film (Paris)

PRICE, NANCY

Sleeping With the Enemy, Novel
Sleeping With the Enemy 1991 d: Joseph Ruben. lps: Julia Roberts, Patrick Bergin, Kevin Anderson. 98M USA.

PRICE, RICHARD

Bloodbrothers, Novel
Bloodbrothers 1978 d: Robert Mulligan. lps: Richard Gere, Paul Sorvino, Tony Lo Bianco. 116M USA. *Blood Brothers*; *Father's Love, A* prod/rel: Warner Bros.

Clockers, Novel
Clockers 1995 d: Spike Lee. lps: Harvey Keitel, John Turturro, Delroy Lindo. 128M USA. prod/rel: Universal, Forty Acres and a Mule

The Wanderers, Novel
Wanderers, The 1979 d: Philip Kaufman. lps: Ken Wahl, John Friedrich, Karen Allen. 113M USA. prod/rel: Aspen

PRICE, WILL

The Barbarians, Story
Tripoli 1950 d: Will Price. lps: John Payne, Maureen O'Hara, Howard Da SilvA. 95M USA. *First Marines* prod/rel: Paramount, Pine-Thomas

PRICHARD, CARADOG

One Full Moon, Novel
Un Nos Ola Leuad 1991 d: Endaf Emlyn. lps: Dyfan Roberts, Tudor Roberts, Betsan Llwyd. 98M UKN. *One Full Moon* prod/rel: Ffilm Cymru, S4C

PRICHARD, HESKETH

Don Q's Love Story, New York 1925, Novel
Don Q, Son of Zorro 1925 d: Donald Crisp. lps: Douglas Fairbanks, Mary Astor, Jack McDonald. 11r USA. prod/rel: Elton Corp., United Artists

PRICHARD, KATE

Don Q, Son of Zorro, 1925, Novel
Don Q, Son of Zorro 1925 d: Donald Crisp. lps: Douglas Fairbanks, Mary Astor, Jack McDonald. 11r USA. prod/rel: Elton Corp., United Artists

PRIESTLEY, J. B. (1894–1984), UKN, Priestley, John Boynton

Story
Foreman Went to France, The 1942 d: Charles Frend. lps: Tommy Trinder, Clifford Evans, Constance Cummings. 87M UKN. *Somewhere in France* (USA) prod/rel: Ealing Studios, United Artists

Angel Pavement, 1930, Novel
Angel Pavement 1958. lps: Maurice Denham, Alec McCowen. MTV. UKN. prod/rel: BBC

Benighted, London 1927, Novel
Old Dark House, The 1932 d: James Whale. lps: Boris Karloff, Melvyn Douglas, Charles Laughton. 74M USA. prod/rel: Universal Pictures Corp.©

Old Dark House, The 1963 d: William Castle. lps: Robert Morley, Janette Scott, Joyce Grenfell. 86M UKN/USA. prod/rel: William Castle Productions, Hammer

Dangerous Corner, London 1932, Play
Dangerous Corner 1934 d: Phil Rosen. lps: Virginia Bruce, Conrad Nagel, Melvyn Douglas. 67M USA. prod/rel: RKO Radio Pictures, Inc.

Eden End, Play
Eden End 1981 d: Donald McWhinnie. lps: Eileen Atkins, Georgina Hale, Frank Middlemass. MTV. 50M UKN. prod/rel: Ytv

The Good Companions, 1929, Novel
Good Companions, The 1933 d: Victor Saville. lps: Jessie Matthews, Edmund Gwenn, John Gielgud. 113M UKN. prod/rel: Gaumont, Welsh-Pearson

Good Companions, The 1957 d: J. Lee Thompson. lps: Eric Portman, Celia Johnson, Hugh Griffith. 104M UKN. prod/rel: Associated British Picture Corporation, Ab-Pathe

Good Companions, The 1980 d: Bill Hays. lps: Judy Cornwell, Jeremy Nicholas, John Stratton. MTV. 450M UKN. prod/rel: Yorkshire Tv

An Inspector Calls, London 1946, Play
Inspector Calls, An 1954 d: Guy Hamilton. lps: Alastair Sim, Arthur Young, Olga Lindo. 79M UKN. prod/rel: Watergate, British Lion

Laburnum Grove, London 1933, Play
Laburnum Grove 1936 d: Carol Reed. lps: Edmund Gwenn, Cedric Hardwicke, Victoria Hopper. 73M UKN. prod/rel: Associated Talking Pictures, Associated British Film Distributors

Let the People Sing, 1939, Novel
Let the People Sing 1942 d: John Baxter. lps: Alastair Sim, Fred Emney, Edward Rigby. 105M UKN. prod/rel: British National, Anglo-American

Now Let Him Go, Play
Now Let Him Go 1957 d: Dennis Vance. lps: Hugh Griffith, June Thorburn, Peter Halliday. MTV. F UKN. prod/rel: ABC

The Scandalous Affair of Mr. Kettle and Mrs. Moon, 1956, Play
..Und Das Am Montagmorgen 1959 d: Luigi Comencini. lps: O. W. Fischer, Ulla Jacobsson, Robert Graf. 92M GRM. *And on Monday Morning at That*

They Came to a City, London 1943, Play
They Came to a City 1944 d: Basil Dearden. lps: John Clements, Googie Withers, Raymond Huntley. 77M UKN. prod/rel: Ealing Studios

Time and the Conways, 1937, Play
Glucklichen Jahre Der Thorwalds, Die 1962 d: Wolfgang Staudte, John Olden. lps: Elisabeth Bergner, Hansjorg Felmy, Johanna Matz. 90M GRM. *The Happy Years of the Thorwalds*; *The Thorwalds' Happy Years* prod/rel: Allgemeine Produktion, Rolei

When We are Married, London 1938, Play
When We are Married 1943 d: Lance Comfort. lps: Sydney Howard, Raymond Huntley, Olga Lindo. 98M UKN. prod/rel: British National, Anglo-American

PRIETO, GENNARO

Il Mio Socio Davis, Novel
Socio Invisibile, Il 1939 d: Roberto Leone Roberti. lps: Evi Maltagliati, Clara Calamai, Carlo Romano. 85M ITL. *Socio, Il* prod/rel: Scalera Film

My Partner Mr. Davis 1936 d: Claude Autant-LarA. lps: Henry Kendall, Kathleen Kelly, Morris Harvey. 58M UKN. *Mysterious Mr. Davis, The* prod/rel: Oxford Films, RKO

Associate, The 1996 d: Donald Petrie. lps: Whoopi Goldberg, Dianne Wiest, Eli Wallach. 113M USA. prod/rel: Polygram Filmed Entertainment, Interscope Communications

Associe, L' 1979 d: Rene Gainville. lps: Michel Serrault, Claudine Auger, Catherine Alric. 94M FRN/GRM. *Associate, The* (USA) prod/rel: Magyar Prod., Maran

PRINCE, PETER

The Good Father, Novel
Good Father, The 1986 d: Mike Newell. lps: Anthony Hopkins, Jim Broadbent, Harriet Walter. 90M UKN. prod/rel: Mainline, Greenpoint Films

Play Things, Novel
Play Things 1976 d: Stephen Frears. lps: Jonathan Pryce, Colin Campbell. MTV. F UKN. prod/rel: BBC

PRINCESS ELSA (STRATENUS, LOUISE)

Gouden Ketenen, Novel
Gouden Ketenen 1917 d: Maurits H. Binger. lps: Annie Bos, Cor Smits, Cecil Ryan. 1620m NTH. *Golden Chains* prod/rel: Filmfabriek-Hollandia

PRINCESSE BIBESCO

Le Perroquet Vert, Novel
Perroquet Vert, Le 1928 d: Jean MilvA. lps: Edith Jehanne, Max Maxudian, Jeanne Berangere. F FRN. prod/rel: Films a.R.C.

PRINETTO, NATALE

La Cicala, Novel
Cicala, La 1980 d: Alberto LattuadA. lps: Virna Lisi, Anthony Franciosa, Clio Goldsmith. 101M ITL. *Cricket, The*; *La Cicada* prod/rel: N.I.R Film, P.I.C.

PRINTZLAU, OLGA

Where the Forest Ends, Story
Where the Forest Ends 1915 d: Joseph de Grasse. lps: Pauline Bush, William C. Dowlan, Lon Chaney. 2r USA. prod/rel: Rex

PRIOLLET, MARCEL

La Petite Mobilisee, Novel
Petite Mobilisee, La 1917 d: Gaston Leprieur. lps: Henri Collen, Jean Toulout, Suzanne Revonne. 1150m FRN. prod/rel: Grands Films Populaires, Lordier

PRISCO, MICHELE

Una Spirale Di Nebbia, Novel
Spirale Di Nebbia, Una 1977 d: Eriprando Visconti. lps: Martine Brochard, Marc Porel, Claude Jade. 110M ITL/FRN. *Caresses Bourgeoises* (FRN) prod/rel: Messapia Film, Serena Film 73

PROAL, JEAN

Bagarres, Novel
Bagarres 1948 d: Henri Calef. lps: Maria Casares, Roger Pigaut, Jean Brochard. 95M FRN. *The Wench* (USA) prod/rel: Georges Legrand

PROCTER, ADELAIDE ANNE (1825–1864), USA

The Legend of Provence, Poem
Broken Rosary, The 1934 d: Harry Hughes. lps: Derek Oldham, Jean Adrienne, Vesta VictoriA. 85M UKN. prod/rel: Butcher's Film Service

The Legend of Provence, London 1858-61, Poem
Legend of Provence, The 1913. lps: Maude Fealy, James Cruze, Lila Chester. 4r USA. prod/rel: Thanhouser Film Corp., Thanhouser "Big" Productions

The Lost Chord, 1877, Poem
Lost Chord, The 1918. 5r USA. prod/rel: Foursquare Pictures

The Trail of the Lost Chord, Poem
Trail of the Lost Chord, The 1913 d: Thomas Ricketts. lps: Ed Coxen, Winnifred Greenwood, Chester Withey. 2000f USA. prod/rel: American

PROCTOR, CHARLES

Pools of the Past, Novel
Notorious Mrs. Carrick, The 1924 d: George Ridgwell. lps: Disa, Cameron Carr, A. B. Imeson. 5500f UKN. *Pools of the Past* prod/rel: Stoll

PROCTOR, MAURICE

Hell Is a City, Novel
Hell Is a City 1960 d: Val Guest. lps: Stanley Baker, John Crawford, Donald Pleasence. 98M UKN. prod/rel: Hammer, Warner-Pathe

Rich Is the Treasure, Novel
Diamond, The 1954 d: Montgomery Tully, Dennis O'Keefe. lps: Dennis O'Keefe, Margaret Sheridan, Philip Friend. 83M UKN. *The Diamond Wizard* (USA); *Million Dollar Diamond* prod/rel: Gibraltar Films, United Artists

PROCTOR, PHILIP

Americathon 1998, Play
Americathon 1979 d: Neal Israel. lps: Peter Riegert, Harvey Korman, Fred Willard. 85M USA/GRM. *1998 - Die Vier Milliarden Dollar Show*; *Americathon 1998* prod/rel: United Artists

PROFFITT, NICHOLAS

Gardens of Stone, Novel
Gardens of Stone 1987 d: Francis Ford CoppolA. lps: James Caan, Anjelica Huston, James Earl Jones. 111M USA. prod/rel: Tri-Star

PROKOFIEVA, SOFIA
Conversation Without Witnesses, Play
Bez Svidetelei 1983 d: Nikita Mikhalkov. lps: Irina Kupchenko, Mikhail Ulyanov. 97M USS. *Without Witnesses*; *Without Witness* (USA); *Bes Svideteley*; *A Private Conversation* prod/rel: Mosfilm

PROKOSCH, FREDERIC (1908–, USA
City of Shadows, Novel
Conspirators, The 1944 d: Jean Negulesco. lps: Paul Henreid, Hedy Lamarr, Sydney Greenstreet. 101M USA. *Give Me This Woman* prod/rel: Warner Bros.

PROTESS, DAVID
Gone in the Night, Book
Gone in the Night 1996 d: B. W. L. Norton. lps: Shannen Doherty, Kevin Dillon, Dixie Carter. TVM. 173M USA. prod/rel: Leonard Hill Films©

PROUST, MARCEL (1871–1922), FRN
A la Recherche du Temps Perdu, 1913, Novel
Amour de Swann, Un 1983 d: Volker Schlondorff. lps: Jeremy Irons, Ornella Muti, Alain Delon. 110M FRN/GRM. *Swann in Love* (UKN); *Eine Liebe von Swann* (GRM) prod/rel: Bioskop, Wdr

PROUTEAU, GILBERT
Tout Est Dans la Fin, Novel
Tout Est Dans la Fin 1986 d: Jean Delannoy. lps: Michel Duchaussoy, Michel Creton, Fiona Gelin. 115M FRN.

PROUTY, OLIVE HIGGINS (1882–, USA
Now, Voyager, Novel
Now, Voyager 1942 d: Irving Rapper. lps: Bette Davis, Paul Henreid, Claude Rains. 117M USA. prod/rel: Warner Bros.

Stella Dallas, Boston 1923, Novel
Stella Dallas 1925 d: Henry King. lps: Ronald Colman, Belle Bennett, Alice Joyce. 11r USA. prod/rel: Samuel Goldwyn, Inc., United Artists
Stella Dallas 1937 d: King Vidor. lps: Barbara Stanwyck, John Boles, Anne Shirley. 104M USA. prod/rel: United Artists Corp., Howard Productions
Stella 1989 d: John Erman. lps: Bette Midler, John Goodman, Trini Alvarado. 109M USA. prod/rel: MGM, Touchstone Pictures

PROVOST, AGNES LOUISE
Her Kingdom of Dreams, 1919, Short Story
Her Kingdom of Dreams 1919 d: Marshall Neilan. lps: Anita Stewart, Mahlon Hamilton, Anna Q. Nilsson. 7287f USA. prod/rel: Anita Stewart Productions, Inc., First National Exhibitors Circuit, Inc.

PRUMBS, LUCILLE S.
Ever the Beginning, Play
My Girl Tisa 1948 d: Elliott Nugent. lps: Lilli Palmer, Sam Wanamaker, Akim Tamiroff. 95M USA. prod/rel: Warner Bros.

PRUS, BOLESLAW (1847–1912), PLN, Glowacki, Aleksander
Emancypantki, 1894, Novel
Pensja Pani Latter 1982 d: Stanislaw Rozewicz. lps: Barbara Horawianka, Halina Labonarska, Hanna Mikuc. 104M PLN. *Mrs. Latter's Boarding School*

Faraon, 1897, Novel
Faraon 1965 d: Jerzy Kawalerowicz. lps: George Zelnik, Barbara Brylska, Krystyna MikolajewskA. 183M PLN. *The Pharaoh* prod/rel: Kadr Film Unit

Grzechy Dziecinstwa, 1883, Short Story
Grzechy Dziecinstwa 1980 d: Krzysztof Nowak. lps: Iwona Bielska, Bohdan Ejmont. MTV. 73M PLN. *Sins of Childhood*

Lalka, 1890, Novel
Lalka 1968 d: Wojciech J. Has. lps: Beata Tyszkiewicz, Andrzej Lapicki, Mariusz Dmochowski. 159M PLN. *The Doll* (UKN)

PRYCE, RICHARD
Op O' Me Thumb, New York 1905, Play
Suds 1920 d: John Francis Dillon. lps: Mary Pickford, William Austin, Theodore Roberts. 5-6r USA. *The Duchess of Suds*; *Op O' Me Thumb* prod/rel: Mary Pickford Co.©, United Artists Corp.

PRYCE-JONES, DAVID (1936–, UKN
Unity Mitford: a Quest, Book
Unity 1981 d: James Cellan Jones. lps: Lesley-Anne Down, Nigel Havers, Jeremy Kemp. MTV. 105M UKN. prod/rel: BBC

PRYDE, ANTHONY
Spanish Sunlight, New York 1925, Novel
Girl from Montmartre, The 1926 d: Alfred E. Green. lps: Barbara La Marr, Lewis Stone, Robert Ellis. 6200f USA. prod/rel: Associated Holding Corp., First National Pictures

PRYOR, F. R.
Marigold, London 1936, Play
Marigold 1938 d: Thomas Bentley. lps: Sophie Stewart, Patrick Barr, Phyllis Dare. 73M UKN. prod/rel: Associated British Picture Corporation

PRZYBYSZEWSKA, STANISLAWA
Danton, Play
Danton 1982 d: Andrzej WajdA. lps: Gerard Depardieu, Wojciech Pszoniak, Patrice Chereau. 136M FRN/PLN. *L'affaire Danton* prod/rel: Films Du Losange, Gaumont

PU SONGLING
Laoshan Daoshi, Short Story
Qing Xumeng 1922 d: Ren Pengnian. lps: Ding Yuanyi, Bao Guirong, Zhang Shengwu. 3r CHN. *Empty Dream of Purity* prod/rel: Commercial Press Motion Picture Section

Liao Zhai Zhi Yi, Story
Gui Mei 1985 d: Sun Yuanxun. lps: Hao Jie, Wang Linghua, Zhang Jing. 9r CHN. *Ghost Girls* prod/rel: XI'an Film Studio

Lu Gong's Daughter, Story
Chi Nan Kuang Nu Liang Shi Qing 1993 d: Huo Zhuang, Ux XIaoxing. lps: Huang Guoqiang, Zhao Xueqin, Wang Shuo. 9r CHN. *Love With a Spirit* prod/rel: Beijing Film Studio

Shanhu, Ss
Xiao Fu Geng 1922 d: Ren Pengnian. lps: Wang Fuqing. 8r CHN. *The Filial Woman's Soup* prod/rel: Commercial Press Motion Picture Section

Yanzhi, Short Story
Yanzhi 1925 d: Li Beihai. lps: Li Minwei, Lin Chuchu. 8r CHN. *Rouge* prod/rel: Minxin Film Company

PUCCINI, GIACOMO (1858–1924), ITL
La Boheme, Turin 1896, Opera
Addio Mimi! 1947 d: Carmine Gallone. lps: Marta Eggerth, Jan Kiepura, Janis Carter. 90M ITL. *Her Wonderful Lie* (USA); *La Boheme* prod/rel: Cineopera, Ceiad
Boheme, La 1965 d: Franco Zeffirelli. lps: Gianni Raimondi, Rolando Panerai, Gianni Maffeo. 107M SWT/ITL. prod/rel: Cosmotel Produktion (Zurich)

PUCCINI, MARIO
La Prigione, Novel
Prigione, La 1942 d: Ferruccio Cerio. lps: Liliana Laine, Gianni Santuccio, Manuel Roero. 80M ITL. *Serenata d'Amore* prod/rel: Bassoli Film, E.N.I.C.

PUDNEY, JOHN (1909–1977), UKN, Pudney, John Sleigh
The Net, Novel
Net, The 1953 d: Anthony Asquith. lps: Phyllis Calvert, James Donald, Robert Beatty. 86M UKN. *Project M 7* (USA) prod/rel: General Film Distributors, Two Cities

Thursday Adventure, London 1955, Novel
Stolen Airliner, The 1955 d: Don Sharp. lps: Fella Edmonds, Diana Day, Peter Dyneley. 59M UKN. prod/rel: Associated British Picture Corporation, Children's Film Foundation

PUGANIGG, INGRID
Martha Dubronsky, Novel
Martha Dubronsky 1984 d: Beat Kuert. lps: Ingrid Puganigg, Peter Wyssbrod, Barbara Freier. 96M SWT. prod/rel: Gruppe Ansia

PUGET, CLAUDE-ANDRE
Les Jours Heureux, Play
Jours Heureux, Les 1941 d: Jean de Marguenat. lps: Pierre Richard-Willm, Francois Perier, Juliette Faber. 90M FRN. prod/rel: Films Roger Richebe
Giorni Felici 1943 d: Gianni Franciolini. lps: Lilia Silvi, Amedeo Nazzari, Vera Carmi. 85M ITL. prod/rel: Excelsa Film, Minerva Film

PUGH, MARSHALL
Commander Crabb, Book
Silent Enemy, The 1958 d: William Fairchild. lps: Laurence Harvey, Dawn Addams, John Clements. 112M UKN. prod/rel: Independent Film Distributors, Romulus

PUGLIESE, SERGIO
L'ippocampo, Play
Ippocampo, L' 1943 d: Gian Paolo Rosmino. lps: Vittorio de Sica, Lida Baarova, Maria Mercader. 70M ITL. prod/rel: Arno Film

PUIG, MANUEL (1932–1990), ARG
Story
Naked Tango 1990 d: Leonard Schrader. lps: Vincent d'Onofrio, Mathilda May, Fernando Rey. 92M USA/ARG. prod/rel: Sugarloaf/Gotan, Towa Production Company (Tokyo)

Kiss of the Spider Woman, Novel
Kiss of the Spider Woman 1984 d: Hector Babenco. lps: William Hurt, Raul Julia, Sonia BragA. 121M BRZ. *Beso de la Mujer Arana, El*; *O Beijo Da Muler Aranha* prod/rel: Hb Filmes, Sugarloaf

PUJMANOVA, MARIE
Pacientka Dr. Hegla, Novel
Pacientka Dr. Hegla 1940 d: Otakar VavrA. lps: Otomar Korbelar, Svetla Svozilova, Zorka Janu. 2433m CZC. *Dr. Hegl's Patient* prod/rel: Slavia-Film

Predtucha, Novel
Predtucha 1947 d: Otakar VavrA. lps: Frantisek Smolik, Natasa TanskA. F CZC. *Premonition*; *Presentiment*; *Forbodings*
Predtucha 1944 d: Miroslav Cikan. lps: Jana Ditetova, Zdenek Dite, Vladimir Salac. UNF. CZC. *Premonition* prod/rel: Nationalfilm

PUJOL, RENE
La Pouponniere, Opera
Pouponniere, La 1932 d: Jean Boyer. lps: Robert Arnoux, Rene Koval, Germaine Roger. 80M FRN. prod/rel: Films Paramount

Yes, Opera
Defense d'Aimer 1942 d: Richard Pottier. lps: Paul Meurisse, Suzy Delair, Andre Gabriello. 90M FRN. *Le Coeur Sur la Main*; *Totte Et Sa Chance* prod/rel: Continental-Film

PULVER, MARY BRECHT
Story
Man Who Was Afraid, The 1917 d: Fred E. Wright. lps: Bryant Washburn, Ernest Maupain, Margaret Watts. 4-5r USA. prod/rel: Essanay Film Mfg. Co.©, K-E-S-E Service

The Man Hater, 1917, Short Story
Man Hater, The 1917 d: Albert Parker. lps: Winifred Allen, Jack Meredith, Harry Neville. 5r USA. prod/rel: Triangle Film Corp., Triangle Distributing Corp.

PUNCH, MONKEY
Kariosutoro No Shiro, Short Story
Kariosutoro No Shiro 1991 d: Hayao Miyazaki. ANM. 110M JPN. *The Castle of Cagliostro* prod/rel: Tms Co.

PURCELL, HAROLD
Lisbon Story, London 1943, Play
Lisbon Story 1946 d: Paul L. Stein. lps: Patricia Burke, David Farrar, Walter RillA. 103M UKN. prod/rel: British National, Anglo-American

PURDUE, VIRGINIA
He Fell Down Dead, Novel
Shadow of a Woman 1946 d: Joseph Santley. lps: Helmut Dantine, Andrea King, Don McGuire. 78M USA. prod/rel: Warner Bros.

PURDUM, HERBERT
Story
Dalton Girls, The 1957 d: Reginald Le Borg. lps: Merry Anders, Lisa Davis, Penny Edwards. 71M USA. prod/rel: United Artists, Bel-Air

PURDY, JAMES
In a Shallow Grave, Novel
In a Shallow Grave 1988 d: Kenneth Bowser. lps: Michael Biehn, Maureen Mueller, Michael Beach. 92M USA. prod/rel: Skouras, American Playhouse Theatrical Films

PUSHKIN, ALEXANDER (1799–1837), RSS, Pushkin, Alexander Sergevich
Novel
Volga En Flammes 1933 d: Victor Tourjansky. lps: Danielle Darrieux, Albert Prejean, Valery Inkijinoff. 86M FRN/CZC. *Volha V Plamenech* (CZC); *Volga En Feu*; *Flames on the Volga* prod/rel: Ab, Charles Philipp
Baryshnya-Krestyanka 1995 d: Alexei Sakharov. lps: Elena Korikova, Leonid Kuravlyov, Vassilli Lanovoi. F RSS. *The Lady Peasant* prod/rel: Ritm Studio (Mosfilm), Roskomkino

Boris Godunov, 1831, Play
Boris Godunov 1986 d: Sergei Bondarchuk. lps: Sergei Bondarchuk, Jura Matjuchin, Adrianna BierdrzynskA. 145M USS/CZC. *Boris Godounov* prod/rel: Mosfilm, Erstes Studio

Dubrovsky, 1841, Short Story
Eagle, The 1925 d: Clarence Brown. lps: Rudolph Valentino, Vilma Banky, Louise Dresser. 6755f USA. *The Lone Eagle* prod/rel: Art Finance Corp.
Dubrovsky 1936 d: Alexander Ivanovsky. 77M USS.
Aquila Nera 1946 d: Riccardo FredA. lps: Irasema Dilian, Rossano Brazzi, Rina Morelli. 97M ITL. *The Black Eagle* prod/rel: Cin.Ca Distributori Indipendenti
Vendicatore, Il 1959 d: William Dieterle. lps: Rosanna Schiaffino, Paul Dahlke, John Forsythe. 117M ITL/YGS. *Revolt of the Volga*; *Dubrovsky*; *L'aigle Noir*; *Revolte Sur la Volga* prod/rel: Hesperia Film (Roma), Vardar Film (Skopje)
Blagorodnie Razboinik Vladimir Dubrovsky 1989 d: Vyatcheslav Nikiforov. 103M USS.

377

Kapitanskaya Dochka, 1836, Short Story
Figlia Del Capitano, La 1947 d: Mario Camerini. lps: Amedeo Nazzari, Irasema Dilian, Vittorio Gassman. 104M ITL. *The Captain's Daughter; Nastro d'Argento; Double Cross* prod/rel: Lux Film

Kapitanskaia Dotshka 1958 d: Vladimir Kaplunovsky. lps: Ilya Arepina, Oleg Strishenov, Sergei Lukyanov. 95M USS. *The Captain's Daughter; Kapitanskaya Dochka* prod/rel: Mosfilm

Tempesta, La 1958 d: Alberto Lattuada, Michelangelo Antonioni (Uncredited). lps: Silvana Mangano, Van Heflin, Viveca Lindfors. 122M ITL/FRN/YGS. *Tempete, La* (FRN); *The Tempest* (UKN) prod/rel: Dino de Laurentiis Cin.Ca (Roma), Gray S.N. (Paris)

Kapitanskayd Dochka, 1836, Short Story
Kapitanskaia Dochka 1928 d: Yuri Tarich. lps: N. Prozorovski, S. Kuznetsov, I. Kliukvin. 86M USS.

Kat'a, Short Story
Krasavice Kata 1919 d: Vaclav Binovec. lps: Suzanne Marwille, Vaclav Vydra St., Jiri Steimar. CZC. *Katia the Beauty; Beautiful Kata* prod/rel: Weteb

Kavkazskij Plennik, 1821, Poem
Prigioniero Del Caucaso, Il 1911 d: Giovanni Vitrotti. lps: M. Tamarov. 385m ITL/USS. *Kavkazskij Plennik; The Prisoner of the Caucaso* (UKN); *A Prisoner of the Caucasus* (USA) prod/rel: Timan-Rejngart, S.A. Ambrosio

Metel', 1831, Short Story
Metelj 1964 d: Vladimir Basov. lps: Valentina Titova, Georgi Martyniuk, Oleg Vidov. 80M USS. *The Blizzard; Metel'*

Und Der Regen Verwischt Jede Spur 1972 d: Alfred Vohrer. lps: Alain Noury, Anita Lochner, Wolfgang Reichmann. 98M GRM/FRN. *And the Rain Erases All Traces* prod/rel: Roxy, Maya

Esli Eto Ne Lyubovto Tchto Zhe.? 1974 d: Daria GurinA. 21M USS.

Motsart I Saleri, 1830, Short Story
Motsart I Salyeri 1962 d: Vladimir Gorikker. lps: Innokenti Smoktunovsky, Pyotr Glebov, A. Milbret. 47M USS. *Requiem for Mozart* (USA); *Mozart and Salieri* prod/rel: Riga Film Studio

Legenda O Salieri 1986 d: Vadim Kurtchevsky. ANM. 19M USS.

Pikovaya Dama, 1834, Short Story
Pique Dame 1918 d: Arthur Wellin. lps: Alexander Moissi. GRM. *Queen of Spades* prod/rel: Amboss-Film Dworsky & Co.

Pique Dame 1927 d: Alexander Rasumny. lps: Rudolf Forster, Alexandra Schmitt, Jenny Jugo. 2426m GRM. *Queen of Spades*

Pique Dame 1937 d: Fedor Ozep. lps: Marguerite Moreno, Madeleine Ozeray, Pierre Blanchar. 87M FRN. *Queen of Spades* (USA); *La Dame de Pique* prod/rel: General Production

Queen of Spades, The 1949 d: Thorold Dickinson. lps: Anton Walbrook, Edith Evans, Ronald Howard. 95M UKN. prod/rel: Associated British-Pathe, Associated British Picture Corporation

Pikovaya Dama 1960 d: Roman Tikhomirov. lps: Oleg Strizhenov, Olga Krasina, Yelena PolevitskayA. 106M USS. *Queen of Spades, The* (USA) prod/rel: Lenfilm

Dame de Pique, La 1965 d: Leonard Keigel. lps: Dita Parlo, Jean Negroni, Katharina Renn. 91M FRN. *The Queen of Spades* prod/rel: Paris-Cite Productions

Eti. Tri Vernye Karty 1988 d: Alexandr Orlov. 86M USS.

Der Postmeister, Short Story
Dunja 1955 d: Josef von Baky. lps: Eva Bartok, Ivan Desny, Walter Richter. 97M AUS. prod/rel: Sascha

I Racconti Della Piccola Russia
Wanda Warenine 1917 d: Riccardo Tolentino. lps: Fabienne Fabreges, Domenico Serra, Bonaventura Ibanez. 1667m ITL. prod/rel: Latina-Ars

Ruslan I Lyudmila, 1820, Poem
Ruslan I Lyudmila 1938 d: Ivan Nikitchenko, Viktor Nevezhin. 52M USS.

Ruslan I Ljudmila 1970 d: Alexander Ptushko. lps: Natalia Petrova, Valery Kalanets, Vladimir Fiodorov. 105M USS. *Rusland I Liudmila*

Skazka O Mertvoy Tsarevne I O Semi Bogatyryakh, 1833, Poem
Skazka O Mertvoy Tsarevne I O Semi Bogatyryakh 1951 d: Ivan Ivanov-Vano. ANM. 32M USS. *The Tale of a Dead Princess*

Skazka O Pope I O Rabotnike Ego Balde, 1831, Short Story
Skazka O Pope I O Rabot Ego Balde 1939 d: Piotr Sazonov. ANM. 22M USS.

Skazka O Pope I O Rabotnike Ego Balde 1956 d: Anatoli Karanovich. ANM. 25M USS.

Skazka O Rybake I Rybke, 1833, Poem
Skazka O Rybake I Rybke 1937 d: Alexander Ptushko. ANM. 28M USS. *Tale of the Fisherman and the Little Fish; Fishmonger and the Fish*

Rybar a Zlata Rybka 1951 d: Jiri TrnkA. ANM. 15M CZC. *The Golden Fish* (USA); *O Zlate Rybce; A Gold Fish; O Zlate Rybce*

Skazka O Tsare Saltane, 1831, Poem
Skazka O Tsare Saltane 1943 d: Valentina Brumberg, Zinaida Brumberg. ANM. 37M USS.

Skazka O Tsare Saltane 1967 d: Alexander Ptushko. lps: Vladimir Andreyev, Larisa Golubkina, Oleg Vidov. 108M USS. *The Tale of Tsar Saltan; Tales of Czar Tsaltan; The Tale of Czar Saltan*

Skazka O Tsare Saltane 1984 d: Ivan Ivanov-Vano, L. Milchin. ANM. 56M USS.

Skazka O Zolotom Petukhe, 1834, Short Story
Skazka O Zolotom Petukhe 1967 d: Alexander Snezhko-BlotskayA. ANM. 32M USS.

Stantsionny Smotritel, 1831, Short Story
Nostalgie 1937 d: Victor Tourjansky. lps: Harry Baur, Jorge Rigaud, Janine Crispin. 97M FRN. *The Postmaster's Daughter* prod/rel: Milo Film Productions

Postmeister, Der 1940 d: Gustav Ucicky. lps: Heinrich George, Hilde Krahl, Siegfried Breuer. 95M AUS. *Her Crime Was Love* prod/rel: Wien

Rakkauden Risti 1946 d: Teuvo Tulio. lps: Regina Linnanheimo. 99M FNL. *The Cross of Love*

Postmeister, Der 1955 d: Josef von Baky. lps: Eva Bartok, Ivan Desny, Karlheinz Bohm. 93M GRM. *Her Crime Was Love* (UKN)

Tsygany, 1824, Poem
Aleko 1953 d: Grigori Roshal, Sergei Sidelev. 60M USS. *Alego*

Vystrel, 1831, Short Story
Coups de Feu 1939 d: Rene Barberis. lps: Mireille Balin, Ginette Leclerc, Aime Clariond. 75M FRN. *Duels* prod/rel: Rex-Film

Colpo Di Pistola, Un 1942 d: Renato Castellani. lps: Assia Noris, Fosco Giachetti, Antonio CentA. 90M ITL. prod/rel: Lux Film

Vystrel 1967 d: Naum Trakhtenberg. lps: Oleg Tabakov, Mikhail Kozakov, Yuri Yakovlev. 78M USS. *The Shot; Vistrel; A Pistol Shot*

PUTER, ALFRED
Play
Zena, Ktera Se Smeje 1931 d: Jan Bor. lps: Olga Scheinpflugova, Antonin Strnad, Marie VackovA. 2280m CZC. *The Laughing Woman* prod/rel: Paramount

PUTNAM, NINA WILCOX
Doubling for Cupid, 1924, Short Story
Beautiful Cheat, The 1926 d: Edward Sloman. lps: Laura La Plante, Harry Myers, Bertram Grassby. 6583f USA. prod/rel: Universal Pictures

The Grandflapper, 1926, Short Story
Slaves of Beauty 1927 d: John G. Blystone. lps: Olive Tell, Holmes Herbert, Earle Foxe. 5412f USA. prod/rel: Fox Film Corp.

In Search of Arcady, Garden City, N.Y. 1912, Novel
In Search of Arcady 1919 d: Bertram Bracken. lps: Billie Rhodes, Wellington Playter, Thomas Santschi. 5r USA. prod/rel: National Film Corp. of America, Robertson-Cole Co.

The Price of Applause, Short Story
Price of Applause, The 1918 d: Thomas N. Heffron. lps: Jack Livingston, Claire Anderson, Joe King. 5r USA. prod/rel: Triangle Film Corp., Triangle Distributing Corp.

Two Weeks With Pay, 1920, Short Story
Two Weeks With Pay 1921 d: Maurice Campbell. lps: Bebe Daniels, Jack Mulhall, James Mason. 4136f USA. prod/rel: Realart Pictures

PUTNAM, WESLEY J.
Playthings of Desire, Story
Playthings of Desire 1924 d: Burton L. King. lps: Estelle Taylor, Mahlon Hamilton, Dagmar Godowsky. 5500f USA. prod/rel: Jans Productions

PUZO, MARIO (1920–), USA
The Godfather, Novel
Godfather, The 1972 d: Francis Ford CoppolA. lps: Al Pacino, Marlon Brando, James Caan. 175M USA. prod/rel: Paramount

The Last Don, Novel
Mario Puzo's the Last Don 1997 d: Graeme Clifford. lps: Danny Aiello, Joe Mantegna, Daryl Hannah. TVM. 360M USA. prod/rel: Konigsberg Sanitsky Prods.

The Sicilian, Novel
Sicilian, The 1987 d: Michael Cimino. lps: Christopher Lambert, Terence Stamp, Barbara SukowA. 146M USA. prod/rel: 20th Century Fox

PYAT, FELIX
Le Chiffonnier de Paris, Novel
Chiffonnier de Paris, Le 1924 d: Serge Nadejdine. lps: Nicolas Koline, Helene Darly, Francine Mussey. 2400m FRN. prod/rel: Films Albatros

PYLE, ERNIE
The Story of G.I. Joe, Book
Story of G.I. Joe, The 1945 d: William A. Wellman. lps: Burgess Meredith, Robert Mitchum, Freddie Steele. 109M USA. *War Correspondent; G.I. Joe* prod/rel: United Artists

PYLE, HOWARD
Men of Iron, 1954, Novel
Black Shield of Falworth, The 1954 d: Rudolph Mate. lps: Tony Curtis, Janet Leigh, David Farrar. 99M USA. prod/rel: Universal-International

PYSZORA, ANNE-FRANCOISE
Expense of Spirit, Novel
Winterschlaefer 1997 d: Tom Tykwer. lps: Ulrich Matthes, Marie-Lou Sellem, Floriane Daniel. 122M GRM. *Wintersleepers* prod/rel: X-Filme Creative Pool, Palladio Film

Q

QIN ZHAOYANG
Novel
Wei Hai Zi Men Zhu Fu 1953 d: Zhao Dan. lps: Huang Zongyin, Wang Longji, Jiang Tianliu. 9r CHN. *Bless the Children* prod/rel: Changjiang, Kunlun Assoc. Film Co.

QIONG YAO
Spray, Novel
Qing Hai Lang Hua 1991 d: Pao Zhifang. lps: Yu Lan, Tong Ruiming, Wu Jing. 10r CHN. *Love Spray* prod/rel: Shanghai Film Studio

Tingyuan Shenshen, Novel
Tingyuan Shenshen 1989 d: Shi Shujun. lps: Song Jia, You Yong, Jin Meng. 18r CHN. *Jiating Shenshen; The Spacious Courtyard* prod/rel: Shanghai Film Studio

QIU WEIMING
High Tide, Low Tide, Novel
Shen Bu You Ji 1993 d: Fu Dongyu. lps: Liu XIaoning, Tian Ge, Li Ping. 9r CHN. *Out of My Control* prod/rel: Shanghai Film Studio

QU BO
Lin Hai Xue Yuan, Novel
Lin Hai Xue Yuan 1960 d: Liu Peiran. lps: Zhang Yongshou, Wang Runsheng, Liang Zhipeng. 12r CHN. *Sea of Forests and Plains of Snow* prod/rel: August First Film Studio

QUARANTA, GIANNI
Tutti Gli Uomini Del Parlamento, Book
Tutti Gli Uomini El Parlamento 1979 d: Claudio RaccA. DOC. F ITL. prod/rel: Norma Film

QUARANTOTTI-GAMBINI, PIER
La Calda Vita, Turin 1958, Novel
Calda Vita, La 1963 d: Florestano Vancini. lps: Catherine Spaak, Gabriele Ferzetti, Jacques Perrin. 110M ITL/FRN. prod/rel: Jolly Film (Roma), Les Films Agiman (Paris)

QUARTULLO, PINO
Le Faremo Tanto Male, Play
Faremo Tanto Male, Le 1998 d: Pino Quartullo. lps: Stefania Sandrelli, Pino Quartullo, Ricky Memphis. 102M ITL. *We'll Really Hurt You* prod/rel: Italian Intl. Film, Blu Film

QUATTROCCHI, FRANK
The Projected Man, Novel
Projected Man, The 1966 d: Ian Curteis. lps: Bryant Halliday, Mary Peach, Norman Wooland. 90M UKN. prod/rel: Compton, Mlc

QUEEN, ELLERY
Calamity Town, Novel
Haitatsu Sarenai Santsu No Tegami 1979 d: Yoshitaro NomurA. lps: Keiko Matsuzaka, Komaki Kurihara, Mayumi OgawA. 130M JPN. *The Three Undelivered Letters; Three Letters Undelivered* prod/rel: Shochiku Co.

Cat O'Nine Tails (Cat of Many Tales), Novel
Ellery Queen: Don't Look Behind You 1971 d: Barry Shear. lps: Peter Lawford, Harry Morgan, E. G. Marshall. TVM. 100M USA. prod/rel: NBC, Universal TV

The Chinese Orange Mystery, New York 1934, Novel
Mandarin Mystery, The 1936 d: Ralph Staub. lps: Eddie Quillan, Charlotte Henry, Rita La Roy. 66M USA. *The Chinese Orange Mystery* prod/rel: Republic Pictures Corp.©

Danger - Men Working, Baltimore, Md. 1936, Play
Crime Nobody Saw, The 1937 d: Charles T. Barton. lps: Lew Ayres, Vivienne Osborne, Eugene Pallette. 60M USA. *Danger, Men Working* prod/rel: Paramount Pictures, Inc.

The Dragon's Teeth, a Problem of Deduction, Story
Close Call for Ellery Queen, A 1942 d: James P. Hogan. lps: William Gargan, Margaret Lindsay, Charley Grapewin. 65M USA. *Close Call, A* (UKN) prod/rel: Columbia

Ellery Queen, Master Detective, Novel
Ellery Queen, Master Detective 1940 d: Kurt Neumann. lps: Ralph Bellamy, Margaret Lindsay, Charley Grapewin. 66M USA. *John Braun's Body* prod/rel: Larry Darmour Productions, Columbia Pictures Corp.©

A Good Samaritan, Radio Play
Desperate Chance for Ellery Queen, A 1942 d: James P. Hogan. lps: William Gargan, Margaret Lindsay, Charley Grapewin. 70M USA. *A Desperate Chance* (UKN) prod/rel: Columbia

The Greek Coffin Mystery, Story
Enemy Agents Meet Ellery Queen 1942 d: James P. Hogan. lps: William Gargan, Margaret Lindsay, Charley Grapewin. 65M USA. *The Lido Mystery* (UKN) prod/rel: Columbia

The Penthouse Mystery, Novel
Ellery Queen's Penthouse Mystery 1941 d: James P. Hogan. lps: Ralph Bellamy, Margaret Lindsay, Charley Grapewin. 69M USA. prod/rel: Columbia

The Perfect Crime, Story
Ellery Queen and the Murder Ring 1941 d: James P. Hogan. lps: Ralph Bellamy, Margaret Lindsa, Charley Grapewin. 65M USA. *The Murder Ring* (UKN) prod/rel: Columbia

The Spanish Cape Mystery, New York 1935, Novel
Spanish Cape Mystery, The 1935 d: Lewis D. Collins. lps: Helen Twelvetrees, Donald Cook, Berton Churchill. 73M USA. prod/rel: Liberty Pictures Corp., M. H. Hoffman Production

A Study in Terror, Novel
Study in Terror, A 1965 d: James Hill. lps: John Neville, Donald Houston, John Fraser. 95M UKN/GRM/USA. *Sherlock Holmes Grosster Fall* (GRM); *Fog* prod/rel: Compton-Tekli, Sir Nigel

QUEFFELEC, HENRI (1910–, FRN
Un Recteur Dans l'Ile de Sein, Novel
Dieu a Besoin Des Hommes 1950 d: Jean Delannoy. lps: Pierre Fresnay, Madeleine Robinson, Daniel Gelin. 100M FRN. *Isle of Sinners* (UKN); *God Needs Man* (USA) prod/rel: Wipf, Louis

QUEFFELEC, YANN
Les Noces Barbares, Novel
Noces Barbares, Les 1987 d: Marion Hansel. lps: Thierry Fremont, Marianne Basler, Yves Cotton. 100M BLG/FRN. *The Cruel Embrace* prod/rel: Man's Film, Flach Film

QUEMENEUR, J. S.
Les Coups Pour Rien, Novel
Coups Pour Rien, Les 1970 d: Pierre Lambert. lps: Pierre Brice, Yanti Somer, Roland Lesaffre. 90M FRN. prod/rel: Rene Thevenet, P.I.P.

QUENEAU, RAYMOND (1903–1976), FRN
Le Dimanche de la Vie, 1951, Novel
Dimanche de la Vie, Le 1967 d: Jean Herman. lps: Danielle Darrieux, Jean-Pierre Moulin, Olivier Hussenot. 100M FRN/GRM/ITL. *The Sunday of Life* (USA) prod/rel: Sofracina, Doxa Films

On Est Toujours Trop Bon Avec Les Femmes, 1947, Novel
On Est Toujours Trop Bon Avec Les Femmes 1970 d: Michel Boisrond. lps: Elisabeth Wiener, Jean-Pierre Marielle, Gerard Lartigau. 77M FRN. prod/rel: Intermondia, Marianne Production

Zazie Dans le Metro, Paris 1959, Novel
Zazie Dans le Metro 1960 d: Louis Malle. lps: Catherine Demongeot, Philippe Noiret, Hubert Deschamps. 88M FRN. *Zazie* (USA); *Zazie in the Underground* prod/rel: Nouvelles Editions De Films

QUENTIN, PATRICK
Fatal Woman, 1952, Novel
Black Widow 1954 d: Nunnally Johnson. lps: Van Heflin, Ginger Rogers, Gene Tierney. 95M USA. prod/rel: 20th Century-Fox

Man in the Net: a Novel of Suspense, 1956, Novel
Man in the Net, The 1959 d: Michael Curtiz. lps: Alan Ladd, Carolyn Jones, Diane Brewster. 97M USA. prod/rel: United Artists, Mirisch-Jaguar

The Man With Two Wives, Novel
Rendez-Vous, Le 1961 d: Jean Delannoy. lps: Annie Girardot, Odile Versois, Jean-Claude Pascal. 128M FRN/ITL. *L'appuntamento* (ITL) prod/rel: Silver Films, Cinetel

Puzzle for Fiends, Novel
Strange Awakening 1958 d: Montgomery Tully. lps: Lex Barker, Carole Mathews, Lisa Gastoni. 69M UKN. *Female Friends* (USA) prod/rel: Anglo-Amalgamated, Merton Park

Puzzle for Puppets, Novel
Homicide for Three 1948 d: George Blair. lps: Audrey Long, Warren Douglas, Grant Withers. 60M USA. *An Interrupted Honeymoon* (UKN) prod/rel: Republic

Shadow of Guilt, Novel
Homme a Femmes, L' 1960 d: Jacques-Gerard Cornu. lps: Mel Ferrer, Danielle Darrieux, Claude Rich. 92M FRN. prod/rel: Films Du Cyclope

QUERI, GEORG
Erbin Vom Rosenhof, Opera
Erbin Vom Rosenhof, Die 1942 d: Franz Seitz. lps: Hansi Knoteck, Paul Klinger, Trude Haefelin. 85M GRM. prod/rel: Germania, Adler

QUERIDO, ISRAEL
Menschenwee, 1903, Novel
Menschenwee 1921 d: Theo Frenkel Sr. lps: Willem Van Der Veer, Kitty Kluppell, Vera Van Haeften. 1800m NTH. *Human Woe*; *Danshuis Op Den Zeedijk, Het*; *The Dance-Hall on the Zeedijk* prod/rel: Amsterdam Film Cie

QUICK, DOROTHY
Enchantment: a Little Girl's Friendship With Mark Twain, Novel
Mark Twain and Me 1991 d: Daniel Petrie. lps: Jason Robards Jr., Talia Shire, R. H. Thomson. TVM. 95M CND.

QUICK, HERBERT
Double Trouble, Indianapolis 1906, Novel
Double Trouble 1915 d: W. Christy Cabanne. lps: Douglas Fairbanks, Margery Wilson, Richard Cummings. 5r USA. prod/rel: Fine Arts Film Co., Triangle Film Corp.©

QUIEN, KRUNO
Kaja, Unit Cu Te
Kaja, Ubit Cu Te! 1967 d: Vatroslav MimicA. lps: Zaim Muzaferija, Ugljesa Kojadinovic, Antun Nalis. 75M YGS. *Kaya, I'll Kill You*; *Kaja, I'll Kill You*; *Kaya* (USA) prod/rel: Jadran Film, Cineastes Associes

QUIGLEY, JOHN
King's Royal, Novel
King's Royal 1982 d: Andrew Morgan, David Reynolds. lps: Tom Bell, Louise Ramsay, Eric Deacon. TVM. 500M UKN. prod/rel: BBC Scotland

QUILICI, FOLCO (1930–, ITL
Oceano, Book
Oceano 1971 d: Folco Quilici. lps: W. M. Reno, Hubert Putigny, K. Imrie. 98M ITL. *Ocean Odyssey* prod/rel: P.E.A. Cin.Ca

QUILLER-COUCH, ARTHUR (1863–1944), UKN
St. Ives, 1898, Novel
Secret of St. Ives, The 1949 d: Phil Rosen. lps: Richard Ney, Vanessa Brown, Henry Daniell. 75M USA. prod/rel: Columbia

True Tilda, Novel
True Tilda 1920 d: Harold Shaw. lps: Edna Flugrath, Teddy Gordon Craig, Edward O'Neill. 4654f UKN. prod/rel: London, Jury

QUIN, JOHN
Shadow of Death, Play
Shadow of Death 1939 d: Harry S. Marks. lps: Donald Calthrop, Ellen Pollock, Simon Lack. 25M UKN. prod/rel: Mm Films, Associated British Film Distributors

QUINDLEN, ANNA
One True Thing, Novel
One True Thing 1998 d: Carl Franklin. lps: Meryl Streep, Renee Zellweger, William Hurt. 127M USA. prod/rel: Universal, Monarch Pictures

QUINDT, WILLIAM
Der Tiger Akbar, Novel
Tiger Akbar, Der 1951 d: Harry Piel. lps: Harry Piel, Friedel Hardt, Helga Wiedenbruck. 114M GRM. *The Tiger Akbar* prod/rel: Ariel, Deutsche Cosmopol

QUINELL, A. J.
Man on Fire, Novel
Man on Fire 1987 d: Elie Chouraqui. lps: Scott Glenn, Jade Malle, Paul Shenar. 93M FRN/ITL. prod/rel: 7-Films, Fr 3

QUINLAN, J.
Play
Test, The 1916 d: George Fitzmaurice. lps: Jane Grey, Lumsden Hare, Claude Fleming. 5r USA. prod/rel: Astra Film Corp., Pathe Exchange, Inc.©

QUINN, ANN
Berg, Novel
Killing Dad 1989 d: Michael Austin. lps: Julie Walters, Richard E. Grant, Denholm Elliott. 93M UKN. *Killing Dad (Or How to Love Your Mother)* prod/rel: Palace, Scottish Tv Film Enterprises

QUINN, PETER
Jeunes Filles En Detresse, Novel
Jeunes Filles En Detresse 1939 d: G. W. Pabst. lps: Marcelle Chantal, Micheline Presle, Jacqueline Delubac. 90M FRN. *La Loi Sacree* prod/rel: Globe Films

QUINN, THEODORA KROEBER
Ishi in Two Worlds, Book
Ishi, the Last of His Tribe 1978 d: Robert Ellis Miller. lps: Dennis Weaver, Devon Ericson, Geno SilvA. TVM. 150M USA. prod/rel: NBC, Edward and Mildred Lewis Production

QUINSON, GUSTAVE
L'arpete, Play
Arpete, L' 1928 d: E. B. Donatien. lps: Lucienne Legrand, Raymond Guerin-Catelain, Louis Ravet. 2500m FRN. prod/rel: Franco-Film

Le Chasseur de Chez Maxim's, Play
Chasseur de Chez Maxim's, Le 1927 d: Roger Lion, Nicolas Rimsky. lps: Nicolas Rimsky, Simone Vaudry, Eric Barclay. F FRN. prod/rel: Films Albatros

Chasseur de Chez Maxim's, Le 1932 d: Karl Anton. lps: Robert Burnier, Mireille Perrey, Felicien Tramel. 65M FRN. prod/rel: Films Paramount

Chasseur de Chez Maxim's, Le 1939 d: Maurice Cammage. lps: Bach, Genevieve Callix, Roger Treville. 95M FRN. prod/rel: Films Stella Productions

Chasseur de Chez Maxim's, Le 1953 d: Henri Diamant-Berger. lps: Pauline Carton, Yves Deniaud, Raymond Bussieres. 96M FRN. prod/rel: Actor Film, Film d'Art

La Merveilleuse Journee, Play
Merveilleuse Journee, La 1928 d: Rene Barberis. lps: Dolly Davis, Andre Roanne, Renee Veller. 2100m FRN. prod/rel: Societe Des Cineromans, Films De France

Merveilleuse Journee, La 1932 d: Robert Wyler, Yves Mirande. lps: Florelle, Milly Mathis, Frederic Duvalles. 87M FRN. prod/rel: Pathe-Natan

QUINTERO, ANTONIO
La Copla Andaluza, Play
Copla Andaluza, La 1928 d: Ernesto Gonzalez. lps: Maria Luz Callejo, Javier de Rivera, Jose Montenegro. F SPN. prod/rel: Ernesto Gonzalez (Madrid)

QUIROGA, ELENA
Viento Del Norte, 1951, Novel
Viento Del Norte 1954 d: Antonio Momplet. lps: Enrique A. Diosdado, Maria Piazzai, Isabel de Pomes. 81M SPN. *North Wind*

QUIROGA, HORACIO (1878–1937), URG
Una Bofetada, 1916, Short Story
Prisioneros de la Tierra 1939 d: Mario Soffici. lps: Francisco Petrone, Angel Magana, Elisa Galve. 85M ARG. *Prisoners of the Earth*; *Prisoners of Earth*

Los Destiladores de Naranja, 1923, Short Story
Prisioneros de la Tierra 1939 d: Mario Soffici. lps: Francisco Petrone, Angel Magana, Elisa Galve. 85M ARG. *Prisoners of the Earth*; *Prisoners of Earth*

QUIROULE, PIERRE
Sexton Blake and the Hooded Terror, Novel
Sexton Blake and the Hooded Terror 1938 d: George King. lps: Tod Slaughter, George Curzon, Greta Gynt. 70M UKN. prod/rel: George King, MGM

QUISLANT, M.
Doloretes, Opera
Doloretes 1922 d: Jose Buchs. lps: Elisa Ruiz Romero, Manuel San German, Maria Comendador. 2100m SPN. prod/rel: Atlantida

R

RAABE, WILHELM (1831–1910), GRM
Die Schwarze Galeere, 1902, Novel
Schwarze Galeere, Die 1962 d: Martin Hellberg. 95M GDR. *The Black Galleon*

RABB, SELWYN (1934–, USA
Justice in the Back Room, Novel
Marcus-Nelson Murders, The 1973 d: Joseph Sargent. lps: Telly Savalas, Marjoe Gortner, Jose Ferrer. TVM. 148M USA. *Kojak and the Marcus-Nelson Murders* prod/rel: Universal

RABE, DAVID (1940–, USA, Rabe, David William
Hurlyburly, 1984, Play
Hurlyburly 1998 d: Anthony Drazan. lps: Sean Penn, Kevin Spacey, Robin Wright. 122M USA. prod/rel: Fine Line, Storm Entertainment
Streamers, Play
Streamers 1983 d: Robert Altman. lps: Matthew Modine, Michael Wright, Mitchell Lichtenstein. 118M USA. prod/rel: United Artists Classics

RABELL, DU VERNET
The Three Cornered Kingdom, Story
If I Were Queen 1922 d: Wesley Ruggles. lps: Ethel Clayton, Andree Lejon, Warner Baxter. 6092f USA. prod/rel: R-C Pictures, Film Booking Offices of America
The White Peacock Feathers, Story
Rage of Paris, The 1921 d: Jack Conway. lps: Miss Du Pont, Elinor Hancock, Jack Perrin. 4968f USA. prod/rel: Universal Film Mfg. Co.
The Woman Michael Married, 1918, Novel
Woman Michael Married, The 1919 d: Henry Kolker. lps: Bessie Barriscale, Jack Holt, Marcia Manon. 5r USA. prod/rel: B. B. Features, Robertson-Cole Co.

RABIER, BENJAMIN
Court-Circuit, Play
Court-Circuit 1929 d: Maurice Champreux. lps: Gabriel Vierge, Charpentier, Laure Savidge. 1800m FRN.

RABL, HANS
Ziel in Den Wolken, Novel
Ziel in Den Wolken 1938 d: Wolfgang Liebeneiner. lps: Leny Marenbach, Brigitte Horney, Albert Matterstock. 98M GRM. *Goal in the Clouds* (USA) prod/rel: Terra

RACEWARD, THOMAS
Sunday, New York 1904, Play
Sunday 1915 d: George W. Lederer. lps: Reine Davies, Charles Trowbridge, Adolph Link. 5r USA. prod/rel: George W. Lederer Filmotions, Inc., World Film Corp.©

RACHILDE
La Tour d'Amour, Novel
Drame Au Phare, Un 1914 d: Georges Pallu. 780m FRN. prod/rel: Minerva, le Film d'Art

RACINE, JEAN (1639–1699), FRN
Athalie, Play
Athalie 1910 d: Michel Carre. lps: Edouard de Max, Philippe Garnier, Rene Hervil. 410m FRN. prod/rel: Scagl
Berenice, 1671, Play
Berenice 1967 d: Pierre-Alain Jolivet. lps: Anna Gael, Josee Destoop, Bernard Verlay. 90M FRN. prod/rel: C.E.P.C.
Britannicus, 1669, Play
Britannicus 1908 d: Andre Calmettes. lps: Mounet-Sully, Madeleine Roch. FRN. prod/rel: Film d'Art
Britannicus 1912 d: Camille de Morlhon. lps: Jean Herve, Romuald Joube, Gabriel Signoret. 700m FRN. prod/rel: Films Valetta
Phedre, 1677, Play
Au Coeur de la Casbah 1951 d: Pierre Cardinal. lps: Viviane Romance, Peter Van Eyck, Claude Laydu. 96M FRN. *Maria-Pilar* prod/rel: Films Paral
Phedre 1968 d: Pierre Jourdan. lps: Marie Bell, Jacques Dacqmine, Jean Chevrier. 92M FRN. prod/rel: Nicole Stephane, Ancinex
Phedre Et Hyppolite, 1677, Play
Fedra (Dramma Mitologico Dell'antica Grecia) 1909 d: Oreste Gherardini. lps: Oreste Gherardini. 295m ITL. *Phaedra* (USA) prod/rel: Societa Italiana Pineschi

RACIOPPI, ANTONIO
Roma Baffuta, Play
Mio Padre Monsignore 1971 d: Antonio Racioppi. lps: Lino Capolicchio, Giancarlo Giannini, Barbara Bach. 105M ITL. prod/rel: Prestano Cin.Ca, P.A.C.

RACKIN, MARTIN
Lisbon, Novel
Lisbon 1956 d: Ray Milland. lps: Ray Milland, Claude Rains, Maureen O'HaraA. 90M USA. prod/rel: Republic
Rock Bottom, Story
Three Secrets 1950 d: Robert Wise. lps: Eleanor Parker, Patricia Neal, Ruth Roman. 98M USA. prod/rel: Warner Bros., United States Pictures

RADICHKOV, YORDAN
Baruten Bukvar, 1969, Novel
Baruten Bukvar 1977 d: Todor Dinov. 77M BUL.

Goreshto Pladne, 1965, Short Story
Gorechto Pladne 1965 d: Zako HeskiyA. lps: Peter Slabakov, Plamak Nakov, Kamil Kyuchukov. 88M BUL. *Torrid Noon*; *Hot Noon*; *High Noon*; *Goreshto Pladne*; *Gorescho Pladne*
Khlyab, 1969, Short Story
Hlyab - Chertichkata 1972 d: Naum Shopov, Rashko Ouzunov. lps: Nikola Hadjiyski, Rumyana Bocheva, Violetta GindevA. 89M BUL. *Bread - the Dash*; *Khlyab*
Privarzaniyat Balon, 1965, Short Story
Privarzaniat Balon 1967 d: Binka ZheljazkovA. lps: Grigor Vachkov, Georgi Kaloyanchev, Ivan Bratanov. 98M BUL. *The Attached Balloon*; *The Captive Balloon*; *The Balloon*; *Privarzaniyat Balon*
Vsichki I Nikoy, 1975, Novel
Vsichki I Nikoy 1978 d: Krikor Azarian. lps: Velko Kunov, Georgi Novakov, Nikola Dadov. 103M BUL. *Everybody and Nobody*

RADIGUET, RAYMOND (1903–1923), FRN
Le Bal du Comte d'Orgel, 1924, Novel
Bal du Comte d'Orgel, Le 1969 d: Marc Allegret. lps: Jean-Claude Brialy, Sylvie Fennec, Bruno Garcin. 100M FRN. prod/rel: Films Marceau
Le Diable Au Corps, 1923, Novel
Diable Au Corps, Le 1946 d: Claude Autant-LarA. lps: Micheline Presle, Gerard Philipe, Denise Grey. 110M FRN. *Devil in the Flesh* prod/rel: Transcontinental
Le Diable du Corps, Novel
Devil in the Flesh 1986 d: Scott Murray. lps: Katia Caballero, Keith Smith, John Morris. 99M ASL. *Beyond Innocence*; *Marie Claire* prod/rel: Jcw Film Management Ltd.©, World Film Alliance

RADOMERSKA, MARYNA
Krb Bez Ohne, Novel
Krb Bez Ohne 1937 d: Karel SpelinA. lps: Marta Majova, R. A. Dvorsky, Jiri Dohnal. 2747m CZC. *A Hearth Without a Fire* prod/rel: Dafa
Kroky V Mlze, Novel
Blahove Devce 1938 d: Vaclav Binovec. lps: Vladimir Borsky, Hana Vitova, Pavla StolzovA. 2844m CZC. *A Foolish Girl* prod/rel: Elekta
Srdce V Soumraku, Novel
Srdce V Soumraku 1936 d: Vladimir Slavinsky. lps: Helena Friedlova, Rolf Wanka, Jiri Vondrovic. 3225m CZC. *Heart at Dusk* prod/rel: Elekta
Svetlo Jeho Oci, Novel
Svetlo Jeho Oci 1936 d: Vaclav Kubasek. lps: Jiri Steimar, Jiri Dohnal, Zita KabatovA. 2393m CZC. *The Light of His Eyes* prod/rel: Dafa
Zena Pod Krizem, Novel
Zena Pod Krizem 1937 d: Vladimir Slavinsky. lps: Gustav Hilmar, Helena Busova, Vera FerbasovA. 3090m CZC. *Woman Below the Cross* prod/rel: Slavia-Film

RAE, JOHN
The Custard Boys, London 1960, Novel
Reach for Glory 1962 d: Philip Leacock. lps: Harry Andrews, Kay Walsh, Michael Anderson Jr. 86M UKN. prod/rel: Blazer Films, Gala

RAEDER, GUSTAV
Robert Und Bertram, Play
Robert Und Bertram 1939 d: Hans H. Zerlett. lps: Rudi Godden, Kurt Seifert, Carla Rust. 93M GRM. prod/rel: Tobis

RAFF, FRIEDRICH
Der Kopfpreis, Short Story
Indiskrete Frau, Die 1927 d: Carl Boese. lps: Jenny Jugo, Maria Paudler, Georg Alexander. 2307m GRM. prod/rel: Phoebus-Film Ag

RAGNI, GEROME
Hair, Musical Play
Hair 1979 d: Milos Forman. lps: John Savage, Treat Williams, Beverly d'Angelo. 121M USA. prod/rel: United Artists

RAGSDALE, LULAH
Miss Dulcie from Dixie, 1917, Novel
Miss Dulcie from Dixie 1919 d: Joseph Gleason. lps: Gladys Leslie, Charles Kent, Arthur Donaldson. 4168f USA. prod/rel: Vitagraph Co. of America©

RAGUSA, ENRICO
Play
Ti Ho Sempre Amato! 1954 d: Mario CostA. lps: Amedeo Nazzari, Myriam Bru, Jacques Sernas. 100M ITL. prod/rel: Rizzoli Film, Royal Film

RAIMUND, FERDINAND (1790–1836), AUS
Der Bauer Als Millionar, 1868, Play
Bauer Als Millionar, Der 1961 d: Rudolf Steinbock. lps: Kathe Gold, Josef Meinrad, Paula Wessely. 94M AUS. prod/rel: Thalia

Der Verschwender, 1868, Play
Verschwender, Der 1953 d: Leopold Hainisch. lps: Josef Meinrad, Attila Horbiger, Senta Wengraf. 96M AUS. prod/rel: Dillenz

RAINE, ALLEN
By Berwin Banks, Novel
By Berwin Banks 1920 d: Sidney Morgan. lps: Langhorne Burton, Eileen Magrath, J. Denton-Thompson. 4900f UKN. *By Berwen Banks* prod/rel: Progress, Butcher's Film Service
Torn Sails, Novel
Torn Sails 1920 d: A. V. Bramble. lps: Milton Rosmer, Mary Odette, Geoffrey Kerr. 5000f UKN. prod/rel: Ideal
A Welsh Singer, Novel
Welsh Singer, A 1915 d: Henry Edwards. lps: Florence Turner, Henry Edwards, Campbell Gullan. 4640f UKN. prod/rel: Turner Films, Butcher

RAINE, LOUIS
Le Cavalier Lafleur, Opera
Cavalier Lafleur, Le 1934 d: Pierre-Jean Ducis. lps: Fernandel, Christiane Delyne, Jacques Louvigny. 85M FRN. prod/rel: Gamma Film

RAINE, NORMAN REILLY
Short Stories
Tugboat Annie 1933 d: Mervyn Leroy. lps: Marie Dressler, Wallace Beery, Robert Young. 88M USA. prod/rel: Metro-Goldwyn-Mayer Corp.©
1938, Serial Story
Tugboat Annie Sails Again 1940 d: Lewis Seiler. lps: Marjorie Rambeau, Alan Hale, Jane Wyman. 77M USA. prod/rel: Warner Bros. Pictures©
Hangman's Whip, New York 1933, Play
White Woman 1933 d: Stuart Walker. lps: Carole Lombard, Charles Laughton, Kent Taylor. 73M USA. prod/rel: Paramount Productions©
Hangman's Whip, New 1933, Play
Island of Lost Men 1939 d: Kurt Neumann. lps: Anna May Wong, J. Carrol Naish, Eric Blore. 63M USA. *North of Singapore*; *King of the River* prod/rel: Paramount Pictures©

RAINE, WILLIAM MACLEOD (1871–1954), UKN
Big-Town Round-Up, Boston 1920, Novel
Big Town Round-Up 1921 d: Lynn Reynolds. lps: Tom Mix, Pee Wee Holmes, Ora Carew. 4249f USA. prod/rel: Fox Film Corp.
A Daughter of the Dons, New York 1914, Novel
Burning the Wind 1929 d: Henry McRae, Herbert Blache. lps: Hoot Gibson, Virginia Brown Faire, Cesare GravinA. 5202f USA. prod/rel: Universal Pictures
The Desert's Price, Garden City, N.Y. 1924, Novel
Desert's Price, The 1925 d: W. S. Van Dyke. lps: Buck Jones, Florence Gilbert, Edna Marion. 5709f USA. prod/rel: Fox Film Corp.
Eastward Ho!, 1919, Serial Story
Eastward Ho! 1919 d: Emmett J. Flynn. lps: William Russell, Lucille Lee Stewart, Mary Hay. 5r USA. prod/rel: Fox Film Corp., William Fox©
The Fighting Edge, Boston 1922, Novel
Fighting Edge, The 1926 d: Henry Lehrman. lps: Kenneth Harlan, Patsy Ruth Miller, David Kirby. 6369f USA. prod/rel: Warner Brothers Pictures
Highgrader, The, New York 1915, Novel
Fighting for Gold 1919 d: Edward J. Le Saint. lps: Tom Mix, Teddy Sampson, Sid Jordan. 5r USA. *The Highgrader* prod/rel: Fox Film Corp., William Fox©
A Man Four-Square, Boston 1919, Novel
Man Four-Square, A 1926 d: R. William Neill. lps: Buck Jones, Marion Harlan, Harry Woods. 4744f USA. prod/rel: Fox Film Corp.
Man Size, New York 1922, Novel
Man's Size 1923 d: Howard M. Mitchell. lps: William Russell, Alma Bennett, Stanton Heck. 4316f USA. prod/rel: Fox Film Corp.
Mavericks, New York 1912, Novel
Ridin' Rascal, The 1926 d: Cliff Smith. lps: Art Acord, Olive Hasbrouck, Al Jennings. 4510f USA. prod/rel: Universal Pictures
A Sacrifice to Mammon, New York 1906, Novel
Ridgeway of Montana 1924 d: Cliff Smith. lps: Jack Hoxie, Olive Hasbrouck, Herbert Fortier. 4843f USA. prod/rel: Universal Pictures
The Sheriff's Son, Boston 1918, Novel
Sheriff's Son, The 1919 d: Victor Schertzinger. lps: Charles Ray, Seena Owen, J. P. Lockney. 5r USA. prod/rel: Thomas H. Ince Corp.©, Famous Players-Lasky Corp.
A Texas Ranger, New York 1911, Novel
Pure Grit 1923 d: Nat Ross. lps: Roy Stewart, Esther Ralston, Jere Austin. 4571f USA. *A Texas Ranger* prod/rel: Universal Pictures

Three Young Texans, Novel
Three Young Texans 1954 d: Henry Levin. lps: Mitzi Gaynor, Keefe Brasselle, Jeffrey Hunter. 78M USA. prod/rel: 20th Century-Fox

Through Troubled Waters, Story
Through Troubled Waters 1915 d: Ulysses Davis. lps: Alfred Vosburgh, Anne Schaefer, Myrtle Gonzales. 3r USA. prod/rel: Broadway Star, Vitagraph Co. of America

Wyoming, a Story of the Outdoor West, New York 1908, Novel
Man from Wyoming, The 1924 d: Robert North Bradbury. lps: Jack Hoxie, Lillian Rich, William Welsh. 4717f USA. prod/rel: Universal Pictures

The Yukon Trail, a Tale of the North, Boston 1917, Novel
Grip of the Yukon, The 1928 d: Ernst Laemmle. lps: Francis X. Bushman, Neil Hamilton, June Marlowe. 6599f USA. prod/rel: Universal Pictures

RAINIER, PETER W.
Green Fire, 1942, Novel
Green Fire 1954 d: Andrew Marton. lps: Stewart Granger, Grace Kelly, Paul Douglas. 100M USA. prod/rel: MGM

RAINS, OLGA
We Became Canadians, Book
Zomer Van '45, de 1991 d: Bram Van Erkel. lps: Will Van Kralingen, Renee Fokker, David Palffy. MTV. 640M NTH.

RAIS, KAREL VACLAV
Pantata Bezousek, Novel
Pantata Bezousek 1941 d: Jiri Slavicek. lps: Jaroslav Vojta, Ladislav Bohac, Zita KabatovA. 2541m CZC. *The Old Man Bezousek* prod/rel: Nationalfilm

Zapadli Vlastenci, Novel
Zapadli Vlastenci 1932 d: M. J. Krnansky. lps: Jaroslav Vojta, Hugo Haas, Hermina VojtovA. 2337m CZC. *Forgotten Patriots* prod/rel: Elekta, Reiter

RAISON, MILTON
The Phantom of 42nd Street, Novel
Phantom of 42nd Street, The 1945 d: Al Herman. lps: Dave O'Brien, Katharine Aldridge, Alan Mowbray. 58M USA. prod/rel: Producers Releasing Corp.

RAIT, SEYMOUR
Casper the Friendly Ghost, Story
Casper 1995 d: Brad Silberling. lps: Christina Ricci, Bill Pullman, Cathy Moriarty. 100M USA. prod/rel: Amblin, Harvey

RAJU, MUNIPALLE
Pujari, Novel
Poojapalam 1964 d: B. N. Reddi. lps: A. Nageshwara Rao, Gummadi Venkateshwara Rao, Relangi Venkatramaiah. 156M IND. *The Fruits of Worship*; *Puja Phalamu* prod/rel: Shri Sambhu Films

RAKESH, MOHAN
Ashad Ka Ek Din, 1958, Play
Ashad Ka Ek Din 1971 d: Mani Kaul. lps: Arun Khopkar, Rekha Sabnis, Om Shivpuri. 114M IND. *One Monsoon Day*; *A Monsoon Day* prod/rel: Ffc

Uski Roti, Short Story
Uski Roti 1969 d: Mani Kaul. lps: Gurdeep Singh, Garima, Richa Vyas. 110M IND. *His Daily Bread*; *Our Daily Bread*; *Day's Bread, A*

RAKOUS, VOJTECH
Modche a Rezi, Short Story
Modche a Rezi 1926 d: Premysl Prazsky. lps: Rudolf Hock, Pepi Glocknerova-Kramerova, Karel Noll. CZC. *Modche and Rezi* prod/rel: Julius Schmitt

RALEIGH, CECIL
The Best of Luck, London 1916, Play
Best of Luck, The 1920 d: Ray C. Smallwood. lps: Kathryn Adams, Jack Holt, Lilie Leslie. 5421f USA. prod/rel: Screen Classics, Inc., Metro Pictures Corp.©

The Derby Winner, London 1894, Play
Derby Winner, The 1915 d: Harold Shaw. lps: Edna Flugrath, Gerald Ames, Mary Dibley. 4900f UKN. prod/rel: London, Jury

The Great Ruby, London 1898, Play
Great Ruby, The 1915 d: Barry O'Neil. lps: Octavia Handworth, George Soule Spencer, Beatrice Morgan. 5r USA. prod/rel: Lubin Mfg. Co.©, V-L-S-E, Inc.

Hearts are Trumps, New York 1900, Play
Hearts are Trumps 1920 d: Rex Ingram. lps: Winter Hall, Frank Brownlee, Alice Terry. 6r USA. prod/rel: Metro Pictures Corp.©

The Hope, London 1911, Play
Hope, The 1920 d: Herbert Blache. lps: Jack Mulhall, Marguerite de La Motte, Ruth Stonehouse. 6r USA. prod/rel: Metro Pictures Corp.©

The King's Minister, Play
King's Minister, The 1914 d: Harold Shaw. lps: Edna Flugrath, Arthur Holmes-Gore, Langhorne Burton. 2922f UKN. prod/rel: London, Globe

The Marriages of Mayfair, London 1908, Play
Fatal Hour, The 1920 d: George W. Terwilliger. lps: Thomas W. Ross, Wilfred Lytell, Francis X. Conlan. 6r USA. *The Marriage of Mayfair* prod/rel: Metro Pictures Corp.©

Sealed Orders, London 1913, Play
Stolen Orders 1918 d: Harley Knoles, George Kelson. lps: Kitty Gordon, Carlyle Blackwell, Montagu Love. 8r USA. prod/rel: William A. Brady, State Rights

The Sins of Society, London 1907, Play
Sins of Society, The 1915 d: Oscar Eagle. lps: Robert Warwick, Alec B. Francis, Ralph Delmore. 5r USA. prod/rel: William A. Brady Picture Plays, Inc., World Film Corp.

The Sporting Duchess, New York 1895, Play
Sporting Duchess, The 1915 d: Barry O'Neil. lps: Rose Coghlan, Ethel Clayton, George Soule Spencer. 6r USA. prod/rel: Lubin Mfg. Co., Lubin Liberty Bell Feature

Sporting Duchess, The 1920 d: George W. Terwilliger. lps: Alice Joyce, Percy Marmont, Gustav von Seyffertitz. 7r USA. prod/rel: Vitagraph Co. of America©

Sporting Life, London 1897, Play
Sporting Life 1918 d: Maurice Tourneur. lps: Ralph Graves, Constance Binney, Warner Richmond. 6032f USA. prod/rel: Maurice Tourneur Productions, Inc.©, State Rights

Sporting Life 1925 d: Maurice Tourneur. lps: Bert Lytell, Marian Nixon, Paulette Duval. 6709f USA. prod/rel: Universal Pictures

The Whip, London 1909, Play
Whip, The 1917 d: Maurice Tourneur. lps: Irving Cummings, Alma Hanlon, Paul McAllister. 8r USA. prod/rel: Paragon Films, Inc.©, State Rights

Whip, The 1928 d: Charles J. Brabin. lps: Dorothy MacKaill, Ralph Forbes, Anna Q. Nilsson. 6056f USA. prod/rel: First National Pictures

The White Heather, London 1897, Play
White Heather, The 1919 d: Maurice Tourneur. lps: Ralph Graves, Mabel Ballin, Holmes Herbert. 6r USA. prod/rel: Maurice Tourneur Productions©, Famous Players-Lasky Corp.

RALEIGH, H. M.
Excess Baggage, Novel
Excess Baggage 1933 d: Redd Davis. lps: Claud Allister, Frank Pettingell, Sydney Fairbrother. 59M UKN. prod/rel: Real Art, Radio

RAMARAO, T. K.
Bangarada Manushya, Novel
Bangarada Manushya 1972 d: Siddalingaiah. lps: Rajkumar, Bharati, BalkrishnA. 180M IND. prod/rel: Rajkamal Arts

RAMASWAMY, CHO
Mohammed-Bin-Tughlaq, Play
Mohammed-Bin-Tughlaq 1971 d: Cho Ramaswamy. lps: Cho Ramaswamy, Sukumari, Ambi. 136M IND. prod/rel: Prestige Prod.

RAMATI, ALEXANDER
Novel
I Skrzypce Przestaly Grac 1988 d: Alexander Ramati. lps: Horst Buchholz, Piotr Polk, Maya Ramati. 118M PLN/USA. *And the Violins Stopped Playing*; *And the Fiddle Fell Silent*

The Assisi Underground, Novel
Assisi Underground, The 1984 d: Alexander Ramati. lps: Ben Cross, James Mason, Irene Papas. 178M USA/ITL. prod/rel: Golan-Globus

Beyond the Mountains, London 1958, Novel
Mas Alla de Las Montanas 1967 d: Alexander Ramati. lps: Maximilian Schell, Raf Vallone, Irene Papas. 104M SPN/USA. *The Desperate Ones* (USA); *Beyond the Mountains* prod/rel: David, Pro-Artis Iberica

Rebel Against the Light, New York 1960, Novel
Sands of Beersheba 1965 d: Alexander Ramati. lps: Diane Baker, David Opatoshu, Tom Bell. 93M USA/ISR. *Mordei Ha'or* (ISR); *Rebel Against the Light* prod/rel: David Productions

RAMEAU, JEAN
L'ami Des Montagnes, Novel
Ami Des Montagnes, L' 1920 d: Guy Du Fresnay. lps: Marguerite Madys, Andre Nox, Jean Devalde. 1550m FRN. prod/rel: Gaumont - Serie Pax

RAMEAU, PAUL H.
Novel
Du Bist Musik 1956 d: Paul Martin. lps: Caterina Valente, Paul Hubschmid, Grethe Weiser. 91M GRM. *You are Musik* prod/rel: Ccc-Filmkunst, Gloria

Story
Munchhausen in Afrika 1958 d: Werner Jacobs. lps: Peter Alexander, Anita Gutwell, Gunther Philipp. 88M GRM. prod/rel: C.C.C., Prisma

RAMOS CARRION, MIGUEL
El Rey Que Rabio, Opera
Rey Que Rabio, El 1929 d: Jose Buchs. lps: Juan de Orduna, Amelia Munoz, Jose Montenegro. F SPN. *King Had Rabies, The* prod/rel: Ediciones Forns-Buchs (Madrid)

RAMOS, GRACILIANO (1892–1953), BRZ
Memorias Do Carcere, 1953, Novel
Memorias Do Carcere 1984 d: Nelson Pereira Dos Santos. lps: Carlos Vereza, Jofre Soares, Nildo Parente. 93M BRZ. *Memories of Imprisonment*; *Memories of Prison*; *Memorias de la Carcel*; *Memoires de Prison*

Sao Bernardo, 1934, Novel
Sao Bernardo 1972 d: Leon Hirszman. lps: Othon Bastos, Isabel Ribeiro, Nildo Parente. 110M BRZ. *Saint Bernard*; *S Bernardo* prod/rel: Saga Filmes

Vidas Secas, 1938, Novel
Vidas Secas 1963 d: Nelson Pereira Dos Santos. lps: Atila Iorio, Maria Ribeiro, Jofre Soares. 135M BRZ. *Barren Lives*; *Drought*; *Secheresse*; *Dry Lives* prod/rel: Luiz Carlos Barreto, Herbert Richers

RAMSEY, ALICE
Bridge, 1917, Play
Social Hypocrites 1918 d: Albert Capellani. lps: May Allison, Frank Currier, Joseph Kilgour. 5-6r USA. prod/rel: Metro Pictures Corp.©

Eve's Daughter, New York 1917, Play
Eve's Daughter 1918 d: James Kirkwood. lps: Billie Burke, Thomas Meighan, Lionel Atwill. 5r USA. prod/rel: Famous Players-Lasky Corp.©, Paramount Pictures

RAMSEY, ALICIA
Byron, Play
Prince of Lovers, A 1922 d: Charles Calvert. lps: Howard Gaye, Marjorie Hume, Mary Clare. 7850f UKN. prod/rel: Gaumont, British Screencraft

RAMSEY, JOHN
Where the Rainbow Ends, London 1911, Play
Where the Rainbow Ends 1921 d: H. Lisle Lucoque. lps: Babs Farren, B. Cave Chinn, Muriel Pointer. 5000f UKN. prod/rel: British Photoplay Productions, Pioneer

RAMSEY, JUDITH
Artic
Long Journey Back 1978 d: Mel Damski. lps: Mike Connors, Cloris Leachman, Stephanie Zimbalist. TVM. 100M USA. prod/rel: Lorimar Productions

RAMSEY, RINA
Barnaby, Novel
Barnaby 1919 d: Jack Denton. lps: Dick Webb, Cyril Vaughan, Athalie Davis. 5000f UKN. prod/rel: Barker

RAMUZ, CHARLES FERDINAND
Le Rapt, Novel
Rapt, Le 1984 d: Pierre Koralnik. lps: Pierre Clementi, Daniela Silverio, Heinz Bennent. 100M FRN/SWT. prod/rel: T.S.R., Antenne 2

RAMUZ, CHARLES-FERDINAND (1878–1947), SWT
Derborence, Lausanne 1934, Novel
Derborence 1946 d: Mattia Pinoli. lps: Valentina Cortese, Vittorio Duse, Egisto Olivieri. SWT/ITL.

Farinet, Paris 1932, Novel
Or Dans la Montagne, L' 1938 d: Max Haufler. lps: Jean-Louis Barrault, Suzy Prim, Janine Crispin. 90M FRN/SWT. *Farinet, Oder Das Falsche Geld*; *Farinet, Ou la Fausse Monnaie*; *Faux Monnayeurs*; *Farinet*; *Farinet Ou l'Or Dans la Montagne* prod/rel: Clarte-Film, Basle, Clarte-Film, Paris

La Guerre Dans le Haut-Pays, 1915, Novel
Guerre Dans le Haut-Pays, La 1999 d: Francis Reusser. lps: Marion Cotillard, Yann Tregouet, Francis Marthouret. 105M SWS/FRN/BLG. *The War in the Highlands* prod/rel: Cab Prods. (Switzerland), Arena Films

Le Regne de l'Esprit Malin, Lausanne 1917, Novel
Regne de l'Esprit Malin, Le 1955 d: Guido Wurth. SWT. *Die Herrschaft Des Ublen Geistes*

La Separation Des Races, 1923, Novel
Rapt 1934 d: Dimitri Kirsanoff. lps: Dita Parlo, Nadia Sibirskaia, Geymond Vital. 102M FRN/GRM/SWT. *The Mystic Mountain*; *La Separation Des Races*; *Races*; *Frauenraub*; *Zweikampf Der Geschlechter* prod/rel: Cinedis, Mentor-Film

Histoire du Soldat, Lausanne 1918, Opera
Soldier's Tale, The 1964 d: Michael Birkett. lps: Robert Helpmann, Brian Phelan, Svetlana BeriosovA. 52M UKN. prod/rel: Ipsilon, British Home Entertainments

RAND, AYN (1905–1982), RSS
The Fountainhead, 1943, Novel
Fountainhead, The 1949 d: King Vidor. lps: Gary Cooper, Patricia Neal, Raymond Massey. 114M USA. prod/rel: Warner Bros.

Night of January 16th, New York 1935, Play
Night of January 16th, The 1941 d: William Clemens. lps: Robert Preston, Ellen Drew, Nils Asther. 79M USA. prod/rel: Paramount

We the Living, 1936, Novel
Addio, Kira! 1942 d: Goffredo Alessandrini. lps: Fosco Giachetti, Alida Valli, Rossano Brazzi. 95M ITL. prod/rel: Scalera-Era Film
Noi Vivi 1942 d: Goffredo Alessandrini. lps: Fosco Giachetti, Alida Valli, Rossano Brazzi. 95M ITL. *We the Living* (UKN) prod/rel: Scalera Film, Era Film

RANDALL, BOB
David's Mother, Play
David's Mother 1994 d: Robert Allan Ackerman. lps: Kirstie Alley, Sam Waterston, Stockard Channing. TVM. 92M USA.

The Fan, Novel
Fan, The 1981 d: Edward Bianchi. lps: Lauren Bacall, James Garner, Maureen Stapleton. 95M USA. prod/rel: Paramount, R.S.O.

RANDALL, FLORENCE ENGEL
The Watcher in the Woods, Novel
Watcher in the Woods, The 1980 d: John Hough. lps: Bette Davis, Carroll Baker, David McCallum. 100M UKN/USA. prod/rel: Walt Disney

RANDLE, KEVIN D.
Ufo Crash at Roswell, Book
Roswell 1994 d: Jeremy Paul Kagan. lps: Kyle MacLachlan, Dwight Yoakam, Kim Greist. 87M USA. *Roswell: the Ufo Cover-Up* prod/rel: Viacom Pictures©, Citadel Entertainment

RANK, CLAUDE
Mission Speciale a Caracas, Novel
Mission Speciale a Caracas 1965 d: Raoul Andre. lps: Rod Carter, Saro Urzi, Jany Clair. 87M FRN/SPN/ITL. *Mision Especial En Caracas* (SPN); *Missione Caracas* (ITL); *Special Mission to Caracas* prod/rel: C.F.F.P., Cine Italia Film

Nick Carter Et le Trefle Rouge, Novel
Nick Carter Et le Trefle Rouge 1965 d: Jean-Paul Savignac. lps: Eddie Constantine, Nicole Courcel, Jeanne Valerie. 85M FRN/ITL. *Nick Carter E Il Trifoglio Rosso* (ITL); *Nick Carter and the Red Club* prod/rel: Chaumiane Productions, Parc Film

La Route de Corinthe, Paris 1966, Novel
Route de Corinthe, La 1967 d: Claude Chabrol. lps: Jean Seberg, Maurice Ronet, Christian Marquand. 90M FRN/ITL/GRC. *Criminal Story* (ITL); *The Road to Corinth*; *Who's Got the Black Box?* (USA) prod/rel: Les Films la Boetie, Compagnia Generale Finanziaria Cin.Ca

RANKIN, MCKEE
The Danites, Play
Danites, The 1912 d: Frank Boggs. lps: Betty Harte, Hobart Bosworth, Eugenie Besserer. 2000f USA. prod/rel: Selig Polyscope Co.

The Runaway Wife, Play
Runaway Wife, The 1915 d: Kenean Buel. lps: Stewart Baird, Justina Wayne, Lowell Stuart. 4r USA. prod/rel: Kalem Co., Broadway Favorites

RANKIN, WILLIAM
Be It Ever So Humble, Story
Hi, Beautiful! 1944 d: Leslie Goodwins. lps: Martha O'Driscoll, Noah Beery Jr., Hattie McDaniel. 66M USA. *Pass to Romance* (UKN); *Be It Ever So Humble* prod/rel: Universal

General Court-Martial, Play
South Sea Woman 1953 d: Arthur Lubin. lps: Burt Lancaster, Chuck Connors, Virginia Mayo. 99M USA. *The Marines Have a Word for It* prod/rel: Warner Bros.

Thanks for the Ride, 1936, Short Story
Time Out for Romance 1937 d: Malcolm St. Clair. lps: Claire Trevor, Michael Whalen, Joan Davis. 75M USA. prod/rel: 20th Century-Fox Film Corp.©

RANSLEY, PETER
The Hawk, Novel
Hawk, The 1992 d: David Hayman. lps: Helen Mirren, George Costigan, Rosemary Leach. 86M UKN. prod/rel: BBC, Feature Film

RANSOME, ARTHUR (1884–1967), UKN
Book
Swallows and Amazons Forever! 1982 d: Andrew Morgan. lps: Henry Dimbleby, John Woodvine, Colin Baker. MTV. 100M UKN. prod/rel: BBC

Swallows and Amazons, 1931, Novel
Swallows and Amazons 1974 d: Claude Whatham. lps: Virginia McKenna, Ronald Fraser, Simon West. 92M UKN. prod/rel: Emi, Theatre Projects

RANSOME, STEPHEN
Hearses Don't Hurry, Novel
Who Is Hope Schuyler? 1942 d: Thomas Z. Loring. lps: Joseph Allen Jr., Mary Howard, Sheila Ryan. 57M USA. prod/rel: 20th Century Fox

RAO, R. NAGENDRA
Bhukailasa, Play
Bhukailasa 1940 d: Sundarao Nadkarni. lps: R. Nagendra Rao, M. V. Subbaiah Naidu, Lakshmibai. 185M IND. prod/rel: Saraswati Cine Films

RAPHAEL, FREDERIC (1931–), USA
Darling, 1965, Novel
Darling. 1965 d: John Schlesinger. lps: Dirk Bogarde, Laurence Harvey, Julie Christie. 127M UKN. prod/rel: Anglo-Amalgamated, Vic

Oxbridge Blues, Novel
Oxbridge Blues 1984 d: James Cellan Jones. lps: Ian Charleson, Malcolm Stoddard, Amanda Redman. SER. UKN. prod/rel: BBC

Richard's Things, Novel
Richard's Things 1980 d: Anthony Harvey. lps: Liv Ullmann, Amanda Redman, Tim Pigott-Smith. 104M UKN.

RAPHAEL, FREDERIC
Sleeps Six, Novel
Oxbridge Blues 1984 d: James Cellan Jones. lps: Ian Charleson, Malcolm Stoddard, Amanda Redman. SER. UKN. prod/rel: BBC

RAPHAELSON, SAMSON
Accent on Youth, New York 1934, Play
Accent on Youth 1935 d: Wesley Ruggles. lps: Herbert Marshall, Sylvia Sidney, Philip Reed. 77M USA. prod/rel: Paramount Productions, Inc.
Mr. Music 1950 d: Richard Haydn. lps: Bing Crosby, Nancy Olson, Richard Haydn. 113M USA. prod/rel: Paramount
But Not for Me 1959 d: Walter Lang. lps: Clark Gable, Carroll Baker, Lilli Palmer. 105M USA. prod/rel: Paramount, Seaton-Perlberg

The Day of Atonement, 1922, Short Story
Jazz Singer, The 1927 d: Alan Crosland. lps: Al Jolson, May McAvoy, Warner Oland. 8117f USA. prod/rel: Warner Brothers Pictures
Jazz Singer, The 1953 d: Michael Curtiz. lps: Danny Thomas, Peggy Lee, Mildred Dunnock. 107M USA. prod/rel: Warner Bros.
Jazz Singer, The 1980 d: Richard Fleischer. lps: Neil Diamond, Laurence Olivier, Lucie Arnaz. 115M USA. prod/rel: Emi

Hilda Crane, New York 1950, Play
Hilda Crane 1956 d: Philip Dunne. lps: Jean Simmons, Guy Madison, Jean-Pierre Aumont. 87M USA. *Many Loves of Hilda Crane, The* prod/rel: 20th Century-Fox

The Perfect Marriage, New York 1944, Play
Perfect Marriage, The 1946 d: Lewis Allen. lps: David Niven, Loretta Young, Nona Griffith. 87M USA. prod/rel: Paramount

A Rose Is Not a Rose, Short Story
Bannerline 1951 d: Don Weis. lps: Keefe Brasselle, Sally Forrest, Lionel Barrymore. 88M USA. prod/rel: Metro-Goldwyn-Mayer Corp.

Skylark, New York 1939, Play
Skylark 1941 d: Mark Sandrich. lps: Claudette Colbert, Ray Milland, Brian Aherne. 94M USA. prod/rel: Paramount

RASCOVICH, MARK
The Bedford Incident, New York 1963, Novel
Bedford Incident, The 1965 d: James B. Harris. lps: Richard Widmark, Sidney Poitier, James MacArthur. 102M UKN/USA. prod/rel: Bedford Productions, Columbia

RASHKE, RICHARD
Escape from Sorbibor, Book
Escape from Sobibor 1987 d: Jack Gold. lps: Alan Arkin, Rutger Hauer, Joanna PaculA. TVM. 165M UKN/USA/YGS. prod/rel: Rule-Starger Productions, Zenith Productions

RASMUS, MIRIAM BODE
The Cross, Poem
Her Life's Story 1914 d: Joseph de Grasse. lps: Lon Chaney, Pauline Bush, Laura Oakley. 2r USA. prod/rel: Rex

RASPUTIN, VALENTIN
Story
Urok Franzuskovo 1978 d: Yevgyeni Tashkov. lps: Mischa Yegerov, Tatjana Vasileva, Valentina TalyzinA. 79M USS. prod/rel: Mosfilm

Proscanie, Novel
Proscanie 1981 d: Elem Klimov, Larissa Shepitko. lps: Stefanija Stanjuta, Lev Durov, Alexei Petrenko. 126M USS. *Farewell to Matjora*; *Farewell*; *Proshchanie* prod/rel: Mosfilm

RASSER, ALFRED
Demokrat Lappli, 1947, Play
Demokrat Lappli 1961 d: Alfred Rasser. lps: Alfred Rasser, Ruedi Walter, Margrit Rainer. 98M SWT. *Le Democrate Lappli*; *Hd Lappli Wird Zivilist* prod/rel: Walter Kagi-Films

Hd-Soldat Lappli. Volksstuck in 16 Bildern, 1945, Play
Hd Lappli 1959 d: Alfred Rasser. lps: Alfred Rasser, Editha Nordberg, Otto Wiesely. 115M SWT. *Le Soldat Auxiliaire Lappli*; *Lappli, Der Etappenheld* prod/rel: Walter Kagi-Filmproduktion

RATEL, SIMONE
La Maison Des Bories, Novel
Maison Des Bories, La 1969 d: Jacques Doniol-Valcroze. lps: Marie Dubois, Mathieu Carriere, Maurice Garrel. 90M FRN. prod/rel: Parc Films, U.G.C.

RATH, E. J.
The Dark Chapter, New York 1924, Novel
Asi Es la Vida 1930 d: George J. Crone. lps: Jose Bohr, Delia Magana, Lola Vendrill. 6486f USA. prod/rel: Sono-Art Productions
Merrily We Live 1938 d: Norman Z. McLeod. lps: Constance Bennett, Brian Aherne, Alan Mowbray. 90M USA. *Take It Easy*; *Love Without Reason*; *Dark Chapter* prod/rel: Metro-Goldwyn-Mayer Corp., Loew's, Inc.©

Elope if You Must, Play
Elope if You Must 1922 d: C. R. Wallace. lps: Eileen Percy, Eddie Sutherland, Joe Bennett. 4995f USA. prod/rel: Fox Film Corp.

Good References, London 1920, Play
Good References 1920 d: R. William Neill. lps: Constance Talmadge, Vincent Coleman, Ned Sparks. 5r USA. prod/rel: First National Exhibitors Circuit, Joseph M. Schenck©

Mister 44, New York 1916, Novel
Mister 44 1916 d: Henry Otto. lps: Harold Lockwood, May Allison, Lester Cuneo. 5r USA. prod/rel: Yorke Film Corp., Metro Pictures Corp.©

The Nervous Wreck, New York 1923, Novel
Nervous Wreck, The 1926 d: Scott Sidney. lps: Harrison Ford, Phyllis Haver, Chester Conklin. 6730f USA. prod/rel: Christie Film Co., Producers Distributing Corp.

Too Many Crooks, New York 1918, Novel
Too Many Crooks 1919 d: Ralph Ince. lps: Gladys Leslie, Jean Paige, Huntley Gordon. 5r USA. prod/rel: Vitagraph Co. of America©
Too Many Crooks 1927 d: Fred Newmeyer. lps: Mildred Davis, Lloyd Hughes, George Bancroft. 5399f USA. prod/rel: Famous Players-Lasky, Paramount Pictures

When the Devil Was Sick, New York 1926, Novel
Clear the Decks 1929 d: Joseph Henabery. lps: Reginald Denny, Olive Hasbrouck, Otis Harlan. 5792f USA. prod/rel: Universal Pictures

RATTIGAN, TERENCE (1911–1977), UKN, Rattigan, Terence Mervyn
A Bequest to the Nation, 1970, Play
Bequest to the Nation, A 1973 d: James Cellan Jones. lps: Peter Finch, Glenda Jackson, Michael Jayston. 116M UKN. *The Nelson Affair* prod/rel: Universal, Hal B. Wallis

The Browning Version, London 1948, Play
Browning Version, The 1951 d: Anthony Asquith. lps: Michael Redgrave, Jean Kent, Nigel Patrick. 90M UKN. prod/rel: General Film Distributors, Javelin
Browning Version, The 1994 d: Mike Figgis. lps: Albert Finney, Greta Scacchi, Matthew Modine. 97M UKN. prod/rel: Percy Main

The Deep Blue Sea, London 1952, Play
Deep Blue Sea, The 1955 d: Anatole Litvak. lps: Vivien Leigh, Kenneth More, Eric Portman. 99M UKN. prod/rel: London Films, 20th Century-Fox

French Without Tears, London 1936, Play
French Without Tears 1939 d: Anthony Asquith. lps: Ray Milland, Ellen Drew, Janine Darcy. 85M UKN. prod/rel: Paramount, Two Cities

Separate Tables, London 1955, Play
Separate Tables 1958 d: Delbert Mann. lps: Burt Lancaster, Rita Hayworth, David Niven. 99M USA. prod/rel: United Artists, Clifton Prods.
Separate Tables 1983 d: John Schlesinger. lps: Alan Bates, Julie Christie, Claire Bloom. TVM. 113M UKN/USA. prod/rel: MGM

The Sleeping Prince, London 1953, Play
Prince and the Showgirl, The 1957 d: Laurence Olivier, Anthony Bushell. lps: Laurence Olivier, Marilyn Monroe, Sybil Thorndike. 114M UKN/USA. prod/rel: Warner Bros., Marilyn Monroe Prods.

While the Sun Shines, London 1943, Play
   While the Sun Shines 1947 d: Anthony Asquith. lps: Barbara White, Ronald Squire, Ronald Howard. 81M UKN. prod/rel: Associated British Picture Corp., International Screenplays

Who Is Sylvia?, London 1950, Play
   Man Who Loved Redheads, The 1955 d: Harold French. lps: Moira Shearer, John Justin, Roland Culver. 90M UKN. prod/rel: British Lion, London Films

The Winslow Boy, London 1946, Play
   Winslow Boy, The 1948 d: Anthony Asquith. lps: Robert Donat, Margaret Leighton, Cedric Hardwicke. 117M UKN. prod/rel: British Lion Production Assets, London Films
   Winslow Boy, The 1999 d: David Mamet. lps: Nigel Hawthorne, Jeremy Northam, Rebecca Pidgeon. 104M USA. prod/rel: Sony Pictures Classic

RATZKA, CLARA
Das Bekenntnis, Novel
   Rutschbahn 1928 d: Richard Eichberg. lps: Fee Malten, Heinrich George, Harry Hardt. 2703m GRM. prod/rel: Richard Eichberg-Film

RAU, MARGARET
I'm Giving Them Up for Good, Novel
   Cold Turkey 1971 d: Norman Lear. lps: Dick Van Dyke, Pippa Scott, Tom Poston. 102M USA. prod/rel: United Artists Corp., Tandem

RAU, NEIL
   Cold Turkey 1971 d: Norman Lear. lps: Dick Van Dyke, Pippa Scott, Tom Poston. 102M USA. prod/rel: United Artists Corp., Tandem

RAUKHVERGER, M.
Cholpon - Utrennyaya Zvezda, 1944, Bal
   Cholpon - Utrennyaya Zvezda 1960 d: Roman Tikhomirov. lps: Reina Chokoyeva, Uran Sarbagishev, Nikolay Tugelov. 75M USS. *Morning Star* (USA); *Cholpon* prod/rel: Lenfilm, Frunze Film Studio

RAUPACH, ERNST
Mlynar a Jeho Dite, Play
   Mlynar a Jeho Dite 1928 d: Zet Molas. lps: Jan Svoboda, Zet Molas, J. Kaspar. 2226m CZC. *The Miller and His Son*; *The Miller and His Child* prod/rel: Molas-Film

Der Muller Und Sein Kind, Play
   Muller Und Sein Kind, Der 1911 d: Adolf Gartner. lps: Henny Porten, Friedrich Zelnik, Robert Garrison. 690m GRM. prod/rel: Messters Projektion

RAVALEC, VINCENT
Cantique de la Racaille, Novel
   Cantique de la Racaille 1998 d: Vincent Ravalec. lps: Yvan Attal, Virginie Lanoue, Yann Collette. 104M FRN. *Melody for a Hustler* prod/rel: April Films, M6 Films

RAVEN, SIMON (1927–, UKN
Doctors Wear Scarlet, Novel
   Incense for the Damned 1970 d: Robert Hartford-Davis. lps: Patrick MacNee, Peter Cushing, Alexander Davion. 87M UKN. *Bloodsuckers* (USA); *Doctors Wear Scarlet*; *Bloodsucker* prod/rel: Grand National, Lucinda

RAVET, E.
La Niece d'Amerique, Play
   Niece d'Amerique, La 1913. lps: Maurice Luguet, Andree Pascal, Berangere. 355m FRN. prod/rel: Scagl

RAVIUS, ERNST LUDWIG
Ich Schwore Und Gelobe, Novel
   Ich Schwore Und Gelobe 1960 d: Geza von Radvanyi. lps: Wolfgang Lukschy, Corny Collins, Hans Christian Blech. 103M GRM. *On My Honor* prod/rel: Omega, N.F.

RAWLINGS, MARJORIE K. (1896–1953), USA, Rawlings, Marjorie Kinnan
Cross Creek, 1942, Book
   Cross Creek 1983 d: Martin Ritt. lps: Mary Steenburgen, Rip Torn, Peter Coyote. 120M USA. prod/rel: Emi

Gal Young 'Un, 1940, Short Story
   Gal Young un 1979 d: Victor Nunez. lps: Dana Preu, David Peck, J. Smith. 105M USA. prod/rel: Nunez Films

RAWLINGS, MARJORIE K., Rawlings, Marjorie Kinnan
Short Stories
   Sun Comes Up, The 1948 d: Richard Thorpe. lps: Jeanette MacDonald, Claude Jarman Jr., Lloyd Nolan. 94M USA. *Sun in the Morning* prod/rel: MGM

RAWLINGS, MARJORIE K. (1896–1953), USA, Rawlings, Marjorie Kinnan
The Yearling, 1938, Novel
   Yearling, The 1946 d: Clarence Brown. lps: Gregory Peck, Jane Wyman, Claude Jarman Jr. 128M USA. prod/rel: MGM
   Yearling, The 1994 d: Rod Hardy. lps: Peter Strauss, Jean Smart, Wil Horneff. TVM. 120M USA. prod/rel: Rhi Entertainment©

RAWLINSON, A. R.
Scarlet Thread, 1949, Play
   Scarlet Thread 1951 d: Lewis Gilbert. lps: Kathleen Byron, Laurence Harvey, Sydney Tafler. 84M UKN. prod/rel: Nettlefold, International Realist

RAWLS, WILSON
Summer of the Monkey, Book
   Summer of the Monkey 1998 d: Michael Anderson. lps: Michael Ontkean, Leslie Hope, Wilford Brimley. 101M CND. prod/rel: Bwe Distribution, Edge Prods.

Where the Red Fern Grows, Novel
   Where the Red Fern Grows 1974 d: Norman Tokar. lps: James Whitmore, Beverly Garland, Jack Ging. 90M USA. prod/rel: Doty-Dayton

RAWSON, CLAYTON
Death from a Top Hat, New York 1938, Novel
   Miracles for Sale 1939 d: Tod Browning. lps: Robert Young, Florence Rice, Henry Hull. 71M USA. prod/rel: Metro-Goldwyn-Mayer Corp., Loew's, Inc.©

No Coffin for the Corpse, Novel
   Man Who Wouldn't Die, The 1942 d: Herbert I. Leeds. lps: Lloyd Nolan, Marjorie Weaver, Helene Reynolds. 75M USA. *Million Dollar Ghost* prod/rel: 20th Century-Fox

RAY, JEAN
Malpertuis, Novel
   Malpertuis 1972 d: Harry Kumel. lps: Orson Welles, Susan Hampshire, Mathieu Carriere. 125M FRN/BLG/GRM. *Malpertuis: Histoire d'une Maison Maudite*; *The Legend of Doom House*; *Maudite: Legend of Doom House* prod/rel: Societe D'expansion Du Spectacle, Sofidoc

RAY, RENE
Strange World of Planet X, Novel
   Strange World of Planet X, The 1958 d: Gilbert Gunn. lps: Forrest Tucker, Gaby Andre, Martin Benson. 75M UKN. *The Cosmic Monster* (USA); *Creatures from Another World*; *Cosmic Monsters*; *The Strange World*; *The Crawling Terror* prod/rel: Eros, Artistes Alliance

RAYMAN, SYLVIA
Women of Twilight, London 1951, Play
   Women of Twilight 1952 d: Gordon Parry. lps: Freda Jackson, Rene Ray, Lois Maxwell. 89M UKN. *Twilight Women* (USA); *Another Chance* prod/rel: Romulus, Daniel M. Angel

RAYMO, CHET
The Dork of Cork, Novel
   Frankie Starlight 1995 d: Michael Lindsay-Hogg. lps: Anne Parillaud, Matt Dillon, Gabriel Byrne. 100M USA. prod/rel: Film Four, Ferndale

RAYMOND, ALLEN
The Heart of Salome, Boston 1925, Novel
   Heart of Salome, The 1927 d: Victor Schertzinger. lps: Alma Rubens, Walter Pidgeon, Holmes Herbert. 5615f USA. prod/rel: Fox Film Corp.

RAYMOND, DEREK, Cook, Raymond
Les Mois d'Avril Sont Meurtriers, Novel
   Mois d'Avril Sont Meurtriers, Les 1986 d: Laurent Heynemann. lps: Jean-Pierre Marielle, Jean-Pierre Bisson, Francois Berleand. 88M FRN. prod/rel: Studio Canal Plus, Little Bear Films

RAYMOND, DEREK
He Died With His Eyes Open, Novel
   On Ne Meurt Que Deux Fois 1986 d: Jacques Deray. lps: Charlotte Rampling, Xavier Duluc, Elisabeth Depardieu. 106M FRN. *He Died With His Eyes Open* prod/rel: Swaine Productions, Tf1 Films

RAYMOND, ERNEST
The Berg, Short Story
   Atlantic 1929 d: E. A. Dupont. lps: Franklin Dyall, Madeleine Carroll, John Stuart. 90M UKN. prod/rel: British International Pictures, Wardour
   Atlantis 1930 d: Jean Kemm, E. A. Dupont. lps: Maxime Desjardins, Constant Remy, Marcel Vibert. F FRN. prod/rel: Etablissements Jacques Haik

For Them That Trespass, Novel
   For Them That Trespass 1949 d: Alberto Cavalcanti. lps: Stephen Murray, Patricia Plunkett, Richard Todd. 95M UKN. prod/rel: Associated British Picture Corporation, Associated British-Pathe

Tell England, Novel
   Tell England 1931 d: Anthony Asquith, Geoffrey Barkas. lps: Fay Compton, Tony Bruce, Carl Harbord. 88M UKN. *Battle of Gallipoli* (USA) prod/rel: British Instructional, Wardour

RAYMOND, FRED
Maske in Blau, Opera
   Maske in Blau 1942 d: Paul Martin. lps: Klari Tabody, Wolf Albach-Retty, Hans Moser. 94M GRM/HNG. *Kek Alarc, A* (HNG); *Mask in Blue* prod/rel: N.F.K., Schorcht
   Maske in Blau 1953 d: Georg Jacoby. lps: Marika Rokk, Paul Hubschmid, Wilfried Seyferth. 100M GRM. *Marika*; *Mask in Blue* prod/rel: Roja, UFA

Die Perle von Tokay, Opera
   Perle von Tokay, Die 1954 d: Hubert MarischkA. lps: Johanna Matz, Karl Hackenberg, Karl Schonbock. 98M AUS. prod/rel: Donau-Papageno

Saison in Salzburg, Opera
   Saison in Salzburg 1952 d: Ernst MarischkA. lps: Adrian Hoven, Walter Muller, Hans Richter. 105M AUS. prod/rel: Wien
   Saison in Salzburg 1961 d: Franz J. Gottlieb. lps: Peter Alexander, Gunther Philipp, Waltraut Haas. 97M AUS. prod/rel: Sascha
   ..Und Die Musik Spielt Dazu 1943 d: Carl Boese. lps: Vivi Gioi, Maria Andergast, Georg Alexander. 88M GRM. *Saison in Salzburg* prod/rel: Deka, Karp

RAYMOND, HIPPOLYTE
Les Vingt-Huit Jours de Clairette, Opera
   Vingt-Huit Jours de Clairette, Les 1933 d: Andre Hugon. lps: Mireille, Janine Guise, Armand Bernard. 98M FRN. prod/rel: Hugon-Films, Gaumont-Franco-Film-Aubert

RAYMOND, MOORE
Smiley, Novel
   Smiley 1956 d: Anthony Kimmins. lps: Ralph Richardson, John McCallum, Chips Rafferty. 97M UKN/ASL. prod/rel: London Films, 20th Century-Fox

Smiley Gets a Gun, Novel
   Smiley Gets a Gun 1958 d: Anthony Kimmins. lps: Keith Calvert, Sybil Thorndike, Chips Rafferty. 90M UKN/ASL. prod/rel: 20th Century-Fox, Canberra Films

RAYNER, B. F.
The Dumb Man of Manchester, London 1837, Play
   Dumb Man of Manchester, The 1908 d: William Haggar. lps: Will Haggar Jr., Jenny Linden, Will Desmond. SHT UKN. prod/rel: Haggar & Sons

RAYNER, D. A.
The Enemy Below, 1956, Novel
   Enemy Below, The 1957 d: Dick Powell. lps: Robert Mitchum, Curd Jurgens, David Hedison. 97M USA. prod/rel: 20th Century-Fox

RAYNER, RICHARD
Los Angeles With a Map, Novel
   L.A. Without a Map 1998 d: Mika Kaurismaki. lps: David Tennant, Vinessa Shaw, Julie Delpy. 106M UKN/FRN/FNL. *Los Angeles Without Maps* prod/rel: Marianna Films, Dan Films

RAYSON, HANNIE
Hotel Sorrento, Play
   Hotel Sorrento 1994 d: Richard Franklin. lps: Joan Plowright, Tara Morice, Caroline Goodall. 112M ASL. prod/rel: Horizon Films, Bayside Pictures

RAZ, ABRAHAM
Play
   Neither By Day Nor By Night 1974 d: Steven Hilliard Stern. lps: Zalman King, Miriam Bernstein-Cohen, Dalia Friedland. 91M USA/ISR. *Lo Bayom Ve'lo Balayla* prod/rel: Motion Pictures International (L.a.), Slonim Film Productions (Tel Aviv)

REA, DOMENICO
Ninfa Plebea, Novel
   Ninfa Plebea 1996 d: Lina Wertmuller. lps: Lucia Cara, Stefania Sandrelli, Raoul BovA. 111M ITL. prod/rel: Italian International Film, Eurolux Produzione

READ, OPIE (1852–1939), USA, Read, Opie Percival
The Jucklins, Chicago 1896, Novel
   Jucklins, The 1920 d: George Melford. lps: Mabel Julienne Scott, Monte Blue, Ruth Renick. 6r USA. *The Fighting Schoolmaster* (UKN) prod/rel: Famous Players-Lasky Corp.©, George Melford Production

A Kentucky Colonel, Chicago 1890, Novel
   Kentucky Colonel, The 1920 d: William A. Seiter. lps: Joseph J. Dowling, Frederick Vroom, Elinor Field. 6r USA. prod/rel: National Film Corp. of America, W. W. Hodkinson Corp.

Old Ebenezer, Chicago 1897, Novel
   Almost a Husband 1919 d: Clarence Badger. lps: Will Rogers, Peggy Wood, Herbert Standing. 4818f USA. prod/rel: Goldwyn Pictures Corp.©, Goldwyn Distributing Corp.

The Tennessee Judge, Play
   Starbucks, The 1912 d: William J. Bowman. lps: Opie Read, Mrs. C. R. Smith, Miss Logan. 2r USA. prod/rel: American

The Wives of the Prophet, Chicago 1894, Novel
   Wives of the Prophet, The 1926 d: J. A. Fitzgerald. lps: Orville Caldwell, Alice Lake, Violet Mersereau. 6560f USA. prod/rel: J. A. Fitzgerald Productions, Lee-Bradford Corp.

A Yankee from the West, Chicago 1879, Novel
Yankee from the West, A 1915 d: George Siegmann. lps: Seena Owen, Wallace Reid, Tom Wilson. 4r USA. prod/rel: Majestic Motion Picture Co., Mutual Film Corp.

READ, PIERS PAUL (1941–, UKN)
A Married Man, Novel
Married Man, A 1983 d: Charles Jarrott. lps: Anthony Hopkins, Ciaran Madden, Lise Hilboldt. TVM. 200M UKN. prod/rel: London Weekend Tv, Lionhearted Productions

Monk Dawson, Novel
Monk Dawson 1997 d: Tom Waller. lps: John Michie, Ben Taylor, Paula Hamilton. 107M UKN. prod/rel: de Warrenne Pictures©

READE, BILL
Novel
Ou Est Passe Tom? 1971 d: Jose Giovanni. lps: Rufus, Alexandra Stewart, Paul Crauchet. 110M FRN/ITL. prod/rel: Profilm, Valoria

READE, CHARLES (1814–1884), UKN
Christie Johnstone, Novel
Christie Johnstone 1921 d: Norman MacDonald. lps: Gertrude McCoy, Stewart Rome, Clive Brook. 5161f UKN. prod/rel: Broadwest, Walturdaw

The Cloister and the Hearth, 1861, Novel
Cloister and the Hearth, The 1913 d: Hay Plumb. lps: Alec Worcester, Alma Taylor, Hay Plumb. 4725f UKN. prod/rel: Hepworth

Foul Play, Novel
Foul Play 1920. lps: Renee Kelly, Henry Hallett, Randolph McLeod. 4594f UKN. prod/rel: Master, British Exhibitors' Films

Hard Cash, 1864, Novel
Hard Cash 1913 d: Charles M. Seay. lps: Charles Ogle, Bigelow Cooper, Barry O'Moore. 2000f USA. prod/rel: Edison

Hard Cash 1921 d: Edwin J. Collins. lps: Dick Webb, Alma Green, Frank Arlton. 5150f UKN. prod/rel: Master Films, Butcher's Film Service

It Is Never Too Late to Mend, 1853, Novel
It Is Never Too Late to Mend 1913 d: Charles M. Seay. lps: Mary Fuller, Harry Beaumont. 2000f USA. prod/rel: Edison

It's Never Too Late to Mend 1917 d: Dave Aylott. lps: George Leyton, Margaret Hope, George Dewhurst. 5492f UKN. prod/rel: Martin's Cinematograph

It's Never Too Late to Mend 1922 d: George Wynn. lps: Russell Thorndike, Ward McAllister, Alec Alexander. 1040f UKN. prod/rel: Master Films, British Exhibitors' Films

It's Never Too Late to Mend 1937 d: David MacDonald. lps: Tod Slaughter, Marjorie Taylor, Jack Livesey. 67M UKN. prod/rel: George King, MGM

The Lyons Mail, London 1877, Play
True Story of the Lyons Mail, The 1915 d: George Pearson. lps: Fred Paul. 2000f UKN. prod/rel: G. B. Samuelson, Moss

Lyons Mail, The 1916 d: Fred Paul. lps: H. B. Irving, Nancy Price, Harry Welchman. 5200f UKN. prod/rel: Ideal

Lyons Mail, The 1931 d: Arthur Maude. lps: John Martin-Harvey, Norah Baring, Ben Webster. 76M UKN. prod/rel: Twickenham, Woolf & Freedman

Peg Woffington, 1852, Novel
Peg Woffington 1910 d: Edwin S. Porter. lps: Florence Turner. 990f USA. prod/rel: Edison

Peg Woffington 1912 d: A. E. Coleby. lps: Leslie Howard Gordon. 2145f UKN. prod/rel: Britannia Films, Pathe

Masks and Faces 1914 d: Lawrence Marston. lps: Alan Hale, Vola Smith, Edward Cecil. 2r USA. prod/rel: Biograph Co.

Masks and Faces 1917 d: Fred Paul. lps: Johnston Forbes-Robertson, Irene Vanbrugh, H. B. Irving. 6200f UKN. prod/rel: Ideal

Peg of Old Drury 1935 d: Herbert Wilcox. lps: Anna Neagle, Cedric Hardwicke, Jack Hawkins. 76M UKN. prod/rel: British and Dominions, United Artists

Put Yourself in His Place, Novel
Put Yourself in His Place 1912 d: Theodore Marston. lps: William Garwood, Marguerite Snow, William Russell. 2r USA. prod/rel: Thanhouser

The Ticket-of-Leave Man, Story
Ticket-of-Leave Man, The 1914 d: Louis J. Gasnier, Donald MacKenzie. lps: Eleanor Woodruff, M. O. Penn, Sheldon Lewis. 3r USA. prod/rel: Wharton

Ticket-of-Leave Man, The, Story
Detective Craig's Coup 1914 d: Donald MacKenzie. lps: Francis Carlyle, Pearl Sindelar, Jack Standing. 5r USA. prod/rel: Pathe Freres, Eclectic Film Co.©

White Lies, Boston 1857, Novel
White Lies 1920 d: Edward J. Le Saint. lps: Gladys Brockwell, William Scott, Josephine Crowell. 4332f USA. prod/rel: Fox Film Corp., William Fox©

REAGE, PAULINE
L'histoire d'O, Novel
Histoire d'O, L' 1975 d: Just Jaeckin. lps: Corinne Clery, Udo Kier, Anthony Steel. 112M FRN/GRM. *Die Geschichte Der O* (GRM); *The Story of O* (USA) prod/rel: Terra Filmkunst, S.N. Prodis

Retour a Roissy, Novel
Shina Ningyo 1981 d: Shuji TerayamA. lps: Klaus Kinski, Isabelle Illiers, Arielle Dombasle. 83M JPN/FRN. *Les Fruits de la Passion* (FRN); *The Fruits of Passion* prod/rel: Argos Films (Paris), Terayama Productions (Tokyo)

REALI, STEFANO
Operations, Play
In Barc a Vela Contromano 1997 d: Stefano Reali. lps: Valerio Mastandrea, Antonio Catania, Emanuela Rossi. 100M ITL. *Physical Jerks* prod/rel: Colorado Film, Medusa Film

REBELO, MARQUES
Estrela Sobe, A, 1939, Novel
Estrela Sobe, A 1974 d: Bruno Barreto. lps: Odete LarA. 90M BRZ.

REBETA-BURDITT, JOYCE
The Cracker Factory, Novel
Cracker Factory, The 1979 d: Burt Brinckerhoff. lps: Natalie Wood, Perry King, Peter Haskell. TVM. 100M USA. prod/rel: ABC, Emi Television

REBOUX, PAUL
Maison de Danses, Novel
Maison de Danses 1930 d: Maurice Tourneur. lps: Charles Vanel, Gaby Morlay, Jose Noguero. 85M FRN. prod/rel: Pathe-Natan

REBREANU, LIVIU
Ciuleandra, 1927, Novel
Verklungene Traume 1930 d: Martin Berger. lps: Maly Delschaft. 90M GRM/RMN. *Ciuleandra* (RMN)
Ciuleandra 1985 d: Sergiu Nicolaescu. lps: Ion Ratiu, Anca Nicola, Gilda Marinescu. 124M RMN. *Kiuleandra*
Ion, 1920, Novel
Ion: Blestemul Pamintului, Blestemul Iubirii 1979 d: Mircea Muresan. 210M RMN. *Ion: the Lust for the Land, the Lust for Love*; *Ion - the Curse of Property, the Curse of Love*
Padurea Spinzuratilor, 1922, Novel
Padurea Spinzuratilor 1965 d: Liviu Ciulei. lps: Victor Rebengiuc, Liviu Ciulei, Ana Szeles. 160M RMN. *The Forest of the Hanged*; *Forest of Hanged Men*; *The Lost Forest* prod/rel: Romania
Rascoala, 1932, Novel
Rascoala 1965 d: Mircea Muresan. lps: Amza Pellea, Ilario Ciabanu. 108M RMN. *Blazing Winter*; *The Uprising*

RECHLIN, EVA
Hosianna, Book
Hosianna 1961 d: Peter Podehl. lps: Thomas Schmidt, Claudia Bartfeld, Gernot DudA. 77M GRM. prod/rel: Schonger

RECK-MALLECZEWEN
Arme Kleine Sif, Novel
Arme Kleine Sif 1927 d: Arthur Bergen. lps: Grete Mosheim, Paul Wegener, Anton Pointner. 2401m GRM. *Das Sif, Das Weib Den Mord Beging* prod/rel: Munchener Lichtspielkunst Ag

Bomben Auf Monte Carlo, Novel
Bomben Auf Monte Carlo 1931 d: Hanns Schwarz. lps: Hans Albers, Anna Sten, Heinz Ruhmann. 111M GRM. prod/rel: UFA-Filmkunst, Transit
Le Capitaine Craddock, Novel
Capitaine Craddock, Le 1931 d: Max de Vaucorbeil, Hanns Schwarz. lps: Kathe von Nagy, Alice Tissot, Jean Murat. 87M FRN. *Un Bombe Sur Monte Carlo*; *Le Croisseur En Folie* prod/rel: U.F.a., a.C.E.
Monte Carlo Madness, Novel
Monte Carlo Madness 1931 d: Hanns Schwarz. lps: Sari Maritza, Hans Albers, Charles Redgie. 83M UKN. prod/rel: UFA, Pathe

REDDI, B. N.
Mangalsutram, Short Story
Vande Mataram 1939 d: B. N. Reddi. lps: Chittor V. Nagaiah, Kanchanmala, Lingamurthy. 222M IND. *Salute the Motherland*; *Mangalsutram* prod/rel: Vauhini Pictures

REDDIN, KEITH
Life During Wartime, Play
Life During Wartime 1997 d: Evan Dunsky. lps: David Arquette, Stanley Tucci, Kate Capshaw. 92M USA. prod/rel: Key Entertainment, Dan Stone, Flynn/Simchowitz

REDDIN, KENNETH
Another Shore, Novel
Another Shore 1948 d: Charles Crichton. lps: Robert Beatty, Stanley Holloway, Moira Lister. 91M UKN. prod/rel: Ealing Studios, General Film Distributors

REDIER, ANTOINE
La Guerre Des Femmes, Poem
Soeurs d'Armes 1937 d: Leon Poirier. lps: Thomy Bourdelle, Jeanne Sully, Josette Day. 125M FRN. prod/rel: S.A.C.I.C.

REDLINSKI, EDWARD
Miracle on Greenpoint, Novel
Szczesliwego Nowego Roku 1997 d: Janusz Zaorski. lps: Boguslaw Linda, Janusz Gajos, Zbigniew Zamachowski. 91M PLN. *Happy New Year*; *Szczesliwego Nowego Jorku*; *Merry Christmas and a Happy New York* prod/rel: Vilm Production, Polish Television

Rat-Poles, Novel
Szczesliwego Nowego Roku 1997 d: Janusz Zaorski. lps: Boguslaw Linda, Janusz Gajos, Zbigniew Zamachowski. 91M PLN. *Happy New Year*; *Szczesliwego Nowego Jorku*; *Merry Christmas and a Happy New York* prod/rel: Vilm Production, Polish Television

REDMOND, FERGUS
A Florida Enchantment, New York 1891, Novel
Florida Enchantment, A 1914 d: Sidney Drew. lps: Sidney Drew, Edith Storey, Ethel Louise Lloyd. 5r USA. prod/rel: Vitagraph Co. of America©, Broadway Star Feature

REDON, JEAN
Les Yeux Sans Visage, Paris 1959, Novel
Yeux Sans Visage, Les 1959 d: Georges Franju. lps: Pierre Brasseur, Alida Valli, Juliette Mayniel. 88M FRN/ITL. *Occhi Senza Volto* (ITL); *Eyes Without a Face* (UKN); *The Horror Chamber of Dr. Faustus* (USA) prod/rel: Champs-Elysees Productions, Lux-Film

REED, BARRY
The Verdict, Novel
Verdict, The 1982 d: Sidney Lumet. lps: Paul Newman, Jack Warden, James Mason. 128M USA. prod/rel: 20th Century Fox

REED, LUTHER
Dear Me, Or April Changes, New York 1921, Play
Purple Highway, The 1923 d: Henry Kolker. lps: Madge Kennedy, Monte Blue, Vincent Coleman. 6574f USA. prod/rel: Kenma Corp., Paramount Pictures

REED, MARK
Petticoat Fever, New York 1935, Play
Petticoat Fever 1936 d: George Fitzmaurice. lps: Robert Montgomery, Myrna Loy, Reginald Owen. 81M USA. prod/rel: Metro-Goldwyn-Mayer Corp.©

Yes, My Darling Daughter, New York 1937, Play
Yes, My Darling Daughter 1939 d: William Keighley. lps: Priscilla Lane, Fay Bainter, Roland Young. 85M USA. prod/rel: Warner Bros. Pictures©, First National Picture

REED, MRS. HAINES W.
The Mother Instinct, Story
Mother Instinct, The 1915 d: Wilfred Lucas. lps: Cleo Madison, Joe King, Edward Sloman. 3r USA. prod/rel: Bison

REED, MYRTLE (1874–1911), USA, Norton, Katherine Lafarge
At the Sign of the Jack O'Lantern, New York 1905, Novel
At the Sign of the Jack O'Lantern 1922 d: Lloyd Ingraham. lps: Betty Ross Clark, Earl Schenck, Wade Boteler. 5193f USA. prod/rel: Renco Film Co., W. W. Hodkinson Corp.

Flower of the Dusk, New York 1908, Novel
Flower of the Dusk 1918 d: John H. Collins. lps: Viola Dana, Guy Coombs, Jack McGowan. 5r USA. prod/rel: Metro Pictures Corp.©

Lavender and Old Lace, New York 1902, Play
Lavender and Old Lace 1921 d: Lloyd Ingraham. lps: Marguerite Snow, Seena Owen, Louis Bennison. 5770f USA. prod/rel: Renco Film Co., W. W. Hodkinson Corp.

A Spinner in the Sun, New York 1906, Novel
Veiled Woman, The 1922 d: Lloyd Ingraham. lps: Marguerite Snow, Ed Coxen, Landers Stevens. 5300f USA. prod/rel: Renco Film Co., W. W. Hodkinson Corp.

A Weaver of Dreams, New York 1911, Novel
Weaver of Dreams, A 1918 d: John H. Collins. lps: Viola Dana, Clifford Bruce, Mildred Davis. 5r USA. prod/rel: Metro Pictures Corp.©

REED, TALBOT BAINES (1852–1893), UKN
The Fifth Form at St. Dominics, London 1881, Novel
Fifth Form at St. Dominic's, The 1921 d: A. E. Coleby. lps: Ralph Forbes, Maurice Thompson, Humberston Wright. 6886f UKN. prod/rel: I. B. Davidson, Granger

REES, R. F. W.
The Second Mate, Novel
Fear Ship, The 1933 d: J. Steven Edwards. lps: Cyril McLaglen, Dorothy Bartlam, Edmund Willard. 66M UKN. prod/rel: Associated Sound Film Industries, Paramount

REES, R. W.
Second Mate, The 1929 d: J. Steven Edwards. lps: David Dunbar, Cecil Barry, Lorna Duveen. SIL. 3960f UKN. prod/rel: H. B. Parkinson, Pioneer

REESE, JOHN
Frontier Frenzy, Serial Story
Young Land, The 1959 d: Ted Tetzlaff. lps: Patrick Wayne, Yvonne Craig, Dennis Hopper. 89M USA. prod/rel: Columbia, C. V. Whitney Pictures

The Looters, Novel
Charley Varrick 1973 d: Don Siegel. lps: Walter Matthau, Joe Don Baker, Felicia Farr. 111M USA. prod/rel: Universal

REEVE, ALICE MEANS
Story
Johnny Doesn't Live Here Any More 1944 d: Joe May. lps: Simone Simon, William Terry, James Ellison. 77M USA. *And So They Were Married* prod/rel: King Bros., Monogram

REEVE, ARTHUR B. (1880–1936), USA
The Clutching Hand, Chicago 1934, Novel
Amazing Exploits of the Clutching Hand, The 1936 d: Al Herman. lps: Jack Mulhall, Rex Lease, Mae Busch. 7r USA. prod/rel: Weiss Productions, Inc.

REEVES, ARNOLD
The Shepherd King, New York 1904, Play
Shepherd King, The 1923 d: J. Gordon Edwards. lps: Violet Mersereau, Edy Darclea, Virginia Lucchetti. 8500f USA. prod/rel: Fox Film Corp.

REEVES, THEODORE
Beggars are Coming to Town, New York 1945, Play
I Walk Alone 1948 d: Byron Haskin. lps: Lizabeth Scott, Burt Lancaster, Kirk Douglas. 98M USA. prod/rel: Paramount

The Harbor, Play
Only Eight Hours 1934 d: George B. Seitz. lps: Chester Morris, Robert Taylor, Virginia Bruce. 68M USA. *Society Doctor*; *After Eight Hours*; *Ambulance Call* prod/rel: Metro-Goldwyn-Mayer Corp.©

REGEILA, ISMET
My Kingdom for a Woman, Short Story
Abdulla the Great 1954 d: Gregory Ratoff. lps: Gregory Ratoff, Kay Kendall, Marina Berti. 92M UKN/USA. *Abdulla's Harem* (USA); *Abdullah's Harem* prod/rel: Sphinx, Independent Film Distributors

REGIO, JOSE
Play
Mon Cas 1986 d: Manoel de OliveirA. lps: Luis Miguel Cintra, Bulle Ogier, Axel Bogousslavsky. 92M FRN/PRT. *O Meu Caso* (PRT); *O Meu Caso: Repeticoes* prod/rel: Filmargem, Les Films Du Passage

Benilde Ou a Virgem-Mae, 1947, Play
Benilde Ou a Virgem Mae 1975 d: Manoel de OliveirA. lps: Maria Amelia Matta, Jorge Rolla, Jacinto Ramos. 112M PRT. *Benilde Or the Virgin Mother*; *Benilde: Virgin and Mother* prod/rel: Tobias Portuguesa, Centro Portugues de Cinema

O Principe Come Orelhas de Burro, 1942, Novel
Principe Com Orelhas de Burro, O 1980 d: Antonio de Macedo. lps: Antonino Solmer, Antonio Cara d'Anjo, Antonio RamA. 105M PRT. *The Prince With a Donkey's Ear*; *The Prince the the Ass's Ears*

O Vestido Cor de Fogo, 1946, Short Story
Vestido Cor de Fogo, O 1984 d: Lauro Antonio. lps: Jorge Vale, Acacia Thiele, Mariana Rey Monteiro. 92M PRT. *The Dress of the Colour of Fire*

REGNIER, MAX
Mort Ou Vif, Play
Mort Ou Vif 1947 d: Jean Tedesco. lps: Max Regnier, Leonce Corne, Nicole Riche. 95M FRN. prod/rel: Pathe

REGNOLI, PIERO
Rebellion, Novel
Sette Baschi Rossi 1968 d: Mario Siciliano. lps: Ivan Rassimov, Sieghardt Rupp, Kirk Morris. 96M ITL/GRM. *Congo Hell* (UKN); *Seven Red Berets*; *Sieben Dreckige Teufel* (GRM); *Seven Dirty Devils* prod/rel: Metheus Film (Roma), Lisa Film (Munich)

Ti Aspettero All'inferno, Novel
Ti Aspettero All'inferno 1960 d: Piero Regnoli. lps: Eva Bartok, Massimo Serato, Antonio Pierfederici. 92M ITL. *I'll See You in Hell* (USA); *I'll Wait for You in Hell* prod/rel: Verdestella Film, Euro International Film

REHFISCH
The Dreyfus Case, Play
Dreyfus 1931 d: F. W. Kraemer, Milton Rosmer. lps: Cedric Hardwicke, Charles Carson, George Merritt. 90M UKN. *The Dreyfus Case* (USA) prod/rel: British International Pictures, Wardour

REHFISCH, HANS
Guilty Melody, Novel
Guilty Melody 1936 d: Richard Pottier. lps: Nils Asther, Gitta Alpar, John Loder. 75M UKN. prod/rel: Franco-London, Associated British Film Distributors

The Guilty Voice, Short Story
Disque 413, Le 1936 d: Richard Pottier. lps: Jules Berry, Jean Galland, Gitta Alpar. 82M FRN. *Symphonie d'Amour* prod/rel: Franco-London Film Production

Wasser Fur Canitoga, Play
Wasser Fur Canitoga 1939 d: Herbert Selpin. lps: Hans Albers, Charlotte Susa, Hilde Sessak. 119M GRM. *Water for Canitoga* prod/rel: Bavaria, Kristall

REHOR, ANTONIN H.
Poprava Josefa Kudrny, Play
Jmenem Jeho Velicenstva 1928 d: Antonin Vojtechovsky. lps: Jaroslav Prucha, Ruza Vechovska-Vojechovska, Josef Skrivan. 1641m CZC. *In the Name of His Majesty*; *Poprava Pesaka Kudrny*; *The Execution of Infantryman Kudrna* prod/rel: Pragafilm

REHOR, VAVRINEC
Dvoji Zivot, Novel
Dvoji Zivot 1924 d: Vaclav Kubasek. lps: Mary Jansova, Sasa Dobrovolna, Jan W. Speerger. 2864m CZC. *Two Lives*; *A Double Life* prod/rel: Pronax-Film
Dvoji Zivot 1939 d: Vaclav Kubasek. lps: Bolek Prchal, Slavka Rosenbergova, Marie GlazrovA. 2295m CZC. *Double Life* prod/rel: Grafo, Moldavia

Valecne Tajnosti Prazske, Novel
Valecne Tajnosti Prazske 1926 d: Vaclav Kubasek. lps: Otto Zahradka, Jan W. Speerger, Marie KopeckA. 2144m CZC. *Prague War Secrecy*; *Military Secrets of Prague* prod/rel: Iris-Film

REICH, WILHELM
La Rivoluzione Sessuale, Book
Rivoluzione Sessuale, La 1968 d: Riccardo Ghione. lps: Riccardo Cucciolla, Marisa Mantovani, Ruggero Miti. 92M ITL. *The Sexual Revolution* prod/rel: West Film, Delta

REICHART, HEINZ
Walzerkreig, Play
Waltzes from Vienna 1933 d: Alfred Hitchcock. lps: Jessie Matthews, Edmund Gwenn, Fay Compton. 81M UKN. *Strauss' Great Waltz* (USA) prod/rel: Tom Arnold, Gaumont-British

REICHENBACK HARRY
Anatomy of Ballyhoo: Phantom Fame, New York 1931, Book
Half-Naked Truth, The 1932 d: Gregory La CavA. lps: Lupe Velez, Lee Tracy, Eugene Pallette. 77M USA. *Phantom Fame*; *The Half-Naked Truth* prod/rel: RKO Radio Pictures©

REID, ED
Artic
Case Against Brooklyn, The 1958 d: Paul Wendkos. lps: Darren McGavin, Margaret Hayes, Warren Stevens. 82M USA. prod/rel: Columbia, Morningside Prods.

REID, HAL
At Cripple Creek, Play
At Cripple Creek 1912 d: Hal Reid. lps: Sue Balfour, Gertrude Robinson, Wallace Reid. SHT USA. prod/rel: Reliance

At the Old Cross Roads, New York 1902, Play
At the Cross Roads 1914 d: Frank L. Dear. lps: Estha Williams, Mrs. Stuart Robson, Rae Ford. 5r USA. *At the Old Crossed Roads* prod/rel: Select Photo Play Producing Co., Alliance Films Corp.

The Confession, New York 1911, Play
Confession, The 1920 d: Bertram Bracken. lps: Henry B. Walthall, Francis McDonald, William Clifford. 7r USA. prod/rel: National Film Corp. of America, State Rights

The Cow Puncher, Play
Cowpuncher, The 1915? d: William Johnson Jossey. lps: C. M. Giffen, Don Williams, Lee Cladwell. 6-8r USA. prod/rel: Reelplays Corp., State Rights

Human Hearts, Play
Human Hearts 1912 d: Otis Turner. lps: King Baggot, Jane Fearnley, Mayme Kelso. 2000f USA. prod/rel: Imp
Human Hearts 1914 d: King Baggot. lps: King Baggot, Arline Pretty. 3r USA. prod/rel: Imp

Human Hearts 1922 d: King Baggot. lps: House Peters, Russell Simpson, Gertrude Claire. 6350f USA. prod/rel: Universal Film Mfg. Co.

Jim and Joe, Poem
Jim and Joe 1911 d: Hal Reid. 1000f USA. prod/rel: Selig Polyscope Co.

The Little Red Schoolhouse, Play
Little Red Schoolhouse, The 1923 d: John G. Adolfi. lps: Martha Mansfield, Harlan Knight, Sheldon Lewis. 5760f USA. *The Greater Law* (UKN) prod/rel: Martin J. Heyl, Arrow Film Corp.

The Peddler, New York 1902, Play
Peddler, The 1917 d: Herbert Blache. lps: Joe Welch, Sidney Mason, Catherine Calvert. 5r USA. prod/rel: U.S. Amusement Corp., Art Dramas, Inc.

Sue, Play
Sue 1912. SHT USA. prod/rel: Champion

REID, MAYNE (1818–1883), IRL, Reid, T. Mayne, Reid, Thomas Mayne
The Quadroon, 1856, Novel
Octoroon, The 1913 d: Kenean Buel. lps: Guy Coombs, Marguerite Courtot, Alice Joyce. 3000f USA. prod/rel: Kalem

REID, P. R.
Colditz Story, Book
Colditz Story, The 1955 d: Guy Hamilton. lps: John Mills, Eric Portman, Frederick Valk. 97M UKN. prod/rel: Ivan Foxwell, British Lion

The Latter Days, Book
Colditz Story, The 1955 d: Guy Hamilton. lps: John Mills, Eric Portman, Frederick Valk. 97M UKN. prod/rel: Ivan Foxwell, British Lion

REILLY, PATRICIA
Big Business Girl, 1930, Story
Big Business Girl 1931 d: William A. Seiter. lps: Loretta Young, Ricardo Cortez, Jack Albertson. 80M USA. prod/rel: First National Pictures, Inc.

REILLY, ROBERT T.
Red Hugh, Prince of Donegal, Milwaukee 1957, Novel
Fighting Prince of Donegal, The 1966 d: Michael O'Herlihy. lps: Peter McEnery, Susan Hampshire, Tom Adams. 104M UKN/USA. prod/rel: Walt Disney Productions, Buena Vista

REIMANN, BRIGITTE
Unser Kurzes Leben, Novel
Unser Kurzes Leben 1980 d: Lothar Warneke. lps: Simone Frost, Gottfried Richter, Hermann Beyer. 113M GDR. *Our Short Life* prod/rel: Defa, Gruppe Roter Kreis

REIMANN, HANS
Das Ekel, Play
Ekel, Das 1939 d: Hans Deppe. lps: Hans Moser, Josefine Dora, Kurt Meisel. 80M GRM. prod/rel: Tobis

Der Haustyrann, Novel
Haustyrann, Der 1959 d: Hans Deppe. lps: Heinz Erhardt, Grethe Weiser, Peter Vogel. 89M GRM. prod/rel: Divina, Gloria

REIMANN, MAX
Familie Hannemann, Play
Tante Jutta Aus Kalkutta 1953 d: Karl G. Kulb. lps: Ida Wust, Ingrid Lutz, Viktor Staal. 90M GRM. *Aunt Jutta from Calcutta* prod/rel: Ariston, N.F.

Der Sprung in Die Ehe, Play
Paprika 1932 d: Carl Boese. lps: Franziska Gaal, Paul Horbiger, Paul Heidemann. F GRM.
Paprika 1933 d: Carl Boese. lps: Elsa Merlini, Renato Cialente, Sergio Tofano. 80M ITL. prod/rel: Italfonosap, Anonima Pittaluga
Paprika 1957 d: Kurt Wilhelm. lps: Violetta Ferrari, Waltraut Haas, Willy HagarA. 91M GRM. prod/rel: Carlton, Eichberg
Paprika 1933 d: Jean de Limur. lps: Rene Lefevre, Pierre Etchepare, Irene de Zilahy. 77M FRN. prod/rel: Societe Internationale De Cinematogrphie

REIMENSNYDER, HELEN
Tillie, a Mennonite Maid, New York 1904, Novel
Tillie 1922 d: Frank Urson. lps: Mary Miles Minter, Noah Beery, Allan Forrest. 5r USA. *Tillie, a Mennonite Maid* prod/rel: Realart Pictures, Paramount Pictures

REINE MARIE DE ROUMANIE, LA
Lily of Life, Novel
Lys de la Vie, Le 1921 d: Loie Fuller, Georgette Sorrere. lps: Loie Fuller, Rene Clair, Jean-Paul Le Tarare. 1650m FRN. *The Lily of Life* prod/rel: Loie Fuller, Georgette Sorrere

REINECKER, HERBERT
Hauen Sie Ab Mit Heldentum, Novel
Kinder, Mutter Und Ein General 1955 d: Laslo Benedek. lps: Therese Giese, Hilde Krahl, Ursula Herking. 105M GRM. *Children, Mother and a General*; *Sons, Mothers and the General* prod/rel: Intercontinental

Some Lie and Some Die, Novel
  Inspector Wexford: Some Lie and Some Die 1990
  d: Sandy Johnson. lps: George Baker, Christopher
  Ravenscroft, Louie Ramsay. TVM. 150M UKN. *Some
  Lie and Some Die* prod/rel: Watch/Grant

The Speaker of Mandarin, Novel
  Inspector Wexford: the Speaker of Mandarin 1992
  d: John Reardon, Herbert Wise. lps: George Baker,
  Christopher Ravenscroft, Louie Ramsay. TVM. 156M
  UKN. *Ruth Rendell Mysteries: the Speaker of Mandarin;
  The Speaker of Mandarin*

The Tree of Hands, Novel
  Tree of Hands 1989 d: Giles Foster. lps: Helen Shaver,
  Paul McGann, Peter Firth. 89M UKN. *Innocent Victim*
  prod/rel: Granada, British Screen

An Unkindness of Ravens, Novel
  Inspector Wexford: an Unkindness of Ravens
  1991 d: John Gorrie. lps: George Baker, Christopher
  Ravenscroft, James Snell. TVM. 99M UKN. *An
  Unkindness of Ravens* prod/rel: Watch/Grant

An Unwanted Woman, Novel
  Inspector Wexford: an Unwanted Woman 1992 d:
  Jenny Wilkes. lps: George Baker, Christopher
  Ravenscroft, Marjorie Sommerville. TVM. 100M UKN.
  *Ruth Rendell Mysteries: an Unwanted Woman; An
  Unwanted Woman*

The Veiled One, Novel
  Inspector Wexford: the Veiled One 1989 d: Mary
  McMurray. lps: George Baker, Christopher
  Ravenscroft, Paola Dionisotti. TVM. 102M UKN. *The
  Veiled One* prod/rel: Watch

Wolf to the Slaughter, Novel
  Inspector Wexford: Wolf to the Slaughter 1987 d:
  John Davies. lps: George Baker, Christopher
  Ravenscroft, Kim Thomson. TVM. 190M UKN. *Wolf to
  the Slaughter* prod/rel: Watch/Grant

RENKER, GUSTAV FRIEDRICH
*Das Verlorene Tal. Ein Roman von Jagd Und
Liebe*, Basle 1931, Novel
  Verlorene Tal, Das 1934 d: Edmund Heuberger. lps:
  Mathias Wieman, Lotte Spira, Marieluise Claudius.
  102M GRM/SWT. *La Vallee Perdue* prod/rel:
  Basilea-Film, Terra-Film

RENN, LUDWIG
Trini, Novel
  Trini 1976 d: Walter Beck. lps: Gunnar Helm, Giso
  Weissbach, Dimitrina SawowA. 83M GDR. *Stirb Fur
  Zapata* prod/rel: Defa

REPACI, LEONIDA
Carne Inquieta, 1930, Novel
  Carne Inquieta 1952 d: Silvestro Prestifilippo, Carlo
  Musso. lps: Marina Berti, Raf Vallone, Luigi CimarA.
  100M ITL. prod/rel: Paolo Montesano

REPP, ED EARL
Cherokee Strip Stampeders, 1936, Short Story
  Cherokee Strip, The 1937 d: Noel Smith. lps: Dick
  Foran, Jane Bryan, Robert Paige. 55M USA. *Strange
  Laws* (UKN); *The Little Buckaroo* prod/rel: Warner
  Bros. Pictures, Inc.

Empty Holsters, New York 1936, Novel
  Empty Holsters 1937 d: B. Reeves Eason. lps: Dick
  Foran, Pat Wathall, Glenn Strange. 62M USA. prod/rel:
  Warner Bros. Pictures©, First National

RESKO, JOHN
Reprieve: the Testament of John Resko, New York
1956, Autob
  Convicts Four 1962 d: Millard Kaufman. lps: Ben
  Gazzara, Stuart Whitman, Ray Walston. 105M USA.
  Reprieve (UKN) prod/rel: Allied Artists,
  Lubin-Kaufman

RESNIK, MURIEL
Any Wednesday, New York 1964, Play
  Any Wednesday 1966 d: Robert Ellis Miller. lps: Jane
  Fonda, Jason Robards Jr., Dean Jones. 109M USA.
  Bachelor Girl Apartment (UKN) prod/rel: Warner Bros.

The Girl in the Turquoise Bikini, New York 1961,
Novel
  How Sweet It Is! 1968 d: Jerry Paris. lps: James
  Garner, Debbie Reynolds, Maurice Ronet. 99M USA.
  prod/rel: Cherokee Productions, National General
  Productions

REUTER, BJARNE
Story
  Busters Verden 1984 d: Bille August. lps: Mads Bugge
  Andersen, Katarina Stenbeck, Peter Schroder. MTV.
  91M DNM. *Buster's World; The World of Buster*
  prod/rel: Crone, Dansk Filminstitutet

REUTER, FRITZ
Kein Husung, 1858, Verse
  Kein Husung 1954 d: Arthur Pohl. 93M GDR.

Ut Mine Stromtid, 1862-64, Novel
  Onkel Brasig 1936 d: Erich Waschneck. lps: Otto
  Wernicke, Harry Hardt, Elga Brink. 88M GRM.
  Livet Pa Landet 1943 d: Bror Bugler. 105M SWD. *Life
  in the Country; Onkel Brasig*

REUZE, ANDRE
Les Cinq Gentlemen Maudits, Novel
  Cinq Gentlemen Maudits, Les 1931 d: Julien
  Duvivier. lps: Harry Baur, Rene Lefevre, Rosine Derean.
  87M FRN. prod/rel: Vandal Et Delac, Societe Generale
  De Cinematographie

REVAL, GABRIELLE
La Fontaine Des Amours, Novel
  Fontaine Des Amours, La 1924 d: Roger Lion. lps:
  Max Maxudian, Gil Clary, Pauline Po. 1800m FRN.
  prod/rel: Films Roger Lion

L'infante a la Rose, Novel
  Infante a la Rose, L' 1921 d: Henry Houry. lps:
  Georges Lannes, Gabrielle Dorziat, Emilio Portes.
  1800m FRN. prod/rel: Dal-Film

REVE, GERARD KORNELIUS VAN HET
Lieve Jongens, 1972, Novel
  Lieve Jongens 1979 d: Paul de Lussanets. lps: Hugo
  Metsers, Hans Dagelet, Bill Van Dijk. 90M NTH. *Dear
  Boys*

Het Lieve Leven, 1974, Novel
  Lieve Jongens 1979 d: Paul de Lussanets. lps: Hugo
  Metsers, Hans Dagelet, Bill Van Dijk. 90M NTH. *Dear
  Boys*

De Taal Der Liefde, 1971, Novel
  Lieve Jongens 1979 d: Paul de Lussanets. lps: Hugo
  Metsers, Hans Dagelet, Bill Van Dijk. 90M NTH. *Dear
  Boys*

De Vierde Man, 1981, Novel
  Vierde Man, de 1983 d: Paul Verhoeven. lps: Jeroen
  Krabbe, Renee Soutendijk, Thom Hoffman. 104M NTH.
  The Fourth Man (UKN) prod/rel: Verenigde
  Nederlandsche Filmcompagnie

REY, ETIENNE
Chantelouve, Play
  Chantelouve 1922 d: Georges Monca, Rose Pansini.
  lps: Yvette Andreyor, Jean Toulout, Charles Boyer.
  1500m FRN. prod/rel: Films Pansini

Miche, Play
  Miche 1931 d: Jean de Marguenat. lps: Suzy Vernon,
  Robert Burnier, Marguerite Moreno. 75M FRN.
  prod/rel: Films Paramount

REY, HENRI-FRANCOIS
La Fete Espagnole, Paris 1958, Novel
  Fete Espagnole, La 1961 d: Jean-Jacques Vierne. lps:
  Peter Van Eyck, Daliah Lavi, Roland Lesaffre. 95M
  FRN. *No Time for Ecstasy* (USA) prod/rel: Les Films
  Univers

Les Pianos Mecaniques, Paris 1962, Novel
  Pianos Mecanicos, Los 1965 d: Juan Antonio
  Bardem. lps: Melina Mercouri, James Mason, Hardy
  Kruger. 100M SPN/ITL/FRN. *Amori Di Una Calda
  Estate* (ITL); *Les Pianos Mecaniques* (FRN); *The
  Uninhibited* (USA); *Los Organillos; The Player Pianos*
  prod/rel: C.I.C.C., Terra Films

REY, JACQUES
Inspecteur Sergil, Novel
  Inspecteur Sergil 1946 d: Jacques Daroy. lps: Paul
  Meurisse, Liliane Bert, Vera Maxime. 95M FRN.
  prod/rel: Les Cigales

REY, MARCOS
O Enterro Da Cafetina, 1967, Novel
  Enterro Da Cafetina, O 1971 d: Alberto Pieralisi.
  90M BRZ.

Memorias de Um Gigolo, 1968, Novel
  Memorias de Um Gigolo 1970 d: Alberto Pieralisi.
  80M BRZ.

REYES, EDGARDO
Maynila, Sa Mga Kuko Ng Liwanag, Novel
  Maynila, Sa Mga Kuko Ng Liwanag 1975 d: Lino
  BrockA. lps: Rafael Roco Jr., Hilda Koronel, Lily
  Gamboa-Mendozy. 125M PHL. *The Nail of Brightness*
  (USA); *Manila* (UKN); *Manila in the Claws of Light;
  Manila: in the Claws of Darkness; Manila: in the Claws
  of Neon* prod/rel: Cinema Artists

REYHER, FERDINAND
I Heard Them Sing, 1946, Novel
  Wait 'Til the Sun Shines, Nellie 1952 d: Henry King.
  lps: David Wayne, Jean Peters, Hugh Marlowe. 109M
  USA. *Wait Till the Sun Shines, Nellie* prod/rel: 20th
  Century-Fox

REYLES, CARLOS (1868–1938), URG
El Embrujo de Sevilla, Novel
  Embrujo de Sevilla, El 1930 d: Benito Perojo. lps:
  Maria de Albaicin, Angel Rivelles, Maria F. Ladron de
  GuevarA. F SPN/GRM. prod/rel: Julio Cesar, UFA
  (Berlin)

Ensorcellement de Seville, L' 1931 d: Benito Perojo.
  lps: Gina Manes, Ginette Maddie, Helene Hallier. 70M
  FRN. prod/rel: Etablissements Braunberger-Richebe

REYMONT, WLADYSLAW STANISLAW
(1867–1925), PLN
Chlopi, 1902-09, Novel
  Chlopi 1973 d: Jan Rybkowski. lps: Wladyslaw Hancza,
  Ignacy Gogolewski, Emilia KrakowskA. 200M PLN.
  Peasants

Komediantka, 1896, Novel
  Komediantka 1987 d: Jerzy SztwiertniA. lps:
  Katarzyna Figura, Malgorzata PieczynskA. 112M PLN.
  Comedienne

Ziemia Obiecana, 1899, Novel
  Ziemia Obiecana 1974 d: Andrzej WajdA. lps: Daniel
  Olbrychski, Wojciech Pszoniak, Andrzej Seweryn. 180M
  PLN. *Land of Promise* (UKN); *Promised Land* (USA)
  prod/rel: Film Polski

REYNAUD-FOURTON, ALAIN
Mystifies, Les, Paris 1962, Novel
  Symphonie Pour un Massacre 1963 d: Jacques
  Deray. lps: Michel Auclair, Claude Dauphin, Jose
  Giovanni. 110M FRN/ITL. *Sinfonia Per un Massacro*
  (ITL); *Symphony for a Massacre* (USA); *The Corrupt*
  (UKN); *The Mystifiers; Les Mystifies* prod/rel: C.I.C.C.,
  P.E.C.F.

REYNOLDS, MRS. BAILLIE
Confession Corner, Novel
  Confessions 1925 d: W. P. Kellino. lps: Ian Hunter,
  Joan Lockton, Eric Bransby Williams. 6324f UKN.
  Confession Corner prod/rel: Stoll

The Daughter Pays, London 1915, Novel
  Daughter Pays, The 1920 d: Robert Ellis. lps: Elaine
  Hammerstein, Norman Trevor, Robert Ellis. 5r USA.
  prod/rel: Selznick Pictures Corp.©, Select Pictures Corp.

The Man Who Won, Novel
  Man Who Won, The 1918 d: Rex Wilson. lps: Isobel
  Elsom, Owen Nares, John Kelt. 6000f UKN. prod/rel: G.
  B. Samuelson, Granger

The Notorious Miss Lisle, New York 1911, Novel
  Notorious Miss Lisle, The 1920 d: James Young. lps:
  Katherine MacDonald, Nigel Barrie, Margaret
  Campbell. 5r USA. prod/rel: Katherine Macdonald
  Pictures Corp.©, Attractions Distributing Corp.

REYNOLDS, QUENTIN
West Side Romance, 1936, Short Story
  Secrets of a Nurse 1938 d: Arthur Lubin. lps: Edmund
  Lowe, Helen Mack, Dick Foran. 75M USA. *West Side
  Miracle* prod/rel: Universal Pictures Co.©

REYNOLDS, STEPHEN ALLEN
The Master Cracksman, Story
  Master Cracksman, The 1913 d: Oscar Apfel. lps:
  Irving Cummings, Irene Howley, Ralph Lewis. 2r USA.
  prod/rel: Reliance

REZAC, VACLAV
Carovne Dedictvi, Novel
  Carovne Dedictvi 1985 d: Zdenek ZelenkA. lps:
  Martin Pert, Rudolf Stedry, Tereza ChudobovA. 80M
  CZC/GDR. *Eine Zauberhafte Erbschaft* (GDR);
  Enchanted Heritage prod/rel: Filmove Studio
  Barrandov, Defa

RHOADES, NINA
The Little Girl Next Door, Story
  Little Girl Next Door, The 1912 d: J. Searle Dawley.
  lps: Marc McDermott, Edna Hammel, Gertrude McCoy.
  1000f USA. prod/rel: Edison

RHODES, DENYS
The Syndicate, New York 1960, Novel
  Syndicate, The 1968 d: Frederic Goode. lps: William
  Sylvester, June Ritchie, Robert Urquhart. 106M UKN.
  Kenya -Country of Treasure prod/rel: Ab-Pathe,
  Warner-Pathe

RHODES, EUGENE MANLOVE
The Girl He Left Behind Him, Story
  Wallop, The 1921 d: John Ford. lps: Harry Carey,
  Mignonne Golden, William Gettinger. 4539f USA. *The
  Homeward Trail* prod/rel: Universal Film Mfg. Co.

The Long Shift, Short Story
  Long Shift, The 1915. lps: Norbert Myles, H. Stanley,
  Edna Payne. 2r USA. prod/rel: Ideal

Paso Por Aqui, Novel
  Four Faces West 1948 d: Alfred E. Green. lps: Joel
  McCrea, Frances Dee, Charles Bickford. 90M USA. *They
  Passed This Way* (UKN); *New Mexico; Wanted* prod/rel:
  United Artists

The Stepsons of Light, Boston 1921, Novel
  Mysterious Witness, The 1923 d: Seymour Zeliff. lps:
  Robert Gordon, Elinor Fair, Nanine Wright. 4850f USA.
  prod/rel: R-C Pictures, Film Booking Offices of America

RHODES, EVAN H.
The Prince of Central Park, Novel
   Prince of Central Park, The 1977 d: Harvey Hart. lps: Ruth Gordon, T. J. Hargrave, Lisa Richard. TVM. 78M USA. prod/rel: Lorimar Productions

RHODES, HARRISON
A Gentleman from Mississippi, New York 1908, Play
   Gentleman from Mississippi, A 1914 d: George L. Sargent. lps: Thomas A. Wise, Chester Barnett, Evelyn Brent. 5r USA. prod/rel: William A. Brady Picture Plays, Inc.©
The Willow Tree, New York 1917, Play
   Willow Tree, The 1920 d: Henry Otto. lps: Viola Dana, Edward Connelly, Pell Trenton. 6r USA. prod/rel: Screen Classics, Metro Pictures Corp.©

RHODES, JOHN
Murders in Praed Street, Novel
   Twelve Good Men 1936 d: Ralph Ince. lps: Henry Kendall, Nancy O'Neil, Joyce Kennedy. 64M UKN. prod/rel: Warner Bros., First National

RHODES, KATHLYN
Afterwards, Novel
   Afterwards 1928 d: W. Lawson Butts. lps: Marjorie Hume, Julie Suedo, J. R. Tozer. 6800f UKN. prod/rel: Bushey Studios, Associated Producers & Distributors

RHYS, JEAN (1890–1979), WIN, Williams, Ella Gwendolen Rees
Quartet, 1929, Novel
   Quartet 1980 d: James Ivory. lps: Alan Bates, Maggie Smith, Isabelle Adjani. 101M UKN/FRN. prod/rel: Twentieth Century Fox, Merchant Ivory
Wide Sargasso Sea, Novel
   Wide Sargasso Sea, The 1992 d: John Duigan. lps: Karina Lombard, Nathaniel Parker, Rachel Ward. 98M ASL. prod/rel: Sargasso, New Line

RIBEIRO, DARCY
Story
   Uira, Um Indio Em Busca de Deus 1973 d: Gustavo Dahl. lps: Enrico Vidal, Ana Maria Magalhaes. 90M BRZ. *Uira, Um Indio a Procura de Dios*; *Uira, an Indian in Search of God* prod/rel: Alter Films, Gustavo Dahl

RIBEIRO, JULIO
A Carne, 1888, Novel
   Carne, A 1976 d: J. Marreco. 90M BRZ.

RIBOT I SERRA, MANUEL
Poem
   Puntaire, La 1928 d: Jose Claramunt, Fructuoso Gelabert. lps: Teresa Pujol, Juan Xucla, Lorenzo AdriA. F SPN. *La Encajera*; *The Lacemaker* prod/rel: Jose Claramunt (Barcelona)

RICARDEL, MOLLY
I Loved You Wednesday, New York 1932, Play
   I Loved You Wednesday 1933 d: Henry King, William Cameron Menzies. lps: Warner Baxter, Elissa Landi, Victor Jory. 77M USA. prod/rel: Fox Film Corp.©

RICCI, FEDERICO (1809–1877), ITL
Crispino E la Comare, Venice 1850, Opera
   Crispino E la Comare 1918 d: Camillo de Riso. lps: Camillo de Riso, Olga Benetti, Lea Giunchi. 1202m ITL. prod/rel: Caesar Film
   Crispino E la Comare 1938 d: Vincenzo Sorelli. lps: Silvana Jachino, Ugo Ceseri, Mario Pisu. 72M ITL. prod/rel: S.C.I.a.

RICCI, LUIGI (1805–1859), ITL
Crispino E la Comare 1918 d: Camillo de Riso. lps: Camillo de Riso, Olga Benetti, Lea Giunchi. 1202m ITL. prod/rel: Caesar Film
   Crispino E la Comare 1938 d: Vincenzo Sorelli. lps: Silvana Jachino, Ugo Ceseri, Mario Pisu. 72M ITL. prod/rel: S.C.I.a.

RICCIARDI, LORENZO
Le Belle Creole Di Melchior de la Cruz, Short Story
   Venere Creola 1961 d: Lorenzo Ricciardi. lps: Calvin Lockhart, Helene Williams, Sheyla Gibson. 98M ITL. prod/rel: Baltea Film, Euro International Film

RICCORA, PAOLA
Fine Mese, Play
   Giorno Di Nozze 1942 d: Raffaello Matarazzo. lps: Armando Falconi, Antonio Gandusio, Roberto VillA. 85M ITL. prod/rel: Lux Film
Sara Stato Giovannino, Play
   Sono Stato Io! 1937 d: Raffaello Matarazzo. lps: Eduardo de Filippo, Peppino de Filippo, Isa PolA. 73M ITL. *It Was I* (USA); *I Did It!* prod/rel: E.I.a., Amato

RICE, ALBERT
Gay Blades, Story
   Gay Blades 1946 d: George Blair. lps: Allan Lane, Jean Rogers, Edward Ashley. 67M USA. *Tournament Tempo* prod/rel: Republic

RICE, ALICE HEGAN (1870–1942), USA, Rice, Alice Caldwell Hegan
Calvary Alley, New York 1917, Novel
   Sunshine Nan 1918 d: Charles Giblyn. lps: Ann Pennington, Johnny Hines, Richard Barthelmess. 5r USA. prod/rel: Famous Players-Lasky Corp.©, Paramount Pictures
Lovey Mary, New York 1903, Novel
   Lovey Mary 1926 d: King Baggot. lps: Bessie Love, William Haines, Mary Alden. 6167f USA. prod/rel: Metro-Goldwyn-Mayer Pictures
   Mrs. Wiggs of the Cabbage Patch 1914 d: Harold Entwhistle. lps: Beatriz Michelena, Blanche Chapman, Andrew Robson. 5r USA. prod/rel: California Motion Picture Corp.©, World Film Corp.
Mr. Opp, New York 1909, Novel
   Mr. Opp 1917 d: Lynn Reynolds. lps: Arthur Hoyt, Neva Gerber, George Chesebro. 5r USA. prod/rel: Bluebird Photoplays, Inc.©
Mrs. Wiggs of the Cabbage Patch, New York 1901, Novel
   Mrs. Wiggs of the Cabbage Patch 1914 d: Harold Entwhistle. lps: Beatriz Michelena, Blanche Chapman, Andrew Robson. 5r USA. prod/rel: California Motion Picture Corp.©, World Film Corp.
   Mrs. Wiggs of the Cabbage Patch 1919 d: Hugh Ford. lps: Marguerite Clark, Mary Carr, Vivia Ogden. 4542f USA. prod/rel: Famous Players-Lasky Corp.©, Paramount Pictures
   Mrs. Wiggs of the Cabbage Patch 1934 d: Norman Taurog. lps: W. C. Fields, Pauline Lord, Zasu Pitts. 80M USA. prod/rel: Paramount Productions©
   Mrs. Wiggs of the Cabbage Patch 1942 d: Ralph Murphy. lps: Fay Bainter, Hugh Herbert, Vera Vague. 80M USA. prod/rel: Paramount
A Romance of Billy-Goat Hill, New York 1912, Novel
   Romance of Billy Goat Hill, A 1916 d: Lynn Reynolds. lps: Myrtle Gonzales, Val Paul, George Hernandez. 5r USA. prod/rel: Universal Film Mfg. Co.©, Red Feather Photoplays
Sandy, New York 1905, Novel
   Sandy 1918 d: George Melford. lps: Jack Pickford, Louise Huff, James Neill. 5r USA. prod/rel: Famous Players-Lasky Corp.©

RICE, CRAIG (1908–1957), USA, Randolph, Georgina Ann
The Big Story, Novel
   Underworld Story, The 1950 d: Cy Endfield. lps: Dan Duryea, Gale Storm, Herbert Marshall. 90M USA. *Whipped, The* prod/rel: United Artists, Film Craft Trading Corp.
Home Sweet Homicide, Novel
   Home, Sweet Homicide 1946 d: Lloyd Bacon. lps: Lynn Bari, Randolph Scott, Peggy Ann Garner. 90M USA. prod/rel: 20th Century-Fox
The Lucky Stiff, Novel
   Lucky Stiff, The 1949 d: Lewis R. Foster. lps: Dorothy Lamour, Brian Donlevy, Claire Trevor. 99M USA. prod/rel: United Artists

RICE, ELMER (1892–1967), USA
The Adding machine, March 1923, Play
   Adding machine, The 1969 d: Jerome Epstein. lps: Phyllis Diller, Milo O'Shea, Billie Whitelaw. 100M UKN/USA. prod/rel: Associated London Films, Universal
Counsellor at Law, New York 1931, Play
   Counsellor at Law 1933 d: William Wyler. lps: John Barrymore, Bebe Daniels, Doris Kenyon. 80M USA. prod/rel: Universal Pictures Corp.©
Dream Girl, New York 1945, Play
   Dream Girl 1948 d: Mitchell Leisen. lps: Betty Hutton, MacDonald Carey, Virginia Field. 85M USA. prod/rel: Paramount
For the Defense, New York 1919, Play
   For the Defense 1922 d: Paul Powell. lps: Ethel Clayton, Vernon Steele, Zasu Pitts. 4905f USA. prod/rel: Famous Players-Lasky, Paramount Pictures
It Is the Law, New York 1922, Play
   It Is the Law 1924 d: J. Gordon Edwards. lps: Arthur Hohl, Herbert Heyes, Mimi Palmeri. 6895f USA. prod/rel: Fox Film Corp.
On Trial, New York 1914, Play
   On Trial 1917 d: James Young. lps: Barbara Castleton, Sidney Ainsworth, James Young. 7r USA. prod/rel: Essanay Film Mfg. Co.©, First National Exhibitors Circuit
   On Trial 1928 d: Archie Mayo. lps: Pauline Frederick, Bert Lytell, Lois Wilson. 9290f USA. prod/rel: Warner Brothers Pictures
   On Trial 1939 d: Terry O. Morse. lps: John Litel, Margaret Lindsay, Edward Norris. 65M USA. *Strickland Case, The* prod/rel: Warner Bros. Pictures©

See Naples and Die, New York 1929, Play
   Oh! Sailor, Behave! 1930 d: Archie Mayo. lps: Irene Delroy, Charles King, Lowell Sherman. 6223f USA. *Nancy from Naples* prod/rel: Warner Brothers Pictures
Street Scene, New York 1929, Play
   Street Scene 1931 d: King Vidor. lps: Sylvia Sidney, William Collier Jr., David Landau. 80M USA. prod/rel: United Artists Corp., Feature Productions©

RICE, LOUISE
The Alien Blood, Short Story
   Alien Blood, The 1917 d: Burton George. lps: Clifford Gray, Winnifred Greenwood. 4r USA. prod/rel: Fortune Photoplay, Balboa Amusement Producing Co.

RICE, TIM
Evita, Musical Play
   Evita 1996 d: Alan Parker. lps: Madonna, Antonio Banderas, Jonathan Pryce. 134M/USA. prod/rel: Cinergi, Robert Stigwood

RICE, TIM (1944–, UKN, Rice, Timothy Miles Bindon
Jesus Christ Superstar, Opera
   Jesus Christ Superstar 1973 d: Norman Jewison. lps: Ted Neeley, Carl Anderson, Yvonne Elliman. 108M USA. prod/rel: Universal Pictures

RICH, ROBERT
Story
   Brave One, The 1956 d: Irving Rapper. lps: Michel Ray, Rodolfo Hoyos Jr., Elsa Cardenas. 100M USA. prod/rel: RKO Radio

RICHARDS, CAROLINE
Novel
   Glykia Patrida 1986 d: Michael Cacoyannis. lps: Jane Alexander, Franco Nero, Carole Laure. 150M GRC/PNM. *Sweet Country* prod/rel: Michael Cacoyannis, Greek Film Centre

RICHARDS, LAURA E. (1850–1943), USA, Richards, Laura Elizabeth Howe
Captain January, New York 1890, Novel
   Captain January 1924 d: Eddie Cline. lps: Hobart Bosworth, Baby Peggy Montgomery, Irene Rich. 6194f USA. prod/rel: Principal Pictures
   Captain January 1936 d: David Butler. lps: Shirley Temple, Guy Kibbee, Slim Summerville. 78M USA. prod/rel: Twentieth Century-Fox Film Corp.

RICHARDS, RENEE
Book
   Second Serve 1986 d: Anthony Page. lps: Vanessa Redgrave, Martin Balsam, William Russ. TVM. 100M USA. *I Change My Life*; *The Renee Richards Story* prod/rel: Linda Yellen, Lorimar

RICHARDS, ROBERT L.
The Last Crooked Mile, Rplay
   Last Crooked Mile, The 1946 d: Philip Ford. lps: Donald Barry, Ann Savage, Adele MarA. 67M USA. prod/rel: Republic

RICHARDS, SILVIA
Gunsight Whitman, Story
   Rancho Notorious 1952 d: Fritz Lang. lps: Marlene Dietrich, Arthur Kennedy, Mel Ferrer. 89M USA. prod/rel: RKO Radio, Fidelity Pictures

RICHARDSON, ABBY
The Pride of Jennico, New York 1900, Play
   Pride of Jennico, The 1914 d: J. Searle Dawley. lps: House Peters, Hal Clarendon, Marie Leonhard. 4r USA. prod/rel: Famous Players Film Co., State Rights

RICHARDSON, ANNA STEESE
Big Hearted Herbert, New York 1934, Play
   Big Hearted Herbert 1934 d: William Keighley. lps: Guy Kibbee, Aline MacMahon, Patricia Ellis. 60M USA. *Big-Hearted Herbert* prod/rel: Warner Bros. Productions Corp.
   Father Is a Prince 1940 d: Noel Smith. lps: Grant Mitchell, Nana Bryant, John Litel. 59M USA. prod/rel: Warner Bros. Pictures©, First National Pictures
A Man's Home, Albany, N.Y. 1917, Play
   Man's Home, A 1921 d: Ralph Ince. lps: Harry T. Morey, Kathlyn Williams, Faire Binney. 6235f USA. prod/rel: Selznick Pictures, Select Pictures

RICHARDSON, ANTHONY
Trouble in the House, Novel
   Twice Branded 1936 d: MacLean Rogers. lps: Robert Rendel, Lucille Lisle, James Mason. 72M UKN. prod/rel: GS Enterprises, Radio

RICHARDSON, ETHEL FLORENCE
The Getting of Wisdom, 1910, Novel
   Getting of Wisdom, The 1977 d: Bruce Beresford. lps: Susannah Fowle, Barry Humphries, Sheila Helpmann. 100M ASL. prod/rel: Souther Cross, Victorian Film
Maurice Guest, 1908, Novel
   Rhapsody 1954 d: Charles Vidor. lps: Elizabeth Taylor, Vittorio Gassman, John Ericson. 115M USA. prod/rel: MGM

RICHARDSON, FRANK
Bait, Play
  Bait 1950 d: Frank Richardson. lps: Diana Napier, John Bentley, John Oxford. 73M UKN. prod/rel: Advance, Adelphi

RICHARDSON, SAMUEL (1689–1761), UKN
Clarissa, 1748, Novel
  Clarissa 1991 d: Robert Bierman. lps: Saskia Wickham, Sean Bean, Cathryn Harrison. TVM. 195M UKN/USA. prod/rel: BBC, Wgbh Boston
Pamela, 1740, Novel
  Mistress Pamela 1973 d: Jim O'Connolly. lps: Julian Barnes, Anna Quayle, Dudley Foster. 91M UKN.

RICHE, DANIEL
Un Million de Dot, Novel
  Million de Dot, Un 1916. lps: Louis Gauthier, Leon Bernard, Gabrielle Robinne. 1176m FRN. prod/rel: Scagl
Sa Conscience, Novel
  Sa Conscience 1919 d: Daniel Riche. lps: Aliette Aubrey, Gilbert Dalleu, Jacques Normand. 1365m FRN. prod/rel: Eclipse

RICHEBOURG, EMILIE
La Dame En Noir, Novel
  Dame En Noir ,la 1913. 1320m FRN.
Dve Matky, Novel
  Dve Matky 1920 d: Premysl Prazsky. lps: Helena Friedlova, Marta Majova, Jiri Myron. CZC. *Two Mothers* prod/rel: Umfilm, Gloriafilm

RICHEPIN, JEAN
Le Chemineau, Play
  Chemineau, Le 1917 d: Henry Krauss. lps: Henry Krauss, Yvonne Sergyl, Charlotte Barbier-Krauss. 1200m FRN. prod/rel: Scagl
  Chemineau, Le 1935 d: Fernand Rivers. lps: Victor Francen, Tania Fedor, Jane Marken. 105M FRN. *Open Road, The* (USA) prod/rel: Films Rivers
Glu, La, Play
  Amante Di un Giorno, L' 1907. 215m ITL. *Innamorato Di un Giorno, L'* prod/rel: Rossi
La Glu, Novel
  Glu, La 1927 d: Henri Fescourt. lps: Germaine Rouer, Henri Maillard, Francois Rozet. F FRN. prod/rel: Societe Des Cineromans
  Glu, La 1938 d: Jean Choux. lps: Marie Bell, Gilbert Gil, Georges Bever. 78M FRN. prod/rel: Films J.L.S.
  Glu, La 1913 d: Albert Capellani. lps: Mistinguett, Henry Krauss, Paul Capellani. 1900m FRN. prod/rel: Scagl
Miarka, la Fille a l'Ourse, Novel
  Miarka, la Fille a l'Ourse 1914 d: Georges-Andre Lacroix. FRN. prod/rel: le Film d'Art
  Miarka, la Fille a l'Ourse 1920 d: Louis Mercanton. lps: Rejane, Jean Richepin, Charles Vanel. F FRN. *Miarka, Daughter of the Bear* (USA); *Gypsy Passion* prod/rel: Societe Des Films Mercanton
  Miarka, la Fille a l'Ourse 1937 d: Jean Choux. lps: Jose Noguero, Suzanne Despres, Rama Tahe. 102M FRN. prod/rel: S.B. Films

RICHER, CLEMENT
Tikoyo and His Shark, Novel
  Beyond the Reef 1981 d: Frank C. Clark. lps: Dayton Ka'ne, Maren Jensen, Kathleen Swan. 91M USA. *Shark Boy of Bora Bora*; *Sea Killer* prod/rel: Universal
Ti-Koyo Et Son Requin, Paris 1941, Novel
  Ti-Koyo E Il Suo Pescecane 1962 d: Folco Quilici. lps: Marlene Among, Al Kauwe, Denis PouirA. 95M ITL/FRN/USA. *Ti-Koyo Et Son Requin* (FRN); *Tiko and the Shark* (USA); *Ti-Koyo and His Shark* prod/rel: Titanus, P.C.M. (Roma)

RICHERT, WILLIAM
Aren't You Even Gonna Kiss Me Goodbye?, Novel
  Night in the Life of Jimmy Reardon, A 1988 d: William Richert. lps: River Phoenix, Ann Magnuson, Meredith Salenger. 90M USA. *Jimmy Reardon* prod/rel: 20th Century Fox

RICHLER, MORDECAI (1931–, CND)
The Apprenticeship of Duddy Kravitz, 1959, Novel
  Apprenticeship of Duddy Kravitz, The 1974 d: Ted Kotcheff. lps: Richard Dreyfuss, Micheline Lanctot, Randy Quaid. 121M CND. *L'apprentissage de Duddy Kravitz* prod/rel: Duddy Kravitz Syndicate, International Cinemedia Center Ltd.
Jacob Two-Two Meets the Hooded Fang, 1975, Novel
  Jacob Two-Two Meets the Hooded Fang 1978 d: Theodore J. Flicker. lps: Stephen Rosenberg, Alex Karras, Guy L'Ecuyer. 81M CND. prod/rel: Gulkin Productions Inc., the Flaxman Film Corporation

Joshua Then and Now, Novel
  Joshua Then and Now 1985 d: Ted Kotcheff. lps: James Woods, Gabrielle Lazure, Alan Arkin. 118M CND. prod/rel: Moviecorp X Inc., Rsl Entertainment Corp.
The Summer My Grandma Was Supposed to Die, 1969, Short Story
  Street, The 1976 d: Caroline Leaf. ANM. 10M CND. *Rue, La*

RICHMAN, ARTHUR
Ambush, New York 1921, Play
  Reckless Hour, The 1931 d: John Francis Dillon. lps: Dorothy MacKaill, Conrad Nagel, Walter Byron. 80M USA. prod/rel: First National Pictures©
The Awful Truth, New York 1922, Play
  Awful Truth, The 1925 d: Paul Powell. lps: Agnes Ayres, Warner Baxter, Phillips Smalley. 5917f USA. *Jealous Sex* prod/rel: Peninsula Studio, Producers Distributing Corp.
  Awful Truth, The 1929 d: Marshall Neilan. lps: Ina Claire, Henry Daniell, Theodore von Eltz. 6129f USA. prod/rel: Pathe Exchange, Inc.
  Awful Truth, The 1937 d: Leo McCarey. lps: Irene Dunne, Cary Grant, Ralph Bellamy. 90M USA. prod/rel: Columbia Pictures Corp.
  Let's Do It Again 1953 d: Alexander Hall. lps: Ray Milland, Jane Wyman, Aldo Ray. 95M USA. *Love Song* prod/rel: Columbia
The Far Cry, New York 1924, Play
  Far Cry, The 1926 d: Silvano Balboni. lps: Blanche Sweet, Jack Mulhall, Myrtle Stedman. 6868f USA. prod/rel: First National Pictures
Not So Long Ago, New York 1924, Play
  Not So Long Ago 1925 d: Sidney Olcott. lps: Betty Bronson, Ricardo Cortez, Edwards Davis. 6943f USA. prod/rel: Famous Players-Lasky, Paramount Pictures

RICHMAN, IRVING BERDINE
The Spanish Conquerors, New Haven 1919, Novel
  Columbus 1923 d: Edwin L. Hollywood. lps: Fred Eric, Paul McAllister, Howard Truesdell. 5r USA. prod/rel: Chronicles of America Pictures, Yale University Press

RICHTER, CONRAD (1890–1968), USA
The Awakening Land, Novel
  Awakening Land, The 1978 d: Boris Sagal. lps: Elizabeth Montgomery, Hal Holbrook, Jane Seymour. TVM. 350M USA. prod/rel: NBC, Warner Bros.
The Light in the Forest, 1953, Novel
  Light in the Forest, The 1958 d: Herschel Daugherty. lps: Fess Parker, Wendell Corey, Joanne Dru. 93M USA. prod/rel: MGM
The Sea of Grass, 1936, Novel
  Sea of Grass, The 1946 d: Elia Kazan. lps: Katharine Hepburn, Spencer Tracy, Melvyn Douglas. 131M USA. prod/rel: MGM
Tacey Cromwell, 1942, Novel
  One Desire 1955 d: Jerry Hopper. lps: Rock Hudson, Anne Baxter, Julie Adams. 94M USA. prod/rel: Universal-International

RICHTER, EGON
Story
  Russen Kommen, Die 1970 d: Heiner Carow. lps: Gerd Krause, Viktor Perevalov, Dorothea Meissner. 95M GDR. *Russians are Coming, The* prod/rel: Defa-Studio Fur Spielfilme

RICHTER, HANS
Der Springer von Pontresina, Berlin 1930, Novel
  Springer von Pontresina, Der 1934 d: Herbert Selpin. lps: Sepp Rist, Vivigenz Eickstedt, Eric Helgar. 95M GRM/SWT. *Le Champion de Saut de Pontresina*; *Liebe in St. Moritz* prod/rel: Terra-Film, Interna-Tonfilm

RICHTER-TERSIK, OSWALD
Ilona Beck, Novel
  Maria Ilona 1939 d: Geza von Bolvary. lps: Paula Wessely, Willy Birgel, Paul Horbiger. 94M GRM. prod/rel: Terra, Siegel

RICK, FRANCIS
Les Jours Ouvrables, Novel
  Souris Chez Les Hommes, Une 1964 d: Jacques Poitrenaud. lps: Dany Saval, Louis de Funes, Dany Carrel. 91M FRN. *Un Drole de Caid* prod/rel: Filmsonor, Procinex
Le Secret, Novel
  Secret, Le 1974 d: Robert Enrico. lps: Jean-Louis Trintignant, Marlene Jobert, Philippe Noiret. 102M FRN/ITL. *Il Segreto* (ITL); *The Secret* prod/rel: President

RICKETTS, CID
Quality, Novel
  Pinky 1949 d: Elia Kazan, John Ford (Uncredited). lps: Jeanne Crain, Ethel Barrymore, Esther Waters. 102M USA. prod/rel: 20th Century-Fox

RIDEAMUS
Der Vetter Aus Dingsda, Opera
  Vetter Aus Dingsda, Der 1934 d: Georg Zoch. lps: Lien Deyers, Lizzi Holzschuh, Walter von Lennep. 75M GRM. *Cousin from Podunk*; *Damenwahl* prod/rel: Victor Klein, Dietz
  Vetter Aus Dingsda, Der 1953 d: Karl Anton. lps: Vera Molnar, Gerhard Riedmann, Grethe Weiser. 95M GRM. prod/rel: Central-Europa, Prisma

RIDGE, ANTONIA
Das Schone Abenteuer, Novel
  Schone Abenteuer, Das 1959 d: Kurt Hoffmann. lps: Liselotte Pulver, Robert Graf, Oliver Grimm. 100M GRM. *The Beautiful Adventure*; *The Great Adventure* prod/rel: Georg Witt, Constantin

RIDGE, W. PETT
The Happy Prisoner, Short Story
  Happy Prisoner, The 1924 d: Hugh Croise. lps: Ben Field, James Knight, Dorothy Easton. 2100f UKN. prod/rel: British & Colonial, Ideal
Love and Hate, Short Story
  Love and Hate 1924 d: Thomas Bentley. lps: George Foley, Eve Chambers, Frank Perfitt. 2000f UKN. prod/rel: British & Colonial, Ideal
Mord Em'ly, Novel
  Mord Em'ly 1922 d: George Pearson. lps: Betty Balfour, Rex Davis, Elsie Craven. 6000f UKN. *Me and My Girl* (USA) prod/rel: Welsh-Pearson, Jury
Wanted, a Boy, Short Story
  Wanted, a Boy 1924 d: Thomas Bentley. lps: Sydney Fairbrother, Lionelle Howard, Pauline Johnson. 1750f UKN. prod/rel: British & Colonial, Ideal

RIDLEY, ARNOLD (1896–1984), UKN
Beggar My Neighbour, 1952, Play
  Meet Mr. Lucifer 1953 d: Anthony Pelissier. lps: Stanley Holloway, Peggy Cummins, Jack Watling. 83M UKN. prod/rel: Ealing Studios, General Film Distributors
East of Ludgate Hill, Play
  East of Ludgate Hill 1937 d: Manning Haynes. lps: Robert Cochran, Nancy O'Neil, Eliot Makeham. 47M UKN. prod/rel: Fox British
Easy Money, 1947, Play
  Easy Money 1948 d: Bernard Knowles. lps: Greta Gynt, Dennis Price, Jack Warner. 94M UKN. prod/rel: General Film Distributors, Gainsborough
The Flying Fool, London 1929, Play
  Flying Fool, The 1931 d: Walter Summers. lps: Henry Kendall, Benita Hume, Wallace Geoffrey. 76M UKN. prod/rel: British International Pictures, Wardour
The Ghost Train, London 1925, Play
  Geisterzug, Die 1927 d: Geza von Bolvary. lps: Ilse Bois, Louis Ralph, Guy Newall. 2072m GRM. prod/rel: F.P.S. Film, Phoebus-Film Ag
  Ghost Train, The 1927 d: Geza von Bolvary. lps: Guy Newall, Ilse Bois, Louis Ralph. 6500f UKN/GRM. prod/rel: Gainsborough, Woolf & Freedman
  Ghost Train, The 1931 d: Walter Forde. lps: Jack Hulbert, Cicely Courtneidge, Donald Calthrop. 72M UKN. prod/rel: Gainsborough, Woolf & Freedman
  Train Dans la Nuit, Un 1934 d: Rene Hervil. lps: Georgius, Dolly Davis, Alice Tissot. 77M FRN. prod/rel: Films Regent
  Ghost Train, The 1941 d: Walter Forde. lps: Arthur Askey, Richard Murdoch, Kathleen Harrison. 85M UKN. prod/rel: Gainsborough, General Film Distributors
Keepers of Youth, London 1929, Play
  Keepers of Youth 1931 d: Thomas Bentley. lps: Garry Marsh, Ann Todd, Robin Irvine. 70M UKN. prod/rel: British International Pictures, Wardour
The Last Chance, Play
  Warren Case, The 1934 d: Walter Summers. lps: Richard Bird, Nancy Burne, Diana Napier. 75M UKN. prod/rel: British International Pictures, Pathe
Recipe for Murder, London 1932, Play
  Blind Justice 1934 d: Bernard Vorhaus. lps: Eva Moore, Frank Vosper, John Stuart. 73M UKN. prod/rel: Real Art, Universal
Tabitha, London 1956, Play
  Who Killed the Cat? 1966 d: Montgomery Tully. lps: Mary Merrall, Ellen Pollock, Amy Dalby. 76M UKN. prod/rel: Grand National, Eternal
Third Time Lucky, London 1929, Play
  Third Time Lucky 1931 d: Walter Forde. lps: Bobby Howes, Gordon Harker, Dorothy Boyd. 85M UKN. prod/rel: Gainsborough, Woolf & Freedman
The Wrecker, London 1927, Play
  Wrecker, The 1928 d: Geza von Bolvary. lps: Carlyle Blackwell, Benita Hume, Joseph Striker. 6670f UKN. prod/rel: Gainsborough, Woolf & Freedman

Seven Sinners 1936 d: Albert de Courville. lps: Edmund Lowe, Constance Cummings, Thomy Bourdelle. 70M UKN. *Doomed Cargo* (USA); *The Wrecker* prod/rel: Gaumont-British

RIDLEY, JOHN
Stray Dogs, Book
   U-Turn 1997 d: Oliver Stone. lps: Sean Penn, Nick Nolte, Jennifer Lopez. 125M USA. prod/rel: Illusion Entertainment Group, Clyde Is Hungry Films

RIECK, HORST
Christiane F., Book
   Christiane F. Wir Kinder Vom Bahnhof Zoo 1981 d: Ulrich Edel. lps: Nadja Brunckhorst, Thomas Haustein, Jens Kuphal. 138M GRM. *We Children from Bahnhof Zoo* (USA); *Christiane F.* (UKN) prod/rel: Solaris, Maran

RIENITS, REX
No Smoking, Television Play
   No Smoking 1955 d: Henry Cass. lps: Reg Dixon, Belinda Lee, Lionel Jeffries. 72M UKN. prod/rel: Tempean, Eros

RIESEBERG, HARRY E.
Port Royal - Ghost City Beneath the Sea, Book
   City Beneath the Sea 1953 d: Budd Boetticher. lps: Robert Ryan, Anthony Quinn, Mala Powers. 87M USA. prod/rel: Universal-International

RIESENBERG, FELIX
East Side, West Side, New York 1927, Novel
   East Side, West Side 1927 d: Allan Dwan. lps: George O'Brien, Virginia Valli, J. Farrell MacDonald. 8154f USA. prod/rel: Fox Film Corp.
   Skyline 1931 d: Sam Taylor. lps: Thomas Meighan, Hardie Albright, Maureen O'Sullivan. 70M USA. prod/rel: Fox Film Corp.©, Sam Taylor Production

RIESS, CURT
Escale a Orly, Novel
   Escale a Orly 1955 d: Jean Dreville. lps: Dany Robin, Francois Perier, Micheline Gary. 107M FRN/GRM. *Zwischenlandung in Paris* (GRM); *Fasten Your Seat Belts* (UKN); *Stopover in Paris* prod/rel: Hoche Production, Marina Films
Roman Eines Frauenarztes, Novel
   Roman Eines Frauenarztes 1954 d: Falk Harnack. lps: Rudolf Prack, Winnie Markus, Anne-Marie Blanc. 92M GRM. *Novel of a Gynecologist* prod/rel: C.C.C., Gloria

RIFBJERG, KLAUS
Den Kroniske Uskyld, 1958, Novel
   Kroniske Uskyld, Den 1985 d: Edward Fleming. lps: Allan Olsen, Lars Simonsen. 100M DNM. *Chronic Innocence*; *Everlasting Innocence*

RIGBY, ARTHUR
Love Lies, Musical Play
   Love Lies 1931 d: Lupino Lane. lps: Stanley Lupino, Dorothy Boyd, Jack Hobbs. 70M UKN. prod/rel: British International Pictures, Wardour

RIGBY, RAY
The Hill, 1965, Novel
   Hill, The 1965 d: Sidney Lumet. lps: Sean Connery, Harry Andrews, Ian Bannen. 123M UKN. prod/rel: Seven Arts Productions, MGM

RIGGS, LYNN (1899–1954), USA
Green Grow the Lilacs, New York 1930, Play
   Oklahoma! 1955 d: Fred Zinnemann. lps: Gordon MacRae, Shirley Jones, Rod Steiger. 145M USA. prod/rel: 20th Century-Fox, Magna Theatre Corp.

RIGSBY, HOWARD
Sundown at Crazy Horse, New York 1957, Novel
   Last Sunset, The 1961 d: Robert Aldrich. lps: Kirk Douglas, Rock Hudson, Dorothy Malone. 112M USA. prod/rel: Bryna Productions

RILEY, EDNA
Before Morning, New York 1933, Play
   Before Morning 1933 d: Arthur Hoerl. lps: Leo Carrillo, Lora Baxter, Taylor Holmes. 56M USA. prod/rel: Stage and Screen Productions, Inc.

RILEY, EDWARD R.
   Before Morning 1933 d: Arthur Hoerl. lps: Leo Carrillo, Lora Baxter, Taylor Holmes. 56M USA. prod/rel: Stage and Screen Productions, Inc.

RILEY, JAMES WHITCOMB (1849–1916), USA
The Girl I Loved, Indianapolis 1910, Novel
   Girl I Loved, The 1923 d: Joseph de Grasse. lps: Charles Ray, Patsy Ruth Miller, Ramsey Wallace. 7100f USA. prod/rel: Charles Ray Productions, United Artists
A Life's Story, Poem
   There, Little Girl, Don't Cry 1910. 1000f USA. prod/rel: Selig Polyscope Co.

Little Orphan Annie, 1908, Poem
   Little Orphan Annie 1919 d: Colin Campbell. lps: Colleen Moore, Thomas Santschi, Harry Lonsdale. 6r USA. prod/rel: William N. Selig, State Rights
The Old Man and Jim, Poem
   Old Man and Jim, The 1911 d: Ulysses Davis. 950f USA. prod/rel: Champion
An Old Sweetheart of Mine, Poem
   Old Sweetheart of Mine, An 1911 d: Bannister Merwin. lps: Marc McDermott, Miriam Nesbitt. 1000f USA. prod/rel: Edison
   Old Sweetheart of Mine, An 1923 d: Harry Garson. lps: Pat Moore, Elliott Dexter, Mary Jane Irving. 5400f USA. prod/rel: Harry Garson Productions, Metro Pictures
The Old Swimmin' Hole, 1883, Poem
   Old Swimmin' Hole, The 1921 d: Joseph de Grasse. lps: Charles Ray, James Gordon, Laura La Plante. 5r USA. prod/rel: Charles Ray Productions, Associated First National Pictures

RILEY, LAWRENCE
Personal Appearance, New York 1934, Play
   Go West Young Man 1936 d: Henry Hathaway. lps: Mae West, Randolph Scott, Warren William. 82M USA. *Personal Appearance* prod/rel: Major Pictures Corp., Emanuel Cohen Production

RILEY, WILLIAM
No.7, Brick Row, Novel
   No. 7 Brick Row 1922 d: Fred W. Durrant. lps: Constance Worth, Marjorie Villis, James Knight. 5500f UKN. prod/rel: Harma, Associated Exhibitors
Peter Pettinger, Novel
   Agitator, The 1945 d: John Harlow. lps: William Hartnell, Mary Morris, John Laurie. 104M UKN. prod/rel: British National, Anglo-American

RILKE, RAINER MARIA (1875–1926), GRM, Rilke, Rene Wilhelm Josef Maria
Die Weise von Liebe Und Tod Des Cornets Christoph Rilke, 1906, Poem
   Cornet, Der 1955 d: Walter Reisch. lps: Gotz von Langheim, Anita Bjork, Wolfgang Preiss. 109M GRM. *Der Cornet - Die Weise von Liebe Und Tod*; *Der Cornet* prod/rel: F.a.M.a.

RIMANELLI, GIOSE
Novel
   Tiro Al Piccione 1961 d: Giuliano Montaldo. lps: Jacques Charrier, Eleonora Rossi-Drago, Francisco Rabal. 114M ITL. prod/rel: Ajace Compagnia Cin.Ca, Euro International Film

RINDI, RUGGERO
I Figli Di Nessuno, Novel
   Figli Di Nessuno, I 1921 d: Ubaldo Maria Del Colle. lps: Leda Gys, Ubaldo Maria Del Colle, Ermanno Roveri. 4173m ITL. prod/rel: Lombardo Film
   Angelo Bianco, L' 1943 d: Giulio Antamoro, Federico Sinibaldi. lps: Emma Gramatica, Beatrice Mancini, Filippo Scelzo. 85M ITL. prod/rel: Titanus
   Figli Di Nessuno, I 1951 d: Raffaello Matarazzo. lps: Amedeo Nazzari, Yvonne Sanson, Francoise Rosay. 105M ITL. prod/rel: Labor Film, Titanus

RINDOM, SVEND
Die Kupferne Hochzeit, Play
   Kupferne Hochzeit, Die 1948 d: Heinz Ruhmann. lps: Hertha Feiler, Peter Pasetti, Sybille von Gymnich. 99M GRM. *Copper Anniversary* prod/rel: Comedia

RINEHARDT, JOHN
The Scales of Justice, Play
   Scales of Justice, The 1914 d: Thomas N. Heffron. lps: Paul McAllister, Harold Lockwood, Mrs. Leslie Carter. 5r USA. prod/rel: Famous Players Film Co., State Rights

RINEHART, MARY ROBERTS (1876–1958), USA
Short Story
   Bab's Matinee Idol 1917 d: J. Searle Dawley. lps: Marguerite Clark, Helen Greene, Nigel Barrie. 5r USA. prod/rel: Famous Players Film Co.©, Paramount Pictures Corp.
Acquitted, 1907, Short Story
   Acquitted 1916 d: Paul Powell. lps: Wilfred Lucas, Mary Alden, Bessie Love. 5r USA. prod/rel: Fine Arts Film Co., Triangle Film Corp.©
Affinities, 1920, Short Story
   Affinities 1922 d: Ward Lascelle. lps: John Bowers, Colleen Moore, Joe Bonner. 5484f USA. prod/rel: Ward Lascelle Productions, W. W. Hodkinson Corp.
Bab's Burglar, 1917, Short Story
   Bab's Burglar 1917 d: J. Searle Dawley. lps: Marguerite Clark, Richard Barthelmess, Guy Coombs. 5r USA. prod/rel: Famous Players Film Co.©, Paramount Pictures

The Bat, New York 1926, Play
   Bat, The 1926 d: Roland West. lps: George Beranger, Charles W. Herzinger, Emily Fitzroy. 8219f USA. prod/rel: Feature Productions, United Artists
   Bat Whispers, The 1930 d: Roland West. lps: Chester Morris, Una Merkel, Chance E. Ward. 70M USA. prod/rel: United Artists Corp., Art Cinema Corp.
The Breaking Point, New York 1922, Novel
   Breaking Point, The 1924 d: Herbert Brenon. lps: Nita Naldi, Patsy Ruth Miller, George Fawcett. 6664f USA. prod/rel: Famous Players-Lasky, Paramount Pictures
The Circular Staircase, Indianapolis 1908, Novel
   Circular Staircase, The 1915 d: Edward J. Le Saint. lps: Eugenie Besserer, Stella Razetto, Guy Oliver. 5r USA. prod/rel: Selig Polyscope Co.©, Selig Red Seal Plays
   Bat, The 1959 d: Crane Wilbur. lps: Vincent Price, Agnes Moorehead, Gavin Gordon. 80M USA. prod/rel: Allied Artists, Liberty Pictures
Dangerous Days, New York 1919, Novel
   Dangerous Days 1920 d: Reginald Barker. lps: W. Lawson Butt, Clarissa Selwynne, Rowland Lee. 6662f USA. prod/rel: Eminent Authors Pictures, Inc., Reginald Barker Production
Empire Builders, 1916, Short Story
   It's a Great Life 1920 d: E. Mason Hopper. lps: Cullen Landis, Molly Malone, Clara Horton. 6r USA. *The Empire Builders*; *This Is the Life* prod/rel: Eminent Authors Pictures, Inc., Goldwyn Distributing Corp.
The G. A. C., Short Story
   Her Country First 1918 d: James Young. lps: Vivian Martin, John Cossar, Florence Oberle. 4232f USA. prod/rel: Famous Players-Lasky Corp.©, Paramount Pictures
Her Diary, 1917, Short Story
   Bab's Diary 1917 d: J. Searle Dawley. lps: Marguerite Clark, Richard Barthelmess, Guy Coombs. 5r USA. prod/rel: Famous Players Film Co.©, Paramount Pictures Corp.
Her Majesty, the Queen, 1924, Short Story
   Her Love Story 1924 d: Allan Dwan. lps: Gloria Swanson, Ian Keith, George Fawcett. 6750f USA. prod/rel: Famous Players-Lasky, Paramount Pictures
In the Pavilion, 1919, Short Story
   Glorious Fool, The 1922 d: E. Mason Hopper. lps: Helene Chadwick, Richard Dix, Vera Lewis. 5392f USA. prod/rel: Goldwyn Pictures
K, New York 1915, Novel
   Doctor and the Woman, The 1918 d: Lois Weber, Phillips Smalley. lps: Mildred Harris, True Boardman, Alan Roscoe. 6r USA. prod/rel: Lois Weber Productions, Jewel Productions©
K, Boston 1915, Novel
   K - the Unknown 1924 d: Harry Pollard. lps: Virginia Valli, Percy Marmont, Margarita Fischer. 8146f USA. prod/rel: Universal Pictures
Long Live the King, Boston 1917, Novel
   Long Live the King 1923 d: Victor Schertzinger. lps: Jackie Coogan, Rosemary Theby, Ruth Renick. 9364f USA. prod/rel: Metro Pictures
Lost Ecstasy, New York 1927, Novel
   I Take This Woman 1931 d: Marion Gering, Slavko Vorkapich. lps: Gary Cooper, Carole Lombard, Lester Vail. 74M USA. *Rodeo Romance*; *Lost Ecstasy*; *Half Angel*; *In Defense of Love* prod/rel: Paramount Publix Corp.©
Make Them Happy, 1919, Short Story
   Finders Keepers 1928 d: Wesley Ruggles. lps: Laura La Plante, John Harron, Edmund Breese. 6081f USA. prod/rel: Universal Pictures
Mind Over Motor, 1912, Short Story
   Mind Over Motor 1923 d: Ward Lascelle. lps: Trixie Friganza, Ralph Graves, Clara Horton. 5r USA. prod/rel: Ward Lascelles Productions, Principal Pictures
Miss Pinkerton: Adventures of a Nurse Detective, New York 1932, Novel
   Miss Pinkerton 1932 d: Lloyd Bacon. lps: Joan Blondell, George Brent, John Wray. 66M USA. prod/rel: First National Pictures©

RINEHART, MARY ROBERTS
   Nurse's Secret, The 1941 d: Noel Smith. lps: Lee Patrick, Regis Toomey, Ann Edmonds. 65M USA. prod/rel: Warner Bros.

RINEHART, MARY ROBERTS (1876–1958), USA
Mr. Cohen Takes a Walk, Novel
   Mr. Cohen Takes a Walk 1935 d: William Beaudine. lps: Paul Graetz, Violet Farebrother, Chili Bouchier. 82M UKN. *Father Takes a Walk* prod/rel: Warner Bros., First National

Seven Days, 1908, Short Story
Seven Days 1925 d: Scott Sidney. lps: Lillian Rich, Creighton Hale, Lilyan Tashman. 6974f USA. prod/rel: Christie Film Corp., Producers Distributing Corp.

The State Versus Elinor Norton, New York 1934, Novel
Elinor Norton 1935 d: Hamilton MacFadden. lps: Claire Trevor, Gilbert Roland, Hugh Williams. 75M USA. *The State Versus Elinor Norton* prod/rel: Fox Film Corp.©

The Street of Seven Stars, Boston 1914, Novel
Street of Seven Stars, The 1918 d: John B. O'Brien. lps: Doris Kenyon, Hugh Thompson, Carey L. Hastings. 6r USA. prod/rel: de Luxe Pictures, Inc., William L. Sherry Service

Twenty-Three and a Half Hours' Leave, 1918, Short Story
23½ Hours Leave 1919 d: Henry King. lps: Douglas MacLean, Doris May, Thomas Guise. 4838f USA. *Twenty-Three and a Half Hours' Leave* prod/rel: Thomas H. Ince Productions, Famous Players-Lasky Corp.
23½ Hours Leave 1937 d: John G. Blystone. lps: James Ellison, Terry Walker, Morgan Hill. 72M USA. prod/rel: Douglas Maclean Productions, Grand National Films©

Twenty-Two, 1919, Short Story
Glorious Fool, The 1922 d: E. Mason Hopper. lps: Helene Chadwick, Richard Dix, Vera Lewis. 5392f USA. prod/rel: Goldwyn Pictures

What Happened to Father, 1909, Short Story
What Happened to Father 1915 d: C. Jay Williams. lps: Frank Daniels, Bernice Berner, Adele Kelly. 5r USA. prod/rel: Vitagraph Co. of America©, Blue Ribbon Feature
What Happened to Father 1927 d: John G. Adolfi. lps: Warner Oland, Flobelle Fairbanks, William Demarest. 5567f USA. prod/rel: Warner Brothers Pictures

RIOS, S. PONDAL
Romance in High C, Story
Romance on the High Seas 1948 d: Michael Curtiz. lps: Jack Carson, Doris Day, Janis Paige. 99M USA. *It's Magic* (UKN) prod/rel: Warner Bros.

RIOS, SIXTO PONDAL
The Gay Senorita, Story
You Were Never Lovelier 1942 d: William A. Seiter. lps: Fred Astaire, Rita Hayworth, Adolphe Menjou. 97M USA. prod/rel: Columbia

RIP
Cognasse, Play
Cognasse 1932 d: Louis Mercanton. lps: Felicien Tramel, Andre Roanne, Therese Dorny. 88M FRN. prod/rel: Films Paramount

RIPLEY, ALEXANDRA (1934–, USA
Scarlett, Novel
Scarlett 1994 d: John Erman. lps: Joanne Whalley-Kilmer, Timothy Dalton, Ann-Margret. TVM. 480M USA/UKN.

RIPLEY, CLEMENTS
Black Moon, New York 1933, Novel
Black Moon 1934 d: R. William Neill. lps: Jack Holt, Fay Wray, Dorothy Burgess. 68M USA. prod/rel: Columbia Pictures Corp.

Dust and Sun, 1928, Short Story
Devil With Women, A 1930 d: Irving Cummings. lps: Victor McLaglen, Mona Maris, Humphrey Bogart. 76M USA. *On the Make* prod/rel: Fox Film Corp.

Gold Is Where You Find It, East Norwalk, Ct. 1936, Novel
Gold Is Where You Find It 1938 d: Michael Curtiz. lps: George Brent, Olivia de Havilland, Claude Rains. 90M USA. prod/rel: Warner Bros. Pictures©, First National Picture

Nor'wester, Story
John Paul Jones 1959 d: John Farrow. lps: Robert Stack, MacDonald Carey, Charles Coburn. 126M USA. prod/rel: Warner Bros., Samuel Bronston

RIPLEY, THOMAS
They Died With Their Boots on, 1937, Book
Lawless Breed, The 1952 d: Raoul Walsh. lps: Rock Hudson, Julie Adams, Mary Castle. 83M USA. prod/rel: Universal-International

RISCO, PADRE
Flores Silvestres, Novel
Floes Silvestres 1926 d: Constantino Dominguez, Antonio LabartA. lps: Maria Antinea, E. Carrasco, Jose Padin. SPN.
Flores Silvestres 1929 d: Jose Ruiz Miron. lps: Antonio Davila, Baby Dane, Dina Montero. SPN. prod/rel: Senores Ansakio (Madrid)

RISING, LAWRENCE IRVING
His Bridal Night, New York 1916, Play
His Bridal Night 1919 d: Kenneth Webb. lps: Alice Brady, Edward Earle, James L. Crane. 5r USA. prod/rel: Select Pictures Corp.©

Proud Flesh, New York 1924, Novel
Proud Flesh 1925 d: King Vidor. lps: Eleanor Boardman, Pat O'Malley, Harrison Ford. 5770f USA. prod/rel: Metro-Goldwyn Pictures

RISKIN, ROBERT
1930, Play
Illicit 1931 d: Archie Mayo. lps: Barbara Stanwyck, James Rennie, Ricardo Cortez. 81M USA. prod/rel: Warner Bros. Pictures©

Bless You Sister, New York 1927, Play
Miracle Woman 1931 d: Frank CaprA. lps: Barbara Stanwyck, David Manners, Sam Hardy. 90M USA. prod/rel: Columbia Pictures Corp.©

Many a Slip, New York 1930, Play
Many a Slip 1931 d: Vin Moore. lps: Joan Bennett, Lew Ayres, Slim Summerville. 74M USA. *Babies Won't Tell* prod/rel: Universal Pictures Corp.©

RISQUE, W. H.
Tally Ho!, London 1901, Play
Tally Ho! 1901 d: Frank Parker. lps: Charles Rock, Hetty Chattell, Douglas Gordon. UKN. prod/rel: Gibbons' Bio-Tableaux

RISS, WENDY
A Darker Purpose, Play
Winner, The 1996 d: Alex Cox. lps: Vincent d'Onofrio, Rebecca de Mornay, Delroy Lindo. 92M USA/ASL. prod/rel: Winner Productions©, Mark Damon Prods.

RISSMANN, CHARLOTTE
Versprich Mir Nichts, Play
Versprich Mir Nichts 1937 d: Wolfgang Liebeneiner. lps: Luise Ullrich, Viktor de Kowa, Heinrich George. 104M GRM. *Promise Me Nothing* (USA) prod/rel: Meteor-Film
Wenn Eine Frau Liebt 1950 d: Wolfgang Liebeneiner. lps: Hilde Krahl, Johannes Heesters, Mathias Wieman. 125M GRM. *When a Woman Gives Her Love* prod/rel: Meteor, UFA

RISTER, CLAUDE
Wolves of Catclaw, 1933, Short Story
Prescott Kid, The 1934 d: David Selman. lps: Tim McCoy, Sheila Bromley, Alden Chase. 58M USA. *Fighting Back*; *Wolves of Catclaw* prod/rel: Columbia Pictures Corp.©

RITA
Calvary, Novel
Calvary 1920 d: Edwin J. Collins. lps: Malvina Longfellow, Henry Victor, Charles Vane. 5200f UKN. prod/rel: Master Films, British Exhibitors' Films

Darby and Joan, Novel
Darby and Joan 1937 d: Syd Courtenay. lps: Peggy Simpson, Ian Fleming, Mickey Brantford. 75M UKN. prod/rel: Rock Studios, MGM

Grim Justice, Novel
Grim Justice 1916 d: Larry Trimble. lps: Florence Turner, Henry Edwards, Malcolm Cherry. 4250f UKN. prod/rel: Turner Films, Butcher

Half a Truth, Novel
Half a Truth 1922 d: Sinclair Hill. lps: Margaret Hope, Lawford Davidson, Miles Mander. 4900f UKN. prod/rel: Stoll

The Iron Stair, Novel
Iron Stair, The 1920 d: F. Martin Thornton. lps: Reginald Fox, Madge Stuart, Frank E. Petley. 5972f UKN. *Branded Soul, The* (USA) prod/rel: Stoll
Iron Stair, The 1933 d: Leslie Hiscott. lps: Henry Kendall, Dorothy Boyd, Michael Hogan. 51M UKN. prod/rel: Real Art, Radio

My Lord Conceit, Novel
My Lord Conceit 1921 d: F. Martin Thornton. lps: Evelyn Boucher, Maresco Marescini, Roland Myles. 6034f UKN. prod/rel: Stoll

Park Lane Scandal, Novel
Park Lane Scandal, A 1915 d: Warwick Buckland. lps: Flora Morris, J. R. Tozer, Austin Camp. 2000f UKN. prod/rel: Michaelson, Lloyd British

Petticoat Loose, Novel
Petticoat Loose 1922 d: George Ridgwell. lps: Dorinea Shirley, Warwick Ward, Lionelle Howard. 4845f UKN. prod/rel: Stoll

The Pointing Finger, Novel
Pointing Finger, The 1922 d: George Ridgwell. lps: Milton Rosmer, Madge Stuart, J. R. Tozer. 5380f UKN. prod/rel: Stoll
Pointing Finger, The 1933 d: George Pearson. lps: John Stuart, Viola Keats, Leslie Perrins. 68M UKN. prod/rel: Real Art, Radio

Sheba, Novel
Sheba 1919 d: Cecil M. Hepworth. lps: Alma Taylor, Gerald Ames, James Carew. 5475f UKN. prod/rel: Hepworth, Butcher's Film Service

RITCH, STEVEN
Plunder Road, Novel
Plunder Road 1957 d: Hubert Cornfield. lps: Gene Raymond, Jeanne Cooper, Wayne Morris. 72M USA. prod/rel: 20th Century-Fox, Regal Films

RITCHEY, WILL M.
The Skein of Life, Story
Skein of Life, The 1915 d: Donald MacDonald. lps: Dorothy Davenport, Lee Hill. 2r USA. prod/rel: Paragon, Mica

RITCHIE, ROBERT WELLES
The Temple of the Giants, Story
Not for Publication 1927 d: Ralph Ince. lps: Ralph Ince, Roy Laidlaw, Rex Lease. 6140f USA. prod/rel: Ralph Ince Productions, Film Booking Offices of America

Trails to Two Moons, Boston 1920, Novel
Two Moons 1920 d: Edward J. Le Saint. lps: Buck Jones, Carol Holloway, Gus Saville. 5r USA. prod/rel: Fox Film Corp., 20th Century Brand

RITTER, EDUARD
Diener Lassen Bitten, Play
Diener Lassen Bitten 1936 d: Hans H. Zerlett. lps: Hans Sohnker, Fita Benkhoff, Joe Stockel. 91M GRM. prod/rel: Euphono, Panorama

RIVERS, JOAN (1933–, USA
The Girl Most Likely to, Novel
Girl Most Likely to., The 1973 d: Lee Philips. lps: Stockard Channing, Edward Asner, Jim Backus. TVM. 73M USA. prod/rel: ABC Circle

RIVES, AMELIE (1863–1945), USA
The Fear Market, New York 1916, Play
Fear Market, The 1920 d: Kenneth Webb. lps: Alice Brady, Frank Losee, Henry Mortimer. 5r USA. prod/rel: Realart Pictures Corp.©

RIVES, HALLIE ERMINIE
The Long Lane's Turning, New York 1917, Novel
Long Lane's Turning, The 1919 d: Louis W. Chaudet. lps: Henry B. Walthall, Mary Charleson, Harry M. O'Connor. 5r USA. prod/rel: National Film Corp. of America, Robertson-Cole Co.

Satan Sanderson, Indianapolis 1907, Novel
Satan Sanderson 1915 d: John W. Noble. lps: Orrin Johnson, Irene Warfield. 5r USA. prod/rel: Rolfe Photoplays, Inc., Metro Pictures Corp.©

The Valiants of Virginia, New York 1912, Novel
Valiants of Virginia, The 1916 d: Thomas N. Heffron. lps: Kathlyn Williams, Arthur Shirley, Edward Peil. 5r USA. prod/rel: Selig Polyscope Co.©, Red Seal Play

RIVKIN, ALLEN
Play
Is My Face Red? 1932 d: William A. Seiter. lps: Ricardo Cortez, Helen Twelvetrees, Jill Esmond. 66M USA. prod/rel: RKO Radio Pictures©

RIVOIRE, ANDRE
Un Homme Heureux, Play
Pour Vivre Heureux 1932 d: Claudio de La Torre. lps: Noel-Noel, Suzet Mais, Pierre Etchepare. 80M FRN. prod/rel: Films Paramount

RIX, GEORGE
Out of the Sunset, 1920, Short Story
Torrent, The 1921 d: Stuart Paton. lps: Eva Novak, Oleta Otis, Jack Perrin. 4855f USA. prod/rel: Universal Film Mfg. Co.

ROA BASTOS, AUGUSTO
Hijo de Hombre, Novel
Hijo de Hombre 1960 d: Lucas Demare. lps: Jacinto Herrera, Francisco Rabal, Olga Zubarry. 89M ARG. *Hijo de Hombre -Choferes Del Chaco (la Sed)*; *Son of Man (Thirst)*; *La Sed* prod/rel: Argentina Sono S.A.C.I., Suevia

ROARK, GARLAND (1904–1985), USA, Garland, George
Fair Wind to Java, Novel
Fair Wind to Java 1953 d: Joseph Kane. lps: Fred MacMurray, Vera Ralston, Robert Douglas. 92M USA. prod/rel: Republic Pictures Corp.

Wake of the Red Witch, Novel
Wake of the Red Witch 1948 d: Edward Ludwig. lps: John Wayne, Gail Russell, Gig Young. 106M USA. prod/rel: Republic

ROBB, JOHN
Punitive Action, 1954, Novel
Desert Sands 1954 d: Lesley Selander. lps: Ralph Meeker, Marla English, J. Carrol Naish. 87M USA. prod/rel: United Artists, Bel-Air

ROBBE-GRILLET, ALAIN (1922–, FRN
Les Gommes, 1953, Novel
　Gommes, Les 1969 d: Lucien Deroisy. lps: Claude Titre, Francoise Brion, Georges Genicot. 100M BLG/FRN. prod/rel: Sofidoc

ROBBINS, CHRISTOPHER
Air America, Book
　Air America 1990 d: Roger Spottiswoode. lps: Mel Gibson, Robert Downey Jr., Nancy Travis. 112M USA. prod/rel: Guild, Indieprod

ROBBINS, CLARENCE AARON
The Unholy Three, New York 1917, Novel
　Unholy Three, The 1925 d: Tod Browning. lps: Lon Chaney, Mae Busch, Matt Moore. 6948f USA. prod/rel: Metro-Goldwyn-Mayer Pictures
　Unholy Three, The 1930 d: Jack Conway. lps: Lon Chaney, Lila Lee, Elliott Nugent. 72M USA. prod/rel: Metro-Goldwyn-Mayer Pictures

ROBBINS, HAROLD (1912–, USA
79 Park Avenue, Novel
　Harold Robbins' 79 Park Avenue 1977 d: Paul Wendkos. lps: Lesley Ann Warren, Marc Singer, David Dukes. TVM. 300M USA. *79 Park Avenue* prod/rel: Universal
The Adventurers, New York 1966, Novel
　Adventurers, The 1970 d: Lewis Gilbert. lps: Bekim Fehmiu, Charles Aznavour, Alan Badel. 171M UKN/USA. prod/rel: Avco-Embassy, Adventurers Film
The Betsy, Novel
　Betsy, The 1978 d: Daniel Petrie. lps: Laurence Olivier, Robert Duvall, Katharine Ross. 125M USA. *Harold Robbins' the Betsy* prod/rel: Allied Artists, Harold Robbins International
The Carpetbaggers, New York 1961, Novel
　Carpetbaggers, The 1964 d: Edward Dmytryk. lps: George Peppard, Alan Ladd, Carroll Baker. 151M USA. prod/rel: Paramount, Embassy
The Dream Merchants, Novel
　Dream Merchants, The 1980 d: Vincent Sherman. lps: Mark Harmon, Morgan Fairchild, Morgan Brittany. TVM. 200M USA. prod/rel: Columbia Pictures
The Lonely Lady, Novel
　Lonely Lady, The 1983 d: Peter Sasdy. lps: Pia Zadora, Lloyd Bochner, Bibi Besch. 92M USA. prod/rel: Universal
Never Love a Stranger, 1948, Novel
　Never Love a Stranger 1958 d: Robert Stevens. lps: John Drew Barrymore, Lita Milan, Robert Bray. 91M USA. prod/rel: Allied Artists, Harold Robbins
The Pirate, Novel
　Pirate, The 1978 d: Ken Annakin. lps: Franco Nero, Anne Archer, Olivia Hussey. TVM. 200M USA. *Harold Robbins' the Pirate* prod/rel: Howard W. Koch Production, Warner Bros.
Stiletto, New York 1969, Novel
　Stiletto 1969 d: Bernard L. Kowalski. lps: Alex Cord, Britt Ekland, Barbara McNair. 99M USA. prod/rel: Harold Robbins Co.
A Stone for Danny Fisher, Novel
　King Creole 1958 d: Michael Curtiz. lps: Elvis Presley, Carolyn Jones, Dolores Hart. 116M USA. prod/rel: Paramount
Where Love Has Gone, New York 1962, Novel
　Where Love Has Gone 1964 d: Edward Dmytryk. lps: Susan Hayward, Bette Davis, Mike Connors. 114M USA. prod/rel: Embassy Pictures, Paramount Pictures

ROBBINS, KATHERINE LEISER
The Gilded Dream, 1920, Novel
　Gilded Dream, The 1920 d: Rollin S. Sturgeon. lps: Carmel Myers, Tom Chatterton, Elsa Lorimer. 5r USA. prod/rel: Universal Film Mfg. Co.©
Her Fling, Short Story
　Risky Road, The 1918 d: Ida May Park. lps: Dorothy Phillips, William Stowell, George Chesebro. 5r USA. *Her Fling* prod/rel: Dorothy Phillips Production, Universal Film Mfg. Co.©
In Folly's Trail, 1920, Short Story
　In Folly's Trail 1920 d: Rollin S. Sturgeon. lps: Carmel Myers, Thomas Holding, Arthur Clayton. 4825f USA. prod/rel: Universal Film Mfg. Co.©
The Scarlet Strain, Novel
　Scarlet Shadow, The 1919 d: Robert Z. Leonard. lps: Mae Murray, Martha Mattox, Frank Elliott. 6r USA. *Scarlet Strain, The* prod/rel: Universal Film Mfg. Co.©

ROBBINS, TOD
Spurs, 1923, Short Story
　Freaks 1932 d: Tod Browning. lps: Wallace Ford, Olga Baclanova, Leila Hyams. 64M USA. *Forbidden Love*; *Nature's Mistakes*; *Barnum*; *The Monster Show*; *Spurs* prod/rel: Metro-Goldwyn-Mayer Corp., Metro-Goldwyn-Mayer Dist. Corp.©

ROBERT, HAROLD G.
Ramsbottom Rides Again, Play
　Ramsbottom Rides Again 1956 d: John Baxter. lps: Arthur Askey, Glenn Melvyn, Sidney James. 93M UKN. prod/rel: Jack Hylton Productions, British Lion

ROBERT, JACQUES
L'appartement Des Filles, Novel
　Appartement Des Filles, L' 1963 d: Michel Deville. lps: Mylene Demongeot, Sylva Koscina, Sami Frey. 90M FRN/GRM/ITL. *L'appartemento Delle Ragazze* (ITL); *Gangster, Gold Und Flotte Madchen* (GRM); *Gangsters, Gold and Cool Chicks* prod/rel: Transcontinental Films, Consul Film
Les Dents Longues, Novel
　Dents Longues, Les 1953 d: Daniel Gelin. lps: Daniel Gelin, Daniele Delorme, Louis Seigner. 95M FRN/ITL. *I Denti Lunghi* (ITL) prod/rel: Jacques Roitfeld, Sirius
Le Desordre Et la Nuit, Paris 1955, Novel
　Desordre Et la Nuit, Le 1958 d: Gilles Grangier. lps: Jean Gabin, Danielle Darrieux, Nadja Tiller. 90M FRN. *Night Affair* (USA) prod/rel: Orex Films
Le Gigolo, Novel
　Gigolo, Le 1960 d: Jacques Deray. lps: Jean-Claude Brialy, Alida Valli, Jean Chevrier. 95M FRN. prod/rel: Orex Films
Marie-Octobre, Novel
　Marie-Octobre 1958 d: Julien Duvivier. lps: Danielle Darrieux, Bernard Blier, Robert Dalban. 102M FRN. *Secret Meeting* (USA); *Marie Octobre* prod/rel: Orex Films, Societe Francaise Theatre Et Cinema
Peau d'Espion, Paris 1966, Novel
　Peau d'Espion 1967 d: Edouard Molinaro. lps: Louis Jourdan, Senta Berger, Bernard Blier. 93M FRN/ITL/GRM. *Congiura Di Spie* (ITL); *To Commit a Murder* (USA); *Der Grausame Job* (GRM); *Brutal Job* prod/rel: Gaumont International, S.N.E. Gaumont
Qualqu'un Derriere la Porte, Novel
　Qualcuno Dietro la Porta 1971 d: Nicolas Gessner. lps: Anthony Perkins, Jill Ireland, Charles Bronson. 97M ITL/FRN. *Quelqu'un Derriere la Porte* (FRN); *Someone Behind the Door* (USA); *Two Minds for Murder* (UKN); *Brainkill* prod/rel: Medusa Distribuzione, Lira Films

ROBERT, JEAN-MARC
L'ami de Vincent, Novel
　Ami de Vincent, L' 1983 d: Pierre Granier-Deferre. lps: Philippe Noiret, Jean Rochefort, Francoise Fabian. 93M FRN. prod/rel: Sara Films, T. Films

ROBERT, YVES
Short Story
　Alexandre le Bienheureux 1968 d: Yves Robert. lps: Philippe Noiret, Marlene Jobert, Francoise Brion. 90M FRN. *Very Happy Alexander* (USA); *Happy Alexander*; *Alexander*; *Alexandre* prod/rel: Productions De La Gueville, Madeleine Film

ROBERTS, ALICE M.
When Fate Leads Trumps, Novel
　When Fate Leads Trumps 1914 d: Harry Handworth. lps: Octavia Handworth, Gordon Demain, William A. Williams. 4r USA. prod/rel: Excelsior Feature Film Co.©, Alliance Films Corp.

ROBERTS, BEN
Portrait in Black, Play
　Portrait in Black 1960 d: Michael Gordon. lps: Lana Turner, Anthony Quinn, Lloyd Nolan. 113M USA. prod/rel: Universal

ROBERTS, BETH
Manganinnie, Novel
　Manganinnie 1980 d: John Honey. lps: Mawuyul Yanthalawuy, Anna Ralph, Philip Hinton. 90M ASL. *Darkening Flame* prod/rel: Tasmanian Film Corporation©, Australian Film Commission

ROBERTS, DENYS
Smugglers' Circuit, Novel
　Law and Disorder 1958 d: Charles Crichton, Henry Cornelius. lps: Michael Redgrave, Robert Morley, Elizabeth Sellars. 76M UKN. prod/rel: British Lion, Hotspur

ROBERTS, EDWARD BARRY
Forsaking All Others, New York 1933, Play
　Forsaking All Others 1934 d: W. S. Van Dyke. lps: Clark Gable, Joan Crawford, Robert Montgomery. 84M USA. prod/rel: Metro-Goldwyn-Mayer Corp.©

ROBERTS, ELIZABETH MADOX (1886–1941), USA
The Great Meadow, New York 1930, Novel
　Great Meadow, The 1931 d: Charles J. Brabin. lps: Johnny Mack Brown, Eleanor Boardman, Guinn (Big Boy) Williams. 78M USA. prod/rel: Metro-Goldwyn-Mayer Corp., Metro-Goldwyn-Mayer Dist. Corp.©

ROBERTS, GEORGE
A Deadly Hate, Play
　Deadly Hate, A 1915 d: Richard Ridgely. lps: Marc MacDermott, Margaret Prussing, Mrs. Wallace Erskine. 3r USA. prod/rel: Edison

ROBERTS, H. W.
La Rubia, Story
　Wife's Romance, A 1923 d: Thomas N. Heffron. lps: Clara Kimball Young, Lewis Dayton, Louise Bates Mortimer. 5169f USA. *Old Madrid* prod/rel: Harry Garson Productions, Metro Pictures

ROBERTS, JEAN-MARC
Une Etrange Affaire, Novel
　Etrange Affaire, Une 1981 d: Pierre Granier-Deferre. lps: Michel Piccoli, Gerard Lanvin, Nathalie Baye. 105M FRN. prod/rel: Sara Films, Antenne 2

ROBERTS, KENNETH LEWIS (1888–1957), USA, Roberts, Kenneth
Captain Caution, a Chronicle of Arundel, New York 1934, Novel
　Captain Caution 1940 d: Richard Wallace. lps: Victor Mature, Louise Platt, Leo Carrillo. 86M USA. prod/rel: Hal Roach Studios, Inc.
Good Will and Almond Shells, 1917, Short Story
　Shell Game, The 1918 d: George D. Baker. lps: Emmy Wehlen, Henry Kolker, Joseph Kilgour. 5r USA. *Good Will and Almond Shells* prod/rel: Metro Pictures Corp.©
Lydia Bailey, 1947, Novel
　Lydia Bailey 1952 d: Jean Negulesco. lps: Dale Robertson, Anne Francis, Charles Korvin. 89M USA. prod/rel: 20th Century-Fox
Northwest Passage, New York 1937, Novel
　Northwest Passage (Book I -Rogers' Rangers) 1939 d: King Vidor. lps: Spencer Tracy, Robert Young, Walter Brennan. 125M USA. *Northwest Passage* prod/rel: Metro-Goldwyn-Mayer Corp., Loew's, Inc.©
Northwest Passage, Novel
　Fury River 1959 d: Jacques Tourneur, George Waggner. lps: Keith Larsen, Buddy Ebsen, Don Burnett. MTV. 74M USA. prod/rel: Loew's, MGM
With Neatness and Dispatch, 1918, Short Story
　With Neatness and Dispatch 1918 d: Will S. Davis. lps: Francis X. Bushman, Beverly Bayne, Frank Currier. 5r USA. prod/rel: Metro Pictures Corp.©

ROBERTS, MORLEY
Holloway's Treasure, Ss
　Holloway's Treasure 1924 d: Sinclair Hill. lps: Dallas Cairns, Kathleen Kilfoyle, Jack Trevor. 1728f UKN. prod/rel: Stoll
A Madonna of the Cells, Short Story
　Madonna of the Cells, A 1925 d: Fred Paul. lps: Fred Paul, Betty Faire, Moore Marriott. 2380f UKN. prod/rel: Stoll

ROBERTS, NORA
Magic Moments, Novel
　Magic Moments 1989 d: Lawrence Gordon Clark. lps: Jenny Seagrove, John Shea, Paul Freeman. TVM. 105M UKN. prod/rel: Arena, Ytv

ROBERTS, RALPH ARTHUR
Ehe in Dosen, Play
　Ehe in Dosen 1939 d: Johannes Meyer. lps: Leny Marenbach, Johannes Riemann, Ralph Arthur Roberts. 96M GRM. prod/rel: Cine-Allianz, Bavaria

ROBERTS, RICHARD EMERY
The Gilded Rooster, 1947, Novel
　Savage Wilderness 1955 d: Anthony Mann. lps: Victor Mature, Guy Madison, Robert Preston. 98M USA. *The Last Frontier* (UKN) prod/rel: Columbia
Star in the West, New York 1951, Novel
　Second Time Around, The 1961 d: Vincent Sherman. lps: Debbie Reynolds, Thelma Ritter, Steve Forrest. 99M USA. *Star in the West*; *The Calico Sheriff*; *Mother Ought to Marry* prod/rel: Cummings-Harman Productions

ROBERTS, WILLIAM L.
The Fighting Parson, New York 1908, Play
　Hell's Oasis 1920 d: Neal Hart. lps: Neal Hart, William Quinn, Hal Wilson. 5r USA. prod/rel: Pinnacle Productions, Independent Film Association

ROBERTSON, DON
The Greatest Thing That Almost Happened, Novel
　Greatest Thing That Almost Happened, The 1977 d: Gilbert Moses. lps: Jimmie Walker, James Earl Jones, Deborah Allen. TVM. 100M USA. prod/rel: Charles Fries Productions, Crestview

ROBERTSON, DOUGAL
Survive the Savage Sea, Book
　Survive the Savage Sea 1992 d: Kevin Dobson. lps: Robert Urich, Ali MacGraw, Danielle von Zemeck. TVM. 96M USA/ASL. prod/rel: Warner Bros., von Zerneck Sertner Films

ROBERTSON, E. ARNOT (1903–1961), UKN, Robertson, Eileen Arbuthnot

Four Frightened People, New York 1931, Novel

Four Frightened People 1934 d: Cecil B. de Mille. lps: Claudette Colbert, Herbert Marshall, Mary Boland. 78M USA. prod/rel: Paramount Productions©

ROBERTSON, MORGAN (1861–1915), USA, Robertston, Morgan Andrew

The Enemies, Story

Enemies, The 1915 d: Harry Davenport. lps: Harry T. Morey, Wilfred North, Edith Storey. 3r USA. prod/rel: Broadway Star, Vitagraph Co. of America

Masters of Men; a Romance of the New Navy, New York 1901, Novel

Masters of Men 1923 d: David Smith. lps: Earle Williams, Alice Calhoun, Cullen Landis. 6740f USA. prod/rel: Vitagraph Co. of America

ROBERTSON, T. W.

Caste, London 1867, Play

Caste 1913 d: C. Jay Williams. lps: William West, Mabel Trunnelle, Gertrude McCoy. 2000f USA. prod/rel: Edison

Caste 1915 d: Larry Trimble. lps: John Hare, Peggy Hyland, Esme Hubbard. 4500f UKN. prod/rel: Turner Films, Ideal

Caste 1930 d: Campbell Gullan. lps: Hermione Baddeley, Nora Swinburne, Alan Napier. 70M UKN. prod/rel: Harry Rowson, United Artists

David Garrick, London 1864, Play

David Garrick 1912 d: Percy Nash. lps: Gerald Lawrence, Mary Dibley, Charles Rock. 1150f UKN. prod/rel: London Films, Cosmopolitan

David Garrick 1913 d: Hay Plumb. lps: Charles Wyndham, Mary Moore, Louis Calvert. 4000f UKN. prod/rel: Hepworth, Ruffell

David Garrick 1913 d: Leedham Bantock. lps: Seymour Hicks, Ellaline Terriss, William Lugg. 2500f UKN. prod/rel: Zenith Films

David Garrick 1914 d: James Young. lps: Clara Kimball Young, James Young, Naomi Childers. 2r USA. prod/rel: Vitagraph Co. of America

David Garrick 1916 d: Frank Lloyd. lps: Dustin Farnum, Winifred Kingston, Herbert Standing. 5r USA. prod/rel: Pallas Pictures, Paramount Pictures Corp.

David Garrick 1922. lps: Milton Rosmer. 1300f UKN. prod/rel: Master Films, British Exhibitors' Films

David Garrick 1928 d: George J. Banfield, Leslie Eveleigh. lps: Gordon McLeod, Gabrielle Morton, Betty Faire. 2046f UKN. prod/rel: British Filmcraft, Ideal

Home, London 1869, Play

Temptress, The 1920 d: George Edwardes Hall. lps: Yvonne Arnaud, Langhorne Burton, John Gliddon. 4585f UKN. prod/rel: British & Colonial, Pathe

The Young Collegian, Play

Fugitive, The 1913 d: Charles H. France. lps: John Lancaster, Lillian Leighton, Palmer Bowman. SHT USA. prod/rel: Selig Polyscope Co.

ROBERTSON, WILLARD

Big Game, New York 1920, Play

Big Game 1921 d: Dallas M. Fitzgerald. lps: May Allison, Forrest Stanley, Edward Cecil. 6r USA. prod/rel: Metro Pictures

Moontide, Novel

Moontide 1942 d: Archie Mayo, Fritz Lang (Uncredited). lps: Jean Gabin, Ida Lupino, Thomas Mitchell. 95M USA. prod/rel: 20th Century-Fox

The Sea Woman, New York 1925, Play

Why Women Love 1925 d: Edwin Carewe. lps: Blanche Sweet, Bert Sprotte, Robert Frazer. 6723f USA. *The Sea Woman*; *Barriers Aflame*; *Dangerous Currents* prod/rel: Edwin Carewe Productions, First National Pictures

ROBESON, KENNETH

Doc Savage, the Man of Bronze, Novel

Doc Savage, the Man of Bronze 1975 d: Michael Anderson. lps: Ron Ely, Pamela Hensley, Paul G. Wexler. 100M USA. prod/rel: George Pal

ROBEY, GEORGE

The Rest Cure, Novel

Rest Cure, The 1923 d: A. E. Coleby. lps: George Robey, Sydney Fairbrother, Gladys Hamer. 4800f UKN. prod/rel: Stoll

ROBIDA, FERDINAND

Novel

Avventure Straordinarissime Di Saturnino Farandola, Le 1914 d: Marcel Fabre, Luigi Maggi (Uncredited). lps: Marcel Fabre, Nilde Baracchi, Filippo CostamagnA. 3660m ITL. *Zingo* (USA) prod/rel: S.A. Ambrosio

ROBINS, ELIZABETH (1865–1952), USA, Raimond, C. E.

A Dark Lantern, New York 1905, Novel

Dark Lantern, A 1920 d: John S. Robertson. lps: Alice Brady, James L. Crane, Reginald Denny. 5956f USA. prod/rel: Realart Pictures Corp.©

My Little Sister, New York 1913, Novel

My Little Sister 1919 d: Kenean Buel. lps: Evelyn Nesbit, Leslie Austen, Lillian Hall. 5r USA. prod/rel: Fox Film Corp., William Fox©

ROBINSON, AMY

Story

Baby It's You 1983 d: John Sayles. lps: Rosanna Arquette, Vincent Spano, Joanna Merlin. 105M USA. prod/rel: Paramount, Double Play

ROBINSON, BARBARA

The Best Christmas Pageant Ever, Book

Best Christmas Pageant Ever, The 1984 d: George Schaefer. lps: Loretta Swit, Jackson Davies, Janet Wright. MTV. 50M USA. prod/rel: Comworld, Schaefer-Karpf

ROBINSON, BERTRAND

Ladies' Day, Play

Ladies' Day 1943 d: Leslie Goodwins. lps: Lupe Velez, Eddie Albert, Patsy Kelly. 62M USA. prod/rel: RKO Radio

Oh, Promise Me, New York 1930, Play

Love, Honor and Oh, Baby! 1933 d: Edward Buzzell. lps: Slim Summerville, Zasu Pitts, George Barbier. 63M USA. prod/rel: Universal Pictures Corp.©

Tommy, New York 1928, Play

She's My Weakness 1930 d: Melville Brown. lps: Arthur Lake, Sue Carol, Lucien Littlefield. 73M USA. prod/rel: RKO Productions

Your Uncle Dudley, New York 1929, Play

Your Uncle Dudley 1935 d: Eugene J. Forde. lps: Edward Everett Horton, Lois Wilson, John McGuire. 70M USA. prod/rel: Twentieth Century-Fox Film Corp.©

Too Busy to Work 1939 d: Otto Brower. lps: Jed Prouty, Spring Byington, Kenneth Howell. 64M USA. *The Little Theater* prod/rel: Twentieth Century-Fox Film Corp.©

ROBINSON, BUDD

The Operator, Novel

Where Does It Hurt? 1972 d: Rod Amateau. lps: Peter Sellers, Jo Ann Pflug, Rick Lenz. 85M USA/UKN. prod/rel: Hemdale

ROBINSON, CHARLES

Sailor Beware, New York 1933, Play

Lady Be Careful 1936 d: Theodore Reed. lps: Lew Ayres, Mary Carlisle, Buster Crabbe. 72M USA. prod/rel: Paramount Pictures©

Fleet's in, The 1942 d: Victor Schertzinger, Hal Walker (Uncredited). lps: Dorothy Lamour, William Holden, Eddie Bracken. 93M USA. prod/rel: Paramount

Sailor Beware 1951 d: Hal Walker. lps: Dean Martin, Jerry Lewis, Corinne Calvet. 108M USA. prod/rel: Paramount, Wallis-Hazen

Swing Your Lady, New York 1936, Play

Swing Your Lady 1938 d: Ray Enright. lps: Humphrey Bogart, Frank McHugh, Louise FazendA. 79M USA. prod/rel: Warner Bros. Pictures©

ROBINSON, CHARLES LARNED

Don't Take a Chance, 1918, Pamph

Scarlet Trail, The 1919 d: John S. Lawrence. lps: Beth Ivins, Vincent Coleman, Margaret Blanc. 6r USA. prod/rel: G. and L. Features, Inc., State Rights

ROBINSON, DAVID

Chaplin - His Life and Art, Book

Chaplin 1992 d: Richard Attenborough. lps: Robert Downey Jr., Geraldine Chaplin, Dan Aykroyd. 145M UKN. prod/rel: Guild, Lambeth

ROBINSON, EDWARD G.

The Kibitzer, New York 1929, Play

Kibitzer, The 1930 d: Edward Sloman. lps: Harry Green, Mary Brian, Neil Hamilton. 7273f USA. *Busybody* (UKN) prod/rel: Paramount Famous Lasky Corp.

ROBINSON, FRANK M.

The Glass Inferno, Novel

Towering Inferno, The 1974 d: Irwin Allen, John Guillermin. lps: Steve McQueen, Paul Newman, William Holden. 165M USA. prod/rel: 20th Century Fox, Warner Bros.

The Power, Philadelphia 1956, Novel

Power, The 1967 d: Byron Haskin. lps: George Hamilton, Suzanne Pleshette, Richard Carlson. 109M USA. prod/rel: Galaxy Productions, MGM

ROBINSON, HENRY MORTON (1898–1961), USA

The Cardinal, New York 1950, Novel

Cardinal, The 1963 d: Otto Preminger. lps: Tom Tryon, Romy Schneider, Raf Vallone. 176M USA. prod/rel: Columbia

ROBINSON, JEAN

The Secret Life of T. K. Dearing, Book

Secret Life of T. K. Dearing, The 1975 d: Harry Harris. lps: Jodie Foster, Eduard Franz, Brian Wood. MTV. 50M USA.

ROBINSON, LEWIS

The General Goes Too Far, Novel

High Command, The 1937 d: Thorold Dickinson. lps: Lionel Atwill, Lucie Mannheim, Steven Geray. 90M UKN. prod/rel: Associated British Film Distributors, Fanfare

ROBINSON, MARILYNNE

Housekeeping, Novel

Housekeeping 1987 d: Bill Forsyth. lps: Christine Lahti, Sara Walker, Andrea Burchill. 116M USA. *Sylvie's Ark* prod/rel: Columbia

ROBINSON, MARTHA

Show Flat, Play

Show Flat 1936 d: Bernerd Mainwaring. lps: Eileen Munro, Anthony Hankey, Clifford Heatherley. 70M UKN. prod/rel: British and Dominions, Paramount British

ROBINSON, PATRICK

True Blue, Book

True Blue 1996 d: Ferdinand Fairfax. lps: Johan Leysen, Dominic West, Dylan Baker. 117M UKN. prod/rel: Rafford Production, Film and General

ROBINSON, PERCY

To What Red Hell, Play

To What Red Hell 1929 d: Edwin Greenwood. lps: Sybil Thorndike, John Hamilton, Bramwell Fletcher. 100M UKN. prod/rel: Strand Films, Twickenham

Wanted for Murder, London 1937, Play

Wanted for Murder 1946 d: Lawrence Huntington. lps: Eric Portman, Dulcie Gray, Derek Farr. 103M UKN. *A Voice in the Night* prod/rel: Excelsior, 20th Century-Fox

ROBINSON, RICHARD

Short Story

High-Ballin' 1978 d: Peter Carter. lps: Peter Fonda, Jerry Reed, Helen Shaver. 98M CND. *High Ballin'*; *Fifth Wheel, The*; *Sacree Balade Pour Les Gros Bras*; *P.F. Flyer* prod/rel: the Pando Co., Jon Slan Productions Inc.

ROBINSON, SIDNEY

Gladstone, Story

Spindle of Life, The 1917 d: George Cochrane. lps: Ben Wilson, Neva Gerber, Jessie Pratt. 5r USA. prod/rel: Universal Film Mfg. Co.©, Butterfly Picture

ROBISON, MARY

Oh, Novel

Twister 1990 d: Michael AlmereydA. lps: Harry Dean Stanton, Suzy Amis, Crispin Glover. 94M USA. prod/rel: Vestron

ROBITAILLE, MARC

Des Histoires d'Hiver, Avec Des Rues, Des Ecoles Et du Hocke, Novel

Histoires d'Hiver 1999 d: Francois Bouvier. lps: Joel Drapeau-Dalpe, Denis Bouchard, Luc Guerin. 105M CND. *Winter Stories* prod/rel: Behaviour Distribution, Aska Film

ROBLES, EMMANUEL (1914–, ALG

Cela S'appelle l'Aurore, 1952, Novel

Cela S'appelle l'Aurore 1955 d: Luis Bunuel. lps: Georges Marchal, Lucia Bose, Gianni Esposito. 120M FRN/ITL. *Gli Amanti Di Domani* (ITL); *That Is Called Dawn*; *When the Sun Rises* prod/rel: Films Marceau, Laetitia Films

ROBSON, MAY

The Three Lights, New York 1911, Play

Night Out, A 1916 d: George D. Baker. lps: May Robson, Flora Finch, Kate Price. 5r USA. prod/rel: Vitagraph Co. of America©, Blue Ribbon Feature

ROBSON, MICHAEL

On Giant's Shoulders, Book

On Giant's Shoulders 1979 d: Anthony Simmons. lps: Bryan Pringle, Judi Dench, Terry Wiles. MTV. 75M UKN. prod/rel: BBC

ROBYN, ALFRED G.

The Yankee Consul, New York 1904, Musical Play

Yankee Consul, The 1924 d: James W. Horne. lps: Arthur Stuart Hull, Douglas MacLean, Patsy Ruth Miller. 6148f USA. prod/rel: Douglas Maclean Productions, Associated Exhibitors

ROCCA, GINO
Nel Caffeuccio Di San Stae, Novel
  Cantante Dell'opera, La 1932 d: Nunzio MalasommA. lps: Gianfranco Giachetti, Germana Paolieri, Isa PolA. 90M ITL. prod/rel: Cines, Anonima Pittaluga

Se No I Xe Mati No Li Volemo, 1926, Play
  Compagnia Dei Matti, La 1928 d: Mario Almirante. lps: Vasco Creti, Celio Bucchi, Alex Bernard. 3250m ITL. prod/rel: S.A. Pittaluga

Se No I Xe Mati No Li Volemo, Play
  Se Non Son Matti No Li Vogliamo 1941 d: Esodo Pratelli. lps: Ruggero Ruggeri, Armando Falconi, Antonio Gandusio. 98M ITL. *Compagnia Dei Matti, La* prod/rel: Cines, E.N.I.C.

ROCCO (MARCO LOMBARDO)
Porci Con le Ali, Book
  Porci Con le Ali 1977 d: Paolo Pietrangeli. lps: Cristiana Mancinelli, Franco Bianchi, Lou Castel. 105M ITL. *If Pigs Had Wings* prod/rel: Eidoscope, Uski Film

ROCHE, ARTHUR SOMERS
Business Is Best, Story
  Girl from Chicago, The 1927 d: Ray Enright. lps: Conrad Nagel, Myrna Loy, William Russell. 5798f USA. prod/rel: Warner Brothers Pictures

The Case Against Mrs. Ames, 1934, Novel
  Case Against Mrs. Ames, The 1936 d: William A. Seiter. lps: Madeleine Carroll, George Brent, Arthur Treacher. 85M USA. prod/rel: Walter Wanger Productions, Inc.

Come to My House, New York 1927, Novel
  Come to My House 1927 d: Alfred E. Green. lps: Olive Borden, Antonio Moreno, Ben Bard. 5430f USA. prod/rel: Fox Film Corp.

The Crimes of the Armchair Club, 1920, Short Story
  Mystery Club, The 1926 d: Herbert Blache. lps: Matt Moore, Edith Roberts, Mildred Harris. 6969f USA. prod/rel: Universal Pictures

The Day of Faith, Boston 1921, Novel
  Day of Faith, The 1923 d: Tod Browning. lps: Eleanor Boardman, Tyrone Power Sr., Raymond Griffith. 6557f USA. prod/rel: Goldwyn Pictures, Goldwyn-Cosmopolitan Distributing Corp.

Fallen Angels, 1927, Short Story
  Man, Woman and Wife 1929 d: Edward Laemmle. lps: Norman Kerry, Pauline Starke, Marion Nixon. 6589f USA. *Fallen Angels* prod/rel: Universal Pictures

Find the Woman, New York 1921, Novel
  Find the Woman 1922 d: Tom Terriss. lps: Alma Rubens, Eileen Huban, Harrison Ford. 5144f USA. prod/rel: Cosmopolitan Productions, Paramount Pictures

Finger Prints, Story
  Finger Prints 1927 d: Lloyd Bacon. lps: Louise Fazenda, John T. Murray, Helene Costello. 7031f USA. prod/rel: Warner Brothers Pictures

Kissed, 1918, Short Story
  Kissed 1922 d: King Baggot. lps: Marie Prevost, Lloyd Whitlock, Lillian Langdon. 4231f USA. prod/rel: Universal Film Mfg. Co.

Loot, Indianapolis 1916, Novel
  Loot 1919 d: William C. Dowlan. lps: Joseph Girard, Ora Carew, Frank Thompson. 5675f USA. prod/rel: Universal Film Mfg. Co.©

Penthouse, New York 1935, Novel
  Penthouse 1933 d: W. S. Van Dyke. lps: Warner Baxter, Myrna Loy, Charles Butterworth. 90M USA. *Crooks in Clover* (UKN); *Penthouse Legend* prod/rel: Metro-Goldwyn-Mayer Corp.©
  Society Lawyer 1939 d: Edwin L. Marin. lps: Walter Pidgeon, Virginia Bruce, Eduardo Ciannelli. 77M USA. *Penthouse*; *Night in Manhattan* prod/rel: Metro-Goldwyn-Mayer Corp., Loew's, Inc.©

The Pleasure Buyers, New York 1925, Novel
  Pleasure Buyers, The 1925 d: Chet Withey. lps: Irene Rich, Clive Brook, Gayne Whitman. 7r USA. prod/rel: Warner Brothers Pictures

Plunder, Indianapolis 1917, Novel
  Living Lies 1922 d: Emile Chautard. lps: Edmund Lowe, Mona Kingsley, Kenneth Hill. 5r USA. prod/rel: Mayflower Photoplay Corp., Clark-Cornelius Corp.

Rich But Honest, 1926, Short Story
  Rich But Honest 1927 d: Albert Ray. lps: Nancy Nash, Clifford Holland, Charles Morton. 5480f USA. prod/rel: Fox Film Corp.

Shadow of Doubt, New York 1935, Novel
  Shadow of Doubt 1935 d: George B. Seitz. lps: Constance Collier, Ricardo Cortez, Virginia Bruce. 75M USA. prod/rel: Metro-Goldwyn-Mayer Corp.©

The Sport of Kings, Indianapolis 1917, Novel
  Sport of Kings, The 1919 d: Frederick A. Thompson. lps: Matt Moore, Aileen Pringle, Margot Kelly. 5r USA. prod/rel: Buffalo Motion Picture Co., State Rights

Star of Midnight, New York 1936, Novel
  Star of Midnight 1935 d: Stephen Roberts. lps: William Powell, Ginger Rogers, Paul Kelly. 90M USA. prod/rel: RKO Radio Pictures©

The Wise Wife, New York 1928, Novel
  Wise Wife, The 1927 d: E. Mason Hopper. lps: Phyllis Haver, Tom Moore, Fred Walton. 5610f USA. prod/rel: de Mille Pictures, Pathe Exchange, Inc.

Wolf's Clothing, 1926, Short Story
  Wolf's Clothing 1927 d: Roy Del Ruth. lps: Monte Blue, Patsy Ruth Miller, John Miljan. 7068f USA. prod/rel: Warner Brothers Pictures

ROCHE, DOMINIC
My Wife's Lodger, London 1951, Play
  My Wife's Lodger 1952 d: Maurice Elvey. lps: Dominic Roche, Olive Sloane, Leslie Dwyer. 80M UKN. prod/rel: Advance, Adelphi

ROCHE, HENRI-PIERRE
Deux Anglaises Et le Continent, 1956, Novel
  Deux Anglaises Et le Continent, Les 1971 d: Francois Truffaut. lps: Jean-Pierre Leaud, Kika Markham, Stacey Tendeter. 108M FRN. *Two English Girls* (USA); *Deux Anglaises, Les*; *Anne and Muriel* prod/rel: Films Du Carosse, Cinetel

Jules Et Jim, Paris 1953, Novel
  Jules Et Jim 1961 d: Francois Truffaut. lps: Jeanne Moreau, Oskar Werner, Henri Serre. 110M FRN. *Jules and Jim* (UKN) prod/rel: Films Du Carrosse, S.E.D.I.F.

ROCHEFORT, CHRISTIANE
Le Repos du Guerrier, Paris 1958, Novel
  Repos du Guerrier, Le 1962 d: Roger Vadim. lps: Brigitte Bardot, Robert Hossein, James Robertson Justice. 102M FRN/ITL. *Il Riposo Del Guerriero* (ITL); *Love on a Pillow* (USA); *Warrior's Rest* prod/rel: Francos Films, I.N.C.E.I. Film

Les Stances a Sophie, 1964, Novel
  Stances a Sophie, Les 1970 d: Moshe Mizrahi. lps: Bernadette Lafont, Bulle Ogier, Virginie Thevenet. 97M FRN/CND. *Sophie's Ways* (USA) prod/rel: Films De La Licorne, Saroy Films

ROCK, C. V.
Herr Borb Besitzt Under Vertrauen, Novel
  Kennwort: MacHin 1939 d: Erich Waschneck. lps: Paul Dahlke, Viktoria von Ballasko, Albert Hehn. 78M GRM. prod/rel: Universum, Nord-Westdeutscher

ROCK, PHILIP
The Steel Monster, Short Story
  Most Dangerous Man Alive, The 1961 d: Allan Dwan. lps: Ron Randell, Debra Paget, Elaine Stewart. 82M USA. *The Steel Monster* prod/rel: Trans-Global Films

ROCKEY, HOWARD P.
Li Ting Lang, Chinese Gentleman, 1916, Short Story
  Li Ting Lang 1920 d: Charles Swickard. lps: Sessue Hayakawa, Doris Pawn, Allan Forrest. 4700f USA. *Traditions Altar* prod/rel: Haworth Pictures Corp.©, Robertson-Cole Distributing Corp.

This Woman, New York 1924, Novel
  This Woman 1924 d: Phil Rosen. lps: Irene Rich, Ricardo Cortez, Louise FazendA. 6842f USA. prod/rel: Warner Brothers Pictures

ROCKFORT, DOROTHY
At the Point of a Gun, Story
  At the Point of a Gun 1919 d: Edward Kull. lps: Pete Morrison, Josephine Hill. 2r USA. prod/rel: Universal Film Mfg. Co.

ROCKWOOD, ROY
Bomba the Jungle Boy, Novel
  Bomba the Jungle Boy 1949 d: Ford Beebe. lps: Johnny Sheffield, Peggy Ann Garner, Onslow Stevens. 71M USA. prod/rel: Monogram

RODARI, GIANNI
La Freccia Azzurra, Novel
  Freccia Azzurra, La 1996 d: Enzo d'Alo. ANM. 97M ITL/SWT/LXM. *The Blue Arrow; The Toys Which Saved Christmas* prod/rel: Monipoly Prods., Lanterna Magica

RODA-RODA
Der Feldherrnhugel, Play
  Feldherrnhugel, Der 1926 d: Erich Schonfelder. lps: Harry Liedtke, Olga Tschechowa, Maria Minzenti. 2259m GRM/ITL. prod/rel: Greenbaum-Film
  Feldherrnhugel, Der 1953 d: Ernst MarischkA. lps: Paul Horbiger, Hans Holt, Gretl Schorg. 100M AUS. prod/rel: Vindobona

RODDY, LEE
In Search of Historic Jesus, Book
  In Search of Historic Jesus 1979 d: Henning Schellerup. lps: John Rubinstein, John Anderson, Nehemiah Persoff. 91M USA. prod/rel: Sunn Classics

RODE, ALFRED
Juanita, Short Story
  Gypsy Melody 1936 d: Edmond T. Greville. lps: Lupe Velez, Alfred Rode, Jerry Verno. 77M UKN. prod/rel: British Artistic, Wardour

RODEN, JOSEF
Irca V Hnizdecku, Novel
  Irca V Hnizdecku 1926 d: Vaclav Binovec. lps: Lexa Jarosin, Ruzena Hofmanova, Betty KysilkovA. CZC. *Irca in Her Little Nest* prod/rel: Weteb, Filmovy Zavody

Ircin Romanek, Novel
  Ircin Romanek I. 1921 d: Vaclav Binovec. lps: Suzanne Marwille, Lexa Jarosin, Bela HorskA. 1992m CZC. *Irca's Little Romance I.* prod/rel: Weteb, Iris-Film
  Ircin Romanek 1936 d: Karel Hasler. lps: Rolf Wanka, Jirina Steimarova, Theodor Pistek. 2511m CZC. *Irca's Romance* prod/rel: Meissner
  Flucht an Die Adria 1936 d: Eugen Schulz-Breiden. lps: Rolf Wanka, Roszi Czikos, Willi Volker. 1972m GRM/CZC. *Sprung Ins Gluck* prod/rel: Meissner

Ircin V Pensionate, Novel
  Ircin Romanek II. 1921 d: Vaclav Binovec. lps: Suzanne Marwille, Lexa Jarosin, Bela HorskA. 2267m CZC. *Irca V Pensionatu*; *Irca's Romance II.*; *Irca in a Boarding School* prod/rel: Weteb, Iris-Film

RODGERS, MARY
A Billion for Boris, Novel
  Billion for Boris, A 1990 d: Alex Grasshoff. lps: Scott Tiler, Mary Tanner, Seth Green. 91M USA. prod/rel: Comworld Pictures

Freaky Friday, Novel
  Freaky Friday 1976 d: Gary Nelson. lps: Jodie Foster, Barbara Harris, John Astin. 100M USA. prod/rel: Walt Disney

RODGERS, RICHARD (1902–1979), USA
Babes in Arms, New York 1937, Musical Play
  Babes in Arms 1939 d: Busby Berkeley. lps: Mickey Rooney, Judy Garland, Charles Winninger. 93M USA. prod/rel: Metro-Goldwyn-Mayer Corp.

Flower Drum Song, New York 1958, Musical Play
  Flower Drum Song 1961 d: Henry Koster. lps: Nancy Kwan, James Shigeta, Juanita Hall. 133M USA. prod/rel: Ross Hunter Productions, Fields Productions

RODGERS, RICHARD
Heads Up, New York 1929, Musical Play
  Heads Up 1930 d: Victor Schertzinger. lps: Charles "Buddy" Rogers, Victor Moore, Helen Kane. 6785f USA. prod/rel: Paramount-Publix Corp.

RODGERS, RICHARD (1902–1979), USA
King and I, The, Musical Play
  King and I, The 1999 d: Richard Rich. ANM. 87M USA. prod/rel: Warner Bros., Morgan Creek

RODGERS, RICHARD
The Melody Man, New York 1924, Musical Play
  Melody Man, The 1930 d: R. William Neill. lps: William Collier Jr., Alice Day, John St. Polis. 68M USA. prod/rel: Columbia Pictures

RODGERS, RICHARD (1902–1979), USA
On Your Toes, New York 1936, Musical Play
  On Your Toes 1939 d: Ray Enright. lps: Vera Zorina, Eddie Albert, Frank McHugh. 93M USA. prod/rel: Warner Bros. Pictures©, First National Picture

RODGERS, RICHARD
Present Arms, New York 1928, Musical Play
  Leathernecking 1930 d: Eddie Cline. lps: Irene Dunne, Ken Murray, Louise FazendA. 80M USA. *Present Arms* (UKN) prod/rel: RKO Productions

RODGERS, RICHARD (1902–1979), USA
The Sound of Music, New York 1959, Musical Play
  Sound of Music, The 1965 d: Robert Wise. lps: Julie Andrews, Christopher Plummer, Eleanor Parker. 174M USA. prod/rel: Argyle Enterprises

RODGERS, RICHARD
Spring Is Here, New York 1929, Musical Play
  Spring Is Here 1930 d: John Francis Dillon. lps: Lawrence Gray, Alexander Gray, Bernice Claire. 6386f USA. prod/rel: First National Pictures

RODGERS, RICHARD (1902–1979), USA
Too Many Girls, New York 1939, Musical Play
  Too Many Girls 1940 d: George Abbott. lps: Lucille Ball, Richard Carlson, Eddie Bracken. 85M USA. prod/rel: RKO Radio Pictures©

RODIO, APOLLONIO
Le Argonautiche, Novel
  Fatiche Di Ercole, Le 1957 d: Pietro Francisci. lps: Steve Reeves, Sylva Koscina, Mimmo PalmarA. 107M ITL. *Hercules* (UKN) prod/rel: Oscar Film, Galatea

RODMAN, DENNIS
Bad As I Wanna Be, Book
Bad As I Wanna Be: the Dennis Rodman Story
1998 d: Jean de Segonzac. lps: Dwayne Adway, John
Terry, Dee Wallace Stone. TVM. 120M USA. prod/rel:
Mandalay Television, Mandalay Sports Entertainment

RODNEY, COLONEL GEORGE B.
Frontier Justice, New York 1936, Novel
Frontier Justice 1935 d: Robert F. McGowan. lps:
Hoot Gibson, Jane Barnes, Richard Cramer. 58M USA.
prod/rel: Wafilms, Walter Futter Production

RODRIGUES, NELSON
Asfalto Selvagem, 1960, Novel
Engracadinha Depois Dos 30 1966 d: J. B. Tanko.
96M BRZ.

Asfalto Selvagem: Livro 2, Rio De Janeiro 1960,
Novel
Asfalto Selvagem 1964 d: J. B. Tanko. lps: Vera
Vianna, Jece Valadao, Maria Helena Dias. 96M BRZ.
Lollipop (USA); *Forbidden Love Affair* prod/rel:
Producoes Cin.Cas Herbert Richers

O Beijo No Asfalto, 1961, Play
Beijo, O 1965 d: Flavio Tambellini. 82M BRZ. *The Kiss*
Beijo No Asfalto, O 1981 d: Bruno Barreto. lps:
Tarcisio Meira, Ney Latorraca, Lidia Brondi. 90M BRZ.

Boca de Ouro, 1959-60, Play
Boca de Ouro, O 1962 d: Nelson Pereira Dos Santos.
lps: Odete Lara, Adriano Lisboa, Maria Pompeu. 103M
BRZ. prod/rel: Copacabana Filmes, Faama Film

Bonitinha, Mas Ordinaria, 1961, Play
Bonitinha, Mas Ordinaria 1963 d: J. P. de Carvalho.
lps: Jece Valadao, Odete Lara, Lia Rossi. 100M BRZ.
Pretty But Wicked (USA) prod/rel: Joffre Rodrigues, Jece
Valadao
Bonitinha, Mas Ordinaria 1981 d: Braz Chediak. lps:
Vera Fischer, Milton Moraes, Lucelia Santos. 103M
BRZ.

O Casamento, 1966, Novel
Casamento, O 1975 d: Arnaldo Jabor. lps: Nelson
Dantas, Camila Amado. 100M BRZ. *The Wedding*

A Falecida, 1953, Play
Falecida, A 1964 d: Leon Hirszman. lps: Fernanda
Montenegro, Ivan Candido, Vanda LacerdA. 98M BRZ.
The Dead Woman; *La Fallecida*

Meu Destino E Pecar, 1944, Novel
Meu Destino E Pecar 1952 d: Manuel Peluffo. 90M
BRZ.

Os Sete Gatinhos, 1958, Play
Sete Gatinhos, Os 1979 d: Neville d'AlmeidA. lps:
Thelma Reston. 95M BRZ.

Toda Nudez Sera Castigada, 1965-66, Play
Toda Nudez Sera Castigada 1973 d: Arnaldo Jabor.
lps: Paulo Porto, Darlene Gloria, Paulo Sacks. 102M
BRZ. *All Nudity Shall Be Punished* (USA); *All Nudity
Will Be Punished*; *Toda Desnudez Sera Castigada*

RODRIGUEZ FLORES, RICARDO
Carceleras, Opera
Carceleras 1922 d: Jose Buchs. lps: Elisa Ruiz Romero,
Jose Romeu, Jose Montenegro. 2170m SPN. *Convicts'
Song* prod/rel: Atlantida

ROE, E. P. (1838–1888), USA, Roe, Edward Payson
He Fell in Love With His Wife, New York 1886, Novel
He Fell in Love With His Wife 1916 d: William D.
Taylor. lps: Florence Rockwell, Forrest Stanley, Page
Peters. 5r USA. prod/rel: Bosworth, Inc., Pallas Pictures

ROE, EDWARD PAYSON
Barriers Burned Away, New York 1872, Novel
Barriers Burned Away 1925 d: W. S. Van Dyke. lps:
Mabel Ballin, Eric Mayne, Frank Mayo. 6474f USA. *The
Chicago Fire* (UKN) prod/rel: Encore Pictures,
Associated Exhibitors

ROE, VINGIE E.
The Alchemy of Love, 1918, Short Story
Twilight 1919 d: J. Searle Dawley. lps: Doris Kenyon,
Frank Mills, Sally Crute. 6r USA. prod/rel: de Luxe
Pictures, Inc., William L. Sherry Service

The Golden Tide, 1940, Novel
Perilous Journey, A 1953 d: R. G. Springsteen. lps:
Vera Ralston, David Brian, Scott Brady. 90M USA. *A
Perilous Voyage* prod/rel: Republic

The Heart of the Night Wind, New York 1913, Novel
Big Timber 1924 d: William James Craft. lps: William
Desmond, Olive Hasbrouck, Betty Francisco. 4650f
USA. prod/rel: Universal Pictures

A Phoenix of the Hills, Story
Her Idol 1915 d: Joseph Smiley. lps: Justina Huff, John
Smiley. SHT USA. prod/rel: Lubin

The Primal Lure: a Romance of Fort Lu Cerne,
New York 1914, Novel
Primal Lure, The 1916 d: William S. Hart. lps: William
S. Hart, Margery Wilson, Robert McKim. 5r USA. *The
Primal Law* prod/rel: New York Motion Picture Corp.,
Kay-Bee

The Splendid Road, New York 1925, Novel
Splendid Road, The 1925 d: Frank Lloyd. lps: Anna Q.
Nilsson, Robert Frazer, Lionel Barrymore. 7646f USA.
prod/rel: Frank Lloyd Productions, First National
Pictures

Tharon of Lost Valley, New York 1919, Novel
Crimson Challenge, The 1922 d: Paul Powell. lps:
Dorothy Dalton, Jack Mower, Frank Campeau. 4942f
USA. prod/rel: Famous Players-Lasky, Paramount
Pictures

Val of Paradise, New York 1921, Novel
North of the Rio Grande 1922 d: Rollin S. Sturgeon,
Joseph Henabery. lps: Jack Holt, Bebe Daniels, Charles
Ogle. 4770f USA. prod/rel: Famous Players-Lasky,
Paramount Pictures

Wild Honey, 1918, Short Story
Wild Honey 1918 d: Francis J. Grandon. lps: Doris
Kenyon, Frank Mills, Edgar Jones. 6r USA. prod/rel: de
Luxe Pictures, Inc., William L. Sherry Service

ROELFZEMA, ERIK HAZELHOFF
Soldaat Van Oranje, Autob
Soldaat Van Oranje 1977 d: Paul Verhoeven. lps:
Rutger Hauer, Jeroen Krabbe, Edward Fox. 165M NTH.
Survival Run (UKN); *Soldier of Orange* (USA)

ROELLINGHOFF, CHARLIE
Book
Weisse Sklaven 1936 d: Karl Anton. lps: Camilla Horn,
Werner Hinz, Agnes Straub. 106M GRM. *Panzerkreuzer
Sebastopol* prod/rel: Lloyd, E.F.U.

ROESSLER, CARL
Die Beiden Seehunde, Play
Beiden Seehunde, Die 1934 d: Fred Sauer. lps: Weiss
Ferdl, Fita Benkhoff, Baby Gray. 94M GRM. *Seine
Hoheit Der Dienstmann* prod/rel: Euphono

ROFFEY, JACK
Hostile Witness, Play
Hostile Witness 1968 d: Ray Milland. lps: Ray Milland,
Sylvia Syms, Felix Aylmer. 101M UKN. prod/rel: United
Artists, Caralan

ROGER
Les Vingt-Huit Jours de Clairette, Opera
Vingt-Huit Jours de Clairette, Les 1933 d: Andre
Hugon. lps: Mireille, Janine Guise, Armand Bernard.
98M FRN. prod/rel: Hugon-Films,
Gaumont-Franco-Film-Aubert

ROGER, GREGORY
Hogan's Alley, Story
Hogan's Alley 1925 d: Roy Del Ruth. lps: Monte Blue,
Patsy Ruth Miller, Willard Louis. 6875f USA. prod/rel:
Warner Brothers Pictures

ROGERS, BETTY BLAKE
Uncle Clem's Boy, 1941, Book
Story of Will Rogers, The 1952 d: Michael Curtiz. lps:
Will Rogers Jr., Jane Wyman, James Gleason. 109M
USA. prod/rel: Warner Bros.

ROGERS, GREGORY
Public Enemy No. 1, Novel
G-Men 1935 d: William Keighley. lps: James Cagney,
Ann Dvorak, Margaret Lindsay. 85M USA. *The Farrell
Case* prod/rel: First National Productions Co., First
National Pictures©

ROGERS, MERRILL
Her First Affaire, London 1930, Play
Her First Affaire 1932 d: Allan Dwan. lps: Ida Lupino,
George Curzon, Diana Napier. 72M UKN. prod/rel: St.
George's Productions, Sterling

ROGERS, THOMAS
The Pursuit of Happiness, Novel
Pursuit of Happiness, The 1971 d: Robert Mulligan.
lps: Michael Sarrazin, Barbara Hershey, Robert Klein.
94M USA. prod/rel: Film-Norton Simon, Columbia

ROGGE, BERNHARD
Schiff 16, Book
Sotto Dieci Bandiere 1960 d: Duilio Coletti, Silvio
Narizzano. lps: Van Heflin, Charles Laughton, Mylene
Demongeot. 112M ITL/UKN/USA. *Under Ten Flags*
(UKN) prod/rel: Dino de Laurentiis Cin.Ca

ROGGER, LOUIS LUCIEN
A Halalkabin, Budapest 1934, Novel
Princess Comes Across 1936 d: William K. Howard.
lps: Carole Lombard, Fred MacMurray, Douglas
Dumbrille. 76M USA. *Concertina* prod/rel: Paramount
Productions©

ROHAN, CRIENA
The Delinquents, Novel
Delinquents, The 1989 d: Chris Thomson. lps: Kylie
Minogue, Charlie Schlatter, Angela Punch-McGregor.
101M ASL. prod/rel: Cutler-Wilcox, Village Roadshow
Corp. Ltd.©

ROHAN, VLADIMIR
Na Ty Louce Zeleny, Opera
Na Ty Louce Zeleny 1936 d: Carl Lamac. lps: Carl
Lamac, Helena Busova, Jara Kohout. 2391m CZC. *On
the Green Meadow* prod/rel: Elekta

Parizanka, Opera
Slecna Matinka 1938 d: Vladimir Slavinsky. lps: Vera
Ferbasova, Stanislav Strnad, Theodor Pistek. 2832m
CZC. *Miss Mother* prod/rel: Lucernafilm

ROHLFS, ANNA KATHARINE GREEN
The Millionaire Baby, Indianapolis 1905, Novel
Millionaire Baby, The 1915 d: Lawrence Marston.
lps: Harry Mestayer, John Charles, Grace Darmond. 6r
USA. prod/rel: Selig Polyscope Co.©, Red Seal Play

ROHMER, ERIC (1920–, FRN, Scherer, Jean-Marie
Maurice
L'amour, l'Apres-Midi, 1974, Short Story
Amour l'Apres-Midi, L' 1972 d: Eric Rohmer. lps:
Bernard Verley, Zouzou, Francoise Verley. 97M FRN.
Love in the Afternoon (UKN); *Chloe in the Afternoon*
(USA) prod/rel: Les Films Du Losange, Barbet
Schroeder

La Boulangere de Monceau, 1974, Short Story
Boulangere de Monceau, La 1962 d: Eric Rohmer.
lps: Barbet Schoeder, Michele Girardon, Claudine
Soubrier. 47M FRN.

La Carriere de Suzanne, 1974, Short Story
Carriere de Suzanne, La 1963 d: Eric Rohmer. lps:
Catherine See, Philippe Beuzen, Christian Charriere.
60M FRN. *Suzanne's Profession*

La Collectionneuse, 1974, Short Story
Collectionneuse, La 1967 d: Eric Rohmer. lps: Patrick
Bauchau, Haydee Politoff, Daniel Pommereulle. 90M
FRN. *Collector, The* (USA) prod/rel: Films Du Losange,
Rome-Paris Films

Le Genou de Claire, 1974, Short Story
Genou de Claire, Le 1970 d: Eric Rohmer. lps:
Jean-Claude Brialy, Beatrice Romand, Aurora Cornu.
110M FRN. *Claire's Knee* (UKN) prod/rel: Films Du
Losange, Pierre Cottrell

Ma Nuit Chez Maud, 1974, Short Story
Ma Nuit Chez Maud 1969 d: Eric Rohmer. lps:
Francoise Fabian, Jean-Louis Trintignant,
Marie-Christine Barrault. 110M FRN. *My Night With
Maud* (UKN); *My Night at Maud's* (USA) prod/rel:
Films Du Losange, F.F.D.

ROHMER, SAX (1883–1959), UKN, Ward, Arthur
Sarsfield
Short Story
Further Mysteries of Dr. Fu Manchu, The 1924 d:
Fred Paul. lps: H. Agar Lyons, Fred Paul, Dorinea
Shirley. SHS. UKN. prod/rel: Stoll
Story
Mysterious Dr. Fu Manchu, The 1929 d: Rowland V.
Lee. lps: Warner Oland, Jean Arthur, Neil Hamilton.
7663f USA. prod/rel: Paramount Famous Lasky Corp.
Novel
Face of Fu Manchu, The 1965 d: Don Sharp. lps:
Christopher Lee, Nigel Green, Joachim Fuchsberger.
94M UKN. *The Mask of Fu Manchu* prod/rel:
Anglo-Emi, Hallam

Aaron's Rod, Short Story
Aaron's Rod 1923 d: A. E. Coleby. lps: H. Agar Lyons,
Fred Paul, Joan Clarkson. 1862f UKN. prod/rel: Stoll

The Cafe l'Egypte, Short Story
Cafe l'Egypte, The 1924 d: Fred Paul. lps: H. Agar
Lyons, Fred Paul, Dorinea Shirley. 2270f UKN. *The
Cafe de l'Egypte* prod/rel: Stoll

The Call of Siva, Short Story
Call of Siva, The 1923 d: A. E. Coleby. lps: H. Agar
Lyons, Fred Paul, Joan Clarkson. 1700f UKN. prod/rel:
Stoll

The Clue of the Pigtail, Short Story
Clue of the Pigtail, The 1923 d: A. E. Coleby. lps: H.
Agar Lyons, Fred Paul, Joan Clarkson. 1700f UKN.
prod/rel: Stoll

The Coughing Horror, Short Story
Coughing Horror, The 1924 d: Fred Paul. lps: H. Agar
Lyons, Fred Paul, Dorinea Shirley. 1800f UKN.
prod/rel: Stoll

Cragmire Tower, Short Story
Cragmire Tower 1924 d: Fred Paul. lps: H. Agar
Lyons, Fred Paul, Dorinea Shirley. 2040f UKN.
prod/rel: Stoll

The Cry of the Nighthawk, Short Story
Cry of the Nighthawk, The 1923 d: A. E. Coleby. lps: H. Agar Lyons, Fred Paul, Joan Clarkson. 1773f UKN. prod/rel: Stoll

Daughter of Fu Manchu, New York 1931, Novel
Daughter of the Dragon 1931 d: Lloyd Corrigan. lps: Warner Oland, Anna May Wong, Sessue HayakawA. 79M USA. prod/rel: Paramount Publix Corp.

The Fiery Hand, Short Story
Fiery Hand, The 1923 d: A. E. Coleby. lps: H. Agar Lyons, Fred Paul, Joan Clarkson. 2174f UKN. prod/rel: Stoll

The Fungi Cellars, Short Story
Fungi Cellars, The 1923 d: A. E. Coleby. lps: H. Agar Lyons, Fred Paul, Joan Clarkson. 1630f UKN. prod/rel: Stoll

The Golden Pomegranates, Short Story
Golden Pomegranates, The 1924 d: Fred Paul. lps: H. Agar Lyons, Fred Paul, Dorinea Shirley. 2100f UKN. prod/rel: Stoll

The Green Mist, Short Story
Green Mist, The 1924 d: Fred Paul. lps: H. Agar Lyons, Fred Paul, Dorinea Shirley. 1734f UKN. prod/rel: Stoll

Greywater Park, Short Story
Greywater Park 1924 d: Fred Paul. lps: H. Agar Lyons, Fred Paul, Dorinea Shirley. 2390f UKN. prod/rel: Stoll

Karamaneh, Short Story
Karamaneh 1924 d: Fred Paul. lps: H. Agar Lyons, Fred Paul, Dorinea Shirley. 2366f UKN. prod/rel: Stoll

The Knocking on the Door, Short Story
Knocking on the Door, The 1923 d: A. E. Coleby. lps: H. Agar Lyons, Fred Paul, Joan Clarkson. 2228f UKN. prod/rel: Stoll

The Man with the Limp, Short Story
Man With the Limp, The 1923 d: A. E. Coleby. lps: H. Agar Lyons, Fred Paul, Joan Clarkson. 2000f UKN. prod/rel: Stoll

The Mask of Fu Manchu, New York 1932, Novel
Mask of Fu Manchu, The 1932 d: Charles J. Brabin, Charles Vidor (Uncredited). lps: Boris Karloff, Lewis Stone, Karen Morley. 72M USA. prod/rel: Metro-Goldwyn-Mayer Corp., Metro-Goldwyn-Mayer Dist. Corp.©

The Midnight Summons, Short Story
Midnight Summons, The 1924 d: Fred Paul. lps: H. Agar Lyons, Fred Paul, Dorinea Shirley. 1791f UKN. prod/rel: Stoll

The Miracle, Short Story
Miracle, The 1923 d: A. E. Coleby. lps: H. Agar Lyons, Fred Paul, Joan Clarkson. 1712f UKN. prod/rel: Stoll

The Queen of Hearts, Short Story
Queen of Hearts, The 1923 d: A. E. Coleby. lps: H. Agar Lyons, Fred Paul, Joan Clarkson. 1750f UKN. prod/rel: Stoll

The Return of Dr. Fu Manchu, New York 1916, Novel
Return of Dr. Fu Manchu, The 1930 d: Rowland V. Lee. lps: Warner Oland, Neil Hamilton, Jean Arthur. 6586f USA. *The New Adventures of Dr. Fu Manchu; The Insidious Dr. Fu Manchu* prod/rel: Paramount-Publix Corp.

The Sacred Order, Short Story
Sacred Order, The 1923 d: A. E. Coleby. lps: H. Agar Lyons, Fred Paul, Joan Clarkson. 1700f UKN. prod/rel: Stoll

The Scented Envelopes, Short Story
Scented Envelopes, The 1923 d: A. E. Coleby. lps: H. Agar Lyons, Fred Paul, Joan Clarkson. 2400f UKN. prod/rel: Stoll

The Shrine of the Seven Lamps, Short Story
Shrine of the Seven Lamps, The 1923 d: A. E. Coleby. lps: H. Agar Lyons, Fred Paul, Joan Clarkson. 1500f UKN. prod/rel: Stoll

The Silver Buddha, Short Story
Silver Buddha, The 1923 d: A. E. Coleby. lps: H. Agar Lyons, Fred Paul, Joan Clarkson. 1570f UKN. prod/rel: Stoll

Sumuru, Novel
Sumuru 1967 d: Lindsay Shonteff. lps: Frankie Avalon, George Nader, Shirley Eaton. 95M UKN. *The 1,000,000 Eyes of Sumuru* (USA); *The Million Eyes of Su-Muru* prod/rel: Anglo-Amalgamated, Sumuru

The West Case, Short Story
West Case, The 1923 d: A. E. Coleby. lps: H. Agar Lyons, Fred Paul, Joan Clarkson. 1800f UKN. prod/rel: Stoll

The Yellow Claw, Novel
Yellow Claw, The 1920 d: Rene Plaissetty. lps: Kitty Fielder, Norman Page, Harvey Braban. 6029f UKN. prod/rel: Stoll

ROHN, NICOLA
Der Fuchs von Glenarvon, Novel
Fuchs von Glenarvon, Der 1940 d: Max W. Kimmich. lps: Olga Tschechowa, Carl Ludwig Diehl, Ferdinand Marian. 91M GRM. prod/rel: Tobis

ROHR, JOHANNES
Die Vom Berghof, Novel
Hammarforsens Brus 1948 d: Ragnar Frisk. lps: Inge Landgre, Peter Lindgren, Arnold Sjostrand. 77M SWD. *The Roar of Hammer Rapids* prod/rel: Kungsfilm

ROIPKE, ANNE RICHARDSON
Up the Sandbox, Novel
Up the Sandbox 1972 d: Irvin Kershner. lps: Barbra Streisand, David Selby, Ariane Heller. 98M USA. prod/rel: First Artists, Barwood

ROJAS GONZALEZ, FRANCISCO
Story
Raices 1953 d: Benito Alazraki. lps: Beatriz Flores, Juan de La Cruz, Antonia Hernandez. 103M MXC. *Roots* prod/rel: Tele-Producciones

ROKA, TOKUTOMI
Buru Gui, Novel
Buru Gui 1926 d: Yang XIaozhong. lps: Wang Fuqing, Shen Huaying, Yang XIaozhang's Mother. 9r CHN. *Better Go Home* prod/rel: Commercial Press Motion Picture Section

ROLIN, DOMINIQUE
Le Lit, Novel
Lit, Le 1982 d: Marion Hansel. lps: Natasha Parry, Heinz Bennent, Francine Blistin. 76M BLG/SWT. *The Bed* prod/rel: Man's Film, Jean-Marc Anchoz

Quai Notre-Dame, Short Story
Quai Notre-Dame 1960 d: Jacques Berthier. lps: Anouk Aimee, Jacques Dacqmine, Christian Pezey. 87M FRN. *Temps d'un Reflet, Le; Eloi* prod/rel: Eloi Films, Gaumont Actualites

ROLLAND, CL.
La Ruse, Play
Ruse, La 1921 d: Edouard-Emile Violet. lps: E. B. Donatien, Marsa Renhardt, Mag Murray. 1455m FRN. prod/rel: Films Lucifer

ROLLAND, CLAUDE
Les Francs-MacOns, Play
Francs-MacOns 1914. lps: Rene Grehan, Vandenne. 835m FRN. prod/rel: Mondial Film

Rien Que Des Mensonges 1932 d: Karl Anton. lps: Robert Burnier, Marguerite Moreno, Jackie Monnier. 84M FRN. *Trois Points C'est Tout; Francs-MacOns; Le Cercle Vicieux* prod/rel: Films Paramount

ROLLAND, ROMAIN (1866-1944), FRN
Pierre Et Luce, 1920, Novel
Mata Au Hi Made 1950 d: Tadashi Imai. lps: Eiji Okada, Osamu Takizawa, Akitake Kono. 111M JPN. *Until the Day We Meet Again; Until We Meet Again* prod/rel: Toho Co.

ROLLENS, JACK
The Tenderfoot, Story
Roaring Adventure, A 1925 d: Cliff Smith. lps: Jack Hoxie, Mary McAllister, Marin Sais. 4800f USA. prod/rel: Universal Pictures

ROLLIN, BETTY (1936–, USA
First You Cry, 1976, Book
First You Cry 1978 d: George Schaefer. lps: Mary Tyler Moore, Anthony Perkins, Richard CrennA. TVM. 100M USA. prod/rel: CBS, Mtm Productions

ROMAINS, JULES (1885-1972), FRN, Farigoule, Louis
Les Copains, 1913, Novel
Copains, Les 1964 d: Yves Robert. lps: Philippe Noiret, Pierre Mondy, Jacques Balutin. 95M FRN. prod/rel: Films de la Gueville

Donogoo, Novel
Donogoo 1936 d: Henri Chomette, Reinhold Schunzel. lps: Raymond Rouleau, Renee Saint-Cyr, Adrien Le Gallo. 89M FRN. prod/rel: U.F.a., a.C.E.

Donogoo-Tonka, Ou Les Miracles la Science, 1920, Short Story
Donogoo Tonka 1936 d: Reinhold Schunzel. lps: Anny Ondra, Viktor Staal, Will Dohm. 100M GRM. *Donogoo Tonka, Die Geheimnisvolle Stadt*

Knock, Ou le Triomphe de la Medecine, 1924, Play
Knock, Ou le Triomphe de la Medecine 1925 d: Rene Hervil. lps: Fernand Fabre, Luce Fabiole, Leon Malavier. 2700m FRN. *Knock* prod/rel: Film d'Art (Vandal Et Delac)

Knock, Ou le Triomphe de la Medecine 1933 d: Louis Jouvet, Roger Goupillieres. lps: Louis Jouvet, Madeleine Ozeray, Robert Le Vigan. 95M FRN. prod/rel: Productions Georges Marret

Knock 1950 d: Guy Lefranc. lps: Louis Jouvet, Jean Brochard, Jane Marken. 98M FRN. *Dr. Knock* (USA) prod/rel: Jacques Roitfeld

Ana Al Doctor 1968 d: Abbas Kamel. lps: Nelly, Farid Shawqi, Mohamed RedA. 100M EGY. *I. the Doctor; I Am the Doctor*

ROMAN, ERIC
After the Trial, Novel
Death Sentence 1975 d: E. W. Swackhamer. lps: Cloris Leachman, Laurence Luckinbill, Nick Nolte. TVM. 78M USA. prod/rel: Spelling-Goldberg Productions

ROMAN, LAWRENCE
Under the Yum Yum Tree, New York 1960, Play
Under the Yum Yum Tree 1963 d: David Swift. lps: Jack Lemmon, Carol Lynley, Dean Jones. 110M USA. prod/rel: Sonnis-Swift Productions

ROMANI, FELICE
L'elisir d'Amore, Opera
Elisir d'Amore, L' 1941 d: Amleto Palermi. lps: Armando Falconi, Margherita Carosio, Roberto VillA. 85M ITL. *Elixir of Love, The* prod/rel: Fono Roma, Lux Film

Norma, 1831, Opera
Norma (Episodio Della Gallia Sotto Il Dominio Di Roma Imperiale) 1911 d: Romolo Bacchini. 332m ITL. prod/rel: Vesuvio Films

Norma, La 1911. lps: Rina Agozzino-Alessio, Bianca Lorenzoni, Alfredo Robert. 267m ITL. *Norma* (UKN) prod/rel: Film d'Arte Italiana

ROMBERG, SIGMUND (1887–1951), HNG
Children of Dreams, 1930, Musical Play
Children of Dreams 1931 d: Alan Crosland. lps: Paul Gregory, Margaret Schilling, Tom PatricolA. 78M USA. prod/rel: Warner Bros. Pictures, Inc.

The Desert Song, New York 1926, Musical Play
Desert Song, The 1929 d: Roy Del Ruth. lps: John Boles, Carlotta King, Louise FazendA. 106M USA. prod/rel: Warner Brothers Pictures

Desert Song, The 1943 d: Robert Florey. lps: Dennis Morgan, Irene Manning, Bruce Cabot. 96M USA. prod/rel: Warner Bros.

Desert Song, The 1953 d: H. Bruce Humberstone. lps: Kathryn Grayson, Gordon MacRae, Steve Cochran. 110M USA. prod/rel: Warner Bros.

New Moon, New York 1928, Mplay
New Moon 1931 d: Jack Conway. lps: Lawrence Tibbett, Grace Moore, Adolphe Menjou. 85M USA. prod/rel: Metro-Goldwyn-Mayer Corp., Metro-Goldwyn-Mayer Dist. Corp.©

New Moon, New York 1928, Musical Play
New Moon 1940 d: Robert Z. Leonard. lps: Jeanette MacDonald, Nelson Eddy, Mary Boland. 105M USA. *Lover Come Back; Parisian Belle* prod/rel: Metro-Goldwyn-Mayer Corp., Loew's, Inc.©

Up in Central Park, New York 1945, Musical Play
Up in Central Park 1948 d: William A. Seiter. lps: Deanna Durbin, Dick Haymes, Vincent Price. 88M USA. prod/rel: Universal-International

ROME, ANTHONY
Lady in Cement, New York 1960, Novel
Lady in Cement 1968 d: Gordon Douglas. lps: Frank Sinatra, Raquel Welch, Richard Conte. 94M USA. prod/rel: Arcola-Millfield Productions

Miami Mayhem, New York 1960, Novel
Tony Rome 1967 d: Gordon Douglas. lps: Frank Sinatra, Jill St. John, Richard Conte. 110M USA. prod/rel: Arcola-Millfield Productions

ROMERO, JOSE RUBEN
Rosenda, 1946, Novel
Rosenda 1948 d: Julio Bracho. lps: Fernando Soler, Rita MacEdo, Nicolas Rodriguez. 103M MXC.

ROMILLY, MME.
Les Hommes de la Cote, Short Story
Hommes de la Cote, Les 1934 d: Andre Pellenc. lps: Aime Simon-Gerard, Pierrette Caillol, Robert Pizani. 69M FRN.

ROMUALDI, GIUSEPPE
Il Piccole Re, Play
Piccole Re, Il 1940 d: Redo Romagnoli. lps: Evi Maltagliati, Egisto Olivieri, Liliana de Mirtis. 70M ITL. prod/rel: Venus Film, Generalcine

L'ultima Carta, Play
Ultima Carta, L' 1939 d: Piero Ballerini. lps: Enzo Biliotti, Isabella Riva, Anna ValpredA. 81M ITL. prod/rel: Comoedia Film

RON, ZDENEK
Vrah, Short Story
Kainovo Znameni 1928 d: Oldrich Kminek. lps: Vaclav Norman, Josef Svab-Malostransky, Antonie NedosinskA. 1901m CZC. *The Mark of Cain; Ve Sparech Hrisne Zeny; In the Clutches of a Sinful Woman* prod/rel: Interfilm

RONALD, JAMES
Death Croons the Blues, Novel
Death Croons the Blues 1937 d: David MacDonald. lps: Hugh Wakefield, Antoinette Cellier, George Hayes. 74M UKN. prod/rel: St. Margarets, MGM

Medal for the General, Novel
Medal for the General 1944 d: Maurice Elvey. lps: Godfrey Tearle, Jeanne de Casalis, Morland Graham. 99M UKN. *The Gay Intruders* (USA) prod/rel: British National, Anglo-American

Murder in the Family, Novel
Murder in the Family 1938 d: Albert Parker. lps: Barry Jones, Jessica Tandy, Evelyn Ankers. 75M UKN. prod/rel: Fox British

The Suspect, Novel
Suspect, The 1944 d: Robert Siodmak. lps: Charles Laughton, Ella Raines, Dean Harens. 85M USA. prod/rel: Universal

They Can't Hang Me, New York 1938, Novel
Witness Vanishes, The 1939 d: Otis Garrett. lps: Edmund Lowe, Wendy Barrie, Bruce Lester. 66M USA. *They Can't Hang Me*; *Eyes of Scotland Yard*; *Escape to London* prod/rel: Crime Club Productions, Universal Pictures Co.©

RONALD, LANDON
Little Miss Nobody, London 1898, Musical Play
Little Miss Nobody 1923 d: Wilfred Noy. lps: Flora Le Breton, John Stuart, Ben Field. 5750f UKN. prod/rel: Carlton Productions, Butcher's Film Service

RONASZEGI, MIKLOS
Kismaszat Es a Gezenguzok, Novel
Kismaszat Es a Gezenguzok 1985 d: Miklos Markos. lps: Zsofi Javor, Sandor Palok, Gabor Csore. 73M HNG.

RONCALLI, ANGELO
John XXiii, Il Giornale Dell'Anima E Altri Scritti Di Pieta, Roma 1964, Book
E Venne un Uomo 1964 d: Ermanno Olmi. lps: Rod Steiger, Adolfo Celi, Rita Bertocchi. 90M ITL. *A Man Named John* (UKN); *And There Came a Man* prod/rel: Majestic, Sol Produzione (Milano)

RONDI, BRUNELLO
Amanti, Play
Amanti 1968 d: Vittorio de SicA. lps: Faye Dunaway, Marcello Mastroianni, Caroline Mortimer. 88M ITL/FRN. *Temps Des Amants, Le* (FRN); *Place for Lovers, A* (USA); *Lovers* prod/rel: C.C. Champion (Roma), Les Films Concordia (Paris)

RON-FEDER, GALILA
Story
B'chinat Bagrut 1983 d: Assaf Dayan. lps: Dan Toren, Irit Frank, Ariella Rabinovich. F ISR. *Final Exams*

El Atzmi, Book
El Atzmi 1988 d: Tamir Paul. lps: Arik Ohana, Tchiya Danon, Roy Bar-Natan. 96M ISR. *On My Own*

Nadia, Book
Nadia 1986 d: Amnon Rubinstein. lps: Hannah Azoulai-Hasfari, Yuval Banai, Meir Banai. F ISR.

RONNS, EDWARD
State Department Murders, New York 1950, Novel
Dead to the World 1960 d: Nicholas Webster. lps: Reedy Talton, Jana Pearce, Ford Rainey. 87M USA.

ROOK, DAVID
The Ballad of the Belstone Fox, Novel
Belstone Fox, The 1973 d: James Hill. lps: Eric Porter, Rachel Roberts, Bill Travers. 103M UKN. *Free Spirit* (USA) prod/rel: Rank, Independent Artists

The White Colt, New York 1967, Novel
Run Wild, Run Free 1969 d: Richard C. Sarafian. lps: John Mills, Mark Lester, Sylvia Syms. 98M UKN. *Philip*; *The White Colt* prod/rel: Irving Allen, Ltd., Columbia

ROONEY, FRANK
The Cyclist's Raid, 1951, Short Story
Wild One, The 1953 d: Laslo Benedek. lps: Marlon Brando, Mary Murphy, Robert Keith. 79M USA. *Hot Blood* prod/rel: Columbia

ROONEY, PHILIP
Captain Boycott, Novel
Captain Boycott 1947 d: Frank Launder. lps: Stewart Granger, Kathleen Ryan, Cecil Parker. 93M UKN. prod/rel: General Film Distributors, Individual

ROOS, KELLEY
Dead Men Tell No Tales, Novel
Dead Men Tell No Tales 1971 d: Walter Grauman. lps: Christopher George, Judy Carne, Patricia Barry. TVM. 73M USA. *To Save His Life* prod/rel: 20th Century-Fox

Valse Blonde, Novel
Voulez-Vous Danser Avec Moi? 1960 d: Michel Boisrond. lps: Brigitte Bardot, Henri Vidal, Dawn Addams. 91M FRN/ITL. *Sexy Girl* (ITL); *Come Dance With Me* (USA) prod/rel: Francos Films, Vides

ROOT, LYNN
Cabin in the Sky, Musical Play
Cabin in the Sky 1942 d: Vincente Minnelli. lps: Ethel Waters, Eddie "Rochester" Anderson, Lena Horne. 100M USA. prod/rel: Metro-Goldwyn-Mayer Corp.

The Milky Way, New York 1934, Play
Kid from Brooklyn, The 1946 d: Norman Z. McLeod. lps: Danny Kaye, Virginia Mayo, Vera-Ellen. 114M USA. prod/rel: Samuel Goldwyn, RKO

Milky Way, The 1936 d: Leo McCarey. lps: Harold Lloyd, Adolphe Menjou, Verree Teasdale. 85M USA. prod/rel: Paramount Productions©

ROOT, WELLS
As You are, Play
Turned Out Nice Again 1941 d: Marcel Varnel. lps: George Formby, Peggy Bryan, Edward Chapman. 81M UKN. prod/rel: Associated Talking Pictures, Ealing Studios

ROOTHAERT, A.
Doctor Vlimmen, Novel
Tierarzt Dr. Vlimmen 1944 d: Boleslav Barlog. lps: Albert Florath, Gustav Knuth, Gunther Luders. 90M GRM. *Dr. Vlimmen, Vet*

Tierarzt Dr. Vlimmen 1956 d: Arthur M. Rabenalt. lps: Bernhard Wicki, Heidemarie Hatheyer, Wolfgang Lukschy. 104M GRM. *Skandal Um Dr. Vlimmen* prod/rel: Real, Rank

Doctor Vlimmen 1976 d: Guido Pieters. lps: Peter Faber, Roger Van Hool, Chris Lomme. 111M NTH/BLG. prod/rel: Cinecentrum, Cine-Ma

Skandal Um Dr. Vlimmen 1956 d: Arthur M. Rabenalt. lps: Bernhard Wicki, Heidemarie Hatheyer, Wolfgang Lukschy. 104M GRM. *Tierarzt Dr. Vlimmen*

ROPER, TONY
The Steamie, Play
Steamie, The 1989 d: Haldane Duncan. lps: Eileen McCallum, Dorothy Paul, Kate Murphy. 85M UKN.

ROPES, BRADFORD
42nd Street, New York 1932, Novel
42nd Street 1933 d: Lloyd Bacon. lps: Warner Baxter, Ruby Keeler, George Brent. 89M USA. *Forty-Second Street* prod/rel: Warner Bros. Pictures©

Go Into Your Dance, New York 1934, Novel
Go Into Your Dance 1935 d: Archie Mayo, Robert Florey (Uncredited). lps: Al Jolson, Ruby Keeler, Glenda Farrell. 97M USA. *Casino de Paree* (UKN) prod/rel: First National Productions Corp., First National Pictures©

Stage Mother, New York 1933, Novel
Stage Mother 1933 d: Charles J. Brabin. lps: Alice Brady, Maureen O'Sullivan, Ted Healy. 87M USA. prod/rel: Metro-Goldwyn-Mayer Corp.©

ROPS, DANIEL
Mort, Ou Est Ta Victoire?, Novel
Mort, Ou Est Ta Victoire? 1962 d: Herve Bromberger. lps: Pascale Audret, Michel Auclair, Laurent Terzieff. 133M FRN. prod/rel: Filmel

ROQUES, RENE
Porte d'Orient, Novel
Porte d'Orient 1950 d: Jacques Daroy. lps: Tilda Thamar, Nathalie Nattier, Yves Vincent. 100M FRN. prod/rel: Protis Films

RORICK, ISABEL SCOTT
Mr. and Mrs. Cugat, Novel
Are Husbands Necessary? 1942 d: Norman Taurog. lps: Ray Milland, Betty Field, Patricia Morison. 79M USA. *Mr. and Mrs. Cugat* prod/rel: Paramount

ROSA, GUIMARAES
Grande Sertao: Veredas, 1956, Novel
Grande Sertao 1964 d: Geraldo Santos Pereira, Renato Santos PereirA. 90M BRZ.

A Hora E Vez de Augusto Matraga, 1946, Short Story
Hora E Vez de Augusto Matraga, A 1965 d: Roberto Santos. lps: Leonardo Villar. 105M BRZ. *The Time and Hour of Augusto Matraga*; *Matraga*; *The Hour and Turn of Augusto Matraga*; *La Hora Y El Momento de Augusto Matraga*

ROSE, ALEXANDER
Four Horse-Players are Missing, New York 1960, Novel
Who's Got the Action? 1962 d: Daniel Mann. lps: Dean Martin, Lana Turner, Eddie Albert. 93M USA. prod/rel: Amro Productions, Claude Productions

ROSE, ANNA PERROTT
Room for One More, 1950, Novel
Room for One More 1952 d: Norman Taurog. lps: Cary Grant, Betsy Drake, Lurene Tuttle. 98M USA. *The Easy Way* prod/rel: Warner Bros.

ROSE, BILLY
That Old Gang of Mine, 1923, Song
That Old Gang of Mine 1925 d: May Tully. lps: MacLyn Arbuckle, Brooke Johns, Tommy Brown. 5r USA. prod/rel: Kerman Films

ROSE, EDWARD E.
Fighting Bob, Book
Fighting Bob 1915 d: John W. Noble. lps: Orrin Johnson, Olive Wyndham, Edward Brenon. prod/rel: Rolfe Photoplays Inc., Metro Pictures Corp.©

The Rear Car, Play
Red Lights 1923 d: Clarence Badger. lps: Marie Prevost, Raymond Griffith, Johnny Walker. prod/rel: Goldwyn Pictures, Goldwyn-Cosmopolitan Distributing Corp.

The Rear Car, Los Angeles 1922, Play
Murder in the Private Car 1934 d: Harry Beaumont. lps: Russell Hardie, Charles Ruggles, Mary Carlisle. 65M USA. *Murder on the Runaway Train* (UKN); *Murder on the Runaway Car*; *The Rear Car*; *Clear the Track* prod/rel: Metro-Goldwyn-Mayer Corp.©

The Rosary, New York 1910, Play
Her Rosary 1913 d: Oscar Apfel. lps: Rosemary Theby, Irving Cummings, Irene Hawley. SHT USA. prod/rel: Reliance

Rosary, The 1915 d: Colin Campbell. lps: Kathlyn Williams, Wheeler Oakman, Charles Clary. 7r USA. prod/rel: Selig Polyscope Co.©, V-L-S-E, Inc.

Rosary, The 1922 d: Jerome Storm. lps: Lewis Stone, Jane Novak, Wallace Beery. 7045f USA. *Romance of the Rosary, The* prod/rel: Selig-Rork Productions, Associated First National Pictures

Turn Back the Hours, Hoboken, N.J. 1917, Play
Turn Back the Hours 1928 d: Howard Bretherton. lps: Myrna Loy, Walter Pidgeon, Sam Hardy. 6500f USA. *The Badge of Courage* prod/rel: Gotham Productions, Lumas Film Corp.

ROSE, FELICITAS
Heideschulmeister Uwe Karsten, Novel
Heideschulmeister Uwe Karsten 1933 d: Carl Heinz Wolff. lps: Paul Henckels, Marianne Hoppe, Brigitte Horney. 94M GRM. *Schoolmaster Karsten*

Heideschulmeister Uwe Karsten 1954 d: Hans Deppe. lps: Barbara Rutting, Katharina Mayberg, Claus Holm. 96M GRM. *Schoolmaster Karsten* prod/rel: H.D. Film, N.F.

ROSE, LOUIS
Me and My Girl, London 1937, Musical Play
Lambeth Walk, The 1939 d: Albert de Courville. lps: Lupino Lane, Sally Gray, Seymour Hicks. 84M UKN. prod/rel: C.a.P.a.D, Pinebrook

ROSE, REGINALD
Story
Stranger on the Run 1967 d: Don Siegel. lps: Henry Fonda, Anne Baxter, Michael Parks. TVM. 100M USA. prod/rel: Universal

12 Angry Men, 1955, Television Play
Twelve Angry Men 1957 d: Sidney Lumet. lps: Henry Fonda, Lee J. Cobb, Ed Begley. 95M USA. *12 Angry Men* prod/rel: United Artists, Orion Prods.

12 Angry Men 1997 d: William Friedkin. lps: Courtney B. Vance, Ossie Davis, George C. Scott. TVM. 120M USA. *Twelve Angry Men* prod/rel: Showtime, MGM Worldwide Tv

Crime in the Streets, 1955, Television Play
Crime in the Streets 1956 d: Don Siegel. lps: James Whitmore, John Cassavetes, Sal Mineo. 81M USA. prod/rel: Allied Artists, Lindbrook Prods.

Dino, 1956, Tplay
Dino 1957 d: Thomas Carr. lps: Sal Mineo, Brian Keith, Susan Kohner. 94M USA. *Killer Dino* (UKN) prod/rel: Allied Artists, Block-Kramarsky

ROSEGGER, PETER
Die Fahneltragerin, 1913, Short Story
Frohliche Wallfahrt, Die 1956 d: Ferdinand Dorfler. lps: Hanna Hutten, Bert Fortell, Richard Romanowsky. 93M GRM. *The Happy Pilgrimage* prod/rel: Dorfler, D.F.H.

Die Forsterbuben, 1908, Short Story
Forsterbuben, Die 1955 d: R. A. Stemmle. lps: Kurt Heintel, Erich Auer, Eva Probst. 100M AUS. prod/rel: Maxim

ROSEN HOA, MME. S.
La Symphonie Des Ombres, Novel
Lian'ai Yu Yiwu 1931 d: Bu Wancang. lps: Ruan Lingyu, Jin Yan, Cheng Yanyan. 13r CHN. *Love and Duty* prod/rel: Lianhua Film Company

ROSENBAUM, ED
A Taste of My Own Medicine, Book
   Doctor, The 1991 d: Randa Haines. lps: William Hurt, Christine Lahti, Elizabeth Perkins. 125M USA. prod/rel: Touchstone Pictures, Silver Screen Partners IV

ROSENBERG, HOWARD L.
Atomic Soldiers, Book
   Nightbreaker 1989 d: Peter Markle. lps: Martin Sheen, Emilio Estevez, Lea Thompson. TVM. 100M USA. *Advance to Ground Zero* prod/rel: Turner Network Tv

ROSENBERG, PHILIP
Badge of the Assassin, Book
   Badge of the Assassin 1985 d: Mel Damski. lps: James Woods, Yaphet Kotto, Alex Rocco. TVM. 100M USA. prod/rel: CBS, Columbia
Contract on Cherry Street, Book
   Contract on Cherry Street 1977 d: William A. Graham. lps: Frank Sinatra, Jay Black, Verna Bloom. TVM. 150M USA. prod/rel: NBC, Artanis
A Question of Honor, Book
   Question of Honor, A 1982 d: Jud Taylor. lps: Ben Gazzara, Paul Sorvino, Robert Vaughn. TVM. 150M USA. prod/rel: CBS, Roger Gimbel

ROSENCRANTZ, PALLE
Ole Opfinders Offer, Novel
   Ole Opfinders Offer 1924 d: Lau Lauritzen. lps: Carl Schenstrom, Harald Madsen, Jutta Lund. 80M DNM. prod/rel: Palladium

ROSENER, GEORGE
Speakeasy, Story
   Speakeasy 1929 d: Ben Stoloff. lps: Lola Lane, Paul Page, Sharon Lynn. 5775f USA. prod/rel: Fox Film Corp.

ROSENER, INGE
Dany, Bitte Schreiben Sie, Novel
   Dany, Bitte Schreiben Sie! 1956 d: Eduard von Borsody. lps: Sonja Ziemann, Rudolf Prack, Fita Benkhoff. 99M GRM. *Please Write, Danny* prod/rel: C.E.O., Prisma

ROSENFELD, HERBERT
Novel
   Telefonista, La 1932 d: Nunzio MalasommA. lps: Isa Pola, Mimi Aylmer, Luigi CimarA. 80M ITL. prod/rel: Cines, Anonima Pittaluga
Fraulein Falsch Verbunden, Play
   Give Her a Ring 1934 d: Arthur Woods. lps: Clifford Mollison, Wendy Barrie, Zelma O'Neal. 79M UKN. *Giving You the Stars* prod/rel: British International Pictures, Pathe
..Und Wer Kusst Mich?, Novel
   Ragazza Dal Livido Azzurro, La 1933 d: E. W. Emo. lps: Hilda Springher, Sergio Tofano, Renato Cialente. 65M ITL. *La Signorina Dal Livido Azzurro* prod/rel: Persic, Itala

ROSENFELD, SETH ZVI
A Brother's Kiss, Play
   Brother's Kiss, A 1997 d: Seth Zvi Rosenfeld. lps: Nick Chinlund, Michael Raynor, Cathy Moriarty. 92M USA. prod/rel: Rosefunk Pictures

ROSENFELD, SYDNEY
Children of Destiny, New York 1910, Play
   Children of Destiny 1920 d: George Irving. lps: Edith Hallor, Arthur Edmund Carewe, William Courtleigh. 6r USA. prod/rel: Weber Productions, Republic Distributing Corp.©
The Purple Lady, New York 1899, Play
   Purple Lady, The 1916 d: George A. Lessey. lps: Ralph Herz, Irene Howley, Alan Hale. 5r USA. prod/rel: Rolfe Photoplays Inc.©, Metro Pictures Corp.

ROSENHAYN, PAUL
Die Gluhende Gasse, Novel
   Gluhende Gasse, Die 1927 d: Paul Sugar. lps: Helga Thomas, Angelo Ferrari, Egon von Jordan. 2379m GRM. prod/rel: Gunsburg-Film Ag
Die Jacht Der Sieben Sunden, Novel
   Jacht Der Sieben Sunden, Die 1928 d: Jacob Fleck, Luise Fleck. lps: Brigitte Helm, Kurt Vespermann, John Stuart. 2212m GRM. *Yacht of the Seven Sins* prod/rel: UFA
Karriere, Berlin 1924, Play
   Careers 1929 d: John Francis Dillon. lps: Billie Dove, Antonio Moreno, Thelma Todd. 8435f USA. prod/rel: First National Pictures
Der Mann Den Niemand Sah, Novel
   Vertauschte Gesichter 1929 d: Rolf Randolf. lps: Marcella Albani, Hanni Weisse, Theodor Loos. 1971m GRM. prod/rel: Omnia-Film
Der Mord Am Karlsbad, Short Story
   Gestandnis Der Drei, Das 1928 d: James Bauer. lps: Hertha von Walther, Olaf Fjord, Angelo Ferrari. 2228m GRM. prod/rel: Internation.Spielfilm

ROSENTHAL, MARGARET
The Honest Courtesan, Biography
   Dangerous Beauty 1998 d: Marshall Herskovitz. lps: Catherine McCormack, Rufus Sewell, Jacqueline Bisset. 111M USA. *The Honest Courtesan* (UKN) prod/rel: Regency Enterprises, Arnon Milchan/ Bedford Falls

ROSINI, GIOVANNI
La Monaca Di Monza, Novel
   Monaca Di Monza, La 1947 d: Raffaello Pacini. lps: Paola Barbara, Rossano Brazzi, Anna Brandimarte. 94M ITL. prod/rel: Artisti Cinematografici Fiorentini, Zeus Film

ROSLER, JO HANNS
Erzahl Mir Nichts, Novel
   Erzahl Mir Nichts 1964 d: Dietrich Haugk. lps: Heidelinde Weis, Karl Michael Vogler, Georg ThomallA. 101M GRM. *Tell Me Nothing* prod/rel: Parnass, Columbia-Bavaria
Philine, Play
   Philine 1945 d: Theo Lingen. lps: Winnie Markus, Siegfried Breuer, Theo Lingen. 73M GRM. *Ein Madel Fur Frohe Stunden*; *A Girl for Happy Hours* prod/rel: Bavaria, Imex

ROSNE, JEAN
La Croix Sur le Rocher, Novel
   Croix Sur le Rocher, La 1927 d: Edmond Levenq, Jean Rosne. lps: Helene Hallier, Maurice de La Mea, Georges Saacke. 2200m FRN. prod/rel: Etoile-Film

ROSNY, JOSEPH HENRI
Dans Les Rues, Novel
   Dans Les Rues 1933 d: Victor Trivas. lps: Jean-Pierre Aumont, Madeleine Ozeray, Vladimir Sokoloff. 82M FRN. prod/rel: Societe Internationale Cinematographique
Les Fiancailles d'Yvonne, Short Story
   Date Fixee, La 1916. 1137m FRN. prod/rel: Scagl
La Guerre du Feu, 1911, Novel
   Guerre du Feu, La 1914 d: Georges DenolA. 490m FRN. prod/rel: Scagl
   Quest for Fire 1981 d: Jean-Jacques Annaud. lps: Everett McGill, Rae Dawn Chong, Ron Perlman. 100M CND/FRN. *La Guerre du Feu* (FRN) prod/rel: International Cinema Corp. (Montreal), Cine Trail Inc. (Montreal)

ROSS, J. MCLAREN
The Key Man, Novel
   Key Man, The 1957 d: Montgomery Tully. lps: Lee Patterson, Hy Hazell, Colin Gordon. 63M UKN. prod/rel: Insignia, Anglo-Amalgamated

ROSS, KENNETH
Breaker Morant, Play
   Breaker Morant 1979 d: Bruce Beresford. lps: Jack Thompson, Bryan Brown, Edward Woodward. 104M ASL. *The Breaker* prod/rel: South Australia Film Corporation©, Australian Film Commission

ROSS, SAM
Le Grand Frere, Novel
   Grand Frere, Le 1982 d: Francis Girod. lps: Gerard Depardieu, Amidou, Hakim Ghanem. 117M FRN. prod/rel: Partners Prods., S.F.P.C.
He Ran All the Way, 1947, Novel
   He Ran All the Way 1951 d: John Berry. lps: John Garfield, Shelley Winters, Wallace Ford. 77M USA. prod/rel: United Artists

ROSS, SUTHERLAND
The Lazy Salmon Mystery, Novel
   Caught in the Net 1960 d: John Haggarty. lps: Jeremy Bulloch, Joanna Horlock, James Luck. 64M UKN. prod/rel: Children's Film Foundation, Wallace

ROSSETTI, PAOLO
Io Il Tebano, Book
   Altri Uomini 1997 d: Claudio Bonivento. lps: Claudio Amendola, Ennio Fantastichini, Veronica Pivetti. 91M ITL. *Other Men* prod/rel: International Dean Film

ROSSI, ANTON GERMANO
Cabine 27, Play
   Famiglia Passaguai, La 1951 d: Aldo Fabrizi. lps: Aldo Fabrizi, Eduardo de Filippo, Tino Scotti. 90M ITL. prod/rel: Alfa Film, Rank Film
Il Ladro, Novel
   Ladro, Il 1940 d: Anton Germano Rossi. lps: Elio Steiner, Silvana Jachino, Giovanni Grasso. 58M ITL. prod/rel: Felix Film, C.I.N.F.
Il Ladro, Short Story
   Biancaneve E I Sette Ladri 1949 d: Giacomo Gentilomo. lps: Peppino de Filippo, Mischa Auer, Silvana Pampanini. 90M ITL. prod/rel: F.C.F., E.N.I.C.

ROSSLER, KARL
Annette Hat Zuviel Geld, Play
   Annette Im Paradies 1934 d: Max Obal. lps: Ursula Grabley, Hans Sohnker, Ida Wust. 2270m GRM/CZC. *Ein Kuss Nach Ladenschluss*; *Anita V Raji* prod/rel: Georg Witt Film, Wolframfilm
   Anita V Raji 1934 d: Jan Svitak. lps: Truda Grosslichtova, Zdenka Baldova, Vladimir Borsky. 2091m CZC. *Anita in Paradise* prod/rel: Wolframfilm
Die Drei Niemandskinder, Novel
   Drei Niemandskinder, Die 1927 d: Fritz Freisler. lps: Greta Graal, Xenia Desni, Willi Forst. 2474m GRM. prod/rel: Greenbaum-Film
Der Feldherrnhugel, Play
   Feldherrnhugel, Der 1926 d: Erich Schonfelder, Hans Otto Lowenstein. lps: Harry Liedtke, Olga Tschechowa, Maria Minzenti. 2259m GRM/ITL. prod/rel: Greenbaum-Film
   Feldherrnhugel, Der 1953 d: Ernst MarischkA. lps: Paul Horbiger, Hans Holt, Gretl Schorg. 100M AUS. prod/rel: Vindobona

ROSSMAN, HERMANN
Flieger, 1931, Play
   Hell in the Heavens 1934 d: John G. Blystone. lps: Warner Baxter, Conchita Montenegro, Russell Hardie. 80M USA. prod/rel: Fox Film Corp.©

ROSSNER, JUDITH (1935–), USA
Looking for Mr. Goodbar, Novel
   Looking for Mr. Goodbar 1977 d: Richard Brooks. lps: Diane Keaton, Richard Gere, William Atherton. 135M USA. prod/rel: Paramount

ROSSNER, KARL
Der Herr Des Todes, Novel
   Herr Des Todes, Der 1913 d: Max Obal. lps: Hugo Flink, Hans Mierendorff, Franz Arndt. 1602m GRM. *The Master of Death* prod/rel: Deutsche Bioscop

ROSSNER, MANFRED
Karl III Und Anna von Osterreich, Play
   Musik, Musik - Und Nur Musik 1955 d: Ernst Matray. lps: Walter Giller, Inge Egger, Eva Schreiber. 83M GRM. *Music, Music, Only Music* prod/rel: Arca, N.F.
Wir machen Musik, Play
   Wir machen Musik 1942 d: Helmut Kautner. lps: Ilse Werner, Viktor de Kowa, Edith Oss. 95M GRM. prod/rel: Terra, Schonger

ROSSNER, ROBERT
L'homme aux Yeux d'Argent, Novel
   Homme aux Yeux d'Argent, L' 1985 d: Pierre Granier-Deferre. lps: Alain Souchon, Tanya Lopert, Jean-Louis Trintignant. 97M FRN. prod/rel: T Films, Antenne 2

ROSSO DI SAN SECONDO, PIER MARIA
La Mia Esistenza d'Acquario
   Due Esistenze, Le 1920 d: Ugo Falena, Giorgio Ricci. lps: Maria Melato, Goffredo d'Andrea, Marion May. 1735m ITL. prod/rel: Bernini Film
La Scala, Play
   Scala, La 1931 d: Gennaro Righelli. lps: Maria Jacobini, Carlo Ninchi, Giorgio Bianchi. 80M ITL. prod/rel: Cines, Anonima Pittaluga
Storiella Di Montagna, Play
   Torrente, Il 1938 d: Marco Elter. lps: Camillo Pilotto, Nelly Corradi, Leo GaravagliA. 70M ITL. *Storiella Di Montagna* prod/rel: Phoebus Film

ROSSO, PIER MARIA
La Bella Addormentata, Play
   Bella Addormentata, La 1942 d: Luigi Chiarini. lps: Luisa Ferida, Amedeo Nazzari, Osvaldo Valenti. 90M ITL. *Sleeping Beauty* (USA) prod/rel: Cines, E.N.I.C.

ROSTAND, EDMOND (1868–1918), FRN
L'aiglon, 1900, Play
   Herzog von Reichstadt, Der 1931 d: Victor Tourjansky. lps: Walter Edhofer, Lien Deyers, Grete Natzler. 109M GRM.
   Aiglon, L' 1931 d: Victor Tourjansky. lps: Jean Weber, Victor Francen, Simone Vaudry. 109M FRN. prod/rel: Societe Des Films Osso
Cyrano de Bergerac, 1897, Play
   Cirano Di Bergerac 1909 d: Ernesto Maria Pasquali. 276m ITL. *Cyrano de Bergerac* (USA) prod/rel: Pasquali E Tempo
   Cirano Di Bergerac 1922 d: Augusto GeninA. lps: Pierre Magnier, Linda Moglia, Angelo Ferrari. 2835m ITL. prod/rel: Extra Film
   Cyrano de Bergerac 1945 d: Fernand Rivers. lps: Claude Dauphin, Ellen Bernsen, Pierre Bertin. 100M FRN. prod/rel: Fernand Rivers
   Cyrano de Bergerac 1950 d: Michael Gordon. lps: Jose Ferrer, Mala Powers, William Prince. 112M USA. prod/rel: United Artists, Stanley Kramer

Cyrano de Bergerac 1960 d: Claude BarmA. lps: Daniel Sorano, Francoise Christophe, Michel Le Royer. MTV. 156M FRN.

Roxanne 1987 d: Fred Schepisi. lps: Steve Martin, Daryl Hannah, Rick Rossovich. 107M USA. prod/rel: Columbia, Daniel Melnick Indieprod and la Films

Cyrano de Bergerac 1989 d: Jean-Paul Rappeneau. lps: Gerard Depardieu, Anne Brochet, Vincent Perez. 138M FRN.

ROSTAND, MAURICE
Un Bon Petit Diable, Paris 1911, Play
Good Little Devil, A 1914 d: Edwin S. Porter, J. Searle Dawley. lps: Mary Pickford, William Norris, Ernest Truex. 5r USA. prod/rel: Famous Players Film Co., State Rights

L'homme Que J'ai Tue, Novel
Pax Domine 1924 d: Rene Leprince. lps: Gaston Nores, Pierre Daltour, Blanche Montel. 1700m FRN. prod/rel: Pathe-Consortium Cinema

L'homme Qui J'ai Tue, Paris 1930, Play
Broken Lullaby 1932 d: Ernst Lubitsch. lps: Lionel Barrymore, Nancy Carroll, Phillips Holmes. 77M USA. *Man I Killed, The* (UKN); *The Fifth Commandment* prod/rel: Paramount Publix Corp.

ROSTAND, ROBERT
Monkey in the Middle, Novel
Killer Elite, The 1975 d: Sam Peckinpah. lps: James Caan, Robert Duvall, Arthur Hill. 123M USA. prod/rel: United Artists

ROSTEN, LEO (1908–, PLN, Rosten, Leo Calvin
Captain Newman, M.D., New York 1961, Novel
Captain Newman M.D. 1963 d: David Miller. lps: Gregory Peck, Tony Curtis, Angie Dickinson. 126M USA. prod/rel: Universal

Dark Corner, 1945, Short Story
Dark Corner, The 1946 d: Henry Hathaway. lps: Mark Stevens, Lucille Ball, William Bendix. 99M USA. prod/rel: 20th Century-Fox

Sleep My Love, 1946, Novel
Sleep My Love 1948 d: Douglas Sirk. lps: Claudette Colbert, Don Ameche, Robert Cummings. 97M USA. prod/rel: United Artists

ROTH, ARTHUR
A Terrible Beauty, Novel
Terrible Beauty, A 1960 d: Tay Garnett. lps: Robert Mitchum, Anne Heywood, Dan O'Herlihy. 89M UKN. *The Night Fighters* (USA) prod/rel: United Artists, Raymond Stross

ROTH, JOSEPH (1894–1939), AUS
Das Falsche Gewicht, 1937, Novel
Falsche Gewicht, Das 1970 d: Bernhard Wicki. lps: Helmut Qualtinger, Agnes Fink, Johannes Schaaf. 146M GRM. *The Wanting Weight; False Weight; Short Weights* prod/rel: Inter Tel, Scotia

Hiob, Roman Eines Ein Fachen Mannes, Berlin 1930, Novel
Sins of Man 1936 d: Gregory Ratoff, Otto Brower. lps: Don Ameche, Allen Jenkins, J. Edward Bromberg. 85M USA. *Turmoil* prod/rel: Twentieth Century-Fox Film Corp.©

Die Kapuzinergruft, 1938, Novel
Trotta 1972 d: Johannes Schaaf. lps: Andras Balint, Rosemarie Fendel, Doris Kunstmann. 95M GRM. prod/rel: Johannes Schaaf, Independent

Die Legende Vom Heiligen Trinker, 1939, Novel
Legende Vom Heiligen Trinker, Die 1963 d: Franz J. Wild. 166M GRM.

Leggenda Del Santo Bevitore, La 1988 d: Ermanno Olmi. lps: Rutger Hauer, Anthony Quayle, Sandrine Dumas. 125M ITL/FRN. *The Legend of the Holy Drinker* (UKN)

Die Rebellion, 1924, Short Story
Rebellion, Die 1962 d: Wolfgang Staudte. lps: Josef Meinrad, Ida Krottendorf, Erna Schickel. 70M GRM.

Das Spinnennetz, Novel
Spinnennetz, Das 1989 d: Bernhard Wicki. lps: Ulrich Muhe, Klaus Maria Brandauer, Armin Mueller-Stahl. 196M GRM. *The Spider's Web* prod/rel: Provobis, ZDF

ROTH, LILLIAN (1910–1980), USA, Rutstein, Lillian
I'll Cry Tomorrow, Book
I'll Cry Tomorrow 1955 d: Daniel Mann. lps: Susan Hayward, Richard Conte, Eddie Albert. 117M USA. prod/rel: MGM

ROTH, LOIS
The Wild Elephant, Short Story
Maya 1966 d: John Berry. lps: Clint Walker, Jay North, I. S. Johar. 91M USA. prod/rel: King Brothers Production

ROTH, MARTY
Story
Boatniks, The 1970 d: Norman Tokar. lps: Robert Morse, Stefanie Powers, Phil Silvers. 100M USA. prod/rel: Buena Vista, Walt Disney

ROTH, PHILIP (1933–, USA, Roth, Philip Milton
The Ghost Writer, Story
Ghost Writer, The 1984 d: Tristram Powell. lps: Rose Arrick, Claire Bloom, MacIntyre Dixon. TVM. 80M USA. prod/rel: Wgbh Boston, Malone Gil

Goodbye, Columbus, Boston 1959, Novel
Goodbye, Columbus 1969 d: Larry Peerce. lps: Richard Benjamin, Ali MacGraw, Jack Klugman. 105M USA. prod/rel: Willow Tree Productions

Portnoy's Complaint, 1969, Novel
Portnoy's Complaint 1972 d: Ernest Lehman. lps: Richard Benjamin, Karen Black, Lee Grant. 99M USA. prod/rel: Warner Bros.

ROTHBERG, MARIE
David, Book
David 1988 d: John Erman. lps: Bernadette Peters, John Glover, Matthew Laurance. TVM. 100M USA.

ROTHE, HANS
Verwehte Spuren, Radio Play
Verwehte Spuren 1938 d: Veit Harlan. lps: Kristina Soderbaum, Frits Van Dongen, Friedrich Kayssler. 81M GRM. *The Footprints Blow Away* prod/rel: Majestic, Panorama

ROTHWELL, TALBOT
Three Spare Wives, Play
Three Spare Wives 1962 d: Ernest Morris. lps: Robin Hunter, Susan Stephen, John Hewer. 70M UKN. prod/rel: United Artists, Danzigers

ROTTER, FRITZ
Story
September Affair 1950 d: William Dieterle. lps: Joseph Cotten, Joan Fontaine, Francoise Rosay. 104M USA. prod/rel: Paramount

ROUECHE, BERTON
Artic
Bigger Than Life 1956 d: Nicholas Ray. lps: James Mason, Barbara Rush, Walter Matthau. 95M USA. *One in a Million* prod/rel: 20th Century-Fox Film Corp., James Mason

ROUIX, JEAN
Le Moussaillon, Novel
Moussaillon, Le 1941 d: Jean Gourguet. lps: Roger Duchesne, Yvette Lebon, Georges Prevost. 80M FRN. prod/rel: Selb Films

ROULAND, J. P.
Tendre Poulet, Novel
Tendre Poulet 1978 d: Philippe de BrocA. lps: Annie Girardot, Philippe Noiret, Catherine Alric. 105M FRN. *Dear Detective* (USA); *Dear Inspector* prod/rel: Ariane, Mondex

ROULET, DOMINIQUE
Une Mort En Trop, Novel
Poulet Au Vinaigre 1984 d: Claude Chabrol. lps: Jean Poiret, Stephane Audran, Michel Bouquet. 110M FRN. *Cop Au Vin* (USA); *Chicken With Vinegar* prod/rel: Mk2, Marin Karmitz

ROUQUETTE, LOUIS FREDERIC
La Bete Errante, Novel
Bete Errante, La 1931 d: Marco de Gastyne. lps: Gabriel Gabrio, Choura Milena, Jacqueline Torrent. 84M FRN. prod/rel: Pathe-Natan

ROURKE, MICKEY (1950–, USA
Story
Homeboy 1989 d: Michael Seresin. lps: Mickey Rourke, Christopher Walken, Debra Feuer. 116M USA. prod/rel: Twentieth Century Fox, Homeboy Productions

ROURKE, THOMAS
Thunder Below, New York 1931, Novel
Thunder Below 1932 d: Richard Wallace. lps: Tallulah Bankhead, Charles Bickford, Paul Lukas. 71M USA. prod/rel: Paramount Publix Corp.©

ROUSE, VIRGINIA
Red Herring, Short Story
Seeing Red 1991 d: Virginia Rouse. lps: Zoe Carides, Anne Louise Lambert, Peta Toppano. F ASL. prod/rel: Goosey

ROUSE, WILLIAM MERRIAM
Jules of the Strong Heart, 1915, Short Story
Jules of the Strong Heart 1918 d: Donald Crisp. lps: George Beban, Helen Jerome Eddy, Guy Oliver. 5r USA. prod/rel: Jesse L. Lasky Feature Play Co.©, Famous Players-Lasky Corp.

ROUSSEAU, JEAN-JACQUES (1712–1778), SWT
Emile; Ou, de l'Education, 1762, Novel
Gai Savoir, Le 1967 d: Jean-Luc Godard. lps: Jean-Pierre Leaud, Juliet Berto, Chantal Jeanson. MTV. 91M FRN/GRM. *Frohliche Wissenschaft, Die* (GRM); *The Joyful Wisdom* prod/rel: Anouchka, Bavaria Atelier

ROUSSEAU, VICTOR
Sunburst Valley, Story
When Dreams Come True 1929 d: Duke Worne. lps: Helene Costello, Rex Lease, Claire McDowell. 6242f USA. *Lost and Won* (UKN) prod/rel: Trem Carr Productions, Rayart Pictures

ROUSSIN, ANDRE (1911–1987), FRN
Bobosse, 1951, Play
Bobosse 1958 d: Etienne Perier. lps: Francois Perier, Micheline Presle, Jean Tissier. 88M FRN. prod/rel: Editions Cinegrafiques

Une Grande Fille Toute Simple, 1943, Play
Grande Fille Toute Simple, Une 1947 d: Jacques Manuel. lps: Raymond Rouleau, Jean Desailly, Madeleine Sologne. 100M FRN. *Just a Big Simple Girl* prod/rel: C.a.P.A.C.

Lorsque l'Enfant Parait, 1952, Play
Lorsque l'Enfant Parait 1956 d: Michel Boisrond. lps: Gaby Morlay, Andre Luguet, Guy Bertil. 85M FRN. *Blessed Events* (UKN) prod/rel: C.F.P.C, Robert De Nesle

Nina, 1951, Play
Nina 1958 d: Jean Boyer. lps: Sophie Desmarets, Jean Poiret, Michel Serrault. 88M FRN. prod/rel: Vauban Productions

Les Oeufs de l'Autruche, 1955, Play
Oeufs de l'Autruche, Les 1957 d: Denys de La Patelliere. lps: Pierre Fresnay, Simone Renant, Yoko Tani. 82M FRN. *The Ostrich Has Two Eggs* prod/rel: Vauban-Productions

La Petite Hutte, 1948, Play
Little Hut, The 1957 d: Mark Robson. lps: Ava Gardner, Stewart Granger, David Niven. 90M USA. prod/rel: MGM

ROUVEROL, AURANIA
Skidding, New York 1928, Play
Family Affair, A 1937 d: George B. Seitz. lps: Lionel Barrymore, Mickey Rooney, Spring Byington. 69M USA. *Skidding; Stand Accused* prod/rel: Metro-Goldwyn-Mayer Corp.©

ROVETTA, GEROLAMO (1851–1910), ITL
La Baraonda
Baraonda, La 1923 d: Orlando Vassallo. lps: Olga Benetti, Carlo Benetti, Pier Camillo Tovagliari. 1800m ITL. *Nora* prod/rel: Flegrea Film

I Disonesti, 1892, Novel
Disonesti, I 1922 d: Giuseppe Sterni. lps: Linda Pini, Giuseppe Sterni, Cesare Dondini. 1486m ITL. prod/rel: Sterni

Le Due Coscienze, 1900, Play
Due Coscienze, Le 1916. lps: Jeanne Nolly. 922m ITL. prod/rel: Italo-Egiziana Film

Mater Dolorosa, 1882, Novel
Mater Dolorosa 1913 d: Mario Caserini. lps: Mary Cleo Tarlarini, Mario Bonnard, Luigi ChiesA. 799m ITL. prod/rel: S.A. Ambrosio

Madonna Di Neve 1919 d: Alfredo de Antoni. lps: Olga Benetti, Giulietta d'Arienzo, Alfredo de Antoni. 1802m ITL. prod/rel: Colosseum

Mater Dolorosa 1943 d: Giacomo Gentilomo. lps: Mariella Lotti, Claudio Gora, Anneliese Uhlig. 82M ITL. prod/rel: E.I.a., Mediterranea

Papa Eccellenza, 1906, Play
Papa Eccellenza 1919 d: Ivo Illuminati. lps: Camillo de Riso, Rina Maggi, Fiorello Giraud. 2161m ITL. prod/rel: Caesar Film

Re Burlone, Play
Re Burlone 1935 d: Enrico Guazzoni. lps: Armando Falconi, Luigi Cimara, Luisa FeridA. 97M ITL. prod/rel: Capitani Film, Consorzio I.C.A.R.

Remigia, Novel
Moglie Di Sua Eccellenza, La 1921 d: Eduardo BencivengA. lps: Fernanda Fassy, Gustavo Serena, Livio Pavanelli. 1809m ITL. prod/rel: U.C.I., Chimera Film

Romanticismo, 1901, Play
Romanticismo 1915 d: Carlo Campogalliani. lps: Tullio Carminati, Helena Makowska, Filippo ButerA. ITL. prod/rel: S.A. Ambrosio

Romanticismo 1951 d: Clemente Fracassi. lps: Amedeo Nazarri, Tamara Lees, Fosco Giachetti. F ITL. prod/rel: Carlo Ponti, Dino de Laurentiis

La Signorina, 1900, Novel
Signorina, La 1920 d: Gian Bistolfi. lps: Isa de Novegradi, Mademoiselle Alexiane, Riccardo Bertacchini. 1741m ITL. prod/rel: U.C.I., D'ambra Film
Signorina, La 1942 d: Ladislao Kish. lps: Loredana, Nino Besozzi, Laura Nucci. 83M ITL. prod/rel: Sabaudia Film, Artisti Associati

La Trilogia Di Dorina, 1889, Play
Trilogia Di Dorina, La 1917 d: Gero Zambuto. lps: Pina Menichelli, Alberto Nepoti, Mary Cleo Tarlarini. 2002m ITL. prod/rel: Itala Film

ROWAN, ANDREW SUMMERS
How I Carried the Message to Garcia, San Francisco 1922, Book
Message to Garcia, A 1936 d: George Marshall. lps: Wallace Beery, Barbara Stanwyck, John Boles. 85M USA. prod/rel: Twentieth Century-Fox Film Corp.©

ROWDEN, WALTER COURTNEY
Fighting Jack, Novel
Corinthian Jack 1921 d: W. C. Rowden. lps: Victor McLaglen, Kathleen Vaughan, Warwick Ward. 5000f UKN. *Fighting Jack* prod/rel: Master Films, Butcher's Film Service

ROWE JR., GARY THOMAS
My Undercover Years With the Ku Klux Klan, Book
Undercover With the Kkk 1979 d: Barry Shear. lps: Don Meredith, James Wainwright, Ed Lauter. TVM. 100M USA. *My Undercover Years With the Ku Klux Klan*; *The Freedom Riders* prod/rel: Columbia Tv

ROWE, NICHOLAS (1674–1718), UKN
Jane Shore, London 1714, Play
Jane Shore 1908. 695f UKN. prod/rel: Gaumont
Jane Shore 1911 d: Frank Powell. lps: Florence Barker. 1238f UKN. prod/rel: Britannia Films, Pathe
Jane Shore 1915 d: Bert Haldane, F. Martin Thornton. lps: Blanche Forsythe, Roy Travers, Robert Purdie. 6300f UKN. *The Strife Eternal* (USA) prod/rel: Barker, Walturdaw
Jane Shore 1922 d: Edwin J. Collins. lps: Sybil Thorndike, Booth Conway, Gordon Hopkirk. 950f UKN. prod/rel: Master Films, British Exhibitors' Films

ROWLAND, HENRY C.
Auld Jeremiah, Short Story
Bonnie, Bonnie Lassie 1919 d: Tod Browning. lps: Mary MacLaren, David Butler, Arthur Edmund Carewe. 6r USA. *Auld Jeremiah* prod/rel: Universal Film Mfg. Co.©

The Closing Net, New York 1912, Novel
Closing Net, The 1915 d: Edward Jose. lps: Howard Estabrook, Bliss Milford, Kathryn Browne-Decker. 5r USA. prod/rel: Pathe Exchange, Inc., Pathe Freres©

Duds, New York 1920, Novel
Duds 1920 d: Thomas R. Mills. lps: Tom Moore, Naomi Childers, Christine Mayo. 4685f USA. *The Dud* prod/rel: Goldwyn Pictures Corp.©, Goldwyn Distributing Corp.

Filling His Own Shoes, Boston 1916, Novel
Filling His Own Shoes 1917 d: Harry Beaumont. lps: Bryant Washburn, Hazel Daly, Rod La Rocque. 5r USA. prod/rel: Essanay Film Mfg. Co.©, K-E-S-E Service

Kidnapping Coline, 1914, Short Story
Conquering the Woman 1922 d: King Vidor. lps: Florence Vidor, Bert Sprotte, Mathilde Brundage. 5887f USA. prod/rel: King W. Vidor Productions, Associated Exhibitors

The Peddler, 1919, Novel
Peddler of Lies, The 1920 d: William C. Dowlan. lps: Frank Mayo, Ora Carew, Ora Devereaux. 5r USA. prod/rel: Universal Film Mfg. Co.©

The Sultana, New York 1914, Novel
Sultana, The 1916 d: Sherwood MacDonald. lps: Ruth Roland, William Conklin, Daniel Gilfether. 5r USA. prod/rel: Balboa Amusement Co., Pathe Exchange, Inc.©

ROWLES, BURTON J.
The Long Way Home, Television Play
That Night 1957 d: John Newland. lps: John Beal, Augusta Dabney, Malcolm Brodrick. 88M USA. prod/rel: Universal-International, RKO

ROWLEY, WILLIAM (c1585–c1637), UKN
The Changeling, Play
Middleton's Changeling 1997 d: Marcus Thompson. lps: Ian Dury, Amanda Ray-King, Colm O Maonlai. 96M UKN. prod/rel: High Time Pictures Ltd.©, United Independent Pictures

ROY, DWIJENDRALAL
Chandragupta, 1911, Play
Mathru Bhoomi 1939 d: H. M. Reddy. lps: T. S. Santhanam, P. U. Chinappa, Kali N. Rathnam. 200M IND. *Motherland*; *Mathrubhoomi* prod/rel: Vel Pictures, Al. Rm. Company, Madras

ROY, GABRIELLE (1909–1983), CND
Bonheur d'Occasion, Novel
Bonheur d'Occasion 1983 d: Claude Fournier. lps: Mireille Deyglun, Martin Neufeld, Marilyn Lightstone. 122M CND. prod/rel: Cine St-Henri Inc., Office National Du Film
Tin Flute, The 1983 d: Claude Fournier. lps: Mireille Deyglun, Martin Neufeld, Marilyn Lightstone. 121M CND. prod/rel: Cine St-Henri Inc., Office National Du Film

Un Vagabond Frappe a Notre Porte, Short Story
Tramp at the Door 1987 d: Allan Kroeker. lps: Ed McNamara, August Schellenberg, Monique Mercure. 81M CND. prod/rel: Canwest Broadcasting (Cknd-Tv) Ltd

ROY, JULIE
Betrayal, Book
Betrayal 1978 d: Paul Wendkos. lps: Lesley Ann Warren, Rip Torn, Richard Masur. TVM. 100M USA. prod/rel: NBC, Emi Television

ROY, JYOTIRMOY
Chheley Kar?, Novel
Bandish 1955 d: Satyen Bose. lps: Ashok Kumar, Meena Kumari, Daisy Irani. 129M IND. *Musical Score* prod/rel: Basu Chitra Mandir

ROY, LOUISE
Une Amie d'Enfance, Play
Amie d'Enfance, Une 1977 d: Francis Mankiewicz. lps: Pauline Martin, Pauline Lapointe, Jean-Guy Viau. 90M CND. prod/rel: Les Productions Du Verseau Inc., Les Films Mutuels

ROY, OLIVIA
The Husband Hunter, Novel
Husband Hunter, The 1920 d: Fred W. Durrant. lps: C. M. Hallard, Madge Titheradge, Tom Reynolds. 6000f UKN. prod/rel: G. B. Samuelson, Granger

ROYER, ALFONSO
La Favorita, Play
Favorita, La 1953 d: Cesare Barlacchi. lps: Gino Sinimberghi, Franca Tamantini, Paolo Silveri. 71M ITL. *The Favourite* prod/rel: Mas Film

ROYLE, EDWIN MILTON
The Silent Call, New York 1910, Novel
Squaw Man's Son, The 1917 d: Edward J. Le Saint. lps: Wallace Reid, Dorothy Davenport, Anita King. 5r USA. prod/rel: Jesse L. Lasky Feature Play Co.©, Paramount Pictures Corp.

The Squaw Man, New York 1905, Play
Squaw Man, The 1914 d: Cecil B. de Mille, Oscar Apfel. lps: Dustin Farnum, Lillian St. Cyr, Winifred Kingston. 6r USA. *The White Man* (UKN) prod/rel: Jesse L. Lasky Feature Play Co.©, State Rights
Squaw Man, The 1918 d: Cecil B. de Mille. lps: Elliott Dexter, Anna Little, Katherine MacDonald. 5897f USA. *The White Man* prod/rel: Famous Players-Lasky Corp.©, Artcraft Pictures
Squaw Man, The 1931 d: Cecil B. de Mille. lps: Warner Baxter, Lupe Velez, Eleanor Boardman. 106M USA. *The White Man* (UKN) prod/rel: Metro-Goldwyn-Mayer Corp., Metro-Goldwyn-Mayer Dist. Corp.©

The Struggle Everlasting, New York 1917, Play
Struggle Everlasting, The 1918 d: James Kirkwood. lps: Florence Reed, Milton Sills, Irving Cummings. 6-7r USA. prod/rel: Harry Rapf Productions, High Art Productions©

The Unwritten Law, New York 1913, Play
Unwritten Law, The 1916 d: George E. Middleton. lps: Beatriz Michelena, William Pike, Andrew Robson. 7r USA. prod/rel: California Motion Picture Corp., State Rights

ROZEK, KAREL
Lasky, Vasne, Zrady, Short Story
Dar Svatebni Noci 1926 d: Oldrich Kminek. lps: Jan W. Speerger, Hermina Rydrychova, Sasa DobrovolnA. 1711m CZC. *The Wedding Night's Gift*; *Lasky - Vasne - Zrady*; *Loves - Passions - Betrayals* prod/rel: Karel Spelina, la Tricolore

ROZOV, VICTOR S.
Vechno Zhivye, 1956, Play
Letyat Zhuravli 1957 d: Mikhail Kalatozov. lps: Alexei Batalov, Tatiana Samoilova, Vasili Merkuriev. 94M USS. *The Cranes are Flying*; *Letiat Jouravly*; *Letjat Zuravli* prod/rel: Mosfilm

RUARK, ROBERT (1915–1965), USA, Ruark, Robert Chester
Something of Value, 1955, Novel
Something of Value 1957 d: Richard Brooks. lps: Rock Hudson, Dana Wynter, Wendy Hiller. 117M USA. *Africa Ablaze* prod/rel: MGM

RUBELL, H. G.
Ta Nase Jedenactka, Novel
Nase XI. 1936 d: Vaclav Binovec. lps: Bedrich Veverka, Natasa Gollova, Anna SteimarovA. 2510m CZC. *Our Eleven* prod/rel: Beda Heller

RUBEN, ALEX
Show Business, Play
Time Out for Rhythm 1941 d: Sidney Salkow. lps: Ann Miller, Rudy Vallee, Rosemary Lane. 74M USA. prod/rel: Columbia

RUBENS, BERNICE (1927–, UKN
Chere Inconnue, Novel
Chere Inconnue 1980 d: Moshe Mizrahi. lps: Simone Signoret, Jean Rochefort, Delphine Seyrig. 112M FRN. *I Sent a Letter to My Love* (USA); *Je T'ai Ecrit une Lettre d'Amour* prod/rel: Paris Studio Cinema

Madame Sousatzka, Novel
Madame Sousatzka 1989 d: John Schlesinger. lps: Shirley MacLaine, Peggy Ashcroft, Navin Chowdhry. 121M UKN. prod/rel: Curzon, Sousatzka Productions

RUBIEN, A. J.
G.I. Honeymoon, Play
G.I. Honeymoon 1945 d: Phil Karlson. lps: Gale Storm, Peter Cookson, Arline Judge. 70M USA. prod/rel: Monogram

RUBIN, DANIEL N.
The Lion Trap, Play
Midnight Madness 1928 d: F. Harmon Weight. lps: Jacqueline Logan, Clive Brook, Walter McGrail. 5659f USA. prod/rel: de Mille Pictures, Pathe Exchange, Inc.

Riddle Me This, New York 1932, Play
Guilty As Hell 1932 d: Erle C. Kenton. lps: Victor McLaglen, Edmund Lowe, Richard Arlen. 81M USA. *Guilty As Charged* (UKN); *Riddle Me This* prod/rel: Paramount Publix Corp.©
Night Club Scandal 1937 d: Ralph Murphy. lps: John Barrymore, Lynne Overman, Louise Campbell. 72M USA. *City Hall Scandal* prod/rel: Paramount Pictures©

Women Go on Forever, New York 1927, Play
Women Go on Forever 1931 d: Walter Lang. lps: Clara Kimball Young, Marian Nixon, Thomas Jackson. 67M USA. prod/rel: James Cruze Productions, Tiffany Productions

RUBIN, THEODORE ISAAC
Lisa and David, New York 1961, Novel
David and Lisa 1962 d: Frank Perry. lps: Keir Dullea, Janet Margolin, Howard Da SilvA. 94M USA. prod/rel: Heller/Perry

RUBY, HARRY
The Life of Marilyn Miller, Book
Look for the Silver Lining 1949 d: David Butler. lps: June Haver, Ray Bolger, Gordon MacRae. 100M USA. *Silver Lining* prod/rel: Warner Bros.

The Ramblers, New York 1926, Musical Play
Cuckoos, The 1930 d: Paul Sloane. lps: Bert Wheeler, Robert Woolsey, June Clyde. 90M USA. *Radio Revels* prod/rel: RKO Productions

Top Speed, New York 1929, Mplay
Top Speed 1930 d: Mervyn Leroy. lps: Joe E. Brown, Bernice Claire, Jack Whiting. 70M USA. prod/rel: First National Pictures

RUCK, BERTA (1878–, UKN
His Official Fiancee, New York 1914, Novel
His Official Fiancee 1919 d: Robert G. VignolA. lps: Vivian Martin, Forrest Stanley, Mollie McConnell. 5r USA. prod/rel: Famous Players-Lasky Corp.©, Paramount-Artcraft Pictures

In Another Girl's Shoes, Novel
In Another Girl's Shoes 1917 d: G. B. Samuelson, Alexander Butler. lps: Mabel Love, Ruby Miller, Leo Belcher. 5000f UKN. prod/rel: G. B. Samuelson

Sir Or Madam, Novel
Ossi Hat Die Hosen an 1928 d: Carl Boese. lps: Ossi Oswalda, Percy Marmont, Annette Benson. 2533m GRM. prod/rel: Carl Boese-Film
Sir Or Madam 1928 d: Carl Boese. lps: Percy Marmont, Ossi Oswalda, Annette Benson. 6421f UKN. prod/rel: Foremost Productions, Warner Bros.

RUD, NILS JOHAN
Ettersokte Er Atten Ar, 1958, Novel
Ung Flukt 1959 d: Edith Kalmar. lps: Liv Ullmann, Atle Merton, Rolf Soder. 91M NRW. *The Wayward Girl* (USA) prod/rel: Carlmar

RUDERMAN, MIKHAIL
Pobyeda, Play
Counter-Attack 1945 d: Zoltan KordA. lps: Paul Muni, Marguerite Chapman, Larry Parks. 90M USA. *One Against Seven* (UKN) prod/rel: Columbia

RUDOLPH, AXEL
Aktenbundel M 2-1706/35, Novel
Polizeifunk Meldet, Der 1939 d: Rudolf Van Der Noss. lps: Lola Muthel, Jasper von Oertzen, Erich Fiedler. 77M GRM. prod/rel: Terra, Knevels

RUDOLPHI, ERNST
Junger Mann, Der Alles Kann, Novel
Junger Mann, Der Alles Kann 1957 d: Thomas Engel. lps: Georg Thomalla, Erik Schumann, Peer Schmidt. 96M GRM. *Young Man, Who Can Do Anything* prod/rel: Bavaria, Terrascope

RUDORF, GUNTER
The First Lesson, Play
Willy 1963 d: Allan A. Buckhantz. lps: Hubert Persicke, Hannelore Schroth, Edith Schultze-Westrum. MTV. 73M GRM/USA. prod/rel: Aba

RUESCH, HANS
Racers, The, 1953, Novel
Racers, The 1955 d: Henry Hathaway. lps: Kirk Douglas, Bella Darvi, Gilbert Roland. 112M USA. *Such Men are Dangerous* (UKN) prod/rel: 20th Century-Fox
Top of the World, New York 1950, Novel
Savage Innocents, The 1959 d: Nicholas Ray, Baccio Bandini. lps: Anthony Quinn, Yoko Tani, Carlo Justini. 111M UKN/FRN/ITL. *Les Dents du Diable* (FRN); *Ombre Bianche* (ITL) prod/rel: Magic Film (Roma), Playart

RUFFINI, GIOVANNI
Il Dottor Antonio, 1855, Novel
Dottor Antonio, Il 1910 d: Mario Caserini. lps: Maria Caserini Gasparini, Mario Monti. 251m ITL. *Doctor Antonio* (UKN) prod/rel: Cines
Dottor Antonio, Il 1914 d: Eleuterio Rodolfi. lps: Hamilton Revelle, Fernanda Negri-Pouget, Alfredo Bertone. 1165m ITL. prod/rel: S.A. Ambrosio
Dottor Antonio, Il 1937 d: Enrico Guazzoni. lps: Ennio Cerlesi, Maria Gambarelli, Lamberto Picasso. 98M ITL. prod/rel: Manderfilm

RUGE, JACK
Joe Butterfly, Play
Joe Butterfly 1957 d: Jesse Hibbs. lps: Audie Murphy, George Nader, Burgess Meredith. 90M USA. prod/rel: Universal-International

RUGGLES, ELEANOR
Prince of Players, 1953, Book
Prince of Players 1955 d: Philip Dunne. lps: Richard Burton, Maggie McNamara, John Derek. 102M USA. prod/rel: 20th Century-Fox

RUIZ DE LA FUENTE, HORACIO
Bandera Negra, Play
Ultima Lamada 1997 d: Carlos Garcia Agraz. lps: Alberto Estrella, Arcelia Ramirez, Imanol GoenagA. F MXC. *Last Call* prod/rel: Televicine

RUIZ IRIARTE, VICTOR
La Guerra Empieza En Cuba, 1957, Play
Guerra Empieza En Cuba, La 1957 d: Mur Oti. lps: Emma Penella, Gustavo Rojo, Roberto Rey. 107M SPN. *The War Begins in Cuba; The War Starts in Cuba*
Juego de Ninos, 1951, Play
Juego de Ninos 1952 d: Enrique Cahen. 85M SPN.

RUIZ, JUAN (c1283–c1350), SPN
Libro de Buen Amor, 1330, Verse
Libro Del Buen Amor I, El 1974 d: Tomas Aznar. lps: Patxi Andion, Blanca Estrada, Monica Randall. 94M SPN. *Book of Good Love, The*

RULE, ANN
Dead By Sunset, Book
Dead By Sunset 1995 d: Karen Arthur. lps: Ken Olin, Lindsay Frost, Annette O'Toole. TVM. 171M USA. prod/rel: Tristar Television©

RULE, JANE
Desert of the Heart, Novel
Desert Hearts 1986 d: Donna Deitch. lps: Helen Shaver, Patricia Charbonneau, Audra Lindley. 93M USA. prod/rel: Goldwyn, Desert Heart Productions

RULFO, JUAN (1918–1986), MXC
Short Story
Pedazo de Noche, Un 1995 d: Roberto Rochin. lps: Dolores Heredia, Eduardo Von, Armando GarciA. F MXC. *A Sliver of Night* prod/rel: IMCine, Dpc
Pedro Parama, 1955, Novel
Pedro Paramo 1966 d: Carlos Velo. lps: John Gavin, Ignacio Lopez Tarso, Pilar Pellicer. 110M MXC.
Pedro Paramo, 1955, Novel
Pedro Paramo 1976 d: Jose Bolanos. 112M MXC.

RULLIER, GASTON
Chantecaille, Novel
Moulin Dans le Soleil, Le 1938 d: Marc Didier. lps: Gaston Rullier, Orane Demazis, Jacqueline Pacaud. 110M FRN. prod/rel: Films F.V.

Troches Et Cie, Play
Intrigante, L' 1939 d: Emile Couzinet. lps: Paul Cambo, Germaine Aussey, Annie France. 98M FRN. *Belle Bordelaise, La* prod/rel: Burgus Film

RUMPFF, HEINRICH
Duell Mit Diamanten, Novel
Blaue Stern Des Sudens, Der 1951 d: Wolfgang Liebeneiner. lps: Viktor de Kowa, Gretl Schorg, Gustav Knuth. 95M AUS. prod/rel: Vindebona, Schorcht

RUNG, OTTO
Kapellmeister Stroganoff, Short Story
Letzte Souper, Das 1928 d: Mario Bonnard. lps: Heinrich George, Marcella Albani, Jean Bradin. 2036m GRM. prod/rel: Nero-Film, Jakob Karol-Film

RUNYON, DAMON (1884–1946), USA, Runyon, Alfred Damon
Story
Bloodhounds of Broadway 1989 d: Howard Brookner. lps: Matt Dillon, Madonna, Jennifer Grey. 101M USA. prod/rel: Vestron
The Big Mitten, Short Story
No Ransom 1934 d: Fred Newmeyer. lps: Edward Nugent, Phillips Holmes, Leila Hyams. 73M USA. *Bonds of Honour* (UKN); *The Quitter* prod/rel: Liberty Pictures Corp.©
Bloodhounds of Broadway, 1931, Short Story
Bloodhounds of Broadway 1952 d: Harmon Jones. lps: Mitzi Gaynor, Scott Brady, Marguerite Chapman. 93M USA. prod/rel: 20th Century-Fox Film Corp.
Butch Minds the Baby, 1931, Short Story
Butch Minds the Baby 1942 d: Albert S. Rogell. lps: Virginia Bruce, Broderick Crawford, Dick Foran. 75M USA. prod/rel: Unviersal, Mayfair-Damon Runyon Productions
Butch Minds the Baby 1980 d: Peter Webb. lps: Zachary Peirce, Jerry O'Shea, Ivan Cotton. 31M UKN.
A Call on the President, 1937, Short Story
Joe and Ethel Turp Call on the President 1939 d: Robert B. Sinclair. lps: Ann Sothern, William Gargan, Lewis Stone. 70M USA. *A Call on the President* prod/rel: Metro-Goldwyn-Mayer Corp., Loew's, Inc.©
Gentlemen, the King, 1931, Short Story
Professional Soldier 1935 d: Tay Garnett. lps: Victor McLaglen, Freddie Bartholomew, Gloria Stuart. 78M USA. prod/rel: Twentieth Century-Fox Film Corp.©
Hold 'Em Yale!, 1931, Short Story
Hold 'Em, Yale 1935 d: Sidney Lanfield. lps: Buster Crabbe, Patricia Ellis, Cesar Romero. 65M USA. *Uniform Lovers* (UKN) prod/rel: Paramount Productions©
The Idyll of Miss Sarah Brown, 1944, Short Story
Guys and Dolls 1955 d: Joseph L. Mankiewicz. lps: Marlon Brando, Jean Simmons, Frank SinatrA. 149M USA. prod/rel: MGM, Samuel Goldwyn Prods., Inc.
Johnny One-Eye, 1944, Short Story
Johnny One-Eye 1950 d: Robert Florey. lps: Pat O'Brien, Wayne Morris, Dolores Moran. 78M USA. prod/rel: United Artists, Benedict Bogeaus
The Lemon Drop Kid, 1934, Short Story
Lemon Drop Kid, The 1934 d: Marshall Neilan. lps: Lee Tracy, Helen Mack, William Frawley. 71M USA. prod/rel: Paramount Productions©
Lemon Drop Kid, The 1951 d: Sidney Lanfield, (Frank) Tashlin (Uncredited). lps: Bob Hope, Marilyn Maxwell, Fred Clark. 91M USA. prod/rel: Paramount
Little Miss Marker, 1932, Short Story
Little Miss Marker 1934 d: Alexander Hall. lps: Adolphe Menjou, Shirley Temple, Dorothy Dell. 80M USA. *The Girl in Pawn* (UKN); *Half Way Decent* prod/rel: Paramount Productions©
Sorrowful Jones 1949 d: Sidney Lanfield. lps: Bob Hope, Lucille Ball, William Demarest. 88M USA. prod/rel: Paramount
Forty Pounds of Trouble 1962 d: Norman Jewison. lps: Tony Curtis, Suzanne Pleshette, Phil Silvers. 106M USA. prod/rel: Curtis Enterprises
Little Miss Marker 1980 d: Walter Bernstein. lps: Walter Matthau, Julie Andrews, Tony Curtis. 103M USA. prod/rel: Universal
Little Pinks, 1940, Short Story
Big Street, The 1942 d: Irving Reis. lps: Henry Fonda, Lucille Ball, Barton MacLane. 88M USA. prod/rel: RKO Radio
Madame la Gimp, 1929, Short Story
Lady for a Day 1933 d: Frank CaprA. lps: Warren William, May Robson, Guy Kibbee. 102M USA. *Apple Annie; Madam la Gimp; Beggar's Holiday* prod/rel: Columbia Pictures Corp.©
Pocketful of Miracles, A 1961 d: Frank CaprA. lps: Glenn Ford, Bette Davis, Hope Lange. 136M USA. prod/rel: Franton, United Artists

Money from Home, 1935, Short Story
Money from Home 1953 d: George Marshall. lps: Dean Martin, Jerry Lewis, Marjie Miller. 100M USA. prod/rel: Paramount
The Old Doll's House, 1933, Short Story
Midnight Alibi 1934 d: Alan Crosland. lps: Richard Barthelmess, Ann Dvorak, Helen Chandler. 59M USA. *The Old Doll's House* prod/rel: First National Pictures©
Princess O'Hara, 1934, Short Story
Princess O'Hara 1935 d: David Burton. lps: Jean Parker, Chester Morris, Leon Errol. 80M USA. prod/rel: Universal Pictures Corp.©
It Ain't Hay 1943 d: Erle C. Kenton. lps: Bud Abbott, Lou Costello, Grace McDonald. 80M USA. *Money for Jam* (UKN) prod/rel: Universal
Ransom, One Million Dollars, Short Story
Million Dollar Ransom 1934 d: Murray Roth. lps: Phillips Holmes, Edward Arnold, Mary Carlisle. 67M USA. *Ransom One Million Dollars* prod/rel: Universal Pictures Corp.©
Saratoga Chips, Play
Straight Place and Show 1938 d: David Butler. lps: The Ritz Brothers, Richard Arlen, Ethel Merman. 68M USA. *They're Off* (UKN) prod/rel: Twentieth Century-Fox Film Corp.©
A Slight Case of Murder, New York 1935, Play
Slight Case of Murder, A 1938 d: Lloyd Bacon. lps: Edward G. Robinson, Jane Bryan, Allen Jenkins. 85M USA. prod/rel: Warner Bros. Pictures©, First National Picture
Stop, You're Killing Me 1952 d: Roy Del Ruth. lps: Broderick Crawford, Claire Trevor, Virginia Gibson. 86M USA. prod/rel: Warner Bros.
Three Wise Guys, 1933, Short Story
Three Wise Guys 1936 d: George B. Seitz. lps: Robert Young, Betty Furness, Raymond Walburn. 75M USA. prod/rel: Metro-Goldwyn-Mayer Corp.©
Tight Shoes, 1938, Short Story
Tight Shoes 1941 d: Albert S. Rogell. lps: John Howard, Binnie Barnes, Broderick Crawford. 68M USA. prod/rel: Universal
A Very Honorable Guy, 1929, Short Story
Very Honorable Guy, A 1934 d: Lloyd Bacon. lps: Joe E. Brown, Alice White, Alan Dinehart. 62M USA. *A Very Honourable Man* (UKN) prod/rel: First National Pictures©

RUSH, CHRISTOPHER
A Twelve-Month and a Day, Book
Venus Peter 1989 d: Ian Sellar. lps: Ray McAnally, Gordon R. Strachan, Caroline Paterson. 94M UKN. prod/rel: Recorded Releasing, British Film Institute

RUSINOL I PRATS, SANTIAGO
La Mere, 1907, Play
Madre, La 1917 d: Giuseppe Sterni. lps: Italia Vitaliani, Giuseppe Sterni, Giuseppe Majone-Diaz. ITL. prod/rel: Milano Film

RUSINOL, SANTIAGO
L'auca Del Senyor Esteve, 1907, Play
Senor Esteve, El 1929 d: Lucas Argiles. lps: Enrique Borras, Josefina Tapias, Gherardo PenA. F SPN. *L'auca Del Senyor Esteve* prod/rel: Troya Films (Madrid)
Senor Esteve, El 1948 d: Edgar Neville. lps: Carlos Munoz, Manuel Arbo, Carmen de Lucio. 108M SPN. *Mister Esteve*
El Mistic, Play
Mistico, El 1926 d: Juan Andreu Moragas. lps: Consuelo Sirera Fos, Jose Ramon Cuevillas, Francisco Priego. SPN. *El Mistic* prod/rel: Ll.a.M.A. Films (Valencia)

RUSKAY, EVERETT S.
The Meanest Man in the World, 1915, Play
Meanest Man in the World, The 1923 d: Eddie Cline. lps: Bert Lytell, Blanche Sweet, Bryant Washburn. 5600f USA. prod/rel: Principal Pictures, Associated First National Pictures

RUSSELL, ELIZABETH
Princess Priscilla's Fortnight, Novel
Runaway Princess, The 1929 d: Anthony Asquith, Frederick Wendhausen. lps: Mady Christians, Paul Cavanagh, Norah Baring. SIL. 7053f UKN/GRM. *Princess Priscilla's Fortnight* prod/rel: British Instructional, Laender Film
Priscillas Fahrt Ins Gluck 1928 d: Anthony Asquith. lps: Mady Christians, Lewis Dayton, Paul Cavanagh. 2908m GRM. prod/rel: Lander-Film

RUSSELL, GLORIA
The Night Life of a Virile Potato, London 1960, Play
Stork Talk 1962 d: Michael Forlong. lps: Tony Britton, Anne Heywood, John Turner. 97M UKN. prod/rel: Unifilms (Feature Productions)

401

RUSSELL, JOHN
The Lost God, 1921, Short Story
  Sea God, The 1930 d: George Abbott. lps: Richard Arlen, Fay Wray, Eugene Pallette. 8054f USA. prod/rel: Paramount-Publix Corp.

Paradise, Boston 1925, Play
  Paradise 1926 d: Irvin V. Willat. lps: Milton Sills, Betty Bronson, Noah Beery. 7090f USA. prod/rel: Ray Rockett Productions, First National Pictures

The Passion Vine, 1919, Short Story
  Where the Pavement Ends 1923 d: Rex Ingram. lps: Edward Connelly, Alice Terry, Ramon Novarro. 7706f USA. prod/rel: Metro Pictures

RUSSELL, MARION
Little Church Around the Corner, 1902, Play
  Little Church Around the Corner, The 1915 d: E. Mason Hopper. lps: Emilie Polini, Madge Evans. 5r USA. prod/rel: World Film Corp.©, Equitable Motion Pictures Corp.
  Little Church Around the Corner 1923 d: William A. Seiter. lps: Claire Windsor, Kenneth Harlan, Hobart Bosworth. 6300f USA. prod/rel: Warner Brothers Pictures

RUSSELL, RAY
Incubus, Novel
  Incubus 1981 d: John Hough. lps: John Cassavetes, Kerrie Keane, Helen Hughes. 92M CND. *Incubus, The* (USA) prod/rel: Incubus Productions Inc., Mark Film Productions Inc.

Sardonicus, 1961, Short Story
  Mr. Sardonicus 1961 d: William Castle. lps: Ronald Lewis, Audrey Dalton, Guy Rolfe. 89M USA. *Sardonicus* prod/rel: William Castle Productions

RUSSELL, ROSALIND (1908–1976), USA
The Gentle Web, Story
  Unguarded Moment, The 1956 d: Harry Keller. lps: Esther Williams, George Nader, Edward Andrews. 95M USA. prod/rel: Universal-International

RUSSELL, SHEILA MACKAY
A Lamp Is Heavy, Novel
  Feminine Touch, The 1956 d: Pat Jackson. lps: George Baker, Belinda Lee, Delphi Lawrence. 91M UKN. *The Gentle Touch* (USA) prod/rel: Ealing Studios, Rank Film Distributors

RUSSELL, SOL SMITH
A Poor Relation, Play
  Poor Relation, A 1915. lps: Thomas Jefferson, Frank Norcross, Mildred Manning. 3r USA. prod/rel: Biograph Co.

RUSSELL, WILLY (1947–, UKN
Educating Rita, 1981, Play
  Educating Rita 1983 d: Lewis Gilbert. lps: Michael Caine, Julie Walters, Michael Williams. 110M UKN. prod/rel: Rank, Acorn

Shirley Valentine, 1988, Play
  Shirley Valentine 1989 d: Lewis Gilbert. lps: Pauline Collins, Tom Conti, Alison Steadman. 108M UKN/USA. prod/rel: Uip, Paramount

Stags and Hens, Play
  Dancin' Through the Dark 1989 d: Mike Ockrent. lps: Claire Hackett, Con O'Neill, Angela Clarke. 95M UKN. *Dancin' Thru the Dark* prod/rel: Palace, BBC Films

RUSSO, ENZO
I Mertedi Del Diavolo, Novel
  Russicum 1989 d: Pasquale Squitieri. lps: F. Murray Abraham, Treat Williams, Danny Aiello. 113M ITL. *Russicum - I Giorni Del Diavolo*; *The Third Solution* prod/rel: Tiger Cinematagrafica, Rai

RUSSO, FERDINANDO
Le Memorie Di un Ladro, 1907
  Buon Ladrone, Il 1917 d: Giulio Antamoro. lps: Tina d'Angelo, Guido Trento, Piero Concialdi. 1391m ITL. prod/rel: Polifilm

RUSSO, JOHN
The Majorettes, Novel
  One By One 1986 d: Bill Hinzman. lps: Kevin Kindlin, Terrie Godfrey, Mark Jevicky. 90M USA. *The Majorettes* prod/rel: Major Films

RUSSO, VITO
Celluloid Closet, The, Book
  Celluloid Closet, The 1995 d: Robert Epstein, Jeffrey Friedman. DOC. 102M USA. prod/rel: Reflective, Telling Pictures

RUSSO-GIUSTI, ANTONINO
L'articolo 1083, Play
  Gatta Ci Cova 1937 d: Gennaro Righelli. lps: Angelo Musco, Rosina Anselmi, Elli Parvo. 73M ITL. prod/rel: Capitani, I.C.A.R.

L'eredita Dello Zio Canonico, Play
  Eredita Dello Zio Buonanima, L' 1934 d: Amleto Palermi. lps: Angelo Musco, Elsa de Giorgi, Rosina Anselmi. 87M ITL. prod/rel: Capitani Film

RUSVA, MEER HADI HASSAN
Umrao Jaan Ada, 1899, Novel
  Umrao Jaan 1979 d: Muzaffar Ali. lps: Rekha, Naseeruddin Shah, Farouque Sheikh. 145M IND. prod/rel: Integrated Films

RUTLEDGE, NANCY
Le Salaire du Peche, Novel
  Salaire du Peche, Le 1956 d: Denys de La Patelliere. lps: Danielle Darrieux, Jean-Claude Pascal, Jeanne Moreau. 110M FRN. prod/rel: Roger De Broin

RUTTER, OWEN
Lucky Star, Novel
  Once in a New Moon 1935 d: Anthony Kimmins. lps: Eliot Makeham, Rene Ray, Morton Selten. 63M UKN. prod/rel: Fox British

RUVALCABA, EUSEBIO
Un Hilito de Sangre, Novel
  Hilito de Sangre, Un 1995 d: Erwin Newmayer. lps: Diego Luna, Jorge Martinez de Hoyos, Aba Castro. F MXC. *A Trace of Blood* prod/rel: Ccc

RYAN, CORNELIUS (1920–1974), IRL, Ryan, Cornelius John
A Bridge Too Far, Book
  Bridge Too Far, A 1977 d: Richard Attenborough. lps: Dirk Bogarde, James Caan, Michael Caine. 175M UKN/USA. prod/rel: United Artists Corp., Joseph Levine

The Longest Day: June 6, 1944, New York 1959, Novel
  Longest Day, The 1962 d: Andrew Marton, Gerd Oswald. lps: Richard Burton, Kenneth More, Peter Lawford. 180M USA. prod/rel: Darryl F. Zanuck Productions

RYAN, J. M.
Brooks Wilson, Ltd., New York 1966, Novel
  Loving 1970 d: Irvin Kershner. lps: George Segal, Eva Marie Saint, Sterling Hayden. 89M USA. *Brooks Wilson Ltd.* prod/rel: Columbia Pictures, Brooks Ltd.

RYAN, MARAH ELLIS
For the Soul of Rafael, Chicago 1906, Novel
  For the Soul of Rafael 1920 d: Harry Garson. lps: Clara Kimball Young, J. Frank Glendon, Bertram Grassby. 7090f USA. prod/rel: Garson Studios, Inc., Equity Pictures Corp.©

That Girl Montana, New York 1901, Novel
  That Girl Montana 1921 d: Robert T. Thornby. lps: Blanche Sweet, Mahlon Hamilton, Frank Lanning. 5r USA. prod/rel: Jesse D. Hampton, Pathe Exchange, Inc.

Told in the Hills, Chicago 1891, Novel
  Told in the Hills 1919 d: George Melford. lps: Robert Warwick, Anna Little, Tom Forman. 5-6r USA. prod/rel: Famous Players-Lasky Corp.©, Paramount-Artcraft Pictures

RYAN, PATRICK
How I Won the War, London 1963, Novel
  How I Won the War 1967 d: Richard Lester. lps: Michael Crawford, John Lennon, Roy Kinnear. 110M UKN. prod/rel: Petersham Films, United Artists

RYCK, FRANCIS
Drole de Pistolet, Novel
  Silencieux, Le 1972 d: Claude Pinoteau. lps: Lino Ventura, Leo Genn, Robert Hardy. 113M FRN/ITL. *Uomo Che Non Seppe Tacere, L'* (ITL); *The Silent One*; *Escape to Nowhere*; *The Man Who Died Twice*; *The Great Manhunt* prod/rel: Medusa Distribuzione

Effraction, Novel
  Effraction 1983 d: Daniel Duval. lps: Marlene Jobert, Jacques Villeret, Bruno Cremer. 95M FRN. prod/rel: a.T.C. 3000

Der Kuss Des Tigers, Novel
  Kuss Des Tigers, Der 1989 d: Petra Haffter. lps: Beate Jensen, Stephane Ferrara, Yves Beneyton. 104M GRM/FRN. *Le Baiser de l'Assassin* (FRN); *The Kiss of the Tiger*; *Voulez-Vous Mourir Avec Moi?* prod/rel: Futura, Pro-Ject

La Peau de Torpedo, Novel
  Peau de Torpedo, La 1970 d: Jean Delannoy. lps: Stephane Audran, Klaus Kinski, Lilli Palmer. 112M FRN/ITL/GRM. *Dossier 212 -Destinazione Morte* (ITL); *Pill of Death* (UKN); *Only the Cool* (USA); *Der Mann Mit Der Torpedohaut* (GRM); *Children of Mata Hari* prod/rel: Ultra Film, Films Copernic

RYER, GEORGE W.
Our New Minister, Play
  Our New Minister 1913. lps: Joseph Conyers, Thomas McGrath, Alice Joyce. 3000f USA. prod/rel: Kalem

---

The Sunshine of Paradise Alley, 1895, Play
  Sunshine of Paradise Alley 1926 d: Jack Nelson. lps: Barbara Bedford, Kenneth McDonald, Max Davidson. 6850f USA. prod/rel: Chadwick Pictures

RYERSON, FLORENCE
Borrowed Love, Story
  Call of the West 1930 d: Albert Ray. lps: Dorothy Revier, Matt Moore, Tom O'Brien. 70M USA. prod/rel: Columbia Pictures

June Mad, Play
  Her First Beau 1941 d: Theodore Reed. lps: Jackie Cooper, Jane Withers, Edith Fellows. 76M USA. prod/rel: Columbia

Notorious Gentleman, Story
  Smooth As Silk 1946 d: Charles T. Barton. lps: Kent Taylor, Virginia Grey, Jane Adams. 65M USA. *Notorious Gentleman*

Willie the Worm, 1926, Short Story
  Love Makes 'Em Wild 1927 d: Albert Ray. lps: John Harron, Sally Phipps, Ben Bard. 5508f USA. prod/rel: Fox Film Corp.

RYLEY, MADELEINE LUCETTE
An American Citizen, New York 1897, Play
  American Citizen, An 1914 d: J. Searle Dawley. lps: John Barrymore, Evelyn Moore, Peter Lang. 4r USA. prod/rel: Famous Players Film Co., State Rights

Mice and Men, Manchester 1901, Play
  Mice and Men 1916 d: J. Searle Dawley. lps: Marguerite Clark, Marshall Neilan, Charles Waldron. 5r USA. prod/rel: Famous Players Film Co.©, Paramount Pictures Corp.

RYSKIND, MORRIE
Louisiana Purchase, New York 1940, Musical Play
  Louisiana Purchase 1941 d: Irving Cummings. lps: Bob Hope, Vera Zorina, Victor Moore. 98M USA. prod/rel: Paramount

RYTON, ROYCE
Crown Matrimonial, Play
  Crown Matrimonial 1973 d: Alan Bridges. lps: Peter Barkworth, Greer Garson, Robert Sansom. MTV. F UKN. prod/rel: Lwt

S

SAAGI, ELI
Eemi Hageneralit, Play
  Eemi Hageneralit 1979 d: Joel Silberg. lps: Gila Almagor, Zachi Noy, Gideon Zinger. 84M ISR. *The General My Mother*; *Imi Hageneralit* prod/rel: Noah

SABA, UMBERTO (1883–1957), ITL
Ernesto, 1975, Novel
  Ernesto 1979 d: Salvatore Samperi. lps: Martin Halm, Virna Lisi, Michele Placido. 95M ITL/SPN/GRM. prod/rel: Clesi Cin.Ca, C.L.I.C. (Roma)

SABATIER, PIERRE
Business, Play
  Venus de l'Or, La 1938 d: Charles Mere, Jean Delannoy. lps: Jacques Copeau, Daniel Lecourtois, Mireille Balin. 95M FRN. prod/rel: Consortium General Du Film

La Puissance du Baiser, Novel
  Et la Femme Crea l'Amour 1964 d: Fabien Collin. lps: Olivier Despax, Juliette Villard, Diana Lepvrier. 90M FRN. *Les Plaisirs de l'Amour* prod/rel: Hoche Productions

La Revoltee, Novel
  Revoltee, La 1947 d: Marcel L'Herbier. lps: Victor Francen, Jacques Berthier, Josette Day. 95M FRN. *Stolen Affections* (USA) prod/rel: Femina, Lux

SABATIER, ROBERT
Alain Et le Negre, Novel
  Gosse de la Butte, Un 1964 d: Maurice Delbez. lps: Madeleine Robinson, Rene Lefevre, Daniel Jacquinot. 87M FRN. *Rue Des Cascades* prod/rel: Films de Mai 1964, Productions de la Gueville

Boulevard, Novel
  Boulevard 1960 d: Julien Duvivier. lps: Jean-Pierre Leaud, Monique Brienne, Magali Noel. 95M FRN. prod/rel: Orex Films

SABATINI, RAFAEL (1875–1950), ITL
Bardelys the Magnificent, Boston 1905, Novel
  Bardelys the Magnificent 1926 d: King Vidor. lps: John Gilbert, Eleanor Boardman, Roy d'Arcy. 8536f USA. prod/rel: Metro-Goldwyn-Mayer Pictures

The Black Swan, Novel
   Black Swan, The 1942 d: Henry King. lps: Tyrone Power, Maureen O'Hara, Laird Cregar. 85M USA. prod/rel: 20th Century-Fox

Bluff, Novel
   Bluff 1921 d: Geoffrey H. Malins. lps: Lewis Willoughby, Marjorie Hume, Lawrence Anderson. 6240f UKN. prod/rel: Hardy, Gaul

Captain Blood; His Odyssey, Boston 1922, Novel
   Captain Blood 1924 d: David Smith. lps: J. Warren Kerrigan, Jean Paige, Charlotte Merriam. 11r USA. prod/rel: Vitagraph Co. of America
   Captain Blood 1935 d: Michael Curtiz. lps: Errol Flynn, Olivia de Havilland, Lionel Atwill. 119M USA. prod/rel: First National Productions Corp., Cosmopolitan Production

Captain Blood Returns, Novel
   Captain Pirate 1952 d: Ralph Murphy. lps: Louis Hayward, Patricia Medina, John Sutton. 85M USA. Fugitive Captain Blood (UKN) prod/rel: Columbia

The Dream, Novel
   Recoil, The 1922 d: Geoffrey H. Malins. lps: Eille Norwood, Phyllis Titmuss, Lawrence Anderson. 5000f UKN. prod/rel: Hardy, Stoll

The Fortunes of Captain Blood, 1936, Novel
   Fortunes of Captain Blood 1950 d: Gordon Douglas. lps: Louis Hayward, Patricia Medina, George MacReady. 90M USA. prod/rel: Columbia

The Gates of Doom, Novel
   Gates of Doom, The 1919 d: Sidney M. Goldin. lps: Maria ZolA. 7000f UKN. prod/rel: Posner Films

The Nuptials of Corbal, Novel
   Marriage of Corbal, The 1936 d: Karl Grune. lps: Nils Asther, Hugh Sinclair, Hazel Terry. 93M UKN. Prisoner of Corbal (USA) prod/rel: Capitol, General Film Distributors

Scaramouche; a Romance of the French Revolution, Boston 1921, Novel
   Scaramouche 1923 d: Rex Ingram. lps: Ramon Novarro, Alice Terry, Lewis Stone. 9850f USA. prod/rel: Metro Pictures
   Scaramouche 1952 d: George Sidney. lps: Stewart Granger, Eleanor Parker, Mel Ferrer. 118M USA. prod/rel: MGM
   Scaramouche 1963 d: Antonio Isasi. lps: Gerard Barray, Michele Girardon, Alberto de MendozA. 98M FRN/SPN/ITL. La Mascara de Scaramouche (SPN); The Adventures of Scaramouche; Le Avventure Di Scaramouche (ITL) prod/rel: Capitole, Fides

The Scourge, Novel
   Scourge, The 1922 d: Geoffrey H. Malins. lps: Madge Stuart, J. R. Tozer, William Stack. 6930f UKN. Fortune's Fools prod/rel: Hardy, H & S

The Sea Hawk, London 1915, Novel
   Sea Hawk, The 1924 d: Frank Lloyd. lps: Milton Sills, Enid Bennett, Lloyd Hughes. 12r USA. prod/rel: Frank Lloyd Productions, Associated First National Pictures
   Sea Hawk, The 1940 d: Michael Curtiz. lps: Errol Flynn, Brenda Marshall, Claude Rains. 127M USA. prod/rel: Warner Bros. Pictures©

The Tavern Knight, Novel
   Tavern Knight, The 1920 d: Maurice Elvey. lps: Eille Norwood, Madge Stuart, Cecil Humphreys. 6735f UKN. prod/rel: Stoll

SABATO, ERNESTO (1911–, ARG
El Tunel, 1948, Novel
   Tunel, El 1952 d: Leon Klimovsky. lps: Maruja Gil QuesadA. 94M ARG.
   Tunel, El 1988 d: Antonio Drove. lps: Peter Weller, Jane Seymour, Fernando Rey. 117M SPN. The Tunnel; Fatal Obsession

SABBATINI, GIOVANNI
I Spaciafornej d'La Val d'Aosta, 1848, Novel
   Spazzacamini Della Val d'Aosta, Gli 1914 d: Umberto Paradisi. lps: Tonino Giolino, Laura Darville, Giovanni CimarA. 1500m ITL. The Chimney-Sweeps of the Valley of Aosta (USA) prod/rel: Pasquali E C.

SABBEN-CLARE, J. W.
The Lure, Play
   Lure, The 1933 d: Arthur Maude. lps: Anne Grey, Cyril Raymond, Alec Fraser. 65M UKN. prod/rel: Maude Productions, Paramount

SABELLO, JULIO
The Virgin of San Blas, Story
   Virgin, The 1924 d: Alvin J. Neitz. lps: Kenneth Harlan, Dorothy Revier, Sam de Grasse. 6r USA. prod/rel: Phil Goldstone Productions, Truart Film Corp.

SABINA, KAREL
Prodana Nevesta, Prague 1866, Opera
   Prodana Nevesta 1913 d: Max Urban. lps: Tadeusz Dura, Marie Slechtova, Adolf Krossing. CZC. The Bartered Bride prod/rel: Asum

Prodana Nevesta 1922 d: Oldrich Kminek. lps: Frantisek Kudlacek, B. Dvorakova, Laura ZelenskA. 1252m CZC. The Bartered Bride prod/rel: Atropos
   Prodana Nevesta 1933 d: Svatopluk Innemann, Jaroslav Kvapil. lps: Jan Konstantin, Dobroslava Sudikova, Ota HorakovA. 3211m CZC. The Bartered Bride prod/rel: Espo

SABINO, FERNANDO TAVARES
A Faca de Dois Gumes, 1985, Novel
   Faca de Dois Gumes 1989 d: Murilo Salles. lps: Paulo Jose, Marieta Severo, Jose Lewgoy. 97M BRZ. Two-Edged Knife

O Grande Mentecapto, 1979, Novel
   Grande Mentecapto, O 1989 d: Oswaldo CaldeirA. lps: Diogo Vilela, Imara Reis, Luis Fernando Guimaraes. 105M BRZ. The Great Madman; The Blissful Misfit

O Homem Nu, 1960, Short Story
   Homem Nu, O 1968 d: Roberto Santos. lps: Paulo Jose, Leila Diniz, Esmeralda Barros. 118M BRZ. The Naked Man; El Hombre Desnudo

SACCHETTONI, DIDO
Le Notti Di Arancia Meccanica, Book
   Odore Della Notte, L' 1999 d: Claudio Caligari. lps: Valerio Mastandrea, Marco Giallini, Giorgio Tirabassi. 99M ITL. The Scent of the Night prod/rel: Filmauro, Sorpasso Film

SACCHI, FILIPPO
La Primadonna, Novel
   Primadonna, La 1943 d: Ivo Perilli. lps: Anneliese Uhlig, Maria Mercader, Renato Bossi. 88M ITL. prod/rel: Artisti Tecnica Associati, Milano, Artisti Associati

SACCOMANNO, GUILLERMO
Bajo Bandera, Book
   Bajo Bandera 1997 d: Juan Jose Jusid. lps: Miguel Angel Sola, Omera Antonutti, Federico Luppi. F ARG/ITL. Under the Flag prod/rel: Prisma Films (Buenos Aires), Surf Film (Roma)

SACCOMARE, EUGENE
Bandits a Marseille, Paris 1968, Novel
   Borsalino 1970 d: Jacques Deray. lps: Jean-Paul Belmondo, Alain Delon, Michel Bouquet. 128M FRN/ITL. prod/rel: Mars Films, Adel Productions

SACHER-MASOCH, LEPOLD
Venus Im Pelz, Novel
   Malizie Di Venere, Le 1969 d: Massimo Dallamano. lps: Laura Antonelli, Wolf Ackva, Werner Pochath. 90M ITL/GRM. Venus Im Pelz (GRM); Venere Nuda; Venus in Furs prod/rel: Roxy Film (Munich), Vip Production (Chiasso)

SACKHEIM, WILLIAM
Story
   Chicago Syndicate 1955 d: Fred F. Sears. lps: Dennis O'Keefe, Abbe Lane, Paul Stewart. 84M USA. prod/rel: Columbia, Clover

Dames Don't Talk, Story
   Smart Girls Don't Talk 1948 d: Richard L. Bare. lps: Virginia Mayo, Bruce Bennett, Robert Hutton. 81M USA. prod/rel: Warner Bros.

Night Beat, Story
   Homicide 1948 d: Felix Jacoves. lps: Robert Douglas, Helen Westcott, Robert AldA. 77M USA. prod/rel: Warner Bros.

SACKLER, HOWARD
The Great White Hope, Washington D.C. 1967, Play
   Great White Hope, The 1970 d: Martin Ritt. lps: James Earl Jones, Jane Alexander, Lou Gilbert. 103M USA. prod/rel: Lawrence Turman Films, Twentieth Century-Fox

SACKS, DR. OLIVER
Awakenings, Book
   Awakenings 1990 d: Penny Marshall. lps: Robert de Niro, Robin Williams, Julie Kavner. 121M USA. prod/rel: Columbia Tristar
   Kind of Alaska, A 1975 d: Kenneth Ives. lps: Paul Scofield, Dorothy Tutin. MTV. 75M UKN. prod/rel: Central

SACKS, OLIVER
To See and Not See, Story
   At First Sight 1999 d: Irwin Winkler. lps: Val Kilmer, Mira Sorvino, Kelly McGillis. 128M USA. prod/rel: Metro-Goldwyn-Mayer

SADE, DONATIEN (1740–1814), FRN, De Sade, Marquis, Sade, Donatien Alphonse Francois
Les 120 Journees de Sodome Ou l'Ecole du Libertinage, 1904, Novel
   Salo O le Centoventi Giornate Di Sodoma 1975 d: Pier Paolo Pasolini. lps: Paolo Bonacelli, Giorgio Cataldi, Umberto P. Quintavalle. 118M ITL/FRN. Salo -the 120 Days of Sodom (USA); Salo Or the 120 Days of

Sodom; Salo Ou Les 120 Journees de Sodome (FRN) prod/rel: P.E.A. (Roma), Les Prods. Artistes Associes (Paris)

Juliette, 1797, Novel
   Marquis de Sade: Justine 1968 d: Jesus Franco. lps: Romina Power, Maria Rohm, Mercedes McCambridge. 104M ITL/FRN. Justine Ovvero le Disavventure Della Vertu (ITL); Justine and Juliet; Les Infortunes de la Vertu (FRN); Justine; Les Deux Beauties
   Vice Et la Vertu, Le 1963 d: Roger Vadim. lps: Annie Girardot, Robert Hossein, Catherine Deneuve. 105M FRN/ITL. Il Vizio E la Virtu (ITL); Vice and Virtue (USA) prod/rel: Trianon Production, S.N.E.G.

Justine; Ou Les Malheurs de la Vertu, 1791, Novel
   Cruel Passion 1977 d: Chris Boger. lps: Koo Stark, Martin Potter, Lydia Lisle. 88M UKN. Marquis de Sade's Justine; Justine; Cruel Star prod/rel: Target International
   Justine 1976 d: Stuart MacKinnon, Clive Myers. 90M UKN.
   Justine de Sade 1970 d: Claude Pierson. lps: Alice Arno, France Verdier, Yves Arcanel. 100M CND/FRN/ITL. The Violation of Justine (UKN); Sade's Justine; Sade Ou Les Malheurs de Justine; Justine prod/rel: Pierson Productions (Paris), I.C.A.R. (Roma)
   Marquis de Sade: Justine 1968 d: Jesus Franco. lps: Romina Power, Maria Rohm, Mercedes McCambridge. 104M GRM/ITL/FRN. Justine Ovvero le Disavventure Della Vertu (ITL); Justine and Juliet; Les Infortunes de la Vertu (FRN); Justine; Les Deux Beauties
   Vice Et la Vertu, Le 1963 d: Roger Vadim. lps: Annie Girardot, Robert Hossein, Catherine Deneuve. 105M FRN/ITL. Il Vizio E la Virtu (ITL); Vice and Virtue (USA) prod/rel: Trianon Production, S.N.E.G.

La Philosophie Dans le Boudoir, Paris 1795, Novel
   Eugenie. the Story of Her Journey Into Perversion 1970 d: Jesus Franco. lps: Marie Liljedahl, Maria Rohm, Jack Taylor. 91M UKN/SPN/GRM. Eugenie; Eugenie de Sade; Eugenie de Franval; Philosophy in the Boudoir prod/rel: Video-Tel International Productions

SADHU, ARUN
Mumbai Dinank, Novel
   Sinhasan 1979 d: Jabbar Patel. lps: Arun Sarnaik, Nilu Phule, Shriram Lagoo. 170M IND. The Throne; Simhasan prod/rel: Sujata Chitra
Simhasan, Novel
   Sinhasan 1979 d: Jabbar Patel. lps: Arun Sarnaik, Nilu Phule, Shriram Lagoo. 170M IND. The Throne; Simhasan prod/rel: Sujata Chitra

SADI-PETY
Le Boudois Japonais, Play
   Boudoir Japonais, Le 1918. lps: Prince, Renee Sylvaire. 400m FRN. prod/rel: Pathe

SADLEIR, MICHAEL (1888–1957), UKN
Fanny By Gaslight, 1940, Novel
   Fanny By Gaslight 1944 d: Anthony Asquith. lps: Phyllis Calvert, James Mason, Wilfred Lawson. 108M UKN. Man of Evil (USA) prod/rel: General Film Distributors, Gainsborough
   Fanny By Gaslight 1981 d: Peter Jeffries. lps: Chloe Salaman, Anthony Bate, Michael Culver. MTV. 200M UKN. prod/rel: BBC

SADOVEAN
Sturmflut Der Liebe, Novel
   Sturmflut Der Liebe 1929 d: Martin Berger. lps: Marcella Albani, Sybill Morel, Werner Fuetterer. 2422m GRM. prod/rel: Mondo-Film-Vertrieb

SADOVEANU, MIHAIL
Baltagul, 1930, Novel
   Baltagul 1969 d: Mircea Muresan. lps: Margarita Lozano, Ernest Maftei. 108M RMN/ITL. La Mazza (ITL); The Hatchet

Dumbrava Minunata, 1926, Novel
   Dumbrava Minunata 1980 d: Gheorghe Naghi. 86M RMN. The Enchanted Grove

Fratii Jderi, 1935, Novel
   Fratii Jderi 1973 d: Mircea Dragan. lps: Gheorghe Cozorici, Sebastian Papaiani, Stefan Velniciuc. 111M RMN. The Captain Martens Brothers; The Jderi Brothers

Locul Unde Nu S-a Intimplat Nimic, 1933, Novel
   Noiembrie, Ultimul Bal 1989 d: Dan PitA. lps: Stefan Iordache, Soimita Lupu, Gabriela Baciu. 110M RMN. The Last Ball in November; The Last Ball November

Mitrea Cocor, 1949, Novel
   Mitrea Cocor 1952 d: Victor Iliu, Marietta SadovA. 105M RMN.

Nada Florilor, 1951, Short Story
   Vacanta Tragica 1978 d: Constantin Vaeni. 87M RMN. Tragic Holiday

Neamul Soimarestilor, 1915, Novel
Neamul Soimarestilor 1965 d: Mircea Dragan. lps: Stefan Ciobotarasu, Amza PelleA. 100M RMN. *The Hawks*

Ochi de Urs, 1938, Short Story
Ochi de Urs 1983 d: Stere GuleA. lps: Dragos Pislaru, Sofia VicoveancA. 100M RMN. *The Bear Eye's Curse*

SAENZ, DALMIRO A.
Setenta Veces Siete, Buenos Aires 1957, Short Story
Setenta Veces Siete 1962 d: Leopoldo Torre-Nilsson. lps: Isabel Sarli, Francisco Rabal, Jardel Filho. 92M ARG. *Female: Seventy Times Seven* (USA); *Seventy Times Seven; The Female* prod/rel: Araucania Films

SAFDIE, OREN
Hyper-Aller-Genic, Play
You Can Thank Me Later 1998 d: Shimon Dotan. lps: Ellen Burstyn, Amanda Plummer, Ted Levine. 110M CND. prod/rel: Danehip Entertainment, Flashpoint Ltd.

SAFFRAY, MARIE EUGENIE
Sepolta Viva, Novel
Sepolta Viva, La 1973 d: Aldo Lado. lps: Agostina Belli, Maurizio Bonuglia, Fred Robsahm. 95M ITL/FRN. prod/rel: Euro International Film (Roma), C.a.P.A.C. (Paris)

SAGAN, CARL (1934–1996), USA, Sagan, Carl Edward
Contact, Novel
Contact 1997 d: Robert Zemeckis. lps: Jodie Foster, Matthew McConaughey, James Woods. 150M USA. prod/rel: South Side Amusement Co., Warner Bros.

SAGAN, FRANCOISE (1935–, FRN, Quoirez, Francoise
Aimez-Vous Brahms?, Paris 1959, Novel
Goodbye Again 1961 d: Anatole Litvak. lps: Ingrid Bergman, Yves Montand, Anthony Perkins. 120M USA/FRN. *Aimez-Vous Brahms?* (FRN) prod/rel: Argus Productions

Bonjour Tristesse, 1954, Novel
Bonjour Tristesse 1958 d: Otto Preminger. lps: Deborah Kerr, David Niven, Jean Seberg. 93M UKN/USA. prod/rel: Columbia, Wheel Productions

Un Certain Sourire, 1956, Novel
Certain Smile, A 1958 d: Jean Negulesco. lps: Rossano Brazzi, Joan Fontaine, Bradford Dillman. 106M USA. prod/rel: 20th Century-Fox

La Chamade, Paris 1965, Novel
Chamade, La 1968 d: Alain Cavalier. lps: Catherine Deneuve, Michel Piccoli, Roger Van Hool. 105M FRN/ITL. *Heartbeat* prod/rel: Films Ariane, Artistes Associes

Chateau En Suede, Paris 1960, Play
Chateau En Suede 1963 d: Roger Vadim. lps: Monica Vitti, Curd Jurgens, Jean-Claude Brialy. 110M FRN/ITL. *Il Castello in Svezia* (ITL); *Naughty Chateau Nutty* (USA); *Castle in Sweden* prod/rel: Les Films Corona, Spectacles Lubroso

Un Peu de Soleil Dans l'Eau Froide, 1969, Novel
Peu de Soleil Dans l'Eau Froide, Un 1971 d: Jacques Deray. lps: Claudine Auger, Marc Porel, Bernard Fresson. 110M FRN/ITL. *Un Po' Di Sole Nell'aqua Gelida* (ITL); *Sunlight on Cold Water* (UKN) prod/rel: Mega Film

La Recreation, Short Story
Recreation, La 1961 d: Francois Moreuil, Fabien Collin. lps: Jean Seberg, Christian Marquand, Francoise Prevost. 89M FRN. *Playtime* (USA); *Love Play; The Recreation* prod/rel: General Productions

SAGARRA, JOSEP MARIA
La Herida Luminosa, Novel
Herida Luminosa, La 1997 d: Jose Luis Garci. lps: Fernando Guillen, Mercedes Sampietro, Julia Gutierrez CabA. 93M SPN. *A Wound of Light* prod/rel: United International Pictures, Nickel Odeon Dos Inc.

SAGREBELNY, PAWLO
Jaroslaw Mudryj, Novel
Jaroslaw Mudryj 1982 d: Grigori Kochan. lps: Juri Murawizki, Ludmila Smorodina, Tatjana KondyrewA. 149M USS. prod/rel: Dovshenko-Studio Kiev, Mosfilm

SAHIA, ALEXANDRU
Intoarcerea Tatii Din Razboi, 1934, Short Story
Viata Nu Iarta 1957 d: Manole Marcus, Iulian Mihu. lps: Nicolae Praida, Marius Rucareanu, Romulus Neacsu. 75M RMN. *When the Mist Is Lifting; Life Doesn't Spare; Pitiless Life*

Moartea Inghititorului de Sabii, 1934, Short Story
Inghititorul de Sabii 1982 d: Alexa Visarion. 113M RMN.

Moartea Tinarului Cu Termen Redus, 1933, Short Story
Viata Nu Iarta 1957 d: Manole Marcus, Iulian Mihu. lps: Nicolae Praida, Marius Rucareanu, Romulus Neacsu. 75M RMN. *When the Mist Is Lifting; Life Doesn't Spare; Pitiless Life*

SAHIN, OSMAN
Derman, Novel
Derman 1983 d: Serif Goren. lps: Hulya Kocyigit, Tarik Akan, Talat Bulut. 90M TRK. *Remedy* prod/rel: Gulsa Film

The White Ox, Novel
Ayna 1984 d: Erden Kiral. lps: Nur Surer, Suavi Eren, Hikmet Celik. 88M GRM/TRK. *The Mirror; Der Spiegel* prod/rel: von Vietinghoff Filmproduktion, ZDF

SAHIWAL
Novel
Mrityudand 1997 d: Prakash JhA. lps: Shabana Azmi, Madhuri Dixit, Om Puri. 120M IND. *Death Sentence* prod/rel: Prakash Jha Prods.

SAHNI, BHISHM
Tamas, Novel
Tamas 1986 d: Govind Nihalani. lps: Surekha Sikri, Om Puri, Deepa Sahi. MTV. 297M IND. *Darkness* prod/rel: Blaze Ents.

SAIA, LOUIS
Une Amie d'Enfance, Play
Amie d'Enfance, Une 1977 d: Francis Mankiewicz. lps: Pauline Martin, Pauline Lapointe, Jean-Guy Viau. 90M CND. prod/rel: Les Productions Du Verseau Inc., Les Films Mutuels

SAIKO, GEORGE EMMANUEL
Der Mann Im Schilf, 1955, Novel
Mann Im Schilf, Der 1978 d: Manfred Purzer. lps: Jean Sorel, Erika Pluhar, Nathalie Delon. 113M GRM. *The Man in the Rushes* prod/rel: Roxy, Neue Constantin

SAINT, H. F.
Memoirs of an Invisible Man, Novel
Memoirs of an Invisible Man 1992 d: John Carpenter. lps: Chevy Chase, Daryl Hannah, Sam Neill. 99M USA. prod/rel: Warner Bros., Cornelius

SAINT-ALBAN, DOMINIQUE
Le Passe Simple, Novel
Passe Simple, Le 1977 d: Michel Drach. lps: Marie-Jose Nat, Victor Lanoux, Anne Lonnberg. 96M FRN. *Replay; The Simple Past* prod/rel: Port Royal, Gaumont

SAINT-ALBIN
Train de Plaisir, 1884, Play
Treno Doria 1924 d: Luciano DoriA. lps: Elena Sangro, Alberto Collo, Lydia QuarantA. 1926m ITL. prod/rel: Fert

SAINT-AMAND
L' Auberge Des Adrets, Play
Auberge Sanglante ,L' 1913 d: Emile Chautard. lps: Andre Liabel, Charles Krauss, Mevisto. FRN. prod/rel: Acad

SAINTE AUBE, ALBERT
La Louve Solitaire, Novel
Louve Solitaire, La 1968 d: Edouard Logereau. lps: Daniele Gaubert, Michel Duchaussoy, Julien Guiomar. 100M FRN/ITL. *La Gatta Dagli Artigli d'Oro* (ITL) prod/rel: Intermondia Films, Films Corona

SAINT-GIL, PHILIPPE
La Meilleure Part, Novel
Meilleure Part, La 1956 d: Yves Allegret. lps: Gerard Philipe, Michele Cordoue, Umberto Spadaro. 90M FRN/ITL. *Gli Anni Che Non Ritornano* (ITL) prod/rel: le Trident, Silver Films

SAINT-HILAIRE
Trois Marins Dans un Couvent, Play
Trois Marins Dans un Couvent 1949 d: Emile Couzinet. lps: Frederic Duvalles, Marcel Vallee, Pierre Brebans. 80M FRN. prod/rel: Burgus Films

SAINT-LAURENT, CECIL (1919–, FRN, Laurent, Jacques
Story
Secret du Chevalier d'Eon, Le 1960 d: Jacqueline Audry. lps: Isa Miranda, Gabriele Ferzetti, Giulia Rubini. 97M FRN/ITL. *Storie d'Amore Proibite* (ITL); *Il Cavaliere E la Czarina; The Secret of the Chevalier d'Eon; Le Chevalier Et la Tzarine* prod/rel: Italia Produzione Film (Roma), Paris Elysees Films

Un Caprice de Caroline Cherie, Novel
Caprice de Caroline Cherie, Un 1952 d: Jean Devaivre. lps: Martine Carol, Jacques Dacqmine, Marthe Mercadier. 98M FRN. *Caprice of "Dear Caroline"* (USA); *Caprice of Caroline* prod/rel: Cinephonic, S.N.E.G.

Caroline Cherie, Novel
Caroline Cherie 1950 d: Richard Pottier. lps: Martine Carol, Jacques Dacqmine, Marie DeA. 140M FRN. *Dear Caroline* (USA) prod/rel: Cinephonic, S.N.E.G.

Caroline Cherie 1967 d: Denys de La Patelliere. lps: France Anglade, Vittorio de Sica, Bernard Blier. 105M FRN/GRM/ITL. *Schon Wie Die Sunde* (GRM); *Pretty As Sin* prod/rel: Cineurop, Norddeutsche Film

Le Fils de Caroline Cherie, Novel
Fils de Caroline Cherie, Le 1954 d: Jean Devaivre. lps: Jean-Claude Pascal, Brigitte Bardot, Micheline Gary. 110M FRN. *The Son of Dear Caroline* (USA) prod/rel: Cinephonic, S.N.E.G.

La Fin de Lamiel, 1966, Novel
Lamiel 1967 d: Jean Aurel. lps: Anna Karina, Michel Bouquet, Denise Gence. 100M FRN/ITL. prod/rel: Rome-Paris-Films, Films Copernic

Lola Montes, Novel
Lola Montes 1955 d: Max Ophuls. lps: Martine Carol, Peter Ustinov, Anton Walbrook. 140M FRN/GRM. *The Sins of Lola Montes* (USA); *The Fall of Lola Montes* (UKN); *Lola Montez* (GRM) prod/rel: Gamma Films, Florida Films

Les Mauvaises Rencontres, Novel
Mauvaises Rencontres, Les 1955 d: Alexandre Astruc. lps: Jean-Claude Pascal, Anouk Aimee, Philippe Lemaire. 84M FRN. prod/rel: Films Marceau

Sophie Et le Crime, Novel
Sophie Et le Crime 1955 d: Pierre Gaspard-Huit. lps: Marina Vlady, Peter Van Eyck, Jean Gaven. 100M FRN. prod/rel: Films Roger Richebe, Synimex

SAINT-MOORE, ADAM
A Coeur Ouvert Pour Face d'Ange, Novel
Killer Per Sua Maesta, Un 1968 d: Federico Chentrens, Maurice Cloche. lps: Kerwin Mathews, Marilu Tolo, Venantino Venantini. 105M ITL/FRN/GRM. *Le Tueur Aime Les Bonbons* (FRN); *Zucker Fur Den Morder* (GRM); *The Killer Likes Candy* (USA); *A Killer of His Majesty; Sugar for the Murderer* prod/rel: Franca Film (Roma), Eichberg (Munich)

SAINT-PAUL
Une Petite Femme En Or, Play
Petite Femme En Or, Une 1933 d: Andre Pellenc. lps: Anthony Gildes, Fernand Rene, Marcel Carpentier. SHT FRN.

SAINT-SAENS, CHARLES (1835–1921), FRN, Saint-Saens, Charles Camille
Samson Et Dalila, Weimar 1877, Opera
Samson and Delilah 1922 d: Edwin J. Collins. lps: Valia, M. D. Waxman. 1100f UKN. prod/rel: Master Films, Gaumont

Samson and Delilah 1927 d: H. B. Parkinson. lps: William Anderson. 2000f UKN. prod/rel: Song Films

SAINT-SORNY
Bicchi, Novel
Ile d'Amour, L' 1927 d: Jean Durand, Berthe Dagmar. lps: Pierre Batcheff, Claude France, Therese Kolb. F FRN. *Bicchi* prod/rel: Franco-Film

L' Ile d'Amour, Novel
Ile d'Amour, L' 1943 d: Maurice Cam. lps: Tino Rossi, Josseline Gael, Edouard Delmont. 106M FRN. prod/rel: Cyrnos, Sigma

Palaces, Novel
Palaces 1927 d: Jean Durand. lps: Huguette Duflos, Leon Bary, Gaston Nores. 2200m FRN. *Bitter Sweets* prod/rel: Natan

SAITO, SHINICHI
Yoshiwara Enjo, Book
Yoshiwara Enjo 1987 d: Hideo GoshA. lps: Yuko Natori, Sayoko Ninomiya, Mariko Fuji. 133M JPN. *Fire Over the Women's Castle; Tokyo Bordello* prod/rel: Toei Co.

SAJBEL, MICHAEL
The Witch, Novel
Superstition 1982 d: James W. Roberson. lps: James Houghton, Albert Salmi, Larry Pennell. 85M USA. *The Witch* prod/rel: Penaria Corporation

SAKAGUCHI, ANGO
Doctor Liver, Book
Kanzo Sensei 1998 d: Shohei ImamurA. lps: Akira Emoto, Kumiko Aso, Jyuro KarA. 129M JPN. *Dr. Akagi* prod/rel: Imamura Prods., Toei Co.

SAKAI, SABURO
Ozora No Samurai, Novel
Ozora No Samurai 1976 d: Seiji MaruyamA. lps: Hiroshi Fujioka, Tetsuro Tamba, Taro Shigaki. 99M JPN. *Zero Pilot* prod/rel: Taikan

SALACROU, ARMAND (1899–1989), FRN
Histoire de Rire, 1940, Play
Histoire de Rire 1941 d: Marcel L'Herbier. lps: Micheline Presle, Fernand Gravey, Pierre Renoir. 117M FRN. *Foolish Husbands* (USA) prod/rel: Discina

SALAMANCA, J. R.
Lilith, New York 1961, Novel
Lilith 1964 d: Robert Rossen. lps: Warren Beatty, Jean Seberg, Peter FondA. 114M USA. prod/rel: Centaur Enterprises, Columbia

The Lost Country, New York 1958, Novel
Wild in the Country 1961 d: Philip Dunne. lps: Elvis Presley, Hope Lange, Tuesday Weld. 114M USA. prod/rel: Company of Artists

SALAS, ANDRE
Latin Boys Go to Hell, Novel
Latin Boys Go to Hell 1997 d: Ela Troyano. lps: Irwin Ossa, John Bryant Davila, Jenifer Lee Simard. 66M USA/GRM/SPN. prod/rel: Jurgen Bruning Filmproduktion, Fernando Colomo P.C.

SALE, CHARLES
The Specialist, Novel
Specialist, The 1966 d: James Hill. lps: Bernard Miles, Colin Ellis, Douglas Milvain. 20M UKN. prod/rel: Ritz, Heald-Samson

SALE, DAVID
Come to Mother, Novel
Live Again, Die Again 1974 d: Richard A. CollA. lps: Cliff Potts, Donna Mills, Walter Pidgeon. TVM. 73M USA. prod/rel: Universal

SALE, RICHARD (1911–1993), USA
Assassination, Novel
Assassination 1987 d: Peter Hunt. lps: Charles Bronson, Jill Ireland, Stephen Elliott. 88M USA. *The President's Wife* prod/rel: Cannon Films, Cannon Films International

The Doctor Doubles in Death, Short Story
This Side of the Law 1950 d: Richard L. Bare. lps: Viveca Lindfors, Kent Smith, Janis Paige. 74M USA. prod/rel: Warner Bros.

Not Too Narrow - Not Too Deep, London 1936, Novel
Strange Cargo 1940 d: Frank Borzage. lps: Joan Crawford, Clark Gable, Ian Hunter. 113M USA. *Not Too Narrow Not Too Deep* prod/rel: Metro-Goldwyn-Mayer Corp., Loew's, Inc.©

The Oscar, New York 1963, Novel
Oscar, The 1966 d: Russell Rouse. lps: Stephen Boyd, Elke Sommer, Milton Berle. 121M USA. prod/rel: Greene-Rouse Productions, Embassy Pictures

The White Buffalo, Novel
White Buffalo, The 1976 d: J. Lee Thompson. lps: Charles Bronson, Jack Warden, Will Sampson. 97M USA. *Hunt to Kill* prod/rel: United Artists

SALEMME, VINCENZO
L' Amico Del Cuore, Play
Amico Del Cuore, L' 1999 d: Vincenzo Salemme. lps: Vincenzo Salemme, Eva Herzigova, Carlo Buccirosso. 98M ITL. *My True Swedish Friend* prod/rel: Cecchi Gori Distribuzione, Cecchi Gori Group Tiger Cin.Ca

SALES, CHARLES
Le Ciffonier de Paris, 1847, Novel
Cenciaiuolo Di Parigi, Il 1917 d: Enrico Vidali. lps: Umberto Mozzato, Liliane de Rosny, Lydia de Roberti. 1413m ITL. prod/rel: Subalpino Film

SALES, HERBERTO
Cascalho, 1944, Novel
Cascalho 1950 d: Leo Marten. 86M BRZ.

SALES, PIERRE
Le Bonhomme Jadis, Short Story
Bonhomme Jadis, Le 1912 d: Emile Chautard. lps: Leon Bernard, Jacques de Feraudy, Renee Sylvaire. 333m FRN. prod/rel: Eclair, Acad

La Danse Heroique, Novel
Danse Heroique, La 1914 d: Ferdinand Zecca, Rene Leprince. lps: Henry Mayer, Gabrielle Robinne, Simone Mareix. 1420m FRN. prod/rel: Scagl

La Mariquita, Novel
Mariquita, La 1913 d: Henri Fescourt. lps: Paul Marcel, Derigal, Augusta Vallee. 1978m FRN. prod/rel: Gaumont

Peine d'Amour, Novel
Peine d'Amour 1914 d: Henri Fescourt. lps: Andre Luguet, Henri Maillard, Madeleine SoriA. 702m FRN. prod/rel: Gaumont

SALGARI, EMILIO
Novel
Cavalieri Del Deserto, I 1942 d: Gino Talamo, Osvaldo Valenti. lps: Osvaldo Valenti, Luisa Ferida, Luigi Pavese. UNF. ITL. *I Predoni Del Deserto*; *Gli Ultimi Taureg*; *I Predoni Del Sahara* prod/rel: a.C.I.

Sandokan Alla Riscossa 1964 d: Luigi Capuano. lps: Ray Danton, Guy Madison, Franca BettojA. 96M ITL. *Sandokan Fights Back* (USA); *Sandokan Strikes Back*; *The Conqueror and the Empress* prod/rel: Liber Film (Roma), Eichberg Gmbh (Munich)

Sandokan Contro Il Leopardo Di Sarawak 1965 d: Luigi Capuano. lps: Ray Danton, Franca Bettoja, Guy Madison. 90M ITL/GRM. *Sandokan Against the Leopard of Sarawak* (USA); *Return of Sandokan*; *Sandokan Und Der Leopard* (GRM) prod/rel: Liber Film (Roma), Eichberg Gmbh (Munich)

Tesoro Del Bengala, Il 1954 d: Gianni Vernuccio. lps: Sabu, Luisella Boni, Amanda Koumar. 90M ITL. prod/rel: Venturini Film
Story
Tigre E Ancora Viva: Sandokan Alla Riscossa, La 1977 d: Sergio SollimA. lps: Massimo Foschi, Kabir Bedi, Philippe Leroy. 130M ITL. *La Tigre E Ancora Viva* prod/rel: Rizzoli Film, Cineriz
Novel
Vendetta Dei Tughs, La 1955 d: Gian Paolo Callegari, Ralph Murphy. lps: Lex Barker, Fiorella Fiori, Paul Muller. 95M ITL. *Killers of the East* (USA) prod/rel: Produzione Venturini

Capitan Tempesta, Novel
Capitan Tempesta 1942 d: Corrado d'Errico. lps: Doris Duranti, Dina Sassoli, Carlo Ninchi. 85M ITL. prod/rel: Scalera Film

Cartagine in Fiamme, Genoa 1908, Novel
Cartagine in Fiamme 1959 d: Carmine Gallone. lps: Pierre Brasseur, Daniel Gelin, Anne Heywood. 120M ITL/FRN. *Carthage En Flammes* (FRN); *Carthage in Flames* (UKN) prod/rel: Lux Film, Produzioni Gallone (Roma)

Il Corsaro Nero, Novel
Corsaro Nero, Il 1936 d: Amleto Palermi. lps: Ciro Verratti, Silvana Jachino, Ada Biagini. 96M ITL. *The Black Corsair* (USA) prod/rel: Artisti Associati

Il Corsaro Verde, Novel
Tre Corsari, I 1952 d: Mario Soldati. lps: Ettore Manni, Barbara Florian, May Britt. 98M ITL. prod/rel: Carlo Ponti, Dino de Laurentiis

Le Due Tigri, 1904, Novel
Due Tigri, Le 1941 d: Giorgio C. Simonelli. lps: Massimo Girotti, Alanova, Sandro Ruffini. 85M ITL. prod/rel: Sol Film, Generalcine

La Figlia Del Corsaro Verde, Novel
Figlia Del Corsaro Verde, La 1941 d: Enrico Guazzoni. lps: Doris Duranti, Fosco Giachetti, Camillo Pilotto. 76M ITL. prod/rel: Manenti Film

Il Figlio Del Corsaro Rosso, Florence 1920, Novel
Figlio Del Corsaro Rosso, Il 1921 d: Vitale de Stefano. lps: Rodolfo Badaloni, Nera Badaloni, Riccardo Tassani. 2941m ITL. prod/rel: Rosa Film

Figlio Del Corsaro Rosso, Il 1942 d: Marco Elter. lps: Luisa Ferida, Loredana, Vittorio Sanni. 80M ITL. prod/rel: Bellamacina E Cuffaro, I.C.I.

Figlio Del Corsaro Rosso, Il 1960 d: Primo Zeglio. lps: Lex Barker, Sylvia Lopez, Vira Silenti. 97M ITL. *Son of the Red Corsair* (USA); *Son of the Red Pirate* prod/rel: Athena Cin.Ca

La Figlia Del Corsaro Nero Iolanda, Novel
Iolanda, la Figlia Del Corsaro Nero 1921 d: Vitale de Stefano. lps: Anita Faraboni, Emilio Liguori. 2785m ITL. *Jolanda la Figlia Del Corsaro Nero* prod/rel: Rosa Film

Il Leone Di Damasco, Novel
Leone Di Damasco, Il 1942 d: Corrado d'Errico. lps: Doris Duranti, Carlo Ninchi, Adriano Rimoldi. 85M ITL. prod/rel: Scalera Film

I Misteri Della Jungla Nera, Genoa 1895, Novel
Misteri Della Giungla Nera, I 1964 d: Luigi Capuano. lps: Guy Madison, Ingeborg Schoner, Giacomo Rossi-Stuart. 90M ITL/GRM. *Das Geheimnis Der Lederschlinge* (GRM); *Secret of the Leather Strap*; *The Mystery of Thug Island* (USA) prod/rel: Liber Film (Roma), Eichberg Film (Munich)

La Montagna Di Luce, Novel
Montagna Di Luce, La 1965 d: Umberto Lenzi. lps: Richard Harrison, Luciana Gilli, Wilbert Bradley. 103M ITL. prod/rel: Filmes, Olimpic Film

I Pirati Della Malesia, Novel
Pirati Della Malesia, I 1941 d: Enrico Guazzoni. lps: Massimo Girotti, Clara Calamai, Camillo Pilotto. 110M ITL/SPN/FRN. *Los Pirates de la Malasia* (SPN); *Les Pirates de Malaisia* (FRN) prod/rel: Sol Film, Generalcine

Pirati Della Malesia, I 1964 d: Umberto Lenzi. lps: Steve Reeves, Genevieve Grad, Rik BattagliA. 110M ITL/SPN/FRN. *Los Pirates de Malasia* (SPN); *Les Pirates de Malaisie* (FRN) prod/rel: Filmes Cin.Ca (Roma), Sirius (Paris)

I Predoni Del Sahara, Novel
Predoni Del Sahara, I 1966 d: Guido MalatestA. lps: George Mikell, Pamela Tudor, Enzo Fiermonte. 92M ITL. prod/rel: King Film Production (Roma), Copro Film (Cairo)

Il Romanzo Della Fiamme, Novel
Cabiria 1914 d: Giovanni Pastrone. lps: Carolina Catena, Lydia Quaranta, Umberto Mozzato. 4000m ITL. prod/rel: Itala Film

Le Tigri Di Mompracem, Genoa 1900, Novel
Sandokan 1964 d: Umberto Lenzi. lps: Steve Reeves, Genevieve Grad, Andrea Bosic. 102M SPN/FRN/ITL. *Sandokan le Tigre de Borneo* (FRN); *Sandokan the Great* (USA); *Sandokan la Tigre Di Mompracem* (ITL) prod/rel: Comptoir Francais Du Film (Paris), Filmes Cin.Ca (Roma)

Tigri Di Mompracem, Le 1970 d: Mario Sequi. lps: Ivan Rassimov, Claudia Gravy, Andrea Bosic. 95M ITL/SPN. *Los Tigres de Mompracem* (SPN); *Yanez - Sandokan - Tremal-Naik* prod/rel: Filmes (Roma), Copercines (Madrid)

Gli Ultimi Filibustieri, Novel
Avventuriero Della Tortuga, L' 1965 d: Luigi Capuano. lps: Rik Battaglia, Guy Madison, Ingeborg Schoner. 97M ITL/GRM. *Adventurer of Tortuga* prod/rel: Liber Film (Roma), Eichberg Film (Munich)

Ultimi Filibustieri, Gli 1921 d: Vitale de Stefano. lps: Riccardo Tassani, Nera Badaloni, La Bella ArgentinA. 2051m ITL. prod/rel: Rosa Film

Ultimi Filibustieri, Gli 1943 d: Marco Elter. lps: Loredana, Vittorio Sanipoli, Osvaldo Valenti. 82M ITL. prod/rel: Bellamacina E Cuffaro, I.C.I.

SALINGER, J.D. (1919–, USA, Salinger, Jerome David
Uncle Wiggily in Connecticut, 1948, Short Story
My Foolish Heart 1949 d: Mark Robson. lps: Susan Hayward, Dana Andrews, Robert Keith. 99M USA. prod/rel: RKO Radio

SALLES, PIERRE
La Tourmente, Novel
Tourmente, La 1912 d: Victorin Jasset. lps: Charles Krauss, Paul Guide, Cecile Guyon. 640m FRN. prod/rel: Eclair

SALMINEN, SALLY
Katrina, 1936, Novel
Katrina 1943 d: Gustaf Edgren. 102M SWD.

SALTEN, FELIX (1869–1945), HNG, Salzmann, Siegmann
Florian - Das Pferd Des Kaisers, Berlin 1933, Novel
Florian 1940 d: Edwin L. Marin. lps: Robert Young, Helen Gilbert, Charles Coburn. 91M USA. prod/rel: Metro-Goldwyn-Mayer Corp., Loew's, Inc.©

The Hound of Florence, 1923, Novel
Shaggy Dog, The 1959 d: Charles T. Barton. lps: Fred MacMurray, Jean Hagen, Tommy Kirk. 101M USA. prod/rel: Buena Vista, Walt Disney Prods.

Shaggy Dog, The 1994 d: Dennis Dugan. lps: Ed Begley Jr., Scott Weinger, Sarah Lassez. TVM. 120M USA. prod/rel: Walt Disney Television

Martin Overbeck, Novel
Schwere Jungens - Leichte Madchen 1927 d: Carl Boese. lps: Lissi Arna, Gustav Frohlich, Karl Falkenberg. 2640m GRM. prod/rel: Carl Boese-Film

Perri, Novel
Perri 1957 d: N. Paul Kenworthy, Ralph Wright. 75M USA. prod/rel: Buena Vista, Walt Disney Prods.

Vorstadtvariete, Play
Vorstadtvariete 1934 d: Werner Hochbaum. lps: Luise Allrich, Mathias Wieman, Olly Gebauer. 93M AUS. *Die Amsel von Lichtental*

SALTER, JAMES
The Hunters, 1957, Novel
Hunters, The 1958 d: Dick Powell. lps: Robert Mitchum, Robert Wagner, Richard Egan. 108M USA. prod/rel: 20th Century-Fox

Twenty Minutes, Short Story
Boys 1996 d: Stacy Cochran. lps: Winona Ryder, Lukas Haas, Skeet Ulrich. 89M USA. prod/rel: Polygram Filmed Entertainment, Interscope Communications

SALTUS, EDGAR (1855–1921), USA, Saltus, Edgar Evertson
Daughters of the Rich, New York 1900, Novel
Daughters of the Rich 1923 d: Louis J. Gasnier. lps: Miriam Cooper, Gaston Glass, Ethel Shannon. 6073f USA. prod/rel: B. P. Schulberg Productions, Al Lichtman Corp.

SALVA, PIERRE
La Main a Couper, Novel
Main a Couper, La 1974 d: Etienne Perier. lps: Lea Massari, Michel Bouquet, Bernard Blier. 95M FRN/ITL. *Un Cadavere Di Troppo* (ITL); *And Hope to Die* prod/rel: Clodio Cin.Ca, Roitfeld

SALVALAGGIO, NANTAS
Il Letto in Piazza, Novel
Letto in Piazza, Il 1976 d: Bruno Alberto Gaburro. lps: Rossana Podesta, Renzo Montagnani, John Ireland. 95M ITL. *Sex Diary* prod/rel: Flaminia Prod.Ni Cin.Che, Fida

SALVAT, PIERRE
Deux de l'Escadrille, Novel
Deux de l'Escadrille 1952 d: Maurice Labro. lps: Jean Richard, Magali Noel, Roland Armontel. 90M FRN. *Les Cochons N'ont Pas d'Ailes* prod/rel: Jason, Latino Consortium Cinema

SALVATORE, ADA
Radio Play
Trent'anni Di Servizio 1945 d: Mario Baffico. lps: Emilio Baldanello, Bianca Doria, Margherita Seglin. F ITL. prod/rel: Cines, E.N.I.C.

SALVICH, SANTIAGO
Duca E Forse Una Duchessa, Play
Idillio a Budapest 1941 d: Giorgio Ansoldi, Gabriele Varriale. lps: Germaine Aussey, Osvaldo Valenti, Sergio Tofano. 78M ITL. *Un Duca E Forse Una Duchessa* prod/rel: Schermi Del Mondo, Cine Tirrenia

SAMAN, E. F.
Novel
Srdce V Celofanu 1939 d: Jan Svitak. lps: Zita Kabatova, Jiri Plachy, Jaroslav Marvan. 2469m CZC. *Heart in Cellophane* prod/rel: Praha-Film, Dafa

SAMBERK, FRANTISEK FERDINAND
Jedenacte Prikazani, Play
Jedenacte Prikazani 1925 d: Vaclav Kubasek. lps: Hugo Haas, Meda Valentova, Jiri Hron. 2716m CZC. *The Eleventh Commandment* prod/rel: Astra, Biografia

Podskalak, Play
Podskalak 1928 d: Premysl Prazsky. lps: Theodor Pistek, Antonie Nedosinska, Mana ZeniskovA. CZC. *The Man from Podskali* prod/rel: Bratri Deglove, Degl a Spol

SAMMIS, EDWARD
Albert R.N., Play
Albert R.N. 1953 d: Lewis Gilbert. lps: Anthony Steel, Jack Warner, Robert Beatty. 88M UKN. *Break to Freedom* (USA); *Spare Man* prod/rel: Dial Films, Eros

SAMS, GIDEON
The Punk, Novel
Punk and the Princess, The 1993 d: Mike Sarne. lps: Charlie Creed-Miles, Vanessa Hadaway, David Shawyer. 96M UKN. *The Punk* prod/rel: Feature Film, Videodrome

SAMSON, BARBARA
You're Not Serious When You're Seventeen, Novel
Mes Dix-Sept Ans 1996 d: Philippe Faucon. lps: Valentine Vidal, Brigitte Rovan, Pierre Beziers. 72M FRN. *I Was Seventeen* prod/rel: France 2, Ellipse Programme

SAMUEL, A.
Poppy Comes to Town, New York 1923, Musical Play
Poppy 1936 d: A. Edward Sutherland, Stuart Heisler (Uncredited). lps: W. C. Fields, Rochelle Hudson, Richard Cromwell. 73M USA. prod/rel: Paramount Productions©

SAMUELS, MAURICE V.
The Wanderer, New York 1917, Play
Wanderer, The 1926 d: Raoul Walsh. lps: Greta Nissen, William Collier Jr., Ernest Torrence. 8173f USA. prod/rel: Famous Players-Lasky, Paramount Pictures

SAN ANTONIO
La Vieille Qui Marchait Dans la Mer, Novel
Vieille Qui Marchait Dans la Mer, La 1991 d: Laurent Heynemann. lps: Jeanne Moreau, Michel Serrault, Luc Thuillier. 97M FRN. *The Old Lady Who Walked in the Sea* (UKN); *The Lady Who Wades in the Sea* prod/rel: Blue Dahlia, Sfc

SANCHEZ, VICENTE
O Passado E O Presente, Play
Passado E O Presente, O 1970 d: Manoel de OliveirA. lps: Maria de Saisset, Manuela de Freitas, Barbara VieirA. 115M PRT. *Past and Present* prod/rel: de Oliveira, Centro Portugues de Cinema

SANCHIS SINISTIERRA, JOSE
Ay Carmela!, Play
Ay, Carmela! 1990 d: Carlos SaurA. lps: Carmen Maura, Andres Pajares, Gabino Diego. 105M SPN/ITL. prod/rel: Iberoamericana Films (Madrid), Ellepi (Roma)

SANCIAUME, JEAN-LOUIS
L' Homme de la Nuit, Novel
Homme de la Nuit, L' 1946 d: Rene Jayet. lps: Albert Prejean, Junie Astor, Maurice Lagrenee. 88M FRN. prod/rel: Codo-Cinema

SAND, GEORGE (1804-1876), FRN, Dupin, Amandine Lucie Aurore
Indiana, 1831, Novel
Indiana 1920 d: Umberto FracchiA. lps: Diana Karenne, Bruno Emanuel Palmi. 2079m ITL. prod/rel: Tespi Film

La Mare Au Diable, Novel
Mare Au Diable, La 1923 d: Pierre Caron. lps: Gladys Rolland, Jean-David Evremond, Gilbert Sambon. 2500m FRN. prod/rel: Films Pierre Caron

Mauprat, Novel
Mauprat 1926 d: Jean Epstein. lps: Sandra Milowanoff, Maurice Schutz, Nino Costantini. 2000m FRN. prod/rel: Films Jean Epstein

La Petite Fadette, Paris 1849, Novel
Fanchon the Cricket 1915 d: James Kirkwood. lps: Mary Pickford, Adele Astaire, Fred Astaire. 5r USA. prod/rel: Famous Players Film Co., Paramount Pictures Corp.

Petite Fadette, La 1921 d: Raphael Adams. lps: Jeanne Van Elsche, Jean Lorette, Jean Adam. F FRN. prod/rel: Eclipse

SANDBURG, CARL (1878-1967), USA
Abraham Lincoln, 1926-1939, Biography
Sandburg's Lincoln 1974-76 d: George Schaefer. lps: Hal Holbrook, Sada Thompson, Roy Poole. MTV. 300M USA.

SANDEAU, JULES
Le Gendre de Monsieur Poirier, 1854, Play
Gendre de Monsieur Poirier, Le 1933 d: Marcel Pagnol. lps: Annie Ducaux, Leon Bernard, Jean Debucourt. 102M FRN. prod/rel: Auteurs Associes

Madeleine, Novel
Madeleine 1916 d: Jean Kemm. lps: Armand Tallier, Maillard, Huguette Duflos. 995m FRN. prod/rel: Scagl

Mademoiselle de la Seigliere, Novel
Mademoiselle de la Seigliere 1920 d: Andre Antoine, Georges DenolA. lps: Felix Huguenet, Huguette Duflos, Charles Granval. 1650m FRN. prod/rel: Scagl, Pathe

La Roche aux Mouettes, Novel
Roche aux Mouettes, La 1932 d: Georges MoncA. lps: Daniel Mendaille, Yvonne Sergyl, Celine James. 73M FRN. prod/rel: Star Film

SANDEL, CORA (1880-1974), NRW, Fabricus, Sara Margarethe
Kranes Konditori - Interior Med Figurer, 1945, Novel
Kranes Konditori 1950 d: Astrid Henning-Jensen. lps: Wenche Foss, Harald Heide-Steen Jr., Erik Hell. 104M NRW. *Krane's Bakery Shop* prod/rel: Norsk Film As

Nina, 1949, Short Story
Hoysommer 1958 d: Arild Brinchmann. 99M NRW.

SANDEMOSE, AKSEL (1899-1965), NRW, Sandemose, Axel
Klabautermannen, 1927, Novel
Klabautermannen 1969 d: Henning Carlsen. lps: Lise Fjeldstad, Hans Stormoen, Claus Nissen. 102M DNM/SWD/NRW. *We are All Dead Demons*; *Klabautermanden*; *We are All Demons*

SANDER, PETER
Doden Kommer Til Middag, Novel
Doden Kommer Til Middag 1964 d: Erik Balling. lps: Poul Reichhardt, Helle Virkner, Birgitte Federspiel. 100M DNM. prod/rel: a/S Nordisk

SANDERS, CHARLES WESLEY
My Arcadian Wife, Short Story
$5,000 Reward 1918 d: Douglas Gerrard. lps: Franklyn Farnum, Gloria Hope, William Lloyd. 5r USA. prod/rel: Bluebird Photoplays, Inc.©

SANDERS, GEORGE
Stranger at Home, Novel
Stranger Came Home, The 1954 d: Terence Fisher. lps: Paulette Goddard, William Sylvester, Patrick Holt. 80M UKN. *The Unholy Four* (USA); *The Stranger* prod/rel: Hammer, Exclusive

SANDERS, HILARY ST. GEORGE
The Red Beret, Book
Red Beret, The 1953 d: Terence Young. lps: Alan Ladd, Leo Genn, Susan Stephen. 88M UKN. *Paratrooper* (USA) prod/rel: Warwick, Columbia

SANDERS, LAWRENCE (1920-), USA
The Anderson Tapes, Novel
Anderson Tapes, The 1972 d: Sidney Lumet. lps: Sean Connery, Dyan Cannon, Martin Balsam. 99M USA. prod/rel: Columbia

The First Deadly Sin, Novel
First Deadly Sin, The 1980 d: Brian G. Hutton. lps: Frank Sinatra, Faye Dunaway, David Dukes. 112M USA. prod/rel: Filmways

SANDGREN, GUSTAV
Maria, 1942, Novel
Maria 1947 d: Gosta Folke. lps: George Fant, Maj-Britt Nilsson, Stig Jarrel. 87M SWD.

..Som Havets Nakna Vind, Stockholm 1965, Novel
Som Havets Nakna Vind 1968 d: Gunnar Hoglund. lps: Hans Gustafsson, Lillemor Ohlsson, Anne Nord. 111M SWD. *One Swedish Summer* (USA); *As the Naked Wind from the Sea*; *The Naked Winds of the Sea*; *Naked As the Wind from the Sea* prod/rel: Swedish Filmproduction

SANDLER, SUSAN
Crossing Delancey, Play
Crossing Delancey 1988 d: Joan Micklin Silver. lps: Amy Irving, Reizl Bozyk, Peter Riegert. 97M USA. prod/rel: Warner Bros.

SANDOZ, MARI (1896-1966), USA, Sandoz, Marie Susette
Cheyenne Autumn, New York 1953, Novel
Cheyenne Autumn 1964 d: John Ford. lps: Richard Widmark, Carroll Baker, Karl Malden. 160M USA. prod/rel: Warner Bros.

SANDRI, SANDRO
Marrabo, Short Story
Sentinelle Di Bronzo 1937 d: Romolo Marcellini. lps: Fosco Giachetti, Giovanni Grasso, Doris Duranti. 83M ITL. prod/rel: Fono Roma

SANDS, LESLIE
Deadlock, Play
Another Man's Poison 1951 d: Irving Rapper. lps: Bette Davis, Gary Merrill, Emlyn Williams. 89M UKN. prod/rel: Daniel Angel, Eros

SANDSTROM, FLORA
Madness of the Heart, Novel
Madness of the Heart 1949 d: Charles Bennett. lps: Margaret Lockwood, Maxwell Reed, Kathleen Byron. 105M UKN. prod/rel: General Film Distributors, Two Cities

The Midwife of Pont Clery, New York 1957, Novel
Jessica 1962 d: Jean Negulesco, Oreste PalellA. lps: Angie Dickinson, Maurice Chevalier, Noel-Noel. 105M USA/FRN/ITL. *La Sage-Femme le Cure Et le Bon Dieu* (FRN) prod/rel: Dear Film (Roma), Les Films Ariane (Paris)

The Milkwhite Unicorn, Novel
White Unicorn, The 1947 d: Bernard Knowles. lps: Margaret Lockwood, Dennis Price, Ian Hunter. 97M UKN. *Bad Sister* (USA) prod/rel: General Film Distributors, John Corfield

SANDY, ISABELLE
Andorra Ou Les Hommes d'Airain, Novel
Andorra Ou Les Hommes d'Airain 1941 d: Emile Couzinet. lps: Jean Chevrier, Jean Galland, Jany Holt. 105M FRN. prod/rel: Burgus-Films

SANDYS, OLIVER
Blinkeyes, Novel
Blinkeyes 1926 d: George Pearson. lps: Betty Balfour, Tom Douglas, Frank Stanmore. 7300f UKN. prod/rel: Welsh-Pearson, Gaumont

Chappy - That's All, Novel
Chappy - That's All 1924 d: Thomas Bentley. lps: Joyce Dearsley, Gertrude McCoy, Francis Lister. 4650f UKN. prod/rel: Stoll

The Green Caravan, Novel
Green Caravan, The 1922 d: Edwin J. Collins. lps: Catherine Calvert, Gregory Scott, ValiA. 5300f UKN. prod/rel: Master, Granger

Mops, Novel
Born Lucky 1932 d: Michael Powell. lps: Talbot O'Farrell, Rene Ray, John Longden. 78M UKN. prod/rel: Westminster, MGM

The Pleasure Garden, Novel
Pleasure Garden, The 1926 d: Alfred Hitchcock. lps: Virginia Valli, Carmelita Geraghty, Miles Mander. 7058f UKN/GRM. *Irrgarten Der Leidenschaft* (GRM); *Der Garten Der Lust* prod/rel: Gainsborough, Emelka

SANFORD, GERALD
Play
Single Room Furnished 1968 d: Matt Cimber. lps: Jayne Mansfield, Dorothy Keller, Fabian Dean. 93M USA. prod/rel: Unifilm Productions

SANFORD, HARRY
Emporia, New York 1961, Novel
Waco 1966 d: R. G. Springsteen. lps: Howard Keel, Jane Russell, Brian Donlevy. 85M USA. prod/rel: A. C. Lyles Productions

Way Station, New York 1961, Book
Apache Uprising 1966 d: R. G. Springsteen. lps: Rory Calhoun, Corinne Calvet, John Russell. 90M USA. prod/rel: A. C. Lyles Productions

SANGSTER, JIMMY (1924-), UKN
Foreign Exchange, Novel
Foreign Exchange 1969 d: Roy Ward Baker. lps: Robert Horton, Sebastian Cabot, Jill St. John. TVM. 74M UKN. prod/rel: ABC, Halsan Productions

Private I, Novel
Spy Killer, The 1969 d: Roy Ward Baker. lps: Robert Horton, Sebastian Cabot, Eleanor Summerfield. TVM. 74M UKN. prod/rel: Halsan Productions, ABC

SANGSTER, MARGARET ELIZABETH
The Island of Faith, New York 1921, Novel
   New Teacher, The 1922 d: Joseph J. Franz. lps: Shirley Mason, Allan Forrest, Earl Metcalfe. 4453f USA. prod/rel: Fox Film Corp.

SANSOM, LESTER A.
Story
   Battle Flame 1959 d: R. G. Springsteen. lps: Scott Brady, Elaine Edwards, Robert Blake. 78M USA. prod/rel: Allied Artists

SANSOM, WILLIAM (1912–1976), UKN
The Last Hours of Sandra Lee, London 1961, Novel
   Wild Affair, The 1963 d: John Krish. lps: Nancy Kwan, Terry-Thomas, Jimmy Logan. 88M UKN. prod/rel: Seven Arts Productions, Bryanston

SANTA, FERENC
Husz Ora, 1964, Novel
   Husz Ora 1964 d: Zoltan Fabri. lps: Antal Pager, Emil Keres, Janos Gorbe. 118M HNG. *Twenty Hours* (UKN) prod/rel: Magyar

Az Otodik Pecset, 1963, Novel
   Otodik Pecset, Az 1977 d: Zoltan Fabri. lps: Lajos Oze, Sandor Horvath, Laszlo Markus. 116M HNG. *The Fifth Seal* prod/rel: Budapest Studio

SANTACROCE, JEAN
Le Voyageur Mort, Novel
   Eclair Au Chocolat 1979 d: Jean-Claude Lord. lps: Lise Thouin, Jean Belzil-Gascon, Jean-Louis Roux. 107M CND. prod/rel: Les Productions Mutuelles Ltee., Les Productions Videofilms Ltee.

SANTARENO, BERNARDO
A Promessa, 1957, Play
   Promessa, A 1973 d: Antonio de Macedo. lps: Sinde Filipe, Guida Maria, Joao RotA. 102M PRT. *The Promise*

SANTI, GIORGIO
Zelmaide; un Colpo in Tre Atti, Novel
   Passi Furtivi in Una Notte Boia 1976 d: Vincenzo Rigo. lps: Walter Chiari, Carmen Villani, Gianni CavinA. 90M ITL. *Zelmaide* prod/rel: R.R. International Film, Euro International Film

SANTLEY, JOSEPH
The House on 56th Street, Story
   Return of Carol Deane, The 1938 d: Arthur Woods. lps: Bebe Daniels, Arthur Margetson, Zena Dare. 77M UKN. prod/rel: Warner Bros., First National

SANTOMI, TON
Higanbana, 1958, Novel
   Higanbana 1958 d: Yasujiro Ozu. lps: Shin Saburi, Fujiko Yamamoto, Kinuyo KanakA. 118M JPN. *Equinox Flower* (USA) prod/rel: Shochiku Co.

SANTONI, TINO
Il Nostro Prossimo, Play
   Nostro Prossimo, Il 1943 d: Gherardo Gherardi, Antonio Rossi. lps: Antonio Gandusio, Maurizio d'Ancora, Michela Belmonte. 90M ITL. prod/rel: I.C.A.R., Generalcine

SANYAL, NARAYAN
Satyakam, Novel
   Satyakam 1969 d: Hrishikesh Mukherjee. lps: Ashok Kumar, Dharmendra, Sharmila Tagore. 160M IND. prod/rel: Panchi Art

SANYAL, PRABODH KUMAR
Mahaprasthaner Pathey, Novel
   Mahaprasthaner Pathey 1952 d: Kartick Chattopadhyay. lps: Basanta Choudhury, Arundhati Devi, Maya Mukherjee. 137M IND. *Maha Prasthaner Pathey; Yatrik* prod/rel: New Theatres

SANYUTEI, ENCHO
Shinkei Kasanegafuchi, Short Story
   Kaidan Kasane-Ga-Fuchi 1957 d: Nobuo NakagawA. lps: Kazuko Wakasugi, Takashi Wada, Tetsuro TambA. 57M JPN. *Ghost of Kasane-Ga-Fuchi; The Depths* prod/rel: Shintoho Co.
   Kaidan Kasane-Ga-Fuchi 1960 d: Kimiyoshi YasudA. lps: Ganjiro Nakamura, Yataro Kitagami. F JPN. *Ghost of Kasane-Ga-Fuchi* prod/rel: Daiei Motion Picture Co.
   Kaidan Kasane Ga Fuchi 1970 d: Kimiyoshi YasudA. lps: Ritsu Ishiyama, Maya Kitajima, Kenjiro IshiyamA. 82M JPN. *Horror of an Ugly Woman; Masseur's Curse* prod/rel: Daiei Motion Picture Co.

SAPERSTEIN, DAVID
Cocoon, Novel
   Cocoon 1985 d: Ron Howard. lps: Don Ameche, Wilford Brimley, Hume Cronyn. 117M USA. prod/rel: 20th Century Fox, Fox-Zanuck-Brown Productions

SAPIR, MICHAEL
La Formation Psychologique du Medecin, Book
   Sur Les Traces de Balint 1977 d: Eric Duvivier. lps: Nadine Alari, Anouk Ferjak, Michael Lonsdale. 87M FRN.

SAPIR, RICHARD
Novel
   Remo Williams: the Adventure Begins 1985 d: Guy Hamilton. lps: Fred Ward, Joel Grey, Wilford Brimley. 99M USA. *Remo Williams .Unarmed and Dangerous; Remo: Unarmed and Dangerous; Remo Williams: the Adventure Continues* prod/rel: Orion Pictures

SAPPER
Bulldog Drummond Again, Play
   Bulldog Drummond Escapes 1937 d: James P. Hogan. lps: Ray Milland, Guy Standing, Heather Angel. 67M USA. *Bulldog Drummond Saves a Lady; Bulldog Drummond's Holiday; Bulldog Drummond's Romance* prod/rel: Paramount Pictures, Inc.

SARAZANI, FABRIZIO
Rosso E Nero Verde, Play
   Ricchezza Senza Domani 1939 d: Ferdinando M. Poggioli. lps: Lamberto Picasso, Doris Duranti, Paola Borboni. 82M ITL. prod/rel: Alfa Film, C.I.N.F.

SARDOU, VICTORIEN (1831–1908), FRN
L' Affaire Des Poisons, 1908, Play
   Affaire Des Poisons, L' 1955 d: Henri Decoin. lps: Danielle Darrieux, Viviane Romance, Marisa Belli. 108M FRN/ITL. *Il Processo Dei Veleni* (ITL); *The Case of Poisons* (USA); *The Poison Affair* prod/rel: Franco-London Films, Excelsa Film

Andrea, 1873, Play
   Andreina 1917 d: Gustavo SerenA. lps: Francesca Bertini, Alfredo de Antoni, Camillo de Riso. 2100m ITL. prod/rel: Caesar Film

Les Bourgeois de Pont-Arcy, 1878, Play
   Borghesi Di Pont-Arcy, I 1920 d: Umberto Mozzato, Emilio Vardannes. lps: Armando Cammarano, Arnaldo Arnaldi, Diana d'Amore. 2264m ITL. prod/rel: Itala

Cleopatre, Paris 1890, Play
   Cleopatra 1912 d: Charles L. Gaskill. lps: Helen Gardner, Robert Gaillord, Harley Knoles. 6r USA. *Helen Gardner in Cleopatra* prod/rel: Helen Gardner Picture Players, United States Film Co.
   Cleopatra 1917 d: J. Gordon Edwards. lps: Theda Bara, Fritz Leiber, Thurston Hall. 11r USA. prod/rel: Fox Film Corp., Fox Standard Picture

Cyprienne Or Divorcons, Paris 1883, Play
   Divorcons 1915 d: Dell Henderson. lps: Dell Henderson, Gertrude Bambrick, Dave Morris. 4r USA. prod/rel: Biograph Co.©, General Film Co.
   Don't Tell the Wife 1927 d: Paul L. Stein. lps: Irene Rich, Huntley Gordon, Lilyan Tashman. 6972f USA. prod/rel: Warner Brothers Pictures
   Kiss Me Again 1925 d: Ernst Lubitsch. lps: Marie Prevost, Monte Blue, John Roche. 6722f USA. prod/rel: Warner Brothers Pictures
   Let's Get a Divorce 1918 d: Charles Giblyn. lps: Billie Burke, John Miltern, Pinna Nesbit. 5r USA. prod/rel: Famous Players-Lasky Corp.©
   That Uncertain Feeling 1941 d: Ernst Lubitsch. lps: Merle Oberon, Melvyn Douglas, Burgess Meredith. 84M USA. prod/rel: United Artists

Diplomacy, New York 1878, Play
   Diplomacy 1926 d: Marshall Neilan. lps: Blanche Sweet, Neil Hamilton, Arlette Marchal. 6950f USA. prod/rel: Famous Players-Lasky, Paramount Pictures

Dora, Paris 1877, Play
   Burden of Proof, The 1918 d: Julius Steger, John G. Adolfi. lps: Marion Davies, John Merkyl, Mary Richards. 5100f USA. prod/rel: Marion Davies Film Corp.©, Select Pictures Corp.
   Diplomacy 1916 d: Sidney Olcott. lps: Marie Doro, Elliott Dexter, Frank Losee. 5r USA. prod/rel: Famous Players Film Co.©, Paramount Pictures Corp.
   Dora O le Spie 1919 d: Roberto Leone Roberti. lps: Vera Vergani, Mina d'Orvella, Gustavo SerenA. 1893m ITL. prod/rel: Giuseppe Barattolo
   Dora, la Espia 1943 d: Raffaello Matarazzo. lps: Adriano Rimoldi, Maruchi Fresno, Francesca Bertini. 99M ITL/SPN. *Dora O le Spie*
   Espionne, L' 1923 d: Henri Desfontaines. lps: Adolphe Cande, Claude Merelle, Marguerite Madys. 2100m FRN. prod/rel: Gaumont

L' Etau, Play
   Morsa, La 1916 d: Emilio Ghione. lps: Hesperia, Emilio Ghione, Alberto Collo. 1628m ITL. prod/rel: Tiber Film

Fedora, Paris 1882, Play
   Fedora 1916 d: Giuseppe de Liguoro. lps: Francesca Bertini, Gustavo Serena, Carlo Benetti. 2042m ITL. prod/rel: Caesar Film
   Fedora 1918 d: Edward Jose. lps: Pauline Frederick, Alfred Hickman, Wilmuth Merkyl. 5r USA. prod/rel: Famous Players-Lasky Corp.©, Paramount Pictures

   Fedora 1934 d: Louis J. Gasnier. lps: Marie Bell, Ernest Ferny, Henri Bosc. 75M FRN. prod/rel: Paris France Production
   Fedora 1942 d: Camillo Mastrocinque. lps: Luisa Ferida, Amedeo Nazzari, Osvaldo Valenti. 90M ITL. prod/rel: I.C.A.R., Generalcine
   Princess Romanoff 1915 d: Frank Powell. lps: Nance O'Neil, Clifford Bruce, Dorothy Bernard. 5r USA. *Fedora* prod/rel: Fox Film Corp., William Fox©
   Woman from Moscow, The 1928 d: Ludwig Berger. lps: Pola Negri, Norman Kerry, Paul Lukas. 6938f USA. prod/rel: Paramount Famous Lasky Corp.

Fernande, 1870, Play
   Beggar Student, The 1931 d: John Harvel, Victor Hanbury. lps: Shirley Dale, Jerry Verno, Lance Fairfax. 66M UKN. prod/rel: Amalgamated Films Associated, British Lion
   Bettelstudent, Der 1927 d: Jacob Fleck, Luise Fleck. lps: Harry Liedtke, Agnes Esterhazy, Maria Paudler. 2623m GRM. prod/rel: Aafa-Film Ag
   Bettelstudent, Der 1931 d: Victor Janson. 92M GRM.
   Bettelstudent, Der 1936 d: Georg Jacoby. lps: Marika Rokk, Johannes Heesters, Carola Hohn. 95M GRM. *The Beggar Student* prod/rel: UFA, Doring
   Bettelstudent, Der 1956 d: Werner Jacobs. lps: Gerhard Riedmann, Waltraut Haas, Elma KarlowA. 98M GRM. *The Beggar Student* (USA); *The Pauper Student* prod/rel: Carlton, Constantin
   Fernanda 1917 d: Gustavo SerenA. lps: Leda Gys, Gustavo Serena, Alfredo de Antoni. 2075m ITL. prod/rel: Caesar Film
   Mazurka Der Liebe 1957 d: Hans Muller. lps: Bert Fortell, Eberhard Krug, Albert Garbe. 86M GDR. *Der Bettelstudent* prod/rel: Defa

Ferreol, Paris 1875, Play
   Ferreol 1916 d: Eduardo BencivengA. lps: Mario Bonnard, Bianchina de Crescenzo, Giovanna Scotto. 1553m ITL. prod/rel: Caesar Film
   Night of Mystery, A 1928 d: Lothar Mendes. lps: Adolphe Menjou, Evelyn Brent, Nora Lane. 5741f USA. *The Code of Honour* prod/rel: Paramount Famous Lasky Corp.

Georgette, 1885, Play
   Giorgina 1919 d: Ubaldo Pittei, Giuseppe Forti. lps: Clarette Rosaj, Noemi de Ferrari. 1896m ITL. prod/rel: Caesar Film

Gismonda, Paris 1894, Play
   Love's Conquest 1918 d: Edward Jose. lps: Lina Cavalieri, Courtenay Foote, Fred Radcliffe. 5r USA. *Gismonda* prod/rel: Famous Players-Lasky Corp.©, Paramount Pictures

Madame Sans-Gene, Paris 1893, Play
   Madame Sans-Gene 1911 d: Andre Calmettes, Henri Desfontaines. lps: Mme. Rejane, Edmond Duquesne, Dorival. FRN. prod/rel: Film d'Art
   Madame Sans-Gene 1925 d: Leonce Perret. lps: Gloria Swanson, Emile Drain, Charles de Rochefort. 9994f USA. prod/rel: Famous Players-Lasky, Paramount Pictures
   Madame Sans-Gene 1941 d: Roger Richebe. lps: Arletty, Albert Dieudonne, Aime Clariond. 100M FRN. prod/rel: Roger Richebe
   Madame Sans-Gene 1961 d: Christian-Jaque. lps: Sophia Loren, Robert Hossein, Julien Bertheau. 118M FRN/ITL/SPN. *Madame* (UKN) prod/rel: Cine-Alliance (Paris), Ge.Si. Cin.Ca

Madame Tallien, Play
   Madame Tallien 1911 d: Camille de Morlhon. lps: Georges Wague, Leon Bernard, Berthe Bovy. 210m FRN. prod/rel: Pathe Freres
   Madame Tallien 1916 d: Enrico Guazzoni. lps: Lyda Borelli, Amleto Novelli, Renzo Fabiani. 1855m ITL. prod/rel: Palatino Film

Marcella, 1895, Play
   Marcella 1915 d: Baldassarre Negroni. lps: Hesperia, Alberto Collo, Attilio de Virgiliis. 1000m ITL. prod/rel: Tiber Film
   Marcella 1937 d: Guido Brignone. lps: Emma Gramatica, Caterina Boratto, Antonio CentA. 76M ITL. prod/rel: S.a.F.a., Appia

Nos Bons Villageois, 1866, Play
   Nostri Buoni Villici, I 1918 d: Camillo de Riso. lps: Camillo de Riso, Tilde Kassaj, Maria Riccardi. 2020m ITL. prod/rel: Caesar Film

Odette, 1881, Play
   Desarroi 1946 d: Robert-Paul Dagan. lps: Jean Mercanton, Jules Berry, Suzy Carrier. 85M FRN. *Odette* prod/rel: Cinema Films Production, Les Moulins D'or

Mein Leben Fur Das Deine 1927 d: Luitz-Morat. lps: Francesca Bertini, Fritz Kortner, Simone Vaudry. 2292m GRM/FRN. *Odette* (FRN) prod/rel: Franco-Deutsch Lichtspiel, F.P.G. Film-Prod.

Odette 1916 d: Giuseppe de Liguoro. lps: Francesca Bertini, Alfredo de Antoni, Carlo Benetti. 1100m ITL. prod/rel: Caesar Film

Odette 1934 d: Jacques Houssin, Giorgio Zambon. lps: Francesca Bertini, Samson Fainsilber, Jacques Maury. 70M FRN/ITL. *Decheance* prod/rel: Caesar Film

Pamela Marchande de Frivolites, 1936, Play
Pamela 1944 d: Pierre de Herain. lps: Renee Saint-Cyr, Fernand Gravey, Georges Marchal. 109M FRN. *Pamela Ou l'Enigma du Temple* prod/rel: S.P.C., Tramichel, Camille

Patrie, 1869, Play
Patrie 1914 d: Albert Capellani. lps: Henry Krauss, Paul Capellani, Vera Sergine. 1885m FRN. prod/rel: Scagl
Patrie 1945 d: Louis Daquin. lps: Pierre Blanchar, Jean Desailly, Lucien Nat. 95M FRN. prod/rel: Filmsonor

Les Pattes de Mouche, Paris 1860, Play
Pattes de Mouche, Les 1936 d: Jean Gremillon. lps: Pierre Brasseur, Renee Saint-Cyr, Charles Dechamps. 85M FRN. *Une Lettre Brulante; Fin de Siecle* prod/rel: U.F.a.
Three Green Eyes 1919 d: Dell Henderson. lps: Carlyle Blackwell, June Elvidge, Evelyn Greeley. 5r USA. *A Scrap of Paper; The Price of Doubt* prod/rel: World Film Corp.©

Rabagas, 1872
Rabagas 1922 d: Gaston Ravel. lps: Helena Makowska, Toto Majorana, Guido Trento. 1793m ITL. prod/rel: U.C.I., Medusa

Le Secret de Delia, Play
Evadee, L' 1928 d: Henri Menessier. lps: Jean Murat, Marcella Albani, Florence Gray. 2500m FRN. *Le Secret de Delia* prod/rel: Rex Ingram

La Sorciere, Paris 1903, Play
Witch, The 1916 d: Frank Powell. lps: Nance O'Neil, Alfred Hickman, Frank Russell. 5r USA. *The Sorceress* prod/rel: Fox Film Corp., William Fox©

Spiritisme, 1897, Play
Spiritismo 1919 d: Camillo de Riso. lps: Francesca Bertini, Amleto Novelli, Ugo Piperno. 1848m ITL. prod/rel: Caesar Film, Bertini Film

Theodora, 1884, Play
Teodora 1922 d: Leopoldo Carlucci. lps: Rita Jolivet, Ferruccio Biancini, Rene Maupre. 2748m ITL. prod/rel: Ambrosio-Zanotta
Teodora, Imperatrice Di Bisanzio 1954 d: Riccardo FredA. lps: Gianna Maria Canale, Georges Marchal, Irene Papas. 88M ITL/FRN. *Theodore Imperatrice de Byzance* (FRN); *Slave Empress Theodora* (USA); *Queen of Byzantium Theodora*; *Theodore Imperatrice Byzantine*; *Teodora, l'Imperatrice Di Bisanzio* prod/rel: Lux Film (Roma), Lux de France (Paris)
Theodora 1912 d: Henri Pouctal. lps: Philippe Garnier, Mancini, Sahari Djelly. FRN. prod/rel: le Film d'Art

La Tosca, Paris 1887, Play
Davanti a Lui Tremava Tutta Roma 1946 d: Carmine Gallone. lps: Anna Magnani, Tito Gobbi, Gino Sinimberghi. 90M ITL. *Before Him All Rome Trembled; Avanti a Lui; Tosca; Innanzi a Lui Tremava Tutta Roma; Avanti a Lui Tremava Tutta Roma* prod/rel: Excelsa Film
Song of Hate, The 1915 d: J. Gordon Edwards. lps: Betty Nansen, Dorothy Bernard, Arthur Hoops. 5-6r USA. prod/rel: Fox Film Corp., William Fox©
Tosca 1918 d: Alfredo de Antoni. lps: Francesca Bertini, Gustavo Serena, Alfredo de Antoni. 2105m ITL. prod/rel: Caesar Film
Tosca 1941 d: Carl Koch, Jean Renoir. lps: Imperio Argentina, Michel Simon, Rossano Brazzi. 100M ITL. *The Story of Tosca* (USA) prod/rel: Era, Scalera Film
Tosca 1956 d: Carmine Gallone. lps: Franca Duval, Afro Poli, Vito de Taranto. 112M ITL. prod/rel: Produzioni Gallone
Tosca, La 1908 d: Andre Calmettes. lps: Sarah Bernhardt, Paul Mounet, Lucien Guitry. 380m FRN. prod/rel: le Film d'Art
Tosca, La 1909 d: Charles Le Bargy. lps: Rene Alexandre, Cecile Sorel, Charles Mosnier. 380m FRN. prod/rel: Film d'Art
Tosca, La 1918 d: Edward Jose. lps: Pauline Frederick, Frank Losee, Jules Raucourt. 5r USA. prod/rel: Famous Players-Lasky Corp.©, Paramount Pictures
Tosca, La 1922. lps: Ethel Irving. 1320f UKN. prod/rel: Master Films, British Exhibitors' Films

Tosca, La 1973 d: Luigi Magni. lps: Monica Vitti, Vittorio Gassman, Luigi Proietti. 104M ITL. prod/rel: Quasars Film Company, Uti Produzioni Associate

SARGENT, E. W.
The Red Cross Seal Story, Story
Price of Human Lives, The 1913 d: Charles H. France. 1000f USA. prod/rel: Edison

SARGENT, HERBERT
Josser on the Farm, Play
Josser on the Farm 1934 d: T. Hayes Hunter. lps: Ernie Lotinga, Betty Astell, Garry Marsh. 63M UKN. prod/rel: Fox British

Love Up the Pole, 1935, Play
Love Up the Pole 1936 d: Clifford Gulliver. lps: Ernie Lotinga, Vivienne Chatterton, Wallace Lupino. 82M UKN. prod/rel: British Comedies, Butcher's Film Service

The Mouse Trap, Play
Acci-Dental Treatment 1929 d: Thomas Bentley. lps: Ernie LotingA. 17M UKN. prod/rel: British Sound Film Production, Bifd

The Naughty Age, Play
Strictly Illegal 1935 d: Ralph Ceder. lps: Leslie Fuller, Betty Astell, Georgie Harris. 69M UKN. *Here Comes a Policeman* prod/rel: Leslie Fuller Films, Gaumont-British

SARKADI, IMRE
Az Elveszett Paradicsom, 1962, Play
Elveszett Paradicsom, Az 1962 d: Karoly Makk. lps: Antal Pager, Mari Torocsik, Gyorgy Palos. 91M HNG. *The Lost Paradise; Paradise Lost*

Kutban, 1971, Short Story
Korhinta 1955 d: Zoltan Fabri. lps: Adam Szirtes, Mari Torocsik, Imre Soos. 101M HNG. *Merry Go Round; Karussell*

Tanyasi Duvad, 1953, Short Story
Duvad 1959 d: Zoltan Fabri. lps: Ferenc Bessenyei, Tibor Bitskey, Maria Medgyesi. 90M HNG. *The Brute; Das Scheusal*

SARKIES, DUNCAN
Saving Grace, Play
Saving Grace 1998 d: Costa Bodes. lps: Kirsty Hamilton, Jim Moriarty, Denise O'Connell. 87M NZL. prod/rel: Kahukura, New Zealand Film Commission

SARMENT, JEAN (1897–, FRN
Leopold le Bien-Aime, 1927, Play
Leopold le Bien-Aime 1933 d: Arno-Charles Brun. lps: Jean Sarment, Marguerite Valmond, Jane Lory. 102M FRN. prod/rel: Auteurs Associes

Mamouret, 1943, Play
Ihr 106 Geburtstag 1958 d: Gunther Luders. lps: Margarete Haagen, Paul Hubschmid, Gerlinde Locker. 97M GRM. *Her 106th Birthday* prod/rel: C.C.C., N.F.
Briseur de Chaines, Le 1941 d: Jacques Daniel-Norman. lps: Pierre Fresnay, Andre Brunot, Marcelle Geniat. 117M FRN. *Mamouret* prod/rel: Pathe-Cinema

Le Voyage a Biarritz, 1936, Play
Voyage a Biarritz 1962 d: Gilles Grangier. lps: Fernandel, Arletty, Rellys. 92M FRN/ITL. prod/rel: Millimax Productions, P.C. Mediterranee

SAROCCHI, MARIO
Short Story
Ich Hab Mein Herz Im Autobus Verloren 1929 d: Domenico M. Gambino, Carlo Campogalliani. lps: Truus Van Aalten, Domenico Gambino, Lydia PotechinA. 2645m GRM. prod/rel: Boston-Film

SAROYAN, WILLIAM (1908–1981), USA
The Human Comedy, 1943, Novel
Human Comedy, The 1943 d: Clarence Brown. lps: Mickey Rooney, Frank Morgan, Butch Jenkins. 118M USA. prod/rel: MGM

The Time of Your Life, New York 1939, Play
Time of Your Life, The 1948 d: H. C. Potter. lps: James Cagney, William Bendix, Wayne Morris. 109M USA. prod/rel: United Artists
Time of Your Life, The 1958 d: Philip Saville. lps: Franchot Tone, Susan Strasberg, Ann Sheridan. MTV. 90M UKN. prod/rel: ABC

SARRAZIN, ALBERTINE
L' Astragale, 1965, Novel
Astragale, L' 1968 d: Guy Casaril. lps: Marlene Jobert, Horst Buchholz, Magali Noel. 102M FRN/GRM. *Astragal* (GRM) prod/rel: Films De La Pleiade, C.C.C.

La Cavale, 1965, Novel
Cavale, La 1971 d: Michel Mitrani. lps: Juliet Berto, Jean-Claude Bouillon, Olga Georges-Picot. 90M FRN.

SARTENE, JEAN
La Griffe, Play
Greep, de 1909. lps: Louis Bouwmeester, Ko Van Sprinkhuijsen, Mien de La Mar. NTH. *La Griffe; The Grip*
Grip, The 1913 d: A. E. Coleby. lps: Louis Bouwmeester, Annesley Healy. 4000f UKN. prod/rel: Britannic Film Producing Syndicate, Martin's

SARTRE, JEAN-PAUL (1905–1980), FRN
Play
In Camera 1964 d: Philip Saville. lps: Harold Pinter, Jane Arden, Catherine Woodville. MTV. UKN. prod/rel: BBC

Huis Clos, Paris 1944, Play
Huis-Clos 1954 d: Jacqueline Audry. lps: Arletty, Gaby Sylvia, Frank Villard. 95M FRN. *Vicious Circle; No Exit* prod/rel: Films Marceau
No Exit 1962 d: Tad Danielewski. lps: Viveca Lindfors, Rita Gam, Morgan Sterne. 91M USA/ARG. *Sinners Go to Hell; Stateless; Huis Clos* (ARG) prod/rel: Aries Cinematografica

Les Mains Sales, 1948, Play
Mains Sales, Les 1951 d: Fernand Rivers. lps: Pierre Brasseur, Daniel Gelin, Claude Nollier. 103M FRN. *Dirty Hands* (USA) prod/rel: Films Fernand Rivers

Le Mur, 1939, Short Story
Mur, Le 1968 d: Serge Roullet. lps: Miguel Del Castillo, Denis Mahaffey, Mathieu Klossowski. 90M FRN. prod/rel: Procinex, Films Niepce

La Putain Respecteuse, 1946, Play
P. Respectueuse, La 1952 d: Marcello Pagliero, Charles Brabant. lps: Barbara Laage, Ivan Desny, Walter Bryant. 95M FRN. *The Respectable Prostitute* (USA); *The Respectful Prostitute; La Putain Respectueuse* prod/rel: Films Agiman, Artes Films

Les Sequestres d'Altona, 1959, Play
Sequestrati Di Altona, I 1962 d: Vittorio de SicA. lps: Fredric March, Maximilian Schell, Sophia Loren. 114M ITL/FRN. *Les Sequestres d'Altona* (FRN); *The Condemned of Altona* (USA); *The Prisoners of Altona* prod/rel: Titanus (Roma), Societe Generale de C.Ie (Paris)

SARVIL, RENE
Au Pays du Soleil, Opera
Au Pays du Soleil 1933 d: Robert Peguy. lps: Henri Alibert, Lisette Lanvin, Fernand Flament. 79M FRN. prod/rel: Films Tellus

Trois de la Canebiere, Opera
Trois de la Canebiere 1955 d: Maurice de Canonge. lps: Jeannette Batti, Colette Dereal, Marcel Merkes. 102M FRN. prod/rel: Films Tellus, Cocinex

Trois de la Marine, Opera
Trois de la Marine 1934 d: Charles Barrois. lps: Armand Bernard, Henri Alibert, Rivers Cadet. 90M FRN. prod/rel: Metropa-Film
Trois de la Marine 1956 d: Maurice de Canonge. lps: Jeannette Batti, Marcel Merkes, Henri Genes. 95M FRN. prod/rel: Cocinex, L.P.C.

SASS, HERBERT RAVENAL
Affair at St. Albans, 1947, Article
Raid, The 1954 d: Hugo Fregonese. lps: Van Heflin, Anne Bancroft, Richard Boone. 83M USA. prod/rel: 20th Century-Fox, Panoramic

SASTRE, ALFONSO (1926–, SPN
La Cornada, 1960, Play
A Las Cinco de la Tarde 1960 d: Juan Antonio Bardem. lps: Francisco Rabal, Enrique A. Diosdado, German Cobos. 108M SPN. *At Five O'Clock in the Afternoon* prod/rel: Union

SASTRI, BELLAVE NARAHARI
Hemareddy Mallamma, Play
Hemareddy Malamamma 1945 d: S. Soundararajan, G. R. Rao. lps: Gubbi Veeranna, Honappa Bhagavathar, C. B. MalappA. F IND. prod/rel: Gubbi Films

SATO, HARUO
Shosetsu Chieko Sho, 1963, Novel
Chieko-Sho 1967 d: Noboru NakamurA. lps: Tetsuro Tamba, Shima Iwashita, Takamaru Sasaki. 125M JPN. *Portrait of Chieko* (USA) prod/rel: Shochiku Co.

SATOMI, TON
Akibiyori, 1960, Novel
Akibiyori 1960 d: Yasujiro Ozu. lps: Setsuko Hara, Yoko Tsukasa, Mariko OkadA. 127M JPN. *Late Autumn* prod/rel: Shochiku Co.

SAUBER, HARRY
Gentlemen are Born, Story
Here Comes Happiness 1941 d: Noel Smith. lps: Mildred Coles, Richard Ainley, Russell Hicks. 56M USA. prod/rel: Warner Bros.

SAUERBRUCH, ERNST FERDINAND
Sauerbruch - Das War Mein Leben, Autobiography
  Sauerbruch 1954 d: Rolf Hansen. lps: Ewald Balser, Heidemarie Hatheyer, Maria Wimmer. 106M GRM. *The Life of Surgeon Sauerbruch; Das War Mein Leben; Sauerbruch - Das War Mein Leben* prod/rel: Corona, Bavaria

SAUL, JOHN
Cry for the Strangers, Novel
  Cry for the Strangers 1982 d: Peter Medak. lps: Patrick Duffy, Cindy Pickett, Lawrence Pressman. TVM. 104M USA. *Cry for Strangers* prod/rel: CBS, MGM-Ua

SAUL, OSCAR
The Dark Side of Love, Novel
  My Kidnapper, My Love 1980 d: Sam Wanamaker. lps: James Stacy, Mickey Rooney, Glynnis O'Connor. TVM. 104M USA.
Road House, Novel
  Road House 1948 d: Jean Negulesco. lps: Ida Lupino, Richard Widmark, Cornel Wilde. 95M USA. prod/rel: 20th Century-Fox
Stalk the Hunter, Story
  Strange Affair 1944 d: Alfred E. Green. lps: Allyn Joslyn, Evelyn Keyes, Marguerite Chapman. 78M USA. prod/rel: Columbia

SAUNDERS, JOHN MONK
Bird of Prey, Story
  Ace of Aces 1933 d: J. Walter Ruben. lps: Richard Dix, Elizabeth Allan, Ralph Bellamy. 74M USA. prod/rel: RKO
The Flight Commander, Story
  Dawn Patrol, The 1930 d: Howard Hawks. lps: Richard Barthelmess, Douglas Fairbanks Jr., Neil Hamilton. 95M USA. *Flight Commander* prod/rel: First National Pictures
A Maker of Gestures, 1923, Short Story
  Too Many Kisses 1925 d: Paul Sloane. lps: Richard Dix, Frances Howard, William Powell. 5759f USA. prod/rel: Famous Players-Lasky, Paramount Pictures
The Shock Punch, Story
  Shock Punch, The 1925 d: Paul Sloane. lps: Richard Dix, Frances Howard, Theodore Babcock. 6151f USA. prod/rel: Famous Players-Lasky, Paramount Pictures

SAUNDERS, LAWRENCE
Snowed Under, Story
  Snowed Under 1936 d: Ray Enright. lps: George Brent, Genevieve Tobin, Glenda Farrell. 68M USA. prod/rel: Warner Bros. Pictures©, First National Picture

SAUNIER, PAUL
Entre le Devoir Et l'Honneur, Short Story
  Entre le Devoiret l'Honneur 1910 d: Emile Chautard. lps: Alexandre Arquilliere, Edmond Duquesne. 254m FRN. prod/rel: Eclair, Acad

SAUREL, PIERRE
Ixe-13, Novel
  Ixe-13 1971 d: Jacques Godbout. lps: Louise Forestier, Andre Dubois, Marc Laurendeau. 115M CND. *Ixe 13* prod/rel: Office National Du Film

SAUVAJON, MARC-GILBERT
L' Amant de Paille, Play
  Amant de Paille, L' 1950 d: Gilles Grangier. lps: Jean-Pierre Aumont, Gaby Sylvia, Lucienne Granier. 86M FRN. prod/rel: Sirius
L' Anatra All'arancia, Play
  Anatra All'arancia, L' 1975 d: Luciano Salce. lps: Monica Vitti, Ugo Tognazzi, Barbara Bouchet. 102M ITL. *Duck in Orange Sauce* (USA); *Duck a la Orange* prod/rel: Capital Film, Cineriz
Au Petit Bonheur, Play
  Au Petit Bonheur 1945 d: Marcel L'Herbier. lps: Danielle Darrieux, Francois Perier, Andre Luguet. 102M FRN. prod/rel: Gibe
Tapage Nocturne, Play
  Tapage Nocturne 1951 d: Marc-Gilbert Sauvajon. lps: Raymond Rouleau, Simone Renant, Elina Labourdette. 86M FRN. prod/rel: Films Modernes
Treize a Table, 1953, Play
  Treize a Table 1955 d: Andre Hunebelle. lps: Micheline Presle, Fernand Gravey, Annie Girardot. 92M FRN. prod/rel: Contact Organisation, Safia
  Treize a Table 1990 d: Philippe Ducrest. lps: Marthe Mercadier, Rene Camoin, Anne Wartel. TVM. 119M FRN.

SAVAGE, COURTENAY
They All Want Something, New York 1926, Play
  Merrily We Live 1938 d: Norman Z. McLeod. lps: Constance Bennett, Brian Aherne, Alan Mowbray. 90M USA. *Take It Easy; Love Without Reason; Dark Chapter* prod/rel: Metro-Goldwyn-Mayer Corp., Loew's, Inc.©

What a Man! 1930 d: George J. Crone. lps: Reginald Denny, Miriam Seegar, Harvey Clark. 7-9r USA. *The Gentleman Chauffeur* (UKN); *His Dark Chapter; They All Want Something* prod/rel: Sono-Art Productions

SAVAGE, GEORGIA
Slate and Wyn and Blanche McBride, Novel
  Slate Wyn and Me 1986 d: Don McLennan. lps: Sigrid Thornton, Simon Burke, Martin Sacks. 91M ASL. *Slate & Wyn and Blanche McBride; Wyn and McBride Slate* prod/rel: Hemdale Film Corporation, Ukiyo Films

SAVAGE JR., LES
The Doctor at Coffin Gap, Novel
  Hills of Utah 1951 d: John English. lps: Gene Autry, Pat Buttram, Elaine Riley. 70M USA. prod/rel: Columbia, Gene Autry Productions
Return to Warbow, 1955, Novel
  Return to Warbow 1958 d: Ray Nazarro. lps: Philip Carey, Catherine McLeod, Andrew Duggan. 67M USA. prod/rel: Columbia

SAVAGE, JUANITA
The Spaniard, New York 1924, Novel
  Spaniard, The 1925 d: Raoul Walsh. lps: Ricardo Cortez, Jetta Goudal, Noah Beery. 6635f USA. *Spanish Love* (UKN) prod/rel: Famous Players-Lasky, Paramount Pictures

SAVAGE, MILDRED
Parrish, New York 1958, Novel
  Parrish 1961 d: Delmer Daves. lps: Troy Donahue, Claudette Colbert, Karl Malden. 137M USA. prod/rel: Warner Bros. Pictures

SAVAGE, RICHARD HENRY
Eskapade, Novel
  Eskapade 1936 d: Erich Waschneck. lps: Renate Muller, Georg Alexander, Walter Franck. 98M GRM. *Seine Offizielle Frau; Geheimagentin Helene* prod/rel: Fanal, Allianz
My Official Wife, New York 1891, Novel
  My Official Wife 1914 d: James Young. lps: Clara Kimball Young, Harry T. Morey, Rose Tapley. 5r USA. prod/rel: Vitagraph Co. of America©, Broadway Star Features

SAVAN, GLENN
White Palace, Novel
  White Palace 1990 d: Luis Mandoki. lps: Susan Sarandon, James Spader, Jason Alexander. 105M USA. *Passion Sin Barreras*

SAVERY, JAMES
In for the Night, New York 1917, Play
  Sic-Em 1920? d: Frederick Sullivan. lps: Betty Francisco, Harry Depp, Irene Wallace. 4200f USA. *In for the Night* prod/rel: William N. Selig, the Export and Import Film Co.

SAVI, ELEANOR MORSE
Joy, Novel
  Zonnetje 1920 d: Maurits H. Binger, B. E. Doxat-Pratt. lps: Annie Bos, Renee Spiljar, Adelqui Millar. NTH/UKN. *Joy* (UKN); *Sunny* prod/rel: Anglo-Hollandia Film

SAVIANE, GIORGIO
Eutanasia Di un Amore, Novel
  Eutanasia Di un Amore 1978 d: Enrico Maria Salerno. lps: Ornella Muti, Tony Musante, Monica Guerritore. 110M ITL. prod/rel: Capital Film, Koral Cin.Ca

SAVILLE, MALCOLM
Story
  Treasure at the Mill 1957 d: Max Anderson. lps: Richard Palmer, John Ruddock, Hilda Fenemore. 60M UKN. prod/rel: Wallace, Children's Film Foundation

SAVIOTTI, GINO
La Casa Sul Mare, Story
  Aurora Sul Mare 1935 d: Giorgio C. Simonelli. lps: Renzo Ricci, Giovanna Scotto, Norma Redivo. 68M ITL. prod/rel: Manenti Film

SAVOIE, JACQUES
Les Portes Tournantes, Novel
  Portes Tournantes, Les 1988 d: Francis Mankiewicz. lps: Monique Spaziani, Gabriel Arcand, Miou-Miou. 102M CND/FRN. *The Revolving Doors* prod/rel: Malofilm, Nation Film Board

SAVOIR, ALFRED (1883–1934), PLN, Posznanski, Alfred
Banco!, Paris 1920, Play
  Lost - a Wife 1925 d: William C. de Mille. lps: Adolphe Menjou, Greta Nissen, Robert Agnew. 6420f USA. prod/rel: Famous Players-Lasky, Paramount Pictures
La Couturiere de Luneville, Paris 1923, Play
  Couturiere de Luneville, La 1931 d: Harry Lachman. lps: Pierre Blanchar, Armand Lurville, Madeleine Renaud. 77M FRN. *The Dressmaker of Luneville* prod/rel: Films Paramount

Dressed to Thrill 1935 d: Harry Lachman. lps: Tutta Rolf, Clive Brook, Robert Barrat. 68M USA. *The Dressmaker* prod/rel: Fox Film Corp.©
Le Demoiselle de Passy, Play
  Ladies Should Listen 1934 d: Frank Tuttle. lps: Cary Grant, Frances Drake, Edward Everett Horton. 63M USA. prod/rel: Paramount Productions©
La Grande-Duchesse Et le Garcon d'Etage, Paris 1924, Play
  Grand Duchess and the Waiter, The 1926 d: Malcolm St. Clair. lps: Adolphe Menjou, Florence Vidor, Lawrence Grant. 6314f USA. prod/rel: Famous Players-Lasky, Paramount Pictures
  Here Is My Heart 1934 d: Frank Tuttle. lps: Bing Crosby, Kitty Carlisle, Roland Young. 80M USA. prod/rel: Paramount Productions©
  His Tiger Lady 1928 d: Hobart Henley. lps: Adolphe Menjou, Evelyn Brent, Rose Dione. 4998f USA. *A Night of Mystery* prod/rel: Paramount Famous Lasky Corp.
La Huitieme Femme de Barbe-Bleue, 1921, Play
  Bluebeard's Eighth Wife 1922 d: Sam Wood. lps: Gloria Swanson, Huntley Gordon, Charles Green. 5960f USA. prod/rel: Famous Players-Lasky Corp., Paramount Pictures
  Bluebeard's Eighth Wife 1938 d: Ernst Lubitsch. lps: Claudette Colbert, Gary Cooper, David Niven. 84M USA. prod/rel: Paramount Pictures, Inc.
La Voie Lactee, Play
  King of Paris, The 1934 d: Jack Raymond. lps: Cedric Hardwicke, Marie Glory, Ralph Richardson. 75M UKN. prod/rel: British and Dominions, United Artists

SAVORY, GERALD (1909–, UKN
George and Margaret, London 1937, Play
  George and Margaret 1940 d: George King. lps: Judy Kelly, Marie Lohr, Oliver Wakefield. 77M UKN. prod/rel: Warner Bros., First National
Hand in Glove, 1944, Play
  Urge to Kill 1960 d: Vernon Sewell. lps: Patrick Barr, Howard Pays, Ruth Dunning. 58M UKN. prod/rel: Anglo-Amalgamated, Merton Park

SAWADA, FUJIKO
Niji No Hashi, Novel
  Niji No Hashi 1993 d: Zenzo MatsuyamA. lps: Emi Wakui, Atsuro Watabe, Masanobu TakashimA. 115M JPN. *Rainbow Bridge* prod/rel: Ogawa Kikaku, Inc.

SAWITZKY, WALTER
Fremdenheim Filoda, Novel
  Fremdenheim Filoda 1937 d: Hans Hinrich. lps: Ida Wust, Richard Romanowsky, Mady Rahl. 102M GRM. *Pension Filoda* prod/rel: Cine-Allianz-Tonfilm

SAWYER, RUTH (1880–1970), USA
The Primrose Ring, New York 1915, Novel
  Primrose Ring, The 1917 d: Robert Z. Leonard. lps: Mae Murray, Tom Moore, Winter Hall. 5r USA. prod/rel: Jesse L. Lasky Feature Play Co.©, Paramount Pictures Corp.

SAXE, TEMPLE
Ice on the Coffin, Play
  Meet the Duke 1949 d: James Corbett. lps: Farnham Baxter, Heather Chasen, Gale Douglas. 64M UKN. prod/rel: New Park, Associated British Film Distributors

SAXO GRAMMATICUS (c1150–c1220), DNM
Gesta Danorum, c1195, Books
  Roda Kappan, Den 1967 d: Gabriel Axel. lps: Gitte Haenning, Oleg Vidov, Gunnar Bjornstrand. 104M SWD/DNM/ICL. *Den Rode Kappe* (DNM); *Hagbard and Signe* (USA); *The Red Mantle; Rautha Skikkjan* (ICL) prod/rel: ASA Film, Movie Art of Europe

SAXON, LYLE
Lafitte the Pirate, New York 1930, Novel
  Buccaneer, The 1938 d: Cecil B. de Mille. lps: Fredric March, Franciska Gaal, Margot Grahame. 126M USA. prod/rel: Paramount Pictures, Inc.
  Buccaneer, The 1958 d: Anthony Quinn. lps: Yul Brynner, Charlton Heston, Claire Bloom. 121M USA. prod/rel: Paramount

SAXON, PETER
The Disoriented Man, London 1966, Novel
  Scream and Scream Again 1969 d: Gordon Hessler. lps: Vincent Price, Christopher Lee, Peter Cushing. 95M UKN/USA. *Screamer* prod/rel: Amicus Productions, American International Pictures

SAYERS, DOROTHY L. (1893–1957), UKN
Busman's Honeymoon, 1937, Novel
  Busman's Honeymoon 1940 d: Arthur Woods. lps: Robert Montgomery, Constance Cummings, Leslie Banks. 99M UKN. *Haunted Honeymoon* (USA) prod/rel: MGM British

The Silent Passenger, Novel
Silent Passenger, The 1935 d: Reginald Denham. lps: John Loder, Peter Haddon, Mary Newland. 75M UKN. prod/rel: Phoenix, Associated British

SAYERS, GALE
I Am Third, Book
Brian's Song 1970 d: Buzz Kulik. lps: James Caan, Billy Dee Williams, Jack Warden. TVM. 73M USA. prod/rel: Columbia, Screen Gems

SAYRE, JOEL
The Man on the Ledge, Story
Fourteen Hours 1951 d: Henry Hathaway. lps: Paul Douglas, Richard Basehart, Barbara Bel Geddes. 92M USA. prod/rel: 20th Century-Fox
Rackety Rax, 1932, Short Story
Rackety Rax 1932 d: Alfred L. Werker. lps: Victor McLaglen, Greta Nissen, Nell O'Day. 75M USA. prod/rel: Fox Film Corp.©

SAYRE, THEODORE BURT
The Commanding Officer, New York 1909, Play
Commanding Officer, The 1915 d: Allan Dwan. lps: Alice Dovey, Marshall Neilan, Donald Crisp. 4r USA. prod/rel: Famous Players Film Co., Paramount Pictures Corp.

SAZIE, LEON
Enfants de Paris, Novel
Enfants de Paris 1924 d: Alberto Francis Bertoni. lps: Felicien Tramel, Marguerite Madys, Simone Sandre. SRL. 5300m FRN. *Enfants de Montmartre* prod/rel: Argus Film
Jacques l'Honneur, Play
Jacques l'Honneur 1913 d: Henri Andreani. lps: Jacques Normand, Jean Toulout, Aimee Tessandier. 1400m FRN. prod/rel: Grands Films Populaires
Zigomar Peau d'Anguille, Novel
Zigomar Peau d'Anguille 1913 d: Victorin Jasset. lps: Alexandre Arquilliere, Andre Liabel, Josette Andriot. 995m FRN. *Zigomar Eelskin* (UKN) prod/rel: Eclair
Roi Des Voleurs Zigomar, Novel
Zigomar, Roi Des Voleurs 1911 d: Victorin Jasset. lps: Alexandre Arquilliere, Andre Liabel, Josette Andriot. 935m FRN. prod/rel: Eclair

SAZIO, GAETANO
The Silver Fox, New York 1921, Play
Rendezvous at Midnight 1935 d: W. Christy Cabanne. lps: Ralph Bellamy, Valerie Hobson, Catherine Doucet. 62M USA. prod/rel: Universal Pictures Corp.©

SCARBERRY, ALMA SIOUX
The Flat Tire, New York 1934, Novel
Hired Wife 1934 d: George Melford. lps: Weldon Heyburn, Molly O'Day, James Kirkwood. 65M USA. *Marriage of Convenience* (UKN) prod/rel: Pinnacle Productions, State Rights
High Hat a Radio Romance, New York 1930, Novel
High Hat 1937 d: Clifford Sanforth. lps: Franklin Pangborn, Dorothy Dare, Lona Andre. 90M USA. prod/rel: Cameo Pictures Corp., Imperial Pictures

SCARBOROUGH, DOROTHY
The Wind, New York 1925, Novel
Wind, The 1928 d: Victor Sjostrom. lps: Lillian Gish, Lars Hanson, Montagu Love. 6721f USA. prod/rel: Metro-Goldwyn-Mayer Corp.

SCARBOROUGH, GEORGE
At Bay, Washington, D.C. 1913, Play
At Bay 1915 d: George Fitzmaurice. lps: Florence Reed, Frank Sheridan, Charles Waldron. 5r USA. prod/rel: Pathe Exchange, Inc., Gold Rooster Play
The Final Judgment, Play
Final Judgment, The 1915 d: Edwin Carewe. lps: Ethel Barrymore, H. Cooper Cliffe, Beatrice Maude. 5r USA. *Her Honor* prod/rel: Rolfe Photoplays, Inc., Metro Pictures Corp.©
The Grail, Play
Grail, The 1923 d: Colin Campbell. lps: Dustin Farnum, Peggy Shaw, Carl Stockdale. 4617f USA. prod/rel: Fox Film Corp.
The Lure, New York 1913, Play
Lure, The 1914 d: Alice Blache. lps: Claire Whitney, Fraunie Fraunholz, Lucia Moore. 5r USA. prod/rel: Blache Features, Inc.
Moonlight and Honeysuckle, New York 1919, Play
Moonlight and Honeysuckle 1921 d: Joseph Henabery. lps: Mary Miles Minter, Monte Blue, Willard Louis. 4294f USA. prod/rel: Realart Pictures
The Son-Daughter, New York 1919, Play
Son-Daughter, The 1932 d: Clarence Brown. lps: Helen Hayes, Ramon Novarro, Lewis Stone. 80M USA. prod/rel: Metro-Goldwyn-Mayer Corp., Metro-Goldwyn-Mayer Dist. Corp.©

SCARPETTA, EDUARDO
Play
Agenzia Matrimoniale 1953 d: Giorgio PastinA. lps: Erminio MacArio, Delia Scala, Aroldo Tieri. 90M ITL. prod/rel: Grazia Film, Di Paolo Film
A' Nutriccia, 1882, Play
Nutrice, La 1914 d: Alessandro Boutet. lps: Eduardo Scarpetta, Nina de Martino, Gennaro Della RossA. ITL. *A' Nutriccia* prod/rel: Musical Film
La Bottigliera Di Rigoletto, 1880, Play
Antico Caffe Napoletano, Un 1914 d: Gino Rossetti. lps: Eduardo ScarpettA. ITL. *Il Non Plus Ultra Della Disperazione* prod/rel: Musical Film
Miseria E Nobilta, 1888, Play
Miseria E Nobilta 1914 d: Enrico Guazzoni?. lps: Eduardo Scarpetta, Rosa Gagliardi, Giuseppe de Martino. 533m ITL. prod/rel: Musical Film
Miseria E Nobilta 1941 d: Corrado d'Errico. lps: Virgilio Riento, Elli Parvo, Luigi Almirante. 62M ITL. prod/rel: Scalera Film
Miseria E Nobilta 1954 d: Mario Mattoli. lps: Toto, Dolores Palumbo, Franca Faldini. 95M ITL. *Poverty and Nobility* (USA) prod/rel: Excelsa Film, Minerva Film
'Na Creatura Sperduta, 1899, Play
Sette Ore Di Guai 1951 d: Vittorio Metz, Marcello Marchesi. lps: Toto, Isa Barzizza, Giulietta MasinA. 85M ITL. prod/rel: Golden Film, Humanitas Film
O' Miedeco d'E Pazze, Play
Medico Dei Pazzi, Il 1954 d: Mario Mattoli. lps: Toto, Carlo Giuffre, Carlo Ninchi. 85M ITL. prod/rel: Carlo Ponti Cin.Ca
O Scarfalietto, 1881, Play
Scaldaletto, Lo 1915 d: Gino Rossetti. lps: Eduardo Scarpetta, Amelia Bottone, Gennaro Della RossA. ITL. prod/rel: Musical Film
Mascherina! Ti Conosco, Play
Ti Conosco, Mascherina! 1944 d: Eduardo de Filippo. lps: Lida Baarova, Eduardo de Filippo, Peppino de Filippo. 78M ITL. prod/rel: Cines, Juventus
Tre Pecore Viziose, 1881, Play
Tre Pecore Viziose 1915 d: Gino Rossetti. lps: Eduardo ScarpettA. 2r ITL. prod/rel: Musical Film
Un Turco Napoletano, Play
Turco Napoletano, Un 1953 d: Mario Mattoli. lps: Toto, Isa Barzizza, Carlo Campanini. 85M ITL. prod/rel: Rosa Film, Lux Film
Vi' Che M'ha Fatto Frateme!, 1881
Tutto Per Mio Fratello 1911. lps: Eduardo ScarpettA. 350m ITL. *Vi' Che M'ha Fatto Frateme!*; *Per Mio Fratello* prod/rel: Latium Film

SCEPANOVIC, BRANIMIR
La Mort de Monsieur Golouga, Novel
Julian Po 1997 d: Alan Wade. lps: Christian Slater, Robin Tunney, Michael Parks. 78M USA. prod/rel: Cypress Films, Mindel/Shaw Prods.

SCERBANENCO, GIORGIO
Novel
Ragazzi Del Massacro, I 1969 d: Fernando Di Leo. lps: Pier Paolo Capponi, Nieves Navarro, Marzio Margine. 99M ITL. *Sex in the Classroom* prod/rel: Daunia Film, Belfagor Cin.Ca
Liberi Armati Pericolosi, Short Story
Liberi Armati Pericolosi 1976 d: Romolo Guerrieri. lps: Tomas Milian, Eleonora Giorgi, Stefano Patrizi. 100M ITL. prod/rel: Centro Di Produzioni Citta Di Milano, Staco Film
I Milanesi Ammazzano Al Sabato, Novel
Morte Risale a Ieri Sera, La 1970 d: Duccio Tessari. lps: Raf Vallone, Eva Renzi, Gabriele Tinti. 102M ITL/GRM. *Das Grauen Kam Aus Dem Nebel* (GRM); *Death Occurred Last Night* (UKN) prod/rel: Lombard Film, Slogan Film (Milano)
Milano Calibro 9, Novel
Milano Calibro 9 1972 d: Fernando Di Leo. lps: Lionel Stander, Gastone Moschin, Barbara Bouchet. 101M ITL. *The Contract* (UKN); *Calibre 9* prod/rel: Cineproduzioni Daunia '70, Lia Film
Venere Privata, Novel
Cran d'Arret 1970 d: Yves Boisset. lps: Bruno Cremer, Renaud Verley, Mario Adorf. 90M FRN/ITL. *Il Caso Venere Privata* (ITL) prod/rel: San Marco, Francos Films

SCHAAF, BARBARA
Shattered Vows, Unpublished
Shattered Promises 1993 d: John Korty. lps: Brian Dennehy, Treat Williams, Embeth Davidtz. TVM. 175M USA. *Deadly Matrimony*

SCHACK, HANS EGEDE
Phantasterne, Copenhagen 1858, Novel
Fantasterne 1967 d: Kirsten Stenbaek. lps: Sisse Reingaard, Per Goldschmidt, Peter Bierlich. 88M DNM. *The Day-Dreamers*; *The Dreamers* prod/rel: Saga Film, ASA Film

SCHADE, JENS AUGUST
Mennesker Modes Og Sod Musik Opstar I Hjertet, Copenhagen 1945, Novel
Mennesker Modes Og Sod Musik Opstar I Hjertet 1968 d: Henning Carlsen. lps: Harriet Andersson, Preben Neergaard, Eva Dahlbeck. 105M DNM/SWD. *Manniskor Mots Och Ljuv Music Uppstar I Hjartet* (SWD); *People Meet* (UKN); *People Meet and Sweet Music Fills the Heart* (USA) prod/rel: Henning Carlsen, Nordisk Films

SCHAEFER, JACK (1907–1991), USA, Schaefer, Jack Warner
The Big Range, 1953, Short Story
Silver Whip, The 1953 d: Harmon Jones. lps: Robert Wagner, Dale Robertson, Rory Calhoun. 73M USA. prod/rel: 20th-Century-Fox
Company of Cowards, 1957, Novel
Advance to the Rear 1964 d: George Marshall. lps: Glenn Ford, Melvyn Douglas, Stella Stevens. 97M USA. *Company of Cowards* prod/rel: MGM, Ted Richmond Productions
Jeremy Rodock (Hanging's for the Lucky), Short Story
Tribute to a Bad Man 1956 d: Robert Wise. lps: James Cagney, Irene Papas, Don Dubbins. 95M USA. prod/rel: MGM
Monte Walsh, Boston 1963, Novel
Monte Walsh 1970 d: William A. Fraker. lps: Lee Marvin, Jack Palance, Jeanne Moreau. 106M USA. prod/rel: Palladian Pictures, National General
Shane, 1949, Novel
Shane 1953 d: George Stevens. lps: Alan Ladd, Jean Arthur, Van Heflin. 118M USA. prod/rel: Paramount
Stubby Pringle's Christmas, Short Story
Stubby Pringle's Christmas 1978 d: Burt Brinckerhoff. lps: Beau Bridges, Julie Harris, Edward Binns. MTV. 50M USA.
Trooper Hook, Story
Trooper Hook 1957 d: Charles Marquis Warren. lps: Barbara Stanwyck, Joel McCrea, Earl Holliman. 81M USA. prod/rel: United Artists, Fielding Prods., Inc.

SCHAEFFER, MAX PIERRE
Vier Schlussel, Novel
Vier Schlussel 1965 d: Jurgen Roland. lps: Gunther Ungeheuer, Hanns Lothar, Walter RillA. 107M GRM. *The Four Keys* prod/rel: Hanns Eckelkamp, Atlas

SCHAETZLE, BUD
Love Can Build a Bridge, Autobiography
Naomi & Wynonna: Love Can Build a Bridge 1995 d: Bobby Roth. lps: Kathleen York, Viveka Davis, Bruce Greenwood. TVM. 240M USA. prod/rel: Avnet/ Korner

SCHAFER, E. W.
Die Reise Nach Paris, Play
Gluck Unterwegs 1944 d: Friedrich Zittau. lps: Dora Komar, Maria von Buchlow, O. W. Fischer. 88M GRM. prod/rel: Prag, D.F.V.

SCHAFER, OTOMAR
Devce Z Tabakove Tovarny, Novel
Devce Z Tabakove Tovarny 1928 d: Vaclav Kubasek. lps: Marie Cerna, Filip Balek-Brodsky, Milka Balek-BrodskA. 2083m CZC. *The Girl from the Tobacco Factory* prod/rel: Poja Film, Karel Votruba
Hrdina Lackmann, Book
Zahadny Pripad Galginuv 1923 d: Vaclav Kubasek. lps: Theodor Pistek, Alois Dvorsky, Xenie Alexandrovna Carelli. 2169m CZC. *Galgin's Mysterious Case* prod/rel: Pronax-Film, Iris-Film
Slecna Konvalinka, Play
Pan Otec Karafiat 1935 d: Jan Svitak. lps: Theodor Pistek, Marie Becvarova, Arno Velecky. 3050m CZC. *The Miller Karafiat*; *Father Karafiat* prod/rel: UFA

SCHANBERG, SYDNEY (1934–), USA
The Death and Life of Dith Pran, Article
Killing Fields, The 1983 d: Roland Joffe. lps: Sam Waterston, Haing S. Ngor, John Malkovich. 142M UKN. prod/rel: Goldcrest, Enigma

SCHANZER, RUDOLPH
Die Frau Im Hermelin, Play
Bride of the Regiment 1930 d: John Francis Dillon. lps: Vivienne Segal, Allan Prior, Walter Pidgeon. 7418f USA. *Lady of the Rose* (UKN) prod/rel: First National Pictures
Lady in Ermine, The 1927 d: James Flood. lps: Corinne Griffith, Einar Hansen, Ward Crane. 6400f USA. prod/rel: Corinne Griffith Productions, First National Pictures

That Lady in Ermine 1948 d: Ernst Lubitsch, Otto Preminger (Uncredited). lps: Douglas Fairbanks Jr., Betty Grable, Cesar Romero. 89M USA. prod/rel: 20th Century Fox

Eine Frau von Format, Operetta
Frau von Format, Eine 1928 d: Fritz Wendhausen. lps: Mady Christians, Peter Leschka, Hans Thimig. 2711m GRM. prod/rel: Terra-Film

Madame Pompadour, Play
Madame Pompadour 1927 d: Herbert Wilcox. lps: Dorothy Gish, Antonio Moreno, Nelson Keys. 7245f UKN. prod/rel: British National, Paramount

Die Tolle Komtess, Operetta
Tolle Komtess, Die 1928 d: Richard Lowenbein. lps: Dina Gralla, Werner Fuetterer, Ralph Arthur Roberts. 2349m GRM. *The Crazy Countess* prod/rel: Richard Eichberg-Film

SCHAUFFLER, ELSIE T.
Parnell, New York 1935, Play
Parnell 1937 d: John M. Stahl. lps: Clark Gable, Myrna Loy, Edna May Oliver. 119M USA. prod/rel: Metro-Goldwyn-Mayer Corp.©

SCHAYE, PAUL-ADRIEN
Mon Ami Sainfoin, Novel
Mon Ami Sainfoin 1949 d: Marc-Gilbert Sauvajon. lps: Pierre Blanchar, Sophie Desmarets, Alfred Adam. 85M FRN. prod/rel: Ariane, Sirius

SCHEFF, WERNER
Ulla Die Tochter, Novel
Zwischen Zwei Herzen 1934 d: Herbert Selpin. lps: Luise Ullrich, Harry Liedtke, Olga TschechowA. 81M GRM. *Between Two Hearts* (USA)

SCHEIDIUS, ERNEST
Ulbo Garvema, Novel
Ulbo Garveema 1917 d: Maurits H. Binger. lps: Frederick Vogeding, Cor Smits, Annie Bos. 1577m NTH. *In Rechten Hersteld*; *Rehabilitated* prod/rel: Filmfabriek-Hollandia

SCHEINHARDT, SALINA
Abschied Vom Falschen Paradies, Novel
Abschied Vom Falschen Paradies 1989 d: Tevfik Baser. lps: Zuhal Olcay, Brigitte Janner, Ruth Olafsdottir. 96M GRM. *Farewell to False Paradise* prod/rel: Ottokar Runze Filmproduktion

SCHEINPFLUGOVA, OLGA
Madla Z Cihelny, Play
Madla Z Cihelny 1933 d: Vladimir Slavinsky. lps: Lida Baarova, Antonie Nedosinska, Hugo Haas. 2976m CZC. *Madla from the Brick-Kiln*; *Madla from the Brickworks* prod/rel: UFA

Okenko, Play
Okenko 1933 d: Vladimir Slavinsky. lps: Hugo Haas, Arno Velecky, Antonie NedosinskA. 3051m CZC. *The Little Window* prod/rel: Ab Vinohrady

SCHELESNIKOW, WLADIMIR
Story
Tschutschelo 1986 d: Rolan Bykov. lps: Kristina Orbakaite, Yuri Nikulin, Yelena SanayevA. 127M USS. *The Scarecrow* prod/rel: Mosfilm

SCHERFIG, HANS
Den Forsvundne Fuldmaegtig, 1938, Novel
Forsvundne Fuldmaegtig, Den 1972 d: Gert Fredholm. lps: Ove Sprogoe, Kim Petersen, Bodil Kjer. 102M DNM. *The Case of the Missing Clerk*; *The Missing Principal*

SCHEU, JUST
Die Schone Lugnerin, Opera
Schone Lugnerin, Die 1959 d: Axel von Ambesser. lps: Romy Schneider, Jean-Claude Pascal, Helmut Lohner. 98M GRM/FRN. *La Belle Et l'Empereur* (FRN); *The Beautiful Liar* prod/rel: Real Film, Regina

Teufel Stellt Mr. Darcy Ein Bein, Play
Damonische Liebe 1951 d: Kurt Meisel. lps: Paul Horbiger, Margot Hielscher, Kurt Meisel. 86M GRM. *Demonic Love* prod/rel: H.M.K., N.F.

SCHILLER, FRIEDRICH
Mary Stuart, Play
Mary Stuart 1913 d: J. Searle Dawley. lps: Mary Fuller, Marc McDermott, Bigelow Cooper. 3000f USA. prod/rel: Edison

Turandot, Play
Turandot, Princesse de Chine 1934 d: Serge Veber, Gerhard Lamprecht. lps: Kathe von Nagy, Pierre Blanchar, Marcel Dalio. 83M FRN. prod/rel: U.F.a., a.C.E.

SCHINE, CATHLEEN
Rameau's Niece, Novel
Misadventures of Margaret, The 1998 d: Brian Skeet. lps: Parker Posey, Jeremy Northam, Craig Chester. 105M UKN/FRN. prod/rel: Tf1 Intl., European Co-Production Fund

SCHIRALDI, VITTORIO
Baciamo le Mani, Novel
Baciamo le Mani 1973 d: Vittorio Schiraldi. lps: Arthur Kennedy, John Saxon, Agostina Belli. 105M ITL. *Family Killer* prod/rel: Aquila Cin.Ca, P.A.C.

SCHIROKAUER, ALFRED
Karriere, Berlin 1924, Play
Careers 1929 d: John Francis Dillon. lps: Billie Dove, Antonio Moreno, Thelma Todd. 8435f USA. prod/rel: First National Pictures

SCHISGAL, MURRAY
Luv, New York 1964, Play
Luv 1967 d: Clive Donner. lps: Jack Lemmon, Peter Falk, Elaine May. 96M USA. prod/rel: Manulis-Jalem Productions

The Tiger, New York 1963, Play
Tiger Makes Out, The 1968 d: Arthur Hiller. lps: Eli Wallach, Anne Jackson, Bob Dishy. 95M USA. *The Tiger* prod/rel: Elan Productions

SCHISGALL, OSCAR
Swastika, Novel
Man I Married, The 1940 d: Irving Pichel. lps: Joan Bennett, Francis Lederer, Lloyd Nolan. 77M USA. *I Married a Nazi* prod/rel: 20th Century-Fox Film Corp.©

SCHLEINITZ, EGON G.
Toller Hecht Auf Krummer Tour, Bad Worishofen 1959, Novel
Toller Hecht Auf Krummen Touren 1961 d: Akos von Rathony. lps: Christine Kaufmann, Michael Hinz, William Bendix. 97M GRM. *The Phony American* (USA); *It's a Great Life*; *Toller Hecht Auf Krummer Tour*; *The Long Way Round* prod/rel: Astra, Filmkunst

SCHLICK, FREDERICK
The Man Who Broke His Heart, Play
Wharf Angel 1934 d: William Cameron Menzies, George Somnes. lps: Victor McLaglen, Dorothy Dell, Preston Foster. 65M USA. *The Man Who Broke His Heart* prod/rel: Paramount Productions©

SCHLINGENSIEF, CHRISTOPH
Hundert Jahre Adolf Hitler, Play
Hundert Jahre Adolf Hitler - Die Letzte Stunde Im Fuhrerbunker 1989 d: Christoph Schlingensief. lps: Volker Spengler, Brigitte Kausch, Margit Carstensen. 60M GRM. prod/rel: D.E.M., Hymen Ii

SCHMIDT, AFONSO
A Caranonha, 1804, Short Story
Cara de Fogo 1960 d: Gallileu GarciA. 93M BRZ.

SCHMIDT, DR. H.
Almenrausch Und Edelweiss, Play
Almenrausch Und Edelweiss 1928 d: Franz Seitz. lps: Charlotte Susa, Leo Peukert, Walter Slezak. 2022m GRM. prod/rel: Munchener Lichtspielkunst Ag

SCHMIDT, LOTHAR
Nur Ein Traum, Munchen 1909, Play
Heure Pres de Toi, Une 1932 d: Ernst Lubitsch. lps: Maurice Chevalier, Jeanette MacDonald, Ernest Ferny. 78M USA. prod/rel: Films Paramount

Marriage Circle, The 1924 d: Ernst Lubitsch. lps: Florence Vidor, Monte Blue, Marie Prevost. 8200f USA. prod/rel: Warner Brothers Pictures

One Hour With You 1932 d: Ernst Lubitsch, George Cukor (Uncredited). lps: Jeanette MacDonald, Maurice Chevalier, Charles Ruggles. 80M USA. prod/rel: Paramount Publix Corp.©, Ernst Lubitsch Production

SCHMIDT, WOLF
Die Familie Hesselbach, Book
Familie Hesselbach, Die 1954 d: Wolf Schmidt. lps: Wolf Schmidt, Else Knott, Irene Marhold. 98M GRM. *The Hesselbach Family* prod/rel: Wolf Schmidt, Union

SCHMIDTBONN, WILHELM
Children of the Night, Novel
Rojo No Reikan 1921 d: Minoru MuratA. lps: Kaoru Osanai, Haruko Sawamura, Koreya Togo. 91M JPN. *Souls on the Road*; *Souls of the Road* prod/rel: Shochiku Co.

SCHMITT, DONALD K.
Ufo Crash at Roswell, Book
Roswell 1994 d: Jeremy Paul Kagan. lps: Kyle MacLachlan, Dwight Yoakam, Kim Greist. 87M USA. *Roswell: the Ufo Cover-Up* prod/rel: Viacom Pictures©, Citadel Entertainment

SCHNECK, STEPHEN
Short Story
High-Ballin' 1978 d: Peter Carter. lps: Peter Fonda, Jerry Reed, Helen Shaver. 98M CND. *High Ballin'*; *The Fifth Wheel*; *Sacree Balade Pour Les Gros Bras*; *P.F. Flyer* prod/rel: the Pando Co., Jon Slan Productions Inc.

SCHNEIDER, HANSJORG
Der Erfinder, Play
Erfinder, Der 1981 d: Kurt Gloor. lps: Bruno Ganz, Walo Luond, Verena Peter. 99M SWT. *The Inventor*; *L' Inventeur* prod/rel: Kurt Gloor Filmprod.

SCHNEIDER, PETER
Der Mann Auf Der Mauer, Novel
Mann Auf Der Mauer, Der 1982 d: Reinhard Hauff. lps: Marius Muller-Westernhagen, Julie Carmen, Patricia von Miseroni. 101M GRM. *The Man on the Wall* prod/rel: Bioskop, Paramount

SCHNEIDER-FOERSTL, J.
Sommerrausch, Play
Warum Lugst Du, Elisabeth? 1944 d: Fritz Kirchhoff. lps: Carola Hohn, Paul Richter, Hansi Wendler. 80M GRM. prod/rel: Universum, Fortuna

SCHNIDER-SCHELDE, RUDOLF
Ein Mann Im Schonsten Alter, Novel
Mann Im Schonsten Alter, Ein 1963 d: Franz Peter Wirth. lps: Karl Michael Vogler, Francoise Prevost, Pascale Audret. 109M GRM. *A Man at the Best Age* prod/rel: Maran, Schorcht

SCHNITZER, I.
Der Zigeunerbaron, Vienna 1885, Operetta
Baron Tzigane, Le 1935 d: Henri Chomette, Karl Hartl. lps: Daniele Parola, Jacqueline Francell, Anton Walbrook. 105M FRN. prod/rel: U.F.a., a.C.E.

Zigeunerbaron, Der 1927 d: Friedrich Zelnik. lps: Lya Mara, Michael Bohnen, Wilhelm Dieterle. 2606m GRM. *The Gypsy Baron* prod/rel: Friedrich Zelnik-Film

Zigeunerbaron, Der 1935 d: Karl Hartl. lps: Anton Walbrook, Hansi Knoteck, Fritz Kampers. 105M GRM. *The Gypsy Baron* prod/rel: UFA, Turck

Zigeunerbaron, Der 1954 d: Arthur M. Rabenalt. lps: Margit Saad, Gerhard Riedmann, Karl Schonbock. 105M GRM. *Gypsy Baron* prod/rel: Berolina, UFA

Zigeunerbaron, Der 1962 d: Kurt Wilhelm. lps: Carlos Thompson, Heidi Bruhl, Willy Millowitsch. 103M GRM/FRN. *Princesse Tzigane* (FRN); *Gypsy Baron* prod/rel: Berolina, Comptoir D'expansion

Zigeunerbaron, Der 1965 d: Arthur M. Rabenalt. lps: Rudolf Schock, Erzsebet Hazy, Benno Kusche. MTV. 113M GRM.

Zigeunerbaron, Der 1976 d: Arthur M. Rabenalt. lps: Siegfried Jerusalem, Ellen Shade, Ivan Rebroff. MTV. 98M GRM.

SCHNITZLER, ARTHUR (1862–1931), AUS
Anatol, 1893, Play
Affairs of Anatol, The 1921 d: Cecil B. de Mille. lps: Wallace Reid, Gloria Swanson, Elliott Dexter. 8806f USA. *A Prodigal Knight* (UKN); *Five Kisses*; *Anatol* prod/rel: Famous Players-Lasky Corp., Paramount Pictures

Casanovas Heimfahrt, Novel
Retour de Casanova, Le 1991 d: Edouard Niermans. lps: Alain Delon, Elsa, Alain Cuny. 90M FRN. *The Return of Casanova*

Ritorno Di Casanova, Il 1978 d: Pasquale Festa Campanile. lps: Piero Vida, Maria Grazia Spina, Giulio Bosetti. MTV. F ITL. prod/rel: Filmes Cin.Ca

Doktor Grasler, 1917, Short Story
Mio Caro Dottor Grasler 1989 d: Roberto FaenzA. lps: Keith Carradine, Miranda Richardson, Max von Sydow. 111M ITL/HNG. *My Dear Doctor Grasler*

Fraulein Else, 1923, Short Story
Angel Desnudo, El 1946 d: Carlos Hugo Christensen. lps: Guillermo Battaglia, Olga Zubarry. 85M ARG. *The Naked Angel*; *O Anjo Nu*

Freiwild, Play
Freiwild 1928 d: Holger-Madsen. lps: Evelyn Holt, Fred Louis Lerch, Bruno Kastner. 2795m GRM. prod/rel: Hegewald-Film

Liebelei, 1895, Play
Christine 1959 d: Pierre Gaspard-Huit. lps: Romy Schneider, Alain Delon, Jean-Claude Brialy. 100M FRN/ITL. *L' Amante Pura* (ITL) prod/rel: Speva Films, Play Art

Liebelei 1927 d: Jacob Fleck, Luise Fleck. lps: Fred Louis Lerch, Henry Stuart, Jaro Furth. 2808m GRM. *Passion's Fool* prod/rel: Hegewald-Film

Liebelei 1932 d: Max Ophuls. lps: Magda Schneider, Luise Ullrich, Wolfgang Liebeneiner. 85M GRM/AUS. *Light Love* (USA) prod/rel: Fred Lissa, Elite

Liebelei 1933 d: Max Ophuls. lps: Wolfgang Liebeneiner, Magda Schneider, Simone Heliard. 90M FRN. *Une Histoire d'Amour*; *Young Love* prod/rel: Alma-Sepic

Der Reigen, 1900, Play
Grosse Liebesspiel, Das 1963 d: Alfred Weidenmann. lps: Lilli Palmer, Hildegard Knef, Daliah Lavi. 138M GRM/AUS. *And So to Bed* (USA); *The Game of Love* prod/rel: Team-Film-Stadthallen Production

New York Nights 1984 d: Simon Nuchtern, Romano Vanderbes. lps: Corinne Alphen, Nicholas Cortland, George Ayer. 109M USA. prod/rel: Bedford

Reigen 1974 d: Otto Schenk. lps: Maria Schneider, Helmut Berger, Sydne Rome. 104M GRM/AUS. *Dance of Love* (UKN); *La Ronde*; *Merry Go Round* prod/rel: Lisa, Divina

Ronde, La 1950 d: Max Ophuls. lps: Anton Walbrook, Simone Signoret, Serge Reggiani. 97M FRN. prod/rel: Sacha Gordine

Ronde, La 1964 d: Roger Vadim. lps: Jean-Claude Brialy, Francine Berge, Marie Dubois. 111M FRN/ITL. *Il Piacere E l'Amore* (ITL); *Circle of Love* (USA) prod/rel: Paris-Film Production, S.N. Pathe

Spiel Im Morgengrauen, 1926, Short Story
Daybreak 1931 d: Jacques Feyder. lps: Ramon Novarro, Helen Chandler, Karen Morley. 76M USA. prod/rel: Metro-Goldwyn-Mayer Corp.

Das Weite Land, 1911, Play
Weite Land, Das 1970 d: Peter Beauvais. lps: Ruth Leuwerik, O. W. Fischer, Walther Reyer. MTV. 102M AUS. prod/rel: Durer, Neue Deutsche Film

Weite Land, Das 1987 d: Luc Bondy. lps: Michel Piccoli, Bulle Ogier, Dominique Blanc. 103M AUS/GRM/FRN. *The Distant Land*; *Terre Etrangere*; *Undiscovered Country* prod/rel: Almaro, Arabella

SCHOENDOERFFER, PIERRE
La 317Eme Section, Novel
317Eme Section, La 1965 d: Pierre Schoendoerffer. lps: Jacques Perrin, Bruno Cremer, Pierre Fabre. 94M FRN/ITL/SPN. *Sangre En Indochina* (SPN); *Trois Cent Dixseptieme*; *Platoon 317* prod/rel: Georges de Beauregard, Rome-Paris Films

L' Adieu a Roi, Novel
Farewell to the King 1988 d: John Milius. lps: Nick Nolte, Nigel Havers, James Fox. 117M USA. prod/rel: Orion

SCHOLEFIELD, ALAN
Venom, Novel
Venom 1981 d: Piers Haggard. lps: Klaus Kinski, Nicol Williamson, Oliver Reed. 98M UKN. prod/rel: Aribage, Morison

SCHOMBING, JASON
Story
Stag 1997 d: Gavin Wilding. lps: Andrew McCarthy, John Stockwell, Kevin Dillon. 92M CND. prod/rel: Cinepix Film Properties, Rampage Entertainment

SCHOMER, ABRAHAM S.
Today, New York 1913, Play
Today 1930 d: William Nigh. lps: Conrad Nagel, Catherine Dale Owen, Sarah Padden. 6660f USA. prod/rel: Majestic Pictures

Today 1917 d: Ralph Ince. lps: Florence Reed, Alice Gale, Gus Weinberg. 5r USA. prod/rel: Today Feature Film Corp., Ralph Ince Production

SCHONER, C.
This Name Is Woman, Play
Thy Name Is Woman 1924 d: Fred Niblo. lps: Ramon Novarro, Barbara La Marr, William V. Mong. 9087f USA. prod/rel: Louis B. Mayer Productions, Metro Pictures

SCHONHERR, KARL (1867–1943), AUS
Erde, 1908, Play
Erde 1947 d: Leopold Hainisch. lps: Eduard Kock, Ilse Exl, Anna Exl. 87M AUS/SWT. *Trotzige Herzen*; *Die Erbin Vom Alpenhof* prod/rel: Omnia-Film (Zurich), Tirol-Film (Innsbruck)

Der Judas von Tirol, 1927, Play
Judas von Tirol, Der 1933 d: Franz Osten. lps: Fritz Rasp, Camilla Spira, Marianne Hoppe. 81M GRM. *Der Ewige Verrat*; *Judas of Tyrol* prod/rel: Lothar Stark-Film

Der Weibsteufel, 1914, Play
Weibsteufel, Der 1951 d: Wolfgang Liebeneiner. lps: Hilde Krahl, Kurt Heintel, Bruno Hubner. 82M AUS. *Devil Woman* prod/rel: Styria

Weibsteufel, Der 1966 d: Georg Tressler. lps: Maria Emo, Sieghardt Rupp, Hugo Gottschlich. 91M AUS. *A Devil of a Woman* prod/rel: Vienna

SCHORSCH, WALTER
Jan Vyrava, Play
Jan Vyrava 1937 d: Vladimir Borsky. lps: Zdenek Stepanek, Stanislav Strnad, Ladislav Brom. 2279m CZC. prod/rel: Projektor

SCHOSTAKOVICH, DIMITRI
Autobiography
Testimony 1988 d: Tony Palmer. lps: Ben Kingsley, Sherry Baines, Terence Rigby. 157M UKN. prod/rel: Isolde Films, the Mandemar Group

SCHOTT, MAX
Murphy's Romance, Novel
Murphy's Romance 1985 d: Martin Ritt. lps: James Garner, Sally Field, Brian Kerwin. 103M USA. prod/rel: Columbia-Delphi V Productions, Martin Ritt/Fogwood Films

SCHRADER, MARIE
So This Is Arizona, 1921, Serial Story
So This Is Arizona 1922 d: Francis Ford. lps: Franklyn Farnum, Francis Ford, Shorty Hamilton. 6r USA. prod/rel: William M. Smith Productions, Merit Film Corp.

SCHREIBER, FLORA RHETA
Sybil, Book
Sybil 1976 d: Daniel Petrie. lps: Joanne Woodward, Sally Field, Brad Davis. TVM. 198M USA. prod/rel: Lorimar Productions

SCHROCK, RAYMOND L.
A Cad, Story
Cad, A 1916 d: Ben Wilson. lps: Ben Wilson, Dorothy Phillips, George W. Girard. SHT USA. *The Cad* prod/rel: Rex

Night Freight, Story
Truck Busters 1943 d: B. Reeves Eason. lps: Richard Travis, Virginia Christine, Don Costello. 58M USA. prod/rel: Warner Bros.

Uncle Sam Awakens, Story
Murder in the Air 1940 d: Lewis Seiler. lps: Ronald Reagan, John Litel, James Stephenson. 55M USA. *The Enemy Within* prod/rel: Warner Bros. Pictures©, First National Picture

SCHTSCHEKOTSCHICHIN, JURI
Minya Zavur Arlekin, Play
Minya Zavut Arlekin 1988 d: Valeri Rybarev. lps: Oleg Fomin, Svetlana Kopylova, Ludmila GavrilovA. 132M USS. prod/rel: Belarus-Film-Studio

SCHUBERT, BERNARD
Song of Love, Play
Song of Love 1947 d: Clarence Brown. lps: Katharine Hepburn, Paul Henreid, Robert Walker. 119M USA. prod/rel: MGM

SCHUBERT, HANS
Hereinspaziert!, Play
Hereinspaziert! 1953 d: Paul Verhoeven. lps: Christl Mardayn, Gardy Granass, Curd Jurgens. 102M AUS. *Tingeltangel*; *Praterherzen*; *Das Leben Ist Starker* prod/rel: Schonbrunn

Mit Besten Empfehlungen, Play
Mit Besten Empfehlungen 1963 d: Kurt Nachmann. lps: Georg Thomalla, Adrian Hoven, Trude Herr. 80M AUS. prod/rel: Wiener Stadthalle

Stadtpark, Play
Kleiner Peter, Grosse Sorgen 1950 d: Hubert MarischkA. lps: Friedl Loor, Peter Czeike, Erik Frey. 99M AUS. prod/rel: Berna-Donau

SCHUEK, PAVEL
Play
Ulice Zpiva 1939 d: Vlasta Burian, Cenek Slegl. lps: Vlasta Burian, Jaroslav Marvan, Antonin Novotny. 2538m CZC. *The Street Sings* prod/rel: Brom, Reiter

SCHULBERG, BUDD (1914–, USA
Across the Everglades, Story
Wind Across the Everglades 1958 d: Nicholas Ray. lps: Burl Ives, Christopher Plummer, Gypsy Rose Lee. 93M USA. prod/rel: Warner Bros., Schulberg

The Harder They Fall, 1947, Novel
Harder They Fall, The 1956 d: Mark Robson. lps: Humphrey Bogart, Rod Steiger, Jan Sterling. 109M USA. prod/rel: Columbia

Waterfront, 1955, Novel
On the Waterfront 1954 d: Elia Kazan. lps: Marlon Brando, Eva Marie Saint, Karl Malden. 108M USA. prod/rel: Columbia, Horizon-American Pictures

Your Arkansas Traveler, 1953, Short Story
Face in the Crowd, A 1957 d: Elia Kazan. lps: Andy Griffith, Patricia Neal, Lee Remick. 121M USA. prod/rel: Warner Bros., Newton Prod.

SCHULLER, VIKTOR
Das Gluck Am Sonntagabend, Novel
Mamitschka 1955 d: Rolf Thiele. lps: Mila Kopp, Jester Naefe, Karl Hackenberg. 96M GRM. prod/rel: Filmaufbau, D.F.H.

SCHULMAN, MAX
The Affairs of Dobie Gillis, Book
Affairs of Dobie Gillis, The 1953 d: Don Weis. lps: Debbie Reynolds, Bobby Van, Barbara Ruick. 74M USA. prod/rel: MGM

SCHULTZ, ALAN BRENER
Private Secretary, New York 1929, Novel
Behind Office Doors 1931 d: Melville Brown. lps: Mary Astor, Robert Ames, Ricardo Cortez. 82M USA. *Private Secretary* prod/rel: RKO Radio Pictures, Inc.

SCHULTZ, JEANNE
La Neuvaine de Colette, Novel
Neuvaine de Colette, La 1925 d: Georges Champavert. lps: Mary Harris, Rene Maupre, Georges Terof. 1800m FRN. prod/rel: Films Champavert

SCHULZ, BRUNO (1892–1942), PLN
Sanatorium Pod Klepsydra, 1937, Short Story
Sanatorium Pod Klepsydra 1973 d: Wojciech J. Has. lps: Jan Nowicki, Tadeusz Kondrat, Halina KowalskA. 120M PLN. *The Hourglass Sanatorium* (USA); *Sanatorium*; *A Sanatorium Beneath the Obituary*; *The Sandglass*

SCHULZ, FRANZ
Die Privatsekretarin, Novel
Sunshine Susie 1932 d: Victor Saville. lps: Renate Muller, Jack Hulbert, Owen Nares. 87M UKN. *The Office Girl* (USA) prod/rel: Gainsborough, Ideal

SCHUNZEL, REINHOLD (1886–1954), GRM
Viktor Und Viktoria, Play
First a Girl 1935 d: Victor Saville. lps: Jessie Matthews, Sonnie Hale, Griffith Jones. 94M UKN. prod/rel: Gaumont-British

SCHUPPLER, BRUNO
Lavendel, Play
Lavendel 1953 d: Arthur M. Rabenalt. lps: Gretl Schorg, Karl Schonbock, Hans Holt. 90M GRM/AUS. *Lavendel Eine Ganz Unmoralische Geschichte* prod/rel: Schonbrunn, Rex

SCHUREK, PAUL
Strassenmusik, Play
Strassenmusik 1936 d: Hans Deppe. lps: Jessie Vihrog, Ernst Legal, Fritz Genschow. 90M GRM. prod/rel: Bavaria

SCHUTT, ROLAND
Kadisbellan, Autobiography
Kadisbellan 1993 d: Ake Sandgren. lps: Jesper Salen, Stellan Skarsgard, Basia Frydman. 102M SWD. *The Slingshot* prod/rel: Ab, Svt Kanal

SCHUTT, WALTER
Tanzanwaltz, Berlin 1912, Play
Lonely Wives 1931 d: Russell MacK. lps: Edward Everett Horton, Esther Ralston, Laura Laplante. 87M USA. prod/rel: Pathe Exchange©, RKO Radio Pictures

SCHUTZ
Le Signal Rouge, Novel
Signal Rouge, Le 1948 d: Ernst Neubach. lps: Erich von Stroheim, Frank Villard, Denise Vernac. 105M FRN. prod/rel: Pen Films, Ernest Neubach

SCHUTZ, ADOLF
Le Grand Bluff, Play
Grand Bluff, Le 1933 d: Maurice Champreux. lps: Jose Noguero, Florelle, Lolita Benavente. 75M FRN. prod/rel: Gaumont-Franco-Film-Aubert

SCHWAB, LAWRENCE
Good News, New York 1927, Musical Play
Good News 1930 d: Nick Grinde, Edgar J. MacGregor. lps: Mary Lawlor, Stanley Smith, Bessie Love. 8100f USA. prod/rel: Metro-Goldwyn-Mayer Pictures

Good News 1947 d: Charles Walters. lps: June Allyson, Peter Lawford, Patricia Marshall. 95M USA. prod/rel: MGM

Take a Chance, New York 1932, Musical Play
Take a Chance 1933 d: Monte Brice, Laurence Schwab. lps: James Dunn, Cliff Edwards, June Knight. 84M USA. prod/rel: Paramount Productions©

SCHWABACH, KURT
Gluckliche Reise, Opera
Gluckliche Reise 1933 d: Alfred Abel. lps: Paul Henckels, Adele Sandrock, Magda Schneider. 78M GRM. *Happy Voyage*

Gluckliche Reise 1954 d: Thomas Engel. lps: Paul Hubschmid, Inge Egger, Paul Klinger. 87M GRM. *Happy Voyage* prod/rel: Capitol, Prisma

SCHWANITZ, DIETRICH
Der Campus, Novel
Campus, Der 1998 d: Sonke Wortmann. lps: Heiner Lauterbach, Axel Milberg, Sibylle CanonicA. 122M GRM. *Campus* prod/rel: Constantin Filmproduktion

SCHWARTZ, ARTHUR
The Band Wagon, New York 1931, Play
Dancing in the Dark 1949 d: Irving Reis. lps: William Powell, Betsy Drake, Mark Stevens. 92M USA. prod/rel: 20th Century Fox

SCHWARTZ, DAVID R.
The Bobo, Novel
Bobo, The 1967 d: Robert Parrish. lps: Peter Sellers, Britt Ekland, Rossano Brazzi. 103M UKN. prod/rel: Gina, Warner-Pathe

SCHWARTZ, OTTO
Familie Hannemann, Play
Tante Jutta Aus Kalkutta 1953 d: Karl G. Kulb. lps: Ida Wust, Ingrid Lutz, Viktor Staal. 90M GRM. *Aunt Jutta from Calcutta* prod/rel: Ariston, N.F.
Der Sprung in Die Ehe, Play
Paprika 1932 d: Carl Boese. lps: Franziska Gaal, Paul Horbiger, Paul Heidemann. F GRM.
Paprika 1933 d: Jean de Limur. lps: Rene Lefevre, Pierre Etchepare, Irene de Zilahy. 77M FRN. prod/rel: Societe Internationale De Cinematogrphie
Paprika 1933 d: Carl Boese. lps: Elsa Merlini, Renato Cialente, Sergio Tofano. 80M ITL. prod/rel: Italfonosap, Anonima Pittaluga
Paprika 1957 d: Kurt Wilhelm. lps: Violetta Ferrari, Waltraut Haas, Willy HagarA. 91M GRM. prod/rel: Carlton, Eichberg

SCHWARTZ, SHEILA
Like Me Like Mom, Novel
Like Mom, Like Me 1978 d: Michael Pressman. lps: Linda Lavin, Kristy McNichol, Patrick O'Neal. TVM. 100M USA. prod/rel: CBS Entertainment

SCHWARTZ, SID
The Electric Man, Story
Man Made Monster 1941 d: George Waggner. lps: Lionel Atwill, Lon Chaney Jr., Anne Nagel. 60M USA. *The Electric Man* (UKN); *The Atomic Monster*; *Mysterious Dr. R.*; *Man-Made Monster* prod/rel: Universal

SCHWARTZ, STEPHEN
Godspell, Musical Play
Godspell 1973 d: David Greene. lps: Victor Garber, David Haskell, Jerry SrokA. 103M USA. prod/rel: Columbia

SCHWARZ, LEW
The Cracksman, Novel
Cracksman, The 1963 d: Peter Graham Scott. lps: Charlie Drake, George Sanders, Dennis Price. 112M UKN. prod/rel: Associated British Picture Corporation, Warner-Pathe

SCHWARZ, TED
False Arrest, Book
False Arrest 1991 d: B. W. L. Norton. lps: Donna Mills, Steven Bauer, Lane Smith. TVM. 182M USA. prod/rel: Leonard Hill Films©, Ron Gilbert Associates

SCHWEIKART, HANS
Ehe Im Schatten, Novel
Ehe Im Schatten 1947 d: Kurt Maetzig. lps: Paul Klinger, Ilse Steppat, Alfred Balthoff. 105M GDR. *Matrimony in the Shadows*; *Marriage in the Shadow* prod/rel: Defa
Ich Brauche Dich, Play
Ich Brauche Dich 1944 d: Hans Schweikart. lps: Marianne Hoppe, Willy Birgel, Paul Dahlke. 81M GRM. prod/rel: George Witt-Film, Schorcht
Lauter Lugen, Play
Lauter Lugen 1938 d: Heinz Ruhmann. lps: Hertha Feiler, Albert Matterstock, Fita Benkhoff. 88M GRM. prod/rel: Terra, Super
Muss Man Sich Gleich Scheiden Lassen? 1953 d: Hans Schweikart. lps: Hardy Kruger, Ruth Leuwerik, Tilda Thamar. 88M GRM. *Is Divorce the Only Answer?* prod/rel: N.F.G., Bavaria
Morder Ohne Mord, Novel
Luge, Die 1950 d: Gustav Frohlich. lps: Otto Gebuhr, Sybille Schmitz, Cornell Borchers. 84M GRM. *The Lie* prod/rel: Junge Film-Union, N.F.

SCHWEIZER, RICHARD
Swiss Tour B Xv, Zurich 1947, Novel
Four Days Leave 1950 d: Leopold Lindtberg. lps: Cornel Wilde, Josette Day, Simone Signoret. 98M SWT/USA. *Ein Seemann Ist Kein Schneemann*; *Swiss Tour*; *Swiss Tour - Suzanne Et Son Marin*; *Herz Geht Vor Anker*; *Swiss Tour B Xv* prod/rel: Praesens-Film, Twentieth Century-Fox

SCHWIEFERT, FRITZ
Margherita Fra I Tre, Play
Margherita Fra I Tre 1942 d: Ivo Perilli. lps: Assia Noris, Carlo Campanini, Giuseppe Porelli. 70M ITL. prod/rel: Realcine, I.C.I.

SCHWITZKE, HEINZ
Der Posaunist, Short Story
Posaunist, Der 1945 d: Carl Boese. lps: Paul Dahlke, Sabine Peters, Ludwig Korner. 79M GRM. *The Trombonist* prod/rel: UFA, Viktoria

SCHWOB, MARCEL
Le Roi a la Masque d'Or, 1893, Novel
Re Della Maschera d'Oro, Il 1920 d: Alfredo Robert. lps: Alfredo Robert, Bianca Maria Hubner. 1485m ITL. prod/rel: Robert Film

SCIASIA, LEONARDO
A Ciascuno Il Suo, Turin 1966, Novel
A Ciascuno Il Suo 1967 d: Elio Petri. lps: Gian Maria Volonte, Irene Papas, Gabriele Ferzetti. 99M ITL. *We Still Kill the Old Way* (USA); *To Each His Own* prod/rel: Cemo Film, Panta
L' Antimonio, 1958, Short Story
Vita Venduta, Una 1977 d: Aldo Florio. lps: Enrico Maria Salerno, Gerardo Amato, Rodolfo Bianchi. 110M ITL. *A Sold Life* prod/rel: Comma 9, Ital Noleggio Cin.Co
Atti Relativi Alla Morte Di Raymond Roussel, Novel
Grand Hotel Des Palmes 1979 d: Meme Perlini. lps: Antonello Aglioti, Bettina Best, Giuliana CalandrA. MTV. F ITL. prod/rel: San Francisco Film, Rai-Tv
Un Caso Di Coscienza, 1973, Short Story
Caso Di Coscienza, Un 1970 d: Gianni Grimaldi. lps: Lando Buzzanca, Francoise Prevost, Antonella Lualdi. 113M ITL. prod/rel: Mars Produzione, Paramount
Il Contesto, 1971, Novel
Cadaveri Eccellenti 1976 d: Francesco Rosi. lps: Lino Ventura, Fernando Rey, Max von Sydow. 120M ITL/FRN. *Cadavres Exquis* (FRN); *Illustrious Corpses* (UKN); *Il Contesto*; *The Context* prod/rel: P.E.A. (Roma), Les Artistes Associes (Paris)
Il Giorno Della Civetta, Turin 1961, Novel
Giorno Della Civetta, Il 1967 d: Damiano Damiani. lps: Claudia Cardinale, Franco Nero, Lee J. Cobb. 113M ITL/FRN. *La Maffia Fait la Loi* (FRN); *The Day of the Owl*; *Mafia* (USA); *La Mafia Fait la Loi* prod/rel: Panda Cin.Ca (Roma), Les Films Corona (Paris)
Porte Aperte, 1987, Novel
Porte Aperte 1989 d: Gianni Amelio. lps: Gian Maria Volonte, Ennio Fantastichini, Renzo Giovampietro. 109M ITL. *Open Doors*
Todo Modo, 1974, Novel
Todo Modo 1976 d: Elio Petri. lps: Gian Maria Volonte, Marcello Mastroianni, Mariangela Melato. 139M ITL. prod/rel: Cinevera

SCIZE, PIERRE
Ludo, Novel
Messieurs Ludovic 1945 d: Jean-Paul Le Chanois. lps: Bernard Blier, Odette Joyeux, Arlette Merry. 105M FRN. *Ludo* prod/rel: Optimax
Le Plus Bel Ivrogne du Quartier, Novel
Ils Sont Dans Les Vignes 1951 d: Robert Vernay. lps: Line Renaud, Lucien Baroux, Albert Prejean. 89M FRN. *Love in the Vineyard* (UKN); *A Votre Sante* prod/rel: U.E.C.

SCLAVI, TIZIANO
Dellamorte Dellamore, Novel
Dellamorte Dellamore 1994 d: Michele Soavi. lps: Rupert Everett, Anna Falchi, Francois Hadji Lazaro. 100M ITL/FRN/GRM. *Cemetery Man* (UKN) prod/rel: Kg, Canal©

SCOGGINS, CHARLES E.
Tycoon, Novel
Tycoon 1947 d: Richard Wallace. lps: John Wayne, Laraine Day, Cedric Hardwicke. 128M USA. prod/rel: RKO Radio
Story
Untamed 1929 d: Jack Conway. lps: Joan Crawford, Robert Montgomery, Ernest Torrence. 88M USA. *Jungle* prod/rel: Metro-Goldwyn-Mayer Pictures

SCORTIA, THOMAS M.
The Glass Inferno, Novel
Towering Inferno, The 1974 d: Irwin Allen, John Guillermin. lps: Steve McQueen, Paul Newman, William Holden. 165M USA. prod/rel: 20th Century Fox, Warner Bros.

SCOTT, ADRIAN
The Great Man's Whiskers, Play
Great Man's Whiskers, The 1971 d: Philip Leacock. lps: Dean Jones, Ann Sothern, Dennis Weaver. TVM. 100M USA. prod/rel: Universal

SCOTT, ALLAN
Goodbye Again, New York 1932, Play
Goodbye Again 1933 d: Michael Curtiz. lps: Warren William, Genevieve Tobin, Joan Blondell. 65M USA. prod/rel: First National Pictures©
Honeymoon for Three 1941 d: Lloyd Bacon. lps: Ann Sheridan, George Brent, Charlie Ruggles. 77M USA. prod/rel: Warner Bros.

SCOTT, CLEMENT
Poppyland, Poem
Poppies 1914 d: Stuart Kinder. 1250f UKN. prod/rel: Climax Films, Browne

SCOTT, DEVALLON (1910–1947), USA
Story
Blackbeard the Pirate 1952 d: Raoul Walsh. lps: Robert Newton, Keith Andes, Linda Darnell. 99M USA. prod/rel: RKO Radio

SCOTT, ERIC CLEMENT
The Fall of a Saint, Novel
Fall of a Saint, The 1920 d: W. P. Kellino. lps: Josephine Earle, Gerald Lawrence, W. T. Ellwanger. 6400f UKN. prod/rel: Gaumont, British Screencraft

SCOTT, EWING
Gator Bait, Story
Untamed Fury 1947 d: Ewing Scott. lps: Gaylord Pendleton, Mikel Conrad, Leigh Whipper. 61M USA. prod/rel: P.R.C., Danches Brothers Prods.
Narana of the North, Novel
Arctic Manhunt 1949 d: Ewing Scott. lps: Mikel Conrad, Carol Thurston, QuiannA. 69M USA. prod/rel: Universal-International

SCOTT, GABRIEL
Fant, 1928, Novel
Fant 1937 d: Tancred Ibsen. lps: Alfred Maurstad, Guri Stormoen, Lars Tvinde. 96M NRW/SWD.
Tante Pose, 1904, Short Story
Tante Pose 1940 d: Leif Sinding. 92M NRW.
De Vergelose; Et Barns Historie, 1938, Novel
Vergelose, de 1939 d: Leif Sinding. 74M NRW.

SCOTT, J. D.
Seawyf and Biscuit, Novel
Sea Wife 1957 d: Bob McNaught. lps: Joan Collins, Richard Burton, Basil Sydney. 82M UKN. *Sea Wyf and Biscuit*; *Seawife* prod/rel: Sumar Films, 20th Century-Fox

SCOTT, JOHN REED
The Colonel of the Red Hussars, Novel
Colonel of the Red Hussars, The 1914 d: Richard Ridgely. lps: Robert Conness, Bigelow Cooper, Miriam Nesbitt. 3r USA. prod/rel: Edison

SCOTT JR., COLONEL ROBERT LEE
God Is My Co-Pilot, Book
God Is My Co-Pilot 1945 d: Robert Florey. lps: Dennis Morgan, Raymond Massey, Dane Clark. 89M USA. prod/rel: Warner Bros.

SCOTT, LEROY
Cordelia the Magnificent, Novel
Cordelia the Magnificent 1923 d: George Archainbaud. lps: Clara Kimball Young, Huntley Gordon, Carol Halloway. 6800f USA. prod/rel: Samuel Zierler Photoplay Corp., Metro Pictures
Counsel for the Defense, New York 1912, Novel
Counsel for the Defense 1925 d: Burton L. King. lps: Jay Hunt, Betty Compson, House Peters. 6622f USA. prod/rel: Burton King, Associated Exhibitors
Counterfeit, Story
Flirting With Love 1924 d: John Francis Dillon. lps: Colleen Moore, Conway Tearle, Bryson Winifred. 6926f USA. prod/rel: First National Pictures
A Daughter of Two Worlds, Boston 1919, Novel
Daughter of Two Worlds, A 1920 d: James Young. lps: Norma Talmadge, Frank Sheridan, Jack Crosby. 6r USA. prod/rel: First National Exhibitors Circuit, Norma Talmadge Film Corp.
In Borrowed Plumes, Short Story
In Borrowed Plumes 1926 d: Victor Hugo Halperin. lps: Marjorie Daw, Niles Welch, Arnold Daly. 5719f USA. *Borrowed Plumes* (UKN) prod/rel: Welcome Pictures, Arrow Pictures
Little Angel, Story
Lady of Chance, A 1928 d: Robert Z. Leonard. lps: Norma Shearer, Lowell Sherman, Gwen Lee. 7126f USA. *The Little Angel* prod/rel: Metro-Goldwyn-Mayer Pictures
Mary Regan, Boston 1918, Novel
Mary Regan 1919 d: Lois Weber. lps: Anita Stewart, Frank Mayo, Carl Miller. 6661f USA. prod/rel: Anita Stewart Productions, First National Exhibitors Circuit
Mother O'Day, 1924, Short Story
City That Never Sleeps, The 1924 d: James Cruze. lps: Louise Dresser, Ricardo Cortez, Kathlyn Williams. 6097f USA. prod/rel: Famous Players-Lasky, Paramount Pictures
The Mother, 1914, Short Story
Poverty of Riches, The 1921 d: Reginald Barker. lps: Richard Dix, Leatrice Joy, John Bowers. 5641f USA. prod/rel: Goldwyn Pictures

No. 13 Washington Square, Boston 1914, Novel
   13 Washington Square 1928 d: Melville Brown. lps: Jean Hersholt, Alice Joyce, George Lewis. 6274f USA. prod/rel: Universal Pictures

The Odalisque, Story
   Odalisque, The 1914 d: W. Christy Cabanne. lps: Blanche Sweet, Henry B. Walthall, Miriam Cooper. 2r USA. prod/rel: Majestic

Partners of the Night, 1916, Short Story
   Partners of the Night 1920 d: Paul Scardon. lps: Pinna Nesbit, William B. Davidson, William Ingersoll. 6r USA. prod/rel: Eminent Authors Pictures, Inc., Goldwyn Distributing Corp.

To Him That Hath, New York 1907, Novel
   Supreme Sacrifice, The 1916 d: Lionel Belmore, Harley Knoles. lps: Robert Warwick, Anna Q. Nilsson, Vernon Steele. 5r USA. *To Him That Hath* prod/rel: Premo Film Corp., World Film Corp.
   To Him That Hath 1918 d: Oscar Apfel. lps: Montagu Love, Gertrude McCoy, Reginald Carrington. 5963f USA. prod/rel: World Film Corp.[C]

SCOTT, MANSFIELD
Behind Red Curtains, Boston 1919, Novel
   One Hour Before Dawn 1920 d: Henry King. lps: H. B. Warner, Anna Q. Nilsson, Augustus Phillips. 4696f USA. *Behind Red Curtains* prod/rel: Jesse D. Hampton Productions, Pathe Exchange, Inc.[C]

SCOTT, MICHAEL (1789–1835), UKN
Tom Cringle's Log, 1836, Novel
   Tom Cringle in Jamaica 1913 d: Charles Raymond. lps: Harry Lorraine, George Melville, Percy Moran. 992f UKN. prod/rel: British and Colonial, Moving Pictures Sales Agency

SCOTT, NOE
The Joker, Novel
   Faschingskonig, Der 1928 d: Georg Jacoby. lps: Gabriel Gabrio, Renee Heribel, Elga Brink. 2866m GRM. prod/rel: Horwa-Goron-Film, Deutsch-Nordischen Film-Union

SCOTT, NOEL
The Trouble, Play
   Ourselves Alone 1936 d: Walter Summers, Brian Desmond Hurst. lps: John Lodge, John Loder, Antoinette Cellier. 68M UKN. *River of Unrest* prod/rel: British International, Wardour

SCOTT, PAUL (1920–1978), UKN, Scott, Paul Mark
Novel
   Alien Sky, The 1956 d: John Jacobs. lps: Stephen Murray, Helen Haye, Roger Delgado. MTV. UKN. prod/rel: BBC

Raj Quartet, Novel
   Jewel in the Crown, The 1984 d: Jim O'Brien, Christopher Morahan. lps: Peggy Ashcroft, Charles Dance, Saeed Jaffrey. MTV. 752M UKN. prod/rel: Granada

Staying on, Novel
   Staying on 1980 d: Silvio Narizzano, Waris Hussein. lps: Trevor Howard, Celia Johnson, Saeed Jaffrey. TVM. 87M UKN. prod/rel: Granada

SCOTT, SIR WALTER (1771–1832), UKN
Anna of Geiersteine, Novel
   Fin de Charles le Temeraire, La 1910 d: Georges DenolA. lps: Louis Ravet, Lemonier, Madeleine Celiat. 160m FRN. prod/rel: Pathe Freres

The Bride of Lammermoor, 1819, Novel
   Bride of Lammermoor, The 1909 d: J. Stuart Blackton. lps: Annette Kellerman, Maurice Costello. 450f USA. prod/rel: Vitagraph Co. of America
   Bride of Lammermoor, The 1922 d: Challis Sanderson. lps: Vivian Gibson, Gordon Hopkirk, Olaf Hytten. 779f UKN. prod/rel: Master Films, Gaumont
   Lucia 1998 d: Don Boyd. lps: Amanda Boyd, Richard Coxon, Mark Holland. 102M UKN. prod/rel: Lexington Films
   Lucia Di Lammermoor 1908. 263m ITL. *Lucy of Lammermoor* (UKN) prod/rel: Itala Film
   Lucia Di Lammermoor 1910 d: Mario Caserini. lps: Aldo Sinimberghi. 299m ITL. *The Bride of Lammermoor* (UKN) prod/rel: Cines

The Fair Maid of Perth, 1828, Novel
   Fair Maid of Perth, The 1923 d: Edwin Greenwood. lps: Russell Thorndike, Sylvia Caine, Lionel d'Aragon. 5500f UKN. prod/rel: Anglia Films, Page

Guy Mannering, 1815, Novel
   Guy Mannering 1912. lps: Hector Dion, Julia Hurley, Irving Cummings. 2r USA. prod/rel: Reliance

The Heart of Midlothian, 1818, Novel
   Heart of Midlothian, The 1914 d: Frank Wilson. lps: Flora Morris, Violet Hopson, Alma Taylor. 4275f UKN. prod/rel: Hepworth, Renters

Woman's Triumph, A 1914 d: J. Searle Dawley. lps: Laura Sawyer, Betty Harte, Hal Clarendon. 4r USA. prod/rel: Famous Players Film Co., State Rights

Ivanhoe, Edinburgh 1819, Novel
   Ivanhoe 1913 d: Leedham Bantock. lps: Lauderdale Maitland, Edith Bracewell, Nancy Bevington. 6000f UKN. *Rebecca the Jewess* (USA) prod/rel: Zenith Films, Big A
   Ivanhoe 1913 d: Herbert Brenon. lps: King Baggot, Leah Baird, Evelyn Hope. 3300f UKN/USA. prod/rel: Independent Moving Pictures, Imp Film Co.
   Ivanhoe 1952 d: Richard Thorpe. lps: Robert Taylor, Elizabeth Taylor, Joan Fontaine. 106M UKN/USA. prod/rel: MGM British
   Ivanhoe 1982 d: Douglas Camfield. lps: James Mason, Anthony Andrews, Sam Neill. TVM. 150M UKN. prod/rel: Columbia
   Ivanhoe 1996 d: Stuart Orme. lps: Steven Waddington, Ciaran Hinds, Susan Lynch. MTV. 100M UKN.
   Rivincita Di Ivanhoe, La 1965 d: Tanio BocciA. lps: Rick Van Nutter, Gilda Lousek, Andrea Aureli. 90M ITL/FRN. *Le Revanche d'Ivanhoe* (FRN); *The Revenge of Ivanhoe* (USA) prod/rel: Tevere Film

Kenilworth, 1821, Novel
   Kenilworth 1909 d: J. Stuart Blackton (Spv). lps: Maurice Costello. 985f USA. prod/rel: Vitagraph Co. of America

The Lady of the Lake, Poem
   Lady of the Lake, The 1912 d: J. Stuart Blackton. lps: Harry T. Morey, Edith Storey, Ralph Ince. 3000f USA. prod/rel: Vitagraph Co. of America
   Lady of the Lake, The 1928 d: James A. Fitzpatrick. lps: Percy Marmont, Benita Hume, Haddon Mason. 5168f UKN/USA. prod/rel: Gainsborough, Select

Marmion a Tale of Flodden Field, 1808, Poem
   Lochinvar 1909 d: J. Searle Dawley. lps: Marc McDermott, Mary Fuller, Harold M. Shaw. 790f USA. prod/rel: Edison
   Lochinvar 1915 d: Leslie Seldon-Truss. lps: Godfrey Tearle, Peggy Hyland. 2100f UKN. prod/rel: Gaumont
   Young Lochinvar 1911. SHT USA. prod/rel: Thanhouser
   Young Lochinvar 1923 d: W. P. Kellino. lps: Owen Nares, Gladys Jennings, Dick Webb. 5300f UKN. prod/rel: Stoll

Quentin Durward, 1823, Novel
   Adventures of Quentin Durward, The 1956 d: Richard Thorpe. lps: Robert Taylor, Kay Kendall, Robert Morley. 100M UKN/USA. *Quentin Durward* (USA) prod/rel: MGM British
   Quentin Durward 1912 d: Adrien Caillard. lps: Claude Garry, Rene Alexandre, Marie VenturA. 390m FRN. prod/rel: Scagl

Rob Roy, Novel
   Rob Roy 1911 d: Arthur Vivian. lps: John Clyde, Theo Henries, Durward Lely. 2500f UKN. prod/rel: United Films, Barker

The Talisman, 1825, Novel
   Richard Lvinoe Serdce 1992 d: Evgenij Gerasimov. lps: Alexander Baluev, Armen Dzhigarkhanjan, Sergej Zhigurov. 92M RSS. *The Lion Heart Richard* prod/rel: Okean, Gorky Studio
   King Richard and the Crusaders 1954 d: David Butler. lps: Rex Harrison, Virginia Mayo, George Sanders. 114M USA. prod/rel: Warner Bros.
   Richard, the Lion-Hearted 1923 d: Chet Withey. lps: Wallace Beery, Charles Gerrard, Kathleen Clifford. 7298f USA. prod/rel: Associated Authors, Allied Producers and Distributors
   Talismano, Il 1911. lps: Amleto Novelli, Emilio Ghione. 623m ITL. *Riccardo Cuor Di Leone; Richard the Lion-Hearted* (USA); *The Talisman* (UKN) prod/rel: Cines

SCOTT, WILL
Fallen Leaves, Story
   Fallen Leaves 1922 d: George A. Cooper. lps: Chris Walker, May Price, Jeff Barlow. 1360f UKN. prod/rel: Quality Plays, Walturdaw

The Limping Man, Croydon 1930, Play
   Creeping Shadows 1931 d: John Orton. lps: Franklin Dyall, Arthur Hardy, Margot Grahame. 79M UKN. *The Limping Man* (USA) prod/rel: British International Pictures, Wardour
   Limping Man, The 1936 d: Walter Summers. lps: Francis L. Sullivan, Hugh Wakefield, Patricia Hilliard. 72M UKN. prod/rel: Welwyn, Pathe

The Queer Fish, Play
   His Wife's Mother 1932 d: Harry Hughes. lps: Gus McNaughton, Jerry Verno, Molly Lamont. 69M UKN. prod/rel: British International Pictures, Wardour

The Umbrella, Play
   London By Night 1937 d: Wilhelm Thiele. lps: George Murphy, Virginia Field, Forrester Harvey. 70M USA. *The Umbrella Man; The Umbrella* prod/rel: Metro-Goldwyn-Mayer Corp.[C]

Untold Gold, Short Story
   Man Who Liked Lemons, The 1923 d: George A. Cooper. lps: Forrester Harvey, Harry J. Worth, W. G. Saunders. 1614f UKN. prod/rel: Quality Plays, Gaumont

SCOTT-ELDER, B.
Smoked Glasses, Play
   Blind Man's Bluff 1936 d: Albert Parker. lps: Basil Sydney, Enid Stamp-Taylor, Barbara Greene. 72M UKN. prod/rel: Fox British

SCOTTO, VINCENT
Trois de la Marine, Opera
   Trois de la Marine 1934 d: Charles Barrois. lps: Armand Bernard, Henri Alibert, Rivers Cadet. 90M FRN. prod/rel: Metropa-Film
   Trois de la Marine 1956 d: Maurice de Canonge. lps: Jeannette Batti, Marcel Merkes, Henri Genes. 95M FRN. prod/rel: Cocinex, L.P.C.

Un de la Canebiere, Opera
   Un de la Canebiere 1938 d: Rene Pujol. lps: Henri Alibert, Rellys, Germaine Roger. 98M FRN. prod/rel: Vondas Films

SCRIBE, EUGENE (1791–1861), FRN, Scribe, Augustin Eugene
Adrienne Lecouvreur, Paris 1849, Play
   Adriana Lecouvreur 1919 d: Ugo FalenA. lps: Bianca Stagno-Bellincioni, Enrico Roma, Marion May. 2196m ITL. prod/rel: Tespi Film
   Adrienne Lecouvreur 1913 d: Louis Mercanton, Henri Desfontaines. lps: Sarah Bernhardt, Max Maxudian, Lou Tellegen. 857m FRN. *An Actress's Romance Adrienne Lecouvreur; Or* prod/rel: Urban Trading
   Adriana Lecouvreur 1956 d: Guido Salvini. lps: Gabriele Ferzetti, Valentina Cortese, Olga Villi. F ITL. prod/rel: Salvini Film
   Dream of Love 1928 d: Fred Niblo. lps: Nils Asther, Joan Crawford, Aileen Pringle. 5764f USA. *Adrienne Lecouvreur* prod/rel: Metro-Goldwyn-Mayer Pictures

La Bataille de Dames; Ou un Duel En Amour, Paris 1851, Novel
   Devil-May-Care 1929 d: Sidney A. Franklin. lps: Ramon Novarro, Dorothy Jordan, Marion Harris. 8782f USA. *Battle of the Ladies; Devil May Care* prod/rel: Metro-Goldwyn-Mayer Pictures

Le Diplomate, Play
   Ambasciatore, L' 1936 d: Baldassarre Negroni. lps: Leda Gloria, Luisa Ferida, Maurizio d'AncorA. 75M ITL. prod/rel: Negroni Film, E.N.I.C.

Les Doigts de Fee, 1858, Play
   Dita Di Fata 1921 d: Nino Giannini. lps: Myriel, Arturo Stinga, Alfredo Martinelli. 1565m ITL. prod/rel: Photodrama

Une Femme Qui Se Jette Par la Fenetre, 1847
   Moglie Che Si Getto Dalla Finestra, La 1920 d: Gian Bistolfi. lps: Rosetta d'Aprile, Mira Terribili, Umberto Zanuccoli. ITL.

Fra Diavolo; Ou l'Hotellerie de Terracine, Paris 1830, Opera
   Devil's Brother, The 1933 d: Hal Roach, Charles Rogers. lps: Stan Laurel, Oliver Hardy, Dennis King. 92M USA. *Fra Diavolo* (UKN); *The Virtuous Tramps; Bogus Bandits* prod/rel: Hal Roach Studios, Inc.
   Fra Diavolo 1908 d: Albert Capellani. lps: Jean Angelo. 245m FRN. prod/rel: Scagl
   Fra Diavolo 1912 d: Alice Blache. lps: Billy Quirk, George Paxton, Fanny Simpson. 3r USA. prod/rel: Solax
   Fra Diavolo 1922 d: Challis Sanderson. lps: Vivian Gibson, Gordon Hopkirk, Lionelle Howard. 1294f UKN. prod/rel: Master Films, Gaumont
   Fra Diavolo 1930 d: Mario Bonnard. lps: Tino Pattiera, Brigitte Horney, Kurt Lilien. F GRM.
   Fra Diavolo 1930 d: Mario Bonnard. lps: Madeleine Breville, Tino Pattiera, Armand Bernard. 82M FRN. prod/rel: Itala Film

Dre Kampf Um Den Mann, Play
   Kampf Um Den Mann, Der 1927 d: Hans Werckmeister. lps: Maria Corda, Georg Alexander. 2555m GRM. prod/rel: Parma-Film

La Muette de Portici, Paris 1828, Opera
   Dumb Girl of Portici, The 1916 d: Lois Weber, Phillips Smalley. lps: Anna Pavlova, Rupert Julian, Wadsworth Harris. 8r USA. *Masaniello* prod/rel: Universal Film Mfg. Co.[C], State Rights

Muta Di Portici, La 1911. lps: Mary Cleo Tarlarini. 272m ITL. *Il Trionfo Di Masaniello* prod/rel: S.A. Ambrosio

Muta Di Portici, La 1924 d: Telemaco Ruggeri. lps: Livio Pavanelli, Cecyl Tryan. 1400m ITL. prod/rel: a.G. Film

La Regina Di Navarra, Play
Regina Di Navarra, La 1942 d: Carmine Gallone. lps: Elsa Merlini, Gino Cervi, Clara Calamai. 86M ITL. *L' Allegra Regina* prod/rel: Juventus Film, E.N.I.C.

Le Verre d'Eau Ou Les Effets Et Les Causes, Paris 1840, Play
Glas Wasser, Das 1960 d: Helmut Kautner. lps: Gustaf Grundgens, Liselotte Pulver, Hilde Krahl. 84M GRM. *A Glass of Water* prod/rel: Deutsche Film Hansa

SCRUGGS, JAN C.
To Heal a Nation, Book
To Heal a Nation 1987 d: Michael Pressman. lps: Eric Roberts, Glynnis O'Connor, Marshall Colt. TVM. 100M USA. prod/rel: Daniuel Films

SCUDDER, KENYON J.
Prisoners are People, 1952, Book
Unchained 1955 d: Hall Bartlett. lps: Elroy Hirsch, Barbara Hale, Chester Morris. 75M USA. prod/rel: Warner Bros., Hall Bartlett Prods.

SCULLIN, GEORGE
The Killer, 1954, Article
Gunfight at the O.K. Corral 1957 d: John Sturges. lps: Burt Lancaster, Kirk Douglas, Rhonda Fleming. 122M USA. prod/rel: Paramount, Wallis-Hazen

SCUTT, W. E.
The Whisper Market, 1918, Short Story
Lady Who Dared, The 1931 d: William Beaudine. lps: Conway Tearle, Billie Dove, Sidney Blackmer. 59M USA. *Devil's Playground* prod/rel: First National Pictures©

SDRAWKOFF, PETKO
Novel
Avantazh 1978 d: Georgi Dyulgerov. lps: Russi Chanev, Maria Statulova, Plamena GetovA. 142M BUL. *Advantage*; *Avantaz* prod/rel: Bulgarische Kinematographie

SEAGALL, HARRY
Halfway to Heaven, Play
Heaven Can Wait 1978 d: Warren Beatty, Buck Henry. lps: Warren Beatty, Julie Christie, Jack Warden. 101M USA. prod/rel: Paramount Pictures

Here Comes Mr. Jordan 1941 d: Alexander Hall. lps: Robert Montgomery, Evelyn Keyes, Claude Rains. 93M USA. *Mr. Jordan Comes to Town* prod/rel: Columbia

SEALS, DAVID
Powwow Highway, Novel
Powwow Highway 1988 d: Jonathan Wacks. lps: Gary Farmer, A Martinez, Amanda Wyss. 91M UKN/USA. prod/rel: Handmade Films

SEAMARK, Small, Austin
Down River, Novel
Down River 1931 d: Peter Godfrey. lps: Charles Laughton, Jane Baxter, Harold Huth. 73M UKN. prod/rel: Gaumont

The Perfect Crime, Short Story
Perfect Crime, The 1925 d: Walter Summers. lps: J. Fisher White. 2000f UKN. prod/rel: Stoll

Query, Novel
Murder in Reverse 1945 d: Montgomery Tully. lps: William Hartnell, Jimmy Hanley, Chili Bouchier. 88M UKN. *Query* prod/rel: British National, Anglo-American

Sailors Don't Care, Novel
Sailors Don't Care 1928 d: W. P. Kellino. lps: Estelle Brody, John Stuart, Alf Goddard. 7500f UKN. prod/rel: Gaumont

SEARLS, HENRY, Searls, Hank
The Crowded Sky, Novel
Crowded Sky, The 1960 d: Joseph Pevney. lps: Anne Francis, Efrem Zimbalist Jr., Troy Donahue. 105M USA. prod/rel: Warner Bros.

The Lost Prince: Young Joe the Forgotten Kennedy, Biography
Young Joe, the Forgotten Kennedy 1977 d: Richard T. Heffron. lps: Peter Strauss, Barbara Parkins, Stephen Elliott. TVM. 100M USA. prod/rel: ABC Circle Films

Overboard, Novel
Overboard 1978 d: John Newland. lps: Angie Dickinson, Cliff Robertson, Andrew Duggan. TVM. 100M USA. prod/rel: Factor-Newland Productions

The Pilgrim Project, New York 1964, Novel
Countdown 1968 d: Robert Altman, William Conrad. lps: James Caan, Joanna Moore, Robert Duvall. 101M USA. *Moonshot* prod/rel: Warner Bros.

SEARS, ZELDA
The Clinging Vine, New York 1922, Play
Clinging Vine, The 1926 d: Paul Sloane. lps: Leatrice Joy, Tom Moore, Toby Claude. 6400f USA. prod/rel: de Mille Pictures, Producers Distributing Corp.

Cornered, New York 1920, Play
Cornered 1924 d: William Beaudine. lps: Marie Prevost, Rockliffe Fellowes, Raymond Hatton. 6500f USA. prod/rel: Warner Brothers Pictures

Road to Paradise 1930 d: William Beaudine. lps: Loretta Young, Jack Mulhall, George Barraud. 6935f USA. *At Bay* prod/rel: First National Pictures

SEATON, GEORGE
The Cockeyed Miracle, Play
Cockeyed Miracle, The 1946 d: S. Sylvan Simon. lps: Frank Morgan, Keenan Wynn, Audrey Totter. 81M USA. *Mr. Griggs Returns* (UKN); *But Not Goodbye* prod/rel: MGM

SEAWELL, MOLLY ELLIOT
Story
Sixteenth Wife, The 1917 d: Charles J. Brabin. lps: Peggy Hyland, Marc MacDermott, George Forth. 5r USA. *His Sixteenth Wife*; *Tina and the Turk*; *Olette the Elusive* prod/rel: Vitagraph Co. of America©, Blue Ribbon Feature

The Fortunes of Fifi, Indianapolis 1903, Play
Fortunes of Fifi, The 1917 d: Robert G. VignolA. lps: Marguerite Clark, William Sorelle, John Sainpolis. 5r USA. prod/rel: Famous Players Film Co., Paramount Pictures Corp.

The Spitfire, Story
Heart of Cerise, The 1915 d: Joseph de Grasse. lps: Pauline Bush, William Clifford, Henry Nelson. 3r USA. prod/rel: Rex

SEBASTIAN, MIHAIL
Jocul de-a Vacanta, 1946, Play
Al Patrulea Stol 1979 d: Timotei Ursu. 101M RMN. *The Fourth Flock*

Steaua Fara Nume, 1946, Play
Mona, l'Etoile Sans Nom 1966 d: Henri Colpi. lps: Marina Vlady, Claude Rich, Chris Avram. 95M FRN/RMN. *Steaua Fara Nume* (RMN); *For a Nameless Star*; *Pour une Etoile Sans Nom* prod/rel: Argos Films, Films Luciana

Ultima Ora, 1956, Play
Afacerea Protar 1956 d: Haralambie Boros. lps: Radu Beligan. 82M RMN. *Protar Affair*

SECCHI, LUCIANO
Agenzia Investigativa Riccardo Finzi, Novel
Agenzia Riccardo Finzi. Praticamente Detective 1979 d: Bruno Corbucci. lps: Renato Pozzetto, Enzo Canavale, Elio Zamuto. 92M ITL. *The Finzi Detective Agency* prod/rel: Cinemaster, Titanus

SECHEHAYE, MARGUERITE ANDREE
Journal d'une Schizofrene, Diary
Diario Di Una Schizofrenica 1968 d: Nelo Risi. lps: Ghislaine d'Orsay, Umberto Raho, Marija Tochinowsky. 100M ITL. *Diary of a Schizophrenic Girl* (USA); *Diary of a Schizophrenic*; *Why Anna?* prod/rel: Idi Cin.Ca, Medusa

SECKLER, HARRY
Yiskor, c1923, Play
Yiskor 1932 d: George Roland. lps: Maurice Schwartz, Oszkar Beregi, Dagny Servaes. 80M USA. *The Prince and the Pauper*; *The Holy Martyr* prod/rel: Gloria Films

SECONDARI, JOHN H.
Coins in a Fountain, Philadelphia 1952, Novel
Pleasure Seekers, The 1964 d: Jean Negulesco. lps: Ann-Margret, Anthony Franciosa, Carol Lynley. 107M USA. prod/rel: 20th Century-Fox Film Corporation

Three Coins in the Fountain 1954 d: Jean Negulesco. lps: Clifton Webb, Dorothy McGuire, Jean Peters. 102M USA. prod/rel: 20th Century-Fox

SECUNDA, SHOLEM
My Sonny, Play
My Son 1939 d: Joseph Seiden. lps: Fabia Rubina, Gustav Berger, Jerry Rosenberg. 90M USA. *Mayn Zundele*; *The Living Orphan*; *Der Lebediker Yusem* prod/rel: Jewish Talking Picture Co.©

SEDGWICK, ANNE DOUGLAS
The Little French Girl, New York 1924, Novel
Little French Girl, The 1925 d: Herbert Brenon. lps: Alice Joyce, Mary Brian, Neil Hamilton. 5628f USA. prod/rel: Famous Players-Lasky, Paramount Pictures

Tante, Novel
Impossible Woman, The 1919 d: Meyrick Milton. lps: Constance Collier, Langhorne Burton, Christine Rayner. 5000f UKN. prod/rel: Ideal

SEDGWICK, MRS. ALFRED
The Kinsman, Novel
Kinsman, The 1919 d: Henry Edwards. lps: Henry Edwards, Chrissie White, James Carew. 5350f UKN. prod/rel: Hepworth, Butcher

SEDLAK, JAN
Milovani Zakazano, Novel
Milovani Zakazano 1938 d: Miroslav Cikan, Carl Lamac. lps: Vaclav Tregl, Hana Vitova, Carl Lamac. 2593m CZC. *Forbidden Love* prod/rel: Reiter

SEELEY, CLINTON
Storm Fear, Novel
Storm Fear 1956 d: Cornel Wilde. lps: Dan Duryea, Cornel Wilde, Jean Wallace. 88M USA. prod/rel: United Artists, Theodora Prods.

SEELIGER, EWALD G.
Peter Voss Der Millionendieb, Book
Peter Voss, Der Millionendieb 1945 d: Karl Anton. lps: Viktor de Kowa, Karl Schonbock, Else von Mollendorff. 89M GRM. prod/rel: Tobis, Doring

Peter Voss, Der Millionendieb 1958 d: Wolfgang Becker. lps: O. W. Fischer, Ingrid Andree, Margit Saad. 112M GRM. prod/rel: Kurt Ulrich, UFA

SEFF, MANUEL
Blessed Event, New York 1932, Play
Blessed Event 1932 d: Roy Del Ruth. lps: Lee Tracy, Mary Brian, Dick Powell. 84M USA. prod/rel: Warner Bros. Pictures, Inc.

SEGAL, ERICH (1937–, USA
Love Story, 1970, Novel
Love Story 1970 d: Arthur Hiller. lps: Ali MacGraw, Ryan O'Neal, John Marley. 100M USA. prod/rel: Paramount

Man Woman and Child, Novel
Man, Woman and Child 1983 d: Dick Richards. lps: Martin Sheen, Blythe Danner, Craig T. Nelson. 100M USA. *A Man a Woman and a Child* prod/rel: Paramount

Oliver's Story, 1977, Novel
Oliver's Story 1978 d: John Korty. lps: Ryan O'Neal, Candice Bergen, Nicola Pagett. 92M USA. prod/rel: Paramount

SEGALL, HARRY
Story
Monkey Business 1952 d: Howard Hawks. lps: Cary Grant, Ginger Rogers, Charles Coburn. 97M USA. *Be Your Age* prod/rel: 20th Century-Fox

The Behavior of Mrs. Crane, New York 1928, Play
Uncertain Lady 1934 d: Karl Freund. lps: Edward Everett Horton, Genevieve Tobin, Renee Gadd. 65M USA. prod/rel: Universal Pictures Corp.©

May We Come in, Play
For Heaven's Sake 1950 d: George Seaton. lps: Robert Cummings, Joan Bennett, Clifton Webb. 92M USA. prod/rel: 20th Century-Fox

SEGERCRANTZ, GOSTA
Watch Your Wife, Story
Watch Your Wife 1926 d: Svend Gade. lps: Virginia Valli, Pat O'Malley, Nat Carr. 6974f USA. prod/rel: Universal Pictures

SEGHERS, ANNA (1900–1983), GRM, Radvanyi, Netty, Reiling, Netty
Der Aufstand Der Fischer von Santa Barbara, 1928, Novel
Vostaniye Rybakov 1934 d: Erwin Piscator. lps: Alexei Diky, Emma Tsesarskaya, Vera YanukovA. 97M USS. *The Revolt of the Fishermen*; *Die Fischer von St. Barbara*

Das Licht Auf Dem Galgen, 1960, Short Story
Licht Auf Dem Galgen, Das 1976 d: Helmut Nitzschke. lps: Erwin Geschonneck, Alexander Lang, Amza PeleA. 112M GDR.

Das Siebte Kreuz, 1939, Novel
Seventh Cross, The 1944 d: Fred Zinnemann. lps: Spencer Tracy, Signe Hasso, Hume Cronyn. 110M USA. prod/rel: MGM

Die Toten Bleiben Jung, 1949, Novel
Toten Bleiben Jung, Die 1968 d: Joachim Kunert. lps: Barbara Dittus, Gunter Wolf, Klaus-Peter Plessow. 108M GDR. *The Dead Remain Young*; *The Dead Stay Young*

Transit, 1944, Novel
Fluchtweg Nach Marseille 1977 d: Ingemo Engstrom, Gerhard Theuring. lps: Katharina Thalbach, Rudiger Vogeler, Francois Mouren-Provensal. TVM. 210M GRM. *Escape Route to Marseilles*; *Flight to Marseille* prod/rel: Theuring-Engstrom

Transit 1990 d: Rene Allio. lps: Sebastian Koch, Claudia Messner, Rudiger Vogler. 123M FRN.

SEIBERT, T. LAWRENCE
Casey Jones, 1909, Song
Casey Jones 1927 d: Charles J. Hunt. lps: Ralph Lewis, Kate Price, Al St. John. 6673f USA. prod/rel: Trem Carr Productions, Rayart Pictures

SEIDLER, TOR
Die Story von Monty Spinnerratz, Book
Story von Monty Spinnerratz, Die 1998 d: Michael F. Huse. lps: Lauren Hutton, Beverly d'Angelo, Jerry Stiller. 89M GRM. *A Rat's Tale* prod/rel: Monty Film

SEILER, HEINRICH
Manner Mussen So Sein, Ebendorf 1938, Novel
Geliebte Bestie 1959 d: Arthur M. Rabenalt. lps: Gerhard Riedmann, Margit Nunke, Willy Birgel. 102M AUS/GRM. *Hippodrome* (USA); *Manner Mussen So Sein; Arena of Fear; Meine Heimat Ist Taglich Woanders; Madchen Im Tigerfell, Das* prod/rel: Sascha Film, Lux-Film
Manner Mussen So Sein 1939 d: Arthur M. Rabenalt. lps: Hertha Feiler, Hans Sohnker, Paul Horbiger. 95M GRM. *Men are That Way* (USA); *Manner Mussen Es Sein* prod/rel: Terra
Truxa, Novel
Truxa 1936 d: Hans H. Zerlett. lps: La Jana, Hannes Stelzer, Rudi Godden. 97M GRM. prod/rel: Tobis, Europa

SEITZ, GEORGE B. (1888–1944), USA, Seitz, George Brackett
The Golden Senorita, Play
Rogues and Romance 1920 d: George B. Seitz. lps: George B. Seitz, June Caprice, Marguerite Courtot. 5827f USA. prod/rel: George B. Seitz Productions, Pathe Exchange, Inc.©
The King's Game, New York 1910, Play
King's Game, The 1916 d: Ashley Miller. lps: Pearl White, George Probert, Sheldon Lewis. 5r USA. prod/rel: Pathe Exchange, Inc.©, Gold Rooster Plays

SEITZ SR., FRANZ
Ehe Fur Eine Nacht, Play
Ehe Fur Eine Nacht 1953 d: Victor Tourjansky. lps: Gustav Frohlich, Adrian Hoven, Hans Leibelt. 92M GRM. *Marriage for a Night* prod/rel: Ariston, N.F.

SEKIZAWA, S.
Dokuritsu Gurentai, Novel
Dokuritsu Gurentai 1959 d: Kihachi Okamoto. lps: Toshiro Mifune, Makoto Sato, Ichiro Nakatani. 109M JPN. *Desperado Outpost* prod/rel: Toho Co.

SELBY, CHARLES
London By Night, Play
London By Night 1913 d: Alexander Butler?. lps: Thomas H. MacDonald, Doreen O'Connor, Roy Travers. 3250f UKN. prod/rel: Barker, Walturdaw
The Marble Heart, New York 1864, Play
Marble Heart, The 1913. lps: James Cruze, Marguerite Snow, Florence Labadie. 2r USA. prod/rel: Thanhouser
Marble Heart, The 1915 d: George A. Lessey. lps: King Baggot, Ned Reardon, Jane Fearnley. 4r USA. prod/rel: Imp, Universal Film Mfg. Co.©

SELBY, HUBERT (1928–, USA, Selby Jr., Hubert
Last Exit to Brooklyn, 1964, Novel
Last Exit to Brooklyn 1989 d: Ulrich Edel. lps: Stephen Lang, Jennifer Jason Leigh, Burt Young. 102M USA/GRM. *Letzte Ausfahrt Brooklyn* (GRM)

SELFE, RAY
Albert's Follies, Story
White Cargo 1974 d: Ray Selfe. lps: David Jason, Hugh Lloyd, Imogen Hassall. 70M UKN. prod/rel: Border Films (London) Ltd

SELINKO, ANNEMARIE
Desiree, Novel
Desiree 1954 d: Henry Koster. lps: Jean Simmons, Marlon Brando, Merle Oberon. 110M USA. prod/rel: 20th Century-Fox
Heute Heiratet Mein Mann, Novel
Heute Heiratet Mein Mann 1956 d: Kurt Hoffmann. lps: Liselotte Pulver, Johannes Heesters, Paul Hubschmid. 95M GRM. *My Husband's Getting Married Today* prod/rel: Georg Witt, Constantin
Ich War Ein Hassliches Madchen, Novel
Ich War Ein Hassliches Madchen 1955 d: Wolfgang Liebeneiner. lps: Sonja Ziemann, Dieter Borsche, Karlheinz Bohm. 96M GRM. *I Was an Ugly Girl* prod/rel: Cine-Allianz, Meteor
Morgen Ist Alles Besser, Novel
Morgen Ist Alles Besser 1948 d: Arthur M. Rabenalt. lps: Ellen Schwanneke, Jacob Tiedtke, Grethe Weiser. 97M GRM. *Everything Will Be Better Tomorrow* prod/rel: Berolina, Herzog

Morgen Wird Alles Besser, Novel
Morgen Gaat Het Beter 1939 d: Friedrich Zelnik. lps: Lily Bouwmeester, Paul Steenbergen, Theo Frenkel. 100M NTH.

SELLIER JR., CHARLES E.
In Search of Historic Jesus, Book
In Search of Historic Jesus 1979 d: Henning Schellerup. lps: John Rubinstein, John Anderson, Nehemiah Persoff. 91M USA. prod/rel: Sunn Classics

SELTZER, CHARLES ALDEN
Short Story
Money Corral, The 1919 d: William S. Hart, Lambert Hillyer. lps: William S. Hart, Jane Novak, Herschal Mayall. 5192f USA. *The Money Corporal* prod/rel: William S. Hart Productions, Inc.©, Famous Players-Lasky Corp.
The Boss of the Lazy Y, New York 1915, Novel
Boss of the Lazy Y, The 1918 d: Cliff Smith. lps: Roy Stewart, Josie Sedgwick, Graham Pettie. 4536f USA. prod/rel: Triangle Film Corp., Triangle Distributing Corp.
The Brass Commandments, New York 1923, Novel
Brass Commandments 1923 d: Lynn Reynolds. lps: William Farnum, Wanda Hawley, Thomas Santschi. 4829f USA. prod/rel: Fox Film Corp.
Chain Lightning 1927 d: Lambert Hillyer. lps: Buck Jones, Diane Ellis, Ted McNamarA. 5333f USA. prod/rel: Fox Film Corp.
The Coming of the Law, New York 1912, Novel
Coming of the Law, The 1919 d: Arthur Rosson. lps: Tom Mix, Agnes Vernon, George Nicholls. 5r USA. prod/rel: Fox Film Corp., William Fox©
Firebrand Trevision, New York 1918, Novel
Firebrand Trevison 1920 d: Thomas N. Heffron. lps: Buck Jones, Winifred Westover, Martha Mattox. 5r USA. *Fire-Brand Trevison* prod/rel: Fox Film Corp., William Fox©
Forbidden Trails, 1919, Short Story
Forbidden Trails 1920 d: Scott R. Dunlap. lps: Buck Jones, Winifred Westover, Stanton Heck. 5r USA. prod/rel: Fox Film Corp., William Fox©
The Range Boss, Chicago 1916, Novel
Range Boss, The 1917 d: W. S. Van Dyke. lps: Jack Gardner, Ruth King, Carl Stockdale. 5r USA. prod/rel: Essanay Film Mfg. Co.©, K-E-S-E Service
Square Deal Sanderson, 1918, Novel
Square Deal Sanderson 1919 d: William S. Hart, Lambert Hillyer. lps: William S. Hart, Anna Little, Frank Whitson. 5003f USA. prod/rel: William S. Hart Productions, Inc.©, Famous Players-Lasky Corp.
The Trail to Yesterday, New York 1913, Novel
Trail to Yesterday, The 1918 d: Edwin Carewe. lps: Bert Lytell, Anna Q. Nilsson, Harry Northrup. 5-6r USA. prod/rel: Metro Pictures Corp.©
The Two-Gun Man, New York 1911, Novel
Treat 'Em Rough 1919 d: Lynn Reynolds. lps: Tom Mix, Jane Novak, Val Paul. 5r USA. *The Two-Gun Man* prod/rel: Fox Film Corp., William Fox©
The Vengeance of Jefferson Gawne, Chicago 1917, Novel
Riddle Gawne 1918 d: William S. Hart, Lambert Hillyer. lps: William S. Hart, Katherine MacDonald, Lon Chaney. 4757f USA. prod/rel: William S. Hart Productions, Inc.©, Famous Players-Lasky Corp.
West!, New York 1922, Novel
Rough Shod 1922 d: B. Reeves Eason. lps: Buck Jones, Helen Ferguson, Ruth Renick. 4486f USA. prod/rel: Fox Film Corp.

SELWYN, EDGAR
The Arab, New York 1911, Play
Arab, The 1915 d: Cecil B. de Mille. lps: Edgar Selwyn, Gertrude Robinson, Theodore Roberts. 5r USA. prod/rel: Jesse L. Lasky Feature Co.©, Paramount Pictures Corp.
Arab, The 1924 d: Rex Ingram. lps: Ramon Novarro, Alice Terry, Max Maxudian. 6710f USA. prod/rel: Metro-Goldwyn Pictures
The Country Boy, New York 1910, Play
Country Boy, The 1915 d: Frederick A. Thompson, Allan Dwan (Spv). lps: Marshall Neilan, Florence Dagmar, Dorothy Green. 4170f USA. prod/rel: Jesse L. Lasky Feature Play Co.©, Paramount Pictures Corp.
The Crowded Hour, New York 1918, Play
Crowded Hour, The 1925 d: E. Mason Hopper. lps: Bebe Daniels, Kenneth Harlan, T. Roy Barnes. 6558f USA. prod/rel: Famous Players-Lasky, Paramount Pictures
Dancing Mothers, New York 1924, Play
Dancing Mothers 1926 d: Herbert Brenon. lps: Alice Joyce, Conway Tearle, Clara Bow. 7169f USA. prod/rel: Famous Players-Lasky, Paramount Pictures

The Divorcee, Play
Primitive Lover, The 1922 d: Sidney A. Franklin. lps: Constance Talmadge, Harrison Ford, Kenneth Harlan. 6172f USA. prod/rel: Constance Talmadge Film Co., Associated First National Pictures
The Mirage, New York 1920, Play
Mirage, The 1924 d: George Archainbaud. lps: Florence Vidor, Clive Brook, Alan Roscoe. 5770f USA. prod/rel: Regal Pictures, Producers Distributing Corp.
Possessed 1931 d: Clarence Brown. lps: Joan Crawford, Clark Gable, Wallace Ford. 72M USA. *The Mirage* prod/rel: Metro-Goldwyn-Mayer Corp.©, Metro-Goldwyn-Mayer Dist. Corp.©
Nearly Married, New York 1913, Play
Nearly Married 1917 d: Chet Withey. lps: Madge Kennedy, Frank Thomas, Mark Smith. 5r USA. prod/rel: Goldwyn Pictures Corp.©, Goldwyn Distributing Corp.
Pierre of the Plains, New York 1908, Play
Heart of the Wilds 1918 d: Marshall Neilan. lps: Elsie Ferguson, Thomas Meighan, Joseph Smiley. 4380f USA. prod/rel: Famous Players-Lasky Corp.©, Artcraft Pictures
Pierre of the Plains 1914 d: Lawrence McGill. lps: Edgar Selwyn, William Conklin, Joseph Rieder. 5r USA. prod/rel: All Star Feature Corp.
Pierre of the Plains 1942 d: George B. Seitz. lps: John Carroll, Ruth Hussey, Bruce Cabot. 66M USA. prod/rel: MGM
Rolling Stones, New York 1915, Play
Rolling Stones 1916 d: Dell Henderson. lps: Owen Moore, Marguerite Courtot, Alan Hale. 5r USA. prod/rel: Famous Players Film Co.©, Paramount Pictures Corp.
Something to Brag About, New York 1925, Play
Baby-Face Harrington 1935 d: Raoul Walsh. lps: Charles Butterworth, Una Merkel, Harvey Stephens. 61M USA. *Baby Face* prod/rel: Metro-Goldwyn-Mayer Corp.

SELZER, CHARLES ALDEN
Slow Burgess, Short Story
Fame and Fortune 1918 d: Lynn Reynolds. lps: Tom Mix, Kathleen O'Connor, George Nicholls. 5r USA. *Mr. Logan* prod/rel: Fox Film Corp., William Fox©

SEMBENE, OUSMANE (1923–, SNL
Le Mandat, 1965, Short Story
Mandat, Le 1968 d: Ousmane Sembene. lps: Mamadou Gueye, Ynousse N'diaye, Issa Niang. 105M SNL/FRN. *The Money Order* (UKN); *Mandabi* (USA) prod/rel: Les Films Domireve, Comptoir Francais Du Film
Voltaique, 1962, Short Story
Noire de., La 1967 d: Ousmane Sembene. lps: Mbissine Therese Diop, Anne-Marie Jelinek, Momar Nar Sene. 70M SNL/FRN. *The Black One from.*; *Black Girl* prod/rel: Les Actualites Francaises, Les Films Domireve
Xala, 1973, Novel
Xala 1974 d: Ousmane Sembene. lps: Tierno Leye, Seune Samb, Myriam Niang. 123M SNL. *The Curse*; *Impotence*; *L' Impuissance Temporaire* prod/rel: Filmi Domireve, Societe Nationale Cinematographique

SEMPLE JR., LORENZO
The Golden Fleecing, 1959, Play
Honeymoon machine, The 1961 d: Richard Thorpe. lps: Steve McQueen, Brigid Bazlen, Jim Hutton. 88M USA. prod/rel: Avon Productions, MGM

SEN, SALIL
Natun Yahudi, Play
Natun Yahudi 1953 d: Salil Sen. lps: Kanu Bannerjee, Bhanu Bannerjee, Bani Ganguly. F IND. prod/rel: Eastern Artists

SENANAYAKE, G. B.
Duwata Mawaka Misa, Short Story
Duwata Mawaka Misa 1997 d: Sumitra Peries. lps: Sangeetha Weeraratne, Tony Ranasinghe, Sanath GunatilakA. 126M SLN. *A Mother Alone* prod/rel: Sumathi Films

SENECA, LUCIUS ANNAEUS (4bc–65ad), ITL
Phaedra, Play
Fedra 1956 d: Mur Oti. lps: Emma Penella, Enrique A. Diosdado, Vicente ParrA. 98M SPN. *Fedra the Devil's Daughter* (USA); *The Stepmother* (UKN); *Phaedra* prod/rel: Suevia

SENESH, HANNA
The Diaries of Hannah Senesh, Book
Hanna's War 1988 d: Menahem Golan. lps: Ellen Burstyn, Maruschka Detmers, Anthony Andrews. 148M USA/ISR. *Hannah Senesh* (ISR); *Innocent Heroes* prod/rel: Cannon

SENGER, VALENTIN
Kaiserhofstrasse 12, Novel
  Kaiserhofstrasse 12 1980 d: Rainer Wolffhardt. lps: Christian Eichhorn, Doris Schade, Sigfrit Steiner. 101M GRM. *Kaiserhof Street 12* prod/rel: Hessischer Rundfunk

SENJE, SIGURD
Feldmann-Saken, Novel
  Feldmann-Saken 1986 d: Bente Erichsen. lps: Bjorn Sundquist, Sverre Anker Ousdal, Ingrid Vardund. 94M NRW. *The Feldmann Case*; *Over Grensen* prod/rel: Jeanette Sundby Prod.

SENTJURC, IGOR
Bumerang, Bad Worishofen 1959, Novel
  Bumerang 1960 d: Alfred Weidenmann. lps: Hardy Kruger, Martin Held, Mario Adorf. 92M GRM. *Cry Double Cross* (UKN); *Boomerang* prod/rel: Roxy, U.F.H.

SEPULVEDA, LUIS
Story of a Seagull and the Cat Who Taught Her to Fly, Novel
  Gabbianella E Il Gatto, La 1998 d: Enzo d'Alo. ANM. 75M ITL. *Zorba and Lucky* prod/rel: Cgg Tiger Cin.Ca, Cecchi Gori Distribuzione

SERAFIMOVICH, ALEKSANDR
Zheleznyi Potok, 1924, Short Story
  Zhelyezny Potok 1967 d: Yefim Dzigan. lps: Vladimir Ivashov, Nikolay Alexeyev, Lev Frichinski. 104M USS. *The Iron Flood*; *Zheleznyi Potok*

SERAO, MATILDE (1856–1927), ITL
Addio Amore!, 1896, Novel
  Addio Amore 1916 d: Alberto Carlo Lolli. lps: Mary Bayma-Riva, Ubaldo Maria Del Colle, Eduardo d'Accursio. 1615m ITL. prod/rel: Floreal
  Addio, Amore! 1944 d: Gianni Franciolini. lps: Jacqueline Laurent, Clara Calamai, Roldano Lupi. 88M ITL. prod/rel: Fauno Film, Lux Film

Castigo, 1893, Novel
  Addio, Amore! 1944 d: Gianni Franciolini. lps: Jacqueline Laurent, Clara Calamai, Roldano Lupi. 88M ITL. prod/rel: Fauno Film, Lux Film
  Castigo 1917 d: Ubaldo Maria Del Colle. lps: Mary Bayma-Riva, Goffredo d'Andrea, Dillo Lombardi. 1774m ITL. prod/rel: Floreal Film

La Mano Tagliata, Novel
  Mano Tagliata, La 1919 d: Alberto Degli Abbati. lps: Mary Bayma-Riva, Eduardo d'Accursio, Enrico Scatizzi. 1577m ITL. prod/rel: Floreal Film

O Giovannino O la Morte!, 1912, Novel
  O Giovannino O. la Morte! 1914 d: Gino Rossetti. lps: Franz Sala, Pina Cicogna, Signora Braccony. 1100m ITL. prod/rel: Musical Film
  Via Delle Cinque Lune 1942 d: Luigi Chiarini. lps: Luisella Beghi, Andrea Checchi, Olga Solbelli. 80M ITL. prod/rel: Centro Sperimentale Di Cinematografica, E.N.I.C.

Tentativo Di Romanzo Cinematografico
  Mia Vita Per la Tua!, La 1914 d: Emilio Ghione. lps: Maria Carmi, Tullio Carminati, Emilio Ghione. ITL. prod/rel: Monopol

SERDAC, ALAIN
La Femme du Bout du Monde, Novel
  Femme du Bout du Monde, La 1937 d: Jean Epstein. lps: Charles Vanel, Jean-Pierre Aumont, Germaine Rouer. 87M FRN. prod/rel: F.R.D.

SERLING, ROBERT J.
The President's Plane Is Missing, Novel
  President's Plane Is Missing, The 1971 d: Daryl Duke. lps: Buddy Ebsen, Peter Graves, Raymond Massey. TVM. 100M USA. prod/rel: ABC Circle Films

SERLING, ROD (1924–1975), USA
Patterns, 1956, Television Play
  Patterns 1956 d: Fielder Cook. lps: Van Heflin, Everett Sloane, Ed Begley. 83M USA. *Patterns of Power* (UKN) prod/rel: United Artists, Jed Harris

The Rack, Television Play
  Rack, The 1956 d: Arnold Laven. lps: Paul Newman, Wendell Corey, Walter Pidgeon. 100M USA. prod/rel: MGM

Requiem for a Heavyweight, 1956, Play
  Requiem for a Heavyweight 1962 d: Ralph Nelson. lps: Anthony Quinn, Jackie Gleason, Mickey Rooney. 86M USA. *Blood Money* (UKN) prod/rel: Paman Productions

SERMET, JULIEN
Le Baiser Supreme, Novel
  Baiser Supreme, Le 1913. lps: Gabriel Signoret, Romuald Joube, Damores. 1000m FRN. prod/rel: Selecta Film

SERNER, WALTER
Die Tigerin, Novel
  Tigress, The 1992 d: Karin Howard. lps: Valentina Vargas, James Remar, Hannes Jaenicke. TVM. 90M USA/GRM. *Die Tigerin* (GRM)

SERRANO, ANTONIO
Sexo Pudor Y Lagrimas, Play
  Sexo, Pudor Y Lagrimas 1999 d: Antonio Serrano. lps: Demian Bichir, Susana Zabaleta, Monic Dionne. 107M MXC. *Shame and Tears Sex* prod/rel: Titan & Spl, IMCino

SERRANO, E.
La Bejarana, Opera
  Bejarana, La 1925 d: Eusebio F. Ardavin. lps: Celia Escudero, Jose Nieto, Maria Luz Callejo. 2508m SPN. *The Girl from Bejar* prod/rel: Producciones Ardavin (Madrid)

SERRANO, J.
La Reina Mora, Opera
  Reina Mora, La 1922 d: Jose Buchs. lps: Carmen de Cordoba, Consuelo Reyes, Jose Montenegro. 2170m SPN. *The Moorish Queen* prod/rel: Atlantida

SERRANO PONCELA, SEGUNDO
El Hombre de la Cruz Verde, 1969, Novel
  Segundo Poder, El 1976 d: Jose Maria Forque. lps: Jon Finch, Juliet Mills, Fernando Rey. 115M SPN. *The Second Power* (USA); *El Hombre de la Cruz Verde*

SERSTEVENS, A. 'T
L' Or du Cristobel, Novel
  Or du Cristobal, L' 1939 d: Jean Stelli, Jacques Becker (Uncredited). lps: Albert Prejean, Charles Vanel, Dita Parlo. 80M FRN. prod/rel: Beryl

SERVICE, ROBERT W. (1874–1958), UKN, Service, Robert William
The Law of the Yukon, 1907, Poem
  Law of the Yukon, The 1920 d: Charles Miller. lps: Edward Earle, Joseph Smiley, Nancy Deaver. 5614f USA. prod/rel: Mayflower Photoplay Corp.©, Realart Pictures Corp.

My Madonna, 1907, Poem
  My Madonna 1915 d: Alice Blache. lps: Olga Petrova, Guy Coombs, Evelyn Dumo. 5r USA. prod/rel: Popular Plays and Players, Inc., Metro Pictures Corp.©

Poisoned Paradise; a Romance of Monte Carlo, New York 1922, Novel
  Poisoned Paradise: the Forbidden Story of Monte Carlo 1924 d: Louis J. Gasnier. lps: Kenneth Harlan, Clara Bow, Barbara Tennant. 6800f USA. prod/rel: Preferred Pictures, Al Lichtman Corp.

The Roughneck, New York 1923, Novel
  Roughneck, The 1924 d: Jack Conway. lps: George O'Brien, Billie Dove, Harry T. Morey. 7619f USA. *Thorns of Passion* (UKN) prod/rel: Fox Film Corp.

The Shooting of Dan McGrew, 1907, Poem
  Shooting of Dan McGrew, The 1915 d: Herbert Blache. lps: Edmund Breese, Evelyn Brent, Kathryn Adams. 5r USA. prod/rel: Popular Play and Players, Inc., Metro Pictures Corp.©
  Shooting of Dan McGrew, The 1924 d: Clarence Badger. lps: Barbara La Marr, Lew Cody, Mae Busch. 6318f USA. prod/rel: S-L Productions, Metro Pictures
  Shooting of Dan McGrew, The 1966 d: Ed Graham. ANM. 7M USA.

Song of the Wage Slave, 1907, Poem
  Song of the Wage Slave, The 1915 d: Herbert Blache. lps: Edmund Breese, Helen Martin, J. Byrnes. 5r USA. prod/rel: Popular Plays and Players, Inc., Metro Pictures Corp.©

The Spell of the Yukon, 1907, Poem
  Lure of Heart's Desire, The 1916 d: Francis J. Grandon. lps: Edmund Breese, Arthur Hoops, John Mahon. 4775f USA. prod/rel: Popular Plays and Players, Inc., Metro Pictures Corp.©
  Spell of the Yukon, The 1916 d: Burton L. King. lps: Edmund Breese, Christine Mayo, William Sherwood. 5r USA. prod/rel: Popular Plays and Players, Inc.©, Metro Pictures Corp.

The Trail of '98, New York 1911, Novel
  Trail of '98, The 1928 d: Clarence Brown. lps: Dolores Del Rio, Harry Carey, Tully Marshall. 8799f USA. prod/rel: Metro-Goldwyn-Mayer Pictures

SERVIN, MICHEL
Deo Gratis, Paris 1961, Novel
  Drole de Paroissien, Un 1963 d: Jean-Pierre Mocky. lps: Bourvil, Jean Yonnel, Veronique Nordey. 82M FRN. *Thank Heaven for Small Favors* (USA); *The Funny Parishioner*; *Heaven Sent* (UKN); *Deo Gratis* prod/rel: le Film d'Art, a.T.I.L.a.

SETON, ANYA (1916–1990), UKN
Dragonwyck, 1944, Novel
  Dragonwyck 1946 d: Joseph L. Mankiewicz. lps: Gene Tierney, Walter Huston, Vincent Price. 103M USA. prod/rel: 20th Century-Fox

Foxfire, 1950, Novel
  Foxfire 1955 d: Joseph Pevney. lps: Jane Russell, Jeff Chandler, Dan DuryeA. 92M USA. prod/rel: Universal-International

SETON, ERNEST THOMPSON (1860–1946), USA
The Barbarian - Ingomar, Short Story
  Barbarian - Ingomar, The 1908 d: D. W. Griffith. lps: Arthur Johnson, Florence Lawrence, Charles Inslee. 1000f USA. prod/rel: Biograph Co.

The Biography of a Grizzly, New York 1903, Novel
  King of the Grizzlies 1970 d: Ron Kelly. lps: Johnny Yesno, Chris Wiggins, Hugh Webster. 93M USA/CND. prod/rel: Walt Disney Productions, Robert Lawrence Productions

SETON, GRAHAM
The "W" Plan, Novel
  "W" Plan, The 1930 d: Victor Saville. lps: Brian Aherne, Madeleine Carroll, Gordon Harker. 105M UKN. *The W Plan* prod/rel: British International Pictures, Burlington

SETOUCHI, HARUMI
Novel
  Tsuma to Onna No Aida 1976 d: Kon Ichikawa, Shiro ToyodA. lps: Akiko Nishina, Yoshiko Mita, Mayumi OzorA. 111M JPN. *Between Women and Wives* (USA); *Between Wife and Lady* (USA) prod/rel: Geiensha Production

SETTI, ATHOS
L' Agonia Di Schizzo, Play
  Lasciate Ogni Speranza 1937 d: Gennaro Righelli. lps: Antonio Gandusio, Rosina Anselmi, Maria Denis. 82M ITL. *Abandon All Hope*; *Leave All Hope* prod/rel: Juventus Film, Astoria Film
  Sogno Di Una Notte Di Mezza Sbornia 1959 d: Eduardo de Filippo. lps: Eduardo de Filippo, Pupella Maggio, Pietro de Vico. 90M ITL. prod/rel: Titanus

SEUREN, GUNTER
Das Gatter, Novel
  Schonzeit Fur Fuchse 1966 d: Peter Schamoni. lps: Helmut Fornbacher, Christian Doermer, Andrea Jonasson. 92M GRM. *Close Time for Foxes*; *Close Season for Foxes* prod/rel: Peter Schamoni, Atlas

SEVERINSEN, HANS
Besaettelse, Copenhagen 1942, Novel
  Kuu on Vaarallinen 1961 d: Toivo SarkkA. lps: Liana Kaarina, Toivo Makela, Esko Salminen. 105M FNL. *Prelude to Ecstasy* (USA) prod/rel: Suomen Filmitcollisuus

SEVIER, ROBERT
Warned Off, Novel
  Warned Off 1928 d: Walter West. lps: Tony Wylde, Chili Bouchier, Queenie Thomas. 6510f UKN. prod/rel: British & Dominions, Jmg

SEWARD, FLORENCE A.
Gold for the Caesars, Englewood Cliffs NJ 1961, Novel
  Oro Per I Cesari 1963 d: Andre de Toth, Sabatino Ciuffini. lps: Jeffrey Hunter, Mylene Demongeot, Ron Randell. 95M ITL/FRN. *Or Pour Les Cesars* (FRN); *L' Or Des Cesars* prod/rel: Adelphia Compagnia Cin.Ca (Roma), C.I.C.C. Borderie (Paris)

SEWELL, ANNA (1820–1878), UKN
Black Beauty, London 1877, Novel
  Black Beauty 1921 d: David Smith. lps: Jean Paige, James Morrison, George Webb. 7r USA. prod/rel: Vitagraph Co. of America
  Black Beauty 1933 d: Phil Rosen. lps: Esther Ralston, Alexander Kirkland, Hale Hamilton. 70M USA. prod/rel: Monogram Pictures Corp.
  Black Beauty 1946 d: Max Nosseck. lps: Mona Freeman, Charles Evans, Richard Denning. 74M USA. prod/rel: 20th Century-Fox
  Black Beauty 1971 d: James Hill. lps: Mark Lester, Walter Slezak, Peter Lee Lawrence. 106M UKN/GRM/SPN. *Belleza Negra* (SPN) prod/rel: Tigon, Chilton
  Black Beauty 1978 d: Daniel Haller. lps: Edward Albert, Eileen Brennan, Lonny Chapman. TVM. 250M USA. prod/rel: Universal TV
  Black Beauty 1994 d: Caroline Thompson. lps: Sean Bean, David Thewlis, Jim Carter. 88M UKN/USA. prod/rel: Warner Bros.
  Your Obedient Servant 1917 d: Edward H. Griffith. lps: Peggy Adams, Pat O'Malley. 5r USA.

SEXTON, LINDA GRAY
Points of Light, Novel
  Reunion 1994 d: Lee Grant. lps: Marlo Thomas, Peter Strauss, Frances Sternhagen. TVM. 120M USA. prod/rel: R.H.I. Entertainment, Hart, Thomas & Berlin Production

SEYLER, CLIFFORD
Squibs, Play
  Squibs 1935 d: Henry Edwards. lps: Betty Balfour, Gordon Harker, Stanley Holloway. 77M UKN. prod/rel: Twickenham, Gaumont-British

SEYMOUR, GERALD (1941–, UKN
Field of Blood, Novel
  Informant, The 1997 d: Jim McBride. lps: Timothy Dalton, Cary Elwes, Anthony Brophy. 105M IRL/USA. prod/rel: Showtime, Jls Prods. (Dublin)

The Glory Boys, Novel
  Glory Boys, The 1982 d: Michael Ferguson. lps: Rod Steiger, Joanna Lumley, Alfred Burke. TVM. 180M USA/UKN. *Operation Terrorist* prod/rel: Ytv, Alan Landsburg Prods.

Harry's Game, 1975, Novel
  Belfast Assassin 1982 d: Lawrence Gordon Clark. lps: Ray Lonnen, Derek Thompson, Benjamin Whitrow. TVM. 156M UKN. *Harry's Game: the Movie; Harry's Game* prod/rel: Ytv

Red Fox, Novel
  Red Fox 1991 d: Ian Toynton. lps: John Hurt, Brian Cox, Jane Birkin. TVM. 180M UKN. prod/rel: Turning Point, Celtic Films

SEYMOUR, HENRY
Infernal Idol, Novel
  Craze 1973 d: Freddie Francis. lps: Jack Palance, Diana Dors, Julie Ege. 96M UKN. *The Infernal Idol* prod/rel: Emi, Harbour

SFORIM, MENDELE MOICHER
Fishke Der Krumer, Short Story
  Klatsche, Die 1939 d: Edgar G. Ulmer. lps: Isidore Cashier, Helen Beverly, David Opatoshu. 110M USA. *The Light Ahead; Di Klyatshe; Fishka Der Krimmer* prod/rel: Cinema Repetory, Carmel Productions

Di Klyatsche, Short Story
  Klatsche, Die 1939 d: Edgar G. Ulmer. lps: Isidore Cashier, Helen Beverly, David Opatoshu. 110M USA. *The Light Ahead; Di Klyatshe; Fishka Der Krimmer* prod/rel: Cinema Repetory, Carmel Productions

Di Takse, Short Story
  Klatsche, Die 1939 d: Edgar G. Ulmer. lps: Isidore Cashier, Helen Beverly, David Opatoshu. 110M USA. *The Light Ahead; Di Klyatshe; Fishka Der Krimmer* prod/rel: Cinema Repetory, Carmel Productions

SGORBANI, MASSIMO
Naja, Play
  Naja 1998 d: Angelo Longoni. lps: Enrico Lo Verso, Stefano Accorsi, Francesco Siciliano. 100M ITL. *The Draft* prod/rel: Cecchi Gor Tiger Cin.Ca

SHADBOLT, MAURICE (1932–, NZL
Among the Cinders, Novel
  Among the Cinders 1983 d: Rolf Hadrich. lps: Paul O'Shea, Derek Hardwick, Yvonne Lawley. 105M NZL. prod/rel: New World

SHAFFER, ANTHONY (1926–, UKN
Sleuth, 1971, Play
  Sleuth 1972 d: Joseph L. Mankiewicz. lps: Laurence Olivier, Michael Caine. 138M UKN/USA. prod/rel: Twentieth Century-Fox, Palomar

SHAFFER, PETER (1926–, UKN, Shaffer, Peter Levin
Amadeus, 1980, Play
  Amadeus 1984 d: Milos Forman. lps: F. Murray Abraham, Tom Hulce, Elizabeth Berridge. 158M USA. prod/rel: Orion, Saul Zaentz Company

Equus, 1973, Play
  Equus 1977 d: Sidney Lumet. lps: Richard Burton, Peter Firth, Colin Blakely. 138M UKN/USA. prod/rel: United Artists, Winkast

Five Finger Exercise, London 1958, Play
  Five Finger Exercise 1962 d: Daniel Mann. lps: Rosalind Russell, Jack Hawkins, Maximilian Schell. 108M USA. prod/rel: Sonnis Corporation, Columbia

The Private Ear, London 1962, Play
  Pad (and How to Use It), The 1966 d: Brian G. Hutton. lps: Brian Bedford, Julie Sommars, James Farentino. 86M USA. prod/rel: Ross Hunter Productions, Universal Pictures

The Public Eye, 1962, Play
  Public Eye, The 1972 d: Carol Reed. lps: Mia Farrow, Topol, Michael Jayston. 95M USA/UKN. *Follow Me* (UKN) prod/rel: Universal, Hal B. Wallis

The Royal Hunt of the Sun, London 1964, Play
  Royal Hunt of the Sun, The 1969 d: Irving Lerner. lps: Robert Shaw, Christopher Plummer, Nigel Davenport. 121M UKN/USA. prod/rel: Royal Films, Benmar Productions

SHAFTEL, JOSEF (1919–1996), USA
Story
  Biggest Bundle of Them All, The 1967 d: Ken Annakin. lps: Vittorio de Sica, Raquel Welch, Robert Wagner. 110M USA. prod/rel: Metro-Goldwyn-Mayer, Inc.

SHAGAN, STEVE
The Formula, Novel
  Formula, The 1980 d: John G. Avildsen. lps: George C. Scott, Marlon Brando, Marthe Keller. 117M USA. prod/rel: MGM

SHAIRP, MORDAUNT
The Crime at Blossoms, Play
  Crime at Blossoms, The 1933 d: MacLean Rogers. lps: Hugh Wakefield, Joyce Bland, Eileen Munro. 77M UKN. prod/rel: British and Dominions, Paramount

  Dark Secret 1949 d: MacLean Rogers. lps: Dinah Sheridan, Emrys Jones, Irene Handl. 85M UKN. prod/rel: Nettlefold, Butcher's Film Service

SHAIWAL
Kaabutra, Story
  Damul 1984 d: Prakash JhA. lps: Manohar Singh, Annu Kapoor, Sreela Majumdar. 141M IND. *Bonded Labour; Bonded Until Death* prod/rel: Prakash Jha Prod.

SHAKESPEARE, WILLIAM (1564–1616), UKN
Play
  Falstaff the Tavern Knight 1923 d: Edwin Greenwood. lps: Roy Byford, Margaret Yarde, Jack Denton. 2493f UKN. prod/rel: British & Colonial, Walturdaw

Antony and Cleopatra, c1607, Play
  Antony and Cleopatra 1908 d: Charles Kent. lps: Paul Panzer, Maurice Costello, Florence Lawrence. 995f USA. prod/rel: Vitagraph Co. of America

  Antony and Cleopatra 1973 d: Charlton Heston. lps: Charlton Heston, Hildegard Neil, Eric Porter. 170M UKN/SPN/SWT. *Marco Antonio Y Cleopatra* (SPN) prod/rel: Todd-Ao 35 Transac, Izaro

  Antony and Cleopatra 1974 d: John Scoffield, Trevor Nunn. lps: Richard Johnson, Janet Suzman, Corin Redgrave. MTV. 100M UKN. prod/rel: Atv

  Antony and Cleopatra 1981 d: Jonathan Miller. lps: Colin Blakely, Jane Lapotaire, John Paul. MTV. 172M UKN.

  Cleopatra 1912 d: Charles L. Gaskill. lps: Helen Gardner, Robert Gaillord, Harley Knoles. 6r USA. *Helen Gardner in Cleopatra* prod/rel: Helen Gardner Picture Players, United States Film Co.

  Cleopatra 1917 d: J. Gordon Edwards. lps: Theda Bara, Fritz Leiber, Thurston Hall. 11r USA. prod/rel: Fox Film Corp., Fox Standard Picture

As You Like It, c1600, Play
  As You Like It 1908 d: Kenean Buel. 915f USA. prod/rel: Kalem

  As You Like It 1912 d: J. Stuart Blackton, James Young. lps: Rose Coghlan, Rosemary Theby, Rose Tapley. 3000f USA. prod/rel: Vitagraph Co. of America

  As You Like It 1936 d: Paul Czinner. lps: Elisabeth Bergner, Laurence Olivier, Sophie Stewart. 96M UKN. prod/rel: Inter-Allied, 20th Century-Fox

  As You Like It 1978 d: Basil Coleman. lps: Helen Mirren, Brian Stirner, Richard Pasco. MTV. 152M UKN.

  As You Like It 1992 d: Christine Edzard. lps: Cyril Cusack, James Fox, Don Henderson. 117M UKN. prod/rel: Squirrel Films, Sands Films

  Love in a Wood 1915 d: Maurice Elvey. lps: Elisabeth Risdon, Gerald Ames, Vera Cunningham. 4189f UKN. prod/rel: London, Diploma

The Comedy of Errors, c1594, Play
  Boys from Syracuse, The 1940 d: A. Edward Sutherland. lps: Allan Jones, Martha Raye, Joe Penner. 73M USA. prod/rel: Mayfair Productions, Inc.

  Comedy of Errors, The 1984 d: James Cellan Jones. lps: Judi Dench, Francesca Annis, Michael Williams. 130M UKN.

Coriolanus, c1608, Play
  Coriolano, Eroe Senza Patria 1965 d: Giorgio Ferroni. lps: Gordon Scott, Alberto Lupo, Lilla Brignone. 97M ITL/FRN. *La Terreur Des Gladiateurs* (FRN); *Thunder of Battle; Coriolanus 'Hero Without a Country* prod/rel: Explorer Film '58, Dorica Film (Roma)

Cymbeline, c1610, Play
  Cymbeline 1913 d: Theodore Marston. lps: Florence Labadie, James Cruze, William Garwood. 2r USA. prod/rel: Thanhouser

Hamlet, c1601, Play
  Amleto 1908 d: Mario Caserini. lps: Fernanda Negri-Pouget. 260m ITL. *Hamlet* (USA) prod/rel: Cines

  Amleto 1908 d: Luca Comerio. 257m ITL. prod/rel: L. Comerio E C.

  Amleto 1917 d: Eleuterio Rodolfi. lps: Ruggero Ruggeri, Helena Makowska, Armand Pouget. 2270m ITL. prod/rel: Rodolfi Film

  Gamlet 1964 d: Grigori Kozintsev. lps: Innokenti Smoktunovsky, Anastasia Virtinskaya, Mikhail Nazvanov. 150M USS. *Hamlet; Hamile* prod/rel: Lenfilm

  Hamlet 1910 d: August Blom. lps: Alwin Neuss, Emilie Sannom, Aage Hertel. 972f DNM. prod/rel: Nordfilm

  Hamlet 1912 d: Charles Raymond. lps: Charles Raymond, Dorothy Foster, Constance Backner. 1525f UKN. prod/rel: Barker

  Hamlet 1913 d: Hay Plumb. lps: Johnston Forbes-Robertson, Gertrude Elliot, Walter Ringham. 5800f UKN. prod/rel: Hepworth, Gaumont

  Hamlet 1914. lps: Eric Williams. UKN. prod/rel: Eric Williams Speaking Pictures

  Hamlet 1920 d: Svend Gade, Heinz Schall. lps: Asta Nielsen, Lilly Jacobsson, Eduard von Winterstein. 2367m GRM. prod/rel: Artfilm

  Hamlet 1948 d: Laurence Olivier. lps: Laurence Olivier, Eileen Herlie, Basil Sydney. 155M UKN. prod/rel: General Film Distributors, Two Cities

  Hamlet 1960 d: Franz Peter Wirth. lps: Maximilian Schell, Hans Caninenberg, Wanda RothA. MTV. 130M GRM. prod/rel: Bavaria Atelier

  Hamlet 1964 d: Bill Colleran, John Gielgud. lps: Richard Burton, Hume Cronyn, Alfred Drake. 186M USA. prod/rel: Electronovision Productions, American Broadcasting

  Hamlet 1969 d: Tony Richardson. lps: Nicol Williamson, Judy Parfitt, Anthony Hopkins. 117M UKN. prod/rel: Woodfall Films, Filmways Ltd.

  Hamlet 1970 d: Peter Wood. lps: Richard Chamberlain, Ciaran Madden, Margaret Leighton. MTV. 100M USA/UKN.

  Hamlet 1971 d: Rene Bonniere. lps: Rick McKenna, Linda Certain, Dan Hennessey. 168M CND.; *The Tragicall Hiftorie of Hamlet Prince of Denmark* prod/rel: Crawley Films Ltd.

  Hamlet 1976 d: Celestino Coronado. 67M UKN.

  Hamlet 1989 d: Pierre Cavassilas. lps: Gerard Desarthe, Nada Stancar, Wladimir Yordanoff. TVM. 270M FRN.

  Hamlet 1990 d: Franco Zeffirelli. lps: Mel Gibson, Glenn Close, Alan Bates. 135M UKN/USA. prod/rel: Carolco

  Hamlet 1996 d: Kenneth Branagh. lps: Kenneth Branagh, Julie Christie, Billy Crystal. 242M UKN/USA. prod/rel: Castle Rock Entertainment, Columbia Pictures

  Hamlet at Elsinore 1964 d: Philip Saville. lps: Christopher Plummer, Robert Shaw, Alec Clunes. 180M UKN/DNM. prod/rel: BBC

  Hamlet Liikemaalimassa 1987 d: Aki Kaurismaki. lps: Pirkka-Pekka Petelius, Esko Salminen, Kati Outinen. 86M FNL. *Hamlet Goes Business; Hamlet Goes to Business* prod/rel: Electric, Villealfa Productions

  Hamlet, Prince of Denmark 1979 d: Rodney Bennett. lps: Derek Jacobi, Claire Bloom, Patrick Stewart. MTV. 217M UKN. *Hamlet*

  Heranca, A 1970 d: Ozualdo Candeias. 87M BRZ. *The Inheritance*

  Ithele Na Yini Vasilias 1967 d: Angelos Theodoropoulos. lps: Angelos Theodoropoulos, Anna Iasonidou, Lykourgos Kallergis. 90M GRC. *He Wanted to Be King*

  Ophelia 1961 d: Claude Chabrol. lps: Andre Jocelyn, Claude Cerval, Alida Valli. 105M FRN/ITL. prod/rel: Boreal Films

  Quella Sporca Storia Del West 1968 d: Enzo G. Castellari. lps: Andrea Giordana, Gabriella Grimaldi, Enio Girolami. 92M ITL. *That Dirty Story of the West; Johnny Hamlet* (USA); *Dirty Story of the West* prod/rel: Leone Film, Daiano Film

  Rest Ist Schweigen, Der 1959 d: Helmut Kautner. lps: Hardy Kruger, Peter Van Eyck, Ingrid Andree. 106M GRM. *The Rest Is Silence* (UKN)

Henry IV, c1597-98, Play

Campanadas a Medianoche 1966 d: Orson Welles. lps: Orson Welles, John Gielgud, Keith Baxter. 119M SPN/SWT. *Falstaff* (UKN); *Chimes at Midnight* prod/rel: International, Alpina

Enrico III 1909 d: Giovanni Pastrone?. 197m ITL. *Henry III* (UKN); *Henry the Third* (USA) prod/rel: Itala Film

Henry IV, Parts 1 & 2 1979 d: David Giles. lps: Jon Finch, Anthony Quayle, David Gwillim. MTV. 301M UKN. prod/rel: BBC

Henry V, c1598-99, Play

Campanadas a Medianoche 1966 d: Orson Welles. lps: Orson Welles, John Gielgud, Keith Baxter. 119M SPN/SWT. *Falstaff* (UKN); *Chimes at Midnight* prod/rel: International, Alpina

England's Warrior King 1915 d: Eric Williams. lps: Eric Williams. UKN. prod/rel: Eric Williams Speaking Pictures, Yorkshire Cinematograph Co.

Henry V 1945 d: Laurence Olivier. lps: Laurence Olivier, Robert Newton, Leslie Banks. 137M UKN. *King Henry V* prod/rel: Eagle-Lion, Two Cities

Henry V 1979 d: David Giles. lps: David Gwillim, Alec McCowen, Jocelyne Boisseau. MTV. 165M UKN.

Henry V 1989 d: Kenneth Branagh. lps: Kenneth Branagh, Derek Jacobi, Brian Blessed. 137M UKN. prod/rel: Curzon, Renaissance Films

Henry VIIi, 1613, Play

Cardinal Wolsey 1912 d: J. Stuart Blackton, Larry Trimble. lps: Hal Reid, Julia Swayne Gordon, Clara Kimball Young. 1000f USA. prod/rel: Vitagraph Co. of America

Henry VIIi 1911 d: Louis N. Parker. lps: Sir Herbert Beerbohm Tree, Arthur Bourchier, Violet Vanbrugh. 2000f UKN. prod/rel: Barker, Globe

Henry VIIi 1978 d: Kevin Billington. lps: Claire Bloom, John Stride, Julian Glover. MTV. 165M UKN.

Julius Caesar, c1599, Play

Bruto 1910 d: Giuseppe de Liguoro. lps: Giuseppe de Liguoro. 163m ITL. *Brutus* (UKN) prod/rel: Milano Films

Bruto 1911 d: Enrico Guazzoni. lps: Amleto Novelli. 362m ITL. *Brutus*

Brutus and Cassius 1918 d: Marshall Moore. lps: Eric Williams. SHT UKN. prod/rel: Eric Williams Speaking Pictures

Giulio Cesare 1909 d: Giovanni Pastrone?. lps: Luigi Mele. 255m ITL. *Julius Caesar* (USA); *Giulio Cesare E Bruto* prod/rel: Itala Film

Honourable Murder, An 1960 d: Godfrey Grayson. lps: Norman Wooland, Margaretta Scott, Lisa Daniely. 69M UKN. prod/rel: the Danzigers, Warner-Pathe

Julius Caesar 1908 d: William V. Ranous. lps: William Shea, Maurice Costello, Florence Lawrence. 980f USA. prod/rel: Vitagraph Co. of America

Julius Caesar 1911. lps: Frank Benson, Constance Benson, Murray Carrington. 990f UKN. prod/rel: Cooperative Cinematograph Co.

Julius Caesar 1926 d: George A. Cooper. lps: Basil Gill, Malcolm Keen. SND. SHT UKN. prod/rel: de Forest Phonofilm

Julius Caesar 1945 d: Compton Bennett. lps: Felix Aylmer, Leo Genn. 19M UKN. prod/rel: Theatrecraft, 20th Century-Fox

Julius Caesar 1950 d: David Bradley. lps: Charlton Heston, Harold Tasker, David Bradley. 96M USA. prod/rel: Brandon, Avon Prods.

Julius Caesar 1953 d: Charles Deane. lps: Young Vic Theatre Company. 13M UKN. *The World's a Stage: Julius Caesar* prod/rel: Emil Katzke, New Realm

Julius Caesar 1953 d: Joseph L. Mankiewicz. lps: Marlon Brando, James Mason, John Gielgud. 120M USA. prod/rel: MGM

Julius Caesar 1970 d: Stuart Burge. lps: Charlton Heston, Jason Robards Jr., John Gielgud. 116M UKN. prod/rel: Commonwealth United

Julius Caesar 1978 d: Herbert Wise. lps: Richard Pasco, Charles Gray, Keith Michell. TVM. 162M UKN.

King John, c1595, Play

Hubert and Arthur 1914. lps: Eric Williams. UKN. prod/rel: Eric Williams Speaking Pictures, Gaumont

King John 1899. lps: Beerbohm Tree, Julia Neilson, Lewis Walker. UKN. prod/rel: Mutoscope & Biograph

King Lear, c1605, Play

Gunsundari Katha 1949 d: K. V. Reddy. lps: Govindrajulu Subbarao, Shantakumari, K. Sivarao. 172M IND. *The Story of Gunsundari* prod/rel: Vauhini

Karol Lir 1969 d: Grigori Kozintsev. lps: Juri Jarvet, Elza Radzina, Galina Volchek. 139M USS. *King Lear*; *Koral Lir*; *Korol Lir*

King Lear 1909 d: William V. Ranous. lps: Maurice Costello, Julia Arthur, Edith Storey. 960f USA. *King Lear Shakespeare's Tragedy* prod/rel: Vitagraph Co. of America

King Lear 1916 d: Ernest C. Warde. lps: Frederick Warde, Ernest C. Warde, Ina Hammer. 5r USA. prod/rel: Thanhouser Film Corp., Pathe Exchange, Inc.

King Lear 1970 d: Peter Brook. lps: Paul Scofield, Irene Worth, Alan Webb. 136M UKN/DNM. prod/rel: Columbia, Filmways

King Lear 1982 d: Jonathan Miller. lps: Michael Hordern, Frank Middlemass, John Shrapnel. TVM. 186M UKN.

King Lear 1983 d: Michael Elliott. lps: Laurence Olivier, Colin Blakely, Anna Calder-Marshall. MTV. 180M UKN. prod/rel: Granada

King Lear 1987 d: Jean-Luc Godard. lps: Burgess Meredith, Peter Sellars, Molly Ringwald. 90M SWT/USA. prod/rel: Cannon

Ran 1985 d: Akira KurosawA. lps: Tatsuya Nakadai, Mieko Harada, Satoshi Terao. 160M JPN/FRN. prod/rel: Greenwich Film Production (Paris), Herald Ace (Tokyo)

Re Lear 1910 d: Giuseppe de Liguoro. lps: Giuseppe de Liguoro, Carlo Campogalliani, Adolfo Padovan. 200m ITL. *King Lear* (UKN)

Re Lear 1910 d: Gerolamo Lo Savio. lps: Ermete Novelli, Francesca Bertini, Giannina Chiantoni. 325m ITL. *King Lear* (UKN) prod/rel: Film d'Arte Italiana

MacBeth, c1606, Play

Joe MacBeth 1955 d: Ken Hughes. lps: Paul Douglas, Ruth Roman, Bonar Colleano. 90M UKN/USA. prod/rel: Film Locations, Columbia

Kumonosu-Jo 1957 d: Akira KurosawA. lps: Toshiro Mifune, Isuzu Yamada, Takashi ShimurA. 109M JPN. *The Castle of the Spider's Web*; *Throne of Blood* (UKN); *Cobweb Castle* prod/rel: Toho Co.

MacBeth 1908 d: J. Stuart Blackton. lps: William V. Ranous, Paul Panzer, Charles Kent. 835f USA. *MacBeth -Shakespeare's Sublime Tragedy*

MacBeth 1909 d: Mario Caserini. lps: Maria Caserini Gasparini, Ettore Pesci. 442m ITL. prod/rel: Cines

MacBeth 1909 d: Andre Calmettes. lps: Paul Mounet, Jeanne Delvair. 325m FRN. prod/rel: Film d'Art

MacBeth 1911. lps: Frank Benson, Constance Benson, Guy Rathbone. 1360f UKN. prod/rel: Cooperative Cinematograph Co.

MacBeth 1916 d: John Emerson. lps: Sir Herbert Beerbohm Tree, Constance Collier, Wilfred Lucas. 8r USA. prod/rel: Reliance Motion Picture Corp., Triangle Film Corp.

MacBeth 1916 d: Gustave Labruyere. lps: Georgette Leblanc. FRN. prod/rel: Eclair

MacBeth 1922 d: H. B. Parkinson. lps: Russell Thorndike, Sybil Thorndike. 1175f UKN. prod/rel: Master Films, British Exhibitors' Films

MacBeth 1945 d: Henry Cass. lps: Wilfred Lawson, Cathleen Nesbitt. 16M UKN. prod/rel: Theatrecraft, 20th Century-Fox

MacBeth 1946 d: David Bradley. lps: David Bradley, Jain Wilimovsky, William Bartholomay. 80M USA. prod/rel: Brandon

MacBeth 1948 d: Orson Welles. lps: Orson Welles, Jeanette Nolan, Dan O'Herlihy. 107M USA. prod/rel: Republic

MacBeth 1953 d: Charles Deane. lps: Young Vic Theatre Company. 13M UKN. *The World's a Stage: MacBeth* prod/rel: Emil Katzke, New Realm

MacBeth 1954 d: George Schaefer. lps: Maurice Evans, Judith Anderson, Staats Cotsworth. MTV. 120M USA.

MacBeth 1961 d: George Schaefer. lps: Maurice Evans, Judith Anderson, Michael Hordern. 108M UKN/USA. prod/rel: Grand Prize Films, British Lion

MacBeth 1966 d: Michael Simpson. lps: Anthony Bate, Donald Eccles, Andrew Keir. MTV. F UKN. prod/rel: BBC

MacBeth 1970 d: John Gorrie. lps: Eric Porter, Janet Suzman, John Thaw. MTV. F UKN. prod/rel: BBC

MacBeth 1971 d: Roman Polanski. lps: Jon Finch, Francesca Annis, Martin Shaw. 140M UKN. prod/rel: Playboy, Caliban

MacBeth 1978 d: Philip Casson. lps: Ian McKellen, Judi Dench. TVM. 146M UKN.

MacBeth 1983 d: Jack Gold. lps: Nicol Williamson, Jane Lapotaire, Tony Doyle. TVM. 149M UKN.

MacBeth 1987 d: Pauli Pentti. 70M FNL.

MacBeth 1988 d: Charles Warren. lps: Barbara Leigh-Hunt, Ralph Nossek, Michael Jayston. 110M UKN.

MacBeth 1997 d: Jeremy Freeston. lps: Jason Connery, Helen Baxendale, Graham McTavish. 129M UKN. prod/rel: Cromwell Productions, Lamancha Productions

Men of Respect 1991 d: William Reilly. lps: John Turturro, Katherine Borowitz, Dennis FarinA. 113M USA. prod/rel: Central City Films, Arthur Goldblatt Productions

Rideau Rouge, Le 1952 d: Andre Barsacq. lps: Michel Simon, Pierre Brasseur, Monelle Valentin. 90M FRN. *Ce Soir on Joue MacBeth*; *Les Rois d'une Nuit* prod/rel: Cinephonic, S.N.E.G.

Measure for Measure, c1604, Play

Dente Per Dente 1943 d: Marco Elter. lps: Carlo Tamberlani, Caterina Boratto, Nelly Corradi. 83M ITL. prod/rel: Atlas, Artisti Associati

Measure for Measure 1978 d: Desmond Davis. lps: Tim Pigott-Smith, Kenneth Colley, Kate Nelligan. TVM. 147M UKN.

The Merchant of Venice, c1595, Play

Marchand de Venise, Le 1952 d: Pierre Billon. lps: Michel Simon, Massimo Serato, Andree Debar. 102M FRN/ITL. *Il Mercante Di Venezia* (ITL) prod/rel: Venturini Film (Roma), Elisee Film (Paris)

Mercante Di Venezia, Il 1910 d: Gerolamo Lo Savio?. lps: Ermete Novelli, Olga Giannini Novelli, Francesca Bertini. 270m ITL. *The Merchant of Venice* (UKN) prod/rel: Film d'Arte Italiana

Merchant of Venice, The 1908 d: William V. Ranous, J. Stuart Blackton (Spv). lps: Julia Swayne Gordon, Florence Turner, Maurice Costello. 980f USA. prod/rel: Vitagraph Co. of America

Merchant of Venice, The 1912 d: Theodore Marston. lps: William Bowman, Florence Labadie, Mignon Anderson. 2r USA. prod/rel: Thanhouser

Merchant of Venice, The 1914 d: Phillips Smalley, Lois Weber. lps: Lois Weber, Phillips Smalley, Rupert Julian. 4r USA. prod/rel: Universal Film Mfg. Co.©, Gold Seal Brand

Merchant of Venice, The 1916 d: Walter West. lps: Matheson Lang, Nellie Hutin Britton, J. R. Tozer. 6000f UKN. prod/rel: Broadwest

Merchant of Venice, The 1922 d: Challis Sanderson. lps: Sybil Thorndike, Ivan Berlyn, R. McLeod. 1170f UKN. prod/rel: Master Films, British Exhibitors' Films

Merchant of Venice, The 1927 d: Widgey R. Newman. lps: Lewis Casson, Joyce Lyons, Christine Murray. SND. SHT UKN. prod/rel: de Forest Phonofilm

Shejlok 1993 d: Boris Blank. lps: K. Kvasadze, Irina Metlickaja, M. Majko. 85M RSS/USA. *Shylock*; *The Merchant of Venice* prod/rel: Mosfilm-Servis, Ameriken Enterprises

Shylock, le Marchand de Venise 1913 d: Henri Desfontaines, Louis Mercanton. lps: Harry Baur, Pepa Bonafe, Romuald Joube. 643m FRN. prod/rel: Eclipse

The Merry Wives of Windsor, c1598, Play

Lustigen Weiber, Die 1935 d: Carl Hoffmann. lps: Magda Schneider, Leo Slezak, Ida Wust. 88M GRM. *Falstaffs Abenteuer*

Lustigen Weiber von Windsor, Die 1950 d: Georg Wildhagen. lps: Paul Esser, Camilla Spire, Sonja Ziemann. 95M GDR. *The Merry Wives of Windsor* prod/rel: Defa

Lustigen Weiber von Windsor, Die 1965 d: Georg Tressler. lps: Norman Foster, Mildred Miler, Colette Boky. 97M AUS/UKN. *The Merry Wives of Windsor* prod/rel: Wien Film

Merry Wives of Windsor, The 1910 d: Frank Boggs. 1000f USA. prod/rel: Selig Polyscope Co.

Merry Wives of Windsor, The 1983 d: David Jones. lps: Richard Griffiths, Prunella Scales, Alan Bennett. MTV. 169M UKN.

A Midsummer Night's Dream, c1594, Play

Midsummer Night's Dream, A 1909 d: Charles Kent, J. Stuart Blackton (Spv). lps: Maurice Costello, Clara Kimball Young, James Young. 991f USA. prod/rel: Vitagraph Co. of America

Midsummer Night's Dream, A 1935 d: Max Reinhardt, William Dieterle. lps: James Cagney, Dick Powell, Joe E. Brown. 132M USA. prod/rel: Warner Bros. Pictures©

Midsummer Night's Dream, A 1953 d: Charles Deane. lps: Young Vic Theatre Company. 12M UKN. *The World's a Stage: a Midsummer Night's Dream* prod/rel: Emil Katzke, New Realm

Midsummer Night's Dream, A 1958 d: Rudolph Cartier. lps: Paul Rogers, Natasha Parry, John Justin. MTV. 104M UKN.

Midsummer Night's Dream, A 1964 d: Joan Kemp-Welch. lps: Jill Bennett, Maureen Beck, Benny Hill. MTV. 120M UKN. prod/rel: Rediffusion

Midsummer Night's Dream, A 1966 d: Dan Eriksen, George Balachine. lps: Suzanne Farrell, Edward Villella, Arthur Mitchell. 93M USA. prod/rel: Oberon Productions

Midsummer Night's Dream, A 1968 d: Peter Hall. lps: Derek Godfrey, Barbara Jefford, Hugh Sullivan. 124M UKN. prod/rel: Eagle, Royal Shakespeare Enterprises

Midsummer Night's Dream, A 1981 d: Elijah Moshinsky. lps: Helen Mirren, Peter McEnery, Nigel Davenport. TVM. 113M UKN.

Midsummer Night's Dream, A 1984 d: Celestino Coronado. lps: Lindsay Kemp, Manuela Vargas, Incredible Orlando. 78M SPN/UKN. *Sueno de Una Noche de Verano* (SPN) prod/rel: Mainline, Cabochon Productions (London)

Midsummer Night's Dream, A 1996 d: Adrian Noble. lps: Lindsay Duncan, Alex Jennings, Desmond Barrit. 105M UKN. prod/rel: Channel 4, Edenwood

Sen Noci Svatojanske 1959 d: Jiri TrnkA. ANM. 80M CZC. *A Midsummer Night's Dream* (UKN) prod/rel: Ceskoslovensky Film

Much Ado About Nothing, c1598, Play

Lyubovyu Za Lyubov 1983 d: Tatyana BerezantsevA. 84M USS.

Mnogo Shuma Iz Nichevo 1956 d: L. Zamkovoy. 94M USS. *Much Ado About Nothing*

Mnogo Suma Iz Nicego 1973 d: Samson Samsonov. 101M USS. *Much Ado About Nothing; Mnogo Shuma Iz Nichevo; Much Noise from Nothing*

Much Ado About Nothing 1978 d: A. J. Anton, Nick HavingA. 180M USA.

Much Ado About Nothing 1984 d: Stuart Burge. lps: Lee Montague, Cherie Lunghi, Katherine Levy. TVM. 150M UKN.

Much Ado About Nothing 1993 d: Kenneth Branagh. lps: Kenneth Branagh, Richard Briers, Michael Keaton. 111M UKN. prod/rel: Samuel Goldwyn, Renaissance

Saty Delaji Clovecka 1912 d: Max Urban, Jara Sedlacek. lps: Andula Sedlackova, Jara Sedlacek, Alois Sedlacek. CZC. *Clothes Make Man; Manners Make Man* prod/rel: Asum

Viel Larm Um Nichts 1964 d: Martin Hellberg. lps: Rolf Ludwig. 101M GDR. *Much Ado About Nothing*

Othello, c1604, Play

Catch My Soul 1974 d: Patrick McGoohan. lps: Richie Havens, Lance Le Gault, Season Hubley. 95M USA. *Santa Fe Satan* prod/rel: Metromedia

Kaliyattam 1998 d: Jayaraj. lps: Jatin Bora, Ashish Vidyarthi, Debashree Roy. 135M IND. *The Play of God* prod/rel: New Generation Cinema (Kerala)

Otello 1906 d: Mario Caserini, Gaston Velle. lps: Ubaldo Maria Del Colle, Mario Caserini. 210m ITL. *Othello* (UKN) prod/rel: Cines

Otello 1909 d: Gerolamo Lo Savio. lps: Ferruccio Garavaglia, Cesare Dondini, Alberto Nepoti. 335m ITL. *Othello* (USA) prod/rel: Film d'Arte Italiana

Otello 1914 d: Luigi Maggi. lps: Paolo Colaci, Cesira Lenard, Ubaldo Stefani. 1491m ITL. *The Moor of Venice* (USA); *Othello; Othello the Moor* (UKN) prod/rel: S.A. Ambrosio

Otello 1951 d: Orson Welles. lps: Orson Welles, Suzanne Cloutier, Michael MacLiammoir. 92M ITL/USA/FRN. *Othello* (USA) prod/rel: United Artists, Mercury (Usa)

Otello 1955 d: Sergei Yutkevich. lps: Sergei Bondarchuk, Irina Skobtseva, Andrey Popov. 108M USS. *Othello* (UKN) prod/rel: Mosfilm

Otello 1986 d: Franco Zeffirelli. lps: Placido Domingo, Katia Ricciarelli, Justino Diaz. 123M ITL/USA. *Othello* prod/rel: Cannon Productions (Roma), Rai

Othello 1946 d: David MacKane. lps: John Slater, Luanne Shaw, Sebastian Cabot. 45M UKN. prod/rel: Henry Halstead, Exclusive

Othello 1953 d: Charles Deane. lps: Young Vic Theatre Company. 13M UKN. *The World's a Stage: Othello* prod/rel: Emil Katzke, New Realm

Othello 1965 d: Stuart Burge. lps: Laurence Olivier, Maggie Smith, Joyce Redman. 166M UKN. prod/rel: B.H.E. Productions, Eagle

Othello 1981 d: Jonathan Miller. lps: Anthony Hopkins, Bob Hoskins, Penelope Wilton. MTV. 207M UKN.

Othello 1982 d: Frank Melton. lps: William Marshall, Ron Moody, Jenny Agutter. 195M USA.

Othello 1989 d: Trevor Nunn. lps: Willard White, Ian McKellen, Imogen Stubbs. 204M USA.

Othello 1990 d: Ted Lange. lps: Ted Lange, Hawthorne James, Mary Otis. 123M USA. prod/rel: Uptown

Othello 1995 d: Oliver Parker. lps: Laurence Fishburne, Irene Jacob, Kenneth Branagh. 124M UKN/USA. prod/rel: Castle Rock, Dakota

Venetsianskiy Mavr 1961 d: Vakhtang Chabukiani. lps: Vera Tsiganadze, Vakhtang Chabukiani, Zarub Kikaleishvili. 95M USS. *Ballet of Othello; Othello* (UKN) prod/rel: Gruziya-Film

Richard II, c1595, Play

Campanadas a Medianoche 1966 d: Orson Welles. lps: Orson Welles, John Gielgud, Keith Baxter. 119M SPN/SWT. *Falstaff* (UKN); *Chimes at Midnight* prod/rel: International, Alpina

Richard II 1978 d: David Giles. MTV. 150M UKN.

Richard III, c1594, Play

Life and Death of Richard III, The 1912 d: James Keane. lps: Frederick Warde, Robert Gemp, Albert Gardner. 5000f USA. *Richard III; Mr. Frederick Warde in Shakespeare's Masterpiece "the Life and Death of King Richard III* prod/rel: Richard III Film, Shakespeare Film Co.

Richard III 1908 d: William V. Ranous, J. Stuart Blackton (Spv). lps: William V. Ranous, Florence Turner, Julia Swayne Gordon. 990f USA. prod/rel: Vitagraph Co. of America

Richard III 1911 d: F. R. Benson. lps: Frank Benson, Constance Benson, Eric Maxon. 1385f UKN. prod/rel: Cooperative Cinematograph Co.

Richard III 1912 d: James Keene. lps: Frederick Warde, Mr. Gomp. 4400f USA. prod/rel: Sterling Camera and Film Co.©, State Rights

Richard III 1955 d: Laurence Olivier, Anthony Bushell. lps: Laurence Olivier, John Gielgud, Claire Bloom. 161M UKN. prod/rel: London Films, Independent Film Distributors

Richard III 1995 d: Richard Loncraine. lps: Ian McKellen, Annette Bening, Jim Broadbent. 105M USA/UKN. prod/rel: United Artists, British Screen

Romeo and Juliet, c1596, Play

Giulietta E Romeo 1908 d: Mario Caserini?. lps: Fernanda Negri-Pouget. 225m ITL. *Romeo E Giulietta; Romeo and Juliet* (USA) prod/rel: Cines

Giulietta E Romeo 1964 d: Riccardo FredA. lps: Geronimo Meynier, Rosemara Dexter, Carlos EstradA. 95M ITL/SPN. *Los Amantes de Verona* (SPN); *Romeo and Juliet* (USA); *Julieta Y Romeo* prod/rel: Imprecine (Roma), Hispamer Films (Madrid)

Romeo and Juliet 1908. lps: Godfrey Tearle, Mary Malone, Gordon Bailey. 1240f UKN. prod/rel: Gaumont

Romeo and Juliet 1908 d: J. Stuart Blackton. lps: Florence Lawrence, Paul Panzer, Harry Salter. 915f USA. *Romeo and Juliette* prod/rel: Vitagraph Co. of America

Romeo and Juliet 1911 d: Theodore Marston. lps: Irma Taylor, George Lessey, Mrs. George W. Walters. 2r USA. prod/rel: Thanhouser

Romeo and Juliet 1914 d: Travers Vale. 508f USA. prod/rel: Biograph Co.

Romeo and Juliet 1916 d: J. Gordon Edwards. lps: Theda Bara, Harry Hilliard, Glenn White. 7r USA. prod/rel: Fox Film Corp., William Fox©

Romeo and Juliet 1916 d: John W. Noble. lps: Francis X. Bushman, Beverly Bayne, John Davidson. 8r USA. prod/rel: Quality Pictures Corp., Metro Pictures Corp.©

Romeo and Juliet 1936 d: George Cukor. lps: Norma Shearer, Leslie Howard, John Barrymore. 130M USA. prod/rel: Metro-Goldwyn-Mayer Corp.©

Romeo and Juliet 1954 d: Renato Castellani. lps: Laurence Harvey, Susan Shentall, Flora Robson. 138M UKN/ITL. *Giulietta E Romeo* (ITL) prod/rel: General Film Distributors, Verona Cin.Ca

Romeo and Juliet 1966 d: Paul Czinner. lps: Margot Fonteyn, Rudolf Nureyev, David Blair. 126M UKN. prod/rel: Poetic Films, Rank Film Distributors

Romeo and Juliet 1968 d: Franco Zeffirelli. lps: Leonard Whiting, Olivia Hussey, Milo O'SheA. 152M UKN/ITL. *Romeo E Giulietta* (ITL) prod/rel: B.H.E. Productions, Verona Produzione

Romeo and Juliet 1979 d: Alvin Rakoff. lps: Patrick Ryecart, Rebecca Saire, Celia Johnson. MTV. 169M UKN.

Romeo and Juliet 1988 d: Joan Kemp-Welch. lps: Christopher Neame, Ann Hasson, Peter Jeffrey. MTV. 360M UKN.

Romeo E Giulietta 1912 d: Ugo FalenA. lps: Francesca Bertini, Gustavo Serena, Giovanni PezzingA. 725m ITL/FRN. *Romeo Et Juliette* (FRN); *Giulietta E Romeo; Romeo and Juliet* (UKN) prod/rel: Pathe Freres, Film d'Arte Italiana

Romeo Et Juliette 1912. 725m FRN. prod/rel: Pathe Freres

Romeo I Dzuletta 1955 d: Leo Arnstam, Leonid Lavrovskiy. lps: Galina Ulanova, Yuriy Zhdanov, Sergei Koren. 90M USS. *The Ballet of Romeo and Juliet; Romeo and Juliet* (UKN) prod/rel: Mosfilm

Romeo Y Julieta 1943 d: Miguel M. Delgado. lps: Cantinflas, Maria Elena Marques, Angel GarasA. 100M MXC.

Tromeo & Juliet 1996 d: Lloyd Kaufman. lps: Will Keenan, Jane Jensen, Debbie Rochon. 107M USA. prod/rel: Troma Inc.

William Shakespeare's Romeo & Juliet 1996 d: Baz Luhrmann. lps: Leonardo Dicaprio, Claire Danes, Brian Dennehy. 120M USA. *Romeo and Juliet* prod/rel: Twentieth Century Fox Film Corporation, Bazmark

The Seven Ages of Man, Poem

Seven Ages of Man, The 1914 d: Charles Vernon. lps: Bransby Williams. 1000f UKN. prod/rel: Planet Films, Hibbert

Sonnets, 1609, Verse

Moods of Love, The 1972 d: David Wickes. 21M UKN.

The Taming of the Shrew, c1593, Play

Bisbetica Domata, La 1908. ITL. prod/rel: Societa Italiana Pineschi

Bisbetica Domata, La 1913. lps: Gigetta Morano, Eleuterio Rodolfi. 910m ITL. *The Taming of the Shrew* (UKN) prod/rel: S.A. Ambrosio

Bisbetica Domata, La 1942 d: Ferdinando M. Poggioli. lps: Lilia Silvi, Amedeo Nazzari, Lauro Gazzolo. 85M ITL. prod/rel: Excelsa Film

Daring Youth 1924 d: William Beaudine. lps: Bebe Daniels, Norman Kerry, Lee Moran. 5795f USA. prod/rel: B. F. Zeidman, Principal Pictures

Fierecilla Domada, La 1955 d: Antonio Roman. lps: Carmen Sevilla, Alberto Closas, Claudine Dupuis. 96M SPN/FRN. *La Megere Apprivoisee* (FRN); *The Taming of the Shrew* prod/rel: Perojo, Buhigas

Kiss Me Kate 1953 d: George Sidney. lps: Howard Keel, Kathryn Grayson, Ann Miller. 109M USA. prod/rel: MGM

Taming of the Shrew 1908 d: D. W. Griffith. lps: Florence Lawrence, Arthur Johnson, Wilfred Lucas. 1048f USA. prod/rel: Biograph Co.

Taming of the Shrew, The 1911. lps: Frank Benson, Constance Benson. 1120f UKN. prod/rel: Cooperative Cinematograph Co.

Taming of the Shrew, The 1915 d: Arthur Backner. lps: Arthur Backner, Constance Backner. 2000f UKN. prod/rel: British and Colonial, Voxograph

Taming of the Shrew, The 1923 d: Edwin J. Collins. lps: Dacia Deane, Lauderdale Maitland, Cynthia Murtagh. 2016f UKN. prod/rel: British & Colonial, Walturdaw

Taming of the Shrew, The 1929 d: Sam Taylor. lps: Mary Pickford, Douglas Fairbanks, Edwin Maxwell. 68M USA. prod/rel: Pickford Corp., Elton Corp.

Taming of the Shrew, The 1967 d: Franco Zeffirelli. lps: Richard Burton, Elizabeth Taylor, Alfred Lynch. 126M USA/ITL. *La Bisbetica Domata* (ITL) prod/rel: Films Artistici Internazionali, Royal Film

Taming of the Shrew, The 1976 d: William Ball, Kirk Browning. 120M USA.

Taming of the Shrew, The 1980 d: Jonathan Miller. lps: John Cleese, Sarah Badel, Susan Penhaligon. TVM. 135M UKN. prod/rel: BBC

Taming of the Shrew, The 1981 d: Peter Dews. 163M USA.

Ukroshchenie Stroptivoy 1961 d: Sergei Kolosov. 92M USS.

The Tempest, c1611, Play

Prospero's Books 1990 d: Peter Greenaway. lps: John Gielgud, Michael Clark, Michel Blanc. 120M NTH/FRN/ITL. prod/rel: Allarts (Amsterdam), Cinea/Camera One (Paris)

Tempest 1983 d: Paul Mazursky. lps: John Cassavetes, Gena Rowlands, Susan Sarandon. 141M USA. prod/rel: Columbia

Tempest, The 1905 d: Charles Urban. lps: Viola Tree, J. Fisher White, S. A. Cookson. 150f UKN. prod/rel: Urban Trading Co.

Tempest, The 1911. SHT USA. prod/rel: Thanhouser

Tempest, The 1960 d: George Schaefer. lps: Richard Burton, Lee Remick, Roddy McDowall. MTV. 80M USA. prod/rel: Hallmark Hall of Fame Prods.

Tempest, The 1969 d: Nicholas Young, David Snasdell. lps: Christopher Scoular, Michael Menaugh, Vanessa Blackmore. 85M UKN. prod/rel: Roger Sherman (P)

Tempest, The 1972 d: Mats Lonnerblad. 80M SWD.

Tempest, The 1979 d: John Gorrie. lps: Michael Hordern, Derek Godfrey, David Waller. TVM. 126M UKN.

Tempest, The 1979 d: Derek Jarman. lps: Heathcote Williams, Elisabeth Welch, Toyah Wilcox. 90M UKN. prod/rel: Boyd's Company

Titus Andronicus, c1590, Play

Titus Andronicus 1985 d: Jane Howell. lps: Edward Hardwicke, Walter Brown, Brian Protheroe. MTV. 170M UKN.

Twelfth Night, c1600, Play

Dvenadtsataya Noch 1955 d: Jan Frid. lps: Klara Luchko, M. Yanshin, A. LarianovA. 87M USS. *Twelfth Night* (UKN)

Nichts Als Sunde 1965 d: Hanus Burger. 105M GDR.

Twelfth Night 1910 d: Charles Kent. lps: Julia Swayne Gordon, Charles Kent, Florence Turner. 970f USA. prod/rel: Vitagraph Co. of America

Twelfth Night 1953 d: Charles Deane. lps: Young Vic Theatre Company. 12M UKN. *The World's a Stage: Twelfth Night* prod/rel: Emil Katzke, New Realm

Twelfth Night 1979 d: John Gorrie. lps: Alec McCowen, Felicity Kendal, Sinead Cusack. MTV. 130M UKN.

Twelfth Night 1986 d: Neil Armfield. lps: Gillian Jones, Ivar Kants, Jacqy Phillips. 117M ASL. prod/rel: Twelfth Night Pty Ltd.©, Greater Union

Twelfth Night 1996 d: Trevor Nunn. lps: Helena Bonham-Carter, Richard E. Grant, Nigel Hawthorne. 134M UKN/USA. prod/rel: Renaissance Films

Viola Und Sebastian 1971 d: Ottokar Runze. lps: Karin Hubner, Frank Glaubrecht, Inken Sommer. 93M GRM. *Viola and Sebastian* prod/rel: Guertler & Runze

The Two Gentlemen of Verona, c1592, Play

Yijian Mei 1931 d: Bu Wancang. lps: Ruan Lingyu, Jin Yan, Gao Zhanfei. 90M CHN. *A Branch of Mei Flowers; A Spray of Plum Blossoms* prod/rel: Lianhua Film Company

The Winter's Tale, c1611, Play

Racconti d'Inverno 1910. 289m ITL. *Racconto d'Inverno; A Winter's Tale* (UKN) prod/rel: Cines

Racconto d'Inverno 1913. lps: Pina Fabbri. 1024m ITL. *Delitto Di un Re; Novella d'Inverno; Una Novella Di Shakespeare; The Winter's Tale* (UKN) prod/rel: Milano Films

Winter's Tale, The 1910 d: Theodore Marston. lps: Miss Rosamonde, Martin Faust, Frank Crane. 1000f USA. prod/rel: Thanhouser

Winter's Tale, The 1953 d: Charles Deane. lps: Young Vic Theatre Company. 13M UKN. *The World's a Stage: the Winter's Tale* prod/rel: Emil Katzke, New Realm

Winter's Tale, The 1968 d: Frank Dunlop. lps: Laurence Harvey, Jane Asher, Diana Churchill. 151M UKN. prod/rel: Cressida, Hurst Park

Winter's Tale, The 1981 d: Jane Howell. lps: Jeremy Kemp, Anna Calder-Marshall, John Welsh. MTV. 117M UKN.

SHAMIR, MOSHE
Play

Hou Halach Basadot 1967 d: Yoseph Millo. lps: Assaf Dayan, Iris Yotvat, Yoseph Millo. 96M ISR. *He Walks Through the Fields; He Walked Through the Fields*

SHAMOSH, AMNON
Novel

Michel Ezra Safra Ve'banav 1983 d: Nissim Dayan. lps: Makram Khoury, Lilith Nagar, David Menachem. F ISR. *Michel Ezra Safra and Sons*

SHANGHAI JOINT STAGE
Hong Yang Haoxia Zhuan, Opera

Hong Yang Haoxia Zhuan 1935 d: Yang XIaozhong. lps: Wang Huchen, Xu Qinfang, Tong Yuejuan. CHN. *The Tale of the Gallant Hong Yang; Story of the Red Sheep Hero* prod/rel: XInhua Film Company

SHANGHAI PUBLIC COMEDY TROUPE
Qi Shi Er Jia Fang Ke, Play

Qi Shi Er Jia Fang Ke 1963 d: Wang Weiyi. lps: XIe Guobi, Shu Yi, Pan Qian. 9r CHN. *Seventy-Two Tenants* prod/rel: Pearl River Film Studio, Hongtu Film Studio

SHANKAR
Jana Aranya, Novel

Jana Aranya 1975 d: Satyajit Ray. lps: Pradip Mukherjee, Satya Bannerjee, Dipankar Dey. 131M IND. *The Masses' Music* (USA); *The Middleman* (UKN); *Dahana-Aranja; The Middle Man* prod/rel: Indus Films

Seemabaddha, Novel

Seemabadha 1971 d: Satyajit Ray. lps: Barun Chanda, Parmita Choudhury, Sharmila Tagore. 112M IND. *Company Limited* (UKN); *The Salesman; Seemabaddha* prod/rel: Chitranjali

SHANNON, ELAINE
Book

Drug Wars: the Kiki Camarena Story, The 1989 d: Brian Gibson. lps: Steven Bauer, Craig T. Nelson, Elizabeth PenA. 134M USA. *The Drugs Wars: Camerena; The Camerena Story* prod/rel: Michael Mann Prods.

SHANNON, ROBERT
Fabulous Ann Medlock, Novel

Adventures of Captain Fabian 1951 d: William Marshall. lps: Errol Flynn, Micheline Presle, Vincent Price. 100M USA/FRN. *La Taverne de Nouvelle-Orleans* (FRN) prod/rel: Republic Pictures Corp., Silver

SHANNON, ROBERT TERRY
The Girl With the Jazz Heart, 1920, Short Story

Girl With the Jazz Heart, The 1920 d: Lawrence C. Windom. lps: Madge Kennedy, Joe King, Pierre Gendron. 5r USA. *The Girl With a Jazz Heart* prod/rel: Goldwyn Pictures Corp.©, Goldwyn Distributing Corp.

The Taxi Dancer, Novel

Taxi Dancer, The 1926 d: Harry Millarde. lps: Joan Crawford, Owen Moore, Marc MacDermott. 6289f USA. prod/rel: Metro-Goldwyn-Mayer Pictures

SHAO HUA
Lang Tao Gun Gun, Novel

Lang Tao Gun Gun 1965 d: Cheng Yin. lps: Qin Yi, Chin Ge, Peng Qiyu. 12r CHN. *Rolling Waves* prod/rel: Beijing Film Studio

SHAPIRO, LIONEL
Sealed Verdict, Novel

Sealed Verdict 1948 d: Lewis Allen. lps: Ray Milland, Florence Marly, Broderick Crawford. 83M USA. prod/rel: Paramount

The Sixth of June, 1955, Novel

D-Day the Sixth of June 1956 d: Henry Koster. lps: Robert Taylor, Dana Wynter, Richard Todd. 106M USA. prod/rel: 20th Century-Fox

SHAPIRO, MEL
The Lay of the Land, Play

Lay of the Land, The 1997 d: Larry Arrick. lps: Sally Kellerman, Ed Begley Jr., Sandra Taylor. 94M USA. prod/rel: Jkg Production, Jonathan D. Krane

SHAPIRO, STANLEY
Me, Natalie, Novel

Me, Natalie 1969 d: Fred Coe. lps: Patty Duke, Salome Jens, Nancy Marchand. 111M USA. prod/rel: Cinema Center

Time to Remember

Running Against Time 1990 d: Bruce Seth Green. lps: Robert Hays, Catherine Hicks, Sam Wanamaker. TVM. 100M USA.

SHAPLEY, HARLOW
Of Stars and Men, Boston 1958, Book

Of Stars and Men 1964 d: John Hubley. ANM. 63M USA. prod/rel: Storyboard Productions

SHARMAN, MAISIE
Death Goes to School, Novel

Death Goes to School 1953 d: Stephen Clarkson. lps: Barbara Murray, Gordon Jackson, Pamela Allan. 65M UKN. prod/rel: Independent Artists, Eros

SHARP, DON
Conflict of Wings, Novel

Conflict of Wings 1954 d: John Eldridge. lps: John Gregson, Muriel Pavlow, Kieron Moore. 84M UKN. *Fuss Over Feathers* (USA) prod/rel: Group Three, British Lion

SHARP, HILDA MARY
The Stars in Their Courses, New York 1917, Novel

Mother's Sin, A 1918 d: Thomas R. Mills. lps: Earle Williams, Miriam Miles, Denton Vane. 5r USA. prod/rel: Vitagraph Co. of America©, Blue Ribbon Feature

SHARP, MARGERY
Britannia Mews, Novel

Britannia Mews 1948 d: Jean Negulesco. lps: Dana Andrews, Maureen O'Hara, Sybil Thorndike. 91M UKN. *Forbidden Street* (USA); *The Affairs of Adelaide* prod/rel: 20th Century Productions, 20th Century-Fox

Cluny Brown, Novel

Cluny Brown 1946 d: Ernst Lubitsch. lps: Charles Boyer, Jennifer Jones, Peter Lawford. 100M USA. prod/rel: 20th Century-Fox

The Notorious Tenant, 1956, Short Story

Notorious Landlady, The 1962 d: Richard Quine. lps: Jack Lemmon, Kim Novak, Fred Astaire. 123M USA. prod/rel: Kohlmar-Quine Production Co.

The Nutmeg Tree, Novel

Julia Misbehaves 1948 d: Jack Conway. lps: Greer Garson, Walter Pidgeon, Elizabeth Taylor. 99M USA. prod/rel: MGM

SHARPE, TOM (1928–, UKN
Blott on the Landscape, Novel

Blott on the Landscape 1989 d: Roger Bamford. lps: George Cole, Geraldine James, David Suchet. MTV. 313M UKN. prod/rel: BBC

Porterhouse Blue, Novel

Porterhouse Blue 1987 d: Robert Knights. lps: David Jason, Ian Richardson, Charles Gray. TVM. 220M UKN.

Wilt, Novel

Wilt 1989 d: Michael Tuchner. lps: Griff Rhys Jones, Mel Smith, Alison Steadman. 92M UKN. *The Misadventures of Mr. Wilt* (USA) prod/rel: Rank, Lwt

SHARROW, ROBERT
Touch It Light, London 1958, Novel

Light Up the Sky 1960 d: Lewis Gilbert. lps: Ian Carmichael, Tommy Steele, Benny Hill. 90M UKN. *Skywatch* (USA) prod/rel: Bryanston, Criterion

SHATTUCK, RICHARD
The Wedding Guest Sat on a Stone, Story

Ghost That Walks Alone, The 1944 d: Lew Landers. lps: Arthur Lake, Lynne Roberts, Janis Carter. 63M USA. prod/rel: Columbia

SHAW, CHARLES
Heaven Knows Mr. Allison, 1952, Novel

Heaven Knows, Mr. Allison 1957 d: John Huston. lps: Deborah Kerr, Robert Mitchum. 106M UKN/USA. prod/rel: 20th Century-Fox

SHAW, DAVID
Night Call, Novel

Take One False Step 1949 d: Chester Erskine. lps: William Powell, Shelley Winters, Marsha Hunt. 94M USA. prod/rel: Universal-International

SHAW, GEORGE BERNARD (1856–1950), IRL
Androcles and the Lion, London 1913, Play

Androcles and the Lion 1952 d: Chester Erskine, Nicholas Ray (Uncredited). lps: Jean Simmons, Alan Young, Victor Mature. 98M USA. prod/rel: RKO Radio

Arms and the Man, 1894, Play

Arms and the Man 1932 d: Cecil Lewis. lps: Barry Jones, Anne Grey, Maurice Colbourne. 85M UKN. prod/rel: British International Pictures, Wardour

Chocolate Soldier, The 1915 d: Walter Morton, Stanislaus Stange. lps: Alice Yorke, Tom Richards, Lucille Saunders. 5r USA. prod/rel: Daisy Feature Film Co., Alliance Films Corp.

Helden 1958 d: Franz Peter Wirth. lps: O. W. Fischer, Liselotte Pulver, Ellen Schwiers. 100M GRM. *Arms and the Man* (USA); *Heroes* prod/rel: Bavaria Filmkunst, H.R. Sokal

Caesar and Cleopatra, 1901, Play

Caesar and Cleopatra 1946 d: Gabriel Pascal, Brian Desmond Hurst. lps: Vivien Leigh, Claude Rains, Stewart Granger. 138M UKN. prod/rel: Eagle-Lion, Gabriel Pascal

Cashel Byron's Profession, Novel

Roman Boxera 1921 d: Vaclav Binovec. lps: Frank Rose-Ruzicka, Suzanne Marwille, V. Ch. Vladimirov. CZC. *Cashel Byron's Profession; The Romance of a Boxer* prod/rel: Weteb, Iris-Film

The Devil's Disciple, London 1899, Play

Devil's Disciple, The 1959 d: Guy Hamilton. lps: Burt Lancaster, Kirk Douglas, Laurence Olivier. 83M UKN/USA. prod/rel: United Artists, Hecht-Hill-Lancaster

The Doctor's Dilemma, London 1906, Play

Doctor's Dilemma, The 1959 d: Anthony Asquith. lps: Leslie Caron, Dirk Bogarde, Alastair Sim. 99M UKN. prod/rel: MGM, Comet

Great Catherine, London 1913, Play

Great Catherine 1967 d: Gordon Flemyng. lps: Peter O'Toole, Jeanne Moreau, Zero Mostel. 98M UKN. prod/rel: Keep Films, Warner-Pathe

Heartbreak House, 1919, Play

Skorbnoe Bescuvstvie 1986 d: Alexander Sokurov. 97M USS. *Heartless Grief; Mournful Unconcern; Scorbnoye Beschuvstvie*

How He Lied to Her Husband, London 1905, Play

How He Lied to Her Husband 1931 d: Cecil Lewis. lps: Edmund Gwenn, Vera Lennox, Robert Harris. 33M UKN. prod/rel: British International Pictures, Wardour

Kak on Lgal Eio Muzhu 1957 d: Tatyana BerezantsevA. 29M USS. *How He Lied to Her Husband*

Love Among the Artists, Novel
Love Among the Artists 1979 d: Howard Baker, Marc Miller. lps: John Stride, Geraldine James, Judy Campbell. MTV. 250M UKN. prod/rel: Granada

Major Barbara, London 1905, Play
Major Barbara 1941 d: Gabriel Pascal, Harold French. lps: Wendy Hiller, Rex Harrison, Robert Morley. 121M UKN. prod/rel: Gabriel Pascal, General Film Distributors

The Millionairess, New York 1936, Play
Millionairess, The 1960 d: Anthony Asquith. lps: Sophia Loren, Peter Sellers, Alastair Sim. 90M UKN. prod/rel: Anatole De Grunwald, Ltd., 2Th Century Fox

Mrs. Warren's Profession, 1898, Play
Frau Warrens Gewerbe 1960 d: Akos von Rathony. lps: Lilli Palmer, O. E. Hasse, Johanna Matz. 102M GRM/SWT. *Mrs. Warren's Trade; Mrs. Warren's Profession* prod/rel: Real, Cinecustodia
Mrs. Warren's Profession 1991 d: Mike Newman. lps: Stephen MacDonald, Debra Gillett, Ann Mitchell. TVM. 85M UKN.

Pygmalion, London 1913, Play
My Fair Lady 1964 d: George Cukor. lps: Audrey Hepburn, Rex Harrison, Wilfrid Hyde-White. 170M USA. prod/rel: Warner Bros. Pictures, First National Pictures
Pigmalion 1957 d: Sergei Alexeyev. 95M USS.
Pygmalion 1935 d: Erich Engel. lps: Jenny Jugo, Gustaf Grundgens, Eugen Klopfer. 93M GRM.
Pygmalion 1937 d: Ludwig Berger. lps: Lily Bouwmeester, Johan de Meester, Emma Morel. 102M NTH.
Pygmalion 1938 d: Anthony Asquith, Leslie Howard. lps: Leslie Howard, Wendy Hiller, Wilfred Lawson. 96M UKN. prod/rel: Gabriel Pascal, General Film Distributors
Pygmalion 1981 d: John Glenister. lps: Twiggy, Robert Powell. MTV. 78M UKN. prod/rel: Ytv

Saint Joan, New York 1923, Play
Saint Joan 1927 d: Widgey R. Newman. lps: Sybil Thorndike. SND. 5M UKN. prod/rel: de Forest Phonofilm
Saint Joan 1957 d: Otto Preminger. lps: Richard Widmark, Richard Todd, Anton Walbrook. 110M UKN/USA. prod/rel: Wheel Films, Preminger Productions
Saint Joan 1977 d: Steven Rumbelow. 45M UKN.

SHAW, IRWIN (1913–, USA
Beggarman, Thief, Novel
Beggarman, Thief 1979 d: Don Chaffey, Lawrence Doheny. lps: Jean Simmons, Glenn Ford, Lynn Redgrave. 200M USA. prod/rel: NBC, Universal

Evening in Byzantium, Novel
Evening in Byzantium 1978 d: Jerry London. lps: Glenn Ford, Eddie Albert, Vince Edwards. TVM. 200M USA. prod/rel: Universal, Operation Prime Time

The Gentle People; a Brooklyn Fable, New York 1939, Play
Out of the Fog 1941 d: Anatole Litvak. lps: Ida Lupino, John Garfield, Thomas Mitchell. 93M USA. *The Gentle People* prod/rel: Warner Bros.

The Girls in Their Summer Dresses, Story
Girls in Their Summer Dresses, The 1982 d: Nick HavingA. TVM. 90M UKN/USA. prod/rel: BBC, Wnet

In the French Style, 1953, Short Story
In the French Style 1963 d: Robert Parrish. lps: Jean Seberg, Stanley Baker, Philippe Forquet. 104M USA/FRN. *A la Francaise* (FRN) prod/rel: Casanna Films, Orsay Films

The Man Who Married a French Wife, Story
Man Who Married a French Wife, The 1982 d: John Glenister. lps: Bob Sherman. TVM. 90M UKN/USA. prod/rel: BBC, Wnet

The Monument, Story
Monument, The 1982 d: Nick HavingA. lps: Charles Durning. TVM. 90M UKN/USA. prod/rel: BBC, Wnet

Night Call, Novel
Take One False Step 1949 d: Chester Erskine. lps: William Powell, Shelley Winters, Marsha Hunt. 94M USA. prod/rel: Universal-International

Rich Man, Poor Man, Novel
Rich Man, Poor Man 1975 d: David Greene, Boris Sagal. lps: Peter Strauss, Nick Nolte, Susan Blakely. MTV. 600M USA. prod/rel: Universal TV

Then We Were Three, 1961, Short Story
Three 1969 d: James Salter. lps: Charlotte Rampling, Robie Porter, Sam Waterston. 95M UKN/ITL. *Noi Tre Soltanto* prod/rel: United Artists, Obelisk

Tip on a Dead Jockey, 1955, Short Story
Tip on a Dead Jockey 1957 d: Richard Thorpe. lps: Robert Taylor, Dorothy Malone, Gia ScalA. 98M USA. *Time for Action* (UKN) prod/rel: MGM

Two Weeks in Another Town, New York 1960, Novel
Two Weeks in Another Town 1962 d: Vincente Minnelli. lps: Kirk Douglas, Edward G. Robinson, Cyd Charisse. 107M USA. prod/rel: John Houseman Productions, MGM

The Young Lions, 1948, Novel
Young Lions, The 1958 d: Edward Dmytryk. lps: Marlon Brando, Montgomery Clift, Dean Martin. 167M USA. prod/rel: 20th Century-Fox

SHAW, ROBERT (1927–1978), UKN
The Hiding Place, London 1959, Novel
Situation Hopeless - But Not Serious 1965 d: Gottfried Reinhardt. lps: Alec Guinness, Mike Connors, Robert Redford. 98M USA. prod/rel: Castle Productions

SHAW, STANLEY
Jungle Heart, 1918, Short Story
Fighting Destiny 1919 d: Paul Scardon. lps: Harry T. Morey, Betty Blythe, Arthur Donaldson. 4301f USA. prod/rel: Vitagraph Co. of America©

SHAWN, WALLACE (1943–), USA
The Designated Mourner, Play
Designated Mourner, The 1997 d: David Hare. lps: Mike Nichols, Miranda Richardson, David de Keyser. 94M UKN. prod/rel: Greenpoint Film

SHEA, TIMOTHY
Sarah and Son, New York 1929, Novel
Richiamo Del Cuore, Il 1930 d: Jack Salvatori. lps: Carmen Boni, Carlo Lombardo, Sandro Salvini. 90M FRN. prod/rel: Paramount
Sarah and Son 1930 d: Dorothy Arzner. lps: Ruth Chatterton, Fredric March, Fuller Mellish Jr. 76M USA. prod/rel: Paramount Famous Lasky Corp.
Toute Sa Vie 1930 d: Alberto Cavalcanti. lps: Marcelle Chantal, Fernand Fabre, Elmire Vautier. 9r FRN/USA. *L' Appel du Coeur* prod/rel: Films Paramount, Paramount-Publix Corp.

SHEARING, JOSEPH
For Her to See, Novel
So Evil My Love 1948 d: Lewis Allen. lps: Ray Milland, Ann Todd, Geraldine Fitzgerald. 109M UKN. prod/rel: Paramount British

Moss Rose, Novel
Moss Rose 1947 d: Gregory Ratoff. lps: Victor Mature, Peggy Cummins, Ethel Barrymore. 82M USA. prod/rel: 20th Century-Fox

SHECKLEY, ROBERT (1928–), USA
Dead Run, New York 1961, Novel
Geheimnisse in Goldenen Nylons 1966 d: Christian-Jaque. lps: Georges Geret, Peter Lawford, Ira Furstenberg. 95M GRM/FRN/ITL. *Deux Billets Pour Mexico* (FRN); *Qui Veut Tuer Carlos?*; *Dead Run* (USA); *Who Wants to Shoot Carlos?*; *Segreti Che Scottano* (ITL) prod/rel: S.N.C., Intermondia Films

The Game of X, Novel
Condorman 1981 d: Charles Jarrott. lps: Michael Crawford, Oliver Reed, Barbara CarrerA. 90M UKN. prod/rel: Walt Disney, Buena Vista

Immortality Inc., Novel
Freejack 1992 d: Geoff Murphy. lps: Emilio Estevez, Mick Jagger, Rene Russo. 108M USA. prod/rel: Morgan Creek, Warner Bros.

The Man in the Water, New York 1962, Novel
Man in the Water, The 1963 d: Mark Stevens. lps: Mark Stevens, Jack Donner, Ann Rouzer. 80M USA. *Escape from Hell Island* prod/rel: Key West Films

The Prize of Peril, Short Story
Prix du Danger, Le 1983 d: Yves Boisset. lps: Gerard Lanvin, Michel Piccoli, Marie-France Pisier. 98M FRN/YGS. *The Prize of Peril* (UKN) prod/rel: Swanie Productions, Tf1

Seventh Victim, 1953, Short Story
Decima Vittima, La 1965 d: Elio Petri. lps: Marcello Mastroianni, Ursula Andress, Elsa Martinelli. 100M ITL/FRN. *La Dixieme Victime* (FRN); *The 10th Victim* (USA) prod/rel: Compagnia Cin.Ca Champion (Roma), Les Films Concordia (Paris)

SHEDD, GEORGE CLIFFORD
In the Shadow of the Hills, New York 1919, Novel
Cold Steel 1921 d: Sherwood MacDonald. lps: J. P. McGowan, Kathleen Clifford, Stanhope Wheatcroft. 5800f USA. prod/rel: L. J. Meyberg, Robertson-Cole Distributing Corp.

The Incorrigible Dukane, Play
Incorrigible Dukane, The 1915 d: James Durkin. lps: John Barrymore, William T. Carleton, Helen Weir. 4-5r USA. prod/rel: Famous Players Film Co.©, Paramount Pictures Corp.

SHEEAN, VINCENT
Personal History, Book
Foreign Correspondent 1940 d: Alfred Hitchcock. lps: Joel McCrea, Laraine Day, Herbert Marshall. 120M USA. *Personal History; Imposter* prod/rel: United Artists, Walter Wanger Productions©

SHEEHAN, NEIL
A Bright Shining Lie, Book
Bright Shining Lie, A 1998 d: Terry George. lps: Bill Paxton, Amy Madigan, Vivian Vu. TVM. 120M USA. prod/rel: Hbo Pictures

SHEEHAN, PERLEY POORE
The Borrowed Duchess, Short Story
Society Sensation, A 1918 d: Paul Powell. lps: Carmel Myers, Rudolph Valentino, Fred Kelsey. 5r USA. *The Borrowed Duchess* prod/rel: Bluebird Photoplays, Inc.©

Four-Forty at Fort Penn, 1917, Short Story
Brave and Bold 1918 d: Carl Harbaugh. lps: George Walsh, Regina Quinn, Francis X. Conlan. 4368f USA. prod/rel: Fox Film Corp., William Fox©

Three Sevens, Novel
Three Sevens 1921 d: Chester Bennett. lps: Antonio Moreno, Jean Calhoun, Emmett King. 5r USA. prod/rel: Vitagraph Co. of America

Upstairs, Short Story
Upstairs 1919 d: Victor Schertzinger. lps: Mabel Normand, Cullen Landis, Hallam Cooley. 5r USA. prod/rel: Goldwyn Pictures Corp.©, Goldwyn Distributing Corp.

The Way of All Flesh, Story
Way of All Flesh, The 1927 d: Victor Fleming. lps: Emil Jannings, Belle Bennett, Phyllis Haver. 8486f USA. prod/rel: Paramount Famous Lasky Corp.
Way of All Flesh, The 1940 d: Louis King. lps: Akim Tamiroff, Gladys George, William Henry. 86M USA. prod/rel: Paramount Pictures©

We are French!, New York 1914, Novel
Bugler of Algiers, The 1916 d: Rupert Julian. lps: Ella Hall, Rupert Julian, Kingsley Benedict. 5r USA. *Comrades* (UKN); *We are French* prod/rel: Bluebird Photoplays, Inc.©
Love and Glory 1924 d: Rupert Julian. lps: Charles de Roche, Wallace MacDonald, Madge Bellamy. 7094f USA. prod/rel: Universal Pictures

The Whispering Chorus, 1918, Short Story
Whispering Chorus, The 1917 d: Cecil B. de Mille. lps: Kathlyn Williams, Raymond Hatton, Elliott Dexter. 6655f USA. prod/rel: Famous Players-Lasky Corp.©, Artcraft Pictures

SHEEHY, GAIL
Hustling, Book
Hustling 1975 d: Joseph Sargent. lps: Lee Remick, Monte Markham, Jill Clayburgh. TVM. 100M USA. prod/rel: Filmways, Lillian Gallo Productions

SHEKLOW, EDNA
The Plant, Play
Promises! Promises! 1963 d: King Donovan. lps: Jayne Mansfield, Marie McDonald, Tommy Noonan. 75M USA. *Promise Her Anything* prod/rel: Noonan-Taylor Productions

SHELDON, CHARLES MONROE (1857–1946), USA
The Crucifixion of Philip Strong, Chicago 1894, Novel
Martyrdom of Philip Strong, The 1916 d: Richard Ridgely. lps: Robert Conness, Mabel Trunnelle, Janet Dawley. 5r USA. *The Martyrdom of Phillip Strong* prod/rel: Thomas A. Edison, Inc., Paramount Pictures Corp.©

In His Steps: "What Would Jesus Do?", New York 1896, Novel
In His Steps 1936 d: Karl Brown. lps: Eric Linden, Cecilia Parker, Olive Tell. 80M USA. *Sins of the Children; Sins of Children* prod/rel: B. F. Zeidman Productions, Grand National Films©
Martyrdom of Philip Strong, The 1916 d: Richard Ridgely. lps: Robert Conness, Mabel Trunnelle, Janet Dawley. 5r USA. *The Martyrdom of Phillip Strong* prod/rel: Thomas A. Edison, Inc., Paramount Pictures Corp.©

SHELDON, E. LLOYD
Story
Beyond the Blue Horizon 1942 d: Alfred Santell. lps: Dorothy Lamour, Richard Denning, Jack Haley. 76M USA. *Malaya* prod/rel: Paramount

Out of the Night, Play
Out of the Night 1918 d: James Kirkwood. lps: Catherine Calvert, Herbert Rawlinson, Frederick Esmelton. 6r USA. prod/rel: Frank A. Kenney Pictures Corp., William L. Sherry Service

SHELDON, EDWARD (1886–1946), USA, Sheldon, Edward Brewster

The Boss, New York 1911, Play
Boss, The 1915 d: Emile Chautard. lps: Holbrook Blinn, Alice Brady, William Marion. 5r USA. prod/rel: William A. Brady Picture Plays, Inc., World Film Corp.©

Dishonored Lady, New York 1930, Play
Dishonored Lady 1947 d: Robert Stevenson. lps: Hedy Lamarr, Dennis O'Keefe, Natalie Schafer. 85M USA. prod/rel: United Artists

Egypt, New York 1912, Play
Call of Her People, The 1917 d: John W. Noble. lps: Ethel Barrymore, Robert Whittier, William B. Davidson. 7r USA. prod/rel: Columbia Pictures Corp., Metro Pictures Corp.

The High Road, New York 1912, Play
High Road, The 1915 d: John W. Noble. lps: Valli Valli, Frank Elliott, C. H. Brennon. 5r USA. prod/rel: Rolfe Photoplays Inc., Metro Pictures Corp.©

My Lulu Belle, 1925, Play
Lulu Belle 1948 d: Leslie Fenton. lps: Dorothy Lamour, George Montgomery, Albert Dekker. 87M USA. prod/rel: Columbia

The Nigger, New York 1909, Play
Nigger, The 1915 d: Edgar Lewis. lps: William Farnum, Claire Whitney, Henry ArmettA. 5r USA. *The New Governor* prod/rel: Fox Film Corp., William Fox©

The Princess Zim-Zim, Albany, Ny. 1911, Play
Coney Island Princess, A 1916 d: Dell Henderson. lps: Irene Fenwick, Owen Moore, Eva Francis. 5r USA. prod/rel: Famous Players Film Co.©, Paramount Pictures Corp.

Romance, New York 1913, Play
Romance 1920 d: Chet Withey. lps: Doris Keane, Basil Sydney, Norman Trevor. 7r USA. prod/rel: United Artists Corp., Doris Keane & Albert L. Grey©

Salvation Nell, New York 1908, Play
Salvation Army Lass, The 1909 d: D. W. Griffith. lps: Florence Lawrence, Marion Leonard, Florence Labadie. 926f USA. prod/rel: Biograph Co.
Salvation Nell 1915 d: George E. Middleton. lps: Beatriz Michelena, William Pike, Andrew Robson. 6r USA. prod/rel: California Motion Picture Corp., World Film Corp.©
Salvation Nell 1921 d: Kenneth Webb. lps: Pauline Starke, Joe King, Gypsy O'Brien. 6384f USA. prod/rel: Associated First National Pictures, Whitman Bennett Productions
Salvation Nell 1931 d: James Cruze. lps: Helen Chandler, Ralph Graves, Sally O'Neil. 85M USA. *Men Women Love* (UKN) prod/rel: James Cruze Productions©, Tiffany Productions

SHELDON, H. S., Sheldon, Harry Sophus

A Bit of Lace, Play
Bit of Lace, A 1915. lps: Edna Mayo, Darwin Karr, Sidney Ainsworth. 3r USA. prod/rel: Essanay

Conscience, Play
Trust Your Wife 1921 d: J. A. Barry. lps: Katherine MacDonald, Dave Winter, Charles Richman. 5-6r USA. prod/rel: Katherine Macdonald Pictures, Associated First National Pictures

A Daughter of the City, Play
Daughter of the City, A 1915 d: E. H. Calvert. lps: Marguerite Clayton, E. H. Calvert, John Junior. 5r USA. prod/rel: Essanay Film Mfg. Co.©, V-L-S-E, Inc.

The Havoc, New York 1911, Play
Havoc, The 1916 d: Arthur Berthelet. lps: Gladys Hanson, Lewis Stone, Bryant Washburn. 5r USA. prod/rel: Essanay Film Mfg. Co.©, V-L-S-E, Inc.

Men, New York 1916, Play
Men 1918 d: Perry N. Vekroff. lps: Anna Lehr, Gertrude McCoy, Huntley Gordon. 6r USA. prod/rel: Bacon-Backer Film Corp., State Rights

SHELDON, SIDNEY (1917–, USA

Bloodline, Novel
Sidney Sheldon's Bloodline 1979 d: Terence Young. lps: Audrey Hepburn, Ben Gazzara, James Mason. 116M USA. *Bloodline* prod/rel: Paramount, Geria

Master of the Game, Novel
Master of the Game 1984 d: Harvey Hart, Kevin Connor. lps: Dyan Cannon, Leslie Caron, Harry Hamlin. TVM. 540M USA/UKN. prod/rel: CBS, Viacom

Memories of Midnight, Novel
Memories of Midnight 1991 d: Gary Nelson. lps: Jane Seymour, Omar Sharif, Taro Meyer. TVM. 186M USA. *Sidney Sheldon's Memories of Midnight*

The Naked Face, Novel
Naked Face, The 1984 d: Bryan Forbes. lps: Roger Moore, Art Carney, Rod Steiger. 105M USA. prod/rel: Cannon

The Other Side of Midnight, Novel
Other Side of Midnight, The 1977 d: Charles Jarrott. lps: Marie-France Pisier, John Beck, Susan Sarandon. 165M USA. prod/rel: 20th Century Fox, Frank Yablans

Rage of Angels, Novel
Rage of Angels 1982 d: Buzz Kulik. lps: Jaclyn Smith, Ken Howard, Armand Assante. TVM. 200M USA. prod/rel: NBC
Rage of Angels: the Story Continues 1986 d: Paul Wendkos. lps: Jaclyn Smith, Ken Howard, Michael Nouri. TVM. 200M USA. *Rage of Angels - Part Two* prod/rel: NBC

The Sands of Time, Novel
Sands of Time, The 1992 d: Gary Nelson. lps: Deborah Raffin, Michael Nouri, Elizabeth Gracen. TVM. 173M USA. *Sidney Sheldon's the Sands of Time* prod/rel: Dove Audio, Jadran Films

Windmills of the Gods, Novel
Windmills of the Gods 1988 d: Lee Philips. lps: Jaclyn Smith, Robert Wagner, Franco Nero. TVM. 200M USA. *Sidney Sheldon's Windmills of the Gods* prod/rel: Dove Productions, Itc Productions

SHELLABARGER, SAMUEL (1888–1954), YSA

Captain from Castile, Novel
Captain from Castile 1947 d: Henry King. lps: Tyrone Power, Jean Peters, Cesar Romero. 140M USA. prod/rel: 20th Century-Fox

Prince of Foxes, Novel
Prince of Foxes 1949 d: Henry King. lps: Tyrone Power, Orson Welles, Wanda Hendrix. 107M USA. prod/rel: 20th Century-Fox

SHELLEY, ELSA

Pickup Girl, London 1946, Play
Too Young to Love 1960 d: Muriel Box. lps: Thomas Mitchell, Pauline Hahn, Joan Miller. 89M UKN. prod/rel: Rank Film Distributors, Beaconsfield

SHELLEY, MARY WOLLSTONECRAFT (1797–1851), UKN

Frankenstein; Or the Modern Prometheus, London 1818, Novel
Bride of Frankenstein 1935 d: James Whale. lps: Boris Karloff, Colin Clive, Valerie Hobson. 80M USA. *Frankenstein Lives Again*; *The Return of Frankenstein* prod/rel: Universal Pictures Corp.
Bride, The 1985 d: Franc Roddam. lps: Sting, Jennifer Beals, Anthony Higgins. 119M UKN/USA. prod/rel: Columbia-Delphi III Productions, Colgems Productions
Curse of Frankenstein, The 1957 d: Terence Fisher. lps: Peter Cushing, Christopher Lee, Hazel Court. 83M UKN. *Birth of Frankenstein* prod/rel: Hammer, Clarion
Frankenstein 1910 d: J. Searle Dawley. lps: Charles Ogle, Augustus Phillips, Mary Fuller. 975f USA. prod/rel: Edison
Frankenstein 1931 d: James Whale. lps: Colin Clive, Mae Clarke, John Boles. 71M USA. prod/rel: Universal Pictures Corp.©
Frankenstein 1973 d: Glenn Jordan. lps: Robert Foxworth, Susan Strasberg, Bo Svenson. TVM. 146M USA. prod/rel: Dan Curtis Productions
Frankenstein 1984 d: James Ormerod. lps: Robert Powell, Carrie Fisher, John Gielgud. TVM. F UKN/USA. prod/rel: Yorkshire Tv
Frankenstein General Hospital 1988 d: Deborah Roberts. lps: Mark Blankfield, Irwin Keyes, Kathy Shower. 92M USA. prod/rel: New Star
Frankenstein: the True Story 1973 d: Jack Smight. lps: Michael Sarrazin, James Mason, David McCallum. TVM. 200M USA/UKN. *Doctor Frankenstein* prod/rel: Universal
Horror of Frankenstein, The 1970 d: Jimmy Sangster. lps: Ralph Bates, Kate O'Mara, Veronica Carlson. 95M UKN. prod/rel: MGM-Emi, Hammer
Life Without Soul 1916 d: Joseph Smiley. lps: Percy Standing, Lucy Cotton, William Cohill. 5r USA. prod/rel: Ocean Film Corp., State Rights
Mary Shelley's Frankenstein 1994 d: Kenneth Branagh. lps: Robert de Niro, Kenneth Branagh, Tom Hulce. 123M UKN/USA.
Mostro Di Frankenstein, Il 1920 d: Eugenio TestA. lps: Luciano Albertini, Umberto Guarracino, Linda Albertini. 1086m ITL. prod/rel: Albertini Film
Son of Frankenstein 1939 d: Rowland V. Lee. lps: Basil Rathbone, Boris Karloff, Bela Lugosi. 95M USA. prod/rel: Universal Pictures Co.©, Rowland V. Lee Production
Victor Frankenstein 1977 d: Calvin Floyd. lps: Leon Vitali, Per Oscarsson, Nicholas Clay. 89M IRL/SWD. *Terror of Frankenstein* (USA); *Terror of Dr. Frankenstein*

SHELLEY, SIDNEY

The Bowmanville Break, New York 1968, Novel
McKenzie Break, The 1970 d: Lamont Johnson. lps: Brian Keith, Helmut Griem, Ian Hendry. 108M UKN. *The MacKenzie Break*; *Wolfpack* prod/rel: Brighton Pictures, United Artists

SHELTON, WILLIAM R.

Stowaway to the Moon: the Camelot Odyssey, Novel
Stowaway to the Moon 1975 d: Andrew V. McLaglen. lps: Lloyd Bridges, Jeremy Slate, Jim McMullan. TVM. 100M USA. prod/rel: 20th Century-Fox

SHEM, SAMUEL

The House of God, Novel
House of God, The 1979 d: Donald Wrye. lps: Tim Matheson, Charles Haid, Michael Sacks. 108M USA. *H.O.G.* prod/rel: United Artists

SHEN CONGWEN

Bian Cheng, 193-, Short Story
Biancheng 1984 d: Ling Zhifeng. lps: Feng Hanyuan, Dai Na, Liu Kui. 101M CHN. *Border Town* prod/rel: Beijing Film Studio

Xiao XIao, 193-, Short Story
Xiangnu XIaoxiao 1987 d: XIe Fei, Wu Lan. lps: Na Renhua, Liu Qing, Deng XIaoguang. 99M CHN. *Xiao XIao -a Girl from Hunan*; *Hunan Girl XIaoxiao*; *Girl from Hunan*; *Married to a Child* prod/rel: Youth Film Studio

SHEN RONG

Ren Dao Zhong Nian, Novel
Ren Dao Zhongnian 1982 d: Wang Qimin, Sun Yu. lps: Pan Hong, Da Shichang, Zhao Kuier. 110M CHN. *At Middle Age* prod/rel: Changchun Film Studio

SHEN SANBAI

Fu Sheng Liu Ji, 18—, Autobiography
Fu Sheng Liu Ji 1947 d: Pei Chong. 110M CHN.

SHEN XIMENG

Ni Hong Deng XIa de Shao Bing, Play
Ni Hong Deng XIa de Shao Bing 1964 d: Wang Ping, Ko Hsin. lps: Xu Linge, Gong Zhipei, Ma Xueshi. 13r CHN. *Sentinels Under the Neon Lights*; *Sentries Under Neon Lights* prod/rel: Tianma Film Studio

SHEN YANBING, Mao Dun

Fu Shi, 1941, Novel
Fushi 1950 d: Zuo Lin. lps: Dan Ni, Shi Hui, Cui Chaoming. 119M CHN. *Corruption* prod/rel: Wenhua Film Company

Linjia Puzi, 1932, Short Story
Linjia Puzhi 1959 d: Shui HuA. lps: XIe Tian, Ma Wei, Han Tao. 9r CHN. *The Lin Family Shop*; *Lin Chia P'tzu* prod/rel: Beijing Film Studio

SHEPARD, KATHLEEN

I Will Be Faithful, New York 1934, Novel
Human Cargo 1936 d: Allan Dwan. lps: Claire Trevor, Brian Donlevy, Alan Dinehart. 66M USA. *I Will Be Faithful* prod/rel: Twentieth Century-Fox Film Corp.©

SHEPARD, SAM (1943–, USA

Curse of the Starving Class, Play
Curse of the Starving Class 1994 d: Michael McClary. lps: James Woods, Kathy Bates, Henry Thomas. TVM. 101M USA.

Fool for Love, 1984, Play
Fool for Love 1986 d: Robert Altman. lps: Sam Shepard, Kim Basinger, Harry Dean Stanton. 108M USA. prod/rel: Cannon

Paris, Texas Motel Chronicles, 1985, Play
Paris, Texas 1984 d: Wim Wenders. lps: Harry Dean Stanton, Sam Berry, Bernhard Wicki. 150M FRN/GRM/USA. prod/rel: Road Movies, Argos

True West, 1980, Play
True West 1983 d: Gary Sinise. MTV. 110M USA.

SHEPHERD, JEAN

In God We Trust - All Others Pay Cash, Novel
Christmas Story, A 1984 d: Bob Clark. lps: Peter Billingsley, Darren McGavin, Melinda Dillon. 98M CND. prod/rel: Christmas Tree Films Inc., MGM/Ua Entertainment

SHEPPARD, STEPHEN

The Artisan, Novel
Georg Elser - Einer Aus Deutschland 1989 d: Klaus Maria Brandauer. lps: Klaus Maria Brandauer, Brian Dennehy, Rebecca Miller. 97M GRM/USA. *Seven Minutes* (USA) prod/rel: Sohnlein, Borman

SHER, JACK

Memo on Kathy O'Rourke, Short Story
Kathy O' 1958 d: Jack Sher. lps: Dan Duryea, Jan Sterling, Patty McCormack. 99M USA. prod/rel: Universal-International

SHERBOURNE, ZOA
A Stranger in the House, Book
Memories Never Die 1982 d: Sandor Stern. lps: Lindsay Wagner, Gerald McRaney, Melissa Michaelsen. TVM. 96M USA. prod/rel: Groverton Productions, Scholastic Productions

SHERBROOKE, NORMAN
Smoke, Short Story
You Can't Believe Everything 1918 d: Jack Conway. lps: Gloria Swanson, Darrel Foss, Jack Richardson. 5r USA. prod/rel: Triangle Film Corp., Triangle Distributing Corp.

The Veil, Story
Who Killed Walton? 1918 d: Thomas N. Heffron. lps: J. Barney Sherry, Mary Mersch, Ed Brady. 5r USA. prod/rel: Triangle Film Corp., Triangle Distributing Corp.

SHERIDAN, RICHARD BRINSLEY (1751–1816), UKN
The Rivals, London 1775, Play
Rivals (Duel Scene), The 1914. lps: Eric Williams. UKN. prod/rel: Eric Williams Speaking Pictures
Rivals, The 1913 d: Theodore Marston. lps: William Jefferson, Gaston Bell, Gilbert Coleman. SHT USA. prod/rel: Kinemacolor

The School for Scandal, London 1777, Play
School for Scandal, The 1914 d: Kenean Buel. lps: Alice Joyce, James B. Ross, Guy Coombs. 4000f USA. prod/rel: Kalem Co., General Film Co.
School for Scandal, The 1923 d: Bertram Phillips. lps: Queenie Thomas, Frank Stanmore, Basil Rathbone. 6350f UKN. prod/rel: B.P. Productions, Butcher's Film Service
School for Scandal, The 1923 d: Edwin Greenwood. lps: Russell Thorndike, Nina Vanna, Florence Wulff. 2386f UKN. prod/rel: British & Colonial, Walturdaw
School for Scandal, The 1930 d: Maurice Elvey. lps: Basil Gill, Madeleine Carroll, Ian Fleming. 76M UKN. prod/rel: Albion Film Syndicate, Paramount
School for Scandal, The 1975 d: Stuart Burge. lps: Jeremy Brett, Pauline Collins, Edward Fox. MTV. UKN. prod/rel: BBC

SHERIE, FENN
Shadow Man, Play
Terror on Tiptoe 1936 d: Louis Renoir. lps: Bernard Nedell, Mabel Poulton, Jasper Maskeleyne. 58M UKN. prod/rel: Mb Productions, New Realm

SHERLOCK, JOHN
The Ordeal of Major Grigsby, London 1964, Novel
Last Grenade, The 1970 d: Gordon Flemyng. lps: Stanley Baker, Alex Cord, Honor Blackman. 93M UKN. *Grigsby* prod/rel: Josef Shaftel Productions, Ciro

SHERMAN, CHARLES
He Comes Up Smiling, Indianapolis 1912, Novel
He Comes Up Smiling 1918 d: Allan Dwan. lps: Douglas Fairbanks, Marjorie Daw, Herbert Standing. 4876f USA. prod/rel: Douglas Fairbanks Pictures Corp., Famous Players-Lasky Corp.©

The Upper Crust, Indianapolis 1913, Novel
Upper Crust, The 1917 d: Rollin S. Sturgeon. lps: Gail Kane, Douglas MacLean, Eugenie Forde. 5r USA. prod/rel: American Film Co., Mutual Film Corp.

A Wise Son, Indianapolis 1914, Novel
Wandering Footsteps 1925 d: Phil Rosen. lps: Alec B. Francis, Estelle Taylor, Bryant Washburn. 5060f USA. prod/rel: Banner Productions, Henry Ginsberg Distributing Corp.

SHERMAN, HAROLD M.
Mark Twain, Play
Adventures of Mark Twain, The 1944 d: Irving Rapper. lps: Fredric March, Alexis Smith, Donald Crisp. 130M USA. prod/rel: Warner Bros.

SHERMAN, MARTIN
Bent, Play
Bent 1997 d: Sean Mathias. lps: Clive Owen, Lothaire Bluteau, Brian Webber. 117M UKN/USA/JPN. prod/rel: Channel Four Films©, Nippon Film Development©

SHERMAN, RICHARD
To Mary - With Love, 1935, Short Story
To Mary -With Love 1936 d: John Cromwell. lps: Warner Baxter, Myrna Loy, Ian Hunter. 92M USA. prod/rel: Twentieth Century-Fox Film Corp.©

SHERRIFF, R. C. (1896–1975), UKN, Sherriff, Robert Cedric
Badger's Green, London 1930, Play
Badger's Green 1934 d: Adrian Brunel. lps: Valerie Hobson, Bruce Lister, Frank (3) Moore. 68M UKN. prod/rel: British and Dominions, Paramount British

Badger's Green 1949 d: John Irwin. lps: Barbara Murray, Brian Nissen, Garry Marsh. 62M UKN. prod/rel: Production Facilities, General Film Distributors

Home at Seven, London 1950, Play
Home at Seven 1952 d: Ralph Richardson. lps: Ralph Richardson, Margaret Leighton, Jack Hawkins. 85M UKN. *Murder on Monday* (USA) prod/rel: British Lion, London Films

Journey's End, London 1929, Play
Aces High 1976 d: Jack Gold. lps: Malcolm McDowell, Christopher Plummer, Peter Firth. 114M UKN/FRN. *Le Tigre du Ciel* (FRN) prod/rel: Emi, S. Benjamin Fisz
Andere Seite, Die 1931 d: Heinz Paul. lps: Viktor de Kowa, Theodor Loos, Wolfgang Liebeneiner. 100M GRM. prod/rel: Cando, Westfalen
Journey's End 1930 d: James Whale. lps: Colin Clive, Ian MacLaren, David Manners. 120M UKN/USA. prod/rel: Gainsborough, Welsh-Pearson
Journey's End 1988 d: Michael Simpson. lps: George Baker, John Forgeham, Dorian Healy. MTV. F UKN.

Windfall, London 1934, Play
Windfall 1935 d: George King. lps: Edward Rigby, Marie Ault, George Carney. 65M UKN. prod/rel: Embassy, Radio

SHERRILL, JOHN & ELIZABETH
The Cross and the Switchblade, New York 1963, Autobiography
Cross and the Switchblade, The 1970 d: Don Murray. lps: Pat Boone, Erik Estrada, Jackie Giroux. 106M USA.

SHERRY, EDNA
Sudden Fear, 1948, Novel
Sudden Fear 1952 d: David Miller. lps: Joan Crawford, Jack Palance, Gloria Grahame. 110M USA. prod/rel: RKO Radio, Joseph Kaufman Prods.

SHERRY, GORDON
Black Limelight, London 1937, Play
Black Limelight 1938 d: Paul L. Stein. lps: Raymond Massey, Joan Marion, Walter Hudd. 70M UKN. prod/rel: Associated British Picture Corporation

SHERRY, JOHN
Pistolero's Progress, New York 1966, Novel
Last Challenge, The 1967 d: Richard Thorpe. lps: Glenn Ford, Angie Dickinson, Chad Everett. 105M USA. *Pistolero of Red River*; *Pistolero* prod/rel: Metro-Goldwyn-Mayer, Inc.

SHERWOOD, R. E. (1896–1955), USA, Sherwood, Robert Emmet
Abe Lincoln of Illinois, New York 1938, Play
Abe Lincoln in Illinois 1940 d: John Cromwell. lps: Raymond Massey, Gene Lockhart, Ruth Gordon. 110M USA. *Spirit of the People* (UKN); *So Great a Man* prod/rel: RKO Radio Pictures, Inc.

Idiot's Delight, New York 1936, Play
Idiot's Delight 1938 d: Clarence Brown. lps: Norma Shearer, Clark Gable, Edward Arnold. 105M USA. prod/rel: Metro-Goldwyn-Mayer Corp., Loew's, Inc.©

Oh, What a Nurse!, Play
Oh, What a Nurse! 1926 d: Charles F. Reisner. lps: Sydney Chaplin, Patsy Ruth Miller, Gayne Whitman. 6930f USA. prod/rel: Warner Brothers Pictures

The Petrified Forest, New York 1935, Play
Escape in the Desert 1945 d: Edward A. Blatt, Robert Florey (Uncredited). lps: Philip Dorn, Helmut Dantine, Jean Sullivan. 81M USA. *Strangers in Our Midst* prod/rel: Warner Bros. Pictures©
Petrified Forest, The 1936 d: Archie Mayo. lps: Leslie Howard, Bette Davis, Dick Foran. 83M USA. prod/rel: Warner Bros. Pictures©

The Queen's Husband, New York 1928, Play
Echec Au Roi 1931 d: Leon d'Usseau, Henri de La Falaise. lps: Francoise Rosay, Pauline Garon, Emile Chautard. 86M USA. *La Mari de la Reine*; *Le Roi S'ennuie* prod/rel: RKO-Radio Pictures
Royal Bed, The 1931 d: Lowell Sherman. lps: Lowell Sherman, Anthony O'Neil, Mary Astor. 73M USA. *The Queen's Husband* (UKN) prod/rel: RKO Radio Pictures©

Reunion in Vienna, New York 1931, Play
Reunion in Vienna 1932 d: Sidney A. Franklin. lps: John Barrymore, Diana Wynyard, Frank Morgan. 100M USA. prod/rel: Metro-Goldwyn-Mayer Corp.©

The Road to Rome, 1927, Play
Jupiter's Darling 1954 d: George Sidney. lps: Esther Williams, Howard Keel, Marge Champion. 96M USA. prod/rel: MGM

This Is New York, New York 1930, Play
Two Kinds of Women 1932 d: William C. de Mille. lps: Phillips Holmes, Miriam Hopkins, Irving Pichel. 73M USA. prod/rel: Paramount Publix Corp.©

Waterloo Bridge, New York 1930, Play
Gaby 1956 d: Curtis Bernhardt. lps: Leslie Caron, John Kerr, Cedric Hardwicke. 97M USA. prod/rel: Metro-Goldwyn-Mayer Corp.
Waterloo Bridge 1931 d: James Whale. lps: Mae Clarke, Douglass Montgomery, Doris Lloyd. 81M USA. prod/rel: Universal Pictures Corp.©
Waterloo Bridge 1940 d: Mervyn Leroy. lps: Vivien Leigh, Robert Taylor, Lucile Watson. 103M USA. prod/rel: Metro-Goldwyn-Mayer Corp., Loew's, Inc.©

SHEVCHENKO, TARAS
Lileya, 1888, Verse
Lileia 1960 d: Vasil Lapoknysh, Vakhtong Vronsky. 88M USS. *Lileya*

SHEVELOVE, BURT
A Funny Thing Happened on the Way to the Forum, New York 1962, Play
Funny Thing Happened on the Way to the Forum, A 1966 d: Richard Lester. lps: Zero Mostel, Phil Silvers, Jack Gifford. 99M UKN/USA. prod/rel: Quadrangle Films, United Artists

SHEWELL, L. R.
The Shadows of a Great City, New York 1884, Play
Shadows of a Great City 1913 d: Frank Wilson. lps: Alec Worcester, Chrissie White, Harry Royston. 3700f UKN. prod/rel: Hepworth
Shadows of a Great City, The 1915. lps: Adelaide Thurston, Thomas Jefferson. 5r USA. prod/rel: Popular Plays and Players, Inc.©, Metro Pictures Corp.

SHI CHENGYUAN
Black Dream, Novel
Da Chongzhuang 1993 d: Zhang XIaomin. lps: Zhang XIaomin, Jie Rui, Zhai Yuguo. 10r CHN. *The Offence*; *Fierce Conflicts* prod/rel: XI'an Film Studio

SHI GUO
Yi Chang Feng Bo, Novel
Yi Chang Feng Bo 1954 d: XIe Jin, Lin Nong. lps: Shu XIuwen, Fu Ke, She Wei. 9r CHN. *Disturbance*; *A Wave of Unrest* prod/rel: Shanghai Film Studio

SHI NAIAN
Shuihu Zhuan, c1500, Novel
Lin Chong 1958 d: Su Shi, Wu Yonggang. lps: Su Shi, Zhang Yi, Lin Bing. 9r CHN. prod/rel: Jiangnan Film Studio
Wu Song 1963 d: Ying Yunwei, Yu Zhongying. 109M CHN.
Wu Song and Pan Jinlian 1938 d: Wu Cun. lps: Jin Yan, Liu Qiong. 90M CHN.
Ye Zhu Lin 1965 d: Wu Cun. 109M CHN.
Yingxiong Bense 1993 d: Chen Huiyi. lps: Liang Jiahui, Wang Zuxian, Xu Jingjiang. 10r CHN/HKG. *Blood of the Leopard*; *True Colors of a Hero* prod/rel: Pearl River Film Studio, Hong Kong Entertainment Film Co.

SHI NAN
Hua Hun, Novel
Hua Hun 1994 d: Huang Shuqin. lps: Gong Li, Er Dongsheng, Da Shichang. 14r CHN/TWN/FRN. *Pan Yu Liang a Woman Painter*; *Soul of a Painter* prod/rel: Shanghai Film Studio, Golden Tripod Film Co.

SHI TIESHENG
Bian Zou Bian Chang, Short Story
Bian Zou Bian Chang 1991 d: Chen Kaige. lps: Liu Zhongyuan, Huang Lei, Xu Qing. 103M CHN/GRM. *Life on a String* (UKN); *Bian Zhou Bian Chang* prod/rel: Beijing Film Studio, Pandora Film (Munich)

SHIBATA, RENZABURO
Kaidan Ruigafuchi, Novel
Kaidan Zankoku Monogatari 1968 d: Kazuo Hase. lps: Sae Kawagushi, Masakazu Tamura, Yusuke Kawazu. 88M JPN. *Curse of the Blood*; *Cruel Ghost Legend* prod/rel: Shochiku Co.

SHIBATA, YOSHIKI
Story
Onna Keiji Riko 2: Seibo No Shinki-En 1998 d: Satoshi IsakA. lps: Ryoko Takizawa, Toshiya Nagasawa, Toru KazamA. 98M JPN. *Detective Riko* prod/rel: Kadokawa Shoten, Ace Pictures

SHIBER, ETTA
Paris Underground, Book
Paris Underground 1945 d: Gregory Ratoff. lps: Constance Bennett, Gracie Fields, Jorge Rigaud. 97M USA. *Madame Pimpernel* (UKN) prod/rel: United Artists

SHIEL, MATTHEW PHIPPS (1865–1947), UKN, Shiel, M. P.
The Purple Cloud, 1902, Novel
World, the Flesh and the Devil, The 1959 d: Ranald MacDougall. lps: Harry Belafonte, Inger Stevens, Mel Ferrer. 95M USA. *End of the World* prod/rel: MGM

SHIELDS, CAROL
Swann, Novel
    Swann 1996 d: Anna Benson Gyles. lps: Miranda Richardson, Brenda Fricker, Michael Ontkean. 98M UKN/CND. prod/rel: Greenpoint (Swann) Films, Shaftesbury (Swann) Films

SHIELDS, JAMES K.
Philip Maynard, Pamphlet
    Stream of Life, The 1919 d: Horace G. Plympton. lps: Douglas Redmond Jr., Allen Willey, Edward Keenan. 7r USA. prod/rel: Plimpton Epic Pictures, Plymouth Film Corp.©

SHIELS, GEORGE
The New Gossoon, Novel
    Sally's Irish Rogue 1958 d: George Pollock. lps: Julie Harris, Tim Seely, Harry Brogan. 74M UKN. *The Poacher's Daughter* (USA) prod/rel: British Lion, Emmett Dalton
Professor Tim, Play
    Professor Tim 1957 d: Henry Cass. lps: Ray McAnally, Maire O'Donnell, Seamus Kavanagh. 57M UKN. prod/rel: Emmett-Dalton-Dublin Films, RKO

SHIFFRIN, A. B.
Cry Murder, Play
    Cry Murder 1950 d: Jack Glenn. lps: Jack Lord, Carole Mathews, Howard Smith. 63M USA. prod/rel: Edward Leven Productions, Film Classics

SHIFFRIN, HERMANN
Der Lugner, Play
    Lugner, Der 1961 d: Ladislao VajdA. lps: Heinz Ruhmann, Annemarie Duringer, Giulia FollinA. 94M GRM. *The Liar* prod/rel: Real, Rolei

SHIGA, NAOYA (1883–1971), JPN
Anya Koro, 1922-37, Novel
    Anya Koro 1959 d: Shiro ToyodA. 140M JPN. *Pilgrimage at Night*

SHIINA, MAKOTO
Musuko, Book
    Musuko 1991 d: Yoji YamadA. lps: Rentaro Mikuni, Masatoshi Nagase, Emi Wakui. 121M JPN. *My Sons; Son* prod/rel: Shochiku Co.

SHIINA, RINZO
Mujakina Hitobito, 1952, Novel
    Entotsu No Mieru Basho 1953 d: Heinosuke Gosho. lps: Ken Uehara, Kinuyo Tanaka, Hiroshi AkutagawA. 108M JPN. *Four Chimneys* (UKN); *From Where Chimneys are Seen; Where Chimneys are Seen; Three Chimneys* prod/rel: Studio Eight, Shintoho Co.

SHILTS, RANDY
And the Band Played on, Book
    And the Band Played on 1993 d: Roger Spottiswoode. lps: Matthew Modine, Alan Alda, Patrick Bauchau. 141M USA. prod/rel: Hbo Pictures, Odyssey

SHIMAZAKI, TOSON (1872–1943), JPN
Hakai, 1906, Novel
    Hakai 1948 d: Keisuke KinoshitA. lps: Osamu Takizawa, Yoshi Rano, Ryo Ikebe. 99M JPN. *Apostasy*
    Hakai 1961 d: Kon IchikawA. lps: Raizo Ichikawa, Shiho Fujimura, Hiroyuki Nagato. 118M JPN. *The Outcast* (UKN); *The Sin* (USA); *Outcasts; The Broken Commandment* prod/rel: Daiei Motion Picture Co.

SHIMOSAWA, KAN
Zato Ichi Monogatari, Novel
    Zato Ichi Monogatari 1962 d: Kenji Misumi. lps: Shintaro Katsu, Shigeru Amachi, Masayo Banri. 96M JPN. *The Life and Opinion of Masseur Ichi; Blind Swordsman; Zatoichi Enters Again* prod/rel: Daiei Motion Picture Co.

SHIN-CHEN WANT
Chin P'inge Mei, 15Th-Century, Novel
    Chin-P'ing-Mei 1969 d: Koji Wakamatsu. lps: Tomoko Mayama, Fumiaki Takashima, Juzo Itami. 90M JPN. *The Notorious Concubines; The Concubines* (USA); *Kinpeibei* prod/rel: Unicorn Productions

SHIPMAN, NELL
The King's Keeper, Story
    Pine's Revenge, The 1915 d: Joseph de Grasse. lps: Cleo Madison, Arthur Shirley, Lon Chaney. 2r USA. prod/rel: Rex

SHIPMAN, SAMUEL
Cheaper to Marry, New York 1926, Novel
    Cheaper to Marry 1924 d: Robert Z. Leonard. lps: Conrad Nagel, Lewis Stone, Paulette Duval. 6500f USA. prod/rel: Metro-Goldwyn-Mayer Pictures
Crime, New York 1927, Play
    Law of the Underworld 1938 d: Lew Landers. lps: Chester Morris, Anne Shirley, Richard Bond. 61M USA. *Crime; See No Evil* prod/rel: RKO Radio Pictures©

East Is West, Play
    East Is West 1922 d: Sidney A. Franklin. lps: Constance Talmadge, Edmund Burns, E. Alyn Warren. 7737f USA. prod/rel: Constance Talmadge Productions, Associated First National Pictures
    East Is West 1930 d: Monta Bell. lps: Lupe Velez, Lew Ayres, Edward G. Robinson. 75M USA. prod/rel: Universal Pictures
Fast Life, New York 1928, Play
    Fast Life 1929 d: John Francis Dillon. lps: Douglas Fairbanks Jr., Loretta Young, William Holden. 7541f USA. prod/rel: First National Pictures
Friendly Enemies, New York 1923, Play
    Friendly Enemies 1925 d: George Melford. lps: Lew Fields, Joe Weber, Virginia Brown Faire. 6288f USA. prod/rel: Belasco Productions, Producers Distributing Corp.
    Friendly Enemies 1942 d: Allan Dwan. lps: Charles Winninger, Charlie Ruggles, James Craig. 95M USA. prod/rel: United Artists
Lawful Larceny, New York 1922, Play
    Lawful Larceny 1923 d: Allan Dwan. lps: Hope Hampton, Conrad Nagel, Nita Naldi. 5503f USA. prod/rel: Famous Players-Lasky, Paramount Pictures
    Lawful Larceny 1930 d: Lowell Sherman. lps: Bebe Daniels, Kenneth Thomson, Lowell Sherman. 6379f USA. prod/rel: RKO Productions
The Lost Game, Short Story
    Law of the Underworld 1938 d: Lew Landers. lps: Chester Morris, Anne Shirley, Richard Bond. 61M USA. *Crime; See No Evil* prod/rel: RKO Radio Pictures©
Scarlet Pages, New York 1929, Play
    Scarlet Pages 1930 d: Ray Enright. lps: Elsie Ferguson, John Halliday, Marion Nixon. 5906f USA. prod/rel: First National Pictures
She Means Business, New York 1931, Play
    Manhattan Parade 1932 d: Lloyd Bacon. lps: Joe Smith, Charles Dale, Luis Alberni. 78M USA. *She Means Business* prod/rel: Warner Bros. Pictures©
The Woman in Room 13, New York 1919, Play
    Woman in Room 13, The 1920 d: Frank Lloyd. lps: Pauline Frederick, Charles Clary, John Bowers. 5r USA. prod/rel: Goldwyn Pictures Corp.©, Goldwyn Distributing Corp.
    Woman in Room 13, The 1932 d: Henry King. lps: Elissa Landi, Ralph Bellamy, Neil Hamilton. 69M USA. prod/rel: Fox Film Corp.©

SHIRK, ADAM HULL
The Ape, Los Angeles 1927, Play
    Ape, The 1940 d: William Nigh. lps: Boris Karloff, Maris Wrixon, Gertrude W. Hoffman. 62M USA. prod/rel: Monogram Pictures Corp.
    House of Mystery, The 1934 d: William Nigh. lps: Ed Lowry, Verna Hillie, John Sheehan. 62M USA. *The Ape; Curse of Kali* prod/rel: Monogram Pictures Corp.©, Paul Malvern Production
The Way Men Love, Story
    By Divine Right 1924 d: R. William Neill. lps: Mildred Harris, Anders Randolf, Elliott Dexter. 6885f USA. *The Way Men Love* prod/rel: Grand-Asher Distributing Corp., Film Booking Offices of America

SHIRKAUER, ALFRED
Paiva Queen of Love, Novel
    Idol of Paris 1948 d: Leslie Arliss. lps: Michael Rennie, Beryl Baxter, Christine Norden. 105M UKN. prod/rel: Premier, Warner Bros.

SHIRLEY, ARTHUR
Her Life in London, Play
    Her Life in London 1915 d: R. Harley West. lps: Alesia Leon, Fred Morgan, Nina Lynn. 4100f UKN. prod/rel: Martin, Dfsa
Her Redemption, Play
    Her Redemption 1924 d: Bertram Phillips. lps: Queenie Thomas, John Stuart, Cecil Humphreys. 5430f UKN. *The Gayest of the Gay* prod/rel: Bp Productions, Mp Sales
Jack Tar, Play
    Jack Tar 1915 d: Bert Haldane. lps: Jack Tessier, Edith Yates, Eve Balfour. 4500f UKN. prod/rel: Barker, Icc
The King of Crime, Play
    King of Crime, The 1914 d: Sidney Northcote. lps: John Lawson, Claudia Guilliot. 3600f UKN. prod/rel: Magnet
My Old Dutch, London 1919, Play
    My Old Dutch 1926 d: Larry Trimble. lps: May McAvoy, Pat O'Malley, Cullen Landis. 7750f USA. prod/rel: Universal Pictures
Saved from the Sea, London 1895, Play
    Saved from the Sea 1908. 815f UKN. prod/rel: Gaumont

    Saved from the Sea 1920 d: W. P. Kellino. lps: Nora Swinburne, Philip Anthony, Cecil Calvert. 5960f UKN. prod/rel: Gaumont, Westminster
Tommy Atkins, London 1895, Play
    Tommy Atkins 1910. 1490f UKN. prod/rel: Gaumont
    Tommy Atkins 1915 d: Bert Haldane. lps: Blanche Forsythe, Jack Tessier, Roy Travers. 3800f UKN. prod/rel: Barker, Icc
    Tommy Atkins 1928 d: Norman Walker. lps: Lillian Hall-Davis, Henry Victor, Walter Butler. 8363f UKN. prod/rel: British International Pictures, Wardour
Two Lancashire Lassies in London, Play
    Two Lancashire Lassies in London 1916 d: Dave Aylott. lps: Lettie Paxton, Dolly Tree, Wingold Lawrence. 5100f UKN. prod/rel: Martin's Cinematograph, Walturdaw
What Money Can Buy, Play
    What Money Can Buy 1928 d: Edwin Greenwood. lps: Madeleine Carroll, Humberston Wright, John Longden. 6400f UKN. prod/rel: Gaumont
Women and Wine, New York 1900, Play
    Model, The 1915 d: Frederick A. Thompson. lps: William Elliott, Cynthia Day, Alec B. Francis. 5r USA. *Women and Wine* prod/rel: William A. Brady Picture Plays, Inc., World Film Corp.©

SHIRLEY, JOHN
Novel
    Specialist, The 1994 d: Luis LlosA. lps: Sylvester Stallone, Sharon Stone, James Woods. 109M USA. prod/rel: Warner Bros.

SHIRREFFS, GORDON D.
Judas Gun, New York 1964, Novel
    Vivo Per la Tua Morte 1968 d: Camillo Bazzoni. lps: Steve Reeves, Wayde Preston, Mimmo PalmarA. 90M ITL. *A Long Ride from Hell* (USA); *I Live for Your Death* prod/rel: B.R.C. Cinematografica, Titanus
Oregon Passage, Novel
    Oregon Passage 1957 d: Paul Landres. lps: John Ericson, Lola Albright, Toni Gerry. 82M USA. prod/rel: Allied Artists, Lindsley Parsons Prods.
Silent Reckoning, Story
    Lonesome Trail, The 1955 d: Richard Bartlett. lps: Wayne Morris, John Agar, Margia Dean. 73M USA. prod/rel: Lippert, L & B Prods.

SHISHI, BUNROKU
Short Story
    Seishun Kaidan 1955 d: Kon IchikawA. lps: Miye Kitahara, So Yamamura, Tatsuya Mihashi. F JPN. *The Youth's Ghost Story; Ghost Story of Youth* prod/rel: Nikkatsu Corp.
Musume to Watashi, 1953-56, Serial
    Musume to Watashi 1962 d: Hiromichi HorikawA. lps: Yuriko Hoshi, So Yamamura, Setsuko HarA. F JPN. *My Daughter and I* (USA) prod/rel: Tokyo Eiga Co.

SHIVERS, LOUISE
Here to Get My Baby Out of Jail, Novel
    Summer Heat 1987 d: Michie Gleason. lps: Lori Singer, Anthony Edwards, Bruce Abbott. 90M USA. prod/rel: Atlantic Entertainment

SHOJI, KAORU
Akazukinchan Kiotsukete, Short Story
    Akazukinchan Kiotsukete 1970 d: Shiro Moritani. lps: Yusuke Okada, Kazuyo Mori, Tetsuo TomikawA. 90M JPN. *Be Careful Red Riding Hood; Take Care Red Riding Hood* prod/rel: Toho Co.

SHOLOKHOV, MIKHAIL (1905–1984), RSS, Sholokhov, Mikhail Aleksandrovich
Chervotochina, 1925, Short Story
    V Lazorevoy Stepi 1970 d: Vitali Koltzov, Oleg Bondarev. USS.
Chuzhaia Krov, 1926, Short Story
    Neproshenaya Lyubov 1964 d: Vladimir Monakhov. 92M USS. *Unwilling Love; Uninvited Love*
Donskie Rasskazy, 1926, Short Story
    Smertelni Vrag 1971 d: Yevgeni Matveyev. lps: Yevgeni Matveyev, Zhanna Prokhorenko, Stanislav Chekan. 86M USS. *Deadly Enemy; Sworn Enemies; Smertnyj Vrag; Smertnyi Vrag*
Kolevert, 1925, Short Story
    V Lazorevoy Stepi 1970 d: Valery Lonskoj, Vladimir Shamshurin. 103M USS. *V Lasurevoi Stepi*
Nakhalenok, 1926, Short Story
    Nakhalenok 1961 d: Yevgyeni Karelov. 57M USS. *The Shame Child; The Bastard*
O Kolchake Krapive I Prochem, 1926, Short Story
    Kogda Kazaki Plachut 1963 d: Eugene Morgunov. 28M USS.

Oni Srazhalis Za Rodinu, 1943-44, Novel
Oni Srajalis Za Rodinou 1974 d: Sergei Bondarchuk. lps: Sergei Bondarchuk, Vyacheslav Tikhonov, Vassili Shukshin. 159M USS. *They Fought for the Motherland* (USA); *They Fought for Their Country*; *Oni Srazhalis Za Rodinu*; *They Fought for Their Motherland*

Podnyataya Tselina, 1932, Novel
Podnyataya Tzelina 1959-61 d: Alexander Ivanov. 303M USS. *Virgin Soil Upturned*

Podnyataya Tzelina 1940 d: Yuli Raizman. 117M USS. *Virgin Soil Upturned*; *Podnjataja Celina*; *Podnyataya Tselina*; *The Soil Upturned*

Prodkomissar, 1925, Short Story
V Lazorevoy Stepi 1970 d: Vitali Koltzov, Oleg Bondarev. USS.

Rodinka, 1924, Short Story
V Lazorevoy Stepi 1970 d: Valery Lonskoj, Vladimir Shamshurin. 103M USS. *V Lasurevoi Stepi*

Shibalkovo Semia, 1926, Short Story
Donskaya Povest 1964 d: Vladimir Fetin. lps: Ljudmilla Tschursina, Yevgeni Leonov, Alexander Blinov. 95M USS. *A Tale of the Don*; *The Don Story* prod/rel: Lenfilm

Sudba Cheloveka, Moscow 1957, Novel
Stranitzy Rasskaza 1957 d: Boris Kryzhanovsky, Mikhail Tereshchenko. 30M USS.

Sudba Cheloveka 1959 d: Sergei Bondarchuk. lps: Sergei Bondarchuk, Pavlik Boriskin, Zoya Kiriyenko. 100M USS. *Fate of a Man* (USA); *Destiny of a Man*; *Sudba Celoveka*; *Soedba Tsjeloveka* prod/rel: Mosfilm

Tikhy Don, 1929, Novel
Tikhii Don 1958 d: Sergei Gerasimov. lps: Elina Bystritskaya, Pyotr Glebov, Zinaida Kirienko. 107M USS. *Quiet Flows the Don* (UKN); *And Quiet Flows the Don*; *Tihij Don*; *Tikhy Don* prod/rel: Gorki

Tikhu Don 1931 d: Olga Preobrazhenskaya, Ivan Pravov. lps: N. Podgorny, Andrei Abrikosov, Yelyena MaximovA. 87M USS. *Cossacks of the Don*; *The Quiet Don*; *Tikhy Don*; *And Quiet Flows the Don*; *Tichi Don*

Zherebenok, 1926, Short Story
Zherebyonok 1960 d: Vladimir Fetin. lps: Yevgeni Matveyev, Leonid Parkhomenko, G. KarelinA. 42M USS. *The Colt* (USA); *Zerebenok*; *The Foal*; *Zherebenok*

SHORE, VIOLA BROTHERS
Notices, Story
Hit of the Show 1928 d: Ralph Ince. lps: Joe E. Brown, Gertrude Olmstead, William Bailey. 6476f USA. prod/rel: Fbo Pictures

On the Shelf, 1922, Short Story
Let Women Alone 1925 d: Paul Powell. lps: Pat O'Malley, Wanda Hawley, Wallace Beery. 5620f USA. *On the Dotted Line*; *On the Shelf*; *The Dotted Line* prod/rel: Peninsula Studios, Producers Distributing Corp.

The Prince of Head Waiters, 1927, Short Story
Prince of Headwaiters, The 1927 d: John Francis Dillon. lps: Lewis Stone, Priscilla Bonner, E. J. Ratcliffe. 6400f USA. prod/rel: Sam E. Rork Productions, First National Pictures

SHORES, DEL
Daddy's Dyin' Who's Got the Will, Play
Daddy's Dyin', Who's Got the Will 1990 d: Jack Fisk. lps: Beau Bridges, Beverly d'Angelo, Tess Harper. 95M USA. prod/rel: Artist Circle Entertainment, Propaganda Films

SHORR, ANSHEL
Shir Hashirim, Play
Shir Hashirim 1935 d: Henry Lynn. lps: Samuel Goldenberg, Dora Weissman, Max Kletter. 70M USA. *Song of Songs* prod/rel: Empire Film Co., Henry Lynn Production

SHORT, LUKE
Story
Hangman, The 1959 d: Michael Curtiz. lps: Robert Taylor, Fess Parker, Tina Louise. 86M USA. Paramount

Albuquerque, Novel
Albuquerque 1948 d: Ray Enright. lps: Randolph Scott, Barbara Britton, George Hayes. 90M USA. *Silver City* (UKN) prod/rel: Paramount

Ambush, Short Story
Ambush 1949 d: Sam Wood. lps: Robert Taylor, John Hodiak, Arlene Dahl. 89M USA. prod/rel: Metro-Goldwyn-Mayer Corp.

Coroner Creek, Novel
Coroner Creek 1948 d: Ray Enright. lps: Randolph Scott, Marguerite Chapman, George MacReady. 90M USA. *Coroner's Creek* prod/rel: Columbia

Gunman's Choice, Novel
Blood on the Moon 1948 d: Robert Wise. lps: Robert Mitchum, Robert Preston, Barbara Bel Geddes. 88M USA. prod/rel: RKO Radio

High Vermilion, 1948, Novel
Silver City 1951 d: Byron Haskin. lps: Yvonne de Carlo, Edmond O'Brien, Barry Fitzgerald. 90M USA. *High Vermilion* (UKN) prod/rel: Paramount

Ramrod, Short Story
Ramrod 1947 d: Andre de Toth. lps: Joel McCrea, Veronica Lake, Donald Crisp. 94M USA. prod/rel: United Artists

Silver Rock, 1953, Novel
Hell's Outpost 1954 d: Joseph Kane. lps: Rod Cameron, John Russell, Joan Leslie. 90M USA. prod/rel: Republic

Station West, Novel
Station West 1948 d: Sidney Lanfield. lps: Dick Powell, Jane Greer, Agnes Moorehead. 92M USA. prod/rel: RKO Radio

Vengeance Valley, 1950, Novel
Vengeance Valley 1950 d: Richard Thorpe. lps: Burt Lancaster, Robert Walker, Joanne Dru. 83M USA. prod/rel: MGM

SHORT, MARION
The Girl from Out Yonder, Baltimore 1914, Play
Out Yonder 1920 d: Ralph Ince. lps: Olive Thomas, Huntley Gordon, Mary Coverdale. 5-6r USA. prod/rel: Selznick Pictures Corp.©, Select Pictures Corp.

The Waiting Soul, 1914, Short Story
Waiting Soul, The 1917 d: Burton L. King. lps: Olga Petrova, Mahlon Hamilton, Mathilde Brundage. 5r USA. prod/rel: Popular Plays and Players, Inc.©, Metro Pictures Corp.

SHOSTAKOVICH, DIMITRIY (1906-1975), RSS, Shostakovich, Dmitry Dmitryevich
Moskva Cheryomushki, Moscow 1959, Opera
Cheryomushki 1963 d: Herbert Rappaport. lps: Olga Zabotkina, Vladimir Vasilyev, M. KhotuntsevA. 92M USS. *Song Over Moscow* (USA); *Wild Cherry Trees*; *Cheremushki* prod/rel: Lenfilm

SHRANK, JOSEPH
Larger Than Life, Springfield, MA. 1936, Play
He Couldn't Say No 1938 d: Lewis Seiler. lps: Frank McHugh, Jane Wyman, Cora Witherspoon. 61M USA. *Larger Than Life* prod/rel: Warner Bros. Pictures©

Page Miss Glory, New York 1934, Play
Page Miss Glory 1935 d: Mervyn Leroy. lps: Marion Davies, Pat O'Brien, Dick Powell. 90M USA. prod/rel: Warner Bros. Productions Corp., Cosmopolitan Production

SHU HUI
Huanghua Ling, Novel
Huanghua Ling 1956 d: Jin Shan. lps: Cui Wei, Zhang Yunfang, Wang Ban. 7r CHN. *Huanghua Mountain Ridge* prod/rel: Central Newsreel & Doc. Film Studio

SHU PING
Evening News, Novel
You Hua Hao Hao Shuo 1997 d: Zhang Yimou. lps: Jiang Wen, Li Baotian, Qu Ying. 94M CHN. *Keep Cool* prod/rel: Guang XI Film Studio

SHU QINGCHUN, Lao She
Cha Guan, 1964, Play
Cha Guan 1982 d: XIe Tian. lps: Yu Shizhi, Zhen Rong, Lan Tianye. 125M CHN. *Ch'a-Kuan*; *Teahouse* prod/rel: Beijing Film Studio

Fang Zhenzhu, 1950, Play
Fang Zhenzhu 1952 d: Xu Changlin. lps: Tao Jin, Little Wang Yurong, Sun Jinglu. 109M CHN. prod/rel: Da Guang Ming Film Company

Gushu Yiren, 194-, Novel
Gushu Yiren 1987 d: Tian Zhuangzhuang. lps: Li Xuejian, Tan Mindi, Chen Qin. 98M CHN. *Travelling Players*; *Gu Shu Yi Ren*; *The Drum Singers* prod/rel: Beijing Film Studio

Longxu Gou, 1950, Play
Longxu Gou 1952 d: XIan Qun. lps: Yu Shizhi, Yu Lan, Zhang FA. 119M CHN. *Dragon Beard Ditch* prod/rel: Beijing Film Studio

Luo Tou XIangzi, 1944, Novel
Luo Tou XIangzi 1982 d: Ling Zhifeng. lps: Zhang Fengyi, Siqin Gaowa, Yan Bide. 117M CHN. *Rickshaw Boy*; *Luotuo XIangzi*; *Camel XIangzi* prod/rel: Beijing Film Studio

Wo Zhe Yibeizi, 1949, Short Story
Wo Zhe Yibeizi 1950 d: Shi Hui. lps: Shi Hui, Wei Heling, Shen Yang. 119M CHN. *This Life of Mine* prod/rel: Wenhua Film Company

Yue Yaer, 194-, Short Story
Yue Yaer 1986 d: Sun Yu. 93M CHN.

SHUKLA, KUMAR
Naukar Ki Kameez, Novel
Naukar Ki Kameez 1999 d: Mani Kaul. lps: Pankaj Sudhir Mishra, Anu Joseph, Om Praksh Dwivedi. 107M IND/NTH. *The Servant's Shirt* prod/rel: Ant Carry the Mountain Films, ZDF-Arte (Germany)

SHULMAN, ARNOLD
The Heart's a Forgotten Hotel, 1955, Television Play
Hole in the Head, A 1959 d: Frank CaprA. lps: Frank Sinatra, Edward G. Robinson, Eleanor Parker. 120M USA. prod/rel: United Artists, Sincap

SHULMAN, IRVING (1913–1995), USA
The Amboy Dukes, Novel
City Across the River 1949 d: Maxwell Shane. lps: Peter Fernandez, Al Ramsen, Joshua Shelley. 90M USA. *The Amboy Dukes* prod/rel: Universal-International

Cry Tough, 1949, Novel
Cry Tough 1959 d: Paul Stanley. lps: John Saxon, Linda Cristal, Joseph CalleiA. 83M USA. prod/rel: United Artists, Canon

Harlow: an Intimate Biography, New York 1964, Book
Harlow 1965 d: Gordon Douglas. lps: Carroll Baker, Martin Balsam, Red Buttons. 126M USA. prod/rel: Paramount Pictures, Embassy Pictures

SHULMAN, MAX
Rally 'Round the Flag Boys!, 1957, Novel
Rally 'Round the Flag, Boys! 1958 d: Leo McCarey. lps: Paul Newman, Joanne Woodward, Joan Collins. 106M USA. prod/rel: 20th Century-Fox

The Tender Trap, New York 1954, Play
Tender Trap, The 1955 d: Charles Walters. lps: Frank Sinatra, Debbie Reynolds, Celeste Holm. 111M USA. prod/rel: MGM

SHULMAN, NEIL B.
What?. Dead Again, Novel
Doc Hollywood 1991 d: Michael Caton-Jones. lps: Michael J. Fox, Julie Warner, Bridget FondA. 104M USA. prod/rel: Warner Bros.

SHUO YUNPING
I Am a Soldier, Play
Gi Lia Hao 1962 d: Yan Jizhou. lps: Zhang Liang, Zhang Yongshou, Zing Jitian. 9r CHN. *Brothers* prod/rel: August First Film Studio

SHUTE, JAMES
Return Engagement, 1936, Play
Fools for Scandal 1938 d: Mervyn Leroy. lps: Carole Lombard, Fernand Gravey, Ralph Bellamy. 85M USA. *Food for Scandal* prod/rel: Warner Bros. Pictures©

SHUTE, NEVIL (1899–1960), UKN, Norway, Nevil Shute
The Far Country, Novel
Far Country, The 1986 d: George Miller. lps: Michael York, Sigrid Thornton, Don Barker. TVM. 205M ASL. *Nevil Shute's the Far Country* prod/rel: Crawford Prod.

Landfall, 1940, Novel
Landfall 1949 d: Ken Annakin. lps: Michael Denison, Patricia Plunkett, Kathleen Harrison. 88M UKN. prod/rel: Associated British-Pathe, Associated British Picture Corporation

The Lonely Road, 1932, Novel
Lonely Road, The 1936 d: James Flood. lps: Clive Brook, Victoria Hopper, Nora Swinburne. 80M UKN. *Scotland Yard Commands* prod/rel: Associated Talking Pictures, Associated British Film Distributors

No Highway, 1948, Novel
No Highway 1951 d: Henry Koster. lps: James Stewart, Marlene Dietrich, Glynis Johns. 99M UKN/USA. *No Highway in the Sky* (USA) prod/rel: 20th Century Productions, 20th Century-Fox

On the Beach, 1957, Novel
On the Beach 1959 d: Stanley Kramer. lps: Gregory Peck, Ava Gardner, Fred Astaire. 135M USA. prod/rel: United Artists, Lomitas Prods.

The Pied Piper, 1942, Novel
Crossing to Freedom 1990 d: Norman Stone. lps: Peter O'Toole, Mare Winningham, Susan Wooldridge. TVM. 100M UKN/USA. *Pied Piper* prod/rel: Granada Films

Pied Piper, The 1942 d: Irving Pichel. lps: Monty Woolley, Roddy McDowall, Anne Baxter. 87M USA. prod/rel: 20th Century-Fox

A Town Like Alice, 1950, Novel
Town Like Alice, A 1956 d: Jack Lee. lps: Virginia McKenna, Peter Finch, Marie Lohr. 117M UKN. *The Rape of Malaya* prod/rel: Vic Films, Rank Film Distributors

Town Like Alice, A 1981 d: David Stevens. lps: Helen Morse, Bryan Brown, Gordon Jackson. MTV. 300M ASL.

SICILIANO, ENZO
La Coppia, Novel
Coppia, La 1968 d: Enzo Siciliano. lps: Anita Sanders, Christian Hay, Massimo Girotti. 91M ITL. *The Couple* prod/rel: Panda

SIDDONS, ANNE RIVERS
Heartbreak Hotel, Novel
  Heart of Dixie 1988 d: Martin Davidson. lps: Ally Sheedy, Virginia Madsen, Phoebe Cates. 95M USA. prod/rel: Orion

SIDHWA, BAPSY (1938–, PKS, Siddhwa, Bapsi
The Ice-Candy Man, Novel
  Earth 1998 d: Deepa MehtA. lps: Nandita Das, Aamir Khan, Rahul KhannA. 108M IND/CND. prod/rel: Kaleidoscope-India, Cracking Earth Films (Canada)

SIDNEY, MARGARET
Five Little Peppers Abroad, Boston 1902, Novel
  Out West With the Peppers 1940 d: Charles T. Barton. lps: Edith Fellows, Dorothy Ann Seese, Dorothy Peterson. 63M USA. prod/rel: Columbia Pictures Corp.©
Five Little Peppers and How They Grew, Boston 1881, Novel
  Five Little Peppers and How They Grew 1939 d: Charles T. Barton. lps: Edith Fellows, Dorothy Ann Seese, Dorothy Peterson. 58M USA. *Five Little Peppers* prod/rel: Columbia Pictures Corp.©
Five Little Peppers at School, Boston 1903, Novel
  Five Little Peppers in Trouble 1940 d: Charles T. Barton. lps: Edith Fellows, Dorothy Ann Seese, Dorothy Peterson. 65M USA. *Five Little Peppers at School* prod/rel: Columbia Pictures Corp.©
Five Little Peppers Midway, Boston 1890, Novel
  Five Little Peppers at Home 1940 d: Charles T. Barton. lps: Edith Fellows, Dorothy Ann Seese, Dorothy Peterson. 67M USA. *Five Little Peppers Midway* prod/rel: Columbia Pictures Corp.©

SIEGAL, WILLIAM
Forgotten Mothers, 1937, Play
  Where Is My Child? 1937 d: Abraham Leff. lps: Celia Adler, Solomon Steinberg, Morris Silberkasten. 95M USA. *Vu Iz Mayn Kind?* prod/rel: Menorah Productions©

SIEGEL, MAX
We Americans, New York 1926, Play
  We Americans 1928 d: Edward Sloman. lps: George Sidney, Patsy Ruth Miller, George Lewis. 8700f USA. *The Heart of a Nation* (UKN) prod/rel: Universal Pictures

SIEKIERSKI, A.
Paciorki Jednego Rozanca, Short Story
  Paciorki Jednego Rozanca 1979 d: Kazimierz Kutz. lps: Marta Strazna, Augustyn Hallota, Ewa WisniewskA. 117M PLN. *A Glass-Bead Rosary*; *The Beads of One Rosary*; *Beads of the Same Rosary* prod/rel: Prf-Zespol Filmowy

SIENKIEWICZ, HENRYK (1846–1916), PLN
Short Story
  Anna 1920 d: Giuseppe de Liguoro. lps: Cecyl Tryan, Guido Trento. 1338m ITL. prod/rel: Gladiator
Janko Muzykant, 1879, Short Story
  Janko Muzykant 1930 d: Ryszard Ordynski. 103M PLN.
Krzyzacy, 1900, Novel
  Krzyzacy 1960 d: Aleksander Ford. lps: Urszula Modrzynska, Mieczyslaw Kalenik, Grazyna StaniszewskA. 175M PLN. *The Knights of the Teutonic Order* (USA); *Knights of the Black Cross*; *Black Cross*; *Teutonic Knights* prod/rel: Studio Film Unit
Ogniem I Mieczem, 1884, Short Story
  Col Ferro E Col Fuoco 1962 d: Fernando Cerchio. lps: Jeanne Crain, John Drew Barrymore, Pierre Brice. 112M FRN/ITL/YGS. *Par le Fer Et Par le Feu* (FRN); *Invasion 1700* (USA); *With Fire and Sword*; *Fire and Sword*; *Daggers of Blood* prod/rel: Europa Cin.Ca (Roma), Comptoir Francais Du Film (Paris)
Pan Wolodyjowski, 1887, Novel
  Pan Wolodyjowski 1969 d: Jerzy Hoffman. lps: Tadeusz Lomnicki, Daniel Olbrychksi, Mieczyslaw Pawlikowski. 155M PLN. *Colonel Wolodyjowski* (UKN); *The Little Knight*; *Pan Michael*
Potop, 1886, Novel
  Potop 1974 d: Jerzy Hoffman. lps: Daniel Olbrychski, Malgorzata Braunek, Tadeusz Lomnicki. 314M PLN. *The Deluge* (USA); *The Flood* prod/rel: Film Polski
Quo Vadis?, 1896, Novel
  Au Temps Des Premiers Chretiens 1910 d: Andre Calmettes. lps: Albert Lambert, Philippe Garnier, Georges Dorival. FRN. prod/rel: Film d'Art
  Quo Vadis? 1913 d: Enrico Guazzoni. lps: Amleto Novelli, Lea Giunchi, Gustavo SerenA. 2250m ITL. prod/rel: Cines
  Quo Vadis? 1924 d: Gabriellino d'Annunzio, Georg Jacoby. lps: Emil Jannings, Elena Sangro, Alfons Fryland. 3308m ITL. prod/rel: Arturo Ambrosio
  Quo Vadis? 1951 d: Mervyn Leroy. lps: Robert Taylor, Deborah Kerr, Leo Genn. 168M USA. prod/rel: MGM

  Quo Vadis? 1985 d: Franco Rossi. lps: Klaus Maria Brandauer, Frederic Forrest, Cristina Raines. TVM. 360M ITL.
Szkice Weglem, 1877, Short Story
  Szkice Weglem 1957 d: Antoni Bohdziewicz. lps: Wieslaw Golas, Barbara WalkownA. 97M PLN. *Charcoal Sketches*; *Sketches in Charcoal*
W Pustyni I W Puszczy, 1911, Novel
  W Pustyni I W Puszczy 1972 d: Wladyslaw Slesicki. lps: Tomasz Medrzak, Monika Rosca, Ahmed Marei. 193M PLN. *In Desert and Jungle*; *In Desert and Wilderness*; *In the Desert and in a Wilderness* prod/rel: Film Polski

SIERRA, DANTE
La Cigarra No Es un Bicho, Buenos Aires 1957, Novel
  Cigarra No Es un Bicho, La 1963 d: Daniel Tinayre. lps: Maria Antinea, Amelia Bence, Elsa Daniel. 107M ARG. *The Games Men Play* (USA); *The Cicada Is Not an Insect*; *The Hotel* prod/rel: Tinayre-Borras S.R.L.

SIFTON, CLAIRE
Midnight, New York 1930, Play
  Midnight 1934 d: Chester Erskine. lps: Sidney Fox, O. P. Heggie, Henry Hull. 80M USA. *Call It Murder* prod/rel: All Star Productions, Universal Pictures Corp.©

SIFTON, PAUL
Midnight, New York 1930, Play
  Midnight 1934 d: Chester Erskine. lps: Sidney Fox, O. P. Heggie, Henry Hull. 80M USA. *Call It Murder* prod/rel: All Star Productions, Universal Pictures Corp.©

SIGNOL, CHRISTIAN
Soleil d'Automne
  Soleil d'Automne 1992 d: Jacques Ertaud. lps: Philippe Rouleau, Catherine Allegret, Anny Romand. TVM. 90M FRN/SWT.

SIGURDARDOTTIR, STEINUNN
Voleur de Vie, Novel
  Voleur de Vie 1998 d: Yves Angelo. lps: Emmanuelle Beart, Sandrine Bonnaire, Andre Dussollier. 104M FRN. *Stolen Life* prod/rel: Film Par France, France 3 Cinema

SILLANPAA, FRANS E. (1888–1964), FNL
Elama Ja Aurinko, 1916, Novel
  Poika Eli Kesaansa 1955 d: Roland Hallstrom. lps: Eila Pieitsalo, Tea Ista, Pertti Weckstrom. 78M FNL. *Hans Forsta Sommar* prod/rel: Fennada-Filmi
Elokuu, 1941, Novel
  Elokuu 1956 d: Matti KassilA. lps: Emma Vaananen, Senni Nieminen. 90M FNL. *August*; *Harvest Month*
Ihmiselon Ihanuus Ja Kurjuus, 1945, Novel
  Ihmiselon Ihanuus Ja Kurjuus 1988 d: Matti KassilA. lps: Liisa-Maija Laaksonen, Tarja Keinanen, Lasse Poysti. 95M FNL. *The Glory and Misery of Human Life*; *The Beauty and Misery of Human Life*
Ihmiset Suviyossa, 1934, Novel
  Ihmiset Suviyossa 1949 d: Valentin VaalA. lps: Martti Katajisto, Kaisu Leppanen, Eero Roine. 66M FNL. *People of the Summer Night*
Miehen Tie, 1932, Novel
  Miehen Tie 1940 d: Nyrki Tapiovaara, Erik Blomberg. lps: Gunnar Hiilloskorpi, Mirjami Kuosmanen, Hugo Hytonen. 93M FNL. *The Way of a Man*; *One Man's Fate*; *En Mans Vag* prod/rel: Eloseppo
Nuorena Nukkunut, 1931, Novel
  Nuorena Nukkunut 1937 d: Teuvo Tulio. lps: Regina Linnanheimo, Otso Pera, Kille Oksanen. 97M FNL. *Silja - Fallen Asleep When Young*; *Silja* prod/rel: Adams Filmi
  Silja - Nuorena Nukkunut 1956 d: Jack WitikkA. lps: Heidi Krohn, Jussi Jurkka, Aku Korhonen. 91M FNL. *Silja - Fallen Asleep When Young*; *Silja* prod/rel: Veikko Itkonen

SILLIPHANT, STIRLING (1918–1996), USA
Huk!, Novel
  Huk! 1956 d: John Barnwell. lps: George Montgomery, Mona Freeman, John Baer. 84M USA. prod/rel: United Artists, Pan Pacific Pictures
Maracaibo, 1955, Novel
  Maracaibo 1958 d: Cornel Wilde. lps: Cornel Wilde, Jean Wallace, Abbe Lane. 88M USA. prod/rel: Paramount, Theodora Prods.

SILLITOE, ALAN (1928–, UKN
The General, 1960, Novel
  Counterpoint 1968 d: Ralph Nelson. lps: Charlton Heston, Maximilian Schell, Kathryn Hays. 107M USA. *The Battle Hours* prod/rel: Universal

The Loneliness of the Long-Distance Runner, London 1959, Short Story
  Loneliness of the Long Distance Runner, The 1962 d: Tony Richardson. lps: Michael Redgrave, Tom Courtenay, Avis Bunnage. 104M UKN. *Rebel With a Cause* prod/rel: Woodfall Film Production, Bryanston
The Ragman's Daughter, 1963, Short Story
  Ragman's Daughter, The 1972 d: Harold Becker. lps: Simon Rouse, Victoria Tennant, Patrick O'Connell. 94M UKN. *The Tea-Leaf* prod/rel: 20th Century Fox, Penelope
Saturday Night and Sunday Morning, London 1958, Novel
  Saturday Night and Sunday Morning 1960 d: Karel Reisz. lps: Albert Finney, Shirley Anne Field, Rachel Roberts. 89M UKN. prod/rel: Woodfall Film Production, Bryanston

SILONE, IGNAZIO (1900–1978), ITL, Tranquilli, Secondo
Fontamara, 1930, Novel
  Fontamara 1980 d: Carlo Lizzani. lps: Michele Placido, Antonella Murgia, Marina Confalone. 135M ITL. prod/rel: Erre, Rai

SILVA, AGUINALDO
Republica Dos Assassinos, 1976, Novel
  Republica Dos Assassinos 1979 d: Miguel Faria Junior. 100M BRZ.

SILVA, MARIO
Song of Love, Play
  Song of Love 1947 d: Clarence Brown. lps: Katharine Hepburn, Paul Henreid, Robert Walker. 119M USA. prod/rel: MGM

SILVER, MURRAY
Book
  Great Balls of Fire 1989 d: Jim McBride. lps: Dennis Quaid, Winona Ryder, Alec Baldwin. 102M USA. prod/rel: Orion, Adam Fields Prods.

SILVERMAN, AL
Foster and Laurie, Book
  Foster and Laurie 1975 d: John Llewellyn Moxey. lps: Perry King, Dorian Harewood, Talia Shire. TVM. 100M USA. prod/rel: Charles Fries Productions

SIMA WENSEN
Stormy Tong River, Novel
  Huanle Yingxiong 1988 d: Wu Ziniu. lps: Tao Zeru, Xu Shouli, Shen Junyi. 18r CHN. *The Joyous Heroes*; *To Die Like a Man* prod/rel: Fujian Film Studio
  Yinyang Jie 1988 d: Wu Ziniu. lps: Tao Zeru, Xu Shouli, Shen Junyi. F CHN. *The Realm Between the Living and the Dead*; *Between Life and Death*; *The Dead and the Living*; *Huang le Ying Xlong Part 2* prod/rel: Fujian Film Studio

SIMACEK, MATEJ ANASTAZIA
Jiny Vzduch, Play
  Jiny Vzduch 1939 d: Martin Fric. lps: Frantisek Smolik, Zdenka Baldova, Hana VitovA. 2365m CZC. *Fresh Air*; *Another Air*; *A Different Air*; *Changing Wind* prod/rel: UFA

SIMENON, GEORGES (1903–1989), BLG
Novel
  Anderer Liebhaber, Ein 1990 d: Xaver Schwarzenberger. lps: Karlheinz Hackl, Friedrich von Thun, Alexander May. TVM. 94M GRM/FRN. prod/rel: Tele-Munchen, Hamster
  Mann, Der Sich Verdachtig machte, Der 1989 d: Yves Boisset. lps: Philippe Leotard, Jean-Pierre Bisson, Claire Nadeau. 77M GRM/FRN. prod/rel: Hamster, ZDF
  Ours En Peluche, L' 1988 d: Edouard Logereau. lps: Claude Rich, Catherine Salvat, Anne-Marie Dreville. TVM. 85M FRN.
  Prison, The 1975 d: David Wickes. lps: James Laurenson, Ann Curthoys, James Maxwell. MTV. 78M UKN. prod/rel: Thames Tv, Euston Films
L' Affaire Saint-Fiacre, 1932, Novel
  Maigret Et l'Affaire Saint-Fiacre 1959 d: Jean Delannoy. lps: Jean Gabin, Michel Auclair, Valentine Tessier. 98M FRN/ITL. prod/rel: Filmsonor, Intermondia Films
L' Aine Des Ferchaux, 1945, Novel
  Aine Des Ferchaux, L' 1963 d: Jean-Pierre Melville. lps: Jean-Paul Belmondo, Charles Vanel, Michele Mercier. 102M FRN/ITL. *Lo Sciacallo* (ITL); *Magnet of Doom*; *Un Jeune Homme*; *Un Jeune Homme Honorable* prod/rel: Spectacles Lumbroso, Ultra Film
Annette Et la Dame Blonde, 1963, Short Story
  Annette Et la Dame Blonde 1941 d: Jean Dreville. lps: Louise Carletti, Henri Garat, Georges Rollin. 85M FRN. prod/rel: Continental-Films

427

L' Assassin, 1937, Novel
Morder, Der 1978 d: Ottokar Runze. lps: Gerhard Olschewski, Johanna Liebeneiner, Wolfgang Wahl. 107M GRM. *The Murderer* prod/rel: Aurora Television, Ottokar Runze

Le Baron de l'Ecluse, 1954, Short Story
Baron de l'Ecluse, Le 1959 d: Jean Delannoy. lps: Jean Gabin, Micheline Presle, Jean Desailly. 95M FRN/ITL. *Il Barone* (ITL) prod/rel: Filmsonor, Intermondia

Le Bateau d'Emile, 1954, Short Story
Bateau d'Emile, Le 1962 d: Denys de La Patelliere. lps: Lino Ventura, Annie Girardot, Pierre Brasseur. 100M FRN/ITL. *Fortuna E Femmine Letto* (ITL) prod/rel: Filmsonor, Intermondia

Betty, 1961, Novel
Betty 1992 d: Claude Chabrol. lps: Marie Trintignant, Stephane Audran, Jean-Francois Garreaud. 103M FRN.

Les Caves du Majestic, 1942, Short Story
Caves du Majestic, Les 1944 d: Richard Pottier. lps: Albert Prejean, Jacques Baumer, Suzy Prim. 100M FRN. prod/rel: Continental-Films

Cecile Est Morte, 1942, Short Story
Cecile Est Morte 1943 d: Maurice Tourneur. lps: Santa Relli, Albert Prejean, Andre Gabriello. 90M FRN. prod/rel: Continental-Films

Le Chat, 1967, Novel
Chat, Le 1971 d: Pierre Granier-Deferre. lps: Jean Gabin, Simone Signoret, Annie Cordy. 97M FRN/ITL. *Le Chat -L'implacabile Uomo Di Saint Germain* (ITL); *The Cat* prod/rel: Unitas Film, Lira Films

Chez Krull, Novel
Mouchoir de Joseph, Le 1988 d: Jacques Fansten. lps: Piotr Shivak, Isabelle Sadoyan, Catherine Frot. TVM. 96M FRN.

Le Chien Jaune, 1931, Novel
Chien Jaune, Le 1932 d: Jean Tarride. lps: Abel Tarride, Rosine Derean, Jane Lory. 88M FRN. prod/rel: Etablissements Petit

La Danseuse du Gai-Moulin, 1931, Novel
Maigret Und Sein Grosster Fall 1966 d: Alfred Weidenmann. lps: Heinz Ruhmann, Francoise Prevost, Alexander Kerst. 90M AUS/ITL/FRN. *Il Caso Difficile Del Commissario Maigret* (ITL); *Maigret Fait Mouche* (FRN); *Enter Inspector Maigret* (USA) prod/rel: Intercontinental, Terra

En Cas de Malheur, 1956, Novel
En Cas de Malheur 1958 d: Claude Autant-LarA. lps: Jean Gabin, Brigitte Bardot, Franco Interlenghi. 122M FRN/ITL. *La Ragazza Del Peccato* (ITL); *Love Is My Profession* (USA) prod/rel: Iena, Raoul-J. Levy
En Plein Coeur 1998 d: Pierre Jolivet. lps: Gerard Lanvin, Virginie Ledoyen, Caroline Bouquet. 101M FRN. *In All Innocence* prod/rel: Bac Films, Legende Enterprises

L' Enterrement de Monsieur Bouvet, Novel
Enterrement de Monsieur Bouvet, L' 1981 d: Guy-Andre Lefranc. lps: Renee Faure, Jacqueline Doyen, Mireille Perrey. 90M FRN. prod/rel: Maintenon, TF 1

Les Fantomes du Chapelier, 1949, Short Story
Fantomes du Chapelier, Les 1981 d: Claude Chabrol. lps: Michel Serrault, Charles Aznavour, Monique Chaumette. 120M FRN. *The Hatter's Ghosts; The Hatmaker* prod/rel: Horizons, S.F.P.C.

Les Fiancailles de Mr. Hire, 1933, Novel
Monsieur Hire 1988 d: Patrice Leconte. lps: Michel Blanc, Sandrine Bonnaire, Luc Thuillier. 88M FRN. *Monsieur Hire's Engagement* prod/rel: Hachette Premiere Et Cie, Cinea
Panique 1946 d: Julien Duvivier. lps: Michel Simon, Paul Bernard, Charles Dorat. 100M FRN. *Panic* (USA) prod/rel: Filmsonor

Le Fils Cardinaud, 1942, Novel
Sang a la Tete, Le 1956 d: Gilles Grangier. lps: Jean Gabin, Paul Frankeur, Claude Sylvain. 83M FRN. prod/rel: Film Fernand Rivers

Le Fond de la Bouteille, 1949, Short Story
Bottom of the Bottle, The 1956 d: Henry Hathaway. lps: Van Johnson, Joseph Cotten, Ruth Roman. 88M USA. *Beyond the River* (UKN) prod/rel: 20th Century-Fox

Les Freres Rico, 1952, Short Story
Brothers Rico, The 1956 d: Phil Karlson. lps: Richard Conte, Dianne Foster, Kathryn Grant. 92M USA. prod/rel: Columbia, William Goetz
Family Rico, The 1972 d: Paul Wendkos. lps: Ben Gazzara, Sal Mineo, Dane Clark. TVM. 73M USA. prod/rel: CBS Inc.

L' Homme de Londres, 1934, Novel
Homme de Londres, L' 1943 d: Henri Decoin. lps: Fernand Ledoux, Jules Berry, Suzy Prim. 98M FRN. prod/rel: S.P.D.F.
Temptation Harbour 1947 d: Lance Comfort. lps: Robert Newton, Simone Simon, William Hartnell. 104M UKN. prod/rel: Associated British, Pathe

L' Homme Qui Regardait Passer Les Trains, 1938, Novel
Man Who Watched Trains Go By, The 1952 d: Harold French. lps: Claude Rains, Marta Toren, Marius Goring. 80M UKN. *Paris Express* (USA); *The Man Who Watched the Trains Go By* prod/rel: Raymond Stross, Eros

L' Horloger d'Everton, 1954, Short Story
Horloger de St. Paul, L' 1973 d: Bertrand Tavernier. lps: Philippe Noiret, Jean Rochefort, Jacques Denis. 105M FRN. *The Watchmaker of St. Paul* (UKN); *The Clockmaker; The Clockmaker of St. Paul* (USA) prod/rel: Lira Films

Les Inconnus Dans la Maison, Paris 1940, Novel
Inconnus Dans la Maison, Les 1941 d: Henri Decoin. lps: Raimu, Juliette Faber, Jacques Baumer. F FRN. *Strangers in the House* prod/rel: Continental-Films
Stranger in the House 1967 d: Pierre Rouve. lps: James Mason, Geraldine Chaplin, Bobby Darin. 104M UKN. *Cop-Out* (USA) prod/rel: Rank Film Distributors, de Grunwald

Lettre a Mon Juge, 1947, Novel
Fruit Defendu, Le 1952 d: Henri Verneuil. lps: Fernandel, Francoise Arnoul, Claude Nollier. 99M FRN. *Forbidden Fruit* prod/rel: Gray Films, A. D'aguiar

Le Locataire, 1934, Novel
Dernier Refuge 1946 d: Marc Maurette. lps: Raymond Rouleau, Giselle Pascal, Mila Parely. 90M FRN. prod/rel: Films Malesherbes
Etoile du Nord, L' 1982 d: Pierre Granier-Deferre. lps: Philippe Noiret, Simone Signoret, Fanny Cottencon. 120M FRN. *The Northern Star* (USA) prod/rel: Sara Films, Antenne 2

Maigret Au "Picratt's", 1951, Novel
Maigret a Pigalle 1966 d: Mario Landi. lps: Gino Cervi, Lila Kedrova, Raymond Pellegrin. 105M ITL/FRN. prod/rel: Riganti Prod. Cin.Ca (Roma), Les Films Number One (Paris)

Maigret, Lognon Et Les Gangsters, 1952, Novel
Maigret Voit Rouge 1963 d: Gilles Grangier. lps: Jean Gabin, Guy Decomble, Paul Carpenter. 90M FRN/ITL. *Maigret E I Gangsters* (ITL) prod/rel: Films Copernic, Ultra

Maigret Tend un Piege, 1955, Novel
Maigret Tend un Piege 1957 d: Jean Delannoy. lps: Jean Gabin, Annie Girardot, Jean Desailly. 116M FRN/ITL. *Maigret Sets a Trap* (UKN); *Inspector Maigret* (USA); *Woman Bait* prod/rel: Jolly Film, Intermondia Films

La Main, Novel
Zweite Leben, Das 1990 d: Carlo RolA. lps: Vadim Glowna, Iris Berben, Monika Lundi. TVM. 76M GRM/FRN.

La Maison Des Sept Jeunes Filles, 1941, Novel
Maison Des Sept Jeunes Filles, La 1941 d: Albert Valentin. lps: Andre Brunot, Jean Paqui, Jacqueline Pagnol. 100M FRN. prod/rel: Regina
Seven Sweethearts 1942 d: Frank Borzage. lps: Kathryn Grayson, Van Heflin, Marsha Hunt. 98M USA. *Seven Girls* prod/rel: MGM

La Marie du Port, 1938, Novel
Marie du Port, La 1949 d: Marcel Carne. lps: Blanchette Brunoy, Nicole Courcel, Jean Gabin. 88M FRN. prod/rel: Sacha Gordine

Monsieur la Souris, 1938, Novel
Midnight Episode 1950 d: Gordon Parry. lps: Stanley Holloway, Leslie Dwyer, Reginald Tate. 78M UKN. prod/rel: Columbia, Triangle
Monsieur la Souris 1942 d: Georges Lacombe. lps: Raimu, Aime Clariond, Charles Granval. 106M FRN. *Midnight in Paris* (USA); *Mr. Mouse* prod/rel: Films Richebe

La Mort de Belle, Paris 1952, Novel
Mort de Belle, La 1961 d: Edouard Molinaro, Terry Curtis. lps: Jean Desailly, Alexandra Stewart, Monique Melinand. 100M FRN. *The Passion of Slow Fire* (USA); *The End of Belle* prod/rel: Cinephonic, Francois Chavane

La Neige Etait Sale, 1948, Novel
Neige Etait Sale, La 1952 d: Luis Saslavsky. lps: Daniel Gelin, Valentine Tessier, Antoine Balpetre. 104M FRN. *The Snow Was Black* (USA); *The Stain on the Snow; La Nieve Estaba Sucia* prod/rel: Tellus Films

La Nuit du Carrefour, 1931, Novel
Nuit du Carrefour, La 1932 d: Jean Renoir. lps: Pierre Renoir, Winna Winfried, Dignimont. 75M FRN. *Night at the Crossroads* prod/rel: Europa-Films

Le Passager Clandestin, 1947, Novel
Passager Clandestin, Le 1960 d: Ralph Habib. lps: Martine Carol, Karlheinz Bohm, Roger Livesey. 98M FRN/ASL. *The Stowaway* prod/rel: Disci Films, Silver Films

Le President, 1958, Novel
President, Le 1960 d: Henri Verneuil. lps: Jean Gabin, Bernard Blier, Renee Faure. 110M FRN/ITL. *Il Presidente* (ITL); *The President* (UKN); *Money Money Money* (USA) prod/rel: Cite Films, Terra Films

Signe Picpus, 1944, Short Story
Picpus 1942 d: Richard Pottier. lps: Albert Prejean, Jean Tissier, Juliette Faber. 95M FRN. *Signe Picpus* prod/rel: Continental Films

La Tete d'un Homme, 1931, Novel
Man on the Eiffel Tower, The 1949 d: Burgess Meredith. lps: Charles Laughton, Franchot Tone, Burgess Meredith. 98M USA/FRN. *L' Homme de la Tour Eiffel* prod/rel: RKO Radio
Tete d'un Homme, La 1932 d: Julien Duvivier. lps: Harry Baur, Valery Inkijinoff, Gina Manes. 100M FRN. prod/rel: Vandal Et Delac

Le Train de Venise, Novel
Train de Vienne, Le 1989 d: Caroline Huppert. lps: Roland Blanche, Therese Liotard, Christophe Odent. TVM. 96M GRM/FRN/SWT.

Le Train, 1961, Novel
Train, Le 1973 d: Pierre Granier-Deferre. lps: Romy Schneider, Jean-Louis Trintignant, Nike Arrighi. 101M FRN/ITL. *Noi Due Senza Domani* (ITL); *The Last Train* prod/rel: Capitolina (Roma), Lira

Trois Chambres a Manhattan, 1946, Novel
Trois Chambres a Manhattan 1965 d: Marcel Carne. lps: Maurice Ronet, Annie Girardot, O. E. Hasse. 112M FRN. prod/rel: Montaigne, F.C.M.

La Verite Sur le Bebe Donge, 1942, Novel
Verite Sur le Bebe Donge, La 1951 d: Henri Decoin. lps: Danielle Darrieux, Jean Gabin, Daniel Lecourtois. 104M FRN. *The Truth About Our Marriage* (UKN); *La Verite Sur Bebe Donge* prod/rel: U.G.C.

La Veuve Couderc, 1942, Novel
Veuve Couderc, Le 1971 d: Pierre Granier-Deferre. lps: Simone Signoret, Alain Delon, Ottavia Piccolo. 89M FRN/ITL. *L' Evaso* (ITL); *The Widow Couderc* (USA) prod/rel: Pegaso, Lira

Le Voyageur de la Toussaint, 1941, Novel
Voyageur de la Toussaint, Le 1942 d: Louis Daquin. lps: Assia Noris, Jean Desailly, Jules Berry. 102M FRN/ITL. *Il Viaggiatore Di Ognissanti* (ITL) prod/rel: Francinex

SIMMEL, JOHANNES MARIO (1924–, GRM

Affaire Nina B., Novel
Affaire Nina B 1961 d: Robert Siodmak. lps: Nadja Tiller, Pierre Brasseur, Walter Giller. 120M GRM/FRN. *The Nina B Affair* (USA) prod/rel: Cine-Alliance, Filmsonor

Alle Menschen Werden Bruder, Novel
Alle Menschen Werden Bruder 1973 d: Alfred Vohrer. lps: Harald Leipnitz, Doris Kunstmann, Rainer von Artenfels. 109M GRM. *All Men Become Brothers* prod/rel: Roxy, Constantin

Die Antwort Kennt Nur Der Wind, Novel
Antwort Kennt Nur Der Wind, Die 1975 d: Alfred Vohrer. lps: Marthe Keller, Maurice Ronet, Karin Dor. 108M GRM/FRN. *Seul le Vent Connait la Response* (FRN); *The Answer's in the Wind; Only the Wind Knows the Answer* prod/rel: Roxy, Paris-Cannes

Bis Zur Bitteren Neige, Novel
Bis Zur Bitteren Neige 1975 d: Gerd Oswald. lps: Maurice Ronet, Suzy Kendall, Susanne Uhlen. 105M AUS/GRM. *To the Bitter End* (USA); *Until the Bitter End* prod/rel: Roxy, Ggb 1.Kg

Bitte Lasst Die Blumen Leben, Novel
Bitte Lasst Die Blumen Leben 1986 d: Duccio Tessari. lps: Klausjurgen Wussow, Birgit Doll, Hannelore Elsner. 99M GRM. *Please Let the Flowers Live* prod/rel: Roxy, Lisa

Diesmal Muss Es Kaviar Sein, Novel
Diesmal Muss Es Kaviar Sein 1961 d: Geza von Radvanyi. lps: O. W. Fischer, Senta Berger, Viktor de KowA. 98M GRM/FRN. *This Time Caviar* prod/rel: C.C.C., C.E.C.

Gott Schutzt Die Liebenden, Novel
Gott Schutzt Die Liebenden 1973 d: Alfred Vohrer. lps: Harald Leipnitz, Gila von Weitershausen, Andrea Jonasson. 106M GRM/SPN/ITL. *Orden Interpol: Sin un*

Moment de Tregua (SPN); *God Protects Lovers*; *Ordine Interpol: Senza un Attimo Di Tregua* (ITL) prod/rel: Zafes (Catania), Roxy

Leben Noch Hurra, Wir, Novel
Wilden Funfziger, Die 1982 d: Peter Zadek. lps: Juraj Kukura, Boy Gobert, Peter Kern. 126M GRM. *The Wild Fifties* prod/rel: Bavaria, ZDF

Lieb Vaterland Magst Ruhig Sein, Novel
Lieb Vaterland, Magst Ruhig Sein 1976 d: Roland Klick. lps: Heinz Domez, Catherine Allegret, Georg MarischkA. 92M GRM. *You Can Rest Easy Dear Fatherland* prod/rel: Solaris, Cotta

Liebe Ist Nur Ein Wort, Novel
Liebe Ist Nur Ein Wort 1971 d: Alfred Vohrer. lps: Judy Winter, Malte Thorsten, Herbert Fleischmann. 115M GRM. *Love Is Only a Word* (UKN) prod/rel: Roxy, Constantin

Mein Schulfreund, Novel
Mein Schulfreund 1960 d: Robert Siodmak. lps: Heinz Ruhmann, Loni von Friedl, Ernst Schroder. 94M GRM. *Der Schulfreund*; *Old School Chum* prod/rel: Divina, Gloria

Mit Himbeergeist Geht Alles Besser, Novel
Mit Himbeergeist Geht Alles Besser 1960 d: Georg MarischkA. lps: O. W. Fischer, Marianne Koch, Jackie Lane. 105M AUS. prod/rel: Sascha

Aus Dem Die Traum Sind, Der Stoff, Novel
Stoff Aus Dem Die Traume Sind, Der 1972 d: Alfred Vohrer. lps: Herbert Fleischmann, Paul Neuhaus, Edith Heerdegen. 142M GRM. *The Stuff of Dreams* prod/rel: Roxy, Constantin

Und Jimmy Ging Zum Regenbogen, Novel
Und Jimmy Ging Zum Regenbogen 1971 d: Alfred Vohrer. lps: Alain Noury, Judy Winter, Horst Frank. 133M GRM/AUS. *And Jimmy Went to the Rainbow's End*; *And Jimmy Went After the Rainbow* prod/rel: Roxy, Wien

SIMMONS, MICHAEL L.
Chuck Connors, Novel
Bowery, The 1933 d: Raoul Walsh. lps: Wallace Beery, George Raft, Jackie Cooper. 92M USA. prod/rel: 20th Century Pictures, Inc., United Artists

SIMO, SANDOR
Franciska Vasarnapjai, Novel
Franciska Vasarnapjai 1997 d: Sandor Simo. lps: Eva Kerekes, Denes Ujlaki, Krisztina Biro. 100M HNG. *Every Sunday*; *The Sundays of Frances* prod/rel: Neuropa Film

SIMON, CHARLES
Zaza, Paris 1898, Play
Zaza 1910. lps: Lydia de Roberti. 232m ITL. prod/rel: Pasquali E C.
Zaza 1913 d: Adrien Caillard. lps: Georges Grand, Marie Ventura, Jules Mondos. 550m FRN. prod/rel: Scagl
Zaza 1915 d: Edwin S. Porter, Hugh Ford. lps: Pauline Frederick, Julian L'Estrange, Ruth Cummings. 5r USA. prod/rel: Famous Players Film Co., Charles Frohman Co.
Zaza 1923 d: Allan Dwan. lps: Gloria Swanson, H. B. Warner, Ferdinand Gottschalk. 7076f USA. prod/rel: Famous Players-Lasky, Paramount Pictures
Zaza 1938 d: George Cukor. lps: Claudette Colbert, Herbert Marshall, Bert Lahr. 87M USA. prod/rel: Paramount Pictures©
Zaza 1942 d: Renato Castellani. lps: Isa Miranda, Antonio Centa, Aldo Silvani. 88M ITL. prod/rel: Lux Film
Zaza 1955 d: Rene Gaveau. lps: Lilo, Maurice Teynac, Pauline Carton. 82M FRN. prod/rel: U.E.C., General Productions

SIMON, NEIL (1927–, USA
Play
Caccia Alla Volpe 1965 d: Vittorio de SicA. lps: Peter Sellers, Victor Mature, Britt Ekland. 103M ITL/UKN. *After the Fox* (UKN) prod/rel: Nancy Enterprises (London), Delegate

Barefoot in the Park, New York 1964, Play
Barefoot in the Park 1967 d: Gene Saks. lps: Jane Fonda, Robert Redford, Mildred Natwick. 105M USA. prod/rel: Nancy Enterprises, Paramount Pictures

Biloxi Blues, 1987, Play
Biloxi Blues 1987 d: Mike Nichols. lps: Matthew Broderick, Christopher Walken, Matt Mulhern. 106M USA. prod/rel: Universal, Rastar

Brighton Beach Memoirs, 1985, Play
Brighton Beach Memoirs 1987 d: Gene Saks. lps: Blythe Danner, Bob Dishy, Jonathan Silverman. 110M USA. prod/rel: Universal, Rastar

Broadway Bound, 1987, Play
Neil Simon's Broadway Bound 1991 d: Paul Bogart. lps: Anne Bancroft, Hume Cronyn, Corey Parker. TVM. 100M USA. *Broadway Bound* prod/rel: Blue Dolphin, ABC Productions

California Suite, 1977, Play
California Suite 1978 d: Herbert Ross. lps: Walter Matthau, Elaine May, Bill Cosby. 103M USA. prod/rel: Columbia

Chapter Two, 1978, Play
Chapter Two 1979 d: Robert Moore. lps: James Caan, Marsha Mason, Joseph BolognA. 124M USA.

Come Blow Your Horn, New York 1961, Play
Come Blow Your Horn 1963 d: Bud Yorkin. lps: Frank Sinatra, Tony Bill, Lee J. Cobb. 113M USA. prod/rel: Paramount

The Gingerbread Lady, 1970, Play
Only When I Laugh 1981 d: Glenn Jordan. lps: Marsha Mason, Kristy McNichol, James Coco. 120M USA. *It Hurts Only When I Laugh* (UKN) prod/rel: Columbia

I Ought to Be in Pictures, 1981, Play
I Ought to Be in Pictures 1982 d: Herbert Ross. lps: Walter Matthau, Ann-Margret, Dinah Manoff. 108M USA. prod/rel: Twentieth Century Fox

Last of the Red Hot Lovers, 1970, Play
Last of the Red Hot Lovers 1972 d: Gene Saks. lps: Alan Arkin, Sally Kellerman, Paula Prentiss. 98M USA. prod/rel: Paramount

London Suite, Play
Neil Simon's London Suite 1996 d: Jay Sandrich. lps: Patricia Clarkson, Kelsey Grammer, Kristen Johnston. TVM. 120M USA. prod/rel: NBC Entertainment, Hallmark Entertainment

The Odd Couple, New York 1965, Play
Odd Couple, The 1968 d: Gene Saks. lps: Jack Lemmon, Walter Matthau, John Fiedler. 105M USA. prod/rel: Paramount Pictures

Plaza Suite, 1969, Play
Plaza Suite 1971 d: Arthur Hiller. lps: Walter Matthau, Maureen Stapleton, Barbara Harris. 115M USA. prod/rel: Paramount

The Prisoner of Second Avenue, 1972, Play
Prisoner of Second Avenue, The 1975 d: Melvin Frank. lps: Jack Lemmon, Anne Bancroft, Gene Saks. 98M USA. prod/rel: Warner Bros.

The Star Spangled Girl, 1967, Play
Star Spangled Girl 1971 d: Jerry Paris. lps: Sandy Duncan, Tony Roberts, Todd Susman. 92M USA. *Star-Spangled Girl*

The Sunshine Boys, 1972, Play
Sunshine Boys, The 1975 d: Herbert Ross. lps: Walter Matthau, George Burns, Richard Benjamin. 112M USA. prod/rel: MGM
Sunshine Boys, The 1997 d: John Erman. lps: Woody Allen, Peter Falk, Sarah Jessica Parker. TVM. 120M USA. prod/rel: Hallmark Entertainment

Sweet Charity, New York 1966, Play
Sweet Charity 1969 d: Bob Fosse. lps: Shirley MacLaine, Sammy Davis Jr., Ricardo Montalban. 152M USA. prod/rel: Universal Pictures

SIMON, ROGER L. (1943–, USA
The Big Fix, Novel
Big Fix, The 1978 d: Jeremy Paul Kagan. lps: Richard Dreyfuss, Susan Anspach, Bonnie BedeliA. 108M USA. prod/rel: Universal

SIMON, S. J.
The Elephant Is White, Novel
Give Us the Moon 1944 d: Val Guest. lps: Margaret Lockwood, Vic Oliver, Peter Graves. 95M UKN. prod/rel: General Film Distributors, Gainsborough

No Nightingales, Novel
Ghosts of Berkeley Square, The 1947 d: Vernon Sewell. lps: Robert Morley, Felix Aylmer, Yvonne Arnaud. 89M UKN. prod/rel: British National, Pathe

Trottie True, Novel
Trottie True 1948 d: Brian Desmond Hurst. lps: Jean Kent, James Donald, Hugh Sinclair. 96M UKN. *The Gay Lady* (USA) prod/rel: General Film Distributors, Two Cities

SIMONETTA, UMBERTO
Il Giovane Normale, Novel
Giovane Normale, Il 1969 d: Dino Risi. lps: Lino Capolicchio, Janet Agren, Jeff Morrow. 105M ITL. *The Normal Young Man* prod/rel: Vides Cin.Ca, Dean Film

I Viaggiatori Della Sera, Novel
Viaggiatori Della Sera, I 1979 d: Ugo Tognazzi. lps: Ugo Tognazzi, Ornella Vanoni, Corinne Clery. 130M ITL/SPN. *Los Viajeros Del Atardecer* (SPN); *Twilight Travellers*; *The Night Visitors* prod/rel: Juppiter Generale Cin.Ca, Il Quadrifoglio S.P.a (Roma)

SIMONI, RENATO
L' Illusione, 1916, Play
Illusione, L' 1917 d: Guglielmo Zorzi. lps: Linda Pini, Paride Sala, Luigi Duse. 1183m ITL. prod/rel: Silentium Film

La Vedova, Play
Vedova, La 1939 d: Goffredo Alessandrini. lps: Isa Pola, Ruggero Ruggeri, Leonardo Cortese. 93M ITL. prod/rel: Scalera Film

SIMONIN, ALBERT
Le Cave Se Rebiffe, Paris 1954, Novel
Cave Se Rebiffe, Le 1961 d: Gilles Grangier. lps: Jean Gabin, Martine Carol, Bernard Blier. 105M FRN/ITL. *The Counterfeiters of Paris* (USA); *Il Re Dei Falsari* (ITL); *The Counterfeiters* (UKN); *Money Money Money* prod/rel: Cite Films, Jacques Bar

Du Mouron Pour Les Petits Oiseaux, Novel
Du Mouron Pour Les Petits Oiseaux 1962 d: Marcel Carne. lps: Dany Saval, Paul Meurisse, Suzy Delair. 107M FRN/ITL. *Dietro la Facciata* (ITL) prod/rel: Champs-Elysees Prods., C.I.C.C.

Les Tontons Flingueurs, Novel
Tontons Flingueurs, Les 1963 d: Georges Lautner. lps: Lino Ventura, Sabine Sinjen, Jacques Dumesnil. 110M FRN/GRM/ITL. *Der Gangster Mein Onkel* (GRM); *Monsieur Gangster* (USA); *Crooks in Clover* (UKN); *In Famiglia Si Spara* (ITL); *My Uncle, the Gangster* prod/rel: S.N.E.G., Sicilia Cinematografica

Touchez Pas Au Grisbi, Novel
Touchez Pas Au Grisbi 1953 d: Jacques Becker. lps: Jean Gabin, Rene Dary, Jeanne Moreau. 94M FRN/ITL. *Grisbi* (ITL); *Honour Among Thieves* (UKN); *Don't Touch the Loot*; *Paris Underground*; *Hands Off the Loot* prod/rel: Del Duca Films, Antares Films

SIMONOV, KONSTANTIN (1915–1979), RSS, Simonov, Konstantin Kirill Mikhailovich
Chetvyorty, 1961, Play
Cetvertyj 1972 d: Alexander Stolper. 71M USS. *The Fourth*; *Chetvyorty*

Dni I Nochi, 1944, Novel
Dni I Noci 1944 d: Alexander Stolper. 90M USS. *Days and Nights*; *Dni I Nochi*

Dvadtsat Dnei Bez Voini, 1973, Short Story
Dvadtsat Dnei Bez Voini 1976 d: Alexei Gherman. lps: Yuri Nikulin, Lyudmila Gurchenko, R. Sadykov. 100M USS. *A Twenty Day Respite from War*; *Twenty Days Without War*; *Dvadcat Dnej Bez Vojny* prod/rel: Lenfilm

Paren Iz Nashego Goroda, 1941, Play
Paren Iz Nashego Goroda 1942 d: Alexander Stolper, Boris Ivanov. 93M USS. *Lad from Our Town* (USA); *A Fellow from Our Town*

Russkiy Vopros, 1946, Play
Russki Voproz 1947 d: Mikhail Romm. 91M USS. *The Russian Question*; *Ruskij Vopros*; *Russkij Voproz*

Russkiye Lyudi, 1942, Play
Vo Imya Rodini 1943 d: V. I. Pudovkin, Dimitri Vasiliev. 96M USS. *In the Name of Our Motherland*; *In the Name of the Fatherland*

Sluchai S Polynnym, 1969, Short Story
Chto Sluchilos S Polinim? 1971 d: Alexei Sakharov. lps: Anastasia Vertinskaya, Oleg Tabakov, Oleg Yefremov. 90M USS. *Sluchai S Polynnym*; *What Happened to Polynin*

Soldatami Ne Rozhdaivtsia, 1964, Novel
Soldatami Nye Rozhdayutsya 1968 d: Alexander Stolper. lps: Kirill Lavrov, Anatoli Papanov, Lyudmila KrylovA. 140M USS. *One Is Not Born a Soldier*; *Soldiers Aren't Born*; *Vengeance*; *None are Born Soldiers*; *Vozmezdie*

Zhdi Menya, 1941, Verse
Zdi Menja 1943 d: Alexander Stolper, Boris Ivanov. 82M USS. *Wait for Me*; *Zhdi Menya*

Zhiviye I Myortviye, 1959, Novel
Zhivye I Mertvye 1964 d: Alexander Stolper. lps: Anatoli Papanov, Mikhail Ulyanov, Kirill Lavrov. 210M USS. *The Living and the Dead*; *Zivye I Mertvye* prod/rel: Mosfilm

SIMONS, LEOPOLD
Le Mystere du 421, Play
Mystere du 421, Le 1937 d: Leopold Simons. lps: Leopold Simons, Line Dariel, Suzanne Christy. 73M FRN.

SIMONTON, IDA VERA
Hell's Playground, 1925, Novel
White Cargo 1942 d: Richard Thorpe. lps: Hedy Lamarr, Walter Pidgeon, Frank Morgan. 90M USA. prod/rel: MGM

White Cargo, 1925, Novel
White Cargo 1929 d: J. B. Williams, Arthur W. Barnes. lps: Leslie Faber, Gypsy Rhouma, John Hamilton. SIL. 7965f UKN. prod/rel: Neo-Art Productions, Williams and Pritchard
White Cargo 1929 d: J. B. Williams, Arthur W. Barnes. lps: Leslie Faber, Gypsy Rhouma, John Hamilton. SND. 88M UKN. prod/rel: Neo-Art Productions, Williams and Pritchard

SIMPSON, HAROLD
The Phantom Picture, Play
Phantom Picture, The 1916 d: Albert Ward. lps: Henry Lonsdale, Violet Campbell, Arthur Poole. 5500f UKN. prod/rel: British Empire Films
The Veiled Woman, Play
Veiled Woman, The 1917 d: Leedham Bantock. lps: Cecil Humphreys, Gladys Mason, Frank Randall. 4450f UKN. prod/rel: British Empire Films

SIMPSON, HELEN
Enter Sir John, London 1928, Play
Murder 1930 d: Alfred Hitchcock. lps: Herbert Marshall, Norah Baring, Phyllis Konstam. 108M UKN. *Mary* prod/rel: British International Pictures, Wardour
Saraband for Dead Lovers, 1935, Novel
Saraband for Dead Lovers 1948 d: Basil Dearden, Michael Relph. lps: Stewart Granger, Joan Greenwood, Francoise Rosay. 96M UKN. *Saraband* (USA) prod/rel: Ealing Studios, General Film Distributors
Under Capricorn, 1937, Novel
Under Capricorn 1949 d: Alfred Hitchcock. lps: Ingrid Bergman, Joseph Cotten, Michael Wilding. 116M USA/UKN. prod/rel: Transatlantic, Capricorn

SIMPSON, N. F.
One Way Pendulum, London 1959, Play
One Way Pendulum 1964 d: Peter Yates. lps: Eric Sykes, George Cole, Julia Foster. 85M UKN. prod/rel: Woodfall Film Productions, United Artists

SIMPSON, REGINALD
Living Dangerously, London 1934, Play
Living Dangerously 1936 d: Herbert Brenon. lps: Otto Kruger, Leonora Corbett, Francis Lister. 72M UKN. prod/rel: British International Pictures, Wardour
The Milky Way, Play
Innocents of Chicago, The 1932 d: Lupino Lane. lps: Henry Kendall, Betty Norton, Margot Grahame. 68M UKN. *Why Saps Leave Home* (USA); *The Milky Way* prod/rel: British International Pictures, Wardour
Who Goes Next?, Play
Who Goes Next? 1938 d: Maurice Elvey. lps: Barry K. Barnes, Sophie Steward, Jack Hawkins. 85M UKN. prod/rel: Fox British

SIMS, DOROTHY RICE
Fog, Boston 1933, Novel
Fog 1934 d: Albert S. Rogell. lps: Donald Cook, Mary Brian, Reginald Denny. 70M USA. prod/rel: Columbia Pictures Corp.©

SIMS, GEORGE R.
Billie's Rose, Poem
Billie's Rose 1922 d: Challis Sanderson. 950f UKN. prod/rel: Master Films, Woolf & Freedman
Christmas Day in the Workhouse, Poem
Christmas Day in the Workhouse 1914 d: George Pearson. lps: Fred Paul. 1000f UKN. prod/rel: G. B. Samuelson, Imperial
The English Rose, London 1890, Play
English Rose, The 1920 d: Fred Paul. lps: Fred Paul, Humberston Wright, Sydney N. Folker. 4890f UKN. prod/rel: British Standard, Whincup
The Ever Open Door, London 1913, Play
Ever-Open Door, The 1920 d: Fred Goodwins. lps: Hayford Hobbs, Daphne Glenne, Margaret Hope. 4850f UKN. prod/rel: Ideal
Fallen By the Way, Poem
Fallen By the Way 1922 d: Challis Sanderson. lps: Judd Green, Jeff Barlow, Kitty Van Loo. 1210f UKN. prod/rel: Master Films, Woolf & Freedman
The Great Day, London 1919, Play
Great Day, The 1920 d: Hugh Ford. lps: Arthur Bourchier, Mary Palfrey, Bertram Burleigh. 3700f UKN/USA. prod/rel: Famous Players-Lasky British Producers, Paramount Pictures
The Harbour Lights, London 1885, Play
Harbour Lights, The 1914 d: Percy Nash. lps: Gerald Lawrence, Mercy Hatton, Daisy Cordell. 3275f UKN. prod/rel: Neptune, Globe
Harbour Lights, The 1923 d: Tom Terriss. lps: Tom Moore, Isobel Elsom, Gerald McCarthy. 5877f UKN. prod/rel: Ideal
His Other Wife, Play
His Other Wife 1921 d: Percy Nash. lps: Eileen Magrath, Jack Raymond, Maria Minetti. 4800f UKN. prod/rel: Screen Plays, British Exhibitors' Films

In the Ranks, London 1883, Play
In the Ranks 1914 d: Percy Nash. lps: Gregory Scott, Daisy Cordell, James Lindsay. 3945f UKN. prod/rel: Neptune, Jury
In the Signal Box, Poem
In the Signal Box 1922 d: H. B. Parkinson. lps: George Wynn, Thelma Murray, Baby Rayner. 1065f UKN. prod/rel: Master Films, Woolf & Freedman
The Lifeboat, Poem
Lifeboat, The 1914. lps: Eric Williams. UKN. prod/rel: Eric Williams Speaking Pictures
The Lights O' London, London 1881, Play
Lights O' London, The 1914 d: Bert Haldane?. lps: Arthur Chesney, Phyllis Relph, Fred Paul. 4000f UKN. prod/rel: Barker, Magnet
Lights O' London, The 1922 d: Edwin J. Collins. lps: Florence Turner, James Knight, Stella Muir. 1000f UKN. prod/rel: Master Films, Woolf & Freedman
Lights of London 1923 d: Charles Calvert. lps: Wanda Hawley, Nigel Barrie, Warburton Gamble. 7386f UKN. prod/rel: Gaumont, British Screencraft
The Lights of Home, London 1892, Play
Lights of Home, The 1920 d: Fred Paul. lps: George Foley, Nora Hayden, Jack Raymond. 5500f UKN. prod/rel: Screen Plays, British Exhibitors' Films
The Magic Wand, Poem
Magic Wand, The 1922 d: George Wynn. lps: Stella Muir, Joan Whalley. 1000f UKN. prod/rel: Master Films, Woolf & Freedman
Master and Man, London 1889, Play
Master and Man 1915 d: Percy Nash. lps: Gregory Scott, Joan Ritz, Douglas Payne. 3612f UKN. prod/rel: Neptune, Walturdaw
The Nightbirds of London, Play
Nightbirds of London, The 1915 d: Frank Wilson. lps: Stewart Rome, Chrissie White, Violet Hopson. 4150f UKN. prod/rel: Hepworth
The Old Actor's Story, Poem
Old Actor's Story, The 1922 d: H. B. Parkinson. lps: Stella Muir, James Knight, Booth Conway. 1000f UKN. prod/rel: Master Films, Woolf & Freedman
'Ostler Joe, Poem
'Ostler Joe 1912 d: J. Searle Dawley. lps: Laura Sawyer, James Gordon, Ben Wilson. 1000f USA. prod/rel: Edison
The Parson's Fight, Poem
Parson's Fight, The 1922 d: Edwin J. Collins. lps: Clive Brook, Lillian Douglas, Ward McAllister. 1000f UKN. prod/rel: Master Films, Woolf & Freedman
The Road to Heaven, Poem
Road to Heaven, The 1922 d: Challis Sanderson. lps: Mickey Brantford, Ida Fane, Miriam Merry. 1000f UKN. prod/rel: Master Films, Woolf & Freedman
The Romany Rye, London 1882, Play
Life Line, The 1919 d: Maurice Tourneur. lps: Jack Holt, Seena Owen, Lew Cody. 5394f USA. *Romany Rye* prod/rel: Maurice Tourneur Productions, Famous Players-Lasky Corp.©
Romany Rye, The 1915 d: Percy Nash. lps: Gerald Lawrence, Gregory Scott, Daisy Cordell. 3030f UKN. prod/rel: Neptune, Bishop, Pessers
Sal Grogan's Face, Poem
Sal Grogan's Face 1922 d: Edwin J. Collins. lps: Ward McAllister, Margaret Dean, Mickey Brantford. 975f UKN. prod/rel: Master Films, Woolf & Freedman
Sir Rupert's Wife, Poem
Sir Rupert's Wife 1922 d: Challis Sanderson. lps: Clive Brook, Maria Minetti, Olaf Hytten. 1000f UKN. prod/rel: Master Films, Woolf & Freedman
The Street Tumblers, Poem
Street Tumblers, The 1922 d: George Wynn. lps: Florence Turner, Tom Morriss. 1000f UKN. prod/rel: Master Films, Woolf & Freedman
Ticket O' Leave, Poem
Ticket O' Leave 1922 d: Edwin J. Collins. lps: Betty Doyle, Ward McAllister, James Knight. 1104f UKN. prod/rel: Master Films, Woolf & Freedman
The Trumpet Call, London 1891, Play
Trumpet Call, The 1915 d: Percy Nash. lps: Gregory Scott, Joan Ritz, Douglas Payne. 4480f UKN. prod/rel: Neptune, Gaumont

SINCLAIR, ANDREW (1935–, UKN
The Breaking of Bumbo, Novel
Breaking of Bumbo, The 1970 d: Andrew Sinclair. lps: Richard Warwick, Joanna Lumley, Natasha Pyne. 90M UKN. prod/rel: Associated British

SINCLAIR, ARTHUR STUART
No Children Allowed, Play
Children Not Wanted 1920 d: Paul Scardon. lps: Edith Day, Ruth Sullivan, Joe King. 6r USA. prod/rel: Crest Pictures Corp., Republic Distributing Corp.

SINCLAIR, BERTHA MUZZY
Chip of the Flying U, New York 1906, Novel
Chip of the Flying U 1939 d: Ralph Staub. lps: Johnny Mack Brown, Bob Baker, Fuzzy Knight. 55M USA. prod/rel: Universal Pictures Co.
Chip of the Flying "U" 1914 d: Colin Campbell. lps: Kathlyn Williams, Tom Mix, Frank Clark. 3r USA.

SINCLAIR, BERTRAND W.
Big Timber, Boston 1916, Novel
Big Timber 1917 d: William D. Taylor. lps: Kathlyn Williams, Wallace Reid, John Burton. 5r USA. prod/rel: Oliver Morosco Photoplay Co.©, Paramount Pictures Corp.
The Whiskey Runners, Story
Raiders, The 1921 d: Nate Watt. lps: Franklyn Farnum, Bud Osborne, Vester Pegg. 4850f USA. prod/rel: William N. Selig Productions, Canyon Pictures

SINCLAIR, HAROLD
The Horse Soldiers, Novel
Horse Soldiers, The 1959 d: John Ford. lps: John Wayne, William Holden, Constance Towers. 119M USA. prod/rel: United Artists, Mirisch Co.

SINCLAIR, MAY (1865–1946), UKN
Kitty Tailleur, 1908, Novel
Kitty Tailleur 1921 d: Frank Richardson. lps: Marjorie Hume, Lewis Dayton, Ivo Dawson. 4900f UKN/NTH. *In de macht Van Het Noodlot* (NTH); *In Fate's Power* prod/rel: Granger-Binger Film

SINCLAIR, UPTON (1878–1968), USA, Sinclair, Upton Beall
Damaged Goods, 1913, Novel
Marriage Forbidden 1936 d: Phil Goldstone. lps: Pedro de Cordoba, Phyllis Barry, Douglas Walton. 61M USA. *Damaged Goods* prod/rel: Criterion Pictures Corp.
The Gnomobile: a Gnice Gnew Gnarrative With Gnonsense., 1962, Novel
Gnome-Mobile, The 1967 d: Robert Stevenson. lps: Walter Brennan, Matthew Garber, Karen Dotrice. 90M USA. prod/rel: Walt Disney Productions, Buena Vista
The Jungle, New York 1906, Novel
Jungle, The 1914 d: Augustus Thomas, George Irving. lps: George Nash, Gail Kane, Alice Marc. 5r USA. prod/rel: All Star Feature Corp., State Rights
The Money Changers, London 1908, Novel
Money-Changers, The 1920 d: Jack Conway. lps: Robert McKim, Claire Adams, Roy Stewart. 6r USA. *What Shall It Profit a Man*; *The Money Changers* prod/rel: Federal Photoplays, Inc. of California, Benjamin B. Hampton Productions
The Wet Parade, New York 1931, Novel
Wet Parade, The 1932 d: Victor Fleming. lps: Walter Huston, Myrna Loy, Neil Hamilton. 122M USA. prod/rel: Metro-Goldwyn-Mayer Corp., Victor Fleming Production

SINCLAIR, WALTER A.
Taxi Hi, Story
Timid Terror, The 1926 d: Del Andrews. lps: George O'Hara, Edith Yorke, Doris Hill. 4892f USA. prod/rel: R-C Pictures, Film Booking Offices of America

SINGER, HOWARD
Wake Me When It's Over, Novel
Wake Me When It's Over 1960 d: Mervyn Leroy. lps: Dick Shawn, Ernie Kovacs, Margo Moore. 126M USA. prod/rel: 20th Century-Fox

SINGER, ISAAC BASHEVIS (1904–1991), PLN
The Beard, 1973, Short Story
Isaac Singer's Nightmare and Mrs. Pupko's Beard 1973 d: Bruce Davidson. 30M USA.
The Cafeteria, 1970, Short Story
Cafeteria, The 1981 d: Amram Nowak. 60M USA.
The Magician of Lublin, 1960, Novel
Hakosem Mi-Lublin 1978 d: Menahem Golan. lps: Alan Arkin, Louise Fletcher, Valerie Perrine. 105M ISR/GRM/CND. *Der Magier* (GRM); *The Magician of Lublin* (USA)
Di Geschichte Fun a Liebe Sonim, 1966, Novel
Enemies, a Love Story 1989 d: Paul Mazursky. lps: Anjelica Huston, Ron Silver, Lena Olin. 119M USA. prod/rel: 20th Century Fox
Stories for Children
Aaron's Magic Village 1997 d: Albert Hanan Kaminski. ANM. 80M USA. *The Real Schlemiel* prod/rel: Benousilio-Volke, Columbia Tristar Home Video
Yentl He Yeshiva Boy, 1964, Short Story
Yentl 1983 d: Barbra Streisand. lps: Barbra Streisand, Mandy Patinkin, Amy Irving. 133M UKN/USA. prod/rel: MGM, United Artists

SINGER, LOREN
The Parallax View, Novel
Parallax View, The 1974 d: Alan J. PakulA. lps: Warren Beatty, Paula Prentiss, William Daniels. 103M USA. prod/rel: Paramount

SINGH, KHUSHWANT (1915–, IND
Train to Pakistan, Novel
Train to Pakistan 1998 d: Pamela Rooks. lps: Nirmal Pandey, Smriti Mishra, Rajit Kapoor. 111M IND. prod/rel: Nfdc of India, Kaleidoscope-India

SINGULAR, STEPHEN
Legacy of Sin, Book
Legacy of Sin - the William Coit Story 1995 d: Steven Schachter. lps: Neil Patrick Harris, Bonnie Bedelia, Meredith Salenger. TVM. 92M USA. prod/rel: Mark Sennet Productions, Citadel Entertainment
Talked to Death: the Life and Murder of Alan Berg, Book
Talk Radio 1988 d: Oliver Stone. lps: Eric Bogosian, Alec Baldwin, Ellen Greene. 110M USA. prod/rel: Universal

SINIAC, PIERRE
Les Morfalous, Novel
Morfalous, Les 1983 d: Henri Verneuil. lps: Jean-Paul Belmondo, Jacques Villeret, Michel Constantin. 105M FRN/TNS. prod/rel: Cerito, Sopro

SINIBALDI, FEDERICO
I Senza Dio, Novel
Orizzonte Di Sangue 1942 d: Gennaro Righelli. lps: Luisa Ferida, Valentina Cortese, Osvaldo Valenti. 83M ITL. *I Senza Dio*; *Orizzonte in Fiamme* prod/rel: Titanus, O.D.I.T.

SIODMAK, CURT (1902–, GRM
Story
Berlin Express 1948 d: Jacques Tourneur. lps: Robert Ryan, Merle Oberon, Charles Korvin. 86M USA. prod/rel: RKO Radio
The Devil's Brood, Story
House of Frankenstein 1944 d: Erle C. Kenton. lps: Boris Karloff, Lon Chaney Jr., John Carradine. 71M USA. *The Devil's Brood*; *Doom of Dracula*; *Destiny*; *Chamber of Horrors* prod/rel: Universal
Donovan's Brain, New York 1943, Novel
Donovan's Brain 1953 d: Felix E. Feist. lps: Lew Ayres, Gene Evans, Nancy Davis. 83M USA. prod/rel: United Artists, Dowling
Lady and the Monster, The 1944 d: George Sherman. lps: Vera Ralston, Erich von Stroheim, Richard Arlen. 86M USA. *The Lady and the Doctor* (UKN); *The Monster and the Lady*; *Tiger Man*; *The Monster* prod/rel: Republic Pictures Corp.
Vengeance 1962 d: Freddie Francis. lps: Anne Heywood, Peter Van Eyck, Cecil Parker. 83M UKN/GRM. *Ein Toter Sucht Seinen Morder* (GRM); *The Brain* (USA); *A Dead Man Seeks His Murderer*; *Over My Dead Body* prod/rel: Garrick, Stross-Ccc
F.P.1 Antwortet Nicht, Novel
F.P.1 1932 d: Karl Hartl. lps: Conrad Veidt, Leslie Fenton, Jill Esmond. 93M UKN. *Secrets of F.P.1* prod/rel: Gaumont, UFA
F.P.1 Antwortet Nicht 1932 d: Karl Hartl. lps: Hans Albers, Sybille Schmitz, Paul Hartmann. 114M GRM. *F.P.1. Does Not Answer; No Answer from F.P.1* prod/rel: UFA, Transit
I.F.1 Ne Repond Plus 1932 d: Karl Hartl. lps: Charles Boyer, Jean Murat, Daniele ParolA. 100M FRN. prod/rel: U.F.a., a.C.E.
Hauser's Memory, Novel
Hauser's Memory 1970 d: Boris Sagal. lps: David McCallum, Susan Strasberg, Lilli Palmer. 100M USA. prod/rel: Universal TV
The Last Lord, Play
Girls Will Be Boys 1934 d: Marcel Varnel. lps: Dolly Haas, Cyril Maude, Esmond Knight. 70M UKN. prod/rel: British International Pictures, Wardour

SIPE, PAUL B.
All Night Long, Play
Outside Woman, The 1921. lps: Wanda Hawley, Clyde Fillmore, Sidney Bracey. 4225f USA. prod/rel: Realart Pictures

SIRAUDIN, PAUL
L' Affaire du Courrier de Lyon, Play
Affaire du Courrier de Lyon, L' 1937 d: Maurice Lehmann, Claude Autant-LarA. lps: Dita Parlo, Pierre Blanchar, Sylvia Bataille. 102M FRN. *The Courier of Lyon* (USA); *L' Affaire Lesurques*; *Le Courrier de Lyon* prod/rel: Productions Maurice Lehmann
Assassinio Del Corriere Di Leone, L' 1916 d: Gabriel Moreau. lps: Cav. Mario Casaleggio, Gabriel Moreau, Liliane de Rosny. 1340m ITL. prod/rel: Subalpina Film

SIRIWARDENE, EILEEN
Ahasin Polawatha, Novel
Ahasin Pola Watha 1976 d: Lester James Peries. lps: Tony Ranasinghe, Sriyani Amarasena, Shanti LekhA. 92M SLN. *White Flowers for the Dead*; *From Heaven to Earth*; *Ahasin Polowata* prod/rel: W. U. Sumathipala

SISTER EILEEN
Ave Maria, Story
Journey's End, The 1921 d: Hugo Ballin. lps: Mabel Ballin, George Bancroft, Wyndham Standing. 7500f USA. prod/rel: Hugo Ballin Productions, W. W. Hodkinson Corp.

SITWELL, OSBERT (1892–1969), UKN, Sitwell, Sir Francis Osbert Sacheverell
A Place of One's Own, 1916, Short Story
Place of One's Own, A 1945 d: Bernard Knowles. lps: Margaret Lockwood, James Mason, Barbara Mullen. 92M UKN. prod/rel: Eagle-Lion, Gainsborough

SIVASANKARA ILLA, TAKAZI
Cemmin, 1956, Novel
Chemmeen 1965 d: Ramu Kariat. lps: Madhu, Sathyan, SheelA. 147M IND. *The Shrimp*; *Red Herrings*; *Wrath of the Sea*; *Chemeen* prod/rel: Kanmani Films

SIWERTZ, SIGFRID
Ett Brott, 1938, Play
Brott, Ett 1940 d: Anders Henrikson. lps: Edvin Adolphson, Karin Ekelund, Anders Henrikson. 93M SWD. *A Crime*; *Ett Brott*
Enhorningen, 1939, Short Story
Enhorningen 1955 d: Gustaf Molander. 98M SWD. *The Unicorn*
Hem Fran Babylon, 1923, Novel
Hem Fran Babylon 1941 d: Alf Sjoberg. 106M SWD. *Home from Babylon*
Malarpirater, 1911, Novel
Malarpirater 1923 d: Gustaf Molander. lps: Einar Hansson, Albert Christiansen, Tom Walter. 2190m SWD. *Pirates on Lake Malar* prod/rel: Ab Svensk Filmindustri
Malarpirater 1959 d: Per Gosta Holmgren. lps: Svenerik Perzon, Carl-Ake Eriksson, Tomas Bolme. 113M SWD. *Pirates on Lake Malar* prod/rel: Omega Film Ab
Vi Arme Syndere, Novel
Vi Arme Syndere 1952 d: Erik Balling, Ole Palsbo. lps: Johannes Meyers, Minna Jorgensen, Karl Stegger. F DNM. prod/rel: Nordisk

SJOBERG, BIRGER
Fridas Andra Bok, 1929, Verse
Fridas Visor 1930 d: Gustaf Molander. lps: Elisabeth Frisk, Bengt Djurberg, Tore Svennberg. 82M SWD. *Frida's Songs* prod/rel: Film Ab Minerva, Ab Svensk Filmindustri
Fridas Bok, 1922, Verse
Fridas Visor 1930 d: Gustaf Molander. lps: Elisabeth Frisk, Bengt Djurberg, Tore Svennberg. 82M SWD. *Frida's Songs* prod/rel: Film Ab Minerva, Ab Svensk Filmindustri
Kvartetten Som Sprangdes, 1924, Novel
Kvartetten Som Sprangdes 1936 d: Arne Bornebusch. lps: Carl Barcklind, Birgit Rosengren, Nils Lundell. 104M SWD. prod/rel: Ab Europa Film
Kvartetten Som Sprangdes 1950 d: Gustaf Molander. lps: Adolf Jahr, Anita Bjork, Inga Landgre. 100M SWD. *The Quartet That Split Up* prod/rel: Ab Svensk Filmindustri

SJOGREN, PEDER
Karlekens Brod, Novel
Karlekens Brod 1953 d: Arne Mattsson. lps: Folke Sundquist, Sissi Kaiser, Georg Rydeberg. 97M SWD. *The Bread of Love* prod/rel: Nordisk-Tonefilm

SJOWALL, MAJ (1935–, SWD
Novel
Laughing Policeman, The 1973 d: Stuart Rosenberg. lps: Walter Matthau, Bruce Dern, Louis Gossett Jr. 112M USA. *An Investigation of Murder* (UKN) prod/rel: 20th Century Fox
Polis Polis Potatismos 1993 d: Pelle Berglund. lps: Gosta Ekman, Kjell Bergqvist, Rolf Lassgard. 91M SWD/GRM.
Polismordaren 1993 d: Peter Keglevic. lps: Gosta Ekman, Kjell Bergqvist, Rolf Lassgard. 97M SWD/GRM.
De Man Op Het Balkon, Novel
Mannen Pa Balkongen 1993 d: Daniel Alfredson. lps: Gosta Ekman, Kjell Bergqvist, Rolf Lassgard. TVM. 94M SWD/GRM. *The Man on the Balcony*
Mannen Pa Taket, Novel
Mannen Pa Taket 1977 d: Bo Widerberg. lps: Carl-Gustaf Lindstedt, Gunnel Wadner, Hakan Serner. 115M SWD. *The Man on the Roof*; *The Abominable Man* prod/rel: Svenska Filminstitut, Svensk Film

Mannen Som Gick Upp I Rok, Novel
Sved Akinek Nyoma Veszett, A 1980 d: Peter Bacso. lps: Derek Jacobi, Judy Winter, Tomas Bolme. 114M HNG/SWD/GRM. *Mannen Som Gick Upp I Rok* (SWD); *The Man Who Went Up in Smoke*; *Der Mann Der Sich in Luft Auflöste* (GRM) prod/rel: Andre Lipik, Europa

SKARMETA, ANTONIO (1940–, CHL
Story
Aus Der Ferne Sehe Ich Dieses Land 1978 d: Christian Ziewer. lps: Pablo Lira, Anibal Reyna, Valeria Villarroel. TVM. 98M GRM. *From Afar I See My Country*; *I See This Land from Afar*; *From the Distance I See This Country* prod/rel: Basis, Wdr
In Der Wuste 1986 d: Rafael Fuster-Pardo. lps: Claudio Caceres Molina, Mustafa Saygili, Adriana Altaras. 74M GRM. *In the Desert* prod/rel: Deutsche Film Und Fernseh
Pequena Revancha 1986 d: Olegario BarrerA. lps: Eduardo Emiro Garcia, Elisa Escamez, Carlos Sanchez. 93M VNZ. *Small Revenge* prod/rel: Cine Seis Ocho C.a.
Radfahrer Vom San Christobal, Der 1987 d: Peter Lilienthal. lps: Rene Baeza, Luz Jimenez, Roberto Navarrete. 87M GRM. prod/rel: Edgar Reitz Film, ZDF
Ardiente Pacienca, Novel
Postino, Il 1995 d: Michael Radford. lps: Massimo Troisi, Philippe Noiret, Maria Grazia CucinottA. 108M ITL/FRN/BLG. *The Postman* (UKN) prod/rel: Cecchi Gori, Tiger

SKELTON, BARBARA
Tears Before Bedtime - Weep No More, Novel
Business Affair, A 1993 d: Charlotte Brandstrom. lps: Christopher Walken, Carole Bouquet, Jonathan Pryce. 102M UKN/FRN/GRM. *D'une Femme a l'Autre* (FRN) prod/rel: Film and General, Osby

SKELTON, JOHN (1460–1529), UKN
The Tunnyng of Elynoure Rummyng, c1520, Verse
Tunnyng of Elinour Rummyng 1976 d: Julien Temple. 33M UKN.

SKEYHILL, TOM
Sergeant York - Last of the Long Hunters, Article
Sergeant York 1941 d: Howard Hawks. lps: Gary Cooper, Walter Brennan, Joan Leslie. 134M USA. prod/rel: Warner Bros.

SKINNER, CONSTANCE LINDSAY
The Noose, 1920, Short Story
Green Temptation, The 1922 d: William D. Taylor. lps: Betty Compson, Mahlon Hamilton, Theodore Kosloff. 6165f USA. prod/rel: Famous Players-Lasky, Paramount Pictures

SKINNER, CORNELIA OTIS (1901–1979), USA
Our Hearts Were Young and Gay, Book
Our Hearts Were Young and Gay 1944 d: Lewis Allen. lps: Gail Russell, Diana Lynn, Charlie Ruggles. 81M USA. prod/rel: Paramount
The Pleasure of His Company, New York 1958, Play
Pleasure of His Company, The 1961 d: George Seaton. lps: Fred Astaire, Debbie Reynolds, Lilli Palmer. 115M USA. prod/rel: Perlsea Co., Paramount Pictures

SKINNER, IRMA
Her Speedy Affair, Story
Her Speedy Affair 1915 d: Horace Davey. lps: Billie Rhodes, George French, Neal Burns. SHT USA. prod/rel: Nestor

SKLAR, GEORGE
Merry-Go-Round, New York 1932, Play
Afraid to Talk 1932 d: Edward L. Cahn. lps: Eric Linden, Sidney Fox, Tully Marshall. 76M USA. *Merry-Go-Round* prod/rel: Universal Pictures Corp.

SKOUEN, ARNE (1913–, NRW
Gategutter, 1948, Novel
Gategutter 1949 d: Arne Skouen, Ulf Greber. lps: Pal Bang-Hansen, Finn Bernhoft, Sven Byhring. 78M NRW. *Gods of the Streets*; *Guttersnipes*; *Boys from the Streets*

SKOWRONNEK, RICHARD
Die Beiden Wildtauben, Novel
Starker Als Die Liebe 1938 d: Joe Stockel. lps: Karin Hardt, Leny Marenbach, Paul Richter. 94M GRM. prod/rel: Rolf Randolf, Bavaria
Das Schweigen Im Walde, Novel
Schweigen Im Walde 1 1918 d: Paul von Woringen. lps: Lotte Neumann, Anton Ernst Ruckert. 1494m GRM. *Ein Erbfolgestreit* prod/rel: Lotte Neumann Film
Schweigen Im Walde 2 1918 d: Paul von Woringen. lps: Lotte Neumann, Anton Ernst Ruckert. 1479m GRM. *Eine Aussergerichtliche Einigung* prod/rel: Lotte Neumann-Film

SKRAM, AMALIE
Lucie, 1888, Novel
Lucie 1979 d: Jan Erik During. lps: Inger Lise Rypdal, Gosta Ekman, Kari Simonsen. 100M NRW.

Pa Sct. Jorgen, 1895, Novel
Formynderne 1978 d: Nicole MacE. lps: Vibeke Lokkeberg, Helge Reiss, Odd Furoy. 104M NRW. *The Guardians; Professoren*

Professor Hieronimus, 1895, Novel
Formynderne 1978 d: Nicole MacE. lps: Vibeke Lokkeberg, Helge Reiss, Odd Furoy. 104M NRW. *The Guardians; Professoren*

SKRUZNY, JOSEF
Denik Kacenky Strnadove, Novel
Lasky Kacenky Strnadove 1926 d: Svatopluk Innemann. lps: Zdena Kavkova, Vlasta Burian, Jiri Sedlacek. 2781m CZC. *The Loves of Kacenka Strnadova* prod/rel: Oceanfilm

Falesna Kocicka, Play
Falesna Kocicka 1937 d: Vladimir Slavinsky. lps: Vera Ferbasova, Karel Jicinsky, Oldrich Novy. 3055m CZC. *The False Pussycat* prod/rel: Elekta
Heiraten - Aber Wen? 1938 d: Carl Boese. lps: Karin Hardt, Fred Hennings, Rolf WankA. 2291m GRM/CZC. *Die Falsche Katze; Verliebte Herzen* prod/rel: Donau-Film, Elekta

Komptoiristka Pana, Play
Komptoiristka 1922 d: Svatopluk Innemann. lps: Zdena Kavkova, H. Fischerova, Theodor Pistek. 1722m CZC. *The Clerk* prod/rel: Atropos, Biografia

Romanek Na Horach, Play
Senkyrka "U Divoke Krasy" 1932 d: Svatopluk Innemann. lps: Jaroslav Marvan, Ludmila Babkova, Lida BaarovA. 2697m CZC. *The Innkeeper "U Divoke Krasy; The Ravishing Barmaid* prod/rel: Meissner

Venousek a Stazicka, Novel
Venousek a Stazicka 1922 d: Svatopluk Innemann. lps: Karel Branald, Zdena Kavkova, Eman FialA. CZC. *Venousek and Stazicka* prod/rel: Ab, Biografia
Venousek a Stazicka 1939 d: Cenek Slegl. lps: Vera Ferbasova, Eva Gerova, Vladimir Salac. 1945m CZC. *Venousek and Stazicka* prod/rel: Brom

Zabec, Play
Zabec 1939 d: Vladimir Slavinsky. lps: Vera Ferbasova, Theodor Pistek, Zita KabatovA. 2780m CZC. *The Little Schoolgirl* prod/rel: Excelsior

Zeleny Automobil, Novel
Zeleny Automobil 1921 d: Svatopluk Innemann. lps: Zdena Kavkova, Luigi Hofman, Milos VavrA. 1410m CZC. *The Green Car* prod/rel: Atropos, Biografia

SKUTECKY, VACLAV
Male Stesti, Play
Vcera Nedele Byla 1938 d: Walter Schorsch. lps: Jiri Stepnickova, Otomar Korbelar, Antonie NedosinskA. 2660m CZC. *Yesterday It Was Sunday; Male Stesti; Yesterday We Had Sunday* prod/rel: Ab

SKUTEZKY, VICTOR
Play
It Happened One Sunday 1944 d: Carl Lamac. lps: Robert Beatty, Barbara White, Marjorie Rhodes. 99M UKN. prod/rel: Associated British Picture Corporation, Pathe

SKVORECKY, JOSEF (1924–, CZC, Skvorecky, Josef Vaclav
Fararuv Konec, Prerov 1969, Novel
Fararuv Konec 1968 d: Evald Schorm. lps: Vlastimil Brodsky, Jana Brejchova, Jan Libicek. 97M CZC. *End of a Priest* (USA); *The Parson's End; Pastor's End; The Priest's End* prod/rel: Barrandov Film Studio

SLADE, BERNARD
Romantic Comedy, Play
Romantic Comedy 1983 d: Arthur Hiller. lps: Dudley Moore, Mary Steenburgen, Frances Sternhagen. 103M USA. prod/rel: MGM, United Artists

Same Time Next Year, Play
Same Time, Next Year 1978 d: Robert Mulligan. lps: Ellen Burstyn, Alan Alda, Ivan Bonar. 120M USA. prod/rel: Universal, Walter Mirisch

Tribute, Play
Tribute 1980 d: Bob Clark. lps: Jack Lemmon, Lee Remick, Robby Benson. 124M CND. *Un Fils Pour l'Ete* prod/rel: Kudos Film Productions Ltd., Tiberius Film Corp.

SLADE, CHRISTINE JOPE
Caretakers Within, 1921, Short Story
Life's Darn Funny 1921 d: Dallas M. Fitzgerald. lps: Viola Dana, Gareth Hughes, Eva Gordon. 6r USA. prod/rel: Metro Pictures

SLATER, BARNEY
The Maverick, Short Story
Three Violent People 1956 d: Rudolph Mate. lps: Charlton Heston, Anne Baxter, Gilbert Roland. 100M USA. prod/rel: Paramount

The Tin Badge, Story
Tin Star, The 1957 d: Anthony Mann. lps: Henry Fonda, Anthony Perkins, Betsy Palmer. 93M USA. prod/rel: Paramount, Perlsea Co.

SLATER, HUMPHREY
Conspirator, Novel
Conspirator 1949 d: Victor Saville. lps: Robert Taylor, Elizabeth Taylor, Robert Flemyng. 87M UKN/USA. prod/rel: MGM British

SLATER, MONTAGUE
Once a Jolly Swagman, Novel
Once a Jolly Swagman 1948 d: Jack Lee. lps: Dirk Bogarde, Bonar Colleano, Renee Asherson. 100M UKN. *Maniacs on Wheels* (USA) prod/rel: General Film Distributors, Wessex

SLATER, NIGEL
The Mad Death, Novel
Mad Death, The 1983 d: Robert Young. lps: Richard Heffer, Barbara Kellerman, Richard Morant. MTV. 165M UKN. prod/rel: BBC Scotland

SLAUGHTER, FRANK G. (1908–, USA
Doctors' Wives, Novel
Doctors' Wives 1971 d: George Schaefer. lps: Dyan Cannon, Richard Crenna, Gene Hackman. 102M USA. prod/rel: Columbia

Sangaree, 1948, Novel
Sangaree 1953 d: Edward Ludwig. lps: Fernando Lamas, Arlene Dahl, Patricia MedinA. 94M USA. prod/rel: Paramount, Pine-Thomas

The Warrior, 1956, Novel
Naked in the Sun 1957 d: R. John Hugh. lps: James Craig, Lita Milan, Barton MacLane. 78M USA. prod/rel: Allied Artists, Empire Studios

SLAVICI, IOAN
Mara, 1906, Novel
Dincolo de Pod 1975 d: Mircea Veroiu. lps: Leopoldina Balanuta, Mircea Albulescu, Ovidiu Iuliu Moldovan. 98M RMN. *The Other Side of the Bridge; Beyond the Bridge; Across the Bridge*

Moara Cu Noroc, 1881, Short Story
Moara Cu Noroc 1956 d: Victor Iliu. lps: Geo Barton, Ioana Bulca, Aurel Cioranu. 116M RMN. *The Mill of Luck and Plenty; The Mill of Good Luck*

Padureanca, 1884, Short Story
Padureanca 1988 d: Nicolae Margineanu. lps: Victor Rebengiuc, Andrian Pintea, Manuela Harabor. 112M RMN. *The Forest Maiden*

SLAYTON, FRANK
The Inferior Sex, New York 1910, Play
Inferior Sex, The 1920 d: Joseph Henabery. lps: Mildred Harris, Milton Sills, Mary Alden. 5685f USA. prod/rel: Chaplin-Mayer Pictures Co., First National Exhibitors Circuit

SLESINGER, TESS
The Answer in the Magnolias, New York 1935, Novel
Girls' School 1938 d: John Brahm. lps: Anne Shirley, Nan Grey, Ralph Bellamy. 73M USA. *The Romantic Age* prod/rel: Columbia Pictures Corp. of California©

SLOANE, A. B.
The Wizard of Oz, 1903, Play
His Majesty, the Scarecrow of Oz 1914 d: L. Frank Baum. lps: Frank Moore, Vivian Reed, Fred Woodward. 5r USA. *The New Wizard of Oz; The Scarecrow of Oz; His Majesty the Scarecrow* prod/rel: Oz Film Manufacturing Co., Alliance Films Corp.

SLOANE, A. BALDWIN
Tillie's Nightmare, New York 1910, Musical Play
Tillie's Punctured Romance 1914 d: MacK Sennett. lps: Marie Dressler, Charles Chaplin, Mabel Normand. 6r USA. *Charlie's Big Romance; For the Love of Tillie; Marie's Millions; Tillie's Nightmare* prod/rel: Keystone Film Co.©, State Rights

SLOANE, EDGAR
Tillie's Punctured Romance 1914 d: MacK Sennett. lps: Marie Dressler, Charles Chaplin, Mabel Normand. 6r USA. *Charlie's Big Romance; For the Love of Tillie; Marie's Millions; Tillie's Nightmare* prod/rel: Keystone Film Co.©, State Rights

SLOANE, ROBERT
Howdy Stranger, New York 1937, Play
Cowboy from Brooklyn 1938 d: Lloyd Bacon. lps: Dick Powell, Pat O'Brien, Priscilla Lane. 80M USA. *Romance and Rhythm* (UKN); *Dude Rancher; Howdy Stranger; The Brooklyn Cowboy* prod/rel: Warner Bros. Pictures, Inc.

SLOANE, WILLIAM
The Edge of Running Water, Story
Devil Commands, The 1941 d: Edward Dmytryk. lps: Boris Karloff, Richard Fiske, Amanda Duff. 65M USA. *When the Devil Commands* prod/rel: Columbia

SLOBODA, CARL
Am Teetisch, Vienna 1915, Play
Tea for Three 1927 d: Robert Z. Leonard. lps: Lew Cody, Aileen Pringle, Owen Moore. 6273f USA. prod/rel: Metro-Goldwyn-Mayer Pictures

Die Hollen Maschine, 1928, Novel
Infernal machine 1933 d: Marcel Varnel. lps: Genevieve Tobin, James Bell, Chester Morris. 66M USA. prod/rel: Fox Film Corp.©

SLOMAN, ROBERT
The Tinker, Stratford 1960, Play
Wild and the Willing, The 1962 d: Ralph Thomas. lps: Virginia Maskell, Paul Rogers, Ian McShane. 122M UKN. *Young and Willing* (USA); *The Young and the Willing* prod/rel: Rank Organisation, Rank Film Distributors

SLOTT, HARRY M.
The Young and the Brave, Novel
Young and the Brave, The 1963 d: Francis D. Lyon. lps: Rory Calhoun, William Bendix, Richard Jaeckel. 84M USA. *Attong* prod/rel: MGM

SLOWACKI, JULIUSZ (1809–1849), PLN
Mazepa, 1840, Play
Blanche 1971 d: Walerian Borowczyk. lps: Ligia Branice, Laurence Trimble, Georges Wilson. 92M FRN. prod/rel: Telepresse Films France, Abel Et Charton
Mazepa 1975 d: Gustaw Holoubek. lps: Zbigniew Zapasiewicz, Magdalena Zawadzka, Jerzy Bonczak. 115M PLN. *Mazeppa*

SMEJKAL, JAROSLAV
Atom Vecnosti a Takova Je Vecna Hra Lasky, Play
Atom Vecnosti 1934 d: Vladimir Smejkal, Cenek Zahradnicek. lps: LakovA. 165m CZC. *Atom of Eternity* prod/rel: Cenek Zahradnicek

SMEJKAL, VLADIMIR
Atom Vecnosti 1934 d: Vladimir Smejkal, Cenek Zahradnicek. lps: LakovA. 165m CZC. *Atom of Eternity* prod/rel: Cenek Zahradnicek

SMETANA, BEDRICH (1824–1884), CZC
Prodana Nevesta, Prague 1866, Opera
Prodana Nevesta 1933 d: Svatopluk Innemann, Jaroslav Kvapil. lps: Jan Konstantin, Dobroslava Sudikova, Ota HorakovA. 3211m CZC. *The Bartered Bride* prod/rel: Espo
Prodana Nevesta 1913 d: Max Urban. lps: Tadeusz Dura, Marie Slechtova, Adolf Krossing. CZC. *The Bartered Bride* prod/rel: Asum
Verkaufte Braut, Die 1932 d: Max Ophuls. lps: Jarmila Novotna, Willi Domgraf-Fassbaender, Liesl Karlstadt. 77M GRM. *The Bartered Bride* prod/rel: Reichsliga Film, Neue Filmkunst

SMILEY, JANE
A Thousand Acres, Novel
Thousand Acres, A 1997 d: Jocelyn Moorhouse. lps: Michelle Pfeiffer, Jessica Lange, Jason Robards Jr. 105M USA. prod/rel: Touchstone Pictures, Beacon Pictures

SMILOVSKY, ALOIS VOJTECH
Parnasie, Novel
Parnasie 1925 d: Josef Kokeisl. lps: Jiri Sedlacek, Marie Fingerova, Milada Jadranska-HrabankovA. 1590m CZC. *The Girl from the Sumava Mountains* prod/rel: Josef Kokeisl

Za Rannich Cervanku, Novel
Za Rannich Cervanku 1934 d: Josef Rovensky. lps: Karel Hasler, Bedrich Vrbsky, Jaroslav PruchA. 2376m CZC. *The Rosy Dawn; In the Red of Morning* prod/rel: Ab

SMITH, ALICE M.
The Strength of the Weak, New York 1906, Play
Strength of the Weak, The 1916 d: Lucius Henderson. lps: Mary Fuller, Edwards Davis, Harry Hilliard. 5r USA. prod/rel: Bluebird Photoplays, Inc.©

SMITH, ALSON JESSE
Brother Van, 1948, Novel
Lawless Eighties, The 1957 d: Joseph Kane. lps: Buster Crabbe, John Smith, Marilyn Saris. 70M USA. prod/rel: Republic, Ventura

SMITH, BETTY (1904–1972), USA
Joy in the Morning, New York 1963, Novel
Joy in the Morning 1965 d: Alex Segal. lps: Richard Chamberlain, Yvette Mimieux, Arthur Kennedy. 103M USA. prod/rel: Metro-Goldwyn-Mayer, Inc.

A Tree Grows in Brooklyn, 1943, Novel
Tree Grows in Brooklyn, A 1945 d: Elia Kazan. lps: Dorothy McGuire, Joan Blondell, James Dunn. 128M USA. prod/rel: 20th Century-Fox
Tree Grows in Brooklyn, A 1974 d: Joseph Hardy. lps: Cliff Robertson, Diane Baker, James Olson. TVM. 78M USA. prod/rel: 20th Century-Fox

SMITH, CRAIG
Ladystinger, Novel
Scam 1993 d: John Flynn. lps: Lorraine Bracco, Christopher Walken, Miguel Ferrer. 102M USA. prod/rel: Viacom Pictures©

SMITH, DODIE (1896–1990), UKN
Call It a Day, New York 1936, Play
Call It a Day 1937 d: Archie Mayo. lps: Olivia de Havilland, Ian Hunter, Alice Brady. 89M USA. prod/rel: Warner Bros. Pictures, Inc.

Dear Octopus, London 1938, Play
Dear Octopus 1943 d: Harold French. lps: Margaret Lockwood, Michael Wilding, Celia Johnson. 86M UKN. *The Randolph Family* (USA) prod/rel: General Film Distributors, Gainsborough

The One Hundred and One Dalmatians, New York 1957, Novel
101 Dalmatians 1996 d: Stephen Herek. lps: Glenn Close, Jeff Daniels, Joely Richardson. 103M USA. prod/rel: Disney Enterprises, Great Oaks
One Hundred and One Dalmatians 1961 d: Wolfgang Reitherman, Hamilton Luske. ANM. 80M USA. prod/rel: Walt Disney Productions, Buena Vista

SMITH, EDGAR
Old Dutch, New York 1909, Musical Play
Old Dutch 1915 d: Frank H. Crane. lps: Lew Fields, Vivian Martin, Charles Judels. 5r USA. prod/rel: Shubert Film Corp., World Film Corp.©

SMITH, F. HOPKINSON, Smith, Francis Hopkinson
Caleb West Master Diver, New York 1899, Novel
Caleb West 1912. lps: E. P. Sullivan, Miss Robinson, Irving Cummings. 2r USA. prod/rel: Reliance
Deep Waters 1920 d: Maurice Tourneur. lps: John Gilbert, Rudolph Christians, Barbara Bedford. 5035f USA. *Master Diver Caleb West* prod/rel: Maurice Tourneur Productions, Inc., Famous Players-Lasky Corp.©

Colonel Carter of Cartersville, New York 1891, Novel
Colonel Carter of Cartersville 1915 d: Howell Hansel. lps: Burr McIntosh, Lily Cahill, Katherine La Salle. 5r USA. prod/rel: Burr Mcintosh Film Corp., World Film Corp.©

Felix O'Day, New York 1915, Novel
Felix O'Day 1920 d: Robert T. Thornby. lps: H. B. Warner, Marguerite Snow, Lillian Rich. 4729f USA. prod/rel: Jesse D. Hampton Productions, Pathe Exchange, Inc.©

Kennedy Square, New York 1911, Novel
Kennedy Square 1916 d: S. Rankin Drew. lps: Antonio Moreno, Charles Kent, Muriel Ostriche. 5r USA. prod/rel: Vitagraph Co. of America©, Blue Ribbon Feature

A Kentucky Cinderella, 1899, Short Story
Desperate Youth 1921 d: Harry B. Harris. lps: Gladys Walton, J. Farrell MacDonald, Lewis Willoughby. 4505f USA. prod/rel: Universal Film Mfg. Co.
Kentucky Cinderella, A 1917 d: Rupert Julian. lps: Harry Carter, Rupert Julian, Ruth Clifford. 5r USA. prod/rel: Bluebird Photoplays, Inc.©

An Old-Fashioned Gentleman, Story
Memories of His Youth 1913 d: Barry O'Neil. lps: Charles Arthur, Marie Weirman, Harry Myers. 1000f USA. prod/rel: Lubin

The Tides of Barnegat, New York 1906, Novel
Tides of Barnegat, The 1917 d: Marshall Neilan. lps: Blanche Sweet, Elliott Dexter, Tom Forman. 5r USA. prod/rel: Jesse L. Lasky Feature Play Co.©, Paramount Pictures Corp.

SMITH, FRANK BERKELEY
Babette, New York 1916, Novel
Babette 1917 d: Charles J. Brabin. lps: Marc McDermott, Peggy Hyland, Templer Saxe. 5r USA. prod/rel: Vitagraph Co. of America©, Blue Ribbon Feature

SMITH, FRANK LEON
The Bells of Waldenbruck, 1933, Story
Melody in Spring 1934 d: Norman Z. McLeod. lps: Lanny Ross, Ann Sothern, Charles Ruggles. 75M USA. prod/rel: Paramount Productions©

SMITH, FREDERICK E.
633 Squadron, London 1958, Novel
633 Squadron 1964 d: Walter Grauman. lps: Cliff Robertson, George Chakiris, Maria Perschy. 101M UKN. prod/rel: Mirisch Corporation, United Artists

SMITH, GARRETT
Old Hutch Lives Up to It, 1920, Short Story
Honest Hutch 1920 d: Clarence Badger. lps: Will Rogers, Mary Alden, Priscilla Bonner. 5r USA. *Old Hutch* prod/rel: Goldwyn Pictures Corp.©, Goldwyn Distributing Corp.

Old Hutch 1936 d: J. Walter Ruben. lps: Wallace Beery, Eric Linden, Cecilia Parker. 80M USA. prod/rel: Metro-Goldwyn-Mayer Corp.©

SMITH, H. ALLEN (1907–, USA, Smith, Harry Allen
Rhubarb, 1946, Novel
Rhubarb 1951 d: Arthur Lubin. lps: Ray Milland, Jan Sterling, Gene Lockhart. 95M USA. prod/rel: Paramount

SMITH, HAROLD JACOB
The Highest Mountain, Story
River's Edge, The 1957 d: Allan Dwan. lps: Ray Milland, Anthony Quinn, Debra Paget. 87M USA. prod/rel: 20th Century-Fox

SMITH, HARRIET LUMMIS
Agatha's Aunt, Indianapolis 1920, Novel
Heart to Let, A 1921 d: Eddie Dillon. lps: Justine Johnstone, Harrison Ford, Marcia Harris. 5349f USA. prod/rel: Realart Pictures

SMITH, HARRY & ROBERT
Sweethearts, New York 1913, Opera
Sweethearts 1938 d: W. S. Van Dyke. lps: Jeanette MacDonald, Nelson Eddy, Frank Morgan. 114M USA. prod/rel: Metro-Goldwyn-Mayer Corp., Loew's, Inc.©

SMITH, HARRY B.
The Billionaire, Story
Billionaire, The 1914 d: James Kirkwood. lps: Dave Morris, Charles Hill Mailes, Gertrude Bambrick. SHT USA. prod/rel: Biograph Co., Klaw & Erlanger

The Fortune Teller, New York 1929, Opera
Buenaventura, La 1934 d: William McGann. lps: Enrico Caruso Jr., Anita Campillo, Luis Alberni. 6907f MXC. prod/rel: First National Pictures, Inc.

Stop Look and Listen, Play
Stop, Look and Listen 1926 d: Larry Semon. lps: Larry Semon, Dorothy Dwan, Mary Carr. 5305f USA. prod/rel: Larry Semon Productions

SMITH, HARRY JAMES
Blackbirds, New York 1913, Play
Blackbirds 1915 d: J. P. McGowan. lps: Laura Hope Crews, Thomas Meighan, George Gebhardt. SHT USA. prod/rel: Jesse L. Lasky Feature Play Co.©, Paramount Pictures Corp.
Blackbirds 1920 d: John Francis Dillon. lps: Justine Johnstone, William "Stage" Boyd, Charles Gerrard. 4979f USA. prod/rel: Realart Pictures Corp.©

SMITH, HILDA HOOKE
Here Will I Nest, Play
Here Will I Nest 1941 d: Melburn E. Turner. lps: John Burton, Robina Richardson, George Simpson. 90M CND. *Talbot of Canada* prod/rel: Melburn E. Turner

SMITH, J. AUGUSTUS
Louisiana, New York 1933, Play
Drums O' Voodoo 1934 d: Arthur Hoerl. lps: J. Augustus Smith, Laura Bowman, Edna Barr. 70M USA. *Voodoo Drums*; *Louisiana*; *Voodoo*; *The Devil*; *Voodoo Devil Drums* prod/rel: International Stageplay Pictures

SMITH, JOAN
Novel
Don't Leave Me This Way 1993 d: Stuart Orme. lps: Moira Williams, Janet McTeer, Imelda Staunton. TVM. 95M UKN. prod/rel: First Choice

A Masculine Ending, Novel
Masculine Ending, A 1992 d: Antonia Bird. lps: Janet McTeer, Imelda Staunton, Paul Brooke. TVM. 95M UKN.

SMITH, LADY ELEANOR
Ballerina, Novel
Men in Her Life, The 1941 d: Gregory Ratoff. lps: Loretta Young, Conrad Veidt, Dean Jagger. 90M USA. *Tonight Belongs to Us*; *Woman of Desire* prod/rel: Columbia

Caravan, Novel
Caravan 1946 d: Arthur Crabtree. lps: Stewart Granger, Jean Kent, Anne Crawford. 122M UKN. prod/rel: Gainsborough, General Film Distributors

The Man in Grey, Novel
Man in Grey, The 1943 d: Leslie Arliss. lps: Margaret Lockwood, Phyllis Calvert, James Mason. 116M UKN. prod/rel: Gainsborough Pictures, General Film Distributors

Red Wagon, Novel
Red Wagon 1934 d: Paul L. Stein. lps: Charles Bickford, Raquel Torres, Greta Nissen. 107M UKN. prod/rel: British International Pictures, Wardour

Tzigane, Novel
Gypsy 1937 d: R. William Neill. lps: Roland Young, Chili Bouchier, Hugh Williams. 78M UKN. *Tzigane* prod/rel: Warner Bros., First National

SMITH, MARTIN
Gypsy in Amber, Novel
Art of Crime, The 1975 d: Richard Irving. lps: Ron Leibman, David Hedison, Jill Clayburgh. TVM. 78M USA. *Roman Grey* prod/rel: Universal

SMITH, MARTIN CRUZ (1942–, USA
Gorky Park, Novel
Gorky Park 1983 d: Michael Apted. lps: William Hurt, Lee Marvin, Brian Dennehy. 128M USA. prod/rel: Orion, Rank

Nightwing, Novel
Nightwing 1979 d: Arthur Hiller. lps: Nick Mancuso, David Warner, Kathryn Harrold. 103M USA/NTH. prod/rel: Columbia, Polyc

SMITH, MAXWELL
Dated, 1920, Short Story
Last Card, The 1921 d: Bayard Veiller. lps: May Allison, Alan Roscoe, James Goethals. 5817f USA. *The Woman Next Door* prod/rel: Metro Pictures

SMITH, MINNA CAROLINE
Rose of the Golden West, Story
Rose of the Golden West 1927 d: George Fitzmaurice. lps: Mary Astor, Gilbert Roland, Gustav von Seyffertitz. 6477f USA. *Rose of Monterey* prod/rel: First National Pictures

SMITH, P. G.
Heads Up, New York 1929, Musical Play
Heads Up 1930 d: Victor Schertzinger. lps: Charles "Buddy" Rogers, Victor Moore, Helen Kane. 6785f USA. prod/rel: Paramount-Publix Corp.

SMITH, PATRICK
Angel City, Novel
Angel City 1980 d: Philip Leacock. lps: Ralph Waite, Mitchell Ryan, Paul Winfield. TVM. 100M USA. prod/rel: CBS, Factor-Newland

SMITH, PAUL GIRARD
Fireman Save My Child, Story
Sandy Gets Her Man 1940 d: Otis Garrett, Paul Gerard Smith. lps: Baby Sandy, Stuart Erwin, Una Merkel. 74M USA. *Fireman Save My Child* prod/rel: Universal Pictures Co.©

Funny Face, London 1928, Play
She Couldn't Say No 1939 d: Graham Cutts. lps: Tommy Trinder, Fred Emney, Googie Withers. 72M UKN. prod/rel: Associated British Picture Corporation
She Knew What She Wanted 1936 d: Thomas Bentley. lps: Albert Burdon, Betty Ann Davies, Claude Dampier. 74M UKN. prod/rel: Rialto, Wardour

SMITH, ROBERT KIMMEL
Jane's House, Novel
Jane's House 1993 d: Glenn Jordan. lps: James Woods, Anne Archer, Missy Crider. TVM. 95M USA. prod/rel: Spelling Television©, Michael Phillips Productions

SMITH, ROBERT PAUL
The Tender Trap, New York 1954, Play
Tender Trap, The 1955 d: Charles Walters. lps: Frank Sinatra, Debbie Reynolds, Celeste Holm. 111M USA. prod/rel: MGM

SMITH, ROSAMUND
Lies of the Twins, Novel
Lies of the Twins 1991 d: Tim Hunter. lps: Isabella Rossellini, Aidan Quinn, Iman. TVM. 93M USA.

SMITH, SARA B.
Ever the Beginning, Play
My Girl Tisa 1948 d: Elliott Nugent. lps: Lilli Palmer, Sam Wanamaker, Akim Tamiroff. 95M USA. prod/rel: Warner Bros.

SMITH, SCOTT B.
A Simple Plan, Novel
Simple Plan, A 1998 d: Sam Raimi. lps: Bill Paxton, Billy Bob Thornton, Brent Briscoe. 121M USA. prod/rel: Paramount, Mutual Film Co.

SMITH, SHELLEY
The Ballad of the Running Man, London 1961, Novel
Running Man, The 1963 d: Carol Reed. lps: Laurence Harvey, Lee Remick, Alan Bates. 103M UKN/USA. prod/rel: Peet Productions, Columbia

SMITH, TERENCE L.
The Thief Who Came to Dinner, Novel
Thief Who Came to Dinner, The 1973 d: Bud Yorkin. lps: Ryan O'Neal, Jacqueline Bisset, Warren Oates. 106M USA. *The Thief Who Came in the Night* prod/rel: Warner Bros.

SMITH, THORNE (1892–1934), USA
The Night Life of the Gods, Garden City, N.Y. 1931, Novel
Night Life of the Gods 1935 d: Lowell Sherman. lps: Alan Mowbray, Florine McKinney, Peggy Shannon. 80M USA. *Private Life of the Gods* prod/rel: Universal Pictures Corp.©

The Passionate Witch, 1941, Novel
I Married a Witch 1942 d: Rene Clair. lps: Fredric March, Veronica Lake, Robert Benchley. 76M USA. *Ma Femme Est une Sorciere* (FRN) prod/rel: United Artists

Topper, New York 1926, Novel
Topper 1937 d: Norman Z. McLeod. lps: Constance Bennett, Cary Grant, Roland Young. 97M USA. prod/rel: Metro-Goldwyn-Mayer Corp., Hal Roach Studios

Topper 1979 d: Charles S. Dubin. lps: Kate Jackson, Andrew Stevens, Jack Warden. TVM. 100M USA.

Topper Returns 1941 d: Roy Del Ruth. lps: Joan Blondell, Roland Young, Carole Landis. 88M USA. prod/rel: United Artists Corp.

Topper Takes a Trip, New York 1932, Novel
Topper Takes a Trip 1939 d: Norman Z. McLeod. lps: Constance Bennett, Roland Young, Billie Burke. 85M USA. prod/rel: Hal Roach Studios©, United Artists Corp.

Turnabout, New York 1931, Novel
Turnabout 1940 d: Hal Roach. lps: John Hubbard, Carole Landis, Adolphe Menjou. 83M USA. prod/rel: Hal Roach Studios©, United Artists Corp.

SMITH, WALLACE
The Captain Hates the Sea, Davison, Mi. 1933, Novel
Captain Hates the Sea, The 1934 d: Lewis Milestone. lps: Victor McLaglen, Helen Vinson, John Gilbert. 80M USA. prod/rel: Columbia Pictures Corp.

The Grouch Bag, Short Story
Not Quite Decent 1929 d: Irving Cummings. lps: Louise Dresser, June Collyer, Allan Lane. 4965f USA. prod/rel: Fox Film Corp.

New York West, 1926, Short Story
West of Broadway 1926 d: Robert T. Thornby. lps: Priscilla Dean, Arnold Gray, Majel Coleman. 5186f USA. prod/rel: Metropolitan Pictures Corp. of Calif., Producers Distributing Corp.

The Snake's Wife, 1926, Short Story
Upstream 1927 d: John Ford. lps: Nancy Nash, Earle Foxe, Grant Withers. 5510f USA. *Footlight Glamour* (UKN) prod/rel: Fox Film Corp.

Strictly Business, 1929, Short Story
Beau Bandit 1930 d: Lambert Hillyer. lps: Rod La Rocque, Doris Kenyon, Tom Keene. 68M USA. prod/rel: RKO Productions

A Woman Decides, Short Story
Delightful Rogue, The 1929 d: Lynn Shores, A. Leslie Pearce. lps: Rod La Rocque, Rita La Roy, Charles Byer. 71M USA. prod/rel: RKO Productions

SMITH, WAYNE
Thor, Novel
Bad Moon 1996 d: Eric Red. lps: Mariel Hemingway, Michael Pare, Mason Gamble. 79M USA. prod/rel: Warner Bros., Morgan Creek Productions

SMITH, WILBUR (1933–, SAF
The Dark of the Sun, London 1965, Novel
Mercenaries, The 1967 d: Jack Cardiff. lps: Rod Taylor, Yvette Mimieux, Peter Carsten. 105M UKN/SAF. *Dark of the Sun* (USA) prod/rel: MGM, Englund Enterprises

Goldmine, Novel
Gold 1974 d: Peter Hunt. lps: Roger Moore, Susannah York, Ray Milland. 120M UKN. prod/rel: Hemdale, Avton

Shout at the Devil, Novel
Shout at the Devil 1976 d: Peter Hunt. lps: Lee Marvin, Roger Moore, Barbara Parkins. 147M UKN. prod/rel: Tonav

SMITH, WILLIAM
The Claw, Novel
Artiglio Del Nibbio, L' 1917 d: Romolo Bacchini. lps: Ettore Mazzanti, Gigi Armandis, Eduardo SenatrA. 1680m ITL. prod/rel: Armenia Film

SMITH, WILLIAM WALLACE
Little Ledna, 1926, Short Story
Big Time 1929 d: Kenneth Hawks. lps: Lee Tracy, Mae Clarke, Daphne Pollard. 7815f USA. prod/rel: Fox Film Corp.

SMITH, WINCHELL (1871–1933), USA
The Boomerang, New York 1915, Play
Love Doctor, The 1929 d: Melville Brown. lps: Richard Dix, June Collyer, Morgan Farley. 5503f USA. prod/rel: Paramount Famous Lasky Corp.

Chicken Feed; Or Wages for Wives, New York 1923, Play
Wages for Wives 1925 d: Frank Borzage. lps: Jacqueline Logan, Creighton Hale, Earle Foxe. 6650f USA. prod/rel: Fox Film Corp.

The Fortune Hunter, New York 1909, Play
Fortune Hunter, The 1914 d: Barry O'Neil. lps: William Elliott, Ethel Clayton, Rosetta Brice. 6r USA. prod/rel: Lubin Mfg. Co.©, General Film Co.

Fortune Hunter, The 1920 d: Tom Terriss. lps: Earle Williams, Jean Paige, Van Dyke Brooke. 7r USA. prod/rel: Vitagraph Co. of America©

Fortune Hunter, The 1927 d: Charles F. Reisner. lps: Sydney Chaplin, Helene Costello, Clara Horton. 6639f USA. prod/rel: Warner Brothers Pictures

Going Crooked, New York 1926, Play
Going Crooked 1926 d: George Melford. lps: Bessie Love, Oscar Shaw, Gustav von Seyffertitz. 5345f USA. prod/rel: Fox Film Corp.

A Holy Terror, New York 1925, Play
Hills of Peril 1927 d: Lambert Hillyer. lps: Buck Jones, Georgia Hale, Albert J. Smith. 4983f USA. prod/rel: Fox Film Corp.

Lightnin', New York 1918, Play
Lightnin' 1925 d: John Ford. lps: Jay Hunt, Madge Bellamy, Wallace MacDonald. 8050f USA. prod/rel: Fox Film Corp.

Lightnin' 1930 d: Henry King. lps: Will Rogers, Louise Dresser, Joel McCreA. 8500f USA. prod/rel: Fox Film Corp.

The New Henrietta, New York 1913, Play
Saphead, The 1920 d: Herbert Blache. lps: Buster Keaton, Carol Holloway, William H. Crane. 6650f USA. prod/rel: Metro Pictures Corp.©

The Only Son, New York 1911, Play
Only Son, The 1914 d: Thomas N. Heffron, Cecil B. de Mille. lps: Thomas W. Ross, Jim Blackwell, Jane Darwell. 4-5r USA. prod/rel: Jesse L. Lasky Feature Play Co.©, State Rights

Thank You, New York 1921, Play
Thank You 1925 d: John Ford. lps: Alec B. Francis, Jacqueline Logan, George O'Brien. 6900f USA. prod/rel: Fox Film Corp.

Three Wise Fools, Ottawa 1919, Play
Three Wise Fools 1923 d: King Vidor. lps: Claude Gillingwater, Eleanor Boardman, William H. Crane. 6946f USA. prod/rel: Goldwyn Pictures

Three Wise Fools 1946 d: Edward Buzzell. lps: Margaret O'Brien, Lewis Stone, Lionel Barrymore. 90M USA. prod/rel: MGM

Turn to the Right, New York 1916, Play
Turn to the Right 1922 d: Rex Ingram. lps: Alice Terry, Jack Mulhall, Harry Myers. 7703f USA. prod/rel: Metro Pictures

Via Wireless, New York 1908, Play
Via Wireless 1915 d: George Fitzmaurice. lps: Gail Kane, Bruce McRae, Brandon Hurst. 5r USA. prod/rel: Pathe Exchange, Inc., Gold Rooster Play

The Wheel, New York 1921, Play
Wheel, The 1925 d: Victor Schertzinger. lps: Margaret Livingston, Harrison Ford, Claire Adams. 7264f USA. prod/rel: Fox Film Corp.

SMITTER, WESSEL
F.O.B. Detroit, Novel
Reaching for the Sun 1941 d: William A. Wellman. lps: Joel McCrea, Ellen Drew, Eddie Bracken. 90M USA. prod/rel: Paramount

SMOLKA, JANOS
Play
Ultimo Addio, L' 1942 d: Ferruccio Cerio. lps: Gino Cervi, Luisa Ferida, Sandro Ruffini. 83M ITL. *Anime Erranti; Diagnosi* prod/rel: Sirena Film, I.N.a.C.

SNAITH, J. C.
The Crime of Constable Kelly, Novel
Romance of Mayfair, A 1925 d: Thomas Bentley. lps: Betty Faire, Henry Victor, Molly Johnson. 4750f UKN. prod/rel: Stoll

SNEIDER, VERN J. (1916–1981), USA, Sneider, Vernon John
The Teahouse of the August Moon, Novel
Teahouse of the August Moon, The 1956 d: Daniel Mann. lps: Glenn Ford, Paul Ford, Marlon Brando. 123M USA. prod/rel: Metro-Goldwyn-Mayer

SNILLOC
Asir of Asirgarh, Novel
Ajit 1948 d: Mohan Dayaram Bhavnani. lps: Monica Desai, Premnath, Yashodhara Katju. 133M IND. *Colourful Life; Rangeen Zamana* prod/rel: Bhavnani Prod.

SNIZEK, JAN
Priklady Tahnou, Play
Priklady Tahnou 1939 d: Miroslav Cikan. lps: Ruzena Naskova, Natasa Gollova, Stella MajovA. 2443m CZC. *Examples Work Wonders* prod/rel: Nationalfilm

SNOW, C. P. (1905–1980), UKN, Snow, Charles Percy
The Affair, Novel
Affair, The 1963 d: John Jacobs. lps: John Clements, Alan Dobie, Michael Goodliffe. MTV. 100M UKN. prod/rel: BBC

SNOWFALL, AMINAL
Le Revenant, Book
Revenant, Le 1979 d: Mahama Johnson Traore. UNF. CND/SNL. prod/rel: Ballon Blanc Inc. (Montreal), Sunu Film (Dakar)

SNYDER, REV. JOHN M.
As Ye Sow, New York 1905, Play
As Ye Sow 1914 d: Frank H. Crane. lps: Alice Brady, Douglas MacLean, Walter Fischter. 5r USA. prod/rel: World Film Corp.©, William A. Brady Picture Plays, Inc.

SOBELL, JACK
Story
Nora Prentiss 1947 d: Vincent Sherman. lps: Ann Sheridan, Kent Smith, Bruce Bennett. 111M USA. prod/rel: Warner Bros.

30 Days Hath September, New York 1938, Play
Thieves Fall Out 1941 d: Ray Enright. lps: Eddie Albert, Joan Leslie, Alan Hale. 72M USA. *Thirty Days Hath September* prod/rel: Warner Bros.

SOD, TED
Satan and Simon Desoto, Play
Crocodile Tears 1998 d: Ann Coppel. lps: Ted Sod, Joanne L. Klein, Wade Madsen. 84M USA. prod/rel: Crocodile Tears

SODERBERG, HJALMAR (1869–1941), SWD
Den Allvarsamma Leken, 1912, Novel
Allvarsamma Leken, Den 1945 d: Rune Carlsten. lps: Viveca Lindfors, John Ekman, Olof Widgren. 106M SWD. *Serious Game* prod/rel: Film Ab Lux

Allvarsamma Leken, Den 1977 d: Anja Breien. lps: Lil Terselius, Stefan Ekman, Palle Granditsky. 100M SWD/NRW. *Games of Love and Loneliness; Love and Loneliness* prod/rel: Stiftelsen Svenska Filminstitutet, Norsk Film a/S

Doktor Glas, 1905, Novel
Doktor Glas 1942 d: Rune Carlsten. lps: Georg Rydeberg, Irma Christenson, Rune Carlsten. 89M SWD. prod/rel: Ab Svensk Talfilm, Svensk Talfilms Distributiosbyra Ab

Doktor Glas 1968 d: Mai Zetterling. lps: Per Oscarsson, Ulf Palme, Lone Hertz. 83M DNM/SWD. *Doctor Glas* (USA) prod/rel: Lanterna Film, Fox Film

Gertrud, 1906, Play
Gertrud 1964 d: Carl T. Dreyer. lps: Nina Pens Rode, Bendt Rothe, Ebbe Rode. 116M DNM. *Gertrude* prod/rel: Palladium

SOEBERG, FINN
Der Bettelstudent, Novel
Bettelstudent Oder: Was MacH' Ich Mit Den Madchen, Der 1969 d: Michael Verhoeven. lps: Christof Wackernagel, Gila von Weitershausen, Hannelore Elsner. 83M GRM. *Der Bettelstudent* prod/rel: Rob Houwer, Constantin

SOEDERHJELM, MARTIN
Skepp Till Indialand, Play
Skepp Till Indialand 1947 d: Ingmar Bergman. lps: Birger Malmsten, Gertrud Fridh, Holger Lowenadler. 104M SWD. *A Ship to India* (UKN); *A Ship Bound for India; Frustration* (USA); *The Land of Desire* prod/rel: Sveriges Folkbiografer

SOHL, JERRY
Night Slaves, Novel
Night Slaves 1970 d: Ted Post. lps: James Franciscus, Lee Grant, Scott Marlowe. TVM. 73M USA. prod/rel: Bing Crosby Productions

SOINI, YRJO
Einmal Eva Zweimal Adam, Novel
2 X Adam - 1 X Eve 1959 d: Franz M. Lang. lps: Heidi Bruhl, Matthias Fuchs, Brigitte Grothum. 89M GRM. *Einmal Eva Zweimal Adam; Two Adams One Eve* prod/rel: Filmaufbau, Pallas

SOKOLOVA-PODPEROVA, ANNA
Neslavna Slava, Short Story
Blahovy Sen 1943 d: J. A. Holman. lps: Jaroslav Marvan, Zdenka Baldova, Natasa GollovA. 2913m CZC. *Fond Dream* prod/rel: Nationalfilm

SOLANO, SOLITA
The Price of Feathers, Story
Beyond the Rainbow 1922 d: W. Christy Cabanne. lps: Harry T. Morey, Billie Dove, Virginia Lee. 6500f USA. prod/rel: R-C Pictures

SOLARI, PIETRO
Due Occhi Per Non Vedere, Play
Due Occhi Per Non Vedere 1939 d: Gennaro Righelli. lps: Loretta Vinci, Renato Cialente, Alma Clark. 75M ITL. prod/rel: Mediterranea Film, C.I.N.F.

SOLDATI, MARIO (1906–, ITL
I Due Maestri, 1957, Short Story
Il Maestro 1989 d: Marion Hansel. lps: Malcolm McDowell, Charles Aznavour, Andrea Ferreol. 90M BLG/FRN. *Maestro*

La Giacca Verde, 1961, Short Story
  Giacca Verde, La 1979 d: Franco Giraldi. lps: Vittorio Sanipoli, Jean-Pierre Cassel, Senta Berger. 103M ITL. prod/rel: C.E.P., Rai-Tv (Roma)

SOLINAS, FRANCO
Squarcio, Novel
  Grande Strada Azzurra, La 1957 d: Gillo Pontecorvo. lps: Yves Montand, Alida Valli, Umberto Spadaro. 100M ITL/YGS/GRM. *Veliki Plavi Put* (YGS); *The Wide Blue Road* (USA); *Squarcia*; *Un Denomme Squarcio*; *Long Blue Road, The* prod/rel: Ge.Si. Cin.Ca (Roma), Play Art (Paris)

SOLOMON, BESSIE R.
Chuck Connors, Novel
  Bowery, The 1933 d: Raoul Walsh. lps: Wallace Beery, George Raft, Jackie Cooper. 92M USA. prod/rel: 20th Century Pictures, Inc., United Artists

SOLOMON, LOUIS
Snafu, New York 1944, Play
  Snafu 1945 d: Jack Moss. lps: Robert Benchley, Vera Vague, Conrad Janis. 82M USA. *Welcome Home* (UKN) prod/rel: Columbia, George Abbott Prods.

SOLOMONS, THEODORE SEIXAS
The Barbarian, 1920, Short Story
  Barbarian, The 1921 d: Donald Crisp. lps: Monroe Salisbury, George Burrell, Barney Sherry. 6r USA. prod/rel: Monroe Salisbury Players, Inc., Pioneer Film Corp.

SOLSER, MICHEL
Revue Artistique, Revue
  Artisten-Revue, de 1926 d: Alex Benno. lps: Isidore Zwaaf, Alex de Meester, Pauline Herve. 1600m NTH. **De Revue-Artistek**; *The Revue of Artistes*; *The Artistice Revue* prod/rel: Alex Benno, Actueel-Film

SOLTIKOW, MICHAEL GRAF
Eine Frau Genugt Nicht?, Novel
  Frau Genugt Nicht?, Eine 1955 d: Ulrich Erfurth. lps: Hilde Krahl, Hans Sohnker, Rudolf Forster. 90M GRM. *Isn't One Wife Enough?* prod/rel: Apollo, D.F.H.

SOLZHENITSYN, ALEXANDER (1918–, RSS
Odin Den Ivana Denisovicha, 1962, Novel
  One Day in the Life of Ivan Denisovich 1971 d: Caspar Wrede. lps: Tom Courtenay, Espen Skjonberg, James Maxwell. 100M UKN/NRW/USA. *En Dag I Ivan Denisoviwich's Liv* (NRW) prod/rel: Group W, Leontes
V Kruge Pervom, 1968, Novel
  Forste Kreds, Den 1971 d: Aleksander Ford. lps: Gunther Malzacher, Elzbieta Czysewska, Vera TschechowA. 100M DNM/GRM/USA. *The First Circle of Hell*; *The First Circle*

SOMERSET, CHARLES
The Mistletoe Bough, Play
  Mistletoe Bough, The 1923 d: Edwin J. Collins. lps: John Stuart, Flora Le Breton, Lionel d'Aragon. 2050f UKN. prod/rel: British & Colonial, Walturdaw

SOMERVILLE, ANDREW W.
No Brakes, 1928, Short Story
  Oh, Yeah! 1929 d: Tay Garnett. lps: Robert Armstrong, James Gleason, Patricia Caron. 6890f USA. *No Brakes* (UKN) prod/rel: Pathe Exchange, Inc.

SOMERVILLE, H. B.
Ashes of Vengeance; a Romance of Old France, New York 1914, Novel
  Ashes of Vengeance 1923 d: Frank Lloyd. lps: Norma Talmadge, Conway Tearle, Wallace Beery. 9893f USA. *Purple Pride* prod/rel: Norma Talmadge Film Co., Associated First National Pictures

SOMMER, EDITH
A Roomful of Roses, Play
  Teenage Rebel 1956 d: Edmund Goulding. lps: Ginger Rogers, Michael Rennie, Mildred Natwick. 94M USA. prod/rel: 20th Century-Fox

SOMMER, HARALD
Ein Unheimlich Starker Abgang, Play
  Unheimlich Starker Abgang, Ein 1973 d: Michael Verhoeven. lps: Katja Rupe, Elmar Wepper, Ingold Platzer. 86M GRM. *A Strangely Powerful Exit*; *Sudden Departure*; *Sonia Scharrt Die Wirklichkeit Ab Oder. Ein Unheimlich Starker Abgang* prod/rel: Sentana, Bavaria

SOMMER, SCOTT
Crisscross, Novel
  Crisscross 1992 d: Chris Menges. lps: Goldie Hawn, Arliss Howard, James Gammon. 100M USA. *Criss Cross* prod/rel: MGM, Hawn-Sylbert

SOMMER, SIEGFRIED
Meine 99 Braute, Novel
  Meine 99 Braute 1958 d: Alfred Vohrer. lps: Claus Wilcke, Horst Frank, Wera Frydtberg. 88M GRM. *My 99 Brides* prod/rel: Interwest, Europa

SOMOGYI TOTH, SANDOR
A Gyerekek Ketszer Szuletnek, 1973, Novel
  Vallald Onmagadat! 1975 d: Frigyes Mamcserov. lps: Istvan Barsony, Marianna Moor, Eva Almasi. 88M HNG. *Be Yourself*
Gyerektukor, 1963, Novel
  Hogy Allunk, Fiatalember? 1963 d: Gyorgy Revesz. lps: Ferenc Kallai, Klari Tolnay, Balazs Kosztolanyi. 85M HNG. *Well Young Man?*
Szivem Profeta Voltal, 1965, Novel
  Profeta Voltal, Szivem 1968 d: Pal Zolnay. lps: Ivan Darvas, Kati Berek, Terry Torday. 86M HNG. *My Dear You've Been a Prophet*; *You Were a Prophet My Dear*

SONDERBY, KNUD
En Kvinde Er Overflodig, 1935, Novel
  Kvinde Er Overflodig, En 1958 d: Gabriel Axel. lps: Clara Pontoppidan. 90M DNM. *Too Much Woman*
Midt I En Jazztid, 1931, Novel
  Midt I En Jazztid 1970 d: Knud Leif Thomsen. lps: Finn Storgaard, Lotte Waever, Annelise Gabold. 101M DNM. *Jazz All Around*

SONDES, WALTER
Faces, Play
  Faces 1934 d: Sidney Morgan. lps: Anna Lee, Harold French, Walter Sondes. 68M UKN. prod/rel: British and Dominions, Paramount British

SONEGO, RODOLFO
Short Story
  Porgi l'Altra Guancia 1974 d: Franco Rossi. lps: Mario Girotti, Carlo Pedersoli, Jean-Pierre Aumont. 95M ITL/FRN. *Les Deux Missionnaires* (FRN); *I Due Missionari*; *Turn the Other Cheek* (USA) prod/rel: Inter Ma.Co. (Roma), Marianne Productions (Paris)

SONG ZHI
Protecting Peace, Play
  Da Ji Qin Lue Zhe 1965 d: Hua Chun. lps: Li Yan, Hu XIaoguang, Yu Chunmian. 10r CHN. *Attacking the Invaders* prod/rel: August First Film Studio

SONNENBLICK, DAVID
From Headquarters, Story
  From Headquarters 1915 d: Ralph Ince. lps: Anita Stewart, Earle Williams, Anders Randolf. 3r USA. prod/rel: Broadway Star, Vitagraph Co. of America

SONO, AYAKO
Satogashi Ga Kowareru Toki, 1965, Novel
  Satogashi Ga Kowareru Toki 1967 d: Tadashi Imai. lps: Ayako Wakao, Chisako Hara, Masahiko TsugawA. 96M JPN. *When the Sugar Cookie Crumbles*; *Satoshi Ga Kowareru Toki*; *When the Sugar Cake Breaks*; *When Sugar Cookies are Broken*; *When the Cookie Crumbles*
Waga Koi No Bohyo, 1959, Novel
  Waga Koi No Tabiji 1961 d: Masahiro ShinodA. 92M JPN. *Epitaph to My Love*

SOPHOCLES (496bc–406bc), GRC
Antigone, c441 bc, Play
  Antigone 1961 d: Georges Tzavellas. lps: Irene Papas, Manos Katrakis, Maro Kontou. 93M GRC. prod/rel: Norma Films Production
  Cannibali, I 1970 d: Liliana Cavani. lps: Britt Ekland, Pierre Clementi, Tomas Milian. 95M ITL. *The Year of the Cannibals* (USA); *The Cannibals Among Us*; *The Cannibals* (UKN) prod/rel: Doria Cin.Ca, San Marco Produzione
Electra, c409 bc, Play
  Elektra 1962 d: Takis Mouzenidis. 110M GRC. *Electra*
Electra, c409 bc., Play
  Elettra 1909. 265m ITL. prod/rel: Aquila Films
Oedipus Rex, c420 bc
  Edipo Re 1910 d: Giuseppe de Liguoro. lps: Giuseppe de Liguoro. 305m ITL. *King Oedipus* (UKN); *Oedipus King* (USA) prod/rel: Milano Films

SOPHOCLES
Oedipus at Colonus, 401 bc, Play
  Edipo Re 1967 d: Pier Paolo Pasolini. lps: Franco Citti, Alida Valli, Julian Beck. 110M ITL/MRC. *Oedipus the King*; *Oedipus Rex* prod/rel: Arco Film (Roma), Somafis (Casablanca)

SOPHOCLES (496bc–406bc), GRC
Oedipus Rex, c420 bc, Play
  Edipo Re 1967 d: Pier Paolo Pasolini. lps: Franco Citti, Alida Valli, Julian Beck. 110M ITL/MRC. *Oedipus the King*; *Oedipus Rex* prod/rel: Arco Film (Roma), Somafis (Casablanca)
  Koning Oedipus 1912. lps: Louis Bouwmeester, Theo Mann-Bouwmeester, Anton Roemer. NTH. *King Oedipus*; *Oedipus* prod/rel: Film-Fabriek F. A. Noggerath
  Oedipus Rex 1957 d: Tyrone Guthrie. lps: Douglas Campbell, Douglas Rain, Eric House. 87M CND. *King Oedipus* prod/rel: Oedipus Rex Productions Ltd.

Oedipus the King 1967 d: Philip Saville. lps: Christopher Plummer, Lilli Palmer, Richard Johnson. 97M UKN. prod/rel: Crossroads Films, World Film Service Productions

SOREL, JEAN-MICHEL
Me Faire Ca a Moi, Novel
  Me Faire Ca a Moi. 1961 d: Pierre Grimblat. lps: Eddie Constantine, Bernadette Lafont, Rita Cadillac. 90M FRN. *It Means That to Me* (USA) prod/rel: Ares Productions, Paris Overseas Films
Y En a Marre, Novel
  Y'en a Marre 1959 d: Yvan Govar. lps: Dominique Wilms, Barbara Laage, Pierre Trabaud. 97M FRN/BLG. *Le Gars d'Anvers*; *Y En a Marre* prod/rel: Yack Films, Belcodiez

SOREL, RENE
Aus Dem Tagebuch Eines Junggesellen, Play
  Aus Dem Tagebuch Eines Junggesellen 1928 d: Erich Schonfelder. lps: Reinhold Schunzel, Iwa Wanja, Grit Haid. 2643m GRM. prod/rel: Reinhold Schunzel Film-Prod.

SORENSEN, VILLY
De Forsvundne Breve, 1955, Short Story
  Forsvundne Breve, de 1967 d: Annelise Hovmand. 15M DNM.

SORIANO, OSVALDO
Das Autogramm, Novel
  Autogramm, Das 1984 d: Peter Lilienthal. lps: Juan Jose Mosalini, Angel Del Villar, Anna LarretA. 94M GRM/FRN. *L' Autographe* (FRN); *The Autograph* prod/rel: Provobis, von Vietinghoff
No Habra Mas Pena Ni Olvido, Novel
  No Habra Mas Pena Ni Olvido 1985 d: Hector OliverA. lps: Federico Luppi, Victor Laplace, Rodolfo Ranni. 80M ARG. *There Will Be No More Sadness Nor Oblivion*; *A Funny Dirty Little War* prod/rel: Aries Cinematografica Argentina

SOSEKI, NATSUME (1867–1916), JPN
Sore Kara, 1910, Novel
  Sorekara 1985 d: Yoshimitsu MoritA. lps: Yusaku Matsuda, Miwako Fujitani, Chishu Ryu. 130M JPN. *And Then*

SOUBIRAN, ANDRE (1910–, FRN
Une Femme En Blanc Se Revolte, Novel
  Nouveau Journal d'une Femme En Blanc, Le 1966 d: Claude Autant-LarA. lps: Danielle Volle, Michel Ruhl, Josee Steiner. 110M FRN. *Une Femme En Blanc Se Revolte* prod/rel: S.O.P.A.C., S.N.E.G.
Les Hommes En Blanc, Novel
  Hommes En Blanc, L' 1955 d: Ralph Habib. lps: Raymond Pellegrin, Jeanne Moreau, Jean Chevrier. 110M FRN. *The Doctors* (USA); *Men in White* prod/rel: Transcontinental
Journal d'une Femme En Blanc, Novel
  Journal d'une Femme En Blanc, Le 1964 d: Claude Autant-LarA. lps: Marie-Jose Nat, Jean Valmont, Claude Gensac. 120M FRN/ITL. *A Woman in White* (USA); *Pelle Di Donna* (ITL) prod/rel: S.O.P.A.C., S.N.E.G.

SOULAINE, PIERRE
Totte Et Sa Chance, Novel
  Sprung Ins Gluck, Der 1927 d: Augusto GeninA. lps: Carmen Boni, Anton Pointner, Hans Junkermann. 2504m GRM/FRN/ITL. *Totte Et Sa Chance* (FRN); *She's a Good Girl* prod/rel: Nero-Film (Berlin), Societe Des Cineromans

SOULIE, FREDERIC
La Closerie Des Genets, Play
  Closerie Des Genets, La 1913 d: Adrien Caillard. lps: Leon Bernard, Jean Herve, Sarah Davids. 805m FRN. prod/rel: Scagl
  Closerie Des Genets, La 1924 d: Andre Liabel. lps: Henry Krauss, Nina Vanna, Helene Darly. SRL. 6EP FRN. prod/rel: Film d'Art (Vandal Et Delac)
Eulalie Pontois, Play
  Autour d'un Testament 1913 d: Emile Chautard. lps: Henry Roussell, Marcel Simon, Mevisto. 780m FRN. prod/rel: Acad

SOUSA, JOHN PHILIP (1854–1932), USA
Marching Along, 1928, Autobiography
  Stars and Stripes Forever 1952 d: Henry Koster. lps: Clifton Webb, Debra Paget, Robert Wagner. 89M USA. *Marching Along* (UKN) prod/rel: 20th Century-Fox

SOUSANDRADE
Guesa Errante, 1868-77, Verse
  Guesa, O 1969 d: Sergio Santeiro. 12M BRZ.

SOUSEDIK, MILOSLAV J.
Papradna Nenarika, Novel
Devcica Z Beskyd 1944 d: Frantisek Cap. lps: Jaroslav Vojta, Marie Nademlejnska, Terezie BrzkovA. 2404m CZC. *The Maiden of Bezkydy; A Girl from the Mountains; The Girl from Beskydy Mountains* prod/rel: Lucernafilm

SOUTAR, ANDREW
Novel
Other Men's Shoes 1920 d: Edgar Lewis. lps: Crauford Kent, Irene Boyle, Stephen Grattan. 6425f USA. prod/rel: Edgar Lewis Productions, Inc., Pathe Exchange, Inc.©

Short Stories
Romances of the Prize Ring 1926 d: H. B. Parkinson, Geoffrey H. Malins. SHS. UKN. prod/rel: H. B. Parkinson, White

Back from the Dead, London 1920, Novel
Back to Life 1925 d: Whitman Bennett. lps: Patsy Ruth Miller, David Powell, Lawford Davidson. 5826f USA. prod/rel: Postman Pictures, Associated Exhibitors

A Beggar in Purple, London 1918, Novel
Beggar in Purple, A 1920 d: Edgar Lewis. lps: Lee Shumway, Ruth King, Charles Arling. 5483f USA. prod/rel: Edgar Lewis Productions, Pathe Exchange, Inc.©

The Black Night, Novel
Black Night, The 1916 d: Harold Weston. lps: Gregory Scott, J. R. Tozer. 4124f UKN. prod/rel: Broadwest

Butterflies in the Rain, Novel
Butterflies in the Rain 1926 d: Edward Sloman. lps: Laura La Plante, James Kirkwood, Robert Ober. 7319f USA. prod/rel: Universal Pictures

The Devil's Triangle, London 1931, Novel
Almost Married 1932 d: William Cameron Menzies. lps: Violet Heming, Ralph Bellamy, Alexander Kirkland. 51M USA. *Circumstance; Circumstances* prod/rel: Fox Film Corp.

The Green Orchard, London 1916, Novel
Green Orchard, The 1916 d: Harold Weston. lps: Gregory Scott, Dora Barton, E. Vassal-Vaughan. 5000f UKN. prod/rel: Broadwest
His Parisian Wife 1919 d: Emile Chautard. lps: Elsie Ferguson, David Powell, Courtenay Foote. 4823f USA. prod/rel: Famous Players-Lasky Corp.©, Artcraft Pictures

High Stakes, 1917, Short Story
High Stakes 1918 d: Arthur Hoyt. lps: J. Barney Sherry, Myrtle Rishell, Harvey Clark. 4923f USA. prod/rel: Triangle Film Corp., Triangle Distributing Corp.

Hornet's Nest, Novel
Hornet's Nest 1923 d: Walter West. lps: Florence Turner, Fred Wright, Nora Swinburne. 6102f UKN. prod/rel: Walter West, Butcher's Film Service

In the Blood, Novel
In the Blood 1923 d: Walter West. lps: Victor McLaglen, Lillian Douglas, Cecil Morton York. 6100f UKN. prod/rel: Walter West, Butcher's Film Service

On Principal, 1918, Short Story
Love's Redemption 1921 d: Albert Parker. lps: Norma Talmadge, Harrison Ford, Montagu Love. 5889f USA. *Regeneration Isle; Playing the Game* prod/rel: Norma Talmadge Film Co., Associated First National Pictures

The Phantom in the House, London 1928, Novel
Phantom in the House, The 1929 d: Phil Rosen. lps: Ricardo Cortez, Nancy Welford, Henry B. Walthall. 5725f USA. prod/rel: Trem Carr Productions, Continental Talking Pictures

The Pruning Knife, Play
Was She Justified? 1922 d: Walter West. lps: Florence Turner, Ivy Close, Lewis Gilbert. 5600f UKN. *The Pruning Knife* prod/rel: Walter West, Butcher's Film Service

Silent Thunder, London 1932, Novel
Man Called Back, The 1932 d: Robert Florey. lps: Conrad Nagel, Doris Kenyon, Reginald Owen. 79M USA. *Silent Thunder* prod/rel: K.B.S. Film Corp., Quadruple Film Corp.

Snow in the Desert, Novel
Snow in the Desert 1919 d: Walter West. lps: Violet Hopson, Stewart Rome, Poppy Wyndham. 7000f UKN. prod/rel: Broadwest, Walturdaw

The Straight Game, Novel
Great Game, The 1918 d: A. E. Coleby. lps: Bdr. Billy Wells, A. E. Coleby, Ernest A. Douglas. 6000f UKN. prod/rel: I. B. Davidson, Ruffells

SOUTHARD, BENNETT
You're in the Army Now, Story
Into No Man's Land 1928 d: Cliff Wheeler. lps: Thomas Santschi, Josephine Norman, Jack Daugherty. 6700f USA. *The Secret Lie* (UKN) prod/rel: Excellent Pictures

SOUTHARD, RUTH
No Sad Songs for Me, Novel
No Sad Songs for Me 1950 d: Rudolph Mate. lps: Margaret Sullavan, Wendell Corey, Viveca Lindfors. 89M USA. prod/rel: Columbia

SOUTHERN, TERRY (1924–, USA
Candy, New York 1964, Novel
Candy 1968 d: Christian Marquand, Giancarlo Zagni. lps: Ewa Aulin, Richard Burton, Walter Matthau. 124M USA/FRN/ITL. *Candy E Il Suo Pazzo Mondo* (ITL) prod/rel: Selmur Pictures (Hollywood), Dear Film (Roma)

The Magic Christian, New York 1960, Novel
Magic Christian, The 1969 d: Joseph McGrath. lps: Peter Sellers, Ringo Starr, Richard Attenborough. 95M UKN. prod/rel: Grand Films, Commonwealth United

SOUTHEY, ROBERT (1774–1843), UKN
The Life of Nelson, Book
Nelson 1918 d: Maurice Elvey. lps: Donald Calthrop, Malvina Longfellow, Ivy Close. 7000f UKN. prod/rel: Master, International Exclusives
Nelson 1926 d: Walter Summers. lps: Cedric Hardwicke, Gertrude McCoy, Frank Perfitt. 7990f UKN. prod/rel: British Instructional, New Era

SOUTHWORTH, E. D. E. N. (1819–1899), USA,
Southworth, Emma Dorothy Eliza, Nevitte, Emma Dorothy Eliza
In the Depths Ishmael; Or, New York 1904, Novel
Hearts of Youth 1921 d: Thomas N. Miranda, Millard Webb. lps: Harold Goodwin, Lillian Hall, Fred Kirby. 5r USA. prod/rel: Fox Film Corp.

SOUVESTRE, PIERRE
Fantomas, Novel
Fantomas 1913 d: Louis Feuillade. lps: Rene Navarre, Georges Melchior, Renee Carl. 1115m FRN. *Fantomas Under the Shadow of the Guillotine* prod/rel: Gaumont
Fantomas 1964 d: Andre Hunebelle. lps: Jean Marais, Louis de Funes, Mylene Demongeot. 105M FRN. *Fantomas 70* prod/rel: P.A.C., S.N.E.G.

Juve Contre Fantomas, Novel
Juve Contre Fantomas 1913 d: Louis Feuillade. lps: Rene Navarre, Edmond Breon, Renee Carl. SRL. 1227m FRN. *Juve Vs. Fantomas; Fantomas II*

Le Magistrat Cambrioleur, Novel
Faux Magistrat, Le 1914 d: Louis Feuillade. lps: Rene Navarre, Edmond Breon, Suzanne Le Bret. 1881m FRN. *The False Magistrate; Fantomas V* prod/rel: Gaumont

Le Policier Apache, Novel
Fantomas Contre Fantomas 1914 d: Louis Feuillade. lps: Rene Navarre, Edmond Breon, Renee Carl. 1274m FRN. *Fantomas the Crook Detective; Fantomas IV* prod/rel: Gaumont

SOYA, CARL ERIK
Bare En Tagsten, 1959, Play
Soyas Tagsten 1966 d: Annelise Meineche. lps: Jytte Abildstrom, Lily Broberg, Poul Bundgaard. 90M DNM. *Soyas En Tagsten I Hovedet* prod/rel: Palladium Film

Efter, 1947, Play
Tre Aar Efter 1948 d: Johan Jacobsen. lps: Ove Sprogoe, Henry Nielsen, Lauritz Olsen. 104M DNM.

Sytten: Erindringer Og Refleksioner, Copenhagen 1953, Novel
Sytten 1965 d: Annelise Meineche. lps: Ole Soltoft, Ghita Norby, Hans Christensen. 89M DNM. *Eric Soya's "17"* (USA); *Seventeen* prod/rel: Palladium

SOYINKA, WOLE (1934–, NGR
Kongi's Harvest, 1967, Play
Kongi's Harvest 1971 d: Ossie Davis. lps: Nina Baden-Semper, Orlando Martins, Wole SoyinkA. 85M USA/NGR/SWD.

SPAGGIARI, ALBERT
Les Egouts du Paradis, Novel
Egouts du Paradis, Les 1978 d: Jose Giovanni. lps: Francis Huster, Jean-Francois Balmer, Lila KedrovA. 115M FRN. *The Sewers of Paris* prod/rel: Alexia Films

SPANG, GUNTER
Mein Onkel Theodor, Novel
Mein Onkel Theodor 1975 d: Gustav Ehmck. lps: Gert Frobe, Barbara Rutting, Wera Frydtberg. 105M GRM. *My Uncle Theodore* prod/rel: Ehmck-Film

SPARK, MURIEL (1918–, UKN
The Abbess of Crewe; a Modern Morality Tale, 1974, Novel
Nasty Habits 1976 d: Michael Lindsay-Hogg. lps: Glenda Jackson, Melina Mercouri, Geraldine Page. 96M UKN/USA. *The Abbess* prod/rel: Brut, Bowden

The Driver's Seat, 1970, Novel
Identikit 1974 d: Giuseppe Patroni Griffi. lps: Elizabeth Taylor, Guido Mannari, Ian Bannen. 105M ITL. *The Driver's Seat* (USA); *Psychotic; Killing Games* prod/rel: Felix Cin.Ca, Rizzoli Film

Memento Mori, Novel
Memento Mori 1992 d: Jack Clayton. lps: Maggie Smith, Michael Hordern, Renee Asherton. TVM. 100M UKN. prod/rel: BBC Tv, BBC Films for Screen Two

The Prime of Miss Jean Brodie, London 1961, Novel
Prime of Miss Jean Brodie, The 1969 d: Ronald Neame. lps: Maggie Smith, Robert Stephens, Pamela Franklin. 116M UKN. prod/rel: 20th Century-Fox

SPARKS, NICHOLAS
Message in a Bottle, Novel
Message in a Bottle 1999 d: Luis Mandoki. lps: Kevin Costner, Robin Wright, Paul Newman. 132M USA. prod/rel: Warner Bros.©, Bel-Air Entertainment Llc©

SPAULDING, SUSAN MARR
Two Shall Be Born, Poem
Two Shall Be Born 1924 d: Whitman Bennett. lps: Jane Novak, Kenneth Harlan, Sigrid Holmquist. 5443f USA. prod/rel: Twin Pictures, Vitagraph Co. of America

SPEARE, DOROTHY
Don't Fall in Love, 1931, Play
One Night of Love 1934 d: Victor Schertzinger. lps: Grace Moore, Tullio Carminati, Lyle Talbot. 84M USA. prod/rel: Columbia Pictures Corp.©

SPEARMAN, FRANK HAMILTON
The Daughter of a Magnate, New York 1903, Novel
Love Special, The 1921 d: Frank Urson. lps: Wallace Reid, Agnes Ayres, Theodore Roberts. 4855f USA. prod/rel: Famous Players-Lasky, Paramount Pictures

The Girl and the Game, Story
Girl and the Game, The 1916 d: J. P. McGowan. lps: Helen Holmes, Leo Maloney, George McDaniel. SRL. 30r USA. prod/rel: Signal Film

Held for Orders, New York 1901, Book
Night Flyer, The 1928 d: Walter Lang. lps: William Boyd, Jobyna Ralston, Philo McCullough. 5954f USA. prod/rel: James Cruze, Inc., Pathe Exchange, Inc.

Nan of Music Mountain, New York 1916, Novel
Nan of Music Mountain 1917 d: George Melford. lps: Wallace Reid, Anna Little, Theodore Roberts. 5r USA. prod/rel: Jesse L. Lasky Feature Play Co.©, Paramount Pictures Corp.

The Nerve of Foley, 1900, Short Story
Runaway Express, The 1926 d: Edward Sedgwick. lps: Jack Daugherty, Blanche Mehaffey, Tom O'Brien. 5865f USA. prod/rel: Universal Pictures

Whispering Smith, New York 1906, Novel
Medicine Bend 1916 d: J. P. McGowan. lps: Helen Holmes, J. P. McGowan, Paul Hurst. 5r USA. *At Medicine Bend* prod/rel: Signal Films Corp., Mutual Film Corp.
Money Madness 1917 d: Henry McRae. lps: Mary MacLaren, Eddie Polo, Don Bailey. 5r USA. prod/rel: Universal Film Mfg. Co.©, Butterfly Picture
Whispering Smith 1916 d: J. P. McGowan. lps: Helen Holmes, J. P. McGowan, Belle Hutchinson. 5r USA. prod/rel: Signal Film Corp., Mutual Film Corp.
Whispering Smith 1926 d: George Melford. lps: H. B. Warner, Lillian Rich, John Bowers. 6187f USA. *The Open Switch* prod/rel: Producers Distributing Corp., Metropolitan Pictures
Whispering Smith 1948 d: Leslie Fenton. lps: Alan Ladd, Robert Preston, Brenda Marshall. 88M USA. prod/rel: Paramount

SPEARS, RAYMOND SMILEY
Hoarded Assets, 1918, Short Story
Hoarded Assets 1918 d: Paul Scardon. lps: Harry T. Morey, Betty Blythe, George Majeroni. 5r USA. prod/rel: Vitagraph Co. of America©, Blue Ribbon Feature

Janie of the Waning Glories, Story
Bar-C Mystery, The 1926 d: Robert F. Hill. lps: Dorothy Phillips, Wallace MacDonald, Ethel Clayton. 4756f USA. prod/rel: Pathe Exchange, Inc.

SPENCE, HARTZELL
Biography
One Foot in Heaven 1941 d: Irving Rapper. lps: Fredric March, Martha Scott, Beulah Bondi. 108M USA. prod/rel: Warner Bros.

SPENCE, RALPH
The Gorilla, New York 1925, Play
Gorilla, The 1927 d: Alfred Santell. lps: Charlie Murray, Fred Kelsey, Alice Day. 8r USA. prod/rel: First National Pictures
Gorilla, The 1930 d: Bryan Foy. lps: Joe Frisco, Harry Gribbon, Walter Pidgeon. 65M USA. prod/rel: First National Pictures

Gorilla, The 1939 d: Allan Dwan. lps: The Ritz Brothers, Anita Louise, Patsy Kelly. 67M USA. prod/rel: Twentieth Century-Fox Film Corp.

Sh! the Octopus, New York 1928, Play
Sh! the Octopus 1937 d: William McGann. lps: Hugh Herbert, Allen Jenkins, Marcia Ralston. 60M USA. prod/rel: Warner Bros. Pictures©, First National Picture

SPENCER, ELIZABETH (1921–, USA
I Maureen, Short Story
I, Maureen 1980 d: Janine Manatis. lps: Colleen Collins, Nellie Salnick, Diane Bigelow. 101M CND. prod/rel: Jandu Productions Ltd., Janspell Communications Inc.

The Light in the Piazza, New York 1960, Novel
Light in the Piazza 1961 d: Guy Green. lps: Olivia de Havilland, Rossano Brazzi, Yvette Mimieux. 101M UKN/USA. prod/rel: MGM British

SPENCER, LAVYRLE
Home Song, Novel
Lavyrle Spencer's Home Song 1996 d: Nancy Malone. lps: Lee Horsley, Polly Draper, Deborah Raffin. TVM. 80M USA. *Home Song*

SPENCER, RICHARD V.
The Gangsters and the Girl, Story
Gangsters and the Girl, The 1914 d: Scott Sidney. lps: Charles Ray, Thomas H. Ince, Elizabeth Burbridge. 2r USA. prod/rel: Kb

SPENCER, SCOTT
Endless Love, Novel
Endless Love 1981 d: Franco Zeffirelli. lps: Martin Hewitt, Brooke Shields, Don Murray. 115M USA. prod/rel: Universal

SPENDER, STEPHEN (1909–1995), UKN, Spender, Stephen Harold
The Fool and the Princess, 1946, Novel
Fool and the Princess, The 1948 d: William C. Hammond. lps: Bruce Lester, Lesley Brook, Adina MandlovA. 72M UKN. prod/rel: Merton Park, General Film Distributors

SPERR, MARTIN
Jagdszenen Aus Niederbayern, Bremen 1966, Play
Jagdszenen Aus Niederbayern 1968 d: Peter Fleischmann. lps: Martin Sperr, Angela Winkler, Else Quecke. 85M GRM. *Hunting Scenes from Bavaria* (USA); *The Hunters are the Hunted*; *Hunting Scenes from Lower Bavaria* prod/rel: Rob Houwer Film, Alpha

SPEWACK, BELLA (1899–, USA
Boy Meets Girl, New York 1935, Play
Boy Meets Girl 1938 d: Lloyd Bacon. lps: James Cagney, Pat O'Brien, Marie Wilson. 86M USA. prod/rel: Warner Bros. Pictures, Inc.

Clear All Wires, New York 1932, Play
Clear All Wires 1933 d: George W. Hill. lps: Lee Tracy, Benita Hume, Una Merkel. 78M USA. prod/rel: Metro-Goldwyn-Mayer Corp.

The Solitaire Man, Boston 1927, Play
Solitaire Man, The 1933 d: Jack Conway. lps: Herbert Marshall, Mary Boland, Lionel Atwill. 65M USA. prod/rel: Metro-Goldwyn-Mayer Corp.©

SPEWACK, SAMUEL (1899–1971), USA
Boy Meets Girl, New York 1935, Play
Boy Meets Girl 1938 d: Lloyd Bacon. lps: James Cagney, Pat O'Brien, Marie Wilson. 86M USA. prod/rel: Warner Bros. Pictures, Inc.

Clear All Wires, New York 1932, Play
Clear All Wires 1933 d: George W. Hill. lps: Lee Tracy, Benita Hume, Una Merkel. 78M USA. prod/rel: Metro-Goldwyn-Mayer Corp.

Murder in the Gilded Cage, New York 1929, Novel
Secret Witness, The 1931 d: Thornton Freeland. lps: William Collier Jr., Una Merkel, Zasu Pitts. 66M USA. *Terror By Night* prod/rel: Columbia Pictures Corp.©

The Solitaire Man, Boston 1927, Play
Solitaire Man, The 1933 d: Jack Conway. lps: Herbert Marshall, Mary Boland, Lionel Atwill. 65M USA. prod/rel: Metro-Goldwyn-Mayer Corp.©

SPEYER, WILHELM
Charlott Etwas Verruckt, Novel
Charlott Etwas Verruckt 1928 d: Adolf Edgar Licho. lps: Lya de Putti, Livio Pavanelli, Alfons Fryland. 2278m GRM. prod/rel: Phoebus-Film Ag

A Hat a Coat a Glove, New York 1934, Play
Hat, Coat and Glove 1934 d: Worthington Miner. lps: Ricardo Cortez, Barbara Robbins, John Beal. 66M USA. prod/rel: RKO Radio Pictures©

Night of Adventure, A 1944 d: Gordon Douglas. lps: Tom Conway, Audrey Long, Edward Brophy. 65M USA. *One Exciting Night* prod/rel: RKO Radio

L' Inconstante, Novel
Inconstante, L' 1931 d: Andre Rigaud, Hans Behrendt. lps: Georges Charlia, Daniele Parola, Georges Peclet. 95M FRN. *Je Sors Et Tu Restes la*; *L' Amour Dispose* prod/rel: Universal-Film

Der Kampf Der Tertia, Novel
Kampf Der Tertia, Der 1928 d: Max Mack. lps: Karl Hoffmann, Fritz Draeger, August Wilhelm Keese. 2978m GRM. *Jugend von Morgen* prod/rel: Terra-Film
Kampf Der Tertia, Der 1953 d: Erik Ode. lps: Brigitte Rau, Wolfgang Jansen, Horst Koppen. 89M GRM. *The Struggle of the Ninth Graders* prod/rel: Cinephon, Saxonia

SPEZIALE, GIOVANNI
La Bella Nipotina, Play
Chi l'Ha Ucciso? 1919 d: Alberto Sannia, Mario GambardellA. lps: Berta Nelson, Mario Gambardella, Max Plemberton. 1547m ITL. prod/rel: Tirrena Film

SPICER, BART
The Adversary, Novel
Aspen 1977 d: Douglas Heyes. lps: Sam Elliott, Perry King, Gene Barry. TVM. 300M USA. *The Innocent and the Damned*; *The Aspen Murder* prod/rel: Universal, Roy Huggins

SPIEGELGASS, LEONHARD
Story
Mystery Street 1950 d: John Sturges. lps: Ricardo Montalban, Sally Forrest, Bruce Bennett. 93M USA. prod/rel: MGM

Miss Wheelwright Discovers America, Story
Million Dollar Baby 1941 d: Curtis Bernhardt. lps: Priscilla Lane, Jeffrey Lynn, Ronald Reagan. 102M USA. *Miss Wheelwright Discovers America* prod/rel: Warner Bros.

SPIELBERG, STEVEN (1946–, USA
Story
Goonies, The 1985 d: Richard Donner. lps: Sean Astin, Josh Brolin, Jeff Cohen. 114M USA. prod/rel: Warner Bros., Amblin Entertainment

SPIERS, K. C.
If Youth But Knew, Play
If Youth But Knew 1926 d: George A. Cooper. lps: Godfrey Tearle, Lillian Hall-Davis, Wyndham Standing. 8095f UKN. prod/rel: Reciprocity Films

SPIGELGASS, LEONARD
A Majority of One, New York 1959, Play
Majority of One, A 1961 d: Mervyn Leroy. lps: Alec Guinness, Rosalind Russell, Ray Danton. 156M USA. prod/rel: Warner Bros. Pictures

SPILAR, VACLAV
Ulicnice, Opera
Ulicnice 1936 d: Vladimir Slavinsky. lps: Vera Ferbasova, Frantisek Sasek, Frantisek Kristof-Vesely. 2931m CZC. *Minx* prod/rel: Slavia-Film

SPILLANE, MICKEY (1918–, USA, Spillane, Frank Morrison
The Delta Factor, New York 1969, Novel
Delta Factor, The 1970 d: Tay Garnett. lps: Yvette Mimieux, Christopher George, Diane McBain. 91M USA.

The Girl Hunters, New York 1962, Novel
Girl Hunters, The 1963 d: Roy Rowland. lps: Mickey Spillane, Shirley Eaton, Lloyd Nolan. 103M UKN. prod/rel: Present Day Productions, Fellane Productions

I the Jury, Novel
I, the Jury 1953 d: Harry Essex. lps: Biff Elliot, Preston Foster, Peggie Castle. 87M USA. prod/rel: United Artists, Parklane
I, the Jury 1982 d: Richard T. Heffron. lps: Armand Assante, Barbara Carrera, Alan King. 111M USA. prod/rel: 20th Century Fox

Kiss Me Deadly, Novel
Kiss Me Deadly 1955 d: Robert Aldrich. lps: Ralph Meeker, Albert Dekker, Paul Stewart. 105M USA. prod/rel: United Artists, Parklane

The Long Wait, 1951, Novel
Long Wait, The 1954 d: Victor Saville. lps: Anthony Quinn, Charles Coburn, Gene Evans. 93M USA. prod/rel: United Artists, Parklane Pictures

My Gun Is Quick, 1950, Novel
My Gun Is Quick 1957 d: George A. White, Phil Victor. lps: Robert Bray, Whitney Blake, Pamela Duncan. 88M USA. prod/rel: United Artists, Parklane Pictures

SPILLMAN, REV. JOSEPH
A Victim to the Seal of Confession, St. Louis 1898, Novel
Victim, The 1917 d: Joseph Levering. lps: Robert T. Haines, Joyce Fair, Inez Marcel. 6r USA. prod/rel: Catholic Art Association, Erbograph Co.

SPILLNER, WOLF
Biologie!, Novel
Biologie! 1990 d: Jorg Foth. lps: Stefanie Stappenbeck, Cornelius Schulz, Carl-Heinz Choynski. 90M GDR. prod/rel: Defa, Gruppe Babelsberg

SPITZ, ERNST
On the Black Sea, Play
World and the Flesh, The 1932 d: John Cromwell. lps: George Bancroft, Miriam Hopkins, Alan Mowbray. 75M USA. *On the Black Sea*; *Red Harvest* prod/rel: Paramount Publix Corp.©

SPITZER, ROBERT
L' Amour a l'Americaine, Play
Amour a l'Americaine, L' 1931 d: Claude Heymann, Paul Fejos. lps: Andre Luguet, Julien Carette, Spinelly. 96M FRN. prod/rel: Etablissements Braunberger-Richebe

L' Homme de Joie, Play
Homme de Joie, L' 1950 d: Gilles Grangier. lps: Jean-Pierre Aumont, Simone Renant, Jacques Morel. 95M FRN. prod/rel: Ariane

SPITZMULLER, GEORGES
Paris Mysterieux, Novel
Paris Mysterieux 1921 d: Louis Paglieri. lps: Philippe Damores, Jeanne Brindeau, Marie Heil. SRL. 10EP FRN. prod/rel: Parisienne-Film

La Tempete, Short Story
Fiancailles Rouges, Les 1926 d: Roger Lion. lps: Jean Murat, Dolly Davis, Gil Clary. F FRN. prod/rel: Films Roger Lion

SPOERL, HEINRICH (1887–1955), GRM
Die Feuerzangenbowle, Novel
Feuerzangenbowle, Die 1944 d: Helmut Weiss. lps: Heinz Ruhmann, Karin Himboldt, Hilde Sessak. 97M GRM. *So Ein Flegel!* prod/rel: Terra, Donau
Feuerzangenbowle, Die 1970 d: Helmut Kautner. lps: Walter Giller, Uschi Glas, Theo Lingen. 100M GRM. *Fire Tong Punch* prod/rel: Rialto, Inter

Die Hochzeitsreise, Novel
Hochzeit Auf Reisen 1953 d: Paul Verhoeven. lps: Gardy Granass, Karlheinz Bohm, Susi Nicoletti. 85M GRM. *Wedding on the Road* prod/rel: Interglobal, Ring

Der Maulkorb, Novel
Maulkorb, Der 1938 d: Erich Engel. lps: Ralph Arthur Roberts, Hilde Weissner, Elisabeth Flickenschildt. 80M GRM. prod/rel: Tobis-Magna, Donau
Maulkorb, Der 1958 d: Wolfgang Staudte. lps: O. E. Hasse, Hertha Feiler, Hansjorg Felmy. 94M GRM. *The Muzzle* prod/rel: Kurt Ulrich, Europa

So Ein Flegel, Novel
So Ein Flegel 1934 d: R. A. Stemmle. lps: Heinz Ruhmann, Rudolf Platte, Inge Konradi. 85M GRM. prod/rel: Cicero, Donau

Wenn Wir Alle Engel Waren, Novel
Wenn Wir Alle Engel Waren 1936 d: Carl Froelich. lps: Heinz Ruhmann, Leny Marenbach, Harald Paulsen. 105M GRM. **If We All Were Angels** (USA) prod/rel: Froelich, Herzog
Wenn Wir Alle Engel Waren 1956 d: Gunther Luders. lps: Dieter Borsche, Marianne Koch, Hans Sohnker. 98M GRM. *If We All Were Angels* prod/rel: Bavaria

SPOLETINI, GUGLIELMO
Ballad of a Champion, Novel
Storia d'Amore E d'Amicizia 1982 d: Franco Rossi. lps: Claudio Amendola, Massimo Bonetti, Barbara de Rossi. 110M ITL.

SPOONER, CECIL
Nell of the Circus, Play
Nell of the Circus 1914. lps: Cecil Spooner. 4r USA. prod/rel: Sawyer, Inc.

SPORTES, MORGAN
L' Appat, Book
Appat, L' 1995 d: Bertrand Tavernier. lps: Marie Gillain, Richard Berry, Olivier Sitruk. 116M FRN. *The Bait* (UKN); *Fresh Bait* prod/rel: Hachette, Little Bear

SPOTA, LUIS
La Estrella Vacia, Mexico City 1950, Novel
Estrella Vacia, La 1958 d: Emilio Gomez Muriel. lps: Maria Felix, Ignacio Lopez Tarso, Enrique Rambal. 105M MXC. *The Empty Star* (USA) prod/rel: Producciones Corsa

SPRING, HOWARD (1889–1965), UKN
Fame Is the Spur, 1940, Novel
Fame Is the Spur 1947 d: Roy Boulting. lps: Michael Redgrave, Rosamund John, Bernard Miles. 116M UKN. prod/rel: General Film Distributors, Two Cities
Fame Is the Spur 1982 d: David Giles. lps: Tim Pigott-Smith, David Hayman, Joanna David. MTV. 400M UKN. prod/rel: BBC

437

My Son, My Son!, London 1938, Novel
  My Son, My Son! 1940 d: Charles Vidor. lps: Madeleine Carroll, Brian Aherne, Louis Hayward. 115M USA. prod/rel: United Artists Corp., Edward Small Productions©

SPRINGER, NORMAN
The Blood Ship, New York 1922, Novel
  Blood Ship, The 1927 d: George B. Seitz. lps: Hobart Bosworth, Jacqueline Logan, Richard Arlen. 6843f USA. prod/rel: Columbia Pictures

  Shanghaied Love 1931 d: George B. Seitz. lps: Richard Cromwell, Noah Beery, Sally Blane. 75M USA. *Shanghai Love* prod/rel: Columbia Pictures Corp.©

SPRINGS, ELLIOTT WHITE
Belated Evidence, 1926, Short Story
  Hard-Boiled Haggerty 1927 d: Charles J. Brabin. lps: Milton Sills, Molly O'Day, Mitchell Lewis. 7443f USA. prod/rel: First National Pictures

Big Eyes and Little Mouth, 1927, Short Story
  Body and Soul 1931 d: Alfred Santell. lps: Charles Farrell, Elissa Landi, Humphrey Bogart. 82M USA. prod/rel: Fox Film Corp.

The One Who Was Clever, 1929, Short Story
  Young Eagles 1930 d: William A. Wellman. lps: Charles "Buddy" Rogers, Jean Arthur, Paul Lukas. 71M USA. prod/rel: Paramount Famous Lasky Corp.

Sky High, 1929, Short Story
  Young Eagles 1930 d: William A. Wellman. lps: Charles "Buddy" Rogers, Jean Arthur, Paul Lukas. 71M USA. prod/rel: Paramount Famous Lasky Corp.

SPYRI, JOHANNA (1827–1901), SWT, Spyri, Johanna Heuser
Gotha 1880, Novel
  Heidi's Song 1982 d: Robert Taylor. ANM. 94M USA. prod/rel: Paramount

Heidi, Zurich 1880, Novel
  Heidi 1937 d: Allan Dwan. lps: Shirley Temple, Jean Hersholt, Arthur Treacher. 88M USA. prod/rel: Twentieth Century-Fox Film Corp.©

  Heidi 1965 d: Werner Jacobs. lps: Eva Maria Singhammer, Gertraud Mittermayr, Gustav Knuth. 103M AUS. prod/rel: Sascha Film

  Heidi 1974 d: June Wyndham-Davis. lps: Emma Blake, Flora Robson, Hans Meyer. MTV. 112M UKN.

  Heidi Kehrt Heim 1967 d: Delbert Mann. lps: Maximilian Schell, Jean Simmons, Jennifer Edwards. TVM. 101M GRM/USA. *Heidi* (USA); *Heidi Goes Home* prod/rel: Omnibus Productions, Studio Hamburg

Was Es Gelernt Hat Heidi Kann Brauchen, Novel
  Heidi Und Peter 1954 d: Franz Schnyder. lps: Heinrich Gretler, Elsbeth Sigmund, Thomas Klameth. 95M SWT. *Heidi and Peter* (USA); *Heidi Et Pietro*; *Heidi Torna a Casa*; *Heidi Kann Brauchen Was Es Gelernt Hat*; *Wiedersehen Mit Heidi* prod/rel: Praesens-Film

Heidi's Lehr- Und Wanderjahre, Gotha 1881, Novel
  Son Tornata Per Te 1953 d: Luigi Comencini. lps: Elsbeth Sigmund, Heinrich Gretler, Thomas Klameth. 100M ITL/SWT. *Heidi* (SWT); *Heidi -Child of the Mountains* (USA); *Heidi - Sehnsucht Nach Der Heimat* prod/rel: Praesens-Film

Rosen-Resli, Novel
  Rosen-Resli 1954 d: Harald Reinl. lps: Christine Kaufmann, Josefin Kipper, Paul Klinger. 85M GRM. *Rose-Girl Resli* prod/rel: Eva, Constantin

Wie Wieseli Seinen Weg Fand, Gotha 1878, Novel
  Bonjour Jeunesse 1956 d: Maurice Cam. lps: Ded Rysel, Alexandre Rignault, Yannick Malloire. 95M FRN/SWT. prod/rel: Felix Beaujon Heimatfilm-Produktion, Les Films Monopole

  Heidemarie 1956 d: Hermann Kugelstadt. lps: Gustav Knuth, Hannes Schmidhauser, Eveline Gruneisen. 97M SWT/FRN. *S'waisechind Vo Engelsberg*; *Tapfere Heidemarie* prod/rel: Beaujon Heimatfilm-Produktion, Elite-Film

SQUIER, EMMA LINDSAY
The Angry God, Short Story
  Angry God, The 1948 d: Van Campel Heilner. lps: Alicia Parla, Casimiro Ortega, Mario Forastieri. 57M USA/MXC. prod/rel: United Artists, Peskay

Glorious Buccaneer, 1930, Short Story
  Dancing Pirate 1936 d: Lloyd Corrigan. lps: Steffi Duna, Charles Collins, Frank Morgan. 85M USA. prod/rel: Pioneer Pictures, Inc.

SREMAC, STEVEN
Pop Cira I Pop Spira, 1898, Novel
  Pop Cira I Pop Spira 1965 d: Soja Jovanovic. lps: Milan Ajvaz, Jovan Gec, Ljubinka Bobic. 81M YGS. *Parson Cira and Parson Spira*; *It's Not Easy to Get Married*

SRIRAMAN, C. V.
Irikkapindam
  Purushartham 1987 d: K. R. Mohanan. lps: Sujata Mehta, Jebin George, Adoor Bhasi. 111M IND. *The Purge*

ST. CLAIRE, ARTHUR
Shotgun Messenger, Story
  Stagecoach Buckaroo 1942 d: Ray Taylor. lps: Johnny Mack Brown, Fuzzy Knight, Nell O'Day. 58M USA. prod/rel: Universal

ST. DENIS, MADELON
The Death Kiss, New York 1932, Novel
  Death Kiss, The 1933 d: Edwin L. Marin. lps: Bela Lugosi, David Manners, Adrienne Ames. 75M USA. prod/rel: K.B.S. Productions, Inc.

ST. JOHNS, ADELA ROGERS
Angle Shooter, 1937, Short Story
  Back in Circulation 1937 d: Ray Enright. lps: Pat O'Brien, Joan Blondell, Margaret Lindsay. 100M USA. *Angle Shooter* prod/rel: Warner Bros. Pictures, Inc.

A Free Soul, New York 1927, Novel
  Free Soul, A 1931 d: Clarence Brown. lps: Norma Shearer, Lionel Barrymore, Clark Gable. 92M USA. prod/rel: Metro-Goldwyn-Mayer Corp., Metro-Goldwyn-Mayer Dist. Corp.©

  Girl Who Had Everything, The 1953 d: Richard Thorpe. lps: Elizabeth Taylor, Fernando Lamas, William Powell. 69M USA. prod/rel: MGM

The Great God Four Flush, Short Story
  Woman's Man, A 1934 d: Edward Ludwig. lps: John Halliday, Marguerite de La Motte, Wallace Ford. 70M USA. prod/rel: Monogram Pictures Corp.©, Ben Verschleiser Production

The Haunted Lady, 1925, Short Story
  Scandal 1929 d: Wesley Ruggles. lps: Laura La Plante, Huntley Gordon, John Boles. 6635f USA. *High Society* (UKN) prod/rel: Universal Pictures

Love O' Women, 1926, Short Story
  Singed 1927 d: John Griffith Wray. lps: Blanche Sweet, Warner Baxter, James Wang. 5790f USA. *Love of Women* prod/rel: Fox Film Corp.

Pretty Ladies, Short Story
  Pretty Ladies 1925 d: Monta Bell. lps: Zasu Pitts, Tom Moore, Ann Pennington. 5828f USA. prod/rel: Metro-Goldwyn Pictures

The Single Standard, New York 1928, Novel
  Single Standard, The 1929 d: John S. Robertson. lps: Greta Garbo, Nils Asther, Johnny Mack Brown. 73M USA. prod/rel: Metro-Goldwyn-Mayer Pictures

The Skyrocket, New York 1925, Novel
  Skyrocket, The 1926 d: Marshall Neilan. lps: Peggy Hopkins Joyce, Owen Moore, Gladys Hulette. 7350f USA. *Love Or Limelight* prod/rel: Celebrity Pictures, Associated Exhibitors

The Worst Woman in Hollywood, 1924, Short Story
  Inez from Hollywood 1924 d: Alfred E. Green. lps: Anna Q. Nilsson, Lewis Stone, Mary Astor. 6919f USA. *The Good Bad Girl* (UKN) prod/rel: Sam E. Rork Productions, First National Pictures

ST. JOSEPH, ELLIS
Story
  Flesh and Fantasy 1943 d: Julien Duvivier. lps: Betty Field, Robert Cummings, Edward G. Robinson. 93M USA. *Obsessions*; *For All We Know* prod/rel: Universal

ST. PIERRE, PAUL
Breaking Smith's Quarter Horse, Chicago 1966, Novel
  Smith! 1969 d: Michael O'Herlihy. lps: Glenn Ford, Nancy Olson, Dean Jagger. 102M USA. prod/rel: Walt Disney Productions

STACKLEBORG, GENE
Double Agent, New York 1959, Novel
  Man Outside, The 1967 d: Samuel Gallu. lps: Van Heflin, Heidelinde Weis, Pinkas Braun. 98M UKN. prod/rel: Trio Films, Group W Films

STACPOOLE, HENRY DE VERE (1863–1951), IRL
The Beach of Dreams, New York 1919, Novel
  Beach of Dreams 1921 d: William Parke. lps: Edith Storey, Noah Beery, Sidney Payne. 5005f USA. prod/rel: Haworth Studios, Robertson-Cole Distributing Corp.

Eileen of the Trees, Novel
  Eileen of the Trees 1928 d: Graham Cutts. lps: Anny Ondra, William Freshman, Randle Ayrton. 7182f UKN. *Glorious Youth* prod/rel: First National, First National-Pathe

The Garden of God, Novel
  Blue Lagoon 1949 d: Frank Launder. lps: Jean Simmons, Donald Houston, Noel Purcell. 103M UKN. prod/rel: General Film Distributors, Individual

  Blue Lagoon, The 1980 d: Randall Kleiser. lps: Brooke Shields, Christopher Atkins, Leo McKern. 104M USA. prod/rel: Columbia

  Return to the Blue Lagoon 1991 d: William A. Graham. lps: Brian Krause, Milla Jovovich, Lisa Pelikan. 100M USA. prod/rel: Price Entertainment

Garryowen, Novel
  Garryowen 1920 d: George Pearson. lps: Fred Groves, Hugh E. Wright, Moyna McGill. 5900f UKN. *Garry Owen* prod/rel: Welsh-Pearson

The Man Who Lost Himself, New York 1918, Novel
  Man Who Lost Himself, The 1920 d: George D. Baker. lps: William Faversham, Hedda Hopper, Violet Reed. 5r USA. prod/rel: Selznick Pictures Corp.©, Faversham Productions

  Man Who Lost Himself, The 1941 d: Edward Ludwig. lps: Brian Aherne, Kay Francis, Henry Stephenson. 71M USA. prod/rel: Universal

Satan; a Romance of the Bahamas, New York 1921, Novel
  Satan's Sister 1925 d: George Pearson. lps: Betty Balfour, Guy Phillips, Philip Stevens. 7800f UKN. prod/rel: B.W.P. Films, Woolf & Freedman

  Truth About Spring, The 1964 d: Richard Thorpe. lps: Hayley Mills, John Mills, James MacArthur. 102M UKN/USA. *The Pirates of Spring Cove*; *Miss Jude* prod/rel: Quota Rentals, Universal-International

The Starlit Garden, Novel
  Starlit Garden, The 1923 d: Guy Newall. lps: Guy Newall, Ivy Duke, ValiA. 6418f UKN. prod/rel: George Clark, Stoll

STADE, O. B.
Viva Villa, New York 1933, Book
  Viva Villa! 1934 d: Jack Conway, Howard Hawks (Uncredited). lps: Wallace Beery, Leo Carrillo, Fay Wray. 115M USA. prod/rel: Metro-Goldwyn-Mayer Corp.©

STADLEY, PAT
The Deadly Hunt, Novel
  Deadly Hunt, The 1971 d: John Newland. lps: Anthony Franciosa, Peter Lawford, Anjanette Comer. TVM. 74M USA. prod/rel: Four Star International

STAGG, CLINTON H.
High Speed, New York 1916, Novel
  High Speed 1920 d: Charles Miller. lps: Edward Earle, Gladys Hulette, L. Rogers Lytton. 5r USA. prod/rel: Hallmark Pictures Corp.©

Teeth, 1917, Short Story
  Teeth 1924 d: John G. Blystone. lps: Tom Mix, Lucy Fox, George Bancroft. 6190f USA. prod/rel: Fox Film Corp.

STAHL, BEN
Blackbeard's Ghost, 1965, Novel
  Blackbeard's Ghost 1968 d: Robert Stevenson. lps: Peter Ustinov, Dean Jones, Suzanne Pleshette. 107M USA. prod/rel: Walt Disney Productions, Buena Vista

STAHL, JERRY
Permanent Midnight, Book
  Permanent Midnight 1998 d: David Veloz. lps: Ben Stiller, Elizabeth Hurley, Maria Bello. 85M USA. prod/rel: Artisan Entertainment, Jd Productions

STALLINGS, LAURENCE (1894–1948), USA
Rainbow, New York 1928, Play
  Song of the West 1930 d: Ray Enright. lps: John Boles, Vivienne Segal, Joe E. Brown. 7185M USA. prod/rel: Warner Brothers Pictures

Tropical Twins, Play
  Cock-Eyed World, The 1929 d: Raoul Walsh. lps: Victor McLaglen, Edmund Lowe, Lili DamitA. 115M USA. prod/rel: Fox Film Corp.

What Price Glory, New York 1924, Play
  What Price Glory 1926 d: Raoul Walsh. lps: Victor McLaglen, Edmund Lowe, Dolores Del Rio. 12r USA. prod/rel: Fox Film Corp.

  What Price Glory 1952 d: John Ford. lps: James Cagney, Dan Dailey, Corinne Calvet. 111M USA. prod/rel: 20th Century-Fox

STAMATOV, GEORGI
Vestovoi Dimo, 1929, Novel
  Slouzhebno -Ordinarets 1979 d: Keran Kolarov. lps: Elefteri Elefterov, Tsvetana Maneva, Peter Despotov. 80M BUL. *Profession - Orderly*; *Status - Orderly*; *Slzhebno Polozhenie - Ordinarets*

STANCU, ZAHARIA
Jocul Cu Moartea, 1962, Novel
  Prin Cenusa Imperiului 1975 d: Andrei Blaier. lps: Cornel Coman, Gheorghe Dinica, Gabriel Marian Oseciuc. 105M RMN. *Through the Ashes of the Empire*

Padurea Nebuna, 1963, Novel
  Padurea Nebuna 1982 d: Nicolae Corjos. 98M RMN.

STANDISH, ROBERT
Elephant Walk, 1949, Novel
　Elephant Walk 1954 d: William Dieterle. lps: Elizabeth Taylor, Dana Andrews, Peter Finch. 103M USA. prod/rel: Paramount

STANEV, EMILIAN
Ivan Kondarev, 1958-64, Novel
　Ivan Kondarev 1973 d: Nicolai Korabov. lps: Anton Gorchev, Katya Paskaleva, Ivan Andonov. 169M BUL.
Kradetsat Na Praskovi, Sofia 1948, Novel
　Kradetsat Na Praskovi 1964 d: Vulo Radev. lps: Nevena Kokanova, Rade Markovic, Mikhail Mikhailov. 103M BUL. *The Peach Thief* (UKN); *Kradecat Na Praskovi* prod/rel: Sofiya Film Studios
Tarnovskata Tsaritsa, 1973, Novel
　Turnovskata Tsaritsa 1981 d: Yanko Yankov. lps: Stefan Danailov, Kamelia Todorova, Elly SkorchevA. 97M BUL. *The Queen of Turnovo*; *Tarnovskata Tsaritsa*; *Tyrnovskata Tzaritsa*
V Tiha Vecher, 1948, Novel
　V Tihata Vecher 1959 d: Borislav Shariliev. lps: Nevena Kokanova, Lyubomir Dimitrov, Borislav Ivanov. 89M BUL. *On a Quiet Evening*; *V Ticha Vetscher*; *V Tiha Vecer*; *V Tikha Vecher*

STANGE, HUGH
After Tomorrow, New York 1931, Play
　After Tomorrow 1932 d: Frank Borzage. lps: Charles Farrell, Marian Nixon, Minna Gombell. 79M USA. prod/rel: Fox Film Corp.
Veneer, New York 1929, Play
　Young Bride 1932 d: William A. Seiter. lps: Helen Twelvetrees, Eric Linden, Arline Judge. 76M USA. *Love Starved*; *Veneer* prod/rel: RKO Pathe Pictures©
Tin Pan Alley, New York 1928, Play
　New York Nights 1929 d: Lewis Milestone. lps: Norma Talmadge, Gilbert Roland, John Wray. 7447f USA. *Tin Pan Alley* prod/rel: United Artists

STANKOVIC, BORISLAV
Necista Krv, 1911, Novel
　Sofka 1948 d: Rados Novakovic. lps: Vera Gregovic, Milivoje Zivanovic, Marija Crnobori. 98M YGS.

STANLEY, ARTHUR
The Tale-Teller Phone, Play
　Tale-Teller Phone, The 1928 d: Arthur Stanley. lps: Philip Desborough, Athalie Davies, Charles Tomlin. SND. 10M UKN. prod/rel: British Sound Film Production, Bifd

STANLEY, CAROL ABBOT
A Modern Madonna, New York 1906, Novel
　Forgotten Law, The 1922 d: James W. Horne. lps: Milton Sills, Jack Mullhall, Cleo Ridgely. 6900f USA. prod/rel: Graf Productions, Metro Pictures

STANLEY, JOSEPH
Murder in a Chinese Theatre, Novel
　Mad Holiday 1936 d: George B. Seitz. lps: Elissa Landi, Edmund Lowe, Zasu Pitts. 72M USA. *The Cockeyed Cruise*; *The White Dragon* prod/rel: Metro-Goldwyn-Mayer Corp.©

STANLEY, MARTHA M.
The First Mrs. Chiverick, Play
　Scrambled Wives 1921 d: Edward H. Griffith. lps: Marguerite Clark, Leon P. Gendron, Ralph Bunker. 6460f USA. prod/rel: Marguerite Clark Productions, Associated First National Pictures
My Son, New York 1924, Play
　My Son 1925 d: Edwin Carewe. lps: Alla Nazimova, Jack Pickford, Hobart Bosworth. 6552f USA. prod/rel: First National Pictures
The Teaser, New York 1921, Play
　Teaser, The 1925 d: William A. Seiter. lps: Laura La Plante, Pat O'Malley, Hedda Hopper. 6800f USA. prod/rel: Universal Pictures

STANTON, CORALIE
Heath Hooken, Novel
　Lotus d'Or, Le 1916 d: Louis Mercanton. lps: Paul Guide, Jean Marie de L'isle, Regina Badet. 1620m FRN. prod/rel: Eclipse
The World's Best Girl, Novel
　Romance of a Movie Star, The 1920 d: Richard Garrick. lps: Violet Hopson, Stewart Rome, Gregory Scott. UKN. prod/rel: Broadwest, Walturdaw

STANTON, WILL
The Golden Evenings of Summer, Novel
　Charley and the Angel 1973 d: Vincent McEveety. lps: Fred MacMurray, Cloris Leachman, Harry Morgan. 93M USA. prod/rel: Walt Disney

STANUSH, CLAUDE
The Newton Boys, Book
　Newton Boys, The 1998 d: Richard Linklater. lps: Matthew McConaughey, Skeet Ulrich, Ethan Hawke. 122M USA. prod/rel: Twentieth Century-Fox, Detour Films

STANWOOD, DONALD A.
The Memory of Eva Ryker, Novel
　Memory of Eva Ryker, The 1980 d: Walter Grauman. lps: Natalie Wood, Robert Foxworth, Ralph Bellamy. TVM. 144M USA. prod/rel: CBS

STAPLETON, JOHN
A Gentleman of Leisure, New York 1911, Play
　Gentleman of Leisure, A 1915 d: George Melford. lps: Wallace Eddinger, Carol Holloway, Billy Elmer. 5r USA. prod/rel: Jesse L. Lasky Feature Play Co.©, Paramount Pictures Corp.
　Gentleman of Leisure, A 1923 d: Joseph Henabery. lps: Jack Holt, Casson Ferguson, Sigrid Holmquist. 5695f USA. prod/rel: Famous Players-Lasky, Paramount Pictures

STAR, MARIA
L' Espagnole, Novel
　Soleil Et Ombre 1922 d: Musidora, Jacques Lasseyne. lps: Musidora, Antonio Canero, Paul Vermoyal. 1325m FRN/SPN. *Sol Y Sombra* (SPN); *Sun and Shadow* prod/rel: Films Musidora

STARACE, FRANCESCO GABRIELLO
Gnesella, 1899, Play
　Gnesella 1918 d: Elvira Notari. lps: Mariu Gleck, Umberto Mucci, Giuseppe de Blasio. 1000m ITL. prod/rel: Films Dora

STARITSKY, MIKHAYLO PETROVICH
Marusia, 1872, Play
　Marusia 1938 d: Leo Bulgakov. lps: Stephania Melnyk, Nicholas Stehnitzky, Peter Chorniuk. 105M USA. prod/rel: Ukra Corp.
Za Dvoma Zaytsyami, 1883, Play
　Za Dvumya Zaytsami 1961 d: V. Ivanov. lps: Oleg Borisov, M. Krinitsyna, N. Yakovchenko. 76M USS. *Chasing Two Hares Kiev Comedy: Or*; *A Kiev Comedy* (USA) prod/rel: Dovzhenko Film Studio

STARK
Causa Kaiser, Play
　Mariage a Responsabilite Limitee 1933 d: Jean de Limur. lps: Pierre Larquey, Florelle, Jean Wall. 75M FRN. prod/rel: Vandor-Film

STARK, WILBUR
Second Level, Short Story
　My Lover, My Son 1970 d: John Newland. lps: Romy Schneider, Donald Houston, Dennis Waterman. 95M UKN/USA. *Don't You Cry*; *Hush-a-Bye Murder* prod/rel: Sagittarius Productions, MGM British

STARKE, ROLAND
The Day, Short Story
　Burning, The 1968 d: Stephen Frears. lps: Gwen Ffrangcon-Davies, Mark Baillie, Isabel Muller. 30M UKN. prod/rel: British Film Institute, Memorial Enterprises

STARLING, LYNN
Meet the Wife, New York 1923, Play
　Meet the Wife 1931 d: A. Leslie Pearce. lps: Laura La Plante, Lew Cody, Joan Marsh. 76M USA. prod/rel: Christie Film Co., Columbia Pictures Corp.©
Weak Sisters, New York 1925, Play
　Dumb-Bells in Ermine 1930 d: John G. Adolfi. lps: Robert Armstrong, Barbara Kent, Beryl Mercer. 6300f USA. *Dumbelles in Ermine* prod/rel: Warner Brothers Pictures

STARR, BLAZE
Blaze Starr: My Life As Told to Huey Perry, Book
　Blaze 1989 d: Ron Shelton. lps: Paul Newman, Lolita Davidovich, Jerry Hardin. 120M USA. prod/rel: Touchstone

STARR, JAMES A.
The Corpse Came C.O.D., Novel
　Corpse Came C.O.D., The 1947 d: Henry Levin. lps: George Brent, Adele Jergens, Joan Blondell. 87M USA. prod/rel: Columbia

STARRETT, VINCENT (1886–1974), CND, Starrett, Charles Vincent Emerson
Recipe for Murder, 1934, Short Story
　Great Hotel Murder, The 1935 d: Eugene J. Forde. lps: Edmund Lowe, Victor McLaglen, Rosemary Ames. 70M USA. *The Great Hotel Mystery*; *Recipe for Murder* prod/rel: Fox Film Corp.©

STAWICKI, JERZY STEFAN
Szesc Wcielen Jana Piszczyka, 1951, Short Story
　Zezowate Szczescie 1960 d: Andrzej Munk. lps: Tadeusz Janczar, Bogumil Kobiela, Maria Ciesielska. 158M PLN. **De la Veine a Revendre**; *Das Schielende Gluck*; *Bad Luck* (USA); *Cockeyed Happiness*
Ucieczka, 1958, Short Story
　Eroica 1958 d: Andrzej Munk. lps: Jozef Nowak, Edward Dziewonski, Barbara PolomskA. 83M PLN. *Heroism*; *Eroica - Polen 44* prod/rel: Zespal Autorow Filmowych Kadr

Wegrzy, 1956, Short Story
　Eroica 1958 d: Andrzej Munk. lps: Jozef Nowak, Edward Dziewonski, Barbara PolomskA. 83M PLN. *Heroism*; *Eroica - Polen 44* prod/rel: Zespal Autorow Filmowych Kadr

STAWINSKI, JERZY STEFAN
Kanal, Warsaw 1956, Novel
　Kanal 1957 d: Andrzej WajdA. lps: Tadeusz Janczar, Teresa Izewska, Wienczyslaw Glinski. 96M PLN. *They Loved Life*; *Sewer* prod/rel: Kadr Film Unit, Polski

STAYTON, FRANK
In Pawn, Play
　Woman in Pawn, A 1927 d: Victor Saville, Edwin Greenwood. lps: Gladys Jennings, John Stuart, Lauderdale Maitland. 6845f UKN. prod/rel: Gaumont
The Joan Danvers, Play
　Gamble in Lives, A 1920 d: George Ridgwell. lps: Malvina Longfellow, Norman McKinnel, Alec Fraser. 5242f UKN. prod/rel: British & Colonial, Pathe
The Last Chance, Play
　Last Chance, The 1937 d: Thomas Bentley. lps: Frank Leighton, Judy Kelly, Billy Milton. 74M UKN. prod/rel: Welwyn, Pathe
Mixed Doubles, London 1925, Play
　Mixed Doubles 1933 d: Sidney Morgan. lps: Jeanne de Casalis, Frederick Lloyd, Molly Johnson. 69M UKN. prod/rel: British and Dominions, Paramount British
The Passionate Adventure, Novel
　Passionate Adventure, The 1924 d: Graham Cutts. lps: Alice Joyce, Marjorie Daw, Clive Brook. 7923f UKN. prod/rel: Gainsborough, Gaumont
Threads, Play
　Threads 1932 d: G. B. Samuelson. lps: Lawrence Anderson, Dorothy Fane, Gerald Rawlinson. 76M UKN. prod/rel: Samuelson, United Artists

STEAD, CHRISTINA (1902–1983), ASL
For Love Alone, Novel
　For Love Alone 1986 d: Stephen Wallace. lps: Helen Buday, Sam Neill, Hugo Weaving. 104M ASL. prod/rel: Uaa, Western Film Prods. No.6 Pty Ltd.©

STEAD, KARL
Smith's Dream, Novel
　Sleeping Dogs 1977 d: Roger Donaldson. lps: Sam Neill, Ian Mune, Warren Oates. 107M NZL. prod/rel: Aardvark, Satori

STEAKLEY, JOHN
Vampire$, Novel
　John Carpenter's Vampires 1998 d: John Carpenter. lps: James Woods, Daniel Baldwin, Sheryl Lee. 104M USA. prod/rel: Largo Entertainment, Film Office

STECH, VACLAV
Treti Zvoneni, Play
　Treti Zvoneni 1938 d: Jan Svitak. lps: Theodor Pistek, Milada Gampeova, Karla OlicovA. 2809m CZC. *The Third Ringing* prod/rel: Elekta

STECK, H. TIPTON
Gift O' Gab, Short Story
　Gift O' Gab 1917 d: W. S. Van Dyke. lps: Jack Gardner, Helen Ferguson, Frank Morris. 5r USA. prod/rel: Essanay Film Mfg. Co.©, George Kleine System
The Great Silence, Novel
　Great Silence, The 1915. lps: Francis X. Bushman, Beverly Bayne, Chester Beery. 3r USA. prod/rel: Essanay

STEDMAN, MARSHALL
Ring of Destiny, Story
　Ring of Destiny, The 1915 d: Cleo Madison. lps: Cleo Madison, Joe King, Hoot Gibson. 2r USA. prod/rel: Rex

STEEBER, MAX
Way Station, New York 1961, Book
　Apache Uprising 1966 d: R. G. Springsteen. lps: Rory Calhoun, Corinne Calvet, John Russell. 90M USA. prod/rel: A. C. Lyles Productions

STEEDMAN, ANDRE
Six Dead Men, Novel
　Riverside Murder, The 1935 d: Albert Parker. lps: Basil Sydney, Judy Gunn, Alastair Sim. 64M UKN. prod/rel: Fox British

STEEL, DANIELLE (1947–, USA, Steel, Danielle Fernande
Crossings, Novel
　Crossings 1985 d: Karen Arthur. lps: Cheryl Ladd, Lee Horsley, Christopher Plummer. TVM. 270M USA. prod/rel: Aaron Spelling, Warner Bros.
Jewels, Novel
　Danielle Steel's Jewels 1992 d: Robert Young. lps: Annette O'Toole, Anthony Andrews, Jurgen Prochnow. TVM. 242M USA. *Jewels*

No Greater Love, Novel
Danielle Steel's No Greater Love 1995 d: Richard T. Heffron. lps: Kelly Rutherford, Chris Sarandon, Nicholas Campbell. TVM. 90M USA. prod/rel: NBC, the Cramer Company

Now and Forever, Novel
Now and Forever 1982 d: Adrian Carr, Richard Cassidy. lps: Cheryl Ladd, Robert Coleby, Carmen Duncan. 93M ASL. prod/rel: Now and Forever Film Partnership©, Roadshow

Vanished, Novel
Danielle Steel's Vanished 1995 d: George Kaczender. lps: George Hamilton, Lisa Rinna, Robert Hays. TVM. 120M USA.

STEEL, KURT
Murder Goes to College, Indianapolis 1936, Novel
Murder Goes to College 1937 d: Charles F. Reisner. lps: Lynne Overman, Roscoe Karns, Marsha Hunt. 77M USA. prod/rel: Paramount Pictures©
Partners in Crime 1937 d: Ralph Murphy. lps: Lynne Overman, Roscoe Karns, Anthony Quinn. 62M USA. *Murder Goes to Jail* prod/rel: Paramount Pictures©

STEELE, AUSTIN
Friends and Neighbours, London 1958, Play
Friends and Neighbours 1959 d: Gordon Parry. lps: Arthur Askey, Megs Jenkins, Tilda Thamar. 79M UKN. *Friends and Neighbors* (USA) prod/rel: Valiant Films, British Lion

STEELE, RUFUS
Article
Hop, the Devil's Brew 1916 d: Phillips Smalley, Lois Weber. lps: Phillips Smalley, Lois Weber, Marie Walcamp. 5r USA. prod/rel: Bluebird Photoplays, Inc., Universal Film Mfg. Co.©
Keeping John Barleycorn Off the Tracks, 1914, Short Story
Rule G 1915 d: George W. Lawrence, G. M. Noble. lps: Harry L. Stevenson, Lawrence Katzenberg, A. C. Posey. 5r USA. prod/rel: Blazon Film Producing Co., Paramount Pictures Corp.

STEELE, WILBUR DANIEL (1886–1970), USA
Ching, Ching, Chinaman, 1917, Short Story
Shadows 1922 d: Tom Forman. lps: Lon Chaney, Marguerite de La Motte, Harrison Ford. 7040f USA. *Ching Ching Chinaman* prod/rel: Preferred Pictures, Al Lichtman Corp.
Footfalls, Short Story
Footfalls 1921 d: Charles J. Brabin. lps: Tyrone Power Sr., Tom Douglas, Estelle Taylor. 8068f USA. prod/rel: Fox Film Corp.
Ropes, 1921, Short Story
False Kisses 1921 d: Paul Scardon. lps: Miss Du Pont, Pat O'Malley, Lloyd Whitlock. 4335f USA. *Ropes* prod/rel: Universal Film Mfg. Co.
Undertow 1930 d: Harry Pollard. lps: Mary Nolan, Johnny Mack Brown, Robert Ellis. 60M USA. *The Girl Who Gave in* prod/rel: Universal Pictures
The Way to the Gold, 1955, Novel
Way to the Gold, The 1957 d: Robert D. Webb. lps: Jeffrey Hunter, Sheree North, Barry Sullivan. 95M USA. prod/rel: 20th Century-Fox

STEEMAN, STANISLAS-ANDRE
L' Assassin Habite Au 21, Novel
Assassin Habite Au 21, L' 1942 d: Henri-Georges Clouzot. lps: Pierre Fresnay, Jean Tissier, Noel Roquevert. 84M FRN. *The Murderer Lives at Number 21* (USA) prod/rel: Continental-Films
Les Atouts de M. Wens, Novel
Atouts de M. Wens, Les 1946 d: E. G. de Meyst. lps: Louis Salou, Marie Dea, Claudine Dupuis. 95M FRN/BLG. *Les Cinq Atouts de M. Wens* prod/rel: Beinapro
Le Dernier Des Six, Novel
Dernier Des Six, Le 1941 d: Georges Lacombe. lps: Pierre Fresnay, Michele Alfa, Suzy Delair. 90M FRN. prod/rel: Continental-Films
Dortoir Des Grandes, Novel
Dortoir Des Grandes 1953 d: Henri Decoin. lps: Jean Marais, Francoise Arnoul, Denise Grey. 98M FRN. *Inside a Girls' Dormitory* (USA); *Girls' Dormitory* prod/rel: C.F.C. Films, E.G.E.
L' Ennemi Sans Visage, Novel
Ennemi Sans Visage, L' 1946 d: Maurice Cammage, Robert-Paul Dagan. lps: Jean Tissier, Frank Villard, Louise Carletti. 105M FRN. prod/rel: Stella
Le Furet, Novel
Furet, Le 1949 d: Raymond Leboursier. lps: Pierre Renoir, Jany Holt, Pierre Larquey. 95M FRN. *Crimes a Vendre* prod/rel: S.P.a.T.

Le Mannequin Assassine, Novel
Mannequin Assassine, Le 1947 d: Pierre de Herain. lps: Blanchette Brunoy, Anne Vernon, Gilbert Gil. 82M FRN. prod/rel: Herve Missir Et Cie, Etendard Films
La Nuit du 13, Novel
Mystere a Shangai 1950 d: Roger Blanc. lps: Paul Bernard, Pierre Jourdan, Helene Perdriere. 85M FRN. *La Nuit du Treize* prod/rel: Rapid Films
Quai Des Orfevres, Novel
Quai Des Orfevres 1947 d: Henri-Georges Clouzot. lps: Louis Jouvet, Bernard Blier, Simone Renart. 105M FRN. *Jenny Lamour* (USA); *Joyeux Noel* prod/rel: Majestic Films
Six Hommes a Tuer, Novel
Que Personne Ne Sorte 1963 d: Yvan Govar. lps: Philippe Nicaud, Jacqueline Maillan, Marie Daems. 90M FRN/BLG. *La Derniere Enquete de Wens* prod/rel: Belcodiex, Japa Films
Le Trajet de la Foudre, Novel
Trajet de la Foudre, Le 1994 d: Jacques Bourton. lps: Jacques Perrin, Elisabeth Bourgine, Beatrice Agenin. TVM. 100M BLG/FRN.

STEFANO, JOSEPH
Television Play
Black Orchid, The 1959 d: Martin Ritt. lps: Sophia Loren, Anthony Quinn, Ina Balin. 96M USA. prod/rel: Paramount, Ponti-Girosi

STEGER, JULIUS
The Fifth Commandment, Play
Fifth Commandment, The 1915. lps: Julius Steger, Forrest Robinson, Kathryn Browne Decker. 5r USA. prod/rel: Cosmos Feature Film Corp.©, World Film Corp.

STEIN, BENJAMIN
Ludes, Novel
Boost, The 1988 d: Harold Becker. lps: James Woods, Sean Young, John Kapelos. 95M USA. prod/rel: Hemdale, Becker-Blatt-Ponicsan

STEIN, DANIEL MICHAEL
Wall of Noise, New York 1960, Novel
Wall of Noise 1963 d: Richard Wilson. lps: Suzanne Pleshette, Ty Hardin, Dorothy Provine. 112M USA. prod/rel: Warner Bros. Pictures

STEIN, GERTRUDE (1874–1946), USA
Things As They are, 1950, Novel
Quest for Love 1987 d: Helena NogueirA. lps: Jana Cilliers, Sandra Prinsloo, Joanna Weinberg. 91M SAF. *Fire in Their Hearts*; *Quest of Truth* prod/rel: Distant Horizon

STEIN, HARRY
Eichmann in My Hands, Book
Man Who Captured Eichmann, The 1996 d: William A. Graham. lps: Robert Duvall, Arliss Howard, Jeffrey Tambor. TVM. 120M USA. prod/rel: Stan Margulies Co., Butchers Run Films

STEIN, JOSEPH
Mrs. Gibbons' Boys, Play
Mrs. Gibbons' Boys 1962 d: Max Varnel. lps: Kathleen Harrison, Lionel Jeffries, Diana Dors. 82M UKN. prod/rel: British Lion, Byron

STEIN, LEO
Die Czardasfurstin, Vienna 1915, Operetta
Czardasfurstin, Die 1927 d: Hanns Schwarz. lps: Liane Haid, Oscar Marion, Imre Raday. 2596m GRM. prod/rel: Ostermayr-Film
Czardasfurstin, Die 1934 d: Georg Jacoby. lps: Marta Eggerth, Hans Sohnker, Paul Horbiger. 85M GRM. *Die Csardasfurstin* prod/rel: UFA
Czardasfurstin, Die 1951 d: Georg Jacoby. lps: Marika Rokk, Johannes Heesters, Franz Schafheitlin. 94M GRM. *The Czardas Princess*; *Die Csardasfurstin* prod/rel: Deutsche Styria, UFA
Princesse Czardas 1934 d: Andre Beucler, Georg Jacoby. lps: Meg Lemonnier, Jacques Pills, Lyne Clevers. 85M FRN. *Serenade* prod/rel: U.F.a., a.C.E.
Die Lustige Witwe, Vienna 1905, Operetta
Merry Widow, The 1925 d: Erich von Stroheim. lps: Mae Murray, John Gilbert, Roy d'Arcy. 10r USA. prod/rel: Metro-Goldwyn-Mayer Pictures
Merry Widow, The 1934 d: Ernst Lubitsch. lps: Maurice Chevalier, Jeanette MacDonald, Edward Everett Horton. 110M USA. *The Lady Dances* prod/rel: Metro-Goldwyn-Mayer Corp.©
Merry Widow, The 1952 d: Curtis Bernhardt. lps: Lana Turner, Fernando Lamas, Una Merkel. 105M USA. prod/rel: MGM
Polska Krev, Opera
Polenblut 1934 d: Carl Lamac. lps: Anny Ondra, Hans Moser, Ivan Petrovich. F GRM/CZC. *Polish Blood* (USA) prod/rel: Ondra-Lamac Film, Elekta

Polska Krev 1934 d: Carl Lamac. lps: Anny Ondra, Theodor Pistek, Stefan HozA. 2375m CZC. *Polish Blood* prod/rel: Elekta, Wolframfilm
Schutzenliesel, Opera
Schutzenliesel 1954 d: Rudolf Schundler. lps: Herta Staal, Helmuth Schneider, Susi Nicoletti. 100M GRM. *Sure-Shot Lisa* prod/rel: Central-Europa, Prisma
La Veuve Joyeuse, Book
Veuve Joyeuse, La 1934 d: Ernst Lubitsch. lps: Maurice Chevalier, Jeanette MacDonald, Daniele ParolA. 105M USA. prod/rel: Metro-Goldwyn-Mayer

STEINBECK, JOHN (1902–1968), USA
Story
Lifeboat 1944 d: Alfred Hitchcock. lps: Tallulah Bankhead, John Hodiak, Hume Cronyn. 97M USA. prod/rel: 20th Century-Fox
Lifepod 1993 d: Ron Silver. lps: Ron Silver, Robert Loggia, Jessica Tuck. TVM. 120M USA.
Medal for Benny, A 1945 d: Irving Pichel. lps: J. Carrol Naish, Dorothy Lamour, Arturo de CordovA. 77M USA. prod/rel: Paramount
Cannery Row, 1945, Novel
Cannery Row 1982 d: David S. Ward. lps: Nick Nolte, Debra Winger, Audra Lindley. 120M USA. prod/rel: United Artists, MGM
East of Eden, 1952, Novel
East of Eden 1955 d: Elia Kazan. lps: James Dean, Julie Harris, Raymond Massey. 115M USA. prod/rel: Warner Bros.
East of Eden 1982 d: Harvey Hart. lps: Jane Seymour, Timothy Bottoms, Bruce Boxleitner. TVM. 640M USA. *John Steinbeck's East of Eden* prod/rel: ABC, Mace Neufeld
Flight, 1945, Short Story
Flight 1960 d: Louis Bispo. 91M USA.
The Grapes of Wrath, New York 1939, Novel
Grapes of Wrath, The 1940 d: John Ford. lps: Henry Fonda, Jane Darwell, John Carradine. 129M USA. prod/rel: 20th Century-Fox Film Corp.©
The Harness, Short Story
Harness, The 1971 d: Boris Sagal. lps: Lorne Greene, Julie Sommars, Murray Hamilton. TVM. 100M USA. prod/rel: Universal
The Long Valley, 1939, Novel
Red Pony, The 1949 d: Lewis Milestone. lps: Myrna Loy, Robert Mitchum, Peter Miles. 89M USA. prod/rel: Republic
Red Pony, The 1973 d: Lewis Totten. lps: Henry Fonda, Maureen O'Hara, Clint Howard. TVM. 100M USA. prod/rel: Universal, Omnibus Productions
The Moon Is Down, 1942, Novel
Moon Is Down, The 1943 d: Irving Pichel. lps: Cedric Hardwicke, Henry Travers, Lee J. Cobb. 90M USA. prod/rel: 20th Century-Fox
Of Mice and Men, New York 1937, Novel
Of Mice and Men 1939 d: Lewis Milestone. lps: Lon Chaney Jr., Burgess Meredith, Betty Field. 104M USA. prod/rel: United Artists Corp.©, Hal Roach Studios
Of Mice and Men 1981 d: Reza Badiyi. lps: Robert Blake, Randy Quaid, Lew Ayres. TVM. 125M USA. prod/rel: NBC
Of Mice and Men 1992 d: Gary Sinise. lps: John Malkovich, Gary Sinise, Ray Walston. 111M USA. prod/rel: Metro-Goldwyn-Mayer
The Pearl, 1945, Novel
Pearl, The 1946 d: Emilio Fernandez. lps: Pedro Armendariz, Fernando Wagner, Maria Elena Marques. 77M USA/MXC. *La Perla* (MXC) prod/rel: RKO, Aguila-Films
Sweet Thursday, 1954, Novel
Cannery Row 1982 d: David S. Ward. lps: Nick Nolte, Debra Winger, Audra Lindley. 120M USA. prod/rel: United Artists, MGM
Tortilla Flat, 1935, Novel
Tortilla Flat 1942 d: Victor Fleming. lps: Spencer Tracy, Hedy Lamarr, John Garfield. 105M USA. prod/rel: MGM
The Wayward Bus, 1947, Novel
Wayward Bus, The 1957 d: Victor Vicas. lps: Joan Collins, Jayne Mansfield, Dan Dailey. 89M USA. prod/rel: 20th Century-Fox

STEINBERG, SAM
Forgotten Mothers, 1937, Play
Where Is My Child? 1937 d: Abraham Leff. lps: Celia Adler, Solomon Steinberg, Morris Silberkasten. 95M USA. *Vu Iz Mayn Kind?* prod/rel: Menorah Productions©

STEINBRECKER, ALEXANDER
Meine Nichte Susanne, Play
    Meine Nichte Susanne 1950 d: Wolfgang Liebeneiner. lps: Hilde Krahl, Inge Meysel, Ingrid Pankow. 92M GRM. *My Niece Susanne* prod/rel: Sphinx, UFA

STEINHARDT, WOLFGANG
Story
    Riviera-Story 1961 d: Wolfgang Becker. lps: Ulla Jacobsson, Wolfgang Preiss, Hartmut Reck. 86M GRM. prod/rel: Cine International, Deutsche Cinevox

STELIBSKY, JOSEF
Nam Je Hej, Opera
    Armadni Dvojcata 1937 d: Jiri Slavicek, Cenek Slegl. lps: Ladislav Pesek, Jindrich Plachta, Frantisek Kreuzmann. 2559m CZC. *Army Twins* prod/rel: Nationalfilm

STELLA, ADORIAN
Die Unentschuldigte Stunde, Play
    Unentschuldigte Stunde, Die 1957 d: Willi Forst. lps: Adrian Hoven, Erika Remberg, Rudolf Forster. 95M AUS. prod/rel: Sascha

STELLA, ENRICO
Una Ragazza Di Nome Francesca, Short Story
    Voglia Matta, La 1962 d: Luciano Salce. lps: Ugo Tognazzi, Catherine Spaak, Gianni Garko. 105M ITL. *Crazy Desire* (USA); *This Crazy Urge* prod/rel: D.D.L., Lux Film

STEMMLE, ROBERT A. (1903–, GRM
Die Schonen Tage von Aranjuez, Play
    Adieu Les Beaux Jours 1933 d: Johannes Meyer, Andre Beucler. lps: Jean Gabin, Brigitte Helm, Henri Bosc. 96M FRN. *Les Beaux Jours d'Aranjuez* prod/rel: U.F.a.
    Desire 1936 d: Frank Borzage. lps: Marlene Dietrich, Gary Cooper, John Halliday. 99M USA. prod/rel: Paramount Productions, Inc.
    Schonen Tage von Aranjuez, Die 1933 d: Johannes Meyer. lps: Brigitte Helm, Gustaf Grundgens, Wolfgang Liebeneiner. F GRM.

STENBERG, BIRGITTA
Chans, Stockholm 1962, Novel
    Chans 1962 d: Gunnar Hellstrom. lps: Lillevi Bergman, Gosta Ekman Jr., Bertil Anderberg. 82M SWD. *Just Once More* (USA); *Chance* prod/rel: Svensk Filmindustri

STENDHAL (1783–1842), FRN, Beyle, Marie Henri
Short Story
    Monache Di Sant'arcangelo, Le 1973 d: Domenico PaolellA. lps: Anne Heywood, Luc Merenda, Ornella Muti. 103M ITL/FRN. *Les Religieuses du Saint Archange* (FRN); *The Nun and the Devil* (UKN) prod/rel: Produzioni Atlas Consorziate (Roma), Splendida Film (Roma)
L' Abbesse de Castro, Short Story
    Badessa Di Castro, La 1974 d: Armando Crispino. lps: Barbara Bouchet, Pier Paolo Capponi, Evelyn Stewart. 102M ITL. prod/rel: Claudia Cin.Ca, Euro International Film
La Chartreuse de Parme, 1839, Novel
    Certosa Di Parma, La 1947 d: Christian-Jaque. lps: Gerard Philipe, Renee Faure, Lucien Coedel. 170M ITL/FRN. *La Chartreuse de Parme* (FRN) prod/rel: Andre Paulve, Scalera Films
    Prima Della Rivoluzione 1964 d: Bernardo Bertolucci. lps: Adriana Asti, Francesco Barilli, Alan Midgette. 112M ITL. *Before the Revolution* (USA) prod/rel: Iride Cinematografica, Cineriz
Le Coffre Et le Revenant, 1867, Short Story
    Amants de Tolede, Les 1953 d: Henri Decoin, Fernando Palacios. lps: Alida Valli, Pedro Armendariz, Francoise Arnoul. 86M FRN/SPN/ITL. *El Tirano de Toledo* (SPN); *Gli Amanti Di Toledo* (ITL); *The Lovers of Toledo* (USA); *Le Coffre Et le Revenant* prod/rel: E.G.E., Athena Films
De l'Amour, Paris 1822, Novel
    De l'Amour 1964 d: Jean Aurel. lps: Michel Piccoli, Elsa Martinelli, Anna KarinA. 94M FRN/ITL. *La Calda Pelle* (ITL); *All About Loving* (UKN); *Concerning Love* prod/rel: Films de la Pleiade, Cocinor-Marceau
Lamiel, 1889, Novel
    Lamiel 1967 d: Jean Aurel. lps: Anna Karina, Michel Bouquet, Denise Gence. 100M FRN/ITL. prod/rel: Rome-Paris-Films, Films Copernic
Mina de Vanghel, 1855, Short Story
    Crimes de l'Amour, Les 1951 d: Alexandre Astruc, Maurice Barry. lps: Odile Versois, Alain Cuny, Jean Servais. 88M FRN. prod/rel: Argos Films, Como Films
Promenades Dans Rome, 1829, Novel
    Interno Di un Convento 1977 d: Walerian Borowczyk. lps: Ligia Branice, Marina Pierro, Gabriella Giaccobe. 95M ITL. *Sex Life in a Convent* (USA); *Behind Convent Walls* (UKN); *Within the Cloister*; *Behind the Convent Walls*; *Unmoralische Novizzinnen* (GRM) prod/rel: Trust International Film (Roma), Lisa Film (Munich)
Le Rouge Et le Noir, 1830, Novel
    Corriere Del Re, Il 1948 d: Gennaro Righelli. lps: Rossano Brazzi, Valentina Cortese, Irasema Dilian. 98M ITL. *Le Rouge Et le Noir* prod/rel: Fincine, Domus Cin.Ca
    Geheime Kurier, Der 1928 d: Gennaro Righelli. lps: Ivan Mosjoukine, Lil Dagover, Jose Davert. 2928m GRM. *Rouge Et Noir*; *The Secret Courier* prod/rel: Greenabaum-Film
    Rouge Et le Noir, Le 1920 d: Mario Bonnard. lps: Mario Bonnard, Vittoria Lepanto, Ugo Piperno. 2345m ITL. prod/rel: Celio Film
    Rouge Et le Noir, Le 1954 d: Claude Autant-LarA. lps: Danielle Darrieux, Gerard Philipe, Antonella Lualdi. 178M FRN/ITL. *L' Uomo E Il Diavolo* (ITL); *Rouge Et Noir* (USA); *Scarlet and Black* prod/rel: Franco-London Films, Documento Films
Vanina Vanini, 1855, Short Story
    Oltre l'Amore 1940 d: Carmine Gallone. lps: Alida Valli, Amedeo Nazzari, Germaine Aussey. 96M ITL. *Passione* prod/rel: Grandi Film Storici, I.C.I.
    Vanina Vanini 1961 d: Roberto Rossellini. lps: Sandra Milo, Laurent Terzieff, Martine Carol. 125M ITL/FRN. *The Betrayer* (USA) prod/rel: Zebra Film (Roma), Orsay Film (Paris)

STENO, FLAVIA
Sissignora, Novel
    Sissignora 1942 d: Ferdinando M. Poggioli. lps: Emma Gramatica, Irma Gramatica, Maria Denis. 80M ITL. *Si Signora* prod/rel: a.T.a., I.C.I.

STENTHOFT, AAGE
Die Ente Klingelt Um ½ Acht, Novel
    Ente Klingelt Um ½ Acht, Die 1968 d: Rolf Thiele. lps: Heinz Ruhmann, Hertha Feiler, Graziella GranatA. 88M GRM/ITL. *The Duck Rings at Seven-Thirty* prod/rel: Roxy, Sancro-International

STEPHENS, HAL
My Wife's Family, Play
    My Wife's Family 1931 d: Monty Banks. lps: Gene Gerrard, Muriel Angelus, Jimmy Godden. 80M UKN. prod/rel: British International Pictures, Wardour
    My Wife's Family 1941 d: Walter C. Mycroft. lps: Charles Clapham, John Warwick, Patricia Roc. 82M UKN. prod/rel: Associated British Picture Corporation, Pathe
    My Wife's Family 1956 d: Gilbert Gunn. lps: Ronald Shiner, Ted Ray, Greta Gynt. 76M UKN. prod/rel: Forth Films, Ab-Pathe

STEPHENS, JOHN A.
Wife for Wife, Play
    Wife for Wife 1915 d: Kenean Buel. lps: Wilmuth Merkyl, John E. MacKin, Regina Richards. 3r USA. prod/rel: Kalem

STEPHENS, ROBERT N.
An Enemy to the King, New York 1896, Play
    Enemy to the King, An 1916 d: Frederick A. Thompson. lps: E. H. Sothern, Edith Storey, John Robertson. 6r USA. prod/rel: Vitagraph Co. of America©, Blue Ribbon Feature

STEPHENSON, B. C.
The Fatal Card, London 1894, Play
    Fatal Card, The 1915 d: James Kirkwood. lps: John Mason, Hazel Dawn, Russell Bassett. 5r USA. prod/rel: Famous Players Film Co., Charles Frohman Co.

STEPHENSON, CARL
Leiningen Vs. the Ants, 1940, Short Story
    Naked Jungle, The 1954 d: Byron Haskin. lps: Charlton Heston, Eleanor Parker, William Conrad. 95M USA. prod/rel: Paramount

STEPT, SAMUEL
Yokel Boy, New York 1939, Musical Play
    Yokel Boy 1942 d: Joseph Santley. lps: Albert Dekker, Joan Davis, Eddie Foy Jr. 69M USA. *Hitting the Headlines* (UKN) prod/rel: Republic

STERN, DAVID
Francis, Novel
    Francis 1949 d: Arthur Lubin. lps: Donald O'Connor, Patricia Medina, Zasu Pitts. 91M USA. prod/rel: Universal

STERN, GLADYS BRONWYN (1890–1973), UKN, Stern, G. B.
Dogs in an Omnibus, London 1942, Novel
    Ugly Dachshund, The 1966 d: Norman Tokar. lps: Dean Jones, Suzanne Pleshette, Charles Ruggles. 93M USA. prod/rel: Walt Disney Productions

Long Lost Father, New York 1933, Novel
    Long Lost Father 1934 d: Ernest B. Schoedsack. lps: John Barrymore, Helen Chandler, Donald Cook. 63M USA. prod/rel: RKO Radio Pictures©
The Woman in the Hall, Novel
    Woman in the Hall, The 1947 d: Jack Lee. lps: Ursula Jeans, Jean Simmons, Cecil Parker. 93M UKN. prod/rel: General Film Distributors, Independent Producers

STERN, HOWARD
Private Parts, Book
    Private Parts 1997 d: Betty Thomas. lps: Howard Stern, Robin Quivers, Mary McCormack. 109M USA. prod/rel: Paramount, Rysher Entertainment

STERN, PHILIP VAN DOREN (1900–1984), USA
The Greatest Gift, Short Story
    It Happened One Christmas 1977 d: Donald Wrye. lps: Marlo Thomas, Orson Welles, Wayne Rogers. TVM. 112M USA. prod/rel: Universal
    It's a Wonderful Life 1946 d: Frank CaprA. lps: James Stewart, Donna Reed, Lionel Barrymore. 130M USA. *The Greatest Gift* prod/rel: RKO Radio

STERN, RICHARD MARTIN
The Tower, Novel
    Towering Inferno, The 1974 d: Irwin Allen, John Guillermin. lps: Steve McQueen, Paul Newman, William Holden. 165M USA. prod/rel: 20th Century Fox, Warner Bros.

STERNE, ELAINE
Sins of the Father, Story
    Fruit of Evil, The 1914 d: Wallace Reid. lps: Wallace Reid, Dorothy Davenport, Ed Brady. SHT USA. prod/rel: Nestor

STERNER, JERRY
Other People's Money, Play
    Other People's Money 1991 d: Norman Jewison. lps: Danny Devito, Gregory Peck, Penelope Ann Miller. 101M USA. prod/rel: Warner Bros., Yorktown

STERNHEIM, CARL
Skandal in Der Residenz, Play
    Hose, Die 1927 d: Hans Behrendt. lps: Werner Krauss, Jenny Jugo, Rudolf Forster. 2425m GRM. *Royal Scandal*; *The Trousers*; *Skandal in Einer Kleinen Residenz* prod/rel: Phoebus-Film Ag, Fidelius

STERRETT, FRANCES ROBERTA
Up the Road With Sallie, New York 1915, Novel
    Up the Road With Sallie 1918 d: William D. Taylor. lps: Constance Talmadge, Norman Kerry, Kate Toncray. 4585f USA. *Up the Road With Sally* prod/rel: Select Pictures Corp.©

STEVENS, C. M.
Cy Perkins in the City of Delusion, Story
    Cy Perkins in the City of Delusion 1915 d: Roy McCray. lps: Ernest Shields. SHT USA. prod/rel: Joker

STEVENS, LESLIE
The Lovers, New York 1956, Play
    War Lord, The 1965 d: Franklin J. Schaffner. lps: Charlton Heston, Richard Boone, Rosemary Forsyth. 130M USA. prod/rel: Court Productions, Universal
Marriage-Go-Round, New York 1958, Play
    Marriage-Go-Round 1961 d: Walter Lang. lps: Susan Hayward, James Mason, Julie Newmar. 98M USA. prod/rel: Daystar

STEVENS, WILLIAM RANDOLPH
Deadly Intentions, Book
    Deadly Intentions 1985 d: Noel Black. lps: Michael Biehn, Madolyn Smith, Morgana King. TVM. 240M USA. prod/rel: ABC, Green-Epstein Productions

STEVENSON, BURTON EGBERT (1872–1962), USA, Stevenson, Burton E.
The Case of the Black Parrot, Play
    Case of the Black Parrot, The 1941 d: Noel Smith. lps: William Lundigan, Maris Wrixon, Eddie Foy Jr. 60M USA. prod/rel: Warner Bros.
Little Comrade: a Tale of the Great War, New York 1915, Novel
    On Dangerous Ground 1917 d: Robert T. Thornby. lps: Gail Kane, Carlyle Blackwell, William Bailey. 5r USA. *Little Comrade* prod/rel: Peerless, World Film Corp.©
The Mystery of the Boule Cabinet, New York 1911, Novel
    In the Next Room 1930 d: Eddie Cline. lps: Jack Mulhall, Alice Day, Robert Emmett O'Connor. 6336f USA. prod/rel: First National Pictures
    Pursuing Vengeance, The 1916 d: Martin Sabine. lps: Sheldon Lewis, Jane Meredith, Henry Mortimer. 5r USA. prod/rel: Unity Pictures Corp., State Rights

STEVENSON, GEORGE
A Little World Apart, Novel
    Fires of Innocence 1922 d: Sidney Morgan. lps: Joan Morgan, Bobbie Andrews, Arthur Lennard. 4700f UKN. prod/rel: Progress, Butcher's Film Service

STEVENSON, JANET (1913–), USA
Counter-Attack, Play
Counter-Attack 1945 d: Zoltan KordA. lps: Paul Muni, Marguerite Chapman, Larry Parks. 90M USA. *One Against Seven* (UKN) prod/rel: Columbia

STEVENSON, PHILIP
Counter-Attack 1945 d: Zoltan KordA. lps: Paul Muni, Marguerite Chapman, Larry Parks. 90M USA. *One Against Seven* (UKN) prod/rel: Columbia

STEVENSON, ROBERT LOUIS (1850–1894), UKN, Stevenson, Robert Louis Balfour
Black Arrow, 1888, Novel
Black Arrow 1985 d: John Hough. lps: Oliver Reed, Benedict Taylor, Stephan Chase. TVM. 93M USA/UKN/SPN. *Flecha Negra* (SPN) prod/rel: Walt Disney, Harry Alan Towers
Black Arrow, The 1911 d: Oscar Apfel. lps: Charles Ogle, Natalie Jerome, Harold M. Shaw. 1000f USA. prod/rel: Edison
Black Arrow, The 1948 d: Gordon Douglas. lps: Louis Hayward, Janet Blair, George MacReady. 76M USA. *The Black Arrow Strikes* (UKN) prod/rel: Columbia
Chernaya Streia 1985 d: Sergei Tarasov. 113M USS. *Black Arrow*

The Body Snatcher, 1894, Short Story
Body Snatcher, The 1945 d: Robert Wise. lps: Boris Karloff, Henry Daniell, Bela Lugosi. 77M USA. prod/rel: RKO Radio

The Bottle Imp, London 1891, Novel
Bottle Imp, The 1917 d: Marshall Neilan. lps: Sessue Hayakawa, Margaret Loomis, George KuwA. 5r USA. prod/rel: Jesse L. Lasky Feature Play Co.©, Paramount Pictures Corp.
Flaschenteufel, Der 1952 d: Ferdinand Diehl. ANM. 75M GRM. *The Bottle Demon* prod/rel: Gebruder Diehl, Hamburg
Liebe, Tod Und Teufel 1934 d: Heinz Hilpert, Reinhart Steinbicker. lps: Kathe von Nagy, Albin Skoda, Brigitte Horney. 104M GRM. *The Devil in a Bottle; The Imp in the Bottle; Love Death and the Devil* prod/rel: UFA

Catriona, 1892, Novel
Schusse Unterm Galgen 1968 d: Horst Seemann. lps: Werner Kanitz, Alena Prochazkova, Thomas Weisgerber. 107M GDR. *Shots Under the Gallows*

David Balfour, New York 1893, Novel
Kidnapped 1938 d: Alfred L. Werker, Otto Preminger (Uncredited). lps: Warner Baxter, Freddie Bartholomew, Arleen Whelan. 93M USA. *Kidnapped - the Adventures of David Balfour* prod/rel: Twentieth Century-Fox Film Corp.©

The Ebb Tide; a Trio and Quartette, 1894, Novel
Adventure Island 1947 d: Sam Newfield. lps: Rory Calhoun, Rhonda Fleming, Paul Kelly. 67M USA. prod/rel: Paramount
Ebb Tide 1915 d: Colin Campbell. lps: Kathlyn Williams, Wheeler Oakman, Harry Lonsdale. 3r USA. prod/rel: Selig Polyscope Co.
Ebb Tide 1922 d: George Melford. lps: Lila Lee, James Kirkwood, Raymond Hatton. 7336f USA. prod/rel: Famous Players-Lasky, Paramount Pictures
Ebb Tide 1937 d: James P. Hogan. lps: Frances Farmer, Ray Milland, Oscar HomolkA. 94M USA. prod/rel: Paramount Pictures©, Lucien Hubbard Production
Reflux, Le 1961 d: Paul Gegauff. lps: Nathalie Tehabe, Roger Vadim, Franco Fabrizi. F FRN. prod/rel: Comacico, Supra Films

Heather Ale: a Galloway Legend, 1890, Verse
Vereskovyi Myod 1974 d: Irina Gurvich. ANM. 9M USS.

Island Nights' Entertainments, Short Story
Diable En Bouteille, Le 1935 d: Heinz Hilpert, Reinhart Steinbicker. lps: Kathe von Nagy, Pierre Blanchar, Paul Azais. 95M FRN. prod/rel: U.F.a., a.CE.

Kidnapped, London 1886, Novel
Kidnapped 1917 d: Alan Crosland. lps: Raymond McKee, Joseph Burke, Robert Cain. 4r USA. prod/rel: Thomas A. Edison, Inc.©, Conquest Pictures
Kidnapped 1938 d: Alfred L. Werker, Otto Preminger (Uncredited). lps: Warner Baxter, Freddie Bartholomew, Arleen Whelan. 93M USA. *Kidnapped - the Adventures of David Balfour* prod/rel: Twentieth Century-Fox Film Corp.©
Kidnapped 1948 d: William Beaudine. lps: Roddy McDowall, Sue England, Dan O'Herlihy. 81M USA. prod/rel: Monogram Pictures Corp.
Kidnapped 1960 d: Robert Stevenson. lps: Peter Finch, James MacArthur, Bernard Lee. 97M UKN. prod/rel: Walt Disney

Kidnapped 1971 d: Delbert Mann. lps: Michael Caine, Trevor Howard, Jack Hawkins. 107M UKN/USA. *David and Catriona* prod/rel: Omnibus
Schusse Unterm Galgen 1968 d: Horst Seemann. lps: Werner Kanitz, Alena Prochazkova, Thomas Weisgerber. 107M GDR. *Shots Under the Gallows*

The Master of Ballantrae, 1888, Novel
Master of Ballantrae, The 1953 d: William Keighley. lps: Errol Flynn, Roger Livesey, Anthony Steel. 88M UKN/USA. prod/rel: Warner Bros., First National
Master of Ballantrae, The 1984 d: Douglas Hickox. lps: Richard Thomas, Michael York, John Gielgud. TVM. 150M USA/UKN. prod/rel: Larry White-High Benson Prods., Htv
Senor de Osanto, El 1972 d: Jaime Humberto Hermosillo. 108M MXC. prod/rel: Churubusco Azteca

The Mirror and Markheim, Short Story
Mirror and Markheim, The 1954 d: John Lemont. lps: Philip Saville, Arthur Lowe, Christopher Lee. 28M UKN. prod/rel: Motley, Exclusive

The Pavilion on the Links, 1882, Short Story
White Circle, The 1920 d: Maurice Tourneur. lps: Spottiswoode Aitken, Janice Wilson, Harry Northrup. 4017f USA. *The Pavilion on the Links* prod/rel: Maurice Tourneur Productions, Inc., Famous Players-Lasky Corp.©

The Rajah's Diamond, Short Story
Tame Cat, The 1921 d: William Bradley. lps: Ray Irwin, Marion Harding. 4943f USA. prod/rel: Dramafilms, Arrow Film Corp.

Silverado Squatters, 1883, Short Story
Adventures in Silverado 1948 d: Phil Karlson. lps: William Bishop, Gloria Henry, Edgar Buchanan. 75M USA. *Above All Laws* (UKN) prod/rel: Columbia

The Sire of Maletroit's Door, 1878, Short Story
Strange Door, The 1951 d: Joseph Pevney. lps: Charles Laughton, Boris Karloff, Sally Forrest. 81M USA. *The Door* prod/rel: Universal-International

St. Ives, 1898, Novel
Secret of St. Ives, The 1949 d: Phil Rosen. lps: Richard Ney, Vanessa Brown, Henry Daniell. 75M USA. prod/rel: Columbia

The Strange Case of Dr. Jekyll and Mr. Hyde, London 1886, Novel
Dottor Jekyll E Gentile Signora 1979 d: Steno. lps: Paolo Villaggio, Edwige Fenech, Gianrico Tedeschi. 107M ITL. *Il Dottor Jekill Jr.; Jekyll Junior* (USA); *Doctor and Mrs. Jeckyll* prod/rel: Medusa Distribuzione
Dr. Jekyll and Mr. Hyde 1912 d: Lucius Henderson. lps: James Cruze, Florence Labadie. SHT USA. prod/rel: Thanhouser
Dr. Jekyll and Mr. Hyde 1913 d: Herbert Brenon. lps: King Baggot, Jane Gail, Matt Snyder. 2r USA. prod/rel: Imp
Dr. Jekyll and Mr. Hyde 1920 d: John S. Robertson. lps: John Barrymore, Martha Mansfield, Nita Naldi. 6355f USA. prod/rel: Famous Players-Lasky Corp.©, Paramount-Artcraft Pictures
Dr. Jekyll and Mr. Hyde 1920 d: Charles J. Hayden. lps: Sheldon Lewis, Alex Shannon, Dora Mills Adams. 5r USA. prod/rel: Pioneer Film Corp.©, State Rights
Dr. Jekyll and Mr. Hyde 1932 d: Rouben Mamoulian. lps: Fredric March, Miriam Hopkins, Rose Hobart. 98M USA. prod/rel: Paramount Publix Corp.
Dr. Jekyll and Mr. Hyde 1941 d: Victor Fleming. lps: Spencer Tracy, Ingrid Bergman, Lana Turner. 114M USA. prod/rel: MGM
Dr. Jekyll and Mr. Hyde 1973 d: David Winters. lps: Kirk Douglas, Susan Hampshire, Michael Redgrave. TVM. 65M UKN.
Dr. Jekyll and Mr. Hyde 1981 d: Alastair Reid. lps: David Hemmings, Lisa Harrow, Ian Bannen. MTV. 115M UKN. prod/rel: ABC
Dr. Jekyll and Mr. Hyde - a Journey Into Fear 1988 d: Gerard Kikoine. lps: Anthony Perkins, Glynis Barber, Sarah Maur-Thorp. 90M UKN. *Edge of Sanity* (USA) prod/rel: Palace, Allied Vision
Duality of Man, The 1910. 580f UKN. prod/rel: Wrench Films
Horrible Hyde 1915 d: Howell Hansel. lps: Jerold T. Hevener. SHT USA. prod/rel: Lubin
I, Monster 1972 d: Stephen Weeks. lps: Christopher Lee, Peter Cushing, Mike Raven. 75M UKN. prod/rel: Amicus
Jekyll and Hyde. Together Again 1982 d: Jerry Belson. lps: Mark Blankfield, Bess Armstrong, Krista Errickson. 87M USA. prod/rel: Paramount
Seltsamer Fall, Ein 1914 d: Max Mack. lps: Alwin Neuss, Hanni Weisse, Lotte Neumann. GRM. *Dr. Jekyll and Mr. Hyde* prod/rel: Vitascope

Strange Case of Dr. Jekyll and Mr. Hyde, The 1967 d: Charles Jarrott. lps: Jack Palance, Denholm Elliott, Billie Whitelaw. TVM. 150M USA/CND. *Dr. Jekyll and Mr. Hyde*
Strange Case of Dr. Jekyll and Mr. Hyde, The 1989 d: Michael Lindsay-Hogg. lps: Anthony Andrews, Gregory Cooke, George Murdoch. TVM. 60M USA.
Strannaya Istoria Doctora Dzhekila I Mistera Khayda 1985 d: Alexandr Orlov. 92M USS.
Testament du Dr. Cordelier, Le 1959 d: Jean Renoir. lps: Jean-Louis Barrault, Teddy Bilis, Michel Vitold. 95M FRN. *The Doctor's Horrible Experiment* (USA); *Experiment in Evil* (UKN); *The Testament of Dr. Cordelier* prod/rel: R.T.F., Sofirad
Two Faces of Dr. Jekyll, The 1960 d: Terence Fisher. lps: Paul Massie, Dawn Addams, Christopher Lee. 88M UKN. *House of Fright* (USA); *Jekyll's Inferno* prod/rel: Hammer Film Productions, Columbia
Ugly Duckling, The 1959 d: Lance Comfort. lps: Bernard Bresslaw, Reginald Beckwith, Jon Pertwee. 84M UKN. prod/rel: Columbia, Hammer

The Suicide Club, London 1882, Short Stories
Geheimnisvolle Klub, Der 1913 d: Joseph Delmont. lps: Joseph Delmont, Fred Sauer, Ilse Bois. GRM. *De Geheime Club; Schaking Van Een Meisje; De Geheimzinnige Club; The Secret Club; Girl's Abduction, A* prod/rel: Eiko-Film
Suicide Club, The 1909 d: D. W. Griffith. lps: Arthur Johnson, MacK Sennett, Charles Craig. 318f USA. prod/rel: Biograph Co.
Suicide Club, The 1914 d: Maurice Elvey. lps: Montagu Love, Elisabeth Risdon, Fred Groves. 3386f UKN. prod/rel: British and Colonial, Renters
Suicide Club, The 1973 d: Bill Glenn. lps: Peter Haskell, Margot Kidder, Joseph Wiseman. TVM. 90M USA.
Suicide Club, The 1988 d: James Bruce. lps: Mariel Hemingway, Robert Joy, Lenny Henry. 90M USA. *Welcome to the Suicide Club* prod/rel: Angelika
Trouble for Two 1936 d: J. Walter Ruben. lps: Robert Montgomery, Rosalind Russell, Frank Morgan. 75M USA. *The Suicide Club* (UKN) prod/rel: Metro-Goldwyn-Mayer Corp.©
Unheimliche Geschichten 1932 d: Richard Oswald. lps: Paul Wegener, Maria Koppenhofer, Blandine Ebinger. 89M GRM. *Tales of the Uncanny* prod/rel: Roto, Dietz

The Superfluous Mansion, Story
Dentro la Casa Della Vecchia Signora 1971 d: Giacomo Battiato. lps: Felice Andreasi, Adriana Alberi, Luigi Carani. MTV. 87M ITL. prod/rel: Politecne Cin.Ca

Treasure Island, London 1883, Novel
Anche Nel West, C'era Una Volta Dio 1968 d: Marino Girolami. lps: Richard Harrison, Gilbert Roland, Enio Girolami. 96M ITL/SPN. *The Devil and a Winchester Between God* (USA); *Entre Dios Y El Diablo* (SPN); *Even in the West There Was God Once Upon a Time; God Was in the West Too at One Time; God Never Walked the West* prod/rel: Circus Film (Roma), R. M. (Madrid)
Ile Au Tresor, L' 1991 d: Raul Ruiz. lps: Melvil Poupaud, Martin Landau, Vic Tayback. 115M FRN/USA. *Treasure Island* (UKN) prod/rel: Les Films Du Passage (Paris), Cannon International (Los Angeles)
Isola Del Tesoro, L' 1973 d: Andrea Bianchi. lps: Orson Welles, Kim Burfield, Walter Slezak. 95M ITL/FRN/SPN. *L' Ile Au Tresor* (FRN); *La Isla Del Tesoro* (SPN); *Die Schatzinsel* (GRM); *L' Ile du Tresor* prod/rel: Seven Film (Roma), C.C.C. Filmkunst (Berlin)
Long John Silver 1954 d: Byron Haskin. lps: Robert Newton, Kit Taylor, Connie Gilchrist. 109M ASL. *Long John Silver Returns to Treasure Island*
Ostrov Sokrovisc 1971 d: Yevgeni Friedman. lps: Boris Andreyev, Aanre Laanemets, L. NoreykA. 85M USS. *Treasure Island; Ostrov Sokrovishch*
Ostrov Sokrovishch 1937 d: Vladimir Vainshtok. 92M USS.
Space Island 1987 d: Antonio Margheriti. lps: Anthony Quinn, Itaco Nardulli, Philippe Leroy. 114M ITL/GRM. *Space Pirates* (GRM); *Treasure Island in Outer Space; L' Isola Del Tesoro* prod/rel: Bavaria, Rai
Treasure Island 1912 d: J. Searle Dawley. lps: Addison Rothermel, Ben Wilson, Charles Ogle. 1050f USA. prod/rel: Edison
Treasure Island 1917 d: Chester M. Franklin, Sidney A. Franklin. lps: Francis Carpenter, Virginia Lee Corbin, Violet Radcliffe. 6r USA. prod/rel: Fox Film Corp., William Fox©

Treasure Island 1920 d: Maurice Tourneur. lps: Shirley Mason, Josie Melville, Al W. Filson. 6r USA. prod/rel: Maurice Tourneur Productions, Famous Players-Lasky Corp.©

Treasure Island 1934 d: Victor Fleming. lps: Wallace Beery, Jackie Cooper, Lewis Stone. 110M USA. prod/rel: Metro-Goldwyn-Mayer Corp.©

Treasure Island 1950 d: Byron Haskin. lps: Bobby Driscoll, Robert Newton, Basil Sydney. 96M UKN/USA. prod/rel: Walt Disney Prods., RKO British

Treasure Island 1970 d: Leif Gram, Zoran Janzic. ANM. 46M ASL.

Treasure Island 1972 d: John Hough, Andrea Bianchi. lps: Orson Welles, Kim Burfield, Lionel Stander. 95M UKN/ITL/SPN. *La Isla Del Tesoro* (SPN); *La Isola Del Tesoro* (ITL); *Die Schatzinsel* (GRM); *L' Ile Au Tresor* (FRN) prod/rel: Massfilms, Fdl

Treasure Island 1977 d: Michael E. Briant. lps: Alfred Burke, Anthony Bate, Patrick Troughton. MTV. 199M UKN. prod/rel: BBC

Treasure Island 1982 d: Dave Heather. lps: Christopher Cazenove, Piers Eady, John Judd. 118M UKN. *Treasure Island: the Musical*

Treasure Island 1987 d: Warwick Gilbert. ANM. 49M ASL.

Treasure Island 1988 d: Kei Ijima, Hiroshi IkedA. 72M JPN.

Treasure Island 1990 d: Fraser C. Heston. lps: Charlton Heston, Christian Bale, Julian Glover. TVM. 131M UKN/USA. *Devil's Treasure* prod/rel: British Lion, Warner Bros.

Treasure of Franchard, 1887, Short Story
Treasure of Lost Canyon, The 1952 d: Ted Tetzlaff. lps: William Powell, Rosemary de Camp, Julie Adams. 82M USA. prod/rel: Universal-International

The Wrecker, 1892, Novel
Tainata Na Apolonia 1984 d: Ivo Toman. lps: David Vejrazka, Jan Pichocinski, Olga ShoberovA. 95M BUL/CZC. *Vrak* (CZC); *Apollonia's Secret*; *The Wreck*; *The Derelict*

The Wrong Box, London 1889, Novel
Wrong Box, The 1966 d: Bryan Forbes. lps: John Mills, Ralph Richardson, Michael Caine. 110M UKN. prod/rel: Salamander Film Productions, Columbia

STEVENSON, WILLIAM
A Man Called Intrepid, Book
Man Called Intrepid, A 1979 d: Peter Carter. lps: David Niven, Michael York, Barbara Hershey. TVM. 300M UKN/CND/USA. prod/rel: Intrepid Productions Ltd. (Montreal), Lorimar Productions Ltd. (U.K.)

STEVENSON, WILLIAM H.
The Bushbabies, Boston 1965, Novel
Bushbaby, The 1970 d: John Trent. lps: Margaret Brooks, Louis Gossett Jr., Donald Houston. 100M UKN. *The Bushbabies*

STEWART, DONALD OGDEN
Mr. & Mrs. Haddick in Paris, New York 1926, Novel
Finn and Hattie 1931 d: Norman Z. McLeod, Norman Taurog. lps: Leon Errol, Zasu Pitts, Regis Toomey. 82M USA. *Finn and Hattie Abroad* prod/rel: Paramount Publix Corp.©

Mr. & Mrs Haddock Abroad, New York 1924, Novel
Finn and Hattie 1931 d: Norman Z. McLeod, Norman Taurog. lps: Leon Errol, Zasu Pitts, Regis Toomey. 82M USA. *Finn and Hattie Abroad* prod/rel: Paramount Publix Corp.©

STEWART, FRED MUSTARD
Ellis Island, Novel
Ellis Island 1984 d: Jerry London. lps: Claire Bloom, Faye Dunaway, Peter Riegert. TVM. 334M USA/UKN. prod/rel: CBS, Telepictures

The Mephisto Waltz, Novel
Mephisto Waltz, The 1971 d: Paul Wendkos. lps: Alan Alda, Jacqueline Bisset, Barbara Parkins. 115M USA. prod/rel: Q.M., 20th Century Fox

Six Weeks, Novel
Six Weeks 1982 d: Tony Bill. lps: Dudley Moore, Mary Tyler Moore, Katherine Healy. 107M USA. prod/rel: Universal

STEWART, GRANT
Arms and the Girl, New York 1916, Play
Arms and the Girl 1917 d: Joseph Kaufman. lps: Billie Burke, Thomas Meighan, Louise Emerald Bates. 5r USA. *Delicate Situation* prod/rel: Famous Players Film Co.©, Paramount Pictures Corp.

STEWART, JAMES
The Only Son, Short Story
Mad Hatters, The 1935 d: Ivar Campbell. lps: Chili Bouchier, Sidney King, Evelyn Foster. 68M UKN. prod/rel: British and Dominions, Paramount British

STEWART, MARY (1916–, UKN, Stewart, Lady Mary Florence Elinor
The Moon-Spinners, New York 1963, Novel
Moonspinners, The 1964 d: James Neilson. lps: Hayley Mills, Eli Wallach, Peter McEnery. 119M UKN. *The Moon-Spinners* prod/rel: Walt Disney Productions

STEWART, MICHAEL
Bye Bye Birdie, New York 1960, Musical Play
Bye Bye Birdie 1963 d: George Sidney. lps: Janet Leigh, Dick Van Dyke, Ann-Margret. 112M USA. prod/rel: Columbia

Ella, Novel
Monkey Shines: an Experiment in Fear 1988 d: George A. Romero. lps: Jason Beghe, John Pankow, Kate McNeil. 115M USA. *Monkey Shines*; *Ella* prod/rel: Orion

Hello, Dolly!, New York 1964, Play
Hello, Dolly! 1969 d: Gene Kelly. lps: Barbra Streisand, Walter Matthau, Michael Crawford. 149M USA. prod/rel: Chenault Productions, 20th Century-Fox

STEWART, RAMONA
Desert Town, Novel
Desert Fury 1947 d: Lewis Allen. lps: Lizabeth Scott, John Hodiak, Burt Lancaster. 95M USA. *Desert Town* prod/rel: Paramount

STEWART, TERRY
La Soupe a la Grimace, Novel
Soupe a la Grimace, La 1954 d: Jean SachA. lps: Maria Mauban, Georges Marchal, Christiane Lenier. 90M FRN. prod/rel: Sonofilm, Ste Generale De Films

STEWART, VEGA
Four Winds Island, Novel
Four Winds Island 1961 d: David Villiers. lps: Amanda Coxell, Annette Robertson, Iain Gregory. SRL. 119M UKN. prod/rel: Children's Film Foundation, Merton Park

STICHTING DE AKTEURS
Broos, Play
Broos 1998 d: Mijke de Jong. lps: Lieneke Le Roux, Maartje Nevejan, Adelheid Roosen. 79M NTH. *Frail* prod/rel: Studio Nieuwe, Vpro Television

STIERNSTEDT, MARIKA
Banketten, Novel
Banketten 1948 d: Hasse Ekman. lps: Eva Henning, Hasse Ekman, Ernst Eklund. 90M SWD. *The Banquet* prod/rel: Terra

STIFTER, ADALBERT (1805–1868), AUS
Bergkristall, 1853, Short Story
Bergkristall 1949 d: Harald Reinl. lps: Franz Eichberger, Hans Renz, Cilli Greif. 86M GRM/AUS. *Der Wildschutz von Tirol*; *The Poacher of Tyrol*; *Rock Crystal* prod/rel: Plesner, Schonger

Der Hochwald, 1841, Short Story
Flucht, Die 1977 d: Hajo Baumgartner. lps: Susanne Flury, Rosemarie Schulz, Werner Brehm. 110M GRM. *The Flight* prod/rel: Hajo Baumgartner

STIGEN, TERJE
Elskere, 1960, Novel
Elskere 1963 d: Nils R. Muller. 103M NRW.

Min Marion, 1972, Novel
Min Marion 1975 d: Nils R. Muller. lps: Ulrikke Greve, Sverre Anker Ousdal. 107M NRW.

STILL, JAMES (1906–, USA
The Velocity of Gary, Play
Velocity of Gary, The 1998 d: Dan Ireland. lps: Salma Hayek, Vincent d'Onofrio, Thomas Jane. 100M USA. prod/rel: Cineville, Ventana Rosa Productions

STINDE, JULIUS
Familie Buchholz, Novel
Familie Buchholz 1944 d: Carl Froelich. lps: Henny Porten, Paul Westermeier, Kathe Dyckhoff. 96M GRM. prod/rel: Universum, Turck

Neigungsehe 1944 d: Carl Froelich. lps: Henny Porten, Paul Westermeier, Kathe Dyckhoff. 94M GRM. prod/rel: UFA, Turck

STINETORF, LOUISE A.
White Witch Doctor, 1950, Novel
White Witch Doctor 1953 d: Henry Hathaway. lps: Susan Hayward, Robert Mitchum, Walter Slezak. 96M USA. prod/rel: 20th Century-Fox

STOCK, RALPH
Black Beach, 1919, Short Story
Love Flower, The 1920 d: D. W. Griffith. lps: Carol Dempster, Richard Barthelmess, George MacQuarrie. 7r USA. *Black Beach*; *The Gamest Girl*; *The Girl Who Dared* prod/rel: D. W. Griffith©, United Artists Corp.

Marama: a Tale of the South Pacific, Boston 1913, Novel
Adorable Savage, The 1920 d: Norman Dawn. lps: Edith Roberts, Jack Perrin, Richard Cummings. 5r USA. prod/rel: Universal Film Mfg. Co.©, Universal Special Attraction

STOCKDALE, JIM
In Love and War, Novel
In Love and War 1987 d: Paul Aaron. lps: Jane Alexander, James Woods, Haing S. Ngor. TVM. 100M USA. *Love and War* prod/rel: Tisch/Avnet

STOCKDALE, SYBIL
In Love and War 1987 d: Paul Aaron. lps: Jane Alexander, James Woods, Haing S. Ngor. TVM. 100M USA. *Love and War* prod/rel: Tisch/Avnet

STOCKING, CHARLES FRANCIS
The Mayor of Filbert, Chicago 1916, Novel
Mayor of Filbert, The 1919 d: W. Christy Cabanne. lps: Jack Richardson, Belle Bennett, J. Barney Sherry. 6-7r USA. prod/rel: Triangle Film Corp., Triangle Distributing Corp.

STOCKLEY, CYNTHIA
April Folly, 1918, Story
April Folly 1920 d: Robert Z. Leonard. lps: Marion Davies, Conway Tearle, Madeline Marshall. 4983f USA. prod/rel: Marion Davies Film Corp., Cosmopolitan Productions

The Claw, New York 1911, Novel
Claw, The 1918 d: Robert G. VignolA. lps: Clara Kimball Young, Milton Sills, Edward M. Kimball. 5r USA. prod/rel: C.K.Y. Film Corp.©, Select Pictures Corp.

Claw, The 1927 d: Sidney Olcott. lps: Norman Kerry, Claire Windsor, Arthur Edmund Carewe. 5252f USA. prod/rel: Universal Pictures

Dalla the Lion Cub, New York 1924, Novel
Female, The 1924 d: Sam Wood. lps: Betty Compson, Warner Baxter, Noah Beery. 6167f USA. prod/rel: Famous Players-Lasky, Paramount Pictures

Pink Gods and Blue Demons, Story
Pink Gods 1922 d: Penrhyn Stanlaws. lps: Bebe Daniels, James Kirkwood, Anna Q. Nilsson. 7180f USA. prod/rel: Famous Players-Lasky, Paramount Pictures

Ponjola, London 1923, Novel
Ponjola 1923 d: Donald Crisp, James Young. lps: Anna Q. Nilsson, James Kirkwood, Tully Marshall. 6960f USA. prod/rel: Sam E. Rork Productions, Associated First National Pictures

Poppy, London 1911, Novel
Poppy 1917 d: Edward Jose. lps: Norma Talmadge, Eugene O'Brien, Frederick Perry. 8r USA. prod/rel: Norma Talmadge Film Corp.©, Lewis J. Selznick Enterprises

Rosanne Ozanne, Short Story
Sins of Rosanne, The 1920 d: Tom Forman. lps: Ethel Clayton, Jack Holt, Fontaine La Rue. 4862f USA. *The Sins of Rozanne*; *Rosanne Ozanne* prod/rel: Famous Players-Lasky Corp.©, Paramount Pictures

Wild Honey, New York 1914, Novel
Wild Honey 1922 d: Wesley Ruggles. lps: Priscilla Dean, Noah Beery, Lloyd Whitlock. 6422f USA. prod/rel: Universal Film Mfg. Co.

STODARD, ROBERT
Up from the Depths, Play
Up from the Depths 1915 d: Paul Powell. lps: Courtenay Foote, Gladys Brockwell, Thomas Jefferson. 4r USA. prod/rel: Reliance Motion Picture Corp., Mutual Film Corp.

STODDARD, G. E.
Listen Lester, Play
Listen Lester 1924 d: William A. Seiter. lps: Louise Fazenda, Harry Myers, Eva Novak. 6242f USA. prod/rel: Sacramento Pictures, Principal Pictures

STODDERT, DAYTON
Prelude to Night, Novel
Ruthless 1948 d: Edgar G. Ulmer. lps: Zachary Scott, Lucille Bremer, Diana Lynn. 104M USA. prod/rel: Eagle-Lion

STOKER, BRAM (1847–1912), IRL, Stoker, Abraham
Dracula, London 1897, Novel
Blacula 1972 d: William Crain. lps: William Marshall, Vonetta McGee, Denise Nicholas. 93M USA.

Conde Dracula, El 1970 d: Jesus Franco. lps: Christopher Lee, Herbert Lom, Klaus Kinski. 100M SPN/GRM/ITL. *Count Dracula* (UKN); *Il Conte Dracula* (ITL); *Bram Stoker's Count Dracula*; *Wenn Dracula Erwacht Nachts* (GRM); *At Night When Dracula Wakes Up* prod/rel: Filmar

Count Dracula 1978 d: Philip Saville. lps: Louis Jourdan, Frank Finlay, Susan Penhaligon. TVM. 145M UKN/USA. prod/rel: Wnet, BBC

Dracula 1931 d: Tod Browning. lps: Bela Lugosi, Helen Chandler, David Manners. 80M USA. prod/rel: Universal Pictures Corp.©

Dracula 1931 d: George Melford. lps: Carlos Villarias, Lupita Tovar, Pablo Alvarez Rubio. 103M USA. prod/rel: Universal Pictures Corp.

Dracula 1958 d: Terence Fisher. lps: Peter Cushing, Christopher Lee, Michael Gough. 82M UKN. *Horror of Dracula* (USA) prod/rel: Hammer, Cadogan

Dracula 1973 d: Dan Curtis. lps: Jack Palance, Simon Ward, Nigel Davenport. TVM. 98M UKN/USA. prod/rel: Universal, Dan Curtis Productions

Dracula 1979 d: John Badham. lps: Frank Langella, Laurence Olivier, Donald Pleasence. 115M UKN/USA. prod/rel: Universal, Mirisch

Dracula 1992 d: Francis Ford CoppolA. lps: Gary Oldman, Winona Ryder, Anthony Hopkins. 127M USA. *Bram Stoker's Dracula* prod/rel: Columbia Tristar, American Zoetrope

Dracula - Prince of Darkness 1965 d: Terence Fisher. lps: Christopher Lee, Barbara Shelley, Andrew Keir. 90M UKN. *The Bloody Scream of Dracula; Revenge of Dracula; Disciple of Dracula* prod/rel: Seven Arts Productions, Hammer Film Productions

Jonathan, Vampire Sterben Nicht 1969 d: Hans W. Geissendorfer. lps: Jurgen Jung, Paul-Albert Krumm, Hertha von Walther. 97M GRM. *Jonathan* (USA)

Nosferatu - Eine Symphonie Des Grauens 1921 d: F. W. Murnau. lps: Max Schreck, Gustav von Wangenheim, Greta Schroder-Matray. 1967m GRM. *Nosferatu a Symphony of Horror; The Vampire Nosferatu* (USA); *The Terror of Dracula; Eine Symphonie Des Grauens; Dracula*

Nosferatu - Phantom Der Nacht 1979 d: Werner Herzog. lps: Klaus Kinski, Isabelle Adjani, Bruno Ganz. 107M GRM/FRN/USA. *Nosferatu the Vampyre* (USA), Werner Herzog

The Jewel of the Seven Stars, 1903, Novel
Awakening, The 1980 d: Mike Newell. lps: Charlton Heston, Susannah York, Jill Townsend. 105M UKN. *The Waking* prod/rel: Emi, Orion

Blood from the Mummy's Tomb 1972 d: Seth Holt, Michael Carreras. lps: Andrew Keir, Valerie Leon, James Villiers. 94M UKN. *Curse of the Mummy* prod/rel: MGM-Emi, Hammer

Tomb, The 1986 d: Fred Olen Ray. lps: Cameron Mitchell, John Carradine, Sybil Danning. 89M USA. prod/rel: Trans World

The Lair of the White Worm, 1911, Novel
Lair of the White Worm, The 1988 d: Ken Russell. lps: Amanda Donohue, Hugh Grant, Catherine Oxenberg. 93M UKN. prod/rel: Vestron Pictures

STOKES, SEWELL
Britannia of Billingsgate, London 1931, Play
Britannia of Billingsgate 1933 d: Sinclair Hill. lps: Violet Loraine, Gordon Harker, Kay Hammond. 99M UKN. prod/rel: Gaumont-British, Ideal

Court Circular, Book
I Believe in You 1952 d: Basil Dearden, Michael Relph. lps: Celia Johnson, Cecil Parker, Godfrey Tearle. 95M UKN. prod/rel: Ealing Studios, General Film Distributors

STOLBA, JOSEF
Morska Panna, Play
Morska Panna 1926 d: Josef Medeotti-Bohac. lps: Lu de Val, Sasa Rasilov, Karel Jicinsky. CZC. *The Mermaid* prod/rel: Biografia

Morska Panna 1939 d: Vaclav Kubasek. lps: Jirina Stepnickova, Bedrich Veverka, Vladimir RepA. 2373m CZC. *The Mermaid* prod/rel: Zdar (Vladimir Posusta)

Na Letnim Byte, Play
Na Letnim Byte 1926 d: Vladimir Slavinsky. lps: Eman Fiala, Antonie Nedosinska, Marie GrossovA. 2116m CZC. *In the Summer Place* prod/rel: Lloydfilm, Bratri Deglove

STOLP, HANNES PETER
Gluck Muss Der Mensch Haben, Novel
Diskretion-Ehrensache 1938 d: Johannes Meyer. lps: Heli Finkenzeller, Hans Holt, Ida Wust. 96M GRM. *Discretion With Honor* (USA) prod/rel: Cine-Allianz, Bavaria

Haus Kiepergass Und Seine Gaste, Novel
Ihr Privatsekretar 1940 d: Charles Klein. lps: Maria Andergast, Gustav Frohlich, Fita Benkhoff. 88M GRM. prod/rel: F.D.F., Bavaria

Die Sache Mit Dem Koffer, Novel
Knall Und Fall Als Detektive 1953 d: Hans Heinrich. lps: Hans Richter, Rudolf Carl, Ludwig Schmitz. 78M AUS/GRM. *Knall and Fall - Detectives* prod/rel: Arena, Mundus

STOLZ, ROBERT
Frauenparadies, Opera
Frauenparadies, Das 1936 d: Arthur M. Rabenalt. lps: Hortense Raky, Iwan Petrovich, Leo Slezak. 86M AUS. *Woman's Paradise* (USA) prod/rel: Donau-Film

Tanz Ins Gluck, Opera
Tanz Ins Gluck 1951 d: Alfred Stoger. lps: Johannes Heesters, Waltraut Haas, Lucie Englisch. 101M AUS. prod/rel: Mundus, UFA

STONE, ARNOLD M.
Secret Honor, Play
Secret Honor 1984 d: Robert Altman. lps: Philip Baker Hall. 90M USA. *Secret Honor: a Political Myth; Lords of Treason; Secret Honor: the Last Testament of Richard M. Nixon* prod/rel: Cinecom, Sandcastle 5

STONE, GENE
Why Not Stay for Breakfast?, Play
Why Not Stay for Breakfast? 1979 d: Terry Marcel. lps: George Chakiris, Gemma Craven, Yvonne Wilder. 95M UKN. prod/rel: Artgrove

STONE, GRACE ZARING
The Bitter Tea of General Yen, Indianapolis 1930, Novel
Bitter Tea of General Yen, The 1933 d: Frank CaprA. lps: Barbara Stanwyck, Nils Asther, Toshia Mori. 89M USA. prod/rel: Columbia Pictures Corp.

STONE, IRVING (1903–1989), USA
The Agony and the Ecstasy, New York 1961, Book
Agony and the Ecstasy, The 1965 d: Carol Reed. lps: Charlton Heston, Rex Harrison, Diane Cilento. 140M USA. prod/rel: 20th Century-Fox, International Classics

False Witness, Story
Arkansas Judge 1941 d: Frank McDonald. lps: Roy Rogers, Spring Byington, Weaver Brothers And Elviry. 72M USA. *False Witness* (UKN) prod/rel: Republic

Lust for Life, 1934, Novel
Lust for Life 1956 d: Vincente Minnelli. lps: Kirk Douglas, Anthony Quinn, James Donald. 120M USA. prod/rel: MGM

The President's Lady, 1951, Novel
President's Lady, The 1953 d: Henry Levin. lps: Susan Hayward, Charlton Heston, John McIntire. 97M USA. prod/rel: 20th Century-Fox

STONE, MARY
A Social Highwayman, New York 1895, Play
Social Highwayman, The 1916 d: Edwin August. lps: Edwin August, Ormi Hawley, John Sainpolis. 5r USA. prod/rel: Shubert Film Corp., World Film Corp.©

STONE, PETER
The Unsuspecting Wife
Charade 1963 d: Stanley Donen. lps: Audrey Hepburn, Cary Grant, Walter Matthau. 116M USA. prod/rel: Universal

STONE, ROBERT (1937–, USA, Stone, Robert Anthony
Dog Soldiers, 1974, Novel
Who'll Stop the Rain 1978 d: Karel Reisz. lps: Nick Nolte, Tuesday Weld, Michael Moriarty. 125M USA. *Dog Soldiers* (UKN) prod/rel: Herb Jaffe, Gabriel Katzka

A Hall of Mirrors, Boston 1966, Novel
Wusa 1970 d: Stuart Rosenberg. lps: Paul Newman, Joanne Woodward, Anthony Perkins. 117M USA. *Hall of Mirrors* prod/rel: Stuart Rosenberg Productions, Coleytown Productions

STONE, WILLIAM C.
The Crooked Lady, Novel
Crooked Lady, The 1932 d: Leslie Hiscott. lps: George Graves, Isobel Elsom, Ursula Jeans. 76M UKN. prod/rel: Real Art, MGM

STONE, WILLIAM S.
Tahiti Landfall, 1946, Novel
Pagan Love Song 1950 d: Robert Alton. lps: Howard Keel, Esther Williams, Minna Gombell. 76M USA. prod/rel: MGM

STONEHAM, CHARLES THURLEY
The Lion's Way; a Story of Men and Lions, London 1931, Novel
King of the Jungle 1933 d: H. Bruce Humberstone, Max Marcin. lps: Buster Crabbe, Frances Dee, Sidney Toler. 73M USA. *The Lion's Way* prod/rel: Paramount Productions©

STONELEY, JACK
Novel
Jenny's War 1985 d: Steve Gethers. lps: Dyan Cannon, Christopher Cazenove, Elke Sommer. TVM. 208M USA/UKN. prod/rel: Htv, Columbia

STONG, PHILIP DUFFIELD (1899–1957), USA
Career, New York 1936, Novel
Career 1939 d: Leigh Jason. lps: Edward Ellis, Anne Shirley, Samuel S. Hinds. 79M USA. prod/rel: RKO Radio Pictures, Inc.

The Farmer in the Dell, New York 1935, Novel
Farmer in the Dell 1936 d: Ben Holmes. lps: Fred Stone, Esther Dale, Jean Parker. 67M USA. prod/rel: RKO Radio Pictures©

State Fair, New York 1932, Novel
State Fair 1933 d: Henry King. lps: Janet Gaynor, Will Rogers, Lew Ayres. 100M USA. prod/rel: Fox Film Corp.©

State Fair 1944 d: Walter Lang. lps: Jeanne Crain, Dana Andrews, Dick Haymes. 100M USA. *It Happened One Summer* prod/rel: Twentieth Century-Fox

State Fair 1962 d: Jose Ferrer. lps: Pat Boone, Bobby Darin, Pamela Tiffin. 118M USA. prod/rel: 20th Century-Fox Film Corporation

State Fair 1976 d: David Lowell Rich. lps: Vera Miles, Tim O'Connor, Mitch Vogel. MTV. 50M USA.

Stranger's Return, New York 1933, Novel
Stranger's Return, The 1933 d: King Vidor. lps: Lionel Barrymore, Miriam Hopkins, Franchot Tone. 89M USA. prod/rel: Metro-Goldwyn-Mayer Corp.©, King Vidor Production

A Village Tale, New York 1934, Novel
Village Tale 1935 d: John Cromwell. lps: Randolph Scott, Kay Johnson, Arthur Hohl. 80M USA. prod/rel: RKO Radio Pictures©

STOPPARD, TOM (1937–, CZC, Strausler, Thomas
Rosencrantz and Guildenstern are Dead, 1968, Play
Rosencrantz and Guildenstern are Dead 1990 d: Tom Stoppard. lps: Gary Oldman, Tim Roth, Richard Dreyfuss. 118M USA. *Rosencrantz and Guildenstern* prod/rel: Brandenberg International

STORCH, EDUARD
Novel
Trilogie Z Praveku: Osada Havranu 1977 d: Jan Schmidt. lps: Jiri Bartoska, Ludvik Hradilek, Maria SykorovA. 91M CZC. *Trilogy from the Primeval Ages* prod/rel: Filmstudio Barrandov

Volani Rodu, Novel
Trilogie Z Praveku: Volani Rodu 1977 d: Jan Schmidt. lps: Jiri Bartoska, Ludvik Hradilek, Gabriele OsvaldovA. 91M CZC. prod/rel: Filmove Studio Barrandov

STOREY, DAVID (1933–, UKN, Storey, David Malcolm
Home, 1970, Play
Home 1972 d: Lindsay Anderson. lps: John Gielgud, Ralph Richardson, Dandy Nichols. MTV. 90M UKN. prod/rel: BBC

In Celebration, 1969, Novel
In Celebration 1974 d: Lindsay Anderson. lps: Alan Bates, James Bolam, Brian Cox. TVM. 110M UKN/CND. prod/rel: Ely Landau, Cinevision

This Sporting Life, 1960, Novel
This Sporting Life 1963 d: Lindsay Anderson. lps: Richard Harris, Rachel Roberts, Alan Badel. 134M UKN. prod/rel: Independent Artists, Rank Film Distributors

STORM, BARRY
Thunder God's Gold, Novel
Lust for Gold 1949 d: S. Sylvan Simon. lps: Glenn Ford, Ida Lupino, Gig Young. 90M USA. *Greed* prod/rel: Columbia

STORM, LESLEY (1903–, UKN
The Day's Mischief, 1951, Play
Personal Affair 1953 d: Anthony Pelissier. lps: Gene Tierney, Leo Genn, Glynis Johns. 83M UKN. prod/rel: General Film Distributors, Two Cities

Discipline, Story
Discipline 1935 d: James Riddell, A. B. Imeson. lps: Charles Mortimer, A. B. Imeson, April Vivian. 18M UKN. prod/rel: Monarch, Zenifilms

Great Day, 1945, Play
Great Day 1945 d: Lance Comfort. lps: Eric Portman, Flora Robson, Sheila Sim. 79M UKN. prod/rel: RKO-Radio British

Tony Draws a Horse, London 1939, Play
Tony Draws a Horse 1950 d: John Paddy Carstairs. lps: Cecil Parker, Anne Crawford, Derek Bond. 91M UKN. prod/rel: Pinnacle, General Film Distributors

STORM, THEODOR (1817–1888), GRM
Aquis Submersus, 1877, Novel
Unsterbliche Geliebte 1951 d: Veit Harlan. lps: Kristina Soderbaum, Franz Schafheitlin, Eduard Marks. 108M GRM. *Eternal Lover* prod/rel: Domnick, UFA

Ein Doppelganger, 1887, Short Story
John Gluckstadt 1975 d: Ulf Miehe. lps: Dieter Laser, Marie-Christine Barrault, Johannes Schaaf. 94M GRM. prod/rel: Independent Film, Filmverlag Der Autoren

Immensee, 1852, Novel
Immensee 1943 d: Veit Harlan. lps: Kristina Soderbaum, Carola Toelle, Carl Raddatz. 94M GRM. *Carnival* prod/rel: UFA

Immensee 1989 d: Klaus Gendries. lps: Maren Schumacher, Axel Wandtke, Dirk Wager. TVM. 84M GDR.

Was Die Schwalbe Sang 1956 d: Geza von Bolvary. lps: Maj-Britt Nilsson, Margit Saad, Claus Biederstaedt. 106M GRM. *What the Swallow Sang; Unsterbliche Liebe*

Pole Poppenspaler, 1874, Short Story
Pole Poppenspaler 1935 d: Curt Oertel. 40M GRM.

Pole Poppenspaler 1955 d: Arthur Pohl. lps: Heliane Bei, Heinz Hoppner, Willi Kleinoschegg. 85M GDR. prod/rel: Defa

Der Schimmelreiter, 1888, Short Story
Schimmelreiter, Der 1934 d: Curt Oertel, Hans Deppe. lps: Marianne Hoppe, Mathias Wieman, Ali Ghito. 86M GRM. *The Rider of the White Horse* (USA); *The Rider on the White Horse* prod/rel: Fritsch

Schimmelreiter, Der 1978 d: Alfred Weidenmann. lps: John Phillip Law, Anita Ekstrom, Gert Frobe. 96M GRM. *The Rider of the White Horse* prod/rel: Schimmelreiter-Albis Film, Studio

Viola Tricolor, 1874, Novel
Ich Werde Dich Auf Handen Tragen 1958 d: Veit Harlan. lps: Kristina Soderbaum, Hans Holt, Hans Nielsen. 89M GRM. *I'll Carry You in My Hands* prod/rel: Arca, Constantin

Serenade 1937 d: Willi Forst. lps: Igo Sym, Walter Janssen, Fritz Odemar. 109M GRM.

STORMQUIST, IRMA
The Woman I Love, Story
Woman I Love, The 1929 d: George Melford. lps: Margaret Morris, Robert Frazer, Leota Lorraine. 6199f USA. prod/rel: Fbo Pictures

STORR, CATHERINE
Marianne Dreams, Novel
Paperhouse 1989 d: Bernard Rose. lps: Charlotte Burke, Glenne Headly, Gemma Jones. 94M UKN. prod/rel: Vestron, Working Title

Ne Reveillez Pas un Flic Qui Dort, Novel
Ne Reveillez Pas un Flic Qui Dort 1988 d: Jose Pinheiro. lps: Alain Delon, Michel Serrault, Patrick Catalifo. 98M FRN. prod/rel: Leda, TF 1

STORY, JACK TREVOR
Mix Me a Person, Novel
Mix Me a Person 1962 d: Leslie Norman. lps: Anne Baxter, Adam Faith, Donald Sinden. 116M UKN. prod/rel: British Lion, Wessex

The Trouble With Harry, 1950, Novel
Trouble With Harry, The 1955 d: Alfred Hitchcock. lps: Edmund Gwenn, Shirley MacLaine, John Forsythe. 99M USA. prod/rel: Paramount, Alfred Hitchcock Prods.

STOSKOPF, GUSTAVE
Monsieur le Maire, Play
Monsieur le Maire 1939 d: Jacques Severac. lps: Georges Maurer, Leonie Bussinger, Eugene Criquipere. F FRN. *D'r Herr Maire* prod/rel: Productions Gloria

STOTHART, H.
Song of the Flame, New York 1925, Musical Play
Song of the Flame 1930 d: Alan Crosland. lps: Alexander Gray, Bernice Claire, Noah Beery. 6501f USA. prod/rel: First National Pictures

STOUT, MRS. E. ALMEZ
Women Who Win, Novel
Women Who Win 1919 d: Percy Nash, Fred W. Durrant. lps: Unity More, Mary Dibley, Mary Forbes. 6000f UKN. prod/rel: T. H. Davidson

STOUT, REX (1886-1975), USA, Stout, Rex Todhunter
The Doorbell Rings, Novel
Nero Wolfe 1977 d: Frank D. Gilroy. lps: Thayer David, Anne Baxter, Tom Mason. TVM. 100M USA. *Rex Stout's Nero Wolfe* prod/rel: Emmett Lavery Jr. Prods., Paramount Tv

Fer-de-Lance, New York 1934, Novel
Meet Nero Wolfe 1936 d: Herbert J. Biberman. lps: Edward Arnold, Joan Perry, Lionel Stander. 73M USA. *Fer-de-Lance* prod/rel: Columbia Pictures Corp. of California©, A. B. P. Schulberg Production

The League of Frightened Men, New York 1935, Novel
League of Frightened Men, The 1937 d: Alfred E. Green. lps: Walter Connolly, Irene Hervey, Lionel Stander. 71M USA. prod/rel: Columbia Pictures Corp. of California©

The President Vanishes, New York 1934, Novel
President Vanishes, The 1934 d: William A. Wellman. lps: Arthur Byron, Edward Arnold, Paul Kelly. 83M USA. *Strange Conspiracy* (UKN) prod/rel: Walter Wanger Productions, Paramount Productions©

STOWE, HARRIET BEECHER (1811-1896), USA
Uncle Tom's Cabin, Boston 1852, Novel
Capanna Dello Zio Tom, La 1918 d: Riccardo Tolentino. lps: Maria Campi, Ermanno Pellegrini, Bruna Ceccatelli. 1518m ITL. prod/rel: Italo-Egiziana Film

Onkel Toms Hutte 1965 d: Geza von Radvanyi. lps: John Kitzmiller, O. W. Fischer, Herbert Lom. 170M GRM/FRN/ITL. *La Case de l'Oncle Tom* (FRN); *Cento Dollari d'Odio* (ITL); *Uncle Tom's Cabin* (USA); *Cica Tomina Koliba* (YGS); *Capanna Del Zio Tom, La* prod/rel: Melodie-Film, Ccc-Filmkunst

Uncle Tom's Cabin 1903 d: Edwin S. Porter. 1068f USA. prod/rel: Edison

Uncle Tom's Cabin 1903. SHT USA. prod/rel: Lubin

Uncle Tom's Cabin 1910. lps: Frank Crane. 1000f USA. prod/rel: Thanhouser

Uncle Tom's Cabin 1910. SHT USA. prod/rel: Pathe

Uncle Tom's Cabin 1910 d: J. Stuart Blackton. lps: E. R. Phillips, Charles Kent, Julia Arthur. 2935f USA. prod/rel: Vitagraph Co. of America

Uncle Tom's Cabin 1913 d: Otis Turner. lps: Margarita Fischer, Gertrude Short, Harry Pollard. 3r USA. prod/rel: Imp

Uncle Tom's Cabin 1913. SHT USA. prod/rel: Powers

Uncle Tom's Cabin 1913 d: Sidney Olcott. lps: Hal Clements, Anna Q. Nilsson. 2r USA. prod/rel: Kalem

Uncle Tom's Cabin 1914 d: William Robert Daly. lps: Irving Cummings, Marie Eline, Sam Lucas. 5r USA. prod/rel: World Producing Corp.©, World Film Corp.

Uncle Tom's Cabin 1918 d: J. Searle Dawley. lps: Marguerite Clark, J. W. Johnston, Florence Carpenter. 5r USA. prod/rel: Famous Players-Lasky Corp.©, Paramount Pictures

Uncle Tom's Cabin 1927 d: Harry Pollard. lps: James Lowe, Virginia Grey, George Siegmann. 13r USA. prod/rel: Universal Pictures

Uncle Tom's Cabin 1987 d: Stan Lathan. lps: Avery Brooks, Kate Burton, Bruce Dern. TVM. 110M USA. prod/rel: Castle Pictures

STRABEL, THELMA
Story
Reap the Wild Wind 1942 d: Cecil B. de Mille. lps: Ray Milland, John Wayne, Paulette Goddard. 124M USA. prod/rel: Paramount

The Forest Rangers, Novel
Forest Rangers, The 1942 d: George Marshall. lps: Fred MacMurray, Paulette Goddard, Susan Hayward. 87M USA. prod/rel: Paramount

You Were There, Book
Undercurrent 1946 d: Vincente Minnelli. lps: Katharine Hepburn, Robert Taylor, Robert Mitchum. 116M USA. prod/rel: MGM

STRAIT, RAYMOND
This for Remembrance, Autobiography
Rosie: the Rosemary Clooney Story 1982 d: Jackie Cooper. lps: Sondra Locke, Tony Orlando, Penelope Milford. TVM. 100M USA.

STRAKER, J. F.
Hell Is Empty, Novel
Hell Is Empty 1967 d: John Ainsworth, Bernard Knowles. lps: Martine Carol, Anthony Steel, James Robertson Justice. 99M UKN/CZC. prod/rel: Rank Film Distributors, Dominion

STRAKOSCH, AVERY
I Married an Artist, 1936, Short Story
She Married an Artist 1937 d: Marion Gering. lps: John Boles, Luli Deste, Frances Drake. 78M USA. *I Married an Artist* prod/rel: Columbia Pictures Corp. of California©

STRANDJEV, KOSTA
Short Story
Kamionat 1980 d: Hristo Hristov. lps: Djoko Rosic, Stefan Dimitrov, Vesselin Vulkov. 107M BUL. *The Lorry; The Truck* prod/rel: Bulgarische Kinematografie

STRANGE, STANISLAUS
The Girl in the Taxi, New York 1910, Play
Girl in the Taxi, The 1921 d: Lloyd Ingraham. lps: Flora Parker de Haven, Carter de Haven, King Baggot. 5420f USA. prod/rel: Carter de Haven Productions, Associated First National Pictures

STRATIEV, STANISLAV
Diva Patitsa Mezhdu Darvetata, 1972, Novel
Pazachat Na Kreposta 1974 d: Milen Nikolov. lps: Yordan Kovachev, Pavel Poppandov, Silvia RangelovA. 74M BUL. *The Fortress Guard; The Fortress Warden; Nazacat Na Krepostta; The Guardian of the Fortress*

Divi Pcheli, 1978, Novel
Ravnovessie 1983 d: Lyudmil Kirkov. lps: Pavel Poppandov, Plamena Getova, Georgi Georgiev-Gets. 140M BUL. *Balance*

Kratko Slantse, 1978, Novel
Kratko Sluntse 1979 d: Lyudmil Kirkov. lps: Vihur Stoychev, Nikola Todev, Anton Gorchev. 106M BUL. *Short Sun; Brief Sunshine; Kratko Slunce; Kratko Slantse*

STRATTON-PORTER, GENE (1886-1924), USA, Porter, Geneva Stratton
Freckles, New York 1904, Novel
Freckles 1917 d: Marshall Neilan. lps: Jack Pickford, Louise Huff, Hobart Bosworth. 5r USA. prod/rel: Jesse L. Lasky Feature Play Co.©, Paramount Pictures Corp.

Freckles 1928 d: James Leo Meehan. lps: John Fox Jr., Gene Stratton Porter, Hobart Bosworth. 6131f USA. prod/rel: Fbo Pictures

Freckles 1935 d: William Hamilton, Edward Killy. lps: Tom Brown, Carol Stone, Virginia Weidler. 69M USA. prod/rel: RKO Radio Pictures©, Pandro S. Berman Production

A Girl of the Limberlost, New York 1909, Novel
Girl of the Limberlost, A 1924 d: James Leo Meehan. lps: Gloria Grey, Emily Fitzroy, Arthur Currier. 5943f USA. prod/rel: Gene Stratton Porter Productions, Film Booking Offices of America

Girl of the Limberlost, A 1934 d: W. Christy Cabanne. lps: Louise Dresser, Ralph Morgan, Marian Marsh. 86M USA. prod/rel: Monogram Pictures Corp.©, William T. Lackey Production

Girl of the Limberlost, A 1945 d: Mel Ferrer. lps: Ruth Nelson, Dorinda Clifton, Loren Tindall. 60M USA. prod/rel: Columbia

Girl of the Limberlost, A 1990 d: Burt Brinckerhoff. lps: Joanna Cassidy, Annette O'Toole, Heather Fairfield. TVM. 115M USA.

Romance of the Limberlost 1938 d: William Nigh. lps: Jean Parker, Eric Linden, Marjorie Main. 81M USA. prod/rel: Monogram Pictures Corp.©

The Harvester, Garden City, N.Y. 1911, Novel
Harvester, The 1927 d: James Leo Meehan. lps: Orville Caldwell, Natalie Kingston, William Walling. 7045f USA. prod/rel: R-C Pictures, Film Booking Offices of America

Harvester, The 1936 d: Joseph Santley. lps: Edward Nugent, Ann Rutherford, Frank Craven. 72M USA. prod/rel: Republic Pictures Corp.©

Her Father's Daughter, New York 1921, Novel
Her First Romance 1940 d: Edward Dmytryk. lps: Edith Fellows, Wilbur Evans, Julie Bishop. 77M USA. *The Right Man; Her Father's Daughter* prod/rel: Monogram Pictures Corp.

The Keeper of the Bees, Garden City, N.Y. 1925, Novel
Keeper of the Bees 1947 d: John Sturges. lps: Harry Davenport, Michael Duane, Gloria Henry. 68M USA. prod/rel: Columbia

Keeper of the Bees, The 1925 d: James Leo Meehan. lps: Robert Frazer, Josef Swickard, Martha Mattox. 6712f USA. prod/rel: Gene Stratton Porter Productions, Film Booking Offices of America

Keeper of the Bees, The 1935 d: W. Christy Cabanne. lps: Neil Hamilton, Betty Furness, Emma Dunn. 75M USA. prod/rel: Monogram Pictures Corp.©

Laddie; a True Blue Story, Garden City, N.Y. 1913, Novel
Laddie 1926 d: James Leo Meehan. lps: John Bowers, Bess Flowers, Theodore von Eltz. 6931f USA. prod/rel: Gene Stratton Porter Productions

Laddie 1934 d: George Stevens. lps: John Beal, Gloria Stuart, Virginia Weidler. 70M USA. prod/rel: RKO Radio Pictures©

Laddie 1940 d: Jack Hively. lps: Tim Holt, Virginia Gilmore, Joan Carroll. 70M USA. prod/rel: RKO Radio Pictures©

The Magic Garden, Novel
Magic Garden, The 1927 d: James Leo Meehan. lps: Joyce Coad, Margaret Morris, Philippe de Lacy. 6807f USA. prod/rel: Gene Stratton Porter Productions, Film Booking Offices of America

Michael O'Halloran, New York 1915, Novel
Michael O'Halloran 1923 d: James Leo Meehan. lps: Virginia True Boardman, Ethelyn Irving, Irene Rich. 7600f USA. prod/rel: Gene Stratton Porter Productions, W. W. Hodkinson Corp.

Michael O'Halloran 1937 d: Karl Brown. lps: Warren Hull, Jackie Moran, Wynne Gibson. 68M USA. *Any Man's Wife* prod/rel: Republic Pictures Corp.©

Michael O'Halloran 1948 d: John Rawlins. lps: Scotty Beckett, Allene Roberts, Tommy Cook. 79M USA. prod/rel: Monogram Pictures Corp.

STRATZ, RUDOLF
Das Paradies Im Schnee, Novel
Paradies Im Schnee, Das 1923 d: Georg Jacoby. lps: Bruno Kastner, Elga Brink, Lona Schmidt. 2575m GRM/SWT. *La Paradis Dans la Neige* prod/rel: Georg Jacoby-Film, Eos-Film

Schloss Vogelod, Novel
 Schloss Vogelod 1921 d: F. W. Murnau. lps: Arnold Korff, Lulu Kyser-Korff, Lothar Mehnert. 1625m GRM. *Haunted Castle* (USA); *Vogelod: the Haunted Castle*; *Vogelod Castle*; *Castle Vogelod* prod/rel: Uco-Film

 Schloss Vogelod 1936 d: Max Obal. lps: Carola Hohn, Hans Stuwe, Hans Zesch-Ballot. 79M GRM. *Vogelod Castle* prod/rel: Tonlicht, UFA

STRAUB, PETER
Ghost Story, Novel
 Ghost Story 1981 d: John Irvin. lps: Fred Astaire, Melvyn Douglas, John Houseman. 110M USA. prod/rel: Universal

Julia, Novel
 Haunting of Julia, The 1976 d: Richard Loncraine. lps: Mia Farrow, Keir Dullea, Tom Conti. 98M UKN/CND. *Full Circle* (CND); *Le Cercle Infernal*; *Where the Wind Blows*; *Hide and Seek*; *Link, The* prod/rel: Paramount, Fetter Productions Ltd. (London)

STRAUS, OSCAR (1870–1954), AUS
Eine Frau Die Weiss Was Sie Will, Operetta
 Frau, Die Weiss, Was Sie Will, Eine 1934 d: Victor Janson. lps: Lil Dagover, Anton Edthofer, Maria Beling. 84M GRM/CZC. prod/rel: Meissner, Slavia-Film

 Frau, Die Weiss, Was Sie Will, Eine 1958 d: Arthur M. Rabenalt. lps: Lilli Palmer, Peter Schutte, Maria Sebaldt. 101M GRM. *A Woman Who Knows What She Wants* prod/rel: Bavaria

 Zena, Ktera Vi Co Chce 1934 d: Vaclav Binovec. lps: Marketa Krausova, Jiri Steimar, Truda GrosslichtovA. 2446m CZC. *A Woman Who Knows What She Wants* prod/rel: Meissner, Slavia-Film

Der Letzte Walzer, Berlin 1920, Operetta
 Derniere Valse, La 1935 d: Leo Mittler. lps: Jean Martinelli, Armand Bernard, Yarmila NovotnA. 90M FRN. prod/rel: Warwick Films

 Last Waltz, The 1936 d: Gerald Barry, Leo Mittler. lps: Jarmila Novotna, Harry Welchman, Gerald Barry. 74M UKN. prod/rel: Warwick, Associated Producers and Distributors

 Letzte Walzer, Der 1927 d: Arthur Robison. lps: Willy Fritsch, Liane Haid, Ida Wust. 2722m GRM. *The Last Waltz* (USA) prod/rel: UFA

 Letzte Walzer, Der 1934 d: Georg Jacoby. lps: Camilla Horn, Ivan Petrovich, Susi Lanner. 94M GRM. *The Last Waltz* prod/rel: Gnom, Panorama

 Letzte Walzer, Der 1953 d: Arthur M. Rabenalt. lps: Eva Bartok, Curd Jurgens, O. E. Hasse. 93M GRM. *The Last Waltz* (USA) prod/rel: Eichberg, Carlton

STRAUSS, BOTHO (1944–, GRM
Gross Und Klein, 1980, Play
 Gross Und Klein 1980 d: Peter Stein. lps: Edith Clever, Gunter Berger, Gerhard Bienert. 270M GRM. *Large and Small* prod/rel: Regina Ziegler, Skylight

Trilogie Des Wiedersehens, 1976, Play
 Trilogie Des Wiedersehens 1978 d: Peter Stein. lps: Libgart Schwarz, Peter Fitz, Otto machtlinger. 128M GRM. *Renewal Trilogy* prod/rel: Schaub Am Halleschen Ufer, Atlas

STRAUSS, JOHANN (1825–1899), AUS
Die Fledermaus, Vienna 1874, Operetta
 Chauve-Souris, La 1931 d: Pierre Billon, Carl Lamac. lps: Anny Ondra, Ivan Petrovitch, Mauricet. 80M FRN. prod/rel: Vandor-Film, Ondra-Lamac-Film

 Fledermaus, Die 1923 d: Max Mack. lps: Eva May, Lya de Putti, Harry Liedtke. 2093m GRM.

 Fledermaus, Die 1931 d: Carl Lamac. lps: Anny Ondra, Georg Alexander, Oskar SimA. 96M GRM.

 Fledermaus, Die 1937 d: Paul Verhoeven. lps: Georg Alexander, Hans Sohnker, Lida BaarovA. 95M GRM.

 Fledermaus, Die 1945 d: Geza von Bolvary. lps: Johannes Heesters, Marte Harell, Hans Brausewetter. 100M GRM. *The Bat* (USA) prod/rel: Terra, Lloyd

 Fledermaus, Die 1955 d: E. W. Fiedler. lps: Jarmila Ksirowa, Sonja Schoner, Erich Arnold. 86M GDR. *Rauschende Melodien* prod/rel: Defa

 Fledermaus, Die 1962 d: Geza von CziffrA. lps: Peter Alexander, Marianne Koch, Marika Rokk. 107M AUS. prod/rel: Sascha-Film

 Fledermaus, Die 1966 d: Annelise Meineche. lps: Poul Reichhardt, Lily Broberg, Holger Jjul-Hansen. 98M DNM. *Flegermusen*

 Oh Rosalinda! 1955 d: Michael Powell, Emeric Pressburger. lps: Michael Redgrave, Ludmilla Tcherina, Anton Walbrook. 101M UKN/GRM. *Fledermaus '55* prod/rel: Powell & Pressburger, Ab-Pathe

 Waltz Time 1933 d: Wilhelm Thiele. lps: Evelyn Laye, Fritz Schultz, Gina Malo. 82M UKN. prod/rel: Gaumont-British, Woolf & Freedman

Eine Nacht in Venedig, Berlin 1883, Operetta
 Nacht in Venedig, Eine 1934 d: Robert Wiene, Carmine Gallone. lps: Tino Pattiera, Tina Eilers, Ludwig Stossel. 82M GRM/ITL. *Una Notte a Venezia* (ITL) prod/rel: Hunnia, Cando

 Nacht in Venedig, Eine 1953 d: Georg Wildhagen. lps: Jeanette Schultze, Peter Pasetti, Marianne Schonauer. 90M AUS. *Komm in Die Gondel* prod/rel: Nova

Wiener Blut, Operetta
 Wiener Blut 1942 d: Willi Forst. lps: Maria Holst, Willy Fritsch, Fred Liewehr. 111M GRM. prod/rel: Forst, Rota

Der Zigeunerbaron, Vienna 1885, Operetta
 Baron Tzigane, Le 1935 d: Henri Chomette, Karl Hartl. lps: Daniele Parola, Jacqueline Francell, Anton Walbrook. 105M FRN. prod/rel: U.F.a., a.C.E.

 Zigeunerbaron, Der 1927 d: Friedrich Zelnik. lps: Lya Mara, Michael Bohnen, Wilhelm Dieterle. 2606m GRM. *The Gypsy Baron* prod/rel: Friedrich Zelnik-Film

 Zigeunerbaron, Der 1935 d: Karl Hartl. lps: Anton Walbrook, Hansi Knoteck, Fritz Kampers. 105M GRM. *The Gypsy Baron* prod/rel: UFA, Turck

 Zigeunerbaron, Der 1954 d: Arthur M. Rabenalt. lps: Margit Saad, Gerhard Riedmann, Karl Schonbock. 105M GRM. *Gypsy Baron* prod/rel: Berolina, UFA

 Zigeunerbaron, Der 1962 d: Kurt Wilhelm. lps: Carlos Thompson, Heidi Bruhl, Willy Millowitsch. 103M GRM/FRN. *Princesse Tzigane* (FRN); *Gypsy Baron* prod/rel: Berolina, Comptoir D'expansion

 Zigeunerbaron, Der 1965 d: Arthur M. Rabenalt. lps: Rudolf Schock, Erzsebet Hazy, Benno Kusche. MTV. 113M GRM.

 Zigeunerbaron, Der 1976 d: Arthur M. Rabenalt. lps: Siegfried Jerusalem, Ellen Shade, Ivan Rebroff. MTV. 98M GRM.

STRAUSS, RALPH
Married Alive, New York 1925, Novel
 Married Alive 1927 d: Emmett J. Flynn. lps: Lou Tellegen, Margaret Livingston, Matt Moore. 4557f USA. prod/rel: Fox Film Corp.

STRAUSS, RICHARD (1864–1949), GRM
Elektra, Dresden 1909, Opera
 Elektra 1970. lps: Gladys Kuchta, Regina Resnik, Ingrid Bjoner. MTV. F GRM. prod/rel: Polyphon Film & Tv Productions

Der Rosenkavalier, Dresden 1911, Opera
 Rosenkavalier, Der 1926 d: Robert Wiene. lps: Michael Bohnen, Huguette Duflos, Paul Hartmann. 75M AUS. prod/rel: Pan-Film

 Rosenkavalier, Der 1962 d: Paul Czinner. lps: Elisabeth Schwarzkopf, Sena Jurinac, Anneliese Rothenberger. 195M UKN. prod/rel: Poetic Films, Rank

STRAUSS, THEODORE
Moonrise, Novel
 Moonrise 1948 d: Frank Borzage. lps: Dane Clark, Gail Russell, Ethel Barrymore. 90M USA. prod/rel: Republic, Marshall Grant Prods.

STRAVINSKY, IGOR (1882–1971), RSS
Histoire du Soldat, Lausanne 1918, Opera
 Soldier's Tale, The 1964 d: Michael Birkett. lps: Robert Helpmann, Brian Phelan, Svetlana BeriosovA. 52M UKN. prod/rel: Ipsilon, British Home Entertainments

STRAWN, ARTHUR
Blossoms for Effie, Short Story
 Affairs of Geraldine, The 1946 d: George Blair. lps: Jane Withers, Jimmy Lydon, Raymond Walburn. 68M USA. prod/rel: Republic Pictures Corp.

STREATFIELD, NOEL
Aunt Clara, Novel
 Aunt Clara 1954 d: Anthony Kimmins. lps: Ronald Shiner, Margaret Rutherford, A. E. Matthews. 84M UKN. prod/rel: London Films, British Lion

Welcome Mr. Washington, Story
 Welcome Mr. Washington 1944 d: Leslie Hiscott. lps: Barbara Mullen, Donald Stewart, Peggy Cummins. 90M UKN. prod/rel: British National, Shaftesbury

STREET, A. G.
Strawberry Roan, Novel
 Strawberry Roan 1945 d: Maurice Elvey. lps: William Hartnell, Carole Raye, Walter Fitzgerald. 84M UKN. prod/rel: British National, Anglo-American

STREET, JAMES H.
The Biscuit Eater, 1939, Short Story
 Biscuit Eater, The 1940 d: Stuart Heisler. lps: Billy Lee, Cordell Hickman, Helene Millard. 83M USA. *God Gave Him a Dog* (UKN) prod/rel: Paramount Pictures, Inc.

 Biscuit Eater, The 1972 d: Vincent McEveety. lps: Earl Holliman, Lew Ayres, Godfrey Cambridge. 90M USA. prod/rel: Buena Vista

Goodbye My Lady, 1954, Novel
 Goodbye, My Lady 1956 d: William A. Wellman. lps: Walter Brennan, Phil Harris, Brandon de Wilde. 95M USA. *The Boy and the Laughing Dog* prod/rel: Warner Bros., Batjac Prods.

Letter to the Editor, 1937, Short Story
 Living It Up 1954 d: Norman Taurog. lps: Dean Martin, Jerry Lewis, Janet Leigh. 95M USA. prod/rel: Paramount, York Pictures

 Nothing Sacred 1937 d: William A. Wellman. lps: Carole Lombard, Fredric March, Walter Connolly. 75M USA. prod/rel: United Artists Corp., Selznick International Pictures©

Tap Roots, Novel
 Tap Roots 1948 d: George Marshall. lps: Van Heflin, Susan Hayward, Boris Karloff. 109M USA. prod/rel: Universal, Walter Wanger

STREET, JULIAN LEONARD
The Country Cousin, New York 1917, Play
 Country Cousin, The 1919 d: Alan Crosland. lps: Elaine Hammerstein, Lumsden Hare, Bigelow Cooper. 5279f USA. prod/rel: Selznick Pictures Corp.©, Select Pictures Corp.

The Goings on of Victorine, Story
 Victorine 1915 d: Paul Powell. lps: Dorothy Gish, Ralph Lewis, William Hinckley. 2r USA. prod/rel: Majestic

Mr. Bisbee's Princess, Short Story
 You're Telling Me 1934 d: Erle C. Kenton. lps: W. C. Fields, Joan Marsh, Buster Crabbe. 70M USA. prod/rel: Paramount Productions©

Need of Change, 1909, Novel
 I'm from Missouri 1939 d: Theodore Reed. lps: Bob "Bazooka" Burns, Gladys George, Gene Lockhart. 77M USA. prod/rel: Paramount Pictures©

Rita Coventry, Garden City, N.Y. 1922, Novel
 Don't Call It Love 1924 d: William C. de Mille. lps: Agnes Ayres, Jack Holt, Nita Naldi. 6450f USA. prod/rel: Famous Players-Lasky, Paramount Pictures

So's Your Old Man, 1925, Short Story
 So's Your Old Man 1926 d: Gregory La CavA. lps: W. C. Fields, Alice Joyce, Charles "Buddy" Rogers. 6347f USA. prod/rel: Famous Players-Lasky, Paramount Pictures

STREETER, EDWARD (1891–1976), USA
Father of the Bride, 1949, Novel
 Father of the Bride 1950 d: Vincente Minnelli. lps: Spencer Tracy, Joan Bennett, Elizabeth Taylor. 93M USA. prod/rel: MGM

 Father of the Bride 1991 d: Charles Shyer. lps: Steve Martin, Diane Keaton, Martin Short. 105M USA. prod/rel: Touchstone Pictures, Touchwood Pacific Partners I

Mr. Hobbs's Vacation, New York 1954, Novel
 Mr. Hobbs Takes a Vacation 1962 d: Henry Koster. lps: James Stewart, Maureen O'Hara, Fabian. 116M USA. prod/rel: Jerry Wald Productions, 20th Century-Fox

STREICHER, FRANZ
Schutt Die Sorgen in Ein Glaschen Wein, Play
 Verlegenheitskind, Das 1938 d: Peter P. Brauer. lps: Ida Wust, Ludwig Schmitz, Paul Klinger. 92M GRM. *Schutt Die Sorgen in Glaschen Wein* prod/rel: UFA, Doring

STRESHINSKY, SHIRLEY
And I Alone Survived, Book
 And I Alone Survived 1978 d: William A. Graham. lps: Blair Brown, Vera Miles, David Ackroyd. TVM. 100M USA. prod/rel: NBC, Jerry Leider Prods.

STRETTON, HESBA
Jessica's First Prayer, Story
 Jessica's First Prayer 1908 d: Dave Aylott?. 490f UKN. prod/rel: Walturdaw

 Jessica's First Prayer 1921 d: Bert Wynne. lps: Joan Griffiths, Peter Coleman, Hargrave Mansell. UKN. prod/rel: Seal

Little Meg's Children, Novel
 Little Meg's Children 1921 d: Bert Wynne. lps: Joan Griffiths, Warwick Ward, Hargrave Mansell. 5000f UKN. prod/rel: Seal, Lester

STREUVELS, STIJN
De Teleurgang Van de Waterhoek, 1927, Novel
 Mira 1971 d: Fons Rademakers. lps: Willeke Van Ammelrooy, Carlos Van Lanckere, Jan Declair. 95M BLG/NTH. *De Teleurgang Van de Waterhoek*

STRIBLING, THOMAS SIGISMUND (1881–1965), USA, Stribling, T. S.
Birthright, New York 1922, Novel
 Birthright 1924 d: Oscar Micheaux. lps: J. Homer Tutt, Evelyn Preer, Salem Tutt Whitney. 9500f USA. prod/rel: Micheaux Film Corp.

Birthright 1939 d: Oscar Micheaux. lps: Ethel Moses, Alec Lovejoy, Carman Newsome. 9r USA. prod/rel: Micheaux Pictures Corp.

STRIEBER, WHITLEY
Communion, Book
Communion 1989 d: Philippe MorA. lps: Christopher Walken, Lindsay Crouse, Frances Sternhagen. 107M USA. prod/rel: Vestron

The Hunger, Novel
Hunger, The 1982 d: Anthony Scott. lps: Catherine Deneuve, David Bowie, Susan Sarandon. 97M USA/UKN. prod/rel: MGM, United Artists

Wolfen, Novel
Wolfen 1981 d: Michael Wadleigh. lps: Albert Finney, Diane Venora, Edward James Olmos. 115M USA. prod/rel: Warner

STRINDBERG, AUGUST (1849–1912), SWD, Strindberg, Johan August
Ett Dockhem, 1884, Short Story
Dockhem, Ett 1955 d: Anders Henrikson. lps: George Fant, Mai Zetterling, Gunnel Brostrom. 78M SWD. prod/rel: Ab Europa Film

Dodsdansen, 1901, Play
Dance of Death, The 1969 d: David Giles. lps: Laurence Olivier, Geraldine McEwan, Carolyn Jones. 149M UKN. prod/rel: Paramount, Bhe-National Theatre

Danse de Mort, La 1946 d: Marcel Cravenne, Erich von Stroheim (Uncredited). lps: Erich von Stroheim, Jean Servais, Denise Vernac. 88M FRN/ITL. *La Prigioniera Dell'isola* (ITL); *The Dance of Death*; *La Danza Della Morte* prod/rel: Alcina

Paarungen 1967 d: Michael Verhoeven. lps: Lilli Palmer, Paul Verhoeven, Karl Michael Vogler. 83M GRM. *Danse MacAbre*; *Couplings*; *Satanic Games*; *Dance of Death* prod/rel: Sentana, Eckelkamp

Erik XIV, 1899, Play
Karin Mansdotter 1954 d: Alf Sjoberg. lps: Ulla Jacobsson, Jarl Kulle, Ulf Palme. 106M SWD. *Karin Daughter of Man*; *Erik XIV*

Fadren, 1887, Play
Fadren 1969 d: Alf Sjoberg. lps: Georg Rydeberg, Gunnel Lindblom, Lena Nyman. 100M SWD. *The Father* (UKN); *Dream of a Father*

Froken Julie, 1888, Play
Froken Julie 1951 d: Alf Sjoberg. lps: Anita Bjork, Ulf Palme, Inger Norberg. 90M SWD. *Miss Julie* (UKN) prod/rel: Sandrew

Miss Julie 1972 d: Robin Philips, John Glenister. lps: Helen Mirren, Donal McCann, Heather Canning. 105M UKN.

Pecado de Julia, El 1947 d: Mario Soffici. 95M ARG.

Hemsoborna, 1887, Novel
Hemsoborna 1919 d: Carl Barcklind. lps: Greta Almroth, Gosta Cederlund. F SWD. *People of Hemso*

Hemsoborna 1944 d: Sigurd Wallen. lps: Sigurd Wallen, Adolf Jahr, Dagmar Ebbesen. 90M SWD. *The People of Hemso* prod/rel: Nordisk

Hemsoborna 1955 d: Arne Mattsson. lps: Erik Strandmark, Hjordis Pettersson, Nils Hallberg. 111M SWD. *The People of Hemso*

Mot Betaining, 1886, Short Story
Giftas 1957 d: Anders Henrikson. lps: Anita Bjork, Mai Zetterling, Anders Henrikson. 132M SWD. *Of Love and Lust* (USA); *Married Life* prod/rel: Europa

Den Starkare, 1890, Play
Stronger, The 1980 d: Ian Knox. 18M UKN.

STRINGER, ARTHUR
The Breaker, 1916, Short Story
Breaker, The 1916 d: Fred E. Wright. lps: Bryant Washburn, Nell Craig, Ernest Maupain. 5r USA. prod/rel: Essanay Film Mfg. Co.©, K-E-S-E Service

The Button Thief, Short Story
From Two to Six 1918 d: Albert Parker. lps: Winifred Allen, Earle Foxe, Forrest Robinson. 5r USA. prod/rel: Triangle Film Corp., Triangle Distributing Corp.

The Coward, 1923, Short Story
Coward, The 1927 d: Alfred Raboch. lps: Warner Baxter, Sharon Lynn, Freeman Wood. 5093f USA. prod/rel: R-C Pictures, Film Booking Offices of America

Empty Hands, Indianapolis 1924, Novel
Empty Hands 1924 d: Victor Fleming. lps: Jack Holt, Norma Shearer, Charles Clary. 6976f USA. prod/rel: Famous Players-Lasky, Paramount Pictures

Fifth Avenue, 1925, Short Story
Fifth Avenue 1926 d: Robert G. VignolA. lps: Marguerite de La Motte, Allan Forrest, Louise Dresser. 5503f USA. *The Octopus* prod/rel: Belasco Productions, Producers Distributing Corp.

The Gun Runner, New York 1909, Novel
Gun Runner, The 1928 d: Edgar Lewis. lps: Ricardo Cortez, Nora Lane, Gino Corrado. 5516f USA. prod/rel: Tiffany-Stahl Productions

The Hand of Peril; a Novel of Adventure, New York 1915, Novel
Hand of Peril, The 1916 d: Maurice Tourneur. lps: House Peters, June Elvidge, Ralph Delmore. 5r USA. prod/rel: Paragon Films, Inc., World Film Corp.©

Heather of the High Hand, New York 1937, Novel
Lady Fights Back, The 1939 d: Milton Carruth. lps: Irene Hervey, Kent Taylor, William Lundigan. 61M USA. prod/rel: Universal Pictures Co.©

The House of Intrigue, Indianapolis 1918, Novel
House of Intrigue, The 1919 d: Lloyd Ingraham. lps: Lloyd Bacon, Donald MacDonald, Mignon Anderson. 5r USA. prod/rel: Haworth Pictures, Robertson-Cole Co.

Manhandled, 1924, Short Story
Manhandled 1924 d: Allan Dwan. lps: Gloria Swanson, Tom Moore, Lilyan Tashman. 6998f USA. prod/rel: Famous Players-Lasky, Paramount Pictures

The Mud Lark, New York 1932, Novel
Purchase Price, The 1932 d: William A. Wellman. lps: Barbara Stanwyck, George Brent, Leila Bennett. 78M USA. *Mud Lark*; *Night Flower* prod/rel: Warner Bros. Pictures©

Snowblind, 1921, Short Story
Unseeing Eyes 1923 d: Edward H. Griffith. lps: Lionel Barrymore, Seena Owen, Louis Wolheim. 8150f USA. prod/rel: Cosmopolitan Productions, Goldwyn-Cosmopolitan Distributing Corp.

The Story Without a Name, New York 1924, Novel
Story Without a Name, The 1924 d: Irvin V. Willat. lps: Agnes Ayres, Antonio Moreno, Tyrone Power Sr. 5912f USA. *Without Warning* prod/rel: Famous Players-Lasky, Paramount Pictures

The Travis Coup, Story
Out of the Storm 1926 d: Louis J. Gasnier. lps: Jacqueline Logan, Tyrone Power Sr., Edmund Burns. 6500f USA. prod/rel: Tiffany Productions

The Waffle Iron, 1920, Short Story
Are All Men Alike? 1920 d: Phil Rosen. lps: May Allison, Wallace MacDonald, John Elliott. 6r USA. prod/rel: Metro Pictures Corp.©, Screen Classics

White Hands, 1927, Short Story
Half a Bride 1928 d: Gregory La CavA. lps: Esther Ralston, Gary Cooper, William Worthington. 6238f USA. prod/rel: Paramount Famous Lasky Corp.

The Wilderness Woman, 1926, Short Story
Wilderness Woman, The 1926 d: Howard Higgin. lps: Aileen Pringle, Lowell Sherman, Chester Conklin. 7553f USA. prod/rel: Robert Kane Productions, First National Pictures

Woman-Handled, 1925, Short Story
Womanhandled 1925 d: Gregory La CavA. lps: Richard Dix, Esther Ralston, Cora Williams. 6765f USA. prod/rel: Famous Players-Lasky, Paramount Pictures

STRINGER, DAVID
Touch Wood, Play
Nearly a Nasty Accident 1961 d: Don Chaffey. lps: Jimmy Edwards, Kenneth Connor, Shirley Eaton. 91M UKN. prod/rel: Marlow Productions, Britannia

STRITTMATTER, THOMAS
Viehjud Levi, Play
Viehjud Levi 1999 d: Didi Danquart. lps: Bruno Cathomas, Caroline Ebner, Ulrich Nothen. 90M GRM/SWT/AUS. *Jew-Boy Levi* prod/rel: Zero Film, Swr-Arte

STRODE, WARREN CHETHAM
Background, London 1950, Play
Background 1953 d: Daniel Birt. lps: Valerie Hobson, Philip Friend, Norman Wooland. 82M UKN. *Edge of Divorce* (USA) prod/rel: Group Three, Associated British Film Distributors

The Guinea Pig, London 1946, Play
Guinea Pig, The 1948 d: Roy Boulting. lps: Richard Attenborough, Sheila Sim, Bernard Miles. 97M UKN. *The Outsider* (USA) prod/rel: Pilgrim, Pathe

STRONG, AUSTIN (1881–1952), USA
Seventh Heaven, New York 1922, Play
7th Heaven 1927 d: Frank Borzage. lps: Janet Gaynor, Charles Farrell, Ben Bard. 12r USA. *Seventh Heaven* prod/rel: Fox Film Corp.

Seventh Heaven 1937 d: Henry King. lps: Simone Simon, James Stewart, Jean Hersholt. 102M USA. prod/rel: Twentieth Century-Fox Film Corp.©

Three Wise Fools, Ottawa 1919, Play
Three Wise Fools 1923 d: King Vidor. lps: Claude Gillingwater, Eleanor Boardman, William H. Crane. 6946f USA. prod/rel: Goldwyn Pictures

Three Wise Fools 1946 d: Edward Buzzell. lps: Margaret O'Brien, Lewis Stone, Lionel Barrymore. 90M USA. prod/rel: MGM

STRONG, HARRINGTON
Saddle Mates, 1924, Short Story
Saddle Mates 1928 d: Richard Thorpe. lps: Wally Wales, Hank Bell, J. Gordon Russell. 4520f USA. prod/rel: Action Pictures, Pathe Exchange, Inc.

STRONG, L. A. G. (1896–1958), IRL, Strong, Leonard Alfred George
The Brothers, 1931, Novel
Brothers, The 1947 d: David MacDonald. lps: Patricia Roc, Will Fyffe, Maxwell Reed. 98M UKN. prod/rel: Triton, General Film Distributors

Dr. O'Dowd, Novel
Dr. O'Dowd 1940 d: Herbert Mason. lps: Shaun Glenville, Peggy Cummins, Mary Merrall. 76M UKN. prod/rel: Warner Bros., First National

Irish for Luck, Novel
Irish for Luck 1936 d: Arthur Woods. lps: Athene Seyler, Margaret Lockwood, Patric Knowles. 68M UKN. *Meet the Duchess* prod/rel: Warner Bros., First National

STRONG, MALCOLM
Father's Helping Hand, Story
Father's Helping Hand 1908 d: Horace Davey. lps: Ray Gallagher, Billie Rhodes, Harry Rattenberry. SHT USA. prod/rel: Nestor

Father's Lucky Escape, Story
Father's Lucky Escape 1915 d: Horace Davey. lps: Billie Rhodes, Ray Gallagher, Neal Burns. SHT USA. prod/rel: Nestor

STROUPEZNICKY, LADISLAV
Nasi Furianti, Play
Nasi Furianti 1937 d: Vladislav Vancura, Vaclav Kubasek. lps: Vaclav Vydra St., Antonie Nedosinska, Zdenek HorA. 2736m CZC. *The Swaggerers*; *Our Defiant Ones*; *Our Swaggerers* prod/rel: P.D.C. (J. V. Musil)

Pan Mincmistrova a Zivkovsky Rarasek, Play
Cech Panen Kutnohorskych 1938 d: Otakar VavrA. lps: Zdenek Stepanek, Ladislav Pesek, Vaclav Vydra St. 2601m CZC. *Guild of the Maidens of Kutna Hora*; *Guild of the Virgins of Kutna*; *Guild of the Kutna Hora Virgins*; *Virgin's Guild of Kutna Hora*; *Merry Wives, The* prod/rel: Lucernafilm

Zkazena Krev, Play
Zkazena Krev 1913 d: Alois Wiesner. lps: Alois Wiesner, Katy Kaclova-Valisova, Otokar Alferi. CZC. *Rotten Blood*; *Spoiled Blood* prod/rel: Illusion

STROUSE, CHARLES
Bye Bye Birdie, New York 1960, Musical Play
Bye Bye Birdie 1963 d: George Sidney. lps: Janet Leigh, Dick Van Dyke, Ann-Margret. 112M USA. prod/rel: Columbia

STRUG, ANDRZEJ
Dzieje Jednego Pocisku, 1910, Novel
Goraczka 1980 d: Agnieszka Holland. lps: Olgierd Lukaszewicz, Barbara Grabowska, Adam Ferency. 122M PLN. *Fever* prod/rel: Zespoly Filmowe X

Fortuna Kasjera Spiewankiewicza, 1928, Novel
Niebezpieczny Romans 1930 d: Michael Waszynski. 98M PLN. *A Dangerous Love Affair*

STRUGATSKY, ARKADI (1925–1991), RSS, Strugatsky, Arkadi Natanovich
Piknik Na Obochine, 1972, Short Story
Stalker 1979 d: Andrei Tarkovsky. lps: Aleksandr Kaidanovsky, Nikolai Grinko, Anatoli Solonitsyn. 161M USS. *The Wish machine*

STRUGATSKY, BORIS (1933–, RSS, Strugatsky, Boris Natanovich
Stalker 1979 d: Andrei Tarkovsky. lps: Aleksandr Kaidanovsky, Nikolai Grinko, Anatoli Solonitsyn. 161M USS. *The Wish machine*

Arkadij Strugatzki, Novel
Es Ist Nicht Leicht, Ein Gott Zu Sein 1988 d: Peter Fleischmann. lps: Edward Zentara, Aleksander Filippenko, Anne Gautier. 119M GRM/USS/FRN. *Trudno Byt Bogom* (USS); *It's Hard to Be God*; *Hard to Be a God* prod/rel: Hallelujah Film, ZDF

STRUTHER, JAN
Mrs. Miniver, Novel
Mrs. Miniver 1942 d: William Wyler. lps: Greer Garson, Walter Pidgeon, Dame May Whitty. 134M USA. prod/rel: MGM

STUART, AIMEE
Her Shop, 1929, Play
Borrowed Clothes 1934 d: Arthur Maude. lps: Anne Grey, Lester Matthews, Sunday Wilshin. 70M UKN. prod/rel: Maude Productions, Columbia

Jeannie, London 1940, Play
  Jeannie 1941 d: Harold French. lps: Michael Redgrave, Barbara Mullen, Wilfred Lawson. 101M UKN. *Girl in Distress* (USA) prod/rel: General Film Distributors, Tansa Films
  Let's Be Happy 1957 d: Henry Levin. lps: Tony Martin, Vera-Ellen, Robert Flemyng. 106M UKN. prod/rel: Ab-Pathe, Marcel Hellman
Nine Till Six, London 1930, Play
  Nine Till Six 1932 d: Basil Dean. lps: Louise Hampton, Elizabeth Allan, Florence Desmond. 75M UKN. prod/rel: Associated Talking Pictures, Radio

STUART, ALEXANDER
The War Zone, 1989, Novel
  War Zone, The 1999 d: Tim Roth. lps: Ray Winstone, Tilda Swinton, Lara Belmont. 98M UKN. prod/rel: Film Four, Sarah Radclyffe

STUART, ANGELA
Story
  Northwest Outpost 1947 d: Allan Dwan. lps: Nelson Eddy, Ilona Massey, Joseph Schildkraut. 91M USA. *End of the Rainbow* (UKN); *One Exciting Kiss* prod/rel: Republic

STUART, DON A.
Who Goes There?, Story
  Thing, The 1951 d: Christian Nyby, Howard Hawks (Uncredited). lps: Margaret Sheridan, Kenneth Tobey, Robert Cornthwaite. 87M USA. *The Thing from Another World* (UKN) prod/rel: RKO Radio, Winchester Pictures
  Thing, The 1982 d: John Carpenter. lps: Kurt Russell, Wilford Brimley, T. K. Carter. 109M USA. prod/rel: Universal

STUART, DONALD
The Shadow, Play
  Shadow, The 1933 d: George A. Cooper. lps: Henry Kendall, Elizabeth Allan, Sam Livesey. 74M UKN. prod/rel: Real Art, United Artists

STUART, IAN
The Satan Bug, New York 1963, Novel
  Satan Bug, The 1965 d: John Sturges. lps: George Maharis, Richard Basehart, Anne Francis. 114M USA. prod/rel: Mirisch Corporation, Kappa Corporation

STUART, JEAN
L' Homme Qui Valait Des Milliards, Novel
  Homme Qui Valait Des Milliards, L' 1967 d: Michel Boisrond. lps: Frederick Stafford, Raymond Pellegrin, Peter Van Eyck. 90M FRN/ITL. *L' Uomo Che Valeva Miliardi* (ITL); *Million Dollar Man* (UKN) prod/rel: France Cinema Productions, S.N.E.G.

STUART, PHILIP
Her Shop, 1929, Play
  Borrowed Clothes 1934 d: Arthur Maude. lps: Anne Grey, Lester Matthews, Sunday Wilshin. 70M UKN. prod/rel: Maude Productions, Columbia
Nine Till Six, London 1930, Play
  Nine Till Six 1932 d: Basil Dean. lps: Louise Hampton, Elizabeth Allan, Florence Desmond. 75M UKN. prod/rel: Associated Talking Pictures, Radio

STUART, WILLIAM L.
Night Cry, 1948, Novel
  Where the Sidewalk Ends 1950 d: Otto Preminger. lps: Dana Andrews, Gene Tierney, Gary Merrill. 95M USA. prod/rel: 20th Century-Fox

STUHLDREHER, HARRY
The Gravy Game, 1933, Short Story
  Band Plays on, The 1934 d: Russell MacK. lps: Robert Young, Stuart Erwin, Preston Foster. 89M USA. *Back Field*; *Kid from College* prod/rel: Metro-Goldwyn-Mayer Corp.

STUMP, AL
Cobb: a Biography, Biography
  Cobb 1994 d: Ron Shelton. lps: Tommy Lee Jones, Robert Wuhl, Lolita Davidovich. 128M USA. prod/rel: Warner Bros., Regency

STUPARICH, GIANNI
Un Anno Di Scuola, Short Story
  Anno Di Scuola, Un 1977 d: Franco Giraldi. lps: Laura Lenzi, Stefano Patrizi, Mario d'Arrigo. MTV. F ITL. *A Year of School* prod/rel: C.E.P., Rai Tv

STURGEON, THEODORE (1918–1985), USA, Sturgeon, Theodore Hamilton, Waldo, Edward Hamilton
Killdozer, Novel
  Killdozer 1974 d: Jerry London. lps: Clint Walker, Carl Betz, Neville Brand. TVM. 78M USA. prod/rel: Universal

STURGES, PRESTON (1898–1959), USA
Child of Manhattan, New York 1932, Play
  Child of Manhattan 1933 d: Edward Buzzell. lps: Nancy Carroll, John Boles, Warburton Gamble. 73M USA. prod/rel: Columbia Pictures Corp.

Strictly Dishonorable, New York 1929, Play
  Strictly Dishonorable 1931 d: John M. Stahl. lps: Paul Lukas, Sidney Fox, Lewis Stone. 94M USA. prod/rel: Universal Pictures Corp.©
  Strictly Dishonorable 1951 d: Norman Panama, Melvin Frank. lps: Ezio Pinza, Janet Leigh, Gale Robbins. 86M USA. prod/rel: Metro-Goldwyn-Mayer Corp.

STURGESS, ARTHUR
La Poupee, London 1897, Opera
  Poupee, La 1920 d: Meyrick Milton. lps: Fred Wright, Flora Le Breton, Richard Scott. 5200f UKN. *La Poupee* prod/rel: Meyrick Milton, Ward

STURM, HANS
Eheringe, Play
  Eheferien 1927 d: Victor Janson. lps: Lilian Harvey, Harry Halm, Ida Perry. 2245m GRM. *Matrimonial Holidays* prod/rel: Richard Eichberg-Film
Liebe Und Trompetenblasen, Play
  Liebe Und Trompetenblasen 1925 d: Richard Eichberg. lps: Lilian Harvey, Harry Liedtke, Harry Halm. 2190m GRM. *Love and Trumpets* prod/rel: Eichberg-Film
  Liebe Und Trompetenblasen 1954 d: Helmut Weiss. lps: Marianne Koch, Hans Holt, Nadja Tiller. 93M GRM. *Love and Trumpets* prod/rel: Oska, Union
Der Ungetreue Eckehart, Play
  Don Juan in Der Madchenschule 1928 d: Reinhold Schunzel. lps: Reinhold Schunzel, Hilde von Stolz, Lydia PotechinA. 2173m GRM. prod/rel: Reinhold Schunzel-Film-Prod.
  Ungetreue Eckehart, Der 1940 d: Hubert MarischkA. lps: Hans Moser, Lucie Englisch, Ethel Reschke. 88M GRM. prod/rel: Algefa, Siegel

STURM, WILLIAM F.
The Drivin' Fool, 1922, Short Story
  Drivin' Fool, The 1923 d: Robert T. Thornby. lps: Alec B. Francis, Patsy Ruth Miller, Wilton Taylor. 5700f USA. prod/rel: Regent Pictures, W. W. Hodkinson Corp.

STURROCK, DUDLEY
Peacetime Spies, Short Story
  Peacetime Spies 1924 d: Lee Morrison. lps: Peggy Worth, Walter Tennyson. 2000f UKN. prod/rel: Phillips
Pixie at the Wheel, Short Story
  Miles Against Minutes 1924 d: Lee Morrison. lps: Peggy Worth, Walter Tennyson. 2000f UKN. prod/rel: Phillips
Speeding Into Trouble, Short Story
  Speeding Into Trouble 1924 d: Lee Morrison. lps: Peggy Worth, Walter Tennyson. 2000f UKN. prod/rel: Phillips
The Trouble, Play
  Ourselves Alone 1936 d: Walter Summers, Brian Desmond Hurst. lps: John Lodge, John Loder, Antoinette Cellier. 68M UKN. *River of Unrest* prod/rel: British International, Wardour

STURZER, RUDOLF
Spitzenhoschen Und Schusterpech, Short Story
  Veteran Votruba 1928 d: Hans Otto Lowenstein. lps: Hans Moser, Milka Balek-Brodska, Jan W. Speerger. CZC/AUS. *Spitzenhoschen Und Schusterpech* (AUS); *Die Lampelgasse* prod/rel: Meteorfilm, Ottol-Film

STYBLOVA, VALJA
Prosim Skalpel, Novel
  Skalpel, Prosim 1986 d: Jiri SvobodA. lps: Miroslav MacHavek, Jana Brejchova, Radoslav Brzobohaty. 114M CZC. *Please Scalpel*

STYNE, JULE
Funny Girl, New York 1964, Musical Play
  Funny Girl 1968 d: William Wyler. lps: Barbra Streisand, Omar Sharif, Kay Medford. 155M USA. prod/rel: Rastar Productions, Columbia

STYRON, WILLIAM (1925–, USA, Styron Jr., William Clark
Short Story
  Shadrach 1998 d: Susanna Styron. lps: Harvey Keitel, Andie MacDowell, John Franklin Sawyer. 86M USA. prod/rel: Millennium Films, Nu Image
Sophie's Choice, 1979, Novel
  Sophie's Choice 1982 d: Alan J. PakulA. lps: Meryl Streep, Kevin Kline, Peter MacNicol. 151M USA. prod/rel: Universal

SU FANGGUI
Story of Adopted Sisters, Novel
  Nuren Hua 1994 d: Wang Jin. lps: Pu Chaoying, Yuan Li, Liu Wei. 105M CHN. *Flower Woman*; *Women Flowers* prod/rel: Pearl River Film Company

SU TONG
Hongfen, Novel
  Hongfen 1994 d: Li Shaohong. lps: Wang Ji, He Saifei, Wang Zhiwen. 119M CHN/HKG. *Rouge*; *Blush* prod/rel: Beijing Film Studio, Ocean Film Co. (Hong Kong)
Wives and Concubines, Novel
  Dahong Denglong Gaogao Gua 1991 d: Zhang Yimou. lps: Gong Li, Ma Jingwa, He Caifei. 125M CHN/TWN/HKG. *Raise the Red Lantern* (UKN) prod/rel: Era International (Hk) Ltd., China Film Co-Production Corporation

SUAREZ Y ROMERO, ANSELMO
Francisco, 1880, Novel
  Otro Francisco, El 1974 d: Sergio Giral, Julio Garcia Espinosa., Miguel Benavides, Alina Sanchez. 100M CUB. *The Other Francisco*

SUASSUNA, ARIANO
Auto Da Compadecida, 1959, Play
  Compadecida, A 1969 d: George Joanas. lps: Regina Duarte, Zozimo Bulbul, Paulo Ribeiro. 104M BRZ. *Our Lady of Compassion*; *The Rogue's Trial*; *The Compassionate One*

SUDERMANN, HERMANN (1857–1928), GRM
La Bonne Reputation, Play
  Mensonges, Les 1927 d: Pierre Marodon. lps: Leon Bary, Germaine Rouer, Lotte Neumann. 2330m FRN/GRM. *Der Gute Ruf* (GRM) prod/rel: Hermes Films
Es War; Roman in Zwei Banden, Stuttgart 1893, Novel
  Flesh and the Devil 1926 d: Clarence Brown. lps: John Gilbert, Greta Garbo, Lars Hanson. 8759f USA. prod/rel: Metro-Goldwyn-Mayer Pictures
Die Frau Des Steffen Tromholt, Stuttgart 1927, Novel
  Wonder of Women 1929 d: Clarence Brown. lps: Lewis Stone, Leila Hyams, Peggy Wood. 8347f USA. prod/rel: Metro-Goldwyn-Mayer Pictures
Frau Sorge, Novel
  Frau Sorge 1928 d: Robert Land. lps: Mary Carr, Grete Mosheim, Wilhelm Dieterle. 3128m GRM. prod/rel: Deutsche Film-Union Ag
Heimat, 1893, Play
  Heimat 1912 d: Adolf Gartner. GRM. prod/rel: Messters Projektion
  Heimat 1938 d: Carl Froelich. lps: Heinrich George, Zarah Leander, Ruth Hellberg. 98M GRM. *Magda*; *Homeland* prod/rel: Carl Froelich, Kristall
  Magda 1917 d: Emile Chautard. lps: Clara Kimball Young, Thomas Holding, Valda Valkyrien. 5r USA., C. K. Y. Film Corp.©
Das Hohe Lied, Berlin 1908, Novel
  Lily of the Dust 1924 d: Dimitri Buchowetzki. lps: Pola Negri, Ben Lyon, Noah Beery. 6811f USA. *Compromised* prod/rel: Famous Players-Lasky, Paramount Pictures
  Song of Songs, The 1918 d: Joseph Kaufman. lps: Elsie Ferguson, Cecil Fletcher, Crauford Kent. 5r USA. prod/rel: Famous Players-Lasky Corp.©, Artcraft Pictures
  Song of Songs, The 1933 d: Rouben Mamoulian. lps: Marlene Dietrich, Brian Aherne, Lionel Atwill. 92M USA. prod/rel: Paramount Productions©, Rouben Mamoulian Production
Johannisfeuer, 1900, Play
  Flames of Johannis, The 1916 d: Edgar Lewis. lps: Nance O'Neil, George Clarke, Eleanor Barry. 5r USA. *The Fires of St. John*; *The Fires of Johannis* prod/rel: Lubin Mfg. Co.©, V-L-S-E, Inc.
  Johannisfeuer 1939 d: Arthur M. Rabenalt. lps: Anna Dammann, Ernst von Klipstein, Gertrud Meyen. 82M GRM. *St. John's Fire* (USA) prod/rel: Terra, Schorcht
  ..Und Ewig Bleibt Die Liebe 1954 d: Wolfgang Liebeneiner. lps: Karlheinz Bohm, Ulla Jacobsson, Ingrid Andree. 96M GRM. *And Love Remains Eternal*; *And Love Lasts Forever* prod/rel: Berolina, Constantin
Jolanthes Hochzeit, 1892, Short Story
  Hochzeit Auf Barenhof 1942 d: Carl Froelich. lps: Heinrich George, Ilse Werner, Paul Wegener. 106M GRM. prod/rel: UFA, Panorama
Jons Und Erdme, 1917, Short Story
  Jons Und Erdme 1959 d: Victor Vicas. lps: Giulietta Masina, Carl Raddatz, Richard Basehart. 101M GRM/ITL. *La Donna Dell'altro* (ITL); *Die Frau Des Anderen*; *Another's Wife* prod/rel: Kurt Ulrich, Nembo
Der Katzensteg, 1889, Novel
  Katzensteg, Der 1915 d: Max Mack. lps: Georg Lengbach, Leontine Kuhnberg, Ludwig Trautmann. 1750m GRM. prod/rel: Projektions-Ag Union
  Katzensteg, Der 1927 d: Gerhard Lamprecht. lps: Lissi Arna, Jack Trevor, A. Behrens-Klausen. 2980m GRM. *Betrayal* prod/rel: National-Film

Katzensteg, Der 1937 d: Fritz Peter Buch. lps: Brigitte Horney, Hannes Stelzer, Fritz Reiff. 87M GRM. *The Cat's Path*

Magda, Berlin 1893, Play
Revelations 1916 d: Arthur Maude. lps: Constance Crawley, Arthur Maude, William Carroll. 5r USA. *Revelation* prod/rel: American Film Co., Mutual Film Corp.

Parmi Les Pierres, Play
Parmi Les Pierres 1912 d: Adrien Caillard. lps: Romuald Joube, Maxime Desjardins, Germaine Dermoz. 365m FRN. prod/rel: Scagl

Die Reise Nach Tilsit, Berlin 1917, Novel
Reise Nach Tilsit, Die 1939 d: Veit Harlan. lps: Frits Van Dongen, Kristina Soderbaum, Anna Dammann. 93M GRM. *The Sun Is Rising*; *The Journey to Tilsit*; *The Trip to Tilsit* prod/rel: Majestic, Panorama

Sunrise - a Song of Two Humans 1927 d: F. W. Murnau. lps: Janet Gaynor, George O'Brien, Bodil Rosing. 11r USA. *Sunrise* (UKN); *Sunrise -a Story of Two Humans* prod/rel: Fox Film Corp.

Stein Unter Steinen, Play
Rehabilitiert 1910. lps: Paul Bildt. 268m GRM. prod/rel: Deutsche Bioscop

SUDRAKA
Mrichchakatikam, c400-500, Play
Utsav 1983 d: Girish Karnad. lps: Shashi Kapoor, Rekha, AnuradhA. 145M IND. *Festivals*; *The Festival*; *Festival of Love* prod/rel: Film Valas

SUE, EUGENE (1804–1857), FRN, Sue, Marie Joseph
Le Juif Errant, 1845, Novel
Ebreo Errante, L' 1912. lps: Renzo Fabiani. 1200m ITL. prod/rel: Roma Film

Ebreo Errante, L' 1916 d: Umberto Paradisi. lps: Mario Cimarra, Egidio Candiani, Enrico Vernier. 1200m ITL. prod/rel: Pasquali E C.

Ebreo Errante, L' 1947 d: Goffredo Alessandrini. lps: Vittorio Gassman, Valentina Cortese, Inge Borg. 99M ITL. *The Wandering Jew* prod/rel: Cin.Ca Distributori Indipendenti

Juif Errant, Le 1913. 1441m FRN. prod/rel: Scf Film

Juif Errant, Le 1926 d: Luitz-Morat. lps: Gabriel Gabrio, Maurice Schutz, Claude Merelle. SRL. FRN. prod/rel: Societe Des Cineromans

Wandering Jew, The 1923 d: Maurice Elvey. lps: Matheson Lang, Hutin Britton, Malvina Longfellow. 8300f UKN. prod/rel: Stoll

Wandering Jew, The 1933 d: Maurice Elvey. lps: Conrad Veidt, Marie Ney, Cicely Oates. 111M UKN. prod/rel: Gaumont-British, Twickenham

Martin Et Bambouche; Ou Les Amis d'Enfance, 1847, Novel
Martino Il Trovatello 1919 d: Alberto A. Capozzi, Ubaldo Maria Del Colle. lps: Alberto A. Capozzi, Piera Bouvier, Nello Carotenuto. 3898m ITL. *I Figli Del Capriccio*; *Le Miserie Dei Trovatelli* prod/rel: Megale Film

Les Mysteres de Paris, 1842-43, Novel
Misteri Di Parigi, I 1958 d: Fernando Cerchio, Giorgio RivaltA. lps: Frank Villard, Lorella de Luca, Matteo SpinolA. 96M ITL/FRN. *Les Mysteres de Paris* (FRN) prod/rel: Prora Film, Faro Film (Roma)

Mysteres de Paris, Les 1909 d: Victorin Jasset. lps: Gilbert Dalleu, Camille Bardou, Suzanne Goldstein. 310m FRN. prod/rel: Eclair

Mysteres de Paris, Les 1912 d: Albert Capellani, Georges DenolA. lps: Edmond Duquesne, Henry Houry, Felix GanderA. 1540m FRN. *The Mysteries of Paris* prod/rel: Scagl

Mysteres de Paris, Les 1922 d: Charles Burguet. lps: Georges Lannes, Huguette Duflos, Roby Guichard. SRL. 12EP FRN. *The Mysteries of Paris* prod/rel: Phocea Film

Mysteres de Paris, Les 1935 d: Felix GanderA. lps: Constant Remy, Madeleine Ozeray, Lucienne Le Marchand. 110M FRN. *The Mysteries of Paris* prod/rel: Productions Felix Gandera

Mysteres de Paris, Les 1943 d: Jacques de Baroncelli. lps: Marcel Herrand, Alexandre Rignault, Lucien Coedel. 89M FRN. *The Mysteries of Paris* prod/rel: Discina

Mysteres de Paris, Les 1962 d: Andre Hunebelle. lps: Jean Marais, Dany Robin, Jill Haworth. 110M FRN/ITL. *I Misteri Di Parigi* (ITL); *Mysteries of Paris* prod/rel: P.A.C., Dama Cinematografica

Mysteries of Paris, The 1920? d: Ed Cornell. lps: Marie Caldwell, Emily Fuller, Robert Carlson. 8r USA. prod/rel: Hub Cinematograph Co. of Boston

Parigi Misteriosa 1917 d: Gustavo SerenA. lps: Gustavo Serena, Enna Saredo, Lea Giunchi. 4966m ITL. *Il Ventre Di Parigi* prod/rel: Caesar Film

Secrets of Paris, The 1922 d: Kenneth Webb. lps: Lew Cody, Gladys Hulette, Effie Shannon. 6481f USA. prod/rel: Whitman Bennett Productions, H. V. Productions

Ventre Di Parigi, Il 1917 d: Ubaldo Maria Del Colle. lps: Mary Bayma-Riva, Ubaldo Maria Del Colle, Nadja Milar. 3443m ITL. *I Misteri Di Parigi* prod/rel: Megale Film

Paula Monti, Novel
Donna Che Fu Molto Amata, La 1922 d: Enrico Vidali. lps: Lydianne, Miss Agar, Jean Berthier. 1613m ITL. prod/rel: Lydianne

SUEIRO, DANIEL
Solo de Moto, 1967, Novel
Puente, El 1977 d: Juan Antonio Bardem. lps: Alfredo Landa, Josele Roman, Victoria Abril. 108M SPN. *The Bridge*; *The Long Weekend*

SUKENICK, RONALD
Out, Novel
Out 1982 d: Eli Hollander. lps: Peter Coyote, O-Lan Shepard, Jim Haynie. 88M USA. prod/rel: Eli Hollander, National Endowment for the Arts

SUKHOVO-KOBYLIN, ALEKSANDR
Smert Tarelkina, 1869, Play
Vesyolyye Rasplyuyevskiye Dni 1966 d: Erast Garin. lps: Anatoli Papanov, Erast Garin, Nikolaj Trofimov. 89M USS. *Those Crazy Rasplyuyev Days*; *Veselye Raspliuyevskie Dni*; *Merry Rasplyuyev Days*; *Gau Rasplyev Days*; *Rasplyuyev's Gay Days*

SULC, BEDRICH
Bila Vrana, Opera
Bila Vrana 1938 d: Vladimir Slavinsky. lps: Jindrich Plachta, Adina Mandlova, Frantisek Kristof-Vesely. 3094m CZC. *White Crow* prod/rel: Elekta

SULLIVAN, ALAN
The Crusader, 1916, Short Story
Crusader, The 1922 d: Howard M. Mitchell, William K. Howard. lps: William Russell, Gertrude Claire, Helen Ferguson. 4780f USA. prod/rel: Fox Film Corp.

The Great Divide, Novel
Great Barrier, The 1937 d: Milton Rosmer. lps: Richard Arlen, Antoinette Cellier, Barry MacKay. 83M UKN. *Silent Barriers* (USA); *Hell's Gateway* prod/rel: Gaumont-British

The Rapids, Novel
Rapids, The 1922 d: David M. Hartford. lps: Mary Astor, Harry T. Morey, Walter Miller. 5r CND. prod/rel: Sault Ste. Marie Films Ltd., Ernest Shipman Film Service

SULLIVAN, ARTHUR (1842–1900), UKN, Sullivan, Arthur Seymour
H.M.S. Pinafore, London 1878, Opera
H.M.S. Pinafore 1950. 70M USA. prod/rel: Hoffberg

The Lost Chord, Song
Lost Battalion, The 1921. lps: Gaston Glass, Blanche Davenport. 6r USA. prod/rel: L. C. Mccallum, Producers Security Corp.

The Mikado, London 1885, Opera
Cool Mikado, The 1963 d: Michael Winner. lps: Frankie Howerd, Stubby Kaye, Tommy Cooper. 81M UKN. prod/rel: Film Production of Gilbert & Sullivan, United Artists

Fan Fan 1918 d: Chester M. Franklin, Sidney A. Franklin. lps: Virginia Lee Corbin, Francis Carpenter, Carmen de Rue. 5r USA. *The Mikado* prod/rel: Fox Film Corp., William Fox©

Mikado, The 1939 d: Victor Schertzinger. lps: Kenny Baker, Jean Colin, Martyn Green. 91M UKN. prod/rel: General Film Distributors, G and S Films

Mikado, The 1967 d: Stuart Burge. lps: Donald Adams, Philip Potter, John Reed. 122M UKN. prod/rel: B.H.E. Productions, Eagle

The Pirates of Penzance, London 1880, Opera
Pirate Movie, The 1982 d: Ken Annakin. lps: Kristy McNichol, Christopher Atkins, Ted Hamilton. 105M ASL/USA. prod/rel: David Joseph, Joseph Hammond Intl. Prods. Pty Ltd.©

Pirates of Penzance, The 1983 d: Wilford Leach. lps: Kevin Kline, Angela Lansbury, Linda Ronstadt. 112M UKN. prod/rel: Universal

SULLIVAN, FRANCIS WILLIAM
Children of Banishment, New York 1914, Novel
Children of Banishment 1919 d: Norval MacGregor. lps: Mitchell Lewis, Bessie Eyton, Herbert Heyes. 4930f USA. prod/rel: Select Pictures Corp.©

The Godson of Jeanette Gontreau, 1917, Short Story
Flames of Chance, The 1918 d: Raymond Wells. lps: Margery Wilson, Jack Mulhall, Anna Hernandez. 5r USA. prod/rel: Triangle Film Corp., Triangle Distributing Corp.

The Wilderness Trail, New York 1913, Novel
Wilderness Trail, The 1919 d: Edward J. Le Saint. lps: Tom Mix, Colleen Moore, Sid Jordan. 5r USA. prod/rel: Fox Film Corp., William Fox©

SULLIVAN, KATE
The Reluctant Grandmother, Play
She Knows Y'know 1962 d: Montgomery Tully. lps: Hylda Baker, Cyril Smith, Joe Gibbons. 72M UKN. prod/rel: Grand National, Eternal

SULLIVAN, TOM
If You Could See What I Hear, Book
If You Could See What I Hear 1981 d: Eric Till. lps: Marc Singer, R. H. Thomson, Sarah Torgov. 103M CND. *Au-Dela du Regard*; *Something Else Again* prod/rel: Cypress Grove Films Ltd., Shelter Films Ltd.

SULLIVAN, WALLACE
No Power on Earth, Short Story
Behind the High Wall 1956 d: Abner Biberman. lps: Tom Tully, Sylvia Sidney, Betty Lynn. 85M USA. prod/rel: Universal-International

Big Guy, The 1940 d: Arthur Lubin. lps: Victor McLaglen, Jackie Cooper, Ona Munson. 78M USA. *No Power on Earth* prod/rel: Universal Pictures Co.

SULTAN, ARNE
Story
Boys' Night Out 1962 d: Michael Gordon. lps: Howard Duff, Tony Randall, Howard Morris. 114M USA. prod/rel: MGM, Filmways

SUMI, SUE
Hashi No Nai Kawa, Novel
Hashi No Nai Kawa 1992 d: Yoichi Higashi. lps: Naoko Otani, Tamao Nakamura, Tetsuta Sugimoto. 139M JPN. *The River With No Bridge* prod/rel: Seiyu Ltd., Galeria

SUMMERS, JARON
Soda Cracker, Novel
Soda Cracker 1989 d: Fred Williamson. lps: Fred Williamson, Maud Adams, Bo Svenson. 90M USA. *The Kill Reflex*; *The Killer Reflex*; *C.C. Action*

SUMMERS, RICHARD ALDRICH
Vigilante, 1949, Novel
San Francisco Story, The 1952 d: Robert Parrish. lps: Joel McCrea, Yvonne de Carlo, Sidney Blackmer. 80M USA. prod/rel: Warner Bros., Fidelity

SUMNER, CID RICKETTS
Tammy Out of Time, Indianapolis 1948, Novel
Tammy and the Bachelor 1957 d: Joseph Pevney. lps: Debbie Reynolds, Leslie Nielsen, Walter Brennan. 89M USA. *Tammy* (UKN) prod/rel: Universal-International

Tammy and the Millionaire 1967 d: Sidney Miller, Ezra C. Stone. lps: Debbie Watson, Donald Woods, Dorothy Green. TVM. 88M USA. prod/rel: Uni-Bet Productions

Tammy Tell Me True, Indianapolis 1959, Novel
Tammy Tell Me True 1961 d: Harry Keller. lps: Sandra Dee, John Gavin, Beulah Bondi. 97M USA. prod/rel: Ross Hunter Productions, Universal-International

SUNDARAM
Vietnam Veedu, Play
Vietnam Veedu 1970 d: P. Madhavan. lps: Sivaji Ganesan, Nagesh, Srikanth. 164M IND. *Vietnam House* prod/rel: Sivaji Prod.

SUNDMAN, OLOF
Ingenjor Andrees Luftfard, Novel
Ingenjor Andrees Luftfard 1982 d: Jan Troell. lps: Max von Sydow, Goran Stangertz, Sverre Anker Ousdal. 140M SWD/NRW/GRM. *The Flight of the Eagle*; *Andrees Luftfard* prod/rel: Bold, Svenska Filminstitut

SUPPER, WALTER
Fruhlingsmarchen, Musical Play
Fruhlingsmarchen 1934 d: Carl Froelich. lps: Claire Fuchs, Maris Wetra, Ida Wust. 86M GRM. *Verlieb' Dich Nicht in Sizilien* prod/rel: Carl Froelich, Europa

Meine Tante - Deine Tante, Play
Meine Tante - Deine Tante 1927 d: Carl Froelich. lps: Henny Porten, Ralph Arthur Roberts, Angelo Ferrari. 2361m GRM. *My Aunt Your Aunt* prod/rel: Henny Porten-Froelich Film Prod.

Meine Tante - Deine Tante 1939 d: Carl Boese. lps: Ralph Arthur Roberts, Johannes Heesters, Olly Holzmann. 90M GRM. *My Aunt Your Aunt*

SURDEZ, GEORGES ARTHUR
The Demon Caravan, 1927, Novel
Desert Legion 1953 d: Joseph Pevney. lps: Alan Ladd, Arlene Dahl, Richard Conte. 86M USA. prod/rel: Universal-International

A Game in the Bush, Short Story
South Sea Love 1927 d: Ralph Ince. lps: Patsy Ruth Miller, Lee Shumway, Alan Brooks. 6388f USA. prod/rel: R-C Pictures, Film Booking Offices of America

SURGUTCHOFF, ILYA
Autumn, Play
　That Dangerous Age 1949 d: Gregory Ratoff. lps: Myrna Loy, Roger Livesey, Peggy Cummins. 99M UKN. *If This Be Sin* (USA); *The Case of Lady Brookes* prod/rel: London Films, British Lion
Igra, Play
　Man Who Broke the Bank at Monte Carlo, The 1935 d: Stephen Roberts. lps: Ronald Colman, Joan Bennett, Colin Clive. 68M USA. prod/rel: Twentieth Century-Fox Film Corp.©

SUSANN, JACQUELINE (1925–1974), USA
The Love machine, Novel
　Love machine, The 1971 d: Jack Haley Jr. lps: John Phillip Law, Dyan Cannon, Robert Ryan. 110M USA. prod/rel: Columbia
Once Is Not Enough, Novel
　Jacqueline Susann's Once Is Not Enough 1975 d: Guy Green. lps: Kirk Douglas, Alexis Smith, David Janssen. 122M USA. *Once Is Not Enough* (UKN) prod/rel: Paramount Pictures
Valley of the Dolls, New York 1966, Novel
　Jacqueline Susann's Valley of the Dolls 1981 d: Walter Grauman. lps: Catherine Hicks, Lisa Hartman, Veronica Hamel. TVM. 240M USA. *Valley of the Dolls*
　Valley of the Dolls 1967 d: Mark Robson. lps: Barbara Parkins, Patty Duke, Paul Burke. 123M USA. prod/rel: Red Lion Productions

SUTHERLAND, DAN
A Breach of Marriage, London 1948, Play
　Question of Adultery, A 1958 d: Don Chaffey. lps: Julie London, Anthony Steel, Basil Sydney. 85M UKN. *The Case of Mrs. Loring* (USA) prod/rel: Eros, Connaught Place

SUTHERLAND, E. G.
The Breed of the Treshams, London 1905, Play
　Breed of the Treshams, The 1920 d: Kenelm Foss. lps: John Martin-Harvey, Mary Odette, Hayford Hobbs. 6000f UKN. prod/rel: Astra Films

SUTHERLAND, EVELYN
The Road to Yesterday, New York 1906, Play
　Road to Yesterday, The 1925 d: Cecil B. de Mille. lps: Joseph Schildkraut, Jetta Goudal, Vera Reynolds. 9980f USA. prod/rel: de Mille Pictures, Producers Distributing Corp.

SUTHERLAND, JOAN
Fettered, Novel
　Fettered 1919 d: Arrigo Bocchi. lps: Manora Thew, Hayford Hobbs, Fred Morgan. 5000f UKN. prod/rel: Windsor, Walturdaw
Wyngate Sahib, Novel
　Fantee 1920 d: Lewis Willoughby. lps: Lewis Willoughby, Olive Valerie, Philip Anthony. UKN. prod/rel: Anglo-Indian Films

SUTHERLAND, RONALD
Snow Lark, Book
　Suzanne 1980 d: Robin Spry. lps: Jennifer Dale, Winston Rekert, Gabriel Arcand. 102M CND. *Mixed Feelings*; *Snow Lark* prod/rel: Moviecorp IV Inc., Rsl Films Ltd.

SUTO, ANDRAS
Csillag a Maglyan, 1976, Play
　Csillag a Maglyan 1979 d: Otto Adam. lps: Istvan Sztankay, Peter Huszti. 101M HNG. *A Bright Star at the Stake*
Felrjaro Salamon, 1955, Short Story
　Mica Intimplare, O 1957 d: Gheorghe Turcu. 68M RMN. *An Unimportant Event*
Zaszlos Demeter, 1960, Short Story
　Doi Barbati Pentru O Moarte 1970 d: Gheorghe Naghi. lps: Stefan Mihailescu-BrailA. 107M RMN. *Two Men for One Death*

SUTRO, ALFRED (1863–1933), UKN
The Builder of Bridges, London 1908, Play
　Builder of Bridges, The 1915 d: George Irving. lps: C. Aubrey Smith, Marie Edith Wells, Jack Sherrill. 5r USA. prod/rel: Frohman Amusement Corp., World Film Corp.©
The Great Well, Play
　Great Well, The 1924 d: Henry Kolker. lps: Thurston Hall, Seena Owen, Lawford Davidson. 6400f UKN. *Neglected Women* (USA) prod/rel: Ideal
John Glayde's Honour, New York 1907, Play
　John Glayde's Honor 1915 d: George Irving. lps: C. Aubrey Smith, Mary Lawton, Richard Hatteras. 5r USA. *The Man's Honor*; *John Glayde's Honour* prod/rel: Frohman Amusement Corp., Pathe Exchange, Inc.
The Laughing Lady, London 1922, Play
　Laughing Lady, The 1929 d: Victor Schertzinger. lps: Ruth Chatterton, Clive Brook, Dan Healy. 7200f USA. prod/rel: Paramount Famous Lasky Corp.

Society Scandal, A 1924 d: Allan Dwan. lps: Gloria Swanson, Rod La Rocque, Ricardo Cortez. 6857f USA. prod/rel: Famous Players-Lasky, Paramount Pictures
The Perfect Lover, London 1905, Play
　For Her Father's Sake 1921 d: Alexander Butler. lps: Owen Nares, Isobel Elsom, James Lindsay. 4983f UKN. prod/rel: G. B. Samuelson, General
The Walls of Jericho, New York 1905, Play
　Walls of Jericho, The 1914 d: Lloyd B. Carleton. lps: Edmund Breese, Claire Whitney, Walter Hitchcock. 5r USA. prod/rel: Box Office Attraction Co., William Fox©

SUTTER, LARABIE
The Gun Witch of Wyoming, Story
　White Squaw, The 1956 d: Ray Nazarro. lps: David Brian, May Wynn, William Bishop. 73M USA. prod/rel: Columbia, Screen Gems, Inc.

SUTTON JR., GEORGE W.
The Dawn of My Tomorrow, Story
　Framed 1927 d: Charles J. Brabin. lps: Milton Sills, Natalie Kingston, E. J. Radcliffe. 5282f USA. *Diamonds in the Rough* prod/rel: First National Pictures

SUTTON, SHELLEY
The Almost Good Man, Story
　Almost Good Man, The 1917 d: Fred A. Kelsey. lps: Harry Carey, Claire Du Brey, Albert MacQuarrie. 3r USA. prod/rel: Gold Seal

SUZUKI, SEIJUN
Kenka Ereji, Novel
　Kenka Serejii 1966 d: Seijun Suzuki. lps: Hideki Takahashi, Junko Asono, Yusuke Kawazu. 86M JPN. *Kenka Elegy*; *Elegy for a Quarrel*; *Fighting Elegy*; *Scuffle Elegy*; *Born Fighter, The* prod/rel: Nikkatsu Corp.

SVATEK, JOSEF
Prazsky Kat, Novel
　Prazsky Kat 1927 d: Rudolf Mestak. lps: Gustav Fristensky, Edmond Trachta, Anna OpplovA. 2420m CZC. *The Prague Executioner* prod/rel: Republikfilm

SVETLA, KAROLINA
Kriz U Potoka, Novel
　Kriz U Potoka 1921 d: J. S. Kolar. lps: Premysl Prazsky, Rudolf Myzet, Karel Noll. 1355m CZC. *The Cross at the Brook*; *The Cross at the Stream* prod/rel: Ab, American
　Kriz U Potoka 1937 d: Miloslav Jares. lps: Jirina Stepnickova, Vitezslav Vejrazka, Mirko Elias. 2338m CZC. *The Cross By the Brook* prod/rel: Excelsior
Nemodlenec, Novel
　Nemodlenec 1927 d: Vaclav Kubasek. lps: H. L. Struna, Marie Cerna, Frantisek Havel. 2817m CZC. *The Man Who Went Out of Fashion*; *The Miscreant* prod/rel: Poja Film, Biografia

SVEVO, ITALO (1861–1928), ITL, Schmitz, Ettore
Senilita, 1898, Novel
　Senilita 1962 d: Mauro Bolognini. lps: Anthony Franciosa, Claudia Cardinale, Betsy Blair. 118M ITL/FRN. *Quand la Chair Succombe* (FRN); *Careless* (USA); *When a Man Grows Old*; *As a Man Grows Older* prod/rel: Zebra Film (Roma), Aera Film (Paris)

SVOBODA, F. X.
Cekanky, Play
　Cekanky 1940 d: Vladimir Borsky. lps: Zorka Janu, Meda Valentova, Anna LetenskA. 2275m CZC. *The Waiting Girls*; *Women in Waiting* prod/rel: Terra
Kasparek, Novel
　Roztomily Clovek 1941 d: Martin Fric. lps: Oldrich Novy, Ladislav Pesek, Natasa GollovA. 2457m CZC. *A Charming Man*; *A Charming Person*; *Sweet Person* prod/rel: Nationalfilm
Posledni Muz, Play
　Posledni Muz 1934 d: Martin Fric. lps: Hugo Haas, Zdenka Baldova, Marie GlazrovA. 2491m CZC. *The Last Man* prod/rel: Moldavia
Smery Zivota, Play
　Smery Zivota 1940 d: Jiri Slavicek. lps: Hana Vitova, Zdenka Baldova, Ladislav Bohac. 2639m CZC. *The Paths of Life* prod/rel: Nationalfilm

SVOBODOVA, RUZENA
Cerni Myslivci, Book
　Cerni Myslivci 1921 d: Vaclav Binovec. lps: Alois Sedlacek, Suzanne Marwille, Marta Marwille. 1392m CZC. *The Black Gamekeepers*; *O Velike Vasni*; *About the Great Passion* prod/rel: Weteb, Iris-Film
　Cerni Myslivci 1945 d: Martin Fric. lps: Dana Medricka, Gustav Nezval, L. H. StrunA. UNF. CZC. *Gamekeepers in Black* prod/rel: Nationalfilm

SWAFFER, GEOFFREY
The Lion and the Lamb, Play
　River Wolves, The 1934 d: George Pearson. lps: Helga Moray, Michael Hogan, John Mills. 56M UKN. prod/rel: Real Art, Radio

SWAIN, JOHN D.
Billy Kane - White and Unmarried, Story
　White and Unmarried 1921 d: Tom Forman. lps: Thomas Meighan, Jacqueline Logan, Grace Darmond. 4458f USA. *The Point of View* prod/rel: Famous Players-Lasky, Paramount Pictures
The Last Man on Earth, 1923, Novel
　It's Great to Be Alive 1933 d: Alfred L. Werker. lps: Gloria Stuart, Joan Marsh, Edna May Oliver. 69M USA. prod/rel: Fox Film Corp.©
　Last Man on Earth, The 1924 d: John G. Blystone. lps: Earle Foxe, Grace Cunard, Gladys Tennyson. 6637f USA. prod/rel: Fox Film Corp.

SWAN, MARK, Swan, Mark Elbert
Her Own Money, New York 1915, Play
　Her Own Money 1922 d: Joseph Henabery. lps: Ethel Clayton, Warner Baxter, Charles K. French. 4981f USA. prod/rel: Famous Players-Lasky, Paramount Pictures
Parlor Bedroom and Bath, New York 1917, Play
　Buster Se Marie 1931 d: Edward Brophy, Claude Autant-LarA. lps: Buster Keaton, Jeanne Helbling, Andre Luguet. 80M USA. prod/rel: Metro-Goldwyn-Mayer
　Casanova Wider Willen 1931 d: Edward Brophy. lps: Buster Keaton, Marion Lessing, Paul Morgan. F USA.
　Parlor, Bedroom and Bath 1920 d: Eddie Dillon. lps: Ruth Stonehouse, Eugene Pallette, Kathleen Kirkham. 6r USA. prod/rel: Metro Pictures Corp.©
　Parlor, Bedroom and Bath 1931 d: Edward Sedgwick. lps: Buster Keaton, Charlotte Greenwood, Reginald Denny. 72M USA. *A Romeo in Pyjamas* (UKN) prod/rel: Metro-Goldwyn-Mayer Corp., Metro-Goldwyn-Mayer Dist. Corp.©
The Princess of Patches, 1901, Play
　Princess of Patches, The 1917 d: Alfred E. Green. lps: Vivian Reed, Burke Wilbur, Hildor Hobert. 5r USA. prod/rel: Selig Polyscope Co., K-E-S-E Service

SWANN, FRANCIS
Out of the Frying Pan, Play
　Young and Willing 1942 d: Edward H. Griffith. lps: William Holden, Eddie Bracken, Barbara Britton. 82M USA. *Out of the Frying Pan* prod/rel: United Artists-Cinema Guild, Paramount

SWANN, FREDERICK A.
Monsieur Andre, Play
　Man Who Broke the Bank at Monte Carlo, The 1935 d: Stephen Roberts. lps: Ronald Colman, Joan Bennett, Colin Clive. 68M USA. prod/rel: Twentieth Century-Fox Film Corp.©

SWANSON, H. N.
Big Business Girl, 1930, Story
　Big Business Girl 1931 d: William A. Seiter. lps: Loretta Young, Ricardo Cortez, Jack Albertson. 80M USA. prod/rel: First National Pictures, Inc.

SWANSON, NEIL HARMON
The First Rebel, New York 1937, Novel
　Allegheny Uprising 1939 d: William A. Seiter. lps: John Wayne, Claire Trevor, Brian Donlevy. 81M USA. *The First Rebel* (UKN); *Pennsylvania Uprising*; *Allegheny Frontier* prod/rel: RKO Radio Pictures, Inc.
The Judas Tree, Novel
　Unconquered 1947 d: Cecil B. de Mille. lps: Gary Cooper, Paulette Goddard, Howard Da SilvA. 147M USA. prod/rel: Paramount

SWARTHOUT, GLENDON (1918–, USA, Swarthout, Glendon Fred
Bless the Beasts and Children, Novel
　Bless the Beasts and Children 1972 d: Stanley Kramer. lps: Bill Mumy, Barry Robins, Miles Chapin. 109M USA. prod/rel: Columbia, Stanley Kramer
A Horse for Mrs. Custer, Story
　Seventh Cavalry 1956 d: Joseph H. Lewis, Raphael J. SevillA. lps: Randolph Scott, Barbara Hale, Jay C. Flippen. 75M USA. *7th Cavalry*; *The Return of Custer*; *El Septimo de Caballeria* prod/rel: Columbia, Producers Actors Corp.
The Melodeon, Novel
　Christmas to Remember, A 1978 d: George Englund. lps: Jason Robards Jr., Eva Marie Saint, George Parry. TVM. 100M USA. prod/rel: CBS, George Englund Enterprises
The Shootist, Novel
　Shootist, The 1976 d: Don Siegel. lps: John Wayne, Lauren Bacall, Ron Howard. 100M USA. prod/rel: Paramount
They Came to Cordura, 1958, Novel
　They Came to Cordura 1959 d: Robert Rossen. lps: Gary Cooper, Rita Hayworth, Van Heflin. 123M USA. prod/rel: Columbia, Goetz Pictures

Where the Boys are, Novel
  Where the Boys are 1960 d: Henry Levin. lps: George Hamilton, Dolores Hart, Yvette Mimieux. 99M USA. prod/rel: MGM, Euterpe
  Where the Boys are '84 1984 d: Hy Averback. lps: Lisa Hartman, Russell Todd, Lorna Luft. 97M USA. prod/rel: Tri-Star

SWAYNE, MARTIN
Lord Richard in the Pantry, Novel
  Lord Richard in the Pantry 1930 d: Walter Forde. lps: Richard Cooper, Dorothy Seacombe, Marjorie Hume. 95M UKN. prod/rel: Twickenham, Warner Bros.

SWERDLOW, JOEL L.
To Heal a Nation, Book
  To Heal a Nation 1987 d: Michael Pressman. lps: Eric Roberts, Glynnis O'Connor, Marshall Colt. TVM. 100M USA. prod/rel: Daniuel Films

SWERLING, JOSEPH
The Kibitzer, New York 1929, Play
  Kibitzer, The 1930 d: Edward Sloman. lps: Harry Green, Mary Brian, Neil Hamilton. 7273f USA. *Busybody* (UKN) prod/rel: Paramount Famous Lasky Corp.
One of Us, New York 1918, Play
  Love Burglar, The 1919 d: James Cruze. lps: Wallace Reid, Anna Q. Nilsson, Raymond Hatton. 4467f USA. prod/rel: Famous Players-Lasky Corp.©, Paramount Pictures
The Understander, Play
  Melody Lane 1929 d: Robert F. Hill. lps: Eddie Leonard, Josephine Dunn, Rose Coe. 6760f USA. prod/rel: Universal Pictures

SWIFT, GRAHAM
Waterland, Novel
  Waterland 1992 d: Stephen Gyllenhaal. lps: Jeremy Irons, Sinead Cusack, Ethan Hawke. 95M UKN. prod/rel: Mayfair Entertainment, Palace Pictures

SWIFT, JONATHAN (1667–1745), IRL
Gulliver's Travels, London 1726, Novel
  Gulliver's Travels 1939 d: Dave Fleischer. ANM. 74M USA. prod/rel: Paramount
  Gulliver's Travels 1977 d: Peter Hunt. lps: Richard Harris, Catherine Schell, Norman Shelley. 80M UKN/BLG. prod/rel: Emi, Valeness-Belvision
  Gulliver's Travels 1979 d: Chris Cuddington. ANM. 47M USA. prod/rel: Hanna-Barbera
  Gulliver's Travels 1996 d: Charles Sturridge. lps: Ted Danson, Mary Steenburgen, James Fox. TVM. 240M USA/UKN.
  Novyi Gulliver 1935 d: Alexander Ptushko. ANM. 85M USS. *A New Gulliver*
  Pripad Pro Zacinajiciho Kata 1969 d: Pavel Juracek. lps: Lubomir Kostelka, Pavel Landovsky, Klara JernekovA. 100M CZC. *A Case for the New Hangman; A Case for a Young Hangman*
  Three Worlds of Gulliver, The 1960 d: Jack Sher. lps: Kerwin Mathews, Jo Morrow, June Thorburn. 98M UKN/USA/SPN. *The 3 Worlds of Gulliver* prod/rel: Columbia, Morningside
  Viajes de Gulliver, Los 1983 d: Cruz Delgado, Antonio de Font. ANM. 77M SPN. *Gulliver's Travels Part 2; Land of the Giants: Gulliver's Travels Part 2*

SWIFT, KAY
Who Could Ask for Anything More, 1943, Novel
  Never a Dull Moment 1950 d: George Marshall. lps: Irene Dunne, Fred MacMurray, William Demarest. 89M USA. *Come Share My Love* prod/rel: RKO Radio

SWIGGETT, HAROLD
The Power and the Prize, 1954, Novel
  Power and the Prize, The 1956 d: Henry Koster. lps: Robert Taylor, Cedric Hardwicke, Elisabeth Muller. 98M USA. prod/rel: MGM

SYKES, PERCIVAL H. T.
An Affair of Honour, Play
  Affair of Honour, An 1904 d: Alf Collins. lps: Percy Murray. 250f UKN. prod/rel: Gaumont

SYLVAINE, VERNON
Aren't Men Beasts!, London 1936, Play
  Aren't Men Beasts! 1937 d: Graham Cutts. lps: Robertson Hare, Alfred Drayton, June Clyde. 66M UKN. prod/rel: British International Pictures, Associated British Picture Corporation
As Long As They're Happy, London 1953, Play
  As Long As They're Happy 1955 d: J. Lee Thompson. lps: Jack Buchanan, Jeannie Carson, Janette Scott. 91M UKN. prod/rel: Group Films, Raymond Stross
Madame Louise, London 1945, Play
  Madame Louise 1951 d: MacLean Rogers. lps: Richard Hearne, Petula Clark, Garry Marsh. 83M UKN. prod/rel: Nettlefold, Butcher's Film Service

One Wild Oat, London 1948, Play
  One Wild Oat 1951 d: Charles Saunders. lps: Robertson Hare, Stanley Holloway, Sam CostA. 78M UKN. prod/rel: Coronet, Eros
A Spot of Bother, London 1937, Play
  Spot of Bother, A 1938 d: David MacDonald. lps: Robertson Hare, Alfred Drayton, Sandra Storme. 70M UKN. prod/rel: Pinebrook, General Film Distributors
Warn That Man, Play
  Warn That Man 1943 d: Lawrence Huntington. lps: Gordon Harker, Raymond Lovell, Finlay Currie. 82M UKN. prod/rel: Associated British Picture Corporation, Pathe
Will Any Gentleman?, London 1950, Play
  Will Any Gentleman? 1953 d: Michael Anderson. lps: George Cole, Veronica Hurst, Jon Pertwee. 84M UKN. prod/rel: Associated British Picture Corporation, Ab-Pathe
Women Aren't Angels, Play
  Women Aren't Angels 1942 d: Lawrence Huntington. lps: Robertson Hare, Alfred Drayton, Polly Ward. 85M UKN. prod/rel: Associated British Picture Corporation, Pathe

SYLVANE, ANDRE
Tire-Au-Flanc!, Paris 1904, Play
  Tire Au Flanc 1912. lps: Armand Morins, Coquet, Andree Coquet. 410m FRN.
  Tire Au Flanc 1928 d: Jean Renoir. lps: Georges Pomies, Michel Simon, Fridette Fatton. 2000m FRN. *Tire-Au-Flanc* prod/rel: Neo Films, Pierre Braunberger
  Tire Au Flanc 1933 d: Henry Wulschleger. lps: Bach, Felix Oudart, Germaine Lix. 103M FRN. prod/rel: Pierre Braunberger, Alex Nalpas
  Tire-Au-Flanc 1961 d: Francois Truffaut, Claude de Givray. lps: Christian de Tiliere, Ricet Barrier, Jacques Balutin. 87M FRN. *The Army Game* (USA); *The Sad Sack; Tire Au Flanc 62* prod/rel: S.E.D.I.F., Films Du Carrosse

SYLVESTER, ROBERT
The Big Boodle, 1954, Novel
  Big Boodle, The 1956 d: Richard Wilson. lps: Errol Flynn, Rossana Rory, Gia ScalA. 83M USA. *Night in Havana* (UKN) prod/rel: United Artists Corp., Monteflor
Rough Sketch, Novel
  We Were Strangers 1949 d: John Huston. lps: Jennifer Jones, John Garfield, Gilbert Roland. 106M USA. *Rough Sketch* prod/rel: Columbia

SYMONS, JULIAN (1912–, UKN, Symons, Julian Gustave
Criss Cross Code, Novel
  Counterspy 1953 d: Vernon Sewell. lps: Dermot Walsh, Hazel Court, Hermione Baddeley. 88M UKN. *Undercover Agent* (USA) prod/rel: Merton Park, Anglo-Amalgamated
The Narrowing Circle, Novel
  Narrowing Circle, The 1956 d: Charles Saunders. lps: Paul Carpenter, Hazel Court, Russell Napier. 66M UKN. prod/rel: Fortress Films, Eros

SYNEK, EMIL
Mimo Proud, Play
  Karel Hynek MacHa 1937 d: Zet Molas. lps: Ladislav Bohac, Karla Olicova, Eva GerovA. 3030m CZC. prod/rel: Triglav, Kinofilm Brno
Vydelecne Zeny, Play
  Vydelecne Zeny 1937 d: Rolf WankA. lps: Rolf Wanka, Marta Majova, Bedrich VeverkA. 2397m CZC. *Working Women* prod/rel: Beda Heller

SYNGE, JOHN MILLINGTON (1871–1909), IRL
The Playboy of the Western World, Dublin 1907, Play
  Playboy of the Western World, The 1962 d: Brian Desmond Hurst. lps: Siobhan McKenna, Gary Raymond, Elspeth March. 100M UKN. prod/rel: Four Provinces Films, British Lion
Riders to the Sea, London 1904, Play
  Riders to the Sea 1935 d: Brian Desmond Hurst. lps: Sara Allgood, Denis Johnstone, Kevin Guthrie. 40M UKN. prod/rel: Flanagan-Hurst, MGM
  Riders to the Sea 1987 d: Ronan O'Leary. 46M IRL.

SYRETT, NETTA
Portrait of a Rebel, New York 1930, Novel
  Woman Rebels, A 1936 d: Mark Sandrich. lps: Katharine Hepburn, Herbert Marshall, Elizabeth Allan. 90M USA. *Portrait of a Rebel* prod/rel: RKO Radio Pictures©, Pandro S. Berman Production

SZABO, PAL
Bolcso, Novel
  Talpalatnyi Fold 1948 d: Frigyes Ban. lps: Adam Szirtes, Agi Meszaros, Viola Orban. 105M HNG. *The Soil Under Your Feet; Treasured Earth*

Keresztelo, 1943, Novel
  Talpalatnyi Fold 1948 d: Frigyes Ban. lps: Adam Szirtes, Agi Meszaros, Viola Orban. 105M HNG. *The Soil Under Your Feet; Treasured Earth*
Lakodalom, 1942, Novel
  Talpalatnyi Fold 1948 d: Frigyes Ban. lps: Adam Szirtes, Agi Meszaros, Viola Orban. 105M HNG. *The Soil Under Your Feet; Treasured Earth*

SZCZEPANSKI, MICHAL
Story
  Girl Guide 1995 d: Juliusz MacHulski. lps: Renata Gabrielska, Pawel Kukiz, Tomasz Tomaszewski. F PLN. prod/rel: Close Up Productions, Tvp S.a.

SZCZEPKOWSKA, MARJA MOROZOWICZ
Play
  Dr. Monica 1934 d: William Keighley, William Dieterle (Uncredited). lps: Kay Francis, Jean Muir, Warren William. 65M USA. *The Affairs of Monica; When Tomorrow Comes* prod/rel: Warner Bros. Pictures, Inc.
Femmes, Novel
  Femmes 1936 d: Bernard-Roland. lps: Jadwiga Andrzejewska, Jeanne Boitel, Henri Rollan. F FRN. prod/rel: Spardice

SZCZYGIEL, JERZY
Milczenie, Novel
  Milczenie 1963 d: Kazimierz Kutz. lps: Zbigniew Cybulski, Kazimierz Fabisiak, Miroslaw Kobierzycki. 94M PLN. *The Silence* (UKN) prod/rel: K.a.D.R.

SZEKELY, HANS
Manolescu, Short Story
  Manolescu 1929 d: Victor Tourjansky. lps: Ivan Mosjoukine, Brigitte Helm, Dita Parlo. 3116m GRM. *Der Konig Der Hochstapler* prod/rel: UFA
Le Mensonge de Nina Petrovna, Novel
  Mensonge de Nina Petrovna, La 1937 d: Victor Tourjansky. lps: Isa Miranda, Gabrielle Dorziat, Fernand Gravey. 108M FRN. *The Lie of Nina Petrovna* (USA); *Nina Petrovna* prod/rel: Solar Films
Die Schonen Tage von Aranjuez, Play
  Adieu Les Beaux Jours 1933 d: Johannes Meyer, Andre Beucler. lps: Jean Gabin, Brigitte Helm, Henri Bosc. 96M FRN. *Les Beaux Jours d'Aranjuez* prod/rel: U.F.a.
  Desire 1936 d: Frank Borzage. lps: Marlene Dietrich, Gary Cooper, John Halliday. 99M USA. prod/rel: Paramount Productions, Inc.
  Schonen Tage von Aranjuez, Die 1933 d: Johannes Meyer. lps: Brigitte Helm, Gustaf Grundgens, Wolfgang Liebeneiner. F GRM.
School of Drama, Play
  Dramatic School 1938 d: Robert B. Sinclair. lps: Luise Rainer, Paulette Goddard, Alan Marshal. 80M USA. prod/rel: MGM, Loew's, Inc.©

SZEKELY-LULOFS, M. H.
Rubber, Novel
  Rubber 1936 d: Gerard Rutten, Johan de Meester. lps: Jules Verstraet, Frits Van Dongen, Enny Meunier. 106M NTH.

SZEP, ERNO
Aranyora, 1931, Play
  Aranyora, Az 1945 d: Akos von Rathony. lps: Eva Szorenyi, Gyula Gozon, Zoltan Varkonyi. 91M HNG. *The Gold Watch*
Lila Akac, 1919, Short Story
  Lila Akac 1934 d: Steve Sekely. lps: Iren Agai, Nusi Somogyi, Gyula Csortos. 76M HNG. *The Girl Who Liked Purple Flowers; Wisteria*
  Lila Akac 1973 d: Steve Sekely. lps: Judit Halasz, Andras Balint, Imre Raday. 89M HNG. *The Girl Who Liked Purple Flowers*
Volegeny, 1922, Play
  Volegeny 1982 d: Laszlo Vamos. 92M HNG. *The Bridegroom*

SZERB, ANTAL
A Pendragon Legenda, 1934, Novel
  Pendragon Legenda, A 1974 d: Gyorgy Revesz. lps: Zoltan Latinovits, Ivan Darvas, Teri Tordai. 101M HNG. *The Pendragon Legend* prod/rel: Mafilm Budapest Filmstudioi

SZIGLIGETI, EDE
Liliomfi, 1849, Play
  Liliomfi 1954 d: Karoly Makk. lps: Samu Balazs, Margit Dayka, Marianne Krencsey. 125M HNG.

SZILAGYI, LADISLAUS
Die Katz' Im Sack, Play
  Quadrille d'Amour 1934 d: Germain Fried, Richard Eichberg. lps: Pierre Brasseur, Irene de Zilahy, Mady Berry. 95M FRN. prod/rel: Societe Internationale Cinematographique

SZILAGYI, STEVE
Photographing Fairies, Book
  Photographing Fairies 1997 d: Nick Willing. lps: Toby Stephens, Emily Woof, Frances Barber. 106M UKN. prod/rel: Starry Night Film Company Ltd., Polygram Filmed Entertainment

SZITNYAI, ZOLTAN NAGYIVANYI
Una Piccola Moglie, Novel
  Piccola Moglie, Una 1944 d: Giorgio Bianchi. lps: Assia Noris, Fosco Giachetti, Clara Calamai. 76M ITL. prod/rel: S.a.N.G.R.a.F.

SZOMAHAZY, STEFAN
Novel
  Dactylo 1931 d: Wilhelm Thiele. lps: Jean Murat, Marie Glory, Armand Bernard. 77M FRN. prod/rel: Pathe-Natan
Die Privatsekretarin, Novel
  Privatsekretarin, Die 1931 d: Wilhelm Thiele. lps: Renate Muller, Hermann Thimig, Felix Bressart. 85M GRM. *The Private Secretary*
  Privatsekretarin, Die 1953 d: Paul Martin. lps: Rudolf Prack, Sonja Ziemann, Paul Horbiger. 90M GRM. *Private Secretary* prod/rel: C.C.C., Gloria
  Segretaria Privata, La 1931 d: Goffredo Alessandrini. lps: Elsa Merlini, Nino Besozzi, Sergio Tofano. 78M ITL. prod/rel: Cines, Anonima Pittaluga
  Sunshine Susie 1932 d: Victor Saville. lps: Renate Muller, Jack Hulbert, Owen Nares. 87M UKN. *The Office Girl* (USA) prod/rel: Gainsborough, Ideal

SZPINER, FRANCIS
Story
  Affaire de Femmes, Une 1988 d: Claude Chabrol. lps: Isabelle Huppert, Francois Cluzet, Marie Trintignant. 110M FRN. *A Story of Women* prod/rel: Mk 2, Films a2

T

TABER, RICHARD
Is Zat So?, New York 1925, Play
  Is Zat So? 1927 d: Alfred E. Green. lps: George O'Brien, Edmund Lowe, Kathryn Perry. 6950f USA. prod/rel: Fox Film Corp.
  Two Fisted 1935 d: James Cruze. lps: Lee Tracy, Grace Bradley, Kent Taylor. 65M USA. *Two-Fisted; Gettin' Smart* prod/rel: Paramount Productions©

TABET, ANDRE
On Demande un Assassin, Play
  On Demande un Assassin 1949 d: Ernst Neubach. lps: Fernandel, Noelle Norman, Felix Oudart. 90M FRN. prod/rel: P.E.N. Films, Cinema Productions

TABORI, GEORGE
The Doubters, Novel
  Crisis 1950 d: Richard Brooks. lps: Cary Grant, Jose Ferrer, Paula Raymond. 96M USA. prod/rel: MGM
My Mother's Courage, Novel
  My Mother's Courage 1995 d: Michael Verhoeven. lps: Pauline Collins, Ulrich Tukur, Natalie Morse. 92M UKN/GRM. *Mutters Courage* (GRM) prod/rel: Sentana Film, Little Bird
The Prince, Play
  Leo the Last 1970 d: John Boorman. lps: Marcello Mastroianni, Billie Whitelaw, Calvin Lockhart. 104M UKN. prod/rel: Char-Wink-Boor Productions, United Artists

TABUCCHI, ANTONIO
Il Fillo Dell'Orizonte, Novel
  Fil de l'Horizon, Le 1993 d: Fernando Lopes. lps: Claude Brasseur, Andrea Ferreol, Antonio Valero. 90M FRN/PRT/SPN. *O Fio Do Horizonte* (PRT); *La Linea Del Horizonte; Line of the Horizon; No Linha Do Horizonte* prod/rel: Films Do Principe Real, Ctn
Nocturne Indienne, Novel
  Nocturne Indien 1988 d: Alain Corneau. lps: Jean-Hugues Anglade, Clementine Celarie, Otto Tausig. 109M FRN. *Indian Nocturne* prod/rel: Sofinergie, Sara
Requiem, Novel
  Requiem 1998 d: Alain Tanner. lps: Francis Frappat, Andre Marcon, Alexandre Zloto. 99M SWT/FRN/PRT. prod/rel: Cab Production, Filmograph

TAGORE, RABINDRANATH (1861–1941), IND
Atithi, 1895, Short Story
  Atithi 1965 d: Tapan SinhA. lps: Partha Mukherji, Basabi Banerji, Samita Biswas. 105M IND. *The Runaway* (UKN); *The Guest*

Balidan, Play
  Balidan 1927 d: Naval Gandhi. lps: Sulochana, Zubeida, Master Vithal. 8282f IND. *Bisarjan; Sacrifice* prod/rel: Orient Pictures
Ghaire Bhaire, 1916, Novel
  Ghare Bhaire 1983 d: Satyajit Ray. lps: Soumitra Chatterjee, Victor Banerjee, Swatilekha Chatterjee. 140M IND. *The Home and the World* (USA) prod/rel: Nfdc
Kabulibala, 1892, Short Story
  Kabuliwala 1956 d: Tapan SinhA. lps: Chhabi Biswas, Tinku Thakur, Radhamohan BhattacharyA. 116M IND. *The Man from Kabul; The Merchant from Kabul* prod/rel: Charuchitra
Kshudhita Pasan, 1910, Short Story
  Kshudita Pashan 1960 d: Tapan SinhA. lps: Soumitra Chatterjee, Arundhati Devi, Radhamohan BhattacharyA. 117M IND. *Hungry Stones* prod/rel: Eastern Circuit
Malyadaan, 1903, Short Story
  Malayadaan 1971 d: Ajay Kar. lps: Bhanu Bannerjee, Soumitra Chatterjee. 113M IND. *The Gift of the Garland; Malyadan; Malaadaan*
Monihara, Short Story
  Teen Kanya 1961 d: Satyajit Ray. lps: Anil Chatterjee, Chandana Bannerjee, Nripati Chatterjee. 171M IND. *Two Daughters* (USA); *Three Daughters; Three Women; Samapti* prod/rel: Satyajit Ray Productions
Nastaneer, 1901, Novel
  Charulata 1964 d: Satyajit Ray. lps: Soumitra Chatterjee, Madhabi Mukherjee, Sailen Mukherjee. 117M IND. *The Lonely Wife* (UKN); *The Lonely Woman; Nashta Neerh* prod/rel: R.D.B.
Nauka Dubi, 1916, Novel
  Milan 1946 d: Nitin Bose. lps: Dilip Kumar, Ranjana, Meera MishrA. 144M IND. *Union* prod/rel: Bombay Talkies
  Nauka Dubi 1946 d: Nitin Bose. lps: Abhi Bhattacharya, Meera Sarkar, Meera MishrA. 147M IND. *Sunken Boat; Naukadubi* prod/rel: Bombay Talkies
Postsmastar, Short Story
  Teen Kanya 1961 d: Satyajit Ray. lps: Anil Chatterjee, Chandana Bannerjee, Nripati Chatterjee. 171M IND. *Two Daughters* (USA); *Three Daughters; Three Women; Samapti* prod/rel: Satyajit Ray Productions
Samapti, Short Story
  Teen Kanya 1961 d: Satyajit Ray. lps: Anil Chatterjee, Chandana Bannerjee, Nripati Chatterjee. 171M IND. *Two Daughters* (USA); *Three Daughters; Three Women; Samapti* prod/rel: Satyajit Ray Productions
Strir Patra, c1916, Short Story
  Streer Patra 1972 d: Purnendu PattreA. lps: Madhabi Mukherjee. 98M IND. *Letter from the Wife; Strir Patra*

TAIJIRO, TAMURA
Shumpu-Den, Novel
  Shunpu-Den 1965 d: Seijun Suzuki. lps: Tamio Kawachi, Yumiko Nogawa, Isao TamagawA. 96M JPN. *Shumpuden; Joy Girls; Story of a Prostitute* prod/rel: Nikkatsu Corporation

TAJ, IMTIAZ ALI
Anarkali, Play
  Loves of a Mughal Prince, The 1928 d: Charu Chandra Roy, Prafulla Roy. lps: Prafulla Roy, Seeta Devi, Maya Devi. 9525f IND. prod/rel: Great Eastern Film

TAKAGI, TOSHIKO
Garasu No Usagi, Novel
  Garasu No Usagi 1979 d: Yuten TachibanA. lps: Yukiko Ebina, Hiroyuki Nagato, Aiko NagayamA. 102M JPN. *Glass Rabbit* prod/rel: Daiei Eizo Co. Ltd.

TAKAYAMA, MICHIO
Biruma No Tategoto, 1948, Novel
  Biruma No Tate Goto 1985 d: Kon IchikawA. lps: Koji Ishizaka, Niichi Nakai, Takuzo Kawatani. MTV. 133M JPN. *The Burmese Harp* prod/rel: Fuji Television Network, Hakuhodo, Inc.
  Biruma No Tategoto 1956 d: Kon IchikawA. lps: Rentaro Mikuni, Shoji Yasui, Tatsuya Mihashi. 143M JPN. *The Burmese Harp* (UKN); *The Harp of Burma* prod/rel: Nikkatsu Corp.

TAKEDA, IZUMO
Kanadehon Chushingura, 1748, Play
  Chushingura 1962 d: Hiroshi Inagaki. lps: Koshiro Matsumoto, Yuzo Kayama, Chusha IchikawA. 204M JPN. *The Loyal Forty-Seven Ronin; The Faithful 47; The 47 Ronin; 47 Samurai* prod/rel: Toho Co.

TAKEDA, TAIJUN
Hakuchu No Torima, 1960, Short Story
  Hakuchu No Torima 1966 d: Nagisa OshimA. lps: Kei Sato, Saeda Kawaguchi, Akiko KoyamA. 99M JPN. *Violence at High Noon; Violence at Noon; Phantom Killer*
Hikarigoke, Novel
  Hikarigoke 1991 d: Kei Kumai. lps: Rentaro Mikuni, Eiji Okada, Kunie TanakA. 118M JPN. *Shiny Moss* prod/rel: Film Crescent, Neo-Life
Runinto Nite, 1953, Short Story
  Shokei No Shima 1966 d: Masahiro ShinodA. lps: Rentaro Mikuni, Shima Iwashita, Akira NittA. 87M JPN. *Punishment Island; Captive's Island*

TAKIGUCHI, YASUHIKO
Haiyo Zuma Shimatsu Yori, Short Story
  Joiuchi - Hairyozuma Shimatsu 1967 d: Masaki Kobayashi. lps: Toshiro Mifune, Takeshi Kato, Tatsuyoshi EharA. 128M JPN. *Samurai Rebellion; Rebellion* (USA); *Joi-Uchi* prod/rel: Toho Co., Mifune Productions
Ibunronin Ki, 1958, Short Story
  Seppuku 1962 d: Masaki Kobayashi. lps: Tatsuya Nakadai, Shima Iwashita, Akira IshihamA. 134M JPN. *Harakiri* (UKN); *Hara-Kiri* prod/rel: Shochiku Co.

TALBOT, HAYDEN
It Is the Law, New York 1922, Play
  It Is the Law 1924 d: J. Gordon Edwards. lps: Arthur Hohl, Herbert Heyes, Mimi Palmeri. 6895f USA. prod/rel: Fox Film Corp.
The Truth Wagon, New York 1912, Play
  Truth Wagon, The 1914 d: Max Figman. lps: Max Figman, Lolita Robertson, Al W. Filson. 5r USA. prod/rel: Masterpiece Film Manufacturing Co., Alliance Films Corp.

TALBOT, MONROE
Last of the Clintons, Short Story
  Last of the Clintons 1935 d: Harry L. Fraser. lps: Harry Carey, Betty MacK, Del Gordon. 64M USA. prod/rel: Astor Pictures Corp., State Rights

TALESE, GAY (1932–, USA
Honor Thy Father, Novel
  Honor Thy Father 1971 d: Paul Wendkos. lps: Joseph Bologna, Brenda Vaccaro, Raf Vallone. TVM. 100M USA. prod/rel: Metromedia Productions

TALEV, DIMITAR
Zhelezniyat Svetilnik, 1952, Novel
  Ikonostasat 1968 d: Hristo Hristov, Todor Dinov. lps: Dimiter Tashev, Emilia Radeva, Violetta GindevA. 100M BUL. *Iconostasis*

TALMI, MENACHEM
Story
  Fille de la Mer Morte, La 1966 d: Menahem Golan. lps: Pierre Brasseur, Saro Urzi, Mike Marshall. 90M FRN/ISR. *Seduced in Sodom* (UKN); *The Girl from the Dead Sea; Fortuna* (ISR)

TAMARO, SUSANNA
Va Dove Ti Porta Il Cuore, Novel
  Va Dove Ti Porta Il Cuore 1996 d: Cristina Comencini. lps: Virna Lisi, Margherita Buy, Galatea Ranzi. 102M ITL/FRN/GRM. *Follow Your Heart* prod/rel: Videa

TAMASI, ARON
Tundoklo Jeromos, 1941, Play
  Mezei Profeta 1947 d: Frigyes Ban. lps: Eva Bartok, Gyula Benko, Jozsef Bihary. 90M HNG. *The Prophet of the Field*

TAMAYO Y BAUS, MANUEL
Un Drama Nuevo, 1867, Play
  Drama Nuevo, Un 1946 d: Juan de OrdunA. lps: Maria Canete, Irasema Dilian, Roberto Font. 92M SPN. *A New Drama*
La Locura de Amor, 1855, Play
  Locura de Amor 1948 d: Juan de OrdunA. lps: Aurora Bautista, Fernando Rey, Sara Montiel. 120M SPN. *The Mad Queen; Madness of Love*

TAMIMI, SARGON
The Hawk, Story
  Captive Hearts 1987 d: Paul Almond. lps: Pat Morita, Chris Makepeace, Mari Sato. 97M USA/CND. *Fate of the Hunter* prod/rel: MGM, United Artists

TAMIYA, TORAHIKO
Ibo Kyodai, 1957, Short Story
  Ibo Kyodai 1957 d: Miyoji Ieki. lps: Kinuyo TanakA. 110M JPN. *Brothers Born of Different Mothers; Stepbrothers*

TAMURA, TAJIRO
Nikutai No Mon, 1947, Novel
  Nikutai No Mon 1948 d: Masahiro Makino. F JPN. *Gate of Flesh*

Nikutai No Mon 1964 d: Seijun Suzuki. lps: Yumiko Nogawa, Kayo Matsuo, Misako TominagA. 90M JPN. *Gate of Flesh* (USA) prod/rel: Nikkatsu Corporation

TAN, AMY
The Joy Luck Club, Novel
Joy Luck Club, The 1993 d: Wayne Wang. lps: Kieu Chinh, Tsai Chin, France Nuyen. 139M USA. prod/rel: Buena Vista Pictures, Hollywood Pictures

TANENBAUM, ROBERT J.
Badge of the Assassin, Book
Badge of the Assassin 1985 d: Mel Damski. lps: James Woods, Yaphet Kotto, Alex Rocco. TVM. 100M USA. prod/rel: CBS, Columbia

TANI, TOSHIHIKO
The Kimura Family, Short Story
Kimura-Ke No Hitobito 1988 d: Yojiro TakitA. lps: Kaori Momoi, Takeshi Kaga, Hiromi Iwasaki. 113M JPN. *The Yen Family*

TANIZAKI, JUNICHIRO (1886–1965), JPN
Alsureba Koso, 1923, Play
Daraku Suru Onna 1967 d: Kozaburo YoshimurA. lps: Miyuki Kuwano, Toshiyuki Hosokawa, Takahiro TamurA. 100M JPN. *A Corrupted Woman*; *A Fallen Woman*

Ashikari, 1932, Novel
Oyu-Sama 1951 d: Kenji Mizoguchi. lps: Kinuyo Tanaka, Yuji Hori, Kiyoko Hirai. 96M JPN. *Miss Oyu* (USA)

Chijin No Ai, 1924, Novel
Chijin No Ai 1967 d: Yasuzo MasumurA. lps: Michiyo Yasuda, Shoichi Ozawa, Masakazu TamurA. 92M JPN. *An Idiot in Love* prod/rel: Daiei

Hakujitsumu Yume, 1926, Short Story
Hakujitsumu 1964 d: Tetsuji Takechi. lps: Kanako Michi, Akira Ishihama, Chojuro HanakawA. 92M JPN. *Day-Dream* (USA) prod/rel: Daisan Productions

Kagi, Tokyo 1956, Novel
Chiave, La 1984 d: Tinto Brass. lps: Stefania Sandrelli, Frank Finlay, Barbara Cupisti. 116M ITL. *The Key* (UKN) prod/rel: San Francisco Film, Selenia Cinematografica
Kagi 1959 d: Kon IchikawA. lps: MacHiko Kyo, Ganjiro Nakamura, Junko Kano. 107M JPN. *Odd Obsessions* (UKN); *The Key* (USA); *Odd Obsession* prod/rel: Daiei Motion Picture Co.
Kagi 1998 d: Toshiharu IkedA. lps: Naomi Kawashima, Akira Emoto, Mikio OsawA. 95M JPN. *The Key* prod/rel: Tohokushinsha Film Co., Toei Co.

Manji, 1930, Novel
Interno Berlinese 1985 d: Liliana Cavani. lps: Gudrun Landgrebe, Kevin McNally, Mio Takaki. 121M ITL/GRM. *Leidenschaften* (GRM); *Affaire Berlinese*; *Berlin Interior*; *Berlin Affair* prod/rel: Cannon Productions (Roma), Kinofilm (Munich)
Manji 1964 d: Yasuzo MasumurA. lps: Ayako Wakao, Kyoko Kishida, Yusuke Kuwasu. 91M JPN. *Passion* (UKN); *All Mixed Up* prod/rel: Daiei Motion Picture Co.

Neko to Shozo to Futari No Onna, 1937, Novel
Neko to Shozo to Futari No Onna 1956 d: Shiro ToyodA. lps: Isuzu YamadA. 107M JPN. *Shozo a Cat and Two Women*; *A Cat Shozo and Two Women*; *A Cat and Two Women*

Okuni to Gohei, 1922, Play
Okuni to Gohei 1952 d: Mikio Naruse. 91M JPN. *Okuni and Gohei*

Sasame Yuki, 1948, Novel
Sasameyuki 1983 d: Kon IchikawA. lps: Yoshiko Sakuma, Keiko Kishi, Sayuri YoshinagA. 140M JPN. *Fine Snow*; *The Makioka Sisters*; *Gentle Snow*; *Sasa Meyuki* prod/rel: Toho-Eizo Co.

Shunkin-Sho, 1933, Novel
Shunkin Monogatari 1954 d: Daisuke Ito. 110M JPN. *Story of Shunkin*

TANNER, JAMES T.
The Broken Melody, London 1892, Play
Broken Melody, The 1929 d: Fred Paul. lps: Georges Galli, Audree Sayre, Enid Stamp-Taylor. SIL. 6414f UKN. prod/rel: Welsh-Pearson-Elder, Paramount

Our Miss Gibbs, London 1909, Musical Play
Gaiety Duet, A 1909 d: Arthur Gilbert. lps: George Grossmith, Madge Melbourne, Edmund Payne. 610f UKN. prod/rel: Gaumont

TANUGI, GILBERT
Saxo, Novel
Saxo 1987 d: Ariel Zeitoun. lps: Gerard Lanvin, Akosua Busia, Richard Brooks. 114M FRN. prod/rel: Partners, Canal Plus

TAO CHENG
My Family, Autobiography
Geming Jiaying 1960 d: Shui HuA. lps: Yu Lan, Sun Daolin, Zhang Liang. 11r CHN. *A Revolutionary Family* prod/rel: Beijing Film Studio

TARCHETTI, IGNIO UGO
Fosca, Novel
Passione d'Amore 1981 d: Ettore ScolA. lps: Bernard Giraudeau, Laura Antonelli, Valeria d'Obici. 118M ITL/FRN. *Passions of Love* (USA); *Passion d'Amour* (FRN); *Passion of Love* prod/rel: Rizzoli Films, Massfilm

TARKINGTON, BOOTH (1869–1946), USA
Story
Geraldine 1929 d: Melville Brown. lps: Marian Nixon, Eddie Quillan, Albert Gran. 5959f USA. prod/rel: Pathe Exchange, Inc.

Alice Adams, New York 1921, Novel
Alice Adams 1923 d: Rowland V. Lee. lps: Florence Vidor, Claude Gillingwater, Harold Goodwin. 6361f USA. *Foolish Daughters* prod/rel: Encore Pictures, Associated Exhibitors
Alice Adams 1935 d: George Stevens. lps: Katharine Hepburn, Fred MacMurray, Fred Stone. 95M USA. prod/rel: RKO Radio Pictures, Inc.

Beasley's Christmas Party, Story
Sophia's Imaginary Visitors 1914 d: Walter Edwin. lps: Marc McDermott, Miriam Nesbitt, Mrs. William Bechtel. 1000f USA. prod/rel: Edison

Beau Brummell, Novel
Beau Brummel 1913 d: James Young. lps: James Young, Julia Swayne Gordon, Clara Kimball Young. 1000f USA. prod/rel: Vitagraph Co. of America

Boy of Mine, Story
Boy of Mine 1923 d: William Beaudine. lps: Ben Alexander, Rockliffe Fellowes, Henry B. Walthall. 6935f USA. prod/rel: J. K. Mcdonald, Associated First National Pictures

Cameo Kirby, New York 1909, Play
Cameo Kirby 1915 d: Oscar Apfel. lps: Dustin Farnum, Frederick Montague, Dick La Reno. 5r USA. prod/rel: Jesse L. Lasky Feature Play Co.©, Paramount Pictures Corp.
Cameo Kirby 1923 d: John Ford. lps: John Gilbert, Gertrude Olmstead, Alan Hale. 6931f USA. prod/rel: Fox Film Corp.
Cameo Kirby 1930 d: Irving Cummings. lps: J. Harold Murray, Norma Terris, Douglas Gilmore. 5910f USA. prod/rel: Fox Film Corp.

Cherry, Short Story
Cherry 1914 d: James Young. lps: Lillian Walker, Billy Quirk, Hughie MacK. SHT USA. prod/rel: Vitagraph Co. of America

Clarence, New York 1919, Play
Clarence 1922 d: William C. de Mille. lps: Wallace Reid, Agnes Ayres, May McAvoy. 6146f USA. prod/rel: Famous Players-Lasky, Paramount Pictures
Clarence 1937 d: George Archainbaud. lps: Roscoe Karns, Johnny Downs, Eleanore Whitney. 64M USA. prod/rel: Paramount Pictures, Inc.

The Conquest of Canaan, New York 1905, Novel
Conquest of Canaan, The 1916 d: George Irving. lps: Edith Taliaferro, Jack Sherill, Ralph Delmore. 5-6r USA. prod/rel: Frohman Amusement Corp., State Rights
Conquest of Canaan, The 1921 d: R. William Neill. lps: Thomas Meighan, Doris Kenyon, Diana Allen. 7r USA. prod/rel: Famous Players-Lasky, Paramount Pictures

The Country Cousin, New York 1917, Play
Country Cousin, The 1919 d: Alan Crosland. lps: Elaine Hammerstein, Lumsden Hare, Bigelow Cooper. 5279f USA. prod/rel: Selznick Pictures Corp.©, Select Pictures Corp.

The Flirt, New York 1913, Novel
Bad Sister 1931 d: Hobart Henley. lps: Conrad Nagel, Sidney Fox, Bette Davis. 71M USA. *Gambling Daughters* prod/rel: Universal Pictures Corp.
Flirt, The 1916 d: Lois Weber, Phillips Smalley. lps: Marie Walcamp, Grace Benham, Antrim Short. 5r USA. prod/rel: Bluebird Photoplays, Inc.©
Flirt, The 1922 d: Hobart Henley. lps: George Nichols, Lydia Knott, Eileen Percy. 8r USA. prod/rel: Universal Pictures

Gentle Julia, New York 1922, Novel
Gentle Julia 1923 d: Rowland V. Lee. lps: Bessie Love, Harold Goodwin, Frank Elliott. 5837f USA. prod/rel: Fox Film Corp.
Gentle Julia 1936 d: John G. Blystone. lps: Jane Withers, Tom Brown, Marsha Hunt. 63M USA. prod/rel: Twentieth Century-Fox Film Corp.©

The Gentleman from Indiana, New York 1899, Novel
Gentleman from Indiana, The 1915 d: Frank Lloyd. lps: Dustin Farnum, Winifred Kingston, Herbert Standing. 5r USA. prod/rel: Pallas Pictures, Pathe Exchange, Inc.

The Gibson Upright, Play
You Find It Everywhere 1921 d: Charles Horan. lps: Catherine Calvert, Herbert Rawlinson, Herbert Standing. 5r USA. *The Gibson Upright* prod/rel: Outlook Photoplays, Jans Film Service

Little Orvie, New York 1934, Novel
Little Orvie 1940 d: Ray McCarey. lps: Johnny Sheffield, Dorothy Tree, Ernest Truex. 66M USA. prod/rel: RKO Radio Pictures©

The Magnificent Ambersons, Garden City, N.Y. 1918, Novel
Magnificent Ambersons, The 1942 d: Orson Welles. lps: Tim Holt, Joseph Cotten, Dolores Costello. 88M USA. prod/rel: RKO Radio Pictures
Pampered Youth 1925 d: David Smith. lps: Cullen Landis, Ben Alexander, Allan Forrest. 6640f USA. *The Magnificent Ambersons* prod/rel: Vitagraph Co. of America

Magnolia, New York 1923, Play
Mississippi 1935 d: A. Edward Sutherland. lps: Bing Crosby, W. C. Fields, Joan Bennett. 80M USA. prod/rel: Paramount Productions©
River of Romance 1929 d: Richard Wallace. lps: Charles "Buddy" Rogers, Mary Brian, June Collyer. 7009f USA. *Magnolia* prod/rel: Paramount Famous Lasky Corp.
Fighting Coward, The 1924 d: James Cruze. lps: Ernest Torrence, Mary Astor, Noah Beery. 6501f USA. prod/rel: Famous Players-Lasky, Paramount Pictures

The Man from Home, Louisville, Ky. 1907, Play
Man from Home, The 1914 d: Cecil B. de Mille, Oscar Apfel. lps: Charles Richman, Theodore Roberts, James Neill. 5r USA. prod/rel: Jesse L. Lasky Feature Play Co.©, Paramount Pictures Corp.
Man from Home, The 1922 d: George Fitzmaurice. lps: James Kirkwood, Anna Q. Nilsson, Norman Kerry. 6700f UKN. prod/rel: Famous Players-Lasky, Paramount Pictures

Mister Antonio, Play
Mister Antonio 1929 d: James Flood, Frank Reicher. lps: Leo Carrillo, Virginia Valli, Gareth Hughes. 6978f USA. prod/rel: Tiffany-Stahl Productions

Monsieur Beaucaire, New York 1900, Short Story
Monsieur Beaucaire 1924 d: Sidney Olcott. lps: Rudolph Valentino, Bebe Daniels, Lois Wilson. 9932f USA. prod/rel: Famous Players-Lasky, Paramount Pictures
Monsieur Beaucaire 1946 d: George Marshall. lps: Bob Hope, Joan Caulfield, Patric Knowles. 93M USA. prod/rel: Paramount
Monte Carlo 1930 d: Ernst Lubitsch. lps: Jack Buchanan, Jeanette MacDonald, Zasu Pitts. 94M USA. prod/rel: Paramount-Publix Corp.

Old Fathers and Young Sons, Story
Father's Son 1931 d: William Beaudine. lps: Lewis Stone, Irene Rich, Leon Janney. 77M USA. prod/rel: First National Pictures©
Father's Son 1941 d: D. Ross Lederman. lps: John Litel, Frieda Inescort, Billy Dawson. 57M USA. prod/rel: Warner Bros.

Penrod, New York 1914, Novel
By the Light of the Silvery Moon 1953 d: David Butler. lps: Doris Day, Gordon MacRae, Leon Ames. 102M USA. prod/rel: Warner Bros.
Penrod 1922 d: Marshall Neilan. lps: Wesley Barry, Tully Marshall, Claire McDowell. 8037f USA. prod/rel: Marshall Neilan Productions, Associated First National Pictures
Penrod and His Twin Brother 1938 d: William McGann. lps: Billy Mauch, Bobby Mauch, Frank Craven. 68M USA. prod/rel: Warner Bros. Pictures©
Penrod's Double Trouble 1938 d: Lewis Seiler. lps: Billy Mauch, Bobby Mauch, Dick Purcell. 65M USA. prod/rel: Warner Bros. Pictures©

Penrod - His Complete Story, 1931, Novel
On Moonlight Bay 1951 d: Roy Del Ruth. lps: Doris Day, Gordon MacRae, Jack (4) Smith. 98M USA. prod/rel: Warner Bros.

Penrod and Sam, New York 1916, Novel
Penrod and His Twin Brother 1938 d: William McGann. lps: Billy Mauch, Bobby Mauch, Frank Craven. 68M USA. prod/rel: Warner Bros. Pictures©
Penrod and Sam 1923 d: William Beaudine. lps: Ben Alexander, Joe Butterworth, Buddy Messinger. 6275f USA. prod/rel: J. K. Mcdonald, Associated First National Pictures

Penrod and Sam 1931 d: William Beaudine. lps: Leon Janney, Junior Coghlan, Matt Moore. 71M USA. *The Adventures of Penrod and Sam* prod/rel: First National Pictures©

Penrod and Sam 1937 d: William McGann. lps: Billy Mauch, Frank Craven, Spring Byington. 64M USA. prod/rel: Warner Bros. Pictures©

Penrod's Double Trouble 1938 d: Lewis Seiler. lps: Billy Mauch, Bobby Mauch, Dick Purcell. 65M USA. prod/rel: Warner Bros. Pictures©

The Plutocrat, New York 1927, Novel
Business and Pleasure 1931 d: David Butler. lps: Will Rogers, Jetta Goudal, Joel McCreA. 76M USA. *The Plutocrat* prod/rel: Fox Film Corp.

Presenting Lily Mars, 1933, Novel
Presenting Lily Mars 1943 d: Norman Taurog. lps: Judy Garland, Van Heflin, Fay Bainter. 104M USA. prod/rel: MGM

Seventeen, New York 1913, Novel
Seventeen 1916 d: Robert G. VignolA. lps: Louise Huff, Jack Pickford, Winifred Allen. 5r USA. prod/rel: Famous Players Film Co.©, Paramount Pictures Corp.

Seventeen 1940 d: Louis King. lps: Jackie Cooper, Betty Field, Otto Kruger. 78M USA. prod/rel: Paramount Pictures©

Springtime, New York 1909, Play
Springtime 1915 d: Will S. Davis. lps: Florence Nash, Adele Ray, William H. Tooker. 5r USA. prod/rel: Life Photo Film Corp., Alco Film Corp.

The Turmoil, New York 1915, Novel
Turmoil, The 1916 d: Edgar Jones. lps: Valli Valli, George Le Guere, Charles Prince. 5r USA. prod/rel: Columbia Pictures Corp., Metro Pictures Corp.©

Turmoil, The 1924 d: Hobart Henley. lps: Emmett Corrigan, George Hackathorne, Edward Hearn. 6741f USA. prod/rel: Universal Pictures

The Two Vanrevels, Novel
Two Vanrevels, The 1914 d: Richard Ridgely. lps: Mabel Trunnelle, Herbert Prior, Bigelow Cooper. 2r USA. prod/rel: Edison

TARLOFF, FRANK
A Guide for the Married Man As Told to Frank Tarloff, Los Angeles 1967, Novel
Guide for the Married Man, A 1967 d: Gene Kelly. lps: Robert Morse, Walter Matthau, Inger Stevens. 89M USA. prod/rel: 20th Century-Fox Film Corporation

TARRIDE, ABEL
Par Habitude, Play
Par Habitude 1932 d: Maurice Cammage. lps: Gaby Basset, Pierre Finaly, Madame Clairval. 31M FRN. prod/rel: Eclair, Nicaea Films

TARSHIS, HAROLD
Rhapsody in Stripes, Story
Jail House Blues 1942 d: Albert S. Rogell. lps: Nat Pendleton, Anne Gwynne, Robert Paige. 62M USA. *Rhapsody in Stripes*; *Big House Blues* prod/rel: Universal

TASSO, TORQUATO (1544–1595), ITL
Aminta, 1573
Aminta 1911 d: Giuseppe Berardi. 350m ITL. prod/rel: Helios Film

La Gerusalemme Liberata, 1575, Poem
Gerusalemme Liberata, La 1911 d: Enrico Guazzoni. lps: Amleto Novelli, Carlo Cattaneo, Emilio Ghione. 1000m ITL. *The Crusaders* (USA); *Jerusalem Delivered* (USA) prod/rel: Cines

Gerusalemme Liberata, La 1918 d: Enrico Guazzoni. lps: Amleto Novelli, Edy Darclea, Olga Benetti. 1908m ITL. prod/rel: Guazzoni Film

Gerusalemme Liberata, La 1935 d: Enrico Guazzoni. lps: Adolfo Geri, Amleto Novelli, Edy DarcleA. 71M ITL. prod/rel: Capitani Film

Gerusalemme Liberata, La 1957 d: Carlo Ludovico BragagliA. lps: Francisco Rabal, Sylva Koscina, Gianna Maria Canale. 93M ITL. *The Mighty Crusaders* (UKN); *The Mighty Invaders* (USA); *Jerusalem Set Free* prod/rel: Max Production Italiana, Euro International Film

TATE, SYLVIA
The Fuzzy Pink Nightgown, 1956, Novel
Fuzzy Pink Nightgown, The 1957 d: Norman Taurog. lps: Jane Russell, Keenan Wynn, Ralph Meeker. 87M USA. prod/rel: United Artists, Russ-Field Corp.

Woman on the Run, 1948, Short Story
Woman on the Run 1950 d: Norman Foster. lps: Ann Sheridan, Dennis O'Keefe, Robert Keith. 77M USA. prod/rel: Universal-International, Fidelity Pictures

TAUBER, CHAIM
Motel the Operator, New York 1936, Play
Motel the Operator 1939 d: Joseph Seiden. lps: Chaim Tauber, Malvina Rappel, Maurice Kroner. 88M USA. prod/rel: Cinema Service Corp.

TAUENTZIEN, THEA
Der Morder Mit Dem Seidenschal, Novel
Morder Mit Dem Seidenschal, Der 1965 d: Adrian Hoven. lps: Susanne Uhlen, Carl Mohner, Folco Lulli. 82M GRM/ITL. *The Murderer With the Silk Scarf* prod/rel: Aquila, Sagittario

TAUNAY, ALFREDO D'ESCRAGNOLLE (1843–1899), BRZ
Inocencia, 1872, Novel
Inocencia 1949 d: Luiz de Barros, Fernando de Barros. 71M BRZ.

Inocencia 1983 d: Walter Lima Jr. lps: Edson Celulari, Fernanda Torres, Rainer Rudolph. 118M BRZ. *Innocence*

TAUPPE, JOE
Und Keiner Schamte Sich, Novel
..Und Keiner Schamte Sich 1960 d: Hans Schott-Schobinger. lps: Gustav Frohlich, Margret Aust, Barbara Frey. 103M GRM. *And Nobody Was Ashamed*; *And No One Was Ashamed* prod/rel: Iso, Adria

Zwei Herzen Und Ein Thron, Novel
Zwei Herzen Und Ein Thron 1955 d: Hans Schott-Schobinger. lps: Hans von Borsody, Elma Karlowa, Gunther Philipp. 105M AUS/GRM. *Hofjagd in Ischl*; *Two Hearts One Throne* prod/rel: Tofi, Patria

TAUSSIG, PAVEL
Story
Kolya 1996 d: Jan Sverak. lps: Zdenek Sverak, Andrej Chalimon, Libuse SafrankovA. 105M CZE/UKN/FRN. prod/rel: Biograf Jan Sverak, Portobello Pictures

TAUT, FRANZ
Conchita Und Der Ingenieur, Novel
Conchita 1954 d: Hans Hinrich, Franz Eichhorn. lps: Robert Freytag, Vanja Orico, Josefin Kipper. 95M GRM/BRZ. *Conchita Und Der Ingenieur*; *Conchita and the Engineer* prod/rel: Franconia, Astra

TAVENER, MARK
In the Red, Novel
In the Red 1998 d: Marcus Mortimer. lps: Warren Clarke, Stephen Fry, Richard Griffiths. TVM. 180M UKN.

TAVES, ISABELLA
Not Bad for a Girl, Book
Rookie of the Year 1973 d: Larry Elikann. lps: Jodie Foster, Dennis McKlernan, Ned Wilson. MTV. 50M USA.

TAVORA, FRANKLIN
O Cabeleira, 1876, Novel
Cabeleira, O 1962 d: Milton Amaral. 90M BRZ.

TAYLOR, BERNARD
The Godsend, Novel
Godsend, The 1979 d: Gabrielle Beaumont. lps: Malcolm Stoddard, Cyd Hayman, Angela Pleasence. 90M UKN. prod/rel: London Cannon

TAYLOR, C. P.
And a Nightingale Sang, Play
And a Nightingale Sang 1989 d: Robert Knights. lps: Phyllis Logan, Tom Watt, Joan Plowright. TVM. 97M UKN. prod/rel: Portman, Tyne Tees Television

TAYLOR, CHAD
Heaven, Novel
Heaven 1998 d: Scott Reynolds. lps: Martin Donovan, Danny Edwards, Richard Schiff. 102M NZL. prod/rel: Midnight Films

TAYLOR, DOMINI
Mother Love, Novel
Mother Love 1989 d: Simon Langton. lps: Diana Rigg, James Wilby, David McCallum. TVM. 220M UKN/USA. prod/rel: BBC Tv, BBC Enterprises

TAYLOR, DWIGHT
Story
Pickup on South Street 1953 d: Samuel Fuller. lps: Richard Widmark, Jean Peters, Thelma Ritter. 81M USA. prod/rel: 20th Century-Fox

Jailbreak, Story
Numbered Men 1930 d: Mervyn Leroy. lps: Conrad Nagel, Bernice Claire, Raymond Hackett. 6480f USA. *Jailbreak* prod/rel: First National Pictures

Two on a Tower, 1934, Play
Paris in Spring 1935 d: Lewis Milestone. lps: Mary Ellis, Tullio Carminati, Ida Lupino. 83M USA. *Paris Love Song* (UKN); *Paris in the Spring*; *Two on a Tower* prod/rel: Paramount Productions©

TAYLOR, GLADYS
Alone in the Australian Outback, Book
Over the Hill 1992 d: George Miller. lps: Olympia Dukakis, Sigrid Thornton, Derek Fowlds. 99M ASL. *Round the Bend* prod/rel: Village Roadshow Pictures (Australia)©, Glasshouse Pictures

TAYLOR, GRANT
Riders of Terror Trail, 1926, Short Story
Terror Trail 1933 d: Armand Schaefer. lps: Tom Mix, Naomi Judge, Raymond Hatton. 57M USA. prod/rel: Universal Pictures Corp.©

TAYLOR, HOWARD P.
Caprice, New York 1884, Play
Caprice 1913 d: J. Searle Dawley. lps: Mary Pickford, Ernest Truex, Owen Moore. 4r USA. prod/rel: Famous Players Film Co., State Rights

TAYLOR, KATHARINE HAVILAND
Cecilia of the Pink Roses, New York 1917, Novel
Cecilia of the Pink Roses 1918 d: Julius Steger. lps: Marion Davies, Harry Benham, Edward O'Connor. 6r USA. prod/rel: Marion Davies Film Co.©, Select Pictures Corp.

TAYLOR, KRESSMAN
Address Unknown, 1938, Novel
Address Unknown 1944 d: William Cameron Menzies. lps: Paul Lukas, Carl Esmond, Peter Van Eyck. 80M USA. prod/rel: Columbia

TAYLOR, MARVIN
Luck in Pawn, New York 1919, Play
Luck in Pawn 1919 d: Walter Edwards. lps: Marguerite Clark, Charles Meredith, Leota Lorraine. 4451f USA. prod/rel: Famous Players-Lasky Corp.©, Paramount Pictures

TAYLOR, MARY IMLAY
Conquest, Story
Conquest 1928 d: Roy Del Ruth. lps: Monte Blue, H. B. Warner, Lois Wilson. 6729f USA. prod/rel: Warner Brothers Pictures

Fate and Pomegranate, Story
In the Shadow of Death 1915 d: Richard Ridgely. lps: Edward Earle, Bessie Learn, George A. Wright. 2r USA. prod/rel: Edison

The Impersonator, Novel
Impersonator, The 1914 d: Charles H. France. lps: Gertrude McCoy, Mrs. William Bechtel. 3000f USA. prod/rel: Edison

The Long Way, Novel
Long Way, The 1914 d: Charles J. Brabin. lps: Miriam Nesbitt, Mabel Trunnelle, Marc McDermott. 3r USA. prod/rel: Edison

The Magnate of Paradise, Novel
Magnate of Paradise, The 1915 d: Charles J. Brabin. lps: Robert Brower, Augustus Phillips, Gertrude Vallon. 2r USA. prod/rel: Edison

The Man in the Street, Novel
Man in the Street, The 1914 d: Charles J. Brabin. lps: Marc MacDermott, Charles Ogle, Gertrude McCoy. 3r USA. prod/rel: Edison

The Man Who Awoke, Short Story
Putting One Over 1919 d: Eddie Dillon. lps: George Walsh, Edith Stockton, Ralph J. Locke. 5r USA. *Chasing a Fortune* prod/rel: Fox Film Corp., Victory Picture

The Wild Fawn, 1920, Short Story
Good-Bad Wife, The 1920 d: Vera McCord. lps: Sidney Mason, Dorothy Green, Moe Lee. 5000f USA. *The Wild Fawn* prod/rel: Vera Mccord Productions, Inc.©, State Rights

The Window That Monsieur Forgot, Story
Question of Identity, A 1914 d: Charles J. Brabin. lps: Julia Calhoun, Augustus Phillips, Carlton King. 2r USA. prod/rel: Edison

TAYLOR, MATT
First Performance, Short Story
Road to Happiness 1941 d: Phil Rosen. lps: John Boles, Mona Barrie, Billy Lee. 83M USA. prod/rel: Monogram

The Knickerbocker Kid, Story
Stepping Along 1926 d: Charles Hines. lps: Johnny Hines, Mary Brian, William Gaxton. 7038f USA. prod/rel: B & H Enterprises

Safari in Manhattan, 1936, Short Story
More Than a Secretary 1936 d: Alfred E. Green. lps: Jean Arthur, George Brent, Lionel Stander. 80M USA. *Safari in Paradise*; *Help Wanted Female* prod/rel: Columbia Pictures Corp. of California©

TAYLOR, RENEE
Lovers and Other Strangers, New York 1968, Play
Lovers and Other Strangers 1970 d: Cy Howard. lps: Gig Young, Bonnie Bedelia, Beatrice Arthur. 106M USA. prod/rel: ABC Pictures

TAYLOR, ROBERT LEWIS
Guns of Diablo, Novel
   Guns of Diablo 1964 d: Boris Sagal. lps: Charles
Bronson, Susan Oliver, Kurt Russell. MTV. 56M USA.
Day of Reckoning prod/rel: MGM

TAYLOR, ROSEMARY
Chicken Every Sunday, Novel
   Chicken Every Sunday 1949 d: George Seaton. lps:
Dan Dailey, Celeste Holm, Colleen Townsend. 91M
USA. prod/rel: 20th Century-Fox

TAYLOR, SAMUEL (1912–, USA
Avanti!, Play
   Avanti! 1972 d: Billy Wilder. lps: Jack Lemmon, Juliet
Mills, Clive Revill. 144M USA/ITL. *Che Cosa E Successo
Tra Mio Padre E Tua Madre?* (ITL) prod/rel: Mirisch
Corporation, P.E.A. (Roma)
The Pleasure of His Company, New York 1958, Play
   Pleasure of His Company, The 1961 d: George
Seaton. lps: Fred Astaire, Debbie Reynolds, Lilli Palmer.
115M USA. prod/rel: Perlsea Co., Paramount Pictures
Sabrina Fair, New York 1953, Play
   Sabrina 1954 d: Billy Wilder. lps: Audrey Hepburn,
William Holden, Humphrey Bogart. 113M USA.
Sabrina Fair (UKN) prod/rel: Paramount
   Sabrina 1995 d: Sydney Pollack. lps: Harrison Ford,
Julia Ormond, Greg Kinnear. 127M USA. prod/rel:
Paramount, Constellation
A Situation of Gravity, 1943, Story
   Absent-Minded Professor, The 1961 d: Robert
Stevenson. lps: Fred MacMurray, Nancy Olson, Keenan
Wynn. 97M USA. prod/rel: Walt Disney Productions,
Buena Vista
   Flubber 1997 d: Les Mayfield. lps: Robin Williams,
Marcia Gay Harden, Christopher McDonald. 94M USA.
prod/rel: Walt Disney Pictures, Greak Oaks

TAYLOR, SAMUEL W.
The Man Who Came to Life, Story
   Man Who Returned to Life, The 1942 d: Lew
Landers. lps: John Howard, Lucille Fairbanks, Ruth
Ford. 61M USA. prod/rel: Columbia
The Man With My Face, 1948, Novel
   Man With My Face, The 1951 d: Edward J. Montague.
lps: Barry Nelson, Lynn Ainley, John Harvey. 86M USA.
prod/rel: United Artists, Edward F. Gardner

TAYLOR, TOM (1817–1880), UKN
Clancarty, London 1907, Play
   Clancarty 1914 d: Harold Shaw. lps: Lillian Logan,
Walter Gay, Charles Rock. 1760f UKN. prod/rel: London
The Fool's Revenge, New York 1864, Play
   Fool's Revenge, The 1916 d: Will S. Davis. lps:
William H. Tooker, Maude Gilbert, Ruth Findlay. 5r
USA. prod/rel: Fox Film Corp., William Fox©
Still Waters Run Deep, London 1855, Play
   Still Waters Run Deep 1916 d: Fred Paul. lps: Lady
Tree, Milton Rosmer, Rutland Barrington. 4500f UKN.
prod/rel: Ideal
   Thundercloud, The 1919 d: Alexander Butler. lps:
Unity More, James Lindsay, Mary Dibley. 4780f UKN.
prod/rel: Barker, Urban
The Ticket-of-Leave Man, London 1863, Play
   Ticket of Leave Man, The 1937 d: George King. lps:
Tod Slaughter, Marjorie Taylor, John Warwick. 71M
UKN. prod/rel: George King Productions, MGM
   Ticket-of-Leave Man, The 1914 d: Travers Vale. lps:
Charles Hill Mailes, George Morgan. 2r USA. prod/rel:
Biograph Co.
   Ticket-of-Leave Man, The 1918 d: Bert Haldane. lps:
Daphne Glenne, George Foley, Aubrey Fitzmaurice.
5800f UKN. prod/rel: Barker, Moss

TAZKY, LADISLAV
Zbehove
   Zbehovia a Putnici 1968 d: Juraj Jakubisko. lps:
Gezja Ferenc, Helena Grodova, Stefan Ladizinsky.
120M CZC/ITL. *The Deserter and the Nomads*; *Il
Disertore E I Nomadi* (ITL); *Deserters and Pilgrims*;
Wanderers; *Zbehovia a Tulaci*

TCHAIKOVSKY, MODEST
Iolanta, St. Petersburg 1892, Opera
   Iolanta 1963 d: Vladimir Gorikker. lps: Natalya
Rudnaya, Fyodor Nikitin, Yuriy Perov. 82M USS.
Yolanta (USA) prod/rel: Riga Film Studio

TCHAIKOVSKY, PETR (1840–1893), RSS
Iolanta
   Iolanta 1963 d: Vladimir Gorikker. lps: Natalya
Rudnaya, Fyodor Nikitin, Yuriy Perov. 82M USS.
Yolanta (USA) prod/rel: Riga Film Studio

TCHONGHADZE, D.
Legenda Suramskoi Kreposti, Book
   Legenda Suramskoi Kreposti 1986 d: Sergei
Paradjanov, Dodo Abachidze. lps: Veriko
Andzhaparidze, David Abashidze, Sofiko Chiaureli.

87M USS. *Legend of the Fortress of Suram*; *Legend of the
Suram Fortress*; *Ambavi Suramis Cikhisa*; *Legenda O
Suramskoj Kreposti* prod/rel: Georgianfilm Studio

TEBELAK, JOHN-MICHAEL
Godspell, Musical Play
   Godspell 1973 d: David Greene. lps: Victor Garber,
David Haskell, Jerry SrokA. 103M USA. prod/rel:
Columbia

TECHNIK, ALFRED
Mlyn Na Ponorne Rece, Prague 1958, Novel
   Dablova Past 1961 d: Frantisek Vlacil. lps: Karla
Chadimova, Vitezslav Vejrazka, Miroslav MacHacek.
88M CZC. *The Devil's Trap* (USA)

TEED, G. H.
They Shall Repay, Novel
   Sexton Blake and the Mademoiselle 1935 d: Alex
Bryce. lps: George Curzon, Lorraine Grey, Tony
Sympson. 63M UKN. prod/rel: Fox British, MGM

TEICHMANN, HOWARD
The Solid Gold Cadillac, New York 1953, Play
   Solid Gold Cadillac, The 1956 d: Richard Quine. lps:
Judy Holliday, Paul Douglas, Fred Clark. 99M USA.
prod/rel: Columbia

TEILHET, DARWIN L.
The Fearmakers, 1945, Novel
   Fearmakers, The 1958 d: Jacques Tourneur. lps:
Dana Andrews, Dick Foran, Mel Torme. 83M USA.
prod/rel: United Artists, Pacemaker
My True Love, Novel
   No Room for the Groom 1952 d: Douglas Sirk. lps:
Tony Curtis, Piper Laurie, Don Defore. 82M USA.
Almost Married prod/rel: Universal-International

TEIRLINCK, HERMAN
Rolande Met de Bles, 1944, Novel
   Rolande Met de Bles 1970 d: Roland Verhavert. lps:
Jan Decleir, Elisabeth Tessier de Cross, Liliane Vincent.
126M BLG. *Roland Or Chronicle of Passion* prod/rel:
Visie

TEJADOR, LUIS
Mia Moglie Mi Piace Di Piu, Play
   Mi Mujer Me Gusta Mas 1960 d: Antonio Roman. lps:
Walter Chiari, Yvonne Bastien, Franco Fabrizi. 99M
SPN/ITL. *La Moglie Di Mio Marito* (ITL); *I Prefer My
Wife*; *My Husband's Wife* prod/rel: Wanguard Film,
Explorer Film

TEJASWI, POORNACHANDRA
Tabarana Kathe, Short Story
   Tabarana Kathe 1986 d: Girish Kasaravalli. lps:
Charuhasan, Ramamoorthy, SavitrammA. 179M IND.
The Story of Tabarana; *The Story of Tabara*;
Tabaranakathe; *Tabara's Tale* prod/rel: Apoorva Chitra

TEJERA OSSAVARRY, SANTIAGO
La Hija Del Mestre, Opera
   Hija Del Mestre, La 1927 d: Carlos Luis Monzon,
Francisco Gonzalez Gonzalez. lps: Antonio Pulido
Rodriguez, Maria Luisa Padron, Francisco Quintero.
1477m SPN. prod/rel: Gran Canaria Films (Las Palmas)

TELFER, DARIEL
The Caretakers, New York 1959, Novel
   Caretakers, The 1963 d: Hall Bartlett. lps: Robert
Stack, Joan Crawford, Herbert Marshall. 97M USA.
Borderlines (UKN) prod/rel: United Artists

TELLADO, CORIN
Mi Boda Contigo, Novel
   Notre Mariage 1984 d: Valeria Sarmiento. lps: Cecilia
Guimaraes, Luis Lucas, Nadege Clair. 100M
FRN/SWT/PRT. *Mi Boda Contigo*

TELLEGEN, LOU (1881–1934), NTH
Blind Youth, New York 1917, Play
   Blind Youth 1920 d: Edward Sloman, Alfred E. Green.
lps: Walter McGrail, Leatrice Joy, Ora Carew. 6r USA.
prod/rel: National Pictures, National Pictures Theatres,
Inc.©

TELLINI, P.
Successo a Paganigua, Story
   Segreto Inviolabile, Il 1939 d: Julio Fleischner. lps:
Tony d'Algy, Maria Mercader, Jose Nieto. 82M
ITL/SPN. *Su Mayor Aventura* (SPN) prod/rel: Nembo
Film

TEMLOW, CLIFFORD
Tuxedo Warrior, Novel
   Tuxedo Warrior 1985 d: Andrew Sinclair. lps: John
Wymann, Carol Royle, Holly Palance. 89M UKN. *The
African Run* prod/rel: Tuxedo Warrior Entertainment

TEMPLE, JOAN
No Room at the Inn, London 1945, Play
   No Room at the Inn 1948 d: Daniel Birt. lps: Freda
Jackson, Joy Shelton, Hermione Baddeley. 82M UKN.
prod/rel: British National, Pathe

The Primrose Path, Story
   Primrose Path, The 1934 d: Reginald Denham. lps:
Isobel Elsom, Whitmore Humphries, Max Adrian. 70M
UKN. prod/rel: British and Dominions, Paramount
British

TEMPLE, WILLIAM F.
Four Sided Triangle, Novel
   Four Sided Triangle 1953 d: Terence Fisher. lps:
Barbara Payton, James Hayter, Stephen Murray. 81M
UKN. prod/rel: Exclusive Films, Hammer

TEMPLETON, CHARLES
The Kidnapping of the President, Novel
   Kidnapping of the President, The 1980 d: George
Menduluk. lps: Hal Holbrook, William Shatner, Miguel
Fernandes. 113M CND. prod/rel: Sefel Pictures
International Ltd., Presidential Productions Ltd.

TEMPLETON, GEORGE
Too Many Parents, Short Story
   Too Many Parents 1936 d: Robert F. McGowan. lps:
Frances Farmer, Lester Matthews, Billy Lee. 73M USA.
prod/rel: Paramount Productions©

TEN BOOM, CORRIE (1892–1983), NTH
The Hiding Place, 1971, Book
   Hiding Place, The 1975 d: James F. Collier. lps: Julie
Harris, Eileen Heckart, Arthur O'Connell. 147M USA.

TENDULKAR, VIJAY
Ghashiram Kotwal, Play
   Ghashiram Kotwal 1976 d: Mani Kaul, K. Hariharan.
lps: Mohan Agashe, Rajani Chavan, Om Puri. 108M
IND. prod/rel: Yukt Film Co-Op

TENGROTH, BIRGIT
Torst, Book
   Torst 1949 d: Ingmar Bergman. lps: Eva Henning,
Birger Malmsten, Birgit Tengroth. 88M SWD. *Three
Strange Loves* (USA); *Thirst* (UKN) prod/rel: Svensk
Filmindustri

TENNO, HELIODORE
The Third Kiss, 1918, Short Story
   Third Kiss, The 1919 d: Robert G. VignolA. lps: Vivian
Martin, Harrison Ford, Robert Ellis. 5r USA. prod/rel:
Famous Players-Lasky Corp.©, Paramount Special
Production

TENNYSON, ALFRED (1809–1892), UKN, Tennyson,
Alfred Lord
Becket, London 1893, Play
   Becket 1923 d: George Ridgwell. lps: Frank Benson,
Gladys Jennings, Mary Clare. 6450f UKN. prod/rel:
Stoll
Break Break Break, Poem
   Day That Is Dead, A 1913 d: Charles H. France. lps:
Laura Sawyer, Mabel Trunnelle, Robert Brower. 1000f
USA. prod/rel: Edison
   Vanished Hand, The 1928 d: George J. Banfield,
Leslie Eveleigh. lps: Cynthia Murtagh, Hugh Dempster,
Annesley Hely. 1911f UKN. prod/rel: British Filmcraft,
Ideal
The Charge of the Light Brigade, 1854, Poem
   Balaclava 1928 d: Maurice Elvey, Milton Rosmer. lps:
Benita Hume, Cyril McLaglen, Alf Goddard. SIL. 8500f
UKN. *Jaws of Hell* (USA) prod/rel: Gainsborough,
Woolf & Freedman
   Balaclava 1930 d: Maurice Elvey, Milton Rosmer. lps:
Benita Hume, Cyril McLaglen, Alf Goddard. SND.
UKN. *Jaws of Hell* (USA) prod/rel: Gainsborough
   Charge of the Light Brigade, The 1914. lps: Eric
Williams. UKN. prod/rel: Eric Williams Speaking
Pictures
   Charge of the Light Brigade, The 1936 d: Michael
Curtiz. lps: Errol Flynn, Olivia de Havilland, Patric
Knowles. 115M USA. prod/rel: Warner Bros. Pictures,
Inc.
Dora, Poem
   Dora 1909 d: Sidney Olcott. 965f USA. prod/rel: Kalem
   Dora 1910 d: Bert Haldane?. 575f UKN. prod/rel:
Hepworth
   Dora 1912 d: H. O. Martinek?. lps: Hetty Johnson, Miss
L. Reeves, E. Lugg. 960f UKN. prod/rel: British and
Colonial, Moving Pictures Sales Agency
   Dora 1912. lps: Florence Barker, Edwin August,
Charles Manley. SHT USA. prod/rel: Powers
   Dora 1913. lps: Marguerite Marsh, Richard Cummings,
William Garwood. SHT USA. prod/rel: Majestic
   Dora 1915 d: Travers Vale. lps: Isabel Rea, Gretchen
Hartman, Jack Mulhall. 3r USA. prod/rel: Biograph Co.
Enoch Arden, 1864, Poem
   Enoch Arden 1914 d: Percy Nash. lps: Gerald
Lawrence, Fay Davis, Ben Webster. 3450f UKN.
prod/rel: Neptune, Renters

Enoch Arden 1915 d: W. Christy Cabanne. lps: Lillian Gish, Alfred Paget, Wallace Reid. 4r USA. *As Fate Ordained* (UKN); *The Fatal Marriage* prod/rel: Majestic Motion Picture Co., Mutual Film Corp.

Enoch Arden Parts I & II 1911 d: D. W. Griffith. lps: Wilfred Lucas, Florence Labadie, Frank Grandon. 2007f USA. prod/rel: Biograph Co.

The Gardener's Daughter, Poem
Gardener's Daughter, The 1913 d: Wilfred Noy. 1000f UKN. prod/rel: Clarendon

Gardener's Daughter, The 1914 d: Wilfred Noy. lps: Norah Chaplin. 1460f UKN. prod/rel: Clarendon

The Lady Clare, Poem
Lady Clare 1911. SHT USA. prod/rel: Thanhouser

Lady Clare, The 1912 d: Ashley Miller. lps: Marc McDermott, Miriam Nesbitt, May Wells. 700f UKN/USA. prod/rel: Edison

Lady Clare, The 1919. lps: Mary Odette, Jack Hobbs, Charles Quartermaine. 6000f UKN. prod/rel: British Actors, Phillips

The Lady of Shallott, 1833, Poem
Lady of Shallott, The 1912 d: Elwin Neame. lps: Ivy Close. 800f UKN. prod/rel: Ivy Close, Hepworth

Lady of Shallott, The 1915 d: C. Jay Williams. lps: Flora Finch, Kate Price, William SheA. SHT USA. prod/rel: Vitagraph Co. of America

Launcelot and Elaine, Poem
Launcelot and Elaine 1909. 1000f USA. prod/rel: Vitagraph

Lover's Tale, Poem
Golden Supper, The 1910 d: D. W. Griffith. lps: Edwin August, Alfred Paget, Dorothy West. 998f USA. prod/rel: Biograph Co.

Maud, Poem
Maud 1911 d: Wilfred Noy. lps: Dorothy Bellew, Charles Calvert. 710f UKN. prod/rel: Clarendon

The May Queen, Poem
May Queen, The 1914. 2300f UKN. prod/rel: Favourite Films, Universal

TERASAKI, GWENDOLYN
Bridge to the Sun, Chapel Hill, Nc. 1957, Novel
Bridge to the Sun 1961 d: Etienne Perier. lps: Carroll Baker, James Shigeta, Emi Florence Hirsch. 112M USA/FRN. *Le Pont Vers le Soleil* (FRN) prod/rel: Cite Films

TERHUNE, ALBERT PAYSON (1872–1942), USA
Caleb Conover - Railroader, New York 1907, Novel
Railroader, The 1919 d: Colin Campbell. lps: Thomas Santschi, Fritzi Brunette, George Fawcett. 5r USA. *The Railroaders* prod/rel: Triangle Film Corp., Triangle Distributing Corp.

Dollars and Cents, New York 1917, Novel
Dollars and the Woman 1916 d: Joseph Kaufman. lps: Ethel Clayton, Tom Moore, Crauford Kent. 6r USA. *Dollars and Cents* prod/rel: Lubin Mfg. Co.©, V-L-S-E, Inc.

Dollars and the Woman 1920 d: George W. Terwilliger. lps: Alice Joyce, Robert Gordon, Crauford Kent. 6052f USA. prod/rel: Vitagraph Co. of America©

Driftwood, 1918, Short Story
Daring Love 1924 d: Roland G. Edwards. lps: Elaine Hammerstein, Huntley Gordon, Walter Long. 5006f USA. prod/rel: Hoffman Productions, Truart Film Corp.

The Fighter, New York 1909, Novel
Fighter, The 1921 d: Henry Kolker. lps: Conway Tearle, Winifred Westover, Arthur Housman. 4943f USA. prod/rel: Selznick Pictures, Select Pictures

The Frontier of the Stars, Story
Frontier of the Stars, The 1921 d: Charles Maigne. lps: Thomas Meighan, Faire Binney, Alphonse Ethier. 5693f USA. prod/rel: Famous Players-Lasky, Paramount Pictures

Grand Larceny, 1920, Short Story
Grand Larceny 1922 d: Wallace Worsley. lps: Claire Windsor, Elliott Dexter, Richard Tucker. 5227f USA. prod/rel: Goldwyn Pictures

The Happiness of Three Women, 1914, Short Story
Happiness of Three Women, The 1917 d: William D. Taylor. lps: House Peters, Myrtle Stedman, Larry Steers. 5r USA. prod/rel: Oliver Morosco Photoplay Co.©, Paramount Pictures Corp.

The Hero, 1928, Short Story
Whom the Gods Destroy 1934 d: Walter Lang. lps: Walter Connolly, Robert Young, Doris Kenyon. 75M USA. prod/rel: Columbia Pictures Corp.©

His Dog, New York 1922, Novel
His Dog 1927 d: Karl Brown. lps: Joseph Schildkraut, Julia Faye, Crauford Kent. 6788f USA. prod/rel: de Mille Pictures, Pathe Exchange, Inc.

The Hunch, 1920, Short Story
Knockout Reilly 1927 d: Malcolm St. Clair. lps: Richard Dix, Mary Brian, Jack Renault. 7080f USA. *Knockout Riley* prod/rel: Famous Players-Lasky, Paramount Pictures

Lad: a Dog, New York 1919, Novel
Lad: a Dog 1962 d: Aram Avakian, Leslie H. Martinson. lps: Peter Breck, Peggy McCay, Carroll O'Connor. 98M USA. prod/rel: Vanguard Productions, Warner Bros.

A Square Deal, 1917, Short Story
Square Deal, The 1918 d: Lloyd Ingraham. lps: Margarita Fischer, Jack Mower, Val Paul. 5r USA. prod/rel: American Film Co., Mutual Film Corp.

A Thief in the Night, Story
Thief in the Night, A 1915. lps: Earl Metcalfe, Herbert Fortier, William H. Turner. 2r USA. prod/rel: Lubin

The Thirtieth Piece of Silver, Novel
Thirtieth Piece of Silver, The 1920 d: George L. Cox. lps: Margarita Fischer, King Baggot, Lillian Leighton. 5-6r USA. prod/rel: American Film Co.©, Pathe Exchange, Inc.

Treve, New York 1925, Novel
Mighty Treve, The 1937 d: Lewis D. Collins. lps: Noah Beery Jr., Barbara Read, Samuel S. Hinds. 70M USA. *Treve* prod/rel: Universal Pictures Co.©

The Years of the Locust, 1915, Short Story
Years of the Locust, The 1916 d: George Melford. lps: Fannie Ward, Walter Long, Jack Dean. 5r USA. *The Years of the Locust* prod/rel: Jesse L. Lasky Feature Play Co.©, Paramount Pictures Corp.

TERRILL, LUCY STONE
Face, 1924, Short Story
Unguarded Women 1924 d: Alan Crosland. lps: Bebe Daniels, Richard Dix, Mary Astor. 6500f USA. prod/rel: Famous Players-Lasky, Paramount Pictures

TERRISS, WILLIAM
The Sword of Honor, Play
Pearl of the Antilles, The 1915 d: Tom Terriss. lps: Tom Terriss, Lionel Pape, Tessie de CordovA. 5r USA. prod/rel: Terriss Feature Film Co., Picture Playhouse Film Co.

TERROT, CHARLES
An Alligator Named Daisy, Novel
Alligator Named Daisy, An 1955 d: J. Lee Thompson. lps: Donald Sinden, Diana Dors, Jeannie Carson. 88M UKN. prod/rel: Group, Raymond Stross Productions

The Angel Who Pawned Her Harp, Television Play
Angel Who Pawned Her Harp, The 1954 d: Alan Bromly. lps: Felix Aylmer, Diane Cilento, Jerry Desmonde. 76M UKN. prod/rel: Group Three, British Lion

Der Engel Der Seine Harfe Versetzte, Novel
Engel, Der Seine Harfe Versetzte, Der 1959 d: Kurt Hoffmann. lps: Matthias Fuchs, Dunja Movar, Ulrich Haupt. 97M GRM. *The Angel Who Pawned His Harp* prod/rel: Goerg Witt, Constantin

TERRY, J. E. HAROLD
Collusion, Play
Midnight Lovers 1926 d: John Francis Dillon. lps: Lewis Stone, Anna Q. Nilsson, John Roche. 6100f USA. prod/rel: John Mccormick Productions, Frist National Pictures

General Post, London 1917, Play
General Post 1920 d: Thomas Bentley. lps: Lilian Braithwaite, R. Henderson Bland, Joyce Dearsley. 5000f UKN. prod/rel: Ideal

The Man Who Stayed at Home, London 1914, Play
Man Who Stayed at Home, The 1915 d: Cecil M. Hepworth. lps: Dennis Eadie, Violet Hopson, Alma Taylor. 3575f UKN. prod/rel: Hepworth, Central

Man Who Stayed at Home, The 1919 d: Herbert Blache. lps: King Baggot, Claire Whitney, Robert Whittier. 6r USA. prod/rel: Screen Classics, Inc., Metro Pictures Corp.©

TERRY, WALLACE
Specialist No.4 Haywood T. "the Kid" Kirkland, Short Story
Dead Presidents 1995 d: Allen Hughes, Albert Hughes. lps: Larenz Tate, Keith David, Chris Tucker. 119M USA. prod/rel: Hollywood Pictures

TERSANSZKY, JOZSI JENO
Kakuk Marci, 1950, Novel
Kakuk Marci 1973 d: Gyorgy Revesz. lps: Gabor Harsanyi, Peter Haumann, Eva Szerencsi. 101M HNG. *Martin Cuckoo*

Legenda a Nyulpaprikasrol, 1936, Novel
Legenda a Nyulpaprikasrol 1975 d: Barna Kabay. lps: Siemion Wojciech, Adam Szirtes, Dezso Garas. 94M HNG. *Legend About the Stewed Hare*; *The Rabbit Stew*

Misi Mokus Kalandjai, 1953, Novel
Misi Mokus Kalandjai 1984 d: Otto Foky. ANM. 72M HNG. *Adventures of Sam the Squirrel*

TERVO, JARI
Rikos & Rakkaus, Novel
Rikos & Rakkaus 1999 d: Pekka Milonoff. lps: Kai Lehtinen, Tiina Lymi, Tomi SalmelA. 109M FNL. *Love & Crime* prod/rel: Kinoproduction Oy

TERZOLI
Le Cadeau, Play
Cadeau, Le 1982 d: Michel Lang. lps: Pierre Mondy, Claudia Cardinale, Clio Goldsmith. 108M FRN/ITL. *Il Regalo* (ITL); *The Gift* prod/rel: Gilbert de Goldschmidt

TERZOLI, ITALO
Amare Significa., Novel
Sera C'incontrammo, Una 1976 d: Piero SchivazappA. lps: Johnny Dorelli, Fran Fullenwider, Lia Tanzi. 100M ITL. prod/rel: Supernova, Euro International Film

Le Braghe Del Padrone, Novel
Braghe Del Padrone, Le 1978 d: Flavio Mogherini. lps: Enrico Montesano, Adolfo Celi, Milena Vukotic. 97M ITL. prod/rel: Zodiac Produzioni, C.I.D.I.F.

TESTONI, ALFREDO
L'Amica Del Cuore, 1914, Play
Ninnola 1920 d: Orlando Vassallo. lps: Elena Lunda, Nora Lucenti, Alfredo Bertone. 1686m ITL. prod/rel: Tacita Film

Il Cardinale Lambertini, Play
Cardinale Lambertini, Il 1934 d: Parsifal Bassi. lps: Ermete Zacconi, Giulietta de Riso, Ernes Zacconi. 72M ITL. prod/rel: Elios Film, E.F.F.E.B.I.

Cardinale Lambertini, Il 1955 d: Giorgio PastinA. lps: Gino Cervi, Nadia Gray, Arnoldo FoA. 101M ITL. prod/rel: Italica Film, Vox Film

La Duchessina, 1903, Play
Duchessina 1921 d: Giovanni PezzingA. lps: Mary Dumont, Domenico Marverti, Delizia PezzingA. 1674m ITL. prod/rel: Tiziano Film

La Modella, 1907, Play
Modella, La 1920 d: Mario Caserini. lps: Vera Vergani, Ida Carloni-Talli, Camillo de Riso. 1337m ITL. prod/rel: Ulpia Film

La Scintilla, 1906, Play
Scintilla, La 1915 d: Eleuterio Rodolfi. lps: Tina Di Lorenzo, Armando Falconi, Oreste BilanciA. ITL. prod/rel: S.A. Ambrosio

Il Successo, Play
Albero Di Adamo, L' 1936 d: Mario Bonnard. lps: Elsa Merlini, Antonio Gandusio, Renato Cialente. 74M ITL. *Adam's Tree* (USA) prod/rel: Manenti Film

TESTORI, GIOVANNI
I Segretti Di Milano: Il Ponte Della Ghisolfa, Milan 1958, Novel
Rocco E I Suoi Fratelli 1960 d: Luchino Visconti. lps: Alain Delon, Renato Salvatori, Annie Girardot. 180M ITL/FRN. *Rocco Et Ses Freres* (FRN); *Rocco and His Brothers* (USA) prod/rel: Titanus (Roma), Les Films Marceau Cocinor (Paris)

TETZNER, LISA (1894–1963), GRM
Was Am See Geschah, Short Story
Zartliches Geheimnis 1956 d: Wolfgang Schleif. lps: Hans Sohnker, Edith Mill, Therese Giehse. 100M GRM. *Ferien in Tirol*; *Tender Secret* prod/rel: H. R. Sokal, Bavaria

TEULE, JEAN
Rainbow Pour Rimbaud, 1991, Novel
Rainbow Pour Rimbaud 1996 d: Jean Teule. lps: Laure Marsac, Robert MacLeod, Bernadette Lafont. 84M FRN. *Rainbow for Rimbaud* prod/rel: la Sept Cinema Prod., Kg Prods.

TEVIS, JAMES H.
Arizona in the '50S, Novel
Tenderfoot, The 1966 d: Byron Paul. lps: Brandon de Wilde, James Whitmore, Richard Long. 80M USA. prod/rel: Walt Disney

TEVIS, WALTER S. (1928–1984), USA
The Color of Money, 1984, Novel
Color of Money, The 1987 d: Martin Scorsese. lps: Paul Newman, Tom Cruise, Mary Elizabeth Mastrantonio. 119M USA. prod/rel: Buena Vista, Touchstone

The Hustler, New York 1959, Novel
Hustler, The 1961 d: Robert Rossen. lps: Paul Newman, Jackie Gleason, Piper Laurie. 135M USA. prod/rel: Rossen Enterprises, 20th Century-Fox

The Man Who Fell to Earth, 1963, Novel
Man Who Fell to Earth, The 1976 d: Nicolas Roeg. lps: David Bowie, Rip Torn, Candy Clark. 140M UKN. prod/rel: British Lion

Man Who Fell to Earth, The 1987 d: Robert J. Roth. lps: Lewis Smith, Beverly d'Angelo, Wil Wheaton. TVM. 100M USA. prod/rel: David Gerber Prods., MGM Television

TEY, JOSEPHINE (1896–1952), UKN, MacKintosh, Elizabeth, Daviot, Gordon
The Franchise Affair, Novel
  Franchise Affair, The 1951 d: Lawrence Huntington. lps: Michael Denison, Dulcie Gray, Anthony Nicholls. 88M UKN. prod/rel: Associated British Picture Corporation, Ab-Pathe
A Shilling for Candles, Novel
  Young and Innocent 1937 d: Alfred Hitchcock. lps: Nova Pilbeam, Derrick de Marney, Percy Marmont. 82M UKN. *The Girl Was Young* (USA); *A Shilling for Candles* prod/rel: General Film Distributors, Gainsborough
Youthful Folly, Play
  Youthful Folly 1934 d: Miles Mander. lps: Irene Vanbrugh, Jane Carr, Mary Lawson. 72M UKN. prod/rel: Sound City, Columbia

THACKERAY, WILLIAM MAKEPEACE (1811–1863), UKN
Story
  George Warrington's Escape 1911 d: Otis Turner. lps: Hobart Bosworth, Thomas Santschi, Betty Harte. 1000f USA. prod/rel: Selig Polyscope Co.
The Memoirs of Barry Lyndon Esq., 1856, Novel
  Barry Lyndon 1975 d: Stanley Kubrick. lps: Ryan O'Neal, Marisa Berenson, Patrick Magee. 185M UKN. *The Luck of Barry Lyndon* prod/rel: Warner Bros., Hawk
The Newcomes, Novel
  Colonel Newcome the Perfect Gentleman 1920 d: Fred Goodwins. lps: Milton Rosmer, Joyce Carey, Temple Bell. 5500f UKN. prod/rel: Ideal
The Rose and the Ring, 1855, Short Story
  Pierscien I Roza 1987 d: Jerzy GruzA. 104M PLN. *The Ring and the Rose*
Vanity Fair, London 1848, Novel
  Becky Sharp 1935 d: Rouben Mamoulian. lps: Miriam Hopkins, Frances Dee, Cedric Hardwicke. 85M USA. prod/rel: Pioneer Pictures, in.C, Rouben Mamoulian Production
  Vanity Fair 1911 d: Charles Kent. lps: Helen Gardner, William V. Ranous, Harry Northrup. 3000f USA. prod/rel: Vitagraph Co. of America
  Vanity Fair 1915 d: Charles J. Brabin, Eugene Nowland. lps: Mrs. Fiske, Shirley Mason, Yale Benner. 6642f USA. prod/rel: Thomas A. Edison, Inc.©, Kleine-Edison Feature Service
  Vanity Fair 1922 d: W. C. Rowden. lps: Cosmo Kyrle Bellew, Clive Brook, Douglas Munro. 1198f UKN. prod/rel: Master Films, British Exhibitors' Films
  Vanity Fair 1923 d: Hugo Ballin. lps: Mabel Ballin, Hobart Bosworth, George Walsh. 7668f USA. prod/rel: Hugo Ballin Productions, Goldwyn Distributing Corp.
  Vanity Fair 1932 d: Chester M. Franklin. lps: Myrna Loy, Barbara Kent, Walter Byron. 78M USA. *Vanity Fair of Today* prod/rel: Allied Pictures Corp., Chester M. Franklin Production

THAYER, E. L. (1863–1940), USA, Thayer, Ernest L.
Casey at the Bat, 1888, Poem
  Casey at the Bat 1916 d: Lloyd Ingraham. lps: De Wolf Hopper, Kate Toncray, May GarciA. 5r USA. prod/rel: Fine Arts Film Co., Triangle Film Corp.
  Casey at the Bat 1927 d: Monte Brice. lps: Wallace Beery, Ford Sterling, Zasu Pitts. 6040f USA. prod/rel: Famous Players-Lasky, Paramount Pictures

THAYER, TIFFANY
Call Her Savage, New York 1931, Novel
  Call Her Savage 1932 d: John Francis Dillon. lps: Clara Bow, Gilbert Roland, Thelma Todd. 87M USA. prod/rel: Fox Film Corp.
The Illustrious Corpse, New York 1930, Novel
  Strangers of the Evening 1932 d: H. Bruce Humberstone. lps: Miriam Seegar, Mahlon Hamilton, Zasu Pitts. 71M USA. *The Hidden Corpse* prod/rel: Quadruple Film Corp.©, Tiffany Productions
One Woman, 1933, Novel
  Chicago Deadline 1949 d: Lewis Allen. lps: Alan Ladd, Donna Reed, Margaret Field. 87M USA. prod/rel: Paramount
  Fame Is the Name of the Game 1966 d: Stuart Rosenberg. lps: Anthony Franciosa, Jill St. John, Jack Klugman. TVM. 100M USA. prod/rel: Universal
Thirteen Women, New York 1932, Novel
  Thirteen Women 1932 d: George Archainbaud. lps: Irene Dunne, Ricardo Cortez, Myrna Loy. 73M USA. *13 Women* prod/rel: RKO Radio Pictures©

THEODOROU, NELLE
He Stephania Sto Anamorphoterio, Athens 1960, Novel
  Stephania 1967 d: Ioannis Dalianidis. lps: Zoe Laskari, Spiros Focas, Lefteris Vournas. 95M GRC. *Stefania* (USA) prod/rel: Finos Films

THEOTOKIS, CONSTANTINOS
Honour and Money, Novel
  Timi Tis Agapis, I 1984 d: Tonia Marketaki. lps: Toula Stathopoulou, Anny Loulou, Stratis Tsopanellis. 110M GRC. *The Price of Love* prod/rel: Andromeda, Greek Film Centre

THERIAULT, YVES (1915–1983), CND
Le Dernier Havre, Novel
  Dernier Havre, Le 1987 d: Denyse Benoit. lps: Paul Hebert, Louisette Dussault, Claude Gauthier. 83M CND. prod/rel: Assoc. Coop. de Prods. Audio-Visuelles
Shadow of the Wolf, Novel
  Shadow of the Wolf 1992 d: Jacques Dorfmann. lps: Donald Sutherland, Lou Diamond Phillips, Toshiro Mifune. 108M CND/FRN. *Agaguk* (FRN) prod/rel: Transfilm, Eiffel

THEROUX, PAUL (1941–, USA, Theroux, Paul Edward
Dr. Slaughter, 1984, Novel
  Half Moon Street 1986 d: Bob Swaim. lps: Michael Caine, Sigourney Weaver, Keith Buckley. 90M UKN/USA. prod/rel: RKO, Geoff Reeve Enterprises
The Mosquito Coast, 1981, Novel
  Mosquito Coast, The 1986 d: Peter Weir. lps: Harrison Ford, Helen Mirren, River Phoenix. 119M USA. prod/rel: Warner Bros., the Saul Zaentz Company
Saint Jack, 1973, Novel
  Saint Jack 1979 d: Peter Bogdanovich. lps: Ben Gazzara, Denholm Elliott, James Villiers. 112M USA. prod/rel: Roger Corman

THERY, JACQUES
Le Fruit Vert, Play
  Between Us Girls 1942 d: Henry Koster. lps: Diana Barrymore, Robert Cummings, Kay Francis. 89M USA. *Boy Meets Baby*; *Love and Kisses*; *What Happened Caroline?*; *Caroline* prod/rel: Universal
  Frutto Acerbo 1934 d: Carlo Ludovico BragagliA. lps: Lotte Menas, Nino Besozzi, Maria WronskA. 76M ITL. prod/rel: Industrice Cin.Che Italiane (I.C.I.)
Josephine, Novel
  Royal Divorce, A 1938 d: Jack Raymond. lps: Ruth Chatterton, Pierre Blanchar, Frank Cellier. 85M UKN. prod/rel: Imperator, Paramount

THEURIET, ANDRE
Au Paradis Des Enfants, Novel
  Au Paradis Des Enfants 1917 d: Charles Burguet. lps: Armand Dutertre, Derive, Fabrice. 1000m FRN. prod/rel: Louis Nalpas Consortium
La Maison Des Deux Barbeaux, Novel
  Maison Sans Amour, L' 1927 d: Emilien Champetier. lps: Jean Coquelin, Marie Glory, Henri Baudin. F FRN. prod/rel: Champetier
Micheline, Novel
  Micheline 1921 d: Jean Kemm. lps: Genevieve Felix, Renee Lemercier, Cesar. 1330m FRN. prod/rel: Scagl
Le Sang Des Finoel, Novel
  Sang Des Finoels, Le 1922 d: Georges Monca, Rose Pansini. lps: Georges Gauthier, Gina Relly, Juliette Boyer. 1770m FRN. prod/rel: Films Pansini

THEVENIN
Barnabe Tignol Et San Baleine, Novel
  Pension Jonas 1941 d: Pierre Caron. lps: Pierre Larquey, Jacques Pills, Suzanne Dehelly. 98M FRN. prod/rel: Films Orange

THEW, HARVEY F.
Mind Your Feet Kitty, Short Story
  Delicious Little Devil, The 1919 d: Robert Z. Leonard. lps: Mae Murray, Harry Rattenberry, Richard Cummings. 5650f USA. prod/rel: Universal Film Mfg. Co.

THIBOUST, LAMBERT
La Voleuse d'Enfants, Play
  Voleuse d'Enfants, La 1912 d: Georges DenolA. lps: Georges Saillard, Lucie Brille. 745m FRN. prod/rel: Scagl

THIELE, COLIN
Blue Fin, 1969, Novel
  Blue Fin 1978 d: Carl Schultz. lps: Hardy Kruger, Greg Rowe, Elspeth Ballantyne. 88M ASL. *Sea Quest* prod/rel: South Australian Film Corp.©, Mcelroy and Mcelroy
A Fire in the Stone, Novel
  Fire in the Stone 1983 d: Gary Conway. lps: Paul Smith, Linda Hartley, Theo Pertsinidis. TVM. 97M ASL. prod/rel: South Australian Film Corp.
Storm Boy, 1963, Novel
  Storm Boy 1976 d: Henri Safran. lps: Greg Rowe, Peter Cummins, David Gulpilil. 88M ASL.

THIER, WALTER
Schweinefleisch in Dosen, Play
  Schuld Allein Ist Der Wein 1949 d: Fritz Kirchhoff. lps: Ernst Waldow, Olga Limburg, Inge Stoldt. 92M GRM. *It's All the Wine's Fault* prod/rel: Pontus, Hamburg

THIERRY, MARIE
Visage d'Aieule, Short Story
  Visage d'Aieule 1926 d: Gaston Roudes. lps: France Dhelia, Jean Gerard, Joachim Carrasco. 1400m FRN. *Portrait d'Aieule Visage de Jeune Fille* prod/rel: Films Roudes

THIES, FRANK
Leggenda Napoletana, Novel
  Enrico Caruso 1951 d: Giacomo Gentilomo. lps: Ermanno Randi, Gina Lollobrigida, Carletto Sposito. 93M ITL. *The Young Caruso* (USA); *Leggenda Di Una Voce* prod/rel: Asso Film

THIESS, FRANK
Weg Zu Isabell, Novel
  Weg Zu Isabell, Der 1939 d: Erich Engel. lps: Hilde Krahl, Ewald Balser, Maria Koppenhofer. 85M GRM. prod/rel: Tobis, N.W.D.F.

THIGPEN M.D., CORBETT
A Case of Multiple Personality, Book
  Three Faces of Eve, The 1957 d: Nunnally Johnson. lps: Joanne Woodward, David Wayne, Lee J. Cobb. 95M USA. prod/rel: 20th Century-Fox

THIJSSEN, FELIX
Wildschut, Novel
  Wildschut 1986 d: Bobby Eerhart. lps: Hidde Maas, Jack Monkau, Annick Christians. 95M BLG/NTH. *Stronghold*; *Gamekeeper* prod/rel: Cannon

THOM, ROBERT
Baby, the Day It All Happened, 1966, Short Story
  Wild in the Streets 1968 d: Barry Shear. lps: Shelley Winters, Christopher Jones, Diane Varsi. 97M USA. prod/rel: American International Pictures
The Legend of Lylah Clare, 1963, Play
  Legend of Lylah Clare, The 1968 d: Robert Aldrich. lps: Kim Novak, Peter Finch, Ernest Borgnine. 130M USA. prod/rel: Associates & Aldrich Co.

THOMA, LUDWIG
Story
  Lausbubengeschichten 1964 d: Helmut Kautner. lps: Hansi Kraus, Michl Lang, Carl Wery. 100M GRM. *Ludwig Thomas Lausbubengeschichten*; *Rascals' Tales* prod/rel: Franz Seitz, Columbia-Bavaria
  Ludwig Auf Freierfuszen 1969 d: Franz Seitz. lps: Hansi Kraus, Harald Juhnke, Kristina Nel. 92M GRM. *Ludwig the Courter* prod/rel: Franz Seitz
  Onkel Filser - Allerneueste Lausbubengeschichten 1966 d: Werner Jacobs. lps: Michl Lang, Hansi Kraus, Fritz Tillmann. 89M GRM. *Uncle Filser* prod/rel: Franz Seitz, Constantin
Play
  Wenn Ludwig Ins Manover Zieht 1967 d: Werner Jacobs. lps: Hansi Kraus, Heidelinde Weis, Rudolf Rhomberg. 91M GRM. *When Ludwig Goes on Manoeuvres* prod/rel: Franz Seitz, Constantin
Erster Klasse, Play
  Weissblaue Lowe, Der 1952 d: Werner Jacobs, Olf Fischer. lps: Wastl Witt, Lore Frisch, Paul Kurzinger. 100M GRM. *The Blue and White Lion* prod/rel: Primus
Der Jagerloisl, Novel
  Heimat, Deine Sterne 1951 d: Hermann Kugelstadt. lps: Adrian Hoven, Hansi Knoteck, Ernst Waldow. 79M GRM. *Stars of the Homeland*; *Jagerloisl Vom Tegersee* prod/rel: Konig, Kopp
Die Medaille, Play
  O Diese Bayern 1960 d: Arnulf Schroeder. lps: Liesl Karlstadt, Rudolf Vogel, Jurgen von Alten. 87M GRM. *Oh These Bavarians* prod/rel: Schonger, Adria
Moral, Play
  Moral 1928 d: Willi Wolff. lps: Ellen Richter, Jacob Tiedtke, Ralph Arthur Roberts. 2216m GRM. prod/rel: Ellen Richter-Film-Prod.
Muncherinnen, Novel
  Munchnerinnen 1944 d: Philipp L. Mayring. lps: Gabriele Reismuller, Heli Finkenzeller, Hans Holt. 86M GRM. *Uber Alles Die Liebe* prod/rel: Bavaria
Der Schusternazi, Play
  Arme Millionar, Der 1939 d: Joe Stockel. lps: Weiss Ferdl, Willy Rosner, Trude Haefelin. 89M GRM. *The Poor Millionaire* (USA) prod/rel: Bavaria, Ring
Tante Frieda, Novel
  Tante Frieda - Neue Lausbubengeschichten 1965 d: Werner Jacobs. lps: Hansi Kraus, Elisabeth Flickenschildt, Gustav Knuth. 87M GRM. *Aunt Frieda* prod/rel: Franz Seitz

THOMACINI, JEAN-PIERRE
Story
Ete d'Enfer, Un 1984 d: Michael Schock. lps: Thierry L'Hermitte, Veronique Jannot, Daniel Duval. 104M FRN/SPN. *Un Verano de Infierno* (SPN) prod/rel: Act 3000, TF 1

THOMAS, A. E.
The Big Pond, New York 1928, Play
Big Pond, The 1930 d: Hobart Henley. lps: Maurice Chevalier, Claudette Colbert, George Barbier. 75M USA. prod/rel: Paramount-Publix Corp.
Grande Mare, La 1930 d: Jacques Bataille-Henri, Hobart Henley. lps: Maurice Chevalier, Claudette Colbert, Henry Mortimer. 78M USA. prod/rel: Films Paramount, Paramount-Publix Corp.
The Champion, New York 1921, Play
World's Champion, The 1922 d: Phil Rosen. lps: Wallace Reid, Lois Wilson, Lionel Belmore. 5030f USA. prod/rel: Famous Players-Lasky, Paramount Pictures
Just Suppose, New York 1923, Play
Just Suppose 1926 d: Kenneth Webb. lps: Richard Barthelmess, Lois Moran, Geoffrey Kerr. 6270f USA. *Golden Youth* (UKN) prod/rel: Inspiration Pictures, First National Pictures
No More Ladies, New York 1934, Play
No More Ladies 1935 d: Edward H. Griffith, George Cukor (Uncredited). lps: Joan Crawford, Robert Montgomery, Charlie Ruggles. 82M USA. prod/rel: Metro-Goldwyn-Mayer Corp.©
Only 38, New York 1921, Play
Only 38 1923 d: William C. de Mille. lps: May McAvoy, Lois Wilson, Elliott Dexter. 6175f USA. prod/rel: Famous Players-Lasky, Paramount Pictures
The Rainbow, New York 1912, Play
Rainbow, The 1917 d: Ralph Dean. lps: Dorothy Bernard, Robert Conness, Jack Sherrill. 6r USA. *After the Storm* prod/rel: William L. Sherrill Feature Corp., Art Dramas, Inc.
Thirty Days; a Farce in Three Acts, 1915, Play
Girl Habit, The 1931 d: Eddie Cline. lps: Charles Ruggles, Sue Conroy, Tamara GevA. 77M USA. prod/rel: Paramount Publix Corp.©
Thirty Days 1922 d: James Cruze. lps: Wallace Reid, Wanda Hawley, Charles Ogle. 4930f USA. prod/rel: Famous Players-Lasky, Paramount Pictures

THOMAS, AMBROISE (1811–1896), FRN
Mignon, Paris 1866, Opera
Mignon 1915 d: William Nigh. lps: Beatriz Michelena, House Peters, Clara Beyers. 5r USA. prod/rel: California Motion Picture Corp.©, World Film Corp.
Mignon 1919 d: Mario Gargiulo. lps: Tina Xeo, Franco Piersanti, Renee de Saint-Leger. 1483m ITL. prod/rel: Flegrea Film

THOMAS, AUGUSTUS
Arizona, Chicago 1899, Play
Arizona 1913 d: Lawrence McGill, Augustus Thomas. lps: Gertrude Shipman, Cyril Scott, Gail Kane. 6r USA. prod/rel: All-Star Feature Corp., State Rights
Arizona 1918 d: Douglas Fairbanks, Albert Parker. lps: Douglas Fairbanks, Marjorie Daw, Marguerite de La Motte. 4213f USA. prod/rel: Douglas Fairbanks Pictures Corp.©, Famous Players-Lasky Corp.
Arizona 1931 d: George B. Seitz. lps: John Wayne, Laura La Plante, Forrest Stanley. 70M USA. *The Virtuous Wife* (UKN); *Men are Like That* prod/rel: Columbia Pictures Corp.
As a Man Thinks, New York 1911, Play
As a Man Thinks 1919 d: George Irving. lps: Leah Baird, Henry Clive, Warburton Gamble. 5r USA. prod/rel: Artco Productions, Inc., Four Star Pictures
The Capitol, New York 1895, Play
Capitol, The 1920 d: George Irving. lps: Leah Baird, Robert T. Haines, Alexander Gaden. 5350f USA. prod/rel: Artco Productions, W. W. Hodkinson Corp.
Colorado, New York 1901, Play
Colorado 1915 d: Norval MacGregor. lps: Hobart Bosworth, Carl von Schiller, Ronald Bradbury. 5r USA. prod/rel: Universal Film Mfg. Co.©
Colorado 1921 d: B. Reeves Eason. lps: Frank Mayo, Charles Newton, Gloria Hope. 4875f USA. prod/rel: Universal Film Mfg. Co.
The Earl of Pawtucket, New York 1903, Play
Earl of Pawtucket, The 1915 d: Harry Myers. lps: Lawrence d'Orsay, Rosemary Theby, Thomas A. Curran. 5r USA. prod/rel: Universal Film Mfg. Co.©
Editha's Burglar, New York 1887, Play
Burglar, The 1917 d: Harley Knoles. lps: Carlyle Blackwell, Madge Evans, Evelyn Greeley. 5r USA. prod/rel: World Film Corp.©

The Education of Mr. Pipp, New York 1905, Play
Education of Mr. Pipp, The 1914 d: Augustus Thomas. lps: Digby Bell, Edna Brun, Belle Daube. 5r USA. prod/rel: All Star Feature Corp., Alco Film Corp.
The Harvest Moon, New York 1909, Play
Harvest Moon, The 1920 d: J. Searle Dawley. lps: Doris Kenyon, Wilfred Lytell, George Lessey. 6r USA. prod/rel: Deitrich-Beck, Inc., Gibraltar Pictures
In Mizzoura, Chicago 1893, Play
In Mizzoura 1914 d: Lawrence McGill. lps: Burr McIntosh, Raymond Bond, Harry Blakemore. 5r USA. prod/rel: All Star Feature Corp.
In Mizzoura 1919 d: Hugh Ford. lps: Robert Warwick, Eileen Percy, Robert Cain. 4475f USA. prod/rel: Famous Players-Lasky Corp.©, Paramount-Artcraft Pictures
The Kentuckian, Play
Kentuckian, The 1908 d: Wallace McCutcheon. lps: Eddie Dillon, Robert Vignola, John Adolfi. 757f USA. prod/rel: Biograph Co.
Mrs. Leffingwell's Boots, 1905, Play
Mrs. Leffingwell's Boots 1919 d: Walter Edwards. lps: Constance Talmadge, Harrison Ford, George Fisher. 4122f USA. *Mrs. Leffingwell's Boot* prod/rel: Select Pictures Corp.©
On the Quiet, New York 1901, Play
On the Quiet 1918 d: Chet Withey. lps: John Barrymore, Lois Meredith, Frank Losee. 4549f USA. prod/rel: Famous Players-Lasky Corp.©, Paramount Pictures
The Other Girl, New York 1903, Play
Other Girl, The 1915 d: Percy Winter. lps: James J. Corbett, Paul Gilmore, Zola Telmzart. 5r USA. prod/rel: Raver Film Corp., State Rights
Rio Grande, New York 1916, Play
Rio Grande 1920 d: Edwin Carewe. lps: Hector V. Sarno, Rosemary Theby, George E. Stone. 7r USA. prod/rel: Edwin Carewe Productions, Inc., Pathe Exchange, Inc.©
The Witching Hour, New York 1907, Play
Witching Hour, The 1916 d: George Irving. lps: C. Aubrey Smith, Robert Conness, Marie Shotwell. 7r USA. prod/rel: Frohman Amusement Corp., State Rights
Witching Hour, The 1921 d: William D. Taylor. lps: Elliott Dexter, Winter Hall, Ruth Renick. 6734f USA. prod/rel: Famous Players-Lasky, Paramount Pictures
Witching Hour, The 1934 d: Henry Hathaway. lps: Guy Standing, John Halliday, Judith Allen. 64M USA. prod/rel: Paramount Productions©

THOMAS, BASIL
Book of the Month, London 1954, Play
Please Turn Over 1959 d: Gerald Thomas. lps: Ted Ray, Jean Kent, Leslie Phillips. 87M UKN. prod/rel: Anglo-Amalgamated, Beaconsfield
The Lovebirds, London 1957, Play
Night We Got the Bird, The 1960 d: Darcy Conyers. lps: Brian Rix, Dora Bryan, Ronald Shiner. 82M UKN. prod/rel: British Lion, Rix-Conyers
Shooting Star, Play
Great Game, The 1953 d: Maurice Elvey. lps: James Hayter, Thora Hird, Diana Dors. 80M UKN. prod/rel: Advance, Adelphi

THOMAS, BOB
Bud and Lou, Book
Bud and Lou 1978 d: Robert C. Thompson. lps: Harvey Korman, Buddy Hackett, Michele Lee. TVM. 100M USA. prod/rel: NBC, Bob Banner Associates
Howard: the Amazing Mr. Hughes, Book
Amazing Howard Hughes, The 1977 d: William A. Graham. lps: Tommy Lee Jones, Ed Flanders, James Hampton. TVM. 215M USA. prod/rel: Emi, Roger Gimbel Productions

THOMAS, BRANDON
Charley's Aunt, London 1892, Play
Charley's Aunt 1925 d: Scott Sidney. lps: Sydney Chaplin, Ethel Shannon, James E. Page. 7243f USA. prod/rel: Christie Film Co., Producers Distributing Corp.
Charley's Aunt 1930 d: Al Christie. lps: Charles Ruggles, June Collyer, Hugh Williams. 88M USA. prod/rel: Christie Film Co., Columbia Pictures
Charley's Aunt 1941 d: Archie Mayo. lps: Jack Benny, Kay Francis, James Ellison. 83M USA. *Charley's American Aunt* (UKN) prod/rel: 20th Century Fox
Charley's Aunt 1969 d: John Gorrie. lps: Danny La Rue, Coral Browne, John Standing. MTV. UKN. prod/rel: BBC
Charley's Aunt 1977 d: Graeme Muir. lps: Eric Sykes, Jimmy Edwards, Barbara Murray. MTV. 75M UKN.

Charley's (Big Hearted) Aunt 1940 d: Walter Forde. lps: Arthur Askey, Richard Murdoch, Moore Marriott. 76M UKN. prod/rel: Gainsborough, General Film Distributors
Charleys Tante 1934 d: R. A. Stemmle. lps: Fita Benkhoff, Paul Henckels, Jan KiepurA. 87M GRM.
Charleys Tante 1956 d: Hans Quest. lps: Heinz Ruhmann, Hertha Feiler, Claus Biederstaedt. 90M GRM. *Charley's Aunt* prod/rel: Berolina
Charleys Tante 1963 d: Geza von CziffrA. lps: Peter Alexander, Maria Sebaldt, Peter Vogel. 91M AUS. prod/rel: Sascha
Marraine de Charley, La 1935 d: Piere Colombier. lps: Lucien Baroux, Claude Lehmann, Olly Flint. 85M FRN. prod/rel: F.E.F.
Marraine de Charley, La 1959 d: Pierre Chevalier. lps: Fernand Raynaud, Claude Vega, Anny Auberson. 83M FRN. prod/rel: Plazza Films Productions
Where's Charley? 1952 d: David Butler. lps: Ray Bolger, Allyn Ann McLerie, Robert Shackleton. 97M UKN/USA. prod/rel: Warner Bros., First National
Zia Di Carlo, La 1911. 188m ITL. *Charley's Aunt* (UKN) prod/rel: Pasquali E C.
Zia Di Carlo, La 1943 d: Alfredo Guarini. lps: Erminio MacArio, Lucia d'Alberti, Carlo Minello. 66M ITL. prod/rel: Cines, Capitani Film
Zio Di Carlo, La 1913 d: Umberto Paradisi. lps: Enrico Bracci, Mario Guaita-Ausonia, Ubaldo Maria Del Colle. 600m ITL. prod/rel: Pasquali E C.

THOMAS, BRUCE
The Safecracker, Book
Safecracker, The 1957 d: Ray Milland. lps: Ray Milland, Barry Jones, Jeannette Sterke. 96M UKN/USA. prod/rel: MGM, Coronado

THOMAS, CRAIG (1942–, UKN, Thomas, Craig D.
Firefox, Novel
Firefox 1982 d: Clint Eastwood. lps: Clint Eastwood, Freddie Jones, David Huffman. 136M USA. prod/rel: Warner

THOMAS, DYLAN (1914–1953), UKN, Thomas, Dylan Marlais
The Mouse and the Woman, 1936, Short Story
In the Afternoon of War 1981 d: Karl Francis. lps: Dafydd Hywel, Karen Archer, Patrick Napier. 105M UKN. *The Mouse and the Woman*; *Afternoon of War* prod/rel: Alvicar, Facelift
Under Milk Wood, 1954, Play
Under Milk Wood 1972 d: Andrew Sinclair. lps: Richard Burton, Peter O'Toole, Elizabeth Taylor. 88M UKN. prod/rel: Timon
Under Milk Wood 1992. ANM. 50M UKN.

THOMAS, EDWARD
House of America, Play
House of America 1997 d: Marc Evans. lps: Sian Phillips, Steven MacKintosh, Matthew Rhys. 96M UKN. prod/rel: September Films, Stichting Bergen

THOMAS, EUGENE
The Man O' Warsman, New York 1898, Play
Man O' Warsman, The 1914 d: Thomas E. SheA. lps: Thomas E. Shea, Dixie Compton. 5r USA. prod/rel: Broadway Picture Producing Co.

THOMAS, GORDON
The Day the Bubble Burst, Book
Day the Bubble Burst, The 1982 d: Joseph Hardy. lps: Richard Crenna, Robert Vaughn, Blanche Baker. TVM. 150M USA. prod/rel: CBS, Twentieth Century Fox
The Day the World Ended, Novel
When Time Ran Out. 1980 d: James Goldstone. lps: Paul Newman, Jacqueline Bisset, William Holden. 121M USA. *The Day the World Ended* prod/rel: Warner
Enola Gay, Book
Enola Gay: the Men, the Mission, the Atomic Bomb 1980 d: David Lowell Rich. lps: Patrick Duffy, Billy Crystal, Kim Darby. TVM. 150M USA. *Enola Gay* (UKN) prod/rel: NBC, the Production Company
Voyage of the Damned, Book
Voyage of the Damned 1976 d: Stuart Rosenberg. lps: Faye Dunaway, Oskar Werner, Max von Sydow. 158M UKN/SPN. prod/rel: Itc, Associated General

THOMAS, HANS
Ferien Wie Noch Nie, Novel
Ferien Wie Noch Nie 1963 d: Wolfgang Schleif. lps: Carlos Thompson, Eva Bartok, Corny Collins. 94M GRM. *Vacation As Never Before* prod/rel: Arca, Kurt Ulrich
Percy Auf Abwegen, Novel
Mann Auf Abwegen, Ein 1940 d: Herbert Selpin. lps: Hans Albers, Hilde Weissner, Charlotte Thiele. 85M GRM. prod/rel: Euphono-Tobis, Kristall

THOMAS, JEAN-LOUIS
Manie de la Persecution, Novel
  Diaboliquement Votre 1967 d: Julien Duvivier. lps: Alain Delon, Senta Berger, Sergio Fantoni. 95M FRN/GRM/ITL. *Mit Teuflischen Grussen* (GRM); *Diabolicamente Tua* (ITL); *Diabolically Yours*; *Devil's Greetings to You* prod/rel: Lira Films, Copernic-Comacico

THOMAS, JOHN
Dry Martini: a Gentleman Turns to Love, New York 1926, Novel
  Dry Martini 1928 d: Harry d'Abbadie d'Arrast. lps: Mary Astor, Matt Moore, Jocelyn Lee. 7176f USA. prod/rel: Fox Film Corp.

THOMAS, LESLIE (1931–, UKN
Novel
  Dangerous Davies - the Last Detective 1979 d: Val Guest. lps: Bernard Cribbins, Bill Maynard, Joss Ackland. TVM. 105M UKN. prod/rel: Atv

Stand Up Virgin Soldiers, Novel
  Stand Up Virgin Soldiers 1977 d: Norman Cohen. lps: Robin Askwith, Nigel Davenport, George Layton. 91M UKN. prod/rel: Warner Bros., Greg Smith

The Tropic of Ruislip, Novel
  Tropic 1979 d: Matthew Robinson. lps: Ronald Pickup, Ronald Lacey, Hilary Tindall. MTV. 300M UKN.

The Virgin Soldiers, London 1966, Novel
  Virgin Soldiers, The 1969 d: John Dexter. lps: Lynn Redgrave, Hywel Bennett, Nigel Davenport. 96M UKN. prod/rel: Open Road Films, Highroad Productions

THOMAS, LOUIS
Les Mauvaises Frequentations, Novel
  Racines du Mal, Les 1967 d: Maurice Cam. lps: Michel Debats, Regine Ginestet, Josette Petit. F FRN. prod/rel: Aiglon Films

THOMAS, MICHAEL
The Dead Heart, Book
  Welcome to Woop Woop 1997 d: Stephan Elliott. lps: Johnathon Schaech, Rod Taylor, Susie Porter. 102M ASL/UKN. prod/rel: Scala, Unthank

THOMAS, PAUL
L' Espion, Paris 1965, Novel
  Espion, L' 1966 d: Raoul J. Levy. lps: Montgomery Clift, Hardy Kruger, Macha Meril. 106M FRN/GRM. *Lautlose Waffen* (GRM); *The Defector* (USA) prod/rel: P.E.C.F., Rhein-Main Films

THOMAS, ROBERT
Piege Pour un Homme Seul, Novel
  Honeymoon With a Stranger 1969 d: John Peyser. lps: Janet Leigh, Rossano Brazzi, Joseph Lenzi. TVM. 74M USA. prod/rel: 20th Century-Fox

Piege Pour un Homme Seul, Play
  Vanishing Act 1986 d: David Greene. lps: Mike Farrell, Margot Kidder, Elliott Gould. TVM. 100M USA. prod/rel: Freemantle International
  One of My Wives Is Missing 1976 d: Glenn Jordan. lps: Jack Klugman, Elizabeth Ashley, James Franciscus. TVM. 100M USA. prod/rel: Spelling/Goldberg Productions

THOMASHEFSKY, BORIS
Bar-Mitzvah, Play
  Bar-Mitzvah 1935 d: Henry Lynn. lps: Boris Thomashefsky, Regina Zuckerberg, Anita Chayes. 81M USA. prod/rel: S & L Film Co.

THOMPSON, ALEX M.
The Arcadians, London 1909, Musical Play
  Arcadians, The 1927 d: Victor Saville. lps: Ben Blue, Jeanne de Casalis, Vesta SylvA. 7000f UKN. *Land of Heart's Desire* prod/rel: Gaumont

THOMPSON, CHARLES S.
The Cavalier, Short Story
  Painted Lady, The 1914 d: Frederick Sullivan. lps: Dorothy Gish, Blanche Sweet, William E. Lawrence. 2r USA. prod/rel: Majestic

THOMPSON, CHARLOTTE
In Search of a Sinner, Play
  In Search of a Sinner 1920 d: David Kirkland. lps: Constance Talmadge, Rockliffe Fellowes, Corliss Giles. 5485f USA. prod/rel: Constance Talmadge Film Co., First National Exhibitors Circuit

The Strength of the Weak, New York 1906, Play
  Strength of the Weak, The 1916 d: Lucius Henderson. lps: Mary Fuller, Edwards Davis, Harry Hilliard. 5r USA. prod/rel: Bluebird Photoplays, Inc.©

THOMPSON, DANIELE
Le Retour, Novel
  Retour, Le 1990 d: Michel Boisrond. lps: Michele Morgan, Marie-France Pisier, Daniel Gelin. TVM. 60M FRN.

THOMPSON, DENMAN
The Old Homestead, Boston 1886, Play
  Old Homestead, The 1916 d: James Kirkwood. lps: Frank Losee, Creighton Hale, Denman Maley. 5r USA. prod/rel: Famous Players Film Co.©, Paramount Pictures Corp.

Our New Minister, Play
  Our New Minister 1913. lps: Joseph Conyers, Thomas McGrath, Alice Joyce. 3000f USA. prod/rel: Kalem

The Sunshine of Paradise Alley, 1895, Play
  Sunshine of Paradise Alley 1926 d: Jack Nelson. lps: Barbara Bedford, Kenneth McDonald, Max Davidson. 6850f USA. prod/rel: Chadwick Pictures

THOMPSON, ERNEST (1950–, USA, Thompson, Richard Ernest
On Golden Pond, Play
  On Golden Pond 1981 d: Mark Rydell. lps: Henry Fonda, Jane Fonda, Katharine Hepburn. 110M USA. prod/rel: Itc, Ipc

THOMPSON, FRED
Funny Face, London 1928, Play
  She Couldn't Say No 1939 d: Graham Cutts. lps: Tommy Trinder, Fred Emney, Googie Withers. 72M UKN. prod/rel: Associated British Picture Corporation
  She Knew What She Wanted 1936 d: Thomas Bentley. lps: Albert Burdon, Betty Ann Davies, Claude Dampier. 74M UKN. prod/rel: Rialto, Wardour

Lady Be Good, New York 1924, Musical Play
  Lady Be Good 1928 d: Richard Wallace. lps: Jack Mulhall, Dorothy MacKaill, John Miljan. 6600f USA. prod/rel: First National Pictures

Rio Rita, New York 1927, Musical Play
  Rio Rita 1929 d: Luther Reed. lps: Bebe Daniels, John Boles, Don Alvarado. 15r USA. prod/rel: RKO Productions
  Rio Rita 1942 d: S. Sylvan Simon. lps: Bud Abbott, Lou Costello, Kathryn Grayson. 91M USA. prod/rel: MGM

This'll Make You Whistle, London 1935, Play
  This'll Make You Whistle 1936 d: Herbert Wilcox. lps: Jack Buchanan, Elsie Randolph, Jean Gillie. 79M UKN. prod/rel: Herbert Wilcox Productions, British International Pictures

Tip-Toes, London 1926, Musical Play
  Tiptoes 1927 d: Herbert Wilcox. lps: Dorothy Gish, Will Rogers, Nelson Keys. 6286f UKN. *Tip Toes* prod/rel: British National, Paramount

A Welcome Wife, Play
  Let's Love and Laugh 1931 d: Richard Eichberg. lps: Gene Gerrard, Muriel Angelus, George Gee. 85M UKN. *Bridegroom for Two* (USA); *The Bridegroom's Widow* prod/rel: British International Pictures, Wardour

THOMPSON, HAMILTON
The Ark Angel, Short Story
  Rowdy, The 1921 d: David Kirkland. lps: Rex de Rosselli, Anna Hernandez, Gladys Walton. 4974f USA. prod/rel: Universal Film Mfg. Co.

THOMPSON, HUNTER S. (1939–, USA, Thompson, Hunter Stockton, Owl, Sebastian
Fear and Loathing in Las Vegas, Book
  Fear and Loathing in Las Vegas 1998 d: Terry Gilliam. lps: Johnny Depp, Benicio Del Toro, Craig Bierko. 119M USA. prod/rel: Universal, Rhino Films

THOMPSON, J. LEE
Double Error, 1935, Play
  Murder Without Crime 1950 d: J. Lee Thompson. lps: Dennis Price, Derek Farr, Patricia Plunkett. 76M UKN. prod/rel: Associated British Picture Corporation, Ab-Pathe
  Price of Folly, The 1937 d: Walter Summers. lps: Leonora Corbett, Colin Keith-Johnston, Leslie Perrins. 52M UKN. *Double Error* prod/rel: Welwyn, Pathe

THOMPSON, JIM (1906–1977), USA
After Dark, My Sweet, Novel
  After Dark, My Sweet 1990 d: James Foley. lps: Jason Patric, Rocky Giordani, Rachel Ward. 114M USA. prod/rel: Avenue Pictures

The Getaway, Novel
  Getaway, The 1972 d: Sam Peckinpah. lps: Steve McQueen, Ali MacGraw, Ben Johnson. 123M USA. prod/rel: Solar, First Artists
  Getaway, The 1994 d: Roger Donaldson. lps: Alec Baldwin, Kim Basinger, Michael Madsen. 115M USA.

The Killer Inside Me, Novel
  Killer Inside Me, The 1976 d: Burt Kennedy. lps: Stacy Keach, Susan Tyrrell, Tisha Sterling. 99M USA. prod/rel: Devi Prod.

The Kill-Off, Novel
  Kill-Off, The 1990 d: Maggie Greenwald. lps: Loretta Gross, Jackson Sims, Steve Monroe. 110M USA. prod/rel: Filmworld International

Pop. 1280, Novel
  Coup de Torchon 1981 d: Bertrand Tavernier. lps: Philippe Noiret, Isabelle Huppert, Stephane Audran. 128M FRN. *Clean Slate* (UKN) prod/rel: Les Films de la Tour, Films a2

A Swell-Looking Babe, Novel
  Hit Me 1996 d: Steven Shainberg. lps: Elias Koteas, Laure Marsac, Jay Leggett. 125M USA. prod/rel: Slough Pond Co.

This World, Then the Fireworks, Short Story
  This World, Then the Fireworks 1997 d: Michael Oblowitz. lps: Billy Zane, Gina Gershon, Sheryl Lee. 100M USA. prod/rel: Largo Entertainment, Muse, Balzac's Shirt, Wyman

THOMPSON, JULIAN
The Warrior's Husband, New York 1932, Play
  Warrior's Husband, The 1933 d: Walter Lang. lps: Elissa Landi, David Manners, Ernest Truex. 75M USA. prod/rel: Fox Film Corp.©

THOMPSON, KEENE
Certain Lee, Story
  Lone Fighter 1923 d: Albert Russell. lps: Vester Pegg, Josephine Hill, Joe Ryan. 4800f USA. prod/rel: Sunset Productions

THOMPSON, MARAVENE
Persuasive Peggy, New York 1916, Novel
  Persuasive Peggy 1917 d: Charles J. Brabin. lps: Peggy Hyland, William B. Davidson, Mary Cecil Parker. 6r USA. prod/rel: Mayfair Film Corp.©, State Rights

The Woman's Law, New York 1914, Novel
  Net, The 1923 d: J. Gordon Edwards. lps: Barbara Castleton, Raymond Bloomer, Alan Roscoe. 6135f USA. prod/rel: Fox Film Corp.
  Woman's Law, The 1916 d: Lawrence McGill. lps: Florence Reed, Duncan McRae, Anita d'Este Scott. 5r USA. prod/rel: Arrow Film Corp., Pathe Exchange, Inc.©

THOMPSON, MARY AGNES
A Call from Mitch Miller, Short Story
  Loving You 1957 d: Hal Kanter. lps: Elvis Presley, Wendell Corey, Lizabeth Scott. 101M USA. prod/rel: Paramount

THOMPSON, MORTON
Joe the Wounded Tennis Player, Novel
  My Brother Talks to Horses 1946 d: Fred Zinnemann. lps: Butch Jenkins, Peter Lawford, Beverly Tyler. 94M USA. prod/rel: MGM

Not As a Stranger, 1954, Novel
  Not As a Stranger 1955 d: Stanley Kramer. lps: Robert Mitchum, Olivia de Havilland, Frank SinatrA. 135M USA. prod/rel: United Artists, Stanley Kramer Pictures Corp.

THOMPSON, PEGGY
A Kiss in the Dark, Novel
  Remous 1934 d: Edmond T. Greville. lps: Jeanne Boitel, Jean Galland, Maurice Maillot. 84M FRN. *Whirlpool* prod/rel: H.O. Films

THOMPSON, STEVEN L.
Recovery, Book
  Honor Bound 1989 d: Jeannot Szwarc. lps: Tom Skerritt, John Philbin, Gabrielle Lazure. 102M USA. prod/rel: Filmaccord Productions

THOMPSON, THOMAS (1933–1982), USA
Celebrity, Novel
  Celebrity 1984 d: Paul Wendkos. lps: Michael Beck, Joseph Bottoms, Ben Masters. TVM. 300M USA. prod/rel: NBC Productions

Richie, Book
  Death of Richie, The 1977 d: Paul Wendkos. lps: Ben Gazzara, Robby Benson, Eileen Brennan. TVM. 100M USA. *Richie* prod/rel: NBC, Henry Jaffe Enterprises

THOMPSON-SETON, ERNEST
The King of the Currampaw Lobo, Novel
  Legend of Lobo, The 1962 d: James Algar. 67M USA. prod/rel: Walt Disney Productions, Cangary, Ltd.

THORN, RONALD SCOTT
The Full Treatment, London 1959, Novel
  Full Treatment, The 1961 d: Val Guest. lps: Claude Dauphin, Diane Cilento, Ronald Lewis. 109M UKN. *Stop Me Before I Kill!* (USA); *The Treatment* prod/rel: Hammer Film Productions, Falcon Films

THORNBURG, NEWTON
Cutter's Way, Novel
  Cutter and Bone 1981 d: Ivan Passer. lps: Jeff Bridges, John Heard, Lisa Eichhorn. 109M USA. *Cutter's Way* prod/rel: United Artists, Gurian Entertainment

THORNDIKE, WILLIAM RUSSELL
Christopher Syn, Novel
  Dr. Syn 1937 d: R. William Neill. lps: George Arliss, John Loder, Margaret Lockwood. 80M UKN. prod/rel: Gaumont-British, General Film Distributors

Dr. Syn - Alias the Scarecrow 1963 d: James Neilson. lps: Patrick McGoohan, George Cole, Tony Britton. 98M UKN. *The Scarecrow of Romney Marsh* prod/rel: Walt Disney

Dr. Syn, Novel
Captain Clegg 1962 d: Peter Graham Scott. lps: Peter Cushing, Yvonne Romain, Patrick Allen. 82M UKN. *Night Creatures* (USA); *Dr. Syn* prod/rel: Hammer, Merlin

THORNE, ANTHONY
The Baby and the Battleship, Novel
Baby and the Battleship, The 1956 d: Jay Lewis. lps: John Mills, Richard Attenborough, Andre Morell. 96M UKN. prod/rel: British Lion, Jay Lewis

So Long at the Fair, Novel
So Long at the Fair 1950 d: Anthony Darnborough, Terence Fisher. lps: Jean Simmons, Dirk Bogarde, David Tomlinson. 86M UKN. prod/rel: General Film Distributors, Gainsborough

THORNE, AUGUSTUS
Beside the Bonnie Brier Bush, London 1895, Play
Beside the Bonnie Brier Bush 1921 d: Donald Crisp. lps: Donald Crisp, Mary Glynne, Langhorne Burton. 4662f UKN/USA. *The Bonnie Brier Bush* (USA); *The Bonnie Briar Bush* prod/rel: Famous Players-Lasky British Producers, Paramount Pictures

THORNE, E. P.
Three Silent Men, Novel
Three Silent Men 1940 d: Thomas Bentley. lps: Sebastian Shaw, Derrick de Marney, Patricia Roc. 72M UKN. prod/rel: Butcher's Film Service

THORNE, GUY
The Disappearance of the Judge, Novel
Disappearance of the Judge, The 1919 d: Alexander Butler. lps: James Lindsay, Florence Nelson, Mark Melford. 5000f UKN. prod/rel: Barker, Globe

When It Was Dark, Novel
When It Was Dark 1919 d: Arrigo Bocchi. lps: Manora Thew, Hayford Hobbs, George Butler. 6700f UKN. prod/rel: Windsor, Walturdaw

THORNE, RONALD SCOTT
Upstairs and Downstairs, Novel
Upstairs and Downstairs 1959 d: Ralph Thomas. lps: Michael Craig, Anne Heywood, Mylene Demongeot. 101M UKN. prod/rel: Rank, Rank Film Distributors

THORNE, VICTOR
Anne Against the World, New York 1925, Novel
Anne Against the World 1929 d: Duke Worne. lps: Shirley Mason, Jack Mower, James Bradbury Jr. 5731f USA. prod/rel: Trem Carr Productions, Rayart Pictures

THORNHILL, ALAN
Decision at Midnight, Novel
Decision at Midnight 1963 d: Lewis Allen. lps: Martin Landau, Nora Swinburne, Walter Fitzgerald. 93M USA. prod/rel: R.a.M.

The Hurricane, London 1960, Novel
Voice of the Hurricane 1964 d: George Fraser. lps: Muriel Smith, Phyllis Konstam, Reginald Owen. 80M USA. *The Hurricane* prod/rel: Ram Productions, Moral Re-Armament

THORP, MOLLY
The Hop Dog, Novel
Adventure in the Hopfields 1954 d: John Guillermin. lps: Mandy Miller, Mona Washbourne, Hilda Fenemore. 60M UKN. prod/rel: Vandyke, Children's Film Foundation

THORP, RODERICK
The Detective, New York 1966, Novel
Detective, The 1968 d: Gordon Douglas. lps: Frank Sinatra, Lee Remick, Ralph Meeker. 114M USA. prod/rel: Arcolla-Millfield, 20th Century-Fox

Nothing Lasts Forever, Novel
Die Hard 1988 d: John McTiernan. lps: Bruce Willis, Alan Rickman, Bonnie BedeliA. 131M USA. prod/rel: 20th Century-Fox, Gordon Company

Rainbow Drive, Novel
Rainbow Drive 1990 d: Bobby Roth. lps: Peter Weller, Sela Ward, Bruce Weitz. TVM. 100M USA.

THORPE, JIM
Jim Thorpe - All American, Autobiography
Jim Thorpe - All American 1951 d: Michael Curtiz. lps: Burt Lancaster, Charles Bickford, Steve Cochran. 107M USA. *Man of Bronze* (UKN) prod/rel: Warner Bros.

THORPE, ROSE H.
Curfew Shall Not Ring Tonight, Poem
Curfew Must Not Ring Tonight 1912 d: Hay Plumb. lps: Alec Worcester, Alma Taylor. 1100f UKN. prod/rel: Hepworth

Curfew Must Not Ring Tonight 1923 d: Edwin J. Collins. lps: Joan Morgan, M. A. Wetherell, Ronald Buchanan. 2700f UKN. prod/rel: British & Colonial, Walturdaw

Curfew Shall Not Ring Tonight 1906 d: Alf Collins. 730f UKN. prod/rel: Gaumont

Curfew Shall Not Ring Tonight 1912 d: Hal Reid. lps: Wallace Reid. SHT USA. prod/rel: Reliance

Curfew Shall Not Ring Tonight 1926 d: Frank Tilley. lps: John Stuart, Ena Evans. 2000f UKN. prod/rel: British Projects, Bsc

THORSTEINSSON, INDRIDI G.
Land Og Synir, Novel
Land Og Synir 1978 d: Agust Gudmundsson. lps: Gudny Sigurjonsson, Janos Trygvason, Jon Sigurbjornsson. 95M ICL. *Land and Sons* prod/rel: Isfilm

THORUP, KIRSTEN
Himmel Og Helvede, 1982, Novel
Himmel Og Helvede 1988 d: Morten Arnfred. lps: Ole Lemmeke, Karina Skands, Erik Mork. 120M DNM. *Heaven and Hell*

THORVALDSON, EINAR
The Match King, New York 1932, Novel
Match King, The 1932 d: Howard Bretherton, William Keighley. lps: Warren William, Lili Damita, Glenda Farrell. 80M USA. prod/rel: First National Pictures©

THORVALL, KERSTIN
I Stallet for En Pappa, 1971, Novel
Maria 1975 d: Mats Arehn. lps: Lis Nilheim, Thomas Hellberg, Ulf Hasseltorp. 97M SWD. prod/rel: Svenska Ab, Nordisk

THOUS, MAXIMILIANO
Moros Y Cristianos, Opera
Moros Y Cristianos 1926 d: Maximiliano Thous. lps: Anita Giner Soler, Leopoldo Pitarch, Ramon Serneguet. 71M SPN. prod/rel: Produccion Artista Cin.Ca Espanola

THRASHER, LESLIE
For the Love O' Lil, Short Story
For the Love O' Lil 1930 d: James Tinling. lps: Jack Mulhall, Elliott Nugent, Sally Starr. 67M USA. prod/rel: Columbia Pictures

THURBER, JAMES (1894–1961), USA, Thurber, James Grover
Story
War Between Men and Women, The 1972 d: Melville Shavelson. lps: Jack Lemmon, Barbara Harris, Jason Robards Jr. 105M USA. prod/rel: Cinema Center

The Catbird Seat, 1943, Short Story
Battle of the Sexes, The 1959 d: Charles Crichton. lps: Peter Sellers, Robert Morley, Constance Cummings. 84M UKN. prod/rel: Bryanston, Prometheus

The Male Animal, New York 1940, Play
Male Animal, The 1942 d: Elliott Nugent. lps: Henry Fonda, Olivia de Havilland, Jack Carson. 101M USA. prod/rel: Warner Bros.

She's Working Her Way Through College 1952 d: H. Bruce Humberstone. lps: Virginia Mayo, Ronald Reagan, Gene Nelson. 101M USA. prod/rel: Warner Bros.

My Life and Hard Times, 1933, Short Story
Rise and Shine 1941 d: Allan Dwan. lps: Jack Oakie, George Murphy, Linda Darnell. 93M USA. prod/rel: 20th Century-Fox

The Night the Ghost Got in, 1945, Short Story
James Thurber's the Night the Ghost Got in 1977 d: Robert Stitzel. 16M USA.

The Secret Life of Walter Mitty, 1945, Short Story
Secret Life of Walter Mitty, The 1947 d: Norman Z. McLeod. lps: Danny Kaye, Virginia Mayo, Boris Karloff. 110M USA. prod/rel: Samuel Goldwyn, RKO

THURSTON, E. TEMPLE (1879–1933), UKN, Thurston, Ernest Temple
Always Tell Your Wife, Play
Always Tell Your Wife 1914 d: Leedham Bantock. lps: Seymour Hicks, Ellaline Terriss. 2000f UKN. prod/rel: Zenith

The Blue Peter, Novel
Blue Peter, The 1928 d: Arthur Rooke. lps: Matheson Lang, Gladys Frazin, Mary Dibley. 7665f UKN. prod/rel: British Filmcraft, Woolf & Freedman

The City of Beautiful Nonsense, 1909, Novel
City of Beautiful Nonsense, The 1919 d: Henry Edwards. lps: Henry Edwards, Chrissie White, James Lindsay. 5725f UKN. prod/rel: Hepworth, Butcher's Film Service
City of Beautiful Nonsense, The 1935 d: Adrian Brunel. lps: Emlyn Williams, Sophie Stesart, Eve Lister. 88M UKN. prod/rel: Butcher's Film Service

World of Wonderful Reality, The 1924 d: Henry Edwards. lps: Henry Edwards, Chrissie White, James Lindsay. 4990f UKN. prod/rel: Hepworth

David and Jonathan, New York 1919, Novel
David and Jonathan 1920 d: Alexander Butler, Dion Titheradge. lps: Madge Titheradge, Geoffrey Webb, Richard Ryan. 6000f UKN/USA. prod/rel: G. B. Samuelson, General

Driven, London 1914, Play
One Precious Year 1933 d: Henry Edwards. lps: Anne Grey, Basil Rathbone, Owen Nares. 76M UKN. prod/rel: British and Dominions, Paramount British

Enchantment, Novel
Enchantment 1920 d: Einar J. Bruun. lps: Henry Krauss, Mary Odette, Eric Barclay. 6000f UKN. prod/rel: London, Jury

The Evolution of Katherine, Play
Driven 1916 d: Maurice Elvey. lps: Elisabeth Risdon, Fred Groves, Guy Newall. 5239f UKN. *Desperation* (USA) prod/rel: London, Diploma

The Garden of Resurrection, Novel
Garden of Resurrection, The 1919 d: Arthur Rooke. lps: Guy Newall, Ivy Duke, Franklin Dyall. 6470f UKN. prod/rel: George Clark Productions, Stoll

The Greatest Wish in the World, Novel
Greatest Wish in the World, The 1918 d: Maurice Elvey. lps: Bransby Williams, Odette Goimbault, Edward Combermere. 5800f UKN. prod/rel: International Exclusives

The Mirage, Novel
Mirage, The 1920 d: Arthur Rooke. lps: Edward O'Neill, Dorothy Holmes-Gore, Douglas Munro. 5500f UKN. prod/rel: George Clark, Stoll

A Roof and Four Walls, London 1923, Play
Discord 1933 d: Henry Edwards. lps: Owen Nares, Benita Hume, Harold Huth. 80M UKN. prod/rel: British and Dominions, Paramount British

Sally Bishop, Novel
Sally Bishop 1916 d: George Pearson. lps: Aurele Sydney, Marjorie Villis, Peggy Hyland. 3752f UKN. prod/rel: Gaumont
Sally Bishop 1923 d: Maurice Elvey. lps: Marie Doro, Henry Ainley, Florence Turner. 7400f UKN. prod/rel: Stoll
Sally Bishop 1932 d: T. Hayes Hunter. lps: Joan Barry, Harold Huth, Isabel Jeans. 82M UKN. prod/rel: British Lion

Traffic, Novel
Traffic 1915 d: Charles Raymond. lps: Marjorie Villis, Charles Vane, Alden Lovett. 3000f UKN. prod/rel: I. B. Davidson, St. George

THURSTON, KATHERINE CECIL (1875–1911), UKN
The Compact, Novel
Compact, The 1912 d: Joseph A. Golden. lps: Crane Wilbur, Octavia Handworth. SHT USA. prod/rel: Pathe Exchange Co.

John Chilcote M.P., 1904, Novel
Masquerader, The 1922 d: James Young. lps: Guy Bates Post, Ruth Cummings, Edward M. Kimball. 7835f USA. *John Chilcote M.P.*; *Jr. Monte Carlo* prod/rel: Richard Walton Tully Productions, Associated First National Pictures

The Masquerader, London 1904, Novel
Masquerader, The 1933 d: Richard Wallace. lps: Ronald Colman, Elissa Landi, Halliwell Hobbes. 78M USA. prod/rel: United Artists Corp., Samuel Goldwyn, Inc.

THURZO, GABOR
A Szent, 1966, Novel
Bekotott Szemmel 1974 d: Andras Kovacs. lps: Andras Kozak, Jozsef Madaras, Sandor Horvath. 85M HNG. *Blindfold*; *With Bound Eyes* prod/rel: Mafilm

THYNNE, ALEXANDER
The Carry-Cot, Novel
Blue Blood 1973 d: Andrew Sinclair. lps: Oliver Reed, Fiona Lewis, Anna Gael. 86M UKN/CND. prod/rel: Mallard Productions Ltd. (London), Impact Films Ltd. (London)

TIAGO, MANUEL
Cinco Dias Cinco Noites, Novel
Cinco Dias, Cinco Noites 1997 d: Jose Fonseca CostA. lps: Victor Norte, Paulo Pires, Ana Padrao. 101M PRT/FRN. *Five Days Five Nights* prod/rel: Madragoa Filmes (Lisbon), Gemini Films

TIAN FEN
Gold, Novel
Lu 1983 d: Chen Lizhou. lps: Wan Yan, Zhang Fengyi, Wang XIanghong. 10r CHN. *The Road* prod/rel: Fujian Film Studio

TIAN HAN
Guan Hanqing, 1958, Play
 Guan Hanqing 1960 d: Xu Tao. lps: Ma Shizeng, Wen
 Juefei, Tan Yuzheng. 138M CHN. prod/rel: Haiyan Film
 Studio, Pearl River Film Studio

Huozhi Taowu, Play
 Lieyan 1933. lps: Peng Fei, Lei Mengna, Pu XI. 11r
 CHN. *Raging Flames* prod/rel: Yihua Film Company

Liren XIng, 1945, Play
 Li Ren XIn 1948 d: Chen Liting. lps: Shangguan
 Yunzhu, Huang Zongying, Sha Li. 100M CHN. *Liren
 XIng*

TICKELL, JERRARD
Appointment With Venus, Novel
 Appointment With Venus 1951 d: Ralph Thomas. lps:
 David Niven, Glynis Johns, George Coulouris. 89M
 UKN. *Island Rescue* (USA) prod/rel: General Film
 Distributors, British Film Makers

The Hand and the Flower, Novel
 Day to Remember, A 1953 d: Ralph Thomas. lps:
 Stanley Holloway, Joan Rice, Odile Versois. 92M UKN.
 prod/rel: Group, General Film Distributors

Odette, Book
 Odette 1950 d: Herbert Wilcox. lps: Anna Neagle,
 Trevor Howard, Marius Goring. 123M UKN. prod/rel:
 Imperadio, British Lion

TIDMARSCH
Mary Gute Nacht, Play
 Gestorte Hochzeitsnacht, Die 1950 d: Helmut
 Weiss, Johannes Riemann. lps: Ilse Werner, Curd
 Jurgens, Paul Dahlke. 88M GRM. *Mary Gute Nacht*;
 Mary Good Night prod/rel: Dornas, Bejohr

TIDMARSH, E. VIVIAN
Is Your Honeymoon Really Necessary?, London
 1944, Play
 Is Your Honeymoon Really Necessary? 1953 d:
 Maurice Elvey. lps: David Tomlinson, Diana Dors,
 Bonar Colleano. 80M UKN. prod/rel: Advance, Adelphi

TIDYMAN, ERNEST
Shaft, Novel
 Shaft 1971 d: Gordon Parks. lps: Richard Roundtree,
 Moses Gunn, Charles Cioffi. 100M USA. prod/rel: MGM

TIE NING
Story
 O! XIang Xue 1989 d: Wang Haowei. lps: Xue Bai,
 Zhuang Li, Tang Ye. 9r CHN. *Oh! Sweet Snow* prod/rel:
 Children's Film Studio

TIECK, LUDWIG (1773–1853), GRM
Des Lebens Uberfluss, 1871, Short Story
 Lebens Uberfluss, Des 1950 d: Wolfgang Liebeneiner.
 lps: Erika Muller, Olaf Torsten, Ingeborg Korner. 82M
 GRM. *The Abundance of Life* prod/rel: Real, Doring

TIERI, VINCENZO
La Sbarra, Play
 Ispettore Vargas, L' 1940 d: Gianni Franciolini. lps:
 Giulio Donadio, Mariella Lotti, Maria Dominiani. 70M
 ITL. *La Sbarra* prod/rel: Produzione Associata
 Sovrania, I.C.A.R.

TIERNEY, HARRY
Dixiana, Story
 Dixiana 1930 d: Luther Reed. lps: Bebe Daniels,
 Everett Marshall, Bert Wheeler. 99M USA. prod/rel:
 RKO Productions

Valkyrie's Armour, Play
 One Brief Summer 1970 d: John MacKenzie. lps:
 Felicity Gibson, Clifford Evans, Jennifer Hilary. 86M
 UKN. prod/rel: 20th Century-Fox, Twickenham Film
 Associates

TIETJENS, PAUL
The Wizard of Oz, 1903, Play
 His Majesty, the Scarecrow of Oz 1914 d: L. Frank
 Baum. lps: Frank Moore, Vivian Reed, Fred Woodward.
 5r USA. *The New Wizard of Oz*; *The Scarecrow of Oz*; *His
 Majesty the Scarecrow* prod/rel: Oz Film Manufacturing
 Co., Alliance Films Corp.

TIGHE, EILEEN
Feature for June, Play
 June Bride 1948 d: Bretaigne Windust. lps: Robert
 Montgomery, Bette Davis, Fay Bainter. 97M USA.
 prod/rel: Warner Bros.

TIKKANEN, MARTA
Novel
 Manrape 1978 d: Jorn Donner. lps: Anna Godenius,
 Gosta Bredefeldt, Toni Regner. 99M SWD/FNL. *Man
 Kan Inte Valdtas* (SWD); *Miesta Ei Voi Raiskata*; *Man
 Cannot Be Raped*; *Men Can't Be Raped* prod/rel:
 Stockholm Films, Jorn Donner

TILAK, LAXMIBAI
Smritichitre, Autobiography
 Smritichitre 1982 d: Vijaya MehtA. lps: Vijaya Mehta,
 Suhas Joshi, Ravindra Mankani. TVM. 135M IND.
 Reminiscences; *Memory Episodes*; *Smriti Chitre*
 prod/rel: Doordarshan

TILDEN, FREEMAN
The Customary Two Weeks, 1917, Short Story
 Customary Two Weeks, The 1917 d: Saul Harrison.
 lps: Craig Ward, Herbert Evans, Robert Ellis. 4114f
 USA. prod/rel: Thomas A. Edison, Inc.©, Conquest
 Picture

Garments of Truth, 1921, Short Story
 Garments of Truth 1921 d: George D. Baker. lps:
 Gareth Hughes, Ethel Grandin, John Steppling. 4968f
 USA. prod/rel: S-L Pictures, Metro Pictures

A Picture of Innocence, 1917, Novel
 Small Town Guy, The 1917 d: Lawrence C. Windom.
 lps: Taylor Holmes, Helen Ferguson, Fred Tilden. 5r
 USA. prod/rel: Essanay Film Mfg. Co.©, Perfection
 Pictures

TILDESLEY, ALICE L.
What Can You Expect?, Short Story
 Short Skirts 1921 d: Harry B. Harris. lps: Gladys
 Walton, Ena Gregory, Jack Mower. 4330f USA. prod/rel:
 Universal Film Mfg. Co.

TILLIER, CLAUDE
Mon Oncle Benjamin, Novel
 Mon Oncle Benjamin 1923 d: Rene Leprince. lps:
 Leon Mathot, Madeleine Erickson, Charles Lamy.
 2500m FRN. prod/rel: Pathe-Consortium-Cinema
 Mon Oncle Benjamin 1969 d: Edouard Molinaro. lps:
 Jacques Brel, Claude Jade, Rosy Varte. 91M FRN/ITL.
 Mio Zio Beniamino (ITL); *L' Uomo Dal Mantello Rosso*;
 The Amorous Adventures of Uncle Benjamin (UKN)
 prod/rel: Euro International Film, Gaumont
 International

TILLINGHAST, A. W.
The Hidden Path, Story
 Discarded Woman, The 1920 d: Burton L. King. lps:
 Grace Darling, James Cooley, Rod La Rocque. 6r USA.
 The Hidden Path prod/rel: Burton King Productions,
 Hallmark Pictures Corp.©

TILSEY, FRANK
Mutiny, London 1958, Novel
 H.M.S. Defiant 1962 d: Lewis Gilbert. lps: Alec
 Guinness, Dirk Bogarde, Anthony Quayle. 101M UKN.
 Damn the Defiant! (USA); *Battle Aboard the Defiant*;
 The Mutineers prod/rel: Columbia, Gw Films

TILTON, DWIGHT
Miss Petticoats, Boston 1902, Novel
 Miss Petticoats 1916 d: Harley Knoles. lps: Alice
 Brady, Arthur Ashley, Isabelle Berwin. 5r USA.
 prod/rel: World Film Corp.©, Peerless

TILTON, GEORGE
The Soul Kiss, New York 1908, Play
 Soldiers and Women 1930 d: Edward Sloman. lps:
 Aileen Pringle, Grant Withers, Judith Wood. 69M USA.
 prod/rel: Columbia Pictures

TIMERMAN, JACOBO (1923–, USS
Cell Without a Number Prisoner Without a Name,
 1981, Book
 Prisoner Without a Name, Cell Without a Number
 1983 d: David Greene, Linda Yellen. lps: Roy Scheider,
 Liv Ullmann, Zach Galligan. TVM. 100M USA.; *Jacobo
 Timerman: Prisoner Without a Name Cell Without a
 Number*

TIMMERMANS, FELIX (1886–1947), BLG
Pallieter, 1916, Novel
 Pallieter 1975 d: Roland Verhavert. lps: Eddy
 Brugman, Jacqueline Rommerts, Sylvia de Leur. 90M
 NTH/BLG. prod/rel: Kunst En Kino, Cine Centrum

TING YI
Bai Mao Nu, Play
 Bai Mao Nu 1950 d: Wang Bin, Shui HuA. lps: Tian
 Hua, Li Baifang, Chen Qiang. 13r CHN. *The
 White-Haired Girl* prod/rel: Northeast Film Studio

TINNISWOOD, PETER
Novel
 Mog 1985 d: Nic Phillips. lps: Enn Reitel. MTV. 390M
 UKN. prod/rel: Witzend, Central

TINSLEY, THEODORE A.
Story
 Manhattan Shakedown 1939 d: Leon BarshA. lps:
 John Gallaudet, Rosalind Keith, George McKay. 57M
 CND. *Manhattan Whirlwind* prod/rel: Central Films
 Ltd.
 Murder Is News 1939 d: Leon BarshA. lps: John
 Gallaudet, Iris Meredith, George McKay. 55M CND.
 prod/rel: Central Films Ltd.

Body Snatcher, 1936, Short Story
 Alibi for Murder 1936 d: D. Ross Lederman. lps:
 William Gargan, Marguerite Churchill, Gene Morgan.
 61M USA. *Two Minute Alibi* prod/rel: Columbia
 Pictures

Five Spot, 1935, Short Story
 Panic on the Air 1936 d: D. Ross Lederman. lps: Lew
 Ayres, Florence Rice, Benny Baker. 60M USA. *Trapped
 By Wireless* prod/rel: Columbia Pictures Corp. of
 California©

TIPPETTE, GILES
The Spikes Gang, Novel
 Spikes Gang, The 1974 d: Richard Fleischer. lps: Lee
 Marvin, Gary Grimes, Ron Howard. 96M USA. prod/rel:
 Mirisch, United Artists

TISSERON, MARCEL
La Rehabilitation
 Affaire Tisseron, L' 1917. FRN. prod/rel: Ruez Films

TITHERADGE, DION
The Crooked Billet, London 1927, Play
 Crooked Billet, The 1929 d: Adrian Brunel. lps:
 Carlyle Blackwell, Madeleine Carroll, Miles Mander.
 SIL. 7226f UKN. prod/rel: Gainsborough, Woolf &
 Freedman

The Fortunate Fool, Play
 Fortunate Fool, The 1933 d: Norman Walker. lps:
 Hugh Wakefield, Joan Wyndham, Jack Raine. 74M
 UKN. prod/rel: Associated British Film Distributors

The K.C., Play
 His Last Defence 1919 d: Geoffrey Wilmer. lps: Dennis
 Neilson-Terry, Mary Glynne, Alfred Bishop. 5000f
 UKN. prod/rel: Vanity Films, Walker

Loose Ends, London 1926, Play
 Loose Ends 1930 d: Norman Walker, Miles Mander.
 lps: Edna Best, Owen Nares, Miles Mander. 95M UKN.
 prod/rel: British International Pictures, Wardour

TITUS, EVE
Basil of Baker Street, Book
 Great Mouse Detective, The 1986 d: John Musker,
 Ron Clements. ANM. 80M USA. *Basil the Great Mouse
 Detective* prod/rel: Buena Vista, Walt Disney

TITUS, HAROLD
Bruce of Circle a, Boston 1918, Novel
 Shod With Fire 1920 d: Emmett J. Flynn. lps: William
 Russell, Helen Ferguson, Betty Schade. 4840f USA.
 Bruce of Circle a prod/rel: Fox Film Corp., William Fox©

The Last Straw, 1920, Serial Story
 Last Straw, The 1920 d: Denison Clift, Charles
 Swickard. lps: Buck Jones, Vivian Rich, Jane Talent.
 4822f USA. prod/rel: Fox Film Corp., William Fox

The Stuff of Heroes, 1924, Short Story
 Great Mr. Nobody, The 1941 d: Ben Stoloff. lps: Eddie
 Albert, Joan Leslie, Alan Hale. 71M USA. *Bashful Hero*;
 Stuff of Heroes prod/rel: Warner Bros.
 How Baxter Butted in 1925 d: William Beaudine. lps:
 Dorothy Devore, Matt Moore, Ward Crane. 6302f USA.
 prod/rel: Warner Brothers Pictures

Timber, Boston 1922, Novel
 Hearts Aflame 1923 d: Reginald Barker. lps: Frank
 Keenan, Anna Q. Nilsson, Craig Ward. 8110f USA.
 prod/rel: Louis B. Mayer Productions, Metro Pictures

TKS BROTHERS
Gumastavin Penn, Play
 Gumastavin Penn 1941 d: Balakrishna Narayan Rao.
 lps: M. V. Rajamma, P. Subbaiah Pillai, T. S.
 Rajalakshmi. 183M IND. *Clerk's Daughter* prod/rel: Tks
 Brothers, Murthy Films-Coimbatore

TOBIAS, CHARLES
Yokel Boy, New York 1939, Musical Play
 Yokel Boy 1942 d: Joseph Santley. lps: Albert Dekker,
 Joan Davis, Eddie Foy Jr. 69M USA. *Hitting the
 Headlines* (UKN) prod/rel: Republic

TOBINO, MARIO (1910–, ITL
Il Deserto de la Libra, Book
 Scemo Di Guerra 1985 d: Dino Risi. lps: Bernard Blier,
 Beppe Grillo, Coluche. 108M ITL. *Madman at War*

Per le Antiche Scale, 1972, Novel
 Per le Antiche Scale 1975 d: Mauro Bolognini. lps:
 Marcello Mastroianni, Francoise Fabian, Marthe
 Keller. 105M ITL/FRN. *Down the Ancient Stairs* (USA);
 Down the Ancient Staircase; *Vertiges* (FRN) prod/rel:
 Italian International Film (Roma), Fox Europa (Paris)

TOBIS, KAREL
Na Ty Louce Zeleny, Opera
 Na Ty Louce Zeleny 1936 d: Carl Lamac. lps: Carl
 Lamac, Helena Busova, Jara Kohout. 2391m CZC. *On
 the Green Meadow* prod/rel: Elekta

Ulicnice, Opera
 Ulicnice 1936 d: Vladimir Slavinsky. lps: Vera
 Ferbasova, Frantisek Sasek, Frantisek Kristof-Vesely.
 2931m CZC. *Minx* prod/rel: Slavia-Film

Sole Anche Di Notte, Il 1990 d: Paolo Taviani, Vittorio Taviani. lps: Julian Sands, Charlotte Gainsbourg, Nastassja Kinski. 113M ITL/FRN/GRM. *Nachtsonne* (GRM); *Night Sun* (USA); *Le Soleil Meme la Nuit* (FRN); *Sunshine Even By Night* prod/rel: Filmtre, Raiuno Radiotelevisione Italiana (Roma)

Polikushka, 1863, Short Story
Polikuska 1958 d: Carmine Gallone. lps: Folco Lulli, Antonella Lualdi, Franco Interlenghi. 88M ITL/FRN/GRM. *Polikuschka* (GRM); *Polijuschka* prod/rel: Lux Film, Produzioni Gallone (Roma)

Sergius Panin
Leben Um Leben 1913 d: Rudolf Meinert. lps: Emil Wittig, Manny Ziener. GRM. prod/rel: Prometheus-Film

Smert Ivana Ilicha, 1886, Short Story
Prostaya Smert 1985 d: Alexander Kaidanovski. lps: Alisa Freyndlikh, Valery Priyemykhov, Vitautas Paukshte. 68M USS.

Tri Medvedya, 1875, Short Story
Tri Medvedya 1958 d: Roman Davydov. ANM. 13M USS.

Voskreseniye, Moscow 1899, Novel
Auferstehung 1958 d: Rolf Hansen. lps: Horst Buchholz, Myriam Bru, Lea Massari. 106M GRM/ITL/FRN. *Resurrection* (FRN); *Resurrezione* (ITL) prod/rel: Bavaria, Rizzoli
Duniya Kya Hai 1938 d: G. P. Pawar. lps: Lalita Pawar, Madhav Kale, Bulbule. 146M IND. *Resurrection* prod/rel: Diamond Pictures
Fu Huo 1941 d: Mei Qian. 90M CHN. *Resurrection*
Fukkatsu 1950 d: Akira Nobuchi. lps: MacHiko Kyo. 93M JPN. *Resurrection; Maslova*
Resurreccion 1931 d: Edwin Carewe. lps: Lupe Velez, Gilbert Roland, Amelia SanisterrA. 9-10r USA. *El Principe Y la Aldeana*
Resurreccion 1943 d: Gilberto Martinez Solares. lps: Emilio Tuero, Lupita Tovar, Sara GarciA. 88M MXC.
Resurrection 1909 d: D. W. Griffith. lps: Florence Lawrence, Arthur Johnson, Clara T. Bracey. 999f USA. prod/rel: Biograph Co.
Resurrection 1909 d: Andre Calmettes, Henri Desfontaines. lps: Dumeny, Philippe Garnier, Henri Etievant. 350m FRN. prod/rel: Pathe Freres
Resurrection 1918 d: Edward Jose. lps: Pauline Frederick, Robert Elliott, John Sainpolis. 4382f USA. prod/rel: Famous Players-Lasky Corp.©, Paramount Pictures
Resurrection 1927 d: Edwin Carewe. lps: Rod La Rocque, Dolores Del Rio, Marc MacDermott. 9120f USA. *Prince Dimitri* prod/rel: Inspiration Pictures, Edwin Carewe Productions
Resurrection 1931 d: Edwin Carewe. lps: John Boles, Lupe Velez, Nance O'Neil. 81M USA. prod/rel: Universal Pictures Corp.©
Resurrezione 1917 d: Mario Caserini. lps: Maria Jacobini, Andrea Habay, Pepa Bonafe. 2106m ITL. prod/rel: Tiber Film
Resurrezione 1944 d: Flavio CalzavarA. lps: Doris Duranti, Claudio Gora, Germana Paolieri. 90M ITL. prod/rel: Incine, Scalera Film
Voskresenie 1961 d: Mikhail Schweitzer. lps: Tamara Syomina, Yevgeni Matveyev, Pavel Massalsky. 207M USS. *Resurrection* (USA) prod/rel: Mosfilm
We Live Again 1934 d: Rouben Mamoulian. lps: Fredric March, Anna Sten, Sam Jaffe. 85M USA. *Resurrection* prod/rel: United Artists Corp., Samuel Goldwyn, Inc.
Woman's Resurrection, A 1915 d: J. Gordon Edwards. lps: Betty Nansen, William J. Kelly, Edward Jose. 5r USA. prod/rel: Fox Film Corp., William Fox©

Voyna I Mir, 1863-69, Novel
Tozhe Lyudi 1960 d: Georgi Daneliya, Igor Talankin. 14M USS. *They are Also People; There are Also People; Toze Ljudi*
Voina I Mir 1967 d: Sergei Bondarchuk. lps: Ludmila Savelieva, Sergei Bondarchuk, Vyacheslav Tikhonov. 507M USS. *War and Peace* (USA); *Voyna I Mir* prod/rel: Mosfilm
War and Peace 1956 d: King Vidor, Mario Soldati. lps: Audrey Hepburn, Henry Fonda, Mel Ferrer. 207M USA/ITL. *Guerra E Pace* (ITL) prod/rel: Paramount, Carlo Ponti
War and Peace 1963 d: Silvio Narizzano. lps: John Franklyn Robbins, Kenneth Griffith, Daniel Massey. MTV. 150M UKN. prod/rel: Granada Tv
War and Peace 1972 d: John Howard Davies. lps: Morag Hood, Alan Dobie, Anthony Hopkins. MTV. 900M UKN. prod/rel: BBC

Zhivoi Trup, Moscow 1911, Play
Atonement 1919 d: William Humphrey. lps: Conway Tearle, Grace Davison, Huntley Gordon. 5r USA. prod/rel: Humphrey Pictures, Inc., State Rights
Cadavere Vivente, Il 1921 d: Pier Angelo Mazzolotti. lps: Franz Sala, Ria Bruna, Enrica MassalA. 1583m ITL. prod/rel: Itala Film
Lebende Leichnam, Der 1918 d: Richard Oswald. lps: Bernd Aldor, Manja Tzatschewa, Olga Engl. GRM. *The Living Corpse; The Living Dead* prod/rel: Richard Oswald-Film
Nuits de Feu 1937 d: Marcel L'Herbier. lps: Victor Francen, Gaby Morlay, Madeleine Robinson. 98M FRN. *The Living Corpse* (USA); *Nights of Fire* prod/rel: Cine-Alliance
Redemption 1930 d: Fred Niblo. lps: John Gilbert, Renee Adoree, Conrad Nagel. 64M USA. prod/rel: Metro-Goldwyn-Mayer Pictures
Weakness of Man, The 1916 d: Barry O'Neil. lps: Holbrook Blinn, Eleanor Woodruff, Richard Wangemann. 5r USA. *The Greater Love* prod/rel: World Film Corp.©, Peerless
Zhivoi Trup 1929 d: Fedor Ozep. lps: Vsevolod I. Pudovkin, Maria Jacobini, Viola Garden. 3532m USS/GRM. *Der Lebende Leichham* (GRM); *The Living Corpse; Zhivoi Trap* prod/rel: Prometheus, Meshrabpomfilm
Zhivoi Trup 1953 d: Vladimir Vengerov. 135M USS. *The Living Corpse; Zivoj Trup*

TOMASETTI, GLEN
Man of Letters, Novel
Man of Letters 1984 d: Chris Thomson. lps: Warren Mitchell, Dinah Shearing, Carol Raye. TVM. F ASL. prod/rel: Australian Broadcasting Corp.

TOMAYANTEE
Khu Gam, Novel
Khu Gam 1996 d: Euthana Mukdasanit. lps: Thongchai McIntyre, Apasiri Nitibhon, Thirapat Sajakul. 131M THL. *Sunset at Chaopraya* prod/rel: Grammy Film Co.

TOMBRAGEL, MAURICE
Rigadoon, Story
Zanzibar 1940 d: Harold Schuster. lps: Lola Lane, James Craig, Eduardo Ciannelli. 70M USA. *Rigadoon* prod/rel: Universal Pictures Co.©

TOMITA, TSUNEO
Sugata Sanshiro, Novel
Sugata Sanshiro 1943 d: Akira KurosawA. lps: Susumu Fujita, Denjiro Okochi, Yukiko Todoroki. 82M JPN. *Sanshiro Sugata; The Legend of Judo; Judo Saga; Judo Story* prod/rel: Toho Co.
Zoku Sugata Sanshiro 1945 d: Akira KurosawA. lps: Susumu Fujita, Denjiro Okochi, Ryunosuke TsukigatA. 83M JPN. *Sugata Sanshiro Part II; Judo Saga II; Sanshiro Sugata Zoku; Sanshiro Sugata Part II* prod/rel: Toho Co.

TOMOJI, ABE
Jinko Teien, 1954, Short Story
Onna No Sono 1954 d: Keisuke KinoshitA. lps: Hideko Takamine, Yoshiko KugA. 141M JPN. *The Garden of Women; The Eternal Generation*

TOMPKINS, JULIET WILBOR
A Girl Named Mary, Indianapolis 1918, Novel
Girl Named Mary, A 1920 d: Walter Edwards. lps: Marguerite Clark, Kathlyn Williams, Wallace MacDonald. 5r USA. prod/rel: Famous Players-Lasky Corp.©, Paramount-Artcraft Pictures
Once There Was a Princess, 1926, Short Story
Misbehaving Ladies 1931 d: William Beaudine. lps: Lila Lee, Ben Lyon, Louise FazendA. 72M USA. *Once There Was a Princess* (UKN); *Queen of Main Street* prod/rel: First National Pictures©
The Two Benjamins, 1918, Serial Story
Little Comrade 1919 d: Chet Withey. lps: Vivian Martin, Niles Welch, Gertrude Claire. 5r USA. prod/rel: Famous Players-Lasky Corp.©, Paramount Pictures

TOMS, BERNARD
The Strange Affair, London 1966, Novel
Strange Affair, The 1968 d: David Greene. lps: Michael York, Jeremy Kemp, Susan George. 106M UKN. prod/rel: Paramount Pictures, Paramount

TONKONOGY, GERTRUDE
Three-Cornered Moon, New York 1932, Play
Three Cornered Moon 1933 d: Elliott Nugent. lps: Claudette Colbert, Richard Arlen, Mary Boland. 72M USA. *Three-Cornered Moon* prod/rel: Paramount Productions©

TOOHEY, JOHN PETER
On the Back Seat, 1925, Short Story
Outcast Souls 1928 d: Louis W. Chaudet. lps: Priscilla Bonner, Charles Delaney, Ralph Lewis. 4866f USA. prod/rel: Sterling Pictures

TOOLE, JOHN KENNEDY (1937–1969), USA
The Neon Bible, Novel
Neon Bible, The 1995 d: Terence Davies. lps: Gena Rowlands, Diana Scarwid, Denis Leary. 92M UKN/USA. prod/rel: Mayfair, Scala

TOOMBS, ALFRED
Raising a Riot, Novel
Raising a Riot 1955 d: Wendy Toye. lps: Kenneth More, Ronald Squire, Mandy Miller. 91M UKN. prod/rel: London Films, Wessex

TOPELIUS, ZACHRIS
Grona Kammarn Pa Linnais Gard, 1859, Novel
Linnaisten Vihrea Kamari 1945 d: Valentin VaalA. lps: Raoul Tuomi, Regina Linnanheimo, Kaija RaholA. 91M FNL. *The Green Room of the Linnaeus Castle; Grona Kammarn Pa Linnais; The Green Chamber of Linnainen* prod/rel: Suomi-Filmi
Prinsessan Tornrosa, 1870, Play
Prinsessa Ruusunen 1949 d: Edvin Laine. lps: Aarne Laine, Mirjam Novero, Pikku-AnnikA. 99M FNL. *Sleeping Beauty; Prinsessan Tornrosa* prod/rel: Suomen Filmiteollisuus

TOPKINS, KATHERINE
Kotch, Novel
Kotch 1971 d: Jack Lemmon. lps: Walter Matthau, Deborah Winters, Felicia Farr. 114M USA. prod/rel: Kotch Company, ABC

TOPOLSKI, DANIEL
True Blue, Book
True Blue 1996 d: Ferdinand Fairfax. lps: Johan Leysen, Dominic West, Dylan Baker. 117M UKN. prod/rel: Rafford Production, Film and General

TOPOR, ROLAND
Le Locataire, 1934, Novel
Tenant, The 1976 d: Roman Polanski. lps: Roman Polanski, Isabelle Adjani, Shelley Winters. 126M USA/FRN. *Le Locataire* (FRN) prod/rel: Marianne

TOPOR, TOM
Nuts, Play
Nuts 1987 d: Martin Ritt. lps: Barbra Streisand, Richard Dreyfuss, Maureen Stapleton. 116M USA. prod/rel: Warner Bros.

TORBERG, FRIEDRICH
'38 - Heim Ins Reich, Novel
38 1986 d: Wolfgang Gluck. lps: Tobias Engel, Sunnyi Melles, Heinz Trixner. 96M AUS/GRM. *'38: Vienna Before the Fall* (USA); *'38 - Heim Ins Reich* prod/rel: Satel, Almaro
Der Schuler Gerber Hat Absolviert, 1930, Novel
Schuler Gerber, Der 1981 d: Wolfgang Gluck. lps: Gabriel Barylli, Werner Kreindl, Romuald Pekny. 99M AUS/GRM. *The Pupil Gerber; Student Gerber* prod/rel: Almaro, Arabella

TORELLI, ACHILLE
I Mariti, Play
Mariti - Tempesta d'Amore, I 1941 d: Camillo Mastrocinque. lps: Amedeo Nazzari, Irma Gramatica, Mariella Lotti. 88M ITL. *La Parabola Dei Mariti; I Mariti* prod/rel: I.C.A.R., Generalcine
Scrollina, 1885, Play
Scrollina 1920 d: Gero Zambuto. lps: Leda Gys, Alberto Nepoti, Leonie Laporte. 1549m ITL. prod/rel: Lombardo Film
Triste Realta, 1871, Play
Triste Realta 1917 d: Franco Dias. lps: Pepa Bonafe, Vittorio Rossi Pianelli, Leo Zanzi-Rissone. 1464m ITL. prod/rel: Dramatica Film

TORELLI, GUGLIELMO
Il Signor Direttore, Play
Promozione Per. Meriti Personali 1914 d: Oreste Gherardini. lps: Bianchina de Crescenzo, Salvatore Papa, Piero Concialdi. ITL. prod/rel: Napoli Film

TOROK, RUDOLF
Teresa Venerdi, Novel
Teresa Venerdi 1941 d: Vittorio de SicA. lps: Adriana Benetti, Irasema Dilian, Anna Magnani. 96M ITL. *Doctor Beware* (USA) prod/rel: a.C.I., Europa

TORRES, EDWIN
After Hours, Novel
Carlito's Way 1993 d: Brian DepalmA. lps: Al Pacino, Sean Penn, Penelope Ann Miller. 145M USA. prod/rel: Universal
Carlito's Way, Novel
Carlito's Way 1993 d: Brian DepalmA. lps: Al Pacino, Sean Penn, Penelope Ann Miller. 145M USA. prod/rel: Universal
Q & A, Novel
Q & A 1990 d: Sidney Lumet. lps: Nick Nolte, Timothy Hutton, Armand Assante. 134M USA. *Questions and Answers* prod/rel: Tri-Star

TORRES, JOSE
Fire and Fear, Book
Tyson: the True Story 1994 d: Ulrich Edel. lps: Michael Jai White, George C. Scott, Paul Winfield. TVM. 105M USA. *Tyson* prod/rel: Edgar J. Scherick Associates, Home Box Office

TOTHEROH, DAN
Deep Valley, Novel
Deep Valley 1947 d: Jean Negulesco. lps: Ida Lupino, Dane Clark, Fay Bainter. 104M USA. prod/rel: Warner Bros.

Mother Lode, New York 1934, Play
Yellow Dust 1936 d: Wallace Fox. lps: Richard Dix, Leila Hyams, Moroni Olsen. 69M USA. *Mother Lode* prod/rel: RKO Radio Pictures©

Wild Birds, New York 1925, Play
Two Alone 1934 d: Elliott Nugent. lps: Jean Parker, Tom Brown, Arthur Byron. 74M USA. *Wild Birds*; *Wild Bird* prod/rel: RKO Radio Pictures©

TOTLIS, SAKIS
Combination Edessa-Zurich, Novel
Valkanisater 1997 d: Sotiris Goritsas. lps: Gerassimos Skiadaressis, Stelios Mainas, Yota FestA. 98M GRC/SWT/BUL. *Balkanisater* prod/rel: Mythos Ltd., Greek Film Centre (Athens)

TOTMAN, WELLYN
The Wildcat, Story
Eternal Woman, The 1929 d: John P. McCarthy. lps: Olive Borden, Ralph Graves, Ruth Clifford. 5812f USA. prod/rel: Columbia Pictures

TOUDOUZE, GEORGES G.
Les Elus de la Mer, Short Story
Elus de la Mer, Les 1921 d: Gaston Roudes, Marcel Dumont. lps: Jean Dehelly, Gaston Modot, Simone Vaudry. 2050m FRN. prod/rel: Films Roudes

Toinon la Ruine, Novel
Toinon la Ruine 1913 d: Alexandre Devarennes. lps: Jean Toulout, Albert Dieudonne, Yvonne Villeroy. FRN. prod/rel: Grands Films Populaires

La Voix de l'Ocean, Novel
Voix de l'Ocean, La 1922 d: Gaston Roudes. lps: Paul Ollivier, Rachel Devirys, Suzanne Marty. 1542m FRN. prod/rel: Gallo-Film

Wolves, Play
Wolves 1930 d: Albert de Courville. lps: Dorothy Gish, Charles Laughton, Malcolm Keen. 56M UKN. *Wanted Men* prod/rel: British and Dominions, Woolf & Freedman

TOULOUSE, DR.
La Double Existence du Docteur Morart, Play
Double Existence du Docteur Morart, La 1919 d: Jacques Gretillat. lps: Jacques Gretillat, Jeanne Delvair, Jean Debucourt. 1230m FRN. prod/rel: Films Pierrot

TOURNIER, JACQUES
Comtesse de Verue Jeanne de Luynes, Novel
King's Whore, The 1990 d: Axel Corti. lps: Timothy Dalton, Valeria Golino, Stephane Freiss. 93M AUS/FRN/UKN. *La Putain du Roi* (FRN) prod/rel: Asc, Fr3

TOURNIER, MICHEL (1924–, FRN
Short Story
Nain Rouge, Le 1998 d: Yvan Le Moine. lps: Jean-Yves Thual, Anita Ekberg, Dyna Gauzy. 104M BLG/FRN/ITL. *The Red Dwarf* prod/rel: a.A. Les Films Belge (Brussels), Mainstream (Paris)

The Erl King, Novel
Unhold, Der 1996 d: Volker Schlondorff. lps: John Malkovich, Armin Mueller-Stahl, Gottfried John. 117M GRM/FRN/UKN. *The Ogre*; *Krol Olch* (PLN) prod/rel: Renn Production (Paris), Studio Babelsberg

TOUSSAINT-SAMAT, JEAN
Reine Des Gitans Cartacalha, Novel
Cartacalha, Reine Des Gitans 1941 d: Leon Mathot. lps: Viviane Romance, Georges Flamant, Roger Duchesne. 95M FRN. prod/rel: Sirius

TOWNBRIDGE, H.
Il Romanzo Di Una Giovane Povera, Novel
Romanzo Di Una Giovane Povera, Il 1920 d: Enrico Vidali. lps: Lydianne, Enrico Vidali. 1713m ITL. prod/rel: Fortuna Film

TOWNE, EDWARD OWINGS
The Madonna in Chains, Story
Woman in Chains, The 1923 d: William P. Burt. lps: E. K. Lincoln, William H. Tooker, Mrs. Rudolph Valentino. 7r USA. *The Women in Chains* prod/rel: Amalgamated Producing Corp.

TOWNEND, W.
The Greater War, Short Story
Greater War, The 1926 d: Jack Raymond. lps: Moore Marriott, Victor Fairley, Joan Vincent. 1725f UKN. prod/rel: Gaumont

A Light for His Pipe, Novel
You Know What Sailors are 1928 d: Maurice Elvey. lps: Alf Goddard, Cyril McLaglen, Chili Bouchier. 7598f UKN. prod/rel: Gaumont

One Crowded Hour, Story
Wishbone, The 1933 d: Arthur Maude. lps: Nellie Wallace, Davy Burnaby, A. Bromley Davenport. 78M UKN. prod/rel: Sound City, MGM

TOWNER, WESLEY
Not for Children, Play
Mad Martindales, The 1942 d: Alfred L. Werker. lps: Jane Withers, Marjorie Weaver, Alan Mowbray. 65M USA. *Not for Children* prod/rel: 20th Century-Fox

TOWNLEY, HOUGHTON
The Bishop's Emeralds, New York 1908, Novel
Bishop's Emeralds, The 1919 d: John B. O'Brien. lps: Virginia Pearson, Sheldon Lewis, Robert Broderick. 5700f USA. prod/rel: Virginia Pearson Photoplays, Inc.©, Pathe Exchange, Inc.

The Gay Lord Waring, New York 1910, Novel
Gay Lord Waring, The 1916 d: Otis Turner. lps: J. Warren Kerrigan, Lois Wilson, Bertram Grassby. 5r USA. prod/rel: Bluebird Photoplays, Inc.©

The Splendid Coward, Novel
Splendid Coward, The 1918 d: F. Martin Thornton. lps: James Knight, Joan Legge, Roy Travers. 5835f UKN. prod/rel: Harma

TOWNSEND, EDWARD WATERMAN
Chimmie Fadden, 1895, Short Story
Chimmie Fadden 1915 d: Cecil B. de Mille. lps: Victor Moore, Camille Astor, Raymond Hatton. 4-5r USA. prod/rel: Jesse L. Lasky Feature Play Co.©, Paramount Pictures Corp.

Chimmie Fadden Out West 1915 d: Cecil B. de Mille. lps: Victor Moore, Camille Astor, Raymond Hatton. 4-5r USA. prod/rel: Jesse L. Lasky Feature Play Co.©, Paramount Pictures Corp.

A Rose of the Tenderloin, Story
Rose of the Tenderloin, A 1909 d: J. Searle Dawley. lps: Mary Fuller, Harold M. Shaw, Robert Brower. 940f USA. prod/rel: Edison

TOWNSHEND, PETER
Tommy, Opera
Tommy 1975 d: Ken Russell. lps: Oliver Reed, Ann-Margret, Roger Daltrey. 111M UKN. prod/rel: Columbia, Hemdale

TRACY, DON
Criss Cross, Novel
Criss Cross 1949 d: Robert Siodmak. lps: Burt Lancaster, Yvonne de Carlo, Dan DuryeA. 87M USA. prod/rel: United Artists

TRACY, LOUIS
One Wonderful Night, New York 1912, Novel
One Wonderful Night 1914 d: E. H. Calvert. lps: Francis X. Bushman, Cyril Leonard, E. H. Calvert. 4r USA. prod/rel: Essanay Film Mfg. Co., General Film Co.

One Wonderful Night 1922 d: Stuart Paton. lps: Herbert Rawlinson, Lillian Rich, Dale Fuller. 4473f USA. prod/rel: Universal Film Mfg. Co.

The Silent Barrier, London 1909, Novel
Silent Barrier, The 1920 d: William Worthington. lps: Sheldon Lewis, Gladys Hulette, Corinne Barker. 6r USA. prod/rel: Louis Tracy Productions, Inc., Gibraltar Pictures

Wings of the Morning, New York 1903, Novel
Wings of the Morning 1919 d: J. Gordon Edwards. lps: William Farnum, Louise Lovely, Herschal Mayall. 6r USA. prod/rel: Fox Film Corp., William Fox©

TRACY, MARGARET
Mrs. White, Novel
White of the Eye 1987 d: Donald Cammell. lps: David Keith, Cathy Moriarty, Alan Rosenberg. 111M UKN. prod/rel: Cannon Classics, Mrs. Whites Production

TRAHEY, JANE
Life With Mother Superior, New York 1962, Novel
Trouble With Angels, The 1966 d: Ida Lupino. lps: Rosalind Russell, Hayley Mills, June Harding. 112M USA. *Mother Superior* prod/rel: William Frye Productions

TRAIL, ARMITAGE
Scarface, New York 1930, Novel
Scarface 1932 d: Howard Hawks. lps: Paul Muni, Ann Dvorak, George Raft. 99M USA. *The Shame of a Nation* (UKN); *Scarface -Shame of a Nation* prod/rel: the Caddo Co.©, United Artists Corp.

The Thirteenth Guest, New York 1929, Novel
Mystery of the 13th Guest, The 1943 d: William Beaudine. lps: Dick Purcell, Helen Parrish, Tim Ryan. 60M USA. prod/rel: Monogram

Thirteenth Guest, The 1932 d: Albert Ray. lps: Ginger Rogers, Lyle Talbot, J. Farrell MacDonald. 68M USA. *Lady Beware* (UKN); *The 13th Guest* prod/rel: Monogram Pictures Corp.©

TRAILL, PETER
The Guilty One, New York 1914, Play
Guilty One, The 1924 d: Joseph Henabery. lps: Agnes Ayres, Edmund Burns, Stanley Taylor. 5365f USA. prod/rel: Famous Players-Lasky, Paramount Pictures

TRAIN, ARTHUR CHENEY (1875–1945), USA, Train, Arthur
The Blind Goddess, New York 1926, Novel
Blind Goddess, The 1926 d: Victor Fleming. lps: Jack Holt, Ernest Torrence, Esther Ralston. 7363f USA. prod/rel: Famous Players-Lasky Corp., Paramount Pictures

His Children's Children, New York 1923, Novel
His Children's Children 1923 d: Sam Wood. lps: Bebe Daniels, Dorothy MacKaill, James Rennie. 8300f USA. prod/rel: Famous Players-Lasky, Paramount Pictures

Illusion, New York 1929, Novel
Illusion 1929 d: Lothar Mendes. lps: Charles "Buddy" Rogers, Nancy Carroll, June Collyer. 7536f USA. prod/rel: Paramount Famous Lasky Corp.

Mortmain, New York 1907, Novel
Mortmain 1915 d: Theodore Marston. lps: Robert Edeson, Donald Hall, Edward Elkas. 5r USA. prod/rel: Vitagraph Co. of America©, Blue Ribbon Feature

Randolph '64, 1905, Short Story
Rose of the South 1916 d: Paul Scardon. lps: Charles Kent, Mary Maurice, Antonio Moreno. 5r USA. *Randolph '64* prod/rel: Vitagraph Co. of America©, Blue Ribbon Feature

TRAKL, GEORG (1887–1914), AUS
Die Junge Magd, 1913, Verse
An Diesen Abenden 1951 d: Herbert Vesely. 10M AUS.

TRANT, JOSEPH H.
Juror Number Seven, Story
Juror Number Seven 1915 d: Ben Wilson. lps: Ben Wilson, Joseph Girard, Frank Benton. 2r USA. prod/rel: Rex

TRANTER, FLORENCE
The Courtneys of Curzon Street, Novel
Courtneys of Curzon Street, The 1947 d: Herbert Wilcox. lps: Anna Neagle, Michael Wilding, Gladys Young. 120M UKN. *The Courtney Affair* (USA); *Kathy's Love Affair* prod/rel: Imperadio, British Lion

TRANTER, NIGEL (1909–, UKN
The Bridal Path, Novel
Bridal Path, The 1959 d: Frank Launder. lps: Bill Travers, George Cole, Bernadette O'Farrell. 95M UKN. prod/rel: British Lion, Vale

TRAPP, MARIA AUGUSTA
The Story of the Trapp Family Singers, Philadelphia 1949, Autobiography
Trapp-Familie, Die 1956 d: Wolfgang Liebeneiner. lps: Ruth Leuwerik, Hans Holt, Maria Holst. 104M GRM. *The Trapp Family* (USA) prod/rel: Divina Film

TRARIEUX, GABRIEL
L' Alibi, Play
Alibi, L' 1914 d: Henri Pouctal. lps: Damores, Jacques Volnys, Albert Mayer. 820m FRN. prod/rel: le Film d'Art

La Brebis Perdue, Play
Brebis Perdue, La 1915 d: Henri Pouctal. lps: Henri Bosc, Cecile Guyon. FRN. prod/rel: Films D'art

TRAVEN, BEN (1890–1969), PLN, Torsvan, Berick Traven, Feige, Albert Otto Max
Die Brucke Im Dschungel, 1929, Novel
Bridge in the Jungle, The 1970 d: Pancho Kohner. lps: John Huston, Charles Robinson, Katy Jurado. 85M MXC/USA.

MacArio, Zurich 1950, Novel
MacArio 1959 d: Roberto Gavaldon. lps: Ignacio Lopez Tarso, Pina Pellicer, Enrique Lucero. 94M MXC. *Le Destin* prod/rel: Clasa Films Mundiales

Die Rebellion Der Gehenkten, 1936, Novel
Rebelion de Los Colgados, La 1953 d: Alfredo B. Crevenna, Emilio Fernandez. lps: Pedro Armendariz, Ariadna Welter, Carlos Lopez MoctezumA. 90M MXC. *Revolt of the Hanged*; *The Rebellion of the Hanged* prod/rel: Jose Kohn

Der Schatz Der Sierra Madre, 1927, Novel
Treasure of the Sierra Madre, The 1948 d: John Huston. lps: Humphrey Bogart, Walter Huston, Tim Holt. 126M USA. *The Treasure of Sierra Madre* prod/rel: Warner Bros.

Das Totenschiff, 1926, Novel
Totenschiff, Das 1959 d: Georg Tressler. lps: Horst Buchholz, Mario Adorf, Helmut Schmid. 97M GRM/MXC. *Ship of the Dead* prod/rel: Universum, Jose Kohn

Die Weisse Rose, 1929, Novel
Rosa Blanca 1961 d: Roberto Gavaldon. lps: Ignacio Lopez Tarso, Christiane Martel, Reinhold Olszewski. 100M MXC. *The White Rose*

TRAVER, ROBERT
Anatomy of a Murder, Novel
Anatomy of a Murder 1959 d: Otto Preminger. lps: James Stewart, Lee Remick, Ben GazzarA. 160M USA. prod/rel: Columbia, Carlyle Prods.

TRAVERS, BEN (1886–1980), UKN
Banana Ridge, London 1938, Play
Banana Ridge 1941 d: Walter C. Mycroft. lps: Robertson Hare, Alfred Drayton, Isabel Jeans. 87M UKN. prod/rel: Associated British Picture Corporation, Pathe
A Cuckoo in the Nest, London 1925, Play
Cuckoo in the Nest, A 1933 d: Tom Walls. lps: Tom Walls, Ralph Lynn, Yvonne Arnaud. 85M UKN. prod/rel: Gaumont-British, Woolf & Freedman
Fast and Loose 1954 d: Gordon Parry. lps: Stanley Holloway, Kay Kendall, Brian Reece. 75M UKN. prod/rel: Group Films, General Film Distributors
A Cup of Kindness, London 1929, Play
Cup of Kindness, A 1934 d: Tom Walls. lps: Tom Walls, Ralph Lynn, Robertson Hare. 81M UKN. prod/rel: Gaumont-British
The Dippers, London 1922, Play
Chance of a Night Time, The 1931 d: Herbert Wilcox, Ralph Lynn. lps: Ralph Lynn, Winifred Shotter, Kenneth Kove. 74M UKN. prod/rel: British and Dominions, Woolf & Freedman
Dirty Work, London 1932, Play
Dirty Work 1934 d: Tom Walls. lps: Ralph Lynn, Gordon Harker, Robertson Hare. 78M UKN. prod/rel: Gaumont-British
Mischief, London 1928, Play
Mischief 1931 d: Jack Raymond. lps: Ralph Lynn, Winifred Shotter, Jeanne Stuart. 69M UKN. prod/rel: British and Dominions, Woolf & Freedman
A Night Like This, London 1930, Play
Night Like This, A 1932 d: Tom Walls. lps: Ralph Lynn, Tom Walls, Winifred Shotter. 74M UKN. prod/rel: British and Dominions, Woolf & Freedman
O Mistress Mine, 1934, Play
Lady in Danger 1934 d: Tom Walls. lps: Tom Walls, Yvonne Arnaud, Leon M. Lion. 68M UKN. *Man Saves the Queen* prod/rel: Gaumont-British
Plunder, London 1928, Play
Plunder 1931 d: Tom Walls. lps: Ralph Lynn, Tom Walls, Winifred Shotter. 98M UKN. prod/rel: Woolf & Freedman, British and Dominions
Rookery Nook, London 1926, Play
Rookery Nook 1930 d: Tom Walls, Byron Haskin. lps: Ralph Lynn, Tom Walls, Winifred Shotter. 76M UKN. *One Embarrassing Night* (USA) prod/rel: British and Dominions, the Gramophone Co.
Thark, London 1927, Play
Thark 1932 d: Tom Walls. lps: Tom Walls, Ralph Lynn, Mary Brough. 80M UKN. *The Haunted House Thark* prod/rel: British and Dominions, Woolf & Freedman
Turkey Time, London 1931, Play
Turkey Time 1933 d: Tom Walls. lps: Tom Walls, Ralph Lynn, Dorothy Hyson. 73M UKN. prod/rel: Gaumont-British

TRAVERS, P. L. (1899–1996), ASL, Travers, Pamela Lyndon
Mary Poppins, Book
Mary Poppins 1964 d: Robert Stevenson. lps: Julie Andrews, Dick Van Dyke, David Tomlinson. 140M USA. prod/rel: Walt Disney Productions

TRAXLER, HANS
Book
Ossegg Oder Die Wahrheit Uber Hansel Und Gretel 1987 d: Thees Klahn. lps: Jean-Pierre Leaud, Alfred Edel, Romy Haag. 82M GRM. prod/rel: Dragon Cine, Studio Hamburg

TREBOR, MICHEL
Visages de Femmes, Play
Visages de Femmes 1938 d: Rene Guissart. lps: Pierre Brasseur, Felicien Tramel, Huguette Duflos. 85M FRN. prod/rel: Societe Du Film Fred

TREGASKIS, RICHARD W. (1916–1973), USA, Tregaskis, Richard William
Guadalcanal Diary, 1943, Novel
Guadalcanal Diary 1943 d: Lewis Seiler. lps: Preston Foster, Lloyd Nolan, William Bendix. 93M USA. prod/rel: 20th Century-Fox
Italian Story, Story
Force of Arms 1951 d: Michael Curtiz. lps: William Holden, Nancy Olson, Frank Lovejoy. 100M USA. *A Girl for Joe* prod/rel: Warner Bros.

TRELL, MAX
Lawyer Man, New York 1932, Novel
Lawyer Man 1932 d: William Dieterle. lps: William Powell, Joan Blondell, Claire Dodd. 72M USA. prod/rel: Warner Bros. Pictures©

TREMAIN, ROSE
Restoration, Novel
Restoration 1995 d: Michael Hoffman. lps: Robert Downey Jr., Meg Ryan, Sam Neill. 118M USA.

TREMAINE, SYDNEY
The Auction Mart, Novel
Auction Mart, The 1920 d: Duncan MacRae. lps: Gertrude McCoy, Charles Quartermaine, Gerald Moore. 5684f UKN. prod/rel: British Actors, Phillips

TREMAYNE, W. A.
The Avalanche, Philadelphia 1912, Play
Avalanche, The 1915 d: Will S. Davis. lps: Catherine Countiss, William H. Tooker, Violet Mersereau. 5r USA. prod/rel: Life Photo Film Corp., State Rights

TREMBLAY, MICHEL (1942–, CND
Cota Ton Teur Laura Cadieux, Novel
C't'a Ton Tour, Laura Cadieux 1998 d: Denise Filatrault. lps: Ginette Reno, Pierette Robitaille, Denise Dubois. 92M CND. *Laura Cadieux It's Your Turn*; *Laura It's Your Turn* prod/rel: Alliance, Cinemaginaire (Montreal)

TREMOIS, ROBERT
Un Tour de Cochon, Play
Tour de Cochon, Un 1934 d: Joseph Tzipine. lps: Romain Bouquet, Mona Goya, Alice Tissot. 85M FRN. prod/rel: Prodis

TREMPER, WILL
Story
Halbstarken, Die 1956 d: Georg Tressler. lps: Horst Buchholz, Karin Baal, Christian Doermer. 88M GRM. *Teenage Wolf Pack* (USA); *Wolfpack* (UKN); *The Wicked Ones*; *Juvenile Toughs* prod/rel: Inter West, Union

TRENCH, HERBERT
Apollo and the Seaman, Poem
Poet and the Soldier, The 1913. lps: Carlyle Blackwell, Lucille Younge, William H. West. 1000f USA. prod/rel: Kalem

TRENKER, LUIS
Schicksal Am Matterhorn, Novel
Von Der Liebe Besiegt 1956 d: Luis Trenker. lps: Marianne Hold, Luis Trenker, Wolfgang Preiss. 93M GRM. *Schicksal Am Matterhorn*; *Conquered By Love* prod/rel: Meteor, Prisma

TRENT, PAUL
Bentley's Conscience, Novel
Bentley's Conscience 1922 d: Denison Clift. lps: Robert Loraine, Betty Faire, Henry Victor. 4120f UKN. prod/rel: Ideal
When Greek Meets Greek, Novel
When Greek Meets Greek 1922 d: Walter West. lps: Violet Hopson, Stewart Rome, Lillian Douglas. 5400f UKN. prod/rel: Walter West, Butcher's Film Service
A Wife By Purchase, London 1909, Novel
God's Law and Man's 1917 d: John H. Collins. lps: Viola Dana, Robert Walker, Augustus Phillips. 5r USA. *A Wife By Purchase* prod/rel: Columbia Pictures Corp., Metro Pictures Corp.©

TRENYOV, KONSTANTIN
Lyubov Yarovaya, 1926, Play
Lyubov Yarovaya 1953 d: Jan Frid. 154M USS. *Ljubov Jarovaja*
Lyubov Yarovaya 1970 d: Vladimir Fetin. lps: Rufina NifontovA. 100M USS. *Ljubov Jarovaja*; *Lubov Yarovaya*

TRESSELL, ROBERT (1868–1911), IRL
The Ragged Trousered Philanthropists, Book
Ragged Trousered Philanthropists, The 1967 d: Christopher Morahan. lps: John Rees, Bryan Pringle. MTV. UKN.

TREVANIAN
The Eiger Sanction, Novel
Eiger Sanction, The 1975 d: Clint Eastwood. lps: Clint Eastwood, George Kennedy, Vonetta McGee. 125M USA. prod/rel: Malpaso

TREVES, SIR FREDERICK (1853–1923), UKN
The Elephant Man and Other Reminiscences, Book
Elephant Man, The 1980 d: David Lynch. lps: John Hurt, Anthony Hopkins, John Gielgud. 125M UKN. prod/rel: Emi, Brooksfilm

TREVOR, ELLESTON (1920–, UKN, Hall, Adam
The Berlin Memorandum, London 1965, Novel
Quiller Memorandum, The 1966 d: Michael Anderson. lps: George Segal, Alec Guinness, Max von Sydow. 103M UKN/USA. prod/rel: Rank Film Distributors, Ivan Foxwell Productions

The Big Pickup, Novel
Dunkirk 1958 d: Leslie Norman. lps: John Mills, Richard Attenborough, Bernard Lee. 135M UKN. prod/rel: MGM, Ealing Films
Dead on Course, Novel
Wings of Danger 1952 d: Terence Fisher. lps: Zachary Scott, Robert Beatty, Kay Kendall. 73M UKN. *Dead on Course* (USA) prod/rel: Exclusive, Hammer
Expressway, Novel
Smash-Up on Interstate Five 1973 d: John Llewellyn Moxey. lps: Robert Conrad, Sian Barbara Allen, Buddy Ebsen. TVM. 100M USA. prod/rel: Filmways Production
The Flight of the Phoenix, New York 1964, Novel
Flight of the Phoenix 1965 d: Robert Aldrich. lps: James Stewart, Richard Attenborough, Peter Finch. 149M USA. prod/rel: Associates & Aldrich Co.
The Pillars of Midnight, Novel
80,000 Suspects 1963 d: Val Guest. lps: Claire Bloom, Richard Johnson, Yolande Donlan. 113M UKN. prod/rel: Rank, Rank Film Distributors
Queen in Danger, Novel
Mantrap 1953 d: Terence Fisher. lps: Paul Henreid, Lois Maxwell, Kieron Moore. 78M UKN. *Man in Hiding* (USA); *Woman in Hiding* prod/rel: Exclusive, Hammer

TREVOR, LEO
Brother Officers, London 1898, Play
Brother Officers 1915 d: Harold Shaw. lps: Henry Ainley, Lettice Fairfax, Gerald Ames. 3975f UKN. prod/rel: London, Jury
The Flag Lieutenant, London 1908, Play
Flag Lieutenant, The 1919 d: Percy Nash. lps: Ivy Close, George Wynn, Dorothy Fane. 5200f UKN. prod/rel: Barker, Jury
Flag Lieutenant, The 1926 d: Maurice Elvey. lps: Henry Edwards, Dorothy Seacombe, Fred Raynham. 8500f UKN. prod/rel: Astra-National
Flag Lieutenant, The 1932 d: Henry Edwards. lps: Henry Edwards, Anna Neagle, Joyce Bland. 85M UKN. prod/rel: British and Dominions, Woolf & Freedman

TREVOR, WILLIAM (1928–, IRL, Cox, William Trevor
Attracta, 1978, Short Story
Attracta 1983 d: Kieran Hickey. lps: Wendy Hiller. 55M IRL.
Fools of Fortune, 1983, Novel
Fools of Fortune 1989 d: Pat O'Connor. lps: Mary Elizabeth Mastrantonio, Iain Glen, Julie Christie. 109M UKN/IRL. prod/rel: Palace, Polygram

TREYMORE, ALBERT M.
The Flash-Light, Short Story
Flashlight, The 1917 d: Ida May Park. lps: Dorothy Phillips, William Stowell, Lon Chaney. 5r USA. *The Flashlight Girl* prod/rel: Bluebird Photoplays, Inc.©

TREYNOR, ALBERT
The Dancing Co-Ed, 1938, Short Story
Dancing Co-Ed 1939 d: S. Sylvan Simon. lps: Lana Turner, Richard Carlson, Leon Errol. 81M USA. *Every Other Inch a Lady* (UKN) prod/rel: Metro-Goldwyn-Mayer Corp.
Highway Robbery, 1934, Short Story
It's a Small World 1935 d: Irving Cummings. lps: Spencer Tracy, Wendy Barrie, Raymond Walburn. 72M USA. prod/rel: Fox Film Corp.©

TRIESTE, LEOPOLDO (1917–, ITL
Cronaca, Play
Febbre Di Vivere 1953 d: Claudio GorA. lps: Massimo Serato, Marina Berti, Anna Maria Ferrero. 110M ITL. *Eager to Live*; *Tempo Di Charleston* prod/rel: Produzione Artistica Cin.Ca, Atlantis Film

TRIFONOV, YURI VALENTINOVICH (1925–1981), RSS
Utolyeniye Zhazhdy, 1963, Novel
Utolyeniye Zhazhdy 1968 d: Bulat Mansurov. lps: Pyotr Aleynikov, Hodzhadurdi Narliyev, Artyk Jalliyev. 83M USS. *Quenching of the Thirst*; *Quenching Thirst*; *Quenched Thirst*

TRIGO, FELIPE
Jarrapellejos, 1914, Novel
Jarrapellejos 1987 d: Antonio Gimenez-Rico. lps: Antonio Ferrandis, Amparo Larranaga, Juan Diego. 108M SPN.

TRILBY
Reve d'Amour, Novel
Lys du Mont Saint-Michel, Le 1920 d: Henry Houry, J. Sheffer. lps: Camille Bert, Agnes Souret, Blanche Altem. F FRN. prod/rel: Dal. Film

TRILBY, T.
Monique - Poupee Francaise, Novel
Faute de Monique, La 1928 d: Maurice Gleize. lps: Victor Vina, Sandra Milowanoff, Rudolf Klein-Rogge. F FRN. *Poupee Francaise Monique* prod/rel: European Films

TRINIAN, JOHN
The Big Grab, New York 1960, Novel
 Melodie En Sous-Sol 1962 d: Henri Verneuil. lps: Jean Gabin, Alain Delon, Viviane Romance. 120M FRN/ITL. *Colpo Grosso Al Casino* (ITL); *Any Number Can Win* (USA); *The Big Snatch*; *The Big Grab* prod/rel: C.C.M., Cipra

TRIPATHI, GOVARDHANRAM
Saraswatichandra, Novel
 Saraswatichandra 1968 d: Govind SaraiyA. lps: Nutan, Manish, Vijaya Choudhury. 156M IND. *Saraswati Chandra* prod/rel: Sarvodaya Pictures

TRIVEDI, SHANKAR
Siddhasansar, Play
 Maya MacHhindra 1932 d: V. Shantaram. lps: Govindrao Tembe, Durga Khote, Winayak. 154M IND. *Maya MacHhindra*; *Illusory World* prod/rel: Prabhat Film

TRIVENI
Hannele Chigurdaga, Novel
 Hannele Chiguridaga 1968 d: M. R. Vittal. lps: R. Nagendra Rao, Rajkumar, KalpanA. 161M IND. prod/rel: Srikanth & Srikanth
Sharapanjara, Novel
 Sharapanjara 1971 d: S. R. Puttana Kanagal. lps: Kalpana, Gangadhar, Chindodi LeelA. 180M IND. *The Cage of Arrows* prod/rel: Vardini Arts

TROLLOPE, ANTHONY (1815–1882), UKN
Barchester Towers, 1857, Novel
 Barchester Chronicles, The 1982 d: David Giles. lps: Donald Pleasence, Nigel Hawthorne, Geraldine McEwan. MTV. 355M UKN. prod/rel: BBC
The Seaweed Children, 1864, Short Story
 Malachi's Cove 1974 d: Henry Herbert. lps: Donald Pleasence, Dai Bradley, Veronica Quilligan. 89M UKN/CND. *The Seaweed Children* prod/rel: Penrith Productions Ltd. (London), Impact Films Ltd. (London)
The Warden, 1855, Novel
 Barchester Chronicles, The 1982 d: David Giles. lps: Donald Pleasence, Nigel Hawthorne, Geraldine McEwan. MTV. 355M UKN. prod/rel: BBC

TROLLOPE, JOANNA (1943–, UKN
The Rector's Wife, Novel
 Rector's Wife, The 1993 d: Giles Foster. lps: Lindsay Duncan, Ronald Pickup, Miles Anderson. MTV. 211M UKN.

TROST, SCOTT
Aaron Gillespie Will Make You a Star, Play
 Aaron Gillespie Will Make You a Star 1996 d: Massimo Mazzucco. lps: Scott Caan, Holly Gagnier, Scott Trust. 94M USA. prod/rel: Maga

TROTTI, LAMAR
Story
 There's No Business Like Show Business 1954 d: Walter Lang. lps: Ethel Merman, Donald O'Connor, Marilyn Monroe. 117M USA. prod/rel: 20th Century-Fox

TROWBRIDGE, J. T.
Roger and I, Poem
 Vagabonds, The 1915. lps: Morris Foster. SHT USA. prod/rel: Thanhouser

TROWBRIDGE, JOHN TOWNSEND (1827–1916), USA, Trowbridge, J. T.
Dorothy in the Garret, Poem
 Old Maid, The 1914 d: John B. O'Brien. lps: Blanche Sweet, Mary Alden, Spottiswoode Aitken. 2r USA. *Dorothy in the Garret* prod/rel: Majestic

TROWBRIDGE, LADY
The Golden Cage, Play
 Golden Cage, The 1933 d: Ivar Campbell. lps: Anne Grey, Anthony Kimmins, Frank Cellier. 62M UKN. prod/rel: Sound City, MGM
His Grace Gives Notice, Novel
 His Grace Gives Notice 1924 d: W. P. Kellino. lps: Nora Swinburne, Henry Victor, John Stuart. 5900f UKN. prod/rel: Stoll
 His Grace Gives Notice 1933 d: George A. Cooper. lps: Arthur Margetson, Viola Keats, Victor Stanley. 57M UKN. prod/rel: Real Art, Radio

TROWBRIDGE, W. H. R.
The White Hope, Novel
 White Hope, The 1915 d: Frank Wilson. lps: Stewart Rome, Violet Hopson, Lionelle Howard. 3650f UKN. prod/rel: Hepworth, Moss
 White Hope, The 1922 d: Frank Wilson. lps: Violet Hopson, Stewart Rome, Frank Wilson. 6300f UKN. prod/rel: Walter West, Butcher's Film Service

TROY, ELIZABETH
No Exit, Story
 Love, Honor and Oh-Baby! 1940 d: Charles Lamont. lps: Donald Woods, Kathryn Adams, Wallace Ford. 60M USA. *No Exit* prod/rel: Universal Pictures Co.©

TROY, UNA
We are Seven, New York 1957, Novel
 She Didn't Say No! 1958 d: Cyril Frankel. lps: Eileen Herlie, Niall MacGinnis, Ray McAnally. 97M UKN. prod/rel: Ab-Pathe, Gw Films
 We are Seven 1991 d: Ken Horn. lps: Helen Roberts, Dafydd Hywel, Christopher Mitchum. MTV. 312M UKN.

TROYAT, HENRI (1911–, RSS, Tarassov, Lev
Grandeur Nature, 1936, Novel
 Feu de Paille, Le 1939 d: Jean Benoit-Levy. lps: Lucien Baroux, Orane Demazis, Florence Luchaire. 117M FRN. *Fire in the Straw* (USA); *L' Enfant Prodige* prod/rel: Societe Des Films Vega
La Neige En Deuil, 1952, Novel
 Mountain, The 1956 d: Edward Dmytryk. lps: Spencer Tracy, Robert Wagner, Claire Trevor. 105M USA. prod/rel: Paramount
Tendre Et Violente Elisabeth, 1957, Novel
 Tendre Et Violente Elisabeth 1960 d: Henri Decoin. lps: Christian Marquand, Lucille Saint-Simon, Jean Hoube. 105M FRN. *Passionate Affair* (UKN) prod/rel: Ceres, Gaumont

TROYEPOLSKIY, G.
U Krutogo Yara, Moscow 1956, Short Story
 U Krutogo Yara 1962 d: Kira Muratova, Alexander Muratov. lps: Valeri Isakov, M. Chebotarenko, V. Markin. 45M USS. *The She-Wolf* (USA); *On the Steep Cliff*; *By the Steep Ravine*; *On a Steep Bank* prod/rel: Gorky Film Studio

TRUESDALE, JUNE
The Strange Deception, Novel
 Accused, The 1948 d: William Dieterle. lps: Loretta Young, Wendell Corey, Robert Cummings. 101M USA. *The Strange Deception* prod/rel: Paramount

TRUMBO, DALTON (1905–1976), USA
Story
 Jealousy 1945 d: Gustav Machaty. lps: John Loder, Jane Randolph, Karen Morley. 71M USA. prod/rel: Republic
Johnny Got His Gun, Novel
 Johnny Got His Gun 1971 d: Dalton Trumbo. lps: Donald Barry, Timothy Bottoms, Craig BoviA. 111M USA. prod/rel: Cinemation
The Remarkable Andrew, Novel
 Remarkable Andrew, The 1942 d: Stuart Heisler. lps: William Holden, Ellen Drew, Brian Donlevy. 80M USA. prod/rel: Paramount
Tugboat Princess, Story
 Tugboat Princess 1936 d: David Selman. lps: Walter C. Kelly, Valerie Hobson, Edith Fellows. 68M CND. prod/rel: Central Films Ltd.

TRUMBULL, ANNIE ELIOT
A Christmas Accident, Story
 Christmas Accident, A 1912 d: Bannister Merwin. lps: William Wadsworth, Mrs. William Bechtel, Augustus Phillips. 1000f USA. prod/rel: Edison

TRUMBULL, WALTER
The Man Who Heard Everything, 1921, Short Story
 Bits of Life 1921 d: Marshall Neilan. lps: Wesley Barry, Rockliffe Fellowes, Lon Chaney. 6339f USA. prod/rel: Marshall Neilan Productions, Associated First National Pictures

TRUSS, SELDON
The Long Night, Novel
 Long Knife, The 1958 d: Montgomery Tully. lps: Joan Rice, Sheldon Lawrence, Dorothy Brewster. 57M UKN. prod/rel: Merton Park, Anglo-Amalgamated

TRYON, THOMAS (1926–1991), USA
Harvest Home, Novel
 Dark Secret of Harvest Home 1978 d: Leo Penn. lps: Bette Davis, David Ackroyd, Rosanna Arquette. TVM. 200M USA. prod/rel: Mca, Universal
The Other, Novel
 Other, The 1972 d: Robert Mulligan. lps: Uta Hagen, Diana Muldaur, Chris Udvarnoky. 100M USA. prod/rel: 20th Century Fox, Rex-Benchmark

TRYZNA, TOMEK
Panna Nikt, Novel
 Panna Nikt 1997 d: Andrzej WajdA. lps: Anna Wielgucka, Anna Mucha, Anna PowierzA. 103M PLN. *Miss Nobody* prod/rel: Studio Filmowe Perspektywa, Telewizja Polska

TRZCINSKI, EDMUND
Stalag 17, New York 1951, Play
 Stalag 17 1953 d: Billy Wilder. lps: William Holden, Don Taylor, Otto Preminger. 120M USA. prod/rel: Paramount

TS'AO CHAN
Hung Lou Meng, 1792
 Hung Lou Meng 1966 d: Wang Ping. lps: Hsu Yu-Lan, Wang Wen-Chuan, Lu Jui-Ying. F CHN. *The Dream of the Red Chamber* (USA) prod/rel: Hayien Film Studio

TSAO YU
Novel
 Sunrise 1986 d: Yu Bun Ching. lps: Fang Shu, Wong See Kwai. 100M TWN.

TSCHCHEIDSE, OTAR
Putchestwie Molodogo Kompozitora, Novel
 Putschestwie Molodogo Kompozitora 1984 d: Georgi ShengelayA. lps: Gija Peradse, Lewan Abaschidse, Surab Kipischidse. 105M USS. *Achalgasrda Komposotoris Mogsautoba*; *A Young Composer's Odyssey*; *Akhalgazrda Kompozitoris Mogzauroba*; *Putesestvie Molodogo Kompozitora*; *Journey of the Young Composer* prod/rel: Grusia-Film

TSCHERNOVITZ, YAMIMA
Book
 Shemona B'ekevot Achat 1964 d: Menahem Golan. lps: Shai K. Ophir, Bomba Tzur, Geula Gill. F ISR. *Eight Against One*

TSEKURAS, NICOS
I Limni Ton Pothon, Play
 Limni Ton Pothon, I 1958 d: Georges Zervos. lps: George Foundas, Jenny Karezi, Sonja Zoidou. 78M GRC. *Le Lac aux Desirs* prod/rel: Anzeros

TSIFOROS, N.
A Shoe from Your Homeland, Play
 Shoe from Your Homeland, A 1980 d: Peter Bernardos. lps: John Chrisoulis, Amalia Vassilliadis, Dennis Dragonas. TVM. F ASL. prod/rel: Aav-Australia

TSIOLKAS, CHRISTOS
Loaded, Book
 Head on 1998 d: Ana Kokkinos. lps: Alex Dimitriades, Paul Capsis, Julian Garner. 104M ASL. prod/rel: Palace Films, Great Scott

TSUBOI, SAKAE
Nijushi No Hitomi, 1952, Novel
 Nijushi No Hitomi 1954 d: Keisuke KinoshitA. lps: Hideko Takamine, Yumeji Tsukioka, Toshiko Kobayashi. 154M JPN. *Twenty-Four Eyes*; *Twenty-Four Hours* prod/rel: Shochiku Co.
 Nijushi No Hitomi 1988 d: Yoshitaka AsamA. lps: Yuko Tanaka, Tetsuya Takeda, Misako Konno. 129M JPN. *Children on the Island* (USA); *24 Eyes* prod/rel: Shochiku Co.

TSURUMA, KAORU
End of Sleepless Nights, Story
 Tsuki to Kyabetsu 1998 d: Tetsuo ShinoharA. lps: Masayoshi Yamazaki, Masumi Sanada, Shingo Tsurumi. 100M JPN. *One More Chance One More Time* prod/rel: Ace Pictures Intl.

TSURUYA, NANBOKU
Shura, Play
 Shura 1970 d: Toshio Matsumoto. lps: Katsuo Nakamura, Yasuko Sanjo, Juro KarA. 134M JPN. *Demons* (USA); *Pandemonium* prod/rel: Matsumoto Productions, Art Theatre Guild
Tokaido Yotsuya Kaidan, 1825, Play
 Tokaido Yotsuya Kaidan 1959 d: Nobuo NakagawA. lps: Shigeru Amachi, Kazuko Wakasugi, Shuntaro Emi. 76M JPN. *Ghost Story of Yotsuya in Tokaido*; *The Ghost of Yotsuya* prod/rel: Shintoho Co.
 Yotsuya Kaidan 1949 d: Keisuke KinoshitA. lps: Kinuyo Tanaka, Ken Uehara, Haruko SugimurA. 158M JPN. *The Yotsuya Ghost Story*; *The Ghost of Yotsuya*; *Shinshaku Yotsuya Kaidan*; *Illusion of Blood*
 Yotsuya Kaidan 1959 d: Kenji Misumi. lps: Kazuo Hasegawa, Yasuko Nakada, Yoko Uraji. 84M JPN. *The Yotsuya Ghost Story*; *The Ghost of Yotsuya*; *Thou Shalt Not Be Jealous* prod/rel: Daiei Motion Picture Co.
 Yotsuya Kaidan 1965 d: Shiro ToyodA. lps: Tatsuya Nakadai, Mariko Okada, Junko Ikeuchi. 107M JPN. *The Yotsuya Ghost Story*; *Illusion of Blood* (USA); *The Ghost of Yotsuya* prod/rel: Tokyo Eiga
Yotsuya Kaidan, Play
 Kaidan Bancho Sarayashiki 1957 d: Juichi Kono. lps: Chiyonosuke Azuma, Hibari MisorA. F JPN. *Ghost Story of Broken Dishes at Bancho Mansion*; *The Ghost of Yotsuya* prod/rel: Toei Co.
 Kaidan Oiwa No Borei 1961 d: Tai Kato. lps: Tomisaburo Wakayama, Hiroko Sakuramachi. F JPN. *The Ghost of Yotsuya*; *Ghost of Oiwa* prod/rel: Toei Co.
 Yotsuya Kaidan -Oiwa No Borei 1969 d: Issei Mori. lps: Kei Sato, Kazuko Inano, Yoshihiko AoyamA. 94M JPN. *The Curse of the Night*; *The Ghost of Yotsuya*; *Oiwa No Borei* prod/rel: Daiei Motion Picture Co.

TSUTSUI, YASUTAKA
Oreno Chi Wa Tanin No Chi, Novel
　Oreno Chi Wa Tanin No Chi 1974 d: Toshio SendA. lps: Shohei Kano, Frankie Sakai, Etsuko Nami. 94M JPN. *Blood* prod/rel: Shochiku Co.

Toki O Kakeru Shojo, Novel
　Toki O Kakeru Shojo 1983 d: Nobuhiko Obayashi. lps: Tomoyo Harada, Ryoichi Takayanagi, Toshinori Omi. 104M JPN. *The Little Girl Who Conquered Time* prod/rel: Haruki Kadokawa Films

TSUUCHI, HANJURO
Narukami, 1742, Play
　Bijo to Kairyu 1955 d: Kozaburo YoshimurA. lps: Chiyonosuke Azuma, Nobuko Otowa, Chojuro Kawarazaki. 100M JPN. *The Beauty and the Dragon; The Lady and the Dragon*

TSUWA-GORMAN, MICHIKO
Autobiography
　My Champion 1981 d: Gwen Arner. lps: Yoko Shimada, Christopher Mitchum, Andy Romero. 105M USA/JPN. *Ritoru Champion* (JPN); *Run Miki Run* prod/rel: Shochiku Co.

TSUZUKI, MICHIO
Ueta Isan, Novel
　Satsujin Kyo Jidai 1967 d: Kihachi Okamoto. lps: Tatsuya Nakadai, Reiko Dan, Hideo SunazukA. 99M JPN. *Epoch of Murder Madness; The Age of Assassins* prod/rel: Toho Co.

TUCHMAN, BARBARA W. (1912–1989), USA, Tuchman, Barbara Wertheim
The Guns of August, New York 1962, Book
　Guns of August, The 1964 d: Nathan Kroll. DOC. 99M USA.

TUCHOLSKY, KURT
Rheinsberg; Ein Bilderbuch Fur Verliebte, 1912, Short Story
　Rheinsberg 1967 d: Kurt Hoffmann. lps: Cornelia Froboess, Christian Wolff, Werner Hinz. 88M GRM. prod/rel: Independent, Constantin

Schloss Gripsholm, 1931, Novel
　Schloss Gripsholm 1963 d: Kurt Hoffmann. lps: Jana Brejchova, Walter Giller, Hanns Lothar. 99M GRM. *Gripsholm Castle* prod/rel: Independent, Gloria

TUCKER, AUGUSTA
Miss Susie Slagle's, Novel
　Miss Susie Slagle's 1945 d: John Berry. lps: Veronica Lake, Joan Caulfield, Lillian Gish. 89M USA. prod/rel: Paramount

TULLY, JIM
Beggars of Life, New York 1924, Novel
　Beggars of Life 1928 d: William A. Wellman. lps: Wallace Beery, Louise Brooks, Richard Arlen. 7560f USA. prod/rel: Paramount Famous Lasky Corp.

Laughter in Hell, New York 1932, Novel
　Laughter in Hell 1933 d: Edward L. Cahn. lps: Pat O'Brien, Tommy Conlon, Merna Kennedy. 68M USA. prod/rel: Universal Pictures Corp.©

TULLY, RICHARD WALTON
The Bird of Paradise, New York 1912, Play
　Bird of Paradise 1932 d: King Vidor. lps: Dolores Del Rio, Joel McCrea, John Halliday. 80M USA. prod/rel: RKO Radio Pictures, Inc.
　Bird of Paradise 1951 d: Delmer Daves. lps: Louis Jourdan, Debra Paget, Jeff Chandler. 100M USA. prod/rel: 20th Century-Fox

Omar the Tentmaker, New York 1914, Play
　Omar the Tentmaker 1922 d: James Young. lps: Post Guy Bates, Virginia Brown Faire, Nigel de Brulier. 8090f USA. prod/rel: Richard Walton Tully Productions, Associated First National Pictures

Rose of the Rancho, New York 1906, Play
　Rose of the Rancho 1914 d: Cecil B. de Mille, Wilfred Buckland. lps: Bessie Barriscale, Monroe Salisbury, Jane Darwell. 5r USA. prod/rel: Jesse L. Lasky Feature Play Co.©, Paramount Pictures Corp.
　Rose of the Rancho 1936 d: Marion Gering, Robert Florey (Uncredited). lps: John Boles, Gladys Swarthout, Charles Bickford. 85M USA. prod/rel: Paramount Pictures

TUMA, KAREL
Z Ceskych Mlynu, Play
　Z Ceskych Mlynu 1925 d: Svatopluk Innemann, Ferry Seidl. lps: Ferry Seidl, Bozena Svobodova, Filip Balek-Brodsky. 2529m CZC. *From the Czech Mills* prod/rel: Elektafilm
　Z Ceskych Mlynu 1929 d: M. J. Krnansky, Ferry Seidl. lps: Frantisek Ruzicka, Nora Ferry, Jiri Hron. 1904m CZC. *From the Czech Mills* prod/rel: Elekta Journal

TUMIATI, DOMENICO
Parisina, 1903, Poem
　Parisina (un Amore Alla Corte Di Ferrara Nel Xv Secolo) 1909 d: Giuseppe de Liguoro. 454m ITL. *Ugo E la Parisina; Ugo E Parisina* prod/rel: Saffi-Comerio

TUMLIR, JAROSLAV
Strasidelna Teticka, Play
　Teticka 1941 d: Martin Fric. lps: Ruzena Naskova, Ferenc Futurista, Frantisek Smolik. 2430m CZC. *Auntie's Fantasies; The Auntie* prod/rel: Lloyd

TUNIS, JOHN R.
American Girl, 1930, Novel
　Hard, Fast and Beautiful 1951 d: Ida Lupino. lps: Sally Forrest, Claire Trevor, Carleton Young. 76M USA. prod/rel: RKO Radio, Filmmakers

TUNSTROM, GORAN
Juloratoriet, Novel
　Juloratoriet 1996 d: Kjelle-Ake Andersson. lps: Peter Haber, Johan Widerberg, Henrik Linnros. 124M SWD. *The Christmas Oratio* prod/rel: Sveriges Tv, Sandrews

TUPPER, EDITH SESSIONS
The House of the Tolling Bell, Novel
　House of the Tolling Bell, The 1920 d: J. Stuart Blackton. lps: May McAvoy, Bruce (4) Gordon, Morgan Thorpe. 6r USA. prod/rel: J. Stuart Blackton Feature Pictures, Pathe Exchange, Inc.©

Whispering Pines, Story
　Wilful Youth 1927 d: Dallas M. Fitzgerald. lps: Edna Murphy, Kenneth Harlan, Jack Richardson. 5900f USA. prod/rel: Dallas M. Fitzgerald Productions, Peerless Pictures

TUPPER, TRISTRAM
Four Brothers, 1928, Short Story
　First Kiss, The 1928 d: Rowland V. Lee. lps: Fay Wray, Gary Cooper, Lane Chandler. 6134f USA. prod/rel: Paramount Famous Lasky Corp.

Klondike, Story
　Klondike 1932 d: Phil Rosen. lps: Lyle Talbot, Thelma Todd, Capt. Frank Hawks. 68M USA. *The Doctor's Sacrifice* (UKN) prod/rel: Monogram Pictures Corp.©
　Klondike Fury 1942 d: William K. Howard. lps: Edmund Lowe, Lucille Fairbanks, William Henry. 68M USA. *Klondike Victory* prod/rel: Monogram, King Brothers

The River, Philadelphia 1928, Novel
　River, The 1928 d: Frank Borzage. lps: Charles Farrell, Mary Duncan, Ivan Linow. 6536f USA. *La Femme Au Corbeau* prod/rel: Fox Film Corp.

Terwilliger, Short Story
　Children of Dust 1923 d: Frank Borzage. lps: Bert Woodruff, Johnny Walker, Frankie Lee. 6228f USA. prod/rel: Arthur H. Jacobs Corp., Associated First National Pictures

Three Episodes in the Life of Timothy Osborn, 1927, Short Story
　Lucky Star 1929 d: Frank Borzage. lps: Charles Farrell, Janet Gaynor, Guinn (Big Boy) Williams. 8784f USA. prod/rel: Fox Film Corp.

TURATI, AUGUSTO
Anime in Tumulto, Novel
　Anime in Tumulto 1942 d: Giulio Del Torre. lps: Gina Falckenberg, Carlo Tamberlani, Leda GloriA. 85M ITL. prod/rel: Stella-Sovrania, Rex

TURGENEV, IVAN (1818–1883), RSS, Turgenev, Ivan Sergeyevich

Pervaya Lyubov 1995 d: Roman Balayan.
Novel
　Summer Lightning 1984 d: Paul Joyce. lps: Paul Scofield, Tom Bell, Edward Rawle-Hicks. TVM. 95M UKN.

Asya, 1858, Short Story
　Asya 1977 d: Josif Heifitz. lps: Elena Koreneva, Vyacheslav Vezerov, Igor Kostolevskij. 96M USS. *Love Should Be Guarded*

Biryuk, 1852, Short Story
　Biryuk 1979 d: Roman Balayan. lps: Mikhail Golubovich, Oleg Tabakov, Lena Chrol. 76M USS. *Birjuk; The Lone Wolf; The Morose Man; The Recluse* prod/rel: Studios Dovjenko

Dvoryanskoe Gnezdo, 1859, Novel
　Chun Can Meng Duan 1947 d: Sun Jing. 100M CHN. *Dream Broken in Late Spring*
　Dvorianskoe Gnezdo 1969 d: Andrei Konchalovsky. lps: Beata Tyszkiewicz, Irina Kupchenko, Viktor Sergachov. 106M USS. *A Nest of Gentlefolk* (UKN); *A Nest of the Gentry; Dvorjanskoe Gnezdo; Dvoryanskoye Gnezdo* prod/rel: Mosfilm

Mesyats V Derevne, 1855, Play
　Month in the Country, A 1955 d: Robert Hamer. lps: Margaret Leighton, Laurence Harvey. MTV. 90M UKN. prod/rel: Itv

　Month in the Country, A 1985 d: Quentin Lawrence. lps: Susannah York, Ian McShane, Linda Thorson. 90M UKN/USA.
　Month in the Country, A 1985 d: Bill Hays. lps: Richard Briers, Eleanor Bron. MTV. F UKN. prod/rel: BBC
　Secrets 1942 d: Pierre Blanchar. lps: Gilbert Gil, Pierre Blanchar, Marie DeA. 100M FRN. *Le Fol Ete* prod/rel: Pathe-Cinema

Mumu, 1854, Short Story
　Mumu 1959 d: Anatoli Bobrovsky, Yevgeniy Teterin. lps: Afanasij Kochetkov, Nina Grebeshkova, Yelena PolevitskayA. 71M USS. prod/rel: Mosfilm
　Mumu 1987 d: V. Karavaev. ANM. 20M USS.
　Mumu 1998 d: Yuri Grymov. lps: Yelena Korikova, Aleksandr Baluyev, Irina ApeksimovA. F RSS.

Nakanune, 1860, Novel
　Nakanunye 1959 d: Vladimir Petrov. lps: Lyubomir Kabakchiev, Irina Milopolskaya, Boris Livanov. 88M USS/BUL. *V Navecherieto* (BUL); *On the Eve; Nakanune*

Nakhlebnik, 1869, Play
　Nakhlebnik 1953 d: Vladimir Basov, M. Korchagin. 100M USS.

Ottsy I Deti, 1862, Novel
　Ottsy I Deti 1958 d: Natalya Rashevskaya, Adolf Bergunkev. 102M USS. *Fathers and Sons*

Pervaya Lyubov, 1860, Short Story
　Erste Liebe 1970 d: Maximilian Schell. lps: John Moulder-Brown, Dominique Sanda, Maximilian Schell. 90M GRM/SWT/UKN. *First Love* (USA) prod/rel: Franz Seitz Filmproduktion, Alfa-Film
　Primer Amor 1942 d: Claudio de La Torre. lps: Rosita Yarza, Mariano Azana, Consuelo NievA. 92M SPN. *First Love*

Rudin, 1856, Novel
　Rudin 1976 d: Konstantin Voinov. lps: Nikolai Figurovsky, Oleg Efremov, Armen Djigarkhanyan. 106M USS. *Roedin*

Veshniye Vody, 1872, Short Story
　Acque Di Primavera 1989 d: Jerzy Skolimowski. lps: Timothy Hutton, Nastassja Kinski, Valeria Golino. 101M ITL/FRN. *Les Eaux Printanieres* (FRN); *Torrents of Spring* prod/rel: Hobo, Erre Produzione
　Jarni Vody 1968 d: Vaclav KrskA. lps: Vit Olmer, Alzbeta Strkulova, Kveta FialovA. 91M CZC. *Spring Waters; Spring Floods*
　Poezdka V Visbaden 1989 d: Evgenij Gerasimov. lps: Sergei Zhigunov, Yelena Seropova, Natalya LapinA. 86M USS/AUS/CZC. *A Trip to Visbaden; A Trip to Wiesbaden; Poyezdka V Visbaden* prod/rel: Bratislava, Klinkart Films

Zavtrak U Predvoditelya, 1856, Play
　Zavtrak U Prevoditelya 1953 d: Anatoly Rybakov. 55M USS.

TURGENEV, S.
Cuzoj Chleb, 1848, Novel
　Pane Altrui, Il 1913 d: Ubaldo Maria Del Colle. lps: Dillo Lombardi, Adriana Costamagna, Mario Roncoroni. 1400m ITL. *Petroff the Vassal (a Russian Romance)* (USA) prod/rel: Savoia Film
　Pane Altrui, Il 1924 d: Telemaco Ruggeri. lps: Gustavo Serena, Cecyl Tryan, Carlo Benetti. 1560m ITL. prod/rel: Film d'Art

TURNBULL, HECTOR
The Cheat, Novel
　Forfaiture 1937 d: Marcel L'Herbier. lps: Victor Francen, Sessue Hayakawa, Lise Delamare. 100M FRN. *The Cheat* prod/rel: Societe Du Cinema Du Pantheon

My American Wife, Story
　My American Wife 1922 d: Sam Wood. lps: Gloria Swanson, Antonio Moreno, Josef Swickard. 6091f USA. *The Count of Arizona* prod/rel: Famous Players-Lasky, Paramount Pictures

TURNBULL, MARGARET
Classmates, New York 1907, Play
　Classmates 1914 d: James Kirkwood. lps: Blanche Sweet, Henry B. Walthall, Lionel Barrymore. 4r USA. prod/rel: Klaw & Erlanger©, Biograph Co.

The Clue, Play
　Clue, The 1915 d: James Neill, Frank Reicher. lps: Blanche Sweet, Gertrude Kellar, Edward MacKaye. 4930f USA. prod/rel: Jesse L. Lasky Feature Play Co.©, Paramount Pictures Corp.

Looking After Sandy, New York 1914, Novel
　Bad Little Angel 1939 d: Wilhelm Thiele. lps: Ian Hunter, Lois Wilson, Virginia Weidler. 77M USA. *Looking After Sandy; Patsy; Runaway Angel* prod/rel: Metro-Goldwyn-Mayer Corp.

TURNER, ALFRED
Missing the Tide, Novel
  Missing the Tide 1918 d: Walter West. lps: Violet Hopson, Basil Gill, Ivy Close. 5063f UKN. prod/rel: Broadwest

TURNER, DAVID
Semi-Detached, 1962, Play
  All the Way Up 1970 d: James MacTaggart. lps: Warren Mitchell, Pat Heywood, Elaine Taylor. 97M UKN. prod/rel: Anglo-Amalgamated, Granada

TURNER, ETHEL
One Way Ticket, New York 1934, Novel
  One Way Ticket 1935 d: Herbert J. Biberman. lps: Lloyd Nolan, Peggy Conklin, Walter Connolly. 72M USA. prod/rel: Columbia Pictures Corp.©

TURNER, GEORGE KIBBE
The Girl in the Glass Cage, New York 1927, Novel
  Girl in the Glass Cage, The 1929 d: Ralph Dawson. lps: Loretta Young, Carroll Nye, Matthew Betz. 7159f USA. prod/rel: First National Pictures

Half Marriage, Story
  Half Marriage 1929 d: William J. Cowen. lps: Olive Borden, Morgan Farley, Ken Murray. 72M USA. prod/rel: RKO Productions

Held in Trust, 1920, Short Story
  Held in Trust 1920 d: John Ince. lps: May Allison, Darrel Foss, Walter Long. 6r USA. prod/rel: Metro Pictures Corp.©, Screen Classics, Inc.

A Passage to Hong Kong, Novel
  Roar of the Dragon 1932 d: Wesley Ruggles. lps: Richard Dix, Gwili Andre, Edward Everett Horton. 76M USA. prod/rel: RKO Radio Pictures©

A Ride in the Country, 1927, Short Story
  Walking Back 1928 d: Rupert Julian. lps: Sue Carol, Richard Walling, Ivan Lebedeff. 5035f USA. prod/rel: de Mille Pictures, Pathe Exchange, Inc.

Street of the Forgotten Men, 1925, Short Story
  Street of Forgotten Men, The 1925 d: Herbert Brenon. lps: Percy Marmont, Mary Brian, Neil Hamilton. 6366f USA. prod/rel: Famous Players-Lasky, Paramount Pictures

Those Who Dance, Story
  Contre-Enquete 1930 d: John Daumery. lps: Daniel Mendaille, Suzy Vernon, Jeanne Helbling. 70M USA. prod/rel: Warner Bros., First National
  Tanz Geht Weiter, Der 1930 d: William Dieterle. lps: Wilhelm Dieterle, Lissi Arna, Anton Pointner. 85M USA. *The Dance Goes on* prod/rel: Warner Brothers Pictures

TURNER, JOHN HASTINGS
Gentleman of Venture, Play
  Gentleman of Venture 1940 d: Paul L. Stein. lps: Wilfred Lawson, Nora Swinburne, Marta Labarr. 80M UKN. *It Happened to One Man* (USA) prod/rel: British Eagle, RKO Radio

A Letter of Warning, Play
  Letter of Warning, A 1932 d: John Daumery. lps: Margot Grahame, Richard Bird, Sydney Fairbrother. 33M UKN. *Undisclosed* prod/rel: First National, Warner Bros.

Lilies of the Field, London 1923, Play
  Lilies of the Field 1934 d: Norman Walker. lps: Winifred Shotter, Ellis Jeffreys, Anthony Bushell. 83M UKN. prod/rel: British and Dominions, United Artists

Lord of the Manor, 1928, Play
  Lord of the Manor 1933 d: Henry Edwards. lps: Betty Stockfeld, Fred Kerr, Henry Wilcoxon. 71M UKN. prod/rel: British and Dominions, Paramount British

The Sea Urchin, 1925, Play
  Sea Urchin, The 1926 d: Graham Cutts. lps: Betty Balfour, George Hackathorne, W. Cronin Wilson. 7340f UKN. prod/rel: Gainsborough, Woolf & Freedman

Simple Souls, New York 1918, Novel
  Simple Souls 1920 d: Robert T. Thornby. lps: Blanche Sweet, Charles Meredith, Kate Lester. 5264f USA. prod/rel: Jesse D. Hampton Productions, Pathe Exchange, Inc.©

TURNER, TINA
I - Tina, Autobiography
  What's Love Got to Do With It 1993 d: Brian Gibson. lps: Angela Bassett, Laurence Fishburne, Vanessa Bell Calloway. 118M USA.

TURNEY, CATHERINE
The Other One, 1952, Novel
  Back from the Dead 1957 d: Charles Marquis Warren. lps: Peggie Castle, Arthur Franz, Marsha Hunt. 79M USA. prod/rel: 20th Century-Fox Film Corp., Regal Films

TURNOVSKY, JOSEF LADISLAV
Zivot a Pusobeni J. K. Tyla
  Josef Kajetan Tyl 1925 d: Svatopluk Innemann. lps: Zdenek Stepanek, Helena Friedlova, Zdena KavkovA. 3178m CZC. prod/rel: Svetofilm

TUROW, SCOTT (1949–, USA
Presumed Innocent, 1990, Novel
  Presumed Innocent 1990 d: Alan J. PakulA. lps: Harrison Ford, Brian Dennehy, Raul JuliA. 127M USA. prod/rel: Warner Bros., Mirage

TUSEK, MIRIAM
Imam Drije Mame I Dva Tate, Novel
  Imam Dvije Mame I Dva Tate 1968 d: Kreso Golik. lps: Relja Basic, Mia Oremovic, Fabijan Sovagovic. 90M YGS. *I Have Two Mummies and Two Daddies; Too Many Parents; I've Got Two Mummies and Two Daddies* prod/rel: Jadran, Alpha

TUTELIER, CHARLES
Marseille Mes Amours, Opera
  Marseille Mes Amours 1939 d: Jacques Daniel-Norman. lps: Leon Belieres, Mireille Ponsard, Janine Roger. 102M FRN. prod/rel: G.a.R.B.

Au Soleil de Marseille, Opera
  Au Soleil de Marseille 1937 d: Pierre-Jean Ducis. lps: Mireille Ponsard, Henri Garat, Gorlett. F FRN. prod/rel: Henri Ullmann

TUTTLE, MARGARET
Feet of Clay, Boston 1923, Novel
  Feet of Clay 1924 d: Cecil B. de Mille. lps: Vera Reynolds, Rod La Rocque, Ricardo Cortez. 9746f USA. prod/rel: Famous Players-Lasky, Paramount Pictures

TUTTLE, W. C.
Assisting Ananias, 1920, Short Story
  Fools of Fortune 1922 d: Louis W. Chaudet. lps: Frank Dill, Russell Simpson, Tully Marshall. 5609f USA. prod/rel: Golden State Films, American Releasing Corp.

Baa Baa Black Sheep, 1921, Short Story
  Black Sheep 1921 d: Paul C. Hurst. lps: Neal Hart, Ted Brooks, George A. Williams. 5r USA. prod/rel: Chaudet-Hurst Productions, Pinnacle Pictures

Blind Trails, Story
  Wild Horse Stampede, The 1926 d: Albert S. Rogell. lps: Jack Hoxie, Fay Wray, William Steele. 4776f USA. prod/rel: Universal Pictures

The Devil's Dooryard, 1921, Short Story
  Devil's Dooryard, The 1923 d: Louis King. lps: William Fairbanks, Ena Gregory, Joseph Girard. 4838f USA. prod/rel: Ben Wilson Productions, Arrow Film Corp.

Fate of the Wolf, 1925, Short Story
  Driftin' Sands 1928 d: Wallace Fox. lps: Bob Steele, Gladys Quartaro, William H. Turner. 4770f USA. prod/rel: Fbo Pictures

The Law Rustlers, 1921, Short Story
  Law Rustlers, The 1923 d: Louis King. lps: William Fairbanks, Edmund Cobb, Joseph Girard. 4849f USA. *Beyond the Law* (UKN); *The Law Hustlers* prod/rel: Ben Wilson Productions, Arrow Film Corp.

No Law in Shadow Valley, 1936, Short Story
  Lawless Valley 1938 d: David Howard. lps: George O'Brien, Kay Sutton, Chill Wills. 59M USA. prod/rel: RKO Radio Pictures©

Peace Medicine, Story
  Fighting Peacemaker, The 1926 d: Cliff Smith. lps: Jack Hoxie, Lola Todd, Ted Oliver. 4500f USA. prod/rel: Universal Pictures

Peaceful, Short Story
  Peaceful Peters 1922 d: Louis King. lps: William Fairbanks, Harry La Mont, W. L. Lynch. 4696f USA. prod/rel: Ben Wilson Productions, Arrow Film Corp.

The Sheriff of Sun-Dog, 1921, Short Story
  Sheriff of Sun-Dog, The 1922 d: Ben Wilson, Louis King. lps: William Fairbanks, Robert McKenzie, James Welch. 4949f USA. prod/rel: Berwilla Film Corp., Arrow Film Corp.

Sir Piegan Passes, New York 1923, Short Story
  Cheyenne Kid, The 1933 d: Robert F. Hill. lps: Tom Keene, Mary Mason, Roscoe Ates. 55M USA. *Land of the Six-Shooter* prod/rel: RKO Radio Pictures, Inc.
  Fargo Kid, The 1940 d: Edward Killy. lps: Tim Holt, Ray Whitley, Emmett Lynn. 63M USA. prod/rel: RKO Radio Pictures©
  Man in the Rough 1928 d: Wallace Fox. lps: Bob Steele, Marjorie King, Thomas Lingham. 4785f USA. prod/rel: Fbo Pictures

Spawn of the Desert, 1922, Short Story
  Spawn of the Desert 1923 d: Ben Wilson, Louis King. lps: William Fairbanks, Florence Gilbert, P. Dempsey Tabler. 4979f USA. prod/rel: Berwilla Film Corp., Arrow Film Corp.

Straight Shooting, 1924, Short Story
  Border Sheriff, The 1926 d: Robert North Bradbury. lps: Jack Hoxie, Olive Hasbrouck, S. E. Jennings. 4440f USA. prod/rel: Universal Pictures

The Yellow Seal, 1925, Short Story
  Prairie Pirate, The 1925 d: Edmund Mortimer. lps: Harry Carey, Jean Dumas, Lloyd Whitlock. 4603f USA. *The Yellow Seal* prod/rel: Hunt Stromberg Corp., Producers Distributing Corp.

TUURI, ANTTI
Pohjanmaa, 1982, Novel
  Pohjanmaa 1988 d: Pekka ParikkA. lps: Esko Nikkari, Esko Salminen, Vesa MakelA. 129M FNL. *Plainlands*

Rukajarven Tie, Novel
  Rukajarven Tie 1999 d: Olli SaarelA. lps: Peter Franzen, Irina Bjorklund, Kari Heiskanen. 100M FNL. *Ambush* prod/rel: Matila & Rohr Prods.

Talvisota, 1984, Novel
  Talvisota 1989 d: Pekka ParikkA. lps: Taneli Makela, Vesa Vierikko, Konsta MakelA. 199M FNL. *The Winter War*

TWAIN, MARK (1835–1920), USA, Clemens, Samuel Langhorne
Story
  Innocents Abroad, The 1982 d: Luciano Salce. lps: Craig Wasson, Brooke Adams, David Ogden Stiers. TVM. 89M USA.
  Life on the Mississippi 1987 d: Peter H. Hunt. lps: Robert Lansing, David Knell, James Keane. TVM. 88M UKN/GRM. *Leben Auf Dem Mississippi* (GRM)
  Mysterious Stranger, The 1982 d: Peter H. Hunt. lps: Chris Makepeace, Lance Kerwin, Bernhard Wicki. TVM. 84M UKN/GRM. *Der Geheimnisvolle Fremde* (GRM); *Number 44 the Mysterious Stranger*
  Private History of a Campaign That Failed, The 1982 d: Peter H. Hunt. lps: Pat Hingle, Edward Herrmann, Harry Crosby. TVM. 90M UKN/GRM. *Geschichte Eines Fehlgeschlagenen Feldzugs* (GRM)

The £1.000.000 Bank-Note, 1893, Short Story
  Million Pound Note, The 1953 d: Ronald Neame. lps: Gregory Peck, Jane Griffiths, Ronald Squire. 91M UKN. *Man With a Million* (USA) prod/rel: Group Films, General Film Distributors
  Million to Juan, A 1994 d: Paul Rodriguez. lps: Paul Rodriguez, Polly Draper, Pepe SernA. 93M USA. *A Million to One*

The Adventures of Huckleberry Finn, New York 1884, Novel
  Adventures of Huck Finn, The 1993 d: Stephen Sommers. lps: Elijah Wood, Courtney B. Vance, Robbie Coltrane. 108M USA. prod/rel: Buena Vista, Walt Disney
  Adventures of Huckleberry Finn 1985 d: Peter H. Hunt. lps: Patrick Day, Jim Dale, Frederic Forrest. TVM. 240M USA.
  Adventures of Huckleberry Finn, The 1938 d: Richard Thorpe. lps: Mickey Rooney, William Frawley, Walter Connolly. 92M USA. *Huckleberry Finn* prod/rel: Metro-Goldwyn-Mayer Corp.
  Adventures of Huckleberry Finn, The 1960 d: Michael Curtiz. lps: Tony Randall, Eddie Hodges, Archie Moore. 107M USA. *Huckleberry Finn* prod/rel: MGM
  Huck and Tom; Or the Further Adventures of Tom Sawyer 1918 d: William D. Taylor. lps: Jack Pickford, Robert Gordon, George Hackathorne. 5r USA. *Huck and Tom* prod/rel: Famous Players-Lasky Corp., Oliver Morosco Photoplay Co.©
  Huckleberry Finn 1920 d: William D. Taylor. lps: Lewis Sargent, Gordon Griffith, Katherine Griffith. 7r USA. prod/rel: Famous Players-Lasky Corp.©, William D. Taylor Production
  Huckleberry Finn 1931 d: Norman Taurog. lps: Jackie Coogan, Mitzi Green, Junior Durkin. 73M USA. prod/rel: Paramount Publix Corp.©
  Huckleberry Finn 1974 d: J. Lee Thompson. lps: Jeff East, Paul Winfield, Harvey Korman. 114M USA.
  Huckleberry Finn 1975 d: Robert Totten. lps: Ron Howard, Donny Most, Royal Dano. TVM. 78M USA. prod/rel: ABC Circle Films
  Huckleberry Finn 1981 d: Bunker Jenkins. ANM. 75M USA.
  Sovsem Propascij 1972 d: Georgi DaneliyA. F USS. *The Adventures of Huckleberry Finn; Hopelessly Lost; Sovsem Propashtshiy; The Hopeless*

Adventures of Tom Sawyer, San Francisco 1876, Novel
  Adventures of Tom Sawyer, The 1938 d: Norman Taurog, H. C. Potter. lps: Tommy Kelly, Jackie Moran, Ann Gillis. 93M USA. prod/rel: Selznick International Pictures, Inc., Warner Bros.

Aventurile Lui Tom Sawyer 1968 d: Mihai Iacob, Wolfgang Liebeneiner. 96M RMN/FRN. *Les Aventures de Tom Sawyer*; *The Adventures of Tom Sawyer*

Huck and Tom; Or the Further Adventures of Tom Sawyer 1918 d: William D. Taylor. lps: Jack Pickford, Robert Gordon, George Hackathorne. 5r USA. *Huck and Tom* prod/rel: Famous Players-Lasky Corp., Oliver Morosco Photoplay Co.©

Moartea Lui Joe Indianul 1968 d: Mihai Iacob, Wolfgang Liebeneiner. 80M RMN/FRN. *The Death of Joe the Indian*

Pani Kluci 1975 d: Vera Plivova-SimkovA. lps: Michal Dymek, Magda Reifova, Petr Vorisek. 87M CZC. *The Boys Gentlemen*; *Boys Will Be Boys*; *Gentlemen Boys* prod/rel: Imbild

Tom Sawyer 1917 d: William D. Taylor. lps: Jack Pickford, George Hackathorne, Alice Marvin. 5r USA. prod/rel: Oliver Morosco Photoplay Co.©, Paramount Pictures Corp.

Tom Sawyer 1930 d: John Cromwell. lps: Jackie Coogan, Junior Durkin, Mitzi Green. 86M USA. prod/rel: Paramount-Publix Corp.

Tom Sawyer 1973 d: Don Taylor. lps: Celeste Holm, Warren Oates, Jeff East. 103M USA.

Tom Sawyer 1973 d: James Neilson. lps: Josh Albee, Jeff Tyler, Buddy Ebsen. TVM. 73M USA. *The Adventures of Tom Sawyer* prod/rel: Universal, Hal Roach Productions

Tom Sawyer 1983 d: Stanislav Govorukhin. lps: Fyodor Stukov, Vladik Suchatschov, Boris Saidenberg. MTV. 159M USS. *The Adventures of Tom Sawyer and Huckleberry Finn* prod/rel: Mosfilm

The Celebrated Jumping Frog of Calaveras County, 1867, Short Story
Best Man Wins 1948 d: John Sturges. lps: Edgar Buchanan, Anna Lee, Robert Shayne. 73M USA. prod/rel: Columbia

A Connecticut Yankee in King Arthur's Court, New York 1889, Novel
Connecticut Yankee, A 1931 d: David Butler. lps: Will Rogers, Maureen O'Sullivan, Myrna Loy. 96M USA. *The Yankee at King Arthur's Court* (UKN); *A Connecticut Yankee in King Arthur's Court* prod/rel: Fox Film Corp.

Connecticut Yankee at King Arthur's Court, A 1920 d: Emmett J. Flynn. lps: Harry Myers, Pauline Starke, Rosemary Theby. 8291f USA. prod/rel: the Mark Twain Co.©, Fox Film Corp.

Connecticut Yankee in King Arthur's Court, A 1948 d: Tay Garnett. lps: Bing Crosby, Rhonda Fleming, Cedric Hardwicke. 107M USA. *A Yankee in King Arthur's Court* (UKN) prod/rel: Paramount

Connecticut Yankee in King Arthur's Court, A 1989 d: Mel Damski. lps: Keshia Knight Pulliam, Jean Marsh, Rene Auberjonois. TVM. 100M USA.

Novye Prikluchenia Janke Pri Dvore Kovola Artura 1989 d: Victor Gres. lps: Sergei Koltakov, Evdokija Germanova, Albert Filozov. 156M USS.; *The New Adventures of a Connecticut Yankee at King Arthur's Court*

Spaceman and King Arthur, The 1979 d: Russ Mayberry. lps: Dennis Dugan, Jim Dale, Ron Moody. 93M UKN/USA. *Unidentified Flying Oddball* (USA) prod/rel: Walt Disney

The Death Disc, Story
Death Disc, The 1909 d: D. W. Griffith. lps: Marion Leonard, Arthur Johnson, MacK Sennett. 995f USA. prod/rel: Biograph Co.

A Dog's Tale, Short Story
Science 1911. lps: Lassie A Dog, King Baggot, Mary Pickford. 750f USA. prod/rel: Imp

A Double Barrelled Detective Story, New York 1902, Novel
Double-Barrelled Detective Story, The 1965 d: Adolfas Mekas. lps: Hurd Hatfield, Greta Thyssen, Jeff Siggins. 90M USA. prod/rel: Saloon Co.

Is He Living Or Is He Dead?, 1900, Short Story
Det Er Ikke Appelsiner -Det Er Heste 1967 d: Ebbe Langberg. lps: Morten Grundwald, Jesper Langberg, Willy Rathnov. 95M DNM. *It Is Not Oranges -But Horses*

The Man That Corrupted Hadleyburg, 1900, Short Story
Man That Corrupted Hadleyburg, The 1980 d: Ralph Rosenblum. lps: Robert Preston, Fred Gwynne, Tom Aldredge. MTV. 38M USA. prod/rel: Learning in Focus

The Prince and the Pauper, New York 1881, Novel
Prince and the Pauper, The 1909 d: J. Searle Dawley. lps: Cecil Spooner, William Sorelle, Charles Ogle. 1070f USA. prod/rel: Edison

Prince and the Pauper, The 1915 d: Edwin S. Porter, Hugh Ford. lps: Marguerite Clark, Robert Broderick, William Sorelle. 5r USA. prod/rel: Famous Players Film Co.©, Paramount Pictures Corp.

Prince and the Pauper, The 1937 d: William Keighley. lps: Errol Flynn, Billy Mauch, Bobby Mauch. 120M USA. prod/rel: Warner Bros. Pictures©, First National Picture

Prince and the Pauper, The 1962 d: Don Chaffey. lps: Guy Williams, Laurence Naismith, Donald Houston. 93M UKN. prod/rel: Walt Disney

Prince and the Pauper, The 1969 d: Elliot Geisinger. lps: Gene Bua, Ken Shaffel. 68M USA. *The Adventures of the Prince and the Pauper* prod/rel: Storyland Films

Prince and the Pauper, The 1971. ANM. 46M ASL.

Prince and the Pauper, The 1978 d: Richard Fleischer. lps: Mark Lester, Oliver Reed, Raquel Welch. 113M UKN/PNM. *Crossed Swords* (USA) prod/rel: International Film Production, Ilya and Alexander Salkind

Seine Majestat, Das Bettlekind 1920 d: Alexander KordA. AUS. *The Prince and the Pauper*; *Prinz Und Bettelknabe*

Pudd'nhead Wilson, Hartford 1894, Novel
Pudd'nhead Wilson 1916 d: Frank Reicher. lps: Theodore Roberts, Alan Hale, Thomas Meighan. 5r USA. *Puddin' Head Wilson* prod/rel: Jesse L. Lasky Feature Play Co.©, Paramount Pictures Corp.

Pudd'nhead Wilson 1984 d: Alan Bridges. lps: Ken Howard, Lise Hilboldt, Stephen Weber. TVM. 90M USA. *The Tragedy of Pudd'nhead Wilson*

Tom Sawyer, Detective, 1897, Short Story
Tom Sawyer, Detective 1938 d: Louis King. lps: Billy Cook, Donald O'Connor, Porter Hall. 68M USA. prod/rel: Paramount Pictures©

TWEED, THOMAS FREDERIC
Gabriel Over the White House; a Novel of the Presidency, New York 1933, Novel
Gabriel Over the White House 1933 d: Gregory La CavA. lps: Walter Huston, Karen Morley, Franchot Tone. 87M USA. prod/rel: Metro-Goldwyn-Mayer Corp.©

TWISS, CLINTON
The Long, Long Trailer, 1951, Novel
Long, Long Trailer, The 1953 d: Vincente Minnelli. lps: Lucille Ball, Desi Arnaz, Marjorie Main. 96M USA. prod/rel: MGM

TWISS, J. O.
The Red Dog, Play
Pyjamas Preferred 1932 d: Val Valentine. lps: Jay Laurier, Betty Amann, Jack Morrison. 46M UKN. prod/rel: British International Pictures, British Instructional

TWIST, JOHN
Across the Panhandle, Story
Fort Worth 1951 d: Edwin L. Marin. lps: Randolph Scott, David Brian, Phyllis Thaxter. 80M USA. prod/rel: Warner Bros.

TYL, JOSEF KAJETAN
Devce Z Predmesti Anebo Vsecko Prijde Na Jevo, Play
Devce Z Predmesti Anebo Vsecko Prijde Na Jevo 1939 d: Theodor Pistek. lps: Frantisek Kreuzmann, Helena Busova, Ladislav Pesek. 2528m CZC. *Suburban Girl Or Everything Comes to Light* prod/rel: Meissner

Fidlovacka Aneb Zadny Hnev a Zadna Rvacka, Play
Fidlovacka 1930 d: Svatopluk Innemann. lps: Antonie Nedosinska, Slavka Tauberova, Ruzena SlemrovA. 2581m CZC. *The Village Festival* prod/rel: Moldavia, Ceskoslovenska MGM

Palicova Dcera, Play
Palicova Dcera 1923 d: Thea CervenkovA. lps: Vojtech Zahorik, Bozena Plecita, Milos VavrA. CZC. *The Fire-Raiser's Daughter*; *The Incendiary's Daughter* prod/rel: Filmovy Ustav, Centrofilm

Palicova Dcera 1941 d: Vladimir Borsky. lps: Zdenek Stepanek, Lida Baarova, Ruzena NaskovA. 2452m CZC. *The Arsonist's Daughter*; *The Incendiary's Daughter* prod/rel: Lucernafilm

Prazsky Flamendr, Play
Prazsky Flamendr 1926 d: Premysl Prazsky. lps: Josef Javorcak, Angelo Ferrari, Sasa DobrovolnA. 2070m CZC. *The Prague Boozer* prod/rel: Karel Spelina, Jan Kyzour

Prazsky Flamendr 1941 d: Karel SpelinA. lps: Frantisek Hanus, Gustav Hilmar, Antonie NedosinskA. 2690m CZC. *The Prague Gallivanter*; *The Prague Boozer* prod/rel: Dafa, Stelibsky, Josef

Strakonicky Dudak Aneb Hody Divych Zen, 1847, Play
Svanda Dudak 1937 d: Svatopluk Innemann. lps: Jiri Dohnal, Helena Busova, Jaroslav Marvan. 2736m CZC. *Svanda the Bagpiper* prod/rel: Kinofilm Brno

TYLER, ANNE (1941–, USA
The Accidental Tourist, 1985, Novel
Accidental Tourist, The 1988 d: Lawrence Kasdan. lps: William Hurt, Kathleen Turner, Geena Davis. 121M USA. prod/rel: Warner Bros.

Earthly Possessions, 1977, Novel
Earthly Possessions 1999 d: James Lapine. lps: Susan Sarandon, Stephen Dorff, Elissabeth Moss. TVM. 105M USA. prod/rel: Rastar Productions, Hbo Pictures

A Slipping-Down Life, 1970, Novel
Slipping-Down Life, A 1999 d: Toni Kalem. lps: Lili Taylor, Guy Pearce, John Hawkes. 111M USA. prod/rel: Dvc/Raddon

TYLER, CHARLES W.
Raggedy Ann, Short Story
Exquisite Thief, The 1919 d: Tod Browning. lps: Priscilla Dean, J. Milton Ross, Sam de Grasse. 6r USA. *Raggedy Ann* prod/rel: Universal Film Mfg. Co.©

With Clear Rights, Story
Across the Great Divide 1915 d: Edward C. Taylor. lps: George M. Wright, Bessie Learn, Frank McGlynn. SHT USA. prod/rel: Edison

TYLER, GEORGE VERE
The Wax Model, 1915, Short Story
Wax Model, The 1917 d: E. Mason Hopper. lps: Vivian Martin, Thomas Holding, Helen Jerome Eddy. 5r USA. prod/rel: Pallas Pictures, Paramount Pictures Corp.

TYLER, POYNTZ
A Garden of Cucumbers, New York 1960, Novel
Fitzwilly 1967 d: Delbert Mann. lps: Dick Van Dyke, Barbara Feldon, Edith Evans. 102M USA. *Fitzwilly Strikes Back* (UKN); *A Garden Full of Cucumbers* prod/rel: Mirisch Corporation, Dramatic Features

TZELKAH, DAN
Story
K'fafot 1986 d: Rafi Adar. lps: Ika Zohar, Ezra Kafri, Sharon Hacohen. F ISR. *Gloves*; *K'fafoth*

U

UCHIDA, YASUO
Tenkawa Densetsu Satsujin Jiken, Novel
Tenkawa Densetsu Satsujin Jiken 1991 d: Kon IchikawA. lps: Takaaki Enoki, Keiko Kishi, Naomi Zaizen. 110M JPN. *The Noh Mask Murders* prod/rel: Kadokawa Shoten Co.

UEBELHOER, MAX
Der Ruf Der Tiefe, Novel
Polizeispionin 77 1929 d: Willi Wolff. lps: Ellen Richter, Ralph Arthur Roberts. 2641m GRM. prod/rel: Ellen Richter Gmbh

UEDA, AKINARI (1734–1809), JPN
Asaji Ga Yado, c1768, Short Story
Ugetsu Monogatari 1953 d: Kenji Mizoguchi. lps: MaCHiko Kyo, Mitsuko Mito, Kinuyo TanakA. 96M JPN. *Tales of the Pale and Silvery Moon After the Rain* (UKN); *Ugetsu* (USA); *Tales After the Rain* prod/rel: Daiei Motion Picture Co.

Jasei No in, c1768, Short Story
Ugetsu Monogatari 1953 d: Kenji Mizoguchi. lps: MaCHiko Kyo, Mitsuko Mito, Kinuyo TanakA. 96M JPN. *Tales of the Pale and Silvery Moon After the Rain* (UKN); *Ugetsu* (USA); *Tales After the Rain* prod/rel: Daiei Motion Picture Co.

UEMURA, NAOMI
Uemura Naomi Monogatari, Autobiography
Uemura Naomi Monogatari 1985 d: Junya Sato. lps: Toshiyuki Nishida, Chieko Baisho, Hideji Otaki. 140M JPN. *Story of an Adventurer Naomi Uemura*; *Lost in the Wilderness* prod/rel: Dentsu/Mainichi Hoso

UGOLINI, LUIGI
Memorie Di un Bracconiere Musoduro, Novel
Musoduro 1954 d: Giuseppe Bennati. lps: Marina Vlady, Fausto Tozzi, Cosetta Greco. 85M ITL. *Amore Selvaggio* prod/rel: Produzione Cin.Ca Mambretti

Il Nido Di Falasco, Novel
Nido Di Falasco, Il 1950 d: Guido Brignone. lps: Umberto Spadaro, Liliana Tellini, Ermanno Randi. 92M ITL. *La Capanna Del Peccato* prod/rel: Romana Film

UHL, RENATE
Die Andere, Novel
  Andere, Die 1949 d: Alfred E. Sistig. lps: Lotte Koch, Wolfgang Luschky, Dagmar Altrichter. 97M GRM. *The Other*; *The Other Woman* prod/rel: Kosmos, Europa

Die Beiden Diersbergs, Novel
  Herz Ohne Heimat 1940 d: Otto Linnekogel. lps: Anneliese Uhlig, Albrecht Schoenhals, Camilla Horn. 87M GRM. prod/rel: F.D.F., Bavaria

UHLIG, OTTO
Books
  Vergessenen Kinder, Die 1981 d: Kurt K. Hieber. lps: Gerhard Gamper, Reinhard Gamper, Stephan Weber. 100M GRM. *Forgotten Children* prod/rel: Badlands-Film

UHLMAN, FRED
Reunion, Novel
  Reunion 1989 d: Jerry Schatzberg. lps: Jason Robards Jr., Christien Anholt, Samuel West. 120M UKN/FRN/GRM. *Der Wiedergefundene Freund* (GRM); *L' Ami Retrouve* (FRN) prod/rel: Rank, Les Films Ariane

UHNAK, DOROTHY (1933–, USA
The Bait, Novel
  Bait, The 1973 d: Leonard Horn. lps: Donna Mills, Michael Constantine, William Devane. TVM. 73M USA. prod/rel: ABC Circle Films

Law and Order, Novel
  Law and Order 1976 d: Marvin J. Chomsky. lps: Darren McGavin, Keir Dullea, Robert Reed. TVM. 150M USA. prod/rel: Paramount

The Ledger, Novel
  Get Christie Love! 1974 d: William A. Graham. lps: Teresa Graves, Harry Guardino, Louise Sorel. TVM. 73M USA. prod/rel: ABC, Wolper Productions

The Price of Justice, Novel
  Kojak: the Price of Justice 1987 d: Alan Metzger. lps: Telly Savalas, Kate Nelligan, Pat Hingle. TVM. 100M USA. *The Price of Justice* prod/rel: Universal

UHRY, ALFRED
Driving Miss Daisy, 1987, Play
  Driving Miss Daisy 1989 d: Bruce Beresford. lps: Morgan Freeman, Jessica Tandy, Dan Aykroyd. 99M USA. prod/rel: Warner Bros.

UKRAINKA, LESYA
Lisova Pisnya: Drama-Feeriya, 1911
  Lesnaya Pesnya 1961 d: Viktor IVchenko. lps: Raisa Nedashkovskaya, V. Sidorchuk, P. Vesklyarov. 95M USS. *Song of the Forest* (USA) prod/rel: Dozhenko Film Studio

ULCELLI, G.
L' Inviolabile, Novel
  Inviolabile, L' 1919 d: Mario Corte. lps: Lido Manetti, Annita Cotic, Ciro Galvani. 1936m ITL. prod/rel: Libertas Film

ULLMAN, A. E.
Rough Stuff, Short Story
  Rough Stuff 1925 d: Dell Henderson. lps: George Larkin. 4764f USA. prod/rel: Dell Henderson Productions, Rayart Pictures

ULLMAN, E. A.
Quick Change, Short Story
  Quick Change 1925 d: Dell Henderson. lps: George Larkin. 4800f USA. prod/rel: Dell Henderson Productions, Rayart Pictures

ULLMAN, JAMES RAMSAY (1907–, USA
Banner in the Sky, Novel
  Third Man on the Mountain 1959 d: Ken Annakin. lps: Michael Rennie, James MacArthur, Janet Munro. 103M UKN/USA. *Banner in the Sky* prod/rel: Walt Disney Prods., Buena Vista

The White Tower, 1945, Novel
  White Tower, The 1950 d: Ted Tetzlaff. lps: Glenn Ford, Claude Rains, Alida Valli. 98M USA. prod/rel: RKO Radio

Windom's Way, Novel
  Windom's Way 1957 d: Ronald Neame. lps: Peter Finch, Mary Ure, Natasha Parry. 108M UKN. prod/rel: Rank, Rank Film Distributors

ULLMAN, JAMES RAMSEY
High Conquest, Novel
  High Conquest 1946 d: Irving Allen. lps: Anna Lee, Gilbert Roland, Warren Douglas. 79M USA. prod/rel: Monogram

ULLMANN, DANIEL B.
Story
  Cattle Empire 1958 d: Charles Marquis Warren. lps: Joel McCrea, Gloria Talbott, Don Haggerty. 83M USA. prod/rel: 20th Century-Fox

ULMER, EDGAR G. (1904–1972), AUS
  From Nine to Nine 1936 d: Edgar G. Ulmer. lps: Ruth Roland, Roland Drew, Doris Covert. 75M CND. *Death Strikes Again*; *The Man With the Umbrella* prod/rel: Coronet Pictures Ltd.

ULRICH, LAUREL THATCHER
Book
  Midwive's Tale, A 1997 d: Richard P. Rogers. lps: Kaiulani Lee, Ron Tough, Kevin Jubinville. 89M USA. prod/rel: Blueberry Hills, National Endownment for the Humanities

UM IN-HEE
Saenggwabu Wijaryo Chyeonggusosong, Play
  Saenggwabu Wijaryo Chyeonggusosong 1998 d: Kang Woo-Suk. lps: Ahn Sung-Ki, Mun Seong-Keun, Hwang Cine. 119M SKR. *Bedroom & Courtroom* prod/rel: Cinema Service Co.

UNDERWOOD, SOPHIE
Big Hearted Herbert, New York 1934, Play
  Big Hearted Herbert 1934 d: William Keighley. lps: Guy Kibbee, Aline MacMahon, Patricia Ellis. 60M USA. *Big-Hearted Herbert* prod/rel: Warner Bros. Productions Corp.
  Father Is a Prince 1940 d: Noel Smith. lps: Grant Mitchell, Nana Bryant, John Litel. 59M USA. prod/rel: Warner Bros. Pictures©, First National Pictures

UNEKIS, RICHARD
Dirty Mary, Crazy Larry, Novel
  Dirty Mary, Crazy Larry 1974 d: John Hough. lps: Peter Fonda, Susan George, Adam Roarke. 93M USA. prod/rel: Academy Pictures

UNGER, GLADYS
The Girl of the Hour, Story
  Fashions for Women 1927 d: Dorothy Arzner. lps: Esther Ralston, Raymond Hatton, Einar Hanson. 6296f USA. prod/rel: Famous Players-Lasky, Paramount Pictures

The Goldfish, New York 1922, Play
  Goldfish, The 1924 d: Jerome Storm. lps: Constance Talmadge, Jack Mulhall, Frank Elliott. 7145f USA. prod/rel: Constance Talmadge Productions, Associated First National Pictures

London Pride, London 1916, Play
  London Pride 1920 d: Harold Shaw. lps: Edna Flugrath, Fred Groves, O. B. Clarence. 5200f UKN. prod/rel: London, Jury

Private Beach, Beverly Hills 1934, Play
  Music Is Magic 1935 d: George Marshall. lps: Alice Faye, Ray Walker, Bebe Daniels. 67M USA. *Private Beach*; *Ball of Fire* prod/rel: Fox Film Corp., Twentieth Century-Fox Film Corp.©

Starlight, New York 1925, Play
  Divine Woman, The 1927 d: Victor Sjostrom. lps: Greta Garbo, Lars Hanson, Lowell Sherman. 7300f USA. prod/rel: Metro-Goldwyn-Mayer Pictures

UNGER, HELLMUTH
Germanin, Novel
  Germanin 1943 d: Max W. Kimmich. lps: Peter Petersen, Lotte Koch, Luis Trenker. 90M GRM. prod/rel: UFA

Sendung Und Gewissen, Novel
  Ich Klage an 1941 d: Wolfgang Liebeneiner. lps: Heidemarie Hatheyer, Paul Hartmann, Mathias Wieman. 124M GRM. *I'm Accusing* prod/rel: Tobis

UNO, CHIYO
Ohan, Novel
  Ohan 1984 d: Kon IchikawA. lps: Sayuri Yoshinaga, Reiko Ohara, Koji IshizakA. 112M JPN. prod/rel: Toho Co.

UNSELT, CARL
Arzt Aus Leidenschaft, Novel
  Arzt Aus Leidenschaft 1936 d: Hans H. Zerlett. lps: Albrecht Schoenhals, Karin Hardt, Hans Sohnker. 82M GRM. prod/rel: Euphono, Bavaria

UNSWORTH, BARRY
Pascali's Island, Novel
  Pascali's Island 1989 d: James Dearden. lps: Ben Kingsley, Charles Dance, Helen Mirren. 106M UKN/USA. prod/rel: Virgin, Avenue

UNTERWEGER, JACK
Autobiography
  Fegefeuer 1988 d: Wilhelm Hengstler. lps: Bobby Prem, Jurgen Goslar, Jeanette Muhlmann. 90M AUS. prod/rel: Epo-Film

UPDEGRAFF, ALLAN EUGENE
Second Youth, New York 1917, Novel
  Second Youth 1924 d: Albert Parker. lps: Alfred Lunt, Dorothy Allen, Jobyna Howland. 6169f USA. prod/rel: Distinctive Pictures, Goldwyn-Cosmopolitan Pictures

UPDIKE, JOHN (1932–, USA, Updike, John Hoyer
Short Stories
  Too Far to Go 1979 d: Fielder Cook. lps: Michael Moriarty, Blythe Danner, Glenn Close. TVM. 100M USA. prod/rel: Sea Cliff Productions

The Music School, 1966, Short Story
  Music School, The 1977 d: John Korty. lps: Ron Weyand, Dana Larson, Tom Dahlgren. MTV. 27M USA. prod/rel: Learning in Focus

Rabbit, Run, New York 1960, Novel
  Rabbit, Run 1970 d: Jack Smight. lps: James Caan, Anjanette Comer, Jack Albertson. 94M USA. prod/rel: Solitaire/Worldcross Productions

The Witches of Eastwick, 1984, Novel
  Witches of Eastwick, The 1987 d: George Miller. lps: Jack Nicholson, Susan Sarandon, Cher. 118M USA. prod/rel: Warner Bros., Guber-Peters Company

UPPDAL, KRISTOFER
Dansen Gjenom Skuggeheim, 1911-24, Novel
  Rallarblod 1978 d: Erik Solbakken. lps: Nils Ole Oftebro, Ragnhild Hilt, Svein Tindberg. 123M NRW. *The Intruders* prod/rel: Norsk Film

UPRIGHT, BLANCHE
The Valley of Content, New York 1922, Novel
  Pleasure Mad 1923 d: Reginald Barker. lps: Huntley Gordon, Mary Alden, Norma Shearer. 7547f USA. prod/rel: Louis B. Mayer Productions, Metro Pictures

UPSON, WILLIAM HAZLETT
Short Story
  Earthworm Tractors 1936 d: Ray Enright. lps: Joe E. Brown, June Travis, Guy Kibbee. 69M USA. *A Natural Born Salesman* (UKN); *Three in Eden* prod/rel: Warner Bros. Pictures©, First National

URATIA, FRED
Story
  Fuerte Perdido 1965 d: Jose Maria ElorrietA. lps: German Cobos, Mariano Vidal, Marta May. 89M SPN. *Massacre at Fort Perdition* (USA); *Massacre at Fort Grant*; *Renegades of Fort Grant*; *Doomed Fort* prod/rel: Alesanco

URBAN, E.
Tanzanwaltz, Berlin 1912, Play
  Lonely Wives 1931 d: Russell MacK. lps: Edward Everett Horton, Esther Ralston, Laura Laplante. 87M USA. prod/rel: Pathe Exchange©, RKO Radio Pictures

URIS, LEON (1924–, USA, Uris, Leon Marcus
Novel
  Sette Contro la Morte 1965 d: Edgar G. Ulmer, Paolo Bianchini. lps: John Saxon, Rosanna Schiaffino, Larry Hagman. 96M ITL/GRM/YGS. *Helden -Himmel Und Holle* (GRM); *The Cavern* (USA); *Neunzig Nachte Und Ein Tag*; *Ninety Nights and One Day* prod/rel: Cine Doris (Roma), Ernst Neubach (Munich)

The Angry Hills, Novel
  Angry Hills, The 1959 d: Robert Aldrich. lps: Robert Mitchum, Stanley Baker, Elisabeth Muller. 105M UKN/USA. prod/rel: MGM, Raymond Stross

Battle Cry, Novel
  Battle Cry 1955 d: Raoul Walsh. lps: Van Heflin, Aldo Ray, Mona Freeman. 149M USA. prod/rel: Warner Bros.

Exodus, 1958, Novel
  Exodus 1960 d: Otto Preminger. lps: Paul Newman, Eva Marie Saint, Ralph Richardson. 220M USA. prod/rel: Otto Preminger, United Artists

QB VII, Novel
  QB VII 1974 d: Tom Gries. lps: Ben Gazzara, Anthony Hopkins, Leslie Caron. TVM. 312M USA. prod/rel: Screen Gems, Columbia

Topaz, New York 1967, Novel
  Topaz 1969 d: Alfred Hitchcock. lps: Frederick Stafford, Karin Dor, Dany Robin. 125M USA. prod/rel: Universal Pictures

URVANTZOV, LEO
Her Private Affair, Play
  Her Private Affair 1929 d: Paul L. Stein. lps: Ann Harding, Harry Bannister, John Loder. 6440f USA. prod/rel: Pathe Exchange, Inc.

USIGLI, RODOLFO (1905–1979), MXC
Ensayo de un Crimen, 1944, Novel
  Ensayo de un Crimen 1955 d: Luis Bunuel. lps: Ernesto Alonso, Miroslava, Rita MacEdo. 91M MXC. *The Criminal Life of Archibaldo de la Cruz* (USA); *Rehearsal for a Crime*; *Archibaldo*; *Practice of a Crime*; *La Vida Criminal de Archibaldo de la Cruz*

USTINOV, PETER (1921–, UKN
Romanoff and Juliet, New York 1957, Play
  Romanoff and Juliet 1961 d: Peter Ustinov. lps: Peter Ustinov, Sandra Dee, John Gavin. 103M USA. *Dig That Juliet* prod/rel: Pavor, S.a.

UTERMANN, WILHELM
Der Kleinstadtpoet, Novel
Kleinstadtpoet, Der 1940 d: Josef von Baky. lps: Paul Kemp, Wilfried Seyferth, Hilde Hildebrand. 96M GRM. prod/rel: UFA

Kollege Kommt Gleich, Play
Kollege Kommt Gleich 1943 d: Karl Anton. lps: Carola Hohn, Albert Matterstock, Elisabeth Markus. 90M GRM. prod/rel: Tobis, Sudwest

UTESILOVA, RUZENA
Klekani, Novel
Druhe Mladi 1938 d: Vaclav Binovec. lps: Jiri Plachy, Ema Hruba, Adina MandlovA. 2867m CZC. *Second Youth; Klekani* prod/rel: Arko

UZZELL, THOMAS H.
Anton the Terrible, 1916, Short Story
Anton the Terrible 1916 d: William C. de Mille. lps: Theodore Roberts, Anita King, Horace B. Carpenter. 5r USA. *The Austrian Spy* prod/rel: Jesse L. Lasky Feature Play Co.©, Paramount Pictures Corp.

V

VACHEK, EMIL
Muz a Stin, Novel
Vrazda V Ostrovni Ulici 1933 d: Svatopluk Innemann. lps: Jindrich Plachta, Zvonimir Rogoz, Theodor Pistek. 2034m CZC. *Murder in Island Street; Murder on Ostrovni Street* prod/rel: Ab

VACHELL, HORACE ANNESLEY (1861–1955), UKN, Vachell, H. a.
The Case of Lady Camber, London 1915, Play
Case of Lady Camber, The 1920 d: Walter West. lps: Violet Hopson, Stewart Rome, Gregory Scott. 6000f UKN. prod/rel: Broadwest, Walturdaw
Lord Camber's Ladies 1932 d: Benn W. Levy. lps: Gerald Du Maurier, Gertrude Lawrence, Benita Hume. 80M UKN. *The Case of Lady Camber* prod/rel: British International Pictures, Wardour
Story of Shirley Yorke, The 1948 d: MacLean Rogers. lps: Derek Farr, Dinah Sheridan, Margaretta Scott. 92M UKN. *Shirley Yorke* prod/rel: Nettlefold, Butcher's Film Service

Her Son, Play
Her Son 1920 d: Walter West. lps: Violet Hopson, Stewart Rome, Mercy Hatton. 6023f UKN. prod/rel: Broadwest, Walturdaw

Humpty Dumpty, 1917, Play
If I Were Rich 1936 d: Randall Faye. lps: Jack Melford, Kay Walsh, Clifford Heatherley. 58M UKN. prod/rel: Randall Faye, Radio

Jelf's, London 1912, Play
Jelf's 1915 d: George Loane Tucker. lps: Henry Ainley, Mary Dibley, Gerald Ames. 5376f UKN. *A Man of His Word* (USA) prod/rel: London, Jury

Quinneys, London 1915, Play
Quinneys 1919 d: Rex Wilson. lps: Henry Ainley, Isobel Elsom, Eric Harrison. 6000f UKN. prod/rel: G. B. Samuelson, Granger
Quinneys 1927 d: Maurice Elvey. lps: Alma Taylor, John Longden, Frances Cuyler. 8600f UKN. prod/rel: Gaumont

VACHEROT, JACQUES
Les Patates, Novel
Patates, Les 1969 d: Claude Autant-LarA. lps: Pierre Perret, Berangere Dautun, Pascale Roberts. 100M FRN. prod/rel: S.O.P.A.C., S.N.E.G.

VAEZ, GUSTAVO
La Favorita, Play
Favorita, La 1953 d: Cesare Barlacchi. lps: Gino Sinimberghi, Franca Tamantini, Paolo Silveri. 71M ITL. *The Favourite* prod/rel: Mas Film

VAILLAND, ROGER (1907–1965), FRN, Vailland, Roger Francois
Beau Masque, 1954, Novel
Beau Masque 1972 d: Bernard Paul. lps: Dominique Labourier, Luigi Diberti, Gaby SylviA. 100M FRN/ITL.

Drole de Jeu, 1945, Novel
Drole de Jeu 1968 d: Pierre Kast. lps: Maurice Garrel, Barbara Laage, Edith Garnier. 90M FRN. *The Most Dangerous Game*

La Loi, 1957, Novel
Loi, La 1958 d: Jules Dassin. lps: Yves Montand, Gina Lollobrigida, Marcello Mastroianni. 126M FRN/ITL. *La Legge* (ITL); *Where the Hot Wind Blows* (USA); *The Law* prod/rel: Cite Films (Paris), Groupe Des Quatre

Les Mauvais Corps, Paris 1948, Novel
Mauvais Coups, Les 1961 d: Francois Leterrier. lps: Simone Signoret, Reginald Kernan, Alexandra Stewart. 103M FRN. *Naked Autumn* (USA) prod/rel: Jean Thuillier, Editions Cinegraphiques

La Truite, 1964, Novel
Truite, La 1982 d: Joseph Losey. lps: Isabelle Huppert, Jean-Pierre Cassel, Jeanne Moreau. 105M FRN. *The Trout* prod/rel: Gaumont, Partner's Prod.

VAIME
Le Cadeau, Play
Cadeau, Le 1982 d: Michel Lang. lps: Pierre Mondy, Claudia Cardinale, Clio Goldsmith. 108M FRN/ITL. *Il Regalo* (ITL); *The Gift* prod/rel: Gilbert de Goldschmidt

VAIME, ENRICO
Amare Significa., Novel
Sera C'incontrammo, Una 1976 d: Piero SchivazappA. lps: Johnny Dorelli, Fran Fullenwider, Lia Tanzi. 100M ITL. prod/rel: Supernova, Euro International Film

Le Braghe Del Padrone, Novel
Braghe Del Padrone, Le 1978 d: Flavio Mogherini. lps: Enrico Montesano, Adolfo Celi, Milena Vukotic. 97M ITL. prod/rel: Zodiac Produzioni, C.I.D.I.F.

VAJDA, ERNEST
Ladies and Gentlemen, London 1937, Play
Great Garrick, The 1937 d: James Whale. lps: Brian Aherne, Olivia de Havilland, Edward Everett Horton. 95M USA. prod/rel: Warner Bros. Pictures©

VAJDA, ERNO
Confession, Play
Woman on Trial, The 1927 d: Mauritz Stiller. lps: Pola Negri, Einar Hanson, Lido Manetti. 5960f USA. prod/rel: Paramount Famous Lasky Corp.

The Head Waiter, Novel
Monsieur Albert 1932 d: Karl Anton. lps: Noel-Noel, Betty Stockfeld, Marcel Barencey. 95M FRN. prod/rel: Films Paramount
Service for Ladies 1932 d: Alexander KordA. lps: Leslie Howard, George Grossmith, Benita Hume. 93M UKN/USA. *Reserved for Ladies* (USA); *The Head Waiter* prod/rel: Paramount Publix Corp.©, Alexander Korda Production

Valoporos Holay, Budapest 1923, Novel
Grounds for Divorce 1925 d: Paul Bern. lps: Florence Vidor, Matt Moore, Harry Myers. 5692f USA. prod/rel: Famous Players-Lasky, Paramount Pictures

VALABREGUE, A.
Coralie Et Cie, 1899, Play
Coralie & C. 1914. lps: Giuseppe Gambardella, Lea Giunchi, Lorenzo Soderini. 1500m ITL. *Madame Coralie E C.* prod/rel: Cines
Coralie Et Cie 1933 d: Alberto Cavalcanti. lps: Josette Day, Jeanne Helbling, Robert Burnier. 90M FRN. prod/rel: Films Jean Dehelly

VALCOURT
I Derelitti Di Valcourt, Play
Derelitti Di Valcourt, I 1921 d: Amedeo Mustacchi. lps: Arnold, Patata, Linda Albertini. 1610m ITL. *I Due Derelitti Di Valcourt* prod/rel: Albertini Film

VALDEZ, LUIS
Zoot Suit, Play
Zoot Suit 1981 d: Luis Valdez. lps: Daniel Valdez, Edward James Olmos, Rose Portillo. 103M USA. prod/rel: Universal

VALE, EUGENE
A Global Affair, Novel
Global Affair, A 1963 d: Jack Arnold. lps: Bob Hope, Liselotte Pulver, Michele Mercier. 84M USA. prod/rel: Hall Bartlett, MGM

VALE, MARTIN
The Two Mrs. Carrolls, Play
Two Mrs. Carrolls, The 1947 d: Peter Godfrey. lps: Barbara Stanwyck, Humphrey Bogart, Alexis Smith. 99M USA. prod/rel: Warner Bros.

VALENS, E. G.
The Other Side of the Mountain, Novel
Other Side of the Mountain, The 1975 d: Larry Peerce. lps: Marilyn Hassett, Beau Bridges, Belinda Montgomery. 104M USA. *A Window to the Sky* (UKN) prod/rel: Universal

VALENSI, THEODORE
Yasmina, Novel
Yasmina 1926 d: Andre Hugon. lps: Huguette Duflos, Leon Mathot, Camille Bert. 2825m FRN. prod/rel: Andre Hugon

VALENTINE, ARTHUR
Tons of Money, London 1922, Play
J'ai une Idee 1934 d: Roger Richebe. lps: Raimu, Georges Morton, Simone Deguyse. 100M FRN. prod/rel: Societe Parisienne Du Film Parlant

Tons of Money 1924 d: Frank H. Crane. lps: Leslie Henson, Flora Le Breton, Mary Brough. 6400f UKN. prod/rel: Walls & Henson, Stoll
Tons of Money 1931 d: Tom Walls. lps: Ralph Lynn, Yvonne Arnaud, Mary Brough. 97M UKN. prod/rel: British and Dominions, Woolf & Freedman

Twilight Hour, Novel
Twilight Hour 1944 d: Paul L. Stein. lps: Mervyn Johns, Basil Radford, Marie Lohr. 85M UKN. prod/rel: British National, Anglo

VALENTINE, JOHN
The Stronger Sex, London 1907, Play
Stronger Sex, The 1931 d: V. Gareth Gundrey. lps: Colin Clive, Adrianne Allen, Gordon Harker. 80M UKN. prod/rel: Gainsborough, Ideal

VALENTINE, VAL
Story
Rake's Progress, The 1945 d: Sidney Gilliat. lps: Rex Harrison, Lilli Palmer, Godfrey Tearle. 123M UKN. *The Notorious Gentleman* (USA) prod/rel: General Film Distributors, Individual

VALENTINETTI, EMERICO
Pignasecca E Pignaverde, Play
Che Tempi! 1948 d: Giorgio Bianchi. lps: Gilberto Govi, Lea Padovani, Walter Chiari. 90M ITL. prod/rel: Taurus Film, Fincine

VALENTINI, N.
Book
Sesso in Confessionale 1974 d: Vittorio de Sisti. lps: Alberto Spinoglio, Pier Maria Rossi, Gloria Serbo. 95M ITL. prod/rel: Supernova

VALERA, JUAN (1824–1905), SPN, Valera Y Alcala Galiano, Juan
Pepita Jimenez, 1874, Novel
Pepita Jimenez 1925 d: Agustin Carrasco. lps: Josefina Tapias, Jose Romeu, Maria AnayA. F SPN. prod/rel: Ediciones Hesperia (Madrid)
Pepita Jimenez 1975 d: Rafael Moreno AlbA. lps: Sarah Miles, Stanley Baker, Pedro Diez Del Corral. 108M SPN/USA. *Bride to Be* (USA)

VALLAND, ROSE
Le Front de l'Art, Novel
Train, Le 1964 d: John Frankenheimer, Bernard Farrel. lps: Burt Lancaster, Paul Scofield, Charles Millot. 140M FRN/ITL. *Il Treno* (ITL); *The Train* (USA) prod/rel: Artistes Associes, Ariane

VALLET, RALF
Mort d'un Pourri, Novel
Mort d'un Pourri 1977 d: Georges Lautner. lps: Alain Delon, Ornella Muti, Stephane Audran. 123M FRN. prod/rel: Adel

VALMAIN, FREDERIC
Le Flamenco Des Assassins, Paris 1961, Novel
Johnny Banco 1967 d: Yves Allegret. lps: Horst Buchholz, Sylva Koscina, Michel de Re. 95M FRN/ITL/GRM. *Jonny Banco -Geliebter Taugenichts* (GRM); *Beloved Good-for-Nothing* prod/rel: Norddeutsche Filmproduktion, Chrysaor Films

VALMIKI
Ramayana, Verse
Lab Kush 1967 d: Ashoke Chatterjee. lps: Master Shanker, Master Sushobhan, Anita GuhA. 140M IND.
Ram Rajya 1967 d: Vijay Bhatt. lps: Kumarsen, Bina Rai, Pt. Badriprasad. 175M IND. *The Kingdom of Ram; The Reign of Lord Ram; Ramrajya*

VALMY, JEAN
Baratin, Opera
Baratin 1957 d: Jean Stelli. lps: Roger Nicolas, Ginette Baudin, Anne-Marie Carrieres. 85M FRN. prod/rel: Films Hergi/ Raymond Horvilleur

Hier Bleib Ich Hier Bin Ich, Play
Hier Bin Ich, Hier Bleib Ich 1959 d: Werner Jacobs. lps: Caterina Valente, Hans Holt, Ruth Stephan. 99M GRM. *I'm Here and I'm Staying* prod/rel: C.C.C., Constantin

J'y Suis. J'y Reste, Play
J'y Suis, J'y Reste 1953 d: Maurice Labro. lps: Robert Pizani, Jane Sourza, Marguerite Pierry. 97M FRN. prod/rel: Champs Elysees Productions, S.G.C.

VALORI, GINO
Novel
Amazzoni Bianche 1936 d: Gennaro Righelli. lps: Paola Barbara, Sandro Ruffini, Luisa FeridA. 83M ITL. prod/rel: Arbor Film, Piemonte Film

VALTINOS, THANASSIS
I Kathodos Ton Enea, Novel
Kathodos Ton Enea, I 1984 d: Christos Shiopachas. lps: Vassilis Tsanglos, Christos Kalavrouzos, Antonis Antoniou. 125M GRC. *Descent of the Nine; Kathodos Ton Ennea* prod/rel: Greek Film Centre, Christos Shiopachas

VAMBA, Bertelli, Luigi
Il Giornalino Di Gian Burrsaca, Novel
  Gian Burrasca 1943 d: Sergio Tofano. lps: Cesco Baseggio, Maria Teresa Le Beau, Giulio Stival. 85M ITL. prod/rel: Faro Film, Cineconsorzio

VAN ATTA, WINFRED
Shock Treatment, New York 1961, Novel
  Shock Treatment 1964 d: Denis Sanders. lps: Stuart Whitman, Carol Lynley, Roddy McDowall. 94M USA. prod/rel: Arcola Pictures

VAN BEETHOVEN, LUDWIG (1770–1827), GRM
Fidelio, Vienna 1805, Opera
  Fidelio 1956 d: Walter Felsenstein. lps: Richard Holm, Claude Nollier, Erwin Gross. 90M AUS. prod/rel: Akkord Film
  Fidelio 1968 d: Joachim Hess. lps: Hans Sotin, Theo Adam, Richard Cassilly. MTV. 119M GRM. prod/rel: Polyphon Film & Tv Productions

VAN BUREN, EVELYN
Left in the Train, Story
  Left in the Train 1914. SHT USA. prod/rel: Thanhouser

VAN DE VELDE, ROGER
Tabula Rasa, Novel
  Tabula Rasa 1979 d: Bert Struys. lps: Daan Van Den Durpel, Romain Deconinck, Diane de Ghouy. MTV. 56M BLG.

VAN DE WATER, VIRGINIA TERHUNE
Story
  If My Country Should Call 1916 d: Joseph de Grasse. lps: Dorothy Phillips, Lon Chaney, Helen Leslie. 5r USA. prod/rel: Universal Film Mfg. Co.©, Red Feather Photoplays

VAN DE WETERING, JANWILLEM
Grijpstra & de Gier, Novel
  Grijpstra & de Gier 1979 d: Wim Verstappen. lps: Rijk de Gooyer, Rutger Hauer, Willeke Van Ammelrooy. 102M NTH. *Outsider in Amsterdam* prod/rel: Verenigade Nederland Filmcompagnie

VAN DEN BROECK, WALTER
Tot Nut Van 'T Algemeen, Novel
  Tot Nut Van 'T Algemeen 1988 d: Lode Verstraete, Raf Verpooten. lps: Dries Wieme, Ugo Prinsen, Denise de Weerdt. TVM. 90M BLG.

VAN DER HEIJDEN, A. F. TH.
Advocaat Van de Hanen, Novel
  Advocaat Van de Hanen 1996 d: Gerrit Van Elst. lps: Pierre Bokma, Margo Dames, Jaap Spijkers. 107M NTH. *Punk Lawyer* prod/rel: Sigma Pictures

VAN DER HURK, PAUL
Die Unheimliche Schachpartie, Novel
  Tat Des Andern, Die 1951 d: Helmut Weiss. lps: Hans Nielsen, Ilse Steppat, Rolf von Nauckhoff. 84M GRM. *Der Unheimliche*; *The Deed of Another* prod/rel: Condor, Falken

VAN DER LAAN, HELEEN
Waar Blijft Het Licht (When the Light Comes), Novel
  When the Light Comes 1999 d: Stijn Coninx. lps: Joachim Krol, Francesca Vanthielen, Reidar Sorensen. 117M NTH/BLG/GRM. prod/rel: Nordic Screen Production (Norway), Tros-Tv (Netherlands)

VAN DER MEERSCH, MAXENCE
Bodies and Souls, Novel
  Doctor and the Girl, The 1949 d: Curtis Bernhardt. lps: Glenn Ford, Charles Coburn, Gloria de Haven. 98M USA. prod/rel: MGM
L' Empreinte du Dieu, Novel
  Empreinte du Dieu, L' 1940 d: Leonide Moguy. lps: Pierre Blanchar, Jacques Dumesnil, Annie Ducaux. 130M FRN. prod/rel: Zama Films
La Maison Dans la Dune, Novel
  Maison Dans la Dune, La 1934 d: Pierre Billon. lps: Pierre Richard-Willm, Madeleine Ozeray, Colette Darfeuil. 100M FRN. *The House on the Dune* (USA) prod/rel: Compagnie Generale De Productions Cine.
  Maison Dans la Dune, La 1952 d: Georges Lampin. lps: Ginette Leclerc, Roger Pigaut, Jean Chevrier. 90M FRN. prod/rel: Films Vendome, Silver Films

VAN DER POST, LAURENS (1906–, SAF
The Seed and the Sower, 1951, Novel
  Merry Christmas, Mr. Lawrence 1982 d: Nagisa OshimaA. lps: Tom Conti, David Bowie, Jack Thompson. 120M UKN/JPN/NZL. prod/rel: Recorded Picture Co. Ltd., Cineventure
A Story Like the Wind and a Far Off Place, Books
  Far Off Place, A 1993 d: Mikael Salomon. lps: Reese Witherspoon, Ethan Randall, Jack Thompson. 116M USA. *Kalahari* prod/rel: Buena Vista, Walt Disney

VAN DER WETERING, JANWILLEM
De Ratelrat, Novel
  Ratelrat, de 1987 d: Wim Verstappen. lps: Rijk de Gooyer, Peter Faber, Annemieke Verdoorn. 90M NTH. *The Rattle Rat* prod/rel: Avroi, Concorde

VAN DINE, S. S. (1888–1939), USA, Wright, Willard Huntingdon
The Benson Murder Case, New York 1926, Novel
  Benson Murder Case, The 1930 d: Frank Tuttle. lps: William Powell, Natalie Moorhead, Eugene Pallette. 69M USA. prod/rel: Paramount Famous Lasky Corp.
The Bishop Murder Case, New York 1917, Novel
  Bishop Murder Case, The 1929 d: Nick Grinde, David Burton. lps: Basil Rathbone, Leila Hyams, Roland Young. 91M USA. prod/rel: Metro-Goldwyn-Mayer Pictures
The Canary Murder Case, New York 1927, Novel
  Canary Murder Case, The 1929 d: Malcolm St. Clair. lps: William Powell, James Hall, Louise Brooks. 81M USA. prod/rel: Paramount Famous Lasky Corp.
The Casino Murder Case, New York 1934, Novel
  Casino Murder Case, The 1935 d: Edwin L. Marin. lps: Paul Lukas, Alison Skipworth, Donald Cook. 88M USA. prod/rel: Metro-Goldwyn-Mayer Corp.
The Dragon Murder Case; a Philo Vance Story, New York 1933, Novel
  Dragon Murder Case, The 1934 d: H. Bruce Humberstone. lps: Warren William, Margaret Lindsay, Lyle Talbot. 68M USA. prod/rel: First National Pictures©
The Garden Murder Case; a Philo Vance Story, New York 1935, Novel
  Garden Murder Case, The 1936 d: Edwin L. Marin. lps: Edmund Lowe, Virginia Bruce, Benita Hume. 62M USA. prod/rel: Metro-Goldwyn-Mayer Corp.©
The Gracie Allen Murder Case, New York 1938, Novel
  Gracie Allen Murder Case, The 1939 d: Alfred E. Green. lps: Gracie Allen, Warren William, Ellen Drew. 74M USA. prod/rel: Paramount Pictures©
The Greene Murder Case, New York 1928, Novel
  Greene Murder Case, The 1929 d: Frank Tuttle. lps: William Powell, Florence Eldridge, Ullrich Haupt. 69M USA. prod/rel: Paramount Famous Lasky Corp.
  Night of Mystery 1937 d: E. A. Dupont. lps: Grant Richards, Roscoe Karns, Helen Burgess. 66M USA. *The Green Murder Case* (UKN) prod/rel: Paramount Pictures
The Kennel Murder Case, New York 1913, Novel
  Calling Philo Vance 1940 d: William Clemens. lps: James Stephenson, Margot Stevenson, Henry O'Neill. 63M USA. *Philo Vance Comes Back*; *Philo Vance Returns* prod/rel: Warner Bros. Pictures, Inc.
  Kennel Murder Case, The 1933 d: Michael Curtiz. lps: William Powell, Mary Astor, Eugene Pallette. 73M USA. prod/rel: Warner Bros. Pictures©
The Scarab Murder Case, Novel
  Scarab Murder Case, The 1936 d: Michael Hankinson. lps: Kathleen Kelly, Wilfrid Hyde-White, Wally Patch. 68M UKN. prod/rel: British and Dominions, Paramount British

VAN DINE, S. S. & OTHERS
The President's Mystery Story, 1935, Novel
  President's Mystery, The 1936 d: Phil Rosen. lps: Henry Wilcoxon, Betty Furness, Evelyn Brent. 81M USA. *One for All* (UKN) prod/rel: Republic Pictures Corp.©

VAN DRUTEN, JOHN (1901–1957), UKN
After All, London 1930, Play
  New Morals for Old 1932 d: Charles J. Brabin. lps: Robert Young, Lewis Stone, Myrna Loy. 72M USA. *After All* prod/rel: Metro-Goldwyn-Mayer Corp., Metro-Goldwyn-Mayer Dist. Corp.©
Behold We Live!, London 1932, Play
  If I Were Free 1933 d: Elliott Nugent. lps: Irene Dunne, Clive Brook, Nils Asther. 66M USA. *Behold We Live* (UKN) prod/rel: RKO Radio Pictures©
Bell Book and Candle, New York 1950, Play
  Bell, Book and Candle 1958 d: Richard Quine. lps: James Stewart, Kim Novak, Jack Lemmon. 103M USA. prod/rel: Columbia, Phoenix Productions
Diversion, London 1928, Play
  Careless Age, The 1929 d: John Griffith Wray. lps: Douglas Fairbanks Jr., Carmel Myers, Holmes Herbert. 6308f USA. prod/rel: First National Pictures
I Am a Camera, 1952, Play
  Cabaret 1972 d: Bob Fosse. lps: Liza Minnelli, Michael York, Helmut Griem. 124M USA. prod/rel: Allied Artists
  I Am a Camera 1955 d: Henry Cornelius. lps: Julie Harris, Laurence Harvey, Shelley Winters. 99M UKN. prod/rel: Romulus, Remus
I Remember Mama, New York 1944, Play
  I Remember Mama 1948 d: George Stevens. lps: Irene Dunne, Barbara Bel Geddes, Oscar HomolkA. 134M USA. prod/rel: RKO Radio
London Wall, London 1931, Play
  After Office Hours 1932 d: Thomas Bentley. lps: Frank Lawton, Heather Angel, Viola Lyel. 78M UKN. prod/rel: British International Pictures, Wardour
Old Acquaintance, New York 1940, Play
  Old Acquaintance 1943 d: Vincent Sherman. lps: Bette Davis, Miriam Hopkins, Gig Young. 110M USA. prod/rel: Warner Bros.
  Rich and Famous 1981 d: George Cukor. lps: Jacqueline Bisset, Candice Bergen, David Selby. 117M USA. prod/rel: MGM, United Artists
There's Always Juliet, New York 1931, Play
  One Night in Lisbon 1941 d: Edward H. Griffith. lps: Fred MacMurray, Madeleine Carroll, Patricia Morison. 97M USA. prod/rel: Paramount
The Voice of the Turtle, New York 1943, Play
  Voice of the Turtle, The 1947 d: Irving Rapper. lps: Ronald Reagan, Eleanor Parker, Eve Arden. 103M USA. *One for the Book* prod/rel: Warner Bros.
Young Woodley, London 1928, Play
  Young Woodley 1929 d: Thomas Bentley. lps: Robin Irvine, Marjorie Hume, Sam Livesey. SIL. 8162f UKN. prod/rel: British International Pictures, Wardour
  Young Woodley 1930 d: Thomas Bentley. lps: Madeleine Carroll, Frank Lawton, Sam Livesey. SND. 79M UKN. prod/rel: Regal, Wardour

VAN DUZER, WINIFRED
The Good Bad Girl, New York 1926, Novel
  Good Bad Girl, The 1931 d: R. William Neill. lps: Mae Clarke, James Hall, Marie Prevost. 73M USA. prod/rel: Columbia Pictures Corp.©

VAN DYKE, CATHERINE
Lincoln the Lover, Story
  Lincoln, the Lover 1914 d: Ralph Ince. lps: Ralph Ince, Anita Stewart, E. K. Lincoln. 1000f USA. prod/rel: Vitagraph Co. of America

VAN DYKE, TOM
Murder at Monte Carlo, Novel
  Murder at Monte Carlo 1935 d: Ralph Ince. lps: Errol Flynn, Eve Gray, Paul Graetz. 70M UKN. prod/rel: Warner Bros., First National

VAN EESLYN, BEN
But Not in Vain, Play
  But Not in Vain 1948 d: Edmond T. Greville. lps: Raymond Lovell, Carol Van Derman, Martin Benson. 73M UKN. prod/rel: Anglo-Dutch, Butcher's Film Service

VAN GREENWAY, PETER
The Medusa Touch, Novel
  Medusa Touch, The 1977 d: Jack Gold. lps: Richard Burton, Lino Ventura, Lee Remick. 109M UKN. prod/rel: Itc, Bulldog

VAN GULICK, ROBERT
Judge Dee at the Haunted Monastery, Novel
  Judge Dee and the Monastery Murders 1974 d: Jeremy Paul Kagan. lps: Khigh Alx Dhiegh, Mako, Sook-Teck Oh. TVM. 100M USA. *Judge Dee in the Monastery Murders*; *Judge Dee* prod/rel: ABC Circle Films
The Lacquer Screen, Novel
  Xue Jian Hua Ping 1986 d: Zhang Qicang. lps: Sun Chongliang, Wun Qian, Zhang Jiumei. 10r CHN. *The Bloodstained Screen* prod/rel: XI'an Film Studio

VAN JAVA, MELATI, Sloot, Marie
La Renzoni, Novel
  Renzoni, La 1916 d: Maurits H. Binger. lps: Annie Bos, Willem Van Der Veer, Paula de Waart. 1765m NTH. *Haar Vader*; *Voor Eer En Deugd*; *Her Father* prod/rel: Filmfabriek-Hollandia

VAN LEEUWEN, JAN
Book
  Velka Syrova Soutez 1987 d: Vaclav Bedrich. ANM. 52M CZC/GRM. *Die Grosse Kaseverschwurung* (GRM) prod/rel: Kratky Film, Wdr

VAN LOAN, CHARLES E.
Buck's Lady Friend, Story
  Buck's Lady Friend 1915 d: William Bertram. lps: Art Acord, Lawrence Peyton, Sylvia Ashton. 3r USA. prod/rel: Mustang, American
Little Sunset, 1912, Short Story
  Little Sunset 1915. lps: Hobart Bosworth, Gordon Griffith, Joseph Ray. 4r USA. prod/rel: Bosworth, Inc.©, Oliver Morosco Photoplay Co.
The Message to Buckshot John, 1912, Novel
  Buckshot John 1915 d: Hobart Bosworth. lps: Hobart Bosworth, Courtenay Foote, Helen Wolcott. 5r USA. prod/rel: Bosworth, Inc., Paramount Pictures Corp.

Scrap Iron, Short Story
   Scrap Iron 1921 d: Charles Ray. lps: Charles Ray, Lydia Knott, Vera Steadman. 6747f USA. prod/rel: Charles Ray Productions, Associated First National Pictures

This Is the Life, Short Story
   This Is the Life 1915 d: William Bertram. lps: Art Acord, Adele Farrington, Lawrence Peyton. 3r USA. prod/rel: Mustang

The Weight of the Last Straw, Story
   Deuce of Spades, The 1922 d: Charles Ray. lps: Charles Ray, Marjorie Maurice, Lincoln Plummer. 4505f USA. prod/rel: Charles Ray Productions, First National Exhibitors Circuit

VAN LOAN, H. H.
The Girl Who Dared, Story
   Winning With Wits 1922 d: Howard M. Mitchell. lps: Barbara Bedford, William Scott, Harry Northrup. 4435f USA. prod/rel: Fox Film Corp.

The Noose, New York 1926, Play
   I'd Give My Life 1936 d: Edwin L. Marin. lps: Guy Standing, Tom Brown, Frances Drake. 82M USA. *The Noose* prod/rel: Paramount Pictures[©]
   Noose, The 1928 d: John Francis Dillon. lps: Richard Barthelmess, Montagu Love, Robert Emmett O'Connor. 7331f USA. *The Governor's Wife* prod/rel: First National Pictures

VAN LOON, HENDRIK WILLEM (1882–1944), NTH
The Story of Mankind, 1921, Book
   Story of Mankind, The 1957 d: Irwin Allen. lps: Ronald Colman, Hedy Lamarr, Virginia Mayo. 100M USA. prod/rel: Warner Bros., Cambridge Prods.

VAN MARISSING, LIDY
Vrouw Die Een Rookspoor Achterliet, Story
   Rooksporen 1992 d: Frans Van de Staak. lps: Marlies Heuer, Peter Blok, Johan Leysen. 105M NTH.

VAN MAURIK, JUSTUS
Krates, 1885, Novel
   Krates 1913 d: Louis H. Chrispijn. lps: Cor Laurentius, Gerard Pilger, Eugenie Krix. 950m NTH. prod/rel: Filmfabriek-Hollandia

VAN NOUHUYS, WILLEM GERARD
Het Goudvischje, 1893, Play
   Goudvischje, Het 1919 d: Maurits H. Binger. lps: Jeanne Van Der Pers, Jan Van Dommelen, Annie Bos. 1818m NTH. *The Little Goldfish* prod/rel: Filmfabriek-Hollandia

VAN NUYS, LAURA BOWER
The Family Band, Lincoln, Nb. 1961, Novel
   One and Only, Genuine, Original Family Band, The 1968 d: Michael O'Herlihy. lps: Walter Brennan, Buddy Ebsen, Lesley Ann Warren. 117M USA. prod/rel: Walt Disney Productions

VAN PEEBLES, MELVIN
Panther, Novel
   Panther 1995 d: Mario Van Peebles. lps: Kadeem Hardison, Bokeem Woodbine, Joe Don Baker. 124M USA. prod/rel: Working Title, Tribeca

La Permission, Paris 1967, Novel
   Permission, La 1968 d: Melvin Van Peebles. lps: Harry Baird, Nicole Berger, Christian Marin. 90M FRN. *The Story of a Three Day Pass* (USA) prod/rel: O.P.E.R.a.

VAN PRAAG, VAN
Combat, 1945, Novel
   Men in War 1957 d: Anthony Mann. lps: Robert Ryan, Aldo Ray, Robert Keith. 101M USA. prod/rel: United Artists, Security Pictures

VAN RIEMSDIJK, JONKHEER A. W. G.
Alexandra, 1922, Novel
   Alexandra 1922 d: Theo Frenkel Sr. lps: Margit Barnay, Paul de Groot, Coen Hissink. 2380M NTH/GRM. prod/rel: Amsterdam Film Cie, Turma-Film Gmbh

Pro Domo, 1914, Play
   Pro Domo 1918 d: Theo Frenkel Sr. lps: Louis Bouwmeester, Theo Mann-Bouwmeester, Jacques Reule. 2100m NTH. *For His Own House* prod/rel: Amsterdam Film Cie

De Sphinx, Play
   Toen 'T Licht Verdween 1918 d: Maurits H. Binger. lps: Jan Van Dommelen, Annie Bos, Lola Cornero. 1871m NTH. *When the Light Vanished; Blind* prod/rel: Filmfabriek-Hollandia

VAN SCHRAEDER, ATREUS
Pearl for Pearl, Story
   Pearl for Pearl 1922 d: George A. Cooper. lps: A. B. Imeson, Dezma Du May, W. G. Saunders. 1600f UKN. prod/rel: Quality Plays, Walturdaw

VAN SLYKE, HELEN (1919–1979), USA, Van Slyke, Helen Lenore Vogt
The Best Place to Be, Novel
   Best Place to Be, The 1979 d: David Miller. lps: Donna Reed, Efrem Zimbalist Jr., Mildred Dunnock. TVM. 200M USA. prod/rel: ABC, Ross Hunter Productions

VAN SLYKE, LUCILLE
Little Miss By-the-Day, New York 1919, Novel
   Stolen Kiss, The 1920 d: Kenneth Webb. lps: Constance Binney, Rod La Rocque, George Backus. 5r USA. prod/rel: Realart Pictures Corp.[©]

VAN STALLE, PAUL
Les Surprises d'une Nuit de Noces, Play
   Surprises d'une Nuit de Noces, Les 1951 d: Jean Vallee. lps: Jacqueline Porel, Andre Claveau, Pierre Stephen. 93M FRN. prod/rel: Rapid Films, J. Deguillaume

VAN STEENWIK, ELIZABETH
Kayla, Novel
   Kayla 1998 d: Nicholas Kendall. lps: Tod Fennell, Henry Czerny, Meredith Henderson. 96M CND. prod/rel: Cine-Action, Telefilm Canada

VAN VECHTEN, CARL (1880–1964), USA
The Tattooed Countess, New York 1924, Novel
   Woman of the World, A 1925 d: Malcolm St. Clair. lps: Pola Negri, Charles Emmett MacK, Holmes Herbert. 6353f USA. prod/rel: Famous Players-Lasky, Paramount Pictures

VAN VEEN, D.
Haar Groote Dag, Novel
   Was She Guilty? 1922 d: George A. Beranger. lps: Gertrude McCoy, Zoe Palmer, Lewis Willoughby. 4891f UKN/NTH. *Gij Zult Niet Dooden; Thou Shalt Not Kill; Haar Groote Dag; Thou Shalt Not* prod/rel: Granger-Binger Film

VAN VORST, MARIE
Big Tremaine, Boston 1914, Novel
   Big Tremaine 1916 d: Henry Otto. lps: Harold Lockwood, May Allison, Lester Cuneo. 5r USA. prod/rel: Yorke Film Corp.[©], Metro Pictures Corp.

The Girl from His Town, Indianapolis 1910, Novel
   Girl from His Town, The 1915 d: Harry Pollard. lps: Margarita Fischer, Carlton Griffin, Lucille Ward. 4r USA. prod/rel: American Film Mfg. Co.[©], Mutual Film Corp.

Mary Moreland, Boston 1915, Novel
   Mary Moreland 1917 d: Frank Powell. lps: Marjorie Rambeau, Robert Elliott, Gene Lamotte. 5r USA. prod/rel: Frank Powell Producing Corp., Mutual Film Corp.

VAN WEIGEN, PETER
I Racconti Fiamminghi, Short Story
   Mulino Delle Donne Di Pietra, Il 1960 d: Giorgio Ferroni. lps: Pierre Brice, Scilla Gabel, Dany Carrel. 100M ITL/FRN. *Le Moulin Des Supplices* (FRN); *Mill of the Stone Women* (USA); *Drops of Blood* (UKN); *Mill of the Stone Maidens; Horror of the Stone Women* prod/rel: Wanguard Film, Faro Film

VANARDY, VARICK
Alias the Night Wind, New York 1913, Novel
   Alias the Night Wind 1923 d: Joseph J. Franz. lps: William Russell, Maude Wayne, Charles K. French. 4145f USA. prod/rel: Fox Film Corp.

The Girl By the Roadside, New York 1917, Novel
   Girl By the Roadside, The 1917 d: Theodore Marston. lps: Violet Mersereau, Cecil Owen, Ann Andrews. 5r USA. prod/rel: Bluebird Photoplays, Inc.[©]
   Girl in the Rain, The 1920 d: Rollin S. Sturgeon. lps: Lloyd Bacon, Anne Cornwall, Jessalyn Van Trump. 4455f USA. prod/rel: Universal Film Mfg. Co.[©]

VANCE, ELMER E.
The Limited Mail, 1889, Play
   Limited Mail, The 1925 d: George W. Hill. lps: Monte Blue, Vera Reynolds, Willard Louis. 7144f USA. prod/rel: Warner Brothers Pictures

VANCE, ETHEL, Stone, Grace Zaring
Escape, Boston 1939, Novel
   Escape 1940 d: Mervyn Leroy. lps: Norma Shearer, Robert Taylor, Conrad Veidt. 104M USA. *When the Door Opened* prod/rel: Metro-Goldwyn-Mayer Corp., Loew's, Inc.[©]

Winter Meeting, 1946, Novel
   Winter Meeting 1948 d: Bretaigne Windust. lps: Bette Davis, Janis Paige, Jim Davis. 104M USA. prod/rel: Warner Bros.

VANCE, HENRY C.
Pin Money, 1921, Short Story
   Diamond Handcuffs 1928 d: John P. McCarthy. lps: Lena Malena, Charles Stevens, Conrad Nagel. 6070f USA. prod/rel: Cosmopolitan Productions, Metro-Goldwyn-Mayer Distributing Corp.

VANCE, JOHN HOLBROOK
Bad Ronald, Novel
   Bad Ronald 1974 d: Buzz Kulik. lps: Scott Jacoby, Pippa Scott, John Larch. TVM. 78M USA. prod/rel: Lorimar Productions

VANCE, LOUIS JOSEPH (1879–1933), USA
Alias the Lone Wolf, Garden City, Ny. 1921, Novel
   Alias the Lone Wolf 1927 d: Edward H. Griffith. lps: Bert Lytell, Lois Wilson, William V. Mong. 6843f USA. prod/rel: Columbia Pictures

The Bandbox, Boston 1912, Novel
   Bandbox, The 1919 d: R. William Neill. lps: Doris Kenyon, Alexander Gaden, Walter McEwen. 6r USA. prod/rel: Deitrich-Beck, Inc., W. W. Hodkinson Corp.

The Black Bag, Indianapolis 1908, Novel
   Black Bag, The 1922 d: Stuart Paton. lps: Herbert Rawlinson, Virginia Valli, Bert Roach. 4343f USA. prod/rel: Universal Film Mfg. Co.

The Brass Bowl, Indianapolis 1907, Novel
   Brass Bowl, The 1914. lps: Ben Wilson. 2000f USA. prod/rel: Edison
   Brass Bowl, The 1924 d: Jerome Storm. lps: Edmund Lowe, Claire Adams, Jack Duffy. 5830f USA. prod/rel: Fox Film Corp.
   Masquerade 1929 d: Russell J. Birdwell. lps: Alan Birmingham, Leila Hyams, Arnold Lucy. 5674f USA. prod/rel: Fox Film Corp.

The Bronze Bell, New York 1909, Novel
   Bronze Bell, The 1921 d: James W. Horne. lps: Courtenay Foote, Doris May, John Davidson. 5507f USA. prod/rel: Thomas H. Ince Productions, Paramount Pictures

Cynthia-of-the-Minute, New York 1911, Novel
   Cynthia-of-the-Minute 1920 d: Perry N. Vekroff. lps: Leah Baird, Hugh Thompson, Burr McIntosh. 6r USA. prod/rel: Gibraltar Pictures, W. W. Hodkinson Corp.

The Dark Mirror, Garden City, N.Y. 1920, Novel
   Dark Mirror, The 1920 d: Charles Giblyn. lps: Dorothy Dalton, Huntley Gordon, Walter Neeland. 5084f USA. prod/rel: Famous Players-Lasky Corp., Paramount-Artcraft Pictures

The Day of Days, Boston 1913, Novel
   Day of Days, The 1914 d: Daniel Frohman. lps: Cyril Scott, David Wall, Hal Clarendon. 4r USA. prod/rel: Famous Players Film Co., State Rights

The Destroying Angel, Boston 1912, Novel
   Destroying Angel, The 1915 d: Richard Ridgely. lps: Mabel Trunnelle, Marc MacDermott, Walter Craven. 5r USA. prod/rel: Thomas A. Edison, Inc.[©], Kleine-Edison Feature Service
   Destroying Angel, The 1923 d: W. S. Van Dyke. lps: Leah Baird, John Bowers, Noah Beery. 5640f USA. prod/rel: Arthur F. Beck, Associated Exhibitors

The False Faces, Garden City, N.Y. 1918, Novel
   False Faces, The 1919 d: Irvin V. Willat. lps: Henry B. Walthall, Mary Anderson, Lon Chaney. 6940f USA. *The Lone Wolf* prod/rel: Thomas H. Ince Corp.[©], Famous Players-Lasky Corp.

His Heart, His Hand and His Sword, Story
   His Heart, His Hand and His Sword 1914 d: Lorimer Johnston, G. P. Hamilton. lps: J. Warren Kerrigan, Vera Sisson. 2r USA. prod/rel: Victor

Joan Thursday, Boston 1913, Novel
   Footlights of Fate, The 1916 d: William Humphrey. lps: Naomi Childers, Marc McDermott, Templer Saxe. 5r USA. prod/rel: Vitagraph Co. of America[©], Blue Ribbon Feature
   Greater Than Marriage 1924 d: Victor Hugo Halperin. lps: Marjorie Daw, Lou Tellegen, Peggy Kelly. 6821f USA. prod/rel: Romance Pictures, Vitagraph Co. of America

The Last of the Lone Wolf, Story
   Last of the Lone Wolf, The 1930 d: Richard Boleslawski. lps: Bert Lytell, Patsy Ruth Miller, Lucien Prival. 6500f USA. prod/rel: Columbia Pictures

The Lone Wolf Returns, New York 1923, Novel
   Lone Wolf in Paris, The 1938 d: Albert S. Rogell. lps: Francis Lederer, Frances Drake, Olaf Hytten. 67M USA. *The Lone Wolf* prod/rel: Columbia Pictures Corp. of California[©]
   Lone Wolf Returns, The 1926 d: Ralph Ince. lps: Bert Lytell, Billie Dove, Freeman Wood. 5750f USA. *Return of the Lone Wolf* prod/rel: Columbia Pictures
   Lone Wolf Returns, The 1935 d: R. William Neill. lps: Melvyn Douglas, Gail Patrick, Tala Birell. 69M USA. prod/rel: Columbia Pictures Corp.[©]

The Lone Wolf, London 1914, Novel
   Lone Wolf, The 1917 d: Herbert Brenon. lps: Bert Lytell, Hazel Dawn, Edward Abeles. 8r USA. prod/rel: Herbert Brenon Film Corp.[©], Lewis J. Selznick Enterprises, Inc.

Lone Wolf, The 1924 d: Stanner E. V. Taylor. lps: Dorothy Dalton, Jack Holt, Wilton Lackaye. 5640f USA. *Lone Wolf's Last Adventure* prod/rel: John Mckeown, Associated Exhibitors

The Lone Wolf's Son, 1931, Story
Cheaters at Play 1932 d: Hamilton MacFadden. lps: Thomas Meighan, Charlotte Greenwood, Ralph Morgan. 58M USA. *First Cabin; The Lone Wolf's Son; Son of the Lone Wolf* prod/rel: Fox Film Corp.

The Mainspring, Short Story
Mainspring, The 1917 d: Henry King. lps: Henry King, Ethel Pepperell, Bert Ensminger. 4r USA. prod/rel: Falcon Features, General Film Co.©

Mainstream, Story
Lost at Sea 1926 d: Louis J. Gasnier. lps: Huntley Gordon, Lowell Sherman, Jane Novak. 6400f USA. prod/rel: Tiffany Productions

No Man's Land, New York 1910, Novel
No Man's Land 1918 d: Will S. Davis. lps: Bert Lytell, Anna Q. Nilsson, Eugene Pallette. 5r USA. prod/rel: Metro Pictures Corp.©

Nobody, New York 1915, Novel
Outsider, The 1917 d: William C. Dowlan. lps: Emmy Whelen, Herbert Heyes, Florence Short. 6r USA. prod/rel: Metro Pictures Corp.©

The Pool of Flame, New York 1909, Novel
Pool of Flame, The 1916 d: Otis Turner. lps: J. Warren Kerrigan, Lois Wilson, Maude George. 5r USA. prod/rel: Universal Film Mfg. Co.©, Red Feather Photoplays

Sheep's Clothing, Novel
Sheep's Clothing 1914 d: Charles M. Seay. lps: Bigelow Cooper, Marjorie Ellison, Elsie Wartemburg. 2r USA. prod/rel: Edison

The Trey O'Hearts, Story
Trey O'Hearts, The 1914 d: Wilfred Lucas, Henry McRae. lps: George Larkin, Edward Sloman, Cleo Madison. SRL. 31r USA. prod/rel: Gold Seal

VANCURA, VLADISLAV (1891–1942), CZC
Konec Starych Casu, 1934, Novel
Konec Starych Casu 1989 d: Jiri Menzel. lps: Josef Abrham, Marian Labuda, Jaromir Hanzlik. 97M CZC. *The End of Old Times* (UKN)

Marketa Lazarova, 1931, Novel
Marketa Lazarova 1967 d: Frantisek Vlacil. lps: Josef Kemr, Magda Vasaryova, Nada HejnA. 162M CZC.

Rozmarne Leto, Prague 1926, Novel
Rozmarne Leto 1967 d: Jiri Menzel. lps: Vlastimil Brodsky, Rudolf Hrusinsky, Mila MyslikovA. 83M CZC. *Capricious Summer* prod/rel: Smida-Fikar, Studio Barrandov

VAND DER HURCK, PAUL
Schuss Im Rampenlicht, Play
Vorhang Fallt, Der 1939 d: Georg Jacoby. lps: Anneliese Uhlig, Hilde Sessak, Elfie Mayerhofer. 91M GRM. prod/rel: Universum, Doring

VANDENBERGHE, PAUL
Gringalet, Play
Gringalet 1946 d: Andre Berthomieu. lps: Paul Vandenberghe, Suzy Carrier, Marguerite Deval. 105M FRN. prod/rel: Pathe Cinema

J'ai Dix-Sept Ans, Play
J'ai 17 Ans 1945 d: Andre Berthomieu. lps: Aime Clariond, Jacqueline Delubac, Madeleine Suffel. 85M FRN. *My First Love* (USA); *J'ai Dix-Sept Ans* prod/rel: Pathe-Cinema, Majestic Films

VANDERBILT JR., CORNELIUS (1898–1974), USA
Reno, New York 1929, Novel
Reno 1930 d: George J. Crone. lps: Ruth Roland, Montagu Love, Kenneth Thomson. 7200f USA. prod/rel: Sono-Art Productions

VANDERBRUCH
Le Gamin de Paris, 1836, Play
Biricchino Di Parigi, Il 1916 d: Ugo FalenA. lps: Bianca Bellincioni-Stagno, Silvia Malinverni, Eric Oulton. 1790m ITL. *Il Birichino Di Parigi* prod/rel: Tespi Film
Gamin de Paris, Le 1923 d: Louis Feuillade. lps: Rene Poyen, Sandra Milowanoff, Adolphe Cande. 1800m FRN. prod/rel: Gaumont
Gamin de Paris, Le 1932 d: Gaston Roudes. lps: Alice Tissot, Arielle, Pierre Arnac. 73M FRN. prod/rel: Consortium Cinematographique Francais

VANDERCOOK, JOHN W. (1902–1963), UKN, Vandercook, John Womack
Murder in Trinidad, New York 1933, Novel
Caribbean Mystery, The 1945 d: Robert D. Webb. lps: James Dunn, Sheila Ryan, Edward Ryan. 65M USA. *Voodoo Mystery* prod/rel: 20th Century-Fox

Mr. Moto in Danger Island 1939 d: Herbert I. Leeds. lps: Peter Lorre, Jean Hersholt, Amanda Duff. 64M USA. *Mr. Moto on Danger Island* (UKN); *Danger Island*; *Mr. Moto in Puerto Rico*; *Mr. Moto in Trinidad* prod/rel: Twentieth Century-Fox Film Corp.©
Murder in Trinidad 1934 d: Louis King. lps: Nigel Bruce, Heather Angel, Victor Jory. 74M USA. prod/rel: Fox Film Corp.©

VANDEREM, FERNAND
La Victime, Novel
Amour Est un Jeu, L' 1957 d: Marc Allegret. lps: Robert Lamoureux, Annie Girardot, Yves Noel. 90M FRN. *Ma Gosse Et Moi Ma Femme* prod/rel: Lambor Films, Gibe

VANDEWATER, VIRGINIA TERHUNE
The Two Sisters, New York 1914, Novel
Two Sisters 1929 d: Scott Pembroke. lps: Viola Dana, Rex Lease, Claire Du Brey. 5161f USA. prod/rel: Trem Carr Productions, Rayart Pictures

VANE, DEREK
Lady Varley, Story
Modern Marriage 1923 d: Lawrence C. Windom. lps: Francis X. Bushman, Beverly Bayne, Roland Bottomley. 6331f USA. prod/rel: F. X. B. Pictures, American Releasing Corp.

VANE, SUTTON (1888–1963), UKN
The Cotton King, London 1894, Play
Cotton King, The 1915 d: Oscar Eagle. lps: George Nash, Julia Hay, Eric Mayne. 5r USA. prod/rel: William A. Brady Picture Plays, Inc., World Film Corp.©

Outward Bound, New York 1924, Play
Between Two Worlds 1944 d: Edward A. Blatt. lps: John Garfield, Paul Henreid, Sydney Greenstreet. 112M USA. *Outward Bound* prod/rel: Warner Bros.
Outward Bound 1930 d: Robert Milton. lps: Leslie Howard, Douglas Fairbanks Jr., Helen Chandler. 83M USA. prod/rel: Warner Bros. Pictures

The Span of Life, New York 1893, Play
Span of Life, The 1914 d: Edward MacKey. lps: Lionel Barrymore, Gladys Wynne, Lester Chambers. 4-5r USA. prod/rel: Kinetophote Corp., State Rights

Two Lancashire Lassies in London, Play
Two Lancashire Lassies in London 1916 d: Dave Aylott. lps: Lettie Paxton, Dolly Tree, Wingold Lawrence. 5100f UKN. prod/rel: Martin's Cinematograph, Walturdaw

VANETT, PETER
Trois Jours a Vivre, Play
Trois Jours a Vivre 1957 d: Gilles Grangier. lps: Daniel Gelin, Jeanne Moreau, Lino VenturA. 85M FRN. prod/rel: International Motion Pictures

VANIO, RALPH
Widow's Island, Novel
Romance in Flanders, A 1937 d: Maurice Elvey. lps: Paul Cavanagh, Marcelle Chantal, Garry Marsh. 73M UKN. *Lost on the Western Front* (USA); *Widow's Island* prod/rel: Franco-London, British Lion

VANLOO, ALBERT
Veronique, Opera
Veronique 1949 d: Robert Vernay. lps: Giselle Pascal, Marina Hotine, Jean Desailly. 100M FRN. prod/rel: Jason, Latino Consortium Cinema

VANLOO, ROLF E.
Diane, Short Story
Diane 1929 d: Erich Waschneck. lps: Olga Tschechowa, Henry Victor, Pierre Blanchar. 2358m GRM. prod/rel: Teschechowa-Film

Gleisdreieck, Novel
Gleisdreieck 1936 d: R. A. Stemmle. lps: Gustav Frohlich, Heli Finkenzeller, Otto Wernicke. 80M GRM. *Alarm Auf Gleis B* prod/rel: F.D.F.

VANNI, ALFREDO
La Vita Puo Ricomciare, Novel
Fatto Di Cronaca 1944 d: Piero Ballerini. lps: Osvaldo Valenti, Luisa Ferida, Anna Capodaglio. F ITL. prod/rel: Larius Film, E.N.I.C.

VAOUX, ALEX
L' Incorrigible, Novel
Incorrigible, L' 1975 d: Philippe de BrocA. lps: Jean-Paul Belmondo, Genevieve Bujold, Julien Guiomar. 99M FRN. prod/rel: Ariane, Mondex

VARA, SIL
Madchenjahre Einer Konigin, Play
Madchenjahre Einer Konigin 1954 d: Ernst MarischA. lps: Romy Schneider, Adrian Hoven, Magda Schneider. 109M AUS/GRM. *The Pursuit and Loves of Queen Victoria*; *The Story of Vickie* (USA) prod/rel: Erma

VARGAS LLOSA, MARIO (1936–, PRU, Vargas Llosa, Jorge Mario Pedro
La Tia Julia Y El Escribidor, 1977, Novel
Aunt Julia and the Scriptwriter 1990 d: Jon Amiel. lps: Barbara Hershey, Keanu Reeves, Peter Falk. 104M USA. *Tune in Tomorrow.*; *On the Air* prod/rel: Polar Films

VARLEY, JOHN
Air Raid, Short Story
Millenium 1989 d: Michael Anderson. lps: Kris Kristofferson, Cheryl Ladd, Robert Joy. 108M CND/USA. prod/rel: 20th Century Fox

VARNLUND, RUDOLF
U 39, 1939, Play
Ubat 39 1952 d: Erik Faustman. lps: Eva Dahlbeck, Karl-Arne Holmsten, Gunnel Brostrom. 85M SWD. *U-Boat 39* prod/rel: Ab Sandrew-Produktion

VARTET, JULIEN
Le Dejeuner Interrompu, Novel
Poison d'Amour 1990 d: Hugues de Laugardiere. lps: Frederic Van Den Driessche, Catherine Wilkening, Clementine Celarie. TVM. 90M FRN.

VASSALLO, ARNALDO LUIGI
La Famiglia De'tappetti, Novel
Policarpo, Ufficiale Di Scittura 1959 d: Mario Soldati. lps: Renato Rascel, Carla Gravina, Romolo Valli. 108M ITL/FRN/SPN. *Policarpo Maitre Calligraphe* (FRN); *Policarpo -Master Writer*; *Oficial Diplomado Policarpo* (SPN), Titanus (Roma)

VASSILIKOS, VASSILIS (1933–, GRC
Z, Athens 1966, Novel
Z 1968 d: Costa-Gavras. lps: Yves Montand, Irene Papas, Jean-Louis Trintignant. 125M FRN/ITL/ALG. *Z (L'orgia Del Potere)* (ITL) prod/rel: Reggane Films, O.N.C.I.C.

VASSILLIADIS, P.
A Shoe from Your Homeland, Play
Shoe from Your Homeland, A 1980 d: Peter Bernardos. lps: John Chrisoulis, Amalia Vassilliadis, Dennis Dragonas. TVM. F ASL. prod/rel: Aav-Australia

VASZARY, JANOS
Play
I Married an Angel 1942 d: W. S. Van Dyke. lps: Jeanette MacDonald, Nelson Eddy, Edward Everett Horton. 84M USA. prod/rel: MGM

VATSYAYANA, MALLANAGA
Kamasutra, Book
Kamasutra - Vollendung Der Liebe 1969 d: Kobi Jaeger. lps: Bruno Dietrich, Barbara Schone, Richard Abbott. DOC. 91M GRM. *Kama Sutra* (USA); *Kamasutra* (UKN); *Kamasutra - Perfection of Love* prod/rel: Conti, Constantin

VAUCAIRE, M.
La Grande Vedette, Play
Grande Vedette, La 1917 d: Edouard-Emile Violet. lps: Mangin, Fred Zorilla, Rachel Devirys. 1120m FRN. prod/rel: Acad

VAUCHER, CHARLES
Hd-Soldat Lappli. Volksstuck in 16 Bildern, 1945, Play
Hd Lappli 1959 d: Alfred Rasser. lps: Alfred Rasser, Editha Nordberg, Otto Wiesely. 115M SWT. *Le Soldat Auxiliaire Lappli*; *Lappli Der Etappenheld* prod/rel: Walter Kagi-Filmproduktion

VAUGHAN, HENRY
Story
Sicario 77 Vivo O Morto 1966 d: Mino Guerrini. lps: Robert Mark, Alicia Brandet, John Stacy. 90M ITL/SPN. *Agente End* (SPN); *Killer 77 Alive Or Dead* prod/rel: Adelphia Compagnia Cin.Ca (Roma), Prod. Cin.Cas Balcazar (Barcelona)

VAUGHAN-THOMAS, WYNFORD
Anzio, New York 1961, Book
Sbarco Di Anzio, Lo 1968 d: Edward Dmytryk, Duilio Coletti. lps: Robert Mitchum, Peter Falk, Arthur Kennedy. 117M ITL. *The Battle for Anzio* (USA); *The Anzio Landing*; *Anzio* prod/rel: Dino de Laurentiis Cin.Ca, Columbia Ceiad

VAUS, JIM
Why I Quit Syndicated Crime, 1956, Book
Wiretapper 1956 d: Dick Ross. lps: Bill Williams, Georgia Lee, Douglas Kennedy. 80M USA. *Wiretappers*; *The Jim Vaus Story* prod/rel: Em-Continental Distributing, Great Commisssion

VAUTEL, CLEMENT
Madame Ne Veut Pas d'Enfants, Novel
Madame Ne Veut Pas d'Enfants 1932 d: Constantin Landau, Hans Steinhoff. lps: Robert Arnoux, Adrien Le Gallo, Marie Glory. 75M FRN. prod/rel: Vandor-Film

Mon Cure Chez Les Pauvres, Novel
Mon Cure Chez Les Pauvres 1925 d: E. B. Donatien. lps: E. B. Donatien, Lucienne Legrand, Louis Kerly. 2400m FRN. prod/rel: Etablissements Louis Aubert

Mon Cure Chez Les Riches, Novel
Mon Cure Chez Les Riches 1926 d: E. B. Donatien. lps: E. B. Donatien, Georges Melchior, Louis Kerny. F FRN. prod/rel: Etablissements Louis Aubert
Mon Cure Chez Les Riches 1932 d: E. B. Donatien. lps: Jim Gerald, Pierre Juvenet, Alice Roberte. 98M FRN. prod/rel: Isis-Film
Mon Cure Chez Les Riches 1938 d: Jean Boyer. lps: Bach, Andre Alerme, Elvire Popesco. 100M FRN. prod/rel: Production U.D.I.F., Joseph Bercholz
Mon Cure Chez Les Riches 1952 d: Henri Diamant-Berger. lps: Yves Deniaud, Lysiane Rey, Robert Arnoux. 98M FRN. prod/rel: U.D.I.F.

VAUTRIN, JEAN, Hermann, Jean
Canicule, Novel
Canicule 1983 d: Yves Boisset. lps: Miou-Miou, Lee Marvin, Jean Carmet. 101M FRN. *Dog Day* (USA); *Dogsday* prod/rel: Swanie, U.G.C.

VAVRINCOVA, FAN
Eva Tropi Hlouposti, Novel
Eva Tropi Hlouposti 1939 d: Martin Fric. lps: Nastasa Gollova, Oldrich Novy, Zdenka BaldovA. 2472m CZC. *Eva Plays the Fool*; *Eva Is Fooling*; *The Escapades of Eva*; *Eva Fools Around* prod/rel: Lucernafilm

VAVRIS, HUGO
Frantisek Lelicek Ve Sluzbach Sherlocka Holmesa, Novel
Lelicek Ve Sluzbach Sherlocka Holmesa 1932 d: Carl Lamac. lps: Vlasta Burian, Martin Fric, Fred Bulin. 2494m CZC. *Lelichek in Sherlock Holmes's Service*; *Lelicek in the Services of Sherlock Holmes* prod/rel: Elekta
Roi Bis, Le 1932 d: Robert Beaudoin. lps: Pierre Bertin, Tania Doll, Henri Kerny. 90M FRN. prod/rel: Elekta-Film

VAYRE, CHARLES
Gossette, Novel
Gossette 1922 d: Germaine Dulac. lps: Regine Bouet, Maurice Schutz, Jean-David Evremont. SRL. 6EP FRN. prod/rel: Societe Des Cineromans
Les Murailles du Silence, Novel
Murailles du Silence, Les 1925 d: Louis de Carbonnat. lps: Rene Navarre, Elmire Vautier, Rene Poyen. 1850m FRN. prod/rel: Films Excelsior

VAZOV, IVAN (1850–1921), BUL
Edna Balgarka, 1899, Short Story
Edna Bulgarka 1956 d: Nikolai Borovishki. lps: Penka Vassileva, Lyuben Bovchevski, Stefan Peichev. 22M BUL. *A Bulgarian Woman*; *Edna Balgarka*
Gramada, 1880, Verse
Gramada 1936 d: Alexander Vazov. lps: Stefan Savov, Nevena Milosheva, Konstantin Kissimov. 91M BUL. *Cairn*
Pod Igoto, 1889-90, Novel
Pod Igoto 1952 d: Dako Dakovski. lps: Apostol Karamitev, Stefan Peichev, Miroslav Mindov. 123M BUL. *Under the Yoke*

VAZQUEZ FIGUEROA, ALBERTO
Novel
Crystal Heart 1987 d: Gil Bettman. lps: Tawny Kitaen, Lee Curreri, Lloyd Bochner. 102M USA/SPN. *Corazon de Cristal* (SPN) prod/rel: New World, Izaro
El Perro, Novel
Perro, El 1977 d: Antonio Isasi. lps: Jason Miller, Lea Massari, Marisa Paredes. 114M SPN. *Vengeance*; *The Dog* prod/rel: Deva
El Ultimo Haren, Novel
Ultimo Harem, L' 1981 d: Sergio Garrone. lps: Corinne Clery, George Lazenby, Daniela Poggi. 92M ITL/GRM/SPN. *Der Letzte Harem* (GRM); *El Ultimo Haren* (SPN) prod/rel: Amakar International, Barbara Seelk Filmprod.

VEBER, FRANCIS (1937–, FRN
Buddy Buddy, Play
Buddy, Buddy 1981 d: Billy Wilder. lps: Jack Lemmon, Walter Matthau, Paula Prentiss. 96M USA. prod/rel: MGM, United Artists
Le Diner de Cons, Play
Diner de Cons, Le 1998 d: Francis Veber. lps: Jacques Villeret, Jacques Lhermitte, Francis Huster. 78M FRN. *The Dinner Game* prod/rel: Gaumont, Tf1 Films Prod.
L' Emmerdeur, Play
Emmerdeur, L' 1973 d: Edouard Molinaro. lps: Lino Ventura, Jacques Brel, Caroline Cellier. 90M FRN/ITL. *Il Rompiballe* (ITL); *A Pain in the a.* (USA); *Allez Vous Pendre Ailleurs* prod/rel: Oceania P.I.C., Ariane

VEBER, PIERRE
Chambre a Part, 1905
Camere Separate 1917 d: Gennaro Righelli. lps: Diomira Jacobini, Ida Carloni-Talli, Alberto Collo. 1446m ITL. prod/rel: Tiber Film
Le Champion de Ces Dames, Play
Champion de Ces Dames, Le 1937 d: Rene Jayet. lps: Alice Tissot, Darman, Roger Treville. SHT FRN.
En Bordee, Play
En Bordee 1931 d: Henry Wulschleger, Joe Francis. lps: Bach, Teddy Parent, Suzette Comte. 87M FRN. prod/rel: Alex Nalpas
Et Moi - J'te Dis Qu'elle T'a Fait de l'Oeil, Play
Et Moi J'te Dis Qu'elle T'a Fait d' l'Oeil 1950 d: Maurice Gleize. lps: Bernard Lancret, Madeleine Lebeau, Frederic Duvalles. 85M FRN. prod/rel: Mondia Films
Et Moi, J'te Dis Qu'elle T'a Fait de l'Oeil 1935 d: Jack Forrester. lps: Colette Darfeuil, Frederic Duvalles, Jules Berry. 80M FRN. *J'te Dis Qu'elle T'a Fait de l'Oeil* prod/rel: Forrester-Parent Productions
Un Fils d'Amerique, Play
Fils d'Amerique, Un 1925 d: Henri Fescourt. lps: Gabriel Gabrio, Marie-Louise Iribe, Alice Tissot. 1750m FRN. prod/rel: Films De France
Fils d'Amerique, Un 1932 d: Carmine Gallone. lps: Annabella, Albert Prejean, Gaston Dubosc. 91M FRN/HNG. *Az Amerikai Flu* (HNG) prod/rel: Societe Des Films Osso
Florette Et Patapon, 1905, Play
Florette E Patapon 1913 d: Mario Caserini. lps: Maria Caserini Gasparini, Gentile Miotti, Camillo de Riso. 2500m ITL. prod/rel: Film Artistica Gloria
Florette E Patapon 1927 d: Amleto Palermi. lps: Ossi Oswalda, Marcel Levesque, Livio Pavanelli. 2080m ITL. prod/rel: Palermi
Florette Et Patapon 1913. 1500m FRN.
La Gamine, 1911, Play
Avventure Di Colette, Le 1916 d: R. Savarese. lps: Anna Fougez, Renato Fabiani, Angelo GallinA. 1741m ITL. prod/rel: Cines
Monella, La 1914 d: Nino OxiliA. lps: Dina Galli, Amerigo Guasti, Stanislao Ciarli. 1107m ITL. prod/rel: Cines
Studio Girl, The 1918 d: Charles Giblyn. lps: Constance Talmadge, Earle Foxe, Johnny Hines. 5r USA. prod/rel: Select Pictures Corp.©
Gonzague, Play
Gonzague 1916. lps: Fernand Rivers, Guyon Fils, Paule Morly. 385m FRN. prod/rel: Eclectic
Les Grands, Play
Grands, Les 1916 d: Georges DenolA. lps: Jean Silvestre, Maurice Lagrenee, Simone Frevalles. 1580m FRN. prod/rel: Scagl
Grands, Les 1924 d: Henri Fescourt. lps: Jeanne Helbling, Max de Rieux, Georges Gauthier. 1900m FRN. prod/rel: Les Films De France
Grands, Les 1936 d: Felix Gandera, Robert Bibal. lps: Charles Vanel, Gaby Morlay, Pierre Larquey. 85M FRN. prod/rel: Productions Felix Gandera
A Kiss in a Taxi, Play
Kiss in a Taxi, A 1927 d: Clarence Badger. lps: Bebe Daniels, Chester Conklin, Douglas Gilmore. 6439f USA. prod/rel: Famous Players-Lasky, Paramount Pictures
Madame la Presidente, Paris C.1898, Play
Madame la Presidente 1916 d: Frank Lloyd. lps: Anna Held, Forrest Stanley, Herbert Standing. 5r USA. *Madame Presidente* prod/rel: Oliver Morosco Photoplay Co.©, Paramount Pictures Corp.
Le Monsieur de 5 Heures, Play
Monsieur de 5 Heures, Le 1938 d: Pierre Caron. lps: Andre Lefaur, Meg Lemonnier, Armand Bernard. 90M FRN. prod/rel: Films Saca
Noblesse Oblige!, 1910, Play
Noblesse Oblige 1918 d: Marcello Dudovich?. lps: Linda Moglia, Lucy Sangermano, Vasco Creti. 1760m ITL. prod/rel: S.A. Ambrosio
On Ne Roule Pas Antoinette, Play
On Ne Roule Pas Antoinette 1936 d: Paul Madeux, Christian-Jaque (Spv). lps: Armand Bernard, Paul Pauley, Simone Renant. 77M FRN. prod/rel: Henri Ullmann
La Presidente, Play
Presidente, La 1938 d: Fernand Rivers. lps: Elvire Popesco, Henri Garat, Andre Lefaur. 85M FRN. prod/rel: Films Fernand Rivers

La Presidentessa, Play
Presidentessa, La 1952 d: Pietro Germi. lps: Silvana Pampanini, Carlo Dapporto, Ave Ninchi. 87M ITL. *Mademoiselle la Presidente* (FRN); *Mademoiselle Gobette*; *The Lady President* prod/rel: Excelsa Film, Giuseppe Amato
Presidentessa, La 1976 d: Luciano Salce. lps: Johnny Dorelli, Mariangela Melato, Gianrico Tedeschi. 105M ITL. *The First Lady* prod/rel: Capital Film, Gold Film
Trois Cents a l'Heure, Play
Trois Cents a l'Heure 1934 d: Willy Rozier. lps: Dorville, Georges Treville, Mona GoyA. 90M FRN. prod/rel: Lumi-Films
Vingt Jours a l'Ombre, 1907, Play
Venti Giorni All'ombra 1918 d: Gennaro Righelli. lps: Diomira Jacobini, Alberto Collo, Ferdinand Guillaume. 1284m ITL. prod/rel: Tiber
Vous N'avez Rien a Declarer?, Play
Vous N'avez Rien a Declarer? 1916. lps: Marcel Simon, Boucot, Jane Renouardt. 1300m FRN. prod/rel: Cinedrama Paz
Vous N'avez Rien a Declarer? 1936 d: Leo Joannon, Yves Allegret. lps: Raimu, Andre Alerme, Germaine Aussey. 102M FRN. prod/rel: Pierre Braunberger
Vous N'avez Rien a Declarer? 1959 d: Clement Duhour. lps: Darry Cowl, Jean Richard, Madeleine Lebeau. 90M FRN. prod/rel: Films Sirius, C.L.M.

VEBER, PIERRE-GILLES
L' Homme Qui Vendit Son Ame, Novel
Homme Qui Vendit Son Ame, L' 1943 d: Jean-Paul Paulin. lps: Andre Luguet, Robert Le Vigan, Michele AlfA. 99M FRN. *L' Homme Qui Vendait Son Ame Au Diable*; *The Man Who Sold His Soul* prod/rel: Minerva
Manon 326, Novel
Route du Bagne, La 1945 d: Leon Mathot. lps: Lucien Coedel, Viviane Romance, Paulette Elambert. 104M FRN. *La Route de Noumea*; *Femmes Pour Noumea*; *Manon 326* prod/rel: Sirius

VEGLIANI, FRANCO
Novel
Frontera, La 1996 d: Franco Giraldi. lps: Raoul Bova, Marco Leonardi, Omero Antonutti. 107M ITL. *The Border* prod/rel: Filmalpha/Factory, Rai-Tv

VEILLER, BAYARD (1869–1943), USA
The Chatterbox, Play
Alias French Gertie 1930 d: George Archainbaud. lps: Bebe Daniels, Ben Lyon, Robert Emmett O'Connor. 6416f USA. *Love Finds a Way* (UKN) prod/rel: RKO Productions
Smooth As Satin 1925 d: Ralph Ince. lps: Evelyn Brent, Bruce Gordon, Fred Kelsey. 6003f USA. prod/rel: R-C Pictures, Film Booking Offices of America
The Fight, New York 1913, Play
Fight, The 1915 d: George W. Lederer. lps: Margaret Wycherly, John E. Kellard, Katherine La Salle. 5-6r USA. prod/rel: George W. Lederer Stage Filmotions, Inc., World Film Corp.©
The Primrose Path, New York 1907, Play
Burnt Wings 1920 d: W. Christy Cabanne. lps: Frank Mayo, Josephine Hill, Betty Blythe. 5r USA. *The Primrose Path* prod/rel: Universal Film Mfg. Co.©
Primrose Path, The 1915 d: Theodore Marston, Lawrence Marston. lps: Gladys Hanson, E. H. Sothern, H. Cooper-Willis. 5r USA. prod/rel: Universal Film Mfg. Co.©, Broadway Universal Feature
The Thirteenth Chair, New York 1916, Play
Thirteenth Chair, The 1919 d: Leonce Perret. lps: Yvonne Delva, Creighton Hale, Marie Shotwell. 5598f USA. prod/rel: Acme Pictures Corp., Pathe Exchange, Inc.©
Thirteenth Chair, The 1929 d: Tod Browning. lps: Conrad Nagel, Leila Hyams, Margaret Wycherly. 71M USA. prod/rel: Metro-Goldwyn-Mayer Pictures
Thirteenth Chair, The 1937 d: George B. Seitz. lps: Dame May Whitty, Elissa Landi, Ralph Forbes. 68M USA. prod/rel: Metro-Goldwyn-Mayer Corp.©
The Trial of Mary Dugan, New York 1927, Play
Proces de Mary Dugan, Le 1931 d: Marcel de Sano. lps: Huguette Duflos, Francoise Rosay, Charles Boyer. 100M USA. prod/rel: Metro-Goldwyn-Mayer
Proceso de Mary Dugan, El 1931 d: Marcel de Sano. lps: Maria F. Ladron de Guevara, Jose Crespo, Rafael Rivelles. 88M SPN. prod/rel: Metro-Goldwyn-Mayer Corp.
Trial of Mary Dugan, The 1929 d: Bayard Veiller. lps: Norma Shearer, Lewis Stone, H. B. Warner. 120M USA. prod/rel: Metro-Goldwyn-Mayer Pictures
Trial of Mary Dugan, The 1940 d: Norman Z. McLeod. lps: Robert Young, Laraine Day, Tom Conway. 90M USA. *The Crime of Mary Andrews*

Within the Law, New York 1912, Play
Paid 1930 d: Sam Wood. lps: Joan Crawford, Robert Armstrong, Marie Prevost. 80M USA. *Within the Law* (UKN) prod/rel: Metro-Goldwyn-Mayer Pictures
Within the Law 1917 d: William P. S. Earle. lps: Alice Joyce, Harry T. Morey, Adele de Garde. 9r USA. *Who Shall Cast the First Stone* prod/rel: Vitagraph Co. of America©, Special Blue Ribbon Feature
Within the Law 1923 d: Frank Lloyd. lps: Norma Talmadge, Lew Cody, Jack Mulhall. 8034f USA. prod/rel: Joseph M. Schenck Productions, Associated First National Pictures
Within the Law 1939 d: Gustav Machaty. lps: Tom Neal, William Gargan, Samuel S. Hinds. 65M USA. prod/rel: Metro-Goldwyn-Mayer Corp., Loew's, Inc.©

The Woman With Four Faces, Play
Woman With Four Faces, The 1923 d: Herbert Brenon. lps: Betty Compson, Richard Dix, George Fawcett. 5700f USA. prod/rel: Famous Players-Lasky, Paramount Pictures

VEILLOT, CLAUDE
Nous N'irons Pas Au Nigeria, Novel
Cent Mille Dollars Au Soleil 1963 d: Henri Verneuil. lps: Jean-Paul Belmondo, Lino Ventura, Reginald Kernan. 130M FRN/ITL. *Centomila Dollari Al Sole* (ITL); *Greed in the Sun* (USA) prod/rel: S.N.E.G., Trianon Productions

VELIE, LESTER
Gangsters in the Dress Business, Article
Garment Jungle, The 1957 d: Vincent Sherman, Robert Aldrich (Uncredited). lps: Lee J. Cobb, Kerwin Mathews, Gia ScalA. 88M USA. *The Garment Center* prod/rel: Columbia

VELTER, JOS M.
Das Gelbe Haus von Rio, Play
Maison Jaune de Rio, La 1930 d: Robert Peguy, Karl Grune. lps: Charles Vanel, Renee Heribel, Jacques Maury. 90M FRN. prod/rel: Pathe-Natan, Emelka-Wochenschau

VELTER, LUIS
La Pantera Nera, Novel
Pantera Nera, La 1942 d: Domenico M. Gambino. lps: Leda Gloria, Dria Paola, Lauro Gazzolo. 77M ITL. prod/rel: Stella Film, Rex

VENANCIO DA SILVA, CIDA
Pixote, the Law of the Strongest, Book
Quem Matou Pixote? 1996 d: Jose Joffily. lps: Cassiano Carneiro, Luciana Rigueira, Joana Fomm. 120M BRZ. *Who Killed Pixote?* prod/rel: Coeves Films

VENATIER, HANS
Der Major Und Die Stiere, Novel
Major Und Die Stiere, Der 1955 d: Eduard von Borsody. lps: Attila Horbiger, Fritz Tillmann, Hans von Borsody. 95M GRM. *The Major and the Bulls* prod/rel: Allianz, Buhne Und Film

VENEZIANI, CARLO
L' Antenato, Play
Antenato, L' 1936 d: Guido Brignone. lps: Antonio Gandusio, Paola Barbara, Olivia Fried. 76M ITL. *The Ancestor* prod/rel: Astra Film, E.N.I.C.

Il Braccialetto Al Piede, 1916, Play
Braccialetto Al Piede, Il 1920 d: Eleuterio Rodolfi. lps: Suzanne Armelle, Eleuterio Rodolfi, Armand Pouget. 1162m ITL. prod/rel: Rodolfi Film

Serenata Al Vento, Play
Serenata Al Vento 1956 d: Luigi de Marchi. lps: Bianca Maria Ferrari, Walter Brandi, Lia Natali. F ITL. prod/rel: Velino Cin.Ca

VENNER, NORMAN
The Imperfect Imposter, New York 1925, Novel
Irish Luck 1925 d: Victor Heerman. lps: Thomas Meighan, Lois Wilson, Cecil Humphreys. 7008f USA. prod/rel: Famous Players-Lasky, Paramount Pictures

VENTURI, MARIA
Una Storia Spezzata, Novel
Seulement Par Amour: Clara 1991 d: Andrea Frazzi, Antonio Frazzi. lps: Barbara de Rossi, Jean Dalric, Pierre Malet. TVM. 170M FRN/ITL.

VERALDI, ATTILIO
La Mazzetta, Novel
Mazzetta, La 1978 d: Sergio Corbucci. lps: Nino Manfredi, Ugo Tognazzi, Paolo StoppA. 115M ITL. *The Payoff* prod/rel: Filmauro, United Artists Europa

VERBITSKY, BERNARDO
Calles de Tango, 1953, Novel
Cita Con la Vida, Una 1957 d: Hugo Del Carril. lps: Gilda Lousek, Pedro Laxalt, Enzo VienA. 89M ARG. *An Appointment With Life* prod/rel: L.E.O.

VERCEL, ROGER (1894-1957), FRN, Cretin, Roger Auguste
Les Eaux Troubles, Short Story
Eaux Troubles, Les 1948 d: Henri Calef. lps: Jean Vilar, Ginette Leclerc, Edouard Delmont. 95M FRN. prod/rel: Euzko Films

Remorques, Novel
Remorques 1940 d: Jean Gremillon. lps: Jean Gabin, Michele Morgan, Fernand Ledoux. 90M FRN. *Stormy Waters* (UKN) prod/rel: M.A.I.C.

VERCORS (1902-1991), FRN, Bruller, Jean Marcel
Les Animaux Denatures, Paris 1952, Novel
Skullduggery 1970 d: Gordon Douglas, Richard Wilson (Uncredited). lps: Burt Reynolds, Susan Clark, Roger C. Carmel. 105M USA. prod/rel: Universal Pictures

Le Silence de la Mer, 1942, Novel
Silence de la Mer, Le 1947 d: Jean-Pierre Melville. lps: Nicole Stephane, Ami Aroe, Howard Vernon. 86M FRN. prod/rel: Melville Productions

VERCOURT, ALFRED
Alcide Pepie, Play
Alcide Pepie 1934 d: Rene Jayet. lps: Alice Tissot, Emile Seylis, Marcel Le Marchand. 26M FRN. prod/rel: Pathe Consortium Cinema

Mam'zelle Culot, Opera
Tampon du Capiston, Le 1930 d: Jean Toulout, Joe Francis. lps: Bach, Helene Hallier, Henry Laverne. F FRN. prod/rel: Alex Nalpas

VERDI, GIUSEPPE (1813-1901), ITL
Aida, Cairo 1871, Opera
Aida 1953 d: Clemente Fracassi. lps: Sophia Loren, Lois Maxwell, Luciano Della MarrA. 96M ITL. prod/rel: Oscar Film, Cei-Incom.

Rigoletto, Venice 1851, Opera
Rigoletto 1947 d: Carmine Gallone. lps: Tito Gobbi, Maria Fillipeschi, Lina Pagliughi. F ITL. prod/rel: Excelsa Film, Minerva Film
Rigoletto E la Sua Tragedia 1956 d: Flavio CalzavarA. lps: Aldo Silvani, Janet Vidor, Gerard Landry. 85M ITL. *Rigoletto* prod/rel: Diva Film

La Traviata, Venice 1853, Opera
Traviata, La 1922 d: Challis Sanderson. lps: Thelma Murray, Clive Brook. 1274f UKN. prod/rel: Master Films, Gaumont
Traviata, La 1927 d: H. B. Parkinson. lps: Anthony Ireland, Peggy Carlisle, Booth Conway. 1605f UKN. prod/rel: Song Films
Traviata, La 1967 d: Mario Lanfranchi. lps: Anna Moffo, Gino Bechi, Franco Bonisolli. 90M ITL. prod/rel: B.L. Vision, I.C.I.T
Traviata, La 1982 d: Franco Zeffirelli. lps: Teresa Stratas, Placido Domingo, Cornell MacNeil. 112M ITL. prod/rel: Accent, Rai

VERDOT, GUY
Madame Et Son Auto, Novel
Madame Et Son Auto 1958 d: Robert Vernay. lps: Sophie Desmarets, Jacques Morel, Jacques Jouanneau. F FRN. prod/rel: Sirius, Films De L'abeille

VERGA, ADA GUARESCHI
Quanto de Me Hanno Tagliato, Autobiography
Immagini Vive (Cio Che Di Me Hanno Lasciato) 1976 d: Ansano Giannarelli. lps: Ada Guareschi Verga, Nicoletta Donati, Gianni Magni. MTV. F ITL. prod/rel: Reiac Film, Rai-Tv

VERGA, GIOVANNI (1840-1922), ITL
L' Amante Di Gramigna, 1880, Short Story
Amante Di Gramigna, L' 1968 d: Carlo Lizzani. lps: Gian Maria Volonte, Stefania Sandrelli, Ivo Garrani. 108M ITL/BUL. *Lyubovnitsata Na Graminya* (BUL); *The Bandit*; *Gramina's Lover*; *Gramigna's Lover* prod/rel: Dino de Laurentiis Cin.Ca (Roma), Studija Za Igralni Film (Sofia)

Caccia Al Lupo, 1901
Caccia Al Lupo 1917 d: Giuseppe Sterni. lps: Ugo Gracci, Emilia Gracci, Vittorio BrombarA. 1155m ITL. prod/rel: Silentium Film

Cavalleria Rusticana, Milan 1880, Short Story
Cavalleria Rusticana 1909 d: Emile Chautard. lps: Charles Krauss, Dupont-Morgan, Marcelle Barry. 308m FRN. prod/rel: Acad
Cavalleria Rusticana 1916 d: Ubaldo Maria Del Colle. lps: Linda Pini, Ubaldo Maria Del Colle, Ugo Gracci. 1014m ITL. prod/rel: Flegrea Film
Cavalleria Rusticana 1916 d: Ugo FalenA. lps: Gemma Stagno-Bellincioni, Bianca Virginia Camagni, Luigi Serventi. 1366m ITL. prod/rel: Tespi Film
Cavalleria Rusticana 1924 d: Mario Gargiulo. lps: Tina Xeo, Giovanni Grasso Sr., Livio Pavanelli. 1894m ITL. prod/rel: Societa Film d'Arte Italiana

Cavalleria Rusticana 1939 d: Amleto Palermi. lps: Isa Pola, Carlo Ninchi, Doris Duranti. 75M ITL. prod/rel: Scalera Film
Cavalleria Rusticana 1953 d: Carmine Gallone. lps: Anthony Quinn, May Britt, Umberto Spadaro. 84M ITL. *Fatal Desire* prod/rel: Excelsa Film, Minerva Film
Cavalleria Rusticana 1953. lps: Marion Rhodes.
Cavalleria Rusticana 1968 d: Ake Falck. lps: Fiorenza Cossotto, Gianfranco Cecchele, Anna Di Stasio. 76M SWT/AUS/GRM.
Cavalleria Rusticana 1986 d: Franco Zeffirelli. lps: Elena Obraztsova, Placido Domingo, Fedora Barbieri. MTV. 70M ITL.

Eva
Eva 1919 d: Ivo Illuminati. lps: Alba Primavera, Attilio de Virgiliis, Giovanni BavierA. 1420m ITL. prod/rel: Silentium Film

La Lupa, 1880, Short Story
Lupa, La 1953 d: Alberto LattuadA. lps: Kerima, May Britt, Ettore Manni. 90M ITL. *The She-Wolf*; *The Vixen*; *The Devil Is a Woman* prod/rel: Ponti-de Laurentiis Cin.Ca, Paramount
Lupa, La 1996 d: Gabriele LaviA. lps: Monica Guerritore, Raoul Bova, Michele Placido. 108M ITL. *She-Wolf* prod/rel: Globe Films, Production Group

Il Marito Di Elena, 1881, Novel
Marito Di Elena, Il 1921 d: Riccardo Cassano. lps: Fernanda Fassy, Nino CamardA. 1503m ITL. prod/rel: Chimera Film

Una Peccatrice, 1866, Novel
Peccatrice, Una 1918 d: Giulio Antamoro. lps: Leda Gys, Goffredo d'Andrea, Ignazio Lupi. 1339m ITL. prod/rel: Polifilm

La Storia Di Una Capinera, 1870, Novel
Storia Di Una Capinera 1943 d: Gennaro Righelli. lps: Marina Berti, Claudio Gora, LoredanA. 82M ITL. prod/rel: Titanus
Storia Di Una Capinera 1993 d: Franco Zeffirelli. lps: Angela Bettis, Johnathon Schaech, Sara-Jane Alexander. 106M ITL. *Sparrow*; *Story of a Blackcap* prod/rel: Polygram, Nippon
Storia Di Una Capinera, La 1917 d: Giuseppe Sterni. lps: Linda Pini, Giuseppe Sterni. 1420m ITL. prod/rel: Silentium Film

Tigre Reale, 1873
Tigre Reale 1916 d: Giovanni Pastrone. lps: Pina Menichelli, Alberto Nepoti, Febo Mari. 1742m ITL. prod/rel: Itala Film

VERGANO, ALESSANDRO MAGGIORA
Baldoria Nei Caraibi, Novel
Baldoria Nei Caraibi 1956 d: Ubaldo Ragona, Jose Luis ZavalA. lps: Wilbert Bradley, Raul Del Castillo, Consuelo VarA. 2200m ITL/SPN. *Fiesta En El Caribe* (SPN) prod/rel: Doxa (Roma), Tarfe Films (Madrid)

VERHAEREN, EMILE (1855-1916), BLG
Les Moines, Belgium 1886, Poem
Monastery 1938 d: Robert Alexander. DOC. 55M USA. prod/rel: State Rights, World Pictures Corp.

VERHOEVEN, PAUL
Das Kleine Hofkonzert, Play
Chanson du Souvenir, La 1936 d: Serge de Poligny, Douglas Sirk. lps: Max Michel, Pierre Magnier, Marta Eggerth. 95M FRN. *Concert a la Cour*; *Song of Remembrance* prod/rel: U.F.a., a.C.E.
Hofkonzert, Das 1936 d: Douglas Sirk. lps: Marta Eggerth, Johannes Heesters, Otto Tressler. 85M GRM. prod/rel: UFA
Kleine Hofkonzert, Das 1945 d: Paul Verhoeven. lps: Elfie Mayerhofer, Erich Ponto, Hans Nielsen. 70M GRM. *A Little Courtly Concert* prod/rel: Tobis, Atlantic

VERHYLLE, ARMAND
Monsieur de Falindor, Play
Monsieur de Falindor 1946 d: Rene Le Henaff. lps: Pierre Jourdan, Jacqueline Dor, Marcelle Duval. 75M FRN. prod/rel: Berton Et Cie, Andre Hugon

VERISSIMO, ERICO (1905-1975), BRZ
Ana Terra, 1949, Short Story
Ana Terra 1972 d: Durval Gomes GarciA. lps: Rossana Ghessa, Geraldo Del Rey, Pereira Dias. 105M BRZ.

Um Certo Capitao Rodrigo, 1949, Short Story
Ana Terra 1972 d: Durval Gomes GarciA. lps: Rossana Ghessa, Geraldo Del Rey, Pereira Dias. 105M BRZ.
Certo Capitao Rodrigo, Um 1970 d: Anselmo Duarte. 100M BRZ. *That Certain Captain Rodrigo*

Noite, 1954, Novel
Noite 1985 d: Gilberto Loureiro. lps: Paulo Cesar Pereio, Otavio Augusto, Cristina Ache. 85M BRZ. *Night*

Olhai Os Lirios Do Campo, 1937, Novel
Mirad Los Lirios Del Campo 1947 d: Ernesto AranctbiA. lps: Francisco de PaulA. 109M ARG. *Behold the Lilies of the Field*

O Sobrado, 1949, Short Story
Ana Terra 1972 d: Durval Gomes GarciA. lps: Rossana Ghessa, Geraldo Del Rey, Pereira Dias. 105M BRZ.
Sobrado, O 1956 d: Cassiano G. Mendes, Walter George Durst. 110M BRZ. *The Second Floor*

VERNAYRE
Par Habitude, Play
Par Habitude 1932 d: Maurice Cammage. lps: Gaby Basset, Pierre Finaly, Madame Clairval. 31M FRN. prod/rel: Eclair, Nicaea Films

VERNBERG, MAXIMILIAN
Article
Letzte Zeuge, Der 1960 d: Wolfgang Staudte. lps: Martin Held, Hanns Lothar, Ellen Schwiers. 102M GRM. *The Last Witness* prod/rel: Kurt Ulrich, Europa

VERNE, JULES (1828–1905), FRN
Novel
Tajemstvi Oceloveho Mesta 1978 d: Ludvik RazA. lps: Jaromir Hanzlik, Martin Ruzek, Josef Vinklar. 89M CZC. *The Secret of the Steel Town* prod/rel: Filmove Studio Barrandov

Un Capitaine de Quinze Ans, 1878, Novel
Pyatnadtzatiletny Kapitan 1945 d: Vasili Zhuravlyov. 82M USS.

Le Chateau Des Carpathes, 1892, Novel
Castelul Din Carpati 1981 d: Stere GuleA. 103M RMN. *The Castle in the Carpathians*
Tajemstvi Hradu V Karpatech 1981 d: Oldrich Lipsky. lps: Jan Hartl, Michal Docolomansky, Milos Kopecky. 99M CZC. *Mystery Castle in the Carpathians*; *Tajemstvi Hradu V Karpatech*; *The Mysterious Castle in the Carpathians*; *Tajemny Hrad V Karpatech* prod/rel: Filmove Studio Barrandov

Cinq Semaines En Ballon, 1863, Novel
Five Weeks in a Balloon 1962 d: Irwin Allen. lps: Red Buttons, Fabian, Barbara Eden. 101M USA. prod/rel: 20th Century-Fox

De la Terre a la Lune; Trajet Direct En 97 Heures, 1865, Novel
From the Earth to the Moon 1958 d: Byron Haskin. lps: Joseph Cotten, George Sanders, Debra Paget. 100M USA. prod/rel: Warner Bros., RKO
Jules Verne's Rocket to the Moon 1967 d: Don Sharp. lps: Burl Ives, Troy Donahue, Gert Frobe. 101M UKN. *Those Fantastic Flying Fools* (USA); *Rocket to the Moon*; *P.T. Barnum's Rocket to the Moon*; *The Journey That Shook the World*; *Blast Off!* prod/rel: Anglo-Amalgamated, Jules Verne

Deux Ans de Vacances, Paris 1888, Novel
Deux Ans de Vacances 1973 d: Gilles Grangier, Sergiu Nicolaescu. lps: Marc Di Napoli, Didier Gaudron, Franz Seidenschwan. MTV. 360M FRN/GRM/RMN. *Two Year Long Holidays*; *Insula Comorilor* (RMN); *Treasure Island*; *Piratti Din Pacific*
Strange Holiday 1970 d: Mende Brown. lps: Jaeme Hamilton, Mark Healey, Jaime Messang. 75M ASL. prod/rel: Mass-Brown Pictures

Les Enfants du Capitaine Grant; Voyage Autour du Monde, Paris 1867-68, Novel
In Search of the Castaways 1961 d: Robert Stevenson. lps: Maurice Chevalier, Hayley Mills, George Sanders. 100M UKN/USA. *The Castaways* prod/rel: Walt Disney Productions

L' Etoile du Sud le Pays de Diamants, Paris 1884, Novel
Etoile du Sud, L' 1918 d: Michel-Jules Verne. 1400m FRN. prod/rel: Film Jules Verne
Southern Star, The 1969 d: Sidney Hayers. lps: George Segal, Ursula Andress, Orson Welles. 105M UKN/FRN/USA. *L' Etoile du Sud* (FRN) prod/rel: Euro France Films, Capitole Films

Face Au Drapeau, 1896, Novel
Vynalez Zkazy 1958 d: Karel Zeman. lps: Lubor Tokos, Arnost Navratil, Miloslav Holub. 83M CZC. *The Fabulous World of Jules Verne* (USA); *Invention for Destruction*; *Weapons of Destruction*; *Invention of Destruction*; *Deadly Invention, The* prod/rel: Kratky Film Praha

Hector Servadac, 1878, Novel
Na Komete 1970 d: Karel Zeman. lps: Emil Horvath, Magda Vasaryova, Frantisek Filipovsky. 85M CZC. *Hector Servadac's Ark*; *Mr. Servadac's Ark*; *Na Comete*; *Archa Pana Servadaca*; *On a Comet* prod/rel: Filmove Studio Barrandov, Kratky Film

Hector Servadac: Voyages Et Aventures a Travers le Monde., Paris 1877, Novel
Valley of the Dragons 1961 d: Edward Bernds. lps: Cesare Danova, Sean McClory, Joan Stanley. 81M USA. *Prehistoric Valley* (UKN) prod/rel: Z.R.B. Productions

L' Ile Mysterieuse, Paris 1874, Novel
Ile Mysterieuse, L' 1973 d: Henri Colpi, Juan Antonio Bardem. lps: Omar Sharif, Philippe Nicaud, Gerard Tichy. 105M FRN/ITL/SPN. *L' Isola Misteriosa E Il Capitano Nemo* (ITL); *The Mysterious Island* (USA); *The Mysterious Island of Captain Nemo*; *La Isla Misteriosa* (SPN) prod/rel: Filmes Cin.Ca (Roma), Copercines (Madrid)
Mysterious Island 1960 d: Cy Endfield. lps: Michael Craig, Joan Greenwood, Michael Callan. 100M UKN/USA. prod/rel: Ameran Films, Columbia

L'isle Mysterieuse, Paris 1874, Novel
Misterio En la Isla de Los Monstruos 1981 d: Piquer Simon. lps: Terence Stamp, Peter Cushing, Ian SerA. 104M SPN/USA. *Mystery on Monster Island*; *Monster Island* prod/rel: Fort Films, Almena

L' Ile Mysterieuse, Paris 1874, Novel
Mysterious Island, The 1929 d: Lucien Hubbard, Maurice Tourneur. lps: Lionel Barrymore, Jane Daly, Lloyd Hughes. 93M USA. prod/rel: Metro-Goldwyn-Mayer Pictures
Tainstvenni Ostrov 1941 d: E. Pentzlin, B. M. Chelintsev. lps: M. V. Commisarov, A. S. Krasnopolski, P. I. Klansky. 92M USS. *Mysterious Island*

Les Indes Noires, Novel
Indes Noires, Les 1917. 1165m FRN. prod/rel: Eclair

La Jangada, 1881, Novel
Ochocientas Mil Leguas Por El Amazonas 1958 d: Emilio Gomez Muriel. lps: Carlos Lopez Moctezuma, Rafael Bertrand, Elvira QuintanA. 95M MXC. *800 Leagues Over the Amazon* (USA); *La Jangada*

Maitre du Monde, Paris 1904, Novel
Master of the World 1961 d: William Witney. lps: Vincent Price, Charles Bronson, Henry Hull. 104M USA. prod/rel: Alta Vista Productions, American International

Mathias Sandorf, 1885, Novel
Mathias Sandorf 1921 d: Henri Fescourt. lps: Romuald Joube, Yvette Andreyor, Jean Toulout. SRL. 9EP FRN. prod/rel: Louis Nalpas
Mathias Sandorf 1962 d: Georges Lampin. lps: Louis Jourdan, Serena Vergano, Francisco Rabal. 105M FRN/ITL/SPN. *Il Grande Ribelle* (ITL); *Mathias Sandorf*; *El Conde Sandorf* (SPN) prod/rel: Societe Francaise de Cinematographie, Procusa

Michel Strogoff, Paris 1876, Novel
Kurier Des Zaren, Der 1935 d: Richard Eichberg. lps: Anton Walbrook, Maria Andergast, Alexander Golling. 93M GRM. *The Tsar's Courier*
Michael Strogoff 1910 d: J. Searle Dawley. lps: Mary Fuller, Charles Ogle, Marc McDermott. 995f USA. prod/rel: Edison Manufacturing Co.
Michael Strogoff 1914 d: Lloyd B. Carleton. lps: Jacob P. Adler, Daniel Makarenko, Eleanor Barry. 5r USA. prod/rel: Popular Plays and Players, Inc.©, Lubin Mfg. Co.
Michel Strogoff 1926 d: Victor Tourjansky. lps: Ivan Mosjoukine, Nathalie Kovanko, Acho Chakatouny. F FRN. *Michael Strogoff* (USA) prod/rel: Cine-France-Fim, Films De France
Michel Strogoff 1935 d: Jacques de Baroncelli, Richard Eichberg. lps: Anton Walbrook, Colette Darfeuil, Yvette Lebon. 100M FRN. prod/rel: Productions Joseph N. Ermolieff, Richard Eichberg-Film
Michel Strogoff 1975 d: Jean-Pierre Decourt. MTV. FRN.
Michele Strogoff 1956 d: Carmine Gallone. lps: Curd Jurgens, Genevieve Page, Sylva KoscinA. 113M ITL/FRN/GRM. *Michel Strogoff* (FRN); *Revolt of the Tartars*; *Michael Strogoff*; *Der Kurier Des Zaren* (GRM); *Courier of the Czar, The* prod/rel: Illia Films, Les Films Modernes
Soldier and the Lady, The 1937 d: George Nicholls Jr. lps: Anton Walbrook, Elizabeth Allan, Margot Grahame. 85M USA. *Michael Strogoff*; *Adventures of Michael Strogoff* prod/rel: RKO Radio Pictures©, Pandro S. Berman Production
Strogoff 1970 d: Eriprando Visconti. lps: Law John Phillip, Mimsy Farmer, Hiram Keller. 101M ITL/FRN/BUL. *Michele Strogoff* (FRN); *Mihail Strogov* (BUL); *Der Kurier Des Zaren* (GRM); *The Courier of the Czar* prod/rel: Nicolo Pomilia, Cineriz
Triomphe de Michel Strogoff, Le 1961 d: Victor Tourjansky. lps: Curd Jurgens, Capucine, Pierre Massimi. 120M FRN/ITL. *Il Trionfo Di Michele Strogoff* (ITL); *Michel Strogoff*; *The Triumph of Michael Strogoff* prod/rel: Films Modernes, Fono Roma

Le Phare du Bout du Monde, 1905, Novel
Luz Del Fin Del Mundo, La 1971 d: Kevin Billington. lps: Kirk Douglas, Yul Brynner, Samantha Eggar. 99M SPN/USA/LCH. *The Light at the Edge of the World* (USA); *Le Phare du Bout du Monde*; *Il Faro in Capo Al Mondo* prod/rel: Jet, Rizzoli

Le Pilote du Danube, 1908, Novel
Dunai Hajos, A 1974 d: Miklos Markos. lps: Gabor Koncz, Gabor Agardy, Istvan Bujtor. 98M HNG. *The Danube Pilot*; *Boatman on the Danube* prod/rel: Hunnia Filmstudio, Magyar Televisio

Robur le Conquerant, Paris 1886, Novel
Master of the World 1961 d: William Witney. lps: Vincent Price, Charles Bronson, Henry Hull. 104M USA. prod/rel: Alta Vista Productions, American International

Le Tour du Monde En Quatre-Vingt Jours, 1873, Novel
Around the World in 80 Days 1956 d: Michael Anderson. lps: David Niven, Cantinflas, Robert Newton. 168M USA. prod/rel: United Artists, Michael Todd Co., Inc.
'Round the World in 80 Days 1914. 6r USA. prod/rel: Lewis Pennant Features Co.©

Les Tribulations d'un Chinois En Chine, Paris 1879, Novel
Tribulations d'un Chinois En Chine, Les 1965 d: Philippe de BrocA. lps: Jean-Paul Belmondo, Ursula Andress, Maria Pacome. 110M FRN/ITL. *L' Uomo Di Hong Kong* (ITL); *Up to His Ears* (USA); *That Man from Hong Kong*; *Chinese Adventures in China* prod/rel: Ariane, Les Productions Artistes Associes

Vingt Mille Lieues Sous Les Mers, 1870, Novel
20,000 Leagues Under the Sea 1916 d: Stuart Paton. lps: Allen Holubar, Jane Gail, Dan Hanlon. 8r USA. prod/rel: Universal Film Mfg. Co.©, Williamson Submarine Film Corp.
20,000 Leagues Under the Sea 1954 d: Richard Fleischer. lps: James Mason, Kirk Douglas, Paul Lukas. 122M USA. *Twenty Thousand Leagues Under the Sea* prod/rel: Buena Vista, Walt Disney Prods.
Twenty Thousand Leagues Under the Sea 1973 d: William Hanna, Joseph BarberA. ANM. 48M USA. *20.000 Leagues Under the Sea*
Vingt Mille Lieues Sous Les Mers 1918. FRN. prod/rel: le Film Jules Verne, Eclair

Voyage Au Centre de la Terre, 1864, Novel
Journey to the Center of the Earth 1959 d: Henry Levin. lps: James Mason, Pat Boone, Arlene Dahl. 130M USA. prod/rel: 20th Century-Fox, Joseph M. Schenck
Journey to the Center of the Earth 1988 d: Rusty Lemorande. lps: Paul Carafotes, Nicola Cooper, Ilan Mitchell-Smith. 86M USA. prod/rel: Cannon
Journey to the Centre of the Earth 1976 d: Richard Slapczynski. ANM. 49M ASL.
Viaje Al Centro de la Tierra 1977 d: Piquer Simon. lps: Kenneth More, Pep Munne, Jack Taylor. 107M SPN. *Fabulous Journey to the Centre of the Earth*; *Where Time Began* (USA); *Journey to the Centre of the Earth* prod/rel: Almena Films

VERNER, GERALD
Whispering Woman, Novel
Noose for a Lady 1953 d: Wolf RillA. lps: Dennis Price, Rona Anderson, Ronald Howard. 73M UKN. prod/rel: Insignia, Anglo-Amalgamated

VERNEUIL, LOUIS
Play
Cross My Heart 1946 d: John Berry. lps: Betty Hutton, Sonny Tufts, Michael Chekhov. 83M USA. prod/rel: Paramount

L' Amant de Madame Vidal, Play
Amant de Madame Vidal, L' 1936 d: Andre Berthomieu. lps: Elvire Popesco, Victor Boucher, Jacques Louvigny. 87M FRN. prod/rel: Societe Des Films Roger Richebe

Arlette Et Ses Papas, Play
Arlette Et Ses Papas 1934 d: Henry Roussell. lps: Renee Saint-Cyr, Christiane Delyne, Jules Berry. 85M FRN. *Avril* prod/rel: Pathe-Nathan

Azais, Play
Azais 1931 d: Rene Hervil. lps: Max Dearly, Simone Rouviere, Jeanne Saint-Bonnet. 102M FRN. prod/rel: Etablissements Jacques Haik

Le Banque Nemo, Play
Banque Nemo, La 1934 d: Marguerite Viel. lps: Mona Goya, Alice Tissot, Victor Boucher. 92M FRN. prod/rel: a.S. Film, Societe Des Films Sonores Tobis

Daniel, Play
Who Is the Man? 1924 d: Walter Summers. lps: Isobel Elsom, Langhorne Burton, Lewis Dayton. 5700f UKN. prod/rel: Napoleon Films

477

Dora Nelson, Play
Dora Nelson 1935 d: Rene Guissart. lps: Elvire Popesco, Micheline Cheirel, Andre Lefaur. 95M FRN. prod/rel: Flores-Film
Dora Nelson 1939 d: Mario Soldati. lps: Assia Noris, Carlo Ninchi, Miretta Mauri. 76M ITL. prod/rel: Urbe Film, Industrie Cin.Che Italiane S.a.

L' Ecole Des Contribuables, Play
Ecole Des Contribuables, L' 1934 d: Rene Guissart. lps: Armand Bernard, Paul Pauley, Mireille Perrey. 75M FRN. prod/rel: France Univers-Films

Le Fauteuil 47, Play
Fauteuil 47, Le 1937 d: Fernand Rivers. lps: Francoise Rosay, Raimu, Andre Lefaur. 93M FRN. prod/rel: Films Fernand Rivers
Parkettsessel 47 1926 d: Gaston Ravel. lps: Erna Morena, Dolly Davis, Otto Tressler. 2277m GRM/FRN. *Le Fauteuil 47* (FRN) prod/rel: Alga, Jean De Merly

Une Femme Ravie, Play
Femme Chipee, Une 1934 d: Piere Colombier. lps: Elvire Popesco, Jules Berry, Marcel Simon. 98M FRN. *Une Femme Ravie* prod/rel: Pathe-Natan

Guignol Ou le Cambrioleur, Play
Flagrant Delit 1930 d: Georges Treville, Hanns Schwarz. lps: Henri Garat, Charles Dechamps, Blanche Montel. 95M FRN. *Le Cambrioleur* prod/rel: U.F.a., a.C.E.

The Lady Is Willing, Play
Lady Is Willing, The 1934 d: Gilbert Miller. lps: Leslie Howard, Cedric Hardwicke, Binnie Barnes. 74M UKN. prod/rel: Columbia British

The Love Habit, Play
Love Habit, The 1930 d: Harry Lachman. lps: Seymour Hicks, Margot Grahame, Edmund Breon. 90M UKN. prod/rel: British International Pictures, Wardour

Ma Cousine de Varsovie, Play
Ma Cousine de Varsovie 1931 d: Carmine Gallone. lps: Andre Roanne, Elvire Popesco, Madeleine Lambert. 95M FRN. prod/rel: Societe Des Films Osso

Ma Soeur Et Moi, Play
Caprice de Princesse 1933 d: Henri-Georges Clouzot, Karl Hartl. lps: Albert Prejean, Armand Bernard, Marie Bell. 85M FRN. prod/rel: U.F.a., a.C.E.
Meine Schwester Und Ich 1929 d: Manfred NoA. lps: Mady Christians, Jack Trevor, Igo Sym. 2475m GRM. *My Sister and I* prod/rel: National-Film Ag
Meine Schwester Und Ich 1954 d: Paul Martin. lps: Sonja Ziemann, Adrian Hoven, Herta Staal. 90M GRM. *My Sister and I* prod/rel: C.C.C., Gloria

Maitre Bolbec Et Son Mari, Play
Maitre Bolbec Et Son Mari 1934 d: Jacques Natanson. lps: Madeleine Soria, Lucien Baroux, Jean Debucourt. 80M FRN. prod/rel: Acta Film
World at Her Feet, The 1927 d: Luther Reed. lps: Florence Vidor, Lido Manetti, Margaret Quimby. 5691f USA. prod/rel: Paramount Famous Lasky Corp.

Mon Crime, Paris 1934, Play
True Confession 1937 d: Wesley Ruggles. lps: Carole Lombard, Fred MacMurray, John Barrymore. 85M USA. *Mon Crime* prod/rel: Paramount Pictures©

Monsieur Lamberthier, Play
Deception 1946 d: Irving Rapper. lps: Bette Davis, Claude Rains, Paul Henreid. 112M USA. prod/rel: Warner Bros.
Jealousy 1929 d: Jean de Limur. lps: Jeanne Eagels, Fredric March, Halliwell Hobbes. 6107f USA. prod/rel: Paramount Famous Lasky Corp.

O Adrienu, Play
O Adrienu 1919 d: Max Urban. lps: Andula Sedlackova, Ludvik VeverkA. CZC. *For Adrien*

Parlez-Moi d'Amour, Play
Parlez-Moi d'Amour 1935 d: Rene Guissart. lps: Roger Treville, Paul Pauley, Germaine Aussey. 75M FRN. prod/rel: Flores-Films

Pile Ou Face, Play
Petite de Montparnasse, La 1931 d: Max de Vaucorbeil, Hanns Schwarz. lps: Pierre Magnier, Grazia Del Rio, Jeanne Cheirel. 89M FRN. *Pile Ou Face* prod/rel: Gaumont-Franco-Film-Aubert

Pour Avoir Adrienne, Play
Vous Serez Ma Femme 1932 d: Serge de Poligny. lps: Alice Field, Roger Treville, Janine Ronceray. 91M FRN. *Pour Avoir Adrienne*; *L' Esbrouffeur* prod/rel: U.F.a., a.C.E.

Le Train Pour Venise, Play
My Life With Caroline 1941 d: Lewis Milestone. lps: Ronald Colman, Anna Lee, Charles Winninger. 81M USA. prod/rel: RKO Radio, United Producers
Train Pour Venise, Le 1938 d: Andre Berthomieu. lps: Victor Boucher, Huguette Duflos, Madeleine Suffel. F FRN. prod/rel: B.U.P.

Tu M'epouseras!, 1927, Play
Get Your Man 1927 d: Dorothy Arzner. lps: Clara Bow, Charles "Buddy" Rogers, Josef Swickard. 5718f USA. prod/rel: Paramount Famous Lasky Corp.
Get Your Man 1934 d: George King. lps: Dorothy Boyd, Sebastian Shaw, Clifford Heatherley. 67M UKN. prod/rel: British and Dominions, Paramount British

VERNON, HARRY M.
Mr. Wu, London 1913, Play
Mister Wu 1920. lps: Amedeo Chiantoni, Alfonsina Pieri, Marcello GiordA. 1203m ITL. prod/rel: Sayta
Mr. Wu 1919 d: Maurice Elvey. lps: Matheson Lang, Lillah McCarthy, Meggie Albanesi. 5170f UKN. prod/rel: Stoll
Mr. Wu 1927 d: William Nigh. lps: Lon Chaney, Louise Dresser, Renee Adoree. 7603f USA. prod/rel: Metro-Goldwyn-Mayer Pictures
Wu Li Chang 1930 d: Nick Grinde. lps: Ernesto Vilches, Jose Crespo, Angelita Benitez. 7r USA. prod/rel: Metro-Goldwyn-Mayer Pictures

VERNOY, JULES H.
La Fille du Regiment, Paris 1840, Opera
Figlia Del Reggimento, La 1911. 243m ITL. *Daughter of the Regiment* (USA) prod/rel: Cines
Fille du Regiment, La 1933 d: Pierre Billon, Carl Lamac. lps: Anny Ondra, Marfa Dhervilly, Pierre Richard-Willm. 90M FRN. prod/rel: Vandor-Film

VERSHININ, ILYA
Pobyeda, Play
Counter-Attack 1945 d: Zoltan KordA. lps: Paul Muni, Marguerite Chapman, Larry Parks. 90M USA. *One Against Seven* (UKN) prod/rel: Columbia

VERVOORT, HANS
Zonder Dollen
Zaak Van Leven of Dood, Een 1983 d: George Schouten. lps: Peter Faber, Carla Hardy, Derek de Lint. 90M NTH. *Silent Fear*

VERY, PIERRE
Les Anciens de Saint-Loup, Novel
Anciens de Saint-Loup, Les 1950 d: Georges Lampin. lps: Bernard Blier, Odile Versois, Francois Perier. 90M FRN. prod/rel: Jacques Roitfeld

L' Assassin a Peur la Nuit, Novel
Assassin a Peur la Nuit, L' 1942 d: Jean Delannoy. lps: Jules Berry, Jean Chevrier, Mireille Balin. 100M FRN. prod/rel: Discina

Les Disparus de Saint-Agil, Novel
Disparus de Saint-Agil, Les 1938 d: Christian-Jaque. lps: Erich von Stroheim, Michel Simon, Aime Clariond. 103M FRN. *Boys' School* (USA) prod/rel: Dimeco Productions

Goupi Mains-Rouges, Novel
Goupi Mains-Rouges 1942 d: Jacques Becker. lps: Fernand Ledoux, Georges Rollin, Blanchette Brunoy. 104M FRN. *It Happened at the Inn* (USA) prod/rel: Minerva

Madame Et le Mort, Novel
Madame Et le Mort 1942 d: Louis Daquin. lps: Renee Saint-Cyr, Henri Guisol, Pierre Renoir. 103M FRN. prod/rel: Sirius

Le Pays Sans Etoiles, Novel
Pays Sans Etoiles, Le 1945 d: Georges Lacombe. lps: Pierre Brasseur, Gerard Philipe, Jany Holt. 100M FRN. *The Country Without Stars* prod/rel: Vog

VESAAS, TARJEI (1897–1970), NRW
Brannen, 1961, Novel
Brannen 1973 d: Hakon Sandoy. lps: Jan Gronli, Bonne Gauguin, Kjell Stormoen. 90M NRW. *The Fire*

Dei Svarte Hestane, 1928, Novel
Dei Svarte Hestane 1951 d: Hans Jacob Nilsen, Sigval Maartmann-Moe. lps: Hans Jacob Nilsen, Eva Sletto, Olav Strandli. 85M NRW.

Fuglane, 1957, Novel
Zywot Mateusza 1968 d: Witold Leszczynski. lps: Franciszek Pieczka, Anna Milewska, Wirgiliusz Gryn. 79M PLN. *The Life of Matthew*; *The Days of Matthew*

Is-Slottet, 1963, Novel
Is-Slottet 1987 d: Per Blom. lps: Line Storesund, Hilde Nyeggen Martinsen, Merete Moen. 78M NRW. *The Ice Palace*

Kimen, 1940, Novel
Kimen 1973 d: Erik Solbakken. lps: Kjell Stormoen, Svein Sturla Hungnes, Ragnhild Michelsen. 95M NRW. *The Seed*

Varnatt, 1954, Novel
Varnatt 1976 d: Erik Solbakken. lps: Espen Skjonberg, Svein Scharffenberg, Anders Mordal. 99M NRW.

VESCEY, GEORGE
Autobiography
Coal Miner's Daughter, The 1980 d: Michael Apted. lps: Sissy Spacek, Tommy Lee Jones, Beverly d'Angelo. 125M USA. *Nashville Lady* prod/rel: Universal

VESTDIJK, SIMON
Op Afbetaling, 1952, Novel
Op Afbetaling 1991 d: Frans Weisz. lps: Renee Soutendijk, Gijs Scholten Van Aschat, Willem Nijholt. TVM. 180M NTH. *In Instalments*; *The Betrayed*

Pastorale 1943, 1967, Novel
Pastorale 1943 1977 d: Wim Verstappen. lps: Frederik de Groot, Renee Soutendijk, Hein Boele. 125M NTH. *Pastorale* prod/rel: Spieghel Filmproductiemij

VESZI, ENDRE
Angi Vera, Novel
Angi Vera 1979 d: Pal Gabor. lps: Veronika Pap, Erzsi Pasztor, Eva Szabo. 96M HNG. *The Education of Vera*; *Vera's Training* prod/rel: Mafilm, Objektiv

VEYRE, CHARLES
L' Amour Qui Doute, Novel
Vol, Le 1925 d: Robert Peguy. lps: Charles Vanel, Denise Legeay, Lucien Dalsace. 1850m FRN. prod/rel: Films Y. Barbaza

VEZHINOV, PAVEL
Barierata, 1977, Novel
Barierata 1979 d: Hristo Hristov. lps: Innokenti Smoktunovsky, Vanya Tsvetkova, Maria DimchevA. 113M BUL. *The Barrier*

Chovekat V Syanka, 1965, Novel
Chovekat V Syanka 1967 d: Yakim Yakimov. lps: Stanyu Mihailov, Ivan Kondov, Mihail Mihailov. 98M BUL. *The Man in the Shade*; *The Man in the Shadow*; *Covekat V Sjanka*

Proizshestvie Na Tikhata Ulitsa, 1960, Novel
Pohishtenie V Zhalto 1980 d: Marianna EvstatievA. lps: Ivailo Vakavliyev, Simeon Mihailov, Mario Philipov. 74M BUL. *Abduction in Yellow*; *Crime in Yellow*

Sinite Peperudi, 1968, Novel
Treta Sled Slantseto 1972 d: Georgi Stoyanov. lps: Kiril Gospodinov, Naum Shopov, Nikolai Nikolov. 124M BUL. *The Third Planet in the Solar System*; *Third After the Sun*; *Third from the Sun*; *Treta Sled Slanceto*; *The Birth of Man*

Sledite Ostavat, 1954, Novel
Sledite Ostavat 1956 d: Peter Vassilev. lps: Krassimir Medarov, Vera Drazhostinova, Stefan Danailov. 100M BUL. *The Traces Remain*

VIALAR, PAUL
La Caille, Novel
On N'aime Qu'une Fois 1949 d: Jean Stelli. lps: Pierre Larquey, Marcel Herrand, Francoise Rosay. 82M FRN. *La Caille* prod/rel: Consortium De Productions De Films, Cine Reportages

Clara Et Les Mechants, Novel
Clara Et Les Mechants 1957 d: Raoul Andre. lps: Minou Drouet, Pierre Destailles, Jacques Morel. 90M FRN. *Bourreaux d'Enfants* prod/rel: Estella Films

La Grande Meute, Novel
Grande Meute, La 1944 d: Jean de Limur. lps: Jacques Dumesnil, Jacqueline Porel, Suzanne Dantes. 105M FRN. prod/rel: Industrie Cinematographique, Pathe Cinema

La Maison Sous la Mer, Novel
Maison Sous la Mer, La 1946 d: Henri Calef. lps: Viviane Romance, Dora Doll, Clement Duhour. 105M FRN. prod/rel: Bervia Films

Le Petit Garcon de l'Ascenseur, Novel
Petit Garcon de l'Enscenseur, Le 1961 d: Pierre Granier-Deferre. lps: Alain Decock, Mireille Negre, Michel de Re. 90M FRN. prod/rel: Films Pomereu, S.N.C.

La Rose de la Mer, Novel
Rose de la Mer, La 1946 d: Jacques de Baroncelli. lps: Fernand Ledoux, Roger Pigaut, Denise Bosc. 85M FRN. prod/rel: Sirius

VIALAR, ROMAN
Le Bon Dieu Sans Confession, Novel
Bon Dieu Sans Confession, Le 1953 d: Claude Autant-LarA. lps: Danielle Darrieux, Henri Vilbert, Myno Burney. 112M FRN. *Les Biens de Ce Monde* prod/rel: Films Gibe

VIAL-LESOU, PIERRE
L' Ardoise, Novel
Ardoise, L' 1969 d: Claude Bernard-Aubert. lps: Salvatore Adamo, Elisabeth Wiener, Michel Constantin. 90M FRN/ITL. prod/rel: Adelfian Compania Cin.Ca, Belles Rives Productions

Un Conde, Novel
Conde, Un 1970 d: Yves Boisset. lps: Michel Bouquet, Francoise Fabian, Gianni Garko. 98M FRN/ITL. *L' Uomo Venuto Da Chicago* (ITL); *Blood on My Hands* (UKN); *Confessions of a Blood Cop; The Prison; Murder Go Round* prod/rel: Empire Film, Stephan Films

Je Vous Salue, Mafia!, Novel
Je Vous Salue, Mafia 1965 d: Raoul J. Levy. lps: Henry Silva, Jack Klugman, Eddie Constantine. 90M FRN/ITL. *Da New York: Mafia Uccide!* (ITL); *Hail! Mafia* (USA) prod/rel: I.T.T.a.C., P.E.C.F.

VIAN, BORIS (1920–1959), FRN
L' Ecume Des Jours, 1947, Novel
Ecume Des Jours, L' 1967 d: Charles Belmont. lps: Jacques Perrin, Annie Buron, Sami Frey. 115M FRN. *The Froth of Time* prod/rel: Chaumiane Productions, Sepic

J'irai Cracher Sur Vos Tombes, Paris 1946, Novel
J'irai Cracher Sur Vos Tombes 1959 d: Michel Gast. lps: Christian Marquand, Antonella Lualdi, Paul Guers. 107M FRN. *I Spit on Your Grave* (USA) prod/rel: C.T.I., S.I.P.R.O.

VIARD
Il Re Dei Mimiduti, Novel
Ettore Lo Fusto 1972 d: Enzo G. Castellari, Pasquale Festa Campanile. lps: Vittorio Caprioli, Vittorio de Sica, Michael Forest. 109M ITL/FRN/SPN. *El Rapto de Elena la Decente Italiana* (SPN); *Hector le Fortiche; Hector the Mighty; The Proxenetes; Humungus Hector* prod/rel: Empire Films (Roma), Labrador Film

VICKER, ANGUS
Fever Heat, New York 1954, Novel
Fever Heat 1968 d: Russell S. Doughton Jr. lps: Nick Adams, Jeannine Riley, Daxson Thomas. 109M USA. prod/rel: Heartland Productions, Fever Heat Ltd.

VICKERS, HAROLD
Discipline and Genevra, 1917, Novel
Talk of the Town, The 1918 d: Allen Holubar. lps: Dorothy Phillips, William Stowell, Lon Chaney. 6r USA. prod/rel: Universal Film Mfg. Co.©

The Ladder, 1918, Novel
Ladder of Lies, The 1920 d: Tom Forman. lps: Ethel Clayton, Clyde Filmore, Jean Acker. 5r USA. *The Ladder* prod/rel: Famous Players-Lasky Corp.©, Paramount-Artcraft Pictures

The Men She Married, 1916, Novel
Men She Married, The 1916 d: Travers Vale. lps: Gail Kane, Muriel Ostriche, Montagu Love. 5r USA. prod/rel: World Film Corp.©, Peerless

VICKERS, ROY
The Girl in the News, Novel
Girl in the News, The 1940 d: Carol Reed. lps: Margaret Lockwood, Barry K. Barnes, Emlyn Williams. 78M UKN. prod/rel: 20th Century Productions, MGM

I'll Never Tell, Novel
False Evidence 1937 d: Donovan Pedelty. lps: Gwenllian Gill, George Pembroke, Michael Hogarth. 71M UKN. prod/rel: Crusade, Paramount

A Question of Suspense, Novel
Question of Suspense, A 1961 d: Max Varnel. lps: Peter Reynolds, Noelle Middleton, Yvonne Buckingham. 63M UKN. prod/rel: Columbia, Bill & Michael Luckwell

VIDAL, G.
L' Aventure Est a Bord, Novel
Croisiere Pour l'Inconnu 1947 d: Pierre Montazel. lps: Claude Dauphin, Sophie Desmarets, Pierre Brasseur. 90M FRN. prod/rel: Gaumont

VIDAL, GORE (1925–, USA
The Best Man; a Play About Politics, 1960, Play
Best Man, The 1964 d: Franklin J. Schaffner. lps: Henry Fonda, Cliff Robertson, Edie Adams. 102M USA. prod/rel: Miller/Turman Productions

The Death of Billy the Kid, 1955, Television Play
Left-Handed Gun, The 1958 d: Arthur Penn. lps: Paul Newman, Lita Milan, John Dehner. 102M USA. prod/rel: Warner Bros., Harroll

Myra Breckenridge, Boston 1968, Novel
Myra Breckenridge 1970 d: Mike Sarne. lps: Mae West, John Huston, Raquel Welch. 94M USA. prod/rel: 20th Century-Fox Film Corporation

Visit to a Small Planet, 1956, Play
Visit to a Small Planet 1960 d: Norman Taurog. lps: Jerry Lewis, Joan Blackman, Earl Holliman. 85M USA. prod/rel: Paramount

VIDAL Y PLANAS, ALFONSO
Play
Santa Isabel de Ceres 1923 d: Jose Sobrado de OnegA. lps: Aurora Redondo, Manuel Sierra, Manuel LunA. SPN. prod/rel: Cinegrafica Espanola (Madrid)

VIDALIE, ALBERT
Bijoutiers du Clair de Lune, Novel
Bijoutiers du Clair de Lune, Les 1958 d: Roger Vadim. lps: Brigitte Bardot, Alida Valli, Stephen Boyd. 90M FRN/ITL. *Gli Amanti Del Chiaro Di Luna* (ITL); *The Night Heaven Fell* (USA); *Heaven Fell That Night* (UKN) prod/rel: Iena, U.C.I.L.

VIDOCQ, FRANCIS EUGENE
Vidocq, Book
Vidocq 1938 d: Jacques Daroy. lps: Andre Brule, Nadine Vogel, Jean Worms. 105M FRN. prod/rel: Societe De Production Du Film Vidocq

VIDYAVINODE, KHIRODE PRASAD
Ali Baba, 1897, Play
Ali Baba 1937 d: Modhu Bose. lps: Sadhona Bose, Suprava Mukherjee, Indira Roy. 119M IND. *Alibaba* prod/rel: Shri Bharatlaxmi Pictures

VIEBIG, CLARA
Kinder Der Eifel, Novel
Delila 1914 d: Eugen Illes. lps: Leontine Kuhnberg. GRM. prod/rel: Literaria-Film

VIEIRA, LUANDINO
Short Story
Sambizanga 1972 d: Sarah Maldoror. lps: Domingos de Oliviera, Elisa de Andrade, Dino Abelino. 102M CNG/FRN. prod/rel: Isabelle

VIERTEL, PETER
Black Heart White Hunter, Novel
White Hunter, Black Heart 1990 d: Clint Eastwood. lps: Clint Eastwood, Jeff Fahey, Charlotte Cornwell. 112M USA. prod/rel: Malpaso, Rastar

VIEWEGH, MICHAL
Novel
Bajecna Leta Pod Psa 1997 d: Petr Nikolaev. lps: Ondrej Vetchy, Libuse Safrankova, Jakub Wehrenberg. 97M CZE. *The Wonderful Years of Lousy Loving; Those Wonderful Years That Sucked* prod/rel: Space Films, Czech Television

Vychova Divek V Cechach, Novel
Vychova Divek V Cechach 1997 d: Petr KohilA. lps: Anna Geislerova, Ondrej Pavelka, Milan LasicA. 119M CZE. *Bringing Up Girls in Bohemia; Educating Girls in Bohemia* prod/rel: Czech Television

VIGANO, RENATA
L' Agnese Va a Morire, Novel
Agnese Va a Morire, L' 1977 d: Giuliano Montaldo. lps: William Berger, Ninetto Davoli, Eleonora Giorgi. 135M ITL. prod/rel: Palamo Film, C.I.D.I.F.

VIGGIANI, FRANCO NAVARRA
Itala Gens, Novel
Fiamma Che Non Si Spegne, La 1949 d: Vittorio Cottafavi. lps: Leonardo Cortese, Gino Cervi, Maria Denis. 95M ITL. prod/rel: Orsa Film, E.N.I.C.

VIGNAL, PIERRE
L' Aventure Amoureuse, Novel
Proie du Vent, La 1926 d: Rene Clair. lps: Sandra Milowanoff, Charles Vanel, Jean Murat. 2200m FRN. *The Prey of the Wind* prod/rel: Films Albatros

VIGNAUD, JEAN
La Maison du Maltais, Novel
Maison du Maltais, La 1927 d: Henri Fescourt. lps: Tina Meller, Sylvio de Pedrelli, Louis Vonelly. 1635m FRN. *Karina the Dancer* prod/rel: Societe Des Cineromans, Films De France

Maison du Maltais, La 1938 d: Pierre Chenal. lps: Viviane Romance, Louis Jouvet, Jany Holt. F FRN. *Sirocco* (USA) prod/rel: Gladiator Films

Sarati le Terrible, Novel
Sarati le Terrible 1923 d: Louis Mercanton, Rene Hervil. lps: Ginette Maddie, Henri Baudin, Arlette Marchal. 2347m FRN. prod/rel: Societe Des Films Mercanton

Sarati le Terrible 1937 d: Andre Hugon. lps: Harry Baur, Jacqueline Laurent, Jorge Rigaud. 102M FRN. prod/rel: Productions Andre Hugon

Venus, Novel
Venus 1929 d: Louis Mercanton. lps: Constance Talmadge, Desdemona Mazza, Jean Murat. 3000m FRN. prod/rel: Succursale Francaise Des Artistes Ass.

VIGNY, BENNO
Amy Jolly - Die Frau Aus Marrakesch, Berlin-Friedenau 1927, Novel
Morocco 1930 d: Josef von Sternberg. lps: Gary Cooper, Marlene Dietrich, Adolphe Menjou. 92M USA. prod/rel: Paramount-Publix Corp.

VIGUS, MARY SPAIN
The House Behind the Hedge, Story
Unknown Treasures 1926 d: Archie Mayo. lps: Gladys Hulette, Robert Agnew, John Miljan. 5643f USA. *The House Behind the Hedge* (UKN) prod/rel: Sterling Pictures

VILAREGUT, SALVADOR
Play
Garra Del Mono, La 1925 d: Juan Andreu Moragas. lps: Jose Fernandez Bayot. SPN. *La Mal Del Mico* prod/rel: Film Artistica Valenciana (Valencia)

VILDRAC, CHARLES (1882–, FRN, Messager, Charles
Le Paquebot Tenacity, Play
Paquebot Tenacity, Le 1934 d: Julien Duvivier. lps: Albert Prejean, Marie Glory, Hubert Prelier. 85M FRN. prod/rel: Vandal Et Delac

VILET
Angel River, Novel
Angel River 1986 d: Sergio Olhovich. lps: Lynn-Holly Johnson, Salvador Sanchez, Janet Sunderland. 91M USA/MXC. prod/rel: Robert Renfield Prod., Dasa

VILFRED, JACQUES
Appelez-Moi Maitre, Play
Monsieur le President-Directeur General 1966 d: Jean Girault. lps: Michel Galabru, Jacqueline Maillan, Claude Rich. 90M FRN. *Appelez-Moi Maitre* prod/rel: Films Copernic, Story Films

VILLAGGIO, PAOLO (1932–, ITL
Fantozzi, Novel
Fantozzi 1975 d: Luciano Salce. lps: Paolo Villaggio, Anna Mazzamauro, Gigi Reder. 97M ITL. prod/rel: Rizzoli Film, Cineriz

Secondo Tragico Fantozzi, Il 1976 d: Luciano Salce. lps: Paolo Villaggio, Anna Mazzamauro, Gigi Reder. 110M ITL. prod/rel: Rizzoli Film, Cineriz

VILLAGGIO, PAOLO
Il Secondo Tragico Fantozzi, Book
Secondo Tragico Fantozzi, Il 1976 d: Luciano Salce. lps: Paolo Villaggio, Anna Mazzamauro, Gigi Reder. 110M ITL. prod/rel: Rizzoli Film, Cineriz

VILLARD, HENRY S.
Hemingway in Love and War, Book
In Love and War 1996 d: Richard Attenborough. lps: Sandra Bullock, Chris O'Donnell, MacKenzie Astin. 115M USA. prod/rel: New Line, Dimitri Villar Productions

VILLAVERDE, CIRILO
Cecilia Valdes O la Loma Del Angel, 1839, Novel
Cecilia 1982 d: Humberto Solas. lps: Daisy Granados, Imanol Arias, Raquel RevueltA. 247M CUB/SPN. *Cecilia Valdes*

Palenques de Negros Cimarrones, 1890, Short Story
Rancheador 1977 d: Sergio Giral. lps: Reynaldo Miravalles, Samuel Claxton, Adolfo Llaurado. 95M CUB. *The Rancher; Slavedriver; Slave-Hunter*

VILLERE, HERVE
Section Speciale, Book
Section Speciale 1975 d: Costa-Gavras. lps: Louis Seigner, Michael Lonsdale, Ivo Garrani. 12OM GRM/ITL/FRN. *L' Affare Della Sezione Speciale* (ITL); *Special Section* (USA) prod/rel: Reggane, Goriz

VILLETARD, PIERRE
Apres Lui, Novel
Apres Lui 1918 d: Maurice de Feraudy, Gaston Leprieur. lps: Maurice de Feraudy, Maurice Varny, Gaston Leprieur. 1160m FRN. prod/rel: Les Films Moliere

VILLIERS, A. J. (1903–1982), ASL, Villiers, Alan John
By Way of Cape Horn, Novel
Windjammer, The 1930 d: John Orton. lps: Tony Bruce, Michael Hogan, Hal Gordon. 58M UKN. prod/rel: Pro Patria

VINCENT, A. L.
Sahara Love, Novel
Sahara Love 1926 d: Sinclair Hill. lps: Marie Colette, John Dehelly, Sybil RhodA. 7300f UKN. prod/rel: Stoll, Espanola

VINCENT, MANUEL
Tram a la Malvarrosa, Novel
Tram a la Malvarrosa 1997 d: Jose Luis Garcia Sanchez. lps: Liberto Rabal, Jorge Merino, Ariadna Gil. 107M SPN. *Tramway to Malvarrosa; Streetcar to Malvarrosa* prod/rel: Sogetel/Lola, Canal Plus (Espana)

VINCI, RAYMOND
Andalousie, Opera
Andalousie 1950 d: Robert Vernay, Luis LuciA. lps: Luis Mariano, Carmen Sevilla, Liliane Bert. 94M FRN/SPN. *El Sueno de Andalucia* (SPN); *Andalusian Dream* prod/rel: C.C.F.C., U.D.I.F.

Au Pays Des Cigales, Opera
Au Pays Des Cigales 1945 d: Maurice Cam. lps: Henri Alibert, Gorlett, Francine Bessy. 85M FRN. prod/rel: D.U.C.

Le Chanteur de Mexico, Opera
Chanteur de Mexico, Le 1956 d: Richard Pottier. lps: Luis Mariano, Bourvil, Annie Cordy. 103M FRN/SPN. *El Cantor de Mejico* (SPN) prod/rel: Benito Perojo, Jason Interprods.

Cinq Millions Comptant, Opera
Cinq Millions Comptant 1956 d: Andre Berthomieu. lps: Ded Rysel, Darry Cowl, Jane SourzA. 90M FRN. prod/rel: Mars, Lyrica

Hier Bin Ich, Hier Bleib Ich, Play
Hier Bin Ich, Hier Bleib Ich 1959 d: Werner Jacobs. lps: Caterina Valente, Hans Holt, Ruth Stephan. 99M GRM. *I'm Here and I'm Staying* prod/rel: C.C.C., Constantin

J'y Suis. J'y Reste, Play
J'y Suis, J'y Reste 1953 d: Maurice Labro. lps: Robert Pizani, Jane Sourza, Marguerite Pierry. 97M FRN. prod/rel: Champs Elysees Productions, S.G.C.

VIOLA, CESARE GIULIO
Prico, Novel
Bambini Ci Guardano, I 1944 d: Vittorio de SicA. lps: Luciano de Ambrosiis, Isa Pola, Emilio Cigoli. 90M ITL. *The Children are Watching Us* prod/rel: Scalera, Invicta

VIOT, JACQUES
Story
Long Night, The 1947 d: Anatole Litvak. lps: Henry Fonda, Vincent Price, Barbara Bel Geddes. 101M USA. prod/rel: RKO Radio

La Choute, Short Story
Air de Paris, L' 1954 d: Marcel Carne. lps: Jean Gabin, Folco Lulli, Arletty. 110M FRN/ITL. *Aria Di Parigi* (ITL) prod/rel: Del Duca Films, Galatea

Une Femme Disparait, Short Story
Femme Disparait, Une 1942 d: Jacques Feyder. lps: Francoise Rosay, Jeanne Provost, Florence Lynn. 110M SWT. *Portrait of a Woman*; *A Woman Disappeared* prod/rel: Les Productions Mondiales D.F.G.

VIOUX, MARCELLE
Belle Jeunesse, Novel
Vie Est Magnifique, La 1938 d: Maurice Cloche. lps: Katia Lova, Jean Servais, Jean Daurand. 84M FRN. prod/rel: Films Albatros

Fleur d'Amour, Novel
Fleur d'Amour 1927 d: Marcel Vandal. lps: Maurice de Feraudy, Rose Mai, Edmond Van Daele. F FRN. prod/rel: Film d'Art

VIRE, PIERRE
S.O.S. Noronha, Novel
S.O.S. Noronha 1956 d: Georges Rouquier. lps: Jean Marais, Ruy Guerra, Daniel Ivernel. 100M FRN/ITL/GRM. prod/rel: Pallas Films, U.G.C.

VIRGIL (70bc–19bc), ITL, Publius Vergilius Maro, Vergil
Aeneid, c20 bc, Verse
Avventure Di Enea, Le 1974 d: Franco Rossi. lps: Giulio Brogi, Olga Karlatos, Marisa Bartoli. MTV. 100M ITL. prod/rel: Leone Film, Daiano Film

Leggenda Di Enea, La 1962 d: Giorgio RivaltA. lps: Steve Reeves, Carla Marlier, Gianni Garko. 105M ITL/FRN. *Les Conquerants Heroiques* (FRN); *The Last Glory of Troy*; *The Avenger* (USA); *The War of the Trojans* prod/rel: Mercury (Roma), Sirius (Paris)

VISHNEVSKY, VSEVOLOD
Nezabyvayemyi 1919 God, 1949, Play
Nezabyvayemi 1919-J God 1951 d: Mikhail Chiaureli. lps: I. Molchanov, Mikhail Gelovani, Boris Andreyev. 108M USS. *The Unforgettable Year of 1919* (USA)

Optimisticheskaya Tragediya, Moscow 1934, Play
Optimisticheskaya Tragediya 1963 d: Samson Samsonov. lps: Boris Andreyev, Vsevolod Sanayev, Vyacheslav Tikhonov. 120M USS. *The Optimistic Tragedy*; *Optimisticeskaja Tragedija* prod/rel: Mosfilm

VITALI, NANDO
Eroismo E Amore, Play
Brigata Firenze 1928 d: Orlando Vassallo. lps: Ugo Gracci, Renato Malavasi, Wanda Tiziani. 1999m ITL. prod/rel: a.D.I.a.

Il Gatto in Cantina, Play
Amo Te Sola 1935 d: Mario Mattoli. lps: Vittorio de Sica, Milly, Enrico Viarisio. 72M ITL. *Idillio 1848*; *Accadde un Giorno* prod/rel: Tiberia Film, S.A. Grandi Films

VITERBO, MAX
La Triezieme Enquete de Grey, Play
Treizieme Enquete de Grey, La 1937 d: Pierre Maudru. lps: Maurice Lagrenee, Paule Dagreve, Raymond Cordy. 85M FRN. prod/rel: Films Regent

VITTORINI, ELIO (1908–1966), ITL
Novel
Jusqu'au Bout du Monde 1962 d: Francois Villiers. lps: Pierre Mondy, Didi Perego, Marietto Angeletti. 88M FRN/ITL. *Un Filo Di Speranza* (ITL); *Un Endroit Reve* prod/rel: Films Caravelle, S.N.E.G.

Garofano Rosso, Novel
Garofano Rosso 1976 d: Luigi Faccini. lps: Miguel Bose, Elsa Martinelli, Denis Karvil. 115M ITL. prod/rel: Filmcoop, I.N.C.

Uomini E No, 1945, Novel
Uomini E No 1979 d: Valentino Orsini. lps: Massimo Foschi, Flavio Bucci, Monica Guerritore. MTV. 103M ITL. *Men are Not Men*; *Men and Others* prod/rel: Ager Cin.Ca, Rai Radiotelevisione Italiana

VITUS, MAXIMILIAN
St. Pauli in St. Peter, Play
Rettende Engel, Der 1940 d: Ferdinand Dorfler. lps: Carla Rust, Sepp Rist, Grethe Weiser. 80M GRM. prod/rel: Arnold & Richter

VIVANT-DENON, DOMINIQUE
Point de Lendemain, Short Story
Amants, Les 1958 d: Louis Malle. lps: Jeanne Moreau, Jean-Marc Bory, Jose Luis de VilallongA. 88M FRN. *The Lovers* prod/rel: Nouvelles Editions De Films

VIVANTI, ANNIE
Astrid, 1911, Novel
Astrid 1917 d: Alberto Carlo Lolli. lps: Mary Bayma-Riva, Franco Piersanti, Mimi. 1850m ITL. prod/rel: Floreal Film

L' Invasore, Novel
Invasori, Gli 1918 d: Gian Paolo Rosmino. lps: Mary Cleo Tarlarini, Gian Paolo Rosmino. 736m ITL. prod/rel: Cleo Film

Vae Victis, Novel
Guai Ai Vinti! 1955 d: Raffaello Matarazzo. lps: Lea Padovani, Anna Maria Ferrero, Clelia MataniA. 95M ITL. prod/rel: G.E.S.I.

VIVES, AMADEO
Doloretes, Opera
Doloretes 1922 d: Jose Buchs. lps: Elisa Ruiz Romero, Manuel San German, Maria Comendador. 2100m SPN. prod/rel: Atlantida

Maruxa, Opera
Maruxa 1923 d: Henri Vorins. lps: Florian Rey, Jose Aguilera, Asuncion Delgado. SPN. prod/rel: Celta Film (Vigo), Ernesto Gonzalez (Madrid)

VIVIANI, RAFFAELE
I Pescatori, Play
Notte Di Tempesta 1946 d: Gianni Franciolini. lps: Marina Berti, Fosco Giachetti, Leonardo Cortese. 90M ITL. prod/rel: Lux Film, Pan Film

La Tavola Dei Poveri, Play
Tavola Dei Poveri, La 1932 d: Alessandro Blasetti. lps: Raffaele Viviani, Leda Gloria, Salvatore CostA. 70M ITL. prod/rel: Cines, Anonima Pittaluga

VIZINCZEY, STEPHEN (1933–, HNG
In Praise of Older Women, Novel
En Brazos de la Mujer Madura 1997 d: Manuel Lombardero. lps: Juan Diego Botto, Miguel A. Garcia, Faye Dunaway. 101M SPN. *In Praise of Older Women* prod/rel: Sogetel, Lola Films

In Praise of Older Women 1978 d: George Kaczender. lps: Tom Berenger, Karen Black, Susan Strasberg. 110M CND. *Hommage aux Femmes. d'un Certain Age*; *Les Femmes de Trente Ans* prod/rel: Rsl Productions Ltd., Astral Bellevue Pathe Ltd.

VIZZOTTO, CARLO
La Duchessa Del Bal Tabarin, 1916, Opera
Duchessa Del Bal Tabarin, La 1917 d: Nino Martinengo. lps: Olga Paradisi, Amerigo Di Giorgio, Edy DarcleA. 1379m ITL. prod/rel: Cyrius Film

VOEGTLIN, ARTHUR
America, 1913, Musical Play
America 1915 d: Lawrence McGill. lps: Bert Shepherd, The Australian Wood Choppers, The Phyllis Equestrians. 6r USA. prod/rel: All Star Feature Corp.©, World Film Corp.

VOGEL, JAROSLAV
Leos Janacek; a Biography, Biography
Leos Janacek: Intimate Excursions 1983 d: Brothers Quay, Keith Griffiths. 27M UKN. prod/rel: Koninck Studios, Channel 4

VOGEL, KLAUS
Virgin Witch, Novel
Virgin Witch 1970 d: Ray Austin. lps: Ann Michelle, Vicki Michelle, Keith Buckley. 89M UKN. *Lesbian Twins* prod/rel: Tigon, Univista

VOJNOVIC, IVO
Ekvinocij, 1895, Play
Nevjera 1953 d: Vladimir Pogacic. lps: Marija Crnobori, Milivoje Zivanovic, Viktor Starcic. 80M YGS. *Equinox*

VOLLMER, LULA
Sun-Up, New York 1925, Play
Sun-Up 1925 d: Edmund Goulding. lps: Pauline Starke, Conrad Nagel, Lucille La Verne. 5819f USA. prod/rel: Metro-Goldwyn-Mayer Corp.

Trigger, New York 1927, Play
Spitfire 1934 d: John Cromwell. lps: Katharine Hepburn, Robert Young, Ralph Bellamy. 88M USA. *Trigger* prod/rel: RKO Radio Pictures©, Pandro S. Berman Production

VOLLMOLLER, KARL
Das Mirakel, 1911, Play
Miracle, The 1959 d: Irving Rapper. lps: Carroll Baker, Roger Moore, Walter Slezak. 120M USA. prod/rel: Warner Bros.

Mirakel, Das 1913 d: Max Reinhardt. lps: Maria Carmi, Douglas Payne, Florence Winston. 4200f GRM/AUS. *The Miracle* prod/rel: Ingenieur Jos. Menchen

La Paiva, Story
Lady of the Pavements 1929 d: D. W. Griffith. lps: Lupe Velez, William Boyd, Jetta Goudal. 8329f USA. *Lady of the Night* (UKN) prod/rel: Art Cinema Corp., United Artists

Schmutziges Geld, Short Story
Song 1928 d: Richard Eichberg. lps: Anna May Wong, Heinrich George, Mary Kid. 2739m GRM. *Schmutziges Geld*; *Show Life* prod/rel: Richard Eichberg-Prod.

VOLODIN, ALEXANDER
Moya Starshaya Sestra, 1961, Play
Starshaya Sestra 1967 d: Georgi Natanson. lps: Tatyana Doronina, Natalya Tenyakova, Mikhail Zharov. 102M USS. *The Elder Sister*; *The Older Sister*

Pyat Vecherov, 1959, Play
Pyat Vecherov 1979 d: Nikita Mikhalkov. lps: Lyudmila Gurchenko, Stanislav Lyubshin, Igor Nefedov. 101M USS. *Five Evenings* (USA); *Pjat Vecerov*; *Pjat Vetsjerov* prod/rel: Mosfilm

VOLPIANA, TALIA
Story
Leggenda Azzurra 1941 d: Joseph Guarino. lps: Neda Naldi, Andrea Checchi, Lauro Gazzolo. 65M ITL. prod/rel: Diana Film, Generalcine

VOLPICELLI, LUIGI
Primavera a Pianabianco, Novel
Rosalba 1945 d: Ferruccio Cerio, Max Calandri. lps: Doris Duranti, Tito Schipa, Luigi Tosi. F ITL. *Primavera a Pianabianco* prod/rel: Scalera Film, Bassoli Film

VOLTAIRE (1694–1778), FRN, Arouet, Francois-Marie
Zaire, 1739
Zaira 1910. 264m ITL. prod/rel: Cines

VON ALTEN, JURGEN
Die Rote Muhle, Play
Rote Muhle, Die 1940 d: Jurgen von Alten. lps: Ida Wust, Grethe Weiser, Theo Lingen. 101M GRM. prod/rel: Aco, Adler

VON ANGERN, MARIANNE
Die Ganz Grossen Torheiten, Novel
Ganz Grossen Torheiten, Die 1937 d: Carl Froelich. lps: Paula Wessely, Rudolf Forster, Hilde Wagener. 95M GRM. prod/rel: Froelich, Herzog

VON ARNIM, BETTINA (1785–1859), GRM, von Arnim, Elizabeth (2)
Story
Gritta Vom Rattenschloss 1985 d: Jurgen Brauer. lps: Nadja Klier, Hermann Beyer, Fred Delmare. 83M GDR. *Gritta of the Castle of Rats*; *Gitta Vom Rattenschloss* prod/rel: Defa

VON ARNIM, ELIZABETH, Elizabeth
Enchanted April, New York 1923, Novel
Enchanted April 1934 d: Harry Beaumont. lps: Ann Harding, Frank Morgan, Katharine Alexander. 66M USA. prod/rel: RKO Radio Pictures©

Enchanted April 1991 d: Mike Newell. lps: Miranda Richardson, Josie Lawrence, Polly Walker. 101M UKN. prod/rel: Hobo, Miramax

VON ARNIM, GISELA
Story
Gritta Vom Rattenschloss 1985 d: Jurgen Brauer. lps: Nadja Klier, Hermann Beyer, Fred Delmare. 83M GDR. *Gritta of the Castle of Rats*; *Gitta Vom Rattenschloss* prod/rel: Defa

VON ARNIM, LUDWIG ACHIM
Der Tolle Invalide Auf Dem Fort Ratonneau, 1818, Short Story
Lebenszeichen 1967 d: Werner Herzog. lps: Peter Brogle, Wolfgang Reichmann, Athina Zacharopoulou. 91M GRM. *Signs of Life* (USA); *Feuerzeichen* prod/rel: Werner Herzog

VON BASEWITZ, GERD
Peterchens Mondfahrt, Book
Peterchens Mondfahrt 1990 d: Wolfgang Urchs. ANM. 80M GRM. prod/rel: Televersal, Iduna Film

VON BELOGH, BELA
Drei Wunsche, Novel
  Jahrmarkt Des Lebens 1927 d: Bela Balogh. lps: Vera Schmiterlow, Gustav Frolich, Alfred Abel. 2614m GRM. prod/rel: Koop-Film-Co

VON BOKAY, JOHANN
Die Gattin, Play
  Gattin, Die 1943 d: Georg Jacoby. lps: Jenny Jugo, Willy Fritsch, Viktor Staal. 89M GRM. prod/rel: Universum, Schorcht
Ich Liebe Vier Frauen, Play
  Gattin, Die 1943 d: Georg Jacoby. lps: Jenny Jugo, Willy Fritsch, Viktor Staal. 89M GRM. prod/rel: Universum, Schorcht

VON BRABENETZ, ANNIE
Brettlfleigen, Novel
  Gehetzte Frauen 1927 d: Richard Oswald. lps: Asta Nielsen, Carmen Boni, Gustav Frohlich. 2447m GRM. *Lebende Ware* prod/rel: Richard Oswald Film-Prod.

VON BROCKDORFF, GERTRUD
Heiratsschwindler, Novel
  Heiratsschwindler 1937 d: Herbert Selpin. lps: Harald Paulsen, Hilde Korber, Fita Benkhoff. 90M GRM. *Die Rote Mutze* prod/rel: ABC-Film

VON CETTO, GITTA
Stefanie, Novel
  Stefanie 1958 d: Josef von Baky. lps: Carlos Thompson, Sabine Sinjen, Rainer Penkert. 100M GRM. prod/rel: UFA

VON CSATHO, CALMAR
Meine Tochter Tut Das Nicht, Play
  Meine Tochter Tut Das Nicht 1940 d: Hans H. Zerlett. lps: Geraldine Katt, Ralph Arthur Roberts, Rolf WankA. 94M GRM. prod/rel: Euphono, Bavaria

VON CZIFFRA, GEZA
Anita Und Der Teufel, Play
  Hollische Liebe 1949 d: Geza von CziffrA. lps: Elfie Mayerhofer, Hans Holt, Petra Trautmann. 97M AUS. prod/rel: Cziffra
Drei Blaue Augen, Play
  Falsche Adam, Der 1955 d: Geza von CziffrA. lps: Rudolf Platte, Waltraut Haas, Oskar SimA. 80M GRM. *The Phony Adam* prod/rel: Arion, D.F.H.
  Oh Diese Manner 1941 d: Hubert MarischkA. lps: Johannes Riemann, Paul Horbiger, Jane Tilden. 100M GRM. prod/rel: F.D.F., Deutsche Commerz
Villa Da Vendere, Play
  Villa Da Vendere 1942 d: Ferruccio Cerio. lps: Amedeo Nazzari, Vera Carmi, Titina de Filippo. 84M ITL. prod/rel: Titanus, S.a.G.I.F

VON DAENIKEN, ERICH (1935–, SWT
Erinnerungen an Die Zukunft, 1968, Book
  Erinnerungen an Die Zukunft 1969 d: Harald Reinl. DOC. 97M GRM. *Chariots of the Gods* (UKN); *Back to the Stars* (USA); *Memories of the Future* prod/rel: Terra Filmkunst

VON DER GRUN, MAX
Vorstadtkrokodile, 1976, Novel
  Vorstadtkrokodile 1978 d: Wolfgang Becker. lps: Wolfgang Sieling, Rita Ramchers, Thomas Bohnen. 88M GRM. *Suburb Crocodiles*; *Crocodiles in the Suburbs* prod/rel: Westdeutscher Rundfunk

VON DER SCHULENBURG, WERNER
Und Die Liebe Lacht Dazu, Play
  ..Und Die Liebe Lacht Dazu 1957 d: R. A. Stemmle. lps: Paul Horbiger, Gerhard Riedmann, Gusti Wolf. 97M GRM. *Schwarzbrot Und Kipferl*; *..and Love Laughs* prod/rel: Maxim, Prisma

VON DER VRING, GEORGE
Schwarzer Jager Johanna, Novel
  Schwarzer Jager Johanna 1934 d: Johannes Meyer. lps: Marianne Hoppe, Paul Hartmann, Gustav Grundgens. 100M GRM. *Der Spione Des Kaisers* prod/rel: Terra-Film

VON EBNER-ESCHENBACH, MARIA
Krambambuli, 1887, Short Story
  Heimatland 1955 d: Franz Antel. lps: Rudolf Prack, Adrian Hoven, Marianne Hold. 99M AUS.
  Krambambuli 1940 d: Karl Kostlin. lps: Viktoria von Ballasko, Rudolf Prack, Sepp Rist. 80M AUS. *Die Geschichte Eines Hundes* prod/rel: Bavaria, Wien-Film
  Sie Nannten Ihn Krambambuli 1972 d: Franz Antel. lps: Michael Schanze, Christian Wolff, Fritz Wepper. 98M GRM/AUS. *They Called Him Krambambuli*

VON EICHENDORFF, JOSEPH (1798–1857), GRN, von Eichendorff, Joseph Freiherr
Aus Dem Leben Eines Taugenichts, 1826, Novel
  Aus Dem Leben Eines Taugenichts 1973 d: Celino Bleiweiss. lps: Dean Reed, Anna Dziadyk, Hannelore Eisner. 95M GDR.

Taugenichts 1978 d: Bernhard Sinkel. lps: Jacques Breuer, Mareike Carriere, Matthias Habich. 90M GRM. *The Good-for-Nothing*; *The Good-for-Nothings*

VON FLOTOW, FRIEDRICH (1812–1883), GRM
Martha, Vienna 1847, Opera
  Martha 1922 d: George Wynn. lps: Dorothy Fane, Leslie Austen, James Knight. 1184f UKN. prod/rel: Master Films, Gaumont
  Martha 1927 d: H. B. Parkinson. lps: Grizelda Hervey, Gerald Rawlinson, Algernon Hicks. 1608f UKN. prod/rel: Song Films
  Martha 1935 d: Karl Anton. lps: Carla Spletter, Helge Roswaenge, Fritz Kampers. 102M GRM. *Letzte Rose* prod/rel: Lloyd, Europa
  Martha 1935 d: Karl Anton. lps: Roger Bourdin, Courteille, Huguette Duflos. 106M FRN. *Les Dernieres Roses* prod/rel: Lloyd-Film

VON GEBHARDT, HERTHA
Und Finden Dereinst Wir Uns Wieder, Novel
  Und Finden Dereinst Wir Uns Wieder 1947 d: Hans Muller. lps: Paul Dahlke, Helmut Heyne, Kurt Langanke. 92M GRM. *And Should We Ever Meet Again* prod/rel: Studio, Herzog

VON GOETHE, JOHANN WOLFGANG (1749–1832), GRM
Aus Meinem Leben. Dichtung Und Wahrheit, 1811-33, Autobiography
  Friedericke 1932 d: Fritz Friedmann-Friedrich. 91M GRM.
  Goethe Lebt.! 1932 d: Eberhard Frowein. 82M GRM.
  Jugendgeliebte, Die 1930 d: Hans Tintner. lps: Elga Brink, Hans Stuwe, Jacob Tiedtke. 88M GRM. *Goethe's Jugendgeliebte* (USA); *Friederike von Sesenheim*
Clavigo, 1774, Play
  Clavigo 1970 d: Marcel Ophuls. MTV. 130M GRM.
Der Erlkonig, 1782, Verse
  Erlkonig, Der 1931 d: Peter P. Brauer, Marie-Louise Iribe. lps: Otto Gebuhr, Rosa Bertens, Joe Hamman. 51M GRM.
  Roi Des Aulnes, Le 1930 d: Marie-Louise Iribe. lps: Joe Hamman, Mary Costes, Otto Gebuhr. 70M FRN. *The Erl King* prod/rel: Les Artistes Reunis
Faust, 1808-32, Play
  Beaute du Diable, La 1950 d: Rene Clair. lps: Michel Simon, Gerard Philipe, Simone Valere. 92M FRN/ITL. *La Bellezza Del Diavolo* (ITL); *Beauty and the Devil* (USA); *Beauty and the Beast* (UKN) prod/rel: E.N.I.C., Franco London Films (Paris)
  Bedazzled 1967 d: Stanley Donen. lps: Peter Cook, Dudley Moore, Raquel Welch. 103M UKN. prod/rel: Stanley Donen Enterprises, 20ᵗʰ Century-Fox
  Faust 1910 d: Enrico Guazzoni. lps: Fernanda Negri-Pouget, Ugo Bazzini, Alfredo Bracci. 361m ITL. prod/rel: Cines
  Faust 1926 d: F. W. Murnau. lps: Gosta Ekman, Camilla Horn, Emil Jannings. 2484m GRM. *Faust - Eine Deutsche Volkssage* prod/rel: Universum, Atlas
  Faust 1960 d: Peter Gorski. lps: Will Quadflieg, Gustaf Grundgens, Ella Buchi. 128M GRM. prod/rel: Divina Film, Gloria
  Faust 1964 d: Michael Susman. 100M USA.
  Faust 1988 d: Dieter Dorn. lps: Helmut Griem, Romuald Pekny, Sunnyi Melles. 169M GRM. prod/rel: Bavaria, S.D.R.
  Faust XX 1966 d: Ion Popescu-Gopo. lps: Emil Botta, Iurie Darie, Jorj Voicu. 85M RMN. *Faustus XX*
  Leggenda Di Faust, La 1949 d: Carmine Gallone. lps: Italo Tajo, Nelly Corradi, Gino MatterA. 90M ITL. *Faust and the Devil*; *Faust E Margherita* prod/rel: Cineopera
  Walpurgis Night 1932 d: Howard Higgin. 20M USA.
Gotz von Berlichingen Mit Der Eisernen Hand, 1773, Play
  Gotz von Berlichingen 1955 d: Alfred Stoger, Josef Gielen. lps: Ewald Balser, Albin Skoda, Judith Holzmeister. 87M GRM. prod/rel: Wiener Mundus
  Gotz von Berlichingen Mit Der Eisernen Hand 1978 d: Wolfgang Liebeneiner. lps: Raimund Harmstorf, Klausjurgen Wassow, Michele Mercier. 103M GRM/YGS. *Gotz von Berlichingen*; *Man With the Iron Fist* prod/rel: Regina, Victoria
  Gotz von Berlichingen Zubenannt Mit Der Eisernen Hand 1925 d: Hubert Moest. lps: Eugen Klopfer, Friedrich Kuhne, Paul Hartmann. 2621m GRM.
Herman Und Dorothea, 1774, Verse
  Liebesleute 1935 d: Erich Waschneck. lps: Renate Muller, Gustav Frohlich, Heinrich Schroth. 96M GRM. *Hermann Und Dorothea von Heute*

Die Leiden Des Jungen Werthers, 1774, Novel
  Begegnung Mit Werther 1949 d: Karl H. Stroux. lps: Horst Caspar, Heidemarie Hatheyer, Paul Klinger. 88M GRM. *Werther Und Lotte*; *Encounter With Werther* prod/rel: Nova, Hamburg
  Leiden Des Jungen Werthers, Die 1976 d: Egon Gunther. lps: Hans-Jurgen Wolf, Katharina Thalbach, Hilmar Baumann. 102M GDR. *Sufferings of Young Werther*; *The Sorrows of Youn Werther* prod/rel: Defa
  Leidenschaftlichen, Die 1981 d: Thomas Koerfer. lps: Lutz Weidlich, Sunnyi Melles, Hanns Zischler. 105M SWT/GRM/AUS. *The Passionate Ones* prod/rel: ZDF, Orf
  Roman de Werther, Le 1938 d: Max Ophuls. lps: Pierre Richard-Willm, Jean Galland, Annie Vernay. 85M FRN. *Werther* prod/rel: Nero-Film
  Werther 1910 d: Henri Pouctal. lps: Andre Brule, Philippe Garnier, Laurence Duluc. 275m FRN. prod/rel: Film d'Art
Reineke Fuchs, 1794, Verse
  Black Fox, The 1962 d: Louis Clyde Stoumen. DOC. 89M USA. prod/rel: Image Productions, Animated Productions
Satyos, 1840, Play
  Rousseauism and the Young Goethe 1972 d: Alasdair Clayre. 25M UKN.
Die Wahlverwandtschaften, 1809, Novel
  Affinita Elettive, Le 1978 d: Gianni Amico. lps: Paolo Graziosi, Veronica Lazar, Francisca Archibugi. 135M ITL. *Elective Affinities* prod/rel: Rai
  Tagebuch 1975 d: Rudolf Thome. lps: Angelika Kettelhack, Cynthia Beatt, Rudolf Thome. 146M GRM. *Diary*
  Tarot 1985 d: Rudolf Thome. lps: Vera Tschechowa, Hanns Zischler, Rudiger Vogler. 120M GRM. prod/rel: Moana, Anthea
  Wahlverwandtschaften, Die 1974 d: Siegfried Kuhn. lps: Beata Tyczkiewicz, Hilmar Thate, Magda VasaryovA. 100M GDR. *Elective Affinities* prod/rel: Defa
Wilhelm Meisters Lehrjahre, 1795, Novel
  Falsche Bewegung 1975 d: Wim Wenders. lps: Rudiger Vogler, Hanna Schygulla, Hans Christian Blech. 103M GRM. *Wrong Movement* (UKN); *The Wrong Move* (USA) prod/rel: Solaris, Filmverlag Der Autoren

VON HACKLANDER, FRIEDRICH WILHELM
Europaisches Sklavenleben, Novel
  Europaisches Sklavenleben 1912 d: Emil Justitz. lps: Ludwig Hartau, Friedrich Zelnik, Carl Beckersachs. GRM. prod/rel: Bonanza-Kunstfilm

VON HARBOU, THEA (1888–1954), GRM
Die Frau Im Mond, Novel
  Frau Im Mond, Die 1929 d: Fritz Lang. lps: Gerda Maurus, Willy Fritsch, Klaus Pohl. 4356m GRM. *By Rocket to the Moon* (UKN); *Woman in the Moon*; *Girl in the Moon* prod/rel: Universum
Das Indische Grabmal, Novel
  Indische Grabmal, Das 1938 d: Richard Eichberg. lps: Kitty Jantzen, Frits Van Dongen, La JanA. F GRM. *The Indian Tomb*
  Indische Grabmal, Das 1959 d: Fritz Lang. lps: Debra Paget, Paul Hubschmid, Walther Reyer. 100M GRM/ITL/FRN. *Il Sepolcro Indiano* (ITL); *Le Tombeau Hindou* (FRN); *Journey to the Lost City*; *The Indian Tomb*
  Indische Grabmal I, Das 1921 d: Joe May. lps: Conrad Veidt, Mia May, Bernhard Goetzke. 2957m GRM. *Die Sendung Des Joghi*
  Indische Grabmal II, Das 1921 d: Joe May. lps: Conrad Veidt, Mia May, Bernhard Goetzke. 2534m GRM. *Der Tiger von Eschnapur*
  Tiger von Eschnapur, Der 1937 d: Richard Eichberg. lps: Kitty Jantzen, Frits Van Dongen, La JanA. F GRM.
  Tiger von Eschnapur, Der 1959 d: Fritz Lang. lps: Debra Paget, Paul Hubschmid, Walther Reyer. 101M GRM/ITL/FRN. *La Tigre Di Eschnapur* (ITL); *Le Tigre du Bengale* (FRN); *Tigress of Bengal*; *Tiger of Bengal* prod/rel: C.C.C., Gloria
  Tigre du Bengale, Le 1937 d: Richard Eichberg. lps: Max Michel, Roger Karl, Alice Field. 180M FRN. prod/rel: Societe Des Films Sonores Tobis
Spione, Novel
  Spione 1928 d: Fritz Lang. lps: Lien Deyers, Lupu Pick, Hertha von Walther. 4364m GRM. *The Spy* (UKN); *Spies* (USA) prod/rel: Universum

VON HEDENSTJERNA, ALFRED
Der Majoratsherr, Novel
  Majoratsherr, Der 1944 d: Hans Deppe. lps: Willy Birgel, Viktoria von Ballasko, Anneliese Uhlig. 87M GRM. prod/rel: UFA, Donau

VON HERZMANOVSKY, FRITZ
Kaiser Joseph Und Die Bahnwartertochter, Play
  Kaiser Joseph Und Die Bahnwartertochter 1962 d: Axel Corti. lps: Inge Konradi, Hans Moser, Hans Holt. 84M AUS. prod/rel: Filmco

VON HILLERN, WILHELMINE
Die Geierwally, Novel
  Geierwally, Die 1940 d: Hans Steinhoff. lps: Eduard Kock, Heidemarie Hatheyer, Winnie Markus. 102M GRM. *Wally and the Vultures* prod/rel: Tobis, Unitas
  Geierwally, Die 1956 d: Frantisek Cap. lps: Barbara Rutting, Carl Mohner, Til Kiwe. 90M GRM. prod/rel: Peter Ostermayr
  Geierwally, Die 1987 d: Walter Bockmayer. lps: Samy Orfgen, Gottfried Lackmann, Christoph Eichhorn. 91M GRM. prod/rel: Entenfilm, Pro-Ject
  Geier-Wally, Die 1921 d: E. A. Dupont. lps: Henny Porten, Wilhelm Dieterle, Albert Steinruck. 2155m GRM. *The Woman Who Killed a Vulture*; *Ein Roman Aus Den Bergen*; *Geierwally* prod/rel: Gloria-Film
  Wally, La 1932 d: Guido Brignone. lps: Germana Paolieri, Carlo Ninchi, Renzo Ricci. 84M ITL. prod/rel: Cines, Anonima Pittaluga
Reis Am Weg, Short Story
  Herz Schlagt Fur Dich, Ein 1955 d: Joe Stockel. lps: Rudolf Prack, Anneliese Reinhold, Curt Baumann. 79M GRM. *A Heart Beats for You* prod/rel: Bavaria, Schorcht

VON HOFMANNSTHAL, HUGO (1874–1929), AUS
Elektra, Dresden 1909, Opera
  Elektra 1970. lps: Gladys Kuchta, Regina Resnik, Ingrid Bjoner. MTV. F GRM. prod/rel: Polyphon Film & Tv Productions
Jedermann: Das Spiel von Sterben Des Reichen Mannes, 1911, Play
  Jedermann 1961 d: Gottfried Reinhardt. lps: Ewald Balser, Walther Reyer, Paula Wessely. 105M AUS. *Everyman* (USA); *The Salzburg Everyman* prod/rel: Durer
Der Rosenkavalier, Dresden 1911, Opera
  Rosenkavalier, Der 1926 d: Robert Wiene. lps: Michael Bohnen, Huguette Duflos, Paul Hartmann. 75M AUS. prod/rel: Pan-Film
  Rosenkavalier, Der 1962 d: Paul Czinner. lps: Elisabeth Schwarzkopf, Sena Jurinac, Anneliese Rothenberger. 195M UKN. prod/rel: Poetic Films, Rank
L' Uomo Difficile, Play
  Uomo Difficile, L' 1978 d: Giancarlo Cobelli. lps: Tino Schirinzi, Anna Maria Gherardi, Ennio GroggiA. MTV. F ITL. prod/rel: Mimika Film

VON HOLLANDER, WALTER
Licht Im Dunklen Haus, Novel
  Anna Favetti 1938 d: Erich Waschneck. lps: Brigitte Horney, Mathias Wieman, Maria Koppenhofer. 99M GRM. prod/rel: Fanal, Kristall

VON HORVATH, ODON (1901–1938), GRM
Geschichten Aus Dem Wiener Wald, 1931, Play
  Geschichten Aus Dem Wienerwald 1979 d: Maximilian Schell. lps: Birgit Doll, Hanno Poschl, Helmut Qualtinger. 90M AUS/GRM. *Tales from the Vienna Woods* (USA); *Stories of the Vienna Woods* prod/rel: M.F.G., Arabella
Hin Und Her, Play
  Hin Und Her 1950 d: Theo Lingen. lps: Theo Lingen, O. W. Fischer, Fritz Eckhardt. 86M AUS. prod/rel: J. A. Hubler-Kahla
Jugend Ohne Gott, 1938, Novel
  Wie Ich Ein Neger Wurde 1970 d: Roland Gall. lps: Gerd Baltus, Walter Ladengast, Wolf EubA. 97M GRM. *How I Became Black*; *How I Became a Negro* prod/rel: Roland Gall

VON KANEL, ROSY
Im Namen Der Liebe. Ein Bekenntnis, Leipzig 1938, Novel
  Fraulein Huser 1940 d: Leonard Steckel. lps: Trudi Stossel, Emil Hegetschweiler, Ellen Widmann. 104M SWT. *Mademoiselle Hauser* prod/rel: Praesens-Film

VON KIRCHBACH, MARIE
Geliebte Feindin, Novel
  Geliebte Feindin 1955 d: Rolf Hansen. lps: Werner Hinz, Ruth Leuwerik, Thomas Holtzmann. 100M GRM. *Beloved Enemy* prod/rel: N.D.F., D.F.H.

VON KLEIST, HEINRICH (1777–1811), GRM
Short Story
  Amour Interdit, L' 1984 d: Jean-Pierre Dougnac. lps: Brigitte Fossey, Fernando Rey, Saverio Marconi. 105M FRN/ITL/CND. prod/rel: Garance, Fr 3

Amphitryon, 1807, Play
  Amphitryon 1935 d: Reinhold Schunzel. lps: Willy Fritsch, Kathe Gold, Paul Kemp. 105M GRM. *Aus Den Wolken Kommt Das Gluck*; *Luck Comes Out of the Clouds* prod/rel: Universum, Transit
  Amphitryon 1981 d: Michael de Groot. 28M GRM.
Der Findling, 1811, Novel
  Findling, Der 1968 d: Georg Moorse. lps: Rudolf Fernau, Julie Felix, Titus Gerhardt. 74M GRM. *The Foundling* prod/rel: Literarisches Colloquium, Bayerischer Rundfunk
Die Marquise von O., 1810, Short Story
  Marquise d'O, La 1976 d: Eric Rohmer. lps: Edith Clever, Bruno Ganz, Peter Luhr. 102M FRN/GRM. *Die Marquise von O.* (GRM); *The Marquise of O.* (USA) prod/rel: Janus, Artemis
  Marquise von O., Die 1989 d: Hans-Jurgen Syberberg. lps: Edith Clever. 225M GRM.
Michel Kohlhaas, 1810, Short Story
  Michael Kohlhaas - Der Rebell 1969 d: Volker Schlondorff. lps: David Warner, Anna Karina, Anita Pallenberg. 99M GRM. *Michael Kohlhaas* (USA); *Michael Kohlhaas - the Rebel* prod/rel: Oceanic, Columbia
Penthesilea, 1808, Play
  Heinrich Penthesilea von Kleist 1983 d: Max Neuenfel. lps: Elisabeth Trissenaar, Hermann Treusch, Berta Drews. 144M GRM. *Traumereien Uber Eine Inszenierung*; *Heinrich von Kleist and Penthesilea* prod/rel: Regina Ziegler Filmprod.
  Penthesilea 1988 d: Hans-Jurgen Syberberg. lps: Edith Clever. 243M GRM. prod/rel: T.M.S.-Film, Schauspielhaus Frankfurt
Prinz Friedrich von Homburg, 1811, Play
  Principe Di Homburg, Il 1997 d: Marco Bellocchio. lps: Andrea Di Stefano, Barbara Bobulova, Toni Bertorelli. 85M ITL. *Heinrich von Kleist's the Prince of Homburg* prod/rel: Filmalbatros, Istituto Luce
Die Verlobung von San Domingo, 1811, Short Story
  San Domingo 1970 d: Hans-Jurgen Syberberg. lps: Michael Konig, Alice Ottawa, Carla Aulaulu. 138M GRM.
  Seduccion, La 1980 d: Arturo Ripstein. lps: Katy Jurado, Virdiana Alatriste, Gonzalo VegA. 85M MXC. *The Seduction*; *Victima de la Seduccion* prod/rel: Conacine
Der Zerbrochene Krug, 1811, Play
  Jungfer, Sie Gefallt Mir 1968 d: Gunter Reisch. 104M GDR. *I Like You Damsel*; *Girl I Like Her*; *The Maid Pleases Me*
  Zerbrochene Krug, Der 1937 d: Gustav Ucicky. lps: Emil Jannings, Angela Salloker, Paul Dahlke. 85M GRM. *The Broken Jug* prod/rel: Tobis-Magna, Donau

VON KRAFFT-EBING, RICHARD
Psychopathia Sexualis: Klinischfornsische Studie, Stuttgart 1886, Book
  On Her Bed of Roses 1966 d: Albert Zugsmith. lps: Ronald Warren, Sandra Lynn, Barbara Hines. 104M USA. prod/rel: Famous Players Corporation

VON KRUSENTJERNA, AGNES
Froknarna von Pahlen, Stockholm 1930-35, Novel
  Alskande Par 1964 d: Mai Zetterling. lps: Harriet Andersson, Gunnel Lindblom, Gio Petre. 118M SWD. *Loving Couples* (USA) prod/rel: Sandrews

VON LE FORT, GERTRUD
Die Letzte Am Schafott, 1931, Short Story
  Dialogue Des Carmelites, Le 1959 d: Philippe Agostini, Raymond-Leopold Bruckberger. lps: Pascale Audret, Jeanne Moreau, Alida Valli. 113M FRN/ITL. *I Dialoghi Delle Carmelitane* (ITL); *The Carmelites* (UKN) prod/rel: Champs-Elysees Productions, Titanus

VON LEHNER, ERICH
Il Pugno Del Potere, Diary
  Rose Di Danzica, Le 1979 d: Alberto BevilacquA. lps: Helmut Berger, Franco Nero, Roberto Posse. MTV. 93M ITL. *The Roses of Danzica* prod/rel: R.P.a., Rai Radiotelevisione Italiana

VON MECK, BARBARA
Beloved Friend, Book
  Music Lovers, The 1970 d: Ken Russell. lps: Richard Chamberlain, Glenda Jackson, Max Adrian. 123M UKN. *The Lonely Heart* prod/rel: United Artists, Russfilms

VON MOLLER
Intermezzo Am Abend, Play
  Alles Fur Gloria 1941 d: Carl Boese. lps: Laura Solari, Johannes Riemann, Lizzi Waldmuller. 94M GRM. prod/rel: Deka, Karp

VON MOLO, WALTER
Der Alte Fritz, Novel
  Alte Fritz 1, Der 1927 d: Gerhard Lamprecht. lps: Otto Gebuhr, Julia Serda, Berthold Reissig. 3404m GRM. *Friede*
  Alte Fritz 2, Der 1927 d: Gerhard Lamprecht. lps: Otto Gebuhr, Julia Serda, Berthold Reissig. 3213m GRM. *Ausklang*
  Alte Fritz, Der 1936 d: Johannes Meyer. lps: Otto Gebuhr, Hilde Korber, Lil Dagover. 98M GRM. *Fridericus* prod/rel: Diana, Turck
Ein Deutscher Ohne Deutschland, Novel
  Unendliche Weg, Der 1943 d: Hans Schweikart. lps: Eugen Klopfer, Eva Immermann, Hedwig Wangel. 99M GRM. *The Endless Way* prod/rel: Bavaria
Luise, Novel
  Luise, Konigin von Preussen 1931 d: Carl Froelich. lps: Henny Porten, Gustaf Grundgens, Ekkehard Arendt. 115M GRM. *Luise Queen of Prussia* prod/rel: Henny Porten-Filmproduktion

VON MOSENTHAL, RITTER
Leah the Forsaken, Short Story
  Leah the Forsaken 1908 d: Van Dyke Brooke. lps: Mary Fuller, Maurice Costello. 850f USA. prod/rel: Vitagraph Co. of America

VON MOSER, GUSTAV
Der Bibliothekar, Play
  Dalles Und Liebe 1914 d: Franz Schmelter. lps: Alfred Heynisch, Ludwig Sachs, Grete Weixler. GRM. prod/rel: Christoph Mulleneisen Sr.
  Private Secretary, The 1935 d: Henry Edwards. lps: Edward Everett Horton, Barry MacKay, Judy Gunn. 70M UKN. prod/rel: Twickenham, Twickenham Film Distributors
Krieg Im Frieden, 1880, Play
  Guerra in Tempo Di Pace 1914 d: Camillo de Riso. lps: Camillo de Riso, Letizia Quaranta, Fanny Ferrari. 2000m ITL. prod/rel: Film Artistica Gloria
  Manovre d'Amore 1941 d: Gennaro Righelli. lps: Antonio Gandusio, Jole Voleri, Clara Calamai. 82M ITL. *Guerra in Tempo Di Pace* prod/rel: I.C.I.

VON OESTEREN, F. W.
Die Pflicht Zu Schweigen, Novel
  Pflicht Zu Schweigen, Die 1927 d: Carl Wilhelm. lps: Marcella Albani, Vivian Gibson, Angelo Ferrari. 1973m GRM. prod/rel: Ama-Film

VON PERFALL, ANTON
Die Finsternis Und Ihr Eigentum, Novel
  Finsternis Und Ihr Eigentum, Die 1914 d: Paul von Woringen. lps: Wladimir Maximoff, Carl Goetz, Robert Garrison. 1889m GRM. prod/rel: Deutsche Mutoskop Und Biograph

VON PETEANI, MARIA
D-Zug 517, Novel
  Sehnsucht Des Herzens 1951 d: Paul Martin. lps: Hans Hotter, Linda Caroll, Rainer Penkert. 78M GRM. *Fruhlingsromanze*; *Yearning of the Heart* prod/rel: Klagemann, Danubia

VON REITZENSTEIN, HANS JOACHIM FREIHERR
Oberwachtmeister Schwenke, Novel
  Oberwachtmeister Schwenke 1935 d: Carl Froelich. lps: Gustav Frohlich, Marianne Hoppe, Emmy Sonnemann. 90M GRM. *Der Vielgeliebte* prod/rel: Carl Froelich
  Oberwachtmeister Borck 1955 d: Gerhard Lamprecht. lps: Gerhard Riedmann, Annemarie Duringer, Ralph Lothar. 99M GRM. *Police Lieutenant Borck* prod/rel: Algefa, N.F.

VON REZNICEK, FELICITAS
Novel
  Zug Fahrt Ab, Ein 1942 d: Johannes Meyer. lps: Leny Marenbach, Ferdinand Marian, Lucie Englisch. 91M GRM. prod/rel: Bavaria, D.F.V.
Shiva Und Die Nacht Der Zwolf, Novel
  Nacht Der Zwolf, Die 1945 d: Hans Schweikart. lps: Ferdinand Marian, Elsa Wagner, Dagny Servaes. 92M GRM. *Die Nacht Der 12* prod/rel: Bavaria, Kristall

VON RHODEN, EMMY
Svehlavicka, Novel
  Svehlavicka 1926 d: Rudolf Mestak. lps: Marie Kalmarova, Karel Jicinsky, Marta Harlasova-SchredrovA. 2496m CZC. *A Self-Willed Girl* prod/rel: Favoritfilm, Republicfilm

VON SACHER-MASOCH, LEOPOLD (1836–1895), AUS
Novel
  Vierte Zeit, Die 1984 d: Klaus Andre. lps: Bernhard Minetti, Ulrich Gehbauer, Katharina Hill. 80M GRM. *The Fourth Time* prod/rel: Berliner Filmladen

Venus in Furs, Novel
Verfuhrung: Die Grausame Frau 1984 d: Elfi Mikesch, Monika Treut. lps: Mechthild Grossmann, Udo Kier, Sheila McLaughlin. 84M GRM. *Seduction: the Cruel Woman* prod/rel: Hyane

VON SCHILLER, FRIEDRICH (1759–1805), GRM, von Schiller, Johan Christoph Friedrich
Die Braut von Messina, 1803, Play
Chamsin 1970 d: Veit Relin. lps: Maria Schell, Gerald Robard, Neda Arneric. 86M GRM/ISR. prod/rel: Schell-Relin
Fidanzata Di Messina, La 1911 d: Mario Caserini. lps: Maria Righelli, Gennaro Righelli. 311m ITL. *The Bride of Messina* (UKN) prod/rel: Cines
Don Carlos, 1787, Play
Carlos 1971 d: Hans W. Geissendorfer. lps: Gottfried John, Bernhard Wicki, Geraldine Chaplin. 105M GRM/ISR. prod/rel: Wdr, B.R.
Don Carlos 1921 d: Giulio Antamoro. lps: Enrico Roma, Elena Lunda, Alfredo Bertone. 1637m ITL. prod/rel: Nova Film
Don Carlos 1950 d: Alfred Stoger. lps: Ewald Balser, Walther Reyer, Aglaja Schmid. 100M AUS. prod/rel: Thalia
Don Carlos 1963 d: Franz Peter Wirth. 190M GRM.
Rival de Son Pere 1909 d: Andre Calmettes. lps: Emile Dehelly, Paul Mounet, Julia Bartet. FRN. prod/rel: le Film d'Art
Fiesco, 1783, Play
Congiura Di Fieschi, La 1911. lps: Francesca Bertini. 375m ITL/FRN. *La Conjuration de Fiesco (1547)* (FRN); *The Genoese Conspiracy* (UKN) prod/rel: Pathe Freres, Film d'Arte Italiana
Der Handschuh, Poem
Guanto, Il 1910 d: Luigi Maggi. lps: Mary Cleo Tarlarini, Alberto A. Capozzi, Mario Voller Buzzi. 225m ITL. *Il Guanto Da Festa*; *The Glove* (USA) prod/rel: S.A. Ambrosio
Kabale Und Liebe, 1784, Play
Kabale Und Liebe 1959 d: Martin Hellberg. lps: Wolf Kaiser, Karola Ebeling. 110M GDR. *Intrigue and Love* prod/rel: Defa
Luisa Miller 1910. 348m ITL. *Louisa Miller* (USA) prod/rel: Itala Film
Luisa Miller 1911 d: Ugo FalenA. 380m ITL. prod/rel: Film d'Arte Italiana
Das Lied von Der Glocke, 1799, Poem
Campana, La 1909. lps: Amleto Novelli, Maria Caserini Gasparini, Giuseppe GambardellA. 232m ITL. *The Bell* (UKN) prod/rel: Cines
Maria Stuart, 1801, Play
Maria Stuart 1959 d: Alfred Stoger, Leopold Lindtberg. lps: Judith Holzmeister, Liselotte Schreiner, Albin SkodA. 104M AUS.
Die Rauber, 1782, Play
Masnadieri, I 1911 d: Mario Caserini. lps: Amleto Novelli. 345m ITL. *The Robbers* (UKN) prod/rel: Cines
VON SCHILLER, FRIEDRICH
Robbers, The 1913 d: Walter Edwin, J. Searle Dawley. lps: Mary Fuller, Barry O'Moore, Robert Brower. 1000f USA. prod/rel: Edison
VON SCHILLER, FRIEDRICH (1759–1805), GRM, von Schiller, Johan Christoph Friedrich
Der Verschworung des Fiesko Zu Genua, 1784, Play
Congiura Dei Fieschi, La 1921 d: Ugo FalenA. lps: Goffredo d'Andrea, Silvia Malinverni, Ignazio Mascalchi. 1435m ITL. prod/rel: Bernini Film
Wahren Geschichte, Play
Verbrecher Aus Verlorener Ehre, Der 1913. GRM. prod/rel: Uranus-Film
Wallenstein, 1800, Play
Wallenstein 1962 d: Franz Peter Wirth. 245M GRM.
Wilhelm Tell, 1804, Play
Guglielmo Tell 1911 d: Ugo FalenA. lps: Giuseppe Kaschmann, Bianca Lorenzoni. 297m ITL. *William Tell* (UKN) prod/rel: Film d'Arte Italiana
Guglielmo Tell 1949 d: Giorgio PastinA. lps: Gino Cervi, Monique Orban, Paul Muller. 86M GRM. *L'Arciere Della Foresta Nera* prod/rel: Fauno Film, Icet
Guillaume Tell 1912 d: Georg Wackerlein. lps: Carl Barbier, August Fluckiger, Hans Aerni. SWT. *Wilhelm Tell* prod/rel: Dramatischer Verein Interlaken
Guillaume Tell 1913 d: Friedrich Feher. lps: Karl Kienlechner, Friedrich Feher, Margarete Wilkens. SWT/GRM. *Wilhelm Tell*; *Die Befreiung Der Schweiz Und Die Sage Vom Wilhelm Tell*; *Wilhelm Tell Oder Die Befreiung Der Schweiz* prod/rel: Deutsche Mutoskop Und Biograph
Guillaume Tell 1914. SWT. prod/rel: Lemania-Film
Wilhelm Tell 1921 d: Friedrich Genhardt. 2000m SWT. prod/rel: Friedrich Genhardt

Wilhelm Tell 1934 d: Heinz Paul. lps: Hans Marr, Conrad Veidt, Emmy Sonnemann. 99M GRM/SWT. *The Legend of William Tell* (USA); *Guillaume Tell* prod/rel: Terra-Film, Schweizer-Produktion Der Terra-Film
Wilhelm Tell 1956 d: Alfred Stoger, Josef Gielen. lps: Ewald Balser, Albin Skoda, Raoul Aslan. 90M AUS.
Wilhelm Tell - Bergen in Flammen 1960 d: Michel Dickoff, Karl Hartl. lps: Robert Freitag, Hannes Schmidthauser, Maria Becker. 90M SWT. *Guillaume Tell*; *Wilhelm Tell - Flammende Berge*; *Bergfeuer Lodern*; *Guglielmo Tell - la Freccia Del Giustiziere*; *Wilhelm Tells Kampf Um Die Freiheit* prod/rel: Urs-Film

VON SCHONTHAN, FRANZ
Krieg Im Frieden, 1880, Play
Guerra in Tempo Di Pace 1914 d: Camillo de Riso. lps: Camillo de Riso, Letizia Quaranta, Fanny Ferrari. 2000m ITL. prod/rel: Film Artistica Gloria
Manovre d'Amore 1941 d: Gennaro Righelli. lps: Antonio Gandusio, Jole Voleri, Clara Calamai. 82M ITL. *Guerra in Tempo Di Pace* prod/rel: I.C.I.
Der Raub Der Sabinerinnen, Play
Raub Der Sabinerinnen, Der 1919 d: Heinrich Bolten-Baeckers. lps: Richard Alexander. 1313m GRM. prod/rel: Bb-Film-Fabrikation
Raub Der Sabinerinnen, Der 1928 d: Robert Land. lps: Ralph Arthur Roberts, Maria Paudler, Wolfgang Zilzer. 2172m GRM. prod/rel: Super-Film
Raub Der Sabinerinnen, Der 1936 d: R. A. Stemmle. lps: Bernhard Wildenhain, Max Gulstorff, Maria Koppenhofer. 93M GRM. prod/rel: Carl Frohlich, Europa
Raub Der Sabinerinnen, Der 1954 d: Kurt Hoffmann. lps: Paul Horbiger, Fita Benkhoff, Gustav Knuth. 90M GRM. *Theft of the Sabines* prod/rel: C.C.C., N.F.

VON SCHONTHAN, PAUL
Raub Der Sabinerinnen, Der 1919 d: Heinrich Bolten-Baeckers. lps: Richard Alexander. 1313m GRM. prod/rel: Bb-Film-Fabrikation
Raub Der Sabinerinnen, Der 1928 d: Robert Land. lps: Ralph Arthur Roberts, Maria Paudler, Wolfgang Zilzer. 2172m GRM. prod/rel: Super-Film
Raub Der Sabinerinnen, Der 1936 d: R. A. Stemmle. lps: Bernhard Wildenhain, Max Gulstorff, Maria Koppenhofer. 93M GRM. prod/rel: Carl Frohlich, Europa
Raub Der Sabinerinnen, Der 1954 d: Kurt Hoffmann. lps: Paul Horbiger, Fita Benkhoff, Gustav Knuth. 90M GRM. *Theft of the Sabines* prod/rel: C.C.C., N.F.

VON SIMPSON, MARGOT
Le Secret Des Woronzeff, Novel
Secret Des Woronzeff, Le 1934 d: Andre Beucler, Arthur Robison. lps: Brigitte Helm, Vladimir Sokoloff, Gaston Dubosc. 85M FRN. prod/rel: U.F.a., a.C.E.

VON SIMPSON, WILLIAM
Die Barrings, Novel
Barrings, Die 1955 d: Rolf Thiele. lps: Dieter Borsche, Nadja Tiller, Paul Hartmann. 108M GRM. *The Barrings* prod/rel: Roxy, Deutsche London

VON SODERHOLM, MARGIT
All'irdisch Freud, Novel
All Jordens Frojd 1953 d: Rolf Husberg. lps: Ulla Jacobsson, Birger Malmsten, Carl-Henrik Fant. 120M SWD. *All the Joy of Earth* prod/rel: Sandrew Baumann

VON SPALLART, JOHANNES
Tintenspritzer, Play
Alltagliche Geschichte, Eine 1945 d: Gunther Rittau. lps: Gustav Frohlich, Marianne Simson, Karl Schonbock. 80M GRM. prod/rel: Tobis

VON STIGLER, KARL
Eine Insel Entdeckt, Play
Pat Und Patachon Im Paradies 1937 d: Carl Lamac. lps: Carl Schenstrom, Harald Madsen, Lucie Englisch. 69M AUS. prod/rel: Atlantis

VON STROHEIM, ERICH (1885–1957), AUS
The Pinnacle, Book
Blind Husbands 1918 d: Erich von Stroheim. lps: Erich von Stroheim, Gibson Gowland, Sam de Grasse. 8r USA. *Pinnacle* prod/rel: Universal Film Mfg. Co.©

VON SUPPE, FRANZ
Boccaccio, Opera
Boccaccio 1940 d: Marcello Albani. lps: Clara Calamai, Osvaldo Valenti, Silvana Jachino. 80M ITL. prod/rel: Venus, Scalera Film

VON TEMPSKI, ARMINE
Hula - a Romance of Hawaii, New York 1927, Novel
Hula 1927 d: Victor Fleming. lps: Clara Bow, Clive Brook, Arlette Marchal. 5862f USA. prod/rel: Paramount Famous Lasky Corp.

VON TILZER, HARRY
The Mansion of Aching Hearts, 1902, Song
Mansion of Aching Hearts, The 1925 d: James P. Hogan. lps: Ethel Clayton, Barbara Bedford, Priscilla Bonner. 6147f USA. prod/rel: B. P. Schulberg Productions

VON UHLAND, BERTHE
Solstizio Di Tenebre, Book
Lunghe Notti Della Gestapo, Le 1977 d: Fabio de Agostini. lps: Ezio Miani, Fred Williams, Isabelle Marchal. 102M ITL. *The Red Nights of the Gestapo* (UKN) prod/rel: Eurogroup Film Dist. of Italy

VON VASZARY, GABOR
Bubusch, Play
Wir Werden Das Kind Schon Schaukeln 1952 d: E. W. Emo. lps: Heinz Ruhmann, Hans Moser, Theo Lingen. 87M AUS. *Brigitte Scham Dich* prod/rel: Styria, Gloria
Heirate Mich Cheri, Novel
Heirate Mich, Cheri 1964 d: Axel von Ambesser. lps: Jana Brejchova, Walter Giller, Paul Hubschmid. 92M GRM/AUS. *Marry Me Cheri* prod/rel: Schlaraffia, Sascha
Ich MacH' Dich Glucklich, Play
Ich MacH' Dich Glucklich 1949 d: Alexander von Szlatinay. lps: Heinz Ruhmann, Hertha Feiler, Karl Schonbock. 92M GRM. *I'll Make You Happy* prod/rel: Comedia, Bavaria
Monpti, Novel
Montpi 1957 d: Helmut Kautner. lps: Romy Schneider, Horst Buchholz, Mara Lane. 101M GRM. *Love from Paris*; *Mon Petit* prod/rel: Neue Deutsche Filmgesellschaft, UFA
Sie, Novel
Sie 1954 d: Rolf Thiele. lps: Marina Vlady, Walter Giller, Nadja Tiller. 92M GRM. *She* prod/rel: Filmaufbau, UFA

VON VASZARY, JOHANN
Ich Vertraue Dir Meine Frau an, Play
Ich Vertraue Dir Meine Frau an 1943 d: Kurt Hoffmann. lps: Heinz Ruhmann, Lil Adina, Else von Mollendorff. 88M GRM. prod/rel: Terra, Donau
Sag Die Wahrheit, Play
Sag' Die Wahrheit 1946 d: Helmut Weiss. lps: Gustav Frohlich, Mady Rahl, Ingeborg von Kusserow. 96M GRM. *Tell the Truth* prod/rel: Studio 45, I.X.a.

VON WEBER, CARL MARIA
Der Freischutz, Berlin 1821, Opera
Freischutz, Der 1968 d: Joachim Hess. lps: Tom Krause, Toni Blankenheim, Arlene Saunders. MTV. 127M GRM. *The Free-Shooter*; *The Marksman* prod/rel: Polyphon Film & Tv Productions

VON WILDENBRUCH, ERNST (1845–1909), GRM
Das Edle Blut, Short Story
Edle Blut, Das 1927 d: Carl Boese. lps: Hanna Ralph, Harry Hardt, Wolfgang Zilzer. 2452m GRM. prod/rel: Phoebus-Film
Die Haubenlerche, Play
Wenn Menschen Reif Zur Liebe Werden 1927 d: Jacob Fleck, Luise Fleck. lps: Evelyn Holt, Henry Stuart, Fritz Kampers. 2145m GRM. *Die Haubenlerche* prod/rel: Hegewald-Film
Das Hexenlied, Poem
Heksenlied, Het 1928 d: Jan Van Dommelen. lps: Mientje Van Kerckhoven-Kling, Jan Van Dommelen, Constant Van Kerckhoven. 600m NTH. **De Bekentenis Van Broeder Medardus**; *The Song of the Witch*; *The Confession of Brother Medardus* prod/rel: Jan Van Dommelen

VON WOEDTKE, FRITZ
Daphne Und Der Diplomat, Novel
Daphne Und Der Diplomat 1937 d: R. A. Stemmle. lps: Karin Hardt, Gerda Maurus, Hans Nielsen. 100M GRM. prod/rel: F.D.F., Fabrikation Deutscher Film
Sophienlund, Play
Sophienlund 1943 d: Heinz Ruhmann. lps: Harry Liedtke, Kathe Haack, Hannelore Schroth. 92M GRM. prod/rel: Terra, D.F.V.

VON WOHL, LUDWIG
Die Englische Heirat, Novel
Englische Heirat, Die 1934 d: Reinhold Schunzel. lps: Adele Sandrock, Hans Richter, Renate Muller. 97M GRM. prod/rel: Cine-Allianz, Neue Filmkunst
Harry McGills Geheime Sendung, Novel
Mein Freund Harry 1928 d: Max Obal. lps: Harry Liedtke, Maria Paudler, Bruno Kastner. 2322m GRM. prod/rel: Aafa-Film Ag

Der Schwerverbrecher Jimmy, Novel
Grosste Gauner Des Jahrhunderts, Der 1927 d: Max Obal. lps: Luciano Albertini, Gritta Ley, Hans Albers. 2459m GRM. prod/rel: Aafa-Film Ag

Lillebil Aus U.S.A., Novel
Madel Mit Temperament, Ein 1928 d: Victor Janson. lps: Maria Paudler, Luigi Serventi, Harry Gondi. 1908m GRM. prod/rel: Erda-Film

Lord Spleen, Novel
Jagd Nach Der Million, Die 1930 d: Max Obal. lps: Luciano Albertini, Gretl Berndt, Elza Temary. 2500m GRM. *The Chase for Millions* prod/rel: Aafa-Film Ag

Der Prasident von Costa Nuova, Novel
Prasident, Der 1928 d: Gennaro Righelli. lps: Ivan Mosjoukine, Suzy Vernon, Nikolai Malikoff. F GRM. *The President* prod/rel: Greenbaum-Film

Punks Kommt Aus Amerika, Novel
Punks Kommt Aus Amerika 1935 d: Karl Heinz Martin. lps: Attila Horbiger, Sybille Schmitz, Oskar SimA. 90M GRM. prod/rel: Robert Neppach, Herzog

Der Vagabund Vom Aquator, Novel
Wenn du Einmal Dein Herz Verschenkst 1929 d: Johannes Guter. lps: Lilian Harvey, Igo Sym, Harry Halm. 2310m GRM. *The Equator Tramp* prod/rel: UFA

Die Weisse Frau Des Maharadscha, Novel
Donna Fra Due Mondi, Una 1936 d: Goffredo Alessandrini, Arthur M. Rabenalt. lps: Isa Miranda, Giulio Donadio, Vasa PrihodA. 80M ITL. *Una Donna Tra Due Mondi* prod/rel: Astra Film, E.N.I.C.

Liebe Des Maharadscha, Die 1936 d: Arthur M. Rabenalt. lps: Isa Miranda, Hilde von Stolz, Gustav Diessl. 87M GRM. *Die Weisse Frau Des Maharadscha*; *Between Two Worlds* (USA); *The Maharaja's Love*

VON WOLZOGEN, ERNST
Der Kraft-Mayr, Novel
Wenn Die Musik Nicht War' 1935 d: Carmine Gallone. lps: Paul Horbiger, Sybille Schmitz, Karin Hardt. 89M GRM. *Das Lied Der Liebe*; *Der Kraft-Mayr*; *Liszt Rhapsody* prod/rel: F.D.F., Bavaria

VON ZELL, F.
Nanon, Play
Nanon 1924 d: Hanns Schwarz. lps: Agnes Esterhazy, Harry Liedtke, Hanni Weisse. 2475m GRM. prod/rel: Trianon-Film Ag

Nanon 1938 d: Herbert Maisch. lps: Erna Sack, Johannes Heesters, Otto Gebuhr. 80M GRM. prod/rel: UFA, Paikert

VON ZOBELTITZ, FEDOR
Drei Madchen Am Spinnrad, Novel
Komplott Auf Erlenhof 1950 d: Carl Froelich. lps: Hans Stuwe, Adelheid Seeck, Georg ThomallA. 110M GRM. *Mutti Muss Heiraten*; *Drei Madchen Spinnen*; *Mom Has to Get Married* prod/rel: Carl Froelich, N.F.

Das Fraulein Und Der Levantiner, Novel
Strafling Aus Stambul, Der 1929 d: Gustav Ucicky. lps: Betty Amann, Heinrich George, Paul Horbiger. 2560m GRM. prod/rel: UFA

VON ZOBELTITZ, H. C.
Kora Terry, Novel
Kora Terry 1940 d: Georg Jacoby. lps: Marika Rokk, Will Quadflieg, Josef Sieber. 106M GRM. prod/rel: UFA, Kristall

VONNEGUT JR., KURT (1922–, USA
Breakfast of Champions, 1976, Novel
Breakfast of Champions 1999 d: Alan Rudolph. lps: Bruce Willis, Albert Finney, Nick Nolte. 110M USA. prod/rel: Summit Entertainment, Flying Heart Films

Happy Birthday, Wanda June, 1971, Play
Happy Birthday, Wanda Jane 1971 d: Mark Robson. lps: Rod Steiger, Susannah York, George Grizzard. 105M USA.

Harrison Bergeron, Short Story
Kurt Vonnegut's Harrison Bergeron 1995 d: Bruce Pittman. lps: Sean Astin, Miranda Depencier, Christopher Plummer. TVM. 90M CND/USA.

Mother Night, Novel
Mother Night 1996 d: Keith Gordon. lps: Nick Nolte, Sheryl Lee, Alan Arkin. 114M USA. prod/rel: New Line Productions, Fine Line Features

Next Door, 1968, Short Story
Next Door 1975 d: Andrew Silver. 24M USA.

Slapstick Or Lonesome No More!, 1976, Novel
Slapstick (of Another Kind) 1984 d: Steven Paul. lps: Jerry Lewis, Madeline Kahn, Marty Feldman. 87M USA. *Slapstick* prod/rel: International Film Marketing, Entertainment Releasing Corp.

Slaughterhouse Five, 1969, Novel
Slaughterhouse Five 1972 d: George Roy Hill. lps: Michael Sacks, Ron Leibman, Eugene Roche. 104M USA. prod/rel: Universal

Who Am I This Time?, 1968, Short Story
Who Am I This Time? 1981 d: Jonathan Demme. lps: Christopher Walken, Susan Sarandon, Robert Ridgely. TVM. 60M USA.

VORSE, MARY HEATON
A Runaway Enchantress, Story
Sea Tiger, The 1927 d: John Francis Dillon. lps: Milton Sills, Mary Astor, Larry Kent. 5606f USA. *The Runaway Enchantress* prod/rel: First National Pictures

VOSKOVEC, JIRI
Rub a Lic, Play
Svet Patri Nam 1937 d: Martin Fric. lps: Jiri Voskovec, Jan Werich, Vladimir Smeral. 2625m CZC. *The World Belongs to Us*; *The World Is Ours* prod/rel: Ab

VOSPER, FRANK
Murder on the Second Floor, London 1929, Play
Murder on the Second Floor 1932 d: William McGann. lps: John Longden, Pat Paterson, Sydney Fairbrother. 70M UKN. prod/rel: Warner Bros., First National

Shadows on the Stairs 1941 d: D. Ross Lederman. lps: Bruce Lester, Frieda Inescort, Heather Angel. 63M USA. prod/rel: Warner Bros.

VOSS, RICHARD
Alexandra, Play
Alexandra 1914 d: Curt A. Stark. lps: Henny Porten, Fritz Feher, Henny Steimann. 1324m GRM. *Die Rache Ist Mein* prod/rel: Messter-Film

Alpentragodie, Novel
Alpentragodie 1927 d: Robert Land. lps: Lucy Doraine, Arnold Korff, Wladimir Gaidarow. 2450m GRM. prod/rel: Deutsche Film-Union Ag

Schuldig, Play
Perjury 1921 d: Harry Millarde. lps: William Farnum, Sally Crute, Wallace Erskine. 8372f USA. prod/rel: Fox Film Corp.

Schuldig 1927 d: Johannes Meyer. lps: Jenny Hasselqvist, Suzy Vernon, Willy Fritsch. 2684m GRM. prod/rel: UFA

Villa Falconieri, Novel
Villa Falconieri 1929 d: Richard Oswald. lps: Maria Jacobini, Hans Stuwe, Clifford McLaglen. 2266m ITL/GRM. *At the Villa Falconer* (UKN) prod/rel: Richard Oswald-Film, S.A. Pittaluga

Zwei Menschen, Novel
Zwei Menschen 1923 d: Hanns Schwarz. lps: Olaf Fjord, Agnes Esterhazy, Prof. Jacoby. 2642m GRM. prod/rel: Trianon-Film Co.

Zwei Menschen 1930 d: Erich Waschneck. lps: Lucie Englisch, Gustav Frohlich, Friedrich Kayssler. F GRM. *Two Lives*; *Two Humans*

Zwei Menschen 1952 d: Paul May. lps: Edith Mill, Helmuth Schneider, Alice Verden. 100M GRM. *Two People* prod/rel: Minerva, D.F.H.

VRBA, JAN
Bozi Mlyny, Novel
Bozi Mlyny 1929 d: Josef Medeotti-Bohac. lps: Alexander Trebovsky, Jan W. Speerger, L. H. StrunA. 2594m CZC. *God's Mills* prod/rel: Starfilm

Bozi Mlyny 1938 d: Vaclav Wasserman. lps: Karel Cerny, Ladislav Bohac, Karel Benisko. 2466m CZC. *God's Mills* prod/rel: Meissner, Gloria

Gottes Muhlen, Die 1938 d: Josef Medeotti-Bohac. lps: Willy Bauer, Viktor Afritsch, Karl Trabauer. 2460m GRM/CZC. *The Mills of the Gods*; *Gottes Muhlen Mahlen Langsam* prod/rel: Meissner, Gloria

VRBSKY, BEDRICH
Zazracny Lekar, Play
Jeji Lekar 1933 d: Vladimir Slavinsky. lps: Hugo Haas, Jindrich Plachta, Antonie NedosinskA. 3021m CZC. *Her Doctor* prod/rel: UFA

VREELAND, SUSAN
What Love Sees, Book
What Love Sees 1996 d: Michael Switzer. lps: Richard Thomas, Annabeth Gish, August Schellenberg. TVM. 93M USA. prod/rel: Rosemont Productions©

VRIGNY, ROGER
Fin de Journee, Novel
Sous le Signe du Taureau 1968 d: Gilles Grangier. lps: Jean Gabin, Suzanne Flon, Colette Dereal. 81M FRN. *Fin de Journee* prod/rel: Gaumont International

VROMAN, MARY ELIZABETH
See How They Run, Short Story
Bright Road 1953 d: Gerald Mayer. lps: Dorothy Dandridge, Philip Hepburn, Harry Belafonte. 68M USA. *See How They Run* prod/rel: MGM

VUILLERMOT, GUILLAUME
Vecchi Sofismi, Play
Non Vendo Mia Figlia! 1920 d: Nicola Fausto Neroni. lps: Fulvia Fulvi, Ignazio Mascalchi, Dante Capelli. 1774m ITL. prod/rel: Capitolium Film

VULLIAMY, C. E.
Don Among the Dead Men, London 1952, Novel
Jolly Bad Fellow, A 1963 d: Don Chaffey. lps: Leo McKern, Janet Munro, Maxine Audley. 96M UKN. *They All Died Laughing* (USA); *For He's a Jolly Bad Fellow* prod/rel: Tower Films, Pax

William Penn, Book
Penn of Pennsylvania 1941 d: Lance Comfort. lps: Clifford Evans, Deborah Kerr, Dennis Arundell. 79M UKN. *The Courageous Mr. Penn* (USA) prod/rel: British National, Anglo-American

VULPUIS, PAUL
Youth at the Helm, Play
Jack of All Trades 1936 d: Jack Hulbert, Robert Stevenson. lps: Jack Hulbert, Gina Malo, Robertson Hare. 76M UKN. *The Two of Us* (USA) prod/rel: Gainsborough, Gaumont-British

VYAS, BHARAT
Ramu Chanana, Play
Mhari Pyari Chanana 1983 d: Jatin Kumar. lps: Satyajit Puri, Pooja Saxena, Ramesh Tiwari. 130M IND. prod/rel: Jayashree Ents.

VYASA
Mahabharata, Poem
Mahabharata 1989 d: Peter Brook. lps: Robert Langdon Lloyd, Antonin Stahly-Vishwanadan, Bruce Myers. 330M FRN/UKN. prod/rel: Les Productions Du 3Eme Etage

VYSKOCIL, QUIDO MARIA
Posledni Vlkodlak, Novel
Vyznavaci Slunce 1925 d: Vaclav Binovec. lps: Luigi Serventi, Vlasta Petrovicova, L. H. StrunA. 1940m CZC. *The Sun Disciples*; *Posledni Vlkodlak*; *The Last Werewolf* prod/rel: Weteb, Elekta

W

WACHTER, F. K.
Kiebich Und Dutz, Play
Kiebich Und Dutz 1987 d: F. K. Wachter. lps: Michael Altmann, Heinz Kraehkamp. 88M GRM. prod/rel: Salina, S.F.B.

WADA, DEN
Iwasigumo, Novel
Iwashigumo 1958 d: Mikio Naruse. lps: Ganjiro Nakamura, Chikage Awashima, Michiyo AratamA. 128M JPN. *Herringbone Clouds*; *Summer Clouds* prod/rel: Toho Co.

WADDE, C. C.
So This Is Arizona, 1921, Serial Story
So This Is Arizona 1922 d: Francis Ford. lps: Franklyn Farnum, Francis Ford, Shorty Hamilton. 6r USA. prod/rel: William M. Smith Productions, Merit Film Corp.

WADDELL, MARTIN
Otley, London 1966, Novel
Otley 1968 d: Dick Clement. lps: Tom Courtenay, Romy Schneider, Alan Badel. 91M UKN. prod/rel: Open Road Films, Bruce Cohn Curtis Films

WADE, PHILIP
Wedding Group, Radio Play
Wedding Group 1936 d: Alex Bryce, Campbell Gullan. lps: Fay Compton, Barbara Greene, Patric Knowles. 70M UKN. *Wrath of Jealousy* (USA) prod/rel: Fox British

WADKA, HANSA
Sangtye Aika, 1970, Autobiography
Bhumika 1977 d: Shyam Benegal. lps: Smita Patil, Anant Nag, Amrish Puri. 142M IND. *The Role* (USA) prod/rel: Blaze Film Ents.

WADLER, JOYCE
My Breast, Autobiography
My Breast 1994 d: Betty Thomas. lps: Meredith Baxter, Jamey Sheridan, James Sutorius. TVM. 88M USA. prod/rel: Diane Kerew Prods., Polone

WADSLEY, OLIVE
Short Story
Stolen Hours 1918 d: Travers Vale. lps: Ethel Clayton, John Bowers, Joseph Herbert. 5r USA. prod/rel: World Film Corp.©

Belonging, New York 1920, Novel
Belonging 1922 d: F. Martin Thornton. lps: Barbara Hoffe, Hugh Buckler, William Lenders. 5253f UKN. prod/rel: Stoll

In Every Woman's Life 1924 d: Irving Cummings. lps: Virginia Valli, Lloyd Hughes, Marc MacDermott. 6300f USA. prod/rel: Associated First National Pictures

The Flame, Novel
Flame, The 1920 d: F. Martin Thornton. lps: Evelyn Boucher, Reginald Fox, Dora de Winton. 6358f UKN. prod/rel: Stoll

Frailty, Novel
Frailty 1921 d: F. Martin Thornton. lps: Madge Stuart, Roland Myles, Sydney Lewis Ransome. 5966f UKN. prod/rel: Stoll

Possession, Novel
Possession 1919 d: Henry Edwards. lps: Henry Edwards, Chrissie White, Gerald Ames. 5275f UKN. prod/rel: Hepworth, Butcher

WAGENHEIM, KARL
Babe Ruth: His Life & Legend, Book
Babe Ruth 1991 d: Mark Tinker. lps: Stephen Lang, Bruce Weitz, Brian Doyle-Murray. TVM. 100M USA. *The Babe*

WAGER, WALTER
58 Minutes, Novel
Die Hard 2 - Die Harder 1990 d: Renny Harlin. lps: Bruce Willis, Bonnie Bedelia, William Atherton. 124M USA. *Die Hard 2* prod/rel: 20ᵗʰ Century-Fox, Gordon Company

Telefon, Novel
Telefon 1977 d: Don Siegel. lps: Charles Bronson, Lee Remick, Donald Pleasence. 102M USA. prod/rel: MGM

Viper Three, Novel
Twilight's Last Gleaming 1977 d: Robert Aldrich. lps: Burt Lancaster, Richard Widmark, Charles Durning. 146M USA/GRM. *Das Ultimatum* (GRM); *Viper Three*; *Nuclear Countdown* prod/rel: N.F. Geria, Lorimar

WAGGERL, KARL HEINRICH
Das Jahr Des Herrn, Novel
Jahr Des Herrn, Das 1950 d: Alfred Stoger. lps: Karl Haberfellner, Kathe Gold, Ewald Balser. 100M AUS. *Kraft Der Liebe*; *Der Wallnerbub* prod/rel: Mundus

WAGNALLS, MABEL
The Rose-Bush of a Thousand Years, 1916, Short Story
Revelation 1918 d: George D. Baker. lps: Alla Nazimova, Charles Bryant, Frank Currier. 7r USA. *God's Message* prod/rel: Metro Pictures Corp.©, Screen Classics, Inc.
Revelation 1924 d: George D. Baker. lps: Viola Dana, Monte Blue, Marjorie Daw. 8752f USA. *In a Monastery Garden* prod/rel: Metro-Goldwyn Pictures

WAGNER, BRUCE
I'm Losing You, 1997, Novel
I'm Losing You 1998 d: Bruce Wagner. lps: Rosanna Arquette, Amanda Donohue, Buck Henry. 102M USA. prod/rel: Lions Gate Films, Killer Films

WAGNER, ELIN
Vandkorset, 1935, Novel
Vandkorset 1944 d: Lauritz Falk, Rune Carlsten. lps: Lauritz Falk, Marianne Aminoff, Irma Christenson. 96M SWD. *Turnstile* prod/rel: Filmo, Ab Svensk Talfilm

Vansklighetens Land, 1917, Novel
Asa-Hanna 1946 d: Anders Henrikson. lps: Aino Taube, Edvin Adolphson, Gosta Pruzelius. 108M SWD. prod/rel: Ab Europa Film

WAGNER, H. L.
Die Kindermorderin, Play
Madchen, Hutet Euch! 1928 d: Valy Arnheim. lps: Gritta Ley, Egon von Jordan, Iwa WanjA. 2324m GRM. prod/rel: William Kahn-Film

WAGNER, JACK
Story
Medal for Benny, A 1945 d: Irving Pichel. lps: J. Carrol Naish, Dorothy Lamour, Arturo de CordovA. 77M USA. prod/rel: Paramount

WAGNER, RICHARD (1813–1883), GRM
Der Fliegende Hollander, Dresden 1843, Opera
Flying Dutchman, The 1923 d: Lloyd B. Carleton. lps: W. Lawson Butt, Nola Luxford, Ella Hall. 5800f USA. prod/rel: R-C Pictures, Film Booking Offices of America

Lohengrin, Weimar 1850, Opera
Lohengrin 1947 d: Max Calandri. lps: Jacqueline Plessis, Antonio Cassinelli, Gianpiero MalaspinA. F ITL. prod/rel: Gennaro Proto, Scalera Film

Die Meistersinger von Nurnberg, Munich 1868, Opera
Meistersinger von Nurnberg, Die 1970 d: Leopold Lindtberg. lps: Giorgio Tozzi, Richard Cassilly, Arlene Saunders. MTV. 251M GRM. prod/rel: Polyphon Film & Tv Productions

Parsifal, Bayreuth 1882, Opera
Parsifal 1981 d: Hans-Jurgen Syberberg. lps: Armin Jordan, Martin Sperr, Robert Lloyd. 255M GRM/FRN. prod/rel: Gaumont, Tms

Der Ring Des Nibelungen, Bayreuth 1876, Opera
Ring, The 1927 d: H. B. Parkinson. 2000f UKN. prod/rel: Song Films

WAGONER, DAVID
The Escape Artist, 1965, Novel
Escape Artist, The 1982 d: Caleb Deschanel. lps: Griffin O'Neal, Raul Julia, Teri Garr. 96M USA. prod/rel: Orion, Warner

WAGSTAFF, H.
Mr. Romeo, New York 1927, Play
Chicken a la King 1928 d: Henry Lehrman. lps: Nancy Carroll, George Meeker, Arthur Stone. 6417f USA. *The Gay Deceiver* prod/rel: Fox Film Corp.

WAHLBERG, GIDEON
Skjaergardsflirt, Play
Skjaergardsflirt 1932 d: Rasmus Breistein. NRW.

WAHLOO, PER (1926–1975), SWD
Novel
Laughing Policeman, The 1973 d: Stuart Rosenberg. lps: Walter Matthau, Bruce Dern, Louis Gossett Jr. 112M USA. *An Investigation of Murder* (UKN) prod/rel: 20ᵗʰ Century Fox
Polis Polis Potatismos 1993 d: Pelle Berglund. lps: Gosta Ekman, Kjell Bergqvist, Rolf Lassgard. 91M SWD/GRM.
Polismordaren 1993 d: Peter Keglevic. lps: Gosta Ekman, Kjell Bergqvist, Rolf Lassgard. 97M SWD/GRM.

Kamikaze, Novel
Kamikaze 1982 d: Wolfgang Gremm. lps: Rainer Werner Fassbinder, Gunther Kaufmann, Boy Gobert. 106M GRM. *Kamikaze '89* prod/rel: Regina Ziegler Filmprod., Trio

De Man Op Het Balkon, Novel
Mannen Pa Balkongen 1993 d: Daniel Alfredson. lps: Gosta Ekman, Kjell Bergqvist, Rolf Lassgard. TVM. 94M SWD/DNM. *The Man on the Balcony*

Mannen Pa Taket, Novel
Mannen Pa Taket 1977 d: Bo Widerberg. lps: Carl-Gustaf Lindstedt, Gunnel Wadner, Hakan Serner. 115M SWD. *The Man on the Roof*; *The Abominable Man* prod/rel: Svenska Filminstitut, Svensk Film

Mannen Som Gick Upp I Rok, Novel
Sved Akinek Nyoma Veszett, A 1980 d: Peter Bacso. lps: Derek Jacobi, Judy Winter, Tomas Bolme. 114M HNG/SWD/GRM. *Mannen Som Gick Upp I Rok* (SWD); *The Man Who Went Up in Smoke*; *Der Mann Der Sich in Luft Aufloste* (GRM) prod/rel: Andre Lipik, Europa

Uppdraget, Novel
Uppdraget 1977 d: Mats Arehn. lps: Christopher Plummer, Thomas Hellberg, Carolyn Seymour. 94M SWD. *The Assignment* prod/rel: Nordisk-Tonefilm

De Vrachtwagen, Novel
Mannen I Skugan 1978 d: Arne Mattsson. lps: Helmut Griem, Gunnel Fred, Slobodan Dimitrijevic. 100M SWD/YGS. *Black Sun*

WAINWRIGHT, JOHN
Garde a Vue, Novel
Garde a Vue 1981 d: Claude Miller. lps: Lino Ventura, Michel Serrault, Romy Schneider. 90M FRN. *The Inquisitor* prod/rel: Les Films Ariane, TF 1

WAITZKIN, FRED
Searching for Bobby Fischer, Book
Searching for Bobby Fischer 1993 d: Steven Zaillian. lps: Max Pomeranc, Joe Mantegna, Joan Allen. 110M USA. *Innocent Moves* (UKN) prod/rel: Paramount, Mirage

WAKEFIELD, DAN (1932–, USA
Going All the Way, Novel
Going All the Way 1997 d: Mark Pellington. lps: Jeremy Davies, Ben Affleck, Amy Locane. 110M USA. prod/rel: Tom Gorai, Lakeshore Entertainment©

WAKEFIELD, GILBERT
Counsel's Opinion, London 1931, Play
Counsel's Opinion 1933 d: Allan Dwan. lps: Henry Kendall, Binnie Barnes, Cyril Maude. 76M UKN. prod/rel: London Films, Paramount
Divorce of Lady X, The 1938 d: Tim Whelan. lps: Merle Oberon, Laurence Olivier, Binnie Barnes. 92M UKN. prod/rel: London Film Productions, Denham Films

Room for Two, London 1938, Play
Room for Two 1940 d: Maurice Elvey. lps: Frances Day, Vic Oliver, Basil Radford. 77M UKN. prod/rel: Hurley, Grand National

WAKEMAN, FREDERIC (1909–
The Hucksters, Novel
Hucksters, The 1947 d: Jack Conway. lps: Clark Gable, Deborah Kerr, Sydney Greenstreet. 115M USA. prod/rel: MGM

WAKEMAN, FREDERIC (1909–, USA
The Saxon Charm, Novel
Saxon Charm, The 1948 d: Claude Binyon. lps: Robert Montgomery, Susan Hayward, John Payne. 88M USA. *The Charming Matt Saxon* prod/rel: Universal-International

Shore Leave, Novel
Kiss Them for Me 1957 d: Stanley Donen. lps: Cary Grant, Jayne Mansfield, Suzy Parker. 103M USA. prod/rel: 20ᵗʰ Century-Fox

The Wastrel, New York 1949, Novel
Relitto, Il 1961 d: Giovanni Paolucci, Michael Cacoyannis. lps: Van Heflin, Elli Lambetti, Franco Fabrizi. 98M ITL. *The Wastrel* (USA); *Hameno Kormi*; *Etsi Esvise I Agapi Mas* prod/rel: Lux Film, Tiberia Film

WALD, JERRY
Hot Air, Story
My Dream Is Yours 1949 d: Michael Curtiz. lps: Jack Carson, Doris Day, Lee Bowman. 101M USA. prod/rel: Warner Bros.
Twenty Million Sweethearts 1934 d: Ray Enright. lps: Dick Powell, Ginger Rogers, Pat O'Brien. 89M USA. *Hot Air*; *Rhythm in the Air*; *On the Air* prod/rel: First National Pictures©

WALD, MALVIN
Man of Fire, Television Play
Man on Fire 1957 d: Ranald MacDougall. lps: Bing Crosby, Inger Stevens, Mary Fickett. 95M USA. prod/rel: MGM

WALES, HUBERT
Cynthia in the Wilderness, Novel
Cynthia in the Wilderness 1916 d: Harold Weston. lps: Eve Balfour, Ben Webster, Milton Rosmer. 4025f UKN. prod/rel: Pioneer Films Agency

The Yoke, Novel
Yoke, The 1915 d: James W. Vickers. lps: Barbara Rutland, Leo Belcher, Jack Hobbs. 4468f UKN. *Love's Legacy* prod/rel: International Cine Corp.

WALES, ROBERT ELLIS
The Penitentes, Novel
Penitentes, The 1915 d: Jack Conway. lps: Orrin Johnson, Seena Owen, Paul Gilmore. 5r USA. *The Penitent*; *The Penitents* prod/rel: Fine Arts Film Co., Triangle Film Corp.©

WALK, CHARLES EDMONDS
The Green Seal, Chicago 1914, Novel
Girl in the Dark, The 1918 d: Stuart Paton. lps: Carmel Myers, Ashton Dearholt, Frank Deshon. 5r USA. prod/rel: Bluebird Photoplays, Inc.©

WALKER, ALICE (1944–, USA
The Color Purple, 1983, Novel
Color Purple, The 1985 d: Steven Spielberg. lps: Danny Glover, Whoopi Goldberg, Margaret Avery. 154M USA. prod/rel: Warner Bros., Amblin Entertainment

WALKER, BRUCE
Master Crook, Play
Cosh Boy 1952 d: Lewis Gilbert. lps: James Kenney, Joan Collins, Hermione Baddeley. 75M UKN. *The Slasher* (USA); *Tough Guy* prod/rel: Romulus, Daniel M. Angel

WALKER, DAVID
Geordie, Novel
Geordie 1955 d: Frank Launder. lps: Alastair Sim, Bill Travers, Norah Gorsen. 99M UKN. *Wee Geordie* (USA) prod/rel: Argonaut, British Lion

Harry Black, Novel
Harry Black 1958 d: Hugo Fregonese. lps: Stewart Granger, Barbara Rush, Anthony Steel. 107M UKN/USA. *Harry Black and the Tiger* (USA) prod/rel: Twentieth Century-Fox, Mersham

WALKER, DAVID E.
Adventure in Diamonds, Novel
Operation Amsterdam 1959 d: Michael McCarthy. lps: Peter Finch, Eva Bartok, Tony Britton. 104M UKN. prod/rel: Rank, Rank Film Distributors

WALKER, DAVID ESDAILE
Diamonds for Danger, New York 1954, Novel
Man Could Get Killed, A 1966 d: Ronald Neame, Cliff Owen. lps: James Garner, Melina Mercouri, Sandra Dee. 99M USA. *Welcome Mr. Beddoes* prod/rel: Universal Pictures, Cherokee Productions

WALKER, GEORGE F.
Better Living, Play
Better Living 1998 d: Max Mayer. lps: Olympia Dukakis, Roy Scheider, Edward Herrmann. 95M USA. prod/rel: Goldheart Pictures

WALKER, GERALD
Cruising, Novel
Cruising 1980 d: William Friedkin. lps: Al Pacino, Paul Sorvino, Karen Allen. 99M USA. prod/rel: United Artists

WALKER, GERTRUDE
Case History, Novel
Damned Don't Cry, The 1950 d: Vincent Sherman. lps: Joan Crawford, David Brian, Steve Cochran. 103M USA. *The Victim* prod/rel: Warner Bros.

WALKER, JOSEPH A.
The River Niger, Play
River Niger, The 1976 d: Krishna Shah. lps: James Earl Jones, Cicely Tyson, Glynn Turman. 105M USA. *The River Niger: Ghetto Warriors* prod/rel: Sidney Beckermann, Isaac L. Jones

WALKER, LESLIE
Sudden Fury, Book
Sudden Fury 1993 d: Craig R. Baxley. lps: Neil Patrick Harris, Johnny Galecki, Linda Kelsey. TVM. 90M USA. *Sudden Fury: a Family Torn Apart* prod/rel: River City Prods., Rhi Entertainment

WALL, DOROTHY
The Complete Adventures of Blinky Bill, Book
Blinky Bill 1992 d: Yoram Gross. ANM. 80M ASL. prod/rel: Yoram Gross, Australian Film Finance Corp.

WALL, HARRY
The Night Porter, Play
Night Porter, The 1930 d: Sewell Collins. lps: Donald Calthrop, Trilby Clark, Gerald Rawlinson. 45M UKN. prod/rel: Gaumont, Ideal

WALL, HENRY
Havoc, Story
Havoc 1925 d: Rowland V. Lee. lps: Madge Bellamy, George O'Brien, Walter McGrail. 9283f USA. prod/rel: Fox Film Corp.

WALL, JUDITH HENRY
Mother Love, Novel
Family Divided, A 1995 d: Donald Wrye. lps: Stephen Collins, Faye Dunaway, Cameron Bancroft. TVM. 90M USA. prod/rel: Citadel Entertainment

WALLACE, BRYAN EDGAR
Novel
Gatto a Nove Code, Il 1971 d: Dario Argento. lps: James Franciscus, Karl Malden, Catherine Spaak. 111M ITL/FRN/GRM. *The Cat O' Nine Tails* (UKN); *Die Neunschwanzige Katze*; *Cat With Nine Tails* prod/rel: Seda Spettacoli, Mondial Te.Fi (Roma)
Story
Geheimnis Der Schwarzen Koffer, Das 1962 d: Werner Klinger. lps: Joachim Hansen, Senta Berger, Hans Reiser. 96M GRM. *The Secret of the Black Trunk* (USA); *Das Schloss Des Schreckens*; *Castle of the Terrified*; *Secret of the Black Suitcases* prod/rel: C.C.C.
Novel
Muerto Hace Las Maletas, El 1970 d: Jesus Franco. lps: Fred Williams, Elisa Montes, Horst Tappert. 82M SPN/GRM. *Der Todesracher von Soho* (GRM); *Death Packs Up*; *Death Avenger*; *The Corpse Packs His Bags*; *The Avenger* prod/rel: Telecine, Fenix
Scotland Yard Jagt Doktor Mabuse 1963 d: Paul May. lps: Peter Van Eyck, Sabine Bethmann, Dieter Borsche. 90M GRM. *Dr. Mabuse Vs. Scotland Yard* (USA); *Die Scharlachrote Dschunke*; *Scotland Yard Vs. Dr. Mabuse*; *The Scarlet Jungle*; *Scotland Yard Hunts Dr. Mabuse* prod/rel: C.C.C., Gloria
Siebente Opfer, Das 1964 d: Franz J. Gottlieb. lps: Hansjorg Felmy, Ann Smyrner, Hans Nielsen. 93M GRM. *Das 7. Opfer*; *The Seventh Victim* prod/rel: C.C.C., Nora
Uccello Dalle Piume de Cristallo, L' 1970 d: Dario Argento. lps: Tony Musante, Suzy Kendall, Eva Renzi. 96M ITL/GRM. *Das Geheimnis Der Schwarzen Handschuhe* (GRM); *The Gallery Murders* (UKN); *The Bird With the Crystal Plumage* (USA); *The Bird With the Glass Feathers*; *Phantom of Terror* prod/rel: Seda Spettacoli (Roma), Ccc-Filmkunst (Berlin)
Wurger von Schloss Blackmoor, Der 1963 d: Harald Reinl. lps: Karin Dor, Ingmar Zeisberg, Harry Riebauer. 87M GRM. *The Strangler of Blackmoor Castle* (USA) prod/rel: C.C.C., Gloria
Murder By Proxy, Novel
Phantom von Soho, Das 1964 d: Franz J. Gottlieb. lps: Hans Sohnker, Dieter Borsche, Peter Vogel. 97M GRM. *The Phantom of Soho* (UKN) prod/rel: Ccc-Filmkunst
White Carpet, Short Story
Henker von London, Der 1963 d: Edwin Zbonek. lps: Hansjorg Felmy, Maria Perschy, Dieter Borsche. 95M GRM. *The Mad Executioners* (USA); *The Hangman of London* prod/rel: Ccc-Filmkunst

WALLACE, EDGAR (1875–1932), UKN
Short Story
£20,000 Kiss, The 1963 d: John Llewellyn Moxey. lps: Dawn Addams, Michael Goodliffe, Richard Thorp. 57M UKN. prod/rel: Anglo-Amalgamated, Merton Park

Novel
A Doppia Faccia 1969 d: Riccardo FredA. lps: Klaus Kinski, Christiane Kruger, Gunther Stoll. 94M ITL/GRM. *Puzzle of Horror* (USA); *Das Gesicht Im Dunkeln* (GRM); *Double Face*; *Face in the Dark* prod/rel: Colt Produzioni Cin.Che, Mega Film (Roma)
Backfire! 1962 d: Paul Almond. lps: Alfred Burke, Zena Marshall, Oliver Johnston. 59M UKN. prod/rel: Anglo-Amalgamated, Merton Park
Circus of Fear 1966 d: John Llewellyn Moxey. lps: Christopher Lee, Leo Genn, Anthony Newlands. 83M UKN. *Psycho-Circus* (USA) prod/rel: Circus Films, David Henley
Death Trap 1962 d: John Llewellyn Moxey. lps: Albert Lieven, Barbara Shelley, John Meillon. 56M UKN. prod/rel: Anglo-Amalgamated, Merton Park
Diamond Man, The 1924 d: Arthur Rooke. lps: Arthur Wontner, Mary Odette, Reginald Fox. 5800f UKN. prod/rel: I. B. Davidson, Butcher's Film Service
Story
Downfall 1964 d: John Llewellyn Moxey. lps: Maurice Denham, Nadja Regin, T. P. McKennA. 59M UKN. prod/rel: Anglo-Amalgamated, Merton Park
Novel
Face of a Stranger 1964 d: John Llewellyn Moxey. lps: Jeremy Kemp, Bernard Archard, Rosemary Leach. 56M UKN. prod/rel: Anglo-Amalgamated, Merton Park
Falscher von London, Der 1961 d: Harald Reinl. lps: Eddi Arent, Viktor de Kowa, Karin Dor. 93M GRM. *The Forger of London* (USA); *The London Counterfeiter* prod/rel: Rialto, Constantin
Gasthaus an Der Themse, Das 1962 d: Alfred Vohrer. lps: Joachim Fuchsberger, Klaus Kinski, Brigitte Grothum. 95M GRM. *The Inn on the River* (USA) prod/rel: Rialto, Constantin
Gorilla von Soho, Der 1968 d: Alfred Vohrer. lps: Horst Tappert, Uschi Glas, Uwe Friedrichsen. 96M GRM. *The Gorilla of Soho* prod/rel: Rialto, Constantin
Grosse Unbekannte, Der 1927 d: Manfred NoA. lps: Andree Lafayette, Jack Trevor, Evi EvA. 2896m GRM. *Der Unheimliche* prod/rel: Noa-Film
Hund von Blackwood Castle, Der 1968 d: Alfred Vohrer. lps: Heinz Drache, Karin Baal, Horst Tappert. 92M GRM. *The Hound of Blackwood Castle* prod/rel: Rialto, Constantin
Im Banne Des Unheimlichen 1968 d: Alfred Vohrer. lps: Joachim Fuchsberger, Siw Mattson, Wolfgang Kieling. 91M GRM. *In the Grip of the Sinister One*; *The Spell of the Uncanny* prod/rel: Rialto, Constantin
Short Story
Incident at Midnight 1963 d: Norman Harrison. lps: Anton Diffring, William Sylvester, Justine Lord. 56M UKN. prod/rel: Anglo-Amalgamated, Merton Park
Novel
Jewel, The 1933 d: Reginald Denham. lps: Hugh Williams, Frances Dean, Jack Hawkins. 67M UKN. prod/rel: Venture Films, Paramount
Story
King Kong 1933 d: Ernest B. Schoedsack, Merian C. Cooper. lps: Fay Wray, Robert Armstrong, Bruce Cabot. 110M USA. *The Eighth Wonder of the World*; *King Ape*; *Kong*; *The Beast* prod/rel: RKO Radio Pictures©
Novel
Lad, The 1935 d: Henry Edwards. lps: Gordon Harker, Betty Stockfeld, Jane Carr. 74M UKN. prod/rel: Universal, Twickenham
Story
Locker 69 1962 d: Norman Harrison. lps: Eddie Byrne, Paul Daneman, Walter Brown. 56M UKN. prod/rel: Anglo-Amalgamated, Merton Park
Novel
Main Chance, The 1964 d: John Knight. lps: Gregoire Aslan, Edward de Souza, Tracy Reed. 61M UKN. prod/rel: Merton Park Studios, Anglo-Amalgamated
Man They Could Not Arrest, The 1931 d: T. Hayes Hunter. lps: Hugh Wakefield, Gordon Harker, Renee ClamA. 74M UKN. *The Man They Couldn't Arrest* (USA) prod/rel: Ideal, Gainsborough
Mann Mit Dem Glasauge, Der 1968 d: Alfred Vohrer. lps: Horst Tappert, Karin Hubner, Hubert von Meyerinck. 87M GRM. *Terror on Half Moon Street* (USA); *The Man With the Glass Eye* prod/rel: Rialto, Constantin
Monch Mit Der Peitsche, Der 1967 d: Alfred Vohrer. lps: Joachim Fuchsberger, Uschi Glas, Siegfried Schurenberg. 88M GRM. *The Monk With the Whip* prod/rel: Rialto, Constantin
Short Story
Never Mention Murder 1964 d: John N. Burton. lps: Maxine Audley, Dudley Foster, Michael Coles. 56M UKN. prod/rel: Anglo-Amalgamated, Merton Park

On the Run 1963 d: Robert Tronson. lps: Emrys Jones, Sarah Lawson, Patrick Barr. 59M UKN. prod/rel: Anglo-Amalgamated, Merton Park
Story
Playback 1962 d: Quentin Lawrence. lps: Margit Saad, Barry Foster, Victor Platt. 62M UKN. prod/rel: Anglo-Amalgamated, Merton Park
Novel
Prison Breaker 1936 d: Adrian Brunel. lps: James Mason, Marguerite Allan, Wally Patch. 69M UKN. prod/rel: GS Enterprises, Columbia
Ratsel Der Roten Orchidee, Das 1961 d: Helmut Ashley. lps: Christopher Lee, Marisa Mell, Klaus Kinski. 94M GRM. *The Puzzle of the Red Orchid* (USA); *The Secret of the Red Orchid* prod/rel: Rialto, Constantin
Short Story
Return to Sender 1963 d: Gordon Hales. lps: Nigel Davenport, Yvonne Romain, Geoffrey Keen. 61M UKN. prod/rel: Anglo-Amalgamated, Merton Park
Set-Up, The 1963 d: Gerald Glaister. lps: Maurice Denham, John Carson, Maria Corvin. 58M UKN. prod/rel: Anglo-Amalgamated, Merton Park
Novel
Teufel Kam Aus Akasawa, Der 1971 d: Jesus Franco. lps: Horst Tappert, Susann Korda, Fred Williams. 84M GRM/SPN. *El Diablo Venia de Akasawa* (SPN); *The Devil Came from Akasawa*; *The Devil Was Coming from Akasawa* prod/rel: C.C.C., Fenix
Tote Aus Der Themse, Die 1971 d: Harald Philipp. lps: Uschi Glas, Hansjorg Felmy, Werner Peters. 89M GRM. *The Dead Woman in the Thames*; *Die Tod Aus Der Themse* prod/rel: Rialto, Constantin
Trygon Factor, The 1967 d: Cyril Frankel. lps: Stewart Granger, Susan Hampshire, Cathleen Nesbitt. 87M UKN. prod/rel: Rank Film Distributors, Rialto Film
Unheimliche Monch, Der 1965 d: Harald Reinl. lps: Harald Leipnitz, Karin Dor, Siegfried Lowitz. 86M GRM. *The Sinister Monk* (USA); *The Mysterious Monk* prod/rel: Rialto, Constantin
Again the Ringer, London 1929, Novel
Neues Vom Hexer 1965 d: Alfred Vohrer. lps: Barbara Rutting, Heinz Drache, Klaus Kinski. 95M GRM. *Again the Wizard*; *Latest Episodes of the Ringer*; *Again the Ringer* prod/rel: Rialto, Constantin
Angel Esquire, London 1908, Novel
Angel Esquire 1919 d: W. P. Kellino. lps: Aurele Sydney, Gertrude McCoy, Dick Webb. 6741f UKN. prod/rel: Gaumont
The Angel of Terror, London 1922, Novel
Ricochet 1963 d: John Llewellyn Moxey. lps: Maxine Audley, Richard Leech, Alex Scott. 64M UKN. prod/rel: Merton Park Studios, Anglo-Amalgamated
The Avenger, London 1926, Novel
Racher, Der 1960 d: Karl Anton. lps: Ingrid Van Bergen, Heinz Drache, Ina DuschA. 102M GRM. *The Avenger* (USA) prod/rel: Kurt Ulrich, Europa
The Best Laid Plans of a Man in Love, Short Story
Candidate for Murder 1962 d: David Villiers. lps: Michael Gough, Erika Remberg, Hans Borsody. 60M UKN. prod/rel: Anglo-Amalgamated, Merton Park
The Big Four, London 1929, Novel
Verdict, The 1964 d: David Eady. lps: Cec Linder, Zena Marshall, Nigel Davenport. 55M UKN. prod/rel: Anglo-Amalgamated, Merton Park
The Black Abbot, London 1926, Novel
Schwarze Abt, Der 1963 d: Franz J. Gottlieb. lps: Joachim Fuchsberger, Dieter Borsche, Grit Bottcher. 95M GRM. *The Black Abbot* (USA) prod/rel: Rialto, Constantin
The Blue Hand, London 1925, Novel
Blaue Hand, Die 1967 d: Alfred Vohrer. lps: Harald Leipnitz, Klaus Kinski, Carl Lange. 87M GRM. *Creature With the Blue Hand* (USA); *The Blue Hand* prod/rel: Rialto, Constantin
Bones, London 1915, Novel
Old Bones of the River 1938 d: Marcel Varnel. lps: Will Hay, Moore Marriott, Graham Moffatt. 90M UKN. prod/rel: General Film Distributors, Gainsborough
The Breaking Point, Short Story
To Have and to Hold 1963 d: Herbert Wise. lps: Ray Barrett, Katharine Blake, Nigel Stock. 71M UKN. prod/rel: Anglo-Amalgamated, Merton Park
The Calendar, London 1930, Novel
Calendar, The 1931 d: T. Hayes Hunter. lps: Herbert Marshall, Edna Best, Gordon Harker. 79M UKN. *Bachelor's Folly* (USA) prod/rel: Gainsborough, British Lion
Calendar, The 1948 d: Arthur Crabtree. lps: Greta Gynt, John McCallum, Raymond Lovell. 80M UKN. prod/rel: Gainsborough, General Film Distributors

The Case of the Frightened Lady, London 1931, Play
Frightened Lady, The 1932 d: T. Hayes Hunter. lps: Norman McKinnel, Cathleen Nesbitt, Emlyn Williams. 87M UKN. *Criminal at Large* (USA) prod/rel: Gainsborough, British Lion
Quelqu'un a Tue 1933 d: Jack Forrester. lps: Pierre Magnier, Andre Burgere, Marcelle Geniat. 90M FRN. *Le Chateau de la Terreur*; *Le Secret du Vieux Prieure*; *La Jeune Fille Effrayee* prod/rel: Forrester-Parant Productions

Chick, London 1923, Novel
Chick 1928 d: A. V. Bramble. lps: Bramwell Fletcher, Trilby Clark, Chili Bouchier. 7215f UKN. prod/rel: British Lion, Ideal
Chick 1936 d: Michael Hankinson. lps: Sydney Howard, Betty Ann Davies, Fred Conyngham. 72M UKN. prod/rel: British and Dominions, United Artists

The Clue of the New Pin, London 1923, Novel
Clue of the New Pin, The 1929 d: Arthur Maude. lps: Benita Hume, Kim Peacock, Donald Calthrop. SIL. 7292f UKN. prod/rel: British Lion, Producers' Distributing Corporation
Clue of the New Pin, The 1961 d: Allan Davis. lps: Paul Daneman, Bernard Archard, James Villiers. 58M UKN. prod/rel: Anglo-Amalgamated, Merton Park

The Clue of the Silver Key, London 1930, Novel
Clue of the Silver Key 1961 d: Gerald Glaister. lps: Bernard Lee, Lyndon Brook, Finlay Currie. 59M UKN. prod/rel: Anglo-Amalgamated, Merton Park

The Clue of the Twisted Candle, London 1918, Novel
Clue of the Twisted Candle 1960 d: Allan Davis. lps: Bernard Lee, David Knight, Colette Wilde. 61M UKN. prod/rel: Anglo-Amalgamated, Merton Park

The Crimson Circle, London 1922, Novel
Crimson Circle, The 1922 d: George Ridgwell. lps: Madge Stuart, Rex Davis, Fred Groves. 5378f UKN. prod/rel: Kinema Club, Granger
Crimson Circle, The 1936 d: Reginald Denham. lps: Hugh Wakefield, Alfred Drayton, Noah Beery. 76M UKN. prod/rel: Wainwright, Universal
Rote Kreis, Der 1928 d: Friedrich Zelnik. lps: Lya Mara, Fred Louis Lerch, Stewart Rome. 3791m GRM/UKN. *The Crimson Circle* (UKN) prod/rel: British Talking Pictures, Bifd
Rote Kreis, Der 1959 d: Jurgen Roland. lps: Fritz Rasp, Karl Saebisch, Renate Ewert. 94M GRM. *The Red Circle* (USA); *The Crimson Circle* prod/rel: Constantin, Rialto

The Daffodil Mystery, London 1920, Novel
Geheimnis Der Gelben Narzissen, Das 1961 d: Akos von Rathony. lps: Christopher Lee, Marius Goring, Albert Lieven. 86M GRM/UKN. *The Devil's Daffodil* (UKN); *Daffodil Killer* prod/rel: Omnia Films, Rialto Film

The Dark Eyes of London, London 1924, Novel
Dark Eyes of London, The 1939 d: Walter Summers. lps: Bela Lugosi, Hugh Williams, Greta Gynt. 75M UKN. *The Human Monster* (USA) prod/rel: Pathe, Argyle Productions
Toten Augen von London, Die 1960 d: Alfred Vohrer. lps: Joachim Fuchsberger, Karin Baal, Dieter Borsche. 100M GRM. *Dead Eyes of London* (USA); *The Dark Eyes of London* prod/rel: Rialto, Constantin

A Dear Liar, Short Story
Dear Liar, A 1925 d: Fred Leroy Granville. lps: Eileen Dennes, James Knight, Edward O'Neill. 2000f UKN. prod/rel: Stoll

Death Watch, 1932, Short Story
Before Dawn 1933 d: Irving Pichel. lps: Stuart Erwin, Dorothy Wilson, Warner Oland. 62M USA. *The Death Watch* prod/rel: RKO Radio Pictures, Inc.

A Debt Discharged, London 1916, Novel
Man Detained 1961 d: Robert Tronson. lps: Bernard Archard, Elvi Hale, Paul Stassino. 59M UKN. prod/rel: Anglo-Amalgamated, Merton Park

The Door With Seven Locks, London 1926, Novel
Door With Seven Locks, The 1940 d: Norman Lee. lps: Leslie Banks, Lilli Palmer, Romilly Lunge. 89M UKN. *Chamber of Horrors* (USA) prod/rel: Rialto, Pathe
Gruft Mit Dem Ratselschloss, Die 1964 d: Franz J. Gottlieb. lps: Harald Leipnitz, Judith Dornys, Rudolf Forster. 90M GRM. *The Curse of the Hidden Vault* (USA); *The Crypt With the Puzzle Lock* prod/rel: Rialto, Constantin
Tur Mit Den Sieben Schlossern, Die 1962 d: Alfred Vohrer. lps: Eddi Arent, Heinz Drache, Klaus Kinski. 96M GRM. *The Door With Seven Locks* (USA) prod/rel: Rialto, Constantin

The Double, London 1928, Novel
Double, The 1963 d: Lionel Harris. lps: Jeannette Sterke, Alan MacNaughton, Robert Brown. 56M UKN. prod/rel: Merton Park Studios, Anglo-Amalgamated

Down Under Donovan, London 1918, Novel
Down Under Donovan 1922 d: Harry Lambart. lps: Cora Goffin, W. H. Benham, Bertram Parnell. 5900f UKN. prod/rel: Stoll

Educated Evans, 1924, Novel
Brotherhood, The 1926 d: Walter West. lps: John MacAndrews, Jameson Thomas. 2230f UKN. prod/rel: Frederick Alfred, Associated Producers & Distributors
Educated Evans 1936 d: William Beaudine. lps: Max Miller, Nancy O'Neil, Clarice Mayne. 86M UKN. prod/rel: Warner Bros., First National

Elegant Edward, London 1928, Novel
Rivals, The 1963 d: Max Varnel. lps: Jack Gwillim, Erica Rogers, Brian Smith. 56M UKN. prod/rel: Anglo-Amalgamated, Merton Park

The Face in the Night, London 1924, Novel
Malpas Mystery, The 1960 d: Sidney Hayers. lps: Maureen Swanson, Allan Cuthbertson, Geoffrey Keen. 60M UKN. prod/rel: Independent Artists, Langton Productions

The Feathered Serpent, London 1927, Novel
Feathered Serpent, The 1934 d: MacLean Rogers. lps: Enid Stamp-Taylor, Tom Helmore, D. A. Clarke-Smith. 72M UKN. prod/rel: GS Enterprises, Columbia
Menace, The 1932 d: R. William Neill. lps: H. B. Warner, Bette Davis, Walter Byron. 71M USA. *The Feathered Serpent* prod/rel: Columbia Pictures Corp.©

The Fellowship of the Frog, London 1925, Novel
Frog, The 1937 d: Jack Raymond. lps: Gordon Harker, Carol Goodner, Noah Beery. 75M UKN. prod/rel: Herbert Wilcox, General Film Distributors
Frosch Mit Der Maske, Der 1959 d: Harald Reinl. lps: Joachim Fuchsberger, Fritz Rasp, Siegfried Lowitz. 92M GRM/DNM. *Fron Med Masken* (DNM); *Face of the Frog* (USA); *Fellowship of the Frog* prod/rel: Rialto, Constantin

Fighting Snub O'Reilly, London 1929, Novel
Fighting Snub Reilly 1924 d: Andrew P. Wilson. lps: David Hawthorne, Ena Evans, Fred Raynham. 2161f UKN. prod/rel: Stoll

Flat Two, London 1927, Novel
Flat Two 1962 d: Alan Cooke. lps: John Le Mesurier, Jack Watling, Bernard Archard. 60M UKN. prod/rel: Anglo-Amalgamated, Merton Park

The Flying Fifty-Five, London 1922, Novel
Flying Fifty-Five 1939 d: Reginald Denham. lps: Derrick de Marney, Nancy Burne, Marius Goring. 72M UKN. prod/rel: Admiral, RKO Radio
Flying Fifty-Five, The 1924 d: A. E. Coleby. lps: Lionelle Howard, Stephanie Stephens, Brian B. Lemon. 4900f UKN. prod/rel: Stoll, Eb

The Flying Squad, London 1928, Novel
Flying Squad, The 1929 d: Arthur Maude. lps: Wyndham Standing, Dorothy Bartlam, John Longden. SIL. 7572f UKN. prod/rel: British Lion, Warner Bros.
Flying Squad, The 1932 d: F. W. Kraemer. lps: Harold Huth, Carol Goodner, Edward Chapman. 80M UKN. prod/rel: British Lion
Flying Squad, The 1940 d: Herbert Brenon. lps: Sebastian Shaw, Phyllis Brooks, Jack Hawkins. 64M UKN. *The Flying Squadron* prod/rel: Associated British Picture Corporation

The Forger, London 1927, Novel
Forger, The 1928 d: G. B. Samuelson. lps: Lillian Rich, James Raglan, Nigel Barrie. 7305f UKN. prod/rel: British Lion, Ideal

The Four Just Men, London 1905, Novel
Four Just Men, The 1921 d: George Ridgwell. lps: Cecil Humphreys, Teddy Arundell, C. H. Croker-King. 4980f UKN. prod/rel: Stoll
Four Just Men, The 1939 d: Walter Forde. lps: Hugh Sinclair, Griffith Jones, Francis L. Sullivan. 85M UKN. *The Secret Four* prod/rel: Ealing Studios, C.a.P.a.D

Four Square Jane, London 1929, Novel
Fourth Square, The 1961 d: Allan Davis. lps: Conrad Phillips, Natasha Parry, Delphi Lawrence. 57M UKN. prod/rel: Anglo-Amalgamated, Merton Park

The Frightened Lady, London 1932, Novel
Case of the Frightened Lady, The 1940 d: George King. lps: Marius Goring, Penelope Dudley-Ward, Helen Haye. 81M UKN. *The Frightened Lady* (USA) prod/rel: Pennant Pictures, British Lion

The Gaunt Stranger, London 1925, Novel
Gaunt Stranger, The 1938 d: Walter Forde. lps: Sonnie Hale, Wilfred Lawson, Louise Henry. 73M UKN. *The Phantom Strikes* (USA) prod/rel: Northwood Enterprises, C.a.P.a.D
Hexer, Der 1964 d: Alfred Vohrer. lps: Joachim Fuchsberger, Eddi Arent, Sophie Hardy. 95M GRM. *The Mysterious Magician* (USA); *The Magician*; *The Wizard*; *The Ringer* prod/rel: Rialto, Constantin
Jugement de Minuit, Le 1932 d: Alexander Esway, Andre Charlot. lps: Jean Galland, Marion Delbo, Janine Merrey. 95M FRN. *Le Mystere de la Dame Blonde*; *Le Vengeur* prod/rel: Pallas Films
Ringer, The 1928 d: Arthur Maude. lps: Leslie Faber, Annette Benson, W. Lawson Butt. 7150f UKN. prod/rel: British Lion, Ideal
Ringer, The 1931 d: Walter Forde. lps: Gordon Harker, Franklin Dyall, John Longden. 75M UKN. prod/rel: Gainsborough, British Lion
Ringer, The 1952 d: Guy Hamilton. lps: Herbert Lom, Donald Wolfit, Mai Zetterling. 78M UKN. prod/rel: British Lion Production Assets, London Films

The Ghost of John Holling, 1924, Short Story
Mystery Liner 1934 d: William Nigh. lps: Noah Beery, Astrid Allwyn, Cornelius Keefe. 62M USA. *The Ghost of John Holling* (UKN); *The Ghost of Mr. Holling* prod/rel: Monogram Pictures Corp.©, Paul Malvern Production

Good Evans, London 1927, Novel
Thank Evans 1938 d: R. William Neill. lps: Max Miller, Hal Walters, Polly Ward. 78M UKN. prod/rel: Warner Bros., First National

The Greek Poropulos, 1911, Short Story
Born to Gamble 1935 d: Phil Rosen. lps: H. B. Warner, Lois Wilson, Ben Alexander. 70M USA. *I'll Bet You* prod/rel: Liberty Pictures Corp.

The Green Archer, London 1923, Novel
Grune Bogenschutze, Der 1960 d: Jurgen Roland. lps: Gert Frobe, Karin Dor, Klausjurgen Wussow. 95M GRM. *The Green Archer* prod/rel: Rialto, Constantin

The Green Pack, London 1933, Novel
Green Pack, The 1934 d: T. Hayes Hunter. lps: John Stuart, Aileen Marson, Hugh Miller. 72M UKN. prod/rel: British Lion

The Green Ribbon, London 1929, Novel
Never Back Losers 1961 d: Robert Tronson. lps: Jack Hedley, Jacqueline Ellis, Patrick Magee. 61M UKN. prod/rel: Anglo-Amalgamated, Merton Park

The Green Rust, London 1919, Novel
Green Terror, The 1919 d: W. P. Kellino. lps: Aurele Sydney, Heather Thatcher, W. T. Ellwanger. 6524f UKN. prod/rel: Gaumont

Grey Timothy, London 1913, Novel
Pallard the Punter 1919 d: J. L. V. Leigh. lps: Jack Leigh, Heather Thatcher, Lionel d'Aragon. 6600f UKN. prod/rel: Gaumont

The Gunner, London 1928, Novel
Solo for Sparrow 1962 d: Gordon Flemyng. lps: Anthony Newlands, Glyn Houston, Nadja Regin. 56M UKN. *Time to Remember* prod/rel: Merton Park, Anglo-Amalgamated

The India Rubber Men, London 1929, Novel
Return of the Frog, The 1938 d: Maurice Elvey. lps: Gordon Harker, Una O'Connor, Rene Ray. 75M UKN. prod/rel: Imperator, British Lion

Jack O' Judgment, London 1920, Novel
Accidental Death 1963 d: Geoffrey Nethercott. lps: John Carson, Jacqueline Ellis, Derrick Sherwin. 57M UKN. prod/rel: Anglo-Amalgamated, Merton Park
Share Out, The 1962 d: Gerald Glaister. lps: Bernard Lee, Alexander Knox, Moira Redmond. 61M UKN. *The Shareout* prod/rel: Merton Park Studios, Anglo-Amalgamated

Kate Plus Ten, London 1919, Novel
Kate Plus Ten 1938 d: Reginald Denham. lps: Jack Hulbert, Genevieve Tobin, Noel Madison. 81M UKN. *Queen of Crime* (USA) prod/rel: Wainwright, General Film Distributors
Wanted at Headquarters 1920 d: Stuart Paton. lps: Eva Novak, Agnes Emerson, Lee Shumway. 4560f USA. *Kate Plus Ten* prod/rel: Universal Film Mfg. Co.©

Lieutenant Bones, London 1918, Novel
Old Bones of the River 1938 d: Marcel Varnel. lps: Will Hay, Moore Marriott, Graham Moffatt. 90M UKN. prod/rel: General Film Distributors, Gainsborough

The Lone House Mystery, London 1929, Novel
Attempt to Kill 1961 d: Royston Morley. lps: Derek Farr, Tony Wright, Richard Pearson. 57M UKN. prod/rel: Merton Park, Anglo-Amalgamated

The Man at the Carlton, London 1931, Novel
Man at the Carlton Tower 1961 d: Robert Tronson. lps: Maxine Audley, Lee Montague, Allan Cuthbertson. 57M UKN. prod/rel: Anglo-Amalgamated, Merton Park

The Man Who Bought London, London 1915, Novel
Man Who Bought London, The 1916 d: F. Martin Thornton. lps: E. J. Arundel, Evelyn Boucher, Roy Travers. 5000f UKN. prod/rel: Windsor, Int-Ex
Time to Remember 1962 d: Charles Jarrott. lps: Yvonne Monlaur, Harry H. Corbett, Robert Rietty. 58M UKN. prod/rel: Anglo-Amalgamated, Merton Park

The Man Who Changed His Name, London 1928, Play
Giallo 1933 d: Mario Camerini. lps: Assia Noris, Sandro Ruffini, Elio Steiner. 67M ITL. prod/rel: Cines, Anonima Pittaluga
Man Who Changed His Name, The 1928 d: A. V. Bramble. lps: Stewart Rome, Betty Faire, James Raglan. 7134f UKN. prod/rel: British Lion
Man Who Changed His Name, The 1934 d: Henry Edwards. lps: Lyn Harding, Betty Stockfeld, Leslie Perrins. 80M UKN. prod/rel: Universal, Real Art

The Man Who Knew, London 1919, Novel
Partners in Crime 1961 d: Peter Duffell. lps: Bernard Lee, John Van Eyssen, Moira Redmond. 54M UKN. prod/rel: Anglo-Amalgamated, Merton Park

The Man Who Was Nobody, London 1927, Novel
Man Who Was Nobody, The 1960 d: Montgomery Tully. lps: Hazel Court, John Crawford, Lisa Daniely. 58M UKN. prod/rel: Anglo-Amalgamated, Merton Park

The Melody of Death, London 1915, Novel
Melody of Death 1922 d: F. Martin Thornton. lps: Philip Anthony, Enid R. Reed, Dick Sutherd. 4771f UKN. prod/rel: Stoll

The Million Dollar Story, London 1926, Novel
Partner, The 1963 d: Gerald Glaister. lps: Yoko Tani, Guy Doleman, Ewan Roberts. 58M UKN. prod/rel: Merton Park Studio, Anglo-Amalgamated

The Mind of Mr. Reeder, London 1925, Novel
Mind of Mr. Reeder, The 1939 d: Jack Raymond. lps: Will Fyffe, Kay Walsh, George Curzon. 75M UKN. *The Mysterious Mr. Reeder* (USA) prod/rel: Jack Raymond, Grand National
Missing People, The 1939 d: Jack Raymond. lps: Will Fyffe, Lyn Harding, Kay Walsh. 71M UKN. prod/rel: Jack Raymond, Grand National

The Missing Million, London 1923, Novel
Missing Million, The 1942 d: Phil Brandon. lps: Linden Travers, John Warwick, Patricia Hilliard. 84M UKN. prod/rel: Signet, Associated British Film Distributors

The Northing Tramp, London 1926, Novel
Strangers on a Honeymoon 1936 d: Albert de Courville. lps: Constance Cummings, Hugh Sinclair, Noah Beery. 70M UKN. *The Northing Tramp* prod/rel: Gaumont-British

Number Six, London 1927, Novel
Number Six 1962 d: Robert Tronson. lps: Ivan Desny, Nadja Regin, Michael Goodliffe. 59M UKN. prod/rel: Anglo-Amalgamated, Merton Park

The Old Man, Play
Old Man, The 1931 d: Manning Haynes. lps: Maisie Gay, Anne Grey, Lester Matthews. 77M UKN. prod/rel: British Lion

On the Spot, London 1930, Play
Dangerous to Know 1938 d: Robert Florey. lps: Akim Tamiroff, Anna May Wong, Gail Patrick. 70M USA. prod/rel: Paramount Pictures, Inc.

Red Aces, London 1929, Novel
Red Aces 1929 d: Edgar Wallace. lps: Janice Adair, Muriel Angelus, Geoffrey Gwyther. SIL. 7200f UKN. prod/rel: British Lion

The River of Stars, London 1913, Novel
River of Stars, The 1921 d: F. Martin Thornton. lps: Philip Anthony, Faith Bevan, Teddy Arundell. 4625f UKN. prod/rel: Stoll

Room 13, London 1924, Novel
Mr. Reeder in Room 13 1938 d: Norman Lee. lps: Gibb McLaughlin, Sara Seegar, Peter Murray Hill. 78M UKN. *Mystery of Room 13* (USA) prod/rel: British National, Associated British Picture Corporation
Zimmer 13 1964 d: Harald Reinl. lps: Joachim Fuchsberger, Karin Dor, Hans Clarin. 89M GRM. *Room 13* (USA) prod/rel: Rialto, Constantin

Sanders of the River, London 1911, Novel
Coast of Skeletons 1964 d: Robert Lynn. lps: Richard Todd, Dale Robertson, Heinz Drache. 91M UKN/SAF. *Sanders* prod/rel: British Lion, Towers of London
Death Drums Along the River 1963 d: Lawrence Huntington. lps: Richard Todd, Marianne Koch, Albert Lieven. 83M UKN. prod/rel: Planet, Big Ben-Hallam

Sanders of the River 1935 d: Zoltan KordA. lps: Paul Robeson, Leslie Banks, Nina Mae McKinney. 98M UKN. *Bosambo* (USA) prod/rel: London Films, United Artists

The Sinister Man, London 1924, Novel
Sinister Man, The 1961 d: Clive Donner. lps: John Bentley, Patrick Allen, Jacqueline Ellis. 60M UKN. prod/rel: Anglo-Amalgamated, Merton Park

The Squeaker, London 1927, Novel
Squeaker, The 1930 d: Edgar Wallace. lps: Percy Marmont, Anne Grey, Gordon Harker. 90M UKN. prod/rel: British Lion
Squeaker, The 1937 d: William K. Howard. lps: Edmund Lowe, Sebastian Shaw, Ann Todd. 77M UKN. *Murder in Diamond Row* (USA) prod/rel: United Artists, Denham Productions
Zinker, Der 1965 d: Alfred Vohrer. lps: Heinz Drache, Eddi Arent, Klaus Kinski. 95M GRM. *The Squeaker* (USA); *The Coronetist* prod/rel: Rialto, Constantin

The Strange Countess, London 1925, Novel
Seltsame Grafin, Die 1961 d: Josef von Baky. lps: Joachim Fuchsberger, Lil Dagover, Marianne Hoppe. 96M GRM. *The Strange Countess* (USA) prod/rel: Rialto, Constantin

The Terrible People, London 1926, Novel
Bande Des Schreckens, Die 1960 d: Harald Reinl. lps: Eddi Arent, Karin Dor, Elisabeth Flickenschildt. 95M GRM. *The Terrible People* (USA); *Hand of the Gallows*; *Terror Band* prod/rel: Rialto, Constantin

The Terror, London 1927, Play
Return of the Terror 1934 d: Howard Bretherton. lps: Mary Astor, Lyle Talbot, John Halliday. 65M USA. prod/rel: First National Pictures
Terror, The 1928 d: Roy Del Ruth. lps: May McAvoy, Louise Fazenda, Edward Everett Horton. 7654f USA. prod/rel: Warner Brothers Pictures
Terror, The 1938 d: Richard Bird. lps: Wilfred Lawson, Arthur Wontner, Linden Travers. 73M UKN. prod/rel: Associated British Picture Corporation

Thief in the Night, London 1928, Novel
Five to One 1963 d: Gordon Flemyng. lps: Lee Montague, Ingrid Hafner, John Thaw. 56M UKN. prod/rel: Anglo-Amalgamated, Merton Park

The Three Oak Mystery, London 1924, Novel
Marriage of Convenience 1960 d: Clive Donner. lps: John Cairney, Harry H. Corbett, Jennifer Daniel. 58M UKN. prod/rel: Merton Park Studios, Anglo-Amalgamated

To Oblige a Lady, Play
To Oblige a Lady 1931 d: Manning Haynes. lps: Maisie Gay, Warwick Ward, Mary Newland. 75M UKN. prod/rel: British Lion

The Traitor's Gate, London 1927, Novel
Yellow Mask, The 1930 d: Harry Lachman. lps: Lupino Lane, Dorothy Seacombe, Warwick Ward. 95M UKN. prod/rel: British International Pictures, Wardour
Traitor's Gate 1964 d: Freddie Francis. lps: Albert Lieven, Gary Raymond, Margot Trooger. 80M UKN/GRM. *Das Verrateror* (GRM) prod/rel: Summit Film Productions, Rialto Film

The Undisclosed Client, Short Story
Who Was Maddox? 1964 d: Geoffrey Nethercott. lps: Bernard Lee, Jack Watling, Suzanne Lloyd. 62M UKN. prod/rel: Anglo-Amalgamated, Merton Park

Valley of the Ghosts, London 1922, Novel
Valley of the Ghosts 1928 d: G. B. Samuelson. lps: Miriam Seegar, Ian Hunter, Leo Sheffield. 5204f UKN. prod/rel: British Lion, Jmg

We Shall See, London 1926, Novel
We Shall See 1964 d: Quentin Lawrence. lps: Maurice Kaufmann, Faith Brook, Alec Mango. 61M UKN. prod/rel: Anglo-Amalgamated, Merton Park

White Face, London 1930, Novel
White Face 1932 d: T. Hayes Hunter. lps: Hugh Williams, Gordon Harker, Norman McKinnel. 70M UKN. prod/rel: Gainsborough, British Lion

WALLACE, FRANCIS
The Big Game, Boston 1936, Novel
Big Game, The 1936 d: George Nicholls Jr. lps: Bruce Cabot, June Travis, James Gleason. 75M USA. prod/rel: RKO Radio Pictures, Inc.

Huddle, New York 1931, Novel
Huddle 1932 d: Sam Wood. lps: Ramon Novarro, Madge Evans, Kane Richmond. 104M USA. *The Impossible Lover* (UKN) prod/rel: Metro-Goldwyn-Mayer Corp., Metro-Goldwyn-Mayer Dist. Corp.©

Kid Galahad, Boston 1936, Novel
Kid Galahad 1937 d: Michael Curtiz. lps: Edward G. Robinson, Bette Davis, Humphrey Bogart. 105M USA. *The Battling Bellhop* prod/rel: Warner Bros. Pictures©

Kid Galahad 1962 d: Phil Karlson. lps: Elvis Presley, Gig Young, Lola Albright. 96M USA. prod/rel: Mirisch Co., United Artists
Wagons Roll at Night, The 1941 d: Ray Enright. lps: Humphrey Bogart, Sylvia Sidney, Eddie Albert. 84M USA. prod/rel: Warner Bros.

O'Reilly of Notre Dame, New York 1931, Novel
Rose Bowl 1936 d: Charles T. Barton. lps: Tom Brown, Eleanore Whitney, Buster Crabbe. 75M USA. *O'Riley's Luck* (UKN) prod/rel: Paramount Pictures

Stadium, New York 1931, Novel
Touchdown 1931 d: Norman Z. McLeod. lps: Richard Arlen, Jack Oakie, Peggy Shannon. 79M USA. *Playing the Game* (UKN) prod/rel: Paramount Publix Corp.©

That's My Boy, New York 1932, Novel
That's My Boy 1932 d: R. William Neill. lps: Richard Cromwell, Dorothy Jordan, Mae Marsh. 71M USA. prod/rel: Columbia Pictures Corp.©

WALLACE, FREDERICK WILLIAM
Blue Water, Novel
Blue Water 1924 d: David M. Hartford. lps: Pierre Gendron, Jane Thomas, Norma Shearer. 5r CND. prod/rel: New Brunswick Films Ltd.

Captain Salvation, New York 1925, Novel
Captain Salvation 1927 d: John S. Robertson. lps: Lars Hanson, Marceline Day, Pauline Starke. 7395f USA. prod/rel: Cosmopolitan Productions, Metro-Goldwyn-Mayer Distributing Corp.

WALLACE, IRVING (1916–1990), USA, Wallechinsky, Irving
The Chapman Report, New York 1960, Novel
Chapman Report, The 1962 d: George Cukor. lps: Efrem Zimbalist Jr., Shelley Winters, Jane FondA. 125M USA. prod/rel: Darryl F. Zanuck

Classmates, Story
West Point Story, The 1950 d: Roy Del Ruth. lps: James Cagney, Virginia Mayo, Doris Day. 107M USA. *Fine and Dandy* (UKN) prod/rel: Warner Bros.

The Prize, New York 1962, Novel
Prize, The 1963 d: Mark Robson. lps: Paul Newman, Edward G. Robinson, Elke Sommer. 135M USA. prod/rel: Roxbury Productions

The Word, Novel
Word, The 1978 d: Richard Lang. lps: David Janssen, James Whitmore, Florinda Bolkan. TVM. 400M USA. prod/rel: Charles Fries Productions, Stonehenge Productions

WALLACE, LEW (1827–1905), USA
Ben Hur, 1880, Novel
Ben-Hur 1925 d: Fred Niblo. lps: Ramon Novarro, Francis X. Bushman, May McAvoy. 12r USA. prod/rel: Metro-Goldwyn-Mayer Pictures
Ben-Hur 1959 d: William Wyler. lps: Charlton Heston, Jack Hawkins, Stephen Boyd. 213M USA. prod/rel: Metro-Goldwyn-Mayer Corp.

The Prince of India, New York 1893, Novel
Prince of India, A 1914 d: Leopold Wharton. lps: Thurlow Bergen, Elsie Esmond, William Riley Hatch. 4r USA. prod/rel: Wharton, Inc., Eclectic Film Co.

WALLACE, LEWIS
The Beauty, Novel
Cuori E Sensi 1917 d: Carlo Farinetti. lps: Liliana Millanva, Amelia Agostoni, Francesco Fazzini. 1170m ITL. prod/rel: Luna-Film

WALLACE, MARJORIE
On Giant's Shoulders, Book
On Giant's Shoulders 1979 d: Anthony Simmons. lps: Bryan Pringle, Judi Dench, Terry Wiles. MTV. 75M UKN. prod/rel: BBC

WALLACE, MICHAEL
Sweet Mystery of Life, New York 1935, Play
Gold Diggers of 1937 1936 d: Lloyd Bacon. lps: Dick Powell, Joan Blondell, Glenda Farrell. 100M USA. prod/rel: Warner Bros. Pictures©

WALLACE, PAMELA
Dreams Lost Dreams Found, Novel
Dreams Lost, Dreams Found 1987 d: Willi Patterson. lps: Willi Patterson, Kathleen Quinlan, David Robb. TVM. 100M UKN/USA. prod/rel: Yorkshire Television

Love With a Perfect Stranger, Novel
Love With a Perfect Stranger 1986 d: Desmond Davis. lps: Marilu Henner, Daniel Massey, Sky Dumont. TVM. 90M UKN. prod/rel: Yorkshire Television

Tears in the Rain, Novel
Tears in the Rain 1988 d: Don Sharp. lps: Sharon Stone, Christopher Cazenove, Leigh Lawson. TVM. 101M UKN.

WALLACE, ROBERT
The Long Way Home, Television Play
That Night 1957 d: John Newland. lps: John Beal, Augusta Dabney, Malcolm Brodrick. 88M USA. prod/rel: Universal-International, RKO

WALLACE, VINCENT (1812–1865), IRL, Wallace, William Vincent
Maritana, London 1845, Opera
Don Caesar de Bazan 1915 d: Robert G. VignolA. lps: W. Lawson Butt, Alice Hollister, Harry Millarde. 4r USA. prod/rel: Kalem Co., Broadway Favorite Special
Maritana 1922 d: George Wynn. lps: Vivian Gibson, Wallace Bosco, Gordon Hopkirk. 1183f UKN. prod/rel: Master Films, Gaumont
Maritana 1927 d: H. B. Parkinson. lps: Herbert Langley, Kathlyn Hilliard. 1652f UKN. prod/rel: Song Films

WALLACH, IRA
Muscle Beach, Boston 1959, Novel
Don't Make Waves 1967 d: Alexander MacKendrick. lps: Tony Curtis, Claudia Cardinale, Robert Webber. 97M USA. prod/rel: Filmways, Inc., Reynard Productions

WALLANT, EDWARD LEWIS (1926–1962), USA
The Pawnbroker, New York 1961, Novel
Pawnbroker, The 1965 d: Sidney Lumet. lps: Rod Steiger, Geraldine Fitzgerald, Brock Peters. 115M USA. prod/rel: Landau/Unger Co., Pawnbroker Co.

WALLER, LESLIE
Book
Hide in Plain Sight 1979 d: James Caan. lps: James Caan, Joe Grifasi, Jill Eikenberry. 92M USA. prod/rel: MGM, United Artists

WALLER, ROBERT JAMES
The Bridges of Madison County, Novel
Bridges of Madison County, The 1995 d: Clint Eastwood. lps: Clint Eastwood, Meryl Streep, Annie Corley. 135M USA. prod/rel: Warner Bros., Amblin

WALLER, TOD
Dudley Does It, Play
Under Proof 1936 d: Roland Gillett. lps: Betty Stockfeld, Tyrrell Davis, Judy Kelly. 50M UKN. prod/rel: Fox British
The Fakers, Play
Find the Lady 1936 d: Burt Gillett. lps: Jack Melford, Althea Henley, George Sanders. 70M UKN. prod/rel: Fox British

WALLERTON, MILES
Another Man's Wife, Play
Another Man's Wife 1915 d: Harold Weston. lps: Elisabeth Risdon, Fred Groves, A. V. Bramble. 3000f UKN. prod/rel: British & Colonial, Renters

WALLIS, A. J.
Thunder Above, Novel
Beyond the Curtain 1960 d: Compton Bennett. lps: Richard Greene, Eva Bartok, Marius Goring. 88M UKN. prod/rel: Rank Film Distributors, Welbeck

WALLIS, J. H.
Once Off Guard, Novel
Woman in the Window, The 1944 d: Fritz Lang. lps: Edward G. Robinson, Joan Bennett, Raymond Massey. 95M USA. prod/rel: RKO Radio

WALLNER, MAX
Die Glucklichste Frau Der Welt, Opera
Bonjour Kathrin 1955 d: Karl Anton. lps: Caterina Valente, Peter Alexander, Silvio Francesco. 96M GRM. *Hello Catherine* prod/rel: Alfred Greven
Der Letzte Walzer, Berlin 1920, Operetta
Derniere Valse, La 1935 d: Leo Mittler. lps: Jean Martinelli, Armand Bernard, Yarmila NovotnA. 90M FRN. prod/rel: Warwick Films
Last Waltz, The 1936 d: Gerald Barry, Leo Mittler. lps: Jarmila Novotna, Harry Welchman, Gerald Barry. 74M UKN. prod/rel: Warwick, Associated Producers and Distributors
Saison in Salzburg, Opera
Lascia Cantare Il Cuore 1943 d: Roberto Savarese. lps: Vivi Gioi, Elena Luber, Loris Gizzi. 84M ITL. prod/rel: Fono Roma, Artisti Associati
Saison in Salzburg 1952 d: Ernst MarischkA. lps: Adrian Hoven, Walter Muller, Hans Richter. 105M AUS. prod/rel: Wien
Saison in Salzburg 1961 d: Franz J. Gottlieb. lps: Peter Alexander, Gunther Philipp, Waltraut Haas. 97M AUS. prod/rel: Sascha
..Und Die Musik Spielt Dazu 1943 d: Carl Boese. lps: Vivi Gioi, Maria Andergast, Georg Alexander. 88M GRM. *Saison in Salzburg* prod/rel: Deka, Karp

WALLOP, DOUGLASS (1920–1985), USA, Wallop III, John Douglass
The Year the Yankees Lost the Pennant, Novel
Damn Yankees 1958 d: George Abbott, Stanley Donen. lps: Tab Hunter, Gwen Verdon, Ray Walston. 110M USA. *What Lola Wants* (UKN) prod/rel: Warner Bros., George Abbott-Stanley Donen

WALMSLEY, LEO
Three Fevers, Novel
Turn of the Tide 1935 d: Norman Walker. lps: John Garrick, Geraldine Fitzgerald, Niall MacGinnis. 80M UKN. prod/rel: British National, Gaumont-British

WALMSLEY, TOM
Paris France, Novel
Paris, France 1993 d: Gerard Ciccoritti. lps: Leslie Hope, Peter Outerbridge, Victor Ertmanis. 112M CND. prod/rel: Alliance, Lightshow

WALPOLE, HUGH (1884–1941), NZL, Walpole, Sir Hugh Seymour
Mr. Perrin and Mr. Traill, 1911, Novel
Mr. Perrin and Mr. Traill 1948 d: Lawrence Huntington. lps: Marius Goring, David Farrar, Greta Gynt. 92M UKN. prod/rel: General Film Distributors, Two Cities
The Silver Mask, 1932, Short Story
Kind Lady 1935 d: George B. Seitz. lps: Aline MacMahon, Basil Rathbone, Mary Carlisle. 76M USA. *House of Menace* prod/rel: Metro-Goldwyn-Mayer Corp.©
Kind Lady 1951 d: John Sturges. lps: Maurice Evans, Ethel Barrymore, Angela Lansbury. 78M USA. prod/rel: MGM
Vanessa, 1933, Novel
Vanessa, Her Love Story 1935 d: William K. Howard. lps: Helen Hayes, Robert Montgomery, Otto Kruger. 78M USA. *Vanessa* (UKN) prod/rel: Metro-Goldwyn-Mayer Corp.©

WALSER, MARTIN (1927–, GRM
Das Einhorn, 1966, Novel
Einhorn, Das 1978 d: Peter Patzak. lps: Peter Vogel, Gila von Weitershausen, Miriam Spoerri. 111M GRM. *The Unicorn* prod/rel: Artus, Sudwestfunk
Der Sturz, 1973, Novel
Sturz, Der 1979 d: Alf Brustellin. lps: Franz Buchrieser, Hannelore Elsner, Wolfgang Kieling. 103M GRM. *The Fall*; *The Plunge* prod/rel: Independent, a.B.S.

WALSER, ROBERT
Les Enfants Tanner, Novel
Simon Tanner 1993 d: Joel Jouanneau. lps: Philippe Demarle, Helene Vincent, Marie Guittier. TVM. 92M FRN/SWT.
Der Gehulfe, Novel
Gehulfe, Der 1976 d: Thomas Koerfer. lps: Paul Burian, Verena Buss, Ingold Wildenauer. 125M SWT. *The Assistant*; *L' Homme a Tout Faire* prod/rel: Thomas Koerfer, ZDF
Jakob von Gunten, Novel
Institute Benjamenta - This Dream People Call Human Life, The 1995 d: Brothers Quay. lps: Mark Rylance, Alice Krige, Gottfried John. 105M UKN. prod/rel: British Screen, Channel 4
Jakob von Gunten 1971 d: Peter Lilienthal. lps: Hanna Schygulla, Hann von Axmann Rezzori, Ludvik Askenazy. MTV. 90M GRM. prod/rel: ZDF

WALSH, MAURICE
Story
Quiet Man, The 1952 d: John Ford. lps: John Wayne, Maureen O'Hara, Victor McLaglen. 129M USA. prod/rel: Republic, Argosy
Trouble in the Glen 1954 d: Herbert Wilcox. lps: Margaret Lockwood, Orson Welles, Forrest Tucker. 91M UKN. prod/rel: Republic, Everest

WALSH, PERCY
Chin Chin Chinaman, Play
Chin Chin Chinaman 1931 d: Guy Newall. lps: Leon M. Lion, Elizabeth Allan, George Curzon. 52M UKN. *Boat from Shanghai* (USA) prod/rel: Real Art, MGM

WALSH, SHEILA
Only a Mill Girl, Play
Only a Mill Girl 1919 d: Lewis Willoughby. lps: Harry Foxwell, Betty Farquhar, Arthur Condy. 5000f UKN. prod/rel: Foxwell Films, Ideal

WALSH, THOMAS
Homecoming, 1936, Short Story
Don't Turn 'Em Loose 1936 d: Ben Stoloff. lps: Lewis Stone, Bruce Cabot, James Gleason. 68M USA. prod/rel: RKO Radio Pictures, Inc.
Husk, 1935, Short Story
We're Only Human 1935 d: James Flood. lps: Preston Foster, Jane Wyatt, James Gleason. 68M USA. *Husk* prod/rel: RKO Radio Pictures©
The Night Watch, Novel
Pushover 1954 d: Richard Quine. lps: Fred MacMurray, Kim Novak, Philip Carey. 88M USA. prod/rel: Columbia

Nightmare in Manhattan, Novel
Union Station 1950 d: Rudolph Mate. lps: William Holden, Nancy Olson, Barry Fitzgerald. 80M USA. prod/rel: Paramount

WALSHE, DOUGLAS
A Girl of London, Novel
Girl of London, A 1925 d: Henry Edwards. lps: Ian Hunter, Harvey Braban, G. H. Mulcaster. 6500f UKN. prod/rel: Stoll
The Wonderful Wooing, Novel
Wonderful Wooing, The 1925 d: Geoffrey H. Malins. lps: Marjorie Hume, G. H. Mulcaster, Eric Bransby Williams. 6250f UKN. *The Way of a Woman* prod/rel: Stoll

WALTARI, MIKA (1908–, FNL, Waltari, Mika Toimi
Ei Koskaan Huomispaivaa, 1942, Novel
Verta Kasissmaame 1958 d: William Markus. lps: Elina Pohjanpaa, Jussi Jurkka, Tauno Palo. 83M FNL. *Blood on Our Hands*; *Blod Pa Vara Hander* prod/rel: Suomen Filmuteollisuus
Ek Koskaan Huomispaivaa, 1942, Novel
Ingen Morgondag 1957 d: Arne Mattsson. lps: Jarl Kulle, Margit Carlqvist, Kolbjorn Knudsen. 105M SWD. *No Tomorrow* prod/rel: Ab Svea Film
Jalkinaytos, 1938, Novel
Vieras Mies 1958 d: Hannu Leminen. lps: Aku Korhonen, Rauni Ikaheimo, Ekso VettenrantA. 105M FNL. *A Stranger Came Home*; *Vieras Mies Tuli Taloon*; *Framlingen* prod/rel: Suomi-Filmi
Vieras Mies Tuli Taloon 1938 d: Wilho Ilmari. lps: Kaisu Leppanen, Eino Kaipainen, Aku Korhonen. 106M FNL. *En Framling Kom Till Garden* prod/rel: Suomen Filmiteollisuus
Jokin Ihmisessa, 1944, Novel
Jokin Ihmisessa 1956 d: Aarne Tarkas. lps: Jussi Jurkka, Anneli Sauli, Emmi JurkkA. 75M FNL. *Nagot I Manniskan* prod/rel: Fennadi-Filmi
Komisario Palmun Erehdys, 1940, Novel
Komisario Plamun Erehdys 1960 d: Matti KassilA. lps: Joel Rinne, Elina Pohjampaa, Matti Ranin. 108M FNL. *Mysteriet Rygseck* prod/rel: Suomen Fimliteollisuus
Kuka Murhasi Rouva Skrofin?, 1939, Novel
Kaasua, Komisario Palmu 1961 d: Matti KassilA. lps: Leo Jokela, Joel Rinne, Matti Rainin. 98M FNL. *Step on the Gas Inspector Palmu*; *Step on It Inspector Palmu*; *Vem Mordale Fru Skrof?* prod/rel: Fennada-Filmi
Kuriton Sukupolvi, 1937, Play
Kuriton Sukupolvi 1937 d: Wilho Ilmari. lps: Ansa Ikonen, Uuno Laakso, Unto Salminen. 110M FNL. *Det Sjalvsvaldiga Slaktet* prod/rel: Suomen Filmiteollisuus
Kuriton Sukupolvi 1957 d: Matti KassilA. lps: Tauno Palo, Irma Seikkula, Jussi JurkkA. 94M FNL. *The Unruly Generation*; *Nutidsungdom* prod/rel: Fennada-Filmi
Noita Palaa Elamaan, 1947, Play
Noita Palaa Elamaan 1952 d: Roland Hallstrom. lps: Toivo Makela, Hillevi Lagerstam, Helge HeralA. 77M FNL. *The Witch* (USA); *The Witch Returns to Life*; *The Witch Reborn* prod/rel: Fennada-Filmi Oy
Egyptilainen Sinuhe, 1946, Novel
Egyptian, The 1954 d: Michael Curtiz. lps: Edmund Purdom, Victor Mature, Jean Simmons. 140M USA. prod/rel: 20th Century-Fox
Suuri Illusioni, 1928, Novel
Suuri Illusioni 1986 d: Tuija-Maija Niskanen. lps: Markku Toikka, Rea Mauranen, Pekka Valkeejarvi. 95M FNL. *Grand Illusion*; *Den Stora Illusionen*
Tanssi Yli Hautojen, 1944, Novel
Tanssi Yli Hautojen 1950 d: Toivo SaakkA. lps: Leif Wager, Eila Peitsalo, Ossi Korhonen. 101M FNL. *Dance Over the Graves*; *Dans Over Gravarna* prod/rel: Suomen Filmiteollisuus
Vieras Mies Tuli Taloon, 1937, Novel
Vieras Mies 1958 d: Hannu Leminen. lps: Aku Korhonen, Rauni Ikaheimo, Ekso VettenrantA. 105M FNL. *A Stranger Came Home*; *Vieras Mies Tuli Taloon*; *Framlingen* prod/rel: Suomi-Filmi
Vieras Mies Tuli Taloon 1938 d: Wilho Ilmari. lps: Kaisu Leppanen, Eino Kaipainen, Aku Korhonen. 106M FNL. *En Framling Kom Till Garden* prod/rel: Suomen Filmiteollisuus

WALTER, EUGENE
Boots and Saddles, Play
Boots and Saddles 1916. lps: R. Henry Grey, Robyn Adair, Norman Luke. 5r USA. prod/rel: Balboa Amusement Producing Co., B. S. Moss Motion Picture Corp.

The Easiest Way, Hartford, Ct. 1908, Play
Easiest Way, The 1917 d: Albert Capellani. lps: Clara Kimball Young, Louise Emerald Bates, Joseph Kilgour. 7r USA. prod/rel: Clara Kimball Young Film Corp.©, Lewis J. Selznick Enterprises
Easiest Way, The 1931 d: Jack Conway. lps: Constance Bennett, Adolphe Menjou, Robert Montgomery. 73M USA. prod/rel: Metro-Goldwyn-Mayer Corp., Metro-Goldwyn-Mayer Dist. Corp.©
Quand on Est Belle 1931 d: Arthur Robison. lps: Lili Damita, Andre Luguet, Andre Burgere. 85M USA. *La Bonne Vie* prod/rel: Metro-Goldwyn-Mayer
Fine Feathers, New York 1913, Play
Fine Feathers 1915 d: Joseph A. Golden. lps: Janet Beecher, David Powell, Lester Chambers. 5r USA. prod/rel: Cosmos Feature Film Corp.©, World Film Corp.
Fine Feathers 1921 d: Fred Sittenham. lps: Eugene Pallette, Claire Whitney, Thomas W. Ross. 6r USA. prod/rel: Metro Pictures
The Flapper, 1923, Play
What Fools Men are 1922 d: George W. Terwilliger. lps: Faire Binney, Lucy Fox, Joseph Striker. 6087f USA. prod/rel: Pyramid Pictures, American Releasing Corp.
Just a Wife, New York 1910, Play
Just a Wife 1920 d: Howard Hickman. lps: Roy Stewart, Leatrice Joy, Kathlyn Williams. 5-6r USA. prod/rel: National Picture Theatres, Inc.©, Select Pictures Corp.
Just a Woman, New York 1916, Play
Just a Woman 1918 d: Julius Steger. lps: Charlotte Walker, Lee Baker, Lorna Volare. 6r USA. prod/rel: S & S Photoplays, Inc., State Rights
Just a Woman 1925 d: Irving Cummings. lps: Claire Windsor, Conway Tearle, Dorothy Brock. 6363f USA. prod/rel: First National Pictures
The Knife, New York 1917, Play
Knife, The 1918 d: Robert G. VignolA. lps: Alice Brady, Frank Morgan, Crauford Kent. 5r USA. prod/rel: Select Pictures Corp.©
Nancy Lee, New York 1918, Play
Way of a Woman, The 1919 d: Robert Z. Leonard. lps: Norma Talmadge, Conway Tearle, Stuart Holmes. 5-6r USA. *Nancy Lee* prod/rel: Norma Talmadge Film Corp.©, Select Pictures Corp.
Paid in Full, New York 1908, Play
Paid in Full 1914 d: Augustus Thomas. lps: William Riley Hatch, Tully Marshall, Caroline French. 5r USA. prod/rel: All Star Feature Corp.
Paid in Full 1919 d: Emile Chautard. lps: Pauline Frederick, Robert Cain, Wyndham Standing. 4112f USA. prod/rel: Famous Players-Lasky Corp.©, Paramount Pictures
The Wolf, New York 1908, Play
Wolf, The 1914 d: Barry O'Neil. lps: George Soule Spencer, Ethel Clayton, Ferdinand Tidmarsh. 6r USA. prod/rel: Lubin Mfg. Co.©, General Film Co.
Wolf, The 1919 d: James Young. lps: Earle Williams, Jane Novak, Brinsley Shaw. 6r USA. prod/rel: Vitagraph Co. of America©

WALTER, JESS
Every Knee Shall Bow, Book
Ruby Ridge: an American Tragedy 1996 d: Roger Young. lps: Laura Dern, Randy Quaid, Kirsten Dunst. TVM. 180M USA. *The Siege of Ruby Ridge*

WALTER, OTTO
Bider Der Flieger, Olten-Freiburg 1938, Book
Bider Der Flieger 1941 d: Leonard Steckel, Max Werner Lenz. lps: Robert Freitag, Lee Ruckstuhl, Rudolf Bernhard. 86M SWT. *Bider l'Aviateur*; *Oskar Bider* prod/rel: Filmkunst-Zurich Ag

WALTERS, MINETTE
The Dark Room, Novel
Dark Room, The 1999 d: Graham Theakston. lps: Dervla Kirwan, James Wilby, Nicholas Gecks. TVM. F UKN.
The Echo, Novel
Echo, The 1998 d: Diarmuid Lawrence. lps: Clive Owen, Joely Richardson, Ian Bartholomew. TVM. 150M UKN. prod/rel: BBC©
The Sculptress, Novel
Sculptress, The 1996. lps: Pauline Quirke, Caroline Goodall, Christopher Fulford. MTV. 180M UKN.

WALTHER, S. P.
Story
Fall Rabanser, Der 1950 d: Kurt Hoffmann. lps: Hans Sohnker, Paul Dahlke, Carola Hohn. 80M GRM. *The Rabanser Case* prod/rel: Junge Film-Union, N.F.

WALTON, FRANCIS
Women in the Wind, New York 1935, Novel
Women in the Wind 1939 d: John Farrow. lps: Kay Francis, William Gargan, Victor Jory. 65M USA. prod/rel: Warner Bros. Pictures©

WALTON, GEORGE
The Devil's Brigade, Philadelphia 1966, Novel
Devil's Brigade, The 1968 d: Andrew V. McLaglen. lps: William Holden, Cliff Robertson, Vince Edwards. 130M USA. prod/rel: United Artists

WALTON, MRS. O. F.
The Old Arm Chair, Novel
Old Arm Chair, The 1920 d: Percy Nash. lps: Manora Thew, Cecil Mannering, Joan Ritz. 5400f UKN. prod/rel: Screen Plays, British Exhibitors' Films
A Peep Behind the Scenes, Novel
Peep Behind the Scenes, A 1918 d: Geoffrey H. Malins, Kenelm Foss. lps: Ivy Close, Gerald Ames, Gertrude Bain. 5000f UKN. prod/rel: Master Films, New Bio
Peep Behind the Scenes, A 1929 d: Jack Raymond. lps: Frances Cuyler, Haddon Mason, H. Saxon-Snell. SIL. 7372f UKN. prod/rel: British & Dominions, Woolf & Freedman

WALTON, TODD
Inside Moves, Novel
Inside Moves 1980 d: Richard Donner. lps: John Savage, David Morse, Diana Scarwid. 113M USA. prod/rel: Goodmark, Associated

WALTYRE, EDWARD
Betta the Gypsy, Opera
Betta the Gypsy 1918 d: Charles Raymond. lps: Marga La Rubia, Malvina Longfellow, George Foley. 4100f UKN. prod/rel: Famous Productions, Butcher
The Laundry Girl, Opera
Laundry Girl, The 1919 d: Albert G. Frenguelli, Edith Mellor. lps: Margaret Campbell, Geoffrey Wilmer, Ida Fane. 4570f UKN. *Because* prod/rel: Hooper, Mellor

WAMBAUGH, JOSEPH (1937–, USA, Wambaugh Jr., Joseph Aloysius
The Black Marble, Novel
Black Marble, The 1980 d: Harold Becker. lps: Robert Foxworth, Paula Prentiss, Harry Dean Stanton. 113M USA. prod/rel: Avco Embassy, the Black Marble
The Blue Knight, 1972, Novel
Blue Knight, The 1973 d: Robert Butler. lps: William Holden, Lee Remick, Joe Santos. TVM. 200M USA. prod/rel: NBC, Lorimar Productions
Blue Knight, The 1975 d: J. Lee Thompson. lps: George Kennedy, Alex Rocco, Glynn Turman. TVM. 78M USA. prod/rel: CBS, Lorimar Productions
The Choirboys, 1975, Novel
Choirboys, The 1977 d: Robert Aldrich. lps: Charles Durning, Louis Gossett Jr., Perry King. 119M USA. prod/rel: Lorimar, Airone
Echoes in the Darkness, Novel
Echoes in the Darkness 1987 d: Glenn Jordan. lps: Peter Coyote, Stockard Channing, Robert LoggiA. TVM. 250M USA. prod/rel: New World
Fugitive Nights, Novel
Fugitive Nights: Danger in the Desert 1993 d: Gary Nelson. lps: Sam Elliott, Teri Garr, Thomas Haden Church. TVM. 95M USA. *Fugitive Nights* prod/rel: Tri-Star Tv, Columbia Pictures
The Glitter Dome, Novel
Glitter Dome, The 1985 d: Stuart Margolin. lps: James Garner, Margot Kidder, John Lithgow. TVM. 95M USA/CND. prod/rel: Hbo, Telepictures Corp. (Los Angeles)
The New Centurions, 1971, Novel
New Centurions, The 1972 d: Richard Fleischer. lps: George C. Scott, Stacy Keach, Jane Alexander. 103M USA. *Precinct 45 - Los Angeles Police* (UKN) prod/rel: Chartoff-Winkler
The Onion Field, Novel
Onion Field, The 1979 d: Harold Becker. lps: John Savage, James Woods, Franklyn Seales. 126M USA. prod/rel: Black Marble

WAN JIABAO
Lei Yu, 1934, Play
Lei Yu 1938 d: Fang Peilin. 98M CHN.
Leiyu 1984 d: Sun Daolin. lps: Sun Daolin, Gu Yongfei, Ma XIaowei. 120M CHN. *Thunderstorm* prod/rel: Shanghai Film Studio
Ri Chu, 1936, Play
Ri Chu 1938 d: Yueh Feng. 106M CHN. *Sunrise*
Richu 1985 d: Yu Bengzheng. lps: Wang Fuli, Fang Shu, Wang Sihuai. 159M CHN. *Sunrise*; *Sunset* prod/rel: Shanghai Film Studio
Yuan Ye, 1939, Play
Shenlin Enchou Ji 1941 d: Yueh Feng. 118M CHN. *Love and Revenge in the Black Forest*

Yuan Ye 1988 d: Ling Zi. lps: Yang Zaibao, Liu XIaoqing, Liu Jian. 109M CHN. *Savage Land* prod/rel: Nanhai Film Company

WANG HONG
Duo Yin, Play
Duo Yin 1963 d: Wang Shaoyan. lps: Li Yan, Tian Hua, Gao Jialin. 9r CHN. *Fighting for Power* prod/rel: August First Film Studio

WANG SHUO
Dongwu XIongmeng, Novel
Yangguang Canlan de Rizi 1994 d: Jiang Wen. lps: XIa Yu, Ning Jing, Geng Le. 139M HKG/CHN/TWN. *In the Heat of the Sun* prod/rel: Dragon Film International, China Film Co-Production Corp.
Emerging from the Sea, Novel
Lunhui 1988 d: Huang Jianxin. lps: Tan XIaoyan, Lei Han, Liu Lijun. 14r CHN. *Samsara* prod/rel: XI'an Film Studio
Wo Shi Ni Ba Ba Ma?, Novel
Wo Shi Hi Ba Ba Ma? 1995 d: Wang Shuo. lps: Feng XIaogang, Hu XIaopei, Xu Fan. F CHN. *Am I Your Father?*; *Baba*; *Father* prod/rel: Beijing Shanhe Film & Tv Art Co. Ltd.
Wuren Hecai, Novel
Wuren Hecai 1993 d: XIa Gang. lps: Ge Ke, XIe Yuan, Ding Jiali. 9r CHN/HKG. *Nobody Applauds*; *No One Cheers* prod/rel: Beijing Film Studio, Yanming International Corp.
Xiao Shi de Nu Ren, Novel
Xiao Shi de Nu Ren 1992 d: He Qun, Liu Baolin. lps: Ge You, You Yong, Geng Ge. 9r CHN. *The Vanished Woman* prod/rel: Fujian Film Studio
Yi Ban Hai Shui Yi Ban Huo Yan, Novel
Yi Ban Huo Yan, Yi Ban Hai Shui 1989 d: XIa Gang. lps: Luo Gang, Ji Ling, Gao Jie. 9r CHN. *Half Brine Half Flame* prod/rel: Beijing Film Studio
Yong Shi Wo Ai, Novel
Yong Shi Wo Ai 1994 d: Feng XIaogang. lps: Guo Tao, Xu Fan, Ju Xue. 10r CHN. *Lost My Love* prod/rel: Hainan Nanyang Film Studio, Beijing Film Studio

WANG WEIZHEN
Hong Chen, Novel
Hong Chen 1994 d: Gu Rong. lps: Xu Songzi, Tao Zeru, Xu Lei. 12r CHN. *An Unwelcome Lady* prod/rel: Beijing Film Studio

WANG XINGPU
Huang He Nu Hou Ba, Play
Nu Hou Ba, Huang He 1979 d: Shen Dan, Jia Shihong. lps: Zhang Ruifang, Liang Yuru, Liu Shangxian. 11r CHN. *Yellow River! Roar* prod/rel: August First Film Studio

WANG XUEBAO
Liu Hao Men, Play
Liu Hao Men 1952 d: Lu Ban. lps: Guo Zhenqing, Li Zhiping, Li XIaogong. 11r CHN. *Gate Number Six* prod/rel: Northeast Film Studio

WANG YAN
Amannisahan, Opera
Amannisahan 1993 d: Wang Yan, Wang XIngjun. lps: Munire, Mulading, Tuerxunjiang. 10r CHN. prod/rel: Tianshan Film Studio, Tianjin Film Studio

WANG YANFEI
The Indigenous Specialist, Play
Cong Ming de Ren 1958 d: Xu Tao. lps: Wun XIying, Zhang Yunxiang, Fan Lai. 10r CHN. *An Intelligent Person* prod/rel: Haiyan Film Studio

WANG YING
Youyi, Play
Youyi 1959 d: Li Jun. lps: Li Jinming, Wang Rui, Xu Yanming. 8r CHN. *Friendship* prod/rel: August First Film Studio

WANG YUANJIAN
Party Membership Dues, Novel
Dang Denuer 1958 d: Lin Nong. lps: Tian Hua, Chen Ge, Li Lin. 10r CHN. *Daughter of the Party* prod/rel: Changchun Film Studio

WANG ZONGYUAN
Novel
Zhi Qu Hua Shan 1953 d: Guo Wei. lps: Li Jinbang, Xu Youxin, Yang Qingwei. 12r CHN. *Capture By Stratagem of Mount Hua* prod/rel: Beijing Film Studio
Hui's Wife, Novel
Kun Lun Shan Shang Yi Ke Cao 1962 d: Dong KenA. lps: Liu Yanjing, Li Mengrao, Wang Zhelan. 6r CHN. *Grass Grows on the Kunlun Mountains* prod/rel: Beijing Film Studio

WARD, BRAD
Marshal of Medicine Bend, 1933, Novel
Lawless Street, A 1955 d: Joseph H. Lewis. lps: Randolph Scott, Angela Lansbury, Warner Anderson. 78M USA. prod/rel: Columbia, Scott-Brown Prods.

WARD, JONAS
The Name's Buchanan, Novel
  Buchanan Rides Alone 1958 d: Budd Boetticher. lps: Randolph Scott, Craig Stevens, Barry Kelley. 78M USA. prod/rel: Columbia, Scott-Brown

WARD, MARY JANE
The Snake Pit, Novel
  Snake Pit, The 1948 d: Anatole Litvak. lps: Olivia de Havilland, Leo Genn, Mark Stevens. 108M USA. prod/rel: 20ᵗʰ Century-Fox

WARD, MRS. HUMPHREY (1851–1920), UKN, Arnold, Mary Augustus
Lady Rose's Daughter, London 1903, Novel
  Lady Rose's Daughter 1920 d: Hugh Ford. lps: Elsie Ferguson, David Powell, Frank Losee. 4585f USA. prod/rel: Famous Players-Lasky Corp.©, Paramount-Artcraft Pictures
The Marriage of William Ashe, New York 1905, Novel
  Marriage of William Ashe, The 1916 d: Cecil M. Hepworth. lps: Henry Ainley, Alma Taylor, Stewart Rome. 5175f UKN. prod/rel: Hepworth, Harma
  Marriage of William Ashe, The 1921 d: Edward Sloman, Bayard Veiller (Spv): lps: May Allison, Wyndham Standing, Zeffie Tilbury. 6r USA.
Missing, New York 1917, Novel
  Missing 1918 d: James Young. lps: Thomas Meighan, Sylvia Breamer, Robert Gordon. 5r USA. prod/rel: J. Stuart Blackton, Famous Players-Lasky Corp.©

WARD, ROBERT
Cattle Annie and Little Britches, Novel
  Cattle Annie and Little Britches 1979 d: Lamont Johnson. lps: Burt Lancaster, John Savage, Rod Steiger. 98M USA. prod/rel: Universal

WARD, ROGER
Reflex, Novel
  Brothers 1982 d: Terry Bourke. lps: Chard Hayward, Margaret Laurence, Ivar Kants. 99M ASL. *Hounds of War* prod/rel: Areflex Pictures

WARDE, ESTRELLA
Cherokee Rose, Short Story
  Fighting Hombre, The 1927 d: Jack Nelson. lps: Bob Custer, Mary O'Day, Bert Sprotte. 4624f USA. prod/rel: Bob Custer Productions, Film Booking Offices of America

WARDE, S.
Trick for Trick, New York 1932, Play
  Trick for Trick 1933 d: Hamilton MacFadden. lps: Ralph Morgan, Victor Jory, Sally Blane. 69M USA. prod/rel: Fox Film Corp.©

WARDEN, FLORENCE
The Dazzling Miss Davison, London 1908, Novel
  Dazzling Miss Davison, The 1917 d: Frank Powell. lps: Marjorie Rambeau, Fred G. Williams, Aubrey Beattie. 5r USA. *On Her Honor* prod/rel: Frank Powell Producing Corp., Mutual Film Corp.
The House on the Marsh, Novel
  House on the Marsh, The 1920 d: Fred Paul. lps: Cecil Humphreys, Peggy Patterson, Harry Welchman. 5250f UKN. prod/rel: London, Jury

WARDEN, ROB
Gone in the Night, Book
  Gone in the Night 1996 d: B. W. L. Norton. lps: Shannen Doherty, Kevin Dillon, Dixie Carter. TVM. 173M USA. prod/rel: Leonard Hill Films©

WARE, DARRELL
Short Stories
  Life Begins in College 1937 d: William A. Seiter. lps: The Ritz Brothers, Joan Davis, Tony Martin. 94M USA. *The Joy Parade* (UKN); *Life Begins at College*; *1937 Pigskin Parade*; *Pigskin Parade of 1937*; *Pigskin Parade of 1938* prod/rel: Twentieth Century-Fox Film Corp.©

WARE, HARLAN
Come Fill the Cup, Novel
  Come Fill the Cup 1951 d: Gordon Douglas. lps: James Cagney, Phyllis Thaxter, Raymond Massey. 113M USA. prod/rel: Warner Bros.
Too Young to Know, Serial Story
  Too Young to Know 1945 d: Frederick de CordovA. lps: Joan Leslie, Robert Hutton, Harry Davenport. 86M USA. prod/rel: Warner Bros.

WARE, LEON
The Boy and the Bridge, Short Story
  Boy and the Bridge, The 1959 d: Kevin McClory. lps: Ian MacLaine, Liam Redmond, James Hayter. 95M UKN. prod/rel: Columbia, Xanadu
Search, Short Story
  Perilous Waters 1948 d: Jack Bernhard. lps: Don Castle, Audrey Long, Peggy Knudsen. 66M USA. *In Self Defense* prod/rel: Monogram

WARGA, WAYNE
Return to Earth, Book
  Return to Earth 1976 d: Jud Taylor. lps: Cliff Robertson, Shirley Knight, Charles Cioffi. TVM. 90M USA. prod/rel: King-Hitzig Production

WARNER, ANNE
The Rejuvenation of Aunt Mary, New York 1907, Play
  Rejuvenation of Aunt Mary, The 1914 d: Eddie Dillon. lps: Dell Henderson, Jack Mulhall, Dave Morris. 4r USA. prod/rel: Klaw & Erlanger©, Biograph Co.
  Rejuvenation of Aunt Mary, The 1916 d: Dell Henderson. lps: Kate Toncray, Audrey Kirby, Dell Henderson. 3r USA.
  Rejuvenation of Aunt Mary, The 1927 d: Erle C. Kenton. lps: May Robson, Harrison Ford, Phyllis Haver. 5844f USA. prod/rel: Metropolitan Pictures Corp. of Calif., Producers Distributing Corp.

WARNER, DOUGLAS
Death of a Snout, London 1961, Novel
  Informers, The 1963 d: Ken Annakin. lps: Nigel Patrick, Margaret Whiting, Harry Andrews. 105M UKN. *Underworld Informers* (USA); *The Snout* prod/rel: Rank Organisation, Rank Film Distributors

WARNER, REX (1905–), UKN
The Aerodrome, Novel
  Aerodrome, The 1983 d: Giles Foster. lps: Jill Bennett, Peter Firth, Richard Johnson. TVM. 91M UKN. prod/rel: BBC

WARNERT, WILLIAM H.
Mothers of Men, New York 1919, Novel
  Mothers of Men 1920 d: Edward Jose. lps: Claire Whitney, Lumsden Hare, Gaston Glass. 6494f USA. prod/rel: Film Specials, Inc.©, Edward Jose Productions

WARRACK, GRAEME
Travel By Dark, Book
  Arnhem: the Story of an Escape 1976 d: Clive Rees. lps: John Hallam, Marie-Louise Stheins, Mark Russel. MTV. 85M UKN. prod/rel: BBC

WARREN, C. E. T.
Above Us the Waves, Book
  Above Us the Waves 1955 d: Ralph Thomas. lps: John Mills, John Gregson, Donald Sinden. 99M UKN. prod/rel: General Film Distributors, London Independent Producers

WARREN, CHARLES MARQUIS (1912–1990), USA
Only the Valiant, 1943, Novel
  Only the Valiant 1951 d: Gordon Douglas. lps: Gregory Peck, Barbara Payton, Ward Bond. 105M USA. prod/rel: Warner Bros.
The Redhead and the Cowboy, Novel
  Redhead and the Cowboy, The 1950 d: Leslie Fenton. lps: Rhonda Fleming, Glenn Ford, Edmond O'Brien. 82M USA. prod/rel: Paramount

WARREN, F. BROOKE
The Face at the Window, Play
  Face at the Window, The 1920 d: Wilfred Noy. lps: C. Aubrey Smith, Gladys Jennings, Jack Hobbs. 5650f UKN. prod/rel: British Actors, Phillips
  Face at the Window, The 1932 d: Leslie Hiscott. lps: Raymond Massey, Isla Bevan, Claude Hulbert. 53M UKN. prod/rel: Real Art, Radio
  Face at the Window, The 1939 d: George King. lps: Tod Slaughter, Marjorie Taylor, John Warwick. 65M UKN. prod/rel: Pennant, British Lion

WARREN, MAUDE RADFORD
The House of Youth, Indianapolis 1923, Novel
  House of Youth, The 1924 d: Ralph Ince. lps: Jacqueline Logan, Malcolm McGregor, Vernon Steele. 6669f USA. prod/rel: Regal Pictures, Producers Distributing Corp.
The Road Through the Dark, 1918, Short Story
  Road Through the Dark, The 1918 d: Edmund Mortimer. lps: Clara Kimball Young, Jack Holt, Henry Woodward. 5r USA. prod/rel: Clara Kimball Young Film Corp.©, Select Pictures Corp.

WARREN, ROBERT PENN (1905–1989), USA
All the King's Men, 1946, Novel
  All the King's Men 1949 d: Robert Rossen. lps: Broderick Crawford, Joanne Dru, John Ireland. 109M USA. prod/rel: Columbia
Band of Angels, 1955, Novel
  Band of Angels 1957 d: Raoul Walsh. lps: Clark Gable, Yvonne de Carlo, Sidney Poitier. 126M USA. prod/rel: Warner Bros.

WARSHAWSKY, CURTIS B.
Girl of the Overland Trail, Novel
  Can't Help Singing 1944 d: Frank Ryan. lps: Deanna Durbin, Robert Paige, Akim Tamiroff. 89M USA. prod/rel: Universal

WARSHAWSKY, SAMUEL J.
  Can't Help Singing 1944 d: Frank Ryan. lps: Deanna Durbin, Robert Paige, Akim Tamiroff. 89M USA. prod/rel: Universal

WARWICK, JAMES
Blind Alley, New York 1935, Play
  Blind Alley 1939 d: Charles Vidor. lps: Chester Morris, Ralph Bellamy, Ann Dvorak. 70M USA. prod/rel: Columbia Pictures Corp.
  Blind Alley 1949 d: Paul Nickell. lps: Jerome Thor, Bramwell Fletcher. MTV. F USA.
  Blind Alley 1952. lps: Roy Hargrove, Beverly Roberts. MTV. F USA.
  Blind Alley 1954. lps: Darren McGavin, Herbert Berghof. MTV. F USA.
  Dark Past, The 1948 d: Rudolph Mate. lps: William Holden, Lee J. Cobb, Nina Foch. 75M USA. prod/rel: Columbia

WASSERMANN, JAKOB (1873–1934), GRM
Der Fall Maurizius, 1928, Novel
  Affaire Maurizius, L' 1953 d: Julien Duvivier. lps: Eleonora Rossi-Drago, Madeleine Robinson, Daniel Gelin. 110M FRN/ITL. *Il Caso Mauritius* (ITL); *The Maurizius Case* (USA); *On Trial* prod/rel: Franco-London Films, Jolly Films
Die Masken Erwin Reiners, Berlin 1910, Novel
  Masks of the Devil, The 1928 d: Victor Sjostrom. lps: John Gilbert, Alma Rubens, Theodore Roberts. 5575f USA. prod/rel: Metro-Goldwyn-Mayer Pictures

WATERHOUSE, KEITH (1929–), UKN
Billy Liar, 1959, Novel
  Billy Liar! 1963 d: John Schlesinger. lps: Tom Courtenay, Julie Christie, Wilfred Pickles. 98M UKN. prod/rel: Vic Films, Waterhall Productions

WATERS, FRANK
River Lady, Novel
  River Lady 1948 d: George Sherman. lps: Yvonne de Carlo, Rod Cameron, Dan DuryeA. 78M USA. prod/rel: Universal-International

WATERSTRADT, BERTA
Wahrend Der Stromsperre, Story
  Buntkarierten, Die 1949 d: Kurt Maetzig. lps: Camilla Spira, Werner Hinz, Carsta Lock. 106M GDR. *The Chequered Bedspread* prod/rel: Defa, Omnium

WATKIN, LAWRENCE EDWARD
On Borrowed Time, New York 1937, Novel
  On Borrowed Time 1939 d: Harold S. Bucquet. lps: Lionel Barrymore, Cedric Hardwicke, Beulah Bondi. 99M USA. prod/rel: Metro-Goldwyn-Mayer Corp., Loew's, Inc.©

WATKINS, MARY T.
Stolen Thunder, 1930, Short Story
  Oh, for a Man! 1930 d: Hamilton MacFadden. lps: Jeanette MacDonald, Reginald Denny, Warren Hymer. 7800f USA. prod/rel: Fox Film Corp.

WATKINS, MAURINE DALLAS
Chicago, New York 1926, Novel
  Chicago 1927 d: Frank Urson. lps: Phyllis Haver, Victor Varconi, Eugene Pallette. 9145f USA. prod/rel: de Mille Pictures, Pathe Exchange, Inc.
Chicago, New York 1926, Play
  Roxie Hart 1942 d: William A. Wellman. lps: Ginger Rogers, Adolphe Menjou, George Montgomery. 75M USA. prod/rel: 20ᵗʰ Century-Fox
Tinsel Girl, 1931, Play
  Strange Love of Molly Louvain, The 1932 d: Michael Curtiz. lps: Ann Dvorak, Richard Cromwell, Lee Tracy. 74M USA. *Tinsel Girl*; *The Tinsel Lady* prod/rel: First National Pictures©

WATKINS, PETER
The War Game, 1967, Play
  War Game, The 1966 d: Peter Watkins. DOC. 50M UKN. prod/rel: BBC, British Film Institute

WATKYN, ARTHUR
For Better. for Worse., London 1948, Play
  For Better, for Worse 1954 d: J. Lee Thompson. lps: Dirk Bogarde, Susan Stephen, Cecil Parker. 84M UKN. *Cocktails in the Kitchen* (USA) prod/rel: Kenwood, Ab-Pathe
The Moonraker, 1952, Play
  Moonraker, The 1958 d: David MacDonald. lps: George Baker, Sylvia Syms, Peter Arne. 82M UKN. prod/rel: Associated British Picture Corporation

WATSON, COLIN (1920–, UKN
Miss Lonelyhearts 4122, Novel
  Crooked Hearts, The 1972 d: Jay Sandrich. lps: Rosalind Russell, Douglas Fairbanks Jr., Ross Martin. TVM. 73M USA. prod/rel: Lorimar Productions

WATSON, DAVID
Fade Out, Play
Fade Out 1970 d: John N. Burton. lps: Stanley Baker, George Sanders, Geoffrey Bayldon. MTV. 96M UKN. prod/rel: Htv

WATSON, E. L. GRANT
The Nun and the Bandit, Novel
Nun and the Bandit, The 1992 d: Paul Cox. lps: Gosia Dobrowolska, Chris Haywood, Victoria Eagger. F ASL. prod/rel: Illumination Films

Priest Island, Novel
Exile 1993 d: Paul Cox. lps: Aden Young, Beth Champion, Claudia Karvan. F ASL. prod/rel: Illumination Films

Where Bonds are Loosed, New York 1918, Novel
Where Bonds are Loosed 1919 d: David G. Fischer. lps: Dixie Lee, Arthur Behrens, David G. Fischer. 5045f USA. prod/rel: Waldorf Photoplays, Inc., World Film Corp.

WATSON, EDWIN B.
Seed of Destruction, Story
Live Fast, Die Young 1958 d: Paul Henreid. lps: Mary Murphy, Norma Eberhardt, Mike Connors. 82M USA. prod/rel: Universal-International, B.R.K., Inc.

WATSON, H. B. MARRIOTT
The Cockerel, Story
Conspiracy Against the King, A 1911 d: J. Searle Dawley. lps: Walter Edwin, Robert Brower, Mary Fuller. 1000f USA. prod/rel: Edison

Her Face, Story
Her Face 1912. lps: Marc McDermott, Miriam Nesbitt, Gertrude McCoy. 1000f USA. prod/rel: Edison

The Interlude, Story
Stanton's Last Fling 1913 d: Charles M. Seay. lps: Charles Vernon, Miriam Nesbitt, William Leonard. 1000f USA. prod/rel: Edison

The Picaroon, Story
On the Isle of Sarne 1914 d: Richard Ridgely. lps: Miriam Nesbitt, Charles Sutton, Mrs. William Bechtel. 2r USA. prod/rel: Edison

WATSON, JOHN, MacLaren, Ian
Doctor of the Old School, 1895, Novel
Hills of Home 1948 d: Fred M. Wilcox. lps: Edmund Gwenn, Donald Crisp, Tom Drake. 97M USA. *Master of Lassie* (UKN) prod/rel: MGM

WATSON, MALCOLM
Sanctuary, Play
Sanctuary 1916 d: Claude Harris. lps: Sylvia Cavalho, Clifford Pembroke. 4000f UKN. prod/rel: Claude Harris, Davison Film Sales Agency

WATTERS, GEORGE MANKER
Burlesque, New York 1927, Play
Dance of Life, The 1929 d: John Cromwell, A. Edward Sutherland. lps: Hal Skelly, Nancy Carroll, Dorothy Revier. 13r USA. *Burlesque* prod/rel: Paramount Famous Lasky Corp.

Swing High, Swing Low 1937 d: Mitchell Leisen. lps: Carole Lombard, Fred MacMurray, Charles Butterworth. 95M USA. *Morning Noon and Night* prod/rel: Paramount Pictures©

When My Baby Smiles at Me 1948 d: Walter Lang. lps: Betty Grable, Dan Dailey, Jack Oakie. 98M USA. *Burlesque* prod/rel: 20th Century-Fox

WATTS, MARY S.
The Rise of Jennie Cushing, New York 1914, Novel
Rise of Jennie Cushing, The 1917 d: Maurice Tourneur. lps: Elsie Ferguson, Elliott Dexter, Fania Marinoff. 5r USA. *The Rise of Jenny Cushing* prod/rel: Artcraft Pictures Corp.©

WATTS, MIKE
The Pot Carriers, Television Play
Pot Carriers, The 1962 d: Peter Graham Scott. lps: Ronald Fraser, Paul Massie, Carole Lesley. 84M UKN. prod/rel: Associated British Picture Corporation, Warner-Pathe

WATTS-DUNTON, THEODORE
Aylwin, Novel
Aylwin 1920 d: Henry Edwards. lps: Henry Edwards, Chrissie White, Gerald Ames. 5485f UKN. prod/rel: Hepworth

WATZLIK, HANS
Die Romantische Reise Des Herrn Carl Maria von Weber, Short Story
Durch Die Walder, Durch Die Auen 1956 d: G. W. Pabst. lps: Eva Bartok, Karl Schonbock, Peter Arens. 98M GRM. prod/rel: Unicorn, N.F.

WAUGH, ALEC (1898–1981), UKN, Waugh, Alexander Raban
Guy Renton, 1953, Novel
Circle of Deception 1960 d: Jack Lee. lps: Bradford Dillman, Suzy Parker, Harry Andrews. 100M UKN. *Destruction Test* prod/rel: 20th Century Fox

Island in the Sun, 1955, Novel
Island in the Sun 1957 d: Robert Rossen. lps: James Mason, Joan Fontaine, Harry Belafonte. 123M UKN/USA. prod/rel: 20th Century-Fox, Darryl F. Zanuck

WAUGH, EVELYN (1903–1966), UKN, Waugh, Evelyn Arthur St. John
Brideshead Revisited, 1945, Novel
Brideshead Revisited 1981 d: Charles Sturridge, Michael Lindsay-Hogg. lps: Jeremy Irons, Anthony Andrews, Diana Quick. MTV. 664M UKN. prod/rel: Granada, Wnet-13

Decline and Fall, London 1928, Novel
Decline and Fall. of a Birdwatcher! 1968 d: John Krish. lps: Robin Philips, Genevieve Page, Donald Wolfit. 113M UKN. *Decline and Fall* prod/rel: 20th Century-Fox, Foxwell Entertainments

A Handful of Dust, 1934, Novel
Handful of Dust, A 1988 d: Charles Sturridge. lps: James Wilby, Kristin Scott-Thomas, Rupert Graves. 118M UKN/USA. prod/rel: Premier

The Loved One, Boston 1948, Novel
Loved One, The 1965 d: Tony Richardson. lps: Robert Morse, Jonathan Winters, Anjanette Comer. 116M USA. prod/rel: Filmways, Inc., United Artists

Scoop, 1938, Novel
Scoop 1987 d: Gavin Millar. lps: Denholm Elliott, Michael Hordern, Michael Maloney. TVM. 120M UKN. prod/rel: London Weekend Tv

Sword of Honour, Novel
Sword of Honour 1967 d: Donald McWhinnie. lps: Freddie Jones, Ronald Fraser, Edward Woodward. MTV. 270M UKN. prod/rel: BBC

WAUGH, HILLARY (1920–, USA, Waugh, Hillary Baldwin
Sleep Long My Love, New York 1959, Novel
Jigsaw 1962 d: Val Guest. lps: Jack Warner, Ronald Lewis, Yolande Donlan. 108M UKN. prod/rel: Figaro Films, Britannia

WAYNE, CHARLES STOKES
Story
Winchester Woman, The 1919 d: Wesley Ruggles. lps: Alice Joyce, Percy Marmont, Robert Middlemass. 5-6r USA. prod/rel: Vitagraph Co. of America©

The Marriage of Little Jeanne Sterling, 1918, Short Story
Midnight Bride, The 1920 d: William J. Humphrey. lps: Gladys Leslie, James Morrison, Gladden James. 4510f USA. *The Marriage of Little Jeanne Sterling* prod/rel: Vitagraph Co. of America©

WAYNE, PRISCILLA
Love Past Thirty, New York 1932, Novel
Love Past Thirty 1934 d: Vin Moore. lps: Aileen Pringle, Theodore von Eltz, Phyllis Barry. 73M USA. prod/rel: Freuler Film Associates, Monarch Productions

Marriage on Approval, New York 1930, Novel
Marriage on Approval 1933 d: Howard Higgin. lps: Barbara Kent, William Farnum, Clarence Geldart. 78M USA. *Married in Haste* (UKN) prod/rel: Freuler Film Associates©, Monarch Production

Rich Relations, Chicago 1934, Novel
Rich Relations 1937 d: Clifford Sanforth. lps: Ralph Forbes, Frances Grant, Barry Norton. 65M USA. prod/rel: Cameo Pictures Corp., Imperial Pictures

WEAD, FRANK (1895–1947), USA, Wead U.S.N., Com. Frank W.
Ceiling Zero, New York 1935, Play
Ceiling Zero 1936 d: Howard Hawks. lps: James Cagney, Pat O'Brien, June Travis. 95M USA. prod/rel: Warner Bros. Pictures, Inc.

International Squadron 1941 d: Lothar Mendes. lps: Ronald Reagan, James Stephenson, Olympe BradnA. 87M USA. *Flight Patrol* prod/rel: Warner Bros.

Wings of Men, Autobiography
Wings of Eagles, The 1956 d: John Ford. lps: John Wayne, Dan Dailey, Maureen O'HarA. 110M USA. prod/rel: MGM

WEATHERLEY, FRED
A Christmas Story, Poem
Christmas Story, A 1918. lps: Eric Williams. 1000f UKN. prod/rel: Eric Williams Speaking Pictures

The Surgeon's Child, Story
Surgeon's Child, The 1912 d: Harry T. Harris. lps: Eric Williams. 1000f UKN. prod/rel: Eric William's Speaking Pictures

WEATHERS, PHILIP
The Hypnotist, 1956, Play
Hypnotist, The 1957 d: Montgomery Tully. lps: Roland Culver, Patricia Roc, Paul Carpenter. 88M UKN. *Scotland Yard Dragnet* (USA) prod/rel: Anglo-Amalgamated, Merton Park

Madame Tictac, 1950, Play
No Road Back 1957 d: Montgomery Tully. lps: Skip Homeier, Paul Carpenter, Patricia Dainton. 83M UKN. prod/rel: Gibraltar, RKO

WEAVER, JOHN D.
A Christmas Gift, Story
Holiday Affair 1949 d: Don Hartman. lps: Janet Leigh, Robert Mitchum, Wendell Corey. 87M USA. prod/rel: RKO Radio

The Love Man, Novel
Dreamboat 1952 d: Claude Binyon. lps: Clifton Webb, Ginger Rogers, Anne Francis. 83M USA. prod/rel: 20th Century-Fox

WEAVER, JOHN V. A. (1893–1938), USA, Weaver, John Van Alstyn
Love 'Em and Leave 'Em, New York 1926, Play
Love 'Em and Leave 'Em 1926 d: Frank Tuttle. lps: Evelyn Brent, Lawrence Gray, Louise Brooks. 6r USA. prod/rel: Famous Players-Lasky, Paramount Pictures

WEAVER, WILL
Red Earth - White Earth, Book
Red Earth, White Earth 1989 d: David Greene. lps: Genevieve Bujold, Timothy Daly, Richard Farnsworth. TVM. 100M USA.

WEAVER, WYN
The Rising Generation, London 1923, Play
Rising Generation, The 1928 d: Harley Knoles, George Dewhurst. lps: Alice Joyce, Jameson Thomas, Robin Irvine. 7200f UKN. prod/rel: Westminster Pictures, Williams & Pritchard

WEBB, CHARLES
Belphegor the Mountebank, Novel
Belphegor the Mountebank 1921 d: Bert Wynne. lps: Milton Rosmer, Kathleen Vaughan, Warwick Ward. 5500f UKN. prod/rel: Ideal

The Graduate, New York 1963, Novel
Graduate, The 1967 d: Mike Nichols. lps: Anne Bancroft, Dustin Hoffman, Katharine Ross. 105M USA. prod/rel: Lawrence Turman, Inc.

Heading for Heaven, Play
Heading for Heaven 1947 d: Lewis D. Collins. lps: Stuart Erwin, Glenda Farrell, Russ Vincent. 71M USA. prod/rel: Eagle-Lion

The Marriage of a Young Stockbroker, 1970, Novel
Marriage of a Young Stockbroker, The 1971 d: Lawrence Turman. lps: Richard Benjamin, Joanna Shimkus, Elizabeth Ashley. 95M USA.

WEBB, GRAHAME
Numunwari, Novel
Dark Age 1986 d: Arch Nicholson. lps: John Jarratt, Nikki Coghill, Max Phipps. 86M ASL. prod/rel: F.G. Film Productions

WEBB, JAMES R.
A Baby for Midge, Story
Close to My Heart 1951 d: William Keighley. lps: Ray Milland, Gene Tierney, Fay Bainter. 90M USA. *As Time Goes By* prod/rel: Warner Bros.

Fugitive Form Terror, Serial Story
Woman in Hiding 1949 d: Michael Gordon. lps: Ida Lupino, Stephen McNally, Peggy Dow. 92M USA. *Fugitive from Terror* prod/rel: Universal-International

WEBB, MARY (1881–1927), UKN
Gone to Earth, 1917, Novel
Gone to Earth 1950 d: Michael Powell, Emeric Pressburger. lps: Jennifer Jones, David Farrar, Cyril Cusack. 110M UKN. *The Wild Heart* (USA) prod/rel: London Films, Vanguard

Precious Bane, 1924, Novel
Precious Bane 1988 d: Christopher Menaul. lps: Janet McTeer, John Bowe, John McEnery. TVM. 120M UKN/USA. prod/rel: BBC, Wgbh Boston

WEBB, WALTER PRESCOTT
The Texas Rangers, Boston 1935, Book
Texas Rangers, The 1936 d: King Vidor. lps: Fred MacMurray, Jack Oakie, Jean Parker. 95M USA. prod/rel: Paramount Pictures©

WEBBER, ANDREW LLOYD (1948–, UKN
Evita, Musical Play
Evita 1996 d: Alan Parker. lps: Madonna, Antonio Banderas, Jonathan Pryce. 134M/USA. prod/rel: Cinergi, Robert Stigwood

Jesus Christ Superstar, Opera
Jesus Christ Superstar 1973 d: Norman Jewison. lps: Ted Neeley, Carl Anderson, Yvonne Elliman. 108M USA. prod/rel: Universal Pictures

WEBBER, ERIC
Separate Vacations, Novel
Separate Vacations 1986 d: Michael Anderson. lps: David Naughton, Jennifer Dale, Mark Keyloun. 94M CND. prod/rel: R.S.L. Entertainment Corp., Moviecorp VIIi Inc.

WEBELS, WILLI

Hochzeit Mit Erika, Play

  Hochzeit Mit Erika 1949 d: Eduard von Borsody. lps: Marianne Schonauer, Wolfgang Lukschy, Dorit Kreysler. 89M GRM. *Wedding With Erika* prod/rel: Euphono, Panorama

WEBER

Les Joies du Foyer, 1894

  Gioie Del Focolare, Le 1920 d: Baldassarre Negroni. lps: Diomira Jacobini, Alberto Collo, Ida Carloni-Talli. 1340m ITL. *Le Gioie Della Famiglia* prod/rel: Film d'Arte Italiana

WEBER, G.

Der Letzte Walzer, Berlin 1920, Operetta

  Derniere Valse, La 1935 d: Leo Mittler. lps: Jean Martinelli, Armand Bernard, Yarmila NovotnA. 90M FRN. prod/rel: Warwick Films

  Last Waltz, The 1936 d: Gerald Barry, Leo Mittler. lps: Jarmila Novotna, Harry Welchman, Gerald Barry. 74M UKN. prod/rel: Warwick, Associated Producers and Distributors

WEBER, PIERRE

Gonzague, Play

  E Arrivato l'Accordatore 1952 d: Duilio Coletti. lps: Nino Taranto, Alberto Sordi, Tamara Lees. 90M ITL. *The Piano Tuner Has Arrived; Zero in Amore* prod/rel: Itala Film, Titanus

WEBER, SERGE

Lycee Des Jeunes Filles, Novel

  Romantic Age, The 1949 d: Edmond T. Greville. lps: Mai Zetterling, Hugh Williams, Margot Grahame. 86M UKN. *Naughty Arlette* (USA) prod/rel: Pinnacle Productions, General Film Distributors

WEBLING, PEGGY

Boundary House, Novel

  Boundary House 1918 d: Cecil M. Hepworth. lps: Alma Taylor, Gerald Ames, William Felton. 5250f UKN. prod/rel: Hepworth, Moss

WEBSTER, HENRY KITCHELL

The Butterfly, New York 1914, Novel

  Butterfly, The 1915 d: O. A. C. Lund. lps: Howard Estabrook, Barbara Tennant, Jessie Lewis. 5r USA. prod/rel: Shubert Film Corp., World Film Corp.©

Comrade John, New York 1907, Novel

  Comrade John 1915 d: T. Hayes Hunter. lps: William Elliott, Ruth Roland, Lew Cody. 5r USA. prod/rel: Balboa Amusement Producing Co., Pathe Exchange, Inc.

Joseph Greer and His Daughter, Indianapolis 1922, Novel

  What Fools Men 1925 d: George Archainbaud. lps: Lewis Stone, Shirley Mason, Ethel Grey Terry. 7349f USA. *Joseph Greer and His Daughter* prod/rel: First National Pictures

A King in Khaki, New York 1909, Novel

  Man of Honor, A 1919 d: Fred J. Balshofer. lps: Harold Lockwood, Bessie Eyton, Stanton Heck. 5r USA. *A King in Khaki* prod/rel: Yorke Film Corp., Metro Pictures Corp.

The Painted Scene, 1916, Short Story

  Great Adventure, The 1918 d: Alice Blache. lps: Bessie Love, Flora Finch, Donald Hall. 5r USA. *Spring of the Year* prod/rel: Pathe Exchange, Inc.©

The Real Adventure, New York 1915, Novel

  Real Adventure, The 1922 d: King Vidor. lps: Florence Vidor, Clyde Fillmore, Nellie Peck Saunders. 4932f USA. prod/rel: Florence Vidor Productions, Cameo Pictures

WEBSTER, JEAN (1876–1916), USA

Daddy Long-Legs, New York 1912, Novel

  Daddy Long Legs 1931 d: Alfred Santell. lps: Janet Gaynor, Warner Baxter, Una Merkel. 80M USA. prod/rel: Fox Film Corp., Alfred Santell Production

  Daddy Long Legs 1955 d: Jean Negulesco. lps: Fred Astaire, Leslie Caron, Terry Moore. 126M USA. prod/rel: 20th Century-Fox

  Daddy-Long-Legs 1919 d: Marshall Neilan. lps: Mary Pickford, Mahlon Hamilton, Milla Davenport. 7200f USA. prod/rel: Mary Pickford Co.©, First National Exhibitors Circuit©

  Vadertje Langbeen 1938 d: Friedrich Zelnik. lps: Lily Bouwmeester, Paul Storm, Jan Retel. 99M NTH.

WEBSTER, PAUL

Story

  Nora Prentiss 1947 d: Vincent Sherman. lps: Ann Sheridan, Kent Smith, Bruce Bennett. 111M USA. prod/rel: Warner Bros.

WEDDING, ALEX

Al Unku Edes Freundin War, Short Story

  Als Unku Edes Freundin War 1980 d: Helmut DziubA. lps: Axel Linder, Jacqueline Ody, Michael Falkenhagen. 72M GDR. *Ede Und Unku* prod/rel: Defa

WEDEKIND, FRANK (1864–1918), GRM

Die Buchse Der Pandora, 1904, Play

  Buchse Der Pandora, Die 1929 d: G. W. Pabst. lps: Louise Brooks, Fritz Kortner, Daisy d'OrA. 131M GRM. *Pandora's Box; Lulu* prod/rel: Nero

  Lulu 1962 d: Rolf Thiele. lps: Nadja Tiller, O. E. Hasse, Hildegard Knef. 100M AUS. *No Orchids for Lulu* (UKN) prod/rel: N.W.D.F.-Unitas

  Lulu 1977 d: Ronald Chase. 96M USA.

  Lulu 1980 d: Walerian Borowczyk. lps: Anne Bennent, Michele Placido, Jean-Jacques Delbo. 95M ITL/GRM/FRN. prod/rel: Capitol, Medusa Distribuzione

Der Erdgeist, 1895, Play

  Buchse Der Pandora, Die 1929 d: G. W. Pabst. lps: Louise Brooks, Fritz Kortner, Daisy d'OrA. 131M GRM. *Pandora's Box; Lulu* prod/rel: Nero

  Lulu 1962 d: Rolf Thiele. lps: Nadja Tiller, O. E. Hasse, Hildegard Knef. 100M AUS. *No Orchids for Lulu* (UKN) prod/rel: N.W.D.F.-Unitas

  Lulu 1980 d: Walerian Borowczyk. lps: Anne Bennent, Michele Placido, Jean-Jacques Delbo. 95M ITL/GRM/FRN. prod/rel: Capitol, Medusa Distribuzione

Fruhlings Erwachen, 1891, Play

  Warm in the Bud 1969 d: Rudolph Caringi. lps: Robert Mont, Dean Stricklin, Toni Hamilton. 57M USA.

Tod Und Teufel, 1909, Play

  Tod Und Teufel 1973 d: Stephen Dwoskin. 90M GRM. *Death and the Devil; Death and Devil*

WEDEKIND, KADIDJA

Story

  Ludwig II 1955 d: Helmut Kautner. lps: O. W. Fischer, Ruth Leuwerik, Paul Bildt. 115M GRM/AUS. *Glanz Und Ende Eines Konigs* prod/rel: Aura, Bavaria

WEFF, CLARENCE

Cent Briques Et Des Tuiles, Paris 1964, Novel

  Cent Briques Et Des Tuiles 1965 d: Pierre Grimblat. lps: Jean-Claude Brialy, Marie Laforet, Sophie Daumier. 95M FRN/ITL. *Colpo Grosso a Parigi* (FRN); *La Jeune de Les Cent Briques; How Not to Rob a Department Store* (USA) prod/rel: France Cinema Productions, P.C.M.

Y'avait un MacChabee, Novel

  Des Pissenlits Par la Racine 1963 d: Georges Lautner. lps: Louis de Funes, Michel Serrault, Mireille Darc. 95M FRN/ITL. *7-9-18 Da Parigi un Cadavere Per Rocky* (ITL) prod/rel: Ardennes Films, Transinter Films

WEGENER, M.

Kommissar X Jagt Den Roten Tiger, Novel

  Kommissar X: Jagt Die Roten Tiger 1971 d: Harald Reinl, Giancarlo Romitelli. lps: Luciano Stella, Brad Harris, Gisela Hahn. 90M GRM/ITL/PKS. *F.B.I. Operazione Pakistan* (ITL); *Tiger Gang; Commissioner X Chases the Red Tigers* prod/rel: Virginia Cin.Ca (Roma), Regina Film (Munich)

WEICHAND, PHILIP

Salvator, Play

  Monche, Madchen Und Panduren 1952 d: Ferdinand Dorfler. lps: Joe Stockel, Erich Ponto, Marianne Schonauer. 85M GRM. *Monks Girls and Hungarian Soldiers* prod/rel: Dorfler, Deutsche Cosmopol

WEICHAND, PHILIPP

Der Scheinheilige Florian, Play

  Scheinheilige Florian, Der 1941 d: Joe Stockel. lps: Joe Stockel, Erna Fentsch, Josef Eichheim. 93M GRM. prod/rel: Bavaria, Nordwest

WEICHERT, ERNST

Regina Amstetten, 1936, Short Story

  Regina Amstetten 1954 d: Kurt Neumann. lps: Luise Ullrich, Willy Eichberger, Paul Hartmann. 97M GRM. prod/rel: Roxy, D.F.H.

WEID, GUSTAV

Slaegten, 1898, Novel

  Slaegten 1978 d: Anders Refn. lps: Jens Okking, Helle Hertz, Bodil Udsen. 119M DNM. *Heritage; The Baron*

WEIDMAN, JEROME (1913–1998), USA

House of Strangers, Novel

  Broken Lance 1954 d: Edward Dmytryk. lps: Spencer Tracy, Robert Wagner, Jean Peters. 96M USA. prod/rel: 20th Century-Fox

  House of Strangers 1949 d: Joseph L. Mankiewicz. lps: Edward G. Robinson, Susan Hayward, Richard Conte. 101M USA. prod/rel: 20th Century Fox

I Can Get It for You Wholesale, 1937, Novel

  I Can Get It for You Wholesale 1951 d: Michael Gordon. lps: Susan Hayward, Dan Dailey, George Sanders. 93M USA. *This Is My Affair* (UKN); *Only the Best* prod/rel: 20th Century-Fox

WEIGALL, ARTHUR

Burning Sands, New York 1921, Novel

  Burning Sands 1922 d: George Melford. lps: Wanda Hawley, Milton Sills, Louise Dresser. 6919f USA. *The Dweller in the Desert* prod/rel: Famous Players-Lasky, Paramount Pictures

WEILL, KURT

Knickerbocker Holiday, New York 1938, Musical Play

  Knickerbocker Holiday 1944 d: Harry J. Brown. lps: Nelson Eddy, Charles Coburn, Constance Dowling. 85M USA. prod/rel: United Artists

One Touch of Venus, 1944, Musical Play

  One Touch of Venus 1948 d: William A. Seiter. lps: Robert Walker, Ava Gardner, Dick Haymes. 81M USA. prod/rel: Universal

WEIMAN, RITA

The Acquittal, New York 1920, Play

  Acquittal, The 1923 d: Clarence Brown. lps: Claire Windsor, Norman Kerry, Richard C. Travers. 6523f USA. prod/rel: Universal Pictures

The Co-Respondent, New York 1916, Play

  Co-Respondent, The 1917 d: Ralph Ince. lps: Elaine Hammerstein, Wilfred Lucas, George Anderson. 5-6r USA. prod/rel: Advanced Motion Pictures, Jewel Productions, Inc.©

  Whispered Name, The 1924 d: King Baggot. lps: Ruth Clifford, Charles Clary, William E. Lawrence. 5196f USA. *Blackmail; The Co-Respondent* prod/rel: Universal Pictures

Curtain, 1919, Short Story

  Curtain 1920 d: James Young. lps: Katherine MacDonald, Edwin Booth Tilton, Earl Whitlock. 5r USA. prod/rel: Katherine Macdonald Pictures Corp.©, First National Exhibitors Circuit

Footlights, 1919, Short Story

  Footlights 1921 d: John S. Robertson. lps: Elsie Ferguson, Reginald Denny, Marc MacDermott. 7078f USA. prod/rel: Famous Players-Lasky, Paramount Pictures

  Spotlight, The 1927 d: Frank Tuttle. lps: Esther Ralston, Neil Hamilton, Nicholas Soussanin. 4866f USA. prod/rel: Paramount Famous Lasky Corp.

Madame Peacock, 1919, Short Story

  Madame Peacock 1920 d: Ray C. Smallwood. lps: Alla Nazimova, George Probert, John Steppling. 5423f USA. prod/rel: the Nazimova Productions, Metro Pictures Corp.©

On Your Back, 1930, Short Story

  Esclavas de la Moda 1931 d: David Howard. lps: Carmen Larrabeiti, Julio Pena, Blanca de Castejon. 75M USA. *Sobre Su Espalda* prod/rel: Fox Film Corp.

  On Your Back 1930 d: Guthrie McClintic. lps: Irene Rich, Raymond Hackett, H. B. Warner. 6600f USA. *Clothes and the Woman* prod/rel: Fox Film Corp.

One Man's Secret, Novel

  Possessed 1947 d: Curtis Bernhardt. lps: Joan Crawford, Van Heflin, Raymond Massey. 108M USA. *One Man's Secret; The Secret* prod/rel: Warner Bros.

The Stage Door, Short Story

  After the Show 1921 d: William C. de Mille. lps: Jack Holt, Lila Lee, Charles Ogle. 5884f USA. prod/rel: Famous Players-Lasky Corp., Paramount Pictures

To Whom It May Concern, 1922, Short Story

  Social Code, The 1923 d: Oscar Apfel. lps: Viola Dana, Malcolm McGregor, Edna Flugrath. 4843f USA. *To Whom It May Concern* prod/rel: Metro Pictures

Upstage, 1922, Short Story

  Rouged Lips 1923 d: Harold Shaw. lps: Viola Dana, Tom Moore, Nola Luxford. 5150f USA. prod/rel: Metro Pictures

The Witness Chair, 1935, Novel

  Witness Chair, The 1936 d: George Nicholls Jr. lps: Ann Harding, Walter Abel, Douglas Dumbrille. 66M USA. prod/rel: RKO Radio Pictures©

WEINBERGER, KARL

Die Schone Tolzerin, Short Story

  Schone Tolzerin, Die 1952 d: Richard Haussler. lps: Franziska Kinz, Ingeborg Cornelius, Richard Haussler. 98M GRM. *The Elector's Woman* prod/rel: Ostermayr, Kopp

WEINER, JACK B.

The Morning After, Novel

  Morning After, The 1974 d: Richard T. Heffron. lps: Dick Van Dyke, Lynn Carlin, Don Porter. TVM. 78M USA. prod/rel: David L. Wolper Productions

WEINERT-WILTON, LOUIS
Das Geheimnis Der Chinesischen Nelke, Novel
   Geheimnis Der Chinesischen Nelke, Das 1964 d:
   Rudolf Zehetgruber. lps: Paul Dahlke, Olly Schoberova,
   Horst Frank. 90M GRM/ITL/SPN. *Il Segreto Del
   Garofano Cinese* (ITL); *The Secret of the Chinese
   Carnation* (USA) prod/rel: Rapid, Jacques Leitienne

Das Geheimnis Der Schwarzen Witwe, Novel
   Geheimnis Der Schwarzen Witwe, Das 1963 d:
   Franz J. Gottlieb. lps: O. W. Fischer, Karin Dor, Werner
   Peters. 100M GRM/SPN. *The Secret of the Black Widow*
   (USA); *Arana Negra* (SPN) prod/rel: International
   Germania, Procusa

Der Teppich Des Grauens, Novel
   Teppich Des Grauens, Der 1962 d: Harald Reinl. lps:
   Eleonora Rossi-Drago, Joachim Fuchsberger, Karin
   Dor. 92M GRM/ITL/SPN. *Il Terrore Di Notte* (ITL); *The
   Carpet of Horror* (USA); *Carpet of Cruelty*; *Terror En la
   Noche* (SPN) prod/rel: International Germania, Epoca

Die Weisse Spinne, Novel
   Weisse Spinne, Die 1963 d: Harald Reinl. lps: Joachim
   Fuchsberger, Karin Dor, Horst Frank. 110M GRM. *The
   White Spider* (USA) prod/rel: Arca, Oppenheimer

WEINTRAUB, WILLIAM
Why Rock the Boat?, Novel
   Why Rock the Boat? 1974 d: John Howe. lps: Stuart
   Gillard, Tiiu Leek, Ken James. 112M CND. prod/rel:
   National Film Board, Columbia Pictures

WEIR, HUGH C.
Dr. Mason's Temptation, Story
   Dr. Mason's Temptation 1915 d: Frank Lloyd. lps:
   Millard K. Wilson, Olive Fuller Golden, Marc Robbins.
   SHT USA. prod/rel: Laemmle

The Woolworth Diamonds, Short Story
   Under Suspicion 1918 d: Will S. Davis. lps: Francis X.
   Bushman, Beverly Bayne, Eva Gordon. 5r USA.
   prod/rel: Metro Pictures Corp.©

WEIRAUCH, ANNA ELISABETH
Das Ratsel Manuela, Novel
   Es Lebe Die Liebe 1944 d: Erich Engel. lps: Johannes
   Heesters, Lizzi Waldmuller, Hilde Seipp. 88M GRM.
   prod/rel: Bavaria, Nord-Westdeutscher

WEISENBORN, GUNTER
Das Madchen von Fano, 1935, Novel
   Madchen von Fano, Das 1940 d: Hans Schweikart.
   lps: Brigitte Horney, Joachim Gottschalk, Gustav
   Knuth. 95M GRM. prod/rel: Bavaria, Astor

WEISER, FRANZ
Das Licht Der Berge
   Licht Der Bergen, Het 1955 d: Gust Geens, Hugo Van
   Den Hoegaerde. lps: Leo Schuermans, Jan Van Brussel,
   Andre Tops. 90M BLG.

WEISKOPF, F. C.
Lissy, Novel
   Lissy 1957 d: Konrad Wolf. lps: Sonja Sutter,
   Hans-Peter Minetti, Horst DrindA. 88M GDR. prod/rel:
   Defa

WEISMAN, MARY-LOU
Intensive Care, Book
   Time to Live, A 1985 d: Rick Wallace. lps: Liza
   Minnelli, Jeffrey Demunn, Swoosie Kurtz. TVM. 100M
   USA. prod/rel: Itc Productions, Blue Andre Productions

WEISS, ERNST
Story
   Franta 1988 d: Mathias Allary. lps: Jan Kurbjuweit,
   Nicole Ansari, Ben Hekker. 96M GRM. prod/rel:
   Mathias Allary Prod., Sudwestfunk

WEISS, HELMUT
Sophienlund, Play
   Sophienlund 1943 d: Heinz Ruhmann. lps: Harry
   Liedtke, Kathe Haack, Hannelore Schroth. 92M GRM.
   prod/rel: Terra, D.F.V.

Talent Zum Gluck, Play
   Geheimnis Einer Ehe, Das 1951 d: Helmut Weiss.
   lps: Olga Tschechowa, Curd Jurgens, Paul Klinger. 94M
   GRM. *Secret of a Marriage* prod/rel: Venus

WEISS, JAN
Story
   Susse Zeit Mit Kalimagdora, Die 1968 d: Leopold
   LaholA. lps: Rudiger Bahr, Monika Zinnenberg, Gisela
   Hahn. 108M GRM/CZC. *The Delectable Time of
   Kalimagdora*; *The Sweet Time of Kalimagdora*; *Sladky
   Cas Kalimagdory* prod/rel: Gala International

WEISS, MARTA
Janken, Novel
   Janken 1970 d: Lars Lennart Forsberg. lps: Anita
   Ekstrom, Lars Green, Mona Dan-Bergman. 95M SWD.
   The Yankee prod/rel: Svenska Filminstitutet

WEISS, PETER (1916–1982), GRM, Weiss, Peter Ulrich
*Die Verfolgung Und Ermordung Jean Paul
Marats*, 1964, Play
   **Persecution and Assassination of Jean-Paul
   Marat As Performed By the Inmates of the
   Asylum.** 1966 d: Peter Brook. lps: Patrick Magee, Ian
   Richardson, Glenda Jackson. 116M UKN. *Marat/de
   Sade* prod/rel: Marat Sade Productions, United Artists

WEITZENKORN, LOUIS
Five Star Final, New York 1930, Play
   Five Star Final 1931 d: Mervyn Leroy. lps: Edward G.
   Robinson, H. B. Warner, Marian Marsh. 89M USA. *One
   Fatal Hour* prod/rel: First National Pictures©
   Two Against the World 1936 d: William McGann. lps:
   Humphrey Bogart, Beverly Roberts, Linda Perry. 64M
   USA. *The Case of Mrs. Pembroke* (UKN); *One Fatal
   Hour*; *The Voice of Life* prod/rel: Warner Bros. Pictures©

WELDON, FAY (1933–, UKN
Novel
   President's Child, The 1992 d: Sam Pillsbury. lps:
   Donna Mills, William Devane, Trevor Eve. TVM. 93M
   USA. prod/rel: CBS©

The Life and Loves of a She-Devil, Novel
   She-Devil 1989 d: Susan Seidelman. lps: Meryl Streep,
   Roseanne Barr, Ed Begley Jr. 99M USA. *The Life and
   Loves of a She-Devil* prod/rel: Orion

WELISCH, ERNST
Die Frau Im Hermelin, Play
   Bride of the Regiment 1930 d: John Francis Dillon.
   lps: Vivienne Segal, Allan Prior, Walter Pidgeon. 7418f
   USA. *Lady of the Rose* (UKN) prod/rel: First National
   Pictures
   Lady in Ermine, The 1927 d: James Flood. lps:
   Corinne Griffith, Einar Hansen, Ward Crane. 6400f
   USA. prod/rel: Corinne Griffith Productions, First
   National Pictures
   That Lady in Ermine 1948 d: Ernst Lubitsch, Otto
   Preminger (Uncredited). lps: Douglas Fairbanks Jr.,
   Betty Grable, Cesar Romero. 89M USA. prod/rel: 20th
   Century Fox

Eine Frau von Format, Operetta
   Frau von Format, Eine 1928 d: Fritz Wendhausen.
   lps: Mady Christians, Peter Leschka, Hans Thimig.
   2711m GRM. prod/rel: Terra-Film

Madame Pompadour, Play
   Madame Pompadour 1927 d: Herbert Wilcox. lps:
   Dorothy Gish, Antonio Moreno, Nelson Keys. 7245f
   UKN. prod/rel: British National, Paramount

WELLAND, COLIN
Kisses at 50, Play
   Twice in a Lifetime 1985 d: Bud Yorkin. lps: Gene
   Hackman, Ann-Margret, Ellen Burstyn. 117M USA.
   prod/rel: the Yorkin Company

WELLARD, JAMES
Action of the Tiger, Novel
   Action of the Tiger 1957 d: Terence Young. lps: Van
   Johnson, Martine Carol, Herbert Lom. 93M UKN/USA.
   prod/rel: MGM, Claridge

WELLEMINSKY, J. M.
The Dubarry, Opera
   I Give My Heart 1935 d: Marcel Varnel. lps: Gitta
   Alpar, Patrick Waddington, Owen Nares. 91M UKN.
   The Loves of Madame Dubarry (USA); *The Dubarry*
   prod/rel: British International Pictures, Wardour

WELLENKAMP, BRUNO
Lauter Sonnentage, Novel
   Annemarie, Die Geschichte Einer Jungen Liebe
   1936 d: Fritz Peter Buch. lps: Gisela Uhlen, Viktor von
   Zitzewitz, Paul Bildt. 95M GRM. *Die Geschichte Einer
   Jungen Liebe*; *Annemarie* prod/rel: Georg Witt-Film

WELLER, ARCHIE
Day of the Dog, Novel
   Blackfellas 1992 d: James Ricketson. lps: John Moore,
   David Ngoombujarra, Jaylene Riley. F ASL. *Day of the
   Dog* prod/rel: Barron Films

WELLERS, MICHAEL
Spoils of War, 1988, Play
   Spoils of War 1994 d: David Greene. lps: Kate Nelligan,
   John Heard, Tobey Maguire. TVM. 110M USA.

WELLERSHOFF, DIETER
Die Schattengrenze, Novel
   Schattengrenze, Die 1978 d: Wolfgang Gremm. lps:
   Gunter Lamprecht, Antje Hagen, Friedrich W.
   Bauschulte. TVM. 105M GRM. *Shadow's Edge* prod/rel:
   C.C.C., ZDF

WELLES, ORSON (1915–1985), USA
Mr. Arkadin, Novel
   Confidential Report 1955 d: Orson Welles. lps: Orson
   Welles, Robert Arden, Paola Mori. 99M
   UKN/SWT/SPN. *Mr. Arkadin* (USA); *Confidential File*;
   Monsieur Arkadin prod/rel: Sevilla Studios, Warner
   Bros.

WELLESLEY, GORDON
Gestapo, Novel
   Night Train to Munich 1940 d: Carol Reed. lps:
   Margaret Lockwood, Rex Harrison, Paul Henreid. 95M
   UKN. *Night Train* (USA); *Gestapo* prod/rel: 20th
   Century Productions, MGM

WELLM, ALFRED
Short Story
   Pferdemadchen, Der 1978 d: Egon Schlegel. lps:
   Martke Wellm, Wolfgang Winkler, Annette Roth. 84M
   GDR. prod/rel: Defa

WELLMAN, PAUL I. (1898–1966), USA, Wellman, Paul
Iselin
Bronco Apache, Novel
   Apache 1954 d: Robert Aldrich. lps: Burt Lancaster,
   Jean Peters, John McIntire. 91M USA. prod/rel: United
   Artists Corp., Hecht-Lancaster

The Comancheros, New York 1952, Novel
   Comancheros, The 1961 d: Michael Curtiz. lps: John
   Wayne, Stuart Whitman, Ina Balin. 107M USA.
   prod/rel: 20th Century-Fox

The Iron Mistress, Novel
   Iron Mistress, The 1952 d: Gordon Douglas. lps: Alan
   Ladd, Virginia Mayo, Don Beddoe. 110M USA. prod/rel:
   Warner Bros.

Jubal Troop, Novel
   Jubal 1956 d: Delmer Daves. lps: Glenn Ford, Ernest
   Borgnine, Rod Steiger. 101M USA. prod/rel: Columbia

Walls of Jericho, 1947, Novel
   Walls of Jericho 1948 d: John M. Stahl. lps: Cornel
   Wilde, Ann Dvorak, Anne Baxter. 106M USA. prod/rel:
   20th Century-Fox

WELLMAN, WILLIAM A. (1896–1975), USA
C'est la Guerre, Story
   Lafayette Escadrille 1958 d: William A. Wellman. lps:
   Tab Hunter, Etchika Choureau, Marcel Dalio. 93M
   USA. *Hell Bent for Glory* (UKN) prod/rel: Warner Bros.,
   William A. Wellman

WELLS, C. R.
Sous Les Cieux d'Arabie, Novel
   Sous le Ciel d'Orient 1927 d: Fred Leroy Granville, H.
   C. Grantham-Hayes. lps: Flora Le Breton, Gaston
   Modot, Joe Hamman. F FRN. prod/rel: Jacques Haik

WELLS, CAROLYN (1869–1942), USA
The Gold Bag, Story
   Mystery of West Sedgwick, The 1913. lps: Gertrude
   McCoy, Augustus Phillips, Bigelow Cooper. 2000f USA.
   prod/rel: Edison

That Winsome Winnie's Smile, Story
   Winnie's Dance 1912. lps: Gertrude McCoy. 1000f
   USA. prod/rel: Edison

The Three Kisses, Story
   Three Kisses, The 1909 d: Edwin S. Porter. lps:
   Florence Turner. 500f USA. prod/rel: Edison

Vicky Van, Philadelphia 1918, Novel
   Woman Next Door, The 1919 d: Robert G. VignolA.
   lps: Ethel Clayton, Emory Johnson, Noah Beery. USA.
   The Girl Next Door; *Vicky Van* prod/rel: Famous
   Players-Lasky Corp.©, Paramount Pictures

WELLS, H. G. (1866–1946), UKN, Wells, Herbert George
Bluebottles, Short Story
   Bluebottles 1928 d: Ivor Montagu. lps: Elsa
   Lanchester, Joe Beckett, Dorice Fordred. 2285f UKN.
   prod/rel: Angle Pictures, Ideal

Daydreams, Short Story
   Daydreams 1928 d: Ivor Montagu. lps: Elsa
   Lanchester, Harold Warrender, Charles Laughton.
   2224f UKN. prod/rel: Angle Pictures, Ideal

The Door in the Wall, 1911, Short Story
   Door in the Wall, The 1956 d: Glenn H. Alvey Jr. lps:
   Stephen Murray, Ian Hunter, Leonard Sachs. 29M
   UKN. prod/rel: British Film Institute, Ab-Pathe

Empire of the Ants, 1913, Short Story
   Empire of the Ants 1977 d: Bert I. Gordon. lps: Joan
   Collins, Robert Lansing, Albert Salmi. 90M USA.
   prod/rel: American International Pictures, Cinema 77

The First Men in the Moon, London 1901, Novel
   First Men in the Moon 1964 d: Nathan Juran. lps:
   Edward Judd, Martha Hyer, Lionel Jeffries. 103M
   UKN/USA. prod/rel: Ameran Films, Columbia
   First Men in the Moon, The 1919 d: J. L. V. Leigh. lps:
   Bruce Gordon, Heather Thatcher, Hector Abbas. 5175f
   UKN. prod/rel: Gaumont

The Food of the Gods and How It Came to Earth,
London 1904, Novel
Food of the Gods, The 1976 d: Bert I. Gordon. lps:
Marjoe Gortner, Pamela Franklin, Ralph Meeker. 88M
USA. prod/rel: American International
Village of the Giants 1965 d: Bert I. Gordon. lps:
Tommy Kirk, Johnny Crawford, Beau Bridges. 80M
USA. prod/rel: Berkeley Productions, Embassy Pictures

The History of Mr. Polly, London 1910, Novel
History of Mr. Polly, The 1949 d: Anthony Pelissier.
lps: John Mills, Sally Ann Howes, Finlay Currie. 95M
UKN. prod/rel: General Film Distributors, Two Cities

The Invisible Man, London 1897, Novel
Gemini Man 1976 d: Alan J. Levi. lps: Ben Murphy,
Katherine Crawford, Richard Dysart. TVM. 100M USA.
Code Name: Minus One prod/rel: NBC, Universal
Giustiziere Invisibile, Il 1916 d: Mario Roncoroni.
lps: Armando Fineschi, Valeria Creti, Vasco Creti. 863m
ITL. prod/rel: Corona Film
Invisible Man Returns, The 1940 d: Joe May. lps:
Cedric Hardwicke, Nan Grey, Vincent Price. 81M USA.
prod/rel: Universal Pictures Co.©
Invisible Man, The 1933 d: James Whale. lps: Claude
Rains, Gloria Stuart, William Harrigan. 71M USA.
prod/rel: Universal Pictures Corp.©
Invisible Man, The 1975 d: Robert Michael Lewis. lps:
David McCallum, Melinda Fee, Jackie Cooper. TVM.
78M USA. prod/rel: Universal
Tomei Ningen 1954 d: Motoyoshi OdA. lps: Seizaburo
Kawazu, Minoru Takada, Yoshio TsuchiyA. 70M JPN.
Invisible Man prod/rel: Toho Co.

The Island of Dr. Moreau, London 1896, Novel
Island of Dr. Moreau, The 1977 d: Don Taylor. lps:
Burt Lancaster, Michael York, Nigel Davenport. 104M
USA.
Island of Dr. Moreau, The 1996 d: John
Frankenheimer. lps: Marlon Brando, Val Kilmer, David
Thewlis. 95M USA. prod/rel: New Line Productions,
Edward R. Pressman Production
Island of Lost Souls 1933 d: Erle C. Kenton. lps:
Charles Laughton, Bela Lugosi, Richard Arlen. 74M
USA. *The Island of Dr. Moreau* prod/rel: Paramount
Productions©
Terror Is a Man 1959 d: Gerardo de Leon. lps: Francis
Lederer, Greta Thyssen, Richard Derr. 89M USA.
*Creature from Blood Island; Blood Creature; The Gory
Creatures* prod/rel: Valiant, Lynn-Romero Prods.

Kipps, London 1905, Novel
Half a Sixpence 1967 d: George Sidney. lps: Tommy
Steele, Julia Foster, Cyril Ritchard. 146M UKN/USA.
prod/rel: Ameran Films, Paramount
Kipps 1921 d: Harold Shaw. lps: George K. Arthur,
Edna Flugrath, Christine Rayner. 6194f UKN. prod/rel:
Stoll
Kipps 1941 d: Carol Reed. lps: Michael Redgrave, Diana
Wynyard, Phyllis Calvert. 112M UKN/USA. *The
Remarkable Mr. Kipps* prod/rel: 20th Century-Fox, 20th
Century Productions

The Magic Shop, 1905, Short Story
Magic Shop, The 1982 d: Ian Emes. 23M UKN.

The Man Who Could Work Miracles, 1899, Short
Story
Man Who Could Work Miracles, The 1936 d: Lothar
Mendes. lps: Roland Young, Ralph Richardson, Edward
Chapman. 82M UKN. prod/rel: London Films, United
Artists

Marriage, London 1912, Novel
Marriage 1927 d: R. William Neill. lps: Virginia Valli,
Allan Durant, Gladys McConnell. 5458f USA. prod/rel:
Fox Film Corp.

The Passionate Friends, 1913, Novel
Passionate Friends, The 1922 d: Maurice Elvey. lps:
Milton Rosmer, Valia, Fred Raynham. 7231f UKN.
prod/rel: Stoll
Passionate Friends, The 1948 d: David Lean. lps:
Ann Todd, Claude Rains, Trevor Howard. 95M UKN.
One Woman's Story (USA) prod/rel: General Film
Distributors, Cineguild

The Shape of Things to Come, 1933, Novel
Shape of Things to Come, The 1979 d: George
McCowan. lps: Jack Palance, Carol Lynley, John
Ireland. 98M CND. *H.G. Wells' the Shape of Things to
Come; Delta III; Alerte Dans le Cosmos* prod/rel:
S.O.T.T.C. Film Productions Ltd., Cfi Investments Inc.
Things to Come 1936 d: William Cameron Menzies.
lps: Raymond Massey, Cedric Hardwicke, Margaretta
Scott. 100M UKN. *The Shape of Things to Come;
Whither Mankind* prod/rel: London Films, United
Artists

The Time machine, 1895, Novel
Time machine, The 1960 d: George Pal. lps: Rod
Taylor, Alan Young, Sebastian Cabot. 101M USA.
prod/rel: George Pal, MGM
Time machine, The 1978 d: Henning Schellerup. lps:
John Beck, Priscilla Barnes, Andrew Duggan. TVM.
100M USA. prod/rel: Schick Sunn Classics

The Tonic, Short Story
Tonic, The 1928 d: Ivor Montagu. lps: Elsa Lanchester,
Renee de Vaux. 2410f UKN. prod/rel: Angle Pictures,
Ideal

War of the Worlds, 1897, Novel
War of the Worlds, The 1953 d: Byron Haskin. lps:
Gene Barry, Ann Robinson, Les Tremayne. 85M USA.
prod/rel: Paramount

The Wheels of Chance, Novel
Wheels of Chance, The 1922 d: Harold Shaw. lps:
George K. Arthur, Olwen Roose, Gordon Parker. 5312f
UKN. prod/rel: Stoll

The Wonderful Visit, 1895, Novel
Merveilleuse Visite, La 1973 d: Marcel Carne. lps:
Gilles Kohler, Deborah Berger, Roland Lesaffre. 100M
FRN/ITL.

WELLS, JOHN
Rafter Romance, New York 1932, Novel
Living on Love 1937 d: Lew Landers. lps: James Dunn,
Whitney Bourne, Joan Woodbury. 61M USA. *Love in a
Basement* prod/rel: RKO Radio Pictures©
Rafter Romance 1934 d: William A. Seiter. lps: Ginger
Rogers, Norman Foster, George Sidney. 70M USA.
prod/rel: RKO Radio Pictures©

WELLS, LEE
Day of the Outlaw, 1955, Novel
Day of the Outlaw 1959 d: Andre de Toth. lps: Robert
Ryan, Tina Louise, Burl Ives. 90M USA. prod/rel:
United Artists, Security Pictures
Night of the Running Man, Novel
Night of the Running Man 1994 d: Mark L. Lester.
lps: Scott Glenn, Andrew McCarthy, Janet Gunn. 93M
USA. prod/rel: Trimark, American World

WELLS, LEILA BURTON
The Naked Truth, 1916, Short Story
Perfect Lover, The 1919 d: Ralph Ince. lps: Eugene
O'Brien, Lucille Lee Stewart, Marguerite Courtot.
4851f USA. *The Naked Truth; The Perfect Love* prod/rel:
Selznick Pictures Corp.©, Select Pictures Corp.

WELLS, LINTON
Suzanna, Story
Suzanna 1922 d: F. Richard Jones. lps: Mabel
Normand, George Nichols, Walter McGrail. 6500f USA.
prod/rel: Mack Sennett Productions, Allied Producers
and Distributors

WELLS, PETER
Of Memory & Desire, Story
Memory & Desire 1998 d: Niki Caro. lps: Yuri
Kinugawa, Eugene Nomura, Yoko Narahashi. 89M
NZL. prod/rel: Newmarket Capital Group, Goldwyn
Films

WELLS, TIFFANY
Shebo, Story
Miss Nobody 1926 d: Lambert Hillyer. lps: Anna Q.
Nilsson, Walter Pidgeon, Louise FazendA. 6859f USA.
prod/rel: First National Pictures

WELLS, W. K.
Manhattan Mary, New York 1927, Musical Play
Follow the Leader 1930 d: Norman Taurog. lps: Ed
Wynn, Ginger Rogers, Stanley Smith. 6851f USA.
Manhattan Mary prod/rel: Paramount-Publix Corp.

WELSH, IRVINE
The Acid House, Short Stories
Acid House, The 1998 d: Paul McGuigan. lps: Stephen
McCole, Maurice Roeves, Garry Sweeney. 118M UKN.
prod/rel: Picture Palace North, Umbrella Prods.
Trainspotting, Novel
Trainspotting 1996 d: Danny Boyle. lps: Ewan
McGregor, Ewen Bremner, Jonny Lee Miller. 94M
UKN. prod/rel: Polygram, Channel 4

WELSKOPF-HENRICH, LIESELOTTE
Die Sohne Der Grossen Barin, Novel
Sohne Der Grossen Barin, Die 1966 d: Josef MacH.
lps: Gojko Mitic, Jiri Vrstala, Rolf Romer. 92M GDR.
Sons of the Great Bear prod/rel: Defa

WELTI, A. J.
Steibruch, Elgg 1939, Play
Steibruch 1942 d: Sigfrit Steiner. lps: Maria Schell,
Heinrich Gretler, Adolf Manz. 99M SWT.
*Gottesmuhlen; Stimme Des Blutes; La Carriere; Spate
Suhne* prod/rel: Zurcher Filmkollektiv Der Gloriafilm

WELTZENKORN, LOUIS
Ten Cent Lady, Short Story
Like Wildfire 1917 d: Stuart Paton. lps: Herbert
Rawlinson, Neva Gerber, L. M. Wells. 5r USA. prod/rel:
Universal Film Mfg. Co.©, Butterfly Picture

WEN DA
Double Bell Watch, Novel
Guo Qing Shi Dian Zhong 1956 d: Wu Tian. lps: Yin
Zhiming, Zhao Lian, Zhao Zhiyue. 10r CHN. *10:00 on the
National Holiday* prod/rel: Changchun Film Studio

WENDT, ALBERT
Flying Fox in a Freedom Tree, Novel
Flying Fox in a Freedom Tree 1989 d: Martyn
Sanderson. lps: Faifua Amiga Jr., Richard von Sturmer,
Peseta Isara IsarA. 92M NZL. prod/rel: Grahame
Mclean Associates, New Zealand Film Commission

WENGER, LISA
Verenas Hochzeit, Novel
Mariage de Verena, Le 1938 d: Jacques Daroy. lps:
Jeanne Boitel, Pierre Larquey, Rene Daix. 95M
FRN/SWT. *La Batarde* prod/rel: Producteurs Associes

WENIG, JAN
Madla Zpiva Evrope, Novel
Madla Zpiva Evrope 1940 d: Vaclav Binovec. lps:
Zdenka Sulanova, Ladislav Bohac, Jaroslav PruchA.
3035m CZC. *Madla Sings to Europe* prod/rel: Europa

WENTWORTH, MARION CRAIG
War Brides, Play
War Brides 1916 d: Herbert Brenon. lps: Alla
Nazimova, Charles Hutchison, Charles Bryant. 8r USA.
Joan of Flanders prod/rel: Herbert Brenon Film Corp.©,
Lewis J. Selznick Enterprises, Inc.

WENTWORTH-JAMES, GERTIE
The Girl Who Wouldn't Work, London 1913, Novel
Girl Who Wouldn't Work, The 1925 d: Marcel de
Sano. lps: Lionel Barrymore, Marguerite de La Motte,
Henry B. Walthall. 5979f USA. prod/rel: B. P. Schulberg
Productions
House of Chance, New York 1912, Novel
Cheating Blondes 1933 d: Joseph Levering. lps:
Thelma Todd, Rolfe Harold, Inez Courtney. 66M USA.
House of Chance (UKN) prod/rel: Equitable Pictures,
Inc.
The Wife Who Wasn't Wanted, London 1923, Novel
Wife Who Wasn't Wanted, The 1925 d: James Flood.
lps: Irene Rich, Huntley Gordon, John Harron. 6858f
USA. prod/rel: Warner Brothers Pictures

WEORES, SANDOR
Psyche: Egy Hajdani Koltono Irasai, 1972, Novel
Narcisz Es Psyche 1980 d: Gabor Body. lps: Patricia
Adriani, Udo Kier, Gyorgy Cserhalmi. 140M HNG.
Narcissus and Psyche prod/rel: Mafilm

WERFEL, FRANZ (1890–1945), AUS
Jacobowsky Und Der Oberst, 1944, Play
Me and the Colonel 1958 d: Peter Glenville. lps:
Danny Kaye, Curd Jurgens, Nicole Maurey. 109M USA.
prod/rel: Columbia, Gourt-Goetz Prods.
Juarez Und Maximilian, Vienna 1924, Play
Juarez 1939 d: William Dieterle. lps: Paul Muni, Bette
Davis, Brian Aherne. 132M USA. *The Phantom Crown;
Maximilian and Carlotta* prod/rel: Warner Bros.
Pictures©
Das Lied von Bernadette, 1941, Novel
Song of Bernadette, The 1943 d: Henry King. lps:
Jennifer Jones, Charles Bickford, Gladys Cooper. 156M
USA. prod/rel: 20th Century-Fox
Verdi. Roman Der Oper, 1924, Novel
Giuseppe Verdi 1953 d: Raffaello Matarazzo. lps:
Pierre Cressoy, Anna Maria Ferrero, Tito Gobbi. 120M
ITL. *The Life and Music of Giuseppe Verdi* (USA); *Verdi*
prod/rel: Consorzio Verdi, P.a.T.
Der Veruntreute Himmel, 1948, Novel
Veruntreute Himmel, Der 1958 d: Ernst MarischkA.
lps: Annie Rosar, Hans Holt, Viktor de KowA. 105M
GRM. *Embezzled Heaven* (USA); *Cheated Heaven*
prod/rel: Rhombus

WERGELAND, HENRIK (1808–1845), NRW
Der Weihnachtsabend, Poem
Isaak, Der Handelsjude 1912 d: Adolf Gartner. lps:
Robert Garrison. 448m GRM. prod/rel: Messters
Projektion

WERICH, JAN
Rub a Lic, Play
Svet Patri Nam 1937 d: Martin Fric. lps: Jiri Voskovec,
Jan Werich, Vladimir Smeral. 2625m CZC. *The World
Belongs to Us; The World Is Ours* prod/rel: Ab

WERNER, ELSIE
You're in the Army Now, Story
Into No Man's Land 1928 d: Cliff Wheeler. lps:
Thomas Santschi, Josephine Norman, Jack Daugherty.
6700f USA. *The Secret Lie* (UKN) prod/rel: Excellent
Pictures

WERNER, VILEM
Lide Na Kre, Play
Lide Na Kre 1937 d: Martin Fric. lps: Frantisek Smolik, Zdenka Baldova, Ladislav Bohac. 2523m CZC. *People on the Iceberg; Lost on the Ice; People on a Glacier; People on an Iceberg* prod/rel: UFA
Pravo Na Hrich, Play
Pravo Na Hrich 1932 d: Vladimir Slavinsky. lps: K. V. Marek, Truda Grosslichtova, Antonin VaverkA. 2847m CZC. *The Title for the Sin; The Right to Sin* prod/rel: Oceanfilm

WERSBY, BARBARA
The Country of the Heart, Book
Matters of the Heart 1990 d: Michael Ray Rhodes. lps: Jane Seymour, Christopher Gartin, James Stacy. TVM. 100M USA.

WESKER, ARNOLD (1932–, UKN
The Kitchen, London 1959, Play
Kitchen, The 1961 d: James Hill. lps: Carl Mohner, Mary Yeomans, Eric Pohlmann. 74M UKN. prod/rel: Act Films, British Lion

WESLEY, MARY
The Camomile Lawn, Novel
Camomile Lawn, The 1991 d: Peter Hall. lps: Felicity Kendal, Paul Eddington, Oliver Cotton. MTV. 258M UKN. prod/rel: Zed Ltd., Channel Four
Harnessing Peacocks, Novel
Harnessing Peacocks 1992 d: James Cellan Jones. lps: Serena Scott Thomas, Peter Davison, Tom Beasley. TVM. 104M UKN. prod/rel: Friday Productions
Jumping the Queue, Novel
Jumping the Queue 1989 d: Claude Whatham. lps: Sheila Hancock, David Threlfall, Don Henderson. TVM. 160M UKN. prod/rel: BBC

WEST, CON
Josser on the Farm, Play
Josser on the Farm 1934 d: T. Hayes Hunter. lps: Ernie Lotinga, Betty Astell, Garry Marsh. 63M UKN. prod/rel: Fox British
Love Up the Pole, 1935, Play
Love Up the Pole 1936 d: Clifford Gulliver. lps: Ernie Lotinga, Vivienne Chatterton, Wallace Lupino. 82M UKN. prod/rel: British Comedies, Butcher's Film Service
The Mouse Trap, Play
Acci-Dental Treatment 1929 d: Thomas Bentley. lps: Ernie LotingA. 17M UKN. prod/rel: British Sound Film Production, Bifd
The Naughty Age, Play
Strictly Illegal 1935 d: Ralph Ceder. lps: Leslie Fuller, Betty Astell, Georgie Harris. 69M UKN. *Here Comes a Policeman* prod/rel: Leslie Fuller Films, Gaumont-British

WEST, DOROTHY
The Wedding, Novel
Oprah Winfrey Presents: the Wedding 1998 d: Charles Burnett. lps: Halle Berry, Eric Thal, Lynn Whitfield. TVM. 240M USA. prod/rel: Harpo Films Inc.

WEST, JESSAMYN
Except for Me and Thee, Book
Friendly Persuasion 1975 d: Joseph Sargent. lps: Richard Kiley, Shirley Knight, Clifton James. TVM. 100M USA. *Except for Me and Thee* prod/rel: Allied Artists, International Television Pruductions
The Friendly Persuasion, 1945, Novel
Friendly Persuasion 1956 d: William Wyler. lps: Gary Cooper, Dorothy McGuire, Marjorie Main. 139M USA. *Thee I Love* prod/rel: Allied Artists, B-M Prod.
The Friendly Persuasion, 1945, Book
Friendly Persuasion 1975 d: Joseph Sargent. lps: Richard Kiley, Shirley Knight, Clifton James. TVM. 100M USA. *Except for Me and Thee* prod/rel: Allied Artists, International Television Pruductions

WEST, M.
Der Vogelhandler, Vienna 1891, Operetta
Vogelhandler, Der 1953 d: Arthur M. Rabenalt. lps: Ilse Werner, Eva Probst, Erni Mangold. 92M GRM. *The Bird Dealer* prod/rel: Berolina, Deutsche Cosmopol
Vogelhandler, Der 1962 d: Geza von CziffrA. lps: Conny Froboess, Peter Weck, Maria Sebaldt. 87M GRM. *The Bird Dealer* prod/rel: Divina, Gloria

WEST, MAE (1892–1980), USA
Diamond Lil, New York 1928, Play
She Done Him Wrong 1933 d: Lowell Sherman. lps: Mae West, Cary Grant, Gilbert Roland. 66M USA. *Honky Tonk; Ruby Red; Lady Lou* prod/rel: Paramount Productions

WEST, MORRIS (1916–, ASL, West, Morris Langlo
The Big Story, London 1957, Novel
Crooked Road, The 1964 d: Don Chaffey. lps: Robert Ryan, Stewart Granger, Nadia Gray. 93M UKN/YGS. *Krivi Put* (YGS) prod/rel: Gala, Argo

The Devil's Advocate, 1959, Novel
Avvocato Del Diavolo, L' 1977 d: Guy Green. lps: John Mills, Stephane Audran, Jason Miller. 109M ITL/GRM. *The Devil's Advocate* (UKN); *Des Teufels Advokat* (GRM) prod/rel: Nf Geria, Bavaria
The Naked Country, Novel
Morris West's the Naked Country 1985 d: Tim Burstall. lps: John Stanton, Rebecca Gilling, Ivar Kants. 92M ASL. *The Naked Country* prod/rel: Naked Country Productions©, Filmpac
The Salamander, Novel
Salamander, The 1981 d: Peter Zinner. lps: Franco Nero, Anthony Quinn, Martin Balsam. 101M USA/UKN/ITL. prod/rel: Grade, William R. Foreman
The Second Victory, Novel
Second Victory, The 1987 d: Gerald Thomas. lps: Anthony Andrews, Helmut Griem, Mario Adorf. 112M UKN/ASL. prod/rel: Lelaleuka, J and M
The Shoes of the Fisherman, New York 1963, Novel
Shoes of the Fisherman, The 1968 d: Michael Anderson. lps: Anthony Quinn, Oskar Werner, David Janssen. 155M USA/ITL. prod/rel: Metro-Goldwyn-Mayer, Inc.

WEST, NATHANAEL (1904–1940), USA, Weinstein, Nathanael Wallenstein
The Day of the Locust, 1939, Novel
Day of the Locust, The 1975 d: John Schlesinger. lps: Karen Black, Donald Sutherland, Burgess Meredith. 145M USA. prod/rel: Paramount
Miss Lonelyhearts, New York 1933, Novel
Advice to the Lovelorn 1933 d: Alfred L. Werker. lps: Lee Tracy, Sally Blane, Sterling Holloway. 62M USA. prod/rel: 20th Century Pictures, Inc., United Artists
I'll Tell the World 1945 d: Leslie Goodwins. lps: Lee Tracy, Brenda Joyce, Raymond Walburn. 61M USA. prod/rel: Universal
Lonelyhearts 1958 d: Vincent J. Donehue. lps: Montgomery Clift, Robert Ryan, Myrna Loy. 101M USA. *Miss Lonelyhearts* prod/rel: United Artists, Schary Prods.

WEST, REBECCA (1892–1983), IRL, Andrews, Cicily Maxwell
Abiding Vision, 1935, Short Story
Life of Her Own, A 1950 d: George Cukor. lps: Lana Turner, Ray Milland, Tom Ewell. 108M USA. prod/rel: MGM
The Return of the Soldier, 1918, Novel
Return of the Soldier 1982 d: Alan Bridges. lps: Alan Bates, Glenda Jackson, Julie Christie. 101M UKN. prod/rel: Brent Walker, Barry R. Cooper

WEST, ROLAND
The Unknown Purple, New York 1918, Play
Unknown Purple, The 1923 d: Roland West. lps: Henry B. Walthall, Alice Lake, Stuart Holmes. 7r USA. prod/rel: Carlos Productions, Truart Film Corp.

WEST, STANLEY
Amos, Novel
Amos 1985 d: Michael Tuchner. lps: Kirk Douglas, Elizabeth Montgomery, Dorothy McGuire. TVM. 100M USA. prod/rel: CBS, the Bryna Company

WEST, WALLACE
Muddy Waters, Short Story
Headline Shooter 1933 d: Otto Brower. lps: William Gargan, Frances Dee, Ralph Bellamy. 65M USA. *Evidence in Camera* (UKN); *Headline Shooters* prod/rel: RKO Radio Pictures©

WEST, WALTER
Big Bend Buckaroo, Short Story
Riding Avenger, The 1936 d: Harry L. Fraser. lps: Hoot Gibson, Ruth Mix, Buzz Barton. 60M USA. prod/rel: Wafilms, State Rights

WEST, WILTON
Short Story
Crimson Trail, The 1935 d: Alfred Raboch. lps: Buck Jones, Polly Ann Young, Carl Stockdale. 58M USA. prod/rel: Universal Pictures Corp.

WESTA, THOMAS
Amor Und Zwirn Himmel, Novel
Himmel, Amor Und Zwirn 1960 d: Ulrich Erfurth. lps: Hartmut Reck, Grit Boettcher, Hannelore Schroth. 86M GRM. *Heaven Love and Twine* prod/rel: D.F.H.

WESTBROOK, HERBERT
Brother Alfred, London 1913, Play
Brother Alfred 1932 d: Henry Edwards. lps: Gene Gerrard, Molly Lamont, Elsie Randolph. 77M UKN. prod/rel: British International Pictures, Wardour

WESTBROOK, ROBERT T.
The Magic Garden of Stanley Sweetheart, New York 1969, Novel
Magic Garden of Stanley Sweetheart, The 1970 d: Leonard Horn. lps: Don Johnson, Linda Gillin, Michael Greer. 117M USA. prod/rel: Metro-Goldwyn-Mayer, Inc.

WESTCOTT, EDWARD NOYES
David Harum, New York 1898, Novel
David Harum 1915 d: Allan Dwan. lps: William H. Crance, Harold Lockwood, Kate Meeks. 5r USA. prod/rel: Famous Players Film Co., Paramount Pictures Corp.
David Harum 1934 d: James Cruze. lps: Will Rogers, Louise Dresser, Evelyn Venable. 83M USA. prod/rel: Fox Film Corp.

WESTCOTT, F. N.
Dabney Todd, New York 1916, Novel
Down Home 1920 d: Irvin V. Willat. lps: James O. Barrows, Edward Hearn, Aggie Herring. 7r USA. prod/rel: Willat Productions, Inc.©, W. W. Hodkinson Corp.

WESTENBERGER, HEDDA
Streit Um Den Knaben Jo, Novel
Streit Um Den Knaben Jo 1937 d: Erich Waschneck. lps: Lil Dagover, Willy Fritsch, Maria von Tasnady. 95M GRM. *Strife Over the Boy Jo* (USA) prod/rel: Fanal-Filmproduktion

WESTERBY, ROBERT
The Small Voice, Novel
Small Voice, The 1948 d: Fergus McDonnell. lps: Valerie Hobson, James Donald, Howard Keel. 85M UKN. *The Hideout* (USA) prod/rel: British Lion, Constellation
Wide Boys Never Work, Novel
Soho Incident 1956 d: Vernon Sewell. lps: Faith Domergue, Lee Patterson, Rona Anderson. 77M UKN. *Spin a Dark Web* (USA); *Forty-Four Soho Square* prod/rel: Film Locations, Columbia

WESTERVELT, LEONIDAS
The Siren's Song, Play
Siren's Song, The 1915 d: George W. Lederer. lps: Charles Trowbridge, Mlle. Diane, Adolph Link. 5r USA. *The Song of the Siren; The Sinner* prod/rel: Shubert Film Corp., World Film Corp.©

WESTHEIMER, DAVID
My Sweet Charlie, New York 1965, Novel
My Sweet Charlie 1970 d: Lamont Johnson. lps: Patty Duke, Al Freeman Jr., Ford Rainey. TVM. 97M USA. prod/rel: Universal
Von Ryan's Express, New York 1964, Novel
Von Ryan's Express 1965 d: Mark Robson. lps: Frank Sinatra, Trevor Howard, Raffaella CarrA. 117M USA. prod/rel: P-R Productions

WESTLAKE, DONALD E. (1933–, USA, Stark, Richard, Westlake, Donald Edwin Edmund
The Bank Shot, Novel
Bank Shot, The 1974 d: Gower Champion. lps: George C. Scott, Joanna Cassidy, Sorrell Brooke. 84M USA. prod/rel: United Artists Corp.
The Busy Body, New York 1966, Novel
Busy Body, The 1967 d: William Castle. lps: Sid Caesar, Robert Ryan, Anne Baxter. 102M USA.
Dancing Aztecs, Novel
Divine Poursuite, La 1997 d: Michel Deville. lps: Antoine de Caunes, Emmanuelle Seigner, Elodie Bouchez. 102M FRN. *The Gods Must Be Dancing* prod/rel: Elefilm, France 3 Cinema
The Hot Rock, Novel
Hot Rock, The 1972 d: Peter Yates. lps: Robert Redford, George Segal, Ron Leibman. 101M USA. *How to Steal a Diamond in Four Uneasy Lessons* (UKN) prod/rel: Landers-Roberts
The Hunter, New York 1963, Novel
Payback 1999 d: Brian Helgeland. lps: Mel Gibson, Gregg Henry, Maria Bello. 101M USA. prod/rel: Paramount Pictures, Icon
Point Blank 1967 d: John Boorman. lps: Lee Marvin, Angie Dickinson, Keenan Wynn. 92M USA. prod/rel: Metro-Goldwyn-Mayer, Inc.
Gli Ineffabili Cinque, Novel
Cinque Furbastri E un Furbacchione 1977 d: Lucio de Caro. lps: Renato Cestie, Walter Chiari, Stefania Casini. 95M ITL. *Un Furbacchione Cinque Furbastri; Come Ti Rapisco Il Pupo* prod/rel: Serena Film, Euro International Film
Jimmy the Kid, Novel
Jimmy the Kid 1983 d: Gary Nelson. lps: Gary Coleman, Paul Lemat, Walter Olkewicz. 85M USA. prod/rel: New World
Mise a Sac, Novel
Mise a Sac 1967 d: Alain Cavalier. lps: Daniel Ivernel, Michel Constantin, Franco Interlenghi. 108M FRN/ITL. *Una Notte Per 5 Rapine* (ITL); *Torn to Bits* prod/rel: Films Ariane, Artistes Associes
The Outfit, Novel
Outfit, The 1973 d: John Flynn. lps: Robert Duvall, Karen Black, Robert Ryan. 103M USA. *The Good Guys Always Win* prod/rel: MGM

Rien Dans le Coffre, Novel
Made in U.S.A. 1966 d: Jean-Luc Godard. lps: Anna Karina, Jean-Pierre Leaud, Laszlo Szabo. 90M FRN. prod/rel: Rome-Paris-Films, Anouchka Films

The Seventh, New York 1966, Novel
Split, The 1968 d: Gordon Flemyng. lps: Jim Brown, Diahann Carroll, Ernest Borgnine. 90M USA. prod/rel: Spectrum Productions

Slayground, Novel
Slayground 1983 d: Terry Bedford. lps: Peter Coyote, Mel Smith, Billie Whitelaw. 89M UKN. prod/rel: Emi, Jennie & Co.

Two Much, Novel
Jumeau, Le 1984 d: Yves Robert. lps: Pierre Richard, Carey More, Camilla More. 110M FRN. prod/rel: la Gueville, Fideline Films

Loco de Amor 1996 d: Fernando TruebA. lps: Antonio Banderas, Melanie Griffith, Daryl Hannah. 115M SPN/USA. *Two Much* (USA) prod/rel: Andres Vicente Gomez, Sogetel

Why Me?, Novel
Why Me? 1990 d: Gene Quintano. lps: Christopher Lambert, Kim Greist, Christopher Lloyd. 88M USA. prod/rel: Carolina, Epic

WESTLEY, GEORGE HEMBERT
Rothschild, 1932, Play
House of Rothschild, The 1934 d: Alfred L. Werker. lps: George Arliss, Boris Karloff, Loretta Young. 94M USA. *Rothschild*; *The Great Rothschilds* prod/rel: United Artists Corp., 20th Century Pictures©

WESTON, CAROLYN
Poor Ophelia Poor, Novel
Streets of San Francisco, The 1972 d: Walter Grauman. lps: Karl Malden, Michael Douglas, Robert Wagner. TVM. 98M USA. prod/rel: Quinn Martin Productions

WESTON, GARNETT
Mounted Patrol, Serial Story
Pony Soldier 1952 d: Joseph M. Newman. lps: Tyrone Power, Cameron Mitchell, Thomas Gomez. 82M USA. *MacDonald of the Canadian Mounties* (UKN) prod/rel: 20th Century-Fox

WESTON, GEORGE
The Apple-Tree Girl, 1917, Story
Apple-Tree Girl, The 1917 d: Alan Crosland. lps: Shirley Mason, Joyce Fair, Jessie Stevens. 4977f USA. prod/rel: Thomas A. Edison, Inc.©, Perfection Pictures

Girls Don't Gamble Anymore, 1920, Short Story
Girls Don't Gamble 1920 d: Fred J. Butler. lps: David Butler, Harry Todd, Elinor Field. 5r USA. prod/rel: D. N. Schwab Productions, Jans Film Service

Jem of the Old Rock, 1918, Short Story
Winning Girl, The 1919 d: Robert G. VignolA. lps: Shirley Mason, Niles Welch, Theodore Roberts. 4290f USA. prod/rel: Famous Players-Lasky Corp.©, Paramount Pictures

The Open Door, 1921, Short Story
Is Life Worth Living? 1921 d: Alan Crosland. lps: Eugene O'Brien, Winifred Westover, Arthur Housman. 5039f USA. prod/rel: Selznick Pictures, Select Pictures

The Salt of the Earth, 1918, Short Story
Eyes of the Soul 1919 d: Emile Chautard. lps: Elsie Ferguson, Wyndham Standing, J. Flannigan. 5r USA. prod/rel: Famous Players-Lasky Corp.©, Artcraft Pictures

Taxi! Taxi!, 1925, Short Story
Taxi! Taxi! 1927 d: Melville Brown. lps: Edward Everett Horton, Marian Nixon, Burr McIntosh. 7173f USA. prod/rel: Universal Pictures

You Never Saw Such a Girl, New York 1919, Story
You Never Saw Such a Girl 1919 d: Robert G. VignolA. lps: Vivian Martin, Harrison Ford, Mayme Kelso. 4512f USA. prod/rel: Famous Players-Lasky Corp.©, Paramount Feature

WESTON, JOHN
Hero! Hail, New York 1968, Novel
Hail, Hero! 1969 d: David Miller. lps: Michael Douglas, Arthur Kennedy, Teresa Wright. 97M USA. prod/rel: Halcyon Productions, National General

WESTON, R. P.
Black Hand George, Play
Black Hand Gang, The 1930 d: Monty Banks. lps: Wee Georgie Wood, Dolly Harmer, Violet Young. 63M UKN. prod/rel: British International Pictures, Wardour

Please Teacher, London 1935, Play
Please Teacher 1937 d: Stafford Dickens. lps: Bobby Howes, Rene Ray, Wylie Watson. 76M UKN. prod/rel: Associated British Picture Corporation, Wardour

WESTOVER, CLYDE C.
The Dragon's Daughter, New York 1912, Novel
Tong Man, The 1919 d: William Worthington. lps: Sessue Hayakawa, Helen Jerome Eddy, Marc Robbins. 4975f USA. prod/rel: Haworth Pictures Corp.©, Robertson-Cole Co.

The Scuttlers, New York 1914, Novel
Scuttlers, The 1920 d: J. Gordon Edwards. lps: William Farnum, Jackie Saunders, Herschal Mayall. 6r USA. prod/rel: Fox Film Corp., William Fox©

WESTRATE, E.
Story
Jesse James Vs. the Daltons 1954 d: William Castle. lps: Brett King, Barbara Lawrence, James Griffith. 65M USA. prod/rel: Columbia

WETJEN, ALBERT RICHARD
Short Story
Wallaby Jim of the Islands 1937 d: Charles Lamont. lps: George Houston, Ruth Coleman, Douglas Walton. 73M USA. prod/rel: Grand National Films©, Bud Barsky Production

Way for a Sailor, New York 1928, Novel
En Cada Puerto un Amor 1931 d: Marcel Silver. lps: Jose Crespo, Conchita Montenegro, Juan de LandA. 91M USA. *Paso Al Marino!*; *La Ruta Del Marino* prod/rel: Metro-Goldwyn-Mayer Corp., Culver Export Co.

Way for a Sailor 1930 d: Sam Wood. lps: John Gilbert, Wallace Beery, Jim Tully. 83M USA. prod/rel: Metro-Goldwyn-Mayer Pictures

WEXLEY, JOHN (1907–, USA
The Last Mile, New York 1930, Play
Last Mile, The 1932 d: Sam Bischoff. lps: Howard Phillips, Preston Foster, George E. Stone. 84M USA. prod/rel: K.B.S. Film Co., World Wide Pictures©

Last Mile, The 1959 d: Howard W. Koch. lps: Mickey Rooney, Clifford David, Harry Millard. 78M USA. prod/rel: United Artists, Vanguard

WEXLEY, JUDITH
Novel
Alcova, L' 1984 d: Joe d'Amato. lps: Lilli Carati, Annie Belle, Pier Luigi Conti. 93M ITL. prod/rel: Filmirage

WEYMAN, STANLEY (1855–1928), UKN, Weyman, Stanley John
A Gentleman of France, 1893, Novel
Gentleman of France, A 1921 d: Maurice Elvey. lps: Eille Norwood, Madge Stuart, Hugh Buckler. 5951f UKN. prod/rel: Stoll

Under the Red Robe, 1894, Novel
Under the Red Robe 1915 d: Wilfred Noy. lps: Owen Roughwood, Dorothy Drake, Jackson Wilcox. 3747f UKN. prod/rel: Clarendon, Gaumont

Under the Red Robe 1923 d: Alan Crosland. lps: Robert B. Mantell, John Charles Thomas, Alma Rubens. 9062f USA. prod/rel: Cosmopolitan Corp., Goldwyn-Cosmopolitan Distributing Corp.

Under the Red Robe 1937 d: Victor Sjostrom. lps: Conrad Veidt, Annabella, Raymond Massey. 82M UKN/USA. prod/rel: New World, 20th Century-Fox

WEYSSENHOFF, JOZEF
Sobol I Panna, 1912, Novel
Sobol I Panna 1983 d: Hubert DrapellA. lps: Jolanta Nowak, Jacek Borkowski, Jan Englert. 92M PLN. *The Sable and the Maiden*

WHALEN, WILLIAM WILFRED
Ill-Starred Babbie, Boston 1912, Novel
Ill-Starred Babbie 1915 d: Sherwood MacDonald. lps: Jackie Saunders. 5r USA. *Ill Starred Babbie* prod/rel: Balboa

WHARTON, ANTHONY
At the Barn, New York 1914, Play
Two Weeks 1920 d: Sidney A. Franklin. lps: Constance Talmadge, Conway Tearle, Reginald Mason. 6r USA. *At the Barn* prod/rel: Joseph M. Schenck Productions, Emerson-Loos Production

WHARTON, EDITH (1862–1937), USA, Wharton, Edith Newbold Jones
The Age of Innocence, New York 1920, Novel
Age of Innocence, The 1924 d: Wesley Ruggles. lps: Edith Roberts, Elliott Dexter, Willard Louis. 6700f USA. prod/rel: Warner Brothers Pictures

Age of Innocence, The 1934 d: Philip Moeller. lps: Irene Dunne, John Boles, Julie Haydon. 82M USA. prod/rel: RKO Radio Pictures, Inc.

Age of Innocence, The 1993 d: Martin Scorsese. lps: Daniel Day-Lewis, Michelle Pfeiffer, Winona Ryder. 138M USA. prod/rel: Columbia

Bread Upon the Waters, 1934, Short Story
Strange Wives 1935 d: Richard Thorpe. lps: Roger Pryor, June Clayworth, Esther Ralston. 75M USA. prod/rel: Universal Pictures Corp.©

The Children, New York 1928, Novel
Children, The 1990 d: Tony Palmer. lps: Ben Kingsley, Kim Novak, Siri Neal. 115M UKN/GRM. prod/rel: Isolde, Arbo Film & Maran

Marriage Playground, The 1929 d: Lothar Mendes. lps: Mary Brian, Fredric March, Lilyan Tashman. 70M USA. *The Children* prod/rel: Paramount Famous Lasky Corp.

Ethan Frome, 1911, Novel
Ethan Frome 1992 d: John Madden. lps: Liam Neeson, Patricia Arquette, Joan Allen. TVM. 99M USA. prod/rel: American Playhouse, BBC

The Glimpses of the Moon, New York 1922, Novel
Glimpses of the Moon, The 1923 d: Allan Dwan. lps: Bebe Daniels, Nita Naldi, David Powell. 6502f USA. prod/rel: Famous Players-Lasky, Paramount Pictures

The House of Mirth, New York 1905, Novel
House of Mirth, The 1918 d: Albert Capellani. lps: Katherine Harris Barrymore, Joseph Kilgour, Henry Kolker. 5640f USA. prod/rel: Metro Pictures Corp.©

The Old Maid, New York 1924, Novel
Old Maid, The 1939 d: Edmund Goulding. lps: Bette Davis, Miriam Hopkins, George Brent. 95M USA. prod/rel: Warner Bros. Pictures©

WHARTON, WILLIAM
Birdy, Novel
Birdy 1984 d: Alan Parker. lps: Matthew Modine, Nicolas Cage, John Harkins. 120M USA. prod/rel: Tri-Star-Delphi III Productions, a & M Films

Dad, Novel
Dad 1989 d: David Goldberg. lps: Jack Lemmon, Ted Danson, Olympia Dukakis. 117M USA. prod/rel: Universal

A Midnight Clear, Novel
Midnight Clear, A 1992 d: Keith Gordon. lps: Peter Berg, Kevin Dillon, Arye Gross. 107M USA. prod/rel: Beacon, a & M

WHEATLEY, DENNIS (1897–1977), UKN
The Devil Rides Out, London 1935, Novel
Devil Rides Out, The 1968 d: Terence Fisher. lps: Christopher Lee, Charles Gray, Nike Arrighi. 95M UKN. *The Devil's Bride* (USA) prod/rel: Hammer, Warner-Pathe

Eunuch of Stamboul, Novel
Secret of Stamboul, The 1936 d: Andrew Marton. lps: Valerie Hobson, Frank Vosper, James Mason. 93M UKN. *The Spy in White* prod/rel: Wainwright, General Film Distributors

Forbidden Territory, Novel
Forbidden Territory 1934 d: Phil Rosen. lps: Gregory Ratoff, Ronald Squire, Binnie Barnes. 82M UKN. prod/rel: Progress Pictures, Gaumont-British

To the Devil a Daughter, Novel
To the Devil a Daughter 1976 d: Peter Sykes. lps: Christopher Lee, Richard Widmark, Nastassja Kinski. 92M UKN/GRM. *Die Braut Des Satans* (GRM); *Satan's Bride* prod/rel: Emi, Hammer-Terra Filmkunst

Uncharted Seas, London 1938, Novel
Lost Continent, The 1968 d: Michael Carreras, Leslie Norman (Uncredited). lps: Eric Porter, Hildegard Knef, Suzanna Leigh. 98M UKN. *The People of Abrimes* prod/rel: Hammer Film Productions, Seven Arts Productions

WHEELER, A. C.
The Great Diamond Robbery, New York 1895, Play
Great Diamond Robbery, The 1914 d: Edward A. Morange, Daniel V. Arthur (Spv). lps: Wallace Eddinger, Gail Kane, Dorothy Arthur. 6r USA. prod/rel: Playgoers Film Co.

The Still Alarm, New York 1887, Play
Still Alarm, The 1926 d: Edward Laemmle. lps: Helene Chadwick, William Russell, Richard C. Travers. 7207f USA. prod/rel: Universal Pictures

WHEELER, GRISWOLD
For Sale, 1918, Short Story
Marriage Price, The 1919 d: Emile Chautard. lps: Elsie Ferguson, Wyndham Standing, Lionel Atwill. 4539f USA. *For Sale* prod/rel: Famous Players-Lasky Corp.©, Artcraft Pictures

WHEELER, HARVEY
Fail-Safe, New York 1962, Novel
Fail-Safe 1964 d: Sidney Lumet. lps: Dan O'Herlihy, Walter Matthau, Frank Overton. 111M USA. prod/rel: Columbia Pictures

WHEELIS, ALLEN
The Illusionless Man and the Visionary Maid, 1964, Novel
Crazy Quilt 1966 d: John Korty. lps: Tom Rosqui, Ina Mela, David Winters. 75M USA. prod/rel: John Korty

WHEELWRIGHT, RALPH
Story
These Wilder Years 1956 d: Roy Rowland. lps: James Cagney, Barbara Stanwyck, Walter Pidgeon. 91M USA. *Somewhere I'll Find Him* prod/rel: MGM

WHERRY, EDITH
The Red Lantern, New York 1911, Novel
Red Lantern, The 1919 d: Albert Capellani. lps: Alla Nazimova, Frank Currier, Darrel Foss. 7r USA. prod/rel: the Nazimova Productions, Metro Pictures Corp.©

WHIPPLE, DOROTHY
They Knew Mr. Knight, Novel
They Knew Mr. Knight 1945 d: Norman Walker. lps: Mervyn Johns, Nora Swinburne, Alfred Drayton. 93M UKN. prod/rel: General Film Distributors, Gregory, Hake & Walker

They Were Sisters, Novel
They Were Sisters 1945 d: Arthur Crabtree. lps: Phyllis Calvert, James Mason, Hugh Sinclair. 115M UKN. prod/rel: Gainsborough Pictures, General Film Distributors

WHISNANT, SCOTT
Innocent Victims, Book
Innocent Victims 1996 d: Gilbert Cates. lps: Ricky Schroder, John Corbett, Tom Irwin. TVM. 240M USA.

WHISTER, OWEN
The Westerner, Novel
Western Romance, A 1910 d: Edwin S. Porter. lps: J. Barney Sherry. 690f USA. prod/rel: Edison

WHITAKER, HERMAN
Over the Border, New York 1917, Novel
Not Exactly Gentlemen 1931 d: Ben Stoloff. lps: Victor McLaglen, Fay Wray, Lew Cody. 60M USA. *Three Rogues* (UKN); *Land Rush*; *Three Rough Diamonds*; *Three Bad Men* prod/rel: Fox Film Corp.©

Three Bad Men 1926 d: John Ford. lps: George O'Brien, Olive Borden, Lou Tellegen. 8710f USA. prod/rel: Fox Film Corp.

The Planter, New York 1909, Novel
Planter, The 1917 d: Thomas N. Heffron. lps: Tyrone Power Sr., Helen Bateman, Mabel Wiles. 10r USA. prod/rel: Nevada Motion Picture Corp., State Rights

WHITCOMB, DANIEL F.
The Golden Gift, Novel
Dangerous Talent, The 1920 d: George L. Cox. lps: Margarita Fischer, Harry Hilliard, Beatrice Van. 5460f USA. *The Golden Gift* prod/rel: American Film Co.©, Pathe Exchange, Inc.

WHITE, ALAN
The Long Day's Dying, London 1965, Novel
Long Day's Dying, The 1968 d: Peter Collinson. lps: David Hemmings, Tom Bell, Tony Beckley. 95M UKN. prod/rel: Junction Films, Paramount

WHITE, BOUCK
Book of Daneile Drew, New York 1910, Book
Toast of New York, The 1937 d: Rowland V. Lee. lps: Edward Arnold, Cary Grant, Frances Farmer. 109M USA. *The Robber Barons* prod/rel: RKO Radio Pictures©

WHITE, E. B.
Charlotte's Web, Novel
Charlotte's Web 1973 d: Iwao Takamoto, Charles Nichols. ANM. 96M USA. *E.B. White's Charlotte's Web* prod/rel: Hanna-Barbera, Sagittarius

WHITE, EDWARD STUART
Two-Gun Man, 1925, Short Story
Under a Texas Moon 1930 d: Michael Curtiz. lps: Frank Fay, Raquel Torres, Myrna Loy. 82M USA. prod/rel: Warner Brothers Pictures

WHITE, ETHEL LINA
Her Heart in Her Throat, Novel
Unseen, The 1945 d: Lewis Allen. lps: Gail Russell, Joel McCrea, Herbert Marshall. 81M USA. *Her Heart in Her Throat* prod/rel: Columbia

Some Must Watch, Novel
Spiral Staircase, The 1946 d: Robert Siodmak. lps: Dorothy McGuire, George Brent, Ethel Barrymore. 83M USA. prod/rel: RKO Radio

Spiral Staircase, The 1975 d: Peter Collinson. lps: Jacqueline Bisset, Christopher Plummer, Sam Wanamaker. 89M UKN. prod/rel: Warner Bros., Raven

The Wheel Spins, Novel
Lady Vanishes, The 1938 d: Alfred Hitchcock. lps: Margaret Lockwood, Michael Redgrave, Paul Lukas. 95M UKN. *Lost Lady* prod/rel: MGM, Gainsborough

Lady Vanishes, The 1979 d: Anthony Page. lps: Elliott Gould, Cybill Shepherd, Angela Lansbury. 97M UKN. prod/rel: Rank

WHITE, GEORGE
Manhattan Mary, New York 1927, Musical Play
Follow the Leader 1930 d: Norman Taurog. lps: Ed Wynn, Ginger Rogers, Stanley Smith. 6851f USA. *Manhattan Mary* prod/rel: Paramount-Publix Corp.

WHITE, GILLIAN
Mothertime, Novel
Mothertime 1997 d: Matthew Jacobs. lps: Kate Maberly, Gina McKee, Anthony Andrews. TVM. 90M UKN. prod/rel: BBC

WHITE, GRACE MILLER
From the Valley of the Missing, New York 1911, Novel
From the Valley of the Missing 1915 d: Frank Powell. lps: Jane Miller, Vivian Tobin, Harry Spingler. 5r USA. *Valley of the Missing* prod/rel: Fox Film Corp., William Fox©

Judy of Rogue's Harbor, New York 1918, Novel
Judy of Rogue's Harbor 1920 d: William D. Taylor. lps: Mary Miles Minter, Charles Meredith, Herbert Standing. 6r USA. prod/rel: Realart Pictures Corp.©

Rose O' Paradise, New York 1915, Novel
Rose O' Paradise 1918 d: James Young. lps: Bessie Barriscale, Norman Kerry, Howard Hickman. 6r USA. prod/rel: Paralta Plays, Inc., W. W. Hodkinson Corp.

The Secret of the Storm Country, New York 1917, Novel
Secret of the Storm Country, The 1917 d: Charles Miller. lps: Norma Talmadge, Herbert Frank, Niles Welch. 5-6r USA. prod/rel: Norma Talmadge Film Corp.©, Select Pictures Corp.

Tess of the Storm Country, New York 1909, Novel
Tess of the Storm Country 1914 d: Edwin S. Porter. lps: Mary Pickford, Mr. W. R. Walters, Olive Fuller Golden. 5r USA. prod/rel: Famous Players Film Co., State Rights

Tess of the Storm Country 1922 d: John S. Robertson. lps: Mary Pickford, Lloyd Hughes, Gloria Hope. 9639f USA. prod/rel: Mary Pickford Co., United Artists Corp.

Tess of the Storm Country 1932 d: Alfred Santell. lps: Janet Gaynor, Charles Farrell, Dudley Digges. 75M USA. prod/rel: Fox Film Corp.©, Alfred Santell Production

Tess of the Storm Country 1961 d: Paul Guilfoyle. lps: Diane Baker, Jack Ging, Lee Philips. 84M USA. prod/rel: Twentieth Century-Fox Film Corp.

WHITE, IRVING
Fly Away Home, Play
Always in My Heart 1942 d: Jo Graham. lps: Kay Francis, Walter Huston, Gloria Warren. 92M USA. prod/rel: Warner Bros.

WHITE, JON MANCHIP
Crack in the World, Novel
Crack in the World 1965 d: Andrew Marton. lps: Dana Andrews, Kieron Moore, Janette Scott. 96M USA. prod/rel: Security

Mask of Dust, Novel
Mask of Dust 1954 d: Terence Fisher. lps: Richard Conte, Mari Aldon, George Coulouris. 79M UKN. *Race for Life* (USA) prod/rel: Hammer, Exclusive

Mystery Submarine, Play
Mystery Submarine 1963 d: C. M. Pennington-Richards. lps: Edward Judd, James Robertson Justice, Laurence Payne. 92M UKN. *Decoy* (USA); *Mystery Submarines* prod/rel: Bertram Ostrer Productions, Britannia

The Obi, Play
Naked Evil 1966 d: Stanley Goulder. lps: Anthony Ainley, Basil Dignam, Suzanne Neve. 79M UKN. *Exorcism at Midnight* prod/rel: Columbia, Gibraltar

WHITE, LESLIE T.
Five Thousand Trojan Soldiers, Story
Northern Pursuit 1943 d: Raoul Walsh. lps: Errol Flynn, Julie Bishop, Helmut Dantine. 94M USA. prod/rel: Warner Bros.

Harness Bull, 1937, Novel
Vice Squad 1953 d: Arnold Laven. lps: Edward G. Robinson, Paulette Goddard, K. T. Stevens. 87M USA. *The Girl in Room 17* (UKN) prod/rel: United Artists, Sequoia Pictures

Six Weeks South of Texas, Serial Story
Americano, The 1955 d: William Castle. lps: Glenn Ford, Ursula Thiess, Frank Lovejoy. 85M USA. prod/rel: RKO

WHITE, LIONEL
Clean Break, 1955, Novel
Killing, The 1956 d: Stanley Kubrick. lps: Sterling Hayden, Coleen Gray, Vince Edwards. 83M USA. *Clean Break* prod/rel: United Artists, Harris-Kubrick

The Money Trap, New York 1963, Novel
Money Trap, The 1965 d: Burt Kennedy. lps: Glenn Ford, Elke Sommer, Rita Hayworth. 92M USA. prod/rel: Metro-Goldwyn-Mayer, Inc.

Obsession, New York 1962, Novel
Pierrot le Fou 1965 d: Jean-Luc Godard. lps: Jean-Paul Belmondo, Anna Karina, Dirk Sanders. 112M FRN/ITL. *Il Bandito Della 11* (ITL); *Le Demon de Onze Heures* prod/rel: Rome Paris Films, Productions Georges De Beauregard

The Snatchers, New York 1953, Novel
Night of the Following Day, The 1969 d: Hubert Cornfield. lps: Marlon Brando, Richard Boone, Jess Hahn. 93M USA. prod/rel: Gina Productions

WHITE, MAUD REEVES
Sue of the South, Novel
Sue of the South 1919 d: W. Eugene Moore. lps: Edith Roberts, James Farley, Ruby Lafayette. 5r USA. prod/rel: Bluebird Photoplays, Inc.©

WHITE, MEL
David, Book
David 1988 d: John Erman. lps: Bernadette Peters, John Glover, Matthew Laurance. TVM. 100M USA.

WHITE, META
The Match Breaker, Story
Match-Breaker, The 1921 d: Dallas M. Fitzgerald. lps: Viola Dana, Jack Perrin, Edward Jobson. 4860f USA. prod/rel: Metro Pictures

WHITE, NELIA GARDNER
The Little Horse, Short Story
Gift of Love, The 1958 d: Jean Negulesco. lps: Lauren Bacall, Robert Stack, Evelyn Rudie. 105M USA. prod/rel: 20th Century-Fox

Sentimental Journey 1946 d: Walter Lang. lps: John Payne, Maureen O'Hara, William Bendix. 94M USA. prod/rel: 20th Century-Fox

Sentimental Journey 1984 d: James Goldstone. lps: Jaclyn Smith, David Dukes, Maureen Stapleton. TVM. 100M USA. prod/rel: Lucille Ball Productions

WHITE, PATRICK (1912–1990), UKN, White, Patrick Victor Martindale
Big Toys, Play
Big Toys 1980 d: Chris Thomson. lps: Diane Cilento, John Gaden, Max Cullen. TVM. F ASL. prod/rel: Australian Broadcasting Corp.

The Night the Prowler, 1974, Short Story
Patrick White's the Night the Prowler 1978 d: Jim Sharman. lps: Ruth Cracknell, John Frawley, Kerry Walker. 90M ASL. *The Night Prowler* (USA); *The Night the Prowler* prod/rel: New South Wales Film Corp., Chariot Films Pty. Ltd.©

WHITE, PAUL
They Also Serve, Short Story
Master Spy 1963 d: Montgomery Tully. lps: Stephen Murray, June Thorburn, Alan Wheatley. 74M UKN. prod/rel: Eternal Films, Grand National

WHITE, ROBB
Story
Up Periscope 1959 d: Gordon Douglas. lps: James Garner, Edmond O'Brien, Andra Martin. 111M USA. prod/rel: Warner Bros., Lakeside

Death Watch, Novel
Savages 1974 d: Lee H. Katzin. lps: Andy Griffith, Sam Bottoms, Noah Beery Jr. TVM. 78M USA. prod/rel: Spelling/Goldberg Productions

Our Virgin Island, Book
Virgin Island 1958 d: Pat Jackson. lps: John Cassavetes, Virginia Maskell, Sidney Poitier. 94M UKN. *Our Virgin Island* prod/rel: British Lion, Countryman

WHITE, STEWART EDWARD
The Conjuror's House, New York 1903, Novel
Call of the North, The 1914 d: Cecil B. de Mille, Oscar Apfel. lps: Robert Edeson, Winifred Kingston, Theodore Roberts. 5r USA. prod/rel: Jesse L. Lasky Feature Play Co.©, State Rights

Call of the North, The 1921 d: Joseph Henabery. lps: Jack Holt, Madge Bellamy, Noah Beery. 4823f USA. *The Conjuror's House* (UKN) prod/rel: Famous Players-Lasky, Paramount Pictures

The Gray Dawn, Garden City, N.Y. 1915, Novel
Gray Dawn, The 1922 d: Eliot Howe?. lps: Carl Gantvoort, Claire Adams, Robert McKim. 5600f USA. *The Grey Dawn* prod/rel: Benjamin B. Hampton Productions

The Killer, Garden City, N.Y. 1920, Novel
Killer, The 1921 d: Howard Hickman. lps: Claire Adams, Jack Conway, Frankie Lee. 6r USA. prod/rel: Benjamin B. Hampton Productions, Pathe Exchange, Inc.

The Killer, 1919, Short Story
Mystery Ranch 1932 d: David Howard. lps: George O'Brien, Cecilia Parker, Charles Middleton. 65M USA. *The Killer; Death Valley* prod/rel: Fox Film Corp.©

The Leopard Woman, New York 1916, Novel
Leopard Woman, The 1920 d: Wesley Ruggles. lps: Louise Glaum, House Peters, Alfred Hollingsworth. 7r USA. prod/rel: J. Parker Read Jr. Productions, Associated Producers, Inc.

The Shepper-Newfounder, 1930, Short Story
Change of Heart 1938 d: James Tinling. lps: Gloria Stuart, Michael Whalen, Lyle Talbot. 66M USA. *Headline Huntress* prod/rel: Twentieth Century-Fox Film Corp.
Part Time Wife 1930 d: Leo McCarey. lps: Edmund Lowe, Leila Hyams, Tom Clifford. 6500f USA. prod/rel: Fox Film Corp.

The Westerners, New York 1901, Novel
Westerners, The 1919 d: Edward Sloman. lps: Roy Stewart, Robert McKim, Mildred Manning. 7r USA. prod/rel: Benjamin B. Hampton Productions, Great Authors Pictures, Inc.

Wild Geese Calling, Novel
Wild Geese Calling 1941 d: John Brahm. lps: Henry Fonda, Joan Bennett, Warren William. 77M USA. prod/rel: 20th Century Fox

WHITE, T. H. (1906–1964), UKN, White, Terence Hanbury
The Once and Future King, London 1958, Novel
Camelot 1967 d: Joshua Logan. lps: Richard Harris, Vanessa Redgrave, Franco Nero. 181M USA. prod/rel: Warner

The Sword in the Stone, London 1938, Novel
Sword in the Stone, The 1963 d: Wolfgang Reitherman. ANM. 75M USA. prod/rel: Walt Disney Productions, Buena Vista

WHITE, TERI
Triangle, Novel
Regard Les Hommes Tomber 1994 d: Jacques Audiard. lps: Jean Yanne, Jean-Louis Trintignant, Mathieu Kassovitz. 100M FRN. *See How They Fall* (UKN) prod/rel: Bloody Mary Productions, France 3 Cinema

WHITE, THEODORE H. (1915–1986), USA, White, Theodore Harold
The Mountain Road, Novel
Mountain Road, The 1960 d: Daniel Mann. lps: James Stewart, Lisa Lu, Glenn Corbett. 102M USA. prod/rel: Columbia

WHITE, W. L.
Article
Lost Boundaries 1949 d: Alfred L. Werker. lps: Mel Ferrer, Beatrice Pearson, Richard Hylton. 99M USA. prod/rel: Film Classics, Rd-Dr Prods.

WHITE, WILLIAM ALLEN (1868–1944), USA
Book
Mary White 1977 d: Jud Taylor. lps: Ed Flanders, Fionnula Flanagan, Tim Matheson. TVM. 100M USA. prod/rel: Radnitz, Mattel Productions

A Certain Rich Man, New York 1909, Novel
Certain Rich Man, A 1921 d: Howard Hickman. lps: Carl Gantvoort, Claire Adams, Robert McKim. 5900f USA. prod/rel: Great Authors Pictures, W. W. Hodkinson Corp.

In the Heart of a Fool, New York 1918, Novel
In the Heart of a Fool 1920 d: Allan Dwan. lps: Mary Thurman, Anna Q. Nilsson, James Kirkwood. 6r USA. *Heart of a Fool* prod/rel: Mayflower Photoplay Corp.©, Allan Dwan Production

WHITE, WILLIAM C.
Matter of Pride, 1937, Short Story
Beg, Borrow Or Steal 1937 d: Wilhelm Thiele. lps: John Beal, Florence Rice, Frank Morgan. 72M USA. *A Matter of Pride* prod/rel: Metro-Goldwyn-Mayer Corp.

WHITE, WILLIAM L.
Journey for Margaret, Book
Journey for Margaret 1942 d: W. S. Van Dyke. lps: Robert Young, Laraine Day, Fay Bainter. 81M USA. prod/rel: MGM

They Were Expendable, Book
They Were Expendable 1945 d: John Ford. lps: Robert Montgomery, John Wayne, Donna Reed. 136M USA. prod/rel: MGM

WHITE, WILLIAM PATTERSON
The Buster, Boston 1920, Novel
Buster, The 1923 d: Colin Campbell. lps: Dustin Farnum, Doris Pawn, Francis McDonald. 4587f USA. prod/rel: Fox Film Corp.

The Heart of the Range, Garden City, N.Y. 1921, Novel
Pardon My Nerve! 1922 d: B. Reeves Eason. lps: Buck Jones, Eileen Percy, Mae Busch. 4093f USA. prod/rel: Fox Film Corp.

High Pockets, 1918, Novel
High Pockets 1919 d: Ira M. Lowry. lps: Louis Bennison, Katherine MacDonald, W. W. Black. 5r USA. prod/rel: Betzwood Film Co., Goldwyn Distributing Corp.

Lynch Lawyers, Boston 192O, Novel
Western Speed 1922 d: Scott R. Dunlap, C. R. Wallace. lps: Buck Jones, Eileen Percy, Jack McDonald. 5002f USA. prod/rel: Fox Film Corp.

WHITEHEAD, DON (1908–1981), USA, Whitehead, Donald Ford
Attack on Terror, Novel
Attack on Terror 1975 d: Marvin J. Chomsky. lps: Ned Beatty, John Beck, Billy "Green" Bush. TVM. 215M USA. *Attack on Terror: the F.B.I. Vs. the Ku Klux Klan* prod/rel: Warner Bros., Quinn Martin Productions

The F.B.I. Story, 1956, Book
F.B.I. Story, The 1959 d: Mervyn Leroy. lps: James Stewart, Vera Miles, Murray Hamilton. 149M USA. prod/rel: Warner Bros.

WHITEHOUSE, ESTHER
The Call of the East, Novel
Call of the East, The 1922 d: Bert Wynne. lps: Doris Eaton, Warwick Ward, Walter Tennyson. 5000f UKN. *His Supreme Sacrifice* prod/rel: International Artists, Curry

WHITEING, RICHARD
No. 5 John Street, Novel
No. 5 John Street 1921 d: Kenelm Foss. lps: Zena Dare, Mary Odette, Lionelle Howard. 5300f UKN. prod/rel: Astra Films

WHITELAW, DAVID
The Big Picture, Novel
It's in the Blood 1938 d: Gene Gerrard. lps: Claude Hulbert, Lesley Brook, James Stephenson. 56M UKN. prod/rel: Warner Bros., First National

The Girl from the East, Novel
Heart of the Hills, The 1916 d: Richard Ridgely. lps: Mabel Trunnelle, Conway Tearle, Bigelow Cooper. 5r USA. *The Girl from the East* prod/rel: Thomas A. Edison, Inc.©, K-E-S-E Service

The Little Hour of Peter Wells, 1913, Novel
Little Hour of Peter Wells, The 1920 d: B. E. Doxat-Pratt, Maurits H. Binger. lps: O. B. Clarence, Heather Thatcher, Hebden Foster. 5000f UKN/NTH. **De Heldendaad Van Peter Wells** (NTH); *The Heroic Deed of Peter Wells* prod/rel: Granger-Binger Film

The Roof, Novel
Roof, The 1933 d: George A. Cooper. lps: Leslie Perrins, Judy Gunn, Russell Thorndike. 58M UKN. prod/rel: Real Art, Radio

WHITEMORE, HUGH
The Best of Friends, Play
Best of Friends, The 1991 d: Alvin Rakoff. lps: John Gielgud, Wendy Hiller, Patrick McGoohan. TVM. 80M UKN. prod/rel: London Films

Pack of Lies, Play
Pack of Lies 1987 d: Anthony Page. lps: Ellen Burstyn, Teri Garr, Alan Bates. TVM. 103M UKN/USA. prod/rel: Robert Halmi Inc.

WHITING, JOHN (1917–1963), UKN, Whiting, John Robert
The Devils, 1961, Play
Devils, The 1971 d: Ken Russell. lps: Vanessa Redgrave, Oliver Reed, Dudley Sutton. 111M UKN. prod/rel: Warner Bros., Russo

WHITING, ROBERT RUDD
The Golden Idiot, 1916, Novel
Golden Idiot, The 1917 d: Arthur Berthelet. lps: Bryant Washburn, Virginia Valli, Arthur Metcalfe. 5r USA. prod/rel: Essanay Film Mfg. Co.©, K-E-S-E Service

WHITMAN, S. E.
Captain Apache, Novel
Captain Apache 1971 d: Alexander Singer. lps: Lee Van Cleef, Carroll Baker, Stuart Whitman. 94M USA/UKN/SPN. *The Gun of April Morning* prod/rel: Benmar

WHITMAN, STEPHEN FRENCH
Isle of Life; a Romance, New York 1913, Novel
Blonde Saint, The 1926 d: Svend Gade. lps: Lewis Stone, Doris Kenyon, Ann Rork. 6800f USA. prod/rel: Sam E. Rork Productions, First National Pictures
Isle of Life, The 1916 d: Burton George. lps: Roberta Wilson, Frank Whitson, Hayward MacK. 5r USA. prod/rel: Universal Film Mfg. Co.©, Red Feather Photoplays

Sacrifice, New York 1922, Novel
Drums of Fate 1923 d: Charles Maigne. lps: Mary Miles Minter, Maurice B. Flynn, George Fawcett. 5716f USA. *Drums of Destiny* prod/rel: Famous Players-Lasky, Paramount Pictures

WHITMORE, VIRGINIA
The Swinging Doors, Story
Swinging Doors, The 1915 d: Murdock MacQuarrie. lps: Murdock MacQuarrie. 2r USA. prod/rel: Big U

WHITSON, BETH SLATER
Wings, Story
Compassion 1927 d: Victor Adamson, Norval MacGregor. lps: Gaston Glass, Alma Bennett, Josef Swickard. 5800f USA. prod/rel: Victor Adamson Productions

WHITTEN, LESLIE H.
Moon of the Wolf, Novel
Moon of the Wolf 1972 d: Daniel Petrie. lps: David Janssen, Barbara Rush, Bradford Dillman. TVM. 73M USA. prod/rel: Filmways

WHITTIER, JOHN GREENLEAF (1807–1892), USA
Barbara Frietchie, 1864, Poem
Barbara Frietchie 1908 d: J. Stuart Blackton. lps: Julia Arthur, Edith Storey, Earle Williams. 505f USA. *Barbara Fritchie*
Barbara Frietchie 1915 d: Herbert Blache. lps: Mary Miles Minter, Mrs. Thomas Whiffen, Guy Coombs. 5r USA. prod/rel: Popular Plays & Players, Metro Pictures Corp.©
Barbara Frietchie 1924 d: Lambert Hillyer. lps: Florence Vidor, Edmund Lowe, Emmett King. 7179f USA. *Love of a Patriot* prod/rel: Regal Pictures, Producers Distributing Corp.

The Barefoot Boy, Boston 1856, Poem
Barefoot Boy 1938 d: Karl Brown. lps: Jackie Moran, Marcia Mae Jones, Ralph Morgan. 63M USA. prod/rel: Monogram Pictures Corp.
Barefoot Boy, The 1923 d: David Kirkland. lps: John Bowers, Marjorie Daw, Sylvia Breamer. 5943f USA. prod/rel: Mission Film Corp., C. B. C. Film Sales

The Battle of Seven Isles, Poem
Bay of Seven Isles, The 1915 d: Frank Lloyd. lps: Frank Lloyd, Helen Leslie, Millard K. Wilson. SHT USA. prod/rel: Laemmle

Maud Muller, 1854, Poem
Maud Muller 1911. lps: Kathlyn Williams, Charles Clary. 1000f USA. prod/rel: Selig Polyscope Co.
Maud Muller 1912 d: Thomas Ricketts. lps: Vivian Rich, Donald MacDonald. 2r USA. prod/rel: Nestor
Maude Muller 1909. 982f USA. prod/rel: Essanay

Mogg Megone, Poem
Mogg Megone 1909 d: J. Stuart Blackton (Spv). lps: Edith Storey. 390f USA. prod/rel: Vitagraph Co. of America

WHITTING, RALPH S.
Girl With an Itch, Novel
Girl With an Itch 1958 d: Ronnie Ashcroft. lps: Kathy Marlowe, Robert Armstrong, Robert Clark. 78M USA. prod/rel: Don-Tru

WHITTINGTON, HARRY
Story
Desire in the Dust 1960 d: William F. Claxton. lps: Ken Scott, Raymond Burr, Martha Hyer. 105M USA. prod/rel: Associated

Adios, Novel
Adios Gringo 1965 d: Giorgio Stegani. lps: Giuliano Gemma, Evelyn Stewart, Roberto Camardiel. 100M ITL/FRN/SPN. prod/rel: Explorer Film '58, Les Films Corona (Paris)

Man in the Shadow, Novel
Man in the Shadow 1956 d: Jack Arnold. lps: Orson Welles, Jeff Chandler, Colleen Miller. 80M USA. *Pay the Devil* (UKN) prod/rel: Universal-International

Wyoming Wildcatters, Short Story
Black Gold 1963 d: Leslie H. Martinson. lps: Philip Carey, Diane McBain, Claude Akins. 99M USA. prod/rel: Warner Bros. Pictures

WIBBERLEY, LEONARD (1915–1983), IRL, Wibberley, Leonard Patrick O'Connor
The Mouse on the Moon, New York 1962, Novel
Mouse on the Moon, The 1963 d: Richard Lester. lps: Margaret Rutherford, Bernard Cribbins, Ron Moody. 85M UKN. *A Rocket from Fenwick* prod/rel: Walter Shenson Films, United Artists

The Wrath of the Grapes, Novel
Mouse That Roared, The 1959 d: Jack Arnold. lps: Peter Sellers, Jean Seberg, William Hartnell. 90M UKN. *The Day New York Was Invaded* prod/rel: Columbia, Open Road

WICHELEGGER, ULRICH
Das Gespensterhaus, Zurich 1943, Novel
  Gespensterhaus, Das 1942 d: Franz Schnyder. lps: Emil Hegetschweiler, Jakob Sulzer, Blanche Aubry. 100M SWT. *La Maison Hantee; Junkerngasse 54* prod/rel: Praesens-Film

WICHELER, FERNAND
Le Mariage de Mademoiselle Beulemans, Play
  Mariage de Mademoiselle Beulemans, Le 1926 d: Julien Duvivier. lps: Andree Brabant, Gustave Libeau, Jean Dehelly. 1800m FRN. prod/rel: Film d'Art (Vandal Et Delac)
  Mariage de Mademoiselle Beulemans, Le 1950 d: Andre Cerf. lps: Christian Alers, Saturnin Fabre, Pierre Larquey. 95M FRN/BLG. prod/rel: Tellus Films
  Mariage de Mademoiselle Beulemans, Le 1983 d: Michel Rochat. lps: Ana Guedroitz, Leonil McCormack, Jacques Lippe. TVM. 110M BLG.
  Mariage de Mlle Beulemans, Le 1932 d: Jean Choux. lps: Lily Bourget, Charles Mahieu, Pierre Alcover. 102M FRN. prod/rel: Films Reingold-Lafitte Et Cie

WICKENBURG-ALMASY, WILHELMINE GRAFIN
Der Geiger Freidel, Poem
  Friedel, Der Geiger 1911 d: Adolf Gartner. lps: Henny Porten. 224m GRM. prod/rel: Messters Projektion

WICKER, TOM (1926–, USA, Wicker, Thomas Grey
A Time to Die, Book
  Attica 1980 d: Marvin J. Chomsky. lps: Charles Durning, George Grizzard, Glynn Turman. TVM. 100M USA. prod/rel: ABC Circle

WICKHAM, SYLVIA
Jim's Gift, Novel
  Jim's Gift 1994 d: Bob Keen. lps: Robert Llewellyn, Chris Jury, Jennifer Calvert. 95M UKN.

WIDDEMER, MARGARET (1890–, USA
The Rose-Garden Husband, Philadelphia 1915, Novel
  Wife on Trial, A 1917 d: Ruth Ann Baldwin. lps: Mignon Anderson, Leo Pierson, L. M. Wells. 5r USA. prod/rel: Universal Film Mfg. Co.©, Butterfly Picture
Why Not?, New York 1915, Novel
  Dream Lady, The 1918 d: Elsie Jane Wilson. lps: Carmel Myers, Thomas Holding, Kathleen Emerson. 5r USA. prod/rel: Bluebird Photoplays, Inc.©
The Wishing Ring Man, New York 1917, Novel
  Wishing Ring Man, The 1919 d: David Smith. lps: Bessie Love, J. Frank Glendon, Jean Hathaway. 5r USA. prod/rel: Vitagraph Co. of America©

WIED, GUSTAV (1858–1914), DNM, Wied, Gustav Johannes
Die Alte Gnadige
  Feuer, Das 1914 d: Urban Gad. lps: Asta Nielsen, Mary Scheller, Max LandA. 1070m GRM. *The Fire* prod/rel: Pagu
Livsens Ondskab, 1899, Novel
  Thummelumsen 1941 d: Emanuel Gregers. lps: Henry Nielsen, Richard Christensen, Paul Holck-Hofmann. 95M DNM. prod/rel: Nordisk Film
Thummelumsen, 1901, Novel
  Thummelumsen 1941 d: Emanuel Gregers. lps: Henry Nielsen, Richard Christensen, Paul Holck-Hofmann. 95M DNM. prod/rel: Nordisk Film

WIENER, WILLARD
Four Boys and a Gun, 1944, Novel
  Four Boys and a Gun 1955 d: William Berke. lps: Frank Sutton, Terry Green, James Franciscus. 73M USA. prod/rel: United Artists, Security Pictures

WIERS-JENSSEN, HANS
Anne Pedersdotter, 1917, Play
  Vredens Dag 1943 d: Carl T. Dreyer. lps: Thorkild Roose, Lisbeth Movin, Sigrid Neiiendam. 110M DNM. *Day of Wrath; Dies Irae*

WIESEL, ELIE (1928–, RMN, Wiesel, Eliezer
L'Aube, Book
  Aube, L' 1986 d: Miklos Jancso. lps: Philippe Leotard, Michael York, Christine Boisson. F FRN/ISR. *Hashachar* (ISR); *Dawn*
Le Testament d'un Poete Juif Assassine, Novel
  Testament d'un Poete Juif Assassine, Le 1987 d: Frank Cassenti. lps: Michel Jonasz, Wojciech Pszoniak, Erland Josephson. 90M FRN. prod/rel: Hubert Niogret Prod.

WIGGIN, KATE DOUGLAS (1856–1923), USA
The Birds' Christmas Carol, San Francisco 1887, Story
  Birds' Christmas Carol, The 1917 d: Lule Warrenton. lps: Little Mary Louise, Harold Skinner, Ella Gilbert. 5r USA. *A Bit O' Heaven* prod/rel: Frieder Film Corp.©, State Rights
Mother Carey's Chickens, Boston 1911, Novel
  Mother Carey's Chickens 1938 d: Rowland V. Lee. lps: Fay Bainter, Anne Shirley, Ruby Keeler. 82M USA. prod/rel: RKO Radio Pictures©

Summer Magic 1963 d: James Neilson. lps: Hayley Mills, Dorothy McGuire, Burl Ives. 109M USA. prod/rel: Walt Disney Productions, Buena Vista
Rebecca of Sunnybrook Farm, New York 1903, Novel
  Rebecca of Sunnybrook Farm 1917 d: Marshall Neilan. lps: Mary Pickford, Eugene O'Brien, Wesley Barry. 6r USA. prod/rel: Artcraft Pictures Corp.©, Mary Pickford Film Corp.
  Rebecca of Sunnybrook Farm 1932 d: Alfred Santell. lps: Marian Nixon, Ralph Bellamy, Mae Marsh. 80M USA. prod/rel: Fox Film Corp.©, Alfred Santell Production
  Rebecca of Sunnybrook Farm 1938 d: Allan Dwan. lps: Shirley Temple, Randolph Scott, Jack Haley. 81M USA. prod/rel: Twentieth Century-Fox Film Corp.©
Rose O' the River, Boston 1905, Novel
  Rose O' the River 1919 d: Robert T. Thornby. lps: Lila Lee, Darrel Foss, George Fisher. 5r USA. *Rose of the River* prod/rel: Famous Players-Lasky Corp.©, Paramount Pictures
Timothy's Quest, New York 1895, Novel
  Timothy's Quest 1922 d: Sidney Olcott. lps: Joseph Depew, Baby Helen Rowland, Marie Day. 6377f USA. prod/rel: Dirigo Films, American Releasing Corp.
  Timothy's Quest 1936 d: Charles T. Barton. lps: Tom Keene, Eleanore Whitney, Dickie Moore. 70M USA. prod/rel: Paramount Productions©

WILBUR, CRANE
Story
  Solomon and Sheba 1959 d: King Vidor. lps: Yul Brynner, Gina Lollobrigida, George Sanders. 139M USA. prod/rel: United Artists, Edward Small
Folsom Story, Book
  Inside the Walls of Folsom Prison 1951 d: Crane Wilbur. lps: Steve Cochran, Philip Carey, Ted de CorsiA. 87M USA. *The Story of Folsom* prod/rel: Warner Bros.
The Monster, New York 1922, Play
  Monster, The 1925 d: Roland West. lps: Lon Chaney, Gertrude Olmstead, Hallam Cooley. 6425f USA. prod/rel: Metro-Goldwyn Pictures
The Song Writer, New York 1928, Play
  Children of Pleasure 1930 d: Harry Beaumont. lps: Lawrence Gray, Wynne Gibson, Judith Wood. 6400f USA. *The Song Writer* prod/rel: Metro-Goldwyn-Mayer Pictures

WILBUR, RICHARD (1921–, USA, Wilbur, Richard Purdy
A Game of Catch, 1954, Short Story
  Game of Catch, A 1974 d: Steven K. Witty. 7M USA.

WILCOX, ELLA WHEELER (1850–1919), USA
Poem
  Belle of the Season, The 1919 d: S. Rankin Drew. lps: Emmy Wehlen, S. Rankin Drew, Louis Wolheim. 4600f USA. prod/rel: Metro Pictures Corp.©
  Man Worth While, The 1921 d: Romaine Fielding. lps: Joan Arliss, Lawrence Johnson, Eugene Acker. 5000f USA. prod/rel: Romaine Fielding Productions
The Price He Paid, Poem
  Price He Paid, The 1914 d: Lawrence McGill. lps: Philip Hahn, Gertrude Shipman, Julia Hurley. 5r USA. prod/rel: Humanology Film Producing Co., United Film Service
Reveries of a Station House, Poem
  Beautiful Lie, The 1917 d: John W. Noble. lps: Frances Nelson, Harry Northrup, Edward Earle. 5r USA. prod/rel: Metro Pictures Corp.©, Rolfe Photoplays, Inc.
The Two Glasses, Poem
  Two Glasses, The 1913. SHT USA. prod/rel: Pilot

WILDE, HAGAR
Bringing Up Baby, 1937, Short Story
  Bringing Up Baby 1938 d: Howard Hawks. lps: Cary Grant, Katharine Hepburn, Charles Ruggles. 102M USA. prod/rel: RKO Radio Pictures, Inc.
Dear Evelyn, Play
  Guest in the House, A 1944 d: John Brahm, Andre de Toth (Uncredited). lps: Anne Baxter, Ralph Bellamy, Aline MacMahon. 121M USA. prod/rel: United Artists, Hunt Stromberg

WILDE, OSCAR (1854–1900), IRL
The Ballad of Reading Gaol, 1898, Verse
  Ballad of Reading Gaol, The 1988 d: Richard Kwietniowski. 12M UKN.
The Birthday of the Infants, 1891, Short Story
  Black and Silver 1982 d: William Raban, Marilyn Raban. 75M UKN.
Bunbury, Play
  Touchons du Bois 1933 d: Maurice Champreux. lps: Armand Bernard, Jeanne Cheirel, Lily Zevaco. 95M FRN. *Soyons Serieux* prod/rel: Gaumont-Franco-Film-Aubert

The Canterville Ghost, 1891, Short Story
  Cacador de Fantasma, O 1975 d: Flavio Migliaccio. 86M BRZ. *Ghost Hunter*
  Canterville Ghost, The 1944 d: Jules Dassin. lps: Charles Laughton, Robert Young, Margaret O'Brien. 96M USA. prod/rel: MGM
  Canterville Ghost, The 1954. lps: Monty Woolley. 15M USA. prod/rel: Dynamic Films
  Canterville Ghost, The 1974 d: Walter C. Miller. lps: David Niven, James Whitmore, Audra Lindley. TVM. 50M USA/UKN. prod/rel: Htv, Polytel
  Canterville Ghost, The 1986 d: Paul Bogart. lps: John Gielgud, Ted Wass, Andrea Marcovicci. TVM. 96M USA. prod/rel: Pound Ridge Prods., Inter-Hemisphere Prods.
  Canterville Ghost, The 1996 d: Sydney MacArtney. lps: Patrick Stewart, Neve Campbell, Joan Sims. TVM. 120M USA/UKN.
  Sandmannchen, Das 1955 d: Emil Surmann. lps: Alice Decarli, Heidi Ewert, Erika Knab. 84M GRM. *The Sandman* prod/rel: Delos, Hamburg
A Florentine Tragedy, Play
  Florentine Tragedy, The 1913. lps: Constance Crawley, Arthur Maude, Edith Bostwick. SHT USA. prod/rel: Warner's Features
The Happy Prince, 1888, Short Story
  Printul Fericit 1968 d: Aurel Miheles. 26M RMN. *The Happy Prince*
An Ideal Husband, London 1895, Play
  Ideal Husband, An 1948 d: Alexander KordA. lps: Paulette Goddard, Michael Wilding, Diana Wynyard. 96M UKN. prod/rel: British Lion, London Films
  Ideal Husband, An 1999 d: Oliver Parker. lps: Rupert Everett, Julianne Moore, Jeremy Northam. 96M UKN/USA. prod/rel: Icon Entertainment Intl., Pathe Pictures
  Idealer Gatte, Ein 1935 d: Herbert Selpin. lps: Karl Ludwig Diehl, Brigitte Helm, Georg Alexander. 86M GRM.
  Idealny Muzh 1981 d: Viktor Georgiev. lps: Yuri Yakovlev, Lyudmila Gurchenko, Anna TvelenyovA. 92M USS. *An Ideal Husband*
The Importance of Being Earnest, London 1895, Play
  Importance of Being Earnest, The 1952 d: Anthony Asquith. lps: Michael Redgrave, Michael Denison, Edith Evans. 95M UKN. prod/rel: British Film Makers, Javelin
  Importance of Being Earnest, The 1964 d: Bill Bain. lps: Ian Carmichael, Susannah York, Patrick MacNee. MTV. UKN. prod/rel: ABC
  Liebe, Scherz Und Ernst 1932 d: Franz Wenzler. 91M GRM. *Bunbury*
Lady Windermere's Fan, London 1892, Play
  Abanico de Lady Windermere, El 1944 d: Juan J. OrtegA. lps: Susana Guizar, Anita Blanch, Rene CardonA. 89M MXC.
  Fan, The 1949 d: Otto Preminger. lps: Madeleine Carroll, Jeanne Crain, George Sanders. 89M USA. *Lady Windermere's Fan* (UKN) prod/rel: 20th Century Fox
  Historia de Una Mala Mujer 1948 d: Luis Saslavsky. lps: Francisco de Paula, Maria Duval, Fernando Lamas. 90M ARG. *The Story of an Unfaithful Woman; Lady Windermere's Fan*
  Lady Windermeres Facher 1935 d: Heinz Hilpert. lps: Lil Dagover, Hanna Waag, Walter RillA. 95M GRM. prod/rel: Georg Witt-Film
  Lady Windermere's Fan 1916 d: Fred Paul. lps: Milton Rosmer, Netta Westcott, Nigel Playfair. 4500f UKN. prod/rel: Ideal
  Lady Windermere's Fan 1925 d: Ernst Lubitsch. lps: Ronald Colman, Irene Rich, May McAvoy. 7815f USA. prod/rel: Warner Brothers Pictures
  Lady Windermere's Fan 1967 d: Joan Kemp-Welch. lps: Barbara Jefford, Joan Benham, Jennie Linden. MTV. UKN. prod/rel: Rediffusion
  Shao Nainai de Shanzi 1938 d: Li Pingqian. 90M CHN. *The Young Lady's Fan*
Lord Arthur Savile's Crime, 1891, Short Story
  Crime de Lord Arthur Savile, Le 1921 d: Rene Hervil. lps: Andre Nox, Catherine Fonteney, Andre Dubosc. 1870m FRN. *Lord Arthur Savile's Crime* (USA) prod/rel: Films Andre Legrand, W. Et F. Film Service Ltd. London
  Flesh and Fantasy 1943 d: Julien Duvivier. lps: Betty Field, Robert Cummings, Edward G. Robinson. 93M USA. *Obsessions; For All We Know* prod/rel: Universal
  Lord Arthur Savile's Crime 1960 d: Alan Cooke. lps: Robert Coote, Terry-Thomas, Eric Pohlmann. MTV. UKN. prod/rel: ABC

The Nightingale and the Rose, 1888, Short Story
Nightingale and the Rose, The 1967 d: Josef Kabrt. ANM. 14M CZC.

The Picture of Dorian Gray, London 1891, Novel
Bildnis Des Dorian Gray, Das 1917 d: Richard Oswald. lps: Bernd Aldor, Ernst Pittschau, Lupu Pick. GRM. *The Picture of Dorian Gray (USA)*
Dio Chiamato Dorian, Il 1970 d: Massimo Dallamano. lps: Helmut Berger, Richard Todd, Herbert Lom. 98M ITL/GRM/LCH. *Das Bildnis Des Dorian Gray* (GRM); *The Secret of Dorian Gray*; *Dorian Gray* (USA); *God Calls Dorian*; *Evils of Dorian Gray, The* prod/rel: Sargon Film (Roma), Terra Filmkunst (Munich)
Picture of Dorian Gray, The 1915 d: Mr. Moore. lps: Harris Gordon, Ernest Howard, Ray Johnston. 2r USA. prod/rel: Thanhouser
Picture of Dorian Gray, The 1916 d: Fred W. Durrant. lps: Henry Victor, Pat O'Malley, Jack Jordan. 5752f UKN. prod/rel: Barker, Neptune
Picture of Dorian Gray, The 1944 d: Albert Lewin. lps: George Sanders, Hurd Hatfield, Donna Reed. 111M USA. prod/rel: MGM, Loews ,Inc.
Picture of Dorian Gray, The 1973 d: Glenn Jordan. lps: Shane Briant, Nigel Davenport, Charles Aidman. TVM. 180M USA. prod/rel: Dan Curtis Productions
Picture of Dorian Gray, The 1976 d: John Gorrie. lps: John Gielgud, Peter Firth, Jeremy Brett. MTV. 100M UKN. prod/rel: BBC
Portrait de Dorian Gray, Le 1977 d: Pierre Boutron. lps: Raymond Gerome, Patrice Alexsandre, Denis Manuel. 95M FRN.

Salome, 1893, Play
Modern Salome, A 1920 d: Leonce Perret. lps: Hope Hampton, Sidney Mason, Percy Standing. 5700f USA. prod/rel: Hope Hampton Productions, Inc.©, Metro Pictures Corp.
Salome 1908 d: Albert Capellani?. lps: Paul Capellani, Stacia Napierkowska, Jean Angelo. FRN. prod/rel: Serie D'art Pathe Freres
Salome 1910 d: Ugo FalenA. lps: Laura Orette, Ciro Galvani, Vittoria Lepanto. 285m ITL. prod/rel: Film d'Arte Italiana
Salome 1922 d: Charles Bryant. lps: Alla Nazimova, Rose Dione, Mitchell Lewis. 5595f USA. prod/rel: Nazimova Productions, Allied Producers and Distributors
Salome 1971 d: Werner Schroeter. lps: Mascha Elm-Rabben, Magdalena Montezuma, Ellen Umlauf. 81M GRM.
Salome 1972 d: Carmelo Bene. lps: Carmelo Bene, Lydia Mancinelli, Alfiero Vincenti. 76M ITL. prod/rel: Carmelo Bene, I.N.C.
Salome 1986 d: Claude d'AnnA. lps: Tomas Milian, Pamela Salem, Tim Woodward. 97M FRN/ITL. prod/rel: Dedalus/TF 1 (Paris), Italian Film International (Roma)
Salome; Or, the Dance of the Seven Veils 1908 d: J. Stuart Blackton. lps: Florence Lawrence, Maurice Costello. 710f USA. *The Dance of the Seven Veils*; *Salome* prod/rel: Vitagraph Co. of America
Salome's Last Dance 1988 d: Ken Russell. lps: Imogen Millais-Scott, Glenda Jackson, Stratford Johns. 89M UKN. prod/rel: Vestron Pictures, Jolly Russell Productions

A Woman of No Importance, London 1893, Play
Femme Sans Importance, Une 1937 d: Jean Choux. lps: Pierre Blanchar, Gilbert Gil, Lisette Lanvin. 90M FRN. *Le Secret d'une Vie* prod/rel: Regina
Frau Ohne Bedeutung, Eine 1936 d: Hans Steinhoff. lps: Kathe Dorsch, Gustaf Grundgens, Marianne Hoppe. 79M GRM. *A Woman of No Importance (USA)* prod/rel: Majestic, Nord-Westdeutscher
Woman of No Importance, A 1921 d: Denison Clift. lps: Fay Compton, Milton Rosmer, Ward McAllister. 5250f UKN. prod/rel: Ideal
Woman of No Importance, A 1960 d: Joan Kemp-Welch. lps: Helen Cherry, Griffith Jones, Charles Lloyd Pack. MTV. UKN. prod/rel: Rediffusion

WILDE, PATRICK
What's Wrong With Angry?, Play
Get Real 1998 d: Simon Shore. lps: Ben Silverstone, Brad Gorton, Charlotte Brittain. 110M UKN/SAF. prod/rel: Graphite Films (Get Real) Ltd.©, British Screen

WILDE, PERCIVAL
The Hunch, 1921, Short Story
Hunch, The 1921 d: George D. Baker. lps: Gareth Hughes, Ethel Grandin, John Steppling. 6r USA. *Tempting Luck* prod/rel: S-L Productions, Metro Pictures

The Woman in Room 13, New York 1919, Play
Woman in Room 13, The 1920 d: Frank Lloyd. lps: Pauline Frederick, Charles Clary, John Bowers. 5r USA. prod/rel: Goldwyn Pictures Corp.©, Goldwyn Distributing Corp.
Woman in Room 13, The 1932 d: Henry King. lps: Elissa Landi, Ralph Bellamy, Neil Hamilton. 69M USA. prod/rel: Fox Film Corp.©

WILDER, LAURA INGALLS (1867–1957), USA, Wilder, Laura Elizabeth Ingalls, Wilder, Mrs. Almanzo James
Little House on the Prairie, Novel
Little House on the Prairie, The 1974 d: Michael Landon. lps: Michael Landon, Karen Grassle, Melissa Gilbert. TVM. 100M USA. prod/rel: NBC Entertainment

WILDER, MARGARET BUELL
Since You Went Away, Book
Since You Went Away 1944 d: John Cromwell, Andre de Toth (Uncredited). lps: Claudette Colbert, Jennifer Jones, Shirley Temple. 172M USA. prod/rel: United Artists, Selznick International

WILDER, ROBERT
And Ride a Tiger, 1951, Novel
Stranger in My Arms 1959 d: Helmut Kautner. lps: June Allyson, Jeff Chandler, Sandra Dee. 88M USA. *And Ride a Tiger* prod/rel: Universal-International
Flamingo Road, Novel
Flamingo Road 1949 d: Michael Curtiz. lps: Joan Crawford, Zachary Scott, Sydney Greenstreet. 94M USA. prod/rel: Warner Bros.
Flamingo Road 1980 d: Gus Trikonis. lps: John Beck, Cristina Raines, Howard Duff. TVM. 100M USA. prod/rel: NBC, Lorimar
Fruit of the Poppy, New York 1965, Novel
Heroin Gang, The 1968 d: Brian G. Hutton. lps: David McCallum, Stella Stevens, Telly Savalas. 90M USA. *Sol Madrid* prod/rel: Gershwin-Kastner Productions, Hall Bartlett Productions
Written on the Wind, 1946, Novel
Written on the Wind 1956 d: Douglas Sirk. lps: Rock Hudson, Lauren Bacall, Robert Stack. 100M USA. prod/rel: Universal Pictures Co.©, Universal-International

WILDER, THORNTON (1897–1975), USA, Wilder, Thornton Niven
The Bridge of San Luis Rey, 1927, Novel
Bridge of San Luis Rey, The 1929 d: Charles J. Brabin. lps: Lili Damita, Ernest Torrence, Raquel Torres. 7890f USA. prod/rel: Metro-Goldwyn-Mayer Pictures
Bridge of San Luis Rey, The 1944 d: Rowland V. Lee. lps: Lynn Bari, Akim Tamiroff, Francis Lederer. 89M USA. prod/rel: United Artists
The Merchant of Yonkers, New York 1938, Play
Matchmaker, The 1958 d: Joseph Anthony. lps: Shirley Booth, Anthony Perkins, Shirley MacLaine. 101M USA. prod/rel: Paramount, Don Hartman Prods.
Our Town, New York 1938, Play
Our Town 1940 d: Sam Wood. lps: William Holden, Martha Scott, Frank Craven. 90M USA. prod/rel: United Artists Corp., Principal Artists Productions
Our Town 1977 d: George Schaefer. lps: Ned Beatty, Barbara Bel Geddes, Robby Benson. TVM. 100M USA.
Theophilus North, 1973, Novel
Mr. North 1988 d: Danny Huston. lps: Anthony Edwards, Robert Mitchum, Lauren Bacall. 92M USA. prod/rel: Columbia Tri-Star, Heritage Entertainment

WILDGANS, ANTON
Kirbisch, 1927, Verse
Cordula 1950 d: Gustav Ucicky. lps: Paula Wessely, Attila Horbiger, Erik Frey. 105M AUS. prod/rel: Paula Wessely

WILEY, HUGH
Hop, 1921, Short Story
Bits of Life 1921 d: Marshall Neilan. lps: Wesley Barry, Rockliffe Fellowes, Lon Chaney. 6339f USA. prod/rel: Marshall Neilan Productions, Associated First National Pictures
The Spoils of War, 1925, Short Story
Behind the Front 1926 d: A. Edward Sutherland. lps: Wallace Beery, Raymond Hatton, Mary Brian. 5555f USA. prod/rel: Famous Players-Lasky Corp., Paramount Pictures

WILHELM, FRANK
Louie the Fourteenth, New York 1925, Play
Wife Savers 1928 d: Ralph Ceder. lps: Wallace Beery, Raymond Hatton, Zasu Pitts. 5434f USA. prod/rel: Paramount Famous Lasky Corp.

WILHELM, JULIUS
Wife Savers 1928 d: Ralph Ceder. lps: Wallace Beery, Raymond Hatton, Zasu Pitts. 5434f USA. prod/rel: Paramount Famous Lasky Corp.
Der Zigeunerprimas, Opera
Zigeunerprimas, Der 1929 d: Carl Wilhelm. lps: Raimondo Van Riel, Margarete Schlegel, Ernst Verebes. 2351m GRM. prod/rel: Aco-Film

WILK, MAX
Don't Raise the Bridge, Lower the River, New York 1960, Novel
Don't Raise the Bridge, Lower the River 1968 d: Jerry Paris. lps: Jerry Lewis, Terry-Thomas, Jacqueline Pearce. 99M UKN/USA. prod/rel: Walter Shenson Films, Columbia

WILKERSON, DAVID
The Cross and the Switchblade, New York 1963, Autobiography
Cross and the Switchblade, The 1970 d: Don Murray. lps: Pat Boone, Erik Estrada, Jackie Giroux. 106M USA.

WILKES, W. ERNEST
Broken Threads, New York 1917, Play
Man from Funeral Range, The 1918 d: Walter Edwards. lps: Wallace Reid, Anna Little, Willis Marks. 4512f USA. prod/rel: Famous Players-Lasky Corp.©, Paramount Pictures

WILKINS, VAUGHAN
A King Reluctant, Novel
Dangerous Exile 1957 d: Brian Desmond Hurst. lps: Louis Jourdan, Belinda Lee, Keith Michell. 90M UKN. prod/rel: Rank, Rank Film Distributors

WILKINSON, G. K.
The Monkeys, London 1962, Novel
Monkeys, Go Home 1967 d: Andrew V. McLaglen. lps: Maurice Chevalier, Dean Jones, Yvette Mimieux. 101M USA. prod/rel: Walt Disney Productions, Buena Vista

WILKINSON, MICHAEL
The Phar Lap Story, Book
Phar Lap 1983 d: Simon Wincer. lps: Tom Burlinson, Ron Leibman, Martin Vaughan. 118M ASL. *Phar Lap: Heart of a Nation* prod/rel: Hoyts, Michael Edgely International

WILLARD, JAMES
The Ace of Hearts, Play
Ace of Hearts, The 1916 d: Charles Calvert. lps: James Willard, Dolly Bishop, Frank Sargent. 3600f UKN. prod/rel: Clarendon
A Woman of Pleasure, Play
Woman of Pleasure, A 1919 d: Wallace Worsley. lps: Blanche Sweet, Wilfred Lucas, Wheeler Oakman. 7r USA. prod/rel: Jesse D. Hampton Productions, Pathe Exchange, Inc.©

WILLARD, JOHN
The Cat and the Canary, New York 1922, Play
Cat and the Canary, The 1927 d: Paul Leni. lps: Laura La Plante, Creighton Hale, Tully Marshall. 7713f USA. prod/rel: Universal Pictures
Cat and the Canary, The 1939 d: Elliott Nugent. lps: Bob Hope, Paulette Goddard, Gale Sondergaard. 72M USA. prod/rel: Paramount Pictures, Inc.
Cat and the Canary, The 1978 d: Radley H. Metzger. lps: Honor Blackman, Michael Callan, Edward Fox. 98M UKN. prod/rel: Gala, Grenadier
Cat Creeps, The 1930 d: Rupert Julian. lps: Helen Twelvetrees, Raymond Hackett, Lilyan Tashman. 75M USA. prod/rel: Universal Pictures
Fog, Play
Black Waters 1929 d: Marshall Neilan. lps: James Kirkwood, Mary Brian, John Loder. 79M UKN. prod/rel: British & Dominions, Sono Art World Wide

WILLAUME, JEAN
L' Uomo Fatale,
Uomo Fatale, L' 1912 d: Mario Caserini. lps: Maria Gasparini Caserini, Febo Mari. 770m ITL. prod/rel: Theatralia Film

WILLEFORD, CHARLES
Cockfighter, Novel
Cockfighter 1974 d: Monte Hellman. lps: Warren Oates, Richard B. Shull, Harry Dean Stanton. 83M USA. *Born to Kill*; *Wild Drifter*; *Gamblin' Man* prod/rel: Rio Pinto, New World
Miami Blues, Novel
Miami Blues 1990 d: George Armitage. lps: Alec Baldwin, Cecilia Perez-Cervera, Georgie Cranford. 97M USA. prod/rel: Tristes Tropiques, Orion

WILLEMETZ, ALBERT
Andalousie, Opera
Andalousie 1950 d: Robert Vernay, Luis LuciA. lps: Luis Mariano, Carmen Sevilla, Liliane Bert. 94M FRN/SPN. *El Sueno de Andalucia* (SPN); *Andalusian Dream* prod/rel: C.C.F.C., U.D.I.F.

Couchette No.3, Opera
Surprises du Sleeping, Les 1933 d: Karl Anton. lps: Claude Dauphin, Florelle, Jacques Louvigny. 92M FRN. *Couchette No.3* prod/rel: S.a.P.E.C.

Dede, Opera
Dede 1934 d: Rene Guissart. lps: Danielle Darrieux, Albert Prejean, Rene Bergeron. 75M FRN. prod/rel: France Univers-Film

Une Grave Erreur, Play
Grave Erreur, Une 1930 d: Joe Francys. lps: Maguy Roche, Max Berger, Meret. 40M FRN. prod/rel: Alex Nalpas

Il Est Charmant, Opera
Il Est Charmant 1931 d: Louis Mercanton. lps: Henri Garat, Meg Lemonnier, Cassive. 80M FRN. *Paris Je T'aime* prod/rel: Films Paramount

Passionnement, Opera
Passionnement 1932 d: Rene Guissart, Louis Mercanton (Uncredited). lps: Florelle, Fernand Gravey, Rene Koval. 80M FRN. prod/rel: Films Paramount

Sidonie Panache, Opera
Sidonie Panache 1934 d: Henry Wulschleger. lps: Bach, Alexandre Mihalesco, Florelle. 120M FRN/ALG. prod/rel: Alex Nalpas, Cie Francaise Cinematographique Lux

Un Soir de Reveillon, Opera
Soir de Reveillon, Un 1933 d: Karl Anton. lps: Henri Garat, Meg Lemonnier, Arletty. 85M FRN. prod/rel: Films Paramount

Toi C'est Moi, Opera
Toi C'est Moi 1936 d: Rene Guissart. lps: Jacques Pills, Georges Tabet, Claude May. 90M FRN. prod/rel: Paris-Cine-Films

Trois Jeunes Filles Nues, Opera
Trois Jeunes Filles Nues 1928 d: Robert Boudrioz. lps: Nicolas Rimsky, Rene Ferte, Jeanne Helbling. 2500m FRN. prod/rel: Integral Films

Yes, Opera
Defense d'Aimer 1942 d: Richard Pottier. lps: Paul Meurisse, Suzy Delair, Andre Gabriello. 90M FRN. *Le Coeur Sur la Main*; *Totte Et Sa Chance* prod/rel: Continental-Film

WILLEMSE, C.W.
Behind the Green Lights, New York 1933, Book
Behind the Green Lights 1935 d: W. Christy Cabanne. lps: Norman Foster, Judith Allen, Sidney Blackmer. 70M USA. prod/rel: Mascot Pictures Corp.

WILLETS, GILSON
The First Law, New York 1911, Novel
First Law, The 1918 d: Lawrence McGill. lps: Irene Castle, Antonio Moreno, Marguerite Snow. 5r USA. prod/rel: Astra Film Corp., Pathe Exchange, Inc.

The Quarry, Novel
Quarry, The 1915 d: Lawrence Marston. 3r USA. prod/rel: Selig Polyscope Co.

WILLIAMS, ALAN (1935–, UKN
The Cockroach Trilogy, Play
Cockroach That Ate Cincinnati, The 1996 d: Michael McNamarA. lps: Alan Williams, Deborah Drakeford, Oliver Dennis. 97M CND. prod/rel: Queen West Prods (Toronto)

The One-Woman Idea, 1927, Short Story
One Woman Idea, The 1929 d: Berthold Viertel. lps: Rod La Rocque, Marceline Day, Shirley Dorman. 6111f USA. prod/rel: Fox Film Corp.

Snake Water, London 1965, Novel
Pink Jungle, The 1968 d: Delbert Mann. lps: James Garner, Eva Renzi, George Kennedy. 104M USA. prod/rel: Cherokee Productions

WILLIAMS, BEN AMES (1889–1953), USA
After His Own Heart, 1919, Short Story
After His Own Heart 1919 d: Harry L. Franklin. lps: Hale Hamilton, Naomi Childers, Mrs. Louis. 5r USA. prod/rel: Metro Pictures Corp.

All the Brothers Were Valiant, New York 1919, Novel
Across to Singapore 1928 d: William Nigh. lps: Ramon Novarro, Joan Crawford, Ernest Torrence. 6805f USA. *China Bound* prod/rel: Metro-Goldwyn-Mayer Pictures

All the Brothers Were Valiant 1923 d: Irvin V. Willat. lps: Malcolm McGregor, Billie Dove, Lon Chaney. 6265f USA. prod/rel: Metro Pictures

All the Brothers Were Valiant 1953 d: Richard Thorpe. lps: Stewart Granger, Robert Taylor, Ann Blyth. 101M USA. prod/rel: MGM

Barber John's Boy, Story
Father and Son 1934 d: Monty Banks. lps: Edmund Gwenn, Esmond Knight, James Finlayson. 48M UKN. prod/rel: Warner Bros., First National

Man to Man 1930 d: Allan Dwan. lps: Phillips Holmes, Grant Mitchell, Lucille Powers. 6281f USA. *Barber John's Boy* prod/rel: Warner Brothers Pictures

Black Pawl, Short Story
Godless Men 1921 d: Reginald Barker. lps: Russell Simpson, James Mason, Helene Chadwick. 6367f USA. *Black Pawl* prod/rel: Reginald Barker Productions, Goldwyn Pictures Corp.©

The Great Accident, New York 1920, Novel
Great Accident, The 1920 d: Harry Beaumont. lps: Tom Moore, Jane Novak, Andrew Robson. 5615f USA. prod/rel: Goldwyn Pictures Corp.©, Goldwyn Distributing Corp.

Jubilo, 1919, Short Story
Jubilo 1919 d: Clarence Badger. lps: Will Rogers, Josie Sedgwick, Charles K. French. 5r USA. prod/rel: Goldwyn Pictures Corp.©, Goldwyn Distributing Corp.

Too Busy to Work 1932 d: John G. Blystone. lps: Will Rogers, Marian Nixon, Dick Powell. 76M USA. *Jubilo* prod/rel: Fox Film Corp.©

Leave Her to Heaven, Novel
Leave Her to Heaven 1945 d: John M. Stahl. lps: Gene Tierney, Cornel Wilde, Jeanne Crain. 111M USA. prod/rel: 20th Century-Fox

The Man Who Had Everything, Short Story
Man Who Had Everything, The 1920 d: Alfred E. Green. lps: Jack Pickford, Priscilla Bonner, Lionel Belmore. 5r USA. prod/rel: Goldwyn Pictures Corp.©, Goldwyn Distributing Corp.

More Stately Mansions, 1920, Short Story
Extravagance 1921 d: Phil Rosen. lps: May Allison, Robert Edeson, Theodore von Eltz. 6r USA. prod/rel: Metro Pictures

Small Town Girl, New York 1935, Novel
Small Town Girl 1936 d: William A. Wellman. lps: Janet Gaynor, Robert Taylor, Binnie Barnes. 106M USA. *One Horse Town* prod/rel: Metro-Goldwyn-Mayer Corp.©

Small Town Girl 1952 d: Leslie Kardos. lps: Jane Powell, Farley Granger, Ann Miller. 93M USA. prod/rel: MGM

A Son of Anak, 1928, Short Story
Masked Emotions 1929 d: David Butler, Kenneth Hawks. lps: George O'Brien, Nora Lane, J. Farrell MacDonald. 5419f USA. prod/rel: Fox Film Corp.

The Strange Woman, Novel
Strange Woman, The 1946 d: Edgar G. Ulmer. lps: Hedy Lamarr, George Sanders, Louis Hayward. 101M USA. prod/rel: United Artists

Three in a Thousand, 1917, Short Story
Fighting Lover, The 1921 d: Fred Leroy Granville. lps: Frank Mayo, Elinor Hancock, Gertrude Olmstead. 4040f USA. prod/rel: Universal Film Mfg. Co.

Too Good to Be True, Novel
Too Good to Be True 1988 d: Christian Nyby II. lps: Loni Anderson, Patrick Duffy, Glynnis O'Connor. TVM. 100M USA. prod/rel: Newland-Raynor Prod.

Toujours de l'Audace, 1920, Short Story
Always Audacious 1920 d: James Cruze. lps: Wallace Reid, Margaret Loomis, Clarence Geldart. 5101f USA. prod/rel: Famous Players-Lasky Corp.©, Paramount Pictures

A Very Practical Joke, 1925, Short Story
Inside Story 1938 d: Ricardo Cortez. lps: Michael Whalen, Jean Rogers, Chick Chandler. 60M USA. *A Very Practical Joke* prod/rel: Twentieth Century-Fox Film Corp.©

Man Trouble 1930 d: Berthold Viertel. lps: Milton Sills, Dorothy MacKaill, Kenneth MacKennA. 7800f USA. *Living for Love* prod/rel: Fox Film Corp.

WILLIAMS, BOB
Story
MacAo 1952 d: Josef von Sternberg, Nicholas Ray (Uncredited). lps: Robert Mitchum, Jane Russell, William Bendix. 80M USA. prod/rel: RKO Radio

WILLIAMS, BROCK
The Earl of Chicago, New York 1937, Novel
Earl of Chicago, The 1939 d: Richard Thorpe. lps: Robert Montgomery, Edward Arnold, Reginald Owen. 85M USA. prod/rel: Metro-Goldwyn-Mayer Corp., Loew's, Inc.©

Uncle Willie and the Bicycle Shop, Novel
Isn't Life Wonderful 1953 d: Harold French. lps: Eileen Herlie, Cecil Parker, Donald Wolfit. 83M UKN. *Uncle Willie's Bicycle Shop* prod/rel: Associated British Picture Corporation, Ab-Pathe

Wanted, Play
Wanted 1937 d: George King. lps: Zasu Pitts, Claude Dampier, Finlay Currie. 71M UKN. prod/rel: Embassy, Sound City

WILLIAMS, CHARLES
All the Way, Novel
Third Voice, The 1960 d: Hubert Cornfield. lps: Laraine Day, Edmond O'Brien, Olga San Juan. 80M USA. prod/rel: 20th Century Fox

L' Arme a Gauche, Novel
Arme a Gauche, L' 1965 d: Claude Sautet. lps: Lino Ventura, Sylva Koscina, Leo Gordon. 103M FRN/ITL/SPN. *Corpo a Corpo* (ITL); *The Dictator's Guns* (USA); *Armas Para El Caribe* (SPN); *Guns for the Dictator* (UKN); *Ont-Ils Des Jambes?* prod/rel: Intermondia, T.C. Production

Avec un Elastique, Novel
Gros Coup, Le 1963 d: Jean Valere. lps: Emmanuelle Riva, Hardy Kruger, Francisco Rabal. 105M FRN/ITL. *Il Triangolo Del Delitto* (ITL) prod/rel: Films Arthur Lesser, Film d'Art

Dead Calm, Novel
Dead Calm 1988 d: Phil Noyce. lps: Sam Neill, Nicole Kidman, Billy Zane. 96M ASL. prod/rel: Roadshow, Kennedy Miller Productions©

Diamond Bikini, Novel
Fantasia Chez Les Ploucs 1970 d: Gerard Pires. lps: Lino Ventura, Jean Yanne, Mireille Darc. 100M FRN/ITL. *Il Rompiballe*. *Rompe Ancora* (ITL) prod/rel: Copro Film, Films De La Pleiade

The Long Saturday Night, Novel
Vivement Dimanche 1983 d: Francois Truffaut. lps: Fanny Ardant, Jean-Louis Trintignant, Philippe Laudenbach. 111M FRN. *The Long Saturday Night* (USA); *Confidentially Yours*; *Finally Sunday* prod/rel: Films Du Carrosse, Soprofilms

Nothing in Her Way, 1953, Novel
Peau de Banane 1964 d: Marcel Ophuls. lps: Jeanne Moreau, Jean-Paul Belmondo, Gert Frobe. 97M FRN/ITL. *Buccia Di Banana* (ITL); *Banana Peel* (USA) prod/rel: Sud-Pacifique Films, Capitole Films

The Wrong Venus, New York 1966, Novel
Don't Just Stand There! 1968 d: Ron Winston. lps: Robert Wagner, Mary Tyler Moore, Glynis Johns. 99M USA. prod/rel: Universal Pictures

WILLIAMS, CHARLES N.
The Second Latchkey, Garden City, N.Y. 1920, Novel
My Lady's Latchkey 1921 d: Edwin Carewe. lps: Katherine MacDonald, Edmund Lowe, Claire Du Brey. 5500f USA. prod/rel: Katherine Macdonald Pictures, Associated First National Pictures

WILLIAMS, CYRUS J.
Into the Light, Story
Things Men Do 1920 d: Robert North Bradbury. lps: Margaret Gibson, Edward Hearn, William Lion West. 5000f USA. *Into the Light*; *Hollyhocks* prod/rel: Bradbury Productions, Mitchell Lewis Corp.

WILLIAMS, DAVID
Second Sight, Novel
Two Worlds of Jennie Logan, The 1979 d: Frank de FelittA. lps: Lindsay Wagner, Marc Singer, Alan Feinstein. TVM. 100M USA.

WILLIAMS, ELIOT CRAWSHAW
Fascination, Play
Fascination 1931 d: Miles Mander. lps: Madeleine Carroll, Carl Harbord, Dorothy Bartlam. 70M UKN. prod/rel: Regina, Wardour

WILLIAMS, EMLYN (1905–1987), UKN, Williams, George Emlyn
Play
Leben Beginnt Um Acht, Das 1962 d: Michael Kehlmann. lps: O. E. Hasse, Johanna Matz, Helmut Wildt. 100M GRM. *Life Begins at Eight* prod/rel: Utz Utermann, Nora

The Corn Is Green, London 1938, Play
Corn Is Green, The 1945 d: Irving Rapper. lps: Bette Davis, John Dall, Joan Lorring. 114M USA. prod/rel: Warner Bros.

Corn Is Green, The 1978 d: George Cukor. lps: Katharine Hepburn, Ian Saynor, Bill Fraser. TVM. 100M USA. prod/rel: CBS, Warner Bros. Tv

Headlong, 1981, Novel
King Ralph 1991 d: David S. Ward. lps: John Goodman, Peter O'Toole, John Hurt. 97M USA. *King Ralph I*; *Headlong* prod/rel: Universal, Mirage/Ibro

The Light of Heart, 1940, Play
Life Begins at 8.30 1942 d: Irving Pichel. lps: Monty Woolley, Ida Lupino, Cornel Wilde. 85M USA. *The Light of Heart* (UKN) prod/rel: 20th Century-Fox

Night Must Fall, London 1935, Play
Night Must Fall 1937 d: Richard Thorpe. lps: Robert Montgomery, Rosalind Russell, Dame May Whitty. 117M USA. prod/rel: Metro-Goldwyn-Mayer Corp.©

Night Must Fall 1964 d: Karel Reisz. lps: Albert Finney, Susan Hampshire, Mona Washbourne. 105M UKN. prod/rel: MGM British

Someone Waiting, London 1953, Play
   Time Without Pity 1957 d: Joseph Losey. lps: Michael Redgrave, Ann Todd, Leo McKern. 88M UKN. *No Time for Pity* prod/rel: Harlequin, Eros

WILLIAMS, ERIC
The Wooden Horse, Book
   Wooden Horse, The 1950 d: Jack Lee. lps: Leo Genn, David Tomlinson, Anthony Steel. 101M UKN. prod/rel: British Lion Production Assets, Wessex

WILLIAMS, ERSKINE
Diary of a Negro Maid
   High Yellow 1965 d: Larry Buchanan. lps: Cynthia Hull, Warren Hammack, Kay Taylor. 83M USA. prod/rel: Dinero Productions
The Paradise of Five Dollars, Short Story
   Acid (Delirio Dei Sensi) 1967 d: Giuseppe Maria Scotese. lps: Jane Tillet, Bud Thompson, Annabella Andreoli. 92M ITL. *Acid (Delirium of the Senses)* prod/rel: Produzioni Scotese, Clodia Cin.Ca

WILLIAMS, GORDON M. (1934–, UKN
The Man Who Had Power Over Women, London 1967, Novel
   Man Who Had Power Over Women, The 1970 d: John Krish. lps: Rod Taylor, Carol White, James Booth. 90M UKN. prod/rel: Kettledrum Productions, Rodlor, Inc.
The Siege of Trencher's Farm, Novel
   Straw Dogs 1971 d: Sam Peckinpah. lps: Dustin Hoffman, Susan George, Peter Vaughan. 118M UKN. prod/rel: Talent Associates, Amerbroco

WILLIAMS, HUGH (1904–1969), UKN
The Grass Is Greener, London 1958, Play
   Grass Is Greener, The 1961 d: Stanley Donen. lps: Cary Grant, Deborah Kerr, Robert Mitchum. 104M UKN. prod/rel: United Artists, Grandon

WILLIAMS, JESSE LYNCH
Not Wanted, 1923, Short Story
   Too Many Parents 1936 d: Robert F. McGowan. lps: Frances Farmer, Lester Matthews, Billy Lee. 73M USA. prod/rel: Paramount Productions©
The Wrong Door, 1917, Serial Story
   Through the Wrong Door 1919 d: Clarence Badger. lps: Madge Kennedy, John Bowers, Herbert Standing. 5r USA. *The Wrong Door* prod/rel: Goldwyn Pictures Corp.©, Goldwyn Distributing Corp.

WILLIAMS, JOHN A. (1925–, USA
The Junior Bachelor Society, 1976, Book
   Sophisticated Gents, The 1981 d: Harry Falk. lps: Bernie Casey, Rosey Grier, Robert Hooks. TVM. 200M USA.
Night Song, New York 1961, Novel
   Sweet Love, Bitter 1967 d: Herbert DanskA. lps: Dick Gregory, Don Murray, Diane Varsi. 92M USA. *Baby! It Won't Rub Off*; *Black Love -White Love*; *Night Song* prod/rel: Film 2 Associates

WILLIAMS JR., HERSHEL V.
Janie, New York 1942, Play
   Janie 1944 d: Michael Curtiz. lps: Joyce Reynolds, Robert Hutton, Edward Arnold. 106M USA. prod/rel: Warner Bros.

WILLIAMS, MARGARET
The Grass Is Greener, London 1958, Play
   Grass Is Greener, The 1961 d: Stanley Donen. lps: Cary Grant, Deborah Kerr, Robert Mitchum. 104M UKN. prod/rel: United Artists, Grandon

WILLIAMS, MONA
May the Best Wife Win, Story
   Woman's World, A 1954 d: Jean Negulesco. lps: Clifton Webb, Van Heflin, Cornel Wilde. 94M USA. prod/rel: 20th Century-Fox

WILLIAMS, NIGEL
Play
   Klassen Feind 1983 d: Peter Stein. lps: Greger Hansen, Stefan Reck, Jean-Paul Raths. 125M GRM. *Class Enemy*; *An Enemy of the Class* prod/rel: Regina Ziegler, Pro-Ject
Witchcraft, Novel
   Witchcraft 1992 d: Peter Sasdy. lps: Peter McEnery, Lisa Harrow, Alan Howard. TVM. 180M UKN. prod/rel: BBC Pebble Mill

WILLIAMS, PAUL
The General, Book
   General, The 1998 d: John Boorman. lps: Brendan Gleeson, Adrian Dunbar, Sean McGinley. 124M IRL/UKN. prod/rel: Merlin Films, J&m Entertainment

WILLIAMS, REBECCA YANCEY
The Vanishing Virginian, Book
   Vanishing Virginian, The 1941 d: Frank Borzage. lps: Frank Morgan, Kathryn Grayson, Spring Byington. 97M USA. prod/rel: MGM

WILLIAMS, ROBERT
The Knife in the Body, Novel
   Lama Nel Corpo, La 1966 d: Elio Scardamaglia, Domenico de Felice. lps: William Berger, Francoise Prevost, Mary Young. 87M ITL/FRN. *Les Nuits de l'Epouvante* (FRN); *The Murder Clinic* (USA); *The Murder Society*; *The Blade in the Body*; *The Night of Terrors* prod/rel: Leone Film, Orphee Productions

WILLIAMS, TENNESSEE (1911–1983), USA, Williams, Thomas Lanier
Story
   Migrants, The 1974 d: Tom Gries. lps: Cloris Leachman, Ron Howard, Sissy Spacek. TVM. 73M USA. prod/rel: CBS Television
27 Wagons Full of Cotton, 1945, Play
   Baby Doll 1956 d: Elia Kazan. lps: Carroll Baker, Eli Wallach, Karl Malden. 114M USA. prod/rel: Warner Bros., Newtown Prods, Inc.
Cat on a Hot Tin Roof, New York 1955, Play
   Cat on a Hot Tin Roof 1958 d: Richard Brooks. lps: Elizabeth Taylor, Paul Newman, Burl Ives. 108M USA. prod/rel: MGM, Avon
   Cat on a Hot Tin Roof 1976 d: Robert Moore. lps: Laurence Olivier, Natalie Wood, Robert Wagner. TVM. 100M UKN. prod/rel: Itv, Granada Tv
   Cat on a Hot Tin Roof 1985 d: Jack Hofsiss. lps: Jessica Lange, Tommy Lee Jones, Rip Torn. TVM. 150M USA.
The Glass Menagerie, New York 1945, Play
   Glass Menagerie, The 1950 d: Irving Rapper. lps: Gertrude Lawrence, Jane Wyman, Kirk Douglas. 107M USA. prod/rel: Warner Bros., Charles K. Feldman Group
   Glass Menagerie, The 1973 d: Anthony Harvey. lps: Katharine Hepburn, Sam Waterston, Joanna Miles. TVM. 100M USA. prod/rel: Norton-Simon, Talent Associates
   Glass Menagerie, The 1987 d: Paul Newman. lps: Joanne Woodward, John Malkovich, Karen Allen. 134M USA. prod/rel: Cineplex Odeon
The Long Stay Cut Short, 1948, Play
   Baby Doll 1956 d: Elia Kazan. lps: Carroll Baker, Eli Wallach, Karl Malden. 114M USA. prod/rel: Warner Bros., Newtown Prods, Inc.
The Milk Train Doesn't Stop Here Any More, New York 1962, Play
   Boom! 1968 d: Joseph Losey. lps: Elizabeth Taylor, Richard Burton, Noel Coward. 113M UKN. *Goforth*; *Sunburst* prod/rel: Rank Film Distributors, World Film Services
The Night of the Iguana, New York 1961, Play
   Night of the Iguana, The 1964 d: John Huston. lps: Richard Burton, Ava Gardner, Deborah Kerr. 125M USA. prod/rel: Seven Arts Productions, MGM
Orpheus Descending, New York 1957, Play
   Fugitive Kind, The 1959 d: Sidney Lumet. lps: Marlon Brando, Anna Magnani, Joanne Woodward. 121M USA. prod/rel: United Artists, Jurow-Shepherd-Pennebaker
Period of Adjustment, New York 1961, Play
   Period of Adjustment 1962 d: George Roy Hill. lps: Anthony Franciosa, Jane Fonda, Jim Hutton. 112M USA. prod/rel: Marten Productions, MGM
The Roman Spring of Mrs. Stone, New York 1950, Novel
   Roman Spring of Mrs. Stone, The 1961 d: Jose Quintero. lps: Vivien Leigh, Warren Beatty, Lotte LenyA. 104M UKN/USA. *The Widow and the Gigolo* prod/rel: a.A. Productions, Seven Arts
The Rose Tattoo, New York 1951, Play
   Rose Tattoo, The 1955 d: Daniel Mann. lps: Anna Magnani, Burt Lancaster, Marisa Pavan. 117M USA. prod/rel: Paramount, Wallis-Hazen
The Seven Descents of Myrtle, New York 1968, Play
   Last of the Mobile Hot-Shots, The 1970 d: Sidney Lumet. lps: James Coburn, Lynn Redgrave, Robert Hooks. 108M USA. *Blood Kin* prod/rel: Sidney Lumet Productions
A Streetcar Named Desire, New York 1947, Play
   Streetcar Named Desire, A 1951 d: Elia Kazan. lps: Vivien Leigh, Marlon Brando, Kim Hunter. 125M USA. prod/rel: Warner Bros., Charles K. Feldman Group
   Streetcar Named Desire, A 1984 d: John Erman. lps: Ann-Margret, Treat Williams, Beverly d'Angelo. TVM. 124M USA.
   Streetcar Named Desire, A 1995 d: Glenn Jordan. lps: Jessica Lange, Alec Baldwin, John Goodman. TVM. 180M USA.
Suddenly, Last Summer, New York 1958, Play
   Suddenly, Last Summer 1959 d: Joseph L. Mankiewicz. lps: Elizabeth Taylor, Montgomery Clift, Katharine Hepburn. 114M UKN/USA. prod/rel: Columbia, Horizon Ltd.

   Suddenly, Last Summer 1992 d: Richard Eyre. lps: Maggie Smith, Natasha Richardson, Rob Lowe. TVM. 83M UKN.
Summer and Smoke, New York 1948, Play
   Summer and Smoke 1961 d: Peter Glenville. lps: Laurence Harvey, Geraldine Page, Rita Moreno. 118M USA. prod/rel: Hal Wallis Productions, Paramount
Sweet Bird of Youth, New York 1959, Play
   Sweet Bird of Youth 1962 d: Richard Brooks. lps: Paul Newman, Geraldine Page, Shirley Knight. 120M USA. prod/rel: Roxbury Productions, Metro-Goldwyn-Mayer, Inc.
   Sweet Bird of Youth 1989 d: Nicolas Roeg. lps: Elizabeth Taylor, Mark Harmon, Rip Torn. TVM. 100M USA.
This Property Is Condemned, New York 1956, Play
   This Property Is Condemned 1966 d: Sydney Pollack. lps: Natalie Wood, Robert Redford, Charles Bronson. 110M USA. prod/rel: Seven Arts Productions, Paramount

WILLIAMS, TERRY
The Cocaine Kids, Novel
   Illtown 1996 d: Nick Gomez. lps: Michael Rapaport, Lili Taylor, Adam Trese. 103M USA. prod/rel: Donald C. Carter, Shooting Gallery

WILLIAMS, THOMAS J.
Turn Him Out, Play
   Turn Him Out 1913. lps: Lillian Leighton, Thomas Flynn. SHT USA. prod/rel: Selig Polyscope Co.

WILLIAMS, VALENTINE
Clubfoot, Novel
   Crouching Beast, The 1935 d: Victor Hanbury. lps: Fritz Kortner, Wynne Gibson, Richard Bird. 80M UKN. prod/rel: Stafford, Radio
Fog, Boston 1933, Novel
   Fog 1934 d: Albert S. Rogell. lps: Donald Cook, Mary Brian, Reginald Denny. 70M USA. prod/rel: Columbia Pictures Corp.©

WILLIAMS, WIRT
Ada Dallas, New York 1959, Novel
   Ada 1961 d: Daniel Mann. lps: Susan Hayward, Dean Martin, Wilfrid Hyde-White. 108M USA. prod/rel: MGM, Avon Productions - Chalmar

WILLIAMSON, ALICE MURIEL
Novel
   Demon, The 1918 d: George D. Baker. lps: Edith Storey, Lew Cody, Charles Gerrard. 5021f USA. prod/rel: Metro Pictures Corp.©
The Guests of Hercules, New York 1912, Novel
   Passion's Playground 1920 d: J. A. Barry. lps: Katherine MacDonald, Norman Kerry, Nell Craig. 5r USA. *The Guests of Hercules* prod/rel: Katherine Macdonald Pictures Corp., First National Exhibitors Circuit
Honeymoon Hate, 1927, Short Story
   Honeymoon Hate 1927 d: Luther Reed. lps: Florence Vidor, Tullio Carminati, William Austin. 5415f USA. prod/rel: Paramount Famous Lasky Corp.
   Principe Gondolero, El 1933 d: Edward D. Venturini. lps: Roberto Rey, Rosita Moreno, Andres de SegurolA. 79M USA. prod/rel: Paramount Publix Corp.
The House of the Lost Court, New York 1908, Novel
   House of the Lost Court, The 1915 d: Charles J. Brabin. lps: Viola Dana, Gertrude McCoy, Robert Conness. 5r USA. prod/rel: Thomas A. Edison, Inc.©, Paramount Pictures Corp.
The Lion's Mouse (Vrouwenlist), 1919, Novel
   Lion's Mouse, The 1923 d: Oscar Apfel. lps: Wyndham Standing, Mary Odette, Rex Davis. 6100f UKN/NTH. *De Leeuw En de Muis* (NTH); *The Lion and the Mouse*; *Een Listige Vrouw*; *Vrouwenlist*; *Cunning Woman, A* prod/rel: Granger-Binger Film
Lord John in New York, 1915, Short Story
   Lord John in New York 1915 d: Edward J. Le Saint. lps: William Garwood, Stella Razetto, Ogden Crane. 4r USA. prod/rel: Universal Film Mfg. Co.©, Gold Seal
Lord Loveland Discovers America, New York 1910, Novel
   Lord Loveland Discovers America 1916 d: Arthur Maude. lps: Arthur Maude, Constance Crawley, William Carroll. 5r USA. prod/rel: American Film Co., Mutual Film Corp.
The Second Latchkey, Garden City, N.Y. 1920, Novel
   My Lady's Latchkey 1921 d: Edwin Carewe. lps: Katherine MacDonald, Edmund Lowe, Claire Du Brey. 5500f USA. prod/rel: Katherine Macdonald Pictures, Associated First National Pictures
The Shop Girl, New York 1916, Novel
   Winifred the Shop Girl 1916 d: George D. Baker. lps: Edith Storey, Antonio Moreno, Lillian Burns. 5r USA. *The Shop Girl* prod/rel: Vitagraph Co. of America©, Blue Ribbon Feature

The Woman Who Dared, London 1903, Novel
Woman Who Dared, The 1916 d: George E. Middleton. lps: Beatriz Michelena, Andrew Robson, William Pike. 7r USA. prod/rel: California Motion Picture Corp., State Rights

WILLIAMSON, CHARLES NORRIS
Novel
Demon, The 1918 d: George D. Baker. lps: Edith Storey, Lew Cody, Charles Gerrard. 5021f USA. prod/rel: Metro Pictures Corp.©

The Guests of Hercules, New York 1912, Novel
Passion's Playground 1920 d: J. A. Barry. lps: Katherine MacDonald, Norman Kerry, Nell Craig. 5r USA. *The Guests of Hercules* prod/rel: Katherine Macdonald Pictures Corp., First National Exhibitors Circuit

The Lighting Conductor, New York 1903, Novel
Lightning Conductor, The 1914 d: Walter Hale. lps: Dustin Farnum, Walter Hale, William Elliott. 6-7r USA/ITL. prod/rel: Hefco Films, Sawyer, Inc.

The Lion's Mouse (Vrouwenlist), 1919, Novel
Lion's Mouse, The 1923 d: Oscar Apfel. lps: Wyndham Standing, Mary Odette, Rex Davis. 6100f UKN/NTH. *De Leeuw En de Muis* (NTH); *The Lion and the Mouse*; *Een Listige Vrouw*; *Vrouwenlist*; *Cunning Woman, A* prod/rel: Granger-Binger Film

Lord John in New York, 1915, Short Story
Lord John in New York 1915 d: Edward J. Le Saint. lps: William Garwood, Stella Razetto, Ogden Crane. 4r USA. prod/rel: Universal Film Mfg. Co.©, Gold Seal

Lord Loveland Discovers America, New York 1910, Novel
Lord Loveland Discovers America 1916 d: Arthur Maude. lps: Arthur Maude, Constance Crawley, William Carroll. 5r USA. prod/rel: American Film Co., Mutual Film Corp.

The Shop Girl, New York 1916, Novel
Winifred the Shop Girl 1916 d: George D. Baker. lps: Edith Storey, Antonio Moreno, Lillian Burns. 5r USA. *The Shop Girl* prod/rel: Vitagraph Co. of America©, Blue Ribbon Feature

WILLIAMSON, DAVID
The Club, 1978, Play
David Williamson's the Club 1980 d: Bruce Beresford. lps: Graham Kennedy, Alan Cassell, Jack Thompson. 96M ASL. *Players*; *The Club* prod/rel: South Australia Film Corp.©, New South Wales Film Corp.

The Coming of Stork, 1974, Play
Stork 1971 d: Tim Burstall. lps: Bruce Spence, Graeme Blundell, Sean McEuan. 90M ASL. *The Coming of Stork*

Don's Party, 1973, Play
Don's Party 1976 d: Bruce Beresford. lps: Ray Barrett, Clare Binney, Pat Bishop. 91M ASL. prod/rel: Double Head, Australian Film Commission

Emerald City, Play
Emerald City 1988 d: Michael Jenkins. lps: John Hargreaves, Robyn Nevin, Chris Haywood. 92M ASL. *David Williamson's Emerald City* prod/rel: Greater Union, Limelight Productions Pty Ltd.

The Removalists, 1972, Play
Removalists, The 1975 d: Tom Jeffrey. lps: John Hargreaves, Peter Cummins, Kate Fitzpatrick. 90M ASL.

Travelling North, 1980, Play
Travelling North 1986 d: Carl Schultz. lps: Leo McKern, Julia Blake, Henri Szeps. 98M ASL. prod/rel: View Pictures Ltd.©, C.E.L.

WILLIAMSON, HENRY (1895–1977), UKN
Tarka the Otto, Novel
Tarka the Otter 1978 d: David Cobham. lps: Peter Bennett, Edward Underdown, Brenda Cavendish. 91M UKN. prod/rel: Rank, Tor

WILLIAMSON, MAUD
The Pruning Knife, Play
Was She Justified? 1922 d: Walter West. lps: Florence Turner, Ivy Close, Lewis Gilbert. 5600f UKN. *The Pruning Knife* prod/rel: Walter West, Butcher's Film Service

WILLINGHAM, CALDER (1922–, USA, Willingham Jr., Calder Baynard)
End As a Man, 1947, Novel
Strange One, The 1957 d: Jack Garfein. lps: Ben Gazzara, Pat Hingle, Peter Mark Richman. 100M USA. *End As a Man* (UKN) prod/rel: Columbia, Horizon

Rambling Rose, 1972, Novel
Rambling Rose 1991 d: Martha Coolidge. lps: Laura Dern, Robert Duvall, Diane Ladd. 112M USA. prod/rel: Seven Arts, Carolco

WILLIS, F. MCGREW
The Man Who Turned White, Short Story
Man Who Turned White, The 1919 d: Park Frame. lps: H. B. Warner, Barbara Castleton, Wedgewood Nowell. 5r USA. *The Sheik of Araby* prod/rel: Jesse D. Hampton Productions, Robertson-Cole Co.

A Secret Service Affair, Story
Under a Shadow 1915 d: Joseph de Grasse. lps: Gretchen Lederer, Arthur Shirley, Lon Chaney. 2r USA. prod/rel: Rex

WILLIS, HOWARD
Manhunt: the Story of Stanley Graham, Book
Bad Blood 1980 d: Mike Newell. lps: Jack Thompson, Carol Burns, Denis Lill. TVM. 104M NZL/UKN. *The Graham Murders*; *The Shooting* prod/rel: Southern, Andrew Brown Production

WILLIS, TED (1918–1992), UKN
Hot Summer Night, London 1958, Play
Flame in the Streets 1961 d: Roy Ward Baker. lps: John Mills, Sylvia Syms, Brenda de Banzie. 93M UKN. prod/rel: Somerset Films, Rank Organisation

Maneater, Book
Maneaters are Loose! 1978 d: Timothy Galfas. lps: Tom Skerritt, Steve Forrest, G. D. Spradlin. TVM. 100M USA. prod/rel: Mona Production, Finnegan Associates

No Trees in the Street, Liverpool 1948, Play
No Trees in the Street 1959 d: J. Lee Thompson. lps: Sylvia Syms, Herbert Lom, Ronald Howard. 96M UKN. *No Tree in the Street* prod/rel: Allegro, Ab-Pathe

Woman in a Dressing Gown, Television Play
Woman in a Dressing Gown 1957 d: J. Lee Thompson. lps: Yvonne Mitchell, Sylvia Syms, Anthony Quayle. 94M UKN. prod/rel: Godwin-Willis, Ab-Pathe

The Young and the Guilty, Television Play
Young and the Guilty, The 1958 d: Peter Cotes. lps: Phyllis Calvert, Andrew Ray, Edward Chapman. 67M UKN. prod/rel: Welwyn, Ab-Pathe

WILLNER, A. M.
Gipsy Love, London 1912, Operetta
Rogue Song, The 1929 d: Lionel Barrymore. lps: Lawrence Tibbett, Catherine Dale Owen, Nance O'Neil. 115M USA. prod/rel: Metro-Goldwyn-Mayer Pictures

WILLOCKS, TIM
Love's Executioners
Sweet Angel Mine 1996 d: Curtis Radclyffe. lps: Oliver Milburn, Margaret Langrick, Anna Massey. 86M UKN/CND. prod/rel: Imagex, Mass Prods.

WILLOUGHBY, BARRETT
Rocking Moon, New York 1925, Novel
Rocking Moon 1926 d: George Melford. lps: Lilyan Tashman, John Bowers, Rockliffe Fellowes. 6013f USA. prod/rel: Metropolitan Pictures, Producers Distributing Corp.

WILLOUGHBY, FLORENCE BARRETT
Spawn of the North, Boston 1932, Novel
Alaska Seas 1954 d: Jerry Hopper. lps: Robert Ryan, Brian Keith, Jan Sterling. 78M USA. prod/rel: Paramount

Spawn of the North 1938 d: Henry Hathaway. lps: George Raft, Henry Fonda, Dorothy Lamour. 112M USA. prod/rel: Paramount Pictures

WILLS, JACK
But There are Always Miracles, Book
Some Kind of Miracle 1979 d: Jerrold Freedman. lps: David Dukes, Andrea Marcovicci, Michael C. Gwynne. TVM. 100M USA. prod/rel: Lorimar Productions

WILLS, MARY
Some Kind of Miracle 1979 d: Jerrold Freedman. lps: David Dukes, Andrea Marcovicci, Michael C. Gwynne. TVM. 100M USA. prod/rel: Lorimar Productions

WILLS, W. G.
A Royal Divorce, London 1891, Play
Royal Divorce, A 1923 d: Alexander Butler. lps: Gwylim Evans, Gertrude McCoy, Lillian Hall-Davis. 10r UKN. prod/rel: Napoleon

WILLSON, DIXIE
God Gave Me Twenty Cents, Short Story
Ebb Tide 1932 d: Arthur Rosson. lps: Chili Bouchier, Joan Barry, George Barraud. 74M UKN. prod/rel: Paramount British

God Gave Me Twenty Cents 1926 d: Herbert Brenon. lps: Lois Moran, Lya de Putti, Jack Mulhall. 6321f USA. *Fate Gave Me Twenty Cents* prod/rel: Famous Players-Lasky, Paramount Pictures

Help Yourself to Hay, Short Story
Three-Ring Marriage 1928 d: Marshall Neilan. lps: Mary Astor, Lloyd Hughes, Lawford Davidson. 5834f USA. *Do It Again* prod/rel: First National Pictures

Here Y'are Brother, 1925, Short Story
Affair of the Follies, An 1927 d: Millard Webb. lps: Lewis Stone, Billie Dove, Lloyd Hughes. 6433f USA. *Three in Love* prod/rel: Al Rockett Productions, First National Pictures

WILLSON, MEREDITH
The Music Man, New York 1957, Musical Play
Music Man, The 1962 d: Morton Da CostA. lps: Robert Preston, Shirley Jones, Buddy Hackett. 151M USA. prod/rel: Warner Bros. Pictures

The Unsinkable Molly Brown, New York 1960, Musical Play
Unsinkable Molly Brown, The 1964 d: Charles Walters. lps: Debbie Reynolds, Harve Presnell, Ed Begley. 128M USA. prod/rel: Marten Productions

WILSIE, HONORE
The Salvation of Nance O'Shaughnessy, Story
Salvation of Nance O'Shaugnessy, The 1914 d: Colin Campbell. lps: Bessie Eyton, Eugenie Besserer, Wheeler Oakman. 2000f USA. prod/rel: Selig Polyscope Co.

WILSON, A. N. (1950–, UKN, Wilson, Andrew Norman)
Blore MP, Novel
Blore MP 1989 d: Robert Young. lps: Timothy West, Jill Baker, Stephen Moore. TVM. 85M UKN. prod/rel: BBC

WILSON, ANGUS (1913–1991), UKN, Johnstone-Wilson, Frank
Anglo-Saxon Attitudes, London 1956, Novel
Anglo-Saxon Attitudes 1992 d: Diarmuid Lawrence. lps: Richard Johnson, Douglas Hodge, Elizabeth Spriggs. TVM. 270M UKN. prod/rel: Euston Films, Thames Television

The Old Men at the Zoo, Novel
Old Men at the Zoo, The 1982 d: Stuart Burge. lps: Marius Goring, Roland Culver, Andrew Cruickshank. MTV. 275M UKN. prod/rel: BBC

WILSON, AUGUSTA JANE EVANS, Evans, Augusta Jane
At the Mercy of Tiberius, New York 1887, Novel
At the Mercy of Tiberius 1920 d: Fred Leroy Granville. lps: Peggy Hyland, Campbell Gullan, Tom Chatterton. 6000f UKN/USA. *The Price of Silence* (USA) prod/rel: G. B. Samuelson, General

God's Witness 1915 d: Eugene W. Moore. lps: Florence Labadie, Harris Gordon, Arthur Bauer. 4r USA. prod/rel: Thanhouser Film Corp., Mutual Film Corp.

Price of Silence, The 1921 d: Fred Leroy Granville. lps: Peggy Hyland, Campbell Gullan, Tom Chatterton. 6r USA. *At the Mercy of Tiberius* prod/rel: Samuelson Film Mfg. Co., State Rights

Beulah, New York 1860, Novel
Beulah 1915 d: Bertram Bracken. lps: Henry B. Walthall, Joyce Moore, Clifford Gray. 6r USA. prod/rel: Balboa Amusement Producing Co., Alliance Films Corp.

Infelice, New York 1876, Novel
Infelice 1915 d: Fred Paul, L. C. MacBean. lps: Peggy Hyland, Fred Paul, Bertram Burleigh. 6000f UKN. prod/rel: G. B. Samuelson, Moss

St. Elmo, New York 1867, Novel
St. Elmo 1910. lps: Frank Crane. 860f USA. prod/rel: Thanhouser

WILSON, AUGUSTA JANE EVANS, Evans, August Jane
St. Elmo 1914 d: J. Gordon Edwards. 6r USA. prod/rel: Balboa Amusement Producing Co., State Rights

WILSON, AUGUSTA JANE EVANS, Evans, Augusta Jane
St. Elmo 1923 d: Jerome Storm. lps: John Gilbert, Barbara La Marr, Bessie Love. 5778f USA. *St. Elmo Murray* prod/rel: Fox Film Corp.

St. Elmo 1923 d: Rex Wilson. lps: Shayle Gardner, Gabrielle Gilroy, Madge Tree. 5840f UKN. prod/rel: R.W. Syndicate, Capitol

WILSON, BURTON
The Connecting Link, Story
Connecting Link, The 1915 d: Joseph J. Franz. lps: Sherman Bainbridge, Rex de Rosselli, Edythe Sterling. 2r USA. prod/rel: Bison

WILSON, CHERRY
The Branded Sombrero, 1927, Short Story
Branded Sombrero, The 1928 d: Lambert Hillyer. lps: Buck Jones, Leila Hyams, J. Thornton Baston. 4612f USA. prod/rel: Fox Film Corp.

Empty Saddles, Novel
Empty Saddles 1936 d: Lesley Selander. lps: Buck Jones, Louise Brooks, Harvey Clark. 67M USA. prod/rel: Buck Jones Productions, Universal Productions©

Starr of the Southwest, 1936, Short Story
Sandflow 1936 d: Lesley Selander. lps: Buck Jones, Lita Chevret, Robert Kortman. 58M USA. prod/rel: Universal Pictures Corp.©

Stormy, New York 1929, Novel
   Stormy 1935 d: Lew Landers. lps: Noah Beery Jr., Jean Rogers, J. Farrell MacDonald. 70M USA. prod/rel: Universal Pictures Corp.©, Henry Macrae Production

WILSON, COLIN (1931–, UKN, Wilson, Colin Henry
The Space Vampires, Novel
   Lifeforce 1985 d: Tobe Hooper. lps: Steve Railsback, Peter Firth, Frank Finlay. 101M UKN. *Space Vampires*; *Life Force* prod/rel: London Cannon Films

WILSON, DONALD POWELL
My Six Convicts, Book
   My Six Convicts 1952 d: Hugo Fregonese. lps: Millard Mitchell, Gilbert Roland, John Beal. 104M USA. prod/rel: Columbia, Stanley Kramer Co.

WILSON, F. PAUL
The Keep, Novel
   Keep, The 1983 d: Michael Mann. lps: Scott Glenn, Ian McKellen, Alberta Watson. 96M UKN/USA. prod/rel: Paramount

WILSON, FORREST
Blessed Event, New York 1932, Play
   Blessed Event 1932 d: Roy Del Ruth. lps: Lee Tracy, Mary Brian, Dick Powell. 84M USA. prod/rel: Warner Bros. Pictures, Inc.

WILSON, FRANK, J.
Undercover Man: He Trapped Capone, Book
   Undercover Man, The 1949 d: Joseph H. Lewis. lps: Glenn Ford, Nina Foch, James Whitmore. 85M USA. *Chicago Story* prod/rel: Columbia

WILSON, H. CROWNIN
Nancy Lee, New York 1918, Play
   Way of a Woman, The 1919 d: Robert Z. Leonard. lps: Norma Talmadge, Conway Tearle, Stuart Holmes. 5-6r USA. *Nancy Lee* prod/rel: Norma Talmadge Film Corp.©, Select Pictures Corp.

WILSON, HARRY LEON
Bunker Bean, New York 1913, Novel
   Bunker Bean 1936 d: William Hamilton, Edward Killy. lps: Owen Davis Jr., Louise Latimer, Robert McWade. 67M USA. *His Majesty Bunker Bean* (UKN) prod/rel: RKO Radio Pictures, Inc.
   His Majesty Bunker Bean 1918 d: William D. Taylor. lps: Jack Pickford, Louise Huff, Jack McDonald. 5r USA. prod/rel: Oliver Morosco Photoplay Co., Famous Players-Lasky Corp.©
   His Majesty, Bunker Bean 1925 d: Harry Beaumont. lps: Matt Moore, Dorothy Devore, David Butler. 7291f USA. prod/rel: Warner Brothers Pictures
Cameo Kirby, New York 1909, Play
   Cameo Kirby 1915 d: Oscar Apfel. lps: Dustin Farnum, Frederick Montague, Dick La Reno. 5r USA. prod/rel: Jesse L. Lasky Feature Play Co.©, Paramount Pictures Corp.
   Cameo Kirby 1923 d: John Ford. lps: John Gilbert, Gertrude Olmstead, Alan Hale. 6931f USA. prod/rel: Fox Film Corp.
   Cameo Kirby 1930 d: Irving Cummings. lps: J. Harold Murray, Norma Terris, Douglas Gilmore. 5910f USA. prod/rel: Fox Film Corp.
The Gibson Upright, Play
   You Find It Everywhere 1921 d: Charles Horan. lps: Catherine Calvert, Herbert Rawlinson, MacEy Harlam. 5r USA. *The Gibson Upright* prod/rel: Outlook Photoplays, Jans Film Service
The Man from Home, Louisville, Ky. 1907, Play
   Man from Home, The 1914 d: Cecil B. de Mille, Oscar Apfel. lps: Charles Richman, Theodore Roberts, James Neill. 5r USA. prod/rel: Jesse L. Lasky Feature Play Co.©, Paramount Pictures Corp.
   Man from Home, The 1922 d: George Fitzmaurice. lps: James Kirkwood, Anna Q. Nilsson, Norman Kerry. 6700f UKN. prod/rel: Famous Players-Lasky, Paramount Pictures
Merton of the Movies, New York 1922, Novel
   Make Me a Star! 1932 d: William Beaudine. lps: Stuart Erwin, Joan Blondell, Zasu Pitts. 80M USA. *Gates of Hollywood*; *Half a Hero* prod/rel: Paramount Publix Corp.©
   Merton of the Movies 1924 d: James Cruze. lps: Glenn Hunter, Charles Sellon, Sadie Gordon. 7655f USA. prod/rel: Famous Players-Lasky, Paramount Pictures
   Merton of the Movies 1947 d: Robert Alton. lps: Red Skelton, Virginia O'Brien, Gloria Grahame. 82M USA. prod/rel: Paramount
Oh Doctor!, New York 1923, Novel
   Oh, Doctor! 1925 d: Harry Pollard. lps: Reginald Denny, Mary Astor, Otis Harlan. 6587f USA. prod/rel: Universal Pictures

Doctor! Oh, New York 1923, Novel
   Oh, Doctor! 1937 d: Ray McCarey. lps: Edward Everett Horton, Drue Leyton, William Hall. 70M USA. prod/rel: Universal Pictures Co.©
Ruggles of Red Gap, New York 1915, Novel
   Fancy Pants 1950 d: George Marshall. lps: Bob Hope, Lucille Ball, Hugh French. 92M USA. prod/rel: Paramount
   Ruggles of Red Gap 1918 d: Lawrence C. Windom. lps: Taylor Holmes, Frederick Burton, Lawrence d'Orsay. 7r USA. prod/rel: Essanay Film Mfg. Co.©, George K. Spoor Ultra Feature
   Ruggles of Red Gap 1923 d: James Cruze. lps: Edward Everett Horton, Ernest Torrence, Lois Wilson. 7590f USA. prod/rel: Famous Players-Lasky
   Ruggles of Red Gap 1935 d: Leo McCarey. lps: Charles Laughton, Mary Boland, Charles Ruggles. 90M USA. prod/rel: Paramount Productions©
The Spenders; a Tale of the Third Generation, Boston 1902, Novel
   Spenders, The 1921 d: Jack Conway. lps: Claire Adams, Robert McKim, Joseph J. Dowling. 5693f USA. *The Respondent* prod/rel: Benjamin B. Hampton Productions, Great Authors Pictures, Inc.
Springtime, New York 1909, Play
   Springtime 1915 d: Will S. Davis. lps: Florence Nash, Adele Ray, William H. Tooker. 5r USA. prod/rel: Life Photo Film Corp., Alco Film Corp.

WILSON, J. FLEMING
Learning to Be a Father, Story
   Learning to Be a Father 1915 d: Jacques Jaccard. lps: Charles Manley. SHT USA. prod/rel: Powers

WILSON, JEROME N.
Invisible Government, Story
   Exclusive Rights 1926 d: Frank O'Connor. lps: Gayne Whitman, Lillian Rich, Gloria Gordon. 6087f USA. prod/rel: Preferred Pictures

WILSON, JOHN B.
Suburban Retreat, Novel
   Key to Harmony 1935 d: Norman Walker. lps: Belle Chrystal, Fred Conyngham, Reginald Purdell. 68M UKN. *Chance at Heaven* prod/rel: British and Dominions, Paramount British

WILSON, JOHN FLEMING
The Man Who Came Back, New York 1912, Novel
   Del Infierno Al Cielo 1931 d: Richard Harlan. lps: Juan Torena, Maria Alba, Carlos Villarias. F USA.
   Man Who Came Back, The 1924 d: Emmett J. Flynn. lps: George O'Brien, Dorothy MacKaill, Cyril Chadwick. 8293f USA. prod/rel: Fox Film Corp.
   Man Who Came Back, The 1931 d: Raoul Walsh. lps: Janet Gaynor, Charles Farrell, Kenneth MacKennA. 85M USA. prod/rel: Fox Film Corp.©
The Man Who Married His Own Wife, 1922, Short Story
   Man Who Married His Own Wife, The 1922 d: Stuart Paton. lps: Frank Mayo, Sylvia Breamer, Marie Crisp. 4313f USA. prod/rel: Universal Film Mfg. Co.
The Master Key, Story
   Master Key, The 1915 d: Robert Z. Leonard. lps: Robert Leonard, Ella Hall, William Higby. SRL. 31r USA. prod/rel: Universal Film Mfg. Co.
The Salving of John Somers, 1920, Short Story
   Bonded Woman, The 1922 d: Phil Rosen. lps: Betty Compson, John Bowers, Richard Dix. 5486f USA. prod/rel: Famous Players-Lasky, Paramount Pictures
The Uncharted Sea, 1920, Short Story
   Uncharted Seas 1921 d: Wesley Ruggles. lps: Alice Lake, Carl Gerard, Rudolph Valentino. 6r USA. *The Uncharted Sea* prod/rel: Metro Pictures

WILSON, JOHN P.
America, 1913, Musical Play
   America 1915 d: Lawrence McGill. lps: Bert Shepherd, The Australian Wood Choppers, The Phyllis Equestrians. 6r USA. prod/rel: All Star Feature Corp.©, World Film Corp.

WILSON, JOHN ROWAN
The Pack, Novel
   Behind the Mask 1958 d: Brian Desmond Hurst. lps: Michael Redgrave, Tony Britton, Carl Mohner. 99M UKN. *The Pack* prod/rel: British Lion, Gw Films

WILSON JR., CHARLES J.
The Code of the Klondyke, Short Story
   Greater Law, The 1917 d: Lynn Reynolds. lps: Myrtle Gonzales, Gretchen Lederer, George Hernandez. 5r USA. prod/rel: Bluebird Photoplays, Inc.©

WILSON, MITCHELL
None So Blind, 1945, Novel
   Woman on the Beach, The 1946 d: Jean Renoir. lps: Joan Bennett, Robert Ryan, Charles Bickford. 71M USA. *La Femme Sur la Plage* (FRN); *Desirable Woman* prod/rel: RKO Radio

WILSON, RATHMELL
When Love Dies, Novel
   Eve's Daughter 1916 d: L. C. MacBean. lps: Eve Balfour, Frank Tennant, Alice de Winton. 4100f UKN. *Love* prod/rel: Eve Balfour Films, Jtr

WILSON, SANDY
The Boy Friend, Musical Play
   Boy Friend, The 1972 d: Ken Russell. lps: Twiggy, Christopher Gable, Barbara Windsor. 137M UKN. prod/rel: Emi-MGM, Russflix

WILSON, SLOAN (1920–, USA
The Man in the Gray Flannel Suit, 1955, Novel
   Man in the Gray Flannel Suit, The 1956 d: Nunnally Johnson. lps: Gregory Peck, Jennifer Jones, Fredric March. 153M USA. prod/rel: 20th Century-Fox
A Summer Place, 1958, Novel
   Summer Place, A 1959 d: Delmer Daves. lps: Richard Egan, Dorothy McGuire, Sandra Dee. 122M USA. prod/rel: Warner Bros.

WILSON, WARREN
Second Honeymoon, Story
   Honeymoon Lodge 1943 d: Edward Lilley. lps: David Bruce, Harriet Hilliard, June Vincent. 63M USA. prod/rel: Universal

WILSTACH, FRANK J.
Wild Bill Hickok the Prince of the Pistoleros, Garden City, N.Y. 1934, Novel
   Plainsman, The 1936 d: Cecil B. de Mille. lps: Gary Cooper, Jean Arthur, James Ellison. 115M USA. prod/rel: Paramount Pictures©

WILSTACH, JOHN
Under Cover Man, New York 1931, Novel
   Under-Cover Man 1932 d: James Flood. lps: George Raft, Nancy Carroll, Roscoe Karns. 74M USA. prod/rel: Paramount Publix Corp.©

WILSTACH, PAUL
What Happened at 22, New York 1914, Play
   What Happened at 22 1916 d: George Irving. lps: Frances Nelson, Arthur Ashley, Gladden James. 5r USA. *A Celebrated Case* prod/rel: Frohman Amusement Corp., World Film Corp.©

WILT, A. M. SINCLAIR
Head Winds, New York 1923, Novel
   Head Winds 1925 d: Herbert Blache. lps: House Peters, Patsy Ruth Miller, Richard C. Travers. 5486f USA. *Overboard* prod/rel: Universal Pictures

WILTSHIRE, MAURICE
Story
   My Brother's Keeper 1948 d: Alfred Roome, Roy Rich. lps: Jack Warner, Jane Hylton, David Tomlinson. 91M UKN. *Double Pursuit* prod/rel: General Film Distributors, Gainsborough

WIMBS, JOHN BECKETT
Memoirs of Johnny Daze, Play
   Memoirs 1984 d: Bachar Chbib. lps: Philip Baylaucq, Norma Jean Sanders, Julia Gilmore. 83M CND. prod/rel: Chbib Productions Inc.

WIMPERIS, A.
Louie the Fourteenth, New York 1925, Play
   Wife Savers 1928 d: Ralph Ceder. lps: Wallace Beery, Raymond Hatton, Zasu Pitts. 5434f USA. prod/rel: Paramount Famous Lasky Corp.

WIMSCHNEIDER, ANNA
Autobiography
   Herbstmilch 1988 d: Joseph Vilsmaier. lps: Dana Vavrova, Werner Stocker, Claude Oliver Rudolph. 111M GRM. *Autumn Milk* (UKN) prod/rel: Perathon, ZDF

WINCH, EVELYN
The Girl in the Flat, Story
   Girl in the Flat, The 1934 d: Redd Davis. lps: Stewart Rome, Belle Chrystal, Vera Bogetti. 66M UKN. prod/rel: British and Dominions, Paramount British

WINDLE, JANICE WOODS
True Women, Book
   True Women 1997 d: Karen Arthur. lps: Dana Delany, Annabeth Gish, Angelina Jolie. TVM. 240M USA. prod/rel: Craig Anderson Productions, Hallmark Entertainment

WING, AVRA
Angie I Says, Novel
   Angie 1994 d: Martha Coolidge. lps: Geena Davis, Stephen Rea, James Gandolfini. 108M USA. prod/rel: Buena Vista, Hollywood Pictures

WING, WILLIAM E.
Danger, Story
   Fighting Stranger, The 1921 d: Webster Cullison. lps: Franklyn Farnum, Flora Hollister, W. A. Alleman. 5r USA. prod/rel: William N. Selig, Canyon Pictures

Desert Madness, Story
  Trail of the Horse Thieves, The 1929 d: Robert de Lacy. lps: Tom Tyler, Bee Amann, Harry O'Connor. 4823f USA. *Double Lives* (UKN) prod/rel: Fbo Pictures, RKO Productions

WINGATE, WILLIAM
Shotgun, Novel
  Malone 1987 d: Harley Cokliss. lps: Burt Reynolds, Cliff Robertson, Kenneth McMillan. 92M USA. prod/rel: Orion

WINGFIELD, R. D.
Novel
  Touch of Frost: Care and Protection, A 1992 d: Don Leaver. lps: David Jason, Bruce Alexander, Matt Bardock. TVM. 102M UKN.

WINKLER, ANTHONY C.
The Lunatic, Novel
  Lunatic, The 1990 d: Lol Creme. lps: Julie T. Wallace, Paul Campbell, Reggie Carter. 94M UKN/JMC. prod/rel: Island Pictures

WINSLOE, CHRISTA
Gestern Und Heute, Play
  Madchen in Uniform 1931 d: Leontine Sagan. lps: Dorothea Wieck, Hertha Thiele, Emilia UndA. 93M GRM. *Maidens in Uniform; Girls in Uniform* prod/rel: Deutsche Film
  Madchen in Uniform 1958 d: Geza von Radvanyi. lps: Lilli Palmer, Romy Schneider, Therese Giehse. 95M GRM/FRN. *Jeune Filles En Uniforme* (FRN); *Children in Uniform* prod/rel: Les Films Modernes, S.N.C.
  Muchachas de Uniforme 1950 d: Alfredo B. CrevennA. lps: Irasema Dilian, Rosaura Revueltas, Marga Lopez. 99M MXC. prod/rel: Fama, Europa

WINSLOW, HERBERT HALL
The Country Girl, Short Story
  Decoy, The 1916 d: George W. Lederer. lps: Frances Nelson, Gladden James, Leonore Harris. 5r USA. *The Faithless Sex* prod/rel: Mutual Film Corp.

What's Your Wife Doing?, New York 1923, Play
  Reckless Romance 1924 d: Scott Sidney. lps: T. Roy Barnes, Harry Myers, Wanda Hawley. 5530f USA. prod/rel: Christie Film Co., Producers Distributing Corp.

WINSOR, KATHLEEN (1919–, USA
Forever Amber, Novel
  Forever Amber 1947 d: Otto Preminger. lps: Linda Darnell, Cornel Wilde, George Sanders. 140M USA. prod/rel: 20th Century-Fox

WINSTOCK, MELVIN G.
The Convict's Parole, Story
  Convict's Parole, The 1912 d: Edwin S. Porter. lps: Marc McDermott, Charles Ogle, Robert Brower. 1000f USA. prod/rel: Edison

WINTER, CHARLES E.
Ben Warman, New York 1917, Novel
  Dangerous Love 1920 d: Charles Bartlett. lps: Pete Morrison, Carol Halloway, Ruth King. 5r USA. *The Vanishing Strain; Broken Promises; Ben Warman; A Good Bad Man* prod/rel: Yellowstone Productions, Inc., State Rights

WINTER, JOHN STRANGE
Beautiful Jim, Novel
  Beautiful Jim 1914 d: Maurice Elvey. lps: Elisabeth Risdon, Fred Groves, Bootles Winter. 3253f UKN. *The Price of Justice* (USA) prod/rel: British and Colonial, Renters

Bootle's Baby, Novel
  Bootle's Baby 1914 d: Harold Shaw. lps: Ben Webster, Edna Flugrath, Langhorne Burton. 3794f UKN. prod/rel: London, Fenning
  Bootle's Baby 1914 d: Ashley Miller. lps: Robert Conness, Herbert Prior, Mabel Trunnelle. 2r USA. prod/rel: Edison

Goodbye, Novel
  Goodbye 1918 d: Maurice Elvey. lps: Margaret Bannerman, Jessie Winter, Donald Calthrop. 4685f UKN. prod/rel: Butcher's Film Service

Grip, Novel
  Grip 1915 d: Maurice Elvey. lps: Leon M. Lion, Elisabeth Risdon, Fred Groves. 3000f UKN. prod/rel: British and Colonial, Renters

Jimmy, Novel
  Jimmy 1916 d: A. V. Bramble, Eliot Stannard. lps: John Astley, George Tully, Lettie Paxton. 4080f UKN. prod/rel: British & Colonial, Gaumont

Lady Jennifer, Novel
  Lady Jennifer 1915 d: James W. Vickers. lps: Barbara Rutland, Harry Royston. 3500f UKN. prod/rel: International Cine Corp.

WINTER, KEITH
The Shining Hour, New York 1934, Play
  Shining Hour, The 1938 d: Frank Borzage. lps: Joan Crawford, Margaret Sullavan, Robert Young. 76M USA. prod/rel: Metro-Goldwyn-Mayer Corp., Loew's, Inc.©

WINTER, LOUISE
The Mad Dancer, 1924, Short Story
  Mad Dancer, The 1925 d: Burton L. King. lps: Ann Pennington, Johnny Walker, Coit Albertson. 5500f USA. prod/rel: Jans Productions

The Magnificent Jacala, 1918, Short Story
  Brazen Beauty, The 1918 d: Tod Browning. lps: Priscilla Dean, Thurston Hall, Katherine Griffith. 5r USA. *The Magnificent Jacala; The Beautiful Jacala* prod/rel: Bluebird Photoplays, Inc.©

Marie Ltd., Short Story
  Marie, Ltd. 1919 d: Kenneth Webb. lps: Alice Brady, Frank Losee, Leslie Austen. 4937f USA. prod/rel: Select Pictures Corp.©

Princess Virtue, Novel
  Princess Virtue 1917 d: Robert Z. Leonard. lps: Mae Murray, Lule Warrenton, Wheeler Oakman. 5r USA. prod/rel: Bluebird Photoplays, Inc.©

The Spite Bride, Novel
  Spite Bride, The 1919 d: Charles Giblyn. lps: Olive Thomas, Robert Ellis, Jack Mulhall. 5r USA. prod/rel: Selznick Pictures Corp.©, Select Pictures Corp.

WINTERSON, JEANETTE
Oranges are Not the Only Fruit, Novel
  Oranges are Not the Only Fruit 1989 d: Beeban Kidron. lps: Geraldine McEwan, Charlotte Coleman, Kenneth Cranham. TVM. 175M UKN. prod/rel: BBC

WINTHER, CHRISTIAN
Short Story
  Zpovednice 1928 d: Norbert Masek. lps: Pavel Ron, Isida Pruszinska, Norbert Masek. 438m CZC. *The Confession Box* prod/rel: Normafilm, Gea-Film

WINTON, JOHN
We Joined the Navy, Novel
  We Joined the Navy 1962 d: Wendy Toye. lps: Kenneth More, Lloyd Nolan, Joan O'Brien. 109M UKN. *We are in the Navy Now* (USA) prod/rel: Dial Films, Warner-Pathe

WINTON, TIM
In the Winter Dark, Novel
  In the Winter Dark 1998 d: James Bogle. lps: Brenda Blethyn, Ray Barrett, Richard Roxburgh. 92M ASL. prod/rel: Globe Films, Australian Film Finance Corp.

WIPPERSBERG, W. J. M.
Story
  Fluchtversuch 1976 d: Vojtech Jasny. lps: Tomislav Savic, Hansjorg Felmy, Ilija Ivezic. 98M GRM/AUS. *Attempt at Flight; Attempted Escape; Ivo; An Attempt to Escape; Attempted Flight* prod/rel: Tatiana

WIRE, HAROLD CHANNING
Nevada Gold, Short Story
  Yellow Mountain, The 1954 d: Jesse Hibbs. lps: Howard Duff, Lex Barker, Mala Powers. 78M USA. prod/rel: Universal-International

WISE, LEONARD
The Diggstown Ringers, Novel
  Diggstown 1992 d: Michael Ritchie. lps: James Woods, Louis Gossett Jr., Bruce Dern. 98M USA. *Midnight Sting* (UKN) prod/rel: Metro-Goldwyn-Mayer, Electric Films

WISE, THOMAS A.
A Gentleman from Mississippi, New York 1908, Play
  Gentleman from Mississippi, A 1914 d: George L. Sargent. lps: Thomas A. Wise, Chester Barnett, Evelyn Brent. 5r USA. prod/rel: William A. Brady Picture Plays, Inc., World Film Corp.©

WISEMAN, NICHOLAS PATRICK
Fabiola Or the Church of the Catacombs, London 1854, Novel
  Fabiola 1918 d: Enrico Guazzoni. lps: Maria Antonietta Bartoli-Avveduti, Valeria Sanfilippo, Amleto Novelli. 2258m ITL. *I Misteri Delle Catacombe* prod/rel: Palatino Film
  Fabiola 1948 d: Alessandro Blasetti. lps: Michele Morgan, Henri Vidal, Michel Simon. 96M ITL. prod/rel: Universalia, Warner Bros.
  Rivolta Degli Schiavi, La 1961 d: Nunzio MalasommA. lps: Lang Jeffries, Rhonda Fleming, Gino Cervi. 105M ITL/SPN/GRM. *La Rebelion de Los Esclavos* (SPN); *Die Sklaven Roms* (GRM); *The Revolt of the Slaves* (USA); *Slaves of Rome* prod/rel: Ambrosiana Cin.Ca (Roma), C.B. Films (Madrid)
  San Sebastiano 1911 d: Enrique Santos. lps: Enna Saredo, Amleto Novelli, Giuseppe GambardellA. 340m ITL. *Il Tribuno Sebastiano; St. Sebastian* (UKN) prod/rel: Cines

WISEMAN, THOMAS (1930–, UKN
The Romantic Englishwoman, Novel
  Romantic Englishwoman, The 1974 d: Joseph Losey. lps: Glenda Jackson, Michael Caine, Helmut Berger. 116M UKN/FRN. *Une Anglaise Romantique* (FRN) prod/rel: Dial, Meric-Matalon

WISSELINCK, ERIKA
Anna Im Goldenen Tor, Novel
  Mirjams Mutter 1992 d: Vera Loebner. lps: Heidi Forster, Sabine Oberhorner, Despina Pajanou. TVM. 100M GRM.

WISTER, OWEN (1860–1938), USA
Lin McLean, New York 1897, Novel
  Woman's Fool, A 1918 d: John Ford. lps: Harry Carey, Molly Malone, Millard K. Wilson. 5r USA. prod/rel: Universal Film Mfg. Co.©

The Virginian, New York 1902, Novel
  Virginian, The 1914 d: Cecil B. de Mille. lps: Dustin Farnum, Winifred Kingston, J. W. Johnston. 5r USA. prod/rel: Jesse L. Lasky Feature Play Co.©, Paramount Pictures Corp.
  Virginian, The 1923 d: Tom Forman. lps: Kenneth Harlan, Florence Vidor, Russell Simpson. 8010f USA. prod/rel: B. P. Schulberg Productions, Preferred Pictures
  Virginian, The 1929 d: Victor Fleming. lps: Gary Cooper, Walter Huston, Richard Arlen. 95M USA. prod/rel: Paramount Famous Lasky Corp.
  Virginian, The 1946 d: Stuart Gilmore. lps: Joel McCrea, Brian Donlevy, Sonny Tufts. 90M USA. prod/rel: Paramount

WITNEY, FREDERICK
Bed and Breakfast, Play
  Bed and Breakfast 1930 d: Walter Forde. lps: Jane Baxter, Richard Cooper, Sari MaritzA. 68M UKN. prod/rel: Gaumont

WITTY, FRANK
No Exit, London 1936, Play
  No Escape 1936 d: Norman Lee. lps: Valerie Hobson, Billy Milton, Robert Cochran. 80M UKN. *No Exit* prod/rel: Welwyn, Pathe

WITWER, HARRY CHARLES
Alex the Great, Boston 1919, Novel
  Alex the Great 1928 d: Dudley Murphy. lps: Skeets Gallagher, Albert Conti, Patricia Avery. 5872f USA. prod/rel: Fbo Pictures

Cain and Mabel, Short Story
  Great White Way, The 1924 d: E. Mason Hopper. lps: Anita Stewart, Tom Lewis, T. Roy Barnes. 10r USA. *Cain and Mabel* prod/rel: Cosmopolitan Productions, Goldwyn-Cosmopolitan Distributing Corp.

The Fourth Musketeer, 1922, Short Story
  Fourth Musketeer, The 1923 d: William K. Howard. lps: Johnny Walker, Eileen Percy, Eddie Gribbon. 5800f USA. prod/rel: R-C Pictures, Film Booking Offices of America

WODEHOUSE, P. G. (1881–1975), UKN, Wodehouse, Pelham Grenville
Anything Goes, New York 1934, Musical Play
  Anything Goes 1936 d: Lewis Milestone. lps: Bing Crosby, Ethel Merman, Charles Ruggles. 92M USA. *Tops Is the Limit* prod/rel: Paramount Productions, Inc.
  Anything Goes 1956 d: Robert Lewis. lps: Bing Crosby, Donald O'Connor, Zizi Jeanmaire. 106M USA. prod/rel: Paramount

Brother Alfred, London 1913, Play
  Brother Alfred 1932 d: Henry Edwards. lps: Gene Gerrard, Molly Lamont, Elsie Randolph. 77M UKN. prod/rel: British International Pictures, Wardour

Chester Forgets Himself, Short Story
  Chester Forgets Himself 1924 d: Andrew P. Wilson. lps: Harry Beasley, Jameson Thomas, Ena Evans. 2160f UKN. prod/rel: Stoll

The Clicking of Cuthbert, Short Story
  Clicking of Cuthbert, The 1924 d: Andrew P. Wilson. lps: Harry Beasley, Peter Haddon, Helena Pickard. 1960f UKN. prod/rel: Stoll

A Damsel in Distress, New York 1919, Novel
  Damsel in Distress, A 1919 d: George Archainbaud. lps: June Caprice, Creighton Hale, William H. Thompson. 5r USA. prod/rel: Albert Capellani Productions, Pathe Exchange, Inc.©
  Damsel in Distress, A 1937 d: George Stevens. lps: Fred Astaire, George Burns, Gracie Allen. 100M USA. prod/rel: RKO Radio Pictures, Inc.

A Gentleman of Leisure, New York 1911, Play
  Gentleman of Leisure, A 1915 d: George Melford. lps: Wallace Eddinger, Carol Holloway, Billy Elmer. 5r USA. prod/rel: Jesse L. Lasky Feature Play Co.©, Paramount Pictures Corp.

Gentleman of Leisure, A 1923 d: Joseph Henabery. lps: Jack Holt, Casson Ferguson, Sigrid Holmquist. 5695f USA. prod/rel: Famous Players-Lasky, Paramount Pictures

The Girl on the Boat, 1922, Novel
Girl on the Boat, The 1961 d: Henry Kaplan. lps: Norman Wisdom, Millicent Martin, Richard Briers. 91M UKN. prod/rel: United Artists, Knightsbridge

Her Cardboard Lover, New York 1927, Play
Passionate Plumber, The 1932 d: Edward Sedgwick. lps: Buster Keaton, Jimmy Durante, Polly Moran. 73M USA. *The Cardboard Lover* prod/rel: Metro-Goldwyn-Mayer Corp., Metro-Goldwyn-Mayer Dist. Corp.©

Plombier Amoreux, Le 1932 d: Claude Autant-LarA. lps: Buster Keaton, Jimmy Durante, Polly Moran. F USA. prod/rel: Buster Keaton

Leave It to Psmith, London 1930, Play
Leave It to Me 1933 d: Monty Banks. lps: Gene Gerrard, Olive Borden, Molly Lamont. 76M UKN. *Help* prod/rel: British International Pictures, Wardour

The Long Hole, Short Story
Long Hole, The 1924 d: Andrew P. Wilson. lps: Harry Beasley, Charles Courtneidge, Roger Keyes. 2450f UKN. *The Moving Hazard* prod/rel: Stoll

Oh Boy!, New York 1917, Musical Play
Oh, Boy! 1919 d: Albert Capellani. lps: June Caprice, Creighton Hale, Zena Keefe. 6r USA. prod/rel: Albert Capellani Productions, Inc., Pathe Exchange, Inc.©

Oh Kay!, New York 1926, Play
Oh, Kay! 1928 d: Mervyn Leroy. lps: Colleen Moore, Lawrence Gray, Alan Hale. 6100f USA. prod/rel: First National Pictures

Oh Lady Lady!, New York 1918, Musical Play
Oh, Lady! Lady! 1920 d: Maurice Campbell. lps: Bebe Daniels, Harrison Ford, Walter Hiers. 4212f USA. *Oh Lady Lady* prod/rel: Realart Pictures Corp.©

Ordeal By Golf, Short Story
Ordeal By Golf 1924 d: Andrew P. Wilson. lps: Harry Beasley, Edwin Underhill, Jean Jay. 2000f UKN. prod/rel: Stoll

Piccadilly Jim, London 1917, Novel
Piccadilly Jim 1920 d: Wesley Ruggles. lps: Owen Moore, Zena Keefe, George Bunny. 5r USA. prod/rel: Selznick Pictures Corp.©, Select Pictures Corp.
Piccadilly Jim 1936 d: Robert Z. Leonard. lps: Robert Montgomery, Madge Evans, Frank Morgan. 100M USA. prod/rel: Metro-Goldwyn-Mayer Corp.©

The Prince and Betty, New York 1912, Novel
Prince and Betty, The 1919 d: Robert T. Thornby. lps: William Desmond, Mary Thurman, Anita Kay. 5r USA. prod/rel: Jesse D. Hampton Productions, Pathe Exchange, Inc.©

Rodney Fails to Qualify, Short Story
Rodney Fails to Qualify 1924 d: Andrew P. Wilson. lps: Harry Beasley, Victor Robson, Lionelle Howard. 2100f UKN. prod/rel: Stoll

Sally, New York 1920, Musical Play
Sally 1925 d: Alfred E. Green. lps: Colleen Moore, Lloyd Hughes, Leon Errol. 8636f USA. prod/rel: First National Pictures
Sally 1929 d: John Francis Dillon. lps: Marilyn Miller, Alexander Gray, Joe E. Brown. 9277f USA. prod/rel: First National Pictures

The Small Bachelor, 1926, Short Story
Small Bachelor, The 1927 d: William A. Seiter. lps: Barbara Kent, George Beranger, William Austin. 6218f USA. prod/rel: Universal Pictures

Summer Lightning, 1929, Novel
Blixt Och Dunder 1938 d: Anders Henrikson. 91M SWD. *Thunder and Lightning*
Summer Lightning 1933 d: MacLean Rogers. lps: Ralph Lynn, Winifred Shotter, Chili Bouchier. 78M UKN. prod/rel: British and Dominions, United Artists

Thank You Jeeves!, London 1934, Novel
Thank You, Jeeves! 1936 d: Arthur G. Collins. lps: Arthur Treacher, Virginia Field, David Niven. 57M USA. *Thank You Mr. Jeeves* prod/rel: Twentieth Century-Fox Film Corp.

Their Mutual Child, New York 1919, Novel
Their Mutual Child 1920 d: George L. Cox. lps: Margarita Fischer, Nigel Barrie, Harvey Clark. 6r USA. prod/rel: American Film Co., Inc.©, Pathe Exchange, Inc.

Uneasy Money, New York 1916, Novel
Uneasy Money 1918 d: Lawrence C. Windom. lps: Taylor Holmes, Virginia Valli, Arthur W. Bates. 5-6r USA. prod/rel: Essanay Film Mfg. Co.©, Perfection Pictures

The Watch Dog, 1910, Short Story
Dizzy Dames 1935 d: William Nigh. lps: Marjorie Rambeau, Inez Courtney, Lawrence Gray. 73M USA. prod/rel: Liberty Pictures Corp.

WOESTYN, H. R.
Policier Monsieur Pinson, Novel
Monsieur Pinson, Policier 1915 d: Jacques Feyder, Gaston Ravel. lps: Andre Roanne, Jacques Feyder, Suzanne Dubost. 950m FRN. prod/rel: Gaumont

WOGATZKI, BENITO
Romanze Mit Amelie, Novel
Romanze Mit Amelie 1981 d: Ulrich Thein. lps: Thomas Stecher, Brit Gulland, Gudrun Ritter. 116M GDR. prod/rel: Defa, Dramaturgengruppe Babelsberg

WOHL, BURTON
Cold Wind in August, New York 1960, Novel
Cold Wind in August, A 1961 d: Alexander Singer. lps: Lola Albright, Scott Marlowe, Herschel Bernardi. 80M USA. prod/rel: United Artists Corp., Troy Films

WOHLBRUCK, OLGA
Das Goldene Bett, Novel
Goldene Bett, Das 1913 d: Walter Schmidthassler. lps: Hanni Weisse, Theodor Loos, Mia Cordes. 1707m GRM. prod/rel: Vitascope

WOJTYLA, KAROL
Brat Naszego Boga, 1949, Play
Our God's Brother 1997 d: Krzysztof Zanussi. lps: Scott Wilson, Christoph Waltz, Wojciech Pszoniak. 123M ITL/PLN/GRM. *Brat Naszego Boga* (PLN) prod/rel: Transworld Films, Rai (Rome), Film Studio Tor, Tvp (Warsaw)

WOLBERT, WILLIAM
Paternal Love, Story
Paternal Love 1915 d: Frank Lloyd. lps: Millard K. Wilson, Gretchen Lederer, Marc Robbins. SHT USA. prod/rel: Laemmle

WOLF, ALEXANDER
Zur Holle Mit Den Paukern, Novel
Lummel von Der Ersten Bank 1. Zur Holle Mit Den Paukern, Die 1968 d: Werner Jacobs. lps: Hansi Kraus, Gila von Weitershausen, Gunther Schramm. 88M GRM.; *The Rascals of the Front Bench I. to Hell With Teachers* prod/rel: Franz Seitz, Constantin

WOLF, CHRISTA (1929–, GRM
Der Geteilte Himmel, 1964, Novel
Geteilte Himmel, Der 1964 d: Konrad Wolf. lps: Hilmar Thate, Eberhard Esche, Renate Blume. 114M GDR. *Divided Heaven*; *Divided Sky* prod/rel: Defa

WOLF, DR. EDMUND
Play
Mad Martindales, The 1942 d: Alfred L. Werker. lps: Jane Withers, Marjorie Weaver, Alan Mowbray. 65M USA. *Not for Children* prod/rel: 20th Century-Fox

WOLF, FRIEDRICH
Story
Haus Am Fluss, Das 1985 d: Roland Graf. lps: Katrin Sass, Sylvester Groth, Manfred Gorr. 89M GDR. *House By the River* prod/rel: Defa, Gruppe Roter Kreis

Cyankali, Play
Cyankali 1930 d: Hans Tintner. lps: Grete Mosheim, Nico Turoff, Claus Clausen. 88M GRM. prod/rel: Atlantis-Film

Professor Mamlock, Play
Professor Mamlock 1961 d: Konrad Wolf. lps: Wolfgang Heinz, Ursula Burg, Hilmar Thate. 100M GDR. prod/rel: Defa

WOLF, JACK
The Big Western Hat, Story
Inherited Passions 1916 d: G. P. Hamilton. lps: Dot Farley, William Conklin, Beatrice Van. 7r USA. *Are Passions Inherited?* prod/rel: Century Film Co., Warner's Features

WOLF, RENNOLD
The Beauty Shop, New York 1914, Play
Beauty Shop, The 1922 d: Eddie Dillon. lps: Raymond Hitchcock, Billy Van, James J. Corbett. 6536f USA. prod/rel: Cosmopolitan Productions, Paramount Pictures

My Best Girl, New York 1912, Musical Play
My Best Girl 1915. lps: Max Figman, Lois Meredith, Lawrence Peyton. 5r USA. prod/rel: Rolfe Photoplays, Inc., Metro Pictures Corp.©

A Perfect Lady, New York 1914, Play
Perfect Lady, A 1918 d: Clarence Badger. lps: Madge Kennedy, Jere Austin, Rod La Rocque. 5r USA. prod/rel: Goldwyn Pictures Corp.©, Goldwyn Distributing Corp.

The Red Widow, New York 1911, Musical Play
Red Widow, The 1916 d: James Durkin. lps: John Barrymore, Flora Zabelle, John Hendricks. 5r USA. prod/rel: Famous Players Film Co.©, Paramount Pictures Corp.

WOLFE, H. ASHTON
Secrets of the Surete, 1931, Article
Secrets of the French Police 1932 d: A. Edward Sutherland. lps: Gregory Ratoff, Murray Kinnell, Gwili Andre. 58M USA. *Mysteries of the French Secret Police* prod/rel: RKO Radio Pictures©

WOLFE, THOMAS (1900–1938), USA, Wolfe, Thomas Clayton
You Can't Go Home Again, 1940, Novel
You Can't Go Home Again 1979 d: Ralph Nelson. lps: Lee Grant, Chris Sarandon, Hurd Hatfield. TVM. 100M USA. prod/rel: CBS Entertainment

WOLFE, TOM (1931–, USA, Wolfe Jr., Thomas Kennerly
The Bonfire of the Vanities, 1989, Novel
Bonfire of the Vanities, The 1990 d: Brian DepalmA. lps: Tom Hanks, Bruce Willis, Melanie Griffith. 125M USA. prod/rel: Warner Bros.

The Right Stuff, 1979, Novel
Right Stuff, The 1983 d: Philip Kaufman. lps: Sam Shepard, Scott Glenn, Ed Harris. 193M USA. *When the Future Began* prod/rel: Warner Bros.

WOLFE, WINIFRED
Ask Any Girl, 1958, Novel
Ask Any Girl 1959 d: Charles Walters. lps: Shirley MacLaine, David Niven, Gig Young. 98M USA. prod/rel: MGM, Euterpe

If a Man Answers, New York 1961, Novel
If a Man Answers 1962 d: Henry Levin. lps: Bobby Darin, Sandra Dee, Micheline Presle. 102M USA. prod/rel: Ross Hunter Productions, Universal

WOLFERT, IRA
An American Guerrilla in the Philippines, Novel
American Guerrilla in the Philippines, An 1950 d: Fritz Lang. lps: Tyrone Power, Micheline Presle, Tom Ewell. 105M USA. *I Shall Return* (UKN) prod/rel: 20th Century-Fox

Tucker's People, Novel
Force of Evil 1948 d: Abraham Polonsky. lps: John Garfield, Beatrice Pearson, Thomas Gomez. 78M USA. prod/rel: MGM

WOLFF, LUDWIG
Ariadne in Hoppegarten, Novel
Ariadne in Hoppegarten 1928 d: Robert Dinesen. lps: Maria Jacobini, Alfred Abel, Jean Bradin. 2162m GRM. prod/rel: Maxim-Film, Ebner & Co.

Dr. Bessels Verwandlung, Novel
Dr. Bessels Verwandlung 1927 d: Richard Oswald. lps: Agnes Esterhazy, Hans Stuwe, Jacob Tiedtke. 3148m GRM. prod/rel: Richard Oswald Film-Prod.

Der Krieg Im Dunkel, Berlin 1915, Novel
Mysterious Lady, The 1928 d: Fred Niblo. lps: Greta Garbo, Conrad Nagel, Gustav von Seyffertitz. 7652f USA. *War in the Dark* prod/rel: Metro-Goldwyn-Mayer Pictures

Smarra, Novel
Folle Aventure, La 1930 d: Andre-Paul Antoine, Carl Froelich. lps: Marie Bell, Jean Murat, Jim Gerald. 103M FRN. prod/rel: Films P.J. De Venloo, Carl Froelich Film

Zwei Unterm Himmelszelt, Novel
Zwei Unterm Himmelszelt 1927 d: Johannes Guter. lps: Margarete Schlegel, Ernst Deutsch, Jean Angelo. 2580m GRM. prod/rel: Kulturfilm Ag

WOLFF, MARITTA MARTIN
The Man I Love, Novel
Man I Love, The 1947 d: Raoul Walsh. lps: Ida Lupino, Robert Alda, Andrea King. 96M USA. prod/rel: Warner Bros.

Whistle Stop, Novel
Whistle Stop 1946 d: Leonide Moguy. lps: Ava Gardner, George Raft, Tom Conway. 85M USA. prod/rel: United Artists, Nero Films

WOLFF, PIERRE
Les Ailes Brisees, Play
Ailes Brisees, Les 1933 d: Andre Berthomieu. lps: Victor Francen, Alice Field, Leon Roger-Maxime. 74M FRN. prod/rel: Algo Film Productions

Apres l'Amour, Play
Apres l'Amour 1924 d: Maurice Champreux. lps: Andre Nox, Blanche Montel, Emile Drain. F FRN. prod/rel: Gaumont
Apres l'Amour 1931 d: Leonce Perret. lps: Gaby Morlay, Victor Francen, Jacques Varennes. 73M FRN. prod/rel: Pathe-Natan
Apres l'Amour 1947 d: Maurice Tourneur. lps: Pierre Blanchar, Simone Renant, Fernand Fabre. 90M FRN. prod/rel: Films Modernes

Belle de Nuit, Play
Belle de Nuit 1933 d: Louis Valray. lps: Vera Korene, Nicole Martel, Aime Clariond. 87M FRN. prod/rel: Metropa Films

Le Lys, Play

Lily, The 1926 d: Victor Schertzinger. lps: Belle Bennett, Ian Keith, Reata Hoyt. 6268f USA. prod/rel: Fox Film Corp.

Les Marionettes, Play

Marionettes, The 1918 d: Emile Chautard. lps: Clara Kimball Young, Ethel Winthrop, Nigel Barrie. 5r USA. prod/rel: C. K. Y. Film Corp.©, Select Pictures Corp.

Martin Roumagnac, Novel

Martin Roumagnac 1946 d: Georges Lacombe. lps: Jean Gabin, Marlene Dietrich, Margo Lion. 95M FRN. *The Room Upstairs* (USA) prod/rel: Alcina

Le Ruisseau, Paris 1907, Play

Ruisseau, Le 1912 d: Georges DenolA. lps: Louis Gauthier, Henri Collen, Germaine Germoz. 760m FRN. prod/rel: Scagl

Ruisseau, Le 1929 d: Rene Hervil. lps: Louise Lagrange, Lucien Dalsace, Olga Day. 2498m FRN. prod/rel: Societe Des Cineromans

Ruisseau, Le 1938 d: Maurice Lehmann, Claude Autant-LarA. lps: Francoise Rosay, Paul Cambo, Michel Simon. 100M FRN. prod/rel: Productions Maurice Lehmann

Virtuous Model, The 1919 d: Albert Capellani. lps: Dolores Cassinelli, Vincent Serrano, Franklyn Farnum. 6606f USA. *The Gutter* prod/rel: Pathe Exchange, Inc.©, Albert Capellani Productions, Inc.

Sacre Leonce, Play

Sacre Leonce 1935 d: Christian-Jaque. lps: Armand Bernard, Monique Rolland, Christiane Delyne. 80M FRN. prod/rel: D.U.F.

Le Secret de Polichinelle, Play

Secret de Polichinelle, Le 1913 d: Henri Desfontaines. lps: Armand Numes, Rene Maupre, Paule Andral. FRN. prod/rel: Scagl

Secret de Polichinelle, Le 1923 d: Rene Hervil. lps: Andree Brabant, Gabriel Signoret, Maurice de Feraudy. 2506m FRN. prod/rel: Film d'Art (Vandal Et Delac)

Secret de Polichinelle, Le 1936 d: Andre Berthomieu. lps: Raimu, Andre Alerme, Francoise Rosay. 90M FRN. prod/rel: Societe Des Films Richebe

WOLFF, RUTH

The Abdication, Play

Abdication, The 1974 d: Anthony Harvey. lps: Liv Ullmann, Peter Finch, Cyril Cusack. 103M UKN. prod/rel: Warner

WOLFF, TOBIAS

This Boy's Life, Book

This Boy's Life 1993 d: Michael Caton-Jones. lps: Robert de Niro, Ellen Barkin, Leonardo Dicaprio. 115M USA. prod/rel: Warner Bros.

WOLFGANG, HANS

Die Botschafterin, Novel

Botschafterin, Die 1960 d: Harald Braun. lps: Nadja Tiller, Hansjorg Felmy, James Robertson Justice. 114M GRM. *The Ambassadress* prod/rel: Filmaufbau, N.F.

Wegen Verfuhrung Minderjahriger, Novel

Wegen Verfuhrung Minderjahriger 1960 d: Hermann Leitner. lps: Hans Sohnker, Marisa Mell, Heli Finkenzeller. 95M AUS. prod/rel: Schonbrunn

WOLFORD, NELSON

The Southern Blade, New York 1961, Novel

Time for Killing, A 1967 d: Phil Karlson, Roger Corman (Uncredited). lps: Glenn Ford, Inger Stevens, Paul Peterson. 88M USA. *The Long Ride Home* (UKN); *Southern Blade* prod/rel: Sage Western Pictures, Columbia

WOLFORD, SHIRLEY

The Southern Blade, New York 1961, Novel

Time for Killing, A 1967 d: Phil Karlson, Roger Corman (Uncredited). lps: Glenn Ford, Inger Stevens, Paul Peterson. 88M USA. *The Long Ride Home* (UKN); *Southern Blade* prod/rel: Sage Western Pictures, Columbia

WOLHEIM, DONALD A.

Mimic, Short Story

Mimic 1997 d: Guillermo Del Toro. lps: Mira Sorvino, Jeremy Northam, Josh Brolin. 106M USA. prod/rel: Dimension Films, Miramax Film Corp.©

WOLHEIM, LOUIS R.

The Lone Dit, Short Story

Together 1918 d: O. A. C. Lund. lps: Violet Mersereau, Chester Barnett, Bernard Randall. 5r USA. prod/rel: Bluebird Photoplays, Inc.©

WOLINSKI, GEORGES

Le Roi Des Cons, Play

Roi Des Cons, Le 1981 d: Claude Confortes. lps: Francis Perrin, Marie-Christine Descouard, Bernadette Lafont. 99M FRN. prod/rel: C.a.P.A.C., Films de la Colombe

WOLITZER, MEG

This Is Your Life, Novel

This Is My Life 1992 d: Nora Ephron. lps: Julie Kavner, Samantha Mathis, Gaby Hoffmann. 105M USA. prod/rel: Fox Film Corp., Twentieth Century-Fox Film Corp.©

WOLKERS, JAN HENDRICK

Kort Amerikaans, 1964, Novel

Kort Amerikaans 1979 d: Guido Pieters. lps: Derek de Lint, Tingue Dongelmans, Christel Braak. 100M NTH. *Crew Cut*

Turks Fruit, 1970, Novel

Turks Fruits 1973 d: Paul Verhoeven. lps: Monique Van de Ven, Rutger Hauer, Tonny Huurdeman. 110M NTH. *Turkish Delight* (USA); *The Shelter of Your Arms*; *The Sensualist* prod/rel: Rob Houwer

WOLLEN, PETER

Short Story

Friendship's Death 1987 d: Peter Wollen. lps: Tilda Swinton, Bill Paterson, Patrick Bauchau. 78M UKN. prod/rel: British Film Institute, Modelmark

WOLPERT, STANLEY

Nine Hours to Rama, New York 1962, Novel

Nine Hours to Rama 1963 d: Mark Robson. lps: Horst Buchholz, Jose Ferrer, Valerie Gearon. 125M UKN/USA. *Nine Hours to Live* prod/rel: Red Lion Productions, 20th Century-Fox

WOLTER, CHRISTINE

Die Alleinseglerin, Novel

Alleinseglerin, Die 1987 d: Hermann Zschoche. lps: Christine Powileit, Johanna Schall, Manfred Gorr. 102M GDR. *The Solo Sailor*; *Woman That Sails Alone* prod/rel: Defa, Gruppe Roter Kreis

WOLTER, UDO

Story

U 47 Kapitanleutnant Prien 1958 d: Harald Reinl. lps: Dieter Eppler, Sabina Sesselmann, Joachim Fuchsberger. 91M GRM. *U-47 Lt. Commander Prien* (USA); *U 47 - Lt. Prien*; *Kapitanleutnant Prien - Der Stier von Scapa Flow* prod/rel: Arca, Constantin

WONDERLY, W. CAREY

Short Story

Price of Silence, The 1916 d: Joseph de Grasse. lps: Dorothy Phillips, Lon Chaney, Vola Vale. 5r USA. prod/rel: Bluebird Photoplays, Inc.©

Broadway Gold, 1922, Short Story

Broadway Gold 1923 d: Eddie Dillon, J. Gordon Cooper. lps: Elaine Hammerstein, Elliott Dexter, Kathlyn Williams. 6779f USA. *A Virtuous Fool* prod/rel: Edward Dillon Productions, Truart Film Corp.

Broadway Love, 1916, Novel

Broadway Love 1918 d: Ida May Park. lps: Dorothy Phillips, William Stowell, Lon Chaney. 5r USA. prod/rel: Bluebird Photoplays, Inc.©

Conscription, 1917, Short Story

Her Boy 1918 d: George Irving. lps: Effie Shannon, Niles Welch, Pauline Curley. 5r USA. prod/rel: Metro Pictures Corp.©

The Infamous Miss Revell, Story

Infamous Miss Revell, The 1921 d: Dallas M. Fitzgerald. lps: Alice Lake, Cullen Landis, Jackie Saunders. 6r USA. prod/rel: Metro Pictures

Myself Becky, Short Story

Rouge and Riches 1920 d: Harry L. Franklin. lps: Mary MacLaren, Alberta Lee, Robert Walker. 6r USA. *Rogue and Riches* prod/rel: Universal Film Mfg. Co.©

Smart Set, Story

Second Mrs. Roebuck, The 1914 d: Jack O'Brien, W. Christy Cabanne. lps: Blanche Sweet, Raoul Walsh, Mary Alden. 2r USA. prod/rel: Majestic

The Viennese Charmer, Story

Four Jacks and a Jill 1941 d: Jack Hively. lps: Ray Bolger, Desi Arnaz, Anne Shirley. 68M USA. *Four Jacks and a Queen* prod/rel: RKO

Street Girl 1929 d: Wesley Ruggles. lps: Betty Compson, John Harron, Ned Sparks. 91M USA. *Barber John's Boy* prod/rel: RKO Productions

That Girl from Paris 1936 d: Leigh Jason. lps: Lily Pons, Jack Oakie, Gene Raymond. 105M USA. *Street Girl* prod/rel: RKO Radio Pictures©, Pandro S. Berman Production

WONG, MARY GILLIGAN

Nun: a Memoir, Autobiography

Shattered Vows 1984 d: Jack Bender. lps: Valerie Bertinelli, David Morse, Caroline McWilliams. TVM. 100M USA. prod/rel: NBC, Bertinelli-Pequod

WOOD, BARI

Doll's Eyes, Novel

In Dreams 1999 d: Neil Jordan. lps: Annette Bening, Aidan Quinn, Robert Downey Jr. 99M USA. prod/rel: Dreamworks Pictures, Dreamworks Llc©

Twins, Book

Twins 1988 d: David Cronenberg. lps: Jeremy Irons, Genevieve Bujold, Heidi von Palleske. 117M CND. *Dead Ringers* prod/rel: Rank, the Mantle Clinic Ii

WOOD, CLEMENT BIDDLE

Welcome to the Club, Novel

Welcome to the Club 1970 d: Walter Shenson. lps: Brian Foley, Jack Warden, Lee Meredith. 88M UKN/USA. prod/rel: Columbia-Wb, Welcome

WOOD, CYRUS

Maytime, New York 1917, Play

Maytime 1923 d: Louis J. Gasnier. lps: Ethel Shannon, Harrison Ford, William Norris. 7500f USA. prod/rel: B. P. Schulberg Productions, Preferred Pictures

Sally Irene and Mary, New York 1922, Play

Sally, Irene and Mary 1925 d: Edmund Goulding. lps: Constance Bennett, Joan Crawford, Sally O'Neil. 5564f USA. prod/rel: Metro-Goldwyn-Mayer Pictures

Sally, Irene and Mary 1938 d: William A. Seiter. lps: Alice Faye, Tony Martin, Fred Allen. 86M USA. prod/rel: Twentieth Century-Fox Film Corp.©

WOOD, DEREK

The Narrow Margin, London 1961, Book

Battle of Britain 1969 d: Guy Hamilton. lps: Laurence Olivier, Robert Shaw, Christopher Plummer. 132M UKN. prod/rel: Spitfire Productions, United Artists

WOOD, HENRY

Within the Maze, Novel

Maison Dans la Foret, La 1922 d: Jean Legrand. lps: Christine Lorraine, Jean Angelo, Constance Worth. 2200m FRN/GRM. *Haus Im Wald* (GRM) prod/rel: Films A. Legrand, Vita Films

WOOD, JOHN

Ranchman Buck Peters, Chicago 1912, Novel

Bar 20 Justice 1938 d: Lesley Selander. lps: William Boyd, George Hayes, Russell Hayden. 65M USA. *Deputy Sheriff* prod/rel: Harry Sherman Productions, Inc.

WOOD JR., EDWARD DAVIS

Orgy of the Dead, Novel

Orgy of the Dead 1965 d: A. C. Stephen. lps: Criswell, Pat Barringer, Fawn Silver. 82M USA. *Orgy of the Vampires* prod/rel: Astra Productions

WOOD, METCALFE

The Elder Miss Blossom, London 1898, Play

Elder Miss Blossom, The 1918 d: Percy Nash. lps: Isobel Elsom, Owen Nares, C. M. Hallard. 5000f UKN. *Wanted a Wife* (USA) prod/rel: G. B. Samuelson, Sun

WOOD, MRS. HENRY (1814–1887), UKN, Price, Ellen

The Channings, Novel

Channings, The 1920 d: Edwin J. Collins. lps: Lionelle Howard, Dick Webb, Dorothy Moody. 4500f UKN. prod/rel: Master, Butcher

East Lynne, London 1861, Novel

East Lynne 1902 d: Dicky Winslow. lps: A. W. Fitzgerald, Mrs. Fitzgerald. 500f UKN. prod/rel: Harrison

East Lynne 1910. 1500f UKN. prod/rel: Precision Films

East Lynne 1912 d: George Nicholls, Theodore Marston. lps: David Thompson, Florence Labadie, James Cruze. 2r USA. prod/rel: Thanhouser

East Lynne 1913 d: Arthur Charrington. lps: Nell Emerald, H. Agar Lyons, Frank E. Petley. 2200f UKN. prod/rel: Brightonia, Moving Pictures Sales Agency

East Lynne 1913 d: Bert Haldane. lps: Blanche Forsythe, Fred Paul, Fred Morgan. 6200f UKN. prod/rel: Barker, Walturdaw

East Lynne 1915 d: Travers Vale. lps: Louise Vale, Franklin Ritchie, Alan Hale. 3r USA. prod/rel: Biograph Co.

East Lynne 1916 d: Bertram Bracken. lps: Theda Bara, Stuart Holmes, William H. Tooker. 5r USA. prod/rel: Fox Film Corp., William Fox©

East Lynne 1921 d: Hugo Ballin. lps: Edward Earle, Mabel Ballin, Gladys Coburn. 6634f USA. prod/rel: Hugo Ballin Productions

East Lynne 1922. lps: Iris Hoey. 1240f UKN. prod/rel: Master Films, British Exhibitors' Films

East Lynne 1925 d: Emmett J. Flynn. lps: Alma Rubens, Edmund Lowe, Lou Tellegen. 8975f USA. prod/rel: Fox Film Corp.

East Lynne 1931 d: Frank Lloyd. lps: Ann Harding, Clive Brook, Conrad Nagel. 104M USA. prod/rel: Fox Film Corp.©

Ex-Flame 1930 d: Victor Hugo Halperin. lps: Neil Hamilton, Marian Nixon, Judith Barrie. 6698f USA. *Mixed Doubles* prod/rel: Liberty Productions

WOOD, WILLIAM P.
Court of Honor, Novel
Broken Trust 1995 d: Geoffrey Sax. lps: Tom Selleck, Elizabeth McGovern, William Atherton. TVM. 95M USA. prod/rel: Fonda/Bonfiglio Films

Rampage, Novel
Rampage 1987 d: William Friedkin. lps: Michael Biehn, Alex McArthur, Nicholas Campbell. 97M USA. prod/rel: D.E.G.

WOODBRIDGE, WILLIAM WITHERSPOON
That Something, Tacoma, Wash. 1914, Short Story
That Something 1921 d: Margery Wilson, Lawrence Underwood. lps: Charles Meredith, Margery Wilson, Nigel de Brulier. 5r USA. prod/rel: Hermann Film Corp., State Rights

WOODBURY, HERBERT A.
Story
Riders in the Sky 1949 d: John English. lps: Gene Autry, Gloria Henry, Pat Buttram. 70M USA. prod/rel: Gene Autry, Columbia

WOODHAM-SMITH, CECIL (1896–, UKN
The Reason Why, London 1953, Book
Charge of the Light Brigade, The 1968 d: Tony Richardson. lps: Trevor Howard, Vanessa Redgrave, John Gielgud. 141M UKN. prod/rel: United Artists, Woodfall

WOODLEY, RICHARD
Donnie Brasco: My Undercover Life in the Mafia, Book
Donnie Brasco 1997 d: Mike Newell. lps: Al Pacino, Johnny Depp, Michael Madsen. 126M USA. prod/rel: Baltimore Pictures, Mark Johnson

WOODROW, MRS. WILSON
The Black Pearl, New York 1912, Novel
Black Pearl, The 1928 d: Scott Pembroke. lps: Lila Lee, Ray Hallor, Carl Stockdale. 5261f USA. prod/rel: Trem Carr Productions, Rayart Pictures

Eyes of Youth, Short Story
Without Children 1935 d: William Nigh. lps: Reginald Denny, Marguerite Churchill, Bruce Cabot. 85M USA. *Penthouse Party* prod/rel: Liberty Pictures Corp.©

The Piper's Price, Short Story
Piper's Price, The 1917 d: Joseph de Grasse. lps: Dorothy Phillips, Maude George, William Stowell. 5r USA. prod/rel: Bluebird Photoplays, Inc.©

The Second Chance, New York 1924, Novel
Her Second Chance 1926 d: Lambert Hillyer. lps: Anna Q. Nilsson, Huntley Gordon, Charlie Murray. 6420f USA. prod/rel: First National Pictures, Vitagraph Co. of America

WOODROW, NANCY MANN WADDEL
The Hornet's Nest, Boston 1917, Novel
Hornet's Nest, The 1919 d: James Young. lps: Earle Williams, Brinsley Shaw, Vola Vale. 5-6r USA. prod/rel: Vitagraph Co. of America©

WOODRUFF, HELEN S.
The Lady of the Lighthouse, Book
Lady of the Lighthouse, The 1915 d: Harry Lambart, George Ridgwell. lps: Lionel Adams, Rose Tapley, Charles Wellesley. 3r USA. prod/rel: Broadway Star, Vitagraph Co. of America

WOODS, DONALD (1933–, SAF
Asking for Trouble, Novel
Cry Freedom 1987 d: Richard Attenborough. lps: Kevin Kline, Penelope Wilton, Denzel Washington. 159M UKN/ZIM. *Asking for Trouble* prod/rel: Marble Arch, Universal

Biko, Book
Cry Freedom 1987 d: Richard Attenborough. lps: Kevin Kline, Penelope Wilton, Denzel Washington. 159M UKN/ZIM. *Asking for Trouble* prod/rel: Marble Arch, Universal

WOODS, ELLA
Her Shattered Idol, Story
Her Shattered Idol 1915 d: John B. O'Brien. lps: Mae Marsh, Robert Harron, Spottiswoode Aitken. 4r USA. prod/rel: Majestic Motion Picture Co., Mutual Film Corp.

WOODS, MADELINE
Scandal House, New York 1933, Novel
Slander House 1938 d: Charles Lamont. lps: Craig Reynolds, Adrienne Ames, Esther Ralston. 65M USA. *Scandal House* prod/rel: Progressive Picture Corp.©

WOODS, STUART
Chiefs, Novel
Chiefs 1985 d: Jerry London. lps: Charlton Heston, Keith Carradine, Paul Sorvino. TVM. 283M USA. *Once Upon a Murder* (UKN) prod/rel: CBS, Highgate

WOODS, WALTER
The Pony Express, New York 1925, Novel
Pony Express, The 1925 d: James Cruze. lps: Betty Compson, Ricardo Cortez, Ernest Torrence. 9949f USA. prod/rel: Famous Players-Lasky, Paramount Pictures

WOODS, WILLIAM
Edge of Darkness, Novel
Edge of Darkness 1943 d: Lewis Milestone. lps: Errol Flynn, Ann Sheridan, Walter Huston. 120M USA. prod/rel: Warner Bros.

Manuela, Novel
Manuela 1957 d: Guy Hamilton. lps: Trevor Howard, Pedro Armendariz, Elsa Martinelli. 95M UKN. *Stowaway Girl* (USA) prod/rel: Foxwell Films, Rank Film Distributors

WOODWARD, BOB (1943–, USA, Wooodward, Robert Upshur
All the President's Men, 1974, Book
All the President's Men 1976 d: Alan J. PakulA. lps: Robert Redford, Dustin Hoffman, Jack Warden. 138M USA. prod/rel: Warner Bros., Wildwood

Wired, Biography
Wired 1989 d: Larry Peerce. lps: Michael Chiklis, Ray Sharkey, J. T. Walsh. 108M USA. prod/rel: Taurus

WOODWARD, EUGENE
Rose of the Golden West, Story
Rose of the Golden West 1927 d: George Fitzmaurice. lps: Mary Astor, Gilbert Roland, Gustav von Seyffertitz. 6477f USA. *Rose of Monterey* prod/rel: First National Pictures

WOODWARD, W. E. (1874–1950), USA, Woodward, William E.
Evelyn Prentice, New York 1933, Novel
Evelyn Prentice 1934 d: William K. Howard. lps: William Powell, Myrna Loy, Una Merkel. 80M USA. prod/rel: Metro-Goldwyn-Mayer Corp.©, Cosmopolitan Production

Stronger Than Desire 1939 d: Leslie Fenton. lps: Walter Pidgeon, Virginia Bruce, Ann Dvorak. 80M USA. prod/rel: Metro-Goldwyn-Mayer Corp., Loew's, Inc.©

WOOLF, EDGAR ALLAN
An April Shower, 1915, Play
April Fool 1926 d: Nat Ross. lps: Alexander Carr, Duane Thompson, Mary Alden. 7100f USA. prod/rel: Chadwick Pictures

WOOLF, LEONARD (1880–1969), UKN
The Village in the Jungle, 1913, Novel
Beddegama 1980 d: Lester James Peries. lps: Joe Abeywickrema, Trilicia Gunawardena, Malini FonsekA. 120M SLN. *The Village in the Jungle*; *Baddegama* prod/rel: Wilfred Pererea, Lester James Peries

WOOLF, VIRGINIA (1882–1941), UKN, Woolf, Adeline Virginia
Mrs. Dalloway, Novel
Mrs. Dalloway 1997 d: Marleen Gorris. lps: Vanessa Redgrave, Natascha McElhone, Rupert Graves. 97M USA/UKN/NTH. prod/rel: First Look Pictures, Bayly/Pare

Orlando, Novel
Orlando 1992 d: Sally Potter. lps: Tilda Swinton, Billy Zane, John Wood. 93M UKN/USS/FRN. prod/rel: Adventure Pictures (London), Lenfilm

The Waves, 1931, Novel
Golven 1982 d: Annette Apon. lps: Aat Ceelen, Thea Korterink, Michel Van Rooy. 92M NTH. *The Waves*

WOOLFOLK, JOSIAH PITTS
City Limits, New York 1932, Novel
City Limits 1934 d: William Nigh. lps: Frank Craven, Sally Blane, Ray Walker. 70M USA. prod/rel: Monogram Pictures Corp.

WOOLL, EDWARD
Libel, Play
Libel 1959 d: Anthony Asquith. lps: Dirk Bogarde, Olivia de Havilland, Paul Massie. 100M UKN. prod/rel: MGM, Anatole De Grunwald

WOOLLARD, KENNETH
Morning Departure, Play
Morning Departure 1949 d: Roy Ward Baker. lps: John Mills, Richard Attenborough, Nigel Patrick. 102M UKN. *Operation Disaster* (USA) prod/rel: General Film Distributors, Jay Lewis

WOOLLCOTT, ALEXANDER (1887–1943), USA, Woollcott, Alexander Humphreys
The Dark Tower, New York 1933, Play
Dark Tower, The 1943 d: John Harlow. lps: Ben Lyon, Anne Crawford, David Farrar. 93M UKN. prod/rel: Warner Bros., First National

Man With Two Faces, The 1934 d: Archie Mayo. lps: Edward G. Robinson, Mary Astor, Ricardo Cortez. 72M USA. *The Mysterious Mr. Chautard*; *The Dark Tower*; *The Strange Case of Mr. Chautard*; *Dark Victory* prod/rel: First National Pictures©

WOOLRICH, CORNELL (1903–1968), USA, Irish, William, Hopley, George
Black Alibi, 1942, Novel
Leopard Man, The 1943 d: Jacques Tourneur. lps: Dennis O'Keefe, Margo, Jean Brooks. 66M USA. prod/rel: RKO Radio

The Black Angel, 1943, Novel
Black Angel 1946 d: R. William Neill. lps: Dan Duryea, June Vincent, Peter Lorre. 80M USA. prod/rel: Universal

The Black Curtain, 1941, Novel
Street of Chance 1942 d: Jack Hively. lps: Burgess Meredith, Claire Trevor, Sheldon Leonard. 74M USA. *The Black Curtain* prod/rel: Paramount

The Black Path of Fear, 1944, Novel
Chase, The 1946 d: Arthur Ripley. lps: Robert Cummings, Steve Cochran, Michele Morgan. 86M USA. prod/rel: United Artists, Nero Pictures

The Boy Cried Murder, 1947, Short Story
Boy Cried Murder, The 1966 d: George Breakston. lps: Veronica Hurst, Phil Brown, Fraser "Fiz" MacIntosh. 86M UKN/GRM/YGS. *Decak Je Vikao Ubistvo* (YGS); *Ein Junge Schrie Mord* (GRM) prod/rel: Ccc, Carlos Avala

Cloak and Dagger 1984 d: Richard Franklin. lps: Henry Thomas, Dabney Coleman, Michael Murphy. 101M USA. prod/rel: Universal

Window, The 1949 d: Ted Tetzlaff. lps: Barbara Hale, Bobby Driscoll, Arthur Kennedy. 73M USA. prod/rel: RKO Radio

The Bride Wore Black, New York 1940, Novel
Mariee Etait En Noir, La 1968 d: Francois Truffaut. lps: Jeanne Moreau, Jean-Claude Brialy, Michel Bouquet. 107M FRN/ITL. *La Sposa in Nero* (ITL); *The Bride Wore Black* (UKN) prod/rel: Films Du Carosse, Contact Editions

Cendrillon Et Les Gangsters, Novel
Escapade 1957 d: Ralph Habib. lps: Louis Jourdan, Dany Carrel, Roger Hanin. 75M FRN. prod/rel: Pathe-Cinema, Prod. Generale De Films

Children of the Ritz, Short Story
Children of the Ritz 1929 d: John Francis Dillon. lps: Dorothy MacKaill, Jack Mulhall, James Ford. 6426f USA. prod/rel: First National Pictures

Cocaine, Story
Fall Guy 1947 d: Reginald Le Borg. lps: Clifford Penn, Teala Loring, Robert Armstrong. 64M USA. prod/rel: Monogram

Collared, Story
Pupa Del Gangster, La 1975 d: Giorgio Capitani. lps: Sophia Loren, Marcello Mastroianni, Aldo MacCione. 110M ITL/FRN. *La Pepee du Gangster* (FRN); *The Gangster's Doll*; *Get Rita*; *Poopsie and Company*; *Lady of the Evening* prod/rel: Compagnia Cin.Ca Champion (Roma), Les Films Concordia (Paris)

The Corpse Next Door, Short Story
Union City 1980 d: Mark Reichert. lps: Dennis Lipscomb, Deborah Harry, Irina MaleevA. 90M USA. prod/rel: Kinesis

Deadline at Dawn, 1944, Novel
Deadline at Dawn 1946 d: Harold Clurman. lps: Susan Hayward, Paul Lukas, Bill Williams. 83M USA. prod/rel: RKO Radio

Face Work, Story
Convicted 1938 d: Leon BarshA. lps: Charles Quigley, Rita Hayworth, Marc Lawrence. 58M CND. *Face Work* prod/rel: Central Films Ltd., Columbia Pictures

He Looked Like Murder, 1946, Short Story
Guilty, The 1947 d: John Reinhardt. lps: Bonita Granville, Don Castle, Wally Cassell. 71M USA. prod/rel: Monogram

I Married a Dead Man, 1948, Novel
J'ai Epouse une Ombre 1983 d: Robin Davis. lps: Nathalie Baye, Francis Huster, Richard Bohringer. 110M FRN. *I Married a Shadow* (USA); *I Married a Dead Man*

Mrs. Winterbourne 1996 d: Richard Benjamin. lps: Shirley MacLaine, Ricki Lake, Brendan Fraser. 104M USA. prod/rel: a & M

No Man of Her Own 1950 d: Mitchell Leisen. lps: Barbara Stanwyck, John Lund, Lyle Bettger. 98M USA. *The Lie* prod/rel: Paramount

I Wouldn't Be in Your Shoes, 1943, Novel
I Wouldn't Be in Your Shoes 1948 d: William Nigh. lps: Don Castle, Elyse Knox, Regis Toomey. 70M USA. prod/rel: Monogram

I'm Dangerous Tonight, 1943, Short Story
I'm Dangerous Tonight 1990 d: Tobe Hooper. lps: Anthony Perkins, Madchen Amick, Daisy Hall. TVM. 100M USA. prod/rel: Universal

Manhattan Love Song, New York 1932, Novel
Manhattan Love Song 1934 d: Leonard Fields. lps: Robert Armstrong, Dixie Lee, Franklin Pangborn. 73M USA. prod/rel: Monogram Pictures Corp.©

Night Has a Thousand Eyes, 1945, Novel
Night Has a Thousand Eyes 1948 d: John Farrow. lps: Edward G. Robinson, Gail Russell, John Lund. 81M USA. prod/rel: Paramount

Nightmare, 1943, Short Story
Fear in the Night 1947 d: Maxwell Shane. lps: Paul Kelly, Kay Scott, Deforest Kelley. 72M USA. prod/rel: Paramount

Nightmare 1956 d: Maxwell Shane. lps: Edward G. Robinson, Kevin McCarthy, Connie Russell. 89M USA. prod/rel: United Artists, P-T-S Prods.

Phantom Lady, 1942, Novel
Phantom Lady 1944 d: Robert Siodmak. lps: Franchot Tone, Ella Raines, Alan Curtis. 87M USA. prod/rel: Universal

Rear Window, 1944, Short Story
Rear Window 1954 d: Alfred Hitchcock. lps: James Stewart, Grace Kelly, Raymond Burr. 112M USA. prod/rel: Paramount, Patron, Inc.

Rear Window 1998 d: Jeff Bleckner. lps: Christopher Reeve, Darryl Hannah, Robert Forster. TVM. 120M USA. prod/rel: Hallmark Entertainment, Cambria Prods.

Silent As the Grave, Novel
Obsession 1954 d: Jean Delannoy. lps: Michele Morgan, Raf Vallone, Jean Gaven. 103M FRN/ITL. *Domanda Di Grazia* (ITL) prod/rel: Films Gibe, Franco-London Films

Waltz Into Darkness, New York 1947, Novel
Sirene du Mississippi, La 1969 d: Francois Truffaut. lps: Jean-Paul Belmondo, Catherine Deneuve, Michel Bouquet. 123M FRN/ITL. *La Mia Droga Si Chiama Julie* (ITL); *Mississippi Mermaid* (USA) prod/rel: Films Du Carrosse, Les Productions Artistes Associes

You'll Never See Me Again, Short Story
You'll Never See Me Again 1973 d: Jeannot Szwarc. lps: David Hartman, Jane Wyatt, Ralph Meeker. TVM. 73M USA. prod/rel: Universal

WOON, BASIL DILLON
Misdeal, Play
Recaptured Love 1930 d: John G. Adolfi. lps: Belle Bennett, John Halliday, Dorothy Burgess. 6120f USA. *Fame* prod/rel: Warner Brothers Pictures

WORDLEY, DICK
A Piece of Paper, Novel
Cathy's Child 1979 d: Donald Crombie. lps: Michele Fawdon, Alan Cassell, Bryan Brown. 90M ASL. *Cathie's Child* prod/rel: Australian Film Commission, Roadshow

WORKER, BARBARA
Escape, Book
Escape 1980 d: Robert Michael Lewis. lps: Timothy Bottoms, Kay Lenz, Colleen Dewhurst. TVM. 100M USA. prod/rel: CBS, Henry Jaffe

WORKER, DWIGHT
Escape, Book
Escape 1980 d: Robert Michael Lewis. lps: Timothy Bottoms, Kay Lenz, Colleen Dewhurst. TVM. 100M USA. prod/rel: CBS, Henry Jaffe

WORLD, JOHN
Il Crisantemo MacChiato Di Sangue, Novel
Crisantemo MacChiato Di Sangue, Il 1921 d: Domenico Di Maggio. lps: Edy Dickson, Nella Togni, Teresa Braccioni-Vitaliani. 1417m ITL. *Il Sacro Testamento* prod/rel: Cellini

WORMSER, ANNE
The Baby's Had a Hard Day, Story
West Point Widow 1941 d: Robert Siodmak. lps: Anne Shirley, Richard Carlson, Cecil Kellaway. 64M USA. prod/rel: Paramount

WORMSER, RICHARD
It's All in the Racket, Short Story
Sworn Enemy 1936 d: Edwin L. Marin. lps: Robert Young, Joseph Calleia, Florence Rice. 80M USA. prod/rel: Metro-Goldwyn-Mayer Corp.©

Love in the Mud, Novel
Carnival Queen 1937 d: Nate Watt. lps: Robert Wilcox, Dorothea Kent, Hobart Cavanaugh. 66M USA. prod/rel: Universal Pictures Co.

Right Guy, 1936, Short Story
Frame-Up, The 1937 d: D. Ross Lederman. lps: Paul Kelly, Julie Bishop, George McKay. 59M USA. *The Frame Up*; *Right Guy* prod/rel: Columbia Pictures Corp. of California©

The Road to Carmichael's, Story
Big Steal, The 1949 d: Don Siegel. lps: Robert Mitchum, William Bendix, Patric Knowles. 71M USA. prod/rel: RKO Radio

Sleep All Winter, Short Story
Showdown, The 1950 d: Dorrell McGowan, Stuart E. McGowan. lps: Bill Elliott, Harry Morgan, Walter Brennan. 86M USA. prod/rel: Republic

WORRALL, LECHMERE
The Man Who Stayed at Home, London 1914, Play
Man Who Stayed at Home, The 1915 d: Cecil M. Hepworth. lps: Dennis Eadie, Violet Hopson, Alma Taylor. 3575f UKN. prod/rel: Hepworth, Central

Man Who Stayed at Home, The 1919 d: Herbert Blache. lps: King Baggot, Claire Whitney, Robert Whittier. 6r USA. prod/rel: Screen Classics, Inc., Metro Pictures Corp.©

WORTH, MARVIN (1926–1998), USA
Story
Boys' Night Out 1962 d: Michael Gordon. lps: Howard Duff, Tony Randall, Howard Morris. 114M USA. prod/rel: MGM, Filmways

WORTS, GEORGE FRANK
Down With Women, Story
For Ladies Only 1927 d: Scott Pembroke, Henry Lehrman. lps: John Bowers, Jacqueline Logan, Edna Marion. 5507f USA. prod/rel: Columbia Pictures

Out Where the Worst Begins, 1924, Short Story
Where the Worst Begins 1925 d: John McDermott. lps: Ruth Roland, Alec B. Francis, Matt Moore. 6139f USA. prod/rel: Co-Artists Productions, Truart Film Corp.

The Phantom President, New York 1932, Novel
Phantom President, The 1932 d: Norman Taurog. lps: George M. Cohan, Claudette Colbert, Jimmy Durante. 70M USA. prod/rel: Paramount Publix Corp.©

Red Darkness, 1922, Short Story
Madness of Youth 1923 d: Jerome Storm. lps: John Gilbert, Billie Dove, Donald Hatswell. 4719f USA. prod/rel: Fox Film Corp.

WOUK, HERMAN (1915–, USA
The Caine Mutiny, 1951, Novel
Caine Mutiny, The 1954 d: Edward Dmytryk. lps: Humphrey Bogart, Van Johnson, Jose Ferrer. 125M USA. prod/rel: Columbia

The City Boy, 1948, Novel
Her First Romance 1951 d: Seymour Friedman. lps: Margaret O'Brien, Allen Martin Jr., Jimmy Hunt. 72M USA. *Girls Never Tell* (UKN); *The Romantic Age* prod/rel: Columbia

Marjorie Morningstar, 1955, Novel
Marjorie Morningstar 1958 d: Irving Rapper. lps: Gene Kelly, Natalie Wood, Claire Trevor. 123M USA. prod/rel: Warner Bros.

Slattery's Hurricane, Novel
Slattery's Hurricane 1949 d: Andre de Toth. lps: Richard Widmark, Veronica Lake, Linda Darnell. 83M USA. prod/rel: 20th Century-Fox

War and Remembrance, Novel
War and Remembrance 1988 d: Dan Curtis. lps: Robert Mitchum, Jane Seymour, Hart Bochner. MTV. 1045M USA.

The Winds of War, Novel
Winds of War, The 1983 d: Dan Curtis. lps: Robert Mitchum, Ali MacGraw, Jan-Michael Vincent. TVM. 458M USA.

Youngblood Hawke, New York 1962, Novel
Youngblood Hawke 1964 d: Delmer Daves. lps: James Franciscus, Suzanne Pleshette, Genevieve Page. 136M USA. prod/rel: Warner Bros. Pictures

WOZENCRAFT, KIM
Rush, Book
Rush 1991 d: Lili Fini Zanuck. lps: Jason Patric, Jennifer Jason Leigh, Sam Elliott. 120M USA. prod/rel: Zanuck Company, MGM-Pathe Communications

WRAY, JOHN
Nightstick, New York 1927, Play
Alibi 1929 d: Roland West. lps: Chester Morris, Harry Stubbs, Mae Busch. 90M USA. *The Perfect Alibi* (UKN); *Nightstick* prod/rel: Feature Productions, United Artists

A Sap from Syracuse, Play
Sap from Syracuse, The 1930 d: A. Edward Sutherland. lps: Jack Oakie, Ginger Rogers, Granville Bates. 6108f USA. *The Sap Abroad* (UKN) prod/rel: Paramount-Publix Corp.

WREN, P. C. (1885–1941), UKN
Beau Geste, London 1924, Novel
Beau Geste 1926 d: Herbert Brenon. lps: Ronald Colman, Neil Hamilton, Ralph Forbes. 11r USA. prod/rel: Famous Players-Lasky Corp., Paramount Pictures

Beau Geste 1939 d: William A. Wellman. lps: Gary Cooper, Ray Milland, Robert Preston. 120M USA. prod/rel: Paramount Pictures, Inc.

Beau Geste 1966 d: Douglas Heyes. lps: Guy Stockwell, Doug McClure, Leslie Nielsen. 104M USA. prod/rel: Universal Pictures

Beau Geste 1982 d: Douglas Camfield. lps: Benedict Taylor, Anthony Calf, Jonathan Morris. TVM. 206M USA.

Beau Ideal, New York 1928, Novel
Beau Ideal 1931 d: Herbert Brenon. lps: Lester Vail, Ralph Forbes, George Regas. 82M USA. prod/rel: RKO Radio Pictures, Inc.

Beau Sabreur, New York 1926, Novel
Beau Sabreur 1928 d: John Waters. lps: Gary Cooper, Evelyn Brent, Noah Beery. 6704f USA. prod/rel: Paramount Famous Lasky Corp.

Wages of Virtue, New York 1917, Novel
Wages of Virtue 1924 d: Allan Dwan. lps: Gloria Swanson, Ben Lyon, Norman Trevor. 7093f USA. prod/rel: Famous Players-Lasky, Paramount Pictures

WRENCH, MRS. STANLEY
Burnt Wings, Novel
Burnt Wings 1916 d: Walter West. lps: Eve Balfour, J. R. Tozer, Thomas H. MacDonald. 3640f UKN. prod/rel: Broadwest, Monopol

WRIGHT, FRED E.
York State Folks, New York 1905, Play
York State Folks 1915 d: Harry Jackson. lps: James Lackaye, Ray L. Royce, Edith Offutt. 5r USA. prod/rel: Dra-Ko Film Co., State Rights

WRIGHT, GENE
Pandora la Croix, Philadelphia 1924, Novel
As Man Desires 1925 d: Irving Cummings. lps: Milton Sills, Viola Dana, Ruth Clifford. 7790f USA. prod/rel: First National Pictures

Yellow Fingers, Philadelphia 1925, Novel
Yellow Fingers 1926 d: Emmett J. Flynn. lps: Olive Borden, Ralph Ince, Claire Adams. 5594f USA. prod/rel: Fox Film Corp.

WRIGHT, HAROLD BELL (1872–1944), USA
The Calling of Dan Matthews, Chicago 1909, Novel
Calling of Dan Matthews, The 1935 d: Phil Rosen. lps: Richard Arlen, Mary Kornman, Douglas Dumbrille. 65M USA. prod/rel: Principal Productions, Inc.

The Eyes of the World, Chicago 1914, Novel
Eyes of the World, The 1917 d: Donald Crisp. lps: Jane Novak, Jack Livingston, Kathleen Kirkham. 7-10r USA. prod/rel: Clune Film Producing Co., State Rights

Eyes of the World, The 1930 d: Henry King. lps: Una Merkel, Nance O'Neil, John Holland. 7272f USA. prod/rel: Inspiration Pictures, United Artists

Helen of the Old House, New York 1921, Novel
Western Gold 1937 d: Howard Bretherton. lps: Smith Ballew, Heather Angel, Leroy Mason. 57M USA. *The Mysterious Stranger* (UKN) prod/rel: Principal Productions©, Twentieth Century-Fox Film Corp.

Massacre River, Novel
Massacre River 1949 d: John Rawlins. lps: Guy Madison, Rory Calhoun, Johnny Sands. 78M USA. prod/rel: Allied Artists, Windson Pictures Corp.

The Mine With the Iron Door, New York 1923, Novel
Mine With the Iron Door, The 1924 d: Sam Wood. lps: Pat O'Malley, Dorothy MacKaill, Raymond Hatton. 6180f USA. prod/rel: Sol Lesser Productions, Principal Pictures

Mine With the Iron Door, The 1936 d: David Howard. lps: Richard Arlen, Cecilia Parker, Henry B. Walthall. 68M USA. prod/rel: Principal Productions, Sol Lesser Production

The Re-Creation of Brian Kent, Chicago 1919, Novel
Re-Creation of Brian Kent, The 1925 d: Sam Wood. lps: Kenneth Harlan, Helene Chadwick, Mary Carr. 6878f USA. prod/rel: Principal Pictures

Wild Brian Kent 1936 d: Howard Bretherton. lps: Ralph Bellamy, Mae Clarke, Helen Lowell. 59M USA. prod/rel: Principal Productions©, Twentieth Century-Fox Film Corp.

The Shepherd of the Hills, New York 1907, Novel
Shepherd of the Hills 1941 d: Henry Hathaway. lps: John Wayne, Betty Field, Harry Carey. 98M USA. prod/rel: Paramount

Shepherd of the Hills, The 1920 d: Harold Bell Wright, L. F. Gottschalk. lps: Harry Lonsdale, Catherine Curtis, George McDaniel. Harold Bell Wright Story Picture Corp.©, State Rights

Shepherd of the Hills, The 1928 d: Albert S. Rogell. lps: Alec B. Francis, Molly O'Day, John Boles. 8188f USA. prod/rel: First National Pictures

Shepherd of the Hills, The 1964 d: Ben Parker. lps: Richard Arlen, James W. Middleton, Sherry Lynn. 110M USA. *Thunder Mountain* prod/rel: Macco Productions

A Son of His Father, New York 1925, Novel
Son of His Father, A 1925 d: Victor Fleming. lps: Bessie Love, Warner Baxter, Raymond Hatton. 6925f USA. prod/rel: Famous Players-Lasky, Paramount Pictures

When a Man's a Man, New York 1916, Novel
When a Man's a Man 1924 d: Eddie Cline. lps: John Bowers, Marguerite de La Motte, Robert Frazer. 6910f USA. prod/rel: Principle Pictures, Associated First National Pictures

When a Man's a Man 1935 d: Eddie Cline. lps: George O'Brien, Dorothy Wilson, Paul Kelly. 68M USA. *Saga of the West* prod/rel: Atherton Productions©, Fox Film Corp.

The Winning of Barbara Worth, Chicago 1911, Novel
Winning of Barbara Worth, The 1926 d: Henry King. lps: Ronald Colman, Vilma Banky, Charles Lane. 8757f USA. prod/rel: Samuel Goldwyn, Inc., United Artists

WRIGHT, LAWRENCE
Article
Forgotten Sins 1995 d: Dick Lowry. lps: William Devane, John Shea, Bess Armstrong. TVM. 90M USA. prod/rel: Patchett Kaufman Entertainment©, Nancy Hardin Productions

WRIGHT, MAURICE
River of Missing Men, Story
Zanzibar 1940 d: Harold Schuster. lps: Lola Lane, James Craig, Eduardo Ciannelli. 70M USA. *Rigadoon* prod/rel: Universal Pictures Co.©

WRIGHT, RICHARD (1908–1960), USA, Wright, Richard Nathaniel
The Man Who Was Almost a Man, 1961, Short Story
Almos' a Man 1977 d: Stan Lathan. lps: Levar Burton, Madge Sinclair, Robert Doqui. MTV. 51M USA. prod/rel: Learning in Focus

Native Son, 1940, Novel
Native Son 1986 d: Jerrold Freedman. lps: Victor Love, Matt Dillon, Elizabeth McGovern. 112M USA. prod/rel: Cinecom

Sangre Negra 1948 d: Pierre Chenal. lps: Richard Wright, Jean Wallace, Gloria Madison. 91M ARG/USA. *Native Son* (USA); *Black Blood* prod/rel: Classic Pictures, Argentina Sono

Savage Holiday, Novel
Passerelle, La 1987 d: Jean-Claude Sussfeld. lps: Pierre Arditi, Mathilda May, Jany Holt. 100M FRN. *The Crossing* (UKN) prod/rel: T. Films, TF 1

WRIGHT, ROBERT
Song of Norway, New York 1944, Play
Song of Norway 1970 d: Andrew L. Stone. lps: Toralv Maurstad, Florence Henderson, Christina Schollin. 142M USA. prod/rel: ABC Pictures

WRIGHT, S. FOWLER
Deluge: a Romance, London 1927, Novel
Deluge 1933 d: Felix E. Feist. lps: Sidney Blackmer, Peggy Shannon, Lois Wilson. 70M USA. prod/rel: K.B.S. Productions, Inc.

Three Witnesses, Novel
Three Witnesses 1935 d: Leslie Hiscott. lps: Henry Kendall, Eve Gray, Sebastian Shaw. 68M UKN. prod/rel: Twickenham, Universal

WU CHENGEN
Xi You Ji, 1592, Novel
Da Nao Tian Gong 1964 d: Wu Yingju. 69M CHN. *Revolt of the Holy Monkey in the Heavenly Palace*
Sun Wukong San Da Baigujing 1960 d: Yang XIao-Zhong, Yu Zhongying. 90M CHN.; *The Holy Monkey Fights the White Boned Devil Three Times*
Xi XIng Ping Yao 1991 d: Zhang Che. lps: Jia Yongquan, Chen Jiming, Du Yumin. 9r CHN. *Journeying West to Kill the Demon* prod/rel: XIaoxiang Film Studio, Changhe Film Company

WU JIANREN
Hen Hai, Novel
Hen Hai 1931 d: Tan Zhiyuan, Gao Lihen. lps: Zheng XIaoqiu, Gao Qianpin. 10r CHN. *Sea of Hate* prod/rel: Mingxing Film Company

WUL, STEPHEN
Oms En Serie, Novel
Planete Sauvage, La 1973 d: Rene Laloux. ANM. 72M FRN/CZC. *Fantastic Planet* (USA); *The Savage Planet* prod/rel: Films Armorial, O.R.T.F.

WUOLIJOKI, HELLA
Entas Nyt Niskavuori?, 1953, Play
Niskavuori Taistelee 1957 d: Edvin Laine. lps: Elsa Turakainen, Mirjam Novera, Tauno Palo. 96M FNL. *Niskavuori Fights*; *Niskavuoris Kamp* prod/rel: Suomien Filmiteollisuus

Herr Puntila Und Sein Knecht Matti, 1948, Play
Herr Puntila Und Sein Knecht Matti 1955 d: Alberto Cavalcanti. lps: Curt Bois, Heinz Engelmann, Maria Emo. 97M AUS. *Mr. Puntila and His Valet Matti*; *Puntila*; *Herr Puntila and His Servant Matti* prod/rel: Wien-Film

Herra Puntila Ja Hanen Renkinsa Matti 1979 d: Ralf LangbackA. lps: Lasse Poysti, Pekka Laiho, Arja SaijonmaA. 109M FNL/SWD. *Mr. Puntila and His Servant Matti*; *Herr Puntila Och Hans Drang* (SWD)

Justina, 1937, Play
Eteenpain-Elamaan 1939 d: Toivo Sarkka, Yrjo NortA. lps: Regina Linnanheimo, Tauno Palo, Emmi JurkkA. 110M FNL. *Forward-Toward Life*; *Framat - Mot Livet* prod/rel: Suomen Filmiteollisuus

Juurakon Hulda, 1937, Play
Farmer's Daughter, The 1947 d: H. C. Potter. lps: Joseph Cotten, Loretta Young, Ethel Barrymore. 97M USA. prod/rel: RKO Radio

Juurakon Hulda 1937 d: Valentin VaalA. lps: Irma Seikkula, Tauno Palo, Topo LeistelA. 88M FNL. *Hulda Fran Juurakko* prod/rel: Suomi Film

Niskavuoren Heta, 1950, Play
Niskavuoren Heta 1952 d: Edvin Laine. lps: Kaarlo Halttunen, Rauni Luoma, Mirjam Novero. 95M FNL. *Heta of Niskavuori Farm*; *Heta from Niskavuori*; *Heta Fran Niskavuori* prod/rel: Suomen Filmiteollisuus

Niskavuoren Leipa, 1938, Play
Niskavuoren Aarne 1954 d: Edvin Laine. lps: Elsa Turakainen, Tauno Paolo, Rauni Ikaheimo. 91M FNL. *Aarne of Niskavuori*; *Aarne Fran Niskavuori* prod/rel: Suomen Filmiteollisuus

Niskavuori 1984 d: Matti KassilA. lps: Rauni Luoma, Maija-Liisa Marton, Esko Salminen. 120M FNL. *Tug of Home: the Famous Niskavuori Saga*; *The Family Niskavuori*

Niskavuoren Naiset, 1936, Play
Niskavuoren Naiset 1938 d: Valentin VaalA. lps: Olga Tainio, Tauno Palo, Irja LautiA. 84M FNL. *Women of Niskavuori*; *Kvinnorna Pa Niskavuori* prod/rel: Suomi-Filmi

Niskavuoren Naiset 1958 d: Valentin VaalA. lps: Emma Vaananen, Teija Sopanen, Hilkka HelinA. 80M FNL. *Women of Niskavuori*; *Kvinnorna Pa Niskavuori* prod/rel: Suomi-Filmi

Niskavuori 1984 d: Matti KassilA. lps: Rauni Luoma, Maija-Liisa Marton, Esko Salminen. 120M FNL. *Tug of Home: the Famous Niskavuori Saga*; *The Family Niskavuori*

Niskavuoren Nuori Emanta, 1940, Play
Loviisa, Niskavuoren Nuoriemanta 1946 d: Valentin VaalA. lps: Emma Vaananen, Tauno Palo, Kirsti Hurme. 91M FNL. *Loviisa - Unga Vardinnan Pa Niskavuori*; *Loviisa* prod/rel: Suomi-Filmi

Vihrea Kulta, 1938, Play
Vihrea Kulta 1939 d: Valentin VaalA. lps: Ahnna Taini, Olavi Reimas, Sven Relander. 86M FNL. *Gront Guld* prod/rel: Suomi-Filmi

WURMBRAND, IRMGARD
Ein Weiter Weg, Novel
Vergiss, Wenn du Kannst 1956 d: Hans H. Konig. lps: Winnie Markus, Gustav Frohlich, Bengt Lindstrom. 90M GRM/AUS. *Forget if You Can* prod/rel: Suddeutsche, Bergland

WUTTIG, H. O.
Funf Tage Und Eine Nacht, Novel
Grossalarm 1938 d: Georg Jacoby. lps: Ursula Grabley, Paul Klinger, Lina Carstens. 93M GRM. prod/rel: F.D.F., UFA

WYATT, FRANK
Mrs. Temple's Telegram, New York 1905, Play
Mrs. Temple's Telegram 1920 d: James Cruze. lps: Bryant Washburn, Wanda Hawley, Carmen Phillips. 4318f USA. prod/rel: Famous Players-Lasky Corp.©, Paramount-Artcraft Pictures

WYLIE, PHILIP
Story
Cinderella Jones 1946 d: Busby Berkeley. lps: Joan Leslie, Robert Alda, S. Z. Sakall. 88M USA. prod/rel: Warner Bros.

WYLIE, EVAN
Nice Little Bank That Should Be Robbed, A 1958 d: Henry Levin. lps: Tom Ewell, Mickey Rooney, Mickey Shaughnessy. 88M USA. *How to Rob a Bank* (UKN) prod/rel: 20th Century-Fox

Joe Butterfly, Play
Joe Butterfly 1957 d: Jesse Hibbs. lps: Audie Murphy, George Nader, Burgess Meredith. 90M USA. prod/rel: Universal-International

WYLIE, I. A. R., Wylie, Ida Alexa Ross
The Daughter of Brahma, Indianapolis 1912, Novel
Shattered Idols 1922 d: Edward Sloman. lps: Marguerite de La Motte, William V. Mong, James Morrison. 5850f USA. *Bride of the Gods* prod/rel: J. L. Frothingham Productions, Associated First National Pictures

A Feather in Her Hat, Garden City, N.Y. 1934, Novel
Feather in Her Hat, A 1935 d: Alfred Santell. lps: Pauline Lord, Basil Rathbone, Louis Hayward. 74M USA. prod/rel: Columbia Pictures Corp.©

The Gay Banditti, 1938, Novel
Young in Heart, The 1938 d: Richard Wallace. lps: Janet Gaynor, Douglas Fairbanks Jr., Paulette Goddard. 90M USA. prod/rel: Selznick International Pictures©, United Artists Corp.

Grandmother Bernle Learns Her Letters, 1926, Short Story
Four Sons 1928 d: John Ford. lps: James Hall, Margaret Mann, Earle Foxe. 9412f USA. prod/rel: Fox Film Corp.

Four Sons 1940 d: Archie Mayo. lps: Don Ameche, Eugenie Leontovich, Mary Beth Hughes. 89M USA. prod/rel: 20th Century-Fox Film Corp.

The Hermit Doctor of Gaya, New York 1916, Novel
Stronger Than Death 1920 d: Herbert Blache, Charles Bryant. lps: Alla Nazimova, Charles Bryant, Charles K. French. 7r USA. *The Hermit Doctor of Gaya* prod/rel: Nazimova Productions, Metro Pictures Corp.©

The Inheritors, 1922, Short Story
Gaiety Girl, The 1924 d: King Baggot. lps: Mary Philbin, Joseph J. Dowling, William Haines. 7419f USA. *The Inheritors* prod/rel: Universal Pictures

Jungle Law, Short Story
Man Must Live, A 1925 d: Paul Sloane. lps: Richard Dix, Jacqueline Logan, George Nash. 6116f USA. prod/rel: Famous Players-Lasky, Paramount Pictures

Keeper of the Flame, Novel
Keeper of the Flame 1942 d: George Cukor. lps: Spencer Tracy, Katharine Hepburn, Richard Whorf. 100M USA. prod/rel: MGM

Melia No-Good, 1917, Short Story
For Valour 1917 d: Albert Parker. lps: Winifred Allen, Richard Barthelmess, Henry Weaver. 5r USA. *Melia No-Good*; *For Valor* prod/rel: Triangle Film Corp., Triangle Distributing Corp.

The Paupers of Portman Square, Novel
Grass Orphan, The 1922 d: Frank H. Crane. lps: Margaret Bannerman, Reginald Owen, Douglas Munro. 6000f UKN. prod/rel: Ideal

Phone Call from a Stranger, Novel
Phone Call from a Stranger, A 1952 d: Jean Negulesco. lps: Shelley Winters, Gary Merrill, Bette Davis. 96M USA. prod/rel: 20th Century-Fox

Pilgrimage, 1932, Short Story
Pilgrimage 1933 d: John Ford. lps: Henrietta Crosman, Heather Angel, Norman Foster. 95M USA. prod/rel: Fox Film Corp.©

The Red Mirage, London 1913, Novel
Foreign Legion, The 1928 d: Edward Sloman. lps: Norman Kerry, Lewis Stone, Crauford Kent. 7828f USA. *The Red Mirage* prod/rel: Universal Pictures
Unknown, The 1915 d: George Melford. lps: Lou Tellegen, Theodore Roberts, Dorothy Davenport. 5r USA. prod/rel: Jesse L. Lasky Feature Play Co.©, Paramount Pictures Corp.

The Road to Reno, 1937, Story
Road to Reno, The 1938 d: S. Sylvan Simon. lps: Randolph Scott, Hope Hampton, Glenda Farrell. 69M USA. prod/rel: Universal Pictures Co.©

The Temple of Dawn, London 1915, Novel
Price of Redemption, The 1920 d: Dallas M. Fitzgerald. lps: Bert Lytell, Seena Owen, Cleo Madison. 7r USA. *The Temple of Dawn* prod/rel: Metro Pictures Corp.©

The Underpup, 1938, Short Story
Underpup, The 1939 d: Richard Wallace. lps: Gloria Jean, Robert Cummings, Nan Grey. 87M USA. *The Under-Pup* prod/rel: Universal Pictures Co.©, Joe Pasternak Production

Vivacious Lady, 1936, Short Story
Vivacious Lady 1938 d: George Stevens. lps: James Stewart, Ginger Rogers, James Ellison. 90M USA. prod/rel: RKO Radio Pictures©

Why Should I Cry?, Story
Torch Song 1953 d: Charles Walters. lps: Joan Crawford, Michael Wilding, Gig Young. 90M USA. prod/rel: MGM

Widow's Evening, 1931, Short Story
Evenings for Sale 1932 d: Stuart Walker. lps: Herbert Marshall, Sari Maritza, Charles Ruggles. 68M USA. prod/rel: Paramount Publix Corp.©

The Wonderful Story, Novel
Wonderful Story, The 1922 d: Graham Cutts. lps: Lillian Hall-Davis, Herbert Langley, Olaf Hytten. 5000f UKN. prod/rel: Graham-Wilcox, Astra-National

Wonderful Story, The 1932 d: Reginald Fogwell. lps: Wyn Clare, John Batten, Eric Bransby Williams. 79M UKN. prod/rel: Reginald Fogwell, Sterling

Young Nowheres, 1927, Short Story
Some Day 1935 d: Michael Powell. lps: Esmond Knight, Margaret Lockwood, Henry Mollison. 68M UKN. *Young Nowheres*; *Someday* prod/rel: Warner Bros., First National

That Man's Here Again 1937 d: Louis King. lps: Tom Brown, Mary Maguire, Hugh Herbert. 60M USA. *Love Begins* prod/rel: Warner Bros. Pictures©, First National Picture

Young Nowheres 1929 d: Frank Lloyd. lps: Richard Barthelmess, Marion Nixon, Bert Roach. 70M USA. prod/rel: First National Pictures

WYLIE, PHILIP (1902–1971), USA, Wylie, Philip Gordon
Death Flies East, 1934, Story
Death Flies East 1935 d: Phil Rosen. lps: Conrad Nagel, Florence Rice, Raymond Walburn. 65M USA. *Mistaken Identity* prod/rel: Columbia Pictures Corp.

The Gladiator, New York 1930, Novel
Gladiator, The 1938 d: Edward Sedgwick. lps: Joe E. Brown, Man Mountain Dean, June Travis. 72M USA. prod/rel: David L. Loew Productions©, Columbia Pictures Corp. of California

Murderers Welcome, 1936, Short Story
Under Suspicion 1937 d: Lewis D. Collins. lps: Jack Holt, Katherine de Mille, Luis Alberni. 68M USA. *Murderers Welcome* prod/rel: Larry Darmour Productions, Columbia Pictures Corp. of California©

Night Unto Night, Novel
Night Unto Night 1949 d: Don Siegel. lps: Ronald Reagan, Viveca Lindfors, Osa Massen. 85M USA. prod/rel: Warner Bros.

Paradise Canyon Mystery, 1936, Short Story
Fair Warning 1937 d: Norman Foster. lps: J. Edward Bromberg, Betty Furness, John Howard Payne. 70M USA. *Death in Paradise Canyon*; *Mr. Jericho*; *Without Warning* prod/rel: Twentieth Century-Fox Film Corp.©

Second Honeymoon, Story
Second Honeymoon 1937 d: Walter Lang. lps: Tyrone Power, Loretta Young, Stuart Erwin. 79M USA. prod/rel: Twentieth Century-Fox Film Corp.©

When Worlds Collide, 1950, Novel
When Worlds Collide 1951 d: Rudolph Mate. lps: Richard Derr, Barbara Rush, Larry Keating. 81M USA. prod/rel: Paramount

WYLLARDE, DOLF
An Out Post of Empire Exile, New York 1916, Novel
Exile 1917 d: Maurice Tourneur. lps: Olga Petrova, Wyndham Standing, Mahlon Hamilton. 5r USA. prod/rel: Jesse L. Lasky Feature Play Co.©, Paramount Pictures Corp.

The Holiday Husband, Novel
Holiday Husband, The 1920 d: A. C. Hunter. lps: Harry Welchman, Irma Royce, Adeline Hayden Coffin. 7090f UKN. prod/rel: Alliance Film Corp., Shaftesbury

The Rat Trap, New York 1904, Novel
Wonderful Wife, A 1922 d: Paul Scardon. lps: Miss Du Pont, Vernon Steele, Landers Stevens. 4668f USA. prod/rel: Universal Film Mfg. Co.

WYNDHAM, JOHN (1903–1969), UKN, Harris, John Wyndham Parkes Lucas Beynon
The Day of the Triffids, 1951, Novel
Day of the Triffids, The 1962 d: Steve Sekely, Freddie Francis. lps: Howard Keel, Nicole Maurey, Janette Scott. 94M UKN. prod/rel: Rank Film Distributors, Security

Day of the Triffids, The 1981 d: Ken Hannam. lps: John Duttine, Robert Robinson, Ian Halliburton. TVM. 180M UKN. prod/rel: BBC

The Midwich Cuckoos, 1957, Novel
Children of the Damned 1963 d: Anton M. Leader. lps: Ian Hendry, Alan Badel, Barbara Ferris. 90M UKN. *Horror!* prod/rel: MGM British

Village of the Damned 1960 d: Wolf RillA. lps: George Sanders, Barbara Shelley, Martin Stephens. 77M UKN. prod/rel: MGM British

Village of the Damned 1995 d: John Carpenter. lps: Christopher Reeve, Kirstie Alley, Linda Kozlowski. 98M USA. prod/rel: Universal, Alphaville

Random Quest, 1961, Short Story
Quest for Love 1971 d: Ralph Thomas. lps: Tom Bell, Joan Collins, Denholm Elliott. 91M UKN. prod/rel: Rank, Peter Rogers Productions

WYNGATE, VALERIE
Her Cardboard Lover, New York 1927, Play
Passionate Plumber, The 1932 d: Edward Sedgwick. lps: Buster Keaton, Jimmy Durante, Polly Moran. 73M USA. *The Cardboard Lover* prod/rel: Metro-Goldwyn-Mayer Corp., Metro-Goldwyn-Mayer Dist. Corp.©

Plombier Amoreux, Le 1932 d: Claude Autant-LarA. lps: Buster Keaton, Jimmy Durante, Polly Moran. F USA. prod/rel: Buster Keaton

WYNN, MAY
The Education of Nicky, Novel
Education of Nicky, The 1921 d: Arthur Rooke. lps: James Knight, Marjorie Villis, Constance Worth. 4200f UKN. prod/rel: Harma, Associated Exhibitors

The Little Mother, Novel
Little Mother, The 1922 d: A. V. Bramble. lps: Florence Turner, John Stuart, Lillian Douglas. 5000f UKN. prod/rel: Ideal

WYNNE, BARRY
The Curse of King Tutenkhamen's Tomb, Novel
Curse of King Tutankhamen's Tomb, The 1980 d: Philip Leacock. lps: Raymond Burr, Eva Marie Saint, Wendy Hiller. TVM. 98M UKN/USA. *The Curse of King Tut's Tomb* (USA) prod/rel: Harlech Tv, NBC

WYNNE, GREVILLE
The Man from Moscow, Book
Wynne and Penkovsky 1987 d: Paul Seed. lps: David Calder, Christopher Rozycki, Fiona Walker. MTV. 165M UKN/USA. prod/rel: BBC, Arts Network

WYNNE, MARY
A Run for His Money, Novel
Big Money 1918 d: Harry Lorraine. lps: Rose Manners, James Knight, Charles Rock. 5320f UKN. prod/rel: Harma Photoplays

WYNNE, PAMELA
Ann's an Idiot, London 1923, Novel
Dangerous Innocence 1925 d: William A. Seiter. lps: Laura La Plante, Eugene O'Brien, Jean Hersholt. 6759f USA. prod/rel: Universal Pictures

A Little Flat in the Temple, New York 1930, Novel
Devotion 1931 d: Robert Milton. lps: Ann Harding, Leslie Howard, Douglas Scott. 84M USA. *A Little Flat in the Temple*; *Alias Mrs. Halifax* prod/rel: RKO Pathe Pictures, Inc.

WYSPIANSKI, STANISLAW (1869–1907), PLN
Wesele, 1901, Play
Wesele 1972 d: Andrzej WajdA. lps: Daniel Olbrychski, Ewa Zietek, Andrzej Lapicki. 110M PLN. *The Wedding* (UKN)

WYSS, JOHANN DAVID (1743–1818), SWT
Der Schweizerische Robinson, 1812-27, Novel
Swiss Family Robinson 1940 d: Edward Ludwig. lps: Thomas Mitchell, Edna Best, Freddie Bartholomew. 93M USA. prod/rel: RKO Radio Pictures©, the Play's the Thing Productions

Swiss Family Robinson 1961 d: Ken Annakin. lps: John Mills, Dorothy McGuire, James MacArthur. 126M UKN/USA. prod/rel: Buena Vista, Walt Disney

Swiss Family Robinson 1971 d: Leif Gram. ANM. 47M ASL.

Swiss Family Robinson 1975 d: Harry Harris. lps: Martin Milner, Pat Delany, Cameron Mitchell. TVM. 100M USA. prod/rel: Irwin Allen Productions, 20th Century-Fox

X

XANROF
Souris Blonde, Opera
Blanc Comme Neige 1931 d: Francisco Elias, Camille Lemoine. lps: Moussia, Betty Stockfeld, Roland Toutain. 91M FRN. *La Souris Blonde*; *White As Snow* prod/rel: Orphea-Film

XANROF, LEON
Le Prince Consort, 1919, Play
Love Parade, The 1929 d: Ernst Lubitsch. lps: Maurice Chevalier, Jeanette MacDonald, Lupino Lane. 110M USA. *Parade d'Amour* prod/rel: Paramount Famous Lasky Corp.

XANTIPPE
Death Catches Up With Mr. Kluck, New York 1935, Novel
Danger on the Air 1938 d: Otis Garrett. lps: Donald Woods, Nan Grey, Berton Churchill. 66M USA. prod/rel: Crime Club Productions, Inc.

XIANG KAIRAN
Jiang Hu Qixia Zhuan, Novel
Huoshao Hongliansi (Part 1) 1928 d: Zhang Shichuan. lps: Zheng XIaoqiu, XIa Peizhen, Tan Zhiyuan. 11r CHN. *Burning the Red Lotus Temple (Part 1)* prod/rel: Mingxing Film Company

XIAO YU
Dai Bing de Ren, Play
Dai Bing de Ren 1964 d: Yan Jizhou. lps: Hong Wansheng, Huo Deji, Zhang Hengli. 11r CHN. *Troop Commander* prod/rel: August First Film Studio

XIONG DABA
Fei Dao Hua, Novel
Fei Dao Hua 1963 d: Xu Suling. lps: Li Wei, Wei Heling, Wang Pei. 10r CHN. *Flying Knife Hua* prod/rel: Haiyan Film Studio

XU BAOQI
Er Mo, Novel
Er Mo 1994 d: Zhou XIaowen. lps: Liu Peiqi, Ai Liya, Ge Zhijun. 98M CHN/HKG. *Ermo* prod/rel: Shanghai Film Studio, Dayang Film Corp. Ltd.

XU DISHAN
Chun Tao, 1927, Short Story
Chun Tao 1988 d: Ling Zhifeng. lps: Liu XIaoqing, Jiang Wen, Cao Qianming. 90M CHN. *A Woman for Two* prod/rel: China Nanhai Films Ltd., Liaoning Film Studio

XU YING
Xiangyang de Gushi, Novel
Xiangyang Yuan de Gushi 1974 d: Yuan Naicheng. lps: Pu Ke, Zhang Zhen, Saihan. 10r CHN. *The Story of XIangyang Compound* prod/rel: Changchun Film Studio

XU ZHENYA
Yu Li Hun, Novel
Yu Li Hun 1924 d: Zhang Shichuan, Xu Hu. lps: Wang Hanlun, Wang XIanzhai, Yang Naimei. 10r CHN. *Soul of Jade and Pear*

Y

YA'ARI, YEHUDA
Novel
Mi Klalah le Brachah 1950 d: Joseph Krumgold. lps: Azaria Rappaport, Nahum Buchman, Esther Margalit-Ben Yoseph. F ISR. *Out of Evil* prod/rel: Urim Film Co.

YADAGV, RAJENDRA
Sara Akas, 1960, Novel
Sara Akash 1969 d: Basu Chatterjee. lps: Rakesh Pandey, Madhu Chakravarty, Tarala MehtA. 100M IND. *The Whole Sky*; *The Big Sky* prod/rel: Cine Eye Films

YAFA, STEPHEN H.
Paxton Quigley's Had the Course, Philadelphia 1967, Novel
Three in the Attic 1968 d: Richard Wilson. lps: Yvette Mimieux, Christopher Jones, Judy Pace. 91M USA. *3 in the Attic* prod/rel: American International Productions, Hermes Productions

YALLOP, DAVID
Beyond Reasonable Doubt, Book
Beyond Reasonable Doubt 1980 d: John Laing. lps: David Hemmings, John Hargreaves, Martyn Sanderson. 127M NZL. prod/rel: Endeavour, New Zealand Film Commission

YAMADA, FUTARO
Shinobi No Manji, Short Story
Shinobi No Manji 1968 d: Noribumi Suzuki. lps: Isao Natsuyagi, Hiroko Sakuramachi, Yukiko KuwabarA. 89M JPN. *The Secret of Fylfot*; *Secret of the Ninja* prod/rel: Toei Co.

YAMADA, HUTARO
Makai Tensho, Novel
Makai Tensho 1981 d: Kinji Fukasaku. lps: Shin-Ichi Chiba, Kenji Sawada, Henry SanadA. 122M JPN. *Samurai Reincarnation* prod/rel: Haruki Kadokawa Films, Inc., Toei Co.

Ninja Wars, Novel
Ninja Wars 1982 d: Mitsumasa Saito. lps: Henry Sanada, Shin-Ichi Chiba, Noriku Watanabe. 96M JPN. prod/rel: Haruki Kadokawa Films, Toei Co.

Satomi Hakkenden, Novel
Satomi Hakken Den 1984 d: Kinji Fukasaku. lps: Shin-Ichi Chiba, Etsuko Shiomi, Hiroko Yakushimaru. 135M JPN. *Legend of the Dogs of Satomi*; *Legend of Eight Samurai*; *Legend of the Eight Samurai* prod/rel: Haruki Kadokawa Films, Toei Co.

YAMAMATO, SHUGORO
Fukagawa Anrakutei, Novel
Inochi Bonifuro 1970 d: Masaki Kobayashi. lps: Tatsuya Nakadai, Komaki Kurihara, Kei Sato. 120M JPN. *At the Risk of My Life*; *Inn of Evil* prod/rel: Haiyuza, Toho Co.

YAMAMOTO, SHUGORO
Akahige Shinryotan, Tokyo 1962, Novel
Akahige 1965 d: Akira KurosawA. lps: Toshiro Mifune, Yuzo Kayama, Yoshio TsuchiyA. 185M JPN. *Red Beard* (UKN) prod/rel: Kurosawa Films, Toho Co.

Aobeka Monogatari, Novel
Aobeka Monogatari 1962 d: Yuzo KawashimA. lps: Hisaya Morishige, Eijiro Tono, Sachiko Hidari. 101M JPN. *This Madding Crowd* (USA) prod/rel: Tokyo Eiga Co.

Goben No Tsubaki, Tokyo 1959, Novel
Goben No Tsubaki 1964 d: Yoshitaro NomurA. lps: Shima Iwashita, Yoshi Kato, Sachiko Hidari. 163M JPN. *The Scarlet Camellia* (USA) prod/rel: Shochiku Co.

Torideyama Non Jushichinichi, Tokyo 1964, Short Story
Kiru 1968 d: Kihachi Okamoto. lps: Tatsuya Nakadai, Etsushi Takahashi, Shigeru KoyamA. 115M JPN. *Kill!* prod/rel: Toho Co.

The Town Without Seasons, Novel
Dodeska Den 1970 d: Akira KurosawA. lps: Yoshitaka Zushi, Tomoko Yamazaki, Hiroshi AkutagawA. 244M JPN. *Sounds of Street Cars*; *Dodesukaden* prod/rel: Yonki No Kai, Toho Co.

Tsubaki Sanjuro, Novel
Tsubaki Sanjuro 1962 d: Akira KurosawA. lps: Toshiro Mifune, Tatsuya Nakadai, Masao Shimizu. 96M JPN. *Sanjuro* (USA) prod/rel: Toho Co., Kurosawa Films

YAMANOUCHI, YUKIO
Novel
Onibi 1997 d: Rokuro Mochizuki. lps: Yoshio Harada, Reiko Kataoka, Sho AikawA. 101M JPN. *Onibi: the Fire Within* prod/rel: Gaga Prods. (Tokyo)

YAMAZAKI, FUMIO
Byoin de Shinu to Iu Koto, Book
Byoin de Shinu to Iu Koto 1993 d: Jun IchikawA. lps: Ittoku Kishibe, Masayuki Shinoya, Akira Yamanouchi. 100M JPN. *Dying at a Hospital* prod/rel: Opt Communications, Inc.

YAMAZAKI, TOYOKO
Bonchi, Novel
Bonchi 1960 d: Kon IchikawA. lps: Raizo Ichikawa, Ayako Wakao, Mitsuko Kusakabe. 104M JPN. *Young Lord*; *The Son* prod/rel: Daiei Motion Picture Co.

YAN GELING
Tian Yu, Novel
Xiu XIu: the Sent-Down Girl 1998 d: Joan Chen. lps: Lu Lu, Lopsang, Qian Zheng. 99M USA. *Tian Yu* prod/rel: Whispering Steppes L.P.

YANAGAWA SHUNYO
Nasanu Naka, 1912-13, Novel
Nasanu Naka 1932 d: Mikio Naruse. 105M JPN. *Not Blood Relations*; *Stepchild*

YANEZ, LEONEL
Play
Martir, La 1921 d: Francesc Xandri. lps: Remei Vilallonga, Federico Llobet, Concha Peris. 1200m SPN. prod/rel: Roxan Film (Barcelona)

YANG RUNSHEN
People Whose Hearts Link With Hearts, Novel
Xin Lian XIn 1958 d: Wu Tian. lps: Huang Zong, Shi Kefu, Lu Xun. 10r CHN. *Hearts Link With Hearts* prod/rel: Changchun Film Studio

YANG XIAO
Hong Yu, Novel
Hong Yu 1975 d: Cui Wei. lps: Zen XIushan, Wun Gang, Chen Guoxi. 12r CHN. *Crimson Rain* prod/rel: Beijing Film Studio

YANG YIYAN
Red Rock, Novel
Lie Huozhong Yongsheng 1965 d: Shui HuA. lps: Zhao Dan, Yu Lan, Li Jian. 15r CHN. *Living Forever in Burning Flames*; *Red Crag* prod/rel: Beijing Film Studio

YARD, LESTER
The Shanghai Story, Novel
Shanghai Story, The 1954 d: Frank Lloyd. lps: Edmond O'Brien, Ruth Roman, Richard Jaeckel. 90M USA. prod/rel: Republic

YARDLEY, MAJOR HERBERT O.
The American Black Chamber, Book
Pacific Rendezvous 1942 d: George Sidney. lps: Jean Rogers, Lee Bowman, Carl Esmond. 76M USA. *Secret Operator* prod/rel: MGM
Rendezvous 1935 d: William K. Howard. lps: William Powell, Rosalind Russell, Binnie Barnes. 96M USA. *The Black Chamber*; *Blonde Countess*; *White Bird*; *Puzzle Man* prod/rel: Metro-Goldwyn-Mayer Corp.©

YASUOKA, SHOTARO
Ah Jonan, Novel
Ah Jonan 1960 d: Toshio Sugie. lps: Frankie Sakai, Hajime Hana, Yoshie Mizutani. 87M JPN. *Weaker Sex* (USA) prod/rel: Toho Co.

YATES, DORNFORD (1880-1960), UKN, Mercer, Cecil William
She Fell Among Thieves, Novel
She Fell Among Thieves 1978 d: Clive Donner. lps: Malcolm McDowell, Eileen Atkins, Michael Jayston. TVM. 80M UKN. prod/rel: BBC

YATES, EDMUND (1831-1894), UKN, Yates, Edmund Hodgson
The Black Sheep, Novel
Black Sheep, The 1915 d: J. Farrell MacDonald. lps: Edward Cecil, Hector V. Sarno, Osmond Nye. 2r USA. prod/rel: Biograph Co.

YATES, ELIZABETH
Skeezer - Dog With a Mission, Novel
Skeezer 1982 d: Peter H. Hunt. lps: Karen Valentine, Dee Wallace Stone, Tom Atkins. TVM. 100M USA.

YE ZI
Star, Novel
Yi Ge Nu Ren de Ming Yun 1984 d: Yuan Ye, Zhang Jinbiao. lps: Yin XIn, Gao Weimin, Wang Bozhao. 10r CHN. *A Woman's Destiny* prod/rel: XIaoxiang Film Studio

YEATS, WILLIAM BUTLER (1865-1939), IRL
The Only Jealousy of Emer, 1919, Play
Only Jealousy of Emer, The 1980 d: John McCormick, Alan Stamford. 26M IRL.

YEATS-BROWN, FRANCIS (1886-1944), UKN
The Lives of a Bengal Lancer, New York 1936, Novel
Lives of a Bengal Lancer, The 1935 d: Henry Hathaway. lps: Gary Cooper, Franchot Tone, Richard Cromwell. 110M USA. *More Lives of a Bengal Lancer* prod/rel: Paramount Productions©

YEDAIDE, OSCAR
Short Story
Revelacion, La 1997 d: Mario David. lps: Daniel Kuzniecka, Maria Valenzuela, Emilia Mazer. F ARG. *The Revelation* prod/rel: Rosebud

YEHOSHUA, A. B.
Novel
Hame'ahev 1985 d: Michal Bat-Adam. lps: Michal Bat-Adam, Roberto Pollack, Yehoram Gaon. 87M ISR. *The Lover*

YELLEN, SHERMAN
Story
Early Frost, An 1985 d: John Erman. lps: Gena Rowlands, Sylvia Sidney, Aidan Quinn. TVM. 100M USA. prod/rel: NBC

YERBY, FRANK (1916-1991), USA, Yerby, Frank Garvin
The Foxes of Harrow, 1946, Novel
Foxes of Harrow, The 1947 d: John M. Stahl. lps: Rex Harrison, Maureen O'Hara, Richard Haydn. 119M USA. prod/rel: 20th Century-Fox
The Golden Hawk, 1948, Novel
Golden Hawk, The 1952 d: Sidney Salkow. lps: Sterling Hayden, Rhonda Fleming, Helena Carter. 83M USA. prod/rel: Columbia
The Saracen Blade, 1952, Novel
Saracen Blade, The 1954 d: William Castle. lps: Ricardo Montalban, Betta St. John, Rick Jason. 76M USA. prod/rel: Columbia

YERKOW, CHARLES
Island Freighter, Short Story
Sea Tiger, The 1952 d: Frank McDonald. lps: Marguerite Chapman, John Archer, Harry Lauter. 71M USA. prod/rel: Monogram

YEZIERSKA, ANZIA (1880?-1970), RSS
Hungry Hearts, Boston 1920, Novel
Hungry Hearts 1922 d: E. Mason Hopper. lps: Bryant Washburn, Helen Ferguson, E. Alyn Warren. 6540f USA. prod/rel: Goldwyn Pictures
Salome of the Tenements, New York 1923, Novel
Salome of the Tenements 1925 d: Sidney Olcott. lps: Jetta Goudal, Godfrey Tearle, Jose Ruben. 7017f USA. prod/rel: Famous Players-Lasky, Paramount Pictures

YISRAELI, SHIMON
Story
Hamartef 1963 d: Natan Gross. lps: Shimon Yisraeli, Hannah Kahane, David Semadar. F ISR. *The Cellar*

YOKOMIZO, SEISHI
Inugamike No Ichizoku, Novel
Inugami-Ke No Ichizoku 1976 d: Kon IchikawA. lps: Mieko Takamine, Koji Ishizaka, Teruhiko Aoi. 146M JPN. *The Inugami Family* prod/rel: Haruki Kadokawa Films

YOLEN, JANE
The Devil's Arithmetic, Novel
Devil's Arithmetic, The 1999 d: Donna Deitch. lps: Karen Dunst, Brittany Murphy, Paul Freeman. TVM. 120M USA. prod/rel: Punch 21 Prods., Millbrook Farm Prods.

YORDAN, PHILIP (1913-, USA
Story
Street of Sinners 1957 d: William Berke. lps: George Montgomery, Geraldine Brooks, Nehemiah Persoff. 76M USA. prod/rel: United Artists, Security Pictures
Anna Lucasta, 1944, Play
Anna Lucasta 1949 d: Irving Rapper. lps: William Bishop, Paulette Goddard, Oscar HomolkA. 86M USA. prod/rel: Columbia, Security
Anna Lucasta 1958 d: Arnold Laven. lps: Eartha Kitt, Sammy Davis Jr., Frederick O'Neal. 97M USA. prod/rel: United Artists, Longridge
Man of the West, 1955, Novel
Gun Glory 1957 d: Roy Rowland. lps: Stewart Granger, Rhonda Fleming, Chill Wills. 89M USA. prod/rel: MGM

YORGASON, BLAINE M.
A Promise Made, Novel
Thanksgiving Promise, The 1986 d: Beau Bridges. lps: Beau Bridges, Lloyd Bridges, Jordan Bridges. TVM. 100M USA. *A Promise Made* prod/rel: Mark H. Ovitz Productions, Walt Disney Tv
Windwalker, Novel
Windwalker 1980 d: Kieth Merrill. lps: Trevor Howard, Nick Ramus, James Remar. 108M USA. prod/rel: Pacific International

YORGASON, BRENTON
A Promise Made, Novel
Thanksgiving Promise, The 1986 d: Beau Bridges. lps: Beau Bridges, Lloyd Bridges, Jordan Bridges. TVM. 100M USA. *A Promise Made* prod/rel: Mark H. Ovitz Productions, Walt Disney Tv

YORK, ANDREW
The Eliminator, London 1966, Novel
Danger Route 1967 d: Seth Holt. lps: Richard Johnson, Carol Lynley, Barbara Bouchet. 92M UKN. *The Eliminator* prod/rel: United Artists, Amicus

YORK, SUSANNAH
The Widow, Novel
Vedova X, La 1956 d: Lewis Milestone. lps: Patricia Roc, Massimo Serato, Akim Tamiroff. 89M ITL/FRN. *The Widow* (USA); *La Veuve* prod/rel: Prod. Venturini, Express

YOSHIKAWA, EIJI
Miyamoto Musashi, 1937-39, Novel
Miyamoto Musashi 1954 d: Hiroshi Inagaki. lps: Toshiro Mifune, Rentaro Mikuni, Karuo YashigusA. 92M JPN. *The Legend of Musashi*; *Samurai* (USA); *The Master Swordsman* prod/rel: Toho Co.
Miyamoto Musashi: Ichijoji No Ketto 1955 d: Hiroshi Inagaki. lps: Toshiro Mifune, Koji Tsuruta, Sachio Sakai. 104M JPN. *Samurai (Part Ii)*; *Ichijoji No Ketto*; *Samurai Ii: Duel at Ichijoji Temple* prod/rel: Toho Co.
Miyamoto Musashi: Ketto Ganryujima 1956 d: Hiroshi Inagaki. lps: Toshiro Mifune, Koji Tsuruta, Sachio Sakai. 105M JPN. *Samurai (Part III)*; *Musashi and Kojiro*; *Samurai III: Duel on Ganryu Island*; *Ketto Ganryujima* prod/rel: Toho Co.
Shin Heike Monogatari, Novel
Shin Heike Monogatari 1955 d: Kenji Mizoguchi. lps: Raizo Ichikawa, Yoshiko Kuga, Naritoshi Hayashi. 108M JPN. *New Tales of the Taira Clan* (UKN); *The Taira Clan* (USA); *The Sacrilegious Hero*; *Tales of the Taira Clan*; *Shin-Heike Monogatari* prod/rel: Daiei Motion Picture Co.

YOSHIMOTO, BANANA
Kitchen, Novel
Wo Ai Chufang 1997 d: Yim Ho. lps: Jordan Chan, Yasuko Tomita, Law Kar-Ying. 126M HKG/JPN. *Kitchen*; *Ngo Oi Chuifong* prod/rel: Golden Harvest (H.K.), Amuse Inc. (Japan)©

YOSHIMURA, AKIRA
Yami Ni Hirameku, Story
  Unagi 1997 d: Shohei ImamurA. lps: Koji Yakusho, Misa Shimizu, Fujio TsunetA. 117M JPN. *The Eel* prod/rel: Kss Films©, Eisei Gekijo Co.©

YOST, DOROTHY
The Untamed Heart, Story
  Hills of Kentucky 1927 d: Howard Bretherton. lps: Rin-Tin-Tin, Jason Robards, Dorothy Dwan. 6271f USA. prod/rel: Warner Brothers Pictures

YOST, TIBOR
Cuba Cabana, Short Story
  Cuba Cabana 1952 d: Fritz Peter Buch. lps: Zarah Leander, Paul Hartmann, O. W. Fischer. 90M GRM. prod/rel: Rhombus, UFA

YOUNG, CHARLES LAWRENCE
Jim the Penman, New York 1886, Play
  Jim the Penman 1921 d: Kenneth Webb. lps: Lionel Barrymore, Doris Rankin, Anders Randolf. 6100f USA. prod/rel: Whitman Bennett Productions, Associated First National Pictures

YOUNG, CLARENCE UPSON
Gun Shy, Short Story
  Gunfight in Abilene 1967 d: William Hale. lps: Bobby Darin, Emily Banks, Leslie Nielsen. 86M USA. *Gunfight at Abilene* prod/rel: Universal Pictures
  Showdown at Abilene 1956 d: Charles Haas. lps: Jock Mahoney, Martha Hyer, Lyle Bettger. 80M USA. prod/rel: Universal-International

YOUNG, COLLIER
Story
  Act of Violence 1948 d: Fred Zinnemann. lps: Van Heflin, Robert Ryan, Janet Leigh. 82M USA. prod/rel: MGM
  Ironside 1967 d: James Goldstone. lps: Raymond Burr, Geraldine Brooks, Wally Cox. TVM. 100M USA. prod/rel: Universal

YOUNG, DESMOND
Rommel - the Desert Fox, 1950, Biography
  Desert Fox, The 1951 d: Henry Hathaway. lps: James Mason, Leo G. Carroll, Cedric Hardwicke. 91M USA. *Rommel - Desert Fox* (UKN) prod/rel: 20th Century-Fox

YOUNG, F. E. MILLS
The Bigamist, Novel
  Bigamist, The 1921 d: Guy Newall. lps: Guy Newall, Ivy Duke, Julian Royce. 10r UKN. prod/rel: George Clark, Stoll
Myles Calthrope I.D.B., London 1913, Novel
  Thou Art the Man 1920 d: Thomas N. Heffron. lps: Robert Warwick, Lois Wilson, J. M. Dumont. 5r USA. prod/rel: Famous Players-Lasky Corp.©

YOUNG, FRANCIS BRETT (1884–1954), UKN
A Man About the House, Novel
  Man About the House, A 1947 d: Leslie Arliss. lps: Margaret Johnston, Dulcie Gray, Kieron Moore. 99M UKN. prod/rel: British Lion, British Lion Production Assets
My Brother Jonathan, Novel
  My Brother Jonathan 1948 d: Harold French. lps: Michael Denison, Dulcie Gray, Ronald Howard. 107M UKN. *Brother Jonathan* prod/rel: Associated British Picture Corporation, Pathe
Portrait of Clare, Novel
  Portrait of Clare 1950 d: Lance Comfort. lps: Margaret Johnston, Richard Todd, Robin Bailey. 98M UKN. prod/rel: Associated British Picture Corporation, Ab-Pathe
Sea Horses, London 1925, Novel
  Sea Horses 1926 d: Allan Dwan. lps: Jack Holt, Florence Vidor, William Powell. 6565f USA. prod/rel: Famous Players-Lasky, Paramount Pictures

YOUNG, GORDON
Captain Calamity, Short Story
  Capitan Tormenta, El 1936 d: John Reinhardt. lps: Lupita Tovar, Fortunio Bonanova, Juan TorenA. 75M USA. prod/rel: Regal Productions, Inc.
  Captain Calamity 1936 d: John Reinhardt. lps: George Houston, Marian Nixon, Vince Barnett. 66M USA. *Captain Hurricane* prod/rel: Regal Productions, Inc.
Hurricane Williams, Novel
  Hurricane Smith 1952 d: Jerry Hopper. lps: Yvonne de Carlo, John Ireland, James Craig. 90M USA. prod/rel: Paramount
Quarter Horse, Novel
  Born to the Saddle 1953 d: William Beaudine. lps: Chuck Courtney, Donald Woods, Leif Erickson. 73M USA. prod/rel: Astor

YOUNG, HOWARD IRVING
Play
  Magie Moderne 1931 d: Dimitri Buchowetzki. lps: Lucien Galas, Fanny Clair, Madeleine Guitty. 65M FRN. *Television* prod/rel: Films Paramount
  Televisione 1931 d: Charles de Rochefort. lps: Anna Maria Dossena, Silvio Orsini, Nino Eller. 66M FRN. *La Canzone Del Mondo* prod/rel: Paramount
Hawk Island, New York 1929, Play
  Midnight Mystery 1930 d: George B. Seitz. lps: Betty Compson, Hugh Trevor, Lowell Sherman. 69M USA. *Hawk Island* prod/rel: RKO Productions
Not Herbert, New York 1926, Play
  Perfect Sap, The 1927 d: Howard Higgin. lps: Ben Lyon, Virginia Lee Corbin, Lloyd Whitlock. 5981f USA. prod/rel: Ray Rockett Productions, First National Pictures
Television, Play
  Svet Bez Hranic 1931 d: Julius Lebl. lps: Theodor Pistek, Mana Zeniskova, Marie PtakovA. 1705m CZC. *World Without Frontiers* prod/rel: Paramount

YOUNG, JAMES R.
Behind the Rising Sun, Novel
  Behind the Rising Sun 1943 d: Edward Dmytryk. lps: Margo, Tom Neal, J. Carrol Naish. 89M USA. prod/rel: RKO Radio

YOUNG, KENDAL
Assault, Novel
  Assault 1971 d: Sidney Hayers. lps: Frank Finlay, Suzy Kendall, James Laurenson. 91M UKN. *In the Devil's Garden* (USA); *Tower of Terror*; *The Creepers* prod/rel: Rank, Peter Rogers

YOUNG, MIRIAM
Mother Wore Tights, Novel
  Mother Wore Tights 1947 d: Walter Lang. lps: Betty Grable, Dan Dailey, Mona Freeman. 107M USA. prod/rel: 20th Century-Fox

YOUNG, RIDA JOHNSON
Play
  Marriage Bond, The 1916 d: Lawrence Marston. lps: Nat C. Goodwin, Margaret Greene, P. J. Rollow. 5r USA. prod/rel: Mirror Films, Inc., State Rights
Brown of Harvard, New York 1906, Play
  Brown of Harvard 1911 d: Colin Campbell. lps: Hobart Bosworth, Bessie Eyton, Kempton Greene. 1000f USA. prod/rel: Selig Polyscope Co.
  Brown of Harvard 1918 d: Harry Beaumont. lps: Tom Moore, Hazel Daly, Warner Richmond. 6r USA. *Brown of Harvard* prod/rel: Selig Polyscope Co.©, Perfection Pictures
  Brown of Harvard 1926 d: Jack Conway. lps: Jack Pickford, Mary Brian, Francis X. Bushman Jr. 7941f USA. prod/rel: Metro-Goldwyn-Mayer Pictures
Captain Kidd Junior, New York 1916, Play
  Captain Kidd, Jr. 1919 d: William D. Taylor. lps: Mary Pickford, Douglas MacLean, Spottiswoode Aitken. 5r USA. prod/rel: Pickford Film Corp.©, Famous Players-Lasky Corp.
Glorious Betsy, New York 1908, Play
  Glorious Betsy 1928 d: Alan Crosland. lps: Dolores Costello, Conrad Nagel, John Miljan. 7091f USA. prod/rel: Warner Brothers Pictures
  Hearts Divided 1936 d: Frank Borzage. lps: Marion Davies, Dick Powell, Charles Ruggles. 87M USA. prod/rel: First National Productions Corp., Frank Borzage Production
Little Old New York, New York 1920, Play
  Little Old New York 1923 d: Sidney Olcott. lps: Marion Davies, Stephen Carr, J. M. Kerrigan. 11r USA. prod/rel: Cosmopolitan Pictures, Goldwyn-Cosmopolitan Distributing Corp.
  Little Old New York 1940 d: Henry King. lps: Alice Faye, Fred MacMurray, Richard Greene. 100M USA. *In Old New York* prod/rel: 20th Century-Fox Film Corp.©
The Lottery Man, New York 1909, Play
  Lottery Man, The 1916. lps: Thurlow Bergen, Caroline Lee, Elsie Esmond. 5r USA. prod/rel: F. Ray Comstock Photoplay Co., Unity Sales Corp.
  Lottery Man, The 1919 d: James Cruze. lps: Wallace Reid, Wanda Hawley, Harrison Ford. 4404f USA. prod/rel: Famous Players-Lasky Corp.©, Paramount-Artcraft Pictures
Maytime, New York 1917, Play
  Maytime 1923 d: Louis J. Gasnier. lps: Ethel Shannon, Harrison Ford, William Norris. 7500f USA. prod/rel: B. P. Schulberg Productions, Preferred Pictures
  Maytime 1937 d: Robert Z. Leonard. lps: Jeanette MacDonald, Nelson Eddy, John Barrymore. 132M USA. prod/rel: Metro-Goldwyn-Mayer Corp.©

Naughty Marietta, London 1910, Operetta
  Naughty Marietta 1935 d: W. S. Van Dyke. lps: Jeanette MacDonald, Nelson Eddy, Frank Morgan. 106M USA. prod/rel: Metro-Goldwyn-Mayer Corp.©
Out of the Night, New York 1925, Novel
  Hell Harbor 1930 d: Henry King. lps: Lupe Velez, Jean Hersholt, John Holland. 8354f USA. prod/rel: Inspiration Pictures, United Artists
The Story of Mother MacHree, 1924, Short Story
  Mother MacHree 1928 d: John Ford. lps: Belle Bennett, Neil Hamilton, Philippe de Lacy. 6807f USA. prod/rel: Fox Film Corp.
The Woman Who Did Not Care, Story
  Woman Who Did Not Care, The 1927 d: Phil Rosen. lps: Lilyan Tashman, Edward Martindel, Arthur Rankin. 5996f USA. prod/rel: Gotham Productions, Lumas Film Corp.

YOUNG, SIR CHARLES L.
Jim the Penman, New York 1886, Play
  Jim the Penman 1915 d: Hugh Ford, Edwin S. Porter. lps: John Mason, Russell Bassett, Harold Lockwood. 5r USA. prod/rel: Famous Players Film Co., Paramount Pictures Corp.

YOUNG, SIR WILLIAM
A Japanese Nightingale, New York 1903, Novel
  Japanese Nightingale, A 1918 d: George Fitzmaurice. lps: Fannie Ward, William E. Lawrence, Yukio AoyamA. 5r USA. prod/rel: Astra Film Corp., Pathe Exchange, Inc.©

YOUNG, STARK
So Red the Rose, New York 1934, Novel
  So Red the Rose 1935 d: King Vidor. lps: Margaret Sullavan, Walter Connolly, Randolph Scott. 91M USA. prod/rel: Paramount Productions©

YOUNG, WALDEMAR
Sky High, Short Story
  Flirting With Death 1917 d: Elmer Clifton. lps: Agnes Vernon, Herbert Rawlinson, Frank MacQuarrie. 5r USA. prod/rel: Bluebird Photoplays, Inc.©

YOUNGER, A. P.
Cyclone Hickey, Story
  Swellhead, The 1930 d: James Flood. lps: James Gleason, Johnny Walker, Marion Shilling. 7040f USA. *Counted Out* (UKN) prod/rel: Tiffany Productions

YOURCENAR, MARGUERITE (1903–1987), BLG, De Crayencour, Marguerite
Le Coup de Grace, 1939, Novel
  Fangschuss, Der 1976 d: Volker Schlondorff. lps: Margarethe von Trotta, Matthias Habich, Rudiger Kirschstein. 96M GRM/FRN. *Coup de Grace* prod/rel: Bioskop, Argos

YOUSSOUPOV, PRINCE
Avant l'Exil, Book
  J'ai Tue Raspoutine 1967 d: Robert Hossein. lps: Gert Frobe, Peter McEnery, Robert Hossein. 100M FRN/ITL. *Addio Lara!* (ITL); *I Killed Rasputin* (UKN); *Rasputin* (USA); *Thunder Over St. Petersburg*; *Tonnerre Sur Saint-Petersburg* prod/rel: Films Copernic, Compagnia Generale Cin.Ca

YOVKOV, YORDAN
Chastniyat Uchitel, 1922, Short Story
  24 Chassa Duzhd 1983 d: Vladislav Ikonomov. lps: Stefan Mavrodiev, Stefan Danailov, Eva CzikulskA. 86M BUL. *Dwadeset I Tchetiri Tchasa Dyshd*; *24 Hours of Rain*
Chiflikat Kray Granitsata, 1933-34, Novel
  Nona 1973 d: Grisha Ostrovski. lps: Dorothea Toncheva, Stefan Danailov, Todor Todorov. 84M BUL. *The Farm on the Frontier*
Shibil, 1925, Short Story
  Shibil 1967 d: Zahari Zhandov. lps: Peter Slabakov, Dorothea Toncheva, Ivan Bratanov. 90M BUL. *Sibil*

YU HUA
Lifetimes, Novel
  Huozhe 1994 d: Zhang Yimou. lps: Gong Li, Ge You, Niu Beng. 125M CHN/HKG. *To Live* prod/rel: Shanghai Film Studio, Era International (H.K.)

YUAN CH'IUNG-CH'IUNG
Wanren Qingfu, Novel
  Wanren Qingfu 1996 d: T'ao Shu-HuA. lps: Joan Chen, Sihung Lung, Tony Leung Kar-Wai. F TWN. *Everyone's Lover*

YUAN JING
Xin Er Nu Ying Xlong Zhuan, Novel
  Xin Er Nu Ying Xlong Zhuan 1951 d: Shi Dongshan, Lu Ban. lps: Jin Xlng, Yao Xiangli, Yan Zhenhe. 14r CHN. *New Heroes and Heroines* prod/rel: Beijing Film Studio

YUKI, SHIGEKO
Yoru No Hada, Novel
Yoru No Hada 1960 d: Yuzo KawashimA. lps: Chikage Awashima, Michiyo Aratama, Tomoko Kawaguchi. 110M JPN. *Soft Touch of Night* (USA) prod/rel: Tokyo Eiga Co., Toho Co.

YUMENO, KYUSAKU
Novel
Yume No Ginga 1997 d: Sogo Ishii. lps: Rena Komine, Tadanobu Asano, Kotomi Kyono. 90M JPN. *Labyrinth of Dreams* prod/rel: Kss Films

YURICK, SOL
The Warriors, Novel
Warriors, The 1979 d: Walter Hill. lps: Michael Beck, James Memar, Thomas G. Waites. 90M USA. prod/rel: Paramount

YUSUF, T. MOHAMMED
Kandam Bacha Coat, Novel
Kandam Bacha Coat 1961 d: T. R. Sundaram. lps: T. S. Muthaiah, Thikkurisi Sukumaran Nair, Prem Nawaz. 156M IND. *Patched Coat; Kandam Becha Kottu; The Patched-Up Coat* prod/rel: Modern Theatres

YVAIN, MAURICE
Pas Sur la Bouche, Opera
Pas Sur la Bouche 1931 d: Nicolas Rimsky, Nicolas Evreinoff. lps: Mireille Perrey, Jeanne Marny, Nicolas Rimsky. 80M FRN. prod/rel: Luna Film

Yes, Opera
Defense d'Aimer 1942 d: Richard Pottier. lps: Paul Meurisse, Suzy Delair, Andre Gabriello. 90M FRN. *Le Coeur Sur la Main; Totte Et Sa Chance* prod/rel: Continental-Film

Z

ZACHA SR., WILLIAM
The Capricorn Man, Novel
Ultimate Impostor, The 1979 d: Paul Stanley. lps: Joseph Hacker, Keith Andes, Erin Gray. TVM. 97M USA. *The Ultimate Imposter* prod/rel: Universal

ZACHARIAS
Il Re Dei Mimiduti, Novel
Ettore Lo Fusto 1972 d: Enzo G. Castellari, Pasquale Festa Campanile. lps: Vittorio Caprioli, Vittorio de Sica, Michael Forest. 109M ITL/FRN/SPN. *El Rapto de Elena la Decente Italiana* (SPN); *Hector le Fortiche; Hector the Mighty; The Proxenetes; Humungus Hector* prod/rel: Empire Films (Roma), Labrador Film

ZAGON, STEFAN
Marili, Play
Marili 1959 d: Josef von Baky. lps: Sabine Sinjen, Paul Hubschmid, Hanne Wieder. 95M GRM. prod/rel: C.C.C., Gloria

ZAHAVI, HELEN
Dirty Weekend, Novel
Dirty Weekend 1992 d: Michael Winner. lps: Lia Williams, Rufus Sewell, Michael Cule. 103M UKN. prod/rel: Uip, Scimitar

ZAHN, ERNST
Frau Sixta, Play
Frau Sixta 1938 d: Gustav Ucicky. lps: Ilse Werner, Franziska Kinz, Gustav Frohlich. 100M GRM. prod/rel: UFA, Unitas

Pietro Der Schmuggler, Berlin 1930, Novel
Fille Au Fouet, La 1952 d: Jean Dreville, Rene Le Henaff (Uncredited). lps: Michel Simon, Gaby Morlay, Michel Barbey. 82M FRN. *Eternel Mensonge* prod/rel: Monopole Films (Paris), Aidal-Beaujon-Films (Zurich)

Geheimnis Vom Bergsee, Das 1951 d: Jean Dreville, Rene Le Henaff (Uncredited). lps: Lil Dagover, Harriet Gessner, Howard Vernon. 84M SWT/FRN/GRM. *Die Jungfrau Mit Der Peitsche; Das Madchen Mit Der Peitsche; Die Ewige Luge; Pietro Angelina* prod/rel: Aidal-Beaujon-Film (Zurich), Les Films Monopole (Paris)

Der Schatten, 1904, Short Story
Violanta 1942 d: Paul May. lps: Anneliese Reinhold, Richard Haussler, Hans Schlenck. 100M GRM. prod/rel: UFA

Violantha 1927 d: Carl Froelich. lps: Henny Porten, Wilhelm Dieterle, Alexander SaschA. 2319m GRM/SWT. *Der Schatten* prod/rel: Henny Porten-Froelich Filmproduktion, Monopol-Films

Verena Stadler, Wiesbaden 1906, Short Story
Verena Stadler 1940 d: Hermann Haller. lps: Ellen Widmann, Robert Wyss, Marianne Kober. 96M SWT.

ZAHRADNIK-BRODSKY, BOHUMIL
Carovne Oci, Novel
Carovne Oci 1923 d: Vaclav Kubasek. lps: Frantisek Havel, Theodor Pistek, Eduard Maly. 1750m CZC. *Bewitching Eyes* prod/rel: Pronax-Film, Iris-Film

Devce Z Hor, Novel
Devce Z Hor 1924 d: Vaclav Kubasek. lps: Mary Jansova, Jan W. Speerger, Gitta d'Amaro. 1886m CZC. *Girl from the Mountains* prod/rel: Pronax-Film

Dum Ztraceneho Stesti, Novel
Dum Ztraceneho Stesti 1927 d: Josef Rovensky. lps: Jan W. Speerger, Suzanne Marwille, Josef Rovensky. 2417m CZC. *The House of Lost Happiness* prod/rel: Bratri Deglove

Zivotem Vedla Je Laska, Novel
Zivotem Vedla Je Laska 1928 d: Josef Rovensky. lps: Suzanne Marwille, Jan W. Speerger, Robert Ford. 2066m CZC. *Love Lead Them Through Life; Love Led Them Through Life* prod/rel: Bratri Deglove, Degl a Spol

ZAK, JAROSLAV
Cesta Do Hlubin Studakovy Duse, Novel
Cesta Do Hublin Studakovy Duse 1939 d: Martin Fric. lps: Jindrich Plachta, Jaroslav Prucha, Jaroslav Marvan. 2485m CZC. *Searching the Hearts of Students; A Journey to the Depths of a Schoolboy's Soul; Journey Into the Depth of the Student's Soul* prod/rel: Elekta

Skola Zaklad Zivota, Book
Skola Zaklad Zivota 1938 d: Martin Fric. lps: Theodor Pistek, Marta Majova, Frantisek Kreuzmann. 2573m CZC. *School -the Beginning of Life; School Where Life Begins; School -the Basis of Life; School Is the Foundation of Life* prod/rel: UFA

ZAMBALDI, SILVIO
La Moglie Del Dottore, 1908, Play
Intrusa, L' 1955 d: Raffaello Matarazzo. lps: Lea Padovani, Amedeo Nazzari, Rina Morelli. 100M ITL. prod/rel: Jolly Film, Diana Cin.Ca

Moglie Del Dottore, La 1916 d: Giovanni Zannini. lps: Giulietta de Riso, Lina Pellegrini, Franz SalA. 1305m ITL. prod/rel: Zannini Film

ZAMFIRESCU, DUILIU
Tanase Scatiu, 1885-86, Novel
Tanase Scatiu 1976 d: Dan PitA. lps: Victor Rebengiuc, Eliza Petrachescu, Vasile Nitulescu. 115M RMN. *A Summer Tale* prod/rel: Romania Film

ZAMFIRESCU, GEORGE MIHAIL
Domnisoara Nastasia, 1928, Play
Dincolo de Bariera 1965 d: Francisc Munteanu. lps: Ion Dichiseanu, Silviu Stanculescu. 85M RMN.

ZAMLOCH, A. F.
The Magician Fisherman, Story
Magician Fisherman, The 1913 d: Charles H. France. SHT USA. prod/rel: Selig Polyscope Co.

ZANGWILL, ISRAEL
The Bachelors' Club, 1891, Novel
Bachelors' Club, The 1921 d: A. V. Bramble. lps: Ben Field, Ernest Thesiger, Mary Brough. 5500f UKN. prod/rel: Ideal

The Big Bow Mystery, London 1892, Novel
Crime Doctor 1934 d: John S. Robertson. lps: Otto Kruger, Karen Morley, Nils Asther. 75M USA. prod/rel: RKO Radio Picture, Inc.

Perfect Crime, The 1928 d: Bert Glennon. lps: Clive Brook, Irene Rich, Ethel Wales. 6331f USA. prod/rel: Fbo Pictures

Verdict, The 1946 d: Don Siegel. lps: Sydney Greenstreet, Peter Lorre, Joan Lorring. 86M USA. prod/rel: Warner Bros.

The Children of the Ghetto; a Study of Peculiar People, London 1892, Novel
Children of the Ghetto 1915 d: Frank Powell. lps: Wilton Lackaye, Ethel Kaufman, Ruby Hoffman. 5r USA. prod/rel: Box Office Attraction Co., Fox Film Corp.

The Melting Pot, London 1908, Novel
Melting Pot, The 1915 d: James Vincent, Oliver D. Bailey. lps: Walker Whiteside, Valentine Grant, Fletcher Harvey. 5-6r USA. prod/rel: Cort Film Corp., State Rights

Merely Mary Ann, London 1893, Novel
Merely Mary Ann 1916 d: John G. Adolfi. lps: Vivian Martin, Sidney Bracey, Harry Hilliard. 5r USA. prod/rel: Fox Film Corp., William Fox©

Merely Mary Ann 1920 d: Edward J. Le Saint. lps: Shirley Mason, Casson Ferguson, Harry Spingler. 4555f USA. prod/rel: Fox Film Corp., William Fox©

Merely Mary Ann 1931 d: Henry King. lps: Janet Gaynor, Charles Farrell, Beryl Mercer. 75M USA. prod/rel: Fox Film Corp.©

The Moment of Death, New York 1900, Play
Moment Before, The 1916 d: Robert G. VignolA. lps: Pauline Frederick, Thomas Holding, J. W. Johnston. 5r USA. prod/rel: Famous Players Film Co.©, Paramount Pictures Corp.

Nurse Marjorie, New York 1906, Play
Nurse Marjorie 1920 d: William D. Taylor. lps: Mary Miles Minter, Clyde Fillmore, George Periolat. 5210f USA. prod/rel: Realart Pictures Corp.©

Too Much Money, London 1924, Play
Too Much Money 1926 d: John Francis Dillon. lps: Lewis Stone, Anna Q. Nilsson, Robert Cain. 7600f USA. prod/rel: First National Pictures

We Moderns, New York 1923, Play
We Moderns 1925 d: John Francis Dillon. lps: Colleen Moore, Jack Mulhall, Carl Miller. 6656f USA. prod/rel: John Mccormick Productions, First National Pictures

ZAPOLSKA, GABRIELA
Moralnosc Pani Dulskiej, 1907, Play
Dulscy 1975 d: Jan Rybkowski. lps: Alina Janowska, Barbara Wrzesinska, Irena Karel. 86M PLN. *Non-Matrimonial Story; The Dulski Family*

Moralnosc Pani Dulskiej 1930 d: Boleslaw Newolyn. 91M PLN. *The Morals of Mrs. Dulska; The Morals of Madame Dulska*

O Czym Sie Nie Mowi, 1909, Novel
O Czym Sie Nie Mowi 1939 d: Mecislas Krawicz. 101M PLN.

ZAPOLSKA, GABRIELE
Die Holle Der Jungfrauen, Novel
Holle Der Jungfrauen, Die 1927 d: Robert Dinesen. lps: Andre Nox, Elizza La Porta, Dagny Servaes. 2468m GRM. prod/rel: Fery-Film

Tamten, Play
Warschauer Zitadelle, Die 1930 d: Jacob Fleck, Luise Fleck. lps: Victor Varconi, Adam Brodzisz, Ferdinand Hart. 2662m GRM. *The Citadel of Warsaw* prod/rel: Hegewald-Film

Warschauer Zitadelle, Die 1938 d: Fritz Peter Buch. lps: Werner Hinz, Viktoria von Ballasko, Paul Hartmann. 86M GRM. prod/rel: A.B.C., Deutsche Commerz

Der Zarewitsch, Play
Zarewitsch, Der 1928 d: Jacob Fleck, Luise Fleck. lps: Ivan Petrovich, Marietta Millner, Albert Steinruck. 2649m GRM. prod/rel: Hegewald-Film

ZAPP, ARTHUR
Das Ehrenwort, Novel
Ehrenwort, Das 1913 d: Emil Albes. lps: Erwin Fichtner, Ilse Oeser, Hans Mierendorff. 908m GRM. prod/rel: Deutsche Bioscop

Joly, Novel
"Joly" 1913 d: Emil Albes. lps: Emil Albes, Ludwig Colani. 610m GRM. *Jolly Der Wunderaffe* prod/rel: Deutsche Bioscop

ZARCHI, MEIR
Nini, Book
Nini 1962 d: Shlomo Suryano. lps: Arik Einstein, Ronit Katz, Nurit Ne'eman. F ISR.

ZAVATTINI, CESARE
Buoni Per un Giorno, 1934, Short Story
Daro un Milione 1935 d: Mario Camerini. lps: Vittorio de Sica, Assia Noris, Luigi Almirante. 76M ITL. *I'll Give a Million* prod/rel: Novella Film, E.I.a.

Ligabue, Poem
Ligabue 1978 d: Salvatore NocitA. lps: Andrea Ferreol, Flavio Bucci, Renzo Palmer. TVM. 195M ITL. *La Vita Di Ligabue* prod/rel: Produzioni O.P.C., Panta

Stazione Termini, Novel
Stazione Termini 1953 d: Vittorio de SicA. lps: Jennifer Jones, Montgomery Clift, Gino Cervi. 93M ITL/USA. *Indiscretions of an American Wife* (USA); *Indiscretion* (UKN); *Terminal Station* prod/rel: Columbia, V. de Sica Produzioni

Toto Il Buono, Story
Miracolo a Milano 1951 d: Vittorio de SicA. lps: Emma Gramatica, Francesco Golisano, Paolo StoppA. 95M ITL. *Miracle in Milan* prod/rel: Produzioni de Sica, E.N.I.C.

ZAVREL, FRANTISEK
Dedeckem Proti Sve Vuli, Play
Dedeckem Proti Sve Vuli 1939 d: Vladimir Slavinsky. lps: Oldrich Novy, Raoul Schranil, Ferenc FuturistA. 2856m CZC. *Grandpa Involuntarily; The Reluctant Grandfather* prod/rel: Slavia-Film

Panna, Play
Panna 1940 d: Frantisek Cap. lps: Vera Ferbasova, Sasa Rasilov, Antonie NedosinskA. 2239m CZC. *The Maiden; The Virgin* prod/rel: Lucernafilm

ZHAO YUXIANG
Guan Bu Zhu, Play
 Guan Bu Zhu 1956 d: Zhang XInshi, Liu Guoquan. lps:
 Li Shugu, Tian Jihai, Wang Yuzhu. 7r CHN. *Cannot Be
 Closed* prod/rel: Changchun Film Studio

ZHENG YI
Lao Jing, Novel
 Lao Jing 1987 d: Wu Tianming. lps: Zhang Yimou,
 Liang Yujin, Lu Liping. 124M CHN. *The Old Well*
 prod/rel: XI'an Film Studio

ZHENG ZHENQIU
Guiren Yu Fanren, Play
 Zimei Hua 1933 d: Zheng Zhengqiu. lps: Hudie, Zheng
 XIaoqiu, Xuan Jinglin. 11r CHN. *Sisters' Flowers*
 prod/rel: Mingxing Film Company
Ma Zhenhua, Play
 Ma Zhenhua 1928 d: Wang Yuanlong, Zhu Shouju. lps:
 Zhou Wenzhu, Wang Cilong, Tang Tianxiu. CHN.
 prod/rel: Da Zhonghua Baihe Film Company

ZHONG AHCHENG
Hai Zi Wang, 1982, Short Story
 Hai Zi Wang 1987 d: Chen Kaige. lps: XIe Yuan, Yang
 Xuewen, Chen ShaohuA. 115M CHN. *King of the
 Children*; *Haizi Wang* prod/rel: XI'an Film Studio
Qi Wang, 1982, Short Story
 Qi Wang 1988 d: Teng Wenji. lps: XIe Yuan, Duan XIu,
 Ren Ming. 168M CHN. *Chess King* prod/rel: XI'an Film
 Studio

ZHOU DAXIN
Story
 Ren Hou Da Lie Bian 1992 d: Pan Peicheng. lps: Xu
 Fan, Zhang Qiuge, Zhang XIaotong. 9r CHN. *A Man Or
 a Monkey* prod/rel: XI'an Film Studio
Fu Niu, Novel
 Chi Nan, Yuan Nu He Niu 1994 d: Yu XIangyuan. lps:
 Liu Guanjun, Ge Nan, Zhu NA. 9r CHN. *Love Me Or
 Love My Cow* prod/rel: Changchun Film Studio

ZHOU ERFU
Baiqiuen Daifu, Book
 Baiqiuen Daifu 1964 d: Zhang Junxiang. lps: Gerald
 Tannenbaum, Chun Li, Yin Nuocheng. 12r CHN. *Doctor
 Bethune*; *Doctor Norman Bethune* prod/rel: Haiyan Film
 Studio, August First Film Studio

ZHOU KEQIN
Xumao He Ta de Nu Er Men, Novel
 Xumao He Ta de Nu Er Men 1981 d: Wang Yan. lps: Li
 XIuming, Zhang Jinling, Li Wei. 10r CHN. *Xumao and
 His Daughters* prod/rel: Beijing Film Studio
 Xumao He Ta de Nu Er Men 1981 d: Li Jun. lps: Jia
 Liu, Tian Hua, Wang Fuli. 9r CHN. *Xumao and His
 Daughters* prod/rel: August First Film Studio

ZHOU LIPO, Zhou Libo
Bao Feng Zhou Yu, 1948, Novel
 Baofeng-Zhouyu 1961 d: XIe Tieli. lps: Yu Yang, Gao
 Baocheng, Lu Fei. 120M CHN. *Hurricane*; *Pao Feng
 Tsou Yu*; *Bao Feng Zhou Yu*; *The Tempest* prod/rel:
 Beijing Film Studio

ZHOU MEISHEN
Da Jie, Novel
 Da Jie 1995 d: Wu Tiange. lps: Lei Luosheng, Yuan
 Yuan, Zhao Shengsheng. F CHN. *Big Victory* prod/rel:
 Shanghai Film Studio

ZHOU SHUREN, Lu Xun
Ah Q Zheng Zhuan, 1921, Short Story
 Ah Q Zhen Zhuan 1982 d: Chen Fan. lps: Shunkai Yan.
 124M CHN. *The True Story of Ah Q*; *The Story of Ah Q*
 prod/rel: Shanghai Film Studio
 Ah Q Zheng Zhuan 1958 d: Yuen Yang-An. 107M
 HKG. *The True Story of Ah Q*
Shang Shi, 1925, Short Story
 Shang Shi 1981 d: Shui HuA. lps: Wang XIngang, Lin
 Ying, Li Liansheng. 103M CHN. *Regret for the Past*
 prod/rel: Beijing Film Studio
Yao, 1923, Short Story
 Yao 1981 d: Yu Yanfu. 89M CHN.
Zhu Fu, 1925, Short Story
 Zhufu 1956 d: Sang Hu. lps: Bai Yang, Wei Heling, Li
 Jingbao. 90M CHN. *New Year Sacrifice*; *Zhu Fu*; *New
 Year's Sacrifice* prod/rel: Beijing Film Studio

ZIAK, KARL
Der Ewige Traum, Novel
 Ewige Traum, Der 1934 d: Arnold Fanck. lps: Sepp
 Rist, Brigitte Horney, Ernst Nansen. 85M GRM. *Der
 Konig Des Mont-Blanc* prod/rel: Cine Allianz
Paccard Wider Balmat, Novel
 Reve Eternel 1934 d: Henri Chomette, Arnold Fanck.
 lps: Brigitte Horney, Jeanne de Carol, Sepp Rist. 78M
 FRN. *Le Roi du Mont Blanc* prod/rel:
 Cine-Allianz-Tonfilm

ZIDAROV, KAMEN
Tsar Ivan Shishman, 1962, Play
 Ivan Shishman 1969 d: Yuri Arnaudov. lps: Stefan
 Getsov, Ruzha Delcheva, Vancha DoychevA. 80M BUL.
 Tsar Ivan Shishman
Tsarka Milost, 1949, Play
 Tsarska Milost 1962 d: Stefan Surchadgiev. lps:
 Ivanka Dimitrova, Ivan Dimov, Tseno Kondov. 92M
 BUL. *Royal Mercy*; *The Tsar's Pardon*

ZIEDNER, EDVIN
Bellman Vaudeville, Stockholm 1922, Musical Play
 Ulla Min Ulla 1930 d: Julius Jaenzon. lps: Torsten
 Winge, Ake Claesson, Greta Soderberg. 75M SWD. *Ulla
 My Ulla* prod/rel: Film Ab Minerva, Ab Svensk
 Filmindustri

ZIEGLER, WOLFGANG
Die Konsequenz, Novel
 Konsequenz, Die 1977 d: Wolfgang Petersen. lps:
 Jurgen Prochnow, Ernst Hannawald, Walo Luond.
 100M GRM. *The Consequence* prod/rel: Solaris, Wdr

ZIEGLOSEROVA, ANNA
Short Story
 Trny a Kvety 1921 d: Theodor Pistek. lps: Olga
 Augustova, Theodor Pistek, Ruzena SlemrovA. CZC.
 Thorns and Flowers; *Zabec*; *The Lassie* prod/rel:
 Thespis, Iris-Film
Adam a Eva, Novel
 Adam a Eva 1940 d: Karel SpelinA. lps: Ruzena
 Slemrova, Hana Vitova, Jiri Steimar. 2730m CZC.
 Adam and Eva prod/rel: Dafa
Cacorka, Play
 Cacorka 1935 d: Jan SvobodA. lps: Josef Prihoda, Ella
 Nollova, Blanka WaleskA. 2139m CZC. prod/rel:
 Kamera, Jan Kyzour

ZIEHRER, C. M.
Die Landstreicher, Opera
 Landstreicher, Die 1937 d: Carl Lamac. lps: Paul
 Horbiger, Lucie Englisch, Rudolf Carl. 85M GRM. *The
 Hoboes* prod/rel: Aco, Adler

ZIEMER, GREGOR
Education for Death, Book
 Hitler's Children 1943 d: Edward Dmytryk. lps: Tim
 Holt, Bonita Granville, Kent Smith. 83M USA. prod/rel:
 RKO Radio

ZIKA, VLADIMIR
Zeny U Benzinu, Novel
 Zeny U Benzinu 1939 d: Vaclav Kubasek. lps: Ruzena
 Slemrova, Frantisek Kreuzmann, Jirina SedlackovA.
 2174m CZC. *Women at the Petrol Station* prod/rel:
 P.D.C. (J. V. Musil)

ZILAHY, LAJOS
A Tabornok, Budapest 1928, Play
 Nacht Der Entscheidung, Die 1931 d: Dimitri
 Buchowetzki. lps: Conrad Veidt, Olga Tschechowa,
 Peter Voss. 76M GRM.
 Rebelle, Le 1930 d: Adelqui Millar. lps: Thomy
 Bourdelle, Pierre Batcheff, Suzy Vernon. 85M FRN. *Le
 General* prod/rel: Films Paramount
 Virtuous Sin, The 1930 d: George Cukor, Louis J.
 Gasnier. lps: Walter Huston, Kay Francis, Kenneth
 MacKennA. 82M USA. *Cast Iron* (UKN); *The General*
 prod/rel: Paramount-Publix Corp.
Tuzmadar, Budapest 1932, Play
 Firebird, The 1934 d: William Dieterle. lps: Ricardo
 Cortez, Verree Teasdale, Lionel Atwill. 75M USA.
 prod/rel: Warner Bros. Productions Corp., Warner Bros.
 Pictures©
Puerta Abierta, La 1957 d: Cesar Ardavin. lps: Marta
 Toren, Amedeo Nazzari, Nadia MarlowA. 103M
 SPN./ITL. *L' Ultima Notte d'Amore* (ITL); *The Open
 Door*; *The Last Night of Love* prod/rel: Hesperia Film
 (Madrid), Mercurfilm (Roma)
Valamit Visz a Viz, 1928, Novel
 Hrst Vody 1969 d: Jan Kadar, Elmar Klos. lps: Antal
 Pager, Rade Markovic, Milena Dravic. 108M CZC/USA.
 Something Is Drifting on the Water; *Neco Nese Voda*;
 Zmitana; *Touha Zvana Anada*; *Anada*

ZIMET, JULIAN
Story
 Saigon 1948 d: Leslie Fenton. lps: Alan Ladd, Veronica
 Lake, Douglas Dick. 94M USA. prod/rel: Paramount

ZIMM, MAURICE
A Question of Time, Radio Play
 Jeopardy 1952 d: John Sturges. lps: Barbara
 Stanwyck, Barry Sullivan, Ralph Meeker. 69M USA.
 prod/rel: MGM

ZIMMER, BERNARD
Le Veau Gras, Play
 Veau Gras, Le 1939 d: Serge de Poligny. lps: Elvire
 Popesco, Gabrielle Fontan, Francois Perier. 85M FRN.
 prod/rel: Dimeco

ZINDEL, PAUL
*The Effect of Gamma Rays on Man-in-the-Moon
Marigolds*, New York 1965, Play
 Effect of Gamma Rays on Man-in-the-Moon
 Marigolds, The 1972 d: Paul Newman. lps: Joanne
 Woodward, Nell Potts, Roberta Wallach. 101M USA.
 prod/rel: Newman, Foreman

ZINK, RALPH SPENCER
Without Warning, New York 1937, Play
 Invisible Menace, The 1938 d: John Farrow. lps:
 Boris Karloff, Marie Wilson, Regis Toomey. 59M USA.
 Without Warning prod/rel: Warner Bros. Pictures©

ZINK, ROBERT SPENCER
 Murder on the Waterfront 1943 d: B. Reeves Eason.
 lps: Warren Douglas, Joan Winfield, John Loder. 49M
 USA. prod/rel: Warner Bros.

ZOBEL, JOSEPH
Ruse Cases Negres, Novel
 Rue Cases-Negres 1983 d: Euzhan Palcy. lps: Garry
 Cadenat, Darling Legitimus, Douta Seck. 106M FRN.
 Sugar Cane Alley (USA); *Black Shack Alley* prod/rel: Su
 Ma Fa, Orca

ZOCH, GEORG
Jenny Und Der Herr Im Frack, Play
 Jenny Und Der Herr Im Frack 1941 d: Paul Martin.
 lps: Gusti Huber, Johannes Heesters, Paul Kemp. 89M
 GRM. prod/rel: Bavaria, Schorcht

ZOLA, EMILE (1840–1902), FRN
L' Argent, 1891, Novel
 Argent, L' 1928 d: Marcel L'Herbier. lps: Brigitte
 Helm, Marie Glory, Alfred Abel. 80M FRN. *Money*;
 Jazz-Bank prod/rel: Cine-Mondial, Cinegraphic
 Argent, L' 1936 d: Pierre Billon. lps: Pierre
 Richard-Willm, Jean Worms, Vera Korene. 107M FRN.
 prod/rel: Sofra
L' Assommoir, 1877, Novel
 Assommoir, L' 1909 d: Albert Capellani. lps: Paul
 Capellani, Alexandre Arquilliere, Harry Baur. 850m
 FRN. prod/rel: Scagl
 Assommoir, L' 1921 d: Charles Maudru, Maurice de
 Marsan. lps: Jean Dax, Georges Lannes, Louise SforzA.
 4800m FRN. prod/rel: Maurice De Marsan
 Assommoir, L' 1933 d: Gaston Roudes. lps: Line Noro,
 France Dhelia, Daniel Mendaille. 105M FRN. prod/rel:
 Compagnie Parisienne Cinematographique
 Drink 1917 d: Sidney Morgan. lps: Fred Groves, Irene
 Browne, Alice O'Brien. 6040f UKN. prod/rel: British
 Pictures, Gaumont
 Gervaise 1956 d: Rene Clement. lps: Maria Schell,
 Francois Perier, Suzy Delair. 102M FRN. prod/rel:
 Agnes Delahaie, Silver Films
L'attaque du Moulin, 1880, Short Story
 Attack on the Mill, The 1910 d: Edwin S. Porter. lps:
 Marc MacDermott, Harold M. Shaw. 1000f USA.
 prod/rel: Edison
L' Attaque du Moulin, 1880, Short Story
 Brollopsnatt, En 1959 d: Erik Blomberg. lps: Harriet
 Andersson, Ignacy Gogolewski. F SWD/FNL/PLN. *Noc
 Poslubna* (PLN); *Haayo* (FNL); *Wedding Night*
Au Bonheur Des Dames, 1883, Novel
 Au Bonheur Des Dames 1929 d: Julien Duvivier. lps:
 Dita Parlo, Pierre de Guingand, Germaine Rouer.
 2000m FRN. prod/rel: Film d'Art (Vandal Et Delac)
 Au Bonheur Des Dames 1943 d: Andre Cayatte. lps:
 Michel Simon, Albert Prejean, Blanchette Brunoy. 88M
 FRN. *Shop-Girls of Paris* (USA) prod/rel: Continental
 Films
La Bete Humaine, 1890, Novel
 Bete Humaine, La 1938 d: Jean Renoir. lps: Jean
 Gabin, Simone Simon, Fernand Ledoux. 100M FRN.
 The Human Beast (USA); *Judas Was a Woman* (UKN)
 prod/rel: Paris-Films-Production
 Human Desire 1954 d: Fritz Lang. lps: Broderick
 Crawford, Gloria Grahame, Glenn Ford. 90M USA. *The
 Human Beast* prod/rel: Columbia
La Curee, Paris 1871, Novel
 Cuccagna, La 1917 d: Baldassarre Negroni. lps:
 Hesperia, Alberto Collo, Ida Carloni-Talli. 2103m ITL.
 prod/rel: Tiber Film
 Curee, La 1966 d: Roger Vadim. lps: Jane Fonda, Peter
 McEnery, Michel Piccoli. 100M FRN/ITL. *La Calda
 Preda* (ITL); *The Game Is Over* (USA) prod/rel: Cocinor,
 Les Films Marceau
La Faute de l'Abbe Mouret, 1875, Novel
 Faute de l'Abbe Mouret, La 1970 d: Georges Franju.
 lps: Francis Huster, Gillian Hills, Andre Lacombe. 100M
 FRN/ITL. *L' Amante Del Prete* (ITL); *The Sin of Father
 Mouret*; *The Demise of Father Mouret* (USA); *C'est la
 Faute de l'Abbe Mouret* prod/rel: Stephan Films, Films
 Du Carrosse

Eine Liebesgeschichte, 1934, Short Story
Liebesgeschichte, Eine 1954 d: Rudolf Jugert. lps: Hildegard Knef, O. W. Fischer, Viktor de KowA. 97M GRM. *A Love Story* prod/rel: Intercontinental, Eric Pommer

Nach Dem Sturm, Short Story
Nach Dem Sturm 1948 d: Gustav Ucicky. lps: Marte Harell, Maria Schell, Nicholas Stuart. 99M AUS/SWT. *Apres l'Orage; Le Concert; Opfer Aus Liebe* prod/rel: Cordial-Filmproduktion

Schinderhannes, 1927, Play
Schinderhannes 1928 d: Curtis Bernhardt. lps: Hans Stuwe, Lissi Arna, Albert Steinruck. 2703m GRM. *The Prince of Rogues* (USA) prod/rel: Prometheus-Film
Schinderhannes 1958 d: Helmut Kautner. lps: Curd Jurgens, Maria Schell, Fritz Tillmann. 115M GRM. *Duel in the Forest* (USA) prod/rel: Real, Europa

Der Seelenbrau, 1945, Novel
Seelenbrau, Der 1950 d: Gustav Ucicky. lps: Paul Horbiger, Heinrich Gretler, Aglaja Schmid. 100M AUS. *Im Wirtshaus Zum "Goldenen Herzen"* prod/rel: Vindobona

ZUKROWSKI, WOJCIECH
Lotna, 1945, Short Story
Lotna 1959 d: Andrzej WajdA. lps: Jerzy Pichelski, Adam Pawlikowski, Jerzy Moes. 89M PLN. prod/rel: Kadr Film Unit

ZULAWSKI, JERZY
Novel
Na Srebrnym Globie 1977 d: Andrzej Zulawski. lps: Andrzej Seweryn, Grazyna Dylag, Jerzy TrelA. 158M PLN. *At the Silver Globe; The Silver Globe; Zwyciezca* prod/rel: Gruppe Pryzmat

ZUMBRO, KARL
Story
Liebe, Luft Und Lauter Lugen 1959 d: Peter Beauvais. lps: Eva-Ingeborg Scholz, Gerhard Riedmann, Doris Kirchner. 94M GRM. *Love Air and a Lot of Lies; Love and Lies in the Air* prod/rel: U.F.H.

Morgen Wirst du Um Mich Weinen, Novel
Morgen Wirst du Um Mich Weinen 1959 d: Alfred Braun. lps: Sabine Bethmann, Sabina Sesselmann, Joachim Hansen. 94M GRM. *You'll Cry for Me Tomorrow* prod/rel: Cinelux, Deutsche Cosmopol

ZUPAN, FRANTA
Pepanek Nezdara, Novel
Pepanek Nezdara 1923 d: Premysl Prazsky. lps: Beda Prazsky, Jarmila Urbankova, Karel Urbanek. 2141m CZC. *Pepanek the Rascal* prod/rel: Lloydfilm

ZUR NEDDEN, O. C. A.
Der Stier Geht Los, Play
Hochzeitsnacht 1941 d: Carl Boese. lps: Heli Finkenzeller, Geraldine Katt, Hans Fidesser. 78M GRM. prod/rel: UFA

ZWEIBEL, ALAN
North, Novel
North 1994 d: Rob Reiner. lps: Elijah Wood, Jason Alexander, Julia Louis-Dreyfus. 87M USA.

ZWEIG, ARNOLD (1887–1968), GRM
Das Beil von Wandsbek, 1947, Novel
Beil von Wandsbek, Das 1951 d: Falk Harnack. lps: Erwin Geschonneck, Kathe Braun, Gefion Helmke. 75M GDR. *The Axe of Wandsbek; The Wandsbek Axe* prod/rel: Defa
Beil von Wandsbek, Das 1981 d: Horst Konigstein, Heinrich Breloer. lps: Roland Schafer, Angelika Thomas, Hildegard Schmahl. TVM. 149M GRM. prod/rel: Ndr, Wdr
Beil von Wandsbek, Das 1983 d: Falk Harnack. 90 GDR. *The Axe of Wandsbek*

Junge Frau von 1914, Novel
Junge Frau von 1914 1969 d: Egon Gunther. lps: Jutta Hoffmann, Klaus Piontek, Inge Keller. 156M GDR. *Young Woman of 1914* prod/rel: Deutscheer Fernsehfunk D.F.F.

Der Streit Um Den Sergeanten Grischa, Potsdam 1927, Novel
Case of Sergeant Grischa, The 1930 d: Herbert Brenon. lps: Chester Morris, Betty Compson, Alec B. Francis. 8261f USA. prod/rel: RKO Productions

ZWEIG, STEFAN (1881–1942), AUS
Amok, 1922, Short Story
Amok 1934 d: Fedor Ozep. lps: Marcelle Chantal, Madeleine Guitty, Jean Yonnel. 92M FRN. prod/rel: Pathe-Natan
Amok 1944 d: Antonio Momplet. lps: Maria Felix, Julian Soler, Stella IndA. 105M MXC.
Zakon I Dolg 1927 d: Konstantin Mardzhanov. lps: Nata Vachnadze, A. Imedashvili, V. GuniA. 68M USS.

Die Angst, 1920, Short Story
Angst 1928 d: Hans Steinhoff. lps: Elga Brink, Henry Edwards, Vivian Gibson. 2642m GRM. prod/rel: Orplid-Film
Paura, La 1954 d: Roberto Rossellini. lps: Ingrid Bergman, Mathias Wieman, Renate Mannhardt. 90M ITL/GRM. *Angst* (GRM); *Non Credo Piu All'amore; Fear* (UKN); *Incubo* prod/rel: Aniene Film (Roma), Ariston Film (Munich)
Peur, La 1936 d: Victor Tourjansky. lps: Charles Vanel, Jorge Rigaud, Gaby Morlay. 90M FRN. *Vertige d'un Soir* prod/rel: Procine Standard

Brennendes Geheimnis, 1929, Short Story
Brennendes Geheimnis 1933 d: Robert Siodmak. lps: Willi Forst, Hilde Wagner, Hans Joachim Schaufuss. 93M GRM. *The Burning Secret*
Burning Secret 1989 d: Andrew Birkin. lps: Faye Dunaway, Klaus Maria Brandauer, Ian Richardson. 106M UKN/USA/GRM. *Brennendes Geheimnis* (GRM) prod/rel: Vestron, Nfh

Brief Einer Unbekannten, 1922, Short Story
Letter from an Unknown Woman 1948 d: Max Ophuls. lps: Joan Fontaine, Louis Jourdan, Mady Christians. 90M USA. prod/rel: Universal

Narkose 1929 d: Alfred Abel. lps: Renee Heribel, Alfred Abel, Jack Trevor. 2426m GRM. *Briefe Einer Unbekannten; Narcosis* prod/rel: G.P. Films
Valkoiset Ruusut 1944 d: Hannu Leminen. 102M FNL. *The White Rose; The White Roses*

Das Gestohlene Jahr, Novel
Gestohlene Jahr, Das 1951 d: Wilfried Frass. lps: Elisabeth Hobarth, Ewald Balser, Oskar Werner. 89M GRM/AUS. *The Stolen Year* prod/rel: Ring, N.F.

Marie Antoinette; Bildnis Eines Mittleren Charakters, Leipzig 1932, Biography
Marie Antoinette 1938 d: W. S. Van Dyke, Julien Duvivier. lps: Norma Shearer, Tyrone Power, John Barrymore. 160M USA. prod/rel: Metro-Goldwyn-Mayer Corp., Loews, Inc.©

Die Mondscheingasse, Short Story
Mondscheingasse, Die 1988 d: Edouard Molinaro. lps: Niels Arestrup, Michel Piccoli, Marthe Keller. 90M GRM/FRN/ITL. prod/rel: Fr 3, Rai Due

La Pitie Dangereuse, Novel
Pitie Dangereuse, La 1979 d: Edouard Molinaro. lps: Mathieu Carriere, Marie-Helene Breillat, Jean Desailly. TVM. 170M FRN.

La Ruelle Au Clair de Lune, Novel
Ruelle Au Clair de Lune, La 1990 d: Edouard Molinaro. lps: Marthe Keller, Michel Piccoli, Niels Arestrup. TVM. 95M FRN.

Schachnovelle, Buenos Aires 1942, Novel
Schachnovelle, Die 1960 d: Gerd Oswald. lps: Curd Jurgens, Claire Bloom, Jorge Felmy. 104M GRM. *Brainwashed* (USA); *Three Moves to Freedom; The Royal Game; Chess Clause* prod/rel: Roxy, N.F.

Ungeduld Des Herzens, 1938, Novel
Beware of Pity 1946 d: Maurice Elvey. lps: Lilli Palmer, Albert Lieven, Cedric Hardwicke. 106M UKN. prod/rel: Two Cities, Eagle-Lion

Vierundzwanzig Stunden Aus Dem Leben Einer Frau, Leipzig 1926, Novel
24 Heures de la Vie d'une Femme 1968 d: Dominique Delouche. lps: Danielle Darrieux, Robert Hoffmann, Romina Power. 87M FRN/GRM. *24 Stunden Im Leben Einer Frau* (GRM); *24 Hours in a Woman's Life; Twenty-Four Hours of a Woman's Life; 24 Hours in the Life of a Woman; Vingt-Quatre Heures de la Vie d'une Femme* prod/rel: Progefi, Roxy-Film
24 Horas de la Vida de Una Mujer 1944 d: Carlos Borcosque. lps: Amelia Bence. 90M ARG. *24 Hours in the Life of a Woman*
24 Hours of a Woman's Life 1952 d: Victor Saville. lps: Merle Oberon, Richard Todd, Leo Genn. 90M UKN. *Affair in Monte Carlo* (USA); *Twenty-Four Hours of a Woman's Life* prod/rel: Associated British Picture Corporation, Ab-Pathe
Schicksal Einer Nacht, Das 1927 d: Erich Schonfelder. lps: Erna Morena, Harry Liedtke, Edda Croy. 1973m GRM. prod/rel: Pan Europa-Film

Literary Source Index

ACROSS THE EVERGLADES, Story see Budd Schulberg

ACROSS THE PACIFIC, New York 1904, Play see Charles E. Blaney

ACROSS THE PANHANDLE, Story see John Twist

ACROSS THE WIDE MISSOURI, 1947, Novel see Bernard de Voto

ACT OF LOVE, Novel see Paige Mitchell

ACT OF MERCY, London 1959, Novel see Francis Clifford

ACT OF WILL, Novel see Barbara Taylor Bradford

ACT ONE, New York 1959, Play see Moss Hart

ACTE SANS PAROLES, 1957, Play see Samuel Beckett

ACTION FOR SLANDER, Novel see Mary Borden

ACTION IMMEDIATE, Novel see Paul Kenny

ACTION MAN, THE, New York 1961, Novel see J. M. Flynn

ACTION OF THE TIGER, Novel see James Wellard

ACTO DA PRIMAVERA, Play see Francisco Vaz de Guimaraes

ACTOR'S BLOOD, 1936, Short Story see Ben Hecht

ADA BEATS THE DRUM, New York 1930, Play see John Alexander Kirkpatrick

ADA DALLAS, New York 1959, Novel see Wirt Williams

ADAM A EVA, Novel see Anna Ziegloserova

ADAM AND EVA, New York 1923, Play see Guy Bolton, George Middleton

ADAM AND EVE, Play see C. E. Munro, Louisa Parr

ADAM BEDE, 1859, Novel see George Eliot

ADAM EST EVE, Novel see Francis Didelot

ADAM'S EVENING, Play see Katharine Kavanaugh

ADAPTIVE ULTIMATE, THE, 1941, Short Story see John Jessel

ADARSHA HINDU HOTEL, 1940, Novel see Bibhutibhushan Bannerjee

ADDICT, THE, Play see John Giminez

ADDIE PRAY, Novel see Joe David Brown

ADDING MACHINE, THE, March 1923, Play see Elmer Rice

ADDIO AMORE!, 1896, Novel see Matilde Serao

ADDIO GIOVINEZZA, 1911, Play see Sandro Camasio, Nino Oxilia

ADDIO MIA BELLA NAPOLI!, 1910, Play see Ernesto Murolo

ADDRESS UNKNOWN, 1938, Novel see Kressman Taylor

ADELA. FRAGMENT DIN JURNALUL LUI EMIL CODRESCU, 1933, Novel see Garabet Ibraileanu

ADELAIDE, Paris 1913, Play see Joseph Arthur de Gobineau

ADIEU A ROI, L', Novel see Pierre Schoendoerffer

ADIEU CHERIE, Short Story see Jacques Companeez, Alex Joffe

ADIEU L'AMI, Novel see Sebastien Japrisot

ADIOS!, New York 1929, Novel see Lanier Bartlett, Virginia S. Bartlett

ADIOS, Novel see Harry Whittington

ADIOS, CORDERA!, 1892, Short Story see Leopoldo Alas

ADIOS MY TEXAS, Story see L. L. Foreman

ADJUNKT VRBA, Novel see Jan Klecanda

AD-MAN, 1932, Play see Charles Curran, Arch A. Gaffney

ADMIRABLE CRICHTON, THE, London 1902, Play see J. M. Barrie

ADMIRALS ALL, London 1934, Play see Ian Hay, Stephen King-Hall

ADMIRAL'S SECRET, THE, 1928, Play see Cyril Campion, Edward Dignon

ADOBE WALLS, 1953, Novel see William Riley Burnett

ADOLPHE, 1816, Novel see Henri-Benjamin Constant de Rebeque

ADOPTED FATHER, 1916, Short Story see Edgar Franklin

ADOPTED SON, THE, 1917, Short Story see Max Brand

ADRIENNE GASCOYNE, 1915, Short Story see William Hamilton Osborne

ADRIENNE LECOUVREUR, Paris 1849, Play see Ernest Legouve, Eugene Scribe

ADULTERIO DECENTE, UN, 1935, Play see Enrique Jardiel Poncela

ADVANCEMENT OF LEARNING, AN, London 1972, Novel see Reginald Hill

ADVENT, 1950, Novel see Jarmila Glazarova

ADVENTURE, Novel see Clyde Brion Davis

ADVENTURE, London 1911, Novel see Jack London

ADVENTURE, AN, Book see Frances Lamont, Elizabeth Morrison

ADVENTURE IN DIAMONDS, Novel see David E. Walker

ADVENTURE OF A READY LETTER WRITER, THE, 1920, Short Story see Blanche Brace

ADVENTURE OF JOE SMITH - AMERICAN, THE, Story see Paul Gallico

ADVENTURE OF THE DANCING MAN, 1903, Short Story see Arthur Conan Doyle

ADVENTURE OF THE EMPTY HOUSE, 1903, Short Story see Arthur Conan Doyle

ADVENTURE OF THE FINAL PROBLEM, 1894, Short Story see Arthur Conan Doyle

ADVENTURE OF THE MUSGRAVE RITUAL, 1893, Short Story see Arthur Conan Doyle

ADVENTURE OF THE SIX NAPOLEONS, 1904, Short Story see Arthur Conan Doyle

ADVENTURERS, THE, New York 1966, Novel see Harold Robbins

ADVENTURES OF CAPTAIN KETTLE, THE, Novel see C. J. Cutcliffe-Hyne

ADVENTURES OF HAJJI BABA, 1954, Novel see James Morier

ADVENTURES OF HUCKLEBERRY FINN, THE, New York 1884, Novel see Mark Twain

ADVENTURES OF KITTY COBB, THE, New York 1912, Book see James Montgomery Flagg

ADVENTURES OF THE SCARLET CAR, New York 1907, Novel see Richard Harding Davis

ADVENTURES OF TOM SAWYER, San Francisco 1876, Novel see Mark Twain

ADVENTURES OF VAN BIBBER, THE, Story see Richard Harding Davis

ADVENTURESS, THE, Story see Ewart Adamson

ADVERSARY, THE, Novel see Bart Spicer

ADVISE AND CONSENT, New York 1959, Novel see Allen Drury

ADVOCAAT VAN DE HANEN, Novel see A. F. Th. Van Der Heijden

ADVOKAT CHUDYCH, see Jakub Arbes

ADVOKATKA VERA, Short Story see Vlasta Zemanova

AENEID, c20 bc, Verse see Virgil

AERODROME, THE, Novel see Rex Warner

AFFAIR AT ST. ALBANS, 1947, Article see Herbert Ravenal Sass

AFFAIR AT THE NOVELTY THEATRE, THE, Short Story see Baroness Orczy

AFFAIR OF HONOUR, AN, Play see Percival H. T. Sykes

AFFAIR, THE, Novel see C. P. Snow

AFFAIRE BLAIREAU, L', 1899, Novel see Alphonse Allais

AFFAIRE CLEMENCEAU, L', Paris 1866, Novel see Alexandre Dumas (fils)

AFFAIRE COFFIN, L', Book see Jacques Hebert

AFFAIRE CRAINQUEBILLE, L', 1901, Short Story see Anatole France

AFFAIRE DE LA RUE DE LOURCINE, L', 1857, Play see Eugene Labiche, A. Monnier

AFFAIRE DES POISONS, L', 1908, Play see Victorien Sardou

AFFAIRE DU COLLIER DE LA REINE, L', Novel see Frantz Funck-Brentano

AFFAIRE DU COURRIER DE LYON, L', Play see Louis-Mathurin Moreau, Paul Siraudin

AFFAIRE DU GRAND-THEATRE, L', Novel see Valentin Mandelstamm

AFFAIRE DU TRAIN 24, L', Novel see Andre Bencey

AFFAIRE D'UNE NUIT, L', Novel see Alain Moury

AFFAIRE INTIME, UNE, Novel see Max Gallo

AFFAIRE NINA B., Novel see Johannes Mario Simmel

AFFAIRE ORCIVAL, L', Novel see Emile Gaboriau

AFFAIRE ROUGE, L', Paris 1866, Novel see Emile Gaboriau

AFFAIRE SAINT-FIACRE, L', 1932, Novel see Georges Simenon

AFFAIRES SONT LES AFFAIRES, LES, Paris 1903, Play see Octave Mirbeau

AFFAIRS OF DOBIE GILLIS, THE, Book see Max Schulman

AFFINITIES, 1920, Short Story see Mary Roberts Rinehart

AFFLICTION, 1989, Novel see Russell Banks

AFRICAN BUSH ADVENTURES, Book see John A. Hunter, Daniel P. Mannix

AFRICAN FURY, Book see George Michaels

AFRICAN QUEEN, THE, 1935, Novel see C. S. Forester

AFRIKANSKE FARM, 1937, Short Story see Karen Blixen

AFTER ALL, London 1930, Play see John Van Druten

AFTER DARK, Short Story see Bertram Atkey

AFTER DARK, 1926, Play see J. Jefferson Farjeon

AFTER DARK, London 1868, Play see Dion Boucicault

AFTER DARK, MY SWEET, Novel see Jim Thompson

AFTER FIVE, New York 1913, Play see Cecil B. de Mille, William C. de Mille

AFTER HIS OWN HEART, 1919, Short Story see Ben Ames Williams

AFTER HIS OWN HEART, 1920, Short Story see William Wallace Cook

AFTER HOURS, Novel see Edwin Torres

AFTER JULIUS, Novel see Elizabeth Jane Howard

AFTER MIDNIGHT, 1929, Play see Charles Bennett

AFTER THE BALL, 1892, Song see Charles K. Harris

AFTER THE FUNERAL, London 1953, Novel see Agatha Christie

AFTER THE MERRYMAKING, 1971, Verse see Roger McGough

AFTER THE PLAY, Story see Robert McGowan

AFTER THE RAIN, 1931, Play see Alfred C. Kennedy

AFTER THE TRIAL, Novel see Eric Roman

AFTER THE VERDICT, Novel see Robert Hichens

AFTER TOMORROW, New York 1931, Play see John Golden, Hugh Stange

AFTERMATH, Play see William Addison Hervey

AFTERNOON MIRACLE, AN, Short Story see O. Henry

AFTERWARDS, Novel see Kathlyn Rhodes

AFTERWARDS, London 1933, Play see Walter Hackett

AGADADZA, L', Short Story see Louis d'Hee

AGAIN THE RINGER, London 1929, Novel see Edgar Wallace

AGAINST HEAVEN'S HAND, Novel see Leonard Bishop

AGATHA'S AUNT, Indianapolis 1920, Novel see Harriet Lummis Smith

AGE FOR LOVE, THE, New York 1930, Novel see Ernest Pascal

AGE OF CONSENT, New York 1938, Novel see Norman Lindsay

AGE OF INDISCRETION, Story see Lenore Coffee

AGE OF INNOCENCE, THE, New York 1920, Novel see Edith Wharton

AGENCE BARNETT, L', Novel see Maurice Leblanc

AGENCY, Novel see Paul Gottlieb

AGENZIA INVESTIGATIVA RICCARDO FINZI, Novel see Luciano Secchi

AGGIE APPLEBY, MAKER OF MEN, 1932, Play see Joseph Kesselring

AGNES, New York 1908, Play see George Cameron, Paul M. Potter

AGNES BERNAUER, 1852, Play see Christian Friedrich Hebbel

AGNES CECILIA, Novel see Maria Gripe

AGNES DE RIEN, Novel see Germaine Beaumont

AGNES OF GOD, Play see John Pielmeier

AGNESE VA A MORIRE, L', Novel see Renata Vigano

AGONIA DI SCHIZZO, L', Play see Athos Setti

AGONY AND THE ECSTASY, THE, New York 1961, Book see Irving Stone

AGONY COLUMN, THE, Indianapolis 1916, Novel see Earl Derr Biggers

AGOSTINO, 1944, Novel see Alberto Moravia

AGRICULTURAL CARESS, 1966, Poem see John Betjeman

AGUILAS DE ACERO, Novel see Rafael Lopez Rienda

AH JONAN, Novel *see* Shotaro Yasuoka

AH Q ZHENG ZHUAN, 1921, Short Story *see* Zhou Shuren

AH WILDERNESS!, New York 1933, Play *see* Eugene O'Neill

AHASIN POLAWATHA, Novel *see* Eileen Siriwardene

AI GALLI PIACCIONO LE STELLE, Play *see* Luciano Martino

AI NO KAWAKI, Tokyo 1950, Novel *see* Yukio Mishima

AIDA, Cairo 1871, Opera *see* Antonio Ghislanzoni, Giuseppe Verdi

AIEULE, L', 1863, Play *see* Adolphe-P. d'Ennery, C. Edmond

AIGLE A DEUX TETES, L', 1946, Play *see* Jean Cocteau

AIGLON, L', 1900, Play *see* Edmond Rostand

AIGRETTE, L', 1912, Play *see* Dario Niccodemi

AILES BRISEES, LES, Play *see* Pierre Wolff

AILES DE JULIEN, LES, Novel *see* Denis Belloc

AIMEE & JAGUAR, Book *see* Erica Fischer

AIMEZ-VOUS BRAHMS?, Paris 1959, Novel *see* Francoise Sagan

AIMEZ-VOUS LES FEMMES?, Paris 1961, Novel *see* Georges Bardawil

AINE DES FERCHAUX, L', 1945, Novel *see* Georges Simenon

AIR AMERICA, Book *see* Christopher Robbins

AIR DE FAMILLE, UN, Play *see* Jean-Pierre Bacri, Agnes Jaoui

AIR HOSTESS, 1933, Short Story *see* Dora Macy

AIR MAIL, THE, Novel *see* Byron Morgan

AIR RAID, Short Story *see* John Varley

AIRING IN A CLOSED CARRIAGE, Novel *see* Gabrielle Margaret Vere Long

AIRMAN AND THE CARPENTER, THE, Book *see* Ludovic Kennedy

AIRPORT, New York 1968, Book *see* Arthur Hailey

AJO NELL'IMBARAZZO, L', 1807, Play *see* Giovanni Giraud

AKAHIGE SHINRYOTAN, Tokyo 1962, Novel *see* Shugoro Yamamoto

AKAZUKINCHAN KIOTSUKETE, Short Story *see* Kaoru Shoji

AKENFIELD, Book *see* Ronald Blythe

AKIBIYORI, 1960, Novel *see* Ton Satomi

AKIRA, Novel *see* Katsuhiro Otomo

AKLI MIKLOS ES. KIR. UDV. MULATTATO TORTENETE, 1903, Novel *see* Kalman Mikszath

AKTE FABREANI, Novel *see* Frank F. Braun

AKTENBUNDEL M 2-1706/35, Novel *see* Axel Rudolph

AKUTARO, Novel *see* Toko Kon

AL UNKU EDES FREUNDIN WAR, Short Story *see* Alex Wedding

ALABASTER BOX, AN, New York 1917, Novel *see* Mary E. Wilkins Freeman, Florence Morse Kingsley

ALADDIN FROM BROADWAY, New York 1913, Novel *see* Frederic Stewart Isham

ALAIN ET LE NEGRE, Novel *see* Robert Sabatier

ALASKAN, THE, New York 1923, Novel *see* James Oliver Curwood

ALBA, UN', *see* Lenin

ALBANILES, LOS, Play *see* Vicente Lenero

ALBASTRA ZARE A MORTII, 1948, Short Story *see* Marin Preda

ALBERGO DEGLI ASSENTI, L', Novel *see* Michelangelo Barricelli

ALBERT R.N., Play *see* Guy Morgan, Edward Sammis

ALBERT'S FOLLIES, Story *see* Ray Selfe

ALBO IL GIORNO LA NOTTE, L', Play *see* Aldo Nicodemi

ALBUQUERQUE, Novel *see* Luke Short

ALCALDE DE ZALAMEA, EL, 1651, Play *see* Pedro Calderon de La Barca

ALCATRAZ, New York 1923, Novel *see* Max Brand

ALCESTI, Play *see* Euripides

ALCHEMY OF LOVE, THE, 1918, Short Story *see* Vingie E. Roe

ALCIDE PEPIE, Play *see* Armand Massard, Alfred Vercourt

ALDEA PERDIDA, LA, 1903, Novel *see* Armando Palacio Valdes

ALEGRETTO. PER BENE MA NON TROPPO, Play *see* Ugo Chiti

ALERTE!, Novel *see* Colonel Driant

ALESSANDRO, SEI GRANDE!, Play *see* Luigi Bonelli

ALEX, Book *see* Tessa Duder

ALEX THE GREAT, Boston 1919, Novel *see* Harry Charles Witwer

ALEXA, Play *see* Harald Bratt

ALEXANDRA, Play *see* Franz Martos, Richard Voss

ALEXANDRA, 1922, Novel *see* Jonkheer A. W. G. Van Riemsdijk

ALEXANDRA SI INFERNUL, 1966, Novel *see* Laurentiu Fulga

ALEXANDRIA QUARTET, THE, 1956-60, Novel *see* Lawrence Durrell

ALFIE, London 1963, Play *see* Bill Naughton

ALFRED THE GREAT, Chicago 1956, Book *see* Eleanor Shipley Duckett

ALF'S BUTTON, 1919, Novel *see* W. A. Darlington

ALF'S CARPET, 1928, Novel *see* W. A. Darlington

ALGONQUIN PROJECT, THE, Novel *see* Frederick Nolan

ALI BABA, 1897, Play *see* Khirode Prasad Vidyavinode

ALIAS JIMMY VALENTINE, New York 1910, Play *see* Paul Armstrong

ALIAS MRS. JESSOP, Short Story *see* Blair Hall

ALIAS THE DEACON, New York 1925, Play *see* Leroy Clemens, John B. Hymer

ALIAS THE DOCTOR, Play *see* Emric Foeldes

ALIAS THE LONE WOLF, Garden City, Ny. 1921, Novel *see* Louis Joseph Vance

ALIAS THE NIGHT WIND, New York 1913, Novel *see* Varick Vanardy

ALIBI IKE, 1915, Short Story *see* Ring Lardner

ALIBI, L', Novel *see* Marcel Achard

ALIBI, L', Play *see* Gabriel Trarieux

ALIBI, THE, Story *see* Frank Condon

ALIBI, THE, Boston 1916, Novel *see* George Allan England

ALICE ADAMS, New York 1921, Novel *see* Booth Tarkington

ALICE IN WONDERLAND, Short Story *see* Henry Payson Dowst

ALICE SIT-BY-THE-FIRE, London 1905, Play *see* J. M. Barrie

ALICE'S ADVENTURES IN WONDERLAND, London 1865, Book *see* Lewis Carroll

ALIEN BLOOD, THE, Short Story *see* Louise Rice

ALIEN CORN, THE, 1940, Short Story *see* W. Somerset Maugham

ALIENISTA, O, 1881, Short Story *see* Joaquim Maria Machado de Assis

ALIMENTE, Short Story *see* Walter Gottfried Lohmeyer

ALIVE AND KICKING, Play *see* William Dinner, William Morum

ALL AT SEA, Play *see* Ian Hay

ALL BRIDES ARE BEAUTIFUL, Novel *see* Thomas Bell

ALL CREATURES GREAT AND SMALL, Novel *see* James Herriot

ALL FALL DOWN, New York 1960, Novel *see* James Leo Herlihy

ALL FOR A GIRL, New York 1908, Play *see* Rupert Hughes

ALL FOR LOVE, 1928, Short Story *see* Peter B. Kyne

ALL FOR MARY, London 1954, Play *see* Kay Bannerman, Harold Brooke

ALL GOOD AMERICANS, New York 1933, Play *see* Laura Perelman, S. J. Perelman

ALL IN GOOD TIME, London 1963, Play *see* Bill Naughton

ALL IS CONFUSION, 1934, Short Story *see* Richard Macauley

ALL KNEELING, 1928, Novel *see* Anne Parrish

ALL MEN ARE ENEMIES, New York 1933, Novel *see* Richard Aldington

ALL MEN ARE LIARS, Novel *see* Joseph Hocking

ALL MEN ARE MORTAL, Novel *see* Simone de Beauvoir

ALL MINE, Play *see* Dorian Neve

ALL MY SONS, New York 1947, Play *see* Arthur Miller

ALL NEAT IN BLACK STOCKINGS, London 1966, Novel *see* Jane Gaskell

ALL NIGHT LONG, Play *see* Philip Bartholomae, Paul B. Sipe

ALL ON A SUMMER'S DAY, Novel *see* John Garden

ALL ON ACCOUNT OF AN EGG, Short Story *see* O. Henry

ALL ON THE NEVER-NEVER, Novel *see* Jack Lindsay

ALL OUR FAULT, Novel *see* Daniel Mornin

ALL ROADS LEAD TO CALVARY, Novel *see* Jerome K. Jerome

ALL SORTS AND CONDITIONS OF MEN, Novel *see* Sir Walter Besant

ALL SOULS, Novel *see* Javier Marias

ALL SOULS' EVE, New York 1920, Play *see* Anne Crawford Flexner

ALL THAT HEAVEN ALLOWS, Novel *see* Edna Lee, Harry Lee

ALL THE BROTHERS WERE VALIANT, New York 1919, Novel *see* Ben Ames Williams

ALL THE KING'S HORSES, New York 1934, Musical Play *see* Frederick Herendeen, Edward A. Horan

ALL THE KING'S MEN, 1946, Novel *see* Robert Penn Warren

ALL THE LITTLE ANIMALS, Novel *see* Walker Hamilton

ALL THE PRESIDENT'S MEN, 1974, Book *see* Carl Bernstein, Bob Woodward

ALL THE RIVERS RUN, Novel *see* Nancy Cato

ALL THE WAY, Novel *see* Charles Williams

ALL THE WORLD TO NOTHING, Boston 1912, Novel *see* Wyndham Martyn

ALL THE WORLD'S A STAGE, Novel *see* Herbert Everett

ALL THIS AND HEAVEN TOO, New York 1938, Novel *see* Rachel Field

ALL THROUGHT THE NIGHT, 1955, Novel *see* Whit Masterson

ALLA MODA!, Play *see* Oreste Biancoli, Dino Falconi

ALLABELI, Play *see* Gunwantrai Acharya

ALL-AMERICAN, THE, Story *see* Leonard Freeman

ALLAN QUARTERMAIN, 1885, Novel *see* H. Rider Haggard

ALLE MENSCHEN WERDEN BRUDER, Novel *see* Johannes Mario Simmel

ALLEINSEGLERIN, DIE, Novel *see* Christine Wolter

ALLER SIMPLE, UN, Novel *see* Edward Helseth

ALLES MOET WEG, Novel *see* Tom Lanoye

ALLEY CAT, THE, Novel *see* Anthony Carlyle

ALLIANCE, L', Novel *see* Jean-Claude Carriere

ALLIGATOR NAMED DAISY, AN, Novel *see* Charles Terrot

ALL'IRDISCH FREUD, Novel *see* Margit von Soderholm

ALL-OF-A-SUDDEN-PEGGY, London 1906, Play *see* Ernest Denny

ALLONS Z'ENFANTS, Novel *see* Yves Gibeau

ALLVARSAMMA LEKEN, DEN, 1912, Novel *see* Hjalmar Soderberg

ALMA DE DIOS, Opera *see* Carlos Arniches, E. Garcia Alvarez

ALMA TRIUNFANTE, 1902, Play *see* Jacinto Benavente y Martinez

ALMA, WHERE DO YOU LIVE?, Musical Play *see* Briquet, George V. Hobart, Paul Harve

ALMENRAUSCH UND EDELWEISS, Play *see* Hans Neuert, Dr. H. Schmidt

ALMODO IFJUSAG, 1946, Novel *see* Bela Balazs

ALMOST A HONEYMOON, London 1930, Play *see* Walter Ellis

ALMOST GOLDEN, Biography *see* Gwenda Blair

ALMOST GOOD MAN, THE, Story *see* Shelley Sutton

ALOHA LE CHANT DES ILES, Novel *see* C. A. Gonnet

ALOHA MEANS GOODBYE, Serial Story *see* Robert Carson

ALOHA MEANS GOODBYE, 1972, Novel *see* Naomi A. Hintze

ALOMA OF THE SOUTH SEAS, New York 1925, Play *see* Leroy Clemens, John B. Hymer

ALONE IN LONDON, London 1885, Play *see* Robert Buchanan, Harriet Jay

ALONE IN THE AUSTRALIAN OUTBACK, Book *see* Gladys Taylor

ALONG CAME JONES, Novel *see* Alan Le May

ALONG THE NAVAJO TRAIL, Novel *see* William Colt MacDonald

ALPENTRAGODIE, Novel *see* Richard Voss

ALRAUNE, Novel *see* Hanns Heinz Ewers

ALS MUTTER STREIKTE, Novel *see* Eric Malpass

ALSACE, Play *see* L. Camille, Gaston Leroux

ALSTER CASE, THE, New York 1914, Novel *see* Rufus Gillmore

ALSUREBA KOSO, 1923, Play *see* Junichiro Tanizaki

ALT HEIDELBERG, New York 1902, Play *see* Wilhelm Meyer-Forster

ALTAR MAYOR, 1926, Novel *see* Concha Espina de Serna

ALTAR OF THE DEAD, THE, 1895, Short Story *see* Henry James

ALTAR ON LITTLE THUNDER, AN, 1912, Short Story *see* Elmore Elliott Peake

ALTAR STAIRS, THE, New York 1908, Novel *see* G. B. Lancaster

ALTE FRITZ, DER, Novel *see* Walter von Molo

ALTE GNADIGE, DIE, *see* Gustav Wied

ALTER EGO, Novel *see* Mel Arrighi

ALTER EGO, Radio Play *see* Arch Oboler

ALTERED STATES, 1978, Novel *see* Paddy Chayefsky

ALTES HERZ GEHT AUF DIE REISE, Novel *see* Hans Fallada

ALTING OG ET POSTNUS, 1969, Play *see* Leif Petersen

ALTITUDE 3200, Play *see* Julien Luchaire

ALTRA FACCIA DELLA LUNA, L', Novel *see* Sergio Donati

ALTRO FIGLIO, L', 1905, Short Story *see* Luigi Pirandello

ALVES & CIA, Novel *see* Eca de Queiroz

ALWAY IN THE WAY, 1903, Song *see* Charles K. Harris

ALWAYS, Book *see* Trevor Meldal-Johnson

ALWAYS A VICTIM, *see* Marilyn Goldstein

ALWAYS OUTNUMBERED, ALWAYS OUTGUNNED, Book *see* Walter Mosley

ALWAYS TELL YOUR WIFE, Play *see* Seymour Hicks, E. Temple Thurston

AM ABEND AUF DER HEIDE, Novel *see* F. B. Cortan

AM TEETISCH, Vienna 1915, Play *see* Carl Sloboda

AMADA BATA, Novel *see* Kumar Pattanayak

AMADEUS, 1980, Play *see* Peter Shaffer

AMALIA, 1851, Novel *see* Jose Pedro Cristologo Marmol

AMANNISAHAN, Opera *see* Wang Yan

AMANT DE BORNEO, L', Play *see* Roger Ferdinand, Jose Germain

AMANT DE CINQ JOURS, L', Novel *see* Francois Parturier

AMANT DE MADAME VIDAL, L', Play *see* Louis Verneuil

AMANT DE PAILLE, L', Play *see* Marc-Gilbert Sauvajon

AMANT DE POCHE, L', Novel *see* Valdemar Lestienne

AMANT, L', Novel *see* Marguerite Duras

AMANT REVE, L', 1925, Play *see* Jacques Deval

AMANTE DELL'ORSA MAGGIORE, L', Novel *see* Sergiusz Piaseki

AMANTE DI GRAMIGNA, L', 1880, Short Story *see* Giovanni Verga

AMANTI, Play *see* Renaldo Cabieri, Brunello Rondi

AMANTS DU TAGE, LES, 1954, Novel *see* Joseph Kessel

AMARE SIGNIFICA., Novel *see* Italo Terzoli, Enrico Vaime

AMARILLY OF CLOTHES-LINE ALLEY, Boston 1915, Novel *see* Belle K. Maniates

AMATEUR ADVENTURESS, THE, 1918, Short Story *see* Thomas Edgelow

AMATEUR CRACKSMAN, THE, London 1899, Novel *see* E. W. Hornung

AMATEUR GENTLEMAN, THE, London 1913, Novel *see* Jeffrey Farnol

AMATEUR IN VIOLENCE, Novel *see* Michael Gilbert

AMATEUR NIGHT, Story *see* Bob Dillon

AMATEUR, THE, Novel *see* Robert Littell

AMATEUR WIDOW, AN, Story *see* Joseph Franklin Poland

AMAYA; O, LOS VASCOS EN EL SIGLO VIII, 1879, Novel *see* Francisco Navarro Villoslada

AMAZING ADVENTURE, AN, Story *see* Eleanor M. Ingram

AMAZING DR. CLITTERHOUSE, THE, New York 1937, Play *see* Barre Lyndon

AMAZING PARTNERSHIP, THE, 1914, Novel *see* E. Phillips Oppenheim

AMAZING QUEST OF MR. ERNEST BLISS, THE, London 1919, Novel *see* E. Phillips Oppenheim

AMAZONS, THE, London 1893, Play *see* Arthur Wing Pinero

AMBITION OF MARK TRUITT, THE, Indianapolis 1913, Novel *see* Henry Russell Miller

AMBOY DUKES, THE, Novel *see* Irving Shulman

AMBUSH, Short Story *see* Luke Short

AMBUSH, New York 1921, Play *see* Arthur Richman

AMBUSH AT BLANCO CANYON, Serial Story *see* Donald Hamilton

AMBUSH MURDERS, THE, Book *see* Ben Bradle Jr.

AMBUSHERS, THE, New York 1963, Book *see* Donald Hamilton

AME DE PIERRE, L', Novel *see* Georges Ohnet

AMELIE BOULE, Novel *see* Michele Angot

AMERE VICTOIRE, Novel *see* Rene Hardy

AMERICA, 1913, Musical Play *see* Arthur Voegtlin, John P. Wilson

AMERICA AMERICA, New York 1962, Book *see* Elia Kazan

AMERICAN ARISTOCRACY, Story *see* Frank Howard Clark

AMERICAN BEAUTY, 1927, Short Story *see* Wallace Irwin

AMERICAN BLACK CHAMBER, THE, Book *see* Major Herbert O. Yardley

AMERICAN BUFFALO, 1975, Play *see* David Mamet

AMERICAN CITIZEN, AN, New York 1897, Play *see* Madeleine Lucette Ryley

AMERICAN DREAM, AN, New York 1965, Novel *see* Norman Mailer

AMERICAN GENTLEMAN, AN, New York 1900, Play *see* William Bonelli

AMERICAN GIRL, 1930, Novel *see* John R. Tunis

AMERICAN GUERRILLA IN THE PHILIPPINES, AN, Novel *see* Ira Wolfert

AMERICAN HERO, Novel *see* Larry Beinhart

AMERICAN PRISONER, THE, Play *see* Eden Philpotts

AMERICAN SEX, THE, 1925, Short Story *see* Frank R. Adams

AMERICAN TRAGEDY, AN, New York 1925, Novel *see* Theodore Dreiser

AMERICAN WIDOW, AN, New York 1909, Play *see* Kellett Chambers

AMERICANIZATION OF EMILY, THE, New York 1959, Novel *see* William Bradford Huie

AMERICATHON 1998, Play *see* Peter Bergman, Philip Proctor

AMERICKA JACHTA VE SPLITU, Short Story *see* Milan Begovic

AMERIKA, 1927, Novel *see* Franz Kafka

AMES ENNEMIES, 1907, Novel *see* P. H. Loyson

AMES NOSTALGIQUES, Novel *see* Gabriel Charand

AMI DE MA FEMME, L', Play *see* Henri Geroule, Yves Mirande

AMI DE VINCENT, L', Novel *see* Jean-Marc Robert

AMI DES FEMMES, L', Play *see* Alexandre Dumas (fils)

AMI DES MONTAGNES, L', Novel *see* Jean Rameau

AMI FRITZ, L', Novel *see* Chatrian, Alexandre, Erckmann, Emile

AMI VIENDRA CE SOIR, UN, Play *see* Jacques Companeez, Yvan Noe

AMI-AMI, *see* Pierre Barillet, Jean-Pierre Gredy

AMICA, Monte Carlo 1905, Opera *see* Pierre Berel, Paul Collin, Pietro Mascagni

AMICA DEL CUORE, L', 1914, Play *see* Alfredo Testoni

AMIC/AMAT, Play *see* Josep M. Benet I Jornet

AMICO DEL CUORE, L', Play *see* Vincenzo Salemme

AMICO, L', 1886, Play *see* Marco Praga

AMIE D'ENFANCE, UNE, Play *see* Louise Roy, Louis Saia

AMINTA, 1573, *see* Torquato Tasso

AMINTIRI DIN COPILARIE, 1881-92, Autobiography *see* Ion Creanga

AMITIE, Play *see* Michel Dura

AMITIES PARTICULIERES, LES, Paris 1945, Novel *see* Roger Peyrefitte

AMMENKONIG, DER, Play *see* Max Dreyer

AMMIE, COME HOME, Novel *see* Barbara Michaels

AMOK, 1922, Short Story *see* Stefan Zweig

AMONG THE CINDERS, Novel *see* Maurice Shadbolt

AMONG THE MARRIED, New York 1929, Play *see* Vincent Lawrence

AMONG THE PATHS TO EDEN, 1960, Short Story *see* Truman Capote

AMONG THOSE PRESENT, Play *see* William Miles, Carrington North

AMOR BRUJO, EL, 1915, Play *see* Gregorio Martinez Sierra

AMOR DE LOS AMORES, EL, 1912, Novel *see* Ricardo Leon Y Roman

AMOR DE PERDICAO, 1862, Novel *see* Camilo Castello Branco

AMOR, VERBO INTRANSITIVO, 1927, Novel *see* Mario de Andrade

AMORE A ROMA, UN, Novel *see* Ercole Patti

AMORE CONIUGALE, L', 1949, Novel *see* Alberto Moravia

AMORE COSI FRAGILE COSI VIOLENTO, UN, Novel *see* Leros Pittoni

AMORE MOLESTO, L', Novel *see* Elena Ferrante

AMORE SENZA STIMA, Play *see* Paolo Ferrari

AMORE SUI TETTI, L', 1890, Play *see* Augusto Novelli

AMORE, UN, 1963, Novel *see* Dino Buzzati

AMORI MIEI, Musical Play *see* Iaia Fiastri

AMOROUS PRAWN, THE, London 1959, Play *see* Anthony Kimmins

AMOS, Novel *see* Stanley West

AMOS JUDD, New York 1895, Novel *see* John Ames Mitchell

AMOUR A L'AMERICAINE, L', Play *see* Andre Mouezy-Eon, Robert Spitzer

AMOUR CHANTE, L', Novel *see* Jacques Bousquet, Henri Falk

AMOUR, L'APRES-MIDI, L', 1974, Short Story *see* Eric Rohmer

AMOUR, MADAME, L', Play *see* Felix Gandera, Claude Gevel

AMOUR MASQUE, L', Short Story *see* Honore de Balzac

AMOUR QUI DOUTE, L', Novel *see* R. Florigny, Charles Veyre

AMOUR TERRE INCONNUE, Novel *see* Martin Maurice

AMOUR VEILLE, L', Paris 1907, Play *see* Gaston Arman de Caillavet, Robert de Flers

AMOUREUSE AVENTURE, L', Play *see* Paul Armont, Marcel Gerbidon

AMOURS DE ROCAMBOLE, LES, Novel *see* Ponson Du Terrail

AMPHITRYON, 1807, Play *see* Heinrich von Kleist

AMRITMANTHAN, Novel *see* Narayan Hari Apte

AMY FOSTER, Short Story *see* Joseph Conrad

AMY JOLLY - DIE FRAU AUS MARRAKESCH, Berlin-Friedenau 1927, Novel *see* Benno Vigny

AN HEILIGEN WASSERN, Stuttgart 1898, Novel *see* Jakob Christoph Heer

AN KLINGENDEN UFERN, Novel *see* Alexander Lernet-Holenia

ANA TERRA, 1949, Short Story *see* Erico Verissimo

ANANDMATH, 1884, Novel *see* Bankimchandra Chatterjee

ANARKALI, Play *see* Imtiaz Ali Taj

ANASTASIA, Play *see* Marcelle Maurette

ANATAHAN, Short Story *see* Michiro Maruyama

ANATOL, 1893, Play *see* Arthur Schnitzler

ANATOMIST, THE, 1931, Play *see* James Bridie

ANATOMY OF A MURDER, Novel *see* Robert Traver

ANATOMY OF AN ILLNESS, Autobiography *see* Norman Cousins

ANATOMY OF BALLYHOO: PHANTOM FAME, New York 1931, Book *see* David Freedman, Reichenback Harry

ANATRA ALL'ARANCIA, L', Play *see* William Douglas Home, Marc-Gilbert Sauvajon

ANCIENS DE SAINT-LOUP, LES, Novel *see* Pierre Very

ANCIENT HIGHWAY: A NOVEL OF HIGH HEARTS AND OPEN ROADS, THE, New York 1925, Novel *see* James Oliver Curwood

AND A NIGHTINGALE SANG, Play *see* C. P. Taylor

AND DELILAH, Short Story *see* Neil Paterson

AND I ALONE SURVIVED, Book *see* Lauren Elder, Shirley Streshinsky

AND LET WHO WILL BE CLEVER, Hollywood 1934, Play *see* Alden Nash

..AND NOW MIGUEL, New York 1953, Novel *see* Joseph Krumgold

AND NOW TOMORROW, Novel *see* Rachel Field

AND RIDE A TIGER, 1951, Novel *see* Robert Wilder

AND THE BAND PLAYED ON, Book *see* Randy Shilts

AND THE BEAT GOES ON, Book *see* Sonny Bono

AND THE BEST MAN WON, Short Story *see* George Marshall

AND THE SEA WILL TELL, Book *see* Vincent Bugliosi, Bruce B. Henderson

AND THEY SHALL WALK, Autobiography *see* Mary Kenny

ANDALOUSIE, Opera *see* Raymond Vinci, Albert Willemetz

ANDAMAN KAITHI, Play *see* Ku. SA. Krishnamurthy

ANDERE, DER, 1893, Play *see* Paul Lindau

ANDERE, DIE, Novel *see* Renate Uhl

ANDERE SEITE, DIE, 1908, Novel *see* Alfred Kubin

ANDERSON TAPES, THE, Novel *see* Lawrence Sanders

ANDERTHALB WEIDINGER, Novel *see* Peter Francke

ANDORRA OU LES HOMMES D'AIRAIN, Novel *see* Isabelle Sandy

ANDRE CORNELIS, Novel *see* Paul Bourget

ANDRE UND URSULA, Novel *see* Polly Maria Hofler

ANDREA, 1873, Play *see* Victorien Sardou

ANDREA CHENIER, Milan 1896, Opera *see* Umberto Giordano, Luigi Illica

ANDREMO IN CITTA, Novel *see* Edith Bruck

ANDROCLES AND THE LION, London 1913, Play *see* George Bernard Shaw

ANDROMEDA STRAIN, THE, Novel *see* Michael Crichton

ANDY M'GEE'S CHORUS GIRL, 1892, Short Story *see* Richard Harding Davis

ANE DE BURIDAN, L', 1909, Play *see* Arman Gaston de Caillavet, Robert de Flers

ANGE DE MINUIT, L', *see* Marcel L'Herbier

ANGE DU FOYER, L', Play *see* Arman Gaston de Caillavet, Robert de Flers

ANGE PASSE, UN, 1924, Short Story *see* Jacques Bousquet, Henri Falk

ANGEL AT MY TABLE, AN, 1984, Autobiography *see* Janet Frame

ANGEL CITY, Novel *see* Patrick Smith

ANGEL ESQUIRE, London 1908, Novel *see* Edgar Wallace

ANGEL ISLAND, Play *see* Bernadine Angus

ANGEL LEVINE, THE, 1955, Short Story *see* Bernard Malamud

ANGEL OF TERROR, THE, London 1922, Novel *see* Edgar Wallace

ANGEL OF THE WARD, THE, Novel *see* Murray Herbert

ANGEL PAVEMENT, 1930, Novel *see* J. B. Priestley

ANGEL RIVER, Novel *see* Vilet

ANGEL SQUARE, Novel *see* Brian Doyle

ANGEL WHO PAWNED HER HARP, THE, Television Play *see* Charles Terrot

ANGEL-FACE MOLLY, Story *see* Fred Kennedy Myton

ANGELINA; O EL HONOR DE UN BRIGADIER, Madrid 1934, Play *see* Enrique Jardiel Poncela

ANGELIQUE ET LE ROI, Novel *see* Anne Golon, Serge Golon

ANGELIQUE ET LE SULTAN, Novel *see* Anne Golon, Serge Golon

ANGELIQUE, MARQUISE DES ANGES, Novel *see* Anne Golon, Serge Golon

ANGELITA, Novel *see* Wendy Kesselman

ANGELS IN THE OUTFIELD, Radio Play *see* Richard Conlin

ANGELS OF DOOM, New York 1931, Novel *see* Leslie Charteris

ANGENT TROUBLE, Novel *see* Malcolm Bosse

ANGES NOIRS, LES, 1936, Novel *see* Francois Mauriac

ANGI VERA, Novel *see* Endre Veszi

ANGIE - UPTOWN WOMAN, 1929, Short Story *see* Vina Delmar

ANGIE I SAYS, Novel *see* Avra Wing

ANGLAIS TEL QU'ON LE PARLE, L', Play *see* Tristan Bernard

ANGLAR, FINNS DOM, PAPPA?, Uppsala 1955, Novel *see* John Einar Aberg

ANGLE SHOOTER, 1937, Short Story *see* Adela Rogers St. Johns

ANGLO-SAXON ATTITUDES, London 1956, Novel *see* Angus Wilson

ANGOISSE, L', Play *see* Celia de Vylars, Pierre Mills

ANGRY GOD, THE, Short Story *see* Emma Lindsay Squier

ANGRY HILLS, THE, Novel *see* Leon Uris

ANGST DES TORMANNS BEIM ELFMETER, DIE, 1970, Novel *see* Peter Handke

ANGST, DIE, 1920, Short Story *see* Stefan Zweig

ANGYAL, Vienna 1932, Play *see* Menyhert Lengyel

ANGYALFOLD, 1929, Novel *see* Marie-Luise Kaschnitz

ANIELLO 'A FFEDE, Novel *see* Rocco Galdieri

ANIKINA VREMENA, 1931, Short Story *see* Ivo Andric

ANIMA DEL DEMI-MONDE, L', Short Story *see* Augusto Genina

ANIMA NERA, Play *see* Giuseppe Patroni Griffi

ANIMA PERSA, Novel *see* Giovanni Arpino

ANIMAL CRACKERS, New York 1928, Musical Play *see* Bert Kalmar, George S. Kaufman

ANIMAL FARM, 1945, Novel *see* George Orwell

ANIMAL KINGDOM, THE, New York 1932, Play *see* Philip Barry

ANIMALE BOLNAVE, 1968, Novel *see* Nicolae Breban

ANIMALS ARE MY HOBBY, Book *see* Gertrude Davies Lintz

ANIMAUX DENATURES, LES, Paris 1952, Novel *see* Vercors

ANIME IN TUMULTO, Novel *see* Augusto Turati

ANITA G, 1962, Short Story *see* Alexander Kluge

ANITA UND DER TEUFEL, Play *see* Geza von Cziffra

ANJO MAL, UM, 1968, Short Story *see* Adonias Filho

ANKEMAN JARL, 1940, Play *see* Vilhelm Moberg

ANN ANNINGTON, Indianapolis 1918, Novel *see* Edgar Jepson

ANN VICKERS, New York 1933, Novel *see* Sinclair Lewis

ANNA AND THE KING OF SIAM, Book *see* Margaret Landon

ANNA ASCENDS, New York 1920, Play *see* Harry Chapman Ford

ANNA CHRISTIE, New York 1922, Play *see* Eugene O'Neill

ANNA IM GOLDENEN TOR, Novel *see* Erika Wisselinck

ANNA KARENINA, Moscow 1876, Novel *see* Lev Nikolayevich Tolstoy

ANNA LEE: HEADCASE, Novel *see* Liza Cody

ANNA LUCASTA, 1944, Play *see* Philip Yordan

ANNA MALLEEN, New York 1911, Novel *see* George Hugh Brennan

ANNA NA SHEE, 1895, Short Story *see* Anton Chekhov

ANNA OF GEIERSTEINE, Novel *see* Sir Walter Scott

ANNA RINGARS, 1925, Play *see* Jarl Hemmer

ANNA THE ADVENTURESS, London 1904, Novel *see* E. Phillips Oppenheim

ANNABEL LEE, 1849, Poem *see* Edgar Allan Poe

ANNE AGAINST THE WORLD, New York 1925, Novel *see* Victor Thorne

ANNE FRANK REMEMBERED, Book *see* Miep Gies

ANNE FRANK: THE DIARY OF A YOUNG GIRL, Book *see* Anne Frank

ANNE OF GREEN GABLES, Boston 1908, Novel *see* L. M. Montgomery

ANNE OF THE THOUSAND DAYS, New York 1948, Play *see* Maxwell Anderson

ANNE OF WINDY WILLOWS, New York 1936, Novel *see* L. M. Montgomery

ANNE PEDERSDOTTER, 1917, Play *see* Hans Wiers-Jenssen

ANNEE DES MEDUSES, L', Novel *see* Christopher Frank

ANNEE DU BAC, L', Play *see* Jose-Andre Lacour

ANNEES LUMIERE, LES, Novel *see* Daniel Odier

ANNELIE, Play *see* Walter Lieck

ANNE'S BRIDGE, New York 1914, Novel *see* Robert W. Chambers

ANNETTE ET LA DAME BLONDE, 1963, Short Story *see* Georges Simenon

ANNETTE HAT ZUVIEL GELD, Play *see* Balder-Olden, Karl Rossler

ANNEXING BILL, Short Story *see* Edgar Franklin

ANNIE FOR SPITE, 1916, Short Story *see* Frederick Jackson

ANNIE LAURIE, Chicago 1897, Play *see* Lottie Blair Parker

ANNIE'S COMING OUT, Book *see* Rosemary Crossley, Anne McDonald

ANNIVERSARY, THE, London 1966, Play *see* Bill MacIlwraith

ANNIVERSARY WALTZ, New York 1954, Play *see* Jerome Chodorov, Joseph Fields

ANNO A PIETRALATA, UN, Book *see* Albino Bernardini

ANNO DI SCUOLA, UN, Short Story *see* Gianni Stuparich

ANNO SULL'ALTOPIANO, UN, Novel *see* Emilio Lussu

ANN'S AN IDIOT, London 1923, Novel *see* Pamela Wynne

ANOMALIES, Short Story *see* Paul Bourget

ANONIMA ROYLOTT, L', Play *see* Guglielmo Giannini

ANONYME BRIEFE, Novel *see* Annemarie Artinger

ANOTHER COUNTRY, 1982, Play *see* Julian Mitchell

ANOTHER LANGUAGE, New York 1932, Play *see* Rose Franken

ANOTHER MAN'S SHOES, New York 1913, Novel *see* Victor Bridges

ANOTHER MAN'S WIFE, Play *see* Miles Wallerton

ANOTHER PART OF THE FOREST, 1947, Play *see* Lillian Hellman

ANOTHER SCANDAL, Boston 1924, Novel *see* Cosmo Hamilton

ANOTHER SHORE, Novel *see* Kenneth Reddin

ANOTHER TIME, ANOTHER PLACE, Novel *see* Jessie Kesson

ANSICHTEN EINES CLOWNS, 1963, Novel *see* Heinrich Boll

ANSTANDIGER MENSCH, EIN, Play *see* Georg Fraser

ANSWER IN GRAND LARCENY, AN, 1919, Short Story *see* Jack Boyle

ANSWER IN THE MAGNOLIAS, THE, New York 1935, Novel *see* Tess Slesinger

ANT & THE GRASSHOPPER, THE, 1936, Short Story *see* W. Somerset Maugham

ANTAR, *see* Chekri Ganem

ANTARJALI JATRA, 1960, Novel *see* Kamal Kumar Majumdar

ANTENATO, L', Play *see* Carlo Veneziani

ANTES, O VERAO, 1964, Novel *see* Carlos Heitor Cony

ANTHONY ADVERSE, New York 1933, Novel *see* Hervey Allen

ANTHONY THE ABSOLUTE, New York 1914, Novel *see* Samuel Merwin

ANTIDOTE, THE, Play *see* Ben Landeck

ANTIGONE, c441 bc, Play *see* Sophocles

ANTIMONIO, L', 1958, Short Story *see* Leonardo Sciasia

ANTIQUITATEN, Play *see* Friedrich Forster

ANTI-SNIPER, Article *see* John Falk

ANTON THE TERRIBLE, 1916, Short Story *see* Thomas H. Uzzell

ANTONIA, Play *see* Melchior Lengyel

ANTONIETA, Novel *see* Andres Henestrosa

ANTONIO DI PADOVA IL SANTO DEI MIRACOLI, Novel *see* Vittorino Facchinetti

ANTONY, 1831, Novel *see* Alexandre Dumas (pere)

ANTONY AND CLEOPATRA, c1607, Play *see* William Shakespeare

ANTRE DE MISERICORDE, L', Novel *see* Pierre MacRolan

ANTWORT KENNT NUR DER WIND, DIE, Novel *see* Johannes Mario Simmel

ANY NUMBER CAN PLAY, Novel *see* Edward Harris Heth

ANY WEDNESDAY, New York 1964, Play *see* Muriel Resnik

ANYA KORO, 1922-37, Novel *see* Naoya Shiga

ANYTHING CAN HAPPEN, Book *see* George Papashvily, Helen Papashvily

ANYTHING GOES, New York 1934, Musical Play *see* Guy Bolton, Cole Porter, P. G. Wodehouse

ANYTHING MIGHT HAPPEN, Novel *see* Lady Evelyn Balfour

ANYUTA, 1886, Short Story *see* Anton Chekhov

ANZIO, New York 1961, Book *see* Wynford Vaughan-Thomas

AOBEKA MONOGATARI, Novel *see* Shugoro Yamamoto

AOI SATSUJINSHA, 1966, Novel *see* Shintaro Ishihara

AOIRO KAKUMEI, 1952-53, Novel *see* Tatsuzo Ishikawa

APA, 1973, Novel *see* Alexandru Ivasiuc

APACHE AGENT, 1936, Biography *see* Woodworth Clum

APACHE LANDING, 1951, Novel *see* Robert J. Hogan

APACHE RISING, Greenwich, Ct. 1957, Novel *see* Marvin H. Albert

APACHE TRAIL, Story *see* Ernest Haycox

APARAJITA, 1931, Novel *see* Bibhuti Bhushan Bandyopadhyay

APARAJITO, Novel *see* Bibhutibhushan Bannerjee

APARECIDOS, LOS, Opera *see* Carlos Arniches, Celso Lucio

APE, THE, Los Angeles 1927, Play *see* Adam Hull Shirk

APHRODITE, Novel *see* Pierre Louys

APOLLO AND THE SEAMAN, Poem *see* Herbert Trench

APOLOGO, UM, 1885, Short Story *see* Joaquim Maria Machado de Assis

APOTHEKERIN, DIE, Novel *see* Ingrid Noll

APPALOOSA, THE, Connecticut 1963, Book *see* Robert MacLeod

APPARTEMENT DES FILLES, L', Novel *see* Jacques Robert

APPASSIONNATA, L', Play *see* Pierre Frondaie

APPAT, L', Book *see* Morgan Sportes

APPEARANCE OF EVIL, THE, Short Story *see* Horace Hazeltine

APPEARANCES, Play *see* Edward Knoblock

APPELEZ-MOI MAITRE, Play *see* Jacques Vilfred

APPLAUSE, New York 1928, Novel *see* Beth Brown

APPLE DUMPLING GANG, THE, Novel *see* James M. Bickham

APPLE PIE IN THE SKY, Novel *see* Marc Lovell

APPLE TREE, THE, 1918, Short Story *see* John Galsworthy

APPLESAUCE, New York 1925, Play *see* Barry Conners

APPLE-TREE GIRL, THE, 1917, Story *see* George Weston

APPOINTMENT IN ZAHRAIN, London 1960, Novel *see* Michael Barrett

APPOINTMENT WITH DEATH, Novel *see* Agatha Christie

APPOINTMENT WITH FEAR, Novel *see* Ross Huggins

APPOINTMENT WITH FEAR, Story *see* Roy Huggins

APPOINTMENT WITH VENUS, Novel *see* Jerrard Tickell

APPRENTI SALAUD, L', Novel *see* Frank Neville

APPRENTICESHIP OF DUDDY KRAVITZ, THE, 1959, Novel *see* Mordecai Richler

APPRENTIE, L', *see* Gustave Geffroy

APPUNTAMENTO AL MARE, 1962, Short Story *see* Alberto Moravia

APPUNTAMENTO COL DISONORE, Novel *see* William Cage

APRE LUTTE, L', Play *see* Robert Boudrioz

APRES L'AMOUR, Play *see* Henri Duvernois, Pierre Wolff

APRES LUI, Novel *see* Pierre Villetard

APRIL FOLLY, 1918, Story *see* Cynthia Stockley

APRIL SHOWER, AN, 1915, Play *see* Alexander Carr, Edgar Allan Woolf

APRIL SHROUD, AN, London 1975, Novel *see* Reginald Hill

APRON STRINGS, 1930, Play *see* Dorrance Davis

APT PUPIL, Novel *see* Stephen King

AQUIS SUBMERSUS, 1877, Novel *see* Theodor Storm

ARAB, THE, Story *see* D. D. Calhoun

ARAB, THE, New York 1911, Play *see* Edgar Selwyn

ARAGOSTE DI SICILIA, Play *see* Bruno Corbucci, Gianni Grimaldi

ARAKURE, 1915, Novel *see* Shusei Tokuda

ARANAZHIKANERAM, Novel *see* Parappuram

ARANYE DINRATRI, Novel *see* Sunil Ganguly

ARANYEMBER, AZ, 1872, Novel *see* Mor Jokai

ARANYORA, 1931, Play *see* Erno Szep

ARANYSARKANY, 1925, Novel *see* Dezso Kosztolanyi

ARAUCANA, LA, 1589, Verse *see* Alonso de Ercilla Y Zuniga

ARBEITSPLATZ ODER IM SCHWEISSE DEINES ANGESICHTS SOLLST DU., 1962, Short Story *see* Bertolt Brecht

ARBOUR, THE, Play *see* Andrea Dunbar

ARBRE DE NOEL, L', Paris 1967, Novel *see* Michel Bataille

ARC DE TRIOMPHE, 1946, Novel *see* Erich Maria Remarque

ARCADIANS, THE, London 1909, Musical Play *see* Mark Ambient, Alex M. Thompson

ARCHDUKE, THE, New York 1967, Book *see* Michael Arnold

ARCHE DE NOE, L', Novel *see* Albert Paraz

ARCHER PLUS 20, Novel *see* Hugh Clevely

ARCIDIAVOLO, L', Play *see* Gherardo Gherardi

ARDH SATYA, Short Story *see* S. D. Panwalkar

ARDIENTE PACIENCA, Novel *see* Antonio Skarmeta

ARDOISE, L', Novel *see* Pierre Vial-Lesou

ARE PARENTS PEOPLE?, 1924, Short Story *see* Alice Duer Miller

ARE YOU A MASON?, New York 1901, Play *see* Leo Ditrichstein, Emmanuel Lederer

ARE YOU IN THE HOUSE ALONE?, Novel *see* Richard Peck

ARE YOU LISTENING?, Boston 1932, Novel *see* Joseph Patrick McEvoy

ARE YOU MY WIFE?, New York 1910, Novel *see* Max Marcin

ARE YOU WITH IT?, Play *see* George Balzer, Sam Perrin

ARENASUL ROMAN, 1893, Short Story *see* Ion Luca Caragiale

AREN'T MEN BEASTS!, London 1936, Play *see* Vernon Sylvaine

AREN'T WE ALL?, London 1923, Play *see* Frederick Lonsdale

AREN'T YOU EVEN GONNA KISS ME GOODBYE?, Novel *see* William Richert

ARGENT, L', 1891, Novel *see* Emile Zola

ARGINE, L', Play *see* Rino Alessi

ARGONAUTICHE, LE, Novel *see* Apollonio Rodio

ARGOW IL PIRATA, 1831, Short Story *see* Honore de Balzac

ARGYLE ALBUM, THE, Radio Play *see* Cy Endfield

ARGYLE CASE, THE, New York 1912, Play *see* Harriet Ford, Harvey J. O'Higgins

ARHANGELII, 1914, Novel *see* Ion Agarbiceanu

ARIA DEL CONTINENTE, L', Play *see* Nino Martoglio

ARIADNE IN HOPPEGARTEN, Novel *see* Ludwig Wolff

ARIANE, 1933, Novel *see* Claude Anet

ARISTOCRACY, New York 1892, Play *see* Bronson Howard

ARISTOCRATES, LES, Novel *see* Michel de Saint-Pierre

ARIZONA, Chicago 1899, Play *see* Augustus Thomas

ARIZONA, New York 1939, Novel *see* Clarence Budington Kelland

ARIZONA AMES, New York 1932, Novel *see* Zane Grey

ARIZONA IN THE '50S, Novel *see* James H. Tevis

ARK ANGEL, THE, Short Story *see* Hamilton Thompson

ARLESIENNE, L', 1872, Play *see* Alphonse Daudet

ARLETTE ET SES PAPAS, Play *see* Georges Berr, Louis Verneuil

ARM, THE, Novel *see* Clark Howard

ARMADALE, Novel *see* Wilkie Collins

ARME A GAUCHE, L', Novel *see* Charles Williams

ARME KLEINE SIF, Novel *see* Reck-Malleczewen

ARMEE DES OMBRES, L', 1943, Novel *see* Joseph Kessel

ARMIAMOCI E. PARTITE, Play *see* Jose Castillo

ARMS AND THE GIRL, New York 1916, Play *see* Robert Baker, Grant Stewart

ARMS AND THE MAN, 1894, Play *see* George Bernard Shaw

ARMY BRAT, Novel *see* Thomas D. Naddleton Jr.

ARMY GIRL, 1935, Short Story *see* Charles L. Clifford

AROUSE AND BEWARE, New York 1936, Novel *see* MacKinlay Kantor

ARPETE, L', Play *see* Yves Mirande, Gustave Quinson

ARRAH-NA-POGUE, 1865, Play *see* Dion Boucicault

ARRANGEMENT, THE, New York 1967, Novel *see* Elia Kazan

ARRIVISTE, L', Novel *see* Felicien Champsaur

ARROW IN THE SUN, New York 1969, Novel *see* Theodore V. Olsen

ARSENAL STADIUM MYSTERY, THE, Novel *see* Leonard Gribble

ARSENE LUPIN, Paris 1907, Novel *see* Maurice Leblanc

ARSENIC AND OLD LACE, New York 1941, Play *see* Joseph Kesselring

ARSHIN MAL ALAN, Opera *see* Uzeir Hajibeyov

ARTHUR, Opera *see* Andre Barde, Henri Christine

ARTICLE 330, L', 1900, Play *see* Georges Courteline

ARTICOLO 1083, L', Play *see* Antonino Russo-Giusti

ARTIE, New York 1907, Play *see* George Ade

ARTIFICIAL MAN, THE, London 1965, Novel *see* L. P. Davies

ARTISAN, THE, Novel *see* Stephen Sheppard

ARTUR A LEONTYNA, Novel *see* Ignat Herrmann

ARVACSKA, 1941, Novel *see* Zsigmond Moricz

ARZIGOGOLO, L', 1922, Play *see* Sem Benelli

ARZT AUS LEIDENSCHAFT, Novel *see* Carl Unselt

ARZTINNEN, 1980, Play *see* Rolf Hochhuth

ARZTLICHES GEHEIMNIS, Play *see* Ladislaus Fodor

AS A MAN THINKS, New York 1911, Play *see* Augustus Thomas

AS GOD MADE HER, 1919, Novel *see* Helen Prothero Lewis

AS GOOD AS NEW, New York 1930, Play *see* Thompson Buchanan

AS HUSBANDS GO, New York 1931, Play *see* Rachel Crothers

AS IN A LOOKING GLASS, New York 1887, Novel *see* Francis Charles Philips

AS, L', Play *see* Blanche Alix, Yvan Noe, C. Poidloue

AS LONG AS THEY'RE HAPPY, London 1953, Play *see* Vernon Sylvaine

AS THE EARTH TURNS, New York 1933, Novel *see* Gladys Hasty Carroll

AS THE SPARKS FLY UPWARDS, Story *see* Cyrus Townsend Brady

AS THE SUN WENT DOWN, Play *see* George D. Baker

AS WE SEE RUSSIA, 1948, Book *see* Overseas Press Club

AS YE SOW, New York 1905, Play *see* Rev. John M. Snyder

AS YOU ARE, Play *see* Hugh Mills, Wells Root

AS YOU LIKE IT, c1600, Play *see* William Shakespeare

ASAJI GA YADO, c1768, Short Story *see* Akinari Ueda

ASAKUSA NO SHIMAI, 1932, Short Story *see* Yasunari Kawabata

ASCENSAO AO MUNDO DE ANUSKA, 1965, Short Story *see* Ignacio de Loyola Brandao

ASCENSEUR POUR L'ECHAFAUD, Paris 1956, Novel *see* Noel Calef

ASCHENBROEDEL, Story *see* Bruno Lessing

ASCHENPUTTEL, Short Story *see* Jacob Grimm, Wilhelm Grimm

ASFALTO SELVAGEM, 1960, Novel *see* Nelson Rodrigues

ASFALTO SELVAGEM: LIVRO 2, Rio De Janeiro 1960, Novel *see* Nelson Rodrigues

ASHA PARAT YETE, Novel *see* Jayant Devkule

ASHAD KA EK DIN, 1958, Play *see* Mohan Rakesh

ASHANI SANKET, 1959, Novel *see* Bibhutibhushan Bannerjee

ASHES, Story *see* Marion Brooks

ASHES OF REVENGE, THE, Novel *see* R. C. Carton

ASHES OF VENGEANCE; A ROMANCE OF OLD FRANCE, New York 1914, Novel *see* H. B. Somerville

ASHIK KERIB, 1837, Short Story *see* Mikhail Lermontov

ASHIKARI, 1932, Novel *see* Junichiro Tanizaki

ASHTON-KIRK, INVESTIGATOR, Philadelphia 1910, Book *see* John Thomas McIntyre

ASHWATHAMA, Novel *see* Madampu Kunjukuttan

ASIR OF ASIRGARH, Novel *see* Snilloc

ASK AGAMEMNON, London 1964, Novel *see* Jenni Hall

ASK ANY GIRL, 1958, Novel *see* Winifred Wolfe

ASK BECCLES, London 1926, Play *see* Cyril Campion, Edward Dignon

ASKING FOR TROUBLE, Book *see* Donald Woods

ASPEN, Novel *see* Burt Hirschfield

ASPERN PAPERS, THE, 1888, Short Story *see* Henry James

ASPHALT JUNGLE, New York 1949, Novel *see* William Riley Burnett

ASSASSIN A PEUR LA NUIT, L', Novel *see* Pierre Very

ASSASSIN EST DANS L'ANNUAIRE, L', Novel *see* Charles Exbrayat

ASSASSIN HABITE AU 21, L', Novel *see* Stanislas-Andre Steeman

ASSASSIN, L', 1937, Novel *see* Georges Simenon

ASSASSIN, UN, 1866, Novel *see* Jules Claretie

ASSASSINATION, Novel *see* Richard Sale

ASSASSINATION BUREAU LTD, THE, 1963, Novel *see* Robert L. Fish, Jack London

ASSASSINS DE L'ORDRE, LES, Novel *see* Jean Laborde

ASSAULT, Novel *see* Kendal Young

ASSAULT ON A QUEEN, New York 1959, Novel *see* Jack Finney

ASSAUT, L', Play *see* Henri Bernstein

ASSIGNMENT IN BRITTANY, Novel *see* Helen MacInnes

ASSISI UNDERGROUND, THE, Novel *see* Alexander Ramati

ASSISTANT, THE, 1957, Novel *see* Bernard Malamud

ASSISTING ANANIAS, 1920, Short Story *see* W. C. Tuttle

ASSIZE OF THE DYING, THE, Novel *see* Edith Pargiter

ASSOLUTO NATIONALE, L', Book *see* Goffredo Parise

ASSOMMOIR, L', 1877, Novel *see* Emile Zola

ASSUNTA SPINA, 1909, Play *see* Salvatore Di Giacomo

ASTONISHED HEART, THE, 1936, Play *see* Noel Coward

ASTORIA, Novel *see* Washington Irving

ASTRAGALE, L', 1965, Novel *see* Albertine Sarrazin

ASTRAKHAN COAT, THE, Play *see* Pauline Macaulay

ASTRID, 1911, Novel *see* Annie Vivanti

ASTRONAUCI, Warsaw 1951, Novel *see* Stanislaw Lem

ASYA, 1858, Short Story *see* Ivan Turgenev

AT BAY, Washington, D.C. 1913, Play *see* George Scarborough

AT CRIPPLE CREEK, Play *see* Hal Reid

AT DAWN, Short Story *see* Frederick Moore

AT DERE TOR!, Novel *see* Espen Haavardsholm

AT GOOD OLD SIWASH, Boston 1911, Novel *see* George Fitch

AT PINEY RIDGE, New York 1897, Play *see* David K. Higgins

AT PLAY IN THE FIELDS OF THE LORD, Novel *see* Peter Mathiessen

AT THE BARN, New York 1914, Play *see* Anthony Wharton

AT THE EARTH'S CORE, 1922, Novel *see* Edgar Rice Burroughs

AT THE END OF THE WORLD, Play *see* Ernest Klein

AT THE MERCY OF TIBERIUS, New York 1887, Novel *see* Augusta Jane Evans Wilson

AT THE OLD CROSS ROADS, New York 1902, Play *see* Hal Reid

AT THE POINT OF A GUN, Story *see* Dorothy Rockfort

AT THE SIGN OF THE JACK O'LANTERN, New York 1905, Novel *see* Myrtle Reed

AT THE SWITCH; OR HER MARRIAGE VOW, Play *see* Owen Davis

AT THE VILLA ROSE, 1910, Novel *see* A. E. W. Mason

AT WAR WITH THE ARMY, New York 1949, Play *see* James B. Allardice

ATADURAS, LAS, 1960, Short Story *see* Carmen Martin Gaite

ATALANTA; A STORY OF ATLANTIS, London 1949, Play *see* Gerald P. Hargreaves

ATAVISM OF JOHN TOM LITTLE BEAR, THE, Short Story *see* O. Henry

ATHALIE, Play *see* Jean Racine

ATHALIE, New York 1915, Novel *see* Robert W. Chambers

ATITHI, 1895, Short Story *see* Rabindranath Tagore

ATLANTIC ADVENTURER, 1934, Short Story *see* Diana Bourbon

ATLANTIDE, L', Paris 1919, Novel *see* Pierre Benoit

ATOM VECNOSTI A TAKOVA JE VECNA HRA LASKY, Play *see* Jaroslav Smejkal, Vladimir Smejkal

ATOMIC SOLDIERS, Book *see* Howard L. Rosenberg

ATOUT-COEUR, Play *see* Felix Gandera

ATOUTS DE M. WENS, LES, Novel *see* Stanislas-Andre Steeman

ATTACK ON TERROR, Novel *see* Don Whitehead

ATTAQUE DU MOULIN, L', 1880, Short Story *see* Emile Zola

ATTAQUE NOCTURNE, Play *see* Andre de Lorde, Masson-Forestier

ATTENTAT DE LA MAISON ROUGE, L', Play *see* Andre de Lorde, Alfred Gragnon

ATTENTI AL BUFFONE, Novel *see* Alberto Bevilacqua

ATTI RELATIVI ALLA MORTE DI RAYMOND ROUSSEL, Novel *see* Leonardo Sciasia

ATTRACTA, 1978, Short Story *see* William Trevor

AU BONHEUR DES DAMES, 1883, Novel *see* Emile Zola

AU BOUT DU MONDE, Novel *see* Gerhard Menzel

AU DELA DES LOIS HUMAINES, *see* Daniel Jourda

AU DIABLE LA VERTU, Play *see* Jean Guitton

AU NOM DE LA LOI, Novel *see* Paul Bringuier

AU PARADIS DES ENFANTS, Novel *see* Andre Theuriet

AU PAYS DES CIGALES, Opera *see* Henri Alibert, Marco Cab, Raymond Vinci

AU PAYS DU SOLEIL, Opera *see* Henri Alibert, Rene Sarvil

AU PETIT BONHEUR, Play *see* Marc-Gilbert Sauvajon

AU PIED DU MUR, Novel *see* Gilles Perrault

AU SOLEIL DE MARSEILLE, Opera *see* Marco Cab, Charles Tutelier

AU TELEPHONE, Play *see* Andre de Lorde, Charles Foley

AUBE, L', Book *see* Elie Wiesel

AUBERGE DE L'ABIME, L', 1933, Novel *see* Andre Chamson

AUBERGE DES ADRETS, L', Play *see* Benjamin Antier, Saint-Amand

AUBERGE DU TOHU-BOHU, L', Play *see* Maurice Ordonneau

AUBERGE, L', Short Story *see* Guy de Maupassant

AUBERGE ROUGE, L', 1831, Short Story *see* Honore de Balzac

AUCA DEL SENYOR ESTEVE, L', 1907, Play *see* Santiago Rusinol

AUCTION BLOCK; A NOVEL OF NEW YORK LIFE, THE, New York 1914, Novel *see* Rex Beach

AUCTION MART, THE, Novel *see* Sydney Tremaine

AUCTIONEER, THE, New York 1913, Play *see* Lee Arthur, Charles Klein

AUDREY, Boston 1902, Novel *see* Mary Johnston

AUDREY ROSE, Novel *see* Frank de Felitta

AUFENTHALT, DER, Novel *see* Hermann Kant

AUFHALTSAME AUFSTIEG DER ARTURO UI, DER, 1958, Play *see* Bertolt Brecht

AUFRUHR IM DAMENSTIFT, Play *see* Axel Breidahl

AUFSTAND DER FISCHER VON SANTA BARBARA, DER, 1928, Novel *see* Anna Seghers

AUGEN, DIE, Short Story *see* Franz Nabl

AUGGIE WREN'S CHRISTMAS STORY, Short Story *see* Paul Auster

AUGUST WEEK-END, 1933, Short Story *see* Faith Baldwin

AUGUSTE, Play *see* Raymond Castans

AULD JEREMIAH, Short Story *see* Henry C. Rowland

AUNT CLARA, Novel *see* Noel Streatfield

AUNT EMMA PAINTS THE TOWN, Story *see* Harry Hervey

AUNT RACHEL, Novel *see* David Christie Murray

AUNTIE MAME, Novel *see* Patrick Dennis

AUNTY'S ROMANCE, Play *see* W. Hanson Durham

AURA, Mexico City 1962, Novel *see* Carlos Fuentes

AURA AND THE KINGFISHER, THE, Novel *see* Tom Hart

AURORA FLOYD, Novel *see* Mary Elizabeth Braddon

AUS DEM LEBEN EINES TAUGENICHTS, 1826, Novel *see* Joseph von Eichendorff

AUS DEM TAGEBUCH EINES JUNGGESELLEN, Play *see* Rene Sorel

AUS EINEM DEUTSCHEN LEBEN, Novel *see* Robert Merle

AUS MEINEM LEBEN. DICHTUNG UND WAHRHEIT, 1811-33, Autobiography *see* Johann Wolfgang von Goethe

AUTHENTIC DEATH OF HENDRY JONES, THE, New York 1956, Novel *see* Charles Neider

AUTO DA COMPADECIDA, 1959, Play *see* Ariano Suassuna

AUTOBIOGRAPHY OF FRANCO ZEFFIRELLI, THE, Autobiography *see* Franco Zefirelli

AUTOBIOGRAPHY OF MALCOLM X, THE, Autobiography *see* Alex Haley, Malcolm X

AUTOBIOGRAPHY OF MISS JANE PITTMAN, THE, 1971, Novel *see* Ernest J. Gaines

AUTOGRAMM, DAS, Novel *see* Osvaldo Soriano

AUTRE AILE, L', Novel *see* Canudo

AUTRE FEMME, L', Novel *see* Maria-Luisa Linares

AUTUMN, Play *see* Ilya Surgutchoff

AUTUMN CROCUS, London 1931, Play *see* C. L. Anthony

AUTUMN OF PRIDE, THE, Novel *see* E. Newton Bungey

AUX ABOIS, Zurich 1953, Novel *see* Walter Blickensdorfer

AUX DEUX COLOMBES, Play *see* Sacha Guitry

AV HJARTANS LUST, 1944, Play *see* Karl Ragnar Gierow

AVALANCHE, Novel *see* Frances Doel, Zane Grey

AVALANCHE, 1944, Novel *see* Kay Boyle

AVALANCHE: A MYSTERY STORY, THE, New York 1919, Play *see* Gertrude Franklin Atherton

AVALANCHE EXPRESS, Novel *see* Colin Forbes

AVALANCHE, THE, Philadelphia 1912, Play *see* Robert Hilliard, W. A. Tremayne

AVANT L'EXIL, Book *see* Prince Youssoupov

AVANTI!, Play *see* Samuel Taylor

AVANTI LA MUSICA, Novel see Charles Exbrayat

AVARE, L', 1668, Play see Moliere

AVARIES, LES, Liege 1902, Play see Eugene Brieux

AVATAR, see Theophile Gautier

AVE MARIA, Story see Sister Eileen

AVEC UN ELASTIQUE, Novel see Charles Williams

AVENGER, THE, London 1926, Novel see Edgar Wallace

AVENGER, THE, New York 1926, Novel see John Goodwin

AVENGING ANGEL, THE, Novel see Rex Burns

AVENTURE AMOUREUSE, L', Novel see A. Mercier, Pierre Vignal

AVENTURE COMMENCERA CE SOIR, L', Novel see Robert Collard

AVENTURE EST A BORD, L', Novel see G. Vidal

AVENTURES COCASSES DE BOULOT AVIATEUR, LES, Novel see Georges de La Fouchardiere

AVENTURES DE LAGARDERE, LES, Novel see Paul Feval

AVENTURES DE ROCAMBOLE, LES, see Pierre-Alexis Ponson Du Terrail

AVENTURES DE SCHWEDENKLEES, LES, Novel see Bernhard Kellermann

AVENTURES DE THOMAS PLUMEPATTE, LES, Play see Gaston Marot

AVENTURES DE TILL ESPIEGLE, LES, Novel see Charles de Coster

AVENTURES DU CAPITAINE CORCORAN, LES, Novel see Alfred Assollant

AVENTURES DU CHEVALIER DE FAUBLAS, LES, Novel see Louvet de Couvray

AVENTURES DU DERNIER ABENCERAGE, 1826, see Francois Rene Chateaubriand

AVENTURES DU ROI PAUSOLE, LES, 1901, Novel see Pierre Louys

AVENTURIER, L', Play see Alfred Capus

AVENTURIERE, L', Play see Emile Paul Augier

AVENTURIERS, LES, Paris 1960, Novel see Jose Giovanni

AVERAGE WOMAN, THE, 1922, Short Story see Dorothy de Jagers

AVEU; DANS L'ENGRENAGE DU PROCES DE PRAGUE, L', Paris 1968, Novel see Artur London

AVEUGLE, L', Play see Anicet Bourgeois, Adolphe-P. d'Ennery

AVIATOR, THE, Novel see Ernest K. Gann

AVIATOR, THE, New York 1910, Play see James Montgomery

AVION DE MINUIT, L', Novel see Roger Labric

AVOCAT, L', 1922, Play see Eugene Brieux

AVVENTURA DI UN UOMO TRANQUILLO, L', Book see Pietro Calderoni

AVVENTURA DI VIAGGIO, 1887, Short Story see Roberto Barocco

AVVENTURE DI PINOCCHIO, LE, 1883, Short Story see Carlo Collodi

AVVOCATO DIFENSORE, L', Play see Mario Morais

AWAKENING LAND, THE, Novel see Conrad Richter

AWAKENING OF HELENA RICHIE, THE, New York 1906, Novel see Margaret Deland

AWAKENING, THE, 1899, Novel see Kate Chopin

AWAKENINGS, Book see Dr. Oliver Sacks

AWAY ALL BOATS, 1954, Novel see Kenneth M. Dodson

AWAY ALONE, Play see Janet Noble

AWFUL TRUTH, THE, New York 1922, Play see Arthur Richman

AWFULLY BIG ADVENTURE, AN, 1989, Novel see Beryl Bainbridge

AXELLE, Paris 1928, Novel see Pierre Benoit

AY CARMELA!, Play see Jose Sanchis Sinistierra

AYLWIN, Novel see Theodore Watts-Dunton

AZ EN MASODIK FELESEGEM, 1907, Novel see Eugene Heltai

AZAIS, Play see Georges Berr, Louis Verneuil

AZURE SHORE, THE, 1923, Short Story see Fanny Hatton, Frederic Hatton

B, 1916, Short Story see Edgar Franklin

B. MONKEY, Novel see Andrew Davies

BA SANG TA-TE TI-ME-MENG, Novel see Dschasi Dawa

BA WANG BIE JI, Novel see Li Bihua

BAA BAA BLACK SHEEP, 1921, Short Story see W. C. Tuttle

BAAL, 1922, Play see Bertolt Brecht

BAAL BABYLONE, 1959, Novel see Fernando Arrabal

BABBITT, New York 1922, Novel see Sinclair Lewis

BABE RUTH: HIS LIFE & LEGEND, Book see Karl Wagenheim

BABE: THE LEGEND COMES TO LIFE, Book see Robert W. Creamer

BABES IN ARMS, New York 1937, Musical Play see Lorenz Hart, Richard Rodgers

BABES IN TOYLAND, New York 1903, Operetta see Victor Herbert, Glen MacDonough

BABETTE, New York 1916, Novel see Frank Berkeley Smith

BABETTE'S FEAST, 1950, Short Story see Karen Blixen

BABICKA, 1846, Novel see Bozena Nemcova

BABOUC, OU LE MONDE COMME IL VA, 1750, Short Story see Francois-Marie Arouet de Voltaire

BAB'S BURGLAR, 1917, Short Story see Mary Roberts Rinehart

BABY, Play see Hans H. Zerlett

BABY, 1891, Short Story see Anton Chekhov

BABY AND THE BATTLESHIP, THE, Novel see Anthony Thorne

BABY CYCLONE, THE, Play see George M. Cohan

BABY DANCE, THE, Play see Jane Anderson

BABY FOR MIDGE, A, Story see James R. Webb

BABY IN THE ICEBOX, 1933, Short Story see James M. Cain

BABY LOVE, London 1968, Novel see Tina Chad Christian

BABY MINE, New York 1910, Play see Margaret Mayo

BABYLON REVISITED, 1931, Short Story see F. Scott Fitzgerald

BABY'S HAD A HARD DAY, THE, Story see Anne Wormser

BABYSITTER, THE, Short Story see Robert Coover

BACCARAT, LA, Play see Frederick H. James

BACCHAE, c495 bc, Play see Euripides

BACHELOR BRIDES, 1925, Play see Charles Horace Malcolm

BACHELOR DADDY, THE, Short Story see Edward Peple

BACHELOR FATHER, Play see Floyd Dell, Thomas Mitchell

BACHELOR FATHER, THE, New York 1928, Play see Edward Childs Carpenter

BACHELOR HUSBAND, A, Novel see Ruby M. Ayres

BACHELOR OF ARTS, Indianapolis 1934, Novel see John Erskine

BACHELOR PARTY, THE, 1955, Television Play see Paddy Chayefsky

BACHELOR, THE, New York 1909, Play see Clyde Fitch

BACHELOR'S BABY, Novel see Rolfe Bennett

BACHELORS' CLUB, THE, 1891, Novel see Israel Zangwill

BACHELOR'S ROMANCE, A, Chicago 1896, Play see Martha Morton

BACIAMO LE MANI, Novel see Vittorio Schiraldi

BACIO DELL'AURORA, IL, Novel see Luciana Peverelli

BACIO DI UNA MORTA, IL, 1903, Novel see Carolina Invernizio

BACK FROM THE DEAD, London 1920, Novel see Andrew Soutar

BACK PAY, Short Story see Fannie Hurst

BACK STREET, New York 1931, Novel see Fannie Hurst

BACK TO GOD'S COUNTRY AND OTHER STORIES, New York 1920, Book see James Oliver Curwood

BACK TO THE RIGHT TRAIL, Short Story see Frederick R. Bechdolf

BACK TO THE TREES, Short Story see H. H. Bashford

BACK TO YELLOW JACKET, Short Story see Peter B. Kyne

BACK TRAIL, Novel see Lewis B. Patten

BACKBONE, 1922, Short Story see Clarence Budington Kelland

BACKGROUND, London 1950, Play see Warren Chetham Strode

BACKLASH, Novel see Frank Gruber

BACKTRACK, Story see George W. George, Burt Kennedy

BAD AS I WANNA BE, Book see Tim Keown, Dennis Rodman

BAD AUF DER TENNE, DAS, Story see Rolf Meyer

BAD BUCK OF SANTA YNEZ, THE, Short Story see Bret Harte

BAD GIRL, New York 1928, Novel see Eugene Delmar, Vina Delmar

BAD MAN, THE, New York 1920, Play see Porter Emerson Browne

BAD RONALD, Novel see John Holbrook Vance

BAD SEED, THE, Novel see William March

BAD TIME AT HONDO, Story see Howard Breslin, Don McGuire

BADGE OF EVIL, 1955, Novel see Whit Masterson

BADGE OF FIGHTING HEARTS, THE, 1921, Short Story see Ralph Cummins

BADGE OF POLICEMAN O'ROON, THE, 1904, Short Story see O. Henry

BADGE OF THE ASSASSIN, Book see Philip Rosenberg, Robert J. Tanenbaum

BADGER'S GREEN, London 1930, Play see R. C. Sherriff

BADGES, New York 1924, Play see Edward Hammond, Max Marcin

BADIA DI MONTENERO, LA, Novel see Nicola Misasi

BADMAN, New York 1957, Novel see Clair Huffaker

BAGACEIRA, A, 1928, Novel see Jose Americo de Almeida

BAGARRES, Novel see Jean Proal

BAGNES D'ENFANTS, Play see Pierre Chaine, Andre de Lorde

BAGNO, IL, Play see Vladimir Majakovskij

BAHAMA PASSAGE, Novel see Nelson Hayes

BAHNO PRAHY, Short Story see Karel Ladislav Kukla

BAI MAO NU, Play see He Jingzhi, Ting Yi

BAILBONDSMAN, THE, 1973, Novel see Stanley Elkin

BAILIFF, THE, Sketch see Fred Karno

BAIQIUEN DAIFU, Book see Zhou Erfu

BAISER SUPREME, LE, Novel see Julien Sermet

BAISHOKU KAMONANBAN, 1920, Novel see Kyoka Izumi

BAIT, Play see Frank Richardson

BAIT, THE, Novel see Dorothy Uhnak

BAJAZZO, DER, Opera see Ruggero Leoncavallo

BAJO BANDERA, Book see Guillermo Saccomanno

BAK HOKERENS DISK, 1918, Novel see Oskar Braaten

BAKARUHABAN, 1935, Short Story see Sandor Hunyady

BAKER'S HAWK, Novel see Jack Bickham

BAKONJA FRA BRNE, 1892, Novel see Simo Matavulj

BAL DES POMPIERS, LE, Play see Jean Nohain

BAL DES SCEAUX, LE, see Honore de Balzac

BAL DU COMTE D'ORGEL, LE, 1924, Novel see Raymond Radiguet

BAL, LE, Short Story see Irene Nemirovsky

BALADA DAS DUAS MOCINHAS DE BOTAFOGO, 1959, Verse see Vinicius de Moraes

BALADA ZA GEORG HENIG, 1987, Novel see Viktor Paskov

BALALAIKA, London 1936, Musical Play see Bernard Grun, Eric Maschwitz, George Posford

BALAOO, Paris 1912, Novel see Gaston Leroux

BALCON, LE, 1956, Play see Jean Genet

BALDEVINS BRYLLUP, Oslo 1900, Play see Vilhelm Krag

BALDORIA NEI CARAIBI, Novel see Alessandro Maggiora Vergano

BALGARI OT STARO VREME, 1867, Novel see Lyuben Karavelov

BALIDAN, Play see Rabindranath Tagore

BALL DER NATIONEN, Opera see Paul Bayer, Heinz Hentschke

BALL IM SAVOY, Play see Alfred Grunwald, Fritz Lohner-Beda

527

BALL OF FORTUNE, THE, Novel *see* Sidney Horler

BALLAD OF A CHAMPION, Novel *see* Guglielmo Spoletini

BALLAD OF CAT BALLOU, THE, Boston 1956, Novel *see* Roy Chanslor

BALLAD OF DINGUS MAGEE, THE, Indianapolis 1965, Novel *see* David Markson

BALLAD OF READING GAOL, THE, 1898, Verse *see* Oscar Wilde

BALLAD OF SPLENDID SILENCE, A, Poem *see* E. Nesbit

BALLAD OF THE BELSTONE FOX, THE, Novel *see* David Rook

BALLAD OF THE FLIM-FLAM MAN, New York 1965, Novel *see* Guy Owen

BALLAD OF THE RUNNING MAN, THE, London 1961, Novel *see* Shelley Smith

BALLAD OF THE SAD CAFE, THE, 1951, Short Story *see* Carson McCullers

BALLERINA, Novel *see* Lady Eleanor Smith

BALLHAUS-ANNA, DIE, Novel *see* Leo Leipziger

BALTAGUL, 1930, Novel *see* Mihail Sadoveanu

BALTHAZAR, Play *see* Leopold Marchand

BAMBOLONA, LA, Novel *see* Alba de Cespedes

BANANA RIDGE, London 1938, Play *see* Ben Travers

BANCA DI MONATE, LA, Short Story *see* Piero Chiara

BANCHARAMER BAGAN, Play *see* Manoj Mitra

BANCO!, Paris 1920, Play *see* Alfred Savoir

BAND OF ANGELS, 1955, Novel *see* Robert Penn Warren

BAND WAGON, THE, New York 1931, Play *see* Howard Dietz, George S. Kaufman, Arthur Schwartz

BANDA DEL SOLE, LA, Novel *see* Enzo Barbieri

BANDBOX, THE, Boston 1912, Novel *see* Louis Joseph Vance

BANDERA, LA, 1931, Novel *see* Pierre Mac Orlan

BANDERA NEGRA, Play *see* Horacio Ruiz de La Fuente

BANDIDO DE LA SIERRA, EL, Play *see* Luis Fernandez Ardavin

BANDITS A MARSEILLE, Paris 1968, Novel *see* Eugene Saccomare

BANDOLERO, THE, New York 1904, Novel *see* Paul Gwynne

BANG THE DRUM SLOWLY, 1956, Novel *see* Mark Harris

BANGARADA MANUSHYA, Novel *see* T. K. Ramarao

BANGIKU, 1948, Short Story *see* Fumiko Hayashi

BANGKWANG, Book *see* Fabrizio Paladini

BANJO, Novel *see* Claude McKay

BANJO ON MY KNEE, Indianapolis 1936, Novel *see* Harry Hamilton

BANK SHOT, THE, Novel *see* Donald E. Westlake

BANKA, Novel *see* Yasuko Harada

BANKER'S DAUGHTER, THE, New York 1878, Play *see* Bronson Howard

BANKETTEN, Novel *see* Marika Stiernstedt

BANNER IN THE SKY, Novel *see* James Ramsay Ullman

BANQUE NEMO, LE, Play *see* Louis Verneuil

BANSHEE, 1988, Short Story *see* Ray Bradbury

BAO FENG ZHOU YU, 1948, Novel *see* Zhou Lipo

BAPTEME DU PETIT OSCAR, LE, Play *see* V. Bernard, Eugene Grange

BAR GIRLS, Play *see* Lauren Hoffman

BAR SINISTER, THE, Novel *see* Richard Harding Davis

BAR-20 THREE, Chicago 1921, Novel *see* Clarence E. Mulford

BARA, Story *see* U. R. Ananthamurthy

BARA EN MOR, 1939, Novel *see* Ivar Lo-Johansson

BARA GASSEN, 1937, Novel *see* Fumio Niwa

BARABBAS, 1950, Novel *see* Par Lagerkvist

BARAONDA, LA, *see* Gerolamo Rovetta

BARATIN, Opera *see* Andre Hornez, Jean Valmy

BARATRO, IL, *see* Carlo Gamberoni

BARB WIRE, New York 1931, Novel *see* Walter J. Coburn

BARBARA, 1939, Novel *see* Jorgen-Franz Jacobsen

BARBARA, New York 1968, Novel *see* Frank Newman

BARBARA COMES TO OXFORD, Novel *see* Oona Ball

BARBARA FRIETCHIE, 1864, Poem *see* John Greenleaf Whittier

BARBARA WINSLOW - REBEL, New York 1906, Novel *see* Elizabeth Ellis

BARBARIAN - INGOMAR, THE, Short Story *see* Ernest Thompson Seton

BARBARIAN, THE, 1920, Short Story *see* Theodore Seixas Solomons

BARBARIANS AT THE GATES, Book *see* Bryan Burrough, John Helyar

BARBARIANS, THE, Story *see* Winston Miller, Will Price

BARBARY SHEEP, London 1907, Novel *see* Robert Hichens

BARBE-BLEUE, 1697, Short Story *see* Charles Perrault

BARBER JOHN'S BOY, Story *see* Ben Ames Williams

BARBER OF STAMFORD HILL, THE, Television Play *see* Ronald Harwood

BARBERINE, Play *see* Alfred de Musset

BARBIER DE SEVILLE, LE, 1775, Play *see* Pierre-Augustin Caron de Beaumarchais

BARCA SIN PESCADOR, LA, 1945, Play *see* Alejandro Casona

BARCA VELLA. DOLORA DEL MAR AZUL, Poem *see* Federico Minana, Fernando Miranda

BARCAIOLO DI AMALFI, IL, Novel *see* Francesco Mastriani

BARCHESTER TOWERS, 1857, Novel *see* Anthony Trollope

BARDELYS THE MAGNIFICENT, Boston 1905, Novel *see* Rafael Sabatini

BARE EN TAGSTEN, 1959, Play *see* Carl Erik Soya

BARE SKYER BEVEGER STJERNENE, Novel *see* Torun Lian

BAREE - SON OF KAZAN, Garden City, Ny. 1917, Novel *see* James Oliver Curwood

BAREFOOT BOY, THE, Boston 1856, Poem *see* John Greenleaf Whittier

BAREFOOT IN THE PARK, New York 1964, Play *see* Neil Simon

BAREFOOT MAILMAN, THE, Novel *see* Theodore Pratt

BARGAIN, THE, Play *see* Henry Edwards, Edward Irwin

BARGAIN TRUE, THE, Boston 1918, Novel *see* Mrs. Nalbro Isadorah Bartley

BARIERATA, 1977, Novel *see* Pavel Vezhinov

BARKER; A PLAY OF CARNIVAL LIFE, THE, New York 1917, Play *see* Kenyon Nicholson

BAR-MITZVAH, Play *see* Boris Thomashefsky

BARN BURNING, 1939, Short Story *see* William Faulkner

BARNABE TIGNOL ET SAN BALEINE, Novel *see* Thevenin

BARNABETTA, New York 1914, Novel *see* Helen R. Martin

BARNABO DELLE MONTAGNE, Novel *see* Dino Buzzati

BARNABY, Novel *see* Rina Ramsey

BARNABY LEE, 1902, Short Story *see* John Bennett

BARNABY RUDGE, London 1841, Novel *see* Charles Dickens

BARNDOMMENS GADE, 1943, Novel *see* Tove Ditlevson

BARNENS O, Novel *see* P. C. Jersild

BARNET, 1936, Play *see* Leck Fischer

BARNUM WAS RIGHT, New York 1923, Play *see* Philip Bartholomae, John Meehan

BARNWARTER THIEL, 1888, Short Story *see* Gerhart Hauptmann

BAROCCO, Novel *see* Georges-Andre Cuel

BARON DE L'ECLUSE, LE, 1954, Short Story *see* Georges Simenon

BARON MYSTERE, LE, Novel *see* Henri Germain

BARON PRASIL, Novel *see* Gottfried Burger

BARONE DI CORBO, IL, Play *see* Luigi Antonelli

BARRACA, LA, 1898, Novel *see* Vicente Blasco Ibanez

BARRAGE CONTRE LE PACIFIQUE, UN, 1950, Novel *see* Marguerite Duras

BARRAQUES, LES, Opera *see* Eduardo Escalante (Hijo)

BARRAQUETA DEL NANO, LA, Play *see* Francisco Barchina

BARRETTS OF WIMPOLE STREET, THE, London 1930, Play *see* Rudolf Besier

BARRIER, THE, New York 1908, Novel *see* Rex Beach

BARRIERA, LA, Novel *see* Anton Giulio Majano, Domenico Meccoli

BARRIERS BURNED AWAY, New York 1872, Novel *see* Edward Payson Roe

BARRINGS, DIE, Novel *see* William von Simpson

BARRY GORDON, New York 1908, Novel *see* William Farquhar Payson

BARS OF IRON, Novel *see* Ethel M. Dell

BAR-T MYSTERY, THE, Story *see* J. F. Natteford

BARTER, 1917, Novel *see* Evelyn Campbell

BARTHOLDI ET SON VIGNERON, Play *see* Leopold Netter

BARTLEBY, 1853, Short Story *see* Herman Melville

BARTON MYSTERY, THE, London 1916, Play *see* Walter Hackett

BARTOVA POMSTA, Play *see* Jiri Hora

BARUFFE CHIOZZOTTE, LE, Play *see* Carlo Goldoni

BARUTEN BUKVAR, 1969, Novel *see* Yordan Radichkov

BASEMENT ROOM, THE, 1935, Short Story *see* Graham Greene

BASIL OF BAKER STREET, Book *see* Eve Titus

BASKETBALL DIARIES, THE, Book *see* Jim Carroll

BASQUERIE, New York 1927, Book *see* Eleanor Mercein

BASTARD, THE, Novel *see* John Jakes

BAT, THE, New York 1926, Play *see* Avery Hopwood, Mary Roberts Rinehart

BAT*21, Book *see* William C. Anderson

BATAILLE DE DAMES; OU UN DUEL EN AMOUR, LA, Paris 1851, Novel *see* Ernest Legouve, Eugene Scribe

BATAILLE, LA, Paris 1908, Novel *see* Claude Farrere

BATAILLON DU CIEL, LE, 1947, Novel *see* Joseph Kessel

BATALION A DIVADELNI HRA BATALION, Novel *see* Josef Hais-Tynecky

BATARD, LE, Zurich 1913, Novel *see* Paul Ilg

BATEAU A SOUPE, LE, Novel *see* Gilbert Dupe

BATEAU DE VERRE, LA, Short Story *see* Rene Bizet

BATEAU D'EMILE, LE, 1954, Short Story *see* Georges Simenon

BATELIERS DE LA VOLGA, LES, Novel *see* Joseph Kessel

BATH COMEDY, THE, 1900, Novel *see* Agnes Castle, Egerton Castle

BATS WITH BABY FACES, Novel *see* John Prebble

BATTANT, LE, Novel *see* Andre Caroff

BATTLE CRY, Novel *see* Leon Uris

BATTLE CRY, THE, New York 1914, Novel *see* Charles Neville Buck

BATTLE HYMN OF THE REPUBLIC, THE, Short Story *see* Julia Ward Howe

BATTLE OF BUNKER HILL, THE, Play *see* Clyde Fitch

BATTLE OF FRENCHMAN'S RUN, THE, Story *see* James Oliver Curwood

BATTLE OF SEVEN ISLES, THE, Poem *see* John Greenleaf Whittier

BATTLE OF THE VILLA FIORITA, London 1963, Novel *see* Rumer Godden

BATTLE, THE, New York 1908, Play *see* Cleveland Moffett

BATTLING BUNYON CEASES TO BE FUNNY, 1924, Short Story *see* Raymond Leslie Goldman

BATTLING THE ENEMY AT HIS HEADQUARTERS, Novel *see* Lu Zheng

BAUER ALS MILLIONAR, DER, 1868, Play *see* Ferdinand Raimund

BAVU, New York 1922, Play *see* Earl Carroll

BAYRISCHE DEKAMERON, DAS, 1928, Novel *see* Oskar Maria Graf

BAZAAR-E-HUSN, 1919, Novel *see* Premchand

BE IT EVER SO HUMBLE, Story *see* Eleanore Griffin, William Rankin

BE PREPARED, 1952, Novel *see* Rice E. Cochran

BE READY WITH BELLS AND DRUMS, New York 1961, Novel *see* Elizabeth Kata

BEACH OF DREAMS, THE, New York 1919, Novel *see* Henry de Vere Stacpoole

BEACH RED, New York 1945, Book *see* Peter Bowman

BEACHCOMBER, THE, 1931, Short Story *see* W. Somerset Maugham

BEACHES, Novel *see* Iris Rainer Dart

BEANS OF EGYPT, MAINE, THE, Novel *see* Carolyn Chute

BEAR ISLAND, 1971, Novel *see* Alistair MacLean

BEAR TAMER'S DAUGHTER, THE, 1921, Short Story *see* Konrad Bercovici

BEARD, THE, 1973, Short Story *see* Isaac Bashevis Singer

BEARDLESS WARRIORS, THE, Boston 1960, Novel *see* Richard Matheson

BEARS AND I, THE, Novel *see* Robert Franklin Leslie

BEAR-TRAP, THE, 1919, Short Story *see* Byron Morgan

BEASLEY'S CHRISTMAS PARTY, Story *see* Booth Tarkington

BEAST IN THE JUNGLE, THE, 1903, Short Story *see* Henry James

BEAST MUST DIE, THE, London 1938, Novel *see* Nicholas Blake

BEAST WITHIN, THE, Novel *see* Edward Levy

BEASTMASTER, THE, Novel *see* Andre Norton

BEAT THE DEVIL, 1951, Novel *see* James Helvick

BEATI PAOLI, I, Novel *see* Luigi Natoli

BEATING BACK, 1913, Story *see* Will Irwin, Al J. Jennings

BEATRICE DEVANT LE DESIR, Novel *see* Pierre Frondaie

BEAU BROCADE, Novel *see* Baroness Orczy

BEAU BRUMMELL, Novel *see* Booth Tarkington

BEAU BRUMMELL, New York 1908, Play *see* Clyde Fitch

BEAU GESTE, London 1924, Novel *see* P. C. Wren

BEAU IDEAL, New York 1928, Novel *see* P. C. Wren

BEAU JAMES, Book *see* Gene Fowler

BEAU MASQUE, 1954, Novel *see* Roger Vailland

BEAU MONSTRE, UN, Novel *see* Dominique Fabre

BEAU SABREUR, New York 1926, Novel *see* P. C. Wren

BEAUMARCHAIS, Play *see* Sacha Guitry

BEAU-PERE, Novel *see* Bertrand Blier

BEAUTIFUL AND DAMNED, THE, New York 1922, Novel *see* F. Scott Fitzgerald

BEAUTIFUL BULLET, THE, 1927, Short Story *see* Harold MacGrath

BEAUTIFUL JIM, Novel *see* John Strange Winter

BEAUTIFUL THING, Play *see* Jonathan Harvey

BEAUTY, New York 1933, Novel *see* Faith Baldwin

BEAUTY AND THE BARGE, London 1904, Play *see* W. W. Jacobs, Louis N. Parker

BEAUTY AND THE BEAST, Story *see* Madame de Villeneuve

BEAUTY AND THE BEAT, 1936, Short Story *see* Julian Brodie, Alan Green

BEAUTY SHOP, THE, New York 1914, Play *see* Channing Pollock, Rennold Wolf

BEAUTY, THE, Novel *see* Lewis Wallace

BEAUTY TO LET, Short Story *see* Frederick Jackson

BEAUTY'S DAUGHTER, New York 1935, Novel *see* Kathleen Norris

BEAUTY'S WORTH, 1920, Short Story *see* Sophie Kerr

BEAUX DIMANCHES, LES, Play *see* Marcel Dube

BEBE, Play *see* Maurice Hennequin, Najac

BEBEE; OR TWO LITTLE WOODEN SHOES, Philadelphia 1874, Novel *see* Ouida

BEBEL QUE A CIDADE COMEU, 1960, Novel *see* Ignacio de Loyola Brandao

BEBERT ET L'OMNIBUS, Novel *see* Francois Boyer

BECKET, London 1893, Play *see* Alfred Tennyson

BECKET OU L'HONNEUR DE DIEU, 1959, Play *see* Jean Anouilh

BED AND BREAKFAST, Play *see* Frederick Witney

BED ROCK, Boston 1924, Novel *see* Jack Bethea

BED SITTING ROOM, THE, 1963, Play *see* John Antrobus, Spike Milligan

BEDARA KANNAPPA, Play *see* G. V. Iyer

BEDELIA, Novel *see* Vera Caspary

BEDFORD INCIDENT, THE, New York 1963, Novel *see* Mark Rascovich

BEDTIME STORY, 1951, Play *see* Sean O'Casey

BEDTIME STORY, London 1937, Play *see* Walter Ellis

BEES AND HONEY, 1928, Play *see* H. F. Maltby

BEETLE, THE, Novel *see* Richard Marsh

BEFEJEZETIEN MONDAT, A, 1947, Novel *see* Tibor Dery

BEFORE AND AFTER, Novel *see* Rosellen Brown

BEFORE I WAKE, Novel *see* Hal Debrett

BEFORE MORNING, New York 1933, Play *see* Edna Riley, Edward R. Riley

BEFORE THE FACT, Novel *see* Francis Iles

BEFREITE HANDE, Novel *see* Erich Ebermayer

BEGGAR GIRL'S WEDDING, THE, Play *see* Walter Melville

BEGGAR IN PURPLE, A, London 1918, Novel *see* Andrew Soutar

BEGGAR MY NEIGHBOUR, 1952, Play *see* Arnold Ridley

BEGGAR ON HORSEBACK, New York 1924, Play *see* Marc Connelly, George S. Kaufman

BEGGARMAN, THIEF, Novel *see* Irwin Shaw

BEGGARS ARE COMING TO TOWN, New York 1945, Play *see* Theodore Reeves

BEGGARS OF LIFE, New York 1924, Novel *see* Jim Tully

BEGGAR'S OPERA, THE, London 1728, Play *see* John Gay

BEGHAR, Novel *see* Shanta Nisal

BEGINNER'S LUCK, Novel *see* Andrew Garve

BEGUILED, THE, Novel *see* Thomas Cullinan

BEHAVIOR OF MRS. CRANE, THE, New York 1928, Play *see* Harry Segall

BEHIND RED CURTAINS, Boston 1919, Novel *see* Mansfield Scott

BEHIND THAT CURTAIN, Indianapolis 1928, Novel *see* Earl Derr Biggers

BEHIND THE CURTAIN, Novel *see* Max Pemberton

BEHIND THE DOOR, 1918, Short Story *see* Gouverneur Morris

BEHIND THE GREEN LIGHTS, New York 1933, Book *see* J. Kofold, G.J. Lemmer, C.W. Willemse

BEHIND THE HEADLINES, Novel *see* Robert Chapman

BEHIND THE HILLS, Novel *see* Charles Chestnutt

BEHIND THE RISING SUN, Novel *see* James R. Young

BEHIND THE SCENES, Play *see* Margaret Mayo

BEHIND THE WHEEL, Story *see* Welford Beaton

BEHOLD WE LIVE!, London 1932, Play *see* John Van Druten

BEIDEN DIERSBERGS, DIE, Novel *see* Renate Uhl

BEIDEN SEEHUNDE, DIE, Play *see* Carl Roessler

BEIDEN WILDTAUBEN ,DIE, Novel *see* Richard Skowronnek

BEIJO NO ASFALTO, O, 1961, Play *see* Nelson Rodrigues

BEIL VON WANDSBEK, DAS, 1947, Novel *see* Arnold Zweig

BEIM NACHSTEN MANN WIRD ALLES ANDERS, Novel *see* Eva Heller

BEING RESPECTABLE, New York 1923, Novel *see* Grace Hodgson Landrau

BEING THERE, 1970, Novel *see* Jerzy Kosinski

BEIRUT, Play *see* Alan Bowne

BEJARANA, LA, Opera *see* Luis Fernandez Ardavin, E. Serrano

BEKENNTNIS, DAS, Novel *see* Clara Ratzka

BEKENNTNIS DER INA KAHR, DAS, Novel *see* Hans Emil Diets

BEKENNTNISSE DES HOCHSTAPLERS FELIX KRULL, 1922, Novel *see* Thomas Mann

BEKENNTNISSE EINES MOBLIERTEN HERRN, Novel *see* Oliver Hassencamp

BEL INDIFFERENT, LE, 1949, Play *see* Jean Cocteau

BEL-AMI, 1885, Novel *see* Guy de Maupassant

BELATED EVIDENCE, 1926, Short Story *see* Elliott White Springs

BELEYET PARUS ODINOKIY, 1936, Novel *see* Valentin Kataev

BELIEVE ME IF ALL THOSE ENDEARING YOUNG CHARMS, 1807, Poem *see* Thomas Moore

BELIEVE ME XANTIPPE, New York 1913, Play *see* John Frederick Ballard

BELL BOOK AND CANDLE, New York 1950, Play *see* John Van Druten

BELL FOR ADANO, A, 1944, Novel *see* John Hersey

BELL JAR, THE, 1963, Novel *see* Sylvia Plath

BELL, THE, Novel *see* Iris Murdoch

BELLA ADDORMENTATA, LA, Play *see* Pier Maria Rosso

BELLA DONNA, London 1909, Novel *see* Robert Hichens

BELLA MAFIA, Novel *see* Lynda La Plante

BELLA NIPOTINA, LA, Play *see* Giovanni Speziale

BELLAMY THE MAGNIFICENT, London 1904, Novel *see* Roy Horniman

BELLAMY TRIAL, THE, New York 1927, Novel *see* Frances Noyes Hart

BELL'ANTONIO, IL, 1949, Novel *see* Vitaliano Brancati

BELLE AU BOIS DORMANT, LA, 1697, Short Story *see* Charles Perrault

BELLE AVENTURE, LA, Paris 1914, Play *see* Gaston Arman de Caillavet, Robert de Flers

BELLE CREOLE DI MELCHIOR DE LA CRUZ, LE, Short Story *see* Lorenzo Ricciardi

BELLE DE JOUR, 1928, Novel *see* Joseph Kessel

BELLE DE NUIT, Play *see* Pierre Wolff

BELLE ET LA BETE, LA, 1785-89, Short Story *see* Marie Leprince de Beaumont

BELLE GARCE, UNE, Novel *see* Charles-Henry Hirsch

BELLE IMAGE, LA, 1941, Novel *see* Marcel Ayme

BELLE JEUNESSE, Novel *see* Marcelle Vioux

BELLE MADAME HEBERT, LA, 1905, Play *see* Abel Hermant

BELLE MARINIERE, LA, 1930, Play *see* Marcel Achard

BELLE NIVERNAISE, LA, Short Story *see* Alphonse Daudet

BELLE OF NEW YORK, THE, New York 1897, Musical Play *see* Gustav Kerker, Hugh Morton

BELLE QUE VOILA, LA, Novel *see* Vicki Baum

BELLE RUSSE, LA, New York 1882, Play *see* David Belasco

BELLED PALM, THE, Short Story *see* Allan Vaughan Elston

BELLES ON THEIR TOES, Book *see* Ernestine G. Carey, Frank Gilbreth Jr.

BELLEZZA D'IPPOLITA, LA, Novel *see* Elio Bartolini

BELLISSIMO NOVEMBRE, UN, Novel *see* Ercole Patti

BELL-LESS PACK TRAIN, THE, Novel *see* Bai Hua

BELLMAN AND TRUE, Novel *see* Dennis Lowder

BELLMAN VAUDEVILLE, Stockholm 1922, Musical Play *see* Edvin Ziedner

BELLS ARE RINGING, THE, Musical Play *see* Betty Comden, Adolph Green

BELLS OF SAN JUAN, New York 1919, Novel *see* Jackson Gregory

BELLS OF WALDENBRUCK, THE, 1933, Story *see* Frank Leon Smith

BELLS, THE, Novel *see* Erkman Chatrian

BELLS, THE, Poem *see* Edgar Allan Poe

BELLS, THE, London 1871, Play *see* Leopold Lewis

BELONGING, New York 1920, Novel *see* Olive Wadsley

BELOVED, 1987, Novel *see* Toni Morrison

BELOVED BRUTE, THE, New York 1923, Novel *see* Kenneth Perkins

BELOVED FRIEND, Book *see* Catherine D. Bowen, Barbara von Meck

BELOVED INFIDEL, Book *see* Gerold Frank, Sheilah Graham

BELOVED TRAITOR, THE, New York 1915, Novel *see* Frank L. Packard

BELOVED VAGABOND, THE, London 1906, Novel *see* William J. Locke

BELOW THE DEADLINE, Short Story *see* Scott Campbell

BELPHEGOR THE MOUNTEBANK, Novel *see* Charles Webb

BELTENEBROS, Novel *see* Antonio Munoz Molina

BELVEDERE, Novel *see* Gwen Davenport

BELYE NOCHI, St. Petersburg 1848, Short Story *see* Fyodor Dostoyevsky

BELYI PAROKHOD, 1970, Short Story *see* Chingiz Aitmatov

BEN BLAIR: THE STORY OF A PLAINSMAN, Chicago 1905, Novel *see* William Otis Lillibridge

BEN HUR, 1880, Novel *see* Lew Wallace

BEN WARMAN, New York 1917, Novel *see* Charles E. Winter

BENCH OF DESOLATION, THE, 1910, Short Story *see* Henry James

BEND OF THE SNAKE, 1950, Novel *see* Bill Gulick

BENEFITS FORGOT, New York 1917, Novel *see* Honore Morrow

BENGAL TIGER, 1952, Novel *see* Hall Hunter

BENIGHTED, London 1927, Novel *see* J. B. Priestley

BENILDE OU A VIRGEM-MAE, 1947, Play *see* Jose Regio

BENITO CERENO, 1855, Short Story *see* Herman Melville

BENSON MURDER CASE, THE, New York 1926, Novel *see* S. S. Van Dine

BENT, Play *see* Martin Sherman

BENTLEY'S CONSCIENCE, Novel *see* Paul Trent

BEOWULF, c750, Verse *see* Anon

BEQUEST TO THE NATION, A, 1970, Play *see* Terence Rattigan

BERCEAU, LE, Paris 1908, Play *see* Eugene Brieux

BERE O AFFOGARE, *see* Leo Di Castelnuovo

BEREKETLI TOPRAKLAR UZERINDE, Novel *see* Orhan Kemal

BERENICE, 1671, Play *see* Jean Racine

BERG, Novel *see* Ann Quinn

BERG, THE, Short Story *see* Ernest Raymond

BERGKRISTALL, 1853, Short Story *see* Adalbert Stifter

BERGWIND, Novel *see* Heinrich Klier

BERKELEY SQUARE, London 1926, Play *see* John L. Balderston

BERLIN MEMORANDUM, THE, London 1965, Novel *see* Elleston Trevor

BERLIN STORIES, THE, 1945, Book *see* Christopher Isherwood

BERLIN TUNNEL 21, Novel *see* Donald Linquist

BERLIN-ALEXANDERPLATZ, 1929, Novel *see* Alfred Doblin

BERNARDINE, 1953, Play *see* Mary Coyle Chase

BERNICE BOBS HER HAIR, 1920, Short Story *see* F. Scott Fitzgerald

BERTHA THE SEWING MACHINE GIRL, Play *see* Theodore Kremer

BERTOLDO BERTOLDINO E CACASENNO, Poem *see* Giulio Cesare Croce

BERU ET CES DAMES, Novel *see* Frederic Dard

BERUSAIYU NO BARA, Novel *see* Riyoko Ikeda

BERYL AND THE CROUCHER, Short Story *see* Thomas Burke

BERYL CORONET, THE, Short Story *see* Arthur Conan Doyle

BESAETTELSE, Copenhagen 1942, Novel *see* Hans Severinsen

BESEIGED HEART, THE, Play *see* Robert Hill

BESHENNYE DENGI, 1870, Play *see* Alexander Ostrovsky

BESIDE THE BONNIE BRIER BUSH, London 1895, Play *see* James MacArthur, Augustus Thorne

BESONDERE, DER, Novel *see* Ludwig Ganghofer

BESPRIDANNITSA, 1878, Play *see* Alexander Ostrovsky

BESSERER HERR, EIN, Play *see* Walter Hasenclever

BEST CHRISTMAS PAGEANT EVER, THE, Book *see* Barbara Robinson

BEST FOOT FORWARD, Play *see* John Cecil Holmes

BEST IN LIFE, THE, New York 1918, Novel *see* Muriel Hine Coxen

BEST LAID PLANS OF A MAN IN LOVE, THE, Short Story *see* Edgar Wallace

BEST LITTLE GIRL IN THE WORLD, THE, Novel *see* Stephen Levenkron

BEST LITTLE WHOREHOUSE IN TEXAS, THE, Play *see* Larry L. King, Peter Masterson

BEST MAN; A PLAY ABOUT POLITICS, THE, 1960, Play *see* Gore Vidal

BEST MAN, THE, 1913, Novel *see* Grace Livingston Hill Lutz

BEST MAN TO DIE, THE, Novel *see* Ruth Rendell

BEST NEWS, THE, Story *see* Liu Dawei

BEST OF EVERYTHING, THE, Novel *see* Rona Jaffe

BEST OF EVERYTHING, THE, 1952, Short Story *see* Stanley Ellin

BEST OF FRIENDS, THE, Play *see* Hugh Whitemore

BEST OF LUCK, THE, London 1916, Play *see* Henry Hamilton, Cecil Raleigh

BEST PEOPLE, THE, New York 1924, Play *see* David Gray, Avery Hopwood

BEST PLACE TO BE, THE, Novel *see* Helen Van Slyke

BESUCH DER ALTEN DAME, DER, Zurich 1956, Play *see* Friedrich Durrenmatt

BESY, 1872, Novel *see* Fyodor Dostoyevsky

BESZELO KONTOS, A, 1889, Novel *see* Kalman Mikszath

BESZTERCE OSTROMA, 1896, Novel *see* Kalman Mikszath

BETA SOM, Novel *see* Pino Belli

BETE A L'AFFUT, LA, Novel *see* Day Keane

BETE AUX SEPT MANTEAUX, LA, Novel *see* P. A. Fernic

BETE ERRANTE, LA, Novel *see* Louis Frederic Rouquette

BETE HUMAINE, LA, 1890, Novel *see* Emile Zola

BETH, Short Story *see* Lawrence McCloskey

BETH THE SHEEPDOG, Novel *see* Ernest Lewis

BETHNAL GREEN, Novel *see* Michael Fisher

BETHSABEE, Novel *see* Pierre Benoit

BETRAYAL, Book *see* Lucy Freeman, Julie Roy

BETRAYAL, 1978, Play *see* Harold Pinter

BETRAYAL FROM THE EAST, Novel *see* Alan Hynd

BETSY, THE, Novel *see* Harold Robbins

BETTA THE GYPSY, Opera *see* Edward Waltyre

BETTELSTUDENT, DER, Novel *see* Finn Soeberg

BETTER ANGELS, THE, Novel *see* Charles McCarry

BETTER LIVING, Play *see* George F. Walker

BETTER MAN, THE, Story *see* George Patullo

BETTER MAN, THE, New York 1910, Novel *see* Cyrus Townsend Brady

BETTER 'OLE; OR THE ROMANCE OF OLD BILL, THE, Oxford 1917, Play *see* Bruce Bairnsfather, Arthur Eliot

BETTER THAN A RODEO, Story *see* Kenneth Perkins

BETTER THAN LIFE, 1936, Short Story *see* Louis Bromfield

BETTER WIFE, THE, Short Story *see* Gouverneur Morris

BETTY, 1961, Novel *see* Georges Simenon

BETTY'S A LADY, 1925, Short Story *see* Gerald Beaumont

BETTY'S DREAM HERO, Story *see* George Ade

BETWEEN FRIENDS, New York 1914, Novel *see* Robert W. Chambers

BETWEEN THE TIDES, Short Story *see* Joseph Conrad

BETWEEN TWO WOMEN, Novel *see* Gillian Martin

BEULAH, New York 1860, Novel *see* Augusta Jane Evans Wilson

BEVERLY OF GRAUSTARK, New York 1904, Novel *see* George Barr McCutcheon

BEVERLY'S BALANCE, New York 1915, Play *see* Paul Kester

BEWARE OF BACHELORS, Short Story *see* Mark Canfield

BEWARE OF CHILDREN, London 1958, Novel *see* Verily Anderson

BEWARE OF THE BRIDE, 1920, Short Story *see* Edgar Franklin

BEWARE OF THE DOG, 1944, Short Story *see* Roald Dahl

BEWARE OF WIDOWS, Play *see* Owen Moore

BEYOND, Novel *see* Erich Maria Remarque

BEYOND BEDLAM, Novel *see* Harry Adam Knight

BEYOND REASONABLE DOUBT, Book *see* David Yallop

BEYOND THE DREAMS OF AVARICE, Novel *see* Sir Walter Besant

BEYOND THE FOREST, Novel *see* Stuart Engstrand

BEYOND THE LIMIT, New York 1916, Novel *see* Emmett Dalton

BEYOND THE MOUNTAINS, London 1958, Novel *see* Alexander Ramati

BEYOND THE RIM, 1916, Short Story *see* J. Allen Dunn

BEYOND THE ROCKS, New York 1906, Novel *see* Elinor Glyn

BEYOND THERAPY, Play *see* Christopher Durang

BEYOND THIS PLACE, 1953, Novel *see* A. J. Cronin

BEZ KRASY, BEZ LIMCE, Prague 1962, Novel *see* Hana Belohradska

BEZ VINI VINOVATIYE, 1884, Play *see* Alexander Ostrovsky

BEZDETNA, Short Story *see* Ignat Herrmann

BEZZAKONIE, 1887, Short Story *see* Anton Chekhov

BFG, Novel *see* Roald Dahl

B.F.'S DAUGHTER, 1946, Novel *see* John Phillips Marquand

BHOWANI JUNCTION, 1954, Novel *see* John Masters

BHUKAILASA, Play *see* R. Nagendra Rao

BI XUE JIAN, Novel *see* Jin Yong

BIAN CHENG, 193-, Short Story *see* Shen Congwen

BIAN ZOU BIAN CHANG, Short Story *see* Shi Tiesheng

BIBERPELZ, DER, 1893, Play *see* Gerhart Hauptmann

BIBI LA PUREE, Play *see* Alexandre Fontanes, Andre Mouezy-Eon

BIBLIOTHEKAR, DER, Play *see* Gustav von Moser

BICCHI, Novel *see* Saint-Sorny

BICHON, Play *see* Jean de Letraz

BID FOR FORTUNE, A, Novel *see* Guy Boothby

BID TIME RETURN, Novel *see* Richard Matheson

BIDDY, 1933, Short Story *see* Travis Ingham

BIDER DER FLIEGER, Olten-Freiburg 1938, Book *see* Otto Walter

BIETUL IOANIDE, 1953, Novel *see* George Calinescu

BIG, 1934, Short Story *see* Owen Francis

BIG BANKROLL; THE LIFE AND TIMES OF ARNOLD ROTHSTEIN, THE, New York 1959, Biography *see* Leo Katcher

BIG BEND BUCKAROO, Short Story *see* Walter West

BIG BIRTHDAY, THE, Play *see* Hugh Leonard

BIG BLUE, THE, Short Story *see* Andrew Horn

BIG BONANZA, THE, Novel *see* Peter B. Kyne

BIG BOODLE, THE, 1954, Novel *see* Robert Sylvester

BIG BOUNCE, New York 1969, Novel *see* Elmore Leonard

BIG BOW MYSTERY, THE, London 1892, Novel *see* Israel Zangwill

BIG BOY, New York 1925, Play *see* Harold Atteridge

BIG BROTHER, 1923, Short Story *see* Rex Beach

BIG BROWN EYES, 1935, Short Story *see* James Edward Grant

BIG BUSINESS GIRL, 1930, Story *see* Patricia Reilly, H. N. Swanson

BIG CAGE, THE, New York 1933, Book *see* Edward S. Anthony, Clyde Beatty

BIG CHANCE, THE, Novel *see* Pamela Barrington

BIG CLOCK, THE, 1946, Novel *see* Kenneth Fearing

BIG DEAL IN LAREDO, 1962, Play *see* Sidney Carroll

BIG EXECUTIVE, 1933, Short Story *see* Alice Duer Miller

BIG EYES AND LITTLE MOUTH, 1927, Short Story *see* Elliott White Springs

BIG FIGHT, THE, New York 1928, Play *see* Milton Herbert Gropper, Max Marcin

BIG FISHERMAN, THE, Novel *see* Lloyd C. Douglas

BIG FIX, THE, Novel *see* Roger L. Simon

BIG FOUR, THE, London 1929, Novel *see* Edgar Wallace

BIG FRAME, THE, Story *see* Arthur T. Horman

BIG GAME, New York 1920, Play *see* Kilbourne Gordon, Willard Robertson

BIG GAME, THE, Boston 1936, Novel *see* Francis Wallace

BIG GRAB, THE, New York 1960, Novel *see* John Trinian

BIG HAPPINESS, London 1917, Novel *see* Pan

BIG HEARTED HERBERT, New York 1934, Play *see* Sophie Underwood, Anna Steese Richardson

BIG HEAT, THE, Serial Story *see* William P. McGivern

BIG HUNT, Short Story *see* James Warner Bellah

BIG JIM GARRITY, New York 1914, Play *see* Owen Davis

BIG KNIFE, THE, New York 1949, Play *see* Clifford Odets

BIG LITTLE PERSON, THE, New York 1917, Novel *see* Rebecca Lane Hooper Eastman

BIG MAN, THE, Novel *see* William McIlvanney

BIG MITTEN, THE, Short Story *see* Damon Runyon

BIG PICKUP, THE, Novel *see* Elleston Trevor

BIG PICTURE, THE, Novel *see* David Whitelaw

BIG POND, THE, New York 1928, Play *see* George Middleton, A. E. Thomas

BIG RAINBOW, THE, Story *see* Robert B. Bailey, Hugh King

BIG RANGE, THE, 1953, Short Story *see* Jack Schaefer

BIG RED, New York 1945, Novel *see* James Arthur Kjelgaard

BIG SKY, THE, 1947, Novel *see* A. B. Guthrie Jr.

BIG SLEEP, THE, 1939, Novel *see* Raymond Chandler

BIG STICK-UP AT BRINK'S, Book *see* Noel Behn

BIG STORY, THE, Novel *see* Craig Rice

BIG STORY, THE, London 1957, Novel *see* Morris West

BIG STRONG MAN, THE, Story *see* Christine Castle

BIG SWEEP, THE, Play *see* Matthew Brennan

BIG TIMBER, Boston 1916, Novel *see* Bertrand W. Sinclair

BIG TOWN, THE, 1938, Novel *see* Ring Lardner

BIG TOYS, Play *see* Patrick White

BIG TREMAINE, Boston 1914, Novel *see* Marie Van Vorst

BIG WAR, THE, Novel *see* Anton Myrer

BIG WAVE, THE, New York 1948, Short Story *see* Pearl Buck

BIG WESTERN HAT, THE, Story *see* Jack Wolf

BIGAMIST, THE, Novel *see* F. E. Mills Young

BIGAMISTS, THE, Story *see* Lewis Allen Browne

BIG-HEARTED JIM, 1926, Short Story *see* Patterson Margoni

BIGORNE - CAPORAL DE FRANCE, LA, Novel *see* Pierre Nord

BIGOTE, LA, 1900, Play *see* Jules Renard

BIG-TOWN ROUND-UP, Boston 1920, Novel *see* William MacLeod Raine

BIJOUTIERS DU CLAIR DE LUNE, Novel *see* Albert Vidalie

BIJOUX, LES, 1884, Short Story *see* Guy de Maupassant

BIKO, Book *see* Donald Woods

BILA NEMOC, 1937, Play *see* Karel Capek

BILA VRANA, Opera *see* Frantisek Ketzek, Bedrich Sulc

BILITIS, Novel *see* Pierre Louys

BILL OF DIVORCEMENT, A, London 1921, Play *see* Clemence Dane

BILLARD UM HALB ZEHN, Cologne 1959, Novel *see* Heinrich Boll

BILLETED, London 1917, Play *see* H. M. Harwood, F. Tennyson Jesse

BILLIE, Short Story *see* James Oppenheim

BILLIE'S ROSE, Poem *see* George R. Sims

BILLION DOLLAR BRAIN, London 1966, Novel *see* Len Deighton

BILLION FOR BORIS, A, Novel *see* Mary Rodgers

BILLIONAIRE, THE, Story *see* Harry B. Smith

BILLY AND THE BIG STICK, 1914, Short Story *see* Richard Harding Davis

BILLY BATHGATE, 1989, Novel *see* E. L. Doctorow

BILLY BUDD, 1924, Novel *see* Herman Melville

BILLY FORTUNE AND THE HARD PROPOSITION, Englewood Cliffs, Nj.1912, Novel *see* William Rheem Lighton

BILLY KANE - WHITE AND UNMARRIED, Story *see* John D. Swain

BILLY LIAR, 1959, Novel *see* Keith Waterhouse

BILOXI BLUES, 1987, Play *see* Neil Simon

BINARY, Novel *see* Michael Crichton

BIND, THE, Novel *see* Stanley Ellin

BING BANG BOOM, 1920, Short Story *see* Raymond Leslie Goldman

BING LIN CHENG XIA, Play *see* Bai Ren

BIOGRAPHY, New York 1932, Play *see* S. N. Behrman

BIOGRAPHY OF A GRIZZLY, THE, New York 1903, Novel *see* Ernest Thompson Seton

BIOLOGIE!, Novel *see* Wolf Spillner

BIONDINA, LA, 1893, Novel *see* Marco Praga

BIRAGHIN, Play *see* Arnaldo Fraccaroli

BIRAJ BAU, 1914, Novel *see* Sarat Candra Cattopadhyay

BIRD IN THE NEST, A, Play *see* Alec Coppel

BIRD MAN, THE, Story *see* J. Frank Clark

BIRD OF PARADISE, THE, New York 1912, Play *see* Richard Walton Tully

BIRD OF PREY, Story *see* John Monk Saunders

BIRDMAN OF ALCATRAZ: THE STORY OF ROBERT STROUD, New York 1955, Book *see* Thomas E. Gaddis

BIRDS AND THE BEES, THE, Play *see* Frederick Kohner, Albert Mannheimer

BIRDS' CHRISTMAS CAROL, THE, San Francisco 1887, Story *see* Kate Douglas Wiggin

BIRD'S NEST, THE, 1954, Novel *see* Shirley Jackson

BIRDS OF PREY; BEING PAGES FROM THE BOOK OF BROADWAY, New York 1918, Novel *see* George Bronson Howard

BIRDS, THE, 1952, Short Story *see* Daphne Du Maurier

BIRDY, Novel *see* William Wharton

BIRIBI, Novel *see* Georges Darien

BIRICHINO DI PAPA, IL, Novel *see* Henny Koch

BIRINCHI BABA, *see* Rajasekhar Bose

BIRTHDAY, Play *see* Ladislaus Bus-Fekete

BIRTHDAY OF THE INFANTS, THE, 1891, Short Story *see* Oscar Wilde

BIRTHDAY PARTY, THE, London 1958, Play *see* Harold Pinter

BIRTHRIGHT, New York 1922, Novel *see* Thomas Sigismund Stribling

BIRUMA NO TATEGOTO, 1948, Novel *see* Michio Takayama

BIRYUK, 1852, Short Story *see* Ivan Turgenev

BIS ZUR BITTEREN NEIGE, Novel *see* Johannes Mario Simmel

BISARCA, LA, Radio Play *see* Pietro Garinei, Sandro Giovannini

BISCUIT EATER, THE, 1939, Short Story *see* James H. Street

BISHOP MISBEHAVES, THE, New York 1935, Play *see* Frederick Jackson

BISHOP MURDER CASE, THE, New York 1917, Novel *see* S. S. Van Dine

BISHOP'S EMERALDS, THE, New York 1908, Novel *see* Houghton Townley

BISHOP'S WIFE, THE, 1928, Novel *see* Robert Nathan

BIT OF LACE, A, Play *see* H. S. Sheldon

BITCH, THE, Novel *see* Jackie Collins

BITTE LASST DIE BLUMEN LEBEN, Novel *see* Johannes Mario Simmel

BITTER APPLES, 1925, Short Story *see* Harold MacGrath

BITTER HARVEST: MURDER IN THE HEARTLAND, Book *see* James Corcoran

BITTER SAGE, 1954, Novel *see* Frank Gruber

BITTER SWEET, London 1929, Operetta *see* Noel Coward

BITTER TEA OF GENERAL YEN, THE, Indianapolis 1930, Novel *see* Grace Zaring Stone

BIXBY GIRLS, THE, Novel *see* Rosamund Marshall

BLA VECKAN, DEN, 1928, Short Story *see* Jarl Hemmer

BLACK ABBOT, THE, London 1926, Novel *see* Edgar Wallace

BLACK ALIBI, 1942, Novel *see* Cornell Woolrich

BLACK ANGEL, THE, 1943, Novel *see* Cornell Woolrich

BLACK ARROW, 1888, Novel *see* Robert Louis Stevenson

BLACK BAG, THE, Indianapolis 1908, Novel *see* Louis Joseph Vance

BLACK BEACH, 1919, Short Story *see* Ralph Stock

BLACK BEAUTY, London 1877, Novel *see* Anna Sewell

BLACK BOOK, THE, New York 1920, Novel *see* George Bronson Howard

BLACK BOX, THE, Boston 1915, Novel *see* E. Phillips Oppenheim

BLACK BUTTERFLIES, New York 1927, Novel *see* Elizabeth Jordan

BLACK BUTTES, New York 1923, Novel *see* Clarence E. Mulford

BLACK CAMEL, THE, Indianapolis 1929, Novel *see* Earl Derr Biggers

BLACK CANDLE, THE, Novel *see* Catherine Cookson

BLACK CAP, THE, 1920, Short Story *see* Wadsworth Camp

BLACK CAT, THE, 1843, Short Story *see* Edgar Allan Poe

BLACK COFFEE, Novel *see* Agatha Christie

BLACK CURTAIN, THE, 1941, Novel *see* Cornell Woolrich

BLACK DOLL, THE, New York 1936, Novel *see* William Edward Hayes

BLACK DREAM, Novel *see* Shi Chengyuan

BLACK FRIDAY, Indianapolis 1904, Novel *see* Frederic Stewart Isham

BLACK GANG, THE, Novel *see* H. C. McNeile ("Sapper")

BLACK HAND GEORGE, Play *see* Bert Lee, R. P. Weston

BLACK IS WHITE, New York 1914, Novel *see* George Barr McCutcheon

BLACK JACK, Novel *see* Leon Garfield

BLACK LIKE ME, 1960, Novel *see* John Howard Griffin

BLACK LIMELIGHT, London 1937, Play *see* Gordon Sherry

BLACK MARBLE, THE, Novel *see* Joseph Wambaugh

BLACK MARRIAGE, Story *see* Frederick Jackson

BLACK MOON, New York 1933, Novel *see* Clements Ripley

BLACK NARCISSUS, Novel *see* Rumer Godden

BLACK NIGHT, THE, Novel *see* Andrew Soutar

BLACK OXEN, New York 1923, Novel *see* Gertrude Franklin Atherton

BLACK PANTHER'S CUB, THE, Story *see* Ethel Donoher

BLACK PATH OF FEAR, THE, 1944, Novel *see* Cornell Woolrich

BLACK PAWL, Short Story *see* Ben Ames Williams

BLACK PEARL, THE, New York 1912, Novel *see* Mrs. Wilson Woodrow

BLACK PETER, Short Story *see* Arthur Conan Doyle

BLACK RIDER, THE, Story *see* Max Brand

BLACK ROBE, 1985, Novel *see* Brian Moore

BLACK ROBE, THE, Novel *see* Guy Morton

BLACK ROSE, THE, 1945, Novel *see* Thomas B. Costain

BLACK SHEEP, Short Story *see* Will J. Payne

BLACK SHEEP AND HOW IT CAME TO WASHINGTON, A, New York 1896, Musical Play *see* Charles Hale Hoyt

BLACK SHEEP, THE, Novel *see* Ruby M. Ayres

BLACK SHEEP, THE, Story *see* Dorothy Howell

BLACK SHEEP, THE, Novel *see* Edmund Yates

BLACK SPIDER, THE, London 1911, Novel *see* Carlton Dawe

BLACK STALLION RETURNS, THE, Novel *see* Walter Farley

BLACK STALLION, THE, Novel *see* Walter Farley

BLACK SUNDAY, Novel *see* Thomas Harris

BLACK SWAN, THE, Novel *see* Rafael Sabatini

BLACK, THE STORY OF A DOG, 1868, Short Story *see* Alexandre Dumas (pere)

BLACK TOWER, THE, Novel *see* P. D. James

BLACK VELVET GOWN, THE, Novel *see* Catherine Cookson

BLACK WOLF, THE, Short Story *see* Jean Barrymore

BLACKBEARD'S GHOST, 1965, Novel *see* Ben Stahl

BLACKBIRDS, New York 1913, Play *see* Harry James Smith

BLACKBOARD JUNGLE, 1954, Novel *see* Evan Hunter

BLACKBURN'S HEADHUNTERS, 1955, Book *see* Philip Harkins

BLACK-EYED SUSAN, London 1829, Play *see* Douglas Jerrold

BLACKGUARD, THE, Novel *see* Raymond Paton

BLACKJACK BARGAINER, A, Short Story *see* O. Henry

BLACKMAIL, London 1928, Play *see* Charles Bennett

BLACKMAIL WITH FEATHERS, Story *see* G. T. Fleming-Roberts

BLACKROCK, Play *see* Nick Enright

BLACKSHIRT, Novel *see* Bruce Graeme

BLACKSMITH'S STORY, THE, Poem *see* Frank Olive

BLADE IN HONG KONG, Novel *see* Terry Becker

BLADYS OF THE STEWPONY, Novel *see* Sabine Baring Gould

BLAGUE DANS LE COIN, Novel *see* Carter Brown

BLAJACKOR, Opera *see* Louis Lajtai

BLANC ET LE NOIR, LE, Play *see* Sacha Guitry

BLANCA POR FUERA Y ROSA POR DENTRO, 1943, Play *see* Enrique Jardiel Poncela

BLANCHE FURY, Novel *see* Gabrielle Margaret Vere Long

BLANCHETTE, 1892, Play *see* Eugene Brieux

BLANK WALL, THE, Novel *see* Elisabeth Sanxay Holding

BLAUBART, 1982, Novel *see* Max Frisch

BLAUE STROHHUT, DER, Play *see* Friedrich Michael

BLAUMILCHKANAL, DER, Novel *see* Ephraim Kishon

BLAZE DERRINGER, New York 1910, Novel *see* Eugene P. Lyle Jr.

BLAZE OF NOON, Novel *see* Ernest K. Gann

BLAZE STARR: MY LIFE AS TOLD TO HUEY PERRY, Book *see* Huey Perry, Blaze Starr

BLAZING GUNS, 1934, Short Story *see* Forbes Parkhill

BLAZING LAUNCH MURDER, THE, Novel *see* Rex Hardinge

BLE EN HERBE, LE, 1923, Novel *see* Sidonie Gabrielle Colette

BLEAK HOUSE, London 1853, Novel *see* Charles Dickens

BLECHTROMMEL, DIE, 1959, Novel *see* Gunter Grass

BLEEDERS, THE, 1919, Short Story *see* Margery Land May

BLEEKE BET, 1917, Play *see* Herman Bouber

BLESS THE BEASTS AND CHILDREN, Novel *see* Glendon Swarthout

BLESS THEIR HEARTS, 1936, Short Story *see* Sarah Addington

BLESS THIS HOUSE, Play *see* E. Eynon Evans

BLESS YOU SISTER, New York 1927, Play *see* John Meehan, Robert Riskin

BLESSED EVENT, New York 1932, Play *see* Manuel Seff, Forrest Wilson

BLESSING, THE, 1951, Novel *see* Nancy Mitford

BLESSURE, LA, 1900, Play *see* Henri Kistemaeckers

BLEUS DE L'AMOUR, LES, Play *see* Romain Coolus

BLIND ALLEY, 1953, Play *see* Jack Popplewell

BLIND ALLEY, New York 1935, Play *see* James Warwick

BLIND AMBITION, Book *see* Jean Dean

BLIND BOY, THE, Play *see* George H. Chirgwin

BLIND CHESS, Novel *see* Joe Gores

BLIND CHUTE, THE, Story *see* Sargeson V. Halstead

BLIND DATE, Novel *see* Leigh Howard

BLIND DATE, New York 1931, Novel *see* Vida Hurst

BLIND GIRL OF CASTLE GUILLE, THE, Poem *see* Henry Wadsworth Longfellow

BLIND GODDESS, THE, London 1947, Play *see* Patrick Hastings

BLIND GODDESS, THE, New York 1926, Novel *see* Arthur Cheney Train

BLIND HEARTS, Story *see* Emilie Johnson

BLIND JUSTICE, Short Story *see* Frank R. Adams

BLIND MAN, THE, Short Story *see* D. H. Lawrence

BLIND MAN'S EYES, THE, Boston 1916, Novel *see* Edwin Balmer, William Briggs MacHarg

BLIND MAN'S HOLIDAY, 1905, Short Story *see* O. Henry

BLIND MICE, New York 1930, Play *see* Vera Caspary, Winifred Lenihan

BLIND TRAILS, Story *see* W. C. Tuttle

BLIND YOUTH, New York 1917, Play *see* Willard Mack, Lou Tellegen

BLINDFOLD, New York 1960, Novel *see* Lucille Fletcher

BLINDNESS, 1919, Serial Story *see* Dana Burnet

BLINDNESS OF VIRTUE, THE, London 1908, Novel *see* Cosmo Hamilton

BLINDSPOT, Play *see* Kenyon Nicholson

BLINKEYES, Novel *see* Oliver Sandys

BLINKY, 1923, Short Story *see* Gene Markey

BLISS, Novel *see* Peter Carey

BLITHE SPIRIT, London 1941, Play *see* Noel Coward

BLIZNA, Short Story *see* Romuald Karas

BLONDE BABY, New York 1931, Book *see* Wilson Collison

BLONDIE WHITE, Play *see* Jeffrey Dell, Ladislaus Fodor, Bernard Merivale

BLOOD ALLEY, Novel *see* Albert Sidney Fleischman

BLOOD BROTHER, Novel *see* Elliott Arnold

BLOOD GAMES, Novel *see* Jerry Bledsoe

BLOOD MONEY, Novel *see* Cecil H. Bullivant

BLOOD OF ISRAEL, THE, Book *see* Serge Groussard

BLOOD ON HER SHOE, 1942, Novel *see* Medora Field

BLOOD ON THE BRANCHES, Novel *see* Oliver Crawford

BLOOD ON THE MOON, Novel *see* James Ellroy

BLOOD ORANGES, THE, Novel *see* John Hawkes

BLOOD RED DAWN, THE, New York 1920, Novel *see* Charles Caldwell Dobie

BLOOD RELATIVES, 1975, Novel *see* Evan Hunter

BLOOD RIGHTS, Novel *see* Mike Phillips

BLOOD SHIP, THE, New York 1922, Novel *see* Norman Springer

BLOODBROTHERS, Novel *see* Richard Price

BLOODHOUNDS OF BROADWAY, 1931, Short Story *see* Damon Runyon

BLOODLINE, Novel *see* Sidney Sheldon

BLOODY BROOD, THE, Story *see* Anne Howard Bailey

BLOODY COUNTESS, THE, Novel *see* V. Penrose

BLOODY SPUR, THE, 1953, Novel *see* Charles Einstein

BLOOMING ANGEL, New York 1919, Novel *see* Wallace Irwin

BLORE MP, Novel *see* A. N. Wilson

BLOSSOM, Short Story *see* Clifford Howard

BLOSSOM BRIDGE, Novel *see* Kenneth Pai

BLOSSOMS FOR EFFIE, Short Story *see* Lee Loeb, Arthur Strawn

BLOT IN THE 'SCUTCHEON, A, Poem *see* Robert Browning

BLOTT ON THE LANDSCAPE, Novel *see* Tom Sharpe

BLOW YOUR OWN HORN, Play *see* Owen Davis

BLUDGEON, THE, New York 1914, Novel *see* Paul Armstrong

BLUDICKA, Play *see* Jaroslav Kvapil

BLUDNE DUSE, Novel *see* Vaclav Benes-Trebizsky

BLUE BLOOD AND THE PIRATES, 1912, Short Story *see* Peter B. Kyne

BLUE CARBUNCLE, THE, Short Story *see* Arthur Conan Doyle

BLUE CITY, Novel *see* Ross MacDonald

BLUE COLLAR JOURNAL, Book *see* John R. Coleman

BLUE CROSS, THE, 1929, Short Story *see* G. K. Chesterton

BLUE DENIM, New York 1958, Play *see* James Leo Herlihy, William Noble

BLUE ENVELOPE, THE, Garden City, N.Y. 1917, Novel *see* Sophie Kerr

BLUE FIN, 1969, Novel *see* Colin Thiele

BLUE GRASS, New York 1908, Play *see* Paul Armstrong

BLUE HAND, THE, London 1925, Novel *see* Edgar Wallace

BLUE HOTEL, THE, 1899, Short Story *see* Stephen Crane

BLUE JEANS, New York 1890, Play *see* Joseph Arthur

BLUE KNIGHT, THE, 1972, Novel *see* Joseph Wambaugh

BLUE MAX, THE, New York 1964, Novel *see* Jack D. Hunter

BLUE MOCCASINS, THE, Short Story *see* D. H. Lawrence

BLUE MOON, A TALE OF THE FLATWOODS, Indianapolis 1919, Novel *see* David Wolf Anderson

BLUE PEARL, THE, New York 1918, Play *see* Anne Crawford Flexner

BLUE PETER, THE, Novel *see* E. Temple Thurston

BLUE TATTOOING, THE, 1915, Short Story *see* Kenneth B. Clarke

BLUE WATER, Novel *see* Frederick William Wallace

BLUE WHITE AND PERFECT, Novel *see* Borden Chase

BLUEBOTTLES, Short Story *see* H. G. Wells

BLUFF, Novel *see* Rafael Sabatini

BLUME VON HAWAII, DIE, Opera *see* Paul Abraham

BLUNDERER, THE, New York 1954, Novel *see* Patricia Highsmith

BOARDED WINDOW, 1891, Short Story *see* Ambrose Bierce

BOARDING PARTY, Novel *see* James Leasor

BOB - SON OF BATTLE, 1898, Novel *see* Alfred Ollivant

BOB GOES TO A PARTY, Story *see* Gene Lewis

BOB HAMPTON OF PLACER, Chicago 1910, Novel *see* Randall Parrish

BOBO DO REI, O, 1932, Play *see* Joracy Camargo

BOBO, O, 1884, Novel *see* Alexandre Herculano

BOBO, THE, Novel *see* David R. Schwartz

BOBOSSE, 1951, Play *see* Andre Roussin

BOCA DE OURO, 1959-60, Play *see* Nelson Rodrigues

BOCCACCIO, Opera *see* Franz von Suppe, F. Zell

BOCHORNO, 1960, Short Story *see* Angel Maria de Lera

BOCK I ORTAGARD, 1933, Novel *see* Fritiof Nilsson Piraten

BOCKERER, DER, Play *see* Ulrich Becher, Peter Preses

BOCKHANDLAREN SOM SLUTADE BADA, 1937, Novel *see* Fritiof Nilsson Piraten

BOCKSHORN, 1973, Novel *see* Christoph Meckel

BODA, LA, 1959, Novel *see* Angel Maria de Lera

BODAS DE SANGRE, 1936, Play *see* Federico Garcia Lorca

BODEGA, LA, Novel *see* Vicente Blasco Ibanez

BODEN'S BOY, Novel *see* Tom Gallon

BODIES AND SOULS, Novel *see* Maxence Van Der Meersch

BODY AND SOUL, Play *see* William Hurlbut

BODY AND SOUL, 1919, Short Story *see* Katharine Newlin Burt

BODY IN THE LIBRARY, THE, Novel *see* Agatha Christie

BODY SNATCHER, 1936, Short Story *see* Theodore A. Tinsley

BODY SNATCHER, THE, 1894, Short Story *see* Robert Louis Stevenson

BODY SNATCHERS, THE, 1954, Novel *see* Jack Finney

BODY, THE, Short Story *see* Stephen King

BOEING-BOEING, 1960, Play *see* Marc Camoletti

BOESMAN AND LENA, 1969, Play *see* Athol Fugard

BOFETADA, UNA, 1916, Short Story *see* Horacio Quiroga

BOGDAN KHMELNYTSKY, 1939, Play *see* Aleksander Korniychuk

BOGIE, Biography *see* Joe Hyams

BOHEME, LA, Turin 1896, Opera *see* Giuseppe Giacosa, Luigi Illica, Giacomo Puccini

BOHEMIAN GIRL, THE, London 1843, Opera *see* Michael William Balfe, Alfred Bunn

BOHUNK, Play *see* Harry R. Irving

BOIKUNTHER WILL, 1916, Novel *see* Saratchandra Chatterjee

BOIS SACRE, LE, Play *see* Gaston Arman de Caillavet, Robert de Flers

BOISSIERE, Novel *see* Pierre Benoit

BOKUTO KIDAN, Tokyo 1952, Novel *see* Kafu Nagai

BOLCSO, Novel *see* Pal Szabo

BOLERO, Play *see* Michel Duran

BOLTED DOOR, THE, New York 1910, Novel *see* George Gibbs

BOLWIESER, 1931, Novel *see* Oskar Maria Graf

BOMBA THE JUNGLE BOY, Novel *see* Roy Rockwood

BOMBAY MAIL, Boston 1934, Novel *see* Lawrence G. Blochman

BRASS; A NOVEL OF MARRIAGE, New York 1921, Novel *see* Charles Gilman Norris

BRASS BOTTLE, THE, London 1900, Novel *see* F. Anstey

BRASS BOWL, THE, Indianapolis 1907, Novel *see* Louis Joseph Vance

BRASS CHECK, THE, 1916, Short Story *see* George Allan England

BRASS COMMANDMENTS, THE, New York 1923, Novel *see* Charles Alden Seltzer

BRAT NASZEGO BOGA, 1949, Play *see* Karol Wojtyla

BRAT, THE, Los Angeles 1916, Play *see* Maude Fulton

BRATYA KARAMAZOVY, 1880, Novel *see* Fyodor Dostoyevsky

BRAUT NR. 68, DIE, Novel *see* Peter Bolt

BRAUT VON MESSINA, DIE, 1803, Play *see* Friedrich von Schiller

BRAUTIGAME DER BABETTE BOMBERLING, DIE, Novel *see* Alice Berend

BRAVADOS, THE, Novel *see* Frank O'Rourke

BRAVE BULLS, THE, Novel *see* Tom Lea

BRAVE COWBOY, New York 1956, Novel *see* Edward Abbey

BRAVE HERO, Novel *see* Liu Liu

BRAVE LITTLE TOASTER, THE, Novel *see* Thomas M. Disch

BRAVE NEW WORLD, 1932, Novel *see* Aldous Huxley

BRAVE, THE, Novel *see* Gregory McDonald

BRAVEHEART, Story *see* William C. de Mille

BRAVEST OF THE BRAVE, THE, Story *see* Thomas Delmar

BRAVO, THE, Short Story *see* W. W. Jacobs

BRAVO TWO ZERO, Book *see* Andy McNab

BREACH OF MARRIAGE, A, London 1948, Play *see* Dan Sutherland

BREAD, New York 1923, Novel *see* Charles Gilman Norris

BREAD AND A STONE, Novel *see* Alva Bessie

BREAD UPON THE WATERS, 1923, Short Story *see* Peter B. Kyne

BREAD UPON THE WATERS, 1934, Short Story *see* Edith Wharton

BREAK BREAK BREAK, Poem *see* Alfred Tennyson

BREAK DOWN THE WALLS, Play *see* Mrs. Alexander Grossman

BREAK IN THE CIRCLE, Novel *see* Philip Lorraine

BREAK THE NEWS TO MOTHER, 1897, Song *see* Charles K. Harris

BREAK THE WALLS DOWN, 1914, Play *see* Mrs. Alexander Gross

BREAKER MORANT, Play *see* Kenneth Ross

BREAKER, THE, 1916, Short Story *see* Arthur Stringer

BREAKFAST AT TIFFANY'S, New York 1958, Novel *see* Truman Capote

BREAKFAST OF CHAMPIONS, 1976, Novel *see* Kurt Vonnegut Jr.

BREAKHEART PASS, 1974, Novel *see* Alistair MacLean

BREAKING OF BUMBO, THE, Novel *see* Andrew Sinclair

BREAKING POINT, THE, Short Story *see* Edgar Wallace

BREAKING POINT, THE, London 1957, Novel *see* Laurence Meynell

BREAKING POINT, THE, New York 1922, Novel *see* Mary Roberts Rinehart

BREAKING SMITH'S QUARTER HORSE, Chicago 1966, Novel *see* Paul St. Pierre

BREAKING STRAIN, Short Story *see* Arthur C. Clarke

BREAKOUT, Book *see* Jim Hawkins, Ron Leflore, Frederick Oughton

BREAKTHROUGH, THE, Short Story *see* Daphne Du Maurier

BREATH OF GOD, THE, Boston 1905, Novel *see* Sidney McCall

BREATH OF SCANDAL, THE, Boston 1922, Novel *see* Edwin Balmer

BREATH OF SPRING, London 1958, Play *see* Peter Coke

BREATHES THERE THE MAN, 1917, Short Story *see* George Charles Hull

BREBIS PERDUE, LA, Play *see* Gabriel Trarieux

BRED IN THE BONE, Story *see* Frank Kinsella

BREED O' THE NORTH, Short Story *see* Bret Harte

BREED OF THE BORDER, THE, Story *see* William Dawson Hoffman

BREED OF THE TRENSHAMS, THE, London 1905, Play *see* Beulah Marie Dix, E. G. Sutherland

BREMER STADTMUSIKANTEN, DIE, Short Story *see* Jacob Grimm, Wilhelm Grimm

BRENNENDES GEHEIMNIS, 1929, Short Story *see* Stefan Zweig

BRETTLFLEIGEN, Novel *see* Annie von Brabenetz

BREVE FRA AFRICA, 1960, Short Story *see* Karen Blixen

BREWSTER'S MILLIONS, New York 1902, Novel *see* George Barr McCutcheon

BRIBE, THE, Short Story *see* Frederick Nebel

BRICK DUST ROW, 1906, Short Story *see* O. Henry

BRICK FOXHOLE, THE, Novel *see* Richard Brooks

BRIDAL PATH, THE, Novel *see* Nigel Tranter

BRIDAL PATH, THE, New York 1913, Play *see* Thompson Buchanan

BRIDE COMES HOME, THE, 1935, Short Story *see* Elisabeth Sanxay Holding

BRIDE COMES TO YELLOW SKY, THE, 1898, Short Story *see* Stephen Crane

BRIDE FOR HENRY, A, 1937, Short Story *see* Josephine Bentham

BRIDE OF LAMMERMOOR, THE, 1819, Novel *see* Sir Walter Scott

BRIDE SAID NO, THE, Story *see* W. Scott Darling, Erna Lazarus

BRIDE, THE, New York 1924, Play *see* George Middleton, Stuart Olivier

BRIDE WORE BLACK, THE, New York 1940, Novel *see* Cornell Woolrich

BRIDE'S PLAY, THE, Short Story *see* Brian Oswald Donn-Byrne

BRIDESHEAD REVISITED, 1945, Novel *see* Evelyn Waugh

BRIDGE, Story *see* Erle C. Kenton

BRIDGE, 1917, Play *see* Alice Ramsey

BRIDGE AT REMAGEN, New York 1957, Novel *see* Kenneth William Hechler

BRIDGE BUILT AT NIGHT, Story *see* Maurice Hanline, Jesse Lasky Jr.

BRIDGE OF SAN LUIS REY, THE, 1927, Novel *see* Thornton Wilder

BRIDGE, THE, Novel *see* Maggie Hemingway, Liu Pengde

BRIDGE, THE, New York 1909, Play *see* Rupert Hughes

BRIDGE TO THE SUN, Chapel Hill, Nc. 1957, Novel *see* Gwendolyn Terasaki

BRIDGE TOO FAR, A, Book *see* Cornelius Ryan

BRIDGES AT TOKO-RI, THE, 1953, Novel *see* James A. Michener

BRIDGES OF MADISON COUNTY, THE, Novel *see* Robert James Waller

BRIEF DEBUT OF TILDY, THE, Short Story *see* O. Henry

BRIEF EINER UNBEKANNTEN, 1922, Short Story *see* Stefan Zweig

BRIEF HISTORY OF TIME, A, 1988, Book *see* Stephen Hawking

BRIEF MOMENT, New York 1931, Play *see* S. N. Behrman

BRIERE, LA, Novel *see* Alphonse de Chateaubriant

BRIG, THE, New York 1963, Play *see* Kenneth H. Brown

BRIGADE ANTI-GANGS, Novel *see* Auguste Le Breton

BRIGADOON, New York 1947, Play *see* Alan Jay Lerner

BRIGAND, A ROMANCE OF THE REIGN OF DON CARLOS, Novel *see* Alexandre Dumas (pere)

BRIGANTE DI TACCA DEL LUPO, IL, 1942, Novel *see* Riccardo Bacchelli

BRIGANTE, IL, 1951, Novel *see* Giuseppe Berto

BRIGANTI ITALIANI, I, Novel *see* Mario Monti

BRIGGEN TRE LILJOR, Book *see* Olle Mattson

BRIGHT LEAF, 1948, Novel *see* Foster Fitz-Simons

BRIGHT LIGHTS, BIG CITY, Novel *see* Jay McInerney

BRIGHT ROAD, PART THREE, Novel *see* Hao Ran

BRIGHT SHAWL, THE, New York 1922, Novel *see* Joseph Hergesheimer

BRIGHT SHINING LIE, A, Book *see* Neil Sheehan

BRIGHT VICTORY, Novel *see* Baynard H. Kendrick

BRIGHTON BEACH MEMOIRS, 1985, Play *see* Neil Simon

BRIGHTON MYSTERY, THE, Short Story *see* Baroness Orczy

BRIGHTON ROCK, 1938, Novel *see* Graham Greene

BRIGHTY OF THE GRAND CANYON, New York 1953, Novel *see* Marguerite Henry

BRILLIANT MARRIAGE, Novel *see* Ursula Parrott

BRIMSTONE AND TREACLE, 1978, Play *see* Dennis Potter

BRING ME HIS EARS, 1922, Short Story *see* Clarence E. Mulford

BRINGING UP BABY, 1937, Short Story *see* Hagar Wilde

BRINGING UP THE BRASS, 1951, Book *see* Nardi Reeder Campion, Martin Maher

BRITANNIA MEWS, Novel *see* Margery Sharp

BRITANNIA OF BILLINGSGATE, London 1931, Play *see* Christine Jope-Slade, Sewell Stokes

BRITANNICUS, 1669, Play *see* Jean Racine

BRITISH AGENT, London 1932, Novel *see* R. H. Bruce Lockhart

BRITTON OF THE SEVENTH, Chicago 1914, Novel *see* Cyrus Townsend Brady

BROADWAY A PLAY, New York 1927, Play *see* George Abbott, Philip Dunning

BROADWAY; A PLAY, New York 1927, Play *see* Jed Harris

BROADWAY AFTER DARK, Play *see* Owen Davis

BROADWAY BOUND, 1987, Play *see* Neil Simon

BROADWAY BROKE, 1922, Short Story *see* Earl Derr Biggers

BROADWAY BUBBLE, THE, 1920, Short Story *see* Leigh Gordon Giltner

BROADWAY GOLD, 1922, Short Story *see* W. Carey Wonderly

BROADWAY JONES, New York 1912, Play *see* George M. Cohan

BROADWAY LOVE, 1916, Novel *see* W. Carey Wonderly

BROADWAY MUSKETEERS, 1928, Short Story *see* Jay Gelzer

BROADWAY VIRGIN, New York 1931, Novel *see* Lois Bull

BRODERNA LEJONHJARTA, Novel *see* Astrid Lindgren

BROEDERWEELDE, Novel *see* Jean Paul Franssens

BROGLIACCIO D'AMORE, Novel *see* Gino Maggiora, Franca Monari

BROKEN BARRIERS, New York 1922, Novel *see* Meredith Nicholson

BROKEN CHAINS, 1921, Short Story *see* Jack Bechdolt

BROKEN COIN, THE, Story *see* Emerson Hough

BROKEN DISHES, New York 1929, Play *see* Martin Flavin

BROKEN DOLLAR, THE, 1927, Short Story *see* Johnston McCulley

BROKEN GATE, THE, New York 1917, Novel *see* Emerson Hough

BROKEN GUN, THE, Novel *see* Louis L'Amour

BROKEN HEARTS, Story *see* Z. Libin

BROKEN LANCE, Novel *see* Frank Gruber

BROKEN MELODY, THE, London 1892, Play *see* Herbert Keen, James T. Tanner

BROKEN PROMISE, Book *see* Kent Hayes, Alex Lazzarino

BROKEN ROAD, THE, Novel *see* A. E. W. Mason

BROKEN SEAL, THE, New York 1967, Book *see* Ladislas Farago

BROKEN THREADS, New York 1917, Play *see* W. Ernest Wilkes

BROKEN WING, THE, New York 1920, Play *see* Paul Dickey, Charles W. Goddard

BROKEN WINGS, THE, New York 1957, Novel *see* Kahlil Gibran

BROLLOPSBESVAR, Stockholm 1949, Novel *see* Stig Dagerman

BRONCO APACHE, Novel *see* Paul I. Wellman

BRONEPOEZD NO.14-69, 1922, Play *see* Vsevolod Ivanov

BRONX TALE, A, Play see Chazz Palminteri

BRONZE BELL, THE, New York 1909, Novel see Louis Joseph Vance

BROOK EVANS, London 1928, Novel see Susan Glaspell

BROOKS WILSON, LTD., New York 1966, Novel see J. M. Ryan

BROOS, Play see Stichting de Akteurs

BROT DER FRUHEN JAHRE, DAS, 1955, Novel see Heinrich Boll

BROTHER ALFRED, London 1913, Play see Herbert Westbrook, P. G. Wodehouse

BROTHER OFFICERS, London 1898, Play see Leo Trevor

BROTHER ORCHID, 1938, Short Story see Richard Connell

BROTHER RAT, New York 1936, Play see Fred F. Finkelhoffe, John Monks Jr.

BROTHER VAN, 1948, Novel see Alson Jesse Smith

BROTHERHOOD OF THE ROSE, Novel see David Morrell

BROTHERS, Play see Herbert Ashton Jr., Edwin Burke
BROTHERS, Story see Elmer Harris

BROTHERS IN LAW, Novel see Henry Cecil

BROTHER'S KISS, A, Play see Seth Zvi Rosenfeld

BROTHER'S TALE, A, Novel see Stan Barstow

BROTHERS, THE, 1931, Novel see L. A. G. Strong

BROTHERS UNDER THEIR SKINS, 1921, Short Story see Peter B. Kyne

BROTT, ETT, 1938, Play see Sigfrid Siwertz

BROWN DERBY, THE, 1925, Play see Brian Marlow, E. S. Merlin

BROWN OF HARVARD, New York 1906, Play see Gilbert P. Coleman, Rida Johnson Young

BROWN ON RESOLUTION, 1929, Novel see C. S. Forester

BROWN SUGAR, London 1920, Play see Lady Arthur Lever

BROWN WALLET, THE, Short Story see Stacy Aumonier

BROWN WOLF, 1906, Short Story see Jack London

BROWNING VERSION, THE, London 1948, Play see Terence Rattigan

BROWN'S REQUIEM, 1981, Novel see James Ellroy

BRUCE OF CIRCLE A, Boston 1918, Novel see Harold Titus

BRUCE PARTINGTON PLANS, THE, Short Story see Arthur Conan Doyle

BRUCKE, DIE, Vienna 1958, Novel see Manfred Gregor

BRUCKE IM DSCHUNGEL, DIE, 1929, Novel see Ben Traven

BRUDER GRIMM, DIE, Munich 1952, Biography see Hermann Gerstner

BRUDER MARTIN, Play see Carl Costa

BRUDER STRAUBINGER, Opera see Edmund Eysler

BRUDER VON ST. BERNHARD, DIE, Play see Ohorn

BRUDERMORD, EIN, 1919, Short Story see Franz Kafka

BRUJA, LA, Opera see Miguel Ramos Carrion, Ruperto Chapi

BRUSKI, 1928-37, Novel see Fyodor Panfyorov

BRUTE BREAKER, THE, 1918, Novel see Johnston McCulley

BRUTE, THE, Novel see Guy Des Cars
BRUTE, THE, New York 1912, Novel see Frederic Arnold Kummer
BRUTE, THE, New York 1924, Novel see W. Douglas Newton

BRUVVER JIM'S BABY, New York 1904, Novel see Philip Verrill Mighels

BRUXINHA QUE ERA BOA, A, 1957, Play see Maria Clara Machado

BRZEZINA, 1933, Short Story see Jaroslaw Iwaszkiewicz

BU NENG ZOU NIE TIAO LU, Novel see Li Zhun

BUBBLES, Short Story see J. Basil Kreider

BUBU DI MONTPARNASSE, Novel see Charles L. Philippe

BUBUSCH, Play see Gabor von Vaszary

BUCHANAN'S WIFE, New York 1906, Novel see Justus Miles Forman

BUCHSE DER PANDORA, DIE, 1904, Play see Frank Wedekind

BUCK PETERS, RANCHMAN, Chicago 1912, Novel see Clarence E. Mulford, John Wood

BUCKIN' IN THE BIG FOUR, Short Story see Christopher B. Booth

BUCKING THE TIGER, New York 1917, Novel see Achmed Abdullah

BUCK'S LADY FRIEND, Story see Charles E. Van Loan

BUCKSKIN EMPIRE, Novel see Harry Sinclair Drago

BUD AND LOU, Book see Bob Thomas

BUDAPESTI TAVASZ, 1953, Novel see Ferenc Karinthy

BUDDENBROOKS, Berlin 1901, Novel see Thomas Mann

BUDDWING, New York 1964, Novel see Evan Hunter

BUDDY BUDDY, Play see Francis Veber

BUDDY HOLLY STORY, THE, Biography see John Goldrosen

BUDDY'S SONG, Novel see Nigel Hinton

BUENA SERA, MRS. CAMPBELL, see Aitken Morewood

BUENOS DIAS PERDIDOS, LOS, 1973, Play see Antonio Gala

BUFFALO GRASS, Novel see Frank Gruber

BUG OUT, Story see James Warner Bellah

BUGIARDA, LA, Milan 1956, Play see Diego Fabbri

BUGLES IN THE AFTERNOON, 1944, Novel see Ernest Haycox

BUGLE'S WAKE, 1952, Novel see Curt Brandon

BUGRINHA, 1922, Novel see Julio Afranio Peixoto

BUILD MY GALLOWS HIGH, Novel see Daniel Mainwaring

BUILDER OF BRIDGES, THE, London 1908, Play see Alfred Sutro

BUILD-UP BOYS, THE, New York 1951, Novel see Jeremy Kirk

BUIO E IL MIELE, IL, Novel see Giovanni Arpino

BULL BOYS, THE, Play see R. F. Delderfield

BULL OF THE WEST, THE, Novel see Dee Linford

BULLDOG DRUMMOND, 1920, Novel see H. C. McNeile ("Sapper")

BULLDOG DRUMMOND AGAIN, Play see Gerard Fairlie, Sapper

BULLDOG DRUMMOND AND THE ORIENTAL MIND, 1937, Short Story see H. C. McNeile ("Sapper")

BULLDOG DRUMMOND AT BAY, Novel see H. C. McNeile ("Sapper")

BULLDOG DRUMMOND STRIKES BACK, New York 1933, Novel see H. C. McNeile ("Sapper")

BULLENKLOSTER, DAS, Novel see Hans Henning Claer

BULLET TO BEIJING, Novel see Len Deighton

BUMERANG, Bad Worishofen 1959, Novel see Igor Sentjurc

BUN SANG YUN, Novel see Eileen Chang

BUNBURY, Play see Oscar Wilde

BUNCH OF KEYS, A, 1882, Play see Charles Hale Hoyt

BUNCH OF VIOLETS, A, London 1894, Play see Sidney Grundy

BUNGA-BUNGA, Novel see Stephen King-Hall

BUNKER BEAN, New York 1913, Novel see Harry Leon Wilson

BUNKER, THE, Book see James O'Donnell

BUNNY LAKE IS MISSING, New York 1957, Novel see Evelyn Piper

BUNTY PULLS THE STRINGS, London 1911, Play see Graham Moffatt

BUON SAMARITANO, IL, Novel see Claude Lemaitre

BUONA FIGLIOLA, LA, 1909, Play see Sabatino Lopez

BUONI PER UN GIORNO, 1934, Short Story see Giaci Mondaini, Cesare Zavattini

BURDEN OF PROOF, THE, Novel see James Barlow

BURE BARUTA, Play see Dejan Dukovski

BURGLAR AND THE GIRL, THE, Play see Matthew Boulton

BURGLAR PROOF, 1920, Novel see William Slavens McNutt

BURGLAR, THE, 1953, Novel see David Goodis

BURGOMASTER OF STILEMONDE, THE, London 1919, Play see Maurice Maeterlinck

BURIDAN - HEROS DE LA TOUR DE NESLE, Novel see Michel Zevaco

BURIED ALIVE, London 1908, Novel see Arnold Bennett

BURIED TREASURE, Short Story see O. Henry
BURIED TREASURE, 1923, Short Story see F. Britten Austin

BURKESES AMY, New York 1915, Novel see Julie Mathilde Lippman

BURLESQUE, New York 1927, Play see Arthur Hopkins, George Manker Watters

BURN THE EVIDENCE, Short Story see Percy Hoskins

BURN, WITCH, BURN!, New York 1933, Novel see Abraham Merritt

BURNING BUSH, THE, Play see Heinz Herald, Geza Herczeg

BURNING COURT, THE, New York 1959, Novel see John Dickson Carr

BURNING DAYLIGHT, New York 1910, Novel see Jack London

BURNING HILLS, THE, Novel see Louis L'Amour

BURNING SANDS, New York 1921, Novel see Arthur Weigall

BURNT IN, Novel see S. B. Hill

BURNT OFFERINGS, Novel see Robert Marasco

BURNT RANCH, 1933, Short Story see Walter J. Coburn

BURNT WINGS, Novel see Mrs. Stanley Wrench

BURTON AND SPEKE, Novel see William Harrison

BURU GUI, Novel see Tokutomi Roka

BUS STOP, New York 1955, Play see William Inge

BUS, THE, Short Story see Shirley Jackson

BUSCA, LA, 1904, Novel see Pio Baroja Y Nessi

BUSCHHEXE, DIE, Novel see Georg Muhlen-Schulte

BUSHBABIES, THE, Boston 1965, Novel see William H. Stevenson

BUSINESS, Play see Pierre Sabatier

BUSINESS BEFORE PLEASURE, New York 1917, Play see Montague Glass, Jules Eckert Goodman

BUSINESS IS BEST, Story see Arthur Somers Roche

BUSINESS OF LIFE, THE, New York 1913, Novel see Robert W. Chambers

BUSMAN'S HONEYMOON, 1937, Novel see Dorothy L. Sayers

BUSTER, THE, Boston 1920, Novel see William Patterson White

BUSY BODY, THE, New York 1966, Novel see Donald E. Westlake

BUT FOR THESE MEN, London 1962, Book see John Drummond

BUT GENTLEMEN MARRY BRUNETTES, 1928, Novel see Anita Loos

BUT NOT IN VAIN, Play see Ben Van Eeslyn

BUT THERE ARE ALWAYS MIRACLES, Book see Jack Wills, Mary Wills

BUTCH MINDS THE BABY, 1931, Short Story see Damon Runyon

BUTCHER BOY, THE, 1992, Novel see Patrick McCabe

BUTLER'S NIGHT OFF, THE, Story see Silvio Narizzano

BUTLEY, 1971, Play see Simon Gray

BUTTER AND EGG MAN, THE, Novel see Arthur Caesar

BUTTER AND EGG MAN, THE, New York 1925, Play see George S. Kaufman

BUTTERBROT, Play see Gabriel Barylli

BUTTERCUP CHAIN, THE, Novel see Janice Elliott

BUTTERFIELD 8, 1935, Novel see John O'Hara

BUTTERFLIES ARE FREE, New York 1969, Play see Leonard Gershe

BUTTERFLIES IN THE RAIN, Novel see Andrew Soutar

BUTTERFLY, 1947, Novel see James M. Cain

BUTTERFLY MAN, THE, New York 1910, Novel see George Barr McCutcheon

BUTTERFLY MYSTERY, Short Story see Arthur Hoerl

BUTTERFLY ON THE WHEEL, A, London 1911, Play see Edward Hemmerde, Francis Neilson

BUTTERFLY REVOLUTION, THE, Novel see William Butler

BUTTERFLY, THE, New York 1914, Novel see Henry Kitchell Webster

BUTTON THIEF, THE, Short Story *see* Arthur Stringer

BUTTSUKE HONBAN, Book *see* Hajime Mizuno, Moto Ogasawara

BUX, Novel *see* Hans Passendorf

BUYER FROM CACTUS CITY, THE, Short Story *see* O. Henry

BWANA, Novel *see* Chris McBride

BY BERWIN BANKS, Novel *see* Allen Raine

BY INJUNCTION, Short Story *see* O. Henry

BY JIMINY, Novel *see* David Scott Daniell

BY LOVE POSSESSED, New York 1957, Novel *see* James Gould Cozzens

BY RIGHT OF CONQUEST, New York 1909, Novel *see* Arthur Hornblow

BY THE GREAT HORN SPOON!, Boston 1963, Novel *see* Albert Sidney Fleischman

BY THE WORLD FORGOT, Chicago 1917, Novel *see* Cyrus Townsend Brady

BY WAY OF CAPE HORN, Novel *see* A. J. Villiers

BY YOUR LEAVE, Wells, Emma B. C., Play *see* Gladys Hurlbut

BYE BYE BIRDIE, New York 1960, Musical Play *see* Michael Stewart, Charles Strouse

BYE-BYE BUDDY, Story *see* Ben Herschfield

BYOIN DE SHINU TO IU KOTO, Book *see* Fumio Yamazaki

BYRON, Play *see* Alicia Ramsey

CA N'ARRIVE QU'AUX VIVANTS, Novel *see* James Hadley Chase

CABAL, Novel *see* Clive Barker

CABALLERO AUDAZ, EL, Novel *see* Jose-Maria Carretero

CABALLERO DE HARMENTAL, EL, Novel *see* Alexandre Dumas (pere)

CABALLERO OF THE LAW, 1933, Short Story *see* Ben Hecht

CABALLERO'S WAY, 1904, Short Story *see* O. Henry

CABANE D'AMOUR, LA, Novel *see* Francis de Miomandre

CABARET, Short Story *see* Whitman Chambers

CABELEIRA, O, 1876, Novel *see* Franklin Tavora

CABIN B-16, Radio Play *see* John Dickson Carr

CABIN CRUISER, 1936, Short Story *see* David Garth

CABIN IN THE COTTON, THE, New York 1931, Novel *see* Harry Harrison Kroll

CABIN IN THE SKY, Musical Play *see* Lynn Root

CABINE 27, Play *see* Anton Germano Rossi

CABRITA QUE TIRA AL MONTE, Play *see* Joaquin Alvarez Quintero, Serafin Alvarez Quintero

CACCIA AL LUPO, 1901, *see* Giovanni Verga

CACORKA, Play *see* Anna Ziegloserova

CACTUS FLOWER, New York 1964, Play *see* Abe Burrows

CAD, A, Story *see* Raymond L. Schrock

CADA QUIEN SU VIDA, Play *see* Luis G. Basurto

CADAVRES EN VACANCES, Novel *see* Jean-Pierre Ferriere

CADEAU, LE, Play *see* Terzoli, Vaime

CAESAR AND CLEOPATRA, 1901, Play *see* George Bernard Shaw

CAESAR'S WIFE, London 1919, Play *see* W. Somerset Maugham

CAFE IN CAIRO, A, 1924, Short Story *see* Izola Forrester

CAFE L'EGYPTE, THE, Short Story *see* Sax Rohmer

CAFE NOIR, Novel *see* Georges-Andre Cuel

CAFETERIA, THE, 1970, Short Story *see* Isaac Bashevis Singer

CAGE AUX FOLLES, LA, Play *see* Jean Poiret

CAGE, THE, Play *see* Rick Cluchey

CAGE, THE, Story *see* Hesketh Pearson

CAGLIOSTRO IL TAUMAUTURGO, Book *see* Piero Carpi

CAGNOTTE, LA, 1864, Play *see* A. Delacour, Eugene Labiche

CAIDA, LA, Novel *see* Beatriz Guido

CAIDS, LES, Novel *see* M. G. Braun

CAILLE, LA, Novel *see* Paul Vialar

CAIN, 1821, Poem *see* Lord Byron

CAIN AND MABEL, Short Story *see* Harry Charles Witwer

CAINE MUTINY, THE, 1951, Novel *see* Herman Wouk

CAL, Novel *see* Bernard MacLaverty

CALAFURIA, Novel *see* Delfino Cinelli

CALAIS-DOUVRES, Novel *see* Julius Berstel

CALAMITY TOWN, Novel *see* Ellery Queen

CALDA VITA, LA, Turin 1958, Novel *see* Pier Quarantotti-Gambini

CALDERON'S PRISONER, New York 1903, Novel *see* Alice Duer Miller

CALEA VICTORIEI, 1932, Novel *see* Cezar Petrescu

CALEB CONOVER - RAILROADER, New York 1907, Novel *see* Albert Payson Terhune

CALEB WEST, New York 1900, Play *see* Michael Morton

CALEB WEST MASTER DIVER, New York 1899, Novel *see* F. Hopkinson Smith

CALEB WILLIAMS, Novel *see* William Godwin

CALENDAR, THE, London 1930, Novel *see* Edgar Wallace

CALF LOVE, Novel *see* Vernon Bartlett

CALICO PONY, Novel *see* Herb Meadow

CALIFFA, LA, Novel *see* Alberto Bevilacqua

CALIFORNIA: ITS HISTORY AND ROMANCE (CHAPTER 8), Book *see* John Steven McGroarty

CALIFORNIA SUITE, 1977, Play *see* Neil Simon

CALIFORNIAN AUNTS, THE, Short Story *see* Cynthia Flood

CALIFORNIO, THE, Greenwich CT. 1967, Novel *see* Robert MacLeod

CALINE OLIVIA, Novel *see* Jean Laborde

CALL FOR THE DEAD, London 1961, Novel *see* John Le Carre

CALL FROM MITCH MILLER, A, Short Story *see* Mary Agnes Thompson

CALL HER SAVAGE, New York 1931, Novel *see* Tiffany Thayer

CALL IT A DAY, New York 1936, Play *see* Dodie Smith

CALL IT TREASON, 1949, Book *see* George Locke Howe

CALL LOAN, THE, Short Story *see* O. Henry

CALL ME MADAM, New York 1950, Musical Play *see* Russel Crouse, Howard Lindsay

CALL OF LIFE, THE, New York 1919, Novel *see* Jeanne Judson

CALL OF SIVA, THE, Short Story *see* Sax Rohmer

CALL OF THE BLOOD, THE, Novel *see* Robert Hichens

CALL OF THE CANYON, THE, New York 1924, Novel *see* Zane Grey

CALL OF THE CUMBERLANDS, THE, 1913, Novel *see* Charles Neville Buck

CALL OF THE EAST, THE, Novel *see* Esther Whitehouse

CALL OF THE NORTH, THE, New York 1908, Play *see* George Broadhurst

CALL OF THE WILD, New York 1903, Novel *see* Jack London

CALL ON KUPRIN, A, Novel *see* Maurice Edelman

CALL ON THE PRESIDENT, A, 1937, Short Story *see* Damon Runyon

CALL, THE, Play *see* Julian Frank

CALLAHANS AND THE MURPHYS, THE, Garden City, N.Y. 1924, Novel *see* Kathleen Norris

CALLED BACK, London 1884, Novel *see* Hugh Conway

CALLES DE TANGO, 1953, Novel *see* Bernardo Verbitsky

CALLING BULLDOG DRUMMOND, Novel *see* Gerard Fairlie

CALLING DR. HOROWITZ, Book *see* Steven Horowitz, Neil Offen

CALLING OF DAN MATTHEWS, THE, Chicago 1909, Novel *see* Harold Bell Wright

CALM YOURSELF!, Indianapolis 1934, Novel *see* Edward Hope

CALTEZ VOLAILLES, Novel *see* Ange Bastiani

CALVAIRE D'AMOUR, Novel *see* Noelle Bazan

CALVAIRE DE CIMIEZ, LE, Novel *see* Henri Bordeaux

CALVAIRE DE MIGNON, LE, Novel *see* Paul Feval (fils)

CALVARY, Novel *see* Rita

CALVARY ALLEY, New York 1917, Novel *see* Alice Hegan Rice

CAMBRIC MASK, THE, New York 1899, Novel *see* Robert W. Chambers

CAME A HOT FRIDAY, Novel *see* Ronald Hugh Morrieson

CAME THE DAWN, 1949, Novel *see* Roger Bax

CAMEO KIRBY, New York 1909, Play *see* Booth Tarkington, Harry Leon Wilson

CAMERON'S CLOSETT, Novel *see* Gary Brandner

CAMI DE LA FELICITAT, EL, Novel *see* Josep Maria Folch I Torres

CAMILLE CLAUDEL, Book *see* Reine-Marie Paris

CAMINO, EL, 1950, Novel *see* Miguel Delibes

CAMOMILE LAWN, THE, Novel *see* Mary Wesley

CAMORRISTA, IL, Novel *see* Giuseppe Marrazzo

CAMPANE DI SAN LUCIO, LE, 1916, Play *see* Giovacchino Forzano

CAMPANILE MURDERS, THE, New York 1933, Novel *see* Whitman Chambers

CAMPBELLS ARE COMING, THE, Short Story *see* Emerson Hough

CAMPBELL'S KINGDOM, Novel *see* Hammond Innes

CAMPUS, DER, Novel *see* Dietrich Schwanitz

CANAA, 1902, Novel *see* Jose Pereira Da Graca Aranha

CANARD EN FER-BLANC, LE, Novel *see* Day Keene

CANARIES SOMETIMES SING, London 1929, Play *see* Frederick Lonsdale

CANARY MURDER CASE, THE, New York 1927, Novel *see* S. S. Van Dine

CANAS Y BARRO, 1902, Novel *see* Vicente Blasco Ibanez

CANAVAN THE MAN WHO HAD HIS WAY, 1909, Short Story *see* Rupert Hughes

CAN-CAN, Play *see* Abe Burrows

CANCION DE CUNA, Madrid 1911, Play *see* Gregorio Martinez Sierra

CANDIDAT LAURISTON, LE, Novel *see* Henri Omessa

CANDIDE, 1759, Short Story *see* Francois-Marie Arouet de Voltaire

CANDLE FOR THE DEAD, A, Novel *see* Hugh Marlowe

CANDY, New York 1964, Novel *see* Mason Hoffenberg, Terry Southern

CANDYLEG, New York 1961, Novel *see* Ovid Demaris

CANDYTUFT - I MEAN VERONICA, Novel *see* Mabel Barnes Grundy

CANICULE, Novel *see* Jean Vautrin

CANNE, LA, *see* Honore de Balzac

CANNERY ROW, 1945, Novel *see* John Steinbeck

CANON WALLS, 1930, Story *see* Zane Grey

CANTANTE MISTERIOSO, IL, Novel *see* R. T. de Angelis

CANTERBURY TALES, THE, c1400, Verse *see* Geoffrey Chaucer

CANTERVILLE GHOST, THE, 1891, Short Story *see* Oscar Wilde

CANTICO FINAL, 1959, Novel *see* Vergilio Ferreira

CANTIQUE DE LA RACAILLE, Novel *see* Vincent Ravalec

CANYON OF LIGHT, THE, Novel *see* Kenneth Perkins

CANYON OF THE FOOLS, THE, New York 1922, Novel *see* Richard Matthews Hallet

CANYON PASSAGE, 1945, Novel *see* Ernest Haycox

CAO YUAN SHANG DE REN MEN, Novel *see* Mala Qinfu

CAPE COD FOLKS, Boston 1881, Novel *see* Sarah P. McLean Greene

CAPE FORLORN, 1930, Play *see* Frank Harvey

CAPE SMOKE, 1925, Play *see* Paul Dickey, Walter Frost

CAPELLI BIONDI, 1876, Novel *see* Salvatore Farina

CAPER OF THE GOLDEN BULLS, THE, New York 1966, Novel *see* William P. McGivern

CAPINERA DEL MULINO, LA, Novel *see* Ponson Du Terrail

CAPITAES DA AREIA, 1937, Novel *see* Jorge Amado

CAPITAINE BENOIT, LE, Novel *see* Charles-Robert Dumas

CAPITAINE BLOMET, Play *see* Emile Bergerat

CAPITAINE CRADDOCK, LE, Novel *see* Reck-Malleczewen

CAPITAINE DE QUINZE ANS, UN, 1878, Novel *see* Jules Verne

CAPITAINE FRACASSE, LE, 1863, Novel *see* Theophile Gautier

CAPITAINE PANTOUFLE, Play *see* Alfred Adam

CAPITAL OFFENSE, Story *see* Edwin P. Hicks

CAPITAN, LE, Novel *see* Michel Zevaco

CAPITAN TEMPESTA, Novel *see* Emilio Salgari

CAPITAN VENENO, EL, 1881, Novel *see* Pedro Antonio de Alarcon

CAPITANO DEGLI USSARI, IL, Play *see* Sandor Hunyady

CAPITOL, THE, New York 1895, Play *see* Augustus Thomas

CAP'N ABE STOREKEEPER: A STORY OF CAPE COD, New York 1917, Novel *see* James A. Cooper

CAP'N ERI; A STORY OF THE COAST, New York 1904, Novel *see* Joseph C. Lincoln

CAPORAL EPINGLE, LE, Paris 1947, Novel *see* Jacques Perret

CAPOTE DE PASEO, EL, Novel *see* Celedonio Jose de Arpe

CAPPELLO DEL PRETE, IL, Novel *see* Emilio de Marchi

CAPPOTTO DI ASTRAKAN, IL, Novel *see* Piero Chiara

CAPPY RICKS, New York 1915, Novel *see* Peter B. Kyne

CAPPY RICKS COMES BACK, New York 1934, Short Story *see* Peter B. Kyne

CAPRA CU TREI IEZI, 1875, Short Story *see* Ion Creanga

CAPRICCI DI SUSANNA, I, Play *see* Alessandro de Stefani

CAPRICCIOSI RAGIONAMENTI, Short Story *see* Pietro L'Arentino

CAPRICE, New York 1884, Play *see* Howard P. Taylor

CAPRICE DE CAROLINE CHERIE, UN, Novel *see* Cecil Saint-Laurent

CAPRICE, UN, Play *see* Alfred de Musset

CAPRICES DE MARIANNE, LES, 1834, Play *see* Alfred de Musset

CAPRICORN MAN, THE, Novel *see* William Zacha Sr.

CAPTAIN ALVAREZ, Play *see* Paul Gilmore

CAPTAIN APACHE, Novel *see* S. E. Whitman

CAPTAIN APPLEJACK, New York 1921, Play *see* Walter Hackett

CAPTAIN BLIGH AND MR. CHRISTIAN, Book *see* Richard Hough

CAPTAIN BLOOD; HIS ODYSSEY, Boston 1922, Novel *see* Rafael Sabatini

CAPTAIN BLOOD RETURNS, Novel *see* Rafael Sabatini

CAPTAIN BOYCOTT, Novel *see* Philip Rooney

CAPTAIN CALAMITY, Short Story *see* Gordon Young

CAPTAIN CAUTION; A CHRONICLE OF ARUNDEL, New York 1934, Novel *see* Kenneth Lewis Roberts

CAPTAIN COURTESY, Philadelphia 1906, Novel *see* Edward Childs Carpenter

CAPTAIN DIEPPE, New York 1900, Novel *see* Anthony Hope

CAPTAIN FLY-BY-NIGHT, Novel *see* Johnston McCulley

CAPTAIN FROM CASTILE, Novel *see* Samuel Shellabarger

CAPTAIN HATES THE SEA, THE, Davison, Mi. 1933, Novel *see* Wallace Smith

CAPTAIN HORATIO HORNBLOWER, 1939, Novel *see* C. S. Forester

CAPTAIN JANUARY, New York 1890, Novel *see* Laura E. Richards

CAPTAIN JINKS OF THE HORSE MARINES, New York 1916, Play *see* Clyde Fitch

CAPTAIN KIDD JUNIOR, New York 1916, Play *see* Rida Johnson Young

CAPTAIN LIGHTFOOT, 1954, Novel *see* William Riley Burnett

CAPTAIN MACKLIN: HIS MEMOIRS, New York 1902, Novel *see* Richard Harding Davis

CAPTAIN NEWMAN, M.D., New York 1961, Novel *see* Leo Rosten

CAPTAIN OF THE GREY HORSE TROOP, London 1902, Novel *see* Hamlin Garland

CAPTAIN SALVATION, New York 1925, Novel *see* Frederick William Wallace

CAPTAIN SAZARAC, Indianapolis 1922, Novel *see* Charles Tenney Jackson

CAPTAIN SWIFT, London 1888, Play *see* C. Haddon Chambers

CAPTAINS ALL, Short Story *see* W. W. Jacobs

CAPTAINS AND THE KINGS, Novel *see* Taylor Caldwell

CAPTAINS COURAGEOUS, London 1897, Novel *see* Rudyard Kipling

CAPTAIN'S DOLL, THE, 1923, Short Story *see* D. H. Lawrence

CAPTAIN'S TABLE, THE, Novel *see* Richard Gordon

CAPTIVATING MARY CARSTAIRS, Boston 1910, Novel *see* Henry Sydnor Harrison

CAPTIVATION, Play *see* Edgar C. Middleton

CAPTIVE CITY, THE, New York 1955, Novel *see* John Appleby

CAPTIVES, THE, Story *see* Elmore Leonard

CAPTURED SANTA CLAUS, A, Book *see* Thomas Nelson Page

CARABINIERI, I, Paris 1958, Play *see* Benjamin Joppolo

CARAMBOLAGES, Novel *see* Fred Kassak

CARANCHOS DE LA FLORIDA, LOS, 1916, Novel *see* Benito Lynch

CARANONHA, A, 1804, Short Story *see* Afonso Schmidt

CARARBINIE, 1892, Play *see* Enrico Gemelli

CARAVAN, Novel *see* Lady Eleanor Smith

CARAVAN TO CAMUL, A, Book *see* John Clou

CARAVAN TO VACCARES, 1970, Novel *see* Alistair MacLean

CARAVANS, 1963, Novel *see* James A. Michener

CARCASSE ET LE TORD-COU, LA, Novel *see* Auguste Bailly

CARCELERAS, Opera *see* V. Peydro, Ricardo Rodriguez Flores

CARD, THE, 1912, Novel *see* Arnold Bennett

CARDBOARD BOX, THE, Short Story *see* Arthur Conan Doyle

CARDELLO, Short Story *see* Luigi Capuana

CARDIGAN, New York 1901, Novel *see* Robert W. Chambers

CARDILLAC, Short Story *see* Ernst Theodor Amadeus Hoffmann

CARDINAL, THE, Montreal 1901, Play *see* Louis N. Parker

CARDINAL, THE, New York 1950, Novel *see* Henry Morton Robinson

CARDINALE LAMBERTINI, IL, Play *see* Alfredo Testoni

CAREER, New York 1936, Novel *see* Philip Duffield Stong

CAREER, New York 1957, Play *see* James Lee

CAREER IN C MAJOR, 1938, Short Story *see* James M. Cain

CAREER OF KATHERINE BUSH, THE, New York 1916, Novel *see* Elinor Glyn

CAREFUL, HE MIGHT HEAR YOU, 1963, Novel *see* Sumner Locke Elliott

CAREFUL MAN, THE, London 1962, Novel *see* Richard Deming

CARETAKER, THE, London 1960, Play *see* Harold Pinter

CARETAKERS, THE, New York 1959, Novel *see* Dariel Telfer

CARETAKERS WITHIN, 1921, Short Story *see* Christine Jope Slade

CARIB GOLD, 1926, Novel *see* Ellery Harding Clark

CARIBBEAN MYSTERY, A, Novel *see* Agatha Christie

CARIBIA, Play *see* Pierre Chamblain de Marivaux

CARICIES, Play *see* Sergi Belbel

CARILLONS SANS JOIE, Novel *see* Charles Brabant

CARLITO'S WAY, Novel *see* Edwin Torres

CARLOTA, 1958, Play *see* Miguel Mihura Santos

CARMELA, LA SARTINA DI MONTESARNO, Novel *see* Davide Galdi

CARMEN, Paris 1846, Novel *see* Prosper Merimee

CARMILLA, London 1872, Short Story *see* Sheridan Le Fanu

CARNAVAL TRAGIQUE, Play *see* Adelqui Millar

CARNE, A, 1888, Novel *see* Julio Ribeiro

CARNE INQUIETA, 1930, Novel *see* Leonida Repaci

CARNETS DU MAJOR THOMPSON, LES, Novel *see* Pierre Daninos

CARNIVAL, London 1912, Novel *see* Compton Mackenzie

CARNIVAL, London 1920, Play *see* H. C. M. Hardinge, Matheson Lang

CARNIVAL, New York 1924, Play *see* William R. Doyle

CARNO SZINMU; HAROM FELVONASBAN, A, Budapest 1913, Play *see* Menyhert Lengyel

CARNO SZINMU: HAROM FELVONASBAN, A, Budapest 1913, Play *see* Lajos Biro

CARNOSAUR, Novel *see* Harry Adam Knight

CARO MICHELE, 1973, Novel *see* Natalia Ginzburg

CAROLINE CHERIE, Novel *see* Cecil Saint-Laurent

CAROLYN OF THE CORNERS, New York 1918, Novel *see* Ruth Belmore Endicott

CAROTTE, LA, Play *see* Georges Berr, Marcel Guillemaud

CAROVNE DEDICTVI, Novel *see* Vaclav Rezac

CAROVNE OCI, Novel *see* Bohumil Zahradnik-Brodsky

CARPET FROM BAGDAD, THE, Indianapolis 1911, Novel *see* Harold MacGrath

CARPETBAGGERS, THE, New York 1961, Novel *see* Harold Robbins

CARRE DE DAMES POUR UN AS, Novel *see* Michael Loggan

CARREFOUR, Short Story *see* Hans Kafka

CARRIAGE ENTRANCE, 1947, Novel *see* Polan Banks

CARRIE, 1974, Novel *see* Stephen King

CARRIERE DE SUZANNE, LA, 1974, Short Story *see* Eric Rohmer

CARRINGTON V.C., London 1953, Play *see* Campbell Christie, Dorothy Christie

CARROSSE DU SAINT-SACREMENT, LE, 1829, Play *see* Prosper Merimee

CARRY-COT, THE, Novel *see* Alexander Thynne

CARTACALHA, REINE DES GITANS, Novel *see* Jean Toussaint-Samat

CARTAGINE IN FIAMME, Genoa 1908, Novel *see* Emilio Salgari

CARTAS CREDENCIALES, 1961, Play *see* Joaquin Calvo Sotelo

CARTERETS, THE, Story *see* Justus Miles Forman

CARTOMANTE, A, 1884, Short Story *see* Joaquim Maria Machado de Assis

CARTOUCHE - ROI DE PARIS, Play *see* Pierre Lestringuez, Leopold Marchand

CARUTA CU MERE, 1962, Short Story *see* Dumitru Radu Popescu

CARVE HER NAME WITH PRIDE, Book *see* R. J. Minney

CARYL OF THE MOUNTAINS, Short Story *see* James Oliver Curwood

CAS DE CONSCIENCE, Play *see* Leopold Gomez

CAS SINGULIER, UN, Play *see* J. P. Feydeau

CASA DE BERNARDA ALBA, LA, 1945, Play *see* Federico Garcia Lorca

CASA DE LA LLUVIA, LA, 1925, Short Story *see* Wenceslao Fernandez Florez

CASA DE LA TROYA, LA, Madrid 1915, Novel *see* Alejandro Perez Lugin

CASA DE TROYA, LA, Novel *see* Alejandro Perez Lugin

CASA DEL BUON RITORNO, LA, Novel *see* Beppe Cino

CASA MALEDETTA, LA, Play *see* Elisa Pezzana

CASA NOVA. VITA NOVA, Play *see* Matteo de Majo, Vinicio Gioli

CASA SUL MARE, LA, Story *see* Ferruccio Cerio, Gino Saviotti

CASABLAN, Tel Aviv 1958, Play *see* Yigal Mossensohn

CASAMENTO, O, 1966, Novel *see* Nelson Rodrigues

CASANOVA A PARMA, Play *see* Alessandro de Stefani

CASANOVA FAREBBE COSI, Play *see* Armando Curcio, Peppino de Filippo

CASANOVAS HEIMFAHRT, Novel *see* Arthur Schnitzler

CASCALHO, 1944, Novel *see* Herberto Sales

CASE AGAINST MRS. AMES, THE, 1934, Novel *see* Arthur Somers Roche

CASE FILE F.B.I., 1953, Novel *see* Gordon Gordon, Mildred Gordon

CASE HISTORY, Novel *see* Gertrude Walker

CASE OF BECKY, THE, New York 1912, Play *see* Edward Locke

CASE OF IDENTITY, A, Short Story *see* Arthur Conan Doyle

CASE OF LADY CAMBER, THE, London 1915, Play *see* Horace Annesley Vachell

CASE OF MR. PELHAM, THE, Novel *see* Anthony Armstrong

CASE OF MULTIPLE PERSONALITY, A, Book *see* Hervey M. Cleckley M.D., Corbett Thigpen M.D.

CASE OF NEED, A, Novel *see* Michael Crichton

CASE OF THE BLACK PARROT, THE, Novel *see* Eleanor Robeson Belmont, Harriet Ford

CASE OF THE BLACK PARROT, THE, Play *see* Burton Egbert Stevenson

CASE OF THE BLIND PILOT, Short Story *see* Com. Harry A. Burns

CASE OF THE CARETAKER'S CAT, THE, New York 1935, Novel *see* Erle Stanley Gardner

CASE OF THE CONSTANT GOD, THE, 1936, Short Story *see* Rufus King

CASE OF THE CURIOUS BRIDE, THE, New York 1935, Novel *see* Erle Stanley Gardner

CASE OF THE DANGEROUS DOWAGER, THE, Novel *see* Erle Stanley Gardner

CASE OF THE FRIGHTENED LADY, THE, London 1931, Play *see* Edgar Wallace

CASE OF THE HOWLING DOG, THE, New York 1935, Novel *see* Erle Stanley Gardner

CASE OF THE LUCKY LEGS, THE, New York 1934, Novel *see* Erle Stanley Gardner

CASE OF THE STUTTERING BISHOP, THE, New York 1936, Novel *see* Erle Stanley Gardner

CASE OF THE THREE WEIRD SISTERS, THE, Novel *see* Charlotte Armstrong

CASE OF THE VELVET CLAWS, THE, New York 1933, Novel *see* Erle Stanley Gardner

CASEY AT THE BAT, 1888, Poem *see* E. L. Thayer

CASEY JONES, 1909, Song *see* Eddie Newton, T. Lawrence Seibert

CASH MCCALL, Novel *see* Cameron Hawley

CASH ON DELIVERY, Short Story *see* Alfred Barrett

CASHEL BYRON'S PROFESSION, Novel *see* George Bernard Shaw

CASINO MURDER CASE, THE, New York 1934, Novel *see* S. S. Van Dine

CASINO ROYALE, London 1953, Novel *see* Ian Fleming

CASK OF AMONTILLADO, THE, 1846, Short Story *see* Edgar Allan Poe

CASO DE F.A., O, 1969, Short Story *see* Rubem Fonseca

CASO DI COSCIENZA, UN, 1973, Short Story *see* Leonardo Sciasia

CASO MORO, IL, Novel *see* Robert Katz

CASOTTO, IL, Short Story *see* Vincenzo Cerami

CASPER THE FRIENDLY GHOST, Story *see* Joseph Oriolo, Seymour Rait

CASS TIMBERLANE, 1945, Novel *see* Sinclair Lewis

CASSANDRA CROSSING, Novel *see* Robert Katz

CASSIDY, 1913, Short Story *see* Larry Evans

CASSILIS ENGAGEMENT, THE, Play *see* St. John Hankin

CAST A GIANT SHADOW, New York 1962, Biography *see* Ted Berkman

CAST A LONG SHADOW, Novel *see* Wayne D. Overholser

CASTAWAY, Book *see* Lucy Irvine

CASTE, London 1867, Play *see* T. W. Robertson

CASTIGO, 1893, Novel *see* Matilde Serao

CASTING THE RUNES, 1911, Short Story *see* M. R. James

CASTLE CRANEYCROW, Chicago 1902, Novel *see* George Barr McCutcheon

CASTLE IN THE AIR, London 1949, Play *see* Alan Melville

CASTLE KEEP, New York 1965, Novel *see* William Eastlake

CASTLE MINERVA, London 1955, Novel *see* Victor Canning

CASTLE OF ADVENTURE, THE, Novel *see* Enid Blyton

CASTLES BURNING, Novel *see* Arthur Lyon

CASTLES IN SPAIN, Novel *see* Ruby M. Ayres

CASUAL SEX?, Play *see* Wendy Goldman, Judy Toll

CASUALTIES OF WAR, Book *see* Daniel Lang

CAT AND MOUSE, Novel *see* Michael Halliday

CAT AND THE CANARY, THE, New York 1922, Play *see* John Willard

CAT AND THE FIDDLE, THE, New York 1931, Musical Play *see* Otto Harbach, Jerome Kern

CAT AND THE MICE, THE, London 1958, Novel *see* Leonard Oswald Mosley

CAT CHASER, Novel *see* Elmore Leonard

CAT FROM HELL, Story *see* Stephen King

CAT ON A HOT TIN ROOF, New York 1955, Play *see* Tennessee Williams

CAT O'NINE TAILS (CAT OF MANY TALES), Novel *see* Ellery Queen

CAT THAT WALKED ALONE, THE, Story *see* John Colton

CATACOMBS, New York 1959, Novel *see* Jay Bennett

CATBIRD SEAT, THE, 1943, Short Story *see* James Thurber

CATCH 22, New York 1961, Novel *see* Joseph Heller

CATCH ME A SPY, Novel *see* George Marton, Tibor Meray

CATERED AFFAIR, THE, 1955, Television Play *see* Paddy Chayefsky

CATHERINE, 1898, Play *see* Henri Lavedan

CATHERINE ET CIE, Novel *see* Edouard de Segonzac

CATHERINE IL SUFFIT D'UN AMOUR, Novel *see* Juliette Benzonni

CATHOLICS, Novel *see* Brian Moore

CATLOW, Novel *see* Louis L'Amour

CATRIONA, 1892, Novel *see* Robert Louis Stevenson

CAT'S PAJAMAS, THE, 1968, Novel *see* Peter de Vries

CATSPAW, New York 1911, Novel *see* William Hamilton Osborne

CAT'S-PAW, THE, New York 1934, Novel *see* Clarence Budington Kelland

CATTLE ANNIE AND LITTLE BRITCHES, Novel *see* Robert Ward

CAUDAL DE LOS HIJOS, EL, Madrid 1921, Play *see* Jose Lopez Pinillos

CAUSA KAISER, Play *see* Eisler, Stark

CAUSE CELEBRE, UNE, Novel *see* Gabriel

CAUSE CELEBRE, UNE, Paris 1877, Play *see* Eugene Cormon, Adolphe-P. d'Ennery

CAUSE ED EFFETTI, 1871, Play *see* Paolo Ferrari

CAUSE FOR ALARM, Radio Play *see* Lawrence B. Marcus

CAUTIOUS AMORIST, THE, Novel *see* Norman Lindsay

CAVALCADE, London 1931, Play *see* Noel Coward

CAVALE, LA, 1965, Novel *see* Albertine Sarrazin

CAVALIER LAFLEUR, LE, Opera *see* Andre Mauprey, Louis Raine

CAVALIER OF THE STREETS, THE, Short Story *see* Michael Arlen

CAVALIER, THE, Short Story *see* Charles S. Thompson

CAVALIERE INESISTENTE, IL, 1959, Novel *see* Italo Calvino

CAVALIERS, LES, 1967, Novel *see* Joseph Kessel

CAVALINHO AZUL, O, 1960, Play *see* Maria Clara Machado

CAVALLA STORNA, Poem *see* Giovanni Pascoli

CAVALLERIA RUSTICANA, Milan 1880, Short Story *see* Giovanni Verga

CAVANAUGH - FOREST RANGER; A ROMANCE OF THE MOUNTAIN WEST, New York 1910, Novel *see* Hamlin Garland

CAVE GIRL, THE, New York 1920, Play *see* Guy Bolton, George Middleton

CAVE MAN, THE, New York 1911, Play *see* Gelett Burgess

CAVE SE REBIFFE, LE, Paris 1954, Novel *see* Albert Simonin

CAVERN SPIDER, THE, Short Story *see* L. J. Beeston

CAVES DU MAJESTIC, LES, 1942, Short Story *see* Georges Simenon

CE COCHON DE MORIN, 1883, Short Story *see* Guy de Maupassant

CECILE EST MORTE, 1942, Short Story *see* Georges Simenon

CECILIA OF THE PINK ROSES, New York 1917, Novel *see* Katharine Haviland Taylor

CECILIA VALDES O LA LOMA DEL ANGEL, 1839, Novel *see* Cirilo Villaverde

CEILING ZERO, New York 1935, Play *see* Frank Wead

CEKANKY, Play *see* F. X. Svoboda

CELA S'APPELLE L'AURORE, 1952, Novel *see* Emmanuel Robles

CELEBRATED JUMPING FROG OF CALAVERAS COUNTY, THE, 1867, Short Story *see* Mark Twain

CELEBRATIONS, LES, Play *see* Michel Garneau

CELEBRITY, Novel *see* Thomas Thompson

CELESTIAL CITY, THE, Novel *see* Baroness Orczy

CELESTINA, LA, 1500, Play *see* Fernando de Rojas

CELLE QUI DOMINE LES HOMMES, Story *see* May Edginton

CELLE QUI N'ETAIT PLUS, Novel *see* Pierre Boileau, Thomas Narcejac

CELLIST, THE, Play *see* Marion Hart

CELLULOID CLOSET, THE, Book *see* Vito Russo

CELLULOIDE, Novel *see* Ugo Pirro

CEMENT GARDEN, THE, Novel *see* Ian McEwan

CEMETERY CLUB, THE, Play *see* Ivan Menchell

CEMMIN, 1956, Novel *see* Takazi Sivasankara Illa

CENA DELLE BEFFE, LA, 1909, Play *see* Sem Benelli

CENCIAIUOLO DELLA SANITA, IL, Novel *see* Davide Galdi

CENDRILLON, 1697, Short Story *see* Charles Perrault

CENDRILLON ET LES GANGSTERS, Novel *see* Cornell Woolrich

CENERE, 1904, Novel *see* Grazia Deledda

CENOMILA LETTERE DI GUERRA - CENSURA MILITARE, Book *see* Bino Bellomo

CENT BRIQUES ET DES TUILES, Paris 1964, Novel *see* Clarence Weff

CENTENNIAL, Novel *see* James A. Michener

CENTENNIAL SUMMER, Novel *see* Albert E. Idell

CENTO GIORNI, I, Play *see* Giovacchino Forzano

CENTOVENTI H.P., 1906, Play *see* Amerigo Guasti

CENTURIONS, LES, Paris 1960, Novel *see* Jean Larteguy

'CEPTION SHOALS, New York 1917, Play *see* H. Austin Adams

CEREMONIA SECRETA, 1955, Short Story *see* Marco Denevi

CEREMONIE D'AMOUR, Novel *see* Andre Pieyre de Mandiargues

CEREMONIE, LA, Paris 1951, Novel *see* Frederic Grendel

CERNI MYSLIVCI, Book *see* Ruzena Svobodova

CERNY MUZ, Novel *see* Alfred Machard

CERROMAIOR, 1943, Novel *see* Manuel Da Fonseca

CERTAIN CODE, UN, Novel *see* Fred Noro

CERTAIN LEE, Story *see* Keene Thompson

CERTAIN MONSIEUR, UN, Novel *see* Jean Le Hallier

CERTAIN RICH MAN, A, New York 1909, Novel *see* William Allen White

CERTAIN SOURIRE, UN, 1956, Novel *see* Francoise Sagan

CERTO CAPITAO RODRIGO, UM, 1949, Short Story *see* Erico Verissimo

CERVANTES, Amsterdam 1934, Novel *see* Bruno Frank

CES DAMES AUX CHAPEAUX VERTS, Novel *see* Germaine Acremant

CES MESSIEURS DE LA SANTE, Play *see* Paul Armont, Leopold Marchand

CES SACREES VACANCES, Novel *see* Anne Drouet

CESAR, 1937, Play *see* Marcel Pagnol

CESAR BIROTTEAU, Novel *see* Honore de Balzac

C'EST ARRIVE A ADEN, Novel *see* Pierre Benoit

C'EST LA FAUTE D'ADAM, Novel *see* Maria-Luisa Linares

C'EST LA GUERRE, Story *see* William A. Wellman

CHERVOTOCHINA, 1925, Short Story *see* Mikhail Sholokhov

CHESSBOARD, THE, Short Story *see* Madeleine Sharpe Buchanan

CHESTER FORGETS HIMSELF, Short Story *see* P. G. Wodehouse

CHETVYORTY, 1961, Play *see* Konstantin Simonov

CHEVAL D'ORGUEIL, LE, Book *see* Pierre-Jakez Helias

CHEVALIER AU MASQUES, LE, Play *see* Paul Armont, Jean Manoussi

CHEVALIER DE MAISON ROUGE, LE, 1846, Novel *see* Alexandre Dumas (pere)

CHEVALIER DE PARDAILLAN, LE, Novel *see* Michel Zevaco

CHEVELURE, LA, 1885, Short Story *see* Guy de Maupassant

CHEVIOT, THE STAG AND THE BLACK, BLACK OIL, THE, 1974, Play *see* John McGrath

CHEVRE AUX PIEDS D'OR, LA, Novel *see* Charles-Henry Hirsch

CHEVRE D'OR, LA, 1888, Novel *see* Paul Arene

CHEVREFEUILLE, LA, 1914, *see* Gabriele D'Annunzio

CHEYENNE AUTUMN, New York 1953, Novel *see* Mari Sandoz

CHEZ KRULL, Novel *see* Georges Simenon

C.H.F.R. 35, Short Story *see* Andre Birabeau

CHHELEY KAR?, Novel *see* Jyotirmoy Roy

CHI HOUSE, 1939, Play *see* Mary Coyle Chase

CHICAGO, New York 1926, Play *see* Maurine Dallas Watkins

CHICAGO AFTER MIDNIGHT, Short Story *see* Edna Mae Baker

CHICAGO CONFIDENTIAL, Book *see* Jack Lait, Lee Mortimer

CHICHINETTE ET CIE, Novel *see* Pierre Custot

CHICK, London 1923, Novel *see* Edgar Wallace

CHICKEN CHRONICLES, THE, Novel *see* Paul Diamond

CHICKEN EVERY SUNDAY, Novel *see* Rosemary Taylor

CHICKEN FEED; OR WAGES FOR WIVES, New York 1923, Play *see* Guy Bolton, Winchell Smith

CHICKEN-WAGON FAMILY, THE, New York 1925, Novel *see* John Barry Benefield

CHICKIE, New York 1925, Novel *see* Elenore Meherin

CHICOS DE LA ESCUELA, LOS, Opera *see* Carlos Arniches, T. Lopez Torregrosa

CHIDIAKHANA, Novel *see* Saradindu Bannerjee

CHIEFS, Novel *see* Stuart Woods

CHIEN DE MONTARGIS, LE, Play *see* Romain Coolus

CHIEN JAUNE, LE, 1931, Novel *see* Georges Simenon

CHIEN QUI RAPPORTE, UN, Play *see* Paul Armont, Marcel Gerbidon

CHIENNE, LA, Play *see* Georges de La Fouchardiere

CHIFFONNIER DE PARIS, LE, Novel *see* Felix Pyat

CHIFLIKAT KRAY GRANITSATA, 1933-34, Novel *see* Yordan Yovkov

CHIGNOLE, Novel *see* Marcel Nadaud

CHIGWELL CHICKEN, THE, Play *see* A. P. Dearsley

CHIJIN NO AI, 1924, Novel *see* Junichiro Tanizaki

CHILD IN THE FOREST, A, Book *see* Winifred Foley

CHILD IN THE HOUSE, Play *see* Janet McNeil

CHILD IN THEIR MIDST, A, Novel *see* May Edginton

CHILD OF MANHATTAN, New York 1932, Play *see* Preston Sturges

CHILDREN CROSSING, Novel *see* Verity Bargate

CHILDREN OF A LESSER GOD, 1980, Play *see* Mark Medoff

CHILDREN OF BANISHMENT, New York 1914, Novel *see* Francis William Sullivan

CHILDREN OF CHANCE, Novel *see* Michael Morton

CHILDREN OF DESTINY, New York 1910, Play *see* Sydney Rosenfeld

CHILDREN OF DIVORCE, Boston 1927, Novel *see* Owen Johnson

CHILDREN OF DREAMS, 1930, Musical Play *see* Oscar Hammerstein II, Sigmund Romberg

CHILDREN OF FATE, Short Story *see* James Oliver Curwood

CHILDREN OF GIBEON, THE, Novel *see* Sir Walter Besant

CHILDREN OF LIGHT, THE, London 1960, Novel *see* Henry Lionel Lawrence

CHILDREN OF PLEASURE, New York 1932, Novel *see* Larry Barretto

CHILDREN OF SANCHEZ, THE, Novel *see* Oscar Lewis

CHILDREN OF THE CORN, Short Story *see* Stephen King

CHILDREN OF THE COVERED WAGON, 1934, Novel *see* Mary Jane Carr

CHILDREN OF THE GHETTO; A STUDY OF PECULIAR PEOPLE, THE, London 1892, Novel *see* Israel Zangwill

CHILDREN OF THE NIGHT, Novel *see* Wilhelm Schmidtbonn

CHILDREN OF THE NIGHT, 1919, Short Story *see* Max Brand

CHILDREN OF THE RITZ, Short Story *see* Cornell Woolrich

CHILDREN, THE, New York 1928, Novel *see* Edith Wharton

CHILDREN'S HOUR, THE, Poem *see* Henry Wadsworth Longfellow

CHILDREN'S HOUR, THE, New York 1934, Play *see* Lillian Hellman

CHILD'S PLAY, Play *see* Robert Marasco

CHILD'S PLAY, London 1987, Novel *see* Reginald Hill

CHILTERN HUNDREDS, THE, London 1947, Play *see* William Douglas Home

CHIMERA, 1982, Novel *see* Steven Gallagher

CHIMES, THE, London 1845, Short Story *see* Charles Dickens

CHIMMIE FADDEN, 1895, Short Story *see* Edward Waterman Townsend

CHIN CHIN CHINAMAN, Play *see* Percy Walsh

CHIN P'INGE MEI, 15Th-Century, Novel *see* Shin-Chen Want

CHINA SEAS, New York 1931, Novel *see* Crosbie Garstin

CHINA SKY, 1942, Novel *see* Pearl Buck

CHINESE BUNGALOW, THE, Novel *see* Marian Osmond

CHINESE FINALE, London 1935, Short Story *see* Norah Lofts

CHINESE ORANGE MYSTERY, THE, New York 1934, Novel *see* Ellery Queen

CHINESE PARROT, THE, Indianapolis 1926, Novel *see* Earl Derr Biggers

CHINESE PUZZLE, THE, London 1918, Play *see* Marion Bower, Leon M. Lion

CHING, CHING, CHINAMAN, 1917, Short Story *see* Wilbur Daniel Steele

CHINK AND THE CHILD, THE, 1916, Short Story *see* Thomas Burke

CHINK IN THE ARMOUR, Novel *see* Mrs. Belloc Lowndes

CHIP, CHIP, CHIP, Play *see* Alec Coppel

CHIP OF THE FLYING U, New York 1906, Novel *see* Bertha Muzzy Sinclair

CHIPEE, Play *see* Alex Madis

CHISHOLM TRAIL, THE, Short Story *see* Borden Chase

CHISHOLMS, THE, Novel *see* Evan Hunter

CHITARRA IN PARADISO, UNA, Short Story *see* Massimo Franciosa

CHITTY CHITTY BANG BANG: THE MAGICAL CAR, London 1964, Novel *see* Ian Fleming

CHLAPI PRECE NEPLACOU, Novel *see* Marie Kubatova

CHLOPI, 1902-09, Novel *see* Wladyslaw Stanislaw Reymont

CHOIR PRACTICE, Radio Play *see* Cliff Gordon

CHOIRBOYS, THE, 1975, Novel *see* Joseph Wambaugh

CHOIX D'ASSASSINS, UN, Novel *see* William P. McGivern

CHOLPON - UTRENNYAYA ZVEZDA, 1944, Ballet *see* L. Kramarevskiy, M. Raukhverger

CHOMANA DUDI, 1933, Novel *see* Shivrama Karanth

CHORUS LADY, THE, New York 1906, Play *see* James Forbes

CHORUS LINE, A, Play *see* Nicholas Dante, James Kirkwood

CHORUS OF DISAPPROVAL, A, 1986, Play *see* Alan Ayckbourn

CHOSEN, Tokyo 1960, Novel *see* Shintaro Ishihara

CHOSEN, THE, Novel *see* Chaim Potok

CHOSES DE LA VIE, LES, Paris 1967, Novel *see* Paul Guimard

CHOTARD ET CIE, Play *see* Roger Ferdinand

CHOUANS, LES, 1834, Novel *see* Honore de Balzac

CHOU-CHOU POIDS-PLUME, Play *see* Jacques Bousquet, Alex Madis

CHOUTE, LA, Short Story *see* Jacques Viot

CHOVEKAT V SYANKA, 1965, Novel *see* Pavel Vezhinov

CHRESTOS, Novel *see* Henri Dupuy-Mazuel

CHRIST DANS LA BANLIEUE, LE, Book *see* Pierre Lhande

CHRIST IN CONCRETE, Novel *see* Pietro Di Donato

CHRISTIAN: A STORY, THE, London 1897, Novel *see* Hall Caine

CHRISTIAN MARTYRS, THE, Novel *see* Edward George Bulwer Lytton

CHRISTIANE F., Book *see* K. Hermann, Horst Rieck

CHRISTIE JOHNSTONE, Novel *see* Charles Reade

CHRISTINE, 1983, Novel *see* Stephen King

CHRISTINE JORGENSEN: A PERSONAL AUTOBIOGRAPHY, New York 1967, Autobiography *see* Christine Jorgensen

CHRISTINE OF THE HUNGRY HEART, 1924, Short Story *see* Kathleen Norris

CHRISTMAS ACCIDENT, A, Story *see* Annie Eliot Trumbull

CHRISTMAS AT CANDLESHOE, Novel *see* Michael Innes

CHRISTMAS BOOKS, 1848, *see* Charles Dickens

CHRISTMAS CAROL, A, London 1843, Novel *see* Charles Dickens

CHRISTMAS DAY IN THE WORKHOUSE, Poem *see* George R. Sims

CHRISTMAS EVE AT PILOT BUTTE, 1921, Short Story *see* Courtney Ryley Cooper

CHRISTMAS GIFT, A, Story *see* John D. Weaver

CHRISTMAS HOLIDAY, 1939, Novel *see* W. Somerset Maugham

CHRISTMAS MEMORY, A, 1946, Short Story *see* Truman Capote

CHRISTMAS STORY, A, Poem *see* Fred Weatherley

CHRISTOPHER BLAKE, New York 1946, Play *see* Moss Hart

CHRISTOPHER STRONG: A ROMANCE, New York 1932, Novel *see* Gilbert Frankau

CHRISTOPHER SYN, Novel *see* William Russell Thorndike

CHRISTOS XANASTAVRONETAI, O, 1948, Novel *see* Nikos Kazantzakis

CHRONICLES OF PRYDAINBY, THE, Novel *see* Lloyd Alexander

CHRYSALIS, New York 1932, Play *see* Rose Albert Porter

CHU CHIN CHOW, London 1916, Musical Play *see* Oscar Asche, Frederick Norton

CHUAN CHANG ZHUI ZONG, Novel *see* Fei Liwen

CHUCK CONNORS, Novel *see* Michael L. Simmons, Bessie R. Solomon

C.H.U.D., Novel *see* Shepard Abbott

CHUDA HOLKA, Novel *see* Vaclav Cech-Stran

CHUEH-TAI SHUANG CHIAO, Novel *see* Ku Lung

CHUKA, Greenwich, Ct. 1961, Novel *see* Richard Jessup

CHUKJE, Novel *see* Le Chung-Joon

CHUN CAN, Short Story *see* Mao Dun

CHUN FENG CUI DAO NUOMING HE, Play *see* An Bo

CHUN TAO, 1927, Short Story *see* Xu Dishan

CHUO KORON, 1915, Short Story *see* Mori Ogai

CHURCH MOUSE, THE, Play *see* Ladislaus Fodor, Paul Franck

CHURCH WITH AN OVERSHOT WHEEL, THE, Short Story *see* O. Henry

CHUTE, LA, 1956, Novel *see* Albert Camus

CHUZHAIA KROV, 1926, Short Story *see* Mikhail Sholokhov

CIBOULETTE, Opera *see* Francis de Croisset, Robert de Flers

CICALA, LA, Novel *see* Marina d'Aunia, Natale Prinetto

CID, LE, 1637, Play *see* Pierre Corneille

CIDER WITH ROSIE, 1959, Autobiography *see* Laurie Lee

CIECA DI SORRENTO, LA, 1826, Novel *see* Francesco Mastriani

CIELO E ROSSO, IL, 1947, Novel *see* Giuseppe Berto

CIEN ANOS DE SOLEDAD, 1967, Novel *see* Gabriel Garcia Marquez

CIFFONIER DE PARIS, LE, 1847, Novel *see* Charles Sales

CIGALE, LA, Story *see* Jean de La Fontaine

CIGALE, LA, Novel *see* Lucie Delarue-Mardrus

CIGARETTE - THAT'S ALL, A, Story *see* Helena Evans

CIGARETTE-MAKER'S ROMANCE, A, Novel *see* Marion Crawford

CIGARRA NO ES UN BICHO, LA, Buenos Aires 1957, Novel *see* Dante Sierra

CIKANI, Short Story *see* Karel Hynek MacHa

CIKLON, 1966, Short Story *see* Ivan Mandy

CIMARRON, New York 1930, Novel *see* Edna Ferber

CINCINNATI KID, THE, Boston 1963, Novel *see* Richard Jessup

CINCO ADVERTENCIAS DE SATANAS, LAS, 1938, Play *see* Enrique Jardiel Poncela

CINCO DIAS CINCO NOITES, Novel *see* Manuel Tiago

CINCO DIAS, CINCO NOITES, Novel *see* Alvaro Cunhal

CINDER PATH, THE, Novel *see* Catherine Cookson

CINDERELLA JANE, Garden City, N.Y. 1917, Novel *see* Marjorie Benton Cooke

CINDERELLA LIBERTY, Novel *see* Darryl Ponicsan

CINDERELLA MAN, THE, New York 1916, Play *see* Edward Childs Carpenter

CINEMA GIRL'S ROMANCE, A, Novel *see* Ladbrooke Black

CINEMA MURDER (THE OTHER ROMILLY), THE, Boston 1917, Novel *see* E. Phillips Oppenheim

CINQ GARS POUR SINGAPOUR, Paris 1959, Novel *see* Jean Bruce

CINQ GENTLEMEN MAUDITS, LES, Novel *see* Andre Heuze

CINQ MILLIONS COMPTANT, Opera *see* Francis Lopez, Raymond Vinci

CINQ SEMAINES EN BALLON, 1863, Novel *see* Jules Verne

CINQ SOUS DE LAVAREDE, LES, Novel *see* Paul d'Ivoi

CINTURA, LA, Novel *see* Alberto Moravia

CIOCIORA, LA, Milan 1957, Novel *see* Alberto Moravia

CIPHER, THE, New York 1961, Book *see* Alex Gordon

CIRCLE IN THE FIRE, A, 1955, Short Story *see* Flannery O'Connor

CIRCLE OF CHILDREN, A, Book *see* Mary MacCracken

CIRCLE OF DANGER, Novel *see* Philip MacDonald

CIRCLE OF FRIENDS, Novel *see* Maeve Binchy

CIRCLE, THE, London 1921, Play *see* W. Somerset Maugham

CIRCLES ROUND THE WAGON, 1949, Novel *see* Fred Gipson

CIRCULAR STAIRCASE, THE, Indianapolis 1908, Novel *see* Mary Roberts Rinehart

CIRCUMSTANCES ALTER DIVORCE CASES, Short Story *see* Lewis Allen Browne

CIRCUS OF DR. LAO, THE, New York 1961, Novel *see* Charles G. Finney

CISKE DE RAT, Amsterdam 1941, Novel *see* Piet Bakker

CITADEL, THE, 1937, Novel *see* A. J. Cronin

CITADELA SFARIMATA, 1955, Play *see* Horia Lovinescu

CITY BOY, THE, 1948, Novel *see* Herman Wouk

CITY FOR CONQUEST, New York 1936, Novel *see* Aben Kandel

CITY IN THE SEA, 1831, Poem *see* Edgar Allan Poe

CITY LIMITS, New York 1932, Novel *see* Josiah Pitts Woolfolk

CITY OF BEAUTIFUL NONSENSE, THE, 1909, Novel *see* E. Temple Thurston

CITY OF COMRADES, THE, New York 1919, Novel *see* Basil King

CITY OF JOY, Novel *see* Dominique Lapierre

CITY OF MASKS, THE, New York 1918, Novel *see* George Barr McCutcheon

CITY OF PURPLE DREAMS, THE, Chicago 1913, Novel *see* Edwin Baird

CITY OF SHADOWS, Novel *see* Frederic Prokosch

CITY OF TERRIBLE NIGHT, THE, Short Story *see* Rudyard Kipling

CITY SPARROW, A, 1917, Serial Story *see* Kate Jordan

CITY, THE, New York 1909, Play *see* Clyde Fitch

CITY'S EDGE, THE, Novel *see* W. A. Harbinson

CIUDAD Y LOS PERROS, LA, Novel *see* Mario Vargas Llosa

CIULEANDRA, 1927, Novel *see* Liviu Rebreanu

CIVIL ACTION, A, Book *see* Jonathan Harr

CIVILIAN CLOTHES, New York 1919, Play *see* Thompson Buchanan

CLAIM NO. Z84, Play *see* Abe Pogos

CLAIM, THE, New York 1917, Play *see* Frank Dare, Charles Kenyon

CLAIR DE FEMME, Novel *see* Romain Gary

CLAIRVOYANT, THE, Novel *see* Ernst Lothar

CLAN DES SICILIENS, LE, Paris 1967, Novel *see* Auguste Le Breton

CLAN OF THE CAVE BEAR, THE, Novel *see* Jean M. Auel

CLANCARTY, London 1907, Play *see* Tom Taylor

CLANDESTINES, LES, Paris 1954, Novel *see* Raymond Caillava

CLANDESTINS, LES, *see* Lucien Barnier

CLANSMAN: AN HISTORICAL ROMANCE OF THE KU KLUX KLAN, THE, New York 1906, Novel *see* Thomas Dixon

CLARA ET LES MECHANTS, Novel *see* Paul Vialar

CLARA'S HEART, Novel *see* Joseph Olshan

CLARENCE, New York 1919, Play *see* Booth Tarkington

CLARINES DEL MIEDO, LOS, 1958, Novel *see* Angel Maria de Lera

CLARION CALL, THE, 1908, Short Story *see* O. Henry

CLARION, THE, Boston 1914, Novel *see* Samuel Hopkins Adams

CLARISSA, 1748, Novel *see* Samuel Richardson

CLARISSA AND THE POST ROAD, 1923, Short Story *see* Grace Sartwell Mason

CLARK'S FIELD, New York 1914, Novel *see* Robert Herrick

CLASH BY NIGHT, London 1962, Novel *see* Rupert Croft-Cooke

CLASH BY NIGHT, New York 1941, Play *see* Clifford Odets

CLASS, 1919, Short Story *see* Grace Lovell Bryan

CLASS AND NO CLASS, Novel *see* E. Newton Bungey

CLASS DE ASEN, LA, 1879, Play *see* Eduardo Ferravilla

CLASS OF MISS MACMICHAEL, THE, Novel *see* Sandy Hutson

CLASS PROPHECY, 1935, Short Story *see* Eleanore Griffin

CLASSIFIED, Short Story *see* Edna Ferber

CLASSMATES, Story *see* Irving Wallace

CLASSMATES, New York 1907, Play *see* William C. de Mille, Margaret Turnbull

CLAUDELLE INGLISH, Boston 1959, Novel *see* Erskine Caldwell

CLAUDIA, Novel *see* Rose Franken

CLAUDINE A L'ECOLE, 1900, Novel *see* Sidonie Gabrielle Colette

CLAUDIUS THE GOD, 1934, Novel *see* Robert Graves

CLAUSTROPHOBIA, 1926, Short Story *see* Abbie Carter Goodloe

CLAVIGO, 1774, Play *see* Johann Wolfgang von Goethe

CLAVO, EL, 1854, Short Story *see* Pedro Antonio de Alarcon

CLAW, THE, Novel *see* William Smith

CLAW, THE, New York 1911, Novel *see* Cynthia Stockley

CLAY OF CA'LINA, 1923, Short Story *see* Calvin Johnston

CLE SUR LA PORTE, LA, Novel *see* Marie Cardinal

CLEAN BREAK, 1955, Novel *see* Lionel White

CLEAN GUN, THE, Short Story *see* Barr Moses

CLEAR ALL WIRES, New York 1932, Play *see* Bella Spewack, Samuel Spewack

CLEAR AND PRESENT DANGER, Novel *see* Tom Clancy

CLEMENTINE, Novel *see* Peggy Goodin

CLEO, ROBES ET MANTEAUX, Novel *see* Guido Da Verona

CLEOPATRE, Paris 1890, Play *see* Victorien Sardou

CLERAMBARD, 1950, Play *see* Marcel Ayme

CLICK OF THE TRIANGLE T, Chicago 1925, Novel *see* Oscar J. Friend

CLICKING OF CUTHBERT, THE, Short Story *see* P. G. Wodehouse

CLIENT SERIEUX, UN, 1897, Play *see* Georges Courteline

CLIENT, THE, Novel *see* John Grisham

CLIMATS, 1928, Novel *see* Andre Maurois

CLIMAX, THE, London 1910, Play *see* Edward Locke

CLIMBERS, THE, New York 1901, Play *see* Clyde Fitch

CLINGING VINE, THE, New York 1922, Play *see* Zelda Sears

CLIPPED WINGS, 1928, Short Story *see* Rita Lambert

CLIQUE DOREE, LA, Paris 1871, Novel *see* Emile Gaboriau

CLIVE OF INDIA, London 1934, Play *see* W. P. Lipscomb, R. J. Minney

CLIVIA, Opera *see* Charles Amberg, Nico Dostal

CLOAK AND DAGGER, Novel *see* Corey Ford, Alastair McBain

CLOCHEMERLE, Novel *see* Gabriel Chevallier

CLOCHES DE CORNEVILLE, LES, Paris 1877, Operetta *see* Robert Planquette

CLOCK STRIKES EIGHT, THE, Short Story *see* John Dickson Carr

CLOCK, THE, Novel *see* Cicely Frazer-Simpson

CLOCKERS, Novel *see* Richard Price

CLOCKWORK ORANGE, A, 1962, Novel *see* Anthony Burgess

CLO-CLO, Operetta *see* Franz Lehar

CLOISTER AND THE HEARTH, THE, 1861, Novel *see* Charles Reade

CLOSE CALL, A, Short Story *see* Frederic Arnold Kummer

CLOSERIE DES GENETS, LA, Play *see* Frederic Soulie

CLOSING CHAPTER, THE, Story *see* Clifford Howard

CLOSING NET, THE, New York 1912, Novel *see* Henry C. Rowland

CLOTHES, New York 1906, Play *see* Avery Hopwood, Channing Pollock

CLOTHES IN THE WARDROBE, Novel *see* Alice Thomas Ellis

CLOTHES MAKE THE PIRATE, New York 1925, Novel *see* Holman Francis Day

CLOUD HOWE, Novel *see* Lewis Grassic Gibbon

CLOUD WALTZ, Novel *see* Tory Cates

CLOUDBURST, Play *see* Leo Marks

CLOWN BUX, LE, Novel *see* Hans Possendorff

CLOWNING AROUND ENCORE, Novel *see* David Martin

CLOWNING SIM, Novel *see* David Martin

CLUB DES 400 COUPS, LE, Novel *see* Pierre Clarel

CLUB DES ARISTOCRATES, LE, Novel *see* Detective Ashelbe

CLUB DES TREIZE, LE, Novel *see* Honore de Balzac

CLUB, THE, 1978, Play *see* David Williamson

CLUBBABLE WOMAN, A, London 1970, Novel *see* Reginald Hill

CLUBFOOT, Novel *see* Valentine Williams

CLUE OF THE NEW PIN, THE, London 1923, Novel *see* Edgar Wallace

CLUE OF THE PIGTAIL, THE, Short Story *see* Sax Rohmer

CLUE OF THE SILVER KEY, THE, London 1930, Novel *see* Edgar Wallace

CLUE OF THE TWISTED CANDLE, THE, London 1918, Novel *see* Edgar Wallace

CLUE, THE, Play *see* Margaret Turnbull

CLUNG, 1920, Serial Story *see* Max Brand

CLUNY BROWN, Novel *see* Margery Sharp

CLUTCH OF CIRCUMSTANCE, THE, New York 1914, Novel *see* Leighton Graves Osmun

CLUTCHING HAND, THE, Chicago 1934, Novel *see* Arthur B. Reeve

COAL KING, THE, Play *see* Fewlass Llewellyn, Ernest Martin

COAST OF FOLLY, THE, New York 1924, Novel *see* Conigsby William Dawson

COBB: A BIOGRAPHY, Biography *see* Al Stump

COBRA, New York 1924, Play *see* Martin Brown

COBWEB, THE, Play *see* Naunton Davies, Leon M. Lion

COBWEB, THE, 1954, Novel *see* William Gibson

COCAGNE, Novel *see* Yvan Audouard

COCAINE, Story *see* Cornell Woolrich

COCAINE KIDS, THE, Novel *see* Terry Williams

COCKEREL, THE, Story *see* H. B. Marriott Watson

COCKEYED MIRACLE, THE, Play *see* George Seaton

COCKFIGHTER, Novel *see* Charles Willeford

COCKLESHELL HEROES, Book *see* George Kent

COCKPIT, 1948, Play *see* Bridget Boland

COCKROACH TRILOGY, THE, Play *see* Alan Williams

COCKTAIL, Book *see* J. Heywood Gould

COCOANUTS, THE, New York 1925, Musical Play *see* Irving Berlin, George S. Kaufman

COCOON, Novel *see* David Saperstein

COCU MAGNIFIQUE, LE, Paris 1920, Play *see* Fernand Crommelynck

C.O.D., New York 1912, Play *see* Frederic Chapin

CODE OF THE KLONDYKE, THE, Short Story *see* Charles J. Wilson Jr.

CODE OF THE MOUNTAINS, THE, New York 1915, Novel *see* Charles Neville Buck

CODE OF THE WEST, New York 1924, Novel *see* Zane Grey

CODE OF VICTOR JALLOT, THE, Philadelphia 1907, Novel *see* Edward Childs Carpenter

CODIN, 1926, Novel *see* Panait Istrati

COEUR BUBE, Play *see* Jacques Natanson

COEUR DE FRANCAISE, Play *see* Arthur Bernede, Aristide Bruant

COEUR D'HEROINE, Novel *see* Marcel Allain

COEUR DISPOSE, LE, Play *see* Francis de Croisset

COEUR EBLOUI, LE, 1926, Play *see* Lucien Descaves

COEUR EN FUITE, LE, Novel *see* Linda La Rosa

COFFRE ET LE REVENANT, LE, 1867, Short Story *see* Stendhal

COGNASSE, Play *see* Rip

COHEN'S LUCK, Play *see* Lee Arthur

COIFFEUR POUR DAMES, Play *see* Paul Armont, Marcel Gerbidon

COINS IN A FOUNTAIN, Philadelphia 1952, Novel *see* John H. Secondari

COLD COMFORT, Play *see* James Garrard

COLD COMFORT FARM, 1933, Novel *see* Stella Gibbons

COLD DOG SOUP, Book *see* Stephen Dobyns

COLD EYE, Novel *see* Giles Blunt

COLD HEAVEN, 1983, Novel *see* Brian Moore

COLD RIVER, Novel *see* William Judson

COLD ROOM, THE, Novel *see* Jeffrey Caine

COLD WIND IN AUGUST, New York 1960, Novel *see* Burton Wohl

COLDITZ STORY, Book *see* P. R. Reid

COLINE DE FANTA, LA, Novel *see* Duyen Ahn

COLLARED, Story *see* Cornell Woolrich

COLLECTIONNEUSE, LA, 1974, Short Story *see* Eric Rohmer

COLLECTOR, THE, London 1963, Novel *see* John Fowles

COLLEEN BAWN, THE, London 1860, Play *see* Dion Boucicault

COLLEGE WIDOW, THE, New York 1904, Play *see* George Ade

COLLIER DE CHANVRE, LE, Novel *see* Charles Lafaurie

COLLIER DE LA REINE, LE, 1849-50, Novel *see* Alexandre Dumas (pere)

COLLIER, LE, Short Story *see* Guy de Maupassant

COLLINE OUBLIEE, LA, Novel *see* Mouloud Mammeri

COLLISION, Play *see* E. C. Pollard

COLLUSION, Play *see* J. E. Harold Terry

COLLUSION, New York 1932, Novel *see* Theodore D. Irwin

COLMENA, LA, 1951, Novel *see* Camilo Jose Cela

COLOMBA, 1841, Novel *see* Prosper Merimee

COLONEL CARTER OF CARTERSVILLE, New York 1891, Novel *see* F. Hopkinson Smith

COLONEL CHABERT, LE, 1844, Novel *see* Honore de Balzac

COLONEL DURAND, LE, Novel *see* Jean Martet

COLONEL EFFINGHAM'S RAID, Novel *see* Berry Fleming

COLONEL OF THE RED HUSSARS, THE, Novel *see* John Reed Scott

COLONEL SMITH, London 1909, Play *see* A. E. W. Mason

COLONEL'S LADY, 1947, Short Story *see* W. Somerset Maugham

COLONNA INFAME, LA, Novel *see* Alessandro Manzoni

COLONNE DE CENDRES, LA, Novel *see* Francoise Lorrain

COLOR OF MONEY, THE, 1984, Novel *see* Walter S. Tevis

COLOR PURPLE, THE, 1983, Novel *see* Alice Walker

COLORADO, New York 1901, Play *see* Augustus Thomas

COLORADO JIM; OR THE TAMING OF ANGELA, London 1920, Novel *see* George Goodchild

COLORS OF THE DAY, THE, 1953, Novel *see* Romain Gary

COLOSSUS, London 1966, Novel *see* D. F. Jones

COLOUR OUT OF SPACE, THE, 1927, Short Story *see* H. P. Lovecraft

COLPA VENDICA LA COLPA, LA, 1854, Play *see* Paolo Giacometti

COLPI DI TIMONE, Play *see* Enzo La Rosa

COLPO DI VENTO, UN, Play *see* Giovacchino Forzano

COLTON U.S.N., Play *see* Cyrus Townsend Brady

COMA, Novel *see* Robin Cook

COMANCHE, 1951, Novel *see* David Appel

COMANCHE CAPTIVES, New York 1960, Novel *see* Will Cook

COMANCHEROS, THE, New York 1952, Novel *see* Paul I. Wellman

COMBAT, 1945, Novel *see* Van Van Praag

COMBAT DE FAUVES AU CREPUSCULE, Novel *see* Henri-Frederic Blanc

COMBAT DE NEGRES, Novel *see* Rene Cambon

COMBINATION EDESSA-ZURICH, Novel *see* Sakis Totlis

COME AGAIN SMITH, Play *see* John H. Blackwood

COME AND GET IT, New York 1935, Novel *see* Edna Ferber

COME ANOTHER DAY, Story *see* Edward Newhouse

COME BACK LITTLE SHEBA, New York 1950, Play *see* William Inge

COME BACK PETER, Play *see* A. P. Dearsley

COME BACK TO AARON, Story *see* Robert Lord

COME BACK TO THE FIVE AND DIME JIMMY DEAN JIMMY DEAN, Play *see* Ed Graczyck

COME BE MY LOVE, Short Story *see* Robert Carson

COME BLOW YOUR HORN, New York 1961, Play *see* Neil Simon

COME EASY - GO EASY, London 1960, Novel *see* James Hadley Chase

COME FILL THE CUP, Novel *see* Harlan Ware

COME LE FOGLIE, 1900, Play *see* Giuseppe Giacosa

COME NOW THE LAWYERS, Novel *see* Ralph B. Potts

COME ON, THE, Novel *see* Whitman Chambers

COME OUT OF THE KITCHEN!, New York 1916, Novel *see* Alice Duer Miller

COME PRIMA MEGLIO DI PRIMA, 1921, Play *see* Luigi Pirandello

COME TO MOTHER, Novel *see* David Sale

COME TO MY HOUSE, New York 1927, Novel *see* Arthur Somers Roche

COME TO THE STABLE, Story *see* Clare Boothe Luce

COME TU MI VUOI, Milan 1930, Play *see* Luigi Pirandello

COMEBACK, THE, Story *see* J. Raleigh Davies

COMEDIA INFANTIL, Novel *see* Henning Mankell

COMEDIANS, 1976, Play *see* Trevor Griffiths

COMEDIANS, THE, New York 1966, Novel *see* Graham Greene

COMEDIE DE CELUI QUI EPOUSA UNE FEMME MUETTE, LA, 1912, Play *see* Anatole France

COMEDIE DU BONHEUR, LA, Play *see* Nicolas Evreinov, Fernand Noziere

COMEDY MAN, THE, Novel *see* Douglas Hayes

COMEDY OF ERRORS, THE, c1594, Play *see* William Shakespeare

COMET OVER BROADWAY, 1937, Story *see* Faith Baldwin

COMEUPPANCE, THE, Play *see* Robert Downey

COMFORT OF STRANGERS, THE, 1981, Novel *see* Ian McEwan

COMFORTS OF HOME, 1955, Short Story *see* Flannery O'Connor

COMIC SUPPLEMENT (OF AMERICAN LIFE), THE, Washington D.C. 1925, Play *see* Joseph Patrick McEvoy

COMIN' THRO' THE RYE, Novel *see* Helen Mathers

COMING HOME, Poem *see* Alfred Berlyn

COMING OF STORK, THE, 1974, Play *see* David Williamson

COMING OF THE LAW, THE, New York 1912, Novel *see* Charles Alden Seltzer

COMING OUT OF MAGGIE, THE, Short Story *see* O. Henry

COMING PLAGUE, THE, Book *see* Laurie Garrett

COMMAND DECISION, New York 1947, Play *see* William Wister Haines

COMMAND PERFORMANCE, THE, New York 1928, Play *see* C. Stafford Dickens

COMMAND TO LOVE, THE, New York 1927, Play *see* Fritz Gottwald, Rudolph Lothar

COMMANDER CRABB, Book *see* Marshall Pugh

COMMANDING OFFICER, THE, New York 1909, Play *see* Theodore Burt Sayre

COMMANDO 44, Novel *see* Piet Legay

COMMANDOS, THE, Novel *see* Elliott Arnold

COMMENT FAIRE L'AMOUR AVEC UN NEGRO SANS SE FATIGUER, Novel *see* Dany Laferriere

COMMENT J'AI TUE MON ENFANT, Novel *see* Pierre L'Ermite

COMMENT QU'ELLE EST, Novel *see* Peter Cheyney

COMMISSAIRE EST BON ENFANT, LE, 1899, Play *see* Georges Courteline

COMMISSARIO DI TORINO, IL, Novel *see* Marcato, Novelli

COMMISSARIO PEPE, IL, Novel *see* Ugo Facco de Lagardo

COMMISSIONER, THE, Novel *see* Stanley Johnson

COMMISSIONER, THE, New York 1962, Novel *see* Richard Dougherty

COMMON CLAY, Boston 1915, Play *see* Cleves Kinkead

COMMON GROUND, 1936, Short Story *see* Gerald Beaumont

COMMON LAW, THE, New York 1911, Novel *see* Robert W. Chambers

COMMON PURSUIT, THE, 1984, Play *see* Simon Gray

COMMON SIN, THE, Story *see* Willard Mack

COMMON TOUCH, THE, Novel *see* Herbert Ayres

COMMUNARD'S PIPE, THE, *see* Ilja Erenburg

COMMUNION, Book *see* Whitley Strieber

COMMUTERS, THE, New York 1910, Play *see* James Forbes

COMO AGUA PARA CHOCOLATE, Novel *see* Laura Esquivel

COMPACT, THE, Novel *see* Katherine Cecil Thurston

COMPAGNO DON CAMILLO, IL, Novel *see* Giovanni Guareschi

COMPAGNONS DE JEHU, LES, 1857, Novel *see* Alexandre Dumas (pere)

COMPAGNONS D'ULYSSE, LES, Novel *see* Pierre Benoit

CRIME, INC., Novel see Martin Mooney

CRIME IS MY BUSINESS, Novel see W. Howard Baker

CRIME OF CONSTABLE KELLY, THE, Novel see J. C. Snaith

CRIME OF THE CENTURY, THE, Story see J. Edgar Hoover

CRIME ON THE HILL, 1932, Play see Jack Celestin, Jack de Leon

CRIME UNLIMITED, Novel see David Hume

CRIMES OF THE ARMCHAIR CLUB, THE, 1920, Short Story see Arthur Somers Roche

CRIMES OF THE HEART, 1982, Play see Beth Henley

CRIMINAL CODE, THE, New York 1929, Play see Martin Flavin

CRIMINAL'S MARK, Short Story see John Hawkins, Ward Hawkins

CRIMINEL, LE, Novel see Andre Corthis

CRIMSON CIRCLE, THE, London 1922, Novel see Edgar Wallace

CRIMSON GARDENIA, THE, New York 1916, Short Story see Rex Beach

CRIMSON WEST, THE, Novel see Alexander Philip

CRIMSON WING, THE, Chicago 1902, Novel see Hobart C. Chatfield-Taylor

CRIPS, Novel see Donald Bakeer

CRISANTEMO MACCHIATO DI SANGUE, IL, Novel see John World

CRISI, LA, 1904, Play see Marco Praga

CRISIS, THE, New York 1901, Novel see Winston Churchill

CRISPINO E LA COMARE, Venice 1850, Opera see Federico Ricci, Luigi Ricci

CRISS CROSS, Novel see Don Tracy

CRISS CROSS CODE, Novel see Julian Symons

CRISSCROSS, Novel see Scott Sommer

CRISTILINDA, New York 1926, Novel see Monckton Hoffe

CRISTO EI E FERMATO A EBOLI, 1945, Novel see Carlo Levi

CRISTO NO LAMA, 1964, Novel see Joao Felicio Dos Santos

CRISTO PROIBITO, IL, Novel see Curzio Malaparte

CRITICAL CARE, Novel see Richard Dooling

CRITICAL LIST, THE, Novel see Marshall Goldberg

CRITICAL YEAR, THE, Story see Hans Bachwitz, Rudolph Lothar

CRITIC'S CHOICE, New York 1960, Play see Ira Levin

CROCHETS DU PERE MARTIN, LES, 1858, Play see Eugene Cormon, Eugene Grange

CROISE DE L'ORDRE, LE, Novel see Didier Daeninckx

CROISEE DES CHEMINS, LA, Novel see Henri Bordeaux

CROIX DE BOIS, LES, Novel see Roland Dorgeles

CROIX DU CERVIN, LA, Lausanne 1919, Novel see Charles Gos

CROIX DU SUD, LA, Novel see Paul Achard

CROIX SUR LE ROCHER, LA, Novel see Edmond Levenq, Jean Rosne

CRONACA, Play see Leopoldo Trieste

CRONACA DI UNA MORTE ANNUNCIATA, 1981, Novel see Gabriel Garcia Marquez

CRONACA FAMILIARE, Florence 1947, Novel see Vasco Pratolini

CRONACHE DEL 1787-1790 A BOTANY BAY IN AUSTRALIA, Book see James Price

CRONACHE DI POVERI AMANTI, 1947, Novel see Vasco Pratolini

CRONICA DA CASA ASSASSINADA, 1959, Novel see Lucio Cardoso

CRONICA DE UN REY PASMADO, Novel see Gonzalo Torrente Ballester

CROOKED BILLET, THE, London 1927, Play see Dion Titheradge

CROOKED LADY, THE, Novel see William C. Stone

CROOKED MAN, THE, Short Story see Arthur Conan Doyle

CROONER, New York 1932, Novel see Rian James

CROQUETTE, Novel see Eric Maschwitz

CROSS AND THE SWITCHBLADE, THE, New York 1963, Autobiography see John & Elizabeth Sherrill, David Wilkerson

CROSS CREEK, 1942, Book see Marjorie K. Rawlings

CROSS PULL, THE, New York 1920, Novel see Hal G. Evarts

CROSS ROADS, New York 1929, Play see Martin Flavin

CROSS, THE, Poem see Miriam Bode Rasmus

CROSSBAR, Story see Bill Boyle

CROSS-COUNTRY, Novel see Herbert Kastle

CROSSFIRE, Book see Jim Marrs

CROSSING DELANCEY, Play see Susan Sandler

CROSSINGS, Novel see Danielle Steel

CROSSTRAP, Novel see John Newton Chance

CROSSWORD PUZZLE, THE, Novel see Philip Hamilton Gibbs

CROULANTS SE PORTENT BIEN, LES, Play see Roger Ferdinand

CROWD, THE, 1943, Short Story see Ray Bradbury

CROWDED HOUR, THE, New York 1918, Play see Channing Pollock, Edgar Selwyn

CROWDED SKY, THE, Novel see Henry Searls

CROWN MATRIMONIAL, Play see Royce Ryton

CROWS OF EDWINA HILL, THE, New York 1961, Novel see Allan R. Bosworth

CROWTHERS OF BANKDAM, THE, Novel see Thomas Armstrong

CROXLEY MASTER, THE, Novel see Arthur Conan Doyle

CRUCIBLE, THE, see Yay Marking

CRUCIBLE, THE, 1953, Play see Arthur Miller

CRUCIBLE, THE, New York 1907, Novel see Mark Lee Luther

CRUCIFIX, LE, Poem see Victor Hugo

CRUCIFIXION, Novel see Newman Flower

CRUCIFIXION OF PHILIP STRONG, THE, Chicago 1894, Novel see Charles Monroe Sheldon

CRUEL SEA, THE, 1951, Novel see Nicholas Monsarrat

CRUEL TOWER, THE, Novel see William B. Hartley

CRUISE OF THE JASPER B, THE, New York 1916, Novel see Don Marquis

CRUISE OF THE MAKE-BELIEVES, THE, Boston 1907, Novel see Tom Gallon

CRUISING, Novel see Gerald Walker

CRUSADER, THE, 1916, Short Story see Alan Sullivan

CRUZ DEL DIABLO, LA, 1860, Short Story see Gustavo Adolfo Becquer

CRY COPPER, Story see Gladys Atwater, J. Robert Bren

CRY FOR HAPPY, New York 1958, Novel see George Campbell

CRY FOR THE STRANGERS, Novel see John Saul

CRY MURDER, Play see A. B. Shiffrin

CRY OF THE BLACK WOLVES, Novel see Jack London

CRY OF THE CHILDREN, THE, Poem see Elizabeth Barrett Browning

CRY OF THE NIGHTHAWK, THE, Short Story see Sax Rohmer

CRY OF THE OWL, THE, 1964, Novel see Patricia Highsmith

CRY THE BELOVED COUNTRY, 1948, Novel see Alan Paton

CRY TOUGH, 1949, Novel see Irving Shulman

CRY WOLF, Novel see Marjorie Carleton

CRYSTAL CUP, THE, New York 1925, Novel see Gertrude Franklin Atherton

CSILLAG A MAGLYAN, 1976, Play see Andras Suto

CSILLAGSZEMU, A, 1953, Novel see Grandpierre Emil Kolozsvari

CSUTAK ES A SZURKE LO, 1959, Novel see Ivan Mandy

CUANDO LLEGUE LA NOCHE, 1944, Play see Joaquin Calvo Sotelo

CUATRO JINETES DEL APOCALIPSIS, LOS, Valencia 1916, Novel see Vicente Blasco Ibanez

CUATRO ROBINSONES, LOS, Play see Enrique G. Alvarez, Pedro Munoz Seca

CUB, THE, New York 1910, Play see Thompson Buchanan

CUBA CABANA, Short Story see Tibor Yost

CUCKOO IN THE NEST, A, London 1925, Play see Ben Travers

CUCOANA CHIRITA IN IASI, 1852, Play see Vasile Alecsandri

CUCOANA CHIRITA IN PROVINCIE, 1852, Play see Vasile Alecsandri

CUDZOZIEMKA, 1935, Novel see Maria Kuncewiczowa

CUGINA, LA, Novel see Ercole Patti

CUISINE DES ANGES, LA, Play see Albert Husson

CUJO, 1981, Novel see Stephen King

CULLENBENBONG, Novel see Bernard O'Reilly

CULTURE OF CITIES, THE, Book see Lewis Mumford

CUNNING AND THE HAUNTED, THE, 1954, Novel see Richard Jessup

CUNNINGHAMES ECONOMISE, THE, Story see Mayell Bannister

CUORE, 1886, Short Story see Edmondo de Amicis

CUORE SEMPLICE, UN, Novel see Gustave Flaubert

CUORI NEGLI ABISSI, Novel see Nino de Maria

CUP AND THE SWORD, THE, Novel see Alice Tisdale Hobart

CUP OF FURY, THE, New York 1919, Novel see Rupert Hughes

CUP OF KINDNESS, A, London 1929, Play see Ben Travers

CUPID RIDES PILLION, Novel see Barbara Cartland

CUPID: THE COW-PUNCH, New York 1907, Novel see Eleanor Gates

CURA DE ALDEA, EL, Novel see Enrique Perez Escrich

CURA DE REPOSO, LA, Madrid 1927, Play see Enrique Garcia Velloso

CURE DE SAINT-AMOUR, LE, Play see Jean Guitton

CURE FOR LOVE, THE, London 1945, Play see Walter Greenwood

CUREE, LA, Paris 1871, Novel see Emile Zola

CURFEW SHALL NOT RING TONIGHT, Poem see Rose H. Thorpe

CURIOUS CONDUCT OF JUDGE LEGARDE, THE, Washington D.C. 1912, Play see Louis Forest, Victor Mapes

CURRITO DE LA CRUZ, Novel see Alejandro Perez Lugin

CURRO VARGAS, Opera see Ruperto Chapi, Joaquin Dicenta, Manuel Paso

CURSE OF CAPISTRANO, THE, 1919, Novel see Johnston McCulley

CURSE OF DRINK, THE, 1904, Play see Charles E. Blaney

CURSE OF KING TUTENKHAMEN'S TOMB, THE, Novel see Barry Wynne

CURSE OF THE STARVING CLASS, Play see Sam Shepard

CURSE OF THE VIKING GRAVE, Novel see Farley Mowat

CURSED, Boston 1919, Novel see George Allan England

CURTAIN, 1919, Short Story see Rita Weiman

CURTIS'S CHARM, Short Story see Jim Carroll

CUSTARD BOYS, THE, London 1960, Novel see John Rae

CUSTARD CUP, THE, New York 1921, Novel see Florence Bingham Livingston

CUSTODE, IL, Play see M. Moscariello

CUSTOMARY TWO WEEKS, THE, 1917, Short Story see Freeman Tilden

CUTTER'S WAY, Novel see Newton Thornburg

CUTTIN' A RUG, Play see John Byrne

CUZOI CHLEB, 1848, Novel see S. Turgenev

CUZOJ CHLEB, 1848, Novel see S. Turgenev

CVRCAK POD VODOPADOM, 1937, Short Story see Miroslav Krieza

CY PERKINS IN THE CITY OF DELUSION, Story see C. M. Stevens

CY WHITTAKER'S PLACE, New York 1908, Novel see Joseph C. Lincoln

CYANKALI, Play see Friedrich Wolf

CYBORG, Novel see Martin Caidin

CYCLE OF THE WEREWOLF, Novel see Stephen King

CYCLE OF VIOLENCE, Novel see Colin Bateman

CYCLIST'S RAID, THE, 1951, Short Story see Frank Rooney

CYCLONE HICKEY, Story see A. P. Younger

CYMBELINE, c1610, Play see William Shakespeare

CYNARA, London 1930, Play see Robert Gore-Browne, H. M. Harwood

CYNIC EFFECT, THE, 1920, Short Story see Nalbro Bartley

CYNTHIA IN THE WILDERNESS, Novel see Hubert Wales

CYNTHIA-OF-THE-MINUTE, New York 1911, Novel see Louis Joseph Vance

CYPRIENNE OR DIVORCONS, Paris 1883, Play see Emile de Najac, Victorien Sardou

CYRANO DE BERGERAC, 1897, Play see Edmond Rostand

CYTHEREA, GODDESS OF LOVE, New York 1922, Novel see Joseph Hergesheimer

CZARDASFURSTIN, DIE, Vienna 1915, Operetta see B. Jenbach, Emmerich Kalman, Leo Stein

CZARINA, THE, Play see Lajos Biro, Melchior Lengyel

CZARNE SKRZYDLA, 1928-29, Novel see Juliusz Kaden-Bandrowski

DA DAO JI, Novel see Guo Chengqing

D.A. DRAWS A CIRCLE, THE, Novel see Erle Stanley Gardner

DA JIE, Novel see Zhou Meishen

DABEL, Short Story see Lev Nikolayevich Tolstoy

DABNEY TODD, New York 1916, Novel see F. N. Westcott

DACHNIKI, 1904, Play see Maxim Gorky

DAD, Novel see William Wharton

DADDIES, Play see John L. Hobble

DADDY AND I, New York 1935, Novel see Elizabeth Jordon

DADDY LONG-LEGS, New York 1912, Novel see Jean Webster

DADDY UND DO, Novel see Robert Pilchowsky

DADDY'S DYIN' WHO'S GOT THE WILL, Play see Del Shores

DADDY'S GONE A-HUNTING, New York 1921, Play see Zoe Akins

DAFFODIL MYSTERY, THE, London 1920, Novel see Edgar Wallace

DAHINTEN IN DER HEIDE, Books see Hermann Lons

DAI BING DE REN, Play see XIao Yu

DAIBOSATSU TOGE, Tokyo 1940, Short Story see Kaizan Nakazato

DAIKYOJI SEKIREKI, 1715, Play see Monzaemon Chikamatsu

DAIN CURSE, THE, Novel see Dashiell Hammett

DAISY, Novel see Judith Krantz

DAISY KENYON, Novel see Elizabeth Janeway

DAISY MILLER, 1877, Short Story see Henry James

DAL TECC ALLA CANTINA, Play see Cletto Arrighi

D-ALE CARNAVALULUI, 1885, Play see Ion Luca Caragiale

DALEKO JE SUNCE, 1951, Novel see Dobrica Cosic

DALILA, 1857, Novel see Octave Feuillet

DALLA THE LION CUB, New York 1924, Novel see Cynthia Stockley

DAM, THE, Novel see Dimitris Plaskovitis

DAMA BIANCA, LA, Play see Aldo de Benedetti, Guglielmo Zorzi

DAMA DEL ALBA, LA, 1944, Play see Alejandro Casona

DAMA DUENDE, LA, 1647, Play see Pedro Calderon de La Barca

DAMA S SOBACHKOY, 1899, Short Story see Anton Chekhov

DAMAGED GOODS, 1913, Novel see Upton Sinclair

DAME AUX CAMELIAS, LA, Paris 1848, Novel see Alexandre Dumas (fils)

DAME AUX PERLES, LA, Novel see Alexandre Dumas (fils)

DAME DANS L'AUTO AVEC DES LUNETTES ET UN FUSIL, LA, Paris 1966, Novel see Sebastien Japrisot

DAME DE BRONZE ET LE MONSIEUR DE CRISTAL, LA, Play see Henri Duvernois

DAME DE CHEZ MAXIM, LA, 1898, Play see Georges Feydeau

DAME DE HAUT-LE-BOIS, LA, Novel see Jean-Jose Frappa

DAME DE MALACCA, LA, Novel see Francis de Croisset

DAME DE MONSOREAU, LA, 1856, Novel see Alexandre Dumas (pere)

DAME D'ONZE HEURES, LA, Novel see Pierre Apesteguy

DAME EN GRIS, LA, 1886, Novel see Georges Ohnet

DAME EN NOIR, LA, Novel see Emilie Richebourg

DAME IN SCHWARZ, DIE, Novel see Garai-Arvay

DAME MIT DEM SCHWARZEN HERZEN, DIE, Short Story see Frank Maraun

DAME MIT DEM TIGERFELL, DIE, Novel see Ernst Klein

DAME OF SARK, THE, Play see William Douglas Home

DAMES DE CROIX-MORT, LES, Novel see Georges Ohnet

DAMES DON'T TALK, Story see William Sackheim

DAMIAAN, DE DEFINITIEVE BIOGRAFIE, Biography see Hilde Eynikel

DAMIGELLA DI BARD, LA, Play see Salvator Gotta

DAMNATION ALLEY, 1969, Novel see Roger Zelazny

DAMNED INNOCENTS, THE, Novel see Richard Neely

DAMON AND PYTHIAS, Novel see Edward George Bulwer Lytton

DAMON AND PYTHIAS, Story see Don McGuire

D'AMORE SI MUORE, Play see Giuseppe Patroni Griffi

DAMSEL IN DISTRESS, A, New York 1919, Novel see P. G. Wodehouse

DAMY, 1886, Short Story see Anton Chekhov

DAN KURRIE'S INNING, Short Story see Russell A. Boggs

DANCE HALL, 1929, Short Story see Vina Delmar

DANCE MAGIC, New York 1927, Novel see Clarence Budington Kelland

DANCE OF DEATH, THE, Story see Phil Lang

DANCE OF GENGHIS COHN, Novel see Romain Gary

DANCE OF THE DWARFS, Novel see Geoffrey Household

DANCE TEAM, New York 1931, Novel see Sarah Addington

DANCER AND THE KING, THE, Play see Charles E. Blaney, J. Searle Dawley

DANCER OF PARIS, THE, 1925, Short Story see Michael Arlen

DANCERS, THE, New York 1923, Novel see Hubert Parsons

DANCIN' FOOL, THE, 1919, Short Story see Henry Payson Dowst

DANCING AT LUGHNASA, 1989, Play see Brian Friel

DANCING AZTECS, Novel see Donald E. Westlake

DANCING BOY, Novel see Ethel Mannin

DANCING CO-ED, THE, 1938, Short Story see Albert Treynor

DANCING DAYS, Story see J. J. Bell

DANCING FEET, New York 1931, Novel see Rob Eden

DANCING GIRL, THE, London 1891, Play see Henry Arthur Jones

DANCING IN THE DARK, Novel see Joan Barfoot

DANCING LADY, New York 1932, Novel see James Warner Bellah

DANCING MASTERS, THE, Novel see George Bricker

DANCING MEN, THE, Short Story see Arthur Conan Doyle

DANCING MOTHERS, New York 1924, Play see Edmund Goulding, Edgar Selwyn

DANCING YEARS, THE, London 1939, Play see Ivor Novello

DANDY DICK, London 1887, Play see Arthur Wing Pinero

DANDY IN ASPIC, A, London 1966, Novel see Derek Marlowe

DANGER, Story see William E. Wing

DANGER - MEN WORKING, Baltimore, Md. 1936, Play see Lowell Brentano, Ellery Queen

DANGER MARK, THE, New York 1909, Novel see Robert W. Chambers

DANGER SIGNAL, Novel see Phyllis Bottome

DANGER TRAIL, THE, Indianapolis 1910, Novel see James Oliver Curwood

DANGER ZONE, Radio Play see Herbert Margolis, Louis Morheim

DANGEROUS ADVENTURE, A, Story see Frances Guihan

DANGEROUS AFTERNOON, Play see Gerald Anstruther

DANGEROUS BUSINESS, New York 1927, Novel see Edwin Balmer

DANGEROUS CARGO, Short Story see Percy Hoskins

DANGEROUS CORNER, London 1932, Play see J. B. Priestley

DANGEROUS DAYS, New York 1919, Novel see Mary Roberts Rinehart

DANGEROUS DAYS OF KIOWA JONES, THE, Novel see Clifton Adams

DANGEROUS INHERITANCE; OR MYSTERY OF THE TITTANI RUBIES, THE, Boston 1920, Novel see Izola Forrester

DANGEROUS MEDICINE, Novel see Edmond Deland

DANGEROUS OBSESSION, Play see N. J. Crisp

DANGEROUS WOMAN, A, Novel see Mary McGarry Morris

DANGEROUSLY YOURS, 1929, Play see Charles Behan

DANIEL, Play see Louis Verneuil

DANIEL DERONDA, 1876, Novel see George Eliot

DANIELE CORTIS, 1885, Novel see Antonio Fogazzaro

DANISCHEFFS, DIE, Play see Pierre Newsky

DANITES, THE, Play see McKee Rankin

DANNY THE CHAMPION OF THE WORLD, Novel see Roald Dahl

DANS LE GOUFFRE, Story see Henri Duvernet

DANS LES RUES, Novel see Joseph Henri Rosny

DANS L'OMBRE DU HAREM, Play see Lucien Besnard

DANS MON JOLI PAVILLON, Novel see Michel Lebrun

DANS SA CANDEUR NAIVE, Paris 1927, Play see Jacques Deval

DANS VAN DE REIGER, DE, 1962, Play see Hugo Claus

DANSE HEROIQUE, LA, Novel see Pierre Sales

DANSE MACABRE, Short Story see Edgar Allan Poe

DANSEN GJENOM SKUGGEHEIM, 1911-24, Novel see Kristofer Uppdal

DANSEUR INCONNU, LE, France 1909, Play see Tristan Bernard

DANSEUSE DU GAI-MOULIN, LA, 1931, Novel see Georges Simenon

DANSEUSE NUE, LE, Novel see Colette Andris

DANSEUSE ORCHIDEE, LA, Novel see Jean-Joseph Renaud

DANTON, Play see Stanislawa Przybyszewska

DANY, BITTE SCHREIBEN SIE, Novel see Inge Rosener

DANZA DELLE LANCETTE, LA, Novel see Emilio de Martino

DAPHNE LAUREOLA, Play see James Bridie

DAPHNE UND DER DIPLOMAT, Novel see Fritz von Woedtke

DAPHNIS AND CHLOE, c200, Novel see Longus

DARBY AND JOAN, Novel see Rita

DARBY'S RANGERS, 1945, Book see Major James Altieri

DARDAMELLE, Play see Emile Mazeaud

DAREDEVIL CONQUEST, Novel see Berkeley Gray

DAREDEVIL KATE, Play see Philip Bartholomae

DAREDEVIL, THE, New York 1916, Novel see Maria Thompson Davies

DARF MAN? DARF MAN NICHT?, Play see Bobby E. Luthge

DARK ANGEL, Novel see Gina Kaus

DARK ANGEL, THE, New York 1925, Play see Guy Bolton

DARK AT THE TOP OF THE STAIRS, THE, New York 1957, Play see William Inge

DARK CHAPTER, THE, New York 1924, Novel see E. J. Rath

DARK COMMAND: A KANSAS ILIAD, New York 1938, Novel see William Riley Burnett

DARK CORNER, 1945, Short Story see Leo Rosten

DARK DAME, New York 1935, Novel see Wilson Collison

DARK EYES OF LONDON, THE, London 1924, Novel see Edgar Wallace

DARK HAZARD, New York 1933, Novel *see* William Riley Burnett

DARK LANTERN, A, New York 1905, Novel *see* Elizabeth Robins

DARK MIRROR, THE, Garden City, N.Y. 1920, Novel *see* Louis Joseph Vance

DARK OF THE SUN, THE, London 1965, Novel *see* Wilbur Smith

DARK PAGE, THE, 1944, Novel *see* Samuel Fuller

DARK PASSAGE, 1946, Novel *see* David Goodis

DARK PURPOSE, New York 1960, Novel *see* Doris Hume

DARK RED ROSES, Short Story *see* Stacy Aumonier

DARK ROOM, THE, Novel *see* Minette Walters

DARK ROSALEEN, 1925, Short Story *see* Max Brand

DARK SIDE OF LOVE, THE, Novel *see* Oscar Saul

DARK STAR, Indianapolis 1929, Novel *see* Lorna Moon

DARK STAR, THE, New York 1917, Novel *see* Robert W. Chambers

DARK SWAN, THE, New York 1924, Novel *see* Ernest Pascal

DARK TOWER, THE, New York 1933, Play *see* George S. Kaufman, Alexander Woollcott

DARK VICTORY, New York 1934, Play *see* Bert Bloch, George Emerson Brewer Jr.

DARK WATERS, Story *see* Frank Cockrell, Marian Cockrell

DARK WIND, THE, Novel *see* Tony Hillerman

DARK WITNESS, Novel *see* Day Keene

DARKENED ROOMS, 1928, Short Story *see* Philip Hamilton Gibbs

DARKER PURPOSE, A, Play *see* Wendy Riss

DARKER THAN AMBER, Greenwich, Ct. 1966, Novel *see* John D. MacDonald

DARKEST HOUR, THE, Serial Story *see* William P. McGivern

DARKEST RUSSIA, New York 1894, Play *see* H. Grattan Donnelly, Sidney R. Ellis

DARKNESS, Short Story *see* Max Brand

DARKNESS I LEAVE YOU, Novel *see* Nina Warner Hooke

DARLING, 1965, Novel *see* Frederic Raphael

DARLING BUDS OF MAY, THE, 1958, Novel *see* H. E. Bates

DARLING FAMILY, THE, Play *see* Linda Griffiths

D'ARTAGNAN OF KANSAS, 1912, Short Story *see* Eugene P. Lyle Jr.

DARTMOUTH MURDERS, THE, New York 1929, Novel *see* Clifford Orr

DAS WASSER DES LEBENS, Short Story *see* Jacob Grimm, Wilhelm Grimm

DASHING, Story *see* Ruth Comfort Mitchell

DATED, 1920, Short Story *see* Maxwell Smith

DAUGHTER IN REVOLT, A, Novel *see* Sidney Gowing

DAUGHTER OF A MAGNATE, THE, New York 1903, Novel *see* Frank Hamilton Spearman

DAUGHTER OF BRAHMA, THE, Indianapolis 1912, Novel *see* I. A. R. Wylie

DAUGHTER OF DIAMOND, THE, Novel *see* Christopher B. Booth

DAUGHTER OF ENGLAND, A, Play *see* P. Barrow, Jose G. Levy, E. V. Miller

DAUGHTER OF FU MANCHU, New York 1931, Novel *see* Sax Rohmer

DAUGHTER OF ISRAEL, A, Novel *see* Bruno Lessing

DAUGHTER OF LOVE, A, Novel *see* Mrs. E. J. Key

DAUGHTER OF MOTHER MCGINN, THE, Story *see* Jack Boyle

DAUGHTER OF THE CITY, A, Play *see* H. S. Sheldon

DAUGHTER OF THE DONS, A, New York 1914, Novel *see* William MacLeod Raine

DAUGHTER OF THE PEOPLE, THE, Play *see* J. Searle Dawley

DAUGHTER OF THE SIOUX; A TALE OF THE INDIAN FRONTIER, A, New York 1903, Novel *see* Gen. Charles King

DAUGHTER OF THE WEST, Novel *see* Robert E. Callahan

DAUGHTER OF THE WOLF, A, 1919, Short Story *see* Hugh Pendexter

DAUGHTER OF TWO WORLDS, A, Boston 1919, Novel *see* Leroy Scott

DAUGHTER PAYS, THE, London 1915, Novel *see* Mrs. Baillie Reynolds

DAUGHTERS OF MEN, THE, New York 1906, Play *see* Charles Klein

DAUGHTERS OF THE RICH, New York 1900, Novel *see* Edgar Saltus

DAUGHTERS OF THE VICAR, Short Story *see* D. H. Lawrence

DAUMESDICK, 1812, Short Story *see* Jacob Grimm, Wilhelm Grimm

DAUTAUN HIROZU, Novel *see* Akira Hayasaka

DAVID, Book *see* Joel Konig, Marie Rothberg, Mel White

DAVID AND JONATHAN, New York 1919, Novel *see* E. Temple Thurston

DAVID BALFOUR, New York 1893, Novel *see* Robert Louis Stevenson

DAVID COPPERFIELD, London 1850, Novel *see* Charles Dickens

DAVID GARRICK, London 1864, Play *see* T. W. Robertson

DAVID GOLDER, Novel *see* Irene Nemirovsky

DAVID HARUM, New York 1898, Novel *see* Edward Noyes Westcott

DAVID'S MOTHER, Play *see* Bob Randall

DAVNYM-DAVNO, 1942, Play *see* Aleksandr Gladkov

DAVY CROCKETT, 1872, Play *see* Frank Murdock

DAWN, Novel *see* H. Rider Haggard

DAWN, New York 1919, Novel *see* Eleanor H. Porter

DAWN, New York 1928, Novel *see* Reginald Berkeley

DAWN OF A TOMORROW, THE, New York 1906, Novel *see* Frances Hodgson Burnett

DAWN OF MY TOMORROW, THE, Story *see* George W. Sutton Jr.

DAWN OF RECKONING, 1925, Novel *see* James Hilton

DAY AT THE BROKERS, 1936, Play *see* David Freedman

DAY IN THE DEATH OF JOE EGG, A, 1967, Play *see* Peter Nichols

DAY IS OURS, THE, Novel *see* Hilda Lewis

DAY IT ALL HAPPENED, BABY, THE, 1966, Short Story *see* Robert Thom

DAY OF ATONEMENT, THE, 1922, Short Story *see* Samson Raphaelson

DAY OF DAYS, THE, Boston 1913, Novel *see* Louis Joseph Vance

DAY OF FAITH, THE, Boston 1921, Novel *see* Arthur Somers Roche

DAY OF SOULS, THE, Indianapolis 1910, Novel *see* Charles Tenney Jackson

DAY OF THE ARROW, New York 1964, Novel *see* Philip Loraine

DAY OF THE DOG, Novel *see* Archie Weller

DAY OF THE DOLPHIN, THE, Novel *see* Robert Merle

DAY OF THE JACKAL, THE, 1971, Novel *see* Frederick Forsyth

DAY OF THE LOCUST, THE, 1939, Novel *see* Nathanael West

DAY OF THE OUTLAW, 1955, Novel *see* Lee Wells

DAY OF THE TRIFFIDS, THE, 1951, Novel *see* John Wyndham

DAY RESURGENT, THE, Short Story *see* O. Henry

DAY, THE, Short Story *see* Roland Starke

DAY THE BUBBLE BURST, THE, Book *see* Max Morgan-Witts, Gordon Thomas

DAY THE CENTURY ENDED, THE, 1955, Novel *see* Francis Gwaltney

DAY THE LOVING STOPPED, THE, Book *see* Julie Autumn List

DAY THE WORLD ENDED, THE, Novel *see* Max Morgan-Witts, Gordon Thomas

DAY THEY ROBBED THE BANK OF ENGLAND, THE, Novel *see* John Brophy

DAYBREAK, Play *see* Monckton Hoffe

DAYBREAK, New York 1917, Play *see* Jane Cowl, Jane Murfin

DAYBREAKERS, THE, Novel *see* Louis L'Amour

DAYDREAMS, Short Story *see* H. G. Wells

DAYS BEFORE LENT, 1939, Novel *see* Hamilton Basso

DAY'S MISCHIEF, THE, 1951, Play *see* Lesley Storm

DAZZLING MISS DAVISON, THE, London 1908, Novel *see* Florence Warden

DE LA TERRE A LA LUNE; TRAJET DIRECT EN 97 HEURES, 1865, Novel *see* Jules Verne

DE L'AMOUR, Paris 1822, Novel *see* Stendhal

DE LUXE ANNIE, New York 1917, Play *see* Edward Clark

DE NOCHE VIENES ESMERALDA, Short Story *see* Elena Poniatowska

DEACON, THE, New York 1925, Play *see* Leroy Clemens, John B. Hymer

DEAD BY SUNSET, Book *see* Ann Rule

DEAD CALM, Novel *see* Charles Williams

DEAD CERT, Novel *see* Dick Francis

DEAD CERTAINTY, A, Novel *see* Nat Gould

DEAD DON'T CARE, THE, New York 1938, Novel *see* Jonathan Latimer

DEAD END, New York 1936, Play *see* Sidney Kingsley

DEAD HEART, Play *see* Nick Parsons

DEAD HEART, THE, Book *see* Michael Thomas

DEAD HEART, THE, London 1859, Play *see* Watts Phillips

DEAD MAN WALKING, Book *see* Sister Helen Prejean

DEAD MAN'S FLOAT, Novel *see* Roger Vaughan Carr

DEAD MAN'S FOLLY, Novel *see* Agatha Christie

DEAD MAN'S GOLD, New York 1920, Novel *see* J. Allen Dunn

DEAD MAN'S LOVE, A, *see* Tom Gallon

DEAD MEN DON'T DIG COAL, Book *see* Wendy Lowenstein

DEAD MEN TELL NO TALES, Novel *see* Kelley Roos

DEAD MEN TELL NO TALES, New York 1899, Novel *see* E. W. Hornung

DEAD OF JERICHO, THE, Novel *see* Colin Dexter

DEAD ON COURSE, Novel *see* Elleston Trevor

DEAD ON NINE, Play *see* Jack Popplewell

DEAD PIGEON, New York 1953, Play *see* Leonard Kantor

DEAD RECKONING, Play *see* Robert Lewis

DEAD ROMANTIC, Novel *see* Simon Brett

DEAD RUN, New York 1961, Novel *see* Robert Sheckley

DEAD SECRET, THE, Novel *see* Wilkie Collins

DEAD TAKE NO BOWS, THE, Novel *see* Richard Burke

DEAD YESTERDAY, 1936, Short Story *see* Mignon G. Eberhart

DEAD ZONE, THE, Novel *see* Stephen King

DEADFALL, London 1965, Novel *see* Desmond Cory

DEADHEADS, London 1983, Novel *see* Reginald Hill

DEADLIER THAN THE MALE, Novel *see* James Gunn

DEADLINE, Novel *see* Tim Heald

DEADLINE AT DAWN, 1944, Novel *see* Cornell Woolrich

DEADLOCK, Play *see* Leslie Sands

DEADLY CITY, THE, Story *see* Paul W. Fairman

DEADLY DUO, THE, New York 1960, Novel *see* Richard Jessup

DEADLY HATE, A, Play *see* George Roberts

DEADLY HUNT, THE, Novel *see* Pat Stadley

DEADLY INTENTIONS, Book *see* William Randolph Stevens

DEADLY RECORD, Novel *see* Nina Warner Hooke

DEADLY SILENCE, A, Book *see* Dena Kleiman

DEADLY TRAP, THE, Novel *see* Arthur Cavanaugh

DEAL A BLOW, 1955, Television Play *see* Robert Dozier

DEALING, Novel *see* Michael Crichton

DEAR EVELYN, Play *see* Dale M. Eunson, Hagar Wilde

DEAR FATHER (THESE CHARMING PEOPLE), 1924, Play *see* Michael Arlen

DEAR FOOL, A, Novel *see* Artemas (Arthur T. Mason)

DEAR LIAR, A, Short Story *see* Edgar Wallace

DEAR LITTLE OLD TIME GIRL, Story *see* Leonora Ainsworth

DEAR ME, OR APRIL CHANGES, New York 1921, Play *see* Hamilton Hale, Luther Reed

DEAR MURDERER, Play *see* St. John Leigh Clowes

DEAR OCTOPUS, London 1938, Play *see* Dodie Smith

DEAR PRETENDER, THE, Philadelphia 1924, Novel *see* Alice Ross Colver

DEAR RUTH, New York 1944, Play *see* Norman Krasna

DEAR SOOKY, New York 1929, Novel *see* Percy Lee Crosby

DEATH AND DELIVERANCE, Book *see* Robert Mason Lee

DEATH AND LIFE OF DITH PRAN, THE, Article *see* Sydney Schanberg

DEATH AND THE MAIDEN, Play *see* Ariel Dorfman

DEATH AND THE SKY ABOVE, Novel *see* Andrew Garve

DEATH AT ATTENTION, Novel *see* Kem Bennett

DEATH AT BROADCASTING HOUSE, Novel *see* Val Gielgud

DEATH BE NOT PROUD, Book *see* John Gunther

DEATH BY DESIGN, Short Story *see* Leonard Gribble

DEATH CATCHES UP WITH MR. KLUCK, New York 1935, Novel *see* Xantippe

DEATH CROONS THE BLUES, Novel *see* James Ronald

DEATH DISC, THE, Story *see* Mark Twain

DEATH FLIES EAST, 1934, Story *see* Philip Wylie

DEATH FROM A TOP HAT, New York 1938, Novel *see* Clayton Rawson

DEATH GOES TO SCHOOL, Novel *see* Maisie Sharman

DEATH HAS DEEP ROOTS, Novel *see* Michael Gilbert

DEATH HOPS THE BELLS, 1938, Short Story *see* Charles Molyneaux Brown

DEATH IN BRUNSWICK, Novel *see* Boyd Oxlade

DEATH IN CALIFORNIA, A, Book *see* Joan Barthel

DEATH IN CANAAN, A, Book *see* Joan Barthel

DEATH IN CAPTIVITY, Novel *see* Michael Gilbert

DEATH IN HIGH HEELS, Novel *see* Christianna Brand

DEATH IN THE DEEP SOUTH, Harrisburg, PA. 1936, Novel *see* Ward Greene

DEATH IN THE DOLL'S HOUSE, 1943, Short Story *see* Hannah Lees

DEATH IN THE FAMILY, A, New York 1957, Novel *see* James Agee

DEATH IN THE HAND, Short Story *see* Max Beerbohm

DEATH IS NOW MY NEIGHBOUR, Novel *see* Colin Dexter

DEATH KEEPS A DATE, Play *see* Maurice Harrison, Sidney Nelson

DEATH KISS, THE, New York 1932, Novel *see* Madelon St. Denis

DEATH OF A CITIZEN, New York 1960, Novel *see* Donald Hamilton

DEATH OF A GUNFIGHTER, New York 1968, Novel *see* Lewis B. Patten

DEATH OF A SALESMAN, New York 1949, Play *see* Arthur Miller

DEATH OF A SNOUT, London 1961, Novel *see* Douglas Warner

DEATH OF A THIN-SKINNED ANIMAL, Novel *see* Patrick Alexander

DEATH OF AN EXPERT WITNESS, Novel *see* P. D. James

DEATH OF BILLY THE KID, THE, 1955, Television Play *see* Gore Vidal

DEATH OF GRASS, THE, London 1956, Novel *see* John Christopher

DEATH OF INNOCENCE, A, Novel *see* Zelda Popkin

DEATH OF IVAN THE TERRIBLE, THE, 1867, Play *see* Alexey Konstantinovich Tolstoy

DEATH OF ME YET, THE, Novel *see* Whit Masterson

DEATH ON A SIDE STREET, Story *see* Lawrence Kimble

DEATH ON THE DIAMOND: A BASEBALL MYSTERY STORY, New York 1934, Novel *see* Cortland Fitzsimmons

DEATH ON THE NILE, Novel *see* Agatha Christie

DEATH ON THE SET, Novel *see* Victor MacClure

DEATH RIDER, THE, Story *see* Harold Amacker

DEATH RIDES THE TRAIL, Short Story *see* Steve Frazee

DEATH STALK, Novel *see* Thomas Chastain

DEATH TRAIN, Novel *see* Alistair MacLean

DEATH WATCH, Novel *see* David Compton, Robb White

DEATH WATCH, 1932, Short Story *see* Edgar Wallace

DEATH WHISTLER, THE, Story *see* E. B. Mann

DEATH WISH, Novel *see* Brian Garfield

DEATHTRAP, Play *see* Ira Levin

DEBDAS, 1910, Novel *see* Sarat Candra Cattopadhyay

DEBT DISCHARGED, A, London 1916, Novel *see* Edgar Wallace

DEBT OF DISHONOR, Short Story *see* Jack Boyle

DEBT OF HONOUR, Short Story *see* H. C. McNeile ("Sapper")

DEBT OF HONOUR, A, Novel *see* Ethel M. Dell

DEBURAU, Play *see* Sacha Guitry

DECADENCE, Play *see* Steven Berkoff

DECAMERON, IL, 1349-50, Book *see* Giovanni Boccaccio

DECEIVERS, THE, Novel *see* John Masters

DECEMBER BRIDE, 1951, Novel *see* Sam Hanna Bell

DECEMBER WITH TRUXA, Novel *see* Heinrich Zeiler

DECENTE, LA, 1969, Play *see* Miguel Mihura Santos

DECEPTIONS, Novel *see* Judith Michael

DECHEANCE, Play *see* Michel Zevaco

DECISION AT MIDNIGHT, Novel *see* Peter Howard, Alan Thornhill

DECISION AT SUNDOWN, Book *see* Vernon I. Fluharty

DECISION TO DIE, 1964, Short Story *see* Shana Alexander

DECISION TO KILL, Novel *see* Karl Brown

DECLASSEE, New York 1923, Play *see* Zoe Akins

DECLINE AND FALL, London 1928, Novel *see* Evelyn Waugh

DECORATION DAY, Novel *see* John William Corrington

DECOY BE DAMNED, Novel *see* T. F. Fotherby

DEDALE, LE, Play *see* Paul Hervieu

DEDE, Opera *see* Henri Christine, Albert Willemetz

DEDE LA MUSIQUE, Novel *see* Gaston Montho

DEDECKEM PROTI SVE VULI, Play *see* Frantisek Zavrel

DEDEE D'ANVERS, Novel *see* Detective Ashelbe

DEEDS OF DR. DEADCERT, THE, Novel *see* Joan Fleming

DEEMSTER, THE, London 1887, Novel *see* Hall Caine

DEEP BLUE SEA, THE, London 1952, Play *see* Terence Rattigan

DEEP END OF THE OCEAN, THE, 1996, Novel *see* Jacquelyn Mitchard

DEEP IN MY HEART, 1949, Book *see* Elliott Arnold

DEEP PURPLE, THE, Chicago 1910, Play *see* Paul Armstrong, Wilson Mizner

DEEP SIX, THE, 1953, Novel *see* Martin Dibner

DEEP, THE, 1976, Novel *see* Peter Benchley

DEEP VALLEY, Novel *see* Dan Totheroh

DEEP WATERS, Short Story *see* W. W. Jacobs

DEERSLAYER, THE, 1841, Novel *see* James Fenimore Cooper

DEFEAT OF THE CITY, THE, 1908, Short Story *see* O. Henry

DEFENCE AND THE LAST DAYS, Novel *see* Borislav Pekic

DEFENCELESS AMERICA, New York 1915, Book *see* Hudson Maxim

DEFINITE OBJECT, THE, Boston 1917, Novel *see* Jeffrey Farnol

DEFRAUDANTEN, DIE, 1931, Play *see* Alfred Polgar

DEGOURDIS DE LA 11E, LES, Play *see* C. Daveillant, Andre Mouezy-Eon

DEGREE OF GUILT, Novel *see* Richard North Paterson

DEI SVARTE HESTANE, 1928, Novel *see* Tarjei Vesaas

DEJEUNER DE SOLEIL, UN, Play *see* Andre Birabeau

DEJEUNER INTERROMPU, LE, Novel *see* Julien Vartet

DEL PALMA, 1948, Novel *see* Pamela Kellino

DEL SOTO DEL PARRAL, LA, Opera *see* Anselmo Carreno Y Sevilla

DELIBERATE STRANGER, THE, Novel *see* Richard W. Larsen

DELICATE BALANCE, A, 1966, Play *see* Edward Albee

DELICATESSEN, 1925, Short Story *see* Brooke Hanlon

DELICE, LA, Novel *see* Maud Frere

DELILA, 1937, Play *see* Ferenc Molnar

DELINQUENTS, THE, Novel *see* Criena Rohan

DELITTO AL CIRCOLO DEL TENNIS, 1952, Short Story *see* Alberto Moravia

DELITTO ALL'ISOLA DELLA CAPRE, 1946, Play *see* Ugo Betti

DELITTO DEL COMMENDATORE, IL, Novel *see* Carlo Dadone

DELITTO DELL'OPERA, IL, Novel *see* De Boisgobey

DELIVERANCE, 1970, Novel *see* James Dickey

DELIVREZ-NOUS DU MAL, Novel *see* Frederic Dard, Claude Jasmin

DELLAMORTE DELLAMORE, Novel *see* Tiziano Sclavi

DELO ARTAMONOVYKH, 1925, Novel *see* Maxim Gorky

DELTA FACTOR, THE, New York 1969, Novel *see* Mickey Spillane

DELUGE: A ROMANCE, London 1927, Novel *see* S. Fowler Wright

DEMETRIOS CONTOS, 1905, Short Story *see* Jack London

DEMI-SOLDES, LES, Novel *see* Georges d'Esparbes

DEMI-VIERGES, LES, 1895, Novel *see* Marcel Prevost

DEMOISELLE DE MAGASIN, LA, Play *see* Jean-Francois Fonson

DEMOISELLE DE PASSY, LE, Play *see* Alfred Savoir

DEMOISELLES DE SAINT-CYR, LES, Play *see* Alexandre Dumas (pere)

DEMOKRAT LAPPLI, 1947, Play *see* Alfred Rasser

DEMON, 1841, Poem *see* Mikhail Lermontov

DEMON CARAVAN, THE, 1927, Novel *see* Georges Arthur Surdez

DEMON SEED, Novel *see* Dean R. Koontz

DEMONIOS, LOS, Novel *see* Jesus Franco

DEMOS, Novel *see* George Gissing

DEMPSEY, Autobiography *see* Barbara Piatteli Dempsey, Jack Dempsey

DENA PAONA, Novel *see* Saratchandra Chatterjee

DENG-BYOD, Novel *see* Kim Yu-Jung

DENIK KACENKY STRNADOVE, Novel *see* Josef Skruzny

DENISE, 1885, Novel *see* Alexandre Dumas (fils)

DENMAN THOMPSON'S THE OLD HOMESTEAD, New York 1889, Novel *see* John Russell Coryell

DENTELLIERE, LA, Novel *see* Pascal Laine

DENTIST IN THE CHAIR, London 1955, Novel *see* Matthew Finch

D'ENTRE LES MORTS, 1954, Novel *see* Pierre Boileau, Thomas Narcejac

DENTS LONGUES, LES, Novel *see* Jacques Robert

DENUNZIANTEN, Book *see* Michael Hatry

DEO GRATIS, Paris 1961, Novel *see* Michel Servin

DEPARTMENT K, London 1964, Novel *see* Hartley Howard

DEPARTMENTAL CASE, A, Short Story *see* O. Henry

DEPUTY MARSHAL, Novel *see* Charles Heckelman

DER VAR ENGANG, 1885, Play *see* Holger Drachman

DERBORENCE, Lausanne 1934, Novel *see* Charles-Ferdinand Ramuz

DERBY WINNER, THE, London 1894, Play *see* Henry Hamilton, Augustus Harris, Cecil Raleigh

DERELICTS, Novel *see* William J. Locke

DERELITTI DI VALCOURT, I, Play *see* Valcourt

DERMAN, Novel *see* Osman Sahin

DERNIER DES CAPENDU, LE, Novel *see* Eugene Barbier

DERNIER DES SIX, LE, Novel *see* Stanislas-Andre Steeman

DERNIER DOMICILE CONNU, Novel *see* Joseph Harrington

DERNIER HAVRE, LE, Novel *see* Yves Theriault

DERNIER PARDON, LE, Novel *see* Gyp

DERNIER QUART D'HEURE, LE, Paris 1955, Novel *see* Jean Bruce

DERNIER SAUT, LE, Novel *see* Bartholome Benassar

DERNIERE AVENTURE DU PRINCE CURACAO, Novel *see* Delphi Fabrice, Oscar Metenier

DERNIERES CARTOUCHES, LES, Novel *see* Jules Mary

DEROBADE, LA, Novel *see* Jeanne Cordelier

DIARY OF A MAD HOUSEWIFE, New York 1967, Novel *see* Sue Kaufman

DIARY OF A MADMAN, 1836, Short Story *see* Nikolay Gogol

DIARY OF A NEGRO MAID, *see* Erskine Williams

DIARY OF A NOBODY, 1892, Book *see* George Grossmith, Weedon Grossmith

DIARY OF ANNE FRANK, THE, Play *see* Frances Goodrich, Albert Hackett

DIARY OF VASLAV NIJINSKY, THE, Book *see* Vaslav Nijinsky

DIBUK, DER, 1916, Play *see* Solomon An-Ski

DICE OF GOD, THE, New York 1956, Novel *see* Hoffman Birney

DICK UND DALLI UND DIE PONIES, Novel *see* Ursula Bruns

DICKE UND ICH, DER, Short Story *see* Jens Bahre

DICK'S FAIRY, Novel *see* Silas K. Hocking

DICKY, Play *see* Paul Armont, Marcel Gerbidon

DICKY MONTEITH, Play *see* Tom Gallon, Leon M. Lion

DICTATOR, THE, New York 1904, Play *see* Richard Harding Davis

DIENER LASSEN BITTEN, Play *see* Toni Impekoven, Eduard Ritter

DIESMAL MUSS ES KAVIAR SEIN, Novel *see* Johannes Mario Simmel

DIEU RECONNAITRA LES SIENS, Novel *see* Jean Bommart

DIFFICULTE D'ETRE INFIDELE, LA, Play *see* Marc Camoletti

DIGGSTOWN RINGERS, THE, Novel *see* Leonard Wise

DIMANCHE AU CHAMP D'HONNEUR, UN, Paris 1958, Novel *see* Jean L'Hote

DIMANCHE DE FLICS, UN, Novel *see* Andrew Coburn

DIMANCHE DE LA VIE, LE, 1951, Novel *see* Raymond Queneau

DIMANCHES DE VILLE D'AVRAY, LES, Paris 1958, Novel *see* Bernard Eschasseriaux

DIMBOOLA, 1974, Play *see* Jack Hibberd

DIMINISHING DRAFT, THE, 1918, Short Story *see* Waldemar Kaempfert

DINAMO DELL'EROISMO, LA, Radio Play *see* Alessandro de Stefani

DINCOLO DE NISIPURI, 1962, Short Story *see* Fanus Neagu

DINDON, LE, 1896, Play *see* Georges Feydeau

DINER DE CONS, LE, Play *see* Francis Veber

DINNER AT EIGHT, 1912, Short Story *see* Samuel Merwin

DINNER AT EIGHT, New York 1932, Play *see* Edna Ferber, George S. Kaufman

DINO, 1956, Television Play *see* Reginald Rose

DIPLOMA, Play *see* Emric Foldes

DIPLOMACY, New York 1878, Play *see* Victorien Sardou

DIPLOMATE, LE, Play *see* Germain Delavigne, Eugene Scribe

DIPLOMATIE, 1899-1909, Short Story *see* Ion Luca Caragiale

DIPPERS, THE, London 1922, Play *see* Ben Travers

DIRECT AU COEUR, Play *see* Paul Nivoix, Marcel Pagnol

DIRITTO DI VIVERE, IL, 1900, Play *see* Roberto Bracco

DIRNENTRAGODIE, Play *see* Wilhelm Braun

DIRTY DOZEN, THE, New York 1965, Novel *see* E. M. Nathanson

DIRTY GAMES, Novel *see* Geoffrey Jenkins

DIRTY MARY CRAZY LARRY, Novel *see* Richard Unekis

DIRTY WEEKEND, Novel *see* Helen Zahavi

DIRTY WORK, London 1932, Play *see* Ben Travers

DIS JOE, 1966, Play *see* Samuel Beckett

DISAPPEARANCE OF DOLAN, THE, Story *see* William Fay

DISAPPEARANCE OF LADY FRANCES CARFAX, THE, Short Story *see* Arthur Conan Doyle

DISAPPEARANCE OF ROGER TREMAYNE, THE, Novel *see* Bruce Graeme

DISAPPEARANCE OF RORY BROPHY, THE, Novel *see* Carl Lombard

DISAPPEARANCE OF THE JUDGE, THE, Novel *see* Guy Thorne

DISCIPLE, LE, 1889, Novel *see* Paul Bourget

DISCIPLINE, Story *see* Lesley Storm

DISCIPLINE AND GENEVRA, 1917, Novel *see* Harold Vickers

DISCOUNTERS OF MONEY, Short Story *see* O. Henry

DISHONORED LADY, New York 1930, Play *see* Margaret Ayer Barnes, Edward Sheldon

DISNEYLAND, Warsaw 1965, Novel *see* Stanislaw Dygat

DISONESTI, I, 1892, Novel *see* Gerolamo Rovetta

DISORIENTED MAN, THE, London 1966, Novel *see* Peter Saxon

DISPARU DE L'ASCENSEUR, LE, Novel *see* Leon Groc

DISPARUS DE SAINT-AGIL, LES, Novel *see* Pierre Very

DISPLACED PERSON, THE, 1955, Short Story *see* Flannery O'Connor

DISPREZZO, IL, Milan 1954, Novel *see* Alberto Moravia

DISPUTED PASSAGE, Boston 1939, Novel *see* Lloyd C. Douglas

DISRAELI, New York 1911, Play *see* Louis N. Parker

DISTANT FIELDS, London 1937, Play *see* S. K. Lauren

DISTANT TRUMPET, A, New York 1960, Novel *see* Paul Horgan

DISTRACTIONS, LES, Novel *see* Jean Bassan

DISTRICT ATTORNEY, THE, New York 1895, Play *see* Harrison Grey Fiske, Charles Klein

DISUBBIDIENZA, LA, Novel *see* Alberto Moravia

DITTE MENNESKEBARN, 1917-21, Novel *see* Martin Andersen Nexo

DIVA, Novel *see* Delacorta

DIVA PATITSA MEZHDU DARVETATA, 1972, Novel *see* Stanislav Stratiev

DIVERSION, London 1928, Play *see* John Van Druten

DIVI PCHELI, 1978, Novel *see* Stanislav Stratiev

DIVINA COMMEDIA, LA, 1310, Verse *see* Dante Alighieri

DIVINA FANCIULLA, LA, Novel *see* Luciano Zuccoli

DIVINE GIFT, THE, Story *see* Merle Johnson

DIVINE, LA, Novel *see* Louis Letang

DIVINE LADY; A ROMANCE OF NELSON AND LADY HAMILTON, THE, New York 1924, Novel *see* E. Barrington

DIVINO E L'UMANO, IL, Short Story *see* Lev Nikolayevich Tolstoy

DIVO, IL, Play *see* Nino Martoglio

DIVOCH, Novel *see* Milos Krenovsky

DIVORCE COUPONS, Story *see* Ethel Watts Mumford

DIVORCED, Play *see* Edwin Archer

DIVORCEE, THE, Play *see* Edgar Selwyn

DIVORCING JACK, Novel *see* Colin Bateman

DIVOTA PRASINE, 1954, Novel *see* Vjekoslav Kaleb

DIX HEURES ET DEMIE DU SOIR EN ETE, Paris 1960, Novel *see* Marguerite Duras

DIXIANA, Story *see* Anne Caldwell, Harry Tierney

DIXIE, 1924, Short Story *see* Gerald Beaumont

DIXON'S RETURN, Short Story *see* W. W. Jacobs

DM-KILLER, Novel *see* Peter Norden

DNI I NOCHI, 1944, Novel *see* Konstantin Simonov

DO ANDROIDS DREAM OF ELECTRIC SHEEP?, 1969, Novel *see* Philip K. Dick

DO BAILON KI KATHA, 1936, Short Story *see* Munshi Premchand

DO NOT FOLD SPINDLE OR MUTILATE, Novel *see* Doris Miles Disney

DO PANSKEHO STAVU, Novel *see* Popelka Bilianova

DO RE MI, Short Story *see* Garson Kanin

DO TAMANHO DE UM DEFUNTO, 1957, Play *see* Millor Fernandes

DOC SAVAGE - THE MAN OF BRONZE, Novel *see* Kenneth Robeson

DOCK BRIEF, THE, London 1958, Play *see* John Mortimer

DOCKHEM, ETT, 1884, Short Story *see* August Strindberg

DOCTEUR FRANCOISE GAILLAND, Novel *see* Noelle Loriot

DOCTEUR RAMEAU, LE, Paris 1889, Novel *see* Georges Ohnet

DOCTOR: A TALE OF THE ROCKIES, THE, New York 1906, Novel *see* Ralph Connor

DOCTOR AT COFFIN GAP, THE, Novel *see* Les Savage Jr.

DOCTOR AT LARGE, Novel *see* Richard Gordon

DOCTOR AT SEA, Novel *see* Richard Gordon

DOCTOR DOUBLES IN DEATH, THE, Short Story *see* Richard Sale

DOCTOR FAUSTUS, 1594, Play *see* Christopher Marlowe

DOCTOR IN CLOVER, London 1960, Novel *see* Richard Gordon

DOCTOR IN LOVE, London 1957, Novel *see* Richard Gordon

DOCTOR IN THE HOUSE, Novel *see* Richard Gordon

DOCTOR LIVER, Book *see* Ango Sakaguchi

DOCTOR NYE OF NORTH OSTABLE, New York 1923, Novel *see* Joseph C. Lincoln

DOCTOR OF THE OLD SCHOOL, 1895, Novel *see* John Watson

DOCTOR ON TOAST, Novel *see* Richard Gordon

DOCTOR VLIMMEN, Novel *see* A. Roothaert

DOCTOR WEARS THREE FACES, THE, 1949, Book *see* Mary Bard

DOCTOR'S DILEMMA, THE, London 1906, Play *see* George Bernard Shaw

DOCTOR'S SECRET, THE, 1938, Short Story *see* W. J. Makin

DOCTOR'S SON, THE, Book *see* John O'Hara

DOCTORS WEAR SCARLET, Novel *see* Simon Raven

DOCTORS' WIVES, Novel *see* Frank G. Slaughter

DOCTORS' WIVES, New York 1930, Play *see* Henry Lieferant, Sylvia Lieferant

DOCUMENTO, IL, Play *see* Guglielmo Zorzi

DOCUMENTS A VENDRE, Novel *see* Jean Bruce

DODEN KOMMER TIL MIDDAG, Novel *see* Peter Sander

DODES TJERN, DE, 1942, Novel *see* Andre Bjerke

DODICI ANNI DOPO, 1917, Play *see* Giovanni Grasso Sr.

DODSDANSEN, 1901, Play *see* August Strindberg

DODSWORTH, New York 1929, Novel *see* Sinclair Lewis

DOG MEAT, Story *see* Peter B. Kyne

DOG OF FLANDERS, A, New York 1872, Novel *see* Ouida

DOG OF THE REGIMENT, A, Story *see* Albert S. Howson

DOG SHOW MURDER, 1938, Short Story *see* Frank Gruber

DOG SOLDIERS, 1974, Novel *see* Robert Stone

DOGKESELYU, Novel *see* Miklos Munkcasi

DOGS IN AN OMNIBUS, London 1942, Novel *see* Gladys Bronwyn Stern

DOGS OF WAR, THE, Novel *see* Frederick Forsyth

DOG'S TALE, A, Short Story *see* Mark Twain

DOIGTS DE FEE, LES, 1858, Play *see* Ernest Legouve, Eugene Scribe

DOKHODNOE MESTO, 1857, Play *see* Alexander Ostrovsky

DOKKOISHO, 1967, Novel *see* Shusaku Endo

DOKTOR FAUSTUS, 1947, Novel *see* Thomas Mann

DOKTOR GLAS, 1905, Novel *see* Hjalmar Soderberg

DOKTOR GRASLER, 1917, Short Story *see* Arthur Schnitzler

DOKTOR VYERA, 1966, Novel *see* Boris Nikolaevich Polevoy

DOKTOR ZHIVAGO, 1957, Novel *see* Boris Pasternak

DOKURITSU GURENTAI, Novel *see* S. Sekizawa

DOLL FACE, Play *see* Louise Hovick

DOLL MAKER, THE, 1954, Novel *see* Harriette Arnow

DOLLAR, 1926, Play *see* Hjalmar Bergman

DOLLAR BOTTOM AND TAYLOR'S FINEST HOUR, Book *see* J. Kennaway

DOLLAR MARK, THE, New York 1909, Play *see* George Broadhurst

DOLLARS, Play *see* Raoul Praxy

DOLLARS AND CENTS, New York 1917, Novel *see* Albert Payson Terhune

DOLL'S EYES, Novel *see* Bari Wood

DOLORES, LA, Opera *see* Tomas Breton, Jose Feliu Y Codina

DOLORETES, Opera *see* Carlos Arniches, M. Quislant, Amadeo Vives

DOLOVAI NABOB LEANYA, A, 1894, Play *see* Ferenc Herczeg

DOM CASMURRO, 1899, Novel *see* Joaquim Maria Machado de Assis

DOM S MEZONINOM, 1896, Short Story *see* Anton Chekhov

DOMANDA DIM MATRIMONIO, UNA, Play *see* Anton Chekhov

DOMAREN, 1957, Play *see* Vilhelm Moberg

DOMBEY AND SON, London 1848, Novel *see* Charles Dickens

DOMENICA DELLA BUONA GENTE, LA, Radio Play *see* Giandomenico Giagni, Vasco Pratolini

DOMINANT SEX, THE, London 1934, Play *see* Michael Egan

DOMINGO A TARDE, 1961, Novel *see* Fernando Namora

DOMINO, 1932, Play *see* Marcel Achard

DOMINO NOIR, LE, Paris 1837, Opera *see* Daniel Francois Auber

DOMINO PRINCIPLE, THE, Novel *see* Adam Kennedy

DOMINQUE, Play *see* Yvan Noe

DOMNISOARA AURICA, 1962, Short Story *see* Eugen Barbu

DOMNISOARA NASTASIA, 1928, Play *see* George Mihail Zamfirescu

DON ALVARO O LA FUERZO DEL SINO, 1835, Play *see* Angelo Perez de Saavedra

DON AMONG THE DEAD MEN, London 1952, Novel *see* C. E. Vulliamy

DON BUONAPARTE, Play *see* Giovacchino Forzano

DON CAMILLO E I GIOVANI D'OGGI, Novel *see* Giovanni Guareschi

DON CARELESS, 1930, Novel *see* Rex Beach

DON CARLOS, 1787, Play *see* Friedrich von Schiller

DON CESAR DE BAZAN, 1844, Play *see* Adolphe-P. d'Ennery, Philippe F. Pinel

DON CHICAGO, Novel *see* C. E. Bechhofer-Roberts

DON D'ADELE, LE, Play *see* Pierre Barillet, Jean-Pierre Gredy

DON GIL DALLE CALZE VERDI, Novel *see* Tirso de Molina

DON GIL VON DEN GRUNEN HOSEN, Story *see* Tirso de Molina

DON GIOVANNI, Prague 1787, Opera *see* Lorenzo Da Ponte, Wolfgang Amadeus Mozart

DON GIOVANNI IN SICILIA, 1941, Novel *see* Vitaliano Brancati

DON, I, Play *see* Pippo Marchese

DON JUAN, 1665, Play *see* Moliere

DON JUAN D'AUTRICHE, Play *see* Casimir Delavigne

DON JUAN TENORIO, 1844, Play *see* Jose Zorrilla Y Moral

DON JUAN UND FAUST, 1829, Play *see* Christian Dietrich Grabbe

DON JUANS DREI NACHTE, Berlin 1917, Novel *see* Ludwig Biro

DON KING: ONLY IN AMERICA, Book *see* Jack Newfield

DON PABLO DON PEDRO A VERA LUKASOVA, Novel *see* Bozena Benesova

DON PASQUALE, Opera *see* Michele Accursi

DON PASQUALE, Paris 1843, Opera *see* Gaetano Donizetti

DON PEON, Novel *see* Johnston McCulley

DON PIETRO CARUSO, 1895, Play *see* Roberto Bracco

DON Q'S LOVE STORY, New York 1925, Novel *see* Hesketh Prichard, Kate Prichard

DON QUINTIN EL AMARGAO, Opera *see* Carlos Arniches, Antonio Estremera

DON SEGUNDO SOMBRA, 1926, Novel *see* Ricardo Guiraldes

DONA BARBARA, 1929, Novel *see* Romulo Gallegos

DONA FLOR E SUE DOIS MARIDOS, 1966, Novel *see* Jorge Amado

DONA MARIA LA BRAVA, 1909, Play *see* Eduardo Marquina

DONA PERFECTA, Madrid 1876, Novel *see* Benito Perez Galdos

DONATIENNE, Novel *see* Rene Bazin

DONG XIE XI DU, Novel *see* Jin Yong

DONGWU XIONGMENG, Novel *see* Wang Shuo

DONKERE KAMER VAN DAMOCLES, DE, 1958, Novel *see* Willem Frederik Hermans

DONNA CHE INVENTO L'AMORE, LA, Novel *see* Guido Da Verona

DONNA DEL LAGO, LA, Novel *see* Giovanni Comisso

DONNA DELLA DOMENICO, LA, Novel *see* Fruttero, Lucentini

DONNA IN GUERRA, Novel *see* Dacia Maraini

DONNA INVISIBILE, 1970, Short Story *see* Alberto Moravia

DONNA PERDUTA, LA, Opera *see* Guglielmo Giannini, Giuseppe Pietri, Guglielmo Zorzi

DONNA, UNA, 1892, Play *see* Roberto Bracco

DONNE ALLA FESTA DI DEMETRA, LA, Play *see* Aristophanes

DONNE MUOIONO, LE, Novel *see* Anna Banti

DONNEGAN, New York 1923, Novel *see* George Owen Baxter

DONNIE BRASCO: MY UNDERCOVER LIFE IN THE MAFIA, Book *see* Joseph D. Pistone, Richard Woodley

DONO DEL MATTINO, IL, Play *see* Giovacchino Forzano

DONOGOO, Novel *see* Jules Romains

DONOGOO-TONKA OU LES MIRACLES LA SCIENCE, 1920, Short Story *see* Jules Romains

DONOVAN AFFAIR, THE, New York 1926, Play *see* Owen Davis

DONOVAN'S BRAIN, New York 1943, Novel *see* Curt Siodmak

DON'S PARTY, 1973, Play *see* David Williamson

DONSKIE RASSKAZY, 1926, Short Story *see* Mikhail Sholokhov

DON'T ANSWER THE PHONE, Novel *see* Michael Curtis

DON'T DRINK THE WATER, New York 1966, Play *see* Woody Allen

DON'T EVER LEAVE ME, Story *see* Ben Barzman, Norma Barzman

DON'T EVER MARRY, 1919, Short Story *see* Edgar Franklin

DON'T FALL IN LOVE, Short Story *see* John B. Clymer

DON'T FALL IN LOVE, 1931, Play *see* Charles Beahan, Dorothy Speare

DON'T GO NEAR THE WATER, Novel *see* William Brinkley

DON'T LOOK AND IT WON'T HURT, Novel *see* Richard Peck

DON'T LOOK NOW, 1971, Short Story *see* Daphne Du Maurier

DON'T PANIC CHAPS, Radio Play *see* Michael Corston, Ronald Holroyd

DON'T RAISE THE BRIDGE - LOWER THE RIVER, New York 1960, Novel *see* Max Wilk

DON'T TAKE A CHANCE, 1918, Pamphlet *see* Charles Larned Robinson

DON'T YOU CARE!, 1914, Short Story *see* Rupert Hughes

DOOMSDAY, London 1927, Novel *see* Warwick Deeping

DOOR IN THE WALL, THE, 1911, Short Story *see* H. G. Wells

DOOR THAT HAS NO KEY, THE, Novel *see* Cosmo Hamilton

DOOR WITH SEVEN LOCKS, THE, London 1926, Novel *see* Edgar Wallace

DOORBELL RINGS, THE, Novel *see* Rex Stout

DOORMAT, THE, New York 1922, Play *see* Ethel Clifton, Brenda Fowler

DOORSTEPS, Play *see* Henry Edwards

DOP DOCTOR, THE, Novel *see* Richard Dehan

DOPE, New York 1909, Play *see* Joseph Medill Patterson

DOPPELGANGER, EIN, 1887, Short Story *see* Theodor Storm

DOPPELMENSCH, DER, Play *see* Wilhelm Jacobi, Arthur Lippschutz

DOPPELSELBSTMORD, 1876, Play *see* Ludwig Anzengruber

DOPPELTE LOTTCHEN, DAS, Vienna 1949, Novel *see* Erich Kastner

DOPPELTE MATTHIAS UND SEINE TOCHTER, DER, Berlin 1929, Novel *see* Meinrad Lienert

DOPPIA MORTE AL GOVERNO VECCHIO, Novel *see* Ugo Moretti

DORA, Poem *see* Alfred Tennyson

DORA, Paris 1877, Play *see* Victorien Sardou

DORA NELSON, Play *see* Louis Verneuil

DORA THORNE, New York 1880, Novel *see* Bertha M. Clay

DORK OF CORK, THE, Novel *see* Chet Raymo

DORMEZ, JE LE VEUX, Play *see* Georges Feydeau

DORNROSCHEN, Short Story *see* Jacob Grimm, Wilhelm Grimm

DORO NO KAWA, Novel *see* Teru Miyamoto

DOROTEJ, 1977, Novel *see* Dobrilo Nenadic

DOROTHEA ANGERMANN, 1926, Play *see* Gerhart Hauptmann

DOROTHY IN THE GARRET, Poem *see* John Townsend Trowbridge

DORP AAN DE RIVIER, Novel *see* Anton Coolen

DORTOIR DES GRANDES, Novel *see* Stanislas-Andre Steeman

DOS HOMBRES Y DOS MUJERES EN MEDIO, 1944, Novel *see* Juan Antonio de Zunzunegui

DOSSIER 51, LE, Novel *see* Gilles Perrault

DOSSIER NR. 113, LE, Paris 1867, Short Story *see* Emile Gaboriau

DOSSIER PROSTITUTION, Book *see* Dominique Dallayrac

DOTTOR ANTONIO, IL, 1855, Novel *see* Giovanni Ruffini

DOU ER YUAN, c1230, Play *see* Guan Hanqing

DOUA LOTURI, 1901, Short Story *see* Ion Luca Caragiale

DOUBLE AGENT, New York 1959, Novel *see* Gene Stackleborg

DOUBLE BARRELLED DETECTIVE STORY, A, New York 1902, Novel *see* Mark Twain

DOUBLE BELL WATCH, Novel *see* Lu Shi, Wen Da

DOUBLE CRIME SUR LA LIGNE MAGINOT, Novel *see* Pierre Nord

DOUBLE DEALING, Short Story *see* W. W. Jacobs

DOUBLE DOOR, New York 1933, Play *see* Elizabeth A. McFadden

DOUBLE ERROR, 1935, Play *see* J. Lee Thompson

DOUBLE EVENT, THE, 1917, Play *see* Sidney Blow, Douglas Hoare

DOUBLE EXISTENCE DE LORD SAMSEY, LA, Novel *see* Georges Le Faure

DOUBLE EXISTENCE DU DOCTEUR MORART, LA, Play *see* Andre de Lorde, Dr. Toulouse

DOUBLE HARNESS, London 1933, Play *see* Edward Poor Montgomery

DOUBLE INDEMNITY, 1943, Novel *see* James M. Cain

DOUBLE LIFE OF MR. ALFRED BURTON, THE, 1914, Novel *see* E. Phillips Oppenheim

DOUBLE PIEGE, LE, Play *see* Berr de Turique

DOUBLE TAKE, Story *see* Roy Huggins

DOUBLE, THE, London 1928, Novel *see* Edgar Wallace

DOUBLE TROUBLE, Indianapolis 1906, Novel *see* Herbert Quick

DOUBLE-DYED DECEIVER, A, 1905, Short Story *see* O. Henry

DOUBLING FOR CUPID, 1924, Short Story *see* Nina Wilcox Putnam

DOUBLING FOR LORA, Story *see* Peggy Gaddis

DOUBTERS, THE, Novel *see* George Tabori

DOUCE, Novel *see* Michel Davet

DOUGHGIRLS, THE, New York 1942, Play *see* Joseph Fields

DOULEUR, LA, Novel *see* E. M. Laumann

DOULOREUSE, LA, 1897, Novel *see* Maurice Donnay

DOULOS, LE, Paris 1957, Novel *see* Pierre Lesou

DOULOUREUSE ARCADIE, Novel *see* Peter Mendelssohn

DOUTE, LE, Play *see* Daniel Jourda

DOVE, THE, Book *see* Derek Gill, Robin Lee Graham

DOVE, THE, New York 1925, Play *see* Willard Mack

DOVER ROAD, THE, New York 1921, Play *see* A. A. Milne

DOWN OUR STREET, Play *see* Ernest George

DOWN RIVER, Novel *see* Seamark

DOWN THERE, New York 1956, Novel *see* David Goodis

DOWN UNDER DONOVAN, London 1918, Novel *see* Edgar Wallace

DOWN WITH WOMEN, Story *see* George Frank Worts

DOWNHILL, London 1926, Play *see* Constance Collier, Ivor Novello

DOWNHILL RACERS, New York 1963, Novel *see* Oakley Hall

DOZIVLJAJI NIKOLETINE BURSACA, 1956, Short Story *see* Branko Copic

DR. BESSELS VERWANDLUNG, Novel *see* Ludwig Wolff

DR. COOK'S GARDEN, Play *see* Ira Levin

DR. FISCHER OF GENEVA; OR THE BOMB PARTY, 1980, Novel *see* Graham Greene

DR. MABUSE, Novel *see* Norbert Jacques

DR. MASON'S TEMPTATION, Story *see* Hugh C. Weir

DR. MED. HIOB PRATORIUS, 1934, Play *see* Curt Goetz

DR. MURKES GESAMMELES SCHWEIGEN, 1958, Short Story *see* Heinrich Boll

DR. NO, London 1958, Novel *see* Ian Fleming

DR. O'DOWD, Novel *see* L. A. G. Strong

DR. SLAUGHTER, 1984, Novel *see* Paul Theroux

DR. SYN, Novel *see* William Russell Thorndike

DRACUA PERE ET FILS, Novel *see* Claude Klotz

DRACULA, London 1897, Novel *see* Bram Stoker

DRAG, Boston 1925, Play *see* William Dudley Pelley

DRAG-NET, THE, Play *see* Willard Mack

DRAGON MURDER CASE; A PHILO VANCE STORY, THE, New York 1933, Novel *see* S. S. Van Dine

DRAGON PAINTER, THE, Boston 1906, Novel *see* Mary McNeil Fenollosa

DRAGON SEED, THE, 1942, Novel *see* Pearl Buck

DRAGONI AZZURRI, I, Novel *see* L. Gramegna

DRAGON'S DAUGHTER, THE, New York 1912, Novel *see* Clyde C. Westover

DRAGON'S TEETH; A PROBLEM OF DEDUCTION, THE, Story *see* Ellery Queen

DRAGONWYCK, 1944, Novel *see* Anya Seton

DRAKE, London 1912, Play *see* Louis N. Parker

DRAMA NA OKHOTE, 1884, Short Story *see* Anton Chekhov

DRAMA NUEVO, UN, 1867, Play *see* Manuel Tamayo Y Baus

DRAME AU BORD DE LA MER, UN, *see* Honore de Balzac

DRAME DE VILLESAUGE, LE, Novel *see* Paul de Garros

DRAME DES CHARMETTES, LE, *see* Henri Demesse

DRAME DU 23, LE, Play *see* A. Bourgain, Paul Gavault

DRAMMA, Short Story *see* Grazia Deledda

DRAMMA BORGHESE, UN, Novel *see* Guido Morselli

DRAPEAU NOIR FLOTTE SUR LA MARMITE, LE, Novel *see* Rene Fallet

DRAUSSEN VON DER TUR, 1947, Play *see* Wolfgang Borchert

DREADFUL SUMMIT, Novel *see* Stanley Ellin

DREAM GIRL, New York 1945, Play *see* Elmer Rice

DREAM GIRL, THE, Play *see* Willard Mack

DREAM MERCHANTS, THE, Novel *see* Harold Robbins

DREAM MONGER, THE, Novel *see* Grant Hinden Miller

DREAM OF EUGENE ARAM, THE, Poem *see* Thomas Hood

DREAM OF KINGS, A, New York 1966, Novel *see* Harry Mark Petrakis

DREAM SHIP, THE, Poem *see* Eugene Field

DREAM, THE, Novel *see* Rafael Sabatini

DREAM, THE, Short Story *see* O. Henry

DREAMHOUSE, Novel *see* Kate Grenville

DREAMLAND, New York 1935, Novel *see* Clarence Budington Kelland

DREAMS LOST DREAMS FOUND, Novel *see* Pamela Wallace

DREAM-WOMAN, THE, Boston 1873, Novel *see* Wilkie Collins

DREI BLAUE AUGEN, Play *see* Geza von Cziffra

DREI KAMERADEN, Switzerland 1937, Novel *see* Erich Maria Remarque

DREI MADCHEN AM SPINNRAD, Novel *see* Fedor von Zobeltitz

DREI MANNER IM SCHNEE, Zurich 1934, Novel *see* Erich Kastner

DREI NIEMANDSKINDER, DIE, Novel *see* Karl Rossler

DREI RINGE, DIE, Short Story *see* Paul Keller

DREI TAGE MITTELARREST, Play *see* Bobby E. Luthge, Karl Noti

DREI UM EDITH, DIE, Novel *see* Walther Harich

DREI WUNSCHE, Novel *see* Bela von Belogh

DREIGROSCHENOPER, DIE, Berlin 1928, Play *see* Bertolt Brecht

DRESSER, THE, Play *see* Ronald Harwood

DRESSMAKER, THE, Novel *see* Beryl Bainbridge

DREYFUS CASE, THE, Play *see* Wilhelm Herzog, Hans Rehfisch

DRIFT FENCE, New York 1932, Novel *see* Zane Grey

DRIFTING, New York 1910, Play *see* Daisy H. Andrews, John Colton

DRIFTWOOD, Play *see* Owen Davis

DRIFTWOOD, Story *see* Richard Harding Davis

DRIFTWOOD, 1918, Short Story *see* Albert Payson Terhune

DRIVE HE SAID, 1964, Novel *see* Jeremy Larner

DRIVE, THE, Play *see* Adam Barken

DRIVEN, London 1914, Play *see* E. Temple Thurston

DRIVER'S SEAT, THE, 1970, Novel *see* Muriel Spark

DRIVIN' FOOL, THE, 1922, Short Story *see* William F. Sturm

DRIVING MISS DAISY, 1987, Play *see* Alfred Uhry

DROIT DE L'ENFANT, LE, Novel *see* Georges Ohnet

DROLE DE JEU, 1945, Novel *see* Roger Vailland

DROLE DE NUMERO, UN, Short Story *see* Georges Dolley

DROLE DE PISTOLET, Novel *see* Francis Ryck

DROOMKONINKJE, 1924, Novel *see* Herman Heijermans

DROWNING POOL, THE, Novel *see* Ross MacDonald

DRUGSTORE COWBOY, Novel *see* James Foyle

DRUM, Novel *see* Kyle Onstott

DRUM, THE, 1923, Short Story *see* F. Britten Austin

DRUM, THE, 1937, Novel *see* A. E. W. Mason

DRUMS ALONG THE MOHAWK, Boston/New York 1936, Novel *see* Walter D. Edmonds

DRUMS OF JEOPARDY, New York 1920, Novel *see* Harold MacGrath

DRUSILLA WITH A MILLION, New York 1916, Novel *see* Elizabeth Cooper

DRUZBA PERE KVRZICE, Novel *see* Marte Lovrak

DRY CHECK CHARLIE, Story *see* George Patullo

DRY MARTINI: A GENTLEMAN TURNS TO LOVE, New York 1926, Novel *see* John Thomas

DRY ROT, London 1954, Play *see* John Chapman

DRY VALLEY JOHNSON, Short Story *see* O. Henry

DRY WHITE SEASON, A, 1979, Novel *see* Andre Brink

DSCHUNGEL, Play *see* Joseph Maria Franck

DU BARRY, New York 1901, Play *see* David Belasco

DU BARRY WAS A LADY, New York 1939, Musical Play *see* Buddy De Sylva, Herbert Fields, Cole Porter

DU GRABUGE CHEZ LES VEUVES, Novel *see* Jean-Pierre Ferniere

DU HAUT EN BAS, Play *see* Ladislaus Bus-Fekete

DU MOURON POUR LES PETITS OISEAUX, Novel *see* Albert Simonin

DU RAISINE DANS LE GAS-OIL, Novel *see* Georges Bayle

DU RIFIFI A PANAME, Paris 1965, Novel *see* Auguste Le Breton

DU RIFIFI CHEZ LES FEMMES, Paris 1957, Novel *see* Auguste Le Breton

DU RIFIFI CHEZ LES HOMMES, Novel *see* Auguste Le Breton

DU SANG SOUS LE CHAPITEAU, Novel *see* Leopold Massiera

DU UND ICH, Novel *see* Eberhard Frowein

DUB, THE, 1916, Short Story *see* Edgar Franklin

DUBARRY, DIE, Operetta *see* Karl Millocker

DUBARRY, THE, Opera *see* Paul Knepler, J. M. Welleminsky

DUBLINERS, 1914, Short Story *see* James Joyce

DUBROVSKY, 1841, Short Story *see* Alexander Pushkin

DUCA E FORSE UNA DUCHESSA, Play *see* Santiago Salvich

DUCHESSA DEL BAL TABARIN, LA, 1916, Opera *see* Arturo Franci, Carlo Vizzotto

DUCHESSE DE LANGEAIS, LA, 1839, Novel *see* Honore de Balzac

DUCHESSE DES FOLIES-BERGERE, LA, Play *see* Georges Feydeau

DUCHESSINA, LA, 1903, Play *see* Alfredo Testoni

DUDE WRANGLER, THE, Garden City, N.Y. 1921, Novel *see* Caroline Lockhart

DUDLEY DOES IT, Play *see* Tod Waller

DUDS, New York 1920, Novel *see* Henry C. Rowland

DUE COSCIENZE, LE, 1900, Play *see* Gerolamo Rovetta

DUE DOZZINE DI ROSE SCARLATTE, Play *see* Aldo de Benedetti

DUE MADRI, LE, Poem *see* Arnaldo Fusinato

DUE MAESTRI, I, 1957, Short Story *see* Mario Soldati

DUE OCCHI PER NON VEDERE, Play *see* Pietro Solari

DUE RIVALI, LE, Novel *see* Georges Ohnet

DUE SERGENTI, I, Novel *see* Paolo Lorenzini

DUE TIGRI, LE, 1904, Novel *see* Emilio Salgari

DUEL, Novel *see* Rene Jeanne

DUEL, Short Story *see* Richard Matheson

DUEL, 1891, Short Story *see* Anton Chekhov

DUEL IN THE SUN, Novel *see* Niven Busch

DUEL, LE, 1905, Play *see* Henri Lavedan

DUEL OF HEARTS, Novel *see* Barbara Cartland

DUEL, THE, 1908, Short Story *see* Joseph Conrad

DUELL MIT DIAMANTEN, Novel *see* Heinrich Rumpff

DUELLO, IL, 1868, *see* Paolo Ferrari

DUET, Play *see* Batty Davies

DUET FOR ONE, 1981, Play *see* Tom Kempinski

DUETT ZU DRITT, Play *see* Beatrice Ferrolli

DUI GENTILUOMINI VENEZIANI ONORATAMENTE DA LE MOGLIE SONO., Novel *see* Matteo Maria Bandello

DUIOS ANASTASIA TRECEA, 1967, Short Story *see* Dumitru Radu Popescu

DUKE COMES BACK, THE, Garden City, N.Y. 1933, Novel *see* Lucian Cary

DUKE OF CHIMNEY BUTTE, THE, Chicago 1920, Novel *see* George Washington Ogden

DUKE'S SON, Novel *see* Cosmo Hamilton

DUKKEHJEM, ET, Copenhagen 1879, Play *see* Henrik Ibsen

DULCE NOMBRE, 1921, Novel *see* Concha Espina de Serna

DULCE OLOR A MUERTE, UN, Novel *see* Guillermo Arriaga

DULCIMA, 1953, Short Story *see* H. E. Bates

DULCINEA, Novel *see* Gaston Baty

DULCY, New York 1921, Play *see* Marc Connelly, George S. Kaufman

DUM NA PREDMESTI, Novel *see* Karel Polacek

DUM ZTRACENEHO STESTI, Novel *see* Bohumil Zahradnik-Brodsky

DUMB MAN OF MANCHESTER, THE, London 1837, Play *see* B. F. Rayner

DUMB WAITER, THE, 1960, Play *see* Harold Pinter

DUMBRAVA MINUNATA, 1926, Novel *see* Mihail Sadoveanu

DUMMY, THE, New York 1914, Play *see* Harriet Ford, Harvey J. O'Higgins

DUNE, 1965, Novel *see* Frank Herbert

DUNUNGEN, 1894, Short Story *see* Selma Lagerlof

DUNWICH HORROR, THE, 1933, Short Story *see* H. P. Lovecraft

DUO, Short Story *see* Sidonie Gabrielle Colette

DUO YIN, Play *see* Wang Hong

DUPLICITY OF HARGRAVES, THE, 1902, Short Story *see* O. Henry

DUQUESA DE BENAMEJI, LA, 1932, Play *see* Antonio Machado Y Ruiz, Manuel Machado Y Ruiz

DURAND BIJOUTIER, Play *see* Leopold Marchand

DURCHGANGERIN, DIE, Play *see* Ludwig Fulda

DURCHLAUCHT RADIESCHEN, Play *see* Julius Freund

DURCHS WILDE KURDISTAN, Novel *see* Karl Friedrich May

DURIAN TREE, THE, New York 1960, Novel *see* Michael Keon

DUST AND SUN, 1928, Short Story *see* Clements Ripley

DUST BE MY DESTINY, Novel *see* Jerome Odlum

DUST OF DESIRE, New York 1922, Novel *see* Margaret Peterson

DUST OF EGYPT, THE, London 1912, Play *see* Alan Campbell

DUSTY, Novel *see* Frank Dalby Davison

DUSTY ERMINE, London 1935, Play *see* Neil Grant

DUTCHMAN, New York 1964, Play *see* Leroi Jones

DUTY AND THE MAN, Novel *see* James Oliver Curwood

DUVIDHA, Short Story *see* Vijaydan Detha

DUWATA MAWAKA MISA, Short Story *see* G. B. Senanayake

DUYEN NGHIEP, Short Story *see* Luu Son Minh

DVADTSAT DNEI BEZ VOINI, 1973, Short Story *see* Konstantin Simonov

DVE MATKY, Novel *see* Emilie Richebourg

DVENADTSAT STULYEV, Moscow 1928, Novel *see* Ilya Ilf, Evgeny Petrov

DVOJI ZIVOT, Novel *see* Vavrinec Rehor

DVORYANSKOE GNEZDO, 1859, Novel *see* Ivan Turgenev

DVOYNIK, 1846, Novel *see* Fyodor Dostoyevsky

DWAALLICHT, HET, 1947, Short Story *see* Willem Elsschot

DWELLING PLACE, THE, Novel *see* Catherine Cookson

DWELLING-PLACE OF LIGHT, THE, New York 1917, Novel *see* Winston Churchill

DYADYA VANYA, 1899, Play *see* Anton Chekhov

DYADYUSHKIN SON, 1859, Short Story *see* Fyodor Dostoyevsky

DYCKERPOTTS ERBEN, Play *see* Robert Grotzach

DYDEN GAR AMOK, Novel *see* Knud Poulsen

DYING DETECTIVE, THE, Short Story *see* Arthur Conan Doyle

DYING ROOM ONLY, Short Story *see* Richard Matheson

DYING YOUNG, Novel *see* Marty Leimbach

DYNAMITE GIRL, Novel *see* Paul Gerrard

DYNASTY, Novel *see* James A. Michener

DYSCOLUS, 316 bc, Play *see* Menander

DZHAMILIA, 1958, Short Story *see* Chingiz Aitmatov

DZHESSI I MORGIANA, 1928, Novel *see* Aleksandr Grin

DZIEJE GRZECHU, 1908, Novel *see* Stefan Zeromski

DZIEJE JEDNOGO POCISKU, 1910, Novel *see* Andrzej Strug

DZIEWCZETA Z NOWOLIPEK, 1935, Novel *see* Pola Gojawiczynska

D-ZUG 517, Novel *see* Maria von Peteani

E CADUTA UNA DONNA, Novel *see* Milly Dandolo

E TORNATO CARNEVALE, Play *see* Guido Cantini

EACH ACCORDING TO HIS GIFTS, Short Story *see* Earl Derr Biggers

EACH DAWN I DIE, Indianapolis 1938, Novel *see* Jerome Odlum

EAGLE HAS LANDED, THE, Novel *see* Jack Higgins

EAGLE ISLAND, Novel *see* Mats Helge

EAGLE SQUADRON, 1942, Short Story *see* C. S. Forester

EAGLE'S MATE, THE, New York 1914, Novel *see* Anna Alice Chapin

EAGLE'S NEST, THE, New York 1887, Play *see* Edwin Arden

EARL OF CHICAGO, THE, New York 1937, Novel *see* Brock Williams

EARL OF PAWTUCKET, THE, New York 1903, Play *see* Augustus Thomas

EARLY BIRD, THE, Play *see* J. MacGregor Douglas

EARLY LIFE AND ADVENTURES OF SYLVIA SCARLETT, THE, New York 1918, Novel *see* Compton Mackenzie

EARTHLY POSSESSIONS, 1977, Novel *see* Anne Tyler

EASIEST WAY, THE, Hartford, Ct. 1908, Play *see* Eugene Walter

EAST IS EAST, Play *see* Philip Hubbard, Gwendolyn Logan

EAST IS EAST, 1920, Short Story *see* Lloyd Osbourne

EAST IS WEST, Play *see* John B. Hymer, Samuel Shipman

EAST LYNNE, London 1861, Novel *see* Mrs. Henry Wood

EAST OF EDEN, 1952, Novel *see* John Steinbeck

EAST OF LUDGATE HILL, Play *see* Arnold Ridley

EAST OF PICCADILLY, Novel *see* Gordon Beckles

EAST OF SUEZ, London 1922, Play *see* W. Somerset Maugham

EAST RIVER, New York 1935, Novel *see* Borden Chase, Edward Doherty

EAST SIDE - WEST SIDE, Novel *see* Marcia Davenport

EAST SIDE - WEST SIDE, Play *see* Henry Hull, Leighton Graves Osmun

EAST SIDE - WEST SIDE, New York 1927, Novel *see* Felix Riesenberg

EASTER DINNER, THE, New York 1960, Novel *see* Donald C. Downes

EASTWARD HO!, 1919, Serial Story *see* William MacLeod Raine

EASY AND HARD WAYS OUT, Novel *see* Robert Grossbach

EASY COME EASY GO, New York 1925, Play *see* Owen Davis

EASY MONEY, Novel *see* K. R. G. Browne

EASY MONEY, 1947, Play *see* Arnold Ridley

EASY PICKINGS, Play *see* Paul A. Cruger

EASY VIRTUE, London 1926, Play *see* Noel Coward

EAT A BOWL OF TEA, Novel *see* Louis Chu

EAU DES COLLINES VOL. 1: JEAN DE FLORETTE, L', 1963, Novel *see* Marcel Pagnol

EAU DES COLLINES VOL. 2: MANON DES SOURCES, L', 1963, Novel *see* Marcel Pagnol

EAU DU NIL, L', Novel *see* Pierre Frondaie

EAUX TROUBLES, LES, Short Story *see* Roger Vercel

EBB TIDE; A TRIO AND QUARTETTE, THE, 1894, Novel *see* Lloyd Osbourne, Robert Louis Stevenson

EBONY TOWER, THE, Novel *see* John Fowles

EBREO FASCISTA, L', Novel *see* Luigi Preti

ECCE HOMO, Play *see* Charles P. Carr, Walter Meyjes

ECHAPPEMENT LIBRE, Novel *see* Clet Coroner

ECHEANCE, L', Short Story *see* Paul Bourget

ECHEC AU PORTEUR, Novel *see* Noel Calef

ECHEC AU ROY, *see* Henri Dupuy-Mazuel

ECHEE AU DESTIN, 1950, Novel *see* Francis d'Autheville

ECHO OF BARBARA, Novel *see* Jonathan Burke

ECHO, THE, Novel *see* Minette Walters

ECHOES IN THE DARKNESS, Novel *see* Joseph Wambaugh

ECHOES OF CELANDINE, Novel *see* Derek Marlowe

ECHOES THAT OLD REFRAIN, 1937, Short Story *see* Corey Ford

ECOLE DE LA CHAIR, L', Novel *see* Yukio Mishima

ECOLE DES COCOTTES, L', Play *see* Paul Armont, Marcel Gerbidon

ECOLE DES CONTRIBUABLES, L', Play *see* Georges Berr, Louis Verneuil

ECORNIFLEUR, L', Novel *see* Jules Renard

ECRAN BRISE, L', Novel *see* Henri Bordeaux

ECUME DES JOURS, L', 1947, Novel *see* Boris Vian

ECUYERE, L', Novel *see* Paul Bourget

EDDIE AND THE CRUISERS, Novel *see* P. F. Kluge

EDDIE CHAPMAN STORY, THE, London 1953, Biography *see* Frank Owen

EDDIE MACON'S RUN, Novel *see* James McLendon

EDELWEISSKONIG, DER, Novel *see* Ludwig Ganghofer

EDEN END, Play *see* J. B. Priestley

EDERA, L', Novel *see* Grazia Deledda

EDES ANNA, 1926, Novel *see* Dezso Kosztolanyi

EDGAR ET SA BONNE, Play *see* Eugene Labiche

EDGE O'BEYOND, Novel *see* Gertrude Page

EDGE OF DARKNESS, Novel *see* William Woods

EDGE OF DOOM, 1949, Novel *see* Leo Brady

EDGE OF RUNNING WATER, THE, Story *see* William Sloane

EDITHA'S BURGLAR, New York 1887, Play *see* Augustus Thomas

EDITH'S BURGLAR, Boston 1878, Novel *see* Frances Hodgson Burnett

EDITH'S DIARY, 1977, Novel *see* Patricia Highsmith

EDLE BLUT, DAS, Short Story *see* Ernst von Wildenbruch

EDNA BALGARKA, 1899, Short Story *see* Ivan Vazov

EDOUARD, Novel *see* Jacques Carton

EDOUARD VII ET SON TEMPS, 1933, Novel *see* Andre Maurois

EDUCATED EVANS, 1924, Novel *see* Edgar Wallace

EDUCATING RITA, 1981, Play *see* Willy Russell

EDUCATION DE PRINCE, 1895, Play *see* Charles Maurice Donnay

EDUCATION FOR DEATH, Book *see* Gregor Ziemer

EDUCATION OF LITTLE TREE, THE, Novel *see* Forrest Carter

EDUCATION OF MR. PIPP, THE, New York 1905, Play *see* Charles Dana Gibson, Augustus Thomas

EDUCATION OF NICKY, THE, Novel *see* May Wynn

EDUCATION SENTIMENTALE, L', 1869, Novel *see* Gustave Flaubert

EDWARD II, 1594, Play *see* Christopher Marlowe

EDWARD MY SON, London 1947, Play *see* Noel Langley, Robert Morley

EEMI HAGENERALIT, Play *see* Eli Saagi

EFFECT OF GAMMA RAYS ON MAN-IN-THE-MOON MARIGOLDS, THE, New York 1965, Play *see* Paul Zindel

EFFI BRIEST, 1894-95, Novel *see* Theodor Fontane

EFFICIENCY EDGAR'S COURTSHIP, 1916, Short Story *see* Clarence Budington Kelland

EFFRACTION, Novel *see* Francis Ryck

EFTER, 1947, Play *see* Carl Erik Soya

EGG AND I, THE, Novel *see* Betty MacDonald

EGI MADAR, 1935, Short Story *see* Zsigmond Moricz

EGOUTS DU PARADIS, LES, Novel *see* Albert Spaggiari

EGRI CSILLAGOK, 1901, Novel *see* Geza Gardonyi

EGY - KETTO - HAROM, Budapest 1929, Play *see* Ferenc Molnar

EGYPT, Story *see* Ernest Pascal

EGYPT, New York 1912, Play *see* Edward Sheldon

EH?, London 1964, Play *see* Henry Livings

EHE DES HERRN MISSISSIPPI, DIE, Zurich 1952, Play *see* Friedrich Durrenmatt

EHE FUR EINE NACHT, Play *see* Josef Berger, Franz Seitz Sr.

EHE IM SCHATTEN, Novel *see* Hans Schweikart

EHE IN DOSEN, Play *see* Leo Lenz, Ralph Arthur Roberts

EHERINGE, Play *see* Alexander Engel, Hans Sturm

EHESKANDAL IM HAUSE FROMONT JUN. UND RISLER SEN., Novel *see* Alphonse Daudet

EHESTREIK, Play *see* Julius Pohl

EHRENWORT, DAS, Novel *see* Arthur Zapp

EI KOSKAAN HUOMISPAIVAA, 1942, Novel *see* Mika Waltari

EICHMANN IN MY HANDS, Book *see* Peter Z. Malkin, Harry Stein

EID DES STEPHAN HULLER, DER, Novel *see* Felix Hollaender

EIGER SANCTION, THE, Novel *see* Trevanian

EIGHT BELLS, 1891, Play *see* John F. Byrne

EIGHT BELLS, New York 1933, Play *see* Percy G. Mandley

EIGHT MEN OUT, Book *see* Eliot Asinof

EIGHT O'CLOCK IN THE MORNING, Story *see* Ray Nelson

EILEEN OF THE TREES, Novel *see* Henry de Vere Stacpoole

EINE DUMME GESCHICHTE, Novel *see* Paul Langenscheidt

EINE FRAU GENUGT NICHT?, Novel *see* Michael Graf Soltikow

EINE SELTSAME NACHT, Novel *see* Laurids Bruun

EINEN JUX WILL ER SICH MACHEN, 1844, Play *see* Johann Nestroy

EINER ZUVIEL AN BORD, Novel *see* Fred Andreas

EINGANG ZUR BUHNE, Novel *see* Vicki Baum

EINHORN, DAS, 1966, Novel *see* Martin Walser

EK KOSKAAN HUOMISPAIVAA, 1942, Novel *see* Mika Waltari

EKEL, DAS, Play *see* Toni Impekoven, Hans Reimann

EKKLISIAZUSAI, c392 bc, Play *see* Aristophanes

EKSZERRABLAS A VACI-UCCABAN, 1931, Play *see* Ladislaus Fodor

EKVINOCIJ, 1895, Play *see* Ivo Vojnovic

EL, Novel *see* Mercedes Pinto

EL ATZMI, Book *see* Galila Ron-Feder

EL CHE GUEVARA, Rome 1967, Book *see* Adriano Bolzoni

EL HAKIM, Novel *see* John Knittel

ELAMA JA AURINKO, 1916, Novel *see* Frans E. Sillanpaa

ELCKERLIJC, c1485, Play *see* Anon

ELDER BROTHER, THE, Novel *see* Anthony Gibbs

ELDER MISS BLOSSOM, THE, London 1898, Play *see* Ernest Hendrie, Metcalfe Wood

ELEANOR AND FRANKLIN, Book *see* Joseph P. Lash

ELECTION, 1998, Novel *see* Tom Perrotta

ELECTRA, 413 bc, Play *see* Euripides

ELECTRA, c409 bc, Play *see* Sophocles

ELECTRIC MAN, THE, Story *see* Len Colos, Harry J. Essex, Sid Schwartz

ELEGANT EDWARD, London 1928, Novel *see* Edgar Wallace

ELEGY WRITTEN IN A COUNTRY CHURCHYARD, 1751, Poem *see* Thomas Gray

ELEKTRA, Dresden 1909, Opera *see* Richard Strauss, Hugo von Hofmannsthal

ELENI, Book *see* Nicholas Gage

ELEPHANT IS WHITE, THE, Novel *see* Caryl Brahms, S. J. Simon

ELEPHANT MAN: A STUDY IN HUMAN DIGNITY, THE, Book *see* Ashley Montagu

ELEPHANT MAN AND OTHER REMINISCENCES, THE, Book *see* Sir Frederick Treves

ELEPHANT MAN, THE, Play *see* Bernard Pomerance

ELEPHANT WALK, 1949, Novel *see* Robert Standish

ELEVATION, L', 1917, Play *see* Henri Bernstein

ELEVENTH COMMANDMENT, THE, Play *see* Brandon Fleming

ELEVENTH HOUR, THE, Play *see* Lincoln J. Carter

ELEVENTH HOUR, THE, Novel *see* Ethel M. Dell

ELEVENTH VIRGIN, THE, New York 1924, Novel *see* Dorothy Day

ELI SJURSDOTTER, 1913, Novel *see* Johan Falkberget

ELIMINATOR, THE, London 1966, Novel *see* Andrew York

ELISE OU LA VRAIE VIE, Novel *see* Claire Etcherelli

ELISIR D'AMORE, L', Milan 1832, Opera *see* Felice Romani, Gaetano Donizetti

ELIXIERE DES TEUFELS, DIE, 1815-16, Novel *see* Ernst Theodor Amadeus Hoffmann

ELIXIR DU PERE GAUCHER, L', 1869, Short Story *see* Alphonse Daudet

ELIZA COMES TO STAY, London 1913, Play *see* H. V. Esmond

ELIZABETH OF LADYMEAD, 1948, Play *see* Frank Harvey

ELIZABETH THE QUEEN, New York 1930, Play *see* Maxwell Anderson

ELLA, Novel *see* Michael Stewart

ELLE COURT ELLE COURT LA BANLIEUE, Novel *see* Brigitte Gros

ELLE ET MOI, Novel *see* Jean Duche

ELLEN FOSTER, Book *see* Kaye Gibbons

ELLEN YOUNG, Play *see* Gabriel Enthoven, Edmund Goulding

ELLERY QUEEN, MASTER DETECTIVE, Novel *see* Ellery Queen

ELLIS ISLAND, Novel *see* Fred Mustard Stewart

ELLY PETERSEN, 1941, Novel *see* Mogens Klitgaard

ELMER GANTRY, 1927, Novel *see* Sinclair Lewis

ELMER THE GREAT, New York 1928, Play *see* George M. Cohan, Ring Lardner

ELOISA ESTA DEBAJO DE UN ALMENDRO, 1943, Play *see* Enrique Jardiel Poncela

ELOKUU, 1941, Novel *see* Frans E. Sillanpaa

ELOPE IF YOU MUST, Play *see* E. J. Rath

ELSIE VENNER, Novel *see* Oliver Wendell Holmes

ELSKERE, 1960, Novel *see* Terje Stigen

ELUS DE LA MER, LES, Short Story *see* Georges G. Toudouze

ELUSIVE GRAFT, THE, Story *see* Rex Beach

ELUSIVE ISABEL, Indianapolis 1909, Novel *see* Jacques Futrelle

ELUSIVE PIMPERNEL, THE, 1908, Novel *see* Baroness Orczy

ELVERHOJ, 1828, Play *see* Johan Ludvig Heiberg

ELVESZETT PARADICSOM, AZ, 1962, Play *see* Imre Sarkadi

EMANCIPATION OF AMBROSE, THE, Play *see* Evadne Price

EMANCYPANTKI, 1894, Novel *see* Boleslaw Prus

EMBARRASSMENT OF RICHES, THE, New York 1906, Play *see* Louis K. Anspacher

EMBER TRAGEDIAJA, AZ, 1863, Verse *see* Imre Madach

EMBEZZLER, THE, 1940, Short Story *see* James M. Cain

EMBRASSEZ-MOI, Play *see* Tristan Bernard, Yves Mirande

EMBRUJO DE SEVILLA, EL, Novel *see* Carlos Reyles

EMBRUJO, UN, Novel *see* Don Eliseo

EMBUSCADE, L', Play *see* Henri Kistemaeckers

EMERALD CITY, Play *see* David Williamson

EMERALD ILLUSION, THE, Novel *see* Ronald Bass

EMERALD OF THE EAST, Novel *see* Jerbanu Kothawala

EMERGENCY HOUSE, Story *see* Sidney Morgan

EMERGING FROM THE SEA, Novel *see* Wang Shuo

EMIGRANTI, GLI, Novel *see* Francesco Pastonchi

EMIL, Novel *see* Arthur Landsberger

EMIL UND DIE DETEKTIVE, Berlin 1928, Novel *see* Erich Kastner

EMILE; OU DE L'EDUCATION, 1762, Novel *see* Jean-Jacques Rousseau

EMILIA GALOTTI, 1772, Play *see* Gotthold Ephraim Lessing

EMMA, 1815, Novel *see* Jane Austen

EMMA AND I, Book *see* Sheila Hockens

EMMA ZUNZ, 1949, Short Story *see* Jorge Luis Borges

EMMANUELLE, Novel *see* Emmanuelle Arsan

EMMERDEUR, L', Play *see* Francis Veber

EMMETT STONE, Play *see* Michael Gurr

EMPEREUR DES PAUVRES, L', Novel *see* Felicien Champsaur

EMPEROR JONES, THE, New York 1920, Play *see* Eugene O'Neill

EMPEROR'S CANDLESTICKS, THE, London 1899, Novel *see* Baroness Orczy

EMPEROR'S SNUFFBOX, THE, Novel *see* John Dickson Carr

EMPFANG BEI DER WELT, 1956, Novel *see* Heinrich Mann

EMPIRE BUILDERS, 1916, Short Story *see* Mary Roberts Rinehart

EMPIRE DU DIAMANT, L', Paris 1914, Novel *see* Valentin Mandelstamm

EMPIRE OF THE ANTS, 1913, Short Story *see* H. G. Wells

EMPIRE OF THE SUN, 1984, Novel *see* J. G. Ballard

EMPIRE OF THEIR OWN: HOW THE JEWS INVENTED HOLLYWOOD, AN, Book *see* Neal Gabler

EMPORIA, New York 1961, Novel *see* Max Lamb, Harry Sanford

EMPREINTE DU DIEU, L', Novel *see* Maxence Van Der Meersch

EMPTY BEACH, THE, Novel *see* Peter Corris

EMPTY HANDS, Indianapolis 1924, Novel *see* Arthur Stringer

EMPTY HEARTS, 1924, Short Story *see* Evelyn Campbell

EMPTY HOLSTERS, New York 1936, Novel *see* Ed Earl Repp

EMPTY HOUSE, THE, 1903, Short Story *see* Arthur Conan Doyle

EMPTY POCKETS, New York 1915, Novel *see* Rupert Hughes

EMPTY SADDLES, Novel *see* Cherry Wilson

EN BORDEE, Play *see* Andre Heuze, Pierre Veber

EN CAS DE MALHEUR, 1956, Novel *see* Georges Simenon

EN DAG I OKTOBER, 1931, Novel *see* Sigurd Hoel

EN DETRESSE, Novel *see* Jules Mary

EN L'AIR! (IN THE AIR), New York 1918, Book *see* Bert Hall

EN LOPPE KAN OGSA GO, Novel *see* Jens Pedar Larsen

EN MASODIK FELESEGEN, AZ, 1907, Novel *see* Eugene Heltai

EN NATT I JULI, 1933, Novel *see* Jan Fridegard

ENCANTADES, THE, 1854, Short Story *see* Herman Melville

ENCHANTED APRIL, New York 1923, Novel *see* Elizabeth von Arnim

ENCHANTED BARN, THE, Philadelphia 1918, Novel *see* Grace Livingston Hill Lutz

ENCHANTED COTTAGE, THE, London 1922, Play *see* Arthur Wing Pinero

ENCHANTED HEARTS, Garden City, N.Y. 1917, Novel *see* Darragh Aldrich

ENCHANTED HILL, THE, New York 1924, Novel *see* Peter B. Kyne

ENCHANTED HOUR, THE, Novel *see* Paul Gallico

ENCHANTED KISS, THE, Short Story *see* O. Henry

ENCHANTED PROFILE, THE, Short Story *see* O. Henry

ENCHANTED VOYAGE, THE, 1936, Novel *see* Robert Nathan

ENCHANTEMENT, L', 1900, Play *see* Henry Bataille

ENCHANTMENT, Novel *see* E. Temple Thurston

ENCHANTMENT; A LITTLE GIRL'S FRIENDSHIP WITH MARK TWAIN, Novel *see* Dorothy Quick

END AS A MAN, 1947, Novel *see* Calder Willingham

END OF SLEEPLESS NIGHTS, Story *see* Kaoru Tsuruma

END OF THE AFFAIR, THE, 1951, Novel *see* Graham Greene

END OF THE GOLDEN WEATHER, THE, Play *see* Bruce Mason

END OF THE RIVER, THE, Novel *see* Desmond Holdridge

END OF THE ROAD, New York 1958, Novel *see* John Barth

END OF THE ROAD, THE, Play *see* H. Grattan Donnelly

END OF TRAGEDY, THE, Novel *see* Rachel Ingalls

ENDA SEGERN, DEN, Novel *see* Jan Guillou

ENDE VOM ANGANG, DAS, Novel *see* Michael Holzner

ENDLESS LOVE, Novel *see* Scott Spencer

ENDLESS NIGHT, Novel *see* Agatha Christie

ENDO, SHUSAKU, 1966, Novel *see* Chinmoku

ENEIDE, *see* Publio Virgilio Marone

ENEK A BUZAMEZOKROL, 1927, Novel *see* Ferenc Mora

ENEMIES, THE, Story *see* Morgan Robertson

ENEMIGOS DE LA MUJER, LOS, Novel *see* Vicente Blasco Ibanez

ENEMY BELOW, THE, 1956, Novel *see* D. A. Rayner

ENEMY COAST AHEAD, Book *see* Paul Brickhill, Guy Gibson

ENEMY MINE, Story *see* Barry Longyear

ENEMY TERRITORY, 1937, Short Story *see* Margaret Culkin Banning

ENEMY, THE, Short Story *see* Charlotte Armstrong

ENEMY, THE, New York 1915, Novel see George Randolph Chester, Lillian Chester

ENEMY, THE, New York 1925, Play see Channing Pollock

ENEMY TO THE KING, AN, New York 1896, Play see Robert N. Stephens

ENEMY WITHIN, THE, Novel see Charles W. Bailey II, Fletcher Knebel

ENFANT DE L'AMOUR, L', 1911, Play see Henry Bataille

ENFANT DE MA SOEUR, L', Play see Robert Francheville, Andre Mouezy-Eon

ENFANT DES HALLES, L', Novel see H. G. Magog

ENFANT DU MIRACLE, L', Play see Robert Charvay, Paul Gavault

ENFANT PRODIGE, L', Novel see Georges Dolley

ENFANT-ROI, L', Novel see Pierre Gilles

ENFANTS DE PARIS, Novel see Leon Sazie

ENFANTS D'EDOUARD, LES, Play see Casimir Delavigne

ENFANTS DU CAPITAINE GRANT; VOYAGE AUTOUR DU MONDE, LES, Paris 1867-68, Novel see Jules Verne

ENFANTS DU MARAIS, LES, Novel see Georges Montforez

ENFANTS TANNER, LES, Novel see Robert Walser

ENFANTS TERRIBLES, LES, 1925, Novel see Jean Cocteau

ENFER, L', Novel see Henri Barbusse

ENGEL DER SEINE HARFE VERSETZTE, DER, Novel see Charles Terrot

ENGEL MIT DEM FLAMMENSCHWERT, DER, Novel see Klaus Hellmer

ENGEL MIT DEM SAITENSPIEL, DER, Novel see Alois Johannes Lippl

ENGEL MIT DER POSAUNE, DER, Novel see Ernst Lothar

ENGELE VON LOEWEN, 1952, Novel see Carl Zuckmayer

ENGINEER'S THUMB, THE, Short Story see Arthur Conan Doyle

ENGLAND MADE ME, 1935, Novel see Graham Greene

ENGLISCHE HEIRAT, DIE, Novel see Ludwig von Wohl

ENGLISH PATIENT, THE, Novel see Michael Ondaatje

ENGLISH ROSE, THE, London 1890, Play see Robert Buchanan, George R. Sims

ENGLISHMAN'S HOME, AN, London 1909, Play see Guy Du Maurier

ENHORNINGEN, 1939, Short Story see Sigfrid Siwertz

ENIGMA OTILIEI, 1938, Novel see George Calinescu

ENIGMA SACRIFICE, Novel see Michael Barak

ENIGMATIQUE GENTLEMAN, L', Play see Alfred Gragnon

ENIGME AUX FOLIES BERGERE, Novel see Leo Malet

ENIGME, L', Play see Paul Hervieu

ENLEVEMENT, L', Story see John Lomax

ENNEMI PUBLIC NO. 2, L', Novel see Gerard Lecas

ENNEMI SANS VISAGE, L', Novel see Stanislas-Andre Steeman

ENNEMIE, L', Play see Andre-Paul Antoine

ENOCH, 1965, Short Story see Robert Bloch

ENOCH ARDEN, 1864, Poem see Alfred Tennyson

ENOLA GAY, Book see Max Morgan-Witts, Gordon Thomas

ENOUGH FOR HAPPINESS, Story see D. D. Beauchamp

ENRICO CARUSO, HIS LIFE AND DEATH, 1945, Biography see Dorothy Caruso

ENRICO IV, 1922, Play see Luigi Pirandello

ENSAYO DE UN CRIMEN, 1944, Novel see Rodolfo Usigli

ENTAS NYT NISKAVUORI?, 1953, Play see Hella Wuolijoki

ENTE KLINGELT UM ½ ACHT, DIE, Novel see Aage Stenthoft

ENTER D'ARCY, 1917, Short Story see Samuel Hopkins Adams

ENTER LAUGHING, New York 1958, Novel see Carl Reiner

ENTER MADAME!, New York 1920, Play see Gilda Archibald, Dorothea Donn-Byrne

ENTER SIR JOHN, London 1928, Play see Clemence Dane, Helen Simpson

ENTERREMENT DE MONSIEUR BOUVET, L', Novel see Georges Simenon

ENTERRO DA CAFETINA, O, 1967, Novel see Marcos Rey

ENTERTAINER, THE, London 1957, Play see John Osborne

ENTERTAINING MR. SLOANE, London 1964, Play see Joe Orton

ENTICEMENT, Novel see Clive Arden

ENTITY, THE, Novel see Frank Defilitta

ENTRE LE DEVOIR ET L'HONNEUR, Short Story see Paul Saunier

ENTRE NARANJOS, Novel see Vicente Blasco Ibanez

ENTRE ONZE HEURES ET MINUIT, Novel see Claude Luxel

ENTRETENIDAS, LAS, 1963, Play see Miguel Mihura Santos

ENVERS DU MUSIC-HALL, L', 1913, Novel see Sidonie Gabrielle Colette

ENVOY FROM MIRROR CITY, 1985, Autobiography see Janet Frame

ENVY MY SIMPLICITY, Novel see Rayner Barton

EPAVES, Novel see David Goodis

EPERVIER, L', 1914, Play see Francis de Croisset

EPHEBE DE SUBIACO, L', 1969, Short Story see Jean-Louis Curtis

EPISODE, Story see Walter Reisch

EPISODE OF SPARROWS, AN, Novel see Rumer Godden

EPISTLE TO BE LEFT IN THE EARTH, 1930, Verse see Archibald McLeish

EPITAPH FOR A SPY, 1938, Novel see Eric Ambler

EPITAPH FOR AN ENEMY, New York 1959, Novel see George Barr

EPOUSEZ-NOUS MONSIEUR, Play see Jean de Letraz

EPOUVANTE, L', Paris 1908, Novel see Maurice Level

EPOUX SCANDALEUX, LES, Novel see Fortune Paillot

EQUATORE, Play see Alessandro de Stefani

EQUIPAGE AU COMPLET, L', Paris 1957, Play see Robert Mallet

EQUIPAGE, L', Paris 1923, Novel see Joseph Kessel

EQUUS, 1973, Play see Peter Shaffer

E.R., Play see Josep M. Benet I Jornet

ER MO, Novel see Xu Baoqi

ER PIU DE ROMA, Novel see Marco Guglielmo, Lucio Mandara

ER YUE, 1930, Novel see Zhao Pingfu

ERASMUS MONTANUS, 1731, Play see Ludvig Holberg

ERASMUS WITH FRECKLES, New York 1963, Novel see John Haase

ERBE, DAS, Play see Felix Philippi

ERBE VON BJORNDAL, DAS, Novel see Trygve Gulbranssnen

ERBFORSTER, DER, 1853, Play see Otto Ludwig

ERBIN VOM ROSENHOF, Opera see Georg Queri

ERBSCHLEICHER, DIE, Play see Hans Alfred Kihn

ERDE, 1908, Play see Karl Schonherr

ERDGEIST, DER, 1895, Play see Frank Wedekind

ERECTIONS, EJACULATIONS, EXHIBITIONS AND TALES OF ORDINARY., Book see Charles Bukowski

EREDITA DELLA ZIO NICOLA, L', Play see Emo Bistolfi

EREDITA DELLO ZIO BUONANIMA, L', Play see Russo Giusti

EREDITA DELLO ZIO CANONICO, L', Play see Antonino Russo-Giusti

EREDITA FERRAMONTI, L', Novel see Gaetano Carlo Chelli

EREDITA, L', Florence 1889, Novel see Mario Pratesi

ERFINDER, DER, Play see Hansjorg Schneider

ERFOLGREICHE, DER, Novel see Hans Kades

ERIC, Book see Doris Lund

ERIK XIV, 1899, Play see August Strindberg

ERIKA, 1956, Novel see James McGovern

ERINNERUNGEN AN DIE ZUKUNFT, 1968, Book see Erich von Daeniken

ERIN'S ISLE, Play see Dion Boucicault

ERL KING, THE, Novel see Michel Tournier

ERLKONIG, DER, 1782, Verse see Johann Wolfgang von Goethe

ERNANI, 1830, see Victor Hugo

ERNEST LE REBELLE, 1937, Novel see Jacques Perret

ERNEST MALTRAVERS, Novel see Edward George Bulwer Lytton

ERNESTO, 1975, Novel see Umberto Saba

EROBERUNG DER ZITADELLE, DIE, 1972, Short Story see Gunter Herburger

EROE DEL NOSTRO TEMPO, UN, Novel see Vasco Pratolini

EROI, GLI, Novel see Rene Haward, Albert Kantof

EROISMO E AMORE, Play see Nando Vitali

ERROR OF JUDGEMENT, AN, Short Story see Anthony Gittins

ERSCHEINEN PFLICHT, Novel see Gerhard Holtz-Baumert

ERSTE POLKA, DIE, 1975, Novel see Horst Bienek

ERSTER KLASSE, Play see Ludwig Thoma

ERSTWHILE SUSAN, New York 1916, Play see Marian de Forest

ERZAHL MIR NICHTS, Novel see Jo Hanns Rosler

ERZHERZOG JOHANNS GROSSE LIEBE, Novel see Hans Gustl Kernmayr

ES FING SO HARMIOS AN, Play see Franz Gribitz

ES FLUSTERT DIE NACHT., Short Story see Guido Kreutzer

ES GESCHAH AM HELLICHTEN TAG, Story see Friedrich Durrenmatt

ES MI HOMBRE!, Play see Carlos Amiches

ES PELIGROSO ASOMARSE AL EXTERIOR, 1944, Play see Enrique Jardiel Poncela

ES WAR; ROMAN IN ZWEI BANDEN, Stuttgart 1893, Novel see Hermann Sudermann

ESCADRILLE AMOUREUSE, L', Novel see Jean-Michel Renaitour

ESCADRON BLANC, L', Novel see Joseph Peyre

ESCALE A ORLY, Novel see Curt Riess

ESCALIER C, Novel see Elvire Murail

ESCANDALO, EL, 1875, Novel see Pedro Antonio de Alarcon

ESCAPADE, London 1953, Play see Roger MacDougall

ESCAPE, Novel see Philip MacDonald

ESCAPE, Book see Barbara Worker, Dwight Worker

ESCAPE, Boston 1939, Novel see Ethel Vance

ESCAPE, London 1926, Play see John Galsworthy

ESCAPE, New York 1924, Novel see Alden Brooks

ESCAPE ARTIST, THE, 1965, Novel see David Wagoner

ESCAPE FROM ALCATRAZ, Novel see J. Campbell Bruce

ESCAPE FROM SORBIBOR, Book see Richard Rashke

ESCAPE ME NEVER, London 1933, Play see Margaret Kennedy

ESCAPE OF THE AMETHYST, Book see Laurence Earl

ESCAPE, THE, Story see Charles Belmont Davis

ESCAPE, THE, Play see E. F. Parr

ESCAPE, THE, New York 1913, Play see Paul Armstrong

ESCAPEMENT, Novel see Charles Eric Maine

ESFINGE MARAGATA, LA, 1914, Novel see Concha Espina de Serna

ESKAPADE, Novel see Richard Henry Savage

ESMERALDA, 1877, Short Story see Frances Hodgson Burnett

ESPAGNOLE, L', Novel see Maria Star

ESPION, L', Paris 1965, Novel see Paul Thomas

ESPION LEVE-TOI, Novel see George Markstein

ESPION OU EST-TU M'ENTENDS-TU?, Novel see Charles Exbrayat

ESPIONAGE, London 1935, Play see Walter Hackett

ESPOIR, L', 1937, Novel see Andre Malraux

ESPRIT DU MAL, L', Play see Henry Deyglun

ESPRIT ES-TU LA, Play see Georges Arnold

ESTADO CIVILE: MARTA, Novel *see* Juan Jose Alonso Millan

ESTATE CON SENTIMENTO, UN', Novel *see* John Harwey

ESTHER, RUTH AND JENNIFER, Novel *see* Jack Davies

ESTHER WATERS, 1894, Novel *see* George Moore

ESTOUFFADE A LA CARAIBE, Novel *see* Albert Conroy

ESTRELA SOBE, A, 1939, Novel *see* Marques Rebelo

ESTRELLA VACIA, LA, Mexico City 1950, Novel *see* Luis Spota

ESTRELLAS, LAS, Play *see* Carlos Arniches

ESTUDIANTES Y MODISTILLAS, Play *see* Antonio Casero

ET LA POLICE N'EN SAVAIT RIEN, Play *see* Jean Guitton

ET L'ON REVIENT TOUJOURS, Short Story *see* Camille Medal

ET MOI - J'TE DIS QU'ELLE T'A FAIT DE L'OEIL, Play *see* Pierre Veber

ET MOI J'TE DIS QU'ELLE T'A FAIT DE L'OEIL, Play *see* Maurice Hennequin

ET PUIS S'EN VONT, Novel *see* F. S. Gilbert

ETA DEL MALESSERE, L', Turin 1963, Novel *see* Dacia Maraini

ETAPPENHASE, DER, Play *see* Karl Bunje

ETAU, L', Play *see* Victorien Sardou

ETE DE LA SAINT-MARTIN, L', Play *see* Ludovic Halevy, Henri Meilhac

ETE MEURTRIER, L', Novel *see* Sebastien Japrisot

ETERNAL CITY, THE, London 1901, Novel *see* Hall Caine

ETERNAL MAGDALENE, THE, New York 1915, Play *see* Robert H. McLaughlin

ETERNAL MASCULINE, THE, Short Story *see* Dorothy Canfield

ETERNITE POUR NOUS, L', Paris 1960, Novel *see* G.-J. Arnaud

ETHAN FROME, 1911, Novel *see* Edith Wharton

ETHEL FUE UNA MUJER INGENUA, Novel *see* Alfonso de Benavides

ETIENNE, 1930, Play *see* Jacques Deval

ETIENNE BRULE - IMMORTAL SCOUNDREL, Book *see* J. Herbert Cranston

ETOILE DU SUD LE PAYS DE DIAMANTS, L', Paris 1884, Novel *see* Jules Verne

ETRANGE AFFAIRE, UNE, Novel *see* Jean-Marc Roberts

ETRANGER, L', Paris 1942, Novel *see* Albert Camus

ETRANGERE, L', 1877, Play *see* Alexandre Dumas (fils)

ETRANGLEURS, LES, Paris 1879, Novel *see* Adolphe Belot

ETTERSOKTE ER ATTEN AR, 1958, Novel *see* Nils Johan Rud

ETTORE FIERAMOSCA O LA DISFIDA DI BARLETTA, 1833, Novel *see* Massimo d'Azeglio

ETUDIANT ETRANGER, L', Book *see* Philippe Labro

EUGENE ARAM, London 1832, Novel *see* Edward George Bulwer Lytton

EUGENIE GRANDET, 1833, Novel *see* Honore de Balzac

EULALIE PONTOIS, Play *see* Frederic Soulie

EUNUCH OF STAMBOUL, Novel *see* Dennis Wheatley

EUROPAISCHES SKLAVENLEBEN, Novel *see* Friedrich Wilhelm von Hacklander

EUROPE GALANTE, L', Short Story *see* Paul Morand

EUROPEANS, THE, 1878, Novel *see* Henry James

EUROPOLIS, 1933, Novel *see* Jean Bart

EUTANASIA DI UN AMORE, Novel *see* Giorgio Saviane

EVA, Operetta *see* Franz Lehar

EVA, *see* Giovanni Verga

EVA THE FIFTH; THE ODYSSEY OF A TOM SHOW, New York 1928, Play *see* John Golden, Kenyon Nicholson

EVA TROPI HLOUPOSTI, Novel *see* Fan Vavrincova

EVANGELINE, 1847, Poem *see* Henry Wadsworth Longfellow

EVANGELIST, THE, New York 1907, Play *see* Henry Arthur Jones

EVE, London 1945, Novel *see* James Hadley Chase

EVE IN EXILE, Novel *see* Cosmo Hamilton

EVE OF ST. MARK, THE, 1942, Play *see* Maxwell Anderson

EVELYN PRENTICE, New York 1933, Novel *see* W. E. Woodward

EVEN STEPHEN, 1925, Short Story *see* Gerald Beaumont

EVENING IN BYZANTIUM, Novel *see* Irwin Shaw

EVENING NEWS, Novel *see* Shu Ping

EVENING STAR, THE, Novel *see* Larry McMurtry

EVENSONG, Novel *see* Beverly Nichols

EVENT 1000, Novel *see* David Lavallee

EVENTS WHILE GUARDING THE BOFORS GUN, 1966, Play *see* John McGrath

EVER GREEN, London 1930, Play *see* Benn W. Levy

EVER OPEN DOOR, THE, London 1913, Play *see* H. H. Herbert, George R. Sims

EVER THE BEGINNING, Play *see* Lucille S. Prumbs, Sara B. Smith

EVERGREEN, Novel *see* Belva Plain

EVERLASTING SECRET FAMILY & OTHER SECRETS, THE, Book *see* Frank Moorhouse

EVERLASTING WHISPER, THE, New York 1922, Novel *see* Jackson Gregory

EVERY KNEE SHALL BOW, Book *see* Jess Walter

EVERY LITTLE CROOK AND NANNY, 1972, Novel *see* Evan Hunter

EVERY SECRET THING, Autobiography *see* Patricia Campbell Hearst, Alvin Moscow

EVERYBODY COMES TO RICK'S, Play *see* Joan Alison, Murray Burnett

EVERYBODY WAS VERY NICE, 1936, Short Story *see* Stephen Vincent Benet

EVERYBODY'S ALL AMERICAN, Novel *see* Frank Deford

EVERYTHING BUT THE TRUTH, 1919, Short Story *see* Edgar Franklin

EVERYTHING IS THUNDER, Novel *see* Jocelyn Hardy

EVERYTHING MONEY CAN BUY, 1924, Short Story *see* Ethel Watts Mumford

EVERYWOMAN, New York 1911, Play *see* Walter Browne

EVE'S DAUGHTER, New York 1917, Play *see* Alice Ramsey

EVE'S LEAVES, New York 1925, Play *see* Harry Chapman Ford

EVE'S LOVERS, 1924, Short Story *see* W. K. Clifford

EVIDENCE, New York 1914, Play *see* Jean Du Rocher MacPherson

EVIDENCE OF LOVE, Book *see* John Bloom

EVIL ANGELS, Book *see* John Bryson

EVIL COME, EVIL GO, New York 1961, Novel *see* Whit Masterson

EVIL THAT MEN DO, THE, Novel *see* R. Lance Hill

EVIL UNDER THE SUN, Novel *see* Agatha Christie

EVITA, Musical Play *see* Tim Rice, Andrew Lloyd Webber

EVOLUTION OF KATHERINE, THE, Play *see* E. Temple Thurston

EWIGE JUNGELING, DER, Play *see* Alexander Engel

EWIGE MASKE, DIE, Zurich 1934, Novel *see* Leo Lapaire

EWIGE NARANIM, Play *see* H. Kalmonowitz

EWIGE QUELL, DER, Novel *see* Johannes Linke

EWIGE TRAUM, DER, Novel *see* Karl Ziak

EX, THE, Novel *see* John Lutz

EXALTED FLAPPER, THE, 1925, Short Story *see* Will Irwin

EXCEPT FOR ME AND THEE, Book *see* Jessamyn West

EXCESS BAGGAGE, Novel *see* H. M. Raleigh

EXCESS BAGGAGE, New York 1927, Play *see* John Wesley McGowan

EXCHANGE OF WIVES, New York 1919, Play *see* Cosmo Hamilton

EXCITERS, THE, Story *see* Martin Brown

EXCOMMUNIE, L', Novel *see* Jose Giovanni

EXCUSE ME, New York 1911, Play *see* Rupert Hughes

EX-DUKE, THE, London 1927, Novel *see* E. Phillips Oppenheim

EXECUTION OF CHARLES HORMAN, THE, Book *see* Thomas Hauser

EXECUTION OF PRIVATE SLOVIK, THE, Book *see* William Bradford Huie

EXECUTION, THE, Novel *see* Oliver Crawford

EXECUTIONER'S SONG, THE, 1979, Book *see* Norman Mailer

EXECUTIONERS, THE, New York 1958, Novel *see* John D. MacDonald

EXECUTIVE SUITE, 1952, Novel *see* Cameron Hawley

EXILE, AN, New York 1967, Novel *see* Madison Jones

EXILE, AN OUT POST OF EMPIRE, New York 1916, Novel *see* Dolf Wyllarde

EXILES, THE, 1894, Short Story *see* Richard Harding Davis

EXIT LINES, London 1984, Novel *see* Reginald Hill

EX-MISTRESS, New York 1930, Novel *see* Dora Macy

EXODUS, 1958, Novel *see* Leon Uris

EXORCIST, THE, Novel *see* William Peter Blatty

EXPENSE OF SPIRIT, Novel *see* Anne-Francoise Pyszora

EXPENSIVE WOMEN, New York 1931, Novel *see* Wilson Collison

EXPERIENCE; A MORALITY PLAY OF TODAY, New York 1915, Novel *see* George V. Hobart

EXPERIMENT, Novel *see* Karel Matej Capek-Chod

EXPERIMENT PERILOUS, Novel *see* Margaret Carpenter

EXPERIMENT, THE, Novel *see* Ethel M. Dell

EXPIATION, London 1887, Novel *see* E. Phillips Oppenheim

EXPLOITS OF BRIGADIER GERARD, THE, London 1896, Novel *see* Arthur Conan Doyle

EXPLORER, THE, London 1909, Novel *see* W. Somerset Maugham

EXPRESSO BONGO, London 1958, Musical Play *see* Wolf Mankowitz, Julian More

EXPRESSWAY, Novel *see* Elleston Trevor

EXTRA DRY - CARNEVALE 1910 - CARNEVALE 1913, 1914, Play *see* Luigi Chiarelli

EXTRAVAGANTE THEODORA, L', Play *see* Jean de Letraz

EXTREME MEASURES, Novel *see* Michael Palmer

EXTREMITIES, Play *see* William Mastrosimone

EX-VOTO, L', Novel *see* Lucie Delarue Mardrus

EX-WIFE, New York 1929, Novel *see* Katherine Ursula Parrott

EYE OF GOD, Play *see* Tom Blake Nelson

EYE OF THE NEEDLE, Novel *see* Ken Follett

EYES IN THE NIGHT, Novel *see* Baynard H. Kendrick

EYES OF FATE, Story *see* Holloway Horn

EYES OF JULIA DEEP, THE, Short Story *see* Kate L. McLaurin

EYES OF LAURA MARS, THE, Novel *see* John Carpenter

EYES OF THE AMARYLLIS, THE, Novel *see* Natalie Babbitt

EYES OF THE WORLD, THE, Chicago 1914, Novel *see* Harold Bell Wright

EYES OF YOUTH, Short Story *see* Mrs. Wilson Woodrow

EYES OF YOUTH, New York 1917, Play *see* Charles Guernon, Max Marcin

EYES WIN, THE, Story *see* Alvin J. Neitz

EYE-WITNESS, Novel *see* Mark Hebden

F. EST UN SALAUD, Novel *see* Martin Frank

FABIAN. DIE GESCHICHTE EINES MORALISTEN, 1931, Novel *see* Erich Kastner

FABIOLA OR THE CHURCH OF THE CATACOMBS, London 1854, Novel *see* Nicholas Patrick Wiseman

FABRICATOR, THE, Novel *see* Hollis Hodges

FABRIK DER OFFIZIERE, Novel *see* Hans Hellmut Kirst

FABULOUS ANN MEDLOCK, Novel *see* Robert Shannon

FACA DE DOIS GUMES, A, 1985, Novel *see* Fernando Tavares Sabino

FACA E O RIO, A, Novel *see* Odylo Costa Filho

FACCIA DI MASCALZONE, 1954, Short Story *see* Alberto Moravia

FACCIAMO PARADISO, Novel *see* Giuseppe Pontiggia

FACE, 1924, Short Story *see* Lucy Stone Terrill

FACE AT THE WINDOW, THE, Play *see* F. Brooke Warren

FACE AU DESTIN, Novel *see* Charles-Robert Dumas

FACE AU DRAPEAU, 1896, Novel *see* Jules Verne

FACE IN THE FOG, THE, 1920, Short Story *see* Jack Boyle

FACE IN THE MOONLIGHT, THE, New York 1892, Play *see* Charles Osborne

FACE IN THE NIGHT, THE, London 1924, Novel *see* Edgar Wallace

FACE OF FEAR, Novel *see* Dean R. Koontz

FACE ON THE BARROOM FLOOR, THE, Poem *see* Hugh Antoine d'Arcy

FACE ON THE MILK CARTON, THE, Novel *see* Caroline B. Cooney

FACE THE FACTS, 1936, Short Story *see* Clarence Budington Kelland

FACE THE MUSIC, Novel *see* Ernest Bornemann

FACE WORK, Story *see* Cornell Woolrich

FACELESS MAN, THE, 1966, Play *see* Harry Kliner

FACEREA LUMII, 1964, Novel *see* Eugen Barbu

FACES, Play *see* Patrick Ludlow, Walter Sondes

FACING THE MUSIC, London 1899, Play *see* James H. Darnley

FACLIE DE PASTE, O, 1890, Short Story *see* Ion Luca Caragiale

FACON DE SE DONNER, LA, Play *see* Felix Gandera

FACTEUR S'EN VA-T-EN GUERRE, LE, Paris 1966, Novel *see* Gaston-Jean Gautier

FACTS IN THE CASE OF M. VALDEMAR, THE, 1845, Short Story *see* Edgar Allan Poe

FACTS OF LIFE, THE, 1940, Short Story *see* W. Somerset Maugham

FADE OUT, Play *see* David Watson

FADREN, 1887, Play *see* August Strindberg

FAHNE, DIE, Play *see* Otto Emmerich Groh

FAHNELTRAGERIN, DIE, 1913, Short Story *see* Peter Rosegger

FAHNLEIN DER SIEBEN AUFRECHTEN, DAS, Liepzig 1861, Short Story *see* Gottfried Keller

FAHNLEIN DER VERSPRENGTEN, DAS, Novel *see* Rudolf Herzog

FAHRENHEIT 451, New York 1953, Novel *see* Ray Bradbury

FAIBLE FEMME, UNE, Play *see* Jacques Deval

FAIL-SAFE, New York 1962, Novel *see* Eugene Burdick, Harvey Wheeler

FAILURE, 1932, Short Story *see* Katharine Haviland-Taylor

FAINT PERFUME, New York 1923, Novel *see* Zona Gale

FAIR AND WARMER, New York 1915, Play *see* Avery Hopwood

FAIR BARBARIAN, THE, New York 1880, Novel *see* Frances Hodgson Burnett

FAIR CO-ED, THE, New York 1909, Play *see* George Ade

FAIR GAME, Novel *see* Paula Gosling

FAIR IMPOSTER, A, Novel *see* Charles Garvice

FAIR MAID OF PERTH, THE, 1828, Novel *see* Sir Walter Scott

FAIR STOOD THE WIND FOR FRANCE, 1944, Novel *see* H. E. Bates

FAIR WIND TO JAVA, Novel *see* Garland Roark

FAIRFAX, New York 1879, Play *see* Bartley Campbell

FAISEUR, LE, Play *see* Honore de Balzac

FAIS-MOI CONFIANCE, Novel *see* James Hadley Chase

FAISON UN REVE, 1917, Play *see* Sacha Guitry

FAITH HEALER, THE, New York 1910, Play *see* William Vaughn Moody

FAITHFUL HEART, THE, London 1921, Play *see* Monckton Hoffe

FAITHLESS LOVER, Story *see* Baroness d'Arville

FAKE, THE, London 1924, Play *see* Frederick Lonsdale

FAKERS, THE, Play *see* Tod Waller

FALCON AND THE SNOWMAN, THE, Book *see* Robert Lindsey

FALCON'S MALTESER, THE, Novel *see* Anthony Horowitz

FALECIDA, A, 1953, Play *see* Nelson Rodrigues

FALESNA KOCICKA, Play *see* Josef Skruzny

FALL CLAASEN, DER, Novel *see* Erich Ebermayer

FALL DERUGA, DER, 1917, Novel *see* Ricarda Huch

FALL GEHRSDORF, DER, Novel *see* Hans Land

FALL GROOTMAN, DER, Play *see* Walter Maria Espe

FALL GUY, THE, New York 1924, Play *see* George Abbott, James Gleason

FALL MAURIZIUS, DER, 1928, Novel *see* Jakob Wassermann

FALL OF A NATION: A SEQUEL TO BIRTH OF A NATION, THE, Chicago 1916, Novel *see* Thomas Dixon

FALL OF A SAINT, THE, Novel *see* Eric Clement Scott

FALL OF THE HOUSE OF USHER, THE, 1839, Short Story *see* Edgar Allan Poe

FALLAIT PAS M'ECRASER, Play *see* Jean Guitton

FALLE CLAASEN, DER, Play *see* Erich Ebermayer

FALLEN ANGEL, Novel *see* Marty Holland

FALLEN ANGEL, Boston 1952, Novel *see* Howard Fast

FALLEN ANGELS, 1927, Short Story *see* Arthur Somers Roche

FALLEN BY THE WAY, Poem *see* George R. Sims

FALLEN LEAVES, Story *see* Will Scott

FALLEN SPARROW, THE, Novel *see* Dorothy B. Hughes

FALLET INGEGERD BREMSSEN, 1937, Novel *see* Dagmar Ingeborg Edqvist

FALLING ANGEL, Novel *see* William Hjortsberg

FALSCHE GEWICHT, DAS, 1937, Novel *see* Joseph Roth

FALSCHE PERLEN, Short Story *see* Guy de Maupassant

FALSCHE PRINZ, DER, Book *see* Harry Domela

FALSCHER FUFFZIGER, EIN, Play *see* Robert Overweg

FALSCHUNG, DIE, 1979, Novel *see* Nicholas Born

FALSE ARREST, Book *see* Joyce Lukezic, Ted Schwarz

FALSE COLORS, Story *see* Edwina Levin

FALSE EVIDENCE, 1896, Novel *see* E. Phillips Oppenheim

FALSE FACES, THE, Garden City, N.Y. 1918, Novel *see* Louis Joseph Vance

FALSE FIRES, Story *see* Octavus Roy Cohen

FALSE WITNESS, Story *see* Irving Stone

FALSHIVYI KUPON, 1911, Short Story *see* Lev Nikolayevich Tolstoy

FAMA, Novel *see* Adrien Johnson

FAME, London 1929, Play *see* Audrey Carter, Waverly Carter

FAME IS THE SPUR, 1940, Novel *see* Howard Spring

FAMIGLIA DE'TAPPETTI, LA, Novel *see* Arnaldo Luigi Vassallo

FAMILIA ALVAREDA, LA, 1856, Novel *see* Fernan Caballero

FAMILIA DE PASCUAL DUARTE, LA, 1945, Novel *see* Camilo Jose Cela

FAMILIE BUCHHOLZ, Novel *see* Julius Stinde

FAMILIE HANNEMANN, Play *see* Max Reimann, Otto Schwartz

FAMILIE HESSELBACH, DIE, Book *see* Wolf Schmidt

FAMILIENANSCHLUSS, Play *see* Karl Bunje

FAMILIENTAG IM HAUSE PRELLSTEIN, Play *see* Anton Herrnfeld, Donath Herrnfeld

FAMILLE BOLERO, Play *see* Maurice Hennequin, Albert Milhaud

FAMILLE CUCUROUX, LA, Play *see* Yves Mirande

FAMILLE HERNANDEZ, LA, Play *see* Genevieve Bailac

FAMILLE PONT-BIQUET, LA, Play *see* Alexandre Bisson

FAMILY BAND, THE, Lincoln, Nb. 1961, Novel *see* Laura Bower Van Nuys

FAMILY BUSINESS, Play *see* Dick Goldenberg

FAMILY CUPBOARD, THE, New York 1913, Play *see* Owen Davis

FAMILY HONEYMOON, Novel *see* Homer Croy

FAMILY NOBODY WANTED, THE, 1954, Book *see* Helen Doss

FAMILY PICTURES, Novel *see* Sue Miller

FAMILY PLOT, Novel *see* Victor Canning

FAMILY SKELETON, 1949, Novel *see* Doris Miles Disney

FAMILY TREE, THE, *see* E. Forst

FAMILY UPSTAIRS, THE, Atlantic City 1925, Play *see* Harry Delf

FAMINE CLUB, Play *see* Marcel Lasseaux

FAMOUS, 1946, Short Story *see* Stephen Vincent Benet

FAMOUS MRS. FAIR, THE, New York 1920, Play *see* James Grant Forbes

FAN, THE, Novel *see* Peter Abrahams, Bob Randall

FANATIK ODER ID TSVEY KUNI LEMELS, DER, 1880, Play *see* Abraham Goldfaden

FANDO ET LIS, Paris 1958, Play *see* Fernando Arrabal

FANFANI RAPITO, Play *see* Dario Fo

FANFARE DE SINT-JANSVRIENDEN, Novel *see* Ernest Claes

FANG AND CLAW, New York 1935, Book *see* Frank Buck, Ferrin Fraser

FANG ZHENZHU, 1950, Play *see* Shu Qingchun

FANNY, Paris 1931, Play *see* Marcel Pagnol

FANNY BALLERINA DELLA SCALA, Novel *see* Giuseppe Adami

FANNY BY GASLIGHT, 1940, Novel *see* Michael Sadleir

FANNY HERSELF, New York 1917, Novel *see* Edna Ferber

FANNY HILL; OR MEMOIRS OF A WOMAN OF PLEASURE, London 1749, Novel *see* John Cleland

FANNY LEAR, Play *see* Ludovic Halevy, Henri Meilhac

FANNY OWEN, 1979, Novel *see* Agustina Bessa-Luis

FAN'S NOTES, A, Novel *see* Frederick Earl Exley

FANT, 1928, Novel *see* Gabriel Scott

FANTASMA, New York 1884, Play *see* The Hanlon Brothers

FANTASMA D'AMORE, Novel *see* Mino Milani

FANTASMAS, 1930, Short Story *see* Wenceslao Fernandez Florez

FANTOMAS, Novel *see* Marcel Allain, Pierre Souvestre

FANTOME DE L'OPERA, LE, Paris 1910, Novel *see* Gaston Leroux

FANTOMES DU CHAPELIER, LES, 1949, Short Story *see* Georges Simenon

FANTOZZI, Novel *see* Paolo Villaggio

FAR CALL, THE, 1928, Short Story *see* Edison Marshall

FAR COUNTRY, THE, Novel *see* Nevil Shute

FAR CRY, THE, New York 1924, Play *see* Arthur Richman

FAR FROM THE MADDING CROWD, London 1874, Novel *see* Thomas Hardy

FAR PAVILIONS, THE, Novel *see* M. M. Kaye

FARADAY'S FLOWERS, Novel *see* Tony Kenrick

FARAON, 1897, Novel *see* Boleslaw Prus

FARARUV KONEC, Prerov 1969, Novel *see* Josef Skvorecky

FARBER UND SEIN ZWILLINGSBRUDER, DER, 1890, Play *see* Johann Nestroy

FAREMO TANTO MALE, LE, Play *see* Claudio Masenza, Pino Quartullo

FAREWELL MY LOVELY, 1940, Novel *see* Raymond Chandler

FAREWELL TO ARMS, A, New York 1929, Novel *see* Ernest Hemingway

FAREWELL TO MANZANAR, Book *see* Jeanne Wakatsuki Houston

FAREWELL TO THE MASTER, Story *see* Harry Bates

FARFUI, 1909, Novel *see* Luciano Zuccoli

FARINET, Paris 1932, Novel *see* Charles-Ferdinand Ramuz

FARM FESTIVALS, Book *see* Will Carleton

FARMER, Novel *see* Jim Harrison

FARMER IN THE DELL, THE, New York 1935, Novel *see* Philip Duffield Stong

FARMER TAKES A WIFE, THE, 1934, Play *see* Walter D. Edmonds

FARMER'S WIFE, THE, London 1924, Play *see* Eden Philpotts

FASCINATION, Play *see* Eliot Crawshaw Williams

FASHIONS FOR MEN, Play *see* Ferenc Molnar

FAST COMPANY, New York 1938, Novel *see* Marco Page

FAST LADY, THE, Short Story *see* Keble Howard

FAST LIFE, New York 1928, Play *see* John B. Hymer, Samuel Shipman

FAST MAIL, THE, Play *see* Lincoln J. Carter

FAST ONE, 1932, Short Story *see* Paul Cain

FAST PACE, THE, Story *see* H. G. Logalton

FAST TIMES AT RIDGEMONT HIGH, Novel *see* Cameron Crowe

FASTEST GUN, THE, Short Story *see* Steve Fisher

FASTEST MAN ON EARTH, THE, Story *see* James Edmiston

FASTNACHTSBEICHTE, DIE, Frankfurt 1959, Novel *see* Carl Zuckmayer

FAT CHANCE, Novel *see* Colin Dexter

FAT CITY, Novel *see* Leonard Gardner

FATAL CARD, THE, London 1894, Play *see* C. Haddon Chambers, B. C. Stephenson

FATAL NOISE, THE, Short Story *see* James Oliver Curwood

FATAL VISION, Book *see* Joe McGinness

FATAL WOMAN, 1952, Novel *see* Patrick Quentin

FATE AND POMEGRANATE, Story *see* Mary Imlay Taylor

FATE IN THE BALANCE, Novel *see* Seward W. Hopkins

FATE IS THE HUNTER, New York 1961, Novel *see* Ernest K. Gann

FATE OF THE WOLF, 1925, Short Story *see* W. C. Tuttle

FATE'S ALIBI, Story *see* C. W. Fassett

FATES AND FLORA FOURFLUSH, THE, Story *see* Charles Brown

FATE'S HONEYMOON, 1917, Short Story *see* Max Brand

FAT-FRUMOS DIN TEI, 1875, Verse *see* Mihai Eminescu

FATHER AND DAUGHTER, Novel *see* Kazuo Hirotsu

FATHER AND SON, 1924, Short Story *see* James Hopper

FATHER AND THE BOYS, New York 1908, Play *see* George Ade

FATHER BROWN, DETECTIVE, Novel *see* G. K. Chesterton

FATHER CHRISTMAS, Book *see* Raymond Briggs

FATHER FIGURE, Book *see* Richard Peck

FATHER KNICKERBOCKER'S HISTORY OF NEW YORK, 1809, Book *see* Washington Irving

FATHER LIU SHIHAI'S WALLET, Novel *see* Bai XIaowen

FATHER OF FRANKENSTEIN, Novel *see* Christopher Bram

FATHER OF THE BRIDE, 1949, Novel *see* Edward Streeter

FATHER SKY, Novel *see* Devery Freeman

FATHERHOOD, Story *see* Julia Crawford Ivers

FATHERLAND, Novel *see* Robert Harris

FATHER'S DAY, Story *see* Elliott Nugent, J. C. Nugent

FATHER'S HELPING HAND, Story *see* Malcolm Strong

FATHER'S LUCKY ESCAPE, Story *see* Malcolm Strong

FATTIGGUBBENS BRUD, 1926, Short Story *see* Jarl Hemmer

FAUBOURG-MONTMARTRE, Novel *see* Henri Duvernois

FAUN; OR THEREBY HANGS A TALE, THE, New York 1911, Play *see* Edward Knoblock

FAUNO DI MARMO, IL, 1860, Novel *see* Nathaniel Hawthorne

FAUSSE MAITRESSE, LA, 1841, Short Story *see* Honore de Balzac

FAUSSE RIVIERE, Book *see* Maurice Denuziere

FAUST, 1808-32, Play *see* Johann Wolfgang von Goethe

FAUST, Paris 1859, Opera *see* Charles Gounod

FAUST A MARKETKA, Paris 1859, Opera *see* Charles Gounod

FAUTE DE L'ABBE MOURET, LA, 1875, Novel *see* Emile Zola

FAUTEUIL 47, LE, Play *see* Louis Verneuil

FAVORIT DER KONIGIN, DER, Frankfurt Am Main 1953, Novel *see* Robert Neumann

FAVORITA, LA, Play *see* Alfonso Royer, Gustavo Vaez

F.B.I. STORY, THE, 1956, Book *see* Don Whitehead

F.D.R.: THE LAST YEAR, Book *see* Jim Bishop

FE, LA, 1892, Novel *see* Armando Palacio Valdes

FEAR AND LOATHING IN LAS VEGAS, Book *see* Hunter S. Thompson

FEAR HAS BLACK WINGS, Novel *see* Hugh Brooke

FEAR IN A HANDFUL OF DUST, Novel *see* Brian Garfield

FEAR IS THE KEY, 1961, Novel *see* Alistair MacLean

FEAR MARKET, THE, New York 1916, Play *see* Amelie Rives

FEAR NO MORE, New York 1946, Novel *see* Leslie Edgley

FEAR ON TRIAL, Autobiography *see* John Henry Faulk

FEAR STRIKES OUT, Autobiography *see* Albert S. Hirschberg, Jimmy Piersall

FEARMAKERS, THE, 1945, Novel *see* Darwin L. Teilhet

FEAST OF JULY, THE, Novel *see* H. E. Bates

FEATHER IN HER HAT, A, Garden City, N.Y. 1934, Novel *see* I. A. R. Wylie

FEATHER, THE, Novel *see* C. M. Matheson

FEATHERED SERPENT, THE, London 1927, Novel *see* Edgar Wallace

FEATHERTOP, 1852, Short Story *see* Nathaniel Hawthorne

FEATURE FOR JUNE, Play *see* Graeme Lorimer, Eileen Tighe

FEBRE, 1963, Play *see* Horia Lovinescu

FEBRUARY HILL, New York 1934, Novel *see* Victoria Lincoln

FECONDITE, Novel *see* Emile Zola

FEDERAL BULLETS, London 1937, Novel *see* George Fielding Eliot

FEDORA, Paris 1882, Play *see* Victorien Sardou

FEEDER, THE, 1926, Short Story *see* Mildred Cram

FEET OF CLAY, Story *see* William Morton

FEET OF CLAY, Boston 1923, Novel *see* Margaret Tuttle

FEFELEAGA, 1908, Short Story *see* Ion Agarbiceanu

FEI DAO HUA, Novel *see* XIong Daba

FEI HU DUI, Novel *see* Liu Zhixia

FEKETE GYEMANTOK, 1870, Novel *see* Mor Jokai

FEKETE SZARU CSERESZYNE, 1931, Play *see* Sandor Hunyady

FEKETE VAROS, A, 1911, Novel *see* Kalman Mikszath

FELDHERRNHUGEL, DER, Play *see* Roda-Roda, Karl Rossler

FELDMANN-SAKEN, Novel *see* Sigurd Senje

FELICITA COLOMBO, Play *see* Giuseppe Adami

FELIX GETS A MONTH, Play *see* Tom Gallon, Leon M. Lion

FELIX HOLT THE RADICAL, 1866, Novel *see* George Eliot

FELIX O'DAY, New York 1915, Novel *see* F. Hopkinson Smith

FELIZ ANO VELHO, 1982, Novel *see* Marcelo Rubens Paiva

FELLOW PRISONERS, 1930, Short Story *see* Philip Hamilton Gibbs

FELLOWSHIP OF THE FROG, THE, London 1925, Novel *see* Edgar Wallace

FELRJARO SALAMON, 1955, Short Story *see* Andras Suto

FELUETTES; OU LA REPETITION D'UN DRAME ROMANTIQUE, LES, 1987, Play *see* Michel Marc Bouchard

FEMALE, New York 1932, Novel *see* Donald Henderson Clarke

FEMALE OF THE SPECIES, THE, Short Story *see* Joseph Gollomb

FEMALE OF THE SPECIES, THE, London 1928, Novel *see* H. C. McNeile ("Sapper")

FEMALE PERVERSIONS; THE TEMPTATIONS OF EMMA BOVARY, Book *see* Louise J. Kaplan

FEMALE SWINDLER, THE, Play *see* Walter Melville

FEME, Novel *see* Vicki Baum

FEMENINAS, 1895, Short Story *see* Ramon Maria Del Valle-Inclan

FEMME A PAPA, LA, Play *see* Maurice Hennequin, Albert Milhaud

FEMME A SA FENETRE, UNE, 1930, Novel *see* Pierre Drieu La Rochelle

FEMME AUX YEUX FERMES, LA, Novel *see* Pierre L'Ermite

FEMME BLONDE, LA, Play *see* Henri Demesse

FEMME DE BERROYER EST PLUS BELLE QUE TOI - CONNASSE!, Novel *see* Jackie Berroyer

FEMME DE CHAMBRE DU TITANIC, LA, Novel *see* Didier Decoin

FEMME DE CLAUDE, LA, 1873, Play *see* Alexandre Dumas (fils)

FEMME DE PAILLE, LA, Paris 1956, Novel *see* Catherine Arley

FEMME DE PAUL, LA, 1881, Short Story *see* Guy de Maupassant

FEMME DE TA JEUNESSE, LA, Play *see* Jacques Deval

FEMME DE TRENTE ANS, LA, 1831, Short Story *see* Honore de Balzac

FEMME DISPARAIT, UNE, Short Story *see* Jacques Viot

FEMME DU BOUT DU MONDE, LA, Novel *see* Alain Serdac

FEMME D'UNE NUIT, LA, Novel *see* Alfred Machard

FEMME EN BLANC SE REVOLTE, UNE, Novel *see* Andre Soubiran

FEMME EN HOMME, LA, Play *see* Ugo Falena

FEMME ET LE PANTIN, LA, Paris 1898, Novel *see* Pierre Louys

FEMME ET LE ROSSIGNOL, LA, Short Story *see* Bela Daniel

FEMME FATALE, LA, Play *see* Andre Birabeau

FEMME FATALE, UNE, Novel *see* David Beaty

FEMME MASQUEE, LA, Paris 1923, Play *see* Charles Mere

FEMME NUE, LA, 1908, Play *see* Henry Bataille

FEMME PUBLIQUE, LA, Novel *see* Dominique Granier

FEMME QUI SE JETTE PAR LA FENETRE, UNE, 1847, *see* G. Lemoine, Eugene Scribe

FEMME RAVIE, UNE, Play *see* Louis Verneuil

FEMME REVEE, LA, Novel *see* J. Perez de Rosas

FEMME X, LA, Paris 1908, Play *see* Alexandre Bisson

FEMMES, Novel *see* Marja Morozowicz Szczepkowska

FEMMES COLLANTES, LES, Play *see* Leon Gandillot

FEMMES SAVANTES, LES, 1673, Play *see* Moliere

FEMMES S'EN BALANCENT, LES, Novel *see* Peter Cheyney

FEMMES SONT DES ANGES, LES, Novel *see* Pierre-Aristide Breal

FENG HUANG QING, Novel *see* Liu XInglong

FENG SHUI CHANG LIU, Novel *see* Hu Zheng

FENGRIFFEN, Novel *see* David Case

FENSTER XUM FLUR, DAS, Play *see* Curt Flatow, Horst Pillau

FENSTER ZUM FLUR, DAS, Play *see* Curt Flatow

FER-DE-LANCE, New York 1934, Novel *see* Rex Stout

FERDINAND LE NOCEUR, Play *see* Leon Gandillot

FERDINAND RAIMUND, Biography *see* Eduard Paul Danskzkys

FERIEN MIT PIROSCHKA, Novel *see* Hugo Hartung

FERIEN VOM ICH, 1916, Novel *see* Paul Keller

FERIEN WIE NOCH NIE, Novel *see* Hans Thomas

FERME DU CHOQUART, LA, Novel *see* Victor Cherbuliez

FERME DU PENDU, LA, Novel *see* Gilbert Dupe

FERNANDE, 1870, Play *see* Victorien Sardou

FERREOL, Paris 1875, Play *see* Victorien Sardou

FERRY TO HONGKONG, London 1957, Novel *see* Max Catto

FESSEE, LA, Play *see* Jean de Letraz

FETE ESPAGNOLE, LA, Paris 1958, Novel *see* Henri-Francois Rey

FETTE WELT, Novel *see* Helmut Krausser

FETTERED, Novel *see* Joan Sutherland

FEU DANS LA PEAU, LE, Novel *see* Rene Bragard

FEU FOLLET, LE, Paris 1931, Novel *see* Pierre Drieu La Rochelle

FEU SOUS LA PEAU, LE, Novel *see* Dominique Labarriere

FEU TOUPINEL, Play *see* Alexandre Bisson, Albert Carre

FEUD OF THE ROCKING U, Short Story *see* Russell A. Bankson

FEUERSCHIFF, DAS, 1960, Short Story *see* Siegfried Lenz

FEUERSCHIFF, DAS, 1960, Novel *see* Siegfried Lenz

FEUERWERK, Play *see* Jurg Amstein, Erik Charell

FEUERZANGENBOWLE, DIE, Novel *see* Heinrich Spoerl

FEUILLETON, LE, *see* Pierre-Alexis Ponson Du Terrail

FEVER HEAT, New York 1954, Novel *see* Angus Vicker

FEVER IN THE BLOOD, A, New York 1959, Novel *see* William Pearson

FEVER PITCH, Book *see* Nick Hornby

FEYSSE SUR MER, Novel *see* Marcel-Eric Grancher

FIACCOLA SOTTO IL MOGGIO, LA, 1904, Play *see* Gabriele D'Annunzio

FIACRE N. 13, LE, 1881, Novel *see* Xavier de Montepin

FIAKERMILLI, Play *see* Martin Costa

FIANCAILLES DE MR. HIRE, LES, 1933, Novel *see* Georges Simenon

FIANCAILLES D'YVONNE, LES, Short Story *see* Joseph Henri Rosny

"FIAT VOLUNTAS DEI", Play *see* Giuseppe Macri

FIDALGOS DA CASA MOURISCA, OS, 1871, Novel *see* Julio Dinis

FIDANZAMENTO, IL, Novel *see* Goffredo Parise

FIDANZATA DEL BERSAGLIERE, LA, Play *see* Edoardo Anton

FIDDLER'S GREEN, 1918, Short Story *see* Donn Byrne
FIDDLER'S GREEN, 1950, Novel *see* Ernest K. Gann

FIDELE BAUER, DER, Mannheim 1907, Operetta *see* Viktor Leon, Leo Fall

FIDELIO, Vienna 1805, Opera *see* Ludwig Van Beethoven

FIDLOVACKA ANEB ZADNY HNEV A ZADNA RVACKA, Play *see* Josef Kajetan Tyl

FIEL INFANTERIA, LA, 1943, Novel *see* Rafael Garcia Serrano

FIELD OF BLOOD, Novel *see* Gerald Seymour

FIELD OF HONOR, 1916, Short Story *see* Irvin S. Cobb

FIELD, THE, 1966, Play *see* John B. Keane

FIERCEST HEART, THE, Boston 1960, Novel *see* Stuart Cloete

FIERY CROSS, THE, Novel *see* Esson Maule

FIERY HAND, THE, Short Story *see* Sax Rohmer

FIERY INTRODUCTION, A, Story *see* Julius G. Furthmann

FIESCO, 1783, Play *see* Friedrich von Schiller

FIEVRE MONTE A EL PAO, LA, Novel *see* Henri Castillou

FIFTEEN STREETS, THE, Novel *see* Catherine Cookson

FIFTH AVENUE, 1925, Short Story *see* Arthur Stringer

FIFTH COMMANDMENT, THE, Play *see* Julius Steger

FIFTH CORD, THE, Novel *see* D. M. Devine

FIFTH FORM AT ST. DOMINICS, THE, London 1881, Novel *see* Talbot Baines Reed

FIFTH MAN, THE, Short Story *see* James Oliver Curwood

FIFTH WHEEL, THE, Short Story *see* O. Henry

FIFTY CANDLES, Indianapolis 1926, Novel *see* Earl Derr Biggers

FIFTY MILLION FRENCHMEN, New York 1929, Play *see* Herbert Fields, E.R. Goetz, Cole Porter

FIFTY ROADS TO TOWN, Boston 1936, Novel *see* Frederick Nebel

FIFTY-FIFTY, London 1932, Play *see* H. F. Maltby

FIFTY-TWO MILES TO TERROR, 1956, Short Story *see* Alex Gaby

FIFTY-TWO WEEKS FOR FLORETTE, 1921, Short Story *see* Elizabeth Alexander

FIGHT FOR LIFE, THE, Book *see* Paul de Kruif

FIGHT, THE, New York 1913, Play *see* Bayard Veiller

FIGHTER, THE, New York 1909, Novel *see* Albert Payson Terhune

FIGHTING BOB, Book *see* Edward E. Rose

FIGHTING CARAVANS, New York 1929, Novel *see* Zane Grey

FIGHTING CHANCE, A, Story *see* James Oliver Curwood

FIGHTING CHANCE, THE, New York 1906, Novel *see* Robert W. Chambers

FIGHTING EDGE, THE, Boston 1922, Novel *see* William MacLeod Raine

FIGHTING HOPE, THE, New York 1908, Play *see* William Hurlbut

FIGHTING JACK, Novel *see* Walter Courtney Rowden

FIGHTING PARSON, THE, Play *see* Chris Davis, George Gray

FIGHTING PARSON, THE, New York 1908, Play *see* William L. Roberts

FIGHTING PEDAGOGUE, THE, Story *see* H. A. Halbert Jr.

FIGHTING SHEPHERDESS, THE, Boston 1919, Novel *see* Caroline Lockhart

FIGHTING SNUB O'REILLY, London 1929, Novel *see* Edgar Wallace

FIGLI DEL MARCHESE LUCERA, I, Play *see* Gherardo Gherardi

FIGLI DI NESSUNO, I, Novel *see* Ruggero Rindi

FIGLIA DEL CORSARO VERDE, LA, Novel *see* Emilio Salgari

FIGLIA DEL MENDICANTE, LA, Novel *see* Carolina Invernizio

FIGLIA DI JORIO, LA, 1904, Play *see* Gabriele D'Annunzio

FIGLIA UNICA, LA, 1853, *see* Teobaldo Ciconi

FIGLIO DEL CORSARO ROSSO, IL, Florence 1920, Novel *see* Emilio Salgari

FIGLIO DI BAKUNIN, IL, Book *see* Sergio Atzeni

FIGURANTE, LA, 1889, Play *see* Francois de Curel

FIGURE DE PROUE, Novel *see* Gilbert Dupe

FIGUREHEAD, THE, Poem *see* Crosbie Garstin

FIGURES DE CIRE, Play *see* Andre de Lorde

FIGURES IN A LANDSCAPE, Novel *see* Barry England

FIGURKY, Short Story *see* Jan Neruda

FIL A LA PATTE, UN, 1899, Play *see* Georges Feydeau

FILLA DEL MAR, LA, 1900, Play *see* Angel Guimera

FILLE BIEN GARDEE, LA, Play *see* Eugene Labiche, Marc-Michel

FILLE DE FEU, LA, Novel *see* John D. Fellow

FILLE DE MADAME ANGOT, LA, Brussels 1872, Operetta *see* Clairville, Koning, Charles Lecocq

FILLE DE PROIE, LA, Paris 1953, Novel *see* Christian Coffinet

FILLE DES CHIFFONNIERS, LA, Play *see* Anicet Bourgeois, Ferdinand Dugue

FILLE DU BOCHE, LA, Novel *see* Henri Germain

FILLE DU BOUIF, LA, Play *see* Rene Bussy, Georges de La Fouchardiere

FILLE DU GARDE-CHASSE, LA, *see* Decori, Fontanes

FILLE DU REGENT, UNE, 1845, Novel *see* Alexandre Dumas (pere)

FILLE DU REGIMENT, LA, Paris 1840, Opera *see* Jean-Francois Bayard, Gaetano Donizetti, Jules H. Vernoy

FILLE ELISA, LA, 1877, Novel *see* Edmond de Goncourt

FILLE ET LE GARCON, LE, Play *see* Andre Birabeau, Georges Dolley

FILLE POUR L'ETE, UNE, Paris 1957, Novel *see* Maurice Clavel

FILLE SAUVAGE, LA, Novel *see* Jules Mary

FILLE SAUVAGE, LA, Paris 1902, Play *see* Francois de Curel

FILLEULE D'AMERIQUE, LA, Play *see* Felix Gandera, Andre Mouezy-Eon

FILLING HIS OWN SHOES, Boston 1916, Novel *see* Henry C. Rowland

FILLO DELL'ORIZONTE, IL, Novel *see* Antonio Tabucchi

FILM DU POILU, LE, Short Story *see* Ascanio, Andre Boghen

FILM STAR'S HOLIDAY, A, Short Story *see* Peter B. Kyne

FILOSOFKA MAJA, Novel *see* Vilem Neubauer

FILOSOFSKA HISTORIE, Novel *see* Alois Jirasek

FILS A PAPA, LE, Play *see* Maurice Desvallieres, Antony Mars

FILS CARDINAUD, LE, 1942, Novel *see* Georges Simenon

FILS D'AMERIQUE, UN, Play *see* Marcel Gerbidon, Pierre Veber

FILS DE CAROLINE CHERIE, LE, Novel *see* Cecil Saint-Laurent

FILS DE LA NUIT, LE, Novel *see* Jules de Gastyne

FILS DE LAGARDERE, LE, *see* Paul Feval (fils)

FILS DU FLIBUSTIER, LE, *see* Louis Cartoux

FILS NATUREL, LE, Play *see* Alexandre Dumas (fils)

FILUMENA MARTURANO, Naples 1946, Play *see* Eduardo de Filippo

FIN DE JOURNEE, Novel *see* Roger Vrigny

FIN DE LAMIEL, LA, 1966, Novel *see* Cecil Saint-Laurent

FIN DE MONTE-CARLO, LA, Novel *see* Paul Poulgy

FIN D'UN JOUEUR, LA, Novel *see* Georges Ohnet

FIN D'UNE IDYLLE, LA, Novel *see* Claude Anet

FINAL CLOSE-UP, THE, 1918, Short Story *see* Royal Brown

FINAL COUNT, THE, London 1926, Novel *see* H. C. McNeile ("Sapper")

FINAL DEL JUEGO, 1964, Short Story *see* Julio Cortazar

FINAL DIAGNOSIS, THE, New York 1959, Novel *see* Arthur Hailey

FINAL GOLD, THE, Story *see* L. V. Jefferson

FINAL JUDGMENT, THE, Play *see* George Scarborough

FINAL NIGHT, Novel *see* Robert Gaines

FINAL PROBLEM, THE, Short Story *see* Arthur Conan Doyle

FINAL PROGRAMME, THE, Novel *see* Michael Moorcock

FINANCIAL EXPERT, THE, 1952, Novel *see* R. K. Narayan

FINANZEN DES GROSSHERZOGS, DIE, Novel *see* Frank Heller

FIND THE WOMAN, Indianapolis 1911, Novel *see* Gelett Burgess

FIND THE WOMAN, New York 1921, Novel *see* Arthur Somers Roche

FINDING MAUBEE, Novel *see* A. H. Z. Carr

FINDING SIGNS, Novel *see* Sharlene Baker

FINDLING, DER, 1811, Novel *see* Heinrich von Kleist

FINE FEATHERS, New York 1913, Play *see* Eugene Walter

FINE MADNESS, A, New York 1964, Novel *see* Elliott Baker

FINE MESE, Play *see* Paola Riccora

FINGER PRINTS, Story *see* Arthur Somers Roche

FINI, Short Story *see* Guy de Maupassant

FINIAN'S RAINBOW, New York 1947, Play *see* E. Y. Harburg, Burton Lane

FINING POT IS FOR SILVER, THE, Novel *see* F. Britten Austin

FINNEGAN'S BALL, 1894, Play *see* George H. Emerick

FINNEGAN'S WAKE, 1939, Novel *see* James Joyce

FINSTERNIS UND IHR EIGENTUM, DIE, Novel *see* Anton von Perfall

FIOR D'AMORE, Play *see* Dario Niccodemi

FIORDALISI D'ORO, Play *see* Giovacchino Forzano

FIORE SOTTO GLI OCCHI, IL, Play *see* Fausto Maria Martini

FIORENZA MIA!, 1912, Play *see* Enrico Novelli

FIORI D'ARANCIO, Play *see* Andre Birabeau

FIRE, *see* T. J. Moller

FIRE AND FEAR, Book *see* Jose Torres

FIRE AND RAIN, Book *see* Jerome Greer Chandler

FIRE BRIGADE, THE, Story *see* Kate Corbaley

FIRE DJAEVLE, DE, Kristiania 1895, Novel *see* Herman Bang

FIRE DOWN BELOW, Novel *see* Max Catto

FIRE FLINGERS, THE, New York 1919, Novel *see* William J. Neidig

FIRE IN THE STONE, A, Novel *see* Colin Thiele

FIRE ON THE MOUNTAIN, Book *see* Edward Abbey

FIRE OVER ENGLAND, 1936, Novel *see* A. E. W. Mason

FIRE PATROL, THE, Worcester 1891, Play *see* Edwin Barbour, James W. Harkins Jr.

FIRE SALE, Novel see Robert Klane

FIREBRAND, THE, New York 1924, Play see Edwin Justus Mayer

FIREBRAND TREVISION, New York 1918, Novel see Charles Alden Seltzer

FIREFLY OF FRANCE, THE, New York 1918, Novel see Marion Polk Angelotti

FIREFLY, THE, New York 1912, Operetta see Rudolf Friml, Otto Harbach

FIREFOX, Novel see Craig Thomas

FIREMAN, SAVE MY CHILD, Story see Paul Girard Smith, Sy Bartlett

FIREMAN'S WEDDING, THE, Poem see W. A. Eaton

FIRESTARTER, 1980, Novel see Stephen King

FIRING LINE, THE, New York 1908, Novel see Robert W. Chambers

FIRM OF GIRDLESTONE, THE, Novel see Arthur Conan Doyle

FIRM, THE, Novel see John Grisham

FIRMIN LE MUET DE SAINT-PATACLET, Novel see Lucien Giudice

FIRST AMONG EQUALS, London 1984, Novel see Jeffrey Archer

FIRST AND THE LAST, THE, 1918, Short Story see John Galsworthy

FIRST BLOOD, Novel see David Morrell

FIRST BORN, THE, New York 1897, Play see Francis Powers

FIRST DEADLY SIN, THE, Novel see Lawrence Sanders

FIRST GENTLEMAN, THE, London 1945, Play see Norman Ginsbury

FIRST LADY, New York 1935, Play see Katharine Dayton, George S. Kaufman

FIRST LAW, THE, New York 1911, Novel see Gilson Willets

FIRST LESSON, THE, Play see Gunter Rudorf

FIRST LOVE LAST RITES, Short Story see Ian McEwan

FIRST MEN IN THE MOON, THE, London 1901, Novel see H. G. Wells

FIRST MONDAY IN OCTOBER, Play see Jerome Lawrence, Robert E. Lee

FIRST MRS. CHIVERICK, THE, Play see Adelaide Matthews, Martha M. Stanley

FIRST MRS. FRASER, THE, London 1929, Play see St. John G. Ervine

FIRST PERFORMANCE, Short Story see Matt Taylor

FIRST REBEL, THE, New York 1937, Novel see Neil Harmon Swanson

FIRST TRAIN TO BABYLON, New York 1955, Novel see Max Simon Ehrlich

FIRST WIFE, THE, Play see Jay Presson Allen

FIRST WIVES CLUB, THE, Novel see Olivia Goldsmith

FIRST YEAR, THE, New York 1920, Play see Frank Craven

FIRST YOU CRY, 1976, Book see Betty Rollin

FISHER-GIRL, THE, Story see Frances Marion

FISHKE DER KRUMER, Short Story see Mendele Moicher Sforim

FIVE AND TEN, New York 1929, Novel see Fannie Hurst

FIVE CHILDREN AND IT, 1902, Novel see E. Nesbit

FIVE FINGER EXERCISE, London 1958, Play see Peter Shaffer

FIVE FORTY-EIGHT, THE, 1955, Short Story see John Cheever

FIVE FRAGMENTS, THE, Boston 1932, Novel see George Dyer

FIVE HAVE A MYSTERY TO SOLVE, Novel see Enid Blyton

FIVE LITTLE PEPPERS ABROAD, Boston 1902, Novel see Margaret Sidney

FIVE LITTLE PEPPERS AND HOW THEY GREW, Boston 1881, Novel see Margaret Sidney

FIVE LITTLE PEPPERS AT SCHOOL, Boston 1903, Novel see Margaret Sidney

FIVE LITTLE PEPPERS MIDWAY, Boston 1890, Novel see Margaret Sidney

FIVE NIGHTS, London 1908, Novel see Victoria Cross

FIVE OF ME, THE, Book see Henry Hawksworth

FIVE OF SPADES, THE, Story see Harry O. Hoyt

FIVE ON A TREASURE ISLAND, Novel see Enid Blyton

FIVE ORANGE PIPS, THE, 1892, Short Story see Arthur Conan Doyle

FIVE SPOT, 1935, Short Story see Theodore A. Tinsley

FIVE STAR FINAL, New York 1930, Play see Louis Weitzenkorn

FIVE THOUSAND AN HOUR, New York 1912, Novel see George Randolph Chester

FIVE THOUSAND TROJAN SOLDIERS, Story see Leslie T. White

FIVE WISHES, THE, Play see Laura Leycester

FIXED BAYONETS, Novel see John Brophy

FIXED BY GEORGE, 1920, Short Story see Edgar Franklin

FIXER, THE, 1966, Novel see Bernard Malamud

FJORTEN DAGER FOR FROSTNETTENE, 1935, Novel see Sigurd Hoel

FLAG LIEUTENANT, THE, London 1908, Play see Maj. W. P. Drury, Leo Trevor

FLAMBEAUX, LES, Play see Henry Bataille

FLAMBEE, LA, 1911, Play see Henri Kistemaeckers

FLAME IS LOVE, THE, Novel see Barbara Cartland

FLAME OF THE TIMBERLINE, Story see Richard Morris

FLAME, THE, Novel see Olive Wadsley

FLAME TREES OF THIKA, THE, Novel see Elspeth Huxley

FLAMENCO DES ASSASSINS, LE, Paris 1961, Novel see Frederic Valmain

FLAMES, Novel see Robert Hichens

FLAMING FOREST; A NOVEL OF THE CANADIAN NORTHWEST, THE, New York 1921, Novel see James Oliver Curwood

FLAMING FORGE, THE, Poem see Henry Wadsworth Longfellow

FLAMING RAMPARTS, THE, 1914, Short Story see Edith Barnard Delano

FLAMING STAR, Novel see Clair Huffaker

FLAMING SWORD, THE, New York 1914, Novel see George Gibbs

FLAMING YOUTH, New York 1923, Novel see Warner Fabian

FLAMINGO ROAD, Novel see Robert Wilder

FLAMME, LA, Play see Charles Mere

FLANAGAN BOY, THE, Novel see Max Catto

FLAPPER, THE, 1923, Play see Eugene Walter

FLAPPER WIFE, THE, New York 1925, Novel see Beatrice Burton

FLASH OF AN EMERALD, THE, Short Story see E. M. Ingleton

FLASH OF GREEN, A, Novel see John D. MacDonald

FLASH THE SHEEPDOG, Novel see Kathleen Fidler

FLASH-LIGHT, THE, Short Story see Albert M. Treymore

FLASHPOINT, Book see George La Fontaine

FLAT GOLD, Short Story see James B. Hendryx

FLAT TIRE, THE, New York 1930, Novel see Alma Sioux Scarberry

FLAT TWO, London 1927, Novel see Edgar Wallace

FLEDERMAUS, DIE, Vienna 1874, Operetta see Henri Meilhac, Johann Strauss

FLESH AND BLOOD, Novel see Pete Hamill

FLETCH, Novel see Gregory McDonald

FLEUR AUX DENTS, LA, Novel see Gilles Archambault

FLEUR D'AMOUR, Novel see Marcelle Vioux

FLEUR D'OMBRE, Novel see Charles Folly

FLEUR D'ORANGER, LA, Play see Andre Birabeau, Georges Dolley

FLIC OU VOYOU, Novel see Michel Grisola

FLIC STORY, Novel see Roger Borniche

FLIEGENDE HOLLANDER, DER, Dresden 1843, Opera see Richard Wagner

FLIEGENDE KLASSENZIMMER, DAS, 1933, Novel see Erich Kastner

FLIEGENDE WINDMUHLE ,DIE, Novel see Gunter Feustel

FLIEGER, 1931, Play see Hermann Rossman

FLIGHT, 1945, Short Story see John Steinbeck

FLIGHT COMMANDER, THE, Story see John Monk Saunders

FLIGHT FROM ASHIYA, New York 1959, Novel see Elliott Arnold

FLIGHT INTO DANGER, Television Play see Arthur Hailey

FLIGHT INTO FREEDOM, Story see Phyllis Parker

FLIGHT OF PIGEONS, A, Short Story see Ruskin Bond

FLIGHT OF THE DUCHESS, THE, 1845, Poem see Robert Browning

FLIGHT OF THE PHOENIX, THE, New York 1964, Novel see Elleston Trevor

FLIGHT TO THE HILLS, THE, Garden City, Ny. 1926, Novel see Charles Neville Buck

FLIRT, THE, New York 1913, Novel see Booth Tarkington

FLITTERWOCHEN, Play see Paul Helwig

FLOATING DUTCHMAN, THE, Novel see Nicolas Bentley

FLOODS OF FEAR, Novel see John Hawkins, Ward Hawkins

FLOR DE MAYO, 1895, Novel see Vicente Blasco Ibanez

FLOR DE SANTIDAD, 1904, Novel see Ramon Maria Del Valle-Inclan

FLORADAS NA SERRA, 1939, Novel see Dinah Silveira de Queiros

FLORENTINE DAGGER, THE, New York 1928, Novel see Ben Hecht

FLORENTINE, THE, Play see Damien Gray, Amy McCarty-Baker

FLORENTINE TRAGEDY, A, Play see T. Sturge Moore, Oscar Wilde

FLORES SILVESTRES, Novel see Padre Risco

FLORETTE ET PATAPON, 1905, Play see Maurice Hennequin, Pierre Veber

FLORIAN - DAS PFERD DES KAISERS, Berlin 1933, Novel see Felix Salten

FLORIDA ENCHANTMENT, A, New York 1891, Novel see Archibald Clavering Gunter, Fergus Redmond

FLORINE LA FLEUR DU VALOIS, Novel see Eugene Barbier

FLOTTA DEGLI EMIGRANTI, LA, 1907, Play see Vincenzo Morello

FLOWER DRUM SONG, New York 1958, Musical Play see Oscar Hammerstein II, Richard Rodgers

FLOWER IN THE WILDERNESS, Novel see Ruika Kuroiwa

FLOWER OF NAPOLI, THE, 1924, Short Story see Gerald Beaumont

FLOWER OF THE DUSK, New York 1908, Novel see Myrtle Reed

FLOWER OF THE FLOCK, THE, 1921, Short Story see Jay Gelzer

FLOWER OF THE NORTH, THE, New York 1912, Novel see James Oliver Curwood

FLOWERS FOR ALGERNON, New York 1966, Novel see Daniel Keyes

FLOWERS IN THE ATTIC, Novel see Virginia Andrews

FLOWING GOLD, New York 1922, Novel see Rex Beach

FLUCHT IN DEN HAREM, DIE, Zurich 1927, Play see Paul Altheer

FLUCHT IN DEN NORDEN, 1934, Novel see Klaus Mann

FLUCHT INS WEISSE LAND, DIE, 1929, Book see Peter Freuchen

FLUCHTLING AUS CHIKAGO, DER, Novel see Curt Johannes Braun

FLUCHTLING, DER, 1945, Play see Fritz Hochwalder

FLUKTEN, 1936, Novel see Arthur Omre

FLUSH OF GOLD, 1910, Short Story see Jack London

FLUSSPIRATEN VOM MISSISSIPPI, DIE, Novel see Friedrich Gerstackers

FLY AWAY HOME, Play see Dorothy Bennett, Irving White

FLY AWAY PETER, London 1947, Play see A. P. Dearsley

FLY, THE, Short Story see George Langelaan

FLYING EYE, THE, Novel see John Newton Chance

FLYING FIFTY-FIVE, THE, London 1922, Novel see Edgar Wallace

FLYING FOOL, THE, London 1929, Play see Bernard Merivale, Arnold Ridley

FOUR WINDS ISLAND, Novel see Vega Stewart

FOURBERIES DE SCAPIN, LES, 1671, Play see Moliere

FOURCHAMBAULT, LES, Play see Emile Paul Augier

FOUR-FLUSHER, THE, New York 1925, Play see Cesar Dunn

FOUR-FORTY AT FORT PENN, 1917, Short Story see Perley Poore Sheehan

FOURMI, LA, Short Story see Guy de Maupassant

FOURPOSTER, THE, New York 1951, Play see Jan de Hartog

FOURTEEN HOURS FROM CHI, Serial Story see William Porter

FOURTEENTH LOVER, THE, Story see Alice D. G. Miller

FOURTH BROTHER, THE, Unpublished, Play see Archibald Forbes

FOURTH COMMANDMENT, THE, Story see Emilie Johnson

FOURTH ESTATE, THE, New York 1909, Play see Harriet Ford, Joseph Medill Patterson

FOURTH IN SALVADOR, THE, Short Story see O. Henry

FOURTH MUSKETEER, THE, 1922, Short Story see Harry Charles Witwer

FOURTH PROTOCOL, THE, Novel see Frederick Forsyth

FOURTH WALL, THE, London 1928, Play see A. A. Milne

FOX AND THE HOUND, THE, Novel see Daniel P. Mannix

FOX FARM, Novel see Warwick Deeping

FOX HOUND, THE, Short Story see Maxwell Grant

FOX, THE, 1922, Short Story see D. H. Lawrence

FOXES OF HARROW, THE, 1946, Novel see Frank Yerby

FOXFIRE, Novel see Joyce Carol Oates

FOXFIRE, 1950, Novel see Anya Seton

FOXHOLE FLICKA, A, Story see Lieut. Marvin Park

FOX-WOMAN, THE, Philadelphia 1900, Novel see John Luther Long

FOYER PERDU, Play see Andre Haguet

F.P.1 ANTWORTET NICHT, Novel see Curt Siodmak

FRA BISTURI E FORBICI, Novel see Andrea Majocchi

FRA DIAVOLO; OU L'HOTELLERIE DE TERRACINE, Paris 1830, Opera see Daniel Francois Auber, Eugene Scribe

FRA FINMARKEN: SKILDRINGER, Kristiania 1881, Novel see Jens Andreas Friis

FRA GIACONE, Poem see Robert Buchanan

FRAGILE FOX, New York 1954, Play see Norman Brooks

FRAGMENT OF FEAR, Novel see John Bingham

FRAGMENTS D'EPAVES, Novel see Bernard Frank

FRAILTY, Novel see Olive Wadsley

FRAM URSUL POLAR, 1932, Novel see Cezar Petrescu

FRAMED, Novel see Mike Misenheimer, Art Powers

FRAN, Indianapolis 1912, Novel see John Breckenridge Ellis

FRANCESCO LANNOIS, 1851, Novel see Francesco Mastriani

FRANCHISE AFFAIR, THE, Novel see Josephine Tey

FRANCIS, Novel see David Stern

FRANCISCAIN DE BOURGES, LE, see Marc Toledano

FRANCISCO, 1880, Novel see Anselmo Suarez Y Romero

FRANCISKA VASARNAPJAI, Novel see Sandor Simo

FRANCS-MACONS, LES, Play see G. Leprince, Claude Rolland

FRANKENSTEIN; OR THE MODERN PROMETHEUS, London 1818, Novel see Mary Wollstonecraft Shelley

FRANKIE AND JOHNNY IN THE CLAIR DE LUNE, 1987, Play see Terrence McNally

FRANTISEK LELICEK VE SLUZBACH SHERLOCKA HOLMESA, Novel see Hugo Vavris

FRATELLI CASTIGLIONI, I, Play see Alberto Colantuoni

FRATERNITY, Short Story see Mary McCall Jr.

FRATII JDERI, 1935, Novel see Mihail Sadoveanu

FRAU AM STEUER, Play see Paul Barabas

FRAU DES KUNSTLERS, DIE, Novel see Frantz Kaver Kappus

FRAU DES STEFFEN TROMHOLT, DIE, Stuttgart 1927, Novel see Hermann Sudermann

FRAU DIE WEISS WAS SIE WILL, EINE, Operetta see Alfred Grunwald, Oscar Straus

FRAU FUR DREI TAGE, EINE, Novel see Elisabeth Gurt

FRAU HOLLE, Short Story see Jacob Grimm, Wilhelm Grimm

FRAU IM HERMELIN, DIE, Play see Rudolph Schanzer, Ernst Welisch

FRAU IM MOND, DIE, Novel see Thea von Harbou

FRAU IM SCHRANK, DIE, Play see Dussieux, Maribeau

FRAU IM TALAR, DIE, Novel see Petter Bendow

FRAU IRENE BESSER, Novel see Hans Habe

FRAU JENNY TREIBEL, 1892, Novel see Theodor Fontane

FRAU LUGT, EINE, 1934, Play see Ladislaus Fodor

FRAU LUNA, Opera see Paul Lincke

FRAU MIT DER MASKE, DIE, Berlin 1922, Novel see Rudolph Lothar

FRAU, NACH DER MAN SICH SEHNT, DIE, Novel see Max Brod

FRAU NACH MASS, Play see Eberhard Forster

FRAU OHNE VERGANGENHEIT, DIE, Novel see Curt Johannes Braun

FRAU RETTICH DIE CZERNI UND ICH, Novel see Simone Borowiak

FRAU SIXTA, Play see Ernst Zahn

FRAU SORGE, Novel see Hermann Sudermann

FRAU UND DER SMARAGD, DIE, Play see Harry Jenkins

FRAU VON FORMAT, EINE, Opera see Rudolph Schanzer, Ernst Welisch

FRAUD, Play see H. F. Maltby

FRAUENDIPLOMAT, DER, Play see Curt Johannes Braun, E. B. Leuthege

FRAUENPARADIES, Opera see Robert Stolz

FRAUENSTATION, Novel see Marie Louise Fischer

FRAULEIN CASANOVA, Novel see Karl Hans Leiter

FRAULEIN ELSE, 1923, Short Story see Arthur Schnitzler

FRAULEIN FALSCH VERBUNDEN, Play see Herbert Rosenfeld

FRAULEIN FORTUNA, Play see Ladislaus Fodor

FRAULEIN FRAU, Play see Ludwig Fulda

FRAULEIN UND DER LEVANTINER, DAS, Novel see Fedor von Zobeltitz

FRAULEIN VON SCUDERI, DAS, 1819, Short Story see Ernst Theodor Amadeus Hoffmann

FREAK THE MIGHTY, Novel see Rodman Philbrick

FREAKY FRIDAY, Novel see Mary Rodgers

FRECCIA AZZURRA, LA, Novel see Gianni Rodari

FRECCIA NEL FIANCO, LA, 1913, Novel see Luciano Zuccoli

FRECKLES, New York 1904, Novel see Gene Stratton-Porter

FREE, 1918, Short Story see Wallace Irwin

FREE AIR, New York 1919, Novel see Sinclair Lewis

FREE RANGE LANNING, New York 1921, Novel see George Owen Baxter

FREE SOUL, A, New York 1927, Novel see Adela Rogers St. Johns

FREE WOMAN, 1936, Short Story see Katharine Brush

FREEDOM OF THE SEAS, London 1918, Play see Walter Hackett

FREEDOM ROAD, 1944, Novel see Howard Fast

FREEDOM TRAP, THE, Novel see Desmond Bagley

FREEWAY, Novel see Deanne Barkley

FREI LUIS DE SOUSA, 1859, Play see Almeida Garrett

FREIDEL, DER GEIGER, Poem see Wilhelmine Grafin Wickenburg-Almasy

FREISCHUTZ, DER, Berlin 1821, Opera see Johann F. Kind, Carl Maria von Weber

FREITAG DER 13, Play see Erich Engels

FREIWILD, Play see Arthur Schnitzler

FREMDENHEIM FILODA, Novel see Walter Sawitzky

FRENCH CONNECTION, THE, Book see Robin Moore

FRENCH DOLL, THE, New York 1922, Play see Paul Armont, Marcel Gerbidou

FRENCH LEAVE, London 1920, Play see Reginald Berkeley

FRENCH LIEUTENANT'S WOMAN, THE, 1959, Novel see John Fowles

FRENCH MISTRESS, A, London 1959, Play see Robert Munro

FRENCH SALAD, 1934, Play see Max Catto

FRENCH WITHOUT TEARS, London 1936, Play see Terence Rattigan

FRENCHMAN'S CREEK, 1941, Novel see Daphne Du Maurier

FRENCHY, Story see George Patullo

FRENTE DE MADRID, Short Story see Edgar Neville

FREQUENCE MEURTRE, Novel see Stuart Kaminsky

FRERES BOUQUINQUANT, LES, Novel see Jean Prevost

FRERES CORSES, LES, 1845, Short Story see Alexandre Dumas (pere)

FRERES RICO, LES, 1952, Short Story see Georges Simenon

FRERES ZEMGANNO, LES, Novel see Edmond de Goncourt

FRESH HORSES, Play see Larry Ketron

FREUDENHAUS, DAS, Novel see Henry Jaeger

FRI OS FRA KAERLIGHEDEN, 1973, Novel see Suzanne Brogger

FRIC-FRAC, 1937, Play see Edouard Bourdet

FRICKAN I FRACK, 1925, Novel see Hjalmar Bergman

FRIDAS ANDRA BOK, 1929, Verse see Birger Sjoberg

FRIDAS BOK, 1922, Verse see Birger Sjoberg

FRIDAY THE RABBI SLEPT LATE, Novel see Harry Kemelman

FRIDAY THE THIRTEENTH, New York 1907, Novel see Thomas William Lawson

FRIED GREEN TOMATOES AT THE WHISTLE STOP CAFE, Novel see Fannie Flagg

FRIEDA, London 1946, Play see Ronald Millar

FRIEND, Novel see Diana Henstell

FRIEND IN NEED, THE, Novel see Elizabeth Coxhead

FRIEND OF NAPOLEON, A, 1923, Short Story see Richard Connell

FRIEND OR FOE, Novel see Michael Morpurgo

FRIEND WIFE, Story see Frank R. Adams

FRIENDLY CALL, THE, Short Story see O. Henry

FRIENDLY ENEMIES, New York 1923, Play see Aaron Hoffman, Samuel Shipman

FRIENDLY FIRE, Book see C. D. B. Bryan

FRIENDLY PERSUASION, THE, 1945, Novel see Jessamyn West

FRIENDS AND NEIGHBOURS, London 1958, Play see Austin Steele

FRIENDS OF EDDIE COYLE, THE, Novel see George V. Higgins

FRIENDS OF MR. SWEENEY, New York 1925, Novel see Elmer Holmes Davis

FRIESE-GREENE, Book see Ray Allister

FRIGHTENED CHILD, THE, 1948, Novel see Dana Lyon

FRIGHTENED LADY, THE, London 1932, Novel see Edgar Wallace

FRINGE DWELLERS, THE, Novel see Nene Gare

FRIQUET, LE, 1894, Novel see Gyp

FRISCHER WIND AUS KANADA, Play see Hans Muller

FRISK, Novel see Dennis Cooper

FRISKY MRS. JOHNSON, THE, New York 1903, Play see Clyde Fitch

FROGGY'S LITTLE BROTHER, Novel see Brenda

FROHLICHE DORF, DAS, Play see August Hinrichs

FROHLICHE WEINBERG, DER, 1925, Play see Carl Zuckmayer

FROKEN JULIE, 1888, Play see August Strindberg

FROKNARNA VON PAHLEN, Stockholm 1930-35, Novel see Agnes von Krusentjerna

FROM DOON WITH DEATH, 1964, Novel see Ruth Rendell

FROM FOUR TO ELEVEN-THREE, 1920, Short Story see Royal Brown

FROM HEADQUARTERS, Story *see* David Sonnenblick

FROM HERE TO ETERNITY, 1951, Novel *see* James Jones

FROM MISSOURI, 1926, Short Story *see* Zane Grey

FROM NOON TILL THREE, 1973, Novel *see* Frank D. Gilroy

FROM RUSSIA WITH LOVE, London 1957, Novel *see* Ian Fleming

FROM SHOPGIRL TO DUCHESS, Play *see* Charles Darrell

FROM THE GROUND UP, 1921, Short Story *see* Rupert Hughes

FROM THE TERRACE, 1958, Novel *see* John O'Hara

FROM THE VALLEY OF THE MISSING, New York 1911, Novel *see* Grace Miller White

FROM THIS DARK STAIRWAY, New York 1931, Novel *see* Mignon G. Eberhart

FROM TYRANNY TO LIBERTY, Short Story *see* Francis Scott Key

FROMME HELENE, DIE, 1872, Short Story *see* Wilhelm Busch

FROMONT JEUNE ET RISLER AINE, 1874, Novel *see* Alphonse Daudet

FRONT, 1942, Play *see* Aleksander Korniychuk

FRONT DE L'ART, LE, Novel *see* Rose Valland

FRONT OF HOUSE, London 1936, Play *see* Charles Landstone

FRONT PAGE, THE, New York 1928, Play *see* Ben Hecht, Charles MacArthur

FRONTGOCKEL, DER, Play *see* Hans Fitz

FRONTIER FEUD, Novel *see* Will Cook

FRONTIER FRENZY, Serial Story *see* John Reese

FRONTIER FURY, Novel *see* Will Henry

FRONTIER JUSTICE, New York 1936, Novel *see* Colonel George B. Rodney

FRONTIER OF THE STARS, THE, Story *see* Albert Payson Terhune

FRONTIERES DU COEUR, LES, Novel *see* Paul Margueritte, Victor Margueritte

FROSCHKONIG ODER DER EISERNE HEINRICH, DER, Short Story *see* Jacob Grimm

FROSCHKONIG ODER DER EISERNE HEINRICH, DER, 1812, Short Story *see* Jacob Grimm, Wilhelm Grimm

FROSCHKONIG ODER DER EISERNE HEINRICH, DER, Short Story *see* Wilhelm Grimm

FROU-FROU, Paris 1869, Play *see* Ludovic Halevy, Henri Meilhac

FRU INGER TIL OSTRAAD, 1857, Play *see* Henrik Ibsen

FRUEN FRAHAVET, 1888, Play *see* Henrik Ibsen

FRUHLINGS ERWACHEN, 1891, Play *see* Frank Wedekind

FRUHLINGSMARCHEN, Musical Play *see* W. Hoffmann-Harnisch, Walter Supper

FRUIT . ET PUIS UN AUTRE FRUIT, UN, Novel *see* Jean Pommerol

FRUIT OF THE POPPY, New York 1965, Novel *see* Robert Wilder

FRUIT VERT, LE, Play *see* Regis Gignoux, Jacques Thery

FRUITFUL VINE, THE, Novel *see* Robert Hichens

FRUITS AMERS, Play *see* Colette Audry

FRUITS DE L'ETE, LES, Short Story *see* Philippe Heriat

FU MATTIA PASCAL, IL, 1904, Novel *see* Luigi Pirandello

FU NIU, Novel *see* Zhou Daxin

FU RONG ZHEN, 1979, Novel *see* Gu Hua

FU SHENG LIU JI, 18—, Autobiography *see* Shen Sanbai

FU SHI, Novel *see* He Wei

FU SHI, 1941, Novel *see* Shen Yanbing

FUCHS VON GLENARVON, DER, Novel *see* Nicola Rohn

FUEFUKI-GAWA, 1958-59, Novel *see* Shichiro Fukazawa

FUENTEOVEJUNA, 1619, Play *see* Lope de Vega

FUERZA BRUTA, LA, 1908, Play *see* Jacinto Benavente y Martinez

FUGGIASCHI, I, Novel *see* Ferdinando Paolieri

FUGGITIVA, LA, Novel *see* Milly Dandolo

FUGITIVE FORM TERROR, Serial Story *see* James R. Webb

FUGITIVE LADY, Novel *see* Doris Miles Disney

FUGITIVE NIGHTS, Novel *see* Joseph Wambaugh

FUGITIVE ROAD, 1935, Story *see* Erle Stanley Gardner

FUGITIVES, 1894, Short Story *see* Richard Harding Davis

FUGITIVES, THE, London 1936, Play *see* Walter Hackett

FUGLANE, 1957, Novel *see* Tarjei Vesaas

FUGLINN I FJORUNNI, 1931-32, Novel *see* Halldor Laxness

FUHRMANN HENSCHEL, 1898, Play *see* Gerhart Hauptmann

FUKAGAWA ANRAKUTEI, Novel *see* Shugoro Yamamato

FUKKATSU NO HI, Novel *see* Sakyo Komatsu

FULL HOUSE, A, New York 1915, Play *see* Frederick Jackson

FULL MEASURE, 1934, Short Story *see* James Edward Grant

FULL OF LIFE, 1952, Book *see* John Fante

FULL TREATMENT, THE, London 1959, Novel *see* Ronald Scott Thorn

FUMED OAK, 1936, Play *see* Noel Coward

FUND, DER, Novel *see* Franz Nabl

FUNDVOGEL, Novel *see* Hanns Heinz Ewers

FUNERAL IN BERLIN, London 1964, Novel *see* Len Deighton

FUNF KANICKEL, DIE, Play *see* Julius Pohl

FUNF MILLIONEN SUCHEN EINEN ERBEN, Novel *see* Harald Baumgarten

FUNF TAGE UND EINE NACHT, Novel *see* H. O. Wuttig

FUNFMADELHAUS, Novel *see* Meinrad Leinert

FUNF-MINUTEN-VATER, DER, Play *see* Karl Fischer

FUNGI CELLARS, THE, Short Story *see* Sax Rohmer

FUNNY FACE, London 1928, Play *see* Paul Girard Smith, Fred Thompson

FUNNY FARM, Book *see* Jay Cronley

FUNNY GIRL, New York 1964, Musical Play *see* Isobel Lennart, Merrill Bob, Jule Styne

FUNNY THING HAPPENED ON THE WAY TO THE FORUM, A, New York 1962, Play *see* Larry Gelbart, Burt Shevelove

FUOCHI D'ARTIFICIO, Play *see* Luigi Chiarelli

FUORI E DENTRO IL BORGO, Short Stories *see* Luciano Ligabue

FUR DIE KATZ, Play *see* August Hinrichs

FURCHTE UND ELEND DES DRITTEN REICHES, 1941, Play *see* Bertolt Brecht

FURDES, 1943, Short Story *see* Dezso Kosztolanyi

FURET, LE, Novel *see* Stanislas-Andre Steeman

FURIA, Novel *see* Vittorio Nino Novarese

FURIES, THE, 1948, Novel *see* Niven Busch

FURIES, THE, New York 1928, Play *see* Zoe Akins

FURIN KAZAN, Tokyo 1955, Novel *see* Yasushi Inoue

FURNACE, THE, London 1920, Novel *see* Pan

FURNISHED ROOM, THE, Short Story *see* O. Henry

FURNISHED ROOM, THE, Novel *see* Laura Del Rivo

FURST ODRE CLOWN, Novel *see* Maurice Dekobra

FURST VON PAPPENHEIM, DER, Opera *see* Franz Robert Arnold, Ernst Bach

FURSTENKIND, DAS, Vienna 1909, Operetta *see* Viktor Leon, Franz Lehar

FURY, THE, Novel *see* John Farris

FUSHIN NO TOKI, 1968, Novel *see* Sawako Ariyoshi

FUSILIER WIPF, Zurich 1915, Short Story *see* Robert Faesi

FUSILLE A L'AUBE, Novel *see* Maurice Dekobra

FUTARI, Novel *see* Jiro Akagawa

FUTZ, New York 1967, Play *see* Rochelle Owens

FUZZ, 1968, Novel *see* Evan Hunter

FUZZY PINK NIGHTGOWN, THE, 1956, Novel *see* Sylvia Tate

FYRTOJET, Copenhagen 1835, Short Story *see* Hans Christian Andersen

G. A. C., THE, Short Story *see* Mary Roberts Rinehart

GABAN, 1930, Novel *see* Munshi Premchand

GABRIEL HORN, THE, Novel *see* Felix Holt

GABRIEL OVER THE WHITE HOUSE; A NOVEL OF THE PRESIDENCY, New York 1933, Novel *see* Thomas Frederic Tweed

GABRIELA, CRAVO E CANELA, 1958, Novel *see* Jorge Amado

GABRIELE DAMBRONE, Play *see* Richard Billinger

GABRIELE IL LAMPIONARO DI PORTO, 1853, Play *see* Nicola de Lise

GABY, Book *see* Gabriella Brimmer, Elena Poniatowska

GAD AALA PAN SINHA GELA, Novel *see* Hari Narayan Apte

GADANO BEL, Play *see* Prabhulal Dwivedi

GADYUKA, 1929, Short Story *see* Alexsey Nikolayevich Tolstoy

GAIETES DE L'ESCADRON, LES, 1886, Play *see* Georges Courteline

GAILY GAILY, New York 1963, Novel *see* Ben Hecht

GAL YOUNG 'UN, 1940, Short Story *see* Marjorie K. Rawlings

GALIA, Novel *see* Vahe Katcha

GALLEGHER, Short Story *see* Richard Harding Davis

GALLEY SLAVE, THE, New York 1879, Play *see* Bartley Campbell

GALLOPER, THE, New York 1906, Play *see* Richard Harding Davis

GALVEZ EN EUSKADI, Novel *see* Jorge Martinez Reverte

GAMBIER'S ADVOCATE, London 1914, Novel *see* Ronald McDonald

GAMBIT, Novel *see* Sidney Carrol

GAMBLE FOR LOVE, A, Novel *see* Nat Gould

GAMBLE WITH HEARTS, A, Novel *see* Anthony Carlyle

GAMBLER OF THE WEST, THE, New York 1906, Play *see* Owen Davis

GAMBLERS ALL, London 1915, Play *see* May Martindale

GAMBLERS SOMETIMES WIN, Novel *see* T. H. Bird

GAMBLERS, THE, New York 1910, Play *see* Charles Klein

GAMBLING, New York 1929, Play *see* George M. Cohan

GAMBLING MAN, Novel *see* Clifton Adams

GAMBLING MAN, THE, Novel *see* Catherine Cookson

GAME FOR THREE LOSERS, Novel *see* Edgar Lustgarten

GAME FOR VULTURES, Novel *see* Michael Hartmann

GAME IN THE BUSH, A, Short Story *see* Georges Arthur Surdez

GAME OF CATCH, A, 1954, Short Story *see* Richard Wilbur

GAME OF LIBERTY, THE, 1915, Novel *see* E. Phillips Oppenheim

GAME OF LIFE, Story *see* James Oliver Curwood

GAME OF LIGHT, THE, 1914, Short Story *see* Richard Washburn Child

GAME OF X, THE, Novel *see* Robert Sheckley

GAMEKEEPER, THE, 1975, Novel *see* Barry Hines

GAMES, THE, London 1967, Novel *see* Hugh Atkinson

GAMESMANSHIP / ONEUPMANSHIP / LIFEMANSHIP, Books *see* Stephen Potter

GAMIANI, Novel *see* Alfred de Musset

GAMIN DE PARIS, LE, 1836, Play *see* Jean-Francois Bayard, Vanderbruch

GAMINE, LA, 1911, Play *see* Henri de Gorsse, Pierre Veber

GAMINS DU ROI DE SICILE, LES, Novel *see* Rene Masson

GAMLE PRAEST, DEN, 1899, Novel *see* Jakob Knudsen

GAN, 1913, Novel *see* Ogai Mori

GANADEVATA, 1942, Novel *see* Tarashankar Banerjee

GANG THAT COULDN'T SHOOT STRAIGHT, THE, Novel *see* Jimmy Breslin

GANGA ZUMBA, REI DOS PALMARES, 1961, Novel *see* Joao Felicio Dos Santos

GANGS OF NEW YORK, New York 1936, Novel *see* Herbert Asbury

GANGSTERS AND THE GIRL, THE, Story *see* Richard V. Spencer

GANGSTERS DU CHATEAU D'IF, LES, Opera *see* Henri Alibert

GANGSTER'S GLORY, Boston 1931, Novel *see* E. Phillips Oppenheim

GANGSTERS IN THE DRESS BUSINESS, Article *see* Lester Velie

GANSEMAGD, DIE, 1812, Short Story *see* Jacob Grimm, Wilhelm Grimm

GANZ GROSSEN TORHEITEN, DIE, Novel *see* Marianne von Angern

GANZER KERL, EIN, Play *see* Fritz Peter Buch

GAP, THE, Play *see* Derek Banham

GAPI ET SULLIVAN, Play *see* Antonine Maillet

GARAM HAWA, Short Story *see* Ismat Chughtai

GARAMBICA BAPU, 1952, Novel *see* Shripad Narayan Pendse

GARASU NO USAGI, Novel *see* Toshiko Takagi

GARCON SAUVAGE, LE, Novel *see* Edouard Peisson

GARCONNE, LA, 1922, Novel *see* Victor Margueritte

GARDE A VUE, Novel *see* John Wainwright

GARDE DU CORPS, LE, Novel *see* Yves Kermorvan

GARDEN CITY, Play *see* Gordon Glennon

GARDEN MURDER CASE; A PHILO VANCE STORY, THE, New York 1935, Novel *see* S. S. Van Dine

GARDEN OF ALLAH, THE, London 1904, Novel *see* Robert Hichens

GARDEN OF CUCUMBERS, A, New York 1960, Novel *see* Poyntz Tyler

GARDEN OF GOD, THE, Novel *see* Henry de Vere Stacpoole

GARDEN OF KARMA, THE, Poem *see* Laurence Hope

GARDEN OF LIES, THE, New York 1902, Novel *see* Justus Miles Forman

GARDEN OF RESURRECTION, THE, Novel *see* E. Temple Thurston

GARDEN OF SLEEP, Poem *see* De Lana

GARDEN OF THE MOON, 1937, Short Story *see* H. Bedford-Jones, John Barton Browne

GARDEN OF WEEDS, THE, New York 1924, Play *see* Leon Gordon, Doris Marquette

GARDENER'S DAUGHTER, THE, Poem *see* Alfred Tennyson

GARDENIA, Story *see* Vera Caspary

GARDENS OF STONE, Novel *see* Nicholas Proffitt

GARDIEN DU FEU, LE, Short Story *see* Anatole Le Braz

GARDIENS DE PHARE, Play *see* Paul Autier, Cloquemin

GARLAN & CO., Story *see* David Graham Phillips

GARMENTS OF TRUTH, 1921, Short Story *see* Freeman Tilden

GAROFANO ROSSO, Novel *see* Elio Vittorini

GARRET IN BOHEMIA, A, Novel *see* G. E. R. Mayne

GARRISON'S FINISH, New York 1907, Novel *see* William Blair Morton Ferguson

GARRYOWEN, Novel *see* Henry de Vere Stacpoole

GARS DU MILIEU, LE, Play *see* Paul Chartrettes, Henri Hubert

GARTEN EDEN, DER, Berlin 1926, Play *see* Rudolf Bernauer, Rudolf Osterreicher

GAS LIGHT, London 1938, Play *see* Patrick Hamilton

GASPARD DE BESSE, Novel *see* Jean Aicard

GASPARONE, Operetta *see* Karl Millocker

GASTON OLAF, New York 1917, Novel *see* Henry Oyen

GASTSPIEL IN KOPENHAGEN, Play *see* Friedrich Forster-Burggraf

GATEGUTTER, 1948, Novel *see* Arne Skouen

GATES OF DOOM, THE, Novel *see* Rafael Sabatini

GATHERING OF OLD MEN, A, 1983, Novel *see* Ernest J. Gaines

GATO MONTES, EL, Opera *see* Manuel Penella

GATOR BAIT, Story *see* Ewing Scott

GATTE DES FRAULEINS, DER, Vienna 1916, Play *see* Gabor Dregely

GATTER, DAS, Novel *see* Gunter Seuren

GATTIN, DIE, Play *see* Johann von Bokay

GATTO IN CANTINA, IL, Play *see* Nando Vitali

GATTO NERO, IL, Short Story *see* Edgar Allan Poe

GATTOPARDO, IL, Milan 1958, Novel *see* Giuseppe Di Lampedusa

GAUCHO, O, 1870, Novel *see* Jose Martiniano de Alencar

GAUNT STRANGER, THE, London 1925, Novel *see* Edgar Wallace

GAUNT WOMAN, THE, 1943, Novel *see* Edmund Gilligan

GAY ADVENTURE, THE, London 1931, Play *see* Walter Hackett

GAY AND FESTIVE CLAVERHOUSE, THE, Boston 1914, Novel *see* Anne Warner French

GAY BANDIT OF THE BORDER, THE, New York 1931, Novel *see* Tom Gill

GAY BANDITTI, THE, 1938, Novel *see* I. A. R. Wylie

GAY BLADES, Story *see* Jack Goodman, Albert Rice

GAY CABALLERO, THE, Story *see* Pierre Couderc, Hal Devitt

GAY CORINTHIAN, THE, Novel *see* Ben Bolt

GAY DECEPTION, Story *see* Jules Furthman, John D. Klorer

GAY DOG, THE, London 1951, Play *see* Joseph Colton

GAY LORD QUEX, THE, London 1899, Play *see* Arthur Wing Pinero

GAY LORD WARING, THE, New York 1910, Novel *see* Houghton Townley

GAY LOVE, London 1933, Play *see* Audrey Carten, Waveney Carten

GAY NINETIES, THE, Story *see* Gene Markey

GAY OLD DOG, THE, 1917, Short Story *see* Edna Ferber

GAY SENORITA, THE, Story *see* Carlos A. Olivari, Sixto Pondal Rios

GAY SISTERS, THE, Novel *see* Stephen Longstreet

GAZEBO, THE, New York 1958, Play *see* Alec Coppel

GEFAHRDETE MADCHEN, Novel *see* Lothar

GEFAHRLICHE ALTER, DAS, Novel *see* Karin Michaelis

GEFAHRTIN MEINES SOMMERS, Novel *see* Claus Erich Boerner

GEFALLT EUCH MEINE FRAU, Play *see* Guglielmo Zorzi

GEFRORENE HERZ, DAS, Short Story *see* Meinrad Inglins

GEGENE LE TATOUE, Novel *see* Alphonse Boudard

GEHEIMNIS DER CHINESISCHEN NELKE, DAS, Novel *see* Louis Weinert-Wilton

GEHEIMNIS DER SCHWARZEN WITWE, DAS, Novel *see* Louis Weinert-Wilton

GEHULFE, DER, Novel *see* Robert Walser

GEIERWALLY, DIE, Novel *see* Wilhelmine von Hillern

GEIGENMACHER VON MITTENWALD, DER, Play *see* Ludwig Ganghofer, Hans Neuert

GEISHA, Book *see* Liza Dalby

GELBE FLAGGE, DIE, Novel *see* Fred Andreas

GELBE HAUS AM PINNASBERG, DAS, Novel *see* Bengta Bischoff

GELBE HAUS VON RIO, DAS, Play *see* Jos M. Velter

GELBE NACHTIGALL, DIE, Berlin 1907, Play *see* Hermann Bahr

GELD UND GEIST, ODER DIE VERSOHNUNG, Soleure 1843, Novel *see* Jeremias Gotthelf

GELIEBTE, DIE, Play *see* Alexander Brody

GELIEBTE FEINDIN, Novel *see* Marie von Kirchbach

GELIEBTE ROSWOLSKYS, DIE, Novel *see* Georg Froschel

GELIEBTE SEINER HOHEIT, DIE, Opera *see* Jean Gilbert

GEMINI, Play *see* Albert Innaurato

GENDARME EST SANS PITIE, LE, 1899, Play *see* Georges Courteline

GENDRE DE MONSIEUR POIRIER, LE, 1854, Play *see* Emile Paul Augier, Jules Sandeau

GENERAL COURT-MARTIAL, Play *see* William Rankin

GENERAL CRACK, London 1928, Novel *see* George Preedy

GENERAL DIED AT DAWN, THE, New York 1936, Novel *see* Charles G. Booth

GENERAL GOES TOO FAR, THE, Novel *see* Lewis Robinson

GENERAL JOHN REGAN, London 1913, Play *see* George A. Birmingham

GENERAL MICKEY, New Rochelle 1952, Novel *see* Peter Lappin

GENERAL POST, London 1917, Play *see* J. E. Harold Terry

GENERAL, THE, Short Story *see* Stephen King

GENERAL, THE, Book *see* Paul Williams

GENERAL, THE, 1960, Novel *see* Alan Sillitoe

GENERATION, New York 1965, Play *see* William Goodhart

GENEVIEVE; MEMOIRE D'UNE SERVANTE, Novel *see* Alphonse Lamartine

GENG ER IN BEIJING, Novel *see* Chen Ruoxi

GENGANGERE, 1881, Play *see* Henrik Ibsen

GENIO ALEGRE, EL, 1906, *see* Fratelli Quintero

GENIUS IN THE FAMILY, A, Biography *see* Hilary Du Pre, Piers Du Pre

GENJI MONOGATARI, c1001-1005, Novel *see* Shikibu Murasaki

GENNARENIELLO, Play *see* Eduardo de Filippo

GENOU DE CLAIRE, LE, 1974, Short Story *see* Eric Rohmer

GENROKU CHUSHINGURA, Play *see* Seika Mayama

GENS NOVA, Play *see* Flaviano C. Mancini

GENSDARM MOBIUS, Novel *see* Victor Bluthgen

GENTE AL BABUINO, Florence 1957, Novel *see* Ugo Moretti

GENTE DI RISPETTO, Novel *see* Giuseppe Fava

GENTLE ANNIE, 1942, Novel *see* MacKinlay Kantor

GENTLE BEN, New York 1965, Novel *see* Walt Morey

GENTLE GUNMAN, THE, Play *see* Roger MacDougall

GENTLE ILL WIND, A, 1916, Short Story *see* Maude Pettus

GENTLE JULIA, New York 1922, Novel *see* Booth Tarkington

GENTLE PEOPLE; A BROOKLYN FABLE, THE, New York 1939, Play *see* Irwin Shaw

GENTLE WEB, THE, Story *see* Lawrence B. Marcus, Rosalind Russell

GENTLE WOLFHOUND, THE, Story *see* E. J. Kahn Jr.

GENTLEMAN DE HONG-KONG, LE, Novel *see* Georges Godefroy

GENTLEMAN FROM AMERICA, THE, Short Story *see* Michael Arlen

GENTLEMAN FROM INDIANA, THE, New York 1899, Novel *see* Booth Tarkington

GENTLEMAN FROM MISSISSIPPI, A, New York 1908, Play *see* Harrison Rhodes, Thomas A. Wise

GENTLEMAN FROM PARIS, Novel *see* John Dickson Carr

GENTLEMAN OF FRANCE, A, 1893, Novel *see* Stanley Weyman

GENTLEMAN OF LEISURE, A, New York 1911, Play *see* John Stapleton, P. G. Wodehouse

GENTLEMAN OF QUALITY, A, New York 1909, Novel *see* Frederic Van Rensselaer Dey

GENTLEMAN OF THE JUNGLE, 1940, Novel *see* Tom Gill

GENTLEMAN OF VENTURE, Play *see* Roland Pertwee, John Hastings Turner

GENTLEMAN'S AGREEMENT, Novel *see* Laura Z. Hobson

GENTLEMAN'S AGREEMENT, 1914, Short Story *see* Wallace Irwin

GENTLEMAN'S FATE, A, 1931, Short Story *see* Ursula Parrott

GENTLEMAN'S GENTLEMAN, A, Play *see* Philip MacDonald

GENTLEMEN ARE BORN, Story *see* Harry Sauber

GENTLEMEN OF THE PRESS, Story *see* Ward Morehouse

GENTLEMEN PREFER BLONDES, New York 1925, Novel *see* Anita Loos

GENTLEMEN THE KING, 1931, Short Story *see* Damon Runyon

GEORDIE, Novel *see* David Walker

GEORG UND DIE ZWISCHENFALLE, 1938, Novel *see* Erich Kastner

GEORGE AND MARGARET, London 1937, Play *see* Gerald Savory

GEORGE BARNWELL, London 1731, Play *see* George Lillo

GEORGE DANDIN, OU LE MARI, 1669, Play *see* Moliere

GEORGE THURSTON, 1891, Short Story *see* Ambrose Bierce

GEORGE WASHINGTON, JR., New York 1906, Play *see* George M. Cohan

GEORGE WASHINGTON SLEPT HERE, 1941, Play *see* Moss Hart, George S. Kaufman

GEORGETTE, 1885, Play *see* Victorien Sardou

GEORGY GIRL, London 1965, Novel *see* Margaret Forster

GERALD CRANSTON'S LADY, New York 1924, Novel *see* Gilbert Frankau

GERALDINE; FOR THE LOVE OF A TRANSVESTITE, Book *see* Monica Jay

GERALDINE'S FIRST YEAR, Story *see* Mayell Bannister

GERATSITE, 1911, Novel *see* Pelin Elin

GERMAINE, Novel *see* Edmond About

GERMANIN, Novel *see* Hellmuth Unger

GERMANS, Novel *see* Leon Kruczkowski

GERMINAL, 1885, Novel *see* Emile Zola

GEROI NASHEGO VREMENI, 1840, Novel *see* Mikhail Lermontov

GERTRUD, 1906, Play *see* Hjalmar Soderberg

GERTRUD, 1956, Novel *see* Erik Aalbaek Jensen

GERUSALEMME LIBERATA, LA, 1575, Poem *see* Torquato Tasso

GESCHAFT MIT AMERIKA, Play *see* Paul Franck, Ludwig Hirschfeld

GESCHAFTE DES HERRN JULIUS CAESAR, DIE, 1957, Novel *see* Bertolt Brecht

GESCHENK DES INDERS, DAS, Novel *see* F. C. Oberg

GESCHICHTE VOM GOLDENEN TALER, DIE, Short Story *see* Hans Fallada

GESCHICHTE VON DEM KLEINEN MUCK, DIE, 1826, Short Story *see* Wilhelm Hauff

GESCHICHTE VON DER HANNERL UND IHREN LIEBHABERN, DIE, Leipzig 1913, Novel *see* Rudolf Hans Bartsch

GESCHICHTEN AUS DEM WIENER WALD, 1931, Play *see* Odon von Horvath

GESCHIEDENE FRAU, DIE, Operetta *see* Leo Fall, Viktor Leon

GESCHWISTER OPPENHEIM, DIE, 1933, Novel *see* Lion Feuchtwanger

GESETZ DER LIEBE, DAS, Novel *see* Fred Andreas

GESOM E KAKO SHIPTA, Novel *see* Im Chul-Woo

GESPENSTERHAUS, DAS, Zurich 1943, Novel *see* Ulrich Wichelegger

GESTA DANORUM, c1195, Books *see* Saxo Grammaticus

GESTANDNIS UNTER VIER AUGEN, Novel *see* Hugo Maria Kritz

GESTAPO, Novel *see* Gordon Wellesley

GESTATTEN MEIN NAME IS COX, Radio Play *see* Rolf Becker

GESTE, LE, Novel *see* Maurice Montegut

GESTERN UND HEUTE, Play *see* Christa Winsloe

GESTIEFELTE KATER, DER, Short Story *see* Jacob Grimm, Wilhelm Grimm

GESTOHLENE GEHEIMVERTRAG, DER, Novel *see* Peter Oldfield

GESTOHLENE JAHR, DAS, Novel *see* Stefan Zweig

GESUNDHEIT: GOOD HEALTH IS A LAUGHING MATTER, 1993, Book *see* Hunter Doherty Adams, Maureen Mylander

GET THAT GIRL, Story *see* Wilson Collison

GETAWAY, Short Story *see* Leslie Charteris

GETAWAY, THE, Novel *see* Jim Thompson

GETEILTE HIMMEL, DER, 1964, Novel *see* Christa Wolf

GET-RICH-QUICK WALLINGFORD, New York 1910, Play *see* George M. Cohan

GETTING A START IN LIFE, Short Story *see* James Oliver Curwood

GETTING EVEN, Manuscript *see* Richard Johnson

GETTING GERTIE'S GARTER, New York 1921, Play *see* Wilson Collison, Avery Hopwood

GETTING HURT, Novel *see* Andrew Davies

GETTING IT RIGHT, Novel *see* Elizabeth Jane Howard

GETTING OF WISDOM, THE, 1910, Novel *see* Ethel Florence Richardson

GETTING OUT, Play *see* Marsha Norman

GETTING STRAIGHT, Philadelphia 1967, Novel *see* Ken Kolb

GETTING TOGETHER, New York 1918, Musical Play *see* Ian Hay, P. Knight, J. Hartley Manners

GEWITTER IM MAI, Novel *see* Ludwig Ganghofer

GHAIRE BHAIRE, 1916, Novel *see* Rabindranath Tagore

GHAR BARI, Novel *see* Dibyendu Palit

GHASHIRAM KOTWAL, Play *see* Vijay Tendulkar

GHOST AND MRS. MUIR, THE, Novel *see* R. A. Dick

GHOST BELONGED TO ME, THE, Novel *see* Richard Park

GHOST BREAKER, THE, New York 1909, Play *see* Paul Dickey, Charles W. Goddard

GHOST CAMERA, THE, Story *see* J. Jefferson Farjeon

GHOST IN MONTE CARLO, THE, Novel *see* Barbara Cartland

GHOST IN THE MACHINE, Play *see* David Gilman

GHOST MOUNTAIN, Story *see* Alan Lemay

GHOST OF A CHANCE, THE, Short Story *see* O. Henry

GHOST OF FLIGHT 401, THE, Book *see* John G. Fuller

GHOST OF JOHN HOLLING, THE, 1924, Short Story *see* Edgar Wallace

GHOST OF ROSY TAYLOR, THE, 1917, Short Story *see* Josephine Daskam Bacon

GHOST OF THE MANOR, THE, 1933, Short Story *see* Maxwell Grant

GHOST PATROL, THE, Short Story *see* Sinclair Lewis

GHOST STORY, Novel *see* Peter Straub

GHOST TRAIN, THE, London 1925, Play *see* Arnold Ridley

GHOST WRITER, THE, Story *see* Philip Roth

GHOSTS OF MR. PIM, THE, Play *see* Basil Mason

GHOST'S STORY, THE, Story *see* Basil King

GHOSTS, THE, Story *see* Antonia Baker

GHOST-TOWN GOLD, New York 1935, Novel *see* William Colt MacDonald

GHOUL, THE, London 1928, Novel *see* Frank King

G.I. HONEYMOON, Play *see* Robert Chapin, Marion Page Johnson, A. J. Rubien

GIACCA VERDE, LA, 1961, Short Story *see* Mario Soldati

GIACOMO L'IDEALISTA, 1897, Novel *see* Emilio de Marchi

GIANT, 1952, Novel *see* Edna Ferber

GIANT SWING, 1932, Novel *see* William Riley Burnett

GIANT WOMAN, THE, Novel *see* John Blackburn

GIARDINO DEI FINZI-CONTINI, IL, 1962, Novel *see* Giorgio Bassani

GIBIER DE POTENCE, 1949, Novel *see* Jean-Louis Curtis

GIBIGIANNA, LA, 1898, Play *see* Carlo Bertolazzi

GIBSON UPRIGHT, THE, Play *see* Booth Tarkington, Harry Leon Wilson

GIDEON'S DAY, Novel *see* John Creasey

GIDGET, 1957, Novel *see* Frederick Kohner

GIDGET GOES TO NEW YORK, Novel *see* Frederick Kohner

GIFT FROM THE BOYS, A, Novel *see* Art Buchwald

GIFT O' GAB, Short Story *see* H. Tipton Steck

GIFT OF COCHISE, THE, Short Story *see* Louis L'Amour

GIFT OF THE MAGI, THE, 1906, Short Story *see* O. Henry

GIFT SUPREME, THE, New York 1916, Novel *see* George Allan England

GIFTGAS UBER BERLIN, Play *see* Peter Martin Lampel

GIGANT, DER, Play *see* Richard Billinger

GIGANTES Y CABEZUDOS, Opera *see* Miguel Echegaray, Fernandez Caballero

GIGANTI INNAMORATI, I, Novel *see* Salvator Gotta

GIGI, 1945, Novel *see* Sidonie Gabrielle Colette

GIGOLETTE, Novel *see* Pierre Decourcelle

GIGOLO, New York 1922, Novel *see* Edna Ferber

GIGOLO AND GIGOLETTE, 1940, Short Story *see* W. Somerset Maugham

GIGOLO, LE, Novel *see* Jacques Robert

GIL BLAS, 1715-35, Novel *see* Alain-Rene Lesage

GILBERT AND SULLIVAN BOOK, THE, Book *see* Leslie Bailey

GILBERTE DE COURGENAY, Zurich 1939, Novel *see* Rudolf Bolo Maglin

GILDED CAGE, THE, New York 1921, Play *see* Anne Nichols

GILDED DREAM, THE, 1920, Novel *see* Katherine Leiser Robbins

GILDED FOOL, A, New York 1892, Play *see* Henry Guy Carleton

GILDED ROOSTER, THE, 1947, Novel *see* Richard Emery Roberts

GILLIGAN'S LAST ELEPHANT, Cleveland 1962, Novel *see* Gerald Hanley

GIMBA: PRESIDENTE DOS VALENTES, 1959, Play *see* Gianfrancesco Guarnieri

GINA OF CHINATOWN, 1916, Short Story *see* Thomas Burke

GINGERBREAD LADY, THE, 1970, Play *see* Neil Simon

GINGHAM GIRL, THE, New York 1922, Musical Play *see* Daniel Kusell

GIOCO PERICOLOSO, Play *see* Ladislaus Fodor, Andreas Hindj

GIOCONDA, LA, Play *see* Victor Hugo

GIOCONDA, LA, Milan 1876, Opera *see* Arrigo Boito, Amilcare Ponchielli

GIOCONDA, LA, Palermo 1899, Play *see* Gabriele D'Annunzio

GIOCONDA SMILE, THE, 1922, Short Story *see* Aldous Huxley

GION BAYASHI, Novel *see* Matsutaro Kawaguchi

GIONMATSURI, Tokyo 1968, Short Story *see* Katsumi Nishiguchi

GIORGIO GANDI, 1861, Play *see* Leopoldo Marenco

GIORNALINO DI GIAN BURRSACA, IL, Novel *see* Vamba

GIORNO A MADERA, UN, 1876, Novel *see* Paolo Mantegazza

GIORNO DELLA CIVETTA, IL, Turin 1961, Novel *see* Leonardo Sciasia

GIOVANE NORMALE, IL, Novel *see* Umberto Simonetta

GIOVANNI DALLE BANDE NERO, Novel *see* Luigi Capranica

GIOVANNI L'EPISCOPO, 1891, Novel *see* Gabriele D'Annunzio

GIOVANNINO, Novel *see* Ercole Patti

GIOVE IN DOPPIOPETTO, Play *see* Pietro Garinei, Sandro Giovannini

GIOVINEZZA, GIOVINEZZA, Novel *see* Luigi Preti

GIPERBOLOID INZHENERA GARINA, 1926, Novel *see* Alexsey Nikolayevich Tolstoy

GIPFELKREUZ, Novel *see* Karl Loven

GIPSY LOVE, London 1912, Operetta *see* Robert Bodansky, Franz Lehar, A. M. Willner

GIPSY TRAIL, THE, New York 1917, Play *see* Robert Housum

GIRL, Novel *see* Blake Nelson

GIRL AND MR. MOTO, THE, 1936, Short Story *see* John Phillips Marquand

GIRL AND THE GAME, THE, Story *see* Frank Hamilton Spearman

GIRL AND THE GORILLA, THE, Story *see* Maurice Conn

GIRL AND THE GRAFT, THE, Short Story *see* O. Henry

GIRL AND THE JUDGE, THE, New York 1901, Play *see* Clyde Fitch

GIRL AUX MAINS FINES, LA, Short Story *see* Maurice Dekobra

GIRL BY THE ROADSIDE, THE, New York 1917, Novel *see* Varick Vanardy

GIRL CALLED FATHOM, A, London 1967, Novel *see* Larry Forrester

GIRL CALLED HATTER FOX, THE, Book *see* Marilyn Harris

GIRL CRAZY, New York 1930, Musical Play *see* Guy Bolton, George Gershwin, John McGowan

GIRL FROM HIS TOWN, THE, Indianapolis 1910, Novel *see* Marie Van Vorst

GIRL FROM OUT YONDER, THE, Baltimore 1914, Play *see* Pauline Phelps, Marion Short

GIRL FROM PETROVKA, THE, Novel *see* George Feifer

GIRL FROM RECTOR'S, THE, New York 1909, Play *see* Paul M. Potter

GIRL FROM THE EAST, THE, Novel *see* David Whitelaw

GIRL HE LEFT BEHIND HIM, THE, Story *see* Eugene Manlove Rhodes

GIRL HE LEFT BEHIND; OR ALL QUIET IN THE THIRD PLATOON, Novel *see* Marion Hargrove

GIRL HUNTERS, THE, New York 1962, Novel *see* Mickey Spillane

GIRL I LEFT BEHIND ME, THE, New York 1893, Play *see* David Belasco, Franklin Fyles

GIRL I LOVED, THE, Indianapolis 1910, Novel *see* James Whitcomb Riley

GIRL IN A SWING, Novel *see* Richard Adams

GIRL IN BOHEMIA, A, Play *see* H. B. Daniel

GIRL IN HIS HOUSE, New York 1918, Novel *see* Harold MacGrath

GIRL IN THE FLAT, THE, Story *see* Evelyn Winch

GIRL IN THE GLASS CAGE, THE, New York 1927, Novel *see* George Kibbe Turner

GIRL IN THE LIMOUSINE, THE, New York 1919, Play *see* Wilson Collison, Avery Hopwood

GIRL IN THE MIRROR, THE, New York 1919, Novel *see* Elizabeth Jordan

GIRL IN THE NEWS, THE, Novel *see* Roy Vickers

GIRL IN THE RED BIKINI, THE, Novel *see* Steve Fisher

GIRL IN THE TAXI, THE, New York 1910, Play *see* Stanislaus Strange

GIRL IN THE TURQUOISE BIKINI, THE, New York 1961, Novel *see* Muriel Resnik

GIRL IN UPPER C, THE, Play *see* Wilson Collison

GIRL LIKE CATHY, A, Short Story *see* Edward D. Hoch

GIRL MOST LIKELY TO, THE, Novel *see* Joan Rivers

GIRL MUST LIVE, A, Novel *see* Emery Bonet

GIRL NAMED MARY, A, Indianapolis 1918, Novel *see* Juliet Wilbor Tompkins

GIRL NAMED SOONER, A, Novel *see* Suzanne Clauser

GIRL NAMED TAMIKO, A, New York 1959, Novel *see* Ronald de Levington Kirkbride

GIRL OF GOLD, THE, 1920, Short Story *see* Anna Alice Chapin, Cleveland Moffett

GIRL OF LONDON, A, Novel *see* Douglas Walshe

GIRL OF MY DREAMS, THE, New York 1911, Musical Play *see* Otto Harbach, K. Hoschna, W. D. Nesbit

GIRL OF MY HEART, THE, Play *see* Herbert Leonard

GIRL OF THE GOLDEN WEST, New York 1905, Play *see* David Belasco

GIRL OF THE HOUR, THE, Story *see* Gladys Unger

GIRL OF THE LIMBERLOST, A, New York 1909, Novel *see* Gene Stratton-Porter

GIRL OF THE NIGHT, Novel *see* Harold Greenwald

GIRL OF THE OVERLAND TRAIL, Novel *see* Curtis B. Warshawsky, Samuel J. Warshawsky

GIRL OF YESTERDAY, A, Story *see* Wesley C. MacDermott

GIRL ON A WING, Novel *see* Bernard Glemser

GIRL ON THE BARGE, THE, 1927, Short Story *see* Rupert Hughes

GIRL ON THE BOAT, THE, 1922, Novel *see* P. G. Wodehouse

GIRL ON THE STAIRS, THE, 1924, Short Story *see* Winston Bouve

GIRL ON THE VIA FLAMINIA, THE, Novel *see* Alfred Hayes

GIRL, THE GOLD WATCH AND EVERYTHING, THE, Novel *see* John D. MacDonald

GIRL WHO ALMOST GOT AWAY, THE, Short Story *see* Pat Frank

GIRL WHO CAME BACK, THE, Hoboken 1920, Play *see* Charles E. Blaney, Samuel Ruskin Golding

GIRL WHO COULDN'T QUITE, THE, London 1947, Play *see* Leo Marks

GIRL WHO DARED (SCANDAL IN BUDAPEST), THE, 1911, Play *see* Alexander Farago, Aladar Laszlo

GIRL WHO DARED, THE, Story *see* H. H. Van Loan

GIRL WHO LIVED IN THE WOODS, THE, Chicago 1910, Novel *see* Marjorie Benton Cooke

GIRL WHO PAID DIVIDENDS, THE, 1921, Short Story *see* Earl Derr Biggers

GIRL WHO SAVED HIS HONOUR, THE, 1913, Novel *see* Arthur Applin

GIRL WHO TOOK THE WRONG TURNING, THE, London 1906, Play *see* Walter Melville

GIRL WHO WAS THE LIFE OF THE PARTY, THE, 1923, Short Story *see* Fanny Kilbourne

GIRL WHO WASN'T WANTED, THE, 1928, Short Story *see* Kenneth B. Clarke

GIRL WHO WOULDN'T WORK, THE, London 1913, Novel *see* Gertie Wentworth-James

GIRL WHO WRECKED HIS HOME, THE, Play *see* Walter Melville

GIRL WITH AN ITCH, Novel *see* Ralph S. Whitting

GIRL WITH THE GREEN EYES, THE, New York 1902, Play *see* Clyde Fitch

GIRL WITH THE JAZZ HEART, THE, 1920, Short Story *see* Robert Terry Shannon

GIRL WITHOUT A ROOM, Short Story *see* Jack Lait

GIRLFRIEND, Play *see* David Percival

GIRLS, New York 1908, Play *see* Clyde Fitch

GIRL'S BEST FRIEND IS WALL STREET, A, Book *see* Jane Allen

GIRLS DON'T GAMBLE ANYMORE, 1920, Short Story *see* George Weston

GIRLS IN THEIR SUMMER DRESSES, THE, Story *see* Irwin Shaw

GIRLS OF HUNTINGTON HOUSE, THE, Novel *see* Blossom Elfman

GIRLS TOGETHER, 1931, Short Story *see* Mildred Cram

GIRO DEL MONDO DEGLI INNAMORATI DI PEYNET, IL, Book *see* Raymond Peynet

GIRO DEL MONDO DI UN BIRICCHINO DI PARIGI, IL, Novel *see* Luigi Boussenard

GISELE ET SON DESTIN, Short Story *see* Madame A. de Lacombe

GISMONDA, Paris 1894, Play *see* Victorien Sardou

GITAN, LE, Novel *see* Jose Giovanni

GITANILLA, LA, 1613, Short Story *see* Miguel de Cervantes Saavedra

GIUOCA PIETRO!, Story *see* Luigi Pirandello

GIVE A DOG A BONE, Play *see* Peter Howard

GIVE AND TAKE, New York 1926, Novel *see* Aaron Hoffman

GIVE THE LITTLE GIRL A HAND, 1929, Short Story *see* Fannie Hurst

GJENBOERNE, 1844, Play *see* Jens Christian Hostrup

GLACE BAY MINER'S MUSEUM, THE, Short Story *see* Sheldon Currie

GLAD GUTT, EN, 1859, Short Story *see* Bjornstjerne Bjornson

GLAD TIDINGS, Play *see* R. F. Delderfield

GLADIATOR, THE, New York 1930, Novel *see* Philip Wylie

GLADSTONE, Novel *see* Sidney Robinson

GLAMOROUS NIGHT, London 1935, Musical Play *see* Ivor Novello

GLAMOUR, 1932, Short Story *see* Edna Ferber

GLASAM ZA LJUBAV, 1953, Novel *see* Grozdana Olujic

GLASBLASARNS BARN, 1964, Novel *see* Maria Gripe

GLASERNE BERG, DER, Novel *see* Hans Gustl Kernmayr

GLASS CELL, THE, 1964, Novel *see* Patricia Highsmith

GLASS HOUSE, THE, Story *see* Truman Capote

GLASS INFERNO, THE, Novel *see* Frank M. Robinson, Thomas M. Scortia

GLASS KEY, THE, New York 1931, Novel *see* Dashiell Hammett

GLASS MENAGERIE, THE, New York 1945, Play *see* Tennessee Williams

GLEAM O'DAWN, New York 1908, Novel *see* Arthur Frederick Goodrich

GLEISDREIECK, Novel *see* Rolf E. Vanloo

GLENDOWER LEGACY, THE, Novel *see* Thomas Gifford

GLENGARRY SCHOOL DAYS, Novel *see* Ralph Connor

GLIMPSES OF THE MOON, THE, New York 1922, Novel *see* Edith Wharton

GLITTER DOME, THE, Novel *see* Joseph Wambaugh

GLITZ, Novel *see* Elmore Leonard

GLOBAL AFFAIR, A, Novel *see* Eugene Vale

GLORIA, Novel *see* Solange Bellegarde

GLORIA SCOTT, THE, Short Story *see* Arthur Conan Doyle

GLORIOUS BETSY, New York 1908, Play *see* Rida Johnson Young

GLORIOUS BUCCANEER, 1930, Short Story *see* Emma Lindsay Squier

GLORIOUS DAYS, THE, London 1953, Musical Play *see* Harry Parr Davies, Robert Nesbitt

GLORY, Play *see* Adelyn Bushnell

GLORY BOYS, THE, Novel *see* Gerald Seymour

GLORY FOR ME, 1945, Novel *see* MacKinlay Kantor

GLORY GULCH, New York 1967, Novel *see* Ray Gaulden

GLORY OF CLEMENTINA, THE, New York 1911, Novel *see* William J. Locke

GLORY OF HIS COUNTRY, THE, 1910, Novel *see* Frederick Landis

GLORY OF LOVE, THE, London 1919, Novel *see* Pan

GLU, LA, Play *see* Jean Richepin

GLUCK AM SONNTAGABEND, DAS, Novel *see* Viktor Schuller

GLUCK AUF KUMPEL ODER DER GROSSE BESCHISS, Novel *see* Henry Jaeger

GLUCK, EIN, 1904, Short Story *see* Thomas Mann

GLUCK IM HINTERHAUS, Novel *see* Gunter de Bruyn

GLUCK MUSS DER MENSCH HABEN, Novel *see* Hannes Peter Stolp

GLUCK WOHNT NEBENAN, DAS, Play *see* F. Griebitz

GLUCKLICHE REISE, Opera *see* Max Bertuch, Eduard Kunneke, Kurt Schwabach

GLUCKLICHSTE EHE DER WELT, DIE, Play *see* Karl Georg Kulb

GLUCKLICHSTE FRAU DER WELT, DIE, Opera *see* Kurt Feltz, Max Wallner

GLUHENDE GASSE, DIE, Novel *see* Paul Rosenhayn

GNANAMBIKA, Novel *see* C. Madhavan Pillai

GNESELLA, 1899, Play *see* Francesco Gabriello Starace

GNOMOBILE: A GNICE GNEW GNARRATIVE WITH GNONSENSE., THE, 1962, Novel *see* Upton Sinclair

GO DOWN DEATH - A FUNERAL SERMON, 1927, Poem *see* James Weldon Johnson

GO INTO YOUR DANCE, New York 1934, Novel *see* Bradford Ropes

GO NAKED IN THE WORLD, New York 1959, Novel *see* Tom T. Chamales

GO TELL IT ON THE MOUNTAIN, 1953, Novel *see* James Baldwin

GO TELL THE SPARTANS, Novel *see* Daniel Ford

GOBEN NO TSUBAKI, Tokyo 1959, Novel *see* Shugoro Yamamoto

GO-BETWEEN, THE, 1953, Novel *see* L. P. Hartley

GOBSECK, 1830, Short Story *see* Honore de Balzac

GOD AND MY COUNTRY, Cleveland 1954, Novel *see* MacKinlay Kantor

GOD AND THE MAN, Novel *see* Robert Buchanan

GOD GAVE ME TWENTY CENTS, Short Story *see* Dixie Willson

GOD IN THE GARDEN, THE, Novel *see* Keble Howard

GOD IS MY CO-PILOT, Book *see* Colonel Robert Lee Scott Jr.

GOD OF HER PEOPLE, Story *see* James Oliver Curwood

GOD ON THE ROCKS, Novel *see* Jane Gardam

GODAN, 1936, Novel *see* Premchand

GODDESS OF SAGEBRUSH GULCH, THE, Short Story *see* Bret Harte

GODELUREAUX, LES, Novel *see* Eric Ollivier

GODFATHER, THE, Novel *see* Mario Puzo

GOD'S CLAY, Novel *see* Alice Askew, Claude Askew

GOD'S COUNTRY - AND THE WOMAN, New York 1915, Novel *see* James Oliver Curwood

GOD'S GIFT TO WOMEN, 1930, Short Story see Frederick Hazlitt Brennan

GOD'S GOOD MAN, Novel see Marie Corelli

GODS, GRAVES AND SCHOLARS, Article see C. W. Ceram

GODS HATE KANSAS, THE, 1941, Short Story see Joseph Millard

GOD'S LITTLE ACRE, 1933, Novel see Erskine Caldwell

GOD'S MAN, New York 1915, Novel see George Bronson Howard

GOD'S PRODIGAL, Novel see Edward Jose

GODS REDEEM, THE, Story see James Oliver Curwood

GODSEND, THE, Novel see Bernard Taylor

GODSON OF JEANETTE GONTREAU, THE, 1917, Short Story see Francis William Sullivan

GODSPELL, Musical Play see Stephen Schwartz, John-Michael Tebelak

GODVAKKER - MAREN, 1927, Play see Oskar Braaten

GO-GETTER, THE, Short Story see Peter B. Kyne

GOGO NO EIKO, 1963, Novel see Yukio Mishima

GOING ALL THE WAY, Novel see Dan Wakefield

GOING CROOKED, New York 1926, Play see William Collier, Winchell Smith

GOING GENTLY, Novel see Robert C. S. Downs

GOING OF THE WHITE SWAN, THE, Story see Gilbert Parker

GOING SOME, New York 1909, Play see Paul Armstrong, Rex Beach

GOING UP, New York 1917, Play see Otto Harbach, Louis A. Hirch

GOINGS ON OF VICTORINE, THE, Story see Julian Leonard Street

GOLD, Novel see Tian Fen

GOLD BAG, THE, Story see Carolyn Wells

GOLD BUG, 1843, Short Story see Edgar Allan Poe

GOLD CURE, THE, Novel see Sara J. Duncan

GOLD DIGGERS OF BROADWAY, THE, New York 1919, Play see Avery Hopwood

GOLD FOR THE CAESARS, Englewood Cliffs NJ 1961, Novel see Florence A. Seward

GOLD HUNTERS, THE, Indianapolis 1909, Novel see James Oliver Curwood

GOLD IN NEW FRISCO, Novel see R. Arden

GOLD INSIDE, THE, London 1960, Play see Jack Gillies

GOLD IS WHERE YOU FIND IT, East Norwalk, Ct. 1936, Novel see Clements Ripley

GOLD RAIDERS OF THE NORTH, Novel see Jack London

GOLD THAT GLITTERED, THE, Short Story see O. Henry

GOLDEN ANCHOR, THE, Novel see Hollister Noble

GOLDEN ARROW, THE, 1935, Short Story see Michael Arlen

GOLDEN BIRD, THE, New York 1918, Novel see Maria Thompson Davies

GOLDEN BOY, New York 1937, Play see Clifford Odets

GOLDEN CAGE, THE, Play see Lady Trowbridge

GOLDEN CALF, THE, 1926, Short Story see Aaron Davis

GOLDEN CHANCE, THE, Play see St. Aubin Miller

GOLDEN COCOON, THE, New York 1924, Novel see Ruth Cross

GOLDEN DAWN, New York 1927, Musical Play see Oscar Hammerstein II, Otto Harbach, Emmerich Kalman

GOLDEN EARRINGS, Novel see Yolanda Foldes

GOLDEN EGG, THE, Novel see Tim Krabbe

GOLDEN EVENINGS OF SUMMER, THE, Novel see Will Stanton

GOLDEN FETTER, THE, Short Story see Charles Tenney Jackson

GOLDEN FLEECE, 1917, Short Story see Fannie Hurst

GOLDEN FLEECE, 1918, Short Story see Frederick Irving Anderson

GOLDEN FLEECING, THE, 1959, Play see Lorenzo Semple Jr.

GOLDEN GALLOWS, THE, 1921, Short Story see Victoria Galland

GOLDEN GIFT, THE, Novel see Daniel F. Whitcomb

GOLDEN GOOSE, THE, Story see Robert Harari

GOLDEN HAWK, THE, 1948, Novel see Frank Yerby

GOLDEN HONEYMOON, THE, 1929, Short Story see Ring Lardner

GOLDEN IDIOT, THE, 1916, Novel see Robert Rudd Whiting

GOLDEN LEGEND OF SHULTS, THE, 1939, Play see James Bridie

GOLDEN PINCE-NEZ, THE, Short Story see Arthur Conan Doyle

GOLDEN POMEGRANATES, THE, Short Story see Sax Rohmer

GOLDEN SALAMANDER, Novel see Victor Canning

GOLDEN SENORITA, THE, Play see George B. Seitz

GOLDEN SNARE, THE, New York 1921, Novel see James Oliver Curwood

GOLDEN TIDE, THE, 1940, Novel see Vingie E. Roe

GOLDEN WEB, THE, Boston 1910, Novel see E. Phillips Oppenheim

GOLDEN YEARS, THE, Play see Arthur Miller

GOLDENE BETT, DAS, Novel see Olga Wohlbruck

GOLDENE GANS, DIE, 1812, Short Story see Jacob Grimm, Wilhelm Grimm

GOLDENGIRL, Novel see Peter Lear

GOLDENROD, Novel see Herbert Harker

GOLDFINGER, London 1959, Novel see Ian Fleming

GOLDFISH BOWL, THE, Boston 1932, Novel see Mary McCall Jr.

GOLDFISH, THE, New York 1922, Play see Gladys Unger

GOLDIE GETS ALONG, New York 1931, Novel see Hawthorne Hurst

GOLDMINE, Novel see Wilbur Smith

GOLEM, DER, 1915, Novel see Gustav Meyrink

GOLEMANOV, 1928, Play see Stefan Kostov

GOLOWIN GEHT DURCH DIE STADT, Novel see Hugo Maria Kritz

GOMMES, LES, 1953, Novel see Alain Robbe-Grillet

GONDOLE AUX CHIMERES, LA, Novel see Maurice Dekobra

GONE DU CHAABA, LE, Novel see Azouz Begag

GONE IN THE NIGHT, Book see David Protess, Rob Warden

GONE TO EARTH, 1917, Novel see Mary Webb

GONE TO TEXAS, Novel see Forrest Carter

GONE TO THE DOGS, Story see Paul Kester

GONE WITH THE WIND, New York 1936, Novel see Margaret Mitchell

GONG CRIED MURDER, THE, Short Story see John Dickson Carr

GONZAGUE, Play see Pierre Veber, Pierre Weber

GOOD BAD GIRL, THE, New York 1926, Novel see Winifred Van Duzer

GOOD BOY, Short Story see Mary McSherry

GOOD COMPANIONS, THE, 1929, Novel see J. B. Priestley

GOOD COMPANY, Play see Lawrence Hazard

GOOD COUNTRY PEOPLE, 1955, Short Story see Flannery O'Connor

GOOD DIE YOUNG, THE, Novel see Richard Macauley

GOOD EARTH, THE, New York 1931, Novel see Pearl Buck

GOOD EVANS, London 1927, Novel see Edgar Wallace

GOOD FATHER, THE, Novel see Peter Prince

GOOD FELLOW, THE, New York 1926, Play see George S. Kaufman, Herman J. Mankiewicz

GOOD GRACIOUS ANNABELLE, New York 1916, Play see Clare Kummer

GOOD LOOKING AND RICH, Short Story see Edgar Franklin

GOOD LUCK, London 1923, Play see Ian Hay, Seymour Hicks

GOOD LUCK MISS WYCKOFF, 1970, Novel see William Inge

GOOD MORNING MISS DOVE, 1954, Novel see Frances Gray Patton

GOOD MOTHER, THE, Novel see Sue Miller

GOOD NEIGHBOR SAM, New York 1963, Novel see Jack Finney

GOOD NEWS, New York 1927, Musical Play see Lew Brown, Frank Mandel, Lawrence Schwab

GOOD NIGHT AND GOOD BYE, Novel see Timothy Harris

GOOD PROVIDER, THE, 1914, Short Story see Fannie Hurst

GOOD REFERENCES, London 1920, Novel see E. J. Rath

GOOD SAMARITAN, A, Radio Play see Ellery Queen

GOOD VIBES, Novel see Jay Cronley

GOOD WILL AND ALMOND SHELLS, 1917, Short Story see Kenneth Lewis Roberts

GOODBYE, Novel see John Strange Winter

GOODBYE AGAIN, New York 1932, Play see George Haight, Allan Scott

GOODBYE CHARLIE, New York 1960, Play see George Axelrod

GOODBYE COLUMBUS, Boston 1959, Novel see Philip Roth

GOODBYE MR. CHIPS, 1934, Novel see James Hilton

GOODBYE MY FANCY, New York 1949, Play see Fay Kanin

GOODBYE MY LADY, 1954, Novel see James H. Street

GOODBYE PEOPLE, THE, Play see Herb Gardner

GOODBYE PICCADILLY, FAREWELL LEICESTER SQUARE, Novel see Arthur La Bern

GOODBYE TO THE HILL, London 1965, Novel see Lee Dunne

GOODNESS HOW SAD, London 1938, Play see Robert Morley

GOODNIGHT MISTER TOM, Novel see Michelle Magorian

GOOSE GIRL, THE, New York 1909, Novel see Harold MacGrath

GOOSE HANGS HIGH, THE, New York 1924, Play see Lewis Beach

GOOSE WOMAN, THE, 1925, Short Story see Rex Beach

GOOSEFOOT, Novel see Patrick McGinley

GORBALS STORY, THE, Play see Robert McLeish

GORDIAN, DER TYRANN, Novel see Rudolf Greinz

GORESHTO PLADNE, 1965, Short Story see Yordan Radichkov

GORGEOUS HUSSY, THE, Boston 1934, Novel see Samuel Hopkins Adams

GORGO, IL, 1913, Short Story see Luigi Pirandello

GORGONA, LA, 1913, Play see Sem Benelli

GORIACHEE SERDTSE, 1869, Play see Alexander Ostrovsky

GORILLA, THE, New York 1925, Play see Ralph Spence

GORILLE A MORDU L'ARCHEVEQUE, LE, Novel see Antoine Dominique

GORILLE VOUS SALUE BIEN, LE, Novel see Antoine Dominique

GORKY PARK, Novel see Martin Cruz Smith

GORODA I GODY, 1924, Novel see Konstantin Fedin

GOSLINGS, THE, Play see Henry Moritz

GOSPODA MINISTARKA, 1929, Play see Branislav Nusic

GOSPODICA, 1945, Novel see Ivo Andric

GOSSAMER WEB, THE, Story see John A. Moroso

GOSSES DANS LES RUINES, LES, Play see Paul Grex, Paul Gsell, M. Poulbot

GOSSES MENENT L'ENQUETE, LES, Novel see Francis Didelot

GOSSETTE, Novel see Charles Vayre

GOSSIP, Story see Edith Barnard Delano

GOSSIP FROM THE FOREST, Novel see Thomas Keneally

GOSTA BERLINGS SAGA, Novel see Selma Lagerlof

GOTT SCHUTZT DIE LIEBENDEN, Novel see Johannes Mario Simmel

GOTZ VON BERLICHINGEN MIT DER EISERNEN HAND, 1773, Play see Johann Wolfgang von Goethe

GOUALEUSE, LA, Play see Ludovic Halevy, Georges Maret

GOUBBIAH, Novel see Jean Martet

GOUDEN KETENEN, Novel see Princess Elsa

GOUDVISCHJE, HET, 1893, Play see Willem Gerard Van Nouhuys

GOUPI MAINS-ROUGES, Novel see Pierre Very

GOURDE D'EAU-DE-VIE, LA, Short Story see Andre Gorbaz

567

GOVERNMENT INSPECTOR, THE, 1836, Play *see* Nikolay Gogol

GOVERNOR'S BOSS, THE, New York 1914, Novel *see* James S. Barcus

GOVERNOR'S LADY, THE, New York 1912, Play *see* Alice Bradley

GOWNS BY ROBERTA, New York 1933, Novel *see* Alice Duer Miller

GOYA; ODER DER ARGE WEG DER ERKENNTNIS, 1951, Novel *see* Lion Feuchtwanger

GOYA QUE VUELVE, Novel *see* Antonio Garcia Guzman

GRAB DES LEBENDIGEN, DAS, 1917, Novel *see* Franz Nabl

GRACE, LA, Novel *see* Marcel Ayme

GRACIE ALLEN MURDER CASE, THE, New York 1938, Novel *see* S. S. Van Dine

GRADUATE, THE, New York 1963, Novel *see* Charles Webb

GRAF SPEE, Book *see* Michael Powell

GRAF VON LUXEMBOURG, DER, Vienna 1909, Operetta *see* Franz Lehar

GRAFIN MARITZA, Vienna 1924, Operetta *see* Julius Brammer, Emmerich Kalman

GRAIL, THE, Play *see* George Scarborough

GRAIN OF DUST, THE, New York 1911, Novel *see* David Graham Phillips

GRAINE AU VENT, Novel *see* Lucie Delarue-Mardrus

GRAMADA, 1880, Verse *see* Ivan Vazov

GRAMERCY GHOST, Play *see* John Cecil Holm

GRAN GALEOTO, EL, Madrid 1881, Play *see* Jose Echegaray

GRAN TEATRO DEL MUNDO, EL, 1645, *see* Pedro Calderon de La Barca

GRANATOVYY BRASLET, 1911, Short Story *see* Aleksander Ivanovich Kuprin

GRAND BABYLON HOTEL, THE, Novel *see* Arnold Bennett

GRAND BLUFF, LE, Play *see* Fred Heller, Adolf Schutz

GRAND CAID, LE, Novel *see* Claude Orval

GRAND CANARY, THE, London 1933, Novel *see* A. J. Cronin

GRAND CENTRAL MURDER, Novel *see* Sue McVeigh

GRAND CEREMONIAL, LE, 1965, Play *see* Fernando Arrabal

GRAND CIRQUE, LE, *see* Pierre Clostermann

GRAND CRI D'AMOUR, UN, Play *see* Josiane Balasko

GRAND CROSS OF THE DESERT, THE, 1927, Short Story *see* Richard Harding Davis

GRAND DADAIS, LE, Novel *see* Bertrand Poirot-Delpech

GRAND DUKE AND MR. PIMM, THE, New York 1959, Novel *see* Lindsay Hardy

GRAND ESCOGRIFFE, LE, Novel *see* Rennie Airth

GRAND FRERE, LE, Novel *see* Sam Ross

GRAND HOMME DE PROVINCE A PARIS, UN, 1839, Novel *see* Honore de Balzac

GRAND LARCENY, 1920, Short Story *see* Albert Payson Terhune

GRAND MEAULNES, LE, 1913, Novel *see* Alain Fournier

GRAND NATIONAL NIGHT, London 1946, Play *see* Campbell Christie, Dorothy Christie

GRAND SLAM; THE RISE AND FALL OF A BRIDGE WIZARD, New York 1932, Novel *see* Benjamin Russell Herts

GRANDE AMIE, LA, Novel *see* Pierre L'Ermite

GRANDE BRETECHE OU LES TROIS VENGEANCES, LA, 1837, Novel *see* Honore de Balzac

GRANDE EPREUVE, LA, Novel *see* Georges Le Faure

GRANDE FILLE TOUTE SIMPLE, UNE, 1943, Play *see* Andre Roussin

GRANDE MARNIERE, LA, 1888, Novel *see* Georges Ohnet

GRANDE MARRADE, LA, Novel *see* Claude Neron

GRANDE MENTECAPTO, O, 1979, Novel *see* Fernando Tavares Sabino

GRANDE MEUTE, LA, Novel *see* Paul Vialar

GRANDE SERTAO: VEREDAS, 1956, Novel *see* Guimaraes Rosa

GRANDE TRAGICA, LA, Book *see* Nino Bolla

GRANDE VEDETTE, LA, Play *see* Rene Peter, M. Vaucaire

GRANDE-DUCHESSE ET LE GARCON D'ETAGE, LA, Paris 1924, Play *see* Alfred Savoir

GRANDE-MAGUET, 1888, Novel *see* Catulle Mendes

GRANDES FAMILLES, LES, 1948, Novel *see* Maurice Druon

GRANDEUR ET DECADENCE DE CESAR BIROTTEAU, 1837, Novel *see* Honore de Balzac

GRANDEUR NATURE, 1936, Novel *see* Henri Troyat

GRANDFLAPPER, THE, 1926, Short Story *see* Nina Wilcox Putnam

GRANDHOTEL NEVADA, Play *see* Frantisek Langer

GRANDMOTHER BERNLE LEARNS HER LETTERS, 1926, Short Story *see* I. A. R. Wylie

GRANDPA AND FRANK, Novel *see* Janet Majerus

GRAND-PERE, LE, Play *see* Jules Mary

GRANDS CHEMINS, LES, Paris 1951, Novel *see* Jean Giono

GRANDS, LES, Play *see* Serge Basset, Pierre Veber

GRANGE MYSTERY, THE, Novel *see* Philip Godfrey

GRANICA, 1936, Novel *see* Zofia Nalkowska

GRANUJAS, LOS, Play *see* Carlos Arniches, Jose Jackson Veyan

GRAPES OF WRATH, THE, New York 1939, Novel *see* John Steinbeck

GRAPPLER, THE, Story *see* Charles A. Logue

GRASS ARENA, THE, Novel *see* John Healy

GRASS HARP, THE, 1951, Novel *see* Truman Capote

GRASS IS ALWAYS GREENER OVER THE SEPTIC TANK, THE, Book *see* Erma Bombeck

GRASS IS GREENER, THE, London 1958, Play *see* Hugh Williams, Margaret Williams

GRASS IS SINGING, THE, 1950, Novel *see* Doris Lessing

GRATTACIELI, Play *see* Guglielmo Giannini

GRAUSTARK, New York 1901, Novel *see* George Barr McCutcheon

GRAVE ERREUR, UNE, Play *see* Albert Willemetz

GRAVEYARD SHIFT, Short Story *see* Stephen King

GRAVY GAME, THE, 1933, Short Story *see* W. Thornton Martin, Harry Stuhldreher

GRAY DAWN, THE, Garden City, N.Y. 1915, Novel *see* Stewart Edward White

GRAY MASK, THE, 1915, Short Story *see* Wadsworth Camp

GRAY PARASOL, THE, 1918, Short Story *see* Frederick Jackson

GRAY PATH, THE, 1922, Short Story *see* Izola Forrester

GRAZIELLA, Novel *see* Ercole Patti

GRAZIELLA, 1852, Poem *see* Alphonse de Lamartine

GREASE, Musical Play *see* Warren Casey, Jim Jacobs

GREAT ACCIDENT, THE, New York 1920, Novel *see* Ben Ames Williams

GREAT ADVENTURE, THE, London 1913, Play *see* Arnold Bennett

GREAT AIR MAIL ROBBERY, THE, Story *see* Jack Lait

GREAT BANK ROBBERY, THE, New York 1969, Novel *see* Frank O'Rourke

GREAT CATHERINE, London 1913, Play *see* George Bernard Shaw

GREAT COMPANIONS, THE, Novel *see* Gene Markey

GREAT COUP, A, Novel *see* Nat Gould

GREAT CROONER, THE, New York 1933, Novel *see* Clarence Budington Kelland

GREAT DAY, 1945, Play *see* Lesley Storm

GREAT DAY IN THE MORNING, 1950, Novel *see* Robert Hardy Andrews

GREAT DAY, THE, London 1919, Play *see* Louis N. Parker, George R. Sims

GREAT DIAMOND ROBBERY, THE, New York 1895, Play *see* Edward M. Alfriend, A. C. Wheeler

GREAT DINOSAUR ROBBERY, THE, Novel *see* David Forrest

GREAT DIVIDE, THE, Novel *see* Alan Sullivan

GREAT DIVIDE, THE, New York 1906, Play *see* William Vaughn Moody

GREAT ESCAPE, THE, 1950, Novel *see* Paul Brickhill

GREAT EXPECTATIONS, London 1861, Novel *see* Charles Dickens

GREAT GATSBY, THE, 1925, Novel *see* F. Scott Fitzgerald

GREAT GAY ROAD, THE, Novel *see* Tom Gallon

GREAT GOD FOUR FLUSH, THE, Short Story *see* Adela Rogers St. Johns

GREAT IMPERSONATION, THE, Boston 1920, Novel *see* E. Phillips Oppenheim

GREAT IMPOSTOR, THE, New York 1959, Novel *see* Robert Crichton

GREAT JASPER, THE, New York 1930, Novel *see* Fulton Oursler

GREAT K & A TRAIN ROBBERY, THE, New York 1897, Novel *see* Paul Leicester Ford

GREAT LOVER, THE, New York 1915, Play *see* Leo Ditrichstein, Fanny Hatton, Frederic Hatton

GREAT MAGOO, THE, New York 1932, Play *see* Gene Fowler, Ben Hecht

GREAT MAN, THE, 1955, Novel *see* Al Morgan

GREAT MAN VOTES, THE, 1931, Short Story *see* Gordon Malherbe Hillman

GREAT MAN'S WHISKERS, THE, Play *see* Adrian Scott

GREAT MEADOW, THE, New York 1930, Novel *see* Elizabeth Madox Roberts

GREAT MONO MIRACLE, THE, Novel *see* Peter B. Kyne

GREAT MR. HANDEL, THE, Radio Play *see* L. Du Garde Peach

GREAT MUSIC, New York 1924, Play *see* Martin Brown

GREAT POWER, THE, New York 1928, Play *see* Myron C. Fagan

GREAT PRINCE SHAN, THE, London 1922, Novel *see* E. Phillips Oppenheim

GREAT RUBY, THE, London 1898, Play *see* Henry Hamilton, Cecil Raleigh

GREAT SANTINI, THE, Novel *see* Pat Conroy

GREAT SILENCE, THE, Novel *see* H. Tipton Steck

GREAT SNAKES, Novel *see* William Caine

GREAT TRAIN ROBBERY, THE, Novel *see* Michael Crichton

GREAT WELL, THE, Play *see* Alfred Sutro

GREAT WEST THAT WAS, THE, Book *see* William F. Cody

GREAT WHITE HOPE, THE, Washington D.C. 1967, Play *see* Howard Sackler

GREAT WIND COMETH, A, Book *see* Yoel Palgi

GREATER HATE, THE, Story *see* Roy Norton

GREATER LOVE HATH NO MAN, New York 1913, Novel *see* Frank L. Packard

GREATER WAR, THE, Short Story *see* W. Townend

GREATER WOMAN, THE, Play *see* Algernon Boyesen

GREATEST GIFT, THE, Short Story *see* Philip Van Doren Stern

GREATEST STORY EVER TOLD, THE, New York 1949, Book *see* Fulton Oursler

GREATEST THING THAT ALMOST HAPPENED, THE, Novel *see* Don Robertson

GREATEST WISH IN THE WORLD, THE, Novel *see* E. Temple Thurston

GREATHEART, Novel *see* Ethel M. Dell

GREEK COFFIN MYSTERY, THE, Story *see* Ellery Queen

GREEK INTERPRETER, THE, Short Story *see* Arthur Conan Doyle

GREEK POROPULOS, THE, 1911, Short Story *see* Edgar Wallace

GREEK TYCOON, THE, Novel *see* Nico Mastorakis

GREEKS BEARING GIFTS, Novel *see* Colin Dexter

GREEKS HAD A WORD FOR IT, THE, New York 1930, Play *see* Zoe Akins

GREEN ARCHER, THE, London 1923, Novel *see* Edgar Wallace

GREEN BERETS, THE, New York 1965, Novel *see* Robin Moore

GREEN CARAVAN, THE, Novel *see* Oliver Sandys

GREEN DICE, 1926, Short Story *see* Anne Cameron

GREEN DOLPHIN STREET, Novel *see* Elizabeth Goudge

GREEN DOOR, THE, Short Story *see* O. Henry

GREEN EYE OF THE YELLOW GOD, THE, Poem *see* J. Milton Hayes

GREEN EYE, THE, Play *see* John McNally

GREEN FANCY, New York 1917, Novel *see* George Barr McCutcheon

GREEN FIRE, 1942, Novel *see* Peter W. Rainier

GREEN FOR DANGER, Novel *see* Christianna Brand

GREEN GOD, THE, New York 1911, Novel *see* Frederic Arnold Kummer

GREEN GODDESS, THE, New York 1921, Play *see* William Archer

GREEN GRASS OF WYOMING, Novel *see* Mary O'Hara

GREEN GROW THE LILACS, New York 1930, Play *see* Lynn Riggs

GREEN GROW THE RUSHES, Novel *see* Howard Clewes

GREEN GULLABALOO, THE, Short Story *see* Harry Conway Fisher

GREEN HAT, THE, New York 1924, Novel *see* Michael Arlen

GREEN HELMET, THE, London 1957, Novel *see* Jon Cleary

GREEN ICE, Novel *see* Gerald A. Browne

GREEN JOURNEY, A, Book *see* John Hassler

GREEN LIGHT, Boston 1935, Novel *see* Lloyd C. Douglas

GREEN MANSIONS, 1904, Novel *see* W. H. Hudson

GREEN MIST, THE, Short Story *see* Sax Rohmer

GREEN MOUNTAINS, Novel *see* Bernard O'Reilly

GREEN ORCHARD, THE, London 1916, Novel *see* Andrew Soutar

GREEN PACK, THE, London 1933, Novel *see* Edgar Wallace

GREEN PASTURES, THE, New York 1930, Play *see* Marc Connelly

GREEN PEARL, Novel *see* Kan Kikuchi

GREEN RIBBON, THE, London 1929, Novel *see* Edgar Wallace

GREEN RUST, THE, London 1919, Novel *see* Edgar Wallace

GREEN SEAL, THE, Chicago 1914, Novel *see* Charles Edmonds Walk

GREEN SHADOW, THE, New York 1935, Novel *see* James Edward Grant

GREEN STOCKINGS, 1909, Play *see* A. E. W. Mason

GREEN YEARS, THE, 1944, Novel *see* A. J. Cronin

GREENE MURDER CASE, THE, New York 1928, Novel *see* S. S. Van Dine

GREEN-EYED DEVIL, THE, Story *see* Daniel Carson Goodwin

GREENGAGE SUMMER, THE, London 1958, Novel *see* Rumer Godden

GREENSEA ISLAND, Novel *see* Victor Bridges

GREETINGS FROM HONG KONG, *see* A. L. Malraux

GRELL MYSTERY, THE, London 1913, Novel *see* Frank Froest

GRELUCHON DELICAT, LE, Play *see* Jacques Natanson

GREMLIN'S CASTLE, THE, Short Story *see* Ernest K. Gann

GRENDEL, Novel *see* John Gardner

GRETCHEN, Play *see* Davis, Lipschutz

GRETE MINDE, 1879, Novel *see* Theodor Fontane

GRET'N ANN, 1922, Short Story *see* Louis Dodge

GRETNA GREEN, New York 1903, Play *see* Grace Livingston Furniss

GREVEN AV GAMLA STA'N, Play *see* Arthur Fischer, Siegfried Fischer

GREY CONTRE X, Short Story *see* Alfred Gragnon

GREY GRANITE, Novel *see* Lewis Grassic Gibbon

GREY TIMOTHY, London 1913, Novel *see* Edgar Wallace

GREYFRIARS BOBBY, New York 1912, Novel *see* Eleanor Atkinson

GREYHOUND, THE, New York 1912, Play *see* Paul Armstrong, Wilson Mizner

GREYWATER PARK, Short Story *see* Sax Rohmer

GRIBICHE, Short Story *see* Frederic Boutet

GRIECHE SUCHT GRIECHIN, 1955, Short Story *see* Friedrich Durrenmatt

GRIFFE, LA, Short Story *see* Jean Makis

GRIFFE, LA, Play *see* Jean Sartene

GRIFFE, LA, Paris 1906, Play *see* Henri Bernstein

GRIFTERS, THE, Story *see* C. D. Lancaster

GRIJPSTRA & DE GIER, Novel *see* Janwillem Van de Wetering

GRILLON DU FOYER, LE, Short Story *see* Charles Dickens

GRIM JUSTICE, Novel *see* Rita

GRIMALDI, Play *see* Dion Boucicault

GRIMME AELLING, DER, 1844, Short Story *see* Hans Christian Andersen

GRINE FELDER, New York 1918, Play *see* Peretz Hirshbein

GRINGA, LA, New York 1928, Play *see* Tom Cushing

GRINGALET, Play *see* Paul Vandenberghe

GRIP, Novel *see* John Strange Winter

GRISOU, Play *see* Pierre Brasseur, Marcel Dalio

GRISSOM GANG, THE, Novel *see* James Hadley Chase

GRIT, Short Story *see* F. Scott Fitzgerald

GRIZZLY KING, THE, Novel *see* James Oliver Curwood

GRONA KAMMARN PA LINNAIS GARD, 1859, Novel *see* Zachris Topelius

GROSS UND KLEIN, 1980, Play *see* Botho Strauss

GROSSE EINMALEINS, DAS, Novel *see* Vicki Baum

GROSSE FLATTER, DIE, Novel *see* Leonie Ossowski

GROSSE KURVE, DIE, Play *see* Curt Johannes Braun

GROSSE UND DIE KLEINE WELT, DIE, Play *see* Rudolf Eger

GROSSE UND DIE KLEINE WELT, DIE, Novel *see* Hugo Maria Kritz

GROSVENOR SQUARE GOODBYE, THE, 1974, Novel *see* Francis Clifford

GROTESQUE, THE, Book *see* Patrick McGrath

GROUCH BAG, THE, Short Story *see* Wallace Smith

GROUNDSTAR CONSPIRACY, THE, Novel *see* L. P. Davies

GROUP, THE, New York 1963, Novel *see* Mary McCarthy

GROZA, 1859, Play *see* Alexander Ostrovsky

GRUMPY, New York 1921, Play *see* Horace Hodges, Thomas Wigney Percyval

GRUNE KAISER, DER, Novel *see* Hans Medin

GRUNE MONOKEL, DAS, Novel *see* Guido Kreutzer

GRUPPENBILD MIT DAME, 1971, Novel *see* Heinrich Boll

GRZECHY DZIECINSTWA, 1883, Short Story *see* Boleslaw Prus

G-STRING MURDERS, THE, Novel *see* Gypsy Rose Lee

GUA PENG NU JIE, Novel *see* Liu Shaotang

GUADALCANAL DIARY, 1943, Novel *see* Richard W. Tregaskis

GUAN BU ZHU, Play *see* Zhao Yuxiang

GUAN HANQING, 1958, Play *see* Tian Han

GUAPO DEL 1900, UN, Play *see* Samuel Eichelbaum

GUAPOS, LOS, Play *see* Carlos Arniches, Jose Jackson Veyan

GUARANI, O, 1857, Novel *see* Jose Martiniano de Alencar

GUARDAFUI, Novel *see* Marcello Orano

GUARDIAN OF THE ACCOLADE, THE, Short Story *see* O. Henry

GUBIJINSO, 1908, Novel *see* Soseki Natsume

GUDRUN, Copenhagen 1936, Novel *see* Johannes Vilhelm Jensen

GUERNICA, 1961, Play *see* Fernando Arrabal

GUERRA EMPIEZA EN CUBA, LA, 1957, Play *see* Victor Ruiz Iriarte

GUERRE DANS LE HAUT-PAYS, LA, 1915, Novel *see* Charles-Ferdinand Ramuz

GUERRE DES BOUTONS, LA, Paris 1912, Novel *see* Louis Pergaud

GUERRE DES FEMMES, LA, Poem *see* Antoine Redier

GUERRE DU FEU, LA, 1911, Novel *see* Joseph Henri Rosny

GUERRIERA NERA, LA, Short Story *see* Mario Piereghin

GUERRILLA, LA, 1936, Play *see* Jose Martinez Ruiz

GUERRRE DES MOMES, LA, Novel *see* Alfred Machard

GUESA ERRANTE, 1868-77, Verse *see* Sousandrade

GUESTS OF HERCULES, THE, New York 1912, Novel *see* Alice Muriel Williamson, Charles Norris Williamson

GUESTS OF THE NATION, 1931, Short Story *see* Frank O'Connor

GUEULE D'AMOUR, Novel *see* Andre Beucler

GUEULE D'ANGE, Play *see* Roger Normand

GUEULE DU LOUP, LA, 1904, Play *see* Pierre Bilhaud, Maurice Hennequin

GUEUX AU PARADIS, LES, Play *see* G. M. Martens

GUIDE FOR THE MARRIED MAN AS TOLD TO FRANK TARLOFF, A, Los Angeles 1967, Novel *see* Frank Tarloff

GUIDE, THE, New York 1957, Novel *see* R. K. Narayan

GUIGNOL, Play *see* Marcel Espiau, Paul Gordeaux

GUIGNOL OU LE CAMBRIOLEUR, Play *see* Louis Verneuil

GUILT, Short Story *see* B. Lambert

GUILTY BYSTANDER, 1947, Novel *see* Wade Miller

GUILTY GENERATION, THE, 1928, Play *see* J. Kirby Hawkes, Jo Milward

GUILTY MELODY, Novel *see* Hans Rehfisch

GUILTY MOTHER, A, Play *see* Ben Landeck

GUILTY ONE, THE, New York 1914, Play *see* Michael Morton, Peter Traill

GUILTY PARTY, THE, Short Story *see* O. Henry

GUILTY THING SURPRISED, A, Novel *see* Ruth Rendell

GUILTY VOICE, THE, Short Story *see* Hans Rehfisch

GUINEA PIG, THE, London 1946, Play *see* Warren Chetham Strode

GUIREN YU FANREN, Play *see* Zheng Zhenqiu

GUITAI, Play *see* Gao Shiguo

GUITARE ET LE JAZZ-BAND, LA, Play *see* Robert Dieudonne, Henri Duvernois

GULDREGN, Novel *see* Anders Bodelsen

GULLIVER'S TRAVELS, London 1726, Novel *see* Jonathan Swift

GUMASTAVIN PENN, Play *see* Tks Brothers

GUMSHOES 4-B, 1919, Short Story *see* Forrest Crissey

GUN AND THE PULPIT, THE, Novel *see* Jack Erlich

GUN CRAZY, 1940, Short Story *see* MacKinlay Kantor

GUN FANNER, THE, New York 1922, Novel *see* Kenneth Perkins

GUN FOR SALE, A, 1936, Novel *see* Graham Greene

GUN GENTLEMEN, Short Story *see* Max Brand

GUN GOSPEL, Chicago 1926, Novel *see* William Dawson Hoffman

GUN RUNNER, THE, New York 1909, Novel *see* Arthur Stringer

GUN SHY, Short Story *see* Clarence Upson Young

GUN, THE, 1933, Novel *see* C. S. Forester

GUN WITCH OF WYOMING, THE, Story *see* Larabie Sutter

GUNG HO, Book *see* W. S. Le Francois

GUNGA DIN, 1890, Poem *see* Rudyard Kipling

GUNMAN, Short Story *see* Percy Hoskins

GUNMAN'S CHOICE, Novel *see* Luke Short

GUNNER, THE, London 1928, Novel *see* Edgar Wallace

GUNS IN THE HEATHER, Novel *see* Lockhart Amerman

GUNS OF AUGUST, THE, New York 1962, Book *see* Barbara W. Tuchman

GUNS OF DIABLO, Novel *see* Robert Lewis Taylor

GUNS OF NAVARONE, THE, London 1957, Novel *see* Alistair MacLean

GUNS OF NORTH TEXAS, New York 1958, Novel *see* Will Cook

GUNS OF RIO CONCHOS, Greenwich CT. 1964, Novel *see* Clair Huffaker

GUNS OF THE TIMBERLAND, Novel *see* Louis L'Amour

GUNSIGHT WHITMAN, Story *see* Silvia Richards

GUNSMOKE CASE FOR MAJOR CAIN, A, Story *see* Norbert Davis

GURAMA-TO NO YUWAKU, Play *see* Tadashi Iizawa

GUSHU YIREN, 194-, Novel *see* Shu Qingchun

GUSTAV ADOLFS PAGE, 1882, Short Story *see* Conrad Ferdinand Meyer

GUTE NACHT, MARY, Play *see* Tidmarsch

GUTTER MAGDALEN, A, Short Story *see* Willard Mack

GUY FAWKES, Novel *see* Harrison Ainsworth

GUY MANNERING, 1815, Novel *see* Sir Walter Scott

GUY RENTON, 1953, Novel *see* Alec Waugh

G'WISSENSWURM, DER, 1905, Novel *see* Ludwig Anzengruber

GWYNETH OF THE WELSH HILLS, Novel *see* Edith Nepean

GYEREKEK KETSZER SZULETNEK, A, 1973, Novel *see* Sandor Somogyi Toth

GYEREKTUKOR, 1963, Novel *see* Sandor Somogyi Toth

GYPSY, New York 1959, Play *see* Arthur Laurents

GYPSY IN AMBER, Novel *see* Martin Smith

GYPSY MELODY, Short Story *see* Melchior Lengyel

GYPSY MOTHS, THE, Norwalk, Ct. 1964, Novel *see* James Drought

HA ENTRADO UN LADRON, 1920, Novel *see* Wenceslao Fernandez Florez

HAAR GROOTE DAG, Novel *see* D. Van Veen

HABIT VERT, L', Play *see* Gaston Arman de Caillavet, Robert de Flers

HABITATION OF DRAGONS, THE, 1988, Play *see* Horton Foote

HABITS NOIRS, LES, Novel *see* Paul Feval

HAERVAERK, 1930, Novel *see* Tom Kristensen

HAHSIT BABE, 1935, Short Story *see* James Edward Grant

HAI ZI WANG, 1982, Short Story *see* Zhong Ahcheng

HAIE AN BORD, Novel *see* Becker-Riepen

HAIE UND KLEINE FISCHE, Novel *see* Wolfgang Ott

HAIL AND FAREWELL, New York 1923, Play *see* William Hurlbut

HAIL, HERO!, New York 1968, Novel *see* John Weston

HAIR, Musical Play *see* Galt MacDermot, Hames Rado, Gerome Ragni

HAIRLESS MEXICAN, THE, 1928, Short Story *see* W. Somerset Maugham

HAIRY APE, THE, 1922, Play *see* Eugene O'Neill

HAISHANG HUA LIEZHUANG, Novel *see* Han Ziyun

HAIYO ZUMA SHIMATSU YORI, Short Story *see* Yasuhiko Takiguchi

HAJKA, 1960, Novel *see* Mihailo Lalic

HAKAI, 1906, Novel *see* Toson Shimazaki

HAKKARI'DE BIR MEVSIM, Novel *see* Ferit Edgu

HAKUCHU NO TORIMA, 1960, Short Story *see* Taijun Takeda

HAKUJITSUMU YUME, 1926, Short Story *see* Junichiro Tanizaki

HAL 5 AND THE HAYWARDS, Novel *see* Henry Donald

HALALKABIN, A, Budapest 1934, Novel *see* Louis Lucien Rogger

HALBERDIER OF THE LITTLE RHEINSCHLOSS, THE, 1907, Short Story *see* O. Henry

HALF A CHANCE, Indianapolis 1909, Novel *see* Frederic Stewart Isham

HALF A ROGUE, Indianapolis 1906, Novel *see* Harold MacGrath

HALF A TRUTH, Novel *see* Rita

HALF AN HOUR, New York 1913, Play *see* J. M. Barrie

HALF BREED, 1906, Play *see* H. D. Cottrell, Oliver Morosco

HALF GODS, New York 1929, Play *see* Sidney Coe Howard

HALF MARRIAGE, Story *see* George Kibbe Turner

HALFWAY TO HEAVEN, Play *see* Harry Seagall

HALL OF MIRRORS, A, Boston 1966, Novel *see* Robert Stone

HALLELUJAH TRAIN, New York 1963, Novel *see* Bill Gulick

HALLMARK OF CAIN, THE, Short Story *see* Nell St. John Montagu

HAMECON, L', Paris 1957, Novel *see* Vahe Katcha

HAMILTON, New York 1917, Play *see* George Arliss, Mary Hamlin

HAMLET, c1601, Play *see* William Shakespeare

HAMLET, THE, 1940, Novel *see* William Faulkner

HAMMER THE TOFF, Novel *see* John Creasey

HAMMERHEAD, London 1964, Novel *see* John Mayo

HAMMERMORDER, DER, Book *see* Fred Breinersdorfer

HAMMERS OVER THE ANVIL, Book *see* Alan Marshall

HAMMETT, Novel *see* Joe Gores

HAN YE, 1944, Novel *see* Li Feigan

HANAOKA SEISHU NO TSUMA, 1966, Novel *see* Sawako Ariyoshi

HAND AND THE FLOWER, THE, Novel *see* Jerrard Tickell

HAND IN GLOVE, 1944, Play *see* Charles Freeman, Gerald Savory

HAND OF A CHILD, THE, Poem *see* Alfred Berlyn

HAND OF MARY CONSTABLE, THE, Novel *see* Paul Gallico

HAND OF PERIL; A NOVEL OF ADVENTURE, THE, New York 1915, Novel *see* Arthur Stringer

HANDCUFFS AND KISSES, 1920, Short Story *see* Thomas Edgelow

HANDELIGT UHELD, 1968, Novel *see* Anders Bodelsen

HANDFUL OF CLOUDS, A, Story *see* Rowland Brown

HANDFUL OF DUST, A, 1934, Novel *see* Evelyn Waugh

HANDFUL OF TANSY (DON'T TELL FATHER), 1959, Play *see* Kay Bannerman, Harold Brooke

HANDLE WITH CARE, Story *see* Charles Belmont Davis

HANDMAID'S TALE, THE, 1986, Novel *see* Margaret Atwood

HANDS OF A STRANGER, Novel *see* Robert Daley

HANDS OF NARA, THE, New York 1922, Novel *see* Richard Washburn Child

HANDSCHUH, DER, Poem *see* Friedrich von Schiller

HANDY ANDY, Novel *see* Samuel Lover

HANGED MAN, THE, Novel *see* Dorothy B. Hughes

HANGING JUDGE, THE, Story *see* Tom Gallon

HANGING TREE, THE, 1957, Novel *see* Dorothy M. Johnson

HANGMAN'S HOUSE, New York 1926, Novel *see* Brian Oswald Donn-Byrne

HANGMAN'S VILLAGE, Story *see* Bart Lytton

HANGMAN'S WHIP, New York 1933, Play *see* Frank Butler, Norman Reilly Raine

HANGOVER MURDERS, New York 1935, Novel *see* Adam Hobhouse

HANGOVER SQUARE, 1941, Novel *see* Patrick Hamilton

HANGYABOLY, 1917, Novel *see* Margit Kaffka

HANK WILLIAMS THE SHOW HE NEVER GAVE, Play *see* Maynard Collins

HANKA A JINDRA, Novel *see* Vilem Neubauer

HANNAH JANE, Poem *see* D. R. Locke

HANNELE CHIGURDAGA, Novel *see* Triveni

HANNELES HIMMELFAHRT, 1893, Play *see* Gerhart Hauptmann

HANNERL UND IHRE LIEBHABER, Novel *see* Rudolf Hans Bartsch

HANNIBAL FOLTAMASZTASA, 1949, Novel *see* Ferenc Mora

HANS IM GLUCK, 1812, Short Story *see* Jacob Grimm, Wilhelm Grimm

HANS LE MARIN, Novel *see* Edouard Peisson

HANS NADS TESTAMENTE, 1910, Novel *see* Hjalmar Bergman

HANSEL UND GRETEL, 1812, Short Story *see* Jacob Grimm, Wilhelm Grimm

HANTISE, Novel *see* Marcel Dupont

HAPPIEST DAYS OF YOUR LIFE, THE, London 1947, Play *see* John Dighton

HAPPIEST MILLIONAIRE, THE, New York 1956, Play *see* Kyle Crichton

HAPPINESS, 1914, Play *see* J. Hartley Manners

HAPPINESS A LA MODE, 1919, Short Story *see* Edwina Levin

HAPPINESS OF THREE WOMEN, THE, 1914, Short Story *see* Albert Payson Terhune

HAPPINESS PREFERRED, 1936, Short Story *see* Frank R. Adams

HAPPY BIRTHDAY, WANDA JUNE, 1971, Play *see* Kurt Vonnegut Jr.

HAPPY DEATHDAY, Play *see* Peter Howard

HAPPY ENDING, THE, London 1922, Play *see* Ian Hay

HAPPY FAMILY, THE, Play *see* Michael Clayton Hutton

HAPPY FAMILY, THE, London 1966, Play *see* Maisie Mosco

HAPPY FAMILY, THE, New York 1910, Novel *see* B. M. Bower

HAPPY HUSBAND, THE, London 1927, Play *see* Harrison Owen

HAPPY LAND, 1943, Novel *see* MacKinlay Kantor

HAPPY NOW I GO, Novel *see* Theresa Charles

HAPPY PRINCE, THE, 1888, Short Story *see* Oscar Wilde

HAPPY PRISONER, THE, Short Story *see* W. Pett Ridge

HAPPY TIME, Novel *see* Robert L. Fontaine

HAPPY WARRIOR, THE, London 1912, Novel *see* A. S. M. Hutchinson

HAPPY-GO-LUCKY, 1913, Novel *see* Ian Hay

HARAM, AL-, Novel *see* Youssef Idris

HARASSED HERO, THE, Novel *see* Ernest Dudley

HARBOR BAR, THE, 1914, Short Story *see* Peter B. Kyne

HARBOR ROAD ,THE, Philadelphia 1919, Novel *see* Sara Ware Bassett

HARBOR, THE, Play *see* Theodore Reeves

HARBOUR LIGHTS, THE, London 1885, Play *see* Henry Pettitt, George R. Sims

HARD CASH, 1864, Novel *see* Charles Reade

HARD FEELINGS, Novel *see* Don Bredes

HARD LUCK DAME, Story *see* Laird Doyle

HARD MAN, THE, 1957, Novel *see* Leo Katcher

HARD ROCK MAN, THE, New York 1910, Novel *see* Frederick R. Bechdolf

HARD TIMES, London 1854, Novel *see* Charles Dickens

HARD WAY, THE, Novel *see* "A Peer"

HARDER THEY FALL, THE, 1947, Novel *see* Budd Schulberg

HARDWICK OF HAMBONE, Short Story *see* W. Bert Foster

HARI KARI, New York 1913, Play *see* Julian Johnson

HARLOW: AN INTIMATE BIOGRAPHY, New York 1964, Book *see* Irving Shulman

HARM'S WAY, Cleveland 1962, Novel *see* James Bassett

HARNESS BULL, 1937, Novel *see* Leslie T. White

HARNESS, THE, Short Story *see* John Steinbeck

HARNESSING PEACOCKS, Novel *see* Mary Wesley

HAROLD AND MAUDE, Novel *see* Colin Higgins

HAROM TESTOR AFRIKABAN, A, Novel *see* Jeno Rejto

HARP IN HOCK, A, Story *see* Evelyn Campbell

HARP THAT ONCE, THE, Novel *see* Patrick Hall

HARRIET AND THE PIPER, New York 1920, Novel *see* Kathleen Norris

HARRIET THE SPY, *see* Louise Fitzhugh

HARRISON BERGERON, Short Story *see* Kurt Vonnegut Jr.

HARRISON HIGH, Novel *see* John Farris

HARROWHOUSE, Novel *see* Gerald A. Browne

HARRY BLACK, Novel *see* David Walker

HARRY MCGILLS GEHEIME SENDUNG, Novel *see* Ludwig von Wohl

HARRY'S GAME, 1975, Novel *see* Gerald Seymour

HARVEST HOME, Novel *see* Thomas Tryon

HARVEST MOON, THE, New York 1909, Play *see* Augustus Thomas

HARVESTER, THE, Garden City, N.Y. 1911, Novel *see* Gene Stratton-Porter

HARVEY, New York 1944, Play *see* Mary Coyle Chase

HARVEY GIRLS, THE, 1942, Novel *see* Samuel Hopkins Adams

HASHI NO NAI KAWA, Novel *see* Sue Sumi

HASHIMURA TOGO, New York 1914, Novel *see* Wallace Irwin

HASSAN, London 1922, Play *see* James Elroy Flecker

HAST NOCH DER SOHNE JA?, Frauenfeld 1956, Novel *see* Erwin Heimann

HASTHANDLARENS FLICKOR, 1935, Short Story *see* Nils Artur Lundkvist

HASTY HEART, THE, London 1945, Play *see* John Patrick

HASTY WEDDING, Novel *see* Mignon G. Eberhart

HAT A COAT A GLOVE, A, New York 1934, Play *see* Wilhelm Speyer

HAT-CHECK GIRL, New York 1932, Novel *see* Rian James

HATE, Short Story *see* Wadsworth Camp

HATE SHIP, THE, Novel *see* Bruce Graeme

HATERS, THE, Story *see* J. G. Hawks

HATFUL OF RAIN, A, New York 1955, Play *see* Michael V. Gazzo

HATTERS CASTLE, 1931, Novel *see* A. J. Cronin

HATTYU, A, Budapest 1921, Play *see* Ferenc Molnar

HAUBENLERCHE, DIE, Play *see* Ernst von Wildenbruch

HAUEN SIE AB MIT HELDENTUM, Novel *see* Herbert Reinecker

HAUNTED, Novel *see* James Herbert

HAUNTED AND THE HAUNTERS; OR THE HOUSE AND THE BRAIN, THE, 1849, Short Story *see* Edward George Bulwer Lytton

HAUNTED HOUSE, THE, New York 1926, Play *see* Owen Davis

HAUNTED LADY, THE, 1925, Short Story *see* Adela Rogers St. Johns

HAUNTED LIGHT, THE, 1928, Play *see* Joan Byford, Evadne Price

HAUNTED PAJAMAS, THE, Indianapolis 1911, Novel *see* Francis Perry Elliott

HAUNTED PALACE, THE, 1839, Short Story *see* Edgar Allan Poe

HAUNTED SUMMER, Novel *see* Anne Edwards

HAUNTING OF HILL HOUSE, THE, New York 1959, Novel *see* Shirley Jackson

HAUNTING OF SARAH HARDY, THE, Novel *see* Jim Flannagan

HAUNTING WINDS, Story *see* G. E. Jenks

HAUPTLEHRER HOFER, 1975, Short Story *see* Gunter Herburger

HAUPTMANN UND SEIN HELD, DER, Novel *see* Claus Hubalek

HAUPTMANN VON KOPENICK, DER, 1930, Play *see* Carl Zuckmayer

HAUPTSTADTISCHES JOURNAL, 1957, Short Story *see* Heinrich Boll

HAU-RUCK, Play *see* Ladislaus Fodor

HAUS AUF DEM HUGEL, DAS, Novel *see* Jules Charpentier

HAUS DES LEBENS, Novel *see* Kathe Lambert

HAUS IN DER KARPFENGASSE, DAS, Novel *see* M. Y. Ben-Gavriel

HAUS IN MONTEVIDEO, DAS, Play *see* Curt Goetz

HAUS KIEPERGASS UND SEINE GASTE, Novel *see* Hannes Peter Stolp

HAUSCHEN IN GRINZING, DAS, Opera *see* Joseph Lanner

HAUSER'S MEMORY, Novel *see* Curt Siodmak

HAUSTYRANN, DER, Novel *see* Hans Reimann

HAUT FER, LE, Paris 1962, Novel *see* Jose Giovanni

HAUTE SURVEILLANCE, Paris 1949, Play *see* Jean Genet

HAVE YOU COME FOR ME, Novel *see* Norma Patterson

HAVEN, THE, Novel *see* Eden Philpotts

HAVET OG MENNESKENE, 1948, Play *see* Kaj Munk

HAVING OUR SAY, 1993, Book *see* A. Elizabeth Delany, Sarah L. Delany, Amy Hill Hearth

HAVING WONDERFUL TIME, New York 1937, Play *see* Arthur Kober

HAVOC, Story *see* Henry Wall

HAVOC, THE, New York 1911, Play *see* H. S. Sheldon

HAWAII, New York 1959, Novel *see* James A. Michener

HAWK ISLAND, New York 1929, Play *see* Howard Irving Young

HAWK OF REDE, THE, Novel *see* Harry Harding

HAWK, THE, Novel *see* Peter Ransley

HAWK, THE, Story *see* Sargon Tamimi

HAWLEYS OF THE HIGH STREET, 1922, Play *see* Walter Ellis

HAWTHORNE OF THE U.S.A., New York 1912, Play *see* James B. Fagan

HAZARD OF HEARTS, A, Novel *see* Barbara Cartland

HAZEL KIRKE, New York 1880, Play *see* Steele MacKaye

HAZSZENTELO, 1977, Short Story *see* Ferenc Karinthy

HAZY OSTERWALD STORY, DIE, Zurich 1961, Book *see* Walter Grieder

HD-SOLDAT LAPPLI. VOLKSSTUCK IN 16 BILDERN, 1945, Play *see* Alfred Rasser, Charles Vaucher

HE AND SKI, Novel *see* F. Dawson Gratix

HE COMES UP SMILING, Indianapolis 1912, Novel *see* Charles Sherman

HE DIED WITH HIS EYES OPEN, Novel *see* Derek Raymond

HE FELL DOWN DEAD, Novel *see* Virginia Purdue

HE FELL IN LOVE WITH HIS WIFE, New York 1886, Novel *see* E. P. Roe

HE FOLLOWS THE SUN AGAIN, Article *see* Frederick Hazlitt Brennan

HE LOOKED LIKE MURDER, 1946, Short Story *see* Cornell Woolrich

HE NEVER KNEW, Story *see* Bessie Boniel

HE RAN ALL THE WAY, 1947, Novel *see* Sam Ross

HE STEPHANIA STO ANAMORPHOTERIO, Athens 1960, Novel *see* Nelle Theodorou

HE STOPPED AT MURDER, Story *see* Arthur Ebenhack

HE WAS FOUND IN THE ROAD, Novel *see* Anthony Armstrong

HEAD AND SHOULDERS, 1920, Short Story *see* F. Scott Fitzgerald

HEAD OF THE FAMILY, THE, Short Story *see* W. W. Jacobs

HEAD OF THE FAMILY, THE, 1912, Short Story *see* George Randolph Chester

HEAD OF THE FAMILY, THE, 1924, Play *see* Katharine Clugston

HEAD OFFICE, Novel *see* Hugh Preston

HEAD OVER HEALS, Novel *see* Ann Beattie

HEAD WAITER, THE, Novel *see* Erno Vajda

HEAD WINDS, New York 1923, Novel *see* A. M. Sinclair Wilt

HEADED FOR A HEARSE, New York 1935, Novel *see* Jonathan Latimer

HEADING FOR HEAVEN, Play *see* Daniel Brown, Charles Webb

HEADLONG, 1981, Novel *see* Emlyn Williams

HEADMASTER, THE, London 1913, Play *see* Wilfred T. Coleby, Edward Knoblock

HEADS UP, New York 1929, Musical Play *see* John McGowan, Richard Rodgers, P. G. Smith

HEALER, THE, Book *see* Daniel P. Mannix

HEALER, THE, New York 1911, Novel *see* Robert Herrick

HEARSES DON'T HURRY, Novel *see* Stephen Ransome

HEART AND HAND, 1927, Short Story *see* Olive Edens

HEART IS A LONELY HUNTER, THE, Boston 1940, Novel *see* Carson McCullers

HEART IS YOUNG, THE, 1930, Short Story *see* May Edginton

HEART LINE, THE, Indianapolis 1907, Novel *see* Gelett Burgess

HEART OF A CHILD, Novel *see* Phyllis Bottome

HEART OF A CHILD, THE, London 1908, Novel *see* Frank Danby

HEART OF A THIEF, THE, New York 1914, Play *see* Paul Armstrong

HEART OF ARIZONA, THE, Novel *see* Clarence E. Mulford

HEART OF DARKNESS, 1899, Novel *see* Joseph Conrad

HEART OF MARYLAND, THE, New York 1895, Play *see* David Belasco

HEART OF MIDLOTHIAN, THE, 1818, Novel *see* Sir Walter Scott

HEART OF RACHAEL, THE, Garden City N.Y. 1916, Novel *see* Kathleen Norris

HEART OF SALLY TEMPLE, THE, New York 1913, Novel *see* Rupert Sargent Holland

HEART OF SALOME, THE, Boston 1925, Novel *see* Allen Raymond

HEART OF SISTER ANN, THE, Novel *see* G. E. R. Mayne

HEART OF THE BLUE RIDGE, THE, New York 1915, Novel *see* Waldron Baily

HEART OF THE DESERT, THE, New York 1913, Novel *see* Honore Morrow

HEART OF THE HILLS, THE, New York 1913, Novel *see* John Fox Jr.

HEART OF THE MATTER, THE, 1948, Novel *see* Graham Greene

HEART OF THE NIGHT WIND, THE, New York 1913, Novel *see* Vingie E. Roe

HEART OF THE NORTH, New York 1930, Novel *see* William Byron Mowery

HEART OF THE RANGE, THE, Garden City, N.Y. 1921, Novel *see* William Patterson White

HEART OF THE SUNSET, New York 1913, Novel *see* Rex Beach

HEARTBEAT, Story *see* Ladislaus Bus-Fekete

HEARTBREAK, 1931, Short Story *see* Llewellyn Hughes

HEARTBREAK HOTEL, Novel *see* Anne Rivers Siddons

HEARTBREAK HOUSE, 1919, Play *see* George Bernard Shaw

HEARTBREAK KID, THE, Play *see* Richard Barrett

HEARTBURN, Novel *see* Nora Ephron

HEARTEASE, New York 1897, Play *see* Joseph I. C. Clarke, Charles Klein

HEART'S A FORGOTTEN HOTEL, THE, 1955, Television Play *see* Arnold Shulman

HEARTS AND FISTS, 1924, Short Story *see* Clarence Budington Kelland

HEARTS AND MASKS, Indianapolis 1905, Novel *see* Harold MacGrath

HEARTS ARE TRUMPS, New York 1900, Play *see* Cecil Raleigh

HEART'S HAVEN, Boston 1918, Novel *see* Clara Louise Burnham

HEARTS IN EXILE, New York 1904, Novel *see* John Oxenham

HEARTS OF MEN, Story *see* James Oliver Curwood

HEARTS OF OAK, New York 1880, Play *see* James A. Herne

HEARTS ON THE HIGHWAY, New York 1911, Novel *see* Cyrus Townsend Brady

HEARTS STEADFAST, New York 1915, Novel *see* Edward Stewart Moffat

HEAT, 1985, Novel *see* William Goldman

HEAT AND DUST, 1975, Novel *see* Ruth Prawer Jhabvala

HEAT LIGHTNING, New York 1933, Play *see* George Abbott, Leon Abrams

HEAT WAVE, Cardiff 1929, Play *see* Roland Pertwee

HEATH HOOKEN, Novel *see* Coralie Stanton

HEATHER ALE: A GALLOWAY LEGEND, 1890, Verse *see* Robert Louis Stevenson

HEATHER OF THE HIGH HAND, New York 1937, Novel *see* Arthur Stringer

HEAT'S ON, THE, 1966, Novel *see* Chester Himes

HEAVEN, Novel *see* Chad Taylor

HEAVEN KNOWS MR. ALLISON, 1952, Novel *see* Charles Shaw

HEAVENBENT, Short Story *see* Gerald Beaumont

HEAVEN'S GATE, 1934, Short Story *see* Florence Leighton Pfalzgraf

HEBISUME TO HAKUHATSUKI, Short Story *see* Kazuo Kozu

HECATE, Novel *see* Paul Morand

HECTOR SERVADAC, 1878, Novel *see* Jules Verne

HECTOR SERVADEC: VOYAGES ET AVENTURES A TRAVERS LE MONDE ., Paris 1877, Novel *see* Jules Verne

HEDDA AND LOUELLA, Book *see* George Eels

HEDDA GABLER, 1890, Play *see* Henrik Ibsen

HEI JUN MA, Novel *see* Zhang Chengzhi

HEIDESCHULMEISTER UWE KARSTEN, Novel *see* Felicitas Rose

HEIDI, Zurich 1880, Novel *see* Johanna Spyri

HEIDI KANN BRAUCHEN, WAS ES GELERNT HAT, Novel *see* Johanna Spyri

HEIDI'S LEHR- UND WANDERJAHRE, Gotha 1881, Novel *see* Johanna Spyri

HEIGHTS OF HAZARD, THE, Story *see* Cyrus Townsend Brady

HESPER: A NOVEL, New York 1903, Novel *see* Hamlin Garland

HET AR MIN LANGTAN, Novel *see* Ingrid Beije

..HEUTE ABEND BEI MIR, Play *see* Hans Jaray

HEUTE HEIRATET MEIN MANN, Novel *see* Annemarie Selinko

HEXE, DIE, Novel *see* Fred Andreas

HEXENLIED, DAS, Poem *see* Ernst von Wildenbruch

HEY, I'M ALIVE!, Book *see* Helen Klaban, Beth Day

HEY, ROOKIE, Play *see* Doris Culvan, K. E. B. Culvan

HI MO TSUKI MO, Tokyo 1953, Novel *see* Yasunari Kawabata

HI NELLIE, Story *see* Roy Chanslor

HI NO ATARU SAKAMICHI, 1958, Novel *see* Yojiro Ishizaka

HI, TAXI, Story *see* Walter A. Sinclair

HIBERNATUS, Novel *see* Jean-Bernard Luc

HIDDEN, Novel *see* H. C. Armstrong

HIDDEN CHILDREN, THE, New York 1914, Novel *see* Robert W. Chambers

HIDDEN FIRES, Novel *see* Bertram Atkey

HIDDEN LIVES, Play *see* Robert Hichens, John Knittell

HIDDEN PATH, THE, Story *see* Lawrence McCloskey, A. W. Tillinghast

HIDDEN SPRING, THE, New York 1915, Novel *see* Clarence Budington Kelland

HIDDEN STAIRCASE, THE, New York 1930, Novel *see* Carolyn Keene

HIDE AND I'LL FIND YOU, Novel *see* Marcus McGill

HIDE AND SEEK, Novel *see* Harold Greene

HIDEAWAY, Novel *see* Dean R. Koontz

HIDEG NAPOK, 1965, Novel *see* Tibor Cseres

HIDEOUS KINKY, Novel *see* Esther Freud

HIDING OF BLACK BILL, THE, Short Story *see* O. Henry

HIDING PLACE, THE, 1971, Book *see* Corrie Ten Boom

HIDING PLACE, THE, London 1959, Novel *see* Robert Shaw

HIER BIN ICH, HIER BLEIB ICH, Play *see* Raymond Vinci, Jean Valmy

HIGANBANA, 1958, Novel *see* Ton Santomi

HIGH AND THE MIGHTY, THE, 1953, Novel *see* Ernest K. Gann

HIGH BARBAREE, 1945, Novel *see* James N. Hall, Charles Nordhoff

HIGH BRIGHT SUN, THE, London 1962, Novel *see* Ian Stuart Black

HIGH COMMISSIONER, THE, London 1966, Novel *see* Jon Cleary

HIGH CONQUEST, Novel *see* James Ramsey Ullman

HIGH HAND, THE, Indianapolis 1911, Novel *see* Jacques Futrelle

HIGH HAT A RADIO ROMANCE, New York 1930, Novel *see* Alma Sioux Scarberry

HIGH HELL, Novel *see* Steve Frazee

HIGH PAVEMENT, Novel *see* Emery Bonnet

HIGH POCKETS, 1918, Novel *see* William Patterson White

HIGH RISE DONKEY, Novel *see* Peter Buchanan

HIGH ROAD, THE, London 1927, Play *see* Frederick Lonsdale

HIGH ROAD, THE, New York 1912, Play *see* Edward Sheldon

HIGH ROAD TO CHINA, Novel *see* Jon Cleary

HIGH SIERRA, 1940, Novel *see* William Riley Burnett

HIGH SPEED, 1918, Short Story *see* Frederick Jackson

HIGH SPEED, New York 1916, Novel *see* Clinton H. Stagg

HIGH SPIRITS, Story *see* Edward Cline, Milton Gross

HIGH STAKES, Novel *see* James Hadley Chase

HIGH STAKES, 1917, Short Story *see* Andrew Soutar

HIGH STAKES, 1920, Short Story *see* Earl Wayland Bowman

HIGH TIDE AT NOON, Novel *see* Elizabeth Oglivie

HIGH TIDE, LOW TIDE, Novel *see* Qiu Weiming

HIGH TREASON, Play *see* Noel Pemberton-Billing

HIGH VERMILION, 1948, Novel *see* Luke Short

HIGH WALL, Play *see* Alan R. Clark, Bradbury Foote

HIGH WIND IN JAMAICA, A, London 1929, Novel *see* Richard Hughes

HIGH WINDOW, THE, 1942, Novel *see* Raymond Chandler

HIGH WRAY, Novel *see* Ken Hughes

HIGHER AND HIGHER, Musical Play *see* Gladys Hurlbut, Joshua Logan

HIGHER LAW, THE, Story *see* George Bronson Howard, George Patullo

HIGHEST MOUNTAIN, THE, Story *see* Harold Jacob Smith

HIGHGRADER, THE, New York 1915, Novel *see* William MacLeod Raine

HIGHWAY ROBBERY, 1934, Short Story *see* Albert Treynor

HIGHWAY TO ROMANCE, New York 1937, Novel *see* Eleanor Browne

HIGHWAYMAN, THE, 1907, Poem *see* Alfred Noyes

HIJA DEL MAR, LA, *see* Angel Guimera

HIJA DEL MESTRE, LA, Opera *see* Santiago Tejera Ossavarry

HIJO DE HOMBRE, Novel *see* Augusto Roa Bastos

HIJOS DE LA NOCHE, LOS, Play *see* Leandro Navarro

HIKARIGOKE, Novel *see* Taijun Takeda

HILDA CRANE, New York 1950, Play *see* Samson Raphaelson

HILDEGARDE WITHERS MAKES THE SCENE, *see* Fletcher Flora, Stuart Palmer

HILITO DE SANGRE, UN, Novel *see* Eusebio Ruvalcaba

HILJA, MAITOTYTTO, 1913, Short Story *see* Johannes Linnankoski

HILL IN KOREA, A, Novel *see* Max Catto

HILL, THE, 1965, Novel *see* Ray Rigby

HILLMAN, THE, London 1917, Novel *see* E. Phillips Oppenheim

HI-LO COUNTRY, THE, 1961, Novel *see* Max Evans

HIMMEL, AMOR UND ZWIRN, Novel *see* Thomas Westa

HIMMEL KENNT KEINE GUNSTLINGE, DER, 1961, Novel *see* Erich Maria Remarque

HIMMEL OG HELVEDE, 1982, Novel *see* Kirsten Thorup

HIMMELDONNERWETTER, VICTORIA, Novel *see* H. W. Loeb

HIMMO MELECH YERUSHALAYAM, Novel *see* Yoram Kaniuk

HIN UND HER, Play *see* Odon von Horvath

HINDENBURG, THE, Book *see* Michael M. Mooney

HINDLE WAKES, London 1912, Play *see* Stanley Houghton

HINTER KLOSTERMAUERN, Play *see* Hans Naderer

HINUBER - HERBUER, 1844, Play *see* Johann Nestroy

HIOB ROMAN EINES EIN FACHEN MANNES, Berlin 1930, Novel *see* Joseph Roth

HIPPOLYTUS, 428 bc, Play *see* Euripides

HIPPOPOTAMUS PARADE, THE, 1919, Short Story *see* Byron Morgan

HIRED GUNS, 1923, Short Story *see* Max Brand

HIRELING, THE, 1957, Novel *see* L. P. Hartley

HIRTETTYJEN KETTUJEN METSA, 1983, Novel *see* Arto Paasilinna

HIS ANSWER, Boston 1905, Poem *see* Bret Harte

HIS APOLOGIES, 1932, Poem *see* Rudyard Kipling

HIS BONES ARE CORAL, London 1955, Novel *see* Victor Canning

HIS BRIDAL NIGHT, New York 1916, Play *see* Lawrence Irving Rising

HIS BUDDY'S WIFE, Story *see* T. Howard Kelly

HIS CHILDREN'S CHILDREN, New York 1923, Novel *see* Arthur Cheney Train

HIS DOG, New York 1922, Novel *see* Albert Payson Terhune

HIS DUTY, Short Story *see* O. Henry

HIS EXCELLENCY, London 1950, Play *see* Campbell Christie, Dorothy Christie

HIS FIGHT, Short Story *see* James Oliver Curwood

HIS FIGHTING BLOOD, Short Story *see* James Oliver Curwood

HIS FIRST OFFENCE, Novel *see* J. Storer Clouston

HIS FRIEND AND HIS WIFE, Boston 1920, Novel *see* Cosmo Hamilton

HIS GOOD NAME, 1922, Short Story *see* William Slavens McNutt

HIS GRACE GIVES NOTICE, Novel *see* Lady Trowbridge

HIS HARVEST, New York 1915, Novel *see* Pearl Doles Bell

HIS HEART HIS HAND AND HIS SWORD, Story *see* Louis Joseph Vance

HIS HONOUR THE JUDGE, Novel *see* Niranjan Pal

HIS HOUR, New York 1910, Novel *see* Elinor Glyn

HIS HOUSE IN ORDER, London 1906, Play *see* Arthur Wing Pinero

HIS LAST BOW, 1917, Short Story *see* Arthur Conan Doyle

HIS LAST DOLLAR, New York 1904, Play *see* Baldwin G. Cooke, David Higgins

HIS LORDSHIP, Short Story *see* W. W. Jacobs

HIS MAJESTY O'KEEFE, 1950, Novel *see* Gerald Green, Lawrence Kingman

HIS MAJESTY THE KING, Novel *see* Cosmo Hamilton

HIS MAJESTY'S PYJAMAS, Novel *see* Gene Markey

HIS MASTERPIECE, Short Story *see* O. Henry

HIS MISJUDGEMENT, Story *see* Thomas W. Henshew

HIS MOTHER'S BIRTHDAY, Poem *see* Henry Wadsworth Longfellow

HIS OFFICIAL FIANCEE, New York 1914, Novel *see* Berta Ruck

HIS OTHER WIFE, Play *see* George R. Sims

HIS PRICELESS TREASURE, Story *see* Hy Mayer

HIS REST DAY, Play *see* Matthew Boulton

HIS ROBE OF HONOR, New York 1916, Novel *see* Ethel Dorrance, James Dorrance

HIS TEMPORARY WIFE, 1917, Short Story *see* Robert Ames Bennet

HIS WIFE IN ARIZONA, Novel *see* Elliott J. Clawson

HISSHOKA, Novel *see* Kei Moriyama

HISTOIRE COMIQUE, 1903, Novel *see* Anatole France

HISTOIRE DE 130 FEMMES, Novel *see* Leon Gozlan

HISTOIRE DE L'OEIL, 1928, Novel *see* Georges Bataille

HISTOIRE DE RIRE, 1940, Play *see* Armand Salacrou

HISTOIRE DE SIX PETITES FILLES, Novel *see* Lucie Delorme Madrousse

HISTOIRE DES TREIZE, L', Paris 1835, Short Story *see* Honore de Balzac

HISTOIRE D'O, L', Novel *see* Pauline Reage

HISTOIRE DU CHEVALIER DES GRIEUX ET DE MANON LESCAUT, L', La Haye 1731, Novel *see* Antoine-Francois Prevost d'Exiles

HISTOIRE DU SOLDAT, Lausanne 1918, Opera *see* Charles-Ferdinand Ramuz, Igor Stravinsky

HISTOIRE D'UN AMOUR, Paris 1953, Novel *see* Roger Nimier

HISTOIRE D'UN PIERROT, 1893, *see* Fernand Beissier

HISTOIRE D'UNE FILLE DE FEMME, 1881, Short Story *see* Guy de Maupassant

HISTOIREN OM EN MODER, 1848, Short Story *see* Hans Christian Andersen

HISTORIA DE LA VIDA DEL BUSCON, LA, 1626, Novel *see* Francisco Gomez de Quevedo Y Villegas

HISTORIA DE LOS TARANTOS, LA, Play *see* Alfredo Manas

HISTORIA DE UNA ESCALERA, 1950, Play *see* Antonio Buero Vallejo

HISTORIA PARA SE OUVIR DE NOITE, 1964, Novel *see* Guilherme Figueiredo

HISTORY MAN, THE, Novel *see* Malcolm Bradbury

HISTORY OF LUMINOUS MOTION, THE, Novel *see* Scott Bradfield

HISTORY OF MR. POLLY, THE, London 1910, Novel *see* H. G. Wells

HIT AND RUN, Novel *see* Tom Alderman, James Hadley Chase

HIT-THE-TRAIL-HOLLIDAY, New York 1915, Play *see* George M. Cohan

HLIDAC C. 47, Novel *see* Josef Kopta

H.M. PULMAN, ESQUIRE, 1941, Novel *see* John Phillips Marquand

H.M.S. PINAFORE, London 1878, Opera *see* W. S. Gilbert, Arthur Sullivan

HO, Novel *see* Jose Giovanni

HO CHATZE MANOUEL: MYSTHISTOREMA, Athens 1956, Novel *see* Thrasos Kastanakes

HO PERDUTO MIO MARITO!, Play *see* Giovanni Cenzato

HO SOGNATO IL PARADISO, Play *see* Guido Cantini

HOARDED ASSETS, 1918, Short Story *see* Raymond Smiley Spears

HOBSON'S CHOICE, London 1916, Play *see* Harold Brighouse

HOCHTOURIST, DER, Play *see* Curt Kraatz, Max Neal

HOCHVERRAT, Play *see* Wenzel Goldbaum

HOCHWALD, DER, 1841, Short Story *see* Adalbert Stifter

HOCHZEIT MIT ERIKA, Play *see* Willi Webels

HOCHZEITSNACHT, Play *see* Noel Coward

HOCHZEITSNACHT IM PARADIES, Opera *see* Heinz Hentschke

HOCHZEITSREIS OHNE MANN, Novel *see* F. B. Cortan

HOCHZEITSREISE, DIE, Novel *see* Heinrich Spoerl

HOCHZEITSREISE OHNE MANN, Play *see* Waldemar Frank, Erwin Kreker

HOCUSSING OF CIGARETTE, THE, Short Story *see* Baroness Orczy

HODJA FRA PJORT, Novel *see* Ole Lund Kirkegaard

HOGAN'S ALLEY, Story *see* Gregory Roger

HOHE LIED, DAS, Berlin 1908, Novel *see* Hermann Sudermann

HOHEIT TANZT WALZER, Operetta *see* Julius Brammer, Alfred Grunwald

HOHENFEUER, Novel *see* Fredi M. Murer

HOKUSPOKUS, Play *see* Curt Goetz

HOLCROFT COVENANT, THE, Novel *see* Robert Ludlum

HOLD AUTUMN IN YOUR HAND, Novel *see* George Sessions Perry

HOLD BACK THE NIGHT, 1952, Novel *see* Pat Frank

HOLD 'EM YALE!, 1931, Short Story *see* Damon Runyon

HOLD EVERYTHING, New York 1928, Musical Play *see* Lew Brown, Buddy De Sylva, John McGowan

HOLD MY HAND, London 1931, Musical Play *see* Noel Gay, Stanley Lupino

HOLE IN THE WALL, THE, New York 1920, Play *see* Frederick Jackson

HOLI, Play *see* Mahesh Elkunchwar

HOLIDAY, New York 1928, Play *see* Philip Barry

HOLIDAY FOR LOVERS, New York 1957, Play *see* Ronald Alexander

HOLIDAY HUSBAND, THE, Novel *see* Dolf Wyllarde

HOLIDAY SONG, *see* Paddy Chayefsky

HOLLE AHOI, Novel *see* Georg Muhlen-Schulte

HOLLE DER JUNGFRAUEN, DIE, Novel *see* Gabriele Zapolska

HOLLEN MASCHINE, DIE, 1928, Novel *see* Carl Sloboda

HOLLOW OF HER HAND, THE, New York 1912, Novel *see* George Barr McCutcheon

HOLLOW REED, Short Story *see* Neville Bolt

HOLLOW TRIUMPH, Novel *see* Murray Forbes

HOLLOWAY'S TREASURE, Short Story *see* Morley Roberts

HOLLY AND THE IVY, THE, London 1950, Play *see* Wynard Browne

HOLLYWOOD GIRL, New York 1929, Novel *see* Joseph Patrick McEvoy

HOLOCAUST, Novel *see* Anthony McCall

HOLY ORDERS, Novel *see* Marie Corelli

HOLY SINNER, THE, Short Story *see* Thomas Mann

HOLY TERROR, A, New York 1925, Play *see* George Abbott, Winchell Smith

HOMBA, 1969, Novel *see* Yukio Mishima

HOMBRE, London 1961, Novel *see* Elmore Leonard

HOMBRE DE LA CRUZ VERDE, EL, 1969, Novel *see* Segundo Serrano Poncela

HOMBRE DE MUNDO, EL, 1845, Play *see* Ventura de La Vega

HOMBRE QUE SE QUISO MATAR, EL, 1930, Short Story *see* Wenceslao Fernandez Florez

HOME, 1970, Play *see* David Storey

HOME, London 1869, Play *see* T. W. Robertson

HOME, New York 1914, Novel *see* George Agnew Chamberlain

HOME AT SEVEN, London 1950, Play *see* R. C. Sherriff

HOME BEFORE DARK, 1957, Novel *see* Eileen Bassing

HOME BEFORE NIGHT, Novel *see* Hugh Leonard

HOME FIRES BURNING, Play *see* Chris Cesaro

HOME FROM THE HILL, 1958, Novel *see* William Humphrey

HOME INVADERS, THE, Novel *see* Frank Hohimer

HOME IS THE HERO, New York 1954, Play *see* Walter MacKen

HOME OF THE BRAVE, New York 1945, Play *see* Arthur Laurents

HOME PLACE, THE, 1950, Novel *see* Fred Gipson

HOME SONG, Novel *see* Lavyrle Spencer

HOME SWEET HOME, Play *see* Frank Lindo

HOME, SWEET HOME, 1823, Song *see* Henry Bishop, John Howard Payne

HOME SWEET HOMICIDE, Novel *see* Craig Rice

HOMECOMING, Book *see* Sidney Kingsley

HOMECOMING, 1936, Short Story *see* Thomas Walsh

HOMECOMING, THE, Short Story *see* Marlena Frick

HOMECOMING, THE, Novel *see* Earl Hamner Jr.

HOMECOMING, THE, 1965, Play *see* Harold Pinter

HOMEFRONT, Play *see* James Duff

HOMEM CELEBRE, UM, 1888, Short Story *see* Joaquim Maria Machado de Assis

HOMEM NU, O, 1960, Short Story *see* Fernando Tavares Sabino

HOME-MAKER, THE, New York 1924, Novel *see* Dorothy Canfield

HOMES OF TIPPERARY, THE, Play *see* Charles Kickham

HOMESTEADER, THE, Sioux City 1917, Novel *see* Oscar Micheaux

HOMETOWNERS, THE, New York 1926, Play *see* George M. Cohan

HOMME A ABATTRE, L', Novel *see* Charles-Robert Dumas

HOMME A LA ROSE, L', 1921, Play *see* Henry Bataille

HOMME A L'HISPANO, L', Novel *see* Pierre Frondaie

HOMME A L'IMPERMEABLE, L', Novel *see* James Hadley Chase

HOMME A L'OREILLE CASSEE, L', 1862, Short Story *see* Edmond About

HOMME AU COMPLET GRIS, L', Novel *see* Arnould Galopin

HOMME AU SANG BLEU, L', Novel *see* Leo Malet

HOMME AUX YEUX D'ARGENT, L', Novel *see* Robert Rossner

HOMME BLEU, L', Novel *see* Georges Le Faure

HOMME DE JOIE, L', Play *see* Paul Geraldy, Robert Spitzer

HOMME DE LA JAMAIQUE, L', Novel *see* Robert Gaillard

HOMME DE LA NUIT, L', Novel *see* Jean-Louis Sanciaume

HOMME DE LONDRES, L', 1934, Novel *see* Georges Simenon

HOMME DE TROP A BORD, UN, Novel *see* Fred Andreas

HOMME DE TROP, UN, Paris 1958, Novel *see* Jean-Pierre Chabrol

HOMME DU NORD, UN, Play *see* Charles Mere

HOMME EN HABIT, L', Paris 1922, Play *see* Yves Mirande, Andre Picard

HOMME EN OR, UN, Play *see* Roger Ferdinand

HOMME HEUREUX, UN, Play *see* Yves Mirande, Andre Rivoire

HOMME MARCHE DANS LA VILLE, UN, Novel *see* Jean Jausion

HOMME PRESSE, L', Novel *see* Paul Morand

HOMME QUE J'AI TUE, L', Novel *see* Maurice Rostand

HOMME QUI ASSASSINA, L', Play *see* Pierre Frondaie

HOMME QUI ASSASSINA, L', Paris 1908, Novel *see* Claude Farrere

HOMME QUI J'AI TUE, L', Paris 1930, Play *see* Maurice Rostand

HOMME QUI MOURRA DEMAIN, L', Novel *see* Henri Champly

HOMME QUI REGARDAIT PASSER LES TRAINS, L', 1938, Novel *see* Georges Simenon

HOMME QUI REVIENT DE LOIN, L', Novel *see* Gaston Leroux

HOMME QUI RIT, L', 1869, Novel *see* Victor Hugo

HOMME QUI VALAIT DES MILLIARDS, L', Novel *see* Jean Stuart

HOMME QUI VENDIT SON AME, L', Novel *see* Pierre-Gilles Veber

HOMME RICHE, L', Paris 1914, Play *see* Henri Dupuy-Mazuel, Jean-Jose Frappa

HOMME SANS COEUR, L', Novel *see* Alfred Machard

HOMME SE PENCHE SUR SON PASSE, UN, Novel *see* Maurice Constantin-Weyer

HOMME TRAQUE, L', 1922, Novel *see* Francis Carco

HOMMES DE LA COTE, LES, Short Story *see* Mme. Romilly

HOMMES DE LAS VEGAS, LES, Paris 1969, Novel *see* Andre Lay

HOMMES EN BLANC, LES, Novel *see* Andre Soubiran

HOMMES NOUVEAUX, LES, Novel *see* Claude Farrere

HOMMES SANS NOM, LES, *see* Jean Desvallieres

HOMO FABER, 1957, Novel *see* Max Frisch

HONEST COURTESAN, THE, Biography *see* Margaret Rosenthal

HONEY BEE, THE, New York 1901, Novel *see* Samuel Merwin

HONEYMOON ADVENTURE, A, Novel *see* Cecily Fraser-Smith

HONEYMOON FLATS, 1927, Short Story *see* Earl Derr Biggers

HONEYMOON HATE, 1927, Short Story *see* Alice Muriel Williamson

HONEYMOON LANE, New York 1926, Play *see* Edward Dowling, James F. Hanley

HONEYMOON LIMITED, New York 1932, Novel *see* Vida Hurst

HONEYPOT, THE, Novel *see* Countess Barcynska

HONG CHEN, Novel *see* Huo Da, Wang Weizhen

HONG GAO LIANG, 1985, Novel *see* Mo Yan

HONG LOU MENG, c1750-92, Novel *see* Cao Zhan

HONG QI GE, Novel *see* Liu Canglang, Lu Mei

HONG YANG HAOXIA ZHUAN, Opera *see* Shanghai Joint Stage

HONG YU, Novel *see* Yang XIao

HONGAKUBO IBUN, Novel *see* Yasushi Inoue

HONGFEN, Novel *see* Su Tong

HONGQI PU, 1958, Novel *see* Liang Bin

HONIGMOND, Play *see* Gabriel Barylli

HONKYTONK MAN, Novel *see* Clancy Carlile

HONNEUR D'ARTISTE, Novel *see* Octave Feuillet

HONNEURS DE LA GUERRE, LES, Novel *see* Georges Conchon

HONOR BOUND, Boston 1927, Novel *see* Jack Bethea

HONOR IN PAWN, Novel *see* William Babington Maxwell

HONOR OF KENNETH MCGRATH, THE, Story *see* Calder Johnstone

HONOR OF THE BIG SNOWS, Indianapolis 1911, Novel *see* James Oliver Curwood

HONOR THY FATHER, Novel *see* Gay Talese

HONORABLE MR. WONG, THE, Play *see* Achmed Abdullah, David Belasco

HONORARY CONSUL, THE, 1973, Novel *see* Graham Greene

HONOUR AND MONEY, Novel *see* Constantinos Theotokis

HONOURABLE GENTLEMAN, THE, 1919, Short Story *see* Achmed Abdullah

HONOURABLE MEMBER FOR OUTSIDE LEFT, THE, Short Story *see* Sidney Horler

HONOURS EASY, London 1930, Play *see* Roland Pertwee

HONRADEZ DE LA CERRADURA, LA, 1943, Play *see* Jacinto Benavente y Martinez

HONTE DE LA FAMILLE, LA, Novel *see* Charles Exbrayat

HOODMAN BLIND, London 1885, Play *see* Wilson Barrett, Henry Arthur Jones

HOODS TAKE OVER, THE, Novel *see* Ovid Demaris

HOODS, THE, Novel *see* Harry Grey

HOOSIER SCHOOLBOY, New York 1883, Novel *see* Edward Eggleston

HOOSIER SCHOOLMASTER, THE, New York 1871, Novel *see* Edward Eggleston

HOP, 1921, Short Story *see* Hugh Wiley

HOP DOG, THE, Novel *see* Nora Lavin, Molly Thorp

HOPALONG CASSIDY, Chicago 1912, Novel *see* Clarence E. Mulford

HOPALONG CASSIDY'S PROTEGE, New York 1926, Novel *see* Clarence E. Mulford

HOPE, Short Story *see* W. S. Gilbert

HOPE CHEST, THE, Boston 1918, Novel *see* Mark Lee Luther

HOPE, THE, London 1911, Play *see* Cecil Raleigh

HOPELESS CASE, THE, Short Story *see* H. C. McNeile ("Sapper")

HOP-FROG, 1849, Short Story *see* Edgar Allan Poe

HOPPER, THE, 1916, Short Story *see* Meredith Nicholson

HOPSCOTCH, Novel *see* Brian Garfield

HORA DA ESTRELA, A, 1977, Novel *see* Clarice Lispector

HORA E VEZ DE AUGUSTO MATRAGA, A, 1946, Short Story *see* Guimaraes Rosa

HORACE, 1641, Play *see* Pierre Corneille

HORDUBAL, 1933, Novel *see* Karel Capek

HORLA, LA, 1886, Short Story *see* Guy de Maupassant

HORLOGER D'EVERTON, L', 1954, Short Story *see* Georges Simenon

HORNET'S NEST, Novel *see* Andrew Soutar

HORNET'S NEST, THE, Boston 1917, Novel *see* Nancy Mann Waddel Woodrow

HOROKI, Tokyo 1928, Biography *see* Fumiko Hayashi

HORS LA VIE, Book *see* Roger Auque, Patrick Forestier

HORSE FLESH, 1930, Short Story *see* Frederick Hazlitt Brennan

HORSE FOR MRS. CUSTER, A, Story *see* Glendon Swarthout

HORSE, LA, Novel *see* Michel Lambesc

HORSE SENSE, Story *see* L. V. Jefferson

HORSE SOLDIERS, THE, Novel *see* Harold Sinclair

HORSE WHISPERER, THE, Novel *see* Nicholas Evans

HORSEMAN, PASS BY, New York 1961, Novel *see* Larry McMurtry

HORSES HEAD, A, 1967, Novel *see* Evan Hunter

HORSE'S MOUTH, THE, 1944, Novel *see* Joyce Cary

HORSIE, 1933, Short Story *see* Dorothy Parker

HO-RUKK, Play *see* Ladislaus Fodor

HOSEKRAEMMEREN, 1829, Short Story *see* Steen Steensen Blicher

HOSIANNA, Book *see* Eva Rechlin

HOSTAGE HEART, THE, Novel *see* Gerald Green

HOSTAGE, THE, Article *see* Jose F. Lacaba

HOSTAGE, THE, New York 1959, Novel *see* Henry Farrell

HOSTAGES, 1942, Novel *see* Stefan Heym

HOSTILE WITNESS, Play *see* Jack Roffey

HOT AIR, Story *see* Paul Finder Moss, Jerry Wald

HOT MONEY, New York 1931, Play *see* Aben Kandel

HOT NEWS, New York 1931, Novel *see* Emile Gauvreau

HOT NOCTURNE, Play *see* Edwin Gilbert

HOT ROCK, THE, Novel *see* Donald E. Westlake

HOT SATURDAY, New York 1926, Novel *see* Harvey Fergusson

HOT SPUR, Novel *see* R. W. Cresse

HOT SUMMER NIGHT, London 1958, Play *see* Ted Willis

HOTARUGAWA, Novel *see* Teru Miyamoto

HOTEL, New York 1965, Novel *see* Arthur Hailey

HOTEL DU LAC, Novel *see* Anita Brookner

HOTEL DU LIBRE-ECHANGE, L', Paris 1894, Play *see* Maurice Desvallieres, Georges Feydeau

HOTEL DU NORD, L', 1929, Novel *see* Eugene Dabit

HOTEL MOUSE, THE, Play *see* Armat, Gerbidon

HOTEL NEW HAMPSHIRE, THE, 1981, Novel *see* John Irving

HOTEL SORRENTO, Play *see* Hannie Rayson

HOTEL ST. PAULI, Novel *see* Erland Kiosterod

HOTTENTOT, THE, New York 1920, Play *see* William Collier Sr., Victor Mapes

HOUND OF FLORENCE, THE, 1923, Novel *see* Felix Salten

HOUND OF THE BASKERVILLES, THE, London 1902, Novel *see* Arthur Conan Doyle

HOUR BEFORE THE DAWN, THE, 1942, Novel *see* W. Somerset Maugham

HOUSE BEHIND THE HEDGE, THE, Story *see* Mary Spain Vigus

HOUSE BY THE RIVER, THE, 1921, Novel *see* A. P. Herbert

HOUSE IN MARSH ROAD, THE, Novel *see* Laurence Meynell

HOUSE IN RUE RAPP, THE, Short Story *see* John Dickson Carr

HOUSE IN THE COUNTRY, A, New York 1937, Play *see* Melvin Levy

HOUSE IN THE MIST, THE, 1917, Short Story *see* Octavus Roy Cohen, John U. Giesy

HOUSE IN THE TIMBERWOODS, THE, Novel *see* Joyce Dingwell

HOUSE IS NOT A HOME, A, New York 1953, Autobiography *see* Polly Adler

HOUSE NEXT DOOR, THE, New York 1914, Play *see* J. Hartley Manners

HOUSE OF A THOUSAND CANDLES, THE, New York 1905, Novel *see* Meredith Nicholson

HOUSE OF A THOUSAND WINDOWS, Novel *see* Louis de Wohl

HOUSE OF AMERICA, Play *see* Edward Thomas

HOUSE OF BONDAGE, THE, New York 1910, Novel *see* Reginald Wright Kaufmann

HOUSE OF CARDS, Novel *see* Michael Dobbs

HOUSE OF CARDS, New York 1967, Novel *see* Stanley Ellin

HOUSE OF CHANCE, New York 1912, Novel *see* Gertie Wentworth-James

HOUSE OF CONNELLY, THE, New York 1931, Play *see* Paul Green

HOUSE OF DR. EDWARDES, THE, Novel *see* Francis Beeding

HOUSE OF DREAMS COME TRUE, Novel *see* Margaret Pedlar

HOUSE OF FEAR, 1910, Short Story *see* John Thomas McIntyre

HOUSE OF FEAR, THE, New York 1916, Novel *see* Wadsworth Camp

HOUSE OF GLASS, THE, New York 1915, Play *see* George M. Cohan, Max Marcin

HOUSE OF GOD, THE, Novel *see* Samuel Shem

HOUSE OF INTRIGUE, THE, Indianapolis 1918, Novel *see* Arthur Stringer

HOUSE OF LYNCH, THE, London 1907, Novel *see* Leonard Merrick

HOUSE OF MARNEY, THE, Novel *see* John Goodwin

HOUSE OF MIRTH, THE, New York 1905, Novel *see* Edith Wharton

HOUSE OF MYSTERY, Novel *see* Oscar Micheaux

HOUSE OF NUMBERS, 1956, Novel *see* Jack Finney

HOUSE OF REFUGE, THE, New York 1932, Novel *see* Grace Sothcote Leake

HOUSE OF SECRETS, Novel *see* Sterling Noel

HOUSE OF SECRETS, THE, London 1926, Novel *see* Sidney Horler

HOUSE OF STRANGERS, Novel *see* Jerome Weidman

HOUSE OF THE ARROW, THE, London 1924, Novel *see* A. E. W. Mason

HOUSE OF THE LITTLE SHOES, THE, Novel *see* Eleanor M. Ingram

HOUSE OF THE LOST COURT, THE, New York 1908, Novel *see* Alice Muriel Williamson

HOUSE OF THE SEVEN FLIES, THE, Novel *see* Victor Canning

HOUSE OF THE SEVEN GABLES, THE, Boston 1851, Novel *see* Nathaniel Hawthorne

HOUSE OF THE SPANIARD, THE, Novel *see* Arthur Behrend

HOUSE OF THE SPIRITS, THE, Novel *see* Isabel Allende

HOUSE OF THE TOLLING BELL, THE, Novel *see* Edith Sessions Tupper

HOUSE OF TOYS, THE, Indianapolis 1914, Novel *see* Henry Russell Miller

HOUSE OF UNREST, THE, Play *see* Leslie Howard Gordon

HOUSE OF WHISPERS, THE, Boston 1918, Novel *see* William Andrew Johnston

HOUSE OF YES, THE, Play *see* Wendy MacLeod

HOUSE OF YOUTH, THE, Indianapolis 1923, Novel *see* Maude Radford Warren

HOUSE ON 56TH STREET, THE, Story *see* Joseph Santley

HOUSE ON GARIBALDI STREET, THE, Book *see* Isser Harel

HOUSE ON GREENAPPLE ROAD, THE, Novel *see* Harold R. Daniels

HOUSE ON THE MARSH, THE, Novel *see* Florence Warden

HOUSE OPPOSITE, THE, Play *see* J. Jefferson Farjeon

HOUSE OPPOSITE, THE, London 1909, Play *see* Percival Landon

HOUSE WHERE EVIL DWELLS, THE, Novel *see* James W. Hardiman

HOUSE WITH THE BLUE DOOR, THE, Novel *see* Mary Cathcart Borer

HOUSE WITHOUT A KEY, THE, Indianapolis 1925, Novel *see* Earl Derr Biggers

HOUSE WITHOUT CHILDREN, THE, Cleveland 1917, Play *see* Robert H. McLaughlin

HOUSEHOLD GHOSTS, Novel *see* James Kennaway

HOUSEHOLDER, THE, London 1960, Novel *see* Ruth Prawer Jhabvala

HOUSEKEEPER'S DAUGHTER, THE, New York 1938, Novel *see* Donald Henderson Clarke

HOUSEKEEPING, Novel *see* Marilynne Robinson

HOUSEMASTER, 1936, Novel *see* Ian Hay

HOW AWFUL ABOUT ALLAN, Novel *see* Henry Farrell

HOW COULD YOU, JEAN?, Garden City N.Y. 1917, Novel *see* Eleanor Hoyt Brainerd

HOW GREEN WAS MY VALLEY, 1939, Novel *see* Richard Llewellyn

HOW HE LIED TO HER HUSBAND, London 1905, Play *see* George Bernard Shaw

HOW I CARRIED THE MESSAGE TO GARCIA, San Francisco 1922, Book *see* Andrew Summers Rowan

HOW I MET MY HUSBAND, Short Story *see* Alice Munro

HOW I WON THE WAR, London 1963, Novel *see* Patrick Ryan

HOW IT HAPPENED, Short Story *see* Arthur Conan Doyle

HOW MANY MILES TO BABYLON?, *see* Jennifer Johnston

HOW SAY YOU?, London 1959, Play *see* Kay Bannerman, Harold Brooke

HOW STELLA GOT HER GROOVE BACK, Novel *see* Terry McMillan

HOW TO SUCCEED IN BUSINESS WITHOUT REALLY TRYING, New York 1952, Novel *see* Shepherd Mead

HOWARD: THE AMAZING MR. HUGHES, Book *see* Noah Dietrich, Bob Thomas

HOWARDS END, 1910, Novel *see* E. M. Forster

HOWDY STRANGER, New York 1937, Play *see* . Louis Pelletier Jr, Robert Sloane

HOWLING II, THE, Novel *see* Gary Brandner

HOWLING III, Novel *see* Gary Brandner

HOWLING IN THE WOODS, A, Novel *see* Velda Johnson

HOWLING, THE, Novel *see* Gary Brandner

HRABENKA Z PODSKALI, Play *see* Alois Koldinsky

HRABINA COSEL, 1874, Novel *see* Joszef Ignacy Kraszewski

HRDINA LACKMANN, Book *see* Otomar Schafer

HRIDAYACHI SHRIMANTI, Novel *see* Narayan Hari Apte

HUA HUN, Novel *see* Shi Nan

HUAI SHU ZHUANG, Play *see* Hu Ke

HUANGHUA LING, Novel *see* Shu Hui

HUANGJIANG NUXIA, Novel *see* Guo Mingdao

HUCKSTERS, THE, Novel *see* Frederic Wakeman

HUDDLE, New York 1931, Novel *see* Francis Wallace

HUE AND CRY, 1933, Short Story *see* Carl Detzer

HUELLA DE LUZ, 1925, Short Story *see* Wenceslao Fernandez Florez

HUELLAS, LAS, Novel *see* Mario Fenelli

HUGE, BLACK ONE-EYED MAN, A, 1917, Short Story *see* Kenyon Gambier

HUIS CLOS, Paris 1944, Play *see* Jean-Paul Sartre

HUI'S WIFE, Novel *see* Wang Zongyuan

HUIT HOMMES DANS UN CHATEAU, Novel *see* Jean Kery

HUITIEME FEMME DE BARBE-BLEUE, LA, 1921, Play *see* Alfred Savoir

HUK!, Novel *see* Stirling Silliphant

HULA - A ROMANCE OF HAWAII, New York 1927, Novel *see* Armine von Tempski

HUMAN COMEDY, THE, 1943, Novel *see* William Saroyan

HUMAN DESIRE, Boston 1913, Novel *see* Violet Irwin

HUMAN FACTOR, THE, 1978, Novel *see* Graham Greene

HUMAN HEARTS, Play *see* Hal Reid

HUMAN KIND; A SEQUENCE, THE, New York 1953, Novel *see* Alexander Baron

HUMAN SIDE, THE, Los Angeles 1933, Play *see* Christine Ames

HUMANITY, Short Story *see* Nan Blair

HUMANITY, Play *see* John Lawson

HUMANITY, Short Story *see* Charles R. Macauley

HUMANIZING MR. WINSBY, 1915, Short Story *see* Peter B. Kyne

HUMBUG, THE, New York 1929, Play *see* Max Marcin

HUMILIDES, LOS, Novel *see* Miguel Angel Pereira

HUMMING BIRD, THE, New York 1923, Play *see* Maude Fulton

HUMMINGBIRD TREE, THE, Novel *see* Ian McDonald

HUMORESKA, Novel *see* Karel Matej Capek-Chod

HUMORESQUE, 1919, Short Story *see* Fannie Hurst

HUMPTY DUMPTY, 1917, Play *see* Horace Annesley Vachell

HUNCH, THE, 1920, Short Story *see* Albert Payson Terhune

HUNCH, THE, 1921, Short Story *see* Percival Wilde

HUNDERT JAHRE ADOLF HITLER, Play *see* Christoph Schlingensief

HUNDERTER IM WESTENTASCHER, DER, Play *see* Max Ferner, Max Neal

HUNDRED MILLION FRANCS, A, Novel *see* Paul Berna

HUNDREDTH CHANCE, THE, Novel *see* Ethel M. Dell

HUNG LOU MENG, 1792, *see* Ts'ao Chan

HUNGER, THE, Novel *see* Whitley Strieber

HUNGERKUNSTLER, EIN, 1924, Short Story *see* Franz Kafka

HUNGRY HEART, THE, New York 1909, Novel *see* David Graham Phillips

HUNGRY HEARTS, Boston 1920, Novel *see* Anzia Yezierska

HUNGRY HILL, 1943, Novel *see* Daphne Du Maurier

HUNT FOR RED OCTOBER, THE, Novel *see* Tom Clancy

HUNT THE WOMAN, Short Story *see* Joseph Gollomb

HUNTED WOMAN, THE, New York 1916, Novel *see* James Oliver Curwood

HUNTER, THE, Story *see* David Chase

HUNTER, THE, Book *see* Christopher Keane

HUNTER, THE, New York 1963, Novel *see* Donald E. Westlake

HUNTER'S BLOOD, Novel *see* Jere Cunningham

HUNTERS, THE, 1957, Novel *see* James Salter

HUNTING THE HIGHWAY PIRATES, 1937, Article *see* William E. Frazer

HUNTINGTOWER, 1922, Novel *see* John Buchan

HUNTRESS, THE, New York 1922, Novel *see* Hubert Footner

HUOLI ZUIREN, Novel *see* Chen Lengxue

HUOZHI TAOWU, Play *see* Tian Han

HURDY-GURDY MAN, THE, 1922, Play *see* Leroy Clemens, John B. Hymer

HURLYBURLY, 1984, Play *see* David Rabe

HURRA - EIN JUNGE!, Play *see* Franz Robert Arnold, Ernst Bach

HURRA, WIR LEBEN NOCH, Novel *see* Johannes Mario Simmel

HURRICANE HUNTERS, Novel *see* William C. Anderson

HURRICANE, THE, Boston 1936, Novel *see* James N. Hall, Charles Nordhoff

HURRICANE, THE, London 1960, Novel *see* Peter Howard, Alan Thornhill

HURRICANE WILLIAMS, Novel *see* Gordon Young

HURRY SUNDOWN, New York 1964, Novel *see* K. B. Gilden

HURRYING FATE AND GERALDINE, New York 1913, Novel *see* Florence Morse Kingsley

HUSBAND AND WIFE, New York 1915, Play *see* Charles Kenyon

HUSBAND HUNTER, THE, Novel *see* Olivia Roy

HUSBAND OF EDITH, New York 1908, Novel *see* George Barr McCutcheon

HUSBANDS PREFERRED, Story *see* Albert Shelby Le Vino

HUSH NOW, SWEET CHARLOTTE, Short Story *see* Henry Farrell

HUSK, 1935, Short Story *see* Thomas Walsh

HUSSARDS, LES, Play *see* Pierre-Aristide Breal

HUSTLER, THE, New York 1959, Novel *see* Walter S. Tevis

HUSTLING, Book *see* Gail Sheehy

HUSZ ORA, 1964, Novel *see* Ferenc Santa

HYDE PARK CORNER, London 1934, Play *see* Walter Hackett

HYGEIA AT THE SOLITO, Short Story *see* O. Henry

HYGIENE DE L'ASSASSIN, Novel *see* Amelie Nothomb

HYMENEE, 1941, Play *see* Edouard Bourdet

HYPER-ALLER-GENIC, Play *see* Oren Safdie

HYPERION; ODER DER EREMIT IN GRIECHENLAND, 1797-99, Novel *see* Friedrich Holderlin

HYPNOTIST, THE, 1956, Play *see* Falkland Cary, Philip Weathers

HYPOCRITES, THE, Story *see* Arthur Edmund Jones

HYPOCRITES, THE, 1906, Play *see* Henry Arthur Jones

I - TINA, Autobiography *see* Tina Turner

I ACCUSE!, Book *see* Nicholas Halasz

I AM A CAMERA, 1952, Play *see* John Van Druten

I AM A FUGITIVE FROM A GEORGIA CHAIN GANG!, 1932, Autobiography *see* Robert E. Burns

I AM A SOLDIER, Play *see* Shuo Yunping

I AM LEGEND, New York 1954, Novel *see* Richard Matheson

I AM THE CHEESE, Novel *see* Robert Cormier

I AM THINKING OF MY DARLING, Novel *see* Vincent McHugh

I AM THIRD, Book *see* Gale Sayers

I ANNA, Novel *see* Elsa Lewin

I CAN GET IT FOR YOU WHOLESALE, 1937, Novel *see* Jerome Weidman

I CAN'T GO HOME, Short Story *see* Jack Lait

I CLAUDIUS, 1934, Novel *see* Robert Graves

I COVER THE WATERFRONT, New York 1932, Book *see* Max Miller

I DIDN'T RAISE MY BOY TO BE A SOLDIER, 1915, Song *see* Alfred Bryan, Al Piantadosi

I HATE ACTORS, 1944, Novel *see* Ben Hecht

I HEARD THE OWL CALL MY NAME, Book *see* Margaret Craven

I HEARD THEM SING, 1946, Novel *see* Ferdinand Reyher

I, JAMES LEWIS, 1932, Novel *see* Gilbert Wolff Gabriel

I JERRY TAKE THEE JOAN, New York 1911, Novel *see* Cleo Lucas

I KILLED THE COUNT, London 1937, Play *see* Alec Coppel

I KNOW WHAT YOU DID LAST SUMMER, Novel *see* Lois Duncan

I KNOW WHY THE CAGED BIRD SINGS, 1969, Autobiography *see* Maya Angelou

I LIVE WITH ME DAD, Short Story *see* Derry Moran

I LIVED WITH YOU, London 1932, Play *see* Ivor Novello

I LOST MY HEART IN HEIDELBERG, Play *see* Beda Neumann, Ernst Neumann

I LOVE A MYSTERY, Novel *see* Carleton E. Morse

I LOVE YOU, New York 1919, Play *see* William Le Baron

I LOVE YOU AGAIN, New York 1937, Novel *see* Octavus Roy Cohen

I LOVE YOU I LOVE YOU NOT, Play *see* Wendy Kesselman

I LOVED YOU WEDNESDAY, New York 1932, Play *see* William Dubois, Molly Ricardel

I MARRIED A DEAD MAN, 1948, Novel *see* Cornell Woolrich

I MARRIED A DOG, Short Story *see* Dorothy Crider

I MARRIED ADVENTURE, New York 1940, Book *see* Osa Johnson

I MARRIED AN ARTIST, 1936, Short Story *see* Avery Strakosch

I MARY MACLANE, New York 1917, Autobiography *see* Mary MacLane

I MAUREEN, Short Story *see* Elizabeth Spencer

I NEVER PROMISED YOU A ROSE GARDEN, Novel *see* Hannah Green

I NEVER SANG FOR MY FATHER, New York 1968, Play *see* Robert Woodruff Anderson

I OUGHT TO BE IN PICTURES, 1981, Play *see* Neil Simon

I PASSED THIS WAY, Book *see* Sylvia Ashton-Warner

I POSED AS A COMMUNIST FOR THE F.B.I., Book *see* Matt Cvetic, Pete Martin

I REMEMBER MAMA, New York 1944, Play *see* John Van Druten

I SAW WHAT YOU DID, New York 1964, Novel *see* Ursula Curtiss

I SENZA DIO, Novel *see* Federico Sinibaldi

I SING THE BODY ELECTRIC!, Short Story *see* Ray Bradbury

I STALLET FOR EN PAPPA, 1971, Novel *see* Kerstin Thorvall

I START COUNTING, Novel *see* Audrey Erskine Lindop

I THANK A FOOL, London 1958, Novel *see* Audrey Erskine Lindop

I THE JURY, Novel *see* Mickey Spillane

I TINA, Autobiography *see* Kurt Loder

I WAKE UP SCREAMING, Novel *see* Steve Fisher

I WAS A SPY, Book *see* Marthe Cnockaert McKenna

I WAS MONTY'S DOUBLE, Book *see* M. E. Clifton-James

I WILL BE FAITHFUL, New York 1934, Novel *see* Kathleen Shepard

I WILL KILL YOU, Novel *see* Jim Murphy

I WILL REPAY, Novel *see* Baroness Orczy

I WOULDN'T BE IN YOUR SHOES, 1943, Novel *see* Cornell Woolrich

IARBA REA, 1949, Play *see* Aurel Baranga

IBIS BLEU, L', Novel *see* Jean Aicard

IBO KYODAI, 1957, Short Story *see* Torahiko Tamiya

IBUNRONIN KI, 1958, Short Story *see* Yasuhiko Takiguchi

ICE COLD IN ALEX, Novel *see* Christopher Landon

ICE HOUSE, Play *see* Bo Brinkman

ICE ON THE COFFIN, Play *see* Temple Saxe

ICE PALACE, 1958, Novel *see* Edna Ferber

ICE STATION ZEBRA, London 1963, Novel *see* Alistair MacLean

ICE STORM, THE, 1994, Novel *see* Rick Moody

ICEBOUND, Boston 1923, Novel *see* Owen Davis

ICEBOUND SUMMER, Novel *see* Sally Carrighar

ICE-CANDY MAN, THE, Novel *see* Bapsy Sidhwa

ICEMAN COMETH, THE, 1946, Play *see* Eugene O'Neill

ICH AN MICH, Novel *see* Dinah Nelken

ICH BRAUCHE DICH, Play *see* Hans Schweikart

ICH DENKE OFT AN PIROSCHKA, Novel *see* Hugo Hartung

ICH HEIRATE HERRN DIREKTOR, Novel *see* H. Krackardt

ICH KOMME NICHT ZUM ABENDESSEN, Novel *see* Alice Lyttkens

ICH LIEBE VIER FRAUEN, Play *see* Johann von Bokay

ICH MACH' DICH GLUCKLICH, Play *see* Gabor von Vaszary

ICH SCHWORE UND GELOBE, Novel *see* Ernst Ludwig Ravius

ICH UND DU, Play *see* Christian Bock

ICH VERTRAUE DIR MEINE FRAU AN, Play *see* Johann von Vaszary

ICH WAR EIN HASSLICHES MADCHEN, Novel *see* Annemarie Selinko

ICH WAR JACK MORTIMER, Novel *see* Alexander Lernet-Holenia

ICH WEISS WOFUR ICH LEBE, Novel *see* Ernst Neubach

ICH ZAHLE TAGLICH MEINE SORGEN, Novel *see* H. B. Fredersdorf

I'D CLIMB THE HIGHEST MOUNTAIN, Novel *see* Corra Harris

IDAHO, New York 1933, Novel *see* Paul Evan Lehman

IDEAL HUSBAND, AN, London 1895, Play *see* Oscar Wilde

IDEAL SEPTIMY, Novel *see* Jaromira Huttlova

IDEE DE FRANCOISE, L', Play *see* Paul Gavault

IDEE FOLLE, UNE, Play *see* Carl Laufs

IDIOT, 1868, Novel *see* Fyodor Dostoyevsky

IDIOT A PARIS, UN, Novel *see* Rene Fallet

IDIOT, L', Paris 1960, Play *see* Marcel Achard

IDIOTA, EL, Play *see* Emilio Gomez de Miguel

IDIOT'S DELIGHT, New York 1936, Play *see* R. E. Sherwood

IDLE HANDS, 1921, Short Story *see* Earl Derr Biggers

IDLE WIVES, New York 1914, Novel *see* James Oppenheim

IDLER, THE, New York 1890, Play *see* C. Haddon Chambers

IDOL OF MOOLAH, THE, Play *see* Syd Courtenay, Lola Harvey

IDOL OF PARIS, THE, Play *see* Charles Darrell

IDOL ON PARADE, Novel *see* William Camp

IDOL, THE, Great Neck, N.Y. 1929, Play *see* Martin Brown

IDOLS, London 1899, Novel *see* William J. Locke

IDYLL OF MISS SARAH BROWN, THE, 1944, Short Story *see* Damon Runyon

IDYLL OF RED GULCH, THE, Story *see* Bret Harte

IDYLLE DANS LA ZONE ROUGE, UNE, Play *see* Pierre Gourdon

IDYLLE TRAGIQUE, UNE, 1896, *see* Paul Bourget

IF A MAN ANSWERS, New York 1961, Novel *see* Winifred Wolfe

IF FOUR WALLS TOLD, London 1922, Play *see* Edward Percy

IF I DIE BEFORE I WAKE, Novel *see* Sherwood King

IF I MARRY AGAIN, Story *see* Gilbert Frankau

IF I SHOULD DIE, Article *see* Hugh Pentecost

IF I WAS ALONE WITH YOU, 1929, Short Story *see* Richard Connell

IF I WAS RICH, New York 1926, Play *see* William Anthony McGuire

IF I WERE KING, London 1901, Novel *see* Justin Huntly McCarthy

IF THE GODS LAUGH, London 1925, Novel *see* Rosita Forbes

IF WINTER COMES, Boston 1921, Novel *see* A. S. M. Hutchinson

IF YOU BREAK MY HEART, 1937, Short Story *see* Steve Fisher

IF YOU COULD SEE WHAT I HEAR, Book *see* Derek Gill, Tom Sullivan

IF YOU WANT TO SEE YOUR WIFE AGAIN, Novel *see* John Craig

IF YOUTH BUT KNEW, Play *see* K. C. Spiers

IFUSAG, SZERELEM, 1957, Short Story *see* Ferenc Karinthy

IGNACE, Opera *see* Jean Manse

IGRA, Play *see* Ilya Surgutchoff

IGROK, 1866, Novel *see* Fyodor Dostoyevsky

IGROKI, 1842, Play *see* Nikolay Gogol

IHMISELON IHANUUS JA KURJUUS, 1945, Novel *see* Frans E. Sillanpaa

IHMISET SUVIYOSSA, 1934, Novel *see* Frans E. Sillanpaa

IKARI NO MACHI, 1949, Novel *see* Fumio Niwa

IKINAI, Novel *see* Fumio Nakahara

IL EST CHARMANT, Opera *see* Albert Willemetz

IL EST MINUIT DR. SCHWEITZER, Play *see* Gilbert Cesbron

IL ETAIT UNE FOIS, Play *see* Francis de Croisset

IL FAUT QU'UNE PORTE SOIT OUVERTE OU FERMEE, 1848, Play *see* Alfred de Musset

IL FAUT TUER JULIE, Play *see* Didier Daix

IL FAUT VIVRE DANGEREUSEMENT, Novel *see* R. Marlot

IL FU MATTIA PASCAL, Novel *see* Luigi Pirandello

ILE D'AMOUR, L', Novel *see* Saint-Sorny

ILE DU BOUT DU MONDE, L', Paris 1954, Novel *see* Henri Crouzat

ILE MYSTERIEUSE, L', Paris 1874, Novel *see* Jules Verne

ILE SANS AMOUR, L', Novel *see* Andre Legrand

ILE SANS RIVAGE, L', Novel *see* Therese Doguet

ILIAD, Verse *see* Homer

I'LL BE SEEING YOU, Novel *see* Charles Martin

I'LL CRY TOMORROW, Book *see* Gerold Frank, Lillian Roth

ILL MET BY MOONLIGHT, Book *see* W. Stanley Moss

I'LL NEVER TELL, Novel *see* Roy Vickers

I'LL SHOW YOU THE TOWN, New York 1924, Novel *see* Elmer Holmes Davis

I'LL TRADE YOU AN ELK, Novel *see* Charles A. Goodman

ILLATSZERTAR, 1936, Play *see* Nikolaus Laszlo

ILL-STARRED BABBIE, Boston 1912, Novel *see* William Wilfred Whalen

ILLUMINATA, Play *see* Brandon Cole

ILLUSION, New York 1929, Novel *see* Arthur Cheney Train

ILLUSIONE, L', 1916, Play *see* Renato Simoni

ILLUSIONLESS MAN AND THE VISIONARY MAID, THE, 1964, Novel *see* Allen Wheelis

ILLUSTRE MAURIN, L', 1908, Novel *see* Jean Aicard

ILLUSTRIOUS CLIENT, THE, Short Story *see* Arthur Conan Doyle

ILLUSTRIOUS CORPSE, THE, New York 1930, Novel *see* Tiffany Thayer

ILLUSTRIOUS PRINCE, THE, Boston 1910, Novel *see* E. Phillips Oppenheim

ILONA BECK, Novel *see* Oswald Richter-Tersik

ILONA LLEGA CON LA LLUVA, Novel *see* Alvaro Mutis

ILS, Novel *see* Andre Hardellet

ILS ONT VINGT ANS, Play *see* Roger Ferdinand

ILS PARTIRONT DANS L'IVRESSE, Book *see* Lucie Aubrac

ILUSTRE FREGONA, LA, *see* Miguel de Cervantes Saavedra

I'M A FOOL, 1923, Short Story *see* Sherwood Anderson

I'M AN EXPLOSIVE, Novel *see* Gordon Phillips

I'M DANCING AS FAST AS I CAN, Book *see* Barbara Gordon

I'M DANGEROUS TONIGHT, 1943, Short Story *see* Cornell Woolrich

I'M GIVING THEM UP FOR GOOD, Novel *see* Margaret Rau, Neil Rau

IM HERBST VERBLUHEN DIE ROSEN, Novel *see* Hans Ernst

IM JAHR DER SCHILDKROTE, Novel *see* Hans Werner Kettenbach

I'M JUMPING OVER PUDDLES AGAIN, Autobiography *see* Alan Marshall

I'M LOSING YOU, 1997, Novel *see* Bruce Wagner

IM LUXUSZUG, Play *see* Abel Hermant

IM NAMEN DER LIEBE. EIN BEKENNTNIS, Leipzig 1938, Novel *see* Rosy von Kanel

IM NAMEN EINER MUTTER, Novel *see* Teda Bork

I'M NOT RAPPAPORT, Play *see* Herb Gardner

IM REICHE DES SILBERNEN LOWEN, Novel *see* Karl Friedrich May

IM SECHSTEN STOCK, Play *see* Alfred Gehri

IM WESTEN NICHTS NEUES, Berlin 1929, Novel *see* Erich Maria Remarque

IMAM DRIJE MAME I DVA TATE, Novel *see* Miriam Tusek

IMITATION GAME, THE, 1981, Play *see* Ian McEwan

IMITATION OF LIFE, New York 1933, Novel *see* Fannie Hurst

IMMACOLATA, Short Story *see* Lina Pietravalle

IMMEDIATE LEE, Short Story *see* Kenneth B. Clarke

IMMENSEE, 1852, Novel *see* Theodor Storm

IMMIGRANTS, THE, Novel *see* Howard Fast

IMMORTAL SERGEANT, THE, Novel *see* John Brophy

IMMORTALE, L', Novel *see* Giuliano Di Guida

IMMORTALITY INC., Novel *see* Robert Sheckley

IMMORTALS, THE, Story *see* James E. Gunn

IMPASSIVE FOOTMAN, THE, Play *see* H. C. McNeile ("Sapper")

IMPATIENT MAIDEN, THE, New York 1931, Novel *see* Donald Henderson Clarke

IMPERFECT IMPOSTER, THE, New York 1925, Novel *see* Norman Venner

IMPERSONATOR, THE, Novel *see* Mary Imlay Taylor

IMPORTANCE OF BEING EARNEST, THE, London 1895, Play *see* Oscar Wilde

IMPORTANT, C'EST DAIMER, L', Novel *see* Christopher Frank

IMPORTANT PEOPLE, Play *see* F. Wyndham Mallock

IMPORTUNO VINCE L'AVARO, L', 1887, Play *see* O. Carlini, A. Consigli

IMPOSSIBLE MRS. BELLEW, THE, New York 1916, Novel *see* David Lisle

IMPOSSIBLE OBJECT, 1968, Novel *see* Nicholas Mosley

IMPOSSIBLE YEARS, THE, New York 1965, Play *see* Bob Fisher, Arthur Marx

IMPOSTER, THE, New York 1910, Play *see* Leonard Merrick, Michael Morton

IMPOSTOR, THE, Play *see* Douglas Murray

IMPRECATEUR, L', Novel *see* Rene-Victor Pilhes

IMPRESARIO, Book *see* Ruth Goode, Sol Horuk

IMPREVU, L', Play *see* Victor Margueritte

IMPROPER DUCHESS, THE, London 1931, Play *see* James B. Fagan

IMPULSES, 1919, Short Story *see* Roger Hartman

IN A LONELY PLACE, Novel *see* Dorothy B. Hughes

IN A REMOTE VILLAGE, Novel *see* Nikolai Domojakov

IN A SHALLOW GRAVE, Novel *see* James Purdy

IN ANOTHER GIRL'S SHOES, Novel *see* Berta Ruck

IN BORROWED PLUMES, Short Story *see* W. W. Jacobs, Leroy Scott

IN CALVERT'S VALLEY, New York 1908, Novel *see* Margaret Prescott Montague

IN CELEBRATION, 1969, Novel *see* David Storey

IN COLD BLOOD, New York 1966, Book *see* Truman Capote

IN DE JONGE JAN, Play *see* Herman Heijermans

IN DER STRAFKOLONIE, 1919, Short Story *see* Franz Kafka

IN FLANDERS FIELDS, Poem *see* John McCrae

IN FOLLY'S TRAIL, 1920, Short Story *see* Katherine Leiser Robbins

IN FOR THE NIGHT, New York 1917, Play *see* James Savery

IN FULL CRY, Novel *see* Richard Marsh

IN GOD WE TRUST - ALL OTHERS PAY CASH, Novel *see* Jean Shepherd

IN HAMBURG SIND DIE NACHTE LANG, Novel *see* Peter Francke

IN HIS GRIP, Novel *see* David Christie Murray

IN HIS STEPS: "WHAT WOULD JESUS DO?", New York 1896, Novel *see* Charles Monroe Sheldon

IN LOVE AND WAR, Novel *see* Jim Stockdale, Sybil Stockdale

IN LOVE WITH LOVE, New York 1923, Play *see* Vincent Lawrence

IN MAREMMA, Novel *see* Ouida

IN MIZZOURA, Chicago 1893, Play *see* Augustus Thomas

IN MY SOLITUDE, Novel *see* David Stuart Leslie

IN NAMEN DER UNSCHULD, Novel *see* Dorothea Kleine

IN NAMEN DES TEUFELS, Novel *see* Hans Habe

IN OLD KENTUCKY, Pittsburgh 1893, Play *see* Charles T. Dazey

IN PAWN, Play *see* Frank Stayton

IN PRAISE OF JOHN CARABINE, 1925, Short Story *see* Brian Oswald Donn-Byrne

IN PRAISE OF OLDER WOMEN, Novel *see* Stephen Vizinczey

IN PRINCIPIO ERANO LE MUTANDE, Novel *see* Rossana Campo

IN SEARCH OF A SINNER, Play *see* Charlotte Thompson

IN SEARCH OF A WIFE, Story *see* Robert McGowan

IN SEARCH OF ARCADY, Garden City, N.Y. 1912, Novel *see* Nina Wilcox Putnam

IN SEARCH OF HISTORIC JESUS, Book *see* Lee Roddy, Charles E. Sellier Jr.

IN SILENZIO, 1905, Short Story *see* Luigi Pirandello

IN SLAVERY DAYS, Story *see* James Dayton

IN SPITE OF ALL, Play *see* Steele MacKaye

IN THE AISLES OF THE WILD, Short Story *see* Bret Harte

IN THE BISHOP'S CARRIAGE, Indianapolis 1904, Novel *see* Miriam Michelson

IN THE BISHOP'S GARDEN, Indianapolis 1904, Novel *see* Miriam Michelson

IN THE BLOOD, Novel *see* Andrew Soutar

IN THE CARQUINEZ WOODS, London 1883, Novel *see* Bret Harte

IN THE COOL OF THE DAY, New York 1960, Novel *see* Susan Ertz

IN THE DAYS OF FANNY, Story *see* James Oliver Curwood

IN THE FIRELIGHT, Poem *see* Marc Edmund Jones

IN THE FOG, Short Story *see* Richard Harding Davis

IN THE FRENCH STYLE, 1953, Short Story *see* Irwin Shaw

IN THE GARDEN OF CHARITY, New York 1903, Novel *see* Basil King

IN THE GLOAMING, 1993, Short Story *see* Alice Elliott Dark

IN THE HANDS OF THE SPOILERS, Novel *see* Sydney Paternoster

IN THE HEART OF A FOOL, New York 1918, Novel *see* William Allen White

IN THE HEART OF THE COUNTRY, 1977, Novel *see* J. M. Coetzee

IN THE HEAT OF SUMMER, Novel *see* John Katzenbach

IN THE HEAT OF THE NIGHT, New York 1965, Novel *see* John Dudley Ball

IN THE MEXICAN QUARTER, 1930, Short Story *see* Tom Gill

IN THE NIGHT, London 1919, Play *see* Cyril Harcourt

IN THE PALACE OF THE KING; A LOVE STORY OF OLD MADRID, New York 1900, Novel *see* F. Marion Crawford

IN THE PAVILION, 1919, Short Story *see* Mary Roberts Rinehart

IN THE RANKS, London 1883, Play *see* Henry Pettitt, George R. Sims

IN THE RED, Novel *see* Mark Tavener

IN THE SHADOW, Novel *see* John B. Hymer

IN THE SHADOW OF THE HILLS, New York 1919, Novel *see* George Clifford Shedd

IN THE SIGNAL BOX, Poem *see* George R. Sims

IN THE SOUP, London 1900, Play *see* Ralph R. Lumley

IN THE SPRING, 1918, Short Story *see* John A. Moroso

IN THE TOWN OF BERDICHEV, Novel *see* Vasily Grossman

IN THE WAKE OF A STRANGER, Novel *see* Ian Stuart Black

IN THE WINTER DARK, Novel *see* Tim Winton

IN THIS HOUSE OF BREDE, Novel *see* Rumer Godden

IN THIS OUR LIFE, 1941, Novel *see* Ellen Glasgow

IN THIS SIGN, Novel *see* Joanne Greenberg

IN TWO MINDS, 1967, Play *see* David Mercer

IN VREME DE RAZBOI, 1898-99, Short Story *see* Ion Luca Caragiale

INADMISSABLE EVIDENCE, London 1964, Play *see* John Osborne

INAZUMA, 1935, Novel *see* Fumiko Hayashi

INCIDENT AT 125TH ST., Story *see* J. E. Brown

INCOMPRESO, Novel *see* Florence Montgomery

INCONNUE, L', Short Story *see* Jack Eden

INCONNUS DANS LA MAISON, LES, Paris 1940, Novel *see* Georges Simenon

INCONSTANTE, L', Novel *see* Wilhelm Speyer

INCORRIGIBLE DUKANE, THE, Play *see* George Clifford Shedd

INCORRIGIBLE, L', Novel *see* Alex Vaoux

INCREDIBLE JOURNEY, THE, Boston 1961, Novel *see* Sheila Burnford

INCUBUS, Novel *see* Ray Russell

INCUBUS, THE, New York 1915, Novel *see* Marjorie Benton Cooke

INDECENT OBSESSION, AN, Novel *see* Colleen McCullough

INDECENT PROPOSAL, Novel *see* Jack Engelhard

INDEMNITY, Novel *see* Sara Paretsky

INDES NOIRES, LES, Novel *see* Jules Verne

INDESTRUCTIBLE WIFE, THE, New York 1918, Play *see* Fanny Hatton, Frederic Hatton

INDIA RUBBER MEN, THE, London 1929, Novel *see* Edgar Wallace

INDIAN PAINT, New York 1942, Novel *see* Glenn Balch

INDIAN SUMMER OF DRY VALLEY JOHNSON, THE, 1907, Short Story *see* O. Henry

INDIANA, 1831, Novel *see* George Sand

INDIANS, 1969, Play *see* Arthur Kopit

INDICT AND CONVICT, Book *see* Bill Davidson

INDIFFERENTI, GLI, Milan 1929, Novel *see* Alberto Moravia

INDIGENOUS SPECIALIST, THE, Play *see* Li Zhun, Wang Yanfei

INDIO, O, 1962, Short Story *see* Carlos Drummond de Andrade

INDISCHE GRABMAL, DAS, Novel *see* Thea von Harbou

INDISCRETION OF THE DUCHESS, THE, New York 1894, Novel *see* Anthony Hope

INDOMPTABLE ANGELIQUE, Novel *see* Anne Golon, Serge Golon

INDOOR GAMES NEAR NEWBURY, 1948, Verse *see* John Betjeman

INDRASABHA, 1853, Play *see* Sayed Aga Hasan Amanat

INDULTO, EL, 1885, Short Story *see* Emilia Pardo Bazan

INEFFABILI CINQUE, GLI, Novel *see* Donald E. Westlake

INEVITABLE MILLIONAIRES, THE, London 1923, Novel *see* E. Phillips Oppenheim

INFAMOUS MISS REVELL, THE, Story *see* W. Carey Wonderly

INFANCIA DOS MORTOS, 1977, Novel *see* Jose Louzeiro

INFANTE A LA ROSE, L', Novel *see* Gabrielle Reval

INFATUATION, Indianapolis 1909, Novel *see* Lloyd Osbourne

INFELICE, Novel *see* Augusta Jane Evans

INFERIOR SEX, THE, New York 1910, Play *see* Frank Slayton

INFERNAL IDOL, Novel *see* Henry Seymour

INFERNO, L', Play *see* Franco Liberati

INFORMATION PLEASE, New York 1918, Play *see* Jane Cowl, Jane Murfin

INFORMATION RECEIVED, Novel *see* Berkeley Mather

INFORMER, THE, London 1925, Novel *see* Liam O'Flaherty

INGEN MANS KVINNA, Novel *see* Bernhard Nordh

INGEN MANS LAND, Novel *see* Jan Guillou

INGENIOSO HIDALGO DON QUIJOTE DE LA MANCHA, EL, 1605-15, Novel *see* Miguel de Cervantes Saavedra

INGENJOR ANDREES LUFTFARD, Novel *see* Olof Sundman

INGENU, L', 1767, Short Story *see* Francois-Marie Arouet de Voltaire

INGENUE LIBERTINE, L', 1909, Novel *see* Sidonie Gabrielle Colette

INGLES DE LOS GUESOS, EL, 1924, Novel *see* Benito Lynch

INHERIT THE WIND, New York 1955, Play *see* Jerome Lawrence, Robert E. Lee

INHERITORS, THE, 1922, Short Story *see* I. A. R. Wylie

INICIADO DO VENTO, O, 1959, Short Story *see* Anibal Machado

INNER SHRINE, THE, New York 1909, Novel *see* Basil King

INNKEEPER'S DIARY, AN, Book *see* John Fothergill

INNOCENT, Novel *see* Marie Corelli

INNOCENT, New York 1914, Play *see* George Broadhurst

INNOCENT EREDIRA AND HER HEARTLESS GRANDMOTHER, Novel *see* Gabriel Garcia Marquez

INNOCENT SINNER, AN, Play *see* Lawrence Marston

INNOCENT, THE, Novel *see* Ian McEwan

INNOCENT VICTIMS, Book *see* Scott Whisnant

INNOCENTE, L', 1891, Novel *see* Gabriele D'Annunzio

INNOCENTS, LES, Novel *see* Francis Carco

INNOCENTS OF PARIS, New York 1928, Novel *see* Clarence Edward Andrews

INNOCENZA, L', Novel *see* Francesco Chiesa

INOCENCIA, 1872, Novel *see* Alfredo d'Escragnolle Taunay

INQUEST, Play *see* Michael Barringer

INQUIETUDES DE SHANTI ANDIA, LAS, 1911, Novel *see* Pio Baroja Y Nessi

INSEL, DIE, Play *see* Harald Bratt

INSEL ENTDECKT, EINE, Play *see* Karl von Stigler

INSIDE DAISY CLOVER, New York 1963, Novel *see* Gavin Lambert

INSIDE MOVES, Novel *see* Todd Walton

INSIDE OF THE CUP, THE, New York 1912, Novel *see* Winston Churchill

INSIDE STORY, Story *see* Scott Littleton

INSIDE THE GESTAPO, *see* Helene Moskiewicz

INSIDE THE LINES, New York 1915, Play *see* Earl Derr Biggers

INSIDE THE ROOM, Play *see* Marten Cumberland

INSIGNIFICANCE, 1982, Play *see* Terry Johnson

INSOUMISE, L', Play *see* Pierre Frondaie

INSPECTEUR SERGIL, Novel *see* Jacques Rey

INSPECTOR CALLS, AN, London 1946, Play *see* J. B. Priestley

INSPECTOR, THE, New York 1960, Novel *see* Jan de Hartog

INSPIRATIONS OF HARRY LARRABEE, THE, Short Story *see* Howard Fielding

INSTINCT, L', Play *see* Henri Kistemaeckers

INSTRUCT MY SORROWS, Novel *see* Clare Jaynes

INSULT, Play *see* Jean Fabricus

INTENSITY, Novel *see* Dean R. Koontz

INTENSIVE CARE, Book *see* Mary-Lou Weisman

INTENT TO KILL, Novel *see* Michael Bryan

INTEREM, Radio Play *see* Thomas Edward O'Connell

INTERFERENCE, London 1927, Play *see* Harold Dearden, Roland Pertwee

INTERLOCUTORY, 1924, Short Story *see* Charles William Brackett

INTERLUDE, THE, Story *see* H. B. Marriott Watson

INTERMEZZO AM ABEND, Play *see* Lorenz, von Moller

INTERNATIONAL INCIDENT, Story *see* Neil Paterson

INTERNATIONAL TEAM, 1935, Short Story *see* Frank Van Wyck Mason

INTERNES CAN'T TAKE MONEY, 1936, Story *see* Max Brand

INTERNS, THE, New York 1960, Novel *see* Richard Frede

INTERPOL, Book *see* A. J. Forrest

INTERPRETER, THE, 1945, Short Story *see* Frederick L. Keefe

INTERPRETER'S HOUSE, THE, New York 1924, Novel *see* Maxwell Struthers Burt

INTERRUPTED JOURNEY, THE, Book *see* John G. Fuller

INTERRUPTED MELODY, Autobiography *see* Marjorie Lawrence

INTERRUPTION, AN, Short Story *see* Bruno Lessing

INTERRUPTION, THE, Novel *see* W. W. Jacobs

INTIMATE EXCHANGES, Play *see* Alan Ayckbourn

INTIMATE RELATIONS, 1932, Play *see* C. Stafford Dickens

INTINIREA DIN PAMINTURI, 1948, Short Story *see* Marin Preda

INTO HER KINGDOM, 1925, Short Story *see* Ruth Comfort Mitchell

INTO IT, Novel *see* Edward Pomerantz

INTO THE BLUE, Novel *see* Robert Goddard

INTO THE CRIMSON WEST, 1930, Short Story *see* George Cory Franklin

INTO THE LIGHT, Story *see* Cyrus J. Williams

INTO THE PRIMITIVE, Chicago 1908, Novel *see* Robert Ames Bennet

INTO THE WEST, Short Story *see* Michael Pearce

INTOARCEREA TATII DIN RAZBOI, 1934, Short Story *see* Alexandru Sahia

INTOARCEREA VLASINILOR, 1979, Novel *see* Ioana Postelnicu

INTRUDER IN THE DUST, 1948, Novel *see* William Faulkner

INTRUDER, THE, 1952, Novel *see* Helen Fowler

INTRUDER, THE, New York 1959, Novel *see* Charles Beaumont

INTRUSA, LA, 1952, Short Story *see* Jorge Luis Borges

INTRUSUL, 1968, Novel *see* Marin Preda

INTUNECARE, 1927-28, Novel *see* Cezar Petrescu

INUGAMIKE NO ICHIZOKU, Novel *see* Seishi Yokomizo

INUTILE ATTESA, Novel *see* Rina Maria Pierazzi

INVADERS, THE, Novel *see* John Lloyd

INVANDRARNA, 1952, Novel *see* Vilhelm Moberg

INVASION, Novel *see* Robin Cook

INVASION OF 1910, THE, Novel *see* William Le Queux

INVASORE, L', Novel *see* Annie Vivanti

INVENCION DI MOREL, LA, 1940, Novel *see* Adolfo Bioy Casares

INVENTIAMO L'AMORE, Play *see* Giuseppe Achille, Bruno Corra

INVENTING THE ABBOTTS, *see* Sue Miller

INVESTIGATION, Story *see* Edith Grafton, Samuel Grafton

INVIOLABILE, L', Novel *see* G. Ulcelli

INVISIBLE GOVERNMENT, Story *see* Jerome N. Wilson

INVISIBLE MAN, THE, London 1897, Novel *see* H. G. Wells

INVISIBLE STRIPES, New York 1938, Novel *see* Lewis E. Lawes

INVISIBLE WOUNDS, New York 1925, Novel *see* Frederick Palmer

INVITATION TO A MURDER, Play *see* Rufus King

INVITATION TO MURDER, 1937, Short Story *see* Kay Krausse

INVITATION TO THE WALTZ, Radio Play *see* Holt Marvel, Eric Maschwitz, George Posford

IO E LUI, Short Story *see* Alberto Moravia

IO IL TEBANO, Book *see* Antonio Carlucci, Paolo Rossetti

IO, SUO PADRE, Novel *see* Alba de Cespedes

IOLANDA, LA FIGLIA DEL CORSARO NERO, Novel *see* Emilio Salgari

IOLANTA, St. Petersburg 1892, Opera *see* Modest Tchaikovsky, Petr Tchaikovsky

ION, 1920, Novel *see* Liviu Rebreanu

IONYCH, 1898, Short Story *see* Anton Chekhov

I.O.U.'S OF DEATH, Story *see* Ciela Jaccard

IPCRESS FILE, THE, London 1962, Novel *see* Len Deighton

IPHIGENIA IN AULIA, c407 bc, Play *see* Euripides

IPPOCAMPO, L', Play *see* Sergio Pugliese

IRACEMA, LENDA DO CEARA, 1865, Novel *see* Jose Martiniano de Alencar

IRCA V HNIZDECKU, Novel *see* Josef Roden

IRCIN ROMANEK, Novel *see* Josef Roden

IRCIN V PENSIONATE, Novel *see* Josef Roden

IRENE, Novel *see* Ronald Marsh

IRENE, New York 1919, Musical Play *see* James H. Montgomery

IRIKKAPINDAM, *see* C. V. Sriraman

IRIS, London 1901, Play *see* Arthur Wing Pinero

IRIS OCH LOJTNANTSHJARTA, 1934, Novel *see* Olle Hedberg

IRIS PERDUE ET RETROUVEE, Novel *see* Pierre Frondaie

IRISH AND PROUD OF IT, Story *see* Dorothea Donn Byrne

IRISH FOR LUCK, Novel *see* L. A. G. Strong

IRISHMAN, THE, Novel *see* Elizabeth O'Conner

IRMA LA DOUCE, Paris 1956, Play *see* Alexandre Breffort

IRON CHALICE, THE, Boston 1925, Novel *see* Octavus Roy Cohen

IRON HEEL, THE, *see* Jack London

IRON MAN, THE, New York 1930, Novel *see* William Riley Burnett

IRON MISTRESS, THE, Novel *see* Paul I. Wellman

IRON RIDER, THE, 1916, Short Story *see* Frank L. Packard

IRON STAIR, THE, Novel *see* Rita

IRON TRAIL, THE, New York 1913, Novel *see* Rex Beach

IRON WOMAN, THE, 1932, Play *see* Frederick Jackson

IRON WOMAN, THE, New York 1911, Novel *see* Margaret Deland

IRONWEED, Novel *see* William Kennedy

IRRESISTIBLE CATHERINE, L', Novel *see* Jean de La Vallieres

IRRESISTIBLE MARMADUKE, THE, London 1918, Play *see* Ernest Denny

IRRUNGEN WIRRUNGEN, 1888, Short Story *see* Theodor Fontane

IS GOD DEAD?, Novel *see* Newman Flower

IS HE LIVING OR IS HE DEAD?, 1900, Short Story *see* Mark Twain

IS PARIS BURNING?, New York 1965, Novel *see* Larry Collins, Dominique Lapierre

IS YOUR HONEYMOON REALLY NECESSARY?, London 1944, Play *see* E. Vivian Tidmarsh

IS ZAT SO?, New York 1925, Play *see* James Gleason, Richard Taber

ISHI IN TWO WORLDS, Book *see* Theodora Kroeber Quinn

ISHINAKA-SENSEI GYOJUKI, 1948-49, Novel *see* Yojiro Ishizaka

ISHMAEL; OR, IN THE DEPTHS, New York 1904, Novel *see* E. D. E. N. Southworth

ISLA DEL DIABLO, L', *see* Vincent Mulberry

ISLAND AT THE TOP OF THE WORLD, THE, Novel *see* Ian Cameron

ISLAND DOCTOR, 1939, Short Story *see* Ray Millholland

ISLAND FREIGHTER, Short Story *see* Charles Yerkow

ISLAND IN THE SKY, Novel *see* Ernest K. Gann

ISLAND IN THE SUN, 1955, Novel *see* Alec Waugh

ISLAND MILITIA WOMEN, Novel *see* Li Ruqin

ISLAND NIGHTS' ENTERTAINMENTS, Short Story *see* Robert Louis Stevenson

ISLAND OF DESPAIR, THE, Novel *see* Margot Neville

ISLAND OF DR. MOREAU, THE, London 1896, Novel *see* H. G. Wells

ISLAND OF FAITH, THE, New York 1921, Novel *see* Margaret Elizabeth Sangster

ISLAND OF INTRIGUE, THE, New York 1918, Novel *see* Isabel Ostrander

ISLAND OF REGENERATION: A STORY OF WHAT OUGHT TO BE, THE, New York 1909, Novel *see* Cyrus Townsend Brady

ISLAND OF SURPRISE, THE, New York 1915, Novel *see* Cyrus Townsend Brady

ISLAND OF THE BLUE DOLPHINS, Boston 1960, Novel *see* Scott O'Dell

ISLAND ON BIRD STREET, THE, Book *see* Uri Orlev

ISLAND, THE, 1948, Short Story *see* L. P. Hartley

ISLAND, THE, 1979, Novel *see* Peter Benchley

ISLANDS IN THE STREAM, 1970, Novel *see* Ernest Hemingway

ISLE OF DEAD SHIPS, THE, Philadelphia 1909, Novel *see* Crittenden Marriott

ISLE OF DESTINY, THE, Short Story *see* MacK Arthur

ISLE OF ESCAPE; A STORY OF THE SOUTH SEAS, London 1926, Novel *see* Jack McLaren

ISLE OF LIFE; A ROMANCE, New York 1913, Novel *see* Stephen French Whitman

ISLE OF RETRIBUTION, THE, Boston 1923, Novel *see* Edison Marshall

ISLE OF TERROR, Play *see* Ladislaus Fodor, Gina Kaus

ISLES OF ROMANCE, 1924, Short Story *see* Richard Connell

ISMERETIEN LANY, AZ, Budapest 1934, Play *see* Ferenc Molnar

ISN'T LIFE WONDERFUL!, 1924, Short Story *see* Geoffrey Moss

ISOBEL: A ROMANCE OF THE NORTHERN TRAIL, Novel *see* James Oliver Curwood

ISOLA DELLE PESCATRICI, L', Bari 1960, Novel *see* Fosco Maraini

ISOLA DI ARTURO, L', 1957, Novel *see* Elsa Morante

ISRAEL, 1908, Play *see* Henri Bernstein

ISRAEL RANK, Novel *see* Roy Horniman

IS-SLOTTET, 1963, Novel *see* Tarjei Vesaas

ISSUE OF THE BISHOP'S BLOOD, THE, Novel *see* Thomas Patrick McMahon

ISTORIYA ODNOY POYEZDKI, 1888, Novel *see* Anton Chekhov

ISTRUTTORIA, L', Play *see* Paul Henriot

ISZONY, 1947, Novel *see* Laszlo Nemeth

IT, Novel *see* Elinor Glyn

IT, 1986, Novel *see* Stephen King

IT ALWAYS RAINS ON SUNDAYS, Novel *see* Arthur La Bern

IT DEPENDS WHAT YOU MEAN, London 1944, Play *see* James Bridie

IT HAPPENED ONE DAY, New York 1932, Novel *see* Marjorie Bartholomew Paradis

IT HAPPENED WHILE HE FISHED, Story *see* Peter B. Kyne

IT HAPPENS EVERY THURSDAY, Novel *see* Jane S. McIlvane

IT IS NEVER TOO LATE TO MEND, 1853, Novel *see* Charles Reade

IT IS THE LAW, New York 1922, Play *see* Elmer Rice, Hayden Talbot

IT ISN'T BEING DONE THIS SEASON, 1918, Short Story *see* Thomas Edgelow

IT MIGHT HAVE HAPPENED, Story *see* Abem Finkel, Bella Muni

IT PAYS TO ADVERTISE, New York 1914, Play *see* Walter Hackett, Roi Cooper Megrue

IT WON'T BE A STYLISH MARRIAGE, Play *see* A. P. Dearsley

ITALA GENS, Novel *see* Franco Navarra Viggiani

ITALIAN JOB, THE, Novel *see* Troy Kennedy Martin

ITALIAN STORY, Story *see* Richard W. Tregaskis

ITALIANE SI CONFESSANO, LE, Book *see* Gabriella Parca

ITALIENREISE - LIEBE INBEGRIFFEN, Novel *see* Barbara Noack

IT'S A 2'6" ABOVE THE GROUND WORLD, Play *see* Kevin Laffan

IT'S A BOY, London 1922, Play *see* Franz Robert Arnold, Ernst Bach

IT'S A VET'S LIFE, London 1961, Novel *see* Alex Duncan

IT'S A WISE CHILD, New York 1929, Play *see* Laurence E. Johnson

IT'S ALL IN THE RACKET, Short Story *see* Richard Wormser

IT'S ALWAYS THE WOMAN, Play *see* Bryant Adair

IT'S GOOD TO BE ALIVE, Book *see* Roy Campanella

IT'S HARD TO FIND MECCA, Short Story *see* Cordelia Baird Gross

IT'S NEVER TOO LATE, London 1952, Play *see* Felicity Douglas

IT'S THE OLD ARMY GAME, Story *see* Joseph Patrick McEvoy

IT'S YOU I WANT, London 1933, Play *see* Maurice Braddell

IUBELEI, 1891, Play *see* Anton Chekhov

IVAN, Moscow 1959, Short Story *see* Vladimir Osipovich Bogomolov

IVAN KONDAREV, 1958-64, Novel *see* Emilian Stanev

IVANHOE, Edinburgh 1819, Novel *see* Sir Walter Scott

I'VE GOT MINE, 1946, Novel *see* Richard G. Hubler

IVORY SNUFF BOX, THE, New York 1912, Novel *see* Frederic Arnold Kummer

IVY, Novel *see* Mrs. Belloc Lowndes

IVY GARLAND, THE, Novel *see* John Hoyland

IWASIGUMO, Novel *see* Den Wada

IXE-13, Novel *see* Pierre Saurel

IZBAVITELJ, Short Story *see* Aleksandr Grin

IZLET U NEBO, 1958, Novel *see* Grozdana Olujic

IZU NO ODORIKO, 1925, Short Story *see* Yasunari Kawabata

IZUMI, 1939, Novel *see* Kunio Kishida

J 3, LES, Play *see* Roger Ferdinand

JA JSEM VINNA!, Novel *see* Otakar Hanus

JA, TRUCHLIVY BUH, 1963, Short Story *see* Milan Kundera

JAAR VAN DE KREEFT, HET, 1972, Novel *see* Hugo Claus

JAB KHET JAAGE, 1948, Novel *see* Krishnan Chander

JABANBANDI, Play *see* Bijon Bhattacharya

JABBERWOCKY, 1872, Verse *see* Lewis Carroll

JACHT DER SIEBEN SUNDEN, DIE, Novel *see* Paul Rosenhayn

JACK, Novel *see* Alphonse Daudet, Ulf Lundell

JACK CHANTY: A STORY OF ATHABASCA, New York 1913, Novel *see* Hubert Footner

JACK FRUSCIANTE E USCITO DAL GRUPPO, Novel *see* Enrico Brizzi

JACK IN THE BOX, Novel *see* William Kotzwinkle

JACK IN THE PULPIT, New York 1925, Play *see* Gordon Morris

JACK O' CLUBS, 1923, Short Story *see* Gerald Beaumont

JACK O' JUDGMENT, London 1920, Novel *see* Edgar Wallace

JACK OF DIAMONDS, Story *see* Frederick Jackson

JACK O'LANTERN, Play *see* George Goodchild

JACK SHEPPARD, London 1839, Novel *see* Harrison Ainsworth

JACK SPURLOCK - PRODIGAL, New York 1908, Novel *see* George Horace Lorimer

JACK STRAW, New York 1908, Play *see* W. Somerset Maugham

JACK TAR, Play *see* Ben Landeck, Arthur Shirley

JACK UND JENNY, Novel *see* Anne Piper

JACK WINTER'S DREAM, 1959, Play *see* James K. Baxter

JACK-A-BOY, 1965, Short Story *see* Willa Cather

JACKDAW'S STRUT, New York 1930, Novel *see* Harriet Henry

JACKIE, New York 1921, Novel *see* Countess Barcynska

JACK-KNIFE MAN, THE, New York 1913, Novel *see* Ellis Parker Butler

JACK'S RETURN HOME, Novel *see* Ted Lewis

JACOB, 1891, Novel *see* Alexander Kielland

JACOB TWO-TWO MEETS THE HOODED FANG, 1975, Novel *see* Mordecai Richler

JACOBOWSKY UND DER OBERST, 1944, Play *see* Franz Werfel

JACQUELINE, 1918, Short Story *see* James Oliver Curwood

JACQUES LE FATALISTE ET SON MAITRE, 1797, Novel *see* Denis Diderot

JACQUES L'HONNEUR, Play *see* Leon Sazie

JAFFERY, New York 1915, Novel *see* William J. Locke

JAG, LARS HARD, 1935, Novel *see* Jan Fridegard

JAGDSZENEN AUS NIEDERBAYERN, Bremen 1966, Play *see* Martin Sperr

JAGER VOM ROTECK, DER, Novel *see* Andre Mairock

JAGER VON FALL, DER, Novel *see* Ludwig Ganghofer

JAGERLOISL, DER, Novel *see* Ludwig Thoma

JAGUAR, 1914, Novel *see* Jeno Heltai

JAHR DES HERRN, DAS, Novel *see* Karl Heinrich Waggerl

J'AI DIX-SEPT ANS, Play *see* Paul Vandenberghe

JAIL BREAKER, 1932, Story *see* William Riley Burnett

JAILBIRDS, Sketch *see* Fred Karno

JAILBREAK, Story *see* Dwight Taylor

JAK BYC KOCHANA, 1960, Short Story *see* Kazimierz Brandys

JAKOB DER LUGNER, 1969, Novel *see* Jurek Becker

JAKOB VON GUNTEN, Novel *see* Robert Walser

JALKINAYTOS, 1938, Novel *see* Mika Waltari

JALMA LA DOUBLE, Novel *see* Paul d'Ivoi

JALNA, Boston 1927, Novel *see* Mazo de La Roche

JALOUSE, Play *see* Alexandre Bisson, A. Leclerq

JALSAGAR, Calcutta 1937, Novel *see* Tarashankar Banerjee

JAMAICA INN, 1936, Novel *see* Daphne Du Maurier

JAMES AND THE GIANT PEACH, Book *see* Roald Dahl

JAMES THE FOGEY, Play *see* Henry Arthur Jones

JAN CIMBURA, Novel *see* Jindrich Simon Baar

JAN DERRIKSENS DIENSTJAHR, Novel *see* Konigsfeld

JAN ROHAC, 1922, Play *see* Alois Jirasek

JAN VOLKANIK, Short Story *see* Judge M. A. Musmanno

JAN VYRAVA, Play *see* Antonin Kubovy, Walter Schorsch

JANA ARANYA, Novel *see* Shankar

JANAIKO KAPURUSER KAHINI, *see* Premendra Mitra

JANDARMUL, 1941, Short Story *see* Ion Agarbiceanu

JANE, London 1890, Play *see* W. H. Lestoq, Harry Nicholls

JANE EYRE, London 1847, Novel *see* Charlotte Bronte

JANE SHORE, London 1714, Play *see* Nicholas Rowe

JANE STEPS OUT, 1934, Play *see* Kenneth Horne

JANE'S HOUSE, Novel *see* Robert Kimmel Smith

JANET OF THE DUNES, Novel *see* Harriet T. Comstock

JANGADA, LA, 1881, Novel *see* Jules Verne

JANICE MEREDITH; A STORY OF THE AMERICAN REVOLUTION, New York 1899, Novel *see* Paul Leicester Ford

JANIE, New York 1942, Play *see* Josephine Bentham, Hershel V. Williams Jr.

JANIE OF THE WANING GLORIES, Story *see* Raymond Smiley Spears

JANIKSEN VUOSI, 1975, Novel *see* Arto Passilinna

JANKEN, Novel *see* Marta Weiss

JANKO MUZYKANT, 1879, Short Story *see* Henryk Sienkiewicz

JANOS VITEZ, 1845, Verse *see* Sandor Petofi

JANOSIK, Play *see* Jiri Mahen

JANTJES, DE, 1920, Play *see* Herman Bouber

JANUARY HEIGHTS, Novel *see* Polan Banks

JANUCK, DER, Short Story *see* Rolf Olsen

JAPANESE NIGHTINGALE, A, New York 1903, Novel *see* Sir William Young

JARDIN DES SUPPLICES, LE, Paris 1899, Novel *see* Octave Mirbeau

JARDINIER D'ARGENTEUIL, LE, Novel *see* Rene Jouglet

JARKA A VERA, Novel *see* Eduard Kucera

JAROSLAW MUDRYJ, Novel *see* Pawlo Sagrebelny

JARRAPELLEJOS, 1914, Novel *see* Felipe Trigo

JASEI NO IN, c1768, Short Story *see* Akinari Ueda

JASSY, Novel *see* Norah Lofts

JATIKAL, Play *see* B. Kannan

JAVA HEAD, New York 1919, Novel *see* Joseph Hergesheimer

JAVELKEMEICHE, Story *see* Robert Byington

JAWS, 1974, Novel *see* Peter Benchley

JAZZ KING, 1928, Play *see* James Ashmore Creelman

JE M'APPELLE JERICO, Paris 1964, Novel *see* Catherine Paysan

JE N'AIME QUE TOI, Play *see* J. Montazel

JE NE SUIS PAS UNE HEROINE, Novel *see* Noelle Henry

JE REVIENDRAI A KANDARA, Novel *see* Jean Hougron

JE VOUS SALUE, MAFIA!, Novel *see* Pierre Vial-Lesou

JEAN, Vienna 1936, Play *see* Ladislaus Bus-Fekete

JEAN D'AGREVE, Novel *see* Melchior de Vogue

JEAN DE LA LUNE, 1929, Play *see* Marcel Achard

JEAN LE BLEU, 1932, Novel *see* Jean Giono

JEAN LE COUCHER, 1852, Novel *see* Jean Bouchardy

JEAN OF THE LAZY A, Boston 1915, Novel *see* B. M. Bower

JEANNE, Play *see* Henri Duvernois

JEANNE D'ARC AU BUCHER, 1939, Play *see* Paul Claudel

JEANNE DE LUYNES, COMTESSE DE VERUE, Novel *see* Jacques Tournier

JEANNE DORE, Play *see* Tristan Bernard

JEANNE LA MAUDITE, Play *see* Delbes, Marquet

JEANNE LA PALE, Novel *see* Honore de Balzac

JEANNE OF THE MARSHES, Boston 1908, Novel *see* E. Phillips Oppenheim

JEANNIE, London 1940, Play *see* Aimee Stuart

JEDE MENGE SCHMIDT, Play *see* John Graham

JEDE NACHT IN EINEM ANDEREN BETT, Play *see* Hans Gustl Kernmayr

JEDENACTE PRIKAZANI, Play *see* Frantisek Ferdinand Samberk

JEDER STIRBT FUR SICH ALLEIN, 1947, Novel *see* Hans Fallada

JEDERMANN: DAS SPIEL VON STERBEN DES REICHEN MANNES, 1911, Play *see* Hugo von Hofmannsthal

JEEVAN YATRA, Novel *see* N. S. Phadke

JEEVANA NATAKA, Play *see* A. N. Krishnarao

JEFE POLITICO, EL, Novel *see* Jose-Maria Carretero

JEFF, *see* Raoul Praxy

JEG - EN ELSKER, Copenhagen 1965, Novel *see* Stiig Holm

JEG - EN KVINNDE, Copenhagen 1961, *see* Siv Holm

JEG - EN KVINNE II, Copenhagen 1968, Novel *see* Siv Holm

JEJI PASTORKYNA, Play *see* Gabriela Preissova

JELF'S, London 1912, Play *see* Horace Annesley Vachell

JEM OF THE OLD ROCK, 1918, Short Story *see* George Weston

JENER SELTENEN FRAUEN, EINE, Play *see* Franz Gribitz

JENIFER HALE, Novel *see* Rob Eden

JENNIE GERHARDT, New York 1911, Novel *see* Theodore Dreiser

JENNIE'S STORY, Play *see* Betty Lambert

JENNY ANGEL, New York 1954, Book *see* Elsie Oakes Barber

JENNY BE GOOD, New York 1919, Novel *see* Wilbur Finley Fauley

JENNY LIND, Novel *see* Dorothy Farnum

JENNY OMROYD OF OLDHAM, Play *see* T. G. Bailey

JENNY UND DER HERR IM FRACK, Play *see* Georg Zoch

JENNYS BUMMEL, Berlin 1926, Play *see* Hans Bachwitz, Fritz Jakobstetter

JENS LANGKNIV, 1915, Novel *see* Jeppe Aakjaer

JEPPE HAABJERGET, 1722, Play *see* Ludvig Holberg

JEREMY RODOCK (HANGING'S FOR THE LUCKY), Short Story *see* Jack Schaefer

JEROME PERREAU, Novel *see* Henri Dupuy-Mazuel

JEROMIN, 1905-07, Novel *see* Luis Coloma

JERRY, Play *see* Catherine Chisholm Cushing

JERRY'S MOTHER-IN-LAW, Play *see* V. D. Brown, H. Lidell

JERUSALEM, Novel *see* Selma Lagerlof

JESS, London 1887, Novel *see* H. Rider Haggard

JESSICA'S FIRST PRAYER, Story *see* Hesba Stretton

JEST OF GOD, A, New York 1966, Novel *see* Margaret Laurence

JESUS CHRIST SUPERSTAR, Opera *see* Tim Rice, Andrew Lloyd Webber

JESUS LA CAILLE, 1914, Novel *see* Francis Carco

JESUS VON OTTAKRING, Play *see* Helmut Korherr, Wilhelm Pellert

JET STREAM, Novel *see* Austin Ferguson

JEU DE L'AMOUR ET DU HASARD, LE, 1730, Play *see* Pierre Carlet de Marivaux

JEUNE COUPLE, UN, 1967, Novel *see* Jean-Louis Curtis

JEUNE FILLE SAVAIT, UNE, Play *see* Andre Haguet

JEUNE HOMME QUI SE TUE, UN, Play *see* Georges Berr

JEUNES FILLES EN DETRESSE, Novel *see* Peter Quinn

JEUNESSE, UNE, Novel *see* Patrick Modiano

JEWEL; A CHAPTER IN HER LIFE, Boston 1903, Novel *see* Clara Louise Burnham

JEWEL OF THE SEVEN STARS, THE, 1903, Novel *see* Bram Stoker

JEWELS, Novel *see* Danielle Steel

JEWELS OF DESIRE, Story *see* Agnes Parsons

JEWISH ANTIQUITIES, THE, 93-94 A.D., Book *see* Flavius Josephus

JEZEBEL, New York 1933, Play *see* Owen Davis Sr.

JEZIORO BODENSKIE, 1946, Novel *see* Stanislaw Dygat

JIA, 1933, Novel *see* Li Feigan

JIA TING WEN TI, Novel *see* Hu Wanchun

JIANG HU QIXIA ZHUAN, Novel *see* XIang Kairan

JIAOTOU LAN'E, Novel *see* Lin Qinnan

JIE HUN, Novel *see* Ma Feng

JIGOKU-HEN, 1918, Novel *see* Ryunosuke Akutagawa

JIGSAW MAN, THE, Novel *see* Dorothea Bennett

JILTING OF GRANNY WEATHERALL, THE, 1930, Short Story *see* Katherine Anne Porter

JIM AND JOE, Poem *see* Hal Reid

JIM BLACKWOOD JOCKEY, Novel *see* Valentin Mandelstamm

JIM BLUDSO OF THE PRAIRIE BELLE, 1871, Poem *see* John Hay

JIM LA HOULETTE, Play *see* Jean Guitton

JIM THE CONQUEROR, Short Story *see* Peter B. Kyne

JIM THE PENMAN, New York 1886, Play *see* Charles Lawrence Young, Sir Charles L. Young

JIM THORPE - ALL AMERICAN, Autobiography *see* Russell G. Birdwell, Jim Thorpe

JIMMY, Novel *see* John Strange Winter

JIMMY AND THE DESPERATE WOMAN, Short Story *see* D. H. Lawrence

JIMMY, DER SCHWERVERBRECHER, Novel *see* Ludwig von Wohl

JIMMY HAYES AND MURIEL, Short Story *see* O. Henry

JIMMY THE KID, Novel *see* Donald E. Westlake

JIM'S GIFT, Novel *see* Sylvia Wickham

JIN GUANG DA DAO, Novel *see* Hao Ran

JINDRA - HRABENKA OSTROVINOVA, Novel *see* Ivan Klicpera

JING HUN TAO HUA DANG, Novel *see* Liu Zongdai

JINKO TEIEN, 1954, Short Story *see* Abe Tomoji

JINY VZDUCH, Play *see* Matej Anastazia Simacek

J'IRAI CRACHER SUR VOS TOMBES, Paris 1946, Novel *see* Boris Vian

JIX, Novel *see* Raleigh King

JIZDNI HLIDKA, Play *see* Frantisek Langer

JO TUNDER, A, Budapest 1931, Play *see* Ferenc Molnar

JOAN DANVERS, THE, Play *see* Frank Stayton

JOAN OF LORRAINE, New York 1946, Play *see* Maxwell Anderson

JOAN OF RAINBOW SPRINGS, Boston 1911, Novel *see* Frances Marian Mitchell

JOAN THURSDAY, Boston 1913, Novel *see* Louis Joseph Vance

JOANNA GODDEN, Novel *see* Sheila Kaye-Smith

JOANNA OF THE SKIRTS TOO SHORT AND THE LIPS TOO RED, New York 1926, Novel *see* Henry Leyford Gates

JOCASTE, *see* Anatole France

JOCELYN, 1836, Verse *see* Alphonse de Lamartine

JOCH, DAS, Novel *see* Vicki Baum

JOCK OF THE BUSHVELD, Book *see* Sir Percy Fitzpatrick

JOCUL CU MOARTEA, 1962, Novel *see* Zaharia Stancu

JOCUL DE-A VACANTA, 1946, Play *see* Mihail Sebastian

JOCUL IELELOR, 1947, Play *see* Camil Petrescu

JODO CARTAMIGLI, Novel *see* Vincenzo Pardini

JOE AND JOSETTE, Play *see* Paul Franck, Georg Fraser

JOE BUTTERFLY, Play *see* Jack Ruge, Evan Wylie

JOE IL ROSSO, Play *see* Dino Falconi

JOE PANTHER, Novel *see* Zachary Ball

JOE THE WOUNDED TENNIS PLAYER, Novel *see* Morton Thompson

JOEY BOY, Novel *see* Eddie Chapman

JOFROI DE LA MAUSSAN, 1930, Short Story *see* Jean Giono

JOHAN ULFSTJERNA, Stockholm 1907, Play *see* Tor Hedberg

JOHANN, Play *see* Theo Lingen

JOHANNES FILS DE JOHANNES, Novel *see* Marcel Girette

JOHANNISFEUER, 1900, Play *see* Hermann Sudermann

JOHANNISNACHT, Novel *see* Werner Hill

JOHN AND MARY, London 1966, Novel *see* Mervyn Jones

JOHN AND THE MISSUS, Novel *see* Gordon Pinsent

JOHN BARLEYCORN, New York 1913, Novel *see* Jack London

JOHN BURNS OF GETTYSBURG, Poem *see* Bret Harte

JOHN BURT, Philadelphia 1903, Novel *see* Frederick Upham Adams

JOHN CHILCOTE M.P., 1904, Novel *see* Katherine Cecil Thurston

JOHN ERMINE OF THE YELLOWSTONE, New York 1902, Novel *see* Frederic Remington

JOHN GABRIEL BORKMAN, 1896, Play *see* Henrik Ibsen

JOHN GILPIN, 1782, Poem *see* William Cowper

JOHN GLAYDE'S HONOUR, New York 1907, Play *see* Alfred Sutro

JOHN HALIFAX - GENTLEMAN, 1857, Novel *see* Dinah Maria Craik

JOHN HENRY AND THE RESTLESS SEX, 1921, Short Story *see* Earl Derr Biggers

JOHN HERIOT'S WIFE, Novel *see* Alice Askew, Claude Askew

JOHN HINTE - GENTLEMAN IN BLUE, Novel *see* Mark Allerton

JOHN LOVES MARY, New York 1947, Play *see* Norman Krasna

JOHN MCARDLE, REFEREE, 1921, Short Story *see* Gerald Beaumont

JOHN NEEDHAM'S DOUBLE; A NOVEL, New York 1885, Novel *see* Joseph Hatton

JOHN OF THE FAIR, London 1950, Novel *see* Arthur William Groom

JOHN OF THE WOODS, Story *see* Alice Farwell Brown

JOHN ROBERT POWERS, Book *see* John R. Powers

JOHN TOM LITTLE BEAR, Short Story *see* O. Henry

JOHN XXIII IL GIORNALE DELL'ANIMA E ALTRI SCRITTI DI PIETA, Roma 1964, Book *see* Angelo Roncalli

JOHNNY BELINDA, New York 1940, Play *see* Elmer Harris

JOHNNY CAVE GOES SUBTLE, 1934, Short Story *see* James Edward Grant

JOHNNY CUCABOD, 1920, Short Story *see* Wilbur Hall

JOHNNY GET YOUR GUN, New York 1917, Novel *see* Edmund Lawrence Burke

JOHNNY GETS HIS GUN, 1934, Short Story *see* Lucian Cary

JOHNNY GOT HIS GUN, Novel *see* Dalton Trumbo

JOHNNY GUITAR, Novel *see* Roy Chanslor

JOHNNY MARCH, Story *see* Richard Newman

JOHNNY ONE-EYE, 1944, Short Story *see* Damon Runyon

JOHNNY TREMAIN, Novel *see* Esther Forbes

JOHNNY WE HARDLY KNEW YE, 1972, Book *see* Kenneth O'Donnell, David F. Powers

JOIE FAIT PEUR, LA, Play *see* Mme de Girardin

JOIES DE LA FAMILLE, LES, Paris 1960, Play *see* Philippe Heriat

JOIES DU FOYER, LES, 1894, *see* Maurice Hennequin, Weber

JOKER, THE, Novel *see* Noe Scott

JOKIN IHMISESSA, 1944, Novel *see* Mika Waltari

JOKYO, Novel *see* Shofu Muramatsu

JOLANTHES HOCHZEIT, 1892, Short Story *see* Hermann Sudermann

JOLLY CORNER, THE, 1908, Short Story *see* Henry James

JOLY, Novel *see* Arthur Zapp

JONATHAN LIVINGSTON SEAGULL, Novel *see* Richard Bach

JONI, Book *see* Joni Eareckson

JONS UND ERDME, 1917, Short Story *see* Hermann Sudermann

JOOK GIRL, Novel *see* Theodore Pratt

JORDAN IS A HARD ROAD, Novel *see* Gilbert Parker

JORGE, UM BRASILEIRO, 1967, Novel *see* Oswaldo Franca Junior

JORUND SMED, 1924, Novel *see* Jacob Breda Bull

JOSE, Novel *see* Armando Palacio Valdes

JOSEIMATSURI, Novel *see* Eijiro Hisaita

JOSEPH ANDREWS, 1742, Novel *see* Henry Fielding

JOSEPH BALSAMO, 1846-48, Novel *see* Alexandre Dumas (pere)

JOSEPH GREER AND HIS DAUGHTER, Indianapolis 1922, Novel *see* Henry Kitchell Webster

JOSEPHINE, Novel *see* Jacques Thery

JOSEPHINE VENDUE PAR SES SOEURS, Opera *see* Fabrice Carre, Paul Ferrier

JOSHUA THEN AND NOW, Novel *see* Mordecai Richler

JOSSELYN'S WIFE, New York 1918, Novel *see* Kathleen Norris

JOSSER, K.C., Play *see* Norman Lee, Ernie Lotinga

JOSSER ON THE FARM, Play *see* Herbert Sargent, Con West

JOUEUR D'ECHECS, LE, Novel *see* Henri Dupuy-Mazuel

JOUEUSE D'ORGUE, LA, Novel *see* Xavier de Montepin

JOU-JOU, 1902, Play *see* Henri Bernstein

JOUR DES PARQUES, LE, Novel *see* Charlotte Armstrong

JOURNAL, 1885, Book *see* Maria Baschkirtzeff

JOURNAL D'UN CURE DE CAMPAGNE, 1936, Novel *see* Georges Bernanos

JOURNAL D'UNE FEMME DE CHAMBRE, LE, Paris 1900, Novel *see* Octave Mirbeau

JOURNAL D'UNE FEMME EN BLANC, Novel *see* Andre Soubiran

JOURNAL D'UNE SCHIZOFRENE, Diary *see* Marguerite Andree Sechehaye

JOURNEY AT SUNRISE, Short Story *see* D. D. Beauchamp

JOURNEY FOR MARGARET, Book *see* William L. White

JOURNEY INTO FEAR, Novel *see* Eric Ambler

JOURNEY OF AUGUST KING, THE, 1971, Novel *see* John Ehle

JOURNEY TO SHILOH, New York 1960, Novel *see* Will Henry

JOURNEY'S END, London 1929, Play *see* R. C. Sherriff

JOURS DE FAMINE ET DETRESSE, Autobiography *see* Neel Doff

JOURS HEUREUX, LES, Play *see* Claude-Andre Puget

JOURS OUVRABLES, LES, Novel *see* Francis Rick

JOVANKA E LE ALTRE, Novel *see* Ugo Pirro

JOY, Novel *see* Joy Laurey, Eleanor Morse Savi

JOY GIRL, THE, 1926, Short Story *see* May Edginton

JOY HOUSE, New York 1954, Novel *see* Day Keene

JOY IN THE MORNING, New York 1963, Novel *see* Betty Smith

JOY LUCK CLUB, THE, Novel *see* Amy Tan

JOY OF LIVING, THE, 1914, Story *see* Peter B. Kyne

JOY OF SEX, THE, Book *see* Alex Comfort

JOYCE OF THE NORTH WOODS, Novel *see* Harriet T. Comstock

JOYFUL BEGGAR, THE, Philadelphia 1958, Novel *see* Louis de Wohl

JOYMATI KUNWARI, Play *see* Lakhindranath Bezbaruah

JOYOUS ADVENTURES OF ARISTIEDE PUJOL, THE, Novel *see* William J. Locke

JOYOUS TROUBLEMAKER, THE, New York 1918, Novel *see* Jackson Gregory

JUAN JOSE, Novel *see* Joaquin Dicenta

JUAN LEON LEGIONARIO, Novel *see* Rafael Lopez Rienda

JUAN MOREIRA, 1879, Novel *see* Eduardo Gutierrez

JUAN QUINQUIN EN PUEBLO MOCHO, 1964, Novel *see* Samuel Feijoo

JUANITA, Short Story *see* Alfred Rode

JUAREZ UND MAXIMILIAN, Vienna 1924, Play *see* Franz Werfel

JUBAL TROOP, Novel *see* Paul I. Wellman

JUBIABA, 1935, Novel *see* Jorge Amado

JUBILEE TRAIL, Novel *see* Gwen Bristow

JUBILO, 1919, Short Story *see* Ben Ames Williams

JUCKLINS, THE, Chicago 1896, Novel *see* Opie Read

JUD SUSS, 1925, Novel *see* Lion Feuchtwanger

JUDAH, London 1890, Play *see* Henry Arthur Jones

JUDAS GUN, New York 1964, Novel *see* Gordon D. Shirreffs

JUDAS TREE, THE, Novel *see* Neil Harmon Swanson

JUDAS VON TIROL, DER, 1927, Play *see* Karl Schonherr

JUDE THE OBSCURE, Novel *see* Thomas Hardy

JUDGE DEE AT THE HAUNTED MONASTERY, Novel *see* Robert Van Gulick

JUDGE SEES THE LIGHT, THE, Short Story *see* Allan MacKinnon

JUDGEMENT, 1924, Short Story *see* May Edginton

JUDGEMENT HOUSE, THE, London 1913, Novel *see* Gilbert Parker

JUDGEMENT IN STONE, A, 1977, Novel *see* Ruth Rendell

JUDGEMENT OF THE WEST, Story *see* Valma Clark

JUDGMENT AT NUREMBERG, 1959, Play *see* Abby Mann

JUDGMENT OF BOLINAS PLAIN, THE, 1893, Short Story *see* Bret Harte

JUDGMENT OF THE HILLS, Short Story *see* Larry Evans

JUDITH, Novel *see* Lawrence Durrell

JUDITH, Short Story *see* Charles Edward Montague

JUDITH, Novel *see* Jean-Joseph Renaud

JUDITH OF BETHULIA, 1904, Play *see* Thomas Bailey Aldrich

JUDITH OF BLUE LAKE RANCH, New York 1919, Novel *see* Jackson Gregory

JUDITH OF THE CUMBERLANDS, New York 1908, Novel *see* Alice MacGowan

JUDITH TRACHTENBERG, New York 1891, Novel *see* Karl Emil Franzos

JUDOKA DANS LA VILLE, LE, Novel *see* Ernie Clerk

JUDOKA EN ENFER, Novel *see* Ernie Clerk

JUDY, Book *see* Jerry Hulse

JUDY FORGOT, New York 1910, Play *see* Avery Hopwood

JUDY OF ROGUE'S HARBOR, New York 1918, Novel *see* Grace Miller White

JUE XIANG, Novel *see* Kong Jiesheng

JUEGO DE NINOS, 1951, Play *see* Victor Ruiz Iriarte

JUGE D'INSTRUCTION, LE, Play *see* Jules de Marthold

JUGEND, 1893, Play *see* Max Halbe

JUGEND OHNE GOTT, 1938, Novel *see* Odon von Horvath

JUGGERNAUT, Novel *see* Alice Campbell

JUGGLER, THE, Novel *see* Michael Blankfort

JUHA, 1911, Novel *see* Juhani Aho

JUIF ERRANT, LE, 1845, Novel *see* Eugene Sue

JUIF POLONAIS, LE, Paris 1869, Play *see* Alexandre Chatrian, Emile Erckmann

JUKYUSAI NO CHIZU, Novel *see* Kenji Nakagami

JULES ET JIM, Paris 1953, Novel *see* Henri-Pierre Roche

JULES OF THE STRONG HEART, 1915, Short Story *see* William Merriam Rouse

JULIA, Novel *see* Peter Straub

JULIE, Short Story *see* Richard Matheson

JULIE, 1869, *see* Octave Feuillet

JULIE DE CARNEILHAN, 1941, Novel *see* Sidonie Gabrielle Colette

JULIETA COMPRA UN HIJO, Madrid 1927, Play *see* Gregorio Martinez Sierra, H. Maura

JULIETTA, Novel *see* Louise de Vilmorin

JULIETTE, 1797, Novel *see* Donatien Sade

JULIETTE OU LA CLE DES SONGES, 1930, Play *see* Georges Neveux

JULIUS CAESAR, c1599, Play *see* William Shakespeare

JULORATORIET, Novel *see* Goran Tunstrom

JULY GROUP, THE, Novel *see* Stanley Ellin

JUMBO, New York 1935, Play *see* Ben Hecht, Charles MacArthur

JUMENT VERTE, LA, Paris 1933, Novel *see* Marcel Ayme

JUMP FOR GLORY, Novel *see* Gordon MacDonnell

JUMPING THE QUEUE, Novel *see* Mary Wesley

JUNE MAD, Play *see* Colin Clements, Florence Ryerson

JUNE MOON, New York 1929, Play *see* George S. Kaufman, Ring Lardner

JUNGE ENGLANDER, DER, 1905, Short Story *see* Wilhelm Hauff

JUNGE FRAU VON 1914, Novel *see* Arnold Zweig

JUNGE LEUTE IN DER STADT, Novel *see* Rudolf Braune

JUNGE LORD; KOMISCHE OPER IN ZWEI AKTEN, DER, Berlin 1965, Opera *see* Hans Werner Henze

JUNGE LORD: KOMISCHE OPER IN ZWEI AKTEN, DER, Berlin 1965, Opera *see* Ingeborg Bachmann

JUNGE MAGD, DIE, 1913, Verse *see* Georg Trakl

JUNGER JESU, DIE, 1949, Novel *see* Leonhard Frank

JUNGER MANN, DER ALLES KANN, Novel *see* Ernst Rudolphi

JUNGER WEIN, Play *see* Raimund Martin

JUNGFERN VOM BISCHOFSBERG, DIE, 1907, Play *see* Gerhart Hauptmann

JUNGFRAUENKRIEG, Novel *see* Hans Matschners

JUNGGESELLENFALLE, DIE, Play *see* Albert Kalkus

JUNGLE BOOK, THE, *see* Rudyard Kipling

JUNGLE HEART, 1918, Short Story *see* Stanley Shaw

JUNGLE LAW, Short Story *see* I. A. R. Wylie

JUNGLE MASTER, THE, Story *see* Rex de Rosselli

JUNGLE PATROL, Play *see* William Bowers

JUNGLE, THE, New York 1906, Novel *see* Upton Sinclair

JUNIOR BACHELOR SOCIETY, THE, 1976, Book *see* John A. Williams

JUNIOR MISS, Novel *see* Sally Benson

JUNIOR MISS, New York 1941, Play *see* Jerome Chodorov, Joseph Fields

JUNK, 1920, Short Story *see* Kenneth Harris

JUNKPILE SWEEPSTAKES, 1918, Short Story *see* Byron Morgan

JUNO AND THE PEACOCK, London 1925, Play *see* Sean O'Casey

JUPITER LAUGHS, 1940, Play *see* A. J. Cronin

JUROR NUMBER SEVEN, Story *see* Joseph H. Trant

JUROR, THE, Book *see* George Dawes Green

JURY, THE, Novel *see* Gerald Bullett

JURYMAN, Novel *see* Frank Galbally, Robert MacKlin

JURY'S EVIDENCE, Play *see* Jack Celestin, Jack de Leon

JUSQU'AU DERNIER, Novel *see* A. Dusquesne

JUST A GIRL, Novel *see* Charles Garvice

JUST A WIFE, New York 1910, Play *see* Eugene Walter

JUST A WOMAN, New York 1916, Play *see* Eugene Walter

JUST AND THE UNJUST, THE, Indianapolis 1912, Novel *see* Vaughan Kester

JUST ANOTHER SUCKER, Novel *see* James Hadley Chase

JUST AROUND THE CORNER, 1914, Short Story *see* Fannie Hurst

JUST CAUSE, Novel *see* John Katzenbach

JUST JUDGE, THE, Short Story *see* Peter B. Kyne

JUST MARRIED, Play *see* Adelaide Matthews, Anne Nichols

JUST MARY, Story *see* Pearl Doles Bell

JUST MEAT, Short Story *see* Jack London

JUST OUT OF COLLEGE, New York 1905, Play *see* George Ade

JUST OUTSIDE THE DOOR, New York 1915, Play *see* Jules Eckert Goodman

JUST SUPPOSE, New York 1923, Play *see* A. E. Thomas

JUST TELL ME WHAT YOU WANT, Novel *see* Jay Presson Allen

JUSTICE, London 1910, Play *see* John Galsworthy

JUSTICE, New York 1915, Play *see* Edgar James

JUSTICE DE FEMME!, Novel *see* Daniel Lesuer

JUSTICE DE SINGE, Novel *see* Paul de Rochefort

JUSTICE IN THE BACK ROOM, Novel *see* Selwyn Rabb

JUSTICIERE, LA, Novel *see* Jean Cassagne

JUSTIN MORGAN HAD A HORSE, Novel *see* Marguerite Henry

JUSTINA, 1937, Play *see* Hella Wuolijoki

JUSTINE; OU LES MALHEURS DE LA VERTU, 1791, Novel *see* Donatien Sade

JUSTINIAN AND THEODORA, Novel *see* Edward George Bulwer Lytton

JUURAKON HULDA, 1937, Play *see* Hella Wuolijoki

JUVE CONTRE FANTOMAS, Novel *see* Marcel Allain, Pierre Souvestre

JUX WILL ER SICH MACHEN, Play *see* Johann Nestroy

J'Y SUIS. J'Y RESTE, Play *see* Jean Valmy, Raymond Vinci

K, Boston 1915, Novel *see* Mary Roberts Rinehart

K 2, Play *see* Patrick Meyers

K. UND K. FELDMARSCHALL, DER, Play *see* Emil Artur Longen

KAABUTRA, Story *see* Shaiwal

KABALE UND LIEBE, 1784, Play *see* Friedrich von Schiller

KABULIBALA, 1892, Short Story *see* Rabindranath Tagore

KACKA VOMACENA, Novel *see* Antonin Jenne

KADISBELLAN, Autobiography *see* Roland Schutt

KAERE FAMILIE, DEN, 1892, Play *see* Gustav Esmann

KAERLIGHED, 1948, Play *see* Kaj Munk

KAFUKU, 1936-37, Novel *see* Kan Kikuchi

KAGERO-ZA, Novel *see* Kyoka Izumi

KAGI, Tokyo 1956, Novel *see* Junichiro Tanizaki

KAHN DER FROHLICHEN LEUTE, DER, Novel *see* Jochen Klepper

KAI VILANGU, *see* Jayakanthan

KAIDAN RUIGAFUCHI, Novel *see* Renzaburo Shibata

KAISER JOSEPH UND DIE BAHNWARTERTOCHTER, Play *see* Fritz von Herzmanovsky

KAISERHOFSTRASSE 12, Novel *see* Valentin Senger

KAITEI GUNKAN / KAITEI OKOKU, Novel *see* Shigeru Komatsuzaki, Shunro Oshikawa

KAJA, UNIT CU TE, *see* Kruno Quien

KAK POSSORILIS IVAN IVANOVICH S IVANOM NIKIFOROVITCHEM, 1835, Short Story *see* Nikolay Gogol

KAK ZAKALYALAS STAL, 1932-34, Novel *see* Alexander Ostrovsky

KAKUK MARCI, 1950, Novel *see* Jozsi Jeno Tersanszky

KALAYA TASMEYA, Play *see* C. T. Khanolkar

KALEIDASCOPE IN K, 1933, Short Story *see* A. J. Cronin

KALEVALA, 1835, Verse *see* Elias Lonnrot

KALKHAS, 1896, Short Story *see* Anton Chekhov

KALLE BLOMKVIST, Novel *see* Astrid Lindgren

KALTE HERZ, DAS, 1828, Short Story *see* Wilhelm Hauff

KAM S NIM?, *see* Jan Neruda

KAMASUTRA, Book *see* Mallanaga Vatsyayana

KAMERA OBSCURA, 1932, Novel *see* Vladimir Nabokov

KAMERAD MUTTER, Novel *see* Christel Broehl-Delhaes

KAMIKAZE, Novel *see* Per Wahloo

KAMOURASKA, Novel *see* Anne Hebert

KAMPF DER TERTIA, DER, Novel *see* Wilhelm Speyer

KAMPF DES DONALD WESTHOF, DER, Novel *see* Felix Hollaender

KAMPF UM DEN MANN, DRE, Play *see* Eugene Scribe

KAMPF UM ROM, Novel *see* Felix Dahn

KAMPF UMS MATTERHORN, DER, Novel *see* Carl Haensel

KAMPFER, Novel *see* Ernst Klein

KAMPFER, DER, Play *see* Max Mohr

KAMRATHUSTRU, 1932, Novel *see* Dagmar Ingeborg Edqvist

KANADEHON CHUSHINGURA, 1748, Play *see* Miyoshi, Senryu Namiki, Izumo Takeda

KANAL, Warsaw 1956, Novel *see* Jerzy Stefan Stawinski

KANDAM BACHA COAT, Novel *see* T. Mohammed Yusuf

KANGAROO, Novel *see* Martin Berkeley

KANGAROO, 1923, Novel *see* D. H. Lawrence

KANGAROO, THE, 1913, Short Story *see* Judge Harris Dickson

KANGAROOS, THE, New York 1926, Play *see* Victor Mapes

KANGELOPORTO, I, Novel *see* Andreas Frangias

KANI-KOSEN, 1929, Novel *see* Takiji Kobayashi

KANJINCHO, 1840, Play *see* Gohei III Namiki

KANSAN, THE, Novel *see* Frank Gruber

KANSKE EN DIKTARE, 1932, Play *see* Ragnar Josephson

KANTO MUSHUKU, Novel *see* Taiko Hirabayashi

KANTOR IDEAL, Novel *see* Adela Cervena

KAPELLMEISTER STROGANOFF, Short Story *see* Otto Rung

KAPITANSKAYA DOCHKA, 1836, Short Story *see* Alexander Pushkin

KAPUZINERGRUFT, DIE, 1938, Novel *see* Joseph Roth

KARAKTER, Novel *see* F. Bordewijk

KARAMANEH, Short Story *see* Sax Rohmer

KARATE KILLERS, THE, Novel *see* Boris Ingster

KARE JOHN, Stockholm 1959, Novel *see* Olle Lansberg

KARIERA PAVLA CAMRDY, Novel *see* Ignat Herrmann

KARIOSUTORO NO SHIRO, Short Story *see* Monkey Punch

KARL DALLEBACH, Biography *see* Hansruedi Lerch

KARL DER GROSSE, Novel *see* Wolfgang Marken

KARL HEINRICH, 1899, Novel *see* Wilhelm Meyer-Forster

KARL III UND ANNA VON OSTERREICH, Play *see* Manfred Rossner

KARL UND ANNA, 1926, Short Story *see* Leonhard Frank

KARLEKEN, Novel *see* Theodor Kallifatides

KARLEKENS BROD, Novel *see* Peder Sjogren

KARLEKS PRIS, Novel *see* Yvonne Gronin

KARLEKS SOMMAR, EN, Novel *see* Ivan Klima

KARNAWAL, 1968, Novel *see* Stanislaw Dygat

KARNFOLK, 1897, Short Story *see* Pelle Molin

KARNFOLKUNNEL, 1897, Short Story *see* Pelle Molin

KARPATHY ZOLTAN, 1854, Novel *see* Mor Jokai

KARRIERE, Berlin 1924, Play *see* Paul Rosenhayn, Alfred Schirokauer

KAR'YER, Novel *see* Valentin Bykov

KASEKI, 1967, Novel *see* Yasushi Inoue

KASEKI NO MORI, 1970, Novel *see* Shintaro Ishihara

KASEREI IN DER VEHFREUDE, DIE, Berlin 1850, Novel *see* Jeremias Gotthelf

KASHTANKA, 1887, Short Story *see* Anton Chekhov

KASPAREK, Novel *see* F. X. Svoboda

KASPER IN DE ONDERWERELD, 1974, Novel *see* Hubert Lampo

KASSABRIT, Stockholm 1925, Play *see* Vilhelm Moberg

KASSBACH, Novel *see* Helmut Zenker

KASTA PRO SEBE, Play *see* Emil Artur Longen

KAT'A, Short Story *see* Alexander Pushkin

KATA A KROKODYL, Book *see* N. V. Gernet, G. B. Jagdfeld

KATE PLUS TEN, London 1919, Novel *see* Edgar Wallace

KATERINA VZDOROVITA, Play *see* Evzen Holly

KATHARINA KNIE, Berlin 1928, Play *see* Carl Zuckmayer

KATHLEEN MAVOURNEEN, Play *see* Dion Boucicault

KATHLEEN MAVOURNEEN, Novel *see* Clara Mulholland

KATHLEEN MAVOURNEEN, 1840, Song *see* Annie Crawford, Frederick Crouch

KATHODOS TON ENEA, I, Novel *see* Thanassis Valtinos

KATIA, Novel *see* Lucile Decaux

KATIA LE DEMON BLEU DU TSAR ALEXANDRE, Paris 1938, Novel *see* Lucile Decaux

KATRINA, 1936, Novel *see* Sally Salminen

KATTORNA, Helsinki 1963, Play *see* Walentin Chorell

KATZ' IM SACK, DIE, Play *see* Michael Eisemann, Ladislaus Szilagyi

KATZ UND MAUS, Neuwid Am Rhein 1961, Short Story *see* Gunter Grass

KATZE, DIE, Novel *see* Uwe Erichsen

KATZENSTEG, DER, 1889, Novel *see* Hermann Sudermann

KAVI, 1942, Novel *see* Tarashankar Banerjee

KAVIK THE WOLF DOG, Novel *see* Walt Morey

KAVKAZSKIJ PLENNIK, 1821, Poem *see* Alexander Pushkin

KAWACHI KARUMEN, Novel *see* Toko Kon

KAWAITA HANA, 1958, Short Story *see* Shintaro Ishihara

KAYLA, Novel *see* Elizabeth Van Steenwik

KAYO! OKE!, 1930, Short Story *see* Sophie Kerr

KAZAKI, 1863, Novel *see* Lev Nikolayevich Tolstoy

KAZAN, THE WOLF DOG, Indianapolis 1914, Novel *see* James Oliver Curwood

K.C., THE, Play *see* Dion Titheradge

KDE SE ZEBRA, Play *see* Edmond Konrad

KDO JSI BEZ VINY, Novel *see* Marie Dolezalova

KDO SE BOJI, UTIKA, Novel *see* Josef Pohl

KE SHAN HONG RI, Opera *see* Chen Qitong

KEAN; OU DESORDRE DU GENIE, 1836, Play *see* Alexandre Dumas (pere)

KEEP, THE, Novel *see* F. Paul Wilson

KEEP THE ASPIDISTRA FLYING, 1936, Novel *see* George Orwell

KEEP THE CHANGE, Novel *see* Thomas McGuane

KEEPER OF THE BEES, THE, Garden City, N.Y. 1925, Novel *see* Gene Stratton-Porter

KEEPER OF THE CITY, Novel *see* Gerald Dipego

KEEPER OF THE DOOR, Novel *see* Ethel M. Dell

KEEPER OF THE FLAME, Novel *see* I. A. R. Wylie

KEEPERS OF YOUTH, London 1929, Play *see* Arnold Ridley

KEEPING IT DARK, Story *see* Gertrude Hynes

KEEPING JOHN BARLEYCORN OFF THE TRACKS, 1914, Short Story *see* Rufus Steele

KEEPING MAN INTERESTED, Story *see* Mayell Bannister

KEEPING UP WITH LIZZIE, New York 1911, Novel *see* Irving Addison Bacheller

KEETJE, Autobiography *see* Neel Doff

KEETJE TROTTIN, Autobiography *see* Neel Doff

KEIN HUSUNG, 1858, Verse *see* Fritz Reuter

KEIN PLATZ FUR WILDE TIERE, Book *see* Dr. Bernhard Grzimek

KEIN REIHENHAUS FUR ROBIN HOOD, Novel *see* Horst Bosetzky

KEIN SCHNAPS FUR TAMARA, Novel *see* Hansjorg Martin

KEITH OF THE BORDER, Chicago 1910, Novel *see* Randall Parrish

KEJSARN AV PORTUGALLIEN, Stockholm 1914, Novel *see* Selma Lagerlof

KEK ROKA, A, 1917, Play *see* Ferenc Herczeg

KEMPY, New York 1922, Play *see* Elliott Nugent, J. C. Nugent

KENILWORTH, 1821, Novel *see* Sir Walter Scott

KENKA EREJI, Novel *see* Seijun Suzuki

KENNEDY SQUARE, New York 1911, Novel *see* F. Hopkinson Smith

KENNEL MURDER CASE, THE, New York 1913, Novel *see* S. S. Van Dine

KENSINGTON MYSTERY, THE, Short Story *see* Baroness Orczy

KENT THE FIGHTING MAN, Novel *see* George Edgar

KENTUCKIAN, THE, Play *see* Augustus Thomas

KENTUCKIANS, THE, New York 1897, Novel *see* John Fox Jr.

KENTUCKY CINDERELLA, A, 1899, Short Story *see* F. Hopkinson Smith

KENTUCKY COLONEL, A, Chicago 1890, Novel *see* Opie Read

KENTUCKY ROMANCE, A, Story *see* Mary O'Connor

KERESZTELO, 1943, Novel *see* Pal Szabo

KERNPUNKT, DER, Play *see* Eugene Labiche

KERRY GOW, THE, Play *see* Joe Murphy

KESA'S HUSBAND, Play *see* Kan Kikuchi

KESTREL FOR A KNAVE, A, London 1968, Novel *see* Barry Hines

KET ASSZONY, 1962, Short Story *see* Tibor Dery

KEUSCHE ADAM, DER, Play *see* Gretl Lowinger, Paul Lowinger

KEUSCHE LEBEMANN, DER, Play *see* Franz Robert Arnold, Ernst Bach

KEY LARGO, 1939, Play *see* Maxwell Anderson

KEY MAN, THE, Play *see* J. McLaren Ross

KEY OF THE WORLD, THE, Novel *see* Dorin Craig

KEY, THE, London 1933, Play *see* Robert Gore-Browne, Joseph Lee Hardy

KEY TO NICHOLAS STREET, THE, New York 1952, Novel *see* Stanley Ellin

KEY TO REBECCA, THE, Novel *see* Ken Follett

KEY TO YESTERDAY, THE, New York 1910, Novel *see* Charles Neville Buck

KEYS OF THE KINGDOM, THE, 1941, Novel *see* A. J. Cronin

KEYS TO TULSA, Novel *see* Brian Fair Berkey

KHADZH-MURAT, 1911, Novel *see* Lev Nikolayevich Tolstoy

KHARTOUM, Book *see* Alan Caillou

KHAVAH, Short Story *see* Shalom Aleichem

KHIRURGIA, 1884, Short Story *see* Anton Chekhov

KHLYAB, 1969, Short Story *see* Yordan Radichkov

KHORISTA, 1886, Short Story *see* Anton Chekhov

KHOZHDENIYE PO MUKAM, 1922-45, Novel *see* Alexsey Nikolayevich Tolstoy

KHU GAM, Novel *see* Tomayantee

KHUDOZHESTVO, 1886, Short Story *see* Anton Chekhov

KHUTOROK V STEPI, 1956, Novel *see* Valentin Kataev

KIALTAS, 1967, Short Story *see* Gyula Hernadi

KIALTAS ES KIALTAS, 1981, Novel *see* Gyula Hernadi

KIBITZER, THE, New York 1929, Play *see* Edward G. Robinson, Joseph Swerling

KICK IN, New York 1914, Play *see* Willard Mack

KID BOOTS, New York 1923, Musical Play *see* Otto Harbach, J. P. McCarthy, William Anthony McGuire

KID FOR TWO FARTHINGS, A, Novel *see* Wolf Mankowitz

KID FROM TEXAS, Novel *see* Robert Hardy Andrews

KID GALAHAD, Boston 1936, Novel *see* Francis Wallace

KID TINSEL, Novel *see* Octavus Roy Cohen

KIDNAPPED, London 1886, Novel *see* Robert Louis Stevenson

KIDNAPPED KING, THE, Play *see* C. Douglas Carlile

KIDNAPPING COLINE, 1914, Short Story *see* Henry C. Rowland

KIDNAPPING OF THE PRESIDENT, THE, Novel *see* Charles Templeton

KIDNAPT, 1933, Short Story *see* Rupert Hughes

KIEBICH UND DUTZ, Play *see* F. K. Wachter

KIEZ - AUFSTIEG UND FALL EINES LUDEN, Play *see* Peter Greiner

KIFF TEBBY, 1923, Novel *see* Luciano Zuccoli

KIHLAUS, 1866, Play *see* Aleksis Kivi

KOMEDIANTKA, 1896, Novel *see* Wladyslaw Stanislaw Reymont

KOMET, DER, Budapest 1922, Play *see* Attila Orbok

KOMISARIO PALMUN EREHDYS, 1940, Novel *see* Mika Waltari

KOMM NUR MEIN LIEBSTES VOGELEIN., Novel *see* Joachim Fernau

KOMMISSAR X: DREI GELBE KATZEN, Novel *see* Bert F. Island

KOMMISSAR X: DREI GOLDENE SCHLANGEN, Novel *see* Bert F. Island

KOMMISSAR X: DREI GRUNE HUNDE, Novel *see* Bert F. Island

KOMMISSAR X: IN DEN KLAUEN DES GOLDENEN DRACHEN, Novel *see* Bert F. Island

KOMMISSAR X: JAGD AUF UNBEKANNT, Novel *see* Bert F. Island

KOMMISSAR X JAGT DEN ROTEN TIGER, Novel *see* M. Wegener

KOMPTOIRISTKA PANA, Play *see* Josef Skruzny

KONA COAST, Short Story *see* John D. MacDonald

KONCHU DAI SENSO, Short Story *see* Kingen Amada

KONDURA, 1966, Novel *see* C. T. Khanolkar

KONEC STARYCH CASU, 1934, Novel *see* Vladislav Vancura

KONFERENZ DER TIERE, DIE, 1930, Short Story *see* Erich Kastner

KONGI'S HARVEST, 1967, Play *see* Wole Soyinka

KONGO, New York 1926, Play *see* Chester de Vonde, Kilbourne Gordon

KONIG DER BERNINA, DER, Stuttgart 1900, Novel *see* Jakob Christoph Heer

KONIG DROSSELBART, 1812, Short Story *see* Jacob Grimm, Wilhelm Grimm

KONIG HARLEKIN, Munich 1904, Play *see* Rudolph Lothar

KONIGIN, DIE, Play *see* Bruno Granichstaedten, Ernst Marischka

KONIGIN EINER NACHT, Opera *see* Will Meisel

KONIGSLICHE HOHEIT, 1909, Novel *see* Thomas Mann

KONJIKI YASHA, Novel *see* Koyo Ozaki

KONRAD AUS DER KONSERVENBUCHSE, Novel *see* Christine Nostlinger

KONSEQUENZ, DIE, Novel *see* Wolfgang Ziegler

KONTO X, Play *see* Rudolf Bernauer, Rudolf Osterreicher

KONZERT, DAS, 1909, Play *see* Hermann Bahr

KOPFPREIS, DER, Short Story *see* Friedrich Raff

KOPPANYI AGA TESTAMENTUMA, A, Novel *see* Istvan Fakete

KORA TERRY, Novel *see* H. C. von Zobeltitz

KORKARLEN, 1912, Novel *see* Selma Lagerlof

KOROL, DAMA, VALET, 1928, Novel *see* Vladimir Nabokov

KORPORAL MOMBOUR, 1941, Short Story *see* Ernst Penzoldt

KORSET, 1896, Novel *see* Sigbjorn Obstfelder

KORT AMERIKAANS, 1964, Novel *see* Jan Hendrick Wolkers

KOSCIOT W SKARYSZEWIE, 1967, Short Story *see* Jaroslaw Iwaszkiewicz

KOSHER KITTY KELLY, New York 1925, Play *see* Leon de Costa

KOSHOKU ICHIDAI ONNA, 1686, Novel *see* Saikaku Ihara

KOSZIVU EMBER FIAI, A, 1869, Novel *see* Mor Jokai

KOTCH, Novel *see* Katherine Topkins

KOTIN AND PLATONIDA, 1867, Short Story *see* Nikolay Semyonovich Leskov

KOTO, Tokyo 1962, Novel *see* Yasunari Kawabata

KOUDENHOFFEN CASE, THE, New York 1925, Book *see* Wainwright Evans, Benjamin B. Lindsey

KOUZELNY DUM, Novel *see* Karel J. Benes

KOYA, Novel *see* Yasushi Inoue

KOYA HIJIRI, Tokyo 1901, Novel *see* Kyoka Izumi

KOZIYAT ROG, 1967, Play *see* Nikolai Haitov

KOZMETIKA, 1933, Play *see* Istvan Bekeffy

KRACH IM HINTERHAUS, Play *see* Maximilian Bottcher

KRACH IM VORDERHAUS, Play *see* Maximilian Bottcher

KRACH UM JOLANTHE, Play *see* August Hinrichs

KRADETSAT NA PRASKOVI, Sofia 1948, Novel *see* Emilian Stanev

KRAFT-MAYR, DER, Novel *see* Ernst von Wolzogen

KRAFTPROBE, Novel *see* Dagmar Kekule

KRAJOBRAZ PO BITWIE, Novel *see* Tadeusz Borowski

KRAKATIT, 1924, Novel *see* Karel Capek

KRAMBAMBULI, 1887, Short Story *see* Maria von Ebner-Eschenbach

KRAMER VS. KRAMER, Novel *see* Avery Corman

KRANES KONDITORI - INTERIOR MED FIGURER, 1945, Novel *see* Cora Sandel

KRASNA VYZVEDACKA, Novel *see* Josef Adler

KRASNOE JABLOKO, 1963, Short Story *see* Chingiz Aitmatov

KRASNOLUDKACH I O SIEROTCE MARYSI, O, 1896, Short Story *see* Maria Konopnicka

KRATES, 1885, Novel *see* Justus Van Maurik

KRATKO SLANTSE, 1978, Novel *see* Stanislav Stratiev

KRB BEZ OHNE, Novel *see* Maryna Radomerska

KREHKE VZTAHY, Novel *see* Vaclav Dusek

KREMLIN LETTER, THE, New York 1966, Novel *see* Noel Behn

KREMLYOVSKIE KURANTY, 1941, Play *see* Nikolay Pogodin

KREUTSEROVA SONATA, 1889, Short Story *see* Lev Nikolayevich Tolstoy

KREUTZER SONATA, THE, New York 1906, Play *see* Jacob Gordin

KREUZ IM MOOR, Novel *see* Fritz Gantzer

KREUZELSCHREIBER, DIE, 1892, Play *see* Ludwig Anzengruber

KRIDTSTREGEN, 1976, Novel *see* Erik Aalbaek Jensen

KRIEG IM DUNKEL, DER, Berlin 1915, Novel *see* Ludwig Wolff

KRIEG IM FRIEDEN, 1880, Play *see* Gustav von Moser, Franz von Schonthan

KRIEGSGERICHT, Munich 1959, Novel *see* Will Berthold

KRIGERNES BORN, Novel *see* Hans Ovesen

KRIGSMANS ERINRAN, Goteberg 1946, Play *see* Herbert Grevenius

KRIPPENDORFF'S TRIBE, Book *see* Frank Parkin

KRISTNIHALD UNDIR JOKLI, Novel *see* Halldor Laxness

KRIZ U POTOKA, Novel *see* Karolina Svetla

KROKY V MLZE, Novel *see* Maryna Radomerska

KRONIKA WYPADKOW MILOSNYCH, Autobiography *see* Tadeusz Konwicki

KRONISKE USKYLD, DEN, 1958, Novel *see* Klaus Rifbjerg

KRONZEUGIN, DIE, Play *see* G. C. Marivale

KROONGETUIGE, DE, Novel *see* Maarten 't Hart

KROSOR 500, *see* Lennart Nielsen

KROTKAYA, 1876, Short Story *see* Fyodor Dostoyevsky

KRU BAN NOK, Novel *see* Kamarn Khonkai

KRZYZACY, 1900, Novel *see* Henryk Sienkiewicz

KSHUDHITA PASAN, 1910, Short Story *see* Rabindranath Tagore

KU CAI HUA, Novel *see* Feng Deying

KUCHIZUKE, 1954, Short Story *see* Yojiro Ishizaka

KU'ER LIULANG JI, Novel *see* Bao Tianxiao

KUKA MURHASI ROUVA SKROFIN?, 1939, Novel *see* Mika Waltari

KULCS, A, 1943, Short Story *see* Dezso Kosztolanyi

KULONC, A, Play *see* Gyula Illyes

KULONOS HAZASSAG, 1901, Novel *see* Kalman Mikszath

KUN SANDHEDEN, 1974, Novel *see* Poul Orum

KUNGSGATAN, 1935, Novel *see* Ivar Lo-Johansson

KUNGSLEDEN, Stockholm 1963, Novel *see* Bosse Gustafson

KUNSTSEIDENE MADCHEN, DAS, Novel *see* Irmgard Keun

KUPFERNE HOCHZEIT, DIE, Play *see* Svend Rindom

KURAISHISU NIJUGOJU NEN, Novel *see* Takeshi Kawata

KURITON SUKUPOLVI, 1937, Play *see* Mika Waltari

KUROBARA NO YAKATA, Play *see* Yukio Mishima

KUROI AME, 1965-66, Novel *see* Masuji Ibuse

KUROKTOKAGE, 1962, Play *see* Yukio Mishima

KURUMEN YUKINU, Play *see* Hideo Nagata

KURUZSLO, A, 1927, Play *see* Emric Foldes

KURZE BRIEF ZUM LANGEN ABSCHIED, DER, 1972, *see* Peter Handke

KURZER PROZESS, Novel *see* J. Ashford

KUSS DES TIGERS, DER, Novel *see* Francis Ryck

KUSS VOR DEM SPIEGEL, DER, Vienna 1932, Play *see* Ladislaus Fodor

KUTBAN, 1971, Short Story *see* Imre Sarkadi

KVARTETTEN SOM SPRANGDES, 1924, Novel *see* Birger Sjoberg

KVINDE ER OVERFLODIG, EN, 1935, Novel *see* Knud Sonderby

KVOCNA, Short Story *see* Edmond Konrad

KWA HERI, Novel *see* Marie-Luise Droop

KWAIDAN, Novel *see* Yakumo Koizumi

KYOFO NIKEI NINGEN, Short Story *see* Rampo Edogawa

KYOKO NO IE, 1959, Novel *see* Yukio Mishima

L' RIMEDI PAR LE DONE, Play *see* Fulberto Alarini

L.A. CONFIDENTIAL, Novel *see* James Ellroy

LA DU BARRY, 1901, Play *see* David Belasco

LA HANUL LUI MINJOALA, 1898, Short Story *see* Ion Luca Caragiale

LA LA LUCILLE, New York 1919, Musical Play *see* George Gershwin, Frederick Jackson

LA O NUNTA, 1909, Short Story *see* Ion Agarbiceanu

LA TERRIBULA, Short Story *see* George L. Knapp

LABOR, Story *see* Will S. Davis

LABURNUM GROVE, London 1933, Play *see* J. B. Priestley

LABYRINTH, Novel *see* Gladys Baker

LABYRINTH, THE, Story *see* Harry Chandlee

LAC AUX DAMES, Novel *see* Vicki Baum

LACE, Novel *see* Shirley Conran

LACHE BAJAZZO!, Novel *see* Arthur Landsberger

LACHE, UN, Play *see* Albert Dieudonne

LACHENDE DRITTE, DER, Play *see* Hans Naderer

LACKEY AND THE LADY, THE, Novel *see* Tom Gallon

LACQUER SCREEN, THE, Novel *see* Robert Van Gulick

LAD: A DOG, New York 1919, Novel *see* Albert Payson Terhune

LAD AND THE LION, THE, 1917, Short Story *see* Edgar Rice Burroughs

LADA, 1910, Short Story *see* Ion Agarbiceanu

LADDER, THE, 1918, Novel *see* Harold Vickers

LADDIE; A TRUE BLUE STORY, Garden City, N.Y. 1913, Novel *see* Gene Stratton-Porter

LADENPRINZ, DER, Novel *see* Karl Munzer

LADIES AND GENTLEMEN, London 1937, Play *see* Ernest Vajda

LADIES' DAY, Play *see* Robert Considine, Edward Clark Lilley, Bertrand Robinson

LADIES IN RETIREMENT, London 1939, Play *see* Reginald Denham, Edward Percy

LADIES' MAN, New York 1930, Novel *see* Rupert Hughes

LADIES MUST LIVE, New York 1917, Novel *see* Alice Duer Miller

LADIES' NIGHT IN A TURKISH BATH, Play *see* Charlton Andrews, Avery Hopwood

LADIES OF THE BIG HOUSE, 1931, Play *see* Ernest Booth

LADIES OF THE EVENING, New York 1924, Play *see* Milton Herbert Gropper

LADIES OF THE JURY, New York 1929, Play *see* John Frederick Ballard

LADIES OF THE MOB, 1927, Short Story *see* Ernest Booth

LADIES THEY TALK ABOUT, Play *see* Dorothy MacKaye, Carlton Miles

LADRI DI BICICLETTE, 1948, Novel *see* Luigi Bartolini

LADRI IN CHIESA, 1954, Short Story *see* Alberto Moravia

LADRO, IL, Short Story *see* Anton Germano Rossi

LADRO SONO IO!, IL, Play *see* Giovanni Cenzato

LADRONE, IL, Novel *see* Pasquale Festa Campanile

LADRONES SOMOS GENTE HONRADA, LOS, 1941, Play *see* Enrique Jardiel Poncela

LADY AND THE TRAMP, THE, 1953, Story *see* Ward Greene

LADY AUDLEY'S SECRET, London 1862, Novel *see* Mary Elizabeth Braddon

LADY BARNACLE, 1917, Short Story *see* Edgar Franklin

LADY BE GOOD, New York 1924, Musical Play *see* Guy Bolton, George Gershwin, Fred Thompson

LADY CHATTERLEY'S LOVER, 1928, Novel *see* D. H. Lawrence

LADY CLARE, THE, Poem *see* Alfred Tennyson

LADY COMES TO BURKBURNETT, A, 1939, Short Story *see* James Edward Grant

LADY EVE, THE, Play *see* Monckton Hoffe

LADY FREDERICK, London 1907, Play *see* W. Somerset Maugham

LADY FROM LONGACRE, THE, New York 1919, Novel *see* Victor Bridges

LADY FROM THE SEA, THE, 1888, Play *see* Henrik Ibsen

LADY GANGSTER, Play *see* Dorothy MacKaye, Carlton Miles

LADY HARRINGTON, Novel *see* Maurice Level

LADY IN CEMENT, New York 1960, Novel *see* Anthony Rome

LADY IN LOVE, A, Play *see* Caroline Duer, Harriet Ford

LADY IN THE DARK, New York 1941, Play *see* Moss Hart

LADY IN THE LAKE, THE, 1943, Novel *see* Raymond Chandler

LADY IN THE LIBRARY, THE, Short Story *see* Frederick Orin Bartlett

LADY IN THE MORGUE, THE, New York 1936, Novel *see* Jonathan Latimer

LADY IS WILLING, THE, Play *see* Louis Verneuil

LADY JENNIFER, Novel *see* John Strange Winter

LADY L, Paris 1963, Novel *see* Romain Gary

LADY LADY I DID IT!, 1961, Novel *see* Evan Hunter

LADY LIES, THE, New York 1928, Play *see* John Meehan

LADY MISLAID, A, 1948, Play *see* Kenneth Horne

LADY NOGGS - PEERESS, Novel *see* Selwyn Jepson

LADY OF LYONS, THE, London 1838, Play *see* Edward George Bulwer Lytton

LADY OF QUALITY, A, New York 1896, Novel *see* Frances Hodgson Burnett

LADY OF SHALLOTT, THE, 1833, Poem *see* Alfred Tennyson

LADY OF THE LAKE, THE, Poem *see* Sir Walter Scott

LADY OF THE LIGHTHOUSE, THE, Book *see* Helen S. Woodruff

LADY OF THE SNOWS, THE, Novel *see* Edith Ogden Harrison

LADY ON A TRAIN, Novel *see* Leslie Charteris

LADY ROSE'S DAUGHTER, London 1903, Novel *see* Mrs. Humphrey Ward

LADY SINGS THE BLUES, Autobiography *see* William Dufty, Billie Holiday

LADY SMITH, 1936, Short Story *see* Myles Connolly

LADY TETLEY'S DECREE, Play *see* Sybil Downing, W. F. Downing

LADY, THE, New York 1923, Play *see* Martin Brown

LADY TUBBS, Novel *see* Homer Croy

LADY VARLEY, Story *see* Derek Vane

LADY WHO PLAYED FIDELE, THE, 1925, Short Story *see* Gerald Beaumont

LADY WINDERMERE'S FAN, London 1892, Play *see* Oscar Wilde

LADY WITH A LAMP, THE, London 1929, Play *see* Reginald Berkeley

LADY WITH A PAST, New York 1931, Novel *see* Harriet Henry

LADYFINGERS, New York 1920, Novel *see* Jackson Gregory

LADY'S NAME, A, New York 1916, Play *see* Cyril Harcourt

LADYSTINGER, Novel *see* Craig Smith

LAFITTE THE PIRATE, New York 1930, Novel *see* Lyle Saxon

LAGARTERANOS, LOS, Opera *see* Luis de Vargas

LAGNA PAHAVE KARUN, Short Story *see* C. V. Joshi

LAGUNA HEAT, Novel *see* T. Jefferson Parker

LAHOMA, Indianapolis 1913, Novel *see* John Breckenridge Ellis

LAIR OF THE WHITE WORM, THE, 1911, Novel *see* Bram Stoker

LAKE OF DARKNESS, Novel *see* Ruth Rendell

LAKE OF LIFE, THE, Play *see* Edwin Greenwood

LAKODALOM, 1942, Novel *see* Pal Szabo

LALKA, 1890, Novel *see* Boleslaw Prus

LALLA ROOKS, 1917, Poem *see* Thomas Moore

LAMB, Novel *see* Bernard MacLaverty

LAMENT FOR THE MOLLY MAGUIRES, New York 1964, Novel *see* Arthur H. Lewis

LAMIEL, 1889, Novel *see* Stendhal

LAMP IN THE DESERT, Novel *see* Ethel M. Dell

LAMP IN THE WINDOW, THE, 1916, Short Story *see* Thomas Burke

LAMP IS HEAVY, A, Novel *see* Sheila MacKay Russell

LAMPADA ALLA FINESTRA, UNA, Play *see* Gino Caprioli

LAMPE DANS LA FENETRE, LA, Novel *see* Pauline Cadieux

LAMPLIGHTER, THE, Boston 1854, Novel *see* Marie Susanna Cummins

LANCER SPY, London 1937, Novel *see* Marthe Cnockhaert McKenna

LAND DES LACHELNS, DAS, Berlin 1929, Operetta *see* Franz Lehar

LAND GIRLS, THE, Novel *see* Angela Huth

LAND JUST OVER YONDER, THE, 1915, Short Story *see* Peter B. Kyne

LAND OF OZ, THE, 1904, Novel *see* L. Frank Baum

LAND OF PROMISE, THE, London 1913, Play *see* W. Somerset Maugham

LAND OF THE BROKEN PROMISE, THE, 1913, Novel *see* Dane Coolidge

LAND OF THE FREE, THE, New York 1917, Play *see* William C. de Mille

LAND OF THE LOST, THE, Story *see* Courtney Ryley Cooper

LAND OG SYNIR, Novel *see* Indridi G. Thorsteinsson

LAND THAT TIME FORGOT, THE, 1924, Novel *see* Edgar Rice Burroughs

LANDFALL, 1940, Novel *see* Nevil Shute

LANDLOPER; THE ROMANCE OF A MAN ON FOOT, THE, New York 1915, Novel *see* Holman Francis Day

LANDLORD, THE, New York 1966, Novel *see* Kristin Hunter

LANDSTREICHER, DIE, Opera *see* C. M. Ziehrer

LANDSTRYKERE, 1927, Novel *see* Knut Hamsun

LANDVOGT VON GRIEFENSEE, DER, 1877, Short Story *see* Gottfried Keller

LANE THAT HAD NO TURNING, THE, 1900, Short Story *see* Gilbert Parker

LANG TAO GUN GUN, Novel *see* Shao Hua

LANGES RADIEUX, Novel *see* John Amila

LANGRISHE, GO DOWN, Novel *see* Aidan Higgins

LANTUL SLABICIUNILOR, 1901, Short Story *see* Ion Luca Caragiale

LAO JING, Novel *see* Zheng Yi

LAOREN HE GOU, Novel *see* Zhang XIanliang

LAOSHAN DAOSHI, Short Story *see* Pu Songling

LARAMIE LADD, Story *see* Ralph Cummins

LARCENY ON THE RIGHT, 1934, Short Story *see* James Edward Grant

LARGER THAN LIFE, Springfield, MA. 1936, Play *see* Joseph Shrank

LARK'S GATE, Novel *see* Rachel McNamara

LASCA, Poem *see* Frank Desprez

LASH, THE, London 1926, Play *see* Cyril Campion

LASKA SLECNY VERY, Novel *see* Otakar Hanus

LASKY VASNE ZRADY, Short Story *see* Karel Rozek

LASS JUCKEN, KUMPEL, Novel *see* Hans Henning Claer

LASS LAUFEN, KUMPEL!, Novel *see* Hans Henning Claer

LASSIE COME HOME, 1940, Novel *see* Eric Knight

LAST ADAM, THE, New York 1933, Novel *see* James Gould Cozzens

LAST ANGRY MAN, THE, 1956, Novel *see* Gerald Green

LAST ASSIGNMENT, THE, 1913, Short Story *see* Peter B. Kyne

LAST BUS TO WOODSTOCK, Novel *see* Colin Dexter

LAST CHANCE, THE, Play *see* Arnold Ridley, Frank Stayton

LAST CHAPTER, Novel *see* Knut Hamsun

LAST COUPON, THE, Play *see* Ernest E. Bryan

LAST CROOKED MILE, THE, Radio Play *see* Robert L. Richards

LAST CROP, THE, 1983, Short Story *see* Elizabeth Jolley

LAST CURTAIN, 1933, Play *see* Alfred Davis

LAST DAYS OF POMPEII, THE, 1834, Novel *see* Edward George Bulwer Lytton

LAST DAYS OF THE CHANCELLERY, THE, Book *see* Gerhardt Boldt

LAST DETAIL, THE, Novel *see* Darryl Ponicsan

LAST DON, THE, Novel *see* Mario Puzo

LAST DROP OF WATER, THE, Short Story *see* Bret Harte

LAST EGYPTIAN, THE, Philadelphia 1908, Novel *see* L. Frank Baum

LAST EXIT TO BROOKLYN, 1964, Novel *see* Hubert Selby

LAST EXPRESS, THE, New York 1937, Novel *see* Baynard H. Kendrick

LAST FRONTIER, THE, Boston 1923, Novel *see* Courtney Ryley Cooper

LAST HARD MEN, THE, Novel *see* Brian Garfield

LAST HOUR, THE, Play *see* Charles Bennett

LAST HOURS OF SANDRA LEE, THE, London 1961, Novel *see* William Sansom

LAST HUNT, THE, Novel *see* Milton Lott

LAST HURRAH, THE, 1956, Novel *see* Edwin O'Connor

LAST INNOCENT MAN, THE, Novel *see* Philip M. Margolin

LAST JEWS IN BERLIN, THE, Novel *see* Leonard Gross

LAST LEAF, THE, 1910, Short Story *see* O. Henry

LAST LORD, THE, Play *see* Curt Siodmak

LAST MAN ON EARTH, THE, 1923, Novel *see* John D. Swain

LAST MILE, THE, New York 1930, Play *see* John Wexley

LAST MOHICAN, THE, Novel *see* Bernard Malamud

LAST NIGHT IN THE WORLD, THE, 1951, Short Story *see* Ray Bradbury

LAST NOTCH, THE, Television Play *see* Frank D. Gilroy

LAST OF MRS. CHEYNEY, THE, London 1925, Play *see* Frederick Lonsdale

LAST OF PHILIP BANTER, THE, Novel *see* John Franklin Bardin

LAST OF THE BADMEN, Novel *see* Jay Monaghan

LAST OF THE CLINTONS, Short Story *see* Monroe Talbot

LAST OF THE DUANES, THE, 1914, Short Story *see* Zane Grey

LAST OF THE HIGH KINGS, THE, Novel *see* Ferdia MacAnna

LAST OF THE KNUCKLEMEN, THE, Play *see* John Powers

LAST OF THE LONE WOLF, THE, Story *see* Louis Joseph Vance

LAST OF THE MOHICANS, THE, Boston 1826, Novel *see* James Fenimore Cooper

LAST OF THE RED HOT LOVERS, 1970, Play *see* Neil Simon

LAST OF THE TROUBADOURS, THE, Short Story *see* O. Henry

LAST PAGE, THE, Play *see* James Hadley Chase

LAST PICTURE SHOW, THE, 1966, Novel *see* Larry McMurtry

LAST ROSE OF SUMMER, THE, Novel *see* Hugh Conway

LAST SENTENCE, THE, London 1893, Novel *see* Maxwell Gray

LAST SLAVER, THE, New York 1933, Novel *see* George S. King

LAST STAND AT PAPAGO WELLS, THE, Novel *see* Louis L'Amour

LAST STAND AT SABER RIVER, Novel *see* Elmore Leonard

LAST STRAW, THE, 1920, Serial Story *see* Harold Titus

LAST SUMMER, New York 1968, Novel *see* Evan Hunter

LAST SUPPER, THE, Play *see* Hillar Liitoja

LAST TESTAMENT, THE, Story *see* Carol Amen

LAST TRAIL, THE, New York 1909, Novel *see* Zane Grey

LAST TRAP; A DETECTIVE STORY, THE, New York 1928, Novel *see* Sinclair Gluck

LAST TYCOON, THE, 1941, Novel *see* F. Scott Fitzgerald

LAST UNICORN, THE, Novel *see* Peter S. Beagle

LAST VALLEY, THE, Novel *see* James Clavell

LAST WARNING, THE, New York 1922, Play *see* Thomas F. Fallon

LAST WITNESS, THE, Novel *see* F. Britten Austin

LAST WOMAN, THE, Short Story *see* Frederic Van Rensselaer Dey

LATE BOY WONDER, THE, London 1969, Novel *see* Angus Hall

LATE EDWINA BLACK, THE, London 1949, Play *see* William Dinner, William Morum

LATE GEORGE APLEY, THE, 1937, Novel *see* John Phillips Marquand

LATHE OF HEAVEN, THE, Novel *see* Ursula K. Leguin

LATIN BOYS GO TO HELL, Novel *see* Andre Salas

LATTER DAYS, THE, Book *see* P. R. Reid

LAUGH CLOWN LAUGH!, New York 1923, Play *see* Tom Cushing

LAUGH, CLOWN, LAUGH!, New York 1923, Play *see* David Belasco

LAUGHING BILL HYDE, 1917, Short Story *see* Rex Beach

LAUGHING BOY, Boston 1929, Novel *see* Oliver La Farge

LAUGHING CAVALIER, THE, Novel *see* Baroness Orczy

LAUGHING LADY, THE, Musical Play *see* Ingram d'Abbes

LAUGHING LADY, THE, London 1922, Play *see* Alfred Sutro

LAUGHS WITH A STRANGER, Short Story *see* Alec Coppel

LAUGHTER IN HELL, New York 1932, Novel *see* Jim Tully

LAUGHTER OF FOOLS, THE, 1909, Play *see* H. F. Maltby

LAULU TULIPUNAISESTA KUKASTA, 1905, Novel *see* Johannes Linnankoski

LAUNCELOT AND ELAINE, Poem *see* Alfred Tennyson

LAUNDRY GIRL, THE, Opera *see* Edward Waltyre

LAURA, Novel *see* Vera Caspary

LAURELS AND THE LADY, 1908, Short Story *see* Leonard Merrick

LAUTER LUGEN, Play *see* Hans Schweikart

LAUTER SONNENTAGE, Novel *see* Bruno Wellenkamp

LAVENDEL, Play *see* Bruno Schuppler

LAVENDER AND OLD LACE, New York 1902, Play *see* Myrtle Reed

LAVINA, 1971, Novel *see* Blaga Dimitrova

LAW AND JAKE WADE, THE, 1956, Novel *see* Marvin H. Albert

LAW AND ORDER, Short Story *see* O. Henry

LAW AND ORDER, Novel *see* Dorothy Uhnak

LAW AT RANDADO, THE, Novel *see* Elmore Leonard

LAW DIVINE, THE, Novel *see* H. V. Esmond

LAW OF THE FORTY-FIVES, New York 1933, Novel *see* William Colt MacDonald

LAW OF THE LAND, THE, New York 1914, Play *see* George Broadhurst

LAW OF THE LAWLESS, THE, 1921, Short Story *see* Konrad Bercovici

LAW OF THE RANGE, THE, Novel *see* Wayne Groves Barrows

LAW OF THE YUKON, THE, 1907, Poem *see* Robert W. Service

LAW RUSTLERS, THE, 1921, Short Story *see* W. C. Tuttle

LAW-BRINGERS, THE, New York 1913, Novel *see* G. B. Lancaster

LAWFUL LARCENY, New York 1922, Play *see* Samuel Shipman

LAWMAN, Novel *see* Lee Leighton

LAWMAN, 1955, Novel *see* Lauran Paine

LAWNMOWER MAN, THE, Short Story *see* Stephen King

LAWRENCEVILLE SCHOOL STORIES, Short Stories *see* Owen Johnson

LAWYER MAN, New York 1932, Novel *see* Max Trell

LAWYER QUINCE, Short Story *see* W. W. Jacobs

LAXDALE HALL, 1951, Novel *see* Eric Linklater

LAY OF THE LAND, THE, Play *see* Mel Shapiro

LAY THIS LAUREL, Book *see* Lincoln Kirstein

LAYLA, Novel *see* Andre Miquel

LAZARILLO DE TORMES, 1554, Novel *see* Anon

LAZARO, Book *see* David Kendall

LAZY SALMON MYSTERY, THE, Novel *see* Sutherland Ross

LAZYBONES, 1930, Play *see* Ernest Denny

LAZYBONES, New York 1924, Play *see* Owen Davis

LEA, 1888, Play *see* Felice Cavallotti

LEA LYON, Play *see* Alexander Brody

LEAD PARTY, 1932, Short Story *see* Paul Cain

LEAGUE OF FRIGHTENED MEN, THE, New York 1935, Novel *see* Rex Stout

LEAGUE OF GENTLEMEN, THE, London 1958, Novel *see* John Boland

LEAH KLESCHNA, New York 1904, Play *see* C. M. S. McLellan

LEAH THE FORSAKEN, Short Story *see* Ritter von Mosenthal

LEANDER CLICKS, 1928, Short Story *see* William Slavens McNutt

LEARNING TO BE A FATHER, Story *see* J. Fleming Wilson

LEARNING TREE, THE, New York 1963, Novel *see* Gordon Parks

LEATHER BOYS, THE, London 1961, Novel *see* Eliot George

LEATHER STOCKING TALES, THE, Novel *see* James Fenimore Cooper

LEATHERFACE; A TALE OF OLD FLANDERS, New York 1916, Novel *see* Baroness Orczy

LEAVE HER TO HEAVEN, Novel *see* Ben Ames Williams

LEAVE IT TO PSMITH, London 1930, Play *see* Ian Hay, P. G. Wodehouse

LEAVENWORTH CASE, THE, New York 1878, Novel *see* Anna Katharine Green

LEAVING CHEYENNE, 1963, Novel *see* Larry McMurtry

LEBEN DES GALILEI, 1949, Play *see* Bertolt Brecht

LEBEN FUR DIE LIPIZZANER, EIN, Munich 1960, Book *see* Alois Podhajsky

LECCIONES DE BUEN AMOR, 1924, Play *see* Jacinto Benavente y Martinez

LEDA SENZA CIGNO, Novel *see* Gabriele D'Annunzio

LEDGE, THE, Short Story *see* Stephen King

LEDGER OF LIFE, THE, 1922, Short Story *see* George Patullo

LEDGER, THE, Novel *see* Dorothy Uhnak

LEDI MAKBET MTENSKOGO UEZDA, 1864, Short Story *see* Nikolay Semyonovich Leskov

LEER OM LEER, Novel *see* Jacques Post

LEFT HAND OF GOD, THE, 1951, Novel *see* William E. Barrett

LEFT HANDED LAW, New York 1936, Novel *see* Charles M. Martin

LEFT IN THE TRAIN, Story *see* Evelyn Van Buren

LEFTY FARRELL, Novel *see* James Edward Grant

LEG, THE, Story *see* W. Faulkner

LEGACY, Novel *see* Charles Bonner

LEGACY OF A SPY, New York 1958, Novel *see* Harry S. Maxfield

LEGACY OF SIN, Book *see* Stephen Singular

LEGEND BEAUTIFUL, THE, Poem *see* Henry Wadsworth Longfellow

LEGEND OF HOLLYWOOD, THE, 1924, Short Story *see* Frank Condon

LEGEND OF LYLAH CLARE, THE, 1963, Play *see* Edward Deblasio, Robert Thom

LEGEND OF PROVENCE, THE, London 1858-61, Poem *see* Adelaide Anne Procter

LEGEND OF SLEEPY HOLLOW, THE, 1820, Short Story *see* Washington Irving

LEGEND OF THE INCAS, Story *see* Sydney Boehm

LEGENDA A NYULPAPRIKASROL, 1936, Novel *see* Jozsi Jeno Tersanszky

LEGENDA SURAMSKOI KREPOSTI, Book *see* D. Tchonghadze

LEGENDE DE LA PRIMITIVE EGLISE, LA, Novel *see* Eugene Barbier

LEGENDE DE SOEUR BEATRICE, LA, *see* Charles Nodier

LEGENDE VOM HEILIGEN TRINKER, DIE, 1939, Novel *see* Joseph Roth

LEGERE ET COURT-VETUE, Play *see* Jean Guitton

LEGGENDA NAPOLETANA, Novel *see* Frank Thies

LEGGENDA PER VIOLINO IN 4 TEMPI, *see* Washington Borg

LEGGENDA SIRACUSANA DELL'ANNO 1000, *see* Victor de Lussac

LEGGERA EUFORIA, UNA, Short Story *see* S. Calanchi, Luigi Collo

LEGION, Novel *see* William Peter Blatty

LEGIONER, DER, Play *see* Lajos Biro

LEGY JO MINDHALALIG, 1921, Novel *see* Zsigmond Moricz

LEI YU, 1934, Play *see* Wan Jiabao

LEICHTE ISABELL, DIE, Opera *see* Jean Gilbert

LEIDEN DES JUNGEN WERTHERS, DIE, 1774, Novel *see* Johann Wolfgang von Goethe

LEIDENSCHAFTLICHE BLUMCHEN, Novel *see* Rosalind Erskine

LEININGEN VS. THE ANTS, 1940, Short Story *see* Carl Stephenson

LEISE GIFT, DAS, Book *see* Marcus P. Nester

LELEJSKA GORA, 1957, Novel *see* Mihailo Lalic

LEMKES SEL. WITWE, Novel *see* Erdmann Graeser

LEMON DROP KID, THE, 1934, Short Story *see* Damon Runyon

LENA RIVERS, New York 1856, Novel *see* Mary Jane Holmes

LEND ME YOUR NAME!, Chicago 1917, Novel *see* Francis Perry Elliott

LEND ME YOUR WIFE, Play *see* Edmund Dalby, Fred Duprez

LENIN AND THE SECOND GENERATION, Play *see* Mi Shateluofu

LENNY, Play *see* Julian Barry

LENORE, Poem *see* Gottfried August Burger

LENTE, Book *see* Cyriel Buysse

LENZ, 1839, Short Story *see* Georg Buchner

LEON MORIN - PRETRE, 1952, Novel *see* Beatrix Beck

LEONARDO'S LAST SUPPER, 1970, Play *see* Peter Barnes

LEONE DI DAMASCO, IL, Novel *see* Emilio Salgari

LEONIE, Play *see* H. V. Esmond

LEONIE EST EN AVANCE, Play *see* Georges Feydeau

LEONTINES EHEMANNER, Play *see* Alfred Capus

LEOPARD IN THE SNOW, Novel *see* Ann Mather

LEOPARD LADY, THE, Play *see* Edward Childs Carpenter

LEOPARD WOMAN, THE, New York 1916, Novel *see* Stewart Edward White

LEOPARDESS, THE, Story *see* Katharine Newlin Burt

LEOPOLD LE BIEN-AIME, 1927, Play *see* Jean Sarment

LIGHTS OUT AT ELEVEN, Play *see* W. Armitage Owen

LIGNE DROITE, LA, Novel *see* Yves Gibeau

LIKE MOM, LIKE ME, Novel *see* Sheila Schwartz

LIKE NORMAL PEOPLE, Book *see* Robert Meyers

LIKENESS OF THE NIGHT, THE, London 1908, Play *see* Mrs. W. K. Clifford

LIKES OF HER, THE, London 1923, Play *see* Charles McEvoy

LILA AKAC, 1919, Short Story *see* Erno Szep

LILA DE CALCUTTA, Paris 1960, Novel *see* Jean Bruce

LILAC DOMINO, THE, Play *see* Rudolf Bernauer, E. Gatti, B. Jenbach

LILAC SUNBONNET, THE, Novel *see* S. R. Crockett

LILAC TIME, New York 1917, Play *see* Jane Cowl, Jane Murfin

LILAS BLANC, Play *see* Ladislaus Fodor

LILEYA, 1888, Verse *see* Taras Shevchenko

LILIES OF THE FIELD, London 1923, Play *see* John Hastings Turner

LILIES OF THE FIELD, New York 1921, Play *see* William Hurlbut

LILIES OF THE FIELD, THE, New York 1962, Novel *see* William E. Barrett

LILIKA, 1967, Short Story *see* Dragoslav Mihailovic

LILIOM, 1910, Play *see* Ferenc Molnar

LILIOMFI, 1849, Play *see* Ede Szigligeti

LILITH, New York 1961, Novel *see* J. R. Salamanca

LILLE EYOLF, 1894, Play *see* Henrik Ibsen

LILLE HAUFRUE, DEN, 1837, Short Story *see* Hans Christian Andersen

LILLE PIGE MED SVOVLSTIKKERNE, DEN, 1846, Short Story *see* Hans Christian Andersen

LILLEBIL AUS U.S.A., Novel *see* Ludwig von Wohl

LILLIAN DAY, Play *see* Lloyd Mearson

LILLY TURNER, New York 1932, Play *see* George Abbott, Philip Dunning

LILY CHRISTINE, Novel *see* Michael Arlen

LILY OF KILLARNEY, THE, Opera *see* Charles Benedict

LILY OF LIFE, Novel *see* La Reine Marie de Roumanie

LIMBO LINE, THE, Novel *see* Victor Canning

LIMITED MAIL, THE, 1889, Play *see* Elmer E. Vance

LIMNI TON POTHON, I, Play *see* Nicos Tsekuras

LIMONADOVY JOE, Prague 1958, Novel *see* Jiri Brdecka

LIMOUSINE LIFE, 1917, Story *see* Ida M. Evans

LIMPING MAN, THE, Croydon 1930, Play *see* Will Scott

LIMPY: THE BOY WHO FELT NEGLECTED, Boston 1917, Novel *see* William Andrew Johnston

LIN HAI XUE YUAN, Novel *see* Qu Bo

LIN MCLEAN, New York 1897, Novel *see* Owen Wister

LINCOLN HIGHWAYMAN, THE, New York 1917, Play *see* Paul Dickey

LINCOLN THE LOVER, Story *see* Catherine Van Dyke

LINDA, Boston 1912, Novel *see* Margaret Prescott Montague

LINDA DI CHAMOUNIX, 1842, Opera *see* Gaetano Donizetti

LINE, Oslo 1959, Novel *see* Axel Jensen

LINE ENGAGED, 1934, Play *see* Jack Celestin, Jack de Leon

LINE ON GINGER, 1949, Novel *see* Robin Maugham

LINGER LONGER LETTY, New York 1919, Play *see* Anne Nichols

LINJIA PUZI, 1932, Short Story *see* Shen Yanbing

LINKED BY FATE, Novel *see* Charles Garvice

LINKSHANDIGE FRAU, DIE, 1976, Novel *see* Peter Handke

LIOLA, Rome 1916, Play *see* Luigi Pirandello

LION AND THE LAMB, THE, Play *see* Edward Dignon, Geoffrey Swaffer

LION AND THE LAMB, THE, New York 1930, Novel *see* E. Phillips Oppenheim

LION AND THE MOUSE, THE, New York 1905, Play *see* Charles Klein

LION IN WINTER, THE, New York 1966, Play *see* James Goldman

LION IS IN THE STREETS, A, 1945, Novel *see* Adria Locke Langley

LION, LE, Paris 1958, Novel *see* Joseph Kessel

LION THE WITCH AND THE WARDROBE, THE, 1950, Novel *see* C. S. Lewis

LION TRAP, THE, Play *see* Daniel N. Rubin

LIONHEART, Novel *see* Alexander Fullerton

LION'S DEN, THE, 1919, Short Story *see* Frederick Orin Bartlett

LION'S MOUSE (VROUWENLIST), THE, 1919, Novel *see* Alice Muriel Williamson, Charles Norris Williamson

LIONS SONT LACHES, LES, Novel *see* Nicole

LION'S WAY; A STORY OF MEN AND LIONS, THE, London 1931, Novel *see* Charles Thurley Stoneham

LIPS OF STEEL, Novel *see* Harry Hervey

LIQUID DYNAMITE, Story *see* Joe King

LIQUIDATOR, THE, New York 1964, Novel *see* John Gardner

LIREN XING, 1945, Play *see* Tian Han

LISA AND DAVID, New York 1961, Novel *see* Theodore Isaac Rubin

LISA, BRIGHT AND DARK, Novel *see* John Neufeld

LISBON, Novel *see* Martin Rackin

LISBON STORY, London 1943, Play *see* Harry Parr Davies, Harold Purcell

LISCA, 1960, Short Story *see* Fanus Neagu

LISOVA PISNYA: DRAMA-FEERIYA, 1911, *see* Lesya Ukrainka

LISSY, Novel *see* F. C. Weiskopf

LIST OF ADRIAN MESSENGER, THE, New York 1959, Novel *see* Philip MacDonald

LISTEN LESTER, Play *see* H. L. Cort, H. Orlog, G. E. Stoddard

LIT A COLONNES, LE, Novel *see* Louise de Vilmorin

LIT, LE, Novel *see* Dominique Rolin

LITEN IDA, Novel *see* Laila Mikkelsen, Margit Paulsen

LITTLE ALIENS, New York 1910, Novel *see* Myra Kelly

LITTLE ANGEL, Story *see* Leroy Scott

LITTLE ANGEL OF CANYON CREEK, THE, New York 1914, Novel *see* Cyrus Townsend Brady

LITTLE ARK, THE, Novel *see* Jan de Hartog

LITTLE BIG MAN, New York 1964, Novel *see* Thomas Berger

LITTLE BIG SHOT, Play *see* Janet Allan

LITTLE BIT OF BROADWAY, A, 1924, Short Story *see* Richard Connell

LITTLE BIT OF FLUFF, A, London 1915, Play *see* Walter Ellis

LITTLE BLONDE IN BLACK, Story *see* Julius G. Furthmann

LITTLE BOY BLUE, Story *see* Maurice Zolotow

LITTLE BOY LOST, 1949, Novel *see* Marghanita Laski

LITTLE BREADWINNER, THE, Play *see* James A. Campbell

LITTLE BREECHES, 1871, Poem *see* John Hay

LITTLE BROTHER OF GOD, Novel *see* Leslie Howard Gordon

LITTLE BROTHER OF THE RICH, A, New York 1908, Novel *see* Joseph Medill Patterson

LITTLE CAESAR, New York 1929, Novel *see* William Riley Burnett

LITTLE CHEVALIER, THE, New York 1903, Novel *see* Mary Evelyn Moore Davis

LITTLE CHURCH AROUND THE CORNER, 1902, Play *see* Marion Russell

LITTLE CLOWN, THE, Play *see* Avery Hopwood

LITTLE COLONEL, THE, New York 1895, Novel *see* Annie Fellows Johnston

LITTLE COMRADE: A TALE OF THE GREAT WAR, New York 1915, Novel *see* Burton Egbert Stevenson

LITTLE DAMOZEL, THE, London 1909, Play *see* Monckton Hoffe

LITTLE DORRIT, London 1857, Novel *see* Charles Dickens

LITTLE DRUMMER GIRL, THE, 1983, Novel *see* John Le Carre

LITTLE EROLINDA, 1916, Short Story *see* Johnston McCulley

LITTLE EVA ASCENDS, 1921, Short Story *see* Thomas Beer

LITTLE EVE EGERTON, New York 1914, Novel *see* Eleanor Hallowell Abbott

LITTLE FARM, THE, Short Story *see* H. E. Bates

LITTLE FIDDLER OF THE OZARKS, Chicago 1913, Novel *see* John Breckenridge Ellis

LITTLE FLAT IN THE TEMPLE, A, New York 1930, Novel *see* Pamela Wynne

LITTLE FOXES, THE, New York 1939, Play *see* Lillian Hellman

LITTLE FRENCH GIRL, THE, New York 1924, Novel *see* Anne Douglas Sedgwick

LITTLE FRIEND, Novel *see* Ernst Lothar

LITTLE GAME, A, Novel *see* Fielden Farrington

LITTLE GIRL IN A BIG CITY, A, 1909, Play *see* James Kyrtle MacCurdy

LITTLE GIRL NEXT DOOR, THE, Story *see* Nina Rhoades

LITTLE GIRL THAT HE FORGOT, THE, Play *see* Beulah Poynter

LITTLE GIRL WHO LIVES DOWN THE LANE, THE, Novel *see* Laird Koenig

LITTLE GLORIA. HAPPY AT LAST, Novel *see* Barbara Goldsmith

LITTLE GOOD, THE, *see* Hapsburg Liebe

LITTLE GRAY LADY, THE, New York 1906, Play *see* Channing Pollock

LITTLE HORSE, THE, Short Story *see* Nelia Gardner White

LITTLE HOUR OF PETER WELLS, THE, 1913, Novel *see* David Whitelaw

LITTLE HOUSE ON THE PRAIRIE, Novel *see* Laura Ingalls Wilder

LITTLE JOHNNY JONES, New York 1904, Play *see* George M. Cohan

LITTLE JOURNEY, A, New York 1923, Play *see* Rachel Crothers

LITTLE LAMBS EAT IVY, London 1948, Play *see* Noel Langley

LITTLE LEDNA, 1926, Short Story *see* William Wallace Smith

LITTLE LORD FAUNTLEROY, New York 1886, Novel *see* Frances Hodgson Burnett

LITTLE LOST SISTER, Chicago 1914, Novel *see* Virginia Brooks

LITTLE MEG AND I, Poem *see* G. C. T. Murphy

LITTLE MEG'S CHILDREN, Novel *see* Hesba Stretton

LITTLE MEN, Boston 1871, Novel *see* Louisa May Alcott

LITTLE MILLINER, THE, Poem *see* Robert Buchanan

LITTLE MINISTER, THE, 1891, Novel *see* J. M. Barrie

LITTLE MISS BLUEBEARD, Play *see* Avery Hopwood, Henry Meyers

LITTLE MISS BROWN, New York 1912, Play *see* Philip Bartholomae

LITTLE MISS BY-THE-DAY, New York 1919, Novel *see* Lucille Van Slyke

LITTLE MISS MARKER, 1932, Short Story *see* Damon Runyon

LITTLE MISS NOBODY, London 1898, Musical Play *see* A. E. Godfrey, H. Graham, Landon Ronald

LITTLE MORE, A, London 1921, Novel *see* William Babington Maxwell

LITTLE MOTHER, THE, Novel *see* May Wynn

LITTLE MR. FIXER, Story *see* Maurice de La Parelle

LITTLE MURDERS, New York 1967, Play *see* Jules Feiffer

LITTLE NELLIE KELLY, New York 1922, Musical Play *see* George M. Cohan

LITTLE OLD NEW YORK, New York 1920, Play *see* Rida Johnson Young

LITTLE ORPHAN ANNIE, 1908, Poem *see* James Whitcomb Riley

LITTLE ORVIE, New York 1934, Novel *see* Booth Tarkington

LITTLE PINKS, 1940, Short Story *see* Damon Runyon

LITTLE RED DECIDES, 1917, Short Story *see* William M. McCoy

LITTLE RED SCHOOLHOUSE, THE, Play *see* Hal Reid

LITTLE ROMANCE, A, Novel *see* Patrick Cauvin

LITTLE SAVAGE, THE, 1848-49, Novel *see* Frederick Marryat

LITTLE SAVIOR, THE, Short Story *see* Mary O'Connor

LITTLE SHEPHERD OF BARGAIN ROW, THE, Chicago 1915, Novel *see* Howard McKent Barnes

LITTLE SHEPHERD OF KINGDOM COME, THE, New York 1903, Novel *see* John Fox Jr.

LITTLE SISTER, THE, Boston 1949, Novel *see* Raymond Chandler

LITTLE SPECK IN GARNERED FRUIT, A, Short Story *see* O. Henry

LITTLE SUNSET, 1912, Short Story *see* Charles E. Van Loan

LITTLE TOMMY TUCKER, Play *see* Desmond Carter, Caswell Garth

LITTLE TURNCOAT, THE, Story *see* Mary O'Connor

LITTLE VULGAR BOY, THE, Poem *see* Thomas Ingoldsby

LITTLE WHITE LIES, Book *see* Elizabeth McGregor

LITTLE WOMEN, Boston 1868, Novel *see* Louisa May Alcott

LITTLE WORLD APART, A, Novel *see* George Stevenson

LITTLE YELLOW HOUSE, THE, Garden City, N.Y. 1928, Novel *see* Beatrice Burton Morgan

LITTLEST COLONEL, THE, New York 1911, Play *see* Edward Peple

LITTLEST REBEL, THE, New York 1911, Play *see* Edward Peple

LITTLEST SCRUB LADY, THE, Short Story *see* Belle K. Maniates

LIU HAO MEN, Play *see* Wang Xuebao

LIU ZHI QIN MO, Novel *see* Ni Kang

LIV, 1866, Short Story *see* Kristofer Janson

LIVE AND LET DIE, Novel *see* Ian Fleming

LIVE FLESH, Novel *see* Ruth Rendell

LIVE WIRE, THE, New York 1950, Play *see* Garson Kanin

LIVELY AFFAIR, A, Story *see* Alice M. Moore

LIVES OF A BENGAL LANCER, THE, New York 1936, Novel *see* Francis Yeats-Brown

LIVET PAA HEGNSGAARD, 1907, Play *see* Jeppe Aakjaer

LIVING CHILD, THE, Story *see* Mary Lerner

LIVING DANGEROUSLY, London 1934, Play *see* Frank Gregory, Reginald Simpson

LIVING FREE, Book *see* Joy Adamson

LIVING UP TO LIZZIE, 1934, Short Story *see* Lillian Day

LIVRE DE GOHA LE SIMPLE, LE, Novel *see* Georges Ades, Josipovici

LIVSENS ONDSKAB, 1899, Novel *see* Gustav Wied

LIZA ANN, Play *see* Oliver D. Bailey

LIZARD'S TAIL, THE, Novel *see* Marc Brandel

LOADED, Book *see* Christos Tsiolkas

LOADED DICE, Indianapolis 1909, Novel *see* Ellery Harding Clark

LOBO, EL, Play *see* Joaquin Dicenta

LOBO EL BOSQUE Y EL HOMBRE NUEVO, EL, Novel *see* Senal Paz

LOBO, THE KING OF THE CURRAMPAW, Novel *see* Ernest Thompson-Seton

LOCA DE LA CASA, LA, Play *see* Benito Perez Galdos

LOCANDIERA, LA, 1753, Play *see* Carlo Goldoni

LOCATAIRE, LE, 1934, Novel *see* Georges Simenon, Roland Topor

LOCK AND THE KEY, THE, 1948, Novel *see* Frank Gruber

LOCK UP YOUR DAUGHTERS, London 1959, Play *see* Lionel Bart, Laurie Johnson, Bernard Miles

LOCKED OUT, Story *see* J. Raleigh Davies

LOCO, New York 1946, Play *see* Kath Albert, Dale M. Eunson

LOCO WEED, Story *see* Raymond Cannon

LOCSOLOKOCSI, A, 1965, Novel *see* Ivan Mandy

LOCUL UNDE NU S-A INTIMPLAT NIMIC, 1933, Novel *see* Mihail Sadoveanu

LOCURA DE AMOR, LA, 1855, Play *see* Manuel Tamayo Y Baus

LODGE IN THE WILDERNESS, THE, 1909, Short Story *see* Gilbert Parker

LODGER, THE, London 1913, Novel *see* Mrs. Belloc Lowndes

LOGAN'S RUN, Novel *see* William F. Nolan

LOGNEREN, 1950, Novel *see* Martin A. Hansen

LOHENGRIN, Play *see* Aldo de Benedetti

LOHENGRIN, Weimar 1850, Opera *see* Richard Wagner

LOI DES RUES, LA, Novel *see* Auguste Le Breton

LOI DU SURVIVANT, LA, Novel *see* Jose Giovanni

LOI, LA, 1957, Novel *see* Roger Vailland

LOIN DES YEUX PRES DU COEUR, Novel *see* Pierre Mael

LOJZICKA, Opera *see* Jiri Balda, Jara Kohout

LOKIS, 1869, Short Story *see* Prosper Merimee

LOLA, New York 1911, Play *see* Owen Davis

LOLA MONTES, Novel *see* Cecil Saint-Laurent

LOLA MONTEZ, Story *see* Adolf Paul

LOLA SE VA A LOS PUERTOS, 1929, Play *see* Antonio Machado Y Ruiz, Manuel Machado Y Ruiz

LOLITA, Paris 1955, Novel *see* Vladimir Nabokov

LOMBARDI, LTD., New York 1917, Play *see* Fanny Hatton, Frederic Hatton

LONDON ASSURANCE, London 1841, Play *see* Dion Boucicault

LONDON BELONGS TO ME, Novel *see* Norman Collins

LONDON BY NIGHT, Play *see* Charles Selby

LONDON CALLING NORTH POLE, Novel *see* H. J. Giskes

LONDON NOBODY KNOWS, THE, Book *see* Geoffrey Fletcher

LONDON PRIDE, London 1916, Play *see* A. Neil Lyons, Gladys Unger

LONDON STORY, Radio Play *see* Leo McKern

LONDON SUITE, Play *see* Neil Simon

LONDON WALL, London 1931, Play *see* John Van Druten

LONDONDERRY AIR, THE, Play *see* Rachel Field

LONE COWBOY, New York 1930, Autobiography *see* Will James

LONE DIT, THE, Short Story *see* Louis R. Wolheim

LONE HOUSE MYSTERY, THE, London 1929, Novel *see* Edgar Wallace

LONE RANGER AND TONTO FISTFIGHT IN HEAVEN, THE, Book *see* Sherman Alexie

LONE STAR RANGER, THE, New York 1915, Novel *see* Zane Grey

LONE STAR RUSH, THE, London 1902, Novel *see* Edmund Mitchell

LONE TEXAN, THE, Novel *see* James Landis

LONE WOLF RETURNS, THE, New York 1923, Novel *see* Louis Joseph Vance

LONE WOLF, THE, London 1914, Novel *see* Louis Joseph Vance

LONE WOLF'S SON, THE, 1931, Story *see* Louis Joseph Vance

LONE WOLVES, Novel *see* Charles Dumas

LONELINESS OF THE LONG-DISTANCE RUNNER, THE, London 1959, Short Story *see* Alan Sillitoe

LONELY GIRL, THE, London 1962, Novel *see* Edna O'Brien

LONELY GUY'S BOOK OF LIFE, THE, Novel *see* Bruce Jay Friedman

LONELY LADY OF GROSVENOR SQUARE, THE, Novel *see* Mrs. Henry de La Pasture

LONELY LADY, THE, Novel *see* Harold Robbins

LONELY PASSION OF JUDITH HEARNE, THE, 1955, Novel *see* Brian Moore

LONELY ROAD, THE, 1932, Novel *see* Nevil Shute

LONELY SKIER, THE, Novel *see* Hammond Innes

LONESOME DOVE, Novel *see* Larry McMurtry

LONESOME ROAD, THE, Short Story *see* O. Henry

LONESOME TRAIL, THE, Book *see* B. M. Bower

LONG AGO LADIES, Boston 1934, Play *see* David Carb

LONG AND THE SHORT AND THE TALL, THE, London 1959, Play *see* Willis Hall

LONG ARM OF MANNISTER, THE, Boston 1908, Novel *see* E. Phillips Oppenheim

LONG CHANCE, THE, New York 1914, Novel *see* Peter B. Kyne

LONG DAY'S DYING, THE, London 1965, Novel *see* Alan White

LONG DAY'S JOURNEY INTO NIGHT, New York 1956, Play *see* Eugene O'Neill

LONG GONE, 1956, Short Story *see* Peter Dawson

LONG GOODBYE, THE, 1953, Novel *see* Raymond Chandler

LONG HAUL, New York 1938, Novel *see* Albert Isaac Bezzerides

LONG HAUL, THE, Novel *see* Mervyn Mills

LONG HOLE, THE, Short Story *see* P. G. Wodehouse

LONG JOURNEY, THE, Story *see* Marvin Borowsky

LONG LANE'S TURNING, THE, New York 1917, Novel *see* Hallie Erminie Rives

LONG LIFE OF MARIANNA UCRIA, THE, Novel *see* Dacia Maraini

LONG LIVE THE KING, Boston 1917, Novel *see* Mary Roberts Rinehart

LONG, LONG TRAIL, THE, Play *see* Charles Chilton

LONG LONG TRAILER, THE, 1951, Novel *see* Clinton Twiss

LONG LOST FATHER, New York 1933, Novel *see* Gladys Bronwyn Stern

LONG MEMORY, THE, Novel *see* Howard Clewes

LONG NIGHT, THE, Novel *see* Seldon Truss

LONG RAIN, THE, 1950, Short Story *see* Ray Bradbury

LONG SATURDAY NIGHT, THE, Novel *see* Charles Williams

LONG SHIFT, THE, Short Story *see* Eugene Manlove Rhodes

LONG SHOT, THE, New York 1925, Short Story *see* Thomas Alexander Boyd

LONG STAY CUT SHORT, THE, 1948, Play *see* Tennessee Williams

LONG STRIKE, THE, Story *see* Dion Boucicault

LONG VALLEY, THE, 1939, Novel *see* John Steinbeck

LONG WAIT, THE, 1951, Novel *see* Mickey Spillane

LONG WAY HOME, THE, Television Play *see* Burton J. Rowles, Robert Wallace

LONG WAY, THE, Novel *see* Mary Imlay Taylor

LONGEST DAY: JUNE 6 1944, THE, New York 1959, Novel *see* Cornelius Ryan

LONGS MANTEAUX, LES, Novel *see* G.-J. Arnaud

LONGUE PISTE, LA, Novel *see* Jean-Louis Cotte

LONGXU GOU, 1950, Play *see* Shu Qingchun

LOOK BACK IN ANGER, London 1956, Play *see* John Osborne

LOOK OF EAGLES, THE, New York 1916, Novel *see* John Taintor Foote

LOOKING AFTER SANDY, New York 1914, Novel *see* Margaret Turnbull

LOOKING FOR MIRACLES, Novel *see* A. E. Hochner

LOOKING FOR MR. GOODBAR, Novel *see* Judith Rossner

LOOKING FOR TROUBLE, Book *see* Virginia Spencer Cowles

LOOKING FORWARD, Short Story *see* James Oliver Curwood

LOOKING GLASS WAR, THE, London 1965, Novel *see* John Le Carre

LOONEY LOVE AFFAIR, A, Story *see* Neal Burns

LOOPHOLE, Novel *see* Robert Pollock

LOOSE ANKLES, New York 1926, Play *see* Sam Janney

LOOSE CHANGE, Novel *see* Sara Davidson

LOOSE ENDS, London 1926, Play *see* Dion Titheradge

LOOT, 1967, Play *see* Joe Orton

LOOT, Indianapolis 1916, Novel *see* Arthur Somers Roche

LOOT BELOW, Story *see* Eustace L. Adams

LOOTERS, THE, Novel *see* John Reese

LORD AND LADY ALGY, New York 1903, Play *see* R. C. Carton

LORD ARTHUR SAVILE'S CRIME, 1891, Short Story *see* Oscar Wilde

LORD BABS, London 1928, Play *see* Keble Howard

LORD BARRINGTON'S ESTATE, Story *see* Leonora Dowlan

LORD BYRON OF BROADWAY, New York 1928, Novel *see* Nell Martin

LORD CHUMLEY, New York 1888, Play *see* David Belasco, Cecil B. de Mille

LORD EDGWARE DIES, Novel *see* Agatha Christie

LORD JIM, London 1900, Novel *see* Joseph Conrad

LORD JOHN IN NEW YORK, 1915, Short Story *see* Alice Muriel Williamson, Charles Norris Williamson

LORD LOVE A DUCK, New York 1961, Novel *see* Al Hine

LORD LOVELAND DISCOVERS AMERICA, New York 1910, Novel *see* Alice Muriel Williamson, Charles Norris Williamson

LORD OF THE FLIES, London 1954, Novel *see* William Golding

LORD OF THE MANOR, 1928, Play *see* John Hastings Turner

LORD OF THE RINGS, 1954-55, Novel *see* J. R. R. Tolkien

LORD PROVIDES, THE, Short Story *see* Irvin S. Cobb

LORD RICHARD IN THE PANTRY, Novel *see* Martin Swayne

LORD SPLEEN, Novel *see* Ludwig von Wohl

LORDS OF DISCIPLINE, THE, Novel *see* Pat Conroy

LORDS OF HIGH DECISION, New York 1909, Novel *see* Meredith Nicholson

LORD'S REFEREE, THE, 1923, Short Story *see* Gerald Beaumont

LORELEI, THE, Novel *see* Lawrence P. Bachmann

LORENZACCIO, 1834, Novel *see* Alfred de Musset

LORNA DOONE, 1869, Novel *see* R. D. Blackmore

LORSQUE L'ENFANT PARAIT, 1952, Play *see* Andre Roussin

LORSQU'UNE FEMME VEUT, Play *see* Octave Pradels

LOS ANGELES WITH A MAP, Novel *see* Richard Rayner

LOS QUE NO FUIMOS A LA GUERRE, 1930, Novel *see* Wenceslao Fernandez Florez

LOSER TAKES ALL, 1955, Novel *see* Graham Greene

LOSS OF ROSES, A, New York 1959, Play *see* William Inge

LOST CHORD, THE, Song *see* Arthur Sullivan

LOST CHORD, THE, 1877, Poem *see* Adelaide Anne Procter

LOST CITY, THE, Short Story *see* Frederic Chapin

LOST COUNTRY, THE, New York 1958, Novel *see* J. R. Salamanca

LOST ECSTASY, New York 1927, Novel *see* Mary Roberts Rinehart

LOST FOR WORDS, Book *see* Deric Longden

LOST GAME, THE, Short Story *see* John B. Hymer, Samuel Shipman

LOST GOD, THE, 1921, Short Story *see* John Russell

LOST HORIZON, New York 1933, Novel *see* James Hilton

LOST HOUSE, THE, Story *see* Dorothy Howell

LOST HOUSE, THE, 1911, Short Story *see* Richard Harding Davis

LOST KING, A, Novel *see* Don Capite

LOST LADY, A, New York 1923, Novel *see* Willa Cather

LOST LANGUAGE OF CRANES, THE, Novel *see* David Leavitt

LOST LEADER, A, London 1906, Novel *see* E. Phillips Oppenheim

LOST MILLIONAIRE, THE, Story *see* James Oliver Curwood

LOST MOON, Book *see* Jeffrey Kluger, Jim Lovell

LOST ON DRESS PARADE, Short Story *see* O. Henry

LOST PHOEBE, THE, 1916, Short Story *see* Theodore Dreiser

LOST PRINCE: YOUNG JOE THE FORGOTTEN KENNEDY, THE, Biography *see* Henry Searls

LOST SQUADRON, THE, New York 1932, Novel *see* Dick Grace

LOST TREASURE OF THE ANDES, Story *see* David Duncan

LOST WEEKEND, THE, 1944, Novel *see* Charles Reginald Jackson

LOST WORLD, THE, Novel *see* Michael Crichton

LOST WORLD, THE, London 1912, Novel *see* Arthur Conan Doyle

LOT 29, Story *see* Arthur Conan Doyle

LOTELING, DE, 1850, Novel *see* Hendrik Conscience

LOTNA, 1945, Short Story *see* Wojciech Zukrowski

LOTTE IN WEIMAR, 1939, Novel *see* Thomas Mann

LOTTERISVENKEN, 1919, Short Story *see* Martin Andersen Nexo

LOTTERY MAN, THE, New York 1909, Play *see* Rida Johnson Young

LOTUS AND THE BOTTLE, THE, 1902, Short Story *see* O. Henry

LOUDWATER MYSTERY, THE, Novel *see* Edgar Jepson

LOUIE THE FOURTEENTH, New York 1925, Play *see* Frank Wilhelm, Julius Wilhelm, A. Wimperis

LOUIS BERETTI, New York 1929, Novel *see* Donald Henderson Clarke

LOUISE, Paris 1900, Opera *see* Gustave Charpentier

LOUISIANA, New York 1919, Novel *see* Frances Hodgson Burnett

LOUISIANA, New York 1933, Play *see* J. Augustus Smith

LOUISIANA PURCHASE, New York 1940, Musical Play *see* Morrie Ryskind

LOUISIANE, Book *see* Maurice Denuziere

LOUPEZNICI NA CHLUMU, Short Story *see* Karel Leger

LOUPEZNIK, Play *see* Karel Capek

LOUP-GAROU, LE, Novel *see* Alfred Machard

LOUPIOTE, LA, Novel *see* Arthur Bernede, Aristide Bruant

LOUPS DANS LA BERGERIE, LA, Novel *see* John Amila

LOUVES, LES, Novel *see* Pierre Boileau, Thomas Narcejac

LOUVRE SOLITAIRE, LA, Novel *see* Albert Sainte Aube

LOVE AFFAIR, 1930, Short Story *see* Ursula Parrott

LOVE AMONG THE ARTISTS, Novel *see* George Bernard Shaw

LOVE AND A WHIRLWIND, Novel *see* Helen Prothero Lewis

LOVE AND DEATH ON LONG ISLAND, Novel *see* Gilbert Adair

LOVE AND HATE, Short Story *see* W. Pett Ridge

LOVE AND KISSES, New York 1963, Play *see* Anita Rowe Block

LOVE AND OTHER NATURAL DISASTERS, Book *see* Allen Hannay III

LOVE AND WAR, Novel *see* John Jakes

LOVE BANDIT, THE, 1921, Play *see* Charles E. Blaney, Norman Houston

LOVE CALL, THE, Short Story *see* Marjorie Benton Cooke

LOVE CAN BUILD A BRIDGE, Autobiography *see* Naomi Judd, Bud Schaetzle

LOVE DOCTOR, THE, Play *see* Eric D. Brand

LOVE 'EM AND LEAVE 'EM, New York 1926, Play *see* George Abbott, John V. A. Weaver

LOVE FIELD, Play *see* Stephen Davis

LOVE FLIES IN THE WINDOW, Stockbridge, MA. 1933, Play *see* Anne Morrison Chapin

LOVE FOR LYDIA, Novel *see* H. E. Bates

LOVE FROM EVERYBODY, London 1959, Novel *see* Clifford Hanley

LOVE HABIT, THE, Play *see* Louis Verneuil

LOVE IN AMSTERDAM, Novel *see* Nicolas Freeling

LOVE IN THE MUD, Novel *see* Richard Wormser

LOVE IN THE WILDERNESS, Novel *see* Gertrude Page

LOVE INSURANCE, Indianapolis 1914, Novel *see* Earl Derr Biggers

LOVE IS A RACKET, New York 1931, Novel *see* Rian James

LOVE LIES, Musical Play *see* Stanley Lupino, Arthur Rigby

LOVE LIES BLEEDING, Story *see* John Patrick

LOVE LIKE THAT, A, New York 1937, Novel *see* David Garth

LOVE MACHINE, THE, Novel *see* Jacqueline Susann

LOVE MAGGY, Novel *see* Countess Barcynska

LOVE MAN, THE, Novel *see* John D. Weaver

LOVE MATCH, THE, London 1953, Play *see* Glenn Melvyn

LOVE ME FOR MYSELF, Novel *see* Francis Perry Elliott

LOVE O' WOMEN, 1926, Short Story *see* Adela Rogers St. Johns

LOVE OF PIERRE LAROSSE, THE, Story *see* J. Herbert Chestnut

LOVE ON THE DOLE, Novel *see* Walter Greenwood

LOVE PAST THIRTY, New York 1932, Novel *see* Priscilla Wayne

LOVE PHILTRE OF IKEY SCHOENSTEIN, THE, Short Story *see* O. Henry

LOVE RACE, THE, London 1930, Musical Play *see* Stanley Lupino

LOVE ROUTE, THE, New York 1906, Play *see* Edward Peple

LOVE STORY, Novel *see* J. W. Drawbell

LOVE STORY, 1970, Novel *see* Erich Segal

LOVE STORY OF A MORMON, THE, Novel *see* Winifred Graham

LOVE STORY OF ALIETTE BRUNTON, THE, Novel *see* Gilbert Frankau

LOVE STREAMS, Play *see* Ted Allan

LOVE THE MAN, NOT HIS POSITION, Story *see* Li Li

LOVE UP THE POLE, 1935, Play *see* Herbert Sargent, Con West

LOVE! VALOUR! COMPASSION!, Play *see* Terrence McNally

LOVE WITH A PERFECT STRANGER, Novel *see* Pamela Wallace

LOVE YOUR BODY, Play *see* Schuyler E. Grey, Paul R. Milton

LOVEBIRDS, THE, London 1957, Play *see* Basil Thomas

LOVED ONE, THE, Boston 1948, Novel *see* Evelyn Waugh

LOVELY REASON, 1916, Serial Story *see* George Agnew Chamberlain

LOVERS AND OTHER STRANGERS, New York 1968, Play *see* Joseph Bologna, Renee Taylor

LOVER'S ISLAND, Short Story *see* T. Howard Kelly

LOVERS' LANE, Boston 1915, Play *see* Clyde Fitch

LOVERS MUST LEARN, New York 1932, Novel *see* Irving Fineman

LOVER'S TALE, Poem *see* Alfred Tennyson

LOVERS, THE, New York 1956, Play *see* Leslie Stevens

LOVE'S A LUXURY, Play *see* Edward V. Hole, Guy Paxton

LOVE'S BLINDNESS, New York 1925, Novel *see* Elinor Glyn

LOVE'S EXECUTIONERS, *see* Tim Willocks

LOVE'S GREATEST MISTAKE, New York 1927, Novel *see* Frederic Arnold Kummer

LOVE'S LOVELY COUNTERFEIT, 1942, Novel *see* James M. Cain

LOVES OF MARGERY, THE, Short Story *see* Thomas Hardy

LOVE'S OPTION, Novel *see* Douglas Newton

LOVEY A VERY SPECIAL CHILD, Book *see* Mary MacCracken

LOVEY MARY, New York 1903, Novel *see* Alice Hegan Rice

LOW COMPANY, Novel *see* Daniel Fuchs

LOWE VON BABYLON, DER, Novel *see* Karl Friedrich May

LOWENSKOLDA RINGEN, 1925, Novel *see* Selma Lagerlof

LOWER DEPTHS, THE, 1902, Play *see* Maxim Gorky

LOWLAND CINDERELLA, A, Novel *see* S. R. Crockett

LOYALTIES, London 1922, Play *see* John Galsworthy

L-SHAPED ROOM, THE, London 1960, Novel *see* Lynne Reid Banks

LU CAVALIERI PIDAGNA, 1909, Play *see* Luigi Capuana

LU GONG'S DAUGHTER, Story *see* Pu Songling

LU LIANG YING XIONG, Novel *see* Ma Feng

LU PARANINFU, Play *see* Luigi Capuana

LU XIAOGANG AND HIS SISTER, Novel *see* Ren Daxing

LUCERNA, Play *see* Alois Jirasek

LUCIA DI LAMMERMOOR, 1835, Opera *see* Salvatore Cammarano, Gaetano Donizetti

LUCIA MCCARTNEY, 1969, Short Story *see* Rubem Fonseca

LUCIE, 1888, Novel *see* Amalie Skram

LUCILE, Short Story *see* Cyril Berger

LUCILE, Poem *see* Owen Meredith

LUCIO FLAVIO, O PASSAGEIRO DA AGONIA, 1975, Novel *see* Jose Louzeiro

LUCIOLA, 1862, Short Story *see* Jose Martiniano de Alencar

LUCK, Short Story *see* Jackson Gregory

LUCK IN PAWN, New York 1919, Play *see* Marvin Taylor

LUCK OF GERALDINE LAIRD, THE, 1919, Novel *see* Kathleen Norris

LUCK OF GINGER COFFEY, THE, Boston 1960, Novel *see* Brian Moore

LUCK OF ROARING CAMP, THE, 1868, Short Story *see* Bret Harte

LUCK OF THE IRISH, THE, Novel *see* Victor Haddick

LUCK OF THE IRISH, THE, New York 1917, Novel *see* Harold MacGrath

LUCK OF THE NAVY, THE, London 1918, Play *see* Clifford Mills

LUCKY DAMAGE, Story *see* Marc Edmund Jones

LUCKY JIM, 1953, Novel *see* Kingsley Amis

LUCKY NIGHT, 1935, Short Story *see* Oliver Claxton

LUCKY SAM MCCARVER, New York 1925, Play *see* Sidney Coe Howard

LUCKY SERUM, THE, Story *see* Gouverneur Morris

LUCKY STAR, Novel *see* Owen Rutter

LUCKY STIFF, THE, Novel *see* Craig Rice

LUCRECE BORGIA, Paris 1833, Play *see* Victor Hugo

LUCRETIA LOMBARD, New York 1922, Novel *see* Kathleen Norris

LUDAS MATYI, 1815, Verse *see* Mihaly Fazekas

LUDES, Novel *see* Benjamin Stein

LUDMILA. A LEGEND OF LIECHTENSTEIN, London 1955, Short Story *see* Paul Gallico

LUDO, Novel *see* Pierre Scize

LUDZIE BEZDOMNI, 1899, Novel *see* Stefan Zeromski

LUELLA'S LOVE STORY, Story *see* Winnifred A. Kirkland

LUGNER, DER, Play *see* Hermann Shiffrin

LUGNER UND DIE NONNE, DER, Play *see* Curt Goetz

LUISE, Novel *see* Walter von Molo

LULLABY, THE, New York 1923, Play *see* Edward Knoblock

LUMIE DI SICILIA, Short Story *see* Luigi Pirandello

LUMMOX, New York 1923, Novel *see* Fannie Hurst

LUNA E I FALO, LA, 1950, Short Story *see* Cesare Pavese

LUNATIC AT LARGE, THE, Novel *see* J. Storer Clouston

LUNATIC, THE, Play *see* H. Kalmon

LUNATIC, THE, Novel *see* Anthony C. Winkler

LUNCH HOUR, London 1961, Play *see* John Mortimer

LUNCHRASTEN, Goteborg 1949, Play *see* Herbert Grevenius

LUNE DE FIEL, Novel *see* Pascal Bruckner

LUNEGARDE, Novel *see* Pierre Benoit

LUO TOU XIANGZI, 1944, Novel *see* Shu Qingchun

LUOXIA GUWU, Novel *see* Zhang Henshui

LUPA, LA, 1880, Short Story *see* Giovanni Verga

LURE OF CROONING WATER, THE, Novel *see* Marion Hill

LURE OF LONDON, THE, Play *see* Arthur Applin

LURE OF THE MASK, THE, Indianapolis 1908, Novel *see* Harold MacGrath

LURE, THE, Play *see* J. W. Sabben-Clare

LURE, THE, New York 1913, Play *see* George Scarborough

LUST FOR LIFE, 1934, Novel *see* Irving Stone

LUSTIGE WITWE, DIE, Vienna 1905, Operetta *see* Franz Lehar, Viktor Leon, Leo Stein

LUTHER, 1961, Play *see* John Osborne

LUTHIER DE CREMONE, LE, Play *see* Francois Coppee

LUTTE POUR LA VIE, LA, 1889, Novel *see* Alphonse Daudet

LUV, New York 1964, Play *see* Murray Schisgal

LUXURY TAX, THE, Story *see* Ethel Donoher

LUZ DE LUNA, 1915, Novel *see* Wenceslao Fernandez Florez

LUZIA, 1962, Short Story *see* Carlos Drummond de Andrade

LYCEE DES JEUNES FILLES, Novel *see* Serge Weber

LYDIA BAILEY, 1947, Novel *see* Kenneth Lewis Roberts

LYDIA GILMORE, New York 1912, Play *see* Henry Arthur Jones

LYNCH LAWYERS, Boston 1920, Novel *see* William Patterson White

LYNX, LE, Novel *see* Michel Corday, Andre Couvreur

LYONS MAIL, THE, London 1877, Play *see* Charles Reade

LYS, LE, Play *see* Gaston Leroux, Pierre Wolff

LYS ROUGE, LE, Novel *see* Anatole France

LYSISTRATA, 411 bc, Play *see* Aristophanes

LYTTON STRACHEY, Book *see* Michael Holroyd

LYUBOV YAROVAYA, 1926, Play *see* Konstantin Trenyov

MA COUSINE DE VARSOVIE, Play *see* Louis Verneuil

MA MORT A DES YEUX BLEUS, Novel *see* Andre Lay

MA NON E UNA COSA SERIA, 1910, Short Story *see* Luigi Pirandello

MA NUIT CHEZ MAUD, 1974, Short Story *see* Eric Rohmer

MA SOEUR ET MOI, Play *see* Georges Berr, Louis Verneuil

MA TANTE D'HONFLEUR, Play *see* Paul Gavault

MA ZHENHUA, Play *see* Zheng Zhenqiu

MAA ON SYNTINEN LAULU, 1964, Novel *see* Timo K Mukka

MACAO - L'ENFER DU JEU, Novel *see* Maurice Dekobra

MACARIO, Zurich 1950, Novel *see* Ben Traven

MACBETH, c1606, Play *see* William Shakespeare

MACCHIE DI BELLETTO, Milan 1968, Novel *see* Ludovico Dentice

MACE, Short Story *see* Stanley L. Hough

MACHIKO, 1928, Novel *see* Yaeko Nogami

MACHINE A PREDIRE LA MORT, LA, Novel *see* Roger-F. Didelot, Robert-Claude Dumas

MACHO CALLAHAN, Novel *see* Richard Carr

MACKENNA'S GOLD, New York 1963, Novel *see* Will Henry

MACSKAJATEK, 1963, Novel *see* Istvan Orkeny

MACUNAIMA, O HEROI SEM NENHUM CARATER, 1928, Novel *see* Mario de Andrade

MAD BALL, THE, Play *see* Arthur Carter

MAD DANCER, THE, 1924, Short Story *see* Louise Winter

MAD DEATH, THE, Novel *see* Nigel Slater

MAD DOG, Novel *see* Margaret Carnegie

MAD WITH MUCH HEART, 1945, Novel *see* Gerald Butler

MADAMA, LA, Novel *see* Massimo Felisatti, Fabio Pittoru

MADAME BO-PEEP OF THE RANCHES, New York 1910, Short Story *see* O. Henry

MADAME BOVARY, Paris 1857, Novel *see* Gustave Flaubert

MADAME BUTTERFLY, New York 1898, Novel *see* John Luther Long

MADAME CHRYSANTHEME, 1888, Novel *see* Pierre Loti

MADAME CIRCE, Novel *see* Ernst Klein

MADAME CLAPAIN, Novel *see* Edouard Estaunie

MADAME CORENTINE, Novel *see* Rene Bazin

MADAME CURIE, 1937, Biography *see* Eve Curie

MADAME DE., Novel *see* Louise de Vilmorin

MADAME ET LE MORT, Novel *see* Pierre Very

MADAME ET SON AUTO, Novel *see* Guy Verdot

MADAME FIRMIANI, Short Story *see* Honore de Balzac

MADAME JULIE, 1930, Play *see* Irving Kaye Davis

MADAME LA GIMP, 1929, Short Story *see* Damon Runyon

MADAME LA PRESIDENTE, Paris C.1898, Play *see* Maurice Hennequin, Jose G. Levy, Pierre Veber

MADAME L'ADMIRALE, Play *see* Antony Mars

MADAME L'AMBASSADRICE, Novel *see* Daniel Le Sueur

MADAME LOUISE, London 1945, Play *see* Vernon Sylvaine

MADAME NE VEUT PAS D'ENFANTS, Novel *see* Clement Vautel

MADAME PEACOCK, 1919, Short Story *see* Rita Weiman

MADAME POMPADOUR, Play *see* Rudolph Schanzer, Ernst Welisch

MADAME ROSA, Novel *see* Emile Ajar

MADAME SANS-GENE, Paris 1893, Play *see* Emile Moreau, Victorien Sardou

MADAME SHERRY, New York 1910, Musical Play *see* Otto Hauerbach, Karl Hoschna

MADAME SOUSATZKA, Novel *see* Bernice Rubens

MADAME TALLIEN, Play *see* Victorien Sardou

MADAME TICTAC, 1950, Play *see* Falkland Cary, Philip Weathers

MADAMOISELLE DE MAUPIN, 1835-36, Novel *see* Theophile Gautier

MADCHEN AUS FRISCO, DAS, Short Story *see* Karl Figdor

MADCHEN FUR ALLES, Play *see* Hans Adler

MADCHEN GEHT AN LAND, EIN, Novel *see* Eva Leidmann

MADCHEN IM FENSTER, DAS, Play *see* Fritz Gottwald

MADCHEN IRENE, DAS, Play *see* Eva Leidmann

MADCHEN MIT DER MUNDHARMONIKA, DAS, Novel *see* Frank F. Braun

MADCHEN OHNE PYJAMA, DAS, Play *see* Christian Bock

MADCHEN VON FANO, DAS, 1935, Novel *see* Gunter Weisenborn

MADCHENJAHRE EINER KONIGIN, Play *see* Sil Vara

MADCHENKRIEG, 1975, Novel *see* Manfred Bieler

MADE IN BRITAIN, Play *see* David Leland

MADEJA DE LANA AZUL CELESTE, UNA, 1952, Play *see* Jose Lopez Rubio

MADEL IN NOT, Novel *see* Alfred Heller

MADEL MIT DER PEITSCHE, DAS, Play *see* Hans H. Zerlett

MADEL WIRBELT DURCH DIE WELT, EIN, Novel *see* Hans Holm

MADELEINE, Novel *see* Jules Sandeau

MADELEINE, 1865, Novel *see* Emile Zola

MADELEINE'S CHRISTMAS, Story *see* Hugh Antoine d'Arcy

MADELINE, Book *see* Ludwig Bemelmans

MADELON, New York 1896, Novel *see* Mary E. Wilkins Freeman

MADEMOISELLE DE LA FERTE, Novel *see* Pierre Benoit

MADEMOISELLE DE LA SEIGLIERE, Novel *see* Jules Sandeau

MADEMOISELLE ET SON GANG, Novel *see* Rodolphe-Marie Arlaud

MADEMOISELLE FIFI, 1881, Short Story *see* Guy de Maupassant

MADEMOISELLE JOSETTE MA FEMME, Play *see* Robert Charvay, Paul Gavault

MADEMOISELLE MIMI PINSON, 1853, Short Story *see* Alfred de Musset

MADEMOISELLE MODISTE; A COMIC OPERA, New York 1905, Musical Play *see* Henry Martyn Blossom, Victor Herbert

MADEMOISELLE MONTECRISTO, Novel *see* Paul Mahalin

MADISON SQUARE ARABIAN NIGHT, A, Short Story *see* O. Henry

MADLA Z CIHELNY, Play *see* Olga Scheinpflugova

MADLA ZPIVA EVROPE, Novel *see* Jan Wenig

MADNESS OF GEORGE III, THE, Play *see* Alan Bennett

MADNESS OF THE HEART, Novel *see* Flora Sandstrom

MADONA DE CEDRO, 1957, Novel *see* Antonio Callado

MADONE DES SLEEPINGS, LA, Novel *see* Maurice Dekobra

MADONNA IN CHAINS, THE, Story *see* Edward Owings Towne

MADONNA OF THE CELLS, A, Short Story *see* Morley Roberts

MADONNA OF THE SEVEN MOONS, Novel *see* Margery Lawrence

MADONNA OF THE TUBS, THE, Story *see* Elizabeth Stuart Phelps

MADONNA: UNAUTHORIZED, Book *see* Christopher Andersen

MADRE, LA, 1920, Novel *see* Grazia Deledda

MADRID DE LOS ABUELOS, EL, Novel *see* Pedro de Repide

MADRUGADA, 1954, Play *see* Antonio Buero Vallejo

MAELSTROM, THE, New York 1916, Novel *see* Frank Froest

MAESTRA NORMAL, LA, Novel *see* Manuel Galvez

MAESTRINA, LA, 1917, Play *see* Dario Niccodemi

MAESTRO DI VIGEVANO, IL, Novel *see* Lucio Mastronardi

MAESTRO LANDI, Play *see* Giovacchino Forzano, Ferdinando Paolieri

MAFIA PRINCESS, Book *see* Antoinette Giancana

MAGASISKOLA, 1967, Short Story *see* Miklos Meszoly

MAGDA, Berlin 1893, Play *see* Hermann Sudermann

MAGDALENA, Novel *see* Josef Svatopluk MacHar

MAGDAT KICSAPJA, Play *see* Laszlo Kadar

MAGE DU CARLTON, LE, Play *see* Georges Dolley, Leopold Marchand

MAGGIE PEPPER, New York 1911, Play *see* Charles Klein

MAGIC, 1976, Novel *see* William Goldman

MAGIC BED-KNOB, THE, Short Story *see* Mary Norton

MAGIC BOW, THE, Novel *see* Manuel Komroff

MAGIC CHRISTIAN, THE, New York 1960, Novel *see* Terry Southern

MAGIC FIRE, 1953, Biography *see* Bertita Harding

MAGIC GARDEN OF STANLEY SWEETHEART, THE, New York 1969, Novel *see* Robert T. Westbrook

MAGIC GARDEN, THE, Novel *see* Gene Stratton-Porter

MAGIC MOMENTS, Novel *see* Nora Roberts

MAGIC SHOP, THE, 1905, Short Story *see* H. G. Wells

MAGIC TOYSHOP, THE, 1967, Novel *see* Angela Carter

MAGIC WAND, THE, Poem *see* George R. Sims

MAGIC WHITE SUIT, THE, 1957, Short Story *see* Ray Bradbury

MAGICIAN FISHERMAN, THE, Story *see* A. F. Zamloch

MAGICIAN OF LUBLIN, THE, 1960, Novel *see* Isaac Bashevis Singer

MAGICIAN, THE, London 1908, Novel *see* W. Somerset Maugham

MAGICIENNES, LES, Novel *see* Pierre Boileau, Thomas Narcejac

MAGICIENS, LES, Novel *see* Frederic Dard

MAGISTRAT CAMBRIOLEUR, LE, Novel *see* Marcel Allain, Pierre Souvestre

MAGISTRATE, THE, London 1885, Play *see* Arthur Wing Pinero

MAGNATE OF PARADISE, THE, Novel *see* Mary Imlay Taylor

MAGNETISORENS FEMTE VINTER, Novel *see* Per Olov Enquist

MAGNIFICENT AMBERSONS, THE, Garden City, N.Y. 1918, Novel *see* Booth Tarkington

MAGNIFICENT BASTARDS, THE, 1954, Novel *see* Lucy Herndon Crockett

MAGNIFICENT JACALA, THE, 1918, Short Story *see* Louise Winter

MAGNIFICENT OBSESSION, New York 1933, Novel *see* Lloyd C. Douglas

MAGNIFICENT RESCUE, THE, Short Story *see* Heidi Hall

MAGNOLIA, New York 1923, Play *see* Booth Tarkington

MAGNUM FOR SCHNEIDER, A, Novel *see* James Mitchell

MAGOKORO, 1939, Short Story *see* Yojiro Ishizaka

MAGOT DE JOSEFA, LE, Novel *see* Catherine Claude

MAGUS, THE, 1965, Novel *see* John Fowles

MAGYAR NABOB, EGY, Budapest 1853, Novel *see* Mor Jokai

MAHABHARATA, Poem *see* Vyasa

MAHANAGAR, 1949, Short Story *see* Naredranath Mitra

MAHAPRASTHANER PATHEY, Novel *see* Prabodh Kumar Sanyal

MAHLIA LA METISSE, Novel *see* Jean Francoux

MAID OF CEFN YDFA, THE, Play *see* James Haggar

MAID OF HONOR, 1932, Short Story *see* Katharine Brush

MAID OF THE MOUNTAINS, THE, London 1917, Musical Play *see* Frederick Lonsdale

MAID OF THE SILVER SEA, A, Novel *see* John Oxenham

MAIDEN, MAIDEN, 1957, Short Story *see* Kay Boyle

MAIFU, Novel *see* Fang Fang

MAIGRET AU "PICRATT'S", 1951, Novel *see* Georges Simenon

MAIGRET, LOGNON ET LES GANGSTERS, 1952, Novel *see* Georges Simenon

MAIGRET TEND UN PIEGE, 1955, Novel *see* Georges Simenon

MAIHIME, 1951, Short Story *see* Yasunari Kawabata

MAIL-ORDER BRIDE, 1951, Short Story *see* Van Cort

MAIN A COUPER, LA, Novel *see* Pierre Salva

MAIN DE GLOIRE, LA, 1832, Short Story *see* Gerard de Nerval

MAIN, LA, Novel *see* Georges Simenon

MAIN PLEINE, Novel *see* Pierre Lesou

MAIN STREET KID, THE, Radio Play *see* Caryl Coleman

MAIN STREET; THE STORY OF CAROL KENNICOTT, New York 1920, Novel *see* Sinclair Lewis

MAINS D'ORLAC, LES, Paris 1920, Novel *see* Maurice Renard

MAINS SALES, LES, 1948, Play *see* Jean-Paul Sartre

MAINSPRING, THE, Short Story *see* Louis Joseph Vance

MAINSTREAM, Story *see* Louis Joseph Vance

MAIS N'TE PROMENE DONC PAS TOUTE NUE!, Play *see* Georges Feydeau

MAISON ASSASSINEE, LA, Novel *see* Pierre Magnan

MAISON AU SOLEIL, LA, Novel *see* Raymond Clauzel

MAISON CERNEE, LA, Novel *see* Pierre Frondaie

MAISON DANS LA DUNE, LA, Novel *see* Maxence Van Der Meersch

MAISON D'ARGILE, LA, Play *see* Emile Fabre

MAISON DE DANSES, Novel *see* Paul Reboux

MAISON DE L'ESPION, LA, Novel *see* Jacques de Baroncelli

MAISON D'EN FACE, LA, Play *see* Paul Nivoix

MAISON DES BORIES, LA, Novel *see* Simone Ratel

MAISON DES DEUX BARBEAUX, LA, Novel *see* Andre Theuriet

MAISON DES HOMMES VIVANTS, LA, Novel *see* Claude Farrere

MAISON DES SEPT JEUNES FILLES, LA, 1941, Novel *see* Georges Simenon

MAISON DU BAIGNEUR, LA, Play *see* Auguste Maquet

MAISON DU MALTAIS, LA, Novel *see* Jean Vignaud

MAISON DU MYSTERE, LA, Novel *see* Jules Mary

MAISON DU PRINTEMPS, LA, Play *see* Fernand Millau

MAISON SOUS LE MER, LA, Novel *see* Paul Vialar

MAISON TELLIER, LA, 1881, Short Story *see* Guy de Maupassant

MAISON VIDE, LA, Novel *see* Claude Gutman

MAITRE APRES DIEU, Play *see* Jan de Hartog

MAITRE BOLBEC ET SON MARI, Play *see* Georges Berr, Louis Verneuil

MAITRE CHAT OU LE CHAT BOTTE, LE, Paris 1697, Short Story *see* Charles Perrault

MAITRE CORNELIUS, *see* Honore de Balzac

MAITRE DE FORGES, LE, Paris 1882, Novel *see* Georges Ohnet

MAITRE DU MONDE, Paris 1904, Novel *see* Jules Verne

MAITRESSE DE PIANO, LA, 1949, Short Story *see* Roger Peyrefitte

MAITRESSE LEGITIME, LA, Book *see* Georges Antequil

MAJESTY OF THE LAW, THE, Play *see* Frank O'Connor

MAJKA TARAKJA, Novel *see* Maria Durickova

MAJO, THE, Short Story *see* Arline Lord

MAJOOR FRANS, 1874, Novel *see* Anna L. G. Bosboom-Toussaint

MAJOR BARBARA, London 1905, Play *see* George Bernard Shaw

MAJOR CHANDRAKANT, Play *see* K. Balachander

MAJOR DENNING'S TRUST ESTATE, Story *see* Gordon Grand

MAJOR UND DIE STIERE, DER, Novel *see* Hans Venatier

MAJORATSHERR, DER, Novel *see* Alfred von Hedenstjerna

MAJORETTES, THE, Novel *see* John Russo

MAJORITY OF ONE, A, New York 1959, Play *see* Leonard Spigelgass

MAKAI TENSHO, Novel *see* Hutaro Yamada

MAKE HASTE TO LIVE, 1950, Novel *see* Gordon Gordon, Mildred Gordon

MAKE LOVE NOT WAR - DIE LIEBESGESCHICHTE UNSERER ZEIT, Novel *see* Gunter Adrian

MAKE ME AN OFFER, Novel *see* Wolf Mankowitz

MAKE ROOM! MAKE ROOM!, 1966, Novel *see* Harry Harrison

MAKE THEM HAPPY, 1919, Short Story *see* Mary Roberts Rinehart

MAKE WAY FOR LOVE, Story *see* Al Martin

MAKE YOU A GOOD WIFE, Novel *see* Yolanda Foldes

MAKE YOUR OWN BED, Play *see* Harriet Ford, Harvey J. O'Higgins

MAKER OF GESTURES, A, 1923, Short Story *see* John Monk Saunders

MAKING HER HIS WIFE, New York 1918, Novel *see* Corra Harris

MAKING IT, Short Story *see* Margaret Gibson Gilboord

MAKING IT, Novel *see* James Leigh

MAKING OF BOBBY BURNIT, THE, New York 1909, Novel *see* George Randolph Chester

MAKING OF MADDALENA; OR THE COMPROMISE, THE, Play *see* Mary E. Lewis, Samuel G. Lewis

MAKING OF O'MALLEY, THE, 1924, Short Story *see* Gerald Beaumont

MAKING THE GRADE, 1928, Short Story *see* George Ade

MAKRA, 1971, Novel *see* Akos Kertesz

MALA CARODEJNICE, Novel *see* Otfried Preussler

MALA LEY, LA, Play *see* Manuel Linares Rivas

MALA NOCHE, Story *see* Walt Curtis

MALA NOVA, 'A, 1902, *see* Libero Bavio

MALA YERBA, 1909, Novel *see* Mariano Azuela

MALADE IMAGINAIRE, LE, 1673, Play *see* Moliere

MALAGUETA, PERUS E BACANACO, 1963, Short Story *see* Joao Antonio

MALAJANHA, Novel *see* Upendra Kishore Dash

MALARPIRATER, 1911, Novel *see* Sigfrid Siwertz

MALATESTA, Play *see* Henry de Montherlant

MALCASADA, LA, Play *see* Jose Luis de Lucio, F. Gomez Hidalgo

MALDONNE, Novel *see* Pierre Boileau, Thomas Narcejac

MALE ANIMAL, THE, New York 1940, Play *see* Elliott Nugent, James Thurber

MALE DI LUNA, 1925, Short Story *see* Luigi Pirandello

MALE STESTI, Play *see* Vaclav Skutecky

MALEFICES, Paris 1961, Novel *see* Pierre Boileau, Thomas Narcejac

MALEFICO ANELLO, IL, 1909, Play *see* Vincenzo Morello

MALENA ES UN NOMBRE DE TANGO, Novel *see* Almudena Grandes

MALENCONTRE, Novel *see* Guy de Chantepleure

MALEVIL, Novel *see* Robert Merle

MALHEURS DE SOPHIE, LES, Novel *see* La Comtesse de Segur

MALIA, 1895, Play *see* Luigi Capuana

MALIBU, Boston 1931, Novel *see* Vance Joseph Hoyt

MALICE AFORETHOUGHT, Novel *see* Francis Iles

MALLEN TRILOGY, THE, Novel *see* Catherine Cookson

MALLOY CAMPEADOR, 1921, Short Story *see* Ralph G. Kirk

MALOM A POKOLBAN, 1968, Novel *see* Gyorgy Moldova

MALOMBRA, 1881, Novel *see* Antonio Fogazzaro

MALPERTUIS, Novel *see* Jean Ray

MALQUERIDA, LA, 1913, Play *see* Jacinto Benavente y Martinez

MALTESE FALCON, THE, New York 1930, Novel *see* Dashiell Hammett

MALVA, 1897, Short Story *see* Maxim Gorky

MALVADO CARABEL, EL, 1931, Novel *see* Wenceslao Fernandez Florez

MALVALOCA, Play *see* Joaquin Alvarez Quintero, Serafin Alvarez Quintero

MALY BOBES VE MESTE, Book *see* J. V. Plevas

MALYADAAN, 1903, Short Story *see* Rabindranath Tagore

MAMA, Spain 1913, Play *see* Gregorio Martinez Sierra

MAMAN, Paris 1924, Play *see* Jose Germain Drouilly

MAMAN COLIBRI, 1904, Play *see* Henry Bataille

MAMAN SABOULEUX, Play *see* Eugene Labiche, Marc-Michel

MAMA'S AFFAIR, New York 1920, Play *see* Rachel Burton Butler

MAMBO KINGS PLAY SONGS OF LOVE, THE, Novel *see* Oscar Hijuelos

MAMMA'S BANK ACCOUNT, Book *see* Kathryn Forbes

MAMMON AND THE ARCHER, Short Story *see* O. Henry

M'AMOUR, 1901, Play *see* Maurice Hennequin

MAMOURET, 1943, Play *see* Jean Sarment

MAM'SELLE JO, Garden City, N.Y. 1918, Novel *see* Harriet T. Comstock

MAM'ZELLE BONAPARTE, Novel *see* Gerard Bourgeois, Pierre Chanlaine

MAM'ZELLE CULOT, Opera *see* Andre Mouezy-Eon, Alfred Vercourt

MAM'ZELLE NITOUCHE, Paris 1882, Operetta *see* Herve, Henri Meilhac, Albert Milhaud

MAN ABOUT A DOG, A, Novel *see* Alec Coppel

MAN ABOUT THE HOUSE, A, Novel *see* Francis Brett Young

MAN ABOUT TOWN, New York 1932, Novel *see* Denison Clift

MAN ALIVE, 1912, Novel *see* G. K. Chesterton

MAN AND HIS KINGDOM, Novel *see* A. E. W. Mason

MAN AND HIS MATE, A, Springfield, MA. 1908, Play *see* Harold Riggs Durant

MAN AND HIS MONEY, A, Indianapolis 1912, Novel *see* Frederic Stewart Isham

MAN AND MAID, Philadelphia 1922, Novel *see* Elinor Glyn

MAN AND THE MOMENT, THE, New York 1914, Novel *see* Elinor Glyn

MAN AND THE SNAKE, THE, 1891, Short Story *see* Ambrose Bierce

MAN AT SIX, THE, London 1928, Play *see* Jack Celestin, Jack de Leon

MAN AT THE CARLTON, THE, London 1931, Novel *see* Edgar Wallace

MAN AT THE GATE, THE, Poem *see* Louise Haskin

MAN BAIT, Story *see* Norman Houston

MAN BEHIND THE DOOR, THE, New York 1907, Novel *see* Archibald Clavering Gunter

MAN BEHIND THE MASK, THE, Short Story *see* Robert Buckner

MAN BETWEEN, THE, 1913, Novel *see* Walter Frost

MAN BRAUCHT KEIN GELD, Play *see* Ferdinand Altenkirch

MAN CALLED HORSE, A, 1950, Short Story *see* Dorothy M. Johnson

MAN CALLED INTREPID, A, Book *see* William Stevenson

MAN CALLED NOON, THE, Novel *see* Louis L'Amour

MAN CALLED PETER, A, Biography *see* Catherine Marshall

MAN DIE ZIJN HAAR LIET KNIPPEN, DE, 1947, Novel *see* Johan Daisne

MAN FOR ALL SEASONS, A, London 1960, Play *see* Robert Bolt

MAN FOUR-SQUARE, A, Boston 1919, Novel *see* William MacLeod Raine

MAN FRIDAY, 1974, Play *see* Adrian Mitchell

MAN FROM ASHALUNA, THE, Boston 1920, Novel *see* Henry Payson Dowst

MAN FROM BAR-20; A STORY OF THE COW COUNTRY, THE, Chicago 1918, Novel *see* Clarence E. Mulford

MAN FROM BLANKLEYS, THE, 1893, Short Story *see* F. Anstey

MAN FROM BRODNEY'S, THE, New York 1908, Novel *see* George Barr McCutcheon

MAN FROM COLORADO, THE, Novel *see* Borden Chase

MAN FROM GLENGARRY, Chicago 1901, Novel *see* Ralph Connor

MAN FROM HOME, THE, Louisville, Ky. 1907, Play *see* Booth Tarkington, Harry Leon Wilson

MAN FROM MAKE BELIEVE, THE, Short Story *see* Byron Morgan

MAN FROM MEXICO, THE, New York 1897, Play *see* Henry A. Du Souchet

MAN FROM MOSCOW, THE, Book *see* Greville Wynne

MAN FROM O.R.G.Y., THE, New York 1965, Novel *see* Ted Mark

MAN FROM SNOWY RIVER, THE, 1895, Poem *see* Andrew Barton Paterson

MAN FROM TEN STRIKE, THE, Story *see* James Oliver Curwood

MAN FROM TEXAS, 1950, Serial Story *see* Bill Gulick

MAN FROM TEXAS, THE, Play *see* E. B. Ginty

MAN FROM THE BITTER ROOTS, THE, New York 1915, Novel *see* Caroline Lockhart

MAN FROM THE DESERT, THE, Short Story *see* Wyndham Martin

MAN FROM TORONTO, THE, London 1918, Play *see* Douglas Murray

MAN HATER, THE, 1917, Short Story *see* Mary Brecht Pulver

MAN HUNT, Novel *see* Vernon Clancey

MAN HUNTER, THE, Novel *see* Wade Miller

MAN HUNTING IN THE JUNGLE, 1930, Book *see* George M. Dyott

MAN I LOVE, THE, Novel *see* Maritta Martin Wolff

MAN IN BLACK, THE, Story *see* Marvin H. Albert

MAN IN EVENING CLOTHES, THE, Story *see* Ruth Chatterton

MAN IN GREY, THE, Novel *see* Lady Eleanor Smith

MAN IN HALF MOON STREET, THE, London 1939, Play *see* Barre Lyndon

MAN IN HOBBLES, THE, 1913, Short Story *see* Peter B. Kyne

MAN IN MOTLEY, THE, Novel *see* Tom Gallon

MAN IN POSSESSION, THE, London 1930, Play *see* H. M. Harwood

MAN IN THE ATTIC, THE, Play *see* Charles McEvoy

MAN IN THE GRAY FLANNEL SUIT, THE, 1955, Novel *see* Sloan Wilson

MAN IN THE MIRROR, THE, Novel *see* William Garrett

MAN IN THE NET; A NOVEL OF SUSPENSE, 1956, Novel *see* Patrick Quentin

MAN IN THE OPEN, A, Indianapolis 1912, Novel *see* Roger S. Pocock

MAN IN THE SADDLE, THE, 1938, Novel *see* Ernest Haycox

MAN IN THE SHADOW, Novel *see* Harry Whittington

MAN IN THE STREET, THE, Novel *see* Mary Imlay Taylor

MAN IN THE WATER, THE, New York 1962, Novel *see* Robert Sheckley

MAN INSIDE, THE, Novel *see* M. E. Chaber

MAN INSIDE, THE, New York 1914, Novel *see* Natalie Sumner Lincoln

MAN IS TEN FEET TALL, A, 1955, Television Play *see* Robert Alan Aurther

MAN IST NUR ZWEIM JUNG, Play *see* Otto F. Beer, Peter Preses

MAN NEXT DOOR, THE, New York 1917, Novel *see* Emerson Hough

MAN NOBODY KNOWS; A DISCOVERY OF JESUS, THE, Indianapolis 1925, Book *see* Bruce Barton

MAN O' WARSMAN, THE, New York 1898, Play *see* Eugene Thomas

MAN OCH HAS SAMVETE, EN, 1931, Novel *see* Jarl Hemmer

MAN OF ACTION, A, Short Story *see* Robert J. Horton

MAN OF FIRE, Television Play *see* Jack Jacobs, Malvin Wald

MAN OF LETTERS, Novel *see* Glen Tomasetti

MAN OF PROPERTY, THE, 1906, Novel *see* John Galsworthy

MAN OF THE FOREST, THE, New York 1920, Novel *see* Zane Grey

MAN OF THE HOUR, THE, New York 1906, Play *see* George Broadhurst

MAN OF THE WEST, 1955, Novel *see* Philip Yordan

MAN OF TWO WORLDS; THE NOVEL OF A STRANGER, New York 1933, Novel *see* Ainsworth Morgan

MAN ON FIRE, Novel *see* A. J. Quinell

MAN ON THE BOX, THE, Indianapolis 1904, Novel *see* Harold MacGrath

MAN ON THE LEDGE, THE, Story *see* Joel Sayre

MAN OP DEN ACHTERGROND, DE, 1918, Novel *see* Ivans

MAN OP HET BALKON, DE, Novel *see* Maj Sjowall, Per Wahloo

MAN OR MOUSE, Story *see* Robert B. Hunt

MAN POWER, Story *see* Byron Morgan

MAN REDE MIR NICHT VON LIEBE, Novel *see* Hugo Maria Kritz

MAN RUNNING, Novel *see* Selwyn Jepson

MAN SIZE, New York 1922, Novel *see* William MacLeod Raine

MAN SPRICHT UBER JACQUELINE, Novel *see* Katrin Holland

MAN STEIGT NACH, Play *see* Jeno Heltai

MAN THAT CORRUPTED HADLEYBURG, THE, 1900, Short Story *see* Mark Twain

MAN, THE, Play *see* Mel Dinelli

MAN, THE MISSION AND THE MAID, THE, Story *see* George Randolph Chester

MAN TO MAN, New York 1920, Novel *see* Jackson Gregory

MAN TRAIL, THE, New York 1915, Novel *see* Henry Oyen

MAN UPSTAIRS, THE, Indianapolis 1916, Novel *see* Earl Derr Biggers

MAN WHO AWOKE, THE, Short Story *see* Mary Imlay Taylor

MAN WHO BOUGHT LONDON, THE, London 1915, Novel *see* Edgar Wallace

MAN WHO BROKE HIS HEART, THE, Play *see* Frederick Schlick

MAN WHO CAME BACK, THE, New York 1912, Novel *see* John Fleming Wilson

MAN WHO CAME TO DINNER, THE, New York 1939, Play *see* Moss Hart, George S. Kaufman

MAN WHO CAME TO LIFE, THE, Story *see* Samuel W. Taylor

MAN WHO CHANGED HIS NAME, THE, London 1928, Play *see* Edgar Wallace

MAN WHO COULD NOT LOSE, THE, New York 1911, Novel *see* Richard Harding Davis

MAN WHO COULD WORK MIRACLES, THE, 1899, Short Story *see* H. G. Wells

MAN WHO DARED, THE, Novel *see* May Edginton

MAN WHO DISAPPEARED, THE, Story *see* Richard Washburn Child

MAN WHO FELL TO EARTH, THE, 1963, Novel *see* Walter S. Tevis

MAN WHO FORGOT, THE, New York 1915, Novel *see* James Hay Jr.

MAN WHO HAD EVERYTHING, THE, Short Story *see* Ben Ames Williams

MAN WHO HAD POWER OVER WOMEN, THE, London 1967, Novel *see* Gordon M. Williams

MAN WHO HATED PEOPLE, THE, Short Story *see* Paul Gallico

MAN WHO HEARD EVERYTHING, THE, 1921, Short Story *see* Walter Trumbull

MAN WHO KNEW, THE, London 1919, Novel *see* Edgar Wallace

MAN WHO KNEW TOO MUCH, THE, 1922, Short Story *see* G. K. Chesterton

MAN WHO LOST HIMSELF, THE, New York 1918, Novel *see* Henry de Vere Stacpoole

MAN WHO LOVED CAT DANCING, THE, Novel *see* Marilyn Durham

MAN WHO MARRIED A FRENCH WIFE, THE, Story *see* Irwin Shaw

MAN WHO MARRIED HIS OWN WIFE, THE, 1922, Short Story *see* Mary Ashe Miller, John Fleming Wilson

MAN WHO NEVER WAS, THE, Book *see* Ewen Montagu

MAN WHO RECLAIMED HIS HEAD, THE, New York 1932, Play *see* Jean Bart

MAN WHO ROCKED THE BOAT, THE, 1956, Novel *see* Richard Carter, William J. Keating

MAN WHO SANK THE NAVY, THE, Short Story *see* William Fay

MAN WHO SHOT LIBERTY VALANCE, THE, New York 1953, Short Story *see* Dorothy M. Johnson

MAN WHO STAYED AT HOME, THE, London 1914, Play *see* J. E. Harold Terry, Lechmere Worrall

MAN WHO STOLE A DREAM, THE, Novel *see* L. S. Goldsmith

MAN WHO STOOD STILL, THE, New York 1908, Play *see* Jules Eckert Goodman

MAN WHO, THE, 1921, Short Story *see* Lloyd Osbourne

MAN WHO TURNED WHITE, THE, Short Story *see* F. McGrew Willis

MAN WHO WAS ALMOST A MAN, THE, 1961, Short Story *see* Richard Wright

MAN WHO WAS NOBODY, THE, London 1927, Novel *see* Edgar Wallace

MAN WHO WON, THE, Novel *see* Mrs. Baillie Reynolds

MAN WHO WON, THE, Chicago 1919, Novel *see* Cyrus Townsend Brady

MAN WHO WOULD BE KING, THE, 1888, Short Story *see* Rudyard Kipling

MAN WHO WOULD BE WHITE, THE, Story *see* Aubrey Bowser

MAN WHO WOULDN'T LOVE, THE, Story *see* Dorothy Farnum

MAN WHO WOULDN'T TAKE OFF HIS HAT, THE, 1922, Short Story *see* Philip Le Noir

MAN WHO WOULDN'T TALK, THE, Novel *see* Stanley Jackson

MAN WITH BOGART'S FACE, THE, Novel *see* Andrew J. Fenady

MAN WITH MY FACE, THE, 1948, Novel *see* Samuel W. Taylor

MAN WITH THE BROODING EYES, THE, Story *see* John Goodwin

MAN WITH THE GOLDEN ARM, THE, 1949, Novel *see* Nelson Algren

MAN WITH THE GOLDEN GUN, THE, Novel *see* Ian Fleming

MAN WITH THE LIMP, THE, Short Story *see* Sax Rohmer

MAN WITH THE MAGNETIC EYES, THE, Novel *see* Roland Daniel

MAN WITH THE TWISTED LIP, THE, 1892, Short Story *see* Arthur Conan Doyle

MAN WITH TWO WIVES, THE, Novel *see* Patrick Quentin

MAN WITHIN, THE, 1929, Novel *see* Graham Greene

MAN WITHOUT A COUNTRY, THE, 1863, Short Story *see* Edward Everett Hale

MAN WITHOUT A HEART, THE, New York 1924, Novel *see* Ruby M. Ayres

MAN WITHOUT A PAST, THE, Short Story *see* Joseph Anthony

MAN WITHOUT A STAR, New York 1952, Novel *see* Dee Linford

MAN WITHOUT FRIENDS, A, 1940, Novel *see* Margaret Echard

MAN WOMAN AND CHILD, Novel *see* Erich Segal

MANAGER OF THE B AND A, THE, New York 1901, Novel *see* Vaughan Kester

MANCHA QUE LIMPIA, Play *see* Jose Echegaray

MANCHE ET LA BELLE, UNE, Novel *see* James Hadley Chase

MANCHESTER MAN, THE, Novel *see* Mrs. Linnaeus Banks

MANCHESTER MARRIAGE, A, Novel *see* Mrs. Gaskell

MANCHURIAN CANDIDATE, THE, New York 1959, Novel *see* Richard Condon

MANDAGARNA MED FANNY, Novel *see* Gunnar Evander

MANDALA, Novel *see* Kim Song Dong

MANDARINO PER TEO, UN, Musical Play *see* Pietro Garinei, Sandro Giovannini

MANDAT, LE, 1965, Short Story *see* Ousmane Sembene

MANDINGO, Novel *see* Kyle Onstott

MANDRAGOLA, LA, 1514, Play *see* Niccolo MacHiavelli

MANEATER, Book *see* Ted Willis

MAN-EATERS OF KUMAON, Story *see* James Corbett

MAN-EATING TIGER, Allentown, PA. 1927, Play *see* Rose Caylor, Ben Hecht

MANEGE, Novel *see* Walter Angel

MANGALSUTRAM, Short Story *see* B. N. Reddi

MANGANESE, Novel *see* Francois Ponthier

MANGANINNIE, Novel *see* Beth Roberts

MANGO TREE, THE, Novel *see* Ronald McKie

MANHA SUBMERSA, 1954, Novel *see* Vergilio Ferreira

MANHANDLED, 1924, Short Story *see* Arthur Stringer

MANHANDLING ETHEL, 1921, Short Story *see* Frank R. Adams

MANHATTAN LOVE SONG, New York 1932, Novel *see* Cornell Woolrich

MANHATTAN LOVE SONG, New York 1934, Novel *see* Kathleen Norris

MANHATTAN MARY, New York 1927, Musical Play *see* Buddy De Sylva, W. K. Wells, George White

MANHATTAN MERRY-GO-ROUND, Musical Play *see* Frank Hummert

MANHUNT: THE STORY OF STANLEY GRAHAM, Book *see* Howard Willis

MANI APERTE SULL'ACQUA, Play *see* Luigi Bruno Di Belmonte

MANIE DE LA PERSECUTION, Novel *see* Jean-Louis Thomas

MANIFESTATIONS OF HENRY ORT, THE, Story *see* Ethel Watts Mumford

MANILA ESPIONAGE, Book *see* Myron G. Goldsmith, Claire Phillips

MANITOU, THE, Novel *see* Graham Masterton

MANJI, 1930, Novel *see* Junichiro Tanizaki

MANJIANG HONG, Novel *see* Zhang Henshui

MANMOYEE GIRLS' SCHOOL, Play *see* Rabindranath Maitra

MANN AUF DER MAUER, DER, Novel *see* Peter Schneider

MANN DEN NIEMAND SAH, DER, Novel *see* Paul Rosenhayn

MANN DER SEINEN MORDER SUCHT, DER, Play *see* Ernst Neubach

MANN IM SCHILF, DER, 1955, Novel *see* George Emmanuel Saiko

MANN IM SCHONSTEN ALTER, EIN, Novel *see* Rudolf Schnider-Schelde

MANN IM STROM, DER, 1957, Novel *see* Siegfried Lenz

MANN IN DER WANNE, DER, Play *see* Karl Fellmar, Ernst Friese

MANN WILL NACH DEUTSCHLAND, EIN, Novel *see* Fred Andreas

MANNEN FRAN MALLORCA, Novel *see* Leif G. W. Persson

MANNEN PA TAKET, Novel *see* Maj Sjowall, Per Wahloo

MANNEN SOM GICK UPP I ROK, Novel *see* Maj Sjowall, Per Wahloo

MANNEQUIN, New York 1926, Novel *see* Fannie Hurst

MANNEQUIN ASSASSINE, LE, Novel *see* Stanislas-Andre Steeman

MANNEQUINS, Opera *see* Jacques Bousquet, Henri Falk

MANNER MUSSEN SO SEIN, Ebendorf 1938, Novel *see* Heinrich Seiler

MANO DELLA MORTA, LA, Novel *see* Carolina Invernizio

MANO EN LA TRAMPA, LA, Buenos Aires 1961, Novel *see* Beatriz Guido

MANO TAGLIATA, LA, Novel *see* Matilde Serao

MANOEUVRES DE NUIT, Play *see* Etienne Arnaud, Andre Heuze

MANOLESCU, Short Story *see* Hans Szekely

MANON 326, Novel *see* Pierre-Gilles Veber

MAN'S CASTLE, 1932, Play *see* Lawrence Hazard

MAN'S HOME, A, Albany, Ny. 1917, Play *see* Edmund Breese

MAN'S HOME, A, Albany, N.Y. 1917, Play *see* Anna Steese Richardson

MANS KVINNA, 1933, Novel *see* Vilhelm Moberg

MAN'S LAW, Story *see* James Oliver Curwood

MAN'S MAN, A, 1917, Serial Story *see* Peter B. Kyne

MAN'S MAN, A, New York 1925, Novel *see* Patrick Kearney

MAN'S SHADOW, A, London 1889, Play *see* Robert Buchanan

MAN'S WORLD, A, New York 1910, Play *see* Rachel Crothers

MANSFIELD PARK, 1814, Novel *see* Jane Austen

MANSION OF ACHING HEARTS, THE, 1902, Song *see* Arthur J. Lamb, Harry von Tilzer

MANSLAUGHTER, New York 1921, Novel *see* Alice Duer Miller

MAN-TAMER, THE, 1918, Short Story *see* John Barton Oxford

MANTRAP, New York 1926, Novel *see* Sinclair Lewis

MANUEL ERKENNT SEINE MACHT, Novel *see* Karl Lerbs

MANUELA, Novel *see* William Woods

MANUSCRIT TROUVE A SARAGOSSE, LE, 1815, Novel *see* Jan Potocki

MANUSCRITO DE UNA MADRE, EL, Story *see* Enrique Perez Escrich

MANXMAN, THE, 1894, Novel *see* Hall Caine

MANY A SLIP, New York 1930, Play *see* Edith Fitzgerald, Robert Riskin

MANY RIVERS TO CROSS, Short Story *see* Steve Frazee

MANY SPLENDORED THING, A, 1952, Book *see* Han Suyin

MANY WATERS (THE UNNAMED PLAY), London 1926, Play *see* Monckton Hoffe

MANZELKA NECO TUSI, Novel *see* Mana Dubska

MAOS VAZIAS, 1938, Short Story *see* Lucio Cardoso

MARA, 1906, Novel *see* Ioan Slavici

MARACAIBO, 1955, Novel *see* Stirling Silliphant

MARAMA: A TALE OF THE SOUTH PACIFIC, Boston 1913, Novel *see* Ralph Stock

MARARIA, Novel *see* Rafael Arozarena

MARATHON MAN, 1974, Novel *see* William Goldman

MARATRE, LA, *see* Honore de Balzac

MARATTAM, Play *see* Kavalam Narayana Panicker

MARAUDERS, THE, Novel *see* Alan Marcus

MARAUDERS, THE, New York 1959, Novel *see* Charlton Ogburn Jr.

MARBLE FOREST, THE, 1951, Novel *see* Theo Durrant

MARBLE HEART, THE, New York 1864, Play *see* Charles Selby

MARCEL LEVIGNET, New York 1906, Novel *see* Elwyn Alfred Barron

MARCELLA, 1895, Play *see* Victorien Sardou

MARCEL'S BIRTHDAY PRESENT, Play *see* Harold Riggs Durant

MARCENE, Novel *see* Penelope Knapp

MARCHAND DE BONHEUR, LE, Play *see* Henri Kistemaeckers

MARCHAND DE SABLE, LE, Novel *see* Georges-Andre Cuel

MARCHE DU FOU, LA, Novel *see* Henriette Jelinck

MARCHE NUPTIALE, LA, 1905, Play *see* Henry Bataille

MARCHEN VOM FALSCHEN PRINZEN, DAS, 1826, Short Story *see* Wilhelm Hauff

MARCHESE DI ROCCAVERDINA, IL, 1901, Novel *see* Luigi Capuana

MARCHESE DI RUVOLITO, IL, Play *see* Nino Martoglio

MARCHEURS DE LA NUIT, LES, Unpublished, Novel *see* Real Giguere

MARCHING ALONG, 1928, Autobiography *see* John Philip Sousa

MARCIA INDIETRO, LA, Short Story *see* Alberto Moravia

MARCO HIMSELF, 1929, Short Story *see* Octavus Roy Cohen

MARCO VISCONTI, 1834, Novel *see* Tommaso Grossi

MARE AU DIABLE, LA, Novel *see* George Sand

MARE NOSTRUM, 1916, Novel *see* Vicente Blasco Ibanez

MARELE SINGURATIC, 1972, Novel *see* Marin Preda

MARENS LILLE UGLE, 1957, Novel *see* Finn Havrevold

MARESI, Novel *see* Alexander Lernet-Holenia

MARGARITA, ARMANDO Y SU PADRE, 1931, Play *see* Enrique Jardiel Poncela

MARGHERE DI CAVOURET, Play *see* L. D. Beccari

MARGHERITA FRA I TRE, Play *see* Fritz Schwiefert

MARGHERITA PUSTERLA, 1838, Novel *see* Cesare Cantu

MARGIN FOR ERROR, New York 1939, Play *see* Clare Boothe

MARGOT, 1838, Short Story *see* Alfred de Musset

MARGUERITE DE LA NUIT, 1925, Short Story *see* Pierre Mac Orlan

MARI A LA CAMPAGNE, LE, 1844, Play *see* Bayard, De Vally

MARI A PRIX FIXE, UN, Novel *see* Maria-Luisa Linares

MARI GARCON, LE, Play *see* Paul Armont, Marcel Gerbidon

MARI SANS FEMME, LE, Play *see* Albert Carre, Antony Mars

MARIA, 1942, Novel *see* Gustav Sandgren

MARIA BONITA, 1914, Novel *see* Julio Afranio Peixoto

MARIA CHAPDELAINE; RECIT DU CANADA FRANCAIS, 1916, Novel *see* Louis Hemon

MARIA DEL CARMEN, Novel *see* Jose Felin Y Codina

MARIA MARTEN, London 1840, Play *see* Anon

MARIA MORZECK ODER DAS KANINCHEN BIN ICH, 1965, Novel *see* Manfred Bieler

MARIA ROSA, Spain 1890, Play *see* Angel Guimera

MARIA STUART, 1801, Play *see* Friedrich von Schiller

MARIA VANDAMME, Novel *see* Jacques Duquesne

MARIA ZEF, 1936, Novel *see* Paola Drigo

MARIAGE DE CHIFFON, LE, 1894, Novel *see* Gyp

MARIAGE DE FIGARO, LE, Paris 1784, Play *see* Pierre-Augustin Caron de Beaumarchais

MARIAGE DE MADEMOISELLE BEULEMANS, LE, Play *see* Franz Fonson, Fernand Wicheler

MARIAGE D'OLYMPE, LE, 1885, Play *see* Emile Paul Augier

MARIAGES, 1936, Novel *see* Charles Plisnier

MARIAN, Play *see* Peter Jones

MARIANDL, Play *see* Martin Costa

MARIANELA, 1878, Novel *see* Benito Perez Galdos

MARIANNA SIRCA, Novel *see* Grazia Deledda

MARIANNE DREAMS, Novel *see* Catherine Storr

MARIBEL Y LA EXTRANA FAMILIA, 1960, Play *see* Miguel Mihura Santos

MARIDO DE IDA Y VUELTA, UN, 1939, Play *see* Enrique Jardiel Poncela

MARIE: A TRUE STORY, Book *see* Peter Maas

MARIE ANTOINETTE; BILDNIS EINES MITTLEREN CHARAKTERS, Leipzig 1932, Biography *see* Stefan Zweig

MARIE DES ANGOISSES, Novel *see* Marcel Prevost

MARIE DES ISLES, Novel *see* Robert Gaillard

MARIE DU PORT, LA, 1938, Novel *see* Georges Simenon

MARIE GALANTE, Paris 1931, Novel *see* Jacques Deval

MARIE LTD., Short Story *see* Louise Winter

MARIE TUDOR, Play *see* Victor Hugo

MARIEE DU REGIMENT, LA, Play *see* Etienne Arnaud, Andre Heuze

MARIEE EST TROP BELLE, LA, Novel *see* Odette Joyeux

MARIEE RECALCITRANTE, LA, Play *see* Leon Gandillot

MARIELLE THIBAUT, *see* Adrien Chabot

MARIE-MADELEINE DE VERCHERES ET LES SIENS, Novel *see* F. A. Baillarge

MARIE-OCTOBRE, Novel *see* Jacques Robert

MARIGOLD, London 1936, Play *see* L. Allen Harker, F. R. Pryor

MARIKEN VAN NIEUMEGHEN, c1485-1510, Play *see* Anon

MARILI, Play *see* Stefan Zagon

MARIN DE GIBRALTAR, LE, Paris 1952, Novel *see* Marguerite Duras

MARIOLLES, LES, Novel *see* Frederic Dard

MARION DELORME, 1831, Play *see* Victor Hugo

MARIONA REBULL, 1944, Novel *see* Ignacio Agusti

MARIONETTES, LES, Play *see* Pierre Wolff

MARIONETTES, THE, Short Story *see* O. Henry

MARIONETTES, THE, Play *see* Oliver W. Geoffreys

MARION'S WALL, Novel *see* Jack Finney

MARIPOSA, London 1924, Novel *see* Henry Baerlein

MARIPOSA, LA, Short Story *see* G. G. Napolitano

MARIPOSA QUE VOLO SOBRE EL MAR, LA, 1926, Play *see* Jacinto Benavente y Martinez

MARIQUITA, LA, Novel *see* Pierre Sales

MARIS DE LEONTINE, LES, Play *see* Alfred Capus

MARITANA, London 1845, Opera *see* Edward Fitzball, Vincent Wallace

MARITI, I, Play *see* Achille Torelli

MARITO DELL'AMICA, IL, 1885, Novel *see* Neera

MARITO DI ELENA, IL, 1881, Novel *see* Giovanni Verga

MARITO IN COLLEGIO, IL, Novel *see* Giovanni Guareschi

MARIUS, Paris 1931, Play *see* Marcel Pagnol

MARJORIE MORNINGSTAR, 1955, Novel *see* Herman Wouk

MARK I LOVE YOU, Book *see* Hal W. Painter

MARK OF THE LEOPARD, Short Story *see* James Eastwood

MARK, THE, New York 1958, Novel *see* Charles Israel

MARK TWAIN, Play *see* Harold M. Sherman

MARKED MAN, A, Short Story *see* W. W. Jacobs

MARKETA LAZAROVA, 1931, Novel *see* Vladislav Vancura

MARKISCHE FORSCHUNGEN, Novel *see* Gunter de Bruyn

MARKURELLS I WADKOPING, 1919, Novel *see* Hjalmar Bergman

MARKUS OG DIANA, Novel *see* Klaus Hagerup

MARMAILLE, LA, Novel *see* Alfred Machard

MARMION A TALE OF FLODDEN FIELD, 1808, Poem *see* Sir Walter Scott

MARNIE, London 1961, Novel *see* Winston Graham

MAROONED, New York 1964, Novel *see* Martin Caidin

MARQUIS AND MISS SALLY, THE, Short Story *see* O. Henry

MARQUISE OF BOLIBAR, THE, Novel *see* Leo Perutz

MARQUISE VON O., DIE, 1810, Short Story *see* Heinrich von Kleist

MARRABO, Short Story *see* Marcello Orano, Sandro Sandri

MARRIAGE, London 1912, Novel *see* H. G. Wells

MARRIAGE BED, THE, New York 1927, Novel *see* Ernest Pascal

MARRIAGE IS A PRIVATE AFFAIR, Novel *see* Judith Kelley

MARRIAGE LINES, THE, Novel *see* J. S. Fletcher

MARRIAGE OF A YOUNG STOCKBROKER, THE, 1970, Novel *see* Charles Webb

MARRIAGE OF LITTLE JEANNE STERLING, THE, 1918, Short Story *see* Charles Stokes Wayne

MARRIAGE OF WILLIAM ASHE, THE, New York 1905, Novel *see* Mrs. Humphrey Ward

MARRIAGE ON APPROVAL, New York 1930, Novel *see* Priscilla Wayne

MARRIAGE-GO-ROUND, New York 1958, Play *see* Leslie Stevens

MARRIAGES OF MAYFAIR, THE, London 1908, Play *see* Cecil Raleigh

MARRIED ALIVE, New York 1925, Novel *see* Ralph Strauss

MARRIED IN HOLLYWOOD, Vienna 1928, Play *see* Bruno Hardt-Warden, Leopold Jacobson

MARRIED LIFE, London 1834, Play *see* J. B. Buckstone

MARRIED MAN, A, Novel *see* Piers Paul Read

MARRY AT LEISURE, New York 1959, Novel *see* Anne Piper

MARRY THE GIRL, 1935, Short Story *see* Edward Hope

MARRY THE GIRL, London 1930, Play *see* George Arthurs, Arthur Miller (2)

MARRY THE POOR GIRL, New York 1920, Play *see* Owen Davis

MARRYING MONEY, New York 1914, Play *see* Bertram Marburgh, Washington Pezet

MARRYING OF EMMY, THE, 1919, Short Story *see* Beulah Poynter

MARSE COVINGTON, 1906, Play *see* George Ade

MARSEILLE MES AMOURS, Opera *see* Audiffred, Marco Cab, Charles Tutelier

MARSHAL OF MEDICINE BEND, 1933, Novel *see* Brad Ward

MARTANDA VARMA, 1891, Novel *see* C. V. Raman Pillai

MARTER DER LIEBE, Short Story *see* Carmine Gallone

MARTHA, Vienna 1847, Opera *see* Friedrich von Flotow

MARTHA DUBRONSKY, Novel *see* Ingrid Puganigg

MARTHE, Play *see* Henri Kistemaeckers

MARTIN ARROWSMITH, 1925, Novel *see* Sinclair Lewis

MARTIN EDEN, 1906, Novel *see* Jack London

MARTIN ET BAMBOUCHE; OU LES AMIS D'ENFANCE, 1847, Novel *see* Eugene Sue

MARTIN FIERRO, 1872-79, Verse *see* Jose Herandez

MARTIN KACUR, 1906, Novel *see* Ivan Cankar

MARTIN LUTHER HIS LIFE AND TIMES, Book *see* P. Kurz

MARTIN OVERBECK, Novel *see* Felix Salten

MARTIN ROUMAGNAC, Novel *see* Pierre Wolff

MARTIN TOCCAFERRO, Play *see* Enzo La Rosa

MARTINIQUE, New York 1920, Play *see* Laurence Eyre

MARTINSKLAUSE, DIE, Novel *see* Ludwig Ganghofer

MARTIRES DEL ARROYO, LOS, Novel *see* Luis de Val

MARTY, 1953, Television Play *see* Paddy Chayefsky

MARTYRE!, Novel *see* Adolphe-P. d'Ennery

MARTYRE DE L'OBESE, LE, Novel *see* Henri Beraud

MARTYRS OF THE ALAMO, Novel *see* Theodosia Harris

MARUJA, Boston 1885, Novel *see* Bret Harte

MARUSIA, 1872, Play *see* Mikhaylo Petrovich Staritsky

MARUXA, Opera *see* Luis Pascual Frutos, Amadeo Vives

MARVEILLEUSE ANGELIQUE, Novel *see* Anne Golon, Serge Golon

MARVELOUS HERO, Novel *see* Liu Liu

MARVELOUS LAND OF OZ, THE, Chicago 1904, Novel *see* L. Frank Baum

MARVIN'S ROOM, Play *see* Scott McPherson

MARY ANN, New York 1958, Novel *see* Alex Karmel

MARY CARY, "FREQUENTLY MARTHA", New York 1910, Novel *see* Kate Langley Bosher

MARY GIRL, Play *see* Hope Merrick

MARY HAD A LITTLE., London 1951, Play *see* Muriel Herman, Arthur Herzog Jr.

MARY JANE'S PA, New York 1908, Play *see* Edith Ellis Furness

MARY KEEP YOUR FEET STILL, Short Story *see* Harris Anson

MARY LATIMER, NUN, Novel *see* Eva Elwen

MARY LAVELLE, Novel *see* Kate O'Brien

MARY MARY, New York 1961, Play *see* Jean Kerr

MARY MORELAND, Boston 1915, Novel *see* Marie Van Vorst

MARY OF SCOTLAND, New York 1933, Play *see* Maxwell Anderson

MARY POPPINS, Book *see* P. L. Travers

MARY REGAN, Boston 1918, Novel *see* Leroy Scott

MARY REILLY, Novel *see* Valerie Martin

MARY STUART, Play *see* Friedrich Schiller

MARY THE THIRD, Boston 1923, Play *see* Rachel Crothers

MARY WAS LOVE, Novel *see* Guy Fletcher

MARY-'GUSTA, New York 1916, Novel *see* Joseph C. Lincoln

MARYLAND, MY MARYLAND, 1920, Short Story *see* James Francis Dwyer

MARY'S LAMB, New York 1908, Play *see* Richard Carle

MARYSA, Play *see* Alois Mrstikove, Vilem Mrstikove

MAS ALLA DE LA MUERTE, Novel *see* Jacinto Benavente y Martinez

MASADA, Novel *see* Ernest K. Gann

MASCHENKA, Novel *see* Vladimir Nabokov

MASCHERA E IL VOLTO, LA, 1916, Play *see* Luigi Chiarelli

MASCOTTE DES POILUS, LA, Novel *see* Arnould Galopin

MASCOTTE, LA, Paris 1880, Operetta *see* Chivot, Duru, Edmond Audran

MASCOTTE OF THE THREE STAR, THE, 1921, Short Story *see* J. Allen Dunn

MASCULINE ENDING, A, Novel *see* Joan Smith

MASH, New York 1968, Novel *see* Richard Hooker

MASK OF DIMITRIOS, THE, 1939, Novel *see* Eric Ambler

MASK OF DUST, Novel *see* Jon Manchip White

MASK OF FU MANCHU, THE, New York 1932, Novel *see* Sax Rohmer

MASK, THE, New York 1913, Novel *see* Arthur Hornblow

MASKARAD, 1836, Play *see* Mikhail Lermontov

MASKE IN BLAU, Opera *see* Heinz Hentschke, Fred Raymond

MASKEE, 1926, Short Story *see* Ernest Paynter

MASKEN ERWIN REINERS, DIE, Berlin 1910, Novel *see* Jakob Wassermann

MASQUE, LA, 1908, Play *see* Henry Bataille

MASQUE, LE, 1890, Short Story *see* Guy de Maupassant

MASQUE OF THE RED DEATH, THE, 1842, Short Story *see* Edgar Allan Poe

MASQUERADER, THE, London 1904, Novel *see* Katherine Cecil Thurston

MASQUERADER, THE, New York 1917, Play *see* John Hunter Booth

MASQUERADERS, THE, Play *see* Cyril Campion

MASQUERADERS, THE, London 1894, Play *see* Henry Arthur Jones

MASS APPEAL, Play *see* Bill C. Davis

MASSACRE, Story *see* James Warner Bellah

MASSACRE RIVER, Novel *see* Harold Bell Wright

MASSINELLI IN VACANZA, Play *see* Eduardo Ferravilla

MASTER AND MAN, London 1889, Play *see* Henry Pettitt, George R. Sims

MASTER BOB GAGNANT DU PRIX DE L'AVENIR, Play *see* Henri de Brisay

MASTER CRACKSMAN, THE, Story *see* Stephen Allen Reynolds

MASTER CROOK, Play *see* Bruce Walker

MASTER HAND, THE, New York 1907, Play *see* Carroll Fleming

MASTER I MARGARITA, 1967, Novel *see* Mikhail Bulgakov

MASTER KEY, THE, Story *see* John Fleming Wilson

MASTER MIND, THE, New York 1913, Play *see* Daniel D. Carter

MASTER MUMMER, THE, London 1905, Novel *see* E. Phillips Oppenheim

MASTER OF BALLANTRAE, THE, 1888, Novel *see* Robert Louis Stevenson

MASTER OF CRAFT, A, Short Story *see* W. W. Jacobs

MASTER OF DRAGONARD HILL, Novel *see* Rupert Galchrist

MASTER OF MEN, A, 1901, Novel *see* E. Phillips Oppenheim

MASTER OF THE GAME, Novel *see* Sidney Sheldon

MASTER OF THE HOUNDS, Novel *see* Algis Budrys

MASTER OF THE HOUSE, THE, New York 1912, Play *see* Edgar James

MASTERDETEKTIVEN OCH RASMUS, Novel *see* Astrid Lindgren

MASTERFUL HIRELING, THE, Story *see* Roy Norton

MASTERS OF MEN; A ROMANCE OF THE NEW NAVY, New York 1901, Novel *see* Morgan Robertson

MAT, 1906, Novel *see* Maxim Gorky

MATCH BREAKER, THE, Story *see* Meta White

MATCH KING, THE, New York 1932, Novel *see* Einar Thorvaldson

MATELOT 512, LE, Novel *see* Emile Guinde

MATER ADMIRABILIS, Novel *see* Lucio d'Ambra

MATER DOLOROSA, 1882, Novel *see* Gerolamo Rovetta

MATERASSO DI MARIA RICCHEZZA, IL, Novel *see* Michele d'Avino

MATERIA DE MEMORIA, 1962, Novel *see* Carlos Heitor Cony

MATERINSKOE POLE, 1963, Short Story *see* Chingiz Aitmatov

MATERNELLE, LA, Novel *see* Leon Frapie

MATERNITA, 1903, Play *see* Roberto Bracco

MATHIAS SANDORF, 1885, Novel *see* Jules Verne

MATHILDE ET SES MITAINES, Novel *see* Tristan Bernard

MATHILDE MOHRING, 1907, Novel *see* Theodor Fontane

MATILDA, Novel *see* Roald Dahl, Paul Gallico

MATILDA SHOUTED FIRE, Play *see* Janet Green

MATING CALL, THE, New York 1927, Novel *see* Rex Beach

MATING OF MARCUS, THE, Novel *see* Mabel Barnes Grundy

MATING OF MILLIE, THE, Novel *see* Adele Comandini

MATIR MANISHA, 1930, Novel *see* Kalindi Charan Panigrahi

MATKA JOANNA OD ANIOLOW, 1946, Short Story *see* Jaroslaw Iwaszkiewicz

MATKA KROLOW, 1957, Novel *see* Kazimierz Brandys

MATOU, LE, Novel *see* Yves Beauchemin

MATRIARKHAT, 1967, Novel *see* Georgi Mishev

MATRICULE 33, Play *see* Robert Bouchard, Alex Madis

MATRIMONIAL BED, THE, New York 1927, Play *see* Seymour Hicks, Yves Mirande, Andre Mouezy-Eon

MATRIMONIO SEGRETO, IL, Opera *see* Giovanni Bertati, Domenico Cimarosa

MATRON'S REPORT, THE, 1928, Short Story *see* Frederick Hazlitt Brennan

MATS-PETER, Novel *see* John Einar Aberg

MATT, Novel *see* Robert Buchanan

MATTER OF CONVICTION, A, New York 1959, Novel *see* Evan Hunter

MATTER OF MEAN ELEVATION, A, 1910, Short Story *see* O. Henry

MATTER OF PRIDE, 1937, Short Story *see* William C. White

MATURA, Budapest 1935, Play *see* Ladislaus Fodor

MATURA-REISE, Berne 1942, Novel *see* Paul Mathies, Paul Matthias

MATURE, Play *see* Ladislaus Fodor

MAUD, Poem *see* Alfred Tennyson

MAUD MULLER, 1854, Poem *see* John Greenleaf Whittier

MAULKORB, DER, Novel *see* Heinrich Spoerl

MAUPRAT, Novel *see* George Sand

MAURICE, 1971, Novel *see* E. M. Forster

MAURICE GUEST, 1908, Novel *see* Ethel Florence Richardson

MAURIN DES MAURES, 1905, Novel *see* Jean Aicard

MAUVAIS CORPS, LES, Paris 1948, Novel *see* Roger Vailland

MAUVAIS GARCON, LE, Play *see* Jacques Deval

MAUVAISES FREQUENTATIONS, LES, Novel *see* Louis Thomas

MAUVAISES RENCONTRES, LES, Novel *see* Cecil Saint-Laurent

MAVERICK QUEEN, THE, 1953, Novel *see* Romer Grey, Zane Grey

MAVERICK, THE, Short Story *see* Leonard Praskins, Barney Slater

MAVERICKS, New York 1912, Novel *see* William MacLeod Raine

MAX ET LES FERRAILLEURS, Novel *see* Claude Neron

MAX HAVELAAR, 1859, Novel *see* Eduard Douwes Dekker

MAX UND MORITZ: EINE BUBENGESCHICHTE IN SIEBEN STREICHEN, 1865, Short Story *see* Wilhelm Busch

MAXIME, Paris 1929, Novel *see* Henri Duvernois

MAY BLOSSOM, New York 1884, Play *see* David Belasco

MAY QUEEN, THE, Poem *see* Alfred Tennyson

MAY THE BEST WIFE WIN, Story *see* Mona Williams

MAY WE COME IN, Play *see* Harry Segall

MAYA, Play *see* Simon Gantillon

MAYBE I'LL PITCH FOREVER, Autobiography *see* Satchel Page

MAYERLING, Paris 1931, Book *see* Claude Anet

MAYNILA, SA MGA KUKO NG LIWANAG, Novel *see* Edgardo Reyes

MAYOR OF CASTERBRIDGE, THE, 1886, Novel *see* Thomas Hardy

MAYOR OF FILBERT, THE, Chicago 1916, Novel *see* Charles Francis Stocking

MAYORDOMIA, LA, Mexico City 1952, Novel *see* Rogelio Barriga Rivas

MAYOR'S WIFE, THE, Indianapolis 1907, Novel *see* Anna Katharine Green

MAYSKAYA NOCH, 1831, Short Story *see* Nikolay Gogol

MAYTIME, New York 1917, Play *see* Cyrus Wood, Rida Johnson Young

MAZEPA, 1840, Play *see* Juliusz Slowacki

MAZEPPA, Poem *see* Lord Byron

MAZES & MONSTERS, Novel *see* Rona Jaffe

MAZHKI VREMENA, 1967, Short Story *see* Nikolai Haitov

MAZZETTA, LA, Novel *see* Attilio Veraldi

MCCABE, Novel *see* Edmund Naughton

MCFADDEN'S ROW OF FLATS, London 1896, Play *see* Gus Hill

MCGLUSKY THE SEA ROVER, Novel *see* A. G. Hales

MCLEOD'S FOLLY, 1939, Short Story *see* Louis Bromfield

MCPHEE'S SENSATIONAL REST, 1917, Short Story *see* George Foxhall

MCTEAGUE; A STORY OF SAN FRANCISCO, New York 1899, Novel *see* Frank Norris

MCVICAR BY HIMSELF, Autobiography *see* John McVicar

ME, Play *see* Martin Kinch

ME AN' SHORTY, New York 1929, Novel *see* Clarence E. Mulford

ME AND MY GIRL, London 1937, Musical Play *see* Douglas Furber, Noel Gay, Louis Rose

ME AND THE ARCH KOOK PETULIA, New York 1966, Novel *see* John Haase

ME AND THE GIRLS, 1965, Short Story *see* Noel Coward

ME FAIRE CA A MOI, Novel *see* Jean-Michel Sorel

ME, GANGSTER, New York 1927, Novel *see* Charles Francis Coe

ME, NATALIE, Novel *see* Stanley Shapiro

ME TOO, Novel *see* Ed Davis

MEANEST MAN IN THE WORLD, THE, 1915, Play *see* Everett S. Ruskay

MEANEST MAN IN THE WORLD, THE, New York 1920, Play *see* George M. Cohan, Augustin MacHugh

MEANS OF EVIL, Novel *see* Ruth Rendell

MEASURE FOR MEASURE, c1604, Play *see* William Shakespeare

MEASURE OF A MAN, THE, New York 1911, Novel *see* Norman Duncan

MEASURE OF LEON DUBRAY, THE, Story *see* Harvey Gates

MECTA LJUBVI, 1911, Play *see* Aleksander Kosotorov

MEDAILLE, DIE, Play *see* Ludwig Thoma

MEDAL FOR THE GENERAL, Novel *see* James Ronald

MEDEA, 431 bc, Play *see* Euripides

MEDEA DI PORTAMEDINA, 1882, Novel *see* Francesco Mastriani

MEDECIN DES ENFANTS, LE, Play *see* Anicet Bourgeois, Adolphe-P. d'Ennery

MEDECIN DES FOLLES, LE, 1891, Novel *see* Xavier de Montepin

MEDECIN MALGRE LUI, LE, 1666, Play *see* Moliere

MEDIATOR, THE, New York 1913, Novel *see* Roy Norton

MEDICINE MAN, THE, Play *see* Elliott Lester

MEDICO A PALOS, EL, Play *see* Leandro Fernandez de Moratin

MEDICO DELLA MUTUA, IL, Novel *see* Giuseppe d'Agata

MEDUSA TOUCH, THE, Novel *see* Peter Van Greenway

MEDVED, 1888, Play *see* Anton Chekhov

MEDVEDI A TANECNICE, Novel *see* Karel Novak

MEEK CREATURE, THE, Story *see* Fyodor Dostoyevsky

MEER, DAS, Novel *see* Bernhard Kellermann

MEET A BODY, Play *see* Sidney Gilliat, Frank Launder

MEET ME IN ST. LOUIS, 1942, Short Story *see* Sally Benson

MEET THE EXECUTIONER, Story *see* Frederick C. Davis

MEET THE TIGER, Novel *see* Leslie Charteris

MEET THE WIFE, New York 1923, Play *see* Lynn Starling

MEFIEZ-VOUS FILLETTES, Novel *see* James Hadley Chase

MEG THE LADY, Novel *see* Tom Gallon

MEGSTONE PLOT, THE, Novel *see* Andrew Garve

MEIDO NO HIKYAKU (THE COURIER TO HELL), Play *see* Monzaemon Chikamatsu

MEILLEURE MAITRESSE, LA, Novel *see* Georges Oudart

MEILLEURE PART, LA, Novel *see* Philippe Saint-Gil

MEIN EIGENES PROPRES GELD, Book *see* Eberhard Frowein

MEIN LEOPOLD, Play *see* Adolphe L'Arronge

MEIN ONKEL THEODOR, Novel *see* Gunter Spang

MEIN SCHULFREUND, Novel *see* Johannes Mario Simmel

MEINE 99 BRAUTE, Novel *see* Siegfried Sommer

MEINE FREUNDIN BARBARA, Play *see* Willi Kollo

MEINE NICHTE SUSANNE, Play *see* Hans Adler, Alexander Steinbrecker

MEINE SCHONE MAMA, Novel *see* Mathilde Malewska

MEINE TANTE - DEINE TANTE, Play *see* Walter Supper

MEINE TOCHTER TUT DAS NICHT, Play *see* Calmar von Csatho

MEINEIDBAUER, DER, 1891, Play *see* Ludwig Anzengruber

MEINES VATERS PFERDE, Novel *see* Clemens Laar

MEISEKEN, Play *see* Hans Alfred Kihn

MEISJE MET HET RODE HAAR, HET, Novel *see* Theun de Vries

MEISTER, DER, 1909, Play *see* Hermann Bahr

MEISTERSINGER VON NURNBERG, DIE, Munich 1868, Opera *see* Richard Wagner

MEJ-DIDI, 1915, Short Story *see* Sarat Candra Cattopadhyay

MEJOR, ALCALDE, EL REY, EL, 1620-23, Play *see* Lope de Vega

MELA MARCIA, LA, Novel *see* Peter Maas

MELANCHOLY HUSSAR OF THE GERMAN LEGION, THE, Short Story *see* Thomas Hardy

MELIA NO-GOOD, 1917, Short Story *see* I. A. R. Wylie

MELO, Play *see* Henri Bernstein

MELOCOTON EN ALMIBAR, 1959, Play *see* Miguel Mihura Santos

MELODEON, THE, Novel *see* Glendon Swarthout

MELODY MAN, THE, New York 1924, Musical Play *see* Herbert Fields, Lorenz Hart, Richard Rodgers

MELODY OF DEATH, THE, London 1915, Novel *see* Edgar Wallace

MELTING POT, THE, London 1908, Novel *see* Israel Zangwill

MELVILLE GOODWIN U.S.A., 1951, Novel *see* John Phillips Marquand

MEMBER OF TATTERSALLS, A, Play *see* H. V. Browning

MEMBER OF THE JURY, Novel *see* John Millard

MEMBER OF THE WEDDING, THE, 1946, Novel *see* Carson McCullers

MEMED MY HAWK, Novel *see* Yashar Kemal

MEMENTO MORI, Novel *see* Muriel Spark

MEMENTO, THE, 1908, Short Story *see* O. Henry

MEMO ON KATHY O'ROURKE, Short Story *see* Jack Sher

MEMOIRE ET RAPPORT SUR VICTOR DE L'AVEYRON, Paris 1801-07, *see* Jean Itard

MEMOIRES DE JACQUES CASANOVA DE SEINGALT, 1826-38, Autobiography *see* Giacomo Casanova

MEMOIRS D'UN MEDECIN, Paris 1848, Novel *see* Alexandre Dumas (pere)

MEMOIRS OF A SURVIVOR, 1974, Novel *see* Doris Lessing

MEMOIRS OF AN INVISIBLE MAN, Novel *see* H. F. Saint

MEMOIRS OF BARRY LYNDON ESQ., THE, 1856, Novel *see* William Makepeace Thackeray

MEMOIRS OF JOHNNY DAZE, Play *see* John Beckett Wimbs

MEMORIAL DE SAINTE-HELENE, Play *see* Jules Barbier, Michel Carre

MEMORIAS DE UM GIGOLO, 1968, Novel *see* Marcos Rey

MEMORIAS DEL SUBDESARROLLO, 1965, Novel *see* Edmundo Desnoes

MEMORIAS DO CARCERE, 1953, Novel *see* Graciliano Ramos

MEMORIAS POSTUMAS DE BRAS CUBAS, 1881, Novel *see* Joaquim Maria Machado de Assis

MEMORIE DEL SOTTOSUOLO, Short Story *see* Fyodor Dostoyevsky

MEMORIE DI UN LADRO, LE, 1907, *see* Ferdinando Russo

MEMORIE DI UNA LADRA, Novel *see* Dacia Maraini

MEMORIES OF MIDNIGHT, Novel *see* Sidney Sheldon

MEMORY OF EVA RYKER, THE, Novel *see* Donald A. Stanwood

MEMORY OF LOVE, New York 1934, Novel *see* Bessie Breuer

MEN, Novel *see* Margaret Diehl
MEN, New York 1916, Play *see* H. S. Sheldon

MEN AGAINST THE SEA, 1934, Novel *see* James N. Hall, Charles Nordhoff

MEN AND WOMEN, Play *see* David Belasco, Henry C. de Mille

MEN ARE SUCH FOOLS, New York 1936, Novel *see* Faith Baldwin

MEN GUM (GANG LAW), Novel *see* Li XIao

MEN IN THE RAW, Short Story *see* W. Bert Foster

MEN IN WHITE, New York 1933, Play *see* Sidney Kingsley

MEN MUST FIGHT, New York 1932, Play *see* S. K. Lauren, Reginald Lawrence

MEN OF IRON, 1954, Novel *see* Howard Pyle

MEN OF STEEL, Novel *see* Douglas Newton

MEN OF ZANZIBAR, THE, 1913, Short Story *see* Richard Harding Davis

MEN SHE MARRIED, THE, 1916, Novel *see* Harold Vickers

MEN WITHOUT A PAST, Play *see* Jacques Maret

MEN WITHOUT COUNTRY, 1944, Novel *see* James N. Hall, Charles Nordhoff

MEN, WOMEN AND MONEY, 1918, Short Story *see* Cosmo Hamilton

MENACE, New York 1933, Novel *see* Philip MacDonald

MENACE, LA, Play *see* Pierre Frondaie

MENACE OF THE MUTE, THE, 1910, Short Story *see* John Thomas McIntyre

MENDEL, INC., New York 1929, Play *see* David Freedman

MENDEL PHILIPSEN AND SON, Novel *see* Henri Nathensen

MENDIANTE DE SAINT-SULPICE, LA, Novel *see* Xavier de Montepin

MENDICANTE DI SASSONIA, LA, Novel *see* Bourgeois

MENESGAZDA, A, Novel *see* Istvan Gall

MENEUR DE JOIES, LE, Novel *see* Georges-Andre Cuel

MENILMONTANT, Novel *see* Roger Devigne

MENINO DE ENGENHO, 1932, Novel *see* Jose Lins Do Rego

MENNESKER MODES OG SOD MUSIK OPSTAR I HJERTET, Copenhagen 1945, Novel *see* Jens August Schade

MEN'S CLUB, THE, Novel *see* Leonard Michaels

MENSCHEN IM HOTEL, Berlin 1929, Novel *see* Vicki Baum

MENSCHEN IM NETZ, Munich 1957, Book *see* Erich Kern

MENSCHENWEE, 1903, Novel *see* Israel Querido

MENSONGE DE NINA PETROVNA, LE, Novel *see* Hans Szekely

MENTIONED IN CONFIDENCE, Short Story *see* Howard Fielding

MENUET, Book *see* Louis Paul Boon

MEO PATACCA, Poem *see* Giuseppe Berneri

MEPHISTO, 1936, Novel *see* Klaus Mann

MEPHISTO WALTZ, THE, Novel *see* Fred Mustard Stewart

MERAVIGLIA DI DAMASCO, LA, Musical Play *see* Joaquin Abati, Manuel Paso

MERCADET, 1851, Play *see* Honore de Balzac

MERCHANT OF VENICE, THE, c1595, Play *see* William Shakespeare

MERCHANT OF YONKERS, THE, New York 1938, Play *see* Thornton Wilder

MERCY ISLAND, Novel *see* Theodore Pratt

MERE, LA, 1907, Play *see* Santiago Rusinol I Prats

MERELY MARY ANN, London 1893, Novel *see* Israel Zangwill

MERMAID, Novel *see* Matsutaro Kawaguchi

MERMAIDS, Novel *see* Patty Dann

MERRY ANDREW, New York 1929, Play *see* Lewis Beach

MERRY WIVES OF GOTHAM; OR TWO AND SIXPENCE, New York 1924, Play *see* Laurence Eyre

MERRY WIVES OF WINDSOR, THE, c1598, Play *see* William Shakespeare

MERRY-GO-ROUND, New York 1932, Play *see* Albert Maltz, George Sklar

MERTEDI DEL DIAVOLO, I, Novel *see* Enzo Russo

MERTON OF THE MOVIES, New York 1922, Novel *see* Harry Leon Wilson

MERVEILLEUSE JOURNEE, LA, Play *see* Yves Mirande, Gustave Quinson

MERY PER SEMPERE, Novel *see* Aurelio Grimaldi

MES, HET, Novel *see* Hugo Claus

MES NUITS SONT PLUS BELLES QUE VOS JOURS, Novel *see* Raphaelle Billetdoux

MESE HABBAL, 1934, Novel *see* Zsigmond Remenyik

MESE MARIANO, 1898, Play *see* Salvatore Di Giacomo

MESHI, 1951, Novel *see* Fumiko Hayashi

MESQUITE JENKINS, TUMBLEWEED, New York 1932, Novel *see* Clarence E. Mulford

MESSAGE FROM MARS, A, London 1899, Play *see* Richard Ganthony

MESSAGE IN A BOTTLE, Novel *see* Nicholas Sparks

MESSAGE, THE, Story *see* Brandon Fleming

MESSAGE TO BUCKSHOT JOHN, THE, 1912, Novel *see* Charles E. Van Loan

MESSAGE TO GARCIA, A, 1899, Essay *see* Elbert Hubbard

MESSAGER, LE, Play *see* Henri Bernstein

MESSIEURS LES RONDS-DE-CUIR, 1893, Novel *see* Georges Courteline

MEST, 1886, Short Story *see* Anton Chekhov

MESTECKO NA DLANI, Novel *see* Jan Drda

MESYATS V DEREVNE, 1855, Play *see* Ivan Turgenev

METAL MESSIAH, Play *see* Stephen Zoller

METAMORPHOSE DES CLOPORTES, LA, Paris 1962, Novel *see* Alphonse Boudard

METAMORPHOSES, c2-8, Verse *see* Ovid

METEL', 1831, Short Story *see* Alexander Pushkin

METELLO, 1955, Novel *see* Vasco Pratolini

METEOR, THE, Short Story *see* Ray Bradbury

METER MAN, THE, London 1964, Play *see* C. Scott Forbes

METHINKS THE LADY, Novel *see* Guy Endore

METHOD FOR MURDER, Short Story *see* Robert Bloch

METIER DE FEMME, Play *see* Andre-Paul Antoine

METROLAND, 1980, Novel *see* Julian Barnes

METTI - UNA SERA A CENA, Play *see* Giuseppe Patroni Griffi

METZENGERSTEIN, 1832, Short Story *see* Edgar Allan Poe

MEU DESTINO E PECAR, 1944, Novel *see* Nelson Rodrigues

MEURTRE D'UN SERIN, Novel *see* Sophie Cathala

MEURTRE EST UN MEURTRE, UN, Novel *see* Dominique Fabre

MEURTRES, Novel *see* Charles Plisnier

MEURTRIER DE THEODORE, LE, Play *see* Bernard, Brot, Clairville

MEUTRE A L'ASILE, Zurich 1936, Novel *see* Friedrich Glauser

MEXICAN HAYRIDE, Musical Play *see* Dorothy Fields, Herbert Fields, Cole Porter

MEXICAN, THE, 1913, Short Story *see* Jack London

MEXICAN VILLAGE, A, 1945, Novel *see* Josefina Niggli

MEYER LANSKY: MOGUL OF THE MOB, Book *see* Uri Dan, Dennis Eisenberg, Eli Landau

MEYER L'IPOCRITA, Novel *see* Charles Burlington

MI BODA CONTIGO, Novel *see* Corin Tellado

MI HERMANA ANTONIA, 1909, Short Story *see* Ramon Maria Del Valle-Inclan

MI IDOLATRADO HIJO SISI, 1953, Novel *see* Miguel Delibes

MIA ESISTENZA D'ACQUARIO, LA, *see* Pier Maria Rosso Di San Secondo

MIA FIA, 1878, Play *see* Giacinto Gallina

MIA MOGLIE MI PIACE DI PIU, Play *see* Luis Alfayate, Luis Tejador

MIA MOGLIE SI E FIDANZATA, 1914, Play *see* Gino Calza-Bini

MIAMI BLUES, Novel *see* Charles Willeford

MIAMI MAYHEM, New York 1960, Novel *see* Anthony Rome

MIARKA, LA FILLE A L'OURSE, Novel *see* Jean Richepin

MICE AND MEN, Manchester 1901, Play *see* Madeleine Lucette Ryley

MICHAEL AND HIS LOST ANGEL, London 1896, Play *see* Henry Arthur Jones

MICHAEL AND MARY, London 1930, Play *see* A. A. Milne

MICHAEL O'HALLORAN, New York 1915, Novel *see* Gene Stratton-Porter

MICHAEL SHAYNE, DETECTIVE, Novel *see* Brett Halliday

MICHAEL SHELI, 1968, Novel *see* Amos Oz

MICHAEL THWAITE'S WIFE, New York 1909, Novel *see* Miriam Michelson

MICHE, Play *see* Etienne Rey

MICHEL KOHLHAAS, 1810, Short Story *see* Heinrich von Kleist

MICHEL STROGOFF, Paris 1876, Novel *see* Jules Verne

MICHELE PERRIN, 1834, Play *see* C. Duveyrier, Melesville

MICHELINE, Novel *see* Andre Theuriet

MICHIGAN KID, THE, 1925, Short Story *see* Rex Beach

MICROBE, THE, 1919, Short Story *see* Henry Altimus

MIDAS TOUCH, THE, Novel *see* Margaret Kennedy

MID-CHANNEL, New York 1910, Play *see* Arthur Wing Pinero

MIDDLE AGE SPREAD, Play *see* Roger Hall

MIDDLE OF THE NIGHT, 1954, Television Play *see* Paddy Chayefsky

MIDDLE WATCH, THE, London 1929, Play *see* Ian Hay, Stephen King-Hall

MIDDLEMAN, THE, London 1889, Play *see* Henry Arthur Jones

MIDDLEMARCH, 1872, Novel *see* George Eliot

MIDLANDERS, THE, Indianapolis 1912, Novel *see* Charles Tenney Jackson

MIDNIGHT, New York 1930, Play *see* Claire Sifton, Paul Sifton

MIDNIGHT ALARM, THE, Play *see* James W. Harkins Jr.

MIDNIGHT AND JEREMIAH, Novel *see* Sterling North

MIDNIGHT BELL, A, Play *see* Charles Hale Hoyt

MIDNIGHT CALL, THE, Story *see* James Oliver Curwood

MIDNIGHT CLEAR, A, Novel *see* William Wharton

MIDNIGHT COWBOY, New York 1965, Novel *see* James Leo Herlihy

MIDNIGHT EXPRESS, Book *see* Billy Hayes, William Hoffer

MIDNIGHT IN ST. PETERSBURG, Novel *see* Len Deighton

MIDNIGHT IN THE GARDEN OF GOOD AND EVIL, Book *see* John Berendt

MIDNIGHT RIDE OF PAUL REVERE, THE, Poem *see* Henry Wadsworth Longfellow

MIDNIGHT ROMANCE, A, Short Story *see* Marion Orth

MIDNIGHT SUMMONS, THE, Short Story *see* Sax Rohmer

MIDNIGHT SUN, THE, Story *see* Lauridas Brunn

MIDSHIPMAID, THE, London 1931, Play *see* Ian Hay, Stephen King-Hall

MIDSUMMER NIGHT'S DREAM, A, c1594, Play *see* William Shakespeare

MIDT I EN JAZZTID, 1931, Novel *see* Knud Sonderby

MIDWICH CUCKOOS, THE, 1957, Novel *see* John Wyndham

MIDWIFE OF PONT CLERY, THE, New York 1957, Novel *see* Flora Sandstrom

MIE PRIGIONI, LE, 1832, Novel *see* Silvio Pellico

MIEHEN TIE, 1932, Novel *see* Frans E. Sillanpaa

MIEI PRIMI QUARANT'ANNI, I, Novel *see* Marina Ripa Di Meana

MIEKO, Serial *see* Saburo Okada

MIGNON, Paris 1866, Opera *see* Ambroise Thomas

MIJNHEER HAT LAUTER TOCHTER, Book *see* Maria Becker

MIKADO, THE, London 1885, Opera *see* W. S. Gilbert, Arthur Sullivan

MIKE, 1933, Short Story *see* Grace Perkins

MILAGRO BEANFIELD WAR, THE, Novel *see* John Nichols

MILAGRO DE LA VEGA DE TOLEDO, EL, Poem *see* Jose Zorrilla Y Moral

MILAGRO EN LA PLAZA DEL PROGRESO, 1954, Play *see* Joaquin Calvo Sotelo

MILANESI AMMAZZANO AL SABATO, I, Novel *see* Giorgio Scerbanenco

MILANO CALIBRO 9, Novel *see* Giorgio Scerbanenco

MILCZENIE, Novel *see* Jerzy Szczygiel

MILDRED PIERCE, 1941, Novel *see* James M. Cain

MILE-A-MINUTE KENDALL, New York 1916, Play *see* Owen Davis

MILECHAN, Short Story *see* Ambai

MILES BREWSTER AND THE SUPER SEX, 1921, Short Story *see* Frank R. Adams

MILESTONES, London 1912, Play *see* Arnold Bennett, Edward Knoblock

MILIONARIO SI RIBELLA, UN, Novel *see* Raffaele Carrieri

MILITIZIA TERRITORIALE, Play *see* Aldo de Benedetti

MILITONA, LA, Novel *see* Theophile Gautier

MILK TRAIN DOESN'T STOP HERE ANY MORE, THE, New York 1962, Play *see* Tennessee Williams

MILKWHITE UNICORN, THE, Novel *see* Flora Sandstrom

MILKY WAY, THE, Play *see* J. W. Drawbell, Reginald Simpson

MILKY WAY, THE, New York 1934, Play *see* Harry Clork, Lynn Root

MILL ON THE FLOSS, THE, London 1860, Novel *see* George Eliot

MILLICENT AND THERESE, Short Story *see* Richard Matheson

MILLIE, New York 1930, Novel *see* Donald Henderson Clarke

MILLIE'S DAUGHTER, Novel *see* Donald Henderson Clarke

MILLION A MINUTE: A ROMANCE OF MODERN NEW YORK AND PARIS, A, New York 1908, Novel *see* Robert Aitken

MILLION DE DOT, UN, Novel *see* Daniel Riche

MILLION DOLLAR MYSTERY, THE, Story *see* Harold MacGrath

MILLION DOLLAR STORY, THE, London 1926, Novel *see* Edgar Wallace

MILLION, LE, Paris 1910, Play *see* Georges Berr, Marcel Guillemaud

MILLION POUND DAY, THE, Short Story *see* Leslie Charteris

MILLIONAIRE BABY, THE, Indianapolis 1905, Novel *see* Anna Katharine Green Rohlfs

MILLIONAIRE POLICEMAN, THE, Story *see* Samuel J. Briskin

MILLIONAIRESS, THE, New York 1936, Play *see* George Bernard Shaw

MILLS OF GOD, THE, Novel *see* Ernst Lothar

MILLS OF THE GODS, THE, Poem *see* Edward Madden

MILLS OF THE GODS, THE, New York 1907, Play *see* George Broadhurst

MILLSTONE, THE, London 1964, Novel *see* Margaret Drabble

MILOVANI ZAKAZANO, Novel *see* Jan Sedlak

MIMI BLUETTE FIORE DEL MIO GIARDINO, Novel *see* Guido Da Verona

MIMI TROTTIN, Novel *see* Marcel Nadaud

MIMIC, Short Story *see* Donald A. Wolheim

MIMO PROUD, Play *see* Emil Synek

MIN MARION, 1972, Novel *see* Terje Stigen

MINA DE VANGHEL, 1855, Short Story *see* Stendhal

MINA DROMMARS STAD, Novel *see* Per Anders Fogelstrom

MIND OF MR. REEDER, THE, London 1925, Novel *see* Edgar Wallace

MIND OF MR. SOAMES, THE, London 1961, Novel *see* Charles Eric Maine

MIND OVER MOTOR, 1912, Short Story *see* Mary Roberts Rinehart

"MIND-THE-PAINT" GIRL, THE, London 1912, Play *see* Arthur Wing Pinero

MINE OWN EXECUTIONER, 1945, Novel *see* Nigel Balchin

MINE WITH THE IRON DOOR, THE, New York 1923, Novel *see* Harold Bell Wright

MINISTRY OF FEAR, 1943, Novel *see* Graham Greene

MINNA VON BARNHEIM; ODER DAS SOLDATENGLUCK, Hamburg 1767, Play *see* Gotthold Ephraim Lessing

MINNIE, Novel *see* Hans Werner Kettenbach

MINUIT PLACE PIGALLE, Novel *see* Maurice Dekobra

MINUIT QUAI DE BERCY, Novel *see* Pierre Lambin

MINUS MAN, THE, 1990, Novel *see* Lew McCreary

MINUTE'S WAIT, A, Play *see* Martin McHugh

MINYA ZAVUR ARLEKIN, Play *see* Juri Schtschekotschichin

MIO, MIN MIO!, Novel *see* Astrid Lindgren

MIO SOCIO DAVIS, IL, Novel *see* Gennaro Prieto

MIO ZIO BARBASSOUS, 1891, Play *see* E. Blavet, Fabrice Carre

MIQUETTE ET SA MERE, Play *see* Gaston Arman de Caillavet, Robert de Flers

MIR LOND NOD LUGG, Play *see* Rudolf Eger

MIRABELLE, Play *see* Guy Bolton

MIRACLE, New York 1925, Novel *see* Clarence Budington Kelland

MIRACLE BABY, THE, 1921, Short Story *see* Frank Richardson Pierce

MIRACLE DES LOUPS, LE, Novel *see* Henri Dupuy-Mazuel

MIRACLE IN THE RAIN, 1943, Novel *see* Ben Hecht

MIRACLE MAN, THE, New York 1914, Novel *see* Frank L. Packard

MIRACLE OF HATE, THE, Story *see* William Blacke, James Shelley Hamilton

MIRACLE OF LOVE, THE, New York 1915, Novel *see* Cosmo Hamilton

MIRACLE OF THE BELLS, THE, Novel *see* Richard Janney

MIRACLE ON GREENPOINT, Novel *see* Edward Redlinski

MIRACLE, THE, Short Story *see* Sax Rohmer

MIRACLE WORKER, THE, New York 1959, Play *see* William Gibson

MIRACOLA, IL, Play *see* Mario Amendola

MIRADA DEL HOMBRE OSCURO, LA, Play *see* Ignacio Del Moral

MIRADA DEL OTRO, LA, Novel *see* Fernando G. Delgado

MIRAGE DU COEUR, LE, Short Story *see* Georges Dolley

MIRAGE, THE, Novel *see* E. Temple Thurston

MIRAGE, THE, New York 1920, Play *see* Edgar Selwyn

MIRAKEL, DAS, 1911, Play *see* Karl Vollmoller

MIRANDA, Play *see* Peter Blackmore

MIRANDA OF THE BALCONY, Novel *see* A. E. W. Mason

MIREILLE, Poem *see* Frederic Mistral

MIRELE EFROS, 1898, Play *see* Jacob Gordin

MIRENTXU, Novel *see* Pierre Lhande

MIRIAM, 1944, Short Story *see* Truman Capote
MIRIAM, 1954, Novel *see* Walentin Chorell

MIRIAM ROZELLA, Novel *see* B. J. Farjeon

MIRROR AND MARKHEIM, THE, Short Story *see* Robert Louis Stevenson

MIRROR CRACK'D FROM SIDE TO SIDE, THE, Novel *see* Agatha Christie

MIRROR IN MY HOUSE, 1956, Autobiography *see* Sean O'Casey

MISANTHROPE, LE, 1666, Play *see* Moliere

MISCHIEF, 1950, Novel *see* Charlotte Armstrong
MISCHIEF, London 1928, Play *see* Ben Travers

MISCONDUCT, Play *see* Graham Hope

MISDEAL, Play *see* Basil Dillon Woon

MISE A SAC, Novel *see* Donald E. Westlake

MISE EN CAISSE, Novel *see* James Hadley Chase

MISERABLES, LES, Paris 1862, Novel *see* Victor Hugo

MISERERE, EL, 1862, Short Story *see* Gustavo Adolfo Becquer

MISERIA E NOBILTA, 1888, Play *see* Eduardo Scarpetta

MISERICORDE, Short Story *see* Octave Pradels

MISERIE DI MONSU TRAVET, LE, 1871, Play *see* Vittorio Bersezio

MISERY, Novel *see* Stephen King

MISFITS, THE, 1961, Short Story *see* Arthur Miller

MISI MOKUS KALANDJAI, 1953, Novel *see* Jozsi Jeno Tersanszky

MISLEADING LADY, THE, New York 1913, Play *see* Paul Dickey, Charles W. Goddard

MISMATES, New York 1925, Play *see* Myron C. Fagan

MISS 318 AND MR. 37, Story *see* Rupert Hughes

MISS ANTIQUE, 1919, Short Story *see* Nalbro Bartley

MISS BENTON R.N., 1930, Play *see* Florence Johns, William Lackaye Jr.

MISS BISHOP, Novel *see* Bess Streeter Aldrich

MISS BRACEGIRDLE DOES HER DUTY, Short Story *see* Stacy Aumonier

MISS CHARITY, Novel *see* Keble Howard

MISS DORIS - SAFE-CRACKER, 1918, Short Story *see* Jack Boyle

MISS DULCIE FROM DIXIE, 1917, Novel *see* Lulah Ragsdale

MISS EVERS' BOYS, Play *see* David Feldshuh

MISS FIRECRACKER CONTEST, THE, 1985, Play *see* Beth Henley

MISS HELYETT, Operetta *see* Edmond Audran, Maxime Boucheron

MISS HOBBS, New York 1899, Play *see* Jerome K. Jerome

MISS I.Q., Story *see* Hurd Barrett

MISS LONELYHEARTS, New York 1933, Novel *see* Nathanael West

MISS LONELYHEARTS 4122, Novel *see* Colin Watson

MISS LULU BETT, New York 1920, Novel *see* Zona Gale

MISS MAITLAND, PRIVATE SECRETARY, New York 1918, Novel *see* Geraldine Bonner

MISS PACIFIC FLEET, 1934, Short Story *see* Frederick Hazlitt Brennan

MISS PETTICOATS, Boston 1902, Novel *see* Dwight Tilton

MISS PINKERTON: ADVENTURES OF A NURSE DETECTIVE, New York 1932, Novel *see* Mary Roberts Rinehart

MISS RAFFLES, Story *see* C. S. Morton

MISS ROVEL, Novel *see* Victor Cherbuliez

MISS SHUMWAY WAVES A WAND, Novel *see* James Hadley Chase

MISS SUSIE SLAGLE'S, Novel *see* Augusta Tucker

MISS WHEELWRIGHT DISCOVERS AMERICA, Story *see* Leonhard Spiegelgass

MISSBRAUCHTEN LIEBESBRIEFE, DIE, Stuttgart 1865, Short Story *see* Gottfried Keller

MISSING, New York 1917, Novel *see* Mrs. Humphrey Ward

MISSING MEN, New York 1932, Book *see* Capt. John H. Ayers, Carol Bird

MISSING MILLION, THE, London 1923, Novel *see* Edgar Wallace

MISSING THE TIDE, Novel *see* Alfred Turner

MISSING THREE QUARTER, THE, Short Story *see* Arthur Conan Doyle

MISSING WITNESS, THE, Short Story *see* John Hawkins, Ward Hawkins

MISSION FOR GENERAL HOUSTON, A, Story *see* Jess Arnold

MISSION SPECIALE A CARACAS, Novel *see* Claude Rank

MISSION IN TO MOSCOW, Book *see* Joseph E. Davis

MISSION TO VENICE, Novel *see* James Hadley Chase

MISSION WITHOUT A RECORD, Story *see* James Warner Bellah

MISSIONER, THE, London 1908, Novel *see* E. Phillips Oppenheim

MISSISSIPPI, New York 1929, Novel *see* Ben Lucien Berman

MISSOURI TRAVELER, THE, 1955, Novel *see* John Burress

MIST IN THE VALLEY, Novel *see* Dorin Craig

MISTER 44, New York 1916, Novel *see* E. J. Rath

MISTER AND MRS. EDGEHILL, 1951, Short Story *see* Noel Coward

MISTER ANTONIO, Play *see* Booth Tarkington

MISTER CINDERS, London 1929, Musical Play *see* Clifford Grey, Greatrex Newman

MISTER DYNAMIT - MORGEN KUSST EUCH DER TOD, Novel *see* C. H. Guenter

MISTER FLOW, Novel *see* Gaston Leroux

MISTER JOHNSON, 1939, Novel *see* Joyce Cary

MISTER MOSES, London 1961, Novel *see* Max Catto

MISTER ROBERTS, 1946, Novel *see* Thomas Heggen

MISTERI DELLA JUNGLA NERA, I, Genoa 1895, Novel *see* Emilio Salgari

MISTIC, EL, Play *see* Santiago Rusinol

MISTIGRI, 1931, Play *see* Marcel Achard

MISTLETOE BOUGH, THE, Poem *see* E. T. Bayley
MISTLETOE BOUGH, THE, Play *see* Charles Somerset

MISTR OSTREHO MECE, Play *see* Karel Krpata

MISTRAL, LE, Novel *see* Jacques Carton

MISTRESS NELL, New York 1900, Play *see* George Cochrane Hazelton

MISTRESS NELL GWYNNE, Novel *see* Gabrielle Margaret Vere Long

MISTRESS OF SHENSTONE, THE, New York 1910, Novel *see* Florence L. Barclay

MISTY OF CHINCOTEAGUE, Chicago 1947, Novel *see* Marguerite Henry

MISUNDERSTOOD, Novel *see* Florence Montgomery

MIT BESTEN EMPFEHLUNGEN, Play *see* Hans Schubert

MIT HIMBEERGEIST GEHT ALLES BESSER, Novel *see* Johannes Mario Simmel

MITASARETA SEIKATSU, Novel *see* Tatsuzo Ishikawa

MITICA POPESCU, 1928, Play *see* Camil Petrescu

MITREA COCOR, 1949, Novel *see* Mihail Sadoveanu

MITSI, Paris 1922, Novel *see* Delly

MITSOU; OU, COMMENT L'ESPRIT VIENT AUX FILLES, 1919, Novel *see* Sidonie Gabrielle Colette

MITT LIV SOM HUND, Autobiography *see* Reidar Jonsson

MIX ME A PERSON, Novel *see* Jack Trevor Story

MIXED DOUBLES, London 1925, Play *see* Frank Stayton

MIXED FACES, New York 1921, Novel *see* Roy Norton

MIXED RELATIONS, Short Story *see* W. W. Jacobs

MIYAMOTO MUSASHI, 1937-39, Novel *see* Eiji Yoshikawa

MIZPAH; OR LOVE'S SACRIFICE, Play *see* Wood Lawrence

MIZUMI, 1954, Short Story *see* Yasunari Kawabata

MLHY NA BLATECH, Novel *see* Karel Klostermann

M'LISS: AN IDYLL OF RED MOUNTAIN, Boston 1869, Novel *see* Bret Harte

MLLE. FIFI, New York 1899, Play *see* Leo Ditrichstein

M'LORD OF THE WHITE ROAD, Novel *see* Cedric D. Fraser

MLYN NA PONORNE RECE, Prague 1958, Novel *see* Alfred Technik

MLYNAR A JEHO DITE, Play *see* Ernst Raupach

MME RECAMIER ET SES AMIS, *see* Edouard Herriot

MNOGO IL CHELOVKA ZEMLI NUZNO?, 1885, Short Story *see* Lev Nikolayevich Tolstoy

MO, Book *see* Maureen Dean

MOARA CU NOROC, 1881, Short Story *see* Ioan Slavici

MOARA LUI CALIFAR, 1902, Short Story *see* Gala Galaction

MOARTEA INGHITITORULUI DE SABII, 1934, Short Story *see* Alexandru Sahia

MOARTEA LUI IPU, 1970, Short Story *see* Titus Popovici

MOARTEA TINARULUI CU TERMEN REDUS, 1933, Short Story *see* Alexandru Sahia

MOARTEA UNUI ARTIST, 1965, Play *see* Horia Lovinescu

MOB FROM MASSAC, THE, Short Story *see* Irvin S. Cobb

MOB, THE, 1928, Short Story *see* Henry La Cossitt

MOBBED UP, Book *see* James Neff

MOBILIZATION OF JOHANNA, THE, 1917, Short Story *see* Rupert Hughes

MOBY DICK OR THE WHALE, New York 1851, Novel *see* Herman Melville

MOCKINGBIRD, 1891, Short Story *see* Ambrose Bierce

MODCHE A REZI, Short Story *see* Vojtech Rakous

MODEL YOUNG MAN, A, Story *see* Jacques Futrelle

MODELE, LA, 1888, Short Story *see* Guy de Maupassant

MODELLA, LA, 1907, Play *see* Alfredo Testoni

MODERATO CANTABILE, Paris 1958, Novel *see* Marguerite Duras

MODERHJERTET, 1943, Play *see* Leck Fischer

MODERN HERO, A, New York 1932, Novel *see* Louis Bromfield

MODERN MADONNA, A, New York 1906, Novel *see* Carol Abbot Stanley

MODERN MAGDALEN, A, New York 1902, Play *see* C. Haddon Chambers

MODERNI MAGDALENA, *see* Jakub Arbes

MODESTA, Short Story *see* Domingo Silas Ortiz

MODIFICATION, LA, 1957, Novel *see* Michel Butor

MOETSUKITA CHIZU, 1967, Novel *see* Abe Kobo

MOGG MEGONE, Poem *see* John Greenleaf Whittier

MOGLIE DEL DOTTORE, LA, 1908, Play *see* Silvio Zambaldi

MOHAMMED-BIN-TUGHLAQ, Play *see* Cho Ramaswamy

MOHICANS DE PARIS, LES, 1864, Novel *see* Alexandre Dumas (pere)

MOI MON CORPS MON AME MONTREAL ETC., Novel *see* Roger Fournier

MOI UNIVERSITETI, 1921-22, Autobiography *see* Maxim Gorky

MOINE, LE, Novel *see* Matthew Gregory Lewis

MOINES, LES, Belgium 1886, Poem *see* Emile Verhaeren

MOIS D'AVRIL SONT MEURTRIERS, LES, Novel *see* Derek Raymond

MOJU, Short Story see Rampo Edogawa

MOLINOFF INDRE-ET-LOIRE, Paris 1928, Novel see Maurice Bedel

MOLL FLANDERS, 1722, Novel see Daniel Defoe

MOLLENARD, Novel see Oscar-Paul Gilbert

MOLLY AND I AND THE SILVER RING, Boston 1915, Novel see Frank R. Adams

MOLLY BAWN, 1878, Novel see Margaret Wolfe Hungerford

MOLLY MAKE-BELIEVE, New York 1910, Novel see Eleanor Hallowell Abbott

MOLLY, THE DRUMMER BOY, Novel see Harriet T. Comstock

MOLODAYA GVARDIYA, 1945, Novel see Alexander Fadeev

MOM FOR CHRISTMAS, A, Novel see Barbara Dillon

MOME, LA, Play see A. Acremont, Michel Carre

MOME VERT-DE-GRIS, LA, Novel see Peter Cheyney

MOMENT OF BLINDNESS, Play see Jane Baker, Pip Baker

MOMENT OF DEATH, THE, New York 1900, Play see Israel Zangwill

MOMENT OF VICTORY, THE, Short Story see O. Henry

MOMENTO MUY LARGO, UN, Novel see Silvina Bullrich

MOMMIE DEAREST, Book see Christina Crawford

MOMO, Novel see Michael Ende

MON AMI LE CAMBIOLEUR, Play see Andre Haguet

MON AMI SAINFOIN, Novel see Paul-Adrien Schaye

MON BEGUIN, Novel see Paul Forro

MON COEUR AU RALENTI, Novel see Maurice Dekobra

MON CRIME, Paris 1934, Play see Georges Berr, Louis Verneuil

MON CURE CHEZ LES PAUVRES, Novel see Clement Vautel

MON CURE CHEZ LES RICHES, Novel see Clement Vautel

MON DEPUTE ET SA FEMME, Play see Robert Bodet

MON GOSSE DE PERE, Play see Leopold Marchand

MON HOMME, Paris 1921, Play see Francis Carco, Andre Picard

MON ONCLE BENJAMIN, Novel see Claude Tillier

MON ONCLE D'ARLES, Play see Raymond Clauzel

MON PERE AVAIT RAISON, Play see Sacha Guitry

MON PETIT PRETRE, Novel see Pierre Lhande

MON PHOQUE ET ELLES, Novel see Charles de Richter

MON PREMIER AMOUR, Novel see Jack-Alain Leger

MON VILLAGE, see Hansi

MONACA DI MONZA, LA, Novel see Giovanni Rosini

MONACA DI MONZA, LA, Milan 1961, Novel see Mario Mazzucchelli

MONDAY TUESDAY WEDNESDAY, Novel see Robert Houston

MONDE OU L'ON S'ENNUIE, LE, Play see Edouard Pailleron

MONDJAGER, Novel see Sigrid Heuck

MONDO, Novel see Jean-Marie Le Clezio

MONDO VUOLE COSI, IL, Play see Aldo de Benedetti, Mario Luciani

MONDSCHEINGASSE, DIE, Short Story see Stefan Zweig

MONETA SPEZZATA, UNA, Short Story see Romolo Marcellini

MONEY, London 1840, Play see Edward George Bulwer Lytton

MONEY BOX, THE, 1931, Short Story see W. W. Jacobs

MONEY BY WIRE, Play see Edward A. Paulton

MONEY CHANGERS, THE, London 1908, Novel see Upton Sinclair

MONEY FOR NOTHING, Play see Arthur Eckersley, Seymour Hicks, Guy Newall

MONEY FROM HOME, 1935, Short Story see Damon Runyon

MONEY HABIT, THE, Novel see Paul M. Potter

MONEY ISN'T EVERYTHING, Novel see Sophie Cole

MONEY, MADNESS & MURDER, Novel see Shana Alexander

MONEY MAGIC, New York 1907, Novel see Hamlin Garland

MONEY MAKER, THE, New York 1918, Novel see Irving Ross Allen

MONEY MASTER, THE, New York 1915, Novel see Gilbert Parker

MONEY MEN, Novel see Gerald Petievich

MONEY MOON, THE, Novel see Jeffrey Farnol

MONEY MOVERS, THE, Book see Devon Minchin

MONEY, POWER, MURDER, Novel see Mike Lupica

MONEY RIDER, THE, 1924, Short Story see Gerald Beaumont

MONEY TO BURN, New York 1924, Novel see Reginald Wright Kauffman

MONEY TRAP, THE, New York 1963, Novel see Lionel White

MONEYCHANGERS, THE, Novel see Arthur Hailey

MONGO'S BACK IN TOWN, Novel see E. Richard Johnson

MONIHARA, Short Story see Rabindranath Tagore

MONIQUE, 1920, Novel see Paul Bourget

MONIQUE - POUPEE FRANCAISE, Novel see T. Trilby

MONITORS, THE, New York 1966, Novel see Keith Laumer

MONK DAWSON, Novel see Piers Paul Read

MONK, THE, Novel see M. G. Lewis

MONKEY GRIP, Novel see Helen Garner

MONKEY IN THE MIDDLE, Novel see Robert Rostand

MONKEY'S PAW, THE, 1902, Short Story see W. W. Jacobs

MONKEYS, THE, London 1962, Novel see G. K. Wilkinson

MONNA VANNA, 1902, Play see Maurice Maeterlinck

MONOCLE NOIR, LE, Novel see Remy

MONPTI, Novel see Gabor von Vaszary

MONSEIGNEUR, Play see Michel Dulud

MONSEIGNEUR, Novel see Jean Martet

MONSIEUR, Play see Claude Gevel

MONSIEUR ABEL, Novel see Alain Demouzon

MONSIEUR ANDRE, Play see Frederick A. Swann

MONSIEUR BADIN, Play see Georges Courteline

MONSIEUR BEAUCAIRE, New York 1900, Short Story see Booth Tarkington

MONSIEUR BEGONIA, Novel see Georges Fagot

MONSIEUR BROTONNEAU, Play see Gaston Arman de Caillavet, Robert de Flers

MONSIEUR CHASSE, 1896, Play see Georges Feydeau

MONSIEUR DE 5 HEURES, LE, Play see Maurice Hennequin, Pierre Veber

MONSIEUR DE COMPAGNIE, UN, Paris 1961, Novel see Andre Couteaux

MONSIEUR DE FALINDOR, Play see Georges Manoir, Armand Verhylle

MONSIEUR DE POURCEAUGNAC, 1670, Play see Moliere

MONSIEUR DES LOURDINES, 1911, Novel see Alphonse de Chateaubriant

MONSIEUR HAWARDEN, 1935, Short Story see Filip de Pillecyn

MONSIEUR LA SOURIS, 1938, Novel see Georges Simenon

MONSIEUR LADMIRAL VA BIENTOT MOURIR, 1945, Novel see Pierre Bost

MONSIEUR LAMBERTHIER, Play see Louis Verneuil

MONSIEUR LE DIRECTEUR, Play see Alexandre Bisson, Fabrice Carre

MONSIEUR LE MAIRE, Play see Gustave Stoskopf

MONSIEUR LECOQ, Paris 1869, Novel see Emile Gaboriau

MONSIEUR MASURE, Paris 1956, Play see Claude Magnier

MONSIEUR PERSONNE, Novel see Marcel Allain

MONSIEUR PINSON, POLICIER, Novel see H. R. Woestyn

MONSIEUR PROUST, Book see Celeste Albaret

MONSIEUR RIPOIS AND NEMESIS, 1925, Novel see Louis Hemon

MONSIEUR SUZUKI, Novel see Pierre Conty

MONSIEUR VERNET, Play see Georges Courteline

MONSIGNOR, Novel see Jack-Alain Leger

MONSIGNOR QUIXOTE, 1982, Novel see Graham Greene

MONSTER FROM THE EARTH'S END, Greenwich CT. 1959, Novel see Murray Leinster

MONSTER, THE, 1899, Short Story see Stephen Crane

MONSTER, THE, New York 1922, Play see Crane Wilbur

MONSTRO, O, 1966, Short Story see Josue Montello

MONT MAUDIT, LE, Play see Georges de Buysieulx

MONTAGNA DI LUCE, LA, Novel see Emilio Salgari

MONTANA RIDES, Novel see Evan Evans

MONT-DRAGON, Novel see Robert Margerit

MONTE CARLO MADNESS, Novel see Reck-Malleczewen

MONTE DE LAS ANIMAS, EL, 1860, Short Story see Gustavo Adolfo Becquer

MONTE WALSH, Boston 1963, Novel see Jack Schaefer

MONTE-CARLO, Novel see E. Phillips Oppenheim

MONTECASSINO, Book see Tommaso Leccisotti

MONTE-CHARGE, LA, Paris 1961, Novel see Frederic Dard

MONTH BY THE LAKE, A, Novel see H. E. Bates

MONTH IN THE COUNTRY, A, Novel see J. L. Carr

MONTMARTRE, Play see C. Delorbe, Pierre Frondaie

MONTPARNOS, LES, Paris 1924, Book see Georges Michel

MONUMENT, THE, Story see Irwin Shaw

MOOI JUULTJE VAN VOLENDAM, 1920, Play see Johan Lemaire

MOON AND SIXPENCE, THE, 1919, Novel see W. Somerset Maugham

MOON IN THE GUTTER, THE, 1954, Novel see David Goodis

MOON IS BLUE, THE, New York 1951, Play see F. Hugh Herbert

MOON IS DOWN, THE, 1942, Novel see John Steinbeck

MOON OF THE WOLF, Novel see Leslie H. Whitten

MOON PILOT, 1960, Short Story see Robert Buckner

MOON WALK, 1962, Short Story see Barbara Luther

MOONDIAL, Novel see Helen Cresswell

MOONFLEET, Novel see J. Meade Falkner

MOON-FLOWER, THE, New York 1924, Play see Zoe Akins, Lajos Biro

MOONLIGHT AND HONEYSUCKLE, New York 1919, Play see George Scarborough

MOONRAKER, Novel see Ian Fleming

MOONRAKER, THE, 1952, Play see Arthur Watkyn

MOONRISE, Novel see Theodore Strauss

MOON'S OUR HOME, THE, New York 1936, Novel see Faith Baldwin

MOONSHINE WAR, THE, New York 1969, Novel see Elmore Leonard

MOON-SPINNERS, THE, New York 1963, Novel see Mary Stewart

MOONSTONE, THE, London 1868, Novel see Wilkie Collins

MOONTIDE, Novel see Willard Robertson

MOONWEBS, Book see Josh Freed

MOORLAND TERROR, Novel see Hugh Broadbridge

MOORLAND TRAGEDY, A, Story see Baroness Orczy

MOOS AUF DEN STEINEN, Novel see Gerhard Fritsch

MOPS, Novel see Oliver Sandys

MORAL, Play see Ludwig Thoma

MORALNOSC PANI DULSKIEJ, 1907, Play see Gabriela Zapolska

MORALS OF MARCUS ORDEYNE, THE, London 1905, Novel see William J. Locke

MORAN OF THE LADY LETTY, New York 1898, Novel see Frank Norris

MORD AM KARLSBAD, DER, Short Story see Paul Rosenhayn

MORD EM'LY, Novel see W. Pett Ridge

MORDER MIT DEM SEIDENSCHAL, DER, Novel see Thea Tauentzien

MORDER OHNE MORD, Novel see Martha Maria Gehrke, Hans Schweikart

MORE DEADLY THAN THE MALE, London 1960, Novel see Paul Chevalier

601

MORE STATELY MANSIONS, 1920, Short Story *see* Ben Ames Williams

MORE TALES OF THE CITY, Novel *see* Armistead Maupin

MORE TO BE PITIED THAN SCORNED; OR DEATH BEFORE DISHONOR, 1903, Novel *see* Charles E. Blaney

MORELLA, 1835, Short Story *see* Edgar Allan Poe

MORENINHA, A, 1844, Novel *see* Joaquim Manuel de Macedo

MORFALOUS, LES, Novel *see* Pierre Siniac

MORGADINHA DOS CANAVIAIS, A, 1868, Novel *see* Julio Dinis

MORGANSON'S FINISH, Short Story *see* Jack London

MORGEN DES LEBENS, Novel *see* Kristman Gudmunsson

MORGEN IST ALLES BESSER, Novel *see* Annemarie Selinko

MORGEN WERDE ICH VERHAFTET, Novel *see* Arno Alexander

MORGEN WIRD ALLES BESSER, Novel *see* Annemarie Selinko

MORGEN WIRST DU UM MICH WEINEN, Novel *see* Karl Zumbro

MORGENGRAUEN, Novel *see* Hubert Miketta

MORGENS UM 7 IST DIE WELT NOCH IN ORDNUNG, Novel *see* Eric Malpass

MORGUE IS ALWAYS OPEN, THE, Novel *see* Jerome Odlum

MORIANERNA, Stockholm 1964, Novel *see* Jan Ekstrom

MORITURI, Bayreuth 1963, Novel *see* Jorg Luddecke

MORITZ IN DER LITFASSAULE, Book *see* Christa Kozik

MORNING AFTER, THE, Novel *see* Jack B. Weiner

MORNING DEPARTURE, Play *see* Kenneth Woollard

MORNING GLORY, Los Angeles 1939, Play *see* Zoe Akins

MORO DE LA ALPUJARRA, EL, *see* Pedro Calderon de La Barca

MOROCCO BOX, 1923, Short Story *see* Frederick Jackson

MOROMETII, 1955, Novel *see* Marin Preda

MOROS Y CRISTIANOS, Opera *see* Enrique Cerda, Maximiliano Thous

MOROSO DE LA NONA, EL, 1875, Play *see* Giacinto Gallina

MORPHO EUGENIA, Novel *see* A. S. Byatt

MORSKA PANNA, Play *see* Josef Stolba

MORT A LES YEUX BLEUS, LA, Novel *see* Andre Lay

MORT DE BELLE, LA, Paris 1952, Novel *see* Georges Simenon

MORT DE MONSIEUR GOLOUGA, LA, Novel *see* Branimir Scepanovic

MORT DE TINTAGILES, 1894, Play *see* Maurice Maeterlinck

MORT DES PIRATES, LA, Novel *see* Rene Morot

MORT DU CYGNE, LA, Story *see* Paul Morand

MORT DU LAC, LE, Novel *see* Henri Lapierre

MORT D'UN JUIF, LA, Novel *see* Vahe Katcha

MORT D'UN POURRI, Novel *see* Ralf Vallet

MORT EN CE JARDIN, LE, Paris 1954, Novel *see* Jose-Andre Lacour

MORT EN FRAUDE, Novel *see* Jean Hougron

MORT EN FUITE, LE, Novel *see* Loic de Gouriadec

MORT EN TROP, UNE, Novel *see* Dominique Roulet

MORT, LE, 1882, Novel *see* Camille Lemonnier

MORT OU EST TA VICTOIRE?, Novel *see* Daniel Rops

MORT OU VIF, Play *see* Max Regnier

MORT SANS IMPORTANCE, UNE, Play *see* Yvan Noe

MORT UN DIMANCHE DE PLUIE, Novel *see* Joan Aiken

MORTAL FEAR, Novel *see* Robin Cook

MORTAL STORM, THE, London 1937, Novel *see* Phyllis Bottome

MORTE A ROMA, Book *see* Robert Katz

MORTE CIVILE, LA, 1861, Play *see* Paolo Giacometti

MORTE D'ARTHUR, LE, 1485, Verse *see* Sir Thomas Malory

MORTE E VIDA SEVERINA, 1955, Verse *see* Joao Cabral de Melo Neto

MORTE IN VACANZA, LA, Play *see* Alberto Casella

MORTELLE RANDONNEE, Novel *see* Marc Behm

MORTGAGE OF LIFE, Novel *see* Vicki Baum

MORTI NON PAGANO TASSE, I, Play *see* Nicola Manzari

MORTMAIN, New York 1907, Novel *see* Arthur Cheney Train

MOSELFAHRT AUS LIEBESKUMMER, 1932, Short Story *see* Rudolf Georg Binding

MOSEN JANOT, *see* Angel Guimera

MOSKVA CHERYOMUSHKI, Moscow 1959, Opera *see* Dimitriy Shostakovich

MOSKVA, CHERYOMUSHKI, Moscow 1959, Opera *see* Vladimir Mass

MOSQUITO COAST, THE, 1981, Novel *see* Paul Theroux

MOSS ROSE, Novel *see* Joseph Shearing

MOST DANGEROUS GAME, THE, 1930, Short Story *see* Richard Connell

MOST IMMORAL LADY, A, New York 1928, Play *see* Townsend Martin

MOSTLY FOOLS, Play *see* G. R. Malloch

MOT BETAINING, 1886, Short Story *see* August Strindberg

MOTEL CHRONICLES, PARIS, TEXAS, 1985, Play *see* Sam Shepard

MOTEL TAPES, THE, Novel *see* Mike McGrady

MOTEL THE OPERATOR, New York 1936, Play *see* Chaim Tauber

MOTH AND RUST, Novel *see* Mary Cholmondeley

MOTH AND THE FLAME, THE, New York 1898, Play *see* Clyde Fitch

MOTH, THE, Novel *see* Catherine Cookson

MOTH, THE, New York 1912, Novel *see* William Dana Orcutt

MOTHER, New York 1910, Play *see* Jules Eckert Goodman

MOTHER, New York 1911, Novel *see* Kathleen Norris

MOTHER AND DAUGHTER, Short Story *see* D. H. Lawrence

MOTHER CAREY'S CHICKENS, Boston 1911, Novel *see* Kate Douglas Wiggin

MOTHER GOOSE, Autobiography *see* Bill Lishman

MOTHER INSTINCT, THE, Story *see* Mrs. Haines W. Reed

MOTHER KNOWS BEST, Garden City, N.Y. 1927, Novel *see* Edna Ferber

MOTHER LODE, New York 1934, Play *see* George O'Neal, Dan Totheroh

MOTHER LOVE, Novel *see* Domini Taylor, Judith Henry Wall

MOTHER NIGHT, Novel *see* Kurt Vonnegut Jr.

MOTHER O'DAY, 1924, Short Story *see* Leroy Scott

MOTHER OF DARTMOOR, THE, Novel *see* Eden Philpotts

MOTHER, THE, Novel *see* Eden Philpotts

MOTHER, THE, 1914, Short Story *see* Leroy Scott

MOTHER WORE TIGHTS, Novel *see* Miriam Young

MOTHER'S BOYS, Story *see* Fred Niblo Jr.

MOTHER'S CRY, New York 1930, Novel *see* Helen Grace Carlisle

MOTHER'S MILLIONS, Play *see* Howard McKent Barnes

MOTHERS OF MEN, New York 1919, Novel *see* De Witte Kaplan, William H. Warnert

MOTHER'S TALE, A, 1952, Short Story *see* James Agee

MOTHERTIME, Novel *see* Gillian White

MOTHS, London 1880, Novel *see* Ouida

MOTION TO ADJOURN, A, 1914, Short Story *see* Peter B. Kyne

MOTOCYCLETTE, LA, Paris 1963, Novel *see* Andre Pieyre de Mandiarguew

MOTS POUR LE DIRE, LES, Novel *see* Marie Cardinal

MOTSART I SALERI, 1830, Short Story *see* Alexander Pushkin

MOTTIGE JANUS, Play *see* Arnold Werumeus Buning

MOUCHE, LA, 1854, Short Story *see* Alfred de Musset

MOULIN ROUGE, Novel *see* Pierre La Mure

MOUNT MARUNGA MYSTERY, THE, Story *see* Harrison Owen

MOUNTAIN EUROPA, A, New York 1899, Novel *see* John Fox Jr.

MOUNTAIN GIRL, THE, Story *see* Mary Rider Mechtold

MOUNTAIN JUSTICE, Story *see* Julius G. Furthmann

MOUNTAIN MADNESS, New York 1917, Novel *see* Anna Alice Chapin

MOUNTAIN MAN, 1965, Novel *see* Vardis Fisher

MOUNTAIN RAT, THE, Story *see* Mary Rider Mechtold

MOUNTAIN ROAD, THE, Novel *see* Theodore H. White

MOUNTAINS ARE MY KINGDOM, THE, New York 1937, Book *see* Stuart Hardy

MOUNTEBANK, THE, London 1921, Novel *see* William J. Locke

MOUNTED PATROL, Serial Story *see* Garnett Weston

MOURNING BECOMES ELECTRA, New York 1931, Play *see* Eugene O'Neill

MOUSE AND THE WOMAN, THE, 1936, Short Story *see* Dylan Thomas

MOUSE IN THE CORNER, THE, Short Story *see* Ruth Rendell

MOUSE ON THE MOON, THE, New York 1962, Novel *see* Leonard Wibberley

MOUSE TRAP, THE, Play *see* Herbert Sargent, Con West

MOUSE WHO WOULDN'T PLAY BALL, THE, Novel *see* Anthony Gilbert

MOUSSAILLON, LE, Novel *see* Jean Rouix

MOUTH OF THE DRAGON, THE, 1923, Short Story *see* Jessie E. Henderson

MOUTHPIECE, THE, New York 1929, Play *see* Frank L. Collins

MOUTON ENRAGE LE, Novel *see* Roger Blondel

MOVE!, New York 1968, Novel *see* Joel Lieber

MOVING TARGET, THE, New York 1949, Novel *see* Ross MacDonald

MOY BEDNYY MARAT, 1965, Play *see* Aleksei Nikolaevich Arbuzov

MOYA STARSHAYA SESTRA, 1961, Play *see* Alexander Volodin

MOZA DEL CANTARO, LA, 1646, Play *see* Lope de Vega

MOZART AUF DER REISE NACH PRAG, 1855, Short Story *see* Eduard Morike

MR. & MRS. HADDICK IN PARIS, New York 1926, Novel *see* Donald Ogden Stewart

MR. & MRS HADDOCK ABROAD, New York 1924, Novel *see* Donald Ogden Stewart

MR. ABDULLA, Play *see* Reginald Berkeley, Douglas Furber

MR. AND MRS. CUGAT, Novel *see* Isabel Scott Rorick

MR. ANGEL COMES ABOARD, Novel *see* Charles Gordon Booth

MR. ARKADIN, Novel *see* Orson Welles

MR. BARNES OF NEW YORK, New York 1887, Novel *see* Archibald Clavering Gunter

MR. BILLINGS SPENDS HIS DIME, 1920, Short Story *see* Dana Burnet

MR. BISBEE'S PRINCESS, Short Story *see* Julian Leonard Street

MR. BLANDING BUILDS HIS DREAM HOUSE, Novel *see* Eric Hodgins

MR. BONES, Musical Play *see* Irving Berlin, James Gleason

MR. BRIDGE, 1969, Novel *see* Evan S. Connell

MR. BROWN COMES DOWN THE HILL, Play *see* Peter Howard

MR. BUNTING, Novel *see* Robert Greenwood

MR. BUNTING AT WAR, Novel *see* Robert Greenwood

MR. BUTTLES, Short Story *see* Frederic Arnold Kummer

MR. CINDERELLA, 1917, Novel *see* Max Brand

MR. COHEN TAKES A WALK, Novel *see* Mary Roberts Rinehart

MR. DENNING DRIVES NORTH, Novel *see* Alec Coppel

MR. DRAKE'S DUCK, Radio Play *see* Ian Messiter

MR. EMMANUEL, Novel *see* Louis Golding

MR. FOX OF VENICE, London 1959, Play *see* Frederick Knott

MR. GILFIL'S LOVE STORY, 1857, Short Story see George Eliot

MR. GILHOOLEY, 1926, Novel see Liam O'Flaherty

MR. GREX OF MONTE CARLO, Boston 1915, Novel see E. Phillips Oppenheim

MR. HOBBS'S VACATION, New York 1954, Novel see Edward Streeter

MR. HOPKINSON, London 1905, Play see R. C. Carton

MR. ISAACS, New York 1882, Novel see F. Marion Crawford

MR. JUSTICE HOLMES, Book see Francis Biddle

MR. JUSTICE RAFFLES, Novel see E. W. Hornung

MR. KNOWALL, 1947, Short Story see W. Somerset Maugham

MR. LEANDER, Short Story see James Francis Dwyer

MR. LEMON OF ORANGE, 1930, Play see Jack Hays

MR. LIMPET, New York 1942, Novel see Theodore Pratt

MR. LYNDON AT LIBERTY, Novel see Victor Bridges

MR. MEESON'S WILL, New York 1888, Novel see H. Rider Haggard

MR. MIDSHIPMAN EASY, 1836, Novel see Frederick Marryat

MR. MORGAN, 1951, Short Story see James A. Michener

MR. MURDER, Novel see Dean R. Koontz

MR. NAPUMOCENO'S LAST WILL AND TESTAMENT, Novel see Germano Almeida

MR. OPP, New York 1909, Novel see Alice Hegan Rice

MR. PERRIN AND MR. TRAILL, 1911, Novel see Hugh Walpole

MR. PIM PASSES BY, London 1920, Play see A. A. Milne

MR. POTTER OF TEXAS, see Archibald Clavering Gunter

MR. PREEDY AND THE COUNTESS, London 1909, Play see R. C. Carton

MR. PROHACK, 1922, Novel see Arnold Bennett

MR. ROMEO, New York 1927, Play see W. A. Mannheimer, I. Paul, H. Wagstaff

MR. SAMPAT, 1949, Novel see R. K. Narayan

MR. SKEFFINGTON, Novel see Elizabeth

MR. STEINWAY, 1954, Short Story see Robert Bloch

MR. WAKE'S PATIENT, Play see W. Gayer MacKey, Robert Ord

MR. WINGRAVE - MILLIONAIRE (THE MALEFACTOR), London 1904, Novel see E. Phillips Oppenheim

MR. WINKLE GOES TO WAR, Novel see Theodore Pratt

MR. WU, London 1913, Play see Harold Owen, Harry M. Vernon

MRICHCHAKATIKAM, c400-500, Play see Sudraka

MRIGAYA, Short Story see Bhagbati Charan Panigrahi

MRS. AND MRS. NORTH, New York 1941, Play see Owen Davis

MRS. 'ARRIS GOES TO PARIS, Short Story see Paul Gallico

MRS. BALFAME, New York 1906, Novel see Gertrude Franklin Atherton

MRS. BLACK IS BACK, New York 1904, Play see George V. Hobart

MRS. BRIDGE, 1959, Novel see Evan S. Connell

MRS. CAPPER'S BIRTHDAY, 1965, Short Story see Noel Coward

MRS. CHRISTOPHER, Novel see Elizabeth Myers

MRS. DALLOWAY, Novel see Virginia Woolf

MRS. DANE'S DEFENCE, London 1900, Play see Henry Arthur Jones

MRS. ERRICKER'S REPUTATION, Novel see Thomas Cobb

MRS. FRISBY AND THE RATS OF N.I.M.H., Novel see Robert C. O'Brien

MRS. GIBBONS' BOYS, Play see Will Glickman, Joseph Stein

MRS. HOYLE AND THE HOTEL ROYALSTON, Novel see Jean Z. Owen

MRS. KINSLEY'S REPORT, Play see Arch Oboler

MRS. LEFFINGWELL'S BOOTS, 1905, Play see Augustus Thomas

MRS. MCGINTY'S DEAD, London 1952, Novel see Agatha Christie

MRS. MIKE, Book see Benedict Freedman, Nancy Freedman

MRS. MINIVER, Novel see Jan Struther

MRS. PARKINGTON, 1943, Novel see Louis Bromfield

MRS. PYM OF SCOTLAND YARD, Novel see Nigel Morland

MRS. ROSS, London 1961, Novel see Robert Nicolson

MRS. TEMPLE'S TELEGRAM, New York 1905, Play see William Morris, Frank Wyatt

MRS. THOMPSON, New York 1911, Novel see William Babington Maxwell

MRS. WARREN'S PROFESSION, 1898, Play see George Bernard Shaw

MRS. WHITE, Novel see Margaret Tracy

MRS. WIGGS OF THE CABBAGE PATCH, New York 1901, Novel see Alice Hegan Rice

MRTVI ZIJI, Novel see Karel Dewetter

MSTITEL, Short Story see Anton Chekhov

MUCH ADO ABOUT NOTHING, c1598, Play see William Shakespeare

MUCHACHA DE LAS BRAGES DE ORO, LA, 1978, Novel see Juan Marse

MUCHACHITA DE VALLADOLID, UNA, 1957, Play see Joaquin Calvo Sotelo

MUD LARK, THE, New York 1932, Novel see Arthur Stringer

MUD TURTLE, THE, New York 1925, Play see Elliott Lester

MUDDY WATERS, Short Story see Wallace West

MUDE THEODOR, DER, Play see Max Ferner, Max Neal

MUDLARK, THE, Novel see Theodore Bonnet

MUEDA, MEMORIA E MASSACRE, Play see Calisto Dos Lagos

MUERTE EN LAS CALLES, LA, 1949, Novel see Manuel Galvez

MUETS, LES, 1957, Short Story see Albert Camus

MUETTE DE PORTICI, LA, Paris 1828, Opera see Daniel Francois Auber, Eugene Scribe, Casimir Delavigne

MUFLES, LES, Novel see Eugene Barbier

MUGGABLE MARY, Book see Mary Glatzle

MUGGER, THE, 1956, Novel see Evan Hunter

MUHOMATSU NO ISSHO, Novel see Shunsaku Iwashita

MUJAKINA HITOBITO, 1952, Novel see Rinzo Shiina

MUJER, Barcelona 1925, Play see Gregorio Martinez Sierra

MUJER EL TORERO Y EL TORO, LA, 1926, Novel see Alberto Insua

MULE FOR THE MARQUESA, A, New York 1964, Novel see Frank O'Rourke

MULINO DEL PO, IL, 1938-46, Novel see Riccardo Bacchelli

MULLAWAY, Novel see Bron Nicholls

MULLER UND SEIN KIND, DER, Play see Ernst Raupach

MULTIPLICITY, Short Story see Chris Miller

MUMBAI DINANK, Novel see Arun Sadhu

MUMMING BIRDS, Sketch see Fred Karno

MUMMY AND THE HUMMING BIRD, THE, New York 1902, Play see Isaac Henderson

MUMSIE, Play see Edward Knoblock

MUMU, 1854, Short Story see Ivan Turgenev

MUNAKATA SHIMAI, 1949, Novel see Jiro Osaragi

MUNCHERINNEN, Novel see Ludwig Thoma

MUNCHNER ILLUSTRIERTEN, Book see Will Berthold

MUNDO SIGUE, EL, 1960, Novel see Juan Antonio de Zunzunegui

MUNICIPAL REPORT, A, 1909, Short Story see O. Henry

MUR, LE, 1939, Short Story see Jean-Paul Sartre

MURAILLES DU SILENCE, LES, Novel see Charles Vayre

MURALLA, LA, 1955, Play see Joaquin Calvo Sotelo

MURAT O LA FINE DI UN RE, 1901, see Giuseppe de Liguoro

MURDER AT COVENT GARDEN, Novel see W. J. Makin

MURDER AT GLEN ATHOL, Garden City, N.Y. 1935, Novel see Norman Lippincott

MURDER AT MONTE CARLO, Novel see Tom Van Dyke

MURDER AT SHINGLESTRAND, Novel see Paul Capon

MURDER AT THE VANITIES, New York 1933, Play see Earl Carroll, Rufus King

MURDER BEING ONCE DONE, Novel see Ruth Rendell

MURDER BY AN ARISTOCRAT, New York 1932, Novel see Mignon G. Eberhart

MURDER BY PROXY, Novel see Helen Neilson, Bryan Edgar Wallace

MURDER BY THE CLOCK, New York 1929, Novel see Rufus King

MURDER FOR THE MILLIONS, Novel see Robert Chapman

MURDER GANG, London 1935, Play see Basil Dean, George Munro

MURDER GOES TO COLLEGE, Indianapolis 1936, Novel see Kurt Steel

MURDER IN A CHINESE THEATRE, Novel see Joseph Stanley

MURDER IN AMITYVILLE, Book see Hans Holzer

MURDER IN COWETA COUNTY, Book see Margaret Anne Barnes

MURDER IN MIND, Play see Michael Cooney

MURDER IN THE CATHEDRAL, London 1935, Play see T. S. Eliot

MURDER IN THE FAMILY, Novel see James Ronald

MURDER IN THE GILDED CAGE, New York 1929, Novel see Samuel Spewack

MURDER IN THE STALLS, Play see Maurice Messenger

MURDER IN THE SURGERY, New York 1935, Novel see James G. Edwards

MURDER IN THREE ACTS, Play see Agatha Christie

MURDER IN TRINIDAD, New York 1933, Novel see John W. Vandercook

MURDER IS ANNOUNCED, A, Novel see Agatha Christie

MURDER MISTAKEN, London 1952, Play see Janet Green

MURDER OF A WANTON, New York 1934, Novel see Whitman Chambers

MURDER OF QUALITY, A, Novel see John Le Carre

MURDER OF ROGER ACKROYD, THE, 1926, Novel see Agatha Christie

MURDER OF STEVEN KESTER, THE, New York 1931, Novel see Harriette Ashbrook

MURDER ON SIDE, see Day Keene

MURDER ON SUNSET BOULEVARD, Short Story see Harold Joyce

MURDER ON THE BLACKBOARD, New York 1932, Novel see Stuart Palmer

MURDER ON THE ORIENT EXPRESS, Novel see Agatha Christie

MURDER ON THE SECOND FLOOR, London 1929, Play see Frank Vosper

MURDER STOLE MY MISSING HOURS, Short Story see Francis K. Allen

MURDER TOMORROW?, London 1938, Play see Frank Harvey

MURDER UNDER TWO FLAGS, Book see Anne Nelson

MURDER WITH MIRRORS, Novel see Agatha Christie

MURDERER, THE, 1953, Short Story see Ray Bradbury

MURDERERS' ROW, New York 1962, Novel see Donald Hamilton

MURDERERS WELCOME, 1936, Short Story see Philip Wylie

MURDERS IN PRAED STREET, Novel see John Rhodes

MURDERS IN THE RUE MORGUE, 1841, Short Story see Edgar Allan Poe

MURPHY'S ROMANCE, Novel see Max Schott

MURPHY'S WAR, Novel see Max Catto

MUSASHINO FUJIN, 1951, Novel see Shohei Oka

MUSCLE BEACH, Boston 1959, Novel see Ira Wallach

MUSEUM PIECE NO. 13, Story see Rufus King

MUSGRAVE RITUAL, THE, Short Story *see* Arthur Conan Doyle

MUSIC IN THE AIR, New York 1932, Operetta *see* Oscar Hammerstein II, Jerome Kern

MUSIC MAN, THE, New York 1957, Musical Play *see* Franklin Lacey, Meredith Willson

MUSIC MASTER, THE, Novel *see* Charles Klein

MUSIC OF CHANCE, THE, Novel *see* Paul Auster

MUSIC SCHOOL, THE, 1966, Short Story *see* John Updike

MUSICA, LA, Play *see* Marguerite Duras

MUSICIENS DU CIEL, LES, Novel *see* Rene Lefevre

MUSIK I MORKER, 1937, Novel *see* Dagmar Ingeborg Edqvist

MUSKETYRI Z KATAKOMB, Play *see* Gustav Davis

MUSODURO, MEMORIE DI UN BRACCONIERE, Novel *see* Luigi Ugolini

MUSOTTE, 1891, *see* Guy de Maupassant

MUSTA RAKKAUS, 1948, Novel *see* Vaino Linna

MUSUKO, Book *see* Makoto Shiina

MUSUME TO WATASHI, 1953-56, Serial *see* Bunroku Shishi

MUTE WITNESS, New York 1963, Novel *see* Robert L. Fish

MUTIGE SEEFAHRER, DER, 1926, Play *see* Georg Kaiser

MUTINY, London 1958, Novel *see* Frank Tilsey

MUTINY OF THE ELSINORE, THE, New York 1914, Novel *see* Jack London

MUTINY ON THE BOUNTY, Boston 1932, Novel *see* James N. Hall, Charles Nordhoff

MUTTER COURAGE UND IHRE KINDER, 1949, Play *see* Bertolt Brecht

MUTTER ERDE, 1898, Play *see* Max Halbe

MUTTER UND KIND, 1859, Poem *see* Christian Friedrich Hebbel

MUZ A STIN, Novel *see* Emil Vachek

MUZ BEZ SRDCE, Novel *see* Ernst Klein

MUZI NESTARNOU, Play *see* Jan Patrny

MUZI V OFFSIDU, Novel *see* Karel Polacek

MUZIKANTSKA LIDUSKA, Short Story *see* Vitezslav Halek

MY AMERICAN WIFE, Story *see* Hector Turnbull

MY ANTONIA, 1918, Novel *see* Willa Cather

MY ARCADIAN WIFE, Short Story *see* Charles Wesley Sanders

MY BABY LOVES MUSIC, Story *see* Patricia Harper

MY BEST GIRL, New York 1912, Musical Play *see* Clifton Crawford, Channing Pollock, Rennold Wolf

MY BEST GIRL, New York 1927, Novel *see* Kathleen Norris

MY BIOGRAPHY, Book *see* Charles Chaplin

MY BREAST, Autobiography *see* Joyce Wadler

MY BRILLIANT CAREER, 1901, Novel *see* Miles Franklin

MY BROTHER DOWN THERE, Story *see* Steve Frazee

MY BROTHER JONATHAN, Novel *see* Francis Brett Young

MY BROTHER PAUL, 1919, Short Story *see* Theodore Dreiser

MY CLIENT CURLY, Radio Play *see* Norman Corwin

MY COUSIN RACHEL, 1951, Novel *see* Daphne Du Maurier

MY DEATH IS A MOCKERY, Novel *see* Douglas Baber

MY EARLY LIFE, Autobiography *see* Winston Spencer Churchill

MY FAMILY, Autobiography *see* Tao Cheng

MY FAMILY AND OTHER ANIMALS, Book *see* Gerald Durrell

MY FATHER'S DRAGON, Book *see* Ruth Stiles Gannett

MY FATHER'S HOUSE, Novel *see* Philip Kunhardt Jr.

MY FATHER'S HOUSE, 1947, Novel *see* Meyer Levin

MY FOUR YEARS IN GERMANY, New York 1917, Book *see* James W. Gerard

MY FRIEND FLICKA, 1941, Novel *see* Mary O'Hara

MY FRIEND FROM INDIA, New York 1912, Play *see* Henry A. Du Souchet

MY GIRL PHILIPPA, New York 1916, Novel *see* Robert W. Chambers

MY GREAT-AUNT APPEARING DAY, Story *see* John Prebble

MY GUN IS QUICK, 1950, Novel *see* Mickey Spillane

MY HUNDRED CHILDREN, Book *see* Lena Kuchler-Silberman

MY HUSBAND, New York 1919, Book *see* Irene Castle

MY IRISH MOLLY, Story *see* Earl Baldwin

MY KINGDOM FOR A WOMAN, Short Story *see* Ismet Regeila

MY LADY APRIL, Novel *see* John Overton

MY LADY FRIENDS, New York 1919, Play *see* Frank Mandel, Emil Nyitray

MY LADY OF THE ISLAND, Chicago 1916, Novel *see* Beatrice Grimshaw

MY LADY'S DRESS, London 1914, Play *see* Edward Knoblock

MY LADY'S GARTER, Chicago 1912, Novel *see* Jacques Futrelle

MY LEFT FOOT, Book *see* Christy Brown

MY LIFE, New York 1927, Autobiography *see* Isadora Duncan

MY LIFE AND HARD TIMES, 1933, Short Story *see* James Thurber

MY LITTLE BROTHER IS COMING TOMORROW, Book *see* Bruce Behrenberg

MY LITTLE SISTER, New York 1913, Novel *see* Elizabeth Robins

MY LORD CONCEIT, Novel *see* Rita

MY LORD OF THE DOUBLE B, Story *see* Norton S. Parker

MY LUKE AND I, Book *see* Joseph Durso, Eleanor Gehrig

MY LULU BELLE, 1925, Play *see* Charles MacArthur, Edward Sheldon

MY MADONNA, 1907, Poem *see* Robert W. Service

MY MAMIE ROSE; THE STORY OF MY REGENERATION, New York 1903, Book *see* Owen Frawley Kildare

MY MAN, New York 1910, Play *see* Edith Ellis, Forrest Halsey

MY MAN GODFREY, Boston 1935, Novel *see* Eric Hatch

MY MEMORIES OF VERNON CASTLE, 1919, Short Story *see* Irene Castle

MY MOTHER'S COURAGE, Novel *see* George Tabori

MY OFFICIAL WIFE, Play *see* Archibald Clavering Gunter

MY OFFICIAL WIFE, New York 1891, Novel *see* Richard Henry Savage

MY OLD DUTCH, Poem *see* Albert Chevalier

MY OLD DUTCH, London 1919, Play *see* Albert Chevalier, Arthur Shirley

MY OLD MAN, 1923, Short Story *see* Ernest Hemingway

MY OWN PAL, Story *see* Gerald Beaumont

MY PARTNER, New York 1879, Play *see* Bartley Campbell

MY POOR WIFE, Novel *see* Bertha M. Clay

MY POSSE DON'T DO HOMEWORK, Book *see* Louanne Johnson

MY QUARREL WITH HERSH RASSEYNER, Autobiography *see* Chaim Grade

MY REMINISCENCES AS A COWBOY, Book *see* Frank Harris

MY SIDE OF THE MOUNTAIN, New York 1969, Novel *see* Jean Craighead George

MY SISTER EILEEN, Book *see* Ruth McKinney

MY SISTER IN THIS HOUSE, Play *see* Wendy Kesselman

MY SIX CONVICTS, Book *see* Donald Powell Wilson

MY SIX LOVES, New York 1963, Novel *see* Peter V. K. Funk

MY SON, New York 1924, Play *see* Martha M. Stanley

MY SON - MY SON!, London 1938, Novel *see* Howard Spring

MY SON THE FANATIC, Short Story *see* Hanif Kureishi

MY SONNY, Play *see* Sholem Secunda

MY SWEET CHARLIE, New York 1965, Novel *see* David Westheimer

MY SWEETHEART, Play *see* Minnie Palmer

MY THIRTY YEARS BACKSTAIRS AT THE WHITE HOUSE, Autobiography *see* Lillian Rogers Parks

MY TRUE LOVE, Novel *see* Darwin L. Teilhet

MY UNDERCOVER YEARS WITH THE KU KLUX KLAN, *see* Gary Thomas Rowe Jr.

MY WICKED, WICKED WAYS, Autobiography *see* Errol Flynn

MY WIFE, New York 1907, Play *see* Michael Morton

MY WIFE'S FAMILY, London 1931, Play *see* Hal Stephens, Harry B. Linton

MY WIFE'S LODGER, London 1951, Play *see* Dominic Roche

MYFANWY, 1940, Poems *see* John Betjeman

MYLES CALTHROPE I.D.B., London 1913, Novel *see* F. E. Mills Young

MYORTVYE DUSHI, 1842, Novel *see* Nikolay Gogol

MYRA BRECKENRIDGE, Boston 1968, Novel *see* Gore Vidal

MYRA MEETS HIS FAMILY, 1920, Short Story *see* F. Scott Fitzgerald

MYSELF BECKY, Short Story *see* W. Carey Wonderly

MYSTERE BARTON, LE, Play *see* William Hackett

MYSTERE DE LA CHAMBRE JAUNE, LE, Paris 1908, Novel *see* Gaston Leroux

MYSTERE DU 421, LE, Play *see* Leopold Simons

MYSTERES DE PARIS, LES, 1842-43, Novel *see* Eugene Sue

MYSTERES DES BOIS, LES, *see* Ponson Du Terrail

MYSTERIE VAN DE MONSCHEINSONATE, HET, Novel *see* Willi Corsari

MYSTERIER, 1892, Novel *see* Knut Hamsun

MYSTERIOUS AFFAIR AT STYLES, THE, Novel *see* Agatha Christie

MYSTERIOUS MR. GARLAND, THE, London 1922, Novel *see* Wyndham Martin

MYSTERIOUS RIDER, THE, New York 1921, Novel *see* Zane Grey

MYSTERIOUS STRANGER, THE, New York 1921, Novel *see* Zane Grey

MYSTERY AT SPANISH HACIENDA, Novel *see* Jackson Gregory

MYSTERY OF A HANSOM CAB, THE, Novel *see* Fergus Hume

MYSTERY OF BOSCOMBE VALE, THE, Short Story *see* Arthur Conan Doyle

MYSTERY OF BRUDENELL COURT, THE, Short Story *see* Baroness Orczy

MYSTERY OF DEAD MAN'S ISLE, Short Story *see* James Oliver Curwood

MYSTERY OF DOGSTOOTH CLIFF, THE, Short Story *see* Baroness Orczy

MYSTERY OF EDWIN DROOD, THE, London 1870, Novel *see* Charles Dickens

MYSTERY OF GREEN PARK, THE, Novel *see* Arnould Galopin

MYSTERY OF HUNTING'S END, New York 1930, Novel *see* Mignon G. Eberhart

MYSTERY OF JACK HILTON, THE, Novel *see* Charles Darlington

MYSTERY OF MARIE ROGET, THE, 1842, Short Story *see* Edgar Allan Poe

MYSTERY OF MR. BERNARD BROWN, THE, 1896, Novel *see* E. Phillips Oppenheim

MYSTERY OF NUMBER 47, THE, New York 1911, Novel *see* J. Storer Clouston

MYSTERY OF THE BOULE CABINET, THE, New York 1911, Novel *see* Burton Egbert Stevenson

MYSTERY OF THE KHAKI TUNIC, THE, Short Story *see* Baroness Orczy

MYSTERY OF THE TAPESTRY ROOM, THE, Story *see* George Edwardes Hall

MYSTERY ROAD, THE, Boston 1923, Novel *see* E. Phillips Oppenheim

MYSTERY SHIP, Short Story *see* Commander Herbert A. Jones

MYSTERY SUBMARINE, Play *see* Jon Manchip White

MYSTIFIES, LES, Paris 1962, Novel *see* Alain Reynaud-Fourton

NA BOIKOM MESTE, 1865, Play *see* Alexander Ostrovsky

'NA CREATURA SPERDUTA, 1899, Play *see* Eduardo Scarpetta

NA DACHE, 1886, Short Story *see* Anton Chekhov

NA DIKOM BEREGYE, 1962, Novel *see* Boris Nikolaevich Polevoy

NERVOUS WRECK, THE, New York 1923, Novel *see* E. J. Rath

NERVOUS WRECK, THE, New York 1926, Play *see* Owen Davis

NERVY, Short Story *see* Anton Chekhov

NESLAVNA SLAVA, Short Story *see* Anna Sokolova-Podperova

NESSUNO TORNA INDIETRO, Novel *see* Alba de Cespedes

NEST EGG, THE, New York 1910, Play *see* Anne Caldwell

NEST IN A FALLING TREE, Novel *see* Joy Cowley

NEST, THE, Novel *see* Eli Cantor

NESTOR BURMA - DETECTIVE DE CHOC, Novel *see* Leo Malet

NESTOR BURMA DANS L'ILE, Novel *see* Leo Malet

NESTOR BURMA ET LE MONSTRE, Novel *see* Leo Malet

NESUT MENYA KONI, Novel *see* Anton Chekhov

NET, THE, Novel *see* John Pudney

NET, THE, New York 1912, Novel *see* Rex Beach

NETOCHKA NEZVANOVA, 1849, Short Story *see* Fyodor Dostoyevsky

NETSUDEICHI, Novel *see* Soju Kimura

NETZ, DAS, Novel *see* Hans Habe

NEUEN LEIDEN DES JUNGEN W., DIE, 1972, Play *see* Ulrich Plenzdorf

NEUES VOM RAUBER HOTZENPLOTZ, Book *see* Otfried Preussler

NEUFE DE TREFLE, Novel *see* Lucien Mayrargue

NEUROTANDEM, Novel *see* Silvano Ambrogi

NEUTRALITE MALVEILLANTE, Novel *see* Jean-Pierre Gattegno

NEUVAINE DE COLETTE, LA, Novel *see* Jeanne Schultz

NEVADA; A ROMANCE OF THE WEST, New York 1928, Novel *see* Zane Grey

NEVADA GOLD, Short Story *see* Harold Channing Wire

NEVER BET YOUR HEAD, 1841, Short Story *see* Edgar Allan Poe

NEVER COME BACK, Novel *see* John Mair

NEVER COME BACK, London 1932, Play *see* Frederick Lonsdale

NEVER CRY WOLF, Book *see* Farley Mowat

NEVER LOVE A STRANGER, 1948, Novel *see* Harold Robbins

NEVER PASS THIS WAY AGAIN, Book *see* Naar Lepere

NEVER SAY DIE, New York 1912, Play *see* William Collier Sr., W. H. Post

NEVER TAKE NO FOR AN ANSWER, Novel *see* Paul Gallico

NEVER THE TWAIN SHALL MEET, New York 1923, Novel *see* Peter B. Kyne

NEVER TOO LATE, New York 1962, Play *see* Sumner Arthur Long

NEVESTA, 1902, Short Story *see* Anton Chekhov

NEVIDELI JSTE BOBIKA?, Novel *see* Vladimir Peroutka

NEVILLE'S ISLAND, Play *see* Tim Firth

NEVTELEN VAR, 1877, Novel *see* Mor Jokai

NEW ADAM AND EVE, THE, Story *see* Nathaniel Hawthorne

NEW BROOMS, New York 1925, Play *see* Frank Craven

NEW CENTURIONS, THE, 1971, Novel *see* Joseph Wambaugh

NEW CLOWN, THE, London 1902, Play *see* H. M. Paull

NEW EVE AND OLD ADAM, Short Story *see* Gerald Dynevor

NEW FREEDOM, THE, Short Story *see* Peter B. Kyne

NEW GIRL IN TOWN, A, 1922, Short Story *see* Hubert Footner

NEW GOSSOON, THE, Novel *see* George Shiels

NEW GUINEA GOLD, Novel *see* Thomson Burtis

NEW HENRIETTA, THE, New York 1913, Play *see* Victor Mapes, Winchell Smith

NEW LADY BANTOCK, THE, 1909, Play *see* Jerome K. Jerome

NEW LEASE OF DEATH, A, Novel *see* Ruth Rendell

NEW MAGDALEN, THE, 1873, Novel *see* Wilkie Collins

NEW MOON, New York 1928, Musical Play *see* Oscar Hammerstein II, Sigmund Romberg

NEW PARDNER, THE, Short Story *see* Peter B. Kyne

NEW SO FEW, 1957, Novel *see* Tom T. Chamales

NEW TOYS, New York 1924, Play *see* Milton Herbert Gropper, Arthur Hammerstein

NEW WIZARD OF OZ, THE, Chicago 1903, Novel *see* L. Frank Baum

NEW YORK, New York 1910, Play *see* William Hurlbut

NEW YORK CONFIDENTIAL, 1948, Book *see* Jack Lait, Lee Mortimer

NEW YORK TOWN, 1932, Play *see* Ward Morehouse

NEW YORK WEST, 1926, Short Story *see* Wallace Smith

NEWCOMES, THE, Novel *see* William Makepeace Thackeray

NEWTON BOYS, THE, Book *see* Claude Stanush

NEWTON LETTER, THE, 1982, Novel *see* John Banville

NEXT CORNER, THE, Boston 1921, Novel *see* Kate Jordan

NEXT DOOR, 1968, Short Story *see* Kurt Vonnegut Jr.

NEXT OF KIN, Play *see* Lonnie Coleman

NEXT TIME WE LIVE, New York 1935, Novel *see* Ursula Parrott

NEXT TO LAST TRAIN RIDE, THE, Novel *see* Charles Dennis

NEZ DE CUIR, Novel *see* Jean de La Varende

NEZ QUI VOGUE, LE, Novel *see* Rejean Ducharme

NEZABYVAYEMYI 1919 GOD, 1949, Play *see* Vsevolod Vishnevsky

NEZNANKA, 1964, Short Story *see* Momcilo Milankov

NGO, Play *see* Acharya Athreya

NI EL TIRO DEL FINAL, Novel *see* Jose Pablo Feinmann

NI HONG DENG XIA DE SHAO BING, Play *see* Shen XImeng

NIAN QING DE YI DAI, Play *see* Chen Yun

NICCOLO DE' LAPI, 1841, Novel *see* Massimo d'Azeglio

NICE GIRL?, Play *see* Phyllis Duganne

NICE ITALIAN GIRL, A, Novel *see* Elizabeth Christman

NICE PEOPLE, New York 1921, Play *see* Rachel Crothers

NICE WOMEN, New York 1929, Play *see* William A. Grew

NICHIREN, Novel *see* Matsutaro Kawaguchi

NICHOLAS AND ALEXANDRIA, Book *see* Robert K. Massie

NICHOLAS NICKLEBY, London 1870, Novel *see* Charles Dickens

NICHTEN DER FRAU OBERST, DIE, Short Story *see* Guy de Maupassant

NICK CARTER ET LE TREFLE ROUGE, Novel *see* Claude Rank

NICKEL MOUNTAIN, Novel *see* John Gardner

NICOLE E SA VERTU, Play *see* Felix Gandera

NIDO DI FALASCO, IL, Novel *see* Luigi Ugolini

NIDO DI FARLOTTI, Poem *see* Giovanni Pascoli

NIE WIEDER LIEBE, Play *see* Julius Berstel

NIEBLA, 1914, Novel *see* Miguel de Unamuno

NIECE D'AMERIQUE, LA, Play *see* E. Ravet

NIGGER, THE, New York 1909, Play *see* Edward Sheldon

NIGHT ALONE, London 1937, Play *see* Jeffrey Dell

NIGHT AND MORNING, Novel *see* Edward George Bulwer Lytton

NIGHT AND THE CITY, 1938, Novel *see* Gerald Kersh

NIGHT BEAT, Story *see* William Sackheim

NIGHT BEFORE CHRISTMAS, THE, 1942, Novel *see* Laura Perelman, S. J. Perelman

NIGHT BUS, 1933, Short Story *see* Samuel Hopkins Adams

NIGHT CALL, Novel *see* David Shaw, Irwin Shaw

NIGHT CALLERS, THE, London 1960, Novel *see* Frank Crisp

NIGHT CLUB QUEEN, 1933, Play *see* Anthony Kimmins

NIGHT COURT, Play *see* Charles Beahan, Mark Hellinger

NIGHT CRY, 1948, Novel *see* William L. Stuart

NIGHT DARKENS THE STREET, Novel *see* Arthur La Bern

NIGHT FLIER, THE, Story *see* Stephen King

NIGHT FREIGHT, Story *see* Robert E. Kent, Raymond L. Schrock

NIGHT GAMES, London 1966, Novel *see* Mai Zetterling

NIGHT HAS A THOUSAND EYES, 1945, Novel *see* Cornell Woolrich

NIGHT HAS EYES, THE, Novel *see* Alan Kennington

NIGHT HORSEMAN, THE, New York 1920, Novel *see* Max Brand

NIGHT HOSTESS, THE, New York 1928, Play *see* Frances Dunning, Philip Dunning

NIGHT IN MONTMARTRE, A, 1926, Play *see* Miles Malleson, Walter Peacock

NIGHT IN NEW ARABIA, A, 1910, Short Story *see* O. Henry

NIGHT LIFE, Story *see* Adele Commandini

NIGHT LIFE OF A VIRILE POTATO, THE, London 1960, Play *see* Gloria Russell

NIGHT LIFE OF THE GODS, THE, Garden City, N.Y. 1931, Novel *see* Thorne Smith

NIGHT LIKE THIS, A, London 1930, Play *see* Ben Travers

NIGHT MAIL, Novel *see* Henry Holt

NIGHT MAIL, 1935, Verse *see* W. H. Auden

'NIGHT, MOTHER, Play *see* Marsha Norman

NIGHT MUST FALL, London 1935, Play *see* Emlyn Williams

NIGHT NURSE, Novel *see* Dr. Johnson Abrahams

NIGHT NURSE, New York 1930, Novel *see* Dora Macy

NIGHT OF CLEAR CHOICE, Novel *see* Doris Miles Disney

NIGHT OF JANUARY 16TH, New York 1935, Play *see* Ayn Rand

NIGHT OF REUNION, Book *see* Michael Allegretto

NIGHT OF THE BIG HEAT, Novel *see* John Lymington

NIGHT OF THE FOX, Novel *see* Jack Higgins

NIGHT OF THE HUNTER, 1953, Novel *see* David Grubb

NIGHT OF THE IGUANA, THE, New York 1961, Play *see* Tennessee Williams

NIGHT OF THE JUGGLER, Novel *see* William P. McGivern

NIGHT OF THE LEPUS, Novel *see* Russell Braddon

NIGHT OF THE PARTY, THE, Play *see* John Hastings, Roland Pertwee

NIGHT OF THE RUNNING MAN, Novel *see* Lee Wells

NIGHT OF THE TIGER, THE, New York 1956, Novel *see* Al Dewlen

NIGHT OF WENCESLAS, London 1960, Novel *see* Lionel Davidson

NIGHT PATROL, 1937, Short Story *see* Kimball Herrick

NIGHT PORTER, THE, Play *see* Harry Wall

NIGHT RIDERS: A ROMANCE OF WESTERN CANADA, THE, London 1911, Novel *see* Ridgwell Cullum

NIGHT SHIFT, 1978, Short Story *see* Stephen King

NIGHT SINS, Novel *see* Tami Hoag

NIGHT SLAVES, Novel *see* Jerry Sohl

NIGHT SONG, New York 1961, Novel *see* John A. Williams

NIGHT THE GHOST GOT IN, THE, 1945, Short Story *see* James Thurber

NIGHT THE PROWLER, THE, 1974, Short Story *see* Patrick White

NIGHT THE WORLD FOLDED, THE, Novel *see* Richard Brooks

NIGHT THEY RAIDED MINSKY'S, THE, New York 1960, Novel *see* Rowland Barber

NIGHT TO REMEMBER, A, Book *see* Walter Lord

NIGHT UNTO NIGHT, Novel *see* Philip Wylie

NIGHT WAS OUR FRIEND, Play *see* Michael Pertwee

NIGHT WATCH, Play *see* Lucille Fletcher

NIGHT WATCH, Novel *see* Alistair MacLean

NIGHT WATCH, THE, Novel *see* Thomas Walsh

NIGHT WITHOUT SLEEP, 1950, Novel *see* Elick Moll

NIGHT WITHOUT STARS, Novel *see* Winston Graham

NIGHTBIRDS OF LONDON, THE, Play *see* George R. Sims

NIGHTCAP, THE, New York 1921, Play see Guy Bolton, Max Marcin

NIGHTFALL, 1947, Novel see David Goodis

NIGHTFLYERS, Novel see George R. R. Martin

NIGHTINGALE AND THE ROSE, THE, 1888, Short Story see Oscar Wilde

NIGHTMARE, see George P. Breakston

NIGHTMARE, 1943, Short Story see Cornell Woolrich

NIGHTMARE, New York 1961, Novel see Anne Blaisdell

NIGHTMARE ALLEY, Novel see William Lindsay Gresham

NIGHTMARE HONEYMOON, Novel see Lawrence Block

NIGHTMARE IN MANHATTAN, Novel see Thomas Walsh

NIGHTSTICK, New York 1927, Play see E.S. Carrington, J. C. Nugent, John Wray

NIGHTWING, Novel see Martin Cruz Smith

NIHON CHINBOTSU, Novel see Shinobu Hashimoto

NIHONBASHI, 1914, Novel see Kyoka Izumi

NIJI NO HASHI, Novel see Fujiko Sawada

NIJINSKY, Book see Romola Nijinsky

NIJUSHI NO HITOMI, 1952, Novel see Sakae Tsuboi

NIKDO SE NEBUDE SMAT, 1963, Short Story see Milan Kundera

NIKLAUS VON FLUE, Leipzig 1928, Book see Heinrich Federer

NIKUTAI NO GAKKO, Tokyo 1964, Novel see Yukio Mishima

NIKUTAI NO MON, 1947, Novel see Tajiro Tamura

NILAMBIRI, Novel see Chandrakant Kakodkar

NILS HOLGERSSONS UNDERBARA RESA, 1906-07, Novel see Selma Lagerlof

NINA, 1949, Short Story see Cora Sandel

NINA, 1951, Play see Andre Roussin

NINA DE LUZMELA, LA, 1909, Novel see Concha Espina de Serna

NINA NON FAR LA STUPIDA, Play see Gian Capo

NINA OF THE THEATRE, Story see Rupert Hughes

NINE DAYS BLUNDER, Novel see Gerald Elliott

NINE DAYS OF FATHER SIERRA, THE, 1951, Novel see Isabelle Gibson Zeigler

NINE FORTY-FIVE, Play see Sewell Collins, Owen Davis

NINE GIRLS, Play see William H. Pettit

NINE HOURS TO RAMA, New York 1962, Novel see Stanley Wolpert

NINE TILL SIX, London 1930, Play see Aimee Stuart, Philip Stuart

NINETEEN EIGHTY-FOUR, 1949, Novel see George Orwell

NINETY AND NINE, THE, New York 1902, Play see Ramsay Morris

NINETY-TWO IN THE SHADE, 1973, Novel see Thomas McGuane

NINFA PLEBEA, Novel see Domenico Rea

NINGEN NO JOKEN VOL. 1 & 2, Kyoto 1958, Novel see Jumpei Gomikawa

NINGEN NO JOKEN VOL. 3 & 4, Novel see Jumpei Gomikawa

NINGEN NO JOKEN VOL. 5 & 6, Novel see Jumpei Gomikawa

NINGEN NO SHOMEI, Novel see Seiichi Morimura

NINI, Book see Meir Zarchi

NINICHE, 1878, Play see A. N. Hennequin, Albert Milhaud

NINJA WARS, Novel see Hutaro Yamada

NINO DE LAS MONJAS, EL, Novel see Juan Lopez Nunez

NINO DE ORO, EL, Play see Jose Maria Granada

NINOS DEL HOSPICIO, LOS, Play see Jover Y Valenti

NINTH CONFIGURATION, THE, Novel see William Peter Blatty

NINTH GUEST, THE, New Orleans 1930, Novel see Gwen Bristow, Bruce Manning

NIOBE, London 1892, Play see Edward A. Paulton, Harry Paulton

NIPPON NO ICHIBAN NAGAI HI, Tokyo 1965, Short Story see Soichi Oya

NISKAVUOREN HETA, 1950, Play see Hella Wuolijoki

NISKAVUOREN LEIPA, 1938, Play see Hella Wuolijoki

NISKAVUOREN NAISET, 1936, Play see Hella Wuolijoki

NISKAVUOREN NUORI EMANTA, 1940, Play see Hella Wuolijoki

NO. 13 WASHINGTON SQUARE, Boston 1914, Novel see Leroy Scott

NO. 5 JOHN STREET, Novel see Richard Whiteing

NO BLADE TOO SHARP, Radio Play see Robert Monroe

NO BRAKES, 1928, Short Story see Andrew W. Somerville

NO CHILDREN ALLOWED, Play see Arthur Stuart Sinclair

NO COFFIN FOR THE CORPSE, Novel see Clayton Rawson

NO CRIME OF PASSION, Play see Hubert Griffith

NO CRYING HE MAKES, Novel see Ruth Rendell

NO DIFFERENCE TO ME, Novel see Phyllis Hambledon

NO DOWN PAYMENT, 1957, Novel see John McPartland

NO ESCAPE, Novel see Lawrence B. Marcus

NO EXIT, Story see Elizabeth Troy

NO EXIT, London 1936, Play see George Goodchild, Frank Witty

NO EXPERIENCE REQUIRED, 1917, Short Story see Frank R. Adams

NO GREATER LOVE, Novel see Danielle Steel

NO HABRA MAS PENA NI OLVIDO, Novel see Osvaldo Soriano

NO HANDS ON THE CLOCK, Novel see Daniel Mainwaring

NO HARD FEELINGS, Story see Frederick Nebel

NO HIGHWAY, 1948, Novel see Nevil Shute

NO HOME OF HIS OWN, Short Story see Jacland Marmur

NO LAW IN SHADOW VALLEY, 1936, Short Story see W. C. Tuttle

NO LOVE FOR JOHNNIE, London 1959, Novel see Wilfred Fienburgh

NO MAN'S LAND, New York 1910, Novel see Louis Joseph Vance

NO MEDALS, London 1944, Play see Esther McCracken

NO MORE DYING THEN, Novel see Ruth Rendell

NO MORE GAS, 1940, Novel see James N. Hall, Charles Nordhoff

NO MORE LADIES, New York 1934, Play see A. E. Thomas

NO MORE ORCHIDS, New York 1932, Novel see Grace Perkins

NO MOTHER TO GUIDE HER, Play see Lillian Mortimer

NO NAMES. NO PACKDRILL, Play see Bob Herbert

NO NIGHTINGALES, Novel see Caryl Brahms, S. J. Simon

NO NO NANETTE, New York 1925, Musical Play see Otto Harbach, Frank Mandel

NO ONE MAN, New York 1931, Novel see Rupert Hughes

NO ONE TO SPARE OR WHICH SHALL IT BE?, Story see Ethel Lynn Beers

NO ONE WAS SAVED, 1970, Play see Howard Barker

NO ORCHIDS FOR MISS BLANDISH, Novel see James Hadley Chase

NO PLACE TO HIDE, Novel see Ted Allbeury

NO POCKETS IN A SHROUD, Novel see Horace McCoy

NO POWER ON EARTH, Short Story see Richard K. Polimer, Wallace Sullivan

NO QUIERO NO QUIERO!, 1928, Play see Jacinto Benavente y Martinez

NO RESTING PLACE, Novel see Ian Niall

NO ROOM AT THE INN, London 1945, Play see Joan Temple

NO SAD SONGS FOR ME, Novel see Ruth Southard

NO SE LO DIGAS A NADIE, Novel see Jaime Bayly

NO SEX PLEASE - WE'RE BRITISH, Play see Alistair Foot, Anthony Marriott

NO SMOKING, Television Play see George Moresby-White, Rex Rienits

NO STORY, Short Story see O. Henry

NO TIME FOR COMEDY, Indianapolis 1939, Play see S. N. Behrman

NO TIME FOR SERGEANTS, Novel see Mac Hyman

NO TREES IN THE STREET, Liverpool 1948, Play see Ted Willis

NO WAY TO TREAT A LADY, New York 1964, Novel see William Goldman

NO.7, BRICK ROW, Novel see William Riley

NOAPTE FURTUNOASA, O, 1879, Play see Ion Luca Caragiale

NOBI, Tokyo 1952, Novel see Shohei Ooka

NOBLE BACHELOR, THE, Short Story see Arthur Conan Doyle

NOBLESSE OBLIGE!, 1910, Play see Maurice Hennequin, Pierre Veber

NOBODY, New York 1915, Novel see Louis Joseph Vance

NOBODY LIVES FOREVER, 1943, Novel see William Riley Burnett

NOBODY LOVES A DRUNKEN INDIAN, New York 1967, Novel see Clair Huffaker

NOBODY MAKES ME CRY, Novel see Shelley List

NOBODY'S BRIDE, Novel see Evelyn Campbell

NOBODY'S MONEY, New York 1921, Play see William Le Baron

NOBODY'S WIDOW, New York 1910, Play see Avery Hopwood

NOC A NADEJE, Prague 1957, Novel see Arnost Lustig

NOCE I DNIE, 1934-35, Novel see Maria Dabrowska

NOCES BARBARES, LES, Novel see Yann Queffelec

NOCES CORINTHIENNES, LES, Play see Anatole France

NOCES D'ARGENT, LES, Paris 1917, Play see Paul Geraldy

NOCES VENITIENNES, LES, Novel see Abel Hermant

NOCH PERED ROZHDESTVOM, 1832, Short Story see Nikolay Gogol

NOCHE DEL SABADO, LA, 1903, Play see Jacinto Benavente y Martinez

NOCHE TERRIBLE, 1933, Short Story see Roberto Arlt

NOCTURNE INDIENNE, Novel see Antonio Tabucchi

NOEUD DE VIPERES, LE, Novel see Francois Mauriac

NOGIKU NO HAKA, 1906, Novel see Sachio Ito

NOIA, LA, Milan 1960, Novel see Alberto Moravia

NOISES OFF, Play see Michael Frayn

NOITA PALAA ELAMAAN, 1947, Play see Mika Waltari

NOITE, 1954, Novel see Erico Verissimo

NOITE DE ALMIRANTE, 1884, Short Story see Joaquim Maria Machado de Assis

NOITE E A MADRUGADA, A, 1950, Novel see Fernando Namora

NOIX DE COCO, 1936, Play see Marcel Achard

NOMADS OF THE NORTH, New York 1919, Novel see James Oliver Curwood

NOME DELLA ROSA, IL, 1980, Novel see Umberto Eco

NON E VERO. MA CI CREDO, Play see Peppino de Filippo

NON HO TROVATO ROSE PER MIA MADRE, Short Story see Jose Antonio Garcia Blasquez

NON SHENANIGANS, Story see Peter B. Kyne

NON TI CONOSCO PIU, Play see Aldo de Benedetti

NON TI PAGO!, Play see Eduardo de Filippo

NON-CONFORMIST PARSON, A, Novel see Roy Horniman

NONE BUT THE BRAVE, Novel see Ruby M. Ayres

NONE BUT THE LONELY HEART, 1943, Novel see Richard Llewellyn

NONE SO BLIND, 1945, Novel see Mitchell Wilson

NONNA FELICITA, Play see Giuseppe Adami

NONNA SABELLA, LA, Novel see Pasquale Festa Campanile

NOOSE, London 1947, Play see Richard Llewellyn

NOOSE, THE, 1920, Short Story see Constance Lindsay Skinner

NOOSE, THE, New York 1926, Play see Willard Mack, H. H. Van Loan

NOR THE MOON BY NIGHT, Novel see Joy Packer

NORD ATLANTIQUE, Novel see Oscar-Paul Gilbert

NORDEN FOR LOV OG RET; EN ALASKA-HISTORIE, Copenhagen 1920, Novel see Ejnar Mikkelsen

NORMA, 1831, Opera see Felice Romani

NORMA, Milan 1831, Opera *see* Vincenzo Bellini

NORMAN CONQUESTS, THE, 1974, Play *see* Alan Ayckbourn

NORMAN VINCENT PEALE: MINISTER TO MILLIONS, Englewood Cliffs NJ. 1958, Biography *see* Arthur Gordon

NORTH, Novel *see* Alan Zweibel

NORTH AVENUE IRREGULARS, THE, Novel *see* Albert Fay Hill

NORTH OF 36, New York 1923, Novel *see* Emerson Hough

NORTH SHORE, Boston 1932, Novel *see* Wallace Irwin

NORTH STAR; A DOG STORY OF THE CANADIAN NORTHWEST, New York 1925, Novel *see* Rufus King

NORTH STAR, THE, Novel *see* Will Henry

NORTH TO BUSHMAN'S ROCK, London 1965, Novel *see* George Harding

NORTH WIND'S MALICE, THE, 1917, Short Story *see* Rex Beach

NORTHANGER ABBEY, 1818, Novel *see* Jane Austen

NORTHERN LIGHTS, Play *see* John Hoffmann

NORTHERN LIGHTS, New York 1895, Play *see* Edwin Barbour, James W. Harkins Jr.

NORTHERN MYSTERY, THE, Short Story *see* Baroness Orczy

NORTHING TRAMP, THE, London 1926, Novel *see* Edgar Wallace

NORTHWEST PASSAGE, New York 1937, Novel *see* Kenneth Lewis Roberts

NOR'WESTER, Story *see* Clements Ripley

NORWICH VICTIMS, THE, Novel *see* Francis Beeding

NORWOOD, New York 1966, Novel *see* Charles Portis

NORWOOD BUILDER, THE, Short Story *see* Arthur Conan Doyle

NOS BONS VILLAGEOIS, 1866, Play *see* Victorien Sardou

NOS DEUX CONSCIENCES, 1902, Play *see* Paul Anthelme

NOSE ON MY FACE, THE, London 1961, Novel *see* Laurence Payne

NOSTRA SIGNORA DEI TURCHI, Novel *see* Carmelo Bene

NOSTRI SOGNI, I, Play *see* Ugo Betti

NOSTRO PROSSIMO, IL, Play *see* Tino Santoni

NOSTROMO, 1904, Novel *see* Joseph Conrad

NOSZTY FIU ESETE TOTH MARIVAL, A, 1908, Novel *see* Kalman Mikszath

NOT A PENNY MORE NOT A PENNY LESS, London 1975, Novel *see* Jeffrey Archer

NOT AS A STRANGER, 1954, Novel *see* Morton Thompson

NOT BAD FOR A GIRL, Book *see* Isabella Taves

NOT FOR CHILDREN, Play *see* Wesley Towner

NOT FOR SALE, Novel *see* Monica Ewer

NOT HERBERT, New York 1926, Play *see* Howard Irving Young

NOT NOW, DARLING, Play *see* Ray Cooney

NOT QUITE JERUSALEM, 1982, Play *see* Paul Kember

NOT SO LONG AGO, New York 1924, Play *see* Arthur Richman

NOT TOO NARROW - NOT TOO DEEP, London 1936, Novel *see* Richard Sale

NOT WANTED, 1923, Short Story *see* Jesse Lynch Williams

NOT WITHOUT MY DAUGHTER, Book *see* William Hoffer, Betty Mahmoody

NOTHING A YEAR, New York 1915, Novel *see* Charles Belmont Davis

NOTHING BUT LIES, New York 1918, Play *see* Aaron Hoffman

NOTHING BUT THE NIGHT, Novel *see* John Blackburn

NOTHING BUT THE TRUTH, Play *see* James Montgomery

NOTHING BUT THE TRUTH, Indianapolis 1914, Novel *see* Frederic Stewart Isham

NOTHING EVER HAPPENS RIGHT, Story *see* L. V. Jefferson

NOTHING IN HER WAY, 1953, Novel *see* Charles Williams

NOTHING LASTS FOREVER, Novel *see* Roderick Thorp

NOTHING TO LOSE, Novel *see* R. J. Minney

NOTICES, Story *see* Viola Brothers Shore

NOTORIOUS GENTLEMAN, Story *see* Colin Clements, Florence Ryerson

NOTORIOUS MISS LISLE, THE, New York 1911, Novel *see* Mrs. Baillie Reynolds

NOTORIOUS SOPHIE LANG, THE, London 1925, Novel *see* Frederick Irving Anderson

NOTORIOUS TENANT, THE, 1956, Short Story *see* Margery Sharp

NOTRE REVE QUI ETES AUX CIEUX, Novel *see* M. Durafour

NOTRE-DAME D'AMOUR, 1896, Novel *see* Jean Aicard

NOTRE-DAME DE PARIS, Paris 1831, Novel *see* Victor Hugo

NOTTE DEL '43, UNA, 1960, Novel *see* Giorgio Bassani

NOTTE DI 21 ORE, UNA, Short Story *see* Renato Pestriniero

NOTTE DI NEVE, 1906, Play *see* Roberto Bracco

NOTTE, LA, Short Story *see* Grazia Deledda

NOTTI DEL CIMITERO, LE, Novel *see* Leon Gozlan

NOTTI DI ARANCIA MECCANICA, LE, Book *see* Dido Sacchettoni

NOUS AVONS TOUT FAIT LA MEME CHOSE, Play *see* Jean de Letraz

NOUS NE SOMMES PLUS DES ENFANTS, Play *see* Leopold Marchand

NOUS N'IRONS PAS AU NIGERIA, Novel *see* Claude Veillot

NOUVEAU LOCATAIRE, LE, 1958, Play *see* Eugene Ionesco

NOUVEAU TESTAMENT, LE, Play *see* Sacha Guitry

NOUVEAUX ARISTOCRATES, LES, Novel *see* Michel de Saint-Pierre

NOUVEAUX MESSIEURS, LES, Play *see* Francis de Croisset, Robert de Flers

NOUVEAUX RICHES, LES, Play *see* Charles d'Abadie, Robert de Cesse

NOUVELLE AURORE, LA, 1918, Novel *see* Gaston Leroux

NOVA CALIFORNIA, A, 1948, Short Story *see* Afonso Henriques de Lima Barreto

NOVECENTO, Play *see* Alessandro Baricco

NOVELLE HISTOIRE DE MOUCHETTE, Paris 1937, Novel *see* Georges Bernanos

NOVELLIERE, *see* Tommaso Guardati

NOVEMBERKATZEN, Novel *see* Mirjam Pressler

NOW AND FOREVER, Novel *see* Danielle Steel

NOW BARABBAS., London 1947, Play *see* William Douglas Home

NOW LET HIM GO, Play *see* J. B. Priestley

NOW, VOYAGER, Novel *see* Olive Higgins Prouty

NOWHERE TO GO, Novel *see* Donald MacKenzie

NOWHERE TO RUN, Novel *see* Charles Einstein

NTH COMMANDMENT, THE, 1916, Short Story *see* Fannie Hurst

NU, Copenhagen 1967, Novel *see* Johannes Allen

NU HOU BA, HUANG HE, Play *see* Wang XIngpu

NUAGES SUR LES BRULES, Novel *see* Herve Biron

NUDA OGNI SERA, Novel *see* Ugo Moretti

NUESTRA NATACHA, 1936, Play *see* Alejandro Casona

NUEVAS AMISTADES, 1959, Novel *see* Juan Garcia Hortelano

NUIT A L'HOTEL, UNE, Novel *see* Eliot Crawshay-Williams

NUIT A MEGEVE, UNE, Play *see* Jean de Letraz

NUIT AUX BALEARES, UNE, Opera *see* Louis Gaste, Jean Guitton

NUIT DE MAI, Play *see* Stephan Kamare

NUIT DE NOCES, UNE, Play *see* Albert Barre, Henri Keroul

NUIT DE SERAIL, LA, Novel *see* Michel de Grece

NUIT DES PERVERSES, LA, Novel *see* Fletcher D. Benson

NUIT DES TRAQUES, LA, Novel *see* Benoit Becker

NUIT DU 13, LA, Novel *see* Stanislas-Andre Steeman

NUIT DU 3, LA, Play *see* Jean Guitton

NUIT DU CARREFOUR, LA, 1931, Novel *see* Georges Simenon

NUIT EST A NOUS, LA, Play *see* Henri Kistemaeckers

NUIT SANS PERMISSION, LA, Zurich 1941, Novel *see* Kurt Guggenheim

NUITS DE MONTMARTRE, LES, Novel *see* Claude Orval

NUITS DE MOSCOU, LES, Novel *see* Pierre Benoit

NUITS DE PRINCES, 1927, Novel *see* Joseph Kessel

NUMBER OF DEATHS, Short Story *see* E. Phillips Oppenheim

NUMBER ONE KILLER IN SHANGHAI, Novel *see* Lu Tieren

NUMBER SEVENTEEN, Play *see* J. Jefferson Farjeon

NUMBER SIX, London 1927, Novel *see* Edgar Wallace

NUMMISUUTARIT, 1864, Play *see* Aleksis Kivi

NUMUNWARI, Novel *see* Grahame Webb

NUN: A MEMOIR, Autobiography *see* Mary Gilligan Wong

NUN AND THE BANDIT, THE, Novel *see* E. L. Grant Watson

NUN'S STORY, THE, Book *see* Kathryn C. Hulme

NUORENA NUKKUNUT, 1931, Novel *see* Frans E. Sillanpaa

NUPTIALS OF CORBAL, THE, Novel *see* Rafael Sabatini

NUR EIN TRAUM, Munchen 1909, Play *see* Lothar Schmidt

NURNBERGISCH EI, DAS, Play *see* Walter Harlan

NURSE, Book *see* Peggy Anderson

NURSE IS A NEIGHBOUR, London 1958, Novel *see* Joanna Jones

NURSE MARJORIE, New York 1906, Play *see* Israel Zangwill

NURSEMAID WHO DISAPPEARED, THE, Novel *see* Philip MacDonald

NURSE'S STORY: IN WHICH REALITY MEETS ROMANCE, THE, Indianapolis 1915, Novel *see* Adele Bleneau

NUSSKNACKER UND MAUSEKONIG, 1816, Short Story *see* Ernst Theodor Amadeus Hoffmann

NUT FARM, THE, New York 1929, Play *see* John C. Brownell

NUT-CRACKER, THE, Indianapolis 1920, Novel *see* Frederic Stewart Isham

NUTMEG TREE, THE, Novel *see* Margery Sharp

NUTS, Play *see* Tom Topor

NUTTCHEN, Novel *see* Ernst Klein

NYBGGARNA, 1956, Novel *see* Vilhelm Moberg

NYCKLAR TILL OKANT RUM, 1950, Novel *see* Walter Ljungquist

O ADRIENU, Play *see* Louis Verneuil

O CZYM SIE NIE MOWI, 1909, Novel *see* Gabriela Zapolska

O GIOVANNINO O LA MORTE!, 1912, Novel *see* Matilde Serao

O KOLCHAKE KRAPIVE I PROCHEM, 1926, Short Story *see* Mikhail Sholokhov

O' MIEDECO D'E PAZZE, Play *see* Eduardo Scarpetta

O MISTRESS MINE, 1934, Play *see* Ben Travers

O PIONEERS, 1913, Novel *see* Willa Cather

'O QUATTO 'E MAGGIO, Play *see* Diego Petriccione

O QUE E ISSO, COMPANHEIRO?, Book *see* Fernando Gabeira

O SCARFALIETTO, 1881, Play *see* Eduardo Scarpetta

O SCHIAFFO, Play *see* Pasquale Ponzillo

O SCRISOARE PIERDUTA, 1885, Play *see* Ion Luca Caragiale

'O VOTO, 1889, Play *see* Salvatore Di Giacomo

OAIE SI AI SAI, 1958, Short Story *see* Eugen Barbu

OAKDALE AFFAIR, THE, 1918, Novel *see* Edgar Rice Burroughs

OATS FOR THE WOMAN, 1917, Short Story *see* Fannie Hurst

OBCAN BRYCH, 1955, Novel *see* Jan Otcenasek

OBCHOD NA KORZE, Prague 1965, Novel *see* Ladislav Grosman

OBERARZT DR. SOLM, Novel *see* Harald Baumgarten

OBERSTEIGER, DER, Operetta *see* Carl Zeller

OBERWACHTMEISTER SCHWENKE, Novel see Hans Joachim Freiherr von Reitzenstein

OBEY THE LAW, Play see Max Marcin

OBI, THE, Play see Jon Manchip White

OBJECT OF MY AFFECTION, THE, Novel see Stephen McCauley

OBLAKA, Play see Jaroslav Kvapil

OBLOMOV, 1859, Novel see Ivan Aleksandrovich Goncharov

OBLONG BOX, THE, 1844, Short Story see Edgar Allan Poe

OBRA DO DOMONIO, Novel see Virginia de Castro

OBRACENI FERDYSE PISTORY, Play see Frantisek Langer

OBSCURITY, Story see Rupert Hughes

OBSESSION, New York 1962, Novel see Lionel White

OBZALOVANY, Short Story see Lenka Haskova

OCCHIALI D'ORO, GLI, 1956, Novel see Giorgio Bassani

OCCIDENT, L', Paris 1913, Play see Henri Kistemaeckers

OCCUPE-TOI D'AMELIE, 1911, Play see Georges Feydeau

OCCURRENCE AT OWL CREEK BRIDGE, 1891, Short Story see Ambrose Bierce

OCEAN GOLD, 1938, Short Story see Augustus Muir

OCEANO, Book see Folco Quilici

OCHI DE URS, 1938, Short Story see Mihail Sadoveanu

OCHSENKRIEG, DER, Novel see Ludwig Ganghofer

OCTAVE, Play see Henri Geroule, Yves Mirande

OCTAVE OF CLAUDIUS, THE, London 1897, Novel see Barry Pain

OCTOBER MAN, THE, Novel see Eric Ambler

OCTOPUS, THE, 1901, Novel see Frank Norris

OCTOPUS, THE, 1917, Short Story see Charles Belmont Davis

OCTOPUSSY, Short Story see Ian Fleming

ODALISQUE, THE, Story see Leroy Scott

ODCHAZETI S PODZIMEM, Novel see Vaclav Krska

ODD ANGRY SHOT, THE, Novel see William Nagle

ODD CHARGES, Short Story see W. W. Jacobs

ODD COUPLE, THE, New York 1965, Play see Neil Simon

ODD MAN OUT, London 1945, Novel see Frederick Lawrence Green

ODDS AGAINST TOMORROW, 1957, Novel see William P. McGivern

ODE TO LIBERTY, Washington, D.C. 1934, Play see Sidney Coe Howard

ODESSA FILE, THE, 1972, Novel see Frederick Forsyth

ODETTE, Book see Jerrard Tickell

ODETTE, 1881, Play see Victorien Sardou

ODIN DEN IVANA DENISOVICHA, 1962, Novel see Alexander Solzhenitsyn

ODISSEA VERDE, Novel see Luigi de Marchi

ODORIKO, 1944, Novel see Kafu Nagai

ODYSSEY OF THE NORTH, AN, 1900, Short Story see Jack London

ODYSSEY, THE, Verse see Homer

OEDIPUS AT COLONUS, 401 bc, Play see Sophocles

OEDIPUS REX, c420 bc, Play see Sophocles

OEIL DE LYNX DETECTIVE, Play see Andre Cuel, Abel Deval, Daniel Poire

OEUF, L', 1957, Play see Felicien Marceau

OEUFS DE L'AUTRUCHE, LES, 1955, Play see Andre Roussin

OF HUMAN BONDAGE, London 1915, Novel see W. Somerset Maugham

OF MEMORY & DESIRE, Story see Peter Wells

OF MICE AND MEN, New York 1937, Novel see John Steinbeck

OF MISSING PERSONS, Novel see David Goodis

OF STARS AND MEN, Boston 1958, Book see Harlow Shapley

OFF THE RECORD, London 1947, Play see Ian Hay, Stephen King-Hall

OFFICE WIFE, THE, New York 1930, Novel see Faith Baldwin

OFFICER 666, New York 1912, Play see Augustin MacHugh

OFFICER'S MESS, THE, London 1918, Play see Sidney Blow, Douglas Hoare

OFFICIAL INTRODUCER, THE, Story see Mary Rider Mechtold

OFFICIAL SECRET, London 1938, Play see Jeffrey Dell

OFF-ISLANDERS, THE, New York 1961, Novel see Nathaniel Benchley

OFFSHORE PIRATE, 1920, Short Story see F. Scott Fitzgerald

OFTEN A BRIDEGROOM, Short Story see Lady Mary Cameron

O-GIN SAMA, Tokyo 1927, Short Story see Toko Kon

OGNIEM I MIECZEM, 1884, Short Story see Henryk Sienkiewicz

OH, Novel see Mary Robison

OH, ANNICE!, 1918, Short Story see Alexine Heyland

OH BOY!, New York 1917, Musical Play see Guy Bolton, Jerome Kern, P. G. Wodehouse

OH! BROTHER, Play see Jacques Deval

OH CHRISTINA, Short Story see J. J. Bell

OH DAD, POOR DAD, MAMMA'S HUNG YOU IN THE CLOSET AND I'M FEELING SO SAD, 1960, Play see Arthur Kopit

OH DADDY!, London 1930, Play see Austin Melford

OH, DOCTOR!, New York 1923, Novel see Harry Leon Wilson

OH GOD!, Novel see Avery Corman

OH KAY!, New York 1926, Play see Guy Bolton, P. G. Wodehouse

OH LADY LADY!, New York 1918, Musical Play see Guy Bolton, Jerome Kern, P. G. Wodehouse

OH MEN! OH WOMEN!, Play see Edward Chodorov

OH PROMISE ME, 1926, Short Story see Peter B. Kyne

OH PROMISE ME, New York 1930, Play see Howard Lindsay, Bertrand Robinson

OH SERAFINA!, 1973, Novel see Giuseppe Berto

OH! WHAT A LOVELY WAR, 1965, Play see Joan Littlewood

OH, WHAT A NURSE!, Play see Bert Bloch, R. E. Sherwood

OHAN, Novel see Chiyo Uno

OHNE MUTTER GEHT ES NICHT, Novel see Hans Nicklisch

OHNE SORGE IN SANSSOUCI, Novel see E. W. Droge

OIL FOR THE LAMPS OF CHINA, New York 1933, Novel see Alice Tisdale Hobart

OISEAU BLESSE, L', Play see Alfred Capus

OISEAU BLEU, L', Moscow 1908, Play see Maurice Maeterlinck

OISEAU DE FEU, L', Play see Louis de Zilahy

OISEAUX DE PASSAGE, Novel see Lucien Descaves, Maurice Donnay

OISEAUX VONT MOURIR AU PEROU, LES, 1962, Short Story see Romain Gary

OJOS PERDIDOS, LOS, 1958, Novel see Rafael Garcia Serrano

OKAY MAMA, Novel see Artinger Annemarie

OKENKO, Play see Olga Scheinpflugova

OKOMASAN, 1941, Novel see Masuji Ibuse

OKOVY, Novel see Jan Kobr

OKTOBERFEST, Novel see Branko Dimitrijevic

OKUNI TO GOHEI, 1922, Play see Junichiro Tanizaki

OLD ACQUAINTANCE, New York 1940, Play see John Van Druten

OLD ACTOR'S STORY, THE, Poem see George R. Sims

OLD ARM CHAIR, THE, Novel see Mrs. O. F. Walton

OLD CODE, THE, Story see James Oliver Curwood

OLD COUNTRY, THE, Play see Dion Clayton Calthrop

OLD CURIOSITY SHOP, THE, London 1841, Novel see Charles Dickens

OLD DAD, New York 1919, Novel see Eleanor Hallowell Abbott

OLD DEVILS, THE, 1986, Novel see Kingsley Amis

OLD DOLL'S HOUSE, THE, 1933, Short Story see Damon Runyon

OLD DUTCH, New York 1909, Musical Play see Victor Herbert, George V. Hobart, Edgar Smith

OLD EBENEZER, Chicago 1897, Novel see Opie Read

OLD EIGHT EIGHTY, Article see St. Clair McKelway

OLD ENGLISH, 1924, Play see John Galsworthy

OLD FASHIONED GIRL, AN, 1870, Novel see Louisa May Alcott

OLD FATHERS AND YOUNG SONS, Story see Booth Tarkington

OLD FISH HAWK, Novel see Mitchell F. Jayne

OLD GANG, THE, Story see Paul Ernest

OLD GRINGO, THE, 1985, Novel see Carlos Fuentes

OLD HOMESTEAD, THE, Boston 1886, Play see Denman Thompson

OLD HUTCH LIVES UP TO IT, 1920, Short Story see Garrett Smith

OLD JEST, THE, 1979, Novel see Jennifer Johnston

OLD LADY 31, New York 1916, Play see Rachel Crothers

OLD LADY SHOWS HER MEDALS, THE, New York 1918, Play see J. M. Barrie

OLD MAID, THE, New York 1924, Novel see Edith Wharton

OLD MAN AND JIM, THE, Poem see James Whitcomb Riley

OLD MAN AND THE SEA, THE, 1952, Novel see Ernest Hemingway

OLD MAN MINICK, 1922, Short Story see Edna Ferber

OLD MAN MURPHY, New York 1931, Play see Harry W. Gribble, Patrick Kearney

OLD MAN, THE, Play see Edgar Wallace

OLD MEN AT THE ZOO, THE, Novel see Angus Wilson

OLD MICK-MACK, Radio Play see James Forsyth

OLD MRS. LEONARD AND THE MACHINE GUNS, 1937, Short Story see George Bradshaw, Price Day

OLD NEST, THE, 1911, Short Story see Rupert Hughes

OLD SHATTERHAND, Novel see Karl Friedrich May

OLD SOAK, THE, New York 1922, Play see Don Marquis

OLD ST. PAUL'S, Novel see Harrison Ainsworth

OLD SUREHAND, Freiberg Im Breisgau 1894, Novel see Karl Friedrich May

OLD SWEETHEART OF MINE, AN, Poem see James Whitcomb Riley

OLD SWIMMIN' HOLE, THE, 1883, Poem see James Whitcomb Riley

OLD WEST PER CONTRACT, THE, Short Story see William Wallace Cook

OLD WIVES FOR NEW, New York 1908, Novel see David Graham Phillips

OLD WIVES' TALE, THE, 1908, Novel see Arnold Bennett

OLD WORLD ROMANCE, AN, 1909, Novel see William J. Locke

OLD YELLER, Novel see Fred Gipson

OLDAS ES KOTES, 1964, Short Story see Jozsef Lengyel

OLDEST CONFESSION, THE, New York 1958, Novel see Richard Condon

OLD-FASHIONED GENTLEMAN, AN, Story see F. Hopkinson Smith

OLD-TIMER, 1935, Short Story see Elmer Holmes Davis

OLE OPFINDERS OFFER, Novel see Palle Rosencrantz

OLEISSA, 1898, Short Story see Aleksander Ivanovich Kuprin

OLHAI OS LIRIOS DO CAMPO, 1937, Novel see Erico Verissimo

OLIMPIA, Play see Bert Cole

OLIVER TWIST, London 1838, Novel see Charles Dickens

OLIVER'S STORY, 1977, Novel see Erich Segal

OLIVIERS DE LA JUSTICE, LES, Paris 1959, Novel see Jean Pelegri

OLMO E L'EDERA, L', Novel see Giuseppe Adami

OLPRINZ, DER, Stuttgart 1893, Novel see Karl Friedrich May

OLYMPIA, Budapest 1928, Play see Ferenc Molnar

OMAR THE TENTMAKER, New York 1914, Play see Richard Walton Tully

OMBRA, L', 1915, Play see Dario Niccodemi

OMBRA NELL'OMBRA, UN', Novel see Piero Carpi

OMBRE, L', 1933, Novel see Francis Carco

OMBRE, LE, 1883, Play see Francesco Mastriani

OMBYE AV TAG, 1933, Novel see Walter Ljungquist

OMOO, 1851, Novel see Herman Melville

OMS EN SERIE, Novel see Stephen Wul

OMTRENT DEEDEE, Novel *see* Hugo Claus

OMUL DIN VIS, 1926, Short Story *see* Cezar Petrescu

ON A CLEAR DAY YOU CAN SEE FOREVER, New York 1965, Play *see* Burton Lane, Alan Jay Lerner

ON A JEHO SESTRA, Play *see* Bernhard Buchbinder

ON A TROUVE UNE FEMME NUE, Play *see* Andre Birabeau, Jean Guitton

ON A TUE PENDANT L'ESCALE, Novel *see* Franz-Rudolf Falk

ON APPROVAL, London 1927, Play *see* Frederick Lonsdale

ON BORROWED TIME, New York 1937, Novel *see* Lawrence Edward Watkin

ON DEMANDE UN ASSASSIN, Play *see* Ernest Neubach, Andre Tabet

ON DEMANDE UN MENAGE, Play *see* Jean de Letraz

ON DESERT ALTARS, New York 1915, Novel *see* Norma Lorimer

ON DONOVAN'S DIVISION, Story *see* W. Hanson Durham

ON EST TOUJOURS TROP BON AVEC LES FEMMES, 1947, Novel *see* Raymond Queneau

ON GIANT'S SHOULDERS, Book *see* Michael Robson, Marjorie Wallace

ON GOLDEN POND, Play *see* Ernest Thompson

ON HER MAJESTY'S SECRET SERVICE, London 1963, Novel *see* Ian Fleming

ON IRISH HILL, Short Story *see* Peter B. Kyne

ON MONDAY NEXT, London 1949, Play *see* Philip King

ON NE BADINE PAS AVEC L'AMOUR, 1834, Play *see* Alfred de Musset

ON NE ROULE PAS ANTOINETTE, Play *see* Maurice Hennequin, Pierre Veber

ON N'ENTERRE PAS LE DIMANCHE, Novel *see* Fred Kassak

ON PAROLE, Story *see* Adolf Bannauer

ON PRINCIPAL, 1918, Short Story *see* Andrew Soutar

ON PURGE BEBE, 1910, Play *see* Georges Feydeau

ON THE BACK SEAT, 1925, Short Story *see* John Peter Toohey

ON THE BANKS OF THE WABASH, Song *see* Paul Dresser

ON THE BEACH, 1957, Novel *see* Nevil Shute

ON THE BLACK HILL, 1982, Novel *see* Bruce Chatwin

ON THE BLACK SEA, Play *see* Ernst Spitz, Philipp Zeska

ON THE NIGHT OF THE FIRE, Novel *see* Frederick Lawrence Green

ON THE QUIET, New York 1901, Play *see* Augustus Thomas

ON THE RUN, Novel *see* Nina Bawden

ON THE SHELF, 1922, Short Story *see* Viola Brothers Shore

ON THE SPOT, London 1930, Play *see* Edgar Wallace

ON THE STROKE OF TWELVE, 1898, Play *see* Joseph Le Brandt

ON THE THRESHOLD, Short Story *see* Wilbur Hall

ON THE TOWN, Musical Play *see* Leonard Bernstein, Betty Comden, Adolph Green

ON THE WINGS OF THE STORM, 1926, Short Story *see* Lawrence William Pedrose

ON THE YARD, Novel *see* Malcolm Braly

ON TRIAL, New York 1914, Play *see* Elmer Rice

ON WITH THE DANCE, New York 1917, Play *see* Michael Morton

ON WITH THE SHOW, Play *see* Humphrey Pearson

ON YOUR BACK, 1930, Short Story *see* Rita Weiman

ON YOUR TOES, New York 1936, Musical Play *see* George Abbott, Lorenz Hart, Richard Rodgers

ONAWANDA, Play *see* Dion Boucicault

ONCE A CROOK, Play *see* Ken Attiwill, Evadne Price

ONCE A JOLLY SWAGMAN, Novel *see* Montague Slater

ONCE A PEDDLER, 1921, Short Story *see* Hugh MacNair Kahler

ONCE ABOARD THE LUGGER, Novel *see* A. S. M. Hutchinson

ONCE AN EAGLE, Novel *see* Anton Myrer

ONCE AND FUTURE KING, THE, London 1958, Novel *see* T. H. White

ONCE IN A LIFETIME, New York 1930, Play *see* Moss Hart, George S. Kaufman

ONCE IS NOT ENOUGH, Novel *see* Jacqueline Susann

ONCE MORE WITH FEELING, Play *see* Harry Kurnitz

ONCE OFF GUARD, Novel *see* J. H. Wallis

ONCE OVER LIGHTLY, Play *see* George Holland

ONCE THERE WAS A PRINCESS, 1926, Short Story *see* Juliet Wilbor Tompkins

ONCE TO EVERY MAN, New York 1913, Novel *see* Larry Evans

ONCE TOO OFTEN, Novel *see* Elwyn Whitman Chambers

ONCE UPON A FOREST, Short Story *see* Rae Lambert

ONCE WERE WARRIORS, Novel *see* Alan Duff

ONCLE BERNAC, Novel *see* Arthur Conan Doyle

ONDE HYRDE, DEN, 1960, Novel *see* Jens Bjorneboe

ONDINA, L', 1903, Play *see* Marco Praga

ONE A MINUTE, Play *see* Frederick Jackson

ONE BRIGHT IDEA, 1918, Short Story *see* Edgar Franklin

ONE CHILD, Book *see* Torey Hayden

ONE CLEAR CALL, Short Story *see* Larry Evans

ONE CLEAR CALL, New York 1914, Novel *see* Frances Nimmo Greene

ONE COLOMBO NIGHT, Novel *see* Austin Phillips

ONE CORPSE TOO MANY, Novel *see* Ellis Peters

ONE CROWDED HOUR, Story *see* W. Townend

ONE DAY; A SEQUEL TO "THREE WEEKS", New York 1909, Novel *see* Elinor Glyn

ONE DAY'S WORK, Short Story *see* Peter B. Kyne

ONE DOLLAR'S WORTH, Short Story *see* O. Henry

ONE EIGHTH APACHE, Short Story *see* Peter B. Kyne

ONE FLEW OVER THE CUCKOO'S NEST, 1962, Novel *see* Ken Kesey

ONE FULL MOON, Novel *see* Caradog Prichard

ONE GALLANT RUSH, Book *see* Peter Burchard

ONE GOOD TURN, 1933, Short Story *see* Carl Detzer

ONE HOUR, Novel *see* Elinor Glyn

ONE HUNDRED AND ONE DALMATIANS, THE, New York 1957, Novel *see* Dodie Smith

ONE INCREASING PURPOSE, Boston 1925, Novel *see* A. S. M. Hutchinson

ONE JUMP AHEAD, Novel *see* Robert Chapman

ONE MAN'S SECRET, Novel *see* Rita Weiman

ONE MILLION FRANCS, New York 1912, Novel *see* Arnold Fredericks

ONE MORE SPRING, New York 1933, Novel *see* Robert Nathan

ONE NIGHT AT SUSIE'S, Story *see* Frederick Hazlitt Brennan

ONE NIGHT STAND, Play *see* Carol Bolt

ONE OF OUR GIRLS, New York 1885, Play *see* Bronson Howard

ONE OF THE BEST, London 1895, Play *see* George Edwardes Hall, Seymour Hicks

ONE OF THE BOSTON BULLERTONS, Short Story *see* Walton Atwater Green

ONE OF US, New York 1918, Play *see* Jack Lait, Joseph Swerling

ONE PAIR OF FEET, Novel *see* Monica Dickens

ONE STEP FROM MURDER, Novel *see* Laurence Meynell

ONE SUMMER'S DAY, London 1897, Play *see* H. V. Esmond

ONE SUNDAY AFTERNOON, New York 1933, Play *see* James Hagan

ONE THAT GOT AWAY, THE, Book *see* Kendall Burt, James Leasor

..ONE THIRD OF A NATION., New York 1937, Play *see* Arthur Arent

ONE THOUSAND DOLLARS, 1908, Short Story *see* O. Henry

ONE TOUCH OF NATURE, 1913, Short Story *see* Peter B. Kyne

ONE TOUCH OF VENUS, 1944, Musical Play *see* Ogden Nash, S. J. Perelman, Kurt Weill

ONE TRUE THING, Novel *see* Anna Quindlen

ONE WAY PENDULUM, London 1959, Play *see* N. F. Simpson

ONE WAY STREET, New York 1924, Novel *see* Beale Davis

ONE WAY TICKET, New York 1934, Novel *see* Ethel Turner

ONE WAY TRAIL, THE, London 1911, Novel *see* Ridgwell Cullum

ONE WEEK-END, New York 1919, Novel *see* Wyndham Martyn

ONE WHO WAS CLEVER, THE, 1929, Short Story *see* Elliott White Springs

ONE WILD OAT, London 1948, Play *see* Vernon Sylvaine

ONE WOMAN, 1933, Novel *see* Tiffany Thayer

ONE WOMAN, THE, New York 1903, Novel *see* Thomas Dixon

ONE WONDERFUL NIGHT, New York 1912, Novel *see* Louis Tracy

O'NEIL OF THE GLEN, Play *see* M. T. Pender

ONE-THING-AT-A-TIME O'DAY, 1917, Short Story *see* William Dudley Pelley

ONE-WOMAN IDEA, THE, 1927, Short Story *see* Alan Williams

ONI SRAZHALIS ZA RODINU, 1943-44, Novel *see* Mikhail Sholokhov

ONION FIELD, THE, Novel *see* Joseph Wambaugh

ONIONHEAD, Novel *see* Weldon Hill

ONLY 38, New York 1921, Play *see* A. E. Thomas

ONLY A FEW OF US LEFT, 1922, Short Story *see* John Phillips Marquand

ONLY A MILL GIRL, Play *see* Sheila Walsh

ONLY A NIGGER, London 1901, Novel *see* Edmund Mitchell

ONLY A SHOPGIRL, Play *see* Charles E. Blaney

ONLY COUPLES NEED APPLY, Novel *see* Doris Miles Disney

ONLY GAME IN TOWN, THE, New York 1968, Play *see* Frank D. Gilroy

ONLY JEALOUSY OF EMER, THE, 1919, Play *see* William Butler Yeats

ONLY SON, THE, Short Story *see* James Stewart

ONLY SON, THE, New York 1911, Play *see* Winchell Smith

ONLY THE VALIANT, 1943, Novel *see* Charles Marquis Warren

ONLY WHEN I LARF, London 1968, Novel *see* Len Deighton

ONNA DOSHI, 1955, Short Story *see* Yojiro Ishizaka

ONNA GOROSHI ABURA NO JIGOKU, 1721, Play *see* Monzaemon Chikamatsu

ONOKO'S VOW, Short Story *see* Bret Harte

ONOREVOLE CAMPODARSEGO, L', 1889, Play *see* Libero Pilotto

OP AFBETALING, 1952, Novel *see* Simon Vestdijk

OP CENTER, Novel *see* Tom Clancy

OP HOOP VAN ZEGEN, 1900, Play *see* Herman Heijermans

OP O' ME THUMB, New York 1905, Play *see* Frederick Fenn, Richard Pryce

OPAD, Play *see* Christian Molbech

OPEN ALL NIGHT, Play *see* John Chancellor

OPEN COUNTRY, Novel *see* Maurice Hewlett

OPEN DOOR, THE, 1921, Short Story *see* George Weston

OPEN HOUSE, THE, *see* William Bates

OPEN RANGE, Story *see* Zane Grey

OPEN SESAME, 1918, Short Story *see* Frederick Orin Bartlett

OPENED SHUTTERS, THE, New York 1906, Novel *see* Clara Louise Burnham

OPERA DO MALANDRO, Play *see* Chico Buarque

OPERA HAT, 1935, Short Story *see* Clarence Budington Kelland

OPERACION EMBAJADA, 1962, Play *see* Joaquin Calvo Sotelo

OPERATION CICERO, 1950, Novel *see* L. C. Moyzisch

OPERATION NORTH STAR, Television Play *see* Harald Bratt

OPERATION OVERFLIGHT, Book *see* Gary Francis Powers

OPERATION TERROR, New York 1961, Novel *see* Gordon Gordon, Mildred Gordon

OPERATIONS, Play *see* Stefano Reali

OPERATOR, THE, Novel see Rod Amateau, Budd Robinson

OPERAZIONE OGRO, Book see Julien Aguirre

OPERNBALL, Vienna 1898, Operetta see Richard Heuberger

OPFERGANG, DER, 1911, Short Story see Rudolf Georg Binding

OPPORTUNITY, 1917, Short Story see Edgar Franklin

OPTIMIST, DER, Play see J. Larric

OPTIMISTICHESKAYA TRAGEDIYA, Moscow 1934, Play see Vsevolod Vishnevsky

OR DU CRISTOBEL, L', Novel see A. 't Serstevens

OR. LA MERVEILLEUSE HISTOIRE DU GENERAL JOHANN AUGUST SUTER, Paris 1925, Novel see Blaise Cendrars

OR MAUDIT, L', see Xavier de Montepin

ORA DELLA FANTASIA, L', Rome 1944, Play see Anna Bonacci

ORAISON DU PLUS FORT, L', Novel see Andre Lay

ORANGES AND LEMONS, 1916, Novel see Mrs. D. C. F. Harding

ORANGES ARE NOT THE ONLY FRUIT, Novel see Jeanette Winterson

ORANGES D'ISRAEL, LES, Novel see Michelle Guerin

ORANJE HEIN, 1918, Play see Herman Bouber

ORCHARD CHILDREN, THE, Book see Rachel Maddux

ORCHARD WALLS, THE, 1953, Play see R. F. Delderfield

ORCHESTRA D-2, 1915, Short Story see Kate Jordan

ORDEAL, New York 1924, Novel see Dale Collins

ORDEAL BY GOLF, Short Story see P. G. Wodehouse

ORDEAL BY INNOCENCE, Novel see Agatha Christie

ORDEAL OF MAJOR GRIGSBY, THE, London 1964, Novel see John Sherlock

ORDER OF DEATH, THE, Novel see Hugh Fleetwood

ORDERLY ROOM, THE, Play see Ernie Lotinga

ORDERS ARE ORDERS, London 1932, Play see Anthony Armstrong, Ian Hay

ORDET, 1932, Play see Kaj Munk

ORDINARY LIFE, THE, see Dulat Isabekov

ORDINARY PEOPLE, Novel see Judith Guest

ORDINATEUR DES POMPES FUNEBRES, L', Novel see Walter Kempley

ORDINI SONO ORDINI, GLI, 1970, Short Story see Alberto Moravia

ORDOG; VIGJATEK HAROM FELVONASBAN, AZ, Budapest 1908, Play see Ferenc Molnar

ORDONNANCE, L', 1889, Short Story see Guy de Maupassant

OREGON PASSAGE, Novel see Gordon D. Shirreffs

OREGON TRAIL, THE, Novel see Frank Gruber

O'REILLY OF NOTRE DAME, New York 1931, Novel see Francis Wallace

ORENO CHI WA TANIN NO CHI, Novel see Yasutaka Tsutsui

ORESTEIA, Play see Agamemnon

ORFANA DEL GHETTO, L', Novel see Carolina Invernizio

ORFEU DEA CONCEICAO, 1956, Play see Vinicius de Moraes

ORFEUS I UNDERGRUNDEN, 1979, Play see Benny Andersen

ORGOLII, 1977, Novel see Augustin Buzura

ORGULLO DE ALBACETE, EL, Play see Joaquin Abati, Antonio Paso

ORGY OF THE DEAD, Novel see Edward Davis Wood Jr.

ORIANA, Novel see Marvel Moreno

ORIAS, AZ, 1948, Short Story see Tibor Dery

ORIONS BELTE, Novel see Jan Michelet

ORIZZONTALE, L', Novel see Augusto Genina

ORLANDO, Novel see Virginia Woolf

ORLANDO FURIOSO, 1516, Verse see Ludovico Ariosto

ORLOVI RANO LETE, 1957, Novel see Branko Copic

ORLOW, DER, Operetta see Bruno Granichstaedten, Ernst Marischka

ORMEN, 1945, Novel see Stig Dagerman

ORNIFLE; OU LE COURANT D'AIR, 1956, Play see Jean Anouilh

ORO DI NAPOLI, L', Book see Giuseppe Marotta

OROLOGIO A CUCU, L', Play see Alberto Donini

ORPHAN, THE, New York 1908, Novel see Clarence E. Mulford

ORPHANS, Play see Lyle Kessler

ORPHEE, 1927, Play see Jean Cocteau

ORPHELIN DU CIRQUE, L', Novel see Pierre Mariel

ORPHEUS, 1916, Short Story see Samuel Hopkins Adams

ORPHEUS DESCENDING, New York 1957, Play see Tennessee Williams

ORSO, L', Play see Anton Chekhov

ORVOS HALALA, AZ, 1963, Novel see Gyula Fekete

ORZOWEI, Novel see Alberto Manzi

OSADA MLADYCH SNU, Novel see Vilem Neubauer

OSADENI DUSHI, 1945, Novel see Dimitar Dimov

OSCAR, Play see Claude Magnier

OSCAR AND LUCINDA, Novel see Peter Carey

OSCAR, THE, New York 1963, Novel see Richard Sale

OSCAR WILDE, Biography see Richard Ellman

OSMY DZIEN TYGODNIA, 1957, Novel see Marek Hlasko

O.S.S. 117 N'EST PAS MORT, Novel see Jean Bruce

O.S.S. 117 PREND LE MAQUIS, Novel see Jean Bruce

OSTERMAN WEEKEND, THE, Novel see Robert Ludlum

OSTRE SLEDOVANE VLAKY, Prague 1965, Novel see Bohumil Hrabal

OSTREGA CHE SBREGO!, Play see Arnaldo Fraccaroli

OSUDY DOBREHO VOJAKA SVEJKA ZA SVETOVE VALKY, Prague 1920-23, Novel see Jaroslav Hasek

OT NECHEGO DELAT, 1885-1888, Short Story see Anton Chekhov

OTAGES, Novel see Jack Murray

OTCHAYANIE, 1937, Novel see Vladimir Nabokov

OTEC KONDELIK A ZENICH VEJVARA, Novel see Ignat Herrmann

OTETS SERGEI, 1898, Short Story see Lev Nikolayevich Tolstoy

OTHELLO, c1604, Play see William Shakespeare

OTHER GIRL, THE, New York 1903, Play see Augustus Thomas

OTHER HALVES, Novel see Sue McCanley

OTHER MAN, THE, Novel see Margaret Lynn

OTHER MAN, THE, 1920, Novel see Fergus Hume

OTHER MAN'S WIFE, THE, 1920, Short Story see James Oliver Curwood

OTHER MEN'S WIVES, Play 1929, Play see Walter Hackett

OTHER ONE, THE, 1952, Novel see Catherine Turney

OTHER PEOPLE'S MONEY, Play see Jerry Sterner

OTHER SIDE OF MIDNIGHT, THE, Novel see Sidney Sheldon

OTHER SIDE OF PARADISE, THE, Novel see Noel Barber

OTHER SIDE OF THE DOOR, THE, Indianapolis 1909, Novel see Lucia Chamberlain

OTHER SIDE OF THE MOUNTAIN, THE, Novel see E. G. Valens

OTHER, THE, Novel see Thomas Tryon

OTHER THING, THE, 1917, Short Story see Blair Hall

OTHER TIMES, Play see Harold Brighouse

OTHER WOMAN, THE, Novel see George Randolph Chester

OTHER WOMAN, THE, 1910, Play see Frederic Arnold Kummer

OTHER WOMAN, THE, New York 1920, Novel see Norah Davis

OTHON, 1665, Play see Pierre Corneille

OTLEY, London 1966, Novel see Martin Waddell

OTODIK PECSET, AZ, 1963, Novel see Ferenc Santa

OTOSHIANA, 1972, Play see Ade Kobo

OTRA ESPERANZA, 1978, Short Story see Adolfo Bioy Casares

OTRA ORILLA, LA, 1955, Play see Jose Lopez Rubio

OTSUKU ROJIN, Toyko 1960, see Yukio Togawa

OTTSY I DETI, 1862, Novel see Ivan Turgenev

OUBLIE, L', Short Story see Pierre Benoit

OUBLIER PALERMO, Novel see Edmonde Charles-Roux

OUBLIETTE, THE, Story see George Bronson Howard

OUCCHIE CUNZACRATE, 1916, Play see Roberto Bracco

OUR BETTERS, New York 1917, Play see W. Somerset Maugham

OUR BOYS, London 1875, Play see H. J. Byron

OUR EXPLOITS AT WEST POLEY, 1892-93, Short Story see Thomas Hardy

OUR HEARTS WERE YOUNG AND GAY, Book see Emily Kimbrough, Cornelia Otis Skinner

OUR LADY THE SIREN, Book see Stratis Myrivilis

OUR LITTLE WIFE, New York 1916, Play see Avery Hopwood

OUR MAN IN HAVANA, 1958, Novel see Graham Greene

OUR MISS GIBBS, London 1909, Musical Play see Cryptos, James T. Tanner

OUR MISS KEANE, 1923, Short Story see Grace Sartwell Mason

OUR MOTHER'S HOUSE, New York 1963, Novel see Julian Gloag

OUR MRS. MCCHESNEY, New York 1915, Play see Edna Ferber, George V. Hobart

OUR MUTUAL FRIEND, London 1864, Novel see Charles Dickens

OUR NEW MINISTER, Play see George W. Ryer, Denman Thompson

OUR PLEASANT SINS, New York 1919, Play see Thomas William Broadhurst

OUR RECOLLECTIONS OF YOUTH, Novel see Liang Man

OUR TOWN, New York 1938, Play see Thornton Wilder

OUR UNDISCIPLINED DAUGHTERS, Short Story see Reginald Wright Kauffman

OUR VINES HAVE TENDER GRAPES, Novel see George Victor Martin

OUR VIRGIN ISLAND, Book see Robb White

OUT, Novel see Ronald Sukenick

OUT OF A CLEAR SKY, New York 1917, Novel see Maria Thompson Davies

OUT OF ORDER, Play see Ray Cooney

OUT OF SIGHT, Novel see Elmore Leonard

OUT OF THE DARK, New York 1964, Novel see Ursula Curtiss

OUT OF THE FRYING PAN, Play see Francis Swann

OUT OF THE NIGHT, Short Story see Josephine Miller

OUT OF THE NIGHT, Play see E. Lloyd Sheldon

OUT OF THE NIGHT, New York 1925, Novel see Rida Johnson Young

OUT OF THE RUINS, London 1927, Novel see Philip Hamilton Gibbs

OUT OF THE SHADOWS, Novel see Andrea Davidson

OUT OF THE SUNSET, 1920, Short Story see George Rix

OUT TO WIN, London 1921, Play see Dion Clayton Calthrop, Roland Pertwee

OUT WHERE THE WORST BEGINS, 1924, Short Story see George Frank Worts

OUTBREAK, Novel see Robin Cook

OUTCAST, New York 1914, Play see Hubert Henry Davies

OUTCAST OF THE ISLANDS, AN, 1896, Novel see Joseph Conrad

OUTCAST, THE, Short Story see Thomas Nelson Page

OUTCASTS OF POKER FLAT, THE, 1868, Short Story see Bret Harte

OUTER GATE, THE, Boston 1927, Novel see Octavus Roy Cohen

OUTFIT, THE, Novel see Donald E. Westlake

OUTLAW, Book see Jeff Long

OUTLAW, THE, New York 1914, Novel see Jackson Gregory

OUTLAWED GUNS, 1934, Short Story see Cliff Farrell

OUTLAWS ARE IN TOWN, THE, 1949, Short Story see Bennett Foster

OUTLAWS OF PALOUSE, Short Story see Zane Grey

OUTSIDE EDGE, Play see Richard Harris

611

OUTSIDE THE SOCCER FIELD, Play *see* Jin Zhengjia

OUTSIDER, THE, London 1923, Play *see* Dorothy Brandon

OUTSIDER, THE, New Britain, Ct. 1916, Play *see* Julie Herne

OUTSIDERS, THE, Novel *see* A. E. Martin

OUTSIDERS, THE, 1967, Novel *see* S. E. Hinton

OUTWARD BOUND, New York 1924, Play *see* Sutton Vane

OVAL DIAMOND, THE, 1915, Novel *see* David S. Foster

OVER MY DEAD BODY, Novel *see* James O'Hanlon

OVER NIGHT, New York 1911, Play *see* Philip Bartholomae

OVER SHE GOES, 1936, Play *see* Stanley Lupino

OVER THE BORDER, New York 1917, Novel *see* Herman Whitaker

OVER THE HILL FROM THE POORHOUSE, 1873, Poem *see* Will Carleton

OVER THE HILL TO THE POORHOUSE, 1873, Poem *see* Will Carleton

OVER THE HILLS TO THE POORHOUSE, Novel *see* E. M. Hutchinson

OVER THE ODDS, Play *see* Rex Howard Arundel

OVER THE RIVER, London 1933, Novel *see* John Galsworthy

OVER THE TOP, New York 1917, Book *see* Arthur Guy Empey

OVER TWENTY-ONE, New York 1944, Play *see* Ruth Gordon

OVERBOARD, Novel *see* Henry Searls

OVERCOAT SAM, Short Story *see* W. J. Makin

OVERLAND RED, Boston 1914, Novel *see* Henry Herbert Knibbs

OVERTURE, Short Story *see* Gu Yu

OWL AND THE PUSSYCAT, THE, New York 1964, Play *see* Bill Manhoff

OWNER OF THE AZTEC, THE, 1926, Short Story *see* Murray Leinster

OX-BOW INCIDENT, THE, 1940, Novel *see* Walter Van Tilburg Clark

OXBRIDGE BLUES, Novel *see* Frederic Raphael

OZMA OF OZ, 1907, Novel *see* L. Frank Baum

OZORA NO SAMURAI, Novel *see* Saburo Sakai

PA GJENGRODDE STIER, 1949, Novel *see* Knut Hamsun

PA SCT. JORGEN, 1895, Novel *see* Amalie Skram

PA SOLSIDEN, 1927, Play *see* Helge Krog

PAAR, Short Story *see* Samaresh Bose

PABO SUNON, Novel *see* Dong-Chul Lee

PACCARD WIDER BALMAT, Novel *see* Karl Ziak

PACE, MIO DIO!., Novel *see* Luigi Clumez

PACIENTKA DR. HEGLA, Novel *see* Marie Pujmanova

PACIORKI JEDNEGO ROZANCA, Short Story *see* A. Siekierski

PACK OF LIES, Play *see* Hugh Whitemore

PACK, THE, Novel *see* David Fisher, John Rowan Wilson

PACKING UP, Play *see* Roland Pertwee

PACSIRTA, 1924, Novel *see* Dezso Kosztolanyi

PADDY, Novel *see* Hamilton Maule

PADDY THE NEXT BEST THING, London 1916, Novel *see* Gertrude Page

PADLOCKED, New York 1926, Novel *see* Rex Beach

PADMA NADIR MAJHI, Novel *see* Manik Bandyyopadhyay

PADRE, A MOCA, O, 1959-62, Verse *see* Carlos Drummond de Andrade

PADRE PADRONE, L'EDUCAZIONE DI UN PASTORE, Novel *see* Gavino Ledda

PADRI ETRUSCHI, I, 1941, Play *see* Tullio Pinelli

PADRONE SONO ME, IL, 1925, Novel *see* Alfredo Panzini

PADUREA, 1962, Short Story *see* Dumitru Radu Popescu

PADUREA NEBUNA, 1963, Novel *see* Zaharia Stancu

PADUREA SPINZURATILOR, 1922, Novel *see* Liviu Rebreanu

PADUREANCA, 1884, Short Story *see* Ioan Slavici

PAGADOR DE PROMESSAS, O, Sao Paolo 1960, Play *see* Alfredo Dias Gomes

PAGAN LADY, THE, New York 1930, Play *see* William Du Bois

PAGAN PASSIONS, Story *see* Grace Sanderson Michie

PAGE AFTER PAGE, Novel *see* Tim Page

PAGE D'AMOUR, UNE, 1878, *see* Emile Zola

PAGE MISS GLORY, New York 1934, Play *see* Philip Dunning, Joseph Shrank

PAGE TIM O'BRIEN, 1922, Short Story *see* John A. Moroso

PAGE VOM DALMASSE-HOTEL, DER, Novel *see* Maria Peteani

PAGINAS DE UNA HISTORIA: MENSAKA, Novel *see* Jose Angel Manas

PAGLIACCI, I, Milan 1892, Opera *see* Ruggero Leoncavallo

PAID IN FULL, Novel *see* Michael Cronin

PAID IN FULL, New York 1908, Play *see* Eugene Walter

PAID WITH TEARS, Story *see* Francis Fenton

PAILLASSE, Play *see* Adolphe-P. d'Ennery, Marc Fournier

PAIN DES JULES, LE, Play *see* Ange Bastiani

PAIN DES PAUVRES, LE, Novel *see* Thyde Monnier

PAINT YOUR WAGON, New York 1951, Musical Play *see* Alan Jay Lerner, Frederick Loewe

PAINTED FLAPPER, THE, Novel *see* Alan Pearl

PAINTED LADY, THE, 1912, Short Story *see* Larry Evans

PAINTED PONIES, Short Story *see* John Harold Hamlin

PAINTED SCENE, THE, 1916, Short Story *see* Henry Kitchell Webster

PAINTED VEIL, THE, New York 1925, Novel *see* W. Somerset Maugham

PAINTED WOMAN, THE, New York 1913, Play *see* Frederic Arnold Kummer

PAINTED WORLD, THE, Story *see* Jacques Futrelle

PAINTING CHURCHES, Play *see* Tina Howe

PAIO D'ALI, UN, Musical Play *see* Pietro Garinei, Sandro Giovannini

PAIR OF CLAWS, A, Play *see* Michael Gurr

PAIR OF SILK STOCKINGS, A, New York 1914, Play *see* Cyril Harcourt

PAIR OF SIXES, A, New York 1914, Play *see* Edward Peple

PAIR OF SPECTACLES, A, London 1890, Play *see* Sidney Grundy

PAIS ABSTRATOS, OS, 1965, Play *see* Pedro Bloch

PAIVA, LA, Story *see* Karl Vollmoller

PAIVA QUEEN OF LOVE, Novel *see* Alfred Shirkauer

PAIX CHEZ SOI, LA, 1903, Play *see* Georges Courteline

PAIX SUR LE RHIN, Novel *see* Pierre Claude

PAIX SUR LES CHAMPS, Novel *see* Marie Gevers

PAJAROS DE BADEN-BADEN, LOS, 1965, Short Story *see* Ignacio Aldecoa

PAKLIC, Novel *see* Eduard Fiker

PAL JOEY, 1939, Short Story *see* John O'Hara

PALACE OF DARKENED WINDOWS, THE, New York 1914, Novel *see* Mary Hastings Bradley

PALACE-HOTEL, Play *see* Paul Franck

PALACES, Novel *see* Saint-Sorny

PALATA NO.6, 1892, Short Story *see* Anton Chekhov

PALENQUES DE NEGROS CIMARRONES, 1890, Short Story *see* Cirilo Villaverde

PALICOVA DCERA, Play *see* Josef Kajetan Tyl

PALIO, Play *see* Luigi Bonelli

PALLA DI NEVE, Novel *see* Emilio Nessi

PALLET ON THE FLOOR, Novel *see* Ronald Hugh Morrieson

PALLIETER, 1916, Novel *see* Felix Timmermans

PALLIO, O, 1906, Play *see* Nino Martoglio

PALMES DE M. SCHUTZ, LES, Play *see* Jean-Noel Fenwick

PALS FIRST, New York 1915, Novel *see* Francis Perry Elliott

PALS IN PARADISE, Story *see* Peter B. Kyne

PAL-UTCAI FIUK, A, 1907, Novel *see* Ferenc Molnar

PALYA SZELEN, A, 1963, Novel *see* Ivan Mandy

PAMELA, 1740, Novel *see* Samuel Richardson

PAMELA MARCHANDE DE FRIVOLITES, 1936, Play *see* Victorien Sardou

PAMPA BARBARA, *see* Homero Manzi, Ulises Petit de Murat

PAN, Kristiania 1894, Novel *see* Knut Hamsun

PAN MINCMISTROVA A ZIVKOVSKY RARASEK, Play *see* Ladislav Stroupeznicky

PAN THEODOR MUNDSTOCK, 1963, Novel *see* Ladislav Fuks

PAN WOLODYJOWSKI, 1887, Novel *see* Henryk Sienkiewicz

PANAMA HATTIE, New York 1940, Musical Play *see* Buddy De Sylva, Herbert Fields, Cole Porter

PANCHO VILLA, Los Angeles 1965, Novel *see* William Douglas Lansford

PANDORA LA CROIX, Philadelphia 1924, Novel *see* Gene Wright

PANDORA'S CLOCK, Novel *see* John J. Nance

PANENSTVI, Novel *see* Marie Majerova

PANI WALEWSKA, Book *see* Waclaw Gasiorowski

PANIC IN NEEDLE PARK, Novel *see* James Mills

PANNA, Play *see* Frantisek Zavrel

PANNA NIKT, Novel *see* Tomek Tryzna

PANNE, DIE, 1956, Short Story *see* Friedrich Durrenmatt

PANNON TOREDEK, Novel *see* Miklos Meszoly

PANNY Z WILKO, 1933, Short Story *see* Jaroslaw Iwaszkiewicz

PANTALASKAS, Novel *see* Rene Masson

PANTATA BEZOUSEK, Novel *see* Karel Vaclav Rais

PANTERA NERA, LA, Novel *see* Luis Velter

PANTHEA, London 1913, Play *see* Monckton Hoffe

PANTHER, Novel *see* Melvin Van Peebles

PANTHER'S MOON, 1948, Novel *see* Victor Canning

PAODA SHUANG DENG, Novel *see* Feng Jicai

PAOLINE, 1850, *see* Xavier de Montepin, Alexandre Dumas (pere)

PAOLO IL CALDO, 1955, Novel *see* Vitaliano Brancati

PAPA, 1911, Play *see* Gaston Arman de Caillavet, Robert de Flers

PAPA ECCELLENZA, 1906, Play *see* Gerolamo Rovetta

PAPA SLOZHI!, 1962, Short Story *see* Vasili Aksyonov

PAPA'S DELICATE CONDITION, Boston 1952, Biography *see* Corinne Griffith

PAPER CHASE, Story *see* Oliver Weld Bayer

PAPER CHASE, THE, Play *see* John McNally

PAPER CHASE, THE, Novel *see* John Jay Osborn Jr.

PAPER DOOR, Short Story *see* Stephen Longstreet

PAPER LION, New York 1966, Biography *see* George Plimpton

PAPER MASK, Novel *see* John Collee

PAPER ORCHID, Novel *see* Arthur La Bern

PAPILLON, Book *see* Henri Charriere

PAPILLON DIT LYONNAIS LE JUSTE, Play *see* Louis Benieres

PAPILLON SUR L'EPAULE, UN, Novel *see* John Gearon

PAPRADNA NENARIKA, Novel *see* Miloslav J. Sousedik

PAPRAT I VATRA, Belgrade 1962, Novel *see* Antonije Isakovic

PAQUEBOT TENACITY, LE, Play *see* Charles Vildrac

PAR HABITUDE, Play *see* Abel Tarride, Vernayre

PAR LA VERITE, Short Story *see* Ernest Daudet

PAR LE BOUT DU NEZ, Opera *see* Henri Hallais, Raoul Praxy

PAR UN BEAT MATIN D'ETE, Novel *see* James Hadley Chase

PARADIES DER JUNGGESELLEN, Novel *see* Johannes Boldt

PARADIES IM SCHNEE, DAS, Novel *see* Rudolf Stratz

PARADIGM RED, *see* Harold King

PARADINE CASE, THE, Novel *see* Robert Hichens

PARADIS DE SATAN, LE, Novel *see* Andre Armandy

PARADIS, LE, Play *see* Paul Bilhaud, Maurice Hennequin

PARADISE, Boston 1925, Play *see* Cosmo Hamilton, John Russell

PARADISE CANYON MYSTERY, 1936, Short Story *see* Philip Wylie

PARADISE GARDEN, New York 1916, Novel *see* George Gibbs

PARADISE LOST, 1667, *see* John Milton

PARADISE OF FIVE DOLLARS, THE, Short Story *see* Erskine Williams

PARADISTORG, Novel *see* Ulla Isaksson

PARAGON, THE, London 1948, Play *see* Michael Pertwee, Roland Pertwee

PARAITRE, 1906, Play *see* Maurice Donnay

PARALLAX VIEW, THE, Novel *see* Loren Singer

PARALLELE LIG, DET, Novel *see* Frits Remar

PARANOIA, 1953, Short Story *see* Willem Frederik Hermans

PARASITE, THE, Philadelphia 1913, Novel *see* Helen Reimensnyder Martin

PARCE QUE JE T'AIME, Play *see* Charles Lafaurie

PARDNERS, New York 1905, Novel *see* Rex Beach

PARDONNEE, Short Story *see* Eugene Barbier

PARDS IN PARADISE, Short Story *see* Eric Howard

PAREN IZ NASHEGO GORODA, 1941, Play *see* Konstantin Simonov

PARENTS TERRIBLES, LES, 1938, Play *see* Jean Cocteau

PARFUM DE LA DAME EN NOIR, LE, Novel *see* Gaston Leroux

PARFUM DE LA PEUR, LE, Paris 1960, Novel *see* Dominique Dorn

PARFUMERIE, Play *see* Miklos Laszlo

PARI, 1888, Short Story *see* Anton Chekhov

PARIAS DE LA GLOIRE, Novel *see* Roger Delpey

PARINITA, 1914, Short Story *see* Sarat Candra Cattopadhyay

PARIS, New York 1928, Musical Play *see* Martin Brown

PARIS AU MOIS D'AOUT, Paris 1964, Novel *see* Rene Fallet

PARIS BLUES, New York 1957, Novel *see* Harold Flender

PARIS BOUND, New York 1927, Play *see* Philip Barry

PARIS FRANCE, Novel *see* Tom Walmsley

PARIS MYSTERIEUX, Novel *see* Georges Spitzmuller

PARIS TROUT, Novel *see* Peter Dexter

PARIS UNDERGROUND, Book *see* Etta Shiber

PARISH PRIEST, THE, New York 1900, Play *see* Daniel L. Hart

PARISIENNE, LA, 1885, Play *see* Henri Becque

PARISINA, 1903, Poem *see* Domenico Tumiati

PARIS-PARIS, *see* Maurice Diamant-Berger, Jean Nohain

PARIZANKA, Opera *see* Jara Benes, Vaclav Mirovsky, Vladimir Rohan

PARK AVENUE LOGGER, 1935, Short Story *see* Bruce Hutchison

PARK IS MINE, THE, Novel *see* Stephen Peters

PARK LANE SCANDAL, Novel *see* Rita

PARKER ADDERSON, PHILOSOPHER, 1891, Short Story *see* Ambrose Bierce

PARKSTRASSE 13, Play *see* Axel Ivers

PARLEZ-MOI D'AMOUR, Play *see* Georges Berr, Louis Verneuil

PARLOR, BEDROOM AND BATH, New York 1917, Play *see* Mark Swan, Charles W. Bell

PARMI LES PIERRES, Play *see* Hermann Sudermann

PARMIGIANA, LA, Novel *see* Bruno Piatti

PARNASIE, Novel *see* Alois Vojtech Smilovsky

PARNELL, New York 1935, Play *see* Elsie T. Schauffler

PARPAILLON; OU A LA RECHERCHE DE L'HOMME A LA POMPE D'URSUS, *see* Alfred Jarry

PARRISH, New York 1958, Novel *see* Mildred Savage

PARROT AND COMPANY, Indianapolis 1913, Novel *see* Harold MacGrath

PARSIFAL, Bayreuth 1882, Opera *see* Richard Wagner

PARSON OF PANAMINT, THE, 1915, Short Story *see* Peter B. Kyne

PARSON'S FIGHT, THE, Poem *see* George R. Sims

PARTED CURTAINS, Short Story *see* Franklyn Hall

PARTIE DE CAMPAGNE, UNE, 1881, Short Story *see* Guy de Maupassant

PARTIR, Novel *see* Roland Dorgeles

PARTIRE, Play *see* Gherardo Gherardi

PARTITA, LA, Novel *see* Alberto Ongaro

PARTIZANY V STEPNAKH UKRAYINY, 1941, Play *see* Aleksander Korniychuk

PARTNERS AGAIN, New York 1922, Play *see* Montague Glass, Jules Eckert Goodman

PARTNERS OF THE NIGHT, 1916, Short Story *see* Leroy Scott

PARTNERS OF THE TIDE, New York 1905, Novel *see* Joseph C. Lincoln

PART-TIME WIFE, THE, 1925, Short Story *see* Peggy Gaddis

PARTY, Play *see* Mahesh Elkunchwar

PARTY GIRL, Novel *see* Leo Katcher

PARTY HUSBAND, New York 1930, Novel *see* Geoffrey Barnes

PARTY MEMBERSHIP DUES, Novel *see* Wang Yuanjian

PARTY, THE, 1973, Play *see* Trevor Griffiths

PARTY WIRE, New York 1934, Novel *see* Bruce Manning

PARTY'S OVER, THE, New York 1933, Play *see* Daniel Kusell

PARURE, LA, Short Story *see* Guy de Maupassant

PAS BESOIN D'ARGENT, Play *see* Ferdinand Altenkirch

PAS DE FEMMES, Play *see* Georgius

PAS DE KADDISH POUR SYLBERSTEIN, Novel *see* Guy Konopnicki

PAS DE PANIQUE, Novel *see* Yvan Audouard

PAS DE PITIE POUR LES FEMMES, Novel *see* Jean Giltene

PAS DE ROSES A ISPAHAN POUR O.S.S. 117, Novel *see* Jean Bruce

PAS PERDUS, LES, Novel *see* Rene Fallet

PAS SUR LA BOUCHE, Opera *see* Andre Barde, Maurice Yvain

PAS UN MOT A LA REINE-MERE, Play *see* Maurice Goudeket, Yves Mirande

PASADO, EL, 1890, Play *see* Manuel Acuna

PASAK HOLEK, Novel *see* Egon Erwin Kisch

PASAZERKA, Novel *see* Zofia Posmysz-Piasecka

PASCALI'S ISLAND, Novel *see* Barry Unsworth

PASHER BARI, *see* Arun Choudhury

PASO POR AQUI, Novel *see* Eugene Manlove Rhodes

PASOS DE MUJER, UNOS, 1934, Short Story *see* Wenceslao Fernandez Florez

PASSADO E O PRESENTE, O, Play *see* Vicente Sanchez

PASSAGE, Novel *see* Karel Pecka

PASSAGE HOME, Novel *see* Richard Armstrong

PASSAGE TO HONG KONG, A, Novel *see* George Kibbe Turner

PASSAGE TO INDIA, A, 1924, Novel *see* E. M. Forster

PASSAGER CLANDESTIN, LE, 1947, Novel *see* Georges Simenon

PASSAGERE, LA, Novel *see* Guy Chantepleure

PASSANTE DU SAN-SOUCI, LA, Novel *see* Joseph Kessel

PASSATORE, IL, Novel *see* Bruno Corra

PASSATORE, IL, Play *see* Alberto Donini, Guglielmo Zorzi

PASSE SIMPLE, LE, Novel *see* Dominique Saint-Alban

PASSEGERE, LA, Novel *see* Madame Guy de Chantepleure

PASSE-MURAILLE, LE, Paris 1943, Short Story *see* Marcel Ayme

PASSEPORT DIPLOMATIQUE, AGENT K8, Novel *see* Maurice Dekobra

PASSERELLE, LA, Paris 1902, Play *see* Francis de Croisset, Fred de Gresac

PASSERS-BY, Boston 1910, Novel *see* E. Phillips Oppenheim

PASSERS-BY, London 1911, Play *see* C. Haddon Chambers

PASSEURS D'HOMMES, Novel *see* Martial Lekeux

PASSING BROMPTON ROAD, London 1928, Play *see* Jevan Brandon-Thomas

PASSING OF BLACK EAGLE, THE, 1909, Short Story *see* O. Henry

PASSING OF EVIL, THE, London 1961, Novel *see* Mark McShane

PASSING OF MR. QUIN, THE, Novel *see* Agatha Christie

PASSING OF THE THIRD FLOOR BACK, THE, London 1908, Play *see* Jerome K. Jerome

PASSION FLOWER, 1929, Short Story *see* Kathleen Norris

PASSION ISLAND, Novel *see* W. W. Jacobs

PASSION OF ANY RAND, THE, Book *see* Barbara Branden

PASSION VINE, THE, 1919, Short Story *see* John Russell

PASSIONATE ADVENTURE, THE, Novel *see* Frank Stayton

PASSIONATE FRIENDS, THE, 1913, Novel *see* H. G. Wells

PASSIONATE PILGRIM, THE, Indianapolis 1919, Novel *see* Samuel Merwin

PASSIONATE QUEST, THE, Boston 1924, Novel *see* E. Phillips Oppenheim

PASSIONATE WITCH, THE, 1941, Novel *see* Thorne Smith

PASSIONNEMENT, Opera *see* Maurice Hennequin, Albert Willemetz

PASSPORT TO OBLIVION, London 1964, Novel *see* James Leasor

PASSPORT TO TREASON, Novel *see* Manning O'Brine

PASSWORD IS COURAGE, THE, 1955, Biography *see* John Castle

PASSWORD TO LARKSPUR LANE, THE, New York 1933, Novel *see* Carolyn Keene

PAST FORGETTING, Autobiography *see* Kay Summersby Morgan

PAST ONE AT ROONEY'S, Short Story *see* O. Henry

PASTOR FIDO, IL, 1590, Poem *see* Giovan Battista Guarini

PASTOR HALL, 1937, Play *see* Ernst Toller

PASTORALE 1943, 1967, Novel *see* Simon Vestdijk

PAT AND ROALD, Book *see* Barry Farrell

PATACHON, Paris 1907, Play *see* Felix Duquesnel, Maurice Hennequin

PATATE, Paris 1957, Play *see* Marcel Achard

PATATES, LES, Novel *see* Jacques Vacherot

PATENT LEATHER KID, 1927, Short Story *see* Rupert Hughes

PATER VOJTECH, Novel *see* Jan Klecanda

PATERNAL LOVE, Story *see* William Wolbert

PATH FORBIDDEN, THE, Novel *see* John B. Hymer

PATH OF GLORY, THE, Radio Play *see* L. Du Garde Peach

PATHER PANCALI, 1929, Novel *see* Bibhutibhushan Bannerjee

PATHFINDER, THE, 1840, Novel *see* James Fenimore Cooper

PATHS OF GLORY, 1935, Novel *see* Humphrey Cobb

PATIENCE SPARHAWK AND HER TIMES, New York 1897, Novel *see* Gertrude Franklin Atherton

PATIENT IN ROOM 18, THE, Garden City, N.Y. 1929, Novel *see* Mignon G. Eberhart

PATIO DE LOS NARANJOS, EL, Novel *see* Guillermo Hernandez Mir

PATRICIA BRENT - SPINSTER, Novel *see* Herbert Jenkins

PATRIE, 1869, Play *see* Louis Gallet, Victorien Sardou

PATRIOT, DER, 1925, Short Story *see* Alfred Neumann

PATRIOT GAMES, Novel *see* Tom Clancy

PATROL, New York 1928, Novel *see* Philip MacDonald

PATRONNE, LA, Play *see* Andre Luguet

PATSY, c1914, Play *see* Er Lawshe

PATSY, THE, New York 1925, Play *see* Barry Connors

PATTE D'ELEPHANT, LA, Novel *see* Pierre Fallot

PATTERN OF ISLANDS, A, Book *see* Sir Arthur Grimble

PATTERN OF ROSES, A, Novel *see* K. M. Peyton

PATTERNS, 1956, Television Play *see* Rod Serling

PATTES DE MOUCHE, LES, Paris 1860, Play *see* Victorien Sardou

PATTON: ORDEAL AND TRIUMPH, New York 1964, Biography *see* Ladislas Farago

PATUVANE KAM SEBE SI, 1965, Novel *see* Blaga Dimitrova

PAUL CLIFFORD, Novel *see* Edward George Bulwer Lytton

PAUL ET VIRGINIE, Novel *see* Bernardin de Saint-Pierre

PAULA, Novel *see* Victoria Cross

PAULA MONTI, Novel *see* Eugene Sue

PAULINA 1880, 1925, Novel *see* Pierre-Jean Jouve

PAUL'S CASE, 1905, Short Story *see* Willa Cather

PAUPER MILLIONAIRE, THE, Novel *see* Austin Fryer

PAUPERS OF PORTMAN SQUARE, THE, Novel *see* I. A. R. Wylie

PAUVRES DE PARIS, LES, Play *see* Brisbarre, Nus

PAUVRES GENS, LES, 1859, Verse *see* Victor Hugo

PAVE DU GORILLE, LE, Novel *see* Antoine Dominique

PAVILION ON THE LINKS, THE, 1882, Short Story *see* Robert Louis Stevenson

PAVILLON BRULE, LE, Play *see* Steve Passeur

PAVLIN, 1874, Novel *see* Nikolay Semyonovich Leskov

PAW, DER INDIANERJUNGE, Cologne 1931, Novel *see* Torry Gredsted

PAWN TICKET NO. 210, Play *see* David Belasco, Clay M. Greene

PAWNBROKER, THE, New York 1961, Novel *see* Edward Lewis Wallant

PAWNED, New York 1921, Novel *see* Frank L. Packard

PAXTON QUIGLEY'S HAD THE COURSE, Philadelphia 1967, Novel *see* Stephen H. Yafa

PAY THE PIPER, Novel *see* Peter Howard

PAY TO LEARN, Story *see* Borden Chase

PAY-DAY, New York 1916, Play *see* Oliver D. Bailey, Lottie M. Meaney

PAYMENT DEFERRED, 1926, Novel *see* C. S. Forester

PAYOFF, THE, Novel *see* Ronald T. Owen

PAYROLL, London 1959, Novel *see* Derek Bickerton

PAYS SANS ETOILES, LE, Novel *see* Pierre Very

PAYSANS, LES, Novel *see* Honore de Balzac

PAYSANS NOIRS, Novel *see* Roger Delavignette

PEABODY'S MERMAID, Novel *see* Constance Jones, Guy Jones

PEACE AND QUIET, Play *see* Ronald Jeans

PEACE MEDICINE, Story *see* W. C. Tuttle

PEACEFUL, Short Story *see* W. C. Tuttle

PEACEFUL INN, THE, Play *see* Denis Ogden

PEACEFUL VALLEY, New York 1893, Play *see* Edward E. Kidder

PEACEMAKER, THE, 1954, Novel *see* Richard Poole

PEACETIME SPIES, Short Story *see* Dudley Sturrock

PEACH FLOWER FAN, Play *see* Ouyang Yuqian

PEACH FLOWER LEGEND, Play *see* Kong Shangren

PEACHES, 1915, Play *see* Sidney Blow, Douglas Hoare

PEACHIE, Story *see* George Marion Jr.

PEACOCK FEATHER, THE, London 1913, Novel *see* Katharine Leslie Moore

PEACOCK FEATHERS, Novel *see* Temple Bailey

PEACOCK SCREEN, THE, 1911, Short Story *see* Fanny Heaslip Lea

PEAKS OF GOLD, Story *see* Guy M. McConnell

PEARL FOR PEARL, Story *see* Atreus Van Schraeder

PEARL, THE, 1945, Novel *see* John Steinbeck

PEARLS AND EMERALDS, Story *see* James K. McGuinness

PEARLS BEFORE CECILY, 1923, Short Story *see* Charles William Brackett

PEASANT JUDGE, THE, 1933, Novel *see* Oskar Jellinek

PEAU D'ANE, 1697, Short Story *see* Charles Perrault

PEAU DE CHAGRIN, LA, Paris 1831, Novel *see* Honore de Balzac

PEAU DE PECHE, Novel *see* Gabriel Mauriere

PEAU DE TORPEDO, LA, Novel *see* Francis Ryck

PEAU D'ESPION, Paris 1966, Novel *see* Jacques Robert

PECCATRICE, UNA, 1866, Novel *see* Giovanni Verga

PECHEUR D'ISLANDE, 1886, Novel *see* Pierre Loti

PECK'S BAD BOY AND HIS PA, Story *see* George Wilbur Peck

PEDDLER, THE, 1919, Novel *see* Henry C. Rowland

PEDDLER, THE, New York 1902, Play *see* Hal Reid

PEDIGREE, Story *see* Calvin Johnston

PEDRO MICO, ZUMBI DO CATACUMBA, 1957, Play *see* Antonio Callado

PEDRO PARAMO, 1955, Novel *see* Juan Rulfo

PEEP BEHIND THE SCENES, A, Novel *see* Mrs. O. F. Walton

PEER GYNT, Copenhagen 1867, Play *see* Henrik Ibsen

PEG LEG AND THE KIDNAPPER, 1925, Short Story *see* Frank R. Buckley

PEG O' MY HEART, New York 1912, Play *see* J. Hartley Manners

PEG WOFFINGTON, 1852, Novel *see* Charles Reade

PEGEEN, New York 1915, Novel *see* Eleanor Hoyt Brainerd

PEGGY DOES HER DARNDEST, 1918, Short Story *see* Royal Brown

PEGGY OF BEACON HILL, Boston 1924, Novel *see* Maysie Greig

PEINE D'AMOUR, Novel *see* Pierre Sales

PEINTRE EXIGEANT, LE, Play *see* Tristan Bernard

PELICAN BRIEF, THE, Novel *see* John Grisham

PELICAN, THE, London 1924, Play *see* H. M. Harwood, F. Tennyson Jesse

PELLE EROBREREN, 1906-10, Novel *see* Martin Andersen Nexo

PELLE, LA, Novel *see* Curzio Malaparte

PELLEAS ET MELISANDE, 1892, Play *see* Maurice Maeterlinck

PELOTON D'EXECUTION, Novel *see* Pierre Nord

PENALTY, THE, Play *see* Martin Berkeley

PENALTY, THE, New York 1910, Play *see* Henry Clifford Colwell

PENALTY, THE, New York 1913, Novel *see* Gouverneur Morris

PENDRAGON LEGENDA, A, 1934, Novel *see* Antal Szerb

PENELOPE, New York 1965, Novel *see* Howard Fast

PENGUIN POOL MURDER, THE, New York 1931, Novel *see* Stuart Palmer

PENITENTES, THE, Novel *see* Robert Ellis Wales

PENMARIC, Novel *see* Susan Howatch

PENNIES FROM HEAVEN, 1981, Play *see* Dennis Potter

PENNILESS MILLIONAIRE, THE, Novel *see* David Christie Murray

PENNY ARCADE, New York 1930, Play *see* Marie Baumer

PENNY OF TOP HILL TRAIL, Novel *see* Belle K. Maniates

PENNY PHILANTHROPIST; A STORY THAT COULD BE TRUE, THE, New York 1912, Novel *see* Clara E. Laughlin

PENROD, New York 1914, Novel *see* Booth Tarkington

PENROD - HIS COMPLETE STORY, 1931, Novel *see* Booth Tarkington

PENROD AND SAM, New York 1916, Novel *see* Booth Tarkington

PENSACI GIACOMINO!, 1910, Short Story *see* Luigi Pirandello

PENSION SCHOLLER, Play *see* Wilhelm Jacoby, Carl Laufs

PENTHESILEA, 1808, Play *see* Heinrich von Kleist

PENTHOUSE, New York 1935, Novel *see* Arthur Somers Roche

PENTHOUSE MYSTERY, THE, Novel *see* Ellery Queen

PENTIMENTO, 1973, Short Story *see* Lillian Hellman

PEOPLE AGAINST NANCY PRESTON, THE, New York 1921, Novel *see* John A. Moroso

PEOPLE AGAINST O'HARA, THE, 1950, Novel *see* Eleazar Lipsky

PEOPLE NEXT DOOR, THE, 1968, Play *see* J. P. Miller

PEOPLE WHOSE HEARTS LINK WITH HEARTS, Novel *see* Yang Runshen

PEOPLES, Book *see* Robert C. S. Downs

PEPA DONCEL, 1928, Play *see* Jacinto Benavente y Martinez

PEPANEK NEZDARA, Novel *see* Franta Zupan

PEPE LE MOKO, Paris 1937, Novel *see* Detective Ashelbe

PEPITA JIMENEZ, 1874, Novel *see* Juan Valera

PEQUENECES, 1890, Novel *see* Luis Coloma

PER CAUSE IMPRECISATE, Short Story *see* Carlo Bernari

PER ESSERE PIU LIBERO, Play *see* Deribers

PER LE ANTICHE SCALE, 1972, Novel *see* Mario Tobino

PER QUESTA NOTTE, Novel *see* Juan Carlos Onetti

PERCH OF THE DEVIL, New York 1914, Novel *see* Gertrude Franklin Atherton

PERCY, Novel *see* Raymond Hitchcock

PERCY AUF ABWEGEN, Novel *see* Hans Thomas

PERE DE MADEMOISELLE, LA, Play *see* Roger Ferdinand

PERE GORIOT, LE, Paris 1834, Novel *see* Honore de Balzac

PERE LEBONNARD, LE, 1889, Play *see* Jean Aicard

PERE MILON, LE, Short Story *see* Guy de Maupassant

PEREJE (PEPA), Play *see* Ladislav Novak

PEREPOLOKH, 1886, Short Story *see* Anton Chekhov

PERESOLIL, 1885, Short Story *see* Anton Chekhov

PEREZ FAMILY, THE, Novel *see* Christine Bell

PERFECT CRIME, A, 1920, Short Story *see* Carl Clausen

PERFECT CRIME, THE, Story *see* Ellery Queen

PERFECT CRIME, THE, Short Story *see* Seamark

PERFECT LADY, A, New York 1914, Play *see* Channing Pollock, Rennold Wolf

PERFECT LOVER, THE, London 1905, Play *see* Alfred Sutro

PERFECT MARRIAGE, THE, New York 1944, Play *see* Samson Raphaelson

PERFECT MURDER, THE, Novel *see* H. R. F. Keating

PERFECT SPECIMEN, THE, New York 1936, Novel *see* Samuel Hopkins Adams

PERFECT SPY, A, Novel *see* John Le Carre

PERFECT WEEKEND, A, 1934, Short Story *see* Frederick Hazlitt Brennan

PERFECT WOMAN, THE, London 1948, Play *see* Wallace Geoffrey, Basil Mitchell

PERFETTO AMORE, IL, 1910, Play *see* Roberto Bracco

PERIL FOR THE GUY, Novel *see* John Kennett

PERILOUS PASSAGE, THE, Novel *see* Bruce Micolaysen

PERIOD OF ADJUSTMENT, New York 1961, Play *see* Tennessee Williams

PERJURIO DE LA NIEVE, EL, 1945, Novel *see* Adolfo Bioy Casares

PERKINS, New York 1918, Play *see* Douglas Murray

PERLE VON TOKAY, DIE, Opera *see* Fred Raymond

PERLENKOMODIE, 1928, Play *see* Bruno Frank

PERMANENT MIDNIGHT, Book *see* Jerry Stahl

PERMISSION, LA, Paris 1967, Novel *see* Melvin Van Peebles

PERMISSION TO KILL, Novel *see* Robin Estridge

PERPETUA; OR THE WAY TO TREAT A WOMAN, New York 1911, Novel *see* Dion Clayton Calthrop

PERRI, Novel *see* Felix Salten

PERRO DEL HORTELANO, EL, Play *see* Felix Lope de Vega Y Carpio

PERRO, EL, Novel *see* Alberto Vazquez Figueroa

PERROQUET VERT, LE, Novel *see* Princesse Bibesco

PERSECUTION OF BOB PRETTY, THE, Short Story *see* W. W. Jacobs

PERSISTENT LOVERS, THE, Novel *see* Arthur Hamilton Gibbs

PERSISTENT WARRIOR, Novel *see* Edith Arundel

PERSONAL APPEARANCE, New York 1934, Play *see* Lawrence Riley

PERSONAL HISTORY, Book *see* Vincent Sheean

PERSONAL MAID, New York 1931, Novel *see* Grace Perkins

PERSONS IN HIDING, Boston 1938, Book *see* J. Edgar Hoover

PERSUASION, 1818, Novel *see* Jane Austen

PERSUASIVE PEGGY, New York 1916, Novel *see* Maravene Thompson

PERTO DO CORACAO SELVAGEM, 1943, Novel *see* Clarice Lispector

PERVAYA LYUBOV, 1860, Short Story *see* Ivan Turgenev

PERVYI UCHITEL, 1963, Short Story *see* Chingiz Aitmatov

PESCATORI, I, Play *see* Raffaele Viviani

PESSI JA ILLUSIA, Novel *see* Yrjo Kokko

PESTE, LA, Paris 1947, Novel *see* Albert Camus

PESTI FELHOJATEK, 1946, Short Story *see* Tibor Dery

PET SEMATARY, Novel *see* Stephen King

PETER GOD, Short Story *see* James Oliver Curwood

PETER IBBETSON, New York 1891, Novel *see* George Du Maurier

PETER PAN, London 1904, Play *see* J. M. Barrie

PETER PETTINGER, Novel *see* William Riley

PETER THE GREAT, Book *see* Robert K. Massie

PETER UND SABINE, Novel *see* Marie Louise Fischer

PETER VOSS DER MILLIONENDIEB, Book *see* Ewald G. Seeliger

PETERCHENS MONDFAHRT, Book *see* Gerd von Basewitz

PETER'S PENCE, Short Story *see* W. W. Jacobs

PETIT CAFE, LE, Paris 1912, Play *see* Tristan Bernard

PETIT CHAPERON ROUGE, LE, Paris 1697, Short Story *see* Charles Perrault

PETIT CHOSE, LE, 1868, Novel *see* Alphonse Daudet

PETIT GARCON DE L'ASCENSEUR, LE, Novel *see* Paul Vialar

PETIT JACQUES, LE, 1881, Novel *see* Jules Claretie

PETIT MATIN, LE, Novel *see* Christine de Rivoyre

PETIT MONDE DE DON CAMILLO, LE, Novel *see* Giovanni Guareschi

PETIT PARADIS, UN, Novel *see* G. J. Arnaud

PETIT POUCET, LE, 1697, Short Story *see* Charles Perrault

PETIT PRINCE, LE, 1943, Novel *see* Antoine de Saint-Exupery

PETIT ROI, LE, Novel *see* Anton Lichtenberger

PETIT TROU PAS CHER, UN, Play *see* Henri Caen, Yves Mirande

PETITE AMIE, LA, Play *see* Eugene Brieux

PETITE APOCALYPSE, LA, Novel *see* Tadeusz Konwicki

PETITE CHOCOLATIERE, LA, Play *see* Paul Gavault

PETITE FADETTE, LA, Paris 1849, Novel *see* George Sand

PETITE FEMME DANS LE LIT, UNE, Play *see* Yves Mirande

PETITE FEMME DANS LE TRAIN, UNE, Play *see* Leo Marches

PETITE FEMME EN OR, UNE, Play *see* Lebreton, Saint-Paul

PETITE FIFI, LA, Novel *see* Henri Demesse

PETITE FONCTIONNAIRE, LA, Play *see* Alfred Capus

PETITE HUTTE, LA, 1948, Play *see* Andre Roussin

PETITE MOBILISEE, LA, Novel *see* Marcel Priollet

PETITE PAROISSE, LA, 1901, Novel *see* Alphonse Daudet

PETITE PESTE, Play *see* Romain Coolus

PETITE RADJAH, LE, Short Story *see* Maurice de Marsan

PETITE SIRENE, LA, Novel *see* Yves Dangerfield

PETITE VERTU, LA, Novel *see* James Hadley Chase

PETITES ALLIEES, LES, Novel *see* Claude Farrere

PETITES CARDINALD, LES, Novel *see* Ludovic Halevy

PETITES FILLES MODELES, LES, Novel *see* La Comtesse de Segur

PETITS, LES, Play *see* Lucien Nepoty

PETLA, 1956, Short Story *see* Marek Hlasko

PETRIFIED FOREST, THE, New York 1935, Play *see* R. E. Sherwood

PETRIJIN VENAC, 1975, Novel *see* Dragoslav Mihailovic

PETROLEJOVE LAMPY, Novel *see* Jaroslav Havlicek

PETRONELLA, 1912, Novel *see* Johannes Jegerlehner

PETRUS, 1934, Play *see* Marcel Achard

PETTICOAT FEVER, New York 1935, Play *see* Mark Reed

PETTICOAT LOOSE, Novel *see* Rita

PETTIGREW'S GIRL, 1918, Short Story *see* Dana Burnet

PEU DE SOLEIL DANS L'EAU FROIDE, UN, 1969, Novel *see* Francoise Sagan

PEUR DES COUPS, LA, 1895, Play *see* Georges Courteline

PEYTON PLACE, 1956, Novel *see* Grace Metalious

PFARRER VON KIRCHFELD, DER, 1897, Play *see* Ludwig Anzengruber

PFARRHAUSKOMEDIE, DIE, Play *see* Heinrich Lautensack

PFINGSTORGEL, DIE, Play *see* Alois Johannes Lippl

PFLICHT ZU SCHWEIGEN, DIE, Novel *see* F. W. von Oesteren

PHAEDRA, Play *see* Lucius Annaeus Seneca

PHALENE, LA, 1913, Play *see* Henry Bataille

PHANTASTERNE, Copenhagen 1858, Novel *see* Hans Egede Schack

PHANTOM CROWN, THE, New York 1934, Play *see* Bertita Harding

PHANTOM FILLY, THE, Novel *see* George Agnew Chamberlain

PHANTOM FORTUNE, THE, Story *see* L. V. Jefferson

PHANTOM IN THE HOUSE, THE, London 1928, Novel *see* Andrew Soutar

PHANTOM LADY, 1942, Novel *see* Cornell Woolrich

PHANTOM OF 42ND STREET, THE, Novel *see* Jack Harvey, Milton Raison

PHANTOM OF THE FOREST, THE, Story *see* Frank Foster Davis

PHANTOM PICTURE, THE, Play *see* Harold Simpson

PHANTOM PRESIDENT, THE, New York 1932, Novel *see* George Frank Worts

PHANTOM TOLLBOOTH, THE, New York 1961, Novel *see* Norman Juster

PHANTOMS, Novel *see* Dean R. Koontz

PHAR LAP STORY, THE, Book *see* Michael Wilkinson

PHARE DU BOUT DU MONDE, LE, 1905, Novel *see* Jules Verne

PHARMACIEN, LE, Play *see* Max Maurey

PHEDRE, 1677, Play *see* Jean Racine

PHEDRE ET HYPPOLITE, 1677, Play *see* Jean Racine

PHFFFT, Unproduced, Play *see* George Axelrod

PHIL BLOOD'S LEAP, Poem *see* Robert Buchanan

PHILADELPHIA STORY, New York 1939, Play *see* Philip Barry

PHILADELPHIAN, THE, 1956, Novel *see* Richard Powell

PHILEMON UND BAUCIS, Play *see* Leopold Ahlsen

PHILINE, Novel *see* Olly Boeheim

PHILINE, Play *see* Jo Hanns Rosler

PHILIP MAYNARD, Pamphlet *see* James K. Shields

PHILISTINE IN BOHEMIA, A, Short Story *see* O. Henry

PHILLY, Novel *see* Dan Greenberg

PHILOMEL COTTAGE, Story *see* Agatha Christie

PHILOSOPHIE DANS LE BOUDOIR, LA, Paris 1795, Novel *see* Donatien Sade

PHI-PHI, Opera *see* Henri Christine

PHOENIX OF THE HILLS, A, Story *see* Vingie E. Roe

PHOENIX, THE, 1955, Novel *see* Lawrence P. Bachmann

PHONE CALL FROM A STRANGER, Novel *see* I. A. R. Wylie

PHOTO FINISH, London 1954, Novel *see* Howard Mason

PHOTOGRAPHING FAIRIES, Book *see* Steve Szilagyi

PHROSO, Novel *see* Anthony Hope

PHYLLIS OF THE SIERRAS, A, Boston 1888, Novel *see* Bret Harte

PHYSICIAN, THE, London 1897, Play *see* Henry Arthur Jones

PHYSIOLOGIE DU MARIAGE, LA, Paris 1830, Novel *see* Honore de Balzac

PIACERE, IL, 1889, Novel *see* Gabriele D'Annunzio

PIACEVOLI RAGIONAMENTI, Short Story *see* Pietro L'Arentino

PIANOS MECANIQUES, LES, Paris 1962, Novel *see* Henri-Francois Rey

PIATTO PIANGE, IL, Novel *see* Piero Chiara

PICADOR, LE, Novel *see* Tony Blas, Henri d'Astler

PICAROON, THE, Novel *see* H. B. Marriott Watson

PICASSO: CREATOR AND DESTROYER, Book *see* Arianna Stassinopoulos Huffington

PICCADILLY JIM, London 1917, Novel *see* P. G. Wodehouse

PICCOLA FONTE, LA, 1905, Play *see* Roberto Bracco

PICCOLA MOGLIE, UNA, Novel *see* Zoltan Nagyivanyi Szitnyai

PICCOLA PRETURA, Novel *see* G. G. Lo Schiavo

PICCOLE RE, IL, Play *see* Giuseppe Romualdi

PICCOLI MARTIRI, Novel *see* Carolina Invernizio

PICCOLO ALPINO, Novel *see* Salvator Gotta

PICCOLO MONDO ANTICO, 1896, Novel *see* Antonio Fogazzaro

PICK UP STICKS, Novel *see* Mickey Phillips

PICKET GUARD, THE, Poem *see* Ethelin Elliot Beers

PICK-UP, 1928, Short Story *see* Vina Delmar

PICKUP GIRL, London 1946, Play *see* Elsa Shelley

PICKWICK PAPERS, THE, London 1836, Novel *see* Charles Dickens

PICNIC, New York 1953, Play *see* William Inge

PICNIC AT HANGING ROCK, 1967, Novel *see* Joan Lindsay

PICTURE OF DORIAN GRAY, THE, London 1891, Novel *see* Oscar Wilde

PICTURE OF INNOCENCE, A, 1917, Novel *see* Freeman Tilden

PICTURE ON THE WALL, THE, Kansas City 1920, Novel *see* John Breckenridge Ellis

PICTURE SHOW MAN, THE, Novel *see* Lyle Penn

PIDGIN ISLAND, Indianapolis 1914, Novel *see* Harold MacGrath

PIECE OF PAPER, A, Novel *see* Dick Wordley

PIECE OF STRING, THE, Novel *see* Guy de Maupassant

PIED PIPER OF HAMELIN, THE, 1842, Poem *see* Robert Browning

PIED PIPER, THE, 1942, Novel *see* Nevil Shute

PIEGE POUR UN HOMME SEUL, Novel *see* Robert Thomas

PIERRE AND HIS PEOPLE, London 1892, Novel *see* Gilbert Parker

PIERRE ET JEAN, 1888, Novel *see* Guy de Maupassant

PIERRE ET LUCE, 1920, Novel *see* Romain Rolland

PIERRE ET THERESE, 1909, Novel *see* Marcel Prevost

PIERRE OF THE PLAINS, New York 1908, Play *see* Edgar Selwyn

PIERRE OU JAC, Play *see* Francis de Croisset

PIERWSZY DZIEN WOLNOSCI, Play *see* Leon Kruczkowski

PIETRO DER SCHMUGGLER, Berlin 1930, Novel *see* Ernst Zahn

PIGBOATS, New York 1931, Novel *see* Edward Ellsberg

PIGNASECCA E PIGNAVERDE, Play *see* Emerico Valentinetti

PIGS, New York 1924, Play *see* Patterson McNutt, Anne Morrison

PIGS IS PIGS, Book *see* Ellis Parker Butler

PIKNIK NA OBOCHINE, 1972, Short Story *see* Arkadi Strugatsky, Boris Strugatsky

PIKOVAYA DAMA, 1834, Short Story *see* Alexander Pushkin

PILAR GUERRA, Novel *see* Guillermo Diaz Caneja

PILE OU FACE, Play *see* Louis Verneuil

PILGRIM PROJECT, THE, New York 1964, Novel *see* Henry Searls

PILGRIMAGE, Novel *see* Zenna Henderson

PILGRIMAGE, 1932, Short Story *see* I. A. R. Wylie

PILGRIMAGE, THE, Poem *see* Heinrich Heine

PILGRIM'S PROGRESS, THE, 1684, Allegory *see* John Bunyan

PILLAR TO POST, New York 1943, Play *see* Rose Simon Kohn

PILLARS OF MIDNIGHT, THE, Novel *see* Elleston Trevor

PILLOLE DI ERCOLE, LE, Play *see* Paul Bilhaud, Maurice Hennequin

PILLORY, THE, Short Story *see* Brandon Fleming

PILOT, THE, Novel *see* Robert P. Davis

PILOTE DU DANUBE, LE, 1908, Novel *see* Jules Verne

PIN MONEY, 1921, Short Story *see* Henry C. Vance

PINES OF LORY, THE, Novel *see* J. A. Mitchell

PINK GODS AND BLUE DEMONS, Story *see* Cynthia Stockley

PINK STRING AND SEALING WAX, London 1943, Play *see* Roland Pertwee

PINNACLE, THE, Book *see* Erich von Stroheim

PINTO BEN, Poem *see* William S. Hart

PIONEER GO HOME!, New York 1959, Novel *see* Richard Powell

PIONEERS OF THE OLD SOUTH, New Haven 1918, Book *see* Mary Johnston

PIONEERS, THE, 1823, Novel *see* James Fenimore Cooper

PIONERE IN INGOLSTADT, 1970, Play *see* Marieluise Fleisser

PIPER'S PRICE, THE, Short Story *see* Mrs. Wilson Woodrow

PIPPA PASSES, London 1841, Poem *see* Robert Browning

PIPPI LANGSTRUMP, 1945, Novel *see* Astrid Lindgren

PIRATE, THE, Novel *see* Harold Robbins

PIRATE, THE, New York 1942, Play *see* S. N. Behrman

PIRATES DU RAIL, LES, Novel *see* Oscar-Paul Gilbert

PIRATES OF PENZANCE, THE, London 1880, Opera *see* W. S. Gilbert, Arthur Sullivan

PIRATI DELLA MALESIA, I, Novel *see* Emilio Salgari

PISITO, EL, Novel *see* Rafael Azcona

PISNE ZAVISOVY, Verse *see* Jan Cervenka

PISTOLA DE MI HERMANO, LA, Novel *see* Ray Loriga

PISTOLERO'S PROGRESS, New York 1966, Novel *see* John Sherry

PIT AND THE PENDULUM, THE, 1845, Short Story *see* Edgar Allan Poe

PIT, THE, New York 1903, Novel *see* Frank Norris

PITFALL, THE, Novel *see* Jay Dratler

PITIE DANGEREUSE, LA, Novel *see* Stefan Zweig

PITTUITI'S, LES, Play *see* Michel Duran

PITVA, Short Story *see* Otakar Hanus

PITY MY SIMPLICITY, Novel *see* Chris Massie

PIU BELLA DONNA DEL MONDO, LA, 1919, Novel *see* Salvator Gotta

PIXIE AT THE WHEEL, Short Story *see* Dudley Sturrock

PIXOTE, THE LAW OF THE STRONGEST, Book *see* Cida Venancio Da Silva

PLACE AT THE COAST, THE, Novel *see* Jane Hyde

PLACE AUX FEMMES!, 1898, Play *see* Maurice Hennequin

PLACE BEYOND THE WINDS, THE, Garden City, N.Y. 1914, Novel *see* Harriet T. Comstock

PLACE IN THE SUN, A, Play *see* Cyril Harcourt

PLACE OF DRAGONS, A, Short Story *see* S. H. Barnett

PLACE OF HONEYMOONS, THE, Indianapolis 1912, Novel *see* Harold MacGrath

PLACE OF HONOUR, THE, Novel *see* Ethel M. Dell

PLACE OF ONE'S OWN, A, 1916, Short Story *see* Osbert Sitwell

PLACE TO HIDE, A, Novel *see* Bill Gillham

PLAGUE DOGS, THE, Novel *see* Richard Adams

PLANET OF JUNIOR BROWN, THE, Novel *see* Virginia Hamilton

PLANETE DES SINGES, LA, Paris 1963, Novel *see* Pierre Boulle

PLANT IN SPRING - HARVEST IN FALL, Novel *see* Kang Qu

PLANT, THE, Play *see* Edna Sheklow

PLANTER, THE, New York 1909, Novel *see* Herman Whitaker

PLASTER SAINTS, New York 1922, Novel *see* Frederic Arnold Kummer

PLASTIC AGE, THE, New York 1924, Novel *see* Percy Marks

PLASTIC NIGHTMARE, THE, Novel *see* Richard Neely

PLATERO Y YO, 1914, Autobiography *see* Juan Ramon Jimenez

PLATONOV, c1890, Play *see* Anton Chekhov

PLATOON LEADER, Book *see* James R. McDonough

PLATT RIVER GAMBLE, Short Story *see* L. L. Foreman

PLAY DIRTY, Novel *see* George Marton

PLAY IT AGAIN SAM, Play *see* Woody Allen

PLAY IT AS IT LAYS, 1970, Novel *see* Joan Didion

PLAY ME SOMETHING, 1987, Short Story *see* John Berger

PLAY THINGS, Novel *see* Peter Prince

PLAY WITH SOULS, New York 1922, Novel *see* Clara Longworth

PLAYBACK, Novel *see* Didier Daeninckx

PLAYBOY OF THE WESTERN WORLD, THE, Dublin 1907, Play *see* John Millington Synge

PLAYER, THE, Novel *see* Michael Tolkin

PLAYGROUND, THE, 1953, Short Story *see* Ray Bradbury

PLAYING BEATIE BOW, Novel *see* Ruth Park

PLAYING DEAD, 1915, Short Story *see* Richard Harding Davis

PLAYING THE GAME, Play *see* Sada Cowan

PLAYING THE SAME GAME, Story *see* Cornelia Bleakney

PLAYING WITH FIRE, Story *see* James Oliver Curwood

PLAYTHINGS, Play *see* Sidney Toler

PLAYTHINGS OF DESIRE, Story *see* Wesley J. Putnam

PLAYTHINGS OF DESIRE, New York 1934, Novel *see* Harry Sinclair Drago

PLAZA DE ORIENTE, 1947, Play *see* Joaquin Calvo Sotelo

PLAZA SUITE, 1969, Play *see* Neil Simon

PLEASE DON'T EAT THE DAISIES, Play *see* Jean Kerr

PLEASE GET MARRIED, New York 1919, Play *see* Lewis Allen Browne, James Cullen

PLEASE HELP EMILY, London 1916, Play *see* H. M. Harwood

PLEASE TEACHER, London 1935, Play *see* K. R. G. Browne, Bert Lee, R. P. Weston

PLEASURE BUYERS, THE, New York 1925, Novel *see* Arthur Somers Roche

PLEASURE CRUISE, London 1932, Play *see* Austen Allen

PLEASURE GARDEN, THE, Novel *see* Oliver Sandys

PLEASURE ISLAND, 1949, Novel *see* William Maier

PLEASURE OF HIS COMPANY, THE, New York 1958, Play *see* Cornelia Otis Skinner, Samuel Taylor

PLECAREA VLASINILOR, 1964, Novel *see* Ioana Postelnicu

PLEIN AUX AS, Short Story *see* Henri Kistemaeckers

PLENENO YATO, 1947, Novel *see* Emil Manov

PLENTY, 1978, Play *see* David Hare

PLOUF A EU PEUR, Short Story *see* Fred Argel

PLOUFFE, LES, Novel *see* Roger Lemelin

PLOUGH AND THE STARS, THE, Dublin 1926, Play *see* Sean O'Casey

PLOW WOMAN, THE, New York 1906, Novel *see* Eleanor Gates

PLUFT, O FANTASMINHA, 1957, Play *see* Maria Clara Machado

PLUKOVNIK SVEC, Play *see* Rudolf Medek

PLUME AU VENT, Opera *see* Jean Nohain

PLUNDER, Story *see* Louis L'Amour

PLUNDER, Indianapolis 1917, Novel *see* Arthur Somers Roche

PLUNDER, London 1928, Play *see* Ben Travers

PLUNDER IN THE AIR, Play *see* C. Stafford Dickens

PLUNDER OF THE SUN, 1949, Novel *see* David Dodge

PLUNDER ROAD, Novel *see* Jack Carney, Steven Ritch

PLUNDERER, THE, New York 1912, Novel *see* Roy Norton

PLUS BEAU GOSSE DE FRANCE, LE, Play *see* Andre Mouezy-Eon

PLUS BEL IVROGNE DU QUARTIER, LE, Novel *see* Pierre Scize

PLUS DE WHISKY POUR CALLAGHAN, Novel *see* Peter Cheyney

PLUS FORTS, LES, Paris 1898, Novel *see* Georges Clemenceau

PLUS HEUREUX DES HOMMES, LE, Play *see* Jean Guitton

PLUS QUE REINE, Novel *see* Pierre Decourcelle

PLUSCH UND PLUMOWSKY, Novel *see* Norbert Jacques

PLUTOCRAT, THE, New York 1927, Novel *see* Booth Tarkington

PLYMOUTH ADVENTURE, 1950, Novel *see* Ernest Gebler

POBRE VALBUENA, EL, Opera *see* Carlos Arniches, E. Garcia Alvarez

POBYEDA, Play *see* Mikhail Ruderman, Ilya Vershinin

POCHARDE, LA, Novel *see* Jules Mary

POCKET MONEY, Novel *see* J. P. S. Brown

POCKETFUL OF RYE, A, Story *see* Agatha Christie

POD IGOTO, 1889-90, Novel *see* Ivan Vazov

POD JEDNOU STRECHOU, Short Story *see* Ignat Herrmann

PODEJ STESTI RUKU, Opera *see* Karel Melisek, Jaroslav Mottl

PODNYATAYA TSELINA, 1932, Novel *see* Mikhail Sholokhov

PODSKALAK, Play *see* Frantisek Ferdinand Samberk

POETIC JUSTICE OF UKO SAN, THE, 1910, Short Story *see* James Oliver Curwood

POETIC LICENSE, Story *see* F. K. Junior

POET'S PUB, 1929, Novel *see* Eric Linklater

POHADKA MAJE, Novel *see* Vilem Mrstik

POHJANMAA, 1982, Novel *see* Antti Tuuri

POHORSKA VESNICE, Novel *see* Bozena Nemcova

POIL DE CAROTTE, 1894, Novel *see* Jules Renard

POILU DE LA VICTOIRE, LE, Play *see* Francois Mair

POILUS DE LA 9E, LES, Novel *see* Arnould Galopin

POINT DE LENDEMAIN, Short Story *see* Dominique Vivant-Denon

POINT OF VIEW, THE, New York 1912, Play *see* Edith Ellis, Jules Eckert Goodman

POINTED HEELS, 1929, Short Story *see* Charles William Brackett

POINTING FINGER, THE, Novel *see* Rita

POINTS OF LIGHT, Novel *see* Linda Gray Sexton

POINTS WEST, Boston 1928, Novel *see* B. M. Bower

POISON, Novel *see* Alice Askew, Claude Askew

POISON PEN, London 1937, Play *see* Richard Llewellyn

POISONED PARADISE; A ROMANCE OF MONTE CARLO, New York 1922, Novel *see* Robert W. Service

POISSON CHINOIS, LE, Novel *see* Jean Bommart

POKER, Novel *see* Edmund Edel

POKER D'AS, Novel *see* Arthur Bernede

POKER FACE, 1926, Short Story *see* Carl Clausen

POKER FACES, 1923, Short Story *see* Edgar Franklin

POKHALO, Novel *see* Kalman Csatho

POKHALO, 1972, Novel *see* Erzsebet Galgoczi

POKHOZDENYA GRAFA NEVZOROVA ILI YBIKUS, 1925, Short Story *see* Alexsey Nikolayevich Tolstoy

POKKERS UNGER, DE, Play *see* Estrid Ott

POKOLENIE, 1951, Novel *see* Bohdan Czeszko

POLAR, Novel *see* Jean-Patrick Manchette

POLDARK, Novel *see* Winston Graham

POLE POPPENSPALER, 1874, Short Story *see* Theodor Storm

POLICE DES MOEURS, Novel *see* Pierre Lucas

POLICE FORCE, THE, Play *see* Ernie Lotinga

POLICE PATROL, THE, Story *see* A. Y. Pearson

POLICHE, 1906, Play *see* Henry Bataille

POLICIER APACHE, LE, Novel *see* Marcel Allain, Pierre Souvestre

POLICING THE PLAINS, Novel *see* R. G. MacBeth

POLIKUSHKA, 1863, Short Story *see* Lev Nikolayevich Tolstoy

POLISH CAR WINDOW CLEANER, THE, Novel *see* E. Albinati

POLISHING UP, Story *see* James Oliver Curwood

POLLY IN THE PANTRY, Story *see* Edward Childs Carpenter

POLLY OF THE CIRCUS, New York 1907, Play *see* Margaret Mayo

POLLY WITH A PAST, New York 1917, Play *see* Guy Bolton, George Middleton

POLLYANNA, Boston 1913, Novel *see* Eleanor H. Porter

PRELUDE TO MURDER, Short Story *see* Walter C. Brown

PRELUDE TO NIGHT, Novel *see* Dayton Stoddert

PREMATURE BURIAL, THE, 1844, Short Story *see* Edgar Allan Poe

PREMATURE COMPROMISE, THE, Short Story *see* Robert Barr

PREMIER DE CORDEE, Novel *see* Roger Frison-Roche

PREMIERE LEGION, LA, New York 1934, Play *see* Emmett Lavery

PREMIERES ARMES DE ROCAMBOLE, LES, Novel *see* Ponson Du Terrail

PRENEZ GARDE A LA PEINTURE, 1932, Play *see* Rene Fauchois

PRESCRIPTION: MURDER, Play *see* Richard Levinson, William Link

PRESCRIPTION: MURDER, Book *see* John McGreevey

PRESENT ARMS, New York 1928, Musical Play *see* Herbert Fields, Lorenz Hart, Richard Rodgers

PRESENT FROM MARGATE, A, London 1933, Play *see* Ian Hay, A. E. W. Mason

PRESENTING LILY MARS, 1933, Novel *see* Booth Tarkington

PRESIDENT HAUDECOEUR, LE, Play *see* Roger Ferdinand

PRESIDENT, LE, 1958, Novel *see* Georges Simenon

PRESIDENT VANISHES, THE, New York 1934, Novel *see* Rex Stout

PRESIDENTE, LA, Play *see* Maurice Hennequin, Pierre Veber

PRESIDENTESSA, LA, Play *see* Maurice Hennequin, Pierre Veber

PRESIDENT'S LADY, THE, 1951, Novel *see* Irving Stone

PRESIDENT'S MISTRESS, THE, Novel *see* Patrick Anderson

PRESIDENT'S MYSTERY STORY, THE, 1935, Novel *see* Rupert Hughes, S. S. Van Dine

PRESIDENT'S PLANE IS MISSING, THE, Novel *see* Robert J. Serling

PRESTUPLENIYE I NAKAZANIYE, 1867, Novel *see* Fyodor Dostoyevsky

PRESUMED INNOCENT, 1990, Novel *see* Scott Turow

PRESUMPTION OF STANLEY HAY M.P., THE, Novel *see* Nowell Kaye

PRETE-MOI TA FEMME, Play *see* Maurice Desvallieres

PRETE-MOI TON HABIT, Play *see* Mme d'Herbeville

PRETTY LADIES, Short Story *see* Adela Rogers St. Johns

PRETTY MAIDS ALL IN A ROW, Novel *see* Francis Pollini

PRETTY MRS. SMITH, New York 1914, Play *see* Elmer Harris, Oliver Morosco

PRETTY POLLY BARLOW, London 1964, Short Story *see* Noel Coward

PRETTY SADIE MCKEE, 1933, Short Story *see* Vina Delmar

PRETTY SISTER OF JOSE, THE, New York 1889, Novel *see* Frances Hodgson Burnett

PREY, Short Story *see* Richard Matheson

PREY OF THE DRAGON, THE, Novel *see* Ethel M. Dell

PRIBEH JEDNOHO DNE, Novel *see* Ignat Herrmann

PRIBEH KRIMINALNIHO RADY, 1971, Novel *see* Ladislav Fuks

PRICE HE PAID, THE, Poem *see* Ella Wheeler Wilcox

PRICE OF A PARTY, THE, Short Story *see* William Briggs MacHarg

PRICE OF APPLAUSE, THE, Short Story *see* Norman Jacobsen, Nina Wilcox Putnam

PRICE OF FEATHERS, THE, Story *see* Solita Solano

PRICE OF JUSTICE, THE, Novel *see* Dorothy Uhnak

PRICE OF THINGS, THE, Novel *see* Elinor Glyn

PRICE OF WISDOM, THE, 1932, Play *see* Lionel Brown

PRICE SHE PAID, THE, New York 1912, Novel *see* David Graham Phillips

PRICE, THE, New York 1911, Play *see* George Broadhurst

PRICK UP YOUR EARS, Biography *see* John Lahr

PRICO, Novel *see* Cesare Giulio Viola

PRIDE AND PREJUDICE, London 1813, Novel *see* Jane Austen

PRIDE OF JENNICO, THE, New York 1900, Play *see* Grace Livingston Furniss, Abby Richardson

PRIDE OF PALOMAR, THE, New York 1921, Novel *see* Peter B. Kyne

PRIDE OF THE FANCY, THE, Novel *see* George Edgar

PRIDE OF THE MARINES, 1921, Story *see* Gerald Beaumont

PRIEST ISLAND, Novel *see* E. L. Grant Watson

PRIEST OF LOVE, THE, Book *see* Harry T. Moore

PRIGIONE, LA, Novel *see* Mario Puccini

PRIKLADY TAHNOU, Play *see* Jan Snizek

PRIMADONNA, LA, Novel *see* Filippo Sacchi

PRIMAL LURE; A ROMANCE OF FORT LU CERNE, THE, New York 1914, Novel *see* Vingie E. Roe

PRIMARY COLORS, Novel *see* Joe Klein

PRIMAVERA A PIANABIANCO, Novel *see* Luigi Volpicelli

PRIMAVERA EN OTONO, Madrid 1911, Play *see* Gregorio Martinez Sierra

PRIME OF MISS JEAN BRODIE, THE, London 1961, Novel *see* Muriel Spark

PRIMEL MACHT IHR HAUS VERRUCKT, Novel *see* Kathe Jaenicke

PRIMEROSE, 1911, Play *see* Gaston Arman de Caillavet, Robert de Flers

PRIMO BASILIO, O, 1878, Novel *see* Jose Maria de Eca de Queiros

PRIMROSE PATH, THE, Story *see* E. Lanning Masters, Joan Temple

PRIMROSE PATH, THE, New York 1907, Play *see* Bayard Veiller

PRIMROSE RING, THE, New York 1915, Novel *see* Ruth Sawyer

PRINC BAJAJA, Short Story *see* Bozena Nemcova

PRINC Z ULICE, Novel *see* Stanislav Kolar

PRINCE AND BETTY, THE, New York 1912, Novel *see* P. G. Wodehouse

PRINCE AND THE BEGGARMAID, THE, London 1908, Play *see* Walter Howard

PRINCE AND THE PAUPER, THE, New York 1881, Novel *see* Mark Twain

PRINCE CHAP, THE, New York 1905, Play *see* Edward Peple

PRINCE CONSORT, LE, 1919, Play *see* Jules Chancel, Leon Xanrof

PRINCE CURACAO, LE, Novel *see* Delphi-Fabrice, Oscar Metenier

PRINCE JEAN, LE, Play *see* Charles Mere

PRINCE OF CENTRAL PARK, THE, Novel *see* Evan H. Rhodes

PRINCE OF FOXES, Novel *see* Samuel Shellabarger

PRINCE OF GRAUSTARK, THE, New York 1914, Novel *see* George Barr McCutcheon

PRINCE OF HEAD WAITERS, THE, 1927, Short Story *see* Garrett Fort, Viola Brothers Shore

PRINCE OF INDIA, THE, New York 1893, Novel *see* Lew Wallace

PRINCE OF PILSEN, THE, New York 1902, Musical Play *see* Gustav Luders, Frank Pixley

PRINCE OF PLAYERS, 1953, Book *see* Eleanor Ruggles

PRINCE OF THE CITY, Book *see* Robert Daley

PRINCE OF TIDES, THE, Novel *see* Pat Conroy

PRINCE, THE, Play *see* George Tabori

PRINCE WHO WAS A THIEF, THE, 1927, Short Story *see* Theodore Dreiser

PRINCE ZILAH, LE, Paris 1885, Play *see* Jules Claretie

PRINCESS AND THE GOBLIN, THE, Novel *see* George MacDonald

PRINCESS AND THE PLUMBER, THE, 1929, Short Story *see* Alice Duer Miller

PRINCESS BRIDE, THE, Novel *see* William Goldman

PRINCESS CLEMENTINA, THE, Novel *see* A. E. W. Mason

PRINCESS FITZ, Novel *see* Winifred Carter

PRINCESS FROM THE POORHOUSE, THE, Short Story *see* Henry Albert Phillips

PRINCESS IN LOVE, Book *see* Anna Pasternak

PRINCESS OF COPPER, THE, New York 1900, Novel *see* Archibald Clavering Gunter

PRINCESS OF HAPPY CHANCE, THE, Novel *see* Tom Gallon

PRINCESS OF NEW YORK, THE, New York 1911, Novel *see* Cosmo Hamilton

PRINCESS OF PATCHES, THE, 1901, Play *see* Mark Swan

PRINCESS OF THE DESERT DREAM, THE, Story *see* Ralph Cummins

PRINCESS O'HARA, 1934, Short Story *see* Damon Runyon

PRINCESS PRISCILLA'S FORTNIGHT, Novel *see* Elizabeth Russell

PRINCESS VIRTUE, Novel *see* Louise Winter

PRINCESS ZIM-ZIM, THE, Albany, Ny. 1911, Play *see* Edward Sheldon

PRINCESSE AUX CLOWNS, LA, Novel *see* Jean-Jose Frappa

PRINCESSE DE BAGDAD, LA, 1881, Play *see* Alexandre Dumas (fils)

PRINCESSE DE CLEVES, LA, 1678, Novel *see* Marie-Madeleine La Fayette

PRINCESSEN SOM INGEN KUNDE MALBINDE FELGESVENDEN, 1910, Short Story *see* Peder Christen Asbjornsen

PRINCIPE COME ORELHAS DE BURRO, O, 1942, Novel *see* Jose Regio

PRINCIPESSA GEORGES, LA, 1871, Novel *see* Alexandre Dumas (fils)

PRINCIPESSA, LA, *see* Roberto Bracco

PRINCIPESSINA, LA, 1908, *see* Carlo Bertolazzi

PRINSESSAN, Stockholm 1960, Novel *see* Gunnar Mattsson

PRINSESSAN TORNROSA, 1870, Play *see* Zachris Topelius

PRINSESSEN PA AERTEN, 1835, Short Story *see* Hans Christian Andersen

PRINTEMPS, Short Story *see* Mme M. L. de Wyttenbach

PRINTEMPS SEXUEL, Story *see* Alfred Machard

PRINZ FRIEDRICH VON HOMBURG, 1811, Play *see* Heinrich von Kleist

PRINZ VON ARKADIEN, DER, Play *see* Walter Reisch

PRINZESSIN DAGMAR, Play *see* Rudolf Brettschneider

PRINZESSIN OLALA, Opera *see* Jean Gilbert

PRINZESSIN VON ST. WOLFGANG, DIE, Short Story *see* Ernst Neubach

PRIORY SCHOOL, THE, Short Story *see* Arthur Conan Doyle

PRISCILLA THE RAKE, Play *see* Fanny Bowker

PRISON SANS BARREAUX, Play *see* Egon Eis, Otto Eis, Thomas B. Forster, Hilde Koveloff

PRISONER OF SECOND AVENUE, THE, 1972, Play *see* Neil Simon

PRISONER OF ZENDA, THE, London 1894, Novel *see* Anthony Hope

PRISONER, THE, London 1954, Play *see* Bridget Boland

PRISONER WITHOUT A NAME, CELL WITHOUT A NUMBER, 1981, Book *see* Jacobo Timerman

PRISONERS, Play *see* Ferenc Molnar

PRISONERS ARE PEOPLE, 1952, Book *see* Kenyon J. Scudder

PRISONS DE FEMMES, 1930, Novel *see* Francis Carco

PRITHVI VALLABH, Novel *see* V. B. Joshi

PRITHVI VALLABH, 1920, Novel *see* K. M. Munshi

PRIVARZANIYAT BALON, 1965, Short Story *see* Yordan Radichkov

PRIVATE ANGELO, 1946, Novel *see* Eric Linklater

PRIVATE BEACH, Beverly Hills 1934, Play *see* Jesse Lasky Jr., Gladys Unger

PRIVATE EAR, THE, London 1962, Play *see* Peter Shaffer

PRIVATE I, Novel *see* Jimmy Sangster

PRIVATE INVESTIGATION, A, Novel *see* Karl Alexander

PRIVATE LIFE, Novel *see* Alan Hackney

PRIVATE LIFE OF HELEN OF TROY, THE, Indianapolis 1925, Novel *see* John Erskine

PRIVATE LIVES, London 1930, Play *see* Noel Coward

PRIVATE PARTS, Book *see* Howard Stern

PRIVATE PEAT, Indianpolis 1917, Book *see* Harold Reginald Peat

PRIVATE POTTER, 1961, Television Play see Ronald Harwood

PRIVATE PRACTICE OF MICHAEL SHAYNE, THE, New York 1940, Novel see Brett Halliday

PRIVATE SECRETARY, New York 1929, Novel see Alan Brener Schultz

PRIVATE WORLDS, Boston 1934, Novel see Phyllis Bottome

PRIVATES ON PARADE, 1977, Play see Peter Nichols

PRIVATE'S PROGRESS, Novel see Alan Hackney

PRIVATSEKRETARIN, DIE, Novel see Franz Schulz, Stefan Szomahazy

PRIVILEGED INFORMATION, Book see Tom Alibrandi, Frank H. Armani

PRIZE OF GOLD, A, Novel see Max Catto

PRIZE OF PERIL, THE, Short Story see Robert Sheckley

PRIZE, THE, New York 1962, Novel see Irving Wallace

PRIZZI'S HONOR, 1982, Novel see Richard Condon

PRO DOMO, 1914, Play see Jonkheer A. W. G. Van Riemsdijk

PRO KAMARADA, Radio Play see Ladislav Jilek

PROBLEM IN GRAND LARCENY, A, 1919, Short Story see Jack Boyle

PROCANE CHRONICLE, THE, Novel see Oliver Bleeck

PROCURA-SE UMA ROSA, Play see Glaucio Gill

PRODANA NEVESTA, Prague 1866, Opera see Karel Sabina, Bedrich Smetana

PRODIGA, LA, 1882, Novel see Pedro Antonio de Alarcon

PRODIGAL DAUGHTERS, New York 1921, Novel see Joseph Hocking

PRODIGAL FATHER, THE, 1924, Short Story see Cosmo Hamilton

PRODIGAL IN UTOPIA, A, Short Story see Donn Byrne

PRODIGAL JUDGE, THE, Indianapolis 1911, Novel see Vaughan Kester

PRODIGAL SON, THE, 1904, Novel see Hall Caine

PRODKOMISSAR, 1925, Short Story see Mikhail Sholokhov

PROFESSIONAL GUEST, THE, Novel see William Garrett

PROFESSOR HIERONIMUS, 1895, Novel see Amalie Skram

PROFESSOR MAMLOCK, Play see Friedrich Wolf

PROFESSOR TIM, Play see George Shiels

PROFESSOR UNRAT, 1905, Novel see Heinrich Mann

PROFETA VOLTAL, SZIVEM, 1965, Novel see Sandor Somogyi Toth

PROFIT - AND THE LOSS, Play see H. F. Maltby

PROFLIGATE, THE, Novel see Arthur Hornblow

PROFLIGATE, THE, London 1889, Play see Arthur Wing Pinero

PROHIBITION STILL AT ITS WORST, 1928, Novel see Irving Fisher

PROIBITION AT ITS WORST, 1926, Novel see Irving Fisher

PROIE, LA, Play see Victor Cyril

PROISSHESTVIYE, 1886, Short Story see Anton Chekhov

PROIZSHESTVIE NA TIKHATA ULITSA, 1960, Novel see Pavel Vezhinov

PROIZVEDENIYE ISKUSSTVA, 1886, Short Story see Anton Chekhov

PROJECTED MAN, THE, Novel see Frank Quattrocchi

PROMENADES DANS ROME, 1829, Novel see Stendhal

PROMESSA, A, 1957, Play see Bernardo Santareno

PROMESSA, LA, Novel see Friedrich Durrenmatt

PROMESSE DE L'AUBE, LA, Paris 1960, Book see Romain Gary

PROMESSI SPOSI, I, 1827, Novel see Alessandro Manzoni

PROMETHEUS VINCTUS, c468 bc, Play see Aeschylus

PROMISE; A TALE OF THE GREAT NORTHWEST, THE, New York 1915, Novel see James B. Hendryx

PROMISE MADE, A, Novel see Blaine M. Yorgason, Brenton Yorgason

PROMISED LAND, Novel see Colin Dexter

PROOF THRO' THE NIGHT, Play see Alan R. Kenward

PROPAVSHAYA GRAMOTA, 1831, Short Story see Nikolay Gogol

PROPERTY OF A LADY, THE, Short Story see Ian Fleming

PROSCANIE, Novel see Valentin Rasputin

PROSHCHAY, GUL'SARY, 1966, Short Story see Chingiz Aitmatov

PROSIM PANE PROFESORE!, Novel see Otto Jun

PROSPETTIVA, LA, Short Story see Nikolay Gogol

PROTECTING PEACE, Play see Song Zhi

PROTECTING PRUE, 1924, Short Story see Edgar Franklin

PROTECTION FOR A TOUGH RACKET, Short Story see Cordelia Baird Gross

PROUD FLESH, New York 1924, Novel see Lawrence Irving Rising

PROUD ONES, THE, 1952, Novel see Verne Athanas

PROVDAM SVOU ZENU, Play see Jindrich Horejsi, Julius Lebl

PROVINCIALE, LA, 1952, Novel see Alberto Moravia

PROXIES, 1920, Short Story see Frank R. Adams

PROZESS BUNTERBART, Play see Max Brod

PROZESS, DER, Berlin 1925, Novel see Franz Kafka

PROZESZ AUF LEBEN UND TOD, Novel see Rudolf Brunngraber

PRUDE, THE, Story see Julie Herne

PRUDENCE AND THE PILL, London 1965, Novel see Hugh Mills

PRUDE'S FALL, THE, London 1920, Play see Rudolf Besier, May Edginton

PRUNELLA; OR LOVE IN A DUTCH GARDEN, London 1904, Play see Harley Granville-Barker, L. Housman

PRUNING KNIFE, THE, Play see Andrew Soutar, Maud Williamson

PRVNI PARTA, 1937, Novel see Karel Capek

PSOHLAVCI, Novel see Alois Jirasek

PSYCHE 58, Paris 1958, Novel see Francoise Des Ligneris

PSYCHE: EGY HAJDANI KOLTONO IRASAI, 1972, Novel see Sandor Weores

PSYCHO, 1959, Novel see Robert Bloch

PSYCHOPATHIA SEXUALIS: KLINISCHFORNSISCHE STUDIE, Stuttgart 1886, Book see Richard von Krafft-Ebing

PT 109, JOHN F. KENNEDY IN WORLD WAR II, New York 1961, Biography see Robert J. Donovan

PU VINVIDUR HREINI, 1931-32, Novel see Halldor Laxness

PUBERTY BLUES, Novel see Gabrielle Carey, Kathy Lette

PUBLIC DEFENDER, THE, New York 1917, Book see Mayer C. Goldman

PUBLIC ENEMY NO. 1, Novel see Gregory Rogers

PUBLIC EYE, THE, 1962, Play see Peter Shaffer

PUBLIC FIGURE, A, Television Play see Harry W. Junkin

PUBLIC PIGEON NO. 1, 1956, Television Play see Devery Freeman

PUCE A L'OREILLE, LA, Paris 1907, Play see Georges Feydeau

PUCHINA, 1866, Play see Alexander Ostrovsky

PUDD'NHEAD WILSON, Hartford 1894, Novel see Mark Twain

PUDELNACKT IN OBERBAYERN, Novel see Peter Ammer

PUGNO DEL POTERE, IL, Diary see Erich von Lehner

PUISSANCE DU BAISER, LA, Novel see Pierre Sabatier

PUITS AUX TROIS VERITES, LE, Paris 1949, Novel see Jean Jacques Gautier

PUITS DE JACOBS, LE, Novel see Pierre Benoit

PUJARI, Novel see Munipalle Raju

PULL-OVER ROUGE, LE, Book see Gilles Perrault

PUMPING IRON II: THE UNPRECEDENTED WOMAN, Book see George Butler, Charles Gaines

PUMPKIN EATER, THE, London 1962, Novel see Penelope Mortimer

PUNAO DE ROSAS, EL, Opera see Carlos Arniches, Ruperto Chapi, A. Mas

PUNGUTA CU DOI BANI, 1876, Short Story see Ion Creanga

PUNITIVE ACTION, 1954, Novel see John Robb

PUNK, THE, Novel see Gideon Sams

PUNKS KOMMT AUS AMERIKA, Novel see Ludwig von Wohl

PUNKTCHEN UND ANTON, 1930, Novel see Erich Kastner

PUNKTUR, PUNKTUR, KOMMA, STRIK, Novel see Petur Gunnarsson

PUPIL, THE, Short Story see Henry James

PUPILAS DO SENHOR REITOR, AS, 1867, Novel see Julio Dinis

PUPPET CROWN, THE, Indianapolis 1901, Novel see Harold MacGrath

PUPPET MAN, THE, Novel see Cosmo Gordon Lennox

PUPPET MASTERS, THE, 1951, Novel see Robert A. Heinlein

PUPPET ON A CHAIN, 1969, Novel see Alistair MacLean

PUPPETS, Play see Frances Lightner

PUREZA, 1937, Novel see Jose Lins Do Rego

PURITAN, THE, 1931, Novel see Liam O'Flaherty

PURLIE VICTORIOUS, New York 1961, Play see Ossie Davis

PURPLE AND FINE LINEN, 1926, Short Story see May Edginton

PURPLE CLOUD, THE, 1902, Novel see Matthew Phipps Shiel

PURPLE DRESS, THE, Short Story see O. Henry

PURPLE HIEROGLYPH, THE, 1920, Short Story see Will F. Jenkins

PURPLE LADY, THE, New York 1899, Play see Sydney Rosenfeld

PURPLE PLAIN, THE, 1947, Novel see H. E. Bates

PURSE STRINGS, THE, Play see Bernard Parry

PURSUIT OF HAPPINESS, THE, Novel see Thomas Rogers

PURSUIT OF HAPPINESS, THE, New York 1933, Play see Lawrence Langner, Armina Marshall

PURSUIT OF PAMELA, THE, London 1913, Play see C. B. Fernald

PUSHER, THE, 1956, Novel see Evan Hunter

PUT ON BY CUNNING, Novel see Ruth Rendell

PUT ON THE SPOT, New York 1930, Novel see Jack Lait

PUT YOURSELF IN HIS PLACE, Novel see Charles Reade

PUTAIN RESPECTEUSE, LA, 1946, Play see Jean-Paul Sartre

PUTCHESTWIE MOLODOGO KOMPOSITORA, Novel see Otar Tschcheidse

PUZZLE FOR FIENDS, Novel see Patrick Quentin

PUZZLE FOR PUPPETS, Novel see Patrick Quentin

PUZZLE OF THE PEPPER TREE, THE, New York 1933, Novel see Susan Palmer

PUZZLE OF THE RED STALLION, THE, New York 1936, Novel see Stuart Palmer

PYASI DHARTI, Play see Narendra Khajuria

PYAT VECHEROV, 1959, Play see Alexander Volodin

PYGMALION, London 1913, Play see George Bernard Shaw

PYLON, 1935, Novel see William Faulkner

PYOTR PERVY, 1929-45, Novel see Alexsey Nikolayevich Tolstoy

PYRAMIDE DES SONNENGOTTES, DIE, Novel see Karl Friedrich May

PYSCHO, Novel see Robert Bloch

PYSCHOGEIST, London 1966, Novel see L. P. Davies

PYX, THE, Novel see John Buell

Q & A, Novel see Edwin Torres

QB VII, Novel see Leon Uris

QI SHI ER JIA FANG KE, Play see Shanghai Public Comedy Troupe

QI WANG, 1982, Novel see Chang Chang Hsi-Kuo

QI WANG, 1982, Short Story see Zhong Ahcheng

QIAN WAN BUY YAO WANG JI, Play see Cong Shen

QINGCHENGZHI LIAN, Novel see Eileen Chang

QINGSONG LING, Play see Zhang Zhongpeng

QUADRILLE, Play see Sacha Guitry

RAINBOW, Book *see* Christopher Finch

RAINBOW, New York 1928, Play *see* Oscar Hammerstein II, Laurence Stallings

RAINBOW DRIVE, Novel *see* Roderick Thorp

RAINBOW POUR RIMBAUD, 1991, Novel *see* Jean Teule

RAINBOW, THE, 1915, Novel *see* D. H. Lawrence

RAINBOW, THE, New York 1912, Play *see* A. E. Thomas

RAINBOW TRAIL, THE, New York 1915, Novel *see* Zane Grey

RAINMAKER, THE, Novel *see* John Grisham

RAINMAKER, THE, 1955, Television Play *see* N. Richard Nash

RAINS CAME, THE, New York 1937, Novel *see* Louis Bromfield

RAINTREE COUNTY, 1948, Novel *see* Ross Lockridge

RAINY THE LION KILLER, Story *see* Leonard Grover

RAISE THE TITANIC!, Novel *see* Clive Cussler

RAISIN IN THE SUN, A, New York 1959, Play *see* Lorraine Hansberry

RAISING A RIOT, Novel *see* Alfred Toombs

RAISING DAISY ROTHSCHILD, Book *see* Betty Lesley-Manville, Jock Lesley-Manville

RAJ QUARTET, Novel *see* Paul Scott

RAJAH'S DIAMOND, THE, Short Story *see* Robert Louis Stevenson

RAJSKA JABLON, 1937, Novel *see* Pola Gojawiczynska

RAKKA SURU YUGATA, Novel *see* Kaori Ekuni

RALLY 'ROUND THE FLAG BOYS!, 1957, Novel *see* Max Shulman

RAMAYANA, Verse *see* Valmiki

RAMBLE IN APHASIA, A, Short Story *see* O. Henry

RAMBLERS, THE, New York 1926, Musical Play *see* Guy Bolton, Bert Kalmar, Harry Ruby

RAMBLIN' KID, THE, Indianapolis 1920, Novel *see* Earl Wayland Bowman

RAMBLING ROSE, 1972, Novel *see* Calder Willingham

RAMEAU'S NIECE, Novel *see* Cathleen Schine

RAMEY, Novel *see* Jack Farris

RAMO PARA LUISA, UM, 1959, Short Story *see* Jose Conde

RAMONA, Boston 1884, Novel *see* Helen Hunt Jackson

RAMPAGE, Novel *see* William P. Wood

RAMPAGE, New York 1961, Novel *see* Alan Caillou

RAMPE, LA, 1909, Play *see* Henri de Rotschild

RAMROD, Short Story *see* Luke Short

RAMSBOTTOM RIDES AGAIN, Play *see* Harold G. Robert

RAMSHACKLE HOUSE, New York 1922, Novel *see* Hubert Footner

RAMU CHANANA, Play *see* Bharat Vyas

RAMUNTCHO, 1896, Novel *see* Pierre Loti

RANCH AT THE WOLVERINE, THE, Boston 1914, Novel *see* B. M. Bower

RANCH DES HOMMES FORTS, LE, Novel *see* Jean Desvallieres

RANCON, LA, Play *see* Leopold Gomez

RANDIDANGAZHI, Novel *see* Thakazhy Shivashankar Pillai

RANDOLPH '64, 1905, Short Story *see* Arthur Cheney Train

RANDOM HARVEST, 1941, Novel *see* James Hilton

RANDOM QUEST, 1961, Short Story *see* John Wyndham

RANGE BOSS, THE, Chicago 1916, Novel *see* Charles Alden Seltzer

RANGE DWELLERS, THE, New York 1906, Novel *see* Bertha Sinclair Muzzy

RANGE WAR, 1949, Novel *see* Thomas W. Blackburn

RANGY PETE, Boston 1922, Novel *see* Guy Morton

RANJU SEPANJANG JALAN, Novel *see* Shahnon Ahmad

RANK OUTSIDER, A, Novel *see* Nat Gould

RANNIE ZHURAVLI, 1975, Short Story *see* Chingiz Aitmatov

RANSOM, Philadelphia 1934, Novel *see* Charles Francis Coe

RANSOM OF MACK, THE, Short Story *see* O. Henry

RANSOM OF RED CHIEF, 1907, Short Story *see* O. Henry

RANSOM, ONE MILLION DOLLARS, Short Story *see* Damon Runyon

RANSON'S FOLLY, New York 1902, Novel *see* Richard Harding Davis

RANTZAU, LES, Play *see* Chatrian, Alexandre, Erckmann, Emile

RAP, THE, Novel *see* Ernest Brawley

RAPACITE, Novel *see* Eugene Barbier

RAPA-NUI, Novel *see* Andre Armandy

RAPIDS, THE, Novel *see* Alan Sullivan

RAPPACINI'S DAUGHTER, 1846, Short Story *see* Nathaniel Hawthorne

RAPT, LE, Novel *see* Charles-Ferdinand Ramuz

RAPTURE IN MY RAGS, London 1964, Novel *see* Phyllis Hastings

RASCAL; A MEMOIR OF A BETTER ERA, New York 1963, Novel *see* Sterling North

RASCOALA, 1932, Novel *see* Liviu Rebreanu

RASHOMON, 1915, Short Story *see* Ryunosuke Akutagawa

RASP, THE, Novel *see* Philip MacDonald

RASSKAZ NEIZVESTNOGO CHELOVEKA, 1893, Short Story *see* Anton Chekhov

RAT D'AMERIQUE, LE, Novel *see* Jacques Lanzmann

RAT, THE, London 1924, Play *see* Constance Collier, Ivor Novello

RAT TRAP, THE, New York 1904, Novel *see* Dolf Wyllarde

RATAI, Tokyo 1954, Novel *see* Kafu Nagai

RATAS, LAS, Novel *see* Miguel Delibes

RATELRAT, DE, Novel *see* Janwillem Van Der Wetering

RATHER ENGLISH MARRIAGE, A, Novel *see* Angela Carter

RATHSKELLER AND THE ROSE, THE, Short Story *see* O. Henry

RATMAN'S NOTEBOOKS, Novel *see* Stephen Gilbert

RATNADEEP, Novel *see* Prabhat Kumar Mukherjee

RATON PASS, 1950, Novel *see* Thomas W. Blackburn

RAT-POLES, Novel *see* Edward Redlinski

RATS, THE, Novel *see* James Herbert

RATSEL MANUELA, DAS, Novel *see* Anna Elisabeth Weirauch

RATSEL UM BEATE, Play *see* Hanz Lorenz, Alfred Moller

RATTEN DER GROSSTADT, Novel *see* Fr. Glaser

RATTEN, DIE, 1911, Play *see* Gerhart Hauptmann

RATTLE OF A SIMPLE MAN, London 1962, Play *see* Charles Dyer

RATTLER ROCK, 1923, Short Story *see* Ralph Cummins

RAUB DER SABINERINNEN, DER, Play *see* Franz von Schonthan, Paul von Schonthan

RAUBER, DIE, 1782, Play *see* Friedrich von Schiller

RAUBER HOTZENPLOTZ, DER, Book *see* Otfried Preussler

RAUBERBANDE, DIE, Novel *see* Leonhard Frank

RAUBFISCHER IN HELLAS, Novel *see* Werner Helwig

RAUSCHGIFT, Play *see* Victor Reingruber

RAVEN, THE, 1845, Poem *see* Edgar Allan Poe

RAVEN; THE LOVE STORY OF EDGAR ALLAN POE, THE, New York 1909, Novel *see* George Cochrane Hazelton

RAVISHED ARMENIA, New York 1918, Book *see* Aurora Mardiganian

RAVISSANTE IDIOTE, UNE, Paris 1962, Novel *see* Charles Exbrayat

RAWHEAD REX, Short Story *see* Clive Barker

RAWHIDE YEARS, THE, 1953, Novel *see* Norman A. Fox

RAYON DES JOUETS, LE, 1951, Play *see* Jacques Deval

RAZORBACK, Novel *see* Peter Brennan

RAZOR'S EDGE, THE, 1944, Novel *see* W. Somerset Maugham

RAZZIA, 1929, Short Story *see* Lajos Nagy

RAZZIA SUR LA CHNOUF, Novel *see* Auguste Le Breton

RE BURLONE, Play *see* Gerolamo Rovetta

RE DEI MIMIDUTI, IL, Novel *see* Viard, Zacharias

REACH FOR THE SKY, 1954, Novel *see* Paul Brickhill

READY MONEY, New York 1912, Play *see* James Montgomery

READY WILLING AND ABLE, Short Story *see* Richard Macauley

REAL ADVENTURE, THE, New York 1915, Novel *see* Henry Kitchell Webster

REAL AGATHA, THE, Novel *see* Edith Huntington Mason

REAL GLORY, THE, London 1938, Novel *see* Charles L. Clifford

REAL MAN, THE, New Ork 1915, Novel *see* Francis Lynde

REAR CAR, THE, Los Angeles 1922, Play *see* Edward E. Rose

REAR WINDOW, 1944, Short Story *see* Cornell Woolrich

REARVIEW MIRROR, Novel *see* Caroline B. Cooney

REASON WHY, THE, London 1911, Novel *see* Elinor Glyn

REASON WHY, THE, London 1953, Book *see* Cecil Woodham-Smith

REBECCA, London 1938, Novel *see* Daphne Du Maurier

REBECCA OF SUNNYBROOK FARM, New York 1903, Novel *see* Kate Douglas Wiggin

REBEL AGAINST THE LIGHT, New York 1960, Novel *see* Alexander Ramati

REBEL HIGH, Novel *see* Evan Keliher

REBEL ISLAND, Story *see* Adele Comandini

REBELLION, Novel *see* Piero Regnoli

REBELLION DER GEHENKTEN, DIE, 1936, Novel *see* Ben Traven

REBELLION, DIE, 1924, Short Story *see* Joseph Roth

REBELS, THE, Novel *see* John Jakes

REBOZO DE SOLEDAD, EL, Novel *see* Dr. Ferrer

RECHTER THOMAS, Novel *see* Francois Pauwels

RECIPE FOR MURDER, 1934, Short Story *see* Vincent Starrett

RECIPE FOR MURDER, London 1932, Play *see* Arnold Ridley

RECKLESS LADY, THE, London 1924, Novel *see* Philip Hamilton Gibbs

RECKLESS YOUTH, Story *see* Cosmo Hamilton

RECKLESSNESS, Boston 1914, Play *see* Eugene O'Neill

RECKONING, THE, Novel *see* Hugh Atkinson

RECKONING, THE, Story *see* Dwight Cummings

RECOIL, 1922, Short Story *see* Rex Beach

RECOLLECTIONS OF VESTA TILLEY, Book *see* Lady de Frece

RECOMPENSE, London 1924, Novel *see* Robert Keable

RECOURS EN GRACE, Novel *see* Noel Calef

RECOVERY, Book *see* Steven L. Thompson

RECREATION, LA, Short Story *see* Francoise Sagan

RE-CREATION OF BRIAN KENT, THE, Chicago 1919, Novel *see* Harold Bell Wright

RECTEUR DANS L'ILE DE SEIN, UN, Novel *see* Henri Queffelec

RECTOR'S WIFE, THE, Novel *see* Joanna Trollope

RECURSO DEL METODO, EL, 1974, Novel *see* Alejo Carpentier

RED ACES, London 1929, Novel *see* Edgar Wallace

RED ALERT, New York 1958, Novel *see* Peter Bryan George

RED BADGE OF COURAGE, THE, 1895, Novel *see* Stephen Crane

RED BERET, THE, Book *see* Hilary St. George Sanders

RED BLOOD OF COURAGE, Short Story *see* James Oliver Curwood

RED CAT, THE, New York 1934, Play *see* Hans Adler, Rudolph Lothar

RED CIRCLE, THE, Short Story *see* Arthur Conan Doyle

RED CROSS SEAL STORY, THE, Story *see* E. W. Sargent

RED DANCER OF MOSCOW, THE, New York 1928, Novel *see* Henry Leyford Gates

RED DARKNESS, 1922, Short Story *see* George Frank Worts

RED DOG, THE, Play *see* J. O. Twiss

RED DRAGON, Novel *see* Thomas Harris

RED DUST, New York 1928, Play *see* Wilson Collison

RED EARTH - WHITE EARTH, Book *see* Will Weaver

RED FOR DANGER, Novel *see* Evadne Price

RED FOX, Novel *see* Gerald Seymour

RED HERRING, Short Story *see* Virginia Rouse

RED HORSE HILL, Boston 1909, Novel *see* Sidney McCall

RED HUGH - PRINCE OF DONEGAL, Milwaukee 1957, Novel *see* Robert T. Reilly

RED KISSES, Play *see* Charles E. Blaney, Harry Clay Blaney

RED LANE; A ROMANCE OF THE BORDER, THE, New York 1912, Novel *see* Holman Francis Day

RED LANTERN, THE, New York 1911, Novel *see* Edith Wherry

RED MEAT, Novel *see* David Karsner

RED MILL, THE, New York 1906, Musical Play *see* Henry Martyn Blossom, Victor Herbert

RED MIRAGE, THE, London 1913, Novel *see* I. A. R. Wylie

RED MOUSE; A MYSTERY ROMANCE, THE, New York 1909, Novel *see* William Hamilton Osborne

RED MOUSE, THE, Philadelphia 1903, Play *see* Henry J. W. Dam

RED PEPPERS, 1936, Play *see* Noel Coward

RED PLANET, 1933, Play *see* John L. Balderston, John Hoare

RED POTTAGE, Novel *see* Mary Cholmondeley

RED ROCK, Novel *see* Luo Guangbing, Yang Yiyan

RED SAUNDERS STORIES, 1902-06, Short Stories *see* Henry Wallace Phillips

RED SKY AT MORNING, 1942, Play *see* Dymphna Cusack

RED WAGON, Novel *see* Lady Eleanor Smith

RED WHEELS ROLLING, 1940, Novel *see* Walter D. Edmonds

RED WIDOW, THE, New York 1911, Musical Play *see* Charles J. Gebest, Channing Pollock, Rennold Wolf

REDEEMING SIN, THE, Story *see* L. V. Jefferson

REDEMPTA, Short Story *see* M. de Mylio

REDEMPTION OF DAVID CORSON, THE, New York 1900, Novel *see* Charles Frederick Goss

REDENZIONE, Play *see* Roberto Farinacci

RED-HAIRED ALIBI, New York 1932, Novel *see* Wilson Collison

RED-HAIRED CUPID, 1901, Short Story *see* Henry Wallace Phillips

REDHEAD, New York 1933, Novel *see* Vera Brown

REDHEAD AND THE COWBOY, THE, Novel *see* Charles Marquis Warren

RED-HEADED HUSBAND, THE, 1926, Short Story *see* Katharine Newlin Burt

RED-HEADED LEAGUE, THE, 1891, Short Story *see* Arthur Conan Doyle

RED-HEADED WOMAN, New York 1931, Novel *see* Katharine Brush

REDMAN AND THE CHILD, THE, Short Story *see* Bret Harte

REDWOOD HIGHWAY, Story *see* Daniel Mainwaring

REETIMATA NATAK, 1936, Play *see* Jaladhar Chattopadhyay

REFLECTIONS IN A GOLDEN EYE, Boston 1941, Novel *see* Carson McCullers

REFLET DE CLAUDE MERCOEUR, LE, Novel *see* Frederic Boutet

REFLEX, Novel *see* Roger Ward

REFUGE, LE, 1909, Play *see* Dario Niccodemi

REGAIN, 1930, Novel *see* Jean Giono

REGATES DE SAN FRANCISCO, LES, Story *see* Quarantotti Gambini

REGENERATION, 1991, Novel *see* Pat Barker

REGENTA, LA, 1884, Novel *see* Leopoldo Alas

REGENT'S PARK MYSTERY, THE, Short Story *see* Baroness Orczy

REGI IDOK MOZIJA, 1967, Short Story *see* Ivan Mandy

REGINA AMSTETTEN, 1936, Short Story *see* Ernst Weichert

REGINA DEL MERCATO, LA, Novel *see* Carolina Invernizio

REGINA DI NAVARRA, LA, Play *see* Eugene Scribe

REGINE, 1872, Short Story *see* Gottfried Keller

REGINETTA DELLE ROSE, LA, 1912, Opera *see* Giovacchino Forzano

REGISTERED WOMAN, THE, Play *see* John Farrow

REGNE DE L'ESPRIT MALIN, LE, Lausanne 1917, Novel *see* Charles-Ferdinand Ramuz

REGULATOREN VON ARKANSAS, Novel *see* Friedrich Gerstackers

REHABILITATION, LA, *see* Marcel Tisseron

REI DA VELA, O, Play *see* Oswald de Andrade

REICH MIR DIE HAND, MEIN LEBEN, Short Story *see* Fritz Habeck

REIFEPRUFUNG, DIE, Play *see* Max Dreyer

REIGATE SQUIRES, THE, Short Story *see* Arthur Conan Doyle

REIGEN, DER, 1900, Play *see* Arthur Schnitzler

REINA MORA, LA, Opera *see* Hermanos Alvarez Quintero, J. Serrano

REINCARNATION OF PETER PROUD, THE, Novel *see* Max Simon Ehrlich

REINE DE BIARRITZ, LA, Play *see* Romain Coolus, Maurice Hennequin

REINE ELISABETH, LA, Play *see* Emile Moreau

REINE MARGOT, LA, 1845, Novel *see* Alexandre Dumas (pere)

REINEKE FUCHS, 1794, Verse *see* Johann Wolfgang von Goethe

REIS AM WEG, Short Story *see* Wilhelmine von Hillern

REISE NACH PARIS, DIE, Play *see* E. W. Schafer

REISE NACH TILSIT, DIE, Berlin 1917, Novel *see* Hermann Sudermann

REIVERS; A REMINISCENCE, THE, New York 1962, Novel *see* William Faulkner

REJAS Y VOTOS, Opera *see* Vicente Diez Peydro

REJUVENATION OF AUNT MARY, THE, New York 1907, Play *see* Anne Warner

REKVIEM, 1957-58, Short Story *see* Istvan Orkeny

RELATIONS ARE BEST APART, Play *see* Edwin Lewis

RELATIVE VALUES, 1923, Short Story *see* Sophie Kerr

RELENTLESS, 1972, Novel *see* Brian Garfield

RELIC, THE, Novel *see* Lincoln Child, Douglas Preston

RELICARIO, EL, Song *see* Castellvi Y Oliveras, Jose Padilla

RELIGEUSE, LA, 1796, Novel *see* Denis Diderot

RELIGION, THE, Novel *see* Nicholas Conde

RELUCTANT DEBUTANTE, THE, London 1956, Play *see* William Douglas Home

RELUCTANT GRANDMOTHER, THE, Play *see* Kate Sullivan

RELUCTANT HANGMAN, THE, Story *see* Jo Carpenter

RELUCTANT HEROES, London 1950, Play *see* Colin Morris

RELUCTANT LANDLORD, THE, 1950, Novel *see* Scott Corbett

RELUCTANT WIDOW, THE, Novel *see* Georgette Heyer

REMAINS OF THE DAY, THE, Novel *see* Kazuo Ishiguro

REMAINS TO BE SEEN, New York 1951, Play *see* Russel Crouse, Howard Lindsay

REMARKABLE ANDREW, THE, Novel *see* Dalton Trumbo

REMARKABLE MR. PENNYPACKER, THE, New York 1953, Play *see* Liam O'Brien

REMEMBER, Novel *see* Barbara Taylor Bradford

REMEMBER THE DAY, Play *see* Philip Dunning, Philo Higley

REMEMBER TOMORROW, Story *see* Marion Parsonnet

REMIGIA, Novel *see* Gerolamo Rovetta

REMITTANCE WOMAN, THE, Garden City, Ny. 1924, Novel *see* Achmed Abdullah

REMORQUES, Novel *see* Roger Vercel

REMOTE CONTROL, New York 1929, Play *see* A. C. Fuller, J. Nelson, Clyde North

REMOVALISTS, THE, 1972, Play *see* David Williamson

REMPART DES BEGUINES, LE, 1951, Novel *see* Francoise Mallet-Joris

REMPARTS DU SILENCE, LES, Book *see* Pierre Fyot

REN DAO ZHONG NIAN, Novel *see* Shen Rong

RENAISSANCE AT CHARLEROI, THE, 1903, Short Story *see* O. Henry

REND MIG I TRADITIONERNE, 1958, Novel *see* Leif Panduro

RENDEZ-VOUS AVEC LA CHANCE, Novel *see* Gilbert Dupe

RENDEZ-VOUS CHAMPS-ELYSEES, Short Story *see* Frank Arnold

RENDEZ-VOUS DE SENLIS, LE, Play *see* Jean Anouilh

RENDEZ-VOUS IN WIEN, Play *see* Fritz Eckhardt

RENDEZVOUS WITH DEATH, Novel *see* John Bentley

RENEGADE POSSE, Novel *see* Marvin H. Albert

RENEGADE, THE, 1942, Novel *see* L. L. Foreman

RENEGADE, THE, New York C.1910, Play *see* Paul Armstrong

RENEGAT, LE, Paris 1929, Novel *see* Andre Armandy

RENFREW OF THE ROYAL MOUNTED, New York 1922, Novel *see* Laurie York Erskine

RENFREW RIDES AGAIN, New York 1927, Novel *see* Laurie York Erskine

RENFREW RIDES NORTH, New York 1931, Novel *see* Laurie York Erskine

RENFREW RIDES THE RANGE, New York 1935, Novel *see* Laurie York Erskine

RENFREW RIDES THE SKY, New York 1928, Novel *see* Laurie York Erskine

RENFREW'S LONG TRAIL, Novel *see* Laurie York Erskine

RENO, New York 1929, Novel *see* Cornelius Vanderbilt Jr.

RENUNCIATION, Story *see* Peter B. Kyne

RENZONI, LA, Novel *see* Melati Van Java

REPEAL, 1934, Novel *see* Charles Francis Coe

REPORT TO THE COMMISSIONER, Novel *see* James Mills

REPORTER, THE, Novel *see* Ken Attiwill

REPOS DU GUERRIER, LE, Paris 1958, Novel *see* Christiane Rochefort

REPRIEVE: THE TESTAMENT OF JOHN RESKO, New York 1956, Autobiography *see* John Resko

REPRISAL!, 1950, Novel *see* Arthur Gordon

REPROACH OF ANNESLEY, THE, Novel *see* Maxwell Gray

REPRODUCTION INTERDITE, Novel *see* Michel Lenoir

REPROUVES, LES, Novel *see* Andre Armandy

REPUBLICA DOS ASSASSINOS, 1976, Novel *see* Aguinaldo Silva

REQUIEM, Novel *see* Antonio Tabucchi

REQUIEM AETERNAM DONA EIS DOMINE!, 1913, Short Story *see* Luigi Pirandello

REQUIEM FOR A HEAVYWEIGHT, 1956, Play *see* Rod Serling

REQUIEM FOR A REDHEAD, London 1953, Novel *see* Al Bocca

RESA DI TITI, LA, Play *see* Aldo de Benedetti, Guglielmo Zorzi

RESCUE, THE, London 1920, Novel *see* Joseph Conrad

RESCUING ANGEL, THE, New York 1917, Play *see* Clare Kummer

RESCUING ANNE, Novel *see* Edgar Franklin

RESIDENT PATIENT, THE, Short Story *see* Arthur Conan Doyle

REST CURE, THE, Novel *see* George Robey

RESTLESS SEX, THE, New York 1918, Novel *see* Robert W. Chambers

RESTLESS SOULS, Short Story *see* Cosmo Hamilton

RESTLESS WIVES, Short Story *see* Izola Forrester

RESTLESS YOUTH, Story *see* Cosmo Hamilton

RESTORATION, Novel *see* Rose Tremain

RESURRECTION MAN, Novel *see* Eoin McNamee

RETAGGIO DI SANGUE, Novel *see* Anna Luce

RETALHOS DA VIDA DE UM MEDICO, 1949, Short Story *see* Fernando Namora

RETOUR A ROISSY, Novel *see* Pauline Reage

RETOUR DE FLAMME, Novel *see* Herve Lauwick

RETOUR DE MANIVELLE, Novel *see* James Hadley Chase

RETOUR DES CENDRES, LE, Paris 1961, Novel *see* Hubert Monteilhet

RETOUR, LE, Novel *see* Daniele Thompson

RISE OF ROSCOE PAINE, THE, New York 1912, Novel *see* Joseph C. Lincoln

RISICO, Short Story *see* Ian Fleming

RISING GENERATION, THE, London 1923, Play *see* Laura Leycester, Wyn Weaver

RISING SUN, Novel *see* Michael Crichton

RITA COVENTRY, Garden City, N.Y. 1922, Novel *see* Julian Leonard Street

RITA HAYWORTH, Book *see* John Kobal

RITA, SUE AND BOB TOO!, Play *see* Andrea Dunbar

RITORNO DI UN'ANIMA, IL, Novel *see* Vittorio Mariani

RITRATTO DI PROVINCIA IN ROSSO, Novel *see* Paolo Levi

RITTMEISTER STYX, Novel *see* Georg Muhlen-Schulte

RIVALS, THE, London 1775, Play *see* Richard Brinsley Sheridan

RIVER LADY, Novel *see* Houston Branch, Frank Waters

RIVER LINE, THE, 1949, Novel *see* Charles Morgan

RIVER NIGER, THE, Play *see* Joseph A. Walker

RIVER OF DEATH, Novel *see* Alistair MacLean

RIVER OF MISSING MEN, Story *see* Maurice Wright

RIVER OF STARS, THE, London 1913, Novel *see* Edgar Wallace

RIVER PIRATE, THE, New York 1928, Novel *see* Charles Francis Coe

RIVER RAN OUT OF EDEN, A, Novel *see* James Vance Marshall

RIVER RED, Play *see* Eric Drilling

RIVER, THE, Novel *see* Rumer Godden

RIVER, THE, Play *see* Patrick Hastings

RIVER, THE, 1955, Short Story *see* Flannery O'Connor

RIVER, THE, Philadelphia 1928, Novel *see* Tristram Tupper

RIVER'S END: A NEW STORY OF GOD'S COUNTRY, THE, New York 1919, Novel *see* James Oliver Curwood

RIVETS, Play *see* John McDermott

RIVIERE DES TROIS JONQUES, LA, Paris 1956, Novel *see* Georges Godefroy

RIVOLUZIONE SESSUALE, LA, Book *see* Wilhelm Reich

ROAD, Play *see* Jim Cartwright

ROAD HOUSE, Novel *see* M. Gruen, Oscar Saul

ROAD HOUSE, London 1932, Play *see* Walter Hackett

ROAD SHOW, Novel *see* Eric Hatch

ROAD THROUGH THE DARK, THE, 1918, Short Story *see* Maude Radford Warren

ROAD TO CARMICHAEL'S, THE, Story *see* Richard Wormser

ROAD TO HEAVEN, THE, Poem *see* George R. Sims

ROAD TO LONDON, THE, New York 1914, Novel *see* David S. Foster

ROAD TO RENO, THE, 1937, Story *see* I. A. R. Wylie

ROAD TO ROME, THE, 1927, Play *see* R. E. Sherwood

ROAD TO RUIN, THE, London 1792, Play *see* Thomas Holcroft

ROAD TO THURSDAY, THE, Story *see* John Barton Oxford

ROAD TO WELLVILLE, THE, Novel *see* G. Cograghessan Boyle

ROAD TO YESTERDAY, THE, New York 1906, Play *see* Beulah Marie Dix, Evelyn Sutherland

ROADHOUSE NIGHTS, 1929, Novel *see* Dashiell Hammett

ROADS OF DESTINY, New York 1918, Novel *see* Channing Pollock

ROADS WE TAKE, THE, Short Story *see* O. Henry

ROAR OF THE CROWD, THE, Book *see* James J. Corbett

ROARING GIRL, THE, Los Angeles 1937, Play *see* John C. Moffitt

ROARING LADY, 1933, Short Story *see* Diana Bourbon

ROARING ROAD, THE, 1918, Short Story *see* Byron Morgan

ROB ROY, Novel *see* Sir Walter Scott

ROBBER BARONS, New York 1934, Book *see* Matthew Josephson

ROBBERS' ROOST, New York 1932, Novel *see* Zane Grey

ROBBERS' TALE; THE REAL STORY OF THE GREAT TRAIN ROBBERY, THE, London 1965, Book *see* Peta Fordham

ROBBERY UNDER ARMS, 1888, Novel *see* Rolf Boldrewood

ROBE ROUGE, LA, 1900, Play *see* Eugene Brieux

ROBE, THE, 1946, Novel *see* Lloyd C. Douglas

ROBERT UND BERTRAM, Play *see* Gustav Raeder

ROBIN HOOD OF EL DORADO, THE, New York 1932, Book *see* Walter Noble Burns

ROBINSON CRUSOE, 1719, Novel *see* Daniel Defoe

ROBINSON SOLL NICHT STERBEN, Berlin 1932, Play *see* Friedrich Forster

ROBUR LE CONQUERANT, Paris 1886, Novel *see* Jules Verne

ROCAMBOLE, Novel *see* Pierre-Alexis Ponson Du Terrail

ROCCA: MORTELS RENDEZ-VOUS, Novel *see* Claude Brami, Marcel Jullian

ROCHE AUX MOUETTES, LA, Novel *see* Jules Sandeau

ROCK BOTTOM, Story *see* Gina Kaus, Martin Rackin

ROCKABYE, 1924, Play *see* Lucia Bronder

ROCKET BOYS, Book *see* Homer H. Hickam Jr.

ROCKET SHIP GALILEO, 1947, Novel *see* Robert A. Heinlein

ROCKETS GALORE, 1957, Novel *see* Compton Mackenzie

ROCKETS IN THE DUNES, Novel *see* Lois Lamplugh

ROCKING HORSE WINNER, THE, 1932, Short Story *see* D. H. Lawrence

ROCKING MOON, New York 1925, Novel *see* Barrett Willoughby

ROCKS OF VALPRE, THE, Novel *see* Ethel M. Dell

ROCKY HORROR SHOW, THE, Play *see* Richard O'Brien

ROCKY'S ROSE, Story *see* Eustace Cockrell

RODE ORM SJOFARARA I VASTERLED, Stockholm 1941, Novel *see* Frans Gunnar Bengtsson

RODE SKOE, DE, 1845, Short Story *see* Hans Christian Andersen

RODINKA, 1924, Short Story *see* Mikhail Sholokhov

RODNEY, 1933, Short Story *see* Leonard Nason

RODNEY FAILS TO QUALIFY, Short Story *see* P. G. Wodehouse

RODNEY STONE, 1896, Novel *see* Arthur Conan Doyle

RODOLPHE ET LE REVOLVEUR, Novel *see* Noel Calef

ROGER AND I, Poem *see* J. T. Trowbridge

ROGER LAROCQUE, Novel *see* Jules Mary

ROGER-LA-HONTE, Novel *see* Jules Mary

ROGUE COP, 1954, Novel *see* William P. McGivern

ROGUE IN LOVE, A, Novel *see* Tom Gallon

ROGUE MALE, 1939, Novel *see* Geoffrey Household

ROGUES OF THE TURF, Play *see* John F. Preston

ROI A LA MASQUE D'OR, LE, 1893, Novel *see* Marcel Schwob

ROI COPHETUA, LE, 1970, Short Story *see* Julien Gracq

ROI DE CAMARGUE, LE, 1890, Novel *see* Jean Aicard

ROI DE LA PEDALE, LE, Novel *see* Paul Cartoux, Henri Decoin

ROI DE PARIS, LE, Novel *see* Georges Ohnet

ROI DES CONS, LE, Play *see* Claude Confortes, Georges Wolinski

ROI DES MONTAGNES, LE, 1857, Short Story *see* Edmond About

ROI DES PALACES, LE, Play *see* Henri Kistemaeckers

ROI KOKO, LE, Play *see* Alexandre Bisson

ROI, LE, 1908, Play *see* Gaston Arman de Caillavet, Robert de Flers

ROI PANDORE, LE, Novel *see* Corriem

ROI S'AMUSE, LE, 1832, Play *see* Victor Hugo

ROI SANS DIVERTISSEMENT, UN, 1947, Novel *see* Jean Giono

ROIS EN EXIL, LES, Paris 1879, Novel *see* Alphonse Daudet

ROKONOK, 1930, Novel *see* Zsigmond Moricz

ROLANDE IMMOLEE, Paris 1914, Novel *see* Louis Letang

ROLANDE MET DE BLES, 1944, Novel *see* Herman Teirlinck

ROLES, Boston 1924, Novel *see* Elizabeth Alexander

ROLLING HOME, Play *see* John Hunter Booth

ROLLING STONES, New York 1915, Play *see* Edgar Selwyn

ROLLTREPPE ABWARTS, Novel *see* Hans-Georg Noack

ROMA - VIA DELLE MANTELLATE, Roma 1953, *see* Isa Mari

ROMA BAFFUTA, Play *see* Antonio Racioppi

ROMAIN KALBRIS, Novel *see* Hector Malot

ROMAN BE'HEMSHACHIM, Novel *see* Yitzhak Ben-Nir

ROMAN DE CARPENTIER, LE, *see* Ed de Perrodil

ROMAN DE LA MOMIE, LE, Novel *see* Theophile Gautier

ROMAN D'UN JEUNE HOMME PAUVRE, LE, 1858, Novel *see* Octave Feuillet

ROMAN D'UN SPAHI, LE, 1881, Novel *see* Pierre Loti

ROMAN EINES FRAUENARZTES, Novel *see* Curt Riess

ROMAN HLOUPEHO HONZY, Novel *see* Jan Barta

ROMAN I KONTRABASOM, 1886, Short Story *see* Anton Chekhov

ROMAN PARISIEN, UN, Paris 1882, Play *see* Octave Feuillet

ROMAN SPRING OF MRS. STONE, THE, New York 1950, Novel *see* Tennessee Williams

ROMAN, THE, Novel *see* Edward George Bulwer Lytton

ROMANA, LA, 1947, Novel *see* Alberto Moravia

ROMANCE, 1903, Novel *see* Joseph Conrad, Ford Madox Ford

ROMANCE, New York 1913, Play *see* Edward Sheldon

ROMANCE AND ARABELLA, New York 1917, Play *see* William Hurlbut

ROMANCE IN HIGH C, Story *see* Carlos A. Olivari, S. Pondal Rios

ROMANCE INCORPORATED, Story *see* Val Burton

ROMANCE OF A HORSETHIEF, Novel *see* Joseph Opatoshu

ROMANCE OF A MILLION DOLLARS, Indianapolis 1922, Novel *see* Elizabeth Dejeans

ROMANCE OF ANNIE LAURIE, THE, Play *see* Alfred Denville

ROMANCE OF BILLY-GOAT HILL, A, New York 1912, Novel *see* Alice Hegan Rice

ROMANCE OF HENRY MENAFEE, THE, Book *see* Paul Gallico

ROMANCE OF NEW YORK YESTERDAY AND TODAY, A, New York 1911, Novel *see* George Bronson Howard

ROMANCE OF OLD BAGDAD, A, Novel *see* Jessie Douglas Kerruish

ROMANCE OF ROSY RIDGE, THE, 1937, Novel *see* MacKinlay Kantor

ROMANCE OF THE BLACK CANNON, Novel *see* Zhang XIanliang

ROMANCE OF THE UNDERWORLD, A, New York 1911, Play *see* Paul Armstrong

ROMANCE OF WASTDALE, A, Novel *see* A. E. W. Mason

ROMANCERO, Novel *see* Jacques Deval

ROMANEK NA HORACH, Play *see* Josef Skruzny

ROMANEN OM OLOF, Stockholm 1945, Novel *see* Eyvind Johnson

ROMANOFF AND JULIET, New York 1957, Play *see* Peter Ustinov

ROMANS TERESY HENNERT, 1927, Novel *see* Zofia Nalkowska

ROMANTIC COMEDY, Play *see* Bernard Slade

ROMANTIC ENGLISHWOMAN, THE, Novel *see* Thomas Wiseman

ROMANTIC MR. HINKLIN, THE, Story *see* Richard Carroll, Ray McCarey

ROMANTICISMO, 1901, Play *see* Gerolamo Rovetta

ROMANTISCHE REISE DES HERRN CARL MARIA VON WEBER, DIE, Short Story *see* Hans Watzlik

ROMANY CALL, THE, Short Story *see* Elizabeth Ethel Donoher

ROMANY RYE, London 1857, Novel *see* George Borrow

RUINED LADY, THE, New York 1920, Play *see* Frances Nordstrom

RUISSEAU, LE, Paris 1907, Play *see* Pierre Wolff

RUITER IN DIE NAG, DIE, Bloemfontein 1936, Novel *see* Mikro

RUKAJARVEN TIE, Novel *see* Antti Tuuri

RULER OF MEN, A, Short Story *see* O. Henry

RULING CLASS, THE, 1969, Play *see* Peter Barnes

RULING PASSION, London 1973, Novel *see* Reginald Hill

RULING PASSION, THE, 1922, Short Story *see* Earl Derr Biggers

RUM PUNCH, Novel *see* Elmore Leonard

RUMBLE FISH, Novel *see* S. E. Hinton

RUMBLE ON THE DOCKS, 1953, Novel *see* Frank Paley

RUMPELSTILZCHEN, 1812, Short Story *see* Jacob Grimm, Wilhelm Grimm

RUN COUGAR RUN, Novel *see* Robert Murphy

RUN FOR HIS MONEY, A, Novel *see* Mary Wynne

RUN OF THE COUNTRY, THE, Novel *see* Shane Connaughton

RUN SILENT, RUN DEEP, 1955, Novel *see* Com. Edward L. Beach

RUNAWAY ENCHANTRESS, A, Story *see* Mary Heaton Vorse

RUNAWAY, THE, New York 1911, Play *see* Michael Morton

RUNAWAY WIFE, THE, Play *see* McKee Rankin

RUNAWAYS, THE, Novel *see* Victor Canning

RUNINTO NITE, 1953, Short Story *see* Taijun Takeda

RUNNING FIGHT, THE, New York 1910, Novel *see* William Hamilton Osborne

RUNNING MAN, THE, Novel *see* Stephen King

RUNNING WATER, Novel *see* A. E. W. Mason

RUNWAY ZERO 8, Novel *see* Arthur Hailey

RUOTA, Play *see* Cesare Vico Lodovico

RUPERT OF HENTZAU, 1898, Novel *see* Anthony Hope

RUSE CASES NEGRES, Novel *see* Joseph Zobel

RUSE, LA, Play *see* Hersent, Claude Rolland

RUSH, Book *see* Kim Wozencraft

RUSH TO JUDGMENT, New York 1966, Book *see* Mark Lane

RUSHYA SHRINGA, Play *see* Chandrasekhar Kambhar

RUSLAN I LYUDMILA, 1820, Verse *see* Alexander Pushkin

RUSSIA HOUSE, THE, 1989, Novel *see* John Le Carre

RUSSIAN ROULETTE, Novel *see* Tom Ardies

RUSSKIY LES, 1953, Novel *see* Leonid Maksimovich Leonov

RUSSKIY VOPROS, 1946, Play *see* Konstantin Simonov

RUSSKIYE LYUDI, 1942, Play *see* Konstantin Simonov

RUSTEGHI, I, 1761, Play *see* Carlo Goldoni

RUSTLE OF SILK, THE, Boston 1922, Novel *see* Cosmo Hamilton

RUSTLER OF WIND RIVER, THE, Chicago 1917, Novel *see* George Washington Ogden

RUSTLER'S VALLEY, New York 1924, Novel *see* Clarence E. Mulford

RUSTLING FOR CUPID, 1926, Short Story *see* Peter B. Kyne

RUTHLESS ONES, THE, Novel *see* Laurence Moody

RUY BLAS, 1838, Play *see* Victor Hugo

RYBA NA SUCHU, Play *see* Karel Konstantin

RYMLINGEN FAST, 1933, Novel *see* Dagmar Ingeborg Edqvist

RYNOX, Novel *see* Philip MacDonald

RYTTARE I BLATT, Novel *see* Folke Mellwig

SA CONSCIENCE, Novel *see* Daniel Riche

SA MAJESTE ARSENE, Short Story *see* Zadoc Monteil

SABATO DOMENICA E LUNEDI, 1959, Play *see* Eduardo de Filippo

SABINE WULFF, Novel *see* Karl-Heinz Kruschel

SABLE LORCHA, THE, Chicago 1912, Novel *see* Horace Hazeltine

SABLIERE, LA, Novel *see* Claude Jasmin

SABOTEURS, THE, Story *see* John Hawkins, Ward Hawkins

SABRINA FAIR, New York 1953, Play *see* Samuel Taylor

SACAJAWEA OF THE SHOSHONES, Novel *see* Della Gould Emmons

SACHE MIT DEM KOFFER, DIE, Novel *see* Hannes Peter Stolp

SACHE MIT SCHORRSIEGEL, DIE, Novel *see* Fred Andreas

SACHERTORTE, DIE, Play *see* Siegfried Geyer, Rudolf Osterreicher

SACI, O, 1921, Short Story *see* Monteiro Lobato

SACKCLOTH AND SCARLET, London 1924, Novel *see* George Gibbs

SACKETT, Novel *see* Louis L'Amour

SACRE LEONCE, Play *see* Pierre Wolff

SACRED AND PROFANE LOVE, London 1919, Play *see* Arnold Bennett

SACRED FLAME, THE, New York 1928, Play *see* W. Somerset Maugham

SACRED ORDER, THE, Short Story *see* Sax Rohmer

SACREE JEUNESSE, Play *see* Andre Mouezy-Eon

SACRIFICE, New York 1922, Novel *see* Stephen French Whitman

SACRIFICE TO MAMMON, A, New York 1906, Novel *see* William MacLeod Raine

SAD HORSE, THE, Unpublished, Novel *see* Zoe Akins

SADDLE MATES, 1924, Short Story *see* Harrington Strong

SADGATI, 1931, Short Story *see* Premchand

SADIE, New York 1907, Novel *see* Karl Harriman

SADIE GOES TO HEAVEN, 1917, Short Story *see* Dana Burnet

SADIE LOVE, New York 1915, Play *see* Avery Hopwood

SADIE OF THE DESERT, 1925, Short Story *see* Mildred Cram

SADISTIC HYPNOTIST, THE, *see* Greg Corarito

SADOUNAH, Novel *see* William Le Queux

SAENGGWABU WIJARYO CHYEONGGUSOSONG, Play *see* Um In-Hee

SAFARI, Novel *see* Robert Buckner

SAFARI IN MANHATTAN, 1936, Short Story *see* Matt Taylor

SAFE HARBOUR, Short Story *see* Barbara Harper

SAFE PASSAGE, Novel *see* Ellen Bache

SAFE, THE, Play *see* W. P. Lipscomb

SAFECRACKER, THE, Book *see* Rhys Davis, Bruce Thomas

SAFETY CURTAIN, THE, 1917, Short Story *see* Ethel M. Dell

SAFETY FIRST, Novel *see* Margot Neville

SAG DIE WAHRHEIT, Play *see* Johann von Vaszary

SAGA OF BILLY THE KID, THE, Garden City, N.Y. 1926, Novel *see* Walter Noble Burns

SAGEBRUSHER, THE, New York 1919, Novel *see* Emerson Hough

SAHARA BRULE, LA, Novel *see* Gilles Perrault

SAHARA LOVE, Novel *see* A. L. Vincent

SAHEB BIBI GOLAM, 1952, Novel *see* Bimal Mitra

SAID WITH SOAP, 1925, Short Story *see* Gerald Beaumont

SAIGON COMMANDOS - MAD MINUTE, Novel *see* Jonathan Cain

SAIL A CROOKED SHIP, New York 1960, Novel *see* Nathaniel Benchley

SAILOR BEWARE, London 1955, Play *see* Philip King

SAILOR BEWARE, New York 1933, Play *see* Kenyon Nicholson, Charles Robinson

SAILOR TRAMP, A, Novel *see* Bart Kennedy

SAILORS DON'T CARE, Novel *see* Seamark

SAILOR'S RETURN, THE, Novel *see* David Garnett

SAILORS' WIVES, New York 1924, Novel *see* Warner Fabian

SAINT A PALM SPRINGS, LE, Novel *see* Leslie Charteris

SAINT IN NEW YORK, THE, London 1935, Novel *see* Leslie Charteris

SAINT JACK, 1973, Novel *see* Paul Theroux

SAINT JOAN, New York 1923, Play *see* George Bernard Shaw

SAINT JOHNSON, New York 1930, Novel *see* William Riley Burnett

SAINT OF CALAMITY GULCH, THE, Short Story *see* Bret Harte

SAINTED SISTERS OF SANDY CREEK, THE, Story *see* Elisa Bialk

SAINTS AND SINNERS, London 1884, Play *see* Henry Arthur Jones

SAISIE, LA, Play *see* Albert Dieudonne

SAISON IN SALZBURG, Opera *see* Kurt Feltz, Fred Raymond, Max Wallner

SAL GROGAN'S FACE, Poem *see* George R. Sims

SALAIRE DE LA PEUR, LE, 1950, Novel *see* Georges Arnaud

SALAIRE DU PECHE, LE, Novel *see* Nancy Rutledge

SALAMANDER, THE, Novel *see* Morris West

SALAMANDER, THE, New York 1913, Novel *see* Owen Johnson

SALAMMBO, 1862, Novel *see* Gustave Flaubert

SALAUDS VONT EN ENFER, LES, Play *see* Frederic Dard

SALBURG CONNECTION, THE, Novel *see* Helen MacInnes

SALEM'S LOT, 1974, Novel *see* Stephen King

SALLY, Novel *see* Howard Fast

SALLY, New York 1920, Musical Play *see* Guy Bolton, Clifford Grey, P. G. Wodehouse

SALLY ANN'S STRATEGY, Story *see* Louise Alvord

SALLY BISHOP, Novel *see* E. Temple Thurston

SALLY IN OUR ALLEY, c1715, Song *see* Henry Carey

SALLY IRENE AND MARY, New York 1922, Play *see* Edward Dowling, Cyrus Wood

SALLY'S SHOULDERS, New York 1927, Novel *see* Beatrice Burton

SALOME, 1893, Play *see* Oscar Wilde

SALOME OF THE TENEMENTS, New York 1923, Novel *see* Anzia Yezierska

SALOMY JANE'S KISS, 1900, Short Story *see* Bret Harte

SALON MEXICO, Short Story *see* Rafael Ramirez Heredia

SALOON BAR, London 1939, Play *see* Frank Harvey Jr.

SALT OF THE EARTH, 1917, Short Story *see* Peter B. Kyne

SALT OF THE EARTH, THE, 1918, Short Story *see* George Weston

SALT WATER, New York 1929, Play *see* Frank Craven, John Golden, Daniel Jarrett

SALTEADOR, LE, 1854, Novel *see* Alexandre Dumas (pere)

SALTIMBANQUES, LES, Opera *see* Louis Ganne, Maurice Ordonneau

SALTO MORTALE, Novel *see* Alfred Machard

SALUTE THE TOFF, Novel *see* John Creasey

SALUTE TO THE GODS, New York 1935, Novel *see* Sir Malcolm Campbell

SALUTE TO THE GREAT MACARTHY, A, 1970, Novel *see* Barry Oakley

SALVAGE, 1924, Short Story *see* Izola Forrester

SALVAGE, New York 1906, Novel *see* Aquila Kempster

SALVAJES EN PUENTE SAN GIL, LAS, 1963, Play *see* Jose Martin Recuerda

SALVATION NELL, New York 1908, Play *see* Edward Sheldon

SALVATION OF NANCE O'SHAUGHNESSY, THE, Story *see* Honore Wilsie

SALVATOR, Play *see* Max Ferner, Philip Weichand

SALVING OF A DERELICT, THE, Novel *see* Maurice Drake

SALVING OF JOHN SOMERS, THE, 1920, Short Story *see* John Fleming Wilson

SAMAPTI, Short Story *see* Rabindranath Tagore

SAME TIME NEXT YEAR, Play *see* Bernard Slade

SAMFUNDETS STOTTER, Odense 1877, Play *see* Henrik Ibsen

SAMMY, 1958, Television Play *see* Ken Hughes

SAMMY GOING SOUTH, London 1961, Novel *see* W. H. Canway

SAM'S BOY, Novel *see* W. W. Jacobs

SAMSKARA, 1966, Novel *see* U. R. Ananthamurthy

SAMSON, 1948, Novel *see* Kazimierz Brandys

SCHATZ DER AZTEKEN, DER, Novel see Karl Friedrich May

SCHATZ DER SIERRA MADRE, DER, 1927, Novel see Ben Traven

SCHATZ IM SILBERSEE, DER, Stuttgart 1890, Novel see Karl Friedrich May

SCHAUKEL, DIE, Novel see Annette Kolb

SCHEIDUNGSGRUND: LIEBE, Novel see Ellinor Hartung

SCHEINHEILIGE FLORIAN, DER, Play see Max Neal, Philipp Weichand

SCHICKSAL AM MATTERHORN, Novel see Luis Trenker

SCHIFF 16, Book see Wolfgang Frank, Bernhard Rogge

SCHIFF DER VERLORENEN MENSCHEN, DAS, Novel see Franzos Keremen

SCHILTEN, Novel see Hermann Burger

SCHIMMELREITER, DER, 1888, Short Story see Theodor Storm

SCHINDERHANNES, 1927, Play see Carl Zuckmayer

SCHIZO, see Louis S. London

SCHLOSS, DAS, Munich 1926, Novel see Franz Kafka

SCHLOSS GRIPSHOLM, 1931, Novel see Kurt Tucholsky

SCHLOSS HUBERTUS, Novel see Ludwig Ganghofer

SCHLOSS KONIGSWALD, Novel see Horst Bienek

SCHLOSS VOGELOD, Novel see Rudolf Stratz

SCHMETTERLINGE WEINEN NICHT, Novel see Willi Heinrich

SCHMINKE, Novel see Guido Kreutzer

SCHMUTZIGES GELD, Short Story see Karl Vollmoller

SCHNEEMANN, DER, Novel see Jorg Fauser

SCHNEESCHUHBANDITEN, Novel see Jonathan Jew

SCHNEEWEISSCHEN UND ROSENROT, 1812, Short Story see Jacob Grimm, Wilhelm Grimm

SCHNEEWITTCHEN, 1812, Short Story see Jacob Grimm, Wilhelm Grimm

SCHNEIDER WIBBEL, Play see Hans Muller-Schlosser

SCHNELLES GELD, Novel see Frank Gohre

SCHONE ABENTEUER, DAS, Novel see Antonia Ridge

SCHONE FLORIAN, DER, Musical Play see Walter Maria Espe, Will Kaufmann

SCHONE FRAULEIN SCHRAGG, DAS, Novel see Fred Andreas

SCHONE LUGNERIN, DIE, Opera see Ernst Nebhut, Just Scheu

SCHONE TOLZERIN, DIE, Short Story see Karl Weinberger

SCHONEN TAGE VON ARANJUEZ, DIE, Play see Robert A. Stemmle, Hans Szekely

SCHOOL BELLS, New York 1915, Play see Charles K. Harris

SCHOOL FOR HUSBANDS, 1932, Play see Frederick Jackson

SCHOOL FOR SCANDAL, THE, London 1777, Play see Richard Brinsley Sheridan

SCHOOL OF DRAMA, Play see Zoltan Egyed, Hans Szekely

SCHOOLS AND SCHOOLS, Short Story see O. Henry

SCHOONER, THE, 1978, Short Story see Michael McLaverty

SCHOPFER, DER, Play see Hans Muller

SCHULD DER GABRIELE ROTTWEIL, DIE, Novel see Hans Gustl

SCHULDIG, Play see Richard Voss

SCHULE FUR EHEGLUCK, Book see Andre Maurois

SCHULER GERBER HAT ABSOLVIERT, DER, 1930, Novel see Friedrich Torberg

SCHULGESPENST, DAS, Novel see Peter Abraham

SCHUSS IM RAMPENLICHT, Play see Paul Vand Der Hurck

SCHUSS VON DER KANZEL, DER, Zurich 1877, Short Story see Conrad Ferdinand Meyer

SCHUSTERNAZI, DER, Play see Ludwig Thoma

SCHUT, DER, Novel see Karl Friedrich May

SCHUTT DIE SORGEN IN EIN GLASCHEN WEIN, Play see Franz Streicher

SCHUTZENFEST, Play see Harald Bratt

SCHUTZENLIESEL, Opera see Edmund Eysler, Carl Lindau, Leo Stein

SCHWAMMERL, Leipzig 1916, Novel see Rudolf Hans Bartsch

SCHWARMER, DIE, 1921, Play see Robert Musil

SCHWARZE GALEERE, DIE, 1902, Novel see Wilhelm Raabe

SCHWARZE TANNER, DER, Short Story see Meinrad Inglin

SCHWARZER JAGER JOHANNA, Novel see George von Der Vring

SCHWARZER NERZ AUF ZARTER HAUT, Novel see Henry Pahlen

SCHWARZWALDMADEL, Opera see Leon Jessel, August Neidhardt

SCHWARZ-WEISS-ROTE HIMMELBETT, DAS, Novel see Hans Rudolf Berndorff

SCHWEIGEN IM WALDE, DAS, Novel see Ludwig Ganghofer, Richard Skowronnek

SCHWEIGENDE MUND, DER, Novel see Oskar Jensen

SCHWEIGEPFLICHT, Short Story see Jacques Companeez

SCHWEINEFLEISCH IN DOSEN, Play see Paul Neuhaus, Walter Thier

SCHWEIZERISCHE ROBINSON, DER, 1812-27, Novel see Johann David Wyss

SCINTILLA, LA, 1906, Play see Alfredo Testoni

SCISSORS CUT PAPER, Novel see Gerard Fairlie

SCOOP, 1938, Novel see Evelyn Waugh

SCOOP, THE, Play see Jack Heming

SCORCHERS, Play see David Beaird

SCORPIO LETTERS, THE, Novel see Victor Canning

SCOTCH VALLEY, New York 1928, Novel see Mildred Cram

SCOTLAND YARD, New York 1929, Play see Denison Clift

SCOTLAND YARD MYSTERY, THE, Play see Wallace Geoffrey

SCOTTSBORO - A TRAGEDY OF THE AMERICAN SOUTH, Book see Dan T. Carter

SCOUMOUNE, LA, Novel see Jose Giovanni

SCOURGE OF FATE, THE, Story see Ewart Adamson

SCOURGE OF THE LITTLE C, THE, New York 1925, Novel see Jesse Edward Grinstead

SCOURGE, THE, Novel see Rafael Sabatini

SCRAP IRON, Short Story see Charles E. Van Loan

SCRATCH A THIEF, New York 1961, Novel see Zekial Marko

SCREAMING MIMI, 1949, Novel see Frederick Brown

SCREAMING WOMAN, THE, 1951, Short Story see Ray Bradbury

SCRINUL NEGRU, 1960, Novel see George Calinescu

SCROLLINA, 1885, Play see Achille Torelli

SCRUPLES, Novel see Judith Krantz

SCUDDA HOO SCUDDA HAY, Novel see George Agnew Chamberlain

SCULPTEUR DE MASQUES, LE, Play see Fernand Crommelynck

SCULPTRESS, THE, Novel see Minette Walters

SCUTTLERS, THE, New York 1914, Novel see Clyde C. Westover

SE NO I XE MATI NO LI VOLEMO, 1926, Play see Gino Rocca

SE QUELL'IDIOTA CI PENSASSE., Play see Silvio Benedetti

SEA AROUND US, THE, 1951, Book see Rachel Carson

SEA CHASE, THE, 1948, Novel see Andrew Geer

SEA FLOWER, THE, Short Story see George Charles Hull

SEA HAWK, THE, London 1915, Novel see Rafael Sabatini

SEA HORSES, London 1925, Novel see Francis Brett Young

SEA OF GRASS, THE, 1936, Novel see Conrad Richter

SEA PANTHER, THE, Short Story see Kenneth B. Clarke

SEA SHALL NOT HAVE THEM, THE, Novel see John Harris

SEA URCHIN, THE, 1925, Play see John Hastings Turner

SEA WOLF, THE, New York 1904, Novel see Jack London

SEA WOMAN, THE, New York 1925, Play see Willard Robertson

SEAGULLS OVER SORRENTO, London 1949, Play see Hugh Hastings

SEAL CALLED ANDRE, A, Novel see Lew Dietz, Harry Goodridge

SEAL OF SILENCE, THE, Story see William Hamilton Osborne

SEALED ORDERS, London 1913, Play see Henry Hamilton, Cecil Raleigh

SEALED TRAIN, THE, Book see Michael Pearson

SEALED VALLEY, THE, New York 1914, Novel see Hubert Footner

SEALED VERDICT, Novel see Lionel Shapiro

SEANCE MYSTERY, Novel see Norton S. Parker

SEANCE ON A WET AFTERNOON, 1964, Novel see Mark McShane

SEARA VERMELHA, 1946, Novel see Jorge Amado

SEARCH, Book see Alex Haley

SEARCH, Short Story see Leon Ware

SEARCH FOR BRIDEY MURPHY, THE, Book see Morey Bernstein

SEARCH FOR THE SPRING, Short Story see Eleanor Gates

SEARCHERS, THE, 1954, Novel see Alan Lemay

SEARCHING FOR BOBBY FISCHER, Book see Fred Waitzkin

SEARCHING WIND, THE, New York 1944, Play see Lillian Hellman

SEASON IN PURGATORY, A, Novel see Dominick Dunne

SEATS OF THE MIGHTY, THE, New York 1894, Novel see Gilbert Parker

SEAWEED CHILDREN, THE, 1864, Short Story see Anthony Trollope

SEAWYF AND BISCUIT, Novel see J. D. Scott

SECOND BEST, Novel see David Cook

SECOND CHANCE, Play see Ella Adkins

SECOND CHANCE, Short Story see Faith Baldwin

SECOND CHANCE, THE, New York 1924, Novel see Mrs. Wilson Woodrow

SECOND CHOICE, New York 1928, Novel see Elizabeth Alexander

SECOND CHOICE, New York 1932, Novel see Rob Eden

SECOND HAND ROSE, 1921, Song see Grant Clarke, James F. Hanley

SECOND HAND WIFE, New York 1932, Novel see Kathleen Norris

SECOND HONEYMOON, Story see Warren Wilson, Philip Wylie

SECOND HONEYMOON, THE, New York 1921, Novel see Ruby M. Ayres

SECOND IN COMMAND, THE, London 1900, Play see Robert Marshall

SECOND JUNGLE BOOK, THE, Book see Rudyard Kipling

SECOND LATCHKEY, THE, Garden City, N.Y. 1920, Novel see Charles N. Williams, Alice Muriel Williamson

SECOND LEVEL, Short Story see Wilbur Stark

SECOND MAN, New York 1927, Play see S. N. Behrman

SECOND MATE, THE, Novel see R. W. Rees

SECOND MR. BUSH, THE, London 1938, Play see C. Stafford Dickens

SECOND MRS. TANQUERAY, THE, London 1893, Play see Arthur Wing Pinero

SECOND SIGHT, Novel see David Williams

SECOND STAIN, THE, Short Story see Arthur Conan Doyle

SECOND VARIETY, Short Story see Philip K. Dick

SECOND VERITE, LA, Novel see Jean Laborde

SECOND VICTORY, THE, Novel see Morris West

SECOND YOUTH, New York 1917, Novel see Allan Eugene Updegraff

SECONDO TRAGICO FANTOZZI, IL, Book see Paolo Villaggio

SECONDS, New York 1963, Novel see David Ely

SECRET ADVERSARY, THE, Novel see Agatha Christie

SECRET AGENT, THE, 1907, Novel see Joseph Conrad

SECRET DE DELIA, LE, Play see Victorien Sardou

SECRET DE POLICHINELLE, LE, Play *see* Pierre Wolff

SECRET DES WORONZEFF, LE, Novel *see* Margot von Simpson

SECRET D'HELENE MARIMON, LE, Novel *see* J.-B. Cherrier

SECRET GARDEN, THE, New York 1909, Novel *see* Frances Hodgson Burnett

SECRET HONOR, Play *see* Donald Freed, Arnold M. Stone

SECRET, LE, Novel *see* Francis Rick

SECRET LIFE OF ALGERNON PENDLETON, THE, Novel *see* Russell H. Greenan

SECRET LIFE OF T. K. DEARING, THE, Book *see* Jean Robinson

SECRET LIFE OF WALTER MITTY, THE, 1945, Short Story *see* James Thurber

SECRET LIVES, Novel *see* Paul de Saint-Colombe

SECRET MATING, THE, Short Story *see* Edward A. Kaufman

SECRET OF BLACK MOUNTAIN, THE, Short Story *see* Jackson Gregory

SECRET OF DR. KILDARE, THE, 1939, Story *see* Max Brand

SECRET OF SANTA VITTORIA, THE, New York 1966, Novel *see* Robert Crichton

SECRET OF THE BLACK CAT, THE, Short Story *see* Edgar Allan Poe

SECRET OF THE HILLS, THE, London 1920, Novel *see* William Garrett

SECRET OF THE MOOR, THE, Novel *see* Maurice Gerard

SECRET OF THE RON MOR SKERRY, Novel *see* Rosalie K. Fry

SECRET OF THE STORM COUNTRY, THE, New York 1917, Novel *see* Grace Miller White

SECRET ORCHARD, THE, New York 1907, Play *see* Channing Pollock

SECRET PLACES, Novel *see* Janice Elliott

SECRET RAPTURE, THE, Play *see* David Hare

SECRET SERVICE, New York 1896, Play *see* William Gillette

SECRET SERVICE AFFAIR, A, Story *see* F. McGrew Willis

SECRET SERVICE OPERATOR, New York 1934, Novel *see* Robert W. Chambers

SECRET SHARER, THE, 1910, Short Story *see* Joseph Conrad

SECRET STRINGS, New York 1914, Play *see* Kate Jordan

SECRET TENT, THE, Play *see* Elizabeth Addeyman

SECRET, THE, Play *see* Robert Brenon

SECRET WAYS, THE, New York 1959, Novel *see* Alistair MacLean

SECRET WOMAN, THE, Novel *see* Eden Philpotts

SECRETARY OF FRIVOLOUS AFFAIRS, Indianapolis 1911, Novel *see* May Peel Futrelle

SECRETS, Play *see* Terry Jones, Michael Palin

SECRETS, London 1922, Play *see* Rudolf Besier, May Edginton

SECRETS OF SCOTLAND YARD, Book *see* Ernest Haigh

SECRETS OF THE SURETE, 1931, Article *see* H. Ashton Wolfe

SECTION SPECIALE, Book *see* Herve Villere

SEE HOW THEY RUN, Short Story *see* Mary Elizabeth Vroman

SEE HOW THEY RUN, London 1945, Play *see* Philip King

SEE JANE RUN, Book *see* Joy Fielding

SEE MY LAWYER, New York 1915, Play *see* Max Marcin

SEE NAPLES AND DIE, New York 1929, Play *see* Elmer Rice

SEE NO EVIL, Play *see* Jack Cunningham

SEE YOU IN JAIL, Story *see* William H. Clifford

SEED; A NOVEL OF BIRTH CONTROL, New York 1930, Novel *see* Charles Gilman Norris

SEED AND THE SOWER, THE, 1951, Novel *see* Laurens Van Der Post

SEED OF DESTRUCTION, Story *see* Ib Melchior, Edwin B. Watson

SEEKERS, THE, Novel *see* John Guthrie

SEELENBRAU, DER, 1945, Novel *see* Carl Zuckmayer

SEEMABADDHA, Novel *see* Shankar

SEE-SAW; A STORY OF TODAY, THE, New York 1919, Novel *see* Sophie Kerr

SEGRETTI DI MILANO: IL PONTE DELLA GHISOLFA, I, Milan 1958, Novel *see* Giovanni Testori

SEGURO SOBRE LA DICHA, UN, 1927, Short Story *see* Arturo S. Mom

SEHNSUCHT, Novel *see* Jirij Koch

SEI PERSONAGGI IN CERCA D'AUTORE, Play *see* Luigi Pirandello

SEINE MAJESTAT GUSTAV KRAUSE, Play *see* Eberhard Foerster

SEITENSPRUNGE, Novel *see* Hellmut Lange

SEITSEMAN VELJESTA, 1870, Novel *see* Aleksis Kivi

SEIZE THE DAY, 1956, Short Story *see* Saul Bellow

SEKATOMU RAI GISHI, Novel *see* Baku Akae

SEKKA TOMURAI ZASHI IREZUMI, Novel *see* Baku Akae

SELF-MADE WIFE, THE, 1922, Short Story *see* Elizabeth Alexander

SELKOR, 1933, Novel *see* Georgi Karaslavov

SELLOUT, Novel *see* M. Haile Chace

SELVA TRAGICA, 1959, Novel *see* Hermani Donati

SEMI-DETACHED, 1962, Play *see* David Turner

SEMINARISTA, O, 1895, Novel *see* Bernardo Guimaraes

SEMI-TOUGH, Book *see* Dan Jenkins

SENATOR'S BROTHER, THE, Story *see* Gouverneur Morris

SENBAZURU, Tokyo 1958, Novel *see* Yasunari Kawabata

SEND ANOTHER COFFIN, New York 1939, Novel *see* Frank G. Presnell

SEND ME NO FLOWERS, New York 1960, Play *see* Norman Barasch, Carroll Moore

SENDUNG UND GEWISSEN, Novel *see* Hellmuth Unger

SENGOKU JIEITAI, Novel *see* Ryo Hanmura

SENILITA, 1898, Novel *see* Italo Svevo

SENOR FEUDAL, EL, Play *see* Joaquin Dicenta

SENOR JINGLE BELLS, 1925, Short Story *see* Max Brand

SENOR MUY VIEJO CON UNAS ALAS ENORMES, UN, 1972, Short Story *see* Gabriel Garcia Marquez

SENOR PRESIDENTE, EL, 1946, Novel *see* Miguel Angel Asturias

SENORA AMA, 1908, Play *see* Jacinto Benavente y Martinez

SENORA, LA, Novel *see* Antoni Mus

SENORITO OCTAVIO, EL, 1881, Novel *see* Armando Palacio Valdes

SENS DE LA MORT, LE, Novel *see* Paul Bourget

SENSATION IN BUDAPEST, Play *see* Karl Georg Kulb

SENSATIONSPROZESS CASILLA, Novel *see* Hans Possendorff

SENSE AND SENSIBILITY, 1811, Novel *see* Jane Austen

SENSE OF FREEDOM, A, Autobiography *see* Jimmy Boyle

SENSITIVE, PASSIONATE MAN, A, Novel *see* Barbara Mahoney

SENSO, Milan 1883, Novel *see* Camillo Boito

SENSO TO NINGEN, Novel *see* Jumpei Gomikawa

SENSUALIST, THE, Novel *see* Saikaku Ihara

SENTENCE OF DEATH, THE, Play *see* Cyril Campion, Edward Dignon

SENTIER, LE, Avignon 1959, Novel *see* Richard Prentout

SENTIMENTAL LADY, THE, Play *see* Owen Davis

SENTIMENTAL TOMMY, 1895, Novel *see* J. M. Barrie

SENTIMENTALISTS, THE, Boston 1927, Novel *see* Dale Collins

SENTIMENTALNYI ROMAN, 1958, Novel *see* Vera Fyodorovna Panova

SENTINEL, THE, Novel *see* Jeffrey Konvitz

SENTINEL, THE, 1951, Short Story *see* Arthur C. Clarke

SEPARATE TABLES, London 1955, Play *see* Terence Rattigan

SEPARATE VACATIONS, Novel *see* Eric Webber

SEPARATION, Play *see* Tom Kempinski

SEPARATION DES RACES, LA, 1923, Novel *see* Charles-Ferdinand Ramuz

SEPARATION, LA, Novel *see* Dan Franck

SEPOLCRO DI CARTA, IL, Story *see* Sergio Donati

SEPOLTA VIVA, Novel *see* Marie Eugenie Saffray

SEPOLTA VIVA, LA, Novel *see* Francesco Mastriani

SEPOLTA VIVA, LA, 1900, Novel *see* Carolina Invernizio

SEPT BRANCHES DE LA RIVIERE OTA, LES, Play *see* Robert Lepage

SEPTEMBER, Novel *see* Rosamunde Pilcher

SEPTEMBER, SEPTEMBER, Novel *see* Shelby Foote

SEPTIEME CIEL, LE, Novel *see* Andre Lang

SEPTIEME JURE, LE, Paris 1958, Novel *see* Francis Didelot

SEQUESTRES D'ALTONA, LES, 1959, Play *see* Jean-Paul Sartre

SERA DI PIOGGIA, Story *see* Peppino Amato

SERENADE, 1937, Novel *see* James M. Cain

SERENATA AL VENTO, Play *see* Carlo Veneziani

SERENTATA, Sketch *see* Billy Merson

SERGE PANINE, Novel *see* Georges Ohnet

SERGEANT BERRY, Novel *see* Robert Arden

SERGEANT MUSGRAVE'S DANCE, 1959, Play *see* John Arden

SERGEANT, THE, New York 1958, Novel *see* Dennis Murphy

SERGEANT YORK - LAST OF THE LONG HUNTERS, Article *see* Tom Skeyhill

SERGIUS PANIN, *see* Lev Nikolayevich Tolstoy

SERIAL, Novel *see* Cyra McFadden

SERIOUS CHARGE, London 1955, Play *see* Philip King

SERPENT, LE, Novel *see* Pierre Nord

SERPENT NOIR, LE, Play *see* Paul Adam

SERPENTE A SONAGLI, IL, Play *see* Edoardo Anton

SERPICO, Book *see* Peter Maas

SERVA AMOROSA, LA, 1752, Play *see* Carlo Goldoni

SERVA PADRONA, LA, Opera *see* G. A. Federico

SERVA PADRONA, LA, Napoli 1733, Opera *see* Giovanni Battista Pergolesi

SERVANT IN THE HOUSE, THE, New York 1908, Play *see* Charles Ryan Kennedy

SERVANT OF GOD, Play *see* Madeleine Masson de Belavalle

SERVANT, THE, London 1948, Novel *see* Robin Maugham

SERVER SUNDARAM, Play *see* K. Balachander

SERVICE, London 1932, Play *see* C. L. Anthony

SERVICE FLAT, THE, Play *see* Marriott Edgar

SERVICE OF LOVE, A, Short Story *see* O. Henry

SERVITUDE ET GRANDEUR MILITAIRES, Short Story *see* Alfred de Vigny

SERVUS PETER, Play *see* Karl Noti

SERYOZHA, Leningrad 1955, Novel *see* Vera Fyodorovna Panova

SEST MUSKETYRU, Novel *see* Jan Klecanda

SETE GATINHOS, OS, 1958, Play *see* Nelson Rodrigues

SETEA, 1958, Novel *see* Titus Popovici

SETENTA VECES SIETE, Buenos Aires 1957, Short Story *see* Dalmiro A. Saenz

SETOUCHI MOONLIGHT SERENADE, Novel *see* Yu Aku

SETOUCHI SHONEN YAKYU DAN, Novel *see* Yu Aku

SETTE GIORNI ALL'ALTRO MONDO, Play *see* Aldo de Benedetti

SETTE PIANI, Short Story *see* Dino Buzzati

SETTIMANA NERA, Novel *see* Enrico Emanuelli

SET-UP, THE, 1928, Poem *see* Joseph Moncure March

SEUL BANDIT DU VILLAGE, LE, Play *see* Tristan Bernard

SEVEN AGES OF MAN, THE, Poem *see* William Shakespeare

SEVEN ALONE, Novel *see* Honore Morrow

SEVEN CHANCES, 1924, Play *see* Roi Cooper Megrue

SEVEN DAYS, 1908, Short Story *see* Mary Roberts Rinehart

SILVER BLAZE, 1894, Short Story *see* Arthur Conan Doyle

SILVER BRIDGE, THE, Novel *see* Helen Prothero Lewis

SILVER BUDDHA, THE, Short Story *see* Sax Rohmer

SILVER CHALICE, THE, 1952, Novel *see* Thomas B. Costain

SILVER CORD, THE, New York 1926, Play *see* Sidney Coe Howard

SILVER DARLINGS, THE, Novel *see* Neil Gunn

SILVER DOLLAR, New York 1932, Book *see* David Karsner

SILVER FOX, THE, New York 1921, Play *see* Gaetano Sazio

SILVER GIRL, THE, New York 1907, Play *see* Edward Peple

SILVER HORDE, THE, New York 1909, Novel *see* Rex Beach

SILVER KING, THE, London 1882, Play *see* Henry Herman, Henry Arthur Jones

SILVER LANTERNS, Story *see* Ethel Donoher

SILVER LOCUSTS, THE, Short Story *see* Ray Bradbury

SILVER MASK, THE, 1932, Short Story *see* Hugh Walpole

SILVER RIVER, Novel *see* Stephen Longstreet

SILVER ROCK, 1953, Novel *see* Luke Short

SILVER ROSARY, THE, Short Story *see* Monckton Hoffe

SILVER SHELL, THE, Novel *see* Henry J. W. Dam

SILVER SLIPPERS, 1916, Short Story *see* Jackson Gregory

SILVER SPOON, Serial Story *see* Clarence Budington Kelland

SILVER SPOON, THE, Radio Play *see* Henrik N. Ege

SILVER THREADS AMONG THE GOLD, Story *see* Pierce Kingsley

SILVER WHISTLE, THE, New York 1948, Play *see* Robert C. McEnroe

SILVERADO SQUATTERS, 1883, Short Story *see* Robert Louis Stevenson

SILVERBELL OU LA NUIT SANS ASTRES, Novel *see* Andre Armandy

SIMBA, Novel *see* Anthony Perry

SIMEON TETLOW'S SHADOW, New York 1909, Novel *see* Jennette Barbour Perry Lee

SIMHASAN, Novel *see* Arun Sadhu

SIMON AND LAURA, London 1954, Play *see* Alan Melville

SIMON DALE, Novel *see* Anthony Hope

SIMON LASH, DETECTIVE, Novel *see* Frank Gruber

SIMON THE JESTER, New York 1909, Novel *see* William J. Locke

SIMONE, Novel *see* Eugene Brieux

SIMOUN, LE, 1921, Play *see* Henri-Rene Lenormand

SIMPLE ERREUR, Play *see* Gaston Dumestre

SIMPLE PLAN, A, Novel *see* Scott B. Smith

SIMPLE SIMON, Novel *see* Ryne Douglas Peardon

SIMPLE SOULS, New York 1918, Novel *see* John Hastings Turner

SIN CARGO, Story *see* Lee Renick Brown

SIN OF SUSAN SLADE, THE, New York 1961, Novel *see* Doris Hume

SIN SNIPER, THE, Novel *see* Hugh Garner

SIN THAT WAS HIS, THE, New York 1917, Novel *see* Frank L. Packard

SINCE YOU WENT AWAY, Book *see* Margaret Buell Wilder

SINCERITY, Indianapolis 1929, Novel *see* John Erskine

SINDACO DEL RIONE SANITA, IL, 1960, Play *see* Eduardo de Filippo

SINDROME DI STENDHAL, LA, Novel *see* Graziella Magherini

SINFONIA PASTORAL, 1931, Novel *see* Armando Palacio Valdes

SING A SONG OF HOMICIDE, Story *see* James R. Langham

SINGE EN HIVER, UN, Paris 1959, Novel *see* Antoine Blondin

SINGE QUI PARLE, LE, Paris 1925, Novel *see* Rene Fauchois

SINGED WINGS, Story *see* Katharine Newlin Burt

SINGER NOT THE SONG, THE, London 1953, Novel *see* Audrey Erskine Lindop

SINGING FOOL, THE, Story *see* Leslie S. Barrows

SINGING GUNS, Novel *see* Max Brand

SINGING IDOL, THE, Television Play *see* Paul Monash

SINGLE LIFE, London 1839, Play *see* J. B. Buckstone

SINGLE MAN, A, London 1910, Play *see* Hubert Henry Davies

SINGLE NIGHT, 1932, Story *see* Louis Bromfield

SINGLE STANDARD, THE, Play *see* Daniel Carson Goodman

SINGLE STANDARD, THE, New York 1928, Novel *see* Adela Rogers St. Johns

SINISTER ERRAND, 1945, Novel *see* Peter Cheyney

SINISTER MAN, THE, London 1924, Novel *see* Edgar Wallace

SINISTER STREET, 1914, Novel *see* Compton Mackenzie

SINITE PEPERUDI, 1968, Novel *see* Pavel Vezhinov

SINK THE BISMARCK!, Book *see* C. S. Forester

SINNERS, New York 1915, Play *see* Owen Davis

SINNERS ALL, Novel *see* Jerome Kingston

SINNERS IN HEAVEN, Indianapolis 1923, Novel *see* Clive Arden

SINS, Novel *see* Judith Gould

SINS OF A FATHER, THE, Novel *see* Mrs. Gaskell

SINS OF SOCIETY, THE, London 1907, Play *see* Henry Hamilton, Cecil Raleigh

SINS OF ST. ANTHONY, THE, Short Story *see* Charles Collins

SINS OF THE CHILDREN, THE, Boston 1916, Novel *see* Cosmo Hamilton

SINS OF THE FATHER, Story *see* Elaine Sterne

SINS YE DO, THE, Novel *see* Emmeline Morrison

SINUHE, EGYPTILAINEN, 1946, Novel *see* Mika Waltari

SIR GAWAIN AND THE GREEN KNIGHT, c1375, Verse *see* Anon

SIR OR MADAM, Novel *see* Berta Ruck

SIR PIEGAN PASSES, New York 1923, Short Story *see* W. C. Tuttle

SIR RUPERT'S WIFE, Poem *see* George R. Sims

SIR TRISTRAM GOES WEST, Story *see* Eric Keown

SIRE OF MALETROIT'S DOOR, THE, 1878, Short Story *see* Robert Louis Stevenson

SIRENA, 1935, Novel *see* Marie Majerova

SIRENA NEGRA, LA, 1908, Novel *see* Emilia Pardo Bazan

SIRENES ET TRITONS; LE ROMAN DU SOUS-MARIN, Paris 1927, Novel *see* Maurice Larrouy

SIREN'S SONG, THE, Play *see* George Middleton, Leonidas Westervelt

SIROKKO, Budapest 1969, Novel *see* Gyula Hernadi

SIS HOPKINS, Buffalo, N.Y. 1899, Play *see* Carroll Fleming, George A. Nichols

SISSI, Novel *see* Marie Blank-Eismann

SISSIGNORA, Novel *see* Flavia Steno

SISSY'S BRAUTFAHRT, Play *see* Ernst Decsey, Gustav Holm

SISTA BREVET TILL SVERIGE, 1959, Novel *see* Vilhelm Moberg

SISTE KAPITEL, 1923, Novel *see* Knut Hamsun

SISTEMA PELEGRIN, EL, 1949, Novel *see* Wenceslao Fernandez Florez

SISTER ACT, 1937, Short Story *see* Fannie Hurst

SISTER CARRIE, 1900, Novel *see* Theodore Dreiser

SISTER CHUN, Novel *see* Liu Zhen

SISTER DORA, Book *see* Jo Manton

SISTER TO ASSIST 'ER, A, Play *see* John Le Breton

SISTERHOOD, Novel *see* Casey Bishop, Betty Black

SISTERS OF JEZEBEL, 1924, Short Story *see* Harold B. Montayne

SISTERS OF THE GOLDEN CIRCLE, Short Story *see* O. Henry

SISTERS, THE, New York 1937, Novel *see* Myron Brinig

SITIO DO PICAPAU AMARELO, O, 1939, Short Story *see* Monteiro Lobato

SITTING ON THE WORLD, 1920, Short Story *see* Sophie Kerr

SITTING TARGET, Novel *see* Lawrence Henderson

SITUATION OF GRAVITY, A, 1943, Story *see* Samuel Taylor

SIVOOKY DEMON, Novel *see* Jakub Arbes

SIX A SIX, Short Story *see* Vicki Baum

SIX A.M., Novel *see* Liu Baiyu

SIX BEST CELLARS, THE, 1919, Short Story *see* Holworthy Hall, Hugh MacNair Kahler

SIX CENT MILLE FRANCS PAR MOIS, Play *see* Albert-Jean, Andre Mouezy-Eon

SIX CHEVAUX BLEUS, Novel *see* Yvonne Esconda

SIX DAYS, Philadelphia 1923, Novel *see* Elinor Glyn

SIX DAYS OF THE CONDOR, Novel *see* James Grady

SIX DEAD MEN, Novel *see* Andre Steedman

SIX DEGREES OF SEPARATION, Play *see* John Guare

SIX FEET FOUR, New York 1918, Novel *see* Jackson Gregory

SIX HOMMES A TUER, Novel *see* Stanislas-Andre Steeman

SIX NAPOLEONS, THE, Short Story *see* Arthur Conan Doyle

SIX WEEKS, Novel *see* Fred Mustard Stewart

SIX WEEKS IN AUGUST, Play *see* Pamela Herbert Chais

SIX WEEKS SOUTH OF TEXAS, Serial Story *see* Leslie T. White

SIX-CYLINDER LOVE, New York 1921, Play *see* William Anthony McGuire

SIX-FIFTY, THE, New York 1921, Play *see* Kate L. McLaurin

SIXIEME ETAGE, Play *see* Alfred Gehri

SIXTEEN FATHOMS UNDER, 1932, Short Story *see* Eustace L. Adams

SIXTEEN HANDS, New York 1938, Novel *see* Homer Croy

SIXTH OF JUNE, THE, 1955, Novel *see* Lionel Shapiro

SKALNI PLEMENO, Novel *see* Jan Moravek

SKALPEL, PROSIM, Novel *see* Valja Styblova

SKANDAL IN DER RESIDENZ, Play *see* Carl Sternheim

SKAREDA DEDINA, Novel *see* Petr Jilemnicky

SKAZKA O MERTVOY TSAREVNE I O SEMI BOGATYRYAKH, 1833, Poem *see* Alexander Pushkin

SKAZKA O POPE I O RABOTNIKE EGO BALDE, 1831, Short Story *see* Alexander Pushkin

SKAZKA O RYBAKE I RYBKE, 1833, Poem *see* Alexander Pushkin

SKAZKA O TSARE SALTANE, 1831, Poem *see* Alexander Pushkin

SKAZKA O ZOLOTOM PETUKHE, 1834, Short Story *see* Alexander Pushkin

SKEEZER - DOG WITH A MISSION, Novel *see* Elizabeth Yates

SKEIN OF LIFE, THE, Story *see* Will M. Ritchey

SKELETONS, Novel *see* Marshall Goldberg

SKEPP TILL INDIALAND, Play *see* Martin Soederhjelm

SKIBSDRENGENS FORTAELLING, Copenhagen 1942, Short Story *see* Karen Blixen

SKIDDING, New York 1928, Play *see* Aurania Rouverol

SKIN DEEP, Short Story *see* Frank R. Adams

SKIN GAME, THE, London 1920, Play *see* John Galsworthy

SKINNER'S BABY, New York 1917, Novel *see* Henry Irving Dodge

SKINNER'S BIG IDEA, New York 1918, Novel *see* Henry Irving Dodge

SKINNER'S DRESS SUIT, 1916, Short Story *see* Henry Irving Dodge

SKIPPER OF THE OSPREY, THE, Short Story *see* W. W. Jacobs

SKIPPER SURPRISED HIS WIFE, THE, Article *see* Com. W. J. Lederer

SKIPPER'S WOOING, THE, Novel *see* W. W. Jacobs

SKIPPY, New York 1929, Novel *see* Percy Lee Crosby

SKIS AGAINST THE ATOM, London 1954, Book *see* Knut Haukelid

SKJAERGARDSFLIRT, Play *see* Gideon Wahlberg

SKLENENY VRCH, Short Story *see* Jaroslav Havlicek

SKOLA ZAKLAD ZIVOTA, Book *see* Jaroslav Zak

SKULL OF THE MARQUIS DE SADE, THE, New York 1965, Short Story *see* Robert Bloch

SKULLDUGGERY, Play *see* Philip Davis

SKVERNY ANEKDOT, 1862, Short Story *see* Fyodor Dostoyevsky

SKY HIGH, Short Story *see* Frank Dazey, Waldemar Young

SKY HIGH, 1929, Short Story *see* Elliott White Springs

SKY IS GRAY, THE, 1966, Short Story *see* Ernest J. Gaines

SKY LIFE, 1929, Short Story *see* Frank Dazey, Agnes Christine Johnston

SKY PILOT, THE, Chicago 1899, Novel *see* Ralph Connor

SKY STEWARD, Novel *see* Ken Attiwill

SKYGGEN, 1847, Short Story *see* Hans Christian Andersen

SKYGGER PAA GRAESSET, 1978, Short Story *see* Karen Blixen

SKYJACKED, Novel *see* David Harper

SKYLARK, New York 1939, Play *see* Samson Raphaelson

SKYLIGHT ROOM, THE, 1906, Short Story *see* O. Henry

SKYLINE OF SPRUCE, THE, Boston 1922, Novel *see* Edison Marshall

SKYROCKET, THE, New York 1925, Novel *see* Adela Rogers St. Johns

SKYSCRAPER, New York 1931, Novel *see* Faith Baldwin

SLAB BOYS, THE, Play *see* John Byrne

SLAEGTEN, 1898, Novel *see* Gustav Weid

SLAPSTICK OR LONESOME NO MORE!, 1976, Novel *see* Kurt Vonnegut Jr.

SLATE AND WYN AND BLANCHE MCBRIDE, Novel *see* Georgia Savage

SLATTERY'S HURRICANE, Novel *see* Herman Wouk

SLAUGHTERHOUSE FIVE, 1969, Novel *see* Kurt Vonnegut Jr.

SLAVE, 1964, Play *see* Leroi Jones

SLAVE BRACELET, THE, Story *see* Olga Hall Brown

SLAVE, THE, Novel *see* Robert Hichens

SLAVE TRADE, THE, London 1961, Book *see* Sean O'Callaghan

SLAVES OF TIMBUKTU, THE, Book *see* Robin Maugham

SLAWA I CHWALA, Novel *see* Jaroslaw Iwaszkiewicz

SLAYGROUND, Novel *see* Donald E. Westlake

SLECNA KONVALINKA, Play *see* Otomar Schafer

SLEDITE OSTAVAT, 1954, Novel *see* Pavel Vezhinov

SLEEP ALL WINTER, Short Story *see* Dan Gordon, Richard Wormser

SLEEP LONG MY LOVE, New York 1959, Novel *see* Hillary Waugh

SLEEP MY LOVE, 1946, Novel *see* Leo Rosten

SLEEPERS, Book *see* Lorenzo Carcaterra

SLEEPERS EAST, Boston 1933, Novel *see* Frederick Nebel

SLEEPING CLERGYMAN, A, London 1933, Play *see* James Bridie

SLEEPING LIFE, A, Novel *see* Ruth Rendell

SLEEPING MEMORY (THE GREAT AWAKENING), A, New York 1902, Novel *see* E. Phillips Oppenheim

SLEEPING PARTNER, THE, London 1961, Novel *see* Winston Graham

SLEEPING PRINCE, THE, London 1953, Play *see* Terence Rattigan

SLEEPING SENTINEL, THE, Poem *see* F. H. de Janvier

SLEEPING TIGER, THE, Novel *see* Maurice Moiseiwitch

SLEEPING WITH THE ENEMY, Novel *see* Nancy Price

SLEEPS SIX, Novel *see* Frederic Raphael

SLEPOY MUSYKANT, Moscow 1888, Novel *see* Vladimir Galaktionovich Korolenko

SLEUTH, 1971, Play *see* Anthony Shaffer

SLIGHT CASE OF MURDER, A, New York 1935, Play *see* Howard Lindsay, Damon Runyon

SLIGHTLY SCARLET, Play *see* Percy Heath

SLIM, Boston 1934, Novel *see* William Wister Haines

SLIM PRINCESS, THE, 1906, Short Story *see* George Ade

SLIMMER, Novel *see* John Brosnan

SLINGS AND ARROWS, Novel *see* Hugh Conway

SLIPPING-DOWN LIFE, A, 1970, Novel *see* Anne Tyler

SLIPPY MCGEE: SOMETIMES KNOWN AS THE BUTTERFLY MAN, Novel *see* Marie Conway Oemler

SLIVER, Novel *see* Ira Levin

SLOW BURGESS, Short Story *see* Charles Alden Selzer

SLOW COMING DARK, Book *see* Doug Magee

SLUCHAI S POLYNNYM, 1969, Short Story *see* Konstantin Simonov

SLUGS, Novel *see* Shaun Hutson

SMALL BACHELOR, THE, 1926, Short Story *see* P. G. Wodehouse

SMALL BACK ROOM, THE, 1943, Novel *see* Nigel Balchin

SMALL HOTEL, Play *see* Rex Frost

SMALL MIRACLE, New York 1934, Play *see* Norman Krasna

SMALL TOWN GIRL, New York 1935, Novel *see* Ben Ames Williams

SMALL VOICE, THE, Novel *see* Robert Westerby

SMALL WOMAN, THE, Book *see* Alan Burgess

SMARRA, Novel *see* Ludwig Wolff

SMART KID LIKE YOU, A, Novel *see* Stella Pevsner

SMART MONEY, Story *see* David Lang

SMART SET, Story *see* W. Carey Wonderly

SMARTY, Philadelphia 1927, Play *see* F. Hugh Herbert

SMASHING THE BOOKIE GANG MARAUDERS, Novel *see* John Bartlow Martin

SMASHING THE RACKETS, 1937-38, Article *see* Forest Davis

SMEMORATO, LO, Play *see* Emilio Caglieri

SMERT IVANA ILICHA, 1886, Short Story *see* Lev Nikolayevich Tolstoy

SMERT TARELKINA, 1869, Play *see* Aleksandr Sukhovo-Kobylin

SMERY ZIVOTA, Play *see* F. X. Svoboda

SMILEY, Novel *see* Moore Raymond

SMILEY GETS A GUN, Novel *see* Moore Raymond

SMILEY'S PEOPLE, Novel *see* John Le Carre

SMILIN' THROUGH, New York 1919, Play *see* Jane Cowl, Jane Murfin

SMILLA'S SENSE OF SNOW, Novel *see* Peter Hoeg

SMITH, London 1909, Play *see* W. Somerset Maugham

SMITHEREENS, Novel *see* B. W. Battin

SMITH'S DREAM, Novel *see* Karl Stead

SMOKE, Short Story *see* Norman Sherbrooke

SMOKE BELLEW, New York 1912, Novel *see* Jack London

SMOKED GLASSES, Play *see* William Foster, B. Scott-Elder

SMOKY THE COWHORSE, New York 1926, Novel *see* Will James

SMOKY VALLEY, Novel *see* Donald Hamilton

SMRITICHITRE, Autobiography *see* Laxmibai Tilak

SMRT KRASNYCH SRNCU, Novel *see* Ota Pavel

SMRT' SA VOLA ENGELCHEN, 1959, Novel *see* Ladislav Mnacko

SMUGGLERS' CIRCUIT, Novel *see* Denys Roberts

SMUGGLERS' COVE, Short Story *see* Talbert Josselyn

SMUGGLERS, THE, Novel *see* Elizabeth Hely

SMUGLERE, 1935, Novel *see* Arthur Omre

SNACK BAR BUDAPEST, Novel *see* Silvia Bre, Marco Lodoli

SNAFU, New York 1944, Play *see* Harold Buchman, Louis Solomon

SNAKE PIT, THE, Novel *see* Mary Jane Ward

SNAKE WATER, London 1965, Novel *see* Alan Williams

SNAKE-BITE, 1919, Short Story *see* Robert Hichens

SNAKE'S WIFE, THE, 1926, Short Story *see* Wallace Smith

SNAKHA, 1942, Novel *see* Georgi Karaslavov

SNAPPER, THE, Novel *see* Roddy Doyle

SNATCHERS, THE, New York 1953, Novel *see* Lionel White

SNEDRONNINGEN, 1845, Short Story *see* Hans Christian Andersen

SNEGUROCHKA, 1873, Play *see* Alexander Ostrovsky

SNIPS AND SNAILS, Novel *see* Louise Baker

SNOB, THE, 1918, Short Story *see* William J. Neidig

SNOB; THE STORY OF A MARRIAGE, THE, New York 1924, Novel *see* Helen Reimensnyder Martin

SNOBS, New York 1911, Play *see* George Bronson Howard

SNORKEL, THE, Novel *see* Anthony Dawson

SNOW AND ICE MELT, Novel *see* Li Zhun

SNOW BIRCH, THE, 1958, Novel *see* John Mantley

SNOW DUST, Story *see* Howard E. Morgan

SNOW GOOSE, THE, *see* Paul Gallico

SNOW IN THE DESERT, Novel *see* Andrew Soutar

SNOW LARK, Book *see* Ronald Sutherland

SNOW TREASURE, New York 1942, Novel *see* Marie McSwigan

SNOWBALL, Novel *see* James Lake

SNOWBLIND, 1921, Short Story *see* Katharine Newlin Burt, Arthur Stringer

SNOW-BURNER, THE, Story *see* Henry Oyen

SNOWDRIFT, New York 1922, Novel *see* James B. Hendryx

SNOWED UNDER, Story *see* Lawrence Saunders

SNOWMAN, THE, Book *see* Raymond Briggs

SNOWS OF KILIMANJARO, THE, 1938, Short Story *see* Ernest Hemingway

SNOWSHOE TRAIL, THE, Boston 1921, Novel *see* Edison Marshall

SO BIG!, Garden City, N.Y. 1924, Novel *see* Edna Ferber

SO EIN FLEGEL, Novel *see* Heinrich Spoerl

SO EIN FRUCHTCHEN, Play *see* Franz Gribitz

SO LITTLE CAUSE FOR CAROLINE, Novel *see* Eric Bercovici

SO LONG AT THE FAIR, Novel *see* Anthony Thorne

SO LONG LETTY, New York 1916, Musical Play *see* Carroll, Earl Carroll, Elmer Harris, Oliver Morosco

SO RED THE ROSE, New York 1934, Novel *see* Stark Young

SO THIS IS ARIZONA, 1921, Serial Story *see* Marie Schrader, C. C. Wadde

SO THIS IS LONDON, London 1923, Play *see* Arthur Frederick Goodrich

SO WELL REMEMBERED, 1947, Novel *see* James Hilton

SOB SISTER, New York 1931, Novel *see* Mildred Gilman

SOB SISTER, THE, Story *see* Harry Care

SOBACH'E SERDTSE, 1968, Short Story *see* Mikhail Bulgakov

SOBBIN' WOMEN, THE, 1937, Short Story *see* Stephen Vincent Benet

SOBOL I PANNA, 1912, Novel *see* Jozef Weyssenhoff

SOBRADO, O, 1949, Short Story *see* Erico Verissimo

SOBRENATURAL, Novel *see* Gabriel Gonzalez Melendez

SOCIAL BUCCANEER, THE, Indianapolis 1910, Novel *see* Frederic Stewart Isham

SOCIAL HIGHWAYMAN, A, New York 1895, Play *see* Mary Stone

SOCIAL REGISTER, THE, New York 1931, Play *see* John Emerson, Anita Loos

SOCIETA DEL MALESSERE, LA, Book *see* Giuseppe Fiori

SOCIETY GIRL, New York 1931, Play *see* Charles Beahan, John Larkin Jr.

SODA CRACKER, Novel *see* Jaron Summers

SOEURETTE, Novel *see* Gyp

SOEURS HORTENSIAS, LES, Novel *see* Henri Duvernois

SOEURS KLEH, LES, Novel *see* Gina Kaus

SOFT SHOULDERS, Story *see* Philip Hurn

SOGEKI, Play *see* Hidekazu Nagahara

SOGNI MUOIONO ALL'ALBA, I, Play *see* Indro Montanelli

SOGNI NEL CASSETTO, I, Novel *see* Adriana Chiaromonte

SOGNO DI GIACOBBE, IL, 1900, Play *see* Ugo Falena

SOGNO DI UN TRAMONTO D'AUTUNNO, 1898, *see* Gabriele D'Annunzio

SOHN DER HAGAR, DER, Novel *see* Paul Keller

SOHNE DER GROSSEN BARIN, DIE, Novel *see* Lieselotte Welskopf-Henrich

SOIR AU FRONT, UN, Play *see* Henri Kistemaeckers

SOIR DE REVEILLON, UN, Opera *see* Marcel Gerbidon, Albert Willemetz

SOLARIS, 1961, Novel *see* Stanislaw Lem

SOLD, 1910, Play *see* George Erastov

SOLD GOLD CADILLAC, THE, New York 1953, Play *see* George S. Kaufman

SOLDAAT VAN ORANJE, Autobiography *see* Erik Hazelhoff Roelfzema

SOLDATAMI NE ROZHDAIVTSIA, 1964, Novel *see* Konstantin Simonov

SOLDATENSENDER CALAIS, Novel *see* Michael Mohr

SOLDATESSE, LE, Novel *see* Ugo Pirro

SOLDIER AND A MAN, A, Play *see* Ben Landeck

SOLDIER FOR CHRISTMAS, A, London 1944, Play *see* Reginald Beckwith

SOLDIER IN THE RAIN, New York 1960, Novel *see* William Goldman

SOLDIER OF FORTUNE, 1954, Novel *see* Ernest K. Gann

SOLDIER'S DAUGHTER NEVER CRIES, A, Novel *see* Kaylie Jones

SOLDIER'S HOME, 1930, Short Story *see* Ernest Hemingway

SOLDIERS OF FORTUNE, New York 1897, Novel *see* Richard Harding Davis

SOLDIER'S PLAY, A, 1982, Play *see* Charles Fuller

SOLDIER'S TALE, A, Novel *see* M. K. Joseph

SOLDIERS THREE, 1888, Short Story *see* Rudyard Kipling

SOLEIL A L'OMBRE, LE, Novel *see* Georges Dolley

SOLEIL DANS L'OEIL, LE, Novel *see* Michele Perrein

SOLEIL D'AUTOMNE, *see* Christian Signol

SOLEIL DE MINUIT, LE, Novel *see* Pierre Benoit

SOLEIL DE PLOMB, UN, Novel *see* Michel Lebrun

SOLEIL ROUGE, Novel *see* Laird Koenig

SOLID GOLD ARTICLE, THE, 1929, Short Story *see* Richard Connell

SOLID GOLD CADILLAC, THE, New York 1953, Play *see* Howard Teichmann

SOLID SAID THE EARL, Novel *see* John Paddy Carstairs

SOLITAIRE MAN, THE, Boston 1927, Play *see* Bella Spewack, Samuel Spewack

SOLITARY CHILD, THE, Novel *see* Nina Bawden

SOLITARY CYCLIST, THE, Short Story *see* Arthur Conan Doyle

SOLO DE MOTO, 1967, Novel *see* Daniel Sueiro

SOLSTIZIO DI TENEBRE, Book *see* Berthe von Uhland

..SOM HAVETS NAKNA VIND, Stockholm 1965, Novel *see* Gustav Sandgren

SOMBRERO DE TRES PICOS, EL, 1874, Short Story *see* Pedro Antonio de Alarcon

SOME CAME RUNNING, 1957, Novel *see* James Jones

SOME FIXER, Story *see* Marjorie Jones

SOME KIND OF HERO, Novel *see* James Kirkwood

SOME KIND OF LOVE STORY, Play *see* Arthur Miller

SOME LIAR, 1918, Short Story *see* James Oliver Curwood

SOME LIE AND SOME DIE, Novel *see* Ruth Rendell

SOME LIKE 'EM COLD, Short Story *see* Edna Anhalt, Edward Anhalt

SOME MUST WATCH, Novel *see* Ethel Lina White

SOME OTHER LOVE, Play *see* William Fairchild

SOMEBODY'S DARLING, Novel *see* Sidney Morgan

SOMEBODY'S WAITING, Novel *see* Judith Kelman

SOMEHOW GOOD, Novel *see* William de Morgan

SOMEONE AND SOMEBODY, New York 1917, Novel *see* Porter Emerson Browne

SOMEONE AT THE DOOR, London 1935, Play *see* Campbell Christie, Dorothy Christie

SOMEONE IN THE HOUSE, New York 1918, Play *see* Larry Evans, George S. Kaufman, W. Percival

SOMEONE IS BLEEDING, Novel *see* Richard Matheson

SOMEONE WAITING, London 1953, Play *see* Emlyn Williams

SOMETHING ABOUT A SAILOR, Play *see* Earle Couttie

SOMETHING BORROWED, Story *see* Elizabeth Dunn

SOMETHING FOR THE BOYS, New York 1943, Musical Play *see* Dorothy Fields, Herbert Fields, Cole Porter

SOMETHING IN DISGUISE, Novel *see* Elizabeth Jane Howard

SOMETHING OF VALUE, 1955, Novel *see* Robert Ruark

SOMETHING TO BRAG ABOUT, New York 1925, Play *see* William Le Baron, Edgar Selwyn

SOMETHING TO HIDE, 1966, Novel *see* Nicholas Monsarrat

SOMETHING WICKED THIS WAY COMES, 1962, Novel *see* Ray Bradbury

SOMETHING'S GOT TO GIVE, Article *see* Darcy Frey

SOMETIMES A GREAT NOTION, 1966, Novel *see* Ken Kesey

SOMETIMES THEY COME BACK, Short Story *see* Stephen King

SOMEWHERE IN FRANCE, New York 1915, Novel *see* Richard Harding Davis

SOMEWHERE IN SONORA, Boston 1925, Novel *see* Will Levington Comfort

SOMMAR OCH SYNDARE, Novel *see* Willy Breinholst, Erik Pouplier

SOMMERDANSEN, Novel *see* Peter Olof Ekstrom

SOMMERGLAEDER, 1902, Novel *see* Herman Bang

SOMMERLIEBE, Novel *see* O. E. Hartleben

SOMMERRAUSCH, Novel *see* J. Schneider-Foerstl

SON FILS, Novel *see* Andre Corthis

SON OF ANAK, A, 1928, Short Story *see* Ben Ames Williams

SON OF FURY, Novel *see* Edison Marshall

SON OF HIS FATHER, A, New York 1925, Novel *see* Harold Bell Wright

SON OF HIS FATHER, THE, London 1915, Novel *see* Ridgwell Cullum

SON OF MAMA POSITA, Story *see* Maxwell Aley

SON OF ROBIN HOOD, Novel *see* Paul A. Castleton

SON OF THE GODS, 1929, Serial Story *see* Rex Beach

SON OF THE HILLS, A, New York 1913, Novel *see* Harriet T. Comstock

SON OF THE MORNING STAR, *see* Evan S. Cornell

SON OF THE SAHARA, Novel *see* Kelman D. Frost

SON OF THE SAHARA, A, New York 1922, Novel *see* Louise Gerard

SON OF THE WOLF, 1900, Short Story *see* Jack London

SON RISE: A MIRACLE OF LOVE, Book *see* Barry Neil Kaufman

SONBAINI CHUNDADI, Play *see* Jagjivan Mehta

SON-DAUGHTER, THE, New York 1919, Play *see* David Belasco, George Scarborough

SONEZAKI SHINJU, 1703, Play *see* Monzaemon Chikamatsu

SONG AND DANCE MAN, THE, New York 1923, Play *see* George M. Cohan

SONG AND THE SERGEANT, THE, Short Story *see* O. Henry

SONG IN HIS HEART, Book *see* Rita Olcott

SONG IS ENDED, THE, Play *see* Walter Reisch

SONG OF HIAWATHA, Boston 1855, Poem *see* Henry Wadsworth Longfellow

SONG OF HIS SOUL, THE, 1916, Short Story *see* William Charles Lengel

SONG OF LOVE, Play *see* Bernard Schubert, Mario Silva

SONG OF NORWAY, New York 1944, Play *see* George Forrest, Milton Lazarus, Robert Wright

SONG OF SIXPENCE, A, New York 1913, Novel *see* Frederic Arnold Kummer

SONG OF SONGS, THE, Story *see* Bruno Lessing

SONG OF THE DRAGON, THE, New York 1923, Novel *see* John Taintor Foote

SONG OF THE FLAME, New York 1925, Musical Play *see* George Gershwin, Otto Harbach, H. Stothart

SONG OF THE LOON, New York 1966, Novel *see* Richard Amory

SONG OF THE SHIRT, THE, 1843, Poem *see* Thomas Hood

SONG OF THE WAGE SLAVE, 1907, Poem *see* Robert W. Service

SONG WRITER, THE, New York 1928, Play *see* Crane Wilbur

SONIA, Novel *see* Stephen McKenna

SONIM, DI GESCHICHTE FUN A LIEBE, 1966, Novel *see* Isaac Bashevis Singer

SONJA, Stockholm 1927, Play *see* Herbert Grevenius

SONNAMBULA, LA, Milan 1831, Opera *see* Vincenzo Bellini

SONNBLICK RUFT, DER, Novel *see* Edmund Josef Bendl

SONNE ANGREIFEN, DIE, Novel *see* Witold Gombrowicz

SONNETS, 1609, Verse *see* William Shakespeare

SONNETTE D'ALARME, LA, Play *see* Romain Coolus, Maurice Hennequin

SONNY, New York 1921, Play *see* George V. Hobart, Raymond Hubbell

SONS AND LOVERS, 1913, Novel *see* D. H. Lawrence

SONS OF SATAN, THE, Novel *see* William Le Queux

SONS OF THE SHEIK, THE, Novel *see* Edith Maude Hull

SON'S RETURN, THE, Short Story *see* Guy de Maupassant

SOOKEY, Novel *see* Douglas Newton

SOPHIE ET LE CRIME, Novel *see* Cecil Saint-Laurent

SOPHIE SEMENOFF, 1920, Short Story *see* Wallace Irwin

SOPHIENLUND, Play *see* Fritz von Woedtke, Helmut Weiss

SOPHIE'S CHOICE, 1979, Novel *see* William Styron

SOPHY OF KRAVONIA, London 1905, Novel *see* Anthony Hope

SOR JUANA; HER LIFE AND WORLD (THE TRAPS OF FAITH), Book *see* Octavio Paz

SORCERER'S VILLAGE, THE, Book *see* Hassoldt Davis

SORCIER, LE, Novel *see* Henri Germain

SORCIERE, LA, Paris 1903, Play *see* Victorien Sardou

SORE KARA, 1910, Novel *see* Natsume Soseki

SORELLE MATERASSI, 1934, Novel *see* Aldo Palazzeschi

SOROCHINSKAYA JAMARKA, 1831, Short Story *see* Nikolay Gogol

SORRELL AND SON, 1925, Novel *see* Warwick Deeping

SORRISO DELLA PITHIA, IL, *see* Janis Maris

SORROWS OF SATAN, THE, New York 1895, Novel *see* Marie Corelli

SORRY WRONG NUMBER, Radio Play *see* Lucille Fletcher

SORRY YOU'VE BEEN TROUBLED, London 1929, Play *see* Walter Hackett

SORT OF TRAITORS, London 1949, Novel *see* Nigel Balchin

SORTILEGES, Novel *see* Claude Boncompain

S.O.S., London 1928, Play *see* Walter Ellis

S.O.S. NORONHA, Novel *see* Pierre Vire

SO'S YOUR OLD MAN, 1925, Short Story *see* Julian Leonard Street

SOSEAUA NORDULUI, 1959, Novel *see* Eugen Barbu

SOSIA, IL, Short Story *see* Fyodor Dostoyevsky

SOSKENDE, 1952, Play *see* Hans Christian Branner

SOTTO IL VESTITO NIENTE, Novel *see* Marco Parma

SOUBOJ S BOHEM, Short Story *see* Mor Jokai

SOUBRETTE, Vienna 1938, Play *see* Jacques Deval

SOUFFLE DU DESIR, LE, Novel *see* Gaston Montho

SOUL KISS, THE, New York 1908, Play *see* Paul Hervey Fox, George Tilton

SOUL OF BRONZE, THE, Story *see* Georges Le Faure

SOUL OF KUNLUN PASS, THE, Novel *see* Chen Dunde

SOUL OF PIERRE, THE, Novel *see* Georges Ohnet

SOULS FOR SALE, New York 1922, Novel *see* Rupert Hughes

SOUND AND THE FURY, THE, 1929, Novel *see* William Faulkner

SOUND OF HUNTING, A, New York 1945, Play *see* Harry Peter M'nab Brown

SOUND OF MURDER, THE, London 1959, Play *see* William Fairchild

SOUND OF MUSIC, THE, New York 1959, Musical Play *see* Oscar Hammerstein II, Richard Rodgers

SOUND OF ONE HAND CLAPPING, THE, Novel *see* Richard Flanagan

SOUNDER, 1969, Novel *see* William Armstrong

SOUNDINGS, Boston 1925, Novel *see* Arthur Hamilton Gibbs

SOUPCONS, Novel *see* Maurice Dekobra

SOUPE A LA GRIMACE, LA, Novel *see* Terry Stewart

SOUPE AUX CHOUX, LA, Novel *see* Rene Fallet

SOUR GRAPES, New York 1926, Play *see* Vincent Lawrence

SOUR SWEET, 1982, Novel *see* Timothy Mo

SOURCE OF IRRITATION, Short Story *see* Stacy Aumonier

SOURCE, THE, New York 1918, Novel *see* Clarence Budington Kelland

SOURD DANS LA VILLE, LE, Novel *see* Marie-Claire Blais

SOURIRE DANS LA TEMPETE, UN, Novel *see* Maurice Constantin-Weyer

SOURIS BLONDE, Opera *see* Monjardin, Xanrof

SOURIS D'HOTEL, Play *see* Paul Armont, Marcel Gerbidon

SOUS LE CASQUE DE CUIR, Novel *see* Rene Chambe

SOUS LE SOLEIL DE SATAN, 1926, Novel *see* Georges Bernanos

SOUS L'EPAULETTE, Play *see* Arthur Bernede

SOUS LES CIEUX D'ARABIE, Novel *see* C. R. Wells

SOUTH OF THE RIO GRANDE, 1936, Novel *see* Max Brand

SOUTH RIDING, 1935, Novel *see* Winifred Holtby

SOUTH SEA BUBBLE, A, Novel *see* Roland Pertwee

SOUTHERN BLADE, THE, New York 1961, Novel *see* Nelson Wolford, Shirley Wolford

SOUTHERN MAID, A, London 1920, Musical Play *see* Dion Clayton Calthrop, Harold Fraser-Simson

SOUTHERN ROSES, Play *see* Rudolf Bernauer

SOUTHERNER, THE, Story *see* Bess Meredyth

SOUTHERNERS, THE, Novel *see* Cyrus Townsend Brady

SOUTHWEST PASS, Story *see* John D. Klorer

SOUVENIRS D'ENFANCE, 1957, Autobiography *see* Marcel Pagnol

SOWERS, THE, New York 1895, Novel *see* Henry Seton Merriman

SOWING GLORY, 1933, Short Story *see* J. D. Newsom

SOWING OF ALDERSON CREE, THE, New York 1907, Novel *see* Margaret Prescott Montague

SOWING THE WIND, London 1893, Play *see* Sidney Grundy

SPACE MOONS, Short Story *see* Jojiro Okami

SPACE VAMPIRES, THE, Novel *see* Colin Wilson

SPACEWAYS, Radio Play *see* Charles Eric Maine

SPACIAFORNEJ D'LA VAL D'AOSTA, I, 1848, Novel *see* Giovanni Sabbatini

SPAGHETTI HOUSE, Play *see* Peter Barnes

SPALOVAC MRTVOL, 1967, Novel *see* Ladislav Fuks

SPAM, Story *see* Sean McNamara

SPAN OF LIFE, THE, New York 1893, Play *see* Sutton Vane

SPANIARD, THE, New York 1924, Novel *see* Juanita Savage

SPANISCHE FLIEGE, DIE, Play *see* Franz Robert Arnold, Ernst Bach

SPANISH ACRES, Boston 1925, Novel *see* Hal G. Evarts

SPANISH CAPE MYSTERY, THE, New York 1935, Novel *see* Ellery Queen

SPANISH CONQUERORS, THE, New Haven 1919, Novel *see* Irving Berdine Richman

SPANISH FARM, THE, Short Story *see* R. H. Mottram

SPANISH FARM TRILOGY, THE, Novel *see* R. H. Mottram

SPANISH GARDENER, THE, 1950, Novel *see* A. J. Cronin

SPANISH JADE, THE, New York 1908, Novel *see* Maurice Hewlett

SPANISH STUDENT, THE, Poem *see* Henry Wadsworth Longfellow

SPANISH SUNLIGHT, New York 1925, Novel *see* Anthony Pryde

SPARE THE ROD, Novel *see* Michael Croft

SPARKINS, Short Story *see* Charles Dickens

SPARKLING CYANIDE, Novel *see* Agatha Christie

SPARRERS CAN'T SING, Stratford 1960, Play *see* Stephen Lewis

SPARROWS, 1909, Novel *see* Horace W. C. Newte

SPARTACUS, 1951, Novel *see* Howard Fast

SPARTIZIONE, LA, Novel *see* Piero Chiara

SPATZEN IN GOTTES HAND, Play *see* L. Bender, Edgar Kahn

SPAWN OF THE DESERT, 1922, Short Story *see* W. C. Tuttle

SPAWN OF THE NORTH, Boston 1932, Novel *see* Florence Barrett Willoughby

SPEAK EASILY, New York 1932, Novel *see* Clarence Budington Kelland

SPEAKEASY, Story *see* Edward Knoblock, George Rosener

SPEAKER OF MANDARIN, THE, Novel *see* Ruth Rendell

SPECIAL ARRANGEMENTS, 1935, Short Story *see* Richard Macauley

SPECIALIST NO.4 HAYWOOD T. "THE KID" KIRKLAND, Short Story *see* Wallace Terry

SPECIALIST, THE, Novel *see* Charles Sale

SPECK ON THE WALL, THE, Novel *see* James Oliver Curwood

SPECKLED BAND, THE, 1892, Short Story *see* Arthur Conan Doyle

SPECTER OF THE ROSE, 1945, Short Story *see* Ben Hecht

SPECTRE BRIDEGROOM, THE, Story *see* Washington Irving

SPECTRE DE MONSIEUR IMBERGER, LE, Play *see* Frederic Boutet, Henri Clerc, Henri Gorsse

SPEED, Play *see* Reginald Berkeley

SPEED BUT NO CONTROL, 1924, Short Story *see* Frank Condon

SPEEDING INTO TROUBLE, Short Story *see* Dudley Sturrock

SPELL OF THE YUKON, THE, 1907, Poem *see* Robert W. Service

SPENCER'S MOUNTAIN, New York 1961, Novel *see* Earl Hammer Jr.

SPEND - SPEND - SPEND, Book *see* Vivian Nicholson

SPENDER, THE, 1916, Short Story *see* Frederick Orin Bartlett

SPENDERS; A TALE OF THE THIRD GENERATION, THE, Boston 1902, Novel *see* Harry Leon Wilson

SPENDLOVE HALL, Play *see* Norman Cannon

SPENDTHRIFT, 1936, Novel *see* Eric Hatch

SPENDTHRIFT, THE, New York 1910, Play *see* Porter Emerson Browne

SPERDUTI NEL BUIO, 1901, Play *see* Roberto Bracco

SPERRBEZIRK, Novel *see* Ernst Neubach

SPHERE, Novel *see* Michael Crichton

SPHINX, Novel *see* Robin Cook

SPHINX A PARLES, LE, Paris 1930, Novel *see* Maurice Dekobra

SPHINX, DE, Play *see* Jonkheer A. W. G. Van Riemsdijk

SPHINX, LE, 1874, Novel *see* Octave Feuillet

SPICE OF LIFE, THE, Story *see* Dorothy Howell

SPIDER, THE, New York 1927, Play *see* Lowell Brentano, Fulton Oursler

SPIDER'S WEB, THE, London 1954, Play *see* Agatha Christie

SPIDER'S WEB, THE, New York 1913, Novel *see* Reginald Wright Kauffman

SPIEL AUF DER TENNE, Novel *see* Hans Matscher

SPIEL IM MORGENGRAUEN, 1926, Short Story *see* Arthur Schnitzler

SPIELER, DER, Play *see* Karel Bachmann

SPIELER, DER, Short Story *see* Ernst Theodor Amadeus Hoffmann

SPIELEREIEN EINER KAISERIN, Play *see* Max Dauthendey

SPIKES GANG, THE, Novel *see* Giles Tippette

SPIN THE GLASS WEB, 1952, Novel *see* Max Simon Ehrlich

SPINNENNETZ, DAS, Novel *see* Joseph Roth

SPINNER IN THE SUN, A, New York 1906, Novel *see* Myrtle Reed

SPINNER O' DREAMS, Play *see* W. Strange Hall, Leon M. Lion

SPINSTER, London 1958, Novel *see* Sylvia Ashton-Warner

SPINSTER DINNER, 1934, Short Story *see* Faith Baldwin

SPIONE, Novel *see* Thea von Harbou

SPIONE AM WERK, Novel *see* Robert Baberske, Georg Kloren

SPIRAL ROAD, THE, New York 1957, Novel *see* Jan de Hartog

SPIRALE DI NEBBIA, UNA, Novel *see* Michele Prisco

SPIRIT OF LAFAYETTE, THE, Garden City, N.Y. 1918, Book *see* James Mott Hallowell

SPIRIT OF ST. LOUIS, THE, 1953, Book *see* Charles A. Lindbergh

SPIRIT OF THE ROAD, THE, Story *see* Kate Jordan

SPIRITISME, 1897, Play *see* Victorien Sardou

SPITE BRIDE, THE, Novel *see* Louise Winter

SPITFIRE, THE, Story *see* Molly Elliot Seawell

SPITFIRE, THE, New York 1910, Play *see* Edward Peple

SPITZENHOSCHEN UND SCHUSTERPECH, Short Story *see* Rudolf Sturzer

SPLENDID COWARD, THE, Novel *see* Houghton Townley

SPLENDID CRIME, THE, London 1930, Novel *see* George Goodchild

SPLENDID FOLLY, Novel *see* Margaret Pedlar

SPLENDID HAZARD, THE, New York 1910, Novel *see* Harold MacGrath

SPLENDID OUTCAST, THE, New York 1920, Novel *see* George Gibbs

SPLENDID ROAD, THE, New York 1925, Novel *see* Vingie E. Roe

SPLINTER FLEET OF THE OTRANTO BARRAGE, THE, Indianapolis 1936, Book *see* Ray Millholland

SPLURGE, 1924, Short Story *see* Evelyn Campbell

SPODNI TONY, Novel *see* Marie Blazkova

SPOILERS, THE, New York 1906, Novel *see* Rex Beach

SPOILS OF WAR, 1988, Play *see* Michael Wellers

SPOILS OF WAR, THE, 1925, Short Story *see* Hugh Wiley

SPOOK HOUSE, Story *see* Richard F. Flournoy

SPOOK VAN MONNIKSVEER, HET, Novel *see* Aster Berkhofs

SPORT OF KINGS, THE, Indianapolis 1917, Novel *see* Arthur Somers Roche

SPORT OF KINGS, THE, London 1924, Play *see* Ian Hay

SPORT OF THE GODS, THE, New York 1902, Novel *see* Paul Laurence Dunbar

SPORTING CLUB, THE, 1968, Novel *see* Thomas McGuane

SPORTING DUCHESS, THE, New York 1895, Play *see* Henry Hamilton, Augustus Harris, Cecil Raleigh

SPORTING LIFE, London 1897, Play *see* Seymour Hicks, Cecil Raleigh

SPORTING LOVE, London 1934, Musical Play *see* Stanley Lupino, Billy Mayerl

SPORTING VENUS, THE, 1924, Short Story *see* Gerald Beaumont

SPOSA DEI RE, LA, Play *see* Ugo Falena

SPOSOB BYCIA, 1963, Novel *see* Kazimierz Brandys

SPOT OF BOTHER, A, London 1937, Play *see* Vernon Sylvaine

SPOTTED HORSES, THE, 1933, Short Story *see* William Faulkner

SPRAY, Novel *see* Qiong Yao

SPREADING DAWN, THE, 1916, Short Story *see* Basil King

SPRING 3100, New York 1928, Play *see* Argyle Campbell, Willard Mack

SPRING AND PORT WINE, London 1964, Play *see* Bill Naughton

SPRING CLEANING, New York 1923, Play *see* Frederick Lonsdale

SPRING DANCE, New York 1936, Play *see* Philip Barry

SPRING FEVER, Story *see* Grace Drew Brown, Katherine Pinkerton

SPRING FEVER, New York 1925, Musical Play *see* Vincent Lawrence

SPRING IS HERE, New York 1929, Musical Play *see* Owen Davis, Lorenz Hart, Richard Rodgers

SPRING MEETING, London 1938, Play *see* M. J. Farrell, John Perry

SPRINGBOARD, THE, Novel *see* John Fores

SPRINGER VON PONTRESINA, DER, Berlin 1930, Novel *see* Hans Richter

SPRINGTIME, New York 1909, Play *see* Booth Tarkington, Harry Leon Wilson

SPRINGTIME A LA CARTE, Short Story *see* O. Henry

SPRINGTIME FOR HENRY, New York 1931, Play *see* Benn W. Levy

SPRUNG IN DIE EHE, DER, Play *see* Max Reimann, Otto Schwartz

SPUR DER STEINE, Novel *see* Erik Neutsch

SPURS, 1923, Short Story *see* Tod Robbins

SPY IN BLACK, THE, Novel *see* J. Storer Clouston

SPY OF NAPOLEON, Novel *see* Baroness Orczy

SPY, THE, New York 1821, Novel *see* James Fenimore Cooper

SPY WHO CAME IN FROM THE COLD, THE, London 1963, Novel *see* John Le Carre

SPY WHO LOVED ME, THE, Novel *see* Ian Fleming

SPYSHIP, Book *see* Brian Haynes, Tom Keene

SQUALL, THE, New York 1926, Play *see* Jean Bart

SQUARCIO, Novel *see* Franco Solinas

SQUARE CIRCLE, THE, Novel *see* Daniel Carney

SQUARE CROOKS, New York 1926, Play *see* James P. Judge

SQUARE DANCE, Novel *see* Alan Hines

SQUARE DEAL, A, 1917, Short Story *see* Albert Payson Terhune

SQUARE DEL SANDERSON, 1918, Novel *see* Charles Alden Seltzer

SQUARE PEG, A, New York 1923, Play *see* Lewis Beach

SQUARE RING, THE, Play *see* Ralph Peterson

SQUAW MAN, THE, New York 1905, Play *see* Edwin Milton Royle

SQUEAKER, THE, London 1927, Novel *see* Edgar Wallace

SQUEALER, THE, New York 1928, Play *see* Mark Linder

SQUEEZE, THE, Novel *see* David Craig

SQUIBS, Play *see* George Pearson, Clifford Seyler

SQUIRE OF LONG HADLEY, THE, Novel *see* E. Newton Bungey

SQUIRE THE AUDACIOUS, Play *see* Sydney Bowkett

SRAZKA VLAKU A UZ MOU MILOU, Play *see* Dr. Buffiel

SRDCE V SOUMRAKU, Novel *see* Maryna Radomerska

S.S. GLENCAIRN, 1919, Plays *see* Eugene O'Neill

ST. ELMO, New York 1867, Novel *see* Augusta Jane Evans Wilson

ST. IVES, 1898, Novel *see* Arthur Quiller-Couch, Robert Louis Stevenson

ST. PAULI IN ST. PETER, Play *see* Maximilian Vitus

STAB OF PAIN, Story *see* Bernard Girard

STADIUM, New York 1931, Novel *see* Francis Wallace

STADT IST VOLLER GEHEIMNISSE, DIE, Play *see* Curt Johannes Braun

STADTPARK, Play *see* Hans Schubert

STAGE DOOR, New York 1936, Play *see* Edna Ferber, George S. Kaufman

STAGE DOOR, THE, Short Story *see* Rita Weiman

STAGE MOTHER, New York 1933, Novel *see* Bradford Ropes

STAGE STATION, Novel *see* Ernest Haycox

STAGE TO LORDSBURG, 1937, Short Story *see* Ernest Haycox

STAGECOACH TO FURY, Novel *see* Earle Lyon, Eric Norden

STAGS AND HENS, Play *see* Willy Russell

STAIN, THE, Novel *see* Robert Hobart Davis, Forrest Halsey

STAIRCASE, London 1966, Play *see* Charles Dyer

STAIRS OF SAND, 1928, Novel *see* Zane Grey

STALAG 17, New York 1951, Play *see* Donald Bevan, Edmund Trzcinski

STALK THE HUNTER, Story *see* Oscar Saul

STALKER'S APPRENTICE, THE, Novel *see* M. S. Power

STALKING MOON, THE, New York 1965, Novel *see* Theodore V. Olsen

STALLION ROAD, Novel *see* Stephen Longstreet

STAMBOUL TRAIN, London 1932, Novel *see* Graham Greene

STAMPEDE, New York 1934, Novel *see* E. B. Mann

STAN WILLIS, COWBOY, Story *see* George M. Johnson

STANCES A SOPHIE, LES, 1964, Novel *see* Christiane Rochefort

STAND ON IT, Novel *see* William Neely, Robert K. Ottum

STAND, THE, 1978, Novel *see* Stephen King

STAND UP VIRGIN SOLDIERS, Novel *see* Leslie Thomas

STANDARTE, DIE, Novel *see* Alexander Lernet-Holenia

STANDHAFTIGE TINSOLDAT, DEN, 1838, Short Story *see* Hans Christian Andersen

STAND-IN, 1937, Story *see* Clarence Budington Kelland

STAND-INS, Play *see* Ed Kelleher

STANLEY AND THE WOMEN, 1984, Novel *see* Kingsley Amis

STANTSIONNY SMOTRITEL, 1831, Short Story *see* Alexander Pushkin

STANZA DEL VESCOVO, LA, Novel *see* Piero Chiara

STAR, Novel *see* Ye Zi

STAR IN THE WEST, New York 1951, Novel *see* Richard Emery Roberts

STAR OF MIDNIGHT, New York 1936, Novel *see* Arthur Somers Roche

STAR ROVER, THE, New York 1915, Novel *see* Jack London

STAR SAPPHIRE, Story *see* Gerald Drayson Adams

STAR SPANGLED GIRL, THE, 1967, Play *see* Neil Simon

STARDUST, New York 1919, Novel *see* Fannie Hurst

STARKARE AN LAGEN, Novel *see* Bernhard Nordhs

STARKARE, DEN, 1890, Play *see* August Strindberg

STARKERE, DIE, Novel *see* Christa Linden

STARKERE LEBEN, DAS, Novel *see* Oskar Gluth

STARLIGHT, New York 1925, Play *see* Gladys Unger

STARLIT GARDEN, THE, Novel *see* Henry de Vere Stacpoole

STARR OF THE SOUTHWEST, 1936, Short Story *see* Cherry Wilson

STARS AND BARS, Novel *see* William Boyd

STARS IN MY CROWN, 1947, Novel *see* Joe David Brown

STARS IN THEIR COURSES, THE, New York 1917, Novel *see* Hilda Mary Sharp

STARS IN THEIR COURSES, THE, New York 1960, Novel *see* Harry Peter M'nab Brown

STARS LOOK DOWN, THE, 1935, Novel *see* A. J. Cronin

STARSHIP TROOPERS, Novel *see* Robert A. Heinlein

STARY HRICH, Novel *see* Jan Klecanda

STATE DEPARTMENT MURDERS, New York 1950, Novel *see* Edward Ronns

STATE FAIR, New York 1932, Novel *see* Philip Duffield Stong

STATE OF SIEGE, A, 1966, Novel *see* Janet Frame

STATE OF THE UNION, New York 1945, Play *see* Russel Crouse, Howard Lindsay

STATE TROOPER, Short Story *see* Arthur Durlam

STATE VERSUS ELINOR NORTON, THE, New York 1934, Novel *see* Mary Roberts Rinehart

STATEMENT OF RANDOLPH CARTER, THE, Short Story *see* H. P. Lovecraft

STATION WEST, Novel *see* Luke Short

STATUA DI CARNE, LA, 1862, Play *see* Teobaldo Ciconi

STAY AWAY, JOE, New York 1953, Novel *see* Dan Cushman

STAY HOME, 1921, Short Story *see* Edgar Franklin

STAY HUNGRY, Novel *see* Charles Gaines

STAYING ON, Novel *see* Paul Scott

STAZIONE TERMINI, Novel *see* Cesare Zavattini

STEADFAST HEART, THE, New York 1924, Novel *see* Clarence Budington Kelland

STEADY COMPANY, Story *see* Julius G. Furthmann

STEALING HEAVEN, Novel *see* Marion Meade

STEAMBOAT 'ROUND THE BEND, New York 1933, Novel *see* Ben Lucien Burman

STEAMIE, THE, Play *see* Tony Roper

STEAMING, 1981, Play *see* Nell Dunn

STEAUA FARA NUME, 1946, Play *see* Mihail Sebastian

STEEL GIANT, Novel *see* Cheng Shuzheng

STEEL MAGNOLIAS, Play *see* Robert Harling

STEEL MONSTER, THE, Short Story *see* Michael Pate, Philip Rock

STEEL PREFERRED, New York 1920, Novel *see* Herschel S. Hall

STEEL SARABAND, Novel *see* Roger Dataller

STEELE OF THE ROYAL MOUNTED, New York 1911, Novel *see* James Oliver Curwood

STEFANIE, Novel *see* Gitta von Cetto

STEIBRUCH, Elgg 1939, Play *see* A. J. Welti

STEIN UNTER STEINEN, Play *see* Hermann Sudermann

STELLA, Novel *see* Jan de Hartog

STELLA DALLAS, Boston 1923, Novel *see* Olive Higgins Prouty

STELLA FREGELIUS, Novel *see* H. Rider Haggard

STELLA LUCENTE, Novel *see* A. Erlande

STELLA MARIS, New York 1913, Novel *see* William J. Locke

STEP, 1888, Short Story *see* Anton Chekhov

STEPCHILD OF THE MOON, New York 1926, Novel *see* Fulton Oursler

STEPFORD WIVES, THE, Novel *see* Ira Levin

STEPPE, THE, Short Story *see* Anton Chekhov

STEPPENWOLF, DER, 1927, Novel *see* Hermann Hesse

STEPPING HIGH, Garden City, N.Y. 1929, Novel *see* Gene Markey

STEPPING OUT, 1984, Play *see* Richard Harris

STEPPING SISTERS, New York 1930, Play *see* Howard Warren Comstock

STEPSONS OF LIGHT, THE, Boston 1921, Novel *see* Eugene Manlove Rhodes

STERILE CUCKOO, THE, New York 1965, Novel *see* John Treadwell Nichols

STERN OHNE HIMMEL, Novel *see* Leonie Ossowski

STERNSTEINHOF, DER, 195-, Novel *see* Ludwig Anzengruber

STESTI MA IMENO JONAS, Novel *see* Elisky Horelove

STEVNEMOTE MED GLEMTE AR, 1954, Novel *see* Sigurd Hoel

STICK, Novel *see* Elmore Leonard

STIER GEHT LOS, DER, Play *see* O. C. A. Zur Nedden

STILETTO, New York 1969, Novel *see* Harold Robbins

STILL ALARM, THE, New York 1887, Play *see* Joseph Arthur, A. C. Wheeler

STILL LIFE, London 1936, Play *see* Noel Coward

STILL SMALL VOICE, 1933, Short Story *see* Carl Detzer

STILL WATERS RUN DEEP, London 1855, Play *see* Tom Taylor

STILLWATCH, Novel *see* Mary Higgins Clark

STINE, 1890, Short Story *see* Theodor Fontane

STINGAREE, New York 1905, Novel *see* E. W. Hornung

STINGAREE STORIES, Story *see* E. W. Hornung

STIRRUP BROTHER, THE, Short Story *see* O. Henry

STITCH IN TIME, A, New York 1918, Play *see* Oliver D. Bailey, Lottie M. Meaney

STOCKBROKER'S CLERK, THE, Short Story *see* Arthur Conan Doyle

STOFF, AUS DEM DIE TRAUM SIND, DER, Novel *see* Johannes Mario Simmel

STOLEN CLAIM, THE, Short Story *see* Bret Harte

STOLEN DEATH, Novel *see* Leo Grex

STOLEN LADY, THE, Story *see* William Dudley Pelley

STOLEN LIFE, Novel *see* Karel J. Benes

STOLEN PAPERS, THE, Short Story *see* Arthur Conan Doyle

STOLEN THUNDER, 1930, Short Story *see* Mary T. Watkins

STOLEN VOICE, THE, Story *see* Paul McAllister

STONE FOR DANNY FISHER, A, Novel *see* Harold Robbins

STONE FOX, Novel *see* John Reynolds Gardiner

STONE OF MAZARIN, THE, Short Story *see* Arthur Conan Doyle

STONES FOR IBARRA, Novel *see* Harriet Doerr

STONEWALL, Book *see* Martin Duberman

STONING, THE, Story *see* James Oppenheim

STOP AT A WINNER, London 1961, Novel *see* R. F. Delderfield

STOP FLIRTING, London 1923, Play *see* Frederick Jackson

STOP LOOK AND LISTEN, Play *see* Irving Berlin, Harry B. Smith

STOP THE WORLD - I WANT TO GET OFF, London 1961, Play *see* Leslie Bricusse, Anthony Newley

STOP THIEF, New York 1912, Play *see* Carlyle Moore

STOPOVER, Novel *see* Carol Brink

STOPOVER TOKYO, 1957, Novel *see* John Phillips Marquand

STOPP! TANK PA NAGOT ANNAT, 1939, Novel *see* Olle Hedberg

STOPPEZ COPLAN, Novel *see* Paul Kenny

STOPSEL, Play *see* Franz Robert Arnold, Ernst Bach

STORE BARNEDAPEN, DEN, 1926, Play *see* Oskar Braaten

STORFANGER, 1927, Book *see* Peter Freuchen

STORIA DI UNA CAPINERA, LA, 1870, Novel *see* Giovanni Verga

STORIA, LA, 1974, Novel *see* Elsa Morante

STORIA SPEZZATA, UNA, Novel *see* Maria Venturi

STORIELLA DI MONTAGNA, Play *see* Pier Maria Rosso Di San Secondo

STORIES FOR CHILDREN, *see* Isaac Bashevis Singer

STORKS DON'T BRING BABIES, Story *see* S. K. Lauren

STORK'S NEST, New York 1905, Novel *see* John Breckenridge Ellis

STORM BOY, 1963, Novel *see* Colin Thiele

STORM FEAR, Novel *see* Clinton Seeley

STORM IN THE CITY, Story *see* Horace McCoy

STORM OVER TJURO, 1942, Novel *see* Gustav Hellstrom

STORM RIDER, THE, Novel *see* L. L. Foreman

STORM, THE, New York 1919, Play *see* Langdon McCormick

STORMY, New York 1929, Novel *see* Cherry Wilson

STORMY TONG RIVER, Novel *see* Sima Wensen

STORY LIKE THE WIND AND A FAR OFF PLACE, A, Books *see* Laurens Van Der Post

STORY OF A COUNTRY BOY, New York 1934, Novel *see* Dawn Powell

STORY OF A SEAGULL AND THE CAT WHO TAUGHT HER TO FLY, Novel *see* Luis Sepulveda

STORY OF ADOPTED SISTERS, Novel *see* Su Fanggui

STORY OF CHRISTOPHER EMMANUEL BALESTRERO, THE, Book *see* Maxwell Anderson

STORY OF DR. WASSELL, THE, 1943, Book *see* James Hilton

STORY OF ESTHER COSTELLO, THE, 1953, Novel *see* Nicholas Monsarrat

STORY OF G.I. JOE, THE, Book *see* Ernie Pyle

STORY OF JEES UCK, THE, 1904, Short Story *see* Jack London

STORY OF LI SHUANGSHUANG, THE, Novel *see* Li Zhun

STORY OF LUO XIAOLIN, THE, Novel *see* Zhang Tianyi

STORY OF MANKIND, THE, 1921, Book *see* Hendrik Willem Van Loon

STORY OF MOTHER MACHREE, THE, 1924, Short Story *see* Rida Johnson Young

STORY OF SAN MICHELE, THE, Book *see* Axel Munthe

STORY OF THE BLOOD-RED ROSE, THE, Story *see* James Oliver Curwood

STORY OF THE ROSARY, THE, London 1913, Play *see* Walter Howard

STORY OF THE TRAPP FAMILY SINGERS, THE, Philadelphia 1949, Autobiography *see* Maria Augusta Trapp

STORY OF WATERLOO, A, London 1894, Play *see* Arthur Conan Doyle

STORY OF ZARAK KHAN, THE, Book *see* A. C. Bevan

STORY VON MONTY SPINNERRATZ, DIE, Book *see* Tor Seidler

STORY WITHOUT A NAME, THE, New York 1924, Novel *see* Arthur Stringer

STOWAWAY TO THE MOON: THE CAMELOT ODYSSEY, Novel *see* William R. Shelton

STRAFBATAILLON 999, Novel *see* H. G. Konsalik

STRAIGHT GAME, THE, Novel *see* Andrew Soutar

STRAIGHT ROAD, THE, New York 1907, Play *see* Clyde Fitch

STRAIGHT SHOOTING, 1924, Short Story *see* W. C. Tuttle

STRAIGHT TIME, Novel *see* Edward Bunker

STRAINUL, 1955, Novel *see* Titus Popovici

STRAKONICKY DUDAK ANEB HODY DIVYCH ZEN, 1847, Play *see* Josef Kajetan Tyl

STRANA, Play *see* Vincenzo Bucci

STRANA LA VITA, Novel *see* Giovanni Pascuto

STRANDED IN ARCADY, New York 1917, Novel *see* Francis Lynde

STRANDGUT, 1940, Novel *see* Erich Maria Remarque

STRANGE AFFAIR, THE, London 1966, Novel *see* Bernard Toms

STRANGE BOARDERS OF PARADISE CRESCENT, London 1935, Novel *see* E. Phillips Oppenheim

STRANGE CASE OF CHARLES DEXTER WARD, THE, *see* H. P. Lovecraft

STRANGE CASE OF DR. JEKYLL AND MR. HYDE, THE, London 1886, Novel *see* Robert Louis Stevenson

STRANGE COUNTESS, THE, London 1925, Novel *see* Edgar Wallace

STRANGE DAYS, Novel *see* Jennifer Potter

STRANGE DECEPTION, THE, Novel *see* June Truesdale

STRANGE DISAPPEARANCE, A, Novel *see* Anna Katharine Green

STRANGE HOLIDAY, Radio Play *see* Arch Oboler

STRANGE INTERLUDE, New York 1928, Play *see* Eugene O'Neill

STRANGE SNOW, Play *see* Stephen Metcalfe

STRANGE WOMAN, THE, Novel *see* Ben Ames Williams

STRANGE WOMAN, THE, New York 1913, Play *see* William Hurlbut

STRANGE WORLD OF PLANET X, Novel *see* Rene Ray

STRANGER AT HOME, Novel *see* George Sanders

STRANGER IN THE HOUSE, A, Book *see* Zoa Sherbourne

STRANGER IN THE KINGDOM, A, Novel *see* Howard Frank Mosher

STRANGER IS WATCHING, A, Novel *see* Mary Higgins Clark

STRANGER WITHIN, THE, Short Story *see* Richard Matheson

STRANGERS ALL; OR SEPARATE LIVES, 1934, Play *see* Marie M. Bercovici

STRANGER'S BANQUET, THE, New York 1919, Novel *see* Brian Oswald Donn-Byrne

STRANGER'S HAND, THE, Novel *see* Graham Greene

STRANGERS IN 7A, THE, Novel *see* Fielden Farrington

STRANGERS MAY KISS, New York 1930, Novel *see* Ursula Parrott

STRANGERS ON A TRAIN, 1950, Novel *see* Patricia Highsmith

STRANGER'S RETURN, New York 1933, Novel *see* Philip Duffield Stong

STRANGERS WHEN WE MEET, 1958, Novel *see* Evan Hunter

STRANITSA DNEVNIKA, 1965, Play *see* Aleksander Korniychuk

STRASIDELNA TETICKA, Play *see* Jaroslav Tumlir

STRASSENMUSIK, Play *see* Paul Schurek

STRATHMORE; OR WROUGHT BY HIS OWN HAND, Philadelphia 1866, Novel *see* Ouida

STRATHMORE; OR WROUGHT BY HIS OWN HAND, Philadelphia 1866, Play *see* Ouida

STRAW MAN, THE, Novel *see* Doris Miles Disney

STRAWBERRY ROAN, Novel *see* A. G. Street

STRAWBERRY ROAN, THE, Los Angeles 1931, Poem *see* Curly Fletcher

STRAWBERRY STATEMENT: NOTES OF A COLLEGE REVOLUTIONARY, THE, New York 1969, Novel *see* James Simon Kunen

STRAY DOGS, Book *see* John Ridley

STREAMERS, Play *see* David Rabe

STREET CALLED STRAIGHT, THE, 1912, Short Story *see* Basil King

STREET OF ADVENTURE, THE, Novel *see* Philip Hamilton Gibbs

STREET OF ILLUSION, THE, Story *see* Channing Pollock

STREET OF NO RETURN, Novel *see* David Goodis

STREET OF SEVEN STARS, THE, Boston 1914, Novel *see* Mary Roberts Rinehart

STREET OF THE FLYING DRAGON, THE, 1920, Short Story *see* Dorothy Goodfellow

STREET OF THE FORGOTTEN MEN, 1925, Short Story *see* George Kibbe Turner

STREET OF WOMEN, THE, New York 1931, Novel *see* Polan Banks

STREET SCENE, New York 1929, Play *see* Elmer Rice

STREET TUMBLERS, THE, Poem *see* George R. Sims

STREETCAR NAMED DESIRE, A, New York 1947, Play *see* Tennessee Williams

STREETS OF LONDON, THE, London 1864, Play *see* Dion Boucicault

STREETS OF NEW YORK, THE, Play *see* Dion Boucicault, Leota Morgan

STREETS OF THE LOST, Article *see* Cheryl McCall

STREETS PAVED WITH GOLD, Novel *see* Raymond Friday Locke

STREIT UM DEN KNABEN JO, Novel *see* Hedda Westenberger

STREIT UM DEN SERGEANTEN GRISCHA, DER, Potsdam 1927, Novel *see* Arnold Zweig

STRENGTH OF MEN, THE, Story *see* James Oliver Curwood

STRENGTH OF THE PINES, THE, Boston 1921, Novel *see* Edison Marshall

STRENGTH OF THE WEAK, THE, New York 1906, Play *see* Alice M. Smith, Charlotte Thompson

STRIBRNA OBLAKA, Novel *see* Jan Drda

STRICH DURCH DIE RECHNUNG, Play *see* Fred A. Angermayer

STRICTLY BUSINESS, Short Story *see* O. Henry

STRICTLY BUSINESS, 1929, Short Story *see* Wallace Smith

STRICTLY DISHONORABLE, New York 1929, Play *see* Preston Sturges

STRIKE PAY AND HER TURN, Short Story *see* D. H. Lawrence

STRIKE, THE, Article *see* Jose F. Lacaba

STRING OF PEARLS, A, Short Story *see* Guy de Maupassant

STRIP TEASE, Novel *see* Carl Hiaasen

STRIPED STOCKING GANG, THE, Novel *see* Irene Miller

STRIPPED FOR A MILLION, Short Story *see* Parker Fischer

STRIR PATRA, c1916, Short Story *see* Rabindranath Tagore

STROM, DER, 1903, Play *see* Max Halbe

STRONG MEDICINE, Novel *see* Arthur Hailey

STRONGER SEX, THE, London 1907, Play *see* John Valentine

STRONGHEART, Play *see* William C. de Mille

STRUGATZKI, ARKADIJ, Novel *see* Boris Strugatsky

STRUGGLE EVERLASTING, THE, New York 1917, Play *see* Edwin Milton Royle

STRUGGLE, THE, Story *see* L. V. Jefferson

STRUKTURA KRYSZTALU, Novel *see* Edward Zebrowski

STRUWWELPETER, DER, Book *see* Heinrich Hoffmann

STUBBORNNESS OF GERALDINE, THE, New York 1902, Play *see* Clyde Fitch

STUBBY PRINGLE'S CHRISTMAS, Short Story *see* Jack Schaefer

STUD. CHEM. HELENE WILLFUER, Novel *see* Vicki Baum

STUD, THE, Novel *see* Jackie Collins

STUDENT GING VORBEI, EIN, Novel *see* Hans Ulrich Horster

STUDENT VON PRAG, DER, Novel *see* Hanns Heinz Ewers

STUDIO MURDER MYSTERY, THE, Chicago 1929, Novel *see* A. Channing Edington, Carmen Edington

STUDS LONIGAN, 1934, Novel *see* James Thomas Farrell

STUDY IN SCARLET, A, London 1887, Novel *see* Arthur Conan Doyle

STUDY IN TERROR, A, Novel *see* Ellery Queen

STUFF OF HEROES, THE, 1924, Short Story *see* Harold Titus

STUFFED SHIRT, 1932, Short Story *see* Stephen Morehouse Avery

STUMBLING HERD, THE, New York 1923, Novel *see* John A. Moroso

STURM IM WASSERGLAS, 1930, Play *see* Bruno Frank

STURMFLUT DER LIEBE, Novel *see* Sadovean

STURZ, DER, 1973, Novel *see* Martin Walser

SUA ECCELLENZA DI FALCONMARZANO, Play *see* Nino Martoglio

SUBALTERN'S LOVE SONG, 1940, Poem *see* John Betjeman

SUBJECT WAS ROSES, THE, New York 1964, Play *see* Frank D. Gilroy

SUBLIME DECISION!, 1960, Play *see* Miguel Mihura Santos

SUBSTANCE OF FIRE, THE, Play *see* Jon Robin Baitz

SUBSTANCE OF HIS HOUSE, THE, Boston 1914, Novel *see* Ruth Holt Boucicault

SUBSTITUTE PRISONER, THE, New York 1911, Play *see* Max Marcin

SUBTERRANEANS, THE, 1958, Novel *see* Jack Kerouac

SUBURBAN RETREAT, Novel *see* John B. Wilson

SUBURBAN, THE, 1902, Play *see* Charles T. Dazey

SUBURBIA, Play *see* Eric Bogosian

SUBWAY EXPRESS, New York 1929, Play *see* Eva Kay Flint, Martha Madison

SUBWAY IN THE SKY, London 1957, Play *see* Ian Main

SUCCESS, New York 1918, Play *see* Adeline Leitzbach, Theodore Liebler

SUCCESS STORY, New York 1932, Play *see* John Howard Lawson

SUCCESSFUL CALAMITY, A, New York 1917, Play *see* Clare Kummer

SUCCESSO A PAGANIGUA, Story *see* Ernesto Lucente, P. Tellini

SUCCESSO, IL, Play *see* Alfredo Testoni

SUCH A LITTLE QUEEN, New York 1909, Play *see* Channing Pollock

SUCH A LONG JOURNEY, Novel *see* Rohinton Mistry

SUCH AS SIT IN JUDGEMENT, London 1923, Novel *see* Margery Land May

SUCH GOOD FRIENDS, Novel *see* Lois Gould

SUCHKIND 312, Novel *see* Hans Ulrich Horster

SUCKER, New York 1933, Play *see* Beulah Marie Dix, Bertram Millhauser

SUDBA CHELOVEKA, Moscow 1957, Novel *see* Mikhail Sholokhov

SUDDEN FEAR, 1948, Novel *see* Edna Sherry

SUDDEN FURY, Book *see* Leslie Walker

SUDDEN JIM, New York 1917, Novel *see* Clarence Budington Kelland

SUDDENLY LAST SUMMER, New York 1958, Play *see* Tennessee Williams

SUDIE AND SIMPSON, Novel *see* Sara Flanigan Carter

SUE, Play *see* Hal Reid

SUE OF THE SOUTH, Novel *see* Maud Reeves White

SUENO DE UNA NOCHE DE AGOSTO, Madrid 1918, Play *see* Gregorio Martinez Sierra

SUFFICIENT CARBOHYDRATE, Play *see* Dennis Potter

SUGAR FACTORY, THE, Novel *see* Robert Carter

SUGATA SANSHIRO, Novel *see* Tsuneo Tomita

SUICIDE CLUB, THE, London 1882, Short Stories *see* Robert Louis Stevenson

SUICIDIO, IL, 1875, Play *see* Paolo Ferrari

SUISEN, 1949, Short Story *see* Fumiko Hayashi

SUITABLE CASE FOR TREATMENT, A, 1966, Television Play *see* David Mercer

SUIVEZ LE VEUF, Novel *see* Alfred Harris

SULLE STRADE DI NOTTE, Play *see* Renato Lelli

SULLIVAN, *see* Melesville

SULT, Kristiania 1890, Novel *see* Knut Hamsun

SULTANA, THE, New York 1914, Novel *see* Henry C. Rowland

SULTANS, LES, Novel *see* Christine de Rivoyre

SUMMER AND SMOKE, New York 1948, Play *see* Tennessee Williams

SUMMER LIGHTNING, Play *see* Ernest Denny

SUMMER LIGHTNING, 1929, Novel *see* P. G. Wodehouse

SUMMER LIGHTNING, New York 1936, Novel *see* Allene Corliss

SUMMER MY GRANDMA WAS SUPPOSED TO DIE, THE, 1969, Short Story *see* Mordecai Richler

SUMMER OF FEAR, Novel *see* Lois Duncan

SUMMER OF MY GERMAN SOLDIER, Novel *see* Bette Greene

SUMMER OF THE MONKEY, Book *see* Wilson Rawls

SUMMER OF THE SEVENTEENTH DOLL, THE, Melbourne 1954, Play *see* Ray Lawler

SUMMER PLACE, A, 1958, Novel *see* Sloan Wilson

SUMMER WIDOWERS, New York 1926, Novel *see* Warner Fabian

SUMMONED, 1923, Short Story *see* Katharine Newlin Burt

SUMMONS, THE, 1914, Short Story *see* George Patullo

SUMNJIVO LICE, 1887, Play *see* Branislav Nusic

SUMRAK NAD DETVOU, Play *see* Josef Hobl

SUMURU, Novel *see* Sax Rohmer

SUN ALSO RISES, THE, 1926, Novel *see* Ernest Hemingway

SUN DANCE KID, THE, Story *see* Walter J. Coburn

SUN SHINES BRIGHT,THE, Short Story *see* Irvin S. Cobb

SUN THE MOON AND THE STARS, THE, Short Story *see* Geraldine Creed

SUNA NO ONNA, Tokyo 1952, Novel *see* Abe Kobo

SUNBURST VALLEY, Story *see* Victor Rousseau

SUNDAY, New York 1904, Play *see* Thomas Raceward

SUNDAY IN NEW YORK, New York 1961, Play *see* Norman Krasna

SUNDAYS, Novel *see* Reidun Nortvedt

SUNDIGE DORF, DAS, Play *see* Max Neal

SUNDOWN, Short Story *see* Barre Lyndon

SUNDOWN AT CRAZY HORSE, New York 1957, Novel *see* Howard Rigsby

SUNDOWN JIM, 1940, Novel *see* Ernest Haycox

SUNDOWN SLIM, Boston 1915, Novel *see* Henry Herbert Knibbs

SUNDOWNERS, THE, Novel *see* Jon Cleary

SUNNY, New York 1925, Musical Play *see* Oscar Hammerstein II, Otto Harbach, Jerome Kern

SUNNY DUCROW, New York 1920, Novel *see* Henry St. John Cooper

SUNNY GOES HOME, Short Story *see* Fanny Kilbourne

SUNSET DERBY, THE, 1926, Short Story *see* William Dudley Pelley

SUNSET PASS, Novel *see* Zane Grey

SUNSET SONG, Novel *see* Lewis Grassic Gibbon

SUNSHINE BOYS, THE, 1972, Play *see* Neil Simon

SUNSHINE OF PARADISE ALLEY, THE, 1895, Play *see* George W. Ryer, Denman Thompson

SUN-UP, New York 1925, Play *see* Lula Vollmer

SUONA LA RITIRATA, Novel *see* Beyerlein

SUONATRICE D'ARPA, LA, 1848, Novel *see* Davide Chiossone

SUOR TERESA, Play *see* Luigi Camoletti

SUPER, EL, Play *see* Ivan Acosta

SUPERFLUOUS MANSION, THE, Story *see* Robert Louis Stevenson

SUPREME TEST, THE, Short Story *see* L. V. Jefferson

SUR LA TERRE COMME AU CIEL, Novel *see* Rene Bellotto

SURAJ KA SATWAN GHODA, Novel *see* Dharamvir Bharati

SURE FIRE FLINT, 1922, Short Story *see* Gerald C. Duffy

SURELY YOU'RE JOKING MR. FEYNMAN?, Autobiography *see* Richard Feynman

SURFACING, Novel *see* Margaret Atwood

SURGEON'S CHILD, THE, Poem *see* Fred Weatherley

SURORILE BOGA, 1959, Play *see* Horia Lovinescu

SURPRISES DU DIVORCE, LES, 1888, Play *see* Alexandre Bisson, Antony Mars

SURPRISES D'UNE NUIT DE NOCES, LES, Play *see* Paul Van Stalle

SURVIVE THE SAVAGE SEA, Book *see* Dougal Robertson

SURVIVOR, THE, Book *see* Jack P. Eisner

SURVIVOR, THE, Novel *see* James Herbert

SUSAN, 1952, Play *see* Steve Fisher, Alex Gottlieb

SUSAN AND GOD, Princeton N.J. 1937, Play *see* Rachel Crothers

SUSAN LENNOX - HER FALL AND RISE, New York 1917, Novel *see* David Graham Phillips

SUSANNAH A LITTLE GIRL OF THE MOUNTIES, New York 1936, Novel *see* Muriel Denison

SUSANNE, 1931, Novel *see* Johannes Buchholtz

SUSANNE IN BERLIN, Novel *see* Walter Ebert

SUSETZ, Book *see* Yoram Kaniuk

SUSPECT, THE, Novel *see* James Ronald

SUSPECTS, LES, Novel *see* Paul Andreota

SUSPENSE, Novel *see* Bruce Graeme

SUSPENSE, Play *see* Patrick MacGill

SUSPENSE, New York 1918, Novel *see* Isabel Ostrander

SUSSEX VAMPIRE, THE, Novel *see* Arthur Conan Doyle

SUTOROBERI ROAD, Novel *see* Yoshimi Ishikawa

SUURI ILLUSIONI, 1928, Novel *see* Mika Waltari

SUZANNA, Story *see* Linton Wells

SUZANNE, *see* Steve Passeur

SUZERAINE, 1906, Play *see* Dario Niccodemi

SUZUKAKE NO SANPOMICHI, Play *see* Yojiro Ishizaka

SUZY, New York 1934, Novel *see* Herbert Gorman

SVADBA, 1889, Play *see* Anton Chekhov

SVADBA, 1962, Novel *see* Mihailo Lalic

SVANTES VISER, 1972, Verse *see* Benny Andersen

SVATEBNI KOSILE ZE SBIRKY KYTICE, Poem *see* Karel Jaromir Erben

SVATEK VERITELU, Play *see* Karel Piskor

SVEHLAVICKA, Novel *see* Emmy von Rhoden

SVETLO JEHO OCI, Novel *see* Maryna Radomerska

SVINEDRENGEN, 1842, Short Story *see* Hans Christian Andersen

SVOGA TELA GOSPODAR, 1942, Play *see* Slavko Kolar

S'VRENELI AM THUNERSEE, Berne 1925, Musical Play *see* Karl Grunder

SWALLOWS AND AMAZONS, 1931, Novel *see* Arthur Ransome

SWAMI, 1918, Novel *see* Saratchandra Chatterjee

SWAMP ANGEL, THE, 1923, Short Story *see* Richard Connell

SWAMP WATER, Novel *see* Vereen Bell

SWAMY AND FRIENDS, 1935, Novel *see* R. K. Narayan

SWAN FLOCK, Novel *see* Vasil Zemljak

SWANN, Novel *see* Carol Shields

SWARM, THE, Novel *see* Arthur Herzog

SWASTIKA, Novel *see* Oscar Schisgall

SWAYAMSIDDHA, Novel *see* Manilal Gangopadhyay

SWEDENHIELMS, 1925, Play *see* Hjalmar Bergman

SWEDISH HEROES, Book *see* Reidar Jonsson

SWEENEY TODD; OR THE FIEND OF FLEET STREET, London 1847, Play *see* George Dibdin-Pitt

SWEEPINGS, New York 1926, Novel *see* Lester Cohen

SWEET ADELINE, 1903, Song *see* Harry Armstrong, Richard H. Gerrard

SWEET ADELINE, New York 1929, Musical Play *see* Oscar Hammerstein II, Jerome Kern

SWEET ALOES, London 1934, Play *see* Jay Mallory

SWEET ALYSSUM; A STORY OF THE INDIANA OILFIELDS, 1911, Short Story *see* Charles Major

SWEET AND TWENTY, London 1901, Play *see* Basil Hood

SWEET BIRD OF YOUTH, New York 1959, Play *see* Tennessee Williams

SWEET CHARITY, New York 1966, Play *see* Cy Coleman, Dorothy Fields, Neil Simon

SWEET HEREAFTER, THE, Novel *see* Russell Banks

SWEET KITTY BELLAIRS, New York 1903, Play *see* David Belasco

SWEET LAVENDER, London 1888, Play *see* Arthur Wing Pinero

SWEET MYSTERY OF LIFE, New York 1935, Play *see* George Haight, Richard Maibaum, Michael Wallace

SWEET PEPPER, Novel *see* Geoffrey Moss

SWEET POISON, Novel *see* Leonard Lee

SWEET RIDE, THE, New York 1967, Novel *see* William Murray

SWEET ROSIE O'GRADY, 1896, Song *see* Maude Nugent

SWEET THURSDAY, 1954, Novel *see* John Steinbeck

SWEET WILLIAM, 1975, Novel *see* Beryl Bainbridge

SWEETHEART, *see* Andrew Coburn

SWEETHEART OF THE SONG TRA BONG, Short Story *see* Tim O'Brien

SWEETHEARTS, New York 1913, Opera *see* Fred de Gresac, Harry & Robert Smith

SWEETIE PEACH, Short Story *see* Sophie Kerr

SWEETS TO THE SWEET, Short Story *see* Robert Bloch

SWELL-LOOKING BABE, A, Novel *see* Jim Thompson

SWF SEEKS SAME, Novel *see* John Lutz

SWIFT LIGHTNING, New York 1926, Novel *see* James Oliver Curwood

SWIFTWATER, New York 1950, Novel *see* Paul Annixter

SWIMMER, THE, 1964, Short Story *see* John Cheever

SWINDLER, THE, Novel *see* Ethel M. Dell

SWING YOUR LADY, New York 1936, Play *see* Kenyon Nicholson, Charles Robinson

SWINGING DOORS, THE, Story *see* Virginia Whitmore

SWISS TOUR B XV, Zurich 1947, Novel *see* Richard Schweizer

SWITCH, Novel *see* William Bayer

SWORD IN THE STONE, THE, London 1938, Novel *see* T. H. White

SWORD OF FATE, THE, Novel *see* Henry Herman

SWORD OF HONOR, THE, Play *see* William Terriss

SWORD OF HONOUR, Novel *see* Evelyn Waugh

SWORDSMAN OF SIENA, Novel *see* Anthony Marshall

S/Y GLADJEN, Novel *see* Inger Alfven

SYBIL, Play *see* Max Bordy, Franz Martos
SYBIL, Book *see* Flora Rheta Schreiber
SYBIL, 1846, Novel *see* Benjamin Disraeli

SYLVESTER, Novel *see* Edward Hyams

SYLVIA, New York 1960, Novel *see* Howard Fast

SYLVIE ET LE FANTOME, Play *see* Alfred Adam

SYMBOL, THE, 1966, Novel *see* Alva Bessie

SYMPHONIE DES OMBRES, LA, Novel *see* Mme. S. Rosen Hoa

SYMPHONIE PASTORALE, LA, 1919, Novel *see* Andre Gide

SYMPHONY IN TWO FLATS, London 1929, Play *see* Ivor Novello

SYNCOPATING SUE, Play *see* Reginald Butler Goode

SYNDAFLODEN, Play *see* Henning Berger

SYNDERE I SOMMERSOL, 1928, Novel *see* Sigurd Hoel

SYNDICATE, THE, New York 1960, Novel *see* Denys Rhodes

SYNNOVE SOLBAKKEN, 1857, Novel *see* Bjornstjerne Bjornson

SYNTHETIC GENTLEMAN, New York 1934, Novel *see* Channing Pollock

SYNTHETIC SIN, New York 1927, Play *see* Fanny Hatton, Frederic Hatton

SYSTEM OF DOCTOR TARR AND PROFESSOR FEATHER, THE, 1845, Short Story *see* Edgar Allan Poe

SYTTEN: ERINDRINGER OG REFLEKSIONER, Copenhagen 1953, Novel *see* Carl Erik Soya

SZEGENY GAZDAGOK, 1860, Novel *see* Mor Jokai

SZELISTYEI ASSZONYOK, A, 1901, Novel *see* Kalman Mikszath

SZENT, A, 1966, Novel *see* Gabor Thurzo

SZENT PETER ESERNYOJE, 1895, Novel *see* Kalman Mikszath

SZERELEM, 1956, Short Story *see* Tibor Dery

SZERELEM HATARAI, A, Novel *see* Judit Fenakel

SZERELMEM, ELEKTRA, 1968, Play *see* Laszlo Gyurko

SZERENCSE FIA, A, Budapest 1908, Play *see* Gabor Dregely

SZESC WCIELEN JANA PISZCZYKA, 1951, Short Story *see* Jerzy Stefan Stawicki

SZINDBAD IFJUSAGA, 1911, Novel *see* Gyula Krudy

SZINDBAD UTAZASAI, 1912, Novel *see* Gyula Krudy

SZINMU NEGY FELVONASBAN, Budapest 1917, Play *see* Lajos Biro

SZKICE WEGLEM, 1877, Short Story *see* Henryk Sienkiewicz

SZPITAL PRZEMIENIENIA, 1975, Novel *see* Stanislaw Lem

TA NASE JEDENACTKA, Novel *see* H. G. Rubell

TA RODINA AKROYIALIA, Novel *see* Alexandros Papadiamantis

TAAFE FANGA, Play *see* Adama Drabo

TAAL DER LIEFDE, DE, 1971, Novel *see* Gerard Kornelius Van Het Reve

TAALLA POHJANTAHDEN ALLA, 1962, Novel *see* Vaino Linna

TABARANA KATHE, Short Story *see* Poornachandra Tejaswi

TABITHA, London 1956, Play *see* Mary Cathcart Borer, Arnold Ridley

TABLE-AUX-CREVES, LA, 1929, Novel *see* Marcel Ayme

TABOR PADLYCH ZIEN, Novel *see* Anton Balaz

TABORNOK, A, Budapest 1928, Play *see* Lajos Zilahy

TABULA RASA, Novel *see* Roger Van de Velde

TABUSSE, 1928, Novel *see* Andre Chamson

TACEY CROMWELL, 1942, Novel *see* Conrad Richter

TACKNAMEN: COQ ROUGE, Novel *see* Jan Guillon

TAENK PA ET TAL (THINK OF A NUMBER), 1968, Novel *see* Anders Bodelsen

TAFFIN, Novel *see* Lyndon Megahy

TAGEBUCH EINER VERLORENEN, Novel *see* Margarethe Boehme

TAGGART, New York 1959, Novel *see* Louis L'Amour

TAGGET, Novel *see* Irving A. Greenfield

TAHITI LANDFALL, 1946, Novel *see* William S. Stone

TAIFUN, Budapest 1909, Play *see* Melchior Lengyel, Menyhert Lengyel

TAIHEIYO HITORIBOTCHI, Book *see* Kenichi Horie

TAILLEUR AU CHATEAU, LE, Paris 1924, Play *see* Paul Armont, Leopold Marchand

TAILOR OF GLOUCESTER, THE, Story *see* Beatrix Potter

TAINT OF THE TIGER, 1958, Short Story *see* John D. MacDonald

TAINTED EVIDENCE, Novel *see* Robert Daley

TAINTED MONEY, Story *see* George Edwardes Hall

TAI-PAN, Novel *see* James Clavell

TAKE A CHANCE, 1931, Play *see* Walter Hackett

TAKE A CHANCE, New York 1932, Musical Play *see* Buddy De Sylva, Lawrence Schwab

TAKE A GIANT STEP, 1954, Play *see* Louis S. Peterson

TAKE A GIRL LIKE YOU, London 1960, Novel *see* Kingsley Amis

TAKE CARE OF MY LITTLE GIRL, 1950, Novel *see* Peggy Goodin

TAKE HER, SHE'S MINE, New York 1961, Play *see* Henry Ephron, Phoebe Ephron

TAKE IT FROM ME, Play *see* Will Anderson, William B. Johnstone

TAKE, THE, Novel *see* G. F. Newman

TAKE THREE TENSES, Novel *see* Rumer Godden

TAKEKURABE, 1896, Novel *see* Ichiyo Higuchi

TAKI NO SHIRAITO, Novel *see* Kyoka Izumi

TAKING OF PELHAM ONE-TWO-THREE, THE, Novel *see* John Godey

TAKSE, DI, Short Story *see* Mendele Moicher Sforim

TALANTY I POKLONNIKI, 1882, Play *see* Alexander Ostrovsky

TALE OF A GYPSY HORSE, THE, Short Story *see* Donn Byrne

TALE OF BEATRIX POTTER, THE, Biography *see* Margaret Lane

TALE OF RED ROSES, A, Indianapolis 1914, Novel *see* George Randolph Chester

TALE OF TRIONA, THE, London 1912, Novel *see* William J. Locke

TALE OF TWO CITIES, A, London 1859, Novel *see* Charles Dickens

TALENT ZUM GLUCK, Play *see* Helmut Weiss

TALENTED MR. RIPLEY, THE, New York 1955, Novel *see* Patricia Highsmith

TALES OF THE SOUTH PACIFIC, 1947, Short Story *see* James A. Michener

TALE-TELLER PHONE, THE, Play *see* Arthur Stanley

TALGO, Novel *see* Vassilis Alexakis

TALION, LE, Play *see* Pierre Maudru

TALISMAN, THE, 1825, Novel *see* Sir Walter Scott

TALISMANS, Play *see* Kennett Harris

TALK ABOUT JACQUELINE, Novel *see* Katherine Holland

TALKED TO DEATH: THE LIFE AND MURDER OF ALAN BERG, Book *see* Stephen Singular

TALKER, THE, New York 1912, Play *see* Marion Fairfax

TALKING IT OVER, Novel *see* Julian Barnes

TALL HEADLINES, THE, Novel *see* Audrey Erskine Lindop

TALL MAN RIDING, 1951, Novel *see* Norman A. Fox

TALL MEN, THE, 1954, Novel *see* Clay Fisher

TALL STORY, New York 1959, Play *see* Russel Crouse, Howard Lindsay

TALLY HO!, London 1901, Play *see* W. H. Risque

TALVISOTA, 1984, Novel *see* Antti Tuuri

TAMAHINE, London 1957, Novel *see* Thelma Nicklaus

TAMANGO, 1829, Short Story *see* Prosper Merimee

TAMARA LA COMPLAISANTE, Novel *see* Georges-Andre Cuel

TAMARIND SEED, THE, Novel *see* Evelyn Anthony

TAMAS, Novel *see* Bhishm Sahni

TAMING OF THE SHREW, THE, c1593, Play *see* William Shakespeare

TAMING OF ZENAS HENRY, THE, New York 1915, Novel *see* Sara Ware Bassett

TAMMY OUT OF TIME, Indianapolis 1948, Novel *see* Cid Ricketts Sumner

TAMMY TELL ME TRUE, Indianapolis 1959, Novel *see* Cid Ricketts Sumner

TAMPICO, New York 1926, Novel *see* Joseph Hergesheimer

TAMPON DU CAPISTON, LE, Play *see* Andre Mouezy-Eon

TAMTEN, Play *see* Gabriele Zapolska

TANAMERA, Novel *see* Noel Barber

TANAR UR, KEREM!, 1916, Short Story *see* Frigyes Karinthy

TANASE SCATIU, 1885-86, Novel *see* Duiliu Zamfirescu

TANGE SAZEN, Novel *see* Fubo Hayashi

TANGLED EVIDENCE, Novel *see* Mrs. Champion de Crespigny

TANGO, 1948, Novel *see* Georgi Karaslavov
TANGO, New York 1935, Novel *see* Vida Hurst

TANIN NO KAO, 1964, Novel *see* Ade Kobo

TANITONO, A, 1908, Play *see* Sandor Brody

TANSSI YLI HAUTOJEN, 1944, Novel *see* Mika Waltari

TANSY, Novel *see* Tickner Edwards

TANT QU'IL Y AURA DES FEMMES, Play *see* Marcel Frank

TANTE, Novel *see* Anne Douglas Sedgwick

TANTE FRIEDA, Novel *see* Ludwig Thoma

TANTE POSE, 1904, Short Story *see* Gabriel Scott

TANTE SBARRE, Novel *see* Leros Pittoni

TANTEI JIMUSHO 2-3: KUTABARE AKUTODOMO, Novel *see* Haruhiko Oyabu

TANTES, 1924, Novel *see* Cyriel Buysse

TANYASI DUVAD, 1953, Short Story *see* Imre Sarkadi

TANZ INS GLUCK, Opera *see* Robert Bodansky, Bruno Hardt-Warden, Robert Stolz

TANZANWALTZ, Berlin 1912, Play *see* Pordes Milo, Walter Schutt, E. Urban

TANZENDE HERZ, DAS, Novel *see* W. F. Fichelscher

TANZERIN, DIE, Novel *see* Melchior Lengyel

TAO, Novel *see* Arnould Galopin

TAO HUA SHAN, c1690, Play *see* Kong Shangren

TAP ROOTS, Novel *see* James H. Street

TAPAGE NOCTURNE, Play *see* Marc-Gilbert Sauvajon

TAPFERE SCHNEIDERLEIN, DAS, Short Story *see* Jacob Grimm, Wilhelm Grimm

TARAKANOVA, Novel *see* Henri Dupuy-Mazuel

TARAS BULBA, St. Petersburg 1835, Novel *see* Nikolay Gogol

TARDE, OUTRA TARDE, UMA, 1968, Novel *see* Josue Montello

TARGET, Short Story *see* Stephen Morehouse Avery

TARKA THE OTTO, Novel *see* Henry Williamson

TARNISH, New York 1923, Play *see* Gilbert Emery

TARNOVSKATA TSARITSA, 1973, Novel *see* Emilian Stanev

TARNSMAN OF GOR, Novel *see* John Norman

TARTARIN DE TARASCON, 1872, Novel *see* Alphonse Daudet

TARTARIN SUR LES ALPES, Novel *see* Alphonse Daudet

TARTUFFE, 1669, Play *see* Moliere

TARZAN AND THE GOLDEN LION, Chicago 1923, Novel *see* Edgar Rice Burroughs

TARZAN OF THE APES, Chicago 1914, Novel *see* Edgar Rice Burroughs

TASSE DE THE, UNE, 1860, *see* N. Desarbres, Charles-Louis Nuitter

TASTE FOR DEATH, A, Novel *see* P. D. James

TASTE FOR HONEY, A, New York 1941, Novel *see* H. F. Heard

TASTE OF HONEY, A, Stratford 1958, Play *see* Shelagh Delaney

TASTE OF MY OWN MEDICINE, A, Book *see* Ed Rosenbaum

TATI, A GAROTA, 1959, Short Story *see* Anibal Machado

TATTENHAM CORNER, 1934, Play *see* Brandon Fleming, Bernard Merivale

TATTERLY - THE STORY OF A DEAD MAN, New York 1897, Novel *see* Tom Gallon

TATTOOED COUNTESS, THE, New York 1924, Novel *see* Carl Van Vechten

TATUL, 1938, Novel *see* Georgi Karaslavov

TAVERN KNIGHT, THE, Novel *see* Rafael Sabatini

TAVOLA DEI POVERI, LA, Play *see* Raffaele Viviani

TAXI!, 1919, Short Story *see* George Agnew Chamberlain

TAXI 313 X 7, LE, Short Story *see* Leonnec

TAXI DANCER, THE, Novel *see* Robert Terry Shannon

TAXI MAUVE, UN, 1973, Novel *see* Michel Deon

TAXI! TAXI!, 1925, Short Story *see* George Weston

T-BONE 'N WEASEL, Novel *see* John Klein

TCHAN KONDELIK A ZET VEJVARA, Novel *see* Ignat Herrmann

TCHAO PANTIN, Novel *see* Alain Page

TEA AND SYMPATHY, New York 1953, Play *see* Robert Woodruff Anderson

TEACH ME HOW TO CRY, Play *see* Patricia Joudry-Steele

TEACHER, Book *see* Sylvia Ashton-Warner

TEAHOUSE OF THE AUGUST MOON, THE, Novel *see* Vern J. Sneider

TEARS BEFORE BEDTIME - WEEP NO MORE, Novel *see* Barbara Skelton

TEARS IN THE RAIN, Novel *see* Pamela Wallace

TEASER, THE, New York 1921, Play *see* Adelaide Matthews, Martha M. Stanley

TECHNIC, 1925, Short Story *see* Dana Burnet

TEDDY AND PARTNER, Play *see* Yvan Noe

TEETH, 1917, Short Story *see* Clinton H. Stagg

TELEMACHUS, FRIEND, Short Story *see* O. Henry

TELEFON, Novel *see* Walter Wager

TELEFTAIOS PEIRASMOS, O, 1955, Novel *see* Nikos Kazantzakis

TELEGRAME, 1899, Short Story *see* Ion Luca Caragiale

TELEURGANG VAN DE WATERHOEK, DE, 1927, Novel *see* Stijn Streuvels

TELEVISION, Play *see* Howard Irving Young

TELL ENGLAND, Novel *see* Ernest Raymond

TELL ME A RIDDLE, Novel *see* Tillie Olsen

TELL ME ABOUT IT TOMORROW, Novel *see* Ernest Lehman

TELL ME MY NAME, Book *see* Mary Carter

TELL ME THAT YOU LOVE ME JUNIE MOON, New York 1968, Novel *see* Marjorie Kellogg

TELLE QU'ELLE ETAIT EN SON VIVANT, Novel *see* Maurice Constantin-Weyer

TELL-TALE HEART, THE, 1843, Short Story *see* Edgar Allan Poe

TEMA DEL TRAIDOR Y DEL HEROE, 1944, Short Story *see* Jorge Luis Borges

TEMPERANCE FETE, THE, Story *see* Herbert Jenkins

TEMPERMENTAL LADY, 1936, Short Story *see* Julian Field

TEMPEST AND SUNSHINE, New York 1844, Novel *see* Mary Jane Holmes

TEMPEST, THE, c1611, Play *see* William Shakespeare

TEMPETE, LA, Short Story *see* Lawrence Arnold, Georges Spitzmuller

TEMPIO DEL SACRIFICIO, IL, Novel *see* Miriam Klington

TEMPLE DUSK, 1920, Short Story *see* Calvin Johnston

TEMPLE OF DAWN, THE, London 1915, Novel *see* I. A. R. Wylie

TEMPLE OF THE GIANTS, THE, Story *see* Robert Welles Ritchie

TEMPLE TOWER, Garden City, N.Y. 1929, Novel *see* H. C. McNeile ("Sapper")

TEMPLOM EGERE, A, Budapest 1927, Play *see* Ladislaus Fodor

TEMPO DI MASSACRO, Novel *see* Franco Enna

TEMPORAL POWER, Novel *see* Marie Corelli

TEMPORALE ROSY, Novel *see* Carlo Brizzolara

TEMPORARY GENTLEMAN, A, London 1919, Play *see* H. F. Maltby

TEMPS DE VIVRE, LE, Novel *see* Andre Remacle

TEMPTATION OF CARLTON EARLYE, THE, Novel *see* Stella During

TEMPTING OF TAVARNAKE, THE, Boston 1911, Novel *see* E. Phillips Oppenheim

TEN AGAINST CAESAR, 1952, Story *see* Kathleen G. George, Robert A. Granger

TEN CENT LADY, Short Story *see* Louis Weltzenkorn

TEN DAYS TO DIE, Novel *see* M. A. Musmano

TEN DOLLAR RAISE, THE, 1909, Short Story *see* Peter B. Kyne

TEN LITTLE NIGGERS, London 1939, Novel *see* Agatha Christie

TEN MINUTE ALIBI, London 1933, Play *see* Anthony Armstrong

TEN NIGHTS IN A BAR-ROOM AND WHAT I SAW THERE, Philadelphia 1839, Novel *see* Timothy Shay Arthur

TEN NORTH FREDERICK, 1955, Novel *see* John O'Hara

TEN PLUS ONE, 1963, Novel *see* Evan Hunter

TEN RILLINGTON PLACE, Book *see* Ludovic Kennedy

TEN SECOND JAILBREAK, Novel *see* Frank Kowalski, Howard B. Kreitsek

TEN YEARS A COUNTERSPY, Book *see* Boris Morros

TENANT OF WILDFELL HALL, THE, 1848, Novel *see* Anne Bronte

TENAPENNY PEOPLE, Novel *see* Jim Phelan

TEN-CENT ADVENTURE, A, Story *see* Anita Loos

TENDA DOS MILAGRES, 1969, Novel *see* Jorge Amado

TENDER IS THE NIGHT, New York 1934, Novel *see* F. Scott Fitzgerald

TENDER TRAP, THE, New York 1954, Play *see* Max Shulman, Robert Paul Smith

TENDERFOOT, THE, Short Story *see* Alfred Henry Lewis

TENDERFOOT, THE, Story *see* Jack Rollens

TENDERFOOT, THE, Chicago 1903, Play *see* Richard Carle

TENDRE ET VIOLENTE ELISABETH, 1957, Novel *see* Henri Troyat

TENDRE POULET, Novel *see* Claude Olivier, J. P. Rouland

TENDRES COUSINS, Novel *see* Pascal Laine

TENDRESSE, LA, 1921, Play *see* Henry Bataille

TENENTE GIORGIO, IL, Novel *see* Nicola Misasi

TENKAWA DENSETSU SATSUJIN JIKEN, Novel *see* Yasuo Uchida

TENNESSEE, Short Story *see* Louis Gusman

TENNESSEE JUDGE, THE, Play *see* Opie Read

TENNESSEE'S PARTNER, 1869, Short Story *see* Bret Harte

TENTACLES OF THE NORTH, 1915, Short Story *see* James Oliver Curwood

TENTATION DE SAINT ANTOINE, LA, 1849, *see* Gustave Flaubert

TENTATION, LA, Play *see* Charles Mere

TENTATIVO DI ROMANZO CINEMATOGRAFICO, *see* Matilde Serao

TENTH AVENUE, New York 1927, Play *see* Lloyd Griscom, John McGowan

TENTH MAN, THE, Novel *see* Graham Greene

TENTH MAN, THE, 1913, Play *see* W. Somerset Maugham

TENTH MONTH, THE, Novel *see* Laura Z. Hobson

TENTH WOMAN, THE, Garden City, N.Y. 1923, Novel *see* Harriet T. Comstock

TENTO GEKIJO, 1957, Novel *see* Toko Kon

TEOREMA, Milan 1968, Novel *see* Pier Paolo Pasolini

TEPPICH DES GRAUENS, DER, Novel *see* Louis Weinert-Wilton

TERESA VENERDI, Novel *see* Rudolf Torok

TERM OF TRIAL, London 1961, Novel *see* James Barlow

TERMINAL MAN, THE, Novel *see* Michael Crichton

TERMINUS, Novel *see* Pierre Boileau, Thomas Narcejac

TERMS OF ENDEARMENT, 1975, Novel *see* Larry McMurtry

TERRA BAIXA, Madrid 1896, Play *see* Angel Guimera

TERRE D'ANGOISSE, Novel *see* Pierre Nord

TERRE INHUMAINE, Paris 1923, Play *see* Francois de Curel

TERRE, LA, Novel *see* Emile Zola

TERRE QUI MEURT, LA, 1899, Novel *see* Rene Bazin

TERRIBLE BEAUTY, A, Novel *see* Arthur Roth

TERRIBLE GAME, THE, Novel *see* Dan Tyler Moore

TERRIBLE PEOPLE, THE, London 1926, Novel *see* Edgar Wallace

TERRIBLE TRUTH, THE, Story *see* Harvey Gates

TERRIBULA, LA, 1915, Short Story *see* George L. Knapp

TERRITORIO COMANCHE, Novel *see* Arturo Perez-Reverte

TERROR AT BLACK FALLS, Novel *see* Charles Martin

TERROR E EXTASE, 1978, Novel *see* Jose Carlos de Oliveira

TERROR IN BEVERLY HILLS, Novel *see* Simon Bibiyan

TERROR OVER HOLLYWOOD, 1957, Short Story *see* Robert Bloch

TERROR, THE, London 1927, Play *see* Edgar Wallace

TERROR, THE, New York 1931, Play *see* Howard Warren Comstock, Allen C. Miller

TERRY ON THE FENCE, Novel *see* Bernard Ashley

TERWILLIGER, Short Story *see* Tristram Tupper

TESHA, Novel *see* Countess Barcynska

TESS OF THE D'URBERVILLES, London 1891, Novel *see* Thomas Hardy

TESS OF THE STORM COUNTRY, New York 1909, Novel *see* Grace Miller White

TESSIE AND THE LITTLE SAP, 1925, Short Story *see* Sewell Ford

TEST OF DONALD NORTON, THE, Chicago 1924, Novel *see* Robert E. Pinkerton

TEST PILOTA PIRXA, Short Story *see* Stanislaw Lem

TEST, THE, Short Story *see* Carl Chapin

TESTAMENT D'UN POETE JUIF ASSASSINE, LE, Novel *see* Elie Wiesel

TESTAMENT OF YOUTH, 1933, Autobiography *see* Vera Brittain

TESTIMONY, Novel *see* Alice Askew, Claude Askew

TESTIMONY OF TWO MEN, Novel *see* Taylor Caldwell

TESTOR, A, Budapest 1910, Play *see* Ferenc Molnar

TETE CONTRE LES MURS, LA, 1949, Novel *see* Herve Bazin

TETE DU CLIENT, LA, Novel *see* Michel Lebrun

TETE D'UN HOMME, LA, 1931, Novel *see* Georges Simenon

TEUFEL IN SEIDE, Gutersloh 1956, Novel *see* Gina Kaus

TEUFEL MIT DEN DREI GOLDENEN HAAREN, DER, Short Story *see* Jacob Grimm, Wilhelm Grimm

TEUFEL STELLT MR. DARCY EIN BEIN, Play *see* Ernst Nebhut, Just Scheu

TEVYE AND HIS DAUGHTERS, Short Story *see* Shalom Aleichem

TEVYE DER MILKHIKER, New York 1919, Play *see* Shalom Aleichem

TEX, Novel *see* S. E. Hinton

TEX, Chicago 1922, Novel *see* Clarence E. Mulford

TEXAN, THE, New York 1918, Novel *see* James B. Hendryx

TEXAS RANGER, A, New York 1911, Novel *see* William MacLeod Raine

TEXAS RANGERS, THE, Boston 1935, Book *see* Walter Prescott Webb

TEXAS STEER, A, 1890, Play *see* Charles Hale Hoyt

TEXASVILLE, 1990, Novel *see* Larry McMurtry

THAIS, Paris 1890, Novel *see* Anatole France

THAKICHA LAGNA, Play *see* Ram Ganesh Gadkari

THANATOS PALACE HOTEL, 1951, Short Story *see* Andre Maurois

THANK YOU, New York 1921, Play *see* Tom Cushing, Winchell Smith

THANK YOU, JEEVES!, London 1934, Novel *see* P. G. Wodehouse

THANK YOU M'AM, 1963, Short Story *see* Langston Hughes

THANK YOU MR. MOTO, Boston 1936, Novel *see* John Phillips Marquand

THANKS FOR THE RIDE, 1936, Short Story *see* Eleanore Griffin, William Rankin

THANKS GOD - I'LL TAKE IT FROM HERE, Novel *see* Mae Livingston

THANKS GOD I'LL TAKE IT FROM HERE, Novel *see* Jane Allen

THARK, London 1927, Play *see* Ben Travers

THARON OF LOST VALLEY, New York 1919, Novel *see* Vingie E. Roe

THAT CERTAIN SUMMER, Play *see* Richard Levinson, William Link

THAT CHAMPIONSHIP SEASON, Play *see* Jason Miller

THAT COLD DAY IN THE PARK, New York 1965, Novel *see* Richard Miles

THAT GIRL MONTANA, New York 1901, Novel *see* Marah Ellis Ryan

THAT LADY, Novel *see* Kate O'Brien

THAT LASS O' LOWRIE'S, New York 1877, Novel *see* Frances Hodgson Burnett

THAT OLD GANG OF MINE, 1923, Song *see* Mort Dixon, Ray Henderson, Billy Rose

THAT ROYLE GIRL, New York 1925, Novel *see* Edwin Balmer

THAT SOMETHING, Tacoma, Wash. 1914, Short Story *see* William Witherspoon Woodbridge

THAT SORT, New York 1914, Play *see* Basil McDonald Hastings

THAT SPOT, 1910, Short Story *see* Jack London

THAT UNCERTAIN FEELING, London 1955, Novel *see* Kingsley Amis

THAT WAS THEN - THIS IS NOW, 1971, Novel *see* S. E. Hinton

THAT WINSOME WINNIE'S SMILE, Story *see* Carolyn Wells

THAT'S A GOOD GIRL, London 1928, Musical Play *see* Douglas Furber

THAT'S GOOD, 1915, Short Story *see* Richard Washburn Child

THAT'S GRATITUDE, New York 1930, Play *see* Frank Craven

THAT'S MY BOY, New York 1932, Novel *see* Francis Wallace

THAW AT SLISCOS, THE, Story *see* Rex Beach

THE AU HAREM D'ARCHIMEDE, LE, Novel *see* Mehdi Charef

THEATRE, 1941, Play *see* Guy Bolton, W. Somerset Maugham

THEIR MUTUAL CHILD, New York 1919, Novel *see* P. G. Wodehouse

THEIR NIGHT OUT, Play *see* George Arthurs, Arthur Miller (2)

THEIR OWN DESIRE, Story *see* Sarita Fuller

THELMA - A NORWEGIAN PRINCESS, London 1887, Novel *see* Marie Corelli

THEN I'LL COME BACK TO YOU, New York 1915, Novel *see* Larry Evans

THEN WE WERE THREE, 1961, Short Story *see* Irwin Shaw

THEODORA, 1884, Play *see* Victorien Sardou

THEODORE CHERCHE DES ALLUMETTES, Play *see* Georges Courteline

THEODORE ET CIE, 1909, Play *see* Robert Armont, Nicolas Nancey

THEOPHILUS NORTH, 1973, Novel *see* Thornton Wilder

THERE AIN'T NO JUSTICE, Novel *see* James Curtis

THERE ARE NO CHILDREN HERE, Book *see* Alex Kotlowitz

THERE ARE NO VILLAINS, Story *see* Frank R. Adams

THERE ARE TWO KINDS OF TERRIBLE, Novel *see* Peggy Mann

THERE GOES THE BRIDE, Play *see* Ray Cooney

THERE SHALL BE NO DARKNESS, Novel *see* James Blish

THERE WAS A KING IN EGYPT, New York 1918, Novel *see* Norma Lorimer

THERE WAS A LITTLE BOY, Book *see* Claire R. Jacobs

THERE WAS A LITTLE MAN, Novel *see* Constance Jones, Guy Jones

THERE YOU ARE, New York 1925, Play *see* F. Hugh Herbert

THERE'S A GIRL IN MY SOUP, London 1966, Play *see* Terence Frisby

THERE'S ALWAYS A WOMAN, 1937, Short Story *see* Wilson Collison

THERE'S ALWAYS JULIET, New York 1931, Play *see* John Van Druten

THERESE DESQUEYROUX, Paris 1927, Novel *see* Francois Mauriac

THERESE ET ISABELLE, Paris 1966, Novel *see* Violette Leduc

THERESE ETIENNE, 1927, Novel *see* John Knittel

THERESE RAQUIN, 1867, Novel *see* Emile Zola

THESE GLAMOUR GIRLS, Short Story *see* Jane Hall

THESE OUR STRANGERS, Novel *see* Adrian Arlington

THESE THOUSAND HILLS, 1956, Novel *see* A. B. Guthrie Jr.

THEY ALL WANT SOMETHING, New York 1926, Play *see* Courtenay Savage

THEY ALSO SERVE, Short Story *see* Gerald Anstruther, Paul White

THEY CALL IT SIN, New York 1933, Novel *see* Alberta Stedman Eagan

THEY CALLED HIM DEATH, Novel *see* David Hume

THEY CAME BY NIGHT, London 1937, Play *see* Barre Lyndon

THEY CAME TO A CITY, London 1943, Play *see* J. B. Priestley

THEY CAME TO CORDURA, 1958, Novel *see* Glendon Swarthout

THEY CAN'T HANG ME, Novel *see* Leonard Moseley

THEY CAN'T HANG ME, New York 1938, Novel *see* James Ronald

THEY CRACKED HER GLASS SLIPPER, Novel *see* Gerald Butler

THEY CREEP IN THE DARK, Story *see* Karl Brown

THEY DIED WITH THEIR BOOTS ON, 1937, Book *see* Thomas Ripley

THEY DREAM OF HOME, Novel *see* Niven Busch

THEY DRIVE BY NIGHT, Novel *see* James Curtis

THEY GAVE HIM A GUN, New York 1936, Novel *see* William Joyce Cowen

THEY GOT WHAT THEY WANTED, Play *see* Louis d'Alton

THEY HAD TO SEE PARIS, New York 1926, Novel *see* Homer Croy

THEY KNEW MR. KNIGHT, Novel *see* Dorothy Whipple

THEY KNEW WHAT THEY WANTED, New York 1924, Play *see* Sidney Coe Howard

THEY SAVED LONDON, Book *see* Bernard Newman

THEY SELL SAILORS ELEPHANTS, Story *see* Frederick Hazlitt Brennan

THEY SHALL REPAY, Novel *see* G. H. Teed

THEY SHOOT HORSES, DON'T THEY?, New York 1935, Novel *see* Horace McCoy

THEY STOLE $2,500,000 - AND GOT AWAY WITH IT, Story *see* Joseph F. Dinneen

THEY WALK ALONE, London 1938, Play *see* Max Catto

THEY WERE EXPENDABLE, Book *see* William L. White

THEY WERE SISTERS, Novel *see* Dorothy Whipple

THEY'RE A WEIRD MOB, Book *see* Nino Culotta

THEY'RE OFF, Story *see* Arthur Hoerl

THICKER THAN WATER, Novel *see* Dylan Jones

THICKER THAN WATER, Story *see* Buckleigh Fritz Oxford

THIEF IN THE NIGHT, London 1928, Novel *see* Edgar Wallace

THIEF IN THE NIGHT, A, Story *see* Albert Payson Terhune

THIEF, THE, Story *see* F. K. Junior

THIEF WHO CAME TO DINNER, THE, Novel *see* Terence L. Smith

THIEVES LIKE US, 1937, Novel *see* Edward Anderson

THIEVES' MARKET, Novel *see* Albert Isaac Bezzerides

THIMBLE, THIMBLE, Short Story *see* O. Henry

THIN AIR, 1934, Short Story *see* Mildred Cram

THIN LINE, THE, Novel *see* Edward Atiyah

THIN MAN, THE, New York 1932, Novel *see* Dashiell Hammett

THIN RED LINE, THE, New York 1962, Novel *see* James Jones

THINGS AS THEY ARE, 1950, Novel *see* Gertrude Stein

THINGS HIDDEN, Short Story *see* B. O. Byass

THINGS THE PLAY, THE, Short Story *see* O. Henry

THINNER, 1984, Novel *see* Stephen King

THIRD DAY, THE, New York 1964, Novel *see* Joseph Hayes

THIRD DEGREE, THE, New York 1909, Play *see* Charles Klein

THIRD GENERATION, THE, Novel *see* Charles McEvoy

THIRD GIRL FROM THE RIGHT, Story *see* Robert Carson

THIRD INGREDIENT, THE, Short Story *see* O. Henry

THIRD KISS, THE, 1918, Short Story *see* Heliodore Tenno

THIRD MAN, THE, 1950, Novel *see* Graham Greene

THIRD PARTY RISK, Novel *see* Nicolas Bentley

THIRD ROUND, THE, London 1924, Novel *see* H. C. McNeile ("Sapper")

THIRD STRING, THE, Short Story *see* W. W. Jacobs

THIRD TIME LUCKY, London 1929, Play *see* Arnold Ridley

THIRD TIME UNLUCKY, Novel *see* Laurence Meynell

THIRD VISITOR, THE, London 1945, Play *see* Gerald Anstruther

TOM JONES A FOUNDLING, 1749, Novel *see* Henry Fielding

TOM SAWYER, DETECTIVE, 1897, Short Story *see* Mark Twain

TOMBOY, Novel *see* Hal Ellison

TOMBSTONE EPITAPH, THE, Albuquerque 1951, Novel *see* Douglas D. Martin

TOMMASO BLU, Novel *see* Tommaso Di Ciaula

TOMMELISE, 1835, Short Story *see* Hans Christian Andersen

TOMMY, Opera *see* Peter Townshend

TOMMY, New York 1928, Play *see* Howard Lindsay, Bertrand Robinson

TOMMY ATKINS, London 1895, Play *see* Ben Landeck, Arthur Shirley

TOMMYKNOCKERS, THE, Novel *see* Stephen King

TOMORROW, 1903, Short Story *see* Joseph Conrad

TOMORROW, 1940, Short Story *see* William Faulkner

TOMORROW AND TOMORROW, New York 1931, Play *see* Philip Barry

TOMORROW IS FOREVER, Novel *see* Gwen Bristow

TOMORROW THE WORLD, New York 1943, Play *see* Arnold d'Usseau, James Gow

TOMORROW'S BREAD, 1924, Short Story *see* Wallace Irwin

TOMORROW'S HARVEST, Play *see* Alfred Maury

TONG WAR, Story *see* Samuel Ornitz

TONGUES OF FLAME, New York 1924, Novel *see* Peter Clark MacFarlane

TONGUES OF MEN, THE, New York 1913, Play *see* Edward Childs Carpenter

TONI, London 1924, Musical Play *see* Douglas Furber, Harry Graham, Hugo Hirsch

TONIC, THE, Short Story *see* H. G. Wells

TONIGHT AT 12, New York 1928, Play *see* Owen Davis

TONIGHT AT 8.30, Play *see* Noel Coward

TONIGHT OR NEVER, New York 1930, Play *see* Lili Hatvany

TONIO, Short Story *see* Guy de Maupassant

TONIO KROGER, Berlin 1903, Short Story *see* Thomas Mann

TONIO SON OF THE SIERRAS; A STORY OF THE APACHE WARS, New York 1906, Novel *see* Gen. Charles King

TONNERRE DE DIEU, LE, Novel *see* Bernard Clavel

TONS OF MONEY, London 1922, Play *see* Will Evans, Arthur Valentine

TONTONS FLINGUEURS, LES, Novel *see* Albert Simonin

TONY DRAWS A HORSE, London 1939, Play *see* Lesley Storm

TOO FAT TO FIGHT, Short Story *see* Rex Beach

TOO GOOD TO BE TRUE, Novel *see* Ben Ames Williams

TOO LATE FOR TEARS, 1947, Serial Story *see* Roy Huggins

TOO MANY COOKS, New York 1914, Play *see* Frank Craven

TOO MANY CROOKS, New York 1918, Novel *see* E. J. Rath

TOO MANY GIRLS, New York 1939, Musical Play *see* Lorenz Hart, George Marion Jr., Richard Rodgers

TOO MANY HUSBANDS, Atlantic City, N.J. 1919, Play *see* W. Somerset Maugham

TOO MANY PARENTS, Short Story *see* George Templeton

TOO MUCH JOHNSON, New York 1894, Play *see* William Gillette

TOO MUCH MONEY, London 1924, Play *see* Israel Zangwill

TOO MUCH SPEED, 1921, Short Story *see* Byron Morgan

TOO MUCH, TOO SOON, 1957, Autobiography *see* Diana Barrymore

TOO YOUNG TO KNOW, Serial Story *see* Harlan Ware

TOOMAI OF THE ELEPHANTS, 1894, Short Story *see* Rudyard Kipling

TOP DOG, THE, Novel *see* Fergus Hume

TOP O' THE MORNIN', c1913, Play *see* Anne Caldwell

TOP OF THE WORLD, New York 1950, Novel *see* Hans Ruesch

TOP OF THE WORLD, THE, London 1920, Novel *see* Ethel M. Dell

TOP SPEED, New York 1929, Musical Play *see* Guy Bolton, Bert Kalmar, Harry Ruby

TOPAZ, New York 1967, Novel *see* Leon Uris

TOPAZE, Paris 1928, Play *see* Marcel Pagnol

TOPOLIOK MOI V KRASNOI KOSYNKE, 1961, Short Story *see* Chingiz Aitmatov

TOPPER, New York 1926, Novel *see* Thorne Smith

TOPPER TAKES A TRIP, New York 1932, Novel *see* Thorne Smith

TOPSY AND EVA, New York 1924, Play *see* Catherine Chisholm Cushing

TORA! TORA! TORA!, New York 1969, Book *see* Gordon W. Prange

TORCH SONG, New York 1930, Play *see* Kenyon Nicholson

TORCH SONG TRILOGY, Play *see* Harvey Fierstein

TORCHBEARERS, THE, New York 1922, Play *see* George Edward Kelly

TORIDEYAMA NON JUSHICHINICHI, Tokyo 1964, Short Story *see* Shugoro Yamamoto

TORMENT, Story *see* William Dudley Pelley

TORMENTO, 1884, Novel *see* Benito Perez Galdos

TORN SAILS, Novel *see* Allen Raine

TORNADO, Novel *see* John Guedel

TORNADO, THE, 1891, Play *see* Lincoln J. Carter

TORRE DI PIETRA, LA, 1913, Play *see* Camillo Antona-Traversi

TORRE SUL POLLAIO, LA, Play *see* Vittorio Calvino

TORRENT, THE, Story *see* Langdon McCormick

TORRENTS, Novel *see* Anne-Marie Desmarets

TORST, Book *see* Birgit Tengroth

TORTILLA FLAT, 1935, Novel *see* John Steinbeck

TORTURE EXECUTION OF A HERO MARINE, 1958, Story *see* William Bradford Huie

TORTURE PAR L'ESPERANCE, LA, Short Story *see* Villiers de L'isle-Adam

TORVENTEN BELUL, 1980, Novel *see* Erzsebet Galgoczi

TOSCA, LA, Paris 1887, Play *see* Victorien Sardou

TOSEN FRAN STORMYRTORPET, Stockholm 1908, Short Story *see* Selma Lagerlof

TOSKA, 1885, Short Story *see* Anton Chekhov

TOSSEDE PARADIS, DET, Copenhagen 1953, Novel *see* Ole Juul

TOT, KTO POLUCHAET POSHCHECHINY, Play *see* Leonid Nikolaevich Andreyev

TOT NUT VAN 'T ALGEMEEN, Play *see* Walter Van Den Broeck

TOTE VON BEVERLY HILLS, DIE, Berlin 1951, Novel *see* Kurt Gotz

TOTEK, 1964, Novel *see* Istvan Orkeny

TOTEN BLEIBEN JUNG, DIE, 1949, Novel *see* Anna Seghers

TOTENINSEL, DIE, Novel *see* Hans Ulrich Horster

TOTENSCHIFF, DAS, 1926, Novel *see* Ben Traven

TOTER TAUCHER NIMMT KEIN GOLD, EIN, Novel *see* Heinz G. Konsalik

TOTO IL BUONO, Story *see* Cesare Zavattini

TOTONIA PACHECO, 1935, Novel *see* Joao Alphonsus

TOTTE ET SA CHANCE, Novel *see* Pierre Soulaine

TOUBIB, LE, Novel *see* Jean Freustie

TOUCH, Novel *see* Elmore Leonard

TOUCH IT LIGHT, London 1958, Novel *see* Robert Sharrow

TOUCH OF A CHILD, THE, Story *see* Tom Gallon

TOUCH OF THE MOON, A, Play *see* Cyril Campion

TOUCH THE LION'S PAW, Novel *see* Derek Lambert

TOUCH WOOD, Play *see* David Carr, David Stringer

TOUCHE-A-TOUT, Play *see* Roger Ferdinand

TOUCHEZ PAS AU GRISBI, Novel *see* Albert Simonin

TOUGH GUYS DON'T DANCE, 1984, Novel *see* Norman Mailer

TOUJOURS DE L'AUDACE, 1920, Short Story *see* Ben Ames Williams

TOUJOURS PROVENCE, Book *see* Peter Mayle

TOUR D'AMOUR, LA, Novel *see* Rachilde

TOUR DE COCHON, UN, Play *see* Raoul Prazy, Robert Tremois

TOUR DE NESLE, LA, 1832, Play *see* Alexandre Dumas (pere), F. Gaillardet

TOUR DU MONDE EN QUATRE-VINGT JOURS, LE, 1873, Novel *see* Jules Verne

TOUR DU MONDE EN QUATRE-VINGT JOURS, LE, France 1873, Novel *see* Jules Verne

TOURMENTE, LA, Novel *see* Pierre Salles

TOUT EST DANS LA FIN, Novel *see* Gilbert Prouteau

TOUT POUR RIEN, Play *see* Andre Mouezy-Eon

TOUTE LA FAMILLE ETAIT LA, Novel *see* Henri Falk

TOVARICH, Paris 1933, Play *see* Jacques Deval

TOWER OF IVORY, New York 1910, Novel *see* Gertrude Franklin Atherton

TOWER OF LONDON, THE, Novel *see* Harrison Ainsworth

TOWER, THE, Novel *see* Richard Martin Stern

TOWN IN HELL'S BACKYARD, THE, Story *see* Robert Lee Johnson

TOWN LIKE ALICE, A, 1950, Novel *see* Nevil Shute

TOWN OF CROOKED WAYS, THE, Novel *see* J. S. Fletcher

TOWN PUMPS AND GOLD LEAF, Story *see* Ida M. Evans

TOWN SCANDAL, THE, Story *see* Frederic Arnold Kummer

TOWN TAMER, New York 1958, Novel *see* Frank Gruber

TOWN WITHOUT SEASONS, THE, Novel *see* Shugoro Yamamoto

TOY SOLDIERS, Novel *see* William P. Kennedy

TOYS IN THE ATTIC, New York 1960, Play *see* Lillian Hellman

TRA DONNE SOLE, Turin 1949, Short Story *see* Cesare Pavese

TRACK OF THE CAT, THE, 1949, Novel *see* Walter Van Tilburg Clark

TRACKED TO EARTH, Short Story *see* William J. Neidig

TRACKING NEW YORK'S CRIME BARONS, 1936, Short Story *see* Fred Allhoff

TRACKS, 1928, Short Story *see* Stephen Payne

TRACY THE OUTLAW, Play *see* Pierce Kingsley

TRADE SECRET, A, 1915, Novel *see* Ernest M. Poate

TRADER HORN, New York 1927, Book *see* Alfred Aloysius Horn, Ethelreda Lewis

TRADING POST, THE, Play *see* Larry Ketron

TRADITION DE MINUIT, LA, 1930, Novel *see* Pierre Mac Orlan

TRAFFIC, Novel *see* E. Temple Thurston

TRAFRACKEN, Novel *see* Jan Ekstrom

TRAGEDIE IMPERIALE, LA, Novel *see* Alfred Neumann

TRAGEDY OF BARNSDALE MANOR, THE, Short Story *see* Baroness Orczy

TRAGEDY OF CHARLECOT MANSIONS, THE, 1914, Short Story *see* E. Phillips Oppenheim

TRAGEDY OF THE KOROSKO, THE, London 1898, Novel *see* Arthur Conan Doyle

TRAGEDY OF WHISPERING CREEK, THE, Story *see* Elliott J. Clawson

TRAGEDY THAT LIVED, THE, Short Story *see* James Oliver Curwood

TRAIL DUST, New York 1934, Novel *see* Clarence E. Mulford

TRAIL OF '98, THE, New York 1911, Novel *see* Robert W. Service

TRAIL OF THE ASSASSINS, Book *see* Jim Garrison

TRAIL OF THE LONESOME PINE, THE, New York 1908, Novel *see* John Fox Jr.

TRAIL OF THE LOST CHORD, THE, Poem *see* Adelaide Anne Procter

TRAIL RIDER, THE, New York 1924, Novel *see* George Washington Ogden

TRAIL STREET, Novel *see* William Corcoran

TRAIL TO YESTERDAY, THE, New York 1913, Novel *see* Charles Alden Seltzer

TRAIL TOWN, 1941, Novel *see* Ernest Haycox

TRAILIN', New York 1920, Novel *see* Max Brand

TRAILMAKERS, THE, Novel *see* Vincent Forte

TRAIL'S END, THE, Novel *see* James Oliver Curwood

TRAILS TO TWO MOONS, Boston 1920, Novel *see* Robert Welles Ritchie

TRAIN DE 8H.47, LE, 1891, Novel *see* Georges Courteline

TRAIN DE PLAISIR, 1884, Play *see* Maurice Hennequin, Mortier, Saint-Albin

TRAIN DE VENISE, LE, Novel *see* Georges Simenon

TRAIN, LE, 1961, Novel *see* Georges Simenon

TRAIN POUR VENISE, LE, Play *see* Georges Berr, Louis Verneuil

TRAIN SANS YEUX, LE, Short Story *see* Louis Delluc

TRAIN TO PAKISTAN, Novel *see* Khushwant Singh

TRAINSPOTTING, Novel *see* Irvine Welsh

TRAIT D'UNION, LE, Short Story *see* Alfred Bernier

TRAITOR SPY, Novel *see* T. C. H. Jacobs

TRAITOR'S GATE, THE, London 1927, Novel *see* Edgar Wallace

TRAJET DE LA FOUDRE, LE, Novel *see* Stanislas-Andre Steeman

TRAM A LA MALVARROSA, Novel *see* Manuel Vincent

TRAMONTANA, Short Story *see* Rina Durante

TRANSATLANTIQUES, LES, Novel *see* Abel Hermant

TRANSIENT LADY, 1934, Short Story *see* Octavus Roy Cohen

TRANSIENTS IN ARCADIA, Short Story *see* O. Henry

TRANSIGEONS, Play *see* Gabriel d'Hervilliez

TRANSIT, 1944, Novel *see* Anna Seghers

TRANSLATION OF A SAVAGE, THE, New York 1893, Novel *see* Gilbert Parker

TRANSPLANT, Book *see* Philip Dossick

TRANSPORT, DER, Novel *see* Wolfgang Altendorf

TRAP THAT FAILED, THE, Story *see* Ben Cohn

TRAP, THE, New York 1915, Play *see* Richard Harding Davis, Jules Eckert Goodman

TRAP, THE, New York 1920, Novel *see* Maximilian Foster

TRAPPOLA, LA, Novel *see* Delfino Cinelli

TRAQUE, LA, Novel *see* Serge Leroy

TRATTATO SCOMPARSO, IL, Play *see* Artu (Riccardo Artuffo), Galar (Leo Galetto)

TRAUM ZERBRICHT, EIN, Novel *see* Josef Maria Frank

TRAUMULUS, 1904, Play *see* Arno Holz, Oskar Jerschke

TRAVAIL, Novel *see* Emile Zola

TRAVAILLEURS DE LA MER, LES, 1866, Novel *see* Victor Hugo

TRAVEL BY DARK, Book *see* Graeme Warrack

TRAVELIN' MAN, 1957, Short Story *see* Peter Matthiessen

TRAVELING LADY, THE, 1954, Play *see* Horton Foote

TRAVELING SALESMAN, THE, New York 1908, Play *see* James Grant Forbes

TRAVELLER'S JOY, London 1948, Play *see* Arthur MacRae

TRAVELLING NORTH, 1980, Play *see* David Williamson

TRAVELS WITH MY AUNT, 1969, Novel *see* Graham Greene

TRAVERSATA NERA, Play *see* Giuseppe Achille, Bruno Corra

TRAVERSEE DE PARIS, LA, 1946, Short Story *see* Marcel Ayme

TRAVESTI, 1971, Play *see* Aurel Baranga

TRAVIATA, LA, Venice 1853, Opera *see* Francesco M. Piave, Giuseppe Verdi

TRAVIS COUP, THE, Story *see* Arthur Stringer

TRE GIORNI IN PARADISO, Novel *see* Franz Franchy

TRE HELLIGAFTENER, DE, 1840, Novel *see* Steen Steensen Blicher

TRE PECORE VIZIOSE, 1881, Play *see* Eduardo Scarpetta

TRE SENTIMENTALI, I, 1918, Play *see* Nino Berrini, Sandro Camasio

TREASURE HUNT, London 1949, Play *see* M. J. Farrell, John Perry

TREASURE ISLAND, London 1883, Novel *see* Robert Louis Stevenson

TREASURE OF DESERT ISLE, THE, Story *see* James Oliver Curwood

TREASURE OF FRANCHARD, 1887, Short Story *see* Robert Louis Stevenson

TREASURE OF HEAVEN, THE, Novel *see* Marie Corelli

TREBLE TROUBLE, Play *see* Heather McIntyre

TREDOWATA, Novel *see* Helena Mniszkowna

TREE GROWS IN BROOKLYN, A, 1943, Novel *see* Betty Smith

TREE OF HANDS, THE, Novel *see* Ruth Rendell

TREE OF KNOWLEDGE, THE, London 1897, Play *see* R. C. Carton

TREE OF LIBERTY, THE, New York 1939, Novel *see* Elizabeth Page

TREGUA, LA, Book *see* Primo Levi

TREGUA, LA, 1960, Novel *see* Mario Benedetti

TREI LADRI, I, 1907, Novel *see* Umberto Notari

TREIBHAUS, DAS, Novel *see* Wolfgang Koeppen

TREIZE A TABLE, 1953, Play *see* Marc-Gilbert Sauvajon

TREIZIEME CAPRICE, LE, Novel *see* Roger Boussinot

TRELAWNY OF THE WELLS, London 1898, Play *see* Arthur Wing Pinero

TREMARNE CASE, THE, Short Story *see* Baroness Orczy

TREMOR OF FORGERY, THE, Novel *see* Patricia Highsmith

TREN EXPRESO, EL, 1872-74, Verse *see* Ramon de Campoamor

TRENCK DER PANDUR, Play *see* Otto Emmerich Groh

TRENCK, DER ROMAN EINES GUNSTLINGS, 1926, Novel *see* Bruno Frank

TRENO DELLE 21.15, IL, Play *see* Alvus, Colin

TRENO DI LUSSO, Novel *see* Umberto Notari

TRENTA SECONDI D'AMORE, Play *see* Aldo de Benedetti

TRENTE ET QUARANTE, 1859, Novel *see* Edmond About

TRENTE MILLIONS DE GLADIATOR, LES, Play *see* Philippe Gilles, Eugene Labiche

TRENT'S LAST CASE, London 1913, Novel *see* E. C. Bentley

TRES PERFECTAS CASADAS, LAS, 1941, Play *see* Alejandro Casona

TRESOR DE KERIOLET, LE, Novel *see* M. Pellerin

TRESPASSER, THE, 1912, Novel *see* D. H. Lawrence

TRETI ROTA, Novel *see* Josef Kopta

TRETI ZVONENI, Play *see* Vaclav Stech

TREVE, New York 1925, Novel *see* Albert Payson Terhune

TREVOSHNYYE OBLAKA, *see* A. Borshchagovskiy

TREY O'HEARTS, THE, Story *see* Louis Joseph Vance

TRHANI, Novel *see* Jan Neruda

TRI MEDVEDYA, 1875, Short Story *see* Lev Nikolayevich Tolstoy

TRI MUZI VE SNEHU, Novel *see* Erich Kastner

TRI SESTRY, Moscow 1901, Play *see* Anton Chekhov

TRI TOLSTYAKA, 1928, Short Story *see* Yury Karlovich Olesha

TRIAL, Book *see* Clifford Irving

TRIAL, 1955, Novel *see* Don M. Mankiewicz

TRIAL BY TERROR, 1952, Book *see* Paul Gallico, Pauline Gallico

TRIAL OF CHAPLAIN JENSEN, THE, Book *see* Martin Abrahamson, Andrew Jensen

TRIAL OF JOHNNY NOBODY, THE, 1950, Short Story *see* Albert Z. Carr

TRIAL OF MARY DUGAN, THE, New York 1927, Play *see* Bayard Veiller

TRIAL OF VIVIENNE WARE, THE, New York 1931, Novel *see* Kenneth M. Ellis

TRIALS OF OSCAR WILDE, THE, Book *see* Montgomery Hyde

TRIANGLE, Novel *see* Teri White

TRIANGOLO MAGICO, IL, Play *see* Alessandro de Stefani

TRIBULATIONS D'UN CHINOIS EN CHINE, LES, Paris 1879, Novel *see* Jules Verne

TRIBULATIONS D'UNE MARRAINE, LES, Play *see* Georges Hugot

TRIBUTE, Play *see* Bernard Slade

TRIBUTE TO MOTHER, A, Story *see* James Elliott

TRICK FOR TRICK, New York 1932, Play *see* V. Cosby, Harry W. Gribble, S. Warde

TRICOCHE ET CACOLET, Play *see* Ludovic Halevy, Henri Meilhac

TRIEZIEME ENQUETE DE GREY, LA, Play *see* Alfred Gragnon, Max Viterbo

TRIFLERS, THE, Boston 1917, Novel *see* Frederick Orin Bartlett

TRIGGER, New York 1927, Play *see* Lula Vollmer

TRIGGER FINGERS, Short Story *see* Harry F. Olmstead

TRILBY, London 1894, Novel *see* George Du Maurier

TRILOGIA DI DORINA, LA, 1889, Play *see* Gerolamo Rovetta

TRILOGIE DES WIEDERSEHENS, 1976, Play *see* Botho Strauss

TRIMMED AND BURNING, 1921, Short Story *see* Hapsburg Liebe

TRIMMED IN SCARLET, New York 1920, Play *see* William Hurlbut

TRIMMED LAMP, THE, Short Story *see* O. Henry

TRIMMED WITH RED, New York 1920, Novel *see* Wallace Irwin

TRINE!, 1940, Novel *see* Hans Geelmuyden

TRINI, Novel *see* Ludwig Renn

TRIO INFERNAL, LE, Novel *see* Solange Fasquelle

TRIP TO BOUNTIFUL, THE, Play *see* Horton Foote

TRIP TO CHICAGO, THE, *see* Walter Gutman

TRIP TO CHINATOWN, A, Short Story *see* Charles Hale Hoyt

TRIPLE CROSS FOR DANGER, Story *see* Walter J. Coburn

TRIPLE CROSS, THE, 1918, Serial Story *see* Octavus Roy Cohen, John U. Giesy

TRIPLE ECHO, THE, 1970, Novel *see* H. E. Bates

TRIPLE TROUBLE, Short Story *see* Harry O. Hoyt

TRIPLEPATTE, Play *see* Tristan Bernard, Andre Godfernaux

TRIPORTEUR, LE, Novel *see* Rene Fallet

TRIQUE - GAMIN DE PARIS, Novel *see* Alfred Machard

TRISTANA, Madrid 1892, Novel *see* Benito Perez Galdos

TRISTE REALTA, 1871, Play *see* Achille Torelli

TRISTI AMORI, 1887, Play *see* Giuseppe Giacosa

TRITON, 1928, Short Story *see* W. Somerset Maugham

TRIUMPH, 1916, Short Story *see* Samuel Hopkins Adams

TRIUMPH, New York 1924, Novel *see* May Edginton

TRIUMPH OF THE SCARLET PIMPERNEL, THE, Novel *see* Baroness Orczy

TRIUMPH OVER PAIN, Book *see* Rene Fulop-Miller

TROCHES ET CIE, Play *see* Gaston Rullier

TROIS CENTS A L'HEURE, Play *see* Victor de Cottens, Pierre Veber

TROIS CHAMBRES A MANHATTAN, 1946, Novel *see* Georges Simenon

TROIS DE LA CANEBIERE, Opera *see* Henri Alibert, Rene Sarvil

TROIS DE LA MARINE, Opera *see* Henri Alibert, Rene Sarvil, Vincent Scotto

TROIS ET UNE, Play *see* Denys Amiel

TROIS ETC. DU COLONEL, LES, Play *see* Jose-Maria Peman

TROIS GARCONS, UNE FILLE, Play *see* Roger Ferdinand

TROIS HOMMES A ABATTRE, Novel *see* Jean-Patrick Manchette

TROIS JEUNES FILLES NUES, Opera *see* Yves Mirande, Albert Willemetz

TROIS JOURS A VIVRE, *see* Peter Vanett

TROIS LYS, LES, Novel *see* Lucie Delarue-Mardrus

TROIS MARINS DANS UN COUVENT, Play *see* Duport, Saint-Hilaire

TROIS MASQUES, LES, Play *see* Charles Mere

TROIS MESSES BASSES, LES, 1869, Short Story *see* Alphonse Daudet

TROIS MILLIONS DE DOT, *see* Xavier de Montepin

TROIS MOUSQUETAIRES, LES, Paris 1844, Novel *see* Alexandre Dumas (pere)

TROIS POUR CENT, Play *see* Roger Ferdinand

TROIS. SIX. NEUF, Play *see* Michel Duran

TROIS SULTANES, LES, Play *see* Favart

TROJAN BROTHERS, THE, Novel *see* Pamela Hansford Johnson

TROJAN WOMEN, THE, 415 bc, Play *see* Euripides

TROMPETTE DE LA BERESINA, LE, Novel *see* Ponson Du Terrail

TRONO PARA CRISTY, UN, 1957, Play *see* Jose Lopez Rubio

TROOP BEVERLY HILLS, *see* Ava Ostern Fries

TROOP TRAIN, THE, 1918, Story *see* William Hamilton Osborne

TROOPER BILLY, Play *see* Frederick Paulding

TROOPER HOOK, Story *see* Jack Schaefer

TROOPER O'NEIL, London 1921, Novel *see* George Goodchild

TROPIC OF CANCER, Paris 1934, Novel *see* Henry Miller

TROPIC OF DESIRE, Novel *see* George Edwards

TROPIC OF RUISLIP, THE, Novel *see* Leslie Thomas

TROPICAL TWINS, Play *see* Maxwell Anderson, Laurence Stallings

TROPPA RICA, Short Story *see* Alberto Moravia

TROTTIE TRUE, Novel *see* Caryl Brahms, S. J. Simon

TROU DANS LE MUR, UN, Play *see* Yves Mirande

TROU, LE, Paris 1957, Novel *see* Jose Giovanni

TROUBLE FOR NOTHING, Play *see* Arthur Eckersley, Guy Newall

TROUBLE IN THE HOUSE, Novel *see* Anthony Richardson

TROUBLE SHOOTER, Garden City, N.Y. 1937, Novel *see* Ernest Haycox

TROUBLE, THE, Play *see* Noel Scott, Dudley Sturrock

TROUBLE WITH HARRY, THE, 1950, Novel *see* Jack Trevor Story

TROUPING WITH ELLEN, 1922, Short Story *see* Earl Derr Biggers

TROVADOR, EL, Madrid 1836, Play *see* Antonio Garcia Gutierrez

TROVATELLA DI MILANO, LA, Novel *see* Carolina Invernizio

TRUANTS, THE, Novel *see* A. E. W. Mason

TRUC DU BRESILIEN, LE, Play *see* Paul Armont, Nicolas Nancey

TRUE AS A TURTLE, Novel *see* John Coates

TRUE AS STEEL, 1923, Short Story *see* Rupert Hughes

TRUE BLUE, Book *see* Patrick Robinson, Daniel Topolski

TRUE CONFESSIONS, 1977, Novel *see* John Gregory Dunne

TRUE CRIME, Novel *see* Andrew Klavan

TRUE GRIT, New York 1968, Novel *see* Charles Portis

TRUE TILDA, Novel *see* Arthur Quiller-Couch

TRUE WEST, 1980, Play *see* Sam Shepard

TRUE WOMEN, Book *see* Janice Woods Windle

TRUFFLERS, THE, Indianapolis 1916, Novel *see* Samuel Merwin

TRUITE, LA, 1964, Novel *see* Roger Vailland

TRUMPET CALL, THE, London 1891, Play *see* Robert Buchanan, George R. Sims

TRUNK CRIME, Play *see* Reginald Denham, Edward Percy

TRUST BERKELY, London 1933, Play *see* Cyril Campion

TRUST DER DIEBE, Novel *see* Ernst Klein

TRUTH GAME, THE, London 1928, Play *see* Ivor Novello

TRUTH, THE, Cleveland 1906, Play *see* Clyde Fitch

TRUTH WAGON, THE, New York 1912, Play *see* Hayden Talbot

TRUTZE AUF TRUTZBERG, DIE, Novel *see* Ludwig Ganghofer

TRUXA, Novel *see* Heinrich Seiler

TRUXTON KING; A STORY OF GRAUSTARK, New York 1909, Novel *see* George Barr McCutcheon

TRY THIS ONE FOR SIZE, Novel *see* James Hadley Chase

TRYING TO GET ARRESTED, Short Story *see* O. Henry

TRYING TO GROW, Novel *see* Firdaus Kanga

TSAR IVAN SHISHMAN, 1962, Play *see* Kamen Zidarov

TSARKA MILOST, 1949, Play *see* Kamen Zidarov

TSARSKAYA NEVESTA, 1849, Play *see* Lev Aleksandrovich Mey

TSUBAKI SANJURO, Novel *see* Shugoro Yamamoto

TSUCHI, 1910, Novel *see* Takashi Nagatsuka

TSUMA NO BARA NO YONI, Play *see* Minoru Nakano

TSYGANY, 1824, Poem *see* Alexander Pushkin

TU ERES LA PAZ, 1906, Novel *see* Gregorio Martinez Sierra

TU M'EPOUSERAS!, 1927, Play *see* Louis Verneuil

TU NOMBRE ENVENENA MIS SUENOS, Novel *see* Joaquin Leguina

TU TAN YU QIAO NIU, Novel *see* Huang Huizhong

TU Y YO SOMOS TRES, 1946, Play *see* Enrique Jardiel Poncela

TUAN YUAN, 1956, Short Story *see* Li Feigan

TUCK EVERLASTING, Novel *see* Natalie Babbitt

TUCKER'S PEOPLE, Novel *see* Ira Wolfert

TUCSON, Novel *see* Paul Leslie Peil

TUENEMENY, A, Budapest 1922, Play *see* Attila Orbok

TUEUR, LE, Story *see* Marcel Archard, Anatole Litvak

TUGBOAT PRINCESS, Story *see* Isadore Bernstein, Dalton Trumbo

TULAK, Opera *see* Emanuel Brozik

TULAK, Poem *see* Karel Hasler

TULIPE NOIRE, LA, 1846, Novel *see* Alexandre Dumas (pere)

TUMBA DES VAMPIRO, LA, Novel *see* David Chase

TUNDOKLO JEROMOS, 1941, Play *see* Aron Tamasi

TUNEL, EL, 1948, Novel *see* Ernesto Sabato

TUNES OF GLORY, 1956, Novel *see* James Kennaway

TUNNEL, DER, Novel *see* Bernhard Kellermann

TUNNEL OF LOVE, 1954, Novel *see* Peter de Vries

TUNNEL UNDER THE WORLD, Novel *see* Frederik Pohl

TUNNYNG OF ELYNOURE RUMMYNG, THE, c1520, Verse *see* John Skelton

TUNTEMATON SOTILAS, 1954, Novel *see* Vaino Linna

TUPEINYI KHUDOZHNIK, 1883, Short Story *see* Nikolay Semyonovich Leskov

TURANDOT, Play *see* Carlo Gozzi, Friedrich Schiller

TURBAMENTO, Play *see* Arturo Cantini

TURBINA, Novel *see* Karel Matej Capek-Chod

TURCO NAPOLETANO, UN, Play *see* Eduardo Scarpetta

TURF CONSPIRACY, A, Novel *see* Nat Gould

TURKEY TIME, London 1931, Play *see* Ben Travers

TURKISH PASSION, Novel *see* Antonio Gala

TURKS FRUIT, 1970, Novel *see* Jan Hendrick Wolkers

TURMOIL, THE, New York 1915, Novel *see* Booth Tarkington

TURN ABOUT, 1932, Short Story *see* William Faulkner

TURN ABOUT ELEANOR, Indianapolis 1917, Novel *see* Ethel May Kelley

TURN BACK THE HOURS, Hoboken, N.J. 1917, Play *see* Edward E. Rose

TURN HIM OUT, Play *see* Thomas J. Williams

TURN HOME, 1945, Novel *see* Eleanor R. Mayo

TURN OF THE SCREW, THE, New York 1898, Short Story *see* Henry James

TURN THE KEY SOFTLY, Novel *see* John Brophy

TURN TO THE RIGHT, New York 1916, Play *see* Jack E. Hazzard, Winchell Smith

TURNABOUT, New York 1931, Novel *see* Thorne Smith

TURNED UP, London 1886, Play *see* Mark Melford

TURNING POINT, THE, 1912, Novel *see* Robert W. Chambers

TURNING POINT, THE, 1977, Novel *see* Arthur Laurents

TURTLE BEACH, Novel *see* Blanche d'Alpuget

TURTLE DIARY, Novel *see* Russell Hoban

TUTTI GIU PER TERRA, Novel *see* Giuseppe Culicchia

TUTTI GLI UOMINI DEL PARLAMENTO, Book *see* Gianni Quaranta

TUTTO PER BENE, 1906, Short Story *see* Luigi Pirandello

TUTTO PER LA DONNA, Play *see* Nicola Manzari

TUXEDO WARRIOR, Novel *see* Clifford Temlow

TUZMADAR, Budapest 1932, Play *see* Lajos Zilahy

TVA SALIGA, DE, Novel *see* Ulla Isaksson

'TWAS THE NIGHT BEFORE CHRISTMAS, Story *see* Annie Hamilton Donnell

'TWAS THE NIGHT BEFORE CHRISTMAS, 1937, Short Story *see* Paul Gallico

TWEE VROUWEN, 1975, Novel *see* Harry Mulisch

TWELFTH NIGHT, c1600, Play *see* William Shakespeare

TWELFTH OF NEVER, THE, Novel *see* Douglas Heyes

TWELVE COINS OF CONFUCIUS, THE, Short Story *see* Harry Stephen Keeler

TWELVE GOLDEN CURLS, Short Story *see* Thomas Burke

TWELVE IN A BOX, 1938, Play *see* Ladislaus Bus-Fekete

TWELVE MILES OUT, New York 1925, Play *see* William Anthony McGuire

TWELVE O'CLOCK HIGH, Novel *see* Sy Bartlett, Beirne Lay Jr.

TWELVE POUND LOOK, THE, 1910, Play *see* J. M. Barrie

TWELVE-MONTH AND A DAY, A, Book *see* Christopher Rush

TWENTIETH CENTURY, New York 1932, Play *see* Ben Hecht, Charles MacArthur

TWENTY MINUTES, Short Story *see* James Salter

TWENTY PLUS TWO, New York 1961, Novel *see* Frank Gruber

TWENTY THOUSAND STREETS UNDER THE SKY; A LONDON TRILOGY, 1935, Novel *see* Patrick Hamilton

TWENTY THOUSAND YEARS IN SING SING, Garden City, N.Y. 1932, Book *see* Lewis E. Lawes

TWENTY-FOUR HOURS, New York 1930, Novel *see* Louis Bromfield

TWENTY-THREE AND A HALF HOURS' LEAVE, 1918, Short Story *see* Mary Roberts Rinehart

TWENTY-TWO, 1919, Short Story *see* Mary Roberts Rinehart

TWICE WED, Novel *see* E. Phillips Oppenheim

TWILIGHT, Novel *see* Dean R. Koontz

TWILIGHT FOR THE GODS, 1956, Novel *see* Ernest K. Gann

TWILIGHT HOUR, Novel *see* Arthur Valentine

TWILIGHT OF HONOUR, New York 1961, Novel *see* Al Dewlen

TWILIGHT OF THE GOLDS, THE, Play *see* Jonathan Tolins

TWIN BEDS, New York 1914, Play *see* Edward Salisbury Field, Margaret Mayo

TWIN SISTER, THE, 1902, Play *see* Ludwig Fulda

TWINKLER, THE, Short Story *see* Henry Leverage

TWINKLETOES, London 1917, Novel *see* Thomas Burke

TWINS, Book *see* Jack Geasland, Bari Wood

TWINS OF SUFFERING CREEK, London 1912, Novel *see* Ridgwell Cullum

TWIST OF FATE, 1978, Novel *see* Robert L. Fish

TWIST OF SAND, A, London 1959, Novel *see* Geoffrey Jenkins

TWO ARABIAN KNIGHTS, Short Story *see* Donald McGibney

TWO BELLS FOR PEGASUS, 1922, Short Story *see* Gerald Beaumont

TWO BENJAMINS, THE, 1918, Serial Story *see* Juliet Wilbor Tompkins

TWO BLACK CROWS IN THE A. E. F. THE, Indianapolis 1928, Novel *see* Charles E. MacK

TWO BLACK SHEEP, New York 1933, Novel *see* Warwick Deeping

TWO BLOCKS AWAY, New York 1925, Play *see* Aaron Hoffman

TWO BLUE BIRDS AND IN LOVE, Short Story *see* D. H. Lawrence

TWO CAN PLAY, 1922, Short Story *see* Gerald Mygatt

TWO DEATHS OF SENORA PUCCINI, THE, Novel *see* Stephen Dobyns

V STEPYAKH UKRAYINY, 1941, Play *see* Aleksander Korniychuk

V SUDE, 1886, Short Story *see* Anton Chekhov

V TIKHA VECHER, 1948, Novel *see* Emilian Stanev

V TLAME VELRYBY, Play *see* Emil Artur Longen

VA DOVE TI PORTA IL CUORE, Novel *see* Susanna Tamaro

VA ET VIENT, 1966, Play *see* Samuel Beckett

VACANCES, Play *see* Rene Besson, Georges Fabret

VACANCES DE XAVIER, LES, Book *see* Elisabeth Mariemy

VACANCES FINISSENT DEMAIN, LES, Novel *see* Yvan Noe

VACANCES POUR O.S.S. 117, Novel *see* Jean Bruce

VACATIONERS, THE, Play *see* Maxim Gorky

VADIM, 1832-34, Novel *see* Mikhail Lermontov

VAE VICTIS, Novel *see* Annie Vivanti

VAGABOND FRAPPE A NOTRE PORTE, UN, Short Story *see* Gabrielle Roy

VAGABONDE, LA, 1910, Novel *see* Sidonie Gabrielle Colette

VAGABUND VOM AQUATOR, DER, Novel *see* Ludwig von Wohl

VAGABUNDEN, Play *see* Juliane Kay

VAGEN TILL KLOCKRIKE, 1948, Novel *see* Harry Martinson

VAISSEAUX DU COEUR, LES, Novel *see* Benoit Groult

VAL D'OLIVI, 1873, Novel *see* Anton Giulio Barrili

VAL OF PARADISE, New York 1921, Novel *see* Vingie E. Roe

VALAMIT VISZ A VIZ, 1928, Novel *see* Lajos Zilahy

VALDEZ HORSES, THE, Novel *see* Lee Hoffmann

VALDEZ IS COMING, Novel *see* Elmore Leonard

VALE ABRAAO, Novel *see* Agustina Bessa-Luis

VALECNE TAJNOSTI PRAZSKE, Novel *see* Vavrinec Rehor

VALENTINA, Play *see* Marcello Marchesi, Vittorio Metz

VALENTINE'S DAY, Play *see* Horton Foote

VALENTINS SUNDENFALL, Play *see* Gretl Lowinger

VALERIE A TYDEN DIVU, 1945, Short Story *see* Vitezslav Nezval

VALET MAITRE, LE, Play *see* Paul Armont, Leopold Marchand

VALIANT IS THE WORD FOR CARRIE, New York 1935, Novel *see* Barry Benefield

VALIANT, THE, 1920, Play *see* Holworthy Hall, Robert M. Middlemass

VALIANTS OF VIRGINIA, THE, New York 1912, Novel *see* Hallie Erminie Rives

VALIDITA GIORNI DIECI, Novel *see* Toddi

VALKYRIE'S ARMOUR, Play *see* Harry Tierney

VALLEE DE LAS ESPADAS, EL, Novel *see* P. R. Diaz

VALLEY OF CONTENT, THE, New York 1922, Novel *see* Blanche Upright

VALLEY OF DECISION, THE, Novel *see* Marcia Davenport

VALLEY OF FEAR, THE, London 1914, Novel *see* Arthur Conan Doyle

VALLEY OF SILENT MEN, THE, New York 1920, Novel *see* James Oliver Curwood

VALLEY OF THE DOLLS, New York 1966, Novel *see* Jacqueline Susann

VALLEY OF THE GHOSTS, London 1922, Novel *see* Edgar Wallace

VALLEY OF THE GIANTS, THE, Garden City, N.Y. 1918, Novel *see* Peter B. Kyne

VALLEY OF THE MOON, New York 1913, Novel *see* Jack London

VALLEY OF THE SUN, Story *see* Clarence Budington Kelland

VALOPOROS HOLAY, Budapest 1923, Novel *see* Erno Vajda

VALSE BLONDE, Novel *see* Kelley Roos

VALSE DES TOREADORS, LA, Paris 1952, Play *see* Jean Anouilh

VALSE DU GORILLE, LA, Novel *see* Antoine Dominique

VALUE FOR MONEY, Novel *see* Derrick Boothroyd

VAMPIRE$, Novel *see* John Steakley

VAMPIRE, THE, New York 1897, Poem *see* Rudyard Kipling

VAMSHA VRIKSHA, Novel *see* S. L. Byrappa

VAN, THE, Novel *see* Roddy Doyle

VANDA, Short Story *see* Vasco Pratolini

VANDINY TRAMPOTY, Novel *see* Milos Krenovsky

VANDKORSET, 1935, Novel *see* Elin Wagner

VANDRING MED MANEN, 1941, Novel *see* Walter Ljungquist

VANESSA, 1933, Novel *see* Hugh Walpole

VANGILA VARDIGA, DET, Story *see* Ulla Isaksson

VANINA, Novel *see* Andre Pieyre de Mandiargues

VANINA VANINI, 1855, Short Story *see* Stendhal

VANISHED, Novel *see* Fletcher Knebel, Danielle Steel

VANISHING AMERICAN, THE, New York 1925, Novel *see* Zane Grey

VANISHING CORPSE, THE, Novel *see* Anthony Gilbert

VANISHING VIRGINIAN, THE, Book *see* Rebecca Yancey Williams

VANITY, London 1913, Play *see* Ernest Denny

VANITY AND SOME SABLES, Short Story *see* O. Henry

VANITY FAIR, London 1848, Novel *see* William Makepeace Thackeray

VANITY POOL, THE, Novel *see* Nalbro Bartley

VANITY ROW, 1952, Novel *see* William Riley Burnett

VANKA, 1884, Short Story *see* Anton Chekhov

VANSKLIGHETENS LAND, 1917, Novel *see* Elin Wagner

VARMINT, THE, New York 1910, Novel *see* Owen Johnson

VARNATT, 1954, Novel *see* Tarjei Vesaas

VASCHI DELLA BUJOSA, I, Novel *see* Nino Ilari

VASSA ZHELEZNOVA, 1910, Play *see* Maxim Gorky

VATER SEIN DAGEGEN SEHR, Novel *see* Horst Biernath

VAUTOUR, LE, Novel *see* John Garrick

VAUTRIN, 1840, Play *see* Honore de Balzac

VAVASOUR BALL, THE, Story *see* Frances Livingstone

VDAVALA SE JEDNA PANNA, Poem *see* Karel Hasler

VDAVKY NANYNKY KULICHOVY, Novel *see* Ignat Herrmann

VEAU GRAS, LE, Play *see* Bernard Zimmer

VECCHI E I GIOVANI, I, 1909, Novel *see* Luigi Pirandello

VECCHI SOFISMI, Play *see* Guillaume Vuillermot

VECCHIO CON GLI STIVALI, IL, 1944, Short Story *see* Vitaliano Brancati

VECHNO ZHIVYE, 1956, Play *see* Victor S. Rozov

VECHNYI MUZH, 1870, Short Story *see* Fyodor Dostoyevsky

VED VEJEN, 1886, Novel *see* Herman Bang

VEDMA, 1886, Short Story *see* Anton Chekhov

VEDOVA, LA, Play *see* Renato Simoni

VEGLIONE, LA, Paris 1893, Play *see* Alexandre Bisson, Albert Carre

VEIL, THE, Story *see* Norman Sherbrooke

VEILED ARISTOCRATS, Novel *see* Charles Chestnutt

VEILED ONE, THE, Novel *see* Ruth Rendell

VEILED WOMAN, THE, Play *see* Harold Simpson

VEILLE D'ARMES, LA, Paris 1917, Play *see* Claude Farrere, Lucien Nepoty

VEINE, LA, Play *see* Alfred Capus

VELAIKKARI, Play *see* C. N. Annadurai

VELBLOUD UCHEM JEHLY, Play *see* Frantisek Langer

VELDT, THE, 1951, Short Story *see* Ray Bradbury

VELKE POKUSENI, Novel *see* Marie Krizova

VELOCITY OF GARY, THE, Play *see* James Still

VELVET, 1932, Short Story *see* Paul Cain

VELVET FLEECE, THE, Novel *see* Lois Eby, John Fleming

VENA D'ORO, LA, 1919, Play *see* Guglielmo Zorzi

VENCEDORES DE LA MUERTE, LOS, Novel *see* Alberto Insua

VENDETTA, 1886, Novel *see* Marie Corelli

VENDETTA DI UNA PAZZA, LA, Novel *see* Carolina Invernizio

VENEER, New York 1929, Play *see* Hugh Stange

VENERE ORGIASTA, LA, Short Story *see* Luigi Chiarelli

VENERE PRIVATA, Novel *see* Giorgio Scerbanenco

VENETIAN AFFAIR, THE, New York 1963, Novel *see* Helen MacInnes

VENETIAN BIRD, Novel *see* Victor Canning

VENGANZA ISLENA, *see* Andres Perez de La Mota

VENGEANCE, Short Story *see* David Fleming

VENGEANCE, Book *see* George Jonas

VENGEANCE A RIO, Novel *see* Maxime Delamare

VENGEANCE IS MINE, Novel *see* John A. Moroso

VENGEANCE OF DURAND, THE, Novel *see* Rex Beach

VENGEANCE OF JEFFERSON GAWNE, THE, Chicago 1917, Novel *see* Charles Alden Seltzer

VENGEANCE OF PRIVATE POOLEY, THE, Novel *see* Cyrill Jolly

VENGEANCE VALLEY, 1950, Novel *see* Luke Short

VENIN, LE, Play *see* Henri Bernstein

VENNER, 1917, Play *see* Arnulf Overland

VENOM, Novel *see* Alan Scholefield

VENOUSEK A STAZICKA, Novel *see* Josef Skruzny

VENTENNI NON SONO DELIQUNETI, I, Book *see* Mino Guerrini

VENTIMILA LEGHE SOPRA I MARI, Novel *see* Goffredo d'Andrea

VENTURERS, THE, Short Story *see* O. Henry

VENUS, Novel *see* Jean Vignaud

VENUS D'ARLES, LE, Short Story *see* Mery

VENUS IM PELZ, Novel *see* Lepold Sacher-Masoch

VENUS IN FURS, Novel *see* Leopold von Sacher-Masoch

VENUS IN THE EAST, New York 1918, Novel *see* Wallace Irwin

VENUS RISING, London 1962, Short Story *see* George Bradshaw

VENUS VOM TIVOLI, DIE, Aarau 1931, Novel *see* Peter Haggenmacher

VERA THE MEDIUM, New York 1908, Novel *see* Richard Harding Davis

VERBENA DE LA PALOMA, LA, Opera *see* Tomas Breton, Ricardo de La Vega

VERBLYUZHII GLAZ, 1961, Short Story *see* Chingiz Aitmatov

VERBRECHEN NACH SCHULSCHLUSS, Baden-Baden 1956, Novel *see* Walter Ebert

VERDAMMT ICH BIN ERWACHSEN, Novel *see* Joachim Novotny

VERDAMMT ZUR SUNDE, Novel *see* Henry Jaeger

VERDE, ROSSO E NERO, Play *see* Fabrizio Sarazani

VERDENS ANSIGT, Copenhagen 1917, Novel *see* Johan Bojer

VERDI. ROMAN DER OPER, 1924, Novel *see* Franz Werfel

VERDICT, LE, Novel *see* Henri Coupon

VERDICT OF THE HEART, THE, Novel *see* Charles Garvice

VERDICT, THE, Novel *see* Barry Reed

VEREDA DA SALVACAO, 1965, Play *see* Jorge Andrade

VERENA STADLER, Wiesbaden 1906, Short Story *see* Ernst Zahn

VERENAS HOCHZEIT, Novel *see* Lisa Wenger

VERFOLGUNG UND ERMORDUNG JEAN PAUL MARATS, DIE, 1964, Play *see* Peter Weiss

VERGELOSE; ET BARNS HISTORIE, DE, 1938, Novel *see* Gabriel Scott

VERGER, THE, 1947, Short Story *see* W. Somerset Maugham

VERGINI DI ROMA, LE, Short Story *see* Luigi Emmanuele, Gaetano Laffredo

VERGINI, LE, 1889, Play *see* Marco Praga

VERGISS NICHT DEINE FRAU ZU KUSSEN, Novel *see* Willy Breinholst

VERGNUGLICHE LEBEN DER DOKTORIN LOHNEFIN, DAS, Short Story *see* Konrad Beste

VERITE SUR BEBE DONGE, LA, 1942, Novel *see* Georges Simenon

VERLOBUNG VON SAN DOMINGO, DIE, 1811, Short Story *see* Heinrich von Kleist

VERLORENE, DER, Novel *see* Peter Lorre

VERLORENE EHRE DER KATHARINA BLUM, DIE, 1974, Novel *see* Heinrich Boll

VERLORENE PARADIES, DAS, 1921, Short Story *see* Stefan Markus

VERLORENE PARADIES, DAS, Berlin 1890, Play *see* Ludwig Fulda

VERLORENE TAL. EIN ROMAN VON JAGD UND LIEBE, DAS, Basle 1931, Novel *see* Gustav Friedrich Renker

VERONICA CYBO, *see* Riccardo Olivieri

VERONIQUE, Opera *see* Georges Duval, Albert Vanloo

VERRE D'EAU OU LES EFFETS ET LES CAUSES, LE, Paris 1840, Play *see* Eugene Scribe

VERS L'EXTASE, Novel *see* Madeleine Alleins

VERSCHLOSSENE HAUS, DAS, Book *see* Curt Johannes Braun

VERSCHOLLENE, DER, Short Story *see* Franz Kafka

VERSCHWENDER, DER, 1868, Play *see* Ferdinand Raimund

VERSCHWORUNG DE FIESKO ZU GENUA, DER, 1784, Play *see* Friedrich von Schiller

VERSCHWUNDENE FRAU, DIE, Novel *see* Max Durr

VERSCHWUNDENE MINIATUR, DIE, 1935, Novel *see* Erich Kastner

VERSPRECHEN, DAS, Zurich 1958, Novel *see* Friedrich Durrenmatt

VERSPRICH MIR NICHTS, Play *see* Charlotte Rissmann

VERTAGTE HOCHZEITSNACHT, DIE, Play *see* Franz Peter Arnold, Ernst Bach

VERTE MOISSON, LA, Novel *see* Henri Brunel

VERTIGE DE MINUIT, LE, Novel *see* Egon Hostovsky

VERTIGE, LE, Play *see* Charles Mere

VERTRAG UM KARAKAT, Play *see* Fritz Peter Buch

VERUNTREUTE HIMMEL, DER, 1948, Novel *see* Franz Werfel

VERWANDLUNG, DIE, 1912, Short Story *see* Franz Kafka

VERWEHTE SPUREN, Radio Play *see* Hans Rothe

VERWIRRUNG UM INGE, Novel *see* Hans Nuchtern

VERWIRRUNGEN DES ZOGLINGS TORLESS, DIE, Berlin 1906, Novel *see* Robert Musil

VERY BRITISH COUP, A, Novel *see* Chris Mullen

VERY GOOD YOUNG MAN, A, New York 1918, Play *see* Martin Brown, Robert Housum

VERY HONORABLE GUY, A, 1929, Short Story *see* Damon Runyon

VERY IDEA, THE, New York 1917, Play *see* William Le Baron

VERY PRACTICAL JOKE, A, 1925, Short Story *see* Ben Ames Williams

VERY WARM FOR MAY, Musical Play *see* Oscar Hammerstein II, Jerome Kern

VERZAUBERTE MADCHEN, DAS, Play *see* Martin Doerhoff

VESHNIYE VODY, 1872, Short Story *see* Ivan Turgenev

VESNA NA ODERE, 1950, Novel *see* Emmanuil Kazakevich

VESPERS IN VIENNA, Novel *see* Bruce Marshall

VESSEL OF WRATH, 1931, Short Story *see* W. Somerset Maugham

VESTIDO COR DE FOGO, O, 1946, Short Story *see* Jose Regio

VESTIRE GLI IGNUDI, 1937, Play *see* Luigi Pirandello

VESTOVOI DIMO, 1929, Novel *see* Georgi Stamatov

VETTER AUS DINGSDA, DER, Opera *see* Hermann Haller, Eduard Kunneke, Rideamus

VEUVE COUDERC, LA, 1942, Novel *see* Georges Simenon

VEUVE JOYEUSE, LA, Book *see* Viktor Leon, Leo Stein

VEUVE, LA, Paris 1958, Novel *see* Michel Lebrun

VI ARME SYNDERE, Novel *see* Sigfrid Siwertz

VI' CHE M'HA FATTO FRATEME!, 1881, *see* Eduardo Scarpetta

VI SOM GAR KJOKKENVEIEN, Oslo 1930, Novel *see* Sigrid Boo

VIA DELLA LUCE, LA, Novel *see* Alfredo Bacchelli

VIA MALA, Novel *see* John Knittel

VIA SATELLITE, Play *see* Anthony McCarten

VIA WIRELESS, New York 1908, Play *see* Paul Armstrong, Winchell Smith

VIAGEM AOS SEIOS DE DUILIA, 1959, Short Story *see* Aribal Machado

VIAGGIATORI DELLA SERA, I, Novel *see* Umberto Simonetta

VIAGGIO DI PIACERE, UN, Novel *see* Enzo Gicca Palli

VIAGGIO, IL, 1910, Short Story *see* Luigi Pirandello

VIAJE DE NOVIOS, UN, 1881, Novel *see* Emilia Pardo Bazan

VICAR OF BRAY, THE, Story *see* Anson Dyer

VICAR OF WAKEFIELD, THE, 1766, Novel *see* Oliver Goldsmith

VICE VERSA, 1882, Novel *see* F. Anstey

VICEROY OF OUIDAH, THE, Novel *see* Bruce Chatwin

VICISSITUDES OF EVANGELINE, THE, New York 1905, Novel *see* Elinor Glyn

VICKY VAN, Philadelphia 1918, Novel *see* Carolyn Wells

VICOMTE DE BRAGELONNE, LE, Paris 1847, Novel *see* Alexandre Dumas (pere)

VICTIM TO THE SEAL OF CONFESSION, A, St. Louis 1898, Novel *see* Rev. Joseph Spillman

VICTIME, LA, Novel *see* Fernand Vanderem

VICTIMES, LES, Novel *see* Pierre Boileau, Thomas Narcejac

VICTIMS OF PERSECUTION, Play *see* David Leonard

VICTOR, Play *see* Henri Bernstein

VICTORIA, 1898, Novel *see* Knut Hamsun

VICTORIA DOCKS AT EIGHT, THE, Novel *see* Charles Beahan, Rufus King

VICTORIA REGINA, London 1937, Play *see* Laurence Houseman

VICTORIAN CHAISE-LONGUE, THE, Short Story *see* Marghanita Laski

VICTORY, London 1915, Novel *see* Joseph Conrad

VIDA CONYUGAL, LA, Novel *see* Sergio Pitol

VIDA ES SUENO, LA, 1647, Play *see* Pedro Calderon de La Barca

VIDAM TEMETES, 1963, Short Story *see* Tibor Dery

VIDAS CRUZADAS, 1929, Play *see* Jacinto Benavente y Martinez

VIDAS SECAS, 1938, Novel *see* Graciliano Ramos

VIDOCQ, Novel *see* Arthur Bernede
VIDOCQ, Book *see* Francis Eugene Vidocq

VIE DE BOHEME, LA, Paris 1848, Play *see* Henri Murger

VIE DE CHIEN, UNE, Novel *see* Andre Mycho

VIE EXECRABLE DE GUILLEMETTE BABIN, LA, *see* Maurice Garcon

VIE: L'HUMBLE VERITE, UNE, Paris 1883, Novel *see* Guy de Maupassant

VIE NORMALE, LA, Novel *see* Micheline Morel

VIE PARISIENNE, LA, Operetta *see* Ludovic Halevy, Henri Meilhac

VIEHJUD LEVI, Play *see* Thomas Strittmatter

VIEIL IMBECILE, UN, *see* Alberto Moravia

VIEILLE QUI MARCHAIT DANS LA MER, LA, Novel *see* San Antonio

VIELE HEISSEN KAIN., Novel *see* Alfred Neumann

VIELLE D'ARMES, LA, Paris 1917, Play *see* Claude Farrere, Lucien Nepoty

VIENNESE CHARMER, THE, Story *see* W. Carey Wonderly

VIENNESE MEDLEY, THE, New York 1924, Novel *see* Edith Louise O'Shaughnessy

VIENT DE PARAITRE, 1928, Play *see* Edouard Bourdet

VIENTO DEL NORTE, 1951, Novel *see* Elena Quiroga

VIENTO NEGRO, Novel *see* Mario Martini

VIER GESELLEN, DIE, Play *see* Jochen Huth

VIER MUSKETIERE, DIE, Play *see* Sigmund Graff

VIER SCHLUSSEL, Novel *see* Max Pierre Schaeffer

VIER VON DER INFANTERIE, Novel *see* Ernst Johannsen

VIERAS MIES TULI TALOON, 1937, Novel *see* Mika Waltari

VIERDE MAN, DE, 1981, Novel *see* Gerard Kornelius Van Het Reve

VIERGE DU RHIN, LA, Novel *see* Pierre Nord

VIERGE FOLLE, LA, 1910, Play *see* Henry Bataille

VIERTE GEBOT, DAS, 1891, Play *see* Ludwig Anzengruber

VIERUNDZWANZIG STUNDEN AUS DEM LEBEN EINER FRAU, Leipzig 1926, Novel *see* Stefan Zweig

VIERZEHNTE AM TISCH, DER, Story *see* Ossi Oswalda

VIETNAM TRILOGY, Play *see* George Fernandez

VIETNAM VEEDU, Play *see* Sundaram

VIEUX DE LA VIEILLE, LES, Novel *see* Rene Fallet

VIEW FROM POMPEY'S HEAD, THE, 1954, Novel *see* Hamilton Basso

VIEW FROM THE BRIDGE, A, New York 1955, Play *see* Arthur Miller

VIGIL IN THE NIGHT, Cleveland 1941, Novel *see* A. J. Cronin

VIGILANTE, 1949, Novel *see* Richard Aldrich Summers

VIGNES DU SEIGNEUR, LES, Play *see* Francis de Croisset, Robert de Flers

VIHREA KULTA, 1938, Play *see* Hella Wuolijoki

VIKING, THE, 1951, Novel *see* Edison Marshall

VIKTOR UND VIKTORIA, Play *see* Reinhold Schunzel

VIKTORIA UND IHR HUSAR, Opera *see* Paul Abraham

VILDANDEN, 1884, Play *see* Henrik Ibsen

VILDE SVANER, DE, 1838, Short Story *see* Hans Christian Andersen

VILLA DA VENDERE, Play *see* Geza von Cziffra

VILLA DEL VENERDI, LA, Novel *see* Alberto Moravia

VILLA FALCONIERI, Novel *see* Richard Voss

VILLA TRISTE, Novel *see* Patrick Modiano

VILLAFRANCA, Play *see* Giovacchino Forzano, Benito Mussolini

VILLAGE BLACKSMITH, THE, 1841, Poem *see* Henry Wadsworth Longfellow

VILLAGE IN THE JUNGLE, THE, 1913, Novel *see* Leonard Woolf

VILLAGE PERDU, LE, Novel *see* Gilbert Dupe

VILLAGE SQUIRE, THE, Play *see* Arthur Jarvis Black

VILLAGE TALE, A, New York 1934, Novel *see* Philip Duffield Stong

VILLAGE WEDDING, Play *see* Charles McEvoy

VILLE DES MILLES JOIES, LA, Novel *see* Arnold Bennett

VILLE ETERNELLE, LA, Novel *see* Alexis Curvers

VILVA BAILOR, 1909, Short Story *see* Ion Agarbiceanu

VINAIGRE DES QUATRE VOLEURS, LE, Novel *see* Albert Jean

VINDINGEVALS, 1956, Novel *see* Nils Artur Lundkvist

VINEGAR TREE, THE, New York 1930, Play *see* Paul Osborn

VINGT ANS APRES; SUITE DE TROIS MOUSQUETAIRES, 1845, Novel *see* Alexandre Dumas (pere)

VINGT JOURS A L'OMBRE, 1907, Play *see* Maurice Hennequin, Pierre Veber

VINGT MILLE LIEUES SOUS LES MERS, 1870, Novel *see* Jules Verne

VINGT-CINQ ANS DE BONHEUR, Play *see* Germaine Lefrancq

VINGT-CINQUIEME HEURE, LA, Novel *see* Virgil Gheorghiu

VINGT-HUIT JOURS DE CLAIRETTE, LES, Opera *see* Antony Mars, Hippolyte Raymond, Roger

VINT, 1884, Short Story *see* Anton Chekhov

VINTAGE, THE, 1953, Novel *see* Ursula Keir

VINTERBORN, 1976, Novel *see* Dea Trier Morch

VIOLA TRICOLOR, 1874, Novel *see* Theodor Storm

VIOLENT PLAYGROUND, Novel *see* James Kennaway

VIOLENT SATURDAY, 1955, Novel *see* William L. Heath

VIOLENTATA SULLA SABBIA, Novel *see* Andre Peyre Mandargues

VIOLENZA A ROMA, Novel *see* Massimo Felisatti, Fabio Pittorru

VIOLENZA E IL FURORE, LA, Novel *see* Peter Kane

VIOLENZA, LA, Play *see* Giuseppe Fava

VIOLETA, Play *see* Nicolas Dorr

VIOLETTE NEI CAPELLI, Novel *see* Luciana Peverelli

VIOLETTE NOZIERE, Novel *see* Jean-Marie Fitere

VIOLIN MAKER OF CREMONA, THE, Story *see* Francois Coppee

VIOS KAI POLITEIA TOU ALEXI ZOBRA, 1946, Novel *see* Nikos Kazantzakis

VIPER THREE, Novel *see* Walter Wager

VIRGIN AND THE GYPSY, THE, London 1930, Novel *see* D. H. Lawrence

VIRGIN OF NUREMBERG, THE, Novel *see* Frank Bogart

VIRGIN OF SAN BLAS, THE, Story *see* Julio Sabello

VIRGIN SOLDIERS, THE, London 1966, Novel *see* Leslie Thomas

VIRGIN WITCH, Novel *see* Klaus Vogel

VIRGINIA, Short Story *see* Ida M. Evans

VIRGINIA FLY IS DROWNING, Novel *see* Angela Huth

VIRGINIAN, THE, New York 1902, Novel *see* Owen Wister

VIRGINIA'S HUSBAND, Play *see* Florence Kilpatrick

VIRGINIUS, 1820, Play *see* James Sheridan Knowles

VIRTUE ITS OWN REWARD, Short Story *see* John Barton Oxford

VIRTUOSO, Book *see* Michael Kerr, Brenda Ogdon

VIRTUOUS WIVES, Boston 1917, Novel *see* Owen Johnson

VISAGE D'AIEULE, Short Story *see* Marie Thierry

VISAGES DE FEMMES, Play *see* A. Germain, Michel Trebor

VISAGES DE L'OMBRE, LES, Paris 1953, Novel *see* Pierre Boileau, Thomas Narcejac

VISION QUEST, Novel *see* Terry Davis

VISIT TO A CHIEF'S SON, Book *see* Robert Halmi

VISIT TO A SMALL PLANET, 1956, Play *see* Gore Vidal

VISITA, LA, 1942, Short Story *see* Carlo Cassola

VISITA QUE NO TOCO EL TIMBRE, LA, 1951, Play *see* Joaquin Calvo Sotelo

VISITACIONES DEL DIABLO, LAS, 1965, Novel *see* Emilio Carballido

VISITOR, THE, Novel *see* Chauncey G. Parker III

VISITORS, THE, New York 1964, Novel *see* Nathaniel Benchley

VITA AGRA, LA, Novel *see* Luciano Bianciardi

VITA DI CHIRURGO, Novel *see* Andrea Majocchi

VITA MILITARE, 1869, Short Story *see* Edmondo de Amicis

VITA NUOVA, Play *see* Bruno Paolinelli

VITA PUO RICOMCIARE, LA, Novel *see* Alfredo Vanni

VITA VIOLENTA, UNA, 1959, Novel *see* Pier Paolo Pasolini

VIUDA DE MONTIEL, LA, 1962, Short Story *see* Gabriel Garcia Marquez

VIUDO RIUS, EL, 1945, Novel *see* Ignacio Agusti

VIVA LA MUSICA, Novel *see* H. F. Kollner

VIVA LO IMPOSIBLE!, 1951, Play *see* Joaquin Calvo Sotelo

VIVA MAX!, New York 1966, Novel *see* James Lehrer

VIVA VILLA, New York 1933, Book *see* Edgcumb Pinchon, O. B. Stade

VIVACIOUS LADY, 1936, Short Story *see* I. A. R. Wylie

VIVANTE EPINGLE, LA, Novel *see* Jean-Joseph Renaud

VIVIETTE, 1910, Novel *see* William J. Locke

VIY, 1835, Short Story *see* Nikolay Gogol

VIZITA, Novel *see* Adolf Branald

VIZITA, 1901, Short Story *see* Ion Luca Caragiale

VLASCHAARD, DE, 1908, Novel *see* Frank Lateur

VLCI JAMA, 1941, Novel *see* Jarmila Glazarova

VLUCHT REGENWULPEN, EEN, Novel *see* Maarten 't Hart

VOCATION, LA, Novel *see* Jean d'Avesne

VOCE DELLA LUNA, LA, Novel *see* Ermanno Cavazzoni

VOCE 'E NOTTE, Song *see* G. B. de Curtis, Eduardo Nicolardi

VOCI DI DENTRO, LE, Milan 1948, Play *see* Eduardo de Filippo

VOGELHANDLER, DER, Vienna 1891, Operetta *see* L. Held, M. West, Carl Zeller

VOICE FROM THE FIREPLACE, A, Short Story *see* Guy de Maupassant

VOICE FROM THE MINARET, THE, London 1919, Play *see* Robert Hichens

VOICE IN THE DARK, A, New York 1919, Play *see* Ralph E. Dyar

VOICE IN THE FOG, THE, Indianapolis 1915, Novel *see* Harold MacGrath

VOICE OF ARMAGEDDON, THE, Novel *see* David Lippincott

VOICE OF BUGLE ANN, THE, New York 1935, Novel *see* MacKinlay Kantor

VOICE OF THE HEART, Novel *see* Barbara Taylor Bradford

VOICE OF THE NIGHT, THE, Short Story *see* W. H. Hodgson

VOICE OF THE TURTLE, THE, New York 1943, Play *see* John Van Druten

VOICES, Play *see* Richard Lortz

VOICES IN THE GARDEN, Short Story *see* Dirk Bogarde

VOIE LACTEE, LA, Play *see* Alfred Savoir

VOIE SANS DISQUE, LA, Novel *see* Andre Armandy

VOILE DU BONHEUR, LE, Play *see* Georges Clemenceau

VOIX DE L'OCEAN, LA, Novel *see* Georges G. Toudouze

VOIX HUMAINE, LA, 1930, Play *see* Jean Cocteau

VOJNARKA, Play *see* Alois Jirasek

VOL DE NUIT, Paris 1931, Novel *see* Antoine de Saint-Exupery

VOL ETRANGE, UN, Novel *see* H. Heywood

VOL SUPREME, LA, Short Story *see* Valentin Mandelstamm

VOLANI RODU, Novel *see* Eduard Storch

VOLANTINO, IL, Novel *see* Pietro Buttitta

VOLATA, LA, 1918, Play *see* Dario Niccodemi

VOLEGENY, 1922, Play *see* Erno Szep

VOLEUR DE FEMMES, LE, Novel *see* Pierre Frondaie

VOLEUR DE VIE, Novel *see* Steinunn Sigurdardottir

VOLEUR, LE, Paris 1898, Novel *see* Georges Darien

VOLEUR, LE, Paris 1907, Play *see* Henri Bernstein

VOLEURS DU GRAND MONDE, LES, *see* Ponson Du Terrail

VOLEUSE D'ENFANTS, LA, Play *see* Eugene Grange, Lambert Thiboust

VOLGA BOATMAN, THE, New York 1926, Novel *see* Konrad Bercovici

VOLKI I OVSTY, 1875, Play *see* Alexander Ostrovsky

VOLONTE, Novel *see* Georges Ohnet

VOLPONE, 1607, Play *see* Ben Jonson

VOLTAIQUE, 1962, Short Story *see* Ousmane Sembene

VOLUNTEER ORGANIST, THE, New York 1902, Novel *see* William B. Gray

VOLUPTE D'ETRE, LA, 1954, Novel *see* Maurice Druon

VOLVORETA, 1917, Novel *see* Wenceslao Fernandez Florez

VOM BERGHOF, DIE, Novel *see* Johannes Rohr

VOM SCHICKSAL VERWEHT, Play *see* Joseph Maria Franck

VON DER LIEBE REDEN WIR SPATER, Novel *see* Frank F. Braun

VON RYAN'S EXPRESS, New York 1964, Novel *see* David Westheimer

VOR REHEN WIRD GEWARNT, Novel *see* Vicki Baum

VOR SONNENAUFGANG, 1889, Play *see* Gerhart Hauptmann

VOR SONNENUNTERGANG, Berlin 1932, Play *see* Gerhart Hauptmann

VOROS REKVIEM, 1975, Short Story *see* Gyula Hernadi

VOROSLAMPAS HAZ, A, 1937, Novel *see* Sandor Hunyady

VORSTADTKROKODILE, 1976, Novel *see* Max von Der Grun

VORSTADTVARIETE, Play *see* Felix Salten

VORTEX, THE, London 1924, Play *see* Noel Coward

VORUNTERSUCHUNG, Play *see* Max Alsberg, Ernst Hesse

VOSKHOZHDENIYE NA FUDZIYAMU, 1978, Play *see* Chingiz Aimatov, Kaltai Mukhamedzhanov

VOSKRESENIYE, Moscow 1899, Novel *see* Lev Nikolayevich Tolstoy

VOTRE SOURIRE, Play *see* Andre Birabeau, Georges Dolley

VOUIVRE, LA, Novel *see* Marcel Ayme

VOUS INTERESSEZ-VOUS A LA CHOSE?, Novel *see* Claude Eymouche

VOUS N'AVEZ RIEN A DECLARER?, Play *see* Maurice Hennequin, Pierre Veber

VOUS PIGEZ?, Novel *see* Peter Cheyney

VOYAGE A BIARRITZ, LE, 1936, Play *see* Jean Sarment

VOYAGE A L'OMBRE, LE, Play *see* Andre Birabeau

VOYAGE A PAIMPOL, LE, Novel *see* Dorothee Letessier

VOYAGE A TROIS, Play *see* Jean de Letraz

VOYAGE AROUND MY FATHER, 1971, Play *see* John Mortimer

VOYAGE AU CENTRE DE LA TERRE, 1864, Novel *see* Jules Verne

VOYAGE D'AGREMENT, 1881, Play *see* Alexandre Bisson, Edmond Gondinet

VOYAGE DE BERLURON, LE, 1893, *see* E. Grenet-Dancourt, Maurice Ordonneau

VOYAGE DE CORBILLON, LE, Play *see* Antony Mars

VOYAGE DE MONSIEUR PERRICHON, LE, 1860, Play *see* Eugene Labiche, Edouard Martin

VOYAGE DU PERE, LE, Novel *see* Bernard Clavel

VOYAGE IMPREVU, LE, Novel *see* Tristan Bernard

VOYAGE OF THE DAMNED, Book *see* Max Morgan-Witts, Gordon Thomas

VOYAGEUR DE LA TOUSSAINT, LE, 1941, Novel *see* Georges Simenon

VOYAGEUR MORT, LE, Novel *see* Jean Santacroce

VOYAGEUR SANS BAGAGE, LE, 1936, Play *see* Jean Anouilh

VOYNA I MIR, 1863-69, Novel *see* Lev Nikolayevich Tolstoy

VPERVYE ZAMUZHEM, 1978, Short Story *see* Pavel Nilin

VRACHTWAGEN, DE, Novel *see* Per Wahloo

VRAGI, 1887, Short Story *see* Anton Chekhov

VRAGI, 1906, Play *see* Maxim Gorky

VRAH, Short Story *see* Zdenek Ron

VRAZDA PRIMADONY, Novel *see* Walter Hauff

VREME RAZDELNO, 1964, Novel *see* Anton Donchev

VROUW DIE EEN ROOKSPOOR ACHTERLIET, Story *see* Lidy Van Marissing

VSICHKI I NIKOY, 1975, Novel *see* Yordan Radichkov

VUCJAK, 1925, Play *see* Miroslav Krieza

VUK, Novel *see* Istvan Fekete

VYCHOVA DIVEK V CECHACH, Novel *see* Michal Viewegh

VYDELECNE ZENY, Play *see* Emil Synek

VYLET PANA BROUCKA NA MARS, Novel *see* Svatopluk Cech

VYSTREL, 1831, Short Story *see* Alexander Pushkin

"W" PLAN, THE, Novel *see* Graham Seton

W PUSTYNI I W PUSZCZY, 1911, Novel *see* Henryk Sienkiewicz

WAAR BLIJFT HET LICHT (WHEN THE LIGHT COMES), Novel *see* Heleen Van Der Laan

WACHTMEISTER STUDER, Zurich 1936, Novel *see* Friedrich Glauser

WAFFLE IRON, THE, 1920, Short Story *see* Arthur Stringer

WAG LADY, THE, 1916, Short Story *see* Rex Beach

WAGA KOI NO BOHYO, 1959, Novel *see* Ayako Sono

WAGAHAI WA NEKO DE ARU, 1905, Novel *see* Soseki Natsume

WAGER, THE, Short Story *see* Jennifer Howard

WAGES OF SIN, THE, Novel *see* Lucas Malet

WAGES OF VIRTUE, New York 1917, Novel *see* P. C. Wren

WAHLVERWANDTSCHAFTEN, DIE, 1809, Novel *see* Johann Wolfgang von Goethe

WAHRE JAKOB, DER, Play *see* Franz Robert Arnold, Fritz Peter Arnold, Ernst Bach

WAHREN GESCHICHTE, Play *see* Friedrich von Schiller

WE MODERNS, New York 1923, Play *see* Israel Zangwill

WE MUST DANCE, Short Story *see* William Heinesen

WE MUST KILL TONI, London 1954, Play *see* Ian Stuart Black

WE OF THE NEVER NEVER, Autobiography *see* Jeannie Gunn

WE ONLY KILL EACH OTHER, Book *see* Dean Jennings

WE SHALL SEE, London 1926, Novel *see* Edgar Wallace

WE THE LIVING, 1936, Novel *see* Ayn Rand

WE THINK THE WORLD OF YOU, Novel *see* J. R. Ackerley

WE THREE AND TRODDLES, Novel *see* R. Andom

WE WHO ARE ABOUT TO DIE, New York 1936, Book *see* David Lamson

WE WOMEN, Novel *see* Countess Barcynska

WEAK SISTERS, New York 1925, Play *see* Lynn Starling

WEAPON, Novel *see* Robert Mason

WEARING THE PANTS, Play *see* Zelda Davees

WEATHER IN THE STREETS, THE, 1936, Novel *see* Rosamund Lehmann

WEAVER OF DREAMS, A, New York 1911, Novel *see* Myrtle Reed

WEB, THE, Short Story *see* Irvin S. Cobb

WEBER, DIE, Play *see* Gerhart Hauptmann

WEDDING BELLS, Play *see* Edward Salisbury Field

WEDDING GROUP, Radio Play *see* Philip Wade

WEDDING GUEST SAT ON A STONE, THE, Story *see* Richard Shattuck

WEDDING PRESENT, 1935, Short Story *see* Paul Gallico

WEDDING, THE, Novel *see* Dorothy West

WEDNESDAY'S CHILD, New York 1934, Play *see* Leopold L. Atlas

WEE WILLIE WINKIE, 1888, Short Story *see* Rudyard Kipling

WEEK-END A ZUYDCOOTE, Novel *see* Robert Merle

WEEKEND AT THRACKLEY, A, Play *see* Alan Melville

WEEK-END GIRL, New York 1932, Novel *see* Warner Fabian

WEEKEND IM PARADIES, Play *see* Franz Robert Arnold, Ernst Bach

WEEKEND MARRIAGE, New York 1932, Novel *see* Faith Baldwin

WEEP NO MORE, Novel *see* Lenore Coffee

WEG DURCH DIE NACHT, DER, Novel *see* John Knittel

WEG ZU ISABELL, Novel *see* Frank Thiess

WEG ZUR HOLLE, DER, Play *see* Gustav Kadelburg

WEG ZURUCK, DER, 1931, Novel *see* Erich Maria Remarque

WEGEN VERFUHRUNG MINDERJAHRIGER, Novel *see* Hans Wolfgang

WEGRZY, 1956, Short Story *see* Jerzy Stefan Stawicki

WEIB IN FLAMMEN, Novel *see* Georg Froschel

WEIBSTEUFEL, DER, 1914, Play *see* Karl Schonherr

WEIGHT OF THE LAST STRAW, THE, Story *see* Charles E. Van Loan

WEIHNACHTSABEND, DER, Poem *see* Henrik Wergeland

WEIL DU ARM BIST MUSST DU FRUHER STERBEN, Novel *see* Hans Gustl Kernmayr

WEIRD NEMESIS, THE, Story *see* G. E. Jenks

WEISE VON LIEBE UND TOD DES CORNETS CHRISTOPH RILKE, DIE, 1906, Verse *see* Rainer Maria Rilke

WEISKOPF UR, HANY ORA?, 1968, Short Story *see* Geza Paskandi

WEISSE FRAU DES MAHARADSCHA, DIE, Novel *see* Ludwig von Wohl

WEISSE HOLLE VON PIZ PALU, DIE, Short Story *see* Arnold Fanck

WEISSE ROSE, DIE, 1929, Novel *see* Ben Traven

WEISSE SCHLEIER, DER, Poem *see* Moritz Hartmann

WEISSE SPINNE, DIE, Novel *see* Louis Weinert-Wilton

WEISSE WOLKE CAROLIN, Novel *see* Klaus Meyer

WEISSEN ROSEN VON RAVENSBERG, DIE, Novel *see* Adlersfeld-Ballestrem

WEITE LAND, DAS, 1911, Play *see* Arthur Schnitzler

WEITER WEG, EIN, Novel *see* Irmgard Wurmbrand

WELCOME MR. WASHINGTON, Story *see* Noel Streatfeild

WELCOME STRANGER, New York 1920, Play *see* Aaron Hoffman

WELCOME TO HARD TIMES, New York 1960, Novel *see* E. L. Doctorow

WELCOME TO OUR CITY, New York 1910, Play *see* George V. Hobart

WELCOME TO THE CLUB, Novel *see* Clement Biddle Wood

WELCOME TO XANADU, Novel *see* Nathaniel Benchley

WELCOME WIFE, A, Play *see* Ernest Paulton, Fred Thompson

WELL OF LONELINESS, THE, London 1928, Novel *see* Radclyffe Hall

WELL, THE, Novel *see* Elizabeth Jolley

WELSH SINGER, A, Novel *see* Allen Raine

WELT IN JENEM SOMMER, DIE, Novel *see* Robert Muller

WELTREKORD IM SEITENSPRUNG, Play *see* Josef Geissler

WEM GOTT EIN AMT GIBT, Play *see* Wilhelm Lichtenberg

WEN DIE GOTTER LIEBEN, Novel *see* Richard Billinger

WENN BEIDE SCHULDIG WERDEN, Novel *see* Hans Nogly

WENN DER HAHN KRAHT, Play *see* August Hinrichs

WENN ES ROSEN SIND WERDEN SIE BLUHEN, 1950, Novel *see* Kasimir Edschmid

WENN SUSS DAS MONDLICHT AUF DEN HUGELN SCHLAFT, Novel *see* Eric Malpass

WENN WIR ALLE ENGEL WAREN, Novel *see* Heinrich Spoerl

WER STIRBT SCHON GERNE UNTER PALMEN?, Novel *see* Heinz G. Konsalik

WEREWOLF OF PARIS, THE, New York 1933, Novel *see* Guy Endore

WERKMEISTER BERTHOLD KRAMP, Novel *see* Rudolf Hoepner

WERTHER, Novel *see* Jaroslav Maria

WESELE, 1901, Play *see* Stanislaw Wyspianski

WESNESITELNA LEHKOST BYTI, 1985, Novel *see* Milan Kundera

WEST!, New York 1922, Novel *see* Charles Alden Seltzer

WEST CASE, THE, Short Story *see* Sax Rohmer

WEST OF THE PECOS, New York 1937, Novel *see* Zane Grey

WEST OF THE WATER TOWER, New York 1923, Novel *see* Homer Croy

WEST SIDE ROMANCE, 1936, Short Story *see* Quentin Reynolds

WEST SIDE STORY, New York 1957, Play *see* Leonard Bernstein, Arthur Laurents

WESTERN UNION, Novel *see* Zane Grey

WESTERNER, THE, Story *see* Stuart N. Lake

WESTERNER, THE, Novel *see* Owen Whister

WESTERNERS, THE, New York 1901, Novel *see* Stewart Edward White

WESTWARD HO!, 1855, Novel *see* Charles Kingsley

WESTWARD PASSAGE, Boston 1931, Novel *see* Margaret Ayer Barnes

WET PARADE, THE, New York 1931, Novel *see* Upton Sinclair

WHALE FOR THE KILLING, A, Novel *see* Farley Mowat

WHALES OF AUGUST, THE, Play *see* David Berry

WHAT A CRAZY WORLD, Play *see* Alan Klein

WHAT A LIFE, New York 1938, Play *see* Clifford Goldsmith

WHAT CAN YOU EXPECT?, Short Story *see* Alice L. Tildesley

WHAT CHILDREN WILL DO, Short Story *see* Charles K. Harris

WHAT?. DEAD AGAIN, Novel *see* Neil B. Shulman

WHAT DREAMS MAY COME, Novel *see* Richard Matheson

WHAT EVER HAPPENED TO BABY JANE HUDSON?, New York 1960, Novel *see* Henry Farrell

WHAT EVERY WOMAN KNOWS, London 1908, Play *see* J. M. Barrie

WHAT HAPPENED AT 22, New York 1914, Play *see* Paul Wilstach

WHAT HAPPENED THEN?, Play *see* Lillian T. Bradley

WHAT HAPPENED TO FATHER, 1909, Short Story *see* Mary Roberts Rinehart

WHAT HAPPENED TO JONES, New York 1897, Play *see* George Broadhurst

WHAT LOVE SEES, Book *see* Susan Vreeland

WHAT MAD PURSUIT?, 1939, Short Story *see* Noel Coward

WHAT MAISIE KNEW, 1897, Novel *see* Henry James

WHAT MONEY CAN BUY, Play *see* Ben Landeck, Arthur Shirley

WHAT MONEY CAN'T BUY, New York 1915, Play *see* George Broadhurst

WHAT PRICE GLORY, New York 1924, Play *see* Maxwell Anderson, Laurence Stallings

WHAT SAY THEY?, 1939, Play *see* James Bridie

WHAT SHOULD A WOMAN DO TO PROMOTE YOUTH AND HAPPINESS, Novel *see* Mrs. Barry MacDonald

WHAT THE BUTLER SAW, London 1905, Play *see* Frederick Mouillot, Edward F. Parry

WHAT THE DEAF-MUTE HEARD, Novel *see* G. D. Gearino

WHAT THE RIVER FORETOLD, Story *see* Peter B. Kyne

WHAT WILL PEOPLE SAY?, New York 1914, Novel *see* Rupert Hughes

WHAT WOULD A GENTLEMAN DO?, Play *see* Gilbert Daylis

WHATEVER GOES UP, New York 1935, Play *see* Milton Lazarus

WHATEVER HAPPENED TO JANIE, Novel *see* Caroline B. Cooney

WHATEVER SHE WANTS, 1921, Short Story *see* Edgar Franklin

WHAT'S A FIXER FOR?, New Haven, Ct. 1928, Play *see* H. C. Potter

WHAT'S BETTER THAN MONEY, *see* James Hadley Chase

WHAT'S BRED IN THE BONE, Novel *see* Grant Allen

WHAT'S EATING GILBERT GRAPE, Novel *see* Peter Hedges

WHAT'S WRONG WITH ANGRY?, Play *see* Patrick Wilde

WHAT'S YOUR WIFE DOING?, New York 1923, Play *see* Emil Nyitray, Herbert Hall Winslow

WHAT'S-HIS-NAME, New York 1911, Novel *see* George Barr McCutcheon

WHEEL OF FATE, Play *see* Alex Atkinson

WHEEL OF LIFE, THE, New York 1923, Play *see* James B. Fagan

WHEEL SPINS, THE, Novel *see* Ethel Lina White

WHEEL, THE, New York 1921, Play *see* Winchell Smith

WHEELER DEALERS, THE, New York 1959, Novel *see* George J. W. Goodman

WHEELS, Novel *see* Arthur Hailey

WHEELS, 1970, Short Story *see* John McGahern

WHEELS OF CHANCE, THE, Novel *see* H. G. Wells

WHEELS OF FATE, *see* James Oliver Curwood

WHEELS OF TERROR, Novel *see* Sven Hassel

WHEN A MAN'S A MAN, New York 1916, Novel *see* Harold Bell Wright

WHEN BEAR CAT WENT DRY, New York 1918, Novel *see* Charles Neville Buck

WHEN CAREY CAME TO TOWN, 1915, Serial Story *see* Edith Barnard Delano

WHEN EIGHT BELLS TOLL, 1966, Novel *see* Alistair MacLean

WHEN FATE LEADS TRUMPS, Novel *see* Alice M. Roberts

WHEN GREEK MEETS GREEK, Novel *see* Paul Trent

WHEN IT WAS DARK, Novel *see* Guy Thorne

WHEN JERRY COMES HOME, Play *see* Roy Briant

WHEN JOHNNY COMES MARCHING HOME, 1914, Short Story *see* Charles Belmont Davis

WHEN KNIGHTHOOD WAS IN FLOWER, Indianapolis 1898, Novel *see* Charles Major

WHEN KNIGHTS WERE BOLD, London 1907, Play *see* Charles Marlowe

653

WHEN LADIES MEET, New York 1932, Play *see* Rachel Crothers

WHEN LEO COMES MARCHING HOME, Story *see* Sy Gomberg

WHEN LONDON SLEEPS, Play *see* Charles Darrell

WHEN LOVE DIES, Novel *see* Rathmell Wilson

WHEN LOVE GROWS COLD, Story *see* Laura Jean Libbey

WHEN MY SHIP COMES IN, New York 1915, Novel *see* Gouverneur Morris

WHEN PARIS SLEEPS, Play *see* Charles Darrell

WHEN RABBIT HOWLS, Book *see* E. Jack Neuman

WHEN SMITH MEETS SMITH, Story *see* Meredith Davis

WHEN STRANGERS MEET, New York 1956, Novel *see* Robert Bloomfield

WHEN TERROR STALKED BEHIND, 1930, Story *see* Walter W. Liggert

WHEN THE BOUGH BREAKS, Novel *see* Jonathan Kellerman

WHEN THE DALTONS RODE, New York 1931, Book *see* Emmett Dalton, Jack Jungmeyer

WHEN THE DESERT CALLS, 1920, Short Story *see* Donald McGibney

WHEN THE DEVIL WAS SICK, New York 1926, Novel *see* E. J. Rath

WHEN THE DOOR OPENED, 1920, Short Story *see* James Oliver Curwood

WHEN THE KISSING HAD TO STOP, Novel *see* Constantine Fitzgibbon

WHEN THE LEGENDS DIE, Novel *see* Hal Borland

WHEN THE MIND HEARS, *see* Harlan Lane

WHEN THE WIND BLOWS, Book *see* Raymond Briggs

WHEN WE ARE MARRIED, Sketch *see* Fred Karno

WHEN WE ARE MARRIED, London 1938, Play *see* J. B. Priestley

WHEN WE RAN, Novel *see* Keith Leopold

WHEN WE WERE TWENTY-ONE, New York 1900, Play *see* H. V. Esmond

WHEN WOMAN HATES, Play *see* Fred Bulmer

WHEN WORLDS COLLIDE, 1950, Novel *see* Edwin Balmer, Philip Wylie

WHEN'S YOUR BIRTHDAY?, 1935, Play *see* John Frederick Ballard

WHERE ANGELS FEAR TO TREAD, 1905, Novel *see* E. M. Forster

WHERE ARE THE CHILDREN, Novel *see* Mary Higgins Clark

WHERE ARE YOU GOING, WHERE HAVE YOU BEEN?, 1967, Short Story *see* Joyce Carol Oates

WHERE BONDS ARE LOOSED, New York 1918, Novel *see* E. L. Grant Watson

WHERE DID LOTTIE GO?, Short Story *see* Frances Aymar Mathews

WHERE EAGLES DARE, London 1966, Novel *see* Alistair MacLean

WHERE IS MY WANDERING BOY TONIGHT?, 1877, Song *see* Robert Lowry

WHERE IT'S AT, Play *see* Garson Kanin

WHERE LOVE HAS GONE, New York 1962, Novel *see* Harold Robbins

WHERE LOVE IS, New York 1903, Novel *see* William J. Locke

WHERE PIGEONS GO TO DIE, Book *see* R. Wright Campbell

WHERE THE BOYS ARE, Novel *see* Glendon Swarthout

WHERE THE FOREST ENDS, Story *see* Olga Printzlau

WHERE THE HEAT LIES, 1922, Short Story *see* Lillian Bennett-Thompson, George Hubbard

WHERE THE LILIES BLOOM, Book *see* Bill Cleaver, Vera Cleaver

WHERE THE RAINBOW ENDS, London 1911, Play *see* Clifford Mills, John Ramsey

WHERE THE RED FERN GROWS, Novel *see* Wilson Rawls

WHERE THE RIVERS FLOW NORTH, Novel *see* Howard Frank Mosher

WHERE THE TRAIL DIVIDES, New York 1907, Novel *see* William Otis Lillibridge

WHERE THERE'S A WILL, 1954, Play *see* R. F. Delderfield

WHERE WAS I?, 1924, Short Story *see* Edgar Franklin

WHERE'S POPPA?, Novel *see* Robert Klane

WHIFF OF HELIOTROPE, A, 1918, Short Story *see* Richard Washburn Child

WHILE PARENTS SLEEP, London 1932, Play *see* Anthony Kimmins

WHILE THE AUTO WAITS, Short Story *see* O. Henry

WHILE THE PATIENT SLEPT, New York 1930, Novel *see* Mignon G. Eberhart

WHILE THE SUN SHINES, London 1943, Play *see* Terence Rattigan

WHIP, THE, London 1909, Play *see* Henry Hamilton, Cecil Raleigh

WHIPPING, THE, New York 1930, Novel *see* Roy Flannagan

WHIPSAW, THE, 1934, Short Story *see* James Edward Grant

WHIRLIGIG OF LIFE, THE, Short Story *see* O. Henry

WHIRLIGIGS, Short Story *see* O. Henry

WHIRLPOOL, THE, Novel *see* Arthur Applin

WHIRLPOOL, THE, Play *see* George Edwardes Hall

WHIRLPOOL, THE, New York 1916, Novel *see* Victoria Morton

WHISKEY RUNNERS, THE, Story *see* Bertrand W. Sinclair

WHISKY GALORE!, 1947, Novel *see* Compton Mackenzie

WHISPER MARKET, THE, 1918, Short Story *see* W. E. Scutt

WHISPERING CANYON, THE, New York 1926, Novel *see* John Mersereau

WHISPERING CHORUS, THE, 1918, Short Story *see* Perley Poore Sheehan

WHISPERING DEATH, Novel *see* Daniel Carney

WHISPERING GABLES, Short Story *see* Agnes Platt

WHISPERING PINES, Story *see* Edith Sessions Tupper

WHISPERING SAGE, New York 1922, Novel *see* Harry Sinclair Drago, Joseph Noel

WHISPERING SMITH, New York 1906, Novel *see* Frank Hamilton Spearman

WHISPERING WINDOW, THE, New York 1936, Novel *see* Cortland Fitzsimmons

WHISPERING WIRES, New York 1918, Novel *see* Henry Leverage

WHISPERING WOMAN, Novel *see* Gerald Verner

WHISPERS, Novel *see* Dean R. Koontz

WHISTLE BLOWER, THE, Novel *see* John Hale

WHISTLE DOWN THE WIND, London 1958, Novel *see* Mary Hayley Bell

WHISTLE STOP, Novel *see* Maritta Martin Wolff

WHISTLING DICK'S CHRISTMAS STOCKING, 1909, Short Story *see* O. Henry

WHISTLING IN THE DARK, New York 1932, Play *see* Edward Childs Carpenter, Laurence Gross

WHITE AND YELLOW, 1905, Short Story *see* Jack London

WHITE BANNERS, Boston 1936, Novel *see* Lloyd C. Douglas

WHITE BIRD PASSES, THE, Autobiography *see* Jessie Kesson

WHITE BUFFALO, THE, Novel *see* Richard Sale

WHITE BUS, Short Story *see* Shelagh Delaney

WHITE CARGO, 1925, Novel *see* Ida Vera Simonton

WHITE CARPET, Short Story *see* Bryan Edgar Wallace

WHITE CAT, THE, New York 1907, Novel *see* Gelett Burgess

WHITE CLIFFS, THE, Poem *see* Alice Duer Miller

WHITE COCKATOO, THE, New York 1933, Novel *see* Mignon G. Eberhart

WHITE COLLARS, New York 1923, Play *see* Edith Ellis

WHITE COLT, THE, New York 1967, Novel *see* David Rook

WHITE COOLIES, Diary *see* Betty Jeffrey

WHITE DESERT, THE, New York 1922, Novel *see* Courtney Ryley Cooper

WHITE DOG, Novel *see* Romain Gary

WHITE DOVE, THE, New York 1899, Novel *see* William J. Locke

WHITE FACE, London 1930, Novel *see* Edgar Wallace

WHITE FANG, New York 1905, Novel *see* Jack London

WHITE FLANNELS, 1925, Short Story *see* Lucian Cary

WHITE FRONTIER, THE, Story *see* Jeffrey Deprend

WHITE GOLD, New York 1925, Play *see* J. Palmer Parsons

WHITE GUARD, THE, Play *see* Mikhail Bulgakov

WHITE HANDS, 1927, Short Story *see* Arthur Stringer

WHITE HEAT, Story *see* Virginia Kellogg

WHITE HEAT, Novel *see* Pan

WHITE HEATHER, THE, London 1897, Play *see* Henry Hamilton, Cecil Raleigh

WHITE HEN, THE, Novel *see* Phyllis Campbell

WHITE HOPE, THE, Novel *see* W. H. R. Trowbridge

WHITE HUNTER, BLACK HEART, Novel *see* Peter Viertel

WHITE INVADER, THE, Novel *see* James Warner Bellah

WHITE LIES, Boston 1857, Novel *see* Charles Reade

WHITE LILAC, Play *see* Ladislaus Fodor

WHITE MAN, THE, Indianapolis 1919, Novel *see* George Agnew Chamberlain

WHITE MAN'S CHANCE, A, Short Story *see* Johnston McCulley

WHITE MICE, New York 1909, Novel *see* Richard Harding Davis

WHITE MISCHIEF, Book *see* James Fox

WHITE MOLL, THE, New York 1920, Novel *see* Frank L. Packard

WHITE MONKEY, THE, London 1924, Novel *see* John Galsworthy

WHITE MOUSE, THE, Story *see* James Oliver Curwood

WHITE OX, THE, Novel *see* Osman Sahin

WHITE PALACE, Novel *see* Glenn Savan

WHITE PANTS WILLIE, Novel *see* Elmer Holmes Davis

WHITE PARADE, THE, New York 1934, Novel *see* Rian James

WHITE PEACOCK FEATHERS, THE, Story *see* Du Vernet Rabell

WHITE PEARL, THE, Story *see* Edith Barnard Delano

WHITE RAT, THE, Story *see* K. R. G. Browne

WHITE ROOK, THE, New York 1918, Novel *see* John Harris-Burland

WHITE ROSE OF THE WILDS, THE, Short Story *see* Bret Harte

WHITE SHADOWS IN THE SOUTH SEAS, New York 1919, Novel *see* Frederick O'Brien

WHITE SILENCE, 1900, Short Story *see* Jack London

WHITE SISTER, THE, New York 1909, Novel *see* F. Marion Crawford

WHITE SLAVE, THE, Play *see* Bartley Campbell

WHITE SLIPPERS, Novel *see* Charles Edholm

WHITE SOUTH, THE, Novel *see* Hammond Innes

WHITE STOCKING, THE, Short Story *see* D. H. Lawrence

WHITE TOWER, THE, 1945, Novel *see* James Ramsay Ullman

WHITE WITCH DOCTOR, 1950, Novel *see* Louise A. Stinetorf

WHITEWASHED WALLS, Short Story *see* Ethel Dorrance, James Dorrance

WHO?, *see* Algis Budrys

WHO AM I?, 1918, Short Story *see* Max Brand

WHO AM I THIS TIME?, 1968, Short Story *see* Kurt Vonnegut Jr.

WHO CARES? A STORY OF ADOLESCENCE, Boston 1919, Novel *see* Cosmo Hamilton

WHO COULD ASK FOR ANYTHING MORE, 1943, Novel *see* Kay Swift

WHO GETS THE DRUMSTICK, New York 1965, Novel *see* Helen Beardsley

WHO GOES NEXT?, Play *see* J. W. Drawbell, Reginald Simpson

WHO GOES THERE?, Play *see* Henry A. Du Souchet

WHO GOES THERE?, Story *see* Don A. Stuart

WHO GOES THERE!, London 1951, Play *see* John Dighton

WHO GOES THERE, New York 1915, Novel *see* Robert W. Chambers

WHO HAS SEEN THE WIND, Novel *see* W. O. Mitchell

WHO IS JULIA?, Novel *see* Barbara S. Harris

WHO IS KILLING THE GREAT CHEFS OF EUROPE?, Novel *see* Ivan Lyons, Nan Lyons

WHO IS SYLVIA?, London 1950, Play *see* Terence Rattigan

WHO KILLED AUNT AGGIE?, New York 1939, Novel *see* Medora Field

WHO KILLED HARRY FIELD?, Novel *see* Colin Dexter

WHO KILLED PIXOTE?, Book *see* Jose Loureiro

WHO KILLED SIR HARRY OAKES?, Book *see* Marshall Houts

WHO KNOWS?, 1916, Short Story *see* Ethel Dorrance, James Dorrance

WHO LIE IN GAOL, Novel *see* Joan Henry

WHO RIDES WITH WYATT?, New York 1955, Novel *see* Will Henry

WHO WAS THAT LADY?, Play *see* Norman Krasna

WHOLE TOWN'S TALKING, THE, New York 1923, Play *see* John Emerson, Anita Loos

WHOLE TRUTH, THE, Television Play *see* Philip MacKie

WHO'S AFRAID OF VIRGINIA WOLF?, New York 1962, Play *see* Edward Albee

WHOSE LIFE IS IT ANYWAY?, 1978, Play *see* Brian Clark

WHOSE WIDOW, Short Story *see* Elinor Chipp

WHOSOEVER SHALL OFFEND, Novel *see* Marion Crawford

WHY HAVE THEY TAKEN OUR CHILDREN?, Book *see* Jackie Bough, Jefferson Morgan

WHY I AM HERE, Story *see* James Oliver Curwood

WHY I QUIT SYNDICATED CRIME, 1956, Book *see* Jim Vaus

WHY ME?, Novel *see* Donald E. Westlake

WHY MEN LEAVE HOME, New York 1922, Play *see* Avery Hopwood

WHY NOT?, New York 1915, Novel *see* Margaret Widdemer

WHY NOT STAY FOR BREAKFAST?, Play *see* Ray Cooney, Gene Stone

WHY ROCK THE BOAT?, Novel *see* William Weintraub

WHY RUSTLERS NEVER WIN, Novel *see* Henry Gregor Felsen

WHY SHOOT THE TEACHER?, Novel *see* Max Braithwaite

WHY SHOULD I CRY?, Story *see* I. A. R. Wylie

WHY SMITH LEFT HOME, New York 1899, Play *see* George Broadhurst

WHY THE WHALES CAME, Novel *see* Michael Morpurgo

WHY WOMEN SIN, New York 1903, Play *see* Will C. Murphy

WICKED, Novel *see* Arthur Applin

WICKED FLEE, THE, Novel *see* Anne Hocking

WICKED WASTER, Novel *see* MacKinlay Kantor

WICKED WOMAN, New York 1933, Novel *see* Anne Austin

WIDE BOYS NEVER WORK, Novel *see* Robert Westerby

WIDE GUY, THE, Novel *see* Anthony Armstrong

WIDE SARGASSO SEA, Novel *see* Jean Rhys

WIDECOMBE FAIR, Novel *see* Eden Philpotts

WIDOW, Novel *see* Lynn Caine

WIDOW BY PROXY, New York 1913, Play *see* Catherine Chisholm Cushing

WIDOW MAKERS, THE, Novel *see* Michael Blankfort

WIDOW, THE, Novel *see* Susannah York

WIDOWING OF MRS. HOLROYD, THE, Play *see* D. H. Lawrence

WIDOWS ARE DANGEROUS, London 1953, Play *see* June Garland

WIDOW'S EVENING, 1931, Short Story *see* I. A. R. Wylie

WIDOW'S ISLAND, Novel *see* Mario Fort, Ralph Vanio

WIDOW'S MIGHT, THE, 1931, Play *see* Frederick Jackson

WIDOW'S MIGHT, THE, 1931, Story *see* Reita Lambert

WIDOW'S WALK, Novel *see* Andrew Coburn

WIE ANNE BABI JOWAGER HAUSHALTET UND WIE ES IHM MIT DEM., Soleure 1843-44, Novel *see* Jeremias Gotthelf

WIE D'WAHRHEIT WURKT, Zurich 1886, Play *see* August Corrodi

WIE EIN STURMWIND, Novel *see* Klaus Hellmer

WIE ULI DER KNECHT GLUCKLICH WIRD, Zurich 1841, Novel *see* Jeremias Gotthelf

WIE WIESELI SEINEN WEG FAND, Gotha 1878, Novel *see* Johanna Spyri

WIENER BLUT, Operetta *see* Johann Strauss

WIERNA RZEKA, 1912, Novel *see* Stefan Zeromski

WIFE BY PURCHASE, A, London 1909, Novel *see* Paul Trent

WIFE FOR WIFE, Play *see* John A. Stephens

WIFE IN NAME ONLY, Story *see* Bertha M. Clay

WIFE OF THE CENTAUR, 1923, Novel *see* Cyril Hume

WIFE OR TWO, A, Play *see* Roland Daniel, C. B. Poultney

WIFE VERSUS SECRETARY, 1935, Short Story *see* Faith Baldwin

WIFE WHO WASN'T WANTED, THE, London 1923, Novel *see* Gertie Wentworth-James

WIFE WHOM GOD FORGOT, THE, Novel *see* Cecil H. Bullivant

WILBY CONSPIRACY, THE, Novel *see* Peter Driscoll

WILCAT HETTY, Play *see* Florence Kilpatrick

WILD AT HEART, Novel *see* Barry Gifford

WILD BEAUTY, New York 1930, Novel *see* Mateel Howe Farnham

WILD BILL HICKOK THE PRINCE OF THE PISTOLEROS, Garden City, N.Y. 1934, Novel *see* Frank J. Wilstach

WILD BIRDS, New York 1925, Play *see* Dan Totheroh

WILD BULL'S LAIR, THE, Story *see* Frank M. Clifton

WILD CALENDAR, Novel *see* Libbie Block

WILD CARGO, New York 1932, Book *see* Edward S. Anthony, Frank Buck

WILD ELEPHANT, THE, Short Story *see* Jalal Din, Lois Roth

WILD FAWN, THE, 1920, Short Story *see* Mary Imlay Taylor

WILD GEESE, New York 1925, Novel *see* Martha Ostenso

WILD GEESE CALLING, Novel *see* Stewart Edward White

WILD GEESE, THE, Novel *see* Daniel Carney

WILD GOOSE CHASE, THE, Play *see* William C. de Mille

WILD GOOSE, GOLDEN GOOSE, Story *see* Lawrence G. Blochman

WILD GOOSE, THE, 1919, Short Story *see* Gouverneur Morris

WILD HARVEST, New York 1960, Novel *see* Stephen Longstreet

WILD HEATHER, Play *see* Dorothy Brandon

WILD HONEY, 1918, Short Story *see* Vingie E. Roe

WILD HONEY, New York 1914, Novel *see* Cynthia Stockley

WILD HORSE KILLERS, THE, Novel *see* Mel Ellis

WILD HORSE MESA, Novel *see* Zane Grey

WILD JUSTICE, 1933, Play *see* James Dale

WILD MAN OF BORNEO, THE, New York 1927, Play *see* Marc Connelly, Herman J. Mankiewicz

WILD OATS LANE, New York 1922, Play *see* George Broadhurst

WILD OLIVE, THE, New York 1910, Novel *see* Basil King

WILD ORANGES, New York 1919, Novel *see* Joseph Hergesheimer

WILD PARTY, THE, 1928, Verse *see* Joseph Moncure March

WILD RIVER, Novel *see* William Bradford Huie

WILD WAVES, New York 1932, Play *see* William Ford Manley

WILD WEED, Novel *see* Arthur Hoerl

WILD, WILD CHILD, THE, 1925, Short Story *see* Steuart M. Emery

WILD YOUTH, Philadelphia 1919, Novel *see* Gilbert Parker

WILDCAT, New York 1921, Play *see* Houston Branch

WILDCAT, THE, Story *see* Wellyn Totman

WILDERNESS, Story *see* Helen Campbell

WILDERNESS, Novel *see* Dennis Danvers

WILDERNESS MAIL, THE, Short Story *see* James Oliver Curwood

WILDERNESS TRAIL, THE, New York 1913, Novel *see* Francis William Sullivan

WILDERNESS WOMAN, THE, 1926, Short Story *see* Arthur Stringer

WILDFIRE, New York 1908, Play *see* George Broadhurst, George V. Hobart

WILDFIRE, New York 1916, Novel *see* Zane Grey

WILDFLOWER, Book *see* Sara Flanigan

WILDFLOWER, Story *see* Mary Germaine

WILDSCHUT, Novel *see* Felix Thijssen

WILDWECHSEL, 1968, Play *see* Franz Xaver Kroetz

WILHELM MEISTERS LEHRJAHRE, 1795, Novel *see* Johann Wolfgang von Goethe

WILHELM TELL, 1804, Play *see* Friedrich von Schiller

WILL AND A WAY, A, Novel *see* W. W. Jacobs

WILL ANY GENTLEMAN?, London 1950, Play *see* Vernon Sylvaine

WILL SUCCESS SPOIL ROCK HUNTER?, New York 1955, Play *see* George Axelrod

WILL, THE, London 1913, Play *see* J. M. Barrie

WILLIAM BALUCHET, ROI DES DETECTIVES, Novel *see* Andre Bancey

WILLIAM PENN, Book *see* C. E. Vulliamy

WILLIAM WILSON, 1839, Short Story *see* Edgar Allan Poe

WILLIE AND JOE, 1945, Book *see* Bill Mauldin

WILLIE BOY; A DESERT MANHUNT, Balboa Island, CA. 1960, Novel *see* Harry Lawton

WILLIE THE WORM, 1926, Short Story *see* Florence Ryerson

WILLING FLESH, THE, Novel *see* Willi Heinrich

WILLKOMMEN IN MERGENTHAL, Play *see* Hans Bruhl

WILLOW TREE, THE, New York 1917, Play *see* J. H. Benrimo, Harrison Rhodes

WILT, Novel *see* Tom Sharpe

WIND ALONG THE WASTE, New York 1910, Novel *see* Maude Annesley

WIND CANNOT READ, THE, Novel *see* Richard Mason

WIND IN THE WILLOWS, THE, 1908, Novel *see* Kenneth Grahame

WIND OF THE PAMPAS, Story *see* Elynor Ewing

WIND, THE, New York 1925, Novel *see* Dorothy Scarborough

WINDFALL, London 1934, Play *see* R. C. Sherriff

WINDFALL, New York 1931, Novel *see* Robert D. Andrews

WINDING STAIR, THE, New York 1923, Novel *see* A. E. W. Mason

WINDMILL, THE, Novel *see* John Drabble

WINDMILLS OF THE GODS, Novel *see* Sidney Sheldon

WINDOM'S WAY, Novel *see* James Ramsay Ullman

WINDOW THAT MONSIEUR FORGOT, THE, Story *see* Mary Imlay Taylor

WINDS OF CHANCE, THE, New York 1918, Novel *see* Rex Beach

WINDS OF WAR, THE, Novel *see* Herman Wouk

WINDWALKER, Novel *see* Blaine M. Yorgason

WINE, 1922, Short Story *see* William Briggs MacHarg

WINE AND THE MUSIC, THE, New York 1968, Novel *see* William E. Barrett

WINE OF LIFE, THE, Novel *see* Maude Annesley

WINGED VICTORY, New York 1943, Play *see* Moss Hart

WINGLESS BIRD, THE, Novel *see* Catherine Cookson

WINGS, Story *see* Beth Slater Whitson

WINGS OF MEN, Autobiography *see* Frank Wead

WINGS OF PRIDE, New York 1913, Novel *see* Louise Kennedy Mabie

WINGS OF THE DOVE, THE, 1902, Novel *see* Henry James

WINGS OF THE HAWK, Novel *see* Gerald Drayson Adams

WINGS OF THE MORNING, New York 1903, Novel *see* Louis Tracy

WINNER TAKE ALL, New York 1920, Novel *see* Larry Evans

WINNETOU DER ROTE GENTLEMAN, Freiberg 1893, Novel *see* Karl Friedrich May

WOMEN AND WINE, New York 1900, Play *see* Ben Landeck, Arthur Shirley

WOMEN ARE BUM NEWSPAPERMEN, 1934, Short Story *see* Richard Macauley

WOMEN AREN'T ANGELS, Play *see* Vernon Sylvaine

WOMEN GO ON FOREVER, New York 1927, Play *see* Daniel N. Rubin

WOMEN IN LOVE, 1920, Novel *see* D. H. Lawrence

WOMEN IN THE WIND, New York 1935, Novel *see* Francis Walton

WOMEN MEN LOVE, Short Story *see* Charles T. Dazey

WOMEN OF BREWSTER PLACE, THE, Book *see* Gloria Naylor

WOMEN OF TWILIGHT, London 1951, Play *see* Sylvia Rayman

WOMEN, THE, New York 1936, Play *see* Clare Boothe Luce

WOMEN WHO WIN, Novel *see* Mrs. E. Almez Stout

WOMEN'S ROOM, THE, Novel *see* Marilyn French

WON BY A HEAD, Novel *see* John Gabriel

WONDERFUL ADVENTURE, THE, Play *see* Captain Wilbur Lawson

WONDERFUL COUNTRY, THE, 1952, Novel *see* Tom Lea

WONDERFUL ONE-HORSE SHAY, THE, Poem *see* Oliver Wendell Holmes

WONDERFUL STORY, THE, Novel *see* I. A. R. Wylie

WONDERFUL THING, THE, New York 1920, Play *see* Lillian T. Bradley, Forrest Halsey

WONDERFUL VISIT, THE, 1895, Novel *see* H. G. Wells

WONDERFUL WIZARD OF OZ, THE, Chicago 1900, Novel *see* L. Frank Baum

WONDERFUL WOOING, THE, Novel *see* Douglas Walshe

WONDERFUL YEAR, THE, Novel *see* William J. Locke

WOODEN HORSE, THE, Book *see* Eric Williams

WOODLANDERS, THE, 1877, Novel *see* Thomas Hardy

WOOLWORTH DIAMONDS, THE, Short Story *see* Hugh C. Weir

WORD, THE, Novel *see* Irving Wallace

WORDS AND MUSIC BY., 1919, Story *see* William Charles Lengel

WORLD ACCORDING TO GARP, THE, 1978, Novel *see* John Irving

WORLD FOR SALE, THE, New York 1916, Novel *see* Gilbert Parker

WORLD IN HIS ARMS, THE, 1946, Novel *see* Rex Beach

WORLD IN HIS CORNER, THE, Short Story *see* Eustace Cockrell

WORLD IN MY POCKET, THE, London 1959, Novel *see* James Hadley Chase

WORLD IS FULL OF MARRIED MEN, THE, Novel *see* Jackie Collins

WORLD OF HENRY ORIENT, THE, Boston 1958, Novel *see* Nora Johnson

WORLD OF SIN, A, Play *see* Walter Melville

WORLD OF STRANGERS, A, 1958, Novel *see* Nadine Gordimer

WORLD OF SUZIE WONG, THE, Novel *see* Richard Mason

WORLD OWES ME A LIVING, THE, Novel *see* John Llewellyn-Rhys

WORLD STRUGGLE FOR OIL, THE, 1924, Article *see* Isaac Frederick Marcosson

WORLD THE FLESH AND THE DEVIL, THE, Play *see* Lawrence Cowen

WORLD WITHOUT END, Story *see* May Edginton

WORLDLINGS, THE, New York 1900, Novel *see* Leonard Merrick

WORLDLY GOODS, 1924, Short Story *see* Sophie Kerr

WORLD'S BEST GIRL, THE, Novel *see* E. Hoskin, Coralie Stanton

WORLD'S GREAT SNARE, THE, London 1896, Novel *see* E. Phillips Oppenheim

WORM'S EYE VIEW, London 1945, Play *see* R. F. Delderfield

WORMWOOD: A DRAMA OF PARIS, London 1890, Novel *see* Marie Corelli

WORST WOMAN IN HOLLYWOOD, THE, 1924, Short Story *see* Adela Rogers St. Johns

WORTH WINNING, Novel *see* Dan Lewandowski

WOUND STRIPE, THE, 1925, Play *see* Nell Blackwell, Rowland G. Edwards

WOUNDED AND THE SLAIN, THE, 1959, Novel *see* David Goodis

WOUNDINGS, Play *see* Jeff Noon

WOYZECK, 1879, Play *see* Georg Buchner

WRATH OF GOD, THE, Novel *see* James Graham

WRATH OF THE GRAPES, THE, Novel *see* Leonard Wibberley

WRECK OF THE HESPERUS, THE, 1841, Poem *see* Henry Wadsworth Longfellow

WRECK OF THE MARY DEARE, THE, 1956, Novel *see* Hammond Innes

WRECKER, THE, 1892, Novel *see* Lloyd Osbourne, Robert Louis Stevenson

WRECKER, THE, London 1927, Play *see* Bernard Merivale, Arnold Ridley

WRECKING BOSS, THE, 1919, Short Story *see* Frank L. Packard

WRECKING CREW, THE, Greenwich, Ct. 1963, Novel *see* Donald Hamilton

WRITING ON THE WALL, THE, New York 1909, Play *see* Olga Nethersole

WRITTEN ON THE WIND, 1946, Novel *see* Robert Wilder

WRONG BOX, THE, London 1889, Novel *see* Lloyd Osbourne, Robert Louis Stevenson

WRONG COAT, THE, Story *see* Harold MacGrath

WRONG DOOR, THE, 1917, Serial Story *see* Jesse Lynch Williams

WRONG MR. WRIGHT, THE, Play *see* George Broadhurst

WRONG NUMBER, Play *see* Norman Edwards

WRONG VENUS, THE, New York 1966, Novel *see* Charles Williams

WRONG WOMAN, THE, Play *see* Fawcett Lomax

WU MING YING XIONG, Play *see* Du Xuan

WUNDER DER LIEBE, DAS, Bielefeld 1969, Book *see* Oswald Kolle

WUNDERBAR, DIE, 1930, Play *see* Karl Farkas, Geza Herczeg, Robert Katscher

WUNDERBAREN JAHRE, DIE, Novel *see* Reiner Kunze

WUREN HECAI, Novel *see* Wang Shuo

WUTHERING HEIGHTS, London 1847, Novel *see* Emily Jane Bronte

WYATT EARP - FRONTIER MARSHAL, New York 1931, Book *see* Stuart N. Lake

WYNGATE SAHIB, Novel *see* Joan Sutherland

WYOMING, A STORY OF THE OUTDOOR WEST, New York 1908, Novel *see* William MacLeod Raine

WYOMING WILDCATTERS, Short Story *see* Harry Whittington

X V REX, London 1933, Novel *see* Philip MacDonald

XALA, 1973, Novel *see* Ousmane Sembene

XI YOU JI, 1592, Novel *see* Wu Chengen

XIANGYANG DE GUSHI, Novel *see* Xu Ying

XIAO BAI QI DE FENG BO, Novel *see* Ji Xuexu

XIAO ERHEI JIEHUN, 1945, Short Story *see* Zhao Shuli

XIAO HUO BAN, Novel *see* Liu Zhen

XIAO SHI DE NU REN, Novel *see* Wang Shuo

XIAO XIAO, 193-, Short Story *see* Shen Congwen

XIN ER NU YING XIONG ZHUAN, Novel *see* Kong Jue, Yuan Jing

XIN JU ZHANG DAO LAI ZHI, Play *see* He Qiu

XUMAO HE TA DE NU ER MEN, Novel *see* Zhou Keqin

Y EN A MARRE, Novel *see* Jean-Michel Sorel

YABU NO NAKA, 1922, Short Story *see* Ryunosuke Akutagawa

YAGYU BUGEICHO, 1956-59, Novel *see* Kosuke Gomi

YAHUDI KI LADKI, 1915, Play *see* Aga Hashr Kashmiri

YAJU NO SEISHUN, Novel *see* Haruhiko Oyabu

YAMA, Novel *see* Aleksander Ivanovich Kuprin

YAMA-NO OTO, 1954, Novel *see* Yasunari Kawabata

YAMI NI HIRAMEKU, Story *see* Akira Yoshimura

YAMILE SOUS LES CEDRES, Novel *see* Henri Bordeaux

YAN BIBIYAN, 1933, Novel *see* Pelin Elin

YAN YANG TIAN, Novel *see* Ao Ran

YANCONA YILLIES, 1920, Short Story *see* Herschel S. Hall

YANKEE CONSUL, THE, New York 1904, Musical Play *see* Henry Martyn Blossom, Alfred G. Robyn

YANKEE DARED, A, 1933, Novel *see* Frank J. Nevins

YANKEE FROM THE WEST, A, Chicago 1879, Novel *see* Opie Read

YANKEE GIRL, THE, New York 1910, Play *see* George V. Hobart

YANKEE GOLD, Novel *see* John M. Cunningham

YANKEE PASHA: THE ADVENTURES OF JASON STARBUCK, 1941, Novel *see* Edison Marshall

YANKEL DE SCHMID, New York 1909, Play *see* David Pinski

YANZHI, Short Story *see* Pu Songling

YANZHI KOU, Novel *see* Lee Bihua

YAO, Story *see* Lu Xun

YAO, 1923, Short Story *see* Zhou Shuren

YARI NO GONZA, Play *see* Monzaemon Chikamatsu

YASHAGAIKE, 1913, Play *see* Kyoka Izumi

YASMINA, Novel *see* Theodore Valensi

Y'AVAIT UN MACCHABEE, Novel *see* Clarence Weff

YE SHAN, Novel *see* Jia Pingao

YEA YEA YEA, Novel *see* Angus McGill

YEAR IN PROVENCE, A, Book *see* Peter Mayle

YEAR OF LIVING DANGEROUSLY, THE, 1978, Novel *see* C. J. Koch

YEAR OF THE DRAGON, Novel *see* Robert Daley

YEAR OF THE GUN, Novel *see* Michael Mewshaw

YEAR OF THE HORSE, THE, New York 1965, Novel *see* Eric Hatch

YEAR THE YANKEES LOST THE PENNANT, THE, Novel *see* Douglass Wallop

YEARLING, THE, 1938, Novel *see* Marjorie K. Rawlings

YEARS AGO, Play *see* Ruth Gordon

YEARS ARE SO LONG, New York 1934, Novel *see* Josephine Lawrence

YEARS BETWEEN, THE, London 1945, Play *see* Daphne Du Maurier

YEARS OF THE LOCUST, THE, 1915, Short Story *see* Albert Payson Terhune

YEGOR BULYCHOV I DRUGIYE, 1932, Play *see* Maxim Gorky

YEGUA LUCERA, LA, Poem *see* Pedro Jara Carrillo

YEH SACH HAI, Short Story *see* Manu Bhandari

YEHOU CHUNFENG DOU GU CHENG, Novel *see* Li Yinru

YEKL, 1896, Novel *see* Abraham Cahan

YELLOW CLAW, THE, Novel *see* Sax Rohmer

YELLOW CORN, Novel *see* Upton Grey

YELLOW DOG, THE, 1918, Short Story *see* Henry Irving Dodge

YELLOW DOOR, THE, New York 1915, Novel *see* George Gibbs

YELLOW DOVE, THE, New York 1915, Novel *see* George Gibbs

YELLOW FACE, THE, Short Story *see* Arthur Conan Doyle

YELLOW FINGERS, Philadelphia 1925, Novel *see* Gene Wright

YELLOW HANDKERCHIEF, Short Story *see* Jack London

YELLOW JACK, New York 1934, Play *see* Paul de Kruif, Sidney Coe Howard

YELLOW MEN AND GOLD, New York 1911, Novel *see* Gouverneur Morris

YELLOW SANDS, London 1926, Play *see* Adelaide Philpotts, Eden Philpotts

YELLOW SEAL, THE, 1925, Short Story *see* W. C. Tuttle

YELLOW STOCKINGS, Novel *see* Wilson McArthur

YELLOW TICKET, THE, New York 1914, Play *see* Michael Morton

YELLOW TYPHOON, THE, New York 1919, Novel *see* Harold MacGrath

YELLOW WALLPAPER, THE, Short Story *see* Charlotte Perkins Gilman

YELLOWLEG, New York 1960, Novel *see* Albert Sidney Fleischman

YELLOWSTONE KELLY, 1957, Novel *see* Clay Fisher

YELLOWSTONE PETE'S ONLY DAUGHTER, Poem *see* Wallace G. Coburn

YENTL HE YESHIVA BOY, 1964, Short Story *see* Isaac Bashevis Singer

YEOMAN'S HOSPITAL, Novel *see* Helen Ashton

YER DEMIR GOT BAKIR, Novel *see* Yashar Kemal

YERMA, 1937, Play *see* Federico Garcia Lorca

YES, Opera *see* Rene Pujol, Albert Willemetz, Maurice Yvain

YES, GIORGIO, Novel *see* Anne Piper

YES MADAM?, Novel *see* K. R. G. Browne

YES, MY DARLING DAUGHTER, New York 1937, Play *see* Mark Reed

YES OR NO, New York 1917, Play *see* Arthur Frederick Goodrich

YESTERDAY'S ENEMY, Television Play *see* Peter Newman

YESTERDAY'S HEROES, 1939, Novel *see* William Brent

YESTERDAY'S WIFE, 1920, Short Story *see* Evelyn Campbell

YEUX DU COEUR, LES, Play *see* Paul Gavault

YEUX QUI CHANGENT, LES, Play *see* Cyril, Froyez

YEUX SANS VISAGE, LES, Paris 1959, Novel *see* Jean Redon

YI BAN HUO YAN, YI BAN HAI SHUI, Novel *see* Wang Shuo

YI CHANG FENG BO, Novel *see* Shi Guo

YI JIAN TIAN, Novel *see* Gu Yu

YIDDISHE KENIGEN LEAR, DER, 1889, Play *see* Jacob Gordin

YIELD TO THE NIGHT, Novel *see* Joan Henry

YISKOR, c1923, Play *see* Harry Seckler

YNGSJOMORDET, Stockholm 1951, Novel *see* Yngve Lyttkens

YOBA, Short Story *see* Ryunosuke Akutagawa

YOKE, THE, Novel *see* Hubert Wales

YOKEL BOY, New York 1939, Musical Play *see* Lew Brown, Samuel Stept, Charles Tobias

YOLANDA, New York 1905, Novel *see* Charles Major

YONDER GROW THE DAISIES, New York 1929, Novel *see* William Lipman

YONG SHI WO AI, Novel *see* Wang Shuo

YORK MYSTERY, THE, Short Story *see* Baroness Orczy

YORK STATE FOLKS, New York 1905, Play *see* Fred E. Wright

YORU NO HADA, Novel *see* Shigeko Yuki

YOSHIWARA, Novel *see* Maurice Dekobra

YOSHIWARA ENJO, Book *see* Shinichi Saito

YOTSUYA KAIDAN, Play *see* Nanboku Tsuruya

YOU AND I, New York 1923, Play *see* Philip Barry

YOU CAN'T ALWAYS TELL, Short Story *see* Harold MacGrath

YOU CAN'T ALWAYS TELL, 1925, Short Story *see* Harold MacGrath

YOU CAN'T GET AWAY WITH IT, 1913, Short Story *see* Gouverneur Morris

YOU CAN'T GO HOME AGAIN, 1940, Novel *see* Thomas Wolfe

YOU CAN'T TAKE IT WITH YOU, New York 1936, Play *see* Moss Hart, George S. Kaufman

YOU GOTTA STAY HAPPY, Serial Story *see* Robert Carson

YOU HAVE YOURSELF A DEAL, London 1966, Novel *see* James Hadley Chase

YOU JUST CAN'T WAIT, 1918, Short Story *see* Oscar Graeve

YOU MUST GET MARRIED, Novel *see* David Evans

YOU NEVER CAN TELL, Story *see* Clarence Budington Kelland

YOU NEVER CAN TELL, 1919, Short Story *see* Grace Lovell Bryan

YOU NEVER KNOW YOUR LUCK, London 1914, Novel *see* Gilbert Parker

YOU NEVER SAW SUCH A GIRL, New York 1919, Novel *see* George Weston

YOU ONLY LIVE TWICE, London 1964, Novel *see* Ian Fleming

YOU PAY YOUR MONEY, Novel *see* Michael Cronin

YOU REMEMBER ELLEN, Poem *see* Thomas Moore

YOU WERE THERE, Book *see* Thelma Strabel

YOU'LL NEVER SEE ME AGAIN, Short Story *see* Cornell Woolrich

YOUNG AMERICA, New York 1915, Play *see* John Frederick Ballard

YOUNG AND THE BRAVE, THE, Novel *see* Ronald Davidson, Harry M. Slott

YOUNG AND THE GUILTY, THE, Television Play *see* Ted Willis

YOUNG APOLLO, Novel *see* Anthony Gibbs

YOUNG APRIL, New York 1899, Novel *see* Egerton Castle

YOUNG ARCHIMEDES, 1924, Novel *see* Aldous Huxley

YOUNG COLLEGIAN, THE, Play *see* T. W. Robertson

YOUNG DIANA, THE, 1918, Novel *see* Marie Corelli

YOUNG EVE AND OLD ADAM, Novel *see* Tom Gallon

YOUNG GOODMAN BROWN, 1846, Short Story *see* Nathaniel Hawthorne

YOUNG LIONS, THE, 1948, Novel *see* Irwin Shaw

YOUNG LORD STRANLEIGH, Story *see* Robert Barr

YOUNG LOVERS, THE, New York 1955, Novel *see* Julian Halevy

YOUNG MAN OF MANHATTAN, New York 1930, Novel *see* Katharine Brush

YOUNG MAN WITH A HORN, 1938, Novel *see* Dorothy Baker

YOUNG MRS. WINTHROP, THE, New York 1882, Play *see* Bronson Howard

YOUNG NOWHERES, 1927, Short Story *see* I. A. R. Wylie

YOUNG NUTS OF AMERICA, THE, 1923, Short Story *see* Irvin S. Cobb

YOUNG PERSON IN PINK, THE, London 1920, Play *see* Gertrude E. Jennings

YOUNG PIONEERS, Novel *see* Rose Wilder Lane

YOUNG ROMANCE, Play *see* William C. de Mille

YOUNG SANCHEZ, 1959, Short Story *see* Ignacio Aldecoa

YOUNG SINNERS, New York 1929, Play *see* Elmer Harris

YOUNG WIDOW, Novel *see* Clarissa Fairchild Cushman

YOUNG WIVES' TALE, London 1949, Play *see* Ronald Jeans

YOUNG WOODLEY, London 1928, Play *see* John Van Druten

YOUNGBLOOD HAWKE, New York 1962, Novel *see* Herman Wouk

YOUNGEST OF THREE, THE, 1905, Play *see* H. F. Maltby

YOUNGEST PROFESSION, THE, 1940, Book *see* Lillian Day

YOUR ARKANSAS TRAVELER, 1953, Short Story *see* Budd Schulberg

YOUR FRIEND AND MINE, Play *see* Willard Mack

YOUR TICKET IS NO LONGER VALID, Novel *see* Romain Gary

YOUR UNCLE DUDLEY, New York 1929, Play *see* Howard Lindsay, Bertrand Robinson

YOUR UNCLE WILLIAM, Short Story *see* Michael Kane

YOU'RE A BIG BOY NOW, London 1963, Novel *see* David Benedictus

YOU'RE BEST ALONE, Novel *see* Peter Curtis

YOU'RE IN THE ARMY NOW, Story *see* Bennett Southard, Elsie Werner

YOU'RE NOT SERIOUS WHEN YOU'RE SEVENTEEN, Novel *see* Barbara Samson

YOU'RE ONLY HUMAN ONCE, 1944, Autobiography *see* Grace Moore

YOUTH AT THE HELM, Play *see* Paul Vulpuis

YOUTH TRIUMPHANT, New York 1921, Novel *see* George Gibbs

YOUTHFUL FOLLY, Play *see* Josephine Tey

YOUYI, Play *see* Wang Ying

YU LI HUN, Novel *see* Xu Zhenya

YUAN YE, 1939, Play *see* Wan Jiabao

YUE YAER, 194-, Short Story *see* Shu Qingchun

YUKI FUJIN EZU, Novel *see* Seiichi Funabashi

YUKIGUNI, 1947, Novel *see* Yasunari Kawabata

YUKI-ONNA, Short Story *see* Lafcadio Hearn

YUKON TRAIL; A TALE OF THE NORTH, THE, Boston 1917, Novel *see* William MacLeod Raine

YUREI-SEN, Novel *see* Jiro Osaragi

YUSHA NOMI, Novel *see* Kikumaru Okuda

YVETTE, 1885, Short Story *see* Guy de Maupassant

Z, Athens 1966, Novel *see* Vassilis Vassilikos

Z CESKYCH MLYNU, Play *see* Karel Tuma

Z LASKY, Novel *see* Marie Kyzlinkova

ZA DVOMA ZAYTSYAMI, 1883, Play *see* Mikhaylo Petrovich Staritsky

ZA RANNICH CERVANKU, Novel *see* Alois Vojtech Smilovsky

ZA VLAST SOVETOV, 1949, Novel *see* Valentin Kataev

ZABEC, Play *see* Josef Skruzny

ZABICIE CIOTKI, Novel *see* Andrzej Bursa

ZABRAVETE TOZI SLOUCHAI, Play *see* Georgi Danailow

ZA-BUM, Musical Play *see* Marcello Marchesi

ZADAH TELA, 1982, Novel *see* Zivojin Pavlovic

ZAHADA HLAVOLAMU, Book *see* Jaroslav Foglar

ZAIRE, 1739, *see* Voltaire

ZALACAIN EL AVENTURERO, 1909, Novel *see* Pio Baroja Y Nessi

ZANDER THE GREAT, New York 1923, Play *see* Edward Salisbury Field

ZANZIBAR, Novel *see* Alfred Andersch

ZAPADLI VLASTENCI, Novel *see* Karel Vaclav Rais

ZAPFENSTREICH, DER, Play *see* Franz Adam Beyerlein

ZAPISKI IZ MYORTVOGO DOMA, 1864, Short Story *see* Fyodor Dostoyevsky

ZAPISKI IZ PODPOLYA, 1864, Short Story *see* Fyodor Dostoyevsky

ZAPISKI SUMASSHEDSHEGO, 1835, Short Story *see* Nikolay Gogol

ZAPOMENUTE SVETLO, Novel *see* Jakub Demi

ZAPOROZHETA ZA DUNAYEM, St. Petersburg 1863, Opera *see* Semen Artemowsky

ZAPPLER, DER, Novel *see* Ernst Klee

ZAR UND ZIMMERMANN, Leipzig 1837, Opera *see* Albert Lortzing

ZAREWITSCH, DER, Play *see* Gabriele Zapolska

ZAREWITSCH, DER, Berlin 1927, Operetta *see* Franz Lehar

ZASZLOS DEMETER, 1960, Short Story *see* Andras Suto

ZATO ICHI MONOGATARI, Novel *see* Kan Shimosawa

ZAUBERBERG, DER, 1924, Novel *see* Thomas Mann

ZAUBERGEIGE, DIE, 1940, Novel *see* Kurt Kluge

ZAUBERMANNCHEN, DAS, Play *see* Gudrun Kaltofen

ZAVTRAK U PREDVODITELYA, 1856, Play *see* Ivan Turgenev

ZAVTRAKI SOROK TRET'EGO GODO, 1962, Short Story *see* Vasili Aksyonov

ZAZA, Paris 1898, Play *see* Pierre Berton, Charles Simon

ZAZDROSC I MEDYCYNA, 1932, Novel *see* Michal Choromanski

ZAZIE DANS LE METRO, Paris 1959, Novel *see* Raymond Queneau

ZAZRACNY LEKAR, Play *see* Bedrich Vrbsky

ZBEHOVE, *see* Ladislav Tazky

ZE SVETA LESNICH SAMOT, Novel *see* Karel Klostermann

ZEBRE, LE, Play *see* Paul Armont

ZEBRE, LE, Novel *see* Alexandre Jardin

ZEBRE, LE, Play *see* Jose G. Levy, Nicolas Nancey

ZEEMANSVROUWEN, 1928, Play *see* Herman Bouber

ZEHARI SAAP, Play *see* Narayan Prasad Betaab

ZEIT DE SCHULDLOSEN, 1962, Play *see* Siegfried Lenz

ZEIT ZU LEBEN UND ZEIT ZU STERBEN, 1954, Novel *see* Erich Maria Remarque

ZEKO, 1948, Short Story *see* Ivo Andric

ZELENY AUTOMOBIL, Novel *see* Josef Skruzny

ZELLE, DIE, 1968, Novel *see* Horst Bienek

ZELMAIDE; UN COLPO IN TRE ATTI, Novel *see* Giorgio Santi

ZEMSTA, 1833, Play *see* Alexander Fredro

ZEMYA, 1922, Novel *see* Pelin Elin

ZENA NA ROZCESTI Z CASOPISU PRAZANKA, Novel *see* Olga Fujerova

Film Index

39 Steps, The see THE THIRTY-NINE STEPS (1978).

4 Gesellen, Die see DIE VIER GESELLEN (1938).

40 Carats see FORTY CARATS (1973).

40 Naughty Girls see FORTY NAUGHTY GIRLS (1937).

40TH DOOR, THE 1924 d: George B. Seitz. USA., *The Fortieth Door*, Mary Hastings Bradley, New York 1920, Novel

42ND STREET 1933 d: Lloyd Bacon. USA., *42nd Street*, Bradford Ropes, New York 1932, Novel

45 Minutes from Broadway see FORTY-FIVE MINUTES FROM BROADWAY (1920).

47 Ronin, The see GENROKU CHUSHINGURA PART I (1941).

47 Ronin, The see CHUSHINGURA (1962).

47 Samurai see CHUSHINGURA (1962).

48 Hours see WENT THE DAY WELL? (1942).

'49 - '17 1917 d: Ruth Ann Baldwin. USA., *The Old West Per Contract*, William Wallace Cook, Short Story

491 see 491 (FYRAHUNDRANITTIOETT) (1964).

491 (FYRAHUNDRANITTIOETT) 1964 d: Vilgot Sjoman. SWD., *491*, Lars Gorling, Stockholm 1962, Novel

5 Advertencias de Satanas, Las see LAS CINCO ADVERTENCIAS DE SATANAS (1938).

5 Advertencias de Satanas, Las see LAS CINCO ADVERTENCIAS DE SATANAS (1969).

5 Avisos de Satanas, Os see LAS CINCO ADVERTENCIAS DE SATANAS (1969).

5 Og Spionerne, de see DE FEM OG SPIONERNE (1969).

50 Million Frenchmen see FIFTY MILLION FRENCHMEN (1931).

50 Roads Back see FIFTY ROADS TO TOWN (1937).

$5,000 REWARD 1918 d: Douglas Gerrard. USA., *My Arcadian Wife*, Charles Wesley Sanders, Short Story

$50000 JEWEL THEFT, THE 1915 d: Murdock MacQuarrie. USA., *The $50.000 Jewel Theft*, George Edwardes Hall, Story

52 Miles to Midnight see HOT RODS TO HELL (1967).

52 Miles to Terror see HOT RODS TO HELL (1967).

52 PICK-UP 1987 d: John Frankenheimer. USA., *52 Pickup*, Elmore Leonard, Novel

5:48, THE 1979 d: James Ivory. USA., *The Five Forty-Eight*, John Cheever, 1955, Short Story

5:5 see CHAMESH CHAMESH (1980).

600,000 Franc Par Mois see SIX CENT MILLE FRANCS PAR MOIS (1925).

633 SQUADRON 1964 d: Walter Grauman. UKN., *633 Squadron*, Frederick E. Smith, London 1958, Novel

7 Faces of Dr. Lao see THE SEVEN FACES OF DR. LAO (1964).

7 Fois. (Par Jour) see SEPT FOIS PAR JOUR. (1971).

7 Kleider Der Katrin, Die see DIE SIEBEN KLEIDER DER KATHRIN (1954).

7. Opfer, Das see DAS SIEBENTE OPFER (1964).

7 Times a Day see SEPT FOIS PAR JOUR. (1971).

70,000 WITNESSES 1932 d: Ralph Murphy. USA., *70.000 Witnesses*, Cortland Fitzsimmons, New York 1931, Novel

77 Park Lane see PARK LANE SEVENTY-SEVEN (1931).

79 Park Avenue see HAROLD ROBBINS' 79 PARK AVENUE (1977).

7-9-18 Da Parigi un Cadavere Per Rocky see DES PISSENLITS PAR LA RACINE (1963).

7th Cavalry see SEVENTH CAVALRY (1956).

7th Dawn, The see THE SEVENTH DAWN (1964).

7TH HEAVEN 1927 d: Frank Borzage. USA., *Seventh Heaven*, Austin Strong, New York 1922, Play

800 Leagues Over the Amazon see OCHOCIENTAS MIL LEGUAS POR EL AMAZONAS (1958).

80,000 SUSPECTS 1963 d: Val Guest. UKN., *The Pillars of Midnight*, Elleston Trevor, Novel

"813" 1920 d: Scott Sidney. USA., *813*, Maurice Leblanc, Short Stories

83 HOURS 'TIL DAWN 1990 d: Donald Wrye. USA., *83 Hours 'Til Dawn*, Barbara Jane Mackle, Book

84 CHARING CROSS ROAD 1987 d: David Jones. USA., *84 Charing Cross Road*, Helene Hanff, Book

8.47 Train, The see LE TRAIN DE 8H.47 (1934).

9½ WEEKS 1984 d: Adrian Lyne. USA., *9½ Weeks*, Elizabeth McNeill, Novel

90 Minutes After Midnight see NEUNZIG MINUTEN NACH MITTERNACHT (1962).

92° IN THE SHADE 1975 d: Thomas McGuane. USA., *Ninety-Two in the Shade*, Thomas McGuane, 1973, Novel

A BUEN JUEZ, MEJOR TESTIGO 1926 d: Federico Dean Sanchez. SPN., *El Milagro de la Vega de Toledo*, Jose Zorrilla Y Moral, Poem

A CHE SERVONO QUESTI QUATTRINI? 1942 d: Esodo Pratelli. ITL., *A Che Servono Questi Quattrini?*, Armando Curcio, Play

A CHI TOCCA..TOCCA! 1978 d: Gianfranco Baldanello, Menahem Golan. ITL/GRM/ISR., Ben Porath, Story

A CIASCUNO IL SUO 1967 d: Elio Petri. ITL., *A Ciascuno Il Suo*, Leonardo Sciasia, Turin 1966, Novel

A Divine Comedy -Purgatory see SKARSELD (1975).

A DOPPIA FACCIA 1969 d: Riccardo FredA. ITL/GRM., Edgar Wallace, Novel

A Doppia Mandata see A DOUBLE TOUR (1959).

A DOUBLE TOUR 1959 d: Claude Chabrol. FRN/ITL., *The Key to Nicholas Street*, Stanley Ellin, New York 1952, Novel

A Duo-Trio see DUETT ZU DRITT (1977).

A Escape Libre see ECHAPPEMENT LIBRE (1964).

A Fleur de Peau see GALIA (1966).

A FUERZA DE ARRASTRARSE 1924 d: Jose Buchs. SPN., Jose Echegaray, Play

A LA BELLE ETOILE 1966 d: Pierre Prevert. FRN., *The Cop and the Anthem*, O. Henry, 1906, Short Story

A la Francaise see IN THE FRENCH STYLE (1963).

A LA GUERRE COMME A LA GUERRE 1971 d: Bernard Borderie. FRN/ITL/GRM., *A la Guerre Comme a la Guerre*, Alexander Lernet-Holenia, Novel

A LAS CINCO DE LA TARDE 1960 d: Juan Antonio Bardem. SPN., *La Cornada*, Alfonso Sastre, 1960, Play

A l'Ombre du Deuxieme Bureau see LA FEMME TRAQUEE NADIA (1939).

A l'Ombre d'une Femme see FORT-DOLORES (1938).

A MI-CHEMIN DU CIEL 1930 d: Alberto Cavalcanti. FRN., *Here Comes the Bandwagon*, Henry Leyford Gates, New York 1928, Novel

A MINUIT, LE 7 1936 d: Maurice de Canonge. FRN., *L' Epouvante*, Maurice Level, Paris 1908, Novel

A MOI LES FEMMES 1915. FRN., *A Moi Les Femmes*, J. de Gramont, Play

A' Nutriccia see LA NUTRICE (1914).

..A PATY JEZDEC JE STRACH 1964 d: Zbynek Brynych. CZC., *Bez Limce Bez Krasy*, Hana Belohradska, Prague 1962, Novel

A Q ZHENGZHUAN 1981 d: Ling Fan. CHN., *A Q Zheng Zhuan*, Lu Xun, Story

A SAN FRANCISCO 1915 d: Gustavo SerenA. ITL., *A San Francisco*, Salvatore Di Giacomo, 1896, Play

A SANTA LUCIA 1917 d: Ugo FalenA. ITL., *A Santa Lucia*, Goffredo Cognetti, 1887, Play

A Te la Mala Pasqua! see MALA PASQUA (1919).

A TEPYER SUDI. 1967 d: Vladimir Dovgan. USS., *Stranitsa Dnevnika*, Aleksander Korniychuk, 1965, Play

A TOI DE FAIRE, MIGNONNE 1963 d: Bernard Borderie. FRN/ITL., Peter Cheyney, Novel

A TOI DE JOUER, CALLAGHAN 1954 d: Willy Rozier. FRN., *Callaghan a Toi de Jouer*, Peter Cheyney, Novel

..A TUTTE LE AUTO DELLA POLIZIA 1975 d: Mario Caiano. ITL., *Violenza a Roma*, Massimo Felisatti, Fabio Pittorru, Novel

A Venezia un Dicembre Rosso Shocking see DON'T LOOK NOW (1973).

A VOS ORDRES, MADAME 1942 d: Jean Boyer. FRN., *C.H.F.R. 35*, Andre Birabeau, Short Story

A Votre Sante see ILS SONT DANS LES VIGNES (1951).

a-009 Missione Hong Kong see DAS GEHEIMNIS DER DREI DSCHUNKEN (1965).

Aakaler Sandhane see AKALER SANDHANEY (1980).

AANDHI 1975 d: Gulzar. IND., *Aandhi*, Kamleshwar, Novel

AANSLAG, DE 1986 d: Fons Rademakers. NTH., **De Aanslag**, Harry Mulisch, 1982, Novel

Aarne Fran Niskavuori see NISKAVUOREN AARNE (1954).

Aarne of Niskavuori see NISKAVUOREN AARNE (1954).

AARON GILLESPIE WILL MAKE YOU A STAR 1996 d: Massimo Mazzucco. USA., *Aaron Gillespie Will Make You a Star*, Michael Capellupo, Scott Trost, Play

AARON SLICK FROM PUNKIN CRICK 1951 d: Claude Binyon. USA., *Aaron Slick from Punkin Crick*, Walter Benjamin Hare, 1919, Play

AARON'S MAGIC VILLAGE 1997 d: Albert Hanan Kaminski. USA., *Stories for Children*, Isaac Bashevis Singer

AARON'S ROD 1923 d: A. E. Coleby. UKN., *Aaron's Rod*, Sax Rohmer, Short Story

AB MITTERNACHT 1938 d: Carl Hoffmann. GRM., *Nuits de Princes*, Joseph Kessel, 1927, Novel

Abandon All Hope see LASCIATE OGNI SPERANZA (1937).

Abandon Superstitions see PO CHU MI XING (1958).

ABANICO DE LADY WINDERMERE, EL 1944 d: Juan J. OrtegA. MXC., *Lady Windermere's Fan*, Oscar Wilde, London 1892, Play

Abbe Constantin, L' see BETTINA LOVED A SOLDIER (1916).

ABBE CONSTANTIN, L' 1925 d: Julien Duvivier. FRN., *L' Abbe Constantin*, Ludovic Halevy, France 1882, Novel

ABBE CONSTANTIN, L' 1933 d: Jean-Paul Paulin. FRN., *L' Abbe Constantin*, Ludovic Halevy, France 1882, Novel

Abbess, The see NASTY HABITS (1976).

ABBEY GRANGE, THE 1922 d: George Ridgwell. UKN., *The Abbey Grange*, Arthur Conan Doyle, Short Story

Abbey Grange, The see THE RETURN OF SHERLOCK HOLMES: THE ABBEY GRANGE (1986).

ABC MURDERS, THE 1966 d: Frank Tashlin. UKN., *The A.B.C. Murders*, Agatha Christie, London 1936, Novel

ABC MURDERS, THE 1992 d: Andrew Grieve. UKN., *The A.B.C. Murders*, Agatha Christie, London 1936, Novel

ABDICATION, THE 1974 d: Anthony Harvey. UKN., *The Abdication*, Ruth Wolff, Play

Abduction in Yellow see POHISHTENIE V ZHALTO (1980).

ABDUCTION OF SAINT ANNE, THE 1975 d: Harry Falk. USA., *The Issue of the Bishop's Blood*, Thomas Patrick McMahon, Novel

ABDUL THE DAMNED 1935 d: Karl Grune. UKN., *Abdul the Damned*, Robert Neumann, Novel

ABDULLA THE GREAT 1954 d: Gregory Ratoff. UKN/USA., *My Kingdom for a Woman*, Ismet Regeila, Short Story

Abdullah's Harem see ABDULLA THE GREAT (1954).

Abdulla's Harem see ABDULLA THE GREAT (1954).

ABE LINCOLN IN ILLINOIS 1940 d: John Cromwell. USA., *Abe Lincoln of Illinois*, R. E. Sherwood, New York 1938, Play

ABEL SANCHEZ 1946 d: Carlos Serrano de OsmA. SPN., *Abel Sanchez: Una Historia de Pasion*, Miguel de Unamuno, 1917, Novel

ABELHA NA CHUVA, UMA 1971 d: Fernando Lopes. PRT., *Uma Abelha Na Chuva*, Carlos Oliveira, 1953, Novel

Abenteuer Aus 1000 Nachts, Ein see DIE GESCHICHTE VOM KLEINEN MUCK (1953).

Abenteuer Des Kleinen Muck see DIE GESCHICHTE VOM KLEINEN MUCK (1953).

Abenteuer Des Til Ulenspiegel, Die see LES AVENTURES DE TILL L'ESPIEGLE (1956).

ABENTEUER DES WERNER HOLT, DIE 1963 d: Joachim Kunert. GDR., *Die Abenteuer Des Werner Holt*, Dieter Noll, Novel

Abenteuer in Wien see GEFAHRLICHES ABENTEUER (1953).

ABENTEURER G.M.B.H., DIE 1929 d: Fred Sauer. GRM., *The Secret Adversary*, Agatha Christie, Novel

ABHIJAN 1962 d: Satyajit Ray. IND., *Abhiyan*, Tarasankar Bandyopadhyay, 1946, Novel

Abhiyan see ABHIJAN (1962).

Abhorrence see ISZONY (1965).

ACTORS AND SIN 1952 d: Ben Hecht. USA., *Actor's Blood*, Ben Hecht, 1936, Short Story, *Concerning a Woman of Sin*, Ben Hecht, 1945, Short Story

Actors, The *see* **KOMODIANTEN** (1941).

Actress and Angel *see* **THE BUTTER AND EGG MAN** (1928).

ACTRESS, THE 1928 d: Sidney A. Franklin. USA., *Trelawny of the Wells*, Arthur Wing Pinero, London 1898, Play

ACTRESS, THE 1953 d: George Cukor. USA., *Years Ago*, Ruth Gordon, Play

Actresses *see* **ACTRIUS** (1996).

ACTRIUS 1996 d: Ventura Pons. SPN., *E.R.*, Josep M. Benet I Jornet, Play

Acts of Love *see* **CARRIED AWAY** (1996).

ADA 1961 d: Daniel Mann. USA., *Ada Dallas*, Wirt Williams, New York 1959, Novel

ADALENS POESI 1928 d: Theodor Berthels. SWD., *Karnfolkunnel*, Pelle Molin, 1897, Short Story

ADALENS POESI 1948 d: Ivar Johansson. SWD., *Karnfolk*, Pelle Molin, 1897, Short Story

ADAM A EVA 1940 d: Karel SpelinA. CZC., *Adam a Eva*, Anna Ziegloserova, Novel

ADAM AND EVA 1923 d: Robert G. VignolA. USA., *Adam and Eva*, Guy Bolton, George Middleton, New York 1923, Play

Adam and Eva *see* **ADAM A EVA** (1940).

Adam and Eva *see* **SEPT FOIS PAR JOUR.** (1971).

ADAM BEDE 1918 d: Maurice Elvey. UKN., *Adam Bede*, George Eliot, 1859, Novel

ADAM BEDE 1991 d: Giles Foster. UKN., *Adam Bede*, George Eliot, 1859, Novel

ADAM EST. EVE 1953 d: Rene Gaveau. FRN., *Adam Est Eve*, Francis Didelot, Novel

Adam Est Eve -la Nouvelle Legende Des Sexes *see* **ADAM EST. EVE** (1953).

ADAM HAD FOUR SONS 1941 d: Gregory Ratoff. USA., *Legacy*, Charles Bonner, Novel

Adam Is Eve -the New Legend of the Sexes *see* **ADAM EST. EVE** (1953).

Adama *see* **ADAMAH** (1947).

ADAMAH 1947 d: Helmar Lerski. ISR., *Ziegfried Lehman*, Story

Adam's Evening *see* **HIS EXCITING NIGHT** (1938).

Adam's Tree *see* **L' ALBERO DI ADAMO** (1936).

Adamson of Africa *see* **KILLERS OF KILIMANJARO** (1959).

ADARSHA HINDU HOTEL 1957 d: Ardhendu Sen. IND., *Adarsha Hindu Hotel*, Bibhutibhushan Bannerjee, 1940, Novel

ADDING MACHINE, THE 1969 d: Jerome Epstein. UKN/USA., *The Adding machine*, Elmer Rice, March 1923, Play

ADDIO AMORE 1916 d: Alberto Carlo Lolli. ITL., *Addio Amore!*, Matilde Serao, 1896, Novel

ADDIO, AMORE! 1944 d: Gianni Franciolini. ITL., *Addio Amore!*, Matilde Serao, 1896, Novel, *Castigo*, Matilde Serao, 1893, Novel

ADDIO FRATELLO CRUDELE 1971 d: Giuseppe Patroni Griffi. ITL., *'Tis Pity She's a Whore*, John Ford, 1633, Play

ADDIO GIOVINEZZA! 1913 d: Sandro Camasio. ITL., *Addio Giovinezza*, Sandro Camasio, Nino Oxilia, 1911, Play

ADDIO GIOVINEZZA 1918 d: Augusto GeninA. ITL., *Addio Giovinezza*, Sandro Camasio, Nino Oxilia, 1911, Play

ADDIO GIOVINEZZA 1927 d: Augusto GeninA. ITL., *Addio Giovinezza*, Sandro Camasio, Nino Oxilia, 1911, Play

ADDIO, GIOVINEZZA! 1940 d: Ferdinando M. Poggioli. ITL., *Addio Giovinezza*, Sandro Camasio, Nino Oxilia, 1911, Play

ADDIO, KIRA! 1942 d: Goffredo Alessandrini. ITL., *We the Living*, Ayn Rand, 1936, Novel

Addio Lara! *see* **J'AI TUE RASPOUTINE** (1967).

ADDIO, MIA BELLA NAPOLI! 1946 d: Mario Bonnard. ITL., *Addio Mia Bella Napoli!*, Ernesto Murolo, 1910, Play

ADDIO MIMI! 1947 d: Carmine Gallone. ITL., *La Boheme*, Giuseppe Giacosa, Luigi Illica, Giacomo Puccini, Turin 1896, Opera

ADDRESS UNKNOWN 1944 d: William Cameron Menzies. USA., *Address Unknown*, Kressman Taylor, 1938, Novel

ADELA 1985 d: Mircea Veroiu. RMN., *AdelA. Fragment Din Jurnalul Lui Emil Codrescu*, Garabet Ibraileanu, 1933, Novel

ADELAIDE 1968 d: Jean-Daniel Simon. FRN/ITL., *Adelaide*, Joseph Arthur de Gobineau, Paris 1913, Play

ADELE 1919 d: Wallace Worsley. USA., *The Nurse's Story: in Which Reality Meets Romance*, Adele Bleneau, Indianapolis 1915, Novel

Adieu *see* **ABSCHIED** (1968).

ADIEU CHERIE 1945 d: Raymond Bernard. FRN., *Adieu Cherie*, Jacques Companeez, Alex Joffe, Short Story

ADIEU L'AMI 1968 d: Jean Herman. FRN/ITL., *Adieu l'Ami*, Sebastien Japrisot, Novel

ADIEU LES BEAUX JOURS 1933 d: Johannes Meyer, Andre Beucler. FRN., *Die Schonen Tage von Aranjuez*, Robert A. Stemmle, Hans Szekely, Play

Adios *see* **THE LASH** (1930).

ADIOS, CORDERA 1966 d: Pedro Mario Herrero. SPN., *Cordera! Adios*, Leopoldo Alas, 1892, Short Story

ADIOS GRINGO 1965 d: Giorgio Stegani. ITL/FRN/SPN., *Adios*, Harry Whittington, Novel

ADJUNKT VRBA 1929 d: M. J. Krnansky. CZC., *Adjunkt Vrba*, Jan Klecanda, Novel

ADJUTANT SEINER HOHEIT, DER 1933 d: Martin Fric. GRM/CZC., *Kasta Pro Sebe*, Emil Artur Longen, Play

Ad-Man *see* **NO MARRIAGE TIES** (1933).

ADMIRABLE CRICHTON, THE 1918 d: G. B. Samuelson. UKN., *The Admirable Crichton*, J. M. Barrie, London 1902, Play

Admirable Crichton, The *see* **MALE AND FEMALE** (1919).

ADMIRABLE CRICHTON, THE 1957 d: Lewis Gilbert. UKN., *The Admirable Crichton*, J. M. Barrie, London 1902, Play

ADMIRALS ALL 1935 d: Victor Hanbury. UKN., *Admirals All*, Ian Hay, Stephen King-Hall, London 1934, Play

ADMIRAL'S SECRET, THE 1934 d: Guy Newall. UKN., *The Admiral's Secret*, Cyril Campion, Edward Dignon, 1928, Play

Adolf Hitler: the Bunker *see* **THE BUNKER** (1981).

Adolfo Hitler Alias Il Mio Zio *see* **ZIO ADOLFO IN ARTE FUHRER** (1978).

Adolphe Or the Awkard Age *see* **ADOLPHE OU L'AGE TENDRE** (1968).

ADOLPHE OU L'AGE TENDRE 1968 d: Bernard Toublanc-Michel. FRN/GRM/PLN., *Adolphe*, Henri-Benjamin Constant de Rebeque, 1816, Novel

Adopted Father, The *see* **THE WORKING MAN** (1933).

ADOPTED SON, THE 1917 d: Charles J. Brabin. USA., *The Adopted Son*, Max Brand, 1917, Short Story

ADORABLE DECEIVER, THE 1926 d: Phil Rosen. USA., *Triple Trouble*, Harry O. Hoyt, Short Story

Adorable Julia *see* **DU BIST ZAUBERHAFT JULIA** (1962).

Adorable Julie *see* **DU BIST ZAUBERHAFT JULIA** (1962).

ADORABLE SAVAGE, THE 1920 d: Norman Dawn. USA., *Marama: a Tale of the South Pacific*, Ralph Stock, Boston 1913, Novel

Adorable Sinner *see* **KATJA** (1959).

Adorobile Idiota, Un' *see* **UNE RAVISSANTE IDIOTE** (1964).

ADRIANA LECOUVREUR 1919 d: Ugo FalenA. ITL., *Adrienne Lecouvreur*, Ernest Legouve, Eugene Scribe, Paris 1849, Play

ADRIANA LECOUVREUR 1956 d: Guido Salvini. ITL., *Adrienne Lecouvreur*, Ernest Legouve, Eugene Scribe, Paris 1849, Play

Adrienne Gascoyne *see* **HEARTS OR DIAMONDS?** (1918).

ADRIENNE LECOUVREUR 1913 d: Louis Mercanton, Henri Desfontaines. FRN., *Adrienne Lecouvreur*, Ernest Legouve, Eugene Scribe, Paris 1849, Play

Adrienne Lecouvreur *see* **DREAM OF LOVE** (1928).

Adrienne Lecouvreur; Or, an Actress's Romance *see* **ADRIENNE LECOUVREUR** (1913).

ADULTERA, L' 1946 d: Duilio Coletti. ITL., *I Padri Etruschi*, Tullio Pinelli, 1941, Play

Adulteress, The *see* **L' ADULTERA** (1946).

Adulteress, The *see* **THERESE RAQUIN** (1953).

ADULTERIO CASI DECENTE, UN 1969 d: Rafael Gil. SPN., *Un Adulterio Decente*, Enrique Jardiel Poncela, 1935, Play

Adulterio Decente, Un *see* **UN ADULTERIO CASI DECENTE** (1969).

Advance to Ground Zero *see* **NIGHTBREAKER** (1989).

ADVANCE TO THE REAR 1964 d: George Marshall. USA., *Company of Cowards*, Jack Schaefer, 1957, Novel

Advantage *see* **AVANTAZH** (1978).

ADVENT 1956 d: Vladimir Vlcek. CZC., *Advent*, Jarmila Glazarova, 1950, Novel

ADVENTURE 1925 d: Victor Fleming. USA., *Adventure*, Jack London, London 1911, Novel

ADVENTURE 1945 d: Victor Fleming. USA., *Adventure*, Clyde Brion Davis, Novel

ADVENTURE GIRL 1934 d: Herman C. Raymaker. USA., *The Cradle of the Deep*, Joan Lowell, New York 1920, Novel

Adventure in Berlin *see* **DIE SPUR FUHRT NACH BERLIN** (1952).

ADVENTURE IN HEARTS, AN 1920 d: James Cruze. USA., *Captain Dieppe*, Anthony Hope, New York 1900, Novel

Adventure in Indo-China *see* **LA RIVIERE DES TROIS JONQUES** (1956).

ADVENTURE IN IRAQ 1943 d: D. Ross Lederman. USA., *The Green Goddess*, William Archer, New York 1921, Play

ADVENTURE IN MANHATTAN 1936 d: Edward Ludwig. USA., *Purple and Fine Linen*, May Edginton, 1926, Short Story

ADVENTURE IN THE HOPFIELDS 1954 d: John Guillermin. UKN., *The Hop Dog*, Nora Lavin, Molly Thorp, Novel

ADVENTURE ISLAND 1947 d: Sam Newfield. USA., *The Ebb Tide; a Trio and Quartette*, Lloyd Osbourne, Robert Louis Stevenson, 1894, Novel

ADVENTURE LIMITED 1934 d: George King. UKN., *Trust Berkely*, Cyril Campion, London 1933, Play

ADVENTURE SHOP, THE 1918 d: Kenneth Webb. USA., *The Green Gullabaloo*, Harry Conway Fisher, Short Story

Adventurer of Tortuga *see* **L' AVVENTURIERO DELLA TORTUGA** (1965).

ADVENTURER, THE 1920 d: J. Gordon Edwards. USA., *Ruy Blas*, Victor Hugo, 1838, Play

ADVENTURERS, THE 1970 d: Lewis Gilbert. UKN/USA., *The Adventurers*, Harold Robbins, New York 1966, Novel

Adventures at Rugby *see* **TOM BROWN'S SCHOOLDAYS** (1940).

ADVENTURES IN DIPLOMACY 1914. USA., *Elusive Isabel*, Jacques Futrelle, Indianapolis 1909, Novel

Adventures in Ontario *see* **AVENTURE EN ONTARIO** (1968).

ADVENTURES IN SILVERADO 1948 d: Phil Karlson. USA., *Silverado Squatters*, Robert Louis Stevenson, 1883, Short Story

Adventures of a Nobleman *see* **REKOPIS ZNALEZIONY W SARAGOSSIE** (1965).

ADVENTURES OF A YOUNG MAN 1962 d: Martin Ritt. USA., Ernest Hemingway, Short Stories

ADVENTURES OF BULLWHIP GRIFFIN, THE 1967 d: James Neilson. USA., *By the Great Horn Spoon!*, Albert Sidney Fleischman, Boston 1963, Novel

ADVENTURES OF CAPTAIN FABIAN 1951 d: William Marshall. USA/FRN., *Fabulous Ann Medlock*, Robert Shannon, Novel

ADVENTURES OF CAPTAIN KETTLE, THE 1922 d: Meyrick Milton. UKN., *The Adventures of Captain Kettle*, C. J. Cutcliffe-Hyne, Novel

Adventures of Chang, The *see* **WEST OF SHANGHAI** (1937).

Adventures of David Gray *see* **VAMPYR** (1931).

Adventures of Don Quixote *see* **DON QUICHOTTE** (1932).

Adventures of Don Quixote, The *see* **DON QUIXOTE** (1972).

ADVENTURES OF GERARD, THE 1970 d: Jerzy Skolimowski. UKN/ITL/SWT., *The Exploits of Brigadier Gerard*, Arthur Conan Doyle, London 1896, Novel

Adventures of Gil Blas *see* **LES AVENTURES DE GIL BLAS DE SANTILLANE** (1955).

ADVENTURES OF HAJJI BABA, THE 1954 d: Don Weis. USA., *Adventures of Hajji Baba*, James Morier, 1954, Novel

ADVENTURES OF HAL 5, THE 1958 d: Don Sharp. UKN., *Hal 5 and the Haywards*, Henry Donald, Novel

ADVENTURES OF HUCK FINN, THE 1993 d: Stephen Sommers. USA., *The Adventures of Huckleberry Finn*, Mark Twain, New York 1884, Novel

ADVENTURES OF HUCKLEBERRY FINN 1985 d: Peter H. Hunt. USA., *The Adventures of Huckleberry Finn*, Mark Twain, New York 1884, Novel

ADVENTURES OF HUCKLEBERRY FINN, THE 1938 d: Richard Thorpe. USA., *The Adventures of Huckleberry Finn*, Mark Twain, New York 1884, Novel

ADVENTURES OF HUCKLEBERRY FINN, THE 1960 d: Michael Curtiz. USA., *The Adventures of Huckleberry Finn*, Mark Twain, New York 1884, Novel

Adventures of Huckleberry Finn, The *see* SOVSEM PROPASCIJ (1972).

Adventures of Ichabod and Mr. Toad, The *see* ICHABOD AND MR. TOAD (1949).

Adventures of Jack London *see* JACK LONDON (1942).

Adventures of Juan Quin Quin, The *see* LAS AVENTURAS DE JUAN QUIN QUIN (1967).

ADVENTURES OF KITTY COBB, THE 1914. USA., *The Adventures of Kitty Cobb*, James Montgomery Flagg, New York 1912, Book

ADVENTURES OF MARK TWAIN, THE 1944 d: Irving Rapper. USA., *Mark Twain*, Harold M. Sherman, Play

ADVENTURES OF MARTIN EDEN, THE 1942 d: Sidney Salkow. USA., *Martin Eden*, Jack London, 1906, Novel

Adventures of Michael Strogoff *see* THE SOLDIER AND THE LADY (1937).

ADVENTURES OF MR. PICKWICK, THE 1921 d: Thomas Bentley. UKN., *The Pickwick Papers*, Charles Dickens, London 1836, Novel

ADVENTURES OF MR. PUSHER LONG, THE 1921 d: Kenneth Graeme. UKN., Derwent Nicol, Short Stories

Adventures of Nikoletina Bursac *see* NIKOLETINA BURSAC (1964).

Adventures of Penrod and Sam, The *see* PENROD AND SAM (1931).

Adventures of Pinocchio, The *see* PRIKLJUCENIJA BURATINO (1959).

Adventures of Pinocchio, The *see* LE AVVENTURE DI PINOCCHIO (1968).

ADVENTURES OF PINOCCHIO, THE 1996 d: Steve Barron. UKN/FRN/GRM., *Le Avventure Di Pinocchio*, Carlo Collodi, 1883, Short Story

ADVENTURES OF QUENTIN DURWARD, THE 1956 d: Richard Thorpe. UKN/USA., *Quentin Durward*, Sir Walter Scott, 1823, Novel

Adventures of Remi, The *see* SANS FAMILLE (1957).

Adventures of Robinson Crusoe, The *see* LAS AVENTURAS DE ROBINSON CRUSOE (1952).

Adventures of Robinson Crusoe, the Sailor of York *see* NAMORNIKA Z YORKU ZIVOT A PODIVUHODNA DOBRODRUZSTVI ROBINSONA CRUSOE (1982).

Adventures of Sadie *see* OUR GIRL FRIDAY (1953).

Adventures of Sam the Squirrel *see* MISI MOKUS KALANDJAI (1984).

Adventures of Scaramouche, The *see* SCARAMOUCHE (1963).

Adventures of Shanti-Andia *see* LAS INQUIETUDES DE SHANTI ANDIA (1946).

ADVENTURES OF SHERLOCK HOLMES: A SCANDAL IN BOHEMIA, THE 1984 d: Paul Annett. UKN., *A Scandal in Bohemia*, Arthur Conan Doyle, Short Story

ADVENTURES OF SHERLOCK HOLMES, THE 1939 d: Alfred L. Werker. USA., *Sherlock Holmes*, William Gillette, Buffalo 1899, Play

ADVENTURES OF SHERLOCK HOLMES: THE BLUE CARBUNCLE, THE 1984 d: David Carson. UKN., *The Blue Carbuncle*, Arthur Conan Doyle, Short Story

ADVENTURES OF SHERLOCK HOLMES: THE COPPER BEECHES, THE 1985 d: Paul Annett. UKN., *The Copper Beeches*, Arthur Conan Doyle, Short Story

ADVENTURES OF SHERLOCK HOLMES: THE CROOKED MAN, THE 1983 d: Alan Grint. UKN., *The Crooked Man*, Arthur Conan Doyle, Short Story

ADVENTURES OF SHERLOCK HOLMES: THE DANCING MEN, THE 1984 d: John Bruce. UKN., *The Dancing Men*, Arthur Conan Doyle, Short Story

ADVENTURES OF SHERLOCK HOLMES: THE ELIGIBLE BACHELOR 1993 d: Peter Hammond. UKN., *The Noble Bachelor*, Arthur Conan Doyle, Short Story

ADVENTURES OF SHERLOCK HOLMES: THE FINAL PROBLEM, THE 1985 d: Alan Grint. UKN., *The Final Problem*, Arthur Conan Doyle, Short Story

ADVENTURES OF SHERLOCK HOLMES: THE GREEK INTERPRETER, THE 1985 d: Derek Marlowe. UKN., *The Greek Interpreter*, Arthur Conan Doyle, Short Story

ADVENTURES OF SHERLOCK HOLMES: THE MASTER BLACKMAILER, THE 1991 d: Peter Hammond. UKN., *Charles Augustus Milverton*, Arthur Conan Doyle, 1904, Short Story

ADVENTURES OF SHERLOCK HOLMES: THE NAVAL TREATY, THE 1984 d: Alan Grint. UKN., *The Naval Treaty*, Arthur Conan Doyle, Short Story

ADVENTURES OF SHERLOCK HOLMES: THE NORWOOD BUILDER, THE 1985 d: Ken Grieve. UKN., *The Norwood Builder*, Arthur Conan Doyle, Short Story

ADVENTURES OF SHERLOCK HOLMES: THE RED-HEADED LEAGUE, THE 1985 d: John Bruce. UKN., *The Red-Headed League*, Arthur Conan Doyle, 1891, Short Story

ADVENTURES OF SHERLOCK HOLMES: THE RESIDENT PATIENT, THE 1985 d: David Carson. UKN., *The Resident Patient*, Arthur Conan Doyle, Short Story

ADVENTURES OF SHERLOCK HOLMES: THE SIGN OF FOUR, THE 1987 d: Peter Hammond. UKN., *The Sign of Four*, Arthur Conan Doyle, London 1890, Novel

ADVENTURES OF SHERLOCK HOLMES: THE SOLITARY CYCLIST, THE 1984 d: Paul Annett. UKN., *The Solitary Cyclist*, Arthur Conan Doyle, Short Story

ADVENTURES OF SHERLOCK HOLMES: THE SPECKLED BAND, THE 1984 d: John Bruce. UKN., *The Speckled Band*, Arthur Conan Doyle, 1892, Short Story

Adventures of the Bengal Lancers *see* I TRE SERGENTI DEL BENGALA (1965).

Adventures of the Prince and the Pauper, The *see* THE PRINCE AND THE PAUPER (1969).

Adventures of Till Eulenspiegel, The *see* LES AVENTURES DE TILL L'ESPIEGLE (1956).

Adventures of Tom Jones, The *see* THE BAWDY ADVENTURES OF TOM JONES (1975).

Adventures of Tom Sawyer and Huckleberry Finn, The *see* TOM SAWYER (1983).

ADVENTURES OF TOM SAWYER, THE 1938 d: Norman Taurog, H. C. Potter. USA., *Adventures of Tom Sawyer*, Mark Twain, San Francisco 1876, Novel

Adventures of Tom Sawyer, The *see* AVENTURILE LUI TOM SAWYER (1968).

Adventures of Tom Sawyer, The *see* TOM SAWYER (1973).

Adventures of Werner Holt, The *see* DIE ABENTEUER DES WERNER HOLT (1963).

Adventures of Young Dink Stover *see* THE HAPPY YEARS (1950).

Adversary, The *see* PRATIDWANDI (1970).

ADVICE TO THE LOVELORN 1933 d: Alfred L. Werker. USA., *Miss Lonelyhearts*, Nathanael West, New York 1933, Novel

ADVISE AND CONSENT 1962 d: Otto Preminger. USA., *Advise and Consent*, Allen Drury, New York 1959, Novel

ADVOCAAT VAN DE HANEN 1996 d: Gerrit Van Elst. NTH., *Advocaat Van de Hanen*, A. F. Th. Van Der Heijden, Novel

ADVOKAT CHUDYCH 1941 d: Vladimir Slavinsky. CZC., *Advokat Chudych*, Jakub Arbes

ADVOKATKA VERA 1937 d: Martin Fric. CZC., *Advokatka Vera*, Vlasta Zemanova, Short Story

Aereo Per Baalbeck, Un *see* F.B.I. OPERAZIONE BAALBECK (1964).

AERODROME, THE 1983 d: Giles Foster. UKN., *The Aerodrome*, Rex Warner, Novel

AFACEREA PROTAR 1956 d: Haralambie Boros. RMN., *Ultima Ora*, Mihail Sebastian, 1956, Play

AFFAIR AT THE NOVELTY THEATRE, THE 1924 d: Hugh Croise. UKN., *The Affair at the Novelty Theatre*, Baroness Orczy, Short Story

Affair at the Villa Fiorita, The *see* THE BATTLE OF THE VILLA FIORITA (1965).

Affair Between the Noszty Boy and Man Toth *see* A NOSZTY FIU ESETE TOTH MARIVAL (1960).

Affair in Monte Carlo *see* 24 HOURS OF A WOMAN'S LIFE (1952).

Affair Lafont, The *see* CONFLIT (1938).

Affair of Dartmoor Terrace, The *see* THE KENSINGTON MYSTERY (1924).

AFFAIR OF HONOUR, AN 1904 d: Alf Collins. UKN., *An Affair of Honour*, Percival H. T. Sykes, Play

Affair of State, An *see* ZWEI GIRLS VOM ROTEN STERN (1966).

AFFAIR OF THE FOLLIES, AN 1927 d: Millard Webb. USA., *Here Y'are Brother*, Dixie Willson, 1925, Short Story

AFFAIR OF THREE NATIONS, AN 1915 d: Arnold Daly, Ashley Miller. USA., *Investigator Ashton-Kirk*, John Thomas McIntyre, Philadelphia 1910, Book

AFFAIR, THE 1963 d: John Jacobs. UKN., *The Affair*, C. P. Snow, Novel

Affaire Berlinese *see* INTERNO BERLINESE (1985).

AFFAIRE BLAIREAU, L' 1923 d: Louis Osmont. FRN., *L' Affaire Blaireau*, Alphonse Allais, 1899, Novel

AFFAIRE BLAIREAU, L' 1931 d: Henry Wulschleger. FRN., *L' Affaire Blaireau*, Alphonse Allais, 1899, Novel

Affaire Blaireau, L' *see* NI CONNU. NI VU (1958).

AFFAIRE COFFIN, L' 1980 d: Jean-Claude Labrecque. CND., *L' Affaire Coffin*, Jacques Hebert, Book

Affaire Danton, L' *see* DANTON (1982).

AFFAIRE DE FEMMES, UNE 1988 d: Claude Chabrol. FRN., Francis Szpiner, Story

AFFAIRE DE LA RUE DE LOURCINE, L' 1932 d: Marcel Dumont. FRN., *L' Affaire de la Rue de Lourcine*, Eugene Labiche, A. Monnier, 1857, Play

AFFAIRE DES POISONS, L' 1955 d: Henri Decoin. FRN/ITL., *L' Affaire Des Poisons*, Victorien Sardou, 1908, Play

AFFAIRE D'ORCIVAL, L' 1914 d: Gerard Bourgeois. FRN., *L' Affaire Orcival*, Emile Gaboriau, Novel

AFFAIRE DU COLLIER DE LA REINE, L' 1911 d: Camille de Morlhon. FRN., *L' Affaire du Collier de la Reine*, Frantz Funck-Brentano, Novel

Affaire du Collier de la Reine, L' *see* LE COLLIER DE LA REINE (1929).

AFFAIRE DU COLLIER DE LA REINE, L' 1945 d: Marcel L'Herbier, Jean Dreville (Uncredited). FRN., *Le Collier de la Reine*, Alexandre Dumas (pere), 1849-50, Novel

AFFAIRE DU COURRIER DE LYON, L' 1937 d: Maurice Lehmann, Claude Autant-LarA. FRN., *L' Affaire du Courrier de Lyon*, Louis-Mathurin Moreau, Paul Siraudin, Play

AFFAIRE DU GRAND THEATRE, L' 1916 d: Henri Pouctal. FRN., *L' Affaire du Grand-Theatre*, Valentin Mandelstamm, Novel

AFFAIRE DU TRAIN 24, L' 1921 d: Gaston Leprieur. FRN., *L' Affaire du Train 24*, Andre Bencey, Novel

AFFAIRE D'UNE NUIT, L' 1960 d: Henri Verneuil. FRN., *L' Affaire d'une Nuit*, Alain Moury, Novel

Affaire Lesurques, L' *see* L' AFFAIRE DU COURRIER DE LYON (1937).

AFFAIRE MAURIZIUS, L' 1953 d: Julien Duvivier. FRN/ITL., *Der Fall Maurizius*, Jakob Wassermann, 1928, Novel

Affaire Molyneux, L' *see* DROLE DE DRAME (1937).

AFFAIRE NINA B 1961 d: Robert Siodmak. GRM/FRN., *Affaire Nina B.*, Johannes Mario Simmel, Novel

AFFAIRE TISSERON, L' 1917. FRN., *La Rehabilitation*, Marcel Tisseron

AFFAIRES SONT LES AFFAIRES, LES 1942 d: Jean Dreville. FRN., *Les Affaires Sont Les Affaires*, Octave Mirbeau, Paris 1903, Play

AFFAIRS OF A GENTLEMAN 1934 d: Edwin L. Marin. USA., *Women*, Edith Ellis, Edward Ellis, 1928, Play

Affairs of a Rogue *see* THE FIRST GENTLEMAN (1948).

Affairs of Adelaide, The *see* BRITANNIA MEWS (1948).

AFFAIRS OF ANATOL, THE 1921 d: Cecil B. de Mille. USA., *Anatol*, Arthur Schnitzler, 1893, Play

Affairs of Annabelle, The see **ANNABELLE'S AFFAIRS** (1931).

AFFAIRS OF CELLINI, THE 1934 d: Gregory La CavA. USA., *The Firebrand*, Edwin Justus Mayer, New York 1924, Play

AFFAIRS OF DOBIE GILLIS, THE 1953 d: Don Weis. USA., *The Affairs of Dobie Gillis*, Max Schulman, Book

AFFAIRS OF GERALDINE, THE 1946 d: George Blair. USA., *Blossoms for Effie*, Lee Loeb, Arthur Strawn, Short Story

Affairs of Julie, The see **DIE ZURCHER VERLOBUNG** (1957).

Affairs of Maupassant, The see **DAS TAGEBUCH DER GELIEBTEN** (1936).

Affairs of Monica, The see **DR. MONICA** (1934).

Affare Della Sezione Speciale, L' see **SECTION SPECIALE** (1975).

AFFARE SI COMPLICA, L' 1941 d: Pier Luigi Faraldo. ITL., Guglielmo Giannini, Play

AFFINITA ELETTIVE, LE 1978 d: Gianni Amico. ITL., *Die Wahlverwandtschaften*, Johann Wolfgang von Goethe, 1809, Novel

AFFINITIES 1922 d: Ward Lascelle. USA., *Affinities*, Mary Roberts Rinehart, 1920, Short Story

AFFLICTION 1997 d: Paul Schrader. USA., *Affliction*, Russell Banks, 1989, Novel

Affondamento Della Valiant, L' see **THE VALIANT** (1962).

Afraid to Live see **DAS BEKENNTNIS DER INA KAHR** (1954).

AFRAID TO LOVE 1927 d: Edward H. Griffith. USA., *La Passerelle*, Francis de Croisset, Fred de Gresac, Paris 1902, Play

Afraid to Love see **DAS BEKENNTNIS DER INA KAHR** (1954).

AFRAID TO TALK 1932 d: Edward L. Cahn. USA., *Merry-Go-Round*, Albert Maltz, George Sklar, New York 1932, Play

Africa Ablaze see **SOMETHING OF VALUE** (1957).

African Fury see **THE BELOVED COUNTRY CRY** (1952).

African Fury see **SKABENGA** (1953).

AFRICAN QUEEN, THE 1951 d: John Huston. UKN/USA., *The African Queen*, C. S. Forester, 1935, Novel

AFRICAN QUEEN, THE 1976 d: Richard C. Sarafian. USA., *The African Queen*, C. S. Forester, 1935, Novel

African Rage see **TIGERS DON'T CRY** (1976).

African Run, The see **TUXEDO WARRIOR** (1985).

After All see **NEW MORALS FOR OLD** (1932).

AFTER BUSINESS HOURS 1925 d: Malcolm St. Clair. USA., *Everything Money Can Buy*, Ethel Watts Mumford, 1924, Short Story

AFTER DARK 1915 d: Frederick A. Thompson. USA., *After Dark*, Dion Boucicault, London 1868, Play

AFTER DARK 1915 d: Warwick Buckland. UKN., *After Dark*, Dion Boucicault, London 1868, Play

AFTER DARK 1924 d: Thomas Bentley. UKN., *After Dark*, Bertram Atkey, Short Story

AFTER DARK 1932 d: Albert Parker. UKN., *After Dark*, J. Jefferson Farjeon, 1926, Play

AFTER DARK, MY SWEET 1990 d: James Foley. USA., *After Dark, My Sweet*, Jim Thompson, Novel

After Darkness, Light see **L' AMORE D'OLTRETOMBA** (1912).

After Eight Hours see **ONLY EIGHT HOURS** (1934).

AFTER FIVE 1915 d: Oscar Apfel, Cecil B. de Mille. USA., *After Five*, Cecil B. de Mille, William C. de Mille, New York 1913, Play

AFTER HIS OWN HEART 1919 d: Harry L. Franklin. USA., *After His Own Heart*, Ben Ames Williams, 1919, Short Story

AFTER JULIUS 1979 d: John Glenister. UKN., *After Julius*, Elizabeth Jane Howard, Novel

After Midnight see **NACH MITTERNACHT** (1981).

After Nightfall see **THE GREAT JEWEL ROBBER** (1950).

AFTER OFFICE HOURS 1932 d: Thomas Bentley. UKN., *London Wall*, John Van Druten, London 1931, Play

After School see **VERBRECHEN NACH SCHULSCHLUSS** (1959).

After Schooldays see **FIRST LOVE** (1939).

AFTER THE BALL 1914 d: Pierce Kingsley. USA., *After the Ball*, Charles K. Harris, 1892, Song

AFTER THE BALL 1924 d: Dallas M. Fitzgerald. USA., *After the Ball*, Charles K. Harris, 1892, Song

AFTER THE BALL 1957 d: Compton Bennett. UKN., *Recollections of Vesta Tilley*, Lady de Frece, Book

After the Fox see **CACCIA ALLA VOLPE** (1965).

AFTER THE PLAY 1916 d: William Worthington. USA., *After the Play*, Robert McGowan, Story

After the Rain see **THE PAINTED WOMAN** (1932).

AFTER THE SHOW 1921 d: William C. de Mille. USA., *The Stage Door*, Rita Weiman, Short Story

After the Storm see **DESERT GOLD** (1914).

After the Storm see **THE RAINBOW** (1917).

AFTER THE VERDICT 1929 d: Henrik Galeen. UKN., *After the Verdict*, Robert Hichens, Novel

AFTER TOMORROW 1932 d: Frank Borzage. USA., *After Tomorrow*, John Golden, Hugh Stange, New York 1931, Play

After Your Decrees see **RUTH** (1983).

AFTER YOUR OWN HEART 1921 d: George Marshall. USA., *After His Own Heart*, William Wallace Cook, 1920, Short Story

AFTERMATH 1914. USA., *Aftermath*, William Addison Hervey, Play

AFTERNOON MIRACLE, AN 1920 d: David Smith. USA., *An Afternoon Miracle*, O. Henry, Short Story

Afternoon of War see **IN THE AFTERNOON OF WAR** (1981).

AFTERWARDS 1928 d: W. Lawson Butts. UKN., *Afterwards*, Kathlyn Rhodes, Novel

Afterwards see **THEIR BIG MOMENT** (1934).

Agaguk see **SHADOW OF THE WOLF** (1992).

Again, Forever see **ROMAN BE'HEMSHACHIM** (1985).

Again the Ringer see **NEUES VOM HEXER** (1965).

Again the Wizard see **NEUES VOM HEXER** (1965).

AGAINST ALL ODDS 1984 d: Taylor Hackford. USA., *Build My Gallows High*, Daniel Mainwaring, Novel

Agatha Christie's a Caribbean Mystery see **A CARIBBEAN MYSTERY** (1983).

AGATHA CHRISTIE'S DEAD MAN'S FOLLY 1986 d: Clive Donner. USA/UKN., *Dead Man's Folly*, Agatha Christie, Novel

Agatha Christie's Death on the Nile see **DEATH ON THE NILE** (1978).

Agatha Christie's Endless Night see **ENDLESS NIGHT** (1971).

Agatha Christie's Evil Under the Sun see **EVIL UNDER THE SUN** (1982).

Agatha Christie's Hercule Poirot: Appointment With Death see **APPOINTMENT WITH DEATH** (1987).

Agatha Christie's Hercule Poirot: the Mysterious Affair at Styles see **THE MYSTERIOUS AFFAIR AT STYLES** (1990).

AGATHA CHRISTIE'S MURDER IN THREE ACTS 1986 d: Gary Nelson. USA., *Murder in Three Acts*, Agatha Christie, Play

Agatha Christie's Murder With Mirrors see **MURDER WITH MIRRORS** (1985).

Agatha Christie's Ordeal By Innocence see **ORDEAL BY INNOCENCE** (1984).

Agatha Christie's Sparkling Cyanide see **SPARKLING CYANIDE** (1983).

AGE FOR LOVE, THE 1931 d: Frank Lloyd. USA., *The Age for Love*, Ernest Pascal, New York 1930, Novel

Age of Assassins, The see **SATSUJIN KYO JIDAI** (1967).

AGE OF CONSENT 1969 d: Michael Powell. ASL., *Age of Consent*, Norman Lindsay, New York 1938, Novel

AGE OF CONSENT, THE 1932 d: Gregory La CavA. USA., *Cross Roads*, Martin Flavin, New York 1929, Play

AGE OF INDISCRETION 1935 d: Edward Ludwig. USA., *Age of Indiscretion*, Lenore Coffee, Story

AGE OF INNOCENCE, THE 1924 d: Wesley Ruggles. USA., *The Age of Innocence*, Edith Wharton, New York 1920, Novel

AGE OF INNOCENCE, THE 1934 d: Philip Moeller. USA., *The Age of Innocence*, Edith Wharton, New York 1920, Novel

AGE OF INNOCENCE, THE 1993 d: Martin Scorsese. USA., *The Age of Innocence*, Edith Wharton, New York 1920, Novel

Age of Love see **THE AGE FOR LOVE** (1931).

Age of Uneasiness, The see **L' ETA DEL MALESSERE** (1968).

Agence de la Peur, L' see **AGENCY** (1979).

AGENCY 1979 d: George Kaczender. CND., *Agency*, Paul Gottlieb, Novel

Agent 3S3 Bets It All see **OMICIDIO PER APPUNTAMENTO** (1967).

Agent 38-24-36 (the Warm-Blooded Spy) see **UNE RAVISSANTE IDIOTE** (1964).

Agent 3S3 Setzt Alles Auf Eine Karte see **OMICIDIO PER APPUNTAMENTO** (1967).

Agent 8 3/4 see **HOT ENOUGH FOR JUNE** (1963).

Agent of Doom see **UN SOIR. PAR HASARD** (1964).

AGENT TROUBLE 1987 d: Jean-Pierre Mocky. FRN., *Angent Trouble*, Malcolm Bosse, Novel

Agente 777 Missione Supergame see **COPLAN FX18 CASSE TOUT** (1965).

Agente Coplan: Missione Spionaggio see **COPLAN PREND DES RISQUES** (1963).

Agente End see **SICARIO 77 VIVO O MORTO** (1966).

Agente Federale Lemmy Caution, L' see **MIGNONNE A TOI DE FAIRE** (1963).

Agente Tigre: Sfida Infernale see **AGENT K8 PASSEPORT DIPLOMATIQUE** (1965).

Agente X77 see **BARAKA SUR X 13** (1965).

Agente X77 Ordine Di Uccidere see **BARAKA SUR X 13** (1965).

Agenten Kennen Keine Tranen see **A CHI TOCCA..TOCCA!** (1978).

AGENZIA MATRIMONIALE 1953 d: Giorgio PastinA. ITL., Eduardo Scarpetta, Play

AGENZIA RICCARDO FINZI. PRATICAMENTE DETECTIVE 1979 d: Bruno Corbucci. ITL., *Agenzia Investigativa Riccardo Finzi*, Luciano Secchi, Novel

AGGIE APPLEBY, MAKER OF MEN 1933 d: Mark Sandrich. USA., *Maker of Men Aggie Appleby*, Joseph Kesselring, 1932, Play

Agguato Sul Grande Fiume see **DIE FLUSSPIRATEN VOM MISSISSIPPI** (1963).

AGI MURAD, IL DIAVOLO BIANCO 1959 d: Riccardo FredA. ITL/YGS., *Khadzh-Murat*, Lev Nikolayevich Tolstoy, 1911, Novel

AGIR ROMAN 1997 d: Mustafa Altioklar. TRK/HNG/FRN., Metin Kacan, Novel

AGITATOR, THE 1945 d: John Harlow. UKN., *Peter Pettinger*, William Riley, Novel

Agnes Cecilia see **AGNES CECILIA - EN SALLSAM HISTORIA** (1991).

AGNES CECILIA - EN SALLSAM HISTORIA 1991 d: Anders Gronros. SWD., *Agnes Cecilia*, Maria Gripe, Novel

AGNES DE RIEN 1949 d: Pierre Billon. FRN., *Agnes de Rien*, Germaine Beaumont, Novel

AGNES OF GOD 1985 d: Norman Jewison. CND/USA., *Agnes of God*, John Pielmeier, Play

AGNESE VA A MORIRE, L' 1977 d: Giuliano Montaldo. ITL., *L' Agnese Va a Morire*, Renata Vigano, Novel

AGONIE DES AIGLES, L' 1921 d: Julien Duvivier, Bernard-Deschamps. FRN., *Les Demi-Soldes*, Georges d'Esparbes, Novel

AGONIE DES AIGLES, L' 1933 d: Roger Richebe. FRN., *Les Demi-Soldes*, Georges d'Esparbes, Novel

AGONIE DES AIGLES, L' 1951 d: Jean Alden-Delos. FRN., *Les Demi-Soldes*, Georges d'Esparbes, Novel

AGONY AND THE ECSTASY, THE 1965 d: Carol Reed. USA., *The Agony and the Ecstasy*, Irving Stone, New York 1961, Book

Agony Column, The see **THE BLIND ADVENTURE** (1918).

AGOSTINO 1962 d: Mauro Bolognini. ITL., *Agostino*, Alberto Moravia, 1944, Novel

AGUAS BAJAN NEGRAS, LAS 1948 d: Jose Luis Saenz de HerediA. SPN., *La Aldea Perdida*, Armando Palacio Valdes, 1903, Novel

Aguicheuse, L' see **LA NOTTE DELL'ALTA MAREA** (1977).

AGUILAS DE ACERO 1927 d: Florian Rey. SPN., *Aguilas de Acero*, Rafael Lopez Rienda, Novel

AH JONAN 1960 d: Toshio Sugie. JPN., *Ah Jonan*, Shotaro Yasuoka, Novel

AH Q ZHEN ZHUAN 1982 d: Chen Fan. CHN., *Ah Q Zheng Zhuan*, Zhou Shuren, 1921, Short Story

AH Q ZHENG ZHUAN 1958 d: Yuen Yang-An. HKG., *Ah Q Zheng Zhuan*, Zhou Shuren, 1921, Short Story

AH! SI MON MOINE VOULAIT. 1973 d: Claude Pierson. FRN/CND., *L' Heptameron*, Marguerite de Navarre, Novel

AH, WILDERNESS! 1935 d: Clarence Brown. USA., *Ah Wilderness!*, Eugene O'Neill, New York 1933, Play

AHASIN POLA WATHA 1976 d: Lester James Peries. SLN., *Ahasin Polawatha*, Eileen Siriwardene, Novel

Ahasin Polowata see **AHASIN POLA WATHA** (1976).

Ahava Asura see **TORN APART** (1990).

Ahead of the Silence see **INAINTE DE TACERE** (1979).

AHMAQ 1992 d: Mani Kaul. IND., *Idiot*, Fyodor Dostoyevsky, 1868, Novel

A.I. see **DEADLY FRIEND** (1987).

AI NO BOREI 1977 d: Nagisa OshimA. JPN/FRN., *Itoko Nakamura*, Story

AI NO KAWAKI 1967 d: Koreyoshi KuraharA. JPN., *Ai No Kawaki*, Yukio Mishima, Tokyo 1950, Novel

AI TO HONOHO TO 1961 d: Eizo SugawA. JPN., *Chosen*, Shintaro Ishihara, Tokyo 1960, Novel

AI VOSTRI ORDINI, SIGNORA! 1939 d: Mario Mattoli. ITL., *Un Dejeuner de Soleil*, Andre Birabeau, Play

AIDA 1953 d: Clemente Fracassi. ITL., *Aida*, Antonio Ghislanzoni, Giuseppe Verdi, Cairo 1871, Opera

AIGLE A DEUX TETES, L' 1948 d: Jean Cocteau. FRN., *L' Aigle a Deux Tetes*, Jean Cocteau, 1946, Play

Aigle Noir, L' see **IL VENDICATORE** (1959).

AIGLON, L' 1931 d: Victor Tourjansky. FRN., *L' Aiglon*, Edmond Rostand, 1900, Play

Aiglon, L' see **NAPOLEON II L'AIGLON** (1961).

AIGRETTE, L' 1917 d: Baldassarre Negroni. ITL., *L' Aigrette*, Dario Niccodemi, 1912, Play

AIGUILLE ROUGE, L' 1950 d: Emile Edwin Reinert. FRN., *Das Joch*, Vicki Baum, Novel

AILES BRISEES, LES 1933 d: Andre Berthomieu. FRN., *Les Ailes Brisees*, Pierre Wolff, Play

AIMEE & JAGUAR 1999 d: Max Farberbock. GRM., *Aimee & Jaguar*, Erica Fischer, Book

Aimez-Vous Brahms? see **GOODBYE AGAIN** (1961).

AIMEZ-VOUS LES FEMMES? 1964 d: Jean Leon. FRN/ITL., *Aimez-Vous Les Femmes?*, Georges Bardawil, Paris 1961, Novel

AINE DES FERCHAUX, L' 1963 d: Jean-Pierre Melville. FRN/ITL., *L' Aine Des Ferchaux*, Georges Simenon, 1945, Novel

AINSI VA LA VIE 1918 d: Pierre Bressol. FRN., *La Condamnee*, Henri de Brisay, Play

AIN'T MISBEHAVIN' 1955 d: Edward Buzzell. USA., *Third Girl from the Right*, Robert Carson, Story

AIR AMERICA 1990 d: Roger Spottiswoode. USA., *Air America*, Christopher Robbins, Book

AIR DE FAMILLE, UN 1996 d: Cedric Klapisch. FRN., *Un Air de Famille*, Jean-Pierre Bacri, Agnes Jaoui, Play

AIR DE PARIS, L' 1954 d: Marcel Carne. FRN/ITL., *La Choute*, Jacques Viot, Short Story

AIR HOSTESS 1933 d: Albert S. Rogell. USA., *Air Hostess*, Dora Macy, 1933, Short Story

AIR MAIL, THE 1925 d: Irvin V. Willat. USA., *The Air Mail*, Byron Morgan, Novel

AIR SI PUR, UN 1997 d: Yves Angelo. FRN/PLN/BLG., *Last Chapter*, Knut Hamsun, Novel

Air So Pure, An see **UN AIR SI PUR** (1997).

Air Torpedo see **VZDUSNE TORPEDO 48** (1936).

Airborne see **SKYJACKED** (1972).

AIRPORT 1970 d: George Seaton, Henry Hathaway (Uncredited). USA., *Airport*, Arthur Hailey, New York 1968, Book

AISURU 1997 d: Kei Kumai. JPN., *The Woman I Abandoned*, Shusaku Endo, Novel

Ajaantrik see **AJANTRIK** (1958).

AJANTRIK 1958 d: Ritwik Ghatak. IND., Subodh Ghosh, Story

AJIT 1948 d: Mohan Dayaram Bhavnani. IND., *Asir of Asirgarh*, Snilloc, Novel

AJO NELL'IMBARAZZO, L' 1911. ITL., *L' Ajo Nell'Imbarazzo*, Giovanni Giraud, 1807, Play

AJO NELL'IMBARAZZO, L' 1963 d: Vasco Ugo Finni. ITL., *L' Ajo Nell'Imbarazzo*, Giovanni Giraud, 1807, Play

AKAHIGE 1965 d: Akira KurosawA. JPN., *Akahige Shinryotan*, Shugoro Yamamoto, Tokyo 1962, Novel

AKALER SANDHANEY 1980 d: Mrinal Sen. IND., Amalendu Chakrborty, Story

AKAZUKINCHAN KIOTSUKETE 1970 d: Shiro Moritani. JPN., *Akazukinchan Kiotsukete*, Kaoru Shoji, Short Story

AKENFIELD 1975 d: Peter Hall. UKN., *Akenfield*, Ronald Blythe, Book

Akes Lilla Felsteg see **MON PHOQUE ET ELLES** (1951).

Akhalgazrda Kompozitoris Mogzauroba see **PUTSCHESTWIE MOLODOGO KOMPOSITORA** (1984).

AKIBIYORI 1960 d: Yasujiro Ozu. JPN., *Akibiyori*, Ton Satomi, 1960, Novel

AKIRA 1988 d: Katsuhiro Otomo. JPN., *Akira*, Katsuhiro Otomo, Novel

AKLI MIKLOS 1986 d: Gyorgy Revesz. HNG., *Akli Miklos Es. Kir. Udv. Mulattato Tortenete*, Kalman Mikszath, 1903, Novel

Akseli and Elina see **AKSELI JA ELINA POHJANTAHDEN** (1970).

Akseli and Elina Under the North Sea see **AKSELI JA ELINA POHJANTAHDEN** (1970).

Akseli Ja Elina see **AKSELI JA ELINA POHJANTAHDEN** (1970).

AKSELI JA ELINA POHJANTAHDEN 1970 d: Edvin Laine. FNL., *Taalla Pohjantahden Alla*, Vaino Linna, 1962, Novel

Akte Odessa, Die see **THE ODESSA FILE** (1974).

AKTENSKAPSBROTTAREN 1964 d: Hasse Ekman. SWD., *L' Hotel du Libre-Echange*, Maurice Desvallieres, Georges Feydeau, Paris 1894, Play

AKUTARO 1963 d: Seijun Suzuki. JPN., *Akutaro*, Toko Kon, Novel

AL BUIO INSIEME 1933 d: Gennaro Righelli. ITL., Alessandro de Stefani, Play

Al Christie's "Madame Behave" see **MADAME BEHAVE** (1925).

AL PATRULEA STOL 1979 d: Timotei Ursu. RMN., *Jocul de-a Vacanta*, Mihail Sebastian, 1946, Play

AL PIACERE DI RIVEDERLA 1976 d: Marco Leto. ITL/FRN., *Ritratto Di Provincia in Rosso*, Paolo Levi, Novel

Al Servizio Dell'imperatore see **SI LE ROI SAVAIT CA** (1956).

Al Vostri Ordina, Signora! see **SIGNORA! AI VOSTRI ORDINI** (1939).

ALABASTER BOX, AN 1917 d: Chet Withey. USA., *An Alabaster Box*, Mary E. Wilkins Freeman, Florence Morse Kingsley, New York 1917, Novel

ALADDIN FROM BROADWAY 1917 d: William Wolbert. USA., *Aladdin from Broadway*, Frederic Stewart Isham, New York 1913, Novel

ALADDIN'S OTHER LAMP 1917 d: John H. Collins. USA., *The Dream Girl*, Willard Mack, Play

Alarm see **PEREPOLOH** (1955).

Alarm Auf Gleis B see **GLEISDREIECK** (1936).

ALASKA 1944 d: George Archainbaud. USA., *Flush of Gold*, Jack London, 1910, Short Story

ALASKA SEAS 1954 d: Jerry Hopper. USA., *Spawn of the North*, Florence Barrett Willoughby, Boston 1932, Novel

ALASKAN, THE 1924 d: Herbert Brenon. USA., *The Alaskan*, James Oliver Curwood, New York 1923, Novel

Alba Di Lenin, Un' see **UN' ALBA** (1920).

ALBA, IL GIORNO, LA NOTTE, L' 1955 d: Fernando Trebitsch. ITL., *L' Albo Il Giorno la Notte*, Aldo Nicodemi, Play

ALBA, UN' 1920 d: Eugenio FontanA. ITL., *Un' Alba*, Lenin

ALBANILES, LOS 1976 d: Jorge Fons. MXC., *Los Albaniles*, Vicente Lenero, Play

ALBERGO DEGLI ASSENTI, L' 1939 d: Raffaello Matarazzo. ITL., *L' Albergo Degli Assenti*, Michelangelo Barricelli, Novel

ALBERGO ROMA 1996 d: Ugo Chiti. ITL., *Alegretto. Per Bene Ma Non Troppo*, Ugo Chiti, Play

ALBERO DI ADAMO, L' 1936 d: Mario Bonnard. ITL., *Il Successo*, Alfredo Testoni, Play

Albero Di Natale, L' see **L' ARBRE DE NOEL** (1969).

Albero Verde see **THE GREEN TREE** (1965).

ALBERT R.N. 1953 d: Lewis Gilbert. UKN., *Albert R.N.*, Guy Morgan, Edward Sammis, Play

Alberto Il Marmittone see **L' ALLEGRO SQUADRONE** (1954).

Albi Di Sangue see **MARE NOSTRUM** (1948).

Albino see **WHISPERING DEATH** (1975).

ALBUQUERQUE 1948 d: Ray Enright. USA., *Albuquerque*, Luke Short, Novel

ALCALDE DE ZALAMEA, EL 1953 d: Jose Gutierrez Maesso. SPN., *El Alcalde de Zalamea*, Pedro Calderon de La Barca, 1651, Play

ALCIDE PEPIE 1934 d: Rene Jayet. FRN., *Alcide Pepie*, Armand Massard, Alfred Vercourt, Play

ALCOVA, L' 1984 d: Joe d'Amato. ITL., Judith Wexley, Novel

Alego see **ALEKO** (1953).

ALEKO 1953 d: Grigori Roshal, Sergei Sidelev. USS., *Tsygany*, Alexander Pushkin, 1824, Poem

ALERTE! 1912 d: Georges Pallu, E. Berny. FRN., *Alerte!*, Colonel Driant, Novel

Alerte Dans le Cosmos see **THE SHAPE OF THINGS TO COME** (1979).

ALESSANDRO, SEI GRANDE! 1941 d: Carlo Ludovico BragagliA. ITL., *Sei Grande! Alessandro*, Luigi Bonelli, Play

ALEX 1992 d: Megan Simpson. ASL/NZL., *Alex*, Tessa Duder, Book

ALEX AND THE GYPSY 1976 d: John Korty. USA., *The Bailbondsman*, Stanley Elkin, 1973, Novel

ALEX THE GREAT 1928 d: Dudley Murphy. USA., *Alex the Great*, Harry Charles Witwer, Boston 1919, Novel

Alexander see **ALEXANDRE LE BIENHEUREUX** (1968).

ALEXANDER HAMILTON 1931 d: John G. Adolfi. USA., *Hamilton*, George Arliss, Mary Hamlin, New York 1917, Play

ALEXANDRA 1914 d: Curt A. Stark. GRM., *Alexandra*, Richard Voss, Play

ALEXANDRA 1922 d: Theo Frenkel Sr. NTH/GRM., *Alexandra*, Jonkheer A. W. G. Van Riemsdijk, 1922, Novel

ALEXANDRA 1991 d: Denis Amar. ITL/FRN/GRM., *Le Coeur En Fuite*, Linda la Rosa, Novel

Alexandra and Hell see **ALEXANDRA SI INFERNUL** (1975).

ALEXANDRA SI INFERNUL 1975 d: Iulian Mihu. RMN., *Alexandra Si Infernul*, Laurentiu Fulga, 1966, Novel

Alexandre see **ALEXANDRE LE BIENHEUREUX** (1968).

ALEXANDRE LE BIENHEUREUX 1968 d: Yves Robert. FRN., Yves Robert, Short Story

Alexis Zorbas see **ZORBA THE GREEK** (1964).

ALFIE 1966 d: Lewis Gilbert. UKN., *Alfie*, Bill Naughton, London 1963, Play

ALFRED THE GREAT 1969 d: Clive Donner. UKN., *Alfred the Great*, Eleanor Shipley Duckett, Chicago 1956, Book

ALF'S BABY 1953 d: MacLean Rogers. UKN., *It Won't Be a Stylish Marriage*, A. P. Dearsley, Play

ALF'S BUTTON 1920 d: Cecil M. Hepworth. UKN., *Alf's Button*, W. A. Darlington, 1919, Novel

ALF'S BUTTON 1930 d: W. P. Kellino. UKN., *Alf's Button*, W. A. Darlington, 1919, Novel

ALF'S BUTTON AFLOAT 1938 d: Marcel Varnel. UKN., *Alf's Button*, W. A. Darlington, 1919, Novel

ALF'S CARPET 1929 d: W. P. Kellino. UKN., *Alf's Carpet*, W. A. Darlington, 1928, Novel

ALGERNON BLACKWOOD STORIES 1949 d: Anthony Gilkison. UKN., Algernon Blackwood, Short Stories

ALGIERS 1938 d: John Cromwell. USA., *Pepe le Moko*, Detective Ashelbe, Paris 1937, Novel

ALI BABA 1937 d: Modhu Bose. IND., *Ali Baba*, Khirode Prasad Vidyavinode, 1897, Play

ALIAS FRENCH GERTIE 1930 d: George Archainbaud. USA., *The Chatterbox*, Bayard Veiller, Play

ALIAS JIMMY VALENTINE 1915 d: Maurice Tourneur. USA., *Alias Jimmy Valentine*, Paul Armstrong, New York 1910, Play

ALIAS JIMMY VALENTINE 1920 d: Edmund Mortimer. USA., *Alias Jimmy Valentine*, Paul Armstrong, New York 1910, Play

ALIAS JIMMY VALENTINE 1929 d: Jack Conway. USA., *Alias Jimmy Valentine*, Paul Armstrong, New York 1910, Play

Alias Ladyfingers see **LADYFINGERS** (1921).

ALIAS MIKE MORAN 1919 d: James Cruze. USA., *Open Sesame*, Frederick Orin Bartlett, 1918, Short Story

Alias Mrs. Halifax see **DEVOTION** (1931).

ALIAS MRS. JESSOP 1917 d: Will S. Davis. USA., *Alias Mrs. Jessop*, Blair Hall, Short Story

ALIAS THE DEACON 1928 d: Edward Sloman. USA., *Alias the Deacon*, Leroy Clemens, John B. Hymer, New York 1925, Play

Alias the Deacon see **HALF A SINNER** (1934).

ALIAS THE DEACON 1940 d: W. Christy Cabanne. USA., *The Deacon*, Leroy Clemens, John B. Hymer, New York 1925, Play

ALIAS THE DOCTOR 1932 d: Michael Curtiz. USA., *A Kuruzslo*, Emric Foldes, 1927, Play

ALIAS THE LONE WOLF 1927 d: Edward H. Griffith. USA., *Alias the Lone Wolf*, Louis Joseph Vance, Garden City, Ny. 1921, Novel

ALIAS THE NIGHT WIND 1923 d: Joseph J. Franz. USA., *Alias the Night Wind*, Varick Vanardy, New York 1913, Novel

Alibaba see **ALI BABA** (1937).

ALIBI 1929 d: Roland West. USA., *Nightstick*, E.S. Carrington, J. C. Nugent, John Wray, New York 1927, Play

ALIBI 1931 d: Leslie Hiscott. UKN., *The Murder of Roger Ackroyd*, Agatha Christie, 1926, Novel

ALIBI 1942 d: Brian Desmond Hurst. UKN., *L' Alibi*, Marcel Achard, Novel

ALIBI FOR MURDER 1936 d: D. Ross Lederman. USA., *Body Snatcher*, Theodore A. Tinsley, 1936, Short Story

ALIBI IKE 1935 d: Ray Enright. USA., *Alibi Ike*, Ring Lardner, 1915, Short Story

ALIBI, L' 1914 d: Henri Pouctal. FRN., *L' Alibi*, Gabriel Trarieux, Play

ALIBI, THE 1915 d: Clem Easton. USA., *The Alibi*, Frank Condon, Story

ALIBI, THE 1916 d: Paul Scardon. USA., *The Alibi*, George Allan England, Boston 1916, Novel

ALICE 1980 d: Jerzy Gruza, Yacek Bromski. BLG/PLN/UKN., *Alice's Adventures in Wonderland*, Lewis Carroll, London 1865, Book, *Through the Looking Glass*, Lewis Carroll, London 1870, Book

Alice see **NECO Z ALENKY** (1987).

ALICE ADAMS 1923 d: Rowland V. Lee. USA., *Alice Adams*, Booth Tarkington, New York 1921, Novel

ALICE ADAMS 1935 d: George Stevens. USA., *Alice Adams*, Booth Tarkington, New York 1921, Novel

ALICE IN WONDERLAND 1951 d: Clyde Geronimi, Hamilton Luske. USA., *Alice's Adventures in Wonderland*, Lewis Carroll, London 1865, Book

ALICE IN WONDERLAND 1903 d: Cecil M. Hepworth, Percy Stow. UKN., *Alice's Adventures in Wonderland*, Lewis Carroll, London 1865, Book

ALICE IN WONDERLAND 1915 d: W. W. Young. USA., *Alice's Adventures in Wonderland*, Lewis Carroll, London 1865, Book, *Through the Looking Glass*, Lewis Carroll, London 1870, Book

ALICE IN WONDERLAND 1931 d: Bud Pollard. USA., *Alice's Adventures in Wonderland*, Lewis Carroll, London 1865, Book

ALICE IN WONDERLAND 1933 d: Norman Z. McLeod. USA., *Alice's Adventures in Wonderland*, Lewis Carroll, London 1865, Book, *Through the Looking Glass*, Lewis Carroll, London 1870, Book

ALICE IN WONDERLAND 1951 d: Louis Bunin. USA., *Alice's Adventures in Wonderland*, Lewis Carroll, London 1865, Book

ALICE IN WONDERLAND 1951 d: Dallas Bower. UKN/FRN/USA., *Alice's Adventures in Wonderland*, Lewis Carroll, London 1865, Book, *Through the Looking Glass*, Lewis Carroll, London 1870, Book

ALICE IN WONDERLAND 1967 d: Jonathan Miller. UKN., *Alice's Adventures in Wonderland*, Lewis Carroll, London 1865, Book

ALICE IN WONDERLAND 1976 d: Bud Townsend. USA., *Alice's Adventures in Wonderland*, Lewis Carroll, London 1865, Book

ALICE IN WONDERLAND 1986 d: Harry Harris. USA., *Alice's Adventures in Wonderland*, Lewis Carroll, London 1865, Book, *Through the Looking Glass*, Lewis Carroll, London 1870, Book

ALICE IN WONDERLAND 1999 d: Nick Willing. USA., *Alice's Adventures in Wonderland*, Lewis Carroll, London 1865, Book

ALICE'S ADVENTURES IN WONDERLAND 1972 d: William Sterling. UKN., *Alice's Adventures in Wonderland*, Lewis Carroll, London 1865, Book

Alicja see **ALICE** (1980).

ALIEN BLOOD, THE 1917 d: Burton George. USA., *The Alien Blood*, Louise Rice, Short Story

ALIEN SKY, THE 1956 d: John Jacobs. UKN., Paul Scott, Novel

ALIEN, THE 1915 d: Thomas H. Ince. USA., *The Sign of the Rose*, George Beban, Charles T. Dazey, New York 1911, Play

Alienist, The see **AZYLO MUITO LOUCO** (1970).

Alienista, O see **AZYLO MUITO LOUCO** (1970).

Alieniste, L' see **AZYLO MUITO LOUCO** (1970).

ALIMENTE 1929 d: Carl Boese. GRM., *Alimente*, Walter Gottfried Lohmeyer, Short Story

Alistair MacLean's Death Train see **DEATH TRAIN** (1992).

ALISTAIR MACLEAN'S NIGHT WATCH 1995 d: David S. Jackson. UKN/USA., *Night Watch*, Alistair MacLean, Novel

ALIVE AND KICKING 1958 d: Cyril Frankel. UKN., *Alive and Kicking*, William Dinner, William Morum, Play

All About Loving see **DE L'AMOUR** (1964).

ALL AT SEA 1935 d: Anthony Kimmins. UKN., *All at Sea*, Ian Hay, Play

All Brides are Beautiful see **FROM THIS DAY FORWARD** (1946).

ALL CREATURES GREAT AND SMALL 1974 d: Claude Whatham. UKN., *All Creatures Great and Small*, James Herriot, Novel

ALL FALL DOWN 1962 d: John Frankenheimer. USA., *All Fall Down*, James Leo Herlihy, New York 1960, Novel

ALL FOR A GIRL 1915 d: Roy Applegate. USA., *All for a Girl*, Rupert Hughes, New York 1908, Play

All for Love see **VALLEY OF WANTED MEN** (1935).

ALL FOR MARY 1955 d: Wendy Toye. UKN., *All for Mary*, Kay Bannerman, Harold Brooke, London 1954, Play

All for the Best see **TODO SEA PARA BIEN** (1957).

All for the Love of a Girl see **ALL FOR A GIRL** (1915).

All Girl see **ALL WOMAN** (1967).

All Good Americans see **PARIS INTERLUDE** (1934).

ALL HANDS ON DECK 1961 d: Norman Taurog. USA., *Warm Bodies*, Donald R. Morris, New York 1957, Novel

ALL I DESIRE 1953 d: Douglas Sirk. USA., *Stopover*, Carol Brink, Novel

ALL IN 1936 d: Marcel Varnel. UKN., *Tattenham Corner*, Brandon Fleming, Bernard Merivale, 1934, Play

All in Good Time see **THE FAMILY WAY** (1966).

All in the Night see **CROOKED STREETS** (1920).

All Is Confusion see **RIDING ON AIR** (1937).

ALL JORDENS FROJD 1953 d: Rolf Husberg. SWD., *All'irdisch Freud*, Margit von Soderholm, Novel

ALL LIVING THINGS 1939 d: Andrew Buchanan. UKN., *The Hallmark of Cain*, Nell St. John Montagu, Short Story

ALL LIVING THINGS 1955 d: Victor M. Gover. UKN., *The Hallmark of Cain*, Nell St. John Montagu, Short Story

ALL MAN 1918 d: Paul Scardon. USA., *Fiddler's Green*, Donn Byrne, 1918, Short Story

ALL MEN ARE ENEMIES 1934 d: George Fitzmaurice. USA., *All Men are Enemies*, Richard Aldington, New York 1933, Novel

ALL MEN ARE LIARS 1919 d: Sidney Morgan. UKN., *All Men are Liars*, Joseph Hocking, Novel

ALL MEN ARE MORTAL 1995 d: Ate de Jong. NTH/UKN/FRN., *All Men are Mortal*, Simone de Beauvoir, Novel

All Men Become Brothers see **ALLE MENSCHEN WERDEN BRUDER** (1973).

All Mixed Up see **MANJI** (1964).

ALL MY SONS 1948 d: Irving Reis. USA., *All My Sons*, Arthur Miller, New York 1947, Play

ALL MY SONS 1986 d: John Power. USA., *All My Sons*, Arthur Miller, New York 1947, Play

ALL NEAT IN BLACK STOCKINGS 1968 d: Christopher Morahan. UKN., *All Neat in Black Stockings*, Jane Gaskell, London 1966, Novel

ALL NIGHT 1918 d: Paul Powell. USA., *One Bright Idea*, Edgar Franklin, 1918, Short Story

All Night Through see **UNRUHIGE NACHT** (1958).

All Nudity Shall be Punished see **TODA NUDEZ SERA CASTIGADA** (1973).

All Nudity Will be Punished see **TODA NUDEZ SERA CASTIGADA** (1973).

ALL OF ME 1934 d: James Flood. USA., *Chrysalis*, Rose Albert Porter, New York 1932, Play

ALL OF ME 1984 d: Carl Reiner. USA., *Me Too*, Ed Davis, Novel

All on a Summer's Day see **DOUBLE CONFESSION** (1950).

ALL ON ACCOUNT OF AN EGG 1913. USA., *All on Account of an Egg*, O. Henry, Short Story

All One Night see **LOVE BEGINS AT 20** (1936).

All Our Fault see **NOTHING PERSONAL** (1995).

ALL QUIET ON THE WESTERN FRONT 1930 d: Lewis Milestone. USA., *Im Westen Nichts Neues*, Erich Maria Remarque, Berlin 1929, Novel

ALL QUIET ON THE WESTERN FRONT 1979 d: Delbert Mann. USA., *Im Westen Nichts Neues*, Erich Maria Remarque, Berlin 1929, Novel

ALL ROADS LEAD TO CALVARY 1921 d: Kenelm Foss. UKN., *All Roads Lead to Calvary*, Jerome K. Jerome, Novel

ALL SORTS AND CONDITIONS OF MEN 1921 d: Georges Treville. UKN., *All Sorts and Conditions of Men*, Sir Walter Besant, Novel

ALL SOULS' EVE 1921 d: Chester M. Franklin. USA., *All Souls' Eve*, Anne Crawford Flexner, New York 1920, Play

ALL THAT HEAVEN ALLOWS 1956 d: Douglas Sirk. USA., *All That Heaven Allows*, Edna Lee, Harry Lee, Novel

ALL THAT MONEY CAN BUY 1941 d: William Dieterle. USA., *The Devil and Daniel Webster*, Stephen Vincent Benet, 1937, Short Story

ALL THE BROTHERS WERE VALIANT 1923 d: Irvin V. Willat. USA., *All the Brothers Were Valiant*, Ben Ames Williams, New York 1919, Novel

ALL THE BROTHERS WERE VALIANT 1953 d: Richard Thorpe. USA., *All the Brothers Were Valiant*, Ben Ames Williams, New York 1919, Novel

ALL THE FINE YOUNG CANNIBALS 1960 d: Michael Anderson. USA., *The Bixby Girls*, Rosamund Marshall, Novel

All the Joy of Earth see **ALL JORDENS FROJD** (1953).

ALL THE KING'S HORSES 1935 d: Frank Tuttle. USA., *All the King's Horses*, Frederick Herendeen, Edward A. Horan, New York 1934, Musical Play

ALL THE KING'S MEN 1949 d: Robert Rossen. USA., *All the King's Men*, Robert Penn Warren, 1946, Novel

ALL THE LITTLE ANIMALS 1998 d: Jeremy Thomas. UKN., *All the Little Animals*, Walker Hamilton, Novel

ALL THE PRESIDENT'S MEN 1976 d: Alan J. Pakula. USA., *All the President's Men*, Carl Bernstein, Bob Woodward, 1974, Book

ALL THE RIVERS RUN 1983 d: George Miller, Pino AmentA. ASL., *All the Rivers Run*, Nancy Cato, Novel

All the Things You are see **A LETTER FOR EVIE** (1945).

All the Way see **THE JOKER IS WILD** (1957).

ALL THE WAY HOME 1963 d: Alex Segal. USA., *A Death in the Family*, James Agee, New York 1957, Novel

ALL THE WAY HOME 1981 d: Delbert Mann. USA., *A Death in the Family*, James Agee, New York 1957, Novel

ALL THE WAY UP 1970 d: James MacTaggart. UKN., *Semi-Detached*, David Turner, 1962, Play

ALL THE WINNERS 1920 d: Geoffrey H. Malins. UKN., *Wicked*, Arthur Applin, Novel

ALL THE WORLD TO NOTHING 1919 d: Henry King. USA., *All the World to Nothing*, Wyndham Martyn, Boston 1912, Novel

ALL THE WORLD'S A STAGE 1917 d: Harold Weston. UKN., *All the World's a Stage*, Herbert Everett, Novel

All Things Bright and Beautiful see **IT SHOULDN'T HAPPEN TO A VET** (1976).

ALL THIS, AND HEAVEN TOO 1940 d: Anatole Litvak. USA., *All This and Heaven Too*, Rachel Field, New York 1938, Novel

All This and Money Too *see* **LOVE IS A BALL** (1962).

All We Children from Bullerbyn *see* **ALLA VI BARN I BULLERBYN** (1960).

ALL WOMAN 1918 d: Hobart Henley. USA., *When Carey Came to Town*, Edith Barnard Delano, 1915, Serial Story

ALL WOMAN 1967 d: Frank Warren. USA., *Schizo*, Louis S. London

All Women *see* **THE MALTESE FALCON** (1931).

Alla Conquista Dell'arkansas *see* **DIE GOLDSUCHER VON ARKANSAS** (1964).

ALLA MIA CARA MAMMA NEL GIORNO DEL SUO COMPLEANNO 1974 d: Luciano Salce. ITL., *Nel Giorno Dell'Onomastico Della Mamma*, Rafael Azcona, Luis Berlanga, Story

ALLA VI BARN I BULLERBYN 1960 d: Olle Hellbom. SWD., Astrid Lindgren, Story

ALLA VI BARN I BULLERBYN 1986 d: Lasse Hallstrom. SWD., Astrid Lindgren, Story

ALL-AMERICAN, THE 1953 d: Jesse Hibbs. USA., *The All-American*, Leonard Freeman, Story

ALLAN QUARTERMAIN AND THE LOST CITY OF GOLD 1986 d: Gary Nelson, Newt Arnold. USA., *Allan Quartermain*, H. Rider Haggard, 1885, Novel

ALLE MENSCHEN WERDEN BRUDER 1973 d: Alfred Vohrer. GRM., *Alle Menschen Werden Bruder*, Johannes Mario Simmel, Novel

Allegheny Frontier *see* **ALLEGHENY UPRISING** (1939).

ALLEGHENY UPRISING 1939 d: William A. Seiter. USA., *The First Rebel*, Neil Harmon Swanson, New York 1937, Novel

Allegra Regina, L' *see* **LA REGINA DI NAVARRA** (1942).

Allegri Veterani, Gli *see* **LES VIEUX DE LA VIEILLE** (1960).

ALLEGRO SQUADRONE, L' 1954 d: Paolo Moffa. ITL/FRN., *Les Gaietes de l'Escadron*, Georges Courteline, 1886, Play

ALLEINSEGLERIN, DIE 1987 d: Hermann Zschoche. GDR., *Die Alleinseglerin*, Christine Wolter, Novel

ALLER SIMPLE, UN 1970 d: Jose Giovanni. FRN/ITL/SPN., *Un Aller Simple*, Edward Helseth, Novel

ALLES FUR GLORIA 1941 d: Carl Boese. GRM., *Intermezzo Am Abend*, Lorenz, von Moller, Play

ALLES MOET WEG 1997 d: Jan Verheyen. BLG., *Alles Moet Weg*, Tom Lanoye, Novel

ALLEY CAT, THE 1929 d: Hans Steinhoff. UKN., *The Alley Cat*, Anthony Carlyle, Novel

Alley Cat, The *see* **LE MATOU** (1985).

Allez Vous Pendre Ailleurs *see* **L' EMMERDEUR** (1973).

ALLIANCE, L' 1970 d: Christian de Chalonge. FRN., *L' Alliance*, Jean-Claude Carriere, Novel

Allies *see* **LOVE IN A HURRY** (1919).

ALLIGATOR NAMED DAISY, AN 1955 d: J. Lee Thompson. UKN., *An Alligator Named Daisy*, Charles Terrot, Novel

ALL-OF-A-SUDDEN-PEGGY 1920 d: Walter Edwards. USA., *All-of-a-Sudden-Peggy*, Ernest Denny, London 1906, Play

All'ombra Del Delitto *see* **LA RUPTURE** (1970).

ALL'OMBRA DI UN TRONO 1921 d: Carmine Gallone. ITL., *Fleur d'Ombre*, Charles Folly, Novel

ALLONS Z'ENFANTS 1980 d: Yves Boisset. FRN., *Allons Z'enfants*, Yves Gibeau, Novel

ALL'OVEST DI SACRAMENTO 1971 d: Federico Chentrens. ITL/FRN., Goscinny, Morris, Novel

ALL'S FAIR IN LOVE 1921 d: E. Mason Hopper. USA., *The Bridal Path*, Thompson Buchanan, New York 1913, Play

ALLTAGLICHE GESCHICHTE, EINE 1945 d: Gunther Rittau. GRM., *Tintenspritzer*, Johannes von Spallart, Play

ALLVARSAMMA LEKEN, DEN 1945 d: Rune Carlsten. SWD., *Den Allvarsamma Leken*, Hjalmar Soderberg, 1912, Novel

ALLVARSAMMA LEKEN, DEN 1977 d: Anja Breien. SWD/NRW., *Den Allvarsamma Leken*, Hjalmar Soderberg, 1912, Novel

ALM AN DER GRENZE, DIE 1951 d: Walter Janssen. GRM., *Der Besondere*, Ludwig Ganghofer, Novel

Alma *see* **OS CONDENADOS** (1974).

ALMA DE DIOS 1923 d: Manuel NoriegA. SPN., *Alma de Dios*, Carlos Arniches, E. Garcia Alvarez, Opera

ALMA, WHERE DO YOU LIVE? 1917 d: Hal Clarendon. USA., *Alma, Where Do You Live?*, Briquet, Musical Play, *Alma - Where Do You Live?*, Paul Harve, George V. Hobart, Musical Play

ALMENRAUSCH UND EDELWEISS 1928 d: Franz Seitz. GRM., *Almenrausch Und Edelweiss*, Hans Neuert, Dr. H. Schmidt, Play

ALMODO IFJUSAG 1974 d: Janos RozsA. HNG., *Almodo Ifjusag*, Bela Balazs, 1946, Novel

ALMOS' A MAN 1977 d: Stan Lathan. USA., *The Man Who Was Almost a Man*, Richard Wright, 1961, Short Story

ALMOST A HONEYMOON 1930 d: Monty Banks. UKN., *Almost a Honeymoon*, Walter Ellis, London 1930, Play

ALMOST A HONEYMOON 1938 d: Norman Lee. UKN., *Almost a Honeymoon*, Walter Ellis, London 1930, Play

ALMOST A HUSBAND 1919 d: Clarence Badger. USA., *Old Ebenezer*, Opie Read, Chicago 1897, Novel

ALMOST A LADY 1926 d: E. Mason Hopper. USA., *Skin Deep*, Frank R. Adams, Short Story

ALMOST GOLDEN - THE JESSICA SAVITCH STORY 1995 d: Peter Werner. USA., *Almost Golden*, Gwenda Blair, Biography

ALMOST GOOD MAN, THE 1917 d: Fred A. Kelsey. USA., *The Almost Good Man*, Shelley Sutton, Story

ALMOST MARRIED 1932 d: William Cameron Menzies. USA., *The Devil's Triangle*, Andrew Soutar, London 1931, Novel

Almost Married *see* **NO ROOM FOR THE GROOM** (1952).

Almost-New Suit, The *see* **UBRANIE PRAWIE NOWE** (1963).

ALOHA, LE CHANT DES ILES 1937 d: Leon Mathot. FRN., *Aloha le Chant Des Iles*, C. A. Gonnet, Novel

ALOHA MEANS GOODBYE 1974 d: David Lowell Rich. USA., *Aloha Means Goodbye*, Naomi A. Hintze, 1972, Novel

ALOMA OF THE SOUTH SEAS 1926 d: Maurice Tourneur. USA., *Aloma of the South Seas*, Leroy Clemens, John B. Hymer, New York 1925, Play

ALOMA OF THE SOUTH SEAS 1941 d: Alfred Santell. USA., *Aloma of the South Seas*, Leroy Clemens, John B. Hymer, New York 1925, Play

ALONE IN LONDON 1915 d: Larry Trimble. UKN., *Alone in London*, Robert Buchanan, Harriet Jay, London 1885, Play

Alone in the Pacific *see* **TAIHEIYO HITORIBOTCHI** (1963).

Alone on the Pacific *see* **TAIHEIYO HITORIBOTCHI** (1963).

ALONG CAME A SPIDER 1969 d: Lee H. Katzin. USA., *Sweet Poison*, Leonard Lee, Novel

ALONG CAME JONES 1945 d: Stuart Heisler. USA., *Along Came Jones*, Alan le May, Novel

ALONG CAME RUTH 1924 d: Eddie Cline. USA., *La Demoiselle de Magasin*, Jean-Francois Fonson, Play

ALONG CAME YOUTH 1930 d: Lloyd Corrigan, Norman Z. McLeod. USA., *Molinoff Indre-Et-Loire*, Maurice Bedel, Paris 1928, Novel

ALONG THE NAVAJO TRAIL 1945 d: Frank McDonald. USA., *Along the Navajo Trail*, William Colt MacDonald, Novel

Alouette, L' *see* **WO DIE LERCHE SINGT** (1936).

ALPENTRAGODIE 1927 d: Robert Land. GRM., *Alpentragodie*, Richard Voss, Novel

ALPHABET CITY 1984 d: Amos Poe. USA., Gregory K. Heller, Novel

Alphabet Murders, The *see* **THE ABC MURDERS** (1966).

Alpine Fire *see* **HOHENFEUER** (1985).

ALRAUNE 1928 d: Henrik Galeen. GRM., *Alraune*, Hanns Heinz Ewers, Novel

ALRAUNE 1930 d: Richard Oswald. GRM., *Alraune*, Hanns Heinz Ewers, Novel

ALRAUNE 1952 d: Arthur M. Rabenalt. GRM., *Alraune*, Hanns Heinz Ewers, Novel

ALS MUTTER STREIKTE 1973 d: Eberhard Schroeder. GRM., *Als Mutter Streikte*, Eric Malpass, Novel

ALS TWEE DRUPPELS WATER 1963 d: Fons Rademakers. NTH., **De Donkere Kamer Van Damocles**, Willem Frederik Hermans, 1958, Novel

ALS UNKU EDES FREUNDIN WAR 1980 d: Helmut DziubA. GDR., *Al Unku Edes Freundin War*, Alex Wedding, Short Story

ALSACE 1916 d: Henri Pouctal. FRN., *Alsace*, L. Camille, Gaston Leroux, Play

ALSKANDE PAR 1964 d: Mai Zetterling. SWD., *Froknarna von Pahlen*, Agnes von Krusentjerna, Stockholm 1930-35, Novel

ALSTER CASE, THE 1915 d: J. Charles Haydon. USA., *The Alster Case*, Rufus Gillmore, New York 1914, Novel

ALT FOR KVINDEN 1964 d: Annelise Reenberg. DNM., *Av Hjartans Lust*, Karl Ragnar Gierow, 1944, Novel

ALTAR MAYOR 1943 d: Gonzalo Delgras. SPN., *Altar Mayor*, Concha Espina de Serna, 1926, Novel

ALTAR STAIRS, THE 1922 d: Lambert Hillyer. USA., *The Altar Stairs*, G. B. Lancaster, New York 1908, Novel

ALTE FRITZ 1, DER 1927 d: Gerhard Lamprecht. GRM., *Der Alte Fritz*, Walter von Molo, Novel

ALTE FRITZ 2, DER 1927 d: Gerhard Lamprecht. GRM., *Der Alte Fritz*, Walter von Molo, Novel

ALTE FRITZ, DER 1936 d: Johannes Meyer. GRM., *Der Alte Fritz*, Walter von Molo, Novel

ALTE KAMERADEN 1934 d: Fred Sauer. GRM., *Das Fahnlein Der Versprengten*, Rudolf Herzog, Novel

ALTE LIED, DAS 1945 d: Fritz Peter Buch. GRM., *Irrungen Wirrungen*, Theodor Fontane, 1888, Short Story, *Stine*, Theodor Fontane, 1890, Short Story

Alter Ego *see* **BEWITCHED** (1945).

Alter Ego *see* **MURDER BY THE BOOK** (1987).

ALTERED STATES 1980 d: Ken Russell. USA., *Altered States*, Paddy Chayefsky, 1978, Novel

ALTES HERZ GEHT AUF DIE REISE 1938 d: Karl Junghans, Felix Lutzkendorf. GRM., *Altes Herz Geht Auf Die Reise*, Hans Fallada, Novel

ALT-HEIDELBERG 1959 d: Ernst MarischkA. GRM., *Karl Heinrich*, Wilhelm Meyer-Forster, 1899, Novel

ALTITUDE 3200 1938 d: Jean Benoit-Levy, Marie Epstein. FRN., *Altitude 3200*, Julien Luchaire, Play

ALTRA META DEL CIELO, L' 1977 d: Franco Rossi. ITL., *Romancero*, Jacques Deval, Novel

ALTRI UOMINI 1997 d: Claudio Bonivento. ITL., *Io Il Tebano*, Antonio Carlucci, Paolo Rossetti, Book

Always *see* **DEJA VU** (1984).

ALWAYS A BRIDE 1940 d: Noel Smith. USA., *Applesauce*, Barry Conners, New York 1925, Play

ALWAYS AUDACIOUS 1920 d: James Cruze. USA., *Toujours de l'Audace*, Ben Ames Williams, 1920, Short Story

Always Honest *see* **TAKE A BOW BABY** (1934).

ALWAYS IN MY HEART 1942 d: Jo Graham. USA., *Fly Away Home*, Dorothy Bennett, Irving White, Play

ALWAYS IN THE WAY 1915 d: J. Searle Dawley. USA., *Always in the Way*, Charles K. Harris, 1903, Song

ALWAYS OUTNUMBERED 1998 d: Michael Apted. USA., *Always Outgunned Always Outnumbered*, Walter Mosley, Book

ALWAYS TELL YOUR WIFE 1914 d: Leedham Bantock. UKN., *Always Tell Your Wife*, E. Temple Thurston, Play

ALWAYS TELL YOUR WIFE 1923 d: Hugh Croise, Alfred Hitchcock. UKN., *Always Tell Your Wife*, Seymour Hicks, Play

AM ABEND AUF DER HEIDE 1941 d: Jurgen von Alten. GRM., *Am Abend Auf Der Heide*, F. B. Cortan, Novel

AM ABEND NACH DER OPER 1944 d: Arthur M. Rabenalt. GRM., *Der Fund*, Franz Nabl, Novel

AM ANFANG WAR ES SUNDE 1954 d: Frantisek Cap. GRM/YGS., *Histoire d'une Fille de Femme*, Guy de Maupassant, 1881, Short Story

AM GALGEN HANGT DIE LIEBE 1960 d: Edwin Zbonek. GRM., *Philemon Und Baucis*, Leopold Ahlsen, Play

Am Gletscher *see* **KRISTNIHALD UNDIR JOKLI** (1989).

Am I Your Father? *see* **WO SHI HI BA BA MA?** (1995).

AM SEIDENEN FADEN 1938 d: R. A. Stemmle. GRM., *Mein Eigenes Propres Geld*, Eberhard Frowein, Book

AMADA BATA 1964 d: Amar Ganguly. IND., *Amada Bata*, Kumar Pattanayak, Novel

AMADEUS 1984 d: Milos Forman. USA., *Amadeus*, Peter Shaffer, 1980, Play

AMALIA 1936 d: Luis Barth-MogliA. ARG., *Amalia*, Jose Pedro Cristologo Marmol, 1851, Novel

AMANDA 1916 d: Giuseppe Sterni. ITL., *La Principessina*, Carlo Bertolazzi, 1908

Amanda see **THE ABC MURDERS** (1966).

AMANNISAHAN 1993 d: Wang Yan, Wang XIngjun. CHN., *Amannisahan*, Wang Yan, Opera

AMANT DE BORNEO, L' 1942 d: Jean-Pierre Feydeau, Rene Le Henaff. FRN., *L' Amant de Borneo*, Roger Ferdinand, Jose Germain, Play

AMANT DE CINQ JOURS, L' 1960 d: Philippe de BrocA. FRN/ITL., *L' Amant de Cinq Jours*, Francois Parturier, Novel

AMANT DE LADY CHATTERLEY, L' 1955 d: Marc Allegret. FRN., *Lady Chatterley's Lover*, D. H. Lawrence, 1928, Novel

Amant de Lady Chatterley, L' see **LADY CHATTERLEY'S LOVER** (1981).

AMANT DE MADAME VIDAL, L' 1936 d: Andre Berthomieu. FRN., *L' Amant de Madame Vidal*, Louis Verneuil, Play

AMANT DE PAILLE, L' 1950 d: Gilles Grangier. FRN., *L' Amant de Paille*, Marc-Gilbert Sauvajon, Play

AMANT DE POCHE, L' 1977 d: Bernard Queysanne. FRN., *L' Amant de Poche*, Valdemar Lestienne, Novel

AMANT, L' 1992 d: Jean-Jacques Annaud. FRN/UKN., *L' Amant*, Marguerite Duras, Novel

Amante Del Prete, L' see **LA FAUTE DE L'ABBE MOURET** (1970).

AMANTE DELL'ORSA MAGGIORE, L' 1971 d: Valentino Orsini. ITL/GRM/FRN., *L' Amante Dell'Orsa Maggiore*, Sergiusz Piaseki, Novel

Amante Di Cinque Giorni, L' see **L' AMANT DE CINQ JOURS** (1960).

AMANTE DI GRAMIGNA, L' 1968 d: Carlo Lizzani. ITL/BUL., *L' Amante Di Gramigna*, Giovanni Verga, 1880, Short Story

AMANTE DI UN GIORNO, L' 1907. ITL., *La Glu*, Jean Richepin, Play

Amante Di Una Notte, L' see **LE CHATEAU DE VERRE** (1950).

Amante Infedele see **LA SECONDE VERITE** (1965).

Amante Italiana, L' see **LES SULTANS** (1966).

Amante, L' see **LES CHOSES DE LA VIE** (1970).

Amante Pura, L' see **CHRISTINE** (1959).

AMANTE SEGRETA, L' 1941 d: Carmine Gallone. ITL., *Madel in Not*, Alfred Heller, Novel

Amantes de Verona, Los see **GIULIETTA E ROMEO** (1964).

AMANTI 1968 d: Vittorio de SicA. ITL/FRN., *Amanti*, Renaldo Cabieri, Brunello Rondi, Play

Amanti Del Chiaro Di Luna, Gli see **LES BIJOUTIERS DU CLAIR DE LUNE** (1958).

Amanti Di Domani, Gli see **CELA S'APPELLE L'AURORE** (1955).

Amanti Di Toledo, Gli see **LES AMANTS DE TOLEDE** (1953).

AMANTI SENZA AMORE 1948 d: Gianni Franciolini. ITL., *Kreutserova Sonata*, Lev Nikolayevich Tolstoy, 1889, Short Story

AMANTS DE TOLEDE, LES 1953 d: Henri Decoin, Fernando Palacios. FRN/SPN/ITL., *Le Coffre Et le Revenant*, Stendhal, 1867, Short Story

AMANTS DU TAGE, LES 1955 d: Henri Verneuil. FRN., *Les Amants du Tage*, Joseph Kessel, 1954, Novel

AMANTS ET VOLEURS 1935 d: Raymond Bernard. FRN., *Le Costaud Des Epinettes*, Alfred Athis, Tristan Bernard, Play

AMANTS, LES 1958 d: Louis Malle. FRN., *Point de Lendemain*, Dominique Vivant-Denon, Short Story

AMANTS TERRIBLES, LES 1936 d: Marc Allegret. FRN., *Private Lives*, Noel Coward, London 1930, Play

Amants Traques, Les see **MISTER FLOW** (1936).

AMARILLY OF CLOTHES-LINE ALLEY 1918 d: Marshall Neilan. USA., *Amarilly of Clothes-Line Alley*, Belle K. Maniates, Boston 1915, Novel

AMATEUR ADVENTURESS, THE 1919 d: Henry Otto. USA., *The Amateur Adventuress*, Thomas Edgelow, 1918, Short Story

AMATEUR DADDY 1932 d: John G. Blystone. USA., *Scotch Valley*, Mildred Cram, New York 1928, Novel

Amateur Detective see **IRISH LUCK** (1939).

AMATEUR DEVIL, AN 1920 d: Maurice Campbell. USA., *Wanted: a Blemish*, Henry J. Buxton, Jessie E. Henderson, 1919, Short Story

AMATEUR GENTLEMAN, THE 1920 d: Maurice Elvey. UKN., *The Amateur Gentleman*, Jeffrey Farnol, London 1913, Novel

AMATEUR GENTLEMAN, THE 1926 d: Sidney Olcott. USA., *The Amateur Gentleman*, Jeffrey Farnol, London 1913, Novel

AMATEUR GENTLEMAN, THE 1936 d: Thornton Freeland. UKN., *The Amateur Gentleman*, Jeffrey Farnol, London 1913, Novel

AMATEUR, THE 1982 d: Charles Jarrott. CND., *The Amateur*, Robert Littell, Novel

AMATEUR WIDOW, AN 1919 d: Oscar Apfel. USA., *An Amateur Widow*, Joseph Franklin Poland, Story

AMATEUR WIFE, THE 1920 d: Eddie Dillon. USA., *Miss Antique*, Nalbro Bartley, 1919, Short Story

AMAYA 1952 d: Luis MarquinA. SPN., *Los Vascos En El Siglo VIIi Amaya; O*, Francisco Navarro Villoslada, 1879, Novel

Amazing Adventure see **THE AMAZING QUEST OF ERNEST BLISS** (1936).

AMAZING ADVENTURE, THE 1917 d: Burton George. USA., *An Amazing Adventure*, Eleanor M. Ingram, Story

Amazing Battalion, The see **BATALION** (1927).

AMAZING DOCTOR CLITTERHOUSE, THE 1938 d: Anatole Litvak. USA., *The Amazing Dr. Clitterhouse*, Barre Lyndon, New York 1937, Play

AMAZING EXPLOITS OF THE CLUTCHING HAND, THE 1936 d: Al Herman. USA., *The Clutching Hand*, Arthur B. Reeve, Chicago 1934, Novel

AMAZING HOWARD HUGHES, THE 1977 d: William A. Graham. USA., *Howard: the Amazing Mr. Hughes*, Noah Dietrich, Bob Thomas, Book

Amazing Lovers, The see **EVEN AS EVE** (1920).

Amazing Mr. Beecham, The see **THE CHILTERN HUNDREDS** (1949).

AMAZING MR. BLUNDEN, THE 1972 d: Lionel Jeffries. UKN., *The Ghosts*, Antonia Baker, Story

AMAZING PARTNERSHIP, THE 1921 d: George Ridgwell. UKN., *The Amazing Partnership*, E. Phillips Oppenheim, 1914, Novel

AMAZING QUEST OF ERNEST BLISS, THE 1936 d: Alfred Zeisler. UKN., *The Amazing Quest of Mr. Ernest Bliss*, E. Phillips Oppenheim, London 1919, Novel

AMAZING QUEST OF MR. ERNEST BLISS, THE 1920 d: Henry Edwards. UKN., *The Amazing Quest of Mr. Ernest Bliss*, E. Phillips Oppenheim, London 1919, Novel

Amazing Quest, The see **THE AMAZING QUEST OF ERNEST BLISS** (1936).

AMAZING WIFE, THE 1919 d: Ida May Park. USA., *Whose Widow*, Elinor Chipp, Short Story

Amazons of Rome see **LE VERGINI DI ROMA** (1960).

AMAZONS, THE 1917 d: Joseph Kaufman. USA., *The Amazons*, Arthur Wing Pinero, London 1893, Play

AMAZZONI BIANCHE 1936 d: Gennaro Righelli. ITL., Gino Valori, Novel

AMBASCIATORE, L' 1936 d: Baldassarre Negroni. ITL., *Le Diplomate*, Germain Delavigne, Eugene Scribe, Play

AMBASSADOR, THE 1984 d: J. Lee Thompson. USA., *52 Pickup*, Elmore Leonard, Novel

Ambassadress, The see **DIE BOTSCHAFTERIN** (1960).

Ambavi Suramis Cikhisa see **LEGENDA SURAMSKOI KREPOSTI** (1986).

Ambiciosos, Los see **LA FIEVRE MONTE A EL PAO** (1959).

AMBITIEUSE, L' 1958 d: Yves Allegret. FRN/ITL/ASL., *Manganese*, Francois Ponthier, Novel

Ambitieux, Les see **L' AMBITIEUSE** (1958).

Ambition see **SCANDAL FOR SALE** (1932).

Ambition of Mark Truitt, The see **THE FRUITS OF DESIRE** (1916).

Ambler's Race, The see **PRASHNAI GULSARA** (1969).

Amboy Dukes, The see **CITY ACROSS THE RIVER** (1949).

Ambrose Applejohn's Adventure see **STRANGERS OF THE NIGHT** (1923).

Ambulance Call see **ONLY EIGHT HOURS** (1934).

AMBUSH 1949 d: Sam Wood. USA., *Ambush*, Luke Short, Short Story

Ambush see **RUKAJARVEN TIE** (1999).

AMBUSH MURDERS, THE 1982 d: Steven Hilliard Stern. USA., *The Ambush Murders*, Ben Bradle Jr., Book

AMBUSHERS, THE 1967 d: Henry Levin. USA., *The Ambushers*, Donald Hamilton, New York 1963, Book

AME D'ARTISTE 1924 d: Germaine Dulac. FRN., *Opad*, Christian Molbech, Play

AME DE CLOWN 1933 d: Marc Didier, Yvan Noe. FRN., *Teddy and Partner*, Yvan Noe, Play

AME DE PIERRE, L' 1928 d: Gaston Roudes. FRN., *L' Ame de Pierre*, Georges Ohnet, Novel

Amelia Or the Time for Love see **AMELIE OU LE TEMPS D'AIMER** (1961).

Amelie see **AMELIE OU LE TEMPS D'AIMER** (1961).

AMELIE OU LE TEMPS D'AIMER 1961 d: Michel Drach. FRN., *Amelie Boule*, Michele Angot, Novel

AMERE VICTOIRE 1957 d: Nicholas Ray. FRN/UKN., *Amere Victoire*, Rene Hardy, Novel

AMERICA 1915 d: Lawrence McGill. USA., *America*, Arthur Voegtlin, John P. Wilson, 1913, Musical Play

AMERICA, AMERICA 1963 d: Elia Kazan. USA., *America America*, Elia Kazan, New York 1962, Book

AMERICAN BEAUTY 1927 d: Richard Wallace. USA., *American Beauty*, Wallace Irwin, 1927, Short Story

AMERICAN BUFFALO 1996 d: Michael Corrente. USA/UKN., *American Buffalo*, David Mamet, 1975, Play

AMERICAN CITIZEN, AN 1914 d: J. Searle Dawley. USA., *An American Citizen*, Madeleine Lucette Ryley, New York 1897, Play

AMERICAN DREAM, AN 1966 d: Robert Gist. USA., *An American Dream*, Norman Mailer, New York 1965, Novel

AMERICAN DREAMER 1984 d: Rick Rosenthal. USA., Ann Biderman, Story

American Family see **FOUR WIVES** (1939).

American Friend, The see **DER AMERIKANISCHE FREUND** (1977).

AMERICAN GEISHA 1986 d: Lee Philips. USA., *Geisha*, Liza Dalby, Book

AMERICAN GENTLEMAN, AN 1915 d: John Gorman. USA., *An American Gentleman*, William Bonelli, New York 1900, Play

AMERICAN GUERRILLA IN THE PHILIPPINES, AN 1950 d: Fritz Lang. USA., *An American Guerrilla in the Philippines*, Ira Wolfert, Novel

American Home, An see **THE BATTLE CRY OF PEACE** (1915).

AMERICAN LIVE WIRE, AN 1918 d: Thomas R. Mills. USA., *The Lotus and the Bottle*, O. Henry, 1902, Short Story

AMERICAN METHODS 1917 d: Frank Lloyd. USA., *Le Maitre de Forges*, Georges Ohnet, Paris 1882, Novel

AMERICAN PLUCK 1925 d: Richard Stanton. USA., *Blaze Derringer*, Eugene P. Lyle Jr., New York 1910, Novel

AMERICAN PRISONER, THE 1929 d: Thomas Bentley. UKN., *The American Prisoner*, Eden Philpotts, Play

American Torso see **AMERIKAI ANZIKSZ** (1976).

AMERICAN TRAGEDY, AN 1931 d: Josef von Sternberg. USA., *An American Tragedy*, Theodore Dreiser, New York 1925, Novel

AMERICAN WIDOW, AN 1918 d: Frank Reicher. USA., *An American Widow*, Kellett Chambers, New York 1909, Play

AMERICAN YAKUZA 1994 d: Frank Cappello. USA/JPN., Taka Ichise, Story

Americanism (Versus Bolshevism) see **DANGEROUS HOURS** (1920).

AMERICANIZATION OF EMILY, THE 1964 d: Arthur Hiller. USA., *The Americanization of Emily*, William Bradford Huie, New York 1959, Novel

AMERICANO, THE 1917 d: John Emerson. USA., *Blaze Derringer*, Eugene P. Lyle Jr., New York 1910, Novel

AMERICANO, THE 1955 d: William Castle. USA., *Six Weeks South of Texas*, Leslie T. White, Serial Story

AMERICATHON 1979 d: Neal Israel. USA/GRM., *Americathon 1998*, Peter Bergman, Philip Proctor, Play

Americathon 1998 see **AMERICATHON** (1979).

AMERIKAI ANZIKSZ 1976 d: Gabor Body. HNG., *George Thurston*, Ambrose Bierce, 1891, Short Story

Amerikai Anzix see **AMERIKAI ANZIKSZ** (1976).

Amerikai Flu, Az see **UN FILS D'AMERIQUE** (1932).

AMERIKANISCHE FREUND, DER 1977 d: Wim Wenders. GRM., *Ripley's Game*, Patricia Highsmith, 1974, Novel

Ames Perdues see **ANIMA PERSA** (1976).

AMI DE VINCENT, L' 1983 d: Pierre Granier-Deferre. FRN., *L' Ami de Vincent*, Jean-Marc Robert, Novel

AMI DES MONTAGNES, L' 1920 d: Guy Du Fresnay. FRN., *L' Ami Des Montagnes*, Jean Rameau, Novel

AMI FRITZ, L' 1933 d: Jacques de Baroncelli. FRN., *L' Ami Fritz*, Erckmann-Chatrian, Novel

Ami Retrouve, L' see **REUNION** (1989).

AMI VIENDRA CE SOIR, UN 1945 d: Raymond Bernard. FRN., *Un Ami Viendra Ce Soir*, Jacques Companeez, Yvan Noe, Play

Amiamoci Cosi see **AL BUIO INSIEME** (1933).

AMICA 1916 d: Enrico Guazzoni. ITL., *Amica*, Pierre Berel, Paul Collin, Pietro Mascagni, Monte Carlo 1905, Opera

AMIC/AMAT 1999 d: Ventura Pons. SPN., *Amic/Amat*, Josep M. Benet I Jornet, Play

AMICHE, LE 1955 d: Michelangelo Antonioni. ITL., *Tra Donne Sole*, Cesare Pavese, Turin 1949, Short Story

AMICIZIA 1938 d: Oreste Biancoli. ITL., *Amitie*, Michel Dura, Play

AMICO DEL CUORE, L' 1999 d: Vincenzo Salemme. ITL., *L' Amico Del Cuore*, Vincenzo Salemme, Play

AMICO DELLE DONNE, L' 1943 d: Ferdinando M. Poggioli. ITL., *L' Ami Des Femmes*, Alexandre Dumas (fils), Play

Amico Di Famiglia, L' see **PATATE** (1964).

AMICO, L' 1921 d: Mario Bonnard. ITL., *L'Amico*, Marco Praga, 1886, Play

Amidst the Night's Silence see **WSROD NOCNEJ CISZY** (1978).

AMIE D'ENFANCE, UNE 1977 d: Francis Mankiewicz. CND., *Une Amie d'Enfance*, Louise Roy, Louis Saia, Play

AMINTA 1911 d: Giuseppe Berardi. ITL., *Aminta*, Torquato Tasso, 1573

AMINTIRI DIN COPILARIE 1964 d: Elisabeta Bostan. RMN., *Amintiri Din Copilarie*, Ion Creanga, 1881-92, Autobiography

AMITIES PARTICULIERES, LES 1964 d: Jean Delannoy. FRN., *Les Amities Particulieres*, Roger Peyrefitte, Paris 1945, Novel

AMITYVILLE HORROR, THE 1979 d: Stuart Rosenberg. USA., Jay Anson, Book

AMITYVILLE II: THE POSSESSION 1982 d: Damiano Damiani. USA., *Murder in Amityville*, Hans Holzer, Book

AMLETO 1908 d: Mario Caserini. ITL., *Hamlet*, William Shakespeare, c1601, Play

AMLETO 1908 d: Luca Comerio. ITL., *Hamlet*, William Shakespeare, c1601, Play

AMLETO 1917 d: Eleuterio Rodolfi. ITL., *Hamlet*, William Shakespeare, c1601, Play

AMMALDAR 1953 d: Keshav Narayan Kale, Madhukar Kulkarni. IND., *The Government Inspector*, Nikolay Gogol, 1836, Play

AMMAZZATINA, L' 1975 d: Ignazio Dolce. ITL., *Folle a Lier*, Ange Bastiani, Novel

AMMENKONIG, DER 1935 d: Hans Steinhoff. GRM., *Der Ammenkonig*, Max Dreyer, Play

Ammie, Come Home see **THE HOUSE THAT WOULD NOT DIE** (1970).

AMMIRAGLIA, L' 1914 d: Nino Oxilia. ITL., *Madame l'Admirale*, Antony Mars, Play

AMO TE SOLA 1935 d: Mario Mattoli. ITL., *Il Gatto in Cantina*, Nando Vitali, Play

AMOK 1934 d: Fedor Ozep. FRN., *Amok*, Stefan Zweig, 1922, Short Story

AMOK 1944 d: Antonio Momplet. MXC., *Amok*, Stefan Zweig, 1922, Short Story

Among Human Wolves see **THE SECRET JOURNEY** (1939).

Among People see **V LYUDKYAKH** (1939).

AMONG THE CINDERS 1983 d: Rolf Hadrich. NZL., *Among the Cinders*, Maurice Shadbolt, Novel

Among the Married see **MEN CALL IT LOVE** (1931).

Among Those Present see **THE HEADLEYS AT HOME** (1938).

Among Vultures see **UNTER GEIERN** (1964).

AMOR & CIA 1999 d: Helvecio Ratton. BRZ., *Alves & Cia*, Eca de Queiroz, Novel

Amor Aos 40, O see **UMA TARDE OUTRA TARDE** (1975).

AMOR BRUJO, EL 1967 d: Francisco Rovira BeletA. SPN., *El Amor Brujo*, Gregorio Martinez Sierra, 1915, Play

Amor Contra Amor see **LA LLAMA SAGRADA** (1931).

AMOR DE LOS AMORES, EL 1960 d: Juan de OrdunA. SPN/MXC., *El Amor de Los Amores*, Ricardo Leon Y Roman, 1912, Novel

AMOR DE PERDICAO 1943 d: Antonio Lopes Ribeiro. PRT., *Amor de Perdicao*, Camilo Castello Branco, 1862, Novel

AMOR DE PERDICAO 1977 d: Manoel de OliveirA. PRT., *Amor de Perdicao*, Camilo Castello Branco, 1862, Novel

AMOR MIO! 1916 d: Eleuterio Rodolfi. ITL., *M'amour*, Maurice Hennequin, 1901, Play

AMOR PROHIBIDO 1955 d: Luis Cesar Amadori. ARG., *Anna Karenina*, Lev Nikolayevich Tolstoy, Moscow 1876, Novel

Amor Solfeando, El see **EL PROFESOR DE MI MUJER** (1930).

AMORE 1948 d: Roberto Rossellini. ITL., *La Voix Humaine*, Jean Cocteau, 1930, Play

AMORE A ROMA, UN 1960 d: Dino Risi. ITL/FRN/GRM., *Un Amore a Roma*, Ercole Patti, Novel

AMORE AMARO 1974 d: Florestano Vancini. ITL., *Per Cause Imprecisate*, Carlo Bernari, Short Story

AMORE CONIUGALE, L' 1970 d: Dacia Maraini. ITL., *L' Amore Coniugale*, Alberto Moravia, 1949, Novel

AMORE COSI FRAGILE COSI VIOLENTO, UN 1973 d: Leros Pittoni. ITL., *Un Amore Cosi Fragile Cosi Violento*, Leros Pittoni, Novel

Amore Di Donna see **FIOR DI LEVANTE** (1925).

AMORE D'OLTRETOMBA, L' 1912. ITL., *La Statua Di Carne*, Teobaldo Ciconi, 1862, Play

Amore E Fango see **PALUDE TRAGICA** (1953).

AMORE E GINNASTICA 1973 d: Luigi Filippo d'Amico. ITL., Edmondo de Amicis, Story

AMORE E LA MASCHERA, L' 1920 d: Mario Gargiulo. ITL., *L' Amour Masque*, Honore de Balzac, Short Story

Amore, L' see **AMORE** (1948).

AMORE MOLESTO, L' 1995 d: Mario Martone. ITL., *L' Amore Molesto*, Elena Ferrante, Novel

Amore Per Appuntamento see **NATALE IN CASA D'APPUNTAMENTO** (1976).

AMORE ROSSO 1921 d: Gennaro Righelli. ITL., *La Militona*, Theophile Gautier, Novel

AMORE ROSSO 1953 d: Aldo Vergano. ITL., *Marianna Sirca*, Grazia Deledda, Novel

Amore Selvaggio see **MUSODURO** (1954).

AMORE SENZA STIMA 1914. ITL., *Amore Senza Stima*, Paolo Ferrari, Play

AMORE SI FA COSI, L' 1939 d: Carlo Ludovico BragagliA. ITL., *Monsieur Begonia*, Georges Fagot, Novel

AMORE SUI TETTI, L' 1915 d: Eleuterio Rodolfi. ITL., *L' Amore Sui Tetti*, Augusto Novelli, 1890, Play

Amore Tragico see **I PAGLIACCI** (1949).

AMORE, UN 1965 d: Gianni Vernuccio. ITL/FRN., *Un Amore*, Dino Buzzati, 1963, Novel

AMORI DEGLI ANGELI, GLI 1910 d: Giuseppe de Liguoro. ITL., Thomas Moore, 1823, Poem

AMORI DI MANON LESCAUT, GLI 1955 d: Mario CostA. ITL/FRN., *L' Histoire du Chevalier Des Grieux Et de Manon Lescaut*, Antoine-Francois Prevost d'Exiles, la haye 1731, Novel

Amori Di Una Calda Estate see **LOS PIANOS MECANICOS** (1965).

Amori Impossibili, Gli see **LE REMPART DES BEGUINES** (1972).

AMORI MIEI 1978 d: Steno. ITL., *Amori Miei*, Iaia Fiastri, Musical Play

AMORI PERICOLOSI 1964 d: Giulio Questi, Carlo Lizzani. ITL/FRN., *Chemin de Ronde*, Robert Francheville, Play

AMOROUS ADVENTURES OF MOLL FLANDERS, THE 1965 d: Terence Young. UKN., *Moll Flanders*, Daniel Defoe, 1722, Novel

Amorous Adventures of Uncle Benjamin, The see **MON ONCLE BENJAMIN** (1969).

Amorous General, The see **WALTZ OF THE TOREADORS** (1962).

Amorous Mr. Prawn, The see **THE AMOROUS PRAWN** (1962).

AMOROUS PRAWN, THE 1962 d: Anthony Kimmins. UKN., *The Amorous Prawn*, Anthony Kimmins, London 1959, Play

AMOS 1985 d: Michael Tuchner. USA., *Amos*, Stanley West, Novel

AMOUR A L'AMERICAINE, L' 1931 d: Claude Heymann, Paul Fejos. FRN., *L' Amour a l'Americaine*, Andre Mouezy-Eon, Robert Spitzer, Play

AMOUR DE POCHE, UN 1957 d: Pierre Kast. FRN., *The Diminishing Draft*, Waldemar Kaempfert, 1918, Short Story

AMOUR DE SWANN, UN 1983 d: Volker Schlondorff. FRN/GRM., *A la Recherche du Temps Perdu*, Marcel Proust, 1913, Novel

Amour Dispose, L' see **L' INCONSTANTE** (1931).

Amour du Mort, L' see **LA FIANCEE DU DISPARU** (1921).

AMOUR EN ALLEMAGNE, UN 1983 d: Andrzej WajdA. FRN/GRM., *Eine Liebe in Deutschland*, Rolf Hochhuth, 1978, Novel

Amour Est le Plus Fort, L' see **VIAGGIO IN ITALIA** (1953).

Amour Est un Chien de l'Enfer see **CRAZY LOVE** (1986).

AMOUR EST UN JEU, L' 1957 d: Marc Allegret. FRN., *La Victime*, Fernand Vanderem, Novel

AMOUR ET DISCIPLINE 1931 d: Jean Kemm. FRN., *French Leave*, Reginald Berkeley, London 1920, Play

Amour, Humour Et France see **LES AMOUREUX DU FRANCE** (1963).

AMOUR INTERDIT, L' 1984 d: Jean-Pierre Dougnac. FRN/ITL/CND., Heinrich von Kleist, Short Story

AMOUR L'APRES-MIDI, L' 1972 d: Eric Rohmer. FRN., *L'apres-Midi, L' Amour*, Eric Rohmer, 1974, Short Story

AMOUR, MADAME, L' 1952 d: Gilles Grangier. FRN., *L'amour Madame*, Felix Gandera, Claude Gevel, Play

AMOUR VEILLE, L' 1937 d: Henry Roussell. FRN., *L' Amour Veille*, Gaston Arman de Caillavet, Robert de Flers, Paris 1907, Play

AMOUREUSE AVENTURE, L' 1931 d: Wilhelm Thiele. FRN., *L' Amoureuse Aventure*, Paul Armont, Marcel Gerbidon, Play

AMOUREUX DU FRANCE, LES 1963 d: Pierre Grimblat, Francois Reichenbach. FRN/ITL., *Le Jeu de l'Amour Et du Hasard*, Pierre Carlet de Marivaux, 1730, Play

Amoureux, Les see **L' EPERVIER** (1933).

AMOURS DE LA REINE ELISABETH, LES 1912 d: Henri Desfontaines, Louis Mercanton. FRN., *La Reine Elisabeth*, Emile Moreau, Play

Amours de Manon Lescaut, Les see **GLI AMORI DI MANON LESCAUT** (1955).

AMOURS DE ROCAMBOLE, LES 1924 d: Charles Maudru. FRN., *Les Amours de Rocambole*, Ponson Du Terrail, Novel

AMPHITRYON 1935 d: Reinhold Schunzel. GRM., *Amphitryon*, Heinrich von Kleist, 1807, Play

AMPHITRYON 1981 d: Michael de Groot. GRM., *Amphitryon*, Heinrich von Kleist, 1807, Play

Amrit Manthan see **AMRITMANTHAN** (1934).

AMRITMANTHAN 1934 d: V. Shantaram. IND., *Amritmanthan*, Narayan Hari Apte, Novel

Amsel von Lichtental, Die see **VORSTADTVARIETE** (1934).

AMSTERDAM AFFAIR 1968 d: Gerry O'HarA. UKN., *Love in Amsterdam*, Nicolas Freeling, Novel

AMY FISHER: MY STORY 1992 d: Bradford May. USA., Maria Eftimiades, Book

Amy Foster see **SWEPT FROM THE SEA** (1997).

AN DIESEN ABENDEN 1951 d: Herbert Vesely. AUS., *Die Junge Magd*, Georg Trakl, 1913, Verse

An Einem Freitag in Las Vegas see **500 MILLONES LAS VEGAS** (1968).

AN EINEM FREITAG UM HALB ZWOLF 1961 d: Alvin Rakoff. GRM/FRN/ITL., *The World in My Pocket*, James Hadley Chase, London 1959, Novel

AN HEILIGEN WASSERN 1932 d: Erich Waschneck. GRM/SWT., *An Heiligen Wassern*, Jakob Christoph Heer, Stuttgart 1898, Novel

AN HEILIGEN WASSERN 1961 d: Alfred Weidenmann. SWT., *An Heiligen Wassern*, Jakob Christoph Heer, Stuttgart 1898, Novel

AN KLINGENDEN UFERN 1948 d: Hans Unterkircher. AUS., *An Klingenden Ufern*, Alexander Lernet-Holenia, Novel

AN OLES I YINEKES TOU KOSMOU 1967 d: Nestor Matsas. GRC., *Ekklisiazusai*, Aristophanes, c392 bc, Play

ANA AL DOCTOR 1968 d: Abbas Kamel. EGY., *Knock; Ou le Triomphe de la Medecine*, Jules Romains, 1924, Play

ANA TERRA 1972 d: Durval Gomes GarciA. BRZ., *Ana Terra*, Erico Verissimo, 1949, Short Story, *Um Certo Capitao Rodrigo*, Erico Verissimo, 1949, Short Story, *O Sobrado*, Erico Verissimo, 1949, Short Story

Anada *see* HRST VODY (1969).

ANANDMATH 1952 d: Hemen GuptA. IND., *Anandmath*, Bankimchandra Chatterjee, 1884, Novel

ANASTASIA 1956 d: Anatole Litvak. UKN/USA., *Anastasia*, Marcelle Maurette, Play

ANASTASIA 1997 d: Don Bluth, Gary Goldman. USA., *Anastasia*, Marcelle Maurette, Play

Anastasia Passed By *see* DUIOS ANASTASIA TRECEA (1979).

Anastasia Passing Gently *see* DUIOS ANASTASIA TRECEA (1979).

ANATAHAN 1954 d: Josef von Sternberg. USA/JPN., *Anatahan*, Michiro Maruyama, Short Story

Anatol *see* THE AFFAIRS OF ANATOL (1921).

Anatolian Smile, The *see* AMERICA AMERICA (1963).

ANATOMIST, THE 1961 d: Leonard William. UKN., *The Anatomist*, James Bridie, 1931, Play

ANATOMY OF A MURDER 1959 d: Otto Preminger. USA., *Anatomy of a Murder*, Robert Traver, Novel

Anatomy of a Syndicate *see* THE BIG OPERATOR (1959).

ANATOMY OF AN ILLNESS 1984 d: Richard T. Heffron. USA., *Anatomy of an Illness*, Norman Cousins, Autobiography

ANATRA ALL'ARANCIA, L' 1975 d: Luciano Salce. ITL., *L' Anatra All'arancia*, William Douglas Home, Marc-Gilbert Sauvajon, Play

Ancestor, The *see* L' ANTENATO (1936).

ANCHE NEL WEST, C'ERA UNA VOLTA DIO 1968 d: Marino Girolami. ITL/SPN., *Treasure Island*, Robert Louis Stevenson, London 1883, Novel

ANCIENS DE SAINT-LOUP, LES 1950 d: Georges Lampin. FRN., *Les Anciens de Saint-Loup*, Pierre Very, Novel

Ancient City *see* KOTO (1980).

Ancient City of Koto, The *see* KOTO (1980).

ANCIENT HIGHWAY, THE 1925 d: Irvin V. Willat. USA., *The Ancient Highway: a Novel of High Hearts and Open Roads*, James Oliver Curwood, New York 1925, Novel

ANCIENT MARINER, THE 1925 d: Henry Otto, Chester Bennett. USA., *The Rime of the Ancient Mariner*, Samuel Taylor Coleridge, 1857, Poem

AND A NIGHTINGALE SANG 1989 d: Robert Knights. UKN., *And a Nightingale Sang*, C. P. Taylor, Play

And Die of Pleasure *see* ET MOURIR DE PLAISIR (1960).

And Hope to Die *see* LA MAIN A COUPER (1974).

AND I ALONE SURVIVED 1978 d: William A. Graham. USA., *And I Alone Survived*, Lauren Elder, Shirley Streshinsky, Book

And It All Came True *see* IT ALL CAME TRUE (1940).

And Jimmy Went After the Rainbow *see* UND JIMMY GING ZUM REGENBOGEN (1971).

And Jimmy Went to the Rainbow's End *see* UND JIMMY GING ZUM REGENBOGEN (1971).

And Love Lasts Forever *see* ..UND EWIG BLEIBT DIE LIEBE (1954).

..and Love Laughs *see* ..UND DIE LIEBE LACHT DAZU (1957).

And Love Remains Eternal *see* ..UND EWIG BLEIBT DIE LIEBE (1954).

And No One Was Ashamed *see* ..UND KEINER SCHAMTE SICH (1960).

And Nobody Was Ashamed *see* ..UND KEINER SCHAMTE SICH (1960).

..and Nothing But the Truth *see* ..UND NICHTS ALS DIE WAHRHEIT (1958).

..AND NOW MIGUEL 1966 d: James B. Clark. USA., *..and Now Miguel*, Joseph Krumgold, New York 1953, Novel

And Now Pass Judgement. *see* A TEPYER SUDI. (1967).

AND NOW THE SCREAMING STARTS! 1973 d: Roy Ward Baker. UKN., *Fengriffen*, David Case, Novel

AND NOW TOMORROW 1944 d: Irving Pichel. USA., *And Now Tomorrow*, Rachel Field, Novel

And on Monday Morning at That *see* ..UND DAS AM MONTAGMORGEN (1959).

And Quiet Flows the Don *see* TIKHU DON (1931).

And Quiet Flows the Don *see* TIKHII DON (1958).

And Quiet Rolls the Dawn *see* EK DIN PRATIDIN (1979).

And Ride a Tiger *see* STRANGER IN MY ARMS (1959).

And Should We Ever Meet Again *see* UND FINDEN DEREINST WIR UNS WIEDER (1947).

AND SO THEY WERE MARRIED 1936 d: Elliott Nugent. USA., *Bless Their Hearts*, Sarah Addington, 1936, Short Story

And So They Were Married *see* JOHNNY DOESN'T LIVE HERE ANY MORE (1944).

And So to Bed *see* DAS GROSSE LIEBESSPIEL (1963).

And Still Breaks the Dawn *see* EK DIN PRATIDIN (1979).

AND THE BAND PLAYED ON 1993 d: Roger Spottiswoode. USA., *And the Band Played on*, Randy Shilts, Book

AND THE BEAT GOES ON: THE SONNY AND CHER STORY 1999 d: David Burton Morris. USA., *And the Beat Goes on*, Sonny Bono, Book

AND THE BEST MAN WON 1915 d: Horace Davey. USA., *And the Best Man Won*, George Marshall, Short Story

And the Fiddle Fell Silent *see* I SKRZYPCE PRZESTALY GRAC (1988).

..and the Fifth Rider Is Fear *see* ..A PATY JEZDEC JE STRACH (1964).

And the People Still Ask *see* MEG KER A NEP (1971).

And the Rain Erases All Traces *see* UND DER REGEN VERWISCHT JEDE SPUR (1972).

AND THE SAME TO YOU 1960 d: George Pollock. UKN., *The Chigwell Chicken*, A. P. Dearsley, Play

AND THE SEA WILL TELL 1991 d: Tommy Lee Wallace. USA., *And the Sea Will Tell*, Vincent Bugliosi, Bruce B. Henderson, Book

And the Violins Stopped Playing *see* I SKRZYPCE PRZESTALY GRAC (1988).

And the Wild, Wild Women *see* NELLA CITTA L'INFERNO (1958).

And Then *see* SOREKARA (1985).

..and Then Kills the Male and Eats It *see* MARTA (1971).

AND THEN THERE WERE NONE 1945 d: Rene Clair. USA., *Ten Little Niggers*, Agatha Christie, London 1939, Novel

AND THEN THERE WERE NONE 1974 d: Peter Collinson. UKN/SPN/GRM., *Ten Little Niggers*, Agatha Christie, London 1939, Novel

And There Came a Man *see* E VENNE UN UOMO (1964).

ANDALOUSIE 1950 d: Robert Vernay, Luis LuciA. FRN/SPN., *Andalousie*, Raymond Vinci, Albert Willemetz, Opera

Andalusian Dream *see* ANDALOUSIE (1950).

ANDALUSISCHE NACHTE 1938 d: Herbert Maisch. GRM/SPN., *Carmen*, Prosper Merimee, Paris 1846, Novel

ANDAMAN KAITHI 1952 d: V. Krishnan. IND., *Andaman Kaithi*, Ku. SA. Krishnamurthy, Play

ANDELICKARKA 1929 d: Oldrich Kminek. CZC., *Ja Jsem Vinna!*, Otakar Hanus, Novel

ANDERE, DER 1913 d: Max Mack. GRM., *Der Andere*, Paul Lindau, 1893, Play

ANDERE, DER 1930 d: Robert Wiene. GRM., *Der Andere*, Paul Lindau, 1893, Play

ANDERE, DIE 1949 d: Alfred E. Sistig. GRM., *Die Andere*, Renate Uhl, Novel

Andere Persoon, de *see* THE OTHER PERSON (1921).

ANDERE SEITE, DIE 1931 d: Heinz Paul. GRM., *Journey's End*, R. C. Sherriff, London 1929, Play

ANDERER LIEBHABER, EIN 1990 d: Xaver Schwarzenberger. GRM/FRN., Georges Simenon, Novel

ANDERSON TAPES, THE 1972 d: Sidney Lumet. USA., *The Anderson Tapes*, Lawrence Sanders, Novel

ANDHI GALI 1984 d: Buddhadeb DasguptA. IND., *Ghar Bari*, Dibyendu Palit, Novel

Andhi Galli *see* ANDHI GALI (1984).

ANDORRA OU LES HOMMES D'AIRAIN 1941 d: Emile Couzinet. FRN., *Andorra Ou Les Hommes d'Airain*, Isabelle Sandy, Novel

ANDRE 1994 d: George Miller. USA., *A Seal Called Andre*, Lew Dietz, Harry Goodridge, Novel

Andre and Ursula *see* ANDRE UND URSULA (1955).

Andre Chenier *see* ANDREA CHENIER (1955).

ANDRE CORNELIS 1915 d: Henri Pouctal. FRN., *Andre Cornelis*, Paul Bourget, Novel

ANDRE CORNELIS 1918 d: Jean Kemm, Georges DenolA. FRN., *Andre Cornelis*, Paul Bourget, Novel

ANDRE CORNELIS 1927 d: Jean Kemm. FRN., *Andre Cornelis*, Paul Bourget, Novel

ANDRE UND URSULA 1955 d: Werner Jacobs. GRM., *Andre Und Ursula*, Polly Maria Hofler, Novel

ANDREA CHENIER 1955 d: Clemente Fracassi. ITL/FRN., *Andrea Chenier*, Umberto Giordano, Luigi Illica, Milan 1896, Opera

Andrees Luftfard *see* INGENJOR ANDREES LUFTFARD (1982).

ANDREINA 1917 d: Gustavo SerenA. ITL., *Andrea*, Victorien Sardou, 1873, Play

ANDREMO IN CITTA 1966 d: Nelo Risi. ITL/YGS., *Andremo in Citta*, Edith Bruck, Novel

ANDREUCCIO DA PERUGIA 1910. ITL., *Il Decameron*, Giovanni Boccaccio, 1349-50, Book

ANDROCLES AND THE LION 1952 d: Chester Erskine, Nicholas Ray (Uncredited). USA., *Androcles and the Lion*, George Bernard Shaw, London 1913, Play

ANDROMEDA STRAIN, THE 1971 d: Robert Wise. USA., *The Andromeda Strain*, Michael Crichton, Novel

Andy of the Flying U *see* THE GALLOPING DEVIL (1920).

ANE DE BURIDAN, L' 1916?., *L' Ane de Buridan*, Gaston Arman de Caillavet, Robert de Flers, 1909, Play

ANE DE BURIDAN, L' 1932 d: Alexandre Ryder. FRN., *L' Ane de Buridan*, Gaston de Caillavet, Robert de Flers, 1909, Play

ANGE DE LA NUIT, L' 1942 d: Andre Berthomieu. FRN., *Famine Club*, Marcel Lasseaux, Play

Ange de Minuit, L' *see* BOUCLETTE (1918).

ANGE DU FOYER, L' 1936 d: Leon Mathot. FRN., *L' Ange du Foyer*, Gaston Arman de Caillavet, Robert de Flers, Play

Angeklagte Hat Das Wort, Der *see* MARESI (1948).

ANGEL 1937 d: Ernst Lubitsch. USA., *Angyal*, Menyhert Lengyel, Vienna 1932, Play

Angel *see* THE GRASSHOPPER (1970).

Angel and Sinner *see* BOULE-DE-SUIF (1945).

ANGEL AT MY TABLE, AN 1990 d: Jane Campion. NZL/ASL., *An Angel at My Table*, Janet Frame, 1984, Autobiography, *Envoy from Mirror City*, Janet Frame, 1985, Autobiography, *To the Is-Land*, Janet Frame, 1982, Autobiography

ANGEL BABY 1961 d: Paul Wendkos, Hubert Cornfield. USA., *Jenny Angel*, Elsie Oakes Barber, New York 1954, Book

ANGEL CITY 1980 d: Philip Leacock. USA., *Angel City*, Patrick Smith, Novel

ANGEL DESNUDO, EL 1946 d: Carlos Hugo Christensen. ARG., *Fraulein Else*, Arthur Schnitzler, 1923, Short Story

ANGEL ESQUIRE 1919 d: W. P. Kellino. UKN., *Angel Esquire*, Edgar Wallace, London 1908, Novel

ANGEL EXTERMINADOR, EL 1962 d: Luis Bunuel. MXC., *Los Naufragos de la Calle de la Providencia*, Jose Bergamin, Play

Angel for Satan, An *see* UN ANGELO PER SATANA (1966).

ANGEL FROM TEXAS, AN 1940 d: Ray Enright. USA., *The Butter and Egg Man*, George S. Kaufman, New York 1925, Play

ANGEL HEART 1987 d: Alan Parker. USA., *Falling Angel*, William Hjortsberg, Novel

ANGEL LEVINE, THE 1970 d: Jan Kadar. USA., *The Angel Levine*, Bernard Malamud, 1955, Short Story

ANGEL OF CONTENTION, THE 1914 d: John B. O'Brien. USA., *The Sheriff of Contention*, Will Levington Comfort, Short Story

Angel of the Dark *see* L' ANGE DE LA NUIT (1942).

ANGEL OF THE WARD, THE 1915 d: Tom Watts. UKN., *The Angel of the Ward*, Murray Herbert, Novel

ANGEL PAVEMENT 1958. UKN., *Angel Pavement*, J. B. Priestley, 1930, Novel

ANGEL RIVER 1986 d: Sergio Olhovich. USA/MXC., *Angel River*, Vilet, Novel

ANGEL SQUARE 1991 d: Anne Wheeler. CND., *Angel Square*, Brian Doyle, Novel

Angel Street *see* GASLIGHT (1940).

Angel Street *see* ANGEL SQUARE (1991).

ANGEL TUVO LA CULPA, UN 1959 d: Luis LuciA. SPN., *Milagro En la Plaza Del Progreso*, Joaquin Calvo Sotelo, 1954, Play

Angel Was to Blame, An *see* UN ANGEL TUVO LA CULPA (1959).

ANGEL WHO PAWNED HER HARP, THE 1954 d: Alan Bromly. UKN., *The Angel Who Pawned Her Harp*, Charles Terrot, Television Play

Angel Who Pawned His Harp, The *see* DER SEINE HARFE VERSETZTE, DER ENGEL (1959).

Angel With a Trumpet *see* THE ANGEL WITH THE TRUMPET (1950).

Angel With the Flaming Sword, The *see* DER ENGEL MIT DEM FLAMMENSCHWERT (1954).

Angel With the Trumpet, The *see* DER ENGEL MIT DER POSAUNE (1948).

ANGEL WITH THE TRUMPET, THE 1950 d: Anthony Bushell. UKN., *Der Engel Mit Der Posaune*, Ernst Lothar, Novel

ANGELE 1934 d: Marcel Pagnol. FRN., *Un de Baumugnes*, Jean Giono, 1929, Novel

Angelic Greeting *see* ANGYALI UDVOZLET (1985).

ANGELICA 1939 d: Jean Choux. FRN/ITL., *Les Compagnons d'Ulysse*, Pierre Benoit, Novel

Angelica *see* MARQUISE DES ANGES ANGELIQUE (1964).

Angelica Alla Corte Del Re *see* ANGELIQUE ET LE ROI (1965).

Angelica E Il Gran Sultano *see* ANGELIQUE ET LE SULTAN (1968).

Angelina *see* ANGELINA O EL HONOR DE UN BRIGADIER (1935).

ANGELINA O EL HONOR DE UN BRIGADIER 1935 d: Louis King. USA., *Angelina; O El Honor de un Brigadier*, Enrique Jardiel Poncela, Madrid 1934, Play

Angelique *see* MARQUISE DES ANGES ANGELIQUE (1964).

Angelique 2.Teil *see* MERVEILLEUSE ANGELIQUE (1964).

ANGELIQUE ET LE ROI 1965 d: Bernard Borderie. FRN/ITL/GRM., *Angelique Et le Roi*, Anne Golon, Serge Golon, Novel

ANGELIQUE ET LE SULTAN 1968 d: Bernard Borderie. FRN/GRM/ITL., *Angelique Et le Sultan*, Anne Golon, Serge Golon, Novel

ANGELIQUE, MARQUISE DES ANGES 1964 d: Bernard Borderie. FRN/ITL/GRM., *Marquise Des Anges Angelique*, Anne Golon, Serge Golon, Novel

Angelique -the Road to Versailles *see* MERVEILLEUSE ANGELIQUE (1964).

Angelique Und Der Konig *see* ANGELIQUE ET LE ROI (1965).

Angelique Und Der Sultan *see* ANGELIQUE ET LE SULTAN (1968).

ANGELO BIANCO, L' 1943 d: Giulio Antamoro, Federico Sinibaldi. ITL., *I Figli Di Nessuno*, Ruggero Rindi, Novel

ANGELO DEL MIRACOLO, L' 1945 d: Piero Ballerini. ITL., Hans Christian Andersen, Story

Angelo Della Rivolta, L' *see* TERESA CONFALONIERI (1934).

ANGELO DELLE ALPI, L' 1957 d: Carlo Campogalliani. ITL., *Rina l'Angelo Delle Alpe*, Carolina Invernizio, 1877, Novel

ANGELO PER SATANA, UN 1966 d: Camillo Mastrocinque. ITL., Luigi Emmanuele, Short Story

Angelo, Tyrant of Padua *see* IL TIRANNO DI PADOVA (1947).

Angels & Insects *see* ANGELS AND INSECTS (1995).

ANGELS AND INSECTS 1995 d: Philip Haas. USA/UKN., *Morpho Eugenia*, A. S. Byatt, Novel

Angels and Pirates *see* ANGELS IN THE OUTFIELD (1951).

Angels and the Pirates *see* ANGELS IN THE OUTFIELD (1951).

ANGELS IN THE OUTFIELD 1951 d: Clarence Brown. USA., *Angels in the Outfield*, Richard Conlin, Radio Play

Angel's Leap *see* LE SAUT DE L'ANGE (1971).

Angels of Darkness *see* DONNE PROIBITE (1953).

ANGES NOIRS, LES 1937 d: Willy Rozier. FRN., *Les Anges Noirs*, Francois Mauriac, 1936, Novel

ANGI VERA 1979 d: Pal Gabor. HNG., *Angi Vera*, Endre Veszi, Novel

ANGIE 1994 d: Martha Coolidge. USA., *Angie I Says*, Avra Wing, Novel

ANGLAIS TEL QU'ON LE PARLE, L' 1930 d: Robert Boudrioz. FRN., *L' Anglais Tel Qu'on le Parle*, Tristan Bernard, Play

Anglaise Romantique, Une *see* THE ROMANTIC ENGLISHWOMAN (1974).

ANGLAR, FINNS DOM? 1961 d: Lars-Magnus Lindgren. SWD., *Finns Dom, Pappa? Anglar*, John Einar Aberg, Uppsala 1955, Novel

Angle Shooter *see* BACK IN CIRCULATION (1937).

ANGLO-SAXON ATTITUDES 1992 d: Diarmuid Lawrence. UKN., *Anglo-Saxon Attitudes*, Angus Wilson, London 1956, Novel

ANGRY GOD, THE 1948 d: Van Campel Heilner. USA/MXC., *The Angry God*, Emma Lindsay Squier, Short Story

ANGRY HILLS, THE 1959 d: Robert Aldrich. UKN/USA., *The Angry Hills*, Leon Uris, Novel

Angry Sea, The *see* CHINOHATE NI IKIRU MONO (1960).

Angry Street, The *see* IKARI NO MACHI (1950).

ANGST 1928 d: Hans Steinhoff. GRM., *Die Angst*, Stefan Zweig, 1920, Short Story

Angst *see* LA PAURA (1954).

ANGST DER TORMANNS BIEN ELFMETER, DIE 1971 d: Wim Wenders. GRM., *Die Angst Des Tormanns Beim Elfmeter*, Peter Handke, 1970, Novel

Anguish *see* TORMENTO (1974).

ANGYALI UDVOZLET 1985 d: Andras Jeles. HNG., *Az Ember Tragediaja*, Imre Madach, 1863, Verse

ANGYALOK FOLDJE 1962 d: Gyorgy Revesz. HNG., *Angyalfold*, Marie-Luise Kaschnitz, 1929, Novel

Anicka, Come Back! *see* VRAT SE! ANICKO (1926).

ANICKO, VRAT SE! 1926 d: Theodor Pistek. CZC., *Tulak*, Emanuel Brozik, Opera

ANIKINA VREMENA 1954 d: Vladimir Pogacic. YGS., *Anikina Vremena*, Ivo Andric, 1931, Short Story

ANIMA ALLEGRA 1919 d: Roberto Leone Roberti. ITL., *El Genio Alegre*, Fratelli Quintero, 1906

ANIMA NERA 1962 d: Roberto Rossellini. ITL., *Anima Nera*, Giuseppe Patroni Griffi, Play

Anima Nostalgica *see* LA DANZATRICE MASCHERATA (1916).

ANIMA PERSA 1976 d: Dino Risi. ITL./FRN., *Anima Persa*, Giovanni Arpino, Novel

ANIMAL CRACKERS 1930 d: Victor Heerman. USA., *Animal Crackers*, Bert Kalmar, George S. Kaufman, New York 1928, Musical Play

ANIMAL FARM 1955 d: John Halas, Joy Batchelor. UKN., *Animal Farm*, George Orwell, 1945, Novel

ANIMAL KINGDOM, THE 1932 d: Edward H. Griffith, George Cukor (Uncredited). USA., *The Animal Kingdom*, Philip Barry, New York 1932, Play

Animal Kingdom, The *see* ONE MORE TOMORROW (1946).

ANIMAS TRUJANO, EL HOMBRE IMPORTANTE 1961 d: Ismael Rodriguez. MXC., *La Mayordomia*, Rogelio Barriga Rivas, Mexico City 1952, Novel

Anime Erranti *see* L' ULTIMO ADDIO (1942).

ANIME IN TUMULTO 1942 d: Giulio Del Torre. ITL., *Anime in Tumulto*, Augusto Turati, Novel

ANIME NEMICHE 1917. ITL., *Ames Ennemies*, P. H. Loyson, 1907, Novel

Anita in Paradise *see* ANITA V RAJI (1934).

ANITA V RAJI 1934 d: Jan Svitak. CZC., *Annette Hat Zuviel Geld*, Balder-Olden, Karl Rossler, Play

Anita V Raji *see* ANNETTE IM PARADIES (1934).

ANIUTA 1960 d: Marija Andjaparidze. USS., *Anyuta*, Anton Chekhov, 1886, Short Story

ANJO DO LODO 1951 d: Luiz de Barros. BRZ., *Luciola*, Jose Martiniano de Alencar, 1862, Short Story

ANJO MAU, UM 1972 d: Roberto Santos. BRZ., *Um Anjo Mal*, Adonias Filho, 1968, Short Story

Anjo Nu, O *see* EL ANGEL DESNUDO (1946).

ANKAHEE 1984 d: Amol Palekar. IND., *Kalaya Tasmeya*, C. T. Khanolkar, Play

ANKEMAN JARL 1945 d: Sigurd Wallen. SWD., *Ankeman Jarl*, Vilhelm Moberg, 1940, Play

AN-MAGRITT 1969 d: Arne Skouen. NRW., *Nattens Brod*, Johan Falkberget, 1940, Novel

ANN VICKERS 1933 d: John Cromwell. USA., *Ann Vickers*, Sinclair Lewis, New York 1933, Novel

ANNA 1920 d: Giuseppe de Liguoro. ITL., Henryk Sienkiewicz, Short Story

Anna *see* EDES ANNA (1958).

ANNA AND THE KING OF SIAM 1946 d: John Cromwell. USA., *Anna and the King of Siam*, Margaret Landon, Book

ANNA ASCENDS 1922 d: Victor Fleming. USA., *Anna Ascends*, Harry Chapman Ford, New York 1920, Play

ANNA CHRISTIE 1923 d: John Griffith Wray. USA., *Anna Christie*, Eugene O'Neill, New York 1922, Play

ANNA CHRISTIE 1929 d: Clarence Brown. USA., *Anna Christie*, Eugene O'Neill, New York 1922, Play

ANNA CHRISTIE 1930 d: Jacques Feyder. USA., *Anna Christie*, Eugene O'Neill, New York 1922, Play

Anna Cross, The *see* ANNA NA SHEE (1954).

ANNA FAVETTI 1938 d: Erich Waschneck. GRM., *Licht Im Dunklen Haus*, Walter von Hollander, Novel

ANNA KARENINA 1915 d: J. Gordon Edwards. USA., *Anna Karenina*, Lev Nikolayevich Tolstoy, Moscow 1876, Novel

Anna Karenina *see* LOVE (1927).

ANNA KARENINA 1935 d: Clarence Brown. USA., *Anna Karenina*, Lev Nikolayevich Tolstoy, Moscow 1876, Novel

ANNA KARENINA 1948 d: Julien Duvivier. UKN., *Anna Karenina*, Lev Nikolayevich Tolstoy, Moscow 1876, Novel

ANNA KARENINA 1953 d: Tatyana Lukashevich. USS., *Anna Karenina*, Lev Nikolayevich Tolstoy, Moscow 1876, Novel

ANNA KARENINA 1961 d: Rudolph Cartier. UKN., *Anna Karenina*, Lev Nikolayevich Tolstoy, Moscow 1876, Novel

Anna Karenina *see* ANNA KARYENINA (1968).

Anna Karenina *see* ANNA KARYENINA (1975).

ANNA KARENINA 1978 d: Basil Coleman. UKN., *Anna Karenina*, Lev Nikolayevich Tolstoy, Moscow 1876, Novel

ANNA KARENINA 1985 d: Simon Langton. USA., *Anna Karenina*, Lev Nikolayevich Tolstoy, Moscow 1876, Novel

Anna Karenina *see* LEO TOLSTOY'S ANNA KARENINA (1997).

ANNA KARENINE 1917 d: Ugo FalenA. ITL., *Anna Karenina*, Lev Nikolayevich Tolstoy, Moscow 1876, Novel

ANNA KARYENINA 1968 d: Alexander Zarkhi. USS., *Anna Karenina*, Lev Nikolayevich Tolstoy, Moscow 1876, Novel

ANNA KARYENINA 1975 d: Margarita PilikhinA. USS., *Anna Karenina*, Lev Nikolayevich Tolstoy, Moscow 1876, Novel

ANNA LEE: HEADCASE 1993 d: Colin Bucksey. UKN., *Anna Lee: Headcase*, Liza Cody, Novel

ANNA LUCASTA 1949 d: Irving Rapper. USA., *Anna Lucasta*, Philip Yordan, 1944, Play

ANNA LUCASTA 1958 d: Arnold Laven. USA., *Anna Lucasta*, Philip Yordan, 1944, Play

ANNA NA SHEE 1954 d: Isider Annensky. USS., *Anna Na Shee*, Anton Chekhov, 1895, Short Story

ANNA THE ADVENTURESS 1920 d: Cecil M. Hepworth. UKN., *Anna the Adventuress*, E. Phillips Oppenheim, London 1904, Novel

ANNABEL LEE 1921 d: William J. Scully. USA., *Annabel Lee*, Edgar Allan Poe, 1849, Poem

ANNABELLE'S AFFAIRS 1931 d: Alfred L. Werker. USA., *Good Gracious Annabelle*, Clare Kummer, New York 1916, Play

Annaluise and Anton *see* PUNKTCHEN UND ANTON (1999).

ANNAPOLIS FAREWELL 1935 d: Alexander Hall. USA., *Target*, Stephen Morehouse Avery, Short Story

ANNE AGAINST THE WORLD 1929 d: Duke Worne. USA., *Anne Against the World*, Victor Thorne, New York 1925, Novel

Anne and Muriel *see* LES DEUX ANGLAISES ET LE CONTINENT (1971).

ANNE BABI JOWAGER 1960 d: Franz Schnyder. SWT., *Wie Anne Babi Jowager Haushaltet Und Wie Es Ihm Mit Dem.*, Jeremias Gotthelf, Soleure 1843-44, Novel

Anne of a Thousand Days *see* ANNE OF THE THOUSAND DAYS (1969).

ANNE OF GREEN GABLES 1919 d: William D. Taylor. USA., *Anne of Green Gables*, L. M. Montgomery, Boston 1908, Novel

ANNE OF GREEN GABLES 1934 d: George Nicholls Jr. USA., *Anne of Green Gables*, L. M. Montgomery, Boston 1908, Novel

ANNE OF GREEN GABLES 1985 d: Kevin Sullivan. CND., *Anne of Green Gables*, L. M. Montgomery, Boston 1908, Novel

ANNE OF THE THOUSAND DAYS 1969 d: Charles Jarrott. UKN., *Anne of the Thousand Days*, Maxwell Anderson, New York 1948, Play

ANNE OF WINDY POPLARS 1940 d: Jack Hively. USA., *Anne of Windy Willows*, L. M. Montgomery, New York 1936, Novel

Anne of Windy Willows *see* ANNE OF WINDY POPLARS (1940).

ANNE ONE HUNDRED 1933 d: Henry Edwards. UKN., *Rescuing Anne*, Edgar Franklin, Novel

ANNEE DES MEDUSES, L' 1984 d: Christopher Frank. FRN., *L' Annee Des Meduses*, Christopher Frank, Novel

ANNEE DU BAC, L' 1963 d: Maurice Delbez, Jose-Andre Lacour. FRN., *L' Annee du Bac*, Jose-Andre Lacour, Play

Annees Lumiere, Les *see* LIGHT YEARS AWAY (1981).

Annelie *see* DIE GESCHICHTE EINES LEBENS ANNELIE (1941).

ANNELIE, DIE GESCHICHTE EINES LEBENS 1941 d: Josef von Baky. GRM., *Annelie*, Walter Lieck, Play

Annelie Vom Berghof *see* DIE KASEREI IN DER VEHFREUDE (1958).

Annemarie *see* DIE GESCHICHTE EINER JUNGEN LIEBE ANNEMARIE (1936).

ANNEMARIE, DIE GESCHICHTE EINER JUNGEN LIEBE 1936 d: Fritz Peter Buch. GRM., *Lauter Sonnentage*, Bruno Wellenkamp, Novel

ANNETTE ET LA DAME BLONDE 1941 d: Jean Dreville. FRN., *Annette Et la Dame Blonde*, Georges Simenon, 1963, Short Story

ANNETTE IM PARADIES 1934 d: Max Obal. GRM/CZC., *Annette Hat Zuviel Geld*, Balder-Olden, Karl Rossler, Play

ANNEXING BILL 1918 d: Albert Parker. USA., *Annexing Bill*, Edgar Franklin, Short Story

Anni Che Non Ritornano, Gli *see* LA MEILLEURE PART (1956).

ANNI DIFFICILI 1948 d: Luigi ZampA. ITL., *Il Vecchio Con Gli Stivali*, Vitaliano Brancati, 1944, Short Story

ANNIE, LEAVE THE ROOM! 1935 d: Leslie Hiscott. UKN., *Spendlove Hall*, Norman Cannon, Play

ANNIE-FOR-SPITE 1917 d: James Kirkwood. USA., *Annie-for Spite*, Frederick Jackson, 1916, Short Story

ANNIE'S COMING OUT 1984 d: Gil Brealey. ASL., *Annie's Coming Out*, Rosemary Crossley, Anne McDonald, Book

ANNIVERSARY, THE 1967 d: Roy Ward Baker. UKN., *The Anniversary*, Bill MacIlwraith, London 1966, Play

ANNO DI SCUOLA, UN 1977 d: Franco Giraldi. ITL., *Un Anno Di Scuola*, Gianni Stuparich, Short Story

Anno Sull'altipiano, Un *see* UOMINI CONTRO (1970).

Annonces Matrimoniales *see* LA VISITA (1963).

Annunciation, The *see* ANGYALI UDVOZLET (1985).

ANONIMA ROYLOTT, L' 1936 d: Raffaello Matarazzo. ITL., *L' Anonima Roylott*, Guglielmo Giannini, Play

ANONYME BRIEFE 1949 d: Arthur M. Rabenalt. GRM., *Anonyme Briefe*, Annemarie Artinger, Novel

Anonymous Letters *see* ANONYME BRIEFE (1949).

Another Air *see* JINY VZDUCH (1939).

Another Chance *see* WOMEN OF TWILIGHT (1952).

ANOTHER COUNTRY 1984 d: Marek KanievskA. UKN., *Another Country*, Julian Mitchell, 1982, Play

ANOTHER DAWN 1937 d: William Dieterle. USA., *Caesar's Wife*, W. Somerset Maugham, London 1919, Play

Another Day *see* EGYMASRA NEZVE (1982).

Another Hope *see* OTRA ESPERANZA (1996).

ANOTHER LANGUAGE 1933 d: Edward H. Griffith. USA., *Another Language*, Rose Franken, New York 1932, Play

ANOTHER MAN'S POISON 1951 d: Irving Rapper. UKN., *Deadlock*, Leslie Sands, Play

ANOTHER MAN'S SHOES 1922 d: Jack Conway. USA., *Another Man's Shoes*, Victor Bridges, New York 1913, Novel

ANOTHER MAN'S WIFE 1915 d: Harold Weston. UKN., *Another Man's Wife*, Miles Wallerton, Play

ANOTHER PART OF THE FOREST 1948 d: Michael Gordon. USA., *Another Part of the Forest*, Lillian Hellman, 1947, Play

ANOTHER SCANDAL 1924 d: Edward H. Griffith. USA., *Another Scandal*, Cosmo Hamilton, Boston 1924, Novel

ANOTHER SHORE 1948 d: Charles Crichton. UKN., *Another Shore*, Kenneth Reddin, Novel

ANOTHER TIME, ANOTHER PLACE 1958 d: Lewis Allen. UKN/USA., *Weep No More*, Lenore Coffee, Novel

ANOTHER TIME, ANOTHER PLACE 1983 d: Michael Radford. UKN., *Another Place Another Time*, Jessie Kesson, Novel

Another Way *see* EGYMASRA NEZVE (1982).

Another's Wife *see* JONS UND ERDME (1959).

ANSCHLUSS UM MITTERNACHT 1929 d: Mario Bonnard. GRM., *Coeur Bube*, Jacques Natanson, Play

ANSICHTEN EINES CLOWNS 1975 d: Vojtech Jasny. GRM., *Ansichten Eines Clowns*, Heinrich Boll, 1963, Novel

Answer of the Sea *see* UNDINE (1916).

ANSWER, THE 1916 d: Walter West. UKN., *Is God Dead?*, Newman Flower, Novel

Answer!, The *see* HANDS OF A STRANGLER (1962).

Answer's in the Wind, The *see* DIE ANTWORT KENNT NUR DER WIND (1975).

Antagonists, The *see* MASADA (1980).

ANTAR 1912. FRN., *Antar*, Chekri Ganem

ANTARJALI JATRA 1988 d: Gautam Ghose. IND., *Antarjali Jatra*, Kamal Kumar Majumdar, 1960, Novel

Antaryali Yatra *see* ANTARJALI JATRA (1988).

ANTENATO, L' 1936 d: Guido Brignone. ITL., *L' Antenato*, Carlo Veneziani, Play

ANTES, O VERAO 1968 d: Gerson Tavares. BRZ., *O Verao Antes*, Carlos Heitor Cony, 1964, Novel

ANTHONY ADVERSE 1936 d: Mervyn Leroy. USA., *Anthony Adverse*, Hervey Allen, New York 1933, Novel

ANTICO CAFFE NAPOLETANO, UN 1914 d: Gino Rossetti. ITL., *La Bottigliera Di Rigoletto*, Eduardo Scarpetta, 1880, Play

ANTIDOTE, THE 1927 d: Thomas Bentley. UKN., *The Antidote*, Ben Landeck, Play

ANTIGONE 1961 d: Georges Tzavellas. GRC., *Antigone*, Sophocles, c441 bc, Play

ANTINEA, L'AMANTE DELLA CITTA SEPOLTA 1961 d: Edgar G. Ulmer, Giuseppe Masini. ITL/FRN., *L' Atlantide*, Pierre Benoit, Paris 1919, Novel

Antoinette *see* MADAME CONDUISEZ-MOI (1932).

ANTOINETTE SABRIER 1927 d: Germaine Dulac. FRN., *Antoinette Sabrier*, Romain Coolus, Play

ANTON SPELEC, OSTROSTRELEC 1932 d: Martin Fric. CZC., *Uz Me Vezou*, Emil Artur Longen, Play

Anton Spelec, Sharp-Shooter *see* OSTROSTRELEC ANTON SPELEC (1932).

Anton Spelec, the Thrower *see* OSTROSTRELEC ANTON SPELEC (1932).

ANTON THE TERRIBLE 1916 d: William C. de Mille. USA., *Anton the Terrible*, Thomas H. Uzzell, 1916, Short Story

ANTONIETA 1982 d: Carlos SaurA. SPN/MXC/FRN., *Antonieta*, Andres Henestrosa, Novel

Antonietta *see* ANTONIETA (1982).

ANTONIO DI PADOVA 1931 d: Giulio Antamoro. ITL., *Antonio Di Padova Il Santo Dei Miracoli*, Vittorino Facchinetti, Novel

Antonio Di Padova, Il Santo Dei Miracoli *see* ANTONIO DI PADOVA (1931).

ANTONY AND CLEOPATRA 1908 d: Charles Kent. USA., *Antony and Cleopatra*, William Shakespeare, c1607, Play

ANTONY AND CLEOPATRA 1973 d: Charlton Heston. UKN/SPN/SWT., *Antony and Cleopatra*, William Shakespeare, c1607, Play

ANTONY AND CLEOPATRA 1974 d: John Scoffield, Trevor Nunn. UKN., *Antony and Cleopatra*, William Shakespeare, c1607, Play

ANTONY AND CLEOPATRA 1981 d: Jonathan Miller. UKN., *Antony and Cleopatra*, William Shakespeare, c1607, Play

ANTRE DE MISERICORDE, L' 1976 d: Bernard d'Albrigeon. FRN., *L' Antre de Misericorde*, Pierre MacRolan, Novel

Ant's Nest *see* HANGYABOLY (1971).

ANTWORT KENNT NUR DER WIND, DIE 1975 d: Alfred Vohrer. GRM/FRN., *Die Antwort Kennt Nur Der Wind*, Johannes Mario Simmel, Novel

Anugharam *see* KONDURA (1977).

Anushka, Model and Woman *see* MANEQUIM E MUHLER ANUSKA (1968).

ANUSKA, MANEQUIM E MUHLER 1968 d: Francisco Ramalho Jr. BRZ., *Ascensao Ao Mundo de Anuska*, Ignacio de Loyola Brandao, 1965, Short Story

Anuska, Manikine and Woman *see* MANEQUIM E MUHLER ANUSKA (1968).

ANWALT DES HERZENS, DER 1927 d: Wilhelm Thiele. GRM., *Die Letzten Nachte Der Mrs. Orchard*, Georg Froschel, Short Story

Anxiety of the Goalkeeper at the Penalty Kick, The *see* DIE ANGST DES TORMANNS BIEN ELFMETER (1971).

Any Man's Wife *see* MICHAEL O'HALLORAN (1937).

ANY NUMBER CAN PLAY 1949 d: Mervyn Leroy. USA., *Any Number Can Play*, Edward Harris Heth, Novel

Any Number Can Win *see* MELODIE EN SOUS-SOL (1962).

Any Special Way *see* WAT ZIEN IK (1971).

ANY WEDNESDAY 1966 d: Robert Ellis Miller. USA., *Any Wednesday*, Muriel Resnik, New York 1964, Play

ANYA KORO 1959 d: Shiro ToyodA. JPN., *Anya Koro*, Naoya Shiga, 1922-37, Novel

ANYBODY'S WAR 1930 d: Richard Wallace. USA., *Two Black Crows in the A. E. F. the*, Charles E. MacK, Indianapolis 1928, Novel

ANYBODY'S WOMAN 1930 d: Dorothy Arzner. USA., *The Better Wife*, Gouverneur Morris, Short Story

Anyone for Sex *see* IT'S A 2'6" ABOVE THE GROUND WORLD (1972).

Anyone for Venice? *see* THE HONEY POT (1967).

ANYTHING CAN HAPPEN 1952 d: George Seaton. USA., *Anything Can Happen*, George Papashvily, Helen Papashvily, Book

Anything for Love *see* 11 HARROWHOUSE (1974).

ANYTHING GOES 1936 d: Lewis Milestone. USA., *Anything Goes*, Guy Bolton, Cole Porter, P. G. Wodehouse, New York 1934, Musical Play

ANYTHING GOES 1956 d: Robert Lewis. USA., *Anything Goes*, Guy Bolton, Cole Porter, P. G. Wodehouse, New York 1934, Musical Play

ANYTHING MIGHT HAPPEN 1934 d: George A. Cooper. UKN., *Anything Might Happen*, Lady Evelyn Balfour, Novel

Anyuta *see* ANIUTA (1960).

Anzio *see* LO SBARCO DI ANZIO (1968).

Anzio Landing, The *see* LO SBARCO DI ANZIO (1968).

AOBEKA MONOGATARI 1962 d: Yuzo KawashimA. JPN., *Aobeka Monogatari*, Shugoro Yamamoto, Novel

AOIRO KAKUMEI 1953 d: Kon IchikawA. JPN., *Aoiro Kakumei*, Tatsuzo Ishikawa, 1952-53, Novel

APACHE 1954 d: Robert Aldrich. USA., *Bronco Apache*, Paul I. Wellman, Novel

Apache Gold *see* WINNETOU I (1963).

APACHE TERRITORY 1958 d: Ray Nazarro. USA., *The Last Stand at Papago Wells*, Louis L'Amour, Novel

APACHE TRAIL 1942 d: Richard Thorpe. USA., *Apache Trail*, Ernest Haycox, Story

APACHE UPRISING 1966 d: R. G. Springsteen. USA., *Way Station*, Harry Sanford, Max Steeber, New York 1961, Book

APACHE WAR SMOKE 1952 d: Harold F. Kress. USA., *Stage Station*, Ernest Haycox, Novel

APACHEN VON PARIS, DIE 1927 d: Nikolai Malikoff. GRM/FRN., *Les Innocents*, Francis Carco, Novel

Apaches' Last Battle *see* OLD SHATTERHAND (1964).

Apaches of Paris *see* DIE APACHEN VON PARIS (1927).

APARAJITO 1956 d: Satyajit Ray. IND., *Aparajita*, Bibhuti Bhushan Bandyopadhyay, 1931, Novel

APARECIDOS, LOS 1927 d: Jose Buchs. SPN., *Los Aparecidos*, Carlos Arniches, Celso Lucio, Opera

APARTMENT FOR PEGGY 1948 d: George Seaton. USA., Faith Baldwin, Story

APE MAN, THE 1943 d: William Beaudine. USA., *They Creep in the Dark*, Karl Brown, Story

Ape, The see THE HOUSE OF MYSTERY (1934).

APE, THE 1940 d: William Nigh. USA., *The Ape*, Adam Hull Shirk, Los Angeles 1927, Play

APHRODITE 1982 d: Robert Fuest. FRN./SWT., *Aphrodite*, Pierre Louys, Novel

APOCALYPSE NOW 1979 d: Francis Ford CoppolA. USA., *Heart of Darkness*, Joseph Conrad, 1899, Novel

APOKAL 1971 d: Paul Anczykowski. GRM., *The Black Cat*, Edgar Allan Poe, 1843, Short Story

APOLLO 13 1995 d: Ron Howard. USA., *Lost Moon*, Jeffrey Kluger, Jim Lovell, Book

Apollonia's Secret see TAINATA NA APOLONIA (1984).

APOLOGO, UM 1936 d: Mauro-Humberto, Lucia Miguel PereirA. BRZ., *Um Apologo*, Joaquim Maria Machado de Assis, 1885, Short Story

APOLOGO, UM 1939 d: Mauro-Humberto, Roquette Pinto. BRZ., *Um Apologo*, Joaquim Maria Machado de Assis, 1885, Short Story

APOORVA SAHODARARGAL 1949 d: T. G. RaghavacharyA. IND., *Les Freres Corses*, Alexandre Dumas (pere), 1845, Short Story

APOORVA SAHODHARALU 1949 d: Chittajalu PullayyA. IND., *Les Freres Corses*, Alexandre Dumas (pere), 1845, Short Story

Apostasy see HAKAI (1948).

APOTHEKERIN, DIE 1998 d: Rainer Kaufmann. GRM., *Die Apothekerin*, Ingrid Noll, Novel

APPALOOSA, THE 1966 d: Sidney J. Furie. USA., *The Appaloosa*, Robert MacLeod, Connecticut 1963, Book

APPARTEMENT DES FILLES, L' 1963 d: Michel Deville. FRN/GRM./ITL., *L' Appartement Des Filles*, Jacques Robert, Novel

Appartemento Delle Ragazze, L' see L' APPARTEMENT DES FILLES (1963).

APPASSIONATAMENTE 1954 d: Giacomo Gentilomo. ITL., *La Signora Di Saint Tropez*, A. Anicet-Bourgeois, Adolphe-P. d'Ennery, Play

APPASSIONNATA, L' 1929 d: Leon Mathot, Andre Liabel. FRN., *L' Appassionnata*, Pierre Frondaie, Play

APPAT, L' 1995 d: Bertrand Tavernier. FRN., *L' Appat*, Morgan Sportes, Book

APPEARANCE OF EVIL, THE 1918 d: Lawrence C. Windom. USA., *The Appearance of Evil*, Horace Hazeltine, Short Story

APPEARANCES 1921 d: Donald Crisp. USA/UKN., *Appearances*, Edward Knoblock, Play

Appel de la Foret, L' see CALL OF THE WILD (1972).

Appel du Coeur, L' see TOUTE SA VIE (1930).

APPEL DU SANG, L' 1919 d: Louis Mercanton. FRN., *The Call of the Blood*, Robert Hichens, Novel

Appelez-Moi Maitre see MONSIEUR LE PRESIDENT-DIRECTEUR GENERAL (1966).

APPLAUSE 1929 d: Rouben Mamoulian. USA., *Applause*, Beth Brown, New York 1928, Novel

Apple Annie see LADY FOR A DAY (1933).

APPLE DUMPLING GANG, THE 1975 d: Norman Tokar. USA., *The Apple Dumpling Gang*, James M. Bickham, Novel

Applesauce see BRIDES ARE LIKE THAT (1936).

APPLE-TREE GIRL, THE 1917 d: Alan Crosland. USA., *The Apple-Tree Girl*, George Weston, 1917, Story

Apple-Tree of Paradise, The see RAJSKA JABLON (1985).

APPOINTMENT FOR LOVE 1941 d: William A. Seiter. USA., *Heartbeat*, Ladislaus Bus-Fekete, Story

APPOINTMENT WITH A SHADOW 1958 d: Richard Carlson. USA., **If I Should Die**, Hugh Pentecost, Article

APPOINTMENT WITH DEATH 1987 d: Michael Winner. UKN., *Appointment With Death*, Agatha Christie, Novel

APPOINTMENT WITH FEAR 1946 d: Ronald Haines. UKN., John Dickson Carr, Short Story

Appointment With Fear: the Clock Strikes Eight see THE CLOCK STRIKES EIGHT (1946).

Appointment With Fear: the Gong Cried Murder see THE GONG CRIED MURDER (1946).

Appointment With Fear: the House in Rue Rapp see THE HOUSE IN RUE RAPP (1946).

Appointment With Life, An see UNA CITA CON LA VIDA (1957).

APPOINTMENT WITH VENUS 1951 d: Ralph Thomas. UKN., *Appointment With Venus*, Jerrard Tickell, Novel

APPRENTI SALAUD, L' 1977 d: Michel Deville. FRN., *L' Apprenti Salaud*, Frank Neville, Novel

APPRENTICESHIP OF DUDDY KRAVITZ, THE 1974 d: Ted Kotcheff. CND., *The Apprenticeship of Duddy Kravitz*, Mordecai Richler, 1959, Novel

APPRENTIE, L' 1914 d: Emile Chautard. FRN., *L' Apprentie*, Gustave Geffroy

Apprentissage de Duddy Kravitz, L' see THE APPRENTICESHIP OF DUDDY KRAVITZ (1974).

APPUNTAMENTO COL DISONORE 1970 d: Adriano Bolzoni. ITL/GRM./YGS., *Appuntamento Col Disonore*, William Cage, Novel

Appuntamento, L' see LE RENDEZ-VOUS (1961).

Appuntamento Per Uccidere, Unn see HORACE 62 (1962).

APRE LUTTE, L' 1917 d: Robert Boudrioz, Jacques de Feraudy. FRN., *L' Apre Lutte*, Robert Boudrioz, Play

APRES L'AMOUR 1924 d: Maurice Champreux. FRN., *Apres l'Amour*, Henri Duvernois, Pierre Wolff, Play

APRES L'AMOUR 1931 d: Leonce Perret. FRN., *Apres l'Amour*, Henri Duvernois, Pierre Wolff, Play

APRES L'AMOUR 1947 d: Maurice Tourneur. FRN., *Apres l'Amour*, Henri Duvernois, Pierre Wolff, Play

Apres l'Orage see NACH DEM STURM (1948).

APRES LUI 1918 d: Maurice de Feraudy, Gaston Leprieur. FRN., *Apres Lui*, Pierre Villetard, Novel

APRES VOUS, DUCHESSE 1954 d: Robert de Nesle. FRN., *Jeff*, Raoul Praxy

April Clouds see BOLOND APRILIS (1957).

APRIL FOLLY 1920 d: Robert Z. Leonard. USA., *April Folly*, Cynthia Stockley, 1918, Story

APRIL FOOL 1926 d: Nat Ross. USA., *An April Shower*, Alexander Carr, Edgar Allan Woolf, 1915, Play

APRIL LOVE 1957 d: Henry Levin. USA., *The Phantom Filly*, George Agnew Chamberlain, Novel

Apron Strings see THE VIRTUOUS HUSBAND (1931).

APT PUPIL 1998 d: Bryan Singer. USA., *Apt Pupil*, Stephen King, Novel

APU SANSAR 1958 d: Satyajit Ray. IND., *Aparajito*, Bibhutibhushan Bannerjee, Novel

Apur Sansar see APU SANSAR (1958).

AQUILA NERA 1946 d: Riccardo FredA. ITL., *Dubrovsky*, Alexander Pushkin, 1841, Short Story

Ara Nazhika Neram see ARANAZHIKANERAM (1970).

ARAB, THE 1915 d: Cecil B. de Mille. USA., *The Arab*, Edgar Selwyn, New York 1911, Play

ARAB, THE 1924 d: Rex Ingram. USA., *The Arab*, Edgar Selwyn, New York 1911, Play

Arabella see WE'RE RICH AGAIN (1934).

ARABESQUE 1966 d: Stanley Donen. UKN/USA., *The Cipher*, Alex Gordon, New York 1961, Book

ARAKURE 1957 d: Mikio Naruse. JPN., *Arakure*, Shusei Tokuda, 1915, Novel

Arana Negra see DAS GEHEIMNIS DER SCHWARZEN WITWE (1963).

ARANAZHIKANERAM 1970 d: K. S. Sethumadhavan. IND., *Aranazhikaneram*, Parappuram, Novel

ARANYE DINRATRI 1969 d: Satyajit Ray. IND., *Aranye Dinratri*, Sunil Ganguly, Novel

ARANYEMBER 1917 d: Alexander KordA. HNG., *Az Aranyember*, Mor Jokai, 1872, Novel

ARANYEMBER, AZ 1962 d: Viktor Gertler. HNG., *Az Aranyember*, Mor Jokai, 1872, Novel

Aranyer Din Raatri see ARANYE DINRATRI (1969).

ARANYORA, AZ 1945 d: Akos von Rathony. HNG., *Aranyora*, Erno Szep, 1931, Play

ARANYSARKANY 1966 d: Laszlo Ranody. HNG., *Aranysarkany*, Dezso Kosztolanyi, 1925, Novel

AraucanA. Conquista de Gigantes, La see LA ARAUCANA (1970).

ARAUCANA, LA 1970 d: Julio Coll. SPN/ITL/CHL., *La Araucana*, Alonso de Ercilla Y Zuniga, 1589, Verse

Araucana Massacro Degli Dei, L' see LA ARAUCANA (1970).

Araucana, The see LA ARAUCANA (1970).

Araucanian Girl, The see LA ARAUCANA (1970).

Arbeit macht Frei see ACCIAIO (1933).

ARBRE DE NOEL, L' 1969 d: Terence Young. FRN/ITL., *L' Arbre de Noel*, Michel Bataille, Paris 1967, Novel

ARCADIANS, THE 1927 d: Victor Saville. UKN., *The Arcadians*, Mark Ambient, Alex M. Thompson, London 1909, Musical Play

ARCH OF TRIUMPH 1948 d: Lewis Milestone. USA., *Arc de Triomphe*, Erich Maria Remarque, 1946, Novel

ARCH OF TRIUMPH 1985 d: Waris Hussein. USA., *Arc de Triomphe*, Erich Maria Remarque, 1946, Novel

Archa Pana Servadaca see NA KOMETE (1970).

ARCHE DE NOE, L' 1946 d: Henry-Jacques. FRN., *L' Arche de Noe*, Albert Paraz, Novel

Archer see THE UNDERGROUND MAN (1974).

Archibaldo see ENSAYO DE UN CRIMEN (1955).

ARCIDIAVOLO, L' 1940 d: Tony Frenguelli. ITL., *L' Arcidiavolo*, Gherardo Gherardi, Play

Arciere Della Foresta Nera, L' see GUGLIELMO TELL (1949).

ARCOLAIO DI BARBERINA, L' 1919 d: Lucio d'AmbrA. ITL., *La Quenouille de Barbarine*, Alfred de Musset, 1835

ARCTIC MANHUNT 1949 d: Ewing Scott. USA., *Narana of the North*, Ewing Scott, Novel

ARDH SATYA 1983 d: Govind Nihalani. IND., *Ardh Satya*, S. D. Panwalkar, Short Story

ARDHANGI 1955 d: P. Pullaiah. IND., *Swayamsiddha*, Manilal Gangopadhyay, Novel

ARDOISE, L' 1969 d: Claude Bernard-Aubert. FRN/ITL., *L' Ardoise*, Pierre Vial-Lesou, Novel

ARE ALL MEN ALIKE? 1920 d: Phil Rosen. USA., *The Waffle Iron*, Arthur Stringer, 1920, Short Story

ARE CHILDREN TO BLAME? 1922 d: Paul Price. USA., *Silas Marner*, George Eliot, London 1861, Novel

Are Husbands Necessary? see HONEYMOON IN BALI (1939).

ARE HUSBANDS NECESSARY? 1942 d: Norman Taurog. USA., *Mr. and Mrs. Cugat*, Isabel Scott Rorick, Novel

ARE PARENTS PEOPLE? 1925 d: Malcolm St. Clair. USA., **Are Parents People?**, Alice Duer Miller, 1924, Short Story

Are Passions Inherited? see INHERITED PASSIONS (1916).

Are the Children to Blame? see ARE CHILDREN TO BLAME? (1922).

Are These Our Children? see THE AGE OF CONSENT (1932).

ARE YOU A MASON? 1915 d: Thomas N. Heffron. USA., **Are You a Mason?**, Leo Ditrichstein, Emmanuel Lederer, New York 1901, Play

ARE YOU A MASON? 1934 d: Henry Edwards. UKN., **Are You a Mason?**, Leo Ditrichstein, Emmanuel Lederer, New York 1901, Play

ARE YOU IN THE HOUSE ALONE? 1978 d: Walter Grauman. USA., **Are You in the House Alone?**, Richard Peck, Novel

Are You Interested? see VOUS INTERESSEZ-VOUS A LA CHOSE? (1973).

ARE YOU LISTENING? 1932 d: Harry Beaumont. USA., **Are You Listening?**, Joseph Patrick McEvoy, Boston 1932, Novel

ARE YOU WITH IT? 1948 d: Jack Hively. USA., **Are You With It?**, George Balzer, Sam Perrin, Play

Arena of Fear see GELIEBTE BESTIE (1959).

ARENDASUL ROMAN 1952 d: Jean Georgescu. RMN., *Arenasul Roman*, Ion Luca Caragiale, 1893, Short Story

ARENES JOYEUSES 1935 d: Karl Anton. FRN., *Zou le Midi Bouge*, Henri Alibert, Opera

ARENES SANGLANTES 1917 d: Max Andre. FRN., *Sangre Y Arena*, Vicente Blasco Ibanez, Buenos Aires 1908, Novel

AREN'T MEN BEASTS! 1937 d: Graham Cutts. UKN., *Aren't Men Beasts!*, Vernon Sylvaine, London 1936, Play

AREN'T WE ALL? 1932 d: Harry Lachman. UKN., *Aren't We All?*, Frederick Lonsdale, London 1923, Play

Aren't We Wonderful? see WIR WUNDERKINDER (1958).

Argent de la Banque, L' see **THE SILENT PARTNER** (1978).

ARGENT, L' 1928 d: Marcel L'Herbier. FRN., *L' Argent*, Emile Zola, 1891, Novel

ARGENT, L' 1936 d: Pierre Billon. FRN., *L' Argent*, Emile Zola, 1891, Novel

ARGENT, L' 1983 d: Robert Bresson. FRN/SWT., *Falshivyi Kupon*, Lev Nikolayevich Tolstoy, 1911, Short Story

ARGENTIER DU ROI LOUIS XI, L' 1910. FRN., *Maitre Cornelius*, Honore de Balzac

Argento Maledetto, L' see **L' ORO MALEDETTO** (1911).

ARGINE, L' 1938 d: Corrado d'Errico. ITL., *L' Argine*, Rino Alessi, Play

ARGONAUTS OF CALIFORNIA - 1849, THE 1916 d: Henry Kabierske. USA., *California: Its History and Romance (Chapter 8)*, John Steven McGroarty, Book

Argonauts, The see **THE ARGONAUTS OF CALIFORNIA - 1849** (1916).

ARGYLE CASE, THE 1917 d: Ralph Ince. USA., *The Argyle Case*, Harriet Ford, Harvey J. O'Higgins, New York 1912, Play

ARGYLE CASE, THE 1929 d: Howard Bretherton. USA., *The Argyle Case*, Harriet Ford, Harvey J. O'Higgins, New York 1912, Play

ARGYLE SECRETS, THE 1948 d: Cy Endfield. USA., *The Argyle Album*, Cy Endfield, Radio Play

ARIA DEL CONTINENTE, L' 1935 d: Gennaro Righelli. ITL., *L' Aria Del Continente*, Nino Martoglio, Play

Aria Di Parigi see **L' AIR DE PARIS** (1954).

ARIADNE IN HOPPEGARTEN 1928 d: Robert Dinesen. GRM., *Ariadne in Hoppegarten*, Ludwig Wolff, Novel

ARIANE 1931 d: Paul Czinner. GRM., *Ariane*, Claude Anet, 1933, Novel

ARIANE 1931 d: Paul Czinner. UKN., *Ariane*, Claude Anet, 1933, Novel

Ariane see **THE LOVES OF ARIANE** (1931).

ARIANE, JEUNE FILLE RUSSE 1931 d: Paul Czinner. FRN., *Ariane - Jeune Fille Russe*, Claude Anet, Novel

Arid Earth, The see **BARA** (1981).

ARISTOCRACY 1914 d: Thomas N. Heffron. USA., *Aristocracy*, Bronson Howard, New York 1892, Play

ARISTOCRATES, LES 1955 d: Denys de La Patelliere. FRN., *Les Aristocrates*, Michel de Saint-Pierre, Novel

Aristocrats, The see **LES ARISTOCRATES** (1955).

ARIZONA 1913 d: Lawrence McGill, Augustus Thomas. USA., *Arizona*, Augustus Thomas, Chicago 1899, Play

ARIZONA 1918 d: Douglas Fairbanks, Albert Parker. USA., *Arizona*, Augustus Thomas, Chicago 1899, Play

ARIZONA 1931 d: George B. Seitz. USA., *Arizona*, Augustus Thomas, Chicago 1899, Play

ARIZONA 1940 d: Wesley Ruggles. USA., *Arizona*, Clarence Budington Kelland, New York 1939, Novel

Arizona Ames see **THUNDER TRAIL** (1937).

ARIZONA MAHONEY 1936 d: James P. Hogan. USA., *Stairs of Sand*, Zane Grey, 1928, Novel

ARIZONA RAIDERS, THE 1936 d: James P. Hogan. USA., *Raiders of the Spanish Peaks*, Zane Grey, 1931-32, Story

Arizona Thunderbolt see **ARIZONA MAHONEY** (1936).

Arizona Wildcat see **LIFE IN THE RAW** (1933).

ARKANSAS JUDGE 1941 d: Frank McDonald. USA., *False Witness*, Irving Stone, Story

ARLESIENNE, L' 1908 d: Albert Capellani. FRN., *L' Arlesienne*, Alphonse Daudet, 1872, Play

ARLESIENNE, L' 1922 d: Andre Antoine. FRN., *L' Arlesienne*, Alphonse Daudet, 1872, Play

ARLESIENNE, L' 1930 d: Jacques de Baroncelli. FRN., *L' Arlesienne*, Alphonse Daudet, 1872, Play

ARLESIENNE, L' 1941 d: Marc Allegret. FRN., *L' Arlesienne*, Alphonse Daudet, 1872, Play

Arlette Conquers Paris see **ARLETTE EROBERT PARIS** (1953).

ARLETTE EROBERT PARIS 1953 d: Victor Tourjansky. GRM., *Das Madchen Mit Der Mundharmonika*, Frank F. Braun, Novel

ARLETTE ET L'AMOUR 1943 d: Robert Vernay. FRN., *Atout-Coeur*, Felix Gandera, Play

ARLETTE ET SES PAPAS 1934 d: Henry Roussell. FRN., *Arlette Et Ses Papas*, Georges Berr, Louis Verneuil, Play

ARM OF THE LAW 1932 d: Louis King. USA., *Butterfly Mystery*, Arthur Hoerl, Short Story

Arm, The see **THE BIG TOWN** (1987).

ARMA BIANCA 1936 d: Ferdinando M. Poggioli. ITL., *Casanova a Parma*, Alessandro de Stefani, Play

Arma de Dos Filos, Un see **SHARK!** (1969).

ARMADALE 1916 d: Richard Garrick. USA., *Armadale*, Wilkie Collins, Novel

ARMADNI DVOJCATA 1937 d: Jiri Slavicek, Cenek Slegl. CZC., *Nam Je Hej*, Josef Stelibsky, Opera

Armageddon see **ARMAGUEDON** (1977).

ARMAGUEDON 1977 d: Alain JessuA. FRN/ITL., *The Voice of Armageddon*, David Lippincott, Novel

Armas Para El Caribe see **L' ARME A GAUCHE** (1965).

Armata Degli Eroi, L' see **L' ARMEE DES OMBRES** (1969).

ARME A GAUCHE, L' 1965 d: Claude Sautet. FRN/ITL/SPN., *L' Arme a Gauche*, Charles Williams, Novel

Arme Kleine Inge see **DIE SEXTANERIN** (1936).

ARME KLEINE SIF 1927 d: Arthur Bergen. GRM., *Arme Kleine Sif*, Reck-Malleczewen, Novel

ARME MILLIONAR, DER 1939 d: Joe Stockel. GRM., *Der Schusternazi*, Ludwig Thoma, Play

Armed Troops Behind Enemy Lines (Parts 1 & 2) see **DI HOU WU GONG DUI** (1995).

ARMEE DES OMBRES, L' 1969 d: Jean-Pierre Melville. FRN/ITL., *L' Armee Des Ombres*, Joseph Kessel, 1943, Novel

Armenia Crucified see **AUCTION OF SOULS** (1919).

ARMI E GLI AMORI, LE 1983 d: Giacomo Battiato. ITL., *Orlando Furioso*, Ludovico Ariosto, 1516, Verse

ARMIAMOCI E. PARTITE 1915 d: Camillo de Riso. ITL., *Armiamoci E. Partite*, Jose Castillo, Play

ARMISTEAD MAUPIN'S MORE TALES OF THE CITY 1998 d: Pierre Gang. USA/CND., *More Tales of the City*, Armistead Maupin, Novel

Armistead Maupin's Tales of the City see **TALES OF THE CITY** (1993).

ARMISTICE 1929 d: Victor Saville. UKN., *In Flanders Fields*, John McCrae, Poem

Arms and Loves see **LE ARMI E GLI AMORI** (1983).

ARMS AND THE GIRL 1917 d: Joseph Kaufman. USA., *Arms and the Girl*, Robert Baker, Grant Stewart, New York 1916, Play

ARMS AND THE MAN 1932 d: Cecil Lewis. UKN., *Arms and the Man*, George Bernard Shaw, 1894, Play

Arms and the Man see **HELDEN** (1958).

Arms and the Woman see **MR. WINKLE GOES TO WAR** (1944).

Army Brat see **LITTLE MR. JIM** (1946).

Army Game, The see **TIRE-AU-FLANC** (1961).

ARMY GIRL 1938 d: George Nicholls Jr. USA., *Army Girl*, Charles L. Clifford, 1935, Short Story

Army in the Shadows, The see **L' ARMEE DES OMBRES** (1969).

Army of the Shadows see **L' ARMEE DES OMBRES** (1969).

Army Radio Calais see **SOLDATENSENDER CALAIS** (1960).

Army Twins see **ARMADNI DVOJCATA** (1937).

ARMY WIVES 1986 d: Denny Lawrence. ASL., Lyndall Crisp, Article

ARNHEM: THE STORY OF AN ESCAPE 1976 d: Clive Rees. UKN., *Travel By Dark*, Graeme Warrack, Book

Around the Corner see **TRANSGRESSION** (1931).

AROUND THE WORLD IN 80 DAYS 1956 d: Michael Anderson. USA., *Le Tour du Monde En Quatre-Vingt Jours*, Jules Verne, 1873, Novel

Arouse and Beware see **THE MAN FROM DAKOTA** (1940).

ARPETE, L' 1928 d: E. B. Donatien. FRN., *L' Arpete*, Yves Mirande, Gustave Quinson, Play

ARRAH-NA-POGUE 1911 d: Sidney Olcott. USA., *Arrah-Na-Pogue*, Dion Boucicault, 1865, Play

ARRANGEMENT, THE 1969 d: Elia Kazan. USA., *The Arrangement*, Elia Kazan, New York 1967, Novel

ARRANGIATEVI! 1959 d: Mauro Bolognini. ITL., *Casa NovA. Vita Nova*, Matteo de Majo, Vinicio Gioli, Play

Arrest at Sundown see **TRAILS OF THE WILD** (1935).

ARREST BULLDOG DRUMMOND 1939 d: James P. Hogan. USA., *The Final Count*, H. C. McNeile ("Sapper"), London 1926, Novel

ARRETEZ LES TAMBOURS 1961 d: Georges Lautner. FRN., *Le Sentier*, Richard Prentout, Avignon 1959, Novel

Arrivederci, Baby see **DARLING DROP DEAD** (1966).

Arrivederci Roma see **THE SEVEN HILLS OF ROME** (1957).

Arrivista, L' see **LA RACE DES SEIGNEURS** (1974).

ARRIVISTE, L' 1914 d: Gaston Leprieur. FRN., *L' Arriviste*, Felicien Champsaur, Novel

ARRIVISTE, L' 1924 d: Andre Hugon. FRN., *L' Arriviste*, Felicien Champsaur, Novel

ARRIVISTES, LES 1960 d: Louis Daquin. FRN/GDR., *La Rabouilleuse*, Honore de Balzac, Paris 1842, Novel

ARROW IN THE DUST 1954 d: Lesley Selander. USA., *Platt River Gamble*, L. L. Foreman, Short Story

Arrow, The see **LA FRECCIA NEL FIANCO** (1943).

ARROWHEAD 1953 d: Charles Marquis Warren. USA., *Adobe Walls*, William Riley Burnett, 1953, Novel

ARROWSMITH 1931 d: John Ford. USA., *Martin Arrowsmith*, Sinclair Lewis, 1925, Novel

ARSENAL STADIUM MYSTERY, THE 1939 d: Thorold Dickinson. UKN., *The Arsenal Stadium Mystery*, Leonard Gribble, Novel

ARSENE LUPIN 1916 d: George Loane Tucker. UKN., *Arsene Lupin*, Maurice Leblanc, Paris 1907, Novel

ARSENE LUPIN 1917 d: Paul Scardon. USA., *Arsene Lupin*, Maurice Leblanc, Paris 1907, Novel

ARSENE LUPIN 1932 d: Jack Conway. USA., *Arsene Lupin*, Maurice Leblanc, Paris 1907, Novel

ARSENE LUPIN, DETECTIVE 1937 d: Henri Diamant-Berger. FRN., *L' Agence Barnett*, Maurice Leblanc, Novel

ARSENIC AND OLD LACE 1944 d: Frank CaprA. USA., *Arsenic and Old Lace*, Joseph Kesselring, New York 1941, Play

ARSENIC AND OLD LACE 1969 d: Robert Scheerer. USA., *Arsenic and Old Lace*, Joseph Kesselring, New York 1941, Play

ARSHIN MAL ALAN 1937 d: Setrag Vartian. USA., *Arshin Mal Alan*, Uzeir Hajibeyov, Opera

Arsonist's Daughter, The see **PALICOVA DCERA** (1941).

Arsule see **REGAIN** (1937).

ART OF CRIME, THE 1975 d: Richard Irving. USA., *Gypsy in Amber*, Martin Smith, Novel

Art of Love, The see **PRINZESSIN OLALA** (1928).

Artamanov Affair, The see **DELO ARTAMANOVICH** (1941).

Artamonov and Sons see **DELO ARTAMANOVICH** (1941).

ARTHUR 1930 d: Leonce Perret. FRN., *Arthur*, Andre Barde, Henri Christine, Opera

Arthur Hailey's the Moneychangers see **THE MONEYCHANGERS** (1976).

ARTHUR HAILEY'S WHEELS 1978 d: Jerry London. USA., *Wheels*, Arthur Hailey, Novel

ARTICLE 330, L' 1934 d: Marcel Pagnol. FRN., *L' Article 330*, Georges Courteline, 1900, Play

ARTIE, THE MILLIONAIRE KID 1916 d: Harry Handworth. USA., *Artie*, George Ade, New York 1907, Play

ARTIGLIO DEL NIBBIO, L' 1917 d: Romolo Bacchini. ITL., *The Claw*, William Smith, Novel

Artist and His Pierrette, The see **LAUGHTER AND TEARS** (1921).

Artist With the Ladies see **COIFFEUR POUR DAMES** (1931).

ARTISTEN-REVUE, DE 1926 d: Alex Benno. NTH., *Revue Artistique*, Michel Solser, Revue

Artistice Revue, The see **DE ARTISTEN-REVUE** (1926).

ARTUR A LEONTYNA 1940 d: M. J. Krnansky. CZC., *Artur a Leontyna*, Ignat Herrmann, Novel

Artur and Leontyna see **ARTUR A LEONTYNA** (1940).

Arturo's Island see **L' ISOLA DI ARTURO** (1962).

ARVACSKA 1976 d: Laszlo Ranody. HNG., *Arvacska*, Zsigmond Moricz, 1941, Novel

ARZIGOGOLO, L' 1924 d: Mario Almirante. ITL., *L' Arzigogolo*, Sem Benelli, 1922, Play

ARZT AUS LEIDENSCHAFT 1936 d: Hans H. Zerlett. GRM., *Arzt Aus Leidenschaft*, Carl Unselt, Novel

ARZTINNEN 1983 d: Horst Seemann. GDR/SWD/GRM., *Arztinnen*, Rolf Hochhuth, 1980, Play

As a Man Grows Older *see* SENILITA (1962).

AS A MAN THINKS 1919 d: George Irving. USA., *As a Man Thinks*, Augustus Thomas, New York 1911, Play

As Fate Ordained *see* ENOCH ARDEN (1915).

As God Made Her *see* ZOOALS IK BEN. (1920).

AS GOOD AS NEW 1933 d: Graham Cutts. UKN., *As Good As New*, Thompson Buchanan, New York 1930, Play

AS HE WAS BORN 1919 d: Wilfred Noy. UKN., *Felix Gets a Month*, Tom Gallon, Leon M. Lion, Play

AS HUSBANDS GO 1934 d: Hamilton MacFadden. USA., *As Husbands Go*, Rachel Crothers, New York 1931, Play

AS IN A LOOKING GLASS 1916 d: Frank H. Crane. USA., *As in a Looking Glass*, Francis Charles Philips, New York 1887, Novel

As It Was Before *see* THIS LOVE OF OURS (1945).

As Long As There are Pretty Girls *see* SOLANG' ES HUBSCHE MADCHEN GIBT (1955).

AS LONG AS THEY'RE HAPPY 1955 d: J. Lee Thompson. UKN., *As Long As They're Happy*, Vernon Sylvaine, London 1953, Play

AS MAN DESIRES 1925 d: Irving Cummings. USA., *Pandora la Croix*, Gene Wright, Philadelphia 1924, Novel

As No Man Has Loved *see* THE MAN WITHOUT A COUNTRY (1925).

AS THE EARTH TURNS 1934 d: Alfred E. Green. USA., *As the Earth Turns*, Gladys Hasty Carroll, New York 1933, Novel

As the Naked Wind from the Sea *see* SOM HAVETS NAKNA VIND (1968).

As the Sea Rages *see* RAUBFISCHER IN HELLAS (1959).

AS THE SUN WENT DOWN 1919 d: E. Mason Hopper. USA., *As the Sun Went Down*, George D. Baker, Play

As Time Goes By *see* CLOSE TO MY HEART (1951).

AS YE SOW 1914 d: Frank H. Crane. USA., *As Ye Sow*, Rev. John M. Snyder, New York 1905, Play

AS YOU DESIRE ME 1932 d: George Fitzmaurice. USA., *Come Tu Mi Vuoi*, Luigi Pirandello, Milan 1930, Play

AS YOU LIKE IT 1908 d: Kenean Buel. USA., *As You Like It*, William Shakespeare, c1600, Play

AS YOU LIKE IT 1912 d: J. Stuart Blackton, James Young. USA., *As You Like It*, William Shakespeare, c1600, Play

AS YOU LIKE IT 1936 d: Paul Czinner. UKN., *As You Like It*, William Shakespeare, c1600, Play

AS YOU LIKE IT 1978 d: Basil Coleman. UKN., *As You Like It*, William Shakespeare, c1600, Play

AS YOU LIKE IT 1992 d: Christine Edzard. UKN., *As You Like It*, William Shakespeare, c1600, Play

AS YOUNG AS YOU FEEL 1951 d: Harmon Jones. USA., Paddy Chayefsky, Story

ASA-HANNA 1946 d: Anders Henrikson. SWD., *Vansklighetens Land*, Elin Wagner, 1917, Novel

Asani Sanket *see* ASHANI SANKET (1973).

ASCENSEUR POUR L'ECHAFAUD, L' 1957 d: Louis Malle. FRN., *Ascenseur Pour l'Echafaud*, Noel Calef, Paris 1956, Novel

Ascent of Fujiyama, The *see* VOSHOZDENIE NA FUDZIJAMU (1988).

Ascent of Mount Fuji, The *see* VOSHOZDENIE NA FUDZIJAMU (1988).

ASCHENBROEDEL 1916 d: Ben Wilson. USA., *Aschenbroedel*, Bruno Lessing, Story

ASCHENPUTTEL 1955 d: Fritz Genschow. GRM., *Aschenputtel*, Jacob Grimm, Wilhelm Grimm, Short Story

ASCHENPUTTEL 1989 d: Karin Brandauer. GRM/FRN/CZC., *Aschenputtel*, Jacob Grimm, Wilhelm Grimm, Short Story

Asesino de Tontos, El *see* THE FOOL KILLER (1963).

Asfalto Che Scottia *see* CLASSE TOUS RISQUES (1959).

ASFALTO SELVAGEM 1964 d: J. B. Tanko. BRZ., *Asfalto Selvagem: Livro 2*, Nelson Rodrigues, Rio De Janeiro 1960, Novel

ASH TREE, THE 1975 d: Lawrence Gordon Clark. UKN., M. R. James, Short Story

Ash Wednesday Confession *see* DIE FASTNACHTSBEICHTE (1960).

ASHAD KA EK DIN 1971 d: Mani Kaul. IND., *Ashad Ka Ek Din*, Mohan Rakesh, 1958, Play

ASHAMED OF PARENTS 1921 d: Horace G. Plympton. USA., *What Children Will Do*, Charles K. Harris, Short Story

ASHANI SANKET 1973 d: Satyajit Ray. IND., *Ashani Sanket*, Bibhutibhushan Bannerjee, 1959, Novel

ASHES 1913 d: Oscar Apfel, Edgar Lewis. USA., *Ashes*, Marion Brooks, Story

Ashes *see* POPIOLY (1966).

Ashes and Diamonds *see* POPIOL I DIAMENT (1958).

ASHES OF REVENGE, THE 1915 d: Harold Shaw. UKN., *The Ashes of Revenge*, R. C. Carton, Novel

Ashes of Time *see* DUNG CHE SAI DUK (1993).

ASHES OF VENGEANCE 1923 d: Frank Lloyd. USA., *Ashes of Vengeance; a Romance of Old France*, H. B. Somerville, New York 1914, Novel

ASHIK KERIB 1988 d: Sergei Paradjanov, Dodo Abachidze. USS., *Ashik Kerib*, Mikhail Lermontov, 1837, Short Story

Ashiya Kara No Hiko *see* FLIGHT FROM ASHIYA (1964).

ASHWATHAMA 1979 d: K. R. Mohanan. IND., *Ashwathama*, Madampu Kunjukuttan, Novel

ASI ES LA VIDA 1930 d: George J. Crone. USA., *The Dark Chapter*, E. J. Rath, New York 1924, Novel

Asik Kerib *see* ASHIK KERIB (1988).

Asilo Muito Louco, Um *see* AZYLO MUITO LOUCO (1970).

ASINO DI BURIDANO, L' 1917 d: Eleuterio Rodolfi. ITL., *L' Ane de Buridan*, Gaston Arman de Caillavet, Robert de Flers, 1909, Play

ASK ANY GIRL 1959 d: Charles Walters. USA., *Ask Any Girl*, Winifred Wolfe, 1958, Novel

ASK BECCLES 1933 d: Redd Davis. UKN., *Ask Beccles*, Cyril Campion, Edward Dignon, London 1926, Play

Asking for Trouble *see* CRY FREEDOM (1987).

ASPEN 1977 d: Douglas Heyes. USA., *Aspen*, Burt Hirschfield, Novel, *The Adversary*, Bart Spicer, Novel

Aspen Murder, The *see* ASPEN (1977).

ASPERN 1981 d: Eduardo de Gregorio. PRT/FRN., *The Aspern Papers*, Henry James, 1888, Short Story

ASPHALT JUNGLE, THE 1950 d: John Huston. USA., *Asphalt Jungle*, William Riley Burnett, New York 1949, Novel

ASSASSIN A PEUR LA NUIT, L' 1942 d: Jean Delannoy. FRN., *L' Assassin a Peur la Nuit*, Pierre Very, Novel

ASSASSIN CONNAIT LA MUSIQUE, L' 1963 d: Pierre Chenal. FRN., *Une Chambre Et un Meurtre*, Fred Kassak

ASSASSIN EST DANS L'ANNUAIRE, L' 1961 d: Leo Joannon. FRN., *L' Assassin Est Dans l'Annuaire*, Charles Exbrayat, Novel

ASSASSIN HABITE AU 21, L' 1942 d: Henri-Georges Clouzot. FRN., *L' Assassin Habite Au 21*, Stanislas-Andre Steeman, Novel

Assassin, The *see* VENETIAN BIRD (1952).

ASSASSINATION 1987 d: Peter Hunt. USA., *Assassination*, Richard Sale, Novel

ASSASSINATION BUREAU, THE 1969 d: Basil Dearden. UKN., *The Assassination Bureau Ltd*, Robert L. Fish, Jack London, 1963, Novel

ASSASSINIO DEL CORRIERE DI LEONE, L' 1916 d: Gabriel Moreau. ITL., *L' Affaire du Courrier de Lyon*, Louis-Mathurin Moreau, Paul Siraudin, Play

Assassino Dei Poliziotti, L' *see* ORDER OF DEATH (1983).

Assassino Di Pietra, L' *see* THE STONE KILLER (1973).

ASSASSINS DE L'ORDRE, LES 1970 d: Marcel Carne. FRN/ITL., *Les Assassins de l'Ordre*, Jean Laborde, Novel

ASSAULT 1971 d: Sidney Hayers. UKN., *Assault*, Kendal Young, Novel

Assault Force *see* NORTH SEA HIJACK (1980).

Assault in Broad Daylight *see* ES GESCHAH AM HELLICHTEN TAG (1958).

ASSAULT ON A QUEEN 1966 d: Jack Donohue. USA., *Assault on a Queen*, Jack Finney, New York 1959, Novel

Assault, The *see* DE AANSLAG (1986).

ASSAUT, L' 1936 d: Pierre-Jean Ducis. FRN., *L' Assaut*, Henri Bernstein, Play

Assedio, L' *see* BESEIGED (1998).

ASSENZA INGIUSTIFICATA 1939 d: Max Neufeld. ITL., Istvan Bekeffy, Play

ASSIGNMENT - PARIS! 1952 d: Robert Parrish, Vincent Sherman (Uncredited). USA., *Trial By Terror*, Paul Gallico, Pauline Gallico, 1952, Book

ASSIGNMENT IN BRITTANY 1943 d: Jack Conway. USA., *Assignment in Brittany*, Helen MacInnes, Novel

ASSIGNMENT K 1967 d: Val Guest. UKN., *Department K*, Hartley Howard, London 1964, Novel

Assignment Paris *see* ASSIGNMENT - PARIS! (1952).

ASSIGNMENT REDHEAD 1956 d: MacLean Rogers. UKN., *Requiem for a Redhead*, Al Bocca, London 1953, Novel

Assignment, The *see* UPPDRAGET (1977).

ASSISI UNDERGROUND, THE 1984 d: Alexander Ramati. USA/ITL., *The Assisi Underground*, Alexander Ramati, Novel

Assistant, The *see* DER GEHULFE (1976).

ASSISTANT, THE 1997 d: Daniel Petrie. CND/UKN., *The Assistant*, Bernard Malamud, 1957, Novel

Assistant to His Highness *see* POBOCNIK JEHO VYSOSTI (1933).

Associate, The *see* L' ASSOCIE (1979).

ASSOCIATE, THE 1996 d: Donald Petrie. USA., *Il Mio Socio Davis*, Gennaro Prieto, Novel

ASSOCIE, L' 1979 d: Rene Gainville. FRN/GRM., *Il Mio Socio Davis*, Gennaro Prieto, Novel

ASSOLUTO NATURALE, L' 1969 d: Mauro Bolognini. ITL., *L' Assoluto Nationale*, Goffredo Parise, Book

ASSOMMOIR, L' 1909 d: Albert Capellani. FRN., *L' Assommoir*, Emile Zola, 1877, Novel

ASSOMMOIR, L' 1921 d: Charles Maudru, Maurice de Marsan. FRN., *L' Assommoir*, Emile Zola, 1877, Novel

ASSOMMOIR, L' 1933 d: Gaston Roudes. FRN., *L' Assommoir*, Emile Zola, 1877, Novel

ASSUNTA SPINA 1915 d: Gustavo Serena, Francesca Bertini (Uncredited). ITL., *Assunta Spina*, Salvatore Di Giacomo, 1909, Play

ASSUNTA SPINA 1929 d: Roberto Leone Roberti. ITL., *Assunta Spina*, Salvatore Di Giacomo, 1909, Play

ASSUNTA SPINA 1948 d: Mario Mattoli. ITL., *Assunta Spina*, Salvatore Di Giacomo, 1909, Play

Asszony a Valaszuton *see* DIE FRAU AM SCHEIDEWEGE (1938).

ASTONISHED HEART, THE 1950 d: Anthony Darnborough, Terence Fisher. UKN., *The Astonished Heart*, Noel Coward, 1936, Play

Astonished King, The *see* EL REY PASMADO (1991).

Astragal *see* L' ASTRAGALE (1968).

ASTRAGALE, L' 1968 d: Guy Casaril. FRN/GRM., *L' Astragale*, Albertine Sarrazin, 1965, Novel

Astrakan Coat, The *see* IL CAPPOTTO DI ASTRAKAN (1979).

ASTRID 1917 d: Alberto Carlo Lolli. ITL., *Astrid*, Annie Vivanti, 1911, Novel

Asug Qaribi *see* ASHIK KERIB (1988).

Aswathama *see* ASHWATHAMA (1979).

ASYA 1977 d: Josif Heifitz. USS., *Asya*, Ivan Turgenev, 1858, Short Story

Asylum of Horror *see* DER STUDENT VON PRAG (1913).

At 7 in the Morning All Is Still Well in the World *see* MORGENS UM 7 IST DIE WELT NOCH IN ORDUNG (1968).

At Any Price *see* GLI INTOCCABILI (1969).

AT BAY 1915 d: George Fitzmaurice. USA., *At Bay*, George Scarborough, Washington, D.C. 1913, Play

At Bay *see* ROAD TO PARADISE (1930).

AT CRIPPLE CREEK 1912 d: Hal Reid. USA., *At Cripple Creek*, Hal Reid, Play

AT DAWN 1914 d: Donald Crisp. USA., *At Dawn*, Frederick Moore, Short Story

At Daybreak *see* MORGENGRAUEN (1954).

AT DERE TOR! 1980 d: Lasse Glomm. NRW., *At Dere Tor!*, Espen Haavardsholm, Novel

At First It Was Sin *see* AM ANFANG WAR ES SUNDE (1954).

At First Sight *see* COUP DE FOUDRE (1983).

AT FIRST SIGHT 1999 d: Irwin Winkler. USA., *To See and Not See*, Oliver Sacks, Story

At Five O'Clock in the Afternoon see **A LAS CINCO DE LA TARDE** (1960).

At Good Old Siwash see **THOSE WERE THE DAYS!** (1940).

At Medicine Bend see **MEDICINE BEND** (1916).

At Middle Age see **REN DAO ZHONGNIAN** (1982).

At Night, When Dracula Wakes Up see **EL CONDE DRACULA** (1970).

AT PINEY RIDGE 1916 d: William Robert Daly. USA., *At Piney Ridge*, David K. Higgins, New York 1897, Play

AT PLAY IN THE FIELDS OF THE LORD 1991 d: Hector Babenco. USA/BRZ., *At Play in the Fields of the Lord*, Peter Mathiessen, Novel

At St. Anthony's see **U SVETEHO ANTONICKA** (1933).

AT SWORD'S POINT 1951 d: Lewis Allen. USA., *Vingt Ans Apres; Suite de Trois Mousquetaires*, Alexandre Dumas (pere), 1845, Novel

At the Barn see **TWO WEEKS** (1920).

At the Blue Gates of the Town see **PORTILE ALBASTRE ALE ORASULUI** (1973).

At the Bottom of the Swimming Pool see **LA ULTIMA SENORA ANDERSON** (1970).

AT THE CROSS ROADS 1914 d: Frank L. Dear. USA., *At the Old Cross Roads*, Hal Reid, New York 1902, Play

AT THE EARTH'S CORE 1976 d: Kevin Connor. UKN., *At the Earth's Core*, Edgar Rice Burroughs, 1922, Novel

AT THE ELEVENTH HOUR 1912 d: William V. Ranous. USA., *A String of Pearls*, Guy de Maupassant, Short Story

AT THE END OF THE WORLD 1921 d: Penrhyn Stanlaws. USA., *At the End of the World*, Ernest Klein, Play

At the House of St. Matej, When the Sun Comes Out see **KDYZ SE SLUNKO ZASMEJE U SVATEHO MATEJE** (1928).

AT THE MERCY OF TIBERIUS 1920 d: Fred Leroy Granville. UKN/USA., *At the Mercy of Tiberius*, Augusta Jane Evans Wilson, New York 1887, Novel

At the Mercy of Tiberius see **THE PRICE OF SILENCE** (1921).

At the Old Crossed Roads see **AT THE CROSS ROADS** (1914).

AT THE POINT OF A GUN 1919 d: Edward Kull. USA., *At the Point of a Gun*, Dorothy Rockfort, Story

At the Ravine see **NA KLANCU** (1971).

At the Risk of My Life see **INOCHI BONIFURO** (1970).

AT THE SIGN OF THE JACK O'LANTERN 1922 d: Lloyd Ingraham. USA., *At the Sign of the Jack O'Lantern*, Myrtle Reed, New York 1905, Novel

AT THE SIGN OF THE KANGAROO 1917 d: Paul C. Hurst. USA., *Stingaree Stories*, E. W. Hornung, Story

At the Silver Globe see **NA SREBRNYM GLOBIE** (1977).

At the Stroke of Nine see **MURDER ON THE CAMPUS** (1934).

At the Villa Falconer see **VILLA FALCONIERI** (1929).

AT THE VILLA ROSE 1920 d: Maurice Elvey. UKN., *At the Villa Rose*, A. E. W. Mason, 1910, Novel

AT THE VILLA ROSE 1929 d: Leslie Hiscott. UKN., *At the Villa Rose*, A. E. W. Mason, 1910, Novel

AT THE VILLA ROSE 1939 d: Walter Summers. UKN., *At the Villa Rose*, A. E. W. Mason, 1910, Novel

AT WAR WITH THE ARMY 1950 d: Hal Walker. USA., *At War With the Army*, James B. Allardice, New York 1949, Play

At Yale see **HOLD 'EM YALE!** (1928).

At Your Orders, Madame see **SIGNORA! AI VOSTRI ORDINI** (1939).

Ataque de Los Kurdos, El see **IM REICHE DES SILBERNEN LOWEN** (1965).

ATAVISM OF JOHN TOM LITTLE BEAR, THE 1917 d: David Smith. USA., *The Atavism of John Tom Little Bear*, O. Henry, Short Story

ATE QUE O CASAMENTO NOS SEPARE 1968 d: Flavio Tambellini. BRZ., *Os Pais Abstratos*, Pedro Bloch, 1965, Play

ATHALIE 1910 d: Michel Carre. FRN., *Athalie*, Jean Racine, Play

Athalie see **UNSEEN FORCES** (1920).

ATHLETE INCOMPLET, L' 1932 d: Claude Autant-LarA. FRN., *The Poor Nut*, Elliott Nugent, J. C. Nugent, New York 1925, Play

Athlete Maigre Lui, L' see **L' ATHLETE INCOMPLET** (1932).

Athuan see **A HALO FOR ATHUAN** (1985).

ATITHI 1965 d: Tapan SinhA. IND., *Atithi*, Rabindranath Tagore, 1895, Short Story

ATLANTIC 1929 d: E. A. Dupont. UKN., *The Berg*, Ernest Raymond, Short Story

ATLANTIC ADVENTURE 1935 d: Albert S. Rogell. USA., *Atlantic Adventurer*, Diana Bourbon, 1934, Short Story

Atlantic City Romance see **CONVENTION GIRL** (1934).

ATLANTIDE, L' 1921 d: Jacques Feyder. FRN., *L' Atlantide*, Pierre Benoit, Paris 1919, Novel

ATLANTIDE, L' 1932 d: G. W. Pabst. FRN., *L' Atlantide*, Pierre Benoit, Paris 1919, Novel

Atlantide, L' see **L'AMANTE DELLA CITTA SEPOLTA ANTINEA** (1961).

ATLANTIDE, L' 1991 d: Bob Swaim. FRN., *L' Atlantide*, Pierre Benoit, Paris 1919, Novel

ATLANTIS 1930 d: Jean Kemm, E. A. Dupont. FRN., *The Berg*, Ernest Raymond, Short Story

Atlantis see **SIREN OF ATLANTIS** (1948).

Atlantis the Lost Continent see **SIREN OF ATLANTIS** (1948).

ATLANTIS, THE LOST CONTINENT 1961 d: George Pal. USA., *Atalanta; a Story of Atlantis*, Gerald P. Hargreaves, London 1949, Play

Atlantis, the Lost Continent see **L'AMANTE DELLA CITTA SEPOLTA ANTINEA** (1961).

Atom of Eternity see **ATOM VECNOSTI** (1934).

ATOM VECNOSTI 1934 d: Vladimir Smejkal, Cenek Zahradnicek. CZC., *Atom Vecnosti a Takova Je Vecna Hra Lasky*, Jaroslav Smejkal, Vladimir Smejkal, Play

Atomic Agent see **NATHALIE AGENT SECRET** (1959).

Atomic Man, The see **TIMESLIP** (1955).

Atomic Monster, The see **MAN MADE MONSTER** (1941).

ATONEMENT 1919 d: William Humphrey. USA., *Zhivoi Trup*, Lev Nikolayevich Tolstoy, Moscow 1911, Play

Atonement of Gosta Berling, The see **GOSTA BERLINGS SAGA** (1924).

Atoragon see **KAITEI GUNKAN** (1963).

Atoragon, the Flying Supersub see **KAITEI GUNKAN** (1963).

Atout Coeur see **ARLETTE ET L'AMOUR** (1943).

ATOUT-COEUR 1931 d: Henry Roussell. FRN., *Atout-Coeur*, Felix Gandera, Play

ATOUTS DE M. WENS, LES 1946 d: E. G. de Meyst. FRN/BLG., *Les Atouts de M. Wens*, Stanislas-Andre Steeman, Novel

Atraco Al Hampa see **LE VICOMTE REGLE SES COMPTES** (1967).

Atragon see **KAITEI GUNKAN** (1963).

Atragon the Flying Sub see **KAITEI GUNKAN** (1963).

Attached Balloon, The see **PRIVARZANIAT BALON** (1967).

ATTACK! 1956 d: Robert Aldrich. USA., *Fragile Fox*, Norman Brooks, New York 1954, Play

Attack By Night see **FIRST COMES COURAGE** (1943).

Attack of the Mushroom People see **MATANGO** (1963).

ATTACK ON FEAR 1984 d: Mel Damski. USA., *The Light on Synanon*, David Mitchell, Book

ATTACK ON TERROR 1975 d: Marvin J. Chomsky. USA., *Attack on Terror*, Don Whitehead, Novel

Attack on Terror: the F.B.I. Vs. the Ku Klux Klan see **ATTACK ON TERROR** (1975).

ATTACK ON THE MILL, THE 1910 d: Edwin S. Porter. USA., *L'attaque du Moulin*, Emile Zola, Short Story

Attacking the Invaders see **DA JI QIN LUE ZHE** (1965).

ATTAQUE NOCTURNE 1931 d: Marc Allegret. FRN., *Attaque Nocturne*, Andre de Lorde, Masson-Forestier, Play

Attempt at Flight see **FLUCHTVERSUCH** (1976).

Attempt to Escape, An see **FLUCHTVERSUCH** (1976).

ATTEMPT TO KILL 1961 d: Royston Morley. UKN., *The Lone House Mystery*, Edgar Wallace, London 1929, Novel

Attempted Escape see **FLUCHTVERSUCH** (1976).

Attempted Flight see **FLUCHTVERSUCH** (1976).

Attendance Compulsory see **ERSCHEINEN PFLICHT** (1983).

ATTENTAT DE LA MAISON ROUGE, L' 1917 d: Gaston Silvestre. FRN., *L' Attentat de la Maison Rouge*, Andre de Lorde, Alfred Gragnon, Play

ATTENTI AL BUFFONE 1975 d: Alberto BevilacquA. ITL., *Attenti Al Buffone*, Alberto Bevilacqua, Novel

ATTENTION LES ENFANTS REGARDENT 1977 d: Serge Leroy. FRN., Peter Dixon, Laird Koenig, Novel

Attic of Felix Bavu, The see **BAVU** (1923).

ATTIC: THE HIDING OF ANNE FRANK, THE 1988 d: John Erman. USA., *Anne Frank Remembered*, Miep Gies, Book

ATTICA 1980 d: Marvin J. Chomsky. USA., *A Time to Die*, Tom Wicker, Book

Attong see **THE YOUNG AND THE BRAVE** (1963).

Attorney for the Defense, The see **L' AVVOCATO DIFENSORE** (1934).

ATTRACTA 1983 d: Kieran Hickey. IRL., *Attracta*, William Trevor, 1978, Short Story

Atunci I-Am Condamnat Pe Toti la Moarte see **MOARTEA LUI IPU** (1972).

AU BONHEUR DES DAMES 1929 d: Julien Duvivier. FRN., *Au Bonheur Des Dames*, Emile Zola, 1883, Novel

AU BONHEUR DES DAMES 1943 d: Andre Cayatte. FRN., *Au Bonheur Des Dames*, Emile Zola, 1883, Novel

AU BOUT DU MONDE 1933 d: Henri Chomette, Gustav Ucicky. FRN., *Au Bout du Monde*, Gerhard Menzel, Novel

AU COEUR DE LA CASBAH 1951 d: Pierre Cardinal. FRN., *Phedre*, Jean Racine, 1677, Play

AU COEUR DE LA VIE 1968 d: Robert Enrico. FRN., *Mockingbird*, Ambrose Bierce, 1891, Short Story, *Occurrence at Owl Creek Bridge*, Ambrose Bierce, 1891, Short Story

AU DIABLE LA VERTU 1952 d: Jean Laviron. FRN., *Au Diable la Vertu*, Jean Guitton, Play

AU NOM DE LA LOI 1931 d: Maurice Tourneur. FRN., *Au Nom de la Loi*, Paul Bringuier, Novel

AU NOM DE TOUS LES MIENS 1983 d: Robert Enrico. FRN/CND., *For Those I Loved*, Max Gallo, Martin Grey, Book

AU PARADIS DES ENFANTS 1917 d: Charles Burguet. FRN., *Au Paradis Des Enfants*, Andre Theuriet, Novel

AU PAYS DES CIGALES 1945 d: Maurice Cam. FRN., *Au Pays Des Cigales*, Henri Alibert, Marco Cab, Raymond Vinci, Opera

AU PAYS DES TENEBRES (LA MINE) 1912 d: Victorin Jasset. FRN., *Germinal*, Emile Zola, 1885, Novel

AU PAYS DU SOLEIL 1933 d: Robert Peguy. FRN., *Au Pays du Soleil*, Henri Alibert, Rene Sarvil, Opera

AU PETIT BONHEUR 1945 d: Marcel L'Herbier. FRN., *Au Petit Bonheur*, Marc-Gilbert Sauvajon, Play

AU REVOIR, A LUNDI 1980 d: Maurice Dugowson. CND/FRN., *Moi Mon Corps Mon Ame Montreal Etc.*, Roger Fournier, Novel

AU SOLEIL DE MARSEILLE 1937 d: Pierre-Jean Ducis. FRN., *Au Soleil de Marseille*, Marco Cab, Charles Tutelier, Opera

AU TELEPHONE 1915?. FRN., *Au Telephone*, Charles Foley, Play

AU TEMPS DES PREMIERS CHRETIENS 1910 d: Andre Calmettes. FRN., *Quo Vadis?*, Henryk Sienkiewicz, 1896, Novel

AUBE, L' 1986 d: Miklos Jancso. FRN/ISR., *L' Aube*, Elie Wiesel, Book

AUBERGE DE L'ABIME, L' 1942 d: Willy Rozier. FRN., *L' Auberge de l'Abime*, Andre Chamson, 1933, Novel

AUBERGE DU PECHE, L' 1949 d: Jean de Marguenat. FRN., *Cafe Noir*, Georges-Andre Cuel, Novel

AUBERGE DU TOHU-BOHU, L' 1912 d: Georges DenolA. FRN., *L' Auberge du Tohu-Bohu*, Maurice Ordonneau, Play

AUBERGE, L' 1922 d: E. B. Donatien, Edouard-Emile Violet. FRN., *L' Auberge*, Guy de Maupassant, Short Story

AUBERGE ROUGE, L' 1912. FRN., *L' Auberge Rouge*, Honore de Balzac, 1831, Short Story

AUBERGE ROUGE, L' 1923 d: Jean Epstein. FRN., *L' Auberge Rouge*, Honore de Balzac, 1831, Short Story

AUBERGE ROUGE, L' 1951 d: Claude Autant-LarA. FRN., *L' Auberge Rouge*, Honore de Balzac, 1831, Short Story

AUBERGE SANGLANTE ,L' 1913 d: Emile Chautard. FRN., *L' Auberge Des Adrets*, Benjamin Antier, Saint-Amand, Play

Auca Del Senyor Esteve, L' *see* EL SENOR ESTEVE (1929).

Auch Eine Franzosische Ehe *see* LE TONNERRE DE DIEU (1965).

AUCTION BLOCK, THE 1917 d: Larry Trimble. USA., *The Auction Block; a Novel of New York Life*, Rex Beach, New York 1914, Novel

AUCTION BLOCK, THE 1926 d: Hobart Henley. USA., *The Auction Block; a Novel of New York Life*, Rex Beach, New York 1914, Novel

Auction in Souls *see* THE CONSTANT WOMAN (1933).

AUCTION MART, THE 1920 d: Duncan MacRae. UKN., *The Auction Mart*, Sydney Tremaine, Novel

AUCTION OF SOULS 1919 d: Oscar Apfel. USA., *Ravished Armenia*, Aurora Mardiganian, New York 1918, Book

AUCTIONEER, THE 1927 d: Alfred E. Green. USA., *The Auctioneer*, Lee Arthur, Charles Klein, New York 1913, Play

AUDACIOUS MR. SQUIRE, THE 1923 d: Edwin Greenwood. UKN., *Squire the Audacious*, Sydney Bowkett, Play

Au-Dela de Cette Limite Votre Ticket N'est Plus Valable *see* YOUR TICKET IS NO LONGER VALID (1980).

Au-Dela de la Mort *see* MAS ALLA DE LA MUERTE (1924).

AU-DELA DES LOIS HUMAINES 1920 d: Gaston Roudes, Marcel Dumont. FRN., *Au Dela Des Lois Humaines*, Daniel Jourda

Au-Dela du Regard *see* IF YOU COULD SEE WHAT I HEAR (1981).

AUDREY 1916 d: Robert G. VignolA. USA., *Audrey*, Mary Johnston, Boston 1902, Novel

AUDREY ROSE 1977 d: Robert Wise. USA., *Audrey Rose*, Frank de Felitta, Novel

AUFENTHALT, DER 1983 d: Frank Beyer. GDR., *Der Aufenthalt*, Hermann Kant, Novel

AUFERSTEHUNG 1958 d: Rolf Hansen. GRM/ITL/FRN., *Voskreseniye*, Lev Nikolayevich Tolstoy, Moscow 1899, Novel

AUFRUHR IM DAMENSTIFT 1941 d: F. D. Andam. GRM., *Aufruhr Im Damenstift*, Axel Breidahl, Play

Aufstand Alter Manner, Ein *see* A GATHERING OF OLD MEN (1987).

Aufzug, Der *see* ABWARTS: DAS DUELL UBER DER TIEFE (1984).

August *see* ELOKUU (1956).

AUGUST 1996 d: Anthony Hopkins. USA/UKN., *Uncle Vanya*, Anton Chekhov, 1900, Play

AUGUST WEEK-END 1936 d: Charles Lamont. USA., *August Week-End*, Faith Baldwin, 1933, Short Story

AUGUSTE 1961 d: Pierre Chevalier. FRN., *Auguste*, Raymond Castans, Play

Auld Jeremiah *see* BONNIE LASSIE BONNIE (1919).

AUNT CLARA 1954 d: Anthony Kimmins. UKN., *Aunt Clara*, Noel Streatfield, Novel

Aunt Emma Paints the Town *see* SO'S YOUR AUNT EMMA! (1942).

Aunt Frieda *see* TANTE FRIEDA - NEUE LAUSBUBENGESCHICHTEN (1965).

AUNT JULIA AND THE SCRIPTWRITER 1990 d: Jon Amiel. USA., *La Tia Julia Y El Escribidor*, Mario Vargas Llosa, 1977, Novel

Aunt Jutta from Calcutta *see* TANTE JUTTA AUS KALKUTTA (1953).

AUNT RACHEL 1920 d: Albert Ward. UKN., *Aunt Rachel*, David Christie Murray, Novel

Aunt Tula *see* LA TIA TULA (1964).

AUNTIE MAME 1958 d: Morton Da CostA. USA., *Auntie Mame*, Patrick Dennis, Novel

Auntie, The *see* TETICKA (1941).

Auntie's Fantasies *see* TETICKA (1941).

AUNTY'S ROMANCE 1912 d: George D. Baker. USA., *Aunty's Romance*, W. Hanson Durham, Play

Aura *see* LA STREGA IN AMORE (1966).

AURORA FLOYD 1912 d: Theodore Marston. USA., *Aurora Floyd*, Mary Elizabeth Braddon, Novel

AURORA FLOYD 1915 d: Travers Vale. USA., *Aurora Floyd*, Mary Elizabeth Braddon, Novel

AURORA SUL MARE 1935 d: Giorgio C. Simonelli. ITL., *La Casa Sul Mare*, Ferruccio Cerio, Gino Saviotti, Story

AUS DEM LEBEN EINES TAUGENICHTS 1973 d: Celino Bleiweiss. GDR., *Aus Dem Leben Eines Taugenichts*, Joseph von Eichendorff, 1826, Novel

AUS DEM TAGEBUCH EINES JUNGGESELLEN 1928 d: Erich Schonfelder. GRM., *Aus Dem Tagebuch Eines Junggesellen*, Rene Sorel, Play

Aus Den Wolken Kommt Das Gluck *see* AMPHITRYON (1935).

AUS DER FERNE SEHE ICH DIESES LAND 1978 d: Christian Ziewer. GRM., Antonio Skarmeta, Story

AUS EINEM DEUTSCHEN LEBEN 1978 d: Theodor KotullA. GRM., *Aus Einem Deutschen Leben*, Robert Merle, Novel

AUS ERSTER EHE 1940 d: Paul Verhoeven. GRM., *Kamerad Mutter*, Christel Broehl-Delhaes, Novel

Ausklang *see* DER ALTE FRITZ 2 (1927).

Aussergerichtliche Einigung, Eine *see* SCHWEIGEN IM WALDE 2 (1918).

Austrian Spy, The *see* ANTON THE TERRIBLE (1916).

AUTOBIOGRAPHY OF MISS JANE PITTMAN, THE 1974 d: John Korty. USA., *The Autobiography of Miss Jane Pittman*, Ernest J. Gaines, 1971, Novel

AUTOGRAMM, DAS 1984 d: Peter Lilienthal. GRM/FRN., *Das Autogramm*, Osvaldo Soriano, Novel

Autograph, The *see* DAS AUTOGRAMM (1984).

Autographe, L' *see* DAS AUTOGRAMM (1984).

AUTOSTOP 1977 d: Pasquale Festa Campanile. ITL., *La Violenza E Il Furore*, Peter Kane, Novel

Autostop Rosso Sangue *see* AUTOSTOP (1977).

AUTOUR D'UN TESTAMENT 1913 d: Emile Chautard. FRN., *Eulalie Pontois*, Frederic Soulie, Play

AUTOUR D'UNE ENQUETE 1931 d: Henri Chomette, Robert Siodmak. FRN., *Voruntersuchung*, Max Alsberg, Ernst Hesse, Play

AUTRE AILE, L' 1924 d: Henri Andreani. FRN., *L'Autre Aile*, Canudo, Novel

AUTRE FEMME, L' 1963 d: Francois Villiers. FRN/ITL/SPN., *L' Autre Femme*, Maria-Luisa Linares, Novel

Autre Qui Est En Nous, L' *see* DIE EWIGE MASKE (1935).

AUTUMN CROCUS 1934 d: Basil Dean. UKN., *Autumn Crocus*, C. L. Anthony, London 1931, Play

Autumn Fever *see* BLONDE FEVER (1944).

Autumn Milk *see* HERBSTMILCH (1988).

AUTUMN OF PRIDE, THE 1921 d: W. P. Kellino. UKN., *The Autumn of Pride*, E. Newton Bungey, Novel

Autumn Roses *see* ROSAS DE OTONO (1943).

Autumn Sunset Dream, An *see* SOGNO DI UN TRAMONTO D'AUTUNNO (1911).

Aux Abois *see* DIE GEJAGTEN (1960).

AUX DEUX COLOMBES 1949 d: Sacha Guitry. FRN., *Aux Deux Colombes*, Sacha Guitry, Play

Aux Portes de la Ville *see* AUX PORTES DE PARIS (1934).

AUX PORTES DE PARIS 1934 d: Charles Barrois, Jacques de Baroncelli (Uncredited). FRN., *Chrestos*, Henri Dupuy-Mazuel, Novel

Aux Yeux du Sort Et Des Humains *see* FORTUNE AND MEN'S EYES (1971).

AV HJARTANS LUST 1960 d: Rolf Husberg. SWD., *Av Hjartans Lust*, Karl Ragnar Gierow, 1944, Play

AVALANCHE 1928 d: Otto Brower. USA., *Avalanche*, Zane Grey, Novel

Avalanche *see* NADARE (1937).

AVALANCHE 1946 d: Irving Allen. USA., *Avalanche*, Kay Boyle, 1944, Novel

AVALANCHE 1978 d: Corey Allen. USA., *Avalanche*, Frances Doel, Novel

Avalanche *see* LAVINA (1981).

AVALANCHE EXPRESS 1979 d: Mark Robson, Monte Hellman (Uncredited). USA., *Avalanche Express*, Colin Forbes, Novel

AVALANCHE, THE 1915 d: Will S. Davis. USA., *The Avalanche*, Robert Hilliard, W. A. Tremayne, Philadelphia 1912, Play

AVALANCHE, THE 1919 d: George Fitzmaurice. USA., *The Avalanche: a Mystery Story*, Gertrude Franklin Atherton, New York 1919, Play

Avantaz *see* AVANTAZH (1978).

AVANTAZH 1978 d: Georgi Dyulgerov. BUL., Petko Sdrawkoff, Novel

AVANTI! 1972 d: Billy Wilder. USA/ITL., *Avanti!*, Samuel Taylor, Play

Avanti a Lui *see* DAVANTI A LUI TREMAVA TUTTA ROMA (1946).

Avanti a Lui Tremava Tutta Roma *see* DAVANTI A LUI TREMAVA TUTTA ROMA (1946).

Avanti la Musica! *see* IL CAMBIO DELLA GUARDIA (1962).

AVARE, L' 1979 d: Louis de Funes, Jean Girault. FRN., *L' Avare*, Moliere, 1668, Play

Avarice *see* SISTERS OF EVE (1928).

AVATAR 1916 d: Carmine Gallone. ITL., *Avatar*, Theophile Gautier

Avec Amour Et Avec Rage *see* LA COSTANZA DELLA RAGIONE (1964).

AVEC LA PEAU DES AUTRES 1966 d: Jacques Deray. FRN/ITL., *Au Pied du Mur*, Gilles Perrault, Novel

Avelha Na Chuva, Uma *see* UMA ABELHA NA CHUVA (1971).

Avenger of the Seven Seas *see* IL GIUSTIZIERE DEI MARI (1962).

Avenger of Venice *see* IL PONTE DEI SOSPIRI (1964).

AVENGER, THE 1933 d: Edwin L. Marin. USA., *The Avenger*, John Goodwin, New York 1926, Novel

Avenger, The *see* DER RACHER (1960).

Avenger, The *see* LA LEGGENDA DI ENEA (1962).

Avenger, The *see* EL MUERTO HACE LAS MALETAS (1970).

AVENGERS, THE 1950 d: John H. Auer. USA/ARG., *Don Careless*, Rex Beach, 1930, Novel

Avenging Angels *see* MESSENGER OF DEATH (1988).

AVENGING CONSCIENCE OR THOU SHALT NOT KILL, THE 1914 d: D. W. Griffith. USA., *Annabel Lee*, Edgar Allan Poe, 1849, Poem, *The Tell-Tale Heart*, Edgar Allan Poe, 1843, Short Story

AVENGING RIDER, THE 1943 d: Sam Nelson. USA., *The Five of Spades*, Harry O. Hoyt, Story

AVENGING TRAIL, THE 1918 d: Francis Ford. USA., *Gaston Olaf*, Henry Oyen, New York 1917, Novel

Aventis *see* SI TE DICEN QUE CAI (1988).

Aventura de Gil Blas, Una *see* LES AVENTURES DE GIL BLAS DE SANTILLANE (1955).

AVENTURAS DE JUAN QUIN QUIN, LAS 1967 d: Julio Garcia EspinosA. CUB., *Juan Quinquin En Pueblo Mocho*, Samuel Feijoo, 1964, Novel

AVENTURAS DE ROBINSON CRUSOE, AS 1978 d: Mozael SilveirA. BRZ., *Robinson Crusoe*, Daniel Defoe, 1719, Novel

AVENTURAS DE ROBINSON CRUSOE, LAS 1952 d: Luis Bunuel. MXC/USA., *Robinson Crusoe*, Daniel Defoe, 1719, Novel

Aventuras Del Vizconde, Las *see* LE VICOMTE REGLE SES COMPTES (1967).

AVENTURE A PARIS 1936 d: Marc Allegret. FRN., *Le Rabatteur*, Henri Falk, Play

Aventure de Vidocq, Une *see* LE CAVALIER DE CROIX-MORT (1947).

AVENTURE EN ONTARIO 1968 d: Jean Dreville, Sergiu Nicolaescu. FRN/RMN., *The Pathfinder*, James Fenimore Cooper, 1840, Novel

Aventurero de la Rosa Roja, El *see* ROSE ROSSE PER ANGELICA (1966).

AVENTURES DE GIL BLAS DE SANTILLANE, LES 1955 d: Rene Jolivet, Ricardo Munoz Suay. FRN/SPN., *Gil Blas*, Alain-Rene Lesage, 1715-35, Novel

AVENTURES DE LAGARDERE, LES 1967 d: Jean-Pierre Decourt. FRN/ITL., *Les Aventures de Lagardere*, Paul Feval, Novel

Aventures de Pinocchio, Les *see* LE AVVENTURE DI PINOCCHIO (1972).

AVENTURES DE ROBINSON CRUSOE, LES 1921 d: Gaston Leprieur, Mario Gargiulo. FRN/ITL., *Robinson Crusoe*, Daniel Defoe, 1719, Novel

AVENTURES DE SALAVIN, LES 1963 d: Pierre Granier-Deferre. FRN., *Confession de Minuit*, Georges Duhamel, 1920, Novel

AVENTURES DE THOMAS PLUMEPATTE, LES 1916?. FRN., *Les Aventures de Thomas Plumepatte*, Gaston Marot, Play

AVENTURES DE TILL L'ESPIEGLE, LES 1956 d: Gerard Philipe, Joris Ivens. FRN/GRM., *Les Aventures de Till Espiegle*, Charles de Coster, Novel

Aventures de Tom Sawyer, Les see **AVENTURILE LUI TOM SAWYER** (1968).

AVENTURES DEU CAPITAINE CORCORAN, LES 1914 d: Charles Krauss. FRN., *Les Aventures du Capitaine Corcoran*, Alfred Assollant, Novel

AVENTURES DU CHEVALIER DE FAUBLAS, LES 1913 d: Henri Pouctal. FRN., *Les Aventures du Chevalier de Faublas*, Louvet de Couvray, Novel

AVENTURES DU ROI PAUSOLE, LES 1933 d: Alexis Granowsky. FRN., *Les Aventures du Roi Pausole*, Pierre Louys, 1901, Novel

Aventures du Vicomte, Les see **LE VICOMTE REGLE SES COMPTES** (1967).

Aventures Extraordinaires de Cervantes, Les see **LE AVVENTURE E GLI AMORI DI MIGUEL CERVANTES** (1967).

Aventuri in Ontario see **AVENTURE EN ONTARIO** (1968).

AVENTURIER, L' 1916 d: Maurice Mariaud. FRN., *L' Aventurier*, Alfred Capus, Play

AVENTURIER, L' 1924 d: Maurice Mariaud, Louis Osmont. FRN., *L' Aventurier*, Alfred Capus, Play

AVENTURIER, L' 1934 d: Marcel L'Herbier. FRN., *L' Aventurier*, Alfred Capus, Play

AVENTURIERS, LES 1966 d: Robert Enrico. FRN/ITL., *Les Aventuriers*, Jose Giovanni, Paris 1960, Novel

AVENTURILE LUI TOM SAWYER 1968 d: Mihai Iacob, Wolfgang Liebeneiner. RMN/FRN., *Adventures of Tom Sawyer*, Mark Twain, San Francisco 1876, Novel

Average Man, An see **UN BORGHESE PICCOLO PICCOLO** (1977).

AVERAGE WOMAN, THE 1924 d: W. Christy Cabanne. USA., *The Average Woman*, Dorothy de Jagers, 1922, Short Story

AVEU, L' 1970 d: Costa-Gavras. FRN/ITL., *L'Aveu; Dans l'Engrenage du Proces de Prague*, Artur London, Paris 1968, Novel

AVEUGLE, L' 1914. FRN., *L' Aveugle*, Anicet Bourgeois, Adolphe-P. d'Ennery, Play

Avia's Summer see **HAKAYITZ SHEL AVIYA** (1988).

AVIATEUR, L' 1931 d: William A. Seiter. USA., *The Aviator*, James Montgomery, New York 1910, Play

AVIATOR, THE 1984 d: George Miller. YGS/USA., *The Aviator*, Ernest K. Gann, Novel

AVION DE MINUIT, L' 1938 d: Dimitri Kirsanoff. FRN., *L' Avion de Minuit*, Roger Labric, Novel

Avo Avvelenatore, L' see **L' AVO** (1909).

AVO, L' 1909. ITL., *L' Aieule*, Adolphe-P. d'Ennery, C. Edmond, 1863, Play

AVOCAT, L' 1925 d: Gaston Ravel. FRN., *L' Avocat*, Eugene Brieux, 1922, Play

Avril see **ARLETTE ET SES PAPAS** (1934).

AVVENTURA DI VIAGGIO 1916 d: Camillo de Riso. ITL., *Avventura Di Viaggio*, Roberto Barocco, 1887, Short Story

AVVENTURE DEI TRE MOSCHETTIERI, LE 1957 d: Joseph Lerner. ITL., *Les Trois Mousquetaires*, Alexandre Dumas (pere), Paris 1844, Novel

AVVENTURE DI COLETTE, LE 1916 d: R. Savarese. ITL., *La Gamine*, Henri de Gorsse, Pierre Veber, 1911, Play

AVVENTURE DI ENEA, LE 1974 d: Franco Rossi. ITL., *Aeneid*, Virgil, c20 bc, Verse

Avventure Di Gerard, Le see **THE ADVENTURES OF GERARD** (1970).

Avventure Di Pinocchio, Le see **PINOCCHIO** (1911).

AVVENTURE DI PINOCCHIO, LE 1935 d: Umberto Spano. ITL., *Le Avventure Di Pinocchio*, Carlo Collodi, 1883, Short Story

AVVENTURE DI PINOCCHIO, LE 1947 d: Giannetto Guardone. ITL., *Le Avventure Di Pinocchio*, Carlo Collodi, 1883, Short Story

AVVENTURE DI PINOCCHIO, LE 1968 d: Giuliano Cenci. ITL., *Le Avventure Di Pinocchio*, Carlo Collodi, 1883, Short Story

AVVENTURE DI PINOCCHIO, LE 1972 d: Luigi Comencini. ITL/FRN/GRM., *Le Avventure Di Pinocchio*, Carlo Collodi, 1883, Short Story

Avventure Di Robinson Crusoe, L' see **LES AVENTURES DE ROBINSON CRUSOE** (1921).

Avventure Di Scaramouche, Le see **SCARAMOUCHE** (1963).

AVVENTURE E GLI AMORI DI MIGUEL CERVANTES, LE 1967 d: Vincent Sherman. ITL/FRN/SPN., *Cervantes*, Bruno Frank, Amsterdam 1934, Novel

AVVENTURE STRAORDINARISSIME DI SATURNINO FARANDOLA, LE 1914 d: Marcel Fabre, Luigi Maggi (Uncredited). ITL., *Ferdinand Robida*, Novel

Avventuriera Del Bal Tabarin, L' see **TRENO DI LUSSO** (1917).

Avventuriera Del Circo, L' see **TRENO DI LUSSO** (1917).

AVVENTURIERO DELLA TORTUGA, L' 1965 d: Luigi Capuano. ITL/GRM., *Gli Ultimi Filibustieri*, Emilio Salgari, Novel

AVVENTURIERO, L' 1967 d: Terence Young. ITL/UKN., *The Rover*, Joseph Conrad, 1923, Novel

AVVOCATO DEL DIAVOLO, L' 1977 d: Guy Green. ITL/GRM., *The Devil's Advocate*, Morris West, 1959, Novel

AVVOCATO DIFENSORE, L' 1934 d: Gero Zambuto. ITL., *L' Avvocato Difensore*, Mario Morais, Play

AWAKENING LAND, THE 1978 d: Boris Sagal. USA., *The Awakening Land*, Conrad Richter, Novel

AWAKENING OF HELENA RICHIE, THE 1916 d: John W. Noble. USA., *The Awakening of Helena Richie*, Margaret Deland, New York 1906, Novel

Awakening of Katrina, The see **THE GIRL DOWNSTAIRS** (1938).

AWAKENING, THE 1915 d: Ralph Ince. USA., James Oliver Curwood, Story

AWAKENING, THE 1980 d: Mike Newell. UKN., *The Jewel of the Seven Stars*, Bram Stoker, 1903, Novel

AWAKENINGS 1990 d: Penny Marshall. USA., *Awakenings*, Dr. Oliver Sacks, Book

AWAY ALL BOATS 1956 d: Joseph Pevney. USA., *Away All Boats*, Kenneth M. Dodson, 1954, Novel

Awful Dr. Orloff, The see **GRITOS EN LA NOCHE** (1961).

Awful Story of the Nun of Monza, The see **LA MONACA DI MONZA** (1968).

AWFUL TRUTH, THE 1925 d: Paul Powell. USA., *The Awful Truth*, Arthur Richman, New York 1922, Play

AWFUL TRUTH, THE 1929 d: Marshall Neilan. USA., *The Awful Truth*, Arthur Richman, New York 1922, Play

AWFUL TRUTH, THE 1937 d: Leo McCarey. USA., *The Awful Truth*, Arthur Richman, New York 1922, Play

AWFULLY BIG ADVENTURE, AN 1995 d: Mike Newell. UKN., *An Awfully Big Adventure*, Beryl Bainbridge, 1989, Novel

Axe of Wandsbek, The see **DAS BEIL VON WANDSBEK** (1951).

Axe of Wandsbek, The see **DAS BEIL VON WANDSBEK** (1983).

AXEL MUNTHE, DER ARZT VON SAN MICHELE 1962 d: Rudolf Jugert, Giorgio Capitani. GRM/ITL/FRN., *The Story of San Michele*, Axel Munthe, Book

AY, CARMELA! 1990 d: Carlos SaurA. SPN/ITL., *Ay Carmela!*, Jose Sanchis Sinistierra, Play

AYLWIN 1920 d: Henry Edwards. UKN., *Aylwin*, Theodore Watts-Dunton, Novel

AYNA 1984 d: Erden Kiral. GRM/TRK., *The White Ox*, Osman Sahin, Novel

AZAIS 1931 d: Rene Hervil. FRN., *Azais*, Georges Berr, Louis Verneuil, Play

AZIT HAKALBA HATZANCHANIT 1972 d: Boaz Davidson. ISR., Mota Gur, Story

Azit the Paratrooper Dog see **AZIT HAKALBA HATZANCHANIT** (1972).

AZYLO MUITO LOUCO 1970 d: Nelson Pereira Dos Santos. BRZ., *O Alienista*, Joaquim Maria Machado de Assis, 1881, Short Story

B MONKEY 1998 d: Michael Radford. UKN., *B. Monkey*, Andrew Davies, Novel

BA SANG TA-TE TI-ME-MENG 1985 d: P'an Hsiao-Yang. CHN., *Ba Sang Ta-Te Ti-Me-Meng*, Dschasi Dawa, Novel

BA WANG BIE JI 1993 d: Chen Kaige. HNG/CHN., *Ba Wang Bie Ji*, Li Bihua, Novel

Baba see **WO SHI HI BA BA MA?** (1995).

BABBITT 1924 d: Harry Beaumont. USA., *Babbitt*, Sinclair Lewis, New York 1922, Novel

BABBITT 1934 d: William Keighley. USA., *Babbitt*, Sinclair Lewis, New York 1922, Novel

BABE 1975 d: Buzz Kulik. USA., *This Life I've Led*, Babe Didrikson, Autobiography

BABE 1995 d: Chris Noonan. ASL., *The Sheep-Pig*, Dick King-Smith, Novel

BABE COMES HOME 1927 d: Ted Wilde. USA., *Said With Soap*, Gerald Beaumont, 1925, Short Story

BABE RUTH 1991 d: Mark Tinker. USA., *Babe: the Legend Comes to Life*, Robert W. Creamer, Book, *Babe Ruth: His Life & Legend*, Karl Wagenheim, Book

Babe, The see **BABE RUTH** (1991).

Babe the Gallant Pig see **BABE** (1995).

BABES IN ARMS 1939 d: Busby Berkeley. USA., *Babes in Arms*, Lorenz Hart, Richard Rodgers, New York 1937, Musical Play

BABES IN THE WOODS, THE 1917 d: Chester M. Franklin, Sidney A. Franklin. USA., *Hansel Und Gretel*, Jacob Grimm, Wilhelm Grimm, 1812, Short Story

BABES IN TOYLAND 1934 d: Charles Rogers, Gus Meins. USA., *Babes in Toyland*, Victor Herbert, Glen MacDonough, New York 1903, Operetta

BABES IN TOYLAND 1961 d: Jack Donohue. USA., *Babes in Toyland*, Victor Herbert, Glen MacDonough, New York 1903, Operetta

BABES IN TOYLAND 1986 d: Clive Donner. USA., *Babes in Toyland*, Victor Herbert, Glen MacDonough, New York 1903, Operetta

BABETTE 1917 d: Charles J. Brabin. USA., *Babette*, Frank Berkeley Smith, New York 1916, Novel

Babette's Feast see **BABETTES GAESTEBUD** (1987).

BABETTES GAESTEBUD 1987 d: Gabriel Axel. DNM/FRN., *Babette's Feast*, Karen Blixen, 1950, Short Story

BABICKA 1921 d: Thea CervenkovA. CZC., *Babicka*, Bozena Nemcova, 1846, Novel

BABICKA 1940 d: Frantisek Cap. CZC., *Babicka*, Bozena Nemcova, 1846, Novel

Babies Won't Tell see **MANY A SLIP** (1931).

BAB'S BURGLAR 1917 d: J. Searle Dawley. USA., *Bab's Burglar*, Mary Roberts Rinehart, 1917, Short Story

BAB'S CANDIDATE 1920 d: Edward H. Griffith. USA., *Gumshoes 4-B*, Forrest Crissey, 1919, Short Story

BAB'S DIARY 1917 d: J. Searle Dawley. USA., *Her Diary*, Mary Roberts Rinehart, 1917, Short Story

BAB'S MATINEE IDOL 1917 d: J. Searle Dawley. USA., Mary Roberts Rinehart, Short Story

BABY 1932 d: Pierre Billon, Carl Lamac. FRN., *Baby*, Hans H. Zerlett, Play

BABY AND THE BATTLESHIP, THE 1956 d: Jay Lewis. UKN., *The Baby and the Battleship*, Anthony Thorne, Novel

BABY CYCLONE, THE 1928 d: A. Edward Sutherland. USA., *The Baby Cyclone*, George M. Cohan, Play

BABY DANCE, THE 1998 d: Jane Anderson. USA., *The Baby Dance*, Jane Anderson, Play

BABY DOLL 1956 d: Elia Kazan. USA., *27 Wagons Full of Cotton*, Tennessee Williams, 1945, Play, *The Long Stay Cut Short*, Tennessee Williams, 1948, Play

Baby Doll see **LA BAMBOLONA** (1968).

Baby Face see **BABY-FACE HARRINGTON** (1935).

Baby in the Ice Box see **SHE MADE HER BED** (1934).

BABY IT'S YOU 1983 d: John Sayles. USA., Amy Robinson, Story

BABY LOVE 1968 d: Alastair Reid. UKN., *Baby Love*, Tina Chad Christian, London 1968, Novel

BABY MINE 1917 d: John S. Robertson, Hugo Ballin. USA., *Baby Mine*, Margaret Mayo, New York 1910, Play

BABY MINE 1927 d: Robert Z. Leonard. USA., *Baby Mine*, Margaret Mayo, New York 1910, Play

BABY, TAKE A BOW 1934 d: Harry Lachman. USA., *Square Crooks*, James P. Judge, New York 1926, Play

Baby, The see **UNGEN** (1974).

BABY, THE RAIN MUST FALL 1965 d: Robert Mulligan. USA., *The Traveling Lady*, Horton Foote, 1954, Play

BABY-FACE HARRINGTON 1935 d: Raoul Walsh. USA., *Something to Brag About*, William le Baron, Edgar Selwyn, New York 1925, Play

Babylon-Xx *see* VAVILON-XX (1980).

BABYSITTER, THE 1995 d: Guy Ferland. USA., *The Babysitter*, Robert Coover, Short Story

BACCANTI, LE 1961 d: Giorgio Ferroni. ITL/FRN., *Le Bacchae*, Euripides, c495 bc, Play

Bacchantes, Les *see* LE BACCANTI (1961).

Bacchantes, The *see* LE BACCANTI (1961).

BACH MILLIONNAIRE 1933 d: Henry Wulschleger. FRN., *Papillon Dit Lyonnais le Juste*, Louis Benieres, Play

Bachelor Affairs *see* AMATEUR DADDY (1932).

BACHELOR BRIDES 1926 d: William K. Howard. USA., *Bachelor Brides*, Charles Horace Malcolm, 1925, Play

BACHELOR DADDY, THE 1922 d: Alfred E. Green. USA., *The Bachelor Daddy*, Edward Peple, Short Story

BACHELOR FATHER, THE 1931 d: Robert Z. Leonard. USA., *The Bachelor Father*, Edward Childs Carpenter, New York 1928, Play

BACHELOR FLAT 1962 d: Frank Tashlin. USA., *Libby*, Budd Grossman, Play

Bachelor Girl *see* LA GARCONNE (1957).

Bachelor Girl Apartment *see* ANY WEDNESDAY (1966).

BACHELOR HUSBAND, A 1920 d: Kenelm Foss. UKN., *A Bachelor Husband*, Ruby M. Ayres, Novel

BACHELOR OF ARTS 1934 d: Louis King. USA., *Bachelor of Arts*, John Erskine, Indianapolis 1934, Novel

BACHELOR PARTY, THE 1957 d: Delbert Mann. USA., *The Bachelor Party*, Paddy Chayefsky, 1955, Television Play

Bachelor Trap, The *see* JUNGGESELLENFALLE (1953).

BACHELOR'S AFFAIRS 1932 d: Alfred L. Werker. USA., *Precious*, James Forbes, New York 1929, Play

BACHELOR'S BABY 1932 d: Harry Hughes. UKN., *Bachelor's Baby*, Rolfe Bennett, Novel

BACHELOR'S BABY, A 1922 d: Arthur Rooke. UKN., *Bachelor's Baby*, Rolfe Bennett, Novel

Bachelor's Brides *see* BACHELOR BRIDES (1926).

Bachelor's Club *see* KLUB KAWALEROW (1962).

BACHELORS' CLUB, THE 1921 d: A. V. Bramble. UKN., *The Bachelors' Club*, Israel Zangwill, 1891, Novel

Bachelor's Folly *see* THE CALENDAR (1931).

Bachelor's Paradise *see* PARADIES DER JUNGGESELLEN (1939).

BACHELOR'S ROMANCE, THE 1915. USA., *A Bachelor's Romance*, Martha Morton, Chicago 1896, Play

BACIAMO LE MANI 1973 d: Vittorio Schiraldi. ITL., *Baciamo le Mani*, Vittorio Schiraldi, Novel

Bacio Dell'aurora, Il *see* FRANCOIS IL CONTRABBANDIERE (1954).

BACIO DI UNA MORTA, IL 1917 d: Enrico Vidali. ITL., *Il Bacio Di Una Morta*, Carolina Invernizio, 1903, Novel

BACIO DI UNA MORTA, IL 1949 d: Guido Brignone. ITL., *Il Bacio Di Una Morta*, Carolina Invernizio, 1903, Novel

BACIO DI UNA MORTA, IL 1974 d: Carlo Infascelli. ITL., *Il Bacio Di Una Morta*, Carolina Invernizio, 1903, Novel

BACIO, IL 1974 d: Mario Lanfranchi. ITL., *Il Bacio Di Una Morta*, Carolina Invernizio, 1903, Novel

Back Field *see* THE BAND PLAYS ON (1934).

BACK FROM THE DEAD 1957 d: Charles Marquis Warren. USA., *The Other One*, Catherine Turney, 1952, Novel

BACK IN CIRCULATION 1937 d: Ray Enright. USA., *Angle Shooter*, Adela Rogers St. Johns, 1937, Short Story

Back in the Country *see* DAHINTEN IN DER HEIDE (1936).

BACK PAY 1922 d: Frank Borzage. USA., *Back Pay*, Fannie Hurst, Short Story

BACK PAY 1930 d: William A. Seiter. USA., *Back Pay*, Fannie Hurst, Short Story

Back Porch *see* IT'S A GIFT (1934).

BACK STREET 1932 d: John M. Stahl. USA., *Back Street*, Fannie Hurst, New York 1931, Novel

BACK STREET 1941 d: Robert Stevenson. USA., *Back Street*, Fannie Hurst, New York 1931, Novel

BACK STREET 1961 d: David Miller. USA., *Back Street*, Fannie Hurst, New York 1931, Novel

BACK TO GOD'S COUNTRY 1919 d: David M. Hartford, Bert Van Tuyle (Uncredited). CND/USA., *Wapi the Walrus*, James Oliver Curwood, Story

BACK TO GOD'S COUNTRY 1927 d: Irvin V. Willat. USA., *Back to God's Country and Other Stories*, James Oliver Curwood, New York 1920, Book

BACK TO GOD'S COUNTRY 1953 d: Joseph Pevney. USA., *Back to God's Country and Other Stories*, James Oliver Curwood, New York 1920, Book

BACK TO LIFE 1925 d: Whitman Bennett. USA., *Back from the Dead*, Andrew Soutar, London 1920, Novel

Back to Nature *see* DAO ZIREN QU (1936).

Back to the Stars *see* ERINNERUNGEN AN DIE ZUKUNFT (1969).

BACK TO THE TREES 1926 d: Edwin Greenwood. UKN., *Back to the Trees*, H. H. Bashford, Short Story

Back to the Wall *see* LE DOS AU MUR (1958).

BACK TO YELLOW JACKET 1922 d: Ben Wilson. USA., *Back to Yellow Jacket*, Peter B. Kyne, Short Story

BACKBONE 1923 d: Edward Sloman. USA., *Backbone*, Clarence Budington Kelland, 1922, Short Story

BACKFIRE! 1962 d: Paul Almond. UKN., Edgar Wallace, Novel

Backfire *see* ECHAPPEMENT LIBRE (1964).

BACKGROUND 1953 d: Daniel Birt. UKN., *Background*, Warren Chetham Strode, London 1950, Play

BACKGROUND TO DANGER 1943 d: Raoul Walsh. USA., *Uncommon Danger*, Eric Ambler, Novel

BACKLASH 1956 d: John Sturges. USA., *Backlash*, Frank Gruber, Novel

BACKSTAIRS AT THE WHITE HOUSE 1979 d: Michael O'Herlihy. USA., *My Thirty Years Backstairs at the White House*, Lillian Rogers Parks, Autobiography

Bad Angel *see* UM ANJO MAU (1972).

BAD AS I WANNA BE: THE DENNIS RODMAN STORY 1998 d: Jean de Segonzac. USA., *Bad As I Wanna Be*, Tim Keown, Dennis Rodman, Book

BAD AUF DER TENNE, DAS 1943 d: Volker von Collande. GRM., *Das Bad Auf Der Tenne*, Rolf Meyer, Story

BAD AUF DER TENNE, DAS 1956 d: Paul Martin. GRM., *Das Bad Auf Der Tenne*, Rolf Meyer, Story

Bad Blonde *see* THE FLANAGAN BOY (1953).

BAD BLOOD 1980 d: Mike Newell. NZL/UKN., *Manhunt: the Story of Stanley Graham*, Howard Willis, Book

BAD BUCK OF SANTA YNEZ, THE 1915 d: William S. Hart. USA., *The Bad Buck of Santa Ynez*, Bret Harte, Short Story

BAD COMPANY 1925 d: Edward H. Griffith. USA., *The Ultimate Good*, John C. Brownell, Story

BAD COMPANY 1931 d: Tay Garnett. USA., *Put on the Spot*, Jack Lait, New York 1930, Novel

BAD DAY AT BLACK ROCK 1955 d: John Sturges. USA., *Bad Time at Hondo*, Howard Breslin, Don McGuire, Story

BAD FOR EACH OTHER 1953 d: Irving Rapper. USA., *Scalpel*, Horace McCoy, 1952, Novel

BAD GIRL 1931 d: Frank Borzage. USA., *Bad Girl*, Eugene Delmar, Vina Delmar, New York 1928, Novel

Bad Girl *see* MANHATTAN HEARTBEAT (1940).

Bad Girls Don't Cry *see* LA NOTTE BRAVA (1959).

Bad Goody, A *see* PLOKHOY KHOROSHYI CHELOVEK (1974).

Bad Joke *see* SKVENEI ANEKDOT (1965).

BAD LITTLE ANGEL 1939 d: Wilhelm Thiele. USA., *Looking After Sandy*, Margaret Turnbull, New York 1914, Novel

Bad Luck *see* ZEZOWATE SZCZESCIE (1960).

BAD MAN, THE 1923 d: Edwin Carewe. USA., *The Bad Man*, Porter Emerson Browne, New York 1920, Play

BAD MAN, THE 1930 d: Clarence Badger. USA., *The Bad Man*, Porter Emerson Browne, New York 1920, Play

BAD MAN, THE 1941 d: Richard Thorpe. USA., *The Bad Man*, Porter Emerson Browne, New York 1920, Play

BAD MANNERS 1997 d: Jonathan Kaufer. USA., *Ghost in the machine*, David Gilman, Play

BAD MEDICINE 1985 d: Harvey Miller. USA., *Calling Dr. Horowitz*, Steven Horowitz, Neil Offen, Book

Bad Men of Arizona *see* THE ARIZONA RAIDERS (1936).

BAD MEN OF MISSOURI 1941 d: Ray Enright. USA., Robert E. Kent, Story

BAD MEN OF TOMBSTONE, THE 1949 d: Kurt Neumann. USA., *Last of the Badmen*, Jay Monaghan, Novel

BAD MOON 1996 d: Eric Red. USA., *Thor*, Wayne Smith, Novel

Bad Night *see* MALA NOCHE (1987).

Bad Road, The *see* LA VIACCIA (1961).

BAD RONALD 1974 d: Buzz Kulik. USA., *Bad Ronald*, John Holbrook Vance, Novel

BAD SEED, THE 1956 d: Mervyn Leroy. USA., *The Bad Seed*, William March, Novel

BAD SEED, THE 1985 d: Paul Wendkos. USA., *The Bad Seed*, William March, Novel

BAD SISTER 1931 d: Hobart Henley. USA., *The Flirt*, Booth Tarkington, New York 1913, Novel

Bad Sister *see* THE WHITE UNICORN (1947).

Bad Thief, The *see* IL LADRONE (1979).

Badaranii *see* BADARINII (1960).

BADARINII 1960 d: Gheorghe Naghi, Sica Alexandrescu. RMN., *I Rusteghi*, Carlo Goldoni, 1761, Play

Baddegama *see* BEDDEGAMA (1980).

BADESSA DI CASTRO, LA 1974 d: Armando Crispino. ITL., *L' Abbesse de Castro*, Stendhal, Short Story

Badge of Courage, The *see* TURN BACK THE HOURS (1928).

BADGE OF POLICEMAN O'ROON, THE 1913. USA., *The Badge of Policeman O'Roon*, O. Henry, 1904, Short Story

Badge of Policeman O'Roon, The *see* DOCTOR RHYTHM (1938).

BADGE OF THE ASSASSIN 1985 d: Mel Damski. USA., *Badge of the Assassin*, Philip Rosenberg, Robert J. Tanenbaum, Book

BADGER'S GREEN 1934 d: Adrian Brunel. UKN., *Badger's Green*, R. C. Sherriff, London 1930, Play

BADGER'S GREEN 1949 d: John Irwin. UKN., *Badger's Green*, R. C. Sherriff, London 1930, Play

BADIA DI MONTENERO, LA 1921 d: Renato Bulla Del Torchio. ITL., *La Badia Di Montenero*, Nicola Misasi, Novel

BADLANDERS, THE 1958 d: Delmer Daves. USA., *Asphalt Jungle*, William Riley Burnett, New York 1949, Novel

BAGARRES 1948 d: Henri Calef. FRN., *Bagarres*, Jean Proal, Novel

Bagdad on the Subway *see* O. HENRY'S FULL HOUSE (1952).

Bagne de Femmes *see* ZU NEUEN UFERN (1937).

BAGNES D'ENFANTS 1914 d: Emile Chautard. FRN., *Bagnes d'Enfants*, Pierre Chaine, Andre de Lorde, Play

BAGNES D'ENFANTS 1933 d: Georges Gauthier. FRN., *Bagnes d'Enfants*, Pierre Chaine, Andre de Lorde, Play

BAGNO, IL 1972 d: Ugo Gregoretti. ITL., *Il Bagno*, Vladimir Majakovskij, Play

BAGNOSTRAFLING, DER 1949 d: Gustav Frohlich. GRM., *Vautrin*, Honore de Balzac, 1840, Play

BAHAMA PASSAGE 1941 d: Edward H. Griffith. USA., *Bahama Passage*, Nelson Hayes, Novel

Bahia de Tous Les Saints *see* JUBIABA (1986).

BAHNO PRAHY 1927 d: M. J. Krnansky. CZC., *Bahno Prahy*, Karel Ladislav Kukla, Short Story

BAHNWARTER THIEL 1982 d: Hans-Joachim Kasprzik. GDR., *Barnwarter Thiel*, Gerhart Hauptmann, 1888, Short Story

BAI MAO NU 1950 d: Wang Bin, Shui HuA. CHN., *Bai Mao Nu*, He Jingzhi, Ting Yi, Play

BAILARIN Y EL TRABAJADOR, EL 1936 d: Luis MarquinA. SPN., *Nadie Sabe Lo Que Quiere; O El Bailarin Y El Trabajador*, Jacinto Benavente y Martinez, 1925, Play

Bailiff of Greifensee, The *see* DER LANDVOGT VON GREIFENSEE (1979).

Bailiff, The *see* SANSHO DAYU (1954).

BAILIFFS, THE 1932 d: Frank Cadman. UKN., *The Bailiff*, Fred Karno, Sketch

Bailli de Greifensee, Le see **DER LANDVOGT VON GREIFENSEE** (1979).

BAIQIUEN DAIFU 1964 d: Zhang Junxiang. CHN., *Baiqiuen Daifu*, Zhou Erfu, Book

Baiser de l'Assassin, Le see **DER KUSS DES TIGERS** (1989).

BAISER SUPREME, LE 1913. FRN., *Le Baiser Supreme*, Julien Sermet, Novel

BAIT 1950 d: Frank Richardson. UKN., *Bait*, Frank Richardson, Play

BAIT, THE 1921 d: Maurice Tourneur. USA., *The Tiger Lady*, Sidney Toler, Play

BAIT, THE 1973 d: Leonard Horn. USA., *The Bait*, Dorothy Uhnak, Novel

Bait, The see **L' APPAT** (1995).

Bajaja see **PRINC BAJAJA** (1950).

BAJECNA LETA POD PSA 1997 d: Petr Nikolaev. CZE., Michal Viewegh, Novel

BAJO BANDERA 1997 d: Juan Jose Jusid. ARG/ITL., *Bajo Bandera*, Guillermo Saccomanno, Book

BAJO EL CIELO DE ASTURIAS 1950 d: Gonzalo Delgras. SPN., *Sinfonia Pastoral*, Armando Palacio Valdes, 1931, Novel

Bajo Otra Bandera see **SHOW OF FORCE** (1989).

BAKARUHABAN 1957 d: Imre Feher. HNG., *Bakaruhaban*, Sandor Hunyady, 1935, Short Story

BAKER'S HAWK 1976 d: Lyman D. Dayton. USA., *Baker's Hawk*, Jack Bickham, Novel

Baker's Wife, The see **LA FEMME DU BOULANGER** (1938).

BAKONJA FRA BRNE 1951 d: Fedor Hanzekovic. YGS., *Bakonja Fra Brne*, Simo Matavulj, 1892, Novel

BAL DES ESPIONS, LE 1960 d: Michel Clement, Umberto Scarpelli. FRN/ITL., *Documents a Vendre*, Jean Bruce, Novel

BAL DES POMPIERS, LE 1948 d: Andre Berthomieu. FRN., *Le Bal Des Pompiers*, Jean Nohain, Play

BAL DU COMTE D'ORGEL, LE 1969 d: Marc Allegret. FRN., *Le Bal du Comte d'Orgel*, Raymond Radiguet, 1924, Novel

BAL, LE 1931 d: Wilhelm Thiele. FRN., *Le Bal*, Irene Nemirovsky, Short Story

BALACLAVA 1928 d: Maurice Elvey, Milton Rosmer. UKN., *The Charge of the Light Brigade*, Alfred Tennyson, 1854, Poem

BALACLAVA 1930 d: Maurice Elvey, Milton Rosmer. UKN., *The Charge of the Light Brigade*, Alfred Tennyson, 1854, Poem

BALALAIKA 1939 d: Reinhold Schunzel. USA., *Balalaika*, Bernard Grun, Eric Maschwitz, George Posford, London 1936, Musical Play

Balance see **RAVNOVESSIE** (1983).

Balaoo see **BALAOO OU DES PAS AU PLAFOND** (1912).

BALAOO OU DES PAS AU PLAFOND 1912 d: Victorin Jasset. FRN., *Balaoo*, Gaston Leroux, Paris 1912, Novel

Balcon Sobre El Infierno, Un see **CONSTANCE AUX ENFERS** (1964).

BALCONY, THE 1963 d: Joseph Strick. USA., *Le Balcon*, Jean Genet, 1956, Play

Bald-Cop and Girl Student see **TU TAN YU QIAO NIU** (1994).

BALDEVINS BROLLOP 1938 d: Gideon Wahlberg, Emil A. Lingheim. SWD., *Baldevins Bryllup*, Vilhelm Krag, Oslo 1900, Play

Baldevin's Wedding see **BALDEVINS BROLLOP** (1938).

BALDORIA NEI CARAIBI 1956 d: Ubaldo Ragona, Jose Luis ZavalA. ITL/SPN., *Baldoria Nei Caraibi*, Alessandro Maggiora Vergano, Novel

Baldwin's Wedding see **BALDEVINS BROLLOP** (1938).

Balgari Ot Staro Vreme see **BULGARI OT STARO VREME** (1945).

BALIDAN 1927 d: Naval Gandhi. IND., *Balidan*, Rabindranath Tagore, Play

Balkanisater see **VALKANISATER** (1997).

BALL AT SAVOY 1936 d: Victor Hanbury. UKN., *Ball Im Savoy*, Alfred Grunwald, Fritz Lohner-Beda, Play

Ball at the Savoy, The see **BALL IM SAVOY** (1955).

BALL DER NATIONEN 1954 d: Karl Ritter. GRM., *Ball Der Nationen*, Paul Bayer, Heinz Hentschke, Opera

BALL IM METROPOL 1937 d: Frank Wisbar. GRM., *Irrungen Wirrungen*, Theodor Fontane, 1888, Short Story

BALL IM SAVOY 1955 d: Paul Martin. GRM., *Ball Im Savoy*, Alfred Grunwald, Fritz Lohner-Beda, Play

Ball of Fire see **MUSIC IS MAGIC** (1935).

BALL OF FORTUNE, THE 1926 d: Hugh Croise. UKN., *The Ball of Fortune*, Sidney Horler, Novel

Ball of Suet, A see **PYSHKA** (1934).

Ballad of a Hussar, The see **GUSARSKAYA BALLADA** (1962).

BALLAD OF GREGORIO CORTEZ, THE 1982 d: Robert M. Young. USA., *With His Pistol in His Hands*, Amerigo Paredes, Novel

Ballad of Narayama see **NARAYAMA BUSHI-KO** (1958).

Ballad of Narayama, The see **NARAYAMA BUSHI-KO** (1983).

BALLAD OF READING GAOL, THE 1988 d: Richard Kwietniowski. UKN., *The Ballad of Reading Gaol*, Oscar Wilde, 1898, Verse

BALLAD OF SPLENDID SILENCE, A 1913. UKN., *A Ballad of Splendid Silence*, E. Nesbit, Poem

Ballad of the Narayama, The see **NARAYAMA BUSHI-KO** (1958).

BALLAD OF THE SAD CAFE, THE 1991 d: Simon Callow. USA/UKN., *The Ballad of the Sad Cafe*, Carson McCullers, 1951, Short Story

Ballad of the Windshield Washers, The see **LA BALLATA DEI LAVAVETRI** (1998).

BALLATA DEI LAVAVETRI, LA 1998 d: Peter Del Monte. ITL., *The Polish Car Window Cleaner*, E. Albinati, Novel

Balle Entre Les Yeux, Une see **SHOOT** (1976).

Ballerina see **LA MORT DU CYNGE** (1937).

BALLERINE 1936 d: Gustav Machaty. ITL., *Fanny Ballerina Della Scala*, Giuseppe Adami, Novel

BALLET GIRL, THE 1916 d: George Irving. USA., *Carnival*, Compton Mackenzie, London 1912, Novel

Ballet of Othello see **VENETSIANSKIY MAVR** (1961).

Ballet of Romeo and Juliet, The see **ROMEO I DZULETTA** (1955).

BALLHAUS-ANNA, DIE 1911 d: Walter Schmidthassler. GRM., *Die Ballhaus-Anna*, Leo Leipziger, Novel

Balloon, The see **PRIVARZANIAT BALON** (1967).

BALLYHOO'S STORY, THE 1913 d: Rollin S. Sturgeon. USA., E. A. Brinistol, Story

BALTAGUL 1969 d: Mircea Muresan. RMN/ITL., *Baltagul*, Mihail Sadoveanu, 1930, Novel

BALTHAZAR 1937 d: Piere Colombier. FRN., *Balthazar*, Leopold Marchand, Play

Baltic Rhapsody see **WIERNA RZEKA** (1936).

Balzac Stories see **DIE TOLLDREISTEN GESCHICHTEN - NACH HONORE DE BALZAC** (1969).

Balzaminov's Marriage see **ZHENITBA BALZAMINOVA** (1965).

BAMBINI CI GUARDANO, I 1944 d: Vittorio de SicA. ITL., *Prico*, Cesare Giulio Viola, Novel

BAMBOLONA, LA 1968 d: Franco Giraldi. ITL., *La Bambolona*, Alba de Cespedes, Novel

Banana Peel see **PEAU DE BANANE** (1964).

BANANA RIDGE 1941 d: Walter C. Mycroft. UKN., *Banana Ridge*, Ben Travers, London 1938, Play

Banc de la Desolation, Le see **DE GRAY -LE BANC DE DESOLATION** (1973).

BANCA DI MONATE, LA 1976 d: Francesco Massaro. ITL., *La Banca Di Monate*, Piero Chiara, Short Story

BANCHARAMER BAGAN 1980 d: Tapan SinhA. IND., *Bancharamer Bagan*, Manoj Mitra, Play

BANCO A BANGKOK 1964 d: Andre Hunebelle. FRN/ITL., *Lila de Calcutta*, Jean Bruce, Paris 1960, Novel

Banco a Bangkok Pour Oss 117 see **BANCO A BANGKOK** (1964).

BANCO DE PRINCE 1950 d: Michel Dulud. FRN., *Monseigneur*, Michel Dulud, Play

BAND OF ANGELS 1957 d: Raoul Walsh. USA., *Band of Angels*, Robert Penn Warren, 1955, Novel

Band of Outsiders see **BANDE A PART** (1964).

BAND PLAYS ON, THE 1934 d: Russell MacK. USA., *The Gravy Game*, W. Thornton Martin, Harry Stuhldreher, 1933, Short Story

BANDBOX, THE 1919 d: R. William Neill. USA., *The Bandbox*, Louis Joseph Vance, Boston 1912, Novel

BANDE A PART 1964 d: Jean-Luc Godard. FRN., *Fool's Gold*, Dolores Hitchens, New York 1958, Novel

BANDE DES SCHRECKENS, DIE 1960 d: Harald Reinl. GRM., *The Terrible People*, Edgar Wallace, London 1926, Novel

BANDERA, LA 1935 d: Julien Duvivier. FRN., *La Bandera*, Pierre Mac Orlan, 1931, Novel

BANDIDO DE LA SIERRA, EL 1926 d: Eusebio F. Ardavin. SPN., *El Bandido de la Sierra*, Luis Fernandez Ardavin, Play

BANDINI 1988 d: Dominique Deruddere. BLG/USA., John Fante, Novel

BANDISH 1955 d: Satyen Bose. IND., *Chheley Kar?*, Jyotirmoy Roy, Novel

BANDIT OF SHERWOOD FOREST, THE 1946 d: George Sherman, Henry Levin. USA., *Son of Robin Hood*, Paul A. Castleton, Novel

Bandit of the Mountains, The see **EL BANDIDO DE LA SIERRA** (1926).

Bandit, The see **L' AMANTE DI GRAMIGNA** (1968).

Bandito Della 11, Il see **PIERROT LE FOU** (1965).

Bandito Si. Ma d'Onore see **LA VENDETTA** (1961).

Bandits in Sardinia see **BARBAGIA** (1969).

BANDOLERO! 1968 d: Andrew V. McLaglen. USA., *MacE*, Stanley L. Hough, Short Story

BANDOLERO, THE 1924 d: Tom Terriss. USA., *The Bandolero*, Paul Gwynne, New York 1904, Novel

BANG THE DRUM SLOWLY 1973 d: John Hancock. USA., *Bang the Drum Slowly*, Mark Harris, 1956, Novel

BANGARADA MANUSHYA 1972 d: Siddalingaiah. IND., *Bangarada Manushya*, T. K. Ramarao, Novel

BANGARU PAPA 1954 d: B. N. Reddi. IND., *Silas Marner*, George Eliot, London 1861, Novel

BANGIKU 1954 d: Mikio Naruse. JPN., *Bangiku*, Fumiko Hayashi, 1948, Short Story, *Shirasagi*, Fumiko Hayashi, 1949, Short Story, *Suisen*, Fumiko Hayashi, 1949, Short Story

Bangkok Story see **KILLING DRUGS** (1988).

BANJO ON MY KNEE 1936 d: John Cromwell. USA., *Banjo on My Knee*, Harry Hamilton, Indianapolis 1936, Novel

Bank in Monate, The see **LA BANCA DI MONATE** (1976).

BANK SHOT, THE 1974 d: Gower Champion. USA., *The Bank Shot*, Donald E. Westlake, Novel

BANKA 1957 d: Heinosuke Gosho. JPN., *Banka*, Yasuko Harada, Novel

BANKER MARGAYYA 1983 d: T. S. NagabharanA. IND., *The Financial Expert*, R. K. Narayan, 1952, Novel

BANKER'S DAUGHTER, THE 1914 d: Edward M. Roskam, William F. Haddock. USA., *The Banker's Daughter*, Bronson Howard, New York 1878, Play

BANKER'S DOUBLE, THE 1915 d: Langdon West. USA., *Below the Deadline*, Scott Campbell, Short Story

BANKETTEN 1948 d: Hasse Ekman. SWD., *Banketten*, Marika Stiernstedt, Novel

Banks of the Wabash see **ON THE BANKS OF THE WABASH** (1923).

Banner in the Sky see **THIRD MAN ON THE MOUNTAIN** (1959).

BANNERLINE 1951 d: Don Weis. USA., *A Rose Is Not a Rose*, Samson Raphaelson, Short Story

BANNING 1967 d: Ron Winston. USA., Hamilton Maule, Story

BANQUE NEMO, LA 1934 d: Marguerite Viel. FRN., *Le Banque Nemo*, Louis Verneuil, Play

Banquet, The see **BANKETTEN** (1948).

BANSHUN 1949 d: Yasujiro Ozu. JPN., *Father and Daughter*, Kazuo Hirotsu, Novel

Banter see **THE LAST OF PHILIP BANTER** (1986).

Bao Feng Zhou Yu see **BAOFENG-ZHOUYU** (1961).

BAO MI JU DE QIANG SHENG 1979 d: Chang Yan. CHN., *Battling the Enemy at His Headquarters*, Lu Zheng, Novel

BAOFENG-ZHOUYU 1961 d: XIe Tieli. CHN., *Bao Feng Zhou Yu*, Zhou Lipo, 1948, Novel

BAPTEME DU PETIT OSCAR, LE 1932 d: Jean Dreville. FRN., *Le Bapteme du Petit Oscar*, V. Bernard, Eugene Grange, Play

BAR 20 JUSTICE 1938 d: Lesley Selander. USA., *Ranchman Buck Peters*, Clarence E. Mulford, John Wood, Chicago 1912, Novel

BAR GIRLS 1994 d: Marita Giovanni. USA., *Bar Girls*, Lauren Hoffman, Play

Bar Sinister, The *see* **IT'S A DOG'S LIFE** (1955).

BARA 1981 d: M. S. Sathyu. IND., *Bara*, U. R. Ananthamurthy, Story

BARA EN MOR 1949 d: Alf Sjoberg. SWD., *Bara En Mor*, Ivar Lo-Johansson, 1939, Novel

BARABBA 1961 d: Richard Fleischer. ITL., *Barabbas*, Par Lagerkvist, 1950, Novel

BARABBAS 1953 d: Alf Sjoberg. SWD., *Barabbas*, Par Lagerkvist, 1950, Novel

Barabbas *see* **BARABBA** (1961).

Baragan Thistles *see* **CIULINII BARAGANULUI** (1957).

BARA-GASSEN 1950 d: Mikio Naruse. JPN., *Bara Gassen*, Fumio Niwa, 1937, Novel

BARAKA SUR X 13 1965 d: Maurice Cloche, Silvio Siano. FRN/ITL/SPN., *Silence Clinique*, Eddy Ghilain, Novel

BARAONDA, LA 1923 d: Orlando Vassallo. ITL., *La Baraonda*, Gerolamo Rovetta

BARATIN 1957 d: Jean Stelli. FRN., *Baratin*, Andre Hornez, Jean Valmy, Opera

BARATRO, IL 1912 d: Mario Bernardi. ITL., *Il Baratro*, Carlo Gamberoni

Barb Wire (the Rawhide Halo) *see* **THE RAWHIDE HALO** (1960).

BARBAGIA 1969 d: Carlo Lizzani. ITL., *La Societa Del Malessere*, Giuseppe Fiori, Book

Barbagia -la Societa Del Malessere *see* **BARBAGIA** (1969).

BARBARA 1961 d: Frank Wisbar. GRM., *Barbara*, Jorgen-Franz Jacobsen, 1939, Novel

BARBARA 1970 d: Walter Burns. USA., *Barbara*, Frank Newman, New York 1968, Novel

BARBARA 1998 d: Nils Malmros. DNM/SWD/NRW., *Barbara*, Jorgen-Franz Jacobsen, 1939, Novel

BARBARA FRIETCHIE 1908 d: J. Stuart Blackton. USA., *Barbara Frietchie*, John Greenleaf Whittier, 1864, Poem

BARBARA FRIETCHIE 1915 d: Herbert Blache. USA., *Barbara Frietchie*, John Greenleaf Whittier, 1864, Poem

BARBARA FRIETCHIE 1924 d: Lambert Hillyer. USA., *Barbara Frietchie*, John Greenleaf Whittier, 1864, Poem

Barbara Fritchie *see* **BARBARA FRIETCHIE** (1908).

Barbara Taylor Bradford's Remember *see* **REMEMBER** (1993).

BARBARIAN - INGOMAR, THE 1908 d: D. W. Griffith. USA., *The Barbarian - Ingomar*, Ernest Thompson Seton, Short Story

BARBARIAN, THE 1921 d: Donald Crisp. USA., *The Barbarian*, Theodore Seixas Solomons, 1920, Short Story

Barbarian, The *see* **SHE** (1983).

BARBARIANS AT THE GATE 1993 d: Glenn Jordan. USA., *Barbarians at the Gates*, Bryan Burrough, John Helyar, Book

BARBARY SHEEP 1917 d: Maurice Tourneur. USA., *Barbary Sheep*, Robert Hichens, London 1907, Novel

Barbassous *see* **MIO ZIO BARBASSOUS** (1921).

BARBE-BLEUE 1951 d: Christian-Jaque. FRN/GRM., *Barbe-Bleue*, Charles Perrault, 1697, Short Story

BARBED WIRE 1927 d: Mauritz Stiller, Rowland V. Lee. USA., *The Woman of Knockaloe*, Hall Caine, New York 1923, Novel

Barber John's Boy *see* **STREET GIRL** (1929).

Barber John's Boy *see* **MAN TO MAN** (1930).

Barber of Seville, The *see* **IL BARBIERE DI SIVIGLIA** (1913).

Barber of Seville, The *see* **EL BARBERO DE SEVILLA** (1938).

Barber of Seville, The *see* **IL BARBIERE DI SIVIGLIA** (1946).

BARBER OF STAMFORD HILL, THE 1962 d: Caspar Wrede. UKN., *The Barber of Stamford Hill*, Ronald Harwood, Television Play

BARBERINE 1910 d: Emile Chautard. FRN., *Barberine*, Alfred de Musset, Play

BARBERO DE SEVILLA, EL 1938 d: Benito Perojo. SPN/GRM., *Le Barbier de Seville*, Pierre-Augustin Caron de Beaumarchais, 1775, Play

BARBIER DE SEVILLE, LE 1933 d: Hubert Bourlon, Jean Kemm. FRN., *Le Barbier de Seville*, Pierre-Augustin Caron de Beaumarchais, 1775, Play

Barbier von Sevilla, Der *see* **EL BARBERO DE SEVILLA** (1938).

BARBIERE DI SIVIGLIA, IL 1913 d: Luigi Maggi. ITL., *Le Barbier de Seville*, Pierre-Augustin Caron de Beaumarchais, 1775, Play

BARBIERE DI SIVIGLIA, IL 1946 d: Mario CostA. ITL., *Le Barbier de Seville*, Pierre-Augustin Caron de Beaumarchais, 1775, Play

BARBORA HLAVSOVA 1942 d: Martin Fric. CZC., *Skleneny Vrch*, Jaroslav Havlicek, Short Story

BAR-C MYSTERY, THE 1926 d: Robert F. Hill. USA., *Janie of the Waning Glories*, Raymond Smiley Spears, Story

BARCA SIN PESCADOR, LA 1964 d: Jose Maria Forn. SPN., *La Barca Sin Pescador*, Alejandro Casona, 1945, Play

Barcaiolo d'Amalfi, Il *see* **IL BARCAIOLO DI AMALFI** (1958).

BARCAIOLO DI AMALFI, IL 1958 d: Mino Roli. ITL., *Il Barcaiolo Di Amalfi*, Francesco Mastriani, Novel

Barcarole *see* **BRAND IN DER OPER** (1930).

BARCHESTER CHRONICLES, THE 1982 d: David Giles. UKN., *Barchester Towers*, Anthony Trollope, 1857, Novel, *The Warden*, Anthony Trollope, 1855, Novel

BARDELYS THE MAGNIFICENT 1926 d: King Vidor. USA., *Bardelys the Magnificent*, Rafael Sabatini, Boston 1905, Novel

BARE SKYER BEVEGER STJERNENE 1998 d: Torun Lian. NRW., *Bare Skyer Beveger Stjernene*, Torun Lian, Novel

BAREE, SON OF KAZAN 1918 d: David Smith. USA., *Baree - Son of Kazan*, James Oliver Curwood, Garden City, Ny. 1917, Novel

BAREE, SON OF KAZAN 1925 d: David Smith. USA., *Baree - Son of Kazan*, James Oliver Curwood, Garden City, Ny. 1917, Novel

BAREFOOT BOY 1914 d: Robert G. VignolA. USA., Mrs. Owen Bronson, Story

BAREFOOT BOY 1938 d: Karl Brown. USA., *The Barefoot Boy*, John Greenleaf Whittier, Boston 1856, Poem

BAREFOOT BOY, THE 1923 d: David Kirkland. USA., *The Barefoot Boy*, John Greenleaf Whittier, Boston 1856, Poem

BAREFOOT IN THE PARK 1967 d: Gene Saks. USA., *Barefoot in the Park*, Neil Simon, New York 1964, Play

BAREFOOT MAILMAN, THE 1951 d: Earl McEvoy. USA., *The Barefoot Mailman*, Theodore Pratt, Novel

BARGAIN, THE 1921 d: Henry Edwards. UKN., *The Bargain*, Henry Edwards, Edward Irwin, Play

BARGAIN, THE 1931 d: Robert Milton. USA., *You and I*, Philip Barry, New York 1923, Play

Bargain True, The *see* **THE LURE OF LUXURY** (1918).

Bargain With Satan, a(?) *see* **DER STUDENT VON PRAG** (1913).

Barge-Keeper's Daughter, The *see* **EDUCATION DE PRINCE** (1938).

BARIERATA 1979 d: Hristo Hristov. BUL., *Barierata*, Pavel Vezhinov, 1977, Novel

BARKER, THE 1928 d: George Fitzmaurice. USA., *The Barker; a Play of Carnival Life*, Kenyon Nicholson, New York 1917, Play

BAR-MITZVAH 1935 d: Henry Lynn. USA., *Bar-Mitzvah*, Boris Thomashefsky, Play

Barn Burner *see* **BARN BURNING** (1980).

BARN BURNING 1980 d: Peter Werner. USA., *Barn Burning*, William Faulkner, 1939, Short Story

BARNABO DELLE MONTAGNE 1993 d: Mario BrentA. ITL/FRN/SWT., *Barnabo Delle Montagne*, Dino Buzzati, Novel

Barnabo from the Mountains *see* **BARNABO DELLE MONTAGNE** (1993).

Barnabo of the Mountains *see* **BARNABO DELLE MONTAGNE** (1993).

BARNABY 1919 d: Jack Denton. UKN., *Barnaby*, Rina Ramsey, Novel

BARNABY LEE 1917 d: Edward H. Griffith. USA., *Barnaby Lee*, John Bennett, 1902, Short Story

BARNABY RUDGE 1915 d: Thomas Bentley. UKN., *Barnaby Rudge*, Charles Dickens, London 1841, Novel

BARNDOMMENS GADE 1986 d: Astrid Henning-Jensen. DNM., *Barndommens Gade*, Tove Ditlevson, 1943, Novel

BARNENS O 1981 d: Kay Pollak. SWD., *Barnens O*, P. C. Jersild, Novel

BARNET 1940 d: Benjamin Christensen. DNM., *Barnet*, Leck Fischer, 1936, Play

Barnet Murder Case, The *see* **THE CONSPIRATORS** (1924).

Barnum *see* **FREAKS** (1932).

BARNUM WAS RIGHT 1929 d: Del Lord. USA., *Barnum Was Right*, Philip Bartholomae, John Meehan, New York 1923, Play

Baro, Il *see* **LES GRANDS CHEMINS** (1963).

BAROCCO 1925 d: Charles Burguet. FRN., *Barocco*, Georges-Andre Cuel, Novel

BARON DE L'ECLUSE, LE 1959 d: Jean Delannoy. FRN/ITL., *Le Baron de l'Ecluse*, Georges Simenon, 1954, Short Story

Baron Munchausen *see* **BARON PRASIL** (1940).

Baron Munchausen *see* **BARON PRASIL** (1961).

Baron Munchhausen *see* **BARON PRASIL** (1940).

Baron Munchhausen *see* **BARON PRASIL** (1961).

BARON MYSTERE, LE 1918 d: Maurice Challiot. FRN., *Le Baron Mystere*, Henri Germain, Novel

BARON OF ARIZONA, THE 1950 d: Samuel Fuller. USA., Homer Croy, Article

BARON PRASIL 1940 d: Martin Fric. CZC., *Deti V Notesu*, Rudolf Kautzky, Play

BARON PRASIL 1961 d: Karel Zeman. CZC., *Baron Prasil*, Gottfried Burger, Novel

Baron, The *see* **SLAEGTEN** (1978).

BARON TZIGANE, LE 1935 d: Henri Chomette, Karl Hartl. FRN., *Der Zigeunerbaron*, I. Schnitzer, Johann Strauss, Vienna 1885, Operetta

BARONE DI CORBO, IL 1939 d: Gennaro Righelli. ITL., *Il Barone Di Corbo*, Luigi Antonelli, Play

Barone, Il *see* **LE BARON DE L'ECLUSE** (1959).

BARONESS AND THE BUTLER, THE 1938 d: Walter Lang. USA., *Jean*, Ladislaus Bus-Fekete, Vienna 1936, Play

BARRA PESADA 1977 d: Reginaldo FariA. BRZ., *Quebradas Da Vida*, Plinio Marcos, 1973, Short Story

BARRACA, LA 1944 d: Roberto Gavaldon. MXC., *La Barraca*, Vicente Blasco Ibanez, 1898, Novel

BARRACAS, LAS 1925 d: Mario Roncoroni. SPN., *Les Barraques*, Eduardo Escalante (Hijo), Opera

BARRAGE CONTRE LE PACIFIQUE 1958 d: Rene Clement. FRN/USA/ITL., *Un Barrage Contre le Pacifique*, Marguerite Duras, 1950, Novel

BARRANCO, LTD. 1932 d: Andre Berthomieu. FRN., *Silverbell Ou la Nuit Sans Astres*, Andre Armandy, Novel

Barraques, Les *see* **LAS BARRACAS** (1925).

Barraques (O Una Tragedia de la Huerta), Les *see* **LAS BARRACAS** (1925).

BARRAQUETA DEL NANO, LA 1924 d: Juan Andreu Moragas. SPN., *La Barraqueta Del Nano*, Francisco Barchina, Play

Barren Lives *see* **VIDAS SECAS** (1963).

BARRETTS OF WIMPOLE STREET, THE 1934 d: Sidney A. Franklin. USA., *The Barretts of Wimpole Street*, Rudolf Besier, London 1930, Play

BARRETTS OF WIMPOLE STREET, THE 1950 d: Donald Davis. USA., *The Barretts of Wimpole Street*, Rudolf Besier, London 1930, Play

BARRETTS OF WIMPOLE STREET, THE 1953 d: Fielder Cook. USA., *The Barretts of Wimpole Street*, Rudolf Besier, London 1930, Play

BARRETTS OF WIMPOLE STREET, THE 1955 d: James Sheldon. USA., *The Barretts of Wimpole Street*, Rudolf Besier, London 1930, Play

BARRETTS OF WIMPOLE STREET, THE 1956 d: Vincent J. Donehue. USA., *The Barretts of Wimpole Street*, Rudolf Besier, London 1930, Play

BARRETTS OF WIMPOLE STREET, THE 1957 d: Sidney A. Franklin. UKN/USA., *The Barretts of Wimpole Street*, Rudolf Besier, London 1930, Play

BARRICADE 1950 d: Peter Godfrey. USA., *The Sea Wolf*, Jack London, New York 1904, Novel

BARRIER, THE 1917 d: Edgar Lewis. USA., *The Barrier*, Rex Beach, New York 1908, Novel

BARRIER, THE 1926 d: George W. Hill. USA., *The Barrier*, Rex Beach, New York 1908, Novel

BARRIER, THE 1937 d: Lesley Selander. USA., *The Barrier*, Rex Beach, New York 1908, Novel

Barrier, The see **BARIERATA** (1979).

Barriers Aflame see **WHY WOMEN LOVE** (1925).

BARRIERS BURNED AWAY 1925 d: W. S. Van Dyke. USA., *Barriers Burned Away*, Edward Payson Roe, New York 1872, Novel

BARRINGS, DIE 1955 d: Rolf Thiele. GRM., *Die Barrings*, William von Simpson, Novel

Barrings, The see **DIE BARRINGS** (1955).

BARROCO 1988 d: Paul Leduc. MXC., *Concierto Barroco*, Louis Carette, 1974, Novel

BARRY LYNDON 1975 d: Stanley Kubrick. UKN., *The Memoirs of Barry Lyndon Esq.*, William Makepeace Thackeray, 1856, Novel

BARS OF IRON 1920 d: F. Martin Thornton. UKN., *Bars of Iron*, Ethel M. Dell, Novel

Bartered Bride, The see **PRODANA NEVESTA** (1913).

Bartered Bride, The see **PRODANA NEVESTA** (1922).

Bartered Bride, The see **DIE VERKAUFTE BRAUT** (1932).

Bartered Bride, The see **PRODANA NEVESTA** (1933).

BARTLEBY 1970 d: Anthony Friedmann. UKN., *Bartleby*, Herman Melville, 1853, Short Story

BARTON MYSTERY, THE 1920 d: Harry Roberts. UKN., *The Barton Mystery*, Walter Hackett, London 1916, Play

BARTON MYSTERY, THE 1932 d: Henry Edwards. UKN., *The Barton Mystery*, Walter Hackett, London 1916, Play

Baruffe Chiozzotte, Le see **IL PAESE SENZA PACE** (1943).

BARUTEN BUKVAR 1977 d: Todor Dinov. BUL., *Baruten Bukvar*, Yordan Radichkov, 1969, Novel

BARYSHNYA-KRESTYANKA 1995 d: Alexei Sakharov. RSS., Alexander Pushkin, Novel

BASEMENTS 1987 d: Robert Altman. USA/UKN., *The Dumb Waiter*, Harold Pinter, 1960, Play, *The Room*, Harold Pinter, Play

BAS-FONDS, LES 1936 d: Jean Renoir. FRN., *Na Dne*, Maxim Gorky, Moscow 1902, Play

Bashful Hero see **THE GREAT MR. NOBODY** (1941).

Basil, the Great Mouse Detective see **THE GREAT MOUSE DETECTIVE** (1986).

Baskerville Curse, The see **SHERLOCK HOLMES: THE BASKERVILLE CURSE** (1983).

BASKETBALL DIARIES, THE 1995 d: Scott Kalvert. USA., *The Basketball Diaries*, Jim Carroll, Book

Bastard, The see **NAKHALENOK** (1961).

Bastard, The see **AKUTARO** (1963).

BASTARD, THE 1978 d: Lee H. Katzin. USA., *The Bastard*, John Jakes, Novel

BASTARDO, IL 1915 d: Emilio Graziani-Walter. ITL., *Antony*, Alexandre Dumas (pere), 1831, Novel

Basterretxe Estate, The see **EL MAYORAZGO DE BASTERRETXE** (1928).

BAT, THE 1926 d: Roland West. USA., *The Bat*, Avery Hopwood, Mary Roberts Rinehart, New York 1926, Play

Bat, The see **DIE FLEDERMAUS** (1945).

BAT, THE 1959 d: Crane Wilbur. USA., *The Circular Staircase*, Mary Roberts Rinehart, Indianapolis 1908, Novel

BAT WHISPERS, THE 1930 d: Roland West. USA., *The Bat*, Avery Hopwood, Mary Roberts Rinehart, New York 1926, Play

BAT*21 1988 d: Peter Markle. USA., *Bat*21*, William C. Anderson, Book

Bat.21 see **BAT*21** (1988).

Bataille de San Sebastian, La see **LOS CANONES DE SAN SEBASTIAN** (1967).

BATAILLE, LA 1923 d: Edouard-Emile Violet, Sessue HayakawA. FRN., *La Bataille*, Claude Farrere, Paris 1908, Novel

BATAILLE, LA 1933 d: Nicolas Farkas. UKN., *La Bataille*, Claude Farrere, Paris 1908, Novel

BATAILLE SILENCIEUSE, LA 1937 d: Pierre Billon. FRN., *Le Poisson Chinois*, Jean Bommart, Novel

BATAILLON DU CIEL, LE 1945 d: Alexander Esway. FRN., *Le Bataillon du Ciel*, Joseph Kessel, 1947, Novel

BATALION 1927 d: Premysl Prazsky. CZC., *Batalion a Divadelni Hra Batalion*, Josef Hais-Tynecky, Novel

BATALION 1937 d: Miroslav Cikan. CZC., *Batalion a Divadelni Hra Batalion*, Josef Hais-Tynecky, Novel

BATARD, LE 1941 d: Edmund Heuberger. SWT., *Le Batard*, Paul Ilg, Zurich 1913, Novel

Batarde, La see **LE MARIAGE DE VERENA** (1938).

BATEAU A SOUPE, LE 1946 d: Maurice Gleize. FRN., *Le Bateau a Soupe*, Gilbert Dupe, Novel

Bateau de Verre, Le see **DAS BRENNENDE SCHIFF** (1927).

BATEAU D'EMILE, LE 1962 d: Denys de La Patelliere. FRN/ITL., *Le Bateau d'Emile*, Georges Simenon, 1954, Short Story

BATELIERS DE LA VOLGA, LES 1936 d: Wladimir von Strischewski. FRN., *Les Bateliers de la Volga*, Joseph Kessel, Novel

Bats With Baby Faces see **SKY WEST AND CROOKED** (1965).

Battaglia Di Fort Apache, La see **OLD SHATTERHAND** (1964).

Battalion see **BATALION** (1927).

Battalion see **BATALION** (1937).

BATTANT, LE 1982 d: Alain Delon. FRN., *Le Battant*, Andre Caroff, Novel

BATTICUORE 1939 d: Mario Camerini. ITL., Lilly Janusse, Novel

Battle Aboard the Defiant see **H.M.S. DEFIANT** (1962).

BATTLE CRY 1955 d: Raoul Walsh. USA., *Battle Cry*, Leon Uris, Novel

BATTLE CRY OF PEACE, THE 1915 d: J. Stuart Blackton, Wilfred North. USA., *Defenceless America*, Hudson Maxim, New York 1915, Book

Battle Cry of War, The see **THE BATTLE CRY OF PEACE** (1915).

Battle Cry, The see **HER MAN** (1918).

BATTLE FLAME 1959 d: R. G. Springsteen. USA., Lester A. Sansom, Story

Battle for Anzio, The see **LO SBARCO DI ANZIO** (1968).

Battle for Rome see **TEIL 1: KOMM NUR, MEIN LIEBSTES VOGELEIN KAMPF UM ROM** (1968).

Battle Hell see **YANGTSE INCIDENT** (1957).

Battle Hours, The see **COUNTERPOINT** (1968).

BATTLE HYMN OF THE REPUBLIC, THE 1911 d: Larry Trimble. USA., *The Battle Hymn of the Republic*, Julia Ward Howe, Short Story

BATTLE OF BRITAIN 1969 d: Guy Hamilton. UKN., *The Narrow Margin*, Derek Dempster, Derek Wood, London 1961, Book

BATTLE OF BUNKER HILL, THE 1911 d: J. Searle Dawley. USA., *The Battle of Bunker Hill*, Clyde Fitch, Play

BATTLE OF FRENCHMAN'S RUN, THE 1915 d: Theodore Marston. USA., *The Battle of Frenchman's Run*, James Oliver Curwood, Story

Battle of Gallipoli see **TELL ENGLAND** (1931).

Battle of Manchuria, The see **SENSO TO NINGEN** (1970).

Battle of Roses, The see **BARA-GASSEN** (1950).

Battle of the Ladies see **DEVIL-MAY-CARE** (1929).

BATTLE OF THE RIVER PLATE 1956 d: Michael Powell, Emeric Pressburger. UKN., *Graf Spee*, Michael Powell, Book

BATTLE OF THE SEXES, THE 1914 d: D. W. Griffith. USA., *The Single Standard*, Daniel Carson Goodman, Play

BATTLE OF THE SEXES, THE 1928 d: D. W. Griffith. USA., *The Single Standard*, Daniel Carson Goodman, Play

BATTLE OF THE SEXES, THE 1959 d: Charles Crichton. UKN., *The Catbird Seat*, James Thurber, 1943, Short Story

BATTLE OF THE V 1 1958 d: Vernon Sewell. UKN., *They Saved London*, Bernard Newman, Book

BATTLE OF THE VILLA FIORITA, THE 1965 d: Delmer Daves. UKN/USA., *Battle of the Villa Fiorita*, Rumer Godden, London 1963, Novel

Battle, The see **THE DANGER LINE** (1924).

BATTLE, THE 1934 d: Nicolas Farkas. UKN., *La Bataille*, Claude Farrere, Paris 1908, Novel

Battle, The see **SANGHARSH** (1968).

Battleflag see **DIE STANDARTE** (1977).

Battling Bellhop, The see **KID GALAHAD** (1937).

Battling British, The see **BLACK-EYED SUSAN** (1914).

BATTLING BUNYON 1925 d: Paul C. Hurst. USA., *Battling Bunyon Ceases to Be Funny*, Raymond Leslie Goldman, 1924, Short Story

BAUER ALS MILLIONAR, DER 1961 d: Rudolf Steinbock. AUS., *Der Bauer Als Millionar*, Ferdinand Raimund, 1868, Play

BAVU 1923 d: Stuart Paton. USA., *Bavu*, Earl Carroll, New York 1922, Play

BAWDY ADVENTURES OF TOM JONES, THE 1975 d: Cliff Owen. UKN., *Tom Jones a Foundling*, Henry Fielding, 1749, Novel

Bawdy Tales of Tom Jones, The see **THE BAWDY ADVENTURES OF TOM JONES** (1975).

Bawdy Women of Balzac, The see **DIE TOLLDREISTEN GESCHICHTEN - NACH HONORE DE BALZAC** (1969).

BAY OF SEVEN ISLES, THE 1915 d: Frank Lloyd. USA., *The Battle of Seven Isles*, John Greenleaf Whittier, Poem

BAYAN KO -KAPIT SA PATALIM 1984 d: Lino BrockA. PHL/FRN., *The Hostage*, Jose F. Lacaba, Article, *The Strike*, Jose F. Lacaba, Article

Bayan Ko: My Own Country see **BAYAN KO -KAPIT SA PATALIM** (1984).

Bayaya see **PRINC BAJAJA** (1950).

BAYO 1985 d: Mort Ransen. CND., *Lightly*, Chipman Hall, Novel

BAZA LUDZI UMARLYCH 1958 d: Czeslaw Petelski. PLN., *Nastepny Do Raju*, Marek Hlasko, 1958, Short Story

B'CHINAT BAGRUT 1983 d: Assaf Dayan. ISR., Galila Ron-Feder, Story

Be Beautiful But Shut Up see **DES GENS SANS IMPORTANCE** (1955).

Be Careful How You Wish see **THE INCREDIBLE MR. LIMPET** (1964).

Be Careful Red Riding Hood see **AKAZUKINCHAN KIOTSUKETE** (1970).

Be Careful, Young Lady see **ALL THE KING'S HORSES** (1935).

Be Faithful Unto Death see **LEGY JO MINDHALALIG** (1960).

Be Good Forever see **LEGY JO MINDHALALIG** (1960).

Be Good Until Death see **LEGY JO MINDHALALIG** (1960).

Be It Ever So Humble see **BEAUTIFUL! HI** (1944).

Be Prepared see **TROOP BEVERLY HILLS** (1989).

Be Sick. It's Free see **IL MEDICO DELLA MUTUA** (1968).

Be Your Age see **MONKEY BUSINESS** (1952).

BE YOURSELF! 1930 d: Thornton Freeland. USA., *The Champ*, Joseph Jackson, Story

Be Yourself see **VALLALD ONMAGADAT!** (1975).

Beach Hut, The see **IL CASOTTO** (1977).

BEACH OF DREAMS 1921 d: William Parke. USA., *The Beach of Dreams*, Henry de Vere Stacpoole, New York 1919, Novel

BEACH RED 1967 d: Cornel Wilde. USA., *Beach Red*, Peter Bowman, New York 1945, Book

Beachcomber, The see **VESSEL OF WRATH** (1938).

BEACHCOMBER, THE 1954 d: Muriel Box. UKN., *Vessel of Wrath*, W. Somerset Maugham, 1931, Short Story

BEACHES 1988 d: Garry Marshall. USA., *Beaches*, Iris Rainer Dart, Novel

BEACHHEAD 1954 d: Stuart Heisler. USA., *I've Got Mine*, Richard G. Hubler, 1946, Novel

Beads of One Rosary, The see **PACIORKI JEDNEGO ROZANCA** (1979).

Beads of the Same Rosary see **PACIORKI JEDNEGO ROZANCA** (1979).

BEANS OF EGYPT, MAINE 1994 d: Jennifer Warren. USA., *Maine, the Beans of Egypt*, Carolyn Chute, Novel

Bear Eye's Curse, The see **OCHI DE URS** (1983).

BEAR ISLAND 1979 d: Don Sharp. UKN/CND., *Bear Island*, Alistair MacLean, 1971, Novel

Bear Lady's Lover, The see **L' AMANTE DELL'ORSA MAGGIORE** (1971).

Bear, The see **LOKIS** (1969).

Bear, The see **L' OURS** (1988).

Bear Trap, The see **EXCUSE MY DUST** (1920).

Beardless Warriors, The *see* THE YOUNG WARRIORS (1967).

BEARS AND I, THE 1974 d: Bernard McEveety. USA., *The Bears and I*, Robert Franklin Leslie, Novel

BEAST FROM 20,000 FATHOMS, THE 1953 d: Eugene Lourie. USA., *The Foghorn*, Ray Bradbury, 1951, Play

BEAST MUST DIE, THE 1974 d: Paul Annett. UKN., *There Shall Be No Darkness*, James Blish, Novel

BEAST OF HOLLOW MOUNTAIN, THE 1956 d: Ismael Rodriguez, Edward Nassour. USA/MXC., Willis O'Brien, Story

Beast of War, The *see* THE BEAST (1988).

Beast, The *see* KING KONG (1933).

BEAST, THE 1988 d: Kevin Reynolds. USA., *Nanawatai*, William Mastrosimone, Play

BEAST WITH FIVE FINGERS, THE 1946 d: Robert Florey. USA., W. F. Harvey, Story

BEAST WITHIN, THE 1982 d: Philippe MorA. USA., *The Beast Within*, Edward Levy, Novel

BEASTMASTER 2: THROUGH THE PORTAL OF TIME 1991 d: Sylvio Tabet. USA., *The Beastmaster*, Andre Norton, Novel

Beasts of Marseilles, The *see* SEVEN THUNDERS (1957).

BEAT THE DEVIL 1953 d: John Huston. USA/ITL/UKN., *Beat the Devil*, James Helvick, 1951, Novel

Beati Paoli, I *see* I CAVALIERI DALLE MASCHERA NERA (1948).

BEATING BACK 1914 d: Carroll Fleming. USA., *Beating Back*, Will Irwin, Al J. Jennings, 1913, Story

BEATING THE ODDS 1919 d: Paul Scardon. USA., *The Money Maker*, Irving Ross Allen, New York 1918, Novel

BEATRICE DEVANT LE DESIR 1943 d: Jean de Marguenat. FRN., *Beatrice Devant le Desir*, Pierre Frondaie, Novel

BEATRIZ 1976 d: Gonzalo Suarez. SPN., *Femeninas*, Ramon Maria Del Valle-Inclan, 1895, Short Story, *Mi Hermana Antonia*, Ramon Maria Del Valle-Inclan, 1909, Short Story

BEAU BANDIT 1930 d: Lambert Hillyer. USA., *Strictly Business*, Wallace Smith, 1929, Short Story

BEAU BROCADE 1916 d: Thomas Bentley. UKN., *Beau Brocade*, Baroness Orczy, Novel

BEAU BRUMMEL 1913 d: James Young. USA., *Beau Brummel*, Booth Tarkington, Novel

Beau Brummel *see* BEAU BRUMMELL (1924).

BEAU BRUMMELL 1924 d: Harry Beaumont. USA., *Beau Brummell*, Clyde Fitch, New York 1908, Play

BEAU BRUMMELL 1954 d: Curtis Bernhardt. UKN/USA., *Beau Brummell*, Clyde Fitch, New York 1908, Play

BEAU GESTE 1926 d: Herbert Brenon. USA., *Beau Geste*, P. C. Wren, London 1924, Novel

BEAU GESTE 1939 d: William A. Wellman. USA., *Beau Geste*, P. C. Wren, London 1924, Novel

BEAU GESTE 1966 d: Douglas Heyes. USA., *Beau Geste*, P. C. Wren, London 1924, Novel

BEAU GESTE 1982 d: Douglas Camfield. USA., *Beau Geste*, P. C. Wren, London 1924, Novel

BEAU IDEAL 1931 d: Herbert Brenon. USA., *Beau Ideal*, P. C. Wren, New York 1928, Novel

BEAU JAMES 1957 d: Melville Shavelson. USA., *Beau James*, Gene Fowler, Book

BEAU MASQUE 1972 d: Bernard Paul. FRN/ITL., *Beau Masque*, Roger Vailland, 1954, Novel

Beau Monstre, Un *see* IL BEL MOSTRO (1971).

BEAU SABREUR 1928 d: John Waters. USA., *Beau Sabreur*, P. C. Wren, New York 1926, Novel

Beaucoup de Nuits Pour Rien *see* INDUSTRIALE COL COMPLESSO DEL GIOCATTOLO PRIMA NOTTE DEL DR. DANIELI (1970).

Beaumarchais *see* BEAUMARCHAIS L'INSOLENT (1996).

BEAUMARCHAIS L'INSOLENT 1996 d: Edouard Molinaro. FRN., *Beaumarchais*, Sacha Guitry, Play

Beaumarchais the Scoundrel *see* BEAUMARCHAIS L'INSOLENT (1996).

BEAU-PERE 1981 d: Bertrand Blier. FRN., *Beau-Pere*, Bertrand Blier, Novel

Beaute d'Hyppolite, La *see* LA BELLEZZA D'IPPOLITA (1962).

BEAUTE DU DIABLE, LA 1950 d: Rene Clair. FRN/ITL., *Faust*, Johann Wolfgang von Goethe, 1808-32, Play

BEAUTIFUL ADVENTURE, THE 1917 d: Dell Henderson. USA., *La Belle Aventure*, Gaston Arman de Caillavet, Robert de Flers, Paris 1914, Play

Beautiful Adventure, The *see* DAS SCHONE ABENTEUER (1959).

BEAUTIFUL AND DAMNED, THE 1922 d: William A. Seiter. USA., *The Beautiful and Damned*, F. Scott Fitzgerald, New York 1922, Novel

Beautiful But Dangerous *see* SHE COULDN'T SAY NO (1954).

BEAUTIFUL CHEAT, THE 1926 d: Edward Sloman. USA., *Doubling for Cupid*, Nina Wilcox Putnam, 1924, Short Story

Beautiful Fraud, The *see* AMERICAN BEAUTY (1927).

Beautiful Girl of Volendam, The *see* MOOI JUULTJE VAN VOLDENDAM (1924).

Beautiful Image, The *see* LA BELLE IMAGE (1950).

Beautiful Jacala, The *see* THE BRAZEN BEAUTY (1918).

BEAUTIFUL JIM 1914 d: Maurice Elvey. UKN., *Beautiful Jim*, John Strange Winter, Novel

Beautiful Julie of Volendam *see* MOOI JUULTJE VAN VOLDENDAM (1924).

Beautiful Kata *see* KRASAVICE KATA (1919).

BEAUTIFUL LIAR, THE 1921 d: Wallace Worsley. USA., *Peachie*, George Marion Jr., Story

Beautiful Liar, The *see* DIE SCHONE LUGNERIN (1959).

BEAUTIFUL LIE, THE 1917 d: John W. Noble. USA., *Reveries of a Station House*, Ella Wheeler Wilcox, Poem

Beautiful People, The *see* YORU NO HENRIN (1964).

Beautiful Rebel, The *see* JANICE MEREDITH (1924).

Beautiful Spy, The *see* KRASNA VYZVEDACKA (1927).

BEAUTIFUL THING 1996 d: Hettie MacDonald. UKN., *Beautiful Thing*, Jonathan Harvey, Play

Beautifully Trimmed *see* GOLDIE GETS ALONG (1933).

Beauty! *see* BEAUTY FOR SALE (1933).

Beauty *see* BEAUTY FOR SALE (1933).

Beauty and Misery of Human Life, The *see* IHMISELON IHANUUS JA KURJUUS (1988).

BEAUTY AND THE BAD MAN 1925 d: William Worthington. USA., *Cornflower Cassie's Concert*, Peter B. Kyne, 1924, Short Story

BEAUTY AND THE BARGE 1914 d: Harold Shaw. UKN., *Beauty and the Barge*, W. W. Jacobs, Louis N. Parker, London 1904, Play

BEAUTY AND THE BARGE 1937 d: Henry Edwards. UKN., *Beauty and the Barge*, W. W. Jacobs, Louis N. Parker, London 1904, Play

Beauty and the Beast *see* LA BELLE ET LA BETE (1945).

Beauty and the Beast *see* LA BEAUTE DU DIABLE (1950).

Beauty and the Beast *see* PANNA A NETVOR (1978).

BEAUTY AND THE BEAST 1987 d: Eugene Marner. USA/ISR., *Beauty and the Beast*, Madame de Villeneuve, Story

BEAUTY AND THE BOSS 1932 d: Roy Del Ruth. USA., *A Templom Egere*, Ladislaus Fodor, Budapest 1927, Play

Beauty and the Bullfighter *see* SANG ET LUMIERE (1954).

Beauty and the Devil *see* LA BEAUTE DU DIABLE (1950).

Beauty and the Dragon, The *see* BIJO TO KAIRYU (1955).

BEAUTY FOR SALE 1933 d: Richard Boleslawski. USA., *Beauty*, Faith Baldwin, New York 1933, Novel

Beauty from Nivernaise, The *see* LA BELLE NIVERNAISE (1923).

BEAUTY IN CHAINS 1918 d: Elsie Jane Wilson. USA., *Dona Perfecta*, Benito Perez Galdos, Madrid 1876, Novel

BEAUTY MARKET, THE 1920 d: Colin Campbell. USA., *The Bleeders*, Margery Land May, 1919, Short Story

Beauty of Volendam, The *see* MOOI JUULTJE VAN VOLDENDAM (1924).

Beauty Parlor *see* BEAUTY FOR SALE (1933).

BEAUTY SHOP, THE 1922 d: Eddie Dillon. USA., *The Beauty Shop*, Channing Pollock, Rennold Wolf, New York 1914, Play

Beauty's Daughter *see* NAVY WIFE (1935).

Beauty's Sorrows, The *see* BIJIN AISHU (1931).

BEAUTY'S WORTH 1922 d: Robert G. VignolA. USA., *Beauty's Worth*, Sophie Kerr, 1920, Short Story

BEAUX DIMANCHES, LES 1974 d: Richard Martin. CND., *Les Beaux Dimanches*, Marcel Dube, Play

Beaux Jours d'Aranjuez, Les *see* ADIEU LES BEAUX JOURS (1933).

Beaver Coat, The *see* DER BIBERPELZ (1928).

Beaver Coat, The *see* DER BIBERPELZ (1937).

BEBE 1913 d: Georges MoncA. FRN., *Bebe*, Maurice Hennequin, Najac, Play

Bebel, Advertising Girl *see* GAROTA PROPAGANDA BEBEL (1968).

BEBEL, GAROTA PROPAGANDA 1968 d: Maurice CapovillA. BRZ., *Bebel Que a Cidade Comeu*, Ignacio de Loyola Brandao, 1960, Novel

Bebel, Propaganda Girl *see* GAROTA PROPAGANDA BEBEL (1968).

Bebert and the Train *see* BEBERT ET L'OMNIBUS (1963).

BEBERT ET L'OMNIBUS 1963 d: Yves Robert. FRN., *Bebert Et l'Omnibus*, Francois Boyer, Novel

Bebo's Girl *see* LA RAGAZZA DI BUBE (1963).

Because *see* THE LAUNDRY GIRL (1919).

Because of a Man *see* FOUR DAUGHTERS (1938).

BECAUSE THEY'RE YOUNG 1960 d: Paul Wendkos. USA., *Harrison High*, John Farris, Novel

Because You are Poor, You Die Sooner *see* MUSST DU FRUHER STERBEN WEIL DU ARM BIST (1956).

BECKET 1923 d: George Ridgwell. UKN., *Becket*, Alfred Tennyson, London 1893, Play

BECKET 1964 d: Peter Glenville. UKN., *Becket Ou l'Honneur de Dieu*, Jean Anouilh, 1959, Play

BECKONING ROADS 1920 d: Howard Hickman. USA., *The Call of Life*, Jeanne Judson, New York 1919, Novel

BECKY SHARP 1935 d: Rouben Mamoulian. USA., *Vanity Fair*, William Makepeace Thackeray, London 1848, Novel

Becoming Middle-Class *see* DO PANSKEHO STAVU (1925).

BED AND BREAKFAST 1930 d: Walter Forde. UKN., *Bed and Breakfast*, Frederick Witney, Play

Bed of Roses *see* NA RUZICH USTLANO (1934).

BED SITTING ROOM, THE 1969 d: Richard Lester. UKN., *The Bed Sitting Room*, John Antrobus, Spike Milligan, 1963, Play

Bed, The *see* LE LIT (1982).

BEDARA KANNAPPA 1954 d: H. L. N. SimhA. IND., *Bedara Kannappa*, G. V. Iyer, Play

BEDAZZLED 1967 d: Stanley Donen. UKN., *Faust*, Johann Wolfgang von Goethe, 1808-32, Play

BEDDEGAMA 1980 d: Lester James Peries. SLN., *The Village in the Jungle*, Leonard Woolf, 1913, Novel

BEDELIA 1946 d: Lance Comfort. UKN., *Bedelia*, Vera Caspary, Novel

BEDFORD INCIDENT, THE 1965 d: James B. Harris. UKN/USA., *The Bedford Incident*, Mark Rascovich, New York 1963, Novel

BEDKNOBS AND BROOMSTICKS 1971 d: Robert Stevenson. USA., *Bonfires and Broomsticks*, Mary Norton, Short Story, *The Magic Bed-Knob*, Mary Norton, Short Story

Bed-Rock *see* UNDER PRESSURE (1935).

Bedroom & Courtroom *see* SAENGGWABU WIJARYO CHYEONGGUSOSONG (1998).

Bedroom Vendetta *see* LA JUMENT VERTE (1959).

BEDROOM WINDOW, THE 1987 d: Curtis Hanson. USA., *The Witnesses*, Anne Holden, Novel

BEDTIME STORY 1938 d: Donovan Pedelty. UKN., *Bedtime Story*, Walter Ellis, London 1937, Play

BEDTIME STORY, A 1933 d: Norman Taurog. USA., *Bellamy the Magnificent*, Roy Horniman, London 1904, Novel

Bee Called Maja, A *see* DIE BIENE MAJA (1977).

Bee in the Rain, A *see* UMA ABELHA NA CHUVA (1971).

Bee Millenium, The *see* TISICROCNA VCELA (1983).

BELLA ADDORMENTATA, LA 1942 d: Luigi Chiarini. ITL., *La Bella Addormentata*, Pier Maria Rosso, Play

BELLA ANTONIA PRIMA MONICA E POI DIMONIA 1972 d: Mariano Laurenti. ITL., *Ragionamenti Amorosi*, Pietro L'Aretino, Story

Bella Di Giorno see BELLE DE JOUR (1967).

BELLA DONNA 1915 d: Edwin S. Porter, Hugh Ford. USA., *Bella Donna*, Robert Hichens, London 1909, Novel

BELLA DONNA 1923 d: George Fitzmaurice. USA., *Bella Donna*, Robert Hichens, London 1909, Novel

BELLA DONNA 1934 d: Robert Milton. UKN., *Bella Donna*, Robert Hichens, London 1909, Novel

Bella Donna see TEMPTATION (1946).

BELLA LOLA, LA 1962 d: Alfonso Balcazar. SPN/ITL/FRN., *La Dame aux Camelias*, Alexandre Dumas (fils), Paris 1848, Novel

BELLA MAFIA - PARTS I & II 1997 d: David Greene. USA., *Bella Mafia*, Lynda la Plante, Novel

BELLA MUGNAIA, LA 1955 d: Mario Camerini. ITL., *El Sombrero de Tres Picos*, Pedro Antonio de Alarcon, 1874, Short Story

Belladonna see KANASHIMI NO BELLADONNA (1973).

BELLAMY TRIAL, THE 1928 d: Monta Bell. USA., *The Bellamy Trial*, Frances Noyes Hart, New York 1927, Novel

BELL'ANTONIO, IL 1960 d: Mauro Bolognini. ITL/FRN., *Il Bell'Antonio*, Vitaliano Brancati, 1949, Novel

BELLE AVENTURE, LA 1932 d: Roger Le Bon, Reinhold Schunzel. FRN., *La Belle Aventure*, Gaston Arman de Caillavet, Robert de Flers, Paris 1914, Play

BELLE AVENTURE, LA 1942 d: Marc Allegret. FRN., *La Belle Aventure*, Gaston Arman de Caillavet, Robert de Flers, Paris 1914, Play

Belle Bordelaise, La see L' INTRIGANTE (1939).

BELLE DE JOUR 1967 d: Luis Bunuel. FRN/ITL., *Belle de Jour*, Joseph Kessel, 1928, Novel

BELLE DE MONTPARNASSE, LA 1937 d: Maurice Cammage. FRN., *Le Paradis*, Paul Bilhaud, Maurice Hennequin, Play

BELLE DE NUIT 1933 d: Louis Valray. FRN., *Belle de Nuit*, Pierre Wolff, Play

Belle de Volendam, La see MOOI JUULTJE VAN VOLDENDAM (1924).

BELLE ET LA BETE, LA 1945 d: Rene Clement, Jean Cocteau. FRN., *La Belle Et la Bete*, Marie Leprince de Beaumont, 1785-89, Short Story

Belle Et l'Empereur, La see DIE SCHONE LUGNERIN (1959).

BELLE FILLE COMME MOI, UNE 1972 d: Francois Truffaut. FRN., Henry Farrell, Novel

Belle from Andalusia, The see LA LOZANA ANDALUZA (1976).

BELLE GARCE, UNE 1930 d: Marco de Gastyne. FRN., *Une Belle Garce*, Charles-Henry Hirsch, Novel

BELLE IMAGE, LA 1950 d: Claude Heymann. FRN., *La Belle Image*, Marcel Ayme, 1941, Novel

Belle Lola, La see LA BELLA LOLA (1962).

BELLE MADAME HEBERT, LA 1921 d: Baldassarre Negroni. ITL., *La Belle Madame Hebert*, Abel Hermant, 1905, Play

BELLE MARINIERE, LA 1932 d: Harry Lachman. FRN., *La Belle Mariniere*, Marcel Achard, 1930, Play

BELLE NIVERNAISE, LA 1923 d: Jean Epstein. FRN., *La Belle Nivernaise*, Alphonse Daudet, Short Story

BELLE NOISEUSE -DIVERTIMENTO 1991 d: Jacques Rivette. FRN., *Le Chef d'Oeuvre Inconnu*, Honore de Balzac, 1831, Short Story

BELLE NOISEUSE, LA 1991 d: Jacques Rivette. FRN., *Le Chef d'Oeuvre Inconnu*, Honore de Balzac, 1831, Short Story

Belle Noiseuse, La see BELLE NOISEUSE -DIVERTIMENTO (1991).

Belle of Atlanta see WHO KILLED AUNT MAGGIE? (1940).

BELLE OF NEW YORK, THE 1919 d: Julius Steger. USA., *The Belle of New York*, Gustav Kerker, Hugh Morton, New York 1897, Musical Play

BELLE OF NEW YORK, THE 1951 d: Charles Walters. USA., *The Belle of New York*, Gustav Kerker, Hugh Morton, New York 1897, Musical Play

BELLE OF THE SEASON, THE 1919 d: S. Rankin Drew. USA., Ella Wheeler Wilcox, Poem

BELLE QUE VOILA, LA 1949 d: Jean-Paul Le Chanois. FRN., *La Belle Que Voila*, Vicki Baum, Novel

BELLE REVANCHE, LA 1938 d: Paul Mesnier. FRN., *Edouard*, Jacques Carton, Novel

Belle Romaine, La see LA ROMANA (1954).

BELLE RUSSE, LA 1914 d: William J. Hanley. USA., *La Belle Russe*, David Belasco, New York 1882, Play

BELLE RUSSE, LA 1919 d: Charles J. Brabin. USA., *La Belle Russe*, David Belasco, New York 1882, Play

BELLES ON THEIR TOES 1952 d: Henry Levin. USA., *Belles on Their Toes*, Ernestine G. Carey, Frank Gilbreth Jr., Book

Belleza Negra see BLACK BEAUTY (1971).

Bellezza Del Diavolo, La see LA BEAUTE DU DIABLE (1950).

BELLEZZA D'IPPOLITA, LA 1962 d: Giancarlo Zagni. ITL/FRN., *La Bellezza d'Ippolita*, Elio Bartolini, Novel

BELLISSIMO NOVEMBRE, UN 1968 d: Mauro Bolognini. ITL/FRN., *Un Bellissimo Novembre*, Ercole Patti, Novel

BELLMAN AND TRUE 1988 d: Richard Loncraine. UKN., *Bellman and True*, Dennis Lowder, Novel

Bellman, The see SORTILEGES (1944).

BELLS ARE RINGING, THE 1960 d: Vincente Minnelli. USA., *The Bells are Ringing*, Betty Comden, Adolph Green, Musical Play

BELLS OF SAN JUAN 1922 d: Scott R. Dunlap. USA., *Bells of San Juan*, Jackson Gregory, New York 1919, Novel

Bells of the Loretto Church, The see LORETANSKE ZVONKY (1929).

BELLS, THE 1913 d: Oscar Apfel. USA., *The Bells*, Erkman Chatrian, Novel

BELLS, THE 1913 d: George A. Lessey. USA., *The Bells*, Edgar Allan Poe, Poem

BELLS, THE 1918 d: Ernest C. Warde. USA., *Le Juif Polonais*, Alexandre Chatrian, Emile Erckmann, Paris 1869, Play

BELLS, THE 1923 d: Edwin Greenwood. UKN., *The Bells*, Leopold Lewis, London 1871, Play

BELLS, THE 1926 d: James Young. USA., *Le Juif Polonais*, Alexandre Chatrian, Emile Erckmann, Paris 1869, Play

BELLS, THE 1931 d: Harcourt Templeman, O. M. Werndorff. UKN/GRM., *Le Juif Polonais*, Alexandre Chatrian, Emile Erckmann, Paris 1869, Play

Belly Up see OS MATADORES (1997).

BELONGING 1922 d: F. Martin Thornton. UKN., *Belonging*, Olive Wadsley, New York 1920, Novel

BELOVED 1998 d: Jonathan Demme. USA., *Beloved*, Toni Morrison, 1987, Novel

BELOVED BACHELOR, THE 1931 d: Lloyd Corrigan. USA., *The Prince Chap*, Edward Peple, New York 1905, Play

BELOVED BRUTE, THE 1924 d: J. Stuart Blackton. USA., *The Beloved Brute*, Kenneth Perkins, New York 1923, Novel

Beloved Corinna see GELIEBTE CORINNA (1956).

Beloved Enemy see GELIEBTE FEINDIN (1955).

Beloved Good-for-Nothing see JOHNNY BANCO (1967).

BELOVED IMPOSTER 1936 d: Victor Hanbury. UKN., *Dancing Boy*, Ethel Mannin, Novel

Beloved Impostor see BELOVED IMPOSTER (1936).

BELOVED INFIDEL 1959 d: Henry King. USA., *Beloved Infidel*, Gerold Frank, Sheilah Graham, Book

BELOVED ROGUE, THE 1927 d: Alan Crosland. USA., *If I Were King*, Justin Huntly McCarthy, London 1901, Novel

Beloved, The see DIE GELIEBTE (1927).

BELOVED TRAITOR, THE 1918 d: William Worthington. USA., *The Beloved Traitor*, Frank L. Packard, New York 1915, Novel

BELOVED VAGABOND, THE 1915 d: Edward Jose. USA., *The Beloved Vagabond*, William J. Locke, London 1906, Novel

BELOVED VAGABOND, THE 1923 d: Fred Leroy Granville. UKN., *The Beloved Vagabond*, William J. Locke, London 1906, Novel

BELOVED VAGABOND, THE 1936 d: Curtis Bernhardt. UKN., *The Beloved Vagabond*, William J. Locke, London 1906, Novel

Beloved/Friend see AMIC/AMAT (1999).

BELOW THE RIO GRANDE 1923 d: Neal Hart. USA., *The Fighting Pedagogue*, H. A. Halbert Jr., Story

BELPHEGOR THE MOUNTEBANK 1921 d: Bert Wynne. UKN., *Belphegor the Mountebank*, Charles Webb, Novel

BELSTONE FOX, THE 1973 d: James Hill. UKN., *The Ballad of the Belstone Fox*, David Rook, Novel

BELTENEBROS 1991 d: Pilar Miro. SPN., *Beltenebros*, Antonio Munoz Molina, Novel

Belyi Klyk see BELISCH KLYK (1946).

Belyi Parokhod see BYELI PAROKHOD (1976).

Belyj Parohod see BYELI PAROKHOD (1976).

BEN BLAIR 1916 d: William D. Taylor. USA., *Ben Blair: the Story of a Plainsman*, William Otis Lillibridge, Chicago 1905, Novel

Ben Warman see DANGEROUS LOVE (1920).

Bench of Desolation, The see DE GRAY -LE BANC DE DESOLATION (1973).

BEND OF THE RIVER 1952 d: Anthony Mann. USA., *Bend of the Snake*, Bill Gulick, 1950, Novel

Beneath the Glacier see KRISTNIHALD UNDIR JOKLI (1989).

Beneath the Thousand Lanterns see UNTER DEN TAUSAND LATERNEN (1952).

BENEFICIARY, THE 1979 d: Carlo Gebler. UKN., *V Ovrage*, Anton Chekhov, 1900, Short Story

BENEFIT OF THE DOUBT 1967 d: Peter Whitehead. UKN., *Us*, Denis Cannan, Play

Benefits Forgot see OF HUMAN HEARTS (1938).

BENGAL BRIGADE 1954 d: Laslo Benedek. USA., *Bengal Tiger*, Hall Hunter, 1952, Novel

Bengal Rifles see BENGAL BRIGADE (1954).

BEN-HUR 1925 d: Fred Niblo. USA., *Ben Hur*, Lew Wallace, 1880, Novel

BEN-HUR 1959 d: William Wyler. USA., *Ben Hur*, Lew Wallace, 1880, Novel

Benilde Or the Virgin Mother see BENILDE OU A VIRGEM MAE (1975).

BENILDE OU A VIRGEM MAE 1975 d: Manoel de OliveirA. PRT., *Benilde Ou a Virgem-Mae*, Jose Regio, 1947, Play

Benilde: Virgin and Mother see BENILDE OU A VIRGEM MAE (1975).

BENITO CERENO 1968 d: Serge Roullet. FRN/ITL/BRZ., *Benito Cereno*, Herman Melville, 1855, Short Story

BENSON MURDER CASE, THE 1930 d: Frank Tuttle. USA., *The Benson Murder Case*, S. S. Van Dine, New York 1926, Novel

BENT 1997 d: Sean Mathias. UKN/USA/JPN., *Bent*, Martin Sherman, Play

BENTLEY'S CONSCIENCE 1922 d: Denison Clift. UKN., *Bentley's Conscience*, Paul Trent, Novel

BENVENUTA 1983 d: Andre Delvaux. BLG/FRN/ITL., *La Confession Anonyme*, Suzanne Lilar, Novel

BEOWULF 1976 d: Don Fairservice. UKN., *Beowulf*, Anon, c750, Verse

BEQUEST TO THE NATION, A 1973 d: James Cellan Jones. UKN., *A Bequest to the Nation*, Terence Rattigan, 1970, Play

BEREKETLI TOPRAKLAR UZERINDE 1980 d: Erden Kiral. TRK., *Bereketli Topraklar Uzerinde*, Orhan Kemal, Novel

BERENICE 1967 d: Pierre-Alain Jolivet. FRN., *Berenice*, Jean Racine, 1671, Play

BERG RUFT, DER 1937 d: Luis Trenker. GRM., *Der Kampf Ums Matterhorn*, Carl Haensel, Novel

Bergfeuer Lodern see WILHELM TELL - BERGEN IN FLAMMEN (1960).

BERGKRISTALL 1949 d: Harald Reinl. GRM/AUS., *Bergkristall*, Adalbert Stifter, 1853, Short Story

BERGWIND 1963 d: Eduard von Borsody. AUS., *Bergwind*, Heinrich Klier, Novel

BERKELEY SQUARE 1933 d: Frank Lloyd. USA., *Berkeley Square*, John L. Balderston, London 1926, Play

BERKELEY SQUARE 1949 d: Paul Nickell. USA., *Berkeley Square*, John L. Balderston, London 1926, Play

BERKELEY SQUARE 1951 d: Donald Davis. USA., *Berkeley Square*, John L. Balderston, London 1926, Play

BERKELEY SQUARE 1959 d: George Schaefer. USA., *Berkeley Square*, John L. Balderston, London 1926, Play

Berlin Affair see INTERNO BERLINESE (1985).

BERLIN EXPRESS 1948 d: Jacques Tourneur. USA., Curt Siodmak, Story

Berlin Interior see INTERNO BERLINESE (1985).

BERLIN TUNNEL 21 1981 d: Richard Michaels. USA., *Berlin Tunnel 21*, Donald Linquist, Novel

BERLIN-ALEXANDERPLATZ 1931 d: Phil Jutzi. GRM., *Berlin-Alexanderplatz*, Alfred Doblin, 1929, Novel

BERNARDINE 1957 d: Henry Levin. USA., *Bernardine*, Mary Coyle Chase, 1953, Play

BERNICE BOBS HER HAIR 1976 d: Joan Micklin Silver. USA., *Bernice Bobs Her Hair*, F. Scott Fitzgerald, 1920, Short Story

Bersagliere's Girl, The *see* LA RAGAZZA DEL BERSAGLIERE (1967).

BERTHA, THE SEWING MACHINE GIRL 1926 d: Irving Cummings. USA., *Bertha the Sewing machine Girl*, Theodore Kremer, Play

BERTOLDO, BERTOLDINO E CACASENNO 1936 d: Giorgio C. Simonelli. ITL., *Bertoldo Bertoldino E Cacasenno*, Giulio Cesare Croce, Poem

BERTOLDO, BERTOLDINO E CACASENNO 1954 d: Mario Amendola, Ruggero MacCari. ITL., *Bertoldo Bertoldino E Cacasenno*, Giulio Cesare Croce, Poem

BERTOLDO, BERTOLDINO E CACASENNO 1984 d: Mario Monicelli, Maurizio Nichetti. ITL., *Bertoldo Bertoldino E Cacasenno*, Giulio Cesare Croce, Poem

BERU ET CES DAMES 1968 d: Guy Lefranc. FRN., *Beru Et Ces Dames*, Frederic Dard, Novel

BERUHMTE FRAU, DIE 1927 d: Robert Wiene. GRM., *Die Tanzerin*, Melchior Lengyel, Novel

BERUSAIYU NO BARA 1978 d: Jacques Demy. JPN/FRN., *Berusaiyu No Bara*, Riyoko Ikeda, Novel

BERYL CORONET, THE 1912 d: Georges Treville. UKN., *The Beryl Coronet*, Arthur Conan Doyle, Short Story

BERYL CORONET, THE 1921 d: Maurice Elvey. UKN., *The Beryl Coronet*, Arthur Conan Doyle, Short Story

Bes Svideteley *see* BEZ SVIDETELEI (1983).

BESEIGED 1998 d: Bernardo Bertolucci. ITL., James Lasdun, Story

BESENYE DENGI 1981 d: Yevgeni Matveyev. USS., *Beshennye Dengi*, Alexander Ostrovsky, 1870, Play

Beshenye Dengi *see* BESENYE DENGI (1981).

BESIDE THE BONNIE BRIER BUSH 1921 d: Donald Crisp. UKN/USA., *Beside the Bonnie Brier Bush*, James MacArthur, Augustus Thorne, London 1895, Play

Besieged *see* IL TAMBURINO SARDO (1911).

Beso de la Mujer Arana, El *see* KISS OF THE SPIDER WOMAN (1984).

Besondere, Der *see* DIE ALM AN DER GRENZE (1951).

BESPOKE OVERCOAT, THE 1955 d: Jack Clayton. UKN., *Shinel*, Nikolay Gogol, 1842, Short Story

BESPRIDANNITSA 1936 d: Yakov Protazanov. USS., *Bespridannitsa*, Alexander Ostrovsky, 1878, Play

BESSERER HERR, EIN 1928 d: Gustav Ucicky. GRM., *Ein Besserer Herr*, Walter Hasenclever, Play

BEST BAD MAN, THE 1925 d: John G. Blystone. USA., *Senor Jingle Bells*, Max Brand, 1925, Short Story

BEST CHRISTMAS PAGEANT EVER, THE 1984 d: George Schaefer. USA., *The Best Christmas Pageant Ever*, Barbara Robinson, Book

Best Defence *see* BEST DEFENSE (1984).

BEST DEFENSE 1984 d: Willard Huyck. USA., *Easy and Hard Ways Out*, Robert Grossbach, Novel

BEST FOOT FORWARD 1943 d: Edward Buzzell. USA., *Best Foot Forward*, John Cecil Holmes, Play

BEST LITTLE GIRL IN THE WORLD, THE 1981 d: Sam O'Steen. USA., *The Best Little Girl in the World*, Stephen Levenkron, Novel

BEST LITTLE WHOREHOUSE IN TEXAS, THE 1982 d: Colin Higgins. USA., *The Best Little Whorehouse in Texas*, Larry L. King, Peter Masterson, Play

BEST MAN, THE 1914 d: Charles J. Brabin. USA., *The Best Man*, Grace Livingston Hill Lutz, 1913, Novel

BEST MAN, THE 1919 d: Thomas N. Heffron. USA., *The Best Man*, Grace Livingston Hill Lutz, 1913, Novel

BEST MAN, THE 1964 d: Franklin J. Schaffner. USA., *The Best Man; a Play About Politics*, Gore Vidal, 1960, Play

Best Man to Die, The *see* INSPECTOR WEXFORD: THE BEST MAN TO DIE (1990).

BEST MAN WINS 1948 d: John Sturges. USA., *The Celebrated Jumping Frog of Calaveras County*, Mark Twain, 1867, Short Story

Best Mayor Is the King, The *see* EL REY, EL MEJOR ALCALDE (1973).

Best Mayor, the King, The *see* EL REY, EL MEJOR ALCALDE (1973).

BEST OF EVERYTHING, THE 1959 d: Jean Negulesco. USA., *The Best of Everything*, Rona Jaffe, Novel

BEST OF FRIENDS, THE 1991 d: Alvin Rakoff. UKN., *The Best of Friends*, Hugh Whitemore, Play

BEST OF LUCK, THE 1920 d: Ray C. Smallwood. USA., *The Best of Luck*, Henry Hamilton, Cecil Raleigh, London 1916, Play

BEST PEOPLE, THE 1925 d: Sidney Olcott. USA., *The Best People*, David Gray, Avery Hopwood, New York 1924, Play

Best People, The *see* FAST AND LOOSE (1930).

BEST PLACE TO BE, THE 1979 d: David Miller. USA., *The Best Place to Be*, Helen Van Slyke, Novel

BEST YEARS OF OUR LIVES, THE 1946 d: William Wyler. USA., *Glory for Me*, MacKinlay Kantor, 1945, Novel

Bestia de la Montana, La *see* THE BEAST OF HOLLOW MOUNTAIN (1956).

BESTIA UMANA, LA 1916 d: Leopoldo Carlucci. ITL., *The Jungle Book*, Rudyard Kipling

BESUCH, DER 1964 d: Bernhard Wicki. GRM/ITL/FRN., *Der Besuch Der Alten Dame*, Friedrich Durrenmatt, Zurich 1956, Play

BESZELO KONTOS, A 1969 d: Tamas Fejer. HNG., *A Beszelo Kontos*, Kalman Mikszath, 1889, Novel

BESZTERCE OSTROMA 1948 d: Marton Keleti. HNG., *Beszterce Ostroma*, Kalman Mikszath, 1896, Novel

BET, THE 1969 d: Ron Waller. USA., *Pari*, Anton Chekhov, 1888, Short Story

Bet, The *see* RAMASAGUL (1985).

Beta Som *see* FINCHE DURA LA TEMPESTA (1962).

BETE A L'AFFUT, LA 1959 d: Pierre Chenal. FRN/ITL., *La Bete a l'Affut*, Day Keane, Novel

BETE AUX SEPT MANTEAUX, LA 1936 d: Jean de Limur. FRN., *La Bete aux Sept Manteaux*, P. A. Fernic, Novel

BETE ERRANTE, LA 1931 d: Marco de Gastyne. FRN., *La Bete Errante*, Louis Frederic Rouquette, Novel

BETE HUMAINE, LA 1938 d: Jean Renoir. FRN., *La Bete Humaine*, Emile Zola, 1890, Novel

BETE TRAQUEE, LA 1922 d: Rene Le Somptier, Michel Carre. FRN., *Marielle Thibaut*, Adrien Chabot

BETHSABEE 1947 d: Leonide Moguy. FRN., *Bethsabee*, Pierre Benoit, Novel

Betragen Ungenugend *see* KANTOR IDEAL (1932).

Betrayal *see* DER KATZENSTEG (1927).

BETRAYAL 1932 d: Reginald Fogwell. UKN., *No Crime of Passion*, Hubert Griffith, Play

Betrayal *see* MANHANDLED (1949).

Betrayal *see* UPTIGHT (1968).

BETRAYAL 1974 d: Gordon Hessler. USA., *Only Couples Need Apply*, Doris Miles Disney, Novel

BETRAYAL 1978 d: Paul Wendkos. USA., *Betrayal*, Lucy Freeman, Julie Roy, Book

BETRAYAL 1983 d: David Jones. UKN., *Betrayal*, Harold Pinter, 1978, Play

BETRAYAL FROM THE EAST 1945 d: William Berke. USA., *Betrayal from the East*, Alan Hynd, Novel

Betrayal, The *see* BOLIBAR (1928).

Betrayed, The *see* OP AFBETALING (1991).

Betrayer, The *see* VANINA VANINI (1961).

Betrothal, The *see* KIHLAUS (1922).

Betrothal, The *see* KIHLAUS (1955).

Betrothed, The *see* I PROMESSI SPOSI (1913).

BETSY, THE 1978 d: Daniel Petrie. USA., *The Betsy*, Harold Robbins, Novel

BETTA THE GYPSY 1918 d: Charles Raymond. UKN., *Betta the Gypsy*, Edward Waltyre, Opera

BETTELSTUDENT, DER 1927 d: Jacob Fleck, Luise Fleck. GRM., *Fernande*, Victorien Sardou, 1870, Play

BETTELSTUDENT, DER 1931 d: Victor Janson. GRM., *Fernande*, Victorien Sardou, 1870, Play

BETTELSTUDENT, DER 1936 d: Georg Jacoby. GRM., *Fernande*, Victorien Sardou, 1870, Play

BETTELSTUDENT, DER 1956 d: Werner Jacobs. GRM., *Fernande*, Victorien Sardou, 1870, Play

Bettelstudent, Der *see* MAZURKA DER LIEBE (1957).

Bettelstudent, Der *see* DER BETTELSTUDENT ODER: WAS MACH' ICH MIT DEN MADCHEN (1969).

BETTELSTUDENT ODER: WAS MACH' ICH MIT DEN MADCHEN, DER 1969 d: Michael Verhoeven. GRM., *Der Bettelstudent*, Finn Soeberg, Novel

BETTER DAYS 1927 d: Frank S. Mattison. USA., Willis P. Ellery, Story

Better Go Home *see* BURU GUI (1926).

BETTER HALF, THE 1918 d: John S. Robertson. USA., *Michael Thwaite's Wife*, Miriam Michelson, New York 1909, Novel

Better Half, The *see* ARDHANGI (1955).

BETTER LIVING 1998 d: Max Mayer. USA., *Better Living*, George F. Walker, Play

BETTER MAN, THE 1914 d: Mr. Powers. USA., *The Better Man*, Cyrus Townsend Brady, New York 1910, Novel

BETTER MAN, THE 1915. USA., *The Better Man*, George Patullo, Story

Better Man, The *see* THE BIGGER MAN (1915).

BETTER 'OLE; OR, THE ROMANCE OF OLD BILL, THE 1918 d: George Pearson. UKN., *The Better 'Ole; Or the Romance of Old Bill*, Bruce Bairnsfather, Arthur Eliot, Oxford 1917, Play

BETTER 'OLE, THE 1926 d: Charles F. Reisner. USA., *The Better 'Ole or The Romance of Old Bill*, Bruce Bairnsfather, Arthur Eliot, Oxford 1917, Play

BETTINA LOVED A SOLDIER 1916 d: Rupert Julian. USA., *L' Abbe Constantin*, Ludovic Halevy, France 1882, Novel

BETTY 1992 d: Claude Chabrol. FRN., *Betty*, Georges Simenon, 1961, Novel

Betty Blue *see* 37°2 LE MATIN (1985).

Betty's a Lady *see* THE COUNT OF TEN (1928).

BETTY'S DREAM HERO 1915 d: Robert Z. Leonard. USA., *Betty's Dream Hero*, George Ade, Story

BETWEEN DANGERS 1927 d: Richard Thorpe. USA., *Ride 'Im Cowboy*, Walter J. Coburn, Short Story

Between Eleven and Midnight *see* ENTRE ONZE HEURES ET MINUIT (1948).

Between Facing Mirrors *see* INTRE OGLINZI PARALELE (1978).

BETWEEN FRIENDS 1924 d: J. Stuart Blackton. USA., *Between Friends*, Robert W. Chambers, New York 1914, Novel

BETWEEN FRIENDS 1983 d: Lou Antonio. USA/CND., *Nobody Makes Me Cry*, Shelley List, Novel

Between God, the Devil and a Winchester *see* C'ERA UNA VOLTA DIO ANCHE NEL WEST (1968).

BETWEEN HEAVEN AND HELL 1956 d: Richard Fleischer. USA., *The Day the Century Ended*, Francis Gwaltney, Novel

Between Life and Death *see* YINYANG JIE (1988).

Between Love and Desire *see* LE BOIS DES AMANTS (1960).

Between Love and Duty *see* TUSSCHEN LIEFDE EN PLICHT (1912).

Between Love and Duty *see* LE BOIS DES AMANTS (1960).

Between Opposite Mirrors *see* INTRE OGLINZI PARALELE (1978).

Between Parallel Mirrors *see* INTRE OGLINZI PARALELE (1978).

Between the Nets *see* MORESQUE OBIETTIVO ALLUCINANTE (1967).

Between Two Hearts *see* ZWISCHEN ZWEI HERZEN (1934).

BETWEEN TWO WOMEN 1986 d: Jon Avnet. USA., *Between Two Women*, Gillian Martin, Novel

Between Two Worlds *see* DIE LIEBE DES MAHARADSCHA (1936).

BETWEEN TWO WORLDS 1944 d: Edward A. Blatt. USA., *Outward Bound*, Sutton Vane, New York 1924, Play

Between Two Worlds *see* HADYBBUK (1968).

Between Us *see* COUP DE FOUDRE (1983).

BETWEEN US GIRLS 1942 d: Henry Koster. USA., *Le Fruit Vert*, Regis Gignoux, Jacques Thery, Play

Between Wife and Lady *see* TSUMA TO ONNA NO AIDA (1976).

Between Women and Wives *see* TSUMA TO ONNA NO AIDA (1976).

BEULAH 1915 d: Bertram Bracken. USA., *Beulah*, Augusta Jane Evans Wilson, New York 1860, Novel

BEULAH LAND 1980 d: Virgil W. Vogel, Harry Falk. USA., Lonnie Coleman, Novel

BEVERLY OF GRAUSTARK 1914. USA., *Beverly of Graustark*, George Barr McCutcheon, New York 1904, Novel

BEVERLY OF GRAUSTARK 1926 d: Sidney A. Franklin. USA., *Beverly of Graustark*, George Barr McCutcheon, New York 1904, Novel

BEWARE MY LOVELY 1952 d: Harry Horner. USA., *The Man*, Mel Dinelli, Play

BEWARE OF BACHELORS 1928 d: Roy Del Ruth. USA., *Beware of Bachelors*, Mark Canfield, Short Story

Beware of Children see NO KIDDING (1960).

BEWARE OF PITY 1946 d: Maurice Elvey. UKN., *Ungeduld Des Herzens*, Stefan Zweig, 1938, Novel

BEWARE OF THE BRIDE 1920 d: Howard M. Mitchell. USA., *Beware of the Bride*, Edgar Franklin, 1920, Short Story

BEWARE OF WIDOWS 1927 d: Wesley Ruggles. USA., *Beware of Widows*, Owen Moore, Play

BEWARE, SPOOKS! 1939 d: Edward Sedgwick. USA., *Spook House*, Richard F. Flournoy, Story

Beware the Woman see UNTAMED YOUTH (1924).

BEWITCHED 1945 d: Arch Oboler. USA., *Alter Ego*, Arch Oboler, Radio Play

Bewitched Love see EL AMOR BRUJO (1967).

Bewitching Eyes see CAROVNE OCI (1923).

BEYOND 1921 d: William D. Taylor. USA., *The Lifted Veil*, Henry Arthur Jones, Play

Beyond All Limits see FLOR DE MAYO (1957).

BEYOND BEDLAM 1993 d: Vadim Jean. UKN., *Beyond Bedlam*, Harry Adam Knight, Novel

Beyond Death see MAS ALLA DE LA MUERTE (1924).

Beyond Innocence see DEVIL IN THE FLESH (1986).

BEYOND LONDON LIGHTS 1928 d: Tom Terriss. USA., *Kitty Carstairs*, J. J. Bell, London 1917, Novel

BEYOND MOMBASA 1956 d: George Marshall. UKN/USA., *Mark of the Leopard*, James Eastwood, Short Story

Beyond Prison Gates see THE OUTER GATE (1937).

BEYOND REASONABLE DOUBT 1980 d: John Laing. NZL., *Beyond Reasonable Doubt*, David Yallop, Book

Beyond Sing the Woods see UND EWIG SINGEN DIE WALDER (1959).

BEYOND THE BLUE HORIZON 1942 d: Alfred Santell. USA., Jack de Witt, E. Lloyd Sheldon, Story

BEYOND THE BORDER 1925 d: Scott R. Dunlap. USA., *When Smith Meets Smith*, Meredith Davis, Story

Beyond the Bridge see DINCOLO DE POD (1975).

BEYOND THE CURTAIN 1960 d: Compton Bennett. UKN., *Thunder Above*, Charles Blair, A. J. Wallis, Novel

BEYOND THE DREAMS OF AVARICE 1920 d: Thomas Bentley. UKN., *Beyond the Dreams of Avarice*, Sir Walter Besant, Novel

BEYOND THE FOREST 1949 d: King Vidor. USA., *Beyond the Forest*, Stuart Engstrand, Novel

Beyond the Garden see MAS ALLA DEL JARDIN (1996).

BEYOND THE LAW 1918 d: Theodore Marston. USA., *Beyond the Limit*, Emmett Dalton, New York 1916, Novel

Beyond the Law see THE LAW RUSTLERS (1923).

BEYOND THE LIMIT 1983 d: John MacKenzie. UKN., *The Honorary Consul*, Graham Greene, 1973, Novel

Beyond the Mountains see MAS ALLA DE LAS MONTANAS (1967).

BEYOND THE RAINBOW 1922 d: W. Christy Cabanne. USA., *The Price of Feathers*, Solita Solano, Story

BEYOND THE REEF 1981 d: Frank C. Clark. USA., *Tikoyo and His Shark*, Clement Richer, Novel

Beyond the River see THE BOTTOM OF THE BOTTLE (1956).

BEYOND THE ROCKS 1922 d: Sam Wood. USA., *Beyond the Rocks*, Elinor Glyn, New York 1906, Novel

Beyond the Sands see DINCOLO DE NISIPURI (1973).

Beyond the Veil see THE SECRET KINGDOM (1925).

BEYOND THERAPY 1987 d: Robert Altman. USA., *Beyond Therapy*, Christopher Durang, Play

BEYOND THIS PLACE 1959 d: Jack Cardiff. UKN., *Beyond This Place*, A. J. Cronin, 1953, Novel

BEZ SVIDETELEI 1983 d: Nikita Mikhalkov. USS., *Conversation Without Witnesses*, Sofia Prokofieva, Play

BEZ VINI VINOVATIYE 1945 d: Vladimir Petrov. USS., *Bez Vini Vinovatiye*, Alexander Ostrovsky, 1884, Play

Bez Viny Vinovatye see BEZ VINI VINOVATIYE (1945).

BEZAUBERNDES ARABELLA 1959 d: Axel von Ambesser. GRM., Georgette Heyer, Novel

BEZDETNA 1935 d: M. J. Krnansky. CZC., *Bezdetna*, Ignat Herrmann, Short Story

BEZZAKONIE 1953 d: Konstantin Yudin. USS., *Bezzakonie*, Anton Chekhov, 1887, Short Story

BFG 1990 d: Brian Cosgrove. UKN., *Bfg*, Roald Dahl, Novel

B.F.'S DAUGHTER 1948 d: Robert Z. Leonard. USA., *B.F.'S Daughter*, John Phillips Marquand, 1946, Novel

BHOWANI JUNCTION 1956 d: George Cukor. UKN/USA., *Bhowani Junction*, John Masters, 1954, Novel

BHUKAILASA 1940 d: Sundarao Nadkarni. IND., *Bhukailasa*, R. Nagendra Rao, Play

BHUMIKA 1977 d: Shyam Benegal. IND., *Sangtye Aika*, Hansa Wadka, 1970, Autobiography

BI XUE JIAN 1993 d: Zhang Haijing. CHN/HKG., *Bi Xue Jian*, Jin Yong, Novel

BIAN CHENG LANG ZI 1993 d: Frankie Chan. HKG/CHN/TWN., Gu Long, Novel

Bian Zhou Bian Chang see BIAN ZOU BIAN CHANG (1991).

BIAN ZOU BIAN CHANG 1991 d: Chen Kaige. CHN/UKN/GRM., *Bian Zou Bian Chang*, Shi Tiesheng, Short Story

BIANCANEVE E I SETTE LADRI 1949 d: Giacomo Gentilomo. ITL., *Il Ladro*, Anton Germano Rossi, Short Story

BIANCHENG 1984 d: Ling Zhifeng. CHN., *Bian Cheng*, Shen Congwen, 193-, Short Story

BIAO 1949 d: Zuo Lin. CHN., L. Pandeleev, Novel

BIBERPELZ, DER 1928 d: Erich Schonfelder. GRM., *Der Biberpelz*, Gerhart Hauptmann, 1893, Play

BIBERPELZ, DER 1937 d: Jurgen von Alten. GRM., *Der Biberpelz*, Gerhart Hauptmann, 1893, Play

BIBERPELZ, DER 1949 d: Erich Engel. GDR., *Der Biberpelz*, Gerhart Hauptmann, 1893, Play

BIBI LA PUREE 1925 d: Maurice Champreux. FRN., *Bibi la Puree*, Alexandre Fontanes, Andre Mouezy-Eon, Play

BIBI LA PUREE 1934 d: Leo Joannon. FRN., *Bibi la Puree*, Alexandre Fontanes, Andre Mouezy-Eon, Play

Bicchi see L' ILE D'AMOUR (1927).

BICHON 1935 d: Fernand Rivers. FRN., *Bichon*, Jean de Letraz, Play

BICHON 1947 d: Rene Jayet. FRN., *Bichon*, Jean de Letraz, Play

Bicycle Thief, The see LADRI DI BICICLETTE (1948).

Bicycle Thieves see LADRI DI BICICLETTE (1948).

BID FOR FORTUNE, A 1917 d: Sidney Morgan. UKN., *A Bid for Fortune*, Guy Boothby, Novel

BIDER DER FLIEGER 1941 d: Leonard Steckel, Max Werner Lenz. SWT., *Bider Der Flieger*, Otto Walter, Olten-Freiburg 1938, Book

Bider l'Aviateur see BIDER DER FLIEGER (1941).

BIENE MAJA, DIE 1977 d: Martin Murphy. AUS/JPN., Waldemar Bonsels, Story

Biens de Ce Monde, Les see LE BON DIEU SANS CONFESSION (1953).

BIETUL IOANIDE 1979 d: Dan PitA. RMN., *Bietul Ioanide*, George Calinescu, 1953, Novel, *Scrinul Negru*, George Calinescu, 1960, Novel

Big see THE MAGNIFICENT BRUTE (1936).

Big Bankroll, The see KING OF THE ROARING TWENTIES -THE STORY OF ARNOLD ROTHSTEIN (1961).

BIG BLUE, THE 1987 d: Andrew Horn. USA/GRM., *The Big Blue*, Andrew Horn, Short Story

BIG BONANZA, THE 1944 d: George Archainbaud. USA., *The Big Bonanza*, Peter B. Kyne, Novel

BIG BOODLE, THE 1956 d: Richard Wilson. USA., *The Big Boodle*, Robert Sylvester, Novel

BIG BOUNCE, THE 1969 d: Alex March. USA., *Big Bounce*, Elmore Leonard, New York 1969, Novel

Big Boy see BOY (1925).

BIG BOY 1930 d: Alan Crosland. USA., *Big Boy*, Harold Atteridge, New York 1925, Play

BIG BROADCAST, THE 1932 d: Frank Tuttle. USA., *Wild Waves*, William Ford Manley, New York 1932, Play

BIG BROTHER 1923 d: Allan Dwan. USA., *Big Brother*, Rex Beach, 1923, Short Story

Big Brother see YOUNG DONOVAN'S KID (1931).

BIG BROWN EYES 1936 d: Raoul Walsh. USA., *Big Brown Eyes*, James Edward Grant, 1935, Short Story, *Hahsit Babe*, James Edward Grant, 1935, Short Story

BIG BUSINESS GIRL 1931 d: William A. Seiter. USA., *Big Business Girl*, Patricia Reilly, H. N. Swanson, 1930, Story

BIG CAGE, THE 1933 d: Kurt Neumann. USA., *The Big Cage*, Edward S. Anthony, Clyde Beatty, New York 1933, Book

BIG CHANCE, THE 1957 d: Peter Graham Scott. UKN., *The Big Chance*, Pamela Barrington, Novel

BIG CITY BLUES 1932 d: Mervyn Leroy. USA., *New York Town*, Ward Morehouse, 1932, Play

Big City, The see MAHANAGAR (1963).

BIG CLOCK, THE 1948 d: John Farrow. USA., *The Big Clock*, Kenneth Fearing, 1946, Novel

BIG COUNTRY, THE 1958 d: William Wyler. USA., *Ambush at Blanco Canyon*, Donald Hamilton, Serial Story

Big Day, A see THIS SIDE OF HEAVEN (1932).

Big Deadly Game see THIRD PARTY RISK (1955).

Big Deal at Dodge City see A BIG HAND FOR THE LITTLE LADY (1966).

Big Doll, The see LA BAMBOLONA (1968).

BIG EXECUTIVE 1933 d: Erle C. Kenton. USA., *Big Executive*, Alice Duer Miller, 1933, Short Story

Big Fall, The see DER GROSSE FALL (1945).

Big Fall, The see UNDER MY SKIN (1950).

BIG FELLA 1937 d: J. Elder Wills. UKN., *Banjo*, Claude McKay, Novel

BIG FIGHT, THE 1930 d: Walter Lang. USA., *The Big Fight*, Milton Herbert Gropper, Max Marcin, New York 1928, Play

BIG FISHERMAN, THE 1959 d: Frank Borzage. USA., *The Big Fisherman*, Lloyd C. Douglas, Novel

BIG FIX, THE 1978 d: Jeremy Paul Kagan. USA., *The Big Fix*, Roger L. Simon, Novel

Big Flutter, The see DIE GROSSE FLATTER (1979).

Big Frame, The see UNDERTOW (1949).

Big Friendly Giant see BFG (1990).

BIG GAMBLE, THE 1931 d: Fred Niblo. USA., *The Iron Chalice*, Octavus Roy Cohen, Boston 1925, Novel

BIG GAME 1921 d: Dallas M. Fitzgerald. USA., *Big Game*, Kilbourne Gordon, Willard Robertson, New York 1920, Play

BIG GAME, THE 1936 d: George Nicholls Jr. USA., *The Big Game*, Francis Wallace, Boston 1936, Novel

Big Grab, The see MELODIE EN SOUS-SOL (1962).

BIG GUY, THE 1940 d: Arthur Lubin. USA., *No Power on Earth*, Richard K. Polimer, Wallace Sullivan, Short Story

Big Haircut see WILD HARVEST (1947).

BIG HAND FOR THE LITTLE LADY, A 1966 d: Fielder Cook. USA., *Big Deal in Laredo*, Sidney Carroll, 1962, Play

BIG HAPPINESS 1920 d: Colin Campbell. USA., *Big Happiness*, Pan, London 1917, Novel

Big Heart, The see MIRACLE ON 34TH STREET (1947).

BIG HEARTED HERBERT 1934 d: William Keighley. USA., *Big Hearted Herbert*, Sophie Underwood, Anna Steese Richardson, New York 1934, Play

BIG HEAT, THE 1953 d: Fritz Lang. USA., *The Big Heat*, William P. McGivern, Serial Story

Big House Blues see JAIL HOUSE BLUES (1942).

BIG JIM GARRITY 1916 d: George Fitzmaurice. USA., *Big Jim Garrity*, Owen Davis, New York 1914, Play

BIG KNIFE, THE 1955 d: Robert Aldrich. USA., *The Big Knife*, Clifford Odets, New York 1949, Play

BIG LAND, THE 1956 d: Gordon Douglas. USA., *Buffalo Grass*, Frank Gruber, Novel

BIG LITTLE PERSON, THE 1919 d: Robert Z. Leonard. USA., *The Big Little Person*, Rebecca Lane Hooper Eastman, New York 1917, Novel

Big Man: Crossing the Line, The *see* THE BIG MAN (1990).

BIG MAN, THE 1990 d: David Leland. UKN., *The Big Man*, William McIlvanney, Novel

BIG MONEY 1918 d: Harry Lorraine. UKN., *A Run for His Money*, Mary Wynne, Novel

Big Night, The *see* HER BIG NIGHT (1926).

BIG NIGHT, THE 1951 d: Joseph Losey. USA., *Dreadful Summit*, Stanley Ellin, Novel

Big North, The *see* THE WILD NORTH (1952).

BIG OPERATOR, THE 1959 d: Charles Haas. USA., *The Adventure of Joe Smith - American*, Paul Gallico, Story

Big Pay-Off, The *see* THE PRIDE OF THE LEGION (1932).

Big People *see* OONCHE LOG (1965).

BIG POND, THE 1930 d: Hobart Henley. USA., *The Big Pond*, George Middleton, A. E. Thomas, New York 1928, Play

Big Race, The *see* THE TEXAN (1930).

BIG RED 1962 d: Norman Tokar. USA., *Big Red*, James Arthur Kjelgaard, New York 1945, Novel

Big Risk, The *see* CLASSE TOUS RISQUES (1959).

Big Shot *see* MY PALIKARI (1982).

BIG SKY, THE 1952 d: Howard Hawks. USA., *The Big Sky*, A. B. Guthrie Jr., 1947, Novel

Big Sky, The *see* SARA AKASH (1969).

BIG SLEEP, THE 1946 d: Howard Hawks. USA., *The Big Sleep*, Raymond Chandler, 1939, Novel

BIG SLEEP, THE 1978 d: Michael Winner. UKN/USA., *The Big Sleep*, Raymond Chandler, 1939, Novel

Big Snatch, The *see* MELODIE EN SOUS-SOL (1962).

Big Softie, The *see* LE GRAND DADAIS (1967).

BIG STAKES 1922 d: Clifford S. Elfelt. USA., *High Stakes*, Earl Wayland Bowman, 1920, Short Story

BIG STEAL, THE 1949 d: Don Siegel. USA., *The Road to Carmichael's*, Richard Wormser, Story

Big Stickup at Brink's *see* THE BRINK'S JOB (1978).

Big Story, The *see* APPOINTMENT WITH A SHADOW (1958).

BIG STREET, THE 1942 d: Irving Reis. USA., *Little Pinks*, Damon Runyon, 1940, Short Story

BIG STRONG MAN, THE 1922 d: George A. Cooper. UKN., *The Big Strong Man*, Christine Castle, Story

BIG TIMBER 1917 d: William D. Taylor. USA., *Big Timber*, Bertrand W. Sinclair, Boston 1916, Novel

BIG TIMBER 1921 d: John W. Noble. CND., John Edmund, Story

BIG TIMBER 1924 d: William James Craft. USA., *The Heart of the Night Wind*, Vingie E. Roe, New York 1913, Novel

BIG TIME 1929 d: Kenneth Hawks. USA., *Little Ledna*, William Wallace Smith, 1926, Short Story

BIG TOWN ROUND-UP 1921 d: Lynn Reynolds. USA., *Big-Town Round-Up*, William MacLeod Raine, Boston 1920, Novel

BIG TOWN, THE 1987 d: Ben Bolt. USA., *The Arm*, Clark Howard, Novel

BIG TOYS 1980 d: Chris Thomson. ASL., *Big Toys*, Patrick White, Play

BIG TREES, THE 1952 d: Felix E. Feist. USA., Kenneth Earl, Story

BIG TREMAINE 1916 d: Henry Otto. USA., *Big Tremaine*, Marie Van Vorst, Boston 1914, Novel

Big Victory *see* DA JIE (1995).

BIG WAVE, THE 1962 d: Tad Danielewski. USA/JPN., *The Big Wave*, Pearl Buck, New York 1948, Short Story

BIGAMIST, THE 1921 d: Guy Newall. UKN., *The Bigamist*, F. E. Mills Young, Novel

BIGGER MAN, THE 1915 d: John W. Noble. USA., *The Bridge*, Rupert Hughes, New York 1909, Play

BIGGER THAN LIFE 1956 d: Nicholas Ray. USA., Berton Roueche, Article

BIGGEST BUNDLE OF THEM ALL, THE 1967 d: Ken Annakin. USA., Josef Shaftel, Story

Big-Hearted Herbert *see* BIG HEARTED HERBERT (1934).

BIGORNE, CAPORAL DE FRANCE, LA 1957 d: Robert Darene. FRN., *La Bigorne - Caporal de France*, Pierre Nord, Novel

Bijeli Davo *see* IL DIAVOLO BIANCO AGI MURAD (1959).

BIJIN AISHU 1931 d: Yasujiro Ozu. JPN., Henri de Regnier, Short Story

BIJO TO KAIRYU 1955 d: Kozaburo YoshimurA. JPN., *Narukami*, Hanjuro Tsuuchi, 1742, Play

BIJOUTIERS DU CLAIR DE LUNE, LES 1958 d: Roger Vadim. FRN/ITL., *Bijoutiers du Clair de Lune*, Albert Vidalie, Novel

BILA JACHTA VE SPLITU 1939 d: Ladislav Brom. CZC., *Americka Jachta Ve Splitu*, Milan Begovic, Short Story

BILA NEMOC 1937 d: Hugo Haas. CZC., *Bila Nemoc*, Karel Capek, 1937, Play

BILA VRANA 1938 d: Vladimir Slavinsky. CZC., *Bila Vrana*, Frantisek Ketzek, Bedrich Sulc, Opera

BILDNIS DES DORIAN GRAY, DAS 1917 d: Richard Oswald. GRM., *The Picture of Dorian Gray*, Oscar Wilde, London 1891, Novel

Bildnis Des Dorian Gray, Das *see* IL DIO CHIAMATO DORIAN (1970).

BILITIS 1977 d: David Hamilton. FRN., *Bilitis*, Pierre Louys, Novel

BILL FOR DIVORCEMENT, A 1922 d: Denison Clift. UKN., *A Bill of Divorcement*, Clemence Dane, London 1921, Play

Bill of Divorcement, A *see* A BILL FOR DIVORCEMENT (1922).

BILL OF DIVORCEMENT, A 1932 d: George Cukor. USA., *A Bill of Divorcement*, Clemence Dane, London 1921, Play

BILL OF DIVORCEMENT, A 1940 d: John Farrow. USA., *A Bill of Divorcement*, Clemence Dane, London 1921, Play

Billeted *see* THE MISLEADING WIDOW (1919).

BILLIE 1912. USA., *Billie*, James Oppenheim, Short Story

BILLIE 1965 d: Don Weis. USA., *Time Out for Ginger*, Ronald Alexander, 1952, Play

BILLIE'S ROSE 1922 d: Challis Sanderson. UKN., *Billie's Rose*, George R. Sims, Poem

BILLION DOLLAR BRAIN 1967 d: Ken Russell. UKN/USA., *Billion Dollar Brain*, Len Deighton, London 1966, Novel

BILLION FOR BORIS, A 1990 d: Alex Grasshoff. USA., *A Billion for Boris*, Mary Rodgers, Novel

BILLIONAIRE, THE 1914 d: James Kirkwood. USA., *The Billionaire*, Harry B. Smith, Story

BILLIONS 1920 d: Ray C. Smallwood. USA., *L' Homme Riche*, Henri Dupuy-Mazuel, Jean-Jose Frappa, Paris 1914, Play

BILLY AND THE BIG STICK 1917 d: Edward H. Griffith. USA., *Billy and the Big Stick*, Richard Harding Davis, 1914, Short Story

BILLY BATHGATE 1991 d: Robert Benton. USA., *Billy Bathgate*, E. L. Doctorow, 1989, Novel

BILLY BUDD 1962 d: Peter Ustinov. UKN., *Billy Budd*, Herman Melville, 1924, Novel

BILLY LIAR! 1963 d: John Schlesinger. UKN., *Billy Liar*, Keith Waterhouse, 1959, Novel

BILLY: PORTRAIT OF A STREET KID 1977 d: Steve Gethers. USA., *Peoples*, Robert C. S. Downs, Book

Billy Rose's Diamond Horseshoe *see* DIAMOND HORSESHOE (1945).

BILLY ROSE'S JUMBO 1962 d: Charles Walters. USA., *Jumbo*, Ben Hecht, Charles MacArthur, New York 1935, Play

BILLY THE KID 1930 d: King Vidor. USA., *The Saga of Billy the Kid*, Walter Noble Burns, Garden City, N.Y. 1926, Novel

BILLY THE KID 1941 d: David Miller. USA., *The Saga of Billy the Kid*, Walter Noble Burns, Garden City, N.Y. 1926, Novel

Billy's Cupidity *see* LITTLE MR. FIXER (1915).

BILLY'S SPANISH LOVE SPASM 1915 d: W. P. Kellino. UKN., *Serenata*, Billy Merson, Sketch

BILOXI BLUES 1987 d: Mike Nichols. USA., *Biloxi Blues*, Neil Simon, 1987, Play

BIMBI LONTANI 1919 d: Baldassarre Negroni. ITL., *Leggenda Per Violino in 4 Tempi*, Washington Borg

Binary *see* PURSUIT (1972).

BINDLE 1926 d: H. B. Parkinson. UKN., Herbert Jenkins, Short Stories

BING BANG BOOM 1922 d: Fred J. Butler. USA., *Bing Bang Boom*, Raymond Leslie Goldman, 1920, Short Story

BING JIAN QIAN JIN 1958 d: Yan Gong. CHN., *Snow and Ice Melt*, Li Zhun, Novel

BING LIN CHENG XIA 1964 d: Lin Nong. CHN., *Bing Lin Cheng XIa*, Bai Ren, Play

Biography of a Bachelor *see* BIOGRAPHY OF A BACHELOR GIRL (1934).

BIOGRAPHY OF A BACHELOR GIRL 1934 d: Edward H. Griffith. USA., *Biography*, S. N. Behrman, New York 1932, Play

BIOLOGIE! 1990 d: Jorg Foth. GDR., *Biologie!*, Wolf Spillner, Novel

Bionda Di Pechino, La *see* LA BLONDE DE PEKIN (1968).

BIONDINA, LA 1923 d: Amleto Palermi. ITL., *La Biondina*, Marco Praga, 1893, Novel

BIRAGHIN 1946 d: Carmine Gallone. ITL., *Biraghin*, Arnaldo Fraccaroli, Play

BIRAJ BAHU 1954 d: Bimal Roy. IND., *Biraj Bau*, Sarat Candra Cattopadhyay, 1914, Novel

Birch Wood, The *see* BRZEZINA (1971).

Birchwood *see* BRZEZINA (1971).

Bird Dealer, The *see* DER VOGELHANDLER (1953).

Bird Dealer, The *see* DER VOGELHANDLER (1962).

Bird of Heaven, A *see* EGI MADAR (1957).

BIRD OF PARADISE 1932 d: King Vidor. USA., *The Bird of Paradise*, Richard Walton Tully, New York 1912, Play

BIRD OF PARADISE 1951 d: Delmer Daves. USA., *The Bird of Paradise*, Richard Walton Tully, New York 1912, Play

Bird of Prey *see* L' EPERVIER (1933).

BIRD OF PREY, THE 1918 d: Edward J. Le Saint. USA., Guy de Maupassant, Story

Bird With the Crystal Plumage, The *see* L' UCCELLO DALLE PIUME DE CRISTALLO (1970).

Bird With the Glass Feathers, The *see* L' UCCELLO DALLE PIUME DE CRISTALLO (1970).

BIRDMAN OF ALCATRAZ 1962 d: John Frankenheimer. USA., *Birdman of Alcatraz: the Story of Robert Stroud*, Thomas E. Gaddis, New York 1955, Book

Birds and the Bees, The *see* THREE DARING DAUGHTERS (1947).

BIRDS AND THE BEES, THE 1956 d: Norman Taurog. USA., *The Lady Eve*, Monckton Hoffe, Play

BIRDS' CHRISTMAS CAROL, THE 1917 d: Lule Warrenton. USA., *The Birds' Christmas Carol*, Kate Douglas Wiggin, San Francisco 1887, Story

Birds Come to Die in Peru, The *see* LES OISEAUX VONT MOURIR AU PEROU (1968).

Birds in Peru *see* LES OISEAUX VONT MOURIR AU PEROU (1968).

BIRDS OF A FEATHER 1935 d: John Baxter. UKN., *A Rift in the Loot*, George Foster, Play

Birds of a Feather *see* LA CAGE AUX FOLLES (1978).

Birds of Baden-Baden, The *see* LOS PAJAROS DE BADEN-BADEN (1974).

BIRDS OF PREY 1927 d: William James Craft. USA., *Birds of Prey; Being Pages from the Book of Broadway*, George Bronson Howard, New York 1918, Novel

BIRDS OF PREY 1930 d: Basil Dean. UKN., *The Fourth Wall*, A. A. Milne, London 1928, Play

Birds of Prey *see* LE RAPACE (1968).

BIRDS, THE 1963 d: Alfred Hitchcock. USA., *The Birds*, Daphne Du Maurier, 1952, Short Story

BIRDY 1984 d: Alan Parker. USA., *Birdy*, William Wharton, Novel

BIRIBI 1970 d: Daniel Moosmann. FRN/TNS., *Biribi*, Georges Darien, Novel

BIRICCHINO DI PARIGI, IL 1916 d: Ugo FalenA. ITL., *Le Gamin de Paris*, Jean-Francois Bayard, Vanderbruch, 1836, Play

BIRICHINO DI PAPA, IL 1943 d: Raffaello Matarazzo. ITL., *Il Birichino Di Papa*, Henny Koch, Novel

Birichino Di Parigi, Il *see* IL BIRICCHINO DI PARIGI (1916).

Birjuk *see* BIRYUK (1979).

BIRTH OF A NATION, THE 1915 d: D. W. Griffith. USA., *The Clansman: an Historical Romance of the Ku Klux Klan*, Thomas Dixon, New York 1906, Novel

Birth of Frankenstein *see* THE CURSE OF FRANKENSTEIN (1957).

Birth of Man, The *see* TRETA SLED SLANTSETO (1972).

BIRTHDAY PARTY, THE 1970 d: William Friedkin. UKN., *The Birthday Party*, Harold Pinter, London 1958, Play

BIRTHRIGHT 1924 d: Oscar MicheauxA. USA., *Birthright*, Thomas Sigismund Stribling, New York 1922, Novel

BIRTHRIGHT 1939 d: Oscar MicheauxA. USA., *Birthright*, Thomas Sigismund Stribling, New York 1922, Novel

BIRUMA NO TATE GOTO 1985 d: Kon IchikawA. JPN., *Biruma No Tategoto*, Michio Takayama, 1948, Novel

BIRUMA NO TATEGOTO 1956 d: Kon IchikawA. JPN., *Biruma No Tategoto*, Michio Takayama, 1948, Novel

BIRYUK 1979 d: Roman Balayan. USS., *Biryuk*, Ivan Turgenev, 1852, Short Story

BIS ZUM ENDE ALLER TAGE 1961 d: Franz Peter Wirth. GRM., *Brackwasser*, Heinrich Hauser, Leipzig 1928, Novel

BIS ZUR BITTEREN NEIGE 1975 d: Gerd Oswald. AUS/GRM., *Bis Zur Bitteren Neige*, Johannes Mario Simmel, Novel

BISARCA, LA 1950 d: Giorgio C. Simonelli. ITL., *La Bisarca*, Pietro Garinei, Sandro Giovannini, Radio Play

Bisarjan see BALIDAN (1927).

BISBETICA DOMATA, LA 1908. ITL., *The Taming of the Shrew*, William Shakespeare, c1593, Play

BISBETICA DOMATA, LA 1913. ITL., *The Taming of the Shrew*, William Shakespeare, c1593, Play

BISBETICA DOMATA, LA 1942 d: Ferdinando M. Poggioli. ITL., *The Taming of the Shrew*, William Shakespeare, c1593, Play

Bisbetica Domata, La see THE TAMING OF THE SHREW (1967).

BISCUIT EATER, THE 1940 d: Stuart Heisler. USA., *The Biscuit Eater*, James H. Street, 1939, Short Story

BISCUIT EATER, THE 1972 d: Vincent McEveety. USA., *The Biscuit Eater*, James H. Street, 1939, Short Story

BISHOP MISBEHAVES, THE 1935 d: E. A. Dupont. USA., *The Bishop Misbehaves*, Frederick Jackson, New York 1935, Play

BISHOP MURDER CASE, THE 1929 d: Nick Grinde, David Burton. USA., *The Bishop Murder Case*, S. S. Van Dine, New York 1917, Novel

Bishop's Bedroom, The see LA STANZA DEL VESCOVO (1977).

BISHOP'S CANDLESTICKS, THE 1913 d: Herbert Brenon. USA., *Les Miserables*, Victor Hugo, Paris 1862, Novel

BISHOP'S EMERALDS, THE 1919 d: John B. O'Brien. USA., *The Bishop's Emeralds*, Houghton Townley, New York 1908, Novel

Bishop's Misadventures, The see THE BISHOP MISBEHAVES (1935).

Bishop's Room, The see LA STANZA DEL VESCOVO (1977).

Bishop's Son, The see THE DEEMSTER (1917).

BISHOP'S WIFE, THE 1947 d: Henry Koster. USA., *The Bishop's Wife*, Robert Nathan, 1928, Novel

Bit O' Heaven, A see THE BIRDS' CHRISTMAS CAROL (1917).

BIT OF LACE, A 1915. USA., *A Bit of Lace*, H. S. Sheldon, Play

BITCH, THE 1979 d: Gerry O'HarA. UKN., *The Bitch*, Jackie Collins, Novel

Bite of the Gorilla, The see LE GORILLE A MORDU L'ARCHEVEQUE (1962).

BITS OF LIFE 1921 d: Marshall Neilan. USA., *The Man Who Heard Everything*, Walter Trumbull, 1921, Short Story, *Hop*, Hugh Wiley, 1921, Short Story

BITTE LASST DIE BLUMEN LEBEN 1986 d: Duccio Tessari. GRM., *Bitte Lasst Die Blumen Leben*, Johannes Mario Simmel, Novel

BITTER APPLES 1927 d: Harry O. Hoyt. USA., *Bitter Apples*, Harold MacGrath, 1925, Short Story

Bitter Cauliflower see KU CAI HUA (1965).

BITTER END, THE 1997 d: Juan Jose CampanellA. USA., *Ni El Tiro Del Final*, Jose Pablo Feinmann, Novel

Bitter Fruit see FRUITS AMERS (1967).

BITTER HARVEST 1963 d: Peter Graham Scott. UKN., *Twenty Thousand Streets Under the Sky; a London Trilogy*, Patrick Hamilton, 1935, Novel

Bitter Life see LA VITA AGRA (1964).

Bitter Love see AMORE AMARO (1974).

Bitter Moon see LUNE DE FIEL (1992).

BITTER SWEET 1933 d: Herbert Wilcox. UKN., *Bitter Sweet*, Noel Coward, London 1929, Operetta

BITTER SWEET 1940 d: W. S. Van Dyke. USA., *Bitter Sweet*, Noel Coward, London 1929, Operetta

Bitter Sweets see PALACES (1927).

BITTER TEA OF GENERAL YEN, THE 1933 d: Frank CaprA. USA., *The Bitter Tea of General Yen*, Grace Zaring Stone, Indianapolis 1930, Novel

Bitter Victory see PAID IN FULL (1950).

Bitter Victory see AMERE VICTOIRE (1957).

Bizarre Bizarre see DROLE DE DRAME (1937).

Bizet's Carmen see CARMEN (1983).

Bla Veckan, Den see SININEN VIIKKO (1954).

BLACK ABBOT, THE 1934 d: George A. Cooper. UKN., *The Grange Mystery*, Philip Godfrey, Novel

Black Abbot, The see DER SCHWARZE ABT (1963).

BLACK AND SILVER 1982 d: William Raban, Marilyn Raban. UKN., *The Birthday of the Infants*, Oscar Wilde, 1891, Short Story

BLACK ANGEL 1946 d: R. William Neill. USA., *The Black Angel*, Cornell Woolrich, 1943, Novel

BLACK ARROW 1985 d: John Hough. USA/UKN/SPN., *Black Arrow*, Robert Louis Stevenson, 1888, Novel

Black Arrow see CHERNAYA STREIA (1985).

Black Arrow Strikes, The see THE BLACK ARROW (1948).

BLACK ARROW, THE 1911 d: Oscar Apfel. USA., *Black Arrow*, Robert Louis Stevenson, 1888, Novel

BLACK ARROW, THE 1948 d: Gordon Douglas. USA., *Black Arrow*, Robert Louis Stevenson, 1888, Novel

BLACK BAG, THE 1922 d: Stuart Paton. USA., *The Black Bag*, Louis Joseph Vance, Indianapolis 1908, Novel

Black Beach see THE LOVE FLOWER (1920).

BLACK BEAUTY 1921 d: David Smith. USA., *Black Beauty*, Anna Sewell, London 1877, Novel

BLACK BEAUTY 1933 d: Phil Rosen. USA., *Black Beauty*, Anna Sewell, London 1877, Novel

BLACK BEAUTY 1946 d: Max Nosseck. USA., *Black Beauty*, Anna Sewell, London 1877, Novel

BLACK BEAUTY 1971 d: James Hill. UKN/GRM/SPN., *Black Beauty*, Anna Sewell, London 1877, Novel

BLACK BEAUTY 1978 d: Daniel Haller. USA., *Black Beauty*, Anna Sewell, London 1877, Novel

BLACK BEAUTY 1994 d: Caroline Thompson. UKN/USA., *Black Beauty*, Anna Sewell, London 1877, Novel

Black Blood see SANGRE NEGRA (1948).

Black Box see KUFSA SHECHORA (1993).

BLACK BOX, THE 1915 d: Otis Turner. USA., *The Black Box*, E. Phillips Oppenheim, Boston 1915, Novel

BLACK BUTTERFLIES 1928 d: James W. Horne. USA., *Black Butterflies*, Elizabeth Jordan, New York 1927, Novel

BLACK CAMEL, THE 1931 d: Hamilton MacFadden. USA., *The Black Camel*, Earl Derr Biggers, Indianapolis 1929, Novel

BLACK CANDLE, THE 1991 d: Roy Battersby. UKN., *The Black Candle*, Catherine Cookson, Novel

Black Cannon Affair, The see HEIPAO SHIJIAN (1985).

Black Cannon Incident, The see HEIPAO SHIJIAN (1985).

BLACK CAT, THE 1934 d: Edgar G. Ulmer. USA., *The Black Cat*, Edgar Allan Poe, 1843, Short Story

BLACK CAT, THE 1941 d: Albert S. Rogell. USA., *The Black Cat*, Edgar Allan Poe, 1843, Short Story

BLACK CAT, THE 1966 d: Harold Hoffman. USA., *The Black Cat*, Edgar Allan Poe, 1843, Short Story

Black Cat, The see IL GATTO NERO (1981).

BLACK CAULDRON, THE 1985 d: Ted Berman, Richard Rich. USA., *The Chronicles of Prydainby*, Lloyd Alexander, Novel

Black Chamber, The see RENDEZVOUS (1935).

BLACK COFFEE 1931 d: Leslie Hiscott. UKN., *Black Coffee*, Agatha Christie, Novel

Black Corsair, The see IL CORSARO NERO (1936).

Black Cross see KRZYZACY (1960).

Black Curtain, The see STREET OF CHANCE (1942).

Black Diamond see DIAMANT NOIR (1940).

Black Diamond see FEKETE GYEMANTOK (1976).

Black Diamonds see FEKETE GYEMANTOK (1976).

BLACK DOLL, THE 1937 d: Otis Garrett. USA., *The Black Doll*, William Edward Hayes, New York 1936, Novel

BLACK EAGLE 1948 d: Robert Gordon. USA., *The Passing of Black Eagle*, O. Henry, 1909, Short Story

Black Eagle, The see AQUILA NERA (1946).

Black Eyes see OCI CIORNIE (1987).

Black Flowers for the Bride see SOMETHING FOR EVERYONE (1970).

Black Forest Girl see SCHWARZWALDMADEL (1950).

BLACK FOX, THE 1962 d: Louis Clyde Stoumen. USA., *Reineke Fuchs*, Johann Wolfgang von Goethe, 1794, Verse

BLACK FRIDAY 1916 d: Lloyd B. Carleton. USA., *Black Friday*, Frederic Stewart Isham, Indianapolis 1904, Novel

BLACK FURY 1935 d: Michael Curtiz. USA., *Bohunk*, Harry R. Irving, Play, *Jan Volkanik*, Judge M. A. Musmanno, Short Story

Black Galleon, The see DIE SCHWARZE GALEERE (1962).

Black Gamekeepers, The see CERNI MYSLIVCI (1921).

BLACK GATE, THE 1919 d: Theodore Marston. USA., *Hilliard Booth*, Short Story

Black Girl see LA NOIRE DE. (1967).

Black Glove, The see FACE THE MUSIC (1954).

BLACK GOLD 1936 d: Russell Hopton. USA., *The Joy of Living*, Peter B. Kyne, 1914, Story

BLACK GOLD 1963 d: Leslie H. Martinson. USA., *Wyoming Wildcatters*, Harry Whittington, Short Story

BLACK HAND GANG, THE 1930 d: Monty Banks. UKN., *Black Hand George*, Bert Lee, R. P. Weston, Play

Black Hell see BLACK FURY (1935).

Black Horse see HEI JUN MA (1995).

Black Humor see UMORISMO NERO (1965).

BLACK IS WHITE 1920 d: Charles Giblyn. USA., *Black Is White*, George Barr McCutcheon, New York 1914, Novel

BLACK JACK 1927 d: Orville O. Dull. USA., *The Broken Dollar*, Johnston McCulley, 1927, Short Story

BLACK JACK 1980 d: Kenneth Loach. UKN., *Black Jack*, Leon Garfield, Novel

Black Lagoon, The see LA LAGUNA NEGRA (1952).

Black Lake, The see LA LAGUNA NEGRA (1952).

BLACK LIKE ME 1964 d: Carl Lerner. USA., *Black Like Me*, John Howard Griffin, 1960, Novel

BLACK LIMELIGHT 1938 d: Paul L. Stein. UKN., *Black Limelight*, Gordon Sherry, London 1937, Play

Black Lizard see KUROTOKAGE (1968).

Black Love see MUSTA RAKKAUS (1957).

Black Love -White Love see BITTER SWEET LOVE (1967).

BLACK MAGIC 1929 d: George B. Seitz. USA., *Cape Smoke*, Paul Dickey, Walter Frost, 1925, Play, *The Man Between*, Walter Frost, 1913, Novel

BLACK MAGIC 1949 d: Gregory Ratoff. USA/ITL., *Joseph Balsamo*, Alexandre Dumas (pere), 1846-48, Novel

Black Man With a White Soul, The see EL NEGRO QUE TENIA EL ALMA BLANCA (1926).

Black Man With the White Soul, The see EL NEGRO QUE TENIA EL ALMA BLANCA (1933).

BLACK MARBLE, THE 1980 d: Harold Becker. USA., *The Black Marble*, Joseph Wambaugh, Novel

BLACK MARKET BABY 1977 d: Robert Day. USA., *A Nice Italian Girl*, Elizabeth Christman, Novel

BLACK MASK 1935 d: Ralph Ince. UKN., *Blackshirt*, Bruce Graeme, Novel

Black Mermaid, The see LA SIRENA NEGRA (1947).

Black Mink on Tender Skin see SCHWARZER NERZ AUF ZARTER HAUT (1969).

BLACK MIRROR 1981 d: Pierre-Alain Jolivet. CND/FRN., *Haute Surveillance*, Jean Genet, Paris 1949, Play

Black Monk, The see TCHIORNI MONAK (1988).

Black Monocle, The see LE MONOCLE NOIR (1961).

BLACK MOON 1934 d: R. William Neill. USA., *Black Moon*, Clements Ripley, New York 1933, Novel

BLACK NARCISSUS 1947 d: Michael Powell, Emeric Pressburger. UKN., *Black Narcissus*, Rumer Godden, Novel

BLACK NIGHT, THE 1916 d: Harold Weston. UKN., *The Black Night*, Andrew Soutar, Novel

Black One from., The see LA NOIRE DE. (1967).

BLACK ORCHID, THE 1959 d: Martin Ritt. USA., Joseph Stefano, Television Play

Black Orpheus see ORFEU NEGRO (1958).

BLACK OXEN 1924 d: Frank Lloyd. USA., *Black Oxen*, Gertrude Franklin Atherton, New York 1923, Novel

BLACK PANTHER'S CUB, THE 1921 d: Emile Chautard. USA., *The Black Panther's Cub*, Ethel Donoher, Story

Black Pawl see GODLESS MEN (1921).

BLACK PEARL, THE 1928 d: Scott Pembroke. USA., *The Black Pearl*, Mrs. Wilson Woodrow, New York 1912, Novel

BLACK PETER 1922 d: George Ridgwell. UKN., *Black Peter*, Arthur Conan Doyle, Short Story

Black Rain see KUROI AME (1988).

Black Robe, The see STRANGERS IN LOVE (1932).

Black Robe, The see SECRETS OF CHINATOWN (1934).

BLACK ROBE, THE 1991 d: Bruce Beresford. CND/ASL., *Black Robe*, Brian Moore, 1985, Novel

Black Rose see KUROBARA NO YAKATA (1969).

Black Rose Inn, The see KUROBARA NO YAKATA (1969).

BLACK ROSE, THE 1950 d: Henry Hathaway. UKN/USA., *The Black Rose*, Thomas B. Costain, 1945, Novel

Black Shack Alley see RUE CASES-NEGRES (1983).

BLACK SHEEP 1921 d: Paul C. Hurst. USA., *Baa Baa Black Sheep*, W. C. Tuttle, 1921, Short Story

BLACK SHEEP, A 1915 d: Thomas N. Heffron. USA., *A Black Sheep and How It Came to Washington*, Charles Hale Hoyt, New York 1896, Musical Play

BLACK SHEEP, THE 1915 d: J. Farrell MacDonald. USA., *The Black Sheep*, Edmund Yates, Novel

BLACK SHEEP, THE 1920 d: Sidney Morgan. UKN., *The Black Sheep*, Ruby M. Ayres, Novel

Black Sheep, The see DAS SCHWARZE SCHAF (1943).

Black Sheep, The see DAS SCHWARZE SCHAF (1960).

BLACK SHIELD OF FALWORTH, THE 1954 d: Rudolph Mate. USA., *Men of Iron*, Howard Pyle, 1954, Novel

BLACK SPIDER, THE 1920 d: William J. Humphrey. UKN., *The Black Spider*, Carlton Dawe, London 1911, Novel

BLACK STALLION RETURNS, THE 1983 d: Robert DalvA. USA., *The Black Stallion Returns*, Walter Farley, Novel

BLACK STALLION, THE 1979 d: Carroll Ballard. USA., *The Black Stallion*, Walter Farley, Novel

Black Star in a White Night see UN HOMME SE PENCHE SUR SON PASSE (1957).

BLACK STUFF, THE 1978 d: Jim Goddard. UKN., *Boys from the Blackstuff*, Alan Bleasdale, 1983, Play

Black Sun see MANNEN I SKUGAN (1978).

Black Sun see TEMNE SLUNCE (1980).

Black Sunday see LA MASCHERA DEL DEMONIO (1960).

BLACK SUNDAY 1977 d: John Frankenheimer. USA., *Black Sunday*, Thomas Harris, Novel

BLACK SWAN, THE 1942 d: Henry King. USA., *The Black Swan*, Rafael Sabatini, Novel

Black Tower, The see DALGLIESH: THE BLACK TOWER (1987).

Black Town, The see A FEKETE VAROS (1971).

BLACK TULIP, THE 1921 d: Frank Richardson, Maurits H. Binger. UKN/NTH., *La Tulipe Noire*, Alexandre Dumas (pere), 1846, Novel

BLACK TULIP, THE 1937 d: Alex Bryce. UKN., *La Tulipe Noire*, Alexandre Dumas (pere), 1846, Novel

Black Tulip, The see LA TULIPE NOIRE (1963).

Black Velvet see RED CANYON (1949).

BLACK VELVET GOWN, THE 1991 d: Norman Stone. UKN., *The Black Velvet Gown*, Catherine Cookson, Novel

BLACK VENUS 1983 d: Claude Mulot. USA/SPN., Honore de Balzac, Story

BLACK WATCH, THE 1929 d: John Ford. USA., *King - of the Khyber Rifles*, Talbot Mundy, New York 1916, Novel

BLACK WATER GOLD 1969 d: Alan Landsburg. USA., Alan Landsburg, Story

BLACK WATERS 1929 d: Marshall Neilan. UKN., *Fog*, John Willard, Play

Black Werewolf see THE BEAST MUST DIE (1974).

Black, White and Red Fourposter, The see DAS SCHWARZ-WEISS-ROTE HIMMELBETT (1962).

Black, White, and Red Wedding Bed, The see DAS SCHWARZ-WEISS-ROTE HIMMELBETT (1962).

BLACK WIDOW 1951 d: Vernon Sewell. UKN., *Return from Darkness*, Lester Powell, Story

BLACK WIDOW 1954 d: Nunnally Johnson. USA., *Fatal Woman*, Patrick Quentin, 1952, Novel

Black Wind see VIENTO NEGRO (1964).

BLACK WINDMILL, THE 1974 d: Don Siegel. UKN., *Seven Days to a Killing*, Clive Egleton, Novel

Black Wings see CZARNE SKRZYDLA (1962).

BLACK WOLF, THE 1916 d: Frank Reicher. USA., *The Black Wolf*, Jean Barrymore, Short Story

Blackamoors see MORIANERNA (1965).

BLACKBEARD THE PIRATE 1952 d: Raoul Walsh. USA., Devallon Scott, Story

BLACKBEARD'S GHOST 1968 d: Robert Stevenson. USA., *Blackbeard's Ghost*, Ben Stahl, 1965, Novel

BLACKBIRDS 1915 d: J. P. McGowan. USA., *Blackbirds*, Harry James Smith, New York 1913, Play

BLACKBIRDS 1920 d: John Francis Dillon. USA., *Blackbirds*, Harry James Smith, New York 1913, Play

BLACKBOARD JUNGLE, THE 1955 d: Richard Brooks. USA., *Blackboard Jungle*, Evan Hunter, 1954, Novel

BLACK-EYED SUSAN 1908. UKN., *Black-Eyed Susan*, Douglas Jerrold, London 1829, Play

BLACK-EYED SUSAN 1914 d: Maurice Elvey. UKN., *Black-Eyed Susan*, Douglas Jerrold, London 1829, Play

BLACKFELLAS 1992 d: James Ricketson. ASL., *Day of the Dog*, Archie Weller, Novel

BLACKGUARD, THE 1925 d: Graham Cutts. UKN., *The Blackguard*, Raymond Paton, Novel

BLACKIE'S REDEMPTION 1919 d: John Ince. USA., *Boston Blackie*, Jack Boyle, New York 1920, Novel

BLACKJACK BARGAINER, A 1918?. USA., *A Blackjack Bargainer*, O. Henry, Short Story

BLACKJACK KETCHUM, DESPERADO 1956 d: Earl Bellamy. USA., *Kilkenny*, Louis L'Amour, Novel

BLACKMAIL 1920 d: Dallas M. Fitzgerald. USA., *The Underside*, Lucia Chamberlain, 1917, Short Story

Blackmail see THE WHISPERED NAME (1924).

BLACKMAIL 1929 d: Alfred Hitchcock. UKN., *Blackmail*, Charles Bennett, London 1928, Play

BLACKMAILED 1951 d: Marc Allegret. UKN., *Mrs. Christopher*, Elizabeth Myers, Novel

Blackmailer see VYDERAC (1937).

Blackmailer, The see BLACKMAILED (1951).

Blackout see MURDER BY PROXY (1955).

BLACKROCK 1997 d: Steve Vidler. ASL., *Blackrock*, Nick Enright, Play

Blacksmith of Lesetin, The see LESETINSKY KOVAR (1924).

BLACKSMITH'S STORY, THE 1913 d: Travers Vale. USA., *The Blacksmith's Story*, Frank Olive, Poem

BLACULA 1972 d: William Crain. USA., *Dracula*, Bram Stoker, London 1897, Novel

BLADE IN HONG KONG 1985 d: Reza Badiyi. USA., *Blade in Hong Kong*, Terry Becker, Novel

Blade in the Body, The see LA LAMA NEL CORPO (1966).

BLADE RUNNER 1982 d: Ridley Scott. USA., *Do Androids Dream of Electric Sheep?*, Philip K. Dick, 1969, Novel

BLADYS OF THE STEWPONY 1919 d: L. C. MacBean. UKN., *Bladys of the Stewpony*, Sabine Baring Gould, Novel

Blago U Srebrnom Jezeru see DER SCHATZ IM SILBERSEE (1962).

BLAGORODNIE RAZBOINIK VLADIMIR DUBROVSKY 1989 d: Vyatcheslav Nikiforov. USS., *Dubrovsky*, Alexander Pushkin, 1841, Short Story

BLAGUE DANS LE COIN 1963 d: Maurice Labro. FRN., *Blague Dans le Coin*, Carter Brown, Novel

BLAHOVE DEVCE 1938 d: Vaclav Binovec. CZC., *Kroky V Mlze*, Maryna Radomerska, Novel

BLAHOVY SEN 1943 d: J. A. Holman. CZC., *Neslavna Slava*, Anna Sokolova-Podperova, Short Story

BLAJACKOR 1945 d: Rolf Husberg. SWD., *Blajackor*, Louis Lajtai, Opera

Blame It on an Angel see UN ANGEL TUVO LA CULPA (1959).

BLANC COMME NEIGE 1931 d: Francisco Elias, Camille Lemoine. FRN., *Souris Blonde*, Monjardin, Xanrof, Opera

BLANC ET LE NOIR, LE 1930 d: Robert Florey, Marc Allegret. FRN., *Le Blanc Et le Noir*, Sacha Guitry, Play

BLANCA 1955 d: Mihai Iacob, Constantin Neagu. RMN., *Fat-Frumos Din Tei*, Mihai Eminescu, 1875, Verse

BLANCA POR FUERA, ROSA POR DENTRO 1971 d: Pedro LazagA. SPN., *Blanca Por Fuera Y Rosa Por Dentro*, Enrique Jardiel Poncela, 1943, Play

BLANCHE 1971 d: Walerian Borowczyk. FRN., *Mazepa*, Juliusz Slowacki, 1840, Play

BLANCHE FURY 1948 d: Marc Allegret. UKN., *Blanche Fury*, Gabrielle Margaret Vere Long, Novel

BLANCHETTE 1912 d: Henri Pouctal. FRN., *Blanchette*, Eugene Brieux, 1892, Play

BLANCHETTE 1921 d: Rene Hervil. FRN., *Blanchette*, Eugene Brieux, 1892, Play

BLANCHETTE 1936 d: Pierre Caron. FRN., *Blanchette*, Eugene Brieux, 1892, Play

Blank Wall, The see THE RECKLESS MOMENT (1949).

BLARNEY 1926 d: Marcel de Sano. USA., *In Praise of John Carabine*, Brian Oswald Donn-Byrne, 1925, Short Story

Blast Off! see JULES VERNE'S ROCKET TO THE MOON (1967).

Blaubart see BARBE-BLEUE (1951).

BLAUBART 1984 d: Krzysztof Zanussi. GRM/SWT., *Blaubart*, Max Frisch, 1982, Novel

BLAUE ENGEL, DER 1930 d: Josef von Sternberg. GRM., *Professor Unrat*, Heinrich Mann, 1905, Novel

BLAUE HAND, DIE 1967 d: Alfred Vohrer. GRM., *The Blue Hand*, Edgar Wallace, London 1925, Novel

BLAUE STERN DES SUDENS, DER 1951 d: Wolfgang Liebeneiner. AUS., *Duell Mit Diamanten*, Heinrich Rumpff, Novel

BLAUE STROHHUT, DER 1949 d: Victor Tourjansky. GRM., *Der Blaue Strohhut*, Friedrich Michael, Play

BLAUFUCHS, DER 1938 d: Victor Tourjansky. GRM., *A Kek Roka*, Ferenc Herczeg, 1917, Play

BLAUMILCHKANAL, DER 1969 d: Ephraim Kishon. GRM/ISR., *Der Blaumilchkanal*, Ephraim Kishon, Novel

BLAZE 1989 d: Ron Shelton. USA., *Blaze Starr: My Life As Told to Huey Perry*, Huey Perry, Blaze Starr, Book

BLAZE O' GLORY 1929 d: Renaud Hoffman, George J. Crone. USA., *The Long Shot*, Thomas Alexander Boyd, New York 1925, Short Story

BLAZE OF NOON 1947 d: John Farrow. USA., *Blaze of Noon*, Ernest K. Gann, Novel

Blazing Arrows see FIGHTING CARAVANS (1930).

Blazing Barriers see OR BLAZING BARRIERS JACQUELINE (1923).

Blazing Continent see MOERU TAIRIKU (1968).

BLAZING GUNS 1935 d: Ray Heinz. USA., *Blazing Guns*, Forbes Parkhill, 1934, Short Story

Blazing Sun see PLEIN SOLEIL (1960).

Blazing Winter see RASCOALA (1965).

BLE EN HERBE, LE 1953 d: Claude Autant-LarA. FRN., *Le Ble En Herbe*, Sidonie Gabrielle Colette, 1923, Novel

BLEAK HOUSE 1920 d: Maurice Elvey. UKN., *Bleak House*, Charles Dickens, London 1853, Novel

BLEAK HOUSE 1922 d: H. B. Parkinson. UKN., *Bleak House*, Charles Dickens, London 1853, Novel

BLEAK HOUSE 1985 d: Ross Devenish. UKN., *Bleak House*, Charles Dickens, London 1853, Novel

Bleak Morning see KHUROYE UTRO (1959).

BLECHTROMMEL, DIE 1979 d: Volker Schlondorff. GRM/FRN., *Die Blechtrommel*, Gunter Grass, 1959, Novel

BLEEKE BET 1923 d: Alex Benno. NTH., *Bleeke Bet*, Herman Bouber, 1917, Play

BLEEKE BET 1934 d: Alex Benno, Richard Oswald. NTH., *Bleeke Bet*, Herman Bouber, 1917, Play

BLESS THE BEASTS AND CHILDREN 1972 d: Stanley Kramer. USA., *Bless the Beasts and Children*, Glendon Swarthout, Novel

Bless the Children see **WEI HAI ZI MEN ZHU FU** (1953).

Bless Their Hearts see **AND SO THEY WERE MARRIED** (1936).

BLESSED EVENT 1932 d: Roy Del Ruth. USA., *Blessed Event*, Manuel Seff, Forrest Wilson, New York 1932, Play

Blessed Events see **LORSQUE L'ENFANT PARAIT** (1956).

BLESSURE, LA 1922 d: Roberto Leone Roberti. ITL., *La Blessure*, Henri Kistemaeckers, 1900, Play

BLEUS DE L'AMOUR, LES 1917 d: Henri Desfontaines. FRN., *Les Bleus de l'Amour*, Romain Coolus, Play

BLEUS DE L'AMOUR, LES 1932 d: Jean de Marguenat. FRN., *Les Bleus de l'Amour*, Romain Coolus, Play

Blind see **TOEN 'T LICHT VERDWEEN** (1918).

BLIND ADVENTURE, THE 1918 d: Wesley Ruggles. USA., *The Agony Column*, Earl Derr Biggers, Indianapolis 1916, Novel

BLIND ALLEY 1939 d: Charles Vidor. USA., *Blind Alley*, James Warwick, New York 1935, Play

BLIND ALLEY 1949 d: Paul Nickell. USA., *Blind Alley*, James Warwick, New York 1935, Play

BLIND ALLEY 1952. USA., *Blind Alley*, James Warwick, New York 1935, Play

BLIND ALLEY 1954. USA., *Blind Alley*, James Warwick, New York 1935, Play

Blind Alley see **ANDHI GALI** (1984).

BLIND AMBITION 1979 d: George Schaefer. USA., *Blind Ambition*, Jean Dean, Book, *Mo*, Maureen Dean, Book

BLIND BARGAIN, A 1922 d: Wallace Worsley. USA., *The Octave of Claudius*, Barry Pain, London 1897, Novel

Blind Beast, The see **MOJU** (1969).

BLIND BOY, THE 1917 d: Edwin J. Collins, Jack Clare. UKN., *The Blind Boy*, George H. Chirgwin, Play

Blind Cargo see **HIS WOMAN** (1931).

BLIND CHESS 1988 d: Jerry Jameson. USA., *Blind Chess*, Joe Gores, Novel

BLIND DATE 1934 d: R. William Neill. USA., *Blind Date*, Vida Hurst, New York 1931, Novel

BLIND DATE 1959 d: Joseph Losey. UKN., *Blind Date*, Leigh Howard, Novel

BLIND FURY 1989 d: Phil Noyce. USA., Ryozo Kasahara, Story

BLIND GIRL OF CASTLE GUILLE, THE 1913. USA., *The Blind Girl of Castle Guille*, Henry Wadsworth Longfellow, Poem

BLIND GODDESS, THE 1926 d: Victor Fleming. USA., *The Blind Goddess*, Arthur Cheney Train, New York 1926, Novel

BLIND GODDESS, THE 1948 d: Harold French. UKN., *The Blind Goddess*, Patrick Hastings, London 1947, Play

BLIND HEARTS 1921 d: Rowland V. Lee. USA., *Blind Hearts*, Emilie Johnson, Story

BLIND HUSBANDS 1918 d: Erich von Stroheim. USA., *The Pinnacle*, Erich von Stroheim, Book

Blind Justice see **THE LAST HOUR** (1923).

BLIND JUSTICE 1934 d: Bernard Vorhaus. UKN., *Recipe for Murder*, Arnold Ridley, London 1932, Play

BLIND LOVE 1920 d: Oliver D. Bailey. USA., *The Substitute Prisoner*, Max Marcin, New York 1911, Play

BLIND MAN, THE 1967 d: Claude Whatham. UKN., *The Blind Man*, D. H. Lawrence, Short Story

BLIND MAN'S BLUFF 1936 d: Albert Parker. UKN., *Smoked Glasses*, William Foster, B. Scott-Elder, Play

Blind Man's Bluff see **GOLEM BEMA'AGAL** (1993).

BLIND MAN'S EYES 1919 d: John Ince. USA., *The Blind Man's Eyes*, Edwin Balmer, William Briggs MacHarg, Boston 1916, Novel

Blind Man's Guide to Tormes, The see **EL LAZARILLO DE TORMES** (1959).

BLIND MAN'S HOLIDAY 1917 d: Martin Justice. USA., *Blind Man's Holiday*, O. Henry, 1905, Short Story

Blind Retribution, A see **SOGNO DI UN TRAMONTO D'AUTUNNO** (1911).

Blind Spot see **WHISPERING DEATH** (1975).

Blind Swordsman see **ZATO ICHI MONOGATARI** (1962).

BLIND WIVES 1920 d: Charles J. Brabin. USA., *My Lady's Dress*, Edward Knoblock, London 1914, Play

Blind Wives see **A LADY SURRENDERS** (1930).

Blind Wives see **FREE LOVE** (1931).

BLIND YOUTH 1920 d: Edward Sloman, Alfred E. Green. USA., *Blind Youth*, Willard Mack, Lou Tellegen, New York 1917, Play

BLINDFOLD 1966 d: Philip Dunne. USA., *Blindfold*, Lucille Fletcher, New York 1960, Novel

Blindfold see **BEKOTOTT SZEMMEL** (1974).

Blindman's Bluff see **GOLEM BEMA'AGAL** (1993).

Blindman's Guide to Tormes, The see **EL LAZARILLO DE TORMES** (1925).

Blindness see **EYES OF THE HEART** (1920).

BLINDNESS OF VIRTUE, THE 1915 d: Joseph Byron Totten. USA., *The Blindness of Virtue*, Cosmo Hamilton, London 1908, Novel

BLINKEYES 1926 d: George Pearson. UKN., *Blinkeyes*, Oliver Sandys, Novel

BLINKY 1923 d: Edward Sedgwick. USA., *Blinky*, Gene Markey, 1923, Short Story

BLINKY BILL 1992 d: Yoram Gross. ASL., *The Complete Adventures of Blinky Bill*, Dorothy Wall, Book

BLISS 1985 d: Ray Lawrence. ASL., *Bliss*, Peter Carey, Novel

BLISS OF MRS. BLOSSOM, THE 1968 d: Joseph McGrath. UKN., *A Bird in the Nest*, Alec Coppel, Play

Blissful Misfit, The see **O GRANDE MENTECAPTO** (1989).

BLITHE SPIRIT 1945 d: David Lean. UKN., *Blithe Spirit*, Noel Coward, London 1941, Play

BLIXT OCH DUNDER 1938 d: Anders Henrikson. SWD., *Summer Lightning*, P. G. Wodehouse, 1929, Novel

BLIZNA 1976 d: Krzysztof Kieslowski. PLN., *Blizna*, Romuald Karas, Short Story

Blizzard, The see **METELJ** (1964).

Blod Pa Vara Hander see **VERTA KASISSMAAME** (1958).

Bloedgeld see **BLOOD MONEY** (1921).

Bloedhond Van Het Geheimzinnige Sanatorium, de see **BULLDOG DRUMMOND** (1923).

Blonde Baby see **THREE WISE GIRLS** (1932).

Blonde Bombshell see **BOMBSHELL** (1933).

Blonde Comme Ca!, Une see **MISS SHUMWAY JETTE UN SORT** (1962).

Blonde Countess see **RENDEZVOUS** (1935).

BLONDE DE PEKIN, LA 1968 d: Nicolas Gessner. FRN/ITL/GRM., *You Have Yourself a Deal*, James Hadley Chase, London 1966, Novel

Blonde Dynamite see **SOME BLONDES ARE DANGEROUS** (1937).

BLONDE FEVER 1944 d: Richard Whorf. USA., *Delila*, Ferenc Molnar, 1937, Play

BLONDE FOR A DAY 1946 d: Sam Newfield. USA., *Detective Michael Shayne*, Brett Halliday, Novel

Blonde from Peking, The see **LA BLONDE DE PEKIN** (1968).

Blonde Hexe, Die see **HAXAN** (1955).

BLONDE ICE 1948 d: Jack Bernhard. USA., *Once Too Often*, Elwyn Whitman Chambers, Novel

Blonde in a White Car see **TOI LE VENIN** (1958).

BLONDE INSPIRATION 1940 d: Busby Berkeley. USA., *Four Cents a Word*, John Cecil Holm, Play

BLONDE OR BRUNETTE 1927 d: Richard Rosson. USA., *Un Ange Passe*, Jacques Bousquet, Henri Falk, 1924, Short Story

Blonde Reporter, The see **SOB SISTER** (1931).

BLONDE SAINT, THE 1926 d: Svend Gade. USA., *Isle of Life; a Romance*, Stephen French Whitman, New York 1913, Novel

Blonde Sinner see **YIELD TO THE NIGHT** (1956).

BLONDE TROUBLE 1937 d: George Archainbaud. USA., *June Moon*, George S. Kaufman, Ring Lardner, New York 1929, Play

Blonde von Peking, Die see **LA BLONDE DE PEKIN** (1968).

Blonde Witch see **HAXAN** (1955).

BLONDES FOR DANGER 1938 d: Jack Raymond. UKN., *Red for Danger*, Evadne Price, Novel

Blood see **ORENO CHI WA TANIN NO CHI** (1974).

BLOOD ALLEY 1955 d: William A. Wellman. USA., *Blood Alley*, Albert Sidney Fleischman, Novel

Blood and Roses see **ET MOURIR DE PLAISIR** (1960).

BLOOD AND SAND 1922 d: Fred Niblo. USA., *Sangre Y Arena*, Vicente Blasco Ibanez, Buenos Aires 1908, Novel

BLOOD AND SAND 1941 d: Rouben Mamoulian. USA., *Sangre Y Arena*, Vicente Blasco Ibanez, Buenos Aires 1908, Novel

Blood Beast from Outer Space see **THE NIGHT CALLER** (1966).

Blood Brothers see **BROTHERS** (1930).

Blood Brothers see **BLOODBROTHERS** (1978).

Blood Creature see **TERROR IS A MAN** (1959).

Blood Demon, The see **DIE SCHLANGENGRUBE UND DAS PENDEL** (1967).

BLOOD FROM THE MUMMY'S TOMB 1972 d: Seth Holt, Michael Carreras. UKN., *The Jewel of the Seven Stars*, Bram Stoker, 1903, Novel

Blood Honeymoon see **ORS AL-DAM** (1977).

BLOOD HUNT 1985 d: Peter Barber-Fleming. UKN., Neil Gunn, Novel

Blood Kin see **THE LAST OF THE MOBILE HOT-SHOTS** (1970).

BLOOD MONEY 1921 d: Fred Goodwins. UKN/NTH., *Blood Money*, Cecil H. Bullivant, Novel

Blood Money see **REQUIEM FOR A HEAVYWEIGHT** (1962).

Blood of Others, The see **LE SANG DES AUTRES** (1983).

Blood of the Leopard see **YINGXIONG BENSE** (1993).

Blood of the Walsungs see **WALSUNGENBLUT** (1964).

Blood on His Sword see **LE MIRACLE DES LOUPS** (1961).

Blood on My Hands see **KISS THE BLOOD OFF MY HANDS** (1948).

Blood on My Hands see **UN CONDE** (1970).

Blood on Our Hands see **VERTA KASISSMAAME** (1958).

BLOOD ON THE MOON 1948 d: Robert Wise. USA., *Gunman's Choice*, Luke Short, Novel

Blood on the Moon see **COP** (1987).

BLOOD ORANGES, THE 1997 d: Philip Haas. USA., *The Blood Oranges*, John Hawkes, Novel

Blood Relatives see **LES LIENS DE SANG** (1978).

BLOOD RIGHTS 1990 d: Lesley Manning. UKN., *Blood Rights*, Mike Phillips, Novel

BLOOD SHIP, THE 1927 d: George B. Seitz. USA., *The Blood Ship*, Norman Springer, New York 1922, Novel

Blood Splattered Bride, The see **LA NOVIA ENSANGRENTADA** (1972).

Blood Vengeance see **LA FIACCOLA SOTTO IL MOGGIO** (1911).

Blood Wedding see **ORS AL-DAM** (1977).

Blood Wedding see **BODAS DE SANGRE** (1980).

Bloodbath see **MARTA** (1971).

BLOODBROTHERS 1978 d: Robert Mulligan. USA., *Bloodbrothers*, Richard Price, Novel

BLOODHOUNDS OF BROADWAY 1952 d: Harmon Jones. USA., *Bloodhounds of Broadway*, Damon Runyon, 1931, Short Story

BLOODHOUNDS OF BROADWAY 1989 d: Howard Brookner. USA., Damon Runyon, Story

Bloodline see **SIDNEY SHELDON'S BLOODLINE** (1979).

BLOODLUST 1961 d: Ralph Brooke. USA., *The Most Dangerous Game*, Richard Connell, 1930, Short Story

Blood-Spattered Bride, The see **LA NOVIA ENSANGRENTADA** (1972).

Bloodstained Screen, The see **XUE JIAN HUA PING** (1986).

BLOODSTREAM 1993 d: Stephen Tolkin. USA., *Beirut*, Alan Bowne, Play

Bloodsucker see **INCENSE FOR THE DAMNED** (1970).

Bloodsuckers see **INCENSE FOR THE DAMNED** (1970).

Bloody Battle at Kunlun Pass see **TIE XUE KUN LUN GUAN** (1994).

Bloody Bride, The see **LA NOVIA ENSANGRENTADA** (1972).

BLOODY BROOD, THE 1959 d: Julian Roffman. CND., *The Bloody Brood*, Anne Howard Bailey, Story

Bloody Che Contra *see* EL CHE GUEVARA (1968).

Bloody Fiancee *see* LA NOVIA ENSANGRENTADA (1972).

Bloody Moon *see* LUNA DE SANGRE (1950).

Bloody Morning, The *see* XUESE QINGCHEN (1991).

Bloody Scream of Dracula, The *see* DRACULA - PRINCE OF DARKNESS (1965).

BLOOMING ANGEL, THE 1920 d: Victor Schertzinger. USA., *Blooming Angel*, Wallace Irwin, New York 1919, Novel

Blooming Flowers and a Full Moon *see* HUA HAO YUE YUAN (1958).

BLORE MP 1989 d: Robert Young. UKN., *Blore MP*, A. N. Wilson, Novel

Blossoms, Crooks and a Night in Nice *see* LE JARDINIER D'ARGENTEUIL (1966).

BLOT IN THE 'SCUTCHEON, A 1912 d: D. W. Griffith. USA., *A Blot in the 'Scutcheon*, Robert Browning, Poem

BLOTT ON THE LANDSCAPE 1989 d: Roger Bamford. UKN., *Blott on the Landscape*, Tom Sharpe, Novel

BLOW YOUR OWN HORN 1923 d: James W. Horne. USA., *Blow Your Own Horn*, Owen Davis, Play

Blown Away *see* NECESSITY (1988).

BLOW-UP 1966 d: Michelangelo Antonioni. UKN/ITL., *Final Del Juego*, Julio Cortazar, 1964, Short Story

BLUDGEON, THE 1915 d: Webster Cullison. USA., *The Bludgeon*, Paul Armstrong, New York 1914, Novel

Bludicka *see* TY PETRINSKE STRANE (1922).

BLUDNE DUSE 1926 d: Jan W. Speerger. CZC., *Bludne Duse*, Vaclav Benes-Trebizsky, Novel

Blue and White Lion, The *see* DER WEISSBLAUE LOWE (1952).

Blue Angel, The *see* DER BLAUE ENGEL (1930).

BLUE ANGEL, THE 1959 d: Edward Dmytryk. USA., *Professor Unrat*, Heinrich Mann, 1905, Novel

Blue Arrow, The *see* LA FRECCIA AZZURRA (1996).

BLUE BIRD, THE 1910. UKN., *L' Oiseau Bleu*, Maurice Maeterlinck, Moscow 1908, Play

Blue Bird, The *see* THE BLUEBIRD (1918).

BLUE BIRD, THE 1940 d: Walter Lang. USA., *L' Oiseau Bleu*, Maurice Maeterlinck, Moscow 1908, Play

Blue Bird, The *see* SINYAYA PTITSA (1975).

BLUE BLOOD 1925 d: Scott R. Dunlap. USA., *American Aristocracy*, Frank Howard Clark, Story

BLUE BLOOD 1951 d: Lew Landers. USA., *Dog Meat*, Peter B. Kyne, Story

BLUE BLOOD 1973 d: Andrew Sinclair. UKN/CND., *The Carry-Cot*, Alexander Thynne, Novel

BLUE CARBUNCLE, THE 1923 d: George Ridgwell. UKN., *The Blue Carbuncle*, Arthur Conan Doyle, Short Story

Blue Carbuncle, The *see* THE ADVENTURES OF SHERLOCK HOLMES: THE BLUE CARBUNCLE (1984).

BLUE CITY 1986 d: Michelle Manning. USA., *Blue City*, Ross MacDonald, Novel

BLUE DAHLIA, THE 1946 d: George Marshall. USA., Raymond Chandler, Story

Blue Days and Green Days *see* THE END OF THE RIVER (1947).

BLUE DENIM 1959 d: Philip Dunne. USA., *Blue Denim*, James Leo Herlihy, William Noble, New York 1958, Play

BLUE EAGLE, THE 1926 d: John Ford. USA., *The Lord's Referee*, Gerald Beaumont, 1923, Short Story

BLUE ENVELOPE MYSTERY, THE 1916 d: Wilfred North. USA., *The Blue Envelope*, Sophie Kerr, Garden City, N.Y. 1917, Novel

BLUE FIN 1978 d: Carl Schultz. ASL., *Blue Fin*, Colin Thiele, 1969, Novel

Blue Fox *see* DER BLAUFUCHS (1938).

BLUE GARDENIA, THE 1953 d: Fritz Lang. USA., *Gardenia*, Vera Caspary, Story

Blue Gates of the City, The *see* PORTILE ALBASTRE ALE ORASULUI (1973).

BLUE GRASS 1915 d: Charles M. Seay. USA., *Blue Grass*, Paul Armstrong, New York 1908, Play

Blue Hand, The *see* DIE BLAUE HAND (1967).

BLUE HOTEL, THE 1977 d: Jan Kadar. USA., *The Blue Hotel*, Stephen Crane, 1899, Short Story

BLUE ICE 1992 d: Russell Mulcahy. USA., Ted Allbeury, Novel

BLUE JEANS 1917 d: John H. Collins. USA., *Blue Jeans*, Joseph Arthur, New York 1890, Play

Blue Jeans *see* BLUE DENIM (1959).

BLUE KNIGHT, THE 1973 d: Robert Butler. USA., *The Blue Knight*, Joseph Wambaugh, 1972, Novel

BLUE KNIGHT, THE 1975 d: J. Lee Thompson. USA., *The Blue Knight*, Joseph Wambaugh, 1972, Novel

BLUE LAGOON, THE 1949 d: Frank Launder. UKN., *The Garden of God*, Henry de Vere Stacpoole, Novel

BLUE LAGOON, THE 1980 d: Randall Kleiser. USA., *The Garden of God*, Henry de Vere Stacpoole, Novel

BLUE MAX, THE 1966 d: John Guillermin. UKN/USA., *The Blue Max*, Jack D. Hunter, New York 1964, Novel

BLUE MOCCASINS, THE 1967 d: Desmond Davis. UKN., *The Blue Moccasins*, D. H. Lawrence, Short Story

BLUE MOON, THE 1920 d: George L. Cox. USA., *A Tale of the Flatwoods Blue Moon*, David Wolf Anderson, Indianapolis 1919, Novel

Blue Mountain Mystery, The *see* THE BLUE MOUNTAINS MYSTERY (1922).

BLUE MOUNTAINS MYSTERY, THE 1922 d: Raymond Longford, Lottie Lyell. ASL., *The Mount Marunga Mystery*, Harrison Owen, Story

BLUE PARROT, THE 1953 d: John Harlow. UKN., *Gunman*, Percy Hoskins, Short Story

BLUE PEARL, THE 1920 d: George Irving. USA., *The Blue Pearl*, Anne Crawford Flexner, New York 1918, Play

BLUE PETER, THE 1928 d: Arthur Rooke. UKN., *The Blue Peter*, E. Temple Thurston, Novel

Blue Revolution, The *see* AOIRO KAKUMEI (1953).

BLUE SKIES 1929 d: Alfred L. Werker. USA., *The Matron's Report*, Frederick Hazlitt Brennan, 1928, Short Story

Blue Straw Hat, The *see* DER BLAUE STROHHUT (1949).

BLUE VEIL, THE 1951 d: Curtis Bernhardt. USA., Francois Campaux, Story

BLUE WATER 1924 d: David M. Hartford. CND., *Blue Water*, Frederick William Wallace, Novel

Blue Week *see* SININEN VIIKKO (1954).

BLUE, WHITE AND PERFECT 1941 d: Herbert I. Leeds. USA., *Blue White and Perfect*, Borden Chase, Novel

BLUEBEARD 1909 d: J. Searle Dawley. USA., *Barbe-Bleue*, Charles Perrault, 1697, Story

Bluebeard *see* BARBE-BLEUE (1951).

Bluebeard *see* BLAUBART (1984).

BLUEBEARD'S EIGHTH WIFE 1922 d: Sam Wood. USA., *La Huitieme Femme de Barbe-Bleue*, Alfred Savoir, 1921, Play

BLUEBEARD'S EIGHTH WIFE 1938 d: Ernst Lubitsch. USA., *La Huitieme Femme de Barbe-Bleue*, Alfred Savoir, 1921, Play

BLUEBIRD, THE 1918 d: Maurice Tourneur. USA., *L' Oiseau Bleu*, Maurice Maeterlinck, Moscow 1908, Play

BLUEBOTTLES 1928 d: Ivor Montagu. UKN., *Bluebottles*, H. G. Wells, Short Story

Blue-Jackets *see* BLAJACKOR (1945).

BLUES IN THE NIGHT 1941 d: Anatole Litvak. USA., *Hot Nocturne*, Edwin Gilbert, Play

BLUFF 1921 d: Geoffrey H. Malins. UKN., *Bluff*, Rafael Sabatini, Novel

BLUFFEUR, LE 1932 d: Andre Luguet, Henry Blanke. USA., *Hot Money*, Aben Kandel, New York 1931, Play

BLUME VON HAWAII, DIE 1933 d: Richard Oswald. GRM., *Die Blume von Hawaii*, Paul Abraham, Opera

BLUME VON HAWAII, DIE 1953 d: Geza von CziffrA. GRM., *Die Blume von Hawaii*, Paul Abraham, Opera

BLUMENFRAU VON LINDENAU, DIE 1931 d: Georg Jacoby. GRM/AUS., *Sturm Im Wasserglas*, Bruno Frank, 1930, Play

Blush *see* HONGFEN (1994).

Bluten, Gauner Und Die Nacht von Nizza *see* LE JARDINIER D'ARGENTEUIL (1966).

Blutiger Schnee (Zu Freiwild Verdammt) *see* RUTH (1983).

BOARDED WINDOW 1973 d: Alan Beattie. USA., *Boarded Window*, Ambrose Bierce, 1891, Short Story

Boarding House for Bachelors *see* PENSION PRO SVOBODNE PANY (1967).

Boarding House for Gentlemen *see* PENSION PRO SVOBODNE PANY (1967).

Boarding House for Single Gentlemen *see* PENSION PRO SVOBODNE PANY (1967).

Boarding School *see* LEIDENSCHAFTLICHE BLUMCHEN (1978).

Boastful Tailor, The *see* SEDEM JEDNOU RANOU (1988).

Boat from Shanghai *see* CHIN CHIN CHINAMAN (1931).

Boat, The *see* DAS BOOT (1981).

Boat Without a Fisherman, A *see* LA BARCA SIN PESCADOR (1964).

Boat Without the Fisherman, The *see* LA BARCA SIN PESCADOR (1964).

Boatman of River Padma *see* PADMA NADIR MANJHI (1992).

Boatman of the River Padma *see* PADMA NADIR MANJHI (1992).

Boatman on the Danube *see* A DUNAI HAJOS (1974).

BOATNIKS, THE 1970 d: Norman Tokar. USA., Marty Roth, Story

BOATSWAIN'S MATE, THE 1924 d: Manning Haynes. UKN., *The Bosun's Mate*, W. W. Jacobs, Short Story

Boatswain's Story, A *see* SHUI SHOU ZHANG DE GU SHI (1963).

BOB HAMPTON OF PLACER 1921 d: Marshall Neilan. USA., *Bob Hampton of Placer*, Randall Parrish, Chicago 1910, Novel

Bob, Son of Battle *see* THUNDER IN THE VALLEY (1947).

Bobby Burnit *see* THE MAKING OF BOBBY BURNIT (1914).

BOBBY DEERFIELD 1977 d: Sydney Pollack. USA., *Der Himmel Kennt Keine Gunstlinge*, Erich Maria Remarque, 1961, Novel

BOBO DO REI, O 1936 d: MesquitinhA. BRZ., *O Bobo Do Rei*, Joracy Camargo, 1932, Play

BOBO, O 1987 d: Jose Alvaro Morais. PRT., *O Bobo*, Alexandre Herculano, 1884, Novel

BOBO, THE 1967 d: Robert Parrish. UKN., *Olimpia*, Bert Cole, Play, *The Bobo*, David R. Schwartz, Novel

BOBOSSE 1958 d: Etienne Perier. FRN., *Bobosse*, Andre Roussin, 1951, Play

BOCA DE OURO, O 1962 d: Nelson Pereira Dos Santos. BRZ., *Boca de Ouro*, Nelson Rodrigues, 1959-60, Play

BOCCACCIO 1940 d: Marcello Albani. ITL., *Boccaccio*, Franz von Suppe, F. Zell, Opera

BOCCACCIO '70 1962 d: Federico Fellini, Luchino Visconti. ITL/FRN., *Il Decameron*, Giovanni Boccaccio, 1349-50, Book

Boccace 70 *see* BOCCACCIO '70 (1962).

BOCHORNO 1962 d: Juan de OrdunA. SPN., *Bochorno*, Angel Maria de Lera, 1960, Short Story

BOCK I ORTAGARD 1958 d: Gosta Folke. SWD., *Bock I Ortagard*, Fritiof Nilsson Piraten, 1933, Novel

BOCKERER, DER 1981 d: Franz Antel. AUS/GRM., *Der Bockerer*, Ulrich Becher, Peter Preses, Play

BOCKSHORN 1983 d: Frank Beyer. GDR., *Bockshorn*, Christoph Meckel, 1973, Novel

BODA, LA 1963 d: Lucas Demare. ARG/SPN., *La Boda*, Angel Maria de Lera, 1959, Novel

BODAS DE SANGRE 1938 d: Edmundo Guibourg. ARG., *Bodas de Sangre*, Federico Garcia Lorca, 1936, Play

BODAS DE SANGRE 1980 d: Carlos SaurA. SPN/FRN., *Bodas de Sangre*, Federico Garcia Lorca, 1936, Play

BODEGA, LA 1930 d: Benito Perojo. SPN/FRN., *La Bodega*, Vicente Blasco Ibanez, Novel

BODEN'S BOY 1923 d: Henry Edwards. UKN., *Boden's Boy*, Tom Gallon, Novel

Bodensee *see* JEZIORO BODENSKIE (1985).

BODY AND SOUL 1915 d: George Irving. USA., *Body and Soul*, William Hurlbut, Play

BODY AND SOUL 1927 d: Reginald Barker. USA., *Body and Soul*, Katharine Newlin Burt, 1919, Short Story

BODY AND SOUL 1931 d: Alfred Santell. USA., *Big Eyes and Little Mouth*, Elliott White Springs, 1927, Short Story

Body and Soul *see* PRIDE OF THE MARINES (1945).

Body in the Library, The *see* MISS MARPLE: THE BODY IN THE LIBRARY (1985).

Body of Diana, The *see* TELO DIANA (1969).

Body Scent *see* ZADAH TELA (1983).

Body Smell *see* ZADAH TELA (1983).

BODY SNATCHER, THE 1945 d: Robert Wise. USA., *The Body Snatcher*, Robert Louis Stevenson, 1894, Short Story

BODY SNATCHERS 1993 d: Abel FerrarA. USA., *The Body Snatchers*, Jack Finney, 1954, Novel

Body, The see RATAI (1962).

Body, The see STAND BY ME (1986).

Body, The see O CORPO (1989).

BOEING BOEING 1965 d: John Rich. USA., *Boeing-Boeing*, Marc Camoletti, 1960, Play

BOESMAN AND LENA 1973 d: Ross Devenish. SAF., *Boesman and Lena*, Athol Fugard, 1969, Play

BOFORS GUN, THE 1968 d: Jack Gold. UKN., *Events While Guarding the Bofors Gun*, John McGrath, 1966, Play

Bog of Prague, The see BAHNO PRAHY (1927).

BOGDAN KHMELNITSKY 1941 d: Igor Savchenko. USS., *Bogdan Khmelnytsky*, Aleksander Korniychuk, 1939, Play

BOGIE 1980 d: Vincent Sherman. USA., *Bogie*, Joe Hyams, Biography

Bogie: the Last Hero see BOGIE (1980).

BOGNOR: DEADLINE 1981 d: Carol Wiseman. UKN., *Deadline*, Tim Heald, Novel

BOGNOR: LET SLEEPING DOGS LIE 1981 d: Neville Green. UKN., *Let Sleeping Dogs Lie*, Tim Heald, Novel

BOGNOR: UNBECOMING HABITS 1981 d: Robert Tronson. UKN., *Unbecoming Habits*, Tim Heald, Novel

Bogumil I Barbara see NOCE I DNIE (1975).

Bogus Bandits see THE DEVIL'S BROTHER (1933).

Bohdan Khmelnytsky see BOGDAN KHMELNITSKY (1941).

BOHEME, LA 1911. ITL., *La Vie de Boheme*, Henri Murger, Paris 1848, Play

Boheme, La see LA VIE DE BOHEME (1916).

BOHEME, LA 1917 d: Amleto Palermi. ITL., *La Vie de Boheme*, Henri Murger, Paris 1848, Play

BOHEME, LA 1926 d: King Vidor. USA., *La Vie de Boheme*, Henri Murger, Paris 1848, Play

Boheme, La see MIMI (1935).

Boheme, La see LA VIE DE BOHEME (1942).

Boheme, La see ADDIO MIMI! (1947).

BOHEME, LA 1965 d: Franco Zeffirelli. SWT/ITL., *La Boheme*, Giuseppe Giacosa, Luigi Illica, Giacomo Puccini, Turin 1896, Opera

BOHEME, LA 1987 d: Luigi Comencini. ITL/FRN., *La Vie de Boheme*, Henri Murger, Paris 1848, Play

BOHEMIAN GIRL, THE 1922 d: Harley Knoles. UKN., *The Bohemian Girl*, Michael William Balfe, Alfred Bunn, London 1843, Opera

BOHEMIAN GIRL, THE 1927 d: H. B. Parkinson. UKN., *The Bohemian Girl*, Michael William Balfe, Alfred Bunn, London 1843, Opera

BOHEMIAN GIRL, THE 1936 d: James W. Horne, Charles Rogers. USA., *The Bohemian Girl*, Michael William Balfe, Alfred Bunn, London 1843, Opera

Bohemian Love see LA FEMME NUE (1926).

Bohemians, The see LA VIE DE BOHEME (1916).

BOIA DI LILLA, IL 1953 d: Vittorio Cottafavi. ITL/FRN., *Les Trois Mousquetaires*, Alexandre Dumas (pere), Paris 1844, Novel

BOILING POINT 1993 d: James B. Harris. USA., *Money Men*, Gerald Petievich, Novel

BOIS DES AMANTS, LE 1960 d: Claude Autant-LarA. FRN/ITL., *Terre Inhumaine*, Francois de Curel, Paris 1923, Play

BOIS SACRE, LE 1939 d: Leon Mathot, Robert Bibal. FRN., *Le Bois Sacre*, Gaston Arman de Caillavet, Robert de Flers, Play

BOISSIERE 1937 d: Fernand Rivers. FRN., *Boissiere*, Pierre Benoit, Novel

BOKHANDLAREN SOM SLUTADE BARA 1969 d: Jarl Kulle. SWD., *Bockhandlaren Som Slutade Bada*, Fritiof Nilsson Piraten, 1937, Novel

BOKUTO KIDAN 1960 d: Shiro ToyodA. JPN., *Bokuto Kidan*, Kafu Nagai, Tokyo 1952, Novel

Bold Adventure, The see LES AVENTURES DE TILL L'ESPIEGLE (1956).

BOLERO 1941 d: Jean Boyer. FRN., *Bolero*, Michel Duran, Play

BOLIBAR 1928 d: Walter Summers. UKN., *The Marquise of Bolibar*, Leo Perutz, Novel

BOLOND APRILIS 1957 d: Zoltan Fabri. HNG., *Szerelem Ifusag*, Ferenc Karinthy, 1957, Short Story

Bolsaja Zizn see BOLSHAYA ZHIZN (I SERIYA) (1940).

BOLSHAYA ZHIZN (I SERIYA) 1940 d: Leonid Lukov. USS., *Chelovek Idyot V Goru*, Pavel Nilin, 1936, Novel

BOLSHAYA ZHIZN (II SERIYA) 1946 d: Leonid Lukov. USS., *Chelovek Idyot V Goru*, Pavel Nilin, 1936, Novel

BOLSHEVISM ON TRIAL 1919 d: Harley Knoles. USA., *Comrades*, Thomas Dixon, New York 1909, Novel

BOLTED DOOR, THE 1923 d: William Worthington. USA., *The Bolted Door*, George Gibbs, New York 1910, Novel

BOLWIESER 1977 d: R. W. Fassbinder. GRM., *Bolwieser*, Oskar Maria Graf, 1931, Novel

BOMBA THE JUNGLE BOY 1949 d: Ford Beebe. USA., *Bomba the Jungle Boy*, Roy Rockwood, Novel

BOMBAY MAIL 1934 d: Edwin L. Marin. USA., *Bombay Mail*, Lawrence G. Blochman, Boston 1934, Novel

Bombe Sur Monte Carlo, Un see LE CAPITAINE CRADDOCK (1931).

BOMBEN AUF MONTE CARLO 1931 d: Hanns Schwarz. GRM., *Bomben Auf Monte Carlo*, Reck-Malleczewen, Novel

Bombi Bitt and I see BOMBI BITT OCH JAG (1936).

BOMBI BITT OCH JAG 1936 d: Gosta Rodin. SWD., *Bombi Bitt Och Jag*, Fritiof Nilsson Piraten, 1932, Novel

BOMBSHELL 1933 d: Victor Fleming. USA., *Bombshell*, MacK Crane, Caroline Francke, Play

Bombsight Stolen see COTTAGE TO LET (1941).

BON DIEU SANS CONFESSION, LE 1953 d: Claude Autant-LarA. FRN., *Le Bon Dieu Sans Confession*, Roman Vialar, Novel

BON JUGE, LE 1913 d: Georges MoncA. FRN., *Le Bon Juge*, Alexandre Bisson, Play

BON PETIT DIABLE, UN 1924 d: Rene Leprince. FRN., *Un Bon Petit Diable*, la Comtesse de Segur, Novel

BON VOYAGE! 1962 d: James Neilson. USA., *Bon Voyage*, Joseph Hayes, Marijane Hayes, New York 1957, Novel

Bonaventure see THUNDER ON THE HILL (1951).

BONCHI 1960 d: Kon IchikawA. JPN., *Bonchi*, Toyoko Yamazaki, Novel

BOND BOY, THE 1922 d: Henry King. USA., *The Bondboy*, George Washington Ogden, Chicago 1922, Novel

Bondage see DIE LEIBEIGENEN (1927).

BONDAGE 1933 d: Alfred Santell. USA., *The House of Refuge*, Grace Sothcote Leake, New York 1932, Novel

Bondage of Evil, The see NINI VERBENA (1913).

Bonded Labour see DAMUL (1984).

Bonded Until Death see DAMUL (1984).

BONDED WOMAN, THE 1922 d: Phil Rosen. USA., *The Salving of John Somers*, John Fleming Wilson, 1920, Short Story

BONDMAN, THE 1916 d: Edgar Lewis. USA., *The Bondman*, Hall Caine, London 1890, Novel

BONDMAN, THE 1929 d: Herbert Wilcox. UKN., *The Bondman*, Hall Caine, London 1890, Novel

Bonds of Honour see NO RANSOM (1934).

Bones, Love and Parrots see AMOR E PAPAGAIOS OSSO (1957).

BONFIRE OF THE VANITIES, THE 1990 d: Brian DepalmA. USA., *The Bonfire of the Vanities*, Tom Wolfe, 1989, Novel

BONGWATER 1998 d: Richard Sears. USA., *Bongwater*, Michael Hornburg, Novel

BONHEUR D'OCCASION 1983 d: Claude Fournier. CND., *Bonheur d'Occasion*, Gabrielle Roy, Novel

BONHEUR DU JOUR, LE 1927 d: Gaston Ravel. FRN., *Le Bonheur du Jour*, Edmond Guiraud, Play

BONHEUR, LE 1935 d: Marcel L'Herbier. FRN., *Le Bonheur*, Henri Bernstein, Play

BONHOMME JADIS, LE 1912 d: Emile Chautard. FRN., *Le Bonhomme Jadis*, Pierre Sales, Short Story

BONITINHA, MAS ORDINARIA 1963 d: J. P. de Carvalho. BRZ., *Bonitinha Mas Ordinaria*, Nelson Rodrigues, 1961, Play

BONITINHA, MAS ORDINARIA 1981 d: Braz Chediak. BRZ., *Bonitinha Mas Ordinaria*, Nelson Rodrigues, 1961, Play

BONJOUR JEUNESSE 1956 d: Maurice Cam. FRN/SWT., *Wie Wieseli Seinen Weg Fand*, Johanna Spyri, Gotha 1878, Novel

BONJOUR KATHRIN 1955 d: Karl Anton. GRM., *Die Glucklichste Frau Der Welt*, Kurt Feltz, Max Wallner, Opera

BONJOUR TRISTESSE 1958 d: Otto Preminger. UKN/USA., *Bonjour Tristesse*, Francoise Sagan, 1954, Novel

Bonne Nuit, Monsieur Masure see CHERIE REVEILLE-TOI (1960).

BONNE SOUPE, LA 1964 d: Robert Thomas. FRN/ITL., *La Bonne Soupe*, Felicien Marceau, 1958, Play

BONNE TISANE, LA 1957 d: Herve Bromberger. FRN., *La Bonne Tisane*, John Amila, Novel

Bonne Vie, La see QUAND ON EST BELLE (1931).

BONNES A TUER 1954 d: Henri Decoin. FRN/ITL., *Bonnes a Tuer*, Pat MacGerr, Novel

BONNES CAUSES, LES 1963 d: Christian-Jaque. FRN/ITL., *Les Bonnes Causes*, Jean Laborde, Paris 1960, Novel

BONNIE, BONNIE LASSIE 1919 d: Tod Browning. USA., *Auld Jeremiah*, Henry C. Rowland, Short Story

Bonnie Briar Bush, The see BESIDE THE BONNIE BRIER BUSH (1921).

Bonnie Brier Bush, The see BESIDE THE BONNIE BRIER BUSH (1921).

BONNIE MAY 1920 d: Joseph de Grasse, Ida May Park. USA., *Bonnie May*, Louis Dodge, New York 1916, Novel

Book and the Sword, The see SHU JIAN EN CHOU LU (1987).

Book of Athuan, The see A HALO FOR ATHUAN (1985).

Book of Good Love, The see EL LIBRO DEL BUEN AMOR I (1974).

Book of Kings, The see SIAVOSH DAR TAKHTE JAMSHID (1967).

BOOK OF LOVE 1990 d: Robert Shaye. USA., *Jack in the Box*, William Kotzwinkle, Novel

Bookseller Who Gave Up Bathing, The see BOKHANDLAREN SOM SLUTADE BARA (1969).

BOOM! 1968 d: Joseph Losey. UKN., *The Milk Train Doesn't Stop Here Any More*, Tennessee Williams, New York 1962, Play

BOOM TOWN 1940 d: Jack Conway. USA., *A Lady Comes to Burkburnett*, James Edward Grant, 1939, Short Story

BOOMERANG! 1947 d: Elia Kazan. USA., Anthony Abbot, Article

BOOMERANG 1934 d: Arthur Maude. UKN., *Boomerang*, David Evans, Play

Boomerang see BUMERANG (1960).

BOOMERANG BILL 1922 d: Tom Terriss. USA., *Boomerang Bill*, Jack Boyle, Story

BOOMERANG, THE 1913 d: Thomas H. Ince. USA., *The Boomerang*, William Hamilton Osborne, New York 1912, Novel

BOOMERANG, THE 1919 d: Bertram Bracken. USA., *The Boomerang*, William Hamilton Osborne, New York 1912, Novel

Boon, The see KONDURA (1977).

BOOR, THE 1955 d: Nathan Zucker. USA., *Medved*, Anton Chekhov, 1888, Play

Boors, The see BADARINII (1960).

BOOST, THE 1988 d: Harold Becker. USA., *Ludes*, Benjamin Stein, Novel

BOOT, DAS 1981 d: Wolfgang Petersen. GRM., *Das Boot*, Lothar Gunther Buchheim, Novel

BOOTLE'S BABY 1914 d: Harold Shaw. UKN., *Bootle's Baby*, John Strange Winter, Novel

BOOTLE'S BABY 1914 d: Ashley Miller. USA., *Bootle's Baby*, John Strange Winter, Novel

BOOTS AND SADDLES 1916. USA., *Boots and Saddles*, Eugene Walter, Play

Boots and Saddles see ARIZONA MAHONEY (1936).

BOPHA! 1993 d: Morgan Freeman. USA., *Bopha!*, Percy Mtwa, Play

BOR BORSON 1938 d: Toralf Sando, Knut Hergel. NRW., *Bor Borson Jr.*, Johan Falkberget, 1920, Novel

BOR BORSON 1973 d: Jan Erik During. NRW., *Bor Borson Jr.*, Johan Falkberget, 1920, Novel

BORDER CAFE 1937 d: Lew Landers. USA., *In the Mexican Quarter*, Tom Gill, 1930, Short Story

BORDER LEGION, THE 1919 d: T. Hayes Hunter. USA., *The Border Legion*, Zane Grey, New York 1916, Novel

BORDER LEGION, THE 1924 d: William K. Howard. USA., *The Border Legion*, Zane Grey, New York 1916, Novel

BORDER LEGION, THE 1930 d: Otto Brower, Edwin H. Knopf. USA., *The Border Legion*, Zane Grey, New York 1916, Novel

Border Legion, The *see* THE LAST ROUND-UP (1934).

BORDER LEGION, THE 1940 d: Joseph Kane. USA., *The Border Legion*, Zane Grey, New York 1916, Novel

Border Patrol *see* FLASHPOINT (1984).

Border Renegade *see* THE LIGHT OF WESTERN STARS (1940).

BORDER SHERIFF, THE 1926 d: Robert North Bradbury. USA., *Straight Shooting*, W. C. Tuttle, 1924, Short Story

BORDER SHOOTOUT 1990 d: C. J. McIntyre. USA., *The Law at Randado*, Elmore Leonard, Novel

BORDER TERROR 1919 d: Harry Harvey. USA., *Caballero's Way*, O. Henry, Short Story

Border, The *see* LA FRONTERA (1996).

Border Town *see* BIANCHENG (1984).

BORDERLAND 1937 d: Nate Watt. USA., *Bring Me His Ears*, Clarence E. Mulford, 1922, Short Story

Borderlines *see* THE CARETAKERS (1963).

BORDERTOWN 1935 d: Archie Mayo. USA., *Border Town*, Carroll Graham, New York 1934, Novel

BORGHESE PICCOLO PICCOLO, UN 1977 d: Mario Monicelli. ITL., *Un Borghese Piccolo Piccolo*, Vincenzo Cerami, Novel

BORGHESI DI PONT-ARCY, I 1920 d: Umberto Mozzato, Emilio Vardannes. ITL., *Les Bourgeois de Pont-Arcy*, Victorien Sardou, 1878, Play

Boris Godounov *see* BORIS GODUNOV (1986).

BORIS GODUNOV 1986 d: Sergei Bondarchuk. USS/CZC., *Boris Godunov*, Alexander Pushkin, 1831, Play

BORN AGAIN 1978 d: Irving Rapper. USA., *Born Again*, Charles W. Colson, Novel

Born Fighter, The *see* KENKA SEREJII (1966).

Born for Glory *see* BROWN ON RESOLUTION (1935).

BORN FREE 1965 d: James Hill. UKN., *Born Free*, Joy Adamson, London 1960, Book

BORN LUCKY 1932 d: Michael Powell. UKN., *Mops*, Oliver Sandys, Novel

Born of the Cyclone *see* UNTAMED YOUTH (1924).

BORN ON THE FOURTH OF JULY 1989 d: Oliver Stone. USA., *Born on the Fourth of July*, Ron Kovic, Book

BORN RECKLESS 1930 d: John Ford. USA., *Louis Beretti*, Donald Henderson Clarke, New York 1929, Novel

BORN RICH 1924 d: William Nigh. USA., *Born Rich*, Hughes Cornell, Philadelphia 1924, Novel

BORN TO BE BAD 1950 d: Nicholas Ray. USA., *All Kneeling*, Anne Parrish, 1928, Novel

Born to Die *see* ROBIN HOOD OF EL DORADO (1936).

BORN TO FIGHT 1932 d: Walter Mayo. USA., *The Cross Pull*, Hal G. Evarts, New York 1920, Novel

Born to Fight *see* MEN OF ACTION (1935).

BORN TO FIGHT 1936 d: Charles Hutchison. USA., *To Him Who Dares*, Peter B. Kyne, 1911, Short Story

BORN TO GAMBLE 1935 d: Phil Rosen. USA., *The Greek Poropulos*, Edgar Wallace, 1911, Short Story

BORN TO HANG 1934 d: Aubrey Scotto. USA., *Born to Hang*, George Bruce, Short Story

BORN TO KILL 1947 d: Robert Wise. USA., *Deadlier Than the Male*, James Gunn, Novel

Born to Kill *see* COCKFIGHTER (1974).

Born to Run *see* HARNESS FEVER (1976).

Born to the Racket *see* YOUNG DONOVAN'S KID (1931).

BORN TO THE SADDLE 1953 d: William Beaudine. USA., *Quarter Horse*, Gordon Young, Novel

BORN TO THE WEST 1926 d: John Waters. USA., *Born to the West*, Zane Grey, Story

Born Winner *see* L' ULTIMA VOLTA (1976).

BORN YESTERDAY 1950 d: George Cukor. USA., *Born Yesterday*, Garson Kanin, New York 1946, Play

BORN YESTERDAY 1993 d: Luis Mandoki. USA., *Born Yesterday*, Garson Kanin, New York 1946, Play

BORROWED CLOTHES 1934 d: Arthur Maude. UKN., *Her Shop*, Aimee Stuart, Philip Stuart, 1929, Play

Borrowed Duchess, The *see* A SOCIETY SENSATION (1918).

Borrowed Plumes *see* IN BORROWED PLUMES (1926).

BORROWERS, THE 1973 d: Walter C. Miller. USA., *The Borrowers*, Mary Norton, Book

BORROWERS, THE 1997 d: Peter Hewitt. UKN., Mary Norton, Novel

BORSALINO 1970 d: Jacques Deray. FRN/ITL., *Bandits a Marseille*, Eugene Saccomare, Paris 1968, Novel

Bosambo *see* SANDERS OF THE RIVER (1935).

Bosco Degli Amanti, Il *see* LE BOIS DES AMANTS (1960).

BOSCOMBE VALLEY MYSTERY, THE 1922 d: George Ridgwell. UKN., *The Boscombe Valley Mystery*, Arthur Conan Doyle, Short Story

Boss Came Up With Something, The *see* ECHAPPEMENT LIBRE (1964).

Boss Hat Sich Was Ausgedacht, Der *see* ECHAPPEMENT LIBRE (1964).

BOSS OF CAMP 4, THE 1922 d: W. S. Van Dyke. USA., *The Boss of Camp Four*, Arthur Preston Hankins, Novel

Boss of Powderville, The *see* THE GRAND PASSION (1918).

BOSS OF THE LAZY Y, THE 1918 d: Cliff Smith. USA., *The Boss of the Lazy Y*, Charles Alden Seltzer, New York 1915, Novel

BOSS, THE 1915 d: Emile Chautard. USA., *The Boss*, Edward Sheldon, New York 1911, Play

BOSSU, LE 1914 d: Andre Heuze. FRN., *Le Bossu*, Paul Feval, 1875, Novel

Bossu, Le *see* OU LE PETIT PARISIEN, LE BOSSU (1925).

BOSSU, LE 1934 d: Rene Sti. FRN., *Le Bossu*, Paul Feval, 1875, Novel

BOSSU, LE 1944 d: Jean Delannoy. FRN., *Le Bossu*, Paul Feval, 1875, Novel

BOSSU, LE 1959 d: Andre Hunebelle. FRN/ITL., *Le Bossu*, Paul Feval, 1875, Novel

Bossu, Le *see* LES AVENTURES DE LAGARDERE (1967).

BOSSU, LE 1997 d: Philippe de BrocA. FRN/ITL/GRM., *Le Bossu*, Paul Feval, 1875, Novel

BOSSU, OU LE PETIT PARISIEN, LE 1925 d: Jean Kemm. FRN., *Le Bossu*, Paul Feval, 1875, Novel

BOSTON BLACKIE 1923 d: Scott R. Dunlap. USA., *The Water Cross*, Jack Boyle, 1919, Short Story

BOSTON BLACKIE'S LITTLE PAL 1918 d: E. Mason Hopper. USA., *Boston Blackie's Little Pal*, Jack Boyle, 1918, Short Story

BOSTON STRANGLER, THE 1968 d: Richard Fleischer. USA., *The Boston Strangler*, Gerold Frank, New York 1966, Book

BOSTONIANS, THE 1984 d: James Ivory. UKN., *The Bostonians*, Henry James, 1886, Novel

BOSUN'S MATE, THE 1914 d: Harold Shaw. UKN., *The Bosun's Mate*, W. W. Jacobs, Short Story

BOSUN'S MATE, THE 1953 d: Richard Warren. UKN., *The Bosun's Mate*, W. W. Jacobs, Short Story

BOTANY BAY 1953 d: John Farrow. USA., *Botany Bay*, James N. Hall, Charles Nordhoff, 1941, Novel

BOTSCHAFTERIN, DIE 1960 d: Harald Braun. GRM., *Die Botschafterin*, Hans Wolfgang, Novel

BOTTEGA DELL'ANTIQUARIO, LA 1921 d: Mario Corsi. ITL., *The Old Curiosity Shop*, Charles Dickens, London 1841, Novel

Bottle Demon, The *see* DER FLASCHENTEUFEL (1952).

BOTTLE IMP, THE 1917 d: Marshall Neilan. USA., *The Bottle Imp*, Robert Louis Stevenson, London 1891, Novel

BOTTOM OF THE BOTTLE, THE 1956 d: Henry Hathaway. USA., *Le Fond de la Bouteille*, Georges Simenon, 1949, Short Story

BOTTOM OF THE WELL, THE 1917 d: John S. Robertson. USA., *The Bottom of the Well*, Frederick Upham Adams, New York 1906, Novel

BOUASSA, EL 1944 d: Kamel Salim. EGY., *Les Miserables*, Victor Hugo, Paris 1862, Novel

BOUBA 1987 d: Ze'ev Revach. ISR., *Bouba*, Hillel Mittelfunkt, Play

Boubah *see* BOUBA (1987).

BOUBOUROCHE 1911 d: Georges MoncA. FRN., *Boubouroche*, Georges Courteline, Play

BOUBOUROCHE 1933 d: Andre Hugon. FRN., *Boubouroche*, Georges Courteline, Play

Boucanier Des Iles, Le *see* IL GIUSTIZIERE DEI MARI (1962).

BOUCLETTE 1918 d: Louis Mercanton, Rene Hervil. FRN., *L' Ange de Minuit*, Marcel L'Herbier

BOUDOIR DIPLOMAT, THE 1930 d: Malcolm St. Clair. USA., *The Command to Love*, Fritz Gottwald, Rudolph Lothar, New York 1927, Play

BOUDOIR JAPONAIS, LE 1918. FRN., *Le Boudois Japonais*, Sadi-Pety, Play

BOUDU SAUVE DES EAUX 1932 d: Jean Renoir. FRN., *Boudu Sauve Des Eaux*, Rene Fauchois, 1919, Play

Boudu Saved from Drowning *see* BOUDU SAUVE DES EAUX (1932).

BOUGHT 1931 d: Archie Mayo. USA., *Jackdaw's Strut*, Harriet Henry, New York 1930, Novel

BOUGHT AND PAID FOR 1916 d: Harley Knoles. USA., *Bought and Paid for*, George Broadhurst, New York 1911, Play

BOUGHT AND PAID FOR 1922 d: William C. de Mille. USA., *Bought and Paid for*, George Broadhurst, New York 1911, Play

BOUIF ERRANT, LE 1926 d: Rene Hervil. FRN., *Le Bouif Errant*, Georges de La Fouchardiere, Novel

BOULANGERE DE MONCEAU, LA 1962 d: Eric Rohmer. FRN., *La Boulangere de Monceau*, Eric Rohmer, 1974, Short Story

BOULE DE GOMME 1931 d: Georges Lacombe. FRN., *L' Enfant Prodige*, Georges Dolley, Novel

Boule de Suif *see* PYSHKA (1934).

BOULE-DE-SUIF 1945 d: Christian-Jaque. FRN., *Boule de Suif*, Guy de Maupassant, 1880, Short Story, *Mademoiselle Fifi*, Guy de Maupassant, 1881, Short Story

BOULEVARD 1960 d: Julien Duvivier. FRN., *Boulevard*, Robert Sabatier, Novel

BOULEVARD DES ASSASSINS 1982 d: Boramy Tioulong. FRN., *Une Affaire Intime*, Max Gallo, Novel

BOULEVARD DU RHUM 1971 d: Robert Enrico. FRN/ITL/SPN., *Boulevard du Rhum*, Jacques Pecherel, Novel

BOULOT AVIATEUR 1937 d: Maurice de Canonge. FRN., *Les Aventures Cocasses de Boulot Aviateur*, Georges de La Fouchardiere, Novel

BOUM-BOUM 1908 d: Maurice de Feraudy. FRN., *Boum-Boum*, Jules Claretie, Short Story

BOUND FOR GLORY 1976 d: Hal Ashby. USA., Woody Guthrie, Autobiography

BOUND ON THE WHEEL 1915 d: Joseph de Grasse. USA., *Bound on the Wheel*, Julius G. Furthmann, Story

BOUNDARY HOUSE 1918 d: Cecil M. Hepworth. UKN., *Boundary House*, Peggy Webling, Novel

Boundary, The *see* GRANICA (1977).

Bounty Killer, The *see* EL PRECIO DE UN HOMBRE (1966).

Bounty, The *see* MUTINY ON THE BOUNTY (1983).

BOUQUET DE FLIRTS, UN 1931 d: Charles de Rochefort. FRN., *Un Bouquet de Flirts*, J. Folister, Short Story

BOUQUETIERE DES INNOCENTS, LA 1922 d: Jacques Robert. FRN., *La Bouquetiere Des Innocents*, Anicet Bourgeois, Ferdinand Dugue, Play

BOURGEOIS GENTILHOMME, LE 1958 d: Jean Meyer. FRN., *Le Bourgeois Gentilhomme*, Moliere, 1670, Play

BOURRACHON 1935 d: Rene Guissart. FRN., *Bourrachon*, Laurent Doillet, Play

BOURRASQUE 1935 d: Pierre Billon. FRN., *Bourrasque*, Leopold Gomez, Play

Bourreaux d'Enfants *see* CLARA ET LES MECHANTS (1957).

BOURSE ET LA VIE, LA 1928 d: Jean Brocher. SWT., *La Gourde d'Eau-de-Vie*, Andre Gorbaz, Short Story

BOUT DE LA ROUTE, LE 1948 d: Emile Couzinet. FRN., *Le Bout de la Route*, Jean Giono, 1937, Play

Boutique Des Miracles, La *see* TENDA DOS MILAGRES (1977).

BOWERY, THE 1933 d: Raoul Walsh. USA., *Chuck Connors*, Michael L. Simmons, Bessie R. Solomon, Novel

BOX OF DELIGHTS, THE 1984 d: Renny Rye. UKN., *The Box of Delights*, John Masefield, Novel

BOY 1925 d: Benito Perojo. SPN/FRN., *Boy*, Luis Coloma, 1910, Novel

BOY 1940 d: Antonio Calvache. SPN., *Boy*, Luis Coloma, 1910, Novel

BOY AND HIS DOG, A 1975 d: L. Q. Jones. USA., Harlan Ellison, Story

BOY AND THE BRIDGE, THE 1959 d: Kevin McClory. UKN., *The Boy and the Bridge*, Leon Ware, Short Story

Boy and the Laughing Dog, The *see* MY LADY GOODBYE (1956).

Boy and the Wind, The *see* O MENINO E O VENTO (1967).

BOY CRIED MURDER, THE 1966 d: George Breakston. UKN/GRM/YGS., *The Boy Cried Murder*, Cornell Woolrich, 1947, Short Story

BOY FRIEND, THE 1926 d: Monta Bell. USA., *The Book of Charm*, John Alexander Kirkpatrick, New York 1925, Play

BOY FRIEND, THE 1972 d: Ken Russell. UKN., *The Boy Friend*, Sandy Wilson, Musical Play

BOY FROM OKLAHOMA, THE 1954 d: Michael Curtiz. USA., *The Boy from Oklahoma*, Michael Fessier, Short Story

Boy from the Plantations, The *see* MENINO DE ENGENHO (1966).

BOY IN THE BUSH, THE 1984 d: Rob Stewart. ASL/UKN., D. H. Lawrence, Novel

Boy Is Ten Feet Tall, A *see* SAMMY GOING SOUTH (1963).

Boy Meets Baby *see* BETWEEN US GIRLS (1942).

BOY MEETS GIRL 1938 d: Lloyd Bacon. USA., *Boy Meets Girl*, Bella Spewack, Samuel Spewack, New York 1935, Play

Boy (O El Marino Espanol) *see* BOY (1925).

BOY OF FLANDERS, A 1924 d: Victor Schertzinger. USA., *A Dog of Flanders*, Ouida, New York 1872, Novel

Boy of Flanders, A *see* A DOG OF FLANDERS (1935).

BOY OF MINE 1923 d: William Beaudine. USA., *Boy of Mine*, Booth Tarkington, Story

Boy of the World *see* PAW (1959).

Boy of Two Worlds *see* PAW (1959).

BOY ON A DOLPHIN 1957 d: Jean Negulesco. USA., *Boy on a Dolphin*, David Divine, 1955, Novel

Boy Ten Feet Tall, A *see* SAMMY GOING SOUTH (1963).

BOY WOODBURN 1922 d: Guy Newall. UKN., *Boy Woodburn*, Alfred Ollivant, Novel

BOYD'S SHOP 1960 d: Henry Cass. UKN., *Boyd's Shop*, St. John G. Ervine, Play

Boyfriend School, The *see* DON'T TELL HER IT'S ME (1990).

Boys *see* MALTCHIKI (1990).

BOYS 1996 d: Stacy Cochran. USA., *Twenty Minutes*, James Salter, Short Story

Boys' Baseball Team of Setouchi *see* SETOUCHI SHONEN YAKYUDAN (1984).

BOYS FROM BRAZIL, THE 1978 d: Franklin J. Schaffner. USA/UKN., *The Boys from Brazil*, Ira Levin, Novel

BOYS FROM SYRACUSE, THE 1940 d: A. Edward Sutherland. USA., *The Comedy of Errors*, William Shakespeare, c1594, Play

Boys from the Streets *see* GATEGUTTER (1949).

BOYS IN BROWN 1949 d: Montgomery Tully. UKN., *Boys in Brown*, Reginald Beckwith, London 1940, Play

BOYS IN THE BAND, THE 1970 d: William Friedkin. USA., *The Boys in the Band*, Mart Crowley, New York 1968, Play

BOYS IN THE ISLAND 1988 d: Geoffrey Bennett. ASL., *Boys in the Island*, Christopher Koch, Novel

BOYS' NIGHT OUT 1962 d: Michael Gordon. USA., Arne Sultan, Marvin Worth, Story

Boys of Paul Street, The *see* A PAL UTCAI FIUK (1968).

BOYS OF THE OTTER PATROL 1918 d: Percy Nash. UKN., *Boys of the Otter Patrol*, E. Lebreton Martin, Novel

Boys' School *see* LES DISPARUS DE SAINT-AGIL (1938).

BOYS, THE 1998 d: Rowan Woods. ASL/UKN., *The Boys*, Gordon Graham, Play

BOYS WILL BE BOYS 1921 d: Clarence Badger. USA., *Boys Will Be Boys*, Irvin S. Cobb, 1917, Short Story

Boys Will Be Boys *see* PANI KLUCI (1975).

BOZI MLYNY 1929 d: Josef Medeotti-Bohac. CZC., *Bozi Mlyny*, Jan Vrba, Novel

BOZI MLYNY 1938 d: Vaclav Wasserman. CZC., *Bozi Mlyny*, Jan Vrba, Novel

BRA MANNINSKOR 1937 d: Leif Sinding. NRW., *Bra Mennesker*, Oskar Braaten, 1930, Play

Bra Mennesker *see* BRA MANNINSKOR (1937).

BRACCIALETTO AL PIEDE, IL 1920 d: Eleuterio Rodolfi. ITL., *Il Braccialetto Al Piede*, Carlo Veneziani, 1916, Play

BRACELETS 1931 d: Sewell Collins. UKN., *Bracelets*, Sewell Collins, Play

BRADFORD'S CLAIM 1910 d: Edwin S. Porter. USA., *Bradford's Claim*, Bret Harte, Short Story

BRAGHE DEL PADRONE, LE 1978 d: Flavio Mogherini. ITL., *Le Braghe Del Padrone*, Italo Terzoli, Enrico Vaime, Novel

BRAIN EATERS, THE 1958 d: Bruno Ve SotA. USA., *The Puppet Masters*, Robert A. Heinlein, 1951, Novel

Brain, The *see* VENGEANCE (1962).

Brainkill *see* QUALCUNO DIETRO LA PORTA (1971).

BRAINWASH 1981 d: Bobby Roth. USA., Conrad D. Carnes, Jean Church, Book

Brainwashed *see* DIE SCHACHNOVELLE (1960).

Bram Stoker's Count Dracula *see* EL CONDE DRACULA (1970).

Bram Stoker's Dracula *see* DRACULA (1992).

BRAMBLE BUSH, THE 1919 d: Tom Terriss. USA., *The Bramble Bush*, Nalbro Bartley, 1914, Serial Story

BRAMBLE BUSH, THE 1960 d: Daniel Petrie. USA., *The Bramble Bush*, Charles Mergendahl, Novel

Bramy Raju *see* VRATA RAJA (1967).

Branch of Mei Flowers, A *see* YIJIAN MEI (1931).

BRANCHE MORTE, LA 1926 d: Joseph Guarino. FRN., *La Branche Morte*, D'arquilliere, Play

BRAND IN DER OPER 1930 d: Carl Froelich. GRM., *Der Brand Im Opernhaus*, Georg Kaiser, 1919, Play

BRAND OF SHAME 1968 d: B. Ron Elliott. USA., *Brand of Shame*, David F. Friedman, Novel

BRAND, THE 1919 d: Reginald Barker. USA., *The Brand*, Rex Beach, 1913, Short Story

Brand, The *see* BRAND OF SHAME (1968).

BRANDED 1920 d: Charles Calvert. UKN., *Branded*, Gerald Biss, Novel

BRANDED 1950 d: Rudolph Mate. USA., *Montana Rides*, Evan Evans, Novel

BRANDED SOMBRERO, THE 1928 d: Lambert Hillyer. USA., *The Branded Sombrero*, Cherry Wilson, 1927, Short Story

Branded Soul, The *see* THE IRON STAIR (1920).

BRANDED WOMAN, THE 1920 d: Albert Parker. USA., *Branded*, Oliver D. Bailey, New York 1917, Play

BRANDING IRON, THE 1920 d: Reginald Barker. USA., *The Branding Iron*, Katharine Newlin Burt, New York 1919, Novel

Branding Iron, The *see* BODY AND SOUL (1927).

BRANDSTELLEN 1977 d: Horst E. Brandt. GDR., *Brandstellen*, Franz-Josef Degenhardt, Novel

Brandy Ashore *see* GREEN GROW THE RUSHES (1951).

BRANDY FOR THE PARSON 1952 d: John Eldridge. UKN., *Brandy for the Parson*, Geoffrey Household, Novel

BRANNEN 1973 d: Hakon Sandoy. NRW., *Brannen*, Tarjei Vesaas, 1961, Novel

BRANT BARN 1967 d: Hans Abramson. SWD., *Brant Barn*, Stig Dagerman, 1948, Novel

BRAS DE LA NUIT, LES 1961 d: Jacques Guymont. FRN., *Le Bras de la Nuit*, Frederic Dard, Novel

BRASHER DOUBLOON, THE 1947 d: John Brahm. USA., *The High Window*, Raymond Chandler, 1942, Novel

BRASS 1923 d: Sidney A. Franklin. USA., *Brass; a Novel of Marriage*, Charles Gilman Norris, New York 1921, Novel

BRASS BOTTLE, THE 1914 d: Sidney Morgan. UKN., *The Brass Bottle*, F. Anstey, London 1900, Novel

BRASS BOTTLE, THE 1923 d: Maurice Tourneur. USA., *The Brass Bottle*, F. Anstey, London 1900, Novel

BRASS BOTTLE, THE 1964 d: Harry Keller. USA., *The Brass Bottle*, F. Anstey, London 1900, Novel

BRASS BOWL, THE 1914. USA., *The Brass Bowl*, Louis Joseph Vance, Indianapolis 1907, Novel

BRASS BOWL, THE 1924 d: Jerome Storm. USA., *The Brass Bowl*, Louis Joseph Vance, Indianapolis 1907, Novel

BRASS CHECK, THE 1918 d: Will S. Davis. USA., *The Brass Check*, George Allan England, 1916, Short Story

BRASS COMMANDMENTS 1923 d: Lynn Reynolds. USA., *The Brass Commandments*, Charles Alden Seltzer, New York 1923, Novel

BRASS TARGET 1978 d: John Hough. USA., *The Algonquin Project*, Frederick Nolan, Novel

Brat Naszego Boga *see* OUR GOD'S BROTHER (1997).

BRAT, THE 1919 d: Herbert Blache. USA., *The Brat*, Maude Fulton, Los Angeles 1916, Play

Brat, The *see* THE NIPPER (1930).

BRAT, THE 1931 d: John Ford. USA., *The Brat*, Maude Fulton, Los Angeles 1916, Play

Brat, The *see* THE GIRL FROM AVENUE A (1940).

Bratia Karamazov *see* BRATYA KARAMAZOVY (1968).

BRATYA KARAMAZOVY 1968 d: Ivan Pyriev. USS., *Bratya Karamazovy*, Fyodor Dostoyevsky, 1880, Novel

Braut Des Satans, Die *see* TO THE DEVIL A DAUGHTER (1976).

BRAUTIGAME DER BABETTE BOMBERLING 1927 d: Victor Janson. GRM., *Die Brautigame Der Babette Bomberling*, Alice Berend, Novel

BRAVADOS, THE 1958 d: Henry King. USA., *The Bravados*, Frank O'Rourke, Novel

BRAVE AND BOLD 1918 d: Carl Harbaugh. USA., *Four-Forty at Fort Penn*, Perley Poore Sheehan, 1917, Short Story

Brave Archer, The *see* CHUEH-TAI SHUANG CHIAO (1979).

BRAVE BULLS, THE 1951 d: Robert Rossen. USA., *The Brave Bulls*, Tom Lea, Novel

Brave Little Tailor *see* SEDEM JEDNOU RANOU (1988).

Brave Little Tailor, The *see* DAS TAPFERE SCHNEIDERLEIN (1956).

BRAVE LITTLE TOASTER, THE 1987 d: Jerry Rees. USA., *The Brave Little Toaster*, Thomas M. Disch, Novel

BRAVE NEW WORLD 1980 d: Burt Brinckerhoff. USA., *Brave New World*, Aldous Huxley, 1932, Novel

BRAVE NEW WORLD 1998 d: Leslie Libman, Larry Williams. USA., *Brave New World*, Aldous Huxley, 1932, Novel

BRAVE ONE, THE 1956 d: Irving Rapper. USA., Robert Rich, Story

BRAVE SOLDAT SCHWEJK, DER 1960 d: Axel von Ambesser. GRM., *Osudy Dobreho Vojaka Svejka Za Svetove Valky*, Jaroslav Hasek, Prague 1920-23, Novel

BRAVE, THE 1997 d: Johnny Depp. USA., *The Brave*, Gregory McDonald, Novel

BRAVEHEART 1925 d: Alan Hale. USA., *Braveheart*, William C. de Mille, Story

BRAVEST OF THE BRAVE 1915 d: Allen Curtis. USA., *The Bravest of the Brave*, Thomas Delmar, Story

BRAVO, THE 1928 d: Geoffrey H. Malins. UKN., *The Bravo*, W. W. Jacobs, Short Story

BRAVO TWO ZERO 1998 d: Tom Clegg. UKN., *Bravo Two Zero*, Andy McNab, Book

Brawny *see* ARAKURE (1957).

BRAZEN BEAUTY, THE 1918 d: Tod Browning. USA., *The Magnificent Jacala*, Louise Winter, 1918, Short Story

Brazen Women of Balzac, The *see* DIE TOLLDREISTEN GESCHICHTEN - NACH HONORE DE BALZAC (1969).

BREACH OF PROMISE 1932 d: Paul L. Stein. USA., *Obscurity*, Rupert Hughes, Story

Breach of Promise, Or the Furnace *see* THE FURNACE (1920).

BREAD 1924 d: Victor Schertzinger. USA., *Bread*, Charles Gilman Norris, New York 1923, Novel

Bread - the Dash *see* HLYAB - CHERTICHKATA (1972).

Bread and Butter *see* BUTTERBROT (1989).

Bread and Stones *see* BROT UND STEINE (1979).

Bread of Love, The *see* KARLEKENS BROD (1953).

Bread of Our Early Years, The *see* DAS BROT DER FRUHEN JAHRE (1962).

Bread of the Early Years, The *see* DAS BROT DER FRUHEN JAHRE (1962).

Bread Peddler, The *see* LA PORTEUSE DE PAIN (1963).

Break in *see* EINBRUCH (1927).

BREAK IN THE CIRCLE 1955 d: Val Guest. UKN., *Break in the Circle*, Philip Lorraine, Novel

BREAK OUT 1984 d: Frank Godwin. UKN., *A Place to Hide*, Bill Gillham, Novel

BREAK THE NEWS 1938 d: Rene Clair. UKN., *Le Mort En Fuite*, Loic de Gouriadec, Novel

BREAK THE NEWS TO MOTHER 1919 d: Julius Steger. USA., *Break the News to Mother*, Charles K. Harris, 1897, Song

Break to Freedom *see* ALBERT R.N. (1953).

BREAKDOWN 1952 d: Edmund Angelo. USA., *The Samson Slasher*, Robert Abel, Play

BREAKER MORANT 1979 d: Bruce Beresford. ASL., *Breaker Morant*, Kenneth Ross, Play

BREAKER, THE 1916 d: Fred E. Wright. USA., *The Breaker*, Arthur Stringer, 1916, Short Story

Breaker, The *see* BREAKER MORANT (1979).

BREAKFAST AT TIFFANY'S 1961 d: Blake Edwards. USA., *Breakfast at Tiffany's*, Truman Capote, New York 1958, Novel

BREAKFAST FOR TWO 1937 d: Alfred Santell. USA., *A Love Like That*, David Garth, New York 1937, Novel

BREAKFAST OF CHAMPIONS 1999 d: Alan Rudolph. USA., *Breakfast of Champions*, Kurt Vonnegut Jr., 1976, Novel

BREAKHEART PASS 1976 d: Tom Gries. USA., *Breakheart Pass*, Alistair MacLean, 1974, Novel

BREAKING OF BUMBO, THE 1970 d: Andrew Sinclair. UKN., *The Breaking of Bumbo*, Andrew Sinclair, Novel

BREAKING POINT, THE 1921 d: Paul Scardon. USA., *The Living Child*, Mary Lerner, Story

BREAKING POINT, THE 1924 d: Herbert Brenon. USA., *The Breaking Point*, Mary Roberts Rinehart, New York 1922, Novel

BREAKING POINT, THE 1950 d: Michael Curtiz. USA., *To Have and Have Not*, Ernest Hemingway, 1937, Novel

BREAKING POINT, THE 1961 d: Lance Comfort. UKN., *The Breaking Point*, Laurence Meynell, London 1957, Novel

Breaking the News *see* THE FOUNTAIN (1934).

BREAKOUT 1959 d: Peter Graham Scott. UKN., *Breakout*, Frederick Oughton, Book

Breakout *see* DANGER WITHIN (1959).

BREAKOUT 1975 d: Tom Gries. USA/SPN/FRN., *Ten Second Jailbreak*, Frank Kowalski, Howard B. Kreitsek, Novel

Breakout *see* BREAK OUT (1984).

BREAKTHROUGH 1950 d: Lewis Seiler. USA., Joseph I. Breen Jr., Story

Breakthrough *see* THE LIFEFORCE EXPERIMENT (1993).

Breakup, The *see* LA RUPTURE (1970).

Breath of Scandal *see* HIS GLORIOUS NIGHT (1929).

BREATH OF SCANDAL, A 1960 d: Michael Curtiz. USA/ITL/AUS., *Olympia*, Ferenc Molnar, Budapest 1928, Play

BREATH OF SCANDAL, THE 1924 d: Louis J. Gasnier. USA., *The Breath of Scandal*, Edwin Balmer, Boston 1922, Novel

BREATH OF THE GODS, THE 1920 d: Rollin S. Sturgeon. USA., *The Breath of God*, Sidney McCall, Boston 1905, Novel

BREATHLESS MOMENT, THE 1924 d: Robert F. Hill. USA., *Richard*, Marguerite Bryant, New York 1922, Novel

BREBIS PERDUE, LA 1915 d: Henri Pouctal. FRN., *La Brebis Perdue*, Gabriel Trarieux, Play

BRED IN THE BONE 1915 d: Paul Powell. USA., *Bred in the Bone*, Frank Kinsella, Story

BREED O' THE NORTH 1914 d: Walter Edwards. USA., *Breed O' the North*, Bret Harte, Short Story

BREED OF THE BORDER, THE 1924 d: Harry Garson. USA., *The Breed of the Border*, William Dawson Hoffman, Story

BREED OF THE SEA 1926 d: Ralph Ince. USA., *Blue Blood and the Pirates*, Peter B. Kyne, 1912, Short Story

BREED OF THE TRESHAMS, THE 1920 d: Kenelm Foss. UKN., *The Breed of the Treshams*, Beulah Marie Dix, E. G. Sutherland, London 1905, Play

Breeding *see* SHIIKU (1961).

Bremen Town Musicians, The *see* DIE BREMER STADTMUSIKANTEN (1959).

BREMER STADTMUSIKANTEN, DIE 1959 d: Rainer Geis. GRM., *Die Bremer Stadtmusikanten*, Jacob Grimm, Wilhelm Grimm, Short Story

Brennende Gericht, Das *see* LA CHAMBRE ARDENTE (1961).

BRENNENDE SCHIFF, DAS 1927 d: Constantin J. David. GRM/FRN., *La Bateau de Verre*, Rene Bizet, Short Story

BRENNENDES GEHEIMNIS 1933 d: Robert Siodmak. GRM., *Brennendes Geheimnis*, Stefan Zweig, 1929, Short Story

Brennendes Geheimnis *see* BURNING SECRET (1989).

Breve Incontro *see* BRIEF ENCOUNTER (1974).

BREWSTER'S MILLIONS 1914 d: Oscar Apfel, Cecil B. de Mille. USA., *Brewster's Millions*, George Barr McCutcheon, New York 1902, Novel

BREWSTER'S MILLIONS 1921 d: Joseph Henabery. USA., *Brewster's Millions*, George Barr McCutcheon, New York 1902, Novel

BREWSTER'S MILLIONS 1935 d: Thornton Freeland. UKN., *Brewster's Millions*, George Barr McCutcheon, New York 1902, Novel

BREWSTER'S MILLIONS 1945 d: Allan Dwan. USA., *Brewster's Millions*, George Barr McCutcheon, New York 1902, Novel

Brewster's Millions *see* THREE ON A SPREE (1961).

BREWSTER'S MILLIONS 1985 d: Walter Hill. USA., *Brewster's Millions*, George Barr McCutcheon, New York 1902, Novel

BRIAN'S SONG 1970 d: Buzz Kulik. USA., *I Am Third*, Gale Sayers, Book

BRIBE, THE 1948 d: Robert Z. Leonard. USA., *The Bribe*, Frederick Nebel, Short Story

Bricklayers, The *see* LOS ALBANILES (1976).

Bridal Path, The *see* ALL'S FAIR IN LOVE (1921).

BRIDAL PATH, THE 1959 d: Frank Launder. UKN., *The Bridal Path*, Nigel Tranter, Novel

BRIDE COMES HOME, THE 1936 d: Wesley Ruggles. USA., *The Bride Comes Home*, Elisabeth Sanxay Holding, 1935, Short Story

Bride for a Night *see* DULHAN EK RAAT KI (1967).

Bride for a Single Night *see* DULHAN EK RAAT KI (1967).

BRIDE FOR HENRY, A 1937 d: William Nigh. USA., *A Bride for Henry*, Josephine Bentham, 1937, Short Story

Bride Is Much Too Beautiful, The *see* LA MARIEE EST TROP BELLE (1956).

Bride Is Too Beautiful, The *see* LA MARIEE EST TROP BELLE (1956).

BRIDE OF FRANKENSTEIN 1935 d: James Whale. USA., *Frankenstein; Or the Modern Prometheus*, Mary Wollstonecraft Shelley, London 1818, Novel

BRIDE OF LAMMERMOOR, THE 1909 d: J. Stuart Blackton. USA., *The Bride of Lammermoor*, Sir Walter Scott, 1819, Novel

Bride of Lammermoor, The *see* LUCIA DI LAMMERMOOR (1910).

BRIDE OF LAMMERMOOR, THE 1922 d: Challis Sanderson. UKN., *The Bride of Lammermoor*, Sir Walter Scott, 1819, Novel

Bride of Messina, The *see* LA FIDANZATA DI MESSINA (1911).

Bride of the Bayou *see* LAZY RIVER (1934).

Bride of the Gods *see* SHATTERED IDOLS (1922).

Bride of the Lake, The *see* LILY OF KILLARNEY (1934).

BRIDE OF THE REGIMENT 1930 d: John Francis Dillon. USA., *Die Frau Im Hermelin*, Rudolph Schanzer, Ernst Welisch, Play

BRIDE OF THE STORM 1926 d: J. Stuart Blackton. USA., *My Maryland Maryland*, James Francis Dwyer, 1920, Short Story

BRIDE, THE 1985 d: Franc Roddam. UKN/USA., *Frankenstein; Or the Modern Prometheus*, Mary Wollstonecraft Shelley, London 1818, Novel

Bride to Be *see* PEPITA JIMENEZ (1975).

Bride Wore Black, The *see* LA MARIEE ETAIT EN NOIR (1968).

BRIDE WORE RED, THE 1937 d: Dorothy Arzner. USA., *Az Ismeretien Lany*, Ferenc Molnar, Budapest 1934, Play

Bridegroom for Two *see* LET'S LOVE AND LAUGH (1931).

Bridegroom, The *see* VOLEGENY (1982).

Bridegroom's Widow, The *see* LET'S LOVE AND LAUGH (1931).

BRIDES ARE LIKE THAT 1936 d: William McGann. USA., *Applesauce*, Barry Conners, New York 1925, Play

BRIDE'S PLAY, THE 1921 d: George W. Terwilliger. USA., *The Bride's Play*, Brian Oswald Donn-Byrne, Short Story

BRIDES TO BE 1934 d: Reginald Denham. UKN., *Sign Please*, Basil Mason, Short Story

BRIDESHEAD REVISITED 1981 d: Charles Sturridge, Michael Lindsay-Hogg. UKN., *Brideshead Revisited*, Evelyn Waugh, 1945, Novel

BRIDGE AT REMAGEN, THE 1969 d: John Guillermin. USA., *Bridge at Remagen*, Kenneth William Hechler, New York 1957, Novel

Bridge Between Two Shores, A *see* UN PONT ENTRE DEUX RIVES (1999).

Bridge Cannot Be Crossed, The *see* MOST PEREYTI NELIEYA (1960).

BRIDGE IN THE JUNGLE, THE 1970 d: Pancho Kohner. MXC/USA., *Die Brucke Im Dschungel*, Ben Traven, 1929, Novel

Bridge of Japan *see* NIHONBASHI (1956).

BRIDGE OF SAN LUIS REY, THE 1929 d: Charles J. Brabin. USA., *The Bridge of San Luis Rey*, Thornton Wilder, 1927, Novel

BRIDGE OF SAN LUIS REY, THE 1944 d: Rowland V. Lee. USA., *The Bridge of San Luis Rey*, Thornton Wilder, 1927, Novel

BRIDGE ON THE RIVER KWAI, THE 1957 d: David Lean. UKN/USA., *Le Pont de la Riviere Kwai*, Pierre Boulle, 1952, Novel

Bridge, Or the Bigger Man, The *see* THE BIGGER MAN (1915).

Bridge, The *see* DIE BRUCKE (1959).

Bridge, The *see* EL PUENTE (1977).

BRIDGE, THE 1990 d: Sydney MacArtney. UKN., *The Bridge*, Maggie Hemingway, Novel

BRIDGE TO THE SUN 1961 d: Etienne Perier. USA/FRN., *Bridge to the Sun*, Gwendolyn Terasaki, Chapel Hill, Nc. 1957, Novel

BRIDGE TOO FAR, A 1977 d: Richard Attenborough. UKN/USA., *A Bridge Too Far*, Cornelius Ryan, Book

BRIDGES AT TOKO-RI, THE 1954 d: Mark Robson. USA., *The Bridges at Toko-Ri*, James A. Michener, 1953, Novel

BRIDGES OF MADISON COUNTY, THE 1995 d: Clint Eastwood. USA., *The Bridges of Madison County*, Robert James Waller, Novel

BRIEF DEBUT OF TILDY, THE 1918 d: George Ridgwell. USA., *The Brief Debut of Tildy*, O. Henry, Short Story

BRIEF ENCOUNTER 1945 d: David Lean. UKN., *Still Life*, Noel Coward, London 1936, Play

BRIEF ENCOUNTER 1974 d: Alan Bridges. UKN/ITL/USA., *Still Life*, Noel Coward, London 1936, Play

BRIEF HISTORY OF TIME, A 1991 d: Errol Morris. UKN/USA., *A Brief History of Time*, Stephen Hawking, 1988, Book

BRIEF MOMENT 1933 d: David Burton. USA., *Brief Moment*, S. N. Behrman, New York 1931, Play

Brief Sunshine *see* KRATKO SLUNTSE (1979).

Briefe Einer Unbekannten *see* NARKOSE (1929).

BRIERE, LA 1924 d: Leon Poirier. FRN., *La Briere*, Alphonse de Chateaubriant, Novel

BRIG, THE 1965 d: Jonas Mekas, Adolfas Mekas. USA., *The Brig*, Kenneth H. Brown, New York 1963, Play

Brig "Three Lilies", The *see* BRIGGEN TRE LILJOR (1961).

Brigade Antigang *see* BRIGADE ANTI-GANGS (1966).

BRIGADE ANTI-GANGS 1966 d: Bernard Borderie. FRN/ITL., *Brigade Anti-Gangs*, Auguste le Breton, Novel

BRIGADIER GERARD 1915 d: Bert Haldane. UKN., *The Exploits of Brigadier Gerard*, Arthur Conan Doyle, London 1896, Novel

Brigadier Gerard see **THE FIGHTING EAGLE** (1927).

Brigadier Studer, Le see **WACHTMEISTER STUDER** (1939).

BRIGADOON 1954 d: Vincente Minnelli. USA., *Brigadoon*, Alan Jay Lerner, New York 1947, Play

BRIGAND GENTILHOMME, LE 1942 d: Emile Couzinet. FRN., *Le Salteador*, Alexandre Dumas (pere), 1854, Novel

Brigand of Tacca Del Lupo, The see **IL BRIGANTE DI TACCA DEL LUPO** (1952).

Brigand, The see **LOUPEZNIK** (1931).

BRIGAND, THE 1952 d: Phil Karlson. USA., *A Romance of the Reign of Don Carlos Brigand*, Alexandre Dumas (pere), Novel

Brigand, The see **IL BRIGANTE** (1961).

BRIGANTE DI TACCA DEL LUPO, IL 1952 d: Pietro Germi. ITL., *Il Brigante Di Tacca Del Lupo*, Riccardo Bacchelli, 1942, Novel

BRIGANTE, IL 1961 d: Renato Castellani. ITL., *Il Brigante*, Giuseppe Berto, 1951, Novel

BRIGANTI ITALIANI, I 1961 d: Mario Camerini. ITL/FRN., *I Briganti Italiani*, Mario Monti, Novel

BRIGATA FIRENZE 1928 d: Orlando Vassallo. ITL., *Eroismo E Amore*, Nando Vitali, Play

BRIGGEN TRE LILJOR 1961 d: Hans Abramson. SWD., *Briggen Tre Liljor*, Olle Mattson, Book

Brigham Young see **BRIGHAM YOUNG - FRONTIERSMAN** (1940).

BRIGHAM YOUNG - FRONTIERSMAN 1940 d: Henry Hathaway. USA., Louis Bromfield, Story

BRIGHT LEAF 1950 d: Michael Curtiz. USA., *Bright Leaf*, Foster Fitz-Simons, 1948, Novel

BRIGHT LIGHTS 1925 d: Robert Z. Leonard. USA., *A Little Bit of Broadway*, Richard Connell, 1924, Short Story

BRIGHT LIGHTS, BIG CITY 1988 d: James Bridges. USA., *Big City Bright Lights*, Jay McInerney, Novel

BRIGHT ROAD 1953 d: Gerald Mayer. USA., *See How They Run*, Mary Elizabeth Vroman, Short Story

Bright Road (Part One) see **JIN GUANG DA DAO** (1975).

Bright Road (Part Two) see **JIN GUANG DA DAO 2** (1976).

BRIGHT SHAWL, THE 1923 d: John S. Robertson. USA., *The Bright Shawl*, Joseph Hergesheimer, New York 1922, Novel

BRIGHT SHINING LIE, A 1998 d: Terry George. USA., *A Bright Shining Lie*, Neil Sheehan, Book

Bright Star at the Stake, A see **CSILLAG A MAGLYAN** (1979).

Bright Sunny Skies see **YAN YANG TIAN** (1973).

BRIGHT VICTORY 1951 d: Mark Robson. USA., *Bright Victory*, Baynard H. Kendrick, Novel

Brighthaven Express see **SALUTE THE TOFF** (1952).

BRIGHTON BEACH MEMOIRS 1987 d: Gene Saks. USA., *Brighton Beach Memoirs*, Neil Simon, 1985, Play

BRIGHTON MYSTERY, THE 1924 d: Hugh Croise. UKN., *The Brighton Mystery*, Baroness Orczy, Short Story

BRIGHTON ROCK 1947 d: John Boulting. UKN., *Brighton Rock*, Graham Greene, 1938, Novel

Brighty see **BRIGHTY OF THE GRAND CANYON** (1967).

Brighty of Grand Canyon see **BRIGHTY OF THE GRAND CANYON** (1967).

BRIGHTY OF THE GRAND CANYON 1967 d: Norman Foster. USA., *Brighty of the Grand Canyon*, Marguerite Henry, New York 1953, Novel

BRILLIANT MARRIAGE 1936 d: Phil Rosen. USA., *Brilliant Marriage*, Ursula Parrott, Novel

BRIMSTONE & TREACLE 1981 d: Richard Loncraine. UKN., *Brimstone and Treacle*, Dennis Potter, 1978, Play

Brincando Nos Campos Do Senhor see **AT PLAY IN THE FIELDS OF THE LORD** (1991).

BRINGIN' HOME THE BACON 1924 d: Richard Thorpe. USA., *Buckin' in the Big Four*, Christopher B. Booth, Short Story

BRINGING UP BABY 1938 d: Howard Hawks. USA., *Bringing Up Baby*, Hagar Wilde, 1937, Short Story

Bringing Up Girls in Bohemia see **VYCHOVA DIVEK V CECHACH** (1997).

Brink of Life see **NARA LIVET** (1958).

BRINK'S JOB, THE 1978 d: William Friedkin. USA., *Big Stick-Up at Brink's*, Noel Behn, Book

BRISEUR DE CHAINES, LE 1941 d: Jacques Daniel-Norman. FRN., *Mamouret*, Jean Sarment, 1943, Play

BRITANNIA MEWS 1948 d: Jean Negulesco. UKN., *Britannia Mews*, Margery Sharp, Novel

BRITANNIA OF BILLINGSGATE 1933 d: Sinclair Hill. UKN., *Britannia of Billingsgate*, Christine Jope-Slade, Sewell Stokes, London 1931, Play

BRITANNICUS 1908 d: Andre Calmettes. FRN., *Britannicus*, Jean Racine, 1669, Play

BRITANNICUS 1912 d: Camille de Morlhon. FRN., *Britannicus*, Jean Racine, 1669, Play

BRITISH AGENT 1934 d: Michael Curtiz. USA., *British Agent*, R. H. Bruce Lockhart, London 1932, Novel

BRITISH INTELLIGENCE 1940 d: Terry O. Morse. USA., *Three Faces East*, Anthony Paul Kelly, New York 1918, Play

BRITTON OF THE SEVENTH 1916 d: Lionel Belmore. USA., *Britton of the Seventh*, Cyrus Townsend Brady, Chicago 1914, Novel

BRIVIDO 1941 d: Giacomo Gentilomo. ITL., *Il Triangolo Magico*, Alessandro de Stefani, Play

BROADWAY 1929 d: Paul Fejos. USA., *Broadway a Play*, George Abbott, Philip Dunning, New York 1927, Play, *Broadway; a Play*, Jed Harris, New York 1927, Play

BROADWAY 1942 d: William A. Seiter. USA., *Broadway a Play*, George Abbott, Philip Dunning, New York 1927, Play, *Broadway; a Play*, Jed Harris, New York 1927, Play

BROADWAY AFTER DARK 1924 d: Monta Bell. USA., *Broadway After Dark*, Owen Davis, Play

BROADWAY BABIES 1929 d: Mervyn Leroy. USA., *Broadway Musketeers*, Jay Gelzer, 1928, Short Story

Broadway Blues see **SYNCOPATING SUE** (1926).

Broadway Bound see **NEIL SIMON'S BROADWAY BOUND** (1991).

BROADWAY BROKE 1923 d: J. Searle Dawley. USA., *Broadway Broke*, Earl Derr Biggers, 1922, Short Story

BROADWAY BUBBLE, THE 1920 d: George L. Sargent. USA., *The Broadway Bubble*, Leigh Gordon Giltner, 1920, Short Story

BROADWAY COWBOY, A 1920 d: Joseph J. Franz. USA., *The Man from Make Believe*, Byron Morgan, Short Story

Broadway Daddies see **BROADWAY BABIES** (1929).

Broadway Dancer, The see **SOUTH SEA LOVE** (1923).

BROADWAY GOLD 1923 d: Eddie Dillon, J. Gordon Cooper. USA., *Broadway Gold*, W. Carey Wonderly, 1922, Short Story

Broadway Hostess, The see **THE PAINTED ANGEL** (1929).

BROADWAY JONES 1917 d: Joseph Kaufman. USA., *Broadway Jones*, George M. Cohan, New York 1912, Play

Broadway Lawyer see **THE MAN WHO TALKED TOO MUCH** (1940).

BROADWAY LOVE 1918 d: Ida May Park. USA., *Broadway Love*, W. Carey Wonderly, 1916, Novel

Broadway Melody of 1944, The see **BROADWAY RHYTHM** (1943).

Broadway Playboy see **TIMES SQUARE PLAYBOY** (1936).

BROADWAY RHYTHM 1943 d: Roy Del Ruth. USA., *Very Warm for May*, Oscar Hammerstein II, Jerome Kern, Musical Play

Broadway Singer see **TORCH SINGER** (1933).

Broadway to Wyoming see **MAISIE** (1939).

Broadway Virgin see **MANHATTAN BUTTERFLY** (1935).

BRODERNA LEJONHJARTA 1977 d: Olle Hellbom. SWD., *Broderna Lejonhjarta*, Astrid Lindgren, Novel

BROGLIACCIO D'AMORE 1976 d: Decio SillA. ITL., *Brogliaccio d'Amore*, Gino Maggiora, Franca Monari, Novel

BROKEN ARROW 1950 d: Delmer Daves. USA., *Blood Brother*, Elliott Arnold, Novel

BROKEN BARRIER 1917 d: George Bellamy. UKN., *A Guilty Mother*, Ben Landeck, Play

Broken Barrier, The see **THE ISLE OF CONQUEST** (1919).

BROKEN BARRIERS 1919 d: Charles E. Davenport. USA., *Khavah*, Shalom Aleichem, Short Story

BROKEN BARRIERS 1924 d: Reginald Barker. USA., *Broken Barriers*, Meredith Nicholson, New York 1922, Novel

BROKEN BLOSSOMS 1919 d: D. W. Griffith. USA., *The Chink and the Child*, Thomas Burke, 1916, Short Story

BROKEN BLOSSOMS 1936 d: John Brahm. UKN., *The Chink and the Child*, Thomas Burke, 1916, Short Story

Broken Blossoms, Or the Yellow Man and the Girl see **BROKEN BLOSSOMS** (1919).

BROKEN BUTTERFLY, THE 1919 d: Maurice Tourneur. USA., *Marcene*, Penelope Knapp, Novel

BROKEN COIN, THE 1915 d: Francis Ford, Grace Cunard. USA., *The Broken Coin*, Emerson Hough, Story

Broken Commandment, The see **HAKAI** (1961).

Broken Dishes see **TOO YOUNG TO MARRY** (1931).

Broken Dishes see **CALLING ALL HUSBANDS** (1940).

BROKEN DOLL, A 1921 d: Allan Dwan. USA., *Johnny Cucabod*, Wilbur Hall, 1920, Short Story

BROKEN GATE, THE 1920 d: Paul Scardon. USA., *The Broken Gate*, Emerson Hough, New York 1917, Novel

BROKEN GATE, THE 1927 d: James C. McKay. USA., *The Broken Gate*, Emerson Hough, New York 1917, Novel

BROKEN HEARTS 1926 d: Maurice Schwartz. USA., *Broken Hearts*, Z. Libin, Story

Broken Jug, The see **DER ZERBROCHENE KRUG** (1937).

BROKEN LANCE 1954 d: Edward Dmytryk. USA., *House of Strangers*, Jerome Weidman, Novel

BROKEN LAW, THE 1915 d: Oscar Apfel. USA., *Romany Rye*, George Borrow, London 1857, Novel

Broken Lives see **UNKNOWN BLONDE** (1934).

BROKEN LULLABY 1932 d: Ernst Lubitsch. USA., *L' Homme Qui J'ai Tue*, Maurice Rostand, Paris 1930, Play

Broken Melody, A see **ZIJN VIOOL** (1914).

BROKEN MELODY, THE 1929 d: Fred Paul. UKN., *The Broken Melody*, Herbert Keen, James T. Tanner, London 1892, Play

BROKEN PROMISE 1981 d: Don Taylor. USA., *Broken Promise*, Kent Hayes, Alex Lazzarino, Book

Broken Promises see **DANGEROUS LOVE** (1920).

BROKEN ROAD, THE 1921 d: Rene Plaissetty. UKN., *The Broken Road*, A. E. W. Mason, Novel

BROKEN ROSARY, THE 1934 d: Harry Hughes. UKN., *The Legend of Provence*, Adelaide Anne Procter, London 1858-61, Poem

BROKEN SILENCE, THE 1922 d: Dell Henderson. USA., *James Oliver Curwood*, Story

BROKEN TRUST 1995 d: Geoffrey Sax. USA., *Court of Honor*, William P. Wood, Novel

BROKEN VIOLIN, THE 1927 d: Oscar Micheaux. USA., *House of Mystery*, Oscar Micheaux, Novel

BROKEN WING, THE 1923 d: Tom Forman. USA., *The Broken Wing*, Paul Dickey, Charles W. Goddard, New York 1920, Play

BROKEN WING, THE 1932 d: Lloyd Corrigan. USA., *The Broken Wing*, Paul Dickey, Charles W. Goddard, New York 1920, Play

Broken Wings, The see **LAL AGHNIHAT ELMOUTAKASRA** (1964).

BROLLOPSBESVAR 1964 d: Ake Falck. SWD., *Brollopsbesvar*, Stig Dagerman, Stockholm 1949, Novel

BROLLOPSNATT, EN 1959 d: Erik Blomberg. SWD/FNL/PLN., *L' Attaque du Moulin*, Emile Zola, 1880, Short Story

BRONCHO BUSTER, THE 1927 d: Ernst Laemmle. USA., *Loco Weed*, Raymond Cannon, Story

BRONX TALE, A 1993 d: Robert de Niro. USA., *A Bronx Tale*, Chazz Palminteri, Play

BRONZE BELL, THE 1921 d: James W. Horne. USA., *The Bronze Bell*, Louis Joseph Vance, New York 1909, Novel

BROODING EYES 1926 d: Edward J. Le Saint. USA., *The Man With the Brooding Eyes*, John Goodwin, Story

Brooklyn Cowboy, The see **COWBOY FROM BROOKLYN** (1938).

Brooks Wilson Ltd. see **LOVING** (1970).

BROOS 1998 d: Mijke de Jong. NTH., *Broos*, Stichting de Akteurs, Play

BROT DER FRUHEN JAHRE, DAS 1962 d: Herbert Vesely. GRM., *Das Brot Der Fruhen Jahre*, Heinrich Boll, 1955, Novel

BROT UND STEINE 1979 d: Mark M. Rissi. SWT/BLG., Otto Locher, Novel

BROTH OF A BOY 1959 d: George Pollock. UKN., *The Big Birthday*, Hugh Leonard, Play

BROTHER ALFRED 1932 d: Henry Edwards. UKN., *Brother Alfred*, Herbert Westbrook, P. G. Wodehouse, London 1913, Play

Brother and Sister *see* **GE GE HE MEI MEI** (1956).

Brother Jonathan *see* **MY BROTHER JONATHAN** (1948).

BROTHER OFFICERS 1915 d: Harold Shaw. UKN., *Brother Officers*, Leo Trevor, London 1898, Play

BROTHER ORCHID 1940 d: Lloyd Bacon. USA., *Brother Orchid*, Richard Connell, 1938, Short Story

BROTHER RAT 1938 d: William Keighley. USA., *Brother Rat*, Fred F. Finkelhoffe, John Monks Jr., New York 1936, Play

BROTHERHOOD OF THE ROSE 1989 d: Marvin J. Chomsky. USA., *Brotherhood of the Rose*, David Morrell, Novel

BROTHERHOOD, THE 1926 d: Walter West. UKN., *Educated Evans*, Edgar Wallace, 1924, Novel

BROTHERLY LOVE 1928 d: Charles F. Reisner. USA., *Big-Hearted Jim*, Patterson Margoni, 1926, Short Story

Brotherly Love *see* **COUNTRY DANCE** (1969).

BROTHERS 1930 d: Walter Lang. USA., *Brothers*, Herbert Ashton Jr., Play

Brothers *see* **GI LIA HAO** (1962).

BROTHERS 1982 d: Terry Bourke. ASL., *Reflex*, Roger Ward, Novel

Brothers Born of Different Mothers *see* **IBO KYODAI** (1957).

BROTHERS IN LAW 1957 d: Roy Boulting. UKN., *Brothers in Law*, Henry Cecil, Novel

BROTHERS IN TROUBLE 1995 d: Udayan Prasad. UKN., *Return Journey*, Abdullah Hussein, Novel

Brothers Karamazov, The *see* **DER MORDER DIMITRI KARAMASOFF** (1931).

Brothers Karamazov, The *see* **I FRATELLI KARAMAZOFF** (1948).

BROTHERS KARAMAZOV, THE 1958 d: Richard Brooks. USA., *Bratya Karamazovy*, Fyodor Dostoyevsky, 1880, Novel

Brothers Karamazov, The *see* **BRATYA KARAMAZOVY** (1968).

BROTHER'S KISS, A 1997 d: Seth Zvi Rosenfeld. USA., *A Brother's Kiss*, Seth Zvi Rosenfeld, Play

Brothers Lionheart, The *see* **BRODERNA LEJONHJARTA** (1977).

BROTHERS RICO, THE 1956 d: Phil Karlson. USA., *Les Freres Rico*, Georges Simenon, 1952, Short Story

BROTHER'S TALE, A 1983 d: Les Chatfield. UKN., *A Brother's Tale*, Stan Barstow, Novel

BROTHERS, THE 1947 d: David MacDonald. UKN., *The Brothers*, L. A. G. Strong, 1931, Novel

Brothers, The *see* **DIE BRUDER** (1976).

BROTHERS UNDER THE SKIN 1922 d: E. Mason Hopper. USA., *Brothers Under Their Skins*, Peter B. Kyne, 1921, Short Story

BROTT, ETT 1940 d: Anders Henrikson. SWD., *Ett Brott*, Sigfrid Siwertz, 1938, Play

BROTT OCH STRAFF 1945 d: Erik Faustman. SWD., *Prestupleniye I Nakazaniye*, Fyodor Dostoyevsky, 1867, Novel

BROWN DERBY, THE 1926 d: Charles Hines. USA., *The Brown Derby*, Brian Marlow, E. S. Merlin, 1925, Play

BROWN OF HARVARD 1911 d: Colin Campbell. USA., *Brown of Harvard*, Gilbert P. Coleman, Rida Johnson Young, New York 1906, Play

BROWN OF HARVARD 1918 d: Harry Beaumont. USA., *Brown of Harvard*, Gilbert P. Coleman, Rida Johnson Young, New York 1906, Play

BROWN OF HARVARD 1926 d: Jack Conway. USA., *Brown of Harvard*, Gilbert P. Coleman, Rida Johnson Young, New York 1906, Play

BROWN ON RESOLUTION 1935 d: Walter Forde, Anthony Asquith. UKN., *Brown on Resolution*, C. S. Forester, 1929, Novel

Brown on Resolution *see* **SINGLE-HANDED** (1953).

BROWN SUGAR 1922 d: Fred Paul. UKN., *Brown Sugar*, Lady Arthur Lever, London 1920, Play

BROWN SUGAR 1931 d: Leslie Hiscott. UKN., *Brown Sugar*, Lady Arthur Lever, London 1920, Play

BROWN WALLET, THE 1936 d: Michael Powell. UKN., *The Brown Wallet*, Stacy Aumonier, Short Story

BROWN WOLF 1971 d: George Kaczender. CND., *Brown Wolf*, Jack London, 1906, Short Story

BROWNING VERSION, THE 1951 d: Anthony Asquith. UKN., *The Browning Version*, Terence Rattigan, London 1948, Play

BROWNING VERSION, THE 1994 d: Mike Figgis. UKN., *The Browning Version*, Terence Rattigan, London 1948, Play

BROWN'S REQUIEM 1998 d: Jason Freeland. USA., *Brown's Requiem*, James Ellroy, 1981, Novel

Bruce of Circle a *see* **SHOD WITH FIRE** (1920).

BRUCE PARTINGTON PLANS, THE 1922 d: George Ridgwell. UKN., *The Bruce Partington Plans*, Arthur Conan Doyle, Short Story

Bruce Partington Plans, The *see* **THE RETURN OF SHERLOCK HOLMES: THE BRUCE PARTINGTON PLANS** (1986).

BRUCKE, DIE 1959 d: Bernhard Wicki. GRM., *Die Brucke*, Manfred Gregor, Vienna 1958, Novel

BRUDER, DIE 1976 d: Wolfgang Gremm. GRM., Septimus Dale, Short Story

Bruder Martin *see* **UND DER HIMMEL LACHT DAZU** (1954).

BRUDERCHEN UND SCHWESTERCHEN 1953 d: Walter Oehmichen. GRM., Jacob Grimm, Wilhelm Grimm, Short Story

BRUDERLEIN FEIN 1942 d: Hans Thimig. GRM., *Ferdinand Raimund*, Eduard Paul Danszkzys, Biography

BRUDERMORD, EIN 1981 d: Brothers Quay. UKN., *Ein Brudermord*, Franz Kafka, 1919, Short Story

BRUJA, LA 1923 d: Maximiliano Thous. SPN., *La Bruja*, Miguel Ramos Carrion, Ruperto Chapi, Opera

BRULES, LES 1958 d: Bernard Devlin. CND., *Nuages Sur Les Brules*, Herve Biron, Novel

Brutal Job *see* **PEAU D'ESPION** (1967).

BRUTE BREAKER, THE 1919 d: Lynn Reynolds. USA., *The Brute Breaker*, Johnston McCulley, 1918, Novel

BRUTE, THE 1914 d: Thomas N. Heffron. USA., *The Brute*, Frederic Arnold Kummer, New York 1912, Novel

BRUTE, THE 1927 d: Irving Cummings. USA., *The Brute*, W. Douglas Newton, New York 1924, Novel

Brute, The *see* **DUVAD** (1959).

Brute, The *see* **YAJU NO SEISHUN** (1963).

BRUTO 1910 d: Giuseppe de Liguoro. ITL., *Julius Caesar*, William Shakespeare, c1599, Play

BRUTO 1911 d: Enrico Guazzoni. ITL., *Julius Caesar*, William Shakespeare, c1599, Play

Brutus *see* **BRUTO** (1910).

Brutus *see* **BRUTO** (1911).

BRUTUS AND CASSIUS 1918 d: Marshall Moore. UKN., *Julius Caesar*, William Shakespeare, c1599, Play

BRZEZINA 1971 d: Andrzej WajdA. PLN., *Brzezina*, Jaroslaw Iwaszkiewicz, 1933, Short Story

BU NENG ZOU NEI TIAO LU 1954 d: Ying Yunwei. CHN., *Bu Neng Zou Nie Tiao Lu*, Li Zhun, Novel

Bu'asa, Al- *see* **EL BOUASSA** (1944).

BUBBLES 1920 d: Wayne MacK. USA., *Bubbles*, J. Basil Kreider, Short Story

BUBU 1971 d: Mauro Bolognini. ITL., *Bubu Di Montparnasse*, Charles L. Philippe, Novel

Bubu Di Montparnasse *see* **BUBU** (1971).

BUCCANEER, THE 1938 d: Cecil B. de Mille. USA., *Lafitte the Pirate*, Lyle Saxon, New York 1930, Novel

BUCCANEER, THE 1958 d: Anthony Quinn. USA., *Lafitte the Pirate*, Lyle Saxon, New York 1930, Novel

Buccia Di Banana *see* **PEAU DE BANANE** (1964).

BUCHANAN RIDES ALONE 1958 d: Budd Boetticher. USA., *The Name's Buchanan*, Jonas Ward, Novel

BUCHANAN'S WIFE 1918 d: Charles J. Brabin. USA., *Buchanan's Wife*, Justus Miles Forman, New York 1906, Novel

BUCHSE DER PANDORA, DIE 1929 d: G. W. Pabst. GRM., *Die Buchse Der Pandora*, Frank Wedekind, 1904, Play, *Der Erdgeist*, Frank Wedekind, 1895, Play

Buckaroo *see* **THUNDER TRAIL** (1937).

BUCKAROO KID, THE 1926 d: Lynn Reynolds. USA., *Oh Promise Me*, Peter B. Kyne, 1926, Short Story

Bucket of Blood *see* **THE TELL-TALE HEART** (1934).

BUCKET OF BLOOD, A 1960 d: Roger Corman. USA., *The Tell-Tale Heart*, Edgar Allan Poe, 1843, Short Story

BUCKING THE LINE 1921 d: Carl Harbaugh. USA., *The Real Man*, Francis Lynde, New Ork 1915, Novel

BUCKING THE TIGER 1921 d: Henry Kolker. USA., *Bucking the Tiger*, Achmed Abdullah, New York 1917, Novel

BUCK'S LADY FRIEND 1915 d: William Bertram. USA., *Buck's Lady Friend*, Charles E. Van Loan, Story

BUCKSHOT JOHN 1915 d: Hobart Bosworth. USA., *The Message to Buckshot John*, Charles E. Van Loan, 1912, Novel

BUCKSKIN FRONTIER 1943 d: Lesley Selander. USA., *Buckskin Empire*, Harry Sinclair Drago, Novel

Buco, Il *see* **LE TROU** (1960).

BUD AND LOU 1978 d: Robert C. Thompson. USA., *Bud and Lou*, Bob Thomas, Book

Budapest Cloudplay *see* **FELHOJATEK!** (1984).

BUDAPESTI TAVASZ 1955 d: Felix Mariassy. HNG., *Budapesti Tavasz*, Ferenc Karinthy, 1953, Novel

BUDDENBROOKS, DIE 1923 d: Gerhard Lamprecht. GRM., *Buddenbrooks*, Thomas Mann, Berlin 1901, Novel

BUDDENBROOKS, DIE 1959 d: Alfred Weidenmann. GRM., *Buddenbrooks*, Thomas Mann, Berlin 1901, Novel

BUDDY 1997 d: Caroline Thompson. USA., *Animals are My Hobby*, Gertrude Davies Lintz, Book

BUDDY, BUDDY 1981 d: Billy Wilder. USA., *Buddy Buddy*, Francis Veber, Play

BUDDY HOLLY STORY, THE 1978 d: Steve Rash. USA., *The Buddy Holly Story*, John Goldrosen, Biography

BUDDY'S SONG 1991 d: Claude Whatham. UKN., *Buddy's Song*, Nigel Hinton, Novel

BUDENJE PACOVA 1967 d: Zivojin Pavlovic. YGS., *Neznanka*, Momcilo Milankov, 1964, Short Story

Budjenje Pacova *see* **BUDENJE PACOVA** (1967).

BUENAVENTURA, LA 1934 d: William McGann. MXC., *The Fortune Teller*, Victor Herbert, Harry B. Smith, New York 1929, Opera

BUENOS DIAS PERDIDOS, LOS 1975 d: Rafael Gil. SPN., *Los Buenos Dias Perdidos*, Antonio Gala, 1973, Play

Buffalo Bill *see* **BUFFALO BILL AND THE INDIANS OR SITTING BULL'S HISTORY LESSON** (1976).

BUFFALO BILL AND THE INDIANS OR SITTING BULL'S HISTORY LESSON 1976 d: Robert Altman. USA., *Indians*, Arthur Kopit, 1969, Play

Buffalo Stampede *see* **THUNDERING HERD** (1933).

BUG 1975 d: Jeannot Szwarc. USA., *The Hephaestus Plague*, Thomas Page, Novel

BUGIARDA, LA 1965 d: Luigi Comencini. ITL/SPN/FRN., *La Bugiarda*, Diego Fabbri, Milan 1956, Play

BUGLER OF ALGIERS, THE 1916 d: Rupert Julian. USA., *We are French!*, Robert Hobart Davis, Perley Poore Sheehan, New York 1914, Novel

BUGLES IN THE AFTERNOON 1952 d: Roy Rowland. USA., *Bugles in the Afternoon*, Ernest Haycox, 1944, Novel

BUGSY 1991 d: Barry Levinson. USA., *We Only Kill Each Other*, Dean Jennings, Book

Build My Gallows High *see* **OUT OF THE PAST** (1947).

BUILDER OF BRIDGES, THE 1915 d: George Irving. USA., *The Builder of Bridges*, Alfred Sutro, London 1908, Play

BULGARI OT STARO VREME 1945 d: Dimiter Minkov. BUL., *Balgari Ot Staro Vreme*, Lyuben Karavelov, 1867, Novel

Bulgarian Woman, A *see* **EDNA BULGARKA** (1956).

Bulgarians of Ancient Times *see* **BULGARI OT STARO VREME** (1945).

Bull Monastery *see* **KUMPEL (2): DAS BULLENKLOSTER LASS JUCKEN** (1972).

BULL OF THE WEST, THE 1971 d: Paul Stanley, Jerry Hopper. USA., *The Bull of the West*, Dee Linford, Novel

BULLDOG DRUMMOND 1923 d: Oscar Apfel. UKN/NTH., *Bulldog Drummond*, H. C. McNeile ("Sapper"), 1920, Novel

BULLDOG DRUMMOND 1929 d: F. Richard Jones. USA., *Bulldog Drummond*, H. C. McNeile ("Sapper"), 1920, Novel

BULLDOG DRUMMOND AT BAY 1937 d: Norman Lee. UKN., *Bulldog Drummond at Bay*, H. C. McNeile ("Sapper"), Novel

BULLDOG DRUMMOND COMES BACK 1937 d: Louis King. USA., *The Female of the Species*, H. C. McNeile ("Sapper"), London 1928, Novel

BULLDOG DRUMMOND ESCAPES 1937 d: James P. Hogan. USA., *Bulldog Drummond Again*, Gerard Fairlie, Sapper, Play

BULLDOG DRUMMOND IN AFRICA 1938 d: Louis King. USA., *Challenge*, H. C. McNeile ("Sapper"), New York 1937, Novel

Bulldog Drummond Interferes see **BULLDOG DRUMMOND'S PERIL** (1938).

Bulldog Drummond Saves a Lady see **BULLDOG DRUMMOND ESCAPES** (1937).

BULLDOG DRUMMOND STRIKES BACK 1934 d: Roy Del Ruth. USA., *Bulldog Drummond Strikes Back*, H. C. McNeile ("Sapper"), New York 1933, Novel

BULLDOG DRUMMOND'S BRIDE 1939 d: James P. Hogan. USA., *Bulldog Drummond and the Oriental Mind*, H. C. McNeile ("Sapper"), 1937, Short Story

Bulldog Drummond's Holiday see **BULLDOG DRUMMOND ESCAPES** (1937).

BULLDOG DRUMMOND'S PERIL 1938 d: James P. Hogan. USA., *The Third Round*, H. C. McNeile ("Sapper"), London 1924, Novel

BULLDOG DRUMMOND'S REVENGE 1937 d: Louis King. USA., *The Return of Bulldog Drummond*, H. C. McNeile ("Sapper"), London 1932, Novel

Bulldog Drummond's Romance see **BULLDOG DRUMMOND ESCAPES** (1937).

BULLDOG DRUMMOND'S SECRET POLICE 1939 d: James P. Hogan. USA., *Temple Tower*, H. C. McNeile ("Sapper"), Garden City, N.Y. 1929, Novel

BULLDOG DRUMMOND'S THIRD ROUND 1925 d: Sidney Morgan. UKN., *The Third Round*, H. C. McNeile ("Sapper"), London 1924, Novel

Bulldog of the Mysterious Sanatorium, The see **BULLDOG DRUMMOND** (1923).

BULLDOG PLUCK 1927 d: Jack Nelson. USA., *Hardwick of Hambone*, W. Bert Foster, Short Story

BULLDOG SEES IT THROUGH 1940 d: Harold Huth. UKN., *Scissors Cut Paper*, Gerard Fairlie, Novel

Bullenkloster, Das see **KUMPEL (2): DAS BULLENKLOSTER LASS JUCKEN** (1972).

BULLET FOR A BADMAN 1964 d: R. G. Springsteen. USA., *Renegade Posse*, Marvin H. Albert, Novel

Bullet for Stefano, A see **IL PASSATORE** (1947).

Bullet Proof see **LAW AND ORDER** (1932).

BULLET SCARS 1942 d: D. Ross Lederman. USA., William Riley Burnett, Story

BULLITT 1968 d: Peter Yates. USA., *Mute Witness*, Robert L. Fish, New York 1963, Novel

BUMERANG 1960 d: Alfred Weidenmann. GRM., *Bumerang*, Igor Sentjurc, Bad Worishofen 1959, Novel

BUN SANG YUN 1997 d: Hsu An-HuA. HKG., *Bun Sang Yun*, Eileen Chang, Novel

Bunbury see **SCHERZ UND ERNST LIEBE** (1932).

BUNCH OF KEYS, A 1915 d: Richard Foster Baker. USA., *A Bunch of Keys*, Charles Hale Hoyt, 1882, Play

BUNCH OF VIOLETS, A 1916 d: Frank Wilson. UKN., *A Bunch of Violets*, Sidney Grundy, London 1894, Play

BUNDLE OF JOY 1957 d: Norman Taurog. USA., Felix Jackson, Story

BUNKER BEAN 1936 d: William Hamilton, Edward Killy. USA., *Bunker Bean*, Harry Leon Wilson, New York 1913, Novel

BUNKER, THE 1981 d: George Schaefer. USA., *The Bunker*, James O'Donnell, Book

BUNNY LAKE IS MISSING 1965 d: Otto Preminger. UKN., *Bunny Lake Is Missing*, Evelyn Piper, New York 1957, Novel

BUNTKARIERTEN, DIE 1949 d: Kurt Maetzig. GDR., *Wahrend Der Stromsperre*, Berta Waterstradt, Story

BUNTY PULLS THE STRINGS 1921 d: Reginald Barker. USA., *Bunty Pulls the Strings*, Graham Moffatt, London 1911, Play

BUON LADRONE, IL 1917 d: Giulio Antamoro. ITL., *Le Memorie Di un Ladro*, Ferdinando Russo, 1907

BUON SAMARITANO, IL 1919 d: Eleuterio Rodolfi. ITL., *Il Buon Samaritano*, Claude Lemaitre, Novel

BUONA FIGLIOLA, LA 1920 d: Mario Caserini. ITL., *La Buona Figliola*, Sabatino Lopez, 1909, Play

BUONA SERA, MRS. CAMPBELL 1969 d: Melvin Frank. USA., *Mrs. Campbell Buena Sera*, Aitken Morewood

BUONGIORNO PRIMO AMORE! 1957 d: Marino Girolami. ITL./SPN., *Valentina*, Marcello Marchesi, Vittorio Metz, Play

BURAIKAN 1970 d: Masahiro ShinodA. JPN., Mokuami Kawatake, Play

BURDEN OF PROOF, THE 1918 d: Julius Steger, John G. Adolfi. USA., *Dora*, Victorien Sardou, Paris 1877, Play

BURE BARUTA 1998 d: Goran Paskaljevic. YGS/FRN/GRC., *Bure Baruta*, Dejan Dukovski, Play

BUREAU OF MISSING PERSONS 1933 d: Roy Del Ruth. USA., *Missing Men*, Capt. John H. Ayers, Carol Bird, New York 1932, Book

BURGLAR 1987 d: Hugh Wilson. USA., Lawrence Block, Book

BURGLAR AND THE GIRL, THE 1928 d: Hugh Croise. UKN., *The Burglar and the Girl*, Matthew Boulton, Play

BURGLAR PROOF 1920 d: Maurice Campbell. USA., *Burglar Proof*, William Slavens McNutt, 1920, Novel

BURGLAR, THE 1917 d: Harley Knoles. USA., *Editha's Burglar*, Augustus Thomas, New York 1887, Play

BURGLAR, THE 1957 d: Paul Wendkos. USA., *The Burglar*, David Goodis, 1953, Novel

Burglar-Proof see **BURGLAR PROOF** (1920).

Burglars, The see **LE CASSE** (1971).

BURGOMASTER OF STILEMONDE, THE 1928 d: George J. Banfield. UKN., *The Burgomaster of Stilemonde*, Maurice Maeterlinck, London 1919, Play

BURIDAN, HEROS DE LA TOUR DE NESLE 1951 d: Emile Couzinet. FRN., *Buridan - Heros de la Tour de Nesle*, Michel Zevaco, Novel

Buried Alive see **LA SEPOLTA VIVA** (1949).

BURIED TREASURE, THE 1919 d: Kenneth Webb. USA., *The Buried Treasure*, O. Henry, Short Story

BURIED TREASURE 1921 d: George D. Baker. USA., *Buried Treasure*, Frederick Britten Austin, 1923, Short Story

Burlesque see **THE DANCE OF LIFE** (1929).

Burlesque see **WHEN MY BABY SMILES AT ME** (1948).

Burlesque on Carmen see **CHARLIE CHAPLIN'S BURLESQUE ON CARMEN** (1916).

Burmese Harp, The see **BIRUMA NO TATEGOTO** (1956).

Burmese Harp, The see **BIRUMA NO TATE GOTO** (1985).

BURN 'EM UP O'CONNOR 1938 d: Edward Sedgwick. USA., *Salute to the Gods*, Sir Malcolm Campbell, New York 1935, Novel

Burn Out see **JOURNEY INTO FEAR** (1975).

Burn, Witch, Burn see **NIGHT OF THE EAGLE** (1962).

Burned Map, The see **MOETSUKITA CHIZU** (1968).

Burning Court, The see **LA CHAMBRE ARDENTE** (1961).

Burning Cross, The see **THE KLANSMAN** (1974).

BURNING DAYLIGHT 1920 d: Edward Sloman. USA., *Burning Daylight*, Jack London, New York 1910, Novel

BURNING DAYLIGHT 1928 d: Charles J. Brabin. USA., *Burning Daylight*, Jack London, New York 1910, Novel

BURNING DAYLIGHT: THE ADVENTURES OF "BURNING DAYLIGHT" IN ALASKA 1914 d: Hobart Bosworth. USA., *Burning Daylight*, Jack London, New York 1910, Novel

BURNING DAYLIGHT: THE ADVENTURES OF "BURNING DAYLIGHT" IN CIVILIZATION 1914 d: Hobart Bosworth. USA., *Burning Daylight*, Jack London, New York 1910, Novel

BURNING HILLS, THE 1956 d: Stuart Heisler. USA., *The Burning Hills*, Louis L'Amour, Novel

BURNING SANDS 1922 d: George Melford. USA., *Burning Sands*, Arthur Weigall, New York 1921, Novel

BURNING SECRET 1989 d: Andrew Birkin. UKN/USA/GRM., *Brennendes Geheimnis*, Stefan Zweig, 1929, Short Story

Burning Secret, The see **BRENNENDES GEHEIMNIS** (1933).

BURNING, THE 1968 d: Stephen Frears. UKN., *The Day*, Roland Starke, Short Story

Burning the Red Lotus Temple (Part 1) see **HUOSHAO HONGLIANSI (PART 1)** (1928).

BURNING THE WIND 1929 d: Henry McRae, Herbert Blache. USA., *A Daughter of the Dons*, William MacLeod Raine, New York 1914, Novel

BURNING TRAIL, THE 1925 d: Arthur Rosson. USA., *Sundown Slim*, Henry Herbert Knibbs, Boston 1915, Novel

Burnt Child see **BRANT BARN** (1967).

BURNT EVIDENCE 1954 d: Daniel Birt. UKN., *Burn the Evidence*, Percy Hoskins, Short Story

Burnt Fingers see **MAMA STEPS OUT** (1937).

BURNT IN 1920 d: Duncan MacRae. UKN., *Burnt in*, S. B. Hill, Novel

BURNT OFFERINGS 1976 d: Dan Curtis. USA., *Burnt Offerings*, Robert Marasco, Novel

BURNT WINGS 1916 d: Walter West. UKN., *Burnt Wings*, Mrs. Stanley Wrench, Novel

BURNT WINGS 1920 d: W. Christy Cabanne. USA., *The Primrose Path*, Bayard Veiller, New York 1907, Play

BURU GUI 1926 d: Yang XIaozhong. CHN., *Buru Gui*, Tokutomi Roka, Novel

BUS STOP 1956 d: Joshua Logan. USA., *Bus Stop*, William Inge, New York 1955, Play

BUSCA, LA 1967 d: Angelino Fons. SPN., *La Busca*, Pio Baroja Y Nessi, 1904, Novel

BUSCON, EL 1974 d: Luciano BerriatuA. SPN., *La Historia de la Vida Del Buscon*, Francisco Gomez de Quevedo Y Villegas, 1626, Novel

BUSH PILOT 1947 d: Sterling Campbell. CND., W. Scott Darling, Story

Bushbabies, The see **THE BUSHBABY** (1970).

BUSHBABY, THE 1970 d: John Trent. UKN., *The Bushbabies*, William H. Stevenson, Boston 1965, Novel

BUSINESS AFFAIR, A 1993 d: Charlotte Brandstrom. UKN/FRN/GRM., *Tears Before Bedtime - Weep No More*, Barbara Skelton, Novel

BUSINESS AND PLEASURE 1931 d: David Butler. USA., *The Plutocrat*, Booth Tarkington, New York 1927, Novel

BUSINESS IS BUSINESS 1915 d: Otis Turner. USA., *Les Affaires Sont Les Affaires*, Octave Mirbeau, Paris 1903, Play

Business Is Business see **WAT ZIEN IK** (1971).

BUSINESS OF LIFE, THE 1918 d: Tom Terriss. USA., *The Business of Life*, Robert W. Chambers, New York 1913, Novel

BUSMAN'S HONEYMOON 1940 d: Arthur Woods. UKN., *Busman's Honeymoon*, Dorothy L. Sayers, 1937, Novel

BUSTER SE MARIE 1931 d: Edward Brophy, Claude Autant-LarA. USA., *Bedroom and Bath Parlor*, Charles W. Bell, New York 1917, Play, *Parlor Bedroom and Bath*, Mark Swan, New York 1917, Play

BUSTER, THE 1923 d: Colin Campbell. USA., *The Buster*, William Patterson White, Boston 1920, Novel

BUSTERS VERDEN 1984 d: Bille August. DNM., Bjarne Reuter, Story

Buster's World see **BUSTERS VERDEN** (1984).

BUSY BODY, THE 1967 d: William Castle. USA., *The Busy Body*, Donald E. Westlake, New York 1966, Novel

Busybody see **THE KIBITZER** (1930).

But It's Nothing Serious see **MA NON E UNA COSA SERIA** (1936).

BUT NOT FOR ME 1959 d: Walter Lang. USA., *Accent on Youth*, Samson Raphaelson, New York 1934, Play

But Not Goodbye see **THE COCKEYED MIRACLE** (1946).

BUT NOT IN VAIN 1948 d: Edmond T. Greville. UKN., *But Not in Vain*, Ben Van Eeslyn, Play

BUT THE FLESH IS WEAK 1932 d: Jack Conway. USA., *The Truth Game*, Ivor Novello, London 1928, Play

BUTCH MINDS THE BABY 1942 d: Albert S. Rogell. USA., *Butch Minds the Baby*, Damon Runyon, 1931, Short Story

BUTCH MINDS THE BABY 1980 d: Peter Webb. UKN., *Butch Minds the Baby*, Damon Runyon, 1931, Short Story

BUTCHER BOY, THE 1997 d: Neil Jordan. USA., *The Butcher Boy*, Patrick McCabe, 1992, Novel

BUTLER'S NIGHT OFF, THE 1950 d: Roger Racine. CND., *The Butler's Night Off*, Silvio Narizzano, Story

BUTLEY 1973 d: Harold Pinter. UKN/USA., *Butley*, Simon Gray, 1971, Play

BUTTER AND EGG MAN, THE 1928 d: Richard Wallace. USA., *The Butter and Egg Man*, George S. Kaufman, New York 1925, Play

BUTTERBROT 1989 d: Gabriel Barylli. GRM., *Butterbrot*, Gabriel Barylli, Play

BUTTERCUP CHAIN, THE 1970 d: Robert Ellis Miller. UKN., *The Buttercup Chain*, Janice Elliott, Novel

BUTTERFIELD 8 1960 d: Daniel Mann. USA., *Butterfield 8*, John O'Hara, 1935, Novel

BUTTERFLIES ARE FREE 1972 d: Milton Katselas. USA., *Butterflies are Free*, Leonard Gershe, New York 1969, Play

Butterflies Don't Cry see **SCHMETTERLINGE WEINEN NICHT** (1970).

BUTTERFLIES IN THE RAIN 1926 d: Edward Sloman. USA., *Butterflies in the Rain*, Andrew Soutar, Novel

BUTTERFLY 1981 d: Matt Cimber. USA., *Butterfly*, James M. Cain, 1947, Novel

BUTTERFLY MAN, THE 1920 d: Ida May Park. USA., *The Butterfly Man*, George Barr McCutcheon, New York 1910, Novel

Butterfly on the Shoulder see **UN PAPILLON SUR L'EPAULE** (1978).

BUTTERFLY ON THE WHEEL, A 1915 d: Maurice Tourneur. USA., *A Butterfly on the Wheel*, Edward Hemmerde, Francis Neilson, London 1911, Play

Butterfly on the Wheel, The see **DIE FRAU AUF DER FOLTER** (1928).

BUTTERFLY REVOLUTION 1985 d: Penelope Spheeris. USA., *William Butler*, Story

Butterfly Revolution, The see **SUMMER CAMP NIGHTMARE** (1987).

Butterfly That Flew Over the Sea ,the see **LA MARIPOSA QUE VOLO SOBRE EL MAR** (1951).

BUTTERFLY, THE 1915 d: O. A. C. Lund. USA., *The Butterfly*, Henry Kitchell Webster, New York 1914, Novel

Buttlerflies see **BLACK BUTTERFLIES** (1928).

BUTTSUKE HONBAN 1958 d: Kozo Saeki. JPN., *Buttsuke Honban*, Hajime Mizuno, Moto Ogasawara, Book

BUWANA TOSHI NO UTA 1965 d: Susumu Hani. JPN., Toshishide Katayori, Novel

BUYER FROM CACTUS CITY, THE 1918 d: Ashley Miller. USA., *The Buyer from Cactus City*, O. Henry, Short Story

Bwana see **THE WHITE LIONS** (1979).

BWANA 1996 d: Imanol Uribe. SPN., *La Mirada Del Hombre Oscuro*, Ignacio Del Moral, Play

Bwana Toshi see **BUWANA TOSHI NO UTA** (1965).

By Berwen Banks see **BY BERWIN BANKS** (1920).

BY BERWIN BANKS 1920 d: Sidney Morgan. UKN., *By Berwin Banks*, Allen Raine, Novel

BY CANDLELIGHT 1933 d: James Whale. USA., *Kleine Komedie*, Siegfried Geyer, Play

By Dint of Crawling see **A FUERZA DE ARRASTRARSE** (1924).

BY DIVINE RIGHT 1924 d: R. William Neill. USA., *The Way Men Love*, Adam Hull Shirk, Story

BY INJUNCTION 1918 d: David Smith. USA., *By Injunction*, O. Henry, Short Story

BY LOVE POSSESSED 1961 d: John Sturges. USA., *By Love Possessed*, James Gould Cozzens, New York 1957, Novel

By Power of Attorney see **IL MISTERO DI JACK HILTON** (1913).

BY PROXY 1918 d: Cliff Smith. USA., *Red Saunders Stories*, Henry Wallace Phillips, 1902-06, Short Stories

By Right of Conquest see **THE ISLE OF CONQUEST** (1919).

By Rocket to the Moon see **DIE FRAU IM MOND** (1929).

By Secret Command see **THE SECRET COMMAND** (1944).

By St. Anthony see **U SVETEHO ANTONICKA** (1933).

By St. Matthias see **KDYZ SE SLUNKO ZASMEJE U SVATEHO MATEJE** (1928).

By the Law see **PO ZAKONU** (1926).

BY THE LIGHT OF THE SILVERY MOON 1953 d: David Butler. USA., *Penrod*, Booth Tarkington, New York 1914, Novel

By the Steep Ravine see **U KRUTOGO YARA** (1962).

BY THE WORLD FORGOT 1918 d: David Smith. USA., *By the World Forgot*, Cyrus Townsend Brady, Chicago 1917, Novel

BY YOUR LEAVE 1934 d: Lloyd Corrigan. USA., *By Your Leave*, Gladys Hurlbut, Wells, Emma B. C., Play

BYAKUYA NO YOJO 1958 d: Eisuke TakizawA. JPN., *Koya Hijiri*, Kyoka Izumi, Tokyo 1901, Novel

BYE BYE BIRDIE 1963 d: George Sidney. USA., *Bye Bye Birdie*, Michael Stewart, Charles Strouse, New York 1960, Musical Play

BYE BYE BRAVERMAN 1968 d: Sidney Lumet. USA., *To an Early Grave*, Wallace Markfield, New York 1964, Novel

Bye, Bye, Jupiter see **SAYONARA JIYUPETA** (1983).

'Bye, See You Monday see **A LUNDI AU REVOIR** (1980).

BYE-BYE BUDDY 1929 d: Frank S. Mattison. USA., *Bye-Bye Buddy*, Ben Herschfield, Story

Byeg Inokhodtsa see **PRASHNAI GULSARA** (1969).

BYELEYET PARUS ODINOKY 1937 d: Vladimir Legoshin. USS., *Beleyet Parus Odinokiy*, Valentin Kataev, 1936, Novel

BYELI PAROKHOD 1976 d: Bolotbek Shamshiev. USS., *Belyi Parokhod*, Chingiz Aitmatov, 1970, Short Story

BYOIN DE SHINU TO IU KOTO 1993 d: Jun IchikawA. JPN., *Byoin de Shinu to Iu Koto*, Fumio Yamazaki, Book

C. A. K. POLNI MARSALEK 1930 d: Carl Lamac. CZC., *Der K. Und K. Feldmarschall*, Emil Artur Longen, Play

CA N'ARRIVE QU'AUX VIVANTS 1958 d: Tony Saytor. FRN., *Ca N'arrive Qu'aux Vivants*, James Hadley Chase, Novel

Ca S'est Passe a Rome see **LA GIORNATA BALORDA** (1960).

Ca S'est Passe En Plein Jour see **ES GESCHAH AM HELLICHTEN TAG** (1958).

Caballero de la Rosa Roja, El see **ROSE ROSSE PER ANGELICA** (1966).

CABALLERO'S WAY, THE 1914. USA., *Caballero's Way*, O. Henry, 1904, Short Story

Caballos Salvajes see **VALDEZ IL MEZZOSANGUE** (1974).

CABANE D'AMOUR, LA 1923 d: Jane Bruno-Ruby. FRN., *La Cabane d'Amour*, Francis de Miomandre, Novel

CABARET 1972 d: Bob Fosse. USA., *The Berlin Stories*, Christopher Isherwood, 1945, Book, *I Am a Camera*, John Van Druten, 1952, Play

CABELEIRA, O 1962 d: Milton Amaral. BRZ., *O Cabeleira*, Franklin Tavora, 1876, Novel

CABEZA DE VACA 1990 d: Nicolas EchevarriA. MXC/SPN/UKN., *Naufragios*, Alvar Nunez Cabeza de Vaca, Book

Cabezas Quemadas see **LES TETES BRULEES** (1967).

CABIN IN THE COTTON 1932 d: Michael Curtiz, William Keighley. USA., *The Cabin in the Cotton*, Harry Harrison Kroll, New York 1931, Novel

CABIN IN THE SKY 1942 d: Vincente Minnelli. USA., *Cabin in the Sky*, Lynn Root, Musical Play

Cabin of Love see **LA CABANE D'AMOUR** (1923).

CABIRIA 1914 d: Giovanni Pastrone. ITL., *Il Romanzo Della Fiamme*, Emilio Salgari, Novel

CABRITA QUE TIRA AL MONTE 1925 d: Fernando Delgado. SPN., *Cabrita Que Tira Al Monte*, Joaquin Alvarez Quintero, Serafin Alvarez Quintero, Play

CACADOR DE FANTASMA, O 1975 d: Flavio Migliaccio. BRZ., *The Canterville Ghost*, Oscar Wilde, 1891, Short Story

CACCIA AL LUPO 1917 d: Giuseppe Sterni. ITL., *Caccia Al Lupo*, Giovanni Verga, 1901

Caccia Al Montone see **L' ORDINATEUR DES POMPES FUNEBRES** (1976).

CACCIA ALLA VOLPE 1965 d: Vittorio de SicA. ITL/UKN., Neil Simon, Play

CACORKA 1935 d: Jan SvobodA. CZC., *Cacorka*, Anna Ziegloserova, Play

CACTUS FLOWER 1969 d: Gene Saks. USA., *Cactus Flower*, Abe Burrows, New York 1964, Play

CAD, A 1916 d: Ben Wilson. USA., *A Cad*, Raymond L. Schrock, Story

Cad, The see **A CAD** (1916).

CADA QUIEN SU VIDA 1959 d: Julio Bracho. MXC., *Cada Quien Su Vida*, Luis G. Basurto, Play

Cadavere Di Troppo, Un see **LA MAIN A COUPER** (1974).

CADAVERE VIVENTE, IL 1921 d: Pier Angelo Mazzolotti. ITL., *Zhivoi Trup*, Lev Nikolayevich Tolstoy, Moscow 1911, Play

CADAVERI ECCELLENTI 1976 d: Francesco Rosi. ITL/FRN., *Il Contesto*, Leonardo Sciasia, 1971, Novel

CADAVRES EN VACANCES 1961 d: Jacqueline Audry. FRN., *Cadavres En Vacances*, Jean-Pierre Ferriere, Novel

Cadavres Exquis see **CADAVERI ECCELLENTI** (1976).

CADEAU, LE 1982 d: Michel Lang. FRN/ITL., *Le Cadeau*, Terzoli, Vaime, Play

CADFAEL: MONKS HOOD 1994 d: Graham Theakston. UKN., Ellis Peters, Story

CADFAEL: ONE CORPSE TOO MANY 1993 d: Graham Theakston. UKN., *One Corpse Too Many*, Ellis Peters, Novel

CADFAEL: THE LEPER OF ST. GILES 1994 d: Graham Theakston. UKN., *Leper of St. Giles*, Ellis Peters, Novel

CADFAEL: THE SANCTUARY SPARROW 1994 d: Graham Theakston. UKN., *The Sanctuary Sparrow*, Ellis Peters, Novel

CAESAR AND CLEOPATRA 1946 d: Gabriel Pascal, Brian Desmond Hurst. UKN., *Caesar and Cleopatra*, George Bernard Shaw, 1901, Play

Caesar's Wife see **ANOTHER DAWN** (1937).

Cafe de l'Egypte, The see **THE CAFE L'EGYPTE** (1924).

CAFE IN CAIRO, A 1924 d: Chet Withey. USA., *A Cafe in Cairo*, Izola Forrester, 1924, Short Story

CAFE L'EGYPTE, THE 1924 d: Fred Paul. UKN., *The Cafe l'Egypte*, Sax Rohmer, Short Story

CAFE LUNCHRASTEN 1954 d: Erik Faustman. SWD., *Lunchrasten*, Herbert Grevenius, Goteborg 1949, Play

CAFETERIA, THE 1981 d: Amram Nowak. USA., *The Cafeteria*, Isaac Bashevis Singer, 1970, Short Story

Cage aux Folles - Birds of a Feather, La see **LA CAGE AUX FOLLES** (1978).

CAGE AUX FOLLES, LA 1978 d: Edouard Molinaro. FRN/ITL., *La Cage aux Folles*, Jean Poiret, Play

Cage Doree, Une see **RAZZIA SUR LE PLAISIR** (1976).

Cage of Arrows, The see **SHARAPANJARA** (1971).

CAGE, THE 1914 d: George Loane Tucker. UKN., *The Cage*, Hesketh Pearson, Story

Caged see **NELLA CITTA L'INFERNO** (1958).

Cagliostro see **BLACK MAGIC** (1949).

CAGLIOSTRO 1975 d: Daniele Pettinari. ITL., *Cagliostro Il Taumauturgo*, Piero Carpi, Book

Caid, Le see **LA DERNIERE CHEVAUCHEE** (1946).

CAID, LE 1960 d: Bernard Borderie. FRN., *Le Grand Caid*, Claude Orval, Novel

CAIDA, LA 1959 d: Leopoldo Torre-Nilsson. ARG., *La Caida*, Beatriz Guido, Novel

CAIDS, LES 1972 d: Robert Enrico. FRN., *Les Caids*, M. G. Braun, Novel

Caille, La see **ON N'AIME QU'UNE FOIS** (1949).

CAIN 1965 d: Pierre Patry. CND., *Les Marcheurs de la Nuit*, Real Giguere, Unpublished, Novel

Cain and Artem see **KAIN I ARTYOM** (1930).

Cain and Mabel see **THE GREAT WHITE WAY** (1924).

Caine see **SHARK!** (1969).

CAINE MUTINY, THE 1954 d: Edward Dmytryk. USA., *The Caine Mutiny*, Herman Wouk, 1951, Novel

CAINO 1910. ITL., *Cain*, Lord Byron, 1821, Poem

Cairn see **GRAMADA** (1936).

CAIRO 1963 d: Wolf RillA. UKN., *Asphalt Jungle*, William Riley Burnett, New York 1949, Novel

Cajka see **CHAIKA** (1971).

CAL 1984 d: Pat O'Connor. UKN., *Cal*, Bernard MacLaverty, Novel

CALAFURIA 1943 d: Flavio CalzavarA. ITL., *Calafuria*, Delfino Cinelli, Novel

CALAIS - DOUVRES 1931 d: Jean Boyer, Anatole Litvak. FRN., *Calais-Douvres*, Julius Berstel, Novel

Calda E Infedele see **UN DIABLO BAJA LA ALMOHADA** (1968).

Calda Pelle, La see **DE L'AMOUR** (1964).

Calda Preda, La see **LA CUREE** (1966).

CALDA VITA, LA 1963 d: Florestano Vancini. ITL/FRN., *La Calda Vita*, Pier Quarantotti-Gambini, Turin 1958, Novel

CALEA VICTORIEI SAU CHEIA VISURILOR 1966 d: Marius Teodorescu. RMN., *Calea Victoriei*, Cezar Petrescu, 1932, Novel

CALEB WEST 1912. USA., *Caleb West Master Diver*, F. Hopkinson Smith, New York 1899, Novel

Caleb West, Master Diver *see* DEEP WATERS (1920).

CALEB WILLIAMS 1983 d: Herbert Wise. UKN/GRM., *Caleb Williams*, William Godwin, Novel

CALENDAR, THE 1931 d: T. Hayes Hunter. UKN., *The Calendar*, Edgar Wallace, London 1930, Novel

CALENDAR, THE 1948 d: Arthur Crabtree. UKN., *The Calendar*, Edgar Wallace, London 1930, Novel

CALF LOVE 1966 d: Gilchrist Calder. UKN., *Calf Love*, Vernon Bartlett, Novel

Calibre 9 *see* MILANO CALIBRO 9 (1972).

Calico Pony, The *see* COUNT THREE AND PRAY (1955).

Calico Sheriff, The *see* THE SECOND TIME AROUND (1961).

Califar's Mill *see* MOARA LUI CALIFAR (1984).

CALIFFA, LA 1970 d: Alberto BevilacquA. ITL/FRN., *La Califfa*, Alberto Bevilacqua, Novel

CALIFORNIA CONQUEST 1952 d: Lew Landers. USA., *Don Peon*, Johnston McCulley, Novel

CALIFORNIA SUITE 1978 d: Herbert Ross. USA., *California Suite*, Neil Simon, 1977, Play

Californian, The *see* THE MARK OF ZORRO (1940).

CALL HER SAVAGE 1932 d: John Francis Dillon. USA., *Call Her Savage*, Tiffany Thayer, New York 1931, Novel

CALL IT A DAY 1937 d: Archie Mayo. USA., *Call It a Day*, Dodie Smith, New York 1936, Play

Call It Murder *see* MIDNIGHT (1934).

CALL LOAN, THE 1920 d: David Smith. USA., *The Call Loan*, O. Henry, Short Story

CALL ME MADAM 1953 d: Walter Lang. USA., *Call Me Madam*, Russel Crouse, Howard Lindsay, New York 1950, Musical Play

CALL NORTHSIDE 777 1948 d: Henry Hathaway. USA., James P. McGuire, Article

CALL OF HER PEOPLE, THE 1917 d: John W. Noble. USA., *Egypt*, Edward Sheldon, New York 1912, Play

CALL OF HIS PEOPLE, THE 1922. USA., *The Man Who Would Be White*, Aubrey Bowser, Story

CALL OF HOME, THE 1922 d: Louis J. Gasnier. USA., *Home*, George Agnew Chamberlain, New York 1914, Novel

Call of Nature, The *see* THE ISLE OF CONQUEST (1919).

CALL OF SIVA, THE 1923 d: A. E. Coleby. UKN., *The Call of Siva*, Sax Rohmer, Short Story

Call of the Blood *see* L' APPEL DU SANG (1919).

CALL OF THE BLOOD 1948 d: John Clements, Ladislao VajdA. UKN/ITL., *The Call of the Blood*, Robert Hichens, Novel

CALL OF THE CANYON, THE 1923 d: Victor Fleming. USA., *The Call of the Canyon*, Zane Grey, New York 1924, Novel

CALL OF THE CUMBERLANDS, THE 1916 d: Julia Crawford Ivers. USA., *The Battle Cry*, Charles Neville Buck, New York 1914, Novel, *The Call of the Cumberlands*, Charles Neville Buck, 1913, Novel

CALL OF THE EAST, THE 1922 d: Bert Wynne. UKN., *The Call of the East*, Esther Whitehouse, Novel

CALL OF THE NORTH, THE 1914 d: Cecil B. de Mille, Oscar Apfel. USA., *The Call of the North*, George Broadhurst, New York 1908, Play, *The Conjuror's House*, Stewart Edward White, New York 1903, Novel

CALL OF THE NORTH, THE 1921 d: Joseph Henabery. USA., *The Conjuror's House*, Stewart Edward White, New York 1903, Novel

CALL OF THE PRAIRIE 1936 d: Howard Bretherton. USA., *Hopalong Cassidy's Protege*, Clarence E. Mulford, New York 1926, Novel

Call of the Ring, The *see* THE DUKE COMES BACK (1937).

Call of the Sun Watch, The *see* DER SONNBLICK RUFT (1952).

CALL OF THE WEST 1930 d: Albert Ray. USA., *Borrowed Love*, Colin Clements, Florence Ryerson, Story

CALL OF THE WILD 1972 d: Ken Annakin. UKN/GRM/ITL., *Call of the Wild*, Jack London, New York 1903, Novel

CALL OF THE WILD 1976 d: Jerry Jameson. USA., *Call of the Wild*, Jack London, New York 1903, Novel

Call of the Wild *see* IL RICHIAMO DELLA FORESTA (1992).

CALL OF THE WILD, THE 1908 d: D. W. Griffith. USA., *Call of the Wild*, Jack London, New York 1903, Novel

CALL OF THE WILD, THE 1923 d: Fred Jackman. USA., *Call of the Wild*, Jack London, New York 1903, Novel

CALL OF THE WILD, THE 1935 d: William A. Wellman. USA., *Call of the Wild*, Jack London, New York 1903, Novel

CALL OF THE YUKON 1938 d: B. Reeves Eason, John T. Coyle (Uncredited). USA., *Swift Lightning*, James Oliver Curwood, New York 1926, Novel

CALL OF YOUTH, THE 1920 d: Hugh Ford. UKN/USA., *James the Fogey*, Henry Arthur Jones, Play

CALL ON KUPRIN, A 1961 d: John Jacobs. UKN., *A Call on Kuprin*, Maurice Edelman, Novel

Call on the President, A *see* JOE AND ETHEL TURP CALL ON THE PRESIDENT (1939).

Call to Arms Against War, A *see* THE BATTLE CRY OF PEACE (1915).

CALLAHANS AND THE MURPHYS, THE 1927 d: George W. Hill. USA., *The Callahans and the Murphys*, Kathleen Norris, Garden City, N.Y. 1924, Novel

CALLAN 1974 d: Don Sharp. UKN., *A Magnum for Schneider*, James Mitchell, Novel

CALLED BACK 1912. USA., *Called Back*, Hugh Conway, London 1884, Novel

CALLED BACK 1914 d: George Loane Tucker. UKN., *Called Back*, Hugh Conway, London 1884, Novel

CALLED BACK 1914 d: Otis Turner. USA., *Called Back*, Hugh Conway, London 1884, Novel

CALLED BACK 1933 d: Reginald Denham, Jack Harris. UKN., *Called Back*, Hugh Conway, London 1884, Novel

CALLING ALL HUSBANDS 1940 d: Noel Smith. USA., *Broken Dishes*, Martin Flavin, New York 1929, Play

CALLING BULLDOG DRUMMOND 1951 d: Victor Saville. UKN/USA., *Calling Bulldog Drummond*, Gerard Fairlie, Novel

Calling Northside 777 *see* CALL NORTHSIDE 777 (1948).

CALLING OF DAN MATTHEWS, THE 1935 d: Phil Rosen. USA., *The Calling of Dan Matthews*, Harold Bell Wright, Chicago 1909, Novel

CALLING PHILO VANCE 1940 d: William Clemens. USA., *The Kennel Murder Case*, S. S. Van Dine, New York 1913, Novel

CALM YOURSELF 1935 d: George B. Seitz. USA., *Calm Yourself!*, Edward Hope, Indianapolis 1934, Novel

CALVAIRE D'AMOUR 1923 d: Victor Tourjansky. FRN., *Calvaire d'Amour*, Noelle Bazan, Novel

CALVAIRE DE CIMIEZ, LE 1934 d: Jacques de Baroncelli, Rene Dalliere. FRN., *Le Calvaire de Cimiez*, Henri Bordeaux, Novel

CALVAIRE DE DONA PIA, LE 1925 d: Henry Krauss. FRN., *Son Fils*, Andre Corthis, Novel

CALVAIRE DE MIGNON, LE 1916 d: Marcel Simon. FRN., *Le Calvaire de Mignon*, Paul Feval (fils), Novel

CALVARY 1920 d: Edwin J. Collins. UKN., *Calvary*, Rita, Novel

Calvert's Folly *see* CALVERT'S VALLEY (1922).

CALVERT'S VALLEY 1922 d: John Francis Dillon. USA., *In Calvert's Valley*, Margaret Prescott Montague, New York 1908, Novel

Calypso *see* MANFISH (1955).

CAMARERA DEL TITANIC, LA 1997 d: Bigas LunA. SPN/FRN/ITL., *La Femme de Chambre du Titanic*, Didier Decoin, Novel

CAMAROTE DE LUJO 1957 d: Rafael Gil. SPN., *Luz de Luna*, Wenceslao Fernandez Florez, 1915, Novel

CAMBIO DELLA GUARDIA, IL 1962 d: Giorgio Bianchi. ITL/FRN., *Avanti la Musica*, Charles Exbrayat, Novel

CAMBRIC MASK, THE 1919 d: Tom Terriss. USA., *The Cambric Mask*, Robert W. Chambers, New York 1899, Novel

Cambrioleur, Le *see* FLAGRANT DELIT (1930).

CAME A HOT FRIDAY 1985 d: Ian Mune. NZL., *Came a Hot Friday*, Ronald Hugh Morrieson, Novel

Came the Hero *see* THE VIOLENT ENEMY (1969).

Camel Through the Eye of a Needle *see* VELBLOUD UCHEM JEHLY (1936).

Camel Through the Needle's Eye *see* VELBLOUD UCHEM JEHLY (1936).

Camel XIangzi *see* LUO TOU XIANGZI (1982).

CAMELIA 1953 d: Roberto Gavaldon. MXC/SPN., *La Dame aux Camelias*, Alexandre Dumas (fils), Paris 1848, Novel

CAMELOT 1967 d: Joshua Logan. USA., *The Once and Future King*, T. H. White, London 1958, Novel

CAMEO KIRBY 1915 d: Oscar Apfel. USA., *Cameo Kirby*, Booth Tarkington, Harry Leon Wilson, New York 1909, Play

CAMEO KIRBY 1923 d: John Ford. USA., *Cameo Kirby*, Booth Tarkington, Harry Leon Wilson, New York 1909, Play

CAMEO KIRBY 1930 d: Irving Cummings. USA., *Cameo Kirby*, Booth Tarkington, Harry Leon Wilson, New York 1909, Play

CAMERE SEPARATE 1917 d: Gennaro Righelli. ITL., *Chambre a Part*, Pierre Veber, 1905

Camerena Story, The *see* THE DRUG WARS: THE KIKI CAMARENA STORY (1989).

CAMERON OF THE ROYAL MOUNTED 1921 d: Henry McRae. CND., *Corporal Cameron of the North West Mounted Police*, Ralph Connor, Novel

CAMERON'S CLOSET 1988 d: Armand Mastroianni. USA., *Cameron's Closett*, Gary Brandner, Novel

CAMI DE LA FELICITAT ,EL 1925 d: Jose G. Barranco. SPN., *El Cami de la Felicitat*, Josep Maria Folch I Torres, Novel

Camicia Nera *see* UN EROE DEL NOSTRO TEMPO (1960).

CAMILLE 1907 d: Viggo Larsen. DNM., *La Dame aux Camelias*, Alexandre Dumas (fils), Paris 1848, Novel

Camille *see* LA SIGNORA DALLE CAMELIE (1909).

Camille *see* LA DAME AUX CAMELIAS (1911).

CAMILLE 1912 d: Herbert Brenon. USA., *La Dame aux Camelias*, Alexandre Dumas (fils), Paris 1848, Novel

CAMILLE 1915 d: Albert Capellani. USA., *La Dame aux Camelias*, Alexandre Dumas (fils), Paris 1848, Novel

CAMILLE 1917 d: J. Gordon Edwards. USA., *La Dame aux Camelias*, Alexandre Dumas (fils), Paris 1848, Novel

CAMILLE 1921 d: Ray C. Smallwood. USA., *La Dame aux Camelias*, Alexandre Dumas (fils), Paris 1848, Novel

CAMILLE 1927 d: Fred Niblo. USA., *La Dame aux Camelias*, Alexandre Dumas (fils), Paris 1848, Novel

CAMILLE 1937 d: George Cukor. USA., *La Dame aux Camelias*, Alexandre Dumas (fils), Paris 1848, Novel

Camille *see* LA DAME AUX CAMELIAS (1953).

Camille *see* CAMILLE 2000 (1969).

CAMILLE 1984 d: Desmond Davis. UKN., *La Dame aux Camelias*, Alexandre Dumas (fils), Paris 1848, Novel

CAMILLE 2000 1969 d: Radley H. Metzger. ITL/USA., *La Dame aux Camelias*, Alexandre Dumas (fils), Paris 1848, Novel

CAMILLE CLAUDEL 1988 d: Bruno Nuytten. FRN., *Camille Claudel*, Reine-Marie Paris, Book

Camille Claudel -Violence and Passion *see* CAMILLE CLAUDEL (1988).

Camille of the Yukon *see* THE SILENT LIE (1917).

Camillo E l'Americano *see* LE NIPOTI D'AMERICA (1921).

Camino de la Felicidad, El *see* EL CAMI DE LA FELICITAT (1925).

CAMINO, EL 1963 d: Ana Mariscal. SPN., *El Camino*, Miguel Delibes, 1950, Novel

Cammino Del Folle, Il *see* ETES-VOUS FIANCEE A UN MARIN GREC OU A UN PILOTE DE LIGNE? (1970).

CAMMINO DELLA SPERANZA, IL 1950 d: Pietro Germi. ITL., *Cuori Negli Abissi*, Nino de Maria, Novel

CAMOMILE LAWN, THE 1991 d: Peter Hall. UKN., *The Camomile Lawn*, Mary Wesley, Novel

Camorra Man, The *see* IL CAMORRISTA (1986).

Camorra Member, The *see* IL CAMORRISTA (1986).

CAMORRISTA, IL 1986 d: Giuseppe Tornatore. ITL., *Il Camorrista*, Giuseppe Marrazzo, Novel

CAMOUFLAGE KISS, A 1918 d: Harry Millarde. USA., Julius G. Furthmann, Short Story

Camp Followers, The *see* LE SOLDATESSE (1965).

Camp of Fallen Women, The *see* TABOR PADLYCH ZIEN (1998).

Campaign Burma *see* NEVER SO FEW (1959).

CAMPANA, LA 1909. ITL., *Das Lied von Der Glocke*, Friedrich von Schiller, 1799, Poem

CAMPANADAS A MEDIANOCHE 1966 d: Orson Welles. SPN/SWT., *Henry IV*, William Shakespeare, c1597-98, Play, *Henry V*, William Shakespeare, c1598-99, Play, *Richard II*, William Shakespeare, c1595, Play

CAMPANE DI SAN LUCIO, LE 1921 d: Guido Brignone. ITL., *Le Campane Di San Lucio*, Giovacchino Forzano, 1916, Play

CAMPBELLS ARE COMING, THE 1915 d: Francis Ford, Grace Cunard. USA., *The Campbells are Coming*, Emerson Hough, Short Story

CAMPBELL'S KINGDOM 1957 d: Ralph Thomas. UKN., *Campbell's Kingdom*, Hammond Innes, Novel

CAMPO DI MAGGIO 1935 d: Giovacchino Forzano. ITL., *Campo Di Maggio*, Giovacchino Forzano, Play

Campus see DER CAMPUS (1998).

CAMPUS, DER 1998 d: Sonke Wortmann. GRM., *Der Campus*, Dietrich Schwanitz, Novel

CANADIAN, THE 1926 d: William Beaudine. USA., *The Land of Promise*, W. Somerset Maugham, London 1913, Play

Canaglie, Le see LES CANAILLES (1959).

CANAILLES, LES 1959 d: Maurice Labro. FRN/ITL., *Fais-Moi Confiance*, James Hadley Chase, Novel

Canal of Blue Milk see DER BLAUMILCHKANAL (1969).

CANARD EN FER BLANC, LE 1967 d: Jacques Poitrenaud. FRN/SPN., *Le Canard En Fer-Blanc*, Day Keene, Novel

CANARIES SOMETIMES SING 1930 d: Tom Walls. UKN., *Canaries Sometimes Sing*, Frederick Lonsdale, London 1929, Play

CANARY MURDER CASE, THE 1929 d: Malcolm St. Clair. USA., *The Canary Murder Case*, S. S. Van Dine, New York 1927, Novel

Canas Y Barro see PALUDE TRAGICA (1953).

Canavan, the Man Who Had His Way see THE DANGER SIGNAL (1915).

CAN-CAN 1960 d: Walter Lang. USA., *Can-Can*, Abe Burrows, Play

CANCEL MY RESERVATION 1972 d: Paul Bogart. USA., *The Broken Gun*, Louis L'Amour, Novel

Cancer Rising see HET JAAR VAN DE KREEFT (1975).

CANCION DE CUNA 1941 d: Gregorio Martinez SierrA. ARG., *Cancion de Cuna*, Gregorio Martinez Sierra, Madrid 1911, Play

CANCION DE CUNA 1961 d: Jose Maria ElorrietA. SPN., *Cancion de Cuna*, Gregorio Martinez Sierra, Madrid 1911, Play

CANDIDATE FOR MURDER 1962 d: David Villiers. UKN., *The Best Laid Plans of a Man in Love*, Edgar Wallace, Short Story

Candide see OU L'OPTIMISME AU XXEME SIECLE CANDIDE (1960).

CANDIDE, OU L'OPTIMISME AU XXEME SIECLE 1960 d: Norbert Carbonnaux. FRN., *Candide*, Francois-Marie Arouet de Voltaire, 1759, Short Story

CANDLES AT NINE 1944 d: John Harlow. UKN., *The Mouse Who Wouldn't Play Ball*, Anthony Gilbert, Novel

CANDLESHOE 1977 d: Norman Tokar. USA/UKN., *Christmas at Candleshoe*, Michael Innes, Novel

CANDY 1968 d: Christian Marquand, Giancarlo Zagni. USA/FRN/ITL., *Candy*, Mason Hoffenberg, Terry Southern, New York 1964, Novel

Candy E Il Suo Pazzo Mondo see CANDY (1968).

CANDYMAN 1992 d: Bernard Rose. USA., *The Forbidden*, Clive Barker, Story

CANDYMAN: FAREWELL TO THE FLESH 1995 d: Bill Condon. USA., Clive Barker, Story

CANDYTUFT, I MEAN VERONICA 1921 d: Frank Richardson. UKN., *Candytuft - I Mean Veronica*, Mabel Barnes Grundy, Novel

CANICULE 1983 d: Yves Boisset. FRN., *Canicule*, Jean Vautrin, Novel

CANNABIS 1969 d: Pierre Koralnik. FRN/GRM/ITL., *Et Puis S'en Vont*, F. S. Gilbert, Novel

Cannabis - Angel of Violence see CANNABIS (1969).

Cannabis - Engel Der Gewalt see CANNABIS (1969).

Canned Conrad see KONRAD AUS DER KONSERVENBUCHSE (1982).

CANNERY ROW 1982 d: David S. Ward. USA., *Cannery Row*, John Steinbeck, 1945, Novel, *Sweet Thursday*, John Steinbeck, 1954, Novel

CANNIBALI, I 1970 d: Liliana Cavani. ITL., *Antigone*, Sophocles, c441 bc, Play

Cannibals Among Us, The see I CANNIBALI (1970).

Cannibals, The see I CANNIBALI (1970).

Cannon Movie Tales: Sleeping Beauty see SLEEPING BEAUTY (1987).

Cannon Movie Tales: Snow White see SNOW WHITE (1987).

Cannon Movie Tales: the Emperor's New Clothes see THE EMPEROR'S NEW CLOTHES (1987).

Cannoni Di San Sebastian, I see LOS CANONES DE SAN SEBASTIAN (1967).

Cannot Be Closed see GUAN BU ZHU (1956).

CANONES DE SAN SEBASTIAN, LOS 1967 d: Henri Verneuil. FRN/ITL/MXC., *A Wall for San Sebastian*, William Barby Faherty, Fresno, CA. 1962, Novel

CAN'T HELP SINGING 1944 d: Frank Ryan. USA., *Girl of the Overland Trail*, Curtis B. Warshawsky, Samuel J. Warshawsky, Novel

CANTANTE DE NAPOLES, EL 1935 d: Howard Bretherton. USA., Arman Chelieu, Novel

CANTANTE DELL'OPERA, LA 1932 d: Nunzio MalasommA. ITL., *Nel Caffeuccio Di San Stae*, Gino Rocca, Novel

CANTANTE MISTERIOSO, IL 1955 d: Marino Girolami. ITL., *Il Cantante Misterioso*, R. T. de Angelis, Novel

Cantata see OLDAS ES KOTES (1963).

CANTATE CON ME! 1940 d: Guido Brignone. ITL., Mura, Novel

Canterbury Tales, The see I RACCONTI DI CANTERBURY (1972).

CANTERVILLE GHOST, THE 1944 d: Jules Dassin. USA., *The Canterville Ghost*, Oscar Wilde, 1891, Short Story

CANTERVILLE GHOST, THE 1954. USA., *The Canterville Ghost*, Oscar Wilde, 1891, Short Story

CANTERVILLE GHOST, THE 1974 d: Walter C. Miller. USA/UKN., *The Canterville Ghost*, Oscar Wilde, 1891, Short Story

CANTERVILLE GHOST, THE 1986 d: Paul Bogart. USA., *The Canterville Ghost*, Oscar Wilde, 1891, Short Story

CANTERVILLE GHOST, THE 1996 d: Sydney MacArtney. USA/UKN., *The Canterville Ghost*, Oscar Wilde, 1891, Short Story

CANTICO FINAL 1976 d: Manuel Guimaraes, Dordio Guimaraes. PRT., *Cantico Final*, Vergilio Ferreira, 1959, Novel

CANTIQUE DE LA RACAILLE 1998 d: Vincent Ravalec. FRN., *Cantique de la Racaille*, Vincent Ravalec, Novel

CANTO DELLA VITA, IL 1945 d: Carmine Gallone. ITL., Gherardo Gherardi, Play

Canto Nella Notte see VOCE 'E NOTTE (1919).

Cantor de Mejico, El see LE CHANTEUR DE MEXICO (1956).

CANYON OF LIGHT, THE 1926 d: Ben Stoloff. USA., *The Canyon of Light*, Kenneth Perkins, Novel

CANYON OF THE FOOLS 1923 d: Val Paul. USA., *The Canyon of the Fools*, Richard Matthews Hallet, New York 1922, Novel

Canyon Pass see RATON PASS (1951).

CANYON PASSAGE 1946 d: Jacques Tourneur. USA., *Canyon Passage*, Ernest Haycox, 1945, Novel

Canyon Walls see SMOKE LIGHTNING (1933).

Canzone Del Mondo, La see TELEVISIONE (1931).

CANZONE DELL'AMORE, LA 1930 d: Gennaro Righelli. ITL., *In Silenzio*, Luigi Pirandello, 1905, Short Story

CAO YUAN SHANG DE REN MEN 1953 d: Xu Tao. CHN., *Cao Yuan Shang De Ren Men*, Mala Qinfu, Novel

CAP PERDU, LE 1931 d: E. A. Dupont. FRN., *Cape Forlorn*, Frank Harvey, 1930, Play

Capanna Del Peccato, La see IL NIDO DI FALASCO (1950).

Capanna Del Zio Tom, La see ONKEL TOMS HUTTE (1965).

CAPANNA DELLO ZIO TOM, LA 1918 d: Riccardo Tolentino. ITL., *Uncle Tom's Cabin*, Harriet Beecher Stowe, Boston 1852, Novel

Cape Cod see CAPTAIN HURRICANE (1935).

CAPE FEAR 1961 d: J. Lee Thompson. USA., *The Executioners*, John D. MacDonald, New York 1958, Novel

CAPE FEAR 1991 d: Martin Scorsese. USA., *The Executioners*, John D. MacDonald, New York 1958, Novel

CAPE FORLORN 1930 d: E. A. Dupont. UKN., *Cape Forlorn*, Frank Harvey, 1930, Play

CAPELLI BIONDI 1919. ITL., *Capelli Biondi*, Salvatore Farina, 1876, Novel

CAPER OF THE GOLDEN BULLS, THE 1966 d: Russell Rouse. USA., *The Caper of the Golden Bulls*, William P. McGivern, New York 1966, Novel

CAPERUCITA ROJA, LA 1960 d: Roberto Rodriguez. MXC., *Le Petit Chaperon Rouge*, Charles Perrault, Paris 1697, Short Story

CAPINERA DEL MULINO, LA 1957 d: Angio Zane. ITL., *La Capinera Del Mulino*, Ponson Du Terrail, Novel

CAPITAINE BENOIT, LE 1938 d: Maurice de Canonge. FRN., *Le Capitaine Benoit*, Charles-Robert Dumas, Novel

CAPITAINE BLOMET 1947 d: Andree Feix. FRN., *Capitaine Blomet*, Emile Bergerat, Play

Capitaine Corsaire see MOLLENARD (1937).

CAPITAINE CRADDOCK, LE 1931 d: Max de Vaucorbeil, Hanns Schwarz. FRN., *Le Capitaine Craddock*, Reck-Malleczewen, Novel

CAPITAINE FRACASSE, LE 1909 d: Victorin Jasset. FRN., *Le Capitaine Fracasse*, Theophile Gautier, 1863, Novel

CAPITAINE FRACASSE, LE 1929 d: Alberto Cavalcanti. FRN., *Le Capitaine Fracasse*, Theophile Gautier, 1863, Novel

CAPITAINE FRACASSE, LE 1942 d: Abel Gance. FRN., *Le Capitaine Fracasse*, Theophile Gautier, 1863, Novel

CAPITAINE FRACASSE, LE 1960 d: Pierre Gaspard-Huit. FRN/ITL., *Le Capitaine Fracasse*, Theophile Gautier, 1863, Novel

Capitaine Mollenard see MOLLENARD (1937).

CAPITAINE PANTOUFLE 1953 d: Guy Lefranc. FRN., *Capitaine Pantoufle*, Alfred Adam, Play

Capital Offense see HOT SUMMER NIGHT (1956).

CAPITAN BLANCO, IL 1914 d: Nino Martoglio, Roberto Danesi. ITL., *O Pallio*, Nino Martoglio, 1906, Play

CAPITAN FRACASSA 1909 d: Ernesto Maria Pasquali. ITL., *Le Capitaine Fracasse*, Theophile Gautier, 1863, Novel

CAPITAN FRACASSA 1919 d: Mario Caserini. ITL., *Le Capitaine Fracasse*, Theophile Gautier, 1863, Novel

CAPITAN FRACASSA 1940 d: Duilio Coletti. ITL., *Le Capitaine Fracasse*, Theophile Gautier, 1863, Novel

Capitan Fracassa see LE CAPITAINE FRACASSE (1960).

CAPITAN, LE 1945 d: Robert Vernay. FRN., *Le Capitan*, Michel Zevaco, Novel

CAPITAN, LE 1960 d: Andre Hunebelle. FRN/ITL., *Le Capitan*, Michel Zevaco, Novel

CAPITAN TEMPESTA 1942 d: Corrado d'Errico. ITL., *Capitan Tempesta*, Emilio Salgari, Novel

CAPITAN TORMENTA, EL 1936 d: John Reinhardt. USA., *Captain Calamity*, Gordon Young, Short Story

CAPITAN VENENO, EL 1950 d: Luis MarquinA. SPN., *El Capitan Veneno*, Pedro Antonio de Alarcon, 1881, Novel

CAPITANO DEGLI USSARI, IL 1941 d: Sandor Szlatinay. ITL., *Il Capitano Degli Ussari*, Sandor Hunyady, Play

Capitano Del Re, Il see LE CAPITAN (1960).

CAPITOL, THE 1920 d: George Irving. USA., *The Capitol*, Augustus Thomas, New York 1895, Play

CAPITU 1968 d: Paulo Cesar Saraceni. BRZ., *Dom Casmurro*, Joaquim Maria Machado de Assis, 1899, Novel

Cap'n Abe's Niece see THE CAPTAIN'S CAPTAIN (1918).

Cap'n Eri see CAPTAIN ERI (1915).

CAPORAL EPINGLE, LE 1961 d: Jean Renoir. FRN., *Le Caporal Epingle*, Jacques Perret, Paris 1947, Novel

CAPOTE DE PASEO, EL 1927 d: Carlos de Arpe. SPN., *El Capote de Paseo*, Celedonio Jose de Arpe, Novel

CAPPELLO A TRE PUNTE, IL 1935 d: Mario Camerini. ITL., *El Sombrero de Tres Picos*, Pedro Antonio de Alarcon, 1874, Short Story

CAPPELLO DA PRETE, IL 1944 d: Ferdinando M. Poggioli. ITL., *Il Cappello Del Prete*, Emilio de Marchi, Novel

CAPPELLO DI PAGLIA DI FIRENZE 1918 d: Enrico Vidali. ITL., *Un Chapeau de Paille d'Italie*, Eugene Labiche, Marc-Michel, 1847, Play

CAPPOTTO DI ASTRAKAN, IL 1979 d: Marco Vicario. ITL., *Il Cappotto Di Astrakan*, Piero Chiara, Novel

CAPPOTTO, IL 1952 d: Alberto LattuadA. ITL., *Shinel*, Nikolay Gogol, 1842, Short Story

CAPPY RICKS 1921 d: Tom Forman. USA., *Cappy Ricks*, Peter B. Kyne, New York 1915, Novel

CAPPY RICKS RETURNS 1935 d: MacK V. Wright. USA., *Cappy Ricks Comes Back*, Peter B. Kyne, New York 1934, Short Story

CAPRICE 1913 d: J. Searle Dawley. USA., *Caprice*, Howard P. Taylor, New York 1884, Play

CAPRICE DE CAROLINE CHERIE, UN 1952 d: Jean Devaivre. FRN., *Un Caprice de Caroline Cherie*, Cecil Saint-Laurent, Novel

CAPRICE DE PRINCESSE 1933 d: Henri-Georges Clouzot, Karl Hartl. FRN., *Ma Soeur Et Moi*, Georges Berr, Louis Verneuil, Play

Caprice Espagnole *see* THE DEVIL IS A WOMAN (1935).

Caprice of Caroline *see* UN CAPRICE DE CAROLINE CHERIE (1952).

Caprice of "Dear Caroline" *see* UN CAPRICE DE CAROLINE CHERIE (1952).

CAPRICE, UN 1946 d: Lucien Gasnier-Raymond. FRN., *Un Caprice*, Alfred de Musset, Play

Caprices de Marianne, Les *see* LA REGLE DU JEU (1939).

Capricious Summer *see* ROZMARNE LETO (1967).

CAPTAIN ALVAREZ 1914 d: Rollin S. Sturgeon. USA., *Captain Alvarez*, Paul Gilmore, Play

Captain and His Hero, The *see* DER HAUPTMANN UND SEIN HELD (1955).

CAPTAIN APACHE 1971 d: Alexander Singer. USA/UKN/SPN., *Captain Apache*, S. E. Whitman, Novel

Captain Applejack *see* STRANGERS OF THE NIGHT (1923).

CAPTAIN BLOOD 1924 d: David Smith. USA., *Captain Blood; His Odyssey*, Rafael Sabatini, Boston 1922, Novel

CAPTAIN BLOOD 1935 d: Michael Curtiz. USA., *Captain Blood; His Odyssey*, Rafael Sabatini, Boston 1922, Novel

Captain Blood *see* LE CAPITAN (1960).

Captain Blood, Fugitive *see* CAPTAIN PIRATE (1952).

CAPTAIN BOYCOTT 1947 d: Frank Launder. UKN., *Captain Boycott*, Philip Rooney, Novel

CAPTAIN CALAMITY 1936 d: John Reinhardt. USA., *Captain Calamity*, Gordon Young, Short Story

CAPTAIN CAUTION 1940 d: Richard Wallace. USA., *Captain Caution; a Chronicle of Arundel*, Kenneth Lewis Roberts, New York 1934, Novel

CAPTAIN CHINA 1949 d: Lewis R. Foster. USA., Gwen Bagni, John Bagni, Story

CAPTAIN CLEGG 1962 d: Peter Graham Scott. UKN., *Dr. Syn*, William Russell Thorndike, Novel

CAPTAIN COURTESY 1915 d: Hobart Bosworth. USA., *Captain Courtesy*, Edward Childs Carpenter, Philadelphia 1906, Novel

Captain Dieppe *see* AN ADVENTURE IN HEARTS (1920).

CAPTAIN ERI 1915 d: George A. Lessey. USA., *Cap'n Eri; a Story of the Coast*, Joseph C. Lincoln, New York 1904, Novel

CAPTAIN FLY-BY-NIGHT 1922 d: William K. Howard. USA., *Captain Fly-By-Night*, Johnston McCulley, Novel

CAPTAIN FROM CASTILE 1947 d: Henry King. USA., *Captain from Castile*, Samuel Shellabarger, Novel

Captain from Kopenick, The *see* DER HAUPTMANN VON KOPENICK (1956).

CAPTAIN HATES THE SEA, THE 1934 d: Lewis Milestone. USA., *The Captain Hates the Sea*, Wallace Smith, Davison, Mi. 1933, Novel

Captain Horatio Hornblower *see* CAPTAIN HORATIO HORNBLOWER R.N. (1951).

CAPTAIN HORATIO HORNBLOWER R.N. 1951 d: Raoul Walsh. UKN/USA., *Captain Horatio Hornblower*, C. S. Forester, 1939, Novel

CAPTAIN HURRICANE 1935 d: John S. Robertson. USA., *The Taming of Zenas Henry*, Sara Ware Bassett, New York 1915, Novel

Captain Hurricane *see* CAPTAIN CALAMITY (1936).

CAPTAIN IS A LADY, THE 1940 d: Robert B. Sinclair. USA., *Old Lady 31*, Rachel Crothers, New York 1916, Play

CAPTAIN JANUARY 1924 d: Eddie Cline. USA., *Captain January*, Laura E. Richards, New York 1890, Novel

CAPTAIN JANUARY 1936 d: David Butler. USA., *Captain January*, Laura E. Richards, New York 1890, Novel

CAPTAIN JINKS OF THE HORSE MARINES 1916 d: Fred E. Wright. USA., *Captain Jinks of the Horse Marines*, Clyde Fitch, New York 1916, Play

CAPTAIN KIDD, JR. 1919 d: William D. Taylor. USA., *Captain Kidd Junior*, Rida Johnson Young, New York 1916, Play

Captain Korda *see* KAPITAN KORDA (1979).

CAPTAIN LIGHTFOOT 1955 d: Douglas Sirk. USA., *Captain Lightfoot*, William Riley Burnett, 1954, Novel

CAPTAIN MACKLIN 1915 d: John B. O'Brien. USA., *Captain MacKlin: His Memoirs*, Richard Harding Davis, New York 1902, Novel

Captain Martens Brothers, The *see* FRATII JDERI (1973).

CAPTAIN NEWMAN M.D. 1963 d: David Miller. USA., *M.D. Captain Newman*, Leo Rosten, New York 1961, Novel

Captain of a Sinking Ship *see* DER HAVARIST (1983).

CAPTAIN OF KOEPENICK 1946 d: Richard Oswald. USA., *Der Hauptmann von Kopenick*, Carl Zuckmayer, 1930, Play

Captain of Kopenick, The *see* DER HAUPTMANN VON KOPENICK (1931).

CAPTAIN OF THE GRAY HORSE TROOP, THE 1917 d: William Wolbert. USA., *Captain of the Grey Horse Troop*, Hamlin Garland, London 1902, Novel

Captain of the Hurricane, The *see* STORMY WATERS (1928).

CAPTAIN PIRATE 1952 d: Ralph Murphy. USA., *Captain Blood Returns*, Rafael Sabatini, Novel

Captain Poison *see* EL CAPITAN VENENO (1950).

CAPTAIN SALVATION 1927 d: John S. Robertson. USA., *Captain Salvation*, Frederick William Wallace, New York 1925, Novel

CAPTAIN SWIFT 1914 d: Edgar Lewis. USA., *Captain Swift*, C. Haddon Chambers, London 1888, Play

CAPTAIN SWIFT 1920 d: Tom Terriss. USA., *Captain Swift*, C. Haddon Chambers, London 1888, Play

CAPTAIN THUNDER 1930 d: Alan Crosland. USA., *The Gay Caballero*, Pierre Couderc, Hal Devitt, Story

Captain Venom *see* EL CAPITAN VENENO (1950).

CAPTAINS AND THE KINGS 1976 d: Douglas Heyes, Allen Reisner. USA., *Captains and the Kings*, Taylor Caldwell, Novel

CAPTAIN'S CAPTAIN, THE 1918 d: Tom Terriss. USA., *Cap'n Abe Storekeeper: a Story of Cape Cod*, James A. Cooper, New York 1917, Novel

CAPTAINS COURAGEOUS 1937 d: Victor Fleming. USA., *Captains Courageous*, Rudyard Kipling, London 1897, Novel

CAPTAINS COURAGEOUS 1977 d: Harvey Hart. USA., *Captains Courageous*, Rudyard Kipling, London 1897, Novel

Captain's Daughter, The *see* LA FIGLIA DEL CAPITANO (1947).

Captain's Daughter, The *see* KAPITANSKAIA DOTSHKA (1958).

CAPTAIN'S DOLL, THE 1983 d: Claude Whatham. UKN., *The Captain's Doll*, D. H. Lawrence, 1923, Short Story

CAPTAIN'S TABLE, THE 1959 d: Jack Lee. UKN., *The Captain's Table*, Richard Gordon, Novel

Captain's Wife, The *see* THE WOMAN FROM MONTE CARLO (1932).

CAPTIVATING MARY CARSTAIRS 1915 d: Bruce Mitchell. USA., *Captivating Mary Carstairs*, Henry Sydnor Harrison, Boston 1910, Novel

CAPTIVATION 1931 d: John Harvel. UKN., *Captivation*, Edgar C. Middleton, Play

Captive Balloon, The *see* PRIVARZANIAT BALON (1967).

Captive City *see* LA CITTA PRIGIONERA (1962).

CAPTIVE HEARTS 1987 d: Paul Almond. USA/CND., *The Hawk*, Sargon Tamimi, Story

Captive Raby *see* RAB RABY (1965).

Captive, The *see* VACANCES EN ENFER (1960).

Captive's Island *see* SHOKEI NO SHIMA (1966).

CAPTIVES, THE 1970 d: Carl Borch. DNM., *Fire*, T. J. Moller

Capture By Stratagem of Mount Hua *see* ZHI QU HUA SHAN (1953).

CAPTURED! 1933 d: Roy Del Ruth. USA., *Fellow Prisoners*, Philip Hamilton Gibbs, 1930, Short Story

Captured Squadron *see* PLENENO YATO (1962).

Capturing of the Citadel, The *see* DIE EROBERUNG DER ZITADELLE (1976).

Car 99 *see* CAR NO.99 (1935).

CAR NO.99 1935 d: Charles T. Barton. USA., *Hue and Cry*, Carl Detzer, 1933, Short Story, *One Good Turn*, Carl Detzer, 1933, Short Story, *Still Small Voice*, Carl Detzer, 1933, Short Story

CARA DE FOGO 1960 d: Gallileu GarciA. BRZ., *A Caranonha*, Afonso Schmidt, 1804, Short Story

Carabina Per Schut, Una *see* DER SCHUT (1964).

Carabinie *see* CARABINIERE (1913).

CARABINIERE 1913 d: Ubaldo Maria Del Colle. ITL., *Cararbinie*, Enrico Gemelli, 1892, Play

CARABINIERS, LES 1962 d: Jean-Luc Godard. FRN/ITL., *I Carabinieri*, Benjamin Joppolo, Paris 1958, Play

CARAMBOLAGES 1963 d: Marcel Bluwal. FRN., *Carambolages*, Fred Kassak, Novel

CARANCHOS DE LA FLORIDA, LOS 1938 d: Alberto de ZavaliA. ARG., *Los Caranchos de la Florida*, Benito Lynch, 1916, Novel

CARAVAN 1946 d: Arthur Crabtree. UKN., *Caravan*, Lady Eleanor Smith, Novel

CARAVAN TO VACCARES 1974 d: Geoffrey Reeve. UKN/FRN., *Caravan to Vaccares*, Alistair MacLean, 1970, Novel

CARAVANE 1934 d: Erik Charell. USA., *Gypsy Melody*, Melchior Lengyel, Short Story

CARAVANS 1978 d: James Fargo. USA/IRN., *Caravans*, James A. Michener, 1963, Novel

Caravans West *see* WAGON WHEELS (1934).

CARCASSE ET LE TORD-COU, LA 1947 d: Rene Chanas. FRN., *La Carcasse Et le Tord-Cou*, Auguste Bailly, Novel

CARCELERAS 1922 d: Jose Buchs. SPN., *Carceleras*, V. Peydro, Ricardo Rodriguez Flores, Opera

Card from the Journey *see* KARTKA Z PODROZY (1983).

CARD, THE 1922 d: A. V. Bramble. UKN., *The Card*, Arnold Bennett, 1912, Novel

CARD, THE 1952 d: Ronald Neame. UKN., *The Card*, Arnold Bennett, 1912, Novel

CARDBOARD BOX, THE 1923 d: George Ridgwell. UKN., *The Cardboard Box*, Arthur Conan Doyle, Short Story

CARDBOARD LOVER, THE 1928 d: Robert Z. Leonard. USA., *Dans Sa Candeur Naive*, Jacques Deval, Paris 1927, Play

Cardboard Lover, The *see* THE PASSIONATE PLUMBER (1932).

CARDIGAN 1922 d: John W. Noble. USA., *Cardigan*, Robert W. Chambers, New York 1901, Novel

CARDILLAC 1969 d: Edgar Reitz. GRM., *Das Fraulein von Scuderi*, Ernst Theodor Amadeus Hoffmann, 1819, Short Story

CARDINAL RICHELIEU 1936 d: Rowland V. Lee. USA., *Richelieu; Or the Conspiracy*, Edward George Bulwer Lytton, London 1839, Play

CARDINAL RICHELIEU'S WARD 1914. USA., *Richelieu; Or the Conspiracy*, Edward George Bulwer Lytton, London 1839, Play

CARDINAL, THE 1936 d: Sinclair Hill. UKN., *The Cardinal*, Louis N. Parker, Montreal 1901, Play

CARDINAL, THE 1963 d: Otto Preminger. USA., *The Cardinal*, Henry Morton Robinson, New York 1950, Novel

CARDINAL WOLSEY 1912 d: J. Stuart Blackton, Larry Trimble. USA., *Henry VIIi*, William Shakespeare, 1613, Play

CARDINALE LAMBERTINI, IL 1934 d: Parsifal Bassi. ITL., *Il Cardinale Lambertini*, Alfredo Testoni, Play

CARDINALE LAMBERTINI, IL 1955 d: Giorgio PastinA. ITL., *Il Cardinale Lambertini*, Alfredo Testoni, Play

Cartas de Amor de Uma Freira Portuguesa see **DIE LIEBESBRIEFE EINER PORTUGIESISCHEN NONNE** (1977).

Carteggio Valachi see **COSA NOSTRA** (1972).

Carthage En Flammes see **CARTAGINE IN FIAMME** (1959).

Carthage in Flames see **CARTAGINE IN FIAMME** (1959).

CARTOMANTE, A 1974 d: Marcos FariA. BRZ., *A Cartomante*, Joaquim Maria Machado de Assis, 1884, Short Story

CARTOUCHE, ROI DE PARIS 1948 d: Guillaume Radot. FRN., *Cartouche - Roi de Paris*, Pierre Lestringuez, Leopold Marchand, Play

CARUTA CU MERE 1983 d: George CorneA. RMN., *Caruta Cu Mere*, Dumitru Radu Popescu, 1962, Short Story

CARVE HER NAME WITH PRIDE 1958 d: Lewis Gilbert. UKN., *Carve Her Name With Pride*, R. J. Minney, Book

Cary and the Bishop's Wife see **THE BISHOP'S WIFE** (1947).

Caryl of the Mountains see **TRAILS OF THE WILD** (1935).

CARYL OF THE MOUNTAINS 1936 d: Bernard B. Ray. USA., *Caryl of the Mountains*, James Oliver Curwood, Short Story

Cas de Conscience see **DIE EWIGE MASKE** (1935).

CAS DE CONSCIENCE 1939 d: Walter Kapps. FRN., *Cas de Conscience*, Leopold Gomez, Play

CAS DU DOCTEUR BRENNER, LE 1932 d: John Daumery. FRN., *Alias the Doctor*, Emric Foeldes, Play

CAS SUR MILLE, UN 1948 d: Jean-Pierre Feydeau. FRN., *Un Cas Singulier*, J. P. Feydeau, Play

CASA ASSASSINADA, A 1971 d: Paulo Cesar Saraceni. BRZ., *Cronica Da Casa Assassinada*, Lucio Cardoso, 1959, Novel

CASA DE BERNARDA ALBA, LA 1987 d: Mario Camus. SPN., *La Casa de Bernarda Alba*, Federico Garcia Lorca, 1945, Play

CASA DE LA LLUVIA, LA 1943 d: Antonio Roman. SPN., *La Casa de la Lluvia*, Wenceslao Fernandez Florez, 1925, Short Story

CASA DE LA TROYA, LA 1924 d: Alejandro Perez Lugin, Manuel NoriegA. SPN., *La Casa de Troya*, Alejandro Perez Lugin, Novel

CASA DE MUNECAS 1943 d: Ernesto ArancibiA. ARG., *Et Dukkehjem*, Henrik Ibsen, Copenhagen 1879, Play

Casa de Troya, La see **LA CASA DE LA TROYA** (1924).

CASA DEL BUON RITORNO, LA 1986 d: Giuseppina Marotta, Beppe Cino. ITL., *La Casa Del Buon Ritorno*, Beppe Cino, Novel

CASA DI BAMBOLA 1919 d: Febo Mari. ITL., *Et Dukkehjem*, Henrik Ibsen, Copenhagen 1879, Play

Casa Di Madame Kora, La see **FILLETTES MEFIEZ-VOUS** (1957).

Casa Sulla Fungaia, La see **CRIMINE A DUE** (1965).

CASABLAN 1964 d: Larry Frisch. GRC/ISR., *Casablan*, Yigal Mossensohn, Tel Aviv 1958, Play

CASABLANCA 1942 d: Michael Curtiz. USA., *Everybody Comes to Rick's*, Joan Alison, Murray Burnett, Play

CASAMENTO, O 1975 d: Arnaldo Jabor. BRZ., *O Casamento*, Nelson Rodrigues, 1966, Novel

Casanova see **VOCAZIONE E PRIMA ESPERIENZE DI GIACOMO CASANOVA, VENEZIANO INFANZIA** (1969).

CASANOVA 1976 d: Federico Fellini. ITL., *Memoires de Jacques Casanova de Seingalt*, Giacomo Casanova, 1826-38, Autobiography

CASANOVA BROWN 1944 d: Sam Wood. USA., *Bachelor Father*, Floyd Dell, Thomas Mitchell, Play

Casanova de Fellini see **CASANOVA** (1976).

Casanova Di Federico Fellini, Il see **CASANOVA** (1976).

CASANOVA FAREBBE COSI! 1942 d: Carlo Ludovico BragagliA. ITL., *Casanova Farebbe Cosi*, Armando Curcio, Peppino de Filippo, Play

CASANOVA WIDER WILLEN 1931 d: Edward Brophy. USA., *Bedroom and Bath Parlor*, Charles W. Bell, New York 1917, Play, *Parlor Bedroom and Bath*, Mark Swan, New York 1917, Play

Casbah see **PEPE LE MOKO** (1936).

CASBAH 1948 d: John Berry. USA., *Pepe le Moko*, Detective Ashelbe, Paris 1937, Novel

CASCALHO 1950 d: Leo Marten. BRZ., *Cascalho*, Herberto Sales, 1944, Novel

CASCARRABIAS 1930. USA., *Grumpy*, Thomas Wigney Percyval, New York 1921, Play

CASE AGAINST BROOKLYN, THE 1958 d: Paul Wendkos. USA., Ed Reid, Article

Case Against Calvin Cooke see **AN ACT OF MURDER** (1948).

CASE AGAINST MRS. AMES, THE 1936 d: William A. Seiter. USA., *The Case Against Mrs. Ames*, Arthur Somers Roche, 1934, Novel

Case de l'Oncle Tom, La see **ONKEL TOMS HUTTE** (1965).

Case for a Young Hangman, A see **PRIPAD PRO ZACINAJICIHO KATA** (1969).

CASE FOR THE CROWN, THE 1934 d: George A. Cooper. UKN., *An Error of Judgement*, Anthony Gittins, Short Story

Case for the Jury, A see **THE DOCK BRIEF** (1962).

Case for the New Hangman, A see **PRIPAD PRO ZACINAJICIHO KATA** (1969).

CASE OF ARSON, A 1913 d: A. E. Coleby. UKN., *In de Jonge Jan*, Herman Heijermans, Play

CASE OF BECKY, THE 1915 d: Frank Reicher. USA., *The Case of Becky*, Edward Locke, New York 1912, Play

CASE OF BECKY, THE 1921 d: Chester M. Franklin. USA., *The Case of Becky*, Edward Locke, New York 1912, Play

Case of Clara Deane see **THE STRANGE CASE OF CLARA DEANE** (1932).

CASE OF GABRIEL PERRY, THE 1935 d: Albert de Courville. UKN., *Wild Justice*, James Dale, 1933, Play

CASE OF IDENTITY, A 1921 d: Maurice Elvey. UKN., *A Case of Identity*, Arthur Conan Doyle, Short Story

Case of Jonathan Drew, The see **THE LODGER: A STORY OF THE LONDON FOG** (1926).

Case of Lady Brookes, The see **THAT DANGEROUS AGE** (1949).

CASE OF LADY CAMBER, THE 1920 d: Walter West. UKN., *The Case of Lady Camber*, Horace Annesley Vachell, London 1915, Play

Case of Lady Camber, The see **LORD CAMBER'S LADIES** (1932).

Case of Lena Christ, The see **DER FALL LENA CHRIST** (1968).

Case of Mrs. Loring, The see **A QUESTION OF ADULTERY** (1958).

Case of Mrs. Pembroke, The see **TWO AGAINST THE WORLD** (1936).

Case of Poisons, The see **L'AFFAIRE DES POISONS** (1955).

CASE OF SERGEANT GRISCHA, THE 1930 d: Herbert Brenon. USA., *Der Streit Um Den Sergeanten Grischa*, Arnold Zweig, Potsdam 1927, Novel

CASE OF THE BLACK CAT, THE 1936 d: William McGann. USA., *The Case of the Caretaker's Cat*, Erle Stanley Gardner, New York 1935, Novel

CASE OF THE BLACK PARROT, THE 1941 d: Noel Smith. USA., *The Case of the Black Parrot*, Eleanor Robeson Belmont, Harriet Ford, Burton Egbert Stevenson, Play

Case of the Caretaker's Cat, The see **THE CASE OF THE BLACK CAT** (1936).

Case of the Constant God, The see **LOVE LETTERS OF A STAR** (1936).

CASE OF THE CURIOUS BRIDE, THE 1935 d: Michael Curtiz. USA., *The Case of the Curious Bride*, Erle Stanley Gardner, New York 1935, Novel

CASE OF THE FRIGHTENED LADY, THE 1940 d: George King. UKN., *The Frightened Lady*, Edgar Wallace, London 1932, Novel

CASE OF THE HOWLING DOG, THE 1934 d: Alan Crosland. USA., *The Case of the Howling Dog*, Erle Stanley Gardner, New York 1935, Novel

Case of the Investigating Magistrate, The see **ZABRAVETE TOZI SLOUCHAI** (1984).

CASE OF THE LUCKY LEGS, THE 1935 d: Archie Mayo. USA., *The Case of the Lucky Legs*, Erle Stanley Gardner, New York 1934, Novel

Case of the Missing Blonde, The see **THE LADY IN THE MORGUE** (1938).

Case of the Missing Clerk, The see **DEN FORSVUNDNE FULDMAEGTIG** (1972).

Case of the Red Monkey, The see **LITTLE RED MONKEY** (1953).

CASE OF THE STUTTERING BISHOP, THE 1937 d: William Clemens. USA., *The Case of the Stuttering Bishop*, Erle Stanley Gardner, New York 1936, Novel

CASE OF THE VANISHED BONDS, THE 1914 d: Langdon West. USA., *Below the Deadline*, Scott Campbell, Short Story

CASE OF THE VELVET CLAWS, THE 1936 d: William Clemens. USA., *The Case of the Velvet Claws*, Erle Stanley Gardner, New York 1933, Novel

CASEBOOK OF SHERLOCK HOLMES: THE BOSCOMBE VALLEY MYSTERY, THE 1990 d: June Howson. UKN., *The Boscombe Valley Mystery*, Arthur Conan Doyle, Short Story

CASEBOOK OF SHERLOCK HOLMES: THE CREEPING MAN, THE 1991 d: Tim Sullivan. UKN., *The Creeping Man*, Arthur Conan Doyle, Short Story

CASEBOOK OF SHERLOCK HOLMES: THE DISAPPEARANCE OF LADY CARFAX, THE 1990 d: John Madden. UKN., *The Disappearance of Lady Frances Carfax*, Arthur Conan Doyle, Short Story

CASEBOOK OF SHERLOCK HOLMES: THE ILLUSTRIOUS CLIENT, THE 1991 d: Tim Sullivan. UKN., *The Illustrious Client*, Arthur Conan Doyle, Short Story

CASEBOOK OF SHERLOCK HOLMES: THE PROBLEM OF THOR BRIDGE, THE 1990 d: Michael Simpson. UKN., *Thor Bridge*, Arthur Conan Doyle, Short Story

CASEBOOK OF SHERLOCK HOLMES: THE SHOSCOMBE OLD PLACE, THE 1990 d: Patrick Lau. UKN., *Shoscombe Old Place*, Arthur Conan Doyle, Short Story

Caseificio Di Vehfreude, Il see **DIE KASEREI IN DER VEHFREUDE** (1958).

CASEY AT THE BAT 1916 d: Lloyd Ingraham. USA., *Casey at the Bat*, E. L. Thayer, 1888, Poem

CASEY AT THE BAT 1927 d: Monte Brice. USA., *Casey at the Bat*, E. L. Thayer, 1888, Poem

CASEY JONES 1927 d: Charles J. Hunt. USA., *Casey Jones*, Eddie Newton, T. Lawrence Seibert, 1909, Song

CASEY'S SHADOW 1977 d: Martin Ritt. USA., *Ruidoso*, John McPhee, Story

CASH MCCALL 1960 d: Joseph Pevney. USA., *Cash McCall*, Cameron Hawley, Novel

CASH ON DELIVERY 1926 d: Milton Rosmer. UKN., *Cash on Delivery*, Alfred Barrett, Short Story

Cash on Delivery see **A SON TO DOROTHY** (1954).

CASH ON DEMAND 1961 d: Quentin Lawrence. UKN., *The Gold Inside*, Jack Gillies, London 1960, Play

Cashel Byron's Profession see **ROMAN BOXERA** (1921).

Casino de Paree see **GO INTO YOUR DANCE** (1935).

CASINO MURDER CASE, THE 1935 d: Edwin L. Marin. USA., *The Casino Murder Case*, S. S. Van Dine, New York 1934, Novel

CASINO ROYALE 1967 d: John Huston, Ken Hughes. UKN., *Casino Royale*, Ian Fleming, London 1953, Novel

CASO CLAUDIO, O 1979 d: Miguel Borges. BRZ., *Porque Claudia Lessin Vai Morrer*, Valerio Meinel, 1978, Novel

Caso Del Giudice Haller, Il see **IL CASO HALLER** (1933).

CASO DI COSCIENZA, UN 1970 d: Gianni Grimaldi. ITL., *Un Caso Di Coscienza*, Leonardo Sciasia, 1973, Short Story

Caso Difficile Del Commissario Maigret, Il see **MAIGRET UND SEIN GROSSTER FALL** (1966).

CASO HALLER, IL 1933 d: Alessandro Blasetti. ITL., *Der Andere*, Paul Lindau, 1893, Play

Caso Mauritius, Il see **L'AFFAIRE MAURIZIUS** (1953).

CASO MORO, IL 1986 d: Giuseppe FerrarA. ITL., *Il Caso Moro*, Robert Katz, Novel

Caso Venere Privata, Il see **CRAN D'ARRET** (1970).

CASOTTO, IL 1977 d: Sergio Citti. ITL., *Il Casotto*, Vincenzo Cerami, Short Story

CASPER 1995 d: Brad Silberling. USA., *Casper the Friendly Ghost*, Joseph Oriolo, Seymour Rait, Story

CASS TIMBERLANE 1947 d: George Sidney. USA., *Cass Timberlane*, Sinclair Lewis, 1945, Novel

CASSANDRA CROSSING, THE 1977 d: George Pan Cosmatos. UKN/GRM/ITL., *Cassandra Crossing*, Robert Katz, Novel

CASSE, LE 1971 d: Henri Verneuil. FRN/ITL., *The Burglar*, David Goodis, 1953, Novel

CASSE-TETE CHINOIS POUR LE JUDOKA 1968 d: Maurice Labro. FRN/ITL/GRM., *Judoka En Enfer*, Ernie Clerk, Novel

CASSIDY 1917 d: Arthur Rosson. USA., *Cassidy*, Larry Evans, 1913, Short Story

Cassidy Bar Twenty see HOPALONG RIDES AGAIN (1937).

CASSIDY OF BAR 20 1938 d: Lesley Selander. USA., *Me An' Shorty*, Clarence E. Mulford, New York 1929, Novel

Cassidy of the Bar 20 see CASSIDY OF BAR 20 (1938).

CAST A DARK SHADOW 1955 d: Lewis Gilbert. UKN., *Murder Mistaken*, Janet Green, London 1952, Play

CAST A GIANT SHADOW 1966 d: Melville Shavelson. USA., *Cast a Giant Shadow*, Ted Berkman, New York 1962, Biography

CAST A LONG SHADOW 1959 d: Thomas Carr. USA., *Cast a Long Shadow*, Wayne D. Overholser, Novel

Cast Iron see THE VIRTUOUS SIN (1930).

CASTAWAY 1987 d: Nicolas Roeg. UKN., *Castaway*, Lucy Irvine, Book

Castaways, The see IN SEARCH OF THE CASTAWAYS (1961).

CASTE 1913 d: C. Jay Williams. USA., *Caste*, T. W. Robertson, London 1867, Play

CASTE 1915 d: Larry Trimble. USA., *Caste*, T. W. Robertson, London 1867, Play

CASTE 1930 d: Campbell Gullan. UKN., *Caste*, T. W. Robertson, London 1867, Play

Castellana Del Libano, La see LA CHATELAINE DU LIBAN (1956).

CASTELLI IN ARIA 1939 d: Augusto GeninA. ITL./GRM., *Tre Giorni in Paradiso*, Franz Franchy, Novel

Castello in Svezia, Il see CHATEAU EN SUEDE (1963).

CASTELUL DIN CARPATI 1981 d: Stere GuleA. RMN., *Le Chateau Des Carpathes*, Jules Verne, 1892, Novel

CASTIGO 1917 d: Ubaldo Maria Del Colle. ITL., *Castigo*, Matilde Serao, 1893, Novel

Castigo see IL CAPPELLO DA PRETE (1944).

Castilian, The see EL VALLE DE LAS ESPADAS (1963).

Casting Swords see ZHU JIAN (1994).

CASTING THE RUNES 1979 d: Lawrence Gordon Clark. UKN., *Casting the Runes*, M. R. James, 1911, Short Story

Castle in Sweden see CHATEAU EN SUEDE (1963).

CASTLE IN THE AIR 1952 d: Henry Cass. UKN., *Castle in the Air*, Alan Melville, London 1949, Play

Castle in the Carpathians, The see CASTELUL DIN CARPATI (1981).

CASTLE KEEP 1969 d: Sydney Pollack. USA., *Castle Keep*, William Eastlake, New York 1965, Novel

CASTLE OF ADVENTURE, THE 1990 d: Terry Marcel. UKN., *The Castle of Adventure*, Enid Blyton, Novel

Castle of Blood see DANZA MACABRA (1964).

Castle of Cagliostro, The see KARIOSUTORO NO SHIRO (1991).

Castle of Crimes see THE HOUSE OF THE ARROW (1940).

Castle of Doom see VAMPYR (1931).

Castle of Terror see LA VERGINE DI NORIMBERGA (1963).

Castle of the Spider's Web, The see KUMONOSU-JO (1957).

Castle of the Terrified see DAS GEHEIMNIS DER SCHWARZEN KOFFER (1962).

Castle of the Walking Dead see DIE SCHLANGENGRUBE UND DAS PENDEL (1967).

CASTLE ON THE HUDSON 1940 d: Anatole Litvak. USA., *Twenty Thousand Years in Sing Sing*, Lewis E. Lawes, Garden City, N.Y. 1932, Book

Castle, The see DAS SCHLOSS (1968).

Castle, The see LINNA (1986).

Castle Vogelod see SCHLOSS VOGELOD (1921).

CASTLES IN SPAIN 1920 d: H. Lisle Lucoque. UKN., *Castles in Spain*, Ruby M. Ayres, Novel

CASTLES IN THE AIR 1919 d: George D. Baker. USA., *Orchestra D-2*, Kate Jordan, 1915, Short Story

Castles, The see THE STORY OF VERNON AND IRENE CASTLE (1939).

CASUAL SEX? 1988 d: Genevieve Robert. USA., *Casual Sex?*, Wendy Goldman, Judy Toll, Play

CASUALTIES OF WAR 1989 d: Brian DepalmA. USA., *Casualties of War*, Daniel Lang, Book

CAT AND MOUSE 1958 d: Paul RothA. UKN., *Cat and Mouse*, Michael Halliday, Novel

Cat and Mouse see KATZ UND MAUS (1967).

CAT AND THE CANARY, THE 1927 d: Paul Leni. USA., *The Cat and the Canary*, John Willard, New York 1922, Play

CAT AND THE CANARY, THE 1939 d: Elliott Nugent. USA., *The Cat and the Canary*, John Willard, New York 1922, Play

CAT AND THE CANARY, THE 1978 d: Radley H. Metzger. UKN., *The Cat and the Canary*, John Willard, New York 1922, Play

CAT AND THE FIDDLE, THE 1933 d: William K. Howard. USA., *The Cat and the Fiddle*, Otto Harbach, Jerome Kern, New York 1931, Musical Play

Cat and Two Women, A see NEKO TO SHOZO TO FUTARI NO ONNA (1956).

CAT BALLOU 1965 d: Elliot Silverstein. USA., *The Ballad of Cat Ballou*, Roy Chanslor, Boston 1956, Novel

CAT CHASER 1989 d: Abel FerrarA. USA., *Cat Chaser*, Elmore Leonard, Novel

CAT CREEPS, THE 1930 d: Rupert Julian. USA., *The Cat and the Canary*, John Willard, New York 1922, Play

Cat O' Nine Tails, The see IL GATTO A NOVE CODE (1971).

CAT ON A HOT TIN ROOF 1958 d: Richard Brooks. USA., *Cat on a Hot Tin Roof*, Tennessee Williams, New York 1955, Play

CAT ON A HOT TIN ROOF 1976 d: Robert Moore. UKN., *Cat on a Hot Tin Roof*, Tennessee Williams, New York 1955, Play

CAT ON A HOT TIN ROOF 1985 d: Jack Hofsiss. USA., *Cat on a Hot Tin Roof*, Tennessee Williams, New York 1955, Play

Cat, Shozo and Two Women, A see NEKO TO SHOZO TO FUTARI NO ONNA (1956).

Cat, The see LA CHATTE (1958).

Cat, The see LE CHAT (1971).

Cat With Nine Tails see IL GATTO A NOVE CODE (1971).

Catacombs see KATAKOMBY (1940).

CATACOMBS 1964 d: Gordon Hessler. UKN., *Catacombs*, Jay Bennett, New York 1959, Novel

Catamount Killing, The see PITTSVILLE - EINE SAFE VOLL BLUT (1974).

CATASTROPHE 1999 - PROPHECIES OF NOSTRADAMUS 1974 d: Shiro Moritani. JPN., Ben Goto, Novel

CATCH ME A SPY 1971 d: Dick Clement. UKN/USA/FRN., *Catch Me a Spy*, George Marton, Tibor Meray, Novel

CATCH MY SMOKE 1922 d: William Beaudine. USA., *Shoe Bar Stratton*, Joseph Bushnell Ames, New York 1922, Novel

CATCH MY SOUL 1974 d: Patrick McGoohan. USA., *Othello*, William Shakespeare, c1604, Play

Catch, The see SHIIKU (1961).

CATCH-22 1970 d: Mike Nichols. USA., *Catch 22*, Joseph Heller, New York 1961, Novel

CATERED AFFAIR, THE 1956 d: Richard Brooks. USA., *The Catered Affair*, Paddy Chayefsky, 1955, Television Play

CATERINA 1921 d: Mario Caserini. ITL., *Catherine*, Henri Lavedan, 1898, Play

Catherine see IL SUFFIT D'UN AMOUR CATHERINE (1968).

Catherine & Co. see CATHERINE ET CIE (1975).

Catherine -a Live for Love see IL SUFFIT D'UN AMOUR CATHERINE (1968).

Catherine -Ein Leben Fur Die Liebe see IL SUFFIT D'UN AMOUR CATHERINE (1968).

CATHERINE ET CIE 1975 d: Michel Boisrond. FRN/ITL., *Catherine Et Cie*, Edouard de Segonzac, Novel

Catherine, Il Suffit d'Amour see IL SUFFIT D'UN AMOUR CATHERINE (1968).

CATHERINE, IL SUFFIT D'UN AMOUR 1968 d: Bernard Borderie. FRN/ITL/GRM., *Catherine Il Suffit d'un Amour*, Juliette Benzonni, Novel

CATHERINE THE GREAT 1934 d: Paul Czinner. UKN., *The Czarina*, Lajos Biro, Melchior Lengyel, Play

Catherine, un Solo Impossibile Amore see IL SUFFIT D'UN AMOUR CATHERINE (1968).

Cathie's Child see CATHY'S CHILD (1979).

CATHOLICS 1973 d: Jack Gold. USA/UKN., *Catholics*, Brian Moore, Novel

Cathy Tippel see KEETJE TIPPEL (1975).

CATHY'S CHILD 1979 d: Donald Crombie. ASL., *A Piece of Paper*, Dick Wordley, Novel

CATLOW 1971 d: Sam Wanamaker. UKN/USA., *Catlow*, Louis L'Amour, Novel

CAT'S EYE 1985 d: Lewis Teague. USA., *The General*, Stephen King, Short Story, *The Ledge*, Stephen King, Short Story, *Quitters Inc.*, Stephen King, Short Story

Cat's Game see MACSKAJATEK (1974).

Cat's Path, The see DER KATZENSTEG (1937).

CAT'S PAW, THE 1934 d: Sam Taylor. USA., *The Cat's-Paw*, Clarence Budington Kelland, New York 1934, Novel

Cat's Play see KATZENSPIEL (1983).

Cats, The see KATTORNA (1965).

CATSPAW, THE 1916 d: George A. Wright. USA., *Catspaw*, William Hamilton Osborne, New York 1911, Novel

Catsplay see MACSKAJATEK (1974).

Catsplay see KATZENSPIEL (1983).

CATTIVO SOGGETTO, UN 1933 d: Carlo Ludovico BragagliA. ITL., *The Devil to Pay*, Frederick Lonsdale, Play

CATTLE ANNIE AND LITTLE BRITCHES 1979 d: Lamont Johnson. USA., *Cattle Annie and Little Britches*, Robert Ward, Novel

CATTLE EMPIRE 1958 d: Charles Marquis Warren. USA., Daniel B. Ullmann, Story

CATTLE QUEEN OF MONTANA 1954 d: Allan Dwan. USA., Thomas W. Blackburn, Story

CAUGHT 1949 d: Max Ophuls. USA., *Wild Calendar*, Libbie Block, Novel

CAUGHT 1996 d: Robert M. Young. USA., *Into It*, Edward Pomerantz, Novel

CAUGHT BLUFFING 1922 d: Lambert Hillyer. USA., *Broken Chains*, Jack Bechdolt, 1921, Short Story

CAUGHT IN THE NET 1960 d: John Haggarty. UKN., *The Lazy Salmon Mystery*, Sutherland Ross, Novel

CAUSE CELEBRE, UNE 1913. FRN., *Une Cause Celebre*, Gabriel, Novel

CAUSE ED EFFETTI 1917 d: Ugo Gracci. ITL., *Cause Ed Effetti*, Paolo Ferrari, 1871, Play

CAUSE FOR ALARM 1950 d: Tay Garnett. USA., *Cause for Alarm*, Lawrence B. Marcus, Radio Play

CAUSE TOUJOURS, MON LAPIN! 1961 d: Guy Lefranc. FRN., *Dark Witness*, Day Keene, Novel

CAVALCADE 1933 d: Frank Lloyd. USA., *Cavalcade*, Noel Coward, London 1931, Play

CAVALCADE 1955 d: Lewis Allen. USA., *Cavalcade*, Noel Coward, London 1931, Play

CAVALE, LA 1971 d: Michel Mitrani. FRN., *La Cavale*, Albertine Sarrazin, 1965, Novel

CAVALERIE LEGERE 1935 d: Roger Vitrac, Werner Hochbaum. FRN., *Umwege Zur Heimat*, Heinz Lorenz-Lambrecht, Novel

CAVALIER DE CROIX-MORT, LE 1947 d: Lucien Gasnier-Raymond. FRN., *Le Vinaigre Des Quatre Voleurs*, Albert Jean, Novel

Cavalier de Riouclare, Le see SORTILEGES (1944).

CAVALIER LAFLEUR, LE 1934 d: Pierre-Jean Ducis. FRN., *Le Cavalier Lafleur*, Andre Mauprey, Louis Raine, Opera

CAVALIER OF THE STREETS, THE 1937 d: Harold French. UKN., *The Cavalier of the Streets*, Michael Arlen, Short Story

CAVALIER PETAGNA, IL 1926 d: Mario Gargiulo. ITL., *Lu Cavalieri Pidagna*, Luigi Capuana, 1909, Play

CAVALIER, THE 1928 d: Irvin V. Willat. USA., *The Black Rider*, Max Brand, Story

CAVALIERE DEL SILENZIO, IL 1916 d: Oreste Visalli. ITL., *When Knights Were Bold*, Charles Marlowe, London 1907, Play

CAVALIERE DI MAISON ROUGE, IL 1953 d: Vittorio Cottafavi. ITL., *Le Chevalier de Maison Rouge*, Alexandre Dumas (pere), 1846, Novel

Cavaliere E la Czarina, Il see LE SECRET DU CHEVALIER D'EON (1960).

CAVALIERE INESISTENTE, IL 1970 d: Pino Zac. ITL., *Il Cavaliere Inesistente*, Italo Calvino, 1959, Novel

707

CAVALIERI DALLE MASCHERA NERA, I 1948 d: Pino Mercanti. ITL., *I Beati Paoli*, Luigi Natoli, Novel

CAVALIERI DEL DESERTO, I 1942 d: Gino Talamo, Osvaldo Valenti. ITL., Emilio Salgari, Novel

CAVALIERI DELLA REGINA, I 1955 d: Mauro Bolognini. ITL., *Les Trois Mousquetaires*, Alexandre Dumas (pere), Paris 1844, Novel

Cavaliers Rouges, Les *see* OLD SHATTERHAND (1964).

CAVALINHO AZUL, O 1985 d: Eduardo Escorel. BRZ., *O Cavalinho Azul*, Maria Clara Machado, 1960, Play

CAVALLERIA RUSTICANA 1909 d: Emile Chautard. FRN., *Cavalleria Rusticana*, Giovanni Verga, Milan 1880, Short Story

CAVALLERIA RUSTICANA 1916 d: Ubaldo Maria Del Colle. ITL., *Cavalleria Rusticana*, Giovanni Verga, Milan 1880, Short Story

CAVALLERIA RUSTICANA 1916 d: Ugo FalenA. ITL., *Cavalleria Rusticana*, Giovanni Verga, Milan 1880, Short Story

CAVALLERIA RUSTICANA 1924 d: Mario Gargiulo. ITL., *Cavalleria Rusticana*, Giovanni Verga, Milan 1880, Short Story

CAVALLERIA RUSTICANA 1939 d: Amleto Palermi. ITL., *Cavalleria Rusticana*, Giovanni Verga, Milan 1880, Short Story

CAVALLERIA RUSTICANA 1953., *Cavalleria Rusticana*, Giovanni Verga, Milan 1880, Short Story

CAVALLERIA RUSTICANA 1953 d: Carmine Gallone. ITL., *Cavalleria Rusticana*, Giovanni Verga, Milan 1880, Short Story

CAVALLERIA RUSTICANA 1968 d: Ake Falck. SWT/AUS/GRM., *Cavalleria Rusticana*, Giovanni Verga, Milan 1880, Short Story

CAVALLERIA RUSTICANA 1986 d: Franco Zeffirelli. ITL., *Cavalleria Rusticana*, Giovanni Verga, Milan 1880, Short Story

CAVALLINA STORNA, LA 1953 d: Giulio Morelli. ITL., *Cavalla Storna*, Giovanni Pascoli, Poem, *Nido Di Farlotti*, Giovanni Pascoli, Poem, *Un Ricordo*, Giovanni Pascoli, Poem

Cavalry Charge *see* THE LAST OUTPOST (1951).

CAVANAUGH OF THE FOREST RANGERS 1918 d: William Wolbert. USA., *Cavanaugh - Forest Ranger; a Romance of the Mountain West*, Hamlin Garland, New York 1910, Novel

CAVE EST PIEGE, LE 1963 d: Victor MerendA. FRN., *Ne Raccrochez Pas*, Yvan Noe, Novel

CAVE GIRL, THE 1921 d: Joseph J. Franz. USA., *The Cave Girl*, Guy Bolton, George Middleton, New York 1920, Play

CAVE MAN, THE 1915 d: Theodore Marston. USA., *The Cave Man*, Gelett Burgess, New York 1911, Play

CAVE SE REBIFFE, LE 1961 d: Gilles Grangier. FRN/ITL., *Le Cave Se Rebiffe*, Albert Simonin, Paris 1954, Novel

Caveman, The *see* THE CAVE MAN (1915).

CAVEMAN, THE 1926 d: Lewis Milestone. USA., *The Cave Man*, Gelett Burgess, New York 1911, Play

CAVERN SPIDER, THE 1924 d: Thomas Bentley. UKN., *The Cavern Spider*, L. J. Beeston, Short Story

Cavern, The *see* SETTE CONTRO LA MORTE (1965).

CAVES DU MAJESTIC, LES 1944 d: Richard Pottier. FRN., *Les Caves du Majestic*, Georges Simenon, 1942, Short Story

C.C. Action *see* SODA CRACKER (1989).

CE COCHON DE MORIN 1932 d: Georges Lacombe. FRN., *Ce Cochon de Morin*, Guy de Maupassant, 1883, Short Story

Ce Cochon de Morin *see* LA TERREUR DES DAMES (1956).

CE SACRE GRAND-PERE 1968 d: Jacques Poitrenaud. FRN., *Je M'appelle Jerico*, Catherine Paysan, Paris 1964, Novel

Ce Soir on Joue MacBeth *see* LE RIDEAU ROUGE (1952).

CEASE FIRE 1985 d: David Nutter. USA., *Vietnam Trilogy*, George Fernandez, Play

Ceasefire *see* CEASE FIRE (1985).

Cebo, El *see* ES GESCHAH AM HELLICHTEN TAG (1958).

CECH PANEN KUTNOHORSKYCH 1938 d: Otakar VavrA. CZC., *Pan Mincmistrova a Zivkovsky Rarasek*, Ladislav Stroupeznicky, Play

CECILE EST MORTE 1943 d: Maurice Tourneur. FRN., *Cecile Est Morte*, Georges Simenon, 1942, Short Story

CECILIA 1982 d: Humberto Solas. CUB/SPN., *Cecilia Valdes O la Loma Del Angel*, Cirilo Villaverde, 1839, Novel

CECILIA OF THE PINK ROSES 1918 d: Julius Steger. USA., *Cecilia of the Pink Roses*, Katharine Haviland Taylor, New York 1917, Novel

Cecilia Valdes *see* CECILIA (1982).

Cedar Madonna, The *see* A MADONA DE CEDRO (1968).

CEI CARE PLATESC CU VIATA 1989 d: Serban Marinescu. RMN., *Jocul Ielelor*, Camil Petrescu, 1947, Play

CEILING ZERO 1936 d: Howard Hawks. USA., *Ceiling Zero*, Frank Wead, New York 1935, Play

CEKANKY 1940 d: Vladimir Borsky. CZC., *Cekanky*, F. X. Svoboda, Play

CELA S'APPELLE L'AURORE 1955 d: Luis Bunuel. FRN/ITL., *Cela S'appelle l'Aurore*, Emmanuel Robles, 1952, Novel

CELEBRATED CASE, A 1914 d: George Melford. USA., *Une Cause Celebre*, Eugene Cormon, Adolphe-P. d'Ennery, Paris 1877, Play

Celebrated Case, A *see* WHAT HAPPENED AT 22 (1916).

Celebrated Scandal, A *see* THE CELEBRATED SCANDAL (1915).

CELEBRATED SCANDAL, THE 1915 d: James Durkin. USA., *El Gran Galeoto*, Jose Echegaray, Madrid 1881, Play

Celebration *see* THE STRIPPER (1963).

CELEBRATIONS, LES 1979 d: Yves Simoneau. CND., *Les Celebrations*, Michel Garneau, Play

CELEBRITY 1984 d: Paul Wendkos. USA., *Celebrity*, Thomas Thompson, Novel

CELESTE 1981 d: Percy Adlon. GRM., *Monsieur Proust*, Celeste Albaret, Book

CELESTIAL CITY, THE 1929 d: John Orton. UKN., *The Celestial City*, Baroness Orczy, Novel

CELESTINA 1977 d: Miguel Sabido. MXC., *La Celestina*, Fernando de Rojas, 1500, Play

Celestina *see* LA CELESTINA (1996).

CELESTINA, LA 1968 d: Cesar Ardavin. SPN/GRM., *La Celestina*, Fernando de Rojas, 1500, Play

CELESTINA, LA 1996 d: Gerardo VerA. SPN., *La Celestina*, Fernando de Rojas, 1500, Play

CELESTINA P. R., LA 1965 d: Carlo Lizzani. ITL., *La Celestina*, Fernando de Rojas, 1500, Play

CELL 2455, DEATH ROW 1955 d: Fred F. Sears. USA., Caryl Chessman, Book

Cell, The *see* DIE ZELLE (1971).

Cellar, The *see* HAMARTEF (1963).

CELLE QUI DOMINE 1927 d: Carmine Gallone. FRN., *Celle Qui Domine Les Hommes*, May Edginton, Story

Celluloid *see* CELLULOIDE (1996).

CELLULOID CLOSET, THE 1995 d: Robert Epstein, Jeffrey Friedman. USA., *The Celluloid Closet*, Vito Russo, Book

CELLULOIDE 1996 d: Carlo Lizzani. ITL., *Celluloide*, Ugo Pirro, Novel

CELOS 1946 d: Mario Soffici. ARG., *Kreutserova Sonata*, Lev Nikolayevich Tolstoy, 1889, Short Story

Celovek S Ruzem *see* CHELOVEK S RUZHYOM (1938).

CELUI QUI DOIT MOURIR 1956 d: Jules Dassin. FRN/ITL., *O Christos Xanastavronetai*, Nikos Kazantzakis, 1948, Novel

CEMENT GARDEN, THE 1992 d: Andrew Birkin. UKN/GRM/FRN., *The Cement Garden*, Ian McEwan, Novel

CEMETERY CLUB, THE 1993 d: Bill Duke. USA., *The Cemetery Club*, Ivan Menchell, Play

Cemetery Man *see* DELLAMORTE DELLAMORE (1994).

Cena de Los Cobardes, La *see* LE REPAS DES FAUVES (1964).

CENA DELLE BEFFE, LA 1941 d: Alessandro Blasetti. ITL., *La Cena Delle Beffe*, Sem Benelli, 1909, Play

CENCIAIUOLO DELLA SANITA, IL 1917 d: Franco Dias. ITL., *Il Cenciaiuolo Della Sanita*, Davide Galdi, Novel

CENCIAIUOLO DI PARIGI, IL 1917 d: Enrico Vidali. ITL., *Le Ciffonier de Paris*, Charles Sales, 1847, Novel

CENERE 1916 d: Febo Mari. ITL., *Cenere*, Grazia Deledda, 1904, Novel

CENERENTOLA 1949 d: Fernando Cerchio. ITL., *Cendrillon*, Charles Perrault, 1697, Short Story

Cenicienta, La *see* ERASE UNA VEZ (1950).

CENT BRIQUES ET DES TUILES 1965 d: Pierre Grimblat. FRN/ITL., *Cent Briques Et Des Tuiles*, Clarence Weff, Paris 1964, Novel

CENT MILLE DOLLARS AU SOLEIL 1963 d: Henri Verneuil. FRN/ITL., *Nous N'irons Pas Au Nigeria*, Claude Veillot, Novel

Cent Rancunes *see* HARD FEELINGS (1982).

CENTENNIAL 1978 d: Virgil W. Vogel, Paul Krasny. USA., *Centennial*, James A. Michener, Novel

CENTENNIAL SUMMER 1946 d: Otto Preminger. USA., *Centennial Summer*, Albert E. Idell, Novel

Cento Dollari d'Odio *see* ONKEL TOMS HUTTE (1965).

Cento Ragazze Per un Playboy *see* BEL AMI 2000 ODER: WIE VERFUHRT MAN EINEN PLAYBOY? (1966).

CENTOMILA DOLLARI 1940 d: Mario Camerini. ITL., Carl Conrad, Play

Centomila Dollari Al Sole *see* CENT MILLE DOLLARS AU SOLEIL (1963).

CENTOVENTI H.P. 1915 d: Oreste Gherardini. ITL., *Centoventi H.P.*, Amerigo Guasti, 1906, Play

Centurions, The *see* LOST COMMAND (1966).

'Ception Shoals *see* OUT OF THE FOG (1919).

C'era Una Volta in America *see* ONCE UPON A TIME IN AMERICA (1983).

CERCASI MODELLA 1932 d: E. W. Emo. ITL., *Diane Au Bain*, Romain Coolus, Maurice Hennequin, Play

Cercle Infernal, Le *see* THE HAUNTING OF JULIA (1976).

Cercle Vicieux, Le *see* RIEN QUE DES MENSONGES (1932).

Ceremonia, La *see* THE CEREMONY (1963).

CEREMONIE D'AMOUR 1988 d: Walerian Borowczyk. FRN., *Ceremonie d'Amour*, Andre Pieyre de Mandiargues, Novel

CEREMONIE, LA 1995 d: Claude Chabrol. FRN., *A Judgement in Stone*, Ruth Rendell, 1977, Novel

CEREMONY, THE 1963 d: Laurence Harvey. USA/SPN., *La Ceremonie*, Frederic Grendel, Paris 1951, Novel

Cerne Slunce *see* TEMNE SLUNCE (1980).

CERNI MYSLIVCI 1921 d: Vaclav Binovec. CZC., *Cerni Myslivci*, Ruzena Svobodova, Book

CERNI MYSLIVCI 1945 d: Martin Fric. CZC., *Cerni Myslivci*, Ruzena Svobodova, Book

CERROMAIOR 1981 d: Luis Filipe RochA. PRT., *Cerromaior*, Manuel Da Fonseca, 1943, Novel

CERTAIN MONSIEUR, UN 1949 d: Yves Ciampi. FRN., *Un Certain Monsieur*, Jean le Hallier, Novel

CERTAIN RICH MAN, A 1921 d: Howard Hickman. USA., *A Certain Rich Man*, William Allen White, New York 1909, Novel

CERTAIN SMILE, A 1958 d: Jean Negulesco. USA., *Un Certain Sourire*, Francoise Sagan, 1956, Novel

CERTO CAPITAO RODRIGO, UM 1970 d: Anselmo Duarte. BRZ., *Um Certo Capitao Rodrigo*, Erico Verissimo, 1949, Short Story

CERTO, CERTISSIMO, ANZI. PROBABILE 1969 d: Marcello Fondato. ITL., *Diario Di Una Telefonista*, Dacia Maraini, Short Story

CERTOSA DI PARMA, LA 1947 d: Christian-Jaque. ITL/FRN., *La Chartreuse de Parme*, Stendhal, 1839, Novel

Cervantes *see* LE AVVENTURE E GLI AMORI DI MIGUEL CERVANTES (1967).

CES DAMES AUX CHAPEAUX VERTS 1929 d: Andre Berthomieu. FRN., *Ces Dames aux Chapeaux Verts*, Germaine Acremant, Novel

CES DAMES AUX CHAPEAUX VERTS 1937 d: Maurice Cloche. FRN., *Ces Dames aux Chapeaux Verts*, Germaine Acremant, Novel

CES DAMES AUX CHAPEAUX VERTS 1948 d: Fernand Rivers. FRN., *Ces Dames aux Chapeaux Verts*, Germaine Acremant, Novel

CES MESSIEURS DE LA SANTE 1933 d: Piere Colombier. FRN., *Ces Messieurs de la Sante*, Paul Armont, Leopold Marchand, Play

CES SACREES VACANCES 1955 d: Robert Vernay. FRN., *Ces Sacrees Vacances*, Anne Drouet, Novel

CESAR 1936 d: Marcel Pagnol. FRN., *Cesar*, Marcel Pagnol, 1937, Play

CESAR BIROTTEAU 1911 d: Emile Chautard. FRN., *Cesar Birotteau*, Honore de Balzac, Novel

CESARE BIROTTEAU 1921 d: Arnaldo Frateili. ITL., *Grandeur Et Decadence de Cesar Birotteau*, Honore de Balzac, 1837, Novel

C'EST ARRIVE A ADEN 1956 d: Michel Boisrond. FRN., *C'est Arrive a Aden*, Pierre Benoit, Novel

C'EST LA FAUTE D'ADAM 1957 d: Jacqueline Audry. FRN., *C'est la Faute d'Adam*, Maria-Luisa Linares, Novel

C'est la Faute de l'Abbe Mouret *see* LA FAUTE DE L'ABBE MOURET (1970).

C'est Moi le Maitre *see* IL PADRONE SONO ME (1956).

C'EST POUR LA BONNE CAUSE 1997 d: Jacques Fansten. FRN/BLG., *C'est Pour la Bonne Cause*, Jacques Fansten, Novel

C'est Toi Que J'aime *see* JE N'AIME QUE TOI (1949).

CESTA DO HUBLIN STUDAKOVY DUSE 1939 d: Martin Fric. CZC., *Cesta Do Hlubin Studakovy Duse*, Jaroslav Zak, Novel

CESTOU KRIZOVOU 1938 d: Jiri Slavicek. CZC., *Cestou Krizovou*, Jindrich Simon Baar, Novel

CET HOMME EST DANGEREUX 1953 d: Jean SachA. FRN., *Cet Homme Est Dangereux*, Peter Cheyney, Novel

CET OBSCUR OBJET DU DESIR 1977 d: Luis Bunuel. FRN/SPN., *La Femme Et le Pantin*, Pierre Louys, Paris 1898, Novel

CETTE NUIT-LA 1933 d: Marc Sorkin. FRN., *L' Oiseau de Feu*, Louis de Zilahy, Play

CETTE NUIT-LA 1958 d: Maurice Cazeneuve. FRN., *Cette Nuit-la*, Michel Lebrun, Novel

CETTE VIEILLE CANAILLE 1933 d: Anatole Litvak. FRN., *Cette Vieille Canaille*, Fernand Noziere, Play

CETVERTYJ 1972 d: Alexander Stolper. USS., *Chetvyorty*, Konstantin Simonov, 1961, Play

CEU DE ESTRELAS, UM 1996 d: Tata Amaral. BRZ., *Fernando Bonassi*, Novel

CEUX DU CIEL 1940 d: Yvan Noe. FRN., *L' As*, Blanche Alix, Yvan Noe, C. Poidloue, Play

CHA GUAN 1982 d: XIe Tian. CHN., *Cha Guan*, Shu Qingchun, 1964, Play

CHA HUA NU 1938 d: Li Pingqian. CHN., *La Dame aux Camelias*, Alexandre Dumas (fils), Paris 1848, Novel

CHACALS 1917 d: Andre Hugon. FRN., *Chacals*, Arnold Day, Novel

CHAD HANNA 1940 d: Henry King. USA., *Red Wheels Rolling*, Walter D. Edmonds, 1940, Novel

CHAIKA 1971 d: Yuli Karasik. USS., *Chayka*, Anton Chekhov, St. Petersburg 1896, Play

CHAIN INVISIBLE, THE 1916 d: Frank Powell. USA., Richard le Gallienne, Book

CHAIN LIGHTNING 1927 d: Lambert Hillyer. USA., *The Brass Commandments*, Charles Alden Seltzer, New York 1923, Novel

CHAIN OF EVENTS 1958 d: Gerald Thomas. UKN., *London Story*, Leo McKern, Radio Play

Chain of Pearls, The *see* DIE PERLENKETTE (1951).

Chain of Weakness *see* LANTUL SLABICIUNILOR (1952).

Chained Prince, The *see* EL PRINCIPE ENCADENADO (1960).

CHAINS OF BONDAGE 1916 d: A. E. Coleby. UKN., *Chains of Bondage*, Paul Howard, Novel

CHAIR ARDENTE 1932 d: Rene Plaissetty. FRN., *La Cigale*, Lucie Delarue-Mardrus, Novel

CHAIR DE POULE 1964 d: Julien Duvivier. FRN/ITL., *Come Easy - Go Easy*, James Hadley Chase, London 1960, Novel

Chair for Martin Rome, The *see* CRY OF THE CITY (1948).

CHAIRMAN, THE 1969 d: J. Lee Thompson. USA/UKN., *The Chairman*, Jay Richard Kennedy, Novel

Chaise Longue, La *see* DIT-ELLE DETRUIRE (1969).

CHAKRA 1979 d: Rabindra Dharmaraj. IND., *Chakra*, Jaywant Dalvi, 1963, Novel

Ch'a-Kuan *see* CHA GUAN (1982).

CHALEUR DU SEIN, LA 1938 d: Jean Boyer. FRN., *La Chaleur du Sein*, Andre Birabeau, Play

CHALICE OF COURAGE, THE 1915 d: Rollin S. Sturgeon. USA., *The Chalice of Courage: a Romance of Colorado*, Cyrus Townsend Brady, New York 1912, Novel

CHALK GARDEN, THE 1963 d: Ronald Neame. UKN., *The Chalk Garden*, Edith Bagnold, London 1956, Play

Chalked Out *see* YOU CAN'T GET AWAY WITH MURDER (1939).

Challenge of the Frontier *see* MAN OF THE FOREST (1933).

CHALLENGE, THE 1916 d: Donald MacKenzie. USA., *The Challenge*, Edward Childs Carpenter, Play

Challenge, The *see* WOMAN HUNGRY (1931).

CHALLENGE TO LASSIE 1949 d: Richard Thorpe. USA., *Greyfriars Bobby*, Eleanor Atkinson, New York 1912, Novel

Challenge to Live *see* AI TO HONOHO TO (1961).

CHAM 1931 d: Jan Nowina-Przybylski. PLN., *Cham*, Eliza Orzeszkowa, 1888, Novel

CHAMADE, LA 1968 d: Alain Cavalier. FRN/ITL., *La Chamade*, Francoise Sagan, Paris 1965, Novel

Chamber of Horrors *see* MAD LOVE (1935).

Chamber of Horrors *see* THE DOOR WITH SEVEN LOCKS (1940).

Chamber of Horrors *see* HOUSE OF FRANKENSTEIN (1944).

CHAMBER, THE 1996 d: James Foley. USA., *The Chamber*, John Grisham, Novel

Chambermaid and the Titanic, The *see* LA CAMARERA DEL TITANIC (1997).

CHAMBRE ARDENTE, LA 1961 d: Julien Duvivier. FRN/ITL/GRM., *The Burning Court*, John Dickson Carr, New York 1959, Novel

CHAMBRE AU JUDAS, LA 1912 d: Henri Desfontaines. FRN., *La Chambre Au Judas*, Charles Foley, Novel

CHAMBRE DE LA BONNE, LA 1918. FRN., *La Chambre de la Bonne*, Ernest Lunel, Play

Chambre de l'Eveque, La *see* LA STANZA DEL VESCOVO (1977).

Chambre En Ville, Une *see* LEUR DERNIERE NUIT (1953).

Chambre Obscure, La *see* LAUGHTER IN THE DARK (1969).

CHAMBRE ROUGE, LA 1973 d: Jean-Pierre Berckmans. BLG/FRN., *La Chambre Rouge*, Francoise Mallet-Joris, 1955, Novel

CHAMBRE VERTE, LA 1978 d: Francois Truffaut. FRN., *The Altar of the Dead*, Henry James, 1895, Short Story, *The Beast in the Jungle*, Henry James, 1903, Short Story

CHAMESH CHAMESH 1980 d: Shmuel Imberman. ISR., Aharon Meged, Play

Champ de Lin, Le *see* DE VLASCHAARD (1983).

CHAMP FOR A DAY 1953 d: William A. Seiter. USA., *The Disappearance of Dolan*, William Fay, Story

Champ Maudit, Le *see* ESPOIRS (1940).

Champ, The *see* BE YOURSELF! (1930).

CHAMPIGNOL MAIGRE LUI 1933 d: Fred Ellis. FRN., *Champignol Malgre Lui*, Maurice Desvallieres, Georges Feydeau, Play

CHAMPIGNOL MALGRE LUI 1913. FRN., *Champignol Malgre Lui*, Maurice Desvallieres, Georges Feydeau, Play

CHAMPION 1949 d: Mark Robson. USA., *Champion*, Ring Lardner, 1929, Short Story

CHAMPION DE CES DAMES, LE 1937 d: Rene Jayet. FRN., *Le Champion de Ces Dames*, Andre Heuze, Pierre Veber, Play

Champion de Saut de Pontresina, Le *see* DER SPRINGER VON PONTRESINA (1934).

CHAMPION DU REGIMENT, LE 1932 d: Henry Wulschleger. FRN., *Le Champion du Regiment*, Beissier, Jacques Bousquet, Felix Celval, Play

CHAMPION OF LOST CAUSES 1925 d: Chester Bennett. USA., *Champion of Lost Causes*, Max Brand, 1924, Short Story

CHAMPIONS 1983 d: John Irvin. UKN., *Champion's Story*, Bob Champion, Jonathan Powell, Book

Championship Season, The *see* THAT CHAMPIONSHIP SEASON (1982).

CHAMPI-TORTU 1920 d: Jacques de Baroncelli. FRN., *Champi-Tortu*, Gaston Cherau, Novel

CHAMSIN 1970 d: Veit Relin. GRM/ISR., *Die Braut von Messina*, Friedrich von Schiller, 1803, Play

Chance *see* CHANS (1962).

CHANCE AT HEAVEN 1933 d: William A. Seiter. USA., *A Chance at Heaven*, Vina Delmar, 1932, Short Story

Chance at Heaven *see* KEY TO HARMONY (1935).

Chance Meeting *see* BLIND DATE (1959).

Chance Meeting *see* THE YOUNG LOVERS (1964).

CHANCE OF A LIFETIME, THE 1916 d: Bertram Phillips. UKN., *The Chance of a Lifetime*, Nat Gould, Novel

CHANCE OF A NIGHT TIME, THE 1931 d: Herbert Wilcox, Ralph Lynn. UKN., *The Dippers*, Ben Travers, London 1922, Play

Chance the Idol *see* DIE SPIELERIN (1927).

CHANCES 1931 d: Allan Dwan. USA., *Chances*, Arthur Hamilton Gibbs, Boston 1930, Novel

CHANDELIER, LE 1912. FRN., *Le Chandelier*, Alfred de Musset, Play

CHANDIKA 1940 d: Raghupathy S. PrakasA. IND., *Les Trois Mousquetaires*, Alexandre Dumas (pere), Paris 1844, Novel

CHANEL SOLITAIRE 1981 d: George Kaczender. USA/FRN., *Chanel Solitaire*, Claude Dulay, Novel

CHANGE 1974 d: Bernd Fischerauer. GRM., *Change*, Wolfgang Bauer, 1969, Play

CHANGE OF HEART 1934 d: John G. Blystone. USA., *Manhattan Love Song*, Kathleen Norris, New York 1934, Novel

CHANGE OF HEART 1938 d: James Tinling. USA., *The Shepper-Newfounder*, Stewart Edward White, 1930, Short Story

Changed Lives *see* HUAN LE REN JIAN (1959).

CHANGELING, THE 1928 d: Geoffrey H. Malins. UKN., *The Changeling*, W. W. Jacobs, Short Story

CHANGELING, THE 1980 d: Peter Medak. CND., *The Changeling*, Russell Hunter, Story

CHANGING HUSBANDS 1924 d: Frank Urson, Paul Iribe. USA., *Roles*, Elizabeth Alexander, Boston 1924, Novel

Changing Trains *see* OMBYTE AV TAG (1943).

Changing Wind *see* JINY VZDUCH (1939).

CHANGING WOMAN, THE 1918 d: David Smith. USA., *A Matter of Mean Elevation*, O. Henry, 1910, Short Story

CHANNINGS, THE 1920 d: Edwin J. Collins. UKN., *The Channings*, Mrs. Henry Wood, Novel

CHANS 1962 d: Gunnar Hellstrom. SWD., *Chans*, Birgitta Stenberg, Stockholm 1962, Novel

Chan's Cruise *see* CHARLIE CHAN'S MURDER CRUISE (1940).

Chan's Murder Cruise *see* CHARLIE CHAN'S MURDER CRUISE (1940).

Chanson de l'Amour, La *see* LA DERNIERE BERCEUSE (1930).

CHANSON DE ROLAND, LA 1979 d: Frank Cassenti. FRN., *Le Chanson de Roland*, Anon, c1125, Verse

CHANSON DU SOUVENIR, LA 1936 d: Serge de Poligny, Douglas Sirk. FRN., *Das Kleine Hofkonzert*, Toni Impekoven, Paul Verhoeven, Play

CHANT DU MONDE, LE 1965 d: Marcel Camus. FRN/ITL., *Le Chant du Monde*, Jean Giono, 1934, Novel

CHANT OF JIMMIE BLACKSMITH, THE 1978 d: Fred Schepisi. ASL., *The Chant of Jimmie Blacksmith*, Thomas Keneally, 1972, Novel

CHANTECOQ 1916 d: Henri Pouctal. FRN., *Chantecoq*, Arthur Bernede, Novel

CHANTELOUVE 1922 d: Georges Monca, Rose Pansini. FRN., *Chantelouve*, Etienne Rey, Play

CHANTEUR DE MEXICO, LE 1956 d: Richard Pottier. FRN/SPN., *Le Chanteur de Mexico*, Felix Gandera, Raymond Vinci, Opera

CHAO BRUTO 1959 d: Dionizio de Azevedo. BRZ., *Chao Bruto*, Hernani Donati, 1956, Novel

CHAPAYEV 1935 d: Sergei Vasiliev, Georgi Vasiliev. USS., *Chapayev*, Dimitriy Furmanov, 1923, Novel

CHAPEAU DE PAILLE D'ITALIE, UN 1927 d: Rene Clair. FRN., *Un Chapeau de Paille d'Italie*, Eugene Labiche, Marc-Michel, 1847, Play

CHAPEAU DE PAILLE D'ITALIE, UN 1940 d: Maurice Cammage. FRN., *Un Chapeau de Paille d'Italie*, Eugene Labiche, Marc-Michel, 1847, Play

CHAPERON, THE 1916 d: Arthur Berthelet. USA., *The Chaperon*, Marion Fairfax, New York 1908, Play

CHAPLIN 1992 d: Richard Attenborough. UKN., *My Biography*, Charles Chaplin, Book, *Chaplin - His Life and Art*, David Robinson, London 1985, Book

CHAPMAN REPORT, THE 1962 d: George Cukor. USA., *The Chapman Report*, Irving Wallace, New York 1960, Novel

CHAPPY - THAT'S ALL 1924 d: Thomas Bentley. UKN., *Chappy - That's All*, Oliver Sandys, Novel

CHAPTER IN HER LIFE, A 1923 d: Lois Weber. USA., *Jewel; a Chapter in Her Life*, Clara Louise Burnham, Boston 1903, Novel

CHAPTER TWO 1979 d: Robert Moore. USA., *Chapter Two*, Neil Simon, 1978, Play

CHAQUE JOUR A SON SECRET 1958 d: Claude Boissol. FRN., *Chaque Jour a Son Secret*, Maria-Luisa Linares, Novel

Character see KARAKTER (1997).

CHARADE 1963 d: Stanley Donen. USA., *The Unsuspecting Wife*, Marc Behm, Peter Stone

Charcoal Sketches see SZKICE WEGLEM (1957).

CHARCUTIER DE MACHONVILLE, LE 1946 d: Vicky Ivernel. FRN., *Le Charcutier de MacHonville*, Marcel-Eric Grancher, Novel

Chardons du Baragan, Les see CIULINII BARAGANULUI (1957).

Charge Is Murder, The see TWILIGHT OF HONOR (1963).

CHARGE OF THE LIGHT BRIGADE, THE 1914. UKN., *The Charge of the Light Brigade*, Alfred Tennyson, 1854, Poem

CHARGE OF THE LIGHT BRIGADE, THE 1936 d: Michael Curtiz. USA., *The Charge of the Light Brigade*, Alfred Tennyson, 1854, Poem

CHARGE OF THE LIGHT BRIGADE, THE 1968 d: Tony Richardson. UKN., *The Reason Why*, Cecil Woodham-Smith, London 1953, Book

CHARING CROSS ROAD 1935 d: Albert de Courville. UKN., *Charing Cross Road*, Clay Keyes, Gladys Keyes, Radio Play

CHARIOTS OF FIRE 1981 d: Hugh Hudson. UKN., *Dollar Bottom and Taylor's Finest Hour*, J. Kennaway, Book

Chariots of the Gods see ERINNERUNGEN AN DIE ZUKUNFT (1969).

CHARLATAN, THE 1916 d: Sidney Morgan. UKN., *The Charlatan*, Robert Buchanan, Play

CHARLATAN, THE 1929 d: George Melford. USA., *The Charlatan*, Ernest Pascal, Leonard Praskins, New York 1922, Play

CHARLES AUGUSTUS MILVERTON 1922 d: George Ridgwell. UKN., *Charles Augustus Milverton*, Arthur Conan Doyle, 1904, Short Story

CHARLEY AND THE ANGEL 1973 d: Vincent McEveety. USA., *The Golden Evenings of Summer*, Will Stanton, Novel

CHARLEY MOON 1956 d: Guy Hamilton. UKN., *Charley Moon*, Reginald Arkell, Novel

CHARLEY VARRICK 1973 d: Don Siegel. USA., *The Looters*, John Reese, Novel

Charley's American Aunt see CHARLEY'S AUNT (1941).

Charley's Aunt see LA ZIA DI CARLO (1911).

CHARLEY'S AUNT 1925 d: Scott Sidney. USA., *Charley's Aunt*, Brandon Thomas, London 1892, Play

CHARLEY'S AUNT 1930 d: Al Christie. USA., *Charley's Aunt*, Brandon Thomas, London 1892, Play

CHARLEY'S AUNT 1941 d: Archie Mayo. USA., *Charley's Aunt*, Brandon Thomas, London 1892, Play

Charley's Aunt see CHARLEYS TANTE (1956).

CHARLEY'S AUNT 1969 d: John Gorrie. UKN., *Charley's Aunt*, Brandon Thomas, London 1892, Play

CHARLEY'S AUNT 1977 d: Graeme Muir. UKN., *Charley's Aunt*, Brandon Thomas, London 1892, Play

CHARLEY'S (BIG HEARTED) AUNT 1940 d: Walter Forde. UKN., *Charley's Aunt*, Brandon Thomas, London 1892, Play

CHARLEYS TANTE 1934 d: R. A. Stemmle. GRM., *Charley's Aunt*, Brandon Thomas, London 1892, Play

CHARLEYS TANTE 1956 d: Hans Quest. GRM., *Charley's Aunt*, Brandon Thomas, London 1892, Play

CHARLEYS TANTE 1963 d: Geza von CziffrA. AUS., *Charley's Aunt*, Brandon Thomas, London 1892, Play

CHARLIE CHAN CARRIES ON 1931 d: Hamilton MacFadden. USA., *Charlie Chan Carries on*, Earl Derr Biggers, Indianapolis 1930, Novel

CHARLIE CHAN'S CHANCE 1932 d: John G. Blystone. USA., *Behind That Curtain*, Earl Derr Biggers, Indianapolis 1928, Novel

Charlie Chan's Cruise see CHARLIE CHAN'S MURDER CRUISE (1940).

CHARLIE CHAN'S GREATEST CASE 1933 d: Hamilton MacFadden. USA., *The House Without a Key*, Earl Derr Biggers, Indianapolis 1925, Novel

CHARLIE CHAN'S MURDER CRUISE 1940 d: Eugene J. Forde. USA., *Charlie Chan Carries on*, Earl Derr Biggers, Indianapolis 1930, Novel

Charlie Chan's Oriental Cruise see CHARLIE CHAN'S MURDER CRUISE (1940).

CHARLIE CHAPLIN'S BURLESQUE ON CARMEN 1916 d: Charles Chaplin. USA., *Carmen*, Prosper Merimee, Paris 1846, Novel

CHARLIE MUFFIN 1979 d: Jack Gold. UKN., *Charlie Muffin*, Brian Freemantle, Novel

Charlie's Big Romance see TILLIE'S PUNCTURED ROMANCE (1914).

CHARLOTT ETWAS VERRUCKT 1928 d: Adolf Edgar Licho. GRM., *Charlott Etwas Verruckt*, Wilhelm Speyer, Novel

Charlotte Lowenskjold see CHARLOTTE LOWENSKOLD (1930).

CHARLOTTE LOWENSKOLD 1930 d: Gustaf Molander. SWD., *Lowenskolda Ringen*, Selma Lagerlof, 1925, Novel

CHARLOTTE LOWENSKOLD 1979 d: Jackie Soderman. SWD., *Charlotte Lowenskold*, Selma Lagerlof, 1925, Novel

CHARLOTTE'S WEB 1973 d: Iwao Takamoto, Charles Nichols. USA., *Charlotte's Web*, E. B. White, Novel

CHARLY 1968 d: Ralph Nelson. USA., *Flowers for Algernon*, Daniel Keyes, New York 1966, Novel

CHARM SCHOOL, THE 1921 d: James Cruze. USA., *The Charm School*, Alice Duer Miller, 1919, Short Story

Charm School, The see COLLEGIATE (1936).

CHARMER, THE 1925 d: Sidney Olcott. USA., *Mariposa*, Henry Baerlein, London 1924, Novel

CHARMING DECEIVER, THE 1921 d: George L. Sargent. USA., *The Charming Deceiver*, Mrs. Owen Bronson, Story

Charming Man, A see ROZTOMILY CLOVEK (1941).

Charming Matt Saxon, The see THE SAXON CHARM (1948).

Charming Person, A see ROZTOMILY CLOVEK (1941).

CHARMING SINNERS 1929 d: Robert Milton, Dorothy Arzner. USA., *The Constant Wife*, W. Somerset Maugham, New York 1926, Play

Charretier de la Mort, Le see LA CHARRETTE FANTOME (1939).

CHARRETTE FANTOME, LA 1939 d: Julien Duvivier. FRN., *Korkarlen*, Selma Lagerlof, 1912, Novel

Chartreuse de Parme, La see LA CERTOSA DI PARMA (1947).

CHARULATA 1964 d: Satyajit Ray. IND., *Nastaneer*, Rabindranath Tagore, 1901, Novel

Chase for Millions, The see DIE JAGD NACH DER MILLION (1930).

CHASE, THE 1946 d: Arthur Ripley. USA., *The Black Path of Fear*, Cornell Woolrich, 1944, Novel

CHASE, THE 1966 d: Arthur Penn. USA., *The Chase*, Horton Foote, New York 1952, Play

Chase, The see HAJKA (1977).

Chasing a Fortune see PUTTING ONE OVER (1919).

CHASING RAINBOWS 1919 d: Frank Beal. USA., *Sadie*, Karl Harriman, New York 1907, Novel

CHASING YESTERDAY 1935 d: George Nicholls Jr. USA., *Le Crime de Sylvestre Bonnard*, Anatole France, Paris 1881, Novel

Chasse a l'Homme see LE CAVE EST PIEGE (1963).

CHASSE AUX CHAMOIS DANS LES ALPES FRIBOURGEOISES, UNE 1926 d: Pierre Lebrun. SWT., Henri Bordeaux, Book

Chasse En Sologne, La see LA REGLE DU JEU (1939).

CHASSE ROYALE, LA 1969 d: Francois Leterrier. FRN/CZC., *La Chasse Royale*, Pierre Moinot, Novel

CHASSEUR DE CHEZ MAXIM'S, LE 1927 d: Roger Lion, Nicolas Rimsky. FRN., *Le Chasseur de Chez Maxim's*, Yves Mirande, Gustave Quinson, Play

CHASSEUR DE CHEZ MAXIM'S, LE 1932 d: Karl Anton. FRN., *Le Chasseur de Chez Maxim's*, Yves Mirande, Gustave Quinson, Play

CHASSEUR DE CHEZ MAXIM'S, LE 1939 d: Maurice Cammage. FRN., *Le Chasseur de Chez Maxim's*, Yves Mirande, Gustave Quinson, Play

CHASSEUR DE CHEZ MAXIM'S, LE 1953 d: Henri Diamant-Berger. FRN., *Le Chasseur de Chez Maxim's*, Yves Mirande, Gustave Quinson, Play

CHASTE SUZANNE, LA 1937 d: Andre Berthomieu. FRN., *La Chaste Suzanne*, Jean Gilbert, Opera

CHAT, LE 1971 d: Pierre Granier-Deferre. FRN/ITL., *Le Chat*, Georges Simenon, 1967, Novel

Chat -L'implacabile Uomo Di Saint Germain, Le see LE CHAT (1971).

CHATEAU DE LA MORT LENTE, LE 1925 d: E. B. Donatien. FRN., *Le Chateau de la Mort Lente*, Henri Bauche, Andre de Lorde, Play

Chateau de la Terreur, Le see QUELQU'UN A TUE (1933).

CHATEAU DE MA MERE, LA 1990 d: Yves Robert. FRN., *Souvenirs d'Enfance*, Marcel Pagnol, 1957, Autobiography

CHATEAU DE VERRE, LE 1950 d: Rene Clement. FRN/ITL., *Das Grosse Einmaleins*, Vicki Baum, Novel

CHATEAU EN SUEDE 1963 d: Roger Vadim. FRN/ITL., *Chateau En Suede*, Francoise Sagan, Paris 1960, Play

CHATEAU HISTORIQUE 1923 d: Henri Desfontaines. FRN., *Chateau Historique*, J. Berr de Turique, Alexandre Bisson, Play

CHATELAINE DU LIBAN, LA 1926 d: Marco de Gastyne. FRN., *La Chatelaine du Liban*, Pierre Benoit, Novel

CHATELAINE DU LIBAN, LA 1933 d: Jean Epstein. FRN., *La Chatelaine du Liban*, Pierre Benoit, Novel

CHATELAINE DU LIBAN, LA 1956 d: Richard Pottier. FRN/ITL., *La Chatelaine du Liban*, Pierre Benoit, Novel

CHATELAINE, LA 1914 d: Louis Feuillade. FRN., *La Chatelaine*, Alfred Capus, Play

CHATTE, LA 1958 d: Henri Decoin. FRN., *La Chatte*, Jacques Remy, Novel

CHATTERBOX 1936 d: George Nicholls Jr. USA., *Long Ago Ladies*, David Carb, Boston 1934, Play

Chaumiere Et un Meurtre, Une see L' ASSASSIN CONNAIT LA MUSIQUE (1963).

CHAUSSEE DES GEANTS, LA 1926 d: Jean Durand, Robert Boudrioz. FRN., *La Chaussee Des Geants*, Pierre Benoit, Novel

Chautauqua see THE TROUBLE WITH GIRLS (1969).

CHAUVE-SOURIS, LA 1931 d: Pierre Billon, Carl Lamac. FRN., *Die Fledermaus*, Henri Meilhac, Johann Strauss, Vienna 1874, Operetta

CHAVALA, LA 1925 d: Florian Rey. SPN., *La Chavala*, Carlos Fernandez Shaw, J. Lopez Silva, Opera

CHAVURA SHE'KA'ZOT 1962 d: Ze'ev Havatzelet. ISR., Y. Ben-Porat, Story

Chayka see CHAIKA (1971).

Che Cosa E Successo Tra Mio Padre E Tua Madre? see AVANTI! (1972).

CHE GUEVARA, EL 1968 d: Paolo Heusch. ITL., *El Che Guevara*, Adriano Bolzoni, Rome 1967, Book

CHE TEMPI! 1948 d: Giorgio Bianchi. ITL., *Pignasecca E Pignaverde*, Emerico Valentinetti, Play

Cheap Sweet and a Kid see KASHI TO KODOMO (1962).

CHEAPER BY THE DOZEN 1950 d: Walter Lang. USA., *Cheaper By the Dozen*, Ernestine G. Carey, Frank Gilbreth Jr., Book

CHEAPER TO MARRY 1924 d: Robert Z. Leonard. USA., *Cheaper to Marry*, Samuel Shipman, New York 1926, Novel

Cheat, The see FORFAITURE (1937).

CHEATED HEARTS 1921 d: Hobart Henley. USA., *Barry Gordon*, William Farquhar Payson, New York 1908, Novel

Cheated Heaven see DER VERUNTREUTE HIMMEL (1958).

CHEATER, THE 1920 d: Henry Otto. USA., *Judah*, Henry Arthur Jones, London 1890, Play

CHEATERS 1934 d: Phil Rosen. USA., *The Peacock Screen*, Fanny Heaslip Lea, 1911, Short Story

CHEATERS AT PLAY 1932 d: Hamilton MacFadden. USA., *The Lone Wolf's Son*, Louis Joseph Vance, 1931, Story

CHEATING BLONDES 1933 d: Joseph Levering. USA., *House of Chance*, Gertie Wentworth-James, New York 1912, Novel

CHEATING CHEATERS 1919 d: Allan Dwan. USA., *Cheating Cheaters*, Max Marcin, New York 1916, Play

CHEATING CHEATERS 1927 d: Edward Laemmle. USA., *Cheating Cheaters*, Max Marcin, New York 1916, Play

CHEATING CHEATERS 1934 d: Richard Thorpe. USA., *Cheating Cheaters*, Max Marcin, New York 1916, Play

CHECHAKO, THE 1914? d: Hobart Bosworth. USA., *Smoke Bellew*, Jack London, New York 1912, Novel

Check to the Queen see SCACCO ALLA REGINA (1969).

CHECKERED FLAG, THE 1926 d: John G. Adolfi. USA., *The Checkered Flag*, John Mersereau, Boston 1925, Novel

CHECKERS 1913 d: Augustus Thomas. USA., *Checkers: a Hard Luck Story*, Henry Martyn Blossom, Chicago 1896, Novel

CHECKERS 1919 d: Richard Stanton. USA., *Checkers: a Hard Luck Story*, Henry Martyn Blossom, Chicago 1896, Novel

CHECKMATE 1935 d: George Pearson. UKN., *Checkmate*, Amy Kennedy Gould, Novel

CHEER UP AND SMILE 1930 d: Sidney Lanfield. USA., **If I Was Alone With You**, Richard Connell, 1929, Short Story

CHEERFUL FRAUD, THE 1927 d: William A. Seiter. USA., *The Cheerful Fraud*, Robert Gordon Browne, New York 1925, Novel

CHEERS FOR MISS BISHOP 1941 d: Tay Garnett. USA., *Miss Bishop*, Bess Streeter Aldrich, Novel

CHEETAH 1989 d: Jeff Blyth. USA., *The Cheetahs*, Alan Caillou, Novel

CHELKASH 1957 d: Fyodor Filippov. USS., *Chelkash*, Maxim Gorky, 1895, Short Story

CHELOVEK S RUZHYOM 1938 d: Sergei Yutkevich. USS., *Chelovek S Ruzhyom*, Nikolay Pogodin, 1937, Play

CHELOVEK V FUTLYARE 1939 d: Isider Annensky. USS., *Chelovek V Futlyare*, Anton Chekhov, 1898, Short Story

CHELOVEK V FUTLYARE 1983 d: Leonid Zarubin. USS., *Chelovek V Futlyare*, Anton Chekhov, 1898, Short Story

Chemeen see CHEMMEEN (1965).

CHEMIN DE ROSELAND, LE 1924 d: Maurice Gleize. FRN., *Le Chemin de Roselande*, Henri Bordeaux, Short Story

CHEMIN DES ECOLIERS, LE 1959 d: Michel Boisrond. FRN/ITL., *Le Chemin Des Ecoliers*, Marcel Ayme, 1946, Novel

CHEMINEAU, LE 1917 d: Henry Krauss. FRN., *Le Chemineau*, Jean Richepin, Play

CHEMINEAU, LE 1935 d: Fernand Rivers. FRN., *Le Chemineau*, Jean Richepin, Play

CHEMMEEN 1965 d: Ramu Kariat. IND., *Cemmin*, Takazi Sivasankara Illa, 1956, Novel

CHENG NAN JIU SHI 1982 d: Wu Yi-Gong. CHN., *Cheng Nan Jiu Shi*, Lin Haiyin, Novel

Chengnan Jiushi see CHENG NAN JIU SHI (1982).

Chequered Bedspread, The see DIE BUNTKARIERTEN (1949).

Chercheurs d'Or de l'Arkansas, Les see DIE GOLDSUCHER VON ARKANSAS (1964).

CHERE INCONNUE 1980 d: Moshe Mizrahi. FRN., *Chere Inconnue*, Bernice Rubens, Story

CHERE LOUISE 1971 d: Philippe de BrocA. FRN/ITL., *L' Ephebe de Subiaco*, Jean-Louis Curtis, 1969, Short Story

Cheremushki see CHERYOMUSHKI (1963).

CHERI 1950 d: Pierre Billon. FRN., *Cheri*, Sidonie Gabrielle Colette, 1920, Novel

CHERI-BIBI 1914 d: Charles Krauss. FRN., *Cheri-Bibi*, Gaston Leroux, Novel

CHERI-BIBI 1931 d: Carlos Borcosque. USA., *Cheri-Bibi Et Cecily*, Gaston Leroux, Paris 1916, Novel

Cheri-Bibi see THE PHANTOM OF PARIS (1931).

CHERI-BIBI 1954 d: Marcello Pagliero. FRN/ITL., *La Nouvelle Aurore*, Gaston Leroux, 1918, Novel

CHERIE 1930 d: Louis Mercanton. FRN., *Come Out of the Kitchen!*, Alice Duer Miller, New York 1916, Novel

CHERNAYA STREIA 1985 d: Sergei Tarasov. USS., *Black Arrow*, Robert Louis Stevenson, 1888, Novel

Chernyi Monakh see TCHIORNI MONAK (1988).

CHEROKEE STRIP, THE 1937 d: Noel Smith. USA., *Cherokee Strip Stampeders*, Ed Earl Repp, 1936, Short Story

CHERRY 1914 d: James Young. USA., *Cherry*, Booth Tarkington, Short Story

CHERRY 2000 1987 d: Steve de Jarnatt. USA., Lloyd Fonveille, Story

Cherry Garden, The see VISHNEVYJ SAD (1993).

Cherry Orchard, The see VISHNEVYJ SAD (1993).

CHERRY PICKER, THE 1973 d: Peter Curran. UKN., *Pick Up Sticks*, Mickey Phillips, Novel

CHERRY RIPE 1921 d: Kenelm Foss. UKN., *Cherry Ripe*, Helen Mathers, Novel

Cherry Time Is Past see LE GRAND DADAIS (1967).

CHERYOMUSHKI 1963 d: Herbert Rappaport. USS., *Cheryomushki Moskva*, Vladimir Mass, Moscow 1959, Opera, *Moskva Cheryomushki*, Dimitriy Shostakovich, Moscow 1959, Opera

Chess Clause see DIE SCHACHNOVELLE (1960).

Chess King see QI WANG (1988).

Chess Player, The see LE JOUEUR D'ECHECS (1938).

Chess Players, The see SHATRANJ KE KHILADI (1977).

CHESTER FORGETS HIMSELF 1924 d: Andrew P. Wilson. UKN., *Chester Forgets Himself*, P. G. Wodehouse, Short Story

Chetvyorty see CETVERTYJ (1972).

CHEVAL D'ORGEUIL, LE 1980 d: Claude Chabrol. FRN., *Le Cheval d'Orgeuil*, Pierre-Jakez Helias, Book

Chevalier a la Rose Rouge, Le see ROSE ROSSE PER ANGELICA (1966).

Chevalier de Maupin, Le see MADAMIGELLA DI MAUPIN (1966).

CHEVALIER DE PARDAILLAN, LE 1962 d: Bernard Borderie. FRN/ITL., *Le Chevalier de Pardaillan*, Michel Zevaco, Novel

Chevalier du Roi, Le see LE CAPITAN (1945).

Chevalier Et la Tzarine, Le see LE SECRET DU CHEVALIER D'EON (1960).

Chevalier Sans Armure, Le see KNIGHT WITHOUT ARMOUR (1937).

CHEVELURE, LA 1961 d: Ado Kyrou. FRN., *La Chevelure*, Guy de Maupassant, 1885, Short Story

CHEVIOT, THE STAG AND THE BLACK, BLACK OIL, THE 1974 d: John MacKenzie. UKN., *The Cheviot, the Stag and the Black, Black Oil*, John McGrath, 1974, Play

CHEVRE AUX PIEDS D'OR, LA 1925 d: Jacques Robert. FRN., *La Chevre aux Pieds d'Or*, Charles-Henry Hirsch, Novel

Chevre aux Pieds d'Or, La see LA DANSEUSE ROUGE (1937).

CHEVRE D'OR, LA 1942 d: Rene Barberis. FRN., *La Chevre d'Or*, Paul Arene, 1888, Novel

CHEYENNE AUTUMN 1964 d: John Ford. USA., *Cheyenne Autumn*, Mari Sandoz, New York 1953, Novel

CHEYENNE KID, THE 1933 d: Robert F. Hill. USA., *Sir Piegan Passes*, W. C. Tuttle, New York 1923, Short Story

CHEZHONG DAO 1920 d: Ren Pengnian. CHN., *Jiaotou Lan'e*, Lin Qinnan, Novel

CHI E SENZA PECCATO. 1953 d: Raffaello Matarazzo. ITL., *Genevieve; Memoire d'une Servante*, Alphonse Lamartine, Novel

Chi House see SORORITY HOUSE (1939).

CHI L'HA UCCISO? 1919 d: Alberto Sannia, Mario GambardellA. ITL., *La Bella Nipotina*, Giovanni Speziale, Play

CHI NAN KUANG NU LIANG SHI QING 1993 d: Huo Zhuang, Ux XIaoxing. CHN., *Lu Gong's Daughter*, Pu Songling, Story

CHI NAN, YUAN NU HE NIU 1994 d: Yu XIangyuan. CHN., *Fu Niu*, Zhou Daxin, Novel

Chi No Hate Ni Ikuru Mono see CHINOHATE NI IKIRU MONO (1960).

Chi Vuol Dormire Nel Mio Letto? see MESDAMES! MEFIEZ-VOUS (1963).

Chiamavano Mezzogiorno, Lo see THE MAN CALLED NOON (1973).

Chiaro Di Donna see CLAIR DE FEMME (1979).

CHIAVE, LA 1984 d: Tinto Brass. ITL., *Kagi*, Junichiro Tanizaki, Tokyo 1956, Novel

CHICA DEL GATO, LA 1926 d: Antonio Calvache. SPN., Carlos Amiches, Play

CHICAGO 1927 d: Frank Urson. USA., *Chicago*, Maurine Dallas Watkins, New York 1926, Novel

CHICAGO CAB 1998 d: Mary Cybulski, John Tintori. USA., *Hellcab*, Will Kern, Play

Chicago, Chicago see GAILY GAILY (1969).

CHICAGO CONFIDENTIAL 1957 d: Sidney Salkow. USA., *Chicago Confidential*, Jack Lait, Lee Mortimer, Book

CHICAGO DEADLINE 1949 d: Lewis Allen. USA., *One Woman*, Tiffany Thayer, 1933, Novel

Chicago Fire, The see BARRIERS BURNED AWAY (1925).

Chicago Story see THE UNDERCOVER MAN (1949).

CHICAGO SYNDICATE 1955 d: Fred F. Sears. USA., William Sackheim, Story

CHICHINETTE ET CIE 1921 d: Henri Desfontaines. FRN., *Chichinette Et Cie*, Pierre Custot, Novel

CHICK 1928 d: A. V. Bramble. UKN., *Chick*, Edgar Wallace, London 1923, Novel

CHICK 1936 d: Michael Hankinson. UKN., *Chick*, Edgar Wallace, London 1923, Novel

CHICKEN A LA KING 1928 d: Henry Lehrman. USA., *Mr. Romeo*, W. A. Mannheimer, I. Paul, H. Wagstaff, New York 1927, Play

CHICKEN CHRONICLES, THE 1977 d: Francis Simon. CND/USA., *The Chicken Chronicles*, Paul Diamond, Novel

CHICKEN EVERY SUNDAY 1949 d: George Seaton. USA., *Chicken Every Sunday*, Rosemary Taylor, Novel

Chicken That Came Home to Roost, The see THE TOWN SCANDAL (1923).

Chicken, The see THE TOWN SCANDAL (1923).

CHICKEN WAGON FAMILY 1939 d: Herbert I. Leeds. USA., *The Chicken-Wagon Family*, John Barry Benefield, New York 1925, Novel

Chicken With Vinegar see POULET AU VINAIGRE (1984).

CHICKENS 1921 d: Jack Nelson. USA., *Yancona Yillies*, Herschel S. Hall, 1920, Short Story

CHICKIE 1925 d: John Francis Dillon. USA., *Chickie*, Elenore Meherin, New York 1925, Novel

CHICOS DE LA ESCUELA, LOS 1925 d: Florian Rey. SPN., *Los Chicos de la Escuela*, Carlos Arniches, T. Lopez Torregrosa, Opera

CHIDIAKHANA 1967 d: Satyajit Ray. IND., *Chidiakhana*, Saradindu Bannerjee, Novel

Chief of the Horse Farm, The see A MENESGAZDA (1978).

CHIEFS 1985 d: Jerry London. USA., *Chiefs*, Stuart Woods, Novel

CHIEKO-SHO 1967 d: Noboru NakamurA. JPN., *Shosetsu Chieko Sho*, Haruo Sato, 1963, Novel

CHIEN DE MONTAGIS, LE 1909 d: Georges MoncA. FRN., *Le Chien de Montargis*, Romain Coolus, Play

CHIEN JAUNE, LE 1932 d: Jean Tarride. FRN., *Le Chien Jaune*, Georges Simenon, 1931, Novel

CHIEN QUI RAPPORTE, UN 1931 d: Jean Choux. FRN., *Un Chien Qui Rapporte*, Paul Armont, Marcel Gerbidon, Play

CHIENS DANS LA NUIT, LES 1965 d: Willy Rozier. FRN/GRC., *Ho Chatze Manouel: Mysthistorema*, Thrasos Kastanakes, Athens 1956, Novel

CHIFFONNIER DE PARIS, LE 1924 d: Serge Nadejdine. FRN., *Le Chiffonnier de Paris*, Felix Pyat, Novel

CHIGNOLE 1917 d: Rene Plaissetty. FRN., *Chignole*, Marcel Nadaud, Novel

CHIJIN NO AI 1967 d: Yasuzo MasumurA. JPN., *Chijin No Ai*, Junichiro Tanizaki, 1924, Novel

CHIKAMATSU MONOGATARI 1954 d: Kenji Mizoguchi. JPN., *Daikyoji Sekireki*, Monzaemon Chikamatsu, 1715, Play

CHILD IN THE HOUSE 1956 d: Cy Endfield, Charles de La Tour. UKN., *Child in the House*, Janet McNeil, Novel

CHILD IS BORN, A 1940 d: Lloyd Bacon. USA., *Life Begins*, Mary McDougal Axelson, New York 1932, Play

CHILD OF DIVORCE 1946 d: Richard Fleischer. USA., *Wednesday's Child*, Leopold L. Atlas, New York 1934, Play

CHILD OF GLASS 1978 d: John Erman. USA., *The Ghost Belonged to Me*, Richard Peck, Novel

CHILD OF MANHATTAN 1933 d: Edward Buzzell. USA., *Child of Manhattan*, Preston Sturges, New York 1932, Play

CHILD OF M'SIEU 1919 d: Harrish Ingraham. USA., *Pippa Passes*, Robert Browning, London 1841, Poem

Child of the Night see NIGHT HAIR CHILD (1971).

Child, The see BARNET (1940).

Childe John see JANOS VITEZ (1973).

Childhood of Gorky see DETSTVO GORKOVO (1938).

Childhood of Ivan see IVANOVO DETSTVO (1962).

Childhood of Maxim Gorki, The see DETSTVO GORKOVO (1938).

Childless see BEZDETNA (1935).

Children are Watching Us, The see I BAMBINI CI GUARDANO (1944).

CHILDREN CROSSING 1990 d: Angela Pope. UKN., Children Crossing, Verity Bargate, Novel

Children in Uniform see MADCHEN IN UNIFORM (1958).

Children, Mother and a General see MUTTER UND EIN GENERAL KINDER (1955).

CHILDREN NOT WANTED 1920 d: Paul Scardon. USA., No Children Allowed, Arthur Stuart Sinclair, Play

CHILDREN OF A LESSER GOD 1986 d: Randa Haines. USA., Children of a Lesser God, Mark Medoff, 1980, Play

CHILDREN OF BANISHMENT 1919 d: Norval MacGregor. USA., Children of Banishment, Francis William Sullivan, New York 1914, Novel

Children of Bullerby Village, The see ALLA VI BARN I BULLERBYN (1986).

Children of Courage see FROGGY'S LITTLE BROTHER (1921).

CHILDREN OF DESTINY 1920 d: George Irving. USA., Children of Destiny, Sydney Rosenfeld, New York 1910, Play

CHILDREN OF DIVORCE 1927 d: Frank Lloyd, Josef von Sternberg (Uncredited). USA., Children of Divorce, Owen Johnson, Boston 1927, Novel

CHILDREN OF DREAMS 1931 d: Alan Crosland. USA., Children of Dreams, Oscar Hammerstein II, Sigmund Romberg, 1930, Musical Play

CHILDREN OF DUST 1923 d: Frank Borzage. USA., Terwilliger, Tristram Tupper, Short Story

CHILDREN OF FATE 1914 d: Wallace Reid. USA., Children of Fate, James Oliver Curwood, Short Story

CHILDREN OF GIBEON, THE 1920 d: Sidney Morgan. UKN., The Children of Gibeon, Sir Walter Besant, Novel

CHILDREN OF JAZZ 1923 d: Jerome Storm. USA., Other Times, Harold Brighouse, Play

CHILDREN OF LONELINESS 1934 d: Richard C. Kahn. USA., The Well of Loneliness, Radclyffe Hall, London 1928, Novel

Children of Mata Hari see LA PEAU DE TORPEDO (1970).

CHILDREN OF PLEASURE 1930 d: Harry Beaumont. USA., The Song Writer, Crane Wilbur, New York 1928, Play

Children of Pleasure see THE CRASH (1932).

CHILDREN OF SANCHEZ, THE 1978 d: Hall Bartlett. USA/MXC., The Children of Sanchez, Oscar Lewis, Novel

CHILDREN OF THE CORN 1984 d: Fritz Kiersch. USA., Night Shift, Stephen King, 1978, Short Story

Children of the Corn: Deadly Harvest see CHILDREN OF THE CORN II: THE FINAL SACRIFICE (1992).

CHILDREN OF THE CORN II: THE FINAL SACRIFICE 1992 d: David F. Price. USA., Children of the Corn, Stephen King, Short Story

CHILDREN OF THE DAMNED 1963 d: Anton M. Leader. UKN., The Midwich Cuckoos, John Wyndham, 1957, Novel

Children of the Earth see DHARTI KE LAL (1946).

CHILDREN OF THE GHETTO 1915 d: Frank Powell. USA., The Children of the Ghetto; a Study of Peculiar People, Israel Zangwill, London 1892, Novel

Children of the Marshland see LES ENFANTS DU MARAIS (1999).

CHILDREN OF THE NIGHT 1921 d: John Francis Dillon. USA., Children of the Night, Max Brand, 1919, Short Story

Children of the Night see I FIGLI DELLA NOTTE (1939).

CHILDREN OF THE RITZ 1929 d: John Francis Dillon. USA., Children of the Ritz, Cornell Woolrich, Short Story

Children on the Island see NIJUSHI NO HITOMI (1988).

Children, The see THE MARRIAGE PLAYGROUND (1929).

CHILDREN, THE 1990 d: Tony Palmer. UKN/GRM., The Children, Edith Wharton, New York 1928, Novel

CHILDREN'S HOUR, THE 1913 d: USA., The Children's Hour, Henry Wadsworth Longfellow, Poem

CHILDREN'S HOUR, THE 1961 d: William Wyler. USA., The Children's Hour, Lillian Hellman, New York 1934, Play

Children's Island see BARNENS O (1981).

Children's War, The see WAR AND LOVE (1985).

CHILD'S PLAY 1972 d: Sidney Lumet. USA., Child's Play, Robert Marasco, Play

Chilly Scenes of Winter see HEAD OVER HEELS (1979).

CHILTERN HUNDREDS, THE 1949 d: John Paddy Carstairs. UKN., The Chiltern Hundreds, William Douglas Home, London 1947, Play

CHIMERA 1991 d: Lawrence Gordon Clark. UKN., Chimera, Steven Gallagher, 1982, Novel

Chimes at Midnight see CAMPANADAS A MEDIANOCHE (1966).

CHIMES, THE 1914 d: Thomas Bentley. UKN., The Chimes, Charles Dickens, London 1845, Short Story

CHIMES, THE 1914 d: Herbert Blache. USA., The Chimes, Charles Dickens, London 1845, Short Story

CHIMMIE FADDEN 1915 d: Cecil B. de Mille. USA., Chimmie Fadden, Edward Waterman Townsend, 1895, Short Story

CHIMMIE FADDEN OUT WEST 1915 d: Cecil B. de Mille. USA., Chimmie Fadden, Edward Waterman Townsend, 1895, Short Story

Chimney-Sweeps of the Valley of Aosta, The see GLI SPAZZACAMINI DELLA VAL D'AOSTA (1914).

CHIN CHIN CHINAMAN 1931 d: Guy Newall. UKN., Chin Chin Chinaman, Percy Walsh, Play

CHINA 1943 d: John Farrow. USA., The Fourth Brother, Archibald Forbes, Unpublished, Play

China Bandit see WEST OF SHANGHAI (1937).

China Bound see ACROSS TO SINGAPORE (1928).

CHINA SEAS 1935 d: Tay Garnett. USA., China Seas, Crosbie Garstin, New York 1931, Novel

CHINA SKY 1945 d: Ray Enright. USA., China Sky, Pearl Buck, 1942, Novel

China Story see SATAN NEVER SLEEPS (1962).

CHINATOWN NIGHTS 1929 d: William A. Wellman. USA., Tong War, Samuel Ornitz, Story

Chinese Adventures in China see LES TRIBULATIONS D'UN CHINOIS EN CHINE (1965).

CHINESE BUNGALOW, THE 1926 d: Sinclair Hill. UKN., The Chinese Bungalow, Marian Osmond, Novel

CHINESE BUNGALOW, THE 1930 d: J. B. Williams, Arthur W. Barnes. UKN., The Chinese Bungalow, Marian Osmond, Novel

CHINESE BUNGALOW, THE 1940 d: George King. UKN., The Chinese Bungalow, Marian Osmond, Novel

Chinese Den, The see THE CHINESE BUNGALOW (1940).

Chinese Gold see THE GENERAL DIED AT DAWN (1936).

Chinese Orange Mystery, The see THE MANDARIN MYSTERY (1936).

CHINESE PARROT, THE 1927 d: Paul Leni. USA., The Chinese Parrot, Earl Derr Biggers, Indianapolis 1926, Novel

Chinese Puzzle for Judoka see CASSE-TETE CHINOIS POUR LE JUDOKA (1968).

CHINESE PUZZLE, THE 1919 d: Fred Goodwins. UKN., The Chinese Puzzle, Marion Bower, Leon M. Lion, London 1918, Play

CHINESE PUZZLE, THE 1932 d: Guy Newall. UKN., The Chinese Puzzle, Marion Bower, Leon M. Lion, London 1918, Play

Ching, Ching, Chinaman see SHADOWS (1922).

CHINGACHGOCK - DIE GROSSE SCHLANGE 1967 d: Richard Groschopp. GDR., The Deerslayer, James Fenimore Cooper, 1841, Novel

Chingachgock - the Big Snake see CHINGACHGOCK - DIE GROSSE SCHLANGE (1967).

Chink and the Child, The see BROKEN BLOSSOMS (1919).

CHINMOKU 1972 d: Masahiro ShinodA. JPN., Shusaku Endo, Chinmoku, 1966, Novel

Chino see VALDEZ IL MEZZOSANGUE (1974).

CHINOHATE NI IKIRU MONO 1960 d: Seiji Hisamatsu. JPN., Otsuku Rojin, Yukio Togawa, Toyko 1960

CHIN-P'ING-MEI 1969 d: Koji Wakamatsu. JPN., Chin P'inge Mei, Shin-Chen Want, 15Th-Century, Novel

CHIP OF THE FLYING U 1939 d: Ralph Staub. USA., Chip of the Flying U, Bertha Muzzy Sinclair, New York 1906, Novel

CHIP OF THE FLYING "U" 1914 d: Colin Campbell. USA., Chip of the Flying U, Bertha Muzzy Sinclair, New York 1906, Novel

CHIPEE 1937 d: Roger Goupillieres. FRN., Chipee, Alex Madis, Play

Chiriakhana see CHIDIAKHANA (1967).

CHIRITA LA LASI 1988 d: Mircea Dragan. RMN., Cucoana Chirita in Iasi, Vasile Alecsandri, 1852, Play

CHISHOLMS, THE 1978 d: Mel Stuart. USA., The Chisholms, Evan Hunter, Novel

CHITTY CHITTY BANG BANG 1968 d: Ken Hughes. UKN., Chitty Chitty Bang Bang: the Magical Car, Ian Fleming, London 1964, Novel

CHI'UCH HAGDI 1985 d: Shimon Dotan. ISR., David Grossman, Novel

Chizuko's Younger Sister see FUTARI (1991).

CHLAPI PRECE NEPLACOU 1980 d: Josef PinkavA. CZC., Chlapi Prece Neplacou, Marie Kubatova, Novel

Chloe in the Afternoon see L' AMOUR L'APRES-MIDI (1972).

CHLOPI 1973 d: Jan Rybkowski. PLN., Chlopi, Wladyslaw Stanislaw Reymont, 1902-09, Novel

Chnouf see RAZZIA SUR LA CHNOUF (1955).

Chnouf -to Take It Is Deadly see RAZZIA SUR LA CHNOUF (1955).

CHOC, LE 1982 d: Robin Davis. FRN., La Position du Tireur Couche, Jean-Patrick Manchette, Novel

CHOCOLATE SOLDIER, THE 1915 d: Walter Morton, Stanislaus Stange. USA., Arms and the Man, George Bernard Shaw, 1894, Play

CHOCOLATE SOLDIER, THE 1941 d: Roy Del Ruth. USA., A Testor, Ferenc Molnar, Budapest 1910, Play

Choir Practice see VALLEY OF SONG (1953).

CHOIRBOYS, THE 1977 d: Robert Aldrich. USA., The Choirboys, Joseph Wambaugh, 1975, Novel

CHOIX D'ASSASSINS, UN 1967 d: Philippe Fourastie. FRN/ITL., Un Choix d'Assassins, William P. McGivern, Novel

Cholera Street see AGIR ROMAN (1997).

Cholpon see CHOLPON - UTRENNYAYA ZVEZDA (1960).

CHOLPON - UTRENNYAYA ZVEZDA 1960 d: Roman Tikhomirov. USS., Cholpon - Utrennyaya Zvezda, L. Kramarevskiy, M. Raukhverger, 1944, Ballet

Chomana Dhudi see CHOMANA DUDI (1975).

CHOMANA DUDI 1975 d: B. V. Karanth. IND., Chomana Dudi, Shivrama Karanth, 1933, Novel

Chomana's Drum see CHOMANA DUDI (1975).

Chong Hui Yao Shan see SHAN NIANG (1994).

Chorus Girl see ODORIKO (1957).

CHORUS GIRL'S ROMANCE, THE 1920 d: William C. Dowlan. USA., Head and Shoulders, F. Scott Fitzgerald, 1920, Short Story

CHORUS LADY, THE 1915 d: Frank Reicher. USA., The Chorus Lady, James Forbes, New York 1906, Play

CHORUS LADY, THE 1924 d: Ralph Ince. USA., The Chorus Lady, James Forbes, New York 1906, Play

CHORUS LINE, A 1985 d: Richard Attenborough. USA., A Chorus Line, Nicholas Dante, James Kirkwood, Play

CHORUS OF DISAPPROVAL, A 1989 d: Michael Winner. UKN., A Chorus of Disapproval, Alan Ayckbourn, 1986, Play

Chorus of Tokyo, The see TOKYO NO GASSHO (1931).

CHOSEN, THE 1981 d: Jeremy Paul Kagan. USA., The Chosen, Chaim Potok, Novel

CHOSES DE LA VIE, LES 1970 d: Claude Sautet. FRN/ITL/SWT., Les Choses de la Vie, Paul Guimard, Paris 1967, Novel

CHOTARD ET CIE 1932 d: Jean Renoir. FRN., Chotard Et Cie, Roger Ferdinand, Play

CHOUANS, LES 1946 d: Henri Calef. FRN., Les Chouans, Honore de Balzac, 1834, Novel

CHOUCHOU POIDS PLUME 1932 d: Robert Bibal. FRN., *Chou-Chou Poids-Plume*, Jacques Bousquet, Alex Madis, Play

CHOU-CHOU POIDS-PLUME 1925 d: Gaston Ravel. FRN., *Chou-Chou Poids-Plume*, Jacques Bousquet, Alex Madis, Play

CHOURINETTE 1933 d: Andre Hugon. FRN., *Un Jeune Homme Qui Se Tue*, Georges Berr, Play

CHOVEKAT V SYANKA 1967 d: Yakim Yakimov. BUL., *Chovekat V Syanka*, Pavel Vezhinov, 1965, Novel

Christ S'est Arrete a Eboli, Le *see* CRISTO SI E FERMATO A EBOLI (1979).

Christ Stopped at Eboli *see* CRISTO SI E FERMATO A EBOLI (1979).

CHRISTIAN MARTYRS, THE 1909 d: Otis Turner. USA., *The Christian Martyrs*, Edward George Bulwer Lytton, Novel

CHRISTIAN, THE 1914 d: Frederick A. Thompson. USA., *The Christian: a Story*, Hall Caine, London 1897, Novel

CHRISTIAN, THE 1915 d: George Loane Tucker. UKN., *The Christian: a Story*, Hall Caine, London 1897, Novel

CHRISTIAN, THE 1923 d: Maurice Tourneur. USA., *The Christian: a Story*, Hall Caine, London 1897, Novel

Christiane F. *see* CHRISTIANE F. WIR KINDER VOM BAHNHOF ZOO (1981).

CHRISTIANE F. WIR KINDER VOM BAHNHOF ZOO 1981 d: Ulrich Edel. GRM., *Christiane F.*, K. Hermann, Horst Rieck, Book

CHRISTIE JOHNSTONE 1921 d: Norman MacDonald. UKN., *Christie Johnstone*, Charles Reade, Novel

Christina McNab *see* THE FORTUNE OF CHRISTINA MCNAB (1921).

Christine *see* ZWEI BLAUE AUGEN (1955).

CHRISTINE 1959 d: Pierre Gaspard-Huit. FRN/ITL., *Liebelei*, Arthur Schnitzler, 1895, Play

Christine *see* THE CHRISTINE JORGENSEN STORY (1970).

CHRISTINE 1983 d: John Carpenter. USA., *Christine*, Stephen King, 1983, Novel

CHRISTINE JORGENSEN STORY, THE 1970 d: Irving Rapper. USA., *Christine Jorgensen: a Personal Autobiography*, Christine Jorgensen, New York 1967, Autobiography

CHRISTINE OF THE HUNGRY HEART 1924 d: George Archainbaud. USA., *Christine of the Hungry Heart*, Kathleen Norris, 1924, Short Story

CHRISTMAS ACCIDENT, A 1912 d: Bannister Merwin. USA., *A Christmas Accident*, Annie Eliot Trumbull, Story

Christmas at the Brothel *see* NATALE IN CASA D'APPUNTAMENTO (1976).

CHRISTMAS CAROL, A 1908. USA., *A Christmas Carol*, Charles Dickens, London 1843, Novel

CHRISTMAS CAROL, A 1911 d: John H. Collins, J. Searle Dawley (Spv). USA., *A Christmas Carol*, Charles Dickens, London 1843, Novel

CHRISTMAS CAROL, A 1914 d: Harold Shaw. UKN., *A Christmas Carol*, Charles Dickens, London 1843, Novel

Christmas Carol, A *see* THE RIGHT TO BE HAPPY (1916).

CHRISTMAS CAROL, A 1938 d: Edwin L. Marin. USA., *A Christmas Carol*, Charles Dickens, London 1843, Novel

Christmas Carol, A *see* SCROOGE (1951).

CHRISTMAS CAROL, A 1956 d: Ralph Levy. USA., *A Christmas Carol*, Charles Dickens, London 1843, Novel

CHRISTMAS CAROL, A 1960 d: Robert Hartford-Davis. UKN., *A Christmas Carol*, Charles Dickens, London 1843, Novel

CHRISTMAS CAROL, A 1979 d: Jean Tych. ASL., *A Christmas Carol*, Charles Dickens, London 1843, Novel

CHRISTMAS CAROL, A 1984 d: Clive Donner. USA., *A Christmas Carol*, Charles Dickens, London 1843, Novel

CHRISTMAS CAROL: BEING A GHOST STORY OF CHRISTMAS, A 19— d: Moira Armstrong. UKN., *A Christmas Carol*, Charles Dickens, London 1843, Novel

CHRISTMAS DAY IN THE WORKHOUSE 1914 d: George Pearson. UKN., *Christmas Day in the Workhouse*, George R. Sims, Poem

Christmas Eve at Pilot Butte *see* DESPERATE TRAILS (1921).

CHRISTMAS HOLIDAY 1944 d: Robert Siodmak. USA., *Christmas Holiday*, W. Somerset Maugham, 1939, Novel

Christmas Oratio, The *see* JULORATORIET (1996).

CHRISTMAS STORY, A 1918. UKN., *A Christmas Story*, Fred Weatherley, Poem

CHRISTMAS STORY, A 1984 d: Bob Clark. CND., *In God We Trust - All Others Pay Cash*, Jean Shepherd, Novel

Christmas Time in a Brothel *see* NATALE IN CASA D'APPUNTAMENTO (1976).

CHRISTMAS TO REMEMBER, A 1978 d: George Englund. USA., *The Melodeon*, Glendon Swarthout, Novel

Christmas Tree, The *see* L' ARBRE DE NOEL (1969).

Christmas Weekend *see* THIS MAN IS MINE (1946).

CHRISTOPHER BEAN 1933 d: Sam Wood. USA., *Prenez Garde a la Peinture*, Rene Fauchois, 1932, Play

Christopher Blake *see* THE DECISION OF CHRISTOPHER BLAKE (1948).

CHRISTOPHER STRONG 1933 d: Dorothy Arzner. USA., *Christopher Strong: a Romance*, Gilbert Frankau, New York 1932, Novel

CHRISTUS 1914 d: Giuseppe de Liguoro. ITL., *Leggenda Siracusana Dell'Anno 1000*, Victor de Lussac

Chronic Innocence *see* DEN KRONISKE USKYLD (1985).

Chronicle of a Death Foretold *see* CRONACA DI UNA MORTE ANNUNCIATA (1987).

Chronicle of a Love Affair *see* KRONIKA WYPADKOW MILOSNYCH (1985).

Chronicle of a Murder *see* CHRONIK EINES MORDES (1965).

Chronicle of Amorous Incidents, A *see* KRONIKA WYPADKOW MILOSNYCH (1985).

Chronicle of Love Affairs *see* KRONIKA WYPADKOW MILOSNYCH (1985).

Chronicle of Poor Lovers *see* CRONACHE DI POVERI AMANTI (1954).

CHRONICLES OF NARNIA: PRINCE CASPIAN, THE 1989 d: Marilyn Fox. UKN., C. S. Lewis, Novel

CHRONICLES OF NARNIA: THE LION, THE WITCH AND THE WARDROBE, THE 1989 d: Marilyn Fox. UKN., *The Lion the Witch and the Wardrobe*, C. S. Lewis, 1950, Novel

CHRONICLES OF NARNIA: THE SILVER CHAIR, THE 1990 d: Alex Kirby. UKN., C. S. Lewis, Novel

CHRONICLES OF NARNIA: THE VOYAGE OF THE DAWN TREADER, THE 1989 d: Alex Kirby. UKN., C. S. Lewis, Novel

CHRONIK EINES MORDES 1965 d: Joachim Hasler. GDR., *Die Junger Jesu*, Leonhard Frank, 1949, Novel

Chronique d'une Saison Paysanne *see* SANGO MALO (1990).

Chrysalis *see* ALL OF ME (1934).

CHTO SLUCHILOS S POLINIM? 1971 d: Alexei Sakharov. USS., *Sluchai S Polynnym*, Konstantin Simonov, 1969, Short Story

CHU CHIN CHOW 1923 d: Herbert Wilcox. UKN., *Chu Chin Chow*, Oscar Asche, Frederick Norton, London 1916, Musical Play

CHU CHIN CHOW 1934 d: Walter Forde. UKN., *Chu Chin Chow*, Oscar Asche, Frederick Norton, London 1916, Musical Play

CHU CHU AND THE PHILLY FLASH 1981 d: David Lowell Rich. USA., Henry Barrow, Story

CHUAN CHANG ZHUI ZONG 1959 d: Lin Nong. CHN., *Chuan Chang Zhui Zong*, Fei Liwen, Novel

C.H.U.D. 1984 d: Douglas Cheek. USA., *C.H.U.D.*, Shepard Abbott, Novel

CHUDA HOLKA 1929 d: Martin Fric. CZC., *Chuda Holka*, Vaclav Cech-Stran, Novel

CHUEH-TAI SHUANG CHIAO 1979 d: Ch'u Yuan. HKG., *Chueh-Tai Shuang Chiao*, Ku Lung, Novel

CHUKA 1967 d: Gordon Douglas. USA., *Chuka*, Richard Jessup, Greenwich, Ct. 1961, Novel

CHUKJE 1997 d: Im Kwon-Taek. SKR., *Chukje*, le Chung-Joon, Novel

CHUN CAN MENG DUAN 1947 d: Sun Jing. CHN., *Dvoryanskoe Gnezdo*, Ivan Turgenev, 1859, Novel

CHUN FENG CUI DAO NUOMING HE 1954 d: Ling Zhifeng. CHN., *Chun Feng Cui Dao Nuoming He*, an Bo, Play

CHUN TAO 1988 d: Ling Zhifeng. CHN., *Chun Tao*, Xu Dishan, 1927, Short Story

CHUNCAN 1933 d: Cheng Bugao. CHN., *Chun Can*, Mao Dun, Short Story

Church Mouse *see* BEAUTY AND THE BOSS (1932).

CHURCH MOUSE, THE 1934 d: Monty Banks. UKN., *The Church Mouse*, Ladislaus Fodor, Paul Franck, Play

CHURCH WITH AN OVERSHOT WHEEL, THE 1919 d: Joseph Byron Totten. USA., *The Church With an Overshot Wheel*, O. Henry, Short Story

Churning for Nectar *see* AMRITMANTHAN (1934).

Churning of the Oceans, The *see* AMRITMANTHAN (1934).

CHUSHINGURA 1962 d: Hiroshi Inagaki. JPN., *Kanadehon Chushingura*, Miyoshi, Senryu Namiki, Izumo Takeda, 1748, Play

CHUTE DE LA MAISON USHER, LA 1928 d: Jean Epstein. FRN., *The Fall of the House of Usher*, Edgar Allan Poe, 1839, Short Story

CHVETI ZAPOZDALIE 1969 d: Abram Room. USS., *Tzvety Zapozdalye*, Anton Chekhov, 1882, Short Story

CIAO, PAIS. 1956 d: Osvaldo Langini. ITL., Bruno Alberton, Story

CIBOULETTE 1933 d: Claude Autant-LarA. FRN., *Ciboulette*, Francis de Croisset, Robert de Flers, Opera

Cica Tomina Koliba *see* ONKEL TOMS HUTTE (1965).

Cicada Is Not an Insect, The *see* LA CIGARRA NO ES UN BICHO (1963).

Cicada, La *see* LA CICALA (1980).

CICALA, LA 1980 d: Alberto LattuadA. ITL., *La Cicala*, Marina d'Aunia, Natale Prinetto, Novel

Cicha Noc *see* WSROD NOCNEJ CISZY (1978).

CICLONE, IL 1916 d: Eugenio Perego. ITL., *Taifun*, Melchior Lengyel, Budapest 1909, Play

CID, IL 1910 d: Mario Caserini. ITL., *Le Cid*, Pierre Corneille, 1637, Play

CIDER WITH ROSIE 1971 d: Claude Whatham. UKN., *Cider With Rosie*, Laurie Lee, 1959, Autobiography

Cider With Rosie *see* LAURIE LEE'S CIDER WITH ROSIE (1998).

CIECA DI SORRENTO, LA 1916 d: Gustavo SerenA. ITL., *La Cieca Di Sorrento*, Francesco Mastriani, 1826, Novel

CIECA DI SORRENTO, LA 1934 d: Nunzio MalasommA. ITL., *La Cieca Di Sorrento*, Francesco Mastriani, 1826, Novel

CIECA DI SORRENTO, LA 1952 d: Giacomo Gentilomo. ITL., *La Cieca Di Sorrento*, Francesco Mastriani, 1826, Novel

Ciel Est Rouge, Le *see* IL CIELO E ROSSO (1950).

CIELO E ROSSO, IL 1950 d: Claudio GorA. ITL., *Il Cielo E Rosso*, Giuseppe Berto, 1947, Novel

Cien Rifles, Los *see* 100 RIFLES (1969).

CIGALE, LA 1913 d: Elwin Neame. UKN., *La Cigale*, Jean de La Fontaine, Story

CIGARETTE - THAT'S ALL, A 1915 d: Phillips Smalley. USA., *A Cigarette - That's All*, Helena Evans, Story

CIGARETTE MAKER'S ROMANCE, A 1920 d: Tom Watts. UKN., *A Cigarette-Maker's Romance*, Marion Crawford, Novel

CIGARETTE-MAKER'S ROMANCE, A 1913 d: Frank Wilson. UKN., *A Cigarette-Maker's Romance*, Marion Crawford, Novel

CIGARRA NO ES UN BICHO, LA 1963 d: Daniel Tinayre. ARG., *La Cigarra No Es un Bicho*, Dante Sierra, Buenos Aires 1957, Novel

CIKANI 1921 d: Karl Anton. CZC., *Cikani*, Karel Hynek MacHa, Short Story

CIMARRON 1931 d: Wesley Ruggles. USA., *Cimarron*, Edna Ferber, New York 1930, Novel

CIMARRON 1960 d: Anthony Mann, Charles Walters. USA., *Cimarron*, Edna Ferber, New York 1930, Novel

CINCINNATI KID, THE 1965 d: Norman Jewison. USA., *The Cincinnati Kid*, Richard Jessup, Boston 1963, Novel

CINCO ADVERTENCIAS DE SATANAS, LAS 1938 d: Isidro Socias. SPN., *Las Cinco Advertencias de Satanas*, Enrique Jardiel Poncela, 1938, Play

CINCO ADVERTENCIAS DE SATANAS, LAS 1969 d: Jose Luis Merino. SPN/PRT., *Las Cinco Advertencias de Satanas*, Enrique Jardiel Poncela, 1938, Play

CINCO DIAS, CINCO NOITES 1997 d: Jose Fonseca CostA. PRT/FRN., *Cinco Noites Cinco Dias*, Alvaro Cunhal, Novel, *Cinco Dias Cinco Noites*, Manuel Tiago, Novel

CINDER PATH, THE 1994 d: Simon Langton. UKN., *The Cinder Path*, Catherine Cookson, Novel

CINDERELLA 1911 d: Theodore Marston. USA., *Cendrillon*, Charles Perrault, 1697, Short Story

CINDERELLA 1914 d: James Kirkwood. USA., *Cendrillon*, Charles Perrault, 1697, Short Story

Cinderella see FIRST LOVE (1939).

CINDERELLA 1949 d: Wilfred Jackson, Hamilton Luske. USA., *Cendrillon*, Charles Perrault, 1697, Short Story

Cinderella see CENERENTOLA (1949).

CINDERELLA 1954 d: Lotte Reiniger. UKN., *Cendrillon*, Charles Perrault, 1697, Short Story

Cinderella see ASCHENPUTTEL (1955).

Cinderella see KHRUSTALNYY BASHMACHOK (1961).

CINDERELLA 1977 d: Michael Pataki, Stanley Long. USA., *Cendrillon*, Charles Perrault, 1697, Short Story

Cinderella see PEPELJUGA (1979).

CINDERELLA AND THE MAGIC SLIPPER 1917 d: Guy W. McConnell. USA., *Cendrillon*, Charles Perrault, 1697, Short Story

CINDERELLA JONES 1946 d: Busby Berkeley. USA., Philip Wylie, Story

CINDERELLA LIBERTY 1973 d: Mark Rydell. USA., *Cinderella Liberty*, Darryl Ponicsan, Novel

CINDERELLA MAN, THE 1918 d: George Loane Tucker. USA., *The Cinderella Man*, Edward Childs Carpenter, New York 1916, Play

CINDERELLA OF THE HILLS 1921 d: Howard M. Mitchell. USA., *Little Fiddler of the Ozarks*, John Breckenridge Ellis, Chicago 1913, Novel

CINDERELLA'S TWIN 1920 d: Dallas M. Fitzgerald. USA., *Cendrillon*, Charles Perrault, 1697, Short Story

CINEMA GIRL'S ROMANCE, A 1915 d: George Pearson. UKN., *A Cinema Girl's Romance*, Ladbrooke Black, Novel

CINEMA MURDER, THE 1920 d: George D. Baker. USA., *The Cinema Murder (the Other Romilly)*, E. Phillips Oppenheim, Boston 1917, Novel

Cinq Atouts de M. Wens, Les see LES ATOUTS DE M. WENS (1946).

Cinq Dernieres Minutes, Les see GLI ULTIMI CINQUE MINUTI (1955).

CINQ GARS POUR SINGAPOUR 1967 d: Bernard Toublanc-Michel. FRN/ITL., *Cinq Gars Pour Singapour*, Jean Bruce, Paris 1959, Novel

CINQ GENTLEMEN MAUDITS, LES 1920 d: Pierre Regnier, Luitz-Morat. FRN., *Les Cinq Gentlemen Maudits*, Andre Heuze, Novel

CINQ GENTLEMEN MAUDITS, LES 1931 d: Julien Duvivier. FRN., *Les Cinq Gentlemen Maudits*, Andre Heuze, Novel

CINQ MILLIONS COMPTANT 1956 d: Andre Berthomieu. FRN., *Cinq Millions Comptant*, Francis Lopez, Raymond Vinci, Opera

CINQ SOUS DE LAVAREDE, LES 1913 d: Henri Andreani. FRN., *Les Cinq Sous de Lavarede*, Paul d'Ivoi, Novel

CINQ SOUS DE LAVAREDE, LES 1928 d: Maurice Champreux. FRN., *Les Cinq Sous de Lavarede*, Paul d'Ivoi, Novel

CINQ SOUS DE LAVAREDE, LES 1939 d: Maurice Cammage. FRN., *Les Cinq Sous de Lavarede*, Paul d'Ivoi, Novel

CINQUE FURBASTRI E UN FURBACCHIONE 1977 d: Lucio de Caro. ITL., *Gli Ineffabili Cinque*, Donald E. Westlake, Novel

Cinque Furbastri, un Furbacchione see CINQUE FURBASTRI E UN FURBACCHIONE (1977).

Cinque Marines Per Singapore see CINQ GARS POUR SINGAPOUR (1967).

CINQUIEME EMPREINTE, LA 1934 d: Karl Anton. FRN., *Lilas Blanc*, Ladislaus Fodor, Play

CINTURA, LA 1988 d: Giuliana GambA. ITL., *La Cintura*, Alberto Moravia, Novel

CIOCIARA, LA 1961 d: Vittorio de SicA. ITL/FRN., *La Ciociara*, Alberto Moravia, Milan 1957, Novel

CIRANO DI BERGERAC 1909 d: Ernesto Maria Pasquali. ITL., *Cyrano de Bergerac*, Edmond Rostand, 1897, Play

CIRANO DI BERGERAC 1922 d: Augusto GeninA. ITL., *Cyrano de Bergerac*, Edmond Rostand, 1897, Play

CIRCE MODERNA 1914 d: Alberto Degli Abbati. ITL., *La Venere Orgiasta*, Luigi Chiarelli, Short Story

CIRCLE IN THE FIRE, A 1975 d: Victor Nunez. USA., *A Circle in the Fire*, Flannery O'Connor, 1955, Short Story

CIRCLE OF CHILDREN, A 1977 d: Don Taylor. USA., *A Circle of Children*, Mary MacCracken, Book

CIRCLE OF DANGER 1951 d: Jacques Tourneur. UKN., *Circle of Danger*, Philip MacDonald, Novel

Circle of Deceit see DIE FALSCHUNG (1981).

CIRCLE OF DECEPTION 1960 d: Jack Lee. UKN., *Guy Renton*, Alec Waugh, 1953, Novel

CIRCLE OF FRIENDS 1994 d: Pat O'Connor. IRL/USA., *Circle of Friends*, Maeve Binchy, Novel

Circle of Love see LA RONDE (1964).

Circle of Power see BRAINWASH (1981).

CIRCLE OF TWO 1980 d: Jules Dassin. CND., *A Lesson in Love*, Marie-Terese Baird, Novel

CIRCLE, THE 1925 d: Frank Borzage. USA., *The Circle*, W. Somerset Maugham, London 1921, Play

Circle, The see STRICTLY UNCONVENTIONAL (1930).

Circle, The see THE VICIOUS CIRCLE (1948).

CIRCO EQUESTRE ZA-BUM 1944 d: Mario Mattoli. ITL., *Za-Bum*, Marcello Marchesi, Musical Play

CIRCONSTANCES ATTENUANTES 1939 d: Jean Boyer. FRN., *A l'Heritage Ou Les Vacances Singulieres*, Marcel Arnac, Novel

CIRCULAR STAIRCASE, THE 1915 d: Edward J. Le Saint. USA., *The Circular Staircase*, Mary Roberts Rinehart, Indianapolis 1908, Novel

Circumstance see ALMOST MARRIED (1932).

Circumstances see ALMOST MARRIED (1932).

CIRCUMSTANTIAL EVIDENCE 1912 d: Otis B. Thayer. USA., *The Little Good*, Hapsburg Liebe

CIRCUMSTANTIAL EVIDENCE 1952 d: Daniel Birt. UKN., *The Judge Sees the Light*, Allan MacKinnon, Short Story

CIRCUS DAYS 1923 d: Eddie Cline. USA., *Toby Tyler; Or Ten Weeks With a Circus*, James Otis Kaler, New York 1881, Novel

CIRCUS GIRL 1937 d: John H. Auer. USA., *Without the Net*, Frank R. Adams, 1922, Short Story

CIRCUS MAN, THE 1914 d: Oscar Apfel. USA., *The Rose in the Ring*, George Barr McCutcheon, New York 1910, Novel

CIRCUS OF FEAR 1966 d: John Llewellyn Moxey. UKN., Edgar Wallace, Novel

Circus Performers see SALTIMBANCII (1981).

Circus Performers at the North Pole see UN SALTIMBANC LA POLUL NORD (1982).

CIRCUS QUEEN MURDER, THE 1933 d: R. William Neill. USA., *About the Murder of a Circus Queen*, Anthony Abbott, New York 1932, Novel

CISARUV SLAVIK 1948 d: Jiri Trnka, Milos Makovec. CZC., *Nattergalen*, Hans Christian Andersen, 1844, Short Story

Ciske see EIN KIND BRAUCHT LIEBE CISKE (1955).

Ciske -a Child Needs Love see EIN KIND BRAUCHT LIEBE CISKE (1955).

Ciske -a Child Wants Love see EIN KIND BRAUCHT LIEBE CISKE (1955).

Ciske de Rat see EIN KIND BRAUCHT LIEBE CISKE (1955).

CISKE DE RAT 1985 d: Guido Pieters. NTH., *Ciske de Rat*, Piet Bakker, Amsterdam 1941, Novel

CISKE, EIN KIND BRAUCHT LIEBE 1955 d: Wolfgang Staudte. GRM/NTH., *Ciske de Rat*, Piet Bakker, Amsterdam 1941, Novel

Ciske the Rat see EIN KIND BRAUCHT LIEBE CISKE (1955).

Ciske the Rat see CISKE DE RAT (1985).

Cissy see THE KING STEPS OUT (1936).

CITA CON LA VIDA, UNA 1957 d: Hugo Del Carril. ARG., *Calles de Tango*, Bernardo Verbitsky, 1953, Novel

Citadel of Warsaw, The see DIE WARSCHAUER ZITADELLE (1930).

CITADEL, THE 1938 d: King Vidor. UKN/USA., *The Citadel*, A. J. Cronin, 1937, Novel

CITADEL, THE 1983 d: Peter Jeffries, Mike Vardy. UKN., *The Citadel*, A. J. Cronin, 1937, Novel

CITADELA SFARIMATA 1957 d: Marc Maurette. RMN/FRN., *Citadela Sfarimata*, Horia Lovinescu, 1955, Play

Cities and Times see GORODA I GODY (1973).

Cities and Years see GORODA I GODY (1973).

Citizen Brych see OBCAN BRYCH (1958).

CITTA PRIGIONERA, LA 1962 d: Joseph Anthony, Mario Chiari. ITL., *The Captive City*, John Appleby, New York 1955, Novel

CITY ACROSS THE RIVER 1949 d: Maxwell Shane. USA., *The Amboy Dukes*, Irving Shulman, Novel

City After Midnight see THAT WOMAN OPPOSITE (1957).

City and the Dogs, The see LA CIUDAD Y LOS PERROS (1985).

CITY BENEATH THE SEA 1953 d: Budd Boetticher. USA., *Port Royal - Ghost City Beneath the Sea*, Harry E. Rieseberg, Book

CITY FOR CONQUEST 1940 d: Anatole Litvak. USA., *City for Conquest*, Aben Kandel, New York 1936, Novel

CITY GIRL 1930 d: F. W. Murnau, A. F. Erickson. USA., *The Mud Turtle*, Elliott Lester, New York 1925, Play

City Hall Scandal see NIGHT CLUB SCANDAL (1937).

City in the Sea see THE CITY UNDER THE SEA (1965).

City Is Dark, The see CRIME WAVE (1954).

City Is Full of Secrets, The see DIE STADT IST VOLLER GEHEIMNISSE (1955).

City Jungle, The see THE YOUNG PHILADELPHIANS (1959).

CITY LIMITS 1934 d: William Nigh. USA., *City Limits*, Josiah Pitts Woolfolk, New York 1932, Novel

CITY OF BEAUTIFUL NONSENSE, THE 1919 d: Henry Edwards. UKN., *The City of Beautiful Nonsense*, E. Temple Thurston, 1909, Novel

CITY OF BEAUTIFUL NONSENSE, THE 1935 d: Adrian Brunel. UKN., *The City of Beautiful Nonsense*, E. Temple Thurston, 1909, Novel

CITY OF COMRADES, THE 1919 d: Harry Beaumont. USA., *The City of Comrades*, Basil King, New York 1919, Novel

City of Dreams see TRAUMSTADT (1973).

CITY OF JOY 1992 d: Roland Joffe. UKN/FRN., *City of Joy*, Dominique Lapierre, Novel

City of Lost Men see CASTLE ON THE HUDSON (1940).

CITY OF MASKS, THE 1920 d: Thomas N. Heffron. USA., *The City of Masks*, George Barr McCutcheon, New York 1918, Novel

City of My Dreams see MINA DROMMARS STAD (1976).

CITY OF PURPLE DREAMS, THE 1918 d: Colin Campbell. USA., *The City of Purple Dreams*, Edwin Baird, Chicago 1913, Novel

City of Secrets see DIE STADT IST VOLLER GEHEIMNISSE (1955).

CITY OF SILENT MEN 1921 d: Tom Forman. USA., *The Quarry*, John A. Moroso, Boston 1913, Novel

CITY OF TERRIBLE NIGHT, THE 1915 d: George A. Lessey. USA., *The City of Terrible Night*, Rudyard Kipling, Short Story

CITY OF YOUTH, THE 1928 d: Charles Calvert. UKN., *Barbara Comes to Oxford*, Oona Ball, Novel

CITY SPARROW, A 1920 d: Sam Wood. USA., *A City Sparrow*, Kate Jordan, 1917, Serial Story

CITY THAT NEVER SLEEPS, THE 1924 d: James Cruze. USA., *Mother O'Day*, Leroy Scott, 1924, Short Story

CITY, THE 1916 d: Theodore Wharton. USA., *The City*, Clyde Fitch, New York 1909, Play

CITY, THE 1926 d: R. William Neill. USA., *The City*, Clyde Fitch, New York 1909, Play

CITY, THE 1939 d: Willard Van Dyke, Ralph Steiner. USA., *The Culture of Cities*, Lewis Mumford, Book

City Under Siege see BING LIN CHENG XIA (1964).

CITY UNDER THE SEA, THE 1965 d: Jacques Tourneur. UKN/USA., *City in the Sea*, Edgar Allan Poe, 1831, Poem, *A Descent Into the Maelstrom*, Edgar Allan Poe, 1841, Poem

CITY'S EDGE, THE 1983 d: Ken Quinnell. ASL., *The City's Edge*, W. A. Harbinson, Novel

CIUDAD Y LOS PERROS, LA 1985 d: Francisco Lombardi. PRU., *La Ciudad Y Los Perros*, Mario Vargas Llosa, Novel

Ciuleandra see VERKLUNGENE TRAUME (1930).

CIULEANDRA 1985 d: Sergiu Nicolaescu. RMN., *Ciuleandra*, Liviu Rebreanu, 1927, Novel

CIULINII BARAGANULUI 1957 d: Louis Daquin, Gheorghe Vitanidis. RMN/FRN., *Les Chardons du Baragan*, Panait Istrati, 1928, Novel

CIVIL ACTION, A 1998 d: Steven Zaillian. USA., *A Civil Action*, Jonathan Harr, Book

CIVILIAN CLOTHES 1920 d: Hugh Ford. USA., *Civilian Clothes*, Thompson Buchanan, New York 1919, Play

Claim No. Z84 *see* **COMPO** (1988).

CLAIM, THE 1918 d: Frank Reicher. USA., *The Claim*, Frank Dare, Charles Kenyon, New York 1917, Play

CLAIR DE FEMME 1979 d: Costa-Gavras. FRN/GRM/ITL., *Clair de Femme*, Romain Gary, Novel

Claire's Knee *see* **LE GENOU DE CLAIRE** (1970).

CLAIRVOYANT, THE 1935 d: Maurice Elvey. UKN., *The Clairvoyant*, Ernst Lothar, Novel

Clan Degli Uomini Violenti, Il *see* **LA HORSE** (1969).

Clan Dei Marsigliesi, Il *see* **LA SCOUMOUNE** (1973).

CLAN DES SICILIENS, LE 1969 d: Henri Verneuil. FRN., *Le Clan Des Siciliens*, Auguste le Breton, Paris 1967, Novel

CLAN OF THE CAVE BEAR, THE 1985 d: Michael Chapman. USA., *The Clan of the Cave Bear*, Jean M. Auel, Novel

CLANCARTY 1914 d: Harold Shaw. UKN., *Clancarty*, Tom Taylor, London 1907, Play

CLANDESTINES, LES 1954 d: Raoul Andre. FRN., *Les Clandestines*, Raymond Caillava, Paris 1954, Novel

CLANDESTINO A TRIESTE 1952 d: Guido Salvini. ITL., *Camillo Del Signore*, Story

CLANDESTINS, LES 1945 d: Andre Chotin. FRN., *Les Clandestins*, Lucien Barnier

Clansman of the North *see* **BIG TIMBER** (1921).

Clansman, The *see* **THE BIRTH OF A NATION** (1915).

Clara Deane *see* **THE STRANGE CASE OF CLARA DEANE** (1932).

CLARA ET LES MECHANTS 1957 d: Raoul Andre. FRN., *Clara Et Les Mechants*, Paul Vialar, Novel

CLARA'S HEART 1988 d: Robert Mulligan. USA., *Clara's Heart*, Joseph Olshan, Novel

CLARENCE 1922 d: William C. de Mille. USA., *Clarence*, Booth Tarkington, New York 1919, Play

CLARENCE 1937 d: George Archainbaud. USA., *Clarence*, Booth Tarkington, New York 1919, Play

CLARINES DEL MIEDO, LOS 1958 d: Antonio Roman. SPN., *Los Clarines Del Miedo*, Angel Maria de Lera, 1958, Novel

CLARION CALL, THE 1918 d: Ashley Miller. USA., *The Clarion Call*, O.Henry, Short Story

CLARION, THE 1916 d: James Durkin. USA., *The Clarion*, Samuel Hopkins Adams, Boston 1914, Novel

Clarissa *see* **GAMBIER'S ADVOCATE** (1915).

CLARISSA 1991 d: Robert Bierman. UKN/USA., *Clarissa*, Samuel Richardson, 1748, Novel

CLASH BY NIGHT 1952 d: Fritz Lang. USA., *Clash By Night*, Clifford Odets, New York 1941, Play

CLASH BY NIGHT 1963 d: Montgomery Tully. UKN., *Clash By Night*, Rupert Croft-Cooke, London 1962, Novel

Clash of Steel *see* **LE CHEVALIER DE PARDAILLAN** (1962).

CLASS AND NO CLASS 1921 d: W. P. Kellino. UKN., *Class and No Class*, E. Newton Bungey, Novel

Class Conditions *see* **KLASSENVERHALTNISSE** (1984).

CLASS DE ASEN, LA 1914 d: Arnaldo Giacomelli. ITL., *La Class de Asen*, Eduardo Ferravilla, 1879, Play

Class Enemy *see* **KLASSEN FEIND** (1983).

CLASS OF MISS MACMICHAEL, THE 1978 d: Silvio Narizzano. UKN., *The Class of Miss MacMichael*, Sandy Hutson, Novel

Class Prophecy *see* **WHEN LOVE IS YOUNG** (1937).

Class Relations *see* **KLASSENVERHALTNISSE** (1984).

Class Relationships *see* **KLASSENVERHALTNISSE** (1984).

CLASSE TOUS RISQUES 1959 d: Claude Sautet. FRN/ITL., *Le Trou*, Jose Giovanni, Paris 1957, Novel

CLASSIFIED 1925 d: Alfred Santell. USA., *Classified*, Edna Ferber, Short Story

CLASSMATES 1914 d: James Kirkwood. USA., *Classmates*, William C. de Mille, Margaret Turnbull, New York 1907, Play

CLAUDELLE INGLISH 1961 d: Gordon Douglas. USA., *Claudelle Inglish*, Erskine Caldwell, Boston 1959, Novel

CLAUDIA 1943 d: Edmund Goulding. USA., *Claudia*, Rose Franken, Novel

Claudia Case, The *see* **O CASO CLAUDIO** (1979).

CLAUDINE A L'ECOLE 1937 d: Serge de Poligny. FRN., *Claudine a l'Ecole*, Sidonie Gabrielle Colette, 1900, Novel

CLAUDINE'S RETURN 1998 d: Antonio Tibaldi. USA., *The Magnificent Rescue*, Heidi Hall, Short Story

CLAVIGO 1970 d: Marcel Ophuls. GRM., *Clavigo*, Johann Wolfgang von Goethe, 1774, Play

CLAVO, EL 1944 d: Rafael Gil. SPN., *El Clavo*, Pedro Antonio de Alarcon, 1854, Short Story

CLAW, THE 1918 d: Robert G. VignolA. USA., *The Claw*, Cynthia Stockley, New York 1911, Novel

CLAW, THE 1927 d: Sidney Olcott. USA., *The Claw*, Cynthia Stockley, New York 1911, Novel

Clay *see* **KORKARLEN** (1921).

Clay *see* **SHATTERED DREAMS** (1922).

CLAYDON TREASURE MYSTERY, THE 1938 d: Manning Haynes. UKN., *The Shakespeare Murders*, Neil Gordon, Novel

CLAYHANGER 1976 d: John Davies, David Reid. UKN., Arnold Bennett, Novel

CLE SUR LA PORTE, LA 1978 d: Yves Boisset. FRN., *La Cle Sur la Porte*, Marie Cardinal, Novel

Clean Break *see* **THE KILLING** (1956).

CLEAN GUN, THE 1917 d: Harry Harvey. USA., *The Clean Gun*, Barr Moses, Short Story

Clean Slate *see* **COUP DE TORCHON** (1981).

CLEAR ALL WIRES 1933 d: George W. Hill. USA., *Clear All Wires*, Bella Spewack, Samuel Spewack, New York 1932, Play

CLEAR AND PRESENT DANGER 1994 d: Phil Noyce. USA., *Clear and Present Danger*, Tom Clancy, Novel

CLEAR THE DECKS 1929 d: Joseph Henabery. USA., *When the Devil Was Sick*, E. J. Rath, New York 1926, Novel

Clear the Track *see* **MURDER IN THE PRIVATE CAR** (1934).

CLEMENCEAU CASE, THE 1915 d: Herbert Brenon. USA., *L' Affaire Clemenceau*, Alexandre Dumas (fils), Paris 1866, Novel

CLEO, ROBES ET MANTEAUX 1933 d: Nunzio MalasommA. ITL., *Robes Et Manteaux Cleo*, Guido Da Verona, Novel

CLEOPATRA 1912 d: Charles L. Gaskill. USA., *Cleopatre*, Victorien Sardou, Paris 1890, Play, *Antony and Cleopatra*, William Shakespeare, c1607, Play

CLEOPATRA 1917 d: J. Gordon Edwards. USA., *Cleopatre*, Victorien Sardou, Paris 1890, Play, *Antony and Cleopatra*, William Shakespeare, c1607, Play

CLERAMBARD 1969 d: Yves Robert. FRN., *Clerambard*, Marcel Ayme, 1950, Play

Clerk and the Coat, The *see* **GARAM COAT** (1955).

Clerk, The *see* **KOMPTOIRISTKA** (1922).

Clerk's Daughter *see* **GUMASTAVIN PENN** (1941).

Cleverest Woman in Berlin, The *see* **DIE RAFFINIERTESTE FRAU BERLINS** (1927).

CLICKING OF CUTHBERT, THE 1924 d: Andrew P. Wilson. UKN., *The Clicking of Cuthbert*, P. G. Wodehouse, Short Story

CLIENT SERIEUX, UN 1918 d: Jacques Gretillat. FRN., *Un Client Serieux*, Georges Courteline, 1897, Play

CLIENT SERIEUX, UN 1932 d: Claude Autant-LarA. FRN., *Un Client Serieux*, Georges Courteline, 1897, Play

CLIENT, THE 1994 d: Joel Schumacher. USA., *The Client*, John Grisham, Novel

CLIENTE PAS SERIEUSE, UNE 1934 d: Rene Gaveau. FRN., *Le Pharmacien*, Max Maurey, Play

Cliffs of Sand *see* **FALEZE DE NISIP** (1983).

Climates of Love *see* **CLIMATS** (1962).

CLIMATS 1962 d: Stellio Lorenzi. FRN., *Climats*, Andre Maurois, 1928, Novel

CLIMAX, THE 1930 d: Renaud Hoffman. USA., *The Climax*, Edward Locke, London 1910, Play

CLIMAX, THE 1944 d: George Waggner. USA., *The Climax*, Edward Locke, London 1910, Play

Climber, The *see* **KLETTERMAXE** (1952).

CLIMBERS, THE 1915 d: Barry O'Neil. USA., *The Climbers*, Clyde Fitch, New York 1901, Play

CLIMBERS, THE 1919 d: Tom Terriss. USA., *The Climbers*, Clyde Fitch, New York 1901, Play

CLIMBERS, THE 1927 d: Paul L. Stein. USA., *The Climbers*, Clyde Fitch, New York 1901, Play

Climbers, The *see* **L' AMBITIEUSE** (1958).

Climbing Mount Fuji *see* **VOSHOZDENIE NA FUDZIJAMU** (1988).

CLINGING VINE, THE 1926 d: Paul Sloane. USA., *The Clinging Vine*, Zelda Sears, New York 1922, Play

Clipped Wings *see* **HELLO SISTER** (1930).

Clipped Wings *see* **SISTER! HELLO** (1933).

Clippings *see* **POSTRIZINY** (1980).

Clique of Gold, The *see* **THE EVIL WOMEN DO** (1916).

CLIVE OF INDIA 1935 d: Richard Boleslawski. USA., *Clive of India*, W. P. Lipscomb, R. J. Minney, England 1933, Play

CLIVIA 1954 d: Karl Anton. GRM., *Clivia*, Charles Amberg, Nico Dostal, Opera

CLOAK AND DAGGER 1946 d: Fritz Lang. USA., *Cloak and Dagger*, Corey Ford, Alastair McBain, Novel

CLOAK AND DAGGER 1984 d: Richard Franklin. USA., *The Boy Cried Murder*, Cornell Woolrich, 1947, Short Story

Cloak, The *see* **SHINEL** (1926).

Cloak, The *see* **SHINEL** (1960).

CLOCHE POUR URSLI, UN 1964 d: Ulrich Kundig, Nicolas Gessner. SWT., *Uorsin de la S-Chella*, Selina Chonz, 1945, Book

CLOCHEMERLE 1947 d: Pierre Chenal. FRN., *Clochemerle*, Gabriel Chevallier, Novel

CLOCHES DE CORNEVILLE, LES 1917 d: Thomas Bentley. UKN., *Les Cloches de Corneville*, Robert Planquette, Paris 1877, Operetta

CLOCK STRIKES EIGHT, THE 1946 d: Ronald Haines. UKN., *The Clock Strikes Eight*, John Dickson Carr, Short Story

CLOCKERS 1995 d: Spike Lee. USA., *Clockers*, Richard Price, Novel

Clockmaker of St. Paul, The *see* **L' HORLOGER DE ST. PAUL** (1973).

Clockmaker, The *see* **L' HORLOGER DE ST. PAUL** (1973).

CLOCKWORK ORANGE, A 1971 d: Stanley Kubrick. UKN., *A Clockwork Orange*, Anthony Burgess, 1962, Novel

CLOISTER AND THE HEARTH, THE 1913 d: Hay Plumb. UKN., *The Cloister and the Hearth*, Charles Reade, 1861, Novel

Cloister's Hunter, The *see* **DER KLOSTERJAGER** (1953).

Cloportes *see* **METAMORPHOSE DES CLOPORTES** (1965).

Close Call, A *see* **A CLOSE CALL FOR ELLERY QUEEN** (1942).

CLOSE CALL FOR ELLERY QUEEN, A 1942 d: James P. Hogan. USA., *The Dragon's Teeth; a Problem of Deduction*, Ellery Queen, Story

Close Season for Foxes *see* **SCHONZEIT FUR FUCHSE** (1966).

Close Time for Foxes *see* **SCHONZEIT FUR FUCHSE** (1966).

CLOSE TO MY HEART 1951 d: William Keighley. USA., *A Baby for Midge*, James R. Webb, Story

Closely Observed Trains *see* **OSTRE SLEDOVANE VLAKY** (1966).

CLOSERIE DES GENETS, LA 1913 d: Adrien Caillard. FRN., *La Closerie Des Genets*, Frederic Soulie, Play

CLOSERIE DES GENETS, LA 1924 d: Andre Liabel. FRN., *La Closerie Des Genets*, Frederic Soulie, Play

CLOSING CHAPTER, THE 1915 d: Murdock MacQuarrie. USA., *The Closing Chapter*, Clifford Howard, Story

CLOSING NET, THE 1915 d: Edward Jose. USA., *The Closing Net*, Henry C. Rowland, New York 1912, Novel

CLOTHES 1914 d: Francis Powers. USA., *Clothes*, Avery Hopwood, Channing Pollock, New York 1906, Play

CLOTHES 1920 d: Fred Sittenham. USA., *Clothes*, Avery Hopwood, Channing Pollock, New York 1906, Play

Clothes and the Woman *see* **ON YOUR BACK** (1930).

CLOTHES IN THE WARDROBE 1992 d: Waris Hussein. UKN., *Clothes in the Wardrobe*, Alice Thomas Ellis, Novel

Clothes Make Man *see* **SATY DELAJI CLOVECKA** (1912).

Clothes Make People *see* **KLEIDER MACHEN LEUTE** (1940).

Clothes Make the Man *see* **KLEIDER MACHEN LEUTE** (1940).

CLOTHES MAKE THE PIRATE 1925 d: Maurice Tourneur. USA., *Clothes Make the Pirate*, Holman Francis Day, New York 1925, Novel

CLOUD HOWE 1982 d: Tom Cotter. UKN., *Cloud Howe*, Lewis Grassic Gibbon, Novel

CLOUD WALTZ 1987 d: Gordon Flemyng. UKN/USA., *Cloud Waltz*, Tory Cates, Novel

Cloud Waltzer *see* **CLOUD WALTZ** (1987).

Cloud Waltzing *see* **CLOUD WALTZ** (1987).

CLOUDBURST 1951 d: Francis Searle. UKN., *Cloudburst*, Leo Marks, Play

CLOWN AND THE KIDS, THE 1968 d: Mende Brown. USA/BUL., Wilhelm Hauff, Short Story

CLOWN BUX, LE 1935 d: Jacques Natanson. FRN., *Le Clown Bux*, Hans Possendorff, Novel

Clown Must Laugh, A *see* **PAGLIACCI** (1936).

Clown, The *see* **ANSICHTEN EINES CLOWNS** (1975).

CLOWNING AROUND 1991 d: George Whaley. ASL., *Clowning Sim*, David Martin, Novel

CLOWNING AROUND ENCORE 1992 d: George Whaley. ASL., *Clowning Around Encore*, David Martin, Novel

Clowning Sim *see* **CLOWNING AROUND** (1991).

Clowns, The *see* **SALTIMBANCII** (1981).

CLUB DES 400 COUPS, LE 1952 d: Jacques Daroy. FRN., *Le Club Des 400 Coups*, Pierre Clarel, Novel

CLUB DES ARISTOCRATES, LE 1937 d: Piere Colombier. FRN., *Le Club Des Aristocrates*, Detective Ashelbe, Novel

Club Des Quatre Cent Coups, Le *see* **LE CLUB DES 400 COUPS** (1952).

CLUB DES TREIZE, LE 1914 d: Henri Andreani. FRN., *Le Club Des Treize*, Honore de Balzac, Novel

Club of Bachelors *see* **KLUB KAWALEROW** (1962).

Club, The *see* **DAVID WILLIAMSON'S THE CLUB** (1980).

CLUE OF THE NEW PIN, THE 1929 d: Arthur Maude. UKN., *The Clue of the New Pin*, Edgar Wallace, London 1923, Novel

CLUE OF THE NEW PIN, THE 1961 d: Allan Davis. UKN., *The Clue of the New Pin*, Edgar Wallace, London 1923, Novel

CLUE OF THE PIGTAIL, THE 1923 d: A. E. Coleby. UKN., *The Clue of the Pigtail*, Sax Rohmer, Short Story

CLUE OF THE SILVER KEY 1961 d: Gerald Glaister. UKN., *The Clue of the Silver Key*, Edgar Wallace, London 1930, Novel

CLUE OF THE TWISTED CANDLE 1960 d: Allan Davis. UKN., *The Clue of the Twisted Candle*, Edgar Wallace, London 1918, Novel

CLUE, THE 1915 d: James Neill, Frank Reicher. USA., *The Clue*, Margaret Turnbull, Play

CLUNY BROWN 1946 d: Ernst Lubitsch. USA., *Cluny Brown*, Margery Sharp, Novel

CLUTCH OF CIRCUMSTANCE, THE 1918 d: Henry Houry. USA., *The Clutch of Circumstance*, Leighton Graves Osmun, New York 1914, Novel

Coachman Henschel *see* **FUHRMANN HENSCHEL** (1956).

COAL KING, THE 1915 d: Percy Nash. UKN., *The Coal King*, Fewlass Llewellyn, Ernest Martin, Play

COAL MINER'S DAUGHTER, THE 1980 d: Michael Apted. USA., Loretta Lynn, George Vescey, Autobiography

COAST OF FOLLY, THE 1925 d: Allan Dwan. USA., *The Coast of Folly*, Conigsby William Dawson, New York 1924, Novel

COAST OF SKELETONS 1964 d: Robert Lynn. UKN/SAF., *Sanders of the River*, Edgar Wallace, London 1911, Novel

COBB 1994 d: Ron Shelton. USA., *Cobb: a Biography*, Al Stump, Biography

COBRA 1925 d: Joseph Henabery. USA., *Cobra*, Martin Brown, New York 1924, Play

Cobra *see* **LE SAUT DE L'ANGE** (1971).

COBRA 1986 d: George Pan Cosmatos. USA., *Fair Game*, Paula Gosling, Novel

COBRA VERDE 1987 d: Werner Herzog. GRM., *The Viceroy of Ouidah*, Bruce Chatwin, Novel

Cobweb *see* **POKHALO** (1974).

Cobweb Castle *see* **KUMONOSU-JO** (1957).

COBWEB, THE 1917 d: Cecil M. Hepworth. UKN., *The Cobweb*, Naunton Davies, Leon M. Lion, Play

COBWEB, THE 1955 d: Vincente Minnelli. USA., *The Cobweb*, William Gibson, 1954, Novel

COCA-COLA KID, THE 1985 d: Dusan Makavejev. ASL., Frank Moorhouse, Short Stories

COCAGNE 1960 d: Maurice Cloche. FRN/ITL., *Cocagne*, Yvan Audouard, Novel

Cochons N'ont Pas d'Ailes, Les *see* **DEUX DE L'ESCADRILLE** (1952).

COCK O' THE WALK 1930 d: R. William Neill, Walter Lang. USA., *Un Seguro Sobre la Dicha*, Arturo S. Mom, 1927, Short Story

Cock of the Walk *see* **DER FRONTGOCKEL** (1955).

Cockeyed Cruise, The *see* **MAD HOLIDAY** (1936).

Cockeyed Happiness *see* **ZEZOWATE SZCZESCIE** (1960).

COCKEYED MIRACLE, THE 1946 d: S. Sylvan Simon. USA., *The Cockeyed Miracle*, George Seaton, Play

COCK-EYED WORLD, THE 1929 d: Raoul Walsh. USA., *Tropical Twins*, Maxwell Anderson, Laurence Stallings, Play

COCKFIGHTER 1974 d: Monte Hellman. USA., *Cockfighter*, Charles Willeford, Novel

COCKLESHELL HEROES 1955 d: Jose Ferrer. UKN., *Cockleshell Heroes*, George Kent, Book

Cockpit, The *see* **THE LOST PEOPLE** (1949).

COCKROACH THAT ATE CINCINNATI, THE 1996 d: Michael McNamarA. CND., *The Cockroach Trilogy*, Alan Williams, Play

COCKTAIL 1988 d: Roger Donaldson. USA., *Cocktail*, J. Heywood Gould, Book

COCKTAIL HOUR 1933 d: Victor Schertzinger. USA., *Pearls and Emeralds*, James K. McGuinness, Story

Cocktails in the Kitchen *see* **FOR WORSE FOR BETTER** (1954).

Coco Chanel *see* **CHANEL SOLITAIRE** (1981).

COCOANUTS, THE 1929 d: Robert Florey, Joseph Santley. USA., *The Cocoanuts*, Irving Berlin, George S. Kaufman, New York 1925, Musical Play

COCOON 1985 d: Ron Howard. USA., *Cocoon*, David Saperstein, Novel

COCU MAGNIFIQUE, LE 1946 d: E. G. de Meyst. FRN/BLG., *Le Cocu Magnifique*, Fernand Crommelynck, Paris 1920, Play

Cocu Magnifique, Le *see* **IL MAGNIFICO CORNUTO** (1964).

C.O.D. 1915 d: Tefft Johnson. USA., *C.O.D.*, Frederic Chapin, New York 1912, Play

Code Criminel, Le *see* **CRIMINEL** (1932).

Code Name: Cobra *see* **LE SAUT DE L'ANGE** (1971).

CODE NAME: EMERALD 1985 d: Jonathan Sanger. USA., *The Emerald Illusion*, Ronald Bass, Novel

Code Name Is Kill *see* **LIEBESNACHTE IN DER TAIGA** (1967).

Code Name: Minus One *see* **GEMINI MAN** (1976).

Code of Honour, The *see* **A NIGHT OF MYSTERY** (1928).

Code of Scotland Yard, The *see* **THE SHOP AT SLY CORNER** (1947).

Code of the Mountains, The *see* **A WOMAN'S POWER** (1916).

CODE OF THE MOUNTED 1935 d: Sam Newfield. USA., *Wheels of Fate*, James Oliver Curwood

CODE OF THE WEST 1925 d: William K. Howard. USA., *Code of the West*, Zane Grey, New York 1924, Novel

Code of the West *see* **HOME ON THE RANGE** (1935).

CODE OF THE WEST 1947 d: William Berke. USA., *Code of the West*, Zane Grey, New York 1924, Novel

Code of Women *see* **JOKYO** (1960).

Code, The *see* **ADIEU L'AMI** (1968).

Codename: Coq Rouge *see* **TACKNAMEN: COQ ROUGE** (1989).

Codename Emerald *see* **CODE NAME: EMERALD** (1985).

CODIGO PENAL, EL 1931 d: Phil Rosen. USA., *The Criminal Code*, Martin Flavin, New York 1929, Play

CODINE 1962 d: Henri Colpi. FRN/RMN., *Codin*, Panait Istrati, 1926, Novel

Coeur aux Levres, La *see* **COL CUORE IN GOLA** (1967).

COEUR DE FRANCAISE 1916 d: Gaston Leprieur. FRN., *Coeur de Francaise*, Arthur Bernede, Aristide Bruant, Play

Coeur de Francaise *see* **CHANTECOQ** (1916).

COEUR D'HEROINE 1918. FRN., *Coeur d'Heroine*, Marcel Allain, Novel

COEUR DISPOSE, LE 1936 d: Georges Lacombe. FRN., *Le Coeur Dispose*, Francis de Croisset, Play

COEUR EBLOUI, LE 1938 d: Jean Vallee. FRN., *Le Coeur Ebloui*, Lucien Descaves, 1926, Play

Coeur Sur la Main, Le *see* **DEFENSE D'AIMER** (1942).

COEUR-SUR-MER 1950 d: Jacques Daniel-Norman. FRN., *Feysse Sur Mer*, Marcel-Eric Grancher, Novel

Coffin *see* **L' AFFAIRE COFFIN** (1980).

Coffin Affair, The *see* **L' AFFAIRE COFFIN** (1980).

Coffin from Hong Kong, A *see* **EIN SARG AUS HONGKONG** (1964).

Coffin of Terror *see* **DANZA MACABRA** (1964).

Coffin, The *see* **TRAFRACKEN** (1966).

Coffin, The *see* **LES COUSINES** (1969).

Coffre Et le Revenant, Le *see* **LES AMANTS DE TOLEDE** (1953).

COFFRET DE LAQUE, LE 1932 d: Jean Kemm. FRN., *Black Coffee*, Agatha Christie, Novel

COGNASSE 1932 d: Louis Mercanton. FRN., *Cognasse*, Rip, Play

Cohens and Kellys, The *see* **THE COHENS AND THE KELLYS** (1926).

COHENS AND THE KELLYS, THE 1926 d: Harry Pollard. USA., *Two Blocks Away*, Aaron Hoffman, New York 1925, Play

COHEN'S LUCK 1915 d: John H. Collins. USA., *Cohen's Luck*, Lee Arthur, Play

COIFFEUR POUR DAMES 1931 d: Rene Guissart. FRN., *Coiffeur Pour Dames*, Paul Armont, Marcel Gerbidon, Play

COILIN AND PLATONIDA 1976 d: James Scott. UKN., *Kotin and Platonida*, Nikolay Semyonovich Leskov, 1867, Short Story

COL CUORE IN GOLA 1967 d: Tinto Brass. ITL/FRN., *Il Sepolcro Di Carta*, Sergio Donati, Story

COL FERRO E COL FUOCO 1962 d: Fernando Cerchio. FRN/ITL/YGS., *Ogniem I Mieczem*, Henryk Sienkiewicz, 1884, Short Story

COLA DI RIENZI 1910 d: Mario Caserini. ITL., *Rienzi*, Edward George Bulwer Lytton, 1835, Novel

COLD COMFORT 1989 d: Vic Sarin. CND., *Cold Comfort*, James Garrard, Play

COLD COMFORT FARM 1968. UKN., *Cold Comfort Farm*, Stella Gibbons, 1933, Novel

COLD COMFORT FARM 1995 d: John Schlesinger. UKN., *Cold Comfort Farm*, Stella Gibbons, 1933, Novel

Cold Days *see* **HIDEG NAPOK** (1966).

COLD DOG SOUP 1989 d: Alan Metter. USA/UKN., *Cold Dog Soup*, Stephen Dobyns, Book

Cold Heart, The *see* **DAS KALTE HERZ** (1923).

Cold Heart, The *see* **DAS KALTE HERZ** (1930).

Cold Heart, The *see* **DAS KALTE HERZ** (1950).

COLD HEAVEN 1992 d: Nicolas Roeg. USA., *Cold Heaven*, Brian Moore, 1983, Novel

COLD LIGHT OF DAY, THE 1995 d: Rudolf Van Den Berg. NTH/UKN., *Es Geschah Am Hellichten Tag*, Friedrich Durrenmatt, Story

COLD RIVER 1981 d: Fred G. Sullivan. USA., *Cold River*, William Judson, Novel

COLD ROOM, THE 1983 d: James Dearden. UKN/USA., *The Cold Room*, Jeffrey Caine, Novel

COLD STEEL 1921 d: Sherwood MacDonald. USA., *In the Shadow of the Hills*, George Clifford Shedd, New York 1919, Novel

COLD SWEAT 1971 d: Terence Young. UKN/FRN/ITL., *Ride the Nightmare*, Richard Matheson, Novel

COLD TURKEY 1971 d: Norman Lear. USA., *I'm Giving Them Up for Good*, Margaret Rau, Neil Rau, Novel

COLD WIND IN AUGUST, A 1961 d: Alexander Singer. USA., *Cold Wind in August*, Burton Wohl, New York 1960, Novel

COLDITZ STORY, THE 1955 d: Guy Hamilton. UKN., *Colditz Story*, P. R. Reid, Book, *The Latter Days*, P. R. Reid, Book

COLE YOUNGER, GUNFIGHTER 1958 d: R. G. Springsteen. USA., *The Desperado*, Clifton Adams, Novel

COLLECTIONNEUSE, LA 1967 d: Eric Rohmer. FRN., *La Collectionneuse*, Eric Rohmer, 1974, Short Story

COLLECTOR, THE 1965 d: William Wyler. UKN/USA., *The Collector*, John Fowles, London 1963, Novel

Collector, The *see* LA COLLECTIONNEUSE (1967).

COLLEEN BAWN, THE 1911 d: Sidney Olcott. USA., *The Colleen Bawn*, Dion Boucicault, London 1860, Play

COLLEEN BAWN, THE 1924 d: W. P. Kellino. UKN., *The Colleen Bawn*, Dion Boucicault, London 1860, Play

COLLEGE WIDOW, THE 1915 d: Barry O'Neil. USA., *The College Widow*, George Ade, New York 1904, Play

COLLEGE WIDOW, THE 1927 d: Archie Mayo. USA., *The College Widow*, George Ade, New York 1904, Play

Collegians in Business *see* THE FOURFLUSHER (1928).

COLLEGIATE 1936 d: Ralph Murphy. USA., *The Charm School*, Alice Duer Miller, 1919, Short Story

COLLIER DE CHANVRE, LE 1940 d: Leon Mathot. FRN., *Le Collier de Chanvre*, Charles Lafaurie, Novel

Collier de la Reine, La *see* L' AFFAIRE DU COLLIER DE LA REINE (1911).

COLLIER DE LA REINE, LE 1929 d: Gaston Ravel, Tony Lekain. FRN., *Le Collier de la Reine*, Alexandre Dumas (pere), 1849-50, Novel

Colline du Bonheur, La *see* DER GLUCKSHOGER (1942).

COLLINE OUBLIEE, LA 1997 d: Abderrahmane Bouguermouh. ALG/FRN., *La Colline Oubliee*, Mouloud Mammeri, Novel

COLLISION 1932 d: G. B. Samuelson. UKN., *Collision*, E. C. Pollard, Play

Collision *see* THIEVES' HIGHWAY (1949).

COLMENA, LA 1983 d: Mario Camus. SPN., *La Colmena*, Camilo Jose Cela, 1951, Novel

Colmillo Blanco *see* ZANNA BIANCA (1973).

COLOMBA 1915 d: Travers Vale. USA., *Colomba*, Prosper Merimee, 1841, Novel

COLOMBA 1920 d: Jean Herve. FRN., *Colomba*, Prosper Merimee, 1841, Novel

COLOMBA 1933 d: Jacques Severac. FRN., *Colomba*, Prosper Merimee, 1841, Novel

COLOMBA 1947 d: Emile Couzinet. FRN., *Colomba*, Prosper Merimee, 1841, Novel

Colombo Night, A *see* ONE COLOMBO NIGHT (1926).

Colonel and the Werewolf, The *see* O CORONEL E O LOBISOMEM (1980).

Colonel and the Wolfman, The *see* O CORONEL E O LOBISOMEM (1980).

COLONEL CARTER OF CARTERSVILLE 1915 d: Howell Hansel. USA., *Colonel Carter of Cartersville*, F. Hopkinson Smith, New York 1891, Novel

Colonel Chabert *see* LE COLONEL CHABERT (1994).

COLONEL CHABERT, LE 1911 d: Andre Calmettes, Henri Pouctal. FRN., *Le Colonel Chabert*, Honore de Balzac, 1844, Novel

COLONEL CHABERT, LE 1943 d: Rene Le Henaff. FRN., *Le Colonel Chabert*, Honore de Balzac, 1844, Novel

COLONEL CHABERT, LE 1994 d: Yves Angelo. FRN., *Le Colonel Chabert*, Honore de Balzac, 1844, Novel

COLONEL DURAND, LE 1948 d: Rene Chanas. FRN., *Le Colonel Durand*, Jean Martet, Novel

COLONEL EFFINGHAM'S RAID 1945 d: Irving Pichel. USA., *Colonel Effingham's Raid*, Berry Fleming, Novel

COLONEL NEWCOME THE PERFECT GENTLEMAN 1920 d: Fred Goodwins. UKN., *The Newcomes*, William Makepeace Thackeray, Novel

COLONEL OF THE RED HUSSARS, THE 1914 d: Richard Ridgely. USA., *The Colonel of the Red Hussars*, John Reed Scott, Novel

Colonel Rowan of Scotland Yard *see* RAFFLES (1940).

Colonel Svec *see* PLUKOVNIK SVEC (1929).

Colonel Wolodyjowski *see* PAN WOLODYJOWSKI (1969).

COLONIA PENAL, LA 1971 d: Raul Ruiz. CHL., *In Der Strafkolonie*, Franz Kafka, 1919, Short Story

COLONNA INFAME, LA 1973 d: Nelo Risi. ITL., *La Colonna Infame*, Alessandro Manzoni, Novel

Colonne de Cendres *see* HOA-BINH (1970).

COLONNELLO BRIDEAU, IL 1917 d: Giuseppe Pinto. ITL., *La Rabouilleuse*, Honore de Balzac, Paris 1842, Novel

COLONNELLO CHABERT, IL 1920 d: Carmine Gallone. ITL., *Le Colonel Chabert*, Honore de Balzac, 1844, Novel

COLOR OF MONEY, THE 1987 d: Martin Scorsese. USA., *The Color of Money*, Walter S. Tevis, 1984, Novel

COLOR PURPLE, THE 1985 d: Steven Spielberg. USA., *The Color Purple*, Alice Walker, 1983, Novel

COLORADO 1915 d: Norval MacGregor. USA., *Colorado*, Augustus Thomas, New York 1901, Play

COLORADO 1921 d: B. Reeves Eason. USA., *Colorado*, Augustus Thomas, New York 1901, Play

COLORADO PLUCK 1921 d: Jules G. Furthman. USA., *Colorado Jim; Or the Taming of Angela*, George Goodchild, London 1920, Novel

COLORADO TERRITORY 1949 d: Raoul Walsh. USA., *High Sierra*, William Riley Burnett, 1940, Novel

Colossus 1980 *see* THE FORBIN PROJECT (1969).

Colossus the Forbin Project *see* THE FORBIN PROJECT (1969).

Colourful Life *see* AJIT (1948).

Colours *see* SZINES TINTAKROL ALMODOM (1980).

COLPA VENDICA LA COLPA, LA 1919 d: Eduardo BencivengA. ITL., *La Colpa Vendica la Colpa*, Paolo Giacometti, 1854, Play

COLPEVOLI, I 1957 d: Turi Vasile. ITL/FRN., *Sulle Strade Di Notte*, Renato Lelli, Play

COLPI DI TIMONE 1942 d: Gennaro Righelli. ITL., *Colpi Di Timone*, Enzo la Rosa, Play

COLPO DI PISTOLA, UN 1942 d: Renato Castellani. ITL., *Vystrel*, Alexander Pushkin, 1831, Short Story

COLPO DI VENTO, UN 1936 d: Charles-Felix Tavano, Jean Dreville. ITL., *Un Colpo Di Vento*, Giovacchino Forzano, Play

Colpo Grosso a Parigi *see* CENT BRIQUES ET DES TUILES (1965).

Colpo Grosso Al Casino *see* MELODIE EN SOUS-SOL (1962).

Colt, The *see* ZHEREBYONOK (1960).

COLTON, U.S.N. 1915 d: Paul Scardon. USA., *Colton U.S.N.*, Cyrus Townsend Brady, Play

Colui Che Deve Morire *see* CELUI QUI DOIT MOURIR (1956).

COLUMBUS 1923 d: Edwin L. Hollywood. USA., *The Spanish Conquerors*, Irving Berdine Richman, New Haven 1919, Novel

COMA 1978 d: Michael Crichton. USA., *Coma*, Robin Cook, Novel

Comanche Territory *see* TERRITORIO COMANCHE (1997).

COMANCHEROS, THE 1961 d: Michael Curtiz. USA., *The Comancheros*, Paul I. Wellman, New York 1952, Novel

Comando Suicida *see* COMMANDO SUICIDA (1968).

Comandos *see* COMMANDO SUICIDA (1968).

COMBAT DE FAUVES 1997 d: Benoit Lamy. BLG/GRM/FRN., *Combat de Fauves Au Crepuscule*, Henri-Frederic Blanc, Novel

COME ACROSS 1929 d: Ray Taylor. USA., *The Stolen Lady*, William Dudley Pelley, Story

COME AGAIN SMITH 1919 d: E. Mason Hopper. USA., *Come Again Smith*, John H. Blackwood, Story

Come Along, My Dearest *see* MEIN LIEBSTES VOGELEIN KOMM NUR (1968).

COME AND GET IT! 1936 d: Howard Hawks, William Wyler. USA., *Come and Get It*, Edna Ferber, New York 1935, Novel

COME AND GO 1986 d: Nik Houghton. UKN., *Va Et Vient*, Samuel Beckett, 1966, Play

Come and See *see* IDI I SMOTRI (1986).

COME BACK, CHARLESTON BLUE 1972 d: Mark Warren. USA., *The Heat's on*, Chester Himes, 1966, Novel

COME BACK, LITTLE SHEBA 1952 d: Daniel Mann. USA., *Come Back Little Sheba*, William Inge, New York 1950, Play

COME BACK, LITTLE SHEBA 1977 d: Silvio Narizzano. UKN., *Come Back Little Sheba*, William Inge, New York 1950, Play

COME BACK PETER 1952 d: Charles Saunders. UKN., *Come Back Peter*, A. P. Dearsley, Play

Come Back to Me *see* DOLL FACE (1945).

COME BACK TO THE FIVE AND DIME, JIMMY DEAN, JIMMY DEAN 1982 d: Robert Altman. USA., *Come Back to the Five and Dime Jimmy Dean Jimmy Dean*, Ed Graczyck, Play

COME BLOW YOUR HORN 1963 d: Bud Yorkin. USA., *Come Blow Your Horn*, Neil Simon, New York 1961, Play

Come Dance With Me *see* VOULEZ-VOUS DANSER AVEC MOI? (1960).

COME FILL THE CUP 1951 d: Gordon Douglas. USA., *Come Fill the Cup*, Harlan Ware, Novel

COME FLY WITH ME 1963 d: Henry Levin. UKN/USA., *Girl on a Wing*, Bernard Glemser, Novel

COME FU CHE MASUCCIO SALERNITANO, FUGGENDO CON LE BRACHE IN MANO, RIUSCI A CONSERVALO SANO 1973 d: Silvio Amadio. ITL., *Novelliere*, Tommaso Guardati

Come Have Coffee With Us *see* VENGA A PRENDERE IL CAFFE DA NOI (1970).

COME LE FOGLIE 1917 d: Gennaro Righelli. ITL., *Come le Foglie*, Giuseppe Giacosa, 1900, Play

COME LE FOGLIE 1934 d: Mario Camerini. ITL., *Come le Foglie*, Giuseppe Giacosa, 1900, Play

Come Now, My Dear Little Bird *see* MEIN LIEBSTES VOGELEIN KOMM NUR (1968).

COME ON, THE 1956 d: Russell J. Birdwell. USA., *The Come on*, Whitman Chambers, Novel

Come Out of Kitchen *see* COME OUT OF THE KITCHEN (1919).

COME OUT OF THE KITCHEN 1919 d: John S. Robertson. USA., *Come Out of the Kitchen!*, Alice Duer Miller, New York 1916, Novel

Come Out of the Kitchen *see* HONEY (1930).

COME OUT OF THE PANTRY 1935 d: Jack Raymond. UKN., *Come Out of the Kitchen!*, Alice Duer Miller, New York 1916, Novel

Come, Quando, Con Chi? *see* QUANDO, PERCHE COME (1968).

COME, QUANDO, PERCHE 1968 d: Antonio Pietrangeli, Valerio Zurlini. ITL., *Amour Terre Inconnue*, Martin Maurice, Novel

Come Share My Love *see* NEVER A DULL MOMENT (1950).

Come Sposare un Primo Ministre *see* COMMENT EPOUSER UN PREMIER MINISTRE (1964).

COME TE MOVI, TE FULMINO! 1958 d: Mario Mattoli. ITL., *Un Paio d'Ali*, Pietro Garinei, Sandro Giovannini, Musical Play

Come Ti Rapisco Il Pupo *see* CINQUE FURBASTRI E UN FURBACCHIONE (1977).

COME TO MY HOUSE 1927 d: Alfred E. Green. USA., *Come to My House*, Arthur Somers Roche, New York 1927, Novel

COME TO THE STABLE 1949 d: Henry Koster. USA., *Come to the Stable*, Clare Boothe Luce, Story

Come Vuoi. *see* KIFF TEBBY (1928).

COMEDIA INFANTIL 1998 d: Solveig Nordlund. SWD/MZM/PRT., *Comedia Infantil*, Henning Mankell, Novel

COMEDIANS 1979 d: Richard Eyre. UKN., *Comedians*, Trevor Griffiths, 1976, Play

COMEDIANS, THE 1967 d: Peter Glenville. USA/FRN., *The Comedians*, Graham Greene, New York 1966, Novel

COMEDIANTE, EL 1931 d: Ernesto Vilches, Leonard Fields. USA., *Sullivan*, Melesville

COMEDIE DU BONHEUR, LA 1940 d: Marcel L'Herbier. FRN., *La Comedie du Bonheur*, Nicolas Evreinov, Play

Comedienne *see* KOMEDIANTKA (1987).

Comediens, Les *see* THE COMEDIANS (1967).

COMEDY AT HAGERSKOG *see* KOMEDI I HAGERSKOG (1968).

COMEDY MAN, THE 1963 d: Alvin Rakoff. UKN., *The Comedy Man*, Douglas Hayes, Novel

COMEDY OF ERRORS, THE 1984 d: James Cellan Jones. UKN., *The Comedy of Errors*, William Shakespeare, c1594, Play

Comedy of Happiness, The *see* LA COMEDIE DU BONHEUR (1940).

Come-on, The *see* THE COME ON (1956).

Comes a Time *see* SILENCE OF THE NORTH (1981).

COMET OVER BROADWAY 1938 d: Busby Berkeley. USA., *Comet Over Broadway*, Faith Baldwin, 1937, Story

717

COMFORT OF STRANGERS, THE 1991 d: Paul Schrader. USA/ITL., *The Comfort of Strangers*, Ian McEwan, 1981, Novel

COMFORTS OF HOME 1974 d: Jerome Shore. USA., *Comforts of Home*, Flannery O'Connor, 1955, Short Story

COMIN' THRO' THE RYE 1916 d: Cecil M. Hepworth. UKN., *Comin' Thro' the Rye*, Helen Mathers, Novel

COMIN' THRO' THE RYE 1923 d: Cecil M. Hepworth. UKN., *Comin' Thro' the Rye*, Helen Mathers, Novel

Coming Back from Hell see **INTOARCEREA DIN IAD** (1984).

COMING HOME 1913 d: Wilfred Noy. UKN., *Coming Home*, Alfred Berlyn, Poem

COMING HOME 1978 d: Hal Ashby. USA., Nancy Dowd, Story

Coming of Stork, The see **STORK** (1971).

COMING OF THE LAW, THE 1919 d: Arthur Rosson. USA., *The Coming of the Law*, Charles Alden Seltzer, New York 1912, Novel

COMING OUT OF MAGGIE, THE 1917 d: Martin Justice. USA., *The Coming Out of Maggie*, O. Henry, Short Story

COMING PLAGUE, THE 1997 d: Ned Judge. USA., *The Coming Plague*, Laurie Garrett, Book

COMING THROUGH 1925 d: A. Edward Sutherland. USA., *Bed Rock*, Jack Bethea, Boston 1924, Novel

COMMAND DECISION 1948 d: Sam Wood. USA., *Command Decision*, William Wister Haines, New York 1947, Play

COMMAND PERFORMANCE 1931 d: Walter Lang. USA., *The Command Performance*, C. Stafford Dickens, New York 1928, Play

COMMAND PERFORMANCE 1937 d: Sinclair Hill. UKN., *The Command Performance*, C. Stafford Dickens, New York 1928, Play

COMMAND, THE 1953 d: David Butler. USA., *The White Invader*, James Warner Bellah, Novel

COMMANDING OFFICER, THE 1915 d: Allan Dwan. USA., *The Commanding Officer*, Theodore Burt Sayre, New York 1909, Play

COMMANDO SUICIDA 1968 d: Camillo Bazzoni. ITL/SPN., *Commando 44*, Piet Legay, Novel

COMMANDOS STRIKE AT DAWN 1942 d: John Farrow. USA., C. S. Forester, Story

Comme En 14 see **LE TATOUE** (1968).

Comme Mars En Careme see **NE JOUEZ PAS AVEC LES MARTIANS** (1967).

Commedia Della Felicita, La see **ECCO LA FELICITA!** (1940).

COMMENT EPOUSER UN PREMIER MINISTRE 1964 d: Michel Boisrond. FRN/ITL., Mari-Luisa de Linares, Short Story

COMMENT FAIRE L'AMOUR AVEC UN NEGRE SANS SE FATIGUER 1988 d: Jacques W. Benoit. CND/FRN., *Comment Faire l'Amour Avec un Negro Sans Se Fatiguer*, Dany Laferriere, Novel

COMMENT J'AI TUE MON ENFANT 1925 d: Alexandre Ryder. FRN., *Comment J'ai Tue Mon Enfant*, Pierre L'Ermite, Novel

COMMENT QU'ELLE EST? 1960 d: Bernard Borderie. FRN., *Comment Qu'elle Est*, Peter Cheyney, Novel

COMMERCE TRANQUILLE, UN 1964 d: Mel Welles, Guido Franco. SWT/UKN., *La Maison Tellier*, Guy de Maupassant, 1881, Short Story

COMMISSAIRE EST BON ENFANT, LE GENDARME EST SANS PITIE, LE 1934 d: Jacques Becker, Pierre Prevert. FRN., *Le Commissaire Est Bon Enfant*, Georges Courteline, 1899, Play

Commissaire X Traque Les Chiens Verts see **KOMMISSAR X: DREI GRUNE HUNDE** (1967).

Commissar see **KOMISSAR** (1967).

Commissario Pellissier, Il see **MAX ET LES FERRAILLEURS** (1970).

COMMISSARIO PEPE, IL 1969 d: Ettore ScolA. ITL., *Il Commissario Pepe*, Ugo Facco de Lagardo, Novel

Commissione Parlamentare d'Inchiesta Sul Fenomeno Della Mafia in Sicilia see **LA VIOLENZA: QUINTO POTERE** (1972).

COMMISSIONER, THE 1998 d: George Sluizer. GRM/UKN/BLG., *The Commissioner*, Stanley Johnson, Novel

Commissioner X - Three Golden Snakes see **KOMMISSAR X: DREI GOLDENE SCHLANGEN** (1968).

Commissioner X - Unknown Prey see **KOMMISSAR X: JAGD AUF UNBEKANNT** (1965).

Commissioner X Chases the Red Tigers see **KOMMISSAR X: JAGT DIE ROTEN TIGER** (1971).

Commissioner X -Three Blue Panthers see **KOMMISSAR X: DREI BLAUE PANTHER** (1968).

Commissioner X -Three Green Dogs see **KOMMISSAR X: DREI GRUNE HUNDE** (1967).

COMMON CAUSE, THE 1918 d: J. Stuart Blackton. USA., *Getting Together*, Ian Hay, P. Knight, J. Hartley Manners, New York 1918, Musical Play

COMMON CLAY 1919 d: George Fitzmaurice. USA., *Common Clay*, Cleves Kinkead, Boston 1915, Play

COMMON CLAY 1930 d: Victor Fleming. USA., *Common Clay*, Cleves Kinkead, Boston 1915, Play

Common Ground, The see **FRISCO JENNY** (1933).

COMMON LAW, THE 1916 d: Albert Capellani. USA., *The Common Law*, Robert W. Chambers, New York 1911, Novel

COMMON LAW, THE 1923 d: George Archainbaud. USA., *The Common Law*, Robert W. Chambers, New York 1911, Novel

COMMON LAW, THE 1931 d: Paul L. Stein. USA., *The Common Law*, Robert W. Chambers, New York 1911, Novel

COMMON PURSUIT 1991 d: Christopher Morahan. UKN., *The Common Pursuit*, Simon Gray, 1984, Play

COMMON SIN, THE 1920 d: Burton L. King. USA., *The Common Sin*, Willard Mack, Story

COMMON TOUCH, THE 1941 d: John Baxter. UKN., *The Common Touch*, Herbert Ayres, Novel

COMMUNION 1989 d: Philippe MorA. USA., *Communion*, Whitley Strieber, Book

COMMUTERS, THE 1915 d: George Fitzmaurice. USA., *The Commuters*, James Forbes, New York 1910, Play

Commutors, The see **THE COMMUTERS** (1915).

COMO AGUA PARA CHOCOLATE 1991 d: Alfonso Arau. MXC., *Como Agua Para Chocolate*, Laura Esquivel, Novel

COMO LEVANTAR 1000 KILOS 1991 d: Antonio Hernandez. SPN., *Galvez En Euskadi*, Jorge Martinez Reverte, Novel

Como Levantar Mil Kilos see **COMO LEVANTAR 1000 KILOS** (1991).

COMPACT, THE 1912 d: Joseph A. Golden. USA., *The Compact*, Katherine Cecil Thurston, Novel

COMPADECIDA, A 1969 d: George Joanas. BRZ., *Auto Da Compadecida*, Ariano Suassuna, 1959, Play

COMPAGNIA DEI MATTI, LA 1928 d: Mario Almirante. ITL., *Se No I Xe Mati No Li Volemo*, Gino Rocca, 1926, Play

Compagnia Dei Matti, La see **SE NON SON MATTI NO LI VOGLIAMO** (1941).

COMPAGNO DON CAMILLO, IL 1965 d: Luigi Comencini. ITL/FRN/GRM., *Il Compagno Don Camillo*, Giovanni Guareschi, Novel

COMPANIONATE MARRIAGE, THE 1928 d: Erle C. Kenton. USA., *The Companionate Marriage*, Wainwright Evans, Benjamin B. Lindsey, New York 1927, Novel

Company Limited see **SEEMABADHA** (1971).

Company of Cowards see **ADVANCE TO THE REAR** (1964).

COMPANY OF WOLVES, THE 1984 d: Neil Jordan. UKN., Angela Carter, Short Story

Comparison of Heights see **TAKEKURABE** (1955).

COMPARTIMENT DE DAMES SEULES 1934 d: Christian-Jaque. FRN., *Compartiment de Dames Seules*, Maurice Hennequin, George Mitchell, Play

COMPARTIMENT TUEURS 1965 d: Costa-Gavras. FRN., *Compartiment Tueurs*, Sebastien Japrisot, Paris 1962, Novel

COMPASSION 1927 d: Victor Adamson, Norval MacGregor. USA., *Wings*, Beth Slater Whitson, Story

Compassionate One, The see **A COMPADECIDA** (1969).

Complete State of Death see **THE STONE KILLER** (1973).

Complete Surrender see **LAUGHING SINNERS** (1931).

Complexe de Philemon, Le see **CHERIE RELAXE-TOI** (1964).

Complicated Girl, A see **UNA RAGAZZA PIUTTOSTA COMPLICATA** (1968).

Compliments of Mr. Flow see **MISTER FLOW** (1936).

COMPLIMENTS OF THE SEASON 1918 d: Ashley Miller. USA., *Compliments of the Season*, O. Henry, Short Story

COMPO 1988 d: Nigel Buesst. ASL., *Claim No. Z84*, Abe Pogos, Play

COMPRADOR DE FAZENDAS, O 1951 d: Alberto Pieralisi. BRZ., *O Comprador de Fazendas*, Monteiro Lobato, 1918, Short Story

COMPRADOR DE FAZENDAS, O 1974 d: Alberto Pieralisi. BRZ., *O Comprador de Fazendas*, Monteiro Lobato, 1918, Short Story

COMPROMISE 1925 d: Alan Crosland. USA., *Compromise*, Jay Gelzer, New York 1923, Novel

Compromised! see **COMPROMISING DAPHNE** (1930).

Compromised see **LILY OF THE DUST** (1924).

COMPROMISED 1931 d: John G. Adolfi. USA., *Compromised*, Edith Fitzgerald, Play

COMPROMISING DAPHNE 1930 d: Thomas Bentley. UKN., *Compromised*, Edith Fitzgerald, Play

COMPROMISING POSITIONS 1985 d: Frank Perry. USA., *Compromising Positions*, Susan Isaacs, Novel

COMPULSION 1959 d: Richard Fleischer. USA., *Compulsion*, Meyer Levin, 1956, Novel

COMPULSORY HUSBAND, THE 1930 d: Monty Banks, Harry Lachman. UKN., *The Compulsory Husband*, John Glyder, Novel

COMPULSORY WIFE, THE 1937 d: Arthur Woods. UKN., *The Compulsory Wife*, John Glyder, Play

COMRADE JOHN 1915 d: T. Hayes Hunter. USA., *Comrade John*, Samuel Merwin, Henry Kitchell Webster, New York 1907, Novel

Comrades see **THE BUGLER OF ALGIERS** (1916).

Comrades of 1918 see **WESTFRONT 1918** (1930).

COMTE DE MONTE-CRISTO, LE 1917 d: Henri Pouctal. FRN., *Le Comte de Monte-Cristo*, Alexandre Dumas (pere), Paris 1845, Novel

Comte de Monte-Cristo, Le see **MONTE-CRISTO** (1928).

COMTE DE MONTE-CRISTO, LE 1942 d: Robert Vernay, Ferruccio Cerio. FRN/ITL., *Le Comte de Monte-Cristo*, Alexandre Dumas (pere), Paris 1845, Novel

COMTE DE MONTE-CRISTO, LE 1953 d: Robert Vernay. FRN/ITL., *Le Comte de Monte-Cristo*, Alexandre Dumas (pere), Paris 1845, Novel

COMTE DE MONTE-CRISTO, LE 1961 d: Claude Autant-LarA. FRN/ITL., *Le Comte de Monte-Cristo*, Alexandre Dumas (pere), Paris 1845, Novel

COMTE DE MONTE-CRISTO, LE 1979 d: Denys de La Patelliere. FRN., *Le Comte de Monte-Cristo*, Alexandre Dumas (pere), Paris 1845, Novel

COMTE KOSTIA, LE 1924 d: Jacques Robert. FRN/GRM., *Le Comte Kostia*, Victor Cherbuliez, Novel

COMTE OBLIGADO, LE 1934 d: Leon Mathot. FRN., *Le Comte Obligado*, Andre Barde, Opera

COMTESSE DE SOMMERIVE, LA 1917 d: Jean Kemm, Georges DenolA. FRN., *La Comtesse de Sommerive*, Theodore Barriere, Play

Comtesse Marie, La see **LA CONDESA MARIA** (1927).

COMTESSE SARAH, LA 1912 d: Henri Pouctal. FRN., *La Comtesse Sarah*, Georges Ohnet, 1887, Novel

CON EL VIENTO SOLANO 1968 d: Mario Camus. SPN., *Con El Viento Solano*, Ignacio Aldecoa, 1956, Novel

Concealment see **SECRET BRIDE** (1934).

Concerning Love see **DE L'AMOUR** (1964).

Concert a la Cour see **LA CHANSON DU SOUVENIR** (1936).

Concert, Le see **NACH DEM STURM** (1948).

CONCERT, THE 1921 d: Victor Schertzinger. USA., *Das Konzert*, Hermann Bahr, 1909, Play

Concertina see **PRINCESS COMES ACROSS** (1936).

Concerto see **I'VE ALWAYS LOVED YOU** (1946).

Concerto de la Peur, La see **LA DROGUE DU VICE** (1963).

CONCHITA 1954 d: Hans Hinrich, Franz Eichhorn. GRM/BRZ., *Conchita Und Der Ingenieur*, Franz Taut, Novel

Conchita and the Engineer see **CONCHITA** (1954).

Conchita Und Der Ingenieur see **CONCHITA** (1954).

CONCIERGE REVIENT DE SUITE, LE 1937 d: Fernand Rivers. FRN., *Le Concierge Revient de Suite*, Leon Belieres, Jean Kolb, Play

Concile d'Amour, Le see **DAS LIEBESKONZIL** (1981).

Concilio d'Amore see **DAS LIEBESKONZIL** (1981).

Concrete Wilderness see **MEDIUM COOL** (1969).

Concubines, The see **CHIN-P'ING-MEI** (1969).

CONDANNATA SENZA COLPA 1954 d: Luigi de Marchi. ITL., *Maria Zef*, Paola Drigo, 1936, Novel

CONDE DE MARAVILLAS, EL 1927 d: Jose Buchs. SPN., *El Caballero de Harmental*, Alexandre Dumas (pere), Novel

CONDE DE MONTECRISTO, EL 1941 d: Chano UruetA. MXC., *Le Comte de Monte-Cristo*, Alexandre Dumas (pere), Paris 1845, Novel

CONDE DE MONTECRISTO, EL 1953 d: Leon Klimovsky. ARG/SPN., *Le Comte de Monte-Cristo*, Alexandre Dumas (pere), Paris 1845, Novel

CONDE DRACULA, EL 1970 d: Jesus Franco. SPN/GRM/ITL., *Dracula*, Bram Stoker, London 1897, Novel

Conde Sandorf, El see **MATHIAS SANDORF** (1962).

CONDE, UN 1970 d: Yves Boisset. FRN/ITL., *Un Conde*, Pierre Vial-Lesou, Novel

CONDEMNED 1929 d: Wesley Ruggles. USA., *Condemned to Devil's Island*, Blair Niles, New York 1928, Novel

Condemned and Possessed see **POSSESSION DU CONDAMNE** (1967).

Condemned of Altona, The see **I SEQUESTRATI DI ALTONA** (1962).

Condemned Row see **WE WHO ARE ABOUT TO DIE** (1936).

Condemned, The see **OS CONDENADOS** (1974).

CONDEMNED TO DEATH 1932 d: Walter Forde. UKN., *Jack O'Lantern*, George Goodchild, Play

Condemned to Devil's Island see **CONDEMNED** (1929).

CONDENADOS, OS 1974 d: Zelito VianA. BRZ., *Os Condenados*, Oswald de Andrade, 1922, Novel

CONDESA MARIA, LA 1927 d: Benito Perojo, Alexandre KamenkA. SPN/FRN., *La Condesa Maria*, Juan Ignacio Luca de Tena, Play

Conditional Bequest, A see **UNA CURIOSA EREDITA** (1914).

CONDOMINIUM 1979 d: Sidney Hayers. USA., *Condiminium*, John D. MacDonald, Novel

Condominium: When the Hurricane Struck see **CONDOMINIUM** (1979).

CONDORMAN 1981 d: Charles Jarrott. UKN., *The Game of X*, Robert Sheckley, Novel

Condor's Nest see **TREASURE OF THE GOLDEN CONDOR** (1953).

Conduct Report of Professor Ishinaka see **ISHINAKA SENSEI GYOJOKI** (1950).

Conduct Report on Professor Ishinawa see **ISHINAKA SENSEI GYOJOKI** (1950).

CONDUCT UNBECOMING 1975 d: Michael Anderson. UKN., *Conduct Unbecoming*, Barry England, Play

Conduct Unsatisfactory see **KANTOR IDEAL** (1932).

CONDUISEZ-MOI, MADAME 1932 d: Herbert Selpin. FRN., *Chauffeur Antoinette*, Blum, Jean de Letraz, Suzette Desty, Play

CONE OF SILENCE 1960 d: Charles Frend. UKN., *Cone of Silence*, David Beaty, London 1959, Novel

CONEY ISLAND PRINCESS, A 1916 d: Dell Henderson. USA., *The Princess Zim-Zim*, Edward Sheldon, Albany, Ny. 1911, Play

CONFESSION 1955 d: Ken Hughes. UKN., *Confession*, Don Martin, Play

Confession Box, The see **ZPOVEDNICE** (1928).

Confession Corner see **CONFESSIONS** (1925).

Confession de Minuit, La see **LES AVENTURES DE SALAVIN** (1963).

Confession of a Child of the Century, A see **SPOWIEDZ DZIECIECIA WIEKU** (1985).

Confession of Brother Medardus, The see **HET HEKSENLIED** (1928).

CONFESSION, THE 1920 d: Bertram Bracken. USA., *The Confession*, Hal Reid, New York 1911, Play

Confession, The see **L' AVEU** (1970).

Confession With One Listener see **GESTANDNIS UNTER VIER AUGEN** (1954).

Confessione, La see **L' AVEU** (1970).

CONFESSIONI DI UN FIGLIO DEL SECOLO, LE 1921 d: Gian Bistolfi. ITL., *La Confession d'un Enfant du Siecle*, Alfred de Musset, 1836, Novel

CONFESSIONS 1925 d: W. P. Kellino. UKN., *Confession Corner*, Mrs. Baillie Reynolds, Novel

CONFESSIONS FROM THE DAVID GALAXY AFFAIR 1979 d: Willy Roe. UKN., *Confessions from the David Galaxy Affair*, George Evans, Novel

Confessions of a Blood Cop see **UN CONDE** (1970).

Confessions of a Counterspy see **MAN ON A STRING** (1960).

CONFESSIONS OF A DRIVING INSTRUCTOR 1976 d: Norman Cohen. UKN., *Confessions of a Driving Instructor*, Timothy Lea, Novel

Confessions of a Gentleman see **BEKENNTNISSE EINES MOBLIERTEN HERRN** (1962).

CONFESSIONS OF A POP PERFORMER 1975 d: Norman Cohen. UKN., *Confessions from the Pop Scene*, Timothy Lea, Novel

CONFESSIONS OF A QUEEN 1925 d: Victor Sjostrom. USA., *Les Rois En Exil*, Alphonse Daudet, Paris 1879, Novel

Confessions of a Servant Girl see **PRIVATE NUMBER** (1936).

CONFESSIONS OF A WIFE 1928 d: Albert Kelley. USA., *Confession of a Wife; Or from Mill to Millions*, Owen Davis, Story

CONFESSIONS OF AN OPIUM EATER 1962 d: Albert Zugsmith. USA., *Confessions of an English Opium Eater*, Thomas de Quincey, 1821, Short Story

Confessions of Felix Krull see **BEKENNTNISSE DES HOCHSTAPLERS FELIX KRULL** (1957).

Confessions of Ina Kahr, The see **DAS BEKENNTNIS DER INA KAHR** (1954).

Confessions of the Con-Man Felix Krull see **BEKENNTNISSE DES HOCHSTAPLERS FELIX KRULL** (1957).

Confessions of the Con-Man Felix Krull see **BEKENNTNISSE DES HOCHSTAPLERS FELIX KRULL** (1981).

CONFIDENCE MAN, THE 1924 d: Victor Heerman. USA., *The Confidence Man*, Laurie York Erskine, New York 1925, Novel

CONFIDENTIAL AGENT 1945 d: Herman Shumlin. USA., *The Confidential Agent*, Graham Greene, 1939, Novel

Confidential File see **CONFIDENTIAL REPORT** (1955).

CONFIDENTIAL REPORT 1955 d: Orson Welles. UKN/SWT/SPN., *Mr. Arkadin*, Orson Welles, Novel

Confidentially Yours see **VIVEMENT DIMANCHE** (1983).

CONFISSOES DE UMA VIUVA MOCA 1975 d: Adnor PitangA. BRZ., *Confissoes de Uma Viuva Moca*, Joaquim Maria Machado de Assis, 1870, Short Story

Conflagration see **ENJO** (1958).

Conflict see **THE WOMAN BETWEEN** (1931).

CONFLICT 1936 d: David Howard. USA., *The Abysmal Brute*, Jack London, New York 1913, Novel

Conflict see **JUDITH** (1966).

Conflict see **SANGHARSH** (1968).

CONFLICT OF WINGS 1954 d: John Eldridge. UKN., *Conflict of Wings*, Don Sharp, Novel

CONFLICT, THE 1921 d: Stuart Paton. USA., *Conflict*, Clarence Budington Kelland, Novel

Conflict, The see **CATHOLICS** (1973).

CONFLIT 1938 d: Leonide Moguy. FRN., *Les Soeurs Kleh*, Gina Kaus, Novel

Conformist, The see **IL CONFORMISTA** (1970).

CONFORMISTA, IL 1970 d: Bernardo Bertolucci. ITL/FRN/GRM., *Il Conformista*, Alberto Moravia, 1951, Novel

Conformiste, Le see **IL CONFORMISTA** (1970).

Confusion see **PEREPOLOH** (1955).

CONG MING DE REN 1958 d: Xu Tao. CHN., *The Indigenous Specialist*, Li Zhun, Wang Yanfei, Play

Congiura Dei Dieci, La see **LE MERCENAIRE** (1962).

CONGIURA DEI FIESCHI, LA 1921 d: Ugo FalenA. ITL., *Der Verschwurung de Fiesko Zu Genua*, Friedrich von Schiller, 1784, Play

Congiura Dei Potenti, La see **LE MIRACLE DES LOUPS** (1961).

CONGIURA DI FIESCHI, LA 1911. ITL/FRN., *Fiesco*, Friedrich von Schiller, 1783, Play

Congiura Di Spie see **PEAU D'ESPION** (1967).

CONGO 1995 d: Frank Marshall. USA., *Congo*, Michael Crichton, Novel

Congo Hell see **SETTE BASCHI ROSSI** (1968).

CONGO MAISIE 1939 d: H. C. Potter. USA., *Congo Landing*, Wilson Collison, New York 1934, Novel

Congres de Clermont-Ferrand, Le see **TANT QU'IL Y AURA DES FEMMES** (1955).

Conjuration de Fiesco (1547), La see **LA CONGIURA DI FIESCHI** (1911).

Conjure Wife see **NIGHT OF THE EAGLE** (1962).

CONJURE WOMAN, THE 1926 d: Oscar Micheaux. USA., *The Conjure Woman*, Charles Chestnutt, Novel

Conjuror's House, The see **THE CALL OF THE NORTH** (1921).

CONNECTICUT YANKEE, A 1931 d: David Butler. USA., *A Connecticut Yankee in King Arthur's Court*, Mark Twain, New York 1889, Novel

CONNECTICUT YANKEE AT KING ARTHUR'S COURT, A 1920 d: Emmett J. Flynn. USA., *A Connecticut Yankee in King Arthur's Court*, Mark Twain, New York 1889, Novel

Connecticut Yankee in King Arthur's Court, A see **A CONNECTICUT YANKEE** (1931).

CONNECTICUT YANKEE IN KING ARTHUR'S COURT, A 1948 d: Tay Garnett. USA., *A Connecticut Yankee in King Arthur's Court*, Mark Twain, New York 1889, Novel

CONNECTICUT YANKEE IN KING ARTHUR'S COURT, A 1989 d: Mel Damski. USA., *A Connecticut Yankee in King Arthur's Court*, Mark Twain, New York 1889, Novel

CONNECTING LINK, THE 1915 d: Joseph J. Franz. USA., *The Connecting Link*, Burton Wilson, Story

CONNECTING ROOMS 1969 d: Franklin Gollings. UKN., *The Cellist*, Marion Hart, Play

CONNECTION, THE 1962 d: Shirley Clarke. USA., *The Connection*, Jack Gelber, New York 1959, Play

Conquerants Heroiques, Les see **LA LEGGENDA DI ENEA** (1962).

Conquered By Love see **VON DER LIEBE BESIEGT** (1956).

Conquered City see **LA CITTA PRIGIONERA** (1962).

CONQUERING HORDE, THE 1931 d: Edward Sloman. USA., *North of 36*, Emerson Hough, New York 1923, Novel

CONQUERING THE WOMAN 1922 d: King Vidor. USA., *Kidnapping Coline*, Henry C. Rowland, 1914, Short Story

Conqueror and the Empress, The see **SANDOKAN ALLA RISCOSSA** (1964).

Conqueror of the Desert see **FORTUNE CARREE** (1954).

CONQUEROR, THE 1956 d: Dick Powell. USA., *A Caravan to Camul*, John Clou, Book

Conqueror Worm see **WITCHFINDER GENERAL** (1968).

Conquerors of Arkansas see **DIE GOLDSUCHER VON ARKANSAS** (1964).

Conquerors, The see **THE FRANCO-GERMAN INVASION, THE WAR OF WARS; OR** (1914).

CONQUEST 1928 d: Roy Del Ruth. USA., *Conquest*, Mary Imlay Taylor, Story

CONQUEST 1937 d: Clarence Brown. USA., *Pani Walewska*, Waclaw Gasiorowski, Book

CONQUEST OF CANAAN, THE 1916 d: George Irving. USA., *The Conquest of Canaan*, Booth Tarkington, New York 1905, Novel

CONQUEST OF CANAAN, THE 1921 d: R. William Neill. USA., *The Conquest of Canaan*, Booth Tarkington, New York 1905, Novel

Conquest of Chile see **LA ARAUCANA** (1970).

CONQUEST OF SPACE 1955 d: Byron Haskin. USA., *Conquest of Space*, Chesley Bonestell, Willy Ley, 1949, Book

Conquest of the Citadel, The see **DIE EROBERUNG DER ZITADELLE** (1976).

CONQUEST OF THE SOUTH POLE 1989 d: Gillies MacKinnon. UKN., *Conquest of the South Pole*, Manfred Karge, Play

Conquests of Peter the Great, The see **PYOTR PERVY** (1937-39).

Conquete Dramatique du Mont Cervin, La see **DER KAMPF UMS MATTERHORN** (1928).

CONRACK 1974 d: Martin Ritt. USA., *The Water Is Wide*, Pat Conroy, Novel

CONRAD IN QUEST OF HIS YOUTH 1920 d: William C. de Mille. USA., *Conrad in Quest of His Youth*, Leonard Merrick, London 1903, Novel

Conscience see DIE SACHE MIT SCHORRSIEGEL (1928).

CONSCIENCE DE PEONES, LA 1917. FRN., *La Conscience de Peones*, Georges le Faure, Short Story

Conscript, The see DE LOTELING (1974).

Conscrit, Le see DE LOTELING (1974).

CONSENTING ADULT 1985 d: Gilbert Cates. USA., *Consenting Adult*, Laura Z. Hobson, Novel

Consequence, The see DIE KONSEQUENZ (1977).

CONSIDER YOUR VERDICT 1938 d: Roy Boulting. UKN., *Consider Your Verdict*, Laurence Houseman, Radio Play

CONSPIRACY 1930 d: W. Christy Cabanne. USA., *Conspiracy*, Robert Melville Baker, John Emerson, New York 1913, Novel

CONSPIRACY AGAINST THE KING, A 1911 d: J. Searle Dawley. USA., *The Cockerel*, H. B. Marriott Watson, Story

CONSPIRACY OF TERROR 1975 d: John Llewellyn Moxey. USA., *Conspiracy of Terror*, David Delman, Book

CONSPIRACY, THE 1914 d: Allan Dwan. USA., *The Conspiracy*, Robert B. Baker, John Emerson, New York 1912, Play

CONSPIRATOR 1949 d: Victor Saville. UKN/USA., *Conspirator*, Humphrey Slater, Novel

CONSPIRATORS, THE 1924 d: Sinclair Hill. UKN., *The Conspirators*, E. Phillips Oppenheim, London 1907, Novel

CONSPIRATORS, THE 1944 d: Jean Negulesco. USA., *City of Shadows*, Frederic Prokosch, Novel

CONSTABLE'S MOVE, THE 1923 d: Manning Haynes. UKN., *Captains All*, W. W. Jacobs, Short Story

CONSTANCE AUX ENFERS 1964 d: Francois Villiers, Alfonso Balcazar. FRN/SPN., *Constance aux Enfers*, Jean-Pierre Ferriere, Paris 1963, Novel

CONSTANT HOT WATER 1923 d: George A. Cooper. UKN., *Constant Hot Water*, P. L. Mannock, Short Story

CONSTANT NYMPH, THE 1928 d: Adrian Brunel, Basil Dean. UKN., *The Constant Nymph*, Margaret Kennedy, 1924, Novel

CONSTANT NYMPH, THE 1933 d: Basil Dean. UKN., *The Constant Nymph*, Margaret Kennedy, 1924, Novel

CONSTANT NYMPH, THE 1943 d: Edmund Goulding. USA., *The Constant Nymph*, Margaret Kennedy, 1924, Novel

Constant Wife, The see CHARMING SINNERS (1929).

Constant Wife, The see DASS CONSTANZE SICH RICHTIG VERHALT? FINDEN SIE (1962).

CONSTANT WOMAN, THE 1933 d: Victor Schertzinger. USA., *Recklessness*, Eugene O'Neill, Boston 1914, Play

CONSUMING PASSIONS 1988 d: Giles Foster. UKN/USA., *Secrets*, Terry Jones, Michael Palin, Play

CONTACT 1997 d: Robert Zemeckis. USA., *Contact*, Carl Sagan, Novel

CONTE AQUILA, IL 1956 d: Guido Salvini. ITL., *Il Conte Aquila*, Rino Alessi, Play

CONTE CRUEL 1930 d: Gaston Modot. FRN., *La Torture Par l'Esperance*, Villiers de L'isle-Adam, Short Story

Conte de Deux Villes, Un see A TALE OF TWO CITIES (1989).

Conte de la Folie Ordinaire see STORIE DI ORDINARIA FOLLIA (1981).

CONTE DI BRECHARD, IL 1938 d: Mario Bonnard. ITL., *Il Conte Di Brechard*, Giovacchino Forzano, Play

CONTE DI MONTECRISTO, IL 1908 d: Luigi Maggi. ITL., *Le Comte de Monte-Cristo*, Alexandre Dumas (pere), Paris 1845, Novel

Conte Di Montecristo, Il see LE COMTE DE MONTE-CRISTO (1942).

Conte Di Montecristo, Il see LE COMTE DE MONTE-CRISTO (1961).

Conte Dracula, Il see EL CONDE DRACULA (1970).

Conte Hermann, Le see HERMANN (1920).

Contempt see LE MEPRIS (1963).

Contempteur, Le see LE DEMONIAQUE (1968).

CONTESSA SARA, LA 1919 d: Roberto Leone Roberti. ITL., *La Comtesse Sarah*, Georges Ohnet, 1887, Novel

Contesto, Il see CADAVERI ECCELLENTI (1976).

Context, The see CADAVERI ECCELLENTI (1976).

Continental Atmosphere see L' ARIA DEL CONTINENTE (1935).

Continental Express see THE SILENT BATTLE (1939).

CONTRABAND 1925 d: Alan Crosland. USA., *Contraband*, Clarence Budington Kelland, New York 1923, Novel

Contraband see THE LUCK OF A SAILOR (1934).

CONTRACT ON CHERRY STREET 1977 d: William A. Graham. USA., *Contract on Cherry Street*, Philip Rosenberg, Book

Contract, The see MILANO CALIBRO 9 (1972).

CONTREBASSE, LA 1962 d: Maurice Fasquel. FRN., *Le Contrebasse*, Anton Chekhov, Short Story

CONTRE-ENQUETE 1930 d: John Daumery. USA., *Those Who Dance*, George Kibbe Turner, Story

CONTROFIGURA, LA 1971 d: Romolo Guerrieri. ITL., *La Controfigura*, Libero Bigiaretti, Novel

Controleur Des Champs-Elysees, Le see RENDEZ-VOUS CHAMPS-ELYSEES (1937).

Controleur Des Wagon-Lits, Le see DER SCHLAFWAGENKONTROLLEUR (1935).

CONTROLLORE DEI VAGONI-LETTO, IL 1922 d: Mario Almirante. ITL., *Le Controleur Des Wagons-Lits*, Alexandre Bisson, 1898, Play

CONVENTION GIRL 1934 d: Luther Reed. USA., *Convention Girl*, George Boyle, New York 1933, Novel

Conversion of Ferdys Pistora, The see OBRACENI FERDYSE PISTORY (1931).

Conversion of St. Anthony see LE TENTAZIONI DI SANT'ANTONIO (1911).

CONVERT, THE 1923 d: Manning Haynes. UKN., *Deep Waters*, W. W. Jacobs, Short Story

CONVICT 99 1909 d: Arthur Gilbert. UKN., *Convict 99*, Marie Connor, Robert Leighton, Play

CONVICT 99 1919 d: G. B. Samuelson. UKN., *Convict 99*, Marie Connor, Robert Leighton, Play

CONVICTED 1938 d: Leon BarshA. CND., *Face Work*, Cornell Woolrich, Story

CONVICTED 1950 d: Henry Levin. USA., *The Criminal Code*, Martin Flavin, New York 1929, Play

CONVICTS FOUR 1962 d: Millard Kaufman. USA., *Reprieve: the Testament of John Resko*, John Resko, New York 1956, Autobiography

CONVICT'S PAROLE, THE 1912 d: Edwin S. Porter. USA., *The Convict's Parole*, Melvin G. Winstock, Story

Convicts' Song see CARCELERAS (1922).

CONVIENE FAR BENE L'AMORE 1975 d: Pasquale Festa Campanile. ITL., *Conviene Dar Bene l'Amore*, Pasquale Festa Campanile, Novel

CONVOY 1927 d: Joseph C. Boyle, Lothar Mendes (Uncredited). USA., *The Song of the Dragon*, John Taintor Foote, New York 1923, Novel

COOGAN'S BLUFF 1968 d: Don Siegel. USA., *Coogan's Bluff*, Herman Miller, Novel

Cook, The see SOMETHING FOR EVERYONE (1970).

COOL BREEZE 1972 d: Barry Pollack. USA., *Asphalt Jungle*, William Riley Burnett, New York 1949, Novel

COOL HAND LUKE 1967 d: Stuart Rosenberg. USA., *Cool Hand Luke*, Donald Pearce, New York 1965, Novel

COOL MIKADO, THE 1963 d: Michael Winner. UKN., *The Mikado*, W. S. Gilbert, Arthur Sullivan, London 1885, Opera

COOL WORLD, THE 1964 d: Shirley Clarke. USA., *The Cool World*, Warren Miller, Boston 1959, Novel

COP 1987 d: James B. Harris. USA., *Blood on the Moon*, James Ellroy, Novel

COP AND THE ANTHEM, THE 1917 d: Thomas R. Mills. USA., *The Cop and the Anthem*, O. Henry, Short Story

Cop Au Vin see POULET AU VINAIGRE (1984).

COP HATER 1958 d: William Berke. USA., *Cop Hater*, Evan Hunter, 1958, Novel

Cop Killers see ORDER OF DEATH (1983).

COPAINS, LES 1964 d: Yves Robert. FRN., *Les Copains*, Jules Romains, 1913, Novel

Copkiller see ORDER OF DEATH (1983).

COPLA ANDALUZA, LA 1928 d: Ernesto Gonzalez. SPN., *La Copla Andaluza*, Pascual Guillen, Antonio Quintero, Play

COPLAN, AGENT SECRET FX18 1964 d: Maurice Cloche. FRN/ITL/SPN., *Coplan Tente Sa Chance*, Paul Kenny, Novel

COPLAN: COUP DURS 1989 d: Gilles Behat. FRN/GRM/SWT., Paul Kenny, Novel

Coplan: Der Vampir Der Karibik see COPLAN: LE VAMPIRE DES CARAIBES (1989).

Coplan: Entfuhrung Nach Berlin see COPLAN: COUP DURS (1989).

COPLAN FX18 CASSE TOUT 1965 d: Riccardo FredA. FRN/ITL., *Stoppez Coplan*, Paul Kenny, Novel

COPLAN: LE VAMPIRE DES CARAIBES 1989 d: Yvan Butler. FRN/GRM/SWT., Paul Kenny, Novel

Coplan Ouvre le Feu a Mexico see MORESQUE OBIETTIVO ALLUCINANTE (1967).

COPLAN PREND DES RISQUES 1963 d: Maurice Labro. FRN/ITL/BLG., *Coplan Prend Des Risques*, Paul Kelly, Novel

Coplan: Rache in Caracas see COPLAN: RETOUR AUX SOURCES (1989).

COPLAN: RETOUR AUX SOURCES 1989 d: Philippe Toledano. FRN/GRM/SWT., Paul Kenny, Novel

COPLAN SAUVE SA PEAU 1967 d: Yves Boisset. FRN/ITL., *Coplan Paie le Cercueil*, Paul Kenny, Novel

Coplan Saves His Skin see COPLAN SAUVE SA PEAU (1967).

COPO DE COLERA, UM 1999 d: Aluizio Abranches. BRZ., *Um Copo de Colera*, Raduan Nassar, Book

Cop-Out see STRANGER IN THE HOUSE (1967).

Copper Anniversary see DIE KUPFERNE HOCHZEIT (1948).

COPPER BEECHES, THE 1912 d: Georges Treville. UKN., *The Copper Beeches*, Arthur Conan Doyle, Short Story

COPPER BEECHES, THE 1921 d: Maurice Elvey. UKN., *The Copper Beeches*, Arthur Conan Doyle, Short Story

Copper Beeches, The see THE ADVENTURES OF SHERLOCK HOLMES: THE COPPER BEECHES (1985).

COPPER CANYON 1950 d: John Farrow. USA., Richard English, Story

COPPERHEAD, THE 1920 d: Charles Maigne. USA., *The Copperhead*, Frederick Landis, 1918, Play, *The Glory of His Country*, Frederick Landis, 1910, Novel

COPPIA, LA 1968 d: Enzo Siciliano. ITL., *La Coppia*, Enzo Siciliano, Novel

Coq du Village, Le see LIOLA (1964).

COQUECIGROLE 1931 d: Andre Berthomieu. FRN., *Coquecigrole*, Alfred Machard, Novel

COQUETTE 1929 d: Sam Taylor. USA., *Coquette*, George Abbott, Anne P. Bridgers, New York 1928, Play

COR, LE 1931 d: Jean Epstein. FRN., *Le Cor*, Alfred de Vigny, Poem

CORA 1915 d: Edwin Carewe. USA., *Cora*, Fred de Gresac, Play

CORALIE & C. 1914. ITL., *Coralie Et Cie*, Maurice Hennequin, A. Valabregue, 1899, Play

CORALIE ET CIE 1933 d: Alberto Cavalcanti. FRN., *Coralie Et Cie*, Maurice Hennequin, A. Valabregue, 1899, Play

CORALIE LANSDOWNE SAY NO 1980 d: Michael Carson. ASL., *Coralie Lansdowne Says No*, Alexander Buzo, Play

Corazon de Cristal see CRYSTAL HEART (1987).

Corazones Sin Rumbo see HERZEN OHNE ZIEL (1928).

CORDE AU COU, LA 1964 d: Pierre Patry. CND., *Le Corde Au Cou*, Claude Jasmin, Novel

CORDE RAIDE, LA 1959 d: Jean-Charles Dudrumet. FRN., *La Veuve*, Michel Lebrun, Paris 1958, Novel

CORDELIA 1980 d: Jean Beaudin. CND., *La Lampe Dans la Fenetre*, Pauline Cadieux, Novel

CORDELIA THE MAGNIFICENT 1923 d: George Archainbaud. USA., *Cordelia the Magnificent*, Leroy Scott, Novel

CORDON-BLEU 1931 d: Karl Anton. FRN., *Cordon-Bleu*, Tristan Bernard, Play

CORDULA 1950 d: Gustav Ucicky. AUS., *Kirbisch*, Anton Wildgans, 1927, Verse

CO-RESPONDENT, THE 1917 d: Ralph Ince. USA., *The Co-Respondent*, Alice Leal Pollock, Rita Weiman, New York 1916, Play

Co-Respondent, The *see* **THE WHISPERED NAME** (1924).

CORINNA SCHMIDT 1951 d: Arthur Pohl. GDR., *Frau Jenny Treibel*, Theodor Fontane, 1892, Novel

CORINTHIAN JACK 1921 d: W. C. Rowden. UKN., *Fighting Jack*, Walter Courtney Rowden, Novel

CORIOLANO, EROE SENZA PATRIA 1965 d: Giorgio Ferroni. ITL/FRN., *Coriolanus*, William Shakespeare, c1608, Play

Coriolanus: Hero Without a Country *see* **EROE SENZA PATRIA CORIOLANO** (1965).

CORLEONE 1978 d: Pasquale Squitieri. ITL., *I Complici: Gli Anni Dell'Antimafia*, Orazio Barrese, Book

Corleone: Father of the Godfathers *see* **CORLEONE** (1978).

CORMORANT, THE 1992 d: Peter Markham. UKN., *The Cormorant*, Stephen Gregory, Novel

CORN IS GREEN, THE 1945 d: Irving Rapper. USA., *The Corn Is Green*, Emlyn Williams, London 1938, Play

CORN IS GREEN, THE 1978 d: George Cukor. USA., *The Corn Is Green*, Emlyn Williams, London 1938, Play

CORNER GROCER, THE 1917 d: George Cowl. USA., *The Corner Grocery*, Adolf Philipp, New York 1894, Play

Corner Grocery, The *see* **THE CORNER GROCER** (1917).

CORNER IN WHEAT, A 1909 d: D. W. Griffith. USA., *The Pit*, Frank Norris, New York 1903, Novel

CORNERED 1924 d: William Beaudine. USA., *Cornered*, Dodson Mitchell, Zelda Sears, New York 1920, Play

Cornered *see* **WEST OF SHANGHAI** (1937).

Cornet - Die Weise von Liebe Und Tod, Der *see* **DER CORNET** (1955).

CORNET, DER 1955 d: Walter Reisch. GRM., *Die Weise von Liebe Und Tod Des Cornets Christoph Rilke*, Rainer Maria Rilke, 1906, Verse

Cornet, The *see* **DER CORNET** (1955).

CORONEL E O LOBISOMEM, O 1980 d: Alcino Diniz. BRZ., *O Coronel E O Lobisomem*, Jose Candido de Carvalho, 1964, Novel

CORONER CREEK 1948 d: Ray Enright. USA., *Coroner Creek*, Luke Short, Novel

Coroner's Creek *see* **CORONER CREEK** (1948).

Coronet of Shame, The *see* **DE KROON DER SCHANDE** (1918).

Coronetist, The *see* **DER ZINKER** (1965).

Corpo a Corpo *see* **L' ARME A GAUCHE** (1965).

CORPO DELLA RAGAZZA, IL 1979 d: Pasquale Festa Campanile. ITL., *Il Corpo Della Ragassa*, Gianni Brera, Novel

CORPO, O 1989 d: Jose Antonio GarciA. BRZ., *O Corpo*, Clarice Lispector, 1974, Short Story

Corps de Diane, Le *see* **TELO DIANA** (1969).

CORPS DE MON ENNEMI, LE 1976 d: Henri Verneuil. FRN., *Le Corps de mon Ennemi*, Felicien Marceau, Novel

CORPSE CAME C.O.D., THE 1947 d: Henry Levin. USA., *The Corpse Came C.O.D.*, James A. Starr, Novel

Corpse in the Morgue *see* **THE LADY IN THE MORGUE** (1938).

Corpse Makers, The *see* **TWICE-TOLD TALES** (1963).

Corpse of Beverly Hills, The *see* **DIE TOTE VON BEVERLY HILLS** (1964).

Corpse Packs His Bags, The *see* **EL MUERTO HACE LAS MALETAS** (1970).

Corpses on Holiday *see* **CADAVRES EN VACANCES** (1961).

CORRIDOR OF MIRRORS 1948 d: Terence Young. UKN., *Corridor of Mirrors*, Chris Massie, Novel

CORRIERE DEL RE, IL 1948 d: Gennaro Righelli. ITL., *Le Rouge Et le Noir*, Stendhal, 1830, Novel

Corringa, Sept Morts Dans Les Yeux du Chat *see* **LA MORTE NEGLI OCCHI DEL GATTO** (1973).

Corrupt *see* **ORDER OF DEATH** (1983).

Corrupt, The *see* **SYMPHONIE POUR UN MASSACRE** (1963).

Corrupted Woman, A *see* **DARAKU SURU ONNA** (1967).

CORRUPTION 1917 d: John Gorman. USA., *Corruption*, Jack Gorman, Play

Corruption *see* **FUSHI** (1950).

Corruption in the Halls of Justice *see* **CORRUZIONE AL PALAZZO DI GIUSTIZIA** (1975).

CORRUZIONE AL PALAZZO DI GIUSTIZIA 1975 d: Marcello Aliprandi. ITL., *Corruzione Al Palazzo Di Giustizia*, Ugo Betti, Play

CORSAIR 1931 d: Roland West. USA., *Corsair*, Walton Atwater Green, New York 1931, Novel

CORSAIR, THE 1914 d: Frank Powell. USA., *The Corsair*, Lord Byron, London 1814, Poem

CORSARO NERO, IL 1936 d: Amleto Palermi. ITL., *Il Corsaro Nero*, Emilio Salgari, Novel

CORSICAN BROTHERS, THE 1902 d: Dicky Winslow. UKN., *Les Freres Corses*, Alexandre Dumas (pere), 1845, Short Story

CORSICAN BROTHERS, THE 1912 d: Oscar Apfel, J. Searle Dawley. USA., *Les Freres Corses*, Alexandre Dumas (pere), 1845, Short Story

CORSICAN BROTHERS, THE 1915 d: George A. Lessey. USA., *Les Freres Corses*, Alexandre Dumas (pere), 1845, Short Story

Corsican Brothers, The *see* **LES FRERES CORSES** (1917).

CORSICAN BROTHERS, THE 1920 d: Colin Campbell. USA., *Les Freres Corses*, Alexandre Dumas (pere), 1845, Short Story

CORSICAN BROTHERS, THE 1941 d: Gregory Ratoff. USA., *Les Freres Corses*, Alexandre Dumas (pere), 1845, Short Story

Corsican Brothers, The *see* **LOS HERMANOS CORSOS** (1954).

Corsican Brothers, The *see* **I FRATELLI CORSI** (1961).

CORSICAN BROTHERS, THE 1985 d: Ian Sharp. UKN., *Les Freres Corses*, Alexandre Dumas (pere), 1845, Short Story

Cortesie Per Gli Ospiti *see* **THE COMFORT OF STRANGERS** (1991).

CORTICO, O 1945 d: Luiz de Barros. BRZ., *O Cortico*, Aluisio de Azevedo, 1890, Novel

CORTICO, O 1978 d: Francisco Ramalho Jr. BRZ., *O Cortico*, Aluisio de Azevedo, 1890, Novel

CORTILE 1931 d: Carlo Campogalliani. ITL., *Cortile*, Fausto Maria Martini, Sketch

COSA BUFFA, LA 1972 d: Aldo Lado. ITL/FRN., *La Cosa Buffa*, Giuseppe Berto, 1966, Novel

COSA NOSTRA 1972 d: Terence Young. FRN/ITL., *La Mela Marcia*, Peter Maas, Novel

COSACCHI, I 1960 d: Victor Tourjansky, Giorgio RivaltA. ITL/FRN., *Kazaki*, Lev Nikolayevich Tolstoy, 1863, Novel

COSH BOY 1952 d: Lewis Gilbert. UKN., *Master Crook*, Bruce Walker, Play

COSI FAN TUTTE 1970 d: Vaclav Kaslik. AUS/GRM., *Cosi Fan Tutte*, Lorenzo Da Ponte, Wolfgang Amadeus Mozart, Vienna 1790, Opera

COSI FAN TUTTE 1991 d: Tinto Brass. ITL., *Cosi Fan Tutte*, Lorenzo Da Ponte, Wolfgang Amadeus Mozart, Vienna 1790, Opera

COSI PARLO BELLAVISTA 1984 d: Luciano de Crescenzo. ITL., *Cosi Parlo Bellavista*, Luciano de Crescenzo, Novel

Cosmetics *see* **KISS AND MAKE UP** (1934).

Cosmic Man Appears in Tokyo, The *see* **UCHUJIN TOKYO NI ARAWARU** (1956).

Cosmic Monster, The *see* **THE STRANGE WORLD OF PLANET X** (1958).

Cosmic Monsters *see* **THE STRANGE WORLD OF PLANET X** (1958).

COSMOPOLIS 1919 d: Gaston Ravel. ITL., *Cosmopolis*, Paul Bourget, Novel

Cossacks Across the Danube *see* **COSSACKS IN EXILE** (1939).

Cossacks Beyond the Danube *see* **ZAPOROZETS ZA DUNAYEM** (1938).

COSSACKS IN EXILE 1939 d: Edgar G. Ulmer. USA., *Zaporozheta Za Dunayem*, Semen Artemowsky, St. Petersburg 1863, Opera

Cossacks in Exile *see* **COSSACKS IN EXILE** (1939).

Cossacks of the Don *see* **TIKHU DON** (1931).

COSSACKS, THE 1928 d: George W. Hill, Clarence Brown (Uncredited). USA., *Kazaki*, Lev Nikolayevich Tolstoy, 1863, Novel

Cossacks, The *see* **I COSACCHI** (1960).

Cossacks, The *see* **KASAKI** (1961).

Cossaques, Les *see* **I COSACCHI** (1960).

COST, THE 1920 d: Harley Knoles. USA., *The Cost*, David Graham Phillips, Indianapolis 1904, Novel

COSTANZA DELLA RAGIONE, LA 1964 d: Pasquale Festa Campanile. ITL/FRN., *La Costanza Della Ragione*, Vasco Pratolini, 1963, Novel

COSTAUD DES EPINETTES, LE 1922 d: Raymond Bernard. FRN., *Le Costaud Des Epinettes*, Alfred Athis, Tristan Bernard, Play

Coster Bill of Paris *see* **CRAINQUEBILLE** (1922).

COTE D'AZUR 1931 d: Roger Capellani. FRN., *Cote d'Azur*, Andre Birabeau, Georges Dolley, Play

Cottage in the Steppe, The *see* **KHUTOROK V STEPI** (1971).

Cottage, The *see* **LA BARRACA** (1944).

COTTAGE TO LET 1941 d: Anthony Asquith. UKN., *Cottage to Let*, Geoffrey Kerr, London 1940, Play

COTTON COMES TO HARLEM 1970 d: Ossie Davis. USA., *Cotton Comes to Harlem*, Chester Himes, New York 1965, Novel

COTTON KING, THE 1915 d: Oscar Eagle. USA., *The Cotton King*, Sutton Vane, London 1894, Play

COUCH TRIP, THE 1988 d: Michael Ritchie. USA., *The Couch Trip*, Ken Kolb, Novel

COUCHE DE LA MARIEE, LE 1933 d: Roger Lion. FRN., *Le Couche de la Mariee*, Felix Gandera, Play

Couchette No.3 *see* **LES SURPRISES DU SLEEPING** (1933).

COUGHING HORROR, THE 1924 d: Fred Paul. UKN., *The Coughing Horror*, Sax Rohmer, Short Story

COULEURS DU DIABLE, LES 1997 d: Alain JessuA. FRN/ITL., *Cold Eye*, Giles Blunt, Novel

COUNSEL FOR THE DEFENSE 1925 d: Burton L. King. USA., *Counsel for the Defense*, Leroy Scott, New York 1912, Novel

COUNSELLOR AT LAW 1933 d: William Wyler. USA., *Counsellor at Law*, Elmer Rice, New York 1931, Play

Counsellor Vera *see* **ADVOKATKA VERA** (1937).

COUNSEL'S OPINION 1933 d: Allan Dwan. UKN., *Counsel's Opinion*, Gilbert Wakefield, London 1931, Play

Count Dracula *see* **EL CONDE DRACULA** (1970).

COUNT DRACULA 1978 d: Philip Saville. UKN/USA., *Dracula*, Bram Stoker, London 1897, Novel

Count from Munkbro *see* **MUNKBROGREVEN** (1935).

Count Maravillas, The *see* **EL CONDE DE MARAVILLAS** (1927).

Count of Arizona, The *see* **MY AMERICAN WIFE** (1922).

Count of Arizona, The *see* **MY AMERICAN WIFE** (1936).

Count of Bragelonne, The *see* **LE VICOMTE DE BRAGELONNE** (1954).

Count of Brechard, The *see* **IL CONTE DI BRECHARD** (1938).

COUNT OF LUXEMBOURG, THE 1926 d: Arthur Gregor. USA., *Der Graf von Luxembourg*, Franz Lehar, Vienna 1909, Operetta

Count of Luxembourg, The *see* **DER GRAF VON LUXEMBURG** (1957).

Count of Monte Cristo, The *see* **MONTE CRISTO** (1912).

COUNT OF MONTE CRISTO, THE 1913 d: Edwin S. Porter, Joseph A. Golden. USA., *Le Comte de Monte-Cristo*, Alexandre Dumas (pere), Paris 1845, Novel

COUNT OF MONTE CRISTO, THE 1934 d: Rowland V. Lee. USA., *Le Comte de Monte-Cristo*, Alexandre Dumas (pere), Paris 1845, Novel

Count of Monte Cristo, The *see* **LE COMTE DE MONTE-CRISTO** (1942).

Count of Monte Cristo, The *see* **LE COMTE DE MONTE-CRISTO** (1953).

Count of Monte Cristo, The *see* **LE COMTE DE MONTE-CRISTO** (1961).

COUNT OF MONTE CRISTO, THE 1973 d: William Hanna, Joseph BarberA. USA/ASL., *Le Comte de Monte-Cristo*, Alexandre Dumas (pere), Paris 1845, Novel

COUNT OF MONTE CRISTO, THE 1975 d: David Greene. USA/UKN., *Le Comte de Monte-Cristo*, Alexandre Dumas (pere), Paris 1845, Novel

COUNT OF MONTE CRISTO, THE 1987 d: Georgij Jungvald-Khilkevich. USS., *Le Comte de Monte-Cristo*, Alexandre Dumas (pere), Paris 1845, Novel

COUNT OF SOLAR, THE 1991 d: Tristram Powell. UKN., *When the Mind Hears*, Harlan Lane

COUNT OF TEN, THE 1928 d: James Flood. USA., *Betty's a Lady*, Gerald Beaumont, 1925, Short Story

Count of the Old Town, The *see* MUNKBROGREVEN (1935).

Count Pete *see* WALKING ON AIR (1936).

COUNT THREE AND PRAY 1955 d: George Sherman. USA., *Calico Pony*, Herb Meadow, Novel

COUNT YOUR BLESSINGS 1959 d: Jean Negulesco. USA., *The Blessing*, Nancy Mitford, 1951, Novel

COUNTDOWN 1968 d: Robert Altman, William Conrad. USA., *The Pilgrim Project*, Henry Searls, New York 1964, Novel

Counted Out *see* THE SWELLHEAD (1930).

Counter, The *see* GUITAI (1965).

COUNTER-ATTACK 1945 d: Zoltan KordA. USA., *Pobyeda*, Mikhail Ruderman, Play, *Counter-Attack*, Janet Stevenson, Philip Stevenson, Play, *Pobyeda*, Ilya Vershinin, Play

COUNTERFEIT KILLER, THE 1968 d: Joseph Leytes, Stuart Rosenberg. USA., *The Faceless Man*, Harry Kliner, 1966, Play

COUNTERFEIT TRAITOR, THE 1962 d: George Seaton. USA., *The Counterfeit Traitor*, Alexander Klein, New York 1958, Novel

Counterfeiters of Paris, The *see* LE CAVE SE REBIFFE (1961).

Counterfeiters, The *see* LE CAVE SE REBIFFE (1961).

COUNTERPOINT 1968 d: Ralph Nelson. USA., *The General*, Alan Sillitoe, 1960, Novel

COUNTERSPY 1953 d: Vernon Sewell. UKN., *Criss Cross Code*, Julian Symons, Novel

Countess Cosel *see* HRABINA COSEL (1968).

COUNTESS DRACULA 1970 d: Peter Sasdy. UKN., *The Bloody Countess*, V. Penrose, Novel

Countess from Podskali, The *see* HRABENKA Z PODSKALI (1925).

Countess Maria *see* LA CONDESA MARIA (1927).

Countess Mariza *see* GRAFIN MARIZA (1925).

Countess Mariza *see* GRAFIN MARIZA (1932).

Countess Mariza *see* GRAFIN MARIZA (1958).

Countess of Monte Cristo, The *see* DIE GRAFIN VON MONTE CHRISTO (1932).

COUNTESS OF MONTE CRISTO, THE 1948 d: Frederick de CordovA. USA., Walter Reisch, Story

COUNTRY 1981 d: Richard Eyre. UKN., *Country: a Tory Story*, Trevor Griffiths, 1981, Play

COUNTRY BEYOND, THE 1926 d: Irving Cummings. USA., *The Country Beyond*, James Oliver Curwood, New York 1922, Short Story

COUNTRY BEYOND, THE 1936 d: Eugene J. Forde. USA., *The Country Beyond*, James Oliver Curwood, New York 1922, Short Story

COUNTRY BOY, THE 1915 d: Frederick A. Thompson, Allan Dwan (Spv.) USA., *The Country Boy*, Edgar Selwyn, New York 1910, Play

COUNTRY COUSIN, THE 1919 d: Alan Crosland. USA., *The Country Cousin*, Julian Leonard Street, Booth Tarkington, New York 1917, Play

COUNTRY DANCE 1969 d: J. Lee Thompson. UKN/USA., *Household Ghosts*, James Kennaway, Novel

Country Doctor *see* A MAN TO REMEMBER (1938).

Country Doctor, The *see* RETALHOS DA VIDA DE UM MEDICO (1962).

Country Excursion *see* UNE PARTIE DE CAMPAGNE (1936).

COUNTRY FLAPPER, THE 1922 d: F. Richard Jones. USA., *The Cynic Effect*, Nalbro Bartley, 1920, Short Story

COUNTRY GIRL, THE 1915. USA., *The Country Girl*, David Garrick, Play

COUNTRY GIRL, THE 1954 d: George Seaton. USA., *The Country Girl*, Clifford Odets, New York 1950, Play

COUNTRY GIRL, THE 1974 d: Paul Bogart. USA., *The Country Girl*, Clifford Odets, New York 1950, Play

COUNTRY GIRLS, THE 1984 d: Desmond Davis. UKN/IRL., *The Country Girls*, Edna O'Brien, 1960, Novel

COUNTRY LIFE 1994 d: Michael Blakemore. ASL., *Uncle Vanya*, Anton Chekhov, 1900, Play

COUNTRY PARSON, THE 1915. USA., Honore de Balzac, Story

Country Teachers *see* FENG HUANG QING (1993).

Country Without Stars, The *see* LE PAYS SANS ETOILES (1945).

COUNTY CHAIRMAN, THE 1914 d: Allan Dwan. USA., *The County Chairman*, George Ade, New York 1903, Play

COUNTY CHAIRMAN, THE 1935 d: John G. Blystone. USA., *The County Chairman*, George Ade, New York 1903, Play

COUNTY FAIR, THE 1920 d: Maurice Tourneur, Edmund Mortimer. USA., *The County Fair*, Charles Barnard, New York 1889, Play

COUP DE FEU A L'AUBE 1932 d: Serge de Poligny. FRN., *Die Frau Und Der Smaragd*, Harry Jenkins, Play

COUP DE FEU DANS LA NUIT 1942 d: Robert Peguy. FRN., *L' Avocat*, Eugene Brieux, 1922, Play

Coup de Feu Dans l'Eglise, Le *see* DER SCHUSS VON DER KANZEL (1942).

Coup de Foudre *see* CHIPEE (1937).

COUP DE FOUDRE 1983 d: Diane Kurys. FRN., *Coup de Foudre*, Diane Kurys, Book

COUP DE FOUET, LE 1913 d: Georges MoncA. FRN., *Le Coup de Fouet*, Georges Duval, Maurice Hennequin, Play

Coup de Gong a Hong-Kong *see* LOTOSBLUTEN FUR MISS QUON (1966).

Coup de Grace *see* DER FANGSCHUSS (1976).

Coup de Maitre *see* LE DESTIN S'AMUSE (1946).

COUP DE MINUIT, LE 1916 d: Maurice Poggi. FRN., *Le Coup de Minuit*, Hugues Delorme, Francis Galley, Play

COUP DE MISTRAL, UN 1933 d: Gaston Roudes. FRN., *Mon Oncle d'Arles*, Raymond Clauzel, Play

COUP DE TELEPHONE, UN 1931 d: Georges Lacombe. FRN., *Un Coup de Telephone*, Georges Berr, Paul Gavault, Play

COUP DE TETE 1978 d: Jean-Jacques Annaud. FRN., *Coup de Tete*, Alain Godard, Novel

COUP DE TORCHON 1981 d: Bertrand Tavernier. FRN., *Pop. 1280*, Jim Thompson, Novel

Coup d'Etat *see* POWER PLAY (1978).

COUP DUR, UN 1949 d: Jean Loubignac. FRN., *Un Coup Dur*, Jean Guitton, Play

COUPABLE? 1950 d: Yvan Noe. FRN., *Coupable?*, Yvan Montfort, Novel

COUPABLE, LE 1908-18. FRN., *Le Coupable*, Francois Coppee, Paris 1896, Play

COUPABLE, LE 1917 d: Andre Antoine. FRN., *Le Coupable*, Francois Coppee, Paris 1896, Play

COUPABLE, LE 1936 d: Raymond Bernard. FRN., *Le Coupable*, Francois Coppee, Paris 1896, Play

Couple, The *see* LA COPPIA (1968).

Couplings *see* PAARUNGEN (1967).

COUPS DE FEU 1939 d: Rene Barberis. FRN., *Vystrel*, Alexander Pushkin, 1831, Short Story

COUPS DE ROULIS 1931 d: Jean de La Cour. FRN., *Coups de Roulis*, Maurice Larrouy, Novel

Coups Durs *see* COPLAN: COUP DURS (1989).

COUPS POUR RIEN, LES 1970 d: Pierre Lambert. FRN., *Les Coups Pour Rien*, J. S. Quemeneur, Novel

COURAGE 1930 d: Archie Mayo. USA., *Courage*, Tom Barry, New York 1928, Play

COURAGE OF KAVIK THE WOLF DOG, THE 1980 d: Peter Carter. CND., *Kavik the Wolf Dog*, Walt Morey, Novel

COURAGE OF MARGE O'DOONE, THE 1920 d: David Smith. USA., *The Courage of Marge O'Doone*, James Oliver Curwood, Garden City, N.Y. 1918, Novel

COURAGE OF THE COMMONPLACE, THE 1917 d: Ben Turbett. USA., *The Courage of the Commonplace*, Mary Raymond Shipman Andrews, New York 1911, Novel

Courageous *see* A LOST LADY (1934).

Courageous Mr. Penn, The *see* PENN OF PENNSYLVANIA (1941).

Courier of Lyon, The *see* L' AFFAIRE DU COURRIER DE LYON (1937).

Courier of the Czar, The *see* MICHELE STROGOFF (1956).

Courier of the Czar, The *see* STROGOFF (1970).

Courrier de Lyon, Le *see* L' AFFAIRE DU COURRIER DE LYON (1937).

Courrier du Roi, Le *see* LES CHOUANS (1946).

COURRIER-SUD 1936 d: Pierre Billon. FRN., *Courrier Sud*, Antoine de Saint-Exupery, 1929, Novel

COURSE A LA VERTU, LA 1936 d: Maurice Gleize. FRN., *La Course a la Vertu*, Tristan Bernard, Henri Keller, Play

COURSE DU FLAMBEAU, LA 1917 d: Charles Burguet. FRN., *La Course du Flambeau*, Paul Hervieu, Play

Court Martial *see* CARRINGTON V.C. (1954).

Court Martial *see* KRIEGSGERICHT (1959).

COURT MARTIAL OF GENERAL GEORGE ARMSTRONG CUSTER, THE 1978 d: Glenn Jordan. USA., *The Court Martial of General George Armstrong Custer*, Douglas C. Jones, Book

Court of God, The *see* SOUD BOZI (1938).

Court of St. Simon, The *see* THE SILENT MASTER (1917).

COURT-CIRCUIT 1929 d: Maurice Champreux. FRN., *Court-Circuit*, Joullot, Benjamin Rabier, Play

COURTIN' WILDCATS 1929 d: Jerome Storm. USA., *Courtin' Calamity*, William Dudley Pelley, Story

Courtney Affair, The *see* THE COURTNEYS OF CURZON STREET (1947).

COURTNEYS OF CURZON STREET, THE 1947 d: Herbert Wilcox. UKN., *The Courtneys of Curzon Street*, Florence Tranter, Novel

COURTSHIP OF EDDIE'S FATHER, THE 1963 d: Vincente Minnelli. USA., *The Courtship of Eddie's Father*, Mark Toby, New York 1961, Novel

COURTSHIP OF MILES STANDISH, THE 1910 d: Otis Turner. USA., *The Courtship of Miles Standish*, Henry Wadsworth Longfellow, 1858, Poem

COURTSHIP OF MILES STANDISH, THE 1923 d: Frederick Sullivan. USA., *The Courtship of Miles Standish*, Henry Wadsworth Longfellow, 1858, Poem

Cousin Basilio *see* O PRIMO BASILIO (1959).

COUSIN BETTE 1972 d: Gareth Davies. UKN., *La Cousine Bette*, Honore de Balzac, 1846, Novel

COUSIN BETTE 1998 d: Des McAnuff. USA/UKN., *La Cousine Bette*, Honore de Balzac, 1846, Novel

Cousin from Podunk *see* DER VETTER AUS DINGSDA (1934).

COUSIN KATE 1920 d: Mrs. Sidney Drew. USA., *Cousin Kate*, Hubert Henry Davies, Boston 1910, Play

COUSIN PONS 1914 d: Travers Vale. USA., *Le Cousin Pons*, Honore de Balzac, Novel

COUSIN PONS, LE 1923 d: Jacques Robert. FRN., *Le Cousin Pons*, Honore de Balzac, Novel

COUSINE BETTE, LA 1928 d: Max de Rieux. FRN., *La Cousine Bette*, Honore de Balzac, 1846, Novel

COUSINE BETTE, LA 1964 d: Yves-Andre Hubert. FRN., *La Cousine Bette*, Honore de Balzac, 1846, Novel

COUSINES, LES 1969 d: Louis Soulanes. FRN., *La Nuit Des Perverses*, Fletcher D. Benson, Novel

Cousins in Love *see* TENDRES COUSINES (1980).

Coute Que Coute *see* DER KAMPF UMS MATTERHORN (1928).

COUTEAU D'OR, LES 1914 d: Jacques Volnys. FRN., *Les Couteau d'Or*, Paul Feval, Novel

COUTURIERE DE LUNEVILLE, LA 1931 d: Harry Lachman. FRN., *La Couturiere de Luneville*, Alfred Savoir, Paris 1923, Play

Covekat V Sjanka *see* CHOVEKAT V SYANKA (1967).

COVENANT WITH DEATH, A 1966 d: Lamont Johnson. USA., *A Covenant With Death*, Stephen Becker, New York 1964, Novel

Cover Her Face *see* DALGLIESH: COVER HER FACE (1985).

COVERED WAGON, THE 1923 d: James Cruze. USA., *The Covered Wagon*, Emerson Hough, New York 1922, Novel

COW COUNTRY 1953 d: Lesley Selander, Curtis Bishop. USA., *Shadow Range*, Curtis Bishop, 1947, Novel

COWARD, A 1909 d: Edwin S. Porter. USA., Guy de Maupassant, Short Story

Coward, The *see* THE MAN WHO FOUND HIMSELF (1915).

COWARD, THE 1927 d: Alfred Raboch. USA., *The Coward*, Arthur Stringer, 1923, Short Story

Coward, The *see* KAPURUSH (1965).

COWARDICE COURT 1919 d: William C. Dowlan. USA., *Cowardice Court*, George Barr McCutcheon, New York 1906, Novel

COWBOY 1958 d: Delmer Daves. USA., *My Reminiscences As a Cowboy*, Frank Harris, Book

COWBOY AND THE LADY, THE 1915 d: Edwin Carewe. USA., *The Cowboy and the Lady*, Clyde Fitch, New York 1899, Play

COWBOY AND THE LADY, THE 1922 d: Charles Maigne. USA., *The Cowboy and the Lady*, Clyde Fitch, New York 1899, Play

COWBOY FROM BROOKLYN 1938 d: Lloyd Bacon. USA., *Howdy Stranger*, . Louis Pelletier Jr, Robert Sloane, New York 1937, Play

COWBOY QUARTERBACK, THE 1939 d: Noel Smith. USA., *Elmer the Great*, George M. Cohan, Ring Lardner, New York 1928, Play

COWBOYS, THE 1972 d: Mark Rydell. USA., *The Cowboys*, William Dale Jennings, Novel

COWPUNCHER, THE 1915? d: William Johnson Jossey. USA., *The Cow Puncher*, Hal Reid, Play

Crab-Canning Boat *see* KANIKOSEN (1953).

Crab-Canning Ship *see* KANIKOSEN (1953).

CRACK IN THE ICE, A 1964 d: Ronald Eyre. UKN., Nikolay Semyonovich Leskov, Story

CRACK IN THE ICE, A 1985 d: Anthony Garner. UKN., Nikolay Semyonovich Leskov, Story

CRACK IN THE MIRROR 1960 d: Richard Fleischer. USA., *Crack in the Mirror*, Marcel Haedrich, Novel

CRACK IN THE WORLD 1965 d: Andrew Marton. USA., *Crack in the World*, Jon Manchip White, Novel

CRACKER FACTORY, THE 1979 d: Burt Brinckerhoff. USA., *The Cracker Factory*, Joyce Rebeta-Burditt, Novel

CRACKERJACK 1938 d: Albert de Courville. UKN., *Crackerjack*, W. B. Ferguson, Novel

Crackshot *see* THE COUNTERFEIT KILLER (1968).

CRACKSMAN, THE 1963 d: Peter Graham Scott. UKN., *The Cracksman*, Lew Schwarz, Novel

CRACK-UP 1936 d: Malcolm St. Clair. USA., *Crack-Up*, John Goodrich, 1936, Short Story

CRADLE SNATCHERS, THE 1927 d: Howard Hawks. USA., *Cradle Snatchers*, Russell G. Medcraft, Norma Mitchell, New York 1925, Play

CRADLE SONG 1933 d: Mitchell Leisen, Mina Moise. USA., *Cancion de Cuna*, Gregorio Martinez Sierra, Madrid 1911, Play

Cradle Song *see* CANCION DE CUNA (1941).

Cradle Song *see* CANCION DE CUNA (1961).

CRADLE, THE 1922 d: Paul Powell. USA., *Le Berceau*, Eugene Brieux, Paris 1908, Play

CRAGMIRE TOWER 1924 d: Fred Paul. UKN., *Cragmire Tower*, Sax Rohmer, Short Story

CRAIG'S WIFE 1928 d: William C. de Mille. USA., *Craig's Wife*, George Edward Kelly, New York 1925, Play

CRAIG'S WIFE 1936 d: Dorothy Arzner. USA., *Craig's Wife*, George Edward Kelly, New York 1925, Play

CRAINQUEBILLE 1922 d: Jacques Feyder. FRN., *L'affaire Crainquebille*, Anatole France, 1901, Short Story

CRAINQUEBILLE 1933 d: Jacques de Baroncelli. FRN., *L'affaire Crainquebille*, Anatole France, 1901, Short Story

CRAINQUEBILLE 1953 d: Ralph Habib. FRN., *L'affaire Crainquebille*, Anatole France, 1901, Short Story

CRAN D'ARRET 1970 d: Yves Boisset. FRN./ITL., *Venere Privata*, Giorgio Scerbanenco, Novel

Cranes are Flying, The *see* LETYAT ZHURAVLI (1957).

Cranes Fly Early, The *see* RANNIE ZHURAVLI (1979).

CRASH 1978 d: Barry Shear. USA., *Crash*, Rob Elder, Sarah Elder, Book

CRASH 1996 d: David Cronenberg. CND., *Crash*, J. G. Ballard, Novel

Crash of Flight 401, The *see* CRASH (1978).

Crash of Silence *see* MANDY (1952).

CRASH, THE 1928 d: Eddie Cline. USA., *The Wrecking Boss*, Frank L. Packard, 1919, Short Story

CRASH, THE 1932 d: William Dieterle. USA., *Children of Pleasure*, Larry Barretto, New York 1932, Novel

Crashin' Thru *see* CRASHING THRU (1939).

CRASHING HOLLYWOOD 1938 d: Lew Landers. USA., *Lights Out*, Paul Dickey, Mann Page, New York 1922, Play

CRASHING THRU 1939 d: Elmer Clifton. USA., *Renfrew Rides the Range*, Laurie York Erskine, New York 1935, Novel

Crawling Terror, The *see* THE STRANGE WORLD OF PLANET X (1958).

CRAWLSPACE 1971 d: John Newland, Buzz Kulik. USA., *Crawlspace*, Herbert Lieberman, Novel

CRAZE 1973 d: Freddie Francis. UKN., *Infernal Idol*, Henry Seymour, Novel

Crazy Countess, The *see* DIE TOLLE KOMTESS (1928).

Crazy Day, A *see* EIN TOLLER TAG (1945).

Crazy Day, A *see* LA GIORNATA BALORDA (1960).

Crazy Desire *see* LA VOGLIA MATTA (1962).

Crazy for You *see* VISION QUEST (1985).

CRAZY LOVE 1986 d: Dominique Deruddere. BLG/FRN., *California, the Copulating Mermaid of Venice*, Charles Bukowski, Short Story

Crazy Paradise *see* DET TOSSEDE PARADIS (1962).

CRAZY PEOPLE 1934 d: Leslie Hiscott. UKN., *Safety First*, Margot Neville, Novel

CRAZY QUILT 1966 d: John Korty. USA., *The Illusionless Man and the Visionary Maid*, Allen Wheelis, 1964, Novel

CRAZY THAT WAY 1930 d: Hamilton MacFadden. USA., *In Love With Love*, Vincent Lawrence, New York 1923, Play

Cream of the Earth *see* RED LIPS (1928).

Creancier, Le *see* CAS DE CONSCIENCE (1939).

CREATION 1922 d: Humberston Wright. UKN., *The Man Who Dared*, May Edginton, Novel

CREATOR 1985 d: Ivan Passer. USA., *Creator*, Jeremy Leven, Novel

Creature from Blood Island *see* TERROR IS A MAN (1959).

Creature With the Blue Hand *see* DIE BLAUE HAND (1967).

Creatures from Another World *see* THE STRANGE WORLD OF PLANET X (1958).

CREDE-MI 1997 d: Bia Lessa, Dany Roland. BRZ., *The Holy Sinner*, Thomas Mann, Short Story

Creditors' Day *see* SVATEK VERITELU (1939).

Creepers, The *see* ASSAULT (1971).

CREEPING SHADOWS 1931 d: John Orton. UKN., *The Limping Man*, Will Scott, Croydon 1930, Play

Creeping Tides *see* THE TIDES OF FATE (1917).

CREEPSHOW 2 1987 d: Michael Gornick. USA., Stephen King, Short Story

Cremator of Corpses, The *see* SPALOVAC MRTVOL (1968).

Cremator, The *see* SPALOVAC MRTVOL (1968).

Crepscule Des Amours *see* LA NOTTE DELL'ALTA MAREA (1977).

Crest of the Wave *see* SEAGULLS OVER SORRENTO (1954).

CREVALCORE 1917 d: Romolo Bacchini. ITL., *Crevalcore*, Neera, 1907, Novel

Crew Cut *see* KORT AMERIKAANS (1979).

Crew, The *see* L' EQUIPAGE (1927).

CRI DE LA CHAIR, LE 1963 d: Jose Benazeraf. FRN., *L'Eternite Pour Nous*, G.-J. Arnaud, Paris 1960, Novel

CRI DU CORMORAN, LE SOIR, AU-DESSUS DES JONGES, LE 1970 d: Michel Audiard. FRN., *A Horses Head*, Evan Hunter, 1967, Novel

Cri du Hibou, Le *see* LE CRI DU L'HIBOU (1988).

CRI DU L'HIBOU, LE 1988 d: Claude Chabrol. FRN., *The Cry of the Owl*, Patricia Highsmith, 1964, Novel

Cri du Papillon, Le *see* POSLEDNI MOTYL (1989).

Cri, Un *see* DOCTEUR FRANCOISE GAILLAND (1975).

CRICKET ON THE HEARTH, THE 1909 d: D. W. Griffith. USA., *The Cricket on the Hearth*, Charles Dickens, London 1845, Novel

CRICKET ON THE HEARTH, THE 1914 d: Lawrence Marston. USA., *The Cricket on the Hearth*, Charles Dickens, London 1845, Novel

CRICKET ON THE HEARTH, THE 1914 d: Lorimer Johnston. USA., *The Cricket on the Hearth*, Charles Dickens, London 1845, Novel

CRICKET ON THE HEARTH, THE 1923 d: Lorimer Johnston. USA., *The Cricket on the Hearth*, Charles Dickens, London 1845, Novel

Cricket, The *see* LA CICALA (1980).

Cries in the Night *see* GRITOS EN LA NOCHE (1961).

CRIEZ-LE SUR LES TOITS 1932 d: Karl Anton. FRN., *It Pays to Advertise*, Walter Hackett, Roi Cooper Megrue, New York 1914, Play

Crime *see* LAW OF THE UNDERWORLD (1938).

Crime, A *see* ETT BROTT (1940).

Crime After School *see* VERBRECHEN NACH SCHULSCHLUSS (1959).

Crime After School *see* VERBRECHEN NACH SCHULSCHLUSS (1975).

CRIME AND PASSION 1975 d: Ivan Passer. USA/UKN/GRM., *Crime and Passion*, James Hadley Chase, Novel

CRIME AND PUNISHMENT 1917 d: Lawrence McGill. USA., *Prestupleniye I Nakazaniye*, Fyodor Dostoyevsky, 1867, Novel

Crime and Punishment *see* RASKOLNIKOW (1923).

CRIME AND PUNISHMENT 1935 d: Josef von Sternberg. USA., *Prestupleniye I Nakazaniye*, Fyodor Dostoyevsky, 1867, Novel

Crime and Punishment *see* CRIME ET CHATIMENT (1935).

Crime and Punishment *see* BROTT OCH STRAFF (1945).

Crime and Punishment *see* CRIMEN Y CASTIGO (1950).

Crime and Punishment *see* CRIME ET CHATIMENT (1956).

Crime and Punishment *see* PRESTUPLENIE I NAKAZANIE (1970).

Crime and Punishment *see* RIKOS JA RANGAISTUS (1983).

CRIME AND PUNISHMENT U.S.A. 1959 d: Denis Sanders. USA., *Prestupleniye I Nakazaniye*, Fyodor Dostoyevsky, 1867, Novel

CRIME AT BLOSSOMS, THE 1933 d: MacLean Rogers. UKN., *The Crime at Blossoms*, Mordaunt Shairp, Play

CRIME BY NIGHT 1944 d: William Clemens. USA., *Forty Whacks*, Daniel Mainwaring, Novel

Crime City *see* WHISPERING CITY (1947).

CRIME DE LORD ARTHUR SAVILE, LE 1921 d: Rene Hervil. FRN., *Lord Arthur Savile's Crime*, Oscar Wilde, 1891, Short Story

CRIME DE MONIQUE, LE 1924 d: Robert Peguy. FRN., *Le Crime de Monique*, Guy de Teramond, Novel

CRIME DE SYLVESTRE BONNARD, LE 1919. FRN., *Le Crime de Sylvestre Bonnard*, Anatole France, Paris 1881, Novel

CRIME DE SYLVESTRE BONNARD, LE 1929 d: Andre Berthomieu. FRN., *Le Crime de Sylvestre Bonnard*, Anatole France, Paris 1881, Novel

Crime de Vera Mirzewa, Le *see* DER FALL DES STAATSANWALTS M.. (1928).

CRIME DES JUSTES, LE 1948 d: Jean Gehret. FRN., *La Crime Des Justes*, Andre Chamson, 1928, Novel

CRIME DOCTOR 1934 d: John S. Robertson. USA., *The Big Bow Mystery*, Israel Zangwill, London 1892, Novel

CRIME D'OVIDE PLOUFFE, LE 1984 d: Denys Arcand. CND/FRN., *Le Crime d'Ovide Plouffe*, Roger Lemelin, Novel

CRIME DU BOUIF, LE 1921 d: Henri Pouctal. FRN., *Le Crime du Bouif*, Georges de La Fouchardiere, Novel

CRIME DU BOUIF, LE 1932 d: Andre Berthomieu. FRN., *Le Crime du Bouif*, Georges de La Fouchardiere, Novel

CRIME DU CHEMIN ROUGE, LE 1932 d: Jacques Severac. FRN., *Les Yeux du Coeur*, Paul Gavault, Play

CRIME D'UNE SAINTE, LE 1923 d: Charles Maudru. FRN., *Le Crime d'une Sainte*, Pierre Decourcelle, Novel

CRIME ET CHATIMENT 1935 d: Pierre Chenal. FRN., *Prestupleniy I Nakazaniye*, Fyodor Dostoyevsky, 1867, Novel

CRIME ET CHATIMENT 1956 d: Georges Lampin. FRN., *Prestupleniy I Nakazaniye*, Fyodor Dostoyevsky, 1867, Novel

Crime Et Ses Plaisirs, Le *see* LES FELINS (1964).

Crime Gives Orders *see* HUNTED MEN (1938).

Crime in the Maginot Line *see* DOUBLE CRIME SUR LA LIGNE MAGINOT (1937).

CRIME IN THE STREETS 1956 d: Don Siegel. USA., *Crime in the Streets*, Reginald Rose, 1955, Television Play

Crime in Yellow *see* POHISHTENIE V ZHALTO (1980).

Crime, Inc. *see* CRIME INCORPORATED (1945).

CRIME INCORPORATED 1945 d: Lew Landers. USA., *Inc. Crime*, Martin Mooney, Novel

Crime Is a Racket *see* YOU CAN'T GET AWAY WITH MURDER (1939).

CRIME NOBODY SAW, THE 1937 d: Charles T. Barton. USA., *Danger - Men Working*, Lowell Brentano, Ellery Queen, Baltimore, Md. 1936, Play

Crime of Dimitri Karamazov, The *see* DER MORDER DIMITRI KARAMASOFF (1931).

CRIME OF DR. CRESPI, THE 1935 d: John H. Auer. USA., *The Premature Burial*, Edgar Allan Poe, 1844, Short Story

Crime of Mary Andrews, The *see* THE TRIAL OF MARY DUGAN (1940).

Crime of Ovide Plouffe, The *see* LE CRIME D'OVIDE PLOUFFE (1984).

Crime of Sylvestre Bonnard *see* CHASING YESTERDAY (1935).

Crime of the Century *see* WALK EAST ON BEACON (1952).

CRIME OF THE CENTURY 1996 d: Mark Rydell. USA., *The Airman and the Carpenter*, Ludovic Kennedy, Book

CRIME OF THE CENTURY, THE 1933 d: William Beaudine. USA., *Der Fall Grootman*, Walter Maria Espe, Play

CRIME ON THE HILL 1933 d: Bernard Vorhaus. UKN., *Crime on the Hill*, Jack Celestin, Jack de Leon, 1932, Play

CRIME OVER LONDON 1936 d: Alfred Zeisler. UKN., *House of a Thousand Windows*, Louis de Wohl, Novel

Crime Passionnel *see* GUILTY? (1956).

CRIME UNLIMITED 1935 d: Ralph Ince. UKN., *Crime Unlimited*, David Hume, Novel

CRIME WAVE 1954 d: Andre de Toth. USA., *Criminal's Mark*, John Hawkins, Ward Hawkins, Short Story

CRIME WITHOUT PASSION 1934 d: Ben Hecht, Charles MacArthur. USA., *Caballero of the Law*, Ben Hecht, 1933, Short Story

CRIMEN DE ORIBE, EL 1950 d: Leopoldo Torre-Nilsson, Leopoldo Torres-Rios. ARG., *El Perjurio de la Nieve*, Adolfo Bioy Casares, 1945, Novel

CRIMEN Y CASTIGO 1950 d: Fernando de Fuentes. MXC., *Prestupleniye I Nakazaniye*, Fyodor Dostoyevsky, 1867, Novel

Crimes a Vendre *see* LE FURET (1949).

CRIMES AT THE DARK HOUSE 1940 d: George King. UKN., *The Woman in White*, Wilkie Collins, London 1860, Novel

CRIMES DE L'AMOUR, LES 1951 d: Alexandre Astruc, Maurice Barry. FRN., *Mina de Vanghel*, Stendhal, 1855, Short Story

Crimes of Dr. Mabuse *see* DAS TESTAMENT DES DR. MABUSE (1933).

CRIMES OF THE HEART 1986 d: Bruce Beresford. USA., *Crimes of the Heart*, Beth Henley, 1982, Play

Criminal at Large *see* THE FRIGHTENED LADY (1932).

CRIMINAL CODE, THE 1931 d: Howard Hawks. USA., *The Criminal Code*, Martin Flavin, New York 1929, Play

Criminal Doctor *see* UNDERCOVER DOCTOR (1939).

Criminal Face *see* HO! (1968).

Criminal Life of Archibaldo de la Cruz, The *see* ENSAYO DE UN CRIMEN (1955).

Criminal Story *see* LA ROUTE DE CORINTHE (1967).

Criminal Within, The *see* MURDER AT GLEN ATHOL (1936).

CRIMINE A DUE 1965 d: Romano FerrarA. ITL., *La Casa Maledetta*, Elisa Pezzana, Play

CRIMINEL 1932 d: Jack Forrester. FRN., *The Criminal Code*, Martin Flavin, New York 1929, Play

Criminel a Peur Des Gosses, Le *see* LES GOSSES MENENT L'ENQUETE (1946).

CRIMINEL, LE 1926 d: Alexandre Ryder. FRN., *Le Criminel*, Andre Corthis, Novel

Criminels *see* CRIMINEL (1932).

CRIMSON CHALLENGE, THE 1922 d: Paul Powell. USA., *Tharon of Lost Valley*, Vingie E. Roe, New York 1919, Novel

CRIMSON CIRCLE, THE 1922 d: George Ridgwell. UKN., *The Crimson Circle*, Edgar Wallace, London 1922, Novel

Crimson Circle, The *see* DER ROTE KREIS (1928).

CRIMSON CIRCLE, THE 1936 d: Reginald Denham. UKN., *The Crimson Circle*, Edgar Wallace, London 1922, Novel

Crimson Circle, The *see* DER ROTE KREIS (1959).

Crimson Curtain, The *see* LE RIDEAU CRAMOISI (1952).

Crimson Dynasty, The *see* KOENIGSMARK (1935).

CRIMSON GARDENIA, THE 1919 d: Reginald Barker. USA., *The Crimson Gardenia*, Rex Beach, New York 1916, Short Story

CRIMSON PARADISE, THE 1933 d: Robert F. Hill. CND., *The Crimson West*, Alexander Philip, Novel

Crimson Rain *see* HONG YU (1975).

CRIMSON TRAIL, THE 1935 d: Alfred Raboch. USA., Wilton West, Short Story

CRIMSON WING, THE 1915 d: E. H. Calvert. USA., *The Crimson Wing*, Hobart C. Chatfield-Taylor, Chicago 1902, Novel

Crippled Devil, The *see* EL DIABLO COJUELO (1970).

CRIPTA E L'INCUBO, LA 1964 d: Camillo Mastrocinque. ITL/SPN., *Carmilla*, Sheridan le Fanu, London 1872, Short Story

CRISANTEMO MACCHIATO DI SANGUE, IL 1921 d: Domenico Di Maggio. ITL., *Il Crisantemo MacChiato Di Sangue*, John World, Novel

CRISI, LA 1922 d: Augusto GeninA. ITL., *La Crisi*, Marco Praga, 1904, Play

Crisis *see* KRIS (1946).

CRISIS 1950 d: Richard Brooks. USA., *The Doubters*, George Tabori, Novel

Crisis 2050 *see* SOLAR CRISIS (1992).

CRISIS AT CENTRAL HIGH 1981 d: Lamont Johnson. USA., Elizabeth Huckaby, Book

CRISIS, THE 1916 d: Colin Campbell. USA., *The Crisis*, Winston Churchill, New York 1901, Novel

CRISPINO E LA COMARE 1918 d: Camillo de Riso. ITL., *Crispino E la Comare*, Federico Ricci, Luigi Ricci, Venice 1850, Opera

CRISPINO E LA COMARE 1938 d: Vincenzo Sorelli. ITL., *Crispino E la Comare*, Federico Ricci, Luigi Ricci, Venice 1850, Opera

CRISS CROSS 1949 d: Robert Siodmak. USA., *Criss Cross*, Don Tracy, Novel

Criss Cross *see* CRISSCROSS (1992).

CRISSCROSS 1992 d: Chris Menges. USA., *Crisscross*, Scott Sommer, Novel

CRISTO PROIBITO, IL 1951 d: Curzio Malaparte. ITL., *Il Cristo Proibito*, Curzio Malaparte, Novel

CRISTO SI E FERMATO A EBOLI 1979 d: Francesco Rosi. ITL/FRN., *Cristo Ei E Fermato a Eboli*, Carlo Levi, 1945, Novel

Critical Age, The *see* GLENGARRY SCHOOL DAYS (1923).

CRITICAL CARE 1997 d: Sidney Lumet. USA., *Critical Care*, Richard Dooling, Novel

CRITICAL LIST, THE 1978 d: Lou Antonio. USA., *The Critical List*, Marshall Goldberg, Novel, *Skeletons*, Marshall Goldberg, Novel

CRITIC'S CHOICE 1963 d: Don Weis. USA., *Critic's Choice*, Ira Levin, New York 1960, Play

Croc-Blanc *see* ZANNA BIANCA (1973).

CROCODILE TEARS 1998 d: Ann Coppel. USA., *Satan and Simon Desoto*, Ted Sod, Play

Crocodiles in the Suburbs *see* VORSTADTKROKODILE (1978).

Croise de l'Ordre, Le *see* NOVACEK: LE CROISE DE L'ORDRE (1994).

Croise Veux-Tu *see* LES VACANCES DE XAVIER (1933).

CROISEE DES CHEMINS, LA 1942 d: Andre Berthomieu. FRN., *La Croisee Des Chemins*, Henri Bordeaux, Novel

CROISIERE POUR L'INCONNU 1947 d: Pierre Montazel. FRN., *L'Aventure Est a Bord*, G. Vidal, Novel

Croisseur En Folie, Le *see* LE CAPITAINE CRADDOCK (1931).

CROIX DE BOIS, LES 1931 d: Raymond Bernard. FRN., *Les Croix de Bois*, Roland Dorgeles, Novel

CROIX DU CERVIN, LA 1922 d: Marcel Grosnier, Jacques Beranger. SWT., *La Croix du Cervin*, Charles Gos, Lausanne 1919, Novel

CROIX DU SUD, LA 1931 d: Andre Hugon. FRN., *La Croix du Sud*, Paul Achard, Novel

CROIX SUR LE ROCHER, LA 1927 d: Edmond Levenq, Jean Rosne. FRN., *La Croix Sur le Rocher*, Edmond Levenq, Jean Rosne, Novel

CROLLO, IL 1920 d: Mario Gargiulo. ITL., *Lumie Di Sicilia*, Luigi Pirandello, Short Story

CRONACA DI UNA MORTE ANNUNCIATA 1987 d: Francesco Rosi. ITL/FRN., *Cronaca Di Una Morte Annunciata*, Gabriel Garcia Marquez, 1981, Novel

CRONACA FAMILIARE 1962 d: Valerio Zurlini. ITL., *Cronaca Familiare*, Vasco Pratolini, Florence 1947, Novel

CRONACHE DI POVERI AMANTI 1954 d: Carlo Lizzani. ITL., *Cronache Di Poveri Amanti*, Vasco Pratolini, 1947, Novel

CRONICA DA CIDADE AMADA 1965 d: Carlos Hugo Christensen. BRZ., *O Indio*, Carlos Drummond de Andrade, 1962, Short Story, *Luzia*, Carlos Drummond de Andrade, 1962, Short Story

CROOKED BILLET, THE 1929 d: Adrian Brunel. UKN., *The Crooked Billet*, Dion Titheradge, London 1927, Play

CROOKED HEARTS, THE 1972 d: Jay Sandrich. USA., *Miss Lonelyhearts 4122*, Colin Watson, Novel

CROOKED LADY, THE 1932 d: Leslie Hiscott. UKN., *The Crooked Lady*, William C. Stone, Novel

CROOKED MAN, THE 1923 d: George Ridgwell. UKN., *The Crooked Man*, Arthur Conan Doyle, Short Story

Crooked Man, The *see* THE ADVENTURES OF SHERLOCK HOLMES: THE CROOKED MAN (1983).

CROOKED ROAD, THE 1964 d: Don Chaffey. UKN/YGS., *The Big Story*, Morris West, London 1957, Novel

CROOKED STREETS 1920 d: Paul Powell. USA., *Dinner at Eight*, Samuel Merwin, 1912, Short Story

CROOKED WAY, THE 1949 d: Robert Florey. USA., *No Blade Too Sharp*, Robert Monroe, Radio Play

Crooks in Clover *see* PENTHOUSE (1933).

Crooks in Clover *see* LES TONTONS FLINGUERS (1963).

CROONER 1932 d: Lloyd Bacon. USA., *Crooner*, Rian James, New York 1932, Novel

CROQUETTE 1927 d: Louis Mercanton. FRN., *Croquette*, Eric Maschwitz, Novel

CROSS AND THE SWITCHBLADE, THE 1970 d: Don Murray. USA., *The Cross and the Switchblade*, John & Elizabeth Sherrill, David Wilkerson, New York 1963, Autobiography

Cross at the Brook, The *see* KRIZ U POTOKA (1921).

Cross at the Stream, The *see* KRIZ U POTOKA (1921).

Cross By the Brook, The *see* KRIZ U POTOKA (1937).

CROSS COUNTRY 1983 d: Paul Lynch. CND., *Cross-Country*, Herbert Kastle, Novel

Cross Country Romance *see* CROSS-COUNTRY ROMANCE (1940).

CROSS CREEK 1983 d: Martin Ritt. USA., *Cross Creek*, Marjorie K. Rawlings, 1942, Book

CROSS CURRENTS 1935 d: Adrian Brunel. UKN., *Nine Days Blunder*, Gerald Elliott, Novel

CROSS MY HEART 1946 d: John Berry. USA., Georges Berr, Louis Verneuil, Play

CROSS OF IRON 1977 d: Sam Peckinpah. UKN/GRM., *The Willing Flesh*, Willi Heinrich, Novel

CROSS OF LORRAINE, THE 1943 d: Tay Garnett. USA., *A Thousand Shall Fall*, Hans Habe, Autobiography

Cross of Love, The *see* RAKKAUDEN RISTI (1946).

Cross Pull *see* BORN TO FIGHT (1932).

Cross Up *see* TIGER BY THE TAIL (1955).

CROSSBAR 1979 d: John Trent. CND., *Crossbar*, Bill Boyle, Story

CROSS-COUNTRY ROMANCE 1940 d: Frank Woodruff. USA., *Highway to Romance*, Eleanor Browne, New York 1937, Novel

Crossed Lives *see* VIDAS CRUZADAS (1942).

Crossed Swords *see* THE PRINCE AND THE PAUPER (1978).

Crossers, The see DER KREUZLSCHREIBER (1950).

CROSSFIRE 1947 d: Edward Dmytryk. USA., *The Brick Foxhole*, Richard Brooks, Novel

Crossing Borders see HERZLICH WILLKOMMEN (1989).

CROSSING DELANCEY 1988 d: Joan Micklin Silver. USA., *Crossing Delancey*, Susan Sandler, Play

Crossing, The see PAAR (1984).

Crossing, The see LA PASSERELLE (1987).

CROSSING TO FREEDOM 1990 d: Norman Stone. UKN/USA., *The Pied Piper*, Nevil Shute, 1942, Novel

CROSSINGS 1985 d: Karen Arthur. USA., *Crossings*, Danielle Steel, Novel

CROSSMAHEART 1998 d: Henry Herbert. UKN., *Cycle of Violence*, Colin Bateman, Novel

Cross-Makers, The see DER KREUZLSCHREIBER (1950).

Crossroads see THE AGE OF CONSENT (1932).

CROSSTRAP 1962 d: Robert Hartford-Davis. UKN., *Crosstrap*, John Newton Chance, Novel

CROSSWINDS 1951 d: Lewis R. Foster. USA., *New Guinea Gold*, Thomson Burtis, Novel

CROUCHING BEAST, THE 1935 d: Victor Hanbury. UKN., *Clubfoot*, Valentine Williams, Novel

CROULANTS SE PORTENT BIEN, LES 1961 d: Jean Boyer. FRN., *Les Croulants Se Portent Bien*, Roger Ferdinand, Play

Crow Killer, The see JEREMIAH JOHNSON (1972).

Crowded Coffin, The see TRAFRACKEN (1966).

CROWDED HOUR, THE 1925 d: E. Mason Hopper. USA., *The Crowded Hour*, Channing Pollock, Edgar Selwyn, New York 1918, Play

CROWDED SKY, THE 1960 d: Joseph Pevney. USA., *The Crowded Sky*, Henry Searls, Novel

CROWN MATRIMONIAL 1973 d: Alan Bridges. UKN., *Crown Matrimonial*, Royce Ryton, Play

Crown of Shame, The see DE KROON DER SCHANDE (1918).

CROWN V STEVENS 1936 d: Michael Powell. UKN., *Third Time Unlucky*, Laurence Meynell, Novel

CROXLEY MASTER, THE 1921 d: Percy Nash. UKN., *The Croxley Master*, Arthur Conan Doyle, Novel

CRUCIBLE OF LIFE, THE 1918 d: Harry Lambart. USA., *Fairfax*, Bartley Campbell, New York 1879, Play

CRUCIBLE, THE 1914 d: Edwin S. Porter, Hugh Ford. USA., *The Crucible*, Mark Lee Luther, New York 1907, Novel

Crucible, The see LES SORCIERES DE SALEM (1957).

CRUCIBLE, THE 1996 d: Nicholas Hytner. USA., *The Crucible*, Arthur Miller, 1953, Play

Crucified Girl, The see UKRIZOVANA (1921).

Crucified Lovers, The see CHIKAMATSU MONOGATARI (1954).

Crucified, The see UKRIZOVANA (1921).

CRUCIFIX, LE 1909 d: Louis Feuillade. FRN., *Le Crucifix*, Victor Hugo, Poem

Cruel Dawn see ZORSTOKI SVITANKI (1966).

Cruel Embrace, The see LES NOCES BARBARES (1987).

Cruel Ghost Legend see KAIDAN ZANKOKU MONOGATARI (1968).

CRUEL INTENTIONS 1999 d: Roger Kumble. USA., *Les Liaisons Dangereuses*, Pierre Ambrose Choderlos de Laclos, 1782, Novel

CRUEL PASSION 1977 d: Chris Boger. UKN., *Justine; Ou Les Malheurs de la Vertu*, Donatien Sade, 1791, Novel

Cruel Romance see ZESTOKIJ ROMANS (1984).

CRUEL SEA, THE 1953 d: Charles Frend. UKN., *The Cruel Sea*, Nicholas Monsarrat, 1951, Novel

Cruel Star see CRUEL PASSION (1977).

CRUEL TOWER, THE 1956 d: Lew Landers. USA., *The Cruel Tower*, William B. Hartley, Novel

CRUISE OF THE JASPER B, THE 1926 d: James W. Horne. USA., *The Cruise of the Jasper B*, Don Marquis, New York 1916, Novel

CRUISE OF THE MAKE-BELIEVES, THE 1918 d: George Melford. USA., *The Cruise of the Make-Believes*, Tom Gallon, Boston 1907, Novel

CRUISING 1980 d: William Friedkin. USA., *Cruising*, Gerald Walker, Novel

Crumbling Citadel, The see CITADELA SFARIMATA (1957).

CRUSADER, THE 1922 d: Howard M. Mitchell, William K. Howard. USA., *The Crusader*, Alan Sullivan, 1916, Short Story

Crusaders, The see LA GERUSALEMME LIBERATA (1911).

CRUSOE 1989 d: Caleb Deschanel. USA/UKN., *Robinson Crusoe*, Daniel Defoe, 1719, Novel

CRUZ DEL DIABLO, LA 1974 d: John Gilling. SPN., *La Cruz Del Diablo*, Gustavo Adolfo Becquer, 1860, Short Story, *El Miserere*, Gustavo Adolfo Becquer, 1862, Short Story, *El Monte de Las Animas*, Gustavo Adolfo Becquer, 1860, Short Story

Cry and Cry Again see KIALTAS ES KIALTAS (1988).

Cry Double Cross see BUMERANG (1960).

CRY FOR HAPPY 1961 d: George Marshall. USA., *Cry for Happy*, George Campbell, New York 1958, Novel

Cry for Strangers see CRY FOR THE STRANGERS (1982).

CRY FOR THE STRANGERS 1982 d: Peter Medak. USA., *Cry for the Strangers*, John Saul, Novel

CRY FREEDOM 1959 d: Lamberto V. Avellana. PHL., *The Crucible*, Yay Marking

CRY FREEDOM 1987 d: Richard Attenborough. UKN/ZIM., *Asking for Trouble*, Donald Woods, Book, *Biko*, Donald Woods, Book

CRY FROM THE STREETS, A 1958 d: Lewis Gilbert. UKN., *The Friend in Need*, Elizabeth Coxhead, Novel

CRY HAVOC 1943 d: Richard Thorpe. USA., *Proof Thro' the Night*, Alan R. Kenward, Play

CRY IN THE DARK, A 1988 d: Fred Schepisi. USA/ASL., *Evil Angels*, John Bryson, Book

CRY IN THE NIGHT, A 1956 d: Frank Tuttle. USA., *All Throught the Night*, Whit Masterson, 1955, Novel

Cry in the Siberian Night see VYKRIK DO SIBIRSKE NOCI (1935).

CRY MURDER 1950 d: Jack Glenn. USA., *Cry Murder*, A. B. Shiffrin, Play

CRY OF BATTLE 1963 d: Irving Lerner. USA/PHL., *Fortress in the Rice*, Benjamin Appel, Indianapolis 1951, Novel

Cry of the Black Wolves see DER SCHREI DER SCHWARZEN WOLFE (1972).

CRY OF THE CHILDREN, THE 1912. USA., *The Cry of the Children*, Elizabeth Barrett Browning, Poem

CRY OF THE CITY 1948 d: Robert Siodmak. USA., *The Chair for Martin Rome*, Henry Helseth, Novel

CRY OF THE NIGHTHAWK, THE 1923 d: A. E. Coleby. UKN., *The Cry of the Nighthawk*, Sax Rohmer, Short Story

Cry of the Owl, The see LE CRI DU L'HIBOU (1988).

Cry of the Swamp see LURE OF THE WILDERNESS (1952).

CRY, THE BELOVED COUNTRY 1952 d: Zoltan KordA. UKN/SAF., *Cry the Beloved Country*, Alan Paton, 1948, Novel

CRY, THE BELOVED COUNTRY 1995 d: Darrell Roodt. USA., *Cry the Beloved Country*, Alan Paton, 1948, Novel

CRY TOUGH 1959 d: Paul Stanley. USA., *Cry Tough*, Irving Shulman, 1949, Novel

CRY WOLF 1947 d: Peter Godfrey. USA., *Cry Wolf*, Marjorie Carleton, Novel

Crypt and the Nightmare, The see LA CRIPTA E L'INCUBO (1964).

Crypt of Horror see LA CRIPTA E L'INCUBO (1964).

Crypt With the Puzzle Lock, The see DIE GRUFT MIT DEM RATSELSCHLOSS (1964).

CRYSTAL CUP, THE 1927 d: John Francis Dillon. USA., *The Crystal Cup*, Gertrude Franklin Atherton, New York 1925, Novel

CRYSTAL HEART 1987 d: Gil Bettman. USA/SPN., Alberto Vazquez Figueroa, Novel

Crystal's Structure see STRUKTURA KRYSZTALU (1970).

C.S. Lewis: Through the Shadowlands see SHADOWLANDS (1985).

Csardas of the Hearts see CZARDAS DER HERZEN (1951).

Csardasfurstin, Die see DIE CZARDASFURSTIN (1934).

Csardasfurstin, Die see DIE CZARDASFURSTIN (1951).

CSEND ES KIALTAS 1968 d: Miklos Jancso. HNG., *Kialtas*, Gyula Hernadi, 1967, Short Story

CSILLAG A MAGLYAN 1979 d: Otto Adam. HNG., *Csillag a Maglyan*, Andras Suto, 1976, Play

CSILLAGSZEMU, A 1977 d: Miklos Markos. HNG., *A Csillagszemu*, Grandpierre Emil Kolozsvari, 1953, Novel

Csutak and the Grey Horse see CSUTAK ES A SZURKE LO (1960).

CSUTAK ES A SZURKE LO 1960 d: Zoltan Varkonyi. HNG., *Csutak Es a Szurke Lo*, Ivan Mandy, 1959, Novel

C'T'A TON TOUR, LAURA CADIEUX 1998 d: Denise Filatrault. CND., *Cota Ton Teur Laura Cadieux*, Michel Tremblay, Novel

CTRNACTY U STOLU 1943 d: Oldrich Novy, Antonin ZelenkA. CZC., *Der Vierzehnte Am Tisch*, Ossi Oswalda, Story

Cuando Estallo la Paz see LOS QUE NO FUIMOS A LA GUERRA (1961).

CUANDO LLEGUE LA NOCHE 1946 d: Jeronimo MihurA. SPN., *Cuando Llegue la Noche*, Joaquin Calvo Sotelo, 1944, Play

Cuando Los Hijos Nos Juzgan see UNA MUJER SIN AMOR (1951).

Cuatro Novias de Augusto Perez, Las see NIEBLA (1975).

CUATRO ROBINSONES, LOS 1926 d: Reinhardt Blothner. SPN., *Los Cuatro Robinsones*, Enrique G. Alvarez, Pedro Munoz Seca, Play

CUB, THE 1915 d: Maurice Tourneur. USA., *The Cub*, Thompson Buchanan, New York 1910, Play

CUBA CABANA 1952 d: Fritz Peter Buch. GRM., *Cuba Cabana*, Tibor Yost, Short Story

CUCCAGNA, LA 1917 d: Baldassarre Negroni. ITL., *La Curee*, Emile Zola, Paris 1871, Novel

Cuckoo Clock, The see L' OROLOGIO A CUCU (1938).

CUCKOO IN THE NEST, A 1933 d: Tom Walls. UKN., *A Cuckoo in the Nest*, Ben Travers, London 1925, Play

CUCKOOS, THE 1930 d: Paul Sloane. USA., *The Ramblers*, Guy Bolton, Bert Kalmar, Harry Ruby, New York 1926, Musical Play

CUCOANA CHIRITA 1987 d: Mircea Dragan. RMN., *Cucoana Chirita in Provincie*, Vasile Alecsandri, 1852, Play

CUDNA DEVOJKA 1961 d: Jovan Zivanovic. YGS., *Izlet U Nebo*, Grozdana Olujic, 1958, Novel

Cudoviti Prah see DIVOTA PRASINE (1976).

CUDZOZIEMKA 1986 d: Ryszard Ber. PLN., *Cudzoziemka*, Maria Kuncewiczowa, 1935, Novel

CUGINA, LA 1974 d: Aldo Lado. ITL., *La Cugina*, Ercole Patti, Novel

CUJO 1984 d: Lewis Teague. USA., *Cujo*, Stephen King, 1981, Novel

Culte de la Beaute, Le see ARTHUR (1930).

CUMBERLAND ROMANCE, A 1920 d: Charles Maigne. USA., *A Mountain Europa*, John Fox Jr., New York 1899, Novel

CUMBRES BORRASCOSAS 1953 d: Luis Bunuel. MXC., *Wuthering Heights*, Emily Jane Bronte, London 1847, Novel

Cunning Woman, A see THE LION'S MOUSE (1923).

CUNNINGHAMES ECONOMISE, THE 1922 d: George A. Cooper. UKN., *The Cunninghames Economise*, Mayell Bannister, Story

CUOR DI VAGABONDO 1936 d: Jean Epstein. ITL., Alfred MacHin, Novel

CUORE 1948 d: Duilio Coletti. ITL., *Cuore*, Edmondo de Amicis, 1886, Short Story

CUORE 1974 d: Romano Scavolini. ITL., *Cuore*, Edmondo de Amicis, 1886, Short Story

CUORE DI CANE 1975 d: Alberto LattuadA. ITL/GRM., *Sobach'e Serdtse*, Mikhail Bulgakov, 1968, Short Story

CUORE SEMPLICE, UN 1976 d: Giorgio FerrarA. ITL., *Un Cuore Semplice*, Gustave Flaubert, Novel

CUORI E SENSI 1917 d: Carlo Farinetti. ITL., *The Beauty*, Lewis Wallace, Novel

CUP OF FURY, THE 1920 d: T. Hayes Hunter. USA., *The Cup of Fury*, Rupert Hughes, New York 1919, Novel

CUP OF KINDNESS, A 1934 d: Tom Walls. UKN., *A Cup of Kindness*, Ben Travers, London 1929, Play

CUPID FORECLOSES 1919 d: David Smith. USA., *Hurrying Fate and Geraldine*, Florence Morse Kingsley, New York 1913, Novel

725

CUPID IN CLOVER 1929 d: Frank Miller. UKN., *Yellow Corn*, Upton Grey, Novel

Cupid in the Rough *see* MAKER OF MEN AGGIE APPLEBY (1933).

CUPID THE COWPUNCHER 1920 d: Clarence Badger. USA., *Cupid: the Cow-Punch*, Eleanor Gates, New York 1907, Novel

CUPID'S FIREMAN 1923 d: William A. Wellman. USA., *Andy M'gee's Chorus Girl*, Richard Harding Davis, 1892, Short Story

Cupid's Understudy *see* CUPID FORECLOSES (1919).

CURA DE ALDEA, EL 1926 d: Florian Rey. SPN., *El Cura de Aldea*, Enrique Perez Escrich, Novel

CURE DE SAINT-AMOUR, LE 1952 d: Emile Couzinet. FRN., *Le Cure de Saint-Amour*, Jean Guitton, Play

CURE FOR LOVE, THE 1950 d: Robert Donat. UKN., *The Cure for Love*, Walter Greenwood, London 1945, Play

Cure for the Blues *see* YOUNG AS YOU FEEL (1931).

CUREE, LA 1966 d: Roger Vadim. FRN/ITL., *La Curee*, Emile Zola, Paris 1871, Novel

CURFEW MUST NOT RING TONIGHT 1912 d: Hay Plumb. UKN., *Curfew Shall Not Ring Tonight*, Rose H. Thorpe, Poem

CURFEW MUST NOT RING TONIGHT 1923 d: Edwin J. Collins. UKN., *Curfew Shall Not Ring Tonight*, Rose H. Thorpe, Poem

CURFEW SHALL NOT RING TONIGHT 1906 d: Alf Collins. UKN., *Curfew Shall Not Ring Tonight*, Rose H. Thorpe, Poem

CURFEW SHALL NOT RING TONIGHT 1912 d: Hal Reid. USA., *Curfew Shall Not Ring Tonight*, Rose H. Thorpe, Poem

CURFEW SHALL NOT RING TONIGHT 1926 d: Frank Tilley. UKN., *Curfew Shall Not Ring Tonight*, Rose H. Thorpe, Poem

CURIOSA EREDITA, UNA 1914. ITL., *Bere O Affogare*, Leo Di Castelnuovo

CURIOSO IMPERTINENTE, EL 1948 d: Flavio CalzavarA. SPN., *El Ingenioso Hidalgo Don Quijote de la Mancha*, Miguel de Cervantes Saavedra, 1605-15, Novel

CURIOUS CONDUCT OF JUDGE LEGARDE, THE 1915 d: Will S. Davis. USA., *The Curious Conduct of Judge Legarde*, Louis Forest, Victor Mapes, Washington D.C. 1912, Play

Curly *see* ONCE UPON A TIME (1944).

CURLYTOP 1924 d: Maurice Elvey. USA., *Twelve Golden Curls*, Thomas Burke, Short Story

CURRITO DE LA CRUZ 1925 d: Fernando Delgado, Alejandro Perez Lugin. SPN., *Currito de la Cruz*, Alejandro Perez Lugin, Novel

CURRO VARGAS 1923 d: Jose Buchs. SPN., *Curro Vargas*, Ruperto Chapi, Joaquin Dicenta, Manuel Paso, Opera

Curse and the Coffin, The *see* LA CHAMBRE ARDENTE (1961).

Curse of Capistrano, The *see* THE MARK OF ZORRO (1920).

CURSE OF DRINK, THE 1922 d: Harry O. Hoyt. USA., *The Curse of Drink*, Charles E. Blaney, 1904, Play

CURSE OF FRANKENSTEIN, THE 1957 d: Terence Fisher. UKN., *Frankenstein; Or the Modern Prometheus*, Mary Wollstonecraft Shelley, London 1818, Novel

Curse of Greed, The *see* THE TWIN PAWNS (1919).

Curse of Kali *see* THE HOUSE OF MYSTERY (1934).

CURSE OF KING TUTANKHAMEN'S TOMB, THE 1980 d: Philip Leacock. UKN/USA., *The Curse of King Tutenkhamen's Tomb*, Barry Wynne, Novel

Curse of King Tut's Tomb, The *see* THE CURSE OF KING TUTANKHAMEN'S TOMB (1980).

Curse of the Blood *see* KAIDAN ZANKOKU MONOGATARI (1968).

Curse of the Demon *see* NIGHT OF THE DEMON (1957).

CURSE OF THE FLY, THE 1965 d: Don Sharp. UKN., *The Fly*, George Langelaan, Short Story

Curse of the Hidden Vault, The *see* DIE GRUFT MIT DEM RATSELSCHLOSS (1964).

Curse of the Karnstein, The *see* LA CRIPTA E L'INCUBO (1964).

Curse of the Mummy *see* BLOOD FROM THE MUMMY'S TOMB (1972).

Curse of the Night, The *see* YOTSUYA KAIDAN -OIWA NO BOREI (1969).

CURSE OF THE STARVING CLASS 1994 d: Michael McClary. USA., *Curse of the Starving Class*, Sam Shepard, Play

CURSE OF THE VIKING GRAVE 1992 d: Michael Scott. CND., *Curse of the Viking Grave*, Farley Mowat, Novel

CURSE OF THE WEREWOLF, THE 1961 d: Terence Fisher. UKN., *The Werewolf of Paris*, Guy Endore, New York 1933, Novel

Curse, The *see* GHOSTS (1915).

Curse, The *see* XALA (1974).

Cursed Tangle, A *see* UN MALEDETTO IMBROGLIO (1959).

CURTAIN 1920 d: James Young. USA., *Curtain*, Rita Weiman, 1919, Short Story

CURTAIN AT EIGHT 1934 d: E. Mason Hopper. USA., Octavus Roy Cohen, Story

CURTAIN UP 1952 d: Ralph Smart. UKN., *On Monday Next*, Philip King, London 1949, Play

CURTIS'S CHARM 1995 d: John L'Ecuyer. CND., *Curtis's Charm*, Jim Carroll, Short Story

CUSTARD CUP, THE 1923 d: Herbert Brenon. USA., *The Custard Cup*, Florence Bingham Livingston, New York 1921, Novel

Custer's Last Stand *see* BOB HAMPTON OF PLACER (1921).

CUSTOMARY TWO WEEKS, THE 1917 d: Saul Harrison. USA., *The Customary Two Weeks*, Freeman Tilden, 1917, Short Story

CUTTER AND BONE 1981 d: Ivan Passer. USA., *Cutter's Way*, Newton Thornburg, Novel

Cutter's Way *see* CUTTER AND BONE (1981).

Cutting It Short *see* POSTRIZINY (1980).

Cuttings *see* POSTRIZINY (1980).

CY PERKINS IN THE CITY OF DELUSION 1915 d: Roy McCray. USA., *Cy Perkins in the City of Delusion*, C. M. Stevens, Story

CY WHITTAKER'S WARD 1917 d: Ben Turbett. USA., *Cy Whittaker's Place*, Joseph C. Lincoln, New York 1908, Novel

CYANKALI 1930 d: Hans Tintner. GRM., *Cyankali*, Friedrich Wolf, Play

Cybele *see* LES DIMANCHES DE VILLE D'AVRAY (1962).

Cybele Ou Les Dimanches de Ville-D'avray *see* LES DIMANCHES DE VILLE D'AVRAY (1962).

Cyborg *see* THE SIX MILLION DOLLAR MAN (1973).

Cycle of Violence *see* CROSSMAHEART (1998).

Cyclops, The *see* KIKLOP (1982).

CYMBELINE 1913 d: Theodore Marston. USA., *Cymbeline*, William Shakespeare, c1610, Play

CYNARA 1932 d: King Vidor. USA., *Cynara*, Robert Gore-Browne, H. M. Harwood, London 1930, Play

Cynic Effect, The *see* THE COUNTRY FLAPPER (1922).

CYNTHIA 1947 d: Robert Z. Leonard. USA., *The Rich Full Life*, Vina Delmar, New York 1945, Play

CYNTHIA IN THE WILDERNESS 1916 d: Harold Weston. UKN., *Cynthia in the Wilderness*, Hubert Wales, Novel

CYNTHIA-OF-THE-MINUTE 1920 d: Perry N. Vekroff. USA., *Cynthia-of-the-Minute*, Louis Joseph Vance, New York 1911, Novel

Cyrano de Bergerac *see* CIRANO DI BERGERAC (1909).

CYRANO DE BERGERAC 1925 d: Fernand Rivers. FRN., *Cyrano de Bergerac*, Edmond Rostand, 1897, Play

CYRANO DE BERGERAC 1950 d: Michael Gordon. USA., *Cyrano de Bergerac*, Edmond Rostand, 1897, Play

CYRANO DE BERGERAC 1960 d: Claude BarmA. FRN., *Cyrano de Bergerac*, Edmond Rostand, 1897, Play

CYRANO DE BERGERAC 1989 d: Jean-Paul Rappeneau. FRN., *Cyrano de Bergerac*, Edmond Rostand, 1897, Play

CYTHEREA 1924 d: George Fitzmaurice. USA., *Goddess of Love Cytherea*, Joseph Hergesheimer, New York 1922, Novel

CZARDAS DER HERZEN 1951 d: Alexander von SlatinA. GRM., *Servus Peter*, Karl Noti, Play

Czardas Princess, The *see* DIE CZARDASFURSTIN (1951).

CZARDASFURSTIN, DIE 1927 d: Hanns Schwarz. GRM., *Die Czardasfurstin*, B. Jenbach, Emmerich Kalman, Leo Stein, Vienna 1915, Operetta

CZARDASFURSTIN, DIE 1934 d: Georg Jacoby. GRM., *Die Czardasfurstin*, B. Jenbach, Emmerich Kalman, Leo Stein, Vienna 1915, Operetta

CZARDASFURSTIN, DIE 1951 d: Georg Jacoby. GRM., *Die Czardasfurstin*, B. Jenbach, Emmerich Kalman, Leo Stein, Vienna 1915, Operetta

Czarina *see* A ROYAL SCANDAL (1945).

CZARNE SKRZYDLA 1962 d: Ewa Petelska, Czeslaw Petelski. PLN., *Czarne Skrzydla*, Juliusz Kaden-Bandrowski, 1928-29, Novel

D. W. Griffith's "That Royle Girl" *see* "THAT ROYLE GIRL" (1925).

DA 1988 d: Matt Clark. USA., *Home Before Night*, Hugh Leonard, Novel

DA BERLINO L'APOCALISSE 1967 d: Mario Maffei. ITL/FRN/GRM., *Caline Olivia*, Jean Laborde, Novel

DA CHONGZHUANG 1993 d: Zhang XIaomin. CHN., *Black Dream*, Shi Chengyuan, Novel

DA DAO JI 1977 d: Tang Huada, Wang XIuwen. CHN., *Da Dao Ji*, Guo Chengqing, Novel

D.A. Draws a Circle, The *see* THEY CALL IT MURDER (1971).

DA HALT DIE WELT DEN ATEM AN 1927 d: Felix Basch. GRM/FRN., *Schminke*, Guido Kreutzer, Novel

DA ISTAMBUL ORDINE DI UCCIDERE 1965 d: Carlo Ferrero. ITL., *The Devil Executor*, Robert Nilsen, Novel

DA JI QIN LUE ZHE 1965 d: Hua Chun. CHN., *Protecting Peace*, Song Zhi, Play

DA JIE 1995 d: Wu Tiange. CHN., *Da Jie*, Zhou Meishen, Novel

DA NAO TIAN GONG 1964 d: Wu Yingju. CHN., *Xi You Ji*, Wu Chengen, 1592, Novel

Da New York: Mafia Uccide! *see* MAFIA JE VOUS SALUE (1965).

Da Parte Degli Amici Firmato Mafia *see* LE SAUT DE L'ANGE (1971).

DA SVANTE FORSVANDT 1975 d: Henning Carlsen. DNM., *Svantes Viser*, Benny Andersen, 1972, Verse

DABLOVA PAST 1961 d: Frantisek Vlacil. CZC., *Mlyn Na Ponorne Rece*, Alfred Technik, Prague 1958, Novel

DACHNIKI 1967 d: Boris Babochkin. USS., *Dachniki*, Maxim Gorky, 1904, Play

DACTYLO 1931 d: Wilhelm Thiele. FRN., Stefan Szomahazy, Novel

DAD 1989 d: David Goldberg. USA., *Dad*, William Wharton, Novel

DADDIES 1924 d: William A. Seiter. USA., *Daddies*, John L. Hobble, Play

Daddy and I *see* MAKE WAY FOR A LADY (1936).

DADDY LONG LEGS 1931 d: Alfred Santell. USA., *Daddy Long-Legs*, Jean Webster, New York 1912, Novel

DADDY LONG LEGS 1955 d: Jean Negulesco. USA., *Daddy Long-Legs*, Jean Webster, New York 1912, Novel

DADDY-LONG-LEGS 1919 d: Marshall Neilan. USA., *Daddy Long-Legs*, Jean Webster, New York 1912, Novel

DADDY'S DYIN', WHO'S GOT THE WILL 1990 d: Jack Fisk. USA., *Daddy's Dyin' Who's Got the Will*, Del Shores, Play

DADDY'S GONE A-HUNTING 1925 d: Frank Borzage. USA., *Daddy's Gone a-Hunting*, Zoe Akins, New York 1921, Play

Daddy's Gone a-Hunting *see* WOMEN LOVE ONCE (1931).

Daffodil Killer *see* DAS GEHEIMNIS DER GELBEN NARZISSEN (1961).

Dag I Ivan Denisoviwich's Liv, En *see* ONE DAY IN THE LIFE OF IVAN DENISOVICH (1971).

Daggers of Blood *see* COL FERRO E COL FUOCO (1962).

DAGLI APPENNINI ALLE ANDE 1916 d: Umberto Paradisi. ITL., *Cuore*, Edmondo de Amicis, 1886, Short Story

DAGLI APPENNINI ALLE ANDE 1943 d: Flavio CalzavarA. ITL., *Cuore*, Edmondo de Amicis, 1886, Short Story

DAGLI APPENNINI ALLE ANDE 1959 d: Folco Quilici. ITL/ARG., *Cuore*, Edmondo de Amicis, 1886, Short Story

Dagora *see* UCHU DAIKAIJU DOGORA (1964).

Dagora the Space Monster *see* UCHU DAIKAIJU DOGORA (1964).

Dahana-Aranja see JANA ARANYA (1975).

DAHINTEN IN DER HEIDE 1936 d: Carl Boese. GRM., *Dahinten in Der Heide*, Hermann Lons, Books

DAHONG DENGLONG GAOGAO GUA 1991 d: Zhang Yimou. CHN/TWN/HKG., *Wives and Concubines*, Su Tong, Novel

DAI BING DE REN 1964 d: Yan Jizhou. CHN., *Dai Bing de Ren*, XIao Yu, Play

DAI TATSUMAKI 1964 d: Hiroshi Inagaki. JPN., *Shikonmado*, Norio Nanjo, Novel

DAIBOSATSU TOGE 1966 d: Kihachi Okamoto. JPN., *Daibosatsu Toge*, Kaizan Nakazato, Tokyo 1940, Short Story

DAIN CURSE, THE 1978 d: E. W. Swackhamer. USA., *The Dain Curse*, Dashiell Hammett, Novel

DAISY KENYON 1947 d: Otto Preminger. USA., *Daisy Kenyon*, Elizabeth Janeway, Novel

DAISY MILLER 1974 d: Peter Bogdanovich. USA., *Daisy Miller*, Henry James, 1877, Short Story

D-ALE CARNAVALULUI 1958 d: Gheorghe Naghi, Aurel Miheles. RMN., *Conul Leonida Fata Cu Reactiunea*, Ion Luca Caragiale, 1880, Play, *D-Ale Carnavalului*, Ion Luca Caragiale, 1885, Play

DALEKO JE SUNCE 1953 d: Rados Novakovic. YGS., *Daleko Je Sunce*, Dobrica Cosic, 1951, Novel

DALGLIESH: A TASTE FOR DEATH 1988 d: John Davies. UKN., *A Taste for Death*, P. D. James, Novel

DALGLIESH: COVER HER FACE 1985 d: John Davies. UKN., *Cover Her Face*, P. D. James, Novel

DALGLIESH: DEATH OF AN EXPERT WITNESS 1983 d: Herbert Wise. UKN., *Death of an Expert Witness*, P. D. James, Novel

DALGLIESH: DEVICES AND DESIRES 1990 d: John Davies. UKN., *Devices and Desires*, P. D. James, Novel

DALGLIESH: SHROUD FOR A NIGHTINGALE 1984 d: John Gorrie. UKN., *Shroud for a Nightingale*, P. D. James, Novel

DALGLIESH: THE BLACK TOWER 1987 d: Ronald Wilson. UKN., *The Black Tower*, P. D. James, Novel

Dalia Idok see DALIAS IDOK (1983).

DALIAS IDOK 1983 d: Jozsef Gemes. HNG., *Toldi*, Janos Arany, 1847, Verse, *Toldi Esteje*, Janos Arany, 1854, Verse, *Toldi Szerelme*, Janos Arany, 1879, Verse

DALILA 1919 d: Guglielmo Braconini. ITL., *Dalila*, Octave Feuillet, 1857, Novel

Dalla Locana Al Trono see GIOACCHINO MURAT (DALLA LOCANDA AL TRONO) (1910).

DALLA NUBE ALLA RESISTENZA 1979 d: Jean-Marie Straub, Daniele Huillet. ITL/GRM/FRN., *Dialoghi Con Leuco*, Cesare Pavese, 1947, Short Story, *La Luna E I Falo*, Cesare Pavese, 1950, Short Story

DALLEBACH KARL 1970 d: Kurt Fruh. SWT., *Karl Dallebach*, Hansruedi Lerch, Biography

DALLES UND LIEBE 1914 d: Franz Schmelter. GRM., *Der Bibliothekar*, Gustav von Moser, Play

DALTON GIRLS, THE 1957 d: Reginald Le Borg. USA., Herbert Purdum, Story

DALZIEL AND PASCOE: A CLUBBABLE WOMAN 1996 d: Ross Devenish. UKN., *A Clubbable Woman*, Reginald Hill, London 1970, Novel

DALZIEL AND PASCOE: A KILLING KINDNESS 1997 d: Edward Bennett. UKN., *A Killing Kindness*, Reginald Hill, London 1980, Novel

DALZIEL AND PASCOE: AN ADVANCEMENT OF LEARNING 1996 d: Maurice Phillips. UKN., *An Advancement of Learning*, Reginald Hill, London 1972, Novel

DALZIEL AND PASCOE: AN AUTUMN SHROUD 1996 d: Richard Standeven. UKN., *An April Shroud*, Reginald Hill, London 1975, Novel

DALZIEL AND PASCOE: BONES AND SILENCE 1998. UKN., *Bones and Silence*, Reginald Hill, Novel

DALZIEL AND PASCOE: CHILD'S PLAY 1998 d: David Wheatley. UKN., *Child's Play*, Reginald Hill, London 1987, Novel

DALZIEL AND PASCOE: DEADHEADS 1997 d: Edward Bennett. UKN., *Deadheads*, Reginald Hill, London 1983, Novel

DALZIEL AND PASCOE: EXIT LINES 1997 d: Ross Devenish. UKN., *Exit Lines*, Reginald Hill, London 1984, Novel

DALZIEL AND PASCOE: RULING PASSION 1997 d: Gareth Davies. UKN., *Ruling Passion*, Reginald Hill, London 1973, Novel

DAM BUSTERS, THE 1955 d: Michael Anderson. UKN., *Enemy Coast Ahead*, Paul Brickhill, Guy Gibson, Book

Dam, The see TO FRAGMA (1982).

DAMA BIANCA, LA 1938 d: Mario Mattoli. ITL., *La Dama Bianca*, Aldo de Benedetti, Guglielmo Zorzi, Play

DAMA DEL ALBA, LA 1965 d: Francisco Rovira BeletA. SPN., *La Dama Del Alba*, Alejandro Casona, 1944, Play

Dama Di Monsereau, La see LA SIGNORA DI MONSERAU (1909).

Dama Di Monsoreau, La see LA SIGNORA DI MONSERAU (1909).

DAMA DUENDE, LA 1945 d: Luis Saslavsky. ARG., *La Dama Duende*, Pedro Calderon de La Barca, 1647, Play

DAMA S BARZOJEM 1912 d: Max Urban. CZC., *Une Idylle Tragique*, Paul Bourget, 1896

DAMA S SOBACHKOI 1960 d: Josif Heifitz. USS., *Dama S Sobachkoy*, Anton Chekhov, 1899, Short Story

Dama S Sobackoj see DAMA S SOBACHKOI (1960).

DAMAGED GOODS 1915 d: Thomas Ricketts. USA., *Les Avaries*, Eugene Brieux, Liege 1902, Play

DAMAGED GOODS 1919 d: Alexander Butler. UKN., *Les Avaries*, Eugene Brieux, Liege 1902, Play

Damaged Goods see MARRIAGE FORBIDDEN (1936).

DAMAGED LOVE 1930 d: Irvin V. Willat. USA., *Our Pleasant Sins*, Thomas William Broadhurst, New York 1919, Play

DAME AUX CAMELIAS, LA 1911 d: Andre Calmettes, Henri Pouctal. FRN., *La Dame aux Camelias*, Alexandre Dumas (fils), Paris 1848, Novel

DAME AUX CAMELIAS, LA 1934 d: Fernand Rivers, Abel Gance. FRN., *La Dame aux Camelias*, Alexandre Dumas (fils), Paris 1848, Novel

DAME AUX CAMELIAS, LA 1953 d: Raymond Bernard. FRN/ITL., *La Dame aux Camelias*, Alexandre Dumas (fils), Paris 1848, Novel

DAME AUX CAMELIAS, LA 1981 d: Mauro Bolognini. FRN/ITL/GRM., *La Dame aux Camelias*, Alexandre Dumas (fils), Paris 1848, Novel

Dame aux Camelias, Une see LA BELLA LOLA (1962).

DAME DANS L'AUTO AVEC DES LUNETTES ET UN FUSIL, LA 1970 d: Anatole Litvak. FRN/UKN., *La Dame Dans l'Auto Avec Des Lunettes Et un Fusil*, Sebastien Japrisot, Paris 1966, Novel

DAME DE BRONZE ET LE MONSIEUR DE CRISTAL, LA 1929 d: Marcel Manchez. FRN., *La Dame de Bronze Et le Monsieur de Cristal*, Henri Duvernois, Play

Dame de Chez Maxim, La see LA DAME DE CHEZ MAXIM'S (1932).

DAME DE CHEZ MAXIM, LA 1950 d: Marcel Aboulker. FRN., *La Dame de Chez Maxim*, Georges Feydeau, 1898, Play

DAME DE CHEZ MAXIM'S, LA 1912 d: Emile Chautard. FRN., *La Dame de Chez Maxim*, Georges Feydeau, 1898, Play

DAME DE CHEZ MAXIM'S, LA 1923 d: Amleto Palermi. ITL., *La Dame de Chez Maxim*, Georges Feydeau, 1898, Play

DAME DE CHEZ MAXIM'S, LA 1932 d: Alexander KordA. FRN., *La Dame de Chez Maxim*, Georges Feydeau, 1898, Play

DAME DE CHEZ MAXIM'S, LA 1990 d: Jean-Paul Roussillon. FRN., *La Dame de Chez Maxim*, Georges Feydeau, 1898, Play

DAME DE HAUT-LE-BOIS, LA 1946 d: Jacques Daroy. FRN., *La Dame de Haut-le-bois*, Jean-Jose Frappa, Novel

DAME DE MALACCA, LA 1937 d: Marc Allegret. FRN., *La Dame de Malacca*, Francis de Croisset, Novel

DAME DE MONSOREAU, LA 1913 d: Emile Chautard?, Charles Krauss?. FRN., *La Dame de Monsoreau*, Alexandre Dumas (pere), 1856, Novel

DAME DE MONSOREAU, LA 1923 d: Rene Le Somptier. FRN., *La Dame de Monsoreau*, Alexandre Dumas (pere), 1856, Novel

Dame de Pique, La see PIQUE DAME (1937).

DAME DE PIQUE, LA 1965 d: Leonard Keigel. FRN., *Pikovaya Dama*, Alexander Pushkin, 1834, Short Story

DAME D'ONZE HEURES, LA 1947 d: Jean Devaivre. FRN., *La Dame d'Onze Heures*, Pierre Apesteguy, Novel

DAME EN GRIS, LA 1919 d: Gian Paolo Rosmino. ITL., *La Dame En Gris*, Georges Ohnet, 1886, Novel

DAME EN NOIR ,LA 1913. FRN., *La Dame En Noir*, Emilie Richebourg, Novel

DAME IN SCHWARZ, DIE 1928 d: Franz Osten. GRM., *Die Dame in Schwarz*, Garai-Arvay, Novel

DAME MIT DEM TIGERFELL, DIE 1927 d: Willi Wolff. GRM., *Die Dame Mit Dem Tigerfell*, Ernst Klein, Novel

DAME OF SARK, THE 1976 d: Alvin Rakoff. UKN., *The Dame of Sark*, William Douglas Home, Play

DAME UND IHR CHAUFFEUR, DIE 1928 d: Manfred NoA. GRM., *Jan Derriksens Dienstjahr*, Konigsfeld, Novel

Damenwahl see DER VETTER AUS DINGSDA (1934).

DAMES DE CROIX-MORT, LES 1916 d: Maurice Mariaud. FRN., *Les Dames de Croix-Mort*, Georges Ohnet, Novel

Dames de Port Royal, Les see LES DAMES DU BOIS DE BOULOGNE (1945).

DAMES DU BOIS DE BOULOGNE, LES 1945 d: Robert Bresson. FRN., *Jacques le Fataliste Et Son Maitre*, Denis Diderot, 1797, Novel

DAMIGELLA DI BARD, LA 1936 d: Mario Mattoli. ITL., *La Damigella Di Bard*, Salvator Gotta, Play

Damn the Defiant! see H.M.S. DEFIANT (1962).

DAMN YANKEES 1958 d: George Abbott, Stanley Donen. USA., *The Year the Yankees Lost the Pennant*, Douglass Wallop, Novel

DAMNATION ALLEY 1977 d: Jack Smight. USA., *Damnation Alley*, Roger Zelazny, 1969, Novel

Damned and the Daring, The see LES LOUPS DANS LA BERGERIE (1959).

DAMNED DON'T CRY, THE 1950 d: Vincent Sherman. USA., *Case History*, Gertrude Walker, Novel

Damned Roads see BAZA LUDZI UMARLYCH (1958).

Damned Souls see OSADENI DUSHI (1975).

Damned, The see TWILIGHT FOR THE GODS (1958).

DAMNED, THE 1962 d: Joseph Losey. UKN., *The Children of Light*, Henry Lionel Lawrence, London 1960, Novel

Damned to Sin see VERDAMMT ZUR SUNDE (1964).

DAMON AND PYTHIAS 1908 d: Otis Turner. USA., *Damon and Pythias*, Edward George Bulwer Lytton, Novel

DAMON AND PYTHIAS 1914 d: Otis Turner. USA., *Damon and Pythias*, Edward George Bulwer Lytton, Novel

DAMON DES MEERES 1931 d: Michael Curtiz, Lloyd Bacon. USA/USA., *Moby Dick Or the Whale*, Herman Melville, New York 1851, Novel

DAMONISCHE LIEBE 1951 d: Kurt Meisel. GRM., *Teufel Stellt Mr. Darcy Ein Bein*, Ernst Nebhut, Just Scheu, Play

D'AMORE SI MUORE 1972 d: Carlo Caruncchio. ITL., *D'amore Si Muore*, Giuseppe Patroni Griffi, Play

D'AMOUR ET D'EAU FRAICHE 1933 d: Felix GanderA. FRN., *La Facon de Se Donner*, Felix Gandera, Play

Damsel, I Like You see SIE GEFALLT MIR JUNGFER (1968).

DAMSEL IN DISTRESS, A 1919 d: George Archainbaud. USA., *A Damsel in Distress*, P. G. Wodehouse, New York 1919, Novel

DAMSEL IN DISTRESS, A 1937 d: George Stevens. USA., *A Damsel in Distress*, P. G. Wodehouse, New York 1919, Novel

DAMUL 1984 d: Prakash JhA. IND., *Kaabutra*, Shaiwal, Story

DAMY 1954 d: Lev Kulidjanov, Genrikh Oganisyan. USS., *Damy*, Anton Chekhov, 1886, Short Story

Danao Baolinsi see HUANGJIANG NUXIA (PART 1) (1930).

DANCA DAS BRUXAS, A 1970 d: Francisco Dreux. BRZ., *A Bruxinha Que Era Boa*, Maria Clara Machado, 1957, Play

DANCE CHARLIE DANCE 1937 d: Frank McDonald. USA., *The Butter and Egg Man*, George S. Kaufman, New York 1925, Play

Dance Goes on, The see DER TANZ GEHT WEITER (1930).

DANCE HALL 1929 d: Melville Brown. USA., *Dance Hall*, Vina Delmar, 1929, Short Story

DANCE HALL 1941 d: Irving Pichel. USA., *Giant Swing*, William Riley Burnett, 1932, Novel

Dance Hall Daisy see LAZY RIVER (1934).

DANCE MAGIC 1927 d: Victor Hugo Halperin. USA., *Dance Magic*, Clarence Budington Kelland, New York 1927, Novel

Dance, Mephisto see THE OBLONG BOX (1969).

Dance of Death see PAARUNGEN (1967).

DANCE OF DEATH, THE 1914 d: Robert G. VignolA. USA., *The Dance of Death*, Phil Lang, Story

Dance of Death, The see LA DANSE DE MORT (1946).

Dance of Death, The see LE SAINT MENE LA DANSE (1960).

DANCE OF DEATH, THE 1969 d: David Giles. UKN., *Dodsdansen*, August Strindberg, 1901, Play

DANCE OF LIFE, THE 1929 d: John Cromwell. A. Edward Sutherland. USA., *Burlesque*, Arthur Hopkins, George Manker Watters, New York 1927, Play

Dance of Love see REIGEN (1974).

Dance of the Dwarfs see JUNGLE HEAT (1984).

Dance of the Heron see DE DANS VAN DE REIGER (1966).

Dance of the Seven Veils, The see THE DANCE OF THE SEVEN VEILS SALOME; OR (1908).

Dance Over the Graves see TANSSI YLI HAUTOJEN (1950).

Dance Palace see DANCERS IN THE DARK (1932).

DANCE PRETTY LADY 1932 d: Anthony Asquith. UKN., *Carnival*, Compton Mackenzie, London 1912, Novel

DANCE TEAM 1932 d: Sidney Lanfield. USA., *Dance Team*, Sarah Addington, New York 1931, Novel

Dance, The see DANSINN (1998).

Dance-Hall on the Zeedijk, The see MENSCHENWEE (1921).

DANCER AND THE KING, THE 1914 d: E. Arnaud. USA., *The Dancer and the King*, Charles E. Blaney, J. Searle Dawley, Play

Dancer and the Worker, The see EL BAILARIN Y EL TRABAJADOR (1936).

Dancer of Barcelona, The see DIE BERUHMTE FRAU (1927).

Dancer of Izu see IZU NO ODORIKO (1933).

DANCER OF PARIS, THE 1926 d: Alfred Santell. USA., *The Dancer of Paris*, Michael Arlen, 1925, Short Story

Dancer, The see MAIHIME (1951).

DANCERS IN THE DARK 1932 d: David Burton. USA., *Jazz King*, James Ashmore Creelman, 1928, Play

DANCERS, THE 1925 d: Emmett J. Flynn. USA., *The Dancers*, Hubert Parsons, New York 1923, Novel

DANCERS, THE 1930 d: Chandler Sprague. USA., *The Dancers*, Hubert Parsons, New York 1923, Novel

DANCIN' FOOL, THE 1920 d: Sam Wood. USA., *The Dancin' Fool*, Henry Payson Dowst, 1919, Short Story

DANCIN' THROUGH THE DARK 1989 d: Mike Ockrent. UKN., *Stags and Hens*, Willy Russell, Play

Dancin' Thru the Dark see DANCIN' THROUGH THE DARK (1989).

DANCING AT LUGHNASA 1998 d: Pat O'Connor. IRL/UKN/USA., *Dancing at Lughnasa*, Brian Friel, 1989, Play

DANCING CHEAT, THE 1924 d: Irving Cummings. USA., *Clay of Ca'lina*, Calvin Johnston, 1923, Short Story

DANCING CO-ED 1939 d: S. Sylvan Simon. USA., *The Dancing Co-Ed*, Albert Treynor, 1938, Short Story

DANCING DAYS 1926 d: Albert Kelley. USA., *Dancing Days*, J. J. Bell, Story

DANCING FEET 1936 d: Joseph Santley. USA., *Dancing Feet*, Rob Eden, New York 1931, Novel

Dancing Girl see MAIHIME (1951).

Dancing Girl see ODORIKO (1957).

Dancing Girl see IZU NO ODORIKO (1960).

DANCING GIRL, THE 1915 d: Allan Dwan. USA., *The Dancing Girl*, Henry Arthur Jones, London 1891, Play

Dancing Girls of Izu see IZU NO ODORIKO (1933).

Dancing Girls of Izu see IZU NO ODORIKO (1960).

Dancing Heart, The see DAS TANZENDE HERZ (1953).

DANCING IN THE DARK 1949 d: Irving Reis. USA., *The Band Wagon*, Howard Dietz, George S. Kaufman, Arthur Schwartz, New York 1931, Play

DANCING IN THE DARK 1986 d: Leon G. Marr. CND., *Dancing in the Dark*, Joan Barfoot, Novel

DANCING LADY 1933 d: Robert Z. Leonard. USA., *Dancing Lady*, James Warner Bellah, New York 1932, Novel

DANCING MASTERS, THE 1943 d: Malcolm St. Clair. USA., *The Dancing Masters*, George Bricker, Novel

Dancing Men, The see THE ADVENTURES OF SHERLOCK HOLMES: THE DANCING MEN (1984).

DANCING MOTHERS 1926 d: Herbert Brenon. USA., *Dancing Mothers*, Edmund Goulding, Edgar Selwyn, New York 1924, Play

Dancing Partner, The see JUST A GIGOLO (1931).

DANCING PIRATE 1936 d: Lloyd Corrigan. USA., *Glorious Buccaneer*, Emma Lindsay Squier, 1930, Short Story

Dancing Princess see MAIHIME (1951).

DANCING SWEETIES 1930 d: Ray Enright. USA., *Three Flights Up*, Harry Fried, Story

DANCING YEARS, THE 1950 d: Harold French. UKN., *The Dancing Years*, Ivor Novello, London 1939, Play

DANDIN GYORGY 1955 d: Zoltan Varkonyi. HNG., *Ou le Mari George Dandin*, Moliere, 1669, Play

Dandin Gyorgy see DANDIN GYORGY (1955).

DANDY DICK 1935 d: William Beaudine. UKN., *Dandy Dick*, Arthur Wing Pinero, London 1887, Play

DANDY IN ASPIC, A 1968 d: Anthony Mann, Laurence Harvey. UKN/USA., *A Dandy in Aspic*, Derek Marlowe, London 1966, Novel

DANG DENUER 1958 d: Lin Nong. CHN., *Party Membership Dues*, Wang Yuanjian, Novel

DANGER AHEAD 1921 d: Rollin S. Sturgeon. USA., *The Harbor Road*, Sara Ware Bassett, Philadelphia 1919, Novel

DANGER AHEAD 1935 d: Al Herman. USA., *One Eighth Apache*, Peter B. Kyne, Short Story

DANGER AHEAD 1940 d: Ralph Staub. USA., *Renfrew's Long Trail*, Laurie York Erskine, Novel

Danger de Mort see LES CLANDESTINS (1945).

Danger Dimensione Morte see TRAIN D'ENFER (1965).

DANGER GIRL, THE 1926 d: Eddie Dillon. USA., *The Bride*, George Middleton, Stuart Olivier, New York 1924, Play

Danger in the Middle East see LE BAL DES ESPIONS (1960).

Danger in the Skies see THE PILOT (1979).

Danger Is a Woman see QUAI DE GRENELLE (1950).

Danger Island see MR. MOTO IN DANGER ISLAND (1939).

DANGER LINE, THE 1924 d: Edouard-Emile Violet. USA., *La Bataille*, Claude Farrere, Paris 1908, Novel

DANGER MARK, THE 1918 d: Hugh Ford. USA., *The Danger Mark*, Robert W. Chambers, New York 1909, Novel

Danger, Men Working see THE CRIME NOBODY SAW (1937).

DANGER ON THE AIR 1938 d: Otis Garrett. USA., *Death Catches Up With Mr. Kluck*, Xantippe, New York 1935, Novel

DANGER ROUTE 1967 d: Seth Holt. UKN., *The Eliminator*, Andrew York, London 1966, Novel

DANGER SIGNAL 1945 d: Robert Florey. USA., *Danger Signal*, Phyllis Bottome, Novel

DANGER SIGNAL, THE 1915 d: Walter Edwin. USA., *Canavan the Man Who Had His Way*, Rupert Hughes, 1909, Short Story

DANGER STREET 1928 d: Ralph Ince. USA., *The Beautiful Bullet*, Harold MacGrath, 1927, Short Story

DANGER TRAIL, THE 1917 d: Frederick A. Thompson. USA., *The Danger Trail*, James Oliver Curwood, Indianapolis 1910, Novel

DANGER WITHIN 1959 d: Don Chaffey. UKN., *Death in Captivity*, Michael Gilbert, Novel

DANGER ZONE 1951 d: William Berke. USA., *Danger Zone*, Herbert Margolis, Louis Morheim, Radio Play

DANGEROUS 1935 d: Alfred E. Green. USA., *Hard Luck Dame*, Laird Doyle, Story

Dangerous Adventure see A GAME OF DEATH (1946).

DANGEROUS ADVENTURE, A 1922 d: Sam Warner, Jack L. Warner. USA., *A Dangerous Adventure*, Frances Guihan, Story

DANGEROUS AFTERNOON 1961 d: Charles Saunders. UKN., *Dangerous Afternoon*, Gerald Anstruther, Play

Dangerous Agent see CET HOMME EST DANGEREUX (1953).

DANGEROUS BEAUTY 1998 d: Marshall Herskovitz. USA., *The Honest Courtesan*, Margaret Rosenthal, Biography

DANGEROUS BLONDE, THE 1924 d: Robert F. Hill. USA., *A New Girl in Town*, Hubert Footner, 1922, Short Story

DANGEROUS BUSINESS 1920 d: R. William Neill. USA., *The Chessboard*, Madeleine Sharpe Buchanan, Short Story

Dangerous Business see PARTY GIRL (1930).

DANGEROUS CARGO 1954 d: John Harlow. UKN., *Dangerous Cargo*, Percy Hoskins, Short Story

DANGEROUS COMPANY 1982 d: Lamont Johnson. USA., Ray Johnson, Book

DANGEROUS CORNER 1934 d: Phil Rosen. USA., *Dangerous Corner*, J. B. Priestley, London 1932, Play

DANGEROUS CROSSING 1953 d: Joseph M. Newman. USA., *Cabin B-16*, John Dickson Carr, Radio Play

Dangerous Currents see WHY WOMEN LOVE (1925).

DANGEROUS DAVIES - THE LAST DETECTIVE 1979 d: Val Guest. UKN., Leslie Thomas, Novel

DANGEROUS DAYS 1920 d: Reginald Barker. USA., *Dangerous Days*, Mary Roberts Rinehart, New York 1919, Novel

DANGEROUS DAYS OF KIOWA JONES, THE 1966 d: Alex March. USA., *The Dangerous Days of Kiowa Jones*, Clifton Adams, Novel

DANGEROUS EXILE 1957 d: Brian Desmond Hurst. UKN., *A King Reluctant*, Vaughan Wilkins, Novel

Dangerous Female see THE MALTESE FALCON (1931).

DANGEROUS FINGERS 1937 d: Norman Lee. UKN., *Man Hunt*, Vernon Clancey, Novel

DANGEROUS FLIRT, THE 1924 d: Tod Browning. USA., *The Prude*, Julie Herne, Story

Dangerous Flirtation, A see THE DANGEROUS FLIRT (1924).

DANGEROUS GAME, A 1922 d: King Baggot. USA., *Gret'n Ann*, Louis Dodge, 1922, Short Story

Dangerous Games see JEUX DANGEREUX (1958).

Dangerous Games see VESZELYES JATEKOK (1979).

DANGEROUS HOURS 1920 d: Fred Niblo. USA., *A Prodigal in Utopia*, Donn Byrne, Short Story

DANGEROUS INNOCENCE 1925 d: William A. Seiter. USA., *Ann's an Idiot*, Pamela Wynne, London 1923, Novel

DANGEROUS LIAISONS 1988 d: Stephen Frears. UKN/USA., *Les Liaisons Dangereuses*, Pierre Ambrose Choderlos de Laclos, 1782, Novel

DANGEROUS LIES 1921 d: Paul Powell. USA/UKN., *Twice Wed*, E. Phillips Oppenheim, Novel

DANGEROUS LOVE 1920 d: Charles Bartlett. USA., *Ben Warman*, Charles E. Winter, New York 1917, Novel

Dangerous Love, A see BLACK MARKET BABY (1977).

Dangerous Love Affair, A see NIEBEZPIECZNY ROMANS (1930).

Dangerous Love Affairs see LES LIAISONS DANGEREUSES (1959).

DANGEROUS MAID, THE 1923 d: Victor Heerman. USA., *Barbara Winslow - Rebel*, Elizabeth Ellis, New York 1906, Novel

DANGEROUS MEDICINE 1938 d: Arthur Woods. UKN., *Dangerous Medicine*, Edmond Deland, Novel

DANGEROUS MINDS 1995 d: John N. Smith. USA., *My Posse Don't Do Homework*, Louanne Johnson, Book

Dangerous Mists see U-BOAT PRISONER (1944).

DANGEROUS MONEY 1924 d: Frank Tuttle. USA., *Clark's Field*, Robert Herrick, New York 1914, Novel

DANGEROUS PARADISE 1930 d: William A. Wellman. USA., *Victory*, Joseph Conrad, London 1915, Novel

DANGEROUS PARTNERS 1945 d: Edward L. Cahn. USA., *Paper Chase*, Oliver Weld Bayer, Story

Dangerous Roads see FARLIGA VAGAR (1942).

DANGEROUS TALENT, THE 1920 d: George L. Cox. USA., *The Golden Gift*, Daniel F. Whitcomb, Novel

Dangerous Temptation see LOCKENDE GEFAHR (1950).

DANGEROUS TO KNOW 1938 d: Robert Florey. USA., *On the Spot*, Edgar Wallace, London 1930, Play

DANGEROUS TO MEN 1920 d: William C. Dowlan. USA., *Eliza Comes to Stay*, H. V. Esmond, London 1913, Play

Dangerous to Women *see* THE LOVE CAPTIVE (1934).

DANGEROUS WOMAN, A 1929 d: Rowland V. Lee. USA., *A Woman Who Needed Killing*, Margery Lawrence, 1927, Short Story

DANGEROUS WOMAN, A 1993 d: Stephen Gyllenhaal. USA., *A Dangerous Woman*, Mary McGarry Morris, Novel

DANGEROUSLY THEY LIVE 1942 d: Robert Florey. USA., *Remember Tomorrow*, Marion Parsonnet, Story

Dangerously They Live *see* STEEL AGAINST THE SKY (1942).

DANIEL 1983 d: Sidney Lumet. USA., *The Book of Daniel*, E. L. Doctorow, 1971, Novel

Daniel and the Devil *see* ALL THAT MONEY CAN BUY (1941).

DANIEL DERONDA 1921 d: W. C. Rowden. UKN., *Daniel Deronda*, George Eliot, 1876, Novel

DANIELE CORTIS 1947 d: Mario Soldati. ITL., *Daniele Cortis*, Antonio Fogazzaro, 1885, Novel

Daniella By Night *see* ZARTE HAUT IN SCHWARZER SEIDE (1961).

DANIELLE STEEL'S JEWELS 1992 d: Robert Young. USA., *Jewels*, Danielle Steel, Novel

DANIELLE STEEL'S NO GREATER LOVE 1995 d: Richard T. Heffron. USA., *No Greater Love*, Danielle Steel, Novel

DANIELLE STEEL'S VANISHED 1995 d: George Kaczender. USA., *Vanished*, Danielle Steel, Novel

DANITES, THE 1912 d: Frank Boggs. USA., *The Danites*, McKee Rankin, Play

DANMARK ER LUKKET 1981 d: Dan TscherniA. DNM., *Orfeus I Undergrunden*, Benny Andersen, 1979, Play

DANNY, CHAMPION OF THE WORLD 1989 d: Gavin Millar. UKN/USA., *Danny the Champion of the World*, Roald Dahl, Novel

Danny the Champion of the World *see* CHAMPION OF THE WORLD DANNY (1989).

DANS LA GUEULE DU LOUP 1961 d: Jean-Charles Dudrumet. FRN., *Mise En Caisse*, James Hadley Chase, Novel

DANS LE GOUFFRE 1916 d: Pierre Bressol. FRN., *Dans le Gouffre*, Henri Duvernet, Story

DANS L'EAU QUI FAIT DES BULLES 1961 d: Maurice Delbez. FRN., *La Chair a Poissons*, Marcel G. Pretre, Novel

DANS LES RUES 1933 d: Victor Trivas. FRN., *Dans Les Rues*, Joseph Henri Rosny, Novel

DANS L'OMBRE DU HAREM 1928 d: Leon Mathot. FRN., *Dans l'Ombre du Harem*, Lucien Besnard, Play

Dans Over Gravarna *see* TANSSI YLI HAUTOJEN (1950).

DANS UNE ILE PERDUE 1930 d: Alberto Cavalcanti. FRN., *Victory*, Joseph Conrad, London 1915, Novel

DANS VAN DE REIGER, DE 1966 d: Fons Rademakers. NTH., *De Dans Van de Reiger*, Hugo Claus, 1962, Play

DANSE DE MORT, LA 1946 d: Marcel Cravenne, Erich von Stroheim (Uncredited). FRN/ITL., *Dodsdansen*, August Strindberg, 1901, Play

DANSE HEROIQUE, LA 1914 d: Ferdinand Zecca, Rene Leprince. FRN., *La Danse Heroique*, Pierre Sales, Novel

Danse MacAbre *see* PAARUNGEN (1967).

Danseur de Jazz, Le *see* EL NEGRO QUE TENIA EL ALMA BLANCA (1926).

DANSEUR INCONNU, LE 1928 d: Rene Barberis. FRN., *Le Danseur Inconnu*, Tristan Bernard, France 1909, Play

DANSEUSE NUE, LA 1952 d: Pierre-Louis. FRN., *Le Danseuse Nue*, Colette Andris, Novel

DANSEUSE ORCHIDEE, LA 1928 d: Leonce Perret. FRN., *La Danseuse Orchidee*, Jean-Joseph Renaud, Novel

DANSEUSE ROUGE, LA 1937 d: Jean-Paul Paulin. FRN., *La Chevre aux Pieds d'Or*, Charles-Henry Hirsch, Novel

Danshuis Op Den Zeedijk, Het *see* MENSCHENWEE (1921).

DANSINN 1998 d: Agust Gudmundsson. ICL., *We Must Dance*, William Heinesen, Short Story

Dante's Inferno *see* L' INFERNO (1911).

Dante's Paradise *see* IL PARADISO (VISIONI DANTESCHE) (1912).

Dante's Purgatorio *see* IL PURGATORIO (1911).

DANTON 1982 d: Andrzej WajdA. FRN/PLN., *Danton*, Stanislawa Przybyszewska, Play

Danube Pilot, The *see* A DUNAI HAJOS (1974).

DANY, BITTE SCHREIBEN SIE! 1956 d: Eduard von Borsody. GRM., *Bitte Schreiben Sie Dany*, Inge Rosener, Novel

DANZA DEI MILIONI, LA 1940 d: Camillo Mastrocinque. ITL., *Ho-Rukk*, Ladislaus Fodor, Play

Danza Della Morte, La *see* LA DANSE DE MORT (1946).

DANZA DELLE LANCETTE, LA 1936 d: Mario Baffico. ITL., *La Danza Delle Lancette*, Emilio de Martino, Novel

DANZA MACABRA 1964 d: Antonio Margheriti, Sergio Corbucci. ITL/FRN., *Danse MacAbre*, Edgar Allan Poe, Short Story

DANZATRICE MASCHERATA, LA 1916 d: Pier Antonio Gariazzo. ITL., *Ames Nostalgiques*, Gabriel Charand, Novel

DAO ZIREN QU 1936 d: Sun Yu. CHN., *The Admirable Crichton*, J. M. Barrie, London 1902, Play

DAPHNE LAUREOLA 1978 d: Waris Hussein. UKN., *Daphne Laureola*, James Bridie, Play

DAPHNE UND DER DIPLOMAT 1937 d: R. A. Stemmle. GRM., *Daphne Und Der Diplomat*, Fritz von Woedtke, Novel

Daphnis and Chloe 66 *see* DHAFNIS KE HLOI 66 (1967).

DAR SVATEBNI NOCI 1926 d: Oldrich Kminek. CZC., *Lasky Vasne Zrady*, Karel Rozek, Short Story

DARAKU SURU ONNA 1967 d: Kozaburo YoshimurA. JPN., *Alsureba Koso*, Junichiro Tanizaki, 1923, Play

DARBY AND JOAN 1937 d: Syd Courtenay. UKN., *Darby and Joan*, Rita, Novel

DARBY O'GILL AND THE LITTLE PEOPLE 1959 d: Robert Stevenson. USA/UKN., H. T. Kavanagh, Short Stories

DARBY'S RANGERS 1958 d: William A. Wellman. USA., *Darby's Rangers*, Major James Altieri, 1945, Book

Dardamelle *see* CARNAVAL (1953).

DAREDEVIL KATE 1916 d: Kenean Buel. USA., *Daredevil Kate*, Philip Bartholomae, Play

Dare-Devil Kate *see* DAREDEVIL KATE (1916).

DAREDEVIL, THE 1918 d: Francis J. Grandon. USA., *The Daredevil*, Maria Thompson Davies, New York 1916, Novel

DARING LOVE 1924 d: Roland G. Edwards. USA., *Driftwood*, Albert Payson Terhune, 1918, Short Story

DARING YOUTH 1924 d: William Beaudine. USA., *The Taming of the Shrew*, William Shakespeare, c1593, Play

DARK AGE 1986 d: Arch Nicholson. ASL., *Numunwari*, Grahame Webb, Novel

DARK ANGEL, THE 1925 d: George Fitzmaurice. USA., *The Dark Angel*, Guy Bolton, New York 1925, Play

DARK ANGEL, THE 1935 d: Sidney A. Franklin. USA., *The Dark Angel*, Guy Bolton, New York 1925, Play

DARK AT THE TOP OF THE STAIRS, THE 1960 d: Delbert Mann. USA., *The Dark at the Top of the Stairs*, William Inge, New York 1957, Play

Dark Chapter *see* MERRILY WE LIVE (1938).

DARK CITY 1950 d: William Dieterle. USA., *No Escape*, Lawrence B. Marcus, Novel

DARK COMMAND 1940 d: Raoul Walsh. USA., *Dark Command: a Kansas Iliad*, William Riley Burnett, New York 1938, Novel

DARK CORNER, THE 1946 d: Henry Hathaway. USA., *Dark Corner*, Leo Rosten, 1945, Short Story

Dark Eyes *see* OCI CIORNIE (1987).

DARK EYES OF LONDON, THE 1939 d: Walter Summers. UKN., *The Dark Eyes of London*, Edgar Wallace, London 1924, Novel

Dark Eyes of London, The *see* DIE TOTEN AUGEN VON LONDON (1960).

DARK HAZARD 1934 d: Alfred E. Green. USA., *Dark Hazard*, William Riley Burnett, New York 1933, Novel

Dark Holiday *see* PASSPORT TO TERROR (1989).

DARK HOUR, THE 1936 d: Charles Lamont. USA., *The Last Trap; a Detective Story*, Sinclair Gluck, New York 1928, Novel

DARK LANTERN, A 1920 d: John S. Robertson. USA., *A Dark Lantern*, Elizabeth Robins, New York 1905, Novel

DARK MIRROR, THE 1920 d: Charles Giblyn. USA., *The Dark Mirror*, Louis Joseph Vance, Garden City, N.Y. 1920, Novel

Dark of the Night *see* MR. WRONG (1986).

Dark of the Sun *see* THE MERCENARIES (1967).

Dark Page, The *see* SCANDAL SHEET (1952).

DARK PASSAGE 1947 d: Delmer Daves. USA., *Dark Passage*, David Goodis, 1946, Novel

DARK PAST, THE 1948 d: Rudolph Mate. USA., *Blind Alley*, James Warwick, New York 1935, Play

Dark Purpose *see* L' INTRIGO (1964).

DARK RED ROSES 1929 d: Sinclair Hill. UKN., *Dark Red Roses*, Stacy Aumonier, Short Story

Dark Room of Damocles *see* ALS TWEE DRUPPELS WATER (1963).

DARK ROOM, THE 1999 d: Graham Theakston. UKN., *The Dark Room*, Minette Walters, Novel

DARK SECRET 1949 d: MacLean Rogers. UKN., *The Crime at Blossoms*, Mordaunt Shairp, Play

DARK SECRET OF HARVEST HOME 1978 d: Leo Penn. USA., *Harvest Home*, Thomas Tryon, Novel

DARK STAIRWAY, THE 1938 d: Arthur Woods. UKN., *From This Dark Stairway*, Mignon G. Eberhart, New York 1931, Novel

Dark Star *see* MIN AND BILL (1930).

DARK STAR, THE 1919 d: Allan Dwan. USA., *The Dark Star*, Robert W. Chambers, New York 1917, Novel

Dark Sun *see* TEMNE SLUNCE (1980).

Dark Swan, The *see* WEDDING RINGS (1929).

Dark to Dawn *see* NIGHT FLIGHT (1933).

Dark Tower, The *see* THE MAN WITH TWO FACES (1934).

DARK TOWER, THE 1943 d: John Harlow. UKN., *The Dark Tower*, George S. Kaufman, Alexander Woollcott, New York 1933, Play

Dark Victory *see* THE MAN WITH TWO FACES (1934).

DARK VICTORY 1939 d: Edmund Goulding. USA., *Dark Victory*, Bert Bloch, George Emerson Brewer Jr., New York 1934, Play

DARK VICTORY 1976 d: Robert Butler. USA., *Dark Victory*, Bert Bloch, George Emerson Brewer Jr., New York 1934, Play

DARK WATERS 1944 d: Andre de Toth. USA., *Dark Waters*, Frank Cockrell, Marian Cockrell, Story

DARK WIND, THE 1991 d: Errol Morris. USA., *The Dark Wind*, Tony Hillerman, Novel

DARKENED ROOMS 1929 d: Louis J. Gasnier. USA., *Darkened Rooms*, Philip Hamilton Gibbs, 1928, Short Story

Darkening Flame *see* MANGANINNIE (1980).

DARKER THAN AMBER 1970 d: Robert Clouse. USA., *Darker Than Amber*, John D. MacDonald, Greenwich, Ct. 1966, Novel

Darkest Hour, The *see* HELL ON FRISCO BAY (1955).

DARKEST RUSSIA 1917 d: Travers Vale. USA., *Darkest Russia*, H. Grattan Donnelly, Sidney R. Ellis, New York 1894, Play

DARKNESS 1923 d: George A. Cooper. UKN., *Darkness*, Max Brand, Short Story

Darkness *see* TAMAS (1986).

Darkness By Daylight *see* NAPPALI SOTETSEG (1963).

DARKNESS FALLS 1998 d: Gerry Lively. UKN., *Dangerous Obsession*, N. J. Crisp, Play

Darkness in Daytime *see* NAPPALI SOTETSEG (1963).

DARLING. 1965 d: John Schlesinger. UKN., *Darling*, Frederic Raphael, 1965, Novel

DARLING FAMILY, THE 1994 d: Alan Zweig. CND., *The Darling Family*, Linda Griffiths, Play

DARLING, HOW COULD YOU? 1951 d: Mitchell Leisen. USA., *Alice Sit-By-the-Fire*, J. M. Barrie, London 1905, Play

Darling, I Am Going to Have to Shoot You *see* ICH MUSS DICH ERSCHIESSEN LIEBLING (1962).

DARLING OF PARIS, THE 1917 d: J. Gordon Edwards. USA., *Notre-Dame de Paris*, Victor Hugo, Paris 1831, Novel

DARLING OF THE RICH, THE 1922 d: John G. Adolfi. USA., *The Imposter*, Leonard Merrick, Michael Morton, New York 1910, Play

DARO UN MILIONE 1935 d: Mario Camerini. ITL., *Buoni Per un Giorno*, Giaci Mondaini, Cesare Zavattini, 1934, Short Story

D'ARTAGNAN 1916 d: Charles Swickard. USA., *Les Trois Mousquetaires*, Alexandre Dumas (pere), Paris 1844, Novel

D'ARTAGNAN AND THE THREE MUSKETEERS 1978 d: Georgij Jungvald-Khilkevich. USS., *Les Trois Mousquetaires*, Alexandre Dumas (pere), Paris 1844, Novel

DAS WAR MEIN LEBEN 1944 d: Paul Martin. GRM., Gustav Kampendock, Story

Das War Mein Leben *see* SAUERBRUCH (1954).

Dasturmoto Talkie *see* TALKIE OF TALKIES (1937).

DATE FIXEE, LA 1916. FRN., *Les Fiancailles d'Yvonne*, Joseph Henri Rosny, Short Story

Date With Death, A *see* THE HIGH BRIGHT SUN (1964).

DAUGHTER IN REVOLT, A 1927 d: Harry Hughes. UKN., *A Daughter in Revolt*, Sidney Gowing, Novel

DAUGHTER OF DARKNESS 1948 d: Lance Comfort. UKN., *They Walk Alone*, Max Catto, London 1938, Play

Daughter of Destiny, A *see* ALRAUNE (1928).

DAUGHTER OF ENGLAND, A 1915 d: Leedham Bantock. UKN., *A Daughter of England*, P. Barrow, Jose G. Levy, E. V. Miller, Play

Daughter of Evil *see* ALRAUNE (1930).

DAUGHTER OF HER PEOPLE, A 1932 d: George Roland. USA., *Judith Trachtenberg*, Karl Emil Franzos, New York 1891, Novel

Daughter of Israel *see* LES PUITS DE JACOB (1925).

DAUGHTER OF LOVE, A 1925 d: Walter West. UKN., *A Daughter of Love*, Mrs. E. J. Key, Novel

Daughter of Luxury *see* FIVE AND TEN (1931).

DAUGHTER OF LUXURY, A 1922 d: Paul Powell. USA., *The Imposter*, Leonard Merrick, Michael Morton, New York 1910, Play

DAUGHTER OF THE CITY, A 1915 d: E. H. Calvert. USA., *A Daughter of the City*, H. S. Sheldon, Play

DAUGHTER OF THE DRAGON 1931 d: Lloyd Corrigan. USA., *Daughter of Fu Manchu*, Sax Rohmer, New York 1931, Novel

DAUGHTER OF THE LAW, A 1921 d: Jack Conway. USA., *The Black Cap*, Wadsworth Camp, 1920, Short Story

DAUGHTER OF THE MIND 1969 d: Walter Grauman. USA., *The Hand of Mary Constable*, Paul Gallico, Novel

Daughter of the Party *see* DANG DENUER (1958).

DAUGHTER OF THE PEOPLE, A 1915 d: J. Searle Dawley. USA., *The Daughter of the People*, J. Searle Dawley, Play

Daughter of the Regiment *see* LA FIGLIA DEL REGGIMENTO (1911).

DAUGHTER OF THE REGIMENT 1927 d: H. B. Parkinson. UKN., *La Fille du Regiment*, Gaetano Donizetti, Paris 1840, Opera

Daughter of the Sea *see* LA HIJA DEL MAR (1953).

DAUGHTER OF THE SEA, A 1915 d: Charles M. Seay. USA., *The Fisher-Girl*, Frances Marion, Story

DAUGHTER OF THE SIOUX, A 1925 d: Ben Wilson. USA., *A Daughter of the Sioux; a Tale of the Indian Frontier*, Gen. Charles King, New York 1903, Novel

DAUGHTER OF THE WEST 1949 d: Harold Daniels. USA., *Daughter of the West*, Robert E. Callahan, Novel

DAUGHTER OF THE WOLF, A 1919 d: Irvin V. Willat. USA., *A Daughter of the Wolf*, Hugh Pendexter, 1919, Short Story

DAUGHTER OF TWO WORLDS, A 1920 d: James Young. USA., *A Daughter of Two Worlds*, Leroy Scott, Boston 1919, Novel

DAUGHTER PAYS, THE 1920 d: Robert Ellis. USA., *The Daughter Pays*, Mrs. Baillie Reynolds, London 1915, Novel

Daughter-in-Law *see* SNAHA (1954).

Daughter-in-Law, The *see* BIRAJ BAHU (1954).

DAUGHTERS OF MEN, THE 1914 d: George W. Terwilliger. USA., *The Daughters of Men*, Charles Klein, New York 1906, Play

DAUGHTERS OF THE RICH 1923 d: Louis J. Gasnier. USA., *Daughters of the Rich*, Edgar Saltus, New York 1900, Novel

DAUGHTERS OF THE VICAR 1967 d: Gerald Dynevor. UKN., *Daughters of the Vicar*, D. H. Lawrence, Short Story

Daughters of Yoshiwara *see* TAKEKURABE (1955).

DAUNTAUN HIROZU 1988 d: Yoji YamadA. JPN., *Dautaun Hirozu*, Akira Hayasaka, Novel

Dauphin Sur la Plage, Le *see* BANCO DE PRINCE (1950).

DAVANTI A LUI TREMAVA TUTTA ROMA 1946 d: Carmine Gallone. ITL., *La Tosca*, Victorien Sardou, Paris 1877, Play

DAVID 1979 d: Peter Lilienthal. GRM., *David*, Joel Konig, Book

DAVID 1988 d: John Erman. USA., *David*, Marie Rothberg, Mel White, Book

David and Catriona *see* KIDNAPPED (1971).

DAVID AND JONATHAN 1920 d: Alexander Butler, Dion Titheradge. UKN/USA., *David and Jonathan*, E. Temple Thurston, New York 1919, Novel

DAVID AND LISA 1962 d: Frank Perry. USA., *Lisa and David*, Theodore Isaac Rubin, New York 1961, Novel

DAVID COPPERFIELD 1911 d: Theodore Marston. USA., *David Copperfield*, Charles Dickens, London 1850, Novel

DAVID COPPERFIELD 1913 d: Thomas Bentley. UKN., *David Copperfield*, Charles Dickens, London 1850, Novel

DAVID COPPERFIELD 1922 d: Anders W. Sandberg. DNM., *David Copperfield*, Charles Dickens, London 1850, Novel

DAVID COPPERFIELD 1935 d: George Cukor. USA., *David Copperfield*, Charles Dickens, London 1850, Novel

David Copperfield *see* DAVID COPPERFIELD (1935).

DAVID COPPERFIELD 1965 d: Marcel Cravenne. FRN., *David Copperfield*, Charles Dickens, London 1850, Novel

DAVID COPPERFIELD 1969 d: Delbert Mann. UKN., *David Copperfield*, Charles Dickens, London 1850, Novel

DAVID COPPERFIELD 1983 d: Alex Nicholas, Ian MacKenzie. ASL., *David Copperfield*, Charles Dickens, London 1850, Novel

DAVID GARRICK 1912 d: Percy Nash. UKN., *David Garrick*, T. W. Robertson, London 1864, Play

DAVID GARRICK 1913 d: Hay Plumb. UKN., *David Garrick*, T. W. Robertson, London 1864, Play

DAVID GARRICK 1913 d: Leedham Bantock. UKN., *David Garrick*, T. W. Robertson, London 1864, Play

DAVID GARRICK 1914 d: James Young. USA., *David Garrick*, T. W. Robertson, London 1864, Play

DAVID GARRICK 1916 d: Frank Lloyd. USA., *David Garrick*, T. W. Robertson, London 1864, Play

DAVID GARRICK 1922. UKN., *David Garrick*, T. W. Robertson, London 1864, Play

DAVID GARRICK 1928 d: George J. Banfield, Leslie Eveleigh. UKN., *David Garrick*, T. W. Robertson, London 1864, Play

DAVID GOLDER 1930 d: Julien Duvivier. FRN., *David Golder*, Irene Nemirovsky, Novel

DAVID HARUM 1915 d: Allan Dwan. USA., *David Harum*, Edward Noyes Westcott, New York 1898, Novel

DAVID HARUM 1934 d: James Cruze. USA., *David Harum*, Edward Noyes Westcott, New York 1898, Novel

David Williamson's Emerald City *see* EMERALD CITY (1988).

DAVID WILLIAMSON'S THE CLUB 1980 d: Bruce Beresford. ASL., *The Club*, David Williamson, 1978, Play

DAVID'S MOTHER 1994 d: Robert Allan Ackerman. USA., *David's Mother*, Bob Randall, Play

Davolji Raj *see* DJAVOLJI RAJ - ONO LJETO BIJELIH RUZA (1989).

DAVY CROCKETT 1916 d: William D. Taylor. USA., *Davy Crockett*, Frank Murdock, 1872, Play

DAWN 1917 d: H. Lisle Lucoque. UKN., *Dawn*, H. Rider Haggard, Novel

DAWN 1919 d: J. Stuart Blackton. USA., *Dawn*, Eleanor H. Porter, New York 1919, Novel

DAWN 1928 d: Herbert Wilcox. UKN., *Dawn*, Reginald Berkeley, New York 1928, Novel

Dawn *see* MADRUGADA (1957).

Dawn *see* L' AUBE (1986).

DAWN OF A TOMORROW, THE 1915 d: James Kirkwood. USA., *The Dawn of a Tomorrow*, Frances Hodgson Burnett, New York 1906, Novel

DAWN OF A TOMORROW, THE 1924 d: George Melford. USA., *The Dawn of a Tomorrow*, Frances Hodgson Burnett, New York 1906, Novel

Dawn of Life, The *see* LIFE BEGINS (1932).

DAWN OF UNDERSTANDING, THE 1918 d: David Smith. USA., *The Judgment of Bolinas Plain*, Bret Harte, 1893, Short Story

Dawn Over France *see* GASPARD DE BESSE (1935).

DAWN PATROL, THE 1930 d: Howard Hawks. USA., *The Flight Commander*, John Monk Saunders, Story

Dawn Rider *see* GALLOPING DYNAMITE (1937).

Dawn, The *see* UMBARTHA (1982).

DAWNING, THE 1988 d: Robert Knights. UKN., *The Old Jest*, Jennifer Johnston, 1979, Novel

Day After, The *see* UP FROM THE BEACH (1965).

Day After Tomorrow, The *see* STRANGE HOLIDAY (1945).

DAY IN SUMMER, A 1989 d: Bob Mahoney. UKN., J. L. Carr, Story

Day in the Country, A *see* UNE PARTIE DE CAMPAGNE (1936).

DAY IN THE DEATH OF JOE EGG, A 1972 d: Peter Medak. UKN., *A Day in the Death of Joe Egg*, Peter Nichols, 1967, Play

Day More Or Less, A *see* PLUSZ MINUSZ EGY NAP (1972).

Day New York Was Invaded, The *see* THE MOUSE THAT ROARED (1959).

Day of Anger *see* I GIORNI DELL'IRA (1967).

DAY OF DAYS, THE 1914 d: Daniel Frohman. USA., *The Day of Days*, Louis Joseph Vance, Boston 1913, Novel

DAY OF FAITH, THE 1923 d: Tod Browning. USA., *The Day of Faith*, Arthur Somers Roche, Boston 1921, Novel

Day of Reckoning *see* GUNS OF DIABLO (1964).

Day of Resurrection, The *see* FUKKATSU NO HI (1979).

Day of Sin, A *see* LA GIORNATA BALORDA (1960).

Day of the Apocalypse *see* SENGOKU JIEITAI (1980).

DAY OF THE BAD MAN 1958 d: Harry Keller. USA., *Raiders Die Hard*, John M. Cunningham, Novel

Day of the Dog *see* BLACKFELLAS (1992).

DAY OF THE DOLPHIN, THE 1973 d: Mike Nichols. USA., *The Day of the Dolphin*, Robert Merle, Novel

DAY OF THE JACKAL, THE 1973 d: Fred Zinnemann. UKN/USA/FRN., *The Day of the Jackal*, Frederick Forsyth, 1971, Novel

DAY OF THE LOCUST, THE 1975 d: John Schlesinger. USA., *The Day of the Locust*, Nathanael West, 1939, Novel

DAY OF THE OUTLAW 1959 d: Andre de Toth. USA., *Day of the Outlaw*, Lee Wells, 1955, Novel

Day of the Owl, The *see* IL GIORNO DELLA CIVETTA (1967).

DAY OF THE TRIFFIDS, THE 1962 d: Steve Sekely, Freddie Francis. UKN., *The Day of the Triffids*, John Wyndham, 1951, Novel

DAY OF THE TRIFFIDS, THE 1981 d: Ken Hannam. UKN., *The Day of the Triffids*, John Wyndham, 1951, Novel

Day of Wrath *see* VREDENS DAG (1943).

Day of Wrath *see* I GIORNI DELL'IRA (1967).

DAY RESURGENT, THE 1920 d: Joseph Byron Totten. USA., *The Day Resurgent*, O. Henry, Short Story

DAY SHE PAID, THE 1919 d: Rex Ingram. USA., *Oats for the Woman*, Fannie Hurst, 1917, Short Story

DAY THAT IS DEAD, A 1913 d: Charles H. France. USA., *Break Break Break*, Alfred Tennyson, Poem

DAY THE BOOKIES WEPT, THE 1939 d: Leslie Goodwins. USA., *Crazy Over Pigeons*, Daniel Fuchs, 1939, Short Story

DAY THE BUBBLE BURST, THE 1982 d: Joseph Hardy. USA., *The Day the Bubble Burst*, Max Morgan-Witts, Gordon Thomas, Book

Day the Earth Froze, The *see* SAMPO (1959).

DAY THE EARTH STOOD STILL, THE 1950 d: Robert Wise. USA., *Farewell to the Master*, Harry Bates, Story

DAY THE LOVING STOPPED, THE 1981 d: Daniel Mann. USA., *The Day the Loving Stopped*, Julie Autumn List, Book

Day the Sun Rose, The *see* GION MATSURI (1968).

Day the World Changed Hands, The *see* THE FORBIN PROJECT (1969).

Day the World Ended, The *see* WHEN TIME RAN OUT. (1980).

DAY THEY ROBBED THE BANK OF ENGLAND, THE 1960 d: John Guillermin. UKN., *The Day They Robbed the Bank of England*, John Brophy, Novel

DAY TO REMEMBER, A 1953 d: Ralph Thomas. UKN., *The Hand and the Flower*, Jerrard Tickell, Novel

Day Without End *see* BEWARE MY LOVELY (1952).

DAYBREAK 1918 d: Albert Capellani. USA., *Daybreak*, Jane Cowl, Jane Murfin, New York 1917, Play

Daybreak *see* THE OUTSIDER (1926).

DAYBREAK 1931 d: Jacques Feyder. USA., *Spiel Im Morgengrauen*, Arthur Schnitzler, 1926, Short Story

DAYBREAK 1946 d: Compton Bennett. UKN., *Daybreak*, Monckton Hoffe, Play

Daybreakers, The *see* THE SACKETTS (1979).

Day-Dream *see* HAKUJITSUMU (1964).

Day-Dreamers, The *see* FANTASTERNE (1967).

DAYDREAMS 1928 d: Ivor Montagu. UKN., *Daydreams*, H. G. Wells, Short Story

Daylight Valley *see* RIGUANG XIAGU (1995).

Days and Nights *see* DNI I NOCI (1944).

Days and Nights in the Forest *see* ARANYE DINRATRI (1969).

Days Before Lent *see* HOLIDAY FOR SINNERS (1952).

Day's Bread, A *see* USKI ROTI (1969).

Days in the Trees *see* DES JOURNEES ENTIERES DANS LES ARBRES (1976).

Days of Hate *see* DIAS DE ODIO (1954).

Days of Hatred *see* DIAS DE ODIO (1954).

Days of Hope *see* ESPOIR (1939).

Days of Matthew, The *see* ZYWOT MATEUSZA (1968).

Dazdnik Svateho Petra *see* SZENT PETER ESERNYOJE (1958).

DAZZLING MISS DAVISON, THE 1917 d: Frank Powell. USA., *The Dazzling Miss Davison*, Florence Warden, London 1908, Novel

Dcery Eviny *see* EVAS TOCHTER (1928).

D-DAY THE SIXTH OF JUNE 1956 d: Henry Koster. USA., *The Sixth of June*, Lionel Shapiro, 1955, Novel

DE CE TRAG CLOPOTELE, MITICA 1981 d: Lucian Pintilie. RMN., *D-Ale Carnavalului*, Ion Luca Caragiale, 1885, Play

DE GRAY -LE BANC DE DESOLATION 1973 d: Claude Chabrol. FRN., *The Bench of Desolation*, Henry James, 1910, Short Story

De la Part Des Copains *see* COLD SWEAT (1971).

De la Veine a Revendre *see* ZEZOWATE SZCZESCIE (1960).

DE L'AMOUR 1964 d: Jean Aurel. FRN/ITL., *De l'Amour*, Stendhal, Paris 1822, Novel

De l'Eau Au Prix de Leur Sang *see* AN HEILIGEN WASSERN (1961).

DE LUXE ANNIE 1918 d: Roland West. USA., *De Luxe Annie*, Edward Clark, New York 1917, Play

DE MUJER A MUJER 1950 d: Luis LuciA. SPN., *Alma Triunfante*, Jacinto Benavente y Martinez, 1902, Play

DE NOCHE VIENES, ESMERALDA 1997 d: Jaime Humberto Hermosillo. MXC., *De Noche Vienes Esmeralda*, Elena Poniatowska, Short Story

De Quoi Tu Te Meles, Daniela! *see* ZARTE HAUT IN SCHWARZER SEIDE (1961).

DE SFASURAREA 1954 d: Paul Calinescu. RMN., *Desfasurarea*, Marin Preda, 1952, Short Story

Dead Among the Living *see* MRTVY MEZI ZIVYMI (1947).

Dead and the Living, The *see* YINYANG JIE (1988).

Dead are Alive, The *see* MRTVI ZIJI (1922).

Dead are Living, The *see* MRTVI ZIJI (1922).

DEAD BY SUNSET 1995 d: Karen Arthur. USA., *Dead By Sunset*, Ann Rule, Book

DEAD CALM 1988 d: Phil Noyce. ASL., *Dead Calm*, Charles Williams, Novel

DEAD CERT 1974 d: Tony Richardson. UKN., *Dead Cert*, Dick Francis, Novel

DEAD CERTAINTY, A 1920 d: George Dewhurst. UKN., *A Dead Certainty*, Nat Gould, Novel

Dead -Die Toten, The *see* THE DEAD (1987).

Dead Divers Get No Gold *see* EIN TOTER TAUCHER NIMMT KEIN GELD (1975).

Dead Don't Care, The *see* THE LAST WARNING (1938).

DEAD END 1937 d: William Wyler. USA., *Dead End*, Sidney Kingsley, New York 1936, Play

Dead End *see* ANDHI GALI (1984).

Dead End Drive in *see* DEAD-END DRIVE-IN (1986).

Dead Eyes of London *see* DIE TOTEN AUGEN VON LONDON (1960).

DEAD HEART 1996 d: Nick Parsons. ASL., *Dead Heart*, Nick Parsons, Play

DEAD HEART, THE 1914 d: Hay Plumb. UKN., *The Dead Heart*, Watts Phillips, London 1859, Play

Dead House, The *see* MYORTVYI DOM (1932).

Dead Husband Returns, The *see* UN MARIDO DE IDA Y VUELTA (1957).

DEAD LUCKY 1987 d: Barbara Rennie. UKN., *Lake of Darkness*, Ruth Rendell, Novel

Dead Man Seeks His Murderer, A *see* VENGEANCE (1962).

DEAD MAN WALKING 1995 d: Tim Robbins. USA., *Dead Man Walking*, Sister Helen Prejean, Book

DEAD MAN'S FLOAT 1980 d: Peter Maxwell. ASL., *Dead Man's Float*, Roger Vaughan Carr, Novel

Dead Man's Folly *see* AGATHA CHRISTIE'S DEAD MAN'S FOLLY (1986).

DEAD MAN'S SHOES 1939 d: Thomas Bentley. UKN., *Carrefour*, Hans Kafka, Short Story

DEAD MEN ARE DANGEROUS 1939 d: Harold French. UKN., *Hidden*, H. C. Armstrong, Novel

DEAD MEN TELL NO TALES 1920 d: Tom Terriss. USA., *Dead Men Tell No Tales*, E. W. Hornung, New York 1899, Novel

DEAD MEN TELL NO TALES 1938 d: David MacDonald. UKN., *The Norwich Victims*, Francis Beeding, Novel

DEAD MEN TELL NO TALES 1971 d: Walter Grauman. USA., *Dead Men Tell No Tales*, Kelley Roos, Novel

Dead Moon, The *see* MALAJANHA (1965).

Dead of Jericho, The *see* INSPECTOR MORSE: THE DEAD OF JERICHO (1989).

Dead on Course *see* WINGS OF DANGER (1952).

Dead on Nine *see* DESILU PLAYHOUSE: DEAD ON NINE (1958-59).

DEAD ON THE MONEY 1991 d: Mark Cullingham. USA., *The End of Tragedy*, Rachel Ingalls, Novel

DEAD PRESIDENTS 1995 d: Allen Hughes, Albert Hughes. USA., *Specialist No.4 Haywood T. "the Kid" Kirkland*, Wallace Terry, Short Story

DEAD RECKONING 1990 d: Robert Lewis. USA., *Dead Reckoning*, Robert Lewis, Play

Dead Remain Young, The *see* DIE TOTEN BLEIBEN JUNG (1968).

Dead Ringers *see* TWINS (1988).

DEAD ROMANTIC 1992 d: Patrick Lau. UKN., *Dead Romantic*, Simon Brett, Novel

Dead Run *see* GEHEIMNISSE IN GOLDENEN NYLONS (1966).

DEAD SECRET, THE 1913 d: Stanner E. V. Taylor. USA., *The Dead Secret*, Wilkie Collins, Novel

DEAD SHOT BAKER 1917 d: William Duncan. USA., *Wolfville: Episodes of Cowboy Life*, Alfred Henry Lewis, New York 1897, Book

DEAD SILENCE 1997 d: Daniel Petrie Jr. CND/USA., Jeffrey Deaver, Book

Dead Souls *see* MERTVIYE DUSHI (1960).

Dead Stay Young, The *see* DIE TOTEN BLEIBEN JUNG (1968).

DEAD, THE 1987 d: John Huston. USA/UKN/GRM., *Dubliners*, James Joyce, 1914, Short Story

DEAD TO THE WORLD 1960 d: Nicholas Webster. USA., *State Department Murders*, Edward Ronns, New York 1950, Novel

Dead Woman from Beverly Hills *see* DIE TOTE VON BEVERLY HILLS (1964).

Dead Woman in the Thames, The *see* DIE TOTE AUS DER THEMSE (1971).

Dead Woman, The *see* A FALECIDA (1964).

Dead Woman's Kiss, A *see* IL BACIO DI UNA MORTA (1949).

Dead Yesterday *see* THE GREAT HOSPITAL MYSTERY (1937).

DEAD ZONE, THE 1983 d: David Cronenberg. USA., *The Dead Zone*, Stephen King, Novel

DEAD-END DRIVE-IN 1986 d: Brian Trenchard-Smith. ASL., *Crabs*, Peter Carey, Short Story

DEADFALL 1967 d: Bryan Forbes. UKN/USA., *Deadfall*, Desmond Cory, London 1965, Novel

Deadliest Sin, The *see* CONFESSION (1955).

Deadline *see* U.S.A. DEADLINE (1952).

Deadline *see* BOGNOR: DEADLINE (1981).

DEADLINE AT DAWN 1946 d: Harold Clurman. USA., *Deadline at Dawn*, Cornell Woolrich, 1944, Novel

DEADLINE, U.S.A. 1952 d: Richard Brooks. USA., *The Night the World Folded*, Richard Brooks, Novel

Deadlock *see* MAN-TRAP (1961).

Deadlock *see* SIKATOR (1966).

DEADLY AFFAIR, THE 1966 d: Sidney Lumet. UKN., *Call for the Dead*, John le Carre, London 1961, Novel

DEADLY BEES, THE 1967 d: Freddie Francis. UKN., *A Taste for Honey*, H. F. Heard, New York 1941, Novel

Deadly Companion *see* DOUBLE NEGATIVE (1980).

DEADLY COMPANIONS, THE 1961 d: Sam Peckinpah. USA., *Yellowleg*, Albert Sidney Fleischman, New York 1960, Novel

Deadly Decoy, The *see* LE GORILLE A MORDU L'ARCHEVEQUE (1962).

Deadly Dreams *see* LIEBESTRAUM (1951).

DEADLY DUO 1962 d: Reginald Le Borg. USA., *The Deadly Duo*, Richard Jessup, New York 1960, Novel

Deadly Enemy *see* SMERTELNI VRAG (1971).

DEADLY EYES 1982 d: Robert Clouse. CND., *The Rats*, James Herbert, Novel

DEADLY FRIEND 1987 d: Wes Craven. USA., *Friend*, Diana Henstell, Novel

Deadly Game, A *see* CHARLIE MUFFIN (1979).

Deadly Game, The *see* THIRD PARTY RISK (1955).

Deadly Game, The *see* SERPICO: THE DEADLY GAME (1976).

DEADLY HARVEST 1972 d: Michael O'Herlihy. USA., *Watcher in the Shadows*, Geoffrey Household, Novel

DEADLY HATE, A 1915 d: Richard Ridgely. USA., *A Deadly Hate*, George Roberts, Play

Deadly Honeymoon *see* NIGHTMARE HONEYMOON (1972).

DEADLY HUNT, THE 1971 d: John Newland. USA., *The Deadly Hunt*, Pat Stadley, Novel

DEADLY INTENTIONS 1985 d: Noel Black. USA., *Deadly Intentions*, William Randolph Stevens, Book

Deadly Invention, The *see* VYNALEZ ZKAZY (1958).

DEADLY IS THE FEMALE 1949 d: Joseph H. Lewis. USA., *Gun Crazy*, MacKinlay Kantor, 1940, Short Story

Deadly Matrimony *see* SHATTERED PROMISES (1993).

Deadly Melody *see* LIU ZHI QIN MO (1993).

Deadly Reactor *see* THE REACTOR (1989).

DEADLY RECORD 1959 d: Lawrence Huntington. UKN., *Deadly Record*, Nina Warner Hooke, Novel

Deadly Run *see* MORTELLE RANDONNEE (1983).

DEADLY SILENCE, A 1989 d: John Patterson. USA., *A Deadly Silence*, Dena Kleiman, Book

Deadly Sweet *see* COL CUORE IN GOLA (1967).

Deadly Trap, The *see* LA MAISON SOUS LES ARBRES (1971).

Dead-Shot Baker *see* DEAD SHOT BAKER (1917).

DEADWOOD COACH, THE 1924 d: Lynn Reynolds. USA., *The Orphan*, Clarence E. Mulford, New York 1908, Novel

Deaf to the City *see* LE SOURD DANS LA VILLE (1986).

DEALING: OR THE BERKELEY-TO-BOSTON FORTY-BRICK LOST-BAG BLUES 1972 d: Paul Williams. USA., *Dealing*, Michael Crichton, Novel

DEAN KOONTZ'S MR. MURDER 1999 d: Dick Lowry. USA., *Mr. Murder*, Dean R. Koontz, Novel

Dean R. Koontz's Servants of Twilight *see* SERVANTS OF TWILIGHT (1991).

Dear Augustine *see* DER LIEBE AUGUSTIN (1940).

Dear Boys *see* LIEVE JONGENS (1979).

DEAR BRIGITTE 1965 d: Henry Koster. USA., *Erasmus With Freckles*, John Haase, New York 1963, Novel

Dear Caroline *see* CAROLINE CHERIE (1950).

Dear Detective *see* TENDRE POULET (1978).

Dear Family *see* DEN KARA FAMILJEN (1962).

DEAR FOOL, A 1921 d: Harold Shaw. UKN., *A Dear Fool*, Arthur T.) Artemas (Mason, Novel

Dear Inspector *see* TENDRE POULET (1978).

Dear John *see* KARE JOHN (1964).

DEAR LIAR, A 1925 d: Fred Leroy Granville. UKN., *A Dear Liar*, Edgar Wallace, Short Story

DEAR LITTLE OLD TIME GIRL 1915 d: William C. Dowlan. USA., *Dear Little Old Time Girl*, Leonora Ainsworth, Story

Dear Michael *see* CARO MICHELE (1976).

DEAR MR. PROHACK 1949 d: Thornton Freeland. UKN., *Mr. Prohack*, Arnold Bennett, 1922, Novel

DEAR MURDERER 1947 d: Arthur Crabtree. UKN., *Dear Murderer*, St. John Leigh Clowes, Play

DEAR OCTOPUS 1943 d: Harold French. UKN., *Dear Octopus*, Dodie Smith, London 1938, Play

DEAR RUTH 1947 d: William D. Russell. USA., *Dear Ruth*, Norman Krasna, New York 1944, Play

DE-AS FI HARAP ALB 1965 d: Ion Popescu-Gopo. RMN., *Povestea Lui Harap Alb*, Ion Creanga, 1877, Short Story

Death and Devil *see* TOD UND TEUFEL (1973).

Death and Resurrection of Wilhelm Hausmann *see* TOD UND AUFERSTEHUNG DES WILHELM HAUSMANN (1977).

Death and the Devil *see* TOD UND TEUFEL (1973).

DEATH AND THE MAIDEN 1994 d: Roman Polanski. USA/FRN/UKN., *Death and the Maiden*, Ariel Dorfman, Play

Death and the River *see* EL RIO Y LA MUERTE (1954).

DEATH AT BROADCASTING HOUSE 1934 d: Reginald Denham. UKN., *Death at Broadcasting House*, Val Gielgud, Novel

Death at the Deep End of the Swimming Pool *see* LA ULTIMA SENORA ANDERSON (1970).

Death Avenger *see* EL MUERTO HACE LAS MALETAS (1970).

DEATH BE NOT PROUD 1975 d: Donald Wrye. USA., *Death Be Not Proud*, John Gunther, Book

DEATH BY DESIGN 1943 d: Geoffrey Faithfull. UKN., *Death By Design*, Leonard Gribble, Short Story

Death By Witchcraft *see* BYAKUYA NO YOJO (1958).

Death Calls Itself Engelchen *see* SMRT SI RIKA ENGELCHEN (1963).

DEATH CROONS THE BLUES 1937 d: David MacDonald. UKN., *Death Croons the Blues*, James Ronald, Novel

DEATH DISC, THE 1909 d: D. W. Griffith. USA., *The Death Disc*, Mark Twain, Story

Death Drive *see* AUTOSTOP (1977).

DEATH DRUMS ALONG THE RIVER 1963 d: Lawrence Huntington. UKN., *Sanders of the River*, Edgar Wallace, London 1911, Novel

DEATH FLIES EAST 1935 d: Phil Rosen. USA., *Death Flies East*, Philip Wylie, 1934, Story

DEATH GOES TO SCHOOL 1953 d: Stephen Clarkson. UKN., *Death Goes to School*, Maisie Sharman, Novel

Death in a French Garden *see* PERIL EN LA DEMEURE (1985).

DEATH IN BRUNSWICK 1991 d: John Ruane. ASL., *Death in Brunswick*, Boyd Oxlade, Novel

DEATH IN CALIFORNIA, A 1986 d: Delbert Mann. USA., *A Death in California*, Joan Barthel, Book

DEATH IN CANAAN, A 1978 d: Tony Richardson. USA., *A Death in Canaan*, Joan Barthel, Book

Death in Full View *see* DEATH WATCH (1979).

DEATH IN GRANADA 1997 d: Marcos ZurinagA. SPN/PRC., Ian Gibson, Books

DEATH IN HIGH HEELS 1947 d: Lionel Tomlinson. UKN., *Death in High Heels*, Christianna Brand, Novel

Death in Paradise Canyon *see* FAIR WARNING (1937).

Death in Persepolis *see* AND THEN THERE WERE NONE (1974).

Death in Rome *see* RAPPRESAGLIA (1973).

DEATH IN SMALL DOSES 1957 d: Joseph M. Newman. USA., Arthur L. Davis, Article

Death in the Deep South *see* THEY WON'T FORGET (1937).

Death in the Doll's House *see* SHADOW ON THE WALL (1949).

Death in the Garden *see* LA MORT EN CE JARDIN (1956).

DEATH IN THE HAND 1948 d: A. Barr-Smith. UKN., *Death in the Hand*, Max Beerbohm, Short Story

Death in the Sun *see* WHISPERING DEATH (1975).

Death in Therapy *see* PASSAGE A L'ACTE (1996).

Death in Venice *see* MORTE A VENEZIA (1971).

Death Is Called Engelchen *see* SMRT SI RIKA ENGELCHEN (1963).

Death Is Child's Play *see* QUIEN PUEDE MATAR A UN NINO? (1975).

Death Is My Trade *see* AUS EINEM DEUTSCHEN LEBEN (1978).

Death Is Now My Neighbour *see* INSPECTOR MORSE: DEATH IS NOW MY NEIGHBOUR (1997).

DEATH KISS, THE 1933 d: Edwin L. Marin. USA., *The Death Kiss*, Madelon St. Denis, New York 1932, Novel

Death Occurred Last Night *see* LA MORTE RISALE A IERI SERA (1970).

DEATH OF A CHAMPION 1939 d: Robert Florey. USA., *Dog Show Murder*, Frank Gruber, 1938, Short Story

Death of a Doctor *see* AZ ORVOS HALALA (1966).

DEATH OF A GUNFIGHTER 1969 d: Robert Totten, Don Siegel. USA., *Death of a Gunfighter*, Lewis B. Patten, New York 1968, Novel

Death of a Jew *see* SABRA (1970).

DEATH OF A SALESMAN 1951 d: Laslo Benedek. USA., *Death of a Salesman*, Arthur Miller, New York 1949, Play

Death of a Salesman *see* MOST PEREYTI NELIEYA (1960).

DEATH OF A SALESMAN 1985 d: Volker Schlondorff. USA/GRM., *Death of a Salesman*, Arthur Miller, New York 1949, Play

Death of a Swan, The *see* LA MORT DU CYNGE (1937).

Death of a Tea Master *see* SEN NO RIKYU - HONGAKUBO IBUN (1989).

DEATH OF AN ANGEL 1952 d: Charles Saunders. UKN., *This Is Mary's Chair*, Frank King, Play

Death of an Expert Witness *see* DALGLIESH: DEATH OF AN EXPERT WITNESS (1983).

Death of Beautiful Roe-Deers *see* SMRT KRASNYCH SRNCU (1987).

Death of Empedocles *see* DER TOD DES EMPEDOKLES (1986).

DEATH OF INNOCENCE, A 1971 d: Paul Wendkos. USA., *A Death of Innocence*, Zelda Popkin, Novel

Death of Joe the Indian, The *see* MOARTEA LUI JOE INDIANUL (1968).

DEATH OF ME YET, THE 1971 d: John Llewellyn Moxey. USA., *The Death of Me Yet*, Whit Masterson, Novel

DEATH OF MINNEHAHA, THE 1910. USA., *The Song of Hiawatha*, Henry Wadsworth Longfellow, Boston 1855, Poem

DEATH OF RICHIE, THE 1977 d: Paul Wendkos. USA., *Richie*, Thomas Thompson, Book

DEATH OF TINTAGILES, THE 1977 d: Malcolm Edwards. UKN., *Mort de Tintagiles*, Maurice Maeterlinck, 1894, Play

Death on a Side Street *see* ONE-WAY STREET (1950).

DEATH ON THE DIAMOND 1934 d: Edward Sedgwick. USA., *Death on the Diamond: a Baseball Mystery Story*, Cortland Fitzsimmons, New York 1934, Novel

DEATH ON THE NILE 1978 d: John Guillermin. USA/UKN., *Death on the Nile*, Agatha Christie, Novel

DEATH ON THE SET 1935 d: Leslie Hiscott. UKN., *Death on the Set*, Victor MacClure, Novel

Death Packs Up *see* EL MUERTO HACE LAS MALETAS (1970).

Death Predicter, The *see* LE MONDE TREMBLERA (1939).

Death Rays of Dr. Mabuse *see* DIE TODESSTRAHLEN DES DR. MABUSE (1964).

Death Rides This Trail *see* WILD HERITAGE (1958).

Death Rode on Tuesdays *see* I GIORNI DELL'IRA (1967).

Death Scream *see* LA MAISON SOUS LES ARBRES (1971).

DEATH SENTENCE 1975 d: E. W. Swackhamer. USA., *After the Trial*, Eric Roman, Novel

Death Sentence *see* MRITYUDAND (1997).

DEATH STALK 1975 d: Robert Day. USA., *Death Stalk*, Thomas Chastain, Novel

Death Strikes Again *see* FROM NINE TO NINE (1936).

DEATH TAKES A HOLIDAY 1934 d: Mitchell Leisen. USA., *La Morte in Vacanza*, Alberto Casella, Play

DEATH TAKES A HOLIDAY 1971 d: Robert Butler. USA., *La Morte in Vacanza*, Alberto Casella, Play

DEATH TRAIN 1992 d: David S. Jackson. USA/UKN/CRT., *Death Train*, Alistair MacLean, Novel

DEATH TRAP 1962 d: John Llewellyn Moxey. UKN., Edgar Wallace, Novel

Death Valley *see* MYSTERY RANCH (1932).

DEATH WATCH 1979 d: Bertrand Tavernier. UKN/FRN/GRM., *Death Watch*, David Compton, Novel

Death Watch -Der Gekaufte Tod *see* DEATH WATCH (1979).

Death Watch, The *see* BEFORE DAWN (1933).

DEATH WISH 1974 d: Michael Winner. USA., *Death Wish*, Brian Garfield, Novel

DEATHTRAP 1982 d: Sidney Lumet. USA., *Deathtrap*, Ira Levin, Play

DEATHWATCH 1965 d: Vic Morrow. USA., *Haute Surveillance*, Jean Genet, Paris 1949, Play

Deathwatch *see* DEATH WATCH (1979).

Debdas *see* DEVDAS (1935).

Debdas *see* DEVDAS (1955).

DEBOUT LES MORTS 1915 d: Henri Pouctal, Leonce Perret. FRN., *Los Cuatro Jinetes Del Apocalipsis*, Vicente Blasco Ibanez, Valencia 1916, Novel

DEBT OF HONOUR 1936 d: Norman Walker. UKN., *Debt of Honour*, H. C. McNeile ("Sapper"), Short Story

DEBT OF HONOUR, A 1922 d: Maurice Elvey. UKN., *A Debt of Honour*, Ethel M. Dell, Novel

DEBURAU 1950 d: Sacha Guitry. FRN., *Deburau*, Sacha Guitry, Play

DECADENCE 1993 d: Steven Berkoff. UKN/GRM., *Decadence*, Steven Berkoff, Play

Decak Je Vikao Ubistvo *see* THE BOY CRIED MURDER (1966).

DECAMERON NIGHTS 1924 d: Herbert Wilcox. UKN/GRM., *Il Decameron*, Giovanni Boccaccio, 1349-50, Book

DECAMERON NIGHTS 1953 d: Hugo Fregonese. UKN/USA., *Il Decameron*, Giovanni Boccaccio, 1349-50, Book

Decameron, The *see* IL DECAMERONE (1971).

DECAMERONE, IL 1912 d: Gennaro Righelli. ITL., *Il Decameron*, Giovanni Boccaccio, 1349-50, Book

DECAMERONE, IL 1971 d: Pier Paolo Pasolini. ITL/FRN/GRM., *Il Decameron*, Giovanni Boccaccio, 1349-50, Book

DECEIT 1923 d: Oscar Micheaux. USA., *Behind the Hills*, Charles Chestnutt, Novel

Deceit *see* UNHOLY LOVE (1932).

Deceit *see* NO WAY OUT (1987).

DECEIVER, THE 1931 d: Louis King. USA., *It Might Have Happened*, Abem Finkel, Bella Muni, Story

DECEIVERS, THE 1988 d: Nicholas Meyer. UKN/IND., *The Deceivers*, John Masters, Novel

DECEMBER BRIDE, THE 1989 d: Thaddeus O'Sullivan. IRL/UKN., *December Bride*, Sam Hanna Bell, 1951, Novel

Decent Woman, The *see* LA DECENTE (1970).

DECENTE, LA 1970 d: Jose Luis Saenz de HerediA. SPN., *La Decente*, Miguel Mihura Santos, 1969, Play

Deception *see* WOMAN OF PASSION DU BARRY (1930).

DECEPTION 1946 d: Irving Rapper. USA., *Monsieur Lamberthier*, Louis Verneuil, Play

Deception *see* DER RICHTER UND SEIN HENKER (1976).

Deception, The *see* DIE FALSCHUNG (1981).

DECEPTIONS 1985 d: Robert Chenault, Melville Shavelson. USA., *Deceptions*, Judith Michael, Novel

DECHEANCE 1918 d: Michel Zevaco. FRN., *Decheance*, Michel Zevaco, Play

Decheance *see* ODETTE (1934).

DECIDING KISS, THE 1918 d: Tod Browning. USA., *Turn About Eleanor*, Ethel May Kelley, Indianapolis 1917, Novel

DECIMA VITTIMA, LA 1965 d: Elio Petri. ITL/FRN., *Seventh Victim*, Robert Sheckley, 1953, Short Story

DECISION AT MIDNIGHT 1963 d: Lewis Allen. USA., *Decision at Midnight*, Peter Howard, Alan Thornhill, Novel

DECISION AT SUNDOWN 1957 d: Budd Boetticher. USA., *Decision at Sundown*, Vernon I. Fluharty, Book

DECISION BEFORE DAWN 1951 d: Anatole Litvak. USA., *Call It Treason*, George Locke Howe, 1949, Book

DECISION OF CHRISTOPHER BLAKE, THE 1948 d: Peter Godfrey. USA., *Christopher Blake*, Moss Hart, New York 1946, Play

DECLASSEE 1925 d: Robert G. VignolA. USA., *Declassee*, Zoe Akins, New York 1921, Play

Decline and Fall see **DECLINE AND FALL. OF A BIRDWATCHER!** (1968).

DECLINE AND FALL. OF A BIRDWATCHER! 1968 d: John Krish. UKN., *Decline and Fall*, Evelyn Waugh, London 1928, Novel

DECORATION DAY 1990 d: Robert Markowitz. USA., *Decoration Day*, John William Corrington, Novel

Decoy see **MYSTERY SUBMARINE** (1963).

DECOY, THE 1916 d: George W. Lederer. USA., *The Country Girl*, Herbert Hall Winslow, Short Story

DEDALE, LE 1912 d: Rene Leprince. FRN., *Le Dedale*, Paul Hervieu, Play

DEDALE, LE 1917 d: Jean Kemm. FRN., *Le Dedale*, Paul Hervieu, Play

DEDALE, LE 1926 d: Gaston Roudes, Marcel Dumont. FRN., *Le Dedale*, Paul Hervieu, Play

DEDE 1934 d: Rene Guissart. FRN., *Dede*, Henri Christine, Albert Willemetz, Opera

Dede de Montmartre see **DEDE LA MUSIQUE** (1939).

DEDE LA MUSIQUE 1939 d: Andre Berthomieu. FRN., *Dede la Musique*, Gaston Montho, Novel

DEDECKEM PROTI SVE VULI 1939 d: Vladimir Slavinsky. CZC., *Dedeckem Proti Sve Vuli*, Frantisek Zavrel, Play

Dedee see **DEDEE D'ANVERS** (1947).

DEDEE D'ANVERS 1947 d: Yves Allegret. FRN., *Dedee d'Anvers*, Detective Ashelbe, Novel

Deed of Another, The see **DIE TAT DES ANDERN** (1951).

DEEMSTER, THE 1917 d: Howell Hansel. USA., *The Deemster*, Hall Caine, London 1887, Novel

DEEP BLUE SEA, THE 1955 d: Anatole Litvak. UKN., *The Deep Blue Sea*, Terence Rattigan, London 1952, Play

DEEP END OF THE OCEAN, THE 1999 d: Ulu Grosbard. USA., *The Deep End of the Ocean*, Jacquelyn Mitchard, 1996, Novel

Deep End, The see **ONE-WAY STREET** (1950).

DEEP IN MY HEART 1954 d: Stanley Donen. USA., *Deep in My Heart*, Elliott Arnold, 1949, Book

DEEP PURPLE, THE 1915 d: James Young. USA., *The Deep Purple*, Paul Armstrong, Wilson Mizner, Chicago 1910, Play

DEEP PURPLE, THE 1920 d: Raoul Walsh. USA., *The Deep Purple*, Paul Armstrong, Wilson Mizner, Chicago 1910, Play

DEEP SIX, THE 1958 d: Rudolph Mate. USA., *The Deep Six*, Martin Dibner, 1953, Novel

Deep South, The see **THEY WON'T FORGET** (1937).

DEEP, THE 1977 d: Peter Yates. USA., *The Deep*, Peter Benchley, 1976, Novel

DEEP VALLEY 1947 d: Jean Negulesco. USA., *Deep Valley*, Dan Totheroh, Novel

DEEP WATERS 1920 d: Maurice Tourneur. USA., *Caleb West*, Michael Morton, New York 1900, Play, *Caleb West Master Diver*, F. Hopkinson Smith, New York 1899, Novel

Deer Hunt see **MRIGAYA** (1976).

DEERSLAYER 1943 d: Lew Landers. USA., *The Deerslayer*, James Fenimore Cooper, 1841, Novel

DEERSLAYER, THE 1913 d: Hal Reid, Larry Trimble. USA., *The Deerslayer*, James Fenimore Cooper, 1841, Novel

DEERSLAYER, THE 1957 d: Kurt Neumann. USA., *The Deerslayer*, James Fenimore Cooper, 1841, Novel

DEERSLAYER, THE 1978 d: Richard Friedenberg. USA., *The Deerslayer*, James Fenimore Cooper, 1841, Novel

DEFEAT OF THE CITY, THE 1917 d: Thomas R. Mills. USA., *The Defeat of the City*, O. Henry, 1908, Short Story

Defector, The see **L' ESPION** (1966).

Defendant, The see **OBZALOVANY** (1964).

DEFENSE D'AIMER 1942 d: Richard Pottier. FRN., *Yes*, Rene Pujol, Albert Willemetz, Maurice Yvain, Opera

Defi a Gibraltar see **FINCHE DURA LA TEMPESTA** (1962).

Defiant, The see **THE WILD PACK** (1971).

DEFINITE OBJECT, THE 1920 d: Edgar J. Camiller. UKN., *The Definite Object*, Jeffrey Farnol, Boston 1917, Novel

Defoule, Le see **CHERIE RELAXE-TOI** (1964).

DEGOURDIS DE LA 11E, LES 1937 d: Christian-Jaque. FRN., *Les Degourdis de la 11E*, C. Daveillant, Andre Mouezy-Eon, Play

DEGREE OF GUILT 1995 d: Mike Robe. USA., *Degree of Guilt*, Richard North Paterson, Novel

DEI SVARTE HESTANE 1951 d: Hans Jacob Nilsen, Sigval Maartmann-Moe. NRW., *Dei Svarte Hestane*, Tarjei Vesaas, 1928, Novel

DEIN LEBEN GEHORT MIR 1939 d: Johannes Meyer. GRM., *Akte Fabreani*, Frank F. Braun, Novel

DEJA VU 1984 d: Anthony Richmond. UKN., *Always*, Trevor Meldal-Johnson, Book

DEJEUNER DE SOLEIL, UN 1937 d: Marcel Cravenne. FRN., *Un Dejeuner de Soleil*, Andre Birabeau, Play

Dekameron-Nachte see **DECAMERON NIGHTS** (1924).

DEL INFIERNO AL CIELO 1931 d: Richard Harlan. USA., *The Man Who Came Back*, John Fleming Wilson, New York 1912, Novel

DEL SOTO DEL PARRAL, LA 1927 d: Leon ArtolA. SPN., *La Del Soto Del Parral*, Anselmo Carreno Y Sevilla, Opera

DELAVINE AFFAIR, THE 1954 d: Douglas Pierce. UKN., *Winter Wears a Shroud*, Robert Chapman, Novel

Delectable Time of Kalimagdora, The see **DIE SUSSE ZEIT MIT KALIMAGDORA** (1968).

DELIBABOK ORSZAGA 1983 d: Marta Meszaros. HNG., *Revizor*, Nikolay Gogol, 1836, Play

DELIBERATE STRANGER, THE 1985 d: Marvin J. Chomsky. USA., *The Deliberate Stranger*, Richard W. Larsen, Novel

DELICATE BALANCE, A 1973 d: Tony Richardson. USA., *A Delicate Balance*, Edward Albee, 1966, Play

DELICATE DELINQUENT, THE 1957 d: Don McGuire. USA., *Damon and Pythias*, Don McGuire, Story

Delicate Situation see **ARMS AND THE GIRL** (1917).

DELICIOUS LITTLE DEVIL, THE 1919 d: Robert Z. Leonard. USA., *Mind Your Feet Kitty*, John B. Clymer, Harvey F. Thew, Short Story

DELIGHTFUL ROGUE, THE 1929 d: Lynn Shores, A. Leslie Pearce. USA., *A Woman Decides*, Wallace Smith, Short Story

Delightful Story see **ROZKOSNY PRIBEH** (1936).

DELILA 1914 d: Eugen Illes. GRM., *Kinder Der Eifel*, Clara Viebig, Novel

DELINQUENTS, THE 1989 d: Chris Thomson. ASL., *The Delinquents*, Criena Rohan, Novel

DELIT DE FUITE 1958 d: Bernard Borderie. FRN/ITL/YGS., *Hit and Run*, James Hadley Chase, Novel

DELITTO AL CIRCOLO DEL TENNIS 1969 d: Franco Rossetti. ITL/YGS., *Delitto Al Circolo Del Tennis*, Alberto Moravia, 1952, Short Story

DELITTO DEL COMMENDATORE, IL 1921 d: Amedeo Mustacchi. ITL., *Il Delitto Del Commendatore*, Carlo Dadone, Novel

DELITTO DELL'OPERA, IL 1917 d: Eleuterio Rodolfi. ITL., *Il Delitto Dell'Opera*, De Boisgobey, Novel

DELITTO DI CASTEL GIUBILEO, IL 1918 d: Nino Martinengo. ITL., *I Vaschi Della Bujosa*, Nino Ilari, Novel

DELITTO DI GIOVANNI EPISCOPO, IL 1947 d: Alberto LattuadA. ITL., *Giovanni l'Episcopo*, Gabriele D'Annunzio, 1891, Novel

Delitto Di un Re see **RACCONTO D'INVERNO** (1913).

Delitto du Pre, Il see **LES BONNES CAUSES** (1963).

Delitto Per Amore see **L' EDERA** (1950).

DELIVERANCE 1928 d: Ben K. Blake. USA., *Prohibition Still at Its Worst*, Irving Fisher, 1928, Novel, *Proibition at Its Worst*, Irving Fisher, 1926, Novel

Deliverance see **MUKHTI** (1970).

DELIVERANCE 1972 d: John Boorman. USA., *Deliverance*, James Dickey, 1970, Novel

Deliverance see **SADGATI** (1981).

Delivery, The see **LA ENTREGA** (1954).

DELIVREZ-NOUS DU MAL 1965 d: Jean-Claude Lord. CND., *Delivrez-Nous du Mal*, Claude Jasmin, Novel

Della Nuba Alla Resistenza see **DALLA NUBE ALLA RESISTENZA** (1979).

DELLAMORTE DELLAMORE 1994 d: Michele Soavi. ITL/FRN/GRM., *Dellamorte Dellamore*, Tiziano Sclavi, Novel

Delmiro Gouveia, O Desconhocido see **O DESCONHECIDO** (1980).

DELO ARTAMANOVICH 1941 d: Grigori Roshal. USS., *Delo Artamonovykh*, Maxim Gorky, 1925, Novel

Delo Artamanovika see **DELO ARTAMANOVICH** (1941).

Delo Artamonovyh see **DELO ARTAMANOVICH** (1941).

DELPHINE 1931 d: Roger Capellani, Jean de Marguenat. FRN., *Das Konzert*, Hermann Bahr, 1909, Play

DELTA FACTOR, THE 1970 d: Tay Garnett. USA., *The Delta Factor*, Mickey Spillane, New York 1969, Novel

Delta III see **THE SHAPE OF THINGS TO COME** (1979).

DELUGE 1933 d: Felix E. Feist. USA., *Deluge: a Romance*, S. Fowler Wright, London 1927, Novel

Deluge, The see **POTOP** (1974).

Demand, The see **LA PETICION** (1976).

DEMANTY NOCI 1964 d: Jan Nemec. CZC., *Tma Ne Ma Stin*, Arnost Lustig, Prague 1958, Short Story

Demasiadas Mujeres Para Layton see **CARRE DE DAMES POUR UN AS** (1966).

Demise of Father Mouret, The see **LA FAUTE DE L'ABBE MOURET** (1970).

Demi-Soldes, Les see **L' AGONIE DES AIGLES** (1951).

Demi-Vierges, Les see **IL ROMANZO DI MAUD** (1917).

DEMI-VIERGES, LES 1924 d: Armand Du Plessis. FRN., *Les Demi-Vierges*, Marcel Prevost, 1895, Novel

DEMI-VIERGES, LES 1936 d: Pierre Caron. FRN., *Les Demi-Vierges*, Marcel Prevost, 1895, Novel

Democrate Lappli, Le see **DEMOKRAT LAPPLI** (1961).

Demoiselle du Tabac, La see **MIQUETTE** (1940).

Demoiselles de Wilko, Les see **PANNY Z WILKO** (1979).

DEMOKRAT LAPPLI 1961 d: Alfred Rasser. SWT., *Demokrat Lappli*, Alfred Rasser, 1947, Play

DEMON 1911 d: Giovanni Vitrotti, F. Kortfus. ITL/USS., *Demon*, Mikhail Lermontov, 1841, Poem

Demon Barber of Fleet Street, The see **THE DEMON BARBER OF FLEET STREET SWEENEY TODD** (1936).

DEMON DE LA HAINE, LE 1921 d: Leonce Perret. FRN/USA., *La Divine*, Louis Letang, Novel, *Rolande Immolee*, Louis Letang, Paris 1914, Novel

Demon de Onze Heures, Le see **PIERROT LE FOU** (1965).

Demon Doctor, The see **JUGGERNAUT** (1936).

Demon Doctor, The see **GRITOS EN LA NOCHE** (1961).

Demon of Gold see **KONJIKI YASHA** (1954).

Demon Pond see **YASHA-GA-IKE** (1979).

DEMON SEED 1977 d: Donald Cammell. USA., *Demon Seed*, Dean R. Koontz, Novel

Demon, The see **DEMON** (1911).

DEMON, THE 1918 d: George D. Baker. USA., Alice Muriel Williamson, Charles Norris Williamson, Novel

Demone, Il see **DEMON** (1911).

Demoniac see **LES LOUVES** (1956).

Demoniaque see **LES LOUVES** (1956).

DEMONIAQUE, LE 1968 d: Rene Gainville. FRN., *A Tenir Au Frais*, James Hadley Chase, Novel

Demonic Love see **DAMONISCHE LIEBE** (1951).

Demonios, Los see **LES DEMONS** (1973).

Demonios, Os see **LES DEMONS** (1973).

Demons see **SHURA** (1970).

Demons du Sexe, Les see **LES DEMONS** (1973).

DEMONS, LES 1973 d: Jesus Franco. FRN/PRT/SPN., *Los Demonios*, Jesus Franco, Novel

Demon's Mask, The see **LA MASCHERA DEL DEMONIO** (1960).

Demons, The see **LES DEMONS** (1973).

DEMONWARP 1988 d: Emmett Alston. USA., John Buechler, Story

DEMOS 1921 d: Denison Clift. UKN., *Demos*, George Gissing, Novel

DEMPSEY 1983 d: Gus Trikonis. USA., *Dempsey*, Barbara Piatteli Dempsey, Jack Dempsey, Autobiography

DENEN KOKYOGAKU 1938 d: Satsuo Yamamoto. JPN., *La Symphonie Pastorale*, Andre Gide, 1919, Novel

DENG-BYOD 1984 d: Hah Myong-Jung. KOR., *Deng-Byod*, Kim Yu-Jung, Novel

DENIAL, THE 1925 d: Hobart Henley. USA., *A Square Peg*, Lewis Beach, New York 1923, Play

Denmark Is Closed see DANMARK ER LUKKET (1981).

Denomme Squarcio, Un see LA GRANDE STRADA AZZURRA (1957).

DENTE PER DENTE 1943 d: Marco Elter. ITL., *Measure for Measure*, William Shakespeare, c1604, Play

DENTELLIERE, LA 1977 d: Claude GorettA. SWT/FRN/GRM., *La Dentelliere*, Pascal Laine, Novel

Denti Lunghi, I see LES DENTS LONGUES (1953).

DENTIST IN THE CHAIR 1960 d: Don Chaffey. UKN., *Dentist in the Chair*, Matthew Finch, London 1955, Novel

DENTRO LA CASA DELLA VECCHIA SIGNORA 1971 d: Giacomo Battiato. ITL., *The Superfluous Mansion*, Robert Louis Stevenson, Story

Dents du Diable, Les see THE SAVAGE INNOCENTS (1959).

DENTS LONGUES, LES 1953 d: Daniel Gelin. FRN/ITL., *Les Dents Longues*, Jacques Robert, Novel

Deo Gratis see UN DROLE DE PAROISSIEN (1963).

Department K see ASSIGNMENT K (1967).

DEPARTMENTAL CASE, A 1917 d: Martin Justice. USA., *A Departmental Case*, O. Henry, Short Story

DEPARTURE 1986 d: Brian Kavanagh. ASL., *A Pair of Claws*, Michael Gurr, Play

Depot of the Dead, The see BAZA LUDZI UMARLYCH (1958).

Depraved, The see ADELAIDE (1968).

Depths, The see KAIDAN KASANE-GA-FUCHI (1957).

DEPUTY MARSHAL 1949 d: William Berke. USA., *Deputy Marshal*, Charles Heckelman, Novel

Deputy Sheriff see BAR 20 JUSTICE (1938).

DER KOM EN SOLDAT 1969 d: Peer Guldbrandsen. DNM., *Fyrtojet*, Hans Christian Andersen, Copenhagen 1835, Short Story

DER VAR ENGANG 1922 d: Carl T. Dreyer. DNM., *Der Var Engang*, Holger Drachman, 1885, Play

DER VAR ENGANG 1966 d: John Price. DNM., *Der Var Engang*, Holger Drachman, 1885, Play

DERBORENCE 1946 d: Mattia Pinoli. SWT/ITL., *Derborence*, Charles-Ferdinand Ramuz, Lausanne 1934, Novel

DERBY WINNER, THE 1915 d: Harold Shaw. UKN., *The Derby Winner*, Henry Hamilton, Augustus Harris, Cecil Raleigh, London 1894, Play

Derelict, The see TAINATA NA APOLONIA (1984).

DERELICTS 1917 d: Sidney Morgan. UKN., *Derelicts*, William J. Locke, Novel

DERELITTI DI VALCOURT, I 1921 d: Amedeo Mustacchi. ITL., *I Derelitti Di Valcourt*, Valcourt, Play

Derivatif, Le see LA FOLLE NUIT (1932).

DERMAN 1983 d: Serif Goren. TRK., *Derman*, Osman Sahin, Novel

DERNIER DES CAPENDU, LE 1923 d: Jean Manoussi. FRN., *Le Dernier Des Capendu*, Eugene Barbier, Novel

DERNIER DES MOHICANS, LE 1968 d: Jean Dreville, Sergiu Nicolaescu. FRN/RMN., *The Last of the Mohicans*, James Fenimore Cooper, Boston 1826, Novel

DERNIER DES SIX, LE 1941 d: Georges Lacombe. FRN., *Le Dernier Des Six*, Stanislas-Andre Steeman, Novel

DERNIER DOMICILE CONNU 1970 d: Jose Giovanni. FRN/ITL., *Dernier Domicile Connu*, Joseph Harrington, Novel

DERNIER HAVRE, LE 1987 d: Denyse Benoit. CND., *Le Dernier Havre*, Yves Theriault, Novel

DERNIER METRO 1945 d: Maurice de Canonge. FRN., *Mathilde Et Ses Mitaines*, Tristan Bernard, Novel

Dernier Papillon, Le see POSLEDNI MOTYL (1989).

DERNIER PARDON, LE 1913 d: Maurice Tourneur. FRN., *Le Dernier Pardon*, Gyp, Novel

DERNIER REFUGE 1946 d: Marc Maurette. FRN., *Le Locataire*, Georges Simenon, 1934, Novel

DERNIER SAUT, LE 1969 d: Edouard Luntz. FRN/ITL., *Le Dernier Saut*, Bartholome Benassar, Novel

DERNIER TOURNANT, LE 1939 d: Pierre Chenal. FRN., *The Postman Always Rings Twice*, James M. Cain, 1934, Novel

DERNIERE AVENTURE 1941 d: Robert Peguy. FRN., *Papa*, Gaston Arman de Caillavet, Robert de Flers, 1911, Play

DERNIERE AVENTURE DU PRINCE CURACAO, LA 1912. FRN., *Derniere Aventure du Prince Curacao*, Delphi Fabrice, Oscar Metenier, Novel

DERNIERE BERCEUSE, LA 1930 d: Jean Cassagne, Gennaro Righelli. FRN., *In Silenzio*, Luigi Pirandello, 1905, Short Story

DERNIERE CHEVAUCHEE, LA 1946 d: Leon Mathot. FRN., *La Rancon*, Leopold Gomez, Play

Derniere Enquete de Wens, La see QUE PERSONNE NE SORTE (1963).

DERNIERE HEURE, EDITION SPECIALE 1949 d: Maurice de Canonge. FRN., *L' Epouvante*, Maurice Level, Paris 1908, Novel

DERNIERE JEUNESSE 1939 d: Jeff Musso. FRN/ITL., *Mr. Gilhooley*, Liam O'Flaherty, 1926, Novel

Derniere Rencontre see ULTIMO INCONTRO (1952).

DERNIERE VALSE, LA 1935 d: Leo Mittler. FRN., *Der Letzte Walzer*, Oscar Straus, Max Wallner, G. Weber, Berlin 1920, Operetta

DERNIERES CARTOUCHES, LES 1912. FRN., *Les Dernieres Cartouches*, Jules Mary, Novel

Dernieres Roses, Les see MARTHA (1935).

DERNIERS JOURS DE POMPEI, LES 1908. FRN., *The Last Days of Pompeii*, Edward George Bulwer Lytton, 1834, Novel

DERNIERS JOURS DE POMPEI, LES 1948 d: Marcel L'Herbier, Paolo MoffA. FRN/ITL., *The Last Days of Pompeii*, Edward George Bulwer Lytton, 1834, Novel

DEROBADE, LA 1979 d: Daniel Duval. FRN., *La Derobade*, Jeanne Cordelier, Novel

Dersu Uzala see DERZU UZALA (1975).

DERZU UZALA 1975 d: Akira KurosawA. JPN/USS., *Okhotnik Dersu*, Vladimir K. Arsenieva, Book

DES FEMMES DISPARAISSENT 1959 d: Edouard Molinaro. FRN., *Des Femmes Disparaissent*, Gilles-Maurice Morris-Dumoulin, Paris 1958, Novel

Des Filles Pour l'Armee see LE SOLDATESSE (1965).

DES GENS SANS IMPORTANCE 1955 d: Henri Verneuil. FRN., *Des Gens Sans Importance*, Serge Groussard, Novel

DES JOURNEES ENTIERES DANS LES ARBRES 1976 d: Marguerite Duras. FRN., *Des Journees Entieres Dans Les Arbres*, Marguerite Duras, 1954, Novel

DES PISSENLITS PAR LA RACINE 1963 d: Georges Lautner. FRN/ITL., *Y'avait un MacChabee*, Clarence Weff, Novel

Des Prisons Et Des Hommes see FORTUNE AND MEN'S EYES (1971).

Des Teufels Advokat see L' AVVOCATO DEL DIAVOLO (1977).

DES TEUFELS GENERAL 1955 d: Helmut Kautner. GRM., *Des Teufels General*, Carl Zuckmayer, 1945, Play

DES TEUFELS PARADIES 1987 d: Vadim GlownA. GRM., Joseph Conrad, Novel

DESARROI 1946 d: Robert-Paul Dagan. FRN., *Odette*, Victorien Sardou, 1881, Play

Desarrois de l'Eleve Torless, Les see DER JUNGE TORLESS (1966).

DESCENDEZ, ON VOUS DEMANDE 1951 d: Jean Laviron. FRN., *Descendez on Vous Demande*, Jean de Letraz, Play

Descent Into Hell see DESCENTE AUX ENFERS (1986).

Descent of the Nine see I KATHODOS TON ENEA (1984).

DESCENTE AUX ENFERS 1986 d: Francis Girod. FRN., *The Wounded and the Slain*, David Goodis, 1959, Novel

DESCONHECIDO, O 1980 d: Ruy Santos. BRZ., *O Desconhecido*, Lucio Cardoso, 1940, Short Story

Deseo Y El Amor, El see LE DESIR ET L'AMOUR (1951).

Desert Attack see ICE COLD IN ALEX (1958).

DESERT BRIDE, THE 1928 d: Walter Lang. USA., *The Adventuress*, Ewart Adamson, Story

Desert Des Tartares, Le see IL DESERTO DEI TARTARI (1976).

DESERT DRIVEN 1923 d: Val Paul. USA., *The Man from the Desert*, Wyndham Martin, Short Story

DESERT FLOWER, THE 1925 d: Irving Cummings. USA., *The Desert Flower*, Don Mullally, New York 1924, Play

DESERT FOX, THE 1951 d: Henry Hathaway. USA., *Rommel - the Desert Fox*, Desmond Young, 1950, Biography

DESERT FURY 1947 d: Lewis Allen. USA., *Desert Town*, Ramona Stewart, Novel

DESERT GOLD 1914 d: Scott Sidney. USA., *McTeague; a Story of San Francisco*, Frank Norris, New York 1899, Novel

DESERT GOLD 1919 d: T. Hayes Hunter. USA., *Desert Gold*, Zane Grey, New York 1913, Novel

DESERT GOLD 1926 d: George B. Seitz. USA., *Desert Gold*, Zane Grey, New York 1913, Novel

DESERT GOLD 1936 d: James P. Hogan. USA., *Desert Gold*, Zane Grey, New York 1913, Novel

Desert Healer, The see OLD LOVES AND NEW (1926).

DESERT HEARTS 1986 d: Donna Deitch. USA., *Desert of the Heart*, Jane Rule, Novel

DESERT LEGION 1953 d: Joseph Pevney. USA., *The Demon Caravan*, Georges Arthur Surdez, 1927, Novel

Desert of the Tartars, The see IL DESERTO DEI TARTARI (1976).

Desert of Wheat, The see RIDERS OF THE DAWN (1920).

Desert Prince, The see LIGHTNING (1927).

DESERT PURSUIT 1952 d: George Blair. USA., *Desert Voices*, Kenneth Perkins, 1937, Novel

Desert Retour see LA CHATELAINE DU LIBAN (1956).

DESERT SANDS 1954 d: Lesley Selander. USA., *Punitive Action*, John Robb, 1954, Novel

DESERT SHEIK, THE 1924 d: Tom Terriss. USA., *The Tragedy of the Korosko*, Arthur Conan Doyle, London 1898, Novel

Desert Song see DAS LIED DER WUSTE (1939).

DESERT SONG, THE 1929 d: Roy Del Ruth. USA., *The Desert Song*, Otto Harbach, Frank Mandel, Sigmund Romberg, New York 1926, Musical Play

DESERT SONG, THE 1943 d: Robert Florey. USA., *The Desert Song*, Otto Harbach, Frank Mandel, Sigmund Romberg, New York 1926, Musical Play

DESERT SONG, THE 1953 d: H. Bruce Humberstone. USA., *The Desert Song*, Otto Harbach, Frank Mandel, Sigmund Romberg, New York 1926, Musical Play

Desert Town see DESERT FURY (1947).

DESERT VALLEY 1926 d: Scott R. Dunlap. USA., *Desert Valley*, Jackson Gregory, New York 1921, Novel

Desert War see QUATTRO NOTTI CON ALBA (1962).

DESERTED AT THE ALTAR 1922 d: William K. Howard, Albert Kelley. USA., *Deserted at the Altar*, Pierce Kingsley, 1922, Play

Deserter and the Nomads, The see ZBEHOVIA A PUTNICI (1968).

Deserters and Pilgrims see ZBEHOVIA A PUTNICI (1968).

DESERTO DEI TARTARI, IL 1976 d: Valerio Zurlini. ITL/FRN/GRM., *Il Deserto Dei Tartari*, Dino Buzzati, 1940, Novel

DESERT'S PRICE, THE 1925 d: W. S. Van Dyke. USA., *The Desert's Price*, William MacLeod Raine, Garden City, N.Y. 1924, Novel

Desesperado, Le see LA LOI DU SURVIVANT (1966).

Desideri Proibiti see LES GRANDES PERSONNES (1961).

Desiderio Perverso see GIORNATA NERA PER L'ARIETE (1971).

DESIGN FOR LIVING 1933 d: Ernst Lubitsch. USA., *Design for Living*, Noel Coward, New York 1933, Play

Design for Murder see TRUNK CRIME (1939).

DESIGNATED MOURNER, THE 1997 d: David Hare. UKN., *The Designated Mourner*, Wallace Shawn, Play

DESILU PLAYHOUSE: DEAD ON NINE 1958-59 d: William F. Claxton. USA., *Dead on Nine*, Jack Popplewell, Play

DESIR ET L'AMOUR, LE 1951 d: Henri Decoin, Luis Maria Delgado. FRN/SPN., *Le Desir Et l'Amour*, Auguste Bailly, Novel

DESIR, LE 1928 d: Albert Durec. FRN., *Un Fruit . Et Puis un Autre Fruit*, Jean Pommerol, Novel

Desirable Woman *see* **THE WOMAN ON THE BEACH** (1946).

DESIRE 1920 d: George Edwardes Hall. UKN., *La Peau de Chagrin*, Honore de Balzac, Paris 1831, Novel

DESIRE 1936 d: Frank Borzage. USA., *Die Schonen Tage von Aranjuez*, Robert A. Stemmle, Hans Szekely, Play

DESIRE 1937 d: Sacha Guitry. FRN., *Desire*, Sacha Guitry, Play

DESIRE IN THE DUST 1960 d: William F. Claxton. USA., *Harry Whittington*, Story

DESIRE ME 1947 d: George Cukor (Uncredited), Mervyn Leroy (Uncredited). USA., *Karl Und Anna*, Leonhard Frank, 1926, Short Story

DESIRE UNDER THE ELMS 1958 d: Delbert Mann. USA., *Desire Under the Elms*, Eugene O'Neill, New York 1924, Play

DESIRED WOMAN, THE 1918 d: Paul Scardon. USA., *The Desired Woman*, William Nathaniel Harben, New York 1913, Novel

DESIREE 1954 d: Henry Koster. USA., *Desiree*, Annemarie Selinko, Novel

Desires *see* **DAS LETZTE REZEPT** (1952).

Desirs Pervers *see* **GLI INDIFFERENTI** (1964).

DESK SET, THE 1957 d: Walter Lang. USA., *The Desk Set*, William Marchant, New York 1955, Play

DESOBEISSANCE, LA 1981 d: Aldo Lado. FRN/ITL., *La Disubbidienza*, Alberto Moravia, Novel

Desordre Et Genie *see* **KEAN** (1922).

DESORDRE ET LA NUIT, LE 1958 d: Gilles Grangier. FRN., *Le Desordre Et la Nuit*, Jacques Robert, Paris 1955, Novel

Despair *see* **EINE REISE IN LICHTS** (1978).

Desperado Outpost *see* **DOKURITSU GURENTAI** (1959).

DESPERADO, THE 1954 d: Thomas Carr. USA., *The Desperado*, Clifton Adams, Novel

Desperado Trail, The *see* **WINNETOU III** (1965).

Desperadoes are in Town, The *see* **THE DESPERADOS ARE IN TOWN** (1956).

DESPERADOS ARE IN TOWN, THE 1956 d: Kurt Neumann. USA., *The Outlaws are in Town*, Bennett Foster, 1949, Short Story

DESPERATE CARGO 1941 d: William Beaudine. USA., *Loot Below*, Eustace L. Adams, Story

Desperate Chance, A *see* **A DESPERATE CHANCE FOR ELLERY QUEEN** (1942).

DESPERATE CHANCE FOR ELLERY QUEEN, A 1942 d: James P. Hogan. USA., *A Good Samaritan*, Ellery Queen, Radio Play

DESPERATE CHARACTERS 1971 d: Frank D. Gilroy. USA., *Desperate Characters*, Paula Fox, Novel

Desperate Encounters *see* **DESPERATE CHARACTERS** (1971).

DESPERATE HOURS 1990 d: Michael Cimino. USA., *The Desperate Hours*, Joseph Hayes, Novel

DESPERATE HOURS, THE 1955 d: William Wyler. USA., *The Desperate Hours*, Joseph Hayes, Novel

DESPERATE MAN, THE 1959 d: Peter Maxwell. UKN., *Beginner's Luck*, Andrew Garve, Novel

Desperate Men, The *see* **CAT AND MOUSE** (1958).

DESPERATE MOMENT 1953 d: Compton Bennett. UKN., *Desperate Moment*, Martha Albrand, Novel

Desperate Ones, The *see* **CAT AND MOUSE** (1958).

Desperate Ones, The *see* **MAS ALLA DE LAS MONTANAS** (1967).

DESPERATE SEARCH 1952 d: Joseph H. Lewis. USA., *The Desperate Search*, Arthur Mayse, Novel

DESPERATE TRAILS 1921 d: John Ford. USA., *Christmas Eve at Pilot Butte*, Courtney Ryley Cooper, 1921, Short Story

Desperate Woman, A *see* **LADIES AT PLAY** (1926).

DESPERATE YOUTH 1921 d: Harry B. Harris. USA., *A Kentucky Cinderella*, F. Hopkinson Smith, 1899, Short Story

Desperation *see* **DRIVEN** (1916).

DESTIN EXECRABLE DE GUILLEMETTE BABIN, LE 1948 d: Guillaume Radot. FRN., *La Vie Execrable de Guillemette Babin*, Maurice Garcon

Destin, Le *see* **MACARIO** (1959).

DESTIN S'AMUSE, LE 1946 d: Emile Edwin Reinert. FRN., *Le Destin S'amuse*, Jacques Companeez, Pierre Galante, Short Story

Destination 13 Sahara *see* **STATION SIX SAHARA** (1962).

Destination Death *see* **DER TRANSPORT** (1961).

DESTINATION GOBI 1953 d: Robert Wise. USA., Edmund G. Love, Short Story

DESTINATION MOON 1950 d: Irving Pichel. USA., *Rocket Ship Galileo*, Robert A. Heinlein, 1947, Novel

Destinazione Marciapiede *see* **LE VOYAGE DU PERE** (1966).

Destinies of Women *see* **NAISKOHTALOITA** (1948).

DESTINO IN TASCA, IL 1938 d: Gennaro Righelli. ITL., *Il Destino in Tasca*, Alberto Colantuoni, Play

DESTINO SE DISCULPA, EL 1944 d: Jose Luis Saenz de HerediA. SPN., *Fantasmas*, Wenceslao Fernandez Florez, 1930, Short Story

DESTINY 1919 d: Rollin S. Sturgeon. USA., *Destiny*, Charles Neville Buck, New York 1913, Novel

Destiny *see* **HOUSE OF FRANKENSTEIN** (1944).

Destiny of a Man *see* **SUDBA CHELOVEKA** (1959).

DESTINY OF A SPY 1969 d: Boris Sagal. USA., *The Giant Woman*, John Blackburn, Novel

Destiny Says Sorry *see* **EL DESTINO SE DISCULPA** (1944).

Destroy, She Said *see* **DIT-ELLE DETRUIRE** (1969).

DESTROYERS, THE 1916 d: Ralph Ince. USA., *Peter God*, James Oliver Curwood, Short Story

DESTROYING ANGEL, THE 1915 d: Richard Ridgely. USA., *The Destroying Angel*, Louis Joseph Vance, Boston 1912, Novel

DESTROYING ANGEL, THE 1923 d: W. S. Van Dyke. USA., *The Destroying Angel*, Louis Joseph Vance, Boston 1912, Novel

DESTRUCTION 1915 d: Will S. Davis. USA., *Labor*, Will S. Davis, Story

Destruction Test *see* **CIRCLE OF DECEPTION** (1960).

DESTRY 1954 d: George Marshall. USA., *Destry Rides Again*, Max Brand, New York 1930, Novel

DESTRY RIDES AGAIN 1932 d: Ben Stoloff, Alan James. USA., *Destry Rides Again*, Max Brand, New York 1930, Novel

DESTRY RIDES AGAIN 1939 d: George Marshall. USA., *Destry Rides Again*, Max Brand, New York 1930, Novel

DET AR MIN MODELL 1946 d: Gustaf Molander. SWD., *Nationalmonumenttet*, Tor Hedberg, Stockholm 1923, Play

DET ER IKKE APPELSINER -DET ER HESTE 1967 d: Ebbe Langberg. DNM., *Is He Living Or Is He Dead?*, Mark Twain, 1900, Short Story

DET ER NAT MED FRU KNUDSEN 1971 d: Henning Ornbak. DNM., *Alting Og Et Postnus*, Leif Petersen, 1969, Play

Det Kom En Sommar *see* **KORT AR SOMMAREN** (1962).

DET REGNAR PA VAR KARLEK 1946 d: Ingmar Bergman. SWD., *Bra Mennesker*, Oskar Braaten, 1930, Play

Detective, A *see* **UN DETECTIVE** (1969).

Detective Belli *see* **UN DETECTIVE** (1969).

Detective Bureau 2-3: Go to Hell, Bastards! *see* **TANTEI JIMUSHO 2-3: KUTABARE AKUTODOMO** (1963).

"Detective Clive", Bart. *see* **SCOTLAND YARD** (1930).

DETECTIVE CRAIG'S COUP 1914 d: Donald MacKenzie. USA., *The Ticket-of-Leave Man*, Charles Reade, Story

Detective Riko *see* **ONNA KEIJI RIKO 2: SEIBO NO SHINKI-EN** (1998).

DETECTIVE STORY 1951 d: William Wyler. USA., *Detective Story*, Sidney Kingsley, New York 1949, Play

Detective, The *see* **FATHER BROWN** (1954).

DETECTIVE, THE 1968 d: Gordon Douglas. USA., *The Detective*, Roderick Thorp, New York 1966, Novel

DETECTIVE, THE 1985 d: Don Leaver. UKN., *The Detective*, Paul Ferris, Novel

DETECTIVE, UN 1969 d: Romolo Guerrieri. ITL., *MacChie Di Belletto*, Ludovico Dentice, Milan 1968, Novel

Detonator *see* **DEATH TRAIN** (1992).

DETRESSE 1929 d: Jean Durand. FRN., *Detresse*, Alexis Bouvier, Short Story

DETRUIRE, DIT-ELLE 1969 d: Marguerite Duras. FRN., *Dit-Elle Detruire*, Marguerite Duras, Paris 1969, Novel

DETSTVO GORKOVO 1938 d: Mark Donskoi. USS., *Detstvo*, Maxim Gorky, 1913, Autobiography

Detstvo Ivana *see* **IVANOVO DETSTVO** (1962).

DETSTVO TEMY 1991 d: Elena StrizhevskajA. RSS., *Detstvo Temy*, N. Garin-Mikhajlovksy

DETTE DE HAINE 1915 d: Henri Pouctal. FRN., *Dette de Haine*, Georges Ohnet, Novel

DETTE, LA 1920 d: Gaston Roudes. FRN., *Crime Et Redemption*, Daniel Jourda, Play

DEUCE OF SPADES, THE 1922 d: Charles Ray. USA., *The Weight of the Last Straw*, Charles E. Van Loan, Story

DEUTSCHE REVOLUTION, EINE 1981 d: Helmut Herbst. GRM., *Wenn Es Rosen Sind Werden Sie Bluhen*, Kasimir Edschmid, 1950, Novel

DEUTSCHSTUNDE 1971 d: Peter Beauvais. GRM., *Deutschstunde*, Siegfried Lenz, 1968, Novel

DEUX AMIS, LES 1946 d: Dimitri Kirsanoff. FRN., *Deux Amis*, Guy de Maupassant, 1883, Short Story

DEUX ANGLAISES ET LE CONTINENT, LES 1971 d: Francois Truffaut. FRN., *Deux Anglaises Et le Continent*, Henri-Pierre Roche, 1956, Novel

Deux Anglaises, Les *see* **LES DEUX ANGLAISES ET LE CONTINENT** (1971).

DEUX ANS DE VACANCES 1973 d: Gilles Grangier, Sergiu Nicolaescu. FRN/GRM/RMN., *Deux Ans de Vacances*, Jules Verne, Paris 1888, Novel

Deux Beauties, Les *see* **MARQUIS DE SADE: JUSTINE** (1968).

Deux Billets Pour Mexico *see* **GEHEIMNISSE IN GOLDENEN NYLONS** (1966).

DEUX CANARDS, LES 1933 d: Erich Schmidt. FRN., *Les Deux Canards*, Alfred Athis, Tristan Bernard, Play

DEUX DE L'ESCADRILLE 1952 d: Maurice Labro. FRN., *Deux de l'Escadrille*, Pierre Salvat, Novel

DEUX FOIS VINGT ANS 1930 d: Charles-Felix Tavano. FRN., *Deux Fois Vingt Ans*, Pierre Frondaie, Novel

DEUX GAMINES, LES 1950 d: Maurice de Canonge. FRN., *Les Deux Gamines*, Louis Feuillade, Novel

DEUX GOSSES, LES 1912 d: Adrien Caillard. FRN., *Les Deux Gosses*, Pierre Decourcelle, Novel

DEUX GOSSES, LES 1914 d: Albert Capellani. FRN., *Les Deux Gosses*, Pierre Decourcelle, Novel

DEUX GOSSES, LES 1924 d: Louis Mercanton. FRN., *Les Deux Gosses*, Pierre Decourcelle, Novel

DEUX GOSSES, LES 1936 d: Fernand Rivers. FRN., *Les Deux Gosses*, Pierre Decourcelle, Novel

Deux Missionnaires, Les *see* **PORGI L'ALTRA GUANCIA** (1974).

DEUX "MONSIEUR" DE MADAME, LES 1933 d: Abel Jacquin, Georges Pallu. FRN., *Les Deux "Monsieur" de Madame*, Felix Gandera, Andre Mouezy-Eon, Play

DEUX "MONSIEUR" DE MADAME, LES 1951 d: Robert Bibal. FRN., *Les Deux "Monsieur" de Madame*, Felix Gandera, Andre Mouezy-Eon, Play

DEUX ORPHELINES, LES 1932 d: Maurice Tourneur. FRN., *Les Deux Orphelines*, Eugene Cormon, Adolphe-P. d'Ennery, 1874, Novel

Deux Orphelines, Les *see* **LE DUE ORFANELLE** (1955).

Deux Orphelines, Les *see* **LE DUE ORFANELLE** (1966).

Deux Rivales, Les *see* **GLI INDIFFERENTI** (1964).

DEUX SOLDATS, LES 1923 d: Jean Herve. FRN., *Les Deux Soldats*, Gustave Guiches, Novel

Deux Solitudes *see* **TWO SOLITUDES** (1978).

DEUX TIMIDES, LES 1928 d: Rene Clair. FRN., *Les Deux Timides*, Eugene Labiche, Marc-Michel, 1860, Play

Deux Timides, Les *see* **JEUNES TIMIDES** (1941).

DEUXIEME BUREAU 1935 d: Pierre Billon. FRN., *Deuxieme Bureau*, Robert-Claude Dumas, Novel

DEUXIEME BUREAU CONTRE KOMMANDANTUR 1939 d: Rene Jayet, Robert Bibal. FRN., *Terre d'Angoisse*, Pierre Nord, Novel

DEUXIEME BUREAU CONTRE TERRORISTES
1959 d: Jean Stelli. FRN., *Deuxieme Bureau Contre Terroristes*, Slim Harrison, Novel

DEUXIEME SOUFFLE, LE 1966 d: Jean-Pierre Melville. FRN., *Le Deuxieme Souffle*, Jose Giovanni, Novel

DEVCE Z HOR 1924 d: Vaclav Kubasek. CZC., *Devce Z Hor*, Bohumil Zahradnik-Brodsky, Novel

DEVCE Z PREDMESTI ANEBO VSECKO PRIJDE NA JEVO 1939 d: Theodor Pistek. CZC., *Devce Z Predmesti Anebo Vsecko Prijde Na Jevo*, Josef Kajetan Tyl, Play

DEVCE Z TABAKOVE TOVARNY 1928 d: Vaclav Kubasek. CZC., *Devce Z Tabakove Tovarny*, Otomar Schafer, Novel

DEVCICA Z BESKYD 1944 d: Frantisek Cap. CZC., *Papradna Nenarika*, Miloslav J. Sousedik, Novel

DEVDAS 1935 d: Pramathesh Chandra BaruA. IND., *Devdas*, Saratchandra Chatterjee, 1917, Novel

DEVDAS 1941 d: Pramathesh Chandra BaruA. IND., *Devdas*, Saratchandra Chatterjee, 1917, Novel

DEVDAS 1955 d: Bimal Roy. IND., *Debdas*, Sarat Candra Cattopadhyay, 1910, Novel

Devices and Desires see **DALGLIESH: DEVICES AND DESIRES** (1990).

Devil and Daniel Webster, The see **ALL THAT MONEY CAN BUY** (1941).

DEVIL AND THE DEEP 1932 d: Marion Gering. USA., *Sirenes Et Tritons; le Roman du Sous-Marin*, Maurice Larrouy, Paris 1927, Novel

Devil and the Nun, The see **MATKA JOANNA OD ANIOLOW** (1961).

DEVIL AT 4 O'CLOCK, THE 1961 d: Mervyn Leroy. USA., *The Devil at Four O'Clock*, Max Catto, London 1958, Novel

DEVIL BEAR, THE 1929 d: Louis W. Chaudet. CND., *The Blind Chute*, Sargeson V. Halstead, Story

Devil Came from Akasawa, The see **DER TEUFEL KAM AUS AKASAWA** (1971).

DEVIL COMMANDS, THE 1941 d: Edward Dmytryk. USA., *The Edge of Running Water*, William Sloane, Story

Devil Doll, The see **THE DEVIL-DOLL** (1936).

DEVIL GIRL FROM MARS 1954 d: David MacDonald. UKN., *Devil Girl from Mars*, James Eastwood, John C. Mahner, Play

DEVIL IN A BLUE DRESS 1995 d: Carl Franklin. USA., *Devil in a Blue Dress*, Walter Mosley, Novel

Devil in a Bottle, The see **TOD UND TEUFEL LIEBE** (1934).

Devil in Amsterdam, The see **DE DUIVEL IN AMSTERDAM** (1919).

Devil in Me, The see **JSEM DEVCE S CERTEM V TELE** (1933).

Devil in Silk see **TEUFEL IN SEIDE** (1956).

Devil in the Flesh see **LE DIABLE AU CORPS** (1946).

DEVIL IN THE FLESH 1986 d: Scott Murray. ASL., *Le Diable du Corps*, Raymond Radiguet, 1923, Novel

DEVIL IS A WOMAN, THE 1935 d: Josef von Sternberg. USA., *La Femme Et le Pantin*, Pierre Louys, Paris 1898, Novel

Devil Is a Woman, The see **LA LUPA** (1953).

Devil Is an Empress, The see **LE JOUEUR D'ECHECS** (1938).

Devil Made a Woman, The see **LA DE RONDA CARMEN** (1959).

Devil May Care see **DEVIL-MAY-CARE** (1929).

Devil Never Sleeps, The see **SATAN NEVER SLEEPS** (1962).

Devil of a Woman, A see **DER WEIBSTEUFEL** (1966).

Devil on Two Sticks, The see **IL DIAVOLO ZOPPO** (1910).

DEVIL RIDES OUT, THE 1968 d: Terence Fisher. UKN., *The Devil Rides Out*, Dennis Wheatley, London 1935, Novel

DEVIL, THE 1915 d: Thomas H. Ince, Reginald Barker. USA., *Az Ordog; Vigjatek Harom Felvonasban*, Ferenc Molnar, Budapest 1908, Play

DEVIL, THE 1921 d: James Young. USA., *Az Ordog; Vigjatek Harom Felvonasban*, Ferenc Molnar, Budapest 1908, Play

Devil, The see **DRUMS O' VOODOO** (1934).

DEVIL THUMBS A RIDE, THE 1947 d: Felix E. Feist. USA., *The Devil Thumbs a Ride*, Robert C. Dusoe, Novel

DEVIL TO PAY, THE 1920 d: Ernest C. Warde. USA., *The Devil to Pay*, Frances Nimmo Greene, New York 1918, Novel

Devil Under the Pillow, A see **UN DIABLO BAJA LA ALMOHADA** (1968).

Devil Under Your Pillow see **UN DIABLO BAJA LA ALMOHADA** (1968).

Devil Was Coming from Akasawa, The see **DER TEUFEL KAM AUS AKASAWA** (1971).

Devil Was Sick, The see **GOD'S GIFT TO WOMEN** (1931).

Devil With the Three Golden Hairs, The see **DER TEUFEL MIT DEN DREI GOLDENEN HAAREN** (1955).

DEVIL WITH WOMEN, A 1930 d: Irving Cummings. USA., *Dust and Sun*, Clements Ripley, 1928, Short Story

DEVIL WITHIN, THE 1921 d: Bernard J. Durning. USA., *Cursed*, George Allan England, Boston 1919, Novel

Devil Woman see **DER WEIBSTEUFEL** (1951).

DEVIL-DOLL, THE 1936 d: Tod Browning. USA., *Witch, Burn! Burn*, Abraham Merritt, New York 1933, Novel

DEVIL-MAY-CARE 1929 d: Sidney A. Franklin. USA., *La Bataille de Dames; Ou un Duel En Amour*, Ernest Legouve, Eugene Scribe, Paris 1851, Novel

DEVIL'S 8, THE 1969 d: Burt Topper. USA., *The Devil's 8*, Larry Gordon, Novel

Devil's Advocate, The see **L' AVVOCATO DEL DIAVOLO** (1977).

DEVIL'S ADVOCATE, THE 1997 d: Taylor Hackford. USA., *The Devil's Advocate*, Andrew Neiderman, Novel

Devil's Agent, The see **IM NAMEN DES TEUFELS** (1962).

DEVIL'S ARITHMETIC, THE 1999 d: Donna Deitch. USA., *The Devil's Arithmetic*, Jane Yolen, Novel

DEVIL'S BOWL, THE 1923 d: Neal Hart. USA., *The Man Who Wouldn't Take Off His Hat*, Philip le Noir, 1922, Short Story

Devil's Bride, The see **THE DEVIL RIDES OUT** (1968).

DEVIL'S BRIGADE, THE 1968 d: Andrew V. McLaglen. USA., *The Devil's Brigade*, Robert H. Adleman, George Walton, Philadelphia 1966, Novel

Devil's Brood, The see **HOUSE OF FRANKENSTEIN** (1944).

DEVIL'S BROTHER, THE 1933 d: Hal Roach, Charles Rogers. USA., *Fra Diavolo Ou l'Hotellerie de Terracine*, Daniel Francois Auber, Paris 1830, Opera, *Fra Diavolo; Ou l'Hotellerie de Terracine*, Eugene Scribe, Paris 1830, Opera

Devil's Canyon of the Wild Wolves see **ZANNA BIANCA** (1973).

DEVIL'S CHAPLAIN 1929 d: Duke Worne. USA., *Devil's Chaplain*, George Bronson Howard, New York 1922, Novel

Devil's Colors, The see **LES COULEURS DU DIABLE** (1997).

Devil's Cross, The see **LA CRUZ DEL DIABLO** (1974).

Devil's Daffodil, The see **DAS GEHEIMNIS DER GELBEN NARZISSEN** (1961).

DEVIL'S DAUGHTER, THE 1915 d: Frank Powell. USA., *La Gioconda*, Gabriele D'Annunzio, Palermo 1899, Play

DEVIL'S DISCIPLE, THE 1959 d: Guy Hamilton. UKN/USA., *The Devil's Disciple*, George Bernard Shaw, London 1899, Play

DEVIL'S DOORYARD, THE 1923 d: Louis King. USA., *The Devil's Dooryard*, W. C. Tuttle, 1921, Short Story

Devil's Eight, The see **THE DEVIL'S 8** (1969).

Devil's Elixirs, The see **DIE ELIXIERE DES TEUFELS** (1976).

DEVIL'S FOOT, THE 1921 d: Maurice Elvey. UKN., *The Devil's Foot*, Arthur Conan Doyle, Short Story

Devil's Foot, The see **THE RETURN OF SHERLOCK HOLMES: THE DEVIL'S FOOT** (1986).

Devil's Garden see **COPLAN SAUVE SA PEAU** (1967).

DEVIL'S GARDEN, THE 1920 d: Kenneth Webb. USA., *The Devil's Garden*, William Babington Maxwell, Indianapolis 1913, Novel

Devil's General, The see **DES TEUFELS GENERAL** (1955).

Devil's Greetings to You see **DIABOLIQUEMENT VOTRE** (1967).

DEVIL'S HAIRPIN, THE 1957 d: Cornel Wilde. USA., *The Fastest Man on Earth*, James Edmiston, Story

Devil's Hand, The see **LA MAIN DU DIABLE** (1942).

Devil's Island see **LA ISLA DEL DIABLO** (1995).

DEVIL'S LOTTERY 1932 d: Sam Taylor. USA., *Devil's Lottery*, Nalbro Bartley, New York 1931, Novel

DEVIL'S MAZE, THE 1929 d: V. Gareth Gundrey. UKN., *Mostly Fools*, G. R. Malloch, Play

Devil's Own, The see **THE WITCHES** (1966).

Devil's Paradise, The see **DES TEUFELS PARADIES** (1987).

DEVIL'S PARTY, THE 1938 d: Ray McCarey. USA., *Hell's Kitchen Has a Pantry*, Borden Chase, Novel

Devil's Playground see **THE LADY WHO DARED** (1931).

DEVIL'S PROFESSION, THE 1915 d: F. C. S. Tudor. UKN., *The Devil's Profession*, Gertrude de S. Wentworth James, Novel

DEVIL'S RIDDLE, THE 1920 d: Frank Beal. USA., *The Devil's Riddle*, Edwina Levin, 1919, Story

DEVIL'S SADDLE, THE 1927 d: Albert S. Rogell. USA., *The Devil's Saddle*, Kenneth Perkins, 1926, Short Story

Devil's Saint, The see **FLOR DE SANTIDAD** (1972).

DEVIL'S SKIPPER, THE 1928 d: John G. Adolfi. USA., *Demetrios Contos*, Jack London, 1905, Short Story

DEVILS, THE 1971 d: Ken Russell. UKN., *The Devils*, John Whiting, 1961, Play

DEVIL'S TOY, THE 1916 d: Harley Knoles. USA., *The Mills of the Gods*, Edward Madden, Poem

DEVIL'S TRADEMARK, THE 1928 d: James Leo Meehan. USA., *Pedigree*, Calvin Johnston, Story

DEVIL'S TRAIL, THE 1942 d: Lambert Hillyer. USA., *The Town in Hell's Backyard*, Robert Lee Johnson, Story

Devil's Trap, The see **DABLOVA PAST** (1961).

Devil's Treasure see **TREASURE ISLAND** (1990).

Devil's Undead, The see **NOTHING BUT THE NIGHT** (1972).

Devil's Visitations, The see **LAS VISITACIONES DEL DIABLO** (1968).

Devil's Weed, The see **WILD WEED** (1949).

DEVOTION 1931 d: Robert Milton. USA., *A Little Flat in the Temple*, Pamela Wynne, New York 1930, Novel

Devotion see **L' EDERA** (1950).

DEVOTION 1995 d: Mindy Kaplan. USA., *Devotion*, Mindy Kaplan, Novel

DEVOYES, LES 1925 d: Henri Vorins. FRN., *La Nuit du 3*, Jean Guitton, Play

DHAFNIS KE HLOI 66 1967 d: Mika Zaharopoulou. GRC., *Daphnis and Chloe*, Longus, c200, Novel

Dharamveer see **DHARMAVEER** (1937).

DHARMAVEER 1937 d: Winayak. IND., *Samfundets Stotter*, Henrik Ibsen, Odense 1877, Play

DHARTI KE LAL 1946 d: Khwaya Ahmad Abbas. IND., *Jabanbandi*, Bijon Bhattacharya, Play, *Nabanna*, Bijon Bhattacharya, Play

DI HOU WU GONG DUI 1995 d: Lei XIanhe, Kang Ning. CHN., *Di Hou Wu Gong Dui*, Feng Zhi, Novel

Di Kraft Fun Lebn see **THE POWER OF LIFE** (1938).

D.I., THE 1957 d: Jack Webb. USA., *The D.I.*, James Lee Barrett, Television Play

DIABLE AU COEUR, LE 1927 d: Marcel L'Herbier. FRN., *L' Ex-Voto*, Lucie Delarue Mardrus, Novel

DIABLE AU CORPS, LE 1946 d: Claude Autant-LarA. FRN., *Le Diable Au Corps*, Raymond Radiguet, 1923, Novel

Diable de Siberie, Le see **LA TRAGEDIE IMPERIALE** (1937).

DIABLE EN BOUTEILLE, LE 1935 d: Heinz Hilpert, Reinhart Steinbicker. FRN., *Island Nights' Entertainments*, Robert Louis Stevenson, Short Story

Diable Sous l'Oreiller, Le see **UN DIABLO BAJA LA ALMOHADA** (1968).

Diablesses, Les see **LA MORTE NEGLI OCCHI DEL GATTO** (1973).

DIABLO BAJA LA ALMOHADA, UN 1968 d: Jose Maria Forque. SPN/FRN/ITL., *El Ingenioso Hidalgo Don Quijote de la Mancha*, Miguel de Cervantes Saavedra, 1605-15, Novel

DIABLO COJUELO, EL 1970 d: Ramon Fernandez. SPN., *El Diablo Cojuelo*, Ventura de La Vega, 1641, Novel

Diablo Venia de Akasawa, El see **DER TEUFEL KAM AUS AKASAWA** (1971).

Diabolica Malicia see NIGHT HAIR CHILD (1971).

Diabolically Yours see DIABOLIQUEMENT VOTRE (1967).

Diabolicamente Tua see DIABOLIQUEMENT VOTRE (1967).

DIABOLICI, I 1921 d: Augusto GeninA. ITL., *Le Notti Del Cimitero*, Leon Gozlan, Novel

Diabolique see LES DIABOLIQUES (1954).

DIABOLIQUE 1996 d: Jeremiah Chechik. USA., *Celle Qui N'etait Plus*, Pierre Boileau, Thomas Narcejac, Novel

DIABOLIQUEMENT VOTRE 1967 d: Julien Duvivier. FRN/GRM/ITL., *Manie de la Persecution*, Jean-Louis Thomas, Novel

DIABOLIQUES, LES 1954 d: Henri-Georges Clouzot. FRN., *Celle Qui N'etait Plus*, Pierre Boileau, Thomas Narcejac, Novel

Diadia Vanya see DYADYA VANYA (1971).

Diagnosi see L' ULTIMO ADDIO (1942).

DIAL 999 1955 d: Montgomery Tully. UKN., *The Way Out*, Bruce Graeme, Novel

DIAL M FOR MURDER 1954 d: Alfred Hitchcock. USA., *Dial M for Murder*, Frederick Knott, New York 1952, Play

DIAL M FOR MURDER 1981 d: Boris Sagal. USA., *Dial M for Murder*, Frederick Knott, New York 1952, Play

Dialoghi Delle Carmelitane, I see LE DIALOGUE DES CARMELITES (1959).

Dialoghi Di Platone, I see PROCESSO E MORTE DI SOCRATE (1940).

DIALOGUE DES CARMELITES, LE 1959 d: Philippe Agostini, Raymond-Leopold Bruckberger. FRN/ITL., *Die Letzte Am Schafott*, Gertrud von le Fort, 1931, Short Story

DIAMANT DES ZAREN, DER 1932 d: Max Neufeld. GRM., *Der Orlow*, Bruno Granichstaedten, Ernst Marischka, Operetta

DIAMANT NOIR 1940 d: Jean Delannoy. FRN., *Le Diamant Noir*, Jean Aicard, 1895, Novel

DIAMANT NOIR, LE 1922 d: Andre Hugon. FRN., *Le Diamant Noir*, Jean Aicard, 1895, Novel

DIAMANTE BRUTO 1977 d: Orlando SennA. BRZ., *Bugrinha*, Julio Afranio Peixoto, 1922, Novel

DIAMANTI 1939 d: Corrado d'Errico. ITL., *A Bocca Nuda*, Salvator Gotta, Novel

Diamond Earrings, The see MADAME DE. (1953).

DIAMOND HANDCUFFS 1928 d: John P. McCarthy. USA., *Pin Money*, Henry C. Vance, 1921, Short Story

DIAMOND HEAD 1962 d: Guy Green. USA., *Diamond Head*, Peter Gilman, New York 1960, Novel

DIAMOND HORSESHOE 1945 d: George Seaton. USA., *The Barker; a Play of Carnival Life*, Kenyon Nicholson, New York 1917, Play

DIAMOND JIM 1935 d: A. Edward Sutherland. USA., *Diamond Jim*, Parker Morell, New York 1934, Book

Diamond machine, The see VOUS PIGEZ? (1955).

DIAMOND MAN, THE 1924 d: Arthur Rooke. UKN., Edgar Wallace, Novel

DIAMOND NECKLACE, THE 1921 d: Denison Clift. UKN., *La Parure*, Guy de Maupassant, Short Story

DIAMOND, THE 1954 d: Montgomery Tully, Dennis O'Keefe. UKN., *Rich Is the Treasure*, Maurice Proctor, Novel

Diamond Walkers, The see JAGD AUF BLAUE DIAMANTEN (1966).

Diamond Wizard, The see THE DIAMOND (1954).

Diamonds and Pearls see HEERA MOTI (1959).

DIAMONDS ARE FOREVER 1971 d: Guy Hamilton. UKN., *Diamonds are Forever*, Ian Fleming, Novel

Diamond's Edge see JUST ASK FOR DIAMOND (1988).

Diamonds in the Rough see FRAMED (1927).

Diamonds of the Night see DEMANTY NOCI (1964).

DIANA 1983 d: David Tucker. UKN., *Diana*, R. F. Delderfield, Novel

DIANA AND DESTINY 1916 d: F. Martin Thornton. UKN., *Diana and Destiny*, Charles Garvice, Novel

Diana Ardway see SATAN JUNIOR (1919).

DIANA, HER TRUE STORY 1993 d: Kevin Connor. USA/GRM/FRN., *Her True Story Diana*, Andrew Morton, Book

DIANA OF DOBSON'S 1917. UKN., *Diana of Dobson's*, Cicely Hamilton, London 1908, Play

DIANA OF THE CROSSWAYS 1922 d: Denison Clift. UKN., *Diana of the Crossways*, George Meredith, Novel

Diana of the Islands see MUTINY (1925).

DIANE 1929 d: Erich Waschneck. GRM., *Diane*, Rolf E. Vanloo, Short Story

DIANE 1955 d: David Miller. USA., *Diane de Poitiers*, John Erskine, Book

DIANE OF STAR HOLLOW 1921 d: Oliver L. Sellers. USA., *Diane of Star Hollow*, David Potter, Story

DIANE OF THE GREEN VAN 1919 d: Wallace Worsley. USA., *Diane of the Green Van*, Leona Dalrymple, Chicago 1914, Novel

DIAO CHAN 1938 d: Bu Wancang. CHN., *San Guo Yanyi*, Luo Guanzhong, 1522, Novel

DIARIO DI UN ITALIANO 1973 d: Sergio CapognA. ITL., *Vanda*, Vasco Pratolini, Short Story

DIARIO DI UN MAESTRO 1973 d: Vittorio de SetA. ITL., *Un Anno a Pietralata*, Albino Bernardini, Book

DIARIO DI UN UOMO DI CINQUANT'ANNI 1980 d: Andrea Frazzi, Antonio Frazzi. ITL., Henry James, Novel

Diario Di Una Cameriera, Il see LE JOURNAL D'UNE FEMME DE CHAMBRE (1963).

DIARIO DI UNA DONNA AMATA, IL 1936 d: Henry Koster. ITL., *Journal*, Maria Baschkirtzeff, 1885, Book

DIARIO DI UNA SCHIZOFRENICA 1968 d: Nelo Risi. ITL., *Journal d'une Schizofrene*, Marguerite Andree Sechehaye, Diary

Diary see TAGEBUCH (1975).

Diary Found in Saragossa, A see REKOPIS ZNALEZIONY W SARAGOSSIE (1965).

DIARY OF A CHAMBERMAID 1946 d: Jean Renoir. USA., *Le Journal d'une Femme de Chambre*, Octave Mirbeau, Paris 1900, Novel

Diary of a Chambermaid see LE JOURNAL D'UNE FEMME DE CHAMBRE (1963).

Diary of a Country Priest see LE JOURNAL D'UN CURE DE CAMPAGNE (1950).

Diary of a Lost Girl see TAGEBUCH EINER VERLORENEN (1929).

Diary of a Lost One see TAGEBUCH EINER VERLORENEN (1929).

DIARY OF A MAD HOUSEWIFE 1970 d: Frank Perry. USA., *Diary of a Mad Housewife*, Sue Kaufman, New York 1967, Novel

DIARY OF A MADMAN 1963 d: Reginald Le Borg. USA., *La Horla*, Guy de Maupassant, 1886, Short Story

Diary of a Madman see SOFI (1967).

Diary of a Madman see DNEVNIKAT NA EDIN LUD (1996).

Diary of a Married Woman see TAGEBUCH EINER VERLIEBTEN (1953).

Diary of a Mistress see TAGEBUCH EINER VERLIEBTEN (1953).

DIARY OF A NOBODY 1964 d: Ken Russell. UKN., *Diary of a Nobody*, George Grossmith, Weedon Grossmith, 1892, Book

Diary of a Schizophrenic see DIARIO DI UNA SCHIZOFRENICA (1968).

Diary of a Schizophrenic Girl see DIARIO DI UNA SCHIZOFRENICA (1968).

Diary of a Schoolteacher see DIARIO DI UN MAESTRO (1973).

Diary of a Teacher see DIARIO DI UN MAESTRO (1973).

Diary of a Tired Man see NIHON NO SEISHUN (1968).

DIARY OF ANNE FRANK, THE 1959 d: George Stevens. USA., *Anne Frank: the Diary of a Young Girl*, Anne Frank, Book

DIARY OF ANNE FRANK, THE 1980 d: Boris Sagal. USA., *The Diary of Anne Frank*, Frances Goodrich, Albert Hackett, Play

DIARY OF ANNE FRANK, THE 1987 d: Gareth Davies. UKN., *The Diary of Anne Frank*, Frances Goodrich, Albert Hackett, Play

Diary of Major Thompson, The see LES CARNETS DU MAJOR THOMPSON (1955).

DIAS DE ODIO 1954 d: Leopoldo Torre-Nilsson. ARG., *Emma Zunz*, Jorge Luis Borges, 1949, Short Story

DIAVOLO BIANCO, IL 1948 d: Nunzio MalasommA. ITL., *Khadzh-Murat*, Lev Nikolayevich Tolstoy, 1911, Novel

DIAVOLO IN CONVENTO, IL 1951 d: Nunzio MalasommA. ITL., *Il Miracola*, Mario Amendola, Play

DIAVOLO VA IN COLLEGIO, IL 1944 d: Jean Boyer. ITL., *Mam'zelle Nitouche*, Herve, Henri Meilhac, Albert Milhaud, Paris 1882, Operetta

DIAVOLO ZOPPO, IL 1910 d: Luigi Maggi. ITL., *Le Diable Boiteaux*, Alain-Rene Lesage, 1707, Novel

DICE OF DESTINY 1920 d: Henry King. USA., *The People Against Nancy Preston*, John A. Moroso, New York 1921, Novel

DICK TURPIN 1933 d: John Stafford, Victor Hanbury. UKN., *Rookwood*, Harrison Ainsworth, London 1834, Novel

Dick Turpin's Ride see THE LADY AND THE BANDIT (1951).

DICK TURPIN'S RIDE TO YORK 1922 d: Maurice Elvey. UKN., *Rookwood*, Harrison Ainsworth, London 1834, Novel

DICKE UND ICH, DER 1981 d: Karl-Heinz Lotz. GDR., *Der Dicke Und Ich*, Jens Bahre, Short Story

DICKENSIAN FANTASY, A 1933 d: Aveling Ginever. UKN., *A Christmas Carol*, Charles Dickens, London 1843, Novel

DICK'S FAIRY 1921 d: Bert Wynne. UKN., *Dick's Fairy*, Silas K. Hocking, Novel

Dicky see TRAPPOLA D'AMORE (1940).

DICKY MONTEITH 1922 d: Kenelm Foss. UKN., *Dicky Monteith*, Tom Gallon, Leon M. Lion, Play

Dictador, El see EL RECURSO DEL METODO (1978).

DICTATOR, THE 1915 d: Oscar Eagle. USA., *The Dictator*, Richard Harding Davis, New York 1904, Play

DICTATOR, THE 1922 d: James Cruze. USA., *The Dictator*, Richard Harding Davis, New York 1904, Play

Dictator's Guns, The see L' ARME A GAUCHE (1965).

Dido Forsaken By Aeneas see DIDONE ABBANDONATA (1910).

DIDONE ABBANDONATA 1910 d: Luigi Maggi. ITL., *Eneide*, Publio Virgilio Marone

Die! Die! My Darling see FANATIC (1965).

DIE HARD 1988 d: John McTiernan. USA., *Nothing Lasts Forever*, Roderick Thorp, Novel

Die Hard 2 see DIE HARD 2 - DIE HARDER (1990).

DIE HARD 2 - DIE HARDER 1990 d: Renny Harlin. USA., *58 Minutes*, Walter Wager, Novel

Die, Monster, Die see MONSTER OF TERROR (1965).

Die Slowly, You'll Enjoy It More see MISTER DYNAMIT - MORGEN KUSST EUCH DER TOD (1967).

DIE VOM SCHICKSAL VERFOLGTEN 1927 d: Henk Kleinmann. GRM/NTH., *Droomkoninkje*, Herman Heijermans, 1924, Novel

DIENER LASSEN BITTEN 1936 d: Hans H. Zerlett. GRM., *Diener Lassen Bitten*, Toni Impekoven, Eduard Ritter, Play

Dies Irae see VREDENS DAG (1943).

DIESEL 1942 d: Gerhard Lamprecht. GRM., *Rudolf Diesel*, Eugen Diesel, Biography

DIESER MANN GEHORT MIR 1950 d: Paul Verhoeven. GRM., *Das Vergnugliche Leben Der Doktorin Lohnefin*, Konrad Beste, Short Story

DIESMAL MUSS ES KAVIAR SEIN 1961 d: Geza von Radvanyi. GRM/FRN., *Diesmal Muss Es Kaviar Sein*, Johannes Mario Simmel, Novel

Dietro la Facciata see DU MOURON POUR LES PETITS OISEAUX (1962).

DIEU A BESOIN DES HOMMES 1950 d: Jean Delannoy. FRN., *Un Recteur Dans l'Ile de Sein*, Henri Queffelec, Novel

Diez Negritos see AND THEN THERE WERE NONE (1974).

Different Air, A see JINY VZDUCH (1939).

Difficult Love, A see OSTRE SLEDOVANE VLAKY (1966).

Difficult Years see ANNI DIFFICILI (1948).

DIFFICULTE D'ETRE INFIDELE, LA 1963 d: Bernard Toublanc-Michel. FRN/ITL., *La Difficulte d'Etre Infidele*, Marc Camoletti, Play

Dig That Juliet see ROMANOFF AND JULIET (1961).

Diga Sul Pacifico, La see BARRAGE CONTRE LE PACIFIQUE (1958).

DIGGSTOWN 1992 d: Michael Ritchie. USA., *The Diggstown Ringers*, Leonard Wise, Novel

DIKIE LEBEDI 1988 d: Helle Karis. USS., *De Vilde Svaner*, Hans Christian Andersen, 1838, Short Story

DILEMMA 1962 d: Henning Carlsen. DNM/SAF., *A World of Strangers*, Nadine Gordimer, 1958, Novel

Dilemma *see* DUVIDHA (1973).

DIMANCHE A LA COMPAGNE, UN 1984 d: Bertrand Tavernier. FRN., *Monsieur Ladmiral Va Bientot Mourir*, Pierre Bost, 1945, Novel

DIMANCHE DE FLICS, UN 1982 d: Michel Vianey. FRN/GRM., *Un Dimanche de Flics*, Andrew Coburn, Novel

DIMANCHE DE LA VIE, LE 1967 d: Jean Herman. FRN/GRM/ITL., *Le Dimanche de la Vie*, Raymond Queneau, 1951, Novel

DIMANCHES DE VILLE D'AVRAY, LES 1962 d: Serge Bourguignon. FRN., *Les Dimanches de Ville d'Avray*, Bernard Eschasseriaux, Paris 1958, Novel

DIMBOOLA 1979 d: John Duigan. ASL., *Dimboola*, Jack Hibberd, 1974, Play

DIMENTICARE PALERMO 1990 d: Francesco Rosi. ITL/FRN., *Oublier Palermo*, Edmonde Charles-Roux, Novel

Dimky *see* DYMKY (1966).

Dinamo Dell'eroismo, La *see* O LA BORSA O LA VITA (1933).

DINCOLO DE BARIERA 1965 d: Francisc Munteanu. RMN., *Domnisoara Nastasia*, George Mihail Zamfirescu, 1928, Play

DINCOLO DE NISIPURI 1973 d: Radu GabreA. RMN., *Dincolo de Nisipuri*, Fanus Neagu, 1962, Short Story

DINCOLO DE POD 1975 d: Mircea Veroiu. RMN., *Mara*, Ioan Slavici, 1906, Novel

DINDON, LE 1913 d: Marcel Simon. FRN., *Le Dindon*, Georges Feydeau, 1896, Play

DINDON, LE 1951 d: Claude BarmA. FRN., *Le Dindon*, Georges Feydeau, 1896, Play

DINER DE CONS, LE 1998 d: Francis Veber. FRN., *Le Diner de Cons*, Francis Veber, Play

DING DONG WILLIAMS 1945 d: William Berke. USA., Richard English, Short Stories

DINNER AT EIGHT 1933 d: George Cukor. USA., *Dinner at Eight*, Edna Ferber, George S. Kaufman, New York 1932, Play

DINNER AT EIGHT 1989 d: Ron Lagomarsino. USA., *Dinner at Eight*, Edna Ferber, George S. Kaufman, New York 1932, Play

Dinner Game, The *see* LE DINER DE CONS (1998).

DINO 1957 d: Thomas Carr. USA., *Dino*, Reginald Rose, 1956, Television Play

DIO CHIAMATO DORIAN, IL 1970 d: Massimo Dallamano. ITL/GRM/LCH., *The Picture of Dorian Gray*, Oscar Wilde, London 1891, Novel

DIONISIA 1921 d: Eduardo BencivengA. ITL., *Denise*, Alexandre Dumas (fils), 1885, Novel

DIONYSUS IN '69 1970 d: Brian Depalma, Robert Fiore. USA., *Bacchae*, Euripides, c495 bc, Play

DIOS SE LO PAGUE 1947 d: Luis Cesar Amadori. ARG., *Deus Lhe Pague*, Joracy Camargo, 193-, Play

DIPLOMACY 1916 d: Sidney Olcott. USA., *Dora*, Victorien Sardou, Paris 1877, Play

DIPLOMACY 1926 d: Marshall Neilan. USA., *Diplomacy*, Victorien Sardou, New York 1878, Play

DIPLOMATIC COURIER 1952 d: Henry Hathaway. USA., *Sinister Errand*, Peter Cheyney, 1945, Novel

Diplomatic Lover, The *see* HOW'S CHANCES (1934).

Diplomatico de Salon *see* DON JUAN DIPLOMATICO (1931).

DIRECT AU COEUR 1932 d: Roger Lion, Arnaudy. FRN., *Direct Au Coeur*, Paul Nivoix, Marcel Pagnol, Play

Director of a Glassworks, The *see* ROMAN HLOUPEHO HONZY (1926).

DIRITTO DI VIVERE, IL 1912 d: Roberto Troncone. ITL., *Il Diritto Di Vivere*, Roberto Bracco, 1900, Play

DIRNENTRAGODIE 1927 d: Bruno Rahn. GRM., *Dirnentragodie*, Wilhelm Braun, Play

DIRTY DINGUS MAGEE 1970 d: Burt Kennedy. USA., *The Ballad of Dingus Magee*, David Markson, Indianapolis 1965, Novel

Dirty Dozen, The *see* EIGHT IRON MEN (1953).

DIRTY DOZEN, THE 1967 d: Robert Aldrich. UKN/USA., *The Dirty Dozen*, E. M. Nathanson, New York 1965, Novel

DIRTY GAMES 1989 d: Gray Hofmeyr. USA/SAF., *Dirty Games*, Geoffrey Jenkins, Novel

Dirty Hands *see* LES MAINS SALES (1951).

Dirty Hands *see* LES INNOCENTS AUX MAINS SALES (1975).

DIRTY MARY, CRAZY LARRY 1974 d: John Hough. USA., *Dirty Mary Crazy Larry*, Richard Unekis, Novel

Dirty Story of the West *see* QUELLA SPORCA STORIA DEL WEST (1968).

DIRTY TRICKS 1980 d: Alvin Rakoff. CND., *The Glendower Legacy*, Thomas Gifford, Novel

DIRTY WEEKEND 1992 d: Michael Winner. UKN., *Dirty Weekend*, Helen Zahavi, Novel

DIRTY WORK 1934 d: Tom Walls. UKN., *Dirty Work*, Ben Travers, London 1932, Play

DISAPPEARANCE OF FINBAR, THE 1996 d: Susan Clayton. UKN/IRL/SWD., *The Disappearance of Rory Brophy*, Carl Lombard, Novel

DISAPPEARANCE OF LADY FRANCES CARFAX, THE 1923 d: George Ridgwell. UKN., *The Disappearance of Lady Frances Carfax*, Arthur Conan Doyle, Short Story

DISAPPEARANCE OF THE JUDGE, THE 1919 d: Alexander Butler. UKN., *The Disappearance of the Judge*, Guy Thorne, Novel

DISAPPEARANCE, THE 1977 d: Stuart Cooper. UKN/CND., *Echoes of Celandine*, Derek Marlowe, Novel

Disappointed Lover, The *see* SHI LIAN ZHE (1987).

DISCARDED WOMAN, THE 1920 d: Burton L. King. USA., *The Hidden Path*, Lawrence McCloskey, A. W. Tillinghast, Story

DISCEPOLO, IL 1917 d: Giuseppe Giusti. ITL., *Le Disciple*, Paul Bourget, 1889, Novel

Disciple of Dracula *see* DRACULA - PRINCE OF DARKNESS (1965).

DISCIPLINE 1935 d: James Riddell, A. B. Imeson. UKN., *Discipline*, Lesley Storm, Story

DISCORD 1933 d: Henry Edwards. UKN., *A Roof and Four Walls*, E. Temple Thurston, London 1923, Play

DISCOUNTERS OF MONEY 1917 d: Martin Justice. USA., *Discounters of Money*, O. Henry, Short Story

Discretion With Honor *see* DISKRETION-EHRENSACHE (1938).

Disertore E I Nomadi, Il *see* ZBEHOVIA A PUTNICI (1968).

Disfida Di Barletta, La *see* ETTORE FIERAMOSCA (1915).

Dishonorable Woman, The *see* NEPOCESTNA ZENA (1930).

DISHONORED LADY 1947 d: Robert Stevenson. USA., *Dishonored Lady*, Margaret Ayer Barnes, Edward Sheldon, New York 1930, Play

Disillusioned *see* WHITE SHOULDERS (1931).

DISKRETION-EHRENSACHE 1938 d: Johannes Meyer. GRM., *Gluck Muss Der Mensch Haben*, Hannes Peter Stolp, Novel

DIS-MOI QUI TUER? 1965 d: Etienne Perier. FRN., *Le Mort du Lac*, Henri Lapierre, Novel

Disobedient *see* INTIMATE RELATIONS (1953).

DISONESTI, I 1922 d: Giuseppe Sterni. ITL., *I Disonesti*, Gerolamo Rovetta, 1892, Novel

DISONORATA SENZA COLPA 1954 d: Giorgio W. Chili. ITL., Victor Hugo Felluan, Story

Disorder and Early Sorrow *see* UNORDNUNG UND FRUHES LEID (1975).

DISPARU DE L'ASCENSEUR, LE 1931 d: Giulio Del Torre. FRN., *Le Disparu de l'Ascenseur*, Leon Groc, Novel

DISPARUS DE SAINT-AGIL, LES 1938 d: Christian-Jaque. FRN., *Les Disparus de Saint-Agil*, Pierre Very, Novel

Disperati Della Gloria, I *see* PARIAS DE LA GLOIRE (1963).

DISPERATO ADDIO 1956 d: Lionello de Felice. ITL., *Fra Bisturi E Forbici*, Andrea Majocchi, Novel, *Vita Di Chirurgo*, Andrea Majocchi, Novel

DISPLACED PERSON, THE 1977 d: Glenn Jordan. USA., *The Displaced Person*, Flannery O'Connor, 1955, Short Story

Dispossessed, The *see* L' AMBITIEUSE (1958).

Disprezzo, Il *see* LE MEPRIS (1963).

DISPUTED PASSAGE 1939 d: Frank Borzage. USA., *Disputed Passage*, Lloyd C. Douglas, Boston 1939, Novel

DISQUE 413, LE 1936 d: Richard Pottier. FRN., *The Guilty Voice*, Hans Rehfisch, Short Story

DISRAELI 1916 d: Percy Nash, Charles Calvert. UKN., *Disraeli*, Louis N. Parker, New York 1911, Play

DISRAELI 1921 d: Henry Kolker. USA., *Disraeli*, Louis N. Parker, New York 1911, Play

DISRAELI 1929 d: Alfred E. Green. USA., *Disraeli*, Louis N. Parker, New York 1911, Play

Distant Fields *see* MARRIED AND IN LOVE (1940).

Distant Land, The *see* DAS WEITE LAND (1987).

Distant Thunder *see* ASHANI SANKET (1973).

DISTANT TRUMPET, A 1964 d: Raoul Walsh. USA., *A Distant Trumpet*, Paul Horgan, New York 1960, Novel

DISTRACTIONS, LES 1960 d: Jacques Dupont. FRN/ITL., *Les Distractions*, Jean Bassan, Novel

Distrazioni, Le *see* LES DISTRACTIONS (1960).

DISTRICT ATTORNEY, THE 1915 d: Barry O'Neil. USA., *The District Attorney*, Harrison Grey Fiske, Charles Klein, New York 1895, Play

Disturbance *see* YI CHANG FENG BO (1954).

Disubbidienza, La *see* LA DESOBEISSANCE (1981).

DIT VINDARNA BAR 1948 d: Ake Ohberg. SWD/NRW., *Jorund Smed*, Jacob Breda Bull, 1924, Novel

DITA DI FATA 1921 d: Nino Giannini. ITL., *Les Doigts de Fee*, Ernest Legouve, Eugene Scribe, 1858, Play

DITES-LUI QUE JE L'AIME 1977 d: Claude Miller. FRN., *This Sweet Sickness*, Patricia Highsmith, 1960, Novel

Ditte: Child of Man *see* DITTE MENNESKEBARN (1946).

DITTE MENNESKEBARN 1946 d: Bjarne Henning-Jensen. DNM., *Ditte Menneskebarn*, Martin Andersen Nexo, 1917-21, Novel

DIVA 1981 d: Jean-Jacques Beineix. FRN., *Diva*, Delacorta, Novel

Divided Heaven *see* DER GETEILTE HIMMEL (1964).

Divided Sky *see* DER GETEILTE HIMMEL (1964).

Divina Commedia: l'Inferno, La *see* L' INFERNO (1911).

DIVINA CREATURA 1975 d: Giuseppe Patroni Griffi. ITL., *La Divina Fanciulla*, Luciano Zuccoli, Novel

DIVINE 1935 d: Max Ophuls. FRN., *L' Envers du Music-Hall*, Sidonie Gabrielle Colette, 1913, Novel

DIVINE LADY, THE 1929 d: Frank Lloyd. USA., *The Divine Lady; a Romance of Nelson and Lady Hamilton*, E. Barrington, New York 1924, Novel

Divine Nymph, The *see* DIVINA CREATURA (1975).

DIVINE POURSUITE, LA 1997 d: Michel Deville. FRN., *Dancing Aztecs*, Donald E. Westlake, Novel

DIVINE WOMAN, THE 1927 d: Victor Sjostrom. USA., *Starlight*, Gladys Unger, New York 1925, Play

Diving Girls' Island, The *see* VIOLATED PARADISE (1963).

Diving Girls of Japan *see* VIOLATED PARADISE (1963).

DIVOCH 1936 d: Jan Svitak. CZC., *Divoch*, Milos Krenovsky, Novel

Divoch *see* DER WILDFANG (1936).

DIVORCE COUPONS 1922 d: Webster Campbell. USA., *Divorce Coupons*, Ethel Watts Mumford, Story

DIVORCE GAME, THE 1917 d: Travers Vale. USA., *Mlle. Fifi*, Leo Ditrichstein, New York 1899, Play

DIVORCE OF LADY X, THE 1938 d: Tim Whelan. UKN., *Counsel's Opinion*, Gilbert Wakefield, London 1931, Play

DIVORCED 1915 d: Joseph A. Golden. USA., *Divorced*, Edwin Archer, Play

Divorced Woman, The *see* DIE GESCHIEDENE FRAU (1953).

DIVORCEE, THE 1919 d: Herbert Blache. USA., *Lady Frederick*, W. Somerset Maugham, London 1907, Play

DIVORCEE, THE 1930 d: Robert Z. Leonard. USA., *Ex-Wife*, Katherine Ursula Parrott, New York 1929, Novel

DIVORCING JACK 1998 d: David Caffrey. UKN/FRN., *Divorcing Jack*, Colin Bateman, Novel

DIVORCONS 1915 d: Dell Henderson. USA., *Cyprienne Or Divorcons*, Emile de Najac, Victorien Sardou, Paris 1883, Play

DIVOTA PRASINE 1976 d: Milan Ljubic. YGS., *Divota Prasine*, Vjekoslav Kaleb, 1954, Novel

Dix Petits Indiens, Les *see* AND THEN THERE WERE NONE (1945).

DIXIANA 1930 d: Luther Reed. USA., *Dixiana*, Anne Caldwell, Harry Tierney, Story

DIXIE HANDICAP, THE 1924 d: Reginald Barker. USA., *Dixie*, Gerald Beaumont, 1924, Short Story

DIXIE MERCHANT, THE 1926 d: Frank Borzage. USA., *The Chicken-Wagon Family*, John Barry Benefield, New York 1925, Novel

Dixieme Victime, La *see* LA DECIMA VITTIMA (1965).

DIXON'S RETURN 1924 d: Manning Haynes. UKN., *Dixon's Return*, W. W. Jacobs, Short Story

DIZZY DAMES 1935 d: William Nigh. USA., *The Watch Dog*, P. G. Wodehouse, 1910, Short Story

Djadja Vanja *see* DYADYA VANYA (1971).

Djamila *see* JAMILYA (1969).

DJAVOLJI RAJ - ONO LJETO BIJELIH RUZA 1989 d: Rajko Grlic. YGS/UKN., *Defence and the Last Days*, Borislav Pekic, Novel

DM-KILLER 1964 d: Rolf Thiele. AUS., *Dm-Killer*, Peter Norden, Novel

DNEVNIKAT NA EDIN LUD 1996 d: Marius Kurkinski. BUL., *Diary of a Madman*, Nikolay Gogol, 1836, Short Story

Dni I Nochi *see* DNI I NOCI (1944).

DNI I NOCI 1944 d: Alexander Stolper. USS., *Dni I Nochi*, Konstantin Simonov, 1944, Novel

Do Daan *see* GODAN (1962).

Do It Again *see* THREE-RING MARRIAGE (1928).

DO NOT DISTURB 1965 d: Ralph Levy. USA., *Some Other Love*, William Fairchild, Play

DO NOT FOLD, SPINDLE OR MUTILATE 1971 d: Ted Post. USA., *Do Not Fold Spindle Or Mutilate*, Doris Miles Disney, Novel

DO PANSKEHO STAVU 1925 d: Karl Anton. CZC., *Do Panskeho Stavu*, Popelka Bilianova, Novel

DO RAASTE 1969 d: Raj KhoslA. IND., *Nilambiri*, Chandrakant Kakodkar, Novel

Do You Believe in Angels? *see* FINNS DOM? ANGLAR (1961).

Do You Like Women? *see* AIMEZ-VOUS LES FEMMES? (1964).

Dobrodruzstvi Robinsona Crusoe *see* NAMORNIKA Z YORKU ZIVOT A PODIVUHODNA DOBRODRUZSTVI ROBINSONA CRUSOE (1982).

DOBRY VOJAK SVEJK 1926 d: Carl Lamac. CZC., *Osudy Dobreho Vojaka Svejka Za Svetove Valky*, Jaroslav Hasek, Prague 1920-23, Novel

DOBRY VOJAK SVEJK 1931 d: Martin Fric. CZC., *Osudy Dobreho Vojaka Svejka Za Svetove Valky*, Jaroslav Hasek, Prague 1920-23, Novel

DOC HOLLYWOOD 1991 d: Michael Caton-Jones. USA., *What?. Dead Again*, Neil B. Shulman, Novel

DOC SAVAGE, THE MAN OF BRONZE 1975 d: Michael Anderson. USA., *Doc Savage - the Man of Bronze*, Kenneth Robeson, Novel

DOCE SILLAS, LOS 1962 d: Tomas Gutierrez AleA. CUB., *Dvenadtsat Stulyev*, Ilya Ilf, Evgeny Petrov, Moscow 1928, Novel

DOCK BRIEF, THE 1962 d: James Hill. UKN., *The Dock Brief*, John Mortimer, London 1958, Play

DOCKHEM, ETT 1955 d: Anders Henrikson. SWD., *Ett Dockhem*, August Strindberg, 1884, Short Story

DOCTEUR FRANCOISE GAILLAND 1975 d: Jean-Louis Bertucelli. FRN., *Docteur Francoise Gailland*, Noelle Loriot, Novel

Doctor and Mrs. Jeckyll *see* DOTTOR JEKYLL E GENTILE SIGNORA (1979).

DOCTOR AND THE GIRL, THE 1949 d: Curtis Bernhardt. USA., *Bodies and Souls*, Maxence Van Der Meersch, Novel

DOCTOR AND THE WOMAN, THE 1918 d: Lois Weber, Phillips Smalley. USA., *K*, Mary Roberts Rinehart, Boston 1915, Novel

Doctor Antonio *see* IL DOTTOR ANTONIO (1910).

DOCTOR AT LARGE 1957 d: Ralph Thomas. UKN., *Doctor at Large*, Richard Gordon, Novel

DOCTOR AT SEA 1955 d: Ralph Thomas. UKN., *Doctor at Sea*, Richard Gordon, Novel

Doctor Bethune *see* BAIQIUEN DAIFU (1964).

Doctor Beware *see* TERESA VENERDI (1941).

DOCTOR BULL 1933 d: John Ford. USA., *The Last Adam*, James Gould Cozzens, New York 1933, Novel

Doctor Demonio, El *see* GRITOS EN LA NOCHE (1961).

DOCTOR DETROIT 1983 d: Michael Pressman. USA., *Detroit Abe*, Jay Friedman, Novel

DOCTOR DOLITTLE 1967 d: Richard Fleischer. USA., Hugh Lofting, Short Stories

DOCTOR DOLITTLE 1998 d: Betty Thomas. USA., Hugh Lofting, Short Stories

DOCTOR FAUSTUS 1967 d: Nevill Coghill, Richard Burton. UKN/ITL., *Doctor Faustus*, Christopher Marlowe, 1594, Play

Doctor Faustus *see* DOKTOR FAUSTUS (1981).

Doctor Frankenstein *see* FRANKENSTEIN: THE TRUE STORY (1973).

Doctor Glas *see* DOKTOR GLAS (1968).

DOCTOR IN CLOVER 1966 d: Ralph Thomas. UKN., *Doctor in Clover*, Richard Gordon, London 1960, Novel

DOCTOR IN LOVE 1960 d: Ralph Thomas. UKN., *Doctor in Love*, Richard Gordon, London 1957, Novel

DOCTOR IN THE HOUSE 1954 d: Ralph Thomas. UKN., *Doctor in the House*, Richard Gordon, Novel

Doctor in the Village *see* DORP AAN DE RIVIER (1958).

DOCTOR IN TROUBLE 1970 d: Ralph Thomas. UKN., *Doctor on Toast*, Richard Gordon, Novel

Doctor Judym *see* DOKTOR JUDYM (1975).

Doctor Norman Bethune *see* BAIQIUEN DAIFU (1964).

Doctor Nye *see* IDLE TONGUES (1924).

Doctor of San Michele, The *see* DER ARZT VON SAN MICHELE AXEL MUNTHE (1962).

Doctor Praetorius *see* PEOPLE WILL TALK (1951).

DOCTOR RHYTHM 1938 d: Frank Tuttle. USA., *The Badge of Policeman O'Roon*, O. Henry, 1904, Short Story

Doctor, The *see* ONE MAN'S JOURNEY (1933).

DOCTOR, THE 1991 d: Randa Haines. USA., *A Taste of My Own Medicine*, Ed Rosenbaum, Book

Doctor Vera *see* DOKTOR VYERA (1968).

DOCTOR VLIMMEN 1976 d: Guido Pieters. NTH/BLG., *Doctor Vlimmen*, A. Roothaert, Novel

DOCTOR X 1932 d: Michael Curtiz. USA., *The Terror*, Howard Warren Comstock, Allen C. Miller, New York 1931, Play

DOCTOR, YOU'VE GOT TO BE KIDDING 1967 d: Peter Tewkesbury. USA., *Three for a Wedding*, Patte Wheat Mahan, New York 1965, Novel

DOCTOR ZHIVAGO 1965 d: David Lean. USA., *Doktor Zhivago*, Boris Pasternak, 1957, Novel

DOCTOR'S DILEMMA, THE 1959 d: Anthony Asquith. UKN., *The Doctor's Dilemma*, George Bernard Shaw, London 1906, Play

Doctor's Horrible Experiment, The *see* LE TESTAMENT DU DR. CORDELIER (1959).

Doctor's Round *see* VIZITA! POZOR (1981).

Doctor's Sacrifice, The *see* KLONDIKE (1932).

DOCTOR'S SECRET, THE 1930 d: William C. de Mille. USA., *Half an Hour*, J. M. Barrie, New York 1913, Play

Doctor's Secret, The *see* TAJEMSTVI LEKAROVO (1930).

Doctors, The *see* L' HOMMES EN BLANC (1955).

Doctors Wear Scarlet *see* INCENSE FOR THE DAMNED (1970).

DOCTORS' WIVES 1931 d: Frank Borzage. USA., *Doctors' Wives*, Henry Lieferant, Sylvia Lieferant, New York 1930, Novel

DOCTORS' WIVES 1971 d: George Schaefer. USA., *Doctors' Wives*, Frank G. Slaughter, Novel

DOCUMENTO, IL 1939 d: Mario Camerini. ITL., *Il Documento*, Guglielmo Zorzi, Play

DODEN KOMMER TIL MIDDAG 1964 d: Erik Balling. DNM., *Doden Kommer Til Middag*, Peter Sander, Novel

DODES TJERN, DE 1958 d: Kare Bergstrom. NRW., **De Dodes Tjern**, Andre Bjerke, 1942, Novel

DODESKA DEN 1970 d: Akira KurosawA. JPN., *The Town Without Seasons*, Shugoro Yamamoto, Novel

Dodesukaden *see* DODESKA DEN (1970).

Dodici Donne d'Oro *see* KOMMISSAR X: JAGD AUF UNBEKANNT (1965).

DODSWORTH 1936 d: William Wyler. USA., *Dodsworth*, Sinclair Lewis, New York 1929, Novel

Does Mother Know Best *see* MOTHER KNOWS BEST (1928).

Dog Day *see* CANICULE (1983).

Dog Eat Dog *see* EINER FRISST DEN ANDEREN (1964).

Dog in the Manger, The *see* EL PERRO DEL HORTELANO (1996).

DOG OF FLANDERS, A 1935 d: Edward Sloman. USA., *A Dog of Flanders*, Ouida, New York 1872, Novel

DOG OF FLANDERS, A 1959 d: James B. Clark. USA., *A Dog of Flanders*, Ouida, New York 1872, Novel

DOG OF FLANDERS, THE 1914. USA., *A Dog of Flanders*, Ouida, New York 1872, Novel

DOG OF THE REGIMENT, A 1927 d: D. Ross Lederman. USA., *A Dog of the Regiment*, Albert S. Howson, Story

Dog Show Murder *see* DEATH OF A CHAMPION (1939).

Dog Soldiers *see* WHO'LL STOP THE RAIN (1978).

Dog, The *see* EL PERRO (1977).

Dogadaj *see* DOGADJAJ (1969).

DOGADJAJ 1969 d: Vatroslav MimicA. YGS., *Proisshestviye*, Anton Chekhov, 1886, Short Story

Dog-Heads, The *see* PSOHLAVCI (1931).

DOGKESELYU 1982 d: Ferenc Andras. HNG., *Dogkeselyu*, Miklos Munkcasi, Novel

Dogora *see* UCHU DAIKAIJU DOGORA (1964).

Dog's Heart *see* CUORE DI CANE (1975).

DOGS OF WAR, THE 1980 d: John Irvin. UKN., *The Dogs of War*, Frederick Forsyth, Novel

Dogsday *see* CANICULE (1983).

DOI BARBATI PENTRU O MOARTE 1970 d: Gheorghe Naghi. RMN., *Zaszlos Demeter*, Andras Suto, 1960, Short Story

Doigts Croises, Les *see* CATCH ME A SPY (1971).

DOING HIS DUTY 1929 d: Hugh Croise. UKN., *The Police Force*, Ernie Lotinga, Play

DOKTOR FAUSTUS 1981 d: Franz Seitz. GRM., *Doktor Faustus*, Thomas Mann, 1947, Novel

DOKTOR GLAS 1942 d: Rune Carlsten. SWD., *Doktor Glas*, Hjalmar Soderberg, 1905, Novel

DOKTOR GLAS 1968 d: Mai Zetterling. DNM/SWD., *Doktor Glas*, Hjalmar Soderberg, 1905, Novel

DOKTOR JUDYM 1975 d: Wlodzimierz Haupe. PLN., *Ludzie Bezdomni*, Stefan Zeromski, 1899, Novel

DOKTOR MURKES SAMLADE TYSTNAD 1968 d: Per Berglund. SWD., *Dr. Murkes Gesammeles Schweigen*, Heinrich Boll, 1958, Short Story

DOKTOR VYERA 1968 d: Damir Vyatich-Berezhnykh. USS., *Doktor Vyera*, Boris Nikolaevich Polevoy, 1966, Novel

DOKUD MAS MAMINKU 1934 d: Jan Svitak. CZC., *Letcova Maminka*, Evzen Holly, Play

DOKURITSU GURENTAI 1959 d: Kihachi Okamoto. JPN., *Dokuritsu Gurentai*, S. Sekizawa, Novel

Dolcezze Del Peccato, Le *see* DER TURM DER VERBOTENEN LIEBE (1968).

DOLL FACE 1945 d: Lewis Seiler. USA., *Doll Face*, Louise Hovick, Play

DOLL MAKER, THE 1983 d: Daniel Petrie. USA., *The Doll Maker*, Harriette Arnow, 1954, Novel

Doll, The *see* LA POUPEE (1962).

Doll, The *see* LALKA (1968).

DOLLAR 1938 d: Gustaf Molander. SWD., *Dollar*, Hjalmar Bergman, 1926, Play

DOLLAR FOR DOLLAR 1920 d: Frank Keenan. USA., Ethel Watts Mumford, Story

DOLLAR MARK, THE 1914 d: O. A. C. Lund. USA., *The Dollar Mark*, George Broadhurst, New York 1909, Play

Dollars and Cents *see* DOLLARS AND THE WOMAN (1916).

DOLLARS AND THE WOMAN 1916 d: Joseph Kaufman. USA., *Dollars and Cents*, Albert Payson Terhune, New York 1917, Novel

DOLLARS AND THE WOMAN 1920 d: George W. Terwilliger. USA., *Dollars and Cents*, Albert Payson Terhune, New York 1917, Novel

Dollhouse, The *see* CASA DE MUNECAS (1943).

Dollmaker, The *see* THE DOLL MAKER (1983).

DOLL'S HOUSE, A 1917 d: Joseph de Grasse. USA., *Et Dukkehjem*, Henrik Ibsen, Copenhagen 1879, Play

DOLL'S HOUSE, A 1918 d: Maurice Tourneur. USA., *Et Dukkehjem*, Henrik Ibsen, Copenhagen 1879, Play

DOLL'S HOUSE, A 1922 d: Charles Bryant. USA., *Et Dukkehjem*, Henrik Ibsen, Copenhagen 1879, Play

Doll's House, A *see* NORA (1944).

DOLL'S HOUSE, A 1961 d: Robert Tronson. UKN., *Et Dukkehjem*, Henrik Ibsen, Copenhagen 1879, Play

DOLL'S HOUSE, A 1972 d: Joseph Losey. UKN/FRN., *Et Dukkehjem*, Henrik Ibsen, Copenhagen 1879, Play

DOLL'S HOUSE, A 1973 d: Patrick Garland. UKN., *Et Dukkehjem*, Henrik Ibsen, Copenhagen 1879, Play

DOLL'S HOUSE, A 1992 d: David Thacker. UKN., *Et Dukkehjem*, Henrik Ibsen, Copenhagen 1879, Play

DOLLY VARDEN 1913 d: Charles J. Brabin. USA., *Barnaby Rudge*, Charles Dickens, London 1841, Novel

DOLORES, LA 1923 d: Maximiliano Thous. SPN., *La Dolores*, Tomas Breton, Jose Feliu Y Codina, Opera

DOLORETES 1922 d: Jose Buchs. SPN., *Doloretes*, Carlos Arniches, M. Quislant, Amadeo Vives, Opera

DOM S MEZONINOM 1961 d: Yakov Bazelyan. USS., *Dom S Mezoninom*, Anton Chekhov, 1896, Short Story

Domanda Di Grazia *see* **OBSESSION** (1954).

DOMANI E TROPPO TARDI 1950 d: Leonide Moguy. ITL., *Printemps Sexuel*, Alfred Machard, Story

DOMAREN 1960 d: Alf Sjoberg. SWD., *Domaren*, Vilhelm Moberg, 1957, Play

DOMBEY AND SON 1917 d: Maurice Elvey. UKN., *Dombey and Son*, Charles Dickens, London 1848, Novel

DOMENICA DELLA BUONA GENTE, LA 1954 d: Anton Giulio Majano. ITL., *La Domenica Della Buona Gente*, Giandomenico Giagni, Vasco Pratolini, Radio Play

DOMINANT SEX, THE 1937 d: Herbert Brenon. UKN., *The Dominant Sex*, Michael Egan, London 1934, Play

DOMINGO A TARDE 1965 d: Antonio de Macedo. PRT., *Domingo a Tarde*, Fernando Namora, 1961, Novel

DOMINIQUE 1950 d: Yvan Noe. FRN., *Dominque*, Yvan Noe, Play

DOMINO 1943 d: Roger Richebe. FRN., *Domino*, Marcel Achard, 1932, Play

Domino Killings, The *see* **THE DOMINO PRINCIPLE** (1977).

Domino Principe, El *see* **THE DOMINO PRINCIPLE** (1977).

DOMINO PRINCIPLE, THE 1977 d: Stanley Kramer. USA/UKN/MXC., *The Domino Principle*, Adam Kennedy, Novel

DOMINO VERT, LE 1935 d: Henri Decoin, Herbert Selpin. FRN., *Der Falle Claasen*, Erich Ebermayer, Play

DOMNISOARA AURICA 1986 d: Serban Marinescu. RMN., *Domnisoara Aurica*, Eugen Barbu, 1962, Short Story

DON BUONAPARTE 1941 d: Flavio CalzavarA. ITL., *Don Buonaparte*, Giovacchino Forzano, Play

DON CAESAR DE BAZAN 1915 d: Robert G. VignolA. USA., *Maritana*, Edward Fitzball, Vincent Wallace, London 1845, Opera

Don Camillo *see* **LE PETIT MONDE DE DON CAMILLO** (1951).

DON CAMILLO E I GIOVANI D'OGGI 1972 d: Mario Camerini. ITL., *Don Camillo E I Giovani d'Oggi*, Giovanni Guareschi, Novel

Don Camillo E l'Americano *see* **LE NIPOTI D'AMERICA** (1921).

Don Camillo En Russie *see* **IL COMPAGNO DON CAMILLO** (1965).

Don Camillo, Monseigneur *see* **DON CAMILLO MONSIGNORE. MA NON TROPPO** (1961).

DON CAMILLO MONSIGNORE. MA NON TROPPO 1961 d: Carmine Gallone. ITL/FRN., Giovanni Guareschi, Story

DON CARLOS 1921 d: Giulio Antamoro. ITL., *Don Carlos*, Friedrich von Schiller, 1787, Play

DON CARLOS 1950 d: Alfred Stoger. AUS., *Don Carlos*, Friedrich von Schiller, 1787, Play

DON CARLOS 1963 d: Franz Peter Wirth. GRM., *Don Carlos*, Friedrich von Schiller, 1787, Play

DON CESARE DI BAZAN 1942 d: Riccardo FredA. ITL., *Don Cesar de Bazan*, Adolphe-P. d'Ennery, Philippe F. Pinel, 1844, Play

DON CHICAGO 1945 d: MacLean Rogers. UKN., *Don Chicago*, C. E. Bechhofer-Roberts, Novel

DON CHISCIOTTE 1911. ITL., *El Ingenioso Hidalgo Don Quijote de la Mancha*, Miguel de Cervantes Saavedra, 1605-15, Novel

DON CHISCIOTTE 1984 d: Maurizio Scaparro. ITL., *El Ingenioso Hidalgo Don Quijote de la Mancha*, Miguel de Cervantes Saavedra, 1605-15, Novel

Don Chisciotte Della Mancia *see* **DON CHISCIOTTE** (1911).

DON CHISCIOTTE E SANCHO PANZA 1968 d: Gianni Grimaldi. ITL., *El Ingenioso Hidalgo Don Quijote de la Mancha*, Miguel de Cervantes Saavedra, 1605-15, Novel

DON D'ADELE, LE 1950 d: Emile Couzinet. FRN., *Le Don d'Adele*, Pierre Barillet, Jean-Pierre Gredy, Play

DON GIOVANNI 1955 d: Paul Czinner, Alfred Travers. UKN., *Don Giovanni*, Lorenzo Da Ponte, Wolfgang Amadeus Mozart, Prague 1787, Opera

DON GIOVANNI 1979 d: Joseph Losey. ITL/FRN/GRM., *Don Giovanni*, Lorenzo Da Ponte, Prague 1787, Opera

DON GIOVANNI IN SICILIA 1967 d: Alberto LattuadA. ITL., *Don Giovanni in Sicilia*, Vitaliano Brancati, 1941, Novel

Don Giovanni in Sicily *see* **DON GIOVANNI IN SICILIA** (1967).

DON JUAN 1908 d: Albert Capellani, Floury. FRN., *Don Juan*, Moliere, 1665, Play

DON JUAN 1922 d: Edwin J. Collins. UKN., *Don Giovanni*, Lorenzo Da Ponte, Wolfgang Amadeus Mozart, Prague 1787, Opera

Don Juan *see* **DON GIOVANNI** (1955).

DON JUAN 1998 d: Jacques Weber. FRN/SPN/GRM., *Don Juan*, Moliere, 1665, Play

DON JUAN DIPLOMATICO 1931 d: George Melford. USA., *The Command to Love*, Fritz Gottwald, Rudolph Lothar, New York 1927, Play

DON JUAN ET FAUST 1922 d: Marcel L'Herbier. FRN., *Don Juan Und Faust*, Christian Dietrich Grabbe, 1829, Play

DON JUAN IN DER MADCHENSCHULE 1928 d: Reinhold Schunzel. GRM., *Der Ungetreue Eckehart*, Hans Sturm, Play

DON JUAN TENORIO 1952 d: Alejandro PerlA. SPN., *Don Juan Tenorio*, Jose Zorrilla Y Moral, 1844, Play

DON JUAN'S THREE NIGHTS 1926 d: John Francis Dillon. USA., *Don Juans Drei Nachte*, Ludwig Biro, Berlin 1917, Novel

DON KIKHOT 1957 d: Grigori Kozintsev. USS., *El Ingenioso Hidalgo Don Quijote de la Mancha*, Miguel de Cervantes Saavedra, 1605-15, Novel

DON KING: ONLY IN AMERICA 1997 d: John Herzfeld. USA., *Don King: Only in America*, Jack Newfield, Book

DON PASQUALE 1940 d: Camillo Mastrocinque. ITL., *Don Pasquale*, Michele Accursi, Gaetano Donizetti, Paris 1843, Opera

DON PIETRO CARUSO 1914 d: Emilio Ghione. ITL., *Don Pietro Caruso*, Roberto Bracco, 1895, Play

DON Q, SON OF ZORRO 1925 d: Donald Crisp. USA., *Don Q's Love Story*, Hesketh Prichard, Kate Prichard, New York 1925, Novel

DON QUICHOTTE 1913 d: Camille de Morlhon. FRN., *El Ingenioso Hidalgo Don Quijote de la Mancha*, Miguel de Cervantes Saavedra, 1605-15, Novel

DON QUICHOTTE 1932 d: G. W. Pabst. FRN., *El Ingenioso Hidalgo Don Quijote de la Mancha*, Miguel de Cervantes Saavedra, 1605-15, Novel

Don Quichotte *see* **DON QUIJOTE** (1966).

DON QUIJOTE 1961 d: Eino Ruutsalo. FNL., *El Ingenioso Hidalgo Don Quijote de la Mancha*, Miguel de Cervantes Saavedra, 1605-15, Novel

DON QUIJOTE 1966 d: Carlo-Rim. SPN/FRN/GRM., *El Ingenioso Hidalgo Don Quijote de la Mancha*, Miguel de Cervantes Saavedra, 1605-15, Novel

DON QUIJOTE AYER Y HOY 1964 d: Cesar Ardavin. SPN., *El Ingenioso Hidalgo Don Quijote de la Mancha*, Miguel de Cervantes Saavedra, 1605-15, Novel

Don Quijote Cabalga de Nueva *see* **DON QUIXOTE CABALGA DE NUEVA** (1972).

Don Quijote de la Mancha *see* **DON QUIXOTE DE LA MANCHA** (1947).

DON QUINTIN EL AMARGAO 1925 d: Manuel NoriegA. SPN., *Don Quintin El Amargao*, Carlos Arniches, Antonio Estremera, Opera

Don Quixot of la Mancha *see* **DON QUIXOTE DE LA MANCHA** (1947).

Don Quixote *see* **DON CHISCIOTTE** (1911).

DON QUIXOTE 1916 d: Eddie Dillon. USA., *El Ingenioso Hidalgo Don Quijote de la Mancha*, Miguel de Cervantes Saavedra, 1605-15, Novel

DON QUIXOTE 1923 d: Maurice Elvey. UKN., *El Ingenioso Hidalgo Don Quijote de la Mancha*, Miguel de Cervantes Saavedra, 1605-15, Novel

DON QUIXOTE 1932 d: John Farrow, G. W. Pabst. UKN., *El Ingenioso Hidalgo Don Quijote de la Mancha*, Miguel de Cervantes Saavedra, 1605-15, Novel

Don Quixote *see* **DON QUICHOTTE** (1932).

Don Quixote *see* **DON QUIXOTE DE LA MANCHA** (1947).

Don Quixote *see* **DON KIKHOT** (1957).

Don Quixote *see* **DON QUIJOTE** (1966).

DON QUIXOTE 1972 d: Alvin Rakoff. UKN/USA., *El Ingenioso Hidalgo Don Quijote de la Mancha*, Miguel de Cervantes Saavedra, 1605-15, Novel

DON QUIXOTE 1973 d: Robert Helpmann, Rudolf Nureyev. ASL., *El Ingenioso Hidalgo Don Quijote de la Mancha*, Miguel de Cervantes Saavedra, 1605-15, Novel

Don Quixote *see* **DON CHISCIOTTE** (1984).

Don Quixote and Sancho Panza *see* **DON CHISCIOTTE E SANCHO PANZA** (1968).

DON QUIXOTE CABALGA DE NUEVA 1972 d: Roberto Gavaldon. MXC., *El Ingenioso Hidalgo Don Quijote de la Mancha*, Miguel de Cervantes Saavedra, 1605-15, Novel

DON QUIXOTE DE LA MANCHA 1947 d: Rafael Gil. SPN., *El Ingenioso Hidalgo Don Quijote de la Mancha*, Miguel de Cervantes Saavedra, 1605-15, Novel

Don Quixote Rides Again *see* **DON QUIXOTE CABALGA DE NUEVA** (1972).

Don Quixote, Then and Now *see* **DON QUIJOTE AYER Y HOY** (1964).

DON SEGUNDO SOMBRA 1969 d: Manuel Antin. ARG., *Don Segundo Sombra*, Ricardo Guiraldes, 1926, Novel

Don Story, The *see* **DONSKAYA POVEST** (1964).

DONA BARBARA 1943 d: Fernando de Fuentes. MXC., *Dona Barbara*, Romulo Gallegos, 1929, Novel

Dona Flor and Her Two Husbands *see* **DONA FLOR E SEUS DOIS MARIDOS** (1978).

DONA FLOR E SEUS DOIS MARIDOS 1978 d: Bruno Barreto. BRZ., *Dona Flor E Sue Dois Maridos*, Jorge Amado, 1966, Novel

Dona Herlinda and Her Son *see* **DONA HERLINDA Y SU HIJO** (1986).

DONA HERLINDA Y SU HIJO 1986 d: Jaime Humberto Hermosillo. MXC., Jorge Lopez Paez, Story

DONA JUANA 1928 d: Paul Czinner. GRM., *Don Gil von Den Grunen Hosen*, Tirso de Molina, Story

DONA MARIA LA BRAVA 1947 d: Luis MarquinA. SPN., *Dona Maria la Brava*, Eduardo Marquina, 1909, Play

Dona Maria the Brave *see* **DONA MARIA LA BRAVA** (1947).

Dona Perfecta *see* **BEAUTY IN CHAINS** (1918).

DONATIENNE 1908-13. FRN., *Donatienne*, Rene Bazin, Novel

Donde Has Pasado la Noche? *see* **NO DEJES LA PUERTA ABIERTA** (1933).

DONG FANG DI YI CHI KE 1993 d: Zhao Wenxin. CHN., *Number One Killer in Shanghai*, Lu Tieren, Novel

Dong XIe XI Du *see* **DUNG CHE SAI DUK** (1993).

Donkey Skin *see* **PEAU D'ANE** (1970).

Donna Alla Finestra, Una *see* **UNE FEMME A SA FENETRE** (1976).

DONNA BIANCA, LA 1931 d: Jack Salvatori. FRN., *The Letter*, W. Somerset Maugham, 1925, Short Story

DONNA CHE FU MOLTO AMATA, LA 1922 d: Enrico Vidali. ITL., *Paula Monti*, Eugene Sue, Novel

DONNA CHE INVENTO L'AMORE, LA 1952 d: Ferruccio Cerio. ITL., *La Donna Che Invento l'Amore*, Guido Da Verona, Novel

Donna Da Uccidere, Una *see* **FOLLE A TUER** (1975).

DONNA DEL LAGO, LA 1965 d: Luigi Bazzoni, Franco Rossellini. ITL., *La Donna Del Lago*, Giovanni Comisso, Novel

DONNA DEL MARE, LA 1922 d: Nino Valentini. ITL., *Fruen Frahavet*, Henrik Ibsen, 1888, Play

DONNA DELLA DOMENICA, LA 1976 d: Luigi Comencini. ITL/FRN., *La Donna Della Domenico*, Fruttero, Lucentini, Novel

DONNA DELLA MONTAGNA, LA 1943 d: Renato Castellani. ITL., *I Giganti Innamorati*, Salvator Gotta, Novel

Donna Dell'altro, La *see* **JONS UND ERDME** (1959).

Donna Di 30 Anni, Una *see* **LA DONNA DI TRENT'ANNI** (1920).

Donna Di Spagna *see* **IL PECCATO DI ROGELIA SANCHEZ** (1939).

DONNA DI TRENT'ANNI, LA 1920 d: Riccardo Molinari, Alessandro Des Varennes. ITL., *La Femme de Trente Ans*, Honore de Balzac, 1831, Short Story

DONNA FRA DUE MONDI, UNA 1936 d: Goffredo Alessandrini, Arthur M. Rabenalt. ITL., *Die Weisse Frau Des Maharadscha*, Ludwig von Wohl, Novel

DONNA FUNESTA, UNA 1919 d: Camillo de Riso. ITL., *Nana*, Emile Zola, Paris 1880, Novel

DONNA INVISIBILE, LA 1969 d: Paolo SpinolA. ITL., *Donna Invisibile*, Alberto Moravia, 1970, Short Story

DONNA NUDA, LA 1914 d: Carmine Gallone. ITL., *La Femme Nue*, Henry Bataille, 1908, Play

DONNA NUDA, LA 1922 d: Roberto Leone Roberti. ITL., *La Femme Nue*, Henry Bataille, 1908, Play

DONNA PERDUTA, LA 1941 d: Domenico M. Gambino. ITL., *La Donna Perduta*, Guglielmo Giannini, Giuseppe Pietri, Guglielmo Zorzi, Opera

Donna Tra Due Mondi, Una see **UNA DONNA FRA DUE MONDI** (1936).

DONNA, UNA 1917 d: Mario Gargiulo. ITL., *Una Donna*, Roberto Bracco, 1892, Play

Donne, Danni E Diamanti see **VOUS PIGEZ?** (1955).

DONNE PROIBITE 1953 d: Giuseppe Amato. ITL., *Vita Nuova*, Bruno Paolinelli, Play

Donne Senza Paradiso see **DER ARZT VON SAN MICHELE AXEL MUNTHE** (1962).

Donne Sono Deboli, Le see **FAIBLES FEMMES** (1959).

DONNER, BLITZ UND SONNENSCHEIN 1936 d: Erich Engels. GRM., *Der Hunderter Im Westentascher*, Max Ferner, Max Neal, Play

DONNIE BRASCO 1997 d: Mike Newell. USA., *Donnie Brasco: My Undercover Life in the Mafia*, Joseph D. Pistone, Richard Woodley, Book

DONO DEL MATTINO, IL 1932 d: Enrico Guazzoni. ITL., *Il Dono Del Mattino*, Giovacchino Forzano, Play

DONOGOO 1936 d: Henri Chomette, Reinhold Schunzel. FRN., *Donogoo*, Jules Romains, Novel

DONOGOO TONKA 1936 d: Reinhold Schunzel. GRM., *Donogoo-Tonka Ou Les Miracles la Science*, Jules Romains, 1920, Short Story

Donogoo Tonka, Die Geheimnisvolle Stadt see **DONOGOO TONKA** (1936).

DONOVAN AFFAIR, THE 1929 d: Frank CaprA. USA., *The Donovan Affair*, Owen Davis, New York 1926, Play

DONOVAN'S BRAIN 1953 d: Felix E. Feist. USA., *Donovan's Brain*, Curt Siodmak, New York 1943, Novel

Donovan's Kid see **YOUNG DONOVAN'S KID** (1931).

DON'S PARTY 1976 d: Bruce Beresford. ASL., *Don's Party*, David Williamson, 1973, Play

DONSKAYA POVEST 1964 d: Vladimir Fetin. USS., *Shibalkovo Semia*, Mikhail Sholokhov, 1926, Short Story

DON'T 1925 d: Alf Goulding. USA., *Don't You Care!*, Rupert Hughes, 1914, Short Story

DON'T ANSWER THE PHONE! 1980 d: Robert Hammer. USA., *Don't Answer the Phone*, Michael Curtis, Novel

Don't Be Afraid, Jacob! see **JAKOB! FURCHTE DICH NICHT** (1981).

DON'T BOTHER TO KNOCK 1952 d: Roy Ward Baker. USA., *Mischief*, Charlotte Armstrong, 1950, Novel

DON'T BOTHER TO KNOCK 1961 d: Cyril Frankel. UKN., *Love from Everybody*, Clifford Hanley, London 1959, Novel

DON'T CALL IT LOVE 1924 d: William C. de Mille. USA., *Rita Coventry*, Julian Leonard Street, Garden City, N.Y. 1922, Novel

DON'T CALL ME LITTLE GIRL 1921 d: Joseph Henabery. USA., *Jerry*, Catherine Chisholm Cushing, Play

DON'T CHANGE YOUR HUSBAND 1919 d: Cecil B. de Mille. USA., David Graham Phillips, Novel

DON'T DRINK THE WATER 1969 d: Howard Morris. USA., *Don't Drink the Water*, Woody Allen, New York 1966, Play

DON'T EVER LEAVE ME 1949 d: Arthur Crabtree. UKN., *The Wide Guy*, Anthony Armstrong, Novel

DON'T EVER MARRY 1920 d: Marshall Neilan, Victor Heerman. USA., *Don't Ever Marry*, Edgar Franklin, 1919, Short Story

Don't Forget to Kiss Your Wife see **VERGISS NICHT DEINE FRAU ZU KUSSEN** (1967).

Don't Forget to Remember see **THERE GOES THE GROOM** (1937).

Don't Get Excited see **GOOD-BY GIRLS!** (1923).

Don't Give a Damn see **LO SAM ZAYIN** (1987).

DON'T GIVE UP THE SHIP 1959 d: Norman Taurog. USA., Ellis Kadison, Story

DON'T GO NEAR THE WATER 1957 d: Charles Walters. USA., *Don't Go Near the Water*, William Brinkley, Novel

DON'T JUST STAND THERE! 1968 d: Ron Winston. USA., *The Wrong Venus*, Charles Williams, New York 1966, Novel

DON'T LEAVE ME THIS WAY 1993 d: Stuart Orme. UKN., Joan Smith, Novel

Don't Leave the Door Open see **NO DEJES LA PUERTA ABIERTA** (1933).

Don't Look Back see **DON'T LOOK BACK: THE STORY OF LEROY "SATCHEL" PAGE** (1981).

DON'T LOOK BACK: THE STORY OF LEROY "SATCHEL" PAGE 1981 d: Richard A. CollA. USA., *Maybe I'll Pitch Forever*, Satchel Page, Autobiography

DON'T LOOK NOW 1973 d: Nicolas Roeg. UKN/ITL., *Don't Look Now*, Daphne Du Maurier, 1971, Short Story

Don't Make Grandpa Angry see **NEZLOBTE DEDECKA** (1934).

DON'T MAKE WAVES 1967 d: Alexander MacKendrick. USA., *Muscle Beach*, Ira Wallach, Boston 1959, Novel

Don't Mess With the Martians see **NE JOUEZ PAS AVEC LES MARTIANS** (1967).

DON'T PANIC CHAPS! 1959 d: George Pollock. UKN., *Don't Panic Chaps*, Michael Corston, Ronald Holroyd, Radio Play

Don't Play With Martians see **NE JOUEZ PAS AVEC LES MARTIANS** (1967).

DON'T RAISE THE BRIDGE, LOWER THE RIVER 1968 d: Jerry Paris. UKN/USA., *Don't Raise the Bridge - Lower the River*, Max Wilk, New York 1960, Novel

DON'T RUSH ME! 1936 d: Norman Lee. UKN., *When We are Married*, Fred Karno, Sketch

Don't Steal My Baby see **BLACK MARKET BABY** (1977).

Don't Tell Anyone see **NO SE LO DIGAS A NADIE** (1998).

DON'T TELL HER IT'S ME 1990 d: Malcolm Mowbray. USA., *The Boyfriend School*, Sarah Bird, Novel

DON'T TELL THE WIFE 1927 d: Paul L. Stein. USA., *Cyprienne Or Divorcons*, Emile de Najac, Victorien Sardou, Paris 1883, Play

DON'T TELL THE WIFE 1937 d: W. Christy Cabanne. USA., *Once Over Lightly*, George Holland, Play

Don't Tell Them I Fell see **SI TE DICEN QUE CAI** (1988).

Don't Tempt the Devil see **LES BONNES CAUSES** (1963).

Don't Touch the Loot see **TOUCHEZ PAS AU GRISBI** (1953).

DON'T TURN 'EM LOOSE 1936 d: Ben Stoloff. USA., *Homecoming*, Thomas Walsh, 1936, Short Story

DON'T WRITE LETTERS 1922 d: George D. Baker. USA., *The Adventure of a Ready Letter Writer*, Blanche Brace, 1920, Short Story

Don't You Cry see **MY SON MY LOVER** (1970).

Don't You Know Mrs. Hadimrska? see **TO NEZNATE HADIMRSKU** (1931).

DONZOKO 1957 d: Akira KurosawA. JPN., *Na Dne*, Maxim Gorky, Moscow 1902, Play

Donzoku see **DONZOKO** (1957).

Doom of Dracula see **HOUSE OF FRANKENSTEIN** (1944).

Doomed Cargo see **SEVEN SINNERS** (1936).

Doomed Fort see **FUERTE PERDIDO** (1965).

Doomed Love see **AMOR DE PERDICAO** (1943).

Doomed Love see **AMOR DE PERDICAO** (1977).

Doomed Souls see **OSADENI DUSHI** (1975).

DOOMSDAY 1928 d: Rowland V. Lee. USA., *Doomsday*, Warwick Deeping, London 1927, Novel

Doomsday Virus see **PANDORA'S CLOCK** (1996).

DOOR BETWEEN, THE 1917 d: Rupert Julian. USA., *Anthony the Absolute*, Samuel Merwin, New York 1914, Novel

DOOR IN THE WALL, THE 1956 d: Glenn H. Alvey Jr. UKN., *The Door in the Wall*, H. G. Wells, 1911, Short Story

DOOR THAT HAS NO KEY, THE 1921 d: Frank H. Crane. UKN., *The Door That Has No Key*, Cosmo Hamilton, Novel

Door, The see **THE STRANGE DOOR** (1951).

Door With Bars, The see **I KANGELOPORTA** (1979).

DOOR WITH SEVEN LOCKS, THE 1940 d: Norman Lee. UKN., *The Door With Seven Locks*, Edgar Wallace, London 1926, Novel

Door with Seven Locks, The see **DIE TUR MIT DEN SIEBEN SCHLOSSERN** (1962).

DOORSTEPS 1916 d: Henry Edwards. UKN., *Doorsteps*, Henry Edwards, Play

DOORWAY TO HELL, THE 1930 d: Archie Mayo. USA., *A Handful of Clouds*, Rowland Brown, Story

DOP DOCTOR, THE 1915 d: Fred Paul, L. C. MacBean. UKN., *The Dop Doctor*, Richard Dehan, Novel

DOPE 1914 d: Herman Lieb. USA., *Dope*, Joseph Medill Patterson, New York 1909, Play

..Dopo Di Che, Uccide Il Maschio E Lo Divora see **MARTA** (1971).

Doppelleben Des Rd. Dumartin, Das see **DIE EWIGE MASKE** (1935).

DOPPELSELBSTMORD 1937 d: Max W. Kimmich. GRM., *Doppelselbstmord*, Ludwig Anzengruber, 1876, Play

DOPPELTE LOTTCHEN, DAS 1950 d: Josef von Baky. GRM., *Das Doppelte Lottchen*, Erich Kastner, Vienna 1949, Novel

DOPPELTE MATTHIAS UND SEINE TOCHTER, DER 1941 d: Sigfrit Steiner, Emile Edwin Reinert. SWT., *Der Doppelte Matthias Und Seine Tochter*, Meinrad Lienert, Berlin 1929, Novel

Doppelte Matthias Und Seine Tochter, Der see **FUNFMADERLHAUS** (1943).

Doppia Morte Al Governo Vecchio see **DOPPIO DELITTO** (1977).

DOPPIO DELITTO 1977 d: Steno. ITL/FRN., *Doppia Morte Al Governo Vecchio*, Ugo Moretti, Novel

DORA 1909 d: Sidney Olcott. USA., *Dora*, Alfred Tennyson, Poem

DORA 1910 d: Bert Haldane?. UKN., *Dora*, Alfred Tennyson, Poem

DORA 1912 d: H. O. Martinek?. UKN., *Dora*, Alfred Tennyson, Poem

DORA 1912. USA., *Dora*, Alfred Tennyson, Poem

DORA 1913. USA., *Dora*, Alfred Tennyson, Poem

DORA 1915 d: Travers Vale. USA., *Dora*, Alfred Tennyson, Poem

DORA, LA ESPIA 1943 d: Raffaello Matarazzo. ITL/SPN., *Dora*, Victorien Sardou, Paris 1877, Play

DORA NELSON 1935 d: Rene Guissart. FRN., *Dora Nelson*, Louis Verneuil, Play

DORA NELSON 1939 d: Mario Soldati. ITL., *Dora Nelson*, Louis Verneuil, Play

DORA O LE SPIE 1919 d: Roberto Leone Roberti. ITL., *Dora*, Victorien Sardou, Paris 1877, Play

Dora O le Spie see **LA ESPIA DORA** (1943).

DORA THORNE 1910. USA., *Dora Thorne*, Bertha M. Clay, New York 1880, Novel

DORA THORNE 1915 d: Lawrence Marston. USA., *Dora Thorne*, Bertha M. Clay, New York 1880, Novel

DORF UNTERM HIMMEL, DAS 1953 d: Richard Haussler. GRM., *Der Januck*, Rolf Olsen, Short Story

Dorian Gray see **IL DIO CHIAMATO DORIAN** (1970).

DORMEZ, JE LE VEUX 1916 d: Marcel Simon. FRN., *Dormez, Je le Veux*, Georges Feydeau, Play

DORNROSCHEN 1955 d: Fritz Genschow. GRM., *Dornroschen*, Jacob Grimm, Wilhelm Grimm, Short Story

DORO NO KAWA 1981 d: Kohei Oguri. JPN., *Doro No Kawa*, Teru Miyamoto, Novel

DOROTEJ 1981 d: Zdravko Velimirovic. YGS., *Dorotej*, Dobrilo Nenadic, 1977, Novel

DOROTHEA ANGERMANN 1959 d: Robert Siodmak. GRM., *Dorothea Angermann*, Gerhart Hauptmann, 1926, Play

Dorothy in the Garret see **THE OLD MAID** (1914).

DOROTHY VERNON OF HADDON HALL 1924 d: Marshall Neilan. USA., *When Knighthood Was in Flower*, Charles Major, Indianapolis 1898, Novel

DORP AAN DE RIVIER 1958 d: Fons Rademakers. NTH., *Dorp Aan de Rivier*, Anton Coolen, Novel

DORTOIR DES GRANDES 1953 d: Henri Decoin. FRN., *Dortoir Des Grandes*, Stanislas-Andre Steeman, Novel

DOS AU MUR, LE 1958 d: Edouard Molinaro. FRN., *Delivrez-Nous du Mal*, Frederic Dard, Novel

DOS HOMBRES Y EN MEDIO DOS MUJERES 1977 d: Rafael Gil. SPN., *Dos Hombres Y Dos Mujeres En Medio*, Juan Antonio de Zunzunegui, 1944, Novel

DOS MUNDOS DE ANGELITA, LOS 1982 d: Jeanne Morrison. USA., *Angelita*, Wendy Kesselman, Novel

Dossier 212 -Destinazione Morte *see* **LA PEAU DE TORPEDO** (1970).

Dossier 51 *see* **LE DOSSIER 51** (1978).

DOSSIER 51, LE 1978 d: Michel Deville. FRN/GRM., *Le Dossier 51*, Gilles Perrault, Novel

DOSSIER PROSTITUTION 1969 d: Jean-Claude Roy. FRN., *Dossier Prostitution*, Dominique Dallayrac, Book

Dot, Dot, Comma, Dash *see* **PUNKTUR, COMMA, STRIK PUNKTUR** (1980).

DOTHEBOYS HALL; OR, NICHOLAS NICKLEBY 1903 d: Alf Collins. UKN., *Nicholas Nickleby*, Charles Dickens, London 1870, Novel

Dotted Line, The *see* **LET WOMEN ALONE** (1925).

DOTTOR ANTONIO, IL 1910 d: Mario Caserini. ITL., *Il Dottor Antonio*, Giovanni Ruffini, 1855, Novel

DOTTOR ANTONIO, IL 1914 d: Eleuterio Rodolfi. ITL., *Il Dottor Antonio*, Giovanni Ruffini, 1855, Novel

DOTTOR ANTONIO, IL 1937 d: Enrico Guazzoni. ITL., *Il Dottor Antonio*, Giovanni Ruffini, 1855, Novel

Dottor Jekill Jr., Il *see* **DOTTOR JEKYLL E GENTILE SIGNORA** (1979).

DOTTOR JEKYLL E GENTILE SIGNORA 1979 d: Steno. ITL., *The Strange Case of Dr. Jekyll and Mr. Hyde*, Robert Louis Stevenson, London 1886, Novel

DOU ER YUAN 1959 d: Zhang XInshi. CHN., *Dou Er Yuan*, Guan Hanqing, c1230, Play

DOUA LOZURI 1957 d: Gheorghe Naghi, Aurel Miheles. RMN., *Doua Loturi*, Ion Luca Caragiale, 1901, Short Story

DOUBLE CONFESSION 1950 d: Ken Annakin. UKN., *All on a Summer's Day*, John Garden, Novel

DOUBLE CRIME SUR LA LIGNE MAGINOT 1937 d: Felix GanderA. FRN., *Double Crime Sur la Ligne Maginot*, Pierre Nord, Novel

Double Cross *see* **LA FIGLIA DEL CAPITANO** (1947).

Double Cross *see* **DOUBLECROSS** (1956).

DOUBLE CROSS ROADS 1930 d: Alfred L. Werker. USA., *Yonder Grow the Daisies*, William Lipman, New York 1929, Novel

Double Daring *see* **FIXER DUGAN** (1939).

Double Deadly *see* **THE SILENT PARTNER** (1978).

DOUBLE DEALING 1928 d: Geoffrey H. Malins. UKN., *Double Dealing*, W. W. Jacobs, Short Story

Double Deception *see* **LES MAGICIENNES** (1960).

Double Destin *see* **DAS ZWEITE LEBEN** (1954).

Double Destiny *see* **DAS ZWEITE LEBEN** (1954).

DOUBLE DOOR 1934 d: Charles Vidor. USA., *Double Door*, Elizabeth A. McFadden, New York 1933, Play

DOUBLE DYED DECEIVER, THE 1920 d: Alfred E. Green. USA., *A Double-Dyed Deceiver*, O. Henry, 1905, Short Story

Double Error *see* **THE PRICE OF FOLLY** (1937).

DOUBLE EVENT, THE 1921 d: Kenelm Foss. UKN., *The Double Event*, Sidney Blow, Douglas Hoare, 1917, Play

DOUBLE EVENT, THE 1934 d: Leslie H. Gordon. UKN., *The Double Event*, Sidney Blow, Douglas Hoare, 1917, Play

DOUBLE EXISTENCE DE LORD SAMSEY, LA 1924 d: Georges Monca, Maurice Keroul. FRN., *La Double Existence de Lord Samsey*, Georges le Faure, Novel

DOUBLE EXISTENCE DU DOCTEUR MORART, LA 1919 d: Jacques Gretillat. FRN., *La Double Existence du Docteur Morart*, Andre de Lorde, Dr. Toulouse, Play

Double Exposure: the Story of Margaret Bourke-White *see* **MARGARET BOURKE-WHITE: THE TRUE STORY** (1989).

Double Face *see* **A DOPPIA FACCIA** (1969).

Double Furlough *see* **I'LL BE SEEING YOU** (1944).

DOUBLE HARNESS 1933 d: John Cromwell. USA., *Double Harness*, Edward Poor Montgomery, London 1933, Play

Double Identity *see* **RIVER'S END** (1940).

DOUBLE INDEMNITY 1944 d: Billy Wilder. USA., *Double Indemnity*, James M. Cain, 1943, Novel

DOUBLE INDEMNITY 1973 d: Jack Smight. USA., *Double Indemnity*, James M. Cain, 1943, Novel

Double Life *see* **DVOJI ZIVOT** (1939).

Double Life, A *see* **DVOJI ZIVOT** (1924).

Double Life, A *see* **DAS ZWEITE LEBEN** (1954).

DOUBLE LIFE OF MR. ALFRED BURTON, THE 1919 d: Arthur Rooke. UKN., *The Double Life of Mr. Alfred Burton*, E. Phillips Oppenheim, 1914, Novel

Double Lives *see* **THE TRAIL OF THE HORSE THIEVES** (1929).

DOUBLE MAN, THE 1967 d: Franklin J. Schaffner. UKN., *Legacy of a Spy*, Harry S. Maxfield, New York 1958, Novel

Double Matthias Et Ses Filles, Le *see* **DER DOPPELTE MATTHIAS UND SEINE TOCHTER** (1941).

Double Murder *see* **DOPPIO DELITTO** (1977).

DOUBLE NEGATIVE 1980 d: George Bloomfield. CND., *The Three Roads*, Ross MacDonald, Novel

DOUBLE PIEGE, LE 1923 d: Gaston Roudes. FRN., *Le Double Piege*, Berr de Turique, Play

Double Play *see* **LILY IN LOVE** (1985).

Double Pursuit *see* **MY BROTHER'S KEEPER** (1948).

Double Suicide *see* **DOPPELSELBSTMORD** (1937).

Double Suicide *see* **SHINJU TEN NO AMIJIMA** (1969).

Double Suicide *see* **SONEZAKI SHINJU** (1978).

Double Suicide at Amijima *see* **SHINJU TEN NO AMIJIMA** (1969).

Double Suicide at Sonezaki *see* **SONEZAKI SHINJU** (1978).

DOUBLE, THE 1963 d: Lionel Harris. UKN., *The Double*, Edgar Wallace, London 1928, Novel

DOUBLE TROUBLE 1915 d: W. Christy Cabanne. USA., *Double Trouble*, Herbert Quick, Indianapolis 1906, Novel

DOUBLE WEDDING 1937 d: Richard Thorpe. USA., *Nagy Szerelem*, Ferenc Molnar, 1935, Play

DOUBLE X 1991 d: Shani S. Grewal. UKN., *Vengeance*, David Fleming, Short Story

Double X: the Name of the Game *see* **DOUBLE X** (1991).

DOUBLE-BARRELLED DETECTIVE STORY, THE 1965 d: Adolfas Mekas. USA., *A Double Barrelled Detective Story*, Mark Twain, New York 1902, Novel

DOUBLECROSS 1956 d: Anthony Squire. UKN., *The Queer Fish*, Kem Bennett, Novel

Double-Dyed Deceiver, A *see* **THE DOUBLE DYED DECEIVER** (1920).

Double-Dyed Deceiver, The *see* **THE LLANO KID** (1939).

DOUBLETAKE 1985 d: Jud Taylor. USA., *Switch*, William Bayer, Novel

Doubt, The *see* **LA DUDA** (1972).

DOUBTING THOMAS 1935 d: David Butler. USA., *The Torchbearers*, George Edward Kelly, New York 1922, Play

DOUCE 1943 d: Claude Autant-LarA. FRN., *Douce*, Michel Davet, Novel

DOUGHGIRLS, THE 1944 d: James V. Kern. USA., *The Doughgirls*, Joseph Fields, New York 1942, Play

DOULEUR, LA 1925 d: Gaston Roudes. FRN., *La Douleur*, E. M. Laumann, Novel

DOULOREUSE, LA 1921 d: Augusto GeninA. ITL., *La Douloureuse*, Maurice Donnay, 1897, Novel

DOULOS, LE 1962 d: Jean-Pierre Melville. FRN/ITL., *Le Doulos*, Pierre Lesou, Paris 1957, Novel

Doulos -the Finger Man *see* **LE DOULOS** (1962).

DOUTE, LE 1920 d: Gaston Roudes. FRN., *Le Doute*, Daniel Jourda, Play

DOVE, THE 1927 d: Roland West. USA., *The Dove*, Willard Mack, New York 1925, Play

Dove, The *see* **GIRL OF THE RIO** (1932).

Dove, The *see* **THE GIRL AND THE GAMBLER** (1939).

DOVE, THE 1974 d: Charles Jarrott. USA/UKN., *The Dove*, Derek Gill, Robin Lee Graham, Book

Dover Road, The *see* **THE LITTLE ADVENTURESS** (1927).

Dover Road, The *see* **WHERE SINNERS MEET** (1934).

Dowerless Bride *see* **ZESTOKIJ ROMANS** (1984).

DOWN AMONG THE SHELTERING PALMS 1953 d: Edmund Goulding. USA., Edward Hope, Serial Story

DOWN AND OUT IN BEVERLY HILLS 1986 d: Paul Mazursky. USA., *Boudu Sauve Des Eaux*, Rene Fauchois, 1919, Play

DOWN HOME 1920 d: Irvin V. Willat. USA., *Dabney Todd*, F. N. Westcott, New York 1916, Novel

DOWN OUR STREET 1932 d: Harry Lachman. UKN., *Down Our Street*, Ernest George, Play

DOWN RIVER 1931 d: Peter Godfrey. UKN., *Down River*, Seamark, Novel

Down the Ancient Staircase *see* **PER LE ANTICHE SCALE** (1975).

Down the Ancient Stairs *see* **PER LE ANTICHE SCALE** (1975).

DOWN THE STRETCH 1927 d: King Baggot. USA., *The Money Rider*, Gerald Beaumont, 1924, Short Story

DOWN THREE DARK STREETS 1954 d: Arnold Laven. USA., *Case File F.B.I.*, Gordon Gordon, Mildred Gordon, 1953, Novel

DOWN UNDER DONOVAN 1922 d: Harry Lambart. UKN., *Down Under Donovan*, Edgar Wallace, London 1918, Novel

Down With the King *see* **WIR PFEIFEN AUF DEN GURKENKONIG** (1974).

DOWNFALL 1964 d: John Llewellyn Moxey. UKN., Edgar Wallace, Story

Downfall of Osen, The *see* **ORIZURU OSEN** (1934).

Downfall, The *see* **ORIZURU OSEN** (1934).

DOWNHILL 1927 d: Alfred Hitchcock. UKN., *Downhill*, Constance Collier, Ivor Novello, London 1926, Play

DOWNHILL RACER 1969 d: Michael Ritchie. USA., *Downhill Racers*, Oakley Hall, New York 1963, Novel

Downhill Racers, The *see* **DOWNHILL RACER** (1969).

Downy Girl *see* **DUNUNGEN** (1941).

Downy Girl, The *see* **DUNUNGEN** (1919).

Dozivljaji Nikoletine Bursaca *see* **NIKOLETINA BURSAC** (1964).

Doznaniye Pilota Pikrsa *see* **TEST PILOTA PIRXA** (1978).

Dr. Akagi *see* **KANZO SENSEI** (1998).

DR. BESSELS VERWANDLUNG 1927 d: Richard Oswald. GRM., *Dr. Bessels Verwandlung*, Ludwig Wolff, Novel

DR. COOK'S GARDEN 1970 d: Ted Post. USA., *Dr. Cook's Garden*, Ira Levin, Play

Dr. Detroit *see* **DOCTOR DETROIT** (1983).

Dr. Dolittle *see* **DOCTOR DOLITTLE** (1998).

DR. FISCHER OF GENEVA 1983 d: Michael Lindsay-Hogg. UKN., *Dr. Fischer of Geneva; Or the Bomb Party*, Graham Greene, 1980, Novel

Dr. Francoise *see* **DOCTEUR FRANCOISE GAILLAND** (1975).

Dr. Hallers *see* **DER ANDERE** (1930).

Dr. Hegl's Patient *see* **PACIENTKA DR. HEGLA** (1940).

D'r Herr Maire *see* **MONSIEUR LE MAIRE** (1939).

DR. JEKYLL AND MR. HYDE 1912 d: Lucius Henderson. USA., *The Strange Case of Dr. Jekyll and Mr. Hyde*, Robert Louis Stevenson, London 1886, Novel

DR. JEKYLL AND MR. HYDE 1913 d: Herbert Brenon. USA., *The Strange Case of Dr. Jekyll and Mr. Hyde*, Robert Louis Stevenson, London 1886, Novel

Dr. Jekyll and Mr. Hyde *see* **EIN SELTSAMER FALL** (1914).

DR. JEKYLL AND MR. HYDE 1920 d: John S. Robertson. USA., *The Strange Case of Dr. Jekyll and Mr. Hyde*, Robert Louis Stevenson, London 1886, Novel

DR. JEKYLL AND MR. HYDE 1920 d: Charles J. Hayden. USA., *The Strange Case of Dr. Jekyll and Mr. Hyde*, Robert Louis Stevenson, London 1886, Novel

DR. JEKYLL AND MR. HYDE 1932 d: Rouben Mamoulian. USA., *The Strange Case of Dr. Jekyll and Mr. Hyde*, Robert Louis Stevenson, London 1886, Novel

DR. JEKYLL AND MR. HYDE 1941 d: Victor Fleming. USA., *The Strange Case of Dr. Jekyll and Mr. Hyde*, Robert Louis Stevenson, London 1886, Novel

Dr. Jekyll and Mr. Hyde *see* **THE STRANGE CASE OF DR. JEKYLL AND MR. HYDE** (1967).

DR. JEKYLL AND MR. HYDE 1973 d: David Winters. UKN., *The Strange Case of Dr. Jekyll and Mr. Hyde*, Robert Louis Stevenson, London 1886, Novel

DR. JEKYLL AND MR. HYDE 1981 d: Alastair Reid. UKN., *The Strange Case of Dr. Jekyll and Mr. Hyde*, Robert Louis Stevenson, London 1886, Novel

DR. JEKYLL AND MR. HYDE - A JOURNEY INTO FEAR 1988 d: Gerard Kikoine. UKN., *The Strange Case of Dr. Jekyll and Mr. Hyde*, Robert Louis Stevenson, London 1886, Novel

Dr. Knock see KNOCK (1950).

DR. MABUSE, DER SPIELER 1921 d: Fritz Lang. GRM., *Dr. Mabuse*, Norbert Jacques, Novel

Dr. Mabuse Vs. Scotland Yard see **SCOTLAND YARD JAGT DOKTOR MABUSE** (1963).

DR. MASON'S TEMPTATION 1915 d: Frank Lloyd. USA., *Dr. Mason's Temptation*, Hugh C. Weir, Story

DR. MED. HIOB PRATORIUS 1965 d: Kurt Hoffmann. GRM., *Dr. Med. Hiob Pratorius*, Curt Goetz, 1934, Play

DR. MONICA 1934 d: William Keighley, William Dieterle (Uncredited). USA., Marja Morozowicz Szczepkowska, Play

Dr. Murkes Collected Silences see **DOKTOR MURKES SAMLADE TYSTNAD** (1968).

Dr. Murkes Samlade Tystnad see **DOKTOR MURKES SAMLADE TYSTNAD** (1968).

DR. NO 1962 d: Terence Young. UKN., *Dr. No*, Ian Fleming, London 1958, Novel

DR. O'DOWD 1940 d: Herbert Mason. UKN., *Dr. O'Dowd*, L. A. G. Strong, Novel

Dr. Pratorius, Gynecologist see **FRAUENARZT DR. PRATORIUS** (1950).

DR. RAMEAU 1915 d: Will S. Davis. USA., *Le Docteur Rameau*, Georges Ohnet, Paris 1889, Novel

Dr. Rhythm see **DOCTOR RHYTHM** (1938).

DR. SOCRATES 1935 d: William Dieterle. USA., William Riley Burnett, 1935, Story

DR. STRANGELOVE 1963 d: Stanley Kubrick. UKN., *Red Alert*, Peter Bryan George, New York 1958, Novel

Dr. Strangelove: Or, How I Learned to Stop Worrying and Love the Bomb see **DR. STRANGELOVE** (1963).

Dr. Sunshine see **POTASH AND PERLMUTTER** (1923).

DR. SYN 1937 d: R. William Neill. UKN., *Christopher Syn*, William Russell Thorndike, Novel

Dr. Syn see **CAPTAIN CLEGG** (1962).

DR. SYN - ALIAS THE SCARECROW 1963 d: James Neilson. UKN., *Christopher Syn*, William Russell Thorndike, Novel

Dr. Tarr's Torture Dungeon see **LA MANSION DE LA LOCURA** (1971).

Dr. Vlimmen, Vet see **TIERARZT DR. VLIMMEN** (1944).

DR. WAKE'S PATIENT 1916 d: Fred Paul. UKN., *Mr. Wake's Patient*, W. Gayer MacKey, Robert Ord, Play

Dr. Zhivago see **DOCTOR ZHIVAGO** (1965).

Dracula see **NOSFERATU - EINE SYMPHONIE DES GRAUENS** (1921).

DRACULA 1931 d: Tod Browning. USA., *Dracula*, Bram Stoker, London 1897, Novel

DRACULA 1931 d: George Melford. USA., *Dracula*, Bram Stoker, London 1897, Novel

DRACULA 1958 d: Terence Fisher. UKN., *Dracula*, Bram Stoker, London 1897, Novel

DRACULA 1973 d: Dan Curtis. UKN/USA., *Dracula*, Bram Stoker, London 1897, Novel

DRACULA 1979 d: John Badham. UKN/USA., *Dracula*, Bram Stoker, London 1897, Novel

DRACULA 1992 d: Francis Ford CoppolA. USA., *Dracula*, Bram Stoker, London 1897, Novel

DRACULA - PRINCE OF DARKNESS 1965 d: Terence Fisher. UKN., *Dracula*, Bram Stoker, London 1897, Novel

Dracula and Son see **DRACULA PERE ET FILS** (1976).

DRACULA PERE ET FILS 1976 d: Edouard Molinaro. FRN., *Dracua Pere Et Fils*, Claude Klotz, Novel

Draft, The see **NAJA** (1998).

DRAG 1929 d: Frank Lloyd. USA., *Drag*, William Dudley Pelley, Boston 1925, Play

Dragnet, The see **THE DRAG-NET** (1936).

DRAG-NET, THE 1936 d: Vin Moore. USA., *The Drag-Net*, Willard Mack, Play

Dragon Beard Ditch see **LONGXU GOU** (1952).

DRAGON MURDER CASE, THE 1934 d: H. Bruce Humberstone. USA., *The Dragon Murder Case; a Philo Vance Story*, S. S. Van Dine, New York 1933, Novel

DRAGON PAINTER, THE 1919 d: William Worthington. USA., *The Dragon Painter*, Mary McNeil Fenollosa, Boston 1906, Novel

DRAGON SEED 1944 d: Jack Conway, Harold S. Bucquet. USA., *The Dragon Seed*, Pearl Buck, 1942, Novel

Dragonard see **MASTER OF DRAGONARD HILL** (1989).

Dragonseed see **DRAGON SEED** (1944).

DRAGONWYCK 1946 d: Joseph L. Mankiewicz. USA., *Dragonwyck*, Anya Seton, 1944, Novel

DRAGOON WELLS MASSACRE 1957 d: Harold Schuster. USA., Oliver Drake, Story

Dragoons of Klatovy, The see **KLATOVSTI DRAGOUNI** (1937).

DRAKE OF ENGLAND 1935 d: Arthur Woods. UKN., *Drake*, Louis N. Parker, London 1912, Play

Drake the Pirate see **DRAKE OF ENGLAND** (1935).

Drama from Olden Times see **DRAMA IZ STARINNOI ZHIZNI** (1971).

DRAMA IZ STARINNOI ZHIZNI 1971 d: Ilya Averbach. USS., *Tupeinyi Khudozhnik*, Nikolay Semyonovich Leskov, 1883, Short Story

Drama Na Okhote see **MOJ LASKOVYJ I NEZNYJ ZVER** (1978).

DRAMA NUEVO, UN 1946 d: Juan de OrdunA. SPN., *Un Drama Nuevo*, Manuel Tamayo Y Baus, 1867, Play

Drama of Former Times, A see **DRAMA IZ STARINNOI ZHIZNI** (1971).

DRAMATIC SCHOOL 1938 d: Robert B. Sinclair. USA., *School of Drama*, Zoltan Egyed, Hans Szekely, Play

Dramatic Tale of Yore, A see **DRAMA IZ STARINNOI ZHIZNI** (1971).

Drame Au College see **LES GOSSES MENENT L'ENQUETE** (1946).

DRAME AU PHARE, UN 1914 d: Georges Pallu. FRN., *La Tour d'Amour*, Rachilde, Novel

DRAME DE SHANGHAI, LE 1938 d: G. W. Pabst. FRN., *Shanghai Chambard Et Cie*, Oscar-Paul Gilbert, Novel

DRAME DE VILLESAUGE, LE 1909 d: Victorin Jasset. FRN., *Le Drame de Villesauge*, Paul de Garros, Novel

DRAME DES CHARMETTES, LE 1909. FRN., *Le Drame Des Charmettes*, Henri Demesse

DRAME DU 23, LE 1914. FRN., *Le Drame du 23*, A. Bourgain, Paul Gavault, Play

Drame du Mont Cervin, Le see **DER KAMPF UMS MATTERHORN** (1928).

DRAME SOUS NAPOLEON, UN 1921 d: Gerard Bourgeois. FRN., *Oncle Bernac*, Arthur Conan Doyle, Novel

DRAMMA BORGHESE, UN 1979 d: Florestano Vancini. ITL., *Un Dramma Borghese*, Guido Morselli, Novel

Dramma Dell'umanita, Il see **SATANA** (1912).

DRAPEAU NOIR FLOTTE SUR LA MARMITE, LE 1971 d: Michel Audiard. FRN., *Le Drapeau Noir Flotte Sur la Marmite*, Rene Fallet, Novel

Dream Broken in Late Spring see **CHUN CAN MENG DUAN** (1947).

DREAM CHEATER, THE 1920 d: Ernest C. Warde. USA., *La Peau de Chagrin*, Honore de Balzac, Paris 1831, Novel

Dream City see **TRAUMSTADT** (1973).

DREAM GIRL 1948 d: Mitchell Leisen. USA., *Dream Girl*, Elmer Rice, New York 1945, Play

DREAM LADY, THE 1918 d: Elsie Jane Wilson. USA., *Why Not?*, Margaret Widdemer, New York 1915, Novel

Dream machine, The see **ESCAPEMENT** (1957).

DREAM MERCHANTS, THE 1980 d: Vincent Sherman. USA., *The Dream Merchants*, Harold Robbins, Novel

Dream of a Father see **FADREN** (1969).

Dream of Butterfly, The see **IL SOGNO DI BUTTERFLY** (1939).

DREAM OF EUGENE ARAM, THE 1923 d: Edwin Greenwood. UKN., *The Dream of Eugene Aram*, Thomas Hood, Poem

Dream of Heroes, The see **EL SUENO DE LOS HEROES** (1997).

Dream of Home, The see **TILL THE END OF TIME** (1946).

DREAM OF KINGS, A 1969 d: Daniel Mann. USA., *A Dream of Kings*, Harry Mark Petrakis, New York 1966, Novel

DREAM OF LOVE 1928 d: Fred Niblo. USA., *Adrienne Lecouvreur*, Ernest Legouve, Eugene Scribe, Paris 1849, Play

Dream of Old Scrooge see **IL SOGNO DELL'USURAIO** (1910).

Dream of Olwen see **WHILE I LIVE** (1947).

DREAM OF PASSION, A 1978 d: Jules Dassin. GRC., *Medea*, Euripides, 431 bc, Play

Dream of Red Mansions, A see **HONG LOU MENG** (1988-89).

Dream of the Red Chamber see **HONG LOU MENG** (1962).

Dream of the Red Chamber, The see **HUNG LOU MENG** (1966).

DREAM SHIP, THE 1914 d: Harry Pollard. USA., *The Dream Ship*, Eugene Field, Poem

DREAM STREET 1921 d: D. W. Griffith. USA., *Gina of Chinatown*, Thomas Burke, 1916, Short Story, *The Lamp in the Window*, Thomas Burke, 1916, Short Story

DREAM, THE 1920 d: Joseph Byron Totten. USA., *The Dream*, O. Henry, Short Story

DREAM WOMAN, THE 1914 d: Alice Blache. USA., *The Dream-Woman*, Wilkie Collins, Boston 1873, Novel

DREAMBOAT 1952 d: Claude Binyon. USA., *The Love Man*, John D. Weaver, Novel

Dreamers, The see **FANTASTERNE** (1967).

DREAMING LIPS 1935 d: Lee Garmes, Paul Czinner. UKN., *Melo*, Henri Bernstein, Play

Dreaming Lips see **DER TRAUMENDE MUND** (1953).

Dreaming Mouth see **DER TRAUMENDE MUND** (1932).

Dreaming Mouth see **DER TRAUMENDE MUND** (1953).

Dreaming Youth see **ALMODO IFJUSAG** (1974).

Dreamland see **STRIKE ME PINK** (1936).

DREAMS COME TRUE 1936 d: Reginald Denham. UKN., *Clo-Clo*, Franz Lehar, Operetta

Dreams Die at Dawn see **I SOGNI MUOIONO ALL'ALBA** (1961).

Dreams in the Drawer see **I SOGNI NEL CASSETTO** (1957).

DREAMS LOST, DREAMS FOUND 1987 d: Willi Patterson. UKN/USA., *Dreams Lost Dreams Found*, Pamela Wallace, Novel

Dreams of an Idiot see **MECHTY IDIOTA** (1993).

Dreams of Death see **LIEBESTRAUM** (1951).

Dreams of Innocence see **SIPUR SHEMATCHIL BELEVAYA SHEL NACHASH** (1993).

Dreams of Love see **REVES D'AMOUR** (1946).

Dreams of the Red Chamber see **HONG LOU MENG** (1988-89).

Dreamtown see **TRAUMSTADT** (1973).

Dreamy Days see **VERTRAUMTE TAGE** (1951).

DREI FRAUEN VON URBAN HELL, DIE 1928 d: Jaap Speyer. GRM., *Hell in Frauensee*, Vicki Baum, Novel

Drei Madchen Spinnen see **KOMPLOTT AUF ERLENHOF** (1950).

DREI MADERL UM SCHUBERT 1936 d: E. W. Emo. GRM., *Schwammerl*, Rudolf Hans Bartsch, Leipzig 1916, Novel

DREI MANN IN EINEM BOOT 1961 d: Helmut Weiss. GRM/AUS., *Three Men in a Boat (to Say Nothing of the Dog)*, Jerome K. Jerome, London 1889, Novel

DREI MANNER IM SCHNEE 1955 d: Kurt Hoffmann. AUS., *Drei Manner Im Schnee*, Erich Kastner, Zurich 1934, Novel

DREI MANNER IM SCHNEE 1973 d: Alfred Vohrer. GRM., *Drei Manner Im Schnee*, Erich Kastner, Zurich 1934, Novel

Drei Menschen Am Piz Palu see **FOHN** (1950).

DREI NIEMANDSKINDER, DIE 1927 d: Fritz Freisler. GRM., *Die Drei Niemandskinder*, Karl Rossler, Novel

DREI TAGE MITTELARREST 1955 d: Georg Jacoby. GRM., *Drei Tage Mittelarrest*, Bobby E. Luthge, Karl Noti, Play

DREI UM EDITH, DIE 1929 d: Erich Waschneck. GRM., *Die Drei Um Edith*, Walther Harich, Novel

DREI VATER UM ANNA 1939 d: Carl Boese. GRM., *Fogg Bringt Ein Madchen Mit*, Walther Kloeppffer, Novel

DREI VOM VARIETE 1954 d: Kurt Neumann. GRM., *Der Eid Des Stephan Huller*, Felix Hollaender, Novel

Drei von Denen Man Spricht see **GLUCK MUSS MAN HABEN** (1953).

743

DREIGROSCHENOPER, DIE 1930 d: G. W. Pabst. GRM., *Die Dreigroschenoper*, Bertolt Brecht, Berlin 1928, Play

DREIGROSCHENOPER, DIE 1963 d: Wolfgang Staudte. GRM/FRN., *Die Dreigroschenoper*, Bertolt Brecht, Berlin 1928, Play

Dreimaderlhaus *see* **DREI MADERL UM SCHUBERT** (1936).

DREIMADERLHAUS, DAS 1958 d: Ernst MarischkA. AUS., *Schwammerl*, Rudolf Hans Bartsch, Leipzig 1916, Novel

DREIZEHN STUHLE 1938 d: E. W. Emo. GRM., *Dvenadtsat Stulyev*, Ilya Ilf, Evgeny Petrov, Moscow 1928, Novel

Dress of the Colour of Fire, The *see* **O VESTIDO COR DE FOGO** (1984).

DRESSED TO KILL 1941 d: Eugene J. Forde. USA., *The Dead Take No Bows*, Richard Burke, Novel

DRESSED TO THRILL 1935 d: Harry Lachman. USA., *La Couturiere de Luneville*, Alfred Savoir, Paris 1923, Play

DRESSER, THE 1983 d: Peter Yates. UKN., *The Dresser*, Ronald Harwood, Play

Dressmaker of Luneville, The *see* **LA COUTURIERE DE LUNEVILLE** (1931).

Dressmaker, The *see* **DRESSED TO THRILL** (1935).

DRESSMAKER, THE 1988 d: Jim O'Brien. UKN., *The Dressmaker*, Beryl Bainbridge, Novel

DREYFUS 1931 d: F. W. Kraemer, Milton Rosmer. UKN., *The Dreyfus Case*, Wilhelm Herzog, Hans Rehfisch, Play

Dreyfus Case, The *see* **DREYFUS** (1931).

DRIFT FENCE 1936 d: Otho Lovering. USA., *Drift Fence*, Zane Grey, New York 1932, Novel

DRIFTIN' SANDS 1928 d: Wallace Fox. USA., *Fate of the Wolf*, W. C. Tuttle, 1925, Short Story

DRIFTING 1923 d: Tod Browning. USA., *Drifting*, Daisy H. Andrews, John Colton, New York 1910, Play

DRIFTWOOD 1916 d: Marshall Farnum. USA., *Driftwood*, Owen Davis, Play

DRIFTWOOD 1928 d: W. Christy Cabanne. USA., *Driftwood*, Richard Harding Davis, Story

Drill Instructor *see* **THE D.I.** (1957).

DRINK 1917 d: Sidney Morgan. UKN., *L' Assommoir*, Emile Zola, 1877, Novel

Drink *see* **THE FACE ON THE BARROOM FLOOR** (1923).

DRITTE, DER 1972 d: Egon Gunther. GDR., Eberhard Panitz, Short Story

DRIVE, HE SAID 1972 d: Jack Nicholson. USA., *Drive He Said*, Jeremy Larner, 1964, Novel

DRIVE, THE 1997 d: Romy Goulem. CND., *The Drive*, Adam Barken, Play

DRIVEN 1916 d: Maurice Elvey. UKN., *The Evolution of Katherine*, E. Temple Thurston, Play

DRIVEN 1923 d: Charles J. Brabin. USA., *The Flower of the Flock*, Jay Gelzer, 1921, Short Story

Driver's Seat, The *see* **IDENTIKIT** (1974).

DRIVIN' FOOL, THE 1923 d: Robert T. Thornby. USA., *The Drivin' Fool*, William F. Sturm, 1922, Short Story

DRIVING MISS DAISY 1989 d: Bruce Beresford. USA., *Driving Miss Daisy*, Alfred Uhry, 1987, Play

DROGUE DU VICE, LA 1963 d: Jose Benazeraf. FRN., *Le Parfum de la Peur*, Dominique Dorn, Paris 1960, Novel

DROIT DE L'ENFANT, LE 1914 d: Henri Pouctal. FRN., *Le Droit de l'Enfant*, Georges Ohnet, Novel

DROIT DE L'ENFANT, LE 1948 d: Jacques Daroy. FRN., *Le Droit de l'Enfant*, Georges Ohnet, Novel

Drole de Caid, Un *see* **UNE SOURIS CHEZ LES HOMMES** (1964).

DROLE DE DRAME 1937 d: Marcel Carne. FRN., *His First Offence*, J. Storer Clouston, Novel

DROLE DE JEU 1968 d: Pierre Kast. FRN., *Drole de Jeu*, Roger Vailland, 1945, Novel

DROLE DE NUMERO, UN 1933 d: Jean Gourguet. FRN., *Un Drole de Numero*, Georges Dolley, Short Story

DROLE DE PAROISSIEN, UN 1963 d: Jean-Pierre Mocky. FRN., *Deo Gratis*, Michel Servin, Paris 1961, Novel

Droomkoninkje *see* **DIE VOM SCHICKSAL VERFOLGTEN** (1927).

DROP DEAD, DARLING 1966 d: Ken Hughes. UKN., *The Careful Man*, Richard Deming, London 1962, Novel

Drop Dead, My Love *see* **IL MARITO E MIO E L'AMMAZZO QUANDO MI PARE** (1967).

Drops of Blood *see* **IL MULINO DELLE DONNE DI PIETRA** (1960).

D'rossliwirtin, Eusere Soldate-Muetter *see* **MOB 39** (1940).

Drought *see* **VIDAS SECAS** (1963).

Drought, The *see* **BARA** (1981).

DROWNING POOL, THE 1975 d: Stuart Rosenberg. USA., *The Drowning Pool*, Ross MacDonald, Novel

DRUG WARS: THE KIKI CAMARENA STORY, THE 1989 d: Brian Gibson. USA., Elaine Shannon, Book

Drugs Wars: Camerena, The *see* **THE DRUG WARS: THE KIKI CAMARENA STORY** (1989).

DRUGSTORE COWBOY 1989 d: Gus Van Sant Jr. USA., *Drugstore Cowboy*, James Foyle, Novel

DRUHE MLADI 1938 d: Vaclav Binovec. CZC., *Klekani*, Ruzena Utesilova, Novel

DRUM 1976 d: Steve Carver. USA., *Drum*, Kyle Onstott, Novel

Drum Singers, The *see* **GUSHU YIREN** (1987).

DRUM, THE 1924 d: Sinclair Hill. UKN., *The Drum*, F. Britten Austin, 1923, Short Story

DRUM, THE 1938 d: Zoltan KordA. UKN., *The Drum*, A. E. W. Mason, 1937, Novel

Drums *see* **THE DRUM** (1938).

DRUMS ALONG THE MOHAWK 1939 d: John Ford. USA., *Drums Along the Mohawk*, Walter D. Edmonds, Boston/New York 1936, Novel

DRUMS IN THE DEEP SOUTH 1951 d: William Cameron Menzies. USA., *Woman With a Sword*, Hollister Noble, 1948, Book

DRUMS O' VOODOO 1934 d: Arthur Hoerl. USA., *Louisiana*, J. Augustus Smith, New York 1933, Play

Drums of Destiny *see* **DRUMS OF FATE** (1923).

DRUMS OF FATE 1923 d: Charles Maigne. USA., *Sacrifice*, Stephen French Whitman, New York 1922, Novel

DRUMS OF JEOPARDY 1931 d: George B. Seitz. USA., *Drums of Jeopardy*, Harold MacGrath, New York 1920, Novel

DRUMS OF JEOPARDY, THE 1923 d: Eddie Dillon. USA., *Drums of Jeopardy*, Harold MacGrath, New York 1920, Novel

DRUMS OF THE DESERT 1927 d: John Waters. USA., *Desert Bound*, Zane Grey, Story

DRUSILLA WITH A MILLION 1925 d: F. Harmon Weight. USA., *Drusilla With a Million*, Elizabeth Cooper, New York 1916, Novel

DRUZBA PERE KVRZICE 1971 d: Vladimir Tadej. YGS., *Druzba Pere Kvrzice*, Marte Lovrak, Novel

Dry Lives *see* **VIDAS SECAS** (1963).

DRY MARTINI 1928 d: Harry d'Abbadie d'Arrast. USA., *Dry Martini: a Gentleman Turns to Love*, John Thomas, New York 1926, Novel

DRY ROT 1956 d: Maurice Elvey. UKN., *Dry Rot*, John Chapman, London 1954, Play

DRY VALLEY JOHNSON 1917. USA., *Dry Valley Johnson*, O. Henry, Short Story

DRY WHITE SEASON, A 1988 d: Euzhan Palcy. USA., *A Dry White Season*, Andre Brink, 1979, Novel

DSCHUNGEL RUFT, DER 1936 d: Harry Piel. GRM., *Die Buschhexe*, Georg Muhlen-Schulte, Novel

Du Ar Inte Klok Madicken *see* **MADICKEN PA JUNIBACKEN** (1979).

DU BARRY 1915 d: George Kleine. USA., *Du Barry*, David Belasco, New York 1901, Play

DU BARRY 1918 d: J. Gordon Edwards. USA., *Memoirs d'un Medecin*, Alexandre Dumas (pere), Paris 1848, Novel

Du Barry *see* **WOMAN OF PASSION DU BARRY** (1930).

DU BARRY, LA 1914 d: Eduardo BencivengA. ITL., *Du Barry*, David Belasco, New York 1901, Play

DU BARRY WAS A LADY 1943 d: Roy Del Ruth. USA., *Du Barry Was a Lady*, Buddy De Sylva, Herbert Fields, Cole Porter, New York 1939, Musical Play

DU BARRY, WOMAN OF PASSION 1930 d: Sam Taylor. USA., *Du Barry*, David Belasco, New York 1901, Play

DU BIST MUSIK 1956 d: Paul Martin. GRM., Paul H. Rameau, Revue

Du Crepuscule a l'Aube *see* **SOIXANTE-DIX-SEPT RUE CHALGRIN** (1931).

DU DARFST NICHT LANGER SCHWEIGEN 1955 d: R. A. Stemmle. GRM., *Morgen Des Lebens*, Kristman Gudmunsson, Novel

DU GRABUGE CHEZ LES VEUVES 1963 d: Jacques Poitrenaud. FRN/ITL., *Du Grabuge Chez Les Veuves*, Jean-Pierre Ferniere, Novel

DU HAUT EN BAS 1933 d: G. W. Pabst. FRN., *Du Haut En Bas*, Ladislaus Bus-Fekete, Play

DU MEIN STILLES TAL 1955 d: Leonard Steckel. GRM., *Schweigepflicht*, Jacques Companeez, Short Story

DU MOURON POUR LES PETITS OISEAUX 1962 d: Marcel Carne. FRN/ITL., *Du Mouron Pour Les Petits Oiseaux*, Albert Simonin, Novel

DU RIFIFI A PANAMA 1966 d: Denys de La Patelliere. FRN/ITL/GRM., *Du Rififi a Paname*, Auguste le Breton, Paris 1965, Novel

DU RIFIFI CHEZ LES FEMMES 1959 d: Alex Joffe. FRN/ITL., *Du Rififi Chez Les Femmes*, Auguste le Breton, Paris 1957, Novel

DU RIFIFI CHEZ LES HOMMES 1955 d: Jules Dassin. FRN., *Du Rififi Chez Les Hommes*, Auguste le Breton, Novel

Du Sang Dans le Soleil *see* **PROIBITO** (1955).

Du Sang Et Des Roses *see* **ET MOURIR DE PLAISIR** (1960).

DU SANG SOUS LE CHAPITEAU 1956 d: Georges Peclet. FRN., *Du Sang Sous le Chapiteau*, Leopold Massiera, Novel

Du Sollst Nicht Ehebrechen! *see* **THERESE RAQUIN** (1928).

Du the Pour Monsieur Jose *see* **L' INVITE DU MARDI** (1949).

DU UND ICH 1938 d: Wolfgang Liebeneiner. GRM., *Du Und Ich*, Eberhard Frowein, Novel

DUALITY OF MAN, THE 1910. UKN., *The Strange Case of Dr. Jekyll and Mr. Hyde*, Robert Louis Stevenson, London 1886, Novel

DUB, THE 1919 d: James Cruze. USA., *The Dub*, Edgar Franklin, 1916, Short Story

Dubarry *see* **DU BARRY** (1915).

DUBARRY, DIE 1951 d: Georg Wildhagen. GRM., *Die Dubarry*, Karl Millocker, Operetta

Dubarry, La *see* **LA DU BARRY** (1914).

Dubarry, The *see* **I GIVE MY HEART** (1935).

DUBROVSKY 1936 d: Alexander Ivanovsky. USS., *Dubrovsky*, Alexander Pushkin, 1841, Short Story

Dubrowsky *see* **IL VENDICATORE** (1959).

Duca E Forse Una Duchessa, Un *see* **IDILLIO A BUDAPEST** (1941).

DUCHACEK TO ZARIDI 1938 d: Carl Lamac. CZC., *Konto X*, Rudolf Bernauer, Rudolf Osterreicher, Play

Duchacek Will Fix It *see* **DUCHACEK TO ZARIDI** (1938).

Duchess of Benameji *see* **LA DUQUESA DE BENAMEJI** (1949).

DUCHESS OF BUFFALO, THE 1926 d: Sidney A. Franklin. USA., *Sybil*, Max Bordy, Franz Martos, Play

Duchess of Langeais, The *see* **THE ETERNAL FLAME** (1922).

Duchess of Suds, The *see* **SUDS** (1920).

DUCHESSA DEL BAL TABARIN, LA 1917 d: Nino Martinengo. ITL., *La Duchessa Del Bal Tabarin*, Arturo Franci, Carlo Vizzotto, 1916, Opera

Duchessa Di Montefiore, La *see* **INUTILE ATTESA** (1919).

DUCHESSE DE LANGEAIS, LA 1942 d: Jacques de Baroncelli. FRN., *La Duchesse de Langeais*, Honore de Balzac, 1839, Novel

DUCHESSE DES FOLIES-BERGERE, LA 1913 d: Emile Chautard. FRN., *La Duchesse Des Folies-Bergere*, Georges Feydeau, Play

DUCHESSINA 1921 d: Giovanni PezzingA. ITL., *La Duchessina*, Alfredo Testoni, 1903, Play

Duchin Story, The *see* **THE EDDY DUCHIN STORY** (1956).

Duck a la Orange *see* **L' ANATRA ALL'ARANCIA** (1975).

Duck in Orange Sauce *see* **L' ANATRA ALL'ARANCIA** (1975).

Duck Rings at Seven-Thirty, The *see* **DIE ENTE KLINGELT UM ½ ACHT** (1968).

Dud, The *see* **DUDS** (1920).

DUDA, LA 1972 d: Rafael Gil. SPN., *El Abuelo*, Benito Perez Galdos, 1897, Novel

Dude Rancher *see* **COWBOY FROM BROOKLYN** (1938).

DUDE WRANGLER, THE 1930 d: Richard Thorpe. USA., *The Dude Wrangler*, Caroline Lockhart, Garden City, N.Y. 1921, Novel

DUDS 1920 d: Thomas R. Mills. USA., *Duds*, Henry C. Rowland, New York 1920, Novel

DUE COSCIENZE, LE 1916. ITL., *Le Due Coscienze*, Gerolamo Rovetta, 1900, Play

DUE CUORI FELICI 1932 d: Baldassarre Negroni. ITL., *Geschaft Mit Amerika*, Paul Franck, Ludwig Hirschfeld, Play

DUE CUORI FRA LE BELVE 1943 d: Giorgio C. Simonelli. ITL., *Ventimila Leghe Sopra I Mari*, Goffredo d'Andrea, Novel

Due Derelitti Di Valcourt, I *see* **I DERELITTI DI VALCOURT** (1921).

DUE DERELITTI, I 1952 d: Flavio CalzavarA. ITL., *Les Deux Gosses*, Pierre Decourcelle, Novel

Due Dozzine Di Rose Scarlatte *see* **ROSE SCARLATTE** (1940).

DUE ESISTENZE, LE 1920 d: Ugo Falena, Giorgio Ricci. ITL., *La Mia Esistenza d'Acquario*, Pier Maria Rosso Di San Secondo

DUE FOSCARI, I 1942 d: Enrico Fulchignoni. ITL., *The Two Foscari*, George Byron, Play

DUE MADRI, LE 1909. ITL., *Le Due Madri*, Arnaldo Fusinato, Poem

Due Matrimoni *see* **GIOVANNA LA PALLIDA** (1911).

Due Missionari, I *see* **PORGI L'ALTRA GUANCIA** (1974).

DUE OCCHI PER NON VEDERE 1939 d: Gennaro Righelli. ITL., *Due Occhi Per Non Vedere*, Pietro Solari, Play

DUE ORFANELLE, LE 1918 d: Eduardo BencivengA. ITL., *Les Deux Orphelines*, Eugene Cormon, Adolphe-P. d'Ennery, 1874, Novel

DUE ORFANELLE, LE 1942 d: Carmine Gallone. ITL., *Les Deux Orphelines*, Eugene Cormon, Adolphe-P. d'Ennery, 1874, Novel

DUE ORFANELLE, LE 1955 d: Giacomo Gentilomo. ITL/FRN., *Les Deux Orphelines*, Adolphe-P. d'Ennery, 1874, Novel

DUE ORFANELLE, LE 1966 d: Riccardo FredA. ITL/FRN., *Les Deux Orphelines*, Eugene Cormon, Adolphe-P. d'Ennery, 1874, Novel

DUE ORFANELLE, LE 1978 d: Leopoldo SavonA. ITL/FRN., *Les Deux Orphelines*, Eugene Cormon, Adolphe-P. d'Ennery, 1874, Novel

Due Sergenti Al Cordone Sanitario Di Porto Vandre, I *see* **I DUE SERGENTI** (1913).

DUE SERGENTI, I 1909. ITL., *Les Deux Sergents*, B. Daubigny, A. Maillard, 1823, Play

DUE SERGENTI, I 1913 d: Ubaldo Maria Del Colle. ITL., *Les Deux Sergents*, B. Daubigny, A. Maillard, 1823, Play

DUE SERGENTI, I 1936 d: Enrico Guazzoni. ITL., *I Due Sergenti*, Paolo Lorenzini, Novel

Due Sporche Carogne *see* **ADIEU L'AMI** (1968).

DUE TIGRI, LE 1941 d: Giorgio C. Simonelli. ITL., *Le Due Tigri*, Emilio Salgari, 1904, Novel

DUEL 1927 d: Jacques de Baroncelli. FRN., *Duel*, Rene Jeanne, Novel

DUEL 1961 d: Tatyana Berezantseva, Lev Rudnik. USS., *Duel*, Anton Chekhov, 1891, Short Story

DUEL 1971 d: Steven Spielberg. USA., *Duel*, Richard Matheson, Short Story

DUEL AT DIABLO 1966 d: Ralph Nelson. USA., *Apache Rising*, Marvin H. Albert, Greenwich, Ct. 1957, Novel

DUEL DU FOU, LE 1913. FRN., *Le Chercheur de Merveilleux*, Jean-Joseph Renaud

Duel in the Forest *see* **SCHINDERHANNES** (1958).

DUEL IN THE SUN 1946 d: King Vidor, Josef von Sternberg (Uncredited). USA., *Duel in the Sun*, Niven Busch, Novel

Duel la Vodka *see* **ZWEI GIRLS VOM ROTEN STERN** (1966).

DUEL, LE 1939 d: Pierre Fresnay. FRN., *Le Duel*, Henri Lavedan, 1905, Play

DUEL OF HEARTS 1992 d: John Hough. UKN., *Duel of Hearts*, Barbara Cartland, Novel

DUEL SCENE FROM "THE TWO ORPHANS" 1902 d: William Haggar. UKN., *Les Deux Orphelines*, Eugene Cormon, Adolphe-P. d'Ennery, 1874, Novel

Duel, The *see* **POEDINOK** (1957).

Duel, The *see* **PLOKHOY KHOROSHYI CHELOVEK** (1974).

Duel With Death *see* **UND EWIG SINGEN DIE WALDER** (1959).

Duel With God *see* **SOUBOJ S BOHEM** (1921).

DUELLISTS, THE 1977 d: Ridley Scott. UKN., *The Duel*, Joseph Conrad, 1908, Short Story

DUELLO, IL 1914. ITL., *Il Duello*, Paolo Ferrari, 1868

Duels *see* **COUPS DE FEU** (1939).

DUET FOR ONE 1986 d: Andrei Konchalovsky. UKN., *Duet for One*, Tom Kempinski, 1981, Play

DUETT ZU DRITT 1977 d: Gerhard JandA. AUS., *Duett Zu Dritt*, Beatrice Ferrolli, Play

DUFFY OF SAN QUENTIN 1954 d: Walter Doniger. USA., *The San Quentin Story*, Clinton T. Duffy, 1950, Book

Dugi Brodovi *see* **THE LONG SHIPS** (1964).

DUHUL AURULUI 1974 d: Mircea Veroiu, Dan PitA. RMN., *Lada*, Ion Agarbiceanu, 1910, Short Story, *Vilva Bailor*, Ion Agarbiceanu, 1909, Short Story

DUIOS ANASTASIA TRECEA 1979 d: Alexandru Tatos. RMN., *Duios Anastasia Trecea*, Dumitru Radu Popescu, 1967, Short Story

DUIVEL IN AMSTERDAM, DE 1919 d: Theo Frenkel Sr. NTH., *Az Ordog; Vigjatek Harom Felvonasban*, Ferenc Molnar, Budapest 1908, Play

DUKE COMES BACK, THE 1937 d: Irving Pichel. USA., *The Duke Comes Back*, Lucian Cary, Garden City, N.Y. 1933, Novel

DUKE OF CHICAGO 1949 d: George Blair. USA., *The Duke Comes Back*, Lucian Cary, Garden City, N.Y. 1933, Novel

DUKE OF CHIMNEY BUTTE, THE 1921 d: Frank Borzage. USA., *The Duke of Chimney Butte*, George Washington Ogden, Chicago 1920, Novel

DUKE'S JESTER, OR A FOOL'S REVENGE, THE 1909 d: J. Stuart Blackton (Spv) USA., *Le Roi S'amuse*, Victor Hugo, 1832, Play

DUKE'S SON 1920 d: Franklyn Dyall. UKN., *Duke's Son*, Cosmo Hamilton, Novel

DULCE NOMBRE 1951 d: Enrique Gomez Bascuas. SPN., *Dulce Nombre*, Concha Espina de Serna, 1921, Novel

DULCE OLOR A MUERTE, UN 1999 d: Gabriel Retes. MXC/SPN/ARG., *Un Dulce Olor a Muerte*, Guillermo Arriaga, Novel

DULCIMA 1971 d: Frank Nesbitt. UKN., *Dulcima*, H. E. Bates, 1953, Short Story

Dulcimer Street *see* **LONDON BELONGS TO ME** (1948).

DULCINEA 1962 d: Vicente EscrivA. SPN/ITL/GRM., *Dulcinea*, Gaston Baty, Novel

DULCY 1923 d: Sidney A. Franklin. USA., *Dulcy*, Marc Connelly, George S. Kaufman, New York 1921, Play

Dulcy *see* **NOT SO DUMB** (1930).

DULCY 1940 d: S. Sylvan Simon. USA., *Dulcy*, Marc Connelly, George S. Kaufman, New York 1921, Play

DULHAN EK RAAT KI 1967 d: D. D. Kashyap. IND., *Tess of the d'Urbervilles*, Thomas Hardy, London 1891, Novel

DULSCY 1975 d: Jan Rybkowski. PLN., *Moralnosc Pani Dulskiej*, Gabriela Zapolska, 1907, Play

Dulski Family, The *see* **DULSCY** (1975).

DUM NA PREDMESTI 1933 d: Miroslav Cikan. CZC., *Dum Na Predmesti*, Karel Polacek, Novel

DUM ZTRACENEHO STESTI 1927 d: Josef Rovensky. CZC., *Dum Ztraceneho Stesti*, Bohumil Zahradnik-Brodsky, Novel

DUMB GIRL OF PORTICI, THE 1916 d: Lois Weber, Phillips Smalley. USA., *La Muette de Portici*, Daniel Francois Auber, Eugene Scribe, Casimir Delavigne, Paris 1828, Opera

DUMB MAN OF MANCHESTER, THE 1908 d: William Haggar. UKN., *The Dumb Man of Manchester*, B. F. Rayner, London 1837, Play

DUMB WAITER, THE 1989 d: Robert Altman. USA., *The Dumb Waiter*, Harold Pinter, 1960, Play

Dumb Wife, The *see* **YA QI** (1948).

DUMB-BELLS IN ERMINE 1930 d: John G. Adolfi. USA., *Weak Sisters*, Lynn Starling, New York 1925, Play

Dumbelles in Ermine *see* **DUMB-BELLS IN ERMINE** (1930).

DUMBRAVA MINUNATA 1980 d: Gheorghe Naghi. RMN., *Dumbrava Minunata*, Mihail Sadoveanu, 1926, Novel

Dummy in a Circle *see* **GOLEM BEMA'AGAL** (1993).

DUMMY, THE 1917 d: Francis J. Grandon. USA., *The Dummy*, Harriet Ford, Harvey J. O'Higgins, New York 1914, Play

DUMMY, THE 1929 d: Robert Milton. USA., *The Dummy*, Harriet Ford, Harvey J. O'Higgins, New York 1914, Play

DUNAI HAJOS, A 1974 d: Miklos Markos. HNG., *Le Pilote du Danube*, Jules Verne, 1908, Novel

DUNE 1984 d: David Lynch. USA., *Dune*, Frank Herbert, 1965, Novel

D'une Femme a l'Autre *see* **A BUSINESS AFFAIR** (1993).

DUNG CHE SAI DUK 1993 d: Wong Kar-Wai. HKG/CHN., *Dong XIe XI Du*, Jin Yong, Novel

Dungche Saiduk *see* **DUNG CHE SAI DUK** (1993).

DUNIYA KYA HAI 1938 d: G. P. Pawar. IND., *Voskreseniye*, Lev Nikolayevich Tolstoy, Moscow 1899, Novel

DUNIYA NA MANE 1937 d: V. Shantaram. IND., *Na Patnari Goshta*, Narayan Hari Apte, 1923, Novel

DUNJA 1955 d: Josef von Baky. AUS., *Der Postmeister*, Alexander Pushkin, Short Story

Dunkel Bei Tageslicht *see* **NAPPALI SOTETSEG** (1963).

DUNKIRK 1958 d: Leslie Norman. UKN., *The Big Pickup*, Elleston Trevor, Novel

DUNUNGEN 1919 d: Ivan Hedqvist. SWD., *Dunungen*, Selma Lagerlof, 1894, Short Story

DUNUNGEN 1941 d: Weyler Hildebrand. SWD., *Dunungen*, Selma Lagerlof, 1894, Short Story

Dunwich *see* **THE DUNWICH HORROR** (1970).

DUNWICH HORROR, THE 1970 d: Daniel Haller. USA., *The Dunwich Horror*, H. P. Lovecraft, 1933, Short Story

DUO YIN 1963 d: Wang Shaoyan. CHN., *Duo Yin*, Wang Hong, Play

DUPLICITY OF HARGRAVES, THE 1917 d: Thomas R. Mills. USA., *The Duplicity of Hargraves*, O. Henry, 1902, Short Story

DUQUESA DE BENAMEJI, LA 1949 d: Luis LuciA. SPN., *La Duquesa de Benameji*, Antonio Machado Y Ruiz, Manuel Machado Y Ruiz, 1932, Play

Dura Lex *see* **PO ZAKONU** (1926).

DURAND BIJOUTIER 1938 d: Jean Stelli. FRN., *Durand Bijoutier*, Leopold Marchand, Play

DURCH DIE WALDER, DURCH DIE AUEN 1956 d: G. W. Pabst. GRM., *Die Romantische Reise Des Herrn Carl Maria von Weber*, Hans Watzlik, Short Story

DURCHGANGERIN, DIE 1928 d: Hanns Schwarz. GRM., *Die Durchgangerin*, Ludwig Fulda, Play

DURCHLAUCHT RADIESCHEN 1927 d: Richard Eichberg. GRM., *Durchlaucht Radieschen*, Julius Freund, Play

DURCHS WILDE KURDISTAN 1965 d: Franz J. Gottlieb. GRM/SPN., *Durchs Wilde Kurdistan*, Karl Friedrich May, Novel

During Quiet Nights *see* **ZA TICHYCH NOCI** (1940).

DURS A CUIRE, LES 1964 d: Jack Pinoteau. FRN., *Dans Mon Joli Pavillon*, Michel Lebrun, Novel

Dushkal *see* **BARA** (1981).

DUSK TO DAWN 1922 d: King Vidor. USA., *The Shuttle Soul*, Katherine Hill, Story

DUST 1985 d: Marion Hansel. BLG/FRN., *In the Heart of the Country*, J. M. Coetzee, 1977, Novel

DUST BE MY DESTINY 1939 d: Lewis Seiler. USA., *Dust Be My Destiny*, Jerome Odlum, Novel

Dust of Desire *see* **THE SONG OF LOVE** (1923).

DUST OF EGYPT, THE 1915 d: George D. Baker. USA., *The Dust of Egypt*, Alan Campbell, London 1912, Play

DUSTY 1982 d: John Richardson. ASL., *Dusty*, Frank Dalby Davison, Novel

DUSTY ERMINE 1936 d: Bernard Vorhaus. UKN., *Dusty Ermine*, Neil Grant, London 1935, Play

DUTCHMAN 1967 d: Anthony Harvey. UKN., *Dutchman*, Leroi Jones, New York 1964, Play

DUTY AND THE MAN 1913 d: Oscar Apfel. USA., *Duty and the Man*, James Oliver Curwood, Novel

Duty Stronger Than Love *see* **TUSSCHEN LIEFDE EN PLICHT** (1912).

DUVAD 1959 d: Zoltan Fabri. HNG., *Tanyasi Duvad*, Imre Sarkadi, 1953, Short Story

DUVIDHA 1973 d: Mani Kaul. IND., *Duvidha*, Vijaydan Detha, Short Story

DUVOD K ROZVODU 1937 d: Carl Lamac. CZC., *Der Spieler*, Karel Bachmann, Play

DUWATA MAWAKA MISA 1997 d: Sumitra Peries. SLN., *Duwata Mawaka Misa*, G. B. Senanayake, Short Story

DUYEN NGHIEP 1998 d: Nguyen Vu Chau. VTN., *Duyen Nghiep*, Luu Son Minh, Short Story

Dvadcat Dnej Bez Vojny see DVADTSAT DNEI BEZ VOINI (1976).

DVADTSAT DNEI BEZ VOINI 1976 d: Alexei Gherman. USS., *Dvadtsat Dnei Bez Voini*, Konstantin Simonov, 1973, Short Story

DVANACT KRESEL 1933 d: Martin Fric, Michael Waszynski. CZC/PLN., *Dvenadtsat Stulyev*, Ilya Ilf, Evgeny Petrov, Moscow 1928, Novel

DVE MATKY 1920 d: Premysl Prazsky. CZC., *Dve Matky*, Emilie Richebourg, Novel

Dvenadcat Stulev see DVINATSAT STULYEV (1971).

DVENADTSATAYA NOCH 1955 d: Jan Frid. USS., *Twelfth Night*, William Shakespeare, c1600, Play

Dvenadtstat Stulyev see DVINATSAT STULYEV (1971).

DVINATSAT STULYEV 1971 d: Leonid Gaidai. USS., *Dvenadtsat Stulyev*, Ilya Ilf, Evgeny Petrov, Moscow 1928, Novel

DVOJI ZIVOT 1924 d: Vaclav Kubasek. CZC., *Dvoji Zivot*, Vavrinec Rehor, Novel

DVOJI ZIVOT 1939 d: Vaclav Kubasek. CZC., *Dvoji Zivot*, Vavrinec Rehor, Novel

DVORIANSKOE GNEZDO 1969 d: Andrei Konchalovsky. USS., *Dvoryanskoe Gnezdo*, Ivan Turgenev, 1859, Novel

Dvorjanskoe Gnezdo see DVORIANSKOE GNEZDO (1969).

Dvoryanskoye Gnezdo see DVORIANSKOE GNEZDO (1969).

DWAALLICHT, HET 1973 d: Frans Buyens. BLG/NTH., *Het Dwaallicht*, Willem Elsschot, 1947, Short Story

Dwadeset I Tchetiri Tchasa Dyshd see 24 CHASSA DUZHD (1983).

Dwanascie Krzesel see DVANACT KRESEL (1933).

Dweller in the Desert, The see BURNING SANDS (1922).

DWELLING PLACE OF LIGHT, THE 1920 d: Jack Conway. USA., *The Dwelling-Place of Light*, Winston Churchill, New York 1917, Novel

DWELLING PLACE, THE 1990 d: Gavin Millar. UKN., *The Dwelling Place*, Catherine Cookson, Novel

DYADYA VANYA 1971 d: Andrei Konchalovsky. USS., *Dyadya Vanya*, Anton Chekhov, 1899, Play

DYADYUSHKIN SON 1967 d: Konstantin Voinov. USS., *Dyadyushkin Son*, Fyodor Dostoyevsky, 1859, Short Story

DYBBUK 1937 d: Michael Waszynski. PLN., *Der Dibuk*, Solomon an-Ski, 1916, Play

Dybbuk, The see DYBBUK (1937).

Dybbuk, The see HADYBBUK (1968).

DYCKERPOTTS ERBEN 1928 d: Hans Behrendt. GRM., *Dyckerpotts Erben*, Robert Grotzach, Play

DYDEN GAR AMOK 1967 d: Sven Methling. DNM., *Dyden Gar Amok*, Knud Poulsen, Novel

Dying at a Hospital see BYOIN DE SHINU TO IU KOTO (1993).

DYING DETECTIVE, THE 1921 d: Maurice Elvey. UKN., *The Dying Detective*, Arthur Conan Doyle, Short Story

DYING ROOM ONLY 1973 d: Philip Leacock. USA., *Dying Room Only*, Richard Matheson, Short Story

DYING YOUNG 1991 d: Joel Schumacher. USA., *Dying Young*, Marty Leimbach, Novel

DYMKY 1966 d: Vojtech Jasny. CZC/AUS., Ilja Ehrenberg, Short Story

Dynamite see MAN POWER (1927).

Dynamite Girl see LES FEMMES D'ABORD (1962).

Dynamite Man from Glory Jail see FOOLS' PARADE (1971).

Dynasty see JAMES MICHENER'S DYNASTY (1976).

Dzhamilia see JAMILYA (1969).

Dzieci Wodne see THE WATER BABIES (1979).

DZIEJE GRZECHU 1933 d: Henryk Szaro. PLN., *Dzieje Grzechu*, Stefan Zeromski, 1908, Novel

DZIEJE GRZECHU 1975 d: Walerian Borowczyk. PLN., *Dzieje Grzechu*, Stefan Zeromski, 1908, Novel

DZIEWCZETA Z NOWOLIPEK 1938 d: Joseph Leytes. PLN., *Dziewczeta Z Nowolipek*, Pola Gojawiczynska, 1935, Novel

DZIEWCZETA Z NOWOLIPEK 1985 d: Barbara Sass. PLN., *Dziewczeta Z Nowolipek*, Pola Gojawiczynska, 1935, Novel

E ARRIVATO L'ACCORDATORE 1952 d: Duilio Coletti. ITL., *Gonzague*, Pierre Weber, Play

E CADUTA UNA DONNA 1941 d: Alfredo Guarini. ITL., *E Caduta Una Donna*, Milly Dandolo, Novel

E NACHTLANG FUURLAND 1982 d: Clemens Klopfenstein, Remo Legnazzi. SWT., Alex Gfeller, Story

E Perigoso Debrucar-Se see ES PELIGROSO ASOMARSE AL EXTERIOR (1945).

E. Phillips Oppenheim's Midnight Club see MIDNIGHT CLUB (1933).

E SBARCATO UN MARINAIO 1940 d: Piero Ballerini. ITL., *L' Uomo Sull'acqua*, Enrico Bassano, Novel

E TORNATO CARNEVALE 1937 d: Raffaello Matarazzo. ITL., *E Tornato Carnevale*, Guido Cantini, Play

E VENNE UN UOMO 1964 d: Ermanno Olmi. ITL., *John XXIii Il Giornale Dell'Anima E Altri Scritti Di Pieta*, Angelo Roncalli, Roma 1964, Book

EACH DAWN I DIE 1939 d: William Keighley. USA., *Each Dawn I Die*, Jerome Odlum, Indianapolis 1938, Novel

Eager to Live see FEBBRE DI VIVERE (1953).

Eager to Work see RARIN' TO GO (1924).

EAGLE AND THE HAWK, THE 1950 d: Lewis R. Foster. USA., *A Mission for General Houston*, Jess Arnold, Story

EAGLE HAS LANDED, THE 1976 d: John Sturges. UKN., *The Eagle Has Landed*, Jack Higgins, Novel

Eagle Has Two Heads, The see L' AIGLE A DEUX TETES (1948).

EAGLE ISLAND 1987 d: Mats Helge Olsson. SWD., *Eagle Island*, Mats Helge, Novel

EAGLE OF THE SEA, THE 1926 d: Frank Lloyd. USA., *Captain Sazarac*, Charles Tenney Jackson, Indianapolis 1922, Novel

EAGLE ROCK 1964 d: Henry Geddes. UKN., Mary Cathcart Borer, Story

EAGLE SQUADRON 1942 d: Arthur Lubin. USA., *Eagle Squadron*, C. S. Forester, 1942, Short Story

EAGLE, THE 1925 d: Clarence Brown. USA., *Dubrovsky*, Alexander Pushkin, 1841, Short Story

Eagle Warriors see THE YOUNG WARRIORS (1967).

Eagle With Two Heads, The see L' AIGLE A DEUX TETES (1948).

Eagles Fly Early, The see ORLOVI RANO LETE (1966).

EAGLE'S MATE, THE 1914 d: James Kirkwood. USA., *The Eagle's Mate*, Anna Alice Chapin, New York 1914, Novel

EAGLE'S NEST, THE 1915 d: Romaine Fielding. USA., *The Eagle's Nest*, Edwin Arden, New York 1887, Play

EARL OF CHICAGO, THE 1939 d: Richard Thorpe. USA., *The Earl of Chicago*, Brock Williams, New York 1937, Novel

EARL OF PAWTUCKET, THE 1915 d: Harry Myers. USA., *The Earl of Pawtucket*, Augustus Thomas, New York 1903, Play

EARLY BIRD, THE 1936 d: Donovan Pedelty. UKN., *The Early Bird*, J. MacGregor Douglas, Play

Early Cranes see RANNIE ZHURAVLI (1979).

EARLY FROST, AN 1985 d: John Erman. USA., Sherman Yellen, Story

Early Spring see ZAOCHUN ERYUE (1963).

Early Spring see BARNDOMMENS GADE (1986).

EARLY TO WED 1926 d: Frank Borzage. USA., *Splurge*, Evelyn Campbell, 1924, Short Story

Earrings of Madame de., The see MADAME DE. (1953).

Earth see ADAMAH (1947).

Earth see ZEMYA (1957).

EARTH 1998 d: Deepa MehtA. IND/CND., *The Ice-Candy Man*, Bapsy Sidhwa, Novel

Earth Is a Sinful Song, The see MAA ON SYNTINEN LAULAU (1973).

Earth Is Flat, The see JORDEN ER FLAD (1976).

Earth Is Our Sinful Song see MAA ON SYNTINEN LAULAU (1973).

Earth, The see TSUCHI (1939).

EARTHBOUND 1940 d: Irving Pichel. USA., *The Ghost's Story*, Basil King, Story

EARTHLY POSSESSIONS 1999 d: James Lapine. USA., *Earthly Possessions*, Anne Tyler, 1977, Novel

EARTHWORM TRACTORS 1936 d: Ray Enright. USA., William Hazlett Upson, Short Story

EASIEST WAY, THE 1917 d: Albert Capellani. USA., *The Easiest Way*, Eugene Walter, Hartford, Ct. 1908, Play

EASIEST WAY, THE 1931 d: Jack Conway. USA., *The Easiest Way*, Eugene Walter, Hartford, Ct. 1908, Play

EAST IS EAST 1916 d: Henry Edwards. UKN., *East Is East*, Philip Hubbard, Gwendolyn Logan, Play

EAST IS WEST 1922 d: Sidney A. Franklin. USA., *East Is West*, John B. Hymer, Samuel Shipman, Play

EAST IS WEST 1930 d: Monta Bell. USA., *East Is West*, John B. Hymer, Samuel Shipman, Play

EAST LYNNE 1902 d: Dicky Winslow. UKN., *East Lynne*, Mrs. Henry Wood, London 1861, Novel

EAST LYNNE 1910. UKN., *East Lynne*, Mrs. Henry Wood, London 1861, Novel

EAST LYNNE 1912 d: George Nicholls, Theodore Marston. USA., *East Lynne*, Mrs. Henry Wood, London 1861, Novel

EAST LYNNE 1913 d: Arthur Charrington. UKN., *East Lynne*, Mrs. Henry Wood, London 1861, Novel

EAST LYNNE 1913 d: Bert Haldane. UKN., *East Lynne*, Mrs. Henry Wood, London 1861, Novel

EAST LYNNE 1915 d: Travers Vale. USA., *East Lynne*, Mrs. Henry Wood, London 1861, Novel

EAST LYNNE 1916 d: Bertram Bracken. USA., *East Lynne*, Mrs. Henry Wood, London 1861, Novel

EAST LYNNE 1921 d: Hugo Ballin. USA., *East Lynne*, Mrs. Henry Wood, London 1861, Novel

EAST LYNNE 1922. UKN., *East Lynne*, Mrs. Henry Wood, London 1861, Novel

EAST LYNNE 1925 d: Emmett J. Flynn. USA., *East Lynne*, Mrs. Henry Wood, London 1861, Novel

EAST LYNNE 1931 d: Frank Lloyd. USA., *East Lynne*, Mrs. Henry Wood, London 1861, Novel

EAST MEETS WEST 1936 d: Herbert Mason. UKN., *The Lake of Life*, Edwin Greenwood, Play

EAST OF EDEN 1955 d: Elia Kazan. USA., *East of Eden*, John Steinbeck, 1952, Novel

EAST OF EDEN 1982 d: Harvey Hart. USA., *East of Eden*, John Steinbeck, 1952, Novel

EAST OF JAVA 1935 d: George Melford. USA., *Tiger Island*, Gouverneur Morris, New York 1934, Novel

EAST OF LUDGATE HILL 1937 d: Manning Haynes. UKN., *East of Ludgate Hill*, Arnold Ridley, Play

EAST OF PICCADILLY 1939 d: Harold Huth. UKN., *East of Piccadilly*, Gordon Beckles, Novel

East of Shanghai see RICH AND STRANGE (1931).

EAST OF SUEZ 1925 d: Raoul Walsh. USA., *East of Suez*, W. Somerset Maugham, London 1922, Play

East River see UNDER PRESSURE (1935).

EAST SIDE - WEST SIDE 1923 d: Irving Cummings. USA., *East Side - West Side*, Henry Hull, Leighton Graves Osmun, Play

EAST SIDE, WEST SIDE 1927 d: Allan Dwan. USA., *East Side - West Side*, Felix Riesenberg, New York 1927, Novel

EAST SIDE, WEST SIDE 1949 d: Mervyn Leroy. USA., *East Side - West Side*, Marcia Davenport, Novel

Easter Dinner, The see THE PIGEON THAT TOOK ROME (1962).

EASTWARD HO! 1919 d: Emmett J. Flynn. USA., *Eastward Ho!*, William MacLeod Raine, 1919, Serial Story

EASY COME, EASY GO 1928 d: Frank Tuttle. USA., *Easy Come Easy Go*, Owen Davis, New York 1925, Play

Easy Going see ON AGAIN -OFF AGAIN (1937).

EASY MILLIONS 1933 d: Fred Newmeyer. USA., *Good Looking and Rich*, Edgar Franklin, Short Story

EASY MONEY 1934 d: Redd Davis. UKN., *The Ghosts of Mr. Pim*, Basil Mason, Play

EASY MONEY 1948 d: Bernard Knowles. UKN., *Easy Money*, Arnold Ridley, 1947, Play

Easy Money see BESENYE DENGI (1981).

EASY PICKINGS 1927 d: George Archainbaud. USA., *Easy Pickings*, Paul A. Cruger, Play

EASY TO LOVE 1934 d: William Keighley. USA., *As Good As New*, Thompson Buchanan, New York 1930, Play

EASY VIRTUE 1927 d: Alfred Hitchcock. UKN., *Easy Virtue*, Noel Coward, London 1926, Play

Easy Way, The *see* ROOM FOR ONE MORE (1952).

EAT A BOWL OF TEA 1989 d: Wayne Wang. USA., *Eat a Bowl of Tea*, Louis Chu, Novel

Eaten Out of House and Home *see* U SNEDENEHO KRAMU (1933).

Eaten-Up Shop, The *see* U SNEDENEHO KRAMU (1933).

EAU DU NIL, L' 1928 d: Marcel Vandal. FRN., *L' Eau du Nil*, Pierre Frondaie, Novel

Eaux Printanieres, Les *see* ACQUE DI PRIMAVERA (1989).

EAUX PROFONDES 1981 d: Michel Deville. FRN., Patricia Highsmith, Novel

Eaux Saintes du Valais, Les *see* AN HEILIGEN WASSERN (1961).

Eaux Saintes, Les *see* AN HEILIGEN WASSERN (1932).

Eaux Saintes, Les *see* AN HEILIGEN WASSERN (1961).

EAUX TROUBLES, LES 1948 d: Henri Calef. FRN., *Les Eaux Troubles*, Roger Vercel, Short Story

E.B. White's Charlotte's Web *see* CHARLOTTE'S WEB (1973).

EBB TIDE 1915 d: Colin Campbell. USA., *The Ebb Tide; a Trio and Quartette*, Lloyd Osbourne, Robert Louis Stevenson, 1894, Novel

EBB TIDE 1922 d: George Melford. USA., *The Ebb Tide; a Trio and Quartette*, Lloyd Osbourne, Robert Louis Stevenson, 1894, Novel

EBB TIDE 1932 d: Arthur Rosson. UKN., *God Gave Me Twenty Cents*, Dixie Willson, Short Story

EBB TIDE 1937 d: James P. Hogan. USA., *The Ebb Tide; a Trio and Quartette*, Lloyd Osbourne, Robert Louis Stevenson, 1894, Novel

Eboli *see* CRISTO SI E FERMATO A EBOLI (1979).

EBONY TOWER, THE 1987 d: Robert Knights. UKN., *The Ebony Tower*, John Fowles, Novel

EBREO ERRANTE, L' 1912. ITL., *Le Juif Errant*, Eugene Sue, 1845, Novel

EBREO ERRANTE, L' 1916 d: Umberto Paradisi. ITL., *Le Juif Errant*, Eugene Sue, 1845, Novel

EBREO ERRANTE, L' 1947 d: Goffredo Alessandrini. ITL., *Le Juif Errant*, Eugene Sue, 1845, Novel

EBREO FASCISTA, L' 1980 d: Franco Mole. ITL., *L' Ebreo Fascista*, Luigi Preti, Novel

Eccitanti Guerre Di Adeleine, Le *see* A LA GUERRE COMME A LA GUERRE (1971).

ECCO LA FELICITA! 1940 d: Marcel L'Herbier. ITL., *La Comedie du Bonheur*, Fernand Noziere, Play

ECHAPPEMENT LIBRE 1964 d: Jean Becker. FRN/ITL/SPN., *Echappement Libre*, Clet Coroner, Novel

ECHEC AU PORTEUR 1957 d: Gilles Grangier. FRN., *Echec Au Porteur*, Noel Calef, Novel

ECHEC AU ROI 1931 d: Leon d'Usseau, Henri de La Falaise. USA., *The Queen's Husband*, R. E. Sherwood, New York 1928, Play

ECHEC AU ROY 1943 d: Jean-Paul Paulin. FRN., *Echec Au Roy*, Henri Dupuy-Mazuel

Echec d'un Assassin, L' *see* PORTRAIT ROBOT (1960).

Echo of a Shot *see* EKKO AF ET SKUD (1970).

ECHO OF BARBARA 1961 d: Sidney Hayers. UKN., *Echo of Barbara*, Jonathan Burke, Novel

Echo, The *see* YAMA NO OTO (1954).

ECHO, THE 1998 d: Diarmuid Lawrence. UKN., *The Echo*, Minette Walters, Novel

ECHOES IN THE DARKNESS 1987 d: Glenn Jordan. USA., *Echoes in the Darkness*, Joseph Wambaugh, Novel

Echoes of the Jungle *see* THE COOL WORLD (1964).

ECLAIR AU CHOCOLAT 1979 d: Jean-Claude Lord. CND., *Le Voyageur Mort*, Jean Santacroce, Novel

ECOLE DE LA CHAIR, L' 1998 d: Benoit Jacquot. FRN., *L' Ecole de la Chair*, Yukio Mishima, Novel

ECOLE DES COCOTTES, L' 1935 d: Piere Colombier. FRN., *L' Ecole Des Cocottes*, Paul Armont, Marcel Gerbidon, Play

ECOLE DES CONTRIBUABLES, L' 1934 d: Rene Guissart. FRN., *L' Ecole Des Contribuables*, Georges Berr, Louis Verneuil, Play

ECRAN BRISE, L' 1922 d: Raoul d'Auchy. FRN., *L' Ecran Brise*, Henri Bordeaux, Novel

ECUME DES JOURS, L' 1967 d: Charles Belmont. FRN., *L' Ecume Des Jours*, Boris Vian, 1947, Novel

ECUYERE, L' 1922 d: Leonce Perret. FRN., *L' Ecuyere*, Paul Reboux, Novel

ED MCBAIN'S 87TH PRECINCT 1995 d: Bruce Paltrow. USA., *Lightning*, Evan Hunter, Novel

EDDIE AND THE CRUISERS 1984 d: Martin Davidson. USA., *Eddie and the Cruisers*, P. F. Kluge, Novel

EDDIE MACON'S RUN 1983 d: Jeff Kanew. USA., *Eddie MacOn's Run*, James McLendon, Novel

EDDY DUCHIN STORY, THE 1956 d: George Sidney. USA., Leo Katcher, Story

Ede Und Unku *see* ALS UNKU EDES FREUNDIN WAR (1980).

EDELWEISSKONIG, DER 1919 d: Peter Ostermayr. GRM., *Der Edelweisskonig*, Ludwig Ganghofer, Novel

EDELWEISSKONIG, DER 1938 d: Paul May. GRM., *Der Edelweisskonig*, Ludwig Ganghofer, Novel

EDELWEISSKONIG, DER 1957 d: Gustav Ucicky. GRM., *Der Edelweisskonig*, Ludwig Ganghofer, Novel

EDELWEISSKONIG, DER 1975 d: Alfred Vohrer. GRM., *Der Edelweisskonig*, Ludwig Ganghofer, Novel

EDEN END 1981 d: Donald McWhinnie. UKN., *Eden End*, J. B. Priestley, Play

EDERA, L' 1950 d: Augusto GeninA. ITL., *L' Edera*, Grazia Deledda, Novel

EDES ANNA 1958 d: Zoltan Fabri. HNG., *Edes Anna*, Dezso Kosztolanyi, 1926, Novel

Edgar Allan Poe's Castle of Blood *see* DANZA MACABRA (1964).

Edgar Allan Poe's Conqueror Worm *see* WITCHFINDER GENERAL (1968).

Edgar Allan Poe's Masque of the Red Death *see* THE MASQUE OF THE RED DEATH (1989).

Edgar Allan Poe's the Oblong Box *see* THE OBLONG BOX (1969).

EDGAR ET SA BONNE 1914. FRN., *Edgar Et Sa Bonne*, Eugene Labiche, Play

EDGE O'BEYOND 1919 d: Fred W. Durrant. UKN., *Edge O'Beyond*, Gertrude Page, Novel

EDGE OF DARKNESS 1943 d: Lewis Milestone. USA., *Edge of Darkness*, William Woods, Novel

Edge of Divorce *see* BACKGROUND (1953).

EDGE OF DOOM 1950 d: Mark Robson. USA., *Edge of Doom*, Leo Brady, 1949, Novel

EDGE OF FURY 1958 d: Irving Lerner, Robert Gurney Jr. USA., *Wisteria Cottage*, Robert M. Coates, 1948, Novel

Edge of Sanity *see* DR. JEKYLL AND MR. HYDE - A JOURNEY INTO FEAR (1988).

EDGE OF THE CITY 1956 d: Martin Ritt. USA., *A Man Is Ten Feet Tall*, Robert Alan Aurther, 1955, Television Play

Edge of the City *see* THE CITY'S EDGE (1983).

EDGE OF THE LAW 1917 d: Louis W. Chaudet. USA., *A Gentle Ill Wind*, Maude Pettus, 1916, Short Story

EDIPO RE 1910 d: Giuseppe de Liguoro. ITL., *Oedipus Rex*, Sophocles, c420 bc

EDIPO RE 1967 d: Pier Paolo Pasolini. ITL/MRC., *Oedipus Rex*, Sophocles, c420 bc, Play, *Oedipus at Colonus*, Sophocles, 401 bc, Play

Edith's Diary *see* EDITHS TAGEBUCH (1983).

EDITHS TAGEBUCH 1983 d: Hans W. Geissendorfer. GRM., *Edith's Diary*, Patricia Highsmith, 1977, Novel

Edkin Pratidin *see* EK DIN PRATIDIN (1979).

EDLE BLUT, DAS 1927 d: Carl Boese. GRM., *Das Edle Blut*, Ernst von Wildenbruch, Short Story

Edmee *see* LES FEMMES SONT DES ANGES (1952).

Edna Balgarka *see* EDNA BULGARKA (1956).

EDNA BULGARKA 1956 d: Nikolai Borovishki. BUL., *Edna Balgarka*, Ivan Vazov, 1899, Short Story

EDUCANDE DI SAINT-CYR, LE 1941 d: Gennaro Righelli. ITL., *Les Demoiselles de Saint-Cyr*, Alexandre Dumas (pere), Play

EDUCATED EVANS 1936 d: William Beaudine. UKN., *Educated Evans*, Edgar Wallace, 1924, Novel

Educating Girls in Bohemia *see* VYCHOVA DIVEK V CECHACH (1997).

EDUCATING RITA 1983 d: Lewis Gilbert. UKN., *Educating Rita*, Willy Russell, 1981, Play

EDUCATION DE PRINCE 1926 d: Henri Diamant-Berger. FRN., *Education de Prince*, Charles Maurice Donnay, 1895, Play

EDUCATION DE PRINCE 1938 d: Alexander Esway. FRN., *Education de Prince*, Charles Maurice Donnay, 1895, Play

EDUCATION OF ELIZABETH, THE 1921 d: Eddie Dillon. USA., Roy Horniman, Play

EDUCATION OF LITTLE TREE, THE 1997 d: Richard Friedenberg. USA., *The Education of Little Tree*, Forrest Carter, Novel

EDUCATION OF MR. PIPP, THE 1914 d: Augustus Thomas. USA., *The Education of Mr. Pipp*, Charles Dana Gibson, Augustus Thomas, New York 1905, Play

EDUCATION OF NICKY, THE 1921 d: Arthur Rooke. UKN., *The Education of Nicky*, May Wynn, Novel

EDUCATION OF SONNY CARSON, THE 1974 d: Michael Campus. USA., Sonny Carson, Autobiography

Education of Vera, The *see* ANGI VERA (1979).

EDUCATION SENTIMENTALE, L' 1961 d: Alexandre Astruc. FRN/ITL., *L' Education Sentimentale*, Gustave Flaubert, 1869, Novel

EDWARD II 1991 d: Derek Jarman. UKN., *Edward II*, Christopher Marlowe, 1594, Play

EDWARD, MY SON 1948 d: George Cukor. UKN/USA., *Edward My Son*, Noel Langley, Robert Morley, London 1947, Play

Eel, The *see* UNAGI (1997).

EEMI HAGENERALIT 1979 d: Joel Silberg. ISR., *Eemi Hageneralit*, Eli Saagi, Play

EFFECT OF GAMMA RAYS ON MAN-IN-THE-MOON MARIGOLDS, THE 1972 d: Paul Newman. USA., *The Effect of Gamma Rays on Man-in-the-Moon Marigolds*, Paul Zindel, New York 1965, Play

Effets de la Verite, Les *see* WIE D'WARRET WURKT (1933).

Effi Briest *see* ROSEN IM HERBST (1955).

EFFI BRIEST 1970 d: Wolfgang Luderer. GDR., *Effi Briest*, Theodor Fontane, 1894-95, Novel

Effi Briest *see* FONTANE EFFI BRIEST (1974).

EFFICIENCY EDGAR'S COURTSHIP 1917 d: Lawrence C. Windom. USA., *Efficiency Edgar's Courtship*, Clarence Budington Kelland, 1916, Short Story

Effie Briest *see* DER SCHRITT VOM WEGE (1939).

EFFRACTION 1983 d: Daniel Duval. FRN., *Effraction*, Francis Ryck, Novel

EGEN INGANG 1956 d: Hasse Ekman. SWD., *En Dag I Oktober*, Sigurd Hoel, 1931, Novel

EGG AND I, THE 1947 d: Chester Erskine. USA., *The Egg and I*, Betty MacDonald, Novel

Egg, The *see* L' OEUF (1971).

EGI MADAR 1957 d: Imre Feher. HNG., *Egi Madar*, Zsigmond Moricz, 1935, Short Story

EGON, DER FRAUENHELD 1957 d: Hans Albin. GRM., *Der Schone Florian*, Walter Maria Espe, Will Kaufmann, Musical Play

Egon the Ladykiller *see* DER FRAUENHELD EGON (1957).

Egor Bulycov I Drugie *see* YEGOR BULYCHOV I DRUGIYE (1971).

Egor Bulytchev and Others *see* YEGOR BULYCHOV I DRUGIYE (1971).

EGOUTS DU PARADIS, LES 1978 d: Jose Giovanni. FRN., *Les Egouts du Paradis*, Albert Spaggiari, Novel

EGRI CSILLAGOK 1968 d: Zoltan Varkonyi. HNG., *Egri Csillagok*, Geza Gardonyi, 1901, Novel

EGYMASRA NEZVE 1982 d: Karoly Makk. HNG., *Torventen Belul*, Erzsebet Galgoczi, 1980, Novel

EGYPTIAN, THE 1954 d: Michael Curtiz. USA., *Egyptilainen Sinuhe*, Mika Waltari, 1946, Novel

EH JOE! 1986 d: Alan Gilsenan. IRL., *Dis Joe*, Samuel Beckett, 1966, Play

EHE DES HERRN MISSISSIPPI, DIE 1961 d: Kurt Hoffmann. GRM/SWT., *Die Ehe Des Herrn Mississippi*, Friedrich Durrenmatt, Zurich 1952, Play

EHE FUR EINE NACHT 1953 d: Victor Tourjansky. GRM., *Ehe Fur Eine Nacht*, Josef Berger, Franz Seitz Sr., Play

747

EHE IM SCHATTEN 1947 d: Kurt Maetzig. GDR., *Ehe Im Schatten*, Hans Schweikart, Novel

EHE IN DOSEN 1939 d: Johannes Meyer. GRM., *Ehe in Dosen*, Leo Lenz, Ralph Arthur Roberts, Play

EHE IN NOT 1929 d: Richard Oswald. GRM., *La Maitresse Legitime*, Georges Antequil, Book

EHE MAN EHEMANN WIRD 1941 d: Alwin Elling. GRM., *Hochzeitsreise Ohne Mann*, Waldemar Frank, Erwin Kreker, Play

EHEFERIEN 1927 d: Victor Janson. GRM., *Eheringe*, Alexander Engel, Hans Sturm, Play

Ehen Zu Dritt see EHE IN NOT (1929).

EHESANATORIUM 1955 d: Franz Antel. AUS., *Willkommen in Mergenthal*, Hans Bruhl, Play

EHESKANDAL IM HAUSE FROMONT JUN. UND RISLER SEN. 1927 d: Anders W. Sandberg. GRM., *Eheskandal Im Hause from Jun. Und Risler Sen.*, Alphonse Daudet, Novel

EHESTREIK, DER 1953 d: Joe Stockel. GRM., *Ehestreik*, Julius Pohl, Play

EHRENWORT, DAS 1913 d: Emil Albes. GRM., *Das Ehrenwort*, Arthur Zapp, Novel

Eichmann see THE HOUSE ON GARIBALDI STREET (1979).

EID DES STEPHAN HULLER 1, DER 1912 d: Viggo Larsen. GRM., *Der Eid Des Stephan Huller*, Felix Hollaender, Novel

EIGER SANCTION, THE 1975 d: Clint Eastwood. USA., *The Eiger Sanction*, Trevanian, Novel

Eight Against One see SHEMONA B'EKEVOT ACHAT (1964).

EIGHT BELLS 1916 d: John F. Byrne. USA., *Eight Bells*, John F. Byrne, 1891, Play

EIGHT BELLS 1935 d: R. William Neill. USA., *Eight Bells*, Percy G. Mandley, New York 1933, Play

EIGHT IRON MEN 1953 d: Edward Dmytryk. USA., *A Sound of Hunting*, Harry Peter M'nab Brown, New York 1945, Play

EIGHT MEN OUT 1989 d: John Sayles. USA., *Eight Men Out*, Eliot Asinof, Book

Eight to Five see PLAY GIRL (1932).

Eighteen Springs see BUN SANG YUN (1997).

Eighteen Years Old see OSMNACTILETA (1939).

Eighteenth Year, The see VOSEMNADCATYJ GOD (1958).

Eighteen-Year Old Girl see OSMNACTILETA (1939).

Eighth Day of the Week, The see OSMY DZIEN TYGODNIA (1958).

Eighth Wonder of the World, The see KING KONG (1933).

Eight-Thirteen see "813" (1920).

EILEEN OF THE TREES 1928 d: Graham Cutts. UKN., *Eileen of the Trees*, Henry de Vere Stacpoole, Novel

EINBRUCH 1927 d: Franz Osten. GRM., *Emil*, Arthur Landsberger, Novel

EINE REISE IN LICHTS 1978 d: R. W. Fassbinder. GRM., *Otchayanie*, Vladimir Nabokov, 1937, Novel

Einen Jux Will Er Sich machen see EINMAL KEINE SORGEN HABEN (1953).

EINEN JUX WILL ER SICH MACHEN 1957 d: Alfred Stoger. AUS., *Einen Jux Will Er sich machen*, Johann Nestroy, 1844, Play

EINER FRISST DEN ANDEREN 1964 d: Ray Nazarro, Gustav Gavrin. GRM/ITL/USA., *When Strangers Meet*, Robert Bloomfield, New York 1956, Novel

EINER ZUVIEL AN BORD 1935 d: Gerhard Lamprecht. GRM., *Einer Zuviel an Bord*, Fred Andreas, Novel

EINGEBILDETE KRANKE, DER 1952 d: Hans H. Konig. GRM., *Le Malade Imaginaire*, Moliere, 1673, Play

EINHORN, DAS 1978 d: Peter Patzak. GRM., *Das Einhorn*, Martin Walser, 1966, Novel

EINMAL KEINE SORGEN HABEN 1953 d: Georg MarischkA. GRM/AUS., *Einen Jux Will Er Sich machen*, Johann Nestroy, 1844, Play

EINMALEINS DER LIEBE, DAS 1935 d: Carl Hoffmann. GRM., *Einen Jux Will Er Sich machen*, Johann Nestroy, 1844, Play

Eisenerde - Kupferhimmel see GOK BAKIR YER DEMIR (1987).

EISZEIT, DIE 1975 d: Peter Zadek, Tankred Dorst. GRM/NRW., *Pa Gjengrodde Stier*, Knut Hamsun, 1949, Novel

Ej Tha Raja see MARMA YOGI (1951).

EK DIN PRATIDIN 1979 d: Mrinal Sen. IND., *Abiroto Chen Mukh*, Amalendu Chakravarty, Story

EKEL, DAS 1939 d: Hans Deppe. GRM., *Das Ekel*, Toni Impekoven, Hans Reimann, Play

EKKO AF ET SKUD 1970 d: Erik Frohn Nielsen. DNM., *Gertrud*, Erik Aalbaek Jensen, 1956, Novel

EL 1952 d: Luis Bunuel. MXC., *El*, Mercedes Pinto, Novel

EL ATZMI 1988 d: Tamir Paul. ISR., *El Atzmi*, Galila Ron-Feder, Book

EL CHE 1997 d: Maurice Dugowson. FRN/SPN., *Ernesto Guevara, une Legende du Siecle Che*, Pierre Kalfon, Book

EL CID 1961 d: Anthony Mann, Giovanni Paolucci. USA/ITL., *Le Cid*, Pierre Corneille, 1637, Play

El Dorado see ELDORADO (1963).

EL DORADO 1967 d: Howard Hawks. USA., *The Stars in Their Courses*, Harry Peter M'nab Brown, New York 1960, Novel

El Guelmouna, Marchand de Sable see LE MARCHAND DE SABLE (1931).

EL HAKIM 1957 d: Rolf Thiele. GRM., *El Hakim*, John Knittel, Novel

El Super see EL SUPER (1979).

El: This Strange Passion see EL (1952).

Elckerlijc see ELCKERLYC (1975).

ELCKERLYC 1975 d: Jos Stelling. NTH., *Elckerlijc*, Anon, c1485, Play

ELDER BROTHER, THE 1937 d: Frederick Hayward. UKN., *The Elder Brother*, Anthony Gibbs, Novel

ELDER MISS BLOSSOM, THE 1918 d: Percy Nash. UKN., *The Elder Miss Blossom*, Ernest Hendrie, Metcalfe Wood, London 1898, Play

Elder Sister, The see STARSHAYA SESTRA (1967).

ELDORADO 1963 d: Menahem Golan. ISR., *Yigal Mossensohn*, Play

ELEANOR AND FRANKLIN 1976 d: Daniel Petrie. USA., *Eleanor and Franklin*, Joseph P. Lash, Book

ELEANOR AND FRANKLIN: THE WHITE HOUSE YEARS 1977 d: Daniel Petrie. USA., *Eleanor and Franklin*, Joseph P. Lash, Book

ELECTION 1999 d: Alexander Payne. USA., *Election*, Tom Perrotta, 1998, Novel

Elective Affinities see DIE WAHLVERWANDTSCHAFTEN (1974).

Elective Affinities see LE AFFINITA ELETTIVE (1978).

Elector's Woman, The see DIE SCHONE TOLZERIN (1952).

Electra see ELEKTRA (1962).

Electra, My Love see SZERELMEM ELEKTRA (1974).

Electric Grandmother, The see RAY BRADBURY'S THE ELECTRIC GRANDMOTHER (1981).

ELECTRIC HORSEMAN, THE 1979 d: Sydney Pollack. USA., Shelly Burton, Story

Electric Man, The see MAN MADE MONSTER (1941).

Electronic Monster, The see ESCAPEMENT (1957).

Elegy, An see BANKA (1957).

Elegy for a Quarrel see KENKA SEREJII (1966).

Elegy of the North see BANKA (1957).

ELEKTRA 1962 d: Michael Cacoyannis. GRC., *Electra*, Euripides, 413 bc, Play

ELEKTRA 1962 d: Takis Mouzenidis. GRC., *Electra*, Sophocles, c409 bc, Play

ELEKTRA 1970. GRM., *Elektra*, Richard Strauss, Hugo von Hofmannsthal, Dresden 1909, Opera

Elektra see SZERELMEM ELEKTRA (1974).

Elektreia see SZERELMEM ELEKTRA (1974).

ELENI 1985 d: Peter Yates. USA., *Eleni*, Nicholas Gage, Book

Eleni - a Son's Revenge see ELENI (1985).

ELEONORA DUSE 1950 d: Filippo Walter Ratti. ITL., *La Grande Tragica*, Nino Bolla, Book

ELEPHANT BOY 1937 d: Robert Flaherty, Zoltan KordA. UKN., *Toomai of the Elephants*, Rudyard Kipling, 1894, Short Story

Elephant Gun see NOR THE MOON BY NIGHT (1958).

ELEPHANT MAN, THE 1980 d: David Lynch. UKN., *The Elephant Man: a Study in Human Dignity*, Ashley Montagu, Book, *The Elephant Man and Other Reminiscences*, Sir Frederick Treves, Book

ELEPHANT MAN, THE 1981 d: Jack Hofsiss. USA., *The Elephant Man*, Bernard Pomerance, Play

ELEPHANT WALK 1954 d: William Dieterle. USA., *Elephant Walk*, Robert Standish, 1949, Novel

Elephants Never Forget see ZENOBIA (1939).

ELETTRA 1909. ITL., *Electra*, Sophocles, c409 bc., Play

Elevator to the Gallows see L' ASCENSEUR POUR L'ECHAFAUD (1957).

ELEVAZIONE 1920 d: Telemaco Ruggeri. ITL., *L' Elevation*, Henri Bernstein, 1917, Play

ELEVE, L' 1996 d: Olivier Schatzky. FRN., *The Pupil*, Henry James, Short Story

Eleven Harrowhouse see 11 HARROWHOUSE (1974).

Eleven Lives see FROM HELL TO HEAVEN (1933).

Eleven Years and a Day see ELF JAHRE UND EIN TAG (1963).

ELEVENTH COMMANDMENT, THE 1924 d: George A. Cooper. UKN., *The Eleventh Commandment*, Brandon Fleming, Play

Eleventh Commandment, The see JEDENACTE PRIKAZANI (1925).

ELEVENTH COMMANDMENT, THE 1933 d: George Melford, W. Christy Cabanne. USA., *The Pillory*, Brandon Fleming, Short Story

Eleventh Commandment, The see THE SWORD OF GIDEON (1986).

ELEVENTH HOUR, THE 1922 d: George Ridgwell. UKN., *The Eleventh Hour*, Ethel M. Dell, Novel

ELEVENTH HOUR, THE 1923 d: Bernard J. Durning. USA., *The Eleventh Hour*, Lincoln J. Carter, Play

ELF JAHRE UND EIN TAG 1963 d: Gottfried Reinhardt. GRM., Nigel Balchin, Novel

ELI SJURSDOTTER 1938 d: Arne Bornebusch, Leif Sinding. SWD/NRW., *Eli Sjursdotter*, Johan Falkberget, 1913, Novel

Eligible Bachelor, The see ADVENTURES OF SHERLOCK HOLMES: THE ELIGIBLE BACHELOR (1993).

Eliminator, The see DANGER ROUTE (1967).

ELINOR NORTON 1935 d: Hamilton MacFadden. USA., *The State Versus Elinor Norton*, Mary Roberts Rinehart, New York 1934, Novel

Elisa see LA FILLE ELISA (1956).

Elisabeth Reine d'Angleterre see LES AMOURS DE LA REINE ELISABETH (1912).

Elise see FILMEN OG ELISE (1986).

ELISE OU LA VRAIE VIE 1970 d: Michel Drach. FRN/ALG., *Elise Ou la Vraie Vie*, Claire Etcherelli, Novel

ELISIR D'AMORE, L' 1941 d: Amleto Palermi. ITL., *L' Elisir d'Amore*, Gaetano Donizetti, Felice Romani, Opera

ELISIR D'AMORE, L' 1947 d: Mario CostA. ITL., *L' Elisir d'Amore*, Gaetano Donizetti, Milan 1832, Opera

Elite Killer, The see THE STALKING MOON (1969).

ELIXIERE DES TEUFELS, DIE 1973 d: Ralf Kirsten. GDR/CZC., *Die Elixiere Des Teufels*, Ernst Theodor Amadeus Hoffmann, 1815-16, Novel

ELIXIERE DES TEUFELS, DIE 1976 d: Manfred Purzer. GRM., *Die Elixiere Des Teufels*, Ernst Theodor Amadeus Hoffmann, 1815-16, Novel

Elixir of Love, The see L' ELISIR D'AMORE (1941).

Eliza Comes to Stay see DANGEROUS TO MEN (1920).

ELIZA COMES TO STAY 1936 d: Henry Edwards. UKN., *Eliza Comes to Stay*, H. V. Esmond, London 1913, Play

Elizabeth and Essex see THE PRIVATE LIVES OF ELIZABETH AND ESSEX (1939).

Elizabeth of England see DRAKE OF ENGLAND (1935).

ELIZABETH OF LADYMEAD 1949 d: Herbert Wilcox. UKN., *Elizabeth of Ladymead*, Frank Harvey, 1948, Play

Elizabeth the Queen see THE PRIVATE LIVES OF ELIZABETH AND ESSEX (1939).

Ella see MONKEY SHINES: AN EXPERIMENT IN FEAR (1988).

Elle Aime Ca see UN AMORE (1965).

ELLE BOIT PAS, ELLE FUME PAS, ELLE DRAGUE PAS, MAIS. ELLE CAUSE! 1969 d: Michel Audiard. FRN., *Bonne Vie Et Meurtres*, Fred Kassak, Novel

ELLE COURT, ELLE COURT, LA BANLIEUE 1973 d: Gerard Pires. FRN/ITL., *Elle Court Elle Court la Banlieue*, Brigitte Gros, Novel

ELLE ET MOI 1952 d: Guy Lefranc. FRN., *Elle Et Moi*, Jean Duche, Novel

ELLEN FOSTER 1997 d: John Erman. USA., *Ellen Foster*, Kaye Gibbons, Book

ELLERY QUEEN AND THE MURDER RING 1941 d: James P. Hogan. USA., *The Perfect Crime*, Ellery Queen, Story

ELLERY QUEEN: DON'T LOOK BEHIND YOU 1971 d: Barry Shear. USA., *Cat O'Nine Tails (Cat of Many Tales)*, Ellery Queen, Novel

ELLERY QUEEN, MASTER DETECTIVE 1940 d: Kurt Neumann. USA., *Master Detective Ellery Queen*, Ellery Queen, Novel

ELLERY QUEEN'S PENTHOUSE MYSTERY 1941 d: James P. Hogan. USA., *The Penthouse Mystery*, Ellery Queen, Novel

ELLIS ISLAND 1984 d: Jerry London. USA/UKN., *Ellis Island*, Fred Mustard Stewart, Novel

ELLY PETERSEN 1944 d: Alice O'Fredericks, Jon Iversen. DNM., *Elly Petersen*, Mogens Klitgaard, 1941, Novel

ELMER AND ELSIE 1934 d: Gilbert Pratt. USA., *To the Ladies!*, Marc Connelly, George S. Kaufman, New York 1922, Play

ELMER GANTRY 1960 d: Richard Brooks. USA., *Elmer Gantry*, Sinclair Lewis, 1927, Novel

ELMER NO BOKEN 1999 d: Masami HatA. JPN., *My Father's Dragon*, Ruth Stiles Gannett, Book

ELMER THE GREAT 1933 d: Mervyn Leroy. USA., *Elmer the Great*, George M. Cohan, Ring Lardner, New York 1928, Play

Eloi *see* **QUAI NOTRE-DAME** (1960).

ELOISA ESTA DEBAJO DE UN ALMENDRO 1943 d: Rafael Gil. SPN., *Eloisa Esta Debajo de un Almendro*, Enrique Jardiel Poncela, 1943, Play

Eloisa Is Under an Almond Tree *see* **ELOISA ESTA DEBAJO DE UN ALMENDRO** (1943).

ELOKUU 1956 d: Matti KassilA. FNL., *Elokuu*, Frans E. Sillanpaa, 1941, Novel

ELOPE IF YOU MUST 1922 d: C. R. Wallace. USA., *Elope if You Must*, E. J. Rath, Play

Els. Din Naeste! *see* **VERGISS NICHT DEINE FRAU ZU KUSSEN** (1967).

ELSIE VENNER 1914. USA., *Elsie Venner*, Oliver Wendell Holmes, Novel

ELSKERE 1963 d: Nils R. Muller. NRW., *Elskere*, Terje Stigen, 1960, Novel

ELUS DE LA MER, LES 1921 d: Gaston Roudes, Marcel Dumont. FRN., *Les Elus de la Mer*, Georges G. Toudouze, Short Story

Elusive Corporal, The *see* **LE CAPORAL EPINGLE** (1961).

ELUSIVE ISABEL 1916 d: Stuart Paton. USA., *Elusive Isabel*, Jacques Futrelle, Indianapolis 1909, Novel

ELUSIVE PIMPERNEL, THE 1919 d: Maurice Elvey. UKN., *The Elusive Pimpernel*, Baroness Orczy, 1908, Novel

ELUSIVE PIMPERNEL, THE 1950 d: Michael Powell, Emeric Pressburger. UKN., *The Scarlet Pimpernel*, Baroness Orczy, 1905, Novel

ELVERHOJ 1939 d: Sven Methling. DNM., *Elverhoj*, Johan Ludvig Heiberg, 1828, Play

ELVESZETT ILLUZIOK 1983 d: Gyula Gazdag. HNG., *Un Grand Homme de Province a Paris*, Honore de Balzac, 1839, Novel

ELVESZETT PARADICSOM, AZ 1962 d: Karoly Makk. HNG., *Az Elveszett Paradicsom*, Imre Sarkadi, 1962, Play

EMBARRASSMENT OF RICHES, THE 1918 d: Eddie Dillon. USA., *The Embarrassment of Riches*, Louis K. Anspacher, New York 1906, Play

Embassy Girl *see* **HAT CHECK GIRL** (1932).

Embezzled Heaven *see* **DER VERUNTREUTE HIMMEL** (1958).

EMBRASSEZ-MOI 1928 d: Robert Peguy, Max de Rieux. FRN., *Embrassez-Moi*, Tristan Bernard, Yves Mirande, Play

EMBRASSEZ-MOI 1932 d: Leon Mathot. FRN., *Embrassez-Moi*, Tristan Bernard, Yves Mirande, Play

EMBRUJO DE SEVILLA, EL 1930 d: Benito Perojo. SPN/GRM., *El Embrujo de Sevilla*, Carlos Reyles, Novel

EMBRUJO, UN 1998 d: Carlos CarrerA. MXC., *Un Embrujo*, Don Eliseo, Novel

---

EMBUSCADE, L' 1939 d: Fernand Rivers. FRN., *L' Embuscade*, Henri Kistemaeckers, Play

Emerald *see* **CODE NAME: EMERALD** (1985).

EMERALD CITY 1988 d: Michael Jenkins. ASL., *Emerald City*, David Williamson, Play

EMERALD OF THE EAST 1928 d: Jean de Kuharski. UKN., *Emerald of the East*, Jerbanu Kothawala, Novel

Emergency Ward *see* **THE CAREY TREATMENT** (1972).

EMIGRANTI, GLI 1915 d: Gino ZaccariA. ITL., *Gli Emigranti*, Francesco Pastonchi, Novel

Emigrants, The *see* **UTVANDRARNA** (1970).

Emil *see* **EMIL AND THE DETECTIVES** (1935).

Emil and the Detectives *see* **EMIL UND DIE DETEKTIVE** (1931).

EMIL AND THE DETECTIVES 1935 d: Milton Rosmer. UKN., *Emil Und Die Detektive*, Erich Kastner, Berlin 1928, Novel

Emil and the Detectives *see* **EMIL UND DIE DETEKTIVE** (1955).

EMIL AND THE DETECTIVES 1964 d: Peter Tewkesbury. USA/GRM., *Emil Und Die Detektive*, Erich Kastner, Berlin 1928, Novel

EMIL UND DIE DETEKTIVE 1931 d: Gerhard Lamprecht. GRM., *Emil Und Die Detektive*, Erich Kastner, Berlin 1928, Novel

EMIL UND DIE DETEKTIVE 1955 d: R. A. Stemmle. GRM., *Emil Und Die Detektive*, Erich Kastner, Berlin 1928, Novel

EMILE L'AFRICAIN 1947 d: Robert Vernay. FRN., *Le Bouillant Achille*, Paul Nivoix, Play

EMILIA GALOTTI 1913 d: Friedrich Feher. GRM., *Emilia Galotti*, Gotthold Ephraim Lessing, 1772, Play

EMILIA GALOTTI 1958 d: Martin Hellberg. GDR., *Emilia Galotti*, Gotthold Ephraim Lessing, 1772, Play

EMILIA GALOTTI 1968 d: Franz Peter Wirth. GRM., *Emilia Galotti*, Gotthold Ephraim Lessing, 1772, Play

EMILIA, PARADA Y FONDA 1976 d: Angelino Fons. SPN., *Las Ataduras*, Carmen Martin Gaite, 1960, Short Story

EmiliA. Roadside Motel *see* **PARADA Y FONDA EMILIA** (1976).

Emily *see* **THE AMERICANIZATION OF EMILY** (1964).

Emily Bronte's Wuthering Heights *see* **WUTHERING HEIGHTS** (1992).

Emily. Halt and Inn *see* **PARADA Y FONDA EMILIA** (1976).

EMMA 1972 d: John Glenister. UKN., *Emma*, Jane Austen, 1815, Novel

EMMA 1996 d: Diarmuid Lawrence. UKN., *Emma*, Jane Austen, 1815, Novel

EMMA 1996 d: Douglas McGrath. UKN/USA., *Emma*, Jane Austen, 1815, Novel

EMMANUELLE 1974 d: Just Jaeckin. FRN., *Emmanuelle*, Emmanuelle Arsan, Novel

EMMERDEUR, L' 1973 d: Edouard Molinaro. FRN/ITL., *L' Emmerdeur*, Francis Veber, Play

EMMETT STONE 1985 d: Elizabeth Alexander. ASL., *Emmett Stone*, Michael Gurr, Play

EMMY OF STORK'S NEST 1915 d: William Nigh. USA., *Stork's Nest*, John Breckenridge Ellis, New York 1905, Novel

EMPEREUR DES PAUVRES, L' 1921 d: Rene Leprince. FRN., *L' Empereur Des Pauvres*, Felicien Champsaur, Novel

Emperor and a General, The *see* **NIHON NO ICHIBAN NAGAI HI** (1967).

Emperor and the Nightingale, The *see* **CISARUV SLAVIK** (1948).

EMPEROR JONES, THE 1933 d: Dudley Murphy. USA., *The Emperor Jones*, Eugene O'Neill, New York 1920, Play

EMPEROR JONES, THE 1958 d: Ted Kotcheff. UKN., *The Emperor Jones*, Eugene O'Neill, New York 1920, Play

Emperor of Portugal, The *see* **KEJSARN AV PORTUGALLIEN** (1944).

EMPEROR'S CANDLESTICKS, THE 1937 d: George Fitzmaurice. USA., *The Emperor's Candlesticks*, Baroness Orczy, London 1899, Novel

EMPEROR'S NEW CLOTHES, THE 1987 d: David Irving. USA., Hans Christian Andersen, Short Story

Emperor's Nightingale, The *see* **CISARUV SLAVIK** (1948).

Empire Builders, The *see* **IT'S A GREAT LIFE** (1920).

Empire Des Caresses, L' *see* **BEL AMI** (1975).

Empire Des Passions, L' *see* **AI NO BOREI** (1977).

Empire du Diamant, L' *see* **THE EMPIRE OF DIAMONDS** (1920).

EMPIRE DU DIAMANT, L' 1922 d: Leonce Perret. FRN., *L' Empire du Diamant*, Valentin Mandelstamm, Paris 1914, Novel

EMPIRE OF DIAMONDS, THE 1920 d: Leonce Perret. USA., *L' Empire du Diamant*, Valentin Mandelstamm, Paris 1914, Novel

Empire of Passion *see* **AI NO BOREI** (1977).

EMPIRE OF THE ANTS 1977 d: Bert I. Gordon. USA., *Empire of the Ants*, H. G. Wells, 1913, Short Story

EMPIRE OF THE SUN 1987 d: Steven Spielberg. USA., *Empire of the Sun*, J. G. Ballard, 1984, Novel

EMPLOYEE'S ENTRANCE 1933 d: Roy Del Ruth. USA., David Boehm, Play

EMPREINTE DU DIEU, L' 1940 d: Leonide Moguy. FRN., *L' Empreinte du Dieu*, Maxence Van Der Meersch, Novel

EMPREINTE ROUGE, L' 1936 d: Maurice de Canonge. FRN., *La Patte d'Elephant*, Pierre Fallot, Novel

Empress of China, The *see* **DIE KAISERIN VON CHINA** (1953).

Emptied-Out Grocer's Shop, The *see* **U SNEDENEHO KRAMU** (1933).

EMPTY BEACH, THE 1985 d: Chris Thomson. ASL., *The Empty Beach*, Peter Corris, Novel

Empty Canvas, The *see* **LA NOIA** (1964).

EMPTY CRADLE, THE 1923 d: Burton L. King. USA., *Cheating Wives*, Leota Morgan, Story

Empty Dream of Purity *see* **QING XUMENG** (1922).

EMPTY HANDS 1924 d: Victor Fleming. USA., *Empty Hands*, Arthur Stringer, Indianapolis 1924, Novel

EMPTY HEARTS 1924 d: Alfred Santell. USA., *Empty Hearts*, Evelyn Campbell, 1924, Short Story

EMPTY HOLSTERS 1937 d: B. Reeves Eason. USA., *Empty Holsters*, Ed Earl Repp, New York 1936, Novel

EMPTY HOUSE, THE 1921 d: Maurice Elvey. UKN., *The Empty House*, Arthur Conan Doyle, 1903, Short Story

Empty House, The *see* **THE RETURN OF SHERLOCK HOLMES: THE EMPTY HOUSE** (1986).

EMPTY POCKETS 1918 d: Herbert Brenon. USA., *Empty Pockets*, Rupert Hughes, New York 1915, Novel

EMPTY SADDLES 1936 d: Lesley Selander. USA., *Empty Saddles*, Cherry Wilson, Novel

Empty Star, The *see* **LA ESTRELLA VACIA** (1958).

En Avant la Musique *see* **IL CAMBIO DELLA GUARDIA** (1962).

EN BORDEE 1931 d: Henry Wulschleger, Joe Francis. FRN., *En Bordee*, Andre Heuze, Pierre Veber, Play

EN BRAZOS DE LA MUJER MADURA 1997 d: Manuel Lombardero. SPN., *In Praise of Older Women*, Stephen Vizinczey, Novel

EN CADA PUERTO UN AMOR 1931 d: Marcel Silver. USA., *Way for a Sailor*, Albert Richard Wetjen, New York 1928, Novel

EN CAS DE MALHEUR 1958 d: Claude Autant-LarA. FRN/ITL., *En Cas de Malheur*, Georges Simenon, 1956, Novel

En Chair Et En Os *see* **CARNE TREMULA** (1997).

EN DETRESSE 1918 d: Henri Pouctal. FRN., *En Detresse*, Jules Mary, Novel

En Framling Kom Till Garden *see* **VIERAS MIES TULI TALOON** (1938).

EN LAS ENTRANAS DE MADRID 1923 d: Rafael Salvador. SPN., *El Madrid de Los Abuelos*, Pedro de Repide, Novel

En Las Entranas de Babilonia *see* **LAS RUINAS DE BABILONIA** (1959).

EN LOPPE KAN OGSA GO 1997 d: Stellan Olsson. DNM., *En Loppe Kan Ogsa Go*, Jens Pedar Larsen, Novel

EN PLEIN CIRAGE 1961 d: Georges Lautner. FRN/ITL., *Le Sang Des Mattioli*, M. G. Braun, Novel

EN PLEIN COEUR 1998 d: Pierre Jolivet. FRN., *En Cas de Malheur*, Georges Simenon, 1956, Novel

EN PLONGEE 1926 d: Jacques Robert. FRN., *Fragments d'Epaves*, Bernard Frank, Novel

En Vagyok a Falu Rossza Egyedul *see* **A KARD** (1976).

Encajera, La *see* **LA PUNTAIRE** (1928).

ENCHANTED APRIL 1934 d: Harry Beaumont. USA., *Enchanted April*, Elizabeth von Arnim, New York 1923, Novel

ENCHANTED APRIL 1991 d: Mike Newell. UKN., *Enchanted April*, Elizabeth von Arnim, New York 1923, Novel

ENCHANTED BARN, THE 1919 d: David Smith. USA., *The Enchanted Barn*, Grace Livingston Hill Lutz, Philadelphia 1918, Novel

ENCHANTED COTTAGE, THE 1924 d: John S. Robertson. USA., *The Enchanted Cottage*, Arthur Wing Pinero, London 1922, Play

ENCHANTED COTTAGE, THE 1945 d: John Cromwell. USA., *The Enchanted Cottage*, Arthur Wing Pinero, London 1922, Play

Enchanted Grove, The *see* **DUMBRAVA MINUNATA** (1980).

Enchanted Heritage *see* **CAROVNE DEDICTVI** (1985).

ENCHANTED HILL, THE 1926 d: Irvin V. Willat. USA., *The Enchanted Hill*, Peter B. Kyne, New York 1924, Novel

Enchanted House, The *see* **KOUZELNY DUM** (1939).

ENCHANTED ISLAND 1958 d: Allan Dwan. USA., *Typee*, Herman Melville, 1846, Novel

Enchanted Isles, The *see* **LES ILES ENCHANTEES** (1964).

Enchanted Kiss, The *Short Story* (1917) d: David Smith. USA., the Enchanted Kiss, O. Henry

Enchanted Profile, The *Short Story* (1918) d: Martin Justice. USA., the Enchanted Profile, O. Henry

Enchanted Voyage *see* **WAKE UP AND DREAM** (1946).

Enchanting Arabella *see* **BEZAUBERNDES ARABELLA** (1959).

Enchanting House, The *see* **KOUZELNY DUM** (1939).

ENCHANTMENT 1920 d: Einar J. Bruun. UKN., *Enchantment*, E. Temple Thurston, Novel

ENCHANTMENT 1921 d: Robert G. VignolA. USA., *Manhandling Ethel*, Frank R. Adams, 1921, Short Story

ENCHANTMENT 1948 d: Irving Reis. USA., *Take Three Tenses*, Rumer Godden, Novel

Enchantment of Love *see* **DULCINEA** (1962).

Enchantress, The *see* **BYAKUYA NO YOJO** (1958).

ENCORE 1951 d: Harold French, Pat Jackson. UKN., *The Ant & the Grasshopper*, W. Somerset Maugham, 1936, Short Story

ENCORE 1951 d: Anthony Pelissier. UKN., *Gigolo and Gigolette*, W. Somerset Maugham, 1940, Short Story

ENCORE 1951 d: Harold French, Pat Jackson. UKN., *Winter Cruise*, W. Somerset Maugham, 1947, Short Story

Encounter *see* **IMBARCO A MEZZANOTTE** (1952).

Encounter in Salzburg *see* **BEGEGNUNG IN SALZBURG** (1964).

Encounter With Werther *see* **BEGEGNUNG MIT WERTHER** (1949).

End As a Man *see* **THE STRANGE ONE** (1957).

End of a Priest *see* **FARARUV KONEC** (1968).

End of Atlantis *see* **L'AMANTE DELLA CITTA SEPOLTA ANTINEA** (1961).

END OF AUGUST, THE 1981 d: Bob Graham. USA., *The Awakening*, Kate Chopin, 1899, Novel

End of Belle, The *see* **LA MORT DE BELLE** (1961).

End of Desire *see* **UNE VIE** (1958).

End of Old Times, The *see* **KONEC STARYCH CASU** (1989).

End of "Saturn", The *see* **KONYETS "SATURNA"** (1968).

END OF THE AFFAIR, THE 1955 d: Edward Dmytryk. UKN., *The End of the Affair*, Graham Greene, 1951, Novel

End of the Beginning, The *see* **DAS ENDE VOM ANFANG** (1981).

End of the Game *see* **DER RICHTER UND SEIN HENKER** (1976).

END OF THE GOLDEN WEATHER, THE 1992 d: Ian Mune. NZL., *The End of the Golden Weather*, Bruce Mason, Play

End of the Rainbow *see* **NORTHWEST OUTPOST** (1947).

END OF THE RIVER, THE 1947 d: Derek Twist. UKN., *The End of the River*, Desmond Holdridge, Novel

END OF THE ROAD 1944 d: George Blair. USA., Alva Johnston, Article

END OF THE ROAD 1970 d: Aram Avakian. USA., *End of the Road*, John Barth, New York 1958, Novel

END OF THE ROAD, THE 1913 d: William Robert Daly. USA., *Ernest Maltravers*, Edward George Bulwer Lytton, Novel

END OF THE ROAD, THE 1915 d: Thomas Ricketts. USA., *The End of the Road*, H. Grattan Donnelly, Play

END OF THE ROAD, THE 1954 d: Wolf RillA. UKN., *Old Mick-MacK*, James Forsyth, Radio Play

END OF THE TRAIL 1936 d: Erle C. Kenton. USA., *Outlaws of Palouse*, Zane Grey, Short Story

End of the World *see* **THE FLESH AND THE DEVIL, THE WORLD** (1959).

ENDE VOM ANFANG, DAS 1981 d: Helmut Christian Gorlitz. GRM., *Das Ende Vom Angang*, Michael Holzner, Novel

ENDLESS LOVE 1981 d: Franco Zeffirelli. USA., *Endless Love*, Scott Spencer, Novel

ENDLESS NIGHT 1971 d: Sidney Gilliat. UKN., *Endless Night*, Agatha Christie, Novel

Endless Way, The *see* **DER UNENDLICHE WEG** (1943).

Endroit Reve, Un *see* **JUSQU'AU BOUT DU MONDE** (1962).

Endstation Dreizehn Sahara *see* **STATION SIX SAHARA** (1962).

Enduring Flame, The *see* **STEEL PREFERRED** (1926).

ENEK A BUZAMEZOKROL 1947 d: Istvan Szots. HNG., *Enek a Buzamezokrol*, Ferenc Mora, 1927, Novel

Enemies *see* **VRAGI** (1960).

ENEMIES, A LOVE STORY 1989 d: Paul Mazursky. USA., *Di Geschichte Fun a Liebe Sonim*, Isaac Bashevis Singer, 1966, Novel

ENEMIES OF CHILDREN 1923 d: Lillian Ducey, John M. Voshell. USA., *Youth Triumphant*, George Gibbs, New York 1921, Novel

ENEMIES OF WOMEN, THE 1923 d: Alan Crosland. USA., *Los Enemigos de la Mujer*, Vicente Blasco Ibanez, Novel

ENEMIES, THE 1915 d: Harry Davenport. USA., *The Enemies*, Morgan Robertson, Story

Enemies, The *see* **VRAGI** (1938).

Enemy Agent *see* **BRITISH INTELLIGENCE** (1940).

ENEMY AGENTS MEET ELLERY QUEEN 1942 d: James P. Hogan. USA., *The Greek Coffin Mystery*, Ellery Queen, Story

ENEMY BELOW, THE 1957 d: Dick Powell. USA., *The Enemy Below*, D. A. Rayner, 1956, Novel

ENEMY MINE 1985 d: Wolfgang Petersen. USA/GRM., *Enemy Mine*, Barry Longyear, Story

Enemy Mine -Geliebter Feind *see* **ENEMY MINE** (1985).

Enemy of the Class, An *see* **KLASSEN FEIND** (1983).

ENEMY OF THE PEOPLE, AN 1978 d: George Schaefer. USA., *En Folkefiende*, Henrik Ibsen, 1882, Play

Enemy of the People, An *see* **GANASHATRU** (1989).

Enemy Territory *see* **WOMAN AGAINST WOMAN** (1938).

ENEMY, THE 1916 d: Paul Scardon. USA., *The Enemy*, George Randolph Chester, Lillian Chester, New York 1915, Novel

ENEMY, THE 1927 d: Fred Niblo. USA., *The Enemy*, Channing Pollock, New York 1925, Play

Enemy, The *see* **TALK ABOUT A STRANGER** (1952).

Enemy, The *see* **HELL IN THE PACIFIC** (1968).

Enemy, the Sea, The *see* **TAIHEIYO HITORIBOTCHI** (1963).

ENEMY TO SOCIETY, AN 1915 d: Edgar Jones. USA., *A Romance of New York Yesterday and Today*, George Bronson Howard, New York 1911, Novel

ENEMY TO THE KING, AN 1916 d: Frederick A. Thompson. USA., *An Enemy to the King*, Robert N. Stephens, New York 1896, Play

Enemy Within, The *see* **MURDER IN THE AIR** (1940).

ENEMY WITHIN, THE 1994 d: Jonathan Darby. USA., *The Enemy Within*, Charles W. Bailey II, Fletcher Knebel, Novel

ENFANT DE L'AMOUR, L' 1916 d: Emilio Ghione. ITL., *L' Enfant de l'Amour*, Henry Bataille, 1911, Play

ENFANT DE L'AMOUR, L' 1930 d: Marcel L'Herbier. FRN., *L' Enfant de l'Amour*, Henry Bataille, 1911, Play

ENFANT DE L'AMOUR, L' 1944 d: Jean Stelli. FRN., *L' Enfant de l'Amour*, Henry Bataille, 1911, Play

ENFANT DE MA SOEUR, L' 1932 d: Henry Wulschleger. FRN., *L' Enfant de Ma Soeur*, Robert Francheville, Andre Mouezy-Eon, Play

ENFANT DES HALLES, L' 1924 d: Rene Leprince. FRN., *L' Enfant Des Halles*, H. G. Magog, Novel

Enfant du Diable, L' *see* **THE CHANGELING** (1980).

ENFANT DU MIRACLE, L' 1932 d: D. B. Maurice. FRN., *L' Enfant du Miracle*, Robert Charvay, Paul Gavault, Play

Enfant Prodige, L' *see* **LE FEU DE PAILLE** (1939).

ENFANT ROI, L' 1924 d: Jean Kemm. FRN., *L' Enfant-Roi*, Pierre Gilles, Novel

ENFANT SAUVAGE, L' 1970 d: Francois Truffaut. FRN., *Memoire Et Rapport Sur Victor de l'Aveyron*, Jean Itard, Paris 1801-07

Enfants de Choeur, Les *see* **GLI EROI** (1973).

Enfants de la Montagne, Les *see* **KINDER DER BERGE** (1958).

Enfants de Montmartre *see* **ENFANTS DE PARIS** (1924).

ENFANTS DE PARIS 1924 d: Alberto Francis Bertoni. FRN., *Enfants de Paris*, Leon Sazie, Novel

ENFANTS D'EDOUARD, LES 1909 d: Andre Calmettes. FRN., *Les Enfants d'Edouard*, Casimir Delavigne, Play

ENFANTS D'EDOUARD, LES 1914 d: Henri Andreani. FRN., *Les Enfants d'Edouard*, Casimir Delavigne, Play

ENFANTS DU MARAIS, LES 1999 d: Jean Becker. FRN., *Les Enfants du Marais*, Georges Montforez, Novel

ENFANTS TERRIBLES, LES 1949 d: Jean-Pierre Melville. FRN., *Les Enfants Terribles*, Jean Cocteau, 1925, Novel

Enfer Dans la Ville, L' *see* **NELLA CITTA L'INFERNO** (1958).

Enfer du Jeu, L' *see* **L'ENFER DU JEU MACAO** (1939).

Engagement Party, The *see* **LA PETICION** (1976).

Engagement, The *see* **LA PETICION** (1976).

ENGEL, DER SEINE HARFE VERSETZTE, DER 1959 d: Kurt Hoffmann. GRM., *Der Engel Der Seine Harfe Versetzte*, Charles Terrot, Novel

ENGEL MIT DEM FLAMMENSCHWERT, DER 1954 d: Gerhard Lamprecht. GRM., *Der Engel Mit Dem Flammenschwert*, Klaus Hellmer, Novel

ENGEL MIT DEM SAITENSPIEL, DER 1944 d: Heinz Ruhmann. GRM., *Der Engel Mit Dem Saitenspiel*, Alois Johannes Lippl, Novel

ENGEL MIT DER POSAUNE, DER 1948 d: Karl Hartl, Anthony Bushell. AUS/UKN., *Der Engel Mit Der Posaune*, Ernst Lothar, Novel

ENGINEER'S THUMB, THE 1923 d: George Ridgwell. UKN., *The Engineer's Thumb*, Arthur Conan Doyle, Short Story

ENGLAND MADE ME 1972 d: Peter Duffell. UKN/USA/YGS., *England Made Me*, Graham Greene, 1935, Novel

ENGLAND'S WARRIOR KING 1915 d: Eric Williams. UKN., *Henry V*, William Shakespeare, c1598-99, Play

ENGLISCHE HEIRAT, DIE 1934 d: Reinhold Schunzel. GRM., *Die Englische Heirat*, Ludwig von Wohl, Novel

ENGLISH NELL 1900. UKN., *Simon Dale*, Anthony Hope, Novel

ENGLISH PATIENT, THE 1996 d: Anthony MinghellA. USA., *The English Patient*, Michael Ondaatje, Novel

ENGLISH ROSE, THE 1920 d: Fred Paul. UKN., *The English Rose*, Robert Buchanan, George R. Sims, London 1890, Play

ENGLISHMAN'S HOME, AN 1914 d: Ernest G. Batley. UKN., *An Englishman's Home*, Guy Du Maurier, London 1909, Play

ENGLISHMAN'S HOME, AN 1939 d: Albert de Courville. UKN., *An Englishman's Home*, Guy Du Maurier, London 1909, Play

ENGRACADINHA DEPOIS DOS 30 1966 d: J. B. Tanko. BRZ., *Asfalto Selvagem*, Nelson Rodrigues, 1960, Novel

ENHORNINGEN 1955 d: Gustaf Molander. SWD., *Enhorningen*, Sigfrid Siwertz, 1939, Short Story

Enigma *see* **NACH DER MAN SICH SEHNT, DIE FRAU** (1929).

ENIGMA 1982 d: Jeannot Szwarc. UKN/FRN., *Enigma Sacrifice*, Michael Barak, Novel

Enigma de Los Cornell, El *see* **HOTEL DER TOTEN GASTE** (1965).

Enigmatique Gentleman, L' *see* **LE SECRET DE L'EMERALDE** (1936).

ENIGMATIQUE MONSIEUR PARKES, L' 1930 d: Louis J. Gasnier. USA., *Slightly Scarlet*, Percy Heath, Play

ENIGME AUX FOLIES BERGERE 1959 d: Jean Mitry. FRN., *Enigme aux Folies Bergere*, Leo Malet, Novel

ENIGME, L' 1918 d: Jean Kemm. FRN., *L' Enigme*, Paul Hervieu, Play

ENJO 1958 d: Kon IchikawA. JPN., *Kinkaku-Ji*, Yukio Mishima, 1956, Novel

ENLEVEMENT, L' 1912. FRN., *L' Enlevement*, John Lomax, Story

ENLEVEZ-MOI 1932 d: Leonce Perret. FRN., *Par le Bout du Nez*, Henri Hallais, Raoul Praxy, Opera

ENNEMI PUBLIC NO. 2, L' 1983 d: Edouard Niermans. FRN/LXM/SWT., *L' Ennemi Public No. 2*, Gerard Lecas, Novel

ENNEMI SANS VISAGE, L' 1946 d: Maurice Cammage, Robert-Paul Dagan. FRN., *L' Ennemi Sans Visage*, Stanislas-Andre Steeman, Novel

Ennemie, L' *see* **LA TENDRE ENNEMIE** (1935).

ENNEMIS, LES 1961 d: Edouard Molinaro. FRN., *Un Certain Code*, Fred Noro, Novel

Ennui *see* **L' ENNUI** (1998).

Ennui Et Sa Diversion, l'Erotisme, L' *see* **LA NOIA** (1964).

ENNUI, L' 1998 d: Cedric Kahn. FRN., *La Noia*, Alberto Moravia, Milan 1960, Novel

ENOCH ARDEN 1914 d: Percy Nash. UKN., *Enoch Arden*, Alfred Tennyson, 1864, Poem

ENOCH ARDEN 1915 d: W. Christy Cabanne. USA., *Enoch Arden*, Alfred Tennyson, 1864, Poem

ENOCH ARDEN PARTS I & II 1911 d: D. W. Griffith. USA., *Enoch Arden*, Alfred Tennyson, 1864, Poem

Enola Gay *see* **THE MISSION, THE ATOMIC BOMB ENOLA GAY: THE MEN** (1980).

ENOLA GAY: THE MEN, THE MISSION, THE ATOMIC BOMB 1980 d: David Lowell Rich. USA., *Enola Gay*, Max Morgan-Witts, Gordon Thomas, Book

Enormous Changes *see* **ENORMOUS CHANGES AT THE LAST MINUTE** (1983).

ENORMOUS CHANGES AT THE LAST MINUTE 1983 d: Mirra Bank, Ellen Hovde. USA., Grace Paley, Story

Enough Rope *see* **LE MEURTRIER** (1962).

Enquete a l'Italienne *see* **DOPPIO DELITTO** (1977).

Enraged Sheep, The *see* **LE MOUTON ENRAGE** (1974).

ENRICO CARUSO 1951 d: Giacomo Gentilomo. ITL., *Leggenda Napoletana*, Frank Thies, Novel

ENRICO III 1909 d: Giovanni Pastrone?. ITL., *Henry IV*, William Shakespeare, c1597-98, Play

ENRICO IV 1944 d: Giorgio PastinA. ITL., *Enrico IV*, Luigi Pirandello, 1922, Play

ENRICO IV 1984 d: Marco Bellocchio. ITL., *Enrico IV*, Luigi Pirandello, 1922, Play

ENSAYO DE UN CRIMEN 1955 d: Luis Bunuel. MXC., *Ensayo de un Crimen*, Rodolfo Usigli, 1944, Novel

ENSIGN PULVER 1964 d: Joshua Logan. USA., *Mister Roberts*, Thomas Heggen, 1946, Novel

ENSORCELLEMENT DE SEVILLE, L' 1931 d: Benito Perojo. FRN., *El Embrujo de Sevilla*, Carlos Reyles, Novel

ENTE KLINGELT UM ½ ACHT, DIE 1968 d: Rolf Thiele. GRM/ITL., *Die Ente Klingelt Um ½ Acht*, Aage Stenthoft, Novel

ENTENTE CORDIALE 1939 d: Marcel L'Herbier. FRN., *Edouard VII Et Son Temps*, Andre Maurois, 1933, Novel

Enter Inspector Maigret *see* **MAIGRET UND SEIN GROSSTER FALL** (1966).

ENTER LAUGHING 1967 d: Carl Reiner. USA., *Enter Laughing*, Carl Reiner, New York 1958, Novel

ENTER MADAME! 1935 d: Elliott Nugent. USA., *Enter Madame!*, Gilda Archibald, Dolores Donn-Byrne, New York 1920, Play

ENTER MADAME 1922 d: Wallace Worsley. USA., *Enter Madame!*, Gilda Archibald, Dolores Donn-Byrne, New York 1920, Play

ENTERREMENT DE MONSIEUR BOUVET, L' 1981 d: Guy-Andre Lefranc. FRN., *L' Enterrement de Monsieur Bouvet*, Georges Simenon, Novel

ENTERRO DA CAFETINA, O 1971 d: Alberto Pieralisi. BRZ., *O Enterro Da Cafetina*, Marcos Rey, 1967, Novel

ENTERTAINER, THE 1960 d: Tony Richardson. UKN., *The Entertainer*, John Osborne, London 1957, Play

ENTERTAINER, THE 1976 d: Donald Wrye. USA., *The Entertainer*, John Osborne, London 1957, Play

ENTERTAINING MR. SLOANE 1970 d: Douglas Hickox. UKN/AUS., *Entertaining Mr. Sloane*, Joe Orton, London 1964, Play

ENTICEMENT 1925 d: George Archainbaud. USA., *Enticement*, Clive Arden, Novel

Entire Days Among the Trees *see* **DES JOURNEES ENTIERES DANS LES ARBRES** (1976).

ENTITY, THE 1982 d: Sidney J. Furie. USA., *The Entity*, Frank Defilitta, Novel

Entmundigt *see* **LISTEN TO MY STORY** (1974).

ENTOTSU NO MIERU BASHO 1953 d: Heinosuke Gosho. JPN., *Mujakina Hitobito*, Rinzo Shiina, 1952, Novel

Entranas de Madrid, Las *see* **EN LAS ENTRANAS DE MADRID** (1923).

Entre Dios Y El Diablo *see* **C'ERA UNA VOLTA DIO ANCHE NEL WEST** (1968).

Entre Las Redes *see* **MORESQUE OBIETTIVO ALLUCINANTE** (1967).

ENTRE LE DEVOIRET L'HONNEUR 1910 d: Emile Chautard. FRN., *Entre le Devoir Et l'Honneur*, Paul Saunier, Short Story

Entre Nous *see* **COUP DE FOUDRE** (1983).

ENTRE ONZE HEURES ET MINUIT 1948 d: Henri Decoin. FRN., *Entre Onze Heures Et Minuit*, Claude Luxel, Novel

ENTREGA, LA 1954 d: Julian Soler. MXC., *Nada Menos Que Todo un Hombre*, Miguel de Unamuno, 1916, Short Story

Entreintes Suedoises *see* **SEX IN SWEDEN** (1977).

Entrevista, La *see* **LA VISITA** (1963).

Environment *see* **ALIAS THE DOCTOR** (1932).

EPAVE, L' 1949 d: Willy Rozier. FRN., *Chanson Flamenca*, Jean Colet, Novel

EPERVIER, L' 1924 d: Robert Boudrioz. FRN., *L' Epervier*, Francis de Croisset, 1914, Play

EPERVIER, L' 1933 d: Marcel L'Herbier. FRN., *L' Epervier*, Francis de Croisset, 1914, Play

Episode *see* **MY LOVE CAME BACK** (1940).

EPISTLE TO BE LEFT IN THE EARTH 1973 d: John Saxton. CND., *Epistle to Be Left in the Earth*, Archibald McLeish, 1930, Verse

EPISTROFI TIS MIDIAS, I 1968 d: Yan Hristian. GRC., *Medea*, Euripides, 431 bc, Play

Epitaph to My Love *see* **WAGA KOI NO TABIJI** (1961).

Epoch of Murder Madness *see* **SATSUJIN KYO JIDAI** (1967).

Epousez Ma Femme *see* **LES EPOUX SCANDALEUX** (1935).

EPOUX SCANDALEUX, LES 1935 d: Georges Lacombe. FRN., *Les Epoux Scandaleux*, Fortune Paillot, Novel

Equator Tramp, The *see* **WENN DU EINMAL DEIN HERZ VERSCHENKST** (1929).

EQUATORE 1939 d: Gino Valori. ITL., *Equatore*, Alessandro de Stefani, Play

Equinox *see* **NEVJERA** (1953).

Equinox *see* **EQUINOZIO** (1971).

Equinox Flower *see* **HIGANBANA** (1958).

EQUINOZIO 1971 d: Maurizio Ponzi. ITL., *Le Donne Muoiono*, Anna Banti, Novel

EQUIPAGE, L' 1927 d: Maurice Tourneur. FRN., *L' Equipage*, Joseph Kessel, Paris 1923, Novel

EQUIPAGE, L' 1935 d: Anatole Litvak. FRN., *L' Equipage*, Joseph Kessel, Paris 1923, Novel

EQUUS 1977 d: Sidney Lumet. UKN/USA., *Equus*, Peter Shaffer, 1973, Play

ER KANN'S NICHT LASSEN 1962 d: Axel von Ambesser. GRM., G. K. Chesterton, Short Stories

ER MO 1994 d: Zhou XIaowen. CHN/HKG., *Er Mo*, Xu Baoqi, Novel

ER UND SEIN SCHWESTER 1931 d: Carl Lamac. GRM/SWT., *On a Jeho Sestra*, Bernhard Buchbinder, Play

ERAN TRECE 1932 d: David Howard. USA., *Charlie Chan Carries on*, Earl Derr Biggers, Indianapolis 1930, Novel

ERASE UNA VEZ 1950 d: Cirici Pellicer, Josep Escobar. SPN., *Cendrillon*, Charles Perrault, 1697, Short Story

Erasmus With Freckles *see* **DEAR BRIGITTE** (1965).

Erbarmungslose, Der *see* **LA HORSE** (1969).

ERBE, DAS 1913. GRM., *Das Erbe*, Felix Philippi, Play

ERBE VOM PRUGGERHOF, DAS 1956 d: Hans H. Konig. GRM., *Das Starkere Leben*, Oskar Gluth, Novel

ERBE VON BJORNDAL, DAS 1960 d: Gustav Ucicky. AUS., *Das Erbe von Bjorndal*, Trygve Gulbrannssen, Novel

Erbfolgestreit, Ein *see* **SCHWEIGEN IM WALDE 1** (1918).

ERBFORSTER, DER 1944 d: Alois J. Lippl. GRM., *Der Erbforster*, Otto Ludwig, 1853, Play

Erbin Vom Alpenhof, Die *see* **ERDE** (1947).

ERBIN VOM ROSENHOF, DIE 1942 d: Franz Seitz. GRM., *Erbin Vom Rosenhof*, Georg Queri, Play

ERBSCHLEICHER, DIE 1937 d: Hans Deppe. GRM., *Die Erbschleicher*, Hans Alfred Kihn, Play

ERDE 1947 d: Leopold Hainisch. AUS/SWT., *Erde*, Karl Schonherr, 1908, Play

EREDE DI JAGO, L' 1913 d: Alberto Carlo Lolli. ITL., *Meyer l'Ipocrita*, Charles Burlington, Novel

EREDITA DELLO ZIO BUONANIMA, L' 1934 d: Amleto Palermi. ITL., *L' Eredita Dello Zio Canonico*, Antonino Russo-Giusti, Play

EREDITA DELLO ZIO BUONANIMA, L' 1975 d: Alfonso BresciA. ITL., *L' Eredita Dello Zio Buonanima*, Russo Giusti, Play

EREDITA FERRAMONTI, L' 1976 d: Mauro Bolognini. ITL., *L' Eredita Ferramonti*, Gaetano Carlo Chelli, Novel

ERENDIRA 1982 d: Ruy GuerrA. MXC/FRN/GRM., *Innocent Eredira and Her Heartless Grandmother*, Gabriel Garcia Marquez, Novel

ERFINDER, DER 1981 d: Kurt Gloor. SWT., *Der Erfinder*, Hansjorg Schneider, Play

ERGOSTASIO, TO 1981 d: Tasos Psarras. GRC., L. Pavlidis, Novel

ERIC 1975 d: James Goldstone. USA., *Eric*, Doris Lund, Book

Eric Soya's "17" *see* **SYTTEN** (1965).

Erik XIv *see* **KARIN MANSDOTTER** (1954).

ERINNERUNGEN AN DIE ZUKUNFT 1969 d: Harald Reinl. GRM., *Erinnerungen an Die Zukunft*, Erich von Daeniken, 1968, Book

ERKOLCSOS EJSZAKA, EGY 1977 d: Karoly Makk. HNG., *A Voroslampas Haz*, Sandor Hunyady, 1937, Novel

Erl King, The *see* **LE ROI DES AULNES** (1930).

Erlebnisse Einer Grossen Liebe *see* **ICH GLAUBE AN DICH** (1945).

ERLKONIG, DER 1931 d: Peter P. Brauer, Marie-Louise Iribe. GRM., *Der Erlkonig*, Johann Wolfgang von Goethe, 1782, Verse

Ermo *see* **ER MO** (1994).

ERNANI 1911 d: Louis J. Gasnier. ITL., *Ernani*, Victor Hugo, 1830

Ernest Hemingway's the Killers *see* **THE KILLERS** (1964).

Ernest Hemingway's the Old Man and the Sea *see* **THE OLD MAN AND THE SEA** (1990).

ERNEST LE REBELLE 1938 d: Christian-Jaque. FRN., *Ernest le Rebelle*, Jacques Perret, 1937, Novel

ERNEST MALTRAVERS 1914 d: Travers Vale. USA., *Ernest Maltravers*, Edward George Bulwer Lytton, Novel

ERNEST MALTRAVERS 1920 d: Jack Denton. UKN., *Ernest Maltravers*, Edward George Bulwer Lytton, Novel

ERNESTO 1979 d: Salvatore Samperi. ITL/SPN/GRM., *Ernesto*, Umberto Saba, 1975, Novel

Ernste Spiele *see* **VESZELYES JATEKOK** (1979).

EROBERUNG DER ZITADELLE, DIE 1976 d: Bernhard Wicki. GRM., *Die Eroberung Der Zitadelle*, Gunter Herburger, 1972, Short Story

EROE DEL NOSTRO TEMPO, UN 1960 d: Sergio CapognA. ITL., *Un Eroe Del Nostro Tempo*, Vasco Pratolini, Novel

Eroe Della Vandea, L' *see* **LES REVOLTES DE LOMANACH** (1953).

EROI, GLI 1973 d: Duccio Tessari. ITL/FRN/SPN., *Gli Eroi*, Rene Haward, Albert Kantof, Novel

EROICA 1958 d: Andrzej Munk. PLN., *Ucieczka*, Jerzy Stefan Stawicki, 1958, Short Story, *Wegrzy*, Jerzy Stefan Stawicki, 1956, Short Story

Eroica - Polen 44 *see* EROICA (1958).

Eroismo Di Ketty, L' *see* PICCOLO MARTIRI (1917).

ERSCHEINEN PFLICHT 1983 d: Helmut DziubA. GDR., *Erscheinen Pflicht*, Gerhard Holtz-Baumert, Novel

Erste Liebe *see* DIE SEXTANERIN (1936).

ERSTE LIEBE 1970 d: Maximilian Schell. GRM/SWT/UKN., *Pervaya Lyubov*, Ivan Turgenev, 1860, Short Story

ERSTE POLKA, DIE 1978 d: Klaus Emmerich. GRM., *Die Erste Polka*, Horst Bienek, 1975, Novel

ERSTWHILE SUSAN 1919 d: John S. Robertson. USA., *Erstwhile Susan*, Marian de Forest, New York 1916, Play, *Barnabetta*, Helen R. Martin, New York 1914, Novel

ERZAHL MIR NICHTS 1964 d: Dietrich Haugk. GRM., *Erzahl Mir Nichts*, Jo Hanns Rosler, Novel

ERZHERZOG JOHANNS GROSSE LIEBE 1950 d: Hans Schott-Schobinger. AUS., *Erzherzog Johanns Grosse Liebe*, Hans Gustl Kernmayr, Novel

ES FING SO HARMLOS AN 1944 d: Theo Lingen. GRM., *Es Fing So Harmlos an*, Franz Gribitz, Play

ES FLUSTERT DIE NACHT. 1929 d: Victor Janson. GRM., *Es Flustert Die Nacht.*, Guido Kreutzer, Short Story

ES GEHT UM MEIN LEBEN 1936 d: Richard Eichberg. GRM., *Der Schweigende Mund*, Oskar Jensen, Novel

ES GESCHAH AM HELLICHTEN TAG 1958 d: Ladislao VajdA. GRM/SWT/SPN., *Das Versprechen*, Friedrich Durrenmatt, Zurich 1958, Novel

Es Geschah Am See *see* A PATTERN OF ROSES (1983).

Es Hilft Nicht, Wo Gewalt Herrscht *see* WO GEWALT HERRSCHT" NICHT VERSOHNT ODER "ES HILFT NUR GEWALT (1965).

ES IST NICHT LEICHT, EIN GOTT ZU SEIN 1988 d: Peter Fleischmann. GRM/USS/FRN., *Arkadij Strugatzki*, Boris Strugatsky, Novel

ES KOMMT EIN TAG 1950 d: Rudolf Jugert. GRM., *Korporal Mombour*, Ernst Penzoldt, 1941, Short Story

ES LEBE DIE LIEBE 1944 d: Erich Engel. GRM., *Das Ratsel Manuela*, Anna Elisabeth Weirauch, Novel

ES MI HOMBRE 1928 d: Carlos Fernandez CuencA. SPN., *Es Mi Hombre!*, Carlos Amiches, Play

ES PELIGROSO ASOMARSE AL EXTERIOR 1945 d: Alejandro Ulloa, Arthur Duarte. SPN/PRT., *Es Peligroso Asomarse Al Exterior*, Enrique Jardiel Poncela, 1944, Play

Esame Di Giuda *see* TEMPO DI ROMA (1964).

Esbrouffeur, L' *see* VOUS SEREZ MA FEMME (1932).

Escadrille *see* THE WOMAN I LOVE (1937).

ESCADRILLE DE LA CHANCE, L' 1937 d: Max de Vaucorbeil. FRN., *L' Escadrille Amoureuse*, Jean-Michel Renaitour, Novel

ESCALE A ORLY 1955 d: Jean Dreville. FRN/GRM., *Escale a Orly*, Curt Riess, Novel

ESCALIER C 1984 d: Jean-Charles TacchellA. FRN., *Escalier C*, Elvire Murail, Novel

ESCANDALO, EL 1943 d: Jose Luis Saenz de HerediA. SPN., *El Escandalo*, Pedro Antonio de Alarcon, 1875, Novel

ESCANDALO, EL 1963 d: Javier Seto. SPN., *El Escandalo*, Pedro Antonio de Alarcon, 1875, Novel

Escapade *see* ONE EXCITING ADVENTURE (1934).

ESCAPADE 1955 d: Philip Leacock. UKN., *Escapade*, Roger MacDougall, London 1953, Play

ESCAPADE 1957 d: Ralph Habib. FRN., *Cendrillon Et Les Gangsters*, Cornell Woolrich, Novel

Escapades of Eva, The *see* EVA TROPI HLOUPOSTI (1939).

ESCAPE 1930 d: Basil Dean. UKN., *Escape*, John Galsworthy, London 1926, Play

ESCAPE 1940 d: Mervyn Leroy. USA., *Escape*, Ethel Vance, Boston 1939, Novel

ESCAPE 1948 d: Joseph L. Mankiewicz. UKN., *Escape*, John Galsworthy, London 1926, Play

Escape *see* UTEK (1967).

ESCAPE 1980 d: Robert Michael Lewis. USA., *Escape*, Barbara Worker, Dwight Worker, Book

ESCAPE ARTIST, THE 1982 d: Caleb Deschanel. USA., *The Escape Artist*, David Wagoner, 1965, Novel

Escape at Dawn *see* RED SKY AT MORNING (1944).

Escape By Night *see* CLASH BY NIGHT (1963).

ESCAPE FROM ALCATRAZ 1979 d: Don Siegel. USA., *Escape from Alcatraz*, J. Campbell Bruce, Novel

Escape from Bataan *see* THE LONGEST HUNDRED MILES (1967).

Escape from Hell Island *see* THE MAN IN THE WATER (1963).

Escape from Love *see* THE LADY ESCAPES (1937).

ESCAPE FROM SOBIBOR 1987 d: Jack Gold. UKN/USA/YGS., *Escape from Sorbibor*, Richard Rashke, Book

Escape from Taiga *see* LIEBESNACHTE IN DER TAIGA (1967).

Escape from Yesterday *see* LA BANDERA (1935).

ESCAPE FROM ZAHRAIN 1962 d: Ronald Neame. USA., *Appointment in Zahrain*, Michael Barrett, London 1960, Novel

ESCAPE IN THE DESERT 1945 d: Edward A. Blatt, Robert Florey (Uncredited). USA., *The Petrified Forest*, R. E. Sherwood, New York 1935, Play

ESCAPE ME NEVER 1935 d: Paul Czinner. UKN., *Escape Me Never*, Margaret Kennedy, London 1933, Play

ESCAPE ME NEVER 1947 d: Peter Godfrey. USA., *Escape Me Never*, Margaret Kennedy, London 1933, Play

Escape of Princess Charming, The *see* PRINCESS CHARMING (1934).

Escape of the Amethyst *see* YANGTSE INCIDENT (1957).

Escape Route to Marseilles *see* FLUCHTWEG NACH MARSEILLE (1977).

ESCAPE, THE 1914 d: D. W. Griffith. USA., *The Escape*, Paul Armstrong, New York 1913, Play

ESCAPE, THE 1926 d: Edwin Greenwood. UKN., *The Escape*, E. F. Parr, Play

ESCAPE, THE 1928 d: Richard Rosson. USA., *The Escape*, Paul Armstrong, New York 1913, Play

ESCAPE TO BURMA 1955 d: Allan Dwan. USA., *Bow Tamely to Me*, Kenneth Perkins, Story

Escape to London *see* THE WITNESS VANISHES (1939).

Escape to Nowhere *see* LE SILENCIEUX (1972).

ESCAPEMENT 1957 d: Montgomery Tully. UKN., *Escapement*, Charles Eric Maine, Novel

ESCLAVAS DE LA MODA 1931 d: David Howard. USA., *On Your Back*, Rita Weiman, 1930, Short Story

Esclaves Existent Toujours, Les *see* LE SCHIAVE ESISTONO ANCORA (1964).

ESCORT WEST 1958 d: Francis D. Lyon. USA., Steven Hayes, Short Story

Esecutore Oltre la Legge *see* LES SEINS DE GLACE (1974).

ESERCITO DI SCIPIONE, L' 1978 d: Giuliana Berlinguer. ITL., Giuseppe d'Agata, Novel

ESFINGE MARAGATA, LA 1948 d: Antonio Obregon. SPN., *La Esfinge Maragata*, Concha Espina de Serna, 1914, Novel

ESHET HAGIBOR 1963 d: Peter Frye. ISR., Margot Klausner, Story

ESKAPADE 1936 d: Erich Waschneck. GRM., *Eskapade*, Richard Henry Savage, Novel

ESKIMO 1933 d: W. S. Van Dyke. USA., *Die Flucht Ins Weisse Land*, Peter Freuchen, 1929, Book, *Storfanger*, Peter Freuchen, 1927, Book

ESLI ETO NE LYUBOVTO TCHTO ZHE.? 1974 d: Daria GurinA. USS., *Metel'*, Alexander Pushkin, 1831, Short Story

ESMERALDA 1915 d: James Kirkwood. USA., *Esmeralda*, Frances Hodgson Burnett, 1877, Short Story

ESMERALDA 1922 d: Edwin J. Collins. UKN., *Notre-Dame de Paris*, Victor Hugo, Paris 1831, Novel

Esmeralda Comes By Night *see* ESMERALDA DE NOCHE VIENES (1997).

ESPION, L' 1966 d: Raoul J. Levy. FRN/GRM., *L' Espion*, Paul Thomas, Paris 1965, Novel

ESPION, LEVE-TOI 1981 d: Yves Boisset. FRN., *Espion Leve-Toi*, George Markstein, Novel

ESPIONAGE 1937 d: Kurt Neumann. USA., *Espionage*, Walter Hackett, London 1935, Play

ESPIONNE, L' 1923 d: Henri Desfontaines. FRN., *Dora*, Victorien Sardou, Paris 1877, Play

Espions Dans la Ville, Les *see* AGENCY (1979).

ESPIONS, LES 1957 d: Henri-Georges Clouzot. FRN/ITL., *Le Vertige de Minuit*, Egon Hostovsky, Novel

ESPIRITISMO 1961 d: Benito Alazraki. MXC., *The Monkey's Paw*, W. W. Jacobs, 1902, Short Story

ESPOIR 1939 d: Andre Malraux. FRN/SPN., *L' Espoir*, Andre Malraux, 1937, Novel

ESPOIRS 1940 d: Willy Rozier. FRN., *Romeo Und Julia Auf Dem Dorfe*, Gottfried Keller, Braunschweig 1865, Short Story

ESPRIT DU MAL, L' 1954 d: Jean-Yves Bigras. CND., *L' Esprit du Mal*, Henry Deyglun, Play

ESPRIT ES-TU LA 1917 d: Fernand Rivers. FRN., *Esprit Es-Tu la*, Georges Arnold, Play

ESSE RIO QUE EU AMO 1961 d: Carlos Hugo Christensen. BRZ., *Noite de Almirante*, Joaquim Maria Machado de Assis, 1884, Short Story

Estado Civil: Martha *see* MARTA (1971).

Estampas de Ayer *see* IL ROMANZO DI UN GIOVANE POVERO (1958).

ESTATE CON SENTIMENTO, UN' 1970 d: Roberto B. ScarsellA. ITL., *Un' Estate Con Sentimento*, John Harwey, Novel

ESTHER REDEEMED 1915 d: Sidney Morgan. UKN., *The Wolf Wife*, Arthur Bertram, Play

Esther, Ruth & Jennifer *see* NORTH SEA HIJACK (1980).

ESTHER WATERS 1948 d: Ian Dalrymple, Peter Proud. UKN., *Esther Waters*, George Moore, 1894, Novel

ESTOUFFADE A LA CARAIBE 1966 d: Jacques Besnard. FRN/ITL., *Estouffade a la Caraibe*, Albert Conroy, Novel

ESTRELA SOBE, A 1974 d: Bruno Barreto. BRZ., *A Estrela Sobe*, Marques Rebelo, 1939, Novel

Estrella Negra *see* LA FRUTA AMARGA (1931).

ESTRELLA VACIA, LA 1958 d: Emilio Gomez Muriel. MXC., *La Estrella Vacia*, Luis Spota, Mexico City 1950, Novel

ESTRELLAS, LAS 1927 d: Luis R. Alonso. SPN., *Las Estrellas*, Carlos Arniches, Play

ESTUDIANTES Y MODISTILLAS 1927 d: Juan Antonio Cabero. SPN., *Estudiantes Y Modistillas*, Antonio Casero, Play

ET LA FEMME CREA L'AMOUR 1964 d: Fabien Collin. FRN., *La Puissance du Baiser*, Pierre Sabatier, Novel

ET L'ON REVIENT TOUJOURS 1917 d: Fernand Rivers. FRN., *Et l'On Revient Toujours*, Camille Medal, Short Story

ET MOI J'TE DIS QU'ELLE T'A FAIT D' L'OEIL 1950 d: Maurice Gleize. FRN., *Et Moi J'te Dis Qu'elle T'a Fait de l'Oeil*, Maurice Hennequin, Play, *Et Moi - J'te Dis Qu'elle T'a Fait de l'Oeil*, Pierre Veber, Play

ET MOI, J'TE DIS QU'ELLE T'A FAIT DE L'OEIL 1935 d: Jack Forrester. FRN., *Et Moi J'te Dis Qu'elle T'a Fait de l'Oeil*, Maurice Hennequin, Play, *Et Moi - J'te Dis Qu'elle T'a Fait de l'Oeil*, Pierre Veber, Play

ET MOURIR DE PLAISIR 1960 d: Roger Vadim. FRN/ITL., *Carmilla*, Sheridan le Fanu, London 1872, Short Story

Et Vient le Jour de Vengeance *see* BEHOLD A PALE HORSE (1964).

ETA CRITICA, L' 1921 d: Amleto Palermi. ITL., *Die Siebzehnjahrigen*, Max Dreyer, 1904, Play

ETA DEL MALESSERE, L' 1968 d: Giuliano Biagetti. ITL., *L' Eta Del Malessere*, Dacia Maraini, Turin 1963, Novel

Etang Tragique, L' *see* SWAMP WATER (1941).

ETAPPENHASE, DER 1937 d: Joe Stockel. GRM., *Der Etappenhase*, Karl Bunje, Play

ETAPPENHASE, DER 1956 d: Wolfgang Becker. GRM., *Der Etappenhase*, Karl Bunje, Play

ETE DE LA SAINT-MARTIN, L' 1920 d: Georges Champavert. FRN., *L' Ete de la Saint-Martin*, Ludovic Halevy, Henri Meilhac, Play

ETE D'ENFER, UN 1984 d: Michael Schock. FRN/SPN., Jean-Pierre Thomacini, Story

ETE MEURTRIER, UN 1983 d: Jean Becker. FRN., *L' Ete Meurtrier*, Sebastien Japrisot, Novel

ETEENPAIN-ELAMAAN 1939 d: Toivo Sarkka. FNL., *Justina*, Hella Wuolijoki, 1937, Novel

ETERNAL CITY, THE 1915 d: Edwin S. Porter, Hugh Ford. USA., *The Eternal City*, Hall Caine, London 1901, Novel

ETERNAL CITY, THE 1923 d: George Fitzmaurice. USA., *The Eternal City*, Hall Caine, London 1901, Novel

ETERNAL FLAME, THE 1922 d: Frank Lloyd. USA., *La Duchesse de Langeais*, Honore de Balzac, 1839, Novel

ETERNAL FOOLS 1930 d: Sidney M. Goldin. USA., *Ewige Naranim*, H. Kalmonowitz, Play

Eternal Generation, The *see* **ONNA NO SONO** (1954).

Eternal Husband, The *see* **L' HOMME AU CHAPEAU ROND** (1946).

ETERNAL LOVE 1929 d: Ernst Lubitsch. USA., *Der Konig Der Bernina*, Jakob Christoph Heer, Stuttgart 1900, Novel

Eternal Lover *see* **UNSTERBLICHE GELIEBTE** (1951).

ETERNAL MAGDALENE, THE 1919 d: Arthur Hopkins. USA., *The Eternal Magdalene*, Robert H. McLaughlin, New York 1915, Play

Eternal Mask, The *see* **DIE EWIGE MASKE** (1935).

ETERNAL MOTHER, THE 1917 d: Frank Reicher. USA., *Red Horse Hill*, Sidney McCall, Boston 1909, Novel

ETERNAL SIN, THE 1917 d: Herbert Brenon. USA., *Lucrece Borgia*, Victor Hugo, Paris 1833, Play

ETERNAL STRUGGLE, THE 1923 d: Reginald Barker. USA., *The Law-Bringers*, G. B. Lancaster, New York 1913, Novel

ETERNAL WOMAN, THE 1929 d: John P. McCarthy. USA., *The Wildcat*, Wellyn Totman, Story

Eternel Mensonge *see* **LA FILLE AU FOUET** (1952).

Eternite Pour Nous, L' *see* **LE CRI DE LA CHAIR** (1963).

Eternity for Us *see* **LE CRI DE LA CHAIR** (1963).

ETES-VOUS FIANCEE A UN MARIN GREC OU A UN PILOTE DE LIGNE? 1970 d: Jean Aurel. FRN/ITL., *La Marche du Fou*, Henriette Jelinck, Novel

ETES-VOUS JALOUSE? 1937 d: Henri Chomette. FRN., *Jalouse*, Alexandre Bisson, A. Leclerq, Play

ETHAN FROME 1992 d: John Madden. USA., *Ethan Frome*, Edith Wharton, 1911, Novel

ETHEL FUE UNA MUJER INGENUA 1926 d: Alfonso de Benavides. SPN., *Ethel Fue Una Mujer Ingenua*, Alfonso de Benavides, Novel

ETI. TRI VERNYE KARTY 1988 d: Alexandr Orlov. USS., *Pikovaya Dama*, Alexander Pushkin, 1834, Short Story

ETIENNE 1933 d: Jean Tarride. FRN., *Etienne*, Jacques Deval, 1930, Play

ETIENNE BRULE GIBIER DE POTENCE 1952 d: Melburn E. Turner. CND., *Etienne Brule - Immortal Scoundrel*, J. Herbert Cranston, Book

ETOILE DU NORD, L' 1982 d: Pierre Granier-Deferre. FRN., *Le Locataire*, Georges Simenon, 1934, Novel

ETOILE DU SUD, L' 1918 d: Michel-Jules Verne. FRN., *L' Etoile du Sud le Pays de Diamants*, Jules Verne, Paris 1884, Novel

Etoile du Sud, L' *see* **THE SOUTHERN STAR** (1969).

Etot Grustnyj Veselyj Cirk *see* **SALTIMBANCII** (1981).

ETRANGE AFFAIRE, UNE 1981 d: Pierre Granier-Deferre. FRN., *Une Etrange Affaire*, Jean-Marc Roberts, Novel

ETRANGE AVENTURE DU DOCTEUR WORKS, L' 1921 d: Robert Saidreau. FRN., *La Porte Close*, Robert Francheville, Novel

ETRANGE DESTIN 1945 d: Louis Cuny. FRN., *Gisele Et Son Destin*, Madame A. de Lacombe, Short Story

ETRANGE FIANCEE, L' 1930 d: Georges Pallu. FRN., *The System of Doctor Tarr and Professor Feather*, Edgar Allan Poe, 1845, Short Story

Etrange Madame Clapain, L' *see* **LE SECRET DE MADAME CLAPAIN** (1943).

ETRANGE MONSIEUR STEVE, L' 1957 d: Raymond Bailly. FRN., *La Revanche Des Mediocres*, Marcel G. Pretre, Novel

Etrange Mort de Monsieur Crauqual, L' *see* **LES GOSSES MENENT L'ENQUETE** (1946).

Etranger, L' *see* **LO STRANIERO** (1967).

ETRANGERE, L' 1917 d: Georges Pallu. FRN., *Deux Femmes*, Charles Foley, Novel

ETRANGERE, L' 1930 d: Gaston Ravel. FRN., *L' Etrangere*, Alexandre Dumas (fils), 1877, Play

ETRANGERS, LES 1968 d: Jean-Pierre Desagnat. FRN/ITL/GRM., *L' Oraison du Plus Fort*, Andre Lay, Novel

Etsi Esvise I Agapi Mas *see* **IL RELITTO** (1961).

Ett Brott *see* **ETT BROTT** (1940).

ETTORE FIERAMOSCA 1915 d: Umberto Paradisi. ITL., *Ettore Fieramosca O la Disfida Di Barletta*, Massimo d'Azeglio, 1833, Novel

ETTORE FIERAMOSCA 1938 d: Alessandro Blasetti. ITL., *Ettore Fieramosca O la Disfida Di Barletta*, Massimo d'Azeglio, 1833, Novel

ETTORE FIERAMOSCA, OVVERO LA DISFIDA DI BARLETTA 1909 d: Ernesto Maria Pasquali. ITL., *Ettore Fieramosca O la Disfida Di Barletta*, Massimo d'Azeglio, 1833, Novel

ETTORE LO FUSTO 1972 d: Enzo G. Castellari, Pasquale Festa Campanile. ITL/FRN/SPN., *Il Re Dei Mimiduti*, Viard, Zacharias, Novel

Etudiant Etranger, L' *see* **THE FOREIGN STUDENT** (1994).

EUGENE ARAM 1914 d: Edwin J. Collins. UKN., *Eugene Aram*, Edward George Bulwer Lytton, London 1832, Novel

EUGENE ARAM 1915 d: Richard Ridgely. USA., *Eugene Aram*, Edward George Bulwer Lytton, London 1832, Novel

EUGENE ARAM 1924 d: Arthur Rooke. UKN., *Eugene Aram*, Edward George Bulwer Lytton, London 1832, Novel

EUGENE GRANDE 1960 d: Sergei Alexeyev. USS., *Eugene Grandet*, Honore de Balzac, 1833, Novel

EUGENE WRAYBURN 1911. USA., *Our Mutual Friend*, Charles Dickens, London 1864, Novel

EUGENIA GRANDET 1947 d: Mario Soldati. ITL., *Eugenie Grandet*, Honore de Balzac, 1833, Novel

EUGENIA GRANDET 1952 d: Emilio Gomez Muriel. MXC., *Eugenie Grandet*, Honore de Balzac, 1833, Novel

EUGENIA GRANDET 1977 d: Pilar Miro. SPN., *Eugenie Grandet*, Honore de Balzac, 1833, Novel

Eugenie *see* **EUGENIE. THE STORY OF HER JOURNEY INTO PERVERSION** (1970).

Eugenie de Franval *see* **EUGENIE. THE STORY OF HER JOURNEY INTO PERVERSION** (1970).

Eugenie de Sade *see* **EUGENIE. THE STORY OF HER JOURNEY INTO PERVERSION** (1970).

EUGENIE GRANDET 1910 d: Emile Chautard. FRN., *Eugenie Grandet*, Honore de Balzac, 1833, Novel

Eugenie Grandet *see* **EUGENIA GRANDET** (1977).

EUGENIE. THE STORY OF HER JOURNEY INTO PERVERSION 1970 d: Jesus Franco. UKN/SPN/GRM., *La Philosophie Dans le Boudoir*, Donatien Sade, Paris 1795, Novel

EUREKA 1982 d: Nicolas Roeg. USA/UKN., *Who Killed Sir Harry Oakes?*, Marshall Houts, Book

EUROPA, EUROPA 1991 d: Agnieszka Holland. GRM/FRN., Salomon Perel, Memoirs

EUROPAISCHES SKLAVENLEBEN 1912 d: Emil Justitz. GRM., *Europaisches Sklavenleben*, Friedrich Wilhelm von Hacklander, Novel

EUROPEANS, THE 1979 d: James Ivory. UKN., *The Europeans*, Henry James, 1878, Novel

EUTANASIA DI UN AMORE 1978 d: Enrico Maria Salerno. ITL., *Eutanasia Di un Amore*, Giorgio Saviane, Novel

EVA 1919 d: Ivo Illuminati. ITL., *Eva*, Giovanni Verga

EVA 1935 d: Johannes Riemann. AUS., *Eva*, Franz Lehar, Operetta

EVA 1962 d: Joseph Losey, Guidarino Guidi. FRN/ITL., *Eve*, James Hadley Chase, London 1945, Novel

Eva, Das Fabriksmadel *see* **EVA** (1935).

Eva Fools Around *see* **EVA TROPI HLOUPOSTI** (1939).

EVA IN SEIDE 1928 d: Carl Boese. GRM., *Nuttchen*, Ernst Klein, Novel

Eva Is Fooling *see* **EVA TROPI HLOUPOSTI** (1939).

Eva Plays the Fool *see* **EVA TROPI HLOUPOSTI** (1939).

Eva (the Devil's Woman) *see* **EVA** (1962).

Eva the Fifth *see* **THE GIRL IN THE SHOW** (1929).

EVA TROPI HLOUPOSTI 1939 d: Martin Fric. CZC., *Eva Tropi Hlouposti*, Fan Vavrincova, Novel

EVADEE, L' 1928 d: Henri Menessier. FRN., *Le Secret de Delia*, Victorien Sardou, Play

EVANGELINE 1911. USA., *Evangeline*, Henry Wadsworth Longfellow, 1847, Poem

EVANGELINE 1913 d: E. P. Sullivan, William H. Cavanaugh. CND., *Evangeline*, Henry Wadsworth Longfellow, 1847, Poem

---

EVANGELINE 1919 d: Raoul Walsh. USA., *Evangeline*, Henry Wadsworth Longfellow, 1847, Poem

EVANGELINE 1929 d: Edwin Carewe. USA., *Evangeline*, Henry Wadsworth Longfellow, 1847, Poem

EVANGELIST, THE 1915 d: Barry O'Neil. USA., *The Evangelist*, Henry Arthur Jones, New York 1907, Play

EVAS TOCHTER 1928 d: Carl Lamac. GRM/CZC., *Princ Z Ulice*, Stanislav Kolar, Novel

Evasion, The *see* **LA DEROBADE** (1979).

Evasive Peace *see* **CAST A GIANT SHADOW** (1966).

Evaso, L' *see* **LE VEUVE COUDERC** (1971).

Eve *see* **EVA** (1962).

EVE IN EXILE 1919 d: Burton George. USA., *Eve in Exile*, Cosmo Hamilton, Novel

EVE KNEW HER APPLES 1945 d: Will Jason. USA., *Night Bus*, Samuel Hopkins Adams, 1933, Short Story

EVE OF ST. MARK, THE 1944 d: John M. Stahl. USA., *The Eve of St. Mark*, Maxwell Anderson, 1942, Play

EVELYN PRENTICE 1934 d: William K. Howard. USA., *Evelyn Prentice*, W. E. Woodward, New York 1933, Novel

Even a French Marriage *see* **LE TONNERRE DE DIEU** (1965).

EVEN AS EVE 1920 d: B. A. Rolfe, Chester M. de Vonde. USA., *The Shining Band*, Robert W. Chambers, London 1901, Novel

Even in the West There Was God Once Upon a Time *see* **C'ERA UNA VOLTA DIO ANCHE NEL WEST** (1968).

EVENING CLOTHES 1927 d: Luther Reed. USA., *L' Homme En Habit*, Yves Mirande, Andre Picard, Paris 1922, Play

EVENING IN BYZANTIUM 1978 d: Jerry London. USA., *Evening in Byzantium*, Irwin Shaw, Novel

EVENING STAR, THE 1996 d: Robert Harling. USA., *The Evening Star*, Larry McMurtry, Novel

EVENINGS FOR SALE 1932 d: Stuart Walker. USA., *Widow's Evening*, I. A. R. Wylie, 1931, Short Story

EVENSONG 1934 d: Victor Saville. UKN., *Evensong*, Beverly Nichols, Novel

Event, An *see* **DOGADJAJ** (1969).

EVER SINCE EVE 1934 d: George Marshall. USA., *The Heir to the Hoorah*, Paul Armstrong, New York 1905, Play

EVERGREEN 1934 d: Victor Saville. UKN., *Ever Green*, Benn W. Levy, London 1930, Play

EVERGREEN 1984 d: Fielder Cook. USA., *Evergreen*, Belva Plain, Novel

Everlasting Innocence *see* **DEN KRONISKE USKYLD** (1985).

EVERLASTING SECRET FAMILY, THE 1987 d: Michael Thornhill. ASL., *The Everlasting Secret Family & Other Secrets*, Frank Moorhouse, Book

EVERLASTING WHISPER, THE 1925 d: John G. Blystone. USA., *The Everlasting Whisper*, Jackson Gregory, New York 1922, Novel

EVER-OPEN DOOR, THE 1920 d: Fred Goodwins. UKN., *The Ever Open Door*, H. H. Herbert, George R. Sims, London 1913, Play

Every Day's a Holiday *see* **L' ORO DI NAPOLI** (1954).

Every Girl for Herself *see* **BRIDES ARE LIKE THAT** (1936).

EVERY LITTLE CROOK AND NANNY 1972 d: Cy Howard. USA., *Every Little Crook and Nanny*, Evan Hunter, 1972, Novel

Every Man's Woman *see* **UNA ROSA PER TUTTI** (1967).

Every Night a Different Bed *see* **JEDE NACHT IN EINEM ANDERN BETT** (1957).

Every Other Inch a Lady *see* **DANCING CO-ED** (1939).

EVERY SATURDAY NIGHT 1936 d: James Tinling. USA., *Let's Get Together*, Katharine Kavanaugh, Hollywood 1935, Play

Every Sunday *see* **FRANCISKA VASARNAPJAI** (1997).

Every Woman's Life *see* **MY BILL** (1938).

Everybody and Nobody *see* **VSICHKI I NIKOY** (1978).

EVERYBODY DOES IT 1949 d: Edmund Goulding. USA., *Career in C Major*, James M. Cain, 1938, Short Story

Everybody Was Very Nice *see* **HONOR AND BEHAVE LOVE** (1938).

EVERYBODY WINS 1990 d: Karel Reisz. UKN/USA., *Some Kind of Love Story*, Arthur Miller, Play

EVERYBODY'S ALL-AMERICAN 1988 d: Taylor Hackford. USA., *Everybody's All American*, Frank Deford, Novel

EVERYBODY'S GIRL 1918 d: Tom Terriss. USA., *Brick Dust Row*, O. Henry, 1906, Short Story

EVERYBODY'S OLD MAN 1936 d: James Flood. USA., *Adopted Father*, Edgar Franklin, 1916, Short Story

Everyman *see* JEDERMANN (1961).

Everyman *see* ELCKERLYC (1975).

Everyman's Woman *see* UNA ROSA PER TUTTI (1967).

Everyone Dies Alone *see* JEDER STIRBT FUR SICH ALLEIN (1976).

EVERYONE'S CHILD 1996 d: Tsitsi DsangarembgA. ZIM., Shimmer Chinodya, Short Story

Everyone's Lover *see* WANREN QINGFU (1996).

EVERYTHING BUT THE TRUTH 1920 d: Eddie Lyons, Lee Moran. USA., *Everything But the Truth*, Edgar Franklin, 1919, Short Story

EVERYTHING IS THUNDER 1936 d: Milton Rosmer. UKN., *Everything Is Thunder*, Jocelyn Hardy, Novel

Everything Must Go *see* ALLES MOET WEG (1997).

Everything Will Be Better Tomorrow *see* MORGEN IST ALLES BESSER (1948).

EVERYWOMAN 1919 d: George Melford. USA., *Everywoman*, Walter Browne, New York 1911, Play

EVE'S DAUGHTER 1916 d: L. C. MacBean. UKN., *When Love Dies*, Rathmell Wilson, Novel

EVE'S DAUGHTER 1918 d: James Kirkwood. USA., *Eve's Daughter*, Alice Ramsey, New York 1917, Play

Eve's Daughters *see* EVAS TOCHTER (1928).

EVE'S LEAVES 1926 d: Paul Sloane. USA., *Eve's Leaves*, Harry Chapman Ford, New York 1925, Play

EVE'S LOVER 1925 d: Roy Del Ruth. USA., *Eve's Lovers*, W. K. Clifford, 1924, Short Story

EVE'S SECRET 1925 d: Clarence Badger. USA., *The Moon-Flower*, Zoe Akins, Lajos Biro, New York 1924, Play

EVIDENCE 1915 d: Edwin August. USA., *Evidence*, Jean Du Rocher MacPherson, New York 1914, Play

EVIDENCE 1929 d: John G. Adolfi. USA., *Evidence*, MacPherson, Jean Du Rocher, New York 1914, Play

Evidence in Camera *see* HEADLINE SHOOTER (1933).

Evidence in Concrete *see* LE DOS AU MUR (1958).

Evidence of Love *see* A KILLING IN A SMALL TOWN (1990).

EVIGE EVA, DEN 1953 d: Rolf Randall. NRW., *Korset*, Sigbjorn Obstfelder, 1896, Novel

Evil Angel, The *see* UM ANJO MAU (1972).

Evil Angels *see* A CRY IN THE DARK (1988).

Evil Come, Evil Go *see* THE YELLOW CANARY (1963).

Evil Eden *see* LA MORT EN CE JARDIN (1956).

Evil Fingers *see* GIORNATA NERA PER L'ARIETE (1971).

Evil Love *see* EL AMOR BRUJO (1967).

Evil Mind, The *see* THE CLAIRVOYANT (1935).

Evil of Eden *see* LA MORT EN CE JARDIN (1956).

Evil Spell *see* MALEFICES (1961).

Evil Spirits *see* MALEFICES (1961).

Evil That Is Eve, The *see* UNE MANCHE ET LA BELLE (1957).

EVIL THAT MEN DO, THE 1983 d: J. Lee Thompson. USA/MXC., *The Evil That Men Do*, R. Lance Hill, Novel

EVIL UNDER THE SUN 1982 d: Guy Hamilton. UKN., *Evil Under the Sun*, Agatha Christie, Novel

EVIL WOMEN DO, THE 1916 d: Rupert Julian. USA., *La Clique Doree*, Emile Gaboriau, Paris 1871, Novel

Evils of Chinatown *see* CONFESSIONS OF AN OPIUM EATER (1962).

Evils of Dorian Gray, The *see* IL DIO CHIAMATO DORIAN (1970).

EVITA 1996 d: Alan Parker./USA., *Evita*, Tim Rice, Andrew Lloyd Webber, Musical Play

EVREISKOIE SCHASTIE 1925 d: Alexis Granowsky. USS., Shalom Aleichem, Story

Ewige Luge, Die *see* DAS GEHEIMNIS VOM BERGSEE (1951).

EWIGE MASKE, DIE 1935 d: Werner Hochbaum. AUS/SWT., *Die Ewige Maske*, Leo Lapaire, Zurich 1934, Novel

Ewige Naranim *see* ETERNAL FOOLS (1930).

EWIGE QUELL, DER 1939 d: Fritz Kirchhoff. GRM., *Der Ewige Quell*, Johannes Linke, Novel

EWIGE TRAUM, DER 1934 d: Arnold Fanck. GRM., *Der Ewige Traum*, Karl Ziak, Novel

Ewige Verrat, Der *see* DER JUDAS VON TIROL (1933).

EX, THE 1996 d: Mark L. Lester. CND., *The Ex*, John Lutz, Novel

EXALTED FLAPPER, THE 1929 d: James Tinling. USA., *The Exalted Flapper*, Will Irwin, 1925, Short Story

Examples Work Wonders *see* PRIKLADY TAHNOU (1939).

EX-BAD BOY 1931 d: Vin Moore. USA., *The Whole Town's Talking*, John Emerson, Anita Loos, New York 1923, Play

EXCALIBUR 1981 d: John Boorman. UKN/USA., *Le Morte d'Arthur*, Sir Thomas Malory, 1485, Verse

Except for Me and Thee *see* FRIENDLY PERSUASION (1975).

EXCESS BAGGAGE 1928 d: James Cruze. USA., *Excess Baggage*, John Wesley McGowan, New York 1927, Play

EXCESS BAGGAGE 1933 d: Redd Davis. UKN., *Excess Baggage*, H. M. Raleigh, Novel

EXCHANGE OF WIVES, AN 1925 d: Hobart Henley. USA., *Exchange of Wives*, Cosmo Hamilton, New York 1919, Play

Excite Me *see* IL TUO VIZIO E UNA STANZA CHIUSA E SOLO IO NE HO LE CHIAVI (1972).

EXCITERS, THE 1923 d: Maurice Campbell. USA., *The Exciters*, Martin Brown, Story

EXCLUSIVE 1937 d: Alexander Hall. USA., *The Roaring Girl*, John C. Moffitt, Los Angeles 1937, Play

EXCLUSIVE RIGHTS 1926 d: Frank O'Connor. USA., *Invisible Government*, Jerome N. Wilson, Story

EXCUSE ME 1916 d: Henry W. Savage. USA., *Excuse Me*, Rupert Hughes, New York 1911, Play

EXCUSE ME 1924 d: Alf Goulding. USA., *Excuse Me*, Rupert Hughes, New York 1911, Play

EXCUSE MY DUST 1920 d: Sam Wood. USA., *The Bear-Trap*, Byron Morgan, 1919, Short Story

Execrable Destiny of Guillemette Babin, The *see* LE DESTIN EXECRABLE DE GUILLEMETTE BABIN (1948).

Execution of Infantryman Kudrna, The *see* JMENEM JEHO VELICENSTVA (1928).

EXECUTION OF PRIVATE SLOVIK, THE 1974 d: Lamont Johnson. USA., *The Execution of Private Slovik*, William Bradford Huie, Book

EXECUTION, THE 1985 d: Paul Wendkos. USA., *The Execution*, Oliver Crawford, Novel

Executioner on the High Seas, The *see* IL GIUSTIZIERE DEI MARI (1962).

Executioner on the Seas, The *see* IL GIUSTIZIERE DEI MARI (1962).

Executioner, The *see* LADY IN THE DEATH HOUSE (1944).

Executioner's Song, The *see* THE EXECUTIONER'S SONG -THE GARY GILMORE STORY (1982).

EXECUTIONER'S SONG -THE GARY GILMORE STORY, THE 1982 d: Lawrence Schiller. USA., *The Executioner's Song*, Norman Mailer, 1979, Book

EXECUTIVE SUITE 1954 d: Robert Wise. USA., *Executive Suite*, Cameron Hawley, 1952, Novel

EX-FLAME 1930 d: Victor Hugo Halperin. USA., *East Lynne*, Mrs. Henry Wood, London 1861, Novel

EXILE 1917 d: Maurice Tourneur. USA., *An Out Post of Empire Exile*, Dolf Wyllarde, New York 1916, Novel

EXILE 1993 d: Paul Cox. ASL., *Priest Island*, E. L. Grant Watson, Novel

Exile, An *see* I WALK THE LINE (1970).

EXILE, THE 1931 d: Oscar Micheaux. USA., *The Conquest*, Oscar Micheaux, Short Story

EXILE, THE 1947 d: Max Ophuls. USA., *His Majesty the King*, Cosmo Hamilton, Novel

EXILES, THE 1923 d: Edmund Mortimer. USA., *The Exiles*, Richard Harding Davis, 1894, Short Story

Ex-Mistress *see* MY PAST (1931).

EXODUS 1960 d: Otto Preminger. USA., *Exodus*, Leon Uris, 1958, Novel

Exorcism at Midnight *see* NAKED EVIL (1966).

EXORCIST III: THE LEGION 1990 d: William Peter Blatty. USA., *Legion*, William Peter Blatty, Novel

EXORCIST, THE 1973 d: William Friedkin. USA., *The Exorcist*, William Peter Blatty, Novel

Expedition, The *see* ABHIJAN (1962).

EXPENSIVE WOMEN 1931 d: Hobart Henley. USA., *Expensive Women*, Wilson Collison, New York 1931, Novel

EXPERIENCE 1921 d: George Fitzmaurice. USA., *Experience; a Morality Play of Today*, George V. Hobart, New York 1915, Novel

EXPERIMENT 1943 d: Martin Fric. CZC., *Experiment*, Karel Matej Capek-Chod, Novel

Experiment in Evil *see* LE TESTAMENT DU DR. CORDELIER (1959).

Experiment in Murder *see* KRONVITTNET (1989).

EXPERIMENT IN TERROR 1962 d: Blake Edwards. USA., *Operation Terror*, Gordon Gordon, Mildred Gordon, New York 1961, Novel

EXPERIMENT PERILOUS 1944 d: Jacques Tourneur. USA., *Experiment Perilous*, Margaret Carpenter, Novel

EXPERIMENT, THE 1922 d: Sinclair Hill. UKN., *The Experiment*, Ethel M. Dell, Novel

EXPERIMENTAL MARRIAGE 1919 d: Robert G. VignolA. USA., *Saturday to Monday*, William Hurlbut, New York 1917, Play

EXPERT, THE 1932 d: Archie Mayo. USA., *Old Man Minick*, Edna Ferber, 1922, Short Story

EXPIATION 1922 d: Sinclair Hill. UKN., *Expiation*, E. Phillips Oppenheim, London 1887, Novel

Expiation *see* PO ZAKONU (1926).

Exploits in West-Poley *see* OUR EXPLOITS AT WEST POLEY (1987).

Explorations in the March of Brandenburg *see* MARKISCHE FORSCHUNGEN (1982).

EXPLORER, THE 1915 d: George Melford. USA., *The Explorer*, W. Somerset Maugham, London 1909, Novel

Exploring the Marches of Brandenberg *see* MARKISCHE FORSCHUNGEN (1982).

Explosion *see* PURSUIT (1972).

EXPRESSO BONGO 1959 d: Val Guest. UKN., *Expresso Bongo*, Wolf Mankowitz, Julian More, London 1958, Musical Play

EXQUISITE SINNER, THE 1926 d: Josef von Sternberg, Phil Rosen. USA., *Escape*, Alden Brooks, New York 1924, Novel

EXQUISITE THIEF, THE 1919 d: Tod Browning. USA., *Raggedy Ann*, Charles W. Tyler, Short Story

Extase, L' *see* VERS L'EXTASE (1960).

Exterminating Angel, The *see* EL ANGEL EXTERMINADOR (1962).

Exterminators, The *see* COPLAN FX18 CASSE TOUT (1965).

EXTRA-DRY - CARNEVALE 1910 - CARNEVALE 1913 1914 d: Gino Calza-Bini. ITL., *Extra Dry - Carnevale 1910 - Carnevale 1913*, Luigi Chiarelli, 1914, Play

EXTRAVAGANCE 1921 d: Phil Rosen. USA., *More Stately Mansions*, Ben Ames Williams, 1920, Short Story

EXTRAVAGANTE THEODORA, L' 1949 d: Henri Lepage. FRN., *L' Extravagante Theodora*, Jean de Letraz, Play

EXTREME MEASURES 1996 d: Michael Apted. UKN/USA., *Extreme Measures*, Michael Palmer, Novel

EXTREMITIES 1986 d: Robert M. Young. USA., *Extremities*, William Mastrosimone, Play

Eye *see* NAZAR (1990).

EYE FOR EYE 1918 d: Albert Capellani. USA., *L' Occident*, Henri Kistemaeckers, Paris 1913, Play

EYE OF GOD 1997 d: Tom Blake Nelson. USA., *Eye of God*, Tom Blake Nelson, Play

Eye of the Black Cat *see* IL TUO VIZIO E UNA STANZA CHIUSA E SOLO IO NE HO LE CHIAVI (1972).

Eye of the Cat *see* ATTENTI AL BUFFONE (1975).

EYE OF THE DEVIL 1966 d: J. Lee Thompson. USA/UKN., *Day of the Arrow*, Philip Loraine, New York 1964, Novel

EYE OF THE NEEDLE 1981 d: Richard Marquand. UKN., *Eye of the Needle*, Ken Follett, Novel

Eyes Do Not Want to Close at All Times Or Perhaps One Day Rome Will Permit Herself to Choose in H.. *see* YEUX NE VEULENT PAS EN TOUT

TEMPS SE FERMER OU PEUT-ETRE QU'UN JOUR ROME SE PERMETTRA DE CHOISIR A. (1970).

EYES IN THE NIGHT 1942 d: Fred Zinnemann. USA., *Eyes in the Night*, Baynard H. Kendrick, Novel

EYES OF FATE 1933 d: Ivar Campbell. UKN., *Eyes of Fate*, Holloway Horn, Story

EYES OF JULIA DEEP, THE 1918 d: Lloyd Ingraham. USA., *The Eyes of Julia Deep*, Kate L. McLaurin, Short Story

EYES OF LAURA MARS, THE 1978 d: Irvin Kershner. USA., *The Eyes of Laura Mars*, John Carpenter, Novel

EYES OF MYSTERY, THE 1918 d: Tod Browning. USA., *The House in the Mist*, Octavus Roy Cohen, John U. Giesy, 1917, Short Story

Eyes of Scotland Yard see THE WITNESS VANISHES (1939).

EYES OF THE AMARYLLIS, THE 1982 d: Frederick King Keller. USA., *The Eyes of the Amaryllis*, Natalie Babbitt, Novel

EYES OF THE HEART 1920 d: Paul Powell. USA., *Blindness*, Dana Burnet, 1919, Serial Story

EYES OF THE SOUL 1919 d: Emile Chautard. USA., *The Salt of the Earth*, George Weston, 1918, Short Story

EYES OF THE WORLD, THE 1917 d: Donald Crisp. USA., *The Eyes of the World*, Harold Bell Wright, Chicago 1914, Novel

EYES OF THE WORLD, THE 1930 d: Henry King. USA., *The Eyes of the World*, Harold Bell Wright, Chicago 1914, Novel

EYES OF YOUTH 1919 d: Albert Parker. USA., *Eyes of Youth*, Charles Guernon, Max Marcin, New York 1917, Play

EYES OF YOUTH 1920. USA., *Eyes of Youth*, Charles Guernon, Max Marcin, New York 1917, Play

Eyes Without a Face see LES YEUX SANS VISAGE (1959).

EYEWITNESS 1970 d: John Hough. UKN., *Eye-Witness*, Mark Hebden, Novel

EZAI PADUM PADU 1950 d: K. Ramnoth. IND., *Les Miserables*, Victor Hugo, Paris 1862, Novel

Ezhai Padum Padi see EZAI PADUM PADU (1950).

F. EST UN SALAUD 1998 d: Marcel Gisler. SWT/FRN., *F. Est un Salaud*, Martin Frank, Novel

F. Is a Bastard see F. EST UN SALAUD (1998).

FABBRICA DELL'IMPREVISTO, LA 1943 d: Jacopo Comin. ITL., *Quello Che Non T'aspetti*, Luigi Barzini, Arnaldo Fraccaroli, Play

FABBRO DEL CONVENTO, IL 1922 d: Vincenzo C. Denizot. ITL., *Le Forgeron de la Cour Dieu*, Pierre-Alexis Ponson Du Terrail, 1869, Novel

FABBRO DEL CONVENTO, IL 1949 d: Max Calandri. ITL., *Le Forgeron de la Cour Dieu*, Pierre-Alexis Ponson Du Terrail, 1869, Novel

FABIAN 1980 d: Wolfgang Gremm. GRM., *Fabian. Die Geschichte Eines Moralisten*, Erich Kastner, 1931, Novel

FABIOLA 1918 d: Enrico Guazzoni. ITL., *Fabiola Or the Church of the Catacombs*, Nicholas Patrick Wiseman, London 1854, Novel

FABIOLA 1948 d: Alessandro Blasetti. ITL., *Fabiola Or the Church of the Catacombs*, Nicholas Patrick Wiseman, London 1854, Novel

FABLE, A 1971 d: Al Freeman Jr. USA., *Slave*, Leroi Jones, 1964, Play

Fable of May see POHADKA MAJE (1940).

FABRIK DER OFFIZIERE 1960 d: Frank Wisbar. GRM., *Fabrik Der Offiziere*, Hans Hellmut Kirst, Novel

FABRIK DER OFFIZIERE 1988 d: Wolf Vollmar. GRM/CZC., *Fabrik Der Offiziere*, Hans Hellmut Kirst, Novel

Fabulous Baron Munchausen, The see BARON PRASIL (1961).

Fabulous Journey to the Centre of the Earth see VIAJE AL CENTRO DE LA TIERRA (1977).

Fabulous World of Jules Verne, The see VYNALEZ ZKAZY (1958).

FACA DE DOIS GUMES 1989 d: Murilo Salles. BRZ., *A Faca de Dois Gumes*, Fernando Tavares Sabino, 1985, Novel

Faca E O Rio, A see JOAO EN HET MES (1972).

FACCIA DA MASCALZONE 1955 d: Raffaele Andreassi, Lance Comfort. ITL., Alberto Moravia, Short Story

FACCIAMO PARADISO 1995 d: Mario Monicelli. ITL., *Facciamo Paradiso*, Giuseppe Pontiggia, Novel

FACE AT THE WINDOW, THE 1920 d: Wilfred Noy. UKN., *The Face at the Window*, F. Brooke Warren, Play

FACE AT THE WINDOW, THE 1932 d: Leslie Hiscott. UKN., *The Face at the Window*, F. Brooke Warren, Play

FACE AT THE WINDOW, THE 1939 d: George King. UKN., *The Face at the Window*, F. Brooke Warren, Play

FACE AU DESTIN 1939 d: Henri Fescourt. FRN., *Face Au Destin*, Charles-Robert Dumas, Novel

FACE BEHIND THE MASK, THE 1941 d: Robert Florey. USA., *Interem*, Thomas Edward O'Connell, Radio Play

Face Behind the Scar, The see RETURN OF A STRANGER (1937).

FACE BETWEEN, THE 1922 d: Bayard Veiller. USA., *The Carterets*, Justus Miles Forman, Story

FACE IN THE CROWD, A 1957 d: Elia Kazan. USA., *Your Arkansas Traveler*, Budd Schulberg, 1953, Short Story

Face in the Dark see A DOPPIA FACCIA (1969).

FACE IN THE DARK, THE 1918 d: Hobart Henley. USA., *The Web*, Irvin S. Cobb, Short Story

FACE IN THE FOG, A 1936 d: Robert F. Hill. USA., *The Great Mono Miracle*, Peter B. Kyne, Novel

FACE IN THE FOG, THE 1922 d: Alan Crosland. USA., *The Face in the Fog*, Jack Boyle, 1920, Short Story

FACE IN THE MOONLIGHT, THE 1915 d: Albert Capellani. USA., *The Face in the Moonlight*, Charles Osborne, New York 1892, Play

FACE IN THE NIGHT 1957 d: Lance Comfort. UKN., *Suspense*, Bruce Graeme, Novel

FACE OF A FUGITIVE 1959 d: Paul Wendkos. USA., *Long Gone*, Peter Dawson, 1956, Short Story

FACE OF A STRANGER 1964 d: John Llewellyn Moxey. UKN., Edgar Wallace, Novel

Face of Another, The see TANIN NO KAO (1966).

FACE OF FEAR 1990 d: Farhad Mann. USA., *Face of Fear*, Dean R. Koontz, Novel

FACE OF FEAR, THE 1971 d: George McCowan. USA., *Sally*, Howard Fast, Novel

Face of Fire see MANNEN UTAN ANSIKTE (1959).

FACE OF FU MANCHU, THE 1965 d: Don Sharp. UKN., Sax Rohmer, Novel

Face of the Cat, The see LA CHATTE (1958).

Face of the Frog see DER FROSCH MIT DER MASKE (1959).

FACE OF THE WORLD 1921 d: Irvin V. Willat. USA., *Verdens Ansigt*, Johan Bojer, Copenhagen 1917, Novel

FACE ON THE BARROOM FLOOR, THE 1908 d: Edwin S. Porter. USA., *The Face on the Barroom Floor*, Hugh Antoine d'Arcy, Poem

FACE ON THE BARROOM FLOOR, THE 1923 d: John Ford. USA., *The Face on the Barroom Floor*, Hugh Antoine d'Arcy, Poem

FACE ON THE BARROOM FLOOR, THE 1936 d: Bertram Bracken. USA., *The Face on the Barroom Floor*, Hugh Antoine d'Arcy, Poem

FACE ON THE MILK CARTON, THE 1995 d: Waris Hussein. USA., *The Face on the Milk Carton*, Caroline B. Cooney, Novel, *Whatever Happened to Janie*, Caroline B. Cooney, Novel

Face the Facts see MR. BOGGS STEPS OUT (1938).

FACE THE MUSIC 1954 d: Terence Fisher. UKN., *Face the Music*, Ernest Bornemann, Novel

FACE TO FACE 1952 d: John Brahm, Bretaigne Windust. USA., *The Secret Sharer*, Joseph Conrad, 1910, Short Story, *The Bride Comes to Yellow Sky*, Stephen Crane, 1898, Short Story

Face Work see CONVICTED (1938).

Faceless Man, The see THE COUNTERFEIT KILLER (1968).

FACEREA LUMII 1971 d: Gheorghe Vitanidis. RMN., *Facerea Lumii*, Eugen Barbu, 1964, Novel

FACES 1934 d: Sidney Morgan. UKN., *Faces*, Patrick Ludlow, Walter Sondes, Play

Faces and Masks see MARATTAM (1989).

FACES IN THE DARK 1960 d: David Eady. UKN., *Les Visages de l'Ombre*, Pierre Boileau, Thomas Narcejac, Paris 1953, Novel

Faces of a Clown see ANSICHTEN EINES CLOWNS (1975).

Facon de Se Donner, La see D'AMOUR ET D'EAU FRAICHE (1934).

FACTEUR S'EN VA-T-EN GUERRE, LE 1966 d: Claude Bernard-Aubert. FRN., *Le Facteur S'en Va-T-En Guerre*, Gaston-Jean Gautier, Paris 1966, Novel

Factory, The see TO ERGOSTASIO (1981).

Facts of Life, The see 29 ACACIA AVENUE (1945).

Facts of Love, The see 29 ACACIA AVENUE (1945).

Facts of Murder, The see UN MALEDETTO IMBROGLIO (1959).

FADE OUT 1970 d: John N. Burton. UKN., *Fade Out*, David Watson, Play

FADREN 1969 d: Alf Sjoberg. SWD., *Fadren*, August Strindberg, 1887, Play

FAGIN 1922 d: H. B. Parkinson. UKN., *Oliver Twist*, Charles Dickens, London 1838, Novel

Fahnlein Der Sieben Aufrechten, Das see HERMIN UND DIE SIEBEN AUFRECTEN (1935).

Fahnlein Der Versprengten, Das see ALTE KAMERADEN (1934).

FAHRENHEIT 451 1966 d: Francois Truffaut. UKN., *Fahrenheit 451*, Ray Bradbury, New York 1953, Novel

FAHRT INS VERDERBEN, DIE 1924 d: James Bauer. GRM/NTH., *Op Hoop Van Zegen*, Herman Heijermans, 1900, Play

FAIBLE FEMME, UNE 1932 d: Max de Vaucorbeil. FRN., *Une Faible Femme*, Jacques Deval, Play

FAIBLES FEMMES 1959 d: Michel Boisrond. FRN., *Meurtre d'un Serin*, Sophie Cathala, Novel

FAIL-SAFE 1964 d: Sidney Lumet. USA., *Fail-Safe*, Eugene Burdick, Harvey Wheeler, New York 1962, Novel

FAINT PERFUME 1925 d: Louis J. Gasnier. USA., *Faint Perfume*, Zona Gale, New York 1923, Novel

FAIR AND WARMER 1919 d: Henry Otto. USA., *Fair and Warmer*, Avery Hopwood, New York 1915, Play

FAIR BARBARIAN, THE 1917 d: Robert T. Thornby. USA., *The Fair Barbarian*, Frances Hodgson Burnett, New York 1880, Story

FAIR CO-ED, THE 1927 d: Sam Wood. USA., *The Fair Co-Ed*, George Ade, New York 1909, Play

FAIR EXCHANGE, A 1909 d: D. W. Griffith. USA., *Silas Marner*, George Eliot, London 1861, Novel

FAIR IMPOSTER, A 1916 d: Alexander Butler. UKN., *A Fair Imposter*, Charles Garvice, Novel

FAIR LADY 1922 d: Kenneth Webb. USA., *The Net*, Rex Beach, New York 1912, Novel

FAIR MAID OF PERTH, THE 1923 d: Edwin Greenwood. UKN., *The Fair Maid of Perth*, Sir Walter Scott, 1828, Novel

Fair Play see LA REGLE DU JEU (1939).

FAIR STOOD THE WIND FOR FRANCE 1981. UKN., *Fair Stood the Wind for France*, H. E. Bates, 1944, Novel

FAIR WARNING 1931 d: Alfred L. Werker. USA., *The Untamed*, Max Brand, New York 1919, Novel

FAIR WARNING 1937 d: Norman Foster. USA., *Paradise Canyon Mystery*, Philip Wylie, 1936, Short Story

FAIR WIND TO JAVA 1953 d: Joseph Kane. USA., *Fair Wind to Java*, Garland Roark, Novel

Fairy Tale of Malicek, The see POHADKA O MALICKOVI (1985).

Fairy Tale of May see POHADKA MAJE (1940).

FAISEUR, LE 1908-18. FRN., *Le Faiseur*, Honore de Balzac, Play

FAISEUR, LE 1936 d: Andre Hugon. FRN., *Mercadet*, Honore de Balzac, 1851, Play

Faith see LA FE (1947).

Faith and Endurin' see FAITH ENDURIN' (1918).

FAITH ENDURIN' 1918 d: Cliff Smith. USA., *The Blue Tattooing*, Kenneth B. Clarke, 1915, Short Story

FAITH HEALER, THE 1921 d: George Melford. USA., *The Faith Healer*, William Vaughn Moody, New York 1910, Play

FAITH OF HER FATHERS, THE 1915 d: Charles Giblyn. USA., *A Daughter of Israel*, Bruno Lessing, Novel

Faithful see A NOTORIOUS AFFAIR (1930).

Faithful 47, The see CHUSHINGURA (1962).

FAITHFUL HEART, THE 1922 d: G. B. Samuelson. UKN., *The Faithful Heart*, Monckton Hoffe, London 1921, Play

FAITHFUL HEART, THE 1932 d: Victor Saville. UKN., *The Faithful Heart*, Monckton Hoffe, London 1921, Play

Faithful Hearts see THE FAITHFUL HEART (1932).

Faithful Infantry, The see LA FIEL INFANTERIA (1959).

Faithful River see WIERNA RZEKA (1936).

Faithful River, The *see* **WIERNA RZEKA** (1983).

FAITHLESS LOVER, THE 1928 d: Lawrence C. Windom. USA., *Faithless Lover*, Baroness d'Arville, Story

Faithless Sex, The *see* **THE DECOY** (1916).

Fake Integrity *see* **LA HONRADEZ DE LA CERRADURA** (1950).

FAKE, THE 1927 d: Georg Jacoby. UKN., *The Fake*, Frederick Lonsdale, London 1924, Play

FAKIR DU GRAND HOTEL, LE 1933 d: Pierre Billon. FRN., *Le Mage du Carlton*, Georges Dolley, Leopold Marchand, Play

FALCO D'ORO, IL 1956 d: Carlo Ludovico BragagliA. ITL., *Don Gil Dalle Calze Verdi*, Tirso de Molina, Novel

FALCON AND THE SNOWMAN, THE 1984 d: John Schlesinger. USA., *The Falcon and the Snowman*, Robert Lindsey, Book

FALCON TAKES OVER, THE 1942 d: Irving Reis. USA., *Farewell My Lovely*, Raymond Chandler, 1940, Novel

Falcon, The *see* **MAGASISKOLA** (1970).

Falcon's Malteser, The *see* **JUST ASK FOR DIAMOND** (1988).

Falcons, The *see* **MAGASISKOLA** (1970).

FALECIDA, A 1964 d: Leon Hirszman. BRZ., *A Falecida*, Nelson Rodrigues, 1953, Play

FALENA, LA 1916 d: Carmine Gallone. ITL., *La Phalene*, Henry Bataille, 1913, Play

FALESNA KOCICKA 1937 d: Vladimir Slavinsky. CZC., *Falesna Kocicka*, Josef Skruzny, Play

FALEZE DE NISIP 1983 d: Dan PitA. RMN., *Zile de Nisip*, Bujor Nedelcovici, 1979, Novel

FALL DERUGA, DER 1938 d: Fritz Peter Buch. GRM., *Der Fall Deruga*, Ricarda Huch, 1917, Novel

FALL DES STAATSANWALTS M.., DER 1928 d: Rudolf Meinert, Giulio Antamoro. GRM/FRN/ITL., *Le Crime de Vera Mirzewa*, Ourmanzoff, Play

FALL GUY 1947 d: Reginald Le Borg. USA., *Cocaine*, Cornell Woolrich, Story

FALL GUY, THE 1930 d: A. Leslie Pearce. USA., *The Fall Guy*, George Abbott, James Gleason, New York 1924, Play

FALL LENA CHRIST, DER 1968 d: Hans W. Geissendorfer. GRM., Peter Benedix, Lena Christ, Documents

FALL OF A NATION, THE 1916 d: Thomas Dixon. USA., *The Fall of a Nation: a Sequel to Birth of a Nation*, Thomas Dixon, Chicago 1916, Novel

FALL OF A SAINT, THE 1920 d: W. P. Kellino. UKN., *The Fall of a Saint*, Eric Clement Scott, Novel

Fall of Lola Montes, The *see* **LOLA MONTES** (1955).

Fall of the House of Usher, The *see* **LA CHUTE DE LA MAISON USHER** (1928).

FALL OF THE HOUSE OF USHER, THE 1950 d: Ivan Barnett. UKN., *The Fall of the House of Usher*, Edgar Allan Poe, 1839, Short Story

FALL OF THE HOUSE OF USHER, THE 1958. USA., *The Fall of the House of Usher*, Edgar Allan Poe, 1839, Short Story

FALL OF THE HOUSE OF USHER, THE 1960 d: Roger Corman. USA., *The Fall of the House of Usher*, Edgar Allan Poe, 1839, Short Story

FALL OF THE HOUSE OF USHER, THE 1979 d: James L. Conway. USA., *The Fall of the House of Usher*, Edgar Allan Poe, 1839, Short Story

Fall of the House of Usher, The *see* **THE HOUSE OF USHER** (1988).

Fall of the Mohicans *see* **EL FIN DE UNA RAZA UNCAS** (1964).

Fall Out *see* **SORTEZ DES RANGS** (1996).

FALL RABANSER, DER 1950 d: Kurt Hoffmann. GRM., S. P. Walther, Story

Fall, The *see* **LA CAIDA** (1959).

Fall, The *see* **DE VAL** (1974).

Fall, The *see* **DER STURZ** (1979).

Fall Wozzeck, Der *see* **WOZZECK** (1947).

Fallecida, La *see* **A FALECIDA** (1964).

FALLEN ANGEL 1945 d: Otto Preminger. USA., *Fallen Angel*, Marty Holland, Novel

FALLEN ANGEL, THE 1918 d: Robert T. Thornby. USA., *You Can't Get Away With It*, Gouverneur Morris, 1913, Short Story

Fallen Angels *see* **WOMAN AND WIFE MAN** (1929).

FALLEN BY THE WAY 1922 d: Challis Sanderson. UKN., *Fallen By the Way*, George R. Sims, Poem

FALLEN IDOL, THE 1948 d: Carol Reed. UKN., *The Basement Room*, Graham Greene, 1935, Short Story

FALLEN LEAVES 1922 d: George A. Cooper. UKN., *Fallen Leaves*, Will Scott, Story

FALLEN SPARROW, THE 1943 d: Richard Wallace. USA., *The Fallen Sparrow*, Dorothy B. Hughes, Novel

Fallen Woman, A *see* **DARAKU SURU ONNA** (1967).

FALLET INGEGERD BREMSSEN 1942 d: Anders Henrikson. SWD., *Fallet Ingegerd Bremssen*, Dagmar Ingeborg Edqvist, 1937, Novel

Falling Into the Evening *see* **RAKKA SURU YUGATA** (1998).

Falling Stars *see* **SVESDOPAD** (1981).

Falpala *see* **NINI FALPALA** (1933).

FALSA AMANTE, LA 1920 d: Carmine Gallone. ITL., *La Fausse Maitresse*, Honore de Balzac, 1841, Short Story

FALSCHE ADAM, DER 1955 d: Geza von CziffrA. GRM., *Drei Blaue Augen*, Geza von Cziffra, Play

FALSCHE BEWEGUNG 1975 d: Wim Wenders. GRM., *Wilhelm Meisters Lehrjahre*, Johann Wolfgang von Goethe, 1795, Novel

FALSCHE FELDMARSCHALL, DER 1930 d: Carl Lamac. GRM/CZC., *Der K. Und K. Feldmarschall*, Emil Artur Longen, Play

FALSCHE GEWICHT, DAS 1970 d: Bernhard Wicki. GRM., *Das Falsche Gewicht*, Joseph Roth, 1937, Novel

Falsche Katze, Die *see* **HEIRATEN - ABER WEN?** (1938).

FALSCHE PRINZ, DER 1927 d: Heinz Paul. GRM., *Der Falsche Prinz*, Harry Domela, Book

Falsche Wittwe, Die *see* **HURRAH! ICH LEBE!** (1928).

FALSCHER FUFFZIGER, EIN 1935 d: Carl Boese. GRM., *Ein Falscher Fuffziger*, Robert Overweg, Play

FALSCHER VON LONDON, DER 1961 d: Harald Reinl. GRM., Edgar Wallace, Novel

FALSCHUNG, DIE 1981 d: Volker Schlondorff. GRM/FRN., *Die Falschung*, Nicholas Born, 1979, Novel

FALSE ARREST 1991 d: B. W. L. Norton. USA., *False Arrest*, Joyce Lukezic, Ted Schwarz, Book

False Colors *see* **REPUTATION** (1921).

False Colors *see* **TRUE HEAVEN** (1929).

FALSE EVIDENCE 1919 d: Edwin Carewe. USA., *Madelon*, Mary E. Wilkins Freeman, New York 1896, Novel

FALSE EVIDENCE 1922 d: Harold Shaw. UKN., *False Evidence*, E. Phillips Oppenheim, 1896, Novel

FALSE EVIDENCE 1937 d: Donovan Pedelty. UKN., *I'll Never Tell*, Roy Vickers, Novel

FALSE FACES, THE 1919 d: Irvin V. Willat. USA., *The False Faces*, Louis Joseph Vance, Garden City, N.Y. 1918, Novel

False Idol, The *see* **THE FALSE MADONNA** (1931).

FALSE KISSES 1921 d: Paul Scardon. USA., *Ropes*, Wilbur Daniel Steele, 1921, Short Story

FALSE MADONNA, THE 1931 d: Stuart Walker. USA., *The Heart Is Young*, May Edginton, 1930, Short Story

False Magistrate, The *see* **LE FAUX MAGISTRAT** (1914).

False Play *see* **THE LONE HAND** (1922).

False Pussycat, The *see* **FALESNA KOCICKA** (1937).

False Step, The *see* **DER SCHRITT VOM WEGE** (1939).

False Weight *see* **DAS FALSCHE GEWICHT** (1970).

False Witness *see* **TRANSIENT LADY** (1935).

False Witness *see* **ARKANSAS JUDGE** (1941).

False Witness *see* **DIE FALSCHUNG** (1981).

Falstaff *see* **CAMPANADAS A MEDIANOCHE** (1966).

FALSTAFF THE TAVERN KNIGHT 1923 d: Edwin Greenwood. UKN., William Shakespeare, Play

Falstaffs Abenteuer *see* **DIE LUSTIGEN WEIBER** (1935).

Fame *see* **RECAPTURED LOVE** (1930).

Fame *see* **THE BARGAIN** (1931).

FAME AND FORTUNE 1918 d: Lynn Reynolds. USA., *Slow Burgess*, Charles Alden Selzer, Short Story

Fame and Glory *see* **SLAWA I CHWALA** (1997).

FAME IS THE NAME OF THE GAME 1966 d: Stuart Rosenberg. USA., *One Woman*, Tiffany Thayer, 1933, Novel

FAME IS THE SPUR 1947 d: Roy Boulting. UKN., *Fame Is the Spur*, Howard Spring, 1940, Novel

FAME IS THE SPUR 1982 d: David Giles. UKN., *Fame Is the Spur*, Howard Spring, 1940, Novel

FAMIGLIA PASSAGUAI, LA 1951 d: Aldo Fabrizi. ITL., *Cabine 27*, Anton Germano Rossi, Play

FAMILIE BUCHHOLZ 1944 d: Carl Froelich. GRM., *Familie Buchholz*, Julius Stinde, Novel

FAMILIE HESSELBACH, DIE 1954 d: Wolf Schmidt. GRM., *Die Familie Hesselbach*, Wolf Schmidt, Book

Familie Swedenhjelm *see* **FAMILIEN SWEDENHJELM** (1947).

FAMILIEN SWEDENHJELM 1947 d: Lau Lauritzen Jr. DNM., *Swedenhielms*, Hjalmar Bergman, 1925, Play

FAMILIENANSCHLUSS 1941 d: Carl Boese. GRM., *Familienanschluss*, Karl Bunje, Play

FAMILIENTAG IM HAUSE PRELLSTEIN 1927 d: Hans Steinhoff. GRM., *Familientag Im Hause Prellstein*, Anton Herrnfeld, Donath Herrnfeld, Play

FAMILLE BOLERO 1914 d: Georges MoncA. FRN., *Famille Bolero*, Maurice Hennequin, Albert Milhaud, Play

Famille Cardinal, La *see* **LES PETITES CARDINAL** (1950).

FAMILLE CUCUROUX, LA 1953 d: Emile Couzinet. FRN., *La Famille Cucuroux*, Yves Mirande, Play

FAMILLE HERNANDEZ, LA 1964 d: Genevieve Bailac. FRN., *La Famille Hernandez*, Genevieve Bailac, Play

FAMILLE PONT-BIQUET, LA 1935 d: Christian-Jaque. FRN., *La Famille Pont-Biquet*, Alexandre Bisson, Play

Family *see* **JIA** (1941).

Family *see* **JIA** (1957).

Family Adventure *see* **VIVA LO IMPOSIBLE!** (1957).

Family Affair *see* **FOUR WIVES** (1939).

Family Affair, A *see* **BUT THE FLESH IS WEAK** (1932).

FAMILY AFFAIR, A 1937 d: George B. Seitz. USA., *Skidding*, Aurania Rouverol, New York 1928, Play

FAMILY BUSINESS 1982 d: John Stix. USA., *Family Business*, Dick Goldenberg, Play

FAMILY CLOSET, THE 1921 d: John B. O'Brien. USA., *Black Sheep*, Will J. Payne, Short Story

FAMILY CUPBOARD, THE 1915 d: Frank H. Crane. USA., *The Family Cupboard*, Owen Davis, New York 1913, Play

Family Diary *see* **CRONACA FAMILIARE** (1962).

FAMILY DIVIDED, A 1995 d: Donald Wrye. USA., *Mother Love*, Judith Henry Wall, Novel

FAMILY DOCTOR 1958 d: Derek Twist. UKN., *The Deeds of Dr. Deadcert*, Joan Fleming, Novel

Family Game, The *see* **KAZOKU GEEMU** (1983).

Family Happiness *see* **SEMEJNOE SCASTE** (1969).

Family History *see* **CRONACA FAMILIARE** (1962).

FAMILY HONEYMOON 1948 d: Claude Binyon. USA., *Family Honeymoon*, Homer Croy, Novel

Family Killer *see* **BACIAMO LE MANI** (1973).

FAMILY LIFE 1971 d: Kenneth Loach. UKN., *In Two Minds*, David Mercer, 1967, Play

Family Matters *see* **JIA TING WEN TI** (1964).

Family Niskavuori, The *see* **NISKAVUORI** (1984).

FAMILY NOBODY WANTED, THE 1975 d: Ralph Senensky. USA., *The Family Nobody Wanted*, Helen Doss, 1954, Book

FAMILY OF STRANGERS 1993 d: Sheldon Larry. USA/CND., *Judy*, Jerry Hulse, Book

FAMILY PICTURES 1992 d: Philip Saville. USA., *Family Pictures*, Sue Miller, Novel

FAMILY PLOT 1976 d: Alfred Hitchcock. USA., *Family Plot*, Victor Canning, Novel

Family Portrait *see* **RETRATO DE FAMILIA** (1976).

Family Reunion *see* **FOUR WIVES** (1939).

FAMILY RICO, THE 1972 d: Paul Wendkos. USA., *Les Freres Rico*, Georges Simenon, 1952, Short Story

Family Scandal, The *see* **THIS SIDE OF HEAVEN** (1932).

FAMILY SECRET, THE 1924 d: William A. Seiter. USA., *Edith's Burglar*, Frances Hodgson Burnett, Boston 1878, Novel

FAMILY STAIN, THE 1915 d: Will S. Davis. USA., *L'Affaire Rouge*, Emile Gaboriau, Paris 1866, Novel

Family Tree, The *see* **VAMSHA VRIKSHA** (1971).

Family Trees, The *see* **FOOLS AND THEIR MONEY** (1919).

FAMILY UPSTAIRS, THE 1926 d: John G. Blystone. USA., *The Family Upstairs*, Harry Delf, Atlantic City 1925, Play

FAMILY WAY, THE 1966 d: Roy Boulting. UKN., *All in Good Time*, Bill Naughton, London 1963, Play

Famine, The *see* **BARA** (1981).

Famoro le Tyran *see* **PAYSANS NOIRS** (1947).

Famous Man, A *see* **O HOMEM CELEBRE** (1974).

FAMOUS MRS. FAIR, THE 1923 d: Fred Niblo. USA., *The Famous Mrs. Fair*, James Grant Forbes, New York 1920, Play

FAN FAN 1918 d: Chester M. Franklin, Sidney A. Franklin. USA., *The Mikado*, W. S. Gilbert, Arthur Sullivan, London 1885, Opera

FAN, THE 1949 d: Otto Preminger. USA., *Lady Windermere's Fan*, Oscar Wilde, London 1892, Play

FAN, THE 1981 d: Edward Bianchi. USA., *The Fan*, Bob Randall, Novel

FAN, THE 1996 d: Anthony Scott. USA., *The Fan*, Peter Abrahams, Novel

FANATIC 1965 d: Silvio Narizzano. UKN., *Nightmare*, Anne Blaisdell, New York 1961, Novel

FANATISME 1934 d: Gaston Ravel, Tony Lekain. FRN., *La Savelli*, Max Maurey, Play

FANCHON THE CRICKET 1915 d: James Kirkwood. USA., *La Petite Fadette*, George Sand, Paris 1849, Novel

FANCIULLA DELL'ALTRO MONDO, LA 1934 d: Gennaro Righelli. ITL., Corrado d'Errico, Novel

Fancy Free *see* **BACHELOR'S AFFAIRS** (1932).

Fancy Jim Sherwood *see* **THE MAN FROM PAINTED POST** (1917).

FANCY PANTS 1950 d: George Marshall. USA., *Ruggles of Red Gap*, Harry Leon Wilson, New York 1915, Novel

Fandango *see* **LOVE UNDER FIRE** (1937).

Fando and Lis *see* **FANDO Y LIS** (1968).

FANDO Y LIS 1968 d: Alejandro Jodorowsky. MXC., *Fando Et Lis*, Fernando Arrabal, Paris 1958, Play

Fando Y Lys *see* **FANDO Y LIS** (1968).

Fanfani Kidnapped *see* **FANFANI RAPITO** (1975).

FANFANI RAPITO 1975 d: Dimitris Makris. ITL., *Fanfani Rapito*, Dario Fo, Play

FANG AND CLAW 1935 d: Frank Buck, Ray Taylor. USA., *Fang and Claw*, Frank Buck, Ferrin Fraser, New York 1935, Book

FANG ZHENZHU 1952 d: Xu Changlin. CHN., *Fang Zhenzhu*, Shu Qingchun, 1950, Play

FANGS OF THE ARCTIC 1953 d: Rex Bailey. USA., James Oliver Curwood, Story

FANGSCHUSS, DER 1976 d: Volker Schlondorff. GRM/FRN., *Le Coup de Grace*, Marguerite Yourcenar, 1939, Novel

Fanion Des Sept Braves, Le *see* **HERMIN UND DIE SIEBEN AUFRECTEN** (1935).

FANNY 1932 d: Marc Allegret. FRN., *Fanny*, Marcel Pagnol, Paris 1931, Play

FANNY 1933 d: Mario Almirante. ITL., *Fanny*, Marcel Pagnol, Paris 1931, Play

Fanny *see* **PORT OF SEVEN SEAS** (1938).

FANNY 1961 d: Joshua Logan. USA., *Fanny*, Marcel Pagnol, Paris 1931, Play

Fanny, Ballerina Della Scala *see* **BALLERINE** (1936).

FANNY BY GASLIGHT 1944 d: Anthony Asquith. UKN., *Fanny By Gaslight*, Michael Sadleir, 1940, Novel

FANNY BY GASLIGHT 1981 d: Peter Jeffries. UKN., *Fanny By Gaslight*, Michael Sadleir, 1940, Novel

Fanny Hawthorne *see* **HINDLE WAKES** (1927).

FANNY HILL 1964 d: Russ Meyer. GRM/USA., *Fanny Hill; Or Memoirs of a Woman of Pleasure*, John Cleland, London 1749, Novel

FANNY HILL 1968 d: Mac Ahlberg. SWD., *Fanny Hill; Or Memoirs of a Woman of Pleasure*, John Cleland, London 1749, Novel

FANNY HILL 1983 d: Gerry O'HarA. UKN., *Fanny Hill; Or Memoirs of a Woman of Pleasure*, John Cleland, London 1749, Novel

Fanny Hill: Memoirs of a Woman of Pleasure *see* **FANNY HILL** (1964).

FANNY LEAR 1919 d: Jean Manoussi, Robert Boudrioz. FRN., *Fanny Lear*, Ludovic Halevy, Henri Meilhac, Play

FAN'S NOTES, A 1972 d: Eric Till. CND/USA., *A Fan's Notes*, Frederick Earl Exley, Novel

FANT 1937 d: Tancred Ibsen. NRW/SWD., *Fant*, Gabriel Scott, 1928, Novel

FANTASIA CHEZ LES PLOUCS 1970 d: Gerard Pires. FRN/ITL., *Diamond Bikini*, Charles Williams, Novel

FANTASIST, THE 1986 d: Robin Hardy. UKN/IRL., *Goosefoot*, Patrick McGinley, Novel

FANTASMA 1914 d: Charles M. Seay. USA., *Fantasma, the Hanlon Brothers*, New York 1884, Play

FANTASMA D'AMORE 1981 d: Dino Risi. ITL/FRN/GRM., *Fantasma d'Amore*, Mino Milani, Novel

FANTASMA DELL'OPERA, IL 1998 d: Dario Argento. ITL., *Le Fantome de l'Opera*, Gaston Leroux, Paris 1910, Novel

FANTASMA, IL 1915. ITL., Gaston Leroux, Novel

FANTASTERNE 1967 d: Kirsten Stenbaek. DNM., *Phantasterne*, Hans Egede Schack, Copenhagen 1858, Novel

Fantastic Planet *see* **LA PLANETE SAUVAGE** (1973).

Fantastique Histoire Vraie d'Eddie Chapman, La *see* **TRIPLE CROSS** (1966).

FANTEE 1920 d: Lewis Willoughby. UKN., *Wyngate Sahib*, Joan Sutherland, Novel

FANTINE; OR, A MOTHER'S LOVE 1909 d: Van Dyke Brooke. USA., *Les Miserables*, Victor Hugo, Paris 1862, Novel

FANTOMAS 1913 d: Louis Feuillade. FRN., *Fantomas*, Marcel Allain, Pierre Souvestre, Novel

FANTOMAS 1964 d: Andre Hunebelle. FRN., *Fantomas*, Marcel Allain, Pierre Souvestre, Novel

Fantomas 70 *see* **FANTOMAS** (1964).

FANTOMAS CONTRE FANTOMAS 1914 d: Louis Feuillade. FRN., *Le Policier Apache*, Marcel Allain, Pierre Souvestre, Novel

Fantomas II *see* **JUVE CONTRE FANTOMAS** (1913).

Fantomas IV *see* **FANTOMAS CONTRE FANTOMAS** (1914).

Fantomas, the Crook Detective *see* **FANTOMAS CONTRE FANTOMAS** (1914).

Fantomas Under the Shadow of the Guillotine *see* **FANTOMAS** (1913).

Fantomas V *see* **LE FAUX MAGISTRAT** (1914).

Fantome a Vendre, Le *see* **THE GHOST GOES WEST** (1935).

Fantome d'Amour *see* **FANTASMA D'AMORE** (1981).

Fantome d'Amour, Le *see* **SIRENE DE PIERRE** (1922).

Fantome Noir, Le *see* **TAO** (1923).

Fantomes a l'Italienne *see* **QUESTI FANTASMI** (1967).

FANTOMES DU CHAPELIER, LES 1981 d: Claude Chabrol. FRN., *Les Fantomes du Chapelier*, Georges Simenon, 1949, Short Story

FANTOZZI 1975 d: Luciano Salce. ITL., *Fantozzi*, Paolo Villaggio, Novel

FAR CALL, THE 1929 d: Allan Dwan. USA., *The Far Call*, Edison Marshall, 1928, Short Story

FAR COUNTRY, THE 1986 d: George Miller. ASL., *The Far Country*, Nevil Shute, Novel

FAR CRY, THE 1926 d: Silvano Balboni. USA., *The Far Cry*, Arthur Richman, New York 1924, Play

FAR FROM THE MADDING CROWD 1915 d: Larry Trimble. UKN., *Far from the Madding Crowd*, Thomas Hardy, London 1874, Novel

FAR FROM THE MADDING CROWD 1967 d: John Schlesinger. UKN., *Far from the Madding Crowd*, Thomas Hardy, London 1874, Novel

FAR HORIZONS, THE 1955 d: Rudolph Mate. USA., *Sacajawea of the Shoshones*, Della Gould Emmons, Novel

FAR OFF PLACE, A 1993 d: Mikael Salomon. USA., *A Story Like the Wind and a Far Off Place*, Laurens Van Der Post, Books

FAR PAVILIONS, THE 1983 d: Peter Duffell. UKN., *The Far Pavilions*, M. M. Kaye, Novel

FARAON 1965 d: Jerzy Kawalerowicz. PLN., *Faraon*, Boleslaw Prus, 1897, Novel

FARARUV KONEC 1968 d: Evald Schorm. CZC., *Fararuv Konec*, Josef Skvorecky, Prerov 1969, Novel

FAREMO TANTO MALE, LE 1998 d: Pino Quartullo. ITL., *Le Faremo Tanto Male*, Claudio Masenza, Pino Quartullo, Play

Farewell *see* **ABSCHIED** (1968).

Farewell *see* **PROSCANIE** (1981).

Farewell Friend *see* **ADIEU L'AMI** (1968).

Farewell My Concubine *see* **BA WANG BIE JI** (1993).

FAREWELL MY LOVELY 1975 d: Dick Richards. USA., *Farewell My Lovely*, Raymond Chandler, 1940, Novel

Farewell, My Lovely *see* **MY SWEET MURDER** (1945).

FAREWELL TO ARMS, A 1932 d: Frank Borzage. USA., *A Farewell to Arms*, Ernest Hemingway, New York 1929, Novel

FAREWELL TO ARMS, A 1957 d: Charles Vidor. USA., *A Farewell to Arms*, Ernest Hemingway, New York 1929, Novel

Farewell to False Paradise *see* **ABSCHIED VOM FALSCHEN PARADIES** (1989).

FAREWELL TO MANZANAR 1976 d: John Korty. USA., *Farewell to Manzanar*, Jeanne Wakatsuki Houston, Book

Farewell to Matjora *see* **PROSCANIE** (1981).

Farewell to My Concubine *see* **BA WANG BIE JI** (1993).

FAREWELL TO THE KING 1988 d: John Milius. USA., *L' Adieu a Roi*, Pierre Schoendoerffer, Novel

Farewells *see* **POZEGNANIA** (1958).

FARFUI 1919 d: Carlo Bondi. ITL., *Farfui*, Luciano Zuccoli, 1909, Novel

FARGO KID, THE 1940 d: Edward Killy. USA., *Sir Piegan Passes*, W. C. Tuttle, New York 1923, Short Story

Farinet *see* **L' OR DANS LA MONTAGNE** (1938).

Farinet, Oder Das Falsche Geld *see* **L' OR DANS LA MONTAGNE** (1938).

Farinet, Ou la Fausse Monnaie *see* **L' OR DANS LA MONTAGNE** (1938).

Farinet Ou l'Or Dans la Montagne *see* **L' OR DANS LA MONTAGNE** (1938).

Farizeeers *see* **THE HYPOCRITES** (1923).

FARLIGA VAGAR 1942 d: Anders Henrikson. SWD., *Kanske En Diktare*, Ragnar Josephson, 1932, Play

Farm Buyer, The *see* **O COMPRADOR DE FAZENDAS** (1951).

Farm on the Frontier, The *see* **NONA** (1973).

FARMER IN THE DELL, THE 1936 d: Ben Holmes. USA., *The Farmer in the Dell*, Philip Duffield Stong, New York 1935, Novel

FARMER TAKES A WIFE, THE 1935 d: Victor Fleming. USA., *The Farmer Takes a Wife*, Walter D. Edmonds, 1934, Play, *Rome Haul*, Walter D. Edmonds, 1929, Novel

FARMER TAKES A WIFE, THE 1953 d: Henry Levin. USA., *The Farmer Takes a Wife*, Walter D. Edmonds, 1934, Play, *Rome Haul*, Walter D. Edmonds, 1929, Novel

FARMER'S DAUGHTER, THE 1947 d: H. C. Potter. USA., *Juurakon Hulda*, Hella Wuolijoki, 1937, Play

FARMER'S WIFE, THE 1928 d: Alfred Hitchcock. UKN., *The Farmer's Wife*, Eden Philpotts, London 1924, Play

FARMER'S WIFE, THE 1941 d: Norman Lee, Leslie Arliss. UKN., *The Farmer's Wife*, Eden Philpotts, London 1924, Play

Faro in Capo al Mondo, Il *see* **LA LUZ DEL FIN DEL MUNDO** (1971).

Farrell Case, The *see* **G-MEN** (1935).

FASCHINGSKONIG, DER 1928 d: Georg Jacoby. GRM., *The Joker*, Noe Scott, Novel

FASCINATION 1931 d: Miles Mander. UKN., *Fascination*, Eliot Crawshaw Williams, Play

Fascination *see* **LOVE IN THE AFTERNOON** (1957).

Fashion for Men *see* **FINE CLOTHES** (1925).

FASHIONS FOR WOMEN 1927 d: Dorothy Arzner. USA., *The Girl of the Hour*, Gladys Unger, Story

FASHIONS IN LOVE 1929 d: Victor Schertzinger. USA., *Das Konzert*, Hermann Bahr, 1909, Play

FAST AND LOOSE 1930 d: Fred Newmeyer. USA., *The Best People*, David Gray, Avery Hopwood, New York 1924, Play

FAST AND LOOSE 1954 d: Gordon Parry. UKN., *A Cuckoo in the Nest*, Ben Travers, London 1925, Play

Fast Break *see* **FASTBREAK** (1979).

FAST COMPANY 1929 d: A. Edward Sutherland. USA., *Elmer the Great*, George M. Cohan, Ring Lardner, New York 1928, Play

FAST COMPANY 1938 d: Edward Buzzell. USA., *Fast Company*, Marco Page, New York 1938, Novel

FAST COMPANY 1953 d: John Sturges. USA., *Rocky's Rose*, Eustace Cockrell, Story

Fast Fortune see 11 HARROWHOUSE (1974).

Fast Gun, The see THE QUICK GUN (1964).

FAST LADY, THE 1962 d: Ken Annakin. UKN., *The Fast Lady*, Keble Howard, Short Story

FAST LIFE 1929 d: John Francis Dillon. USA., *Fast Life*, John B. Hymer, Samuel Shipman, New York 1928, Play

FAST MAIL, THE 1922 d: Bernard J. Durning. USA., *The Fast Mail*, Lincoln J. Carter, Play

Fast Money see SCHNELLES GELD (1981).

FAST SET, THE 1924 d: William C. de Mille. USA., *Spring Cleaning*, Frederick Lonsdale, New York 1923, Play

Fast Times see FAST TIMES AT RIDGEMONT HIGH (1982).

FAST TIMES AT RIDGEMONT HIGH 1982 d: Amy Heckerling. USA., *Fast Times at Ridgemont High*, Cameron Crowe, Novel

FAST WORKER, THE 1924 d: William A. Seiter. USA., *Husband of Edith*, George Barr McCutcheon, New York 1908, Novel

FAST WORKERS 1933 d: Tod Browning. USA., *Rivets*, John McDermott, Play

FASTBREAK 1979 d: Jack Smight. USA., Marc Kaplan, Story

Fasten Your Seat Belts see ESCALE A ORLY (1955).

FASTEST GUN ALIVE, THE 1956 d: Russell Rouse. USA., *The Last Notch*, Frank D. Gilroy, Television Play

Fastest Gun, The see THE QUICK GUN (1964).

FASTNACHTSBEICHTE, DIE 1960 d: William Dieterle. GRM., *Die Fastnachtsbeichte*, Carl Zuckmayer, Frankfurt 1959, Novel

FAST-WALKING 1981 d: James B. Harris. USA., *The Rap*, Ernest Brawley, Novel

Fat Chance see INSPECTOR MORSE: FAT CHANCE (1989).

FAT CITY 1972 d: John Huston. USA., *Fat City*, Leonard Gardner, Novel

Fat World see FETTE WELT (1998).

Fata Di Borgo Loreto, La see IL NANO ROSSO (1917).

FATAL CARD, THE 1915 d: James Kirkwood. USA., *The Fatal Card*, C. Haddon Chambers, B. C. Stephenson, London 1894, Play

Fatal Desire see CAVALLERIA RUSTICANA (1953).

FATAL HOUR, THE 1920 d: George W. Terwilliger. USA., *The Marriages of Mayfair*, Cecil Raleigh, London 1908, Play

FATAL HOUR, THE 1937 d: George Pearson. UKN., *The Clock*, Cicely Frazer-Simpson, Novel

Fatal Marriage, The see ENOCH ARDEN (1915).

FATAL NIGHT, THE 1948 d: Mario Zampi. UKN., *The Gentleman from America*, Michael Arlen, Short Story

Fatal Obsession see EL TUNEL (1988).

FATAL VISION 1984 d: David Greene. USA., *Fatal Vision*, Joe McGinness, Book

FATALITA 1947 d: Giorgio Bianchi. ITL., *Aniello 'A Ffede*, Rocco Galdieri, Novel

Fatalite du Destin, La see EL NEGRO QUE TENIA EL ALMA BLANCA (1926).

Fate Gave Me Twenty Cents see GOD GAVE ME TWENTY CENTS (1926).

Fate in the Balance see THE GRAY TOWERS MYSTERY (1919).

FATE IS THE HUNTER 1964 d: Ralph Nelson. USA., *Fate Is the Hunter*, Ernest K. Gann, New York 1961, Novel

Fate Largo Ai Moschettieri! see LES TROIS MOUSQUETAIRES (1953).

Fate of a Man see SUDBA CHELOVEKA (1959).

Fate of the Hunter see CAPTIVE HEARTS (1987).

Fated Vocation see DUYEN NGHIEP (1998).

Fateful Nights see OSUDNE NOCI (1928).

FATE'S ALIBI 1915 d: Frank Lloyd. USA., *Fate's Alibi*, C. W. Fassett, Story

FATES AND FLORA FOURFLUSH, THE 1914 d: Wally Van. USA., *The Fates and Flora Fourflush*, Charles Brown, Story

Fate's Plaything see WAT EEUWIG BLIJFT (1920).

Father see WO SHI HI BA BA MA? (1995).

Father and Son see MARKURELLS I WADKOPING (1930).

FATHER AND SON 1934 d: Monty Banks. UKN., *Barber John's Boy*, Ben Ames Williams, Story

FATHER AND THE BOYS 1915 d: Joseph de Grasse. USA., *Father and the Boys*, George Ade, New York 1908, Play

Father and the Boys see YOUNG AS YOU FEEL (1931).

FATHER BROWN 1954 d: Robert Hamer. UKN., *The Blue Cross*, G. K. Chesterton, 1929, Short Story

Father Brown see SANCTUARY OF FEAR (1979).

FATHER BROWN, DETECTIVE 1935 d: Edward Sedgwick. USA., *The Wisdom of Father Brown*, G. K. Chesterton, New York 1915, Short Story

Father Brown, Detective see SANCTUARY OF FEAR (1979).

FATHER CHRISTMAS 1992 d: Dave Unwin. UKN., *Father Christmas*, Raymond Briggs, Book

FATHER DAMIEN 1999 d: Paul Cox. BLG/NTH., **De Definitieve Biografie Damiaan**, Hilde Eynikel, Biography

FATHER FIGURE 1980 d: Jerry London. USA., *Father Figure*, Richard Peck, Book

FATHER GOOSE 1964 d: Ralph Nelson. USA., *A Place of Dragons*, S. H. Barnett, Short Story

FATHER IS A PRINCE 1940 d: Noel Smith. USA., *Big Hearted Herbert*, Anna Steese Richardson, Sophie Underwood, New York 1934, Play

Father Karafiat see PAN OTEC KARAFIAT (1935).

Father Kondelik and Bridegroom Vejvara see OTEC KONDELIK A ZENICH VEJVARA (1937).

Father Kondelik and Bridegroom Vejvara I. see OTEC KONDELIK A ZENICH VEJVARA I. (1926).

Father Kondelik and Bridegroom Vejvara II see OTEC KONDELIK A ZENICH VEJVARA II. (1926).

FATHER MAKES GOOD 1950 d: Jean Yarbrough. USA., *Journey at Sunrise*, D. D. Beauchamp, Short Story

Father Malachy's Miracle see DAS WUNDER DES MALACHIAS (1961).

Father Master see PADRE PADRONE (1977).

FATHER OF THE BRIDE 1950 d: Vincente Minnelli. USA., *Father of the Bride*, Edward Streeter, 1949, Novel

FATHER OF THE BRIDE 1991 d: Charles Shyer. USA., *Father of the Bride*, Edward Streeter, 1949, Novel

Father of the Girl, The see LE PERE DE MADEMOISELLE (1953).

Father Sergi see OTYETS SERGII (1978).

Father Sergius see OTYETS SERGII (1978).

Father Sergy see OTYETS SERGII (1978).

Father Takes a Walk see MR. COHEN TAKES A WALK (1935).

Father, The see FADREN (1969).

FATHER, THE 1970 d: Mark Fine. USA., *Toska*, Anton Chekhov, 1885, Short Story

Father Vojtech see PATER VOJTECH (1928).

Father Vojtech see PATER VOJTECH (1936).

FATHER WAS A FULLBACK 1949 d: John M. Stahl. USA., Clifford Goldsmith, Play

FATHERHOOD 1915 d: Hobart Bosworth. USA., *Fatherhood*, Julia Crawford Ivers, Story

Father-in-Law Kondelik and His Son-in-Law Vejvara see TCHAN KONDELIK A ZET VEJVARA (1929).

FATHERLAND 1994 d: Christopher Menaul. USA., *Fatherland*, Robert Harris, Novel

Fathers and Sons see OTTSY I DETI (1958).

Father's Day see THE RICHEST MAN IN THE WORLD (1930).

FATHER'S DOING FINE 1952 d: Henry Cass. UKN., *Little Lambs Eat Ivy*, Noel Langley, London 1948, Play

Father's Heart, A see LA GERLA DI PAPA MARTIN (1909).

FATHER'S HELPING HAND 1908 d: Horace Davey. USA., *Father's Helping Hand*, Malcolm Strong, Story

Father's Love, A see BLOODBROTHERS (1978).

FATHER'S LUCKY ESCAPE 1915 d: Horace Davey. USA., *Father's Lucky Escape*, Malcolm Strong, Story

FATHER'S SON 1931 d: William Beaudine. USA., *Old Fathers and Young Sons*, Booth Tarkington, Story

FATHER'S SON 1941 d: D. Ross Lederman. USA., *Old Fathers and Young Sons*, Booth Tarkington, Story

FATHER'S WILD GAME 1950 d: Herbert I. Leeds. USA., *A Hunting We Will Go*, D. D. Beauchamp, Story

FATHOM 1967 d: Leslie H. Martinson. UKN., *A Girl Called Fathom*, Larry Forrester, London 1967, Novel

Fatia Negra see SZEGENY GAZDAGOK (1959).

FATICHE DI ERCOLE, LE 1957 d: Pietro Francisci. ITL., *Le Argonautiche*, Apollonio Rodio, Novel

FATTO DI CRONACA 1944 d: Piero Ballerini. ITL., *La Vita Puo Ricomciare*, Alfredo Vanni, Novel

Fatty and Me, The see DER DICKE UND ICH (1981).

FAUBOURG-MONTMARTRE 1924 d: Charles Burguet. FRN., *Faubourg-Montmartre*, Henri Duvernois, Novel

FAUBOURG-MONTMARTRE 1931 d: Raymond Bernard. FRN., *Faubourg-Montmartre*, Henri Duvernois, Novel

Faun, The see BOUGHT AND PAID FOR (1916).

Faun, The see THE MARRIAGE MAKER (1923).

FAUNO DI MARMO, IL 1920 d: Mario Bonnard. ITL., *Il Fauno Di Marmo*, Nathaniel Hawthorne, 1860, Novel

FAUNOVO VELMI POZDNI ODPOLEDNE 1984 d: Vera ChytilovA. CZC., Jiri Brdecka, Story

Faun's Very Late Afternoon, A see FAUNOVO VELMI POZDNI ODPOLEDNE (1984).

Faussaire, Le see DIE FALSCHUNG (1981).

FAUSSE MAITRESSE, LA 1942 d: Andre Cayatte. FRN., *La Fausse Maitresse*, Honore de Balzac, 1841, Short Story

Fausses Nouvelles see BREAK THE NEWS (1938).

FAUST 1909 d: Edwin S. Porter, J. Searle Dawley. USA., *Faust*, Charles Gounod, Paris 1859, Opera

FAUST 1910 d: Enrico Guazzoni. ITL., *Faust*, Johann Wolfgang von Goethe, 1808-32, Play

FAUST 1911 d: Cecil M. Hepworth. UKN., *Faust*, Charles Gounod, Paris 1859, Opera

FAUST 1913 d: Stanislav HlavsA. CZC., *Faust a Marketka*, Charles Gounod, Paris 1859, Opera

FAUST 1922 d: Challis Sanderson. UKN., *Faust*, Charles Gounod, Paris 1859, Opera

FAUST 1926 d: F. W. Murnau. GRM., *Faust*, Johann Wolfgang von Goethe, 1808-32, Play

FAUST 1927 d: H. B. Parkinson. UKN., *Faust*, Charles Gounod, Paris 1859, Opera

FAUST 1936 d: Albert Hopkins. UKN., *Faust*, Charles Gounod, Paris 1859, Opera

FAUST 1960 d: Peter Gorski. GRM., *Faust*, Johann Wolfgang von Goethe, 1808-32, Play

FAUST 1964 d: Michael Susman. USA., *Faust*, Johann Wolfgang von Goethe, 1808-32, Play

FAUST 1988 d: Dieter Dorn. GRM., *Faust*, Johann Wolfgang von Goethe, 1808-32, Play

Faust - Eine Deutsche Volkssage see FAUST (1926).

Faust and the Devil see LA LEGGENDA DI FAUST (1949).

Faust E Margherita see LA LEGGENDA DI FAUST (1949).

Faust Fantasy see FAUST (1936).

FAUST XX 1966 d: Ion Popescu-Gopo. RMN., *Faust*, Johann Wolfgang von Goethe, 1808-32, Play

Faustus XX see FAUST XX (1966).

FAUTE DE L'ABBE MOURET, LA 1970 d: Georges Franju. FRN/ITL., *La Faute de l'Abbe Mouret*, Emile Zola, 1875, Novel

FAUTE DE MONIQUE, LA 1928 d: Maurice Gleize. FRN., *Monique - Poupee Francaise*, T. Trilby, Novel

Fauteuil 47, Le see PARKETTSESSEL 47 (1926).

FAUTEUIL 47, LE 1937 d: Fernand Rivers. FRN., *Le Fauteuil 47*, Louis Verneuil, Play

FAUX MAGISTRAT, LE 1914 d: Louis Feuillade. FRN., *Le Magistrat Cambrioleur*, Marcel Allain, Pierre Souvestre, Novel

Faux Monnayeurs see L' OR DANS LA MONTAGNE (1938).

FAVORITA, LA 1953 d: Cesare Barlacchi. ITL., *La Favorita*, Alfonso Royer, Gustavo Vaez, Play

Favorite Piece of Music see JUE XIANG (1985).

Favorite, The see O PREDILETO (1975).

FAVORITE, THE 1989 d: Jack (4) Smith. USA/SWT., *La Nuit de Serail*, Michel de Grece, Novel

FAVOUR, THE WATCH AND THE VERY BIG FISH, THE 1991 d: Ben Lewin. UKN/FRN., *Rue Saint-Sulpice*, Marcel Ayme, Short Story

Favourite, The see LA FAVORITA (1953).

FAZIL 1928 d: Howard Hawks. USA., *L' Insoumise*, Pierre Frondaie, Play

F.B.I. OPERAZIONE BAALBECK 1964 d: Marcello Giannini. ITL/FRN/LBN., *Una Moneta Spezzata*, Romolo Marcellini, Short Story

F.B.I. Operazione Pakistan see KOMMISSAR X: JAGT DIE ROTEN TIGER (1971).

F.B.I. STORY, THE 1959 d: Mervyn Leroy. USA., *The F.B.I. Story*, Don Whitehead, 1956, Book

F.D.R., THE LAST YEAR 1980 d: Anthony Page. USA., *F.D.R.: the Last Year*, Jim Bishop, Book

FE, LA 1947 d: Rafael Gil. SPN., *La Fe*, Armando Palacio Valdes, 1892, Novel

Fear see LA PAURA (1954).

FEAR AND LOATHING IN LAS VEGAS 1998 d: Terry Gilliam. USA., *Fear and Loathing in Las Vegas*, Hunter S. Thompson, Book

Fear in a Handful of Dust see FLESHBURN (1983).

FEAR IN THE NIGHT 1947 d: Maxwell Shane. USA., *Nightmare*, Cornell Woolrich, 1943, Short Story

FEAR IS THE KEY 1972 d: Michael Tuchner. UKN., *Fear Is the Key*, Alistair MacLean, 1961, Novel

FEAR MARKET, THE 1920 d: Kenneth Webb. USA., *The Fear Market*, Amelie Rives, New York 1916, Play

FEAR NO EVIL 1969 d: Paul Wendkos. USA., Guy Endore, Story

FEAR NO MORE 1961 d: Bernard Wiesen. USA., *Fear No More*, Leslie Edgley, New York 1946, Novel

Fear of Little Men, The see THE LUCK OF THE IRISH (1948).

FEAR ON TRIAL 1975 d: Lamont Johnson. USA., *Fear on Trial*, John Henry Faulk, Autobiography

FEAR SHIP, THE 1933 d: J. Steven Edwards. UKN., *The Second Mate*, R. W. Rees, Novel

FEAR STRIKES OUT 1957 d: Robert Mulligan. USA., *Fear Strikes Out*, Albert S. Hirschberg, Jimmy Piersall, Autobiography

FEARMAKERS, THE 1958 d: Jacques Tourneur. USA., *The Fearmakers*, Darwin L. Teilhet, 1945, Novel

FEAST OF JULY 1995 d: Christopher Menaul. UKN/USA., *The Feast of July*, H. E. Bates, Novel

Feast of St. Jorgen, The see PRAZDNIK SVYATOVO IORGENE (1930).

Feast of the Dove, The see LA VERBENA DE LA PALOMA (1921).

FEATHER IN HER HAT, A 1935 d: Alfred Santell. USA., *A Feather in Her Hat*, I. A. R. Wylie, Garden City, N.Y. 1934, Novel

FEATHER, THE 1929 d: Leslie Hiscott. UKN., *The Feather*, C. M. Matheson, Novel

FEATHER TOP 1912. USA., *Feathertop*, Nathaniel Hawthorne, 1852, Short Story

Feathered Serpent, The see THE MENACE (1932).

FEATHERED SERPENT, THE 1934 d: MacLean Rogers. UKN., *The Feathered Serpent*, Edgar Wallace, London 1927, Novel

Feathered Shadows, The see OPERENE STINY (1930).

Feathertop see FEATHER TOP (1912).

FEATHERTOP 1913. USA., *Feathertop*, Nathaniel Hawthorne, 1852, Short Story

FEATHERTOP 1916 d: Henry J. Vernot. USA., *Feathertop*, Nathaniel Hawthorne, 1852, Short Story

Febbre see ACCADDE A DAMASCO E FEBBRE (1943).

FEBBRE DI VIVERE 1953 d: Claudio GorA. ITL., *Cronaca*, Leopoldo Trieste, Play

FECONDITE 1929 d: Henri Etievant, Nicolas Evreinoff. FRN., *Fecondite*, Emile Zola, Novel

FEDERAL BULLETS 1937 d: Karl Brown. USA., *Federal Bullets*, George Fielding Eliot, London 1937, Novel

Federal Offense see UNDERCOVER DOCTOR (1939).

FEDERICA D'ILLIRIA 1919 d: Eleuterio Rodolfi. ITL., *Les Rois En Exil*, Alphonse Daudet, Paris 1879, Novel

Fedora see PRINCESS ROMANOFF (1915).

FEDORA 1916 d: Giuseppe de Liguoro. ITL., *Fedora*, Victorien Sardou, Paris 1882, Play

FEDORA 1918 d: Edward Jose. USA., *Fedora*, Victorien Sardou, Paris 1882, Play

FEDORA 1934 d: Louis J. Gasnier. FRN., *Fedora*, Victorien Sardou, Paris 1882, Play

FEDORA 1942 d: Camillo Mastrocinque. ITL., *Fedora*, Victorien Sardou, Paris 1882, Play

FEDRA 1956 d: Mur Oti. SPN., *Phaedra*, Lucius Annaeus Seneca, Play

FEDRA (DRAMMA MITOLOGICO DELL'ANTICA GRECIA) 1909 d: Oreste Gherardini. ITL., *Phedre Et Hyppolite*, Jean Racine, 1677, Play

Fedra, the Devil's Daughter see FEDRA (1956).

FEET OF CLAY 1917 d: Harry Harvey. USA., *Feet of Clay*, William Morton, Story

FEET OF CLAY 1924 d: Cecil B. de Mille. USA., *Feet of Clay*, Margaret Tuttle, Boston 1923, Novel

FEGEFEUER 1988 d: Wilhelm Hengstler. AUS., Jack Unterweger, Autobiography

FEI DAO HUA 1963 d: Xu Suling. CHN., *Fei Dao Hua*, XIong Daba, Novel

FEI HU DUI 1995 d: Wang Jixing. CHN., *Fei Hu Dui*, Liu Zhixia, Novel

FEKETE GYEMANTOK 1976 d: Zoltan Varkonyi. HNG., *Fekete Gyemantok*, Mor Jokai, 1870, Novel

FEKETE VAROS, A 1971 d: Eva Zsurzs. HNG., *A Fekete Varos*, Kalman Mikszath, 1911, Novel

Feld Marechal see MONSIEUR LE MARECHAL (1931).

FELDHERRNHUGEL, DER 1926 d: Erich Schonfelder, Hans Otto Lowenstein. GRM/ITL., *Der Feldherrnhugel*, Roda-Roda, Karl Rossler, Play

FELDHERRNHUGEL, DER 1953 d: Ernst MarischkA. AUS., *Der Feldherrnhugel*, Roda-Roda, Karl Rossler, Play

Feldmann Case, The see FELDMANN-SAKEN (1986).

FELDMANN-SAKEN 1986 d: Bente Erichsen. NRW., *Feldmann-Saken*, Sigurd Senje, Novel

FELHOJATEK! 1984 d: Gyula Maar. HNG., *Pesti Felhojatek*, Tibor Dery, 1946, Short Story

FELICIE NANTEUIL 1942 d: Marc Allegret. FRN., *Histoire Comique*, Anatole France, 1903, Novel

FELICITA COLOMBO 1937 d: Mario Mattoli. ITL., *Felicita Colombo*, Giuseppe Adami, Play

FELINS, LES 1964 d: Rene Clement. FRN., *Joy House*, Day Keene, New York 1954, Novel

Felipe Derblay see IL PADRONE DELLE FERRIERE (1959).

Felix and Otilia see FELIX SI OTILIA (1972).

FELIX HOLT 1915 d: Travers Vale. USA., *Felix Holt the Radical*, George Eliot, 1866, Novel

FELIX O'DAY 1920 d: Robert T. Thornby. USA., *Felix O'Day*, F. Hopkinson Smith, New York 1915, Novel

FELIX SI OTILIA 1972 d: Iulian Mihu. RMN., *Enigma Otiliei*, George Calinescu, 1938, Novel

FELIZ ANO VELHO 1988 d: Roberto Gervitz. BRZ., *Feliz Ano Velho*, Marcelo Rubens Paiva, 1982, Novel

Fellini's Casanova see CASANOVA (1976).

FELLINI-SATYRICON 1969 d: Federico Fellini. ITL/FRN., *Satyricon*, Petronius Arbiter, c50-66 a.D., Manuscript

Fellow from Our Town, A see PAREN IZ NASHEGO GORODA (1942).

Fellow Prisoners see CAPTURED! (1933).

Fellowship of the Frog see DER FROSCH MIT DER MASKE (1959).

FEM OG SPIONERNE, DE 1969 d: Trine Hedman. DNM/GRM., Enid Blyton, Novel

FEMALE 1933 d: Michael Curtiz, William Dieterle (Uncredited). USA., *Female*, Donald Henderson Clarke, New York 1932, Novel

Female Friends see STRANGE AWAKENING (1958).

Female Is the Deadliest of the Species, The see ATTENTI AL BUFFONE (1975).

FEMALE ON THE BEACH 1955 d: Joseph Pevney. USA., *The Beseiged Heart*, Robert Hill, Play

FEMALE PERVERSIONS 1996 d: Susan Streitfeld. USA/GRM., *Female Perversions; the Temptations of Emma Bovary*, Louise J. Kaplan, Book

Female: Seventy Times Seven see SETENTA VECES SIETE (1962).

FEMALE SWINDLER, THE 1916 d: Albert Ward. UKN., *The Female Swindler*, Walter Melville, Play

FEMALE, THE 1924 d: Sam Wood. USA., *Dalla the Lion Cub*, Cynthia Stockley, New York 1924, Novel

Female, The see LA FEMME ET LE PANTIN (1958).

Female, The see SETENTA VECES SIETE (1962).

FEME 1927 d: Richard Oswald. GRM., *Feme*, Vicki Baum, Novel

Feminine Touch see THE DUDE WRANGLER (1930).

FEMININE TOUCH, THE 1956 d: Pat Jackson. UKN., *A Lamp Is Heavy*, Sheila MacKay Russell, Novel

FEMME A PAPA, LA 1914 d: Georges MoncA. FRN., *La Femme a Papa*, Maurice Hennequin, Albert Milhaud, Play

FEMME A SA FENETRE, UNE 1976 d: Pierre Granier-Deferre. FRN., *Une Femme a Sa Fenetre*, Pierre Drieu la Rochelle, 1930, Novel

Femme Au Corbeau, La see THE RIVER (1928).

FEMME AUX YEUX FERMES, LA 1925 d: Alexandre Ryder. FRN., *La Femme aux Yeux Fermes*, Pierre L'Ermite, Novel

FEMME BLONDE, LA 1916 d: Henry Roussell. FRN., *La Femme Blonde*, Henri Demesse, Play

FEMME CHIPEE, UNE 1934 d: Piere Colombier. FRN., *Une Femme Ravie*, Louis Verneuil, Play

FEMME COQUETTE, UNE 1955 d: Jean-Luc Godard. SWT., *Le Signe*, Guy de Maupassant, 1887, Short Story

Femme de Chambre du Titanic, La see LA CAMARERA DEL TITANIC (1997).

FEMME DE CLAUDE, LA 1918 d: M. Maurice?. FRN., *La Femme de Claude*, Alexandre Dumas (fils), 1873, Play

Femme de Mes Amours, La see IL FRULLO DEL PASSERO (1988).

FEMME DE MES REVES, LA 1931 d: Jean Bertin. FRN., *Palace-Hotel*, Paul Franck, Play

FEMME DISPARAIT, UNE 1942 d: Jacques Feyder. SWT., *Une Femme Disparait*, Jacques Viot, Short Story

FEMME DOUCE, UNE 1969 d: Robert Bresson. FRN., *Krotkaya*, Fyodor Dostoyevsky, 1876, Short Story

FEMME DU BOULANGER, LA 1938 d: Marcel Pagnol. FRN., *Jean le Bleu*, Jean Giono, 1932, Novel

FEMME DU BOUT DU MONDE, LA 1937 d: Jean Epstein. FRN., *La Femme du Bout du Monde*, Alain Serdac, Novel

Femme du Dimanche, La see LA DONNA DELLA DOMENICA (1976).

FEMME DU SALTIMBANQUE, LA 1910 d: Georges DenolA. FRN., *Paillasse*, Adolphe-P. d'Ennery, Marc Fournier, Play

FEMME D'UNE NUIT, LA 1930 d: Marcel L'Herbier. FRN., *La Femme d'une Nuit*, Alfred Machard, Novel

Femme En Blanc Se Revolte, Une see LE NOUVEAU JOURNAL D'UNE FEMME EN BLANC (1966).

FEMME EN HOMME, LA 1932 d: Augusto GeninA. FRN., *La Femme En Homme*, Ugo Falena, Play

Femme Et le Diamant, La see COUP DE FEU A L'AUBE (1932).

FEMME ET LE PANTIN, LA 1929 d: Jacques de Baroncelli. FRN., *La Femme Et le Pantin*, Pierre Louys, Paris 1898, Play

FEMME ET LE PANTIN, LA 1958 d: Julien Duvivier. FRN/ITL., *La Femme Et le Pantin*, Pierre Louys, Paris 1898, Novel

FEMME ET LE ROSSIGNOL, LA 1930 d: Andre Hugon. FRN., *La Femme Et le Rossignol*, Bela Daniel, Short Story

FEMME FATALE, LA 1945 d: Jean Boyer. FRN., *La Femme Fatale*, Andre Birabeau, Play

FEMME FATALE, UNE 1976 d: Jacques Doniol-Valcroze. FRN/GRM., *Une Femme Fatale*, David Beaty, Novel

FEMME FIDELE, UNE 1976 d: Roger Vadim. FRN., *Les Liaisons Dangereuses*, Pierre Ambrose Choderlos de Laclos, 1782, Novel

FEMME IDEALE, LA 1933 d: Andre Berthomieu. FRN., *La Meilleure Maitresse*, Georges Oudart, Novel

Femme la Plus Riche du Monde, La see L' EAU DU NIL (1928).

Femme Libre, Une see LE FILS DE L'AUTRE (1931).

FEMME NUE, LA 1926 d: Leonce Perret. FRN., *La Femme Nue*, Henry Bataille, 1908, Play

FEMME NUE, LA 1932 d: Jean-Paul Paulin. FRN., *La Femme Nue*, Henry Bataille, 1908, Play

FEMME NUE, LA 1949 d: Andre Berthomieu. FRN., *La Femme Nue*, Henry Bataille, 1908, Play

FEMME PUBLIQUE, LA 1984 d: Andrzej Zulawski. FRN., *La Femme Publique*, Dominique Granier, Novel

Femme Ravie, Une see UNE FEMME CHIPEE (1934).

FEMME REVEE, LA 1929 d: Jean Durand. FRN., *La Femme Revee*, J. Perez de Rosas, Novel

FEMME SANS IMPORTANCE, UNE 1937 d: Jean Choux. FRN., *A Woman of No Importance*, Oscar Wilde, London 1893, Play

Femme Sur la Plage, La see **THE WOMAN ON THE BEACH** (1946).

FEMMES 1936 d: Bernard-Roland. FRN., *Femmes*, Marja Morozowicz Szczepkowska, Novel

FEMMES COLLANTES, LES 1920 d: Georges MoncA. FRN., *Les Femmes Collantes*, Leon Gandillot, Play

FEMMES COLLANTES, LES 1938 d: Pierre Caron. FRN., *Les Femmes Collantes*, Leon Gandillot, Play

FEMMES D'ABORD, LES 1962 d: Raoul Andre. FRN., *Dynamite Girl*, Paul Gerrard, Novel

Femmes de Trente Ans, Les see **IN PRAISE OF OLDER WOMEN** (1978).

Femmes Menent le Jeu, Les see **SCAMPOLO '53** (1954).

Femmes Pour Noumea see **LA ROUTE DU BAGNE** (1945).

FEMMES SAVANTES, LES 1965 d: Jean Meyer. FRN., *Les Femmes Savantes*, Moliere, 1673, Play

FEMMES S'EN BALANCENT, LES 1953 d: Bernard Borderie. FRN., *Les Femmes S'en Balancent*, Peter Cheyney, Novel

FEMMES SONT DES ANGES, LES 1952 d: Marcel Aboulker. FRN., *Les Femmes Sont Des Anges*, Pierre-Aristide Breal, Novel

FEMMES SONT FOLLES, LES 1950 d: Gilles Grangier. FRN., *Chateau Historique*, J. Berr de Turique, Alexandre Bisson, Play

FEMMES SONT MARRANTES, LES 1958 d: Andre Hunebelle. FRN., *Ami-Ami*, Pierre Barillet, Jean-Pierre Gredy

Femmina see **LA FEMME ET LE PANTIN** (1958).

FENDETESTAS 1975 d: Antonio F. Simon. SPN., *El Bosque Animado*, Wenceslao Fernandez Florez, 1943, Novel

FENG HUANG QING 1993 d: He Qun. CHN., *Feng Huang Qing*, Liu XInglong, Novel

Feng River Flows Far, The see **FENG SHUI CHANG LIU** (1963).

FENG SHUI CHANG LIU 1963 d: Sha Meng. CHN., *Feng Shui Chang Liu*, Hu Zheng, Novel

Fengriffen see **AND NOW THE SCREAMING STARTS!** (1973).

Fenster Zum Flur, Das see **IM PARTERRE LINKS** (1963).

Ferat Vampire see **UPIR Z FERATU** (1982).

Fer-de-Lance see **MEET NERO WOLFE** (1936).

FERDINAND LE NOCEUR 1913 d: Georges MoncA. FRN., *Ferdinand le Noceur*, Leon Gandillot, Play

FERDINAND LE NOCEUR 1935 d: Rene Sti. FRN., *Ferdinand le Noceur*, Leon Gandillot, Play

Ferdys Pistora Turns Over a New Leaf see **OBRACENI FERDYSE PISTORY** (1931).

Ferien in Tirol see **ZARTLICHES GEHEIMNIS** (1956).

FERIEN MIT PIROSCHKA 1965 d: Franz J. Gottlieb. GRM/AUS/HNG., *Ferien Mit Piroschka*, Hugo Hartung, Novel

FERIEN VOM ICH 1934 d: Hans Deppe. GRM., *Ferien Vom Ich*, Paul Keller, 1916, Novel

FERIEN VOM ICH 1952 d: Hans Deppe. GRM., *Ferien Vom Ich*, Paul Keller, 1916, Novel

FERIEN VOM ICH 1963 d: Hans Grimm. GRM., *Ferien Vom Ich*, Paul Keller, 1916, Novel

FERIEN WIE NOCH NIE 1963 d: Wolfgang Schleif. GRM., *Ferien Wie Noch Nie*, Hans Thomas, Novel

Ferita, La see **LA BLESSURE** (1922).

Fermati Coplan see **COPLAN FX18 CASSE TOUT** (1965).

FERME DU CHOQUART, LA 1921 d: Jean Kemm. FRN., *La Ferme du Choquart*, Victor Cherbuliez, Novel

Ferme du Maudit, La see **LA FERME DU PENDU** (1945).

FERME DU PENDU, LA 1945 d: Jean Dreville. FRN., *La Ferme du Pendu*, Gilbert Dupe, Novel

FERMIN Y PAULINA 1927. SPN., *L'Abric de Pell*, Jordi Catala, Story

FERNANDA 1917 d: Gustavo SerenA. ITL., *Fernande*, Victorien Sardou, 1870, Play

Fernandel, Scopa E Pennel see **COCAGNE** (1960).

FERRAGUS 1920 d: Enrico Vidali. ITL., *L'Histoire Des Treize*, Honore de Balzac, Paris 1835, Short Story

FERRAGUS 1923 d: Gaston Ravel. FRN., *L'Histoire Des Treize*, Honore de Balzac, Paris 1835, Short Story

FERREOL 1916 d: Eduardo BencivengA. ITL., *Ferreol*, Victorien Sardou, Paris 1875, Play

Ferris Wheel see **DAS RIESENRAD** (1961).

FERRO, IL 1918 d: Ugo FalenA. ITL., *La Chevrefeuille*, Gabriele D'Annunzio, 1914

FERRY TO HONG KONG 1959 d: Lewis Gilbert. UKN., *Ferry to Hongkong*, Max Catto, London 1957, Novel

Fertility God, The see **RUSHYA SHRINGA** (1976).

FESSEE, LA 1937 d: Pierre Caron. FRN., *La Fessee*, Jean de Letraz, Play

Festin de Babette, Le see **BABETTES GAESTEBUD** (1987).

Festival see **CHUKJE** (1997).

Festival at St. Jurgen see **PRAZDNIK SVYATOVO IORGENE** (1930).

Festival of Colour see **HOLI** (1983).

Festival of Fire, The see **HOLI** (1983).

Festival of Gion see **GION MATSURI** (1968).

Festival of Love see **UTSAV** (1983).

Festival, The see **UTSAV** (1983).

Festivals see **UTSAV** (1983).

Festung, Die see **VERDAMMT ZUR SUNDE** (1964).

FETE ESPAGNOLE, LA 1961 d: Jean-Jacques Vierne. FRN., *La Fete Espagnole*, Henri-Francois Rey, Paris 1958, Novel

FETITA CU CHIBRITURI 1967 d: Aurel Miheles. RMN., *Den Lille Pige Med Svovlstikkerne*, Hans Christian Andersen, 1846, Short Story

FETTE WELT 1998 d: Jan Schutte. GRM., *Fette Welt*, Helmut Krausser, Novel

FETTERED 1919 d: Arrigo Bocchi. UKN., *Fettered*, Joan Sutherland, Novel

FETTERED WOMAN, THE 1917 d: Tom Terriss. USA., *Anne's Bridge*, Robert W. Chambers, New York 1914, Novel

Fetters see **OKOVY** (1925).

FEU DANS LA PEAU, LE 1953 d: Marcel Blistene. FRN/ITL., *Le Feu Dans la Peau*, Rene Bragard, Novel

FEU DE PAILLE, LE 1939 d: Jean Benoit-Levy. FRN., *Grandeur Nature*, Henri Troyat, 1936, Novel

FEU FOLLET, LE 1963 d: Louis Malle. FRN/ITL., *Le Feu Follet*, Pierre Drieu la Rochelle, Paris 1931, Novel

FEU MATHIAS PASCAL 1925 d: Marcel L'Herbier. FRN., *Il Fu Mattia Pascal*, Luigi Pirandello, 1904, Novel

FEU SOUS LA PEAU, LE 1985 d: Gerard Kikoine. FRN., *Le Feu Sous la Peau*, Dominique Labarriere, Novel

FEU TOUPINEL 1933 d: Roger Capellani. FRN., *Feu Toupinel*, Alexandre Bisson, Albert Carre, Play

Feud of the Range see **FEUD OF THE WEST** (1936).

FEUD OF THE WEST 1936 d: Harry L. Fraser. USA., *Feud of the Rocking U*, Russell A. Bankson, Short Story

FEUDALISMO (SCENE SICILIANE) 1912 d: Alfredo Robert. ITL., *Terra Baixa*, Angel Guimera, Madrid 1896, Play

FEUER, DAS 1914 d: Urban Gad. GRM., *Die Alte Gnadige*, Gustav Wied

FEUERSCHIFF, DAS 1963 d: Ladislao VajdA. GRM., *Das Feuerschiff*, Siegfried Lenz, 1960, Short Story

FEUERWERK 1956 d: Kurt Hoffmann. GRM., *Feuerwerk*, Jurg Amstein, Erik Charell, Play

FEUERZANGENBOWLE, DIE 1944 d: Helmut Weiss. GRM., *Die Feuerzangenbowle*, Heinrich Spoerl, Novel

FEUERZANGENBOWLE, DIE 1970 d: Helmut Kautner. GRM., *Die Feuerzangenbowle*, Heinrich Spoerl, Novel

Feuerzeichen see **LEBENSZEICHEN** (1967).

FEUERZEUG, DAS 1959 d: Siegfried Hartmann. GDR., *Fyrtojet*, Hans Christian Andersen, Copenhagen 1835, Short Story

Feux de la Sarakina, Les see **CELUI QUI DOIT MOURIR** (1956).

Fever see **GORACZKA** (1980).

FEVER HEAT 1968 d: Russell S. Doughton Jr. USA., *Fever Heat*, Angus Vicker, New York 1954, Novel

FEVER IN THE BLOOD, A 1961 d: Vincent Sherman. USA., *A Fever in the Blood*, William Pearson, New York 1959, Novel

Fever Mounts at El Pao, The see **LA FIEVRE MONTE A EL PAO** (1959).

FEVER PITCH 1996 d: David Evans. UKN., *Fever Pitch*, Nick Hornby, Book

Few Days in the Life of I.I. Oblomov, A see **NESKOLKO DNEI IZ ZHIZNI I.I. OBLOMOV** (1980).

Ffolkes see **NORTH SEA HIJACK** (1980).

FIACCOLA SOTTO IL MOGGIO, LA 1911 d: Luigi Maggi. ITL., *La Fiaccola Sotto Il Moggio*, Gabriele D'Annunzio, 1904, Play

FIACCOLA SOTTO IL MOGGIO, LA 1916 d: Eleuterio Rodolfi. ITL., *La Fiaccola Sotto Il Moggio*, Gabriele D'Annunzio, 1904, Play

FIACRE 13 1947 d: Raoul Andre, Andre Hugon. FRN., *Le Fiacre N. 13*, Xavier de Montepin, 1881, Novel

FIACRE N. 13, IL 1917 d: Alberto A. Capozzi, Gero Zambuto. ITL., *Le Fiacre N. 13*, Xavier de Montepin, 1881, Novel

FIACRE N. 13, IL 1947 d: Mario Mattoli. ITL/FRN., *Le Fiacre N. 13*, Xavier de Montepin, 1881, Novel

Fiakermilli - Liebling von Wien see **DIE FIAKERMILLI** (1953).

FIAKERMILLI, DIE 1953 d: Arthur M. Rabenalt. AUS., *Fiakermilli*, Martin Costa, Play

FIAMMA CHE NON SI SPEGNE, LA 1949 d: Vittorio Cottafavi. ITL., *Itala Gens*, Franco Navarra Viggiani, Novel

FIAMMATA, LA 1922 d: Carmine Gallone. ITL., *La Flambee*, Henri Kistemaeckers, 1911, Play

FIAMMATA, LA 1952 d: Alessandro Blasetti. ITL., *La Flambee*, Henri Kistemaeckers, 1911, Play

FIANCAILLES ROUGES, LES 1926 d: Roger Lion. FRN., *La Tempete*, Lawrence Arnold, Georges Spitzmuller, Short Story

FIANCEE DU DISPARU, LA 1921 d: Charles Maudru. FRN., *A Dead Man's Love*, Tom Gallon

Fiancee, The see **DIE VERLOBTE** (1980).

"FIAT VOLUNTAS DEI" 1935 d: Amleto Palermi. ITL., *"Fiat Voluntas Dei"*, Giuseppe Macri, Play

FICKLE WOMEN 1920 d: Fred J. Butler, Hugh McClung. USA., *Sitting on the World*, Sophie Kerr, 1920, Short Story

FIDALGOS DA CASA MOURISCA, OS 1938 d: Arthur Duarte. PRT., *Os Fidalgos Da Casa Mourisca*, Julio Dinis, 1871, Novel

FIDANZAMENTO, IL 1975 d: Gianni Grimaldi. ITL., *Il Fidanzamento*, Goffredo Parise, Novel

FIDANZATA DI MESSINA, LA 1911 d: Mario Caserini. ITL., *Die Braut von Messina*, Friedrich von Schiller, 1803, Play

FIDDLER ON THE ROOF 1971 d: Norman Jewison. USA., *Tevye and His Daughters*, Shalom Aleichem, Short Story

FIDELE BAUER, DER 1927 d: Franz Seitz. GRM., *Der Fidele Bauer*, Leo Fall, Viktor Leon, Opera

FIDELE BAUER, DER 1951 d: Georg MarischkA. AUS., *Der Fidele Bauer*, Leo Fall, Viktor Leon, Opera

FIDELIO 1956 d: Walter Felsenstein. AUS., *Fidelio*, Ludwig Van Beethoven, Vienna 1805, Opera

FIDELIO 1968 d: Joachim Hess. GRM., *Fidelio*, Ludwig Van Beethoven, Vienna 1805, Opera

Fidget, The see **POPRYGUNYA** (1955).

FIDLOVACKA 1930 d: Svatopluk Innemann. CZC., *Fidlovacka Aneb Zadny Hnev a Zadna Rvacka*, Josef Kajetan Tyl, Play

Fiebre see **ACCADDE A DAMASCO E FEBBRE** (1943).

FIEL INFANTERIA, LA 1959 d: Pedro LazagA. SPN., *La Fiel Infanteria*, Rafael Garcia Serrano, 1943, Novel

Field Marshall, The see **DER FALSCHE FELDMARSCHALL** (1930).

FIELD OF DREAMS 1989 d: Phil Alden Robinson. USA., *Shoeless Joe*, W. P. Kinsella, Book

Field of Honor see **FIELDS OF HONOR** (1918).

Field Poppy, The see **GUBIJINSO** (1935).

FIELD, THE 1990 d: Jim Sheridan. UKN/IRL., *The Field*, John B. Keane, 1966, Play

FIELDS OF HONOR 1918 d: Ralph Ince. USA., *Field of Honor*, Irvin S. Cobb, 1916, Short Story

FIEND WHO WALKED THE WEST, THE 1958 d: Gordon Douglas. USA., *Kiss of Death*, Eleazar Lipsky, Novel

FIEND WITHOUT A FACE 1958 d: Arthur Crabtree. UKN., *The Thought Monster*, Amelia Reynolds Long, Short Story

Fiends, The see **LES DIABOLIQUES** (1954).

Fieras Humanas see SELVA TRAGICA (1964).

Fierce Conflicts see DA CHONGZHUANG (1993).

FIERCEST HEART, THE 1961 d: George Sherman. USA., *The Fiercest Heart*, Stuart Cloete, Boston 1960, Novel

FIERECILLA DOMADA, LA 1955 d: Antonio Roman. SPN/FRN., *The Taming of the Shrew*, William Shakespeare, c1593, Play

FIERY HAND, THE 1923 d: A. E. Coleby. UKN., *The Fiery Hand*, Sax Rohmer, Short Story

FIERY INTRODUCTION, A 1915 d: Charles Giblyn. USA., *A Fiery Introduction*, Julius G. Furthmann, Story

Fiery Spur see HOT SPUR (1968).

Fiery Summer see OHNIVE LETO (1939).

Fiesta En El Caribe see BALDORIA NEI CARAIBI (1956).

Fievre du Pouvoir, La see MACHTRAUSCH - ABER DIE LIEBE SIEGT (1942).

FIEVRE MONTE A EL PAO, LA 1959 d: Luis Bunuel. FRN/MXC., *La Fievre Monte a El Pao*, Henri Castillou, Novel

FIFTEEN STREETS, THE 1989 d: David Wheatley. UKN., *The Fifteen Streets*, Catherine Cookson, Novel

FIFTH AVENUE 1926 d: Robert G. VignolA. USA., *Fifth Avenue*, Arthur Stringer, 1925, Short Story

FIFTH AVENUE MODELS 1925 d: Svend Gade. USA., *The Best in Life*, Muriel Hine Coxen, New York 1918, Novel

Fifth Chair, The see IT'S IN THE BAG (1945).

FIFTH COMMANDMENT, THE 1915. USA., *The Fifth Commandment*, Julius Steger, Play

Fifth Commandment, The see BROKEN LULLABY (1932).

Fifth Cord, The see GIORNATA NERA PER L'ARIETE (1971).

FIFTH FORM AT ST. DOMINIC'S, THE 1921 d: A. E. Coleby. UKN., *The Fifth Form at St. Dominics*, Talbot Baines Reed, London 1881, Novel

Fifth Horseman Is Fear, The see ..A PATY JEZDEC JE STRACH (1964).

FIFTH MAN, THE 1914 d: Francis J. Grandon. USA., *The Fifth Man*, James Oliver Curwood, Short Story

FIFTH MUSKETEER, THE 1977 d: Ken Annakin. UKN/AUS., *Le Vicomte de Bragelonne*, Alexandre Dumas (pere), Paris 1847, Novel

Fifth of November, The see HENNESSY (1975).

Fifth Rider Is Fear, The see ..A PATY JEZDEC JE STRACH (1964).

Fifth Seal, The see AZ OTODIK PECSET (1977).

FIFTH WHEEL, THE 1918 d: David Smith. USA., *The Fifth Wheel*, O. Henry, Short Story

Fifth Wheel, The see HIGH-BALLIN' (1978).

FIFTY CANDLES 1921 d: Irvin V. Willat. USA., *Fifty Candles*, Earl Derr Biggers, Indianapolis 1926, Novel

FIFTY MILLION FRENCHMEN 1931 d: Lloyd Bacon. USA., *Fifty Million Frenchmen*, Herbert Fields, E.R. Goetz, Cole Porter, New York 1929, Play

FIFTY ROADS TO TOWN 1937 d: Norman Taurog. USA., *Fifty Roads to Town*, Frederick Nebel, Boston 1936, Novel

Fifty-Two Pick-Up see 52 PICK-UP (1987).

FIGARO 1928 d: Gaston Ravel. FRN., *Le Mariage de Figaro*, Pierre-Augustin Caron de Beaumarchais, Paris 1784, Play

Figaro, Barbiere Di Siviglia see FIGARO IL BARBIERE DI SIVIGLIA (1955).

FIGARO E LA SUA GRAN GIORNATA 1931 d: Mario Camerini. ITL., *Ostrega Che Sbrego!*, Arnaldo Fraccaroli, Play

FIGARO IL BARBIERE DI SIVIGLIA 1955 d: Camillo Mastrocinque. ITL., *Le Barbier de Seville*, Pierre-Augustin Caron de Beaumarchais, 1775, Play

Figaros Hochzeit see DIE HOCHZEIT DES FIGARO (1968).

Fight for Freedom see THE AUTOBIOGRAPHY OF MISS JANE PITTMAN (1974).

FIGHT FOR LIFE, THE 1940 d: Pare Lorentz. USA., *The Fight for Life*, Paul de Kruif, Book

FIGHT FOR LOVE, A 1919 d: John Ford. USA., *Hell's Neck*, Eugene B. Lewis, Story

FIGHT, THE 1915 d: George W. Lederer. USA., *The Fight*, Bayard Veiller, New York 1913, Play

FIGHTER, THE 1921 d: Henry Kolker. USA., *The Fighter*, Albert Payson Terhune, New York 1909, Novel

FIGHTER, THE 1952 d: Herbert Kline. USA., *The Mexican*, Jack London, 1913, Short Story

FIGHTIN' COMEBACK, THE 1927 d: Tenny Wright. USA., *The Sun Dance Kid*, Walter J. Coburn, Story

Fighting Back see THE PRESCOTT KID (1934).

FIGHTING BACK 1980 d: Robert Lieberman. USA., Rocky Bleier, Terry O'Neil, Biography

FIGHTING BACK 1982 d: Michael Caulfield. ASL., *Tom*, John Embling, Novel

FIGHTING BOB 1915 d: John W. Noble. USA., *Fighting Bob*, Edward E. Rose, Book

FIGHTING CARAVANS 1930 d: David Burton, Otto Brower. USA., *Fighting Caravans*, Zane Grey, New York 1929, Novel

Fighting Caravans see WAGON WHEELS (1934).

FIGHTING CHANCE, A 1913 d: Ralph Ince. USA., *A Fighting Chance*, James Oliver Curwood, Story

FIGHTING CHANCE, THE 1916?. USA., *The Fighting Chance*, Robert W. Chambers, New York 1906, Novel

FIGHTING CHANCE, THE 1920 d: Charles Maigne. USA., *The Fighting Chance*, Robert W. Chambers, New York 1906, Novel

FIGHTING COWARD 1935 d: Dan Milner. USA., *The Last Assignment*, Peter B. Kyne, 1913, Short Story

FIGHTING COWARD, THE 1924 d: James Cruze. USA., *Magnolia*, Booth Tarkington, New York 1923, Play

FIGHTING CRESSY 1919 d: Robert T. Thornby. USA., *Cressy*, Bret Harte, Boston 1889, Novel

FIGHTING DESTINY 1919 d: Paul Scardon. USA., *Jungle Heart*, Stanley Shaw, 1918, Short Story

FIGHTING EAGLE, THE 1927 d: Donald Crisp. USA., *The Exploits of Brigadier Gerard*, Arthur Conan Doyle, London 1896, Novel

FIGHTING EDGE, THE 1926 d: Henry Lehrman. USA., *The Fighting Edge*, William MacLeod Raine, Boston 1922, Novel

Fighting Elegy see KENKA SEREJII (1966).

FIGHTING FOR GOLD 1919 d: Edward J. Le Saint. USA., *The Highgrader*, William MacLeod Raine, New York 1915, Novel

Fighting for Power see DUO YIN (1963).

FIGHTING FURY 1924 d: Cliff Smith. USA., *Triple Cross for Danger*, Walter J. Coburn, Story

FIGHTING GUARDSMAN, THE 1945 d: Henry Levin. USA., *Les Compagnons de Jehu*, Alexandre Dumas (pere), 1857, Novel

FIGHTING HEART, THE 1925 d: John Ford. USA., *Once to Every Man*, Larry Evans, New York 1913, Novel

FIGHTING HOMBRE, THE 1927 d: Jack Nelson. USA., *Cherokee Rose*, Estrella Warde, Short Story

FIGHTING HOPE, THE 1915 d: George Melford. USA., *The Fighting Hope*, William Hurlbut, New York 1908, Play

Fighting Jack see CORINTHIAN JACK (1921).

FIGHTING LADY, THE 1935 d: Carlos Borcosque. USA., Robert Ober, Play

FIGHTING LOVE 1927 d: Nils Chrisander. USA., **If the Gods Laugh**, Rosita Forbes, London 1925, Novel

FIGHTING LOVER, THE 1921 d: Fred Leroy Granville. USA., *Three in a Thousand*, Ben Ames Williams, 1917, Short Story

FIGHTING MAD 1939 d: Sam Newfield. USA., *Renfrew Rides Again*, Laurie York Erskine, New York 1927, Novel

FIGHTING ODDS 1917 d: Allan Dwan. USA., *Under Sentence*, Irvin S. Cobb, Roi Cooper Megrue, New York 1916, Play

FIGHTING PARSON, THE 1912 d: Bert Haldane, George Gray. UKN., *The Fighting Parson*, Chris Davis, George Gray, Play

FIGHTING PEACEMAKER, THE 1926 d: Cliff Smith. USA., *Peace Medicine*, W. C. Tuttle, Story

Fighting Phantom see THE MYSTERIOUS RIDER (1933).

Fighting Pimpernel, The see THE ELUSIVE PIMPERNEL (1950).

Fighting Playboy see THE CRIMSON PARADISE (1933).

FIGHTING PRINCE OF DONEGAL, THE 1966 d: Michael O'Herlihy. UKN/USA., *Red Hugh - Prince of Donegal*, Robert T. Reilly, Milwaukee 1957, Novel

Fighting Schoolmaster, The see THE JUCKLINS (1920).

FIGHTING SHEPHERDESS, THE 1920 d: Edward Jose. USA., *The Fighting Shepherdess*, Caroline Lockhart, Boston 1919, Novel

FIGHTING SNUB REILLY 1924 d: Andrew P. Wilson. UKN., *Fighting Snub O'Reilly*, Edgar Wallace, London 1929, Novel

FIGHTING STRANGER, THE 1921 d: Webster Cullison. USA., *Danger*, William E. Wing, Story

FIGHTING STREAK, THE 1922 d: Arthur Rosson. USA., *Free Range Lanning*, George Owen Baxter, New York 1921, Novel

FIGHTING TEXAN, THE 1937 d: Charles Abbott. USA., *The Tragedy That Lived*, James Oliver Curwood, Short Story

FIGHTING TROOPER, THE 1934 d: Ray Taylor. USA., *Footprints*, James Oliver Curwood, Short Story

Figli Del Capriccio, I see MARTINO IL TROVATELLO (1919).

FIGLI DEL MARCHESE LUCERA, I 1938 d: Amleto Palermi. ITL., *I Figli Del Marchese Lucera*, Gherardo Gherardi, Play

FIGLI DELLA NOTTE, I 1939 d: Benito Perojo, Aldo Vergano. ITL/SPN., *Los Hijos de la Noche*, Leandro Navarro, Play

FIGLI DI NESSUNO, I 1921 d: Ubaldo Maria Del Colle. ITL., *I Figli Di Nessuno*, Ruggero Rindi, Novel

FIGLI DI NESSUNO, I 1951 d: Raffaello Matarazzo. ITL., *I Figli Di Nessuno*, Ruggero Rindi, Novel

FIGLIA DEL CAPITANO, LA 1947 d: Mario Camerini. ITL., *Kapitanskaya Dochka*, Alexander Pushkin, 1836, Short Story

FIGLIA DEL CORSARO VERDE, LA 1941 d: Enrico Guazzoni. ITL., *La Figlia Del Corsaro Verde*, Emilio Salgari, Novel

FIGLIA DEL FORZATO, LA 1955 d: Gaetano AmatA. ITL., *La Morte Civile*, Paolo Giacometti, 1861, Play

FIGLIA DEL MENDICANTE, LA 1950 d: Carlo Campogalliani. ITL., *La Figlia Del Mendicante*, Carolina Invernizio, Novel

FIGLIA DEL REGGIMENTO, LA 1911. ITL., *La Fille du Regiment*, Jean-Francois Bayard, Jules H. Vernoy, Paris 1840, Opera

FIGLIA DEL REGGIMENTO, LA 1920 d: Enrico Vidali. ITL., *La Fille du Regiment*, Jean-Francois Bayard, Gaetano Donizetti, Paris 1840, Opera

FIGLIA DELL'AVARO, LA 1913. ITL., *Eugenie Grandet*, Honore de Balzac, 1833, Novel

FIGLIA DI JORIO, LA 1911. ITL., *La Figlia Di Jorio*, Gabriele D'Annunzio, 1904, Play

FIGLIA DI JORIO, LA 1917 d: Eduardo BencivengA. ITL., *La Figlia Di Jorio*, Gabriele D'Annunzio, 1904, Play

FIGLIA UNICA, LA 1919 d: Camillo de Riso. ITL., *La Figlia Unica*, Teobaldo Ciconi, 1853

FIGLIO DEL CORSARO ROSSO, IL 1921 d: Vitale de Stefano. ITL., *Il Figlio Del Corsaro Rosso*, Emilio Salgari, Florence 1920, Novel

FIGLIO DEL CORSARO ROSSO, IL 1942 d: Marco Elter. ITL., *Il Figlio Del Corsaro Rosso*, Emilio Salgari, Florence 1920, Novel

FIGLIO DEL CORSARO ROSSO, IL 1960 d: Primo Zeglio. ITL., *Il Figlio Del Corsaro Rosso*, Emilio Salgari, Florence 1920, Novel

FIGLIO DI BAKUNIN, IL 1998 d: Gianfranco Cabiddu. ITL., *Il Figlio Di Bakunin*, Sergio Atzeni, Book

FIGLIO DI LAGARDERE, IL 1952 d: Fernando Cerchio. ITL/FRN., *Le Fil de Lagardere*, Paul Feval (fils), Novel

FIGURANTE, LA 1922 d: Gian Bistolfi. ITL., *La Figurante*, Francois de Curel, 1889, Play

FIGURE DE PROUE 1947 d: Christian Stengel. FRN., *Figure de Proue*, Gilbert Dupe, Novel

FIGUREHEAD, THE 1953 d: John Halas, Joy Batchelor. UKN., *The Figurehead*, Crosbie Garstin, Poem

FIGURES DE CIRE 1912 d: Maurice Tourneur. FRN., *Figures de Cire*, Andre de Lorde, Play

FIGURES IN A LANDSCAPE 1970 d: Joseph Losey. UKN., *Figures in a Landscape*, Barry England, Novel

FIL A LA PATTE, UN 1914 d: Henri Pouctal, Marcel Simon. FRN., *Un Fil a la Patte*, Georges Feydeau, 1899, Play

FIL A LA PATTE, UN 1924 d: Robert Saidreau. FRN., *Un Fil a la Patte*, Georges Feydeau, 1899, Play

FIL A LA PATTE, UN 1933 d: Karl Anton. FRN., *Un Fil a la Patte*, Georges Feydeau, 1899, Play

FIL A LA PATTE, UN 1954 d: Guy Lefranc. FRN., *Un Fil a la Patte*, Georges Feydeau, 1899, Play

FIRE BRIGADE, THE 1926 d: William Nigh. USA., *The Fire Brigade*, Kate Corbaley, Story

FIRE DOWN BELOW 1957 d: Robert Parrish. UKN., *Fire Down Below*, Max Catto, Novel

FIRE EATER, THE 1921 d: B. Reeves Eason. USA., *The Badge of Fighting Hearts*, Ralph Cummins, 1921, Short Story

FIRE FLINGERS, THE 1919 d: Rupert Julian. USA., *The Fire Flingers*, William J. Neidig, New York 1919, Novel

Fire in the Flesh *see* LA FILLE DE FEU (1958).

Fire in the Opera House *see* BRAND IN DER OPER (1930).

Fire in the Skin *see* LE FEU DANS LA PEAU (1953).

FIRE IN THE SKY, A 1978 d: Jerry Jameson. USA., Paul Gallico, Story

FIRE IN THE STONE 1983 d: Gary Conway. ASL., *A Fire in the Stone*, Colin Thiele, Novel

Fire in the Straw *see* LE FEU DE PAILLE (1939).

Fire in Their Hearts *see* QUEST FOR LOVE (1987).

FIRE ON THE MOUNTAIN 1981 d: Donald Wrye. USA., *Fire on the Mountain*, Edward Abbey, Book

FIRE OVER ENGLAND 1937 d: William K. Howard. UKN., *Fire Over England*, A. E. W. Mason, 1936, Novel

Fire Over the Women's Castle *see* YOSHIWARA ENJO (1987).

FIRE PATROL, THE 1924 d: Hunt Stromberg. USA., *The Fire Patrol*, Edwin Barbour, James W. Harkins Jr., Worcester 1891, Play

FIRE SALE 1977 d: Alan Arkin. USA., *Fire Sale*, Robert Klane, Novel

Fire, The *see* DAS FEUER (1914).

Fire, The *see* BRANNEN (1973).

Fire Tong Punch *see* DIE FEUERZANGENBOWLE (1970).

Fire Under Her Skin *see* LE FEU DANS LA PEAU (1953).

Fire Within, The *see* LE FEU FOLLET (1963).

FIREBIRD, THE 1934 d: William Dieterle. USA., *Tuzmadar*, Lajos Zilahy, Budapest 1932, Play

Firebrand, The *see* THE AFFAIRS OF CELLINI (1934).

FIREBRAND TREVISON 1920 d: Thomas N. Heffron. USA., *Firebrand Trevison*, Charles Alden Seltzer, New York 1918, Novel

Fire-Brand Trevison *see* FIREBRAND TREVISON (1920).

FIRE-FIGHTER'S LOVE, THE 1912 d: Oscar Eagle. USA., *The Test*, Carl Chapin, Short Story

FIREFLY OF FRANCE, THE 1918 d: Donald Crisp. USA., *The Firefly of France*, Marion Polk Angelotti, New York 1918, Novel

FIREFLY, THE 1937 d: Robert Z. Leonard. USA., *The Firefly*, Rudolf Friml, Otto Harbach, New York 1912, Operetta

FIREFOX 1982 d: Clint Eastwood. USA., *Firefox*, Craig Thomas, Novel

Fireman Save My Child *see* SANDY GETS HER MAN (1940).

FIREMAN'S WEDDING, THE 1918. UKN., *The Fireman's Wedding*, W. A. Eaton, Poem

Fire-Raiser's Daughter, The *see* PALICOVA DCERA (1923).

FIRES OF FATE 1923 d: Tom Terriss. UKN., *The Tragedy of the Korosko*, Arthur Conan Doyle, London 1898, Novel

FIRES OF FATE 1932 d: Norman Walker. UKN., *The Tragedy of the Korosko*, Arthur Conan Doyle, London 1898, Novel

FIRES OF INNOCENCE 1922 d: Sidney Morgan. UKN., *A Little World Apart*, George Stevenson, Novel

Fires of Johannis, The *see* THE FLAMES OF JOHANNIS (1916).

Fires of St. John, The *see* THE FLAMES OF JOHANNIS (1916).

Fires on the Plain *see* NOBI (1959).

FIRESTARTER 1984 d: Mark L. Lester. USA., *Firestarter*, Stephen King, 1980, Novel

FIRING LINE, THE 1919 d: Charles Maigne. USA., *The Firing Line*, Robert W. Chambers, New York 1908, Novel

FIRM OF GIRDLESTONE, THE 1915 d: Harold Shaw. UKN., *The Firm of Girdlestone*, Arthur Conan Doyle, Novel

FIRM, THE 1993 d: Sydney Pollack. USA., *The Firm*, John Grisham, Novel

FIRMIN, LE MUET DE SAINT-PATACLET 1938 d: Jacques Severac. FRN., *Firmin le Muet de Saint-Pataclet*, Lucien Giudice, Novel

FIRST A GIRL 1935 d: Victor Saville. UKN., *Viktor Und Viktoria*, Reinhold Schunzel, Play

FIRST AMONG EQUALS 1986 d: John Gorrie, Brian Mills. UKN., *First Among Equals*, Jeffrey Archer, London 1984, Novel

FIRST AND THE LAST, THE 1937 d: Basil Dean, Alexander Korda (Uncredited). UKN., *The First and the Last*, John Galsworthy, 1918, Short Story

FIRST BLOOD 1982 d: Ted Kotcheff. USA., *First Blood*, David Morrell, Novel

FIRST BORN, THE 1921 d: Colin Campbell. USA., *The First Born*, Francis Powers, New York 1897, Play

FIRST BORN, THE 1928 d: Miles Mander. UKN., *Those Common People*, Miles Mander, Play

First Cabin *see* CHEATERS AT PLAY (1932).

First Circle of Hell, The *see* DEN FORSTE KREDS (1971).

First Circle, The *see* DEN FORSTE KREDS (1971).

FIRST COMES COURAGE 1943 d: Dorothy Arzner. USA., *The Commandos*, Elliott Arnold, Novel

First Day of Freedom, The *see* PIERWSZY DZIEN WOLNOSCI (1964).

FIRST DEADLY SIN, THE 1980 d: Brian G. Hutton. USA., *The First Deadly Sin*, Lawrence Sanders, Novel

FIRST DEGREE 1923 d: Edward Sedgwick. USA., *The Summons*, George Patullo, 1914, Short Story

FIRST GENTLEMAN, THE 1948 d: Alberto Cavalcanti. UKN., *The First Gentleman*, Norman Ginsbury, London 1945, Play

FIRST GREAT TRAIN ROBBERY, THE 1979 d: Michael Crichton. UKN/USA., *The Great Train Robbery*, Michael Crichton, Novel

FIRST KISS, THE 1928 d: Rowland V. Lee. USA., *Four Brothers*, Tristram Tupper, 1928, Short Story

First Kiss, The *see* PRVNI POLIBENI (1935).

First Kiss, The *see* KUCHIZUKE III: ONNA DOSHI (1955).

FIRST LADY 1937 d: Stanley Logan. USA., *First Lady*, Katharine Dayton, George S. Kaufman, New York 1935, Play

First Lady, The *see* LA PRESIDENTESSA (1952).

FIRST LAW, THE 1918 d: Lawrence McGill. USA., *The First Law*, Gilson Willets, New York 1911, Novel

FIRST LEGION, THE 1951 d: Douglas Sirk. USA., *La Premiere Legion*, Emmett Lavery, New York 1934, Play

First Love *see* DIE SEXTANERIN (1936).

FIRST LOVE 1939 d: Henry Koster. USA., *Cendrillon*, Charles Perrault, 1697, Short Story

First Love *see* PRIMER AMOR (1942).

First Love *see* ERSTE LIEBE (1970).

FIRST LOVE 1977 d: Joan Darling. USA., Harold Brodkey, Story

First Love *see* PERVAYA LYUBOV (1995).

FIRST LOVE, LAST RITES 1997 d: Jesse Peretz. USA., *First Love Last Rites*, Ian McEwan, Short Story

First Marines *see* TRIPOLI (1950).

FIRST MEN IN THE MOON 1964 d: Nathan Juran. UKN/USA., *The First Men in the Moon*, H. G. Wells, London 1901, Novel

FIRST MEN IN THE MOON, THE 1919 d: J. L. V. Leigh. UKN., *The First Men in the Moon*, H. G. Wells, London 1901, Novel

FIRST MONDAY IN OCTOBER 1981 d: Ronald Neame. USA., *First Monday in October*, Jerome Lawrence, Robert E. Lee, Play

FIRST MRS. FRASER, THE 1932 d: Sinclair Hill. UKN., *The First Mrs. Fraser*, St. John G. Ervine, London 1929, Play

First Night, The *see* LA PRIMA NOTTE (1959).

First Polka, The *see* DIE ERSTE POLKA (1978).

First Rebel, The *see* ALLEGHENY UPRISING (1939).

First Rescue Party, The *see* PRVNI PARTA (1959).

FIRST SETTLER'S STORY, THE 1912. USA., *Farm Festivals*, Will Carleton, Book

First Spaceship on Venus *see* DER SCHWEIGENDE STERN (1960).

First Teacher, The *see* PERVYI UCHITEL (1965).

First, the Summer *see* O VERAO ANTES (1968).

First Time With Feeling *see* VOUS INTERESSEZ-VOUS A LA CHOSE? (1973).

First Wife *see* WIVES AND LOVERS (1963).

FIRST WIVES CLUB, THE 1996 d: Hugh Wilson. USA., *The First Wives Club*, Olivia Goldsmith, Novel

FIRST YEAR, THE 1926 d: Frank Borzage. USA., *The First Year*, Frank Craven, New York 1920, Play

FIRST YEAR, THE 1932 d: William K. Howard. USA., *The First Year*, Frank Craven, New York 1920, Play

FIRST YOU CRY 1978 d: George Schaefer. USA., *First You Cry*, Betty Rollin, 1976, Book

Fischer von St. Barbara, Die *see* VOSTANIYE RYBAKOV (1934).

FISCHIO AL NASO, IL 1967 d: Ugo Tognazzi. ITL., *Sette Piani*, Dino Buzzati, Short Story

FISH HAWK 1980 d: Donald Shebib. CND., *Old Fish Hawk*, Mitchell F. Jayne, Novel

Fish Out of Water *see* RYBA NA SUCHU (1942).

Fish Poachers of the Greek Isles *see* RAUBFISCHER IN HELLAS (1959).

Fish, The *see* NALIM (1938).

Fisher Girl, The *see* A DAUGHTER OF THE SEA (1915).

Fishka Der Krimmer *see* DIE KLATSCHE (1939).

Fishmonger and the Fish *see* SKAZKA O RYBAKE I RYBKE (1937).

Fit of Rage, A *see* UM COPO DE COLERA (1999).

Fitz and Lily *see* LILY IN LOVE (1985).

FITZWILLY 1967 d: Delbert Mann. USA., *A Garden of Cucumbers*, Poyntz Tyler, New York 1960, Novel

Fitzwilly Strikes Back *see* FITZWILLY (1967).

Five Accursed Gentlemen, The *see* LES CINQ GENTLEMEN MAUDITS (1920).

FIVE AGAINST THE HOUSE 1955 d: Phil Karlson. USA., Jack Finney, Short Story

Five and Five Musical *see* CHAMESH CHAMESH (1980).

FIVE AND TEN 1931 d: Robert Z. Leonard, Jack Conway (Uncredited). USA., *Five and Ten*, Fannie Hurst, New York 1929, Novel

Five Ashore in Singapore *see* CINQ GARS POUR SINGAPOUR (1967).

Five Branded Women *see* JOVANKA E LE ALTRE (1960).

FIVE CARD STUD 1968 d: Henry Hathaway. USA., *Glory Gulch*, Ray Gaulden, New York 1967, Novel

Five Characters in Search of an Exit *see* TWILIGHT ZONE: FIVE CHARACTERS IN SEARCH OF AN EXIT (1959-63).

FIVE CHILDREN AND IT 198- d: Marilyn Fox. UKN., *Five Children and It*, E. Nesbit, 1902, Novel

Five Day Lover, The *see* L' AMANT DE CINQ JOURS (1960).

Five Days, Five Nights *see* CINCO NOITES CINCO DIAS (1997).

FIVE DAYS ONE SUMMER 1982 d: Fred Zinnemann. USA., *Maiden Maiden*, Kay Boyle, 1957, Short Story

FIVE DAYS TO LIVE 1922 d: Norman Dawn. USA., *The Street of the Flying Dragon*, Dorothy Goodfellow, 1920, Short Story

Five Doomed Gentlemen *see* LES CINQ GENTLEMEN MAUDITS (1920).

Five Evenings *see* PYAT VECHEROV (1979).

FIVE FINGER EXERCISE 1962 d: Daniel Mann. USA., *Five Finger Exercise*, Peter Shaffer, London 1958, Play

FIVE FINGERS 1952 d: Joseph L. Mankiewicz. USA., *Operation Cicero*, L. C. Moyzisch, 1950, Novel

Five Five *see* CHAMESH CHAMESH (1980).

Five Forty-Eight, The *see* THE 5:48 (1979).

Five Friends in a Jam *see* DE FEM OG SPIONERNE (1969).

Five Go Adventuring *see* DE FEM OG SPIONERNE (1969).

FIVE GRAVES TO CAIRO 1943 d: Billy Wilder. USA., *Szinmu Negy Felvonasban*, Lajos Biro, Budapest 1917, Play

FIVE HAVE A MYSTERY TO SOLVE 1964 d: Ernest Morris. UKN., *Five Have a Mystery to Solve*, Enid Blyton, Novel

Five Kisses *see* THE AFFAIRS OF ANATOL (1921).

Five Little Peppers *see* FIVE LITTLE PEPPERS AND HOW THEY GREW (1939).

FIVE LITTLE PEPPERS AND HOW THEY GREW 1939 d: Charles T. Barton. USA., *Five Little Peppers and How They Grew*, Margaret Sidney, Boston 1881, Novel

FIVE LITTLE PEPPERS AT HOME 1940 d: Charles T. Barton. USA., *Five Little Peppers Midway*, Margaret Sidney, Boston 1890, Novel

Five Little Peppers at School *see* **FIVE LITTLE PEPPERS IN TROUBLE** (1940).

FIVE LITTLE PEPPERS IN TROUBLE 1940 d: Charles T. Barton. USA., *Five Little Peppers at School*, Margaret Sidney, Boston 1903, Novel

Five Little Peppers Midway *see* **FIVE LITTLE PEPPERS AT HOME** (1940).

Five Millions Seek an Heir *see* **FUNF MILLIONEN SUCHEN EINEN ERBEN** (1938).

FIVE NIGHTS 1915 d: Bert Haldane ?. UKN., *Five Nights*, Victoria Cross, London 1908, Novel

FIVE NIGHTS 1918. USA., *Five Nights*, Victoria Cross, London 1908, Novel

FIVE OF ME, THE 1981 d: Paul Wendkos. USA., *The Five of Me*, Henry Hawksworth, Book

FIVE ON A TREASURE ISLAND 1957 d: Gerald Landau. UKN., *Five on a Treasure Island*, Enid Blyton, Novel

FIVE STAR FINAL 1931 d: Mervyn Leroy. USA., *Five Star Final*, Louis Weitzenkorn, New York 1930, Play

FIVE STEPS TO DANGER 1957 d: Henry S. Kesler. USA., Donald Hamilton, Serial Story

FIVE THOUSAND AN HOUR 1918 d: Ralph Ince. USA., *Five Thousand an Hour*, George Randolph Chester, New York 1912, Novel

FIVE TO ONE 1963 d: Gordon Flemyng. UKN., *Thief in the Night*, Edgar Wallace, London 1928, Novel

FIVE WEEKS IN A BALLOON 1962 d: Irwin Allen. USA., *Cinq Semaines En Ballon*, Jules Verne, 1863, Novel

FIVE WISHES, THE 1916 d: Wilfred Noy?. UKN., *The Five Wishes*, Laura Leycester, Play

Five Women Around Utamaro *see* **UTAMARO O MEGURU GONIN NO ONNA** (1946).

FIXED BAYONETS 1951 d: Samuel Fuller. USA., *Fixed Bayonets*, John Brophy, Novel

FIXED BY GEORGE 1920 d: Eddie Lyons, Lee Moran. USA., *Fixed By George*, Edgar Franklin, 1920, Short Story

FIXER DUGAN 1939 d: Lew Landers. USA., *What's a Fixer for?*, H. C. Potter, New Haven, Ct. 1928, Play

FIXER, THE 1915. USA., *Hello Bill*, Willis Maxwell Goodhue, Play

FIXER, THE 1968 d: John Frankenheimer. USA., *The Fixer*, Bernard Malamud, 1966, Novel

Fixing It *see* **THE LOVE HUNGER** (1919).

FLACARI PE COMORI 1988 d: Nicolae Margineanu. RMN., *Arhangelii*, Ion Agarbiceanu, 1914, Novel

Flachsacker, Der *see* **WENN DIE SONNE WIEDER SCHEINT** (1943).

FLAG LIEUTENANT, THE 1919 d: Percy Nash. UKN., *The Flag Lieutenant*, Maj. W. P. Drury, Leo Trevor, London 1908, Play

FLAG LIEUTENANT, THE 1926 d: Maurice Elvey. UKN., *The Flag Lieutenant*, Maj. W. P. Drury, Leo Trevor, London 1908, Play

FLAG LIEUTENANT, THE 1932 d: Henry Edwards. UKN., *The Flag Lieutenant*, Maj. W. P. Drury, Leo Trevor, London 1908, Play

FLAGRANT DELIT 1930 d: Georges Treville, Hanns Schwarz. FRN., *Guignol Ou le Cambrioleur*, Louis Verneuil, Play

FLAMBARDS 1980 d: Lawrence Gordon Clark, Michael Ferguson. UKN., K. M. Peyton, Novel

FLAMBEAUX, LES 1914 d: Henri Pouctal. FRN., *Les Flambeaux*, Henry Bataille, Play

FLAMBEE, LA 1934 d: Jean de Marguenat. FRN., *La Flambee*, Henri Kistemaeckers, 1911, Play

Flamberge Au Vent *see* **LE CAPITAN** (1945).

FLAME AND THE FLESH, THE 1954 d: Richard Brooks. USA., *Naples Au Baiser de Feu*, Auguste Bailly, Novel

FLAME IN THE HEATHER 1935 d: Donovan Pedelty. UKN., *The Fiery Cross*, Esson Maule, Novel

FLAME IN THE STREETS 1961 d: Roy Ward Baker. UKN., *Hot Summer Night*, Ted Willis, London 1958, Play

FLAME IS LOVE, THE 1979 d: Michael O'Herlihy. USA/UKN., *The Flame Is Love*, Barbara Cartland, Novel

Flame of Life, The *see* **SANGEN OM DEN ELDRODA BLOMMAN** (1918).

Flame of My Love *see* **WAGA KOI WA MOENU** (1949).

Flame of the Flesh *see* **WOMAN OF PASSION DU BARRY** (1930).

FLAME OF THE ISLANDS 1955 d: Edward Ludwig. USA., *Rebel Island*, Adele Comandini, Story

Flame of Torment *see* **ENJO** (1958).

FLAME, THE 1920 d: F. Martin Thornton. UKN., *The Flame*, Olive Wadsley, Novel

FLAME TREES OF THIKA, THE 1981 d: Roy Ward Baker. UKN., *The Flame Trees of Thika*, Elspeth Huxley, Novel

FLAMES 1917 d: Maurice Elvey. UKN., *Flames*, Robert Hichens, Novel

Flames Above Treasures *see* **FLACARI PE COMORI** (1988).

FLAMES OF CHANCE, THE 1918 d: Raymond Wells. USA., *The Godson of Jeanette Gontreau*, Francis William Sullivan, 1917, Short Story

FLAMES OF DESIRE 1924 d: Denison Clift. USA., *Strathmore; Or Wrought By His Own Hand*, Ouida, Philadelphia 1866, Play

FLAMES OF JOHANNIS, THE 1916 d: Edgar Lewis. USA., *Johannisfeuer*, Hermann Sudermann, 1900, Play

Flames on the Treasures *see* **FLACARI PE COMORI** (1988).

Flames on the Volga *see* **VOLGA EN FLAMMES** (1933).

FLAMING FOREST, THE 1926 d: Reginald Barker. USA., *The Flaming Forest; a Novel of the Canadian Northwest*, James Oliver Curwood, New York 1921, Novel

FLAMING FORGE, THE 1913 d: Lanier Bartlett. USA., *The Flaming Forge*, Henry Wadsworth Longfellow, Poem

FLAMING FORTIES, THE 1924 d: Tom Forman. USA., *Tennessee's Partner*, Bret Harte, 1869, Short Story

Flaming Frontier *see* **OLD SUREHAND I** (1965).

FLAMING FURY 1926 d: James P. Hogan. USA., *The Scourge of Fate*, Ewart Adamson, Story

FLAMING GUNS 1932 d: Arthur Rosson. USA., *Oh Promise Me*, Peter B. Kyne, 1926, Short Story

Flaming Passion *see* **LUCRETIA LOMBARD** (1923).

FLAMING STAR 1960 d: Don Siegel. USA., *Flaming Star*, Clair Huffaker, Novel

FLAMING SWORD, THE 1915 d: Edwin Middleton. USA., *The Flaming Sword*, George Gibbs, New York 1914, Novel

FLAMING YOUTH 1923 d: John Francis Dillon. USA., *Flaming Youth*, Warner Fabian, New York 1923, Novel

FLAMINGO ROAD 1949 d: Michael Curtiz. USA., *Flamingo Road*, Robert Wilder, Novel

FLAMINGO ROAD 1980 d: Gus Trikonis. USA., *Flamingo Road*, Robert Wilder, Novel

FLAMME, LA 1925 d: Rene Hervil. FRN., *La Flamme*, Charles Mere, Play

FLAMME, LA 1936 d: Andre Berthomieu. FRN., *La Flamme*, Charles Mere, Play

FLANAGAN BOY, THE 1953 d: Reginald Le Borg. UKN., *The Flanagan Boy*, Max Catto, Novel

FLAP 1969 d: Carol Reed. USA., *Nobody Loves a Drunken Indian*, Clair Huffaker, New York 1967, Novel

FLASCHENTEUFEL, DER 1952 d: Ferdinand Diehl. GRM., *The Bottle Imp*, Robert Louis Stevenson, London 1891, Novel

FLASH OF AN EMERALD, THE 1915 d: Albert Capellani. USA., *The Flash of an Emerald*, E. M. Ingleton, Short Story

FLASH OF GREEN, A 1984 d: Victor Nunez. USA., *A Flash of Green*, John D. MacDonald, Novel

Flash of Lightning, A *see* **INAZUMA** (1967).

FLASH THE SHEEPDOG 1967 d: Laurence Henson. UKN., *Flash the Sheepdog*, Kathleen Fidler, Novel

Flashlight Girl, The *see* **THE FLASHLIGHT** (1917).

FLASHLIGHT, THE 1917 d: Ida May Park. USA., *The Flash-Light*, Albert M. Treymore, Short Story

FLASHPOINT 1984 d: William Tannen. USA., *Flashpoint*, George la Fontaine, Book

FLAT TWO 1962 d: Alan Cooke. UKN., *Flat Two*, Edgar Wallace, London 1927, Novel

Flaxfield, The *see* **DE VLASCHAARD** (1983).

FLAXY MARTIN 1949 d: Richard L. Bare. USA., *Smart Money*, David Lang, Story

FLEA IN HER EAR, A 1968 d: Jacques Charon. USA/FRN., *La Puce a l'Oreille*, Georges Feydeau, Paris 1907, Play

Fleas Bark Too, Don't They? *see* **EN LOPPE KAN OGSA GO** (1997).

Flecha Negra *see* **BLACK ARROW** (1985).

Fledermaus '55 *see* **OH ROSALINDA!** (1955).

FLEDERMAUS, DIE 1923 d: Max Mack. GRM., *Die Fledermaus*, Henri Meilhac, Johann Strauss, Vienna 1874, Operetta

FLEDERMAUS, DIE 1931 d: Carl Lamac. GRM., *Die Fledermaus*, Henri Meilhac, Johann Strauss, Vienna 1874, Operetta

FLEDERMAUS, DIE 1937 d: Paul Verhoeven. GRM., *Die Fledermaus*, Henri Meilhac, Johann Strauss, Vienna 1874, Operetta

FLEDERMAUS, DIE 1945 d: Geza von Bolvary. GRM., *Die Fledermaus*, Henri Meilhac, Johann Strauss, Vienna 1874, Operetta

FLEDERMAUS, DIE 1955 d: E. W. Fiedler. GDR., *Die Fledermaus*, Henri Meilhac, Johann Strauss, Vienna 1874, Operetta

FLEDERMAUS, DIE 1962 d: Geza von CziffrA. AUS., *Die Fledermaus*, Henri Meilhac, Johann Strauss, Vienna 1874, Operetta

FLEDERMAUS, DIE 1966 d: Annelise Meineche. DNM., *Die Fledermaus*, Henri Meilhac, Johann Strauss, Vienna 1874, Operetta

Fledged Shadows *see* **OPERENE STINY** (1930).

FLEET'S IN, THE 1942 d: Victor Schertzinger, Hal Walker (Uncredited). USA., *Sailor Beware*, Kenyon Nicholson, Charles Robinson, New York 1933, Play

Flegermusen *see* **DIE FLEDERMAUS** (1966).

Flesh & Blood *see* **FLESH AND BLOOD** (1979).

FLESH AND BLOOD 1951 d: Anthony Kimmins. UKN., *A Sleeping Clergyman*, James Bridie, London 1933, Play

FLESH AND BLOOD 1979 d: Jud Taylor. USA., *Flesh and Blood*, Pete Hamill, Novel

FLESH AND FANTASY 1943 d: Julien Duvivier. USA., Ellis St. Joseph, Story, *Lord Arthur Savile's Crime*, Oscar Wilde, 1891, Short Story

FLESH AND THE DEVIL 1926 d: Clarence Brown. USA., *Es War; Roman in Zwei Banden*, Hermann Sudermann, Stuttgart 1893, Novel

Flesh of Eve *see* **DANGEROUS PARADISE** (1930).

Flesh Will Surrender *see* **IL DELITTO DI GIOVANNI EPISCOPO** (1947).

FLESHBURN 1983 d: George Gage. USA., *Fear in a Handful of Dust*, Brian Garfield, Novel

FLETCH 1985 d: Michael Ritchie. USA., *Fletch*, Gregory McDonald, Novel

Fleur Au Fusil, La *see* **NI TROMPETTE SANS TAMBOUR** (1949).

FLEUR AUX DENTS, LA 1975 d: Thomas Vamos. CND., *La Fleur aux Dents*, Gilles Archambault, Novel

FLEUR D'AMOUR 1927 d: Marcel Vandal. FRN., *Fleur d'Amour*, Marcelle Vioux, Novel

Fleur de l'Age, La *see* **RAPTURE** (1965).

Fleur d'Epine *see* **FLEUR D'OSEILLE** (1967).

FLEUR D'ORANGER, LA 1932 d: Henry Roussell. FRN., *La Fleur d'Oranger*, Andre Birabeau, Georges Dolley, Play

FLEUR D'OSEILLE 1967 d: Georges Lautner. FRN., *Langes Radieux*, John Amila, Novel

Fleuve, Le *see* **THE RIVER** (1951).

Flibustieri Della Martinica, I *see* **MARIE DES ISLES** (1959).

FLIC OU VOYOU? 1979 d: Georges Lautner. FRN., *Flic Ou Voyou*, Michel Grisola, Novel

FLIC STORY 1975 d: Jacques Deray. FRN/ITL., *Flic Story*, Roger Borniche, Novel

FLICKAN I FRACK 1956 d: Arne Mattsson. SWD., *Frickan I Frack*, Hjalmar Bergman, 1925, Novel

FLICKORNA GYURKOVICS 1926 d: Ragnar Hylten-Cavallius. SWD/GRM., *Die Sieben Tochter Dre Frau Gyurkovics*, Franz Herczeg, Novel

FLIEGENDE KLASSENZIMMER, DAS 1954 d: Kurt Hoffmann. GRM., *Das Fliegende Klassenzimmer*, Erich Kastner, 1933, Novel

FLIEGENDE KLASSENZIMMER, DAS 1973 d: Werner Jacobs. GRM., *Das Fliegende Klassenzimmer*, Erich Kastner, 1933, Novel

FLIEGENDE WINDMUHLE, DIE 1981 d: Gunter Ratz. GRM., *Die Fliegende Windmuhle*, Gunter Feustel, Novel

Flies Hunting *see* POLOWANIE NA MUCHY (1969).

FLIGHT 1960 d: Louis Bispo. USA., *Flight*, John Steinbeck, 1945, Short Story

Flight Commander *see* THE DAWN PATROL (1930).

FLIGHT FROM ASHIYA 1964 d: Michael Anderson. USA/JPN., *Flight from Ashiya*, Elliott Arnold, New York 1959, Novel

Flight from Terror *see* SATAN NEVER SLEEPS (1962).

Flight of Pigeons, A *see* JUNOON (1978).

Flight of Rainbirds, A *see* EEN VLUCHT REGENWULPEN (1981).

FLIGHT OF THE DUCHESS, THE 1916 d: Eugene Nowland. USA., *The Flight of the Duchess*, Robert Browning, 1845, Poem

Flight of the Eagle, The *see* INGENJOR ANDREES LUFTFARD (1982).

FLIGHT OF THE PHOENIX 1965 d: Robert Aldrich. USA., *The Flight of the Phoenix*, Elleston Trevor, New York 1964, Novel

Flight of the White Stallions, The *see* THE MIRACLE OF THE WHITE STALLIONS (1962).

Flight Patrol *see* INTERNATIONAL SQUADRON (1941).

Flight, The *see* DIE FLUCHT (1977).

FLIGHT TO BERLIN 1983 d: Christopher Petit. UKN/GRM., *Strange Days*, Jennifer Potter, Novel

Flight to Marseille *see* FLUCHTWEG NACH MARSEILLE (1977).

FLIM-FLAM MAN, THE 1967 d: Irvin Kershner. USA., *Ballad of the Flim-Flam Man*, Guy Owen, New York 1965, Novel

FLIPPER 1963 d: James B. Clark. USA., Ricou Browning, Jack Cowden, Story

FLIRT, THE 1916 d: Lois Weber, Phillips Smalley. USA., *The Flirt*, Booth Tarkington, New York 1913, Novel

FLIRT, THE 1922 d: Hobart Henley. USA., *The Flirt*, Booth Tarkington, New York 1913, Novel

FLIRTING WIDOW, THE 1930 d: William A. Seiter. USA., *Green Stockings*, A. E. W. Mason, 1909, Play

FLIRTING WITH DEATH 1917 d: Elmer Clifton. USA., *Sky High*, Frank Dazey, Waldemar Young, Short Story

FLIRTING WITH LOVE 1924 d: John Francis Dillon. USA., *Counterfeit*, Leroy Scott, Story

Floating Clouds *see* UKIGUMO (1955).

FLOATING DUTCHMAN, THE 1953 d: Vernon Sewell. UKN., *The Floating Dutchman*, Nicolas Bentley, Novel

Floating Trouble *see* GAMBLING ON THE HIGH SEAS (1940).

FLOES SILVESTRES 1926 d: Constantino Dominguez, Antonio LabartA. SPN., *Flores Silvestres*, Padre Risco, Novel

Flood, The *see* POTOP (1974).

FLOODS OF FEAR 1958 d: Charles Crichton. UKN., *Floods of Fear*, John Hawkins, Ward Hawkins, Novel

FLOOR ABOVE, THE 1914 d: James Kirkwood. USA., *The Tragedy of Charlecot Mansions*, E. Phillips Oppenheim, 1914, Short Story

FLOR DE MAYO 1957 d: Roberto Gavaldon. MXC., *Flor de Mayo*, Vicente Blasco Ibanez, 1895, Novel

FLOR DE SANTIDAD 1972 d: Adolfo Marsillach. SPN., *Flor de Santidad*, Ramon Maria Del Valle-Inclan, 1904, Novel

Flor de Valencia *see* TIERRA VALENCIANA (1926).

FLORADAS NA SERRA 1954 d: Luciano Salce. BRZ., *Floradas Na Serra*, Dinah Silveira de Queiros, 1939, Novel

FLORENCE NIGHTINGALE 1915 d: Maurice Elvey. UKN., *The Life of Florence Nightingale*, Edward Cook, Book

FLORENTINE DAGGER, THE 1935 d: Robert Florey. USA., *The Florentine Dagger*, Ben Hecht, New York 1928, Novel

FLORENTINE, THE 1999 d: Nick Stagliano. USA., *The Florentine*, Damien Gray, Amy McCarty-Baker, Play

FLORENTINE TRAGEDY, THE 1913. USA., *A Florentine Tragedy*, T. Sturge Moore, Oscar Wilde, Play

FLORENTINER HUT, DER 1939 d: Wolfgang Liebeneiner. GRM., *Un Chapeau de Paille d'Italie*, Eugene Labiche, Marc-Michel, 1847, Play

FLORES SILVESTRES 1929 d: Jose Ruiz Miron. SPN., *Flores Silvestres*, Padre Risco, Novel

FLORETTE E PATAPON 1913 d: Mario Caserini. ITL., *Florette Et Patapon*, Maurice Hennequin, Pierre Veber, 1905, Play

FLORETTE E PATAPON 1927 d: Amleto Palermi. ITL., *Florette Et Patapon*, Maurice Hennequin, Pierre Veber, 1905, Play

FLORETTE ET PATAPON 1913. FRN., *Florette Et Patapon*, Maurice Hennequin, Pierre Veber, 1905, Play

FLORIAN 1940 d: Edwin L. Marin. USA., *Florian - Das Pferd Des Kaisers*, Felix Salten, Berlin 1933, Novel

FLORIDA ENCHANTMENT, A 1914 d: Sidney Drew. USA., *A Florida Enchantment*, Archibald Clavering Gunter, Fergus Redmond, New York 1891, Novel

FLORINE, LA FLEUR DU VALOIS 1926 d: E. B. Donatien. FRN., *Florine la Fleur du Valois*, Eugene Barbier, Novel

FLORODORA GIRL, THE 1930 d: Harry Beaumont. USA., *The Gay Nineties*, Gene Markey, Story

Flotsam *see* SO ENDS OUR NIGHT (1941).

FLOTTA DEGLI EMIGRANTI, LA 1917 d: Leopoldo Carlucci. ITL., *La Flotta Degli Emigranti*, Vincenzo Morello, 1907, Play

Flower Blooms, A *see* HANA HIRAKU (1948).

FLOWER DRUM SONG 1961 d: Henry Koster. USA., *Flower Drum Song*, Oscar Hammerstein II, Richard Rodgers, New York 1958, Musical Play

Flower in His Mouth, The *see* GENTE DI RISPETTO (1975).

Flower of Hawaii, The *see* DIE BLUME VON HAWAII (1953).

FLOWER OF THE DUSK 1918 d: John H. Collins. USA., *Flower of the Dusk*, Myrtle Reed, New York 1908, Novel

Flower of the Forest *see* DIE FORSTERCHRISTL (1926).

FLOWER OF THE NORTH 1921 d: David Smith. USA., *The Flower of the North*, James Oliver Curwood, New York 1912, Novel

FLOWERS IN THE ATTIC 1987 d: Jeffrey Bloom. USA., *Flowers in the Attic*, Virginia Andrews, Novel

Flowers of May *see* FLOR DE MAYO (1957).

Flowers of Shanghai *see* HAISHANG HUA (1998).

FLOWING GOLD 1924 d: Joseph de Grasse. USA., *Flowing Gold*, Rex Beach, New York 1922, Novel

FLOWING GOLD 1940 d: Alfred E. Green. USA., *Flowing Gold*, Rex Beach, New York 1922, Novel

FLUBBER 1997 d: Les Mayfield. USA., *A Situation of Gravity*, Samuel Taylor, 1943, Story

FLUCHT AN DIE ADRIA 1936 d: Eugen Schulz-Breiden. GRM/CZC., *Ircin Romanek*, Josef Roden, Novel

FLUCHT, DIE 1977 d: Hajo Baumgartner. GRM., *Der Hochwald*, Adalbert Stifter, 1841, Short Story

FLUCHT IN DEN NORDEN 1986 d: Ingemo Engstrom. GRM/FNL., *Flucht in Den Norden*, Klaus Mann, 1934, Novel

FLUCHT INS PARADIES, DIE 1923 d: Charles Erik Schneider. GRM/SWT., *Helena*, Stefan Markus, 1921, Short Story, *Das Verlorene Paradies*, Stefan Markus, 1921, Short Story

FLUCHTLING AUS CHIKAGO, DER 1934 d: Johannes Meyer. GRM., *Der Fluchtling Aus Chikago*, Curt Johannes Braun, Novel

Fluchtpunkt Berlin *see* FLIGHT TO BERLIN (1983).

FLUCHTVERSUCH 1976 d: Vojtech Jasny. GRM/AUS., W. J. M. Wippersberg, Story

FLUCHTWEG NACH MARSEILLE 1977 d: Ingemo Engstrom, Gerhard Theuring. GRM., *Transit*, Anna Seghers, 1944, Novel

FLUSSPIRATEN VOM MISSISSIPPI, DIE 1963 d: Jurgen Roland. GRM/FRN/ITL., *Die Flusspiraten Vom Mississippi*, Friedrich Gerstackers, Novel

Flusternde Tod, Der *see* WHISPERING DEATH (1975).

Fluttering of a Sparrow, The *see* IL FRULLO DEL PASSERO (1988).

FLY AWAY HOME 1996 d: Carroll Ballard. USA., *Mother Goose*, Bill Lishman, Autobiography

FLY AWAY PETER 1948 d: Charles Saunders. UKN., *Fly Away Peter*, A. P. Dearsley, London 1947, Play

Fly Hunt, The *see* POLOWANIE NA MUCHY (1969).

FLY, THE 1958 d: Kurt Neumann. USA., George Langelaan, Short Story

FLY, THE 1986 d: David Cronenberg. USA., George Langelaan, Short Story

Flying Classroom, The *see* DAS FLIEGENDE KLASSENZIMMER (1954).

Flying Classroom, The *see* DAS FLIEGENDE KLASSENZIMMER (1973).

FLYING DUTCHMAN, THE 1923 d: Lloyd B. Carleton. USA., *Der Fliegende Hollander*, Richard Wagner, Dresden 1843, Opera

FLYING EYE, THE 1955 d: William C. Hammond. UKN., *The Flying Eye*, John Newton Chance, Novel

FLYING FIFTY-FIVE 1939 d: Reginald Denham. UKN., *The Flying Fifty-Five*, Edgar Wallace, London 1922, Novel

FLYING FIFTY-FIVE, THE 1924 d: A. E. Coleby. UKN., *The Flying Fifty-Five*, Edgar Wallace, London 1922, Novel

FLYING FOOL 1925 d: Frank S. Mattison. USA., *The Ace and the Queen*, Putnam Hoover, Story

FLYING FOOL, THE 1931 d: Walter Summers. UKN., *The Flying Fool*, Bernard Merivale, Arnold Ridley, London 1929, Play

FLYING FOX IN A FREEDOM TREE 1989 d: Martyn Sanderson. NZL., *Flying Fox in a Freedom Tree*, Albert Wendt, Novel

FLYING FROM JUSTICE 1913 d: Arthur Charrington. UKN., *Flying from Justice*, Mark Melford, London 1891, Play

FLYING FROM JUSTICE 1915 d: Percy Nash. UKN., *Flying from Justice*, Mark Melford, London 1891, Play

Flying Fury *see* STRAWBERRY ROAN (1933).

FLYING HIGH 1931 d: Charles F. Reisner. USA., *Flying High*, Lew Brown, Buddy De Sylva, Ray Henderson, New York 1930, Musical Play

FLYING HORSEMAN, THE 1926 d: Orville O. Dull. USA., *Dark Rosaleen*, Max Brand, 1925, Short Story

Flying Knife Hua *see* FEI DAO HUA (1963).

FLYING LEATHERNECKS 1951 d: Nicholas Ray. USA., Kenneth Gamet, Story

Flying Matchmaker, The *see* SHNEI KUNI LEMEL (1965).

FLYING SQUAD, THE 1929 d: Arthur Maude. UKN., *The Flying Squad*, Edgar Wallace, London 1928, Novel

FLYING SQUAD, THE 1932 d: F. W. Kraemer. UKN., *The Flying Squad*, Edgar Wallace, London 1928, Novel

FLYING SQUAD, THE 1940 d: Herbert Brenon. UKN., *The Flying Squad*, Edgar Wallace, London 1928, Novel

Flying Squadron, The *see* THE FLYING SQUAD (1940).

Flying Tiger Brigade *see* FEI HU DUI (1995).

FLYING U RANCH, THE 1927 d: Robert de Lacy. USA., *The Flying U Ranch*, B. M. Bower, New York 1914, Novel

Flyktingar *see* FARLIGA VAGAR (1942).

Flyktingarna Fran Murman *see* MUURMANNIN PAKOLAISET (1926).

Foal, The *see* ZHEREBYONOK (1960).

FOG 1934 d: Albert S. Rogell. USA., *Fog*, Dorothy Rice Sims, Valentine Williams, Boston 1933, Novel

Fog *see* A STUDY IN TERROR (1965).

FOG BOUND 1923 d: Irvin V. Willat. USA., *Fog Bound*, Jack Bechdolt, 1921, Short Story

FOG ISLAND 1945 d: Terry O. Morse. USA., *Angel Island*, Bernadine Angus, Play

FOG OVER FRISCO 1934 d: William Dieterle. USA., *The Five Fragments*, George Dyer, Boston 1932, Novel

Fog Over San Francisco *see* FOG OVER FRISCO (1934).

FOG, THE 1923 d: Paul Powell. USA., *The Fog*, William Dudley Pelley, Boston 1921, Novel

FOGO MORTO 1976 d: Marcos FariA. BRZ., *Fogo Morto*, Jose Lins Do Rego, 1943, Novel

FOHN 1950 d: Rolf Hansen. GRM/SWT., *Die Weisse Holle von Piz Palu*, Arnold Fanck, Short Story

Fohn - Sturm in Der Ostwand *see* FOHN (1950).

FOIRE AUX CANCRES, LA 1963 d: Louis Daquin. FRN., *La Foire aux Cancres*, Jean-Charles, Book

Fol Ete, Le *see* SECRETS (1942).

Folies Bergere *see* FOLIES BERGERE DE PARIS (1935).

FOLIES BERGERE DE PARIS 1935 d: Roy Del Ruth. USA., *The Red Cat*, Hans Adler, Rudolph Lothar, New York 1934, Play

FOLIES D'ELODIE, LES 1981 d: Andre Genoves. FRN., *Les Folies d'Elodie*, Ayme Dubois-Jollet, Novel

FOLIES-BERGERE 1935 d: Marcel Achard. FRN., *Folies-Bergere*, Hans Adler, Rudolph Lothar, Play

Folies-Bergere *see* FOLIES BERGERE DE PARIS (1935).

FOLLE A TUER 1975 d: Yves Boisset. FRN/ITL., *Folle a Tuer*, Jean-Patrick Manchette, Novel

FOLLE AVENTURE, LA 1930 d: Andre-Paul Antoine, Carl Froelich. FRN., *Smarra*, Ludwig Wolff, Novel

FOLLE NUIT, LA 1932 d: Robert Bibal. FRN., *Le Conte Galant*, Felix Gandera, Andre Mouezy-Eon

Folles Etreintes de Jennifer see **SEX IN SWEDEN** (1977).

FOLLIE DEL SECOLO 1939 d: Amleto Palermi. ITL., *I Capricci Di Susanna*, Alessandro de Stefani, Play

Follies of Elodie, The see **LES FOLIES D'ELODIE** (1981).

Follow Me see **THE PUBLIC EYE** (1972).

FOLLOW ME, BOYS 1966 d: Norman Tokar. USA., *God and My Country*, MacKinlay Kantor, Cleveland 1954, Novel

FOLLOW THAT DREAM 1962 d: Gordon Douglas. USA., *Pioneer Go Home!*, Richard Powell, New York 1959, Novel

FOLLOW THAT HORSE! 1960 d: Alan Bromly. UKN., *Photo Finish*, Howard Mason, London 1954, Novel

FOLLOW THE BAND 1943 d: Jean Yarbrough. USA., Richard English, Story

FOLLOW THE FLEET 1936 d: Mark Sandrich. USA., *Shore Leave*, Hubert Osborne, New York 1922, Play

FOLLOW THE LEADER 1930 d: Norman Taurog. USA., *Manhattan Mary*, Buddy De Sylva, W. K. Wells, George White, New York 1927, Musical Play

FOLLOW THE SUN 1951 d: Sidney Lanfield. USA., *He Follows the Sun Again*, Frederick Hazlitt Brennan, Article

FOLLOW THRU 1930 d: Laurence Schwab, Lloyd Corrigan. USA., *Follow Thru*, Lew Brown, Buddy De Sylva, Ray Henderson, New York 1929, Musical Play

Follow Your Heart see **VA DOVE TI PORTA IL CUORE** (1996).

Following, The see **PATHLAAG** (1964).

FOLLY OF ANNE, THE 1914 d: John B. O'Brien. USA., *The Folly of Anne*, Ellen Farley, Story

FOLLY TO BE WISE 1952 d: Frank Launder. UKN., *It Depends What You Mean*, James Bridie, London 1944, Play

FOMA GORDEEV 1959 d: Mark Donskoi. USS., *Foma Gordeyev*, Maxim Gorky, St. Petersburg 1899, Novel

Foma Gordeyev see **FOMA GORDEEV** (1959).

FOME DE AMOR 1968 d: Nelson Pereira Dos Santos. BRZ., *Historia Para Se Ouvir de Noite*, Guilherme Figueiredo, 1964, Novel

Fome de Amor. Voce Nunca Tomou Bauho de Sol Inteiramente Nua? see **FOME DE AMOR** (1968).

Fond Dream see **BLAHOVY SEN** (1943).

FONTAINE DES AMOURS, LA 1924 d: Roger Lion. FRN., *La Fontaine Des Amours*, Gabrielle Reval, Novel

FONTAMARA 1980 d: Carlo Lizzani. ITL., *Fontamara*, Ignazio Silone, 1930, Novel

FONTANE EFFI BRIEST 1974 d: R. W. Fassbinder. GRM., *Effi Briest*, Theodor Fontane, 1894-95, Novel

FOOD FOR SCANDAL 1920 d: James Cruze. USA., *Beverly's Balance*, Paul Kester, New York 1915, Play

Food for Scandal see **FOOLS FOR SCANDAL** (1938).

FOOD OF THE GODS, THE 1976 d: Bert I. Gordon. USA., *The Food of the Gods and How It Came to Earth*, H. G. Wells, London 1904, Novel

FOOL AND HIS MONEY, A 1920 d: Robert Ellis. USA., *A Fool and His Money*, George Barr McCutcheon, New York 1913, Novel

FOOL AND HIS MONEY, A 1925 d: Erle C. Kenton. USA., *A Fool and His Money*, George Barr McCutcheon, New York 1913, Novel

FOOL AND THE PRINCESS, THE 1948 d: William C. Hammond. UKN., *The Fool and the Princess*, Stephen Spender, 1946, Novel

Fool for Blondes, A see **THE MAGNIFICENT BRUTE** (1936).

FOOL FOR LOVE 1986 d: Robert Altman. USA., *Fool for Love*, Sam Shepard, 1984, Play

FOOL KILLER, THE 1963 d: Servando Gonzalez. USA/MXC., *The Fool Filler*, Helen Eustis, New York 1954, Novel

FOOL, THE 1913 d: George Pearson. UKN., *A Fool There Was*, Rudyard Kipling, Poem

FOOL, THE 1925 d: Harry Millarde. USA., *The Fool*, Channing Pollock, New York 1922, Play

Fool, The see **O BOBO** (1987).

FOOL, THE 1990 d: Christine Edzard. UKN., Henry Mayhew, Books

FOOL THERE WAS, A 1915 d: Frank Powell. USA., *A Fool There Was*, Porter Everson Brown, 1909, Play, *The Vampire*, Rudyard Kipling, New York 1897, Poem

FOOL THERE WAS, A 1922 d: Emmett J. Flynn. USA., *A Fool There Was*, Porter Emerson Browne, New York 1909, Play

Foolish Daughters see **ALICE ADAMS** (1923).

Foolish Girl, A see **BLAHOVE DEVCE** (1938).

Foolish Husbands see **HISTOIRE DE RIRE** (1941).

FOOLISH MATRONS, THE 1921 d: Maurice Tourneur, Clarence Brown. USA., *The Foolish Matrons*, Brian Oswald Donn-Byrne, New York 1920, Novel

FOOLISH MONTE CARLO 1922 d: William Humphrey. USA., *The Black Spider*, Carlton Dawe, London 1911, Novel

FOOLISH VIRGIN, THE 1917 d: Albert Capellani. USA., *The Foolish Virgin*, Thomas Dixon, New York 1915, Novel

FOOLISH VIRGIN, THE 1924 d: George W. Hill. USA., *The Foolish Virgin*, Thomas Dixon, New York 1915, Novel

FOOLS 1997 d: Ramadan Suleman. FRN/SAF/MZM., *Fools*, Njabulo S. Ndebele, Novel

FOOLS AND THEIR MONEY 1919 d: Herbert Blache. USA., *The Family Tree*, E. Forst

FOOL'S AWAKENING, A 1924 d: Harold Shaw. USA., *The Tale of Triona*, William J. Locke, London 1912, Novel

FOOLS DIE FAST 1996 d: James Purcell. CND., *Fools Die Fast*, David Blackwood, Play

FOOLS FIRST 1922 d: Marshall Neilan. USA., *Fool's First*, Hugh MacNair Kahler, 120, Short Story

FOOLS FOR LUCK 1917 d: Lawrence C. Windom. USA., *Talismans*, Kennett Harris, Play

FOOLS FOR SCANDAL 1938 d: Mervyn Leroy. USA., *Return Engagement*, Rosemary Casey, Nancy Hamilton, James Shute, 1936, Play

FOOLS' HIGHWAY 1924 d: Irving Cummings. USA., *My Mamie Rose; the Story of My Regeneration*, Owen Frawley Kildare, New York 1903, Book

FOOLS OF FASHION 1926 d: James C. McKay. USA., *The Other Woman*, George Randolph Chester, Novel

FOOLS OF FORTUNE 1922 d: Louis W. Chaudet. USA., *Assisting Ananias*, W. C. Tuttle, 1920, Short Story

FOOLS OF FORTUNE 1989 d: Pat O'Connor. UKN/IRL., *Fools of Fortune*, William Trevor, 1983, Novel

FOOLS' PARADE 1971 d: Andrew V. McLaglen. USA., *Fool's Parade*, Davis Grubb, Novel

FOOL'S PARADISE 1921 d: Cecil B. de Mille. USA., *Laurels and the Lady*, Leonard Merrick, 1908, Short Story

FOOL'S REVENGE, A 1909 d: D. W. Griffith. USA., *Le Roi S'amuse*, Victor Hugo, 1832, Play

Fool's Revenge, A see **OR A FOOL'S REVENGE, THE DUKE'S JESTER** (1909).

FOOL'S REVENGE, THE 1916 d: Will S. Davis. USA., *The Fool's Revenge*, Tom Taylor, New York 1864, Play

Fools Rush in see **BLONDE INSPIRATION** (1940).

FOOLS RUSH IN 1949 d: John Paddy Carstairs. UKN., *Fools Rush in*, Kenneth Horne, London 1946, Play

FOOLS STEP IN 1938 d: Nigel Byass. UKN., *Things Hidden*, B. O. Byass, Short Story

Football of the Good Old Days see **REGI IDOK FOCIJA** (1973).

Footbridge, The see **LEVIATHAN** (1966).

FOOTFALLS 1921 d: Charles J. Brabin. USA., *Footfalls*, Wilbur Daniel Steele, Short Story

Footlight Glamour see **UPSTREAM** (1927).

FOOTLIGHTS 1921 d: John S. Robertson. USA., *Footlights*, Rita Weiman, 1919, Short Story

Footlights see **SUNNY SIDE UP** (1926).

FOOTLIGHTS AND FOOLS 1929 d: William A. Seiter. USA., *Footlights and Fools*, Katharine Brush, Story

FOOTLIGHTS AND SHADOWS 1920 d: John W. Noble. USA., *Out of the Night*, Josephine Miller, Short Story

FOOTLIGHTS OF FATE, THE 1916 d: William Humphrey. USA., *Joan Thursday*, Louis Joseph Vance, Boston 1913, Novel

FOOTLOOSE WIDOWS 1926 d: Roy Del Ruth. USA., *Footloose*, Beatrice Burton, Novel

Footprints Blow Away, The see **VERWEHTE SPUREN** (1938).

FOOTSTEPS 1972 d: Paul Wendkos. USA., *Paddy*, Hamilton Maule, Novel

FOOTSTEPS IN THE DARK 1941 d: Lloyd Bacon. USA., *Blondie White*, Jeffrey Dell, Ladislaus Fodor, Bernard Merivale, Play

FOOTSTEPS IN THE FOG 1955 d: Arthur Lubin. UKN., *The Interruption*, W. W. Jacobs, Novel

Footsteps in the Night see **A HONEYMOON ADVENTURE** (1931).

Footsteps: Nice Guys Finish Last see **FOOTSTEPS** (1972).

For a Friend see **PRO KAMARADA** (1940).

For a Nameless Star see **L'ETOILE SANS NOM MONA** (1966).

For Adrien see **O ADRIENU** (1919).

For All We Know see **FLESH AND FANTASY** (1943).

For an Entire Life see **POUR TOUTE LA VIE** (1924).

FOR ANOTHER WOMAN 1924 d: David Kirkland. USA., *Just Mary*, Pearl Doles Bell, Story

FOR BEAUTY'S SAKE 1941 d: Shepard Traube. USA., *For Beauty's Sake*, Clarence Budington Kelland, Short Story

FOR BETTER, FOR WORSE 1954 d: J. Lee Thompson. UKN., *For Better. for Worse.*, Arthur Watkyn, London 1948, Play

For Forest Loneliness see **ZE SVETA LESNICH SAMOT** (1933).

FOR FROSTNETTENE 1966 d: Arnljot Berg. NRW., *Fjorten Dager for Frostnettene*, Sigurd Hoel, 1935, Novel

FOR HEAVEN'S SAKE 1950 d: George Seaton. USA., *May We Come in*, Harry Segall, Play

FOR HER FATHER'S SAKE 1921 d: Alexander Butler. UKN., *The Perfect Lover*, Alfred Sutro, London 1905, Play

For He's a Jolly Bad Fellow see **A JOLLY BAD FELLOW** (1963).

For His Honour see **MADAME PINKETTE & CO.** (1917).

For His Own House see **PRO DOMO** (1918).

FOR LADIES ONLY 1927 d: Scott Pembroke, Henry Lehrman. USA., *Down With Women*, George Frank Worts, Story

For Love see **Z LASKY** (1928).

FOR LOVE ALONE 1986 d: Stephen Wallace. ASL., *For Love Alone*, Christina Stead, Novel

FOR LOVE OF GOLD 1908 d: D. W. Griffith. USA., *Just Meat*, Jack London, Short Story

FOR LOVE OF IVY 1968 d: Daniel Mann. USA., Sidney Poitier, Story

For Love Or Money see **THIS HAPPY FEELING** (1958).

For Lovers Only see **HARD TO GET** (1938).

For Men Only see **SOLO PARA HOMBRES** (1960).

For Men Only see **BEL AMI** (1975).

For My Fellow see **PRO KAMARADA** (1940).

For Our Vines Have Tender Grapes see **OUR VINES HAVE TENDER GRAPES** (1945).

For Sale see **THE MARRIAGE PRICE** (1919).

For Soviet Power see **ZA VLAST SOVETOV** (1956).

FOR THE DEFENSE 1922 d: Paul Powell. USA., *For the Defense*, Elmer Rice, New York 1919, Play

FOR THE LOVE O' LIL 1930 d: James Tinling. USA., *For the Love O' Lil*, Leslie Thrasher, Short Story

FOR THE LOVE OF MIKE 1927 d: Frank CaprA. USA., *Hell's Kitchen*, John A. Moroso, Story

FOR THE LOVE OF MIKE 1932 d: Monty Banks. UKN., *For the Love of Mike*, Clifford Grey, H. F. Maltby, London 1931, Play

For the Love of Tillie see **TILLIE'S PUNCTURED ROMANCE** (1914).

For the Sake of a Dog see **SIMPATYA BISHVIEL KELEV** (1981).

For the Sake of the Revolution see **YI GE MING DE MING YI** (1960).

FOR THE SOUL OF RAFAEL 1920 d: Harry Garson. USA., *For the Soul of Rafael*, Marah Ellis Ryan, Chicago 1906, Novel

FOR THE TERM OF HIS NATURAL LIFE 1927 d: Norman Dawn. ASL., *For the Term of His Natural Life*, Marcus Clarke, Novel

FOR THE TERM OF HIS NATURAL LIFE 1983 d: Rob Stewart. ASL., *For the Term of His Natural Life*, Marcus Clarke, Novel

FOR THEM THAT TRESPASS 1949 d: Alberto Cavalcanti. UKN., *For Them That Trespass*, Ernest Raymond, Novel

FOR THOSE I LOVED 1983 d: Robert Enrico. FRN/CND., *For Those I Loved*, Max Gallo, Martin Grey, Book

FOR US THE LIVING 1982 d: Michael Schultz. USA., *For Us the Living*, Myrlie Evers, Book

For Us the Living: the Medgar Evers Story see **FOR US THE LIVING** (1982).

For Valor see **FOR VALOUR** (1917).

FOR VALOUR 1917 d: Albert Parker. USA., *Melia No-Good*, I. A. R. Wylie, 1917, Short Story

FOR WHOM THE BELL TOLLS 1943 d: Sam Wood. USA., *For Who the Bell Tolls*, Ernest Hemingway, 1940, Novel

FOR WIVES ONLY 1926 d: Victor Heerman. USA., *The Critical Year*, Hans Bachwitz, Rudolph Lothar, Story

FOR YOUR EYES ONLY 1981 d: John Glen. UKN., *For Your Eyes Only*, Ian Fleming, Short Story, *Risico*, Ian Fleming, Short Story

Forbidden see **PROIBITO** (1955).

FORBIDDEN 1986 d: Anthony Page. UKN/GRM/USA., *The Last Jews in Berlin*, Leonard Gross, Novel

Forbidden Adventure see **NEWLY RICH** (1931).

Forbidden Alliance, A see **THE BARRETTS OF WIMPOLE STREET** (1934).

Forbidden Cargo see **THE QUEEN WAS IN THE PARLOUR** (1927).

Forbidden Choices see **MAINE BEANS OF EGYPT** (1994).

Forbidden Christ see **IL CRISTO PROIBITO** (1951).

Forbidden Dreams see **SMRT KRASNYCH SRNCU** (1987).

Forbidden Fruit see **LE FRUIT DEFENDU** (1952).

Forbidden Lips see **SPRINGTIME FOR HENRY** (1934).

Forbidden Love see **THE QUEEN WAS IN THE PARLOUR** (1927).

Forbidden Love see **FREAKS** (1932).

Forbidden Love see **MILOVANI ZAKAZANO** (1938).

Forbidden Love see **TORN APART** (1990).

Forbidden Love Affair see **ASFALTO SELVAGEM** (1964).

FORBIDDEN PARADISE 1924 d: Ernst Lubitsch. USA., *A Carno Szinmu: Harom Felvonasban*, Lajos Biro, Budapest 1913, Play, *A Carno Szinmu; Harom Felvonasban*, Menyhert Lengyel, Budapest 1913, Play

Forbidden Paradise see **HURRICANE** (1979).

Forbidden Room, The see **LA STANZA DEL VESCOVO** (1977).

Forbidden Street see **BRITANNIA MEWS** (1948).

FORBIDDEN TERRITORY 1934 d: Phil Rosen. UKN., *Forbidden Territory*, Dennis Wheatley, Novel

FORBIDDEN THING, THE 1920 d: Allan Dwan. USA., *The Forbidden Thing*, Mary Mears, 1920, Short Story

FORBIDDEN TRAILS 1920 d: Scott R. Dunlap. USA., *Forbidden Trails*, Charles Alden Seltzer, 1919, Short Story

FORBIDDEN VALLEY 1938 d: Wyndham Gittens. USA., *The Mountains are My Kingdom*, Stuart Hardy, New York 1937, Book

Forbidden Way, The see **CYTHEREA** (1924).

FORBIDDEN WOMAN, THE 1927 d: Paul L. Stein. USA., *Brothers*, Elmer Harris, Story

Forbidden Women see **DONNE PROIBITE** (1953).

FORBIN PROJECT, THE 1969 d: Joseph Sargent. USA., *Colossus*, D. F. Jones, London 1966, Novel

Forbodings see **PREDTUCHA** (1947).

FORCE 10 FROM NAVARONE 1978 d: Guy Hamilton. UKN/USA., *Force Ten from Navarone*, Alistair MacLean, 1968, Novel

Force Brutale, La see **LA FORZA BRUTA** (1941).

Force Et le Droit, La see **LES ASSASSINS DE L'ORDRE** (1970).

FORCE OF ARMS 1951 d: Michael Curtiz. USA., *Italian Story*, Richard W. Tregaskis, Story

Force of Destiny, The see **LA FORZA DEL DESTINO** (1950).

FORCE OF EVIL 1948 d: Abraham Polonsky. USA., *Tucker's People*, Ira Wolfert, Novel

Force Ten from Navarone see **FORCE 10 FROM NAVARONE** (1978).

FORDINGTON TWINS, THE 1920 d: W. P. Kellino. UKN., *The Fordington Twins*, E. Newton-Bungey, Novel

FOREIGN BODY 1987 d: Ronald Neame. UKN., *Foreign Body*, Roderick Mann, Novel

FOREIGN CORRESPONDENT 1940 d: Alfred Hitchcock. USA., *Personal History*, Vincent Sheean, Book

FOREIGN EXCHANGE 1969 d: Roy Ward Baker. UKN., *Foreign Exchange*, Jimmy Sangster, Novel

FOREIGN LEGION, THE 1928 d: Edward Sloman. USA., *The Red Mirage*, I. A. R. Wylie, London 1913, Novel

FOREIGN STUDENT, THE 1994 d: Eva Sereny. USA/FRN., *L'Etudiant Etranger*, Philippe Labro, Book

Foreigner, The see **GOD'S CRUCIBLE** (1921).

FOREMAN WENT TO FRANCE, THE 1942 d: Charles Frend. UKN., J. B. Priestley, Story

Forest see **LES** (1980).

Forest Maiden, The see **PADUREANCA** (1988).

Forest of Hanged Men see **PADUREA SPINZURATILOR** (1965).

Forest of Hanging Foxes see **HIRTETTYJEN KETTUJEN METSA** (1986).

Forest of the Hanged, The see **PADUREA SPINZURATILOR** (1965).

FOREST ON THE HILL, THE 1919 d: Cecil M. Hepworth. UKN., *The Forest on the Hill*, Eden Philpotts, Novel

FOREST RANGERS, THE 1942 d: George Marshall. USA., *The Forest Rangers*, Thelma Strabel, Novel

FOREST ROSE, THE 1912 d: Theodore Marston. USA., *The Forest Rose*, Emerson Bennett, Novel

Forest Rush see **WALDRAUSCH** (1977).

Forest Silence see **DAS SCHWEIGEN IM WALDE** (1955).

Forest Silence see **DAS SCHWEIGEN IM WALDE** (1976).

Forest, The see **LES** (1953).

Forest Winter see **WALDWINTER** (1936).

Forest Winter see **WALDWINTER** (1956).

Forester's Daughter, The see **DIE FORSTERCHRISTL** (1926).

Forester's Daughter, The see **DIE FORSTERCHRISTL** (1931).

Forester's Daughter, The see **DIE FORSTERCHRISTL** (1952).

Forester's Daughter, The see **DIE FORSTERCHRISTL** (1962).

FOREVER 1921 d: George Fitzmaurice. USA., *Peter Ibbetson*, George Du Maurier, New York 1891, Novel

FOREVER 1978 d: John Korty. USA., *Forever*, Judy Blume, Novel

FOREVER AFTER 1926 d: F. Harmon Weight. USA., *Forever After*, Owen Davis, Play

FOREVER AMBER 1947 d: Otto Preminger. USA., *Forever Amber*, Kathleen Winsor, Novel

Forever England see **BROWN ON RESOLUTION** (1935).

FOREVER FEMALE 1953 d: Irving Rapper. USA., *Rosalind*, J. M. Barrie, London 1912, Play

Forever in Love see **PRIDE OF THE MARINES** (1945).

Forever Mary see **MERY PER SEMPRE** (1988).

Forever My Love see **SISSI** (1956).

FORFAITURE 1937 d: Marcel L'Herbier. FRN., *The Cheat*, Hector Turnbull, Novel

FORFEIT, THE 1919 d: Frank Powell. USA., *The Forfeit*, Ridgwell Cullum, Philadelphia 1917, Novel

Forger of London, The see **DER FALSCHER VON LONDON** (1961).

FORGER, THE 1928 d: G. B. Samuelson. UKN., *The Forger*, Edgar Wallace, London 1927, Novel

Forgery, The see **DIE FALSCHUNG** (1981).

Forget, if You Can see **WENN DU KANNST VERGISS** (1956).

FORGET-ME-NOT 1917 d: Emile Chautard. USA., *Forget-Me-Not*, F. C. Grove, Herman Merivale, London 1879, Play

Forget-Me-Nots see **FORGET-ME-NOT** (1917).

FORGING AHEAD 1933 d: Norman Walker. UKN., *Easy Money*, K. R. G. Browne, Novel

Forgiven; Or, the Jack O'Diamonds see **THE JACK OF DIAMONDS FORGIVEN; OR** (1914).

FORGIVEN; OR, THE JACK OF DIAMONDS 1914 d: William Robert Daly. USA., *Forgiven; Or the Jack of Diamonds*, Clay M. Greene, New York 1886, Play

Forgiven Sinner, The see **PRETRE LEON MORIN** (1961).

Forgotten see **RIP VAN WINKLE** (1914).

Forgotten Children see **DIE VERGESSENEN KINDER** (1981).

FORGOTTEN FACES 1928 d: Victor Schertzinger. USA., *A Whiff of Heliotrope*, Richard Washburn Child, 1918, Short Story

FORGOTTEN FACES 1936 d: E. A. Dupont. USA., *A Whiff of Heliotrope*, Richard Washburn Child, 1918, Short Story

Forgotten Hero see **THE HOOSIER SCHOOLBOY** (1937).

Forgotten Hill, The see **LA COLLINE OUBLIEE** (1997).

FORGOTTEN LAW, THE 1922 d: James W. Horne. USA., *A Modern Madonna*, Carol Abbot Stanley, New York 1906, Novel

Forgotten Light see **ZAPOMENUTE SVETLO** (1997).

Forgotten Patriots see **ZAPADLI VLASTENCI** (1932).

FORGOTTEN SINS 1995 d: Dick Lowry. USA., Lawrence Wright, Article

Forgotten Vows see **THE ROSE OF KILDARE** (1927).

FORLORN RIVER 1926 d: John Waters. USA., *Forlorn River*, Zane Grey, New York 1927, Novel

FORLORN RIVER 1937 d: Charles T. Barton. USA., *Forlorn River*, Zane Grey, New York 1927, Novel

Forlovningen see **KIHLAUS** (1922).

Forlvningen see **KIHLAUS** (1955).

Formula for Death see **ROBIN COOK'S FORMULA FOR DEATH** (1995).

FORMULA, THE 1980 d: John G. Avildsen. USA., *The Formula*, Steve Shagan, Novel

FORMYNDERNE 1978 d: Nicole MacE. NRW., *Pa Sct. Jorgen*, Amalie Skram, 1895, Novel, *Professor Hieronimus*, Amalie Skram, 1895, Novel

FORNARETTO DI VENEZIA, IL 1907 d: Mario Caserini. ITL., *Il Fornaretto*, Francesco Dall'ongaro, 1846, Play

FORNARETTO DI VENEZIA, IL 1914 d: Luigi Maggi. ITL., *Il Fornaretto*, Francesco Dall'ongaro, 1846, Play

FORNARETTO DI VENEZIA, IL 1923 d: Mario Almirante. ITL., *Il Fornaretto*, Francesco Dall'ongaro, 1846, Play

FORNARETTO DI VENEZIA, IL 1939 d: Duilio Coletti. ITL., *Il Fornaretto*, Francesco Dall'ongaro, 1846, Play

FORNARETTO DI VENEZIA, IL 1963 d: Duccio Tessari. ITL/FRN., *Il Fornaretto*, Francesco Dall'ongaro, 1846, Play

FORNARINA, LA 1944 d: Enrico Guazzoni. ITL., *La Fornarina*, Tullo Gramantieri, Novel

FORRAEDERNE 1984 d: Ole Roos. DNM., *Kridtstregen*, Erik Aalbaek Jensen, 1976, Novel

FORSAKING ALL OTHERS 1934 d: W. S. Van Dyke. USA., *Forsaking All Others*, Frank Cavett, Edward Barry Roberts, New York 1933, Play

FORSE CHE SI, FORSE CHE NO 1921 d: Gaston Ravel. ITL., *Forse Che No Forse Che Si*, Gabriele D'Annunzio, Novel

FORSE ERI TU L'AMORE 1940 d: Gennaro Righelli. ITL., Gherardo Gherardi, Play

FORSTE KREDS, DEN 1971 d: Aleksander Ford. DNM/GRM/USA., *V Kruge Pervom*, Alexander Solzhenitsyn, 1968, Novel

FORSTERBUBEN, DIE 1955 d: R. A. Stemmle. AUS., *Die Forsterbuben*, Peter Rosegger, 1908, Short Story

FORSTERCHRISTL, DIE 1926 d: Friedrich Zelnik. GRM., *Die Forsterchristl*, Bernhard Buchbinder, Georg Jarno, Opera

FORSTERCHRISTL, DIE 1931 d: Friedrich Zelnik. GRM., *Die Forsterchristl*, Bernhard Buchbinder, Georg Jarno, Opera

FORSTERCHRISTL, DIE 1952 d: Arthur M. Rabenalt. GRM., *Die Forsterchristl*, Bernhard Buchbinder, Georg Jarno, Opera

767

FORSTERCHRISTL, DIE 1962 d: Franz J. Gottlieb. GRM., *Die Forsterchristl*, Bernhard Buchbinder, Georg Jarno, Opera

FORSVUNDNE BREVE, DE 1967 d: Annelise Hovmand. DNM., **De Forsvundne Breve**, Villy Sorensen, 1955, Short Story

FORSVUNDNE FULDMAEGTIG, DEN 1972 d: Gert Fredholm. DNM., *Den Forsvundne Fuldmaegtig*, Hans Scherfig, 1938, Novel

FORT APACHE 1948 d: John Ford. USA., *Massacre*, James Warner Bellah, Story

FORT DE LA SOLITUDE 1947 d: Robert Vernay. FRN., *Fort de la Solitude*, Rene Guillot, Story

FORT DOBBS 1958 d: Gordon Douglas. USA., *Backtrack*, George W. George, Burt Kennedy, Story

FORT FRAYNE 1926 d: Ben Wilson. USA., *Fort Frayne*, Gen. Charles King, Philadelphia 1901, Novel

FORT WORTH 1951 d: Edwin L. Marin. USA., *Across the Panhandle*, John Twist, Story

FORT-DOLORES 1938 d: Rene Le Henaff. FRN., *Le Ranch Des Hommes Forts*, Jean Desvallieres, Novel

FORTE, O 1974 d: Olney Sao Paulo. BRZ., *O Forte*, Adonias Filho, 1965, Novel

FORTERESSE, LA 1947 d: Fedor Ozep. CND., Michael Lennox, George Zuckerman, Story

FORTRESS 1985 d: Arch Nicholson. ASL/USA., *Fortress*, Gabrielle Lord, Novel

Fortress Guard, The see **PAZACHAT NA KREPOSTA** (1974).

Fortress Warden, The see **PAZACHAT NA KREPOSTA** (1974).

Fortsyte Saga, The see **THAT FORTSYTE WOMAN** (1949).

Fortuna see **LA FILLE DE LA MER MORTE** (1966).

Fortuna in Tasca, La see **IL DESTINO IN TASCA** (1938).

Fortunata and Jacinta see **FORTUNATA Y JACINTA** (1969).

FORTUNATA Y JACINTA 1969 d: Angelino Fons. SPN., *Fortunata Y Jacinta*, Benito Perez Galdos, 1887, Novel

FORTUNATE FOOL, THE 1933 d: Norman Walker. UKN., *The Fortunate Fool*, Dion Titheradge, Play

Fortunate Fugitive, The see **JR. OLIVER TWIST** (1921).

FORTUNATE YOUTH, THE 1916 d: Joseph Smiley. USA., *The Fortunate Youth*, William J. Locke, New York 1914, Novel

FORTUNE AND MEN'S EYES 1971 d: Harvey Hart. CND., *Fortune and Men's Eyes*, John Herbert, Play

FORTUNE AT STAKE, A 1918 d: Walter West. UKN., *A Fortune at Stake*, Nat Gould, Novel

FORTUNE CARREE 1954 d: Bernard Borderie. FRN./ITL., *Fortune Carree*, Joseph Kessel, Novel

FORTUNE DE MARSEILLE 1951 d: Henri Lepage, Pierre Mere. FRN., *Un Homme du Nord*, Charles Mere, Play

FORTUNE HUNTER, THE 1914 d: Barry O'Neil. USA., *The Fortune Hunter*, Winchell Smith, New York 1909, Play

FORTUNE HUNTER, THE 1920 d: Tom Terriss. USA., *The Fortune Hunter*, Winchell Smith, New York 1909, Play

FORTUNE HUNTER, THE 1927 d: Charles F. Reisner. USA., *The Fortune Hunter*, Winchell Smith, New York 1909, Play

Fortune Hunter, The see **THE OUTCAST** (1954).

FORTUNE IS A WOMAN 1957 d: Sidney Gilliat. UKN., *Fortune Is a Woman*, Winston Graham, Novel

FORTUNE, LA 1931 d: Jean Hemard. FRN., *Que le Monde Est Petit!*, Tristan Bernard, Play

FORTUNE OF CHRISTINA MCNAB, THE 1921 d: W. P. Kellino. UKN., *The Fortune of Christina McNab*, Sarah McNaughton, Novel

FORTUNE TELLER, THE 1920 d: Albert Capellani. USA., *The Fortune Teller*, Leighton Graves Osmun, New York 1919, Play

Fortunes and Misfortunes of Moll Flanders, The see **MOLL FLANDERS** (1996).

FORTUNE'S CHILD 1919 d: Joseph Gleason. USA., *Beth*, Lawrence McCloskey, Short Story

Fortune's Fools see **THE SCOURGE** (1922).

FORTUNE'S MASK 1922 d: Robert Ensminger. USA., *Fortune's Mask*, O. Henry, 1904, Short Story

FORTUNES OF CAPTAIN BLOOD 1950 d: Gordon Douglas. USA., *The Fortunes of Captain Blood*, Rafael Sabatini, 1936, Novel

FORTUNES OF FIFI, THE 1917 d: Robert G. VignolA. USA., *The Fortunes of Fifi*, Molly Elliot Seawell, Indianapolis 1903, Play

FORTUNES OF WAR 1987 d: James Cellan Jones. UKN., *Fortunes of War*, Olivia Manning, Novel

FORTY CARATS 1973 d: Milton Katselas. USA., *Forty Carats*, Pierre Barillet, Jean-Pierre Gredy, Play

FORTY DEUCE 1981 d: Paul Morrissey. USA., *Forty Deuce*, Alan Browne, Play

FORTY NAUGHTY GIRLS 1937 d: Eddie Cline. USA., *The Riddle of the Forty Naughty Girls*, Stuart Palmer, 1934, Short Story

FORTY POUNDS OF TROUBLE 1962 d: Norman Jewison. USA., *Little Miss Marker*, Damon Runyon, 1932, Short Story

FORTY WINKS 1925 d: Frank Urson, Paul Iribe. USA., *Lord Chumley*, David Belasco, Cecil B. de Mille, New York 1888, Play

FORTY-FIVE MINUTES FROM BROADWAY 1920 d: Joseph de Grasse. USA., *Forty-Five Minutes from Broadway*, George M. Cohan, 1906, Musical Play

Forty-Four Soho Square see **SOHO INCIDENT** (1956).

Forty-Second Street see **42ND STREET** (1933).

FORVANDLINGEN 1975 d: Ivo Dvorak. SWD., *Die Verwandlung*, Franz Kafka, 1912, Short Story

Forward-Toward Life see **ETEENPAIN-ELAMAAN** (1939).

FORZA BRUTA, LA 1941 d: Carlo Ludovico BragagliA. ITL/SPN., *La Fuerza Bruta*, Jacinto Benavente y Martinez, 1908, Play

FORZA DEL DESTINO, LA 1911. ITL., *Don Alvaro O la Fuerzo Del Sino*, Angelo Perez de Saavedra, 1835, Play

FORZA DEL DESTINO, LA 1950 d: Carmine Gallone. ITL., *Don Alvaro O la Fuerzo Del Sino*, Angelo Perez de Saavedra, 1835, Play

Forzato Della Guiana, Il see **CHERI-BIBI** (1954).

Fossils see **KASEKI** (1975).

FOSTER AND LAURIE 1975 d: John Llewellyn Moxey. USA., *Foster and Laurie*, Al Silverman, Book

FOTHERGILL 1981 d: Claude Whatham. UKN., *An Innkeeper's Diary*, John Fothergill, Book

FOTOGLIFOS. ESPEJISMOS DEL CARIBE 1990 d: Fernando Birri. SPN., *Un Senor Muy Viejo Con Unas Alas Enormes*, Gabriel Garcia Marquez, 1972, Short Story

FOU DU LABO 4, LE 1967 d: Jacques Besnard. FRN., *Le Fou du Labo 4*, Rene Cambon, Novel

FOUL PLAY 1920. UKN., *Foul Play*, Charles Reade, Novel

Foundling, The see **DER FINDLING** (1968).

FOUNTAIN, THE 1934 d: John Cromwell. USA., *The Fountain*, Charles Morgan, 1932, Novel

Fountain, The see **IZUMI** (1956).

FOUNTAINHEAD, THE 1949 d: King Vidor. USA., *The Fountainhead*, Ayn Rand, 1943, Novel

Fountainhead, The see **IZUMI** (1956).

Four Bags Full see **LA TRAVERSEE DE PARIS** (1956).

FOUR BOYS AND A GUN 1955 d: William Berke. USA., *Four Boys and a Gun*, Willard Wiener, 1944, Novel

Four Cents a Word see **BLONDE INSPIRATION** (1940).

Four Chimneys see **ENTOTSU NO MIERU BASHO** (1953).

FOUR DARK HOURS 1937 d: William Cameron Menzies. UKN., *Graham Greene*, Short Story

FOUR DAUGHTERS 1938 d: Michael Curtiz. USA., *Sister Act*, Fannie Hurst, 1937, Short Story

FOUR DAYS 1951 d: John Guillermin. UKN., *Four Days*, Monckton Hoffe, Play

Four Days in September see **COMPANHEIRO? O QUE E ISSO** (1997).

FOUR DAYS LEAVE 1950 d: Leopold Lindtberg. SWT/USA., *Swiss Tour B Xv*, Richard Schweizer, Zurich 1947, Novel

FOUR DAYS' WONDER 1936 d: Sidney Salkow. USA., *Four Days' Wonder*, A. A. Milne, New York 1933, Novel

FOUR DEVILS 1929 d: F. W. Murnau. USA., *De Fire Djaevle*, Herman Bang, Kristiania 1895, Novel

FOUR FACES WEST 1948 d: Alfred E. Green. USA., *Paso Por Aqui*, Eugene Manlove Rhodes, Novel

FOUR FEATHERS 1915 d: J. Searle Dawley. USA., *The Four Feathers*, A. E. W. Mason, London 1902, Novel

FOUR FEATHERS, THE 1929 d: Merian C. Cooper, Ernest B. Schoedsack. USA., *The Four Feathers*, A. E. W. Mason, London 1902, Novel

FOUR FEATHERS, THE 1921 d: Rene Plaissetty. UKN., *The Four Feathers*, A. E. W. Mason, London 1902, Novel

FOUR FEATHERS, THE 1939 d: Zoltan KordA. UKN., *The Four Feathers*, A. E. W. Mason, London 1902, Novel

Four Feathers, The see **STORM OVER THE NILE** (1955).

FOUR FEATHERS, THE 1978 d: Don Sharp. UKN/USA., *The Four Feathers*, A. E. W. Mason, London 1902, Novel

FOUR FRIGHTENED PEOPLE 1934 d: Cecil B. de Mille. USA., *Four Frightened People*, E. Arnot Robertson, New York 1931, Novel

Four from the Infantry see **WESTFRONT 1918** (1930).

FOUR HORSEMEN OF THE APOCALYPSE, THE 1921 d: Rex Ingram. USA., *Los Cuatro Jinetes Del Apocalipsis*, Vicente Blasco Ibanez, Valencia 1916, Novel

FOUR HORSEMEN OF THE APOCALYPSE, THE 1961 d: Vincente Minnelli. USA., *Los Cuatro Jinetes Del Apocalipsis*, Vicente Blasco Ibanez, Valencia 1916, Novel

FOUR HOURS TO KILL! 1935 d: Mitchell Leisen. USA., *Small Miracle*, Norman Krasna, New York 1934, Play

FOUR JACKS AND A JILL 1941 d: Jack Hively. USA., *The Viennese Charmer*, W. Carey Wonderly, Story

Four Jacks and a Queen see **FOUR JACKS AND A JILL** (1941).

FOUR JUST MEN, THE 1921 d: George Ridgwell. UKN., *The Four Just Men*, Edgar Wallace, London 1905, Novel

FOUR JUST MEN, THE 1939 d: Walter Forde. UKN., *The Four Just Men*, Edgar Wallace, London 1905, Novel

Four Keys, The see **VIER SCHLUSSEL** (1965).

Four Marys, The see **MAN-PROOF** (1937).

FOUR MASKED MEN 1934 d: George Pearson. UKN., *The Masqueraders*, Cyril Campion, Play

FOUR MEN AND A PRAYER 1938 d: John Ford. USA., *Four Men and a Prayer*, David Garth, New York 1937, Novel

FOUR MEN IN A VAN 1921 d: Hugh Croise. UKN., *We Three and Troddles*, R. Andom, Novel

Four Musketeers, The see **DIE VIER MUSKETIERE** (1935).

FOUR MUSKETEERS, THE 1975 d: Richard Lester. UKN/SPN/PNM., *Les Trois Mousquetaires*, Alexandre Dumas (pere), Paris 1844, Novel

Four Musketeers: the Revenge of Milady see **THE FOUR MUSKETEERS** (1975).

Four Nights of a Dreamer see **QUATRE NUITS D'UN REVEUR** (1971).

FOUR SIDED TRIANGLE 1953 d: Terence Fisher. UKN., *Four Sided Triangle*, William F. Temple, Novel

FOUR SONS 1928 d: John Ford. USA., *Grandmother Bernle Learns Her Letters*, I. A. R. Wylie, 1926, Short Story

FOUR SONS 1940 d: Archie Mayo. USA., *Grandmother Bernle Learns Her Letters*, I. A. R. Wylie, 1926, Short Story

FOUR WALLS 1928 d: William Nigh. USA., *Four Walls*, George Abbott, Dana Burnet, New York 1927, Play

Four Walls see **STRAIGHT IS THE WAY** (1934).

FOUR WINDS ISLAND 1961 d: David Villiers. UKN., *Four Winds Island*, Vega Stewart, Novel

FOUR WIVES 1939 d: Michael Curtiz. USA., *Sister Act*, Fannie Hurst, 1937, Short Story

FOURBERIES DE SCAPIN, LES 1980 d: Roger Coggio. FRN., *Les Fourberies de Scapin*, Moliere, 1671, Play

FOURCHAMBAULT, LES 1929 d: Georges MoncA. FRN., *Les Fourchambault*, Emile Paul Augier, Play

FOURFLUSHER, THE 1928 d: Wesley Ruggles. USA., *The Four-Flusher*, Cesar Dunn, New York 1925, Play

FOURPOSTER, THE 1952 d: Irving Reis. USA., *The Fourposter*, Jan de Hartog, New York 1951, Play

FOURTEEN HOURS 1951 d: Henry Hathaway. USA., *The Man on the Ledge*, Joel Sayre, Story

Fourteenth at the Table, The see **CTRNACTY U STOLU** (1943).

FOURTEENTH LOVER, THE 1922 d: Harry Beaumont. USA., *The Fourteenth Lover*, Alice D. G. Miller, Story

FOURTH COMMANDMENT, THE 1927 d: Emory Johnson. USA., *The Fourth Commandment*, Emilie Johnson, Story

FOURTH ESTATE, THE 1916 d: Frank Powell. USA., *The Fourth Estate*, Harriet Ford, Joseph Medill Patterson, New York 1909, Play

Fourth Flock, The *see* AL PATRULEA STOL (1979).

FOURTH IN SALVADOR, THE 1918 d: David Smith. USA., *The Fourth in Salvador*, O. Henry, Short Story

Fourth Man, The *see* DE VIERDE MAN (1983).

FOURTH MUSKETEER, THE 1923 d: William K. Howard. USA., *The Fourth Musketeer*, Harry Charles Witwer, 1922, Short Story

FOURTH PROTOCOL, THE 1987 d: John MacKenzie. UKN., *The Fourth Protocol*, Frederick Forsyth, Novel

FOURTH SQUARE, THE 1961 d: Allan Davis. UKN., *Four Square Jane*, Edgar Wallace, London 1929, Novel

Fourth, The *see* CETVERTYJ (1972).

Fourth Time, The *see* DIE VIERTE ZEIT (1984).

FOX AND THE HOUND, THE 1981 d: Art Stevens, Ted Berman. USA., *The Fox and the Hound*, Daniel P. Mannix, Novel

FOX FARM 1922 d: Guy Newall. UKN., *Fox Farm*, Warwick Deeping, Novel

Fox Fire *see* LE FEU FOLLET (1963).

FOX, THE 1968 d: Mark Rydell. USA., *The Fox*, D. H. Lawrence, 1922, Short Story

FOX WOMAN, THE 1915 d: Lloyd Ingraham. USA., *The Fox-Woman*, John Luther Long, Philadelphia 1900, Novel

FOXES OF HARROW, THE 1947 d: John M. Stahl. USA., *The Foxes of Harrow*, Frank Yerby, 1946, Novel

FOXFIRE 1955 d: Joseph Pevney. USA., *Foxfire*, Anya Seton, 1950, Novel

FOXFIRE 1996 d: Annette Haywood-Carter. USA., *Foxfire*, Joyce Carol Oates, Novel

FOXHOLE IN CAIRO 1960 d: John Llewellyn Moxey. UKN., *The Cat and the Mice*, Leonard Oswald Mosley, London 1958, Novel

Foxiest Girl in Paris, The *see* NATHALIE (1957).

FOYER PERDU 1952 d: Jean Loubignac. FRN., *Foyer Perdu*, Andre Haguet, Play

F.P.1 1932 d: Karl Hartl. UKN., *F.P.1 Antwortet Nicht*, Curt Siodmak, Novel

F.P.1 ANTWORTET NICHT 1932 d: Karl Hartl. GRM., *F.P.1 Antwortet Nicht*, Curt Siodmak, Novel

F.P.1. Does Not Answer *see* F.P.1 ANTWORTET NICHT (1932).

FRA DIAVOLO 1908 d: Albert Capellani. FRN., *Fra Diavolo ou l'Hotellerie de Terracine*, Daniel Francois Auber, Paris 1830, Opera, *Fra Diavolo; Ou l'Hotellerie de Terracine*, Eugene Scribe, Paris 1830, Opera

FRA DIAVOLO 1912 d: Alice Blache. USA., *Fra Diavolo Ou l'Hotellerie de Terracine*, Daniel Francois Auber, Paris 1830, Opera, *Fra Diavolo; Ou l'Hotellerie de Terracine*, Eugene Scribe, Paris 1830, Opera

FRA DIAVOLO 1922 d: Challis Sanderson. UKN., *Fra Diavolo Ou l'Hotellerie de Terracine*, Daniel Francois Auber, Paris 1830, Opera, *Fra Diavolo; Ou l'Hotellerie de Terracine*, Eugene Scribe, Paris 1830, Opera

FRA DIAVOLO 1930 d: Mario Bonnard. GRM., *Fra Diavolo ou l'Hotellerie de Terracine*, Daniel Francois Auber, Paris 1830, Opera

FRA DIAVOLO 1930 d: Mario Bonnard. FRN., *Fra Diavolo ou l'Hotellerie de Terracine*, Daniel Francois Auber, Paris 1830, Opera

FRA DIAVOLO 1930 d: Mario Bonnard. GRM., *Fra Diavolo; Ou l'Hotellerie de Terracine*, Eugene Scribe, Paris 1830, Opera

FRA DIAVOLO 1930 d: Mario Bonnard. FRN., *Fra Diavolo; Ou l'Hotellerie de Terracine*, Eugene Scribe, Paris 1830, Opera

Fra Diavolo *see* THE DEVIL'S BROTHER (1933).

FRA GIACONE 1913. UKN., *Fra Giacone*, Robert Buchanan, Poem

Fra le Spire Del Destino *see* MUSOTTE (1920).

Fragile Relationship *see* KREHKE VZTAHY (1979).

FRAGMA, TO 1982 d: Dimitris Makris. GRC., *The Dam*, Dimitris Plaskovitis, Novel

FRAGMENT OF FEAR 1970 d: Richard C. Sarafian. UKN., *Fragment of Fear*, John Bingham, Novel

Fragments d'Epaves *see* EN PLONGEE (1926).

Fragments from the Life of a Physician *see* RETALHOS DA VIDA DE UM MEDICO (1962).

Frail *see* BROOS (1998).

Fraile, El *see* THE MONK (1990).

FRAILTY 1921 d: F. Martin Thornton. UKN., *Frailty*, Olive Wadsley, Novel

Framat - Mot Livet *see* ETEENPAIN-ELAMAAN (1939).

Frame of Mind, A *see* SPOSOB BYCIA (1966).

Frame Up, The *see* THE FRAME-UP (1937).

FRAMED 1927 d: Charles J. Brabin. USA., *The Dawn of My Tomorrow*, George W. Sutton Jr., Story

Framed *see* RIO GRANDE ROMANCE (1936).

FRAMED 1975 d: Phil Karlson. USA., *Framed*, Mike Misenheimer, Art Powers, Novel

FRAME-UP, THE 1937 d: D. Ross Lederman. USA., *Right Guy*, Richard Wormser, 1936, Short Story

Framlingen *see* VIERAS MIES (1958).

Francesca *see* FRANCISCA (1981).

Francesca Da Rimini *see* PAOLO E FRANCESCA (1950).

FRANCHISE AFFAIR, THE 1951 d: Lawrence Huntington. UKN., *The Franchise Affair*, Josephine Tey, Novel

FRANCINE 1911 d: Oreste Gherardini. ITL., *La Vie de Boheme*, Henri Murger, Paris 1848, Play

FRANCIS 1949 d: Arthur Lubin. USA., *Francis*, David Stern, Novel

FRANCIS GARY POWERS:THE TRUE STORY OF THE U-2 SPY INCIDENT 1976 d: Delbert Mann. USA., *Operation Overflight*, Gary Francis Powers, Book

FRANCIS OF ASSISI 1961 d: Michael Curtiz. USA., *The Joyful Beggar*, Louis de Wohl, Philadelphia 1958, Novel

FRANCISCA 1981 d: Manoel de OliveirA. PRT., *Fanny Owen*, Agustina Bessa-Luis, 1979, Novel

FRANCISCAIN DE BOURGES, LE 1968 d: Claude Autant-LarA. FRN., *Le Franciscain de Bourges*, Marc Toledano

FRANCISKA VASARNAPJAI 1997 d: Sandor Simo. HNG., *Franciska Vasarnapjai*, Sandor Simo, Novel

Franco-German Invasion, The *see* THE FRANCO-GERMAN INVASION, THE WAR OF WARS; OR (1914).

FRANCOIS IL CONTRABBANDIERE 1954 d: Gianfranco Parolini. ITL., *Il Bacio Dell'Aurora*, Luciana Peverelli, Novel

FRANCS-MACONS 1914. FRN., *Les Francs-MacOns*, G. Leprince, Claude Rolland, Play

Francs-MacOns *see* RIEN QUE DES MENSONGES (1932).

Frank Costello Faccia d'Angelo *see* LE SAMOURAI (1967).

FRANKENSTEIN 1910 d: J. Searle Dawley. USA., *Frankenstein; Or the Modern Prometheus*, Mary Wollstonecraft Shelley, London 1818, Novel

FRANKENSTEIN 1931 d: James Whale. USA., *Frankenstein; Or the Modern Prometheus*, Mary Wollstonecraft Shelley, London 1818, Novel

FRANKENSTEIN 1973 d: Glenn Jordan. USA., *Frankenstein; Or the Modern Prometheus*, Mary Wollstonecraft Shelley, London 1818, Novel

FRANKENSTEIN 1984 d: James Ormerod. UKN/USA., *Frankenstein; Or the Modern Prometheus*, Mary Wollstonecraft Shelley, London 1818, Novel

FRANKENSTEIN GENERAL HOSPITAL 1988 d: Deborah Roberts. USA., *Frankenstein; Or the Modern Prometheus*, Mary Wollstonecraft Shelley, London 1818, Novel

Frankenstein Lives Again *see* BRIDE OF FRANKENSTEIN (1935).

FRANKENSTEIN: THE TRUE STORY 1973 d: Jack Smight. USA/UKN., *Frankenstein; Or the Modern Prometheus*, Mary Wollstonecraft Shelley, London 1818, Novel

Frankenstein's Haunted Castle *see* CRIME AND PASSION (1975).

Frankensteins Spukschloss *see* CRIME AND PASSION (1975).

FRANKIE & JOHNNY 1991 d: Garry Marshall. USA., *Frankie and Johnny in the Clair de Lune*, Terrence McNally, 1987, Play

Frankie and Johnny *see* FRANKIE & JOHNNY (1991).

FRANKIE STARLIGHT 1995 d: Michael Lindsay-Hogg. USA., *The Dork of Cork*, Chet Raymo, Novel

FRANKIE'S HOUSE 1991 d: Peter Fisk. ASL/UKN/USA., *Page After Page*, Tim Page, Novel

Frankie's War *see* FRANKIE'S HOUSE (1991).

FRANTA 1988 d: Mathias Allary. GRM., Ernst Weiss, Story

Frantic *see* L' ASCENSEUR POUR L'ECHAFAUD (1957).

Frantic *see* LES MAGICIENNES (1960).

FRANZ 1974 d: John Sweeney, Paul Aspland. CND., *Woyzeck*, Georg Buchner, 1879, Play

FRATELLI CASTIGLIONI, I 1937 d: Corrado d'Errico. ITL., *I Fratelli Castiglioni*, Alberto Colantuoni, Play

FRATELLI CORSI, I 1961 d: Anton Giulio Majano. ITL/FRN., *Les Freres Corses*, Alexandre Dumas (pere), 1845, Short Story

FRATELLI KARAMAZOFF, I 1948 d: Giacomo Gentilomo. ITL., *Bratya Karamazovy*, Fyodor Dostoyevsky, 1880, Novel

Fraternity House *see* THE AGE OF CONSENT (1932).

FRATII JDERI 1973 d: Mircea Dragan. RMN., *Fratii Jderi*, Mihail Sadoveanu, 1935, Novel

FRAU AM DUNKLEN FENSTER, EINE 1960 d: Franz Peter Wirth. GRM., Hugo Maria Kritz, Story

Frau Am Fenster, Die *see* UNE FEMME A SA FENETRE (1976).

FRAU AM SCHEIDEWEGE, DIE 1938 d: Josef von Baky. GRM/HNG., *Ich Komme Nicht Zum Abendessen*, Alice Lyttkens, Novel

FRAU AM STEUER 1939 d: Paul Martin. GRM., *Frau Am Steuer*, Paul Barabas, Play

FRAU AM WEGE, DIE 1948 d: Eduard von Borsody. AUS., *Der Fluchtling*, Fritz Hochwalder, 1945, Play

FRAU AUF DER FOLTER, DIE 1928 d: Robert Wiene. GRM., *A Butterfly on the Wheel*, E. G. Hemmerde, Francis Neilson, Play

FRAU CHENEYS ENDE 1961 d: Franz J. Wild. GRM/SWT., *The Last of Mrs. Cheyney*, Frederick Lonsdale, London 1925, Play

Frau Cheneys Ende *see* FRAU CHENEYS ENDE (1961).

Frau Des Anderen, Die *see* JONS UND ERDME (1959).

FRAU, DIE WEISS, WAS SIE WILL, EINE 1934 d: Victor Janson. GRM/CZC., *Eine Frau Die Weiss Was Sie Will*, Alfred Grunwald, Oscar Straus, Operetta

FRAU, DIE WEISS, WAS SIE WILL, EINE 1958 d: Arthur M. Rabenalt. GRM., *Eine Frau Die Weiss Was Sie Will*, Alfred Grunwald, Oscar Straus, Operetta

Frau Fur 3 Tage, Eine *see* EINE FRAU FUR DREI TAGE (1944).

FRAU FUR DREI TAGE, EINE 1944 d: Fritz Kirchhoff. GRM., *Eine Frau Fur Drei Tage*, Elisabeth Gurt, Novel

Frau Furs Leben, Eine *see* DAS LEBEN KANN SO SCHON SEIN (1938).

FRAU GENUGT NICHT?, EINE 1955 d: Ulrich Erfurth. GRM., *Eine Frau Genugt Nicht?*, Michael Graf Soltikow, Novel

FRAU HOLLE 1954 d: Fritz Genschow. GRM., *Frau Holle*, Jacob Grimm, Wilhelm Grimm, Short Story

FRAU HOLLE 1964 d: Gottfried Kolditz. GDR., *Frau Holle*, Jacob Grimm, Wilhelm Grimm, Short Story

FRAU HOLLE 1985 d: Juraj Jakubisko. GRM/AUS/CZC., *Frau Holle*, Jacob Grimm, Wilhelm Grimm, Short Story

FRAU IM MOND, DIE 1929 d: Fritz Lang. GRM., *Die Frau Im Mond*, Thea von Harbou, Novel

FRAU IM SCHRANK, DIE 1927 d: Rudolf Biebrach. GRM., *Die Frau Im Schrank*, Dussieux, Maribeau, Play

FRAU IM TALAR, DIE 1929 d: Adolf Trotz. GRM., *Die Frau Im Talar*, Petter Bendow, Novel

FRAU IRENE BESSER 1960 d: John Olden. GRM., *Frau Irene Besser*, Hans Habe, Novel

FRAU LUNA 1941 d: Theo Lingen. GRM., *Frau Luna*, Paul Lincke, Opera

FRAU, NACH DER MAN SICH SEHNT, DIE 1929 d: Curtis Bernhardt. GRM., *Nach Der Man Sich Sehnt, Die Frau*, Max Brod, Novel

FRAU NACH MASS 1940 d: Helmut Kautner. GRM., *Frau Nach Mass*, Eberhard Forster, Play

FRAU OHNE BEDEUTUNG, EINE 1936 d: Hans Steinhoff. GRM., *A Woman of No Importance*, Oscar Wilde, London 1893, Play

FRAU OHNE VERGANGENHEIT, DIE 1939 d: Nunzio MalasommA. GRM., *Die Frau Ohne Vergangenheit*, Curt Johannes Braun, Novel

FRAU RETTICH, DIE CZERNI UND ICH 1998 d: Markus Imboden. GRM., *Frau Rettich Die Czerni Und Ich*, Simone Borowiak, Novel

FRAU SIXTA 1938 d: Gustav Ucicky. GRM., *Frau Sixta*, Ernst Zahn, Play

FRAU SORGE 1928 d: Robert Land. GRM., *Frau Sorge*, Hermann Sudermann, Novel

FRAU UND DER FREMDE, DIE 1984 d: Rainer Simon. GDR., *Karl Und Anna*, Leonhard Frank, 1926, Short Story

FRAU VON FORMAT, EINE 1928 d: Fritz Wendhausen. GRM., *Eine Frau von Format*, Rudolph Schanzer, Ernst Welisch, Play

FRAU WARRENS GEWERBE 1960 d: Akos von Rathony. GRM/SWT., *Mrs. Warren's Profession*, George Bernard Shaw, 1898, Play

Frau Weiser Und Ihre Kinder see IM PARTERRE LINKS (1963).

Frau Wera's Schwarze Perlen see ZWEIERLEI MORAL (1930).

FRAU WIE DU, EINE 1939 d: Victor Tourjansky. GRM., *Ich an Mich*, Dinah Nelken, Novel

FRAUENARZT DR. PRATORIUS 1950 d: Curt Goetz. Karl P. Gillmann. GRM., *Dr. Med. Hiob Pratorius*, Curt Goetz, 1934, Play

FRAUENHAUS VON RIO, DAS 1927 d: Hans Steinhoff. GRM., *Plusch Und Plumowsky*, Norbert Jacques, Novel

FRAUENPARADIES, DAS 1936 d: Arthur M. Rabenalt. AUS., *Frauenparadies*, Robert Stolz, Opera

Frauenraub see RAPT (1934).

FRAUENSTATION 1975 d: Rolf Thiele. GRM., *Frauenstation*, Marie Louise Fischer, Novel

FRAULEIN 1958 d: Henry Koster. USA., *Erika*, James McGovern, 1956, Novel

FRAULEIN CASANOVA 1953 d: E. W. Emo. AUS., *Fraulein Casanova*, Karl Hans Leiter, Novel

Fraulein, Das see GOSPODJICA (1980).

FRAULEIN FRAU 1934 d: Carl Boese. GRM., *Fraulein Frau*, Ludwig Fulda, Play

FRAULEIN HUSER 1940 d: Leonard Steckel. SWT., *Im Namen Der Liebe. Ein Bekenntnis*, Rosy von Kanel, Leipzig 1938, Novel

Fraulein Smillas Gespur Fur Schnee see SMILLA'S SENSE OF SNOW (1997).

FRAULEIN VON BARNHELM, DAS 1940 d: Hans Schweikart. GRM., *Minna von Barnhelm; Oder Das Soldatengluck*, Gotthold Ephraim Lessing, Hamburg 1767, Play

FRAULEIN VON SCUDERI, DAS 1955 d: Eugen York. GDR., *Das Fraulein von Scuderi*, Ernst Theodor Amadeus Hoffmann, 1819, Short Story

FREAKS 1932 d: Tod Browning. USA., *Spurs*, Tod Robbins, 1923, Short Story

FREAKY FRIDAY 1976 d: Gary Nelson. USA., *Freaky Friday*, Mary Rodgers, Novel

FRECCIA AZZURRA, LA 1996 d: Enzo d'Alo. ITL/SWT/LXM., *La Freccia Azzurra*, Gianni Rodari, Novel

Freccia, La see LA FRECCIA NEL FIANCO (1943).

FRECCIA NEL FIANCO, LA 1943 d: Alberto LattuadA. ITL., *La Freccia Nel Fianco*, Luciano Zuccoli, 1913, Novel

FRECKLES 1917 d: Marshall Neilan. USA., *Freckles*, Gene Stratton-Porter, New York 1904, Novel

FRECKLES 1928 d: James Leo Meehan. USA., *Freckles*, Gene Stratton-Porter, New York 1904, Novel

FRECKLES 1935 d: William Hamilton, Edward Killy. USA., *Freckles*, Gene Stratton-Porter, New York 1904, Novel

Fredda Alba Del Commissario Joss, La see LE PACHA (1968).

Freddy - Ein Mann Kehrt Heim see HAIE AN BORD (1970).

FREDERICA 1942 d: Jean Boyer. FRN., *Epousez-Nous Monsieur*, Jean de Letraz, Play

Free see THE UPLIFTERS (1919).

FREE AIR 1922 d: Edward H. Griffith. USA., *Free Air*, Sinclair Lewis, New York 1919, Novel

FREE AND EASY 1941 d: George Sidney. USA., *The Truth Game*, Ivor Novello, London 1928, Play

FREE FOR ALL 1949 d: Charles T. Barton. USA., Herbert Clyde Lewis, Story

FREE LOVE 1931 d: Hobart Henley. USA., *Half Gods*, Sidney Coe Howard, New York 1929, Play

FREE SOUL, A 1931 d: Clarence Brown. USA., *A Free Soul*, Adela Rogers St. Johns, New York 1927, Novel

Free Spirit see THE BELSTONE FOX (1973).

Free Spirit see MAXIE (1985).

Free to Live see HOLIDAY (1938).

Freed Hands see BEFREITE HANDE (1939).

FREEDOM OF THE SEAS 1934 d: Marcel Varnel. UKN., *Freedom of the Seas*, Walter Hackett, London 1918, Play

Freedom Riders, The see UNDERCOVER WITH THE KKK (1979).

FREEDOM ROAD 1979 d: Jan Kadar. USA., *Freedom Road*, Howard Fast, 1944, Novel

FREEJACK 1992 d: Geoff Murphy. USA., *Immortality Inc.*, Robert Sheckley, Novel

Free-Shooter, The see DER FREISCHUTZ (1968).

FREEWAY 1988 d: Francis DeliA. USA., *Freeway*, Deanne Barkley, Novel

FREI LUIS DE SOUSA 1949 d: Antonio Lopes Ribeiro. PRT., *Frei Luis de Sousa*, Almeida Garrett, 1859, Play

Freibeuter Der Liebe see PETRUS (1946).

FREISCHUTZ, DER 1968 d: Joachim Hess. GRM., *Der Freischutz*, Johann F. Kind, Carl Maria von Weber, Berlin 1821, Opera

FREITAG DER 13 1944 d: Erich Engels. GRM., *Freitag Der 13*, Erich Engels, Play

FREIWILD 1928 d: Holger-Madsen. GRM., *Freiwild*, Arthur Schnitzler, Play

FREMDENHEIM FILODA 1937 d: Hans Hinrich. GRM., *Fremdenheim Filoda*, Walter Sawitzky, Novel

FRENCH CONNECTION, THE 1971 d: William Friedkin. USA., *The French Connection*, Robin Moore, Book

French Cousins, The see LES COUSINES (1969).

FRENCH DOLL, THE 1923 d: Robert Z. Leonard. USA., *The French Doll*, Paul Armont, Marcel Gerbidou, New York 1922, Play

FRENCH HEELS 1922 d: Edwin L. Hollywood. USA., *Knots and Windshakes*, Clarence Budington Kelland, 1920, Short Story

FRENCH LEAVE 1930 d: Jack Raymond. UKN., *French Leave*, Reginald Berkeley, London 1920, Play

FRENCH LEAVE 1937 d: Norman Lee. UKN., *French Leave*, Reginald Berkeley, London 1920, Play

FRENCH LIEUTENANT'S WOMAN, THE 1981 d: Karel Reisz. UKN., *The French Lieutenant's Woman*, John Fowles, 1959, Novel

FRENCH LINE, THE 1953 d: Lloyd Bacon. USA., Matty Kemp, Story

FRENCH MISTRESS, A 1960 d: Roy Boulting. UKN., *A French Mistress*, Robert Munro, London 1959, Play

French They are a Funny Race, The see LES CARNETS DU MAJOR THOMPSON (1955).

French Way, The see LE MOUTON ENRAGE (1974).

FRENCH WITHOUT TEARS 1939 d: Anthony Asquith. UKN., *French Without Tears*, Terence Rattigan, London 1936, Play

FRENCHMAN'S CREEK 1944 d: Mitchell Leisen. USA., *Frenchman's Creek*, Daphne Du Maurier, 1941, Novel

FRENCHMAN'S CREEK 1998 d: Ferdinand Fairfax. UKN., *Frenchman's Creek*, Daphne Du Maurier, 1941, Novel

FRENCHY 1914. USA., *Frenchy*, George Patullo, Story

FRENESIA 1939 d: Mario Bonnard. ITL., *Alla Moda!*, Oreste Biancoli, Dino Falconi, Play

Frente de Madrid see CARMEN FRA I ROSSI (1939).

Frenzy see FRENESIA (1939).

Frenzy see LATIN QUARTER (1945).

FRENZY 1972 d: Alfred Hitchcock. UKN/USA., *Goodbye Piccadilly, Farewell Leicester Square*, Arthur la Bern, Novel

FREQUENCE MEURTRE 1988 d: Elisabeth Rappeneau. FRN., *Frequence Meurtre*, Stuart Kaminsky, Novel

FRERES BOUQUINQUANT, LES 1947 d: Louis Daquin. FRN., *Les Freres Bouquinquant*, Jean Prevost, Novel

FRERES CORSES 1938 d: Geo Kelber. FRN., *Les Freres Corses*, Alexandre Dumas (pere), 1845, Short Story

FRERES CORSES, LES 1917 d: Andre Antoine. FRN., *Les Freres Corses*, Alexandre Dumas (pere), 1845, Short Story

Freres Corses, Les see I FRATELLI CORSI (1961).

FRERES KARAMAZOFF, LES 1931 d: Fedor Ozep. FRN., *Bratya Karamazovy*, Fyodor Dostoyevsky, 1880, Novel

FRERES ZEMGANNO, LES 1925 d: Alberto Francis Bertoni. FRN., *Les Freres Zemganno*, Edmond de Goncourt, Novel

FRESA Y CHOCOLATE 1993 d: Tomas Gutierrez Alea, Juan Carlos Tabio. CUB., *El Lobo El Bosque Y El Hombre Nuevo*, Senal Paz, Novel

Fresh Air see JINY VZDUCH (1939).

Fresh Bait see L' APPAT (1995).

FRESH HORSES 1988 d: David Anspaugh. USA., *Fresh Horses*, Larry Ketron, Play

FRESHMAN LOVE 1936 d: William McGann. USA., *The College Widow*, George Ade, New York 1904, Play

FREUDENHAUS, DAS 1971 d: Alfred Weidenmann. GRM., *Das Freudenhaus*, Henry Jaeger, Novel

Friar Luis de Sousa see FREI LUIS DE SOUSA (1949).

Fric Met Les Voiles, Le see FLEUR D'OSEILLE (1967).

FRIC-FRAC 1939 d: Maurice Lehmann, Claude Autant-LarA. FRN., *Fric-Frac*, Edouard Bourdet, 1937, Play

Frida's Songs see FRIDAS VISOR (1930).

FRIDAS VISOR 1930 d: Gustaf Molander. SWD., *Fridas Andra Bok*, Birger Sjoberg, 1929, Verse, *Fridas Bok*, Birger Sjoberg, 1922, Verse

Friday the 13th see FRIDAY THE THIRTEENTH (1916).

Friday the 13th see FREITAG DER 13 (1944).

Friday the Rabbi Slept Late see LANIGAN'S RABBI (1976).

FRIDAY THE THIRTEENTH 1916 d: Emile Chautard. USA., *Friday the Thirteenth*, Thomas William Lawson, New York 1907, Novel

Friday Villa, The see LA VILLA DEL VENERDI (1992).

Fridericus see DER ALTE FRITZ (1936).

FRIED GREEN TOMATOES 1991 d: Jon Avnet. USA., *Fried Green Tomatoes at the Whistle Stop Cafe*, Fannie Flagg, Novel

Fried Green Tomatoes at the Whistle Stop Cafe see FRIED GREEN TOMATOES (1991).

FRIEDA 1947 d: Basil Dearden. UKN., *Frieda*, Ronald Millar, London 1946, Play

Friede see DER ALTE FRITZ 1 (1927).

FRIEDEL, DER GEIGER 1911 d: Adolf Gartner. GRM., *Der Geiger Freidel*, Wilhelmine Grafin Wickenburg-Almasy, Poem

FRIEDERICKE 1932 d: Fritz Friedmann-Friedrich. GRM., *Aus Meinem Leben. Dichtung Und Wahrheit*, Johann Wolfgang von Goethe, 1811-33, Autobiography

Friederike von Sesenheim see DIE JUGENDGELIEBTE (1930).

Friend of the Family see PATATE (1964).

FRIEND OR FOE 1982 d: John Krish. UKN., *Friend Or Foe*, Michael Morpurgo, Novel

Friend Will Come Tonight, A see UN AMI VIENDRA CE SOIR (1945).

FRIENDLY CALL, THE 1920 d: Thomas R. Mills. USA., *The Friendly Call*, O. Henry, Short Story

FRIENDLY ENEMIES 1925 d: George Melford. USA., *Friendly Enemies*, Aaron Hoffman, Samuel Shipman, New York 1923, Play

FRIENDLY ENEMIES 1942 d: Allan Dwan. USA., *Friendly Enemies*, Aaron Hoffman, Samuel Shipman, New York 1923, Play

FRIENDLY FIRE 1979 d: David Greene. USA., *Friendly Fire*, C. D. B. Bryan, Book

FRIENDLY PERSUASION 1956 d: William Wyler. USA., *The Friendly Persuasion*, Jessamyn West, 1945, Novel

FRIENDLY PERSUASION 1975 d: Joseph Sargent. USA., *Except for Me and Thee*, Jessamyn West, Book, *The Friendly Persuasion*, Jessamyn West, 1945, Book

Friends see VENNER (1960).

Friends see BEACHES (1988).

FRIENDS AND LOVERS 1931 d: Victor Schertzinger. USA., *Le Sphinx a Parles*, Maurice Dekobra, Paris 1930, Novel

Friends and Neighbors see **FRIENDS AND NEIGHBOURS** (1959).

FRIENDS AND NEIGHBOURS 1959 d: Gordon Parry. UKN., *Friends and Neighbours*, Austin Steele, London 1958, Play

FRIENDS OF EDDIE COYLE, THE 1973 d: Peter Yates. USA., *The Friends of Eddie Coyle*, George V. Higgins, Novel

FRIENDS OF MR. SWEENEY 1934 d: Edward Ludwig. USA., *Friends of Mr. Sweeney*, Elmer Holmes Davis, New York 1925, Novel

Friendship see **AMICIZIA** (1938).

Friendship see **YOUYI** (1959).

FRIENDSHIP'S DEATH 1987 d: Peter Wollen. UKN., Peter Wollen, Short Story

FRIENDSHIPS, SECRETS AMD LIES 1979 d: Ann Zane Shanks, Marlena Laird. USA., *The Walls Came Tumbling Down*, Babs H. Deal, Novel

Frightened Bride, The see **THE TALL HEADLINES** (1952).

Frightened City, The see **THE KILLER THAT STALKED NEW YORK** (1950).

FRIGHTENED LADY, THE 1932 d: T. Hayes Hunter. UKN., *The Case of the Frightened Lady*, Edgar Wallace, London 1931, Play

Frightened Lady, The see **THE CASE OF THE FRIGHTENED LADY** (1940).

FRINGE DWELLERS, THE 1986 d: Bruce Beresford. ASL., *The Fringe Dwellers*, Nene Gare, Novel

Fripons, Voleurs Et Cie see **BOULOT AVIATEUR** (1937).

FRIQUET 1919 d: Gero Zambuto. ITL., *Le Friquet*, Gyp, 1894, Novel

FRIQUET, LE 1912 d: Maurice Tourneur. FRN., *Le Friquet*, Gyp, 1894, Novel

FRISCHER WIND AUS KANADA 1935 d: Heinz Kenter, Erich Holder. GRM., *Frischer Wind Aus Kanada*, Hans Muller, Play

FRISCO JENNY 1933 d: William A. Wellman. USA., *Common Ground*, Gerald Beaumont, 1936, Short Story

Frisco Waterfront see **I COVER THE WATERFRONT** (1933).

FRISK 1995 d: Todd Verow. USA., *Frisk*, Dennis Cooper, Novel

FRISKY MRS. JOHNSON, THE 1920 d: Eddie Dillon. USA., *The Frisky Mrs. Johnson*, Clyde Fitch, New York 1903, Play

Frog King, The see **DER FROSCHKONIG** (1940).

Frog King, The see **DER FROSCHKONIG** (1954).

FROG PRINCE, THE 1987 d: Jackson Hunsicker. USA., *Der Froschkonig Oder Der Eiserne Heinrich*, Jacob Grimm, Wilhelm Grimm, 1812, Short Story

FROG, THE 1937 d: Jack Raymond. UKN., *The Fellowship of the Frog*, Edgar Wallace, London 1925, Novel

FROGGY'S LITTLE BROTHER 1921 d: A. E. Coleby. UKN., *Froggy's Little Brother*, Brenda, Novel

FROGMEN, THE 1951 d: Lloyd Bacon. USA., Oscar Millard, Story

FROHLICHE DORF, DAS 1955 d: Rudolf Schundler. GRM., *Das Frohliche Dorf*, August Hinrichs, Play

FROHLICHE WALLFAHRT, DIE 1956 d: Ferdinand Dorfler. GRM., *Die Fahneltragerin*, Peter Rosegger, 1913, Short Story

FROHLICHE WEINBERG, DER 1927 d: Jacob Fleck, Luise Fleck. GRM., *Der Frohliche Weinberg*, Carl Zuckmayer, 1925, Play

FROHLICHE WEINBERG, DER 1952 d: Erich Engel. GRM., *Der Frohliche Weinberg*, Carl Zuckmayer, 1925, Play

Frohliche Wissenschaft, Die see **LE GAI SAVOIR** (1967).

FROKEN JULIE 1951 d: Alf Sjoberg. SWD., *Froken Julie*, August Strindberg, 1888, Play

From a German Life see **AUS EINEM DEUTSCHEN LEBEN** (1978).

From a Roman Balcony see **LA GIORNATA BALORDA** (1960).

From Afar I See My Country see **AUS DER FERNE SEHE ICH DIESES LAND** (1978).

From Another Planet see **VOM ANDEREN STERN** (1982).

From Doon With Death see **INSPECTOR WEXFORD: FROM DOON WITH DEATH** (1991).

From Ear to Ear see **LES COUSINES** (1969).

FROM HEADQUARTERS 1915 d: Ralph Ince. USA., *From Headquarters*, David Sonnenblick, Story

From Heaven to Earth see **AHASIN POLA WATHA** (1976).

FROM HELL TO HEAVEN 1933 d: Erle C. Kenton. USA., *Good Company*, Lawrence Hazard, Play

FROM HELL TO TEXAS 1958 d: Henry Hathaway. USA., *The Hell-Bent Kid*, Charles O. Locke, 1957, Book

FROM HERE TO ETERNITY 1953 d: Fred Zinnemann. USA., *From Here to Eternity*, James Jones, 1951, Novel

FROM HERE TO ETERNITY 1978 d: Buzz Kulik. USA., *From Here to Eternity*, James Jones, 1951, Novel

From Istanbul - Orders to Kill see **DA ISTAMBUL ORDINE DI UCCIDERE** (1965).

From Missouri see **LIFE IN THE RAW** (1933).

FROM NINE TO NINE 1936 d: Edgar G. Ulmer. CND., Shirley Castle, Edgar G. Ulmer, Story

FROM NOON TILL THREE 1975 d: Frank D. Gilroy. USA., *From Noon Till Three*, Frank D. Gilroy, 1973, Novel

FROM RUSSIA WITH LOVE 1963 d: Terence Young. UKN., *From Russia With Love*, Ian Fleming, London 1957, Novel

FROM SHOPGIRL TO DUCHESS 1915 d: Maurice Elvey. UKN., *From Shopgirl to Duchess*, Charles Darrell, Play

From the Cloud to the Resistance see **DALLA NUBE ALLA RESISTENZA** (1979).

From the Czech Mills see **Z CESKYCH MLYNU** (1925).

From the Czech Mills see **Z CESKYCH MLYNU** (1929).

From the Czech Mills see **Z CESKYCH MLYNU** (1941).

From the Distance I See This Country see **AUS DER FERNE SEHE ICH DIESES LAND** (1978).

FROM THE EARTH TO THE MOON 1958 d: Byron Haskin. USA., **De la Terre a la Lune; Trajet Direct En 97 Heures**, Jules Verne, 1865, Novel

FROM THE GROUND UP 1921 d: E. Mason Hopper. USA., *From the Ground Up*, Rupert Hughes, 1921, Short Story

From the Other Side see **LA OTRA ORILLA** (1966).

FROM THE TERRACE 1960 d: Mark Robson. USA., *From the Terrace*, John O'Hara, 1958, Novel

FROM THE VALLEY OF THE MISSING 1915 d: Frank Powell. USA., *From the Valley of the Missing*, Grace Miller White, New York 1911, Novel

From the World of Forest Solitude see **ZE SVETA LESNICH SAMOT** (1933).

From the World of Wood Cottages see **ZE SVETA LESNICH SAMOT** (1933).

FROM THIS DAY FORWARD 1946 d: John Berry. USA., *All Brides are Beautiful*, Thomas Bell, Novel

FROM TWO TO SIX 1918 d: Albert Parker. USA., *The Button Thief*, Arthur Stringer, Short Story

FROM TYRANNY TO LIBERTY 1910 d: J. Searle Dawley. USA., *From Tyranny to Liberty*, Francis Scott Key, Short Story

From Where Chimneys are Seen see **ENTOTSU NO MIERU BASHO** (1953).

From de Fefreude, La see **DIE KASEREI IN DER VEHFREUDE** (1958).

FROMME HELENE, DIE 1965 d: Axel von Ambesser. GRM., *Die from Helene*, Wilhelm Busch, 1872, Short Story

FROMONT JEUNE ET RISLER AINE 1921 d: Henry Krauss. FRN., *From Jeune Et Risler Aine*, Alphonse Daudet, 1874, Novel

FROMONT JEUNE ET RISLER AINE 1941 d: Leon Mathot. FRN., *From Jeune Et Risler Aine*, Alphonse Daudet, 1874, Novel

Fron Med Masken see **DER FROSCH MIT DER MASKE** (1959).

FRONT 1943 d: Georgi Vasiliev, Sergei Vasiliev. USS., *Front*, Aleksander Korniychuk, 1942, Play

Front and Center see **WHEN WILLIE COMES MARCHING HOME** (1950).

FRONT PAGE STORY 1954 d: Gordon Parry. UKN., *Final Night*, Robert Gaines, Novel

FRONT PAGE, THE 1931 d: Lewis Milestone. USA., *The Front Page*, Ben Hecht, Charles MacArthur, New York 1928, Play

FRONT PAGE, THE 1974 d: Billy Wilder. USA., *The Front Page*, Ben Hecht, Charles MacArthur, New York 1928, Play

FRONT PAGE WOMAN 1935 d: Michael Curtiz. USA., *Women are Bum Newspapermen*, Richard Macauley, 1934, Short Story

Front, The see **FRONT** (1943).

FRONTERA, LA 1996 d: Franco Giraldi. ITL., Franco Vegliani, Novel

FRONTGOCKEL, DER 1955 d: Ferdinand Dorfler. GRM., *Der Frontgockel*, Hans Fitz, Play

Frontier Hellcat see **UNTER GEIERN** (1964).

FRONTIER JUSTICE 1935 d: Robert F. McGowan. USA., *Frontier Justice*, Colonel George B. Rodney, New York 1936, Novel

FRONTIER MARSHAL 1934 d: Lewis Seiler. USA., *Wyatt Earp - Frontier Marshal*, Stuart N. Lake, New York 1931, Book

FRONTIER MARSHAL 1939 d: Allan Dwan. USA., *Wyatt Earp - Frontier Marshal*, Stuart N. Lake, New York 1931, Book

Frontier Marshal, the Saga of Tombstone, Arizona see **FRONTIER MARSHAL** (1939).

FRONTIER OF THE STARS, THE 1921 d: Charles Maigne. USA., *The Frontier of the Stars*, Albert Payson Terhune, Story

Frontier Scout see **FRONTIER SCOUT QUINCANNON** (1956).

FRONTIER UPRISING 1961 d: Edward L. Cahn. USA., *Kit Carson*, George Bruce, Short Story

FRONTIERES DU COEUR, LES 1914 d: Bernard-Deschamps. FRN., *Les Frontieres du Coeur*, Paul Margueritte, Victor Margueritte, Novel

FROSCH MIT DER MASKE, DER 1959 d: Harald Reinl. GRM/DNM., *The Fellowship of the Frog*, Edgar Wallace, London 1925, Novel

FROSCHKONIG, DER 1940 d: Alf Zengerling. GRM., *Der Froschkonig Oder Der Eiserne Heinrich*, Jacob Grimm

Froschkonig, Der 1812 (1940) d: Alf Zengerling. GRM., Wilhelm Grimm, Short Story

FROSCHKONIG, DER 1954 d: Otto Meyer. GRM., *Der Froschkonig Oder Der Eiserne Heinrich*, Jacob Grimm, Wilhelm Grimm, 1812, Short Story

Froth of Time, The see **L' ECUME DES JOURS** (1967).

FROU FROU 1914. USA., *Frou-Frou*, Ludovic Halevy, Henri Meilhac, Paris 1869, Play

Frou Frou see **A HUNGRY HEART** (1917).

Frou Frou see **THE TOY WIFE** (1938).

FROU-FROU 1918 d: Alfredo de Antoni. ITL., *Frou-Frou*, Ludovic Halevy, Henri Meilhac, Paris 1869, Play

FROU-FROU 1923 d: Guy Du Fresnay. FRN., *Frou-Frou*, Ludovic Halevy, Henri Meilhac, Paris 1869, Play

Frozen Heart, The see **DAS GEFRORENE HERZ** (1979).

FROZEN JUSTICE 1929 d: Allan Dwan. USA., *Norden for Lov Og Ret; En Alaska-Historie*, Ejnar Mikkelsen, Copenhagen 1920, Novel

FRU INGER TOL OSTRAT 1975 d: Sverre Udnaes. NRW., *Fru Inger Til Ostraad*, Henrik Ibsen, 1857, Play

FRUHLINGSMARCHEN 1934 d: Carl Froelich. GRM., *Fruhlingsmarchen*, W. Hoffmann-Harnisch, Walter Supper, Musical Play

Fruhlingsromanze see **SEHNSUCHT DES HERZENS** (1951).

Fruit de Passion, La see **IL FRULLO DEL PASSERO** (1988).

FRUIT DEFENDU, LE 1952 d: Henri Verneuil. FRN., *Lettre a Mon Juge*, Georges Simenon, 1947, Novel

FRUIT OF EVIL, THE 1914 d: Wallace Reid. USA., *Sins of the Father*, Elaine Sterne, Story

FRUITFUL VINE, THE 1921 d: Maurice Elvey. UKN., *The Fruitful Vine*, Robert Hichens, Novel

FRUITS AMERS 1967 d: Jacqueline Audry. FRN/ITL/YGS., *Fruits Amers*, Colette Audry, Play

Fruits de la Passion, Les see **SHINA NINGYO** (1981).

FRUITS DE L'ETE, LES 1954 d: Raymond Bernard. FRN/GRM., *Les Fruits de l'Ete*, Philippe Heriat, Short Story

FRUITS OF DESIRE, THE 1916 d: Oscar Eagle. USA., *The Ambition of Mark Truitt*, Henry Russell Miller, Indianapolis 1913, Novel

FRUITS OF PASSION 1919 d: George Ridgwell. USA., *The Ambition of Mark Truitt*, Henry Russell Miller, Indianapolis 1913, Novel

Fruits of Passion, The see **SHINA NINGYO** (1981).

Fruits of Summer see **LES FRUITS DE L'ETE** (1954).

Fruits of Worship, The see **POOJAPALAM** (1964).

FRUITS SAUVAGES, LES 1953 d: Herve Bromberger. FRN., *Notre Reve Qui Etes aux Cieux*, M. Durafour, Novel

FRULLO DEL PASSERO, IL 1988 d: Gianfranco Mingozzi. ITL/FRN., Tonino Guerra, Short Story

Frustration see **SKEPP TILL INDIALAND** (1947).

FRUTA AMARGA, LA 1931 d: Arthur Gregor. USA., *Dark Star*, Lorna Moon, Indianapolis 1929, Novel

Frutti Amari, I see **FRUITS AMERS** (1967).

FRUTTO ACERBO 1934 d: Carlo Ludovico BragagliA. ITL., *Le Fruit Vert*, Regis Gignoux, Jacques Thery, Play

FU HUO 1941 d: Mei Qian. CHN., *Voskreseniye*, Lev Nikolayevich Tolstoy, Moscow 1899, Novel

FU MATTIA PASCAL, IL 1937 d: Pierre Chenal. ITL., *Il Fu Mattia Pascal*, Luigi Pirandello, Novel

FU SHENG LIU JI 1947 d: Pei Chong. CHN., *Fu Sheng Liu Ji*, Shen Sanbai, 18—, Autobiography

FU SHI 1957 d: Ren Sun. CHN., *Fu Shi*, He Wei, Novel

FUCHS VON GLENARVON, DER 1940 d: Max W. Kimmich. GRM., *Der Fuchs von Glenarvon*, Nicola Rohn, Novel

FUEFUKI-GAWA 1960 d: Keisuke KinoshitA. JPN., *Fuefuki-Gawa*, Shichiro Fukazawa, 1958-59, Novel

FUENTEOVEJUNA 1947 d: Antonio Roman. SPN., *Fuenteovejuna*, Lope de Vega, 1619, Play

FUERTE PERDIDO 1965 d: Jose Maria ElorrietA. SPN., Fred Uratia, Story

Fuga Nel Sole see **GOUBBIAH MON AMOUR** (1956).

FUGGITIVA, LA 1941 d: Piero Ballerini. ITL., *La Fuggitiva*, Milly Dandolo, Novel

Fugitifs, Les see **AU BOUT DU MONDE** (1933).

Fugitive from Terror see **WOMAN IN HIDING** (1949).

Fugitive Gold see **SPECIAL INVESTIGATOR** (1936).

Fugitive in Saigon see **MORT EN FRAUDE** (1956).

FUGITIVE KIND, THE 1959 d: Sidney Lumet. USA., *Orpheus Descending*, Tennessee Williams, New York 1957, Play

Fugitive Lady see **LA STRADA BUIA** (1949).

Fugitive Nights see **FUGITIVE NIGHTS: DANGER IN THE DESERT** (1993).

FUGITIVE NIGHTS: DANGER IN THE DESERT 1993 d: Gary Nelson. USA., *Fugitive Nights*, Joseph Wambaugh, Novel

FUGITIVE, THE 1913 d: Charles H. France. USA., *The Young Collegian*, T. W. Robertson, Play

Fugitive, The see **ON THE NIGHT OF THE FIRE** (1939).

FUGITIVE, THE 1946 d: John Ford, Emilio Fernandez. USA/MXC., *The Power and the Glory*, Graham Greene, 1940, Novel

FUGITIVES 1929 d: William Beaudine. USA., *Fugitives*, Richard Harding Davis, 1894, Short Story

Fugitives, Les see **GAMIN DE PARIS TRIQUE** (1960).

Fugitivo, El see **THE FUGITIVE** (1946).

Fugue Pour Clarinette see **L' HOMME A L'IMPERMEABLE** (1957).

FUHRMANN HENSCHEL 1956 d: Josef von Baky. GRM., *Fuhrmann Henschel*, Gerhart Hauptmann, 1898, Play

Fuite a l'Anglaise, La see **AMOUR ET DISCIPLINE** (1931).

FUKKATSU 1950 d: Akira Nobuchi. JPN., *Voskreseniye*, Lev Nikolayevich Tolstoy, Moscow 1899, Novel

FUKKATSU NO HI 1979 d: Kinji Fukasaku. JPN., *Fukkatsu No Hi*, Sakyo Komatsu, Novel

FUKUSHU NO UTA GA KIKOERU 1968 d: Yoshihisa Sadanaga, Shigeyuki Yamane. JPN., *Aoi Satsujinsha*, Shintaro Ishihara, 1966, Novel

Full Circle see **THE HAUNTING OF JULIA** (1976).

FULL HOUSE, A 1920 d: James Cruze. USA., *A Full House*, Frederick Jackson, New York 1915, Play

Full Life, A see **MITASARETA SEIKATSU** (1962).

FULL METAL JACKET 1987 d: Stanley Kubrick. UKN., *The Short-Timers*, Gustav Hasford, Novel

FULL OF LIFE 1956 d: Richard Quine. USA., *Full of Life*, John Fante, 1952, Book

FULL TREATMENT, THE 1961 d: Val Guest. UKN., *The Full Treatment*, Ronald Scott Thorn, London 1959, Novel

Fun Life of an Amsterdam Streetwalker see **WAT ZIEN IK** (1971).

FUNDVOGEL 1930 d: Wolfgang Hoffmann-Harnisch. GRM., *Fundvogel*, Hanns Heinz Ewers, Novel

FUNEBRAK 1932 d: Carl Lamac. CZC., *Srazka Vlaku a Uz Mou Milou*, Dr. Buffiel, Play

FUNERAL IN BERLIN 1966 d: Guy Hamilton. UKN., *Funeral in Berlin*, Len Deighton, London 1964, Novel

Funeral Rites see **SAMSKARA** (1970).

Funf Freunde in Der Tinte see **DE FEM OG SPIONERNE** (1969).

FUNF KARNICKEL, DIE 1953 d: Kurt Steinwendner, Paul Lowinger. AUS., *Die Funf Kanickel*, Julius Pohl, Play

FUNF MILLIONEN SUCHEN EINEN ERBEN 1938 d: Carl Boese. GRM., *Funf Millionen Suchen Einen Erben*, Harald Baumgarten, Novel

FUNFMADERLHAUS 1943 d: Sigfrit Steiner. SWT., *Funfmadelhaus*, Meinrad Leinert, Novel

FUNF-MINUTEN-VATER, DER 1951 d: J. A. Hubler-KahlA. AUS., *Der Funf-Minuten-Vater*, Karl Fischer, Play

FUNGI CELLARS, THE 1923 d: A. E. Coleby. UKN., *The Fungi Cellars*, Sax Rohmer, Short Story

Funny Dirty Little War, A see **NO HABRA MAS PENA NI OLVIDO** (1985).

FUNNY FARM 1988 d: George Roy Hill. USA., *Funny Farm*, Jay Cronley, Book

FUNNY GIRL 1968 d: William Wyler. USA., *Funny Girl*, Isobel Lennart, Merrill Bob, Jule Styne, New York 1964, Musical Play

Funny Parishioner, The see **UN DROLE DE PAROISSIEN** (1963).

FUNNY THING HAPPENED ON THE WAY TO THE FORUM, A 1966 d: Richard Lester. UKN/USA., *A Funny Thing Happened on the Way to the Forum*, Larry Gelbart, Burt Shevelove, New York 1962, Play

FUOCHI D'ARTIFICIO 1938 d: Gennaro Righelli. ITL., *Fuochi d'Artificio*, Luigi Chiarelli, Play

Fuoco Fatuo see **LE FEU FOLLET** (1963).

FUR DIE KATZ 1940 d: Hermann Pfeiffer. GRM., *Fur Die Katz*, August Hinrichs, Play

FURCHTE DICH NICHT, JAKOB! 1981 d: Radu GabreA. GRM/PRT., *O Faclie de Paste*, Ion Luca Caragiale, 1890, Short Story

Furchten Und Lieben see **PAURA E AMORE** (1987).

FURET, LE 1949 d: Raymond Leboursier. FRN., *Le Furet*, Stanislas-Andre Steeman, Novel

FURIA 1946 d: Goffredo Alessandrini. ITL., *Furia*, Vittorio Nino Novarese, Novel

FURIA A BAHIA POUR OSS 117 1965 d: Andre Hunebelle, Jacques Besnard. FRN/ITL., *Le Dernier Quart d'Heure*, Jean Bruce, Paris 1955, Novel

Furia Degli Uomini, La see **GERMINAL** (1963).

Furia Selvaggia a Maracaibo see **INDIOS A NORD-OVEST** (1964).

FURIES, THE 1930 d: Alan Crosland. USA., *The Furies*, Zoe Akins, New York 1928, Play

Furies, The see **PLAYING AROUND** (1930).

FURIES, THE 1950 d: Anthony Mann. USA., *The Furies*, Niven Busch, 1948, Novel

FURIN KAZAN 1969 d: Hiroshi Inagaki. JPN., *Furin Kazan*, Yasushi Inoue, Tokyo 1955, Novel

Furlough on Word of Honor see **URLAUB AUF EHRENWORT** (1937).

FURNACE, THE 1920 d: William D. Taylor. USA., *The Furnace*, Pan, London 1920, Novel

FURNISHED ROOM, THE 1917 d: Thomas R. Mills. USA., *The Furnished Room*, O. Henry, Short Story

Furong Garrison see **FURONG ZHEN** (1985).

FURONG ZHEN 1985 d: XIe Jin. CHN., *Fu Rong Zhen*, Gu Hua, 1979, Novel

Furore Di Vivere see **LE CHEMIN DES ECOLIERS** (1959).

FURST ODER CLOWN 1927 d: Alexander Rasumny. GRM., *Furst Odre Clown*, Maurice Dekobra, Novel

FURST VON PAPPENHEIM, DER 1927 d: Richard Eichberg. GRM., *Der Furst von Pappenheim*, Franz Robert Arnold, Ernst Bach, Opera

FURST VON PAPPENHEIM, DER 1952 d: Hans Deppe. GRM., *Der Furst von Pappenheim*, Franz Robert Arnold, Ernst Bach, Opera

FURSTENKIND, DAS 1927 d: Jacob Fleck, Luise Fleck. GRM., *Das Furstenkind*, Franz Lehar, Viktor Leon, Opera

FURTHER MYSTERIES OF DR. FU MANCHU, THE 1924 d: Fred Paul. UKN., Sax Rohmer, Short Story

Fury see **IL GIORNO DEL FURORE** (1973).

FURY AT SHOWDOWN 1957 d: Gerd Oswald. USA., *Showdown Creek*, Lucas Todd, 1955, Novel

Fury Is a Woman see **SIBIRSKA LEDI MAGBET** (1962).

FURY RIVER 1959 d: Jacques Tourneur, George Waggner. USA., *Northwest Passage*, Kenneth Lewis Roberts, New York 1937, Novel

FURY, THE 1978 d: Brian DepalmA. USA., *The Fury*, John Farris, Novel

FUSHI 1950 d: Zuo Lin. CHN., *Fu Shi*, Shen Yanbing, 1941, Novel

FUSHIN NO TOKI 1968 d: Tadashi Imai. JPN., *Fushin No Toki*, Sawako Ariyoshi, 1968, Novel

FUSILIER WIPF 1938 d: Leopold Lindtberg, Hermann Haller. SWT., *Fusilier Wipf*, Robert Faesi, Zurich 1915, Short Story

Fusilier Wipf, Le see **FUSILIER WIPF** (1938).

FUSILLE A L'AUBE 1950 d: Andre Haguet. FRN., *Fusille a l'Aube*, Maurice Dekobra, Novel

Fuss Over Feathers see **CONFLICT OF WINGS** (1954).

Fusspot, The see **DER BOCKERER** (1981).

FUTARI 1991 d: Nobuhiko Obayashi. JPN., *Futari*, Jiro Akagawa, Novel

Futarizuma see **TSUMA YO BARA NO YONI** (1935).

Future Belongs to You, The see **THE RIGHT TO LIVE** (1935).

FUTURES VEDETTES 1955 d: Marc Allegret. FRN., *Eingang Zur Buhne*, Vicki Baum, Novel

FUTZ 1969 d: Tom O'Horgan. USA., *Futz*, Rochelle Owens, New York 1967, Play

FUZZ 1972 d: Richard A. CollA. USA., *Fuzz*, Evan Hunter, 1968, Novel

FUZZY PINK NIGHTGOWN, THE 1957 d: Norman Taurog. USA., *The Fuzzy Pink Nightgown*, Sylvia Tate, 1956, Novel

Fx-18 Superspy see **COPLAN FX18 CASSE TOUT** (1965).

FYRTOJET 1946 d: Allan Johnsen, Sven Methling. DNM., *Fyrtojet*, Hans Christian Andersen, Copenhagen 1835, Short Story

GABAN 1966 d: Krishan Chopra, Hrishikesh Mukherjee. IND., *Gaban*, Munshi Premchand, 1930, Novel

GABBIANELLA E IL GATTO, LA 1998 d: Enzo d'Alo. ITL., *Story of a Seagull and the Cat Who Taught Her to Fly*, Luis Sepulveda, Novel

GABBIANO, IL 1977 d: Marco Bellocchio. ITL., *Chayka*, Anton Chekhov, St. Petersburg 1896, Play

Gables Mystery, The see **THE MAN AT SIX** (1931).

GABLES MYSTERY, THE 1938 d: Harry Hughes. UKN., *The Man at Six*, Jack Celestin, Jack de Leon, London 1928, Play

GABRIEL OVER THE WHITE HOUSE 1933 d: Gregory La CavA. USA., *Gabriel Over the White House; a Novel of the Presidency*, Thomas Frederic Tweed, New York 1933, Novel

GABRIELA 1984 d: Bruno Barreto. BRZ/ITL., *Cravo E Canela Gabriela*, Jorge Amado, 1958, Novel

Gabriela, Cravo E Canela see **GABRIELA** (1984).

GABRIELE DAMBRONE 1943 d: Hans Steinhoff. GRM., *Gabriele Dambrone*, Richard Billinger, Play

GABRIELE IL LAMPIONARO DI PORTO 1919 d: Elvira Notari. ITL., *Gabriele Il Lampionaro Di Porto*, Nicola de Lise, 1853, Play

GABY 1956 d: Curtis Bernhardt. USA., *Waterloo Bridge*, R. E. Sherwood, New York 1930, Play

GABY 1987 d: Luis Mandoki. MXC/UKN/USA., *Gaby*, Gabriella Brimmer, Elena Poniatowska, Book

Gaby, a True Story see **GABY** (1987).

Gaby, Una Historia Verdadera see **GABY** (1987).

GADANO BEL 1950 d: Ratibhai Punatar. IND., *Gadano Bel*, Prabhulal Dwivedi, Play

Gadfly, The see **POPRYGUNYA** (1955).

GADYUKA 1966 d: Viktor IVchenko. USS., *Gadyuka*, Alexsey Nikolayevich Tolstoy, 1929, Short Story

Gai, Gai, Demarions-Nous see **SOYONS GAIS** (1931).

GAI SAVOIR, LE 1967 d: Jean-Luc Godard. FRN/GRM., *Emile; Ou de l'Education*, Jean-Jacques Rousseau, 1762, Novel

GAIETES DE L'ESCADRON, LES 1932 d: Maurice Tourneur. FRN., *Les Gaietes de l'Escadron*, Georges Courteline, 1886, Play

GAIETY DUET, A 1909 d: Arthur Gilbert. UKN., *Our Miss Gibbs*, Cryptos, James T. Tanner, London 1909, Musical Play

GAIETY GIRL, THE 1924 d: King Baggot. USA., *The Inheritors*, I. A. R. Wylie, 1922, Short Story

GAILY, GAILY 1969 d: Norman Jewison. USA., *Gaily Gaily*, Ben Hecht, New York 1963, Novel

Gaites de l'Escadron, Les see **L' ALLEGRO SQUADRONE** (1954).

GAL YOUNG UN 1979 d: Victor Nunez. USA., *Gal Young 'Un*, Marjorie K. Rawlings, 1940, Short Story

Galgin's Mysterious Case see **ZAHADNY PRIPAD GALGINUV** (1923).

GALIA 1966 d: Georges Lautner. FRN/ITL., *Galia*, Vahe Katcha, Novel

Galia Ou Duel a Fleur de Peau see **GALIA** (1966).

GALILEO 1975 d: Joseph Losey. UKN/CND., *Leben Des Galilei*, Bertolt Brecht, 1949, Play

GALLAN HOYIAN BEETIYAN 1966 d: Kumar Kuldip. IND., *Pyasi Dharti*, Narendra Khajuria, Play

GALLANT BESS 1946 d: Andrew Marton. USA., *A Foxhole Flicka*, Lieut. Marvin Park, Story

Gallant Rebel see **THE VANQUISHED** (1953).

GALLEGHER 1910 d: Edwin S. Porter. USA., *Gallegher*, Richard Harding Davis, Short Story

Gallery Murders, The see **L' UCCELLO DALLE PIUME DE CRISTALLO** (1970).

GALLEY SLAVE, THE 1909 d: J. Stuart Blackton (Spv). USA., *Les Miserables*, Victor Hugo, Paris 1862, Novel

GALLEY SLAVE, THE 1915 d: J. Gordon Edwards. USA., *The Galley Slave*, Bartley Campbell, New York 1879, Play

Gallon Hoyian Beetiyan see **GALLAN HOYIAN BEETIYAN** (1966).

GALLOPER, THE 1915 d: Donald MacKenzie. USA., *The Galloper*, Richard Harding Davis, New York 1906, Play

GALLOPING DEVIL, THE 1920 d: Nate Watt. USA., *The Happy Family*, B. M. Bower, New York 1910, Novel

Galloping Devils see **THE GALLOPING DEVIL** (1920).

GALLOPING DYNAMITE 1937 d: Harry L. Fraser. USA., *Mystery of Dead Man's Isle*, James Oliver Curwood, Short Story

GALLOPING FISH 1924 d: Thomas H. Ince, Del Andrews. USA., *Friend Wife*, Frank R. Adams, Story

GALLOPING FURY 1927 d: B. Reeves Eason. USA., *Tidy Toreador*, Peter B. Kyne, 1927, Short Story

GAMBIER'S ADVOCATE 1915 d: James Kirkwood. USA., *Gambier's Advocate*, Ronald McDonald, London 1914, Novel

GAMBIT 1966 d: Ronald Neame. USA., *Gambit*, Sidney Carrol, Novel

GAMBLE FOR LOVE, A 1917 d: Frank Wilson. UKN., *A Gamble for Love*, Nat Gould, Novel

GAMBLE IN LIVES, A 1920 d: George Ridgwell. UKN., *The Joan Danvers*, Frank Stayton, Play

Gamble, The see **LA PARTITA** (1991).

GAMBLE WITH HEARTS, A 1923 d: Edwin J. Collins. UKN., *A Gamble With Hearts*, Anthony Carlyle, Novel

GAMBLER OF THE WEST, THE 1915. USA., *The Gambler of the West*, Owen Davis, New York 1906, Play

Gambler, The see **THE MICHIGAN KID** (1928).

Gambler, The see **LE JOUEUR** (1958).

Gambler, The see **IGROK** (1972).

GAMBLER WORE A GUN, THE 1961 d: Edward L. Cahn. USA., L. L. Foreman, Story

GAMBLERS ALL 1919 d: Dave Aylott. UKN., *Gamblers All*, May Martindale, London 1915, Play

GAMBLERS, THE 1914 d: George W. Terwilliger. USA., *The Gamblers*, Charles Klein, New York 1910, Play

GAMBLERS, THE 1919 d: Paul Scardon. USA., *The Gamblers*, Charles Klein, New York 1910, Play

GAMBLERS, THE 1929 d: Michael Curtiz. USA., *The Gamblers*, Charles Klein, New York 1910, Play

GAMBLERS, THE 1970 d: Ron Winston. USA., *Igroki*, Nikolay Gogol, 1842, Play

Gamblin' Man see **COCKFIGHTER** (1974).

GAMBLING 1934 d: Rowland V. Lee. USA., *Gambling*, George M. Cohan, New York 1929, Play

Gambling Daughters see **BAD SISTER** (1931).

Gambling Hell see **L'ENFER DU JEU MACAO** (1939).

GAMBLING MAN, THE 1994. UKN., *The Gambling Man*, Catherine Cookson, Novel

GAMBLING ON THE HIGH SEAS 1940 d: George Amy. USA., Roy Chanslor, Story

GAMBLING SHIP 1933 d: Louis J. Gasnier, Max Marcin. USA., *Fast One*, Paul Cain, 1932, Short Story, *Lead Party*, Paul Cain, 1932, Short Story, *Velvet*, Paul Cain, 1932, Short Story

GAME FOR THREE LOSERS 1965 d: Gerry O'HarA. UKN., *Game for Three Losers*, Edgar Lustgarten, Novel

GAME FOR VULTURES 1980 d: James Fargo. UKN/SWT/SAF., *Game for Vultures*, Michael Hartmann, Novel

Game Is Over, The see **LA CUREE** (1966).

GAME OF CATCH, A 1974 d: Steven K. Witty. USA., *A Game of Catch*, Richard Wilbur, 1954, Short Story

GAME OF DEATH, A 1946 d: Robert Wise. USA., *The Most Dangerous Game*, Richard Connell, 1930, Short Story

GAME OF LIBERTY, THE 1916 d: George Loane Tucker. UKN., *The Game of Liberty*, E. Phillips Oppenheim, 1915, Novel

Game of Life, The see **O JOGO DA VIDA** (1977).

Game of Love, The see **LE BLE EN HERBE** (1953).

Game of Love, The see **DAS GROSSE LIEBESSPIEL** (1963).

Game Pass see **WILDWECHSEL** (1972).

Gamekeeper see **WILDSCHUT** (1986).

Gamekeeper, The see **DER KLOSTERJAGER** (1920).

GAMEKEEPER, THE 1980 d: Kenneth Loach. UKN., *The Gamekeeper*, Barry Hines, 1975, Novel

Gamekeepers in Black see **CERNI MYSLIVCI** (1945).

Games Men Play, The see **LA CIGARRA NO ES UN BICHO** (1963).

Games of Love and Loneliness see **DEN ALLVARSAMMA LEKEN** (1977).

GAMES, THE 1969 d: Michael Winner. UKN., *The Games*, Hugh Atkinson, London 1967, Novel

Gamest Girl, The see **THE LOVE FLOWER** (1920).

Gamiani see **POURVU QU'ON AIT L'IVRESSE** (1974).

GAMIN DE PARIS, LE 1923 d: Louis Feuillade. FRN., *Le Gamin de Paris*, Jean-Francois Bayard, Vanderbruch, 1836, Play

GAMIN DE PARIS, LE 1932 d: Gaston Roudes. FRN., *Le Gamin de Paris*, Jean-Francois Bayard, Vanderbruch, 1836, Play

GAMLE PRAEST, DEN 1939 d: Jon Iversen. DNM., *Den Gamle Praest*, Jakob Knudsen, 1899, Novel

GAMLET 1964 d: Grigori Kozintsev. USS., *Hamlet*, William Shakespeare, c1601, Play

GAN 1953 d: Shiro ToyodA. JPN., *Gan*, Ogai Mori, 1913, Novel

GANADEVATA 1978 d: Tarun Majumdar. IND., *Ganadevata*, Tarashankar Banerjee, 1942, Novel

Ganasatru see **GANASHATRU** (1989).

GANASHATRU 1989 d: Satyajit Ray. IND., *En Folkefiende*, Henrik Ibsen, 1882, Play

Gang see **WALK PROUD** (1979).

GANG THAT COULDN'T SHOOT STRAIGHT, THE 1971 d: James Goldstone. USA., *The Gang That Couldn't Shoot Straight*, Jimmy Breslin, Novel

GANG TIE JU REN 1974 d: Yan Gong. CHN., *Steel Giant*, Cheng Shuzheng, Novel

Gang War see **ODD MAN OUT** (1947).

GANG WAR 1958 d: Gene Fowler Jr. USA., *The Hoods Take Over*, Ovid Demaris, Novel

GANGA ZUMBA 1963 d: Carlos Diegues. BRZ., *Rei Dos Palmares Ganga Zumba*, Joao Felicio Dos Santos, 1961, Novel

Ganga Zumba, O Rei Dos Palmares see **GANGA ZUMBA** (1963).

GANGS OF NEW YORK 1938 d: James Cruze. USA., *Gangs of New York*, Herbert Asbury, New York 1936, Novel

Gangster, Gold Und Flotte Madchen see **L' APPARTEMENT DES FILLES** (1963).

GANGSTER, THE 1947 d: Gordon Wiles. USA., *Low Company*, Daniel Fuchs, Novel

GANGSTERS AND THE GIRL, THE 1914 d: Scott Sidney. USA., *The Gangsters and the Girl*, Richard V. Spencer, Story

Gangster's Doll, The see **LA PUPA DEL GANGSTER** (1975).

GANGSTERS DU CHATEAU D'IF, LES 1939 d: Rene Pujol. FRN., *Les Gangsters du Chateau d'If*, Henri Alibert, Opera

Gangsters, Gold and Cool Chicks see **L' APPARTEMENT DES FILLES** (1963).

Gangsters Per un Massacro see **KOMMISSAR X: DREI BLAUE PANTHER** (1968).

Gangster's Wife, The see **BAD COMPANY** (1931).

GANS VON SEDAN, DIE 1959 d: Helmut Kautner. GRM/FRN., *Un Dimanche Au Champ d'Honneur*, Jean L'Hote, Paris 1958, Novel

GANSEMAGD, DIE 1958 d: Fritz Genschow. GRM., *Die Gansemagd*, Jacob Grimm, Wilhelm Grimm, 1812, Short Story

GANZ GROSSEN TORHEITEN, DIE 1937 d: Carl Froelich. GRM., *Die Ganz Grossen Torheiten*, Marianne von Angern, Novel

GANZER KERL, EIN 1935 d: Carl Boese. GRM., *Karl Der Grosse*, Wolfgang Marken, Novel

GANZER KERL, EIN 1939 d: Fritz Peter Buch. GRM., *Ein Ganzer Kerl*, Fritz Peter Buch, Play

GAPI 1982 d: Paul Blouin. CND., *Gapi Et Sullivan*, Antonine Maillet, Play

GARAM COAT 1955 d: Amar Kumar. IND., *Shinel*, Nikolay Gogol, 1842, Short Story

Garam Hava see **GARAM HAWA** (1973).

GARAM HAWA 1973 d: M. S. Sathyu. IND., *Garam Hawa*, Ismat Chughtai, Short Story

GARAMBICA BAPU 1980 d: Baba Mazgonkar. IND., *Garambica Bapu*, Shripad Narayan Pendse, 1952, Novel

Garambicha Bapu see **GARAMBICA BAPU** (1980).

GARASU NO USAGI 1979 d: Yuten TachibanA. JPN., *Garasu No Usagi*, Toshiko Takagi, Novel

Garce Inconsciente, Une see **UN AMORE** (1965).

Garcon Divorce, Le see **LE MARI GARCON** (1933).

GARCON SAUVAGE, LE 1951 d: Jean Delannoy. FRN., *Le Garcon Sauvage*, Edouard Peisson, Novel

GARCONNE, LA 1924 d: Armand Du Plessis. FRN., *La Garconne*, Victor Margueritte, 1922, Novel

GARCONNE, LA 1936 d: Jean de Limur. FRN., *La Garconne*, Victor Margueritte, 1922, Novel

GARCONNE, LA 1957 d: Jacqueline Audry. FRN., *La Garconne*, Victor Margueritte, 1922, Novel

Garcons, Les see **LA NOTTE BRAVA** (1959).

GARDE A VUE 1981 d: Claude Miller. FRN., *Garde a Vue*, John Wainwright, Novel

GARDE DU CORPS, LE 1983 d: Francois Leterrier. FRN., *Le Garde du Corps*, Yves Kermorvan, Novel

Garde-Champetre Mene l'Enquete, Le see **DANS L'EAU QUI FAIT DES BULLES** (1961).

Garden Full of Cucumbers, A see **FITZWILLY** (1967).

GARDEN MURDER CASE, THE 1936 d: Edwin L. Marin. USA., *The Garden Murder Case; a Philo Vance Story*, S. S. Van Dine, New York 1935, Novel

GARDEN OF ALLAH, THE 1916 d: Colin Campbell. USA., *The Garden of Allah*, Robert Hichens, London 1904, Novel

GARDEN OF ALLAH, THE 1927 d: Rex Ingram. USA., *The Garden of Allah*, Robert Hichens, London 1904, Novel

GARDEN OF ALLAH, THE 1936 d: Richard Boleslawski. USA., *The Garden of Allah*, Robert Hichens, London 1904, Novel

Garden of Bancharam see **BANCHARAMER BAGAN** (1980).

GARDEN OF EDEN, THE 1928 d: Lewis Milestone. USA., *Der Garten Eden*, Rudolf Bernauer, Rudolf Osterreicher, Berlin 1926, Play

GARDEN OF LIES, THE 1915 d: Augustus Thomas. USA., *The Garden of Lies*, Justus Miles Forman, New York 1902, Novel

GARDEN OF REDEMPTION, THE 1997 d: Thomas Michael Donnelly. USA., Anthony Difranco, Short Story

GARDEN OF RESURRECTION, THE 1919 d: Arthur Rooke. UKN., *The Garden of Resurrection*, E. Temple Thurston, Novel

Garden of the Finzi-Continis, The see **IL GIARDINO DEI FINZI-CONTINI** (1970).

GARDEN OF THE MOON 1938 d: Busby Berkeley. USA., *Garden of the Moon*, H. Bedford-Jones, John Barton Browne, 1937, Short Story

GARDEN OF WEEDS, THE 1924 d: James Cruze. USA., *The Garden of Weeds*, Leon Gordon, Doris Marquette, New York 1924, Play

Garden of Women, The *see* ONNA NO SONO (1954).

GARDENER'S DAUGHTER, THE 1913 d: Wilfred Noy. UKN., *The Gardener's Daughter*, Alfred Tennyson, Poem

GARDENER'S DAUGHTER, THE 1914 d: Wilfred Noy. UKN., *The Gardener's Daughter*, Alfred Tennyson, Poem

GARDENS OF STONE 1987 d: Francis Ford CoppolA. USA., *Gardens of Stone*, Nicholas Proffitt, Novel

GARDIAN, LE 1945 d: Jean de Marguenat. FRN., *Le Roi de Camargue*, Jean Aicard, 1890, Novel

GARDIEN DU FEU, LE 1924 d: Gaston Ravel. FRN., *Le Gardien du Feu*, Anatole le Braz, Short Story

GARDIENS DE PHARE 1928 d: Jean Gremillon. FRN., *Gardiens de Phare*, Paul Autier, Cloquemin, Play

Garibaldi *see* I MILLE DI GARIBALDI (1933).

Garm Coat *see* GARAM COAT (1955).

Garm Hawa *see* GARAM HAWA (1973).

Garment Center, The *see* THE GARMENT JUNGLE (1957).

GARMENT JUNGLE, THE 1957 d: Vincent Sherman, Robert Aldrich (Uncredited). USA., *Gangsters in the Dress Business*, Lester Velie, Article

GARMENTS OF TRUTH 1921 d: George D. Baker. USA., *Garments of Truth*, Freeman Tilden, 1921, Short Story

Garnet Bracelet, The *see* GRANATOVYY BRASLET (1965).

GAROFANO ROSSO 1976 d: Luigi Faccini. ITL., *Garofano Rosso*, Elio Vittorini, Novel

GAROU-GAROU LE PASSE-MURAILLE 1950 d: Jean Boyer. FRN., *Le Passe-Muraille*, Marcel Ayme, Paris 1943, Short Story

GARRA DEL MONO, LA 1925 d: Juan Andreu Moragas. SPN., Salvador Vilaregut, Play

GARRET IN BOHEMIA, A 1915 d: Harold Shaw. UKN., *A Garret in Bohemia*, G. E. R. Mayne, Novel

GARRISON'S FINISH 1914 d: Francis J. Grandon. USA., *Garrison's Finish*, William Blair Morton Ferguson, New York 1907, Novel

GARRISON'S FINISH 1923 d: Arthur Rosson. USA., *Garrison's Finish*, William Blair Morton Ferguson, New York 1907, Novel

Garry Owen *see* GARRYOWEN (1920).

GARRYOWEN 1920 d: George Pearson. UKN., *Garryowen*, Henry de Vere Stacpoole, Novel

Gars d'Anvers, Le *see* Y'EN A MARRE (1959).

Garten Der Finzi Contini, Der *see* IL GIARDINO DEI FINZI-CONTINI (1970).

Garten Der Lust, Der *see* THE PLEASURE GARDEN (1926).

GARTER GIRL, THE 1920 d: Edward H. Griffith. USA., *The Memento*, O. Henry, 1908, Short Story

GAS FOOD LODGINGS 1991 d: Allison Anders. USA., *Don't Look and It Won't Hurt*, Richard Peck, Novel

GASLIGHT 1940 d: Thorold Dickinson. UKN., *Gas Light*, Patrick Hamilton, London 1938, Play

GASLIGHT 1944 d: George Cukor. USA., *Gas Light*, Patrick Hamilton, London 1938, Play

GAS-OIL 1955 d: Gilles Grangier. FRN., *Du Raisine Dans le Gas-Oil*, Georges Bayle, Novel

GASOLINE GUS 1921 d: James Cruze. USA., *Dry Check Charlie*, George Patullo, Story

GASPARD DE BESSE 1935 d: Andre Hugon. FRN., *Gaspard de Besse*, Jean Aicard, Novel

GASPARONE 1937 d: Georg Jacoby. GRM., *Gasparone*, Karl Millocker, Operetta

GASTHAUS AN DER THEMSE, DAS 1962 d: Alfred Vohrer. GRM., Edgar Wallace, Novel

Gate Number Six *see* LIU HAO MEN (1952).

Gate of Flesh *see* NIKUTAI NO MON (1948).

Gate of Flesh *see* NIKUTAI NO MON (1964).

Gate of Hell *see* JIGOKUMON (1953).

Gate of Lilacs *see* PORTE DES LILAS (1957).

Gate to Paradise, The *see* DIE SELTSAME GESCHICHTE DES BRANDNER KASPER (1949).

GATEGUTTER 1949 d: Arne Skouen, Ulf Greber. NRW., *Gategutter*, Arne Skouen, 1948, Novel

Gates of Dawn, The *see* ADVENT (1956).

GATES OF DOOM, THE 1919 d: Sidney M. Goldin. UKN., *The Gates of Doom*, Rafael Sabatini, Novel

Gates of Hollywood *see* MAKE ME A STAR! (1932).

Gates of Paradise *see* VRATA RAJA (1967).

Gates of Paris *see* PORTE DES LILAS (1957).

Gates to Paradise *see* VRATA RAJA (1967).

GATEWAY OF THE MOON, THE 1928 d: John Griffith Wray. USA., *Upstream*, Clifford Bax, London 1923, Novel

Gathering Clouds *see* INTUNECARE (1985).

GATHERING OF OLD MEN, A 1987 d: Volker Schlondorff. USA/GRM., *A Gathering of Old Men*, Ernest J. Gaines, 1983, Novel

GATO CON BOTAS, EL 1961 d: Roberto Rodriguez. MXC., *Le Maitre Chat Ou le Chat Botte*, Charles Perrault, Paris 1697, Short Story

GATTA CI COVA 1937 d: Gennaro Righelli. ITL., *L'Articolo 1083*, Antonino Russo-Giusti, Play

Gatta Dagli Artigli d'Oro, La *see* LA LOUVE SOLITAIRE (1968).

GATTIN, DIE 1943 d: Georg Jacoby. GRM., *Die Gattin*, Johann von Bokay, Play, *Ich Liebe Vier Frauen*, Johann von Bokay, Play

GATTO A NOVE CODE, IL 1971 d: Dario Argento. ITL/FRN/GRM., Bryan Edgar Wallace, Novel

Gatto Di Park Lane, Il *see* IL GATTO NERO (1981).

GATTO NERO, IL 1981 d: Lucio Fulci. ITL., *The Black Cat*, Edgar Allan Poe, 1843, Short Story

GATTOPARDO, IL 1963 d: Luchino Visconti. ITL/FRN., *Il Gattopardo*, Giuseppe Di Lampedusa, Milan 1958, Novel

Gau Rasplyev Days *see* VESYOLYYE RASPLYUYEVSKIYE DNI (1966).

Gaucho Passion *see* PAIXAO DE GAUCHO (1958).

Gaukler *see* LES SALTIMBANQUES (1930).

GAUNT STRANGER, THE 1938 d: Walter Forde. UKN., *The Gaunt Stranger*, Edgar Wallace, London 1925, Novel

Gaunt Woman, The *see* SEALED CARGO (1951).

Gaunt Woman, The *see* DESTINY OF A SPY (1969).

Gauntlet of Greed, The *see* THE GAUNTLET (1920).

GAUNTLET, THE 1920 d: Edwin L. Hollywood. USA., Lillian Bennett-Thompson, George Hubbard, Short Story

GAVROSH 1937 d: Tatyana Lukashevich. USS., *Les Miserables*, Victor Hugo, Paris 1862, Novel

GAWAIN AND THE GREEN KNIGHT 1973 d: Stephen Weeks. UKN., *Sir Gawain and the Green Knight*, Anon, c1375, Verse

GAY ADVENTURE, THE 1936 d: Sinclair Hill. UKN., *The Gay Adventure*, Walter Hackett, London 1931, Play

GAY AND FESTIVE CLAVERHOUSE 1918? d: Charles J. Brabin. USA., *The Gay and Festive Claverhouse*, Anne Warner French, Boston 1914, Novel

Gay Bandit, The *see* THE GAY CABALLERO (1932).

GAY BLADES 1946 d: George Blair. USA., *Gay Blades*, Jack Goodman, Albert Rice, Story

GAY BRIDE, THE 1934 d: Jack Conway. USA., *Repeal*, Charles Francis Coe, 1934, Novel

Gay Caballero, The *see* CAPTAIN THUNDER (1930).

GAY CABALLERO, THE 1932 d: Alfred L. Werker. USA., *The Gay Bandit of the Border*, Tom Gill, New York 1931, Novel

GAY CORINTHIAN, THE 1924 d: Arthur Rooke. UKN., *The Gay Corinthian*, Ben Bolt, Novel

GAY DECEIVER, THE 1926 d: John M. Stahl. USA., *Patachon*, Felix Duquesnel, Maurice Hennequin, Paris 1907, Play

Gay Deceiver, The *see* CHICKEN A LA KING (1928).

GAY DOG, THE 1954 d: Maurice Elvey. UKN., *The Gay Dog*, Joseph Colton, London 1951, Play

Gay Duellist, The *see* MEET ME AT DAWN (1947).

Gay Intruders, The *see* MEDAL FOR THE GENERAL (1944).

Gay Lady, The *see* LADY TUBBS (1935).

Gay Lady, The *see* TROTTIE TRUE (1948).

GAY LORD QUEX, THE 1917 d: Maurice Elvey. UKN., *The Gay Lord Quex*, Arthur Wing Pinero, London 1899, Play

GAY LORD QUEX, THE 1919 d: Harry Beaumont. USA., *The Gay Lord Quex*, Arthur Wing Pinero, London 1899, Play

GAY LORD WARING, THE 1916 d: Otis Turner. USA., *The Gay Lord Waring*, Houghton Townley, New York 1910, Novel

GAY LOVE 1934 d: Leslie Hiscott. UKN., *Gay Love*, Audrey Carten, Waveney Carten, London 1933, Play

Gay Mrs. Trexel, The *see* SUSAN AND GOD (1940).

Gay Nineties, The *see* THE FLORODORA GIRL (1930).

GAY OLD DOG, THE 1919 d: Hobart Henley. USA., *The Gay Old Dog*, Edna Ferber, 1917, Short Story

GAY SISTERS, THE 1942 d: Irving Rapper. USA., *The Gay Sisters*, Stephen Longstreet, Novel

Gay Vineyard, The *see* DER FROHLICHE WEINBERG (1927).

Gay Vineyard, The *see* DER FROHLICHE WEINBERG (1952).

Gayest of the Gay, The *see* HER REDEMPTION (1924).

Gaze, The *see* NAZAR (1990).

GAZEBO, THE 1959 d: George Marshall. USA., *The Gazebo*, Alec Coppel, New York 1958, Play

GE GE HE MEI MEI 1956 d: Su Li. CHN., *Lu XIaogang and His Sister*, Ren Daxing, Novel

GEFAHRDETE MADCHEN 1927 d: Heinz Schall. GRM., *Gefahrdete Madchen*, Lothar, Novel

GEFAHRLICHE ALTER, DAS 1927 d: Eugen Illes. GRM., *Das Gefahrliche Alter*, Karin Michaelis, Novel

GEFAHRLICHES ABENTEUER 1953 d: Emile Edwin Reinert. AUS., *Ich War Jack Mortimer*, Alexander Lernet-Holenia, Novel

GEFAHRTIN MEINES SOMMERS 1943 d: Fritz Peter Buch. GRM., *Gefahrtin Meines Sommers*, Claus Erich Boerner, Novel

GEFRORENE HERZ, DAS 1979 d: Xavier Koller. SWT., *Das Gefrorene Herz*, Meinrad Inglins, Short Story

Geheimagentin Helene *see* ESKAPADE (1936).

Geheime Club, de *see* DER GEHEIMNISVOLLE KLUB (1913).

GEHEIME KURIER, DER 1928 d: Gennaro Righelli. GRM., *Le Rouge Et le Noir*, Stendhal, 1830, Novel

Geheimnis Der Berge, Das *see* PETRONELLA (1927).

GEHEIMNIS DER CHINESISCHEN NELKE, DAS 1964 d: Rudolf Zehetgruber. GRM/ITL/SPN., *Das Geheimnis Der Chinesischen Nelke*, Louis Weinert-Wilton, Novel

GEHEIMNIS DER DREI DSCHUNKEN, DAS 1965 d: Ernst Hofbauer. GRM/ITL., *La Riviere Des Trois Jonques*, Georges Godefroy, Paris 1956, Novel

GEHEIMNIS DER GELBEN NARZISSEN, DAS 1961 d: Akos von Rathony. GRM/UKN., *The Daffodil Mystery*, Edgar Wallace, London 1920, Novel

Geheimnis Der Lederschlinge, Das *see* I MISTERI DELLA GIUNGLA NERA (1964).

Geheimnis Der Schwarzen Handschuhe, Das *see* L'UCCELLO DALLE PIUME DE CRISTALLO (1970).

GEHEIMNIS DER SCHWARZEN KOFFER, DAS 1962 d: Werner Klinger. GRM., Bryan Edgar Wallace, Story

GEHEIMNIS DER SCHWARZEN WITWE, DAS 1963 d: Franz J. Gottlieb. GRM/SPN., *Das Geheimnis Der Schwarzen Witwe*, Louis Weinert-Wilton, Novel

GEHEIMNIS EINER AERZTIN, DAS 1955 d: August Rieger, Karl Stanzl. AUS/GRM., *Rauschgift*, Victor Reingruber, Play

Geheimnis Einer Arztin *see* DAS GEHEIMNIS EINER AERZTIN (1955).

GEHEIMNIS EINER EHE, DAS 1951 d: Helmut Weiss. GRM., *Talent Zum Gluck*, Helmut Weiss, Play

GEHEIMNIS VOM BERGSEE, DAS 1951 d: Jean Dreville, Rene (#u/C#) Le Henaff. SWT/FRN/GRM., *Pietro Der Schmuggler*, Ernst Zahn, Berlin 1930, Novel

GEHEIMNIS VON GENF, DAS 1927 d: Willy Reiber. GRM., *Der Gestohlene Geheimvertrag*, Peter Oldfield, Novel

Geheimnis von Oberwald, Das *see* IL MISTERO DI OBERWALD (1979).

GEHEIMNISSE IN GOLDENEN NYLONS 1966 d: Christian-Jaque. GRM/FRN/ITL., *Dead Run*, Robert Sheckley, New York 1961, Novel

Geheimnisvolle Fremde, Der *see* THE MYSTERIOUS STRANGER (1982).

GEHEIMNISVOLLE KLUB, DER 1913 d: Joseph Delmont. GRM., *The Suicide Club*, Robert Louis Stevenson, London 1882, Short Stories

Geheimzinnige Club, de *see* DER GEHEIMNISVOLLE KLUB (1913).

Geheimzinnige Sanatorium, Het *see* BULLDOG DRUMMOND (1923).

GEHETZTE FRAUEN 1927 d: Richard Oswald. GRM., *Brettlfleigen*, Annie von Brabenetz, Novel

GEHETZTE MENSCHEN 1932 d: Friedrich Feher. GRM/CZC., *Cerny Muz*, Alfred Machard, Novel

GEHULFE, DER 1976 d: Thomas Koerfer. SWT., *Der Gehulfe*, Robert Walser, Novel

Geier Konnen Warten *see* LES ETRANGERS (1968).

Geierwally *see* DIE GEIER-WALLY (1921).

GEIERWALLY, DIE 1940 d: Hans Steinhoff. GRM., *Die Geierwally*, Wilhelmine von Hillern, Novel

GEIERWALLY, DIE 1956 d: Frantisek Cap. GRM., *Die Geierwally*, Wilhelmine von Hillern, Novel

GEIERWALLY, DIE 1987 d: Walter Bockmayer. GRM., *Die Geierwally*, Wilhelmine von Hillern, Novel

GEIER-WALLY, DIE 1921 d: E. A. Dupont. GRM., *Die Geierwally*, Wilhelmine von Hillern, Novel

GEIGENMACHER VON MITTENWALD, DER 1950 d: Rudolf Schundler. GRM., *Der Geigenmacher von Mittenwald*, Ludwig Ganghofer, Hans Neuert, Play

Geisha *see* AMERICAN GEISHA (1986).

Geisha, A *see* GION BAYASHI (1953).

GEISHA BOY, THE 1958 d: Frank Tashlin. USA., Rudy Makoul, Story

GEISTERZUG, DIE 1927 d: Geza von Bolvary. GRM., *The Ghost Train*, Arnold Ridley, London 1925, Play

GEJAGTEN, DIE 1960 d: Max Michel. SWT., **Aux Abois**, Walter Blickensdorfer, Zurich 1953, Novel

GEKKO KAMEN 1981 d: Yukihiro SawadA. JPN., Kohan Kawauchi, Novel

GELBE FLAGGE, DIE 1937 d: Gerhard Lamprecht. GRM., *Die Gelbe Flagge*, Fred Andreas, Novel

GELBE HAUS AM PINNASBERG, DAS 1970 d: Alfred Vohrer. GRM., *Das Gelbe Haus Am Pinnasberg*, Bengta Bischoff, Novel

Geld, Das *see* L' ARGENT (1983).

GELD UND GEIST 1964 d: Franz Schnyder. SWT., *Oder Die Versohnung Geld Und Geist*, Jeremias Gotthelf, Soleure 1843, Novel

GELIEBTE BESTIE 1959 d: Arthur M. Rabenalt. AUS/GRM., *Manner Mussen So Sein*, Heinrich Seiler, Ebendorf 1938, Novel

GELIEBTE CORINNA 1956 d: Eduard von Borsody. GRM., *Constanze*, Robert Pilchowsky, Novel

Geliebte de Grossen Barin, Der *see* L' AMANTE DELL'ORSA MAGGIORE (1971).

GELIEBTE, DIE 1927 d: Robert Wiene. GRM., *Die Geliebte*, Alexander Brody, Play

GELIEBTE FEINDIN 1955 d: Rolf Hansen. GRM., *Geliebte Feindin*, Marie von Kirchbach, Novel

GELIEBTE SEINER HOHEIT, DIE 1928 d: Jacob Fleck, Luise Fleck. GRM., *Die Geliebte Seiner Hoheit*, Jean Gilbert, Opera

Gelik de Vogelen Des Hemels *see* VOGELVRIJ (1916).

GELOSIA 1943 d: Ferdinando M. Poggioli. ITL., *Il Marchese Di Roccaverdina*, Luigi Capuana, 1901, Novel

GELOSIA 1953 d: Pietro Germi. ITL., *Il Marchese Di Roccaverdina*, Luigi Capuana, 1901, Novel

GEMING JIAYING 1960 d: Shui HuA. CHN., *My Family*, Tao Cheng, Autobiography

GEMINI MAN 1976 d: Alan J. Levi. USA., *The Invisible Man*, H. G. Wells, London 1897, Novel

Gemsjagd in Den Freiburger Alpen, Eine *see* UNE CHASSE AUX CHAMOIS DANS LES ALPES FRIBOURGEOISES (1926).

GENBOERNE 1939 d: Arne Weel. DNM., *Gjenboerne*, Jens Christian Hostrup, 1844, Play

GENDARME EST SAN PITIE, LE 1932 d: Claude Autant-LarA. FRN., *Le Gendarme Est Sans Pitie*, Georges Courteline, 1899, Play

GENDRE DE MONSIEUR POIRIER, LE 1933 d: Marcel Pagnol. FRN., *Le Gendre de Monsieur Poirier*, Emile Paul Augier, Jules Sandeau, 1854, Play

GENERAL CRACK 1929 d: Alan Crosland. USA., *General Crack*, George Preedy, London 1928, Novel

General Della Rovere, Le *see* IL GENERALE DELLA ROVERE (1959).

GENERAL DIED AT DAWN, THE 1936 d: Lewis Milestone. USA., *The General Died at Dawn*, Charles G. Booth, New York 1936, Novel

GENERAL JOHN REGAN 1921 d: Harold Shaw. UKN., *General John Regan*, George A. Birmingham, London 1913, Play

GENERAL JOHN REGAN 1933 d: Henry Edwards. UKN., *General John Regan*, George A. Birmingham, London 1913, Play

General, Le *see* LE REBELLE (1930).

GENERAL POST 1920 d: Thomas Bentley. UKN., *General Post*, J. E. Harold Terry, London 1917, Play

General, The *see* THE VIRTUOUS SIN (1930).

GENERAL, THE 1998 d: John Boorman. IRL/UKN., *The General*, Paul Williams, Book

GENERALE DELLA ROVERE, IL 1959 d: Roberto Rossellini. ITL/FRN., Indro Montanelli, Story

Generals Without Buttons *see* LA GUERRE DES GOSSES (1936).

GENERATION 1969 d: George Schaefer. USA., *Generation*, William Goodhart, New York 1965, Play

Generation, A *see* POKOLENIE (1954).

GENGHIS COHN 1993 d: Elijah Moshinsky. UKN., *Dance of Genghis Cohn*, Romain Gary, Novel

Genio, Il *see* LE GRAND ESCOGRIFFE (1976).

GENJI MONOGATARI 1951 d: Kozaburo YoshimurA. JPN., *Genji Monogatari*, Shikibu Murasaki, c1001-1005, Novel

Genocide *see* KONCHU DAISENSO (1968).

Genoese Conspiracy, The *see* LA CONGIURA DI FIESCHI (1911).

GENOU DE CLAIRE, LE 1970 d: Eric Rohmer. FRN., *Le Genou de Claire*, Eric Rohmer, 1974, Short Story

Genoveffa Di Brabante *see* GENOVEVA DE BRABANTE (1967).

GENOVEVA DE BRABANTE 1967 d: Jose Luis Monter. SPN/ITL., *Leyenda Aurea*, Jacopo Di Voraza, Novel

GENROKU CHUSHINGURA PART I 1941 d: Kenji Mizoguchi. JPN., *Genroku Chushingura*, Seika Mayama, Play

Gens de la Riziere, Les *see* NEAK SRI (1992).

GENS NOVA 1920 d: Luigi Maggi. ITL., *Gens Nova*, Flaviano C. Mancini, Play

Gens, Qui Passent *see* MENSCHEN DIE VORUBERZIEHN (1942).

GENSDARM MOBIUS 1913 d: Stellan Rye. GRM., *Gensdarm Mobius*, Victor Bluthgen, Novel

GENTE DI RISPETTO 1975 d: Luigi ZampA. ITL., *Gente Di Rispetto*, Giuseppe Fava, Novel

Gentiluomo d'Amore *see* NEZ-DE-CUIR (1952).

GENTLE ANNIE 1944 d: Andrew Marton. USA., *Gentle Annie*, MacKinlay Kantor, 1942, Novel

Gentle Creature, A *see* UNE FEMME DOUCE (1969).

GENTLE CYCLONE, THE 1926 d: W. S. Van Dyke. USA., *Peg Leg and the Kidnapper*, Frank R. Buckley, 1925, Short Story

GENTLE GIANT 1967 d: James Neilson. USA., *Gentle Ben*, Walt Morey, New York 1965, Novel

GENTLE GUNMAN, THE 1952 d: Basil Dearden, Michael Relph. UKN., *The Gentle Gunman*, Roger MacDougall, Play

GENTLE JULIA 1923 d: Rowland V. Lee. USA., *Gentle Julia*, Booth Tarkington, New York 1922, Novel

GENTLE JULIA 1936 d: John G. Blystone. USA., *Gentle Julia*, Booth Tarkington, New York 1922, Novel

Gentle People, The *see* OUT OF THE FOG (1941).

Gentle Sergeant, The *see* THREE STRIPES IN THE SUN (1955).

Gentle Snow *see* SASAMEYUKI (1983).

Gentle Thief of Love *see* DEN UNDERBARA LOGNEN (1955).

Gentle Touch, The *see* THE FEMININE TOUCH (1956).

GENTLEMAN AFTER DARK, A 1942 d: Edwin L. Marin. USA., *A Whiff of Heliotrope*, Richard Washburn Child, 1918, Short Story

Gentleman Chauffeur, The *see* WHAT A MAN! (1930).

Gentleman for a Day *see* UNION DEPOT (1932).

Gentleman from Big Bend, The *see* TIMES SQUARE PLAYBOY (1936).

GENTLEMAN FROM INDIANA, THE 1915 d: Frank Lloyd. USA., *The Gentleman from Indiana*, Booth Tarkington, New York 1899, Novel

GENTLEMAN FROM MISSISSIPPI, A 1914 d: George L. Sargent. USA., *A Gentleman from Mississippi*, Harrison Rhodes, Thomas A. Wise, New York 1908, Play

Gentleman from San Francisco, The *see* FOG OVER FRISCO (1934).

Gentleman Goes to Town, A *see* MR. DEEDS GOES TO TOWN (1936).

Gentleman Has Only Daughters, The *see* MIJNHEER HAT LAUTER TOCHTER (1967).

GENTLEMAN IN BLUE, THE 1917. UKN., *John Hinte - Gentleman in Blue*, Mark Allerton, Novel

GENTLEMAN JIM 1942 d: Raoul Walsh. USA., *The Roar of the Crowd*, James J. Corbett, Book

GENTLEMAN OF FRANCE, A 1921 d: Maurice Elvey. UKN., *A Gentleman of France*, Stanley Weyman, 1893, Novel

GENTLEMAN OF LEISURE, A 1915 d: George Melford. USA., *A Gentleman of Leisure*, John Stapleton, P. G. Wodehouse, New York 1911, Play

GENTLEMAN OF LEISURE, A 1923 d: Joseph Henabery. USA., *A Gentleman of Leisure*, John Stapleton, P. G. Wodehouse, New York 1911, Play

GENTLEMAN OF PARIS, A 1927 d: Harry d'Abbadie d'Arrast. USA., *Bellamy the Magnificent*, Roy Horniman, London 1904, Novel

GENTLEMAN OF PARIS, A 1931 d: Sinclair Hill. UKN., *His Honour the Judge*, Niranjan Pal, Novel

GENTLEMAN OF QUALITY, A 1919 d: James Young. USA., *A Gentleman of Quality*, Frederic Van Rensselaer Dey, New York 1909, Novel

GENTLEMAN OF VENTURE 1940 d: Paul L. Stein. UKN., *Gentleman of Venture*, Roland Pertwee, John Hastings Turner, Play

GENTLEMAN'S AGREEMENT 1935 d: George Pearson. UKN., *The Wager*, Jennifer Howard, Short Story

GENTLEMAN'S AGREEMENT 1947 d: Elia Kazan. USA., *Gentleman's Agreement*, Laura Z. Hobson, Novel

GENTLEMAN'S AGREEMENT, A 1918 d: David Smith. USA., *Gentleman's Agreement*, Wallace Irwin, 1914, Short Story

GENTLEMAN'S FATE 1931 d: Mervyn Leroy. USA., *A Gentleman's Fate*, Ursula Parrott, 1931, Short Story

GENTLEMAN'S GENTLEMAN, A 1939 d: R. William Neill. UKN., *A Gentleman's Gentleman*, Philip MacDonald, Play

GENTLEMEN BITTEN ZUR KASSE, DIE 1965 d: John Olden, Claus Peter Witt. GRM., *Th Robbers' Tale; the Real Story of the Great Train Robbery*, Peta Fordham, London 1965, Book

Gentlemen Boys *see* PANI KLUCI (1975).

Gentlemen Don't Eat Poets *see* THE GROTESQUE (1995).

GENTLEMEN MARRY BRUNETTES 1955 d: Richard Sale. USA., *But Gentlemen Marry Brunettes*, Anita Loos, 1928, Novel

Gentlemen of the Navy *see* ANNAPOLIS FAREWELL (1935).

GENTLEMEN OF THE PRESS 1929 d: Millard Webb. USA., *Gentlemen of the Press*, Ward Morehouse, Story

GENTLEMEN PREFER BLONDES 1928 d: Malcolm St. Clair. USA., *Gentlemen Prefer Blondes*, Anita Loos, New York 1925, Novel

GENTLEMEN PREFER BLONDES 1953 d: Howard Hawks. USA., *Gentlemen Prefer Blondes*, Anita Loos, New York 1925, Novel

Gentlemen, the Boys *see* PANI KLUCI (1975).

Gently Passed Anastasia *see* DUIOS ANASTASIA TRECEA (1979).

Gently Was Anastasia Passing *see* DUIOS ANASTASIA TRECEA (1979).

Gentry Skylarking *see* URI MURI (1949).

GEORDIE 1955 d: Frank Launder. UKN., *Geordie*, David Walker, Novel

GEORG ELSER - EINER AUS DEUTSCHLAND 1989 d: Klaus Maria Brandauer. GRM/USA., *The Artisan*, Stephen Sheppard, Novel

GEORGE AND MARGARET 1940 d: George King. UKN., *George and Margaret*, Gerald Savory, London 1937, Play

GEORGE BARNWELL THE LONDON APPRENTICE 1913 d: Hay Plumb. UKN., *George Barnwell*, George Lillo, London 1731, Play

GEORGE WALLACE 1997 d: John Frankenheimer, Gary Sinise. USA., *Wallace*, Marshall Frady, Biography

GEORGE WARRINGTON'S ESCAPE 1911 d: Otis Turner. USA., William Makepeace Thackeray, Story

GEORGE WASHINGTON COHEN 1928 d: George Archainbaud. USA., *The Cherry Tree*, Aaron Hoffman, Play

GEORGE WASHINGTON, JR. 1924 d: Malcolm St. Clair. USA., *Jr. George Washington*, George M. Cohan, New York 1906, Play

GEORGE WASHINGTON SLEPT HERE 1942 d: William Keighley. USA., *George Washington Slept Here*, Moss Hart, George S. Kaufman, 1941, Play

Georges Dandin see **DANDIN GYORGY** (1955).

GEORGY GIRL 1966 d: Silvio Narizzano. UKN., *Georgy Girl*, Margaret Forster, London 1965, Novel

Gerak Family, The see **GERATSITE** (1958).

Geraks, The see **GERATSITE** (1958).

GERALD CRANSTON'S LADY 1924 d: Emmett J. Flynn. USA., *Gerald Cranston's Lady*, Gilbert Frankau, New York 1924, Novel

GERALDINE 1929 d: Melville Brown. USA., Booth Tarkington, Story

GERALDINE'S FIRST YEAR 1922 d: George A. Cooper. UKN., *Geraldine's First Year*, Mayell Bannister, Story

GERATSITE 1958 d: Anton Marinovich. BUL., *Geratsite*, Pelin Elin, 1911, Novel

GERLA DI PAPA MARTIN, LA 1909 d: Mario Caserini. ITL., *Les Crochets du Pere Martin*, Eugene Cormon, Eugene Grange, 1858, Play

GERLA DI PAPA MARTIN, LA 1914 d: Eleuterio Rodolfi. ITL., *Les Crochets du Pere Martin*, Eugene Cormon, Eugene Grange, 1858, Play

GERLA DI PAPA MARTIN, LA 1923 d: Mario Bonnard. ITL., *Les Crochets du Pere Martin*, Eugene Cormon, Eugene Grange, 1858, Play

GERLA DI PAPA MARTIN, LA 1940 d: Mario Bonnard. ITL., *Les Crochets du Pere Martin*, Eugene Cormon, Eugene Grange, 1858, Play

German Lesson see **DEUTSCHSTUNDE** (1971).

German Revolution, A see **EINE DEUTSCHE REVOLUTION** (1981).

Germana see **PER UN FIGLIO** (1920).

GERMANIN 1943 d: Max W. Kimmich. GRM., *Germanin*, Hellmuth Unger, Novel

GERMINAL 1913 d: Albert Capellani. FRN., *Germinal*, Emile Zola, 1885, Novel

GERMINAL 1963 d: Yves Allegret. FRN/ITL/HNG., *Germinal*, Emile Zola, 1885, Novel

GERMINAL 1993 d: Claude Berri. FRN/BLG/ITL., *Germinal*, Emile Zola, 1885, Novel

Geroi Nashego Vremeni Part 1 see **MAXIM MAXIMYCH TAMAN** (1967).

Geroi Nashego Vremeni Part 2 see **BELA** (1967).

GERTRUD 1964 d: Carl T. Dreyer. DNM., *Gertrud*, Hjalmar Soderberg, 1906, Play

Gertrude see **GERTRUD** (1964).

GERUSALEMME LIBERATA, LA 1911 d: Enrico Guazzoni. ITL., *La Gerusalemme Liberata*, Torquato Tasso, 1575, Poem

GERUSALEMME LIBERATA, LA 1918 d: Enrico Guazzoni. ITL., *La Gerusalemme Liberata*, Torquato Tasso, 1575, Poem

GERUSALEMME LIBERATA, LA 1935 d: Enrico Guazzoni. ITL., *La Gerusalemme Liberata*, Torquato Tasso, 1575, Poem

GERUSALEMME LIBERATA, LA 1957 d: Carlo Ludovico BragagliA. ITL., *La Gerusalemme Liberata*, Torquato Tasso, 1575, Poem

GERVAISE 1956 d: Rene Clement. FRN., *L' Assommoir*, Emile Zola, 1877, Novel

GERVAL, LE MAITRE DE FORGES 1912. FRN., *Le Maitre de Forges*, Georges Ohnet, Paris 1882, Novel

GESCHENK DES INDERS 1913 d: Louis Ralph. GRM., *Das Geschenk Des Inders*, F. C. Oberg, Novel

GESCHICHTE DER DIENERIN, DIE 1989 d: Volker Schlondorff. GRM/USA., *The Handmaid's Tale*, Margaret Atwood, 1986, Novel

Geschichte Der O, Die see **L' HISTOIRE D'O** (1975).

Geschichte Einer Jungen Liebe, Die see **DIE GESCHICHTE EINER JUNGEN LIEBE ANNEMARIE** (1936).

Geschichte Eines Fehlgeschlagenen Feldzugs see **THE PRIVATE HISTORY OF A CAMPAIGN THAT FAILED** (1982).

Geschichte Eines Hundes, Die see **KRAMBAMBULI** (1940).

Geschichte Eines Lebens, Die see **DIE GESCHICHTE EINES LEBENS ANNELIE** (1941).

GESCHICHTE VOM GOLDENEN TALER, DIE 1985 d: Bodo Furneisen. GDR., *Die Geschichte Vom Goldenen Taler*, Hans Fallada, Short Story

GESCHICHTE VOM KLEINEN MUCK, DIE 1953 d: Wolfgang Staudte. GDR., *Die Geschichte von Dem Kleinen Muck*, Wilhelm Hauff, 1826, Short Story

GESCHICHTEN AUS DEM WIENERWALD 1979 d: Maximilian Schell. AUS/GRM., *Geschichten Aus Dem Wiener Wald*, Odon von Horvath, 1931, Play

GESCHICHTSUNTERRICHT 1972 d: Jean-Marie Straub, Daniele Huillet. GRM., *Die Geschafte Des Herrn Julius Caesar*, Bertolt Brecht, 1957, Novel

GESCHIEDENE FRAU, DIE 1926 d: Victor Janson. GRM., *Die Geschiedene Frau*, Leo Fall, Viktor Leon, Opera

GESCHIEDENE FRAU, DIE 1953 d: Georg Jacoby. GRM., *Die Geschiedene Frau*, Leo Fall, Viktor Leon, Opera

Geschiedenes Fraulein see **ICH HAB MICH SO AN DICH GEWOHNT** (1952).

GESETZ DER LIEBE, DAS 1945 d: Hans Schweikart. GRM., *Das Gesetz Der Liebe*, Fred Andreas, Novel

GESETZ OHNE GNADE 1951 d: Harald Reinl. GRM/AUS., *Gipfelkreuz*, Karl Loven, Novel

GESHER TZAR ME'OD 1985 d: Nissim Dayan. ISR., Haim Hefer, Story

Gesicht Im Dunkeln, Das see **A DOPPIA FACCIA** (1969).

GESOM E KAKO SHIPTA 1993 d: Park Gwang-Su. SKR., *Gesom E Kako Shipta*, Im Chul-Woo, Novel

GESPENSTERHAUS, DAS 1942 d: Franz Schnyder. SWT., *Das Gespensterhaus*, Ulrich Wichelegger, Zurich 1943, Novel

GESTANDNIS DER DREI, DAS 1928 d: James Bauer. GRM., *Der Mord Am Karlsbad*, Paul Rosenhayn, Short Story

GESTANDNIS UNTER VIER AUGEN 1954 d: Andre Michel. GRM., *Gestandnis Unter Vier Augen*, Hugo Maria Kritz, Novel

Gestapo see **NIGHT TRAIN TO MUNICH** (1940).

GESTATTEN, MEIN NAME IST COX 1955 d: Georg Jacoby. GRM., *Gestatten Mein Name Is Cox*, Rolf Becker, Radio Play

GESTE, LE 1916 d: Georges DenolA. FRN., *Le Geste*, Maurice Montegut, Novel

GESTIEFELTE KATER, DER 1955 d: Herbert B. Fredersdorf. GRM., *Der Gestiefelte Kater*, Jacob Grimm, Wilhelm Grimm, Short Story

GESTOHLENE JAHR, DAS 1951 d: Wilfried Frass. GRM/AUS., *Das Gestohlene Jahr*, Stefan Zweig, Novel

GESTORTE HOCHZEITSNACHT, DIE 1950 d: Helmut Weiss, Johannes Riemann. GRM., *Mary Gute Nacht*, Tidmarsch, Play

Gesuzza, la Sposa Garibaldina see **I MILLE DI GARIBALDI** (1933).

GET CARTER 1970 d: Mike Hodges. UKN., *Jack's Return Home*, Ted Lewis, Novel

GET CHRISTIE LOVE! 1974 d: William A. Graham. USA., *The Ledger*, Dorothy Uhnak, Novel

Get Married and See see **LAGNA PAHAVA KARUN** (1940).

GET OFF MY FOOT 1935 d: William Beaudine. UKN., *Money By Wire*, Edward A. Paulton, Play

GET REAL 1998 d: Simon Shore. UKN/SAF., *What's Wrong With Angry?*, Patrick Wilde, Play

Get Rita see **LA PUPA DEL GANGSTER** (1975).

Get Sick. It's Free! see **IL MEDICO DELLA MUTUA** (1968).

Get That Girl see **CARYL OF THE MOUNTAINS** (1936).

GET YOUR MAN 1927 d: Dorothy Arzner. USA., *Tu M'epouseras!*, Louis Verneuil, 1927, Play

GET YOUR MAN 1934 d: George King. UKN., *Tu M'epouseras!*, Louis Verneuil, 1927, Play

Getaway Life, The see **LA DEROBADE** (1979).

GETAWAY, THE 1972 d: Sam Peckinpah. USA., *The Getaway*, Jim Thompson, Novel

Getaway, The see **LA DEROBADE** (1979).

GETAWAY, THE 1994 d: Roger Donaldson. USA., *The Getaway*, Jim Thompson, Novel

GETEILTE HIMMEL, DER 1964 d: Konrad Wolf. GDR., *Der Geteilte Himmel*, Christa Wolf, 1964, Novel

GET-RICH-QUICK WALLINGFORD 1921 d: Frank Borzage. USA., *Get-Rich-Quick Wallingford*, George M. Cohan, New York 1910, Play

Get-Rich-Quick Wallingford see **THE NEW ADVENTURES OF GET RICH QUICK WALLINGFORD** (1931).

Gettin' Smart see **TWO FISTED** (1935).

Getting Away With Murder see **DER RICHTER UND SEIN HENKER** (1976).

GETTING GERTIE'S GARTER 1927 d: E. Mason Hopper. USA., *Getting Gertie's Garter*, Wilson Collison, Avery Hopwood, New York 1921, Play

GETTING GERTIE'S GARTER 1945 d: Allan Dwan. USA., *Getting Gertie's Garter*, Wilson Collison, Avery Hopwood, New York 1921, Play

GETTING HURT 1998 d: Ben Bolt. UKN., *Getting Hurt*, Andrew Davies, Novel

GETTING IT RIGHT 1989 d: Randall Kleiser. UKN/USA., *Getting It Right*, Elizabeth Jane Howard, Novel

Getting Married see **JIE HUN** (1953).

GETTING OF WISDOM, THE 1977 d: Bruce Beresford. ASL., *The Getting of Wisdom*, Ethel Florence Richardson, 1910, Novel

GETTING OUT 1993 d: John Korty. USA., *Getting Out*, Marsha Norman, Play

GETTING STRAIGHT 1970 d: Richard Rush. USA., *Getting Straight*, Ken Kolb, Philadelphia 1967, Novel

GETTING TO KNOW YOU 1999 d: Lisanne Skyler. USA., Joyce Carol Oates, Short Stories

Getting Up and Going Home see **UNFAITHFUL** (1992).

GEVATTER TOD 1980 d: Wolfgang Hubner. GDR., Jacob Grimm, Wilhelm Grimm, Novel

GEWITTER IM MAI 1919 d: Ludwig Beck. GRM., *Gewitter Im Mai*, Ludwig Ganghofer, Novel

GEWITTER IM MAI 1937 d: Hans Deppe. GRM., *Gewitter Im Mai*, Ludwig Ganghofer, Novel

GEWITTER IM MAI 1988 d: Xaver Schwarzenberger. AUS/GRM., *Gewitter Im Mai*, Ludwig Ganghofer, Novel

GHARBAR 1963 d: James Ivory. IND/USA., *The Householder*, Ruth Prawer Jhabvala, London 1960, Novel

GHARE BHAIRE 1983 d: Satyajit Ray. IND., *Ghaire Bhaire*, Rabindranath Tagore, 1916, Novel

GHASHIRAM KOTWAL 1976 d: Mani Kaul, K. Hariharan. IND., *Ghashiram Kotwal*, Vijay Tendulkar, Play

Ghenga E Nuda Ogni Sera, La see **GIOVENTU DI NOTTE** (1962).

GHOST AND MRS. MUIR, THE 1947 d: Joseph L. Mankiewicz. USA., *The Ghost and Mrs. Muir*, R. A. Dick, Novel

GHOST BREAKER, THE 1914 d: Cecil B. de Mille, Oscar Apfel. USA., *The Ghost Breaker*, Paul Dickey, Charles W. Goddard, New York 1909, Play

GHOST BREAKER, THE 1922 d: Alfred E. Green. USA., *The Ghost Breaker*, Paul Dickey, Charles W. Goddard, New York 1909, Play

GHOST BREAKERS, THE 1940 d: George Marshall. USA., *The Ghost Breaker*, Paul Dickey, Charles W. Goddard, New York 1909, Play

GHOST CAMERA, THE 1933 d: Bernard Vorhaus. UKN., *The Ghost Camera*, J. Jefferson Farjeon, Story

GHOST CATCHERS 1944 d: Eddie Cline. USA., *High Spirits*, Edward Cline, Milton Gross, Story

GHOST COMES HOME, THE 1940 d: Wilhelm Thiele. USA., *Der Mutige Seefahrer*, Georg Kaiser, 1926, Play

Ghost Girls see **GUI MEI** (1985).

GHOST GOES WEST, THE 1935 d: Rene Clair. UKN., *Sir Tristram Goes West*, Eric Keown, Story

Ghost Hunter see **O CACADOR DE FANTASMA** (1975).

GHOST IN MONTE CARLO, THE 1990 d: John Hough. UKN., *The Ghost in Monte Carlo*, Barbara Cartland, Novel

Ghost Man, The see **THE GHOST COMES HOME** (1940).

GHOST OF A CHANCE, THE 1919 d: Kenneth Webb. USA., *The Ghost of a Chance*, O. Henry, Short Story

GHOST OF FLIGHT 401, THE 1978 d: Steven Hilliard Stern. USA., *The Ghost of Flight 401*, John G. Fuller, Book

Ghost of John Holling, The see MYSTERY LINER (1934).

Ghost of Kasane-Ga-Fuchi see KAIDAN KASANE-GA-FUCHI (1957).

Ghost of Kasane-Ga-Fuchi see KAIDAN KASANE-GA-FUCHI (1960).

Ghost of Love see FANTASMA D'AMORE (1981).

Ghost of Mr. Holling, The see MYSTERY LINER (1934).

Ghost of Oiwa see KAIDAN OIWA NO BOREI (1961).

Ghost of Rashmon Hall, The see NIGHT COMES TOO SOON (1948).

Ghost of Rosie Taylor, The see THE GHOST OF ROSY TAYLOR (1918).

GHOST OF ROSY TAYLOR, THE 1918 d: Edward Sloman. USA., The Ghost of Rosy Taylor, Josephine Daskam Bacon, 1917, Short Story

Ghost of Snow-Girl Prostitute see KAIDAN YUKIJORO (1968).

Ghost of Wolfpack, The see A TWIST OF SAND (1967).

Ghost of Yotsuya, The see YOTSUYA KAIDAN (1949).

Ghost of Yotsuya, The see KAIDAN BANCHO SARAYASHIKI (1957).

Ghost of Yotsuya, The see TOKAIDO YOTSUYA KAIDAN (1959).

Ghost of Yotsuya, The see YOTSUYA KAIDAN (1959).

Ghost of Yotsuya, The see KAIDAN OIWA NO BOREI (1961).

Ghost of Yotsuya, The see YOTSUYA KAIDAN (1965).

Ghost of Yotsuya, The see YOTSUYA KAIDAN -OIWA NO BOREI (1969).

GHOST PATROL, THE 1923 d: Nat Ross. USA., The Ghost Patrol, Sinclair Lewis, Short Story

Ghost Ship see YUREISEN (1957).

Ghost Steps Out, The see THE TIME OF THEIR LIVES (1946).

Ghost Stories see KWAIDAN (1964).

GHOST STORY 1981 d: John Irvin. USA., Ghost Story, Peter Straub, Novel

Ghost Story of Broken Dishes at Bancho Mansion see KAIDAN BANCHO SARAYASHIKI (1957).

Ghost Story of Yotsuya in Tokaido see TOKAIDO YOTSUYA KAIDAN (1959).

Ghost Story of Youth see SEISHUN KAIDAN (1955).

GHOST TALKS, THE 1929 d: Lewis Seiler. USA., Badges, Edward Hammond, Max Marcin, New York 1924, Play

GHOST THAT WALKS ALONE, THE 1944 d: Lew Landers. USA., The Wedding Guest Sat on a Stone, Richard Shattuck, Story

GHOST TRAIN, THE 1927 d: Geza von Bolvary. UKN/GRM., The Ghost Train, Arnold Ridley, London 1925, Play

GHOST TRAIN, THE 1931 d: Walter Forde. UKN., The Ghost Train, Arnold Ridley, London 1925, Play

GHOST TRAIN, THE 1941 d: Walter Forde. UKN., The Ghost Train, Arnold Ridley, London 1925, Play

GHOST WRITER, THE 1984 d: Tristram Powell. USA., The Ghost Writer, Philip Roth, Story

Ghostly Inn, The see THE HALFWAY HOUSE (1944).

GHOSTS 1915 d: George Nicholls. USA., Gengangere, Henrik Ibsen, 1881, Play

Ghosts -Italian Style see QUESTI FANTASMI (1967).

GHOSTS OF BERKELEY SQUARE, THE 1947 d: Vernon Sewell. UKN., No Nightingales, Caryl Brahms, S. J. Simon, Novel

GHOSTS OF YESTERDAY, THE 1918 d: Charles Miller. USA., Two Women, Rupert Hughes, New York 1910, Play

Ghosts, The see LOS APARECIDOS (1927).

GHOST-TOWN GOLD 1936 d: Joseph Kane. USA., Ghost-Town Gold, William Colt MacDonald, New York 1935, Novel

GHOUL, THE 1933 d: T. Hayes Hunter. UKN., The Ghoul, Frank King, Novel

G.I. HONEYMOON 1945 d: Phil Karlson. USA., G.I. Honeymoon, Robert Chapin, Marion Page Johnson, A. J. Rubien, Play

G.I. Joe see THE STORY OF G.I. JOE (1945).

GI LIA HAO 1962 d: Yan Jizhou. CHN., I Am a Soldier, Shuo Yunping, Play

GIACCA VERDE, LA 1979 d: Franco Giraldi. ITL., La Giacca Verde, Mario Soldati, 1961, Short Story

GIACOMO L'IDEALISTA 1943 d: Alberto LattuadA. ITL., Giacomo l'Idealista, Emilio de Marchi, 1897, Novel

GIALLO 1933 d: Mario Camerini. ITL., The Man Who Changed His Name, Edgar Wallace, London 1928, Play

GIAN BURRASCA 1943 d: Sergio Tofano. ITL., Il Giornalino Di Gian Burrsaca, Vamba, Novel

GIANT 1956 d: George Stevens. USA., Giant, Edna Ferber, 1952, Novel

Giants and Bigheads see GIGANTES Y CABEZUDOS (1925).

GIARDINO DEI FINZI-CONTINI, IL 1970 d: Vittorio de SicA. ITL/GRM., Il Giardino Dei Finzi-Contini, Giorgio Bassani, 1962, Novel

Gibbsville: the Turning Point of Jim Malloy see THE TURNING POINT OF JIM MALLOY (1975).

GIBIER DE POTENCE 1951 d: Roger Richebe. FRN., Gibier de Potence, Jean-Louis Curtis, 1949, Novel

GIBIGIANNA, LA 1919 d: Luigi Maggi. ITL., La Gibigianna, Carlo Bertolazzi, 1898, Play

Gibigianna, La see VANITA (1947).

Gibson Upright, The see YOU FIND IT EVERYWHERE (1921).

Gideon of Scotland Yard see GIDEON'S DAY (1959).

GIDEON'S DAY 1959 d: John Ford. UKN., Gideon's Day, John Creasey, Novel

GIDGET 1959 d: Paul Wendkos. USA., Gidget, Frederick Kohner, 1957, Novel

GIDGET GROWS UP 1970 d: James Sheldon. USA., Gidget Goes to New York, Frederick Kohner, Novel

GIFT GIRL, THE 1917 d: Rupert Julian. USA., Marcel's Birthday Present, Harold Riggs Durant, Play

GIFT O' GAB 1917 d: W. S. Van Dyke. USA., Gift O' Gab, H. Tipton Steck, Short Story

Gift of Fury see THE GREAT SANTINI (1980).

GIFT OF LOVE, THE 1958 d: Jean Negulesco. USA., The Little Horse, Nelia Gardner White, Short Story

GIFT OF LOVE, THE 1978 d: Don Chaffey. USA., The Gift of the Magi, O. Henry, 1906, Short Story

Gift of the Garland, The see MALAYADAAN (1971).

GIFT OF THE MAGI, THE 1917 d: Brinsley Shaw. USA., The Gift of the Magi, O. Henry, Short Story

GIFT SUPREME, THE 1920 d: Oliver L. Sellers. USA., The Gift Supreme, George Allan England, New York 1916, Novel

Gift, The see LE CADEAU (1982).

GIFTAS 1957 d: Anders Henrikson. SWD., Mot Betaining, August Strindberg, 1886, Short Story

GIFTGAS 1929 d: Michael Dubson. GRM., Giftgas Uber Berlin, Peter Martin Lampel, Play

GIGANTES Y CABEZUDOS 1925 d: Florian Rey. SPN., Gigantes Y Cabezudos, Miguel Echegaray, Fernandez Caballero, Opera

GIGI 1948 d: Jacqueline Audry. FRN., Gigi, Sidonie Gabrielle Colette, 1945, Novel

GIGI 1958 d: Vincente Minnelli. USA., Gigi, Sidonie Gabrielle Colette, 1945, Novel

GIGLIO INFRANTO, IL 1956 d: Giorgio W. Chili. ITL., I Congiurati Di Belfiore, Victor Hugo Feluan, Alfred Niblo, Play

GIGOLETTE 1921 d: Henri Pouctal. FRN., Gigolette, Pierre Decourcelle, Novel

GIGOLETTE 1936 d: Yvan Noe. FRN., Gigolette, Pierre Decourcelle, Novel

GIGOLO 1926 d: William K. Howard. USA., Gigolo, Edna Ferber, New York 1922, Novel

GIGOLO, LE 1960 d: Jacques Deray. FRN., Le Gigolo, Jacques Robert, Novel

Gij Zult Niet Dooden see WAS SHE GUILTY? (1922).

Gil Blas de Santillane see LES AVENTURES DE GIL BLAS DE SANTILLANE (1955).

Gilbert and Sullivan see THE STORY OF GILBERT AND SULLIVAN (1953).

Gilbert Grape see WHAT'S EATING GILBERT GRAPE (1993).

GILBERTE DE COURGENAY 1941 d: Franz Schnyder. SWT., Gilberte de Courgenay, Rudolf Bolo Maglin, Zurich 1939, Novel

GILDA 1946 d: Charles Vidor. USA., E. A. Ellington, Story

GILDED DREAM, THE 1920 d: Rollin S. Sturgeon. USA., The Gilded Dream, Katherine Leiser Robbins, 1920, Novel

GILDED FOOL, A 1915 d: Edgar Lewis. USA., A Gilded Fool, Henry Guy Carleton, New York 1892, Play

GILDED HIGHWAY, THE 1926 d: J. Stuart Blackton. USA., A Little More, William Babington Maxwell, London 1921, Novel

GIMBA 1962 d: Flavio Rangel. BRZ., Gimba: Presidente Dos Valentes, Gianfrancesco Guarnieri, 1959, Play

Gina see LA MORT EN CE JARDIN (1956).

GINGERBREAD MAN, THE 1998 d: Robert Altman. USA., John Grisham, Story

GINGHAM GIRL, THE 1927 d: David Kirkland. USA., The Gingham Girl, Daniel Kusell, New York 1922, Musical Play

GIOACCHINO MURAT (DALLA LOCANDA AL TRONO) 1910 d: Giuseppe de Liguoro. ITL., Murat O la Fine Di un Re, Giuseppe de Liguoro, 1901

Giocatore, Il see LE JOUEUR (1958).

Giochi Di Societa see SIGNORA! AI VOSTRI ORDINI (1939).

GIOCHI PROIBITI DELL'ARETINO PIETRO, I 1972 d: Piero Regnoli. ITL., I Ragionamenti, Pietro L'Arentino, Book

Gioco Degli Innamorati, Il see LES AMOUREUX DU FRANCE (1963).

GIOCO PERICOLOSO 1942 d: Nunzio MalasommA. ITL., Gioco Pericoloso, Ladislaus Fodor, Andreas Hindj, Play

GIOCONDA, LA 1912 d: Luigi Maggi. ITL., La Gioconda, Gabriele D'Annunzio, Palermo 1899, Play

GIOCONDA, LA 1916 d: Eleuterio Rodolfi. ITL., La Gioconda, Gabriele D'Annunzio, Palermo 1899, Play

GIOCONDA, LA 1953 d: Giacinto Solito. ITL., La Gioconda, Arrigo Boito, Amilcare Ponchielli, Milan 1876, Opera

GIOIE DEL FOCOLARE, LE 1920 d: Baldassarre Negroni. ITL., Les Joies du Foyer, Maurice Hennequin, Weber, 1894

Gioie Della Famiglia, Le see LE GIOIE DEL FOCOLARE (1920).

Gioielli Di Madame de., I see MADAME DE. (1953).

GIOIELLI, I 1913. ITL., Le Collier, Guy de Maupassant, Short Story

GION BAYASHI 1953 d: Kenji Mizoguchi. JPN., Gion Bayashi, Matsutaro Kawaguchi, Novel

Gion Festival see GION MATSURI (1968).

Gion Festival Music see GION BAYASHI (1953).

GION MATSURI 1968 d: Daisuke Ito, Tetsuya Yamanouchi. JPN., Gionmatsuri, Katsumi Nishiguchi, Tokyo 1968, Short Story

Gion Music see GION BAYASHI (1953).

Gion Music Festival see GION BAYASHI (1953).

GION NO SHIMAI 1936 d: Kenji Mizoguchi. JPN., Yama, Aleksander Ivanovich Kuprin, Novel

GIORGINA 1919 d: Ubaldo Pittei, Giuseppe Forti. ITL., Georgette, Victorien Sardou, 1885, Play

GIORGIO GANDI 1916 d: Emilio Graziani-Walter. ITL., Giorgio Gandi, Leopoldo Marenco, 1861, Play

GIORNATA BALORDA, LA 1960 d: Mauro Bolognini. ITL/FRN., Racconti Romani, Alberto Moravia, Milan 1954, Short Stories

GIORNATA NERA PER L'ARIETE 1971 d: Luigi Bazzoni. ITL., The Fifth Cord, D. M. Devine, Novel

GIORNI DELL'IRA, I 1967 d: Tonino Valerii. ITL/GRM., Der Tod Ritt Dienstags, Ron Barker, 1963, Novel

Giorni Di Fuoco see WINNETOU II (1964).

GIORNI FELICI 1943 d: Gianni Franciolini. ITL., Les Jours Heureux, Claude-Andre Puget, Play

Giorni Felici a Clichy see JOURS TRANQUILLES A CLICHY (1989).

GIORNO A MADERA, UN 1924 d: Mario Gargiulo. ITL., Un Giorno a Madera, Paolo Mantegazza, 1876, Novel

GIORNO DEL FURORE, IL 1973 d: Antonio CalendA. ITL/UKN., Vadim, Mikhail Lermontov, 1832-34, Novel

GIORNO DELLA CIVETTA, IL 1967 d: Damiano Damiani. ITL/FRN., Il Giorno Della Civetta, Leonardo Sciasia, Turin 1961, Novel

GIORNO DI NOZZE 1942 d: Raffaello Matarazzo. ITL., Fine Mese, Paola Riccora, Play

Giorno in Caserna, Un see L' ALLEGRO SQUADRONE (1954).

GIOVANE NORMALE, IL 1969 d: Dino Risi. ITL., *Il Giovane Normale*, Umberto Simonetta, Novel

GIOVANNA D'ARCO AL ROGO 1954 d: Roberto Rossellini. ITL/FRN., *Jeanne d'Arc Au Bucher*, Paul Claudel, 1939, Play

GIOVANNA LA PALLIDA 1911 d: Mario Caserini. ITL., *Jeanne la Pale*, Honore de Balzac, Novel

GIOVANNI DALLE BANDE NERE 1957 d: Sergio Grieco. ITL., *Giovanni Dalle Bande Nero*, Luigi Capranica, Novel

GIOVANNI EPISCOPO 1916 d: Mario Gargiulo. ITL., *Giovanni l'Episcopo*, Gabriele D'Annunzio, 1891, Novel

Giovanni Episcopo *see* **IL DELITTO DI GIOVANNI EPISCOPO** (1947).

Giovanni Episcopo's Crime *see* **IL DELITTO DI GIOVANNI EPISCOPO** (1947).

GIOVANNINO 1976 d: Paolo Nuzzi. ITL., *Giovannino*, Ercole Patti, Novel

GIOVE IN DOPPIOPETTO 1955 d: Daniele d'AnzA. ITL., *Giove in Doppiopetto*, Pietro Garinei, Sandro Giovannini, Play

GIOVENTU DI NOTTE 1962 d: Mario Sequi. ITL/FRN., *Nuda Ogni Sera*, Ugo Moretti, Novel

Gioventu Nuda *see* **TERRAIN VAGUE** (1960).

GIOVINEZZA, GIOVINEZZA 1969 d: Franco Rossi. ITL., *Giovinezza Giovinezza*, Luigi Preti, Novel

GIPERBOLOID INZHENERA GARINA 1966 d: Alexander Ginzburg. USS., *Giperboloid Inzhenera Garina*, Alexsey Nikolayevich Tolstoy, 1926, Novel

Gipfelkreuz, Das *see* **GESETZ OHNE GNADE** (1951).

Gipsies, The *see* **CIKANI** (1921).

Gipsy Blood *see* **GYPSY BLOOD** (1931).

GIPSY CAVALIER, A 1922 d: J. Stuart Blackton. UKN., *My Lady April*, John Overton, Novel

Gipsy Trail, The *see* **THE GYPSY TRAIL** (1918).

GIRL 1998 d: Jonathan Kahn. USA., *Girl*, Blake Nelson, Novel

Girl Against Napoleon, A *see* **LA DE RONDA CARMEN** (1959).

Girl and the Boy, The *see* **LA FILLE ET LE GARCON** (1931).

GIRL AND THE GAMBLER, THE 1939 d: Lew Landers. USA., *The Dove*, Willard Mack, New York 1925, Play

GIRL AND THE GAME, THE 1916 d: J. P. McGowan. USA., *The Girl and the Game*, Frank Hamilton Spearman, Story

Girl and the Gorilla, The *see* **ZAMBA** (1949).

GIRL AND THE GRAFT, THE 1918 d: William P. S. Earle. USA., *The Girl and the Graft*, O. Henry, Short Story

GIRL AND THE JUDGE, THE 1918 d: John B. O'Brien. USA., *The Girl and the Judge*, Clyde Fitch, New York 1901, Play

Girl and the Legend, The *see* **ROBINSON SOLL NICHT STERBEN** (1957).

Girl and the Palio, The *see* **LA RAGAZZA DEL PALIO** (1957).

GIRL AT BAY, A 1919 d: Thomas R. Mills. USA., *Hunt the Woman*, Joseph Gollomb, Short Story

Girl aux Mains Fines, La *see* **LIEBE GEHT SELTSAME WEGE** (1927).

GIRL BY THE ROADSIDE, THE 1918 d: Theodore Marston. USA., *The Girl By the Roadside*, Varick Vanardy, New York 1917, Novel

Girl Called Fathom, A *see* **FATHOM** (1967).

GIRL CALLED HATTER FOX, THE 1977 d: George Schaefer. USA., *The Girl Called Hatter Fox*, Marilyn Harris, Book

Girl Called Jules, A *see* **LA RAGAZZA DI NOME GIULIO** (1970).

GIRL CAN'T HELP IT, THE 1956 d: Frank Tashlin. USA., *Do Re Mi*, Garson Kanin, Short Story

Girl Can't Stop, The *see* **LES CHIENS DANS LA NUIT** (1965).

GIRL CRAZY 1932 d: William A. Seiter. USA., *Girl Crazy*, Guy Bolton, George Gershwin, John McGowan, New York 1930, Musical Play

GIRL CRAZY 1943 d: Norman Taurog. USA., *Girl Crazy*, Guy Bolton, John McGowan, New York 1930, Musical Play

Girl Crazy *see* **WHEN THE BOYS MEET THE GIRLS** (1965).

GIRL DOWNSTAIRS, THE 1938 d: Norman Taurog. USA., *Bakaruhaban*, Sandor Hunyady, 1935, Short Story

Girl for Happy Hours, A *see* **PHILINE** (1945).

Girl for Joe, A *see* **FORCE OF ARMS** (1951).

Girl for the Summer, A *see* **UNE FILLE POUR L'ETE** (1960).

Girl Friends, The *see* **LE AMICHE** (1955).

GIRL FROM 10TH AVENUE, THE 1935 d: Alfred E. Green. USA., *Outcast*, Hubert Henry Davies, New York 1914, Play

GIRL FROM AVENUE A, THE 1940 d: Otto Brower. USA., *The Brat*, Maude Fulton, Los Angeles 1916, Play

Girl from Bejar, The *see* **LA BEJARANA** (1925).

Girl from Beskydy Mountains, The *see* **DEVCICA Z BESKYD** (1944).

GIRL FROM CHICAGO, THE 1927 d: Ray Enright. USA., *Business Is Best*, Arthur Somers Roche, Story

Girl from China, The *see* **SHANGHAI LADY** (1929).

Girl from Coney Island, The *see* **JUST ANOTHER BLONDE** (1926).

Girl from Flanders, The *see* **EIN MADCHEN AUS FLANDERN** (1956).

Girl from Georgia, The *see* **HER SECRET** (1933).

GIRL FROM GOD'S COUNTRY, THE 1940 d: Sidney Salkow. USA., *Island Doctor*, Ray Millholland, 1939, Short Story

GIRL FROM HIS TOWN, THE 1915 d: Harry Pollard. USA., *The Girl from His Town*, Marie Van Vorst, Indianapolis 1910, Novel

Girl from Hong Kong *see* **BIS ZUM ENDE ALLER TAGE** (1961).

Girl from Hunan *see* **XIANGNU XIAOXIAO** (1987).

Girl from Ireland, The *see* **KATHLEEN MAVOURNEEN** (1930).

Girl from la Mancha *see* **DULCINEA** (1962).

GIRL FROM MANDALAY, THE 1936 d: Howard Bretherton. USA., *Tiger Valley*, Reginald Campbell, New York 1931, Novel

GIRL FROM MAXIM'S, THE 1932 d: Alexander KordA. UKN., *La Dame de Chez Maxim*, Georges Feydeau, 1898, Play

GIRL FROM MONTMARTRE, THE 1926 d: Alfred E. Green. USA., *Spanish Sunlight*, Anthony Pryde, New York 1925, Novel

GIRL FROM OUTSIDE, THE 1919 d: Reginald Barker. USA., *The Wag Lady*, Rex Beach, 1916, Story

Girl from Parma, The *see* **LA PARMIGIANA** (1963).

GIRL FROM PETROVKA, THE 1974 d: Robert Ellis Miller. USA., *The Girl from Petrovka*, George Feifer, Novel

GIRL FROM RECTOR'S, THE 1917. USA., *The Girl from Rector's*, Paul M. Potter, New York 1909, Play

Girl from Stormy Croft *see* **TOSEN FRAN STORMYRTORPET** (1918).

Girl from Tenth Avenue, The *see* **THE GIRL FROM 10TH AVENUE** (1935).

Girl from the Dead Sea, The *see* **LA FILLE DE LA MER MORTE** (1966).

Girl from the East, The *see* **THE HEART OF THE HILLS** (1916).

Girl from the Marsh Croft, A *see* **TOSEN FRAN STORMYRTORPET** (1918).

Girl from the Marsh Croft, A *see* **TOSEN FRAN STORMYRTORPET** (1947).

Girl from the Moor Estate, The *see* **DAS MADCHEN VOM MOORHOF** (1958).

Girl from the Mountains *see* **DEVCE Z HOR** (1924).

Girl from the Mountains, A *see* **DEVCICA Z BESKYD** (1944).

Girl from the Outside, The *see* **THE GIRL FROM OUTSIDE** (1919).

Girl from the Stormy Croft, A *see* **TOSEN FRAN STORMYRTORPET** (1918).

Girl from the Sumava Mountains, The *see* **PARNASIE** (1925).

Girl from the Tobacco Factory, The *see* **DEVCE Z TABAKOVE TOVARNY** (1928).

Girl from Trieste, The *see* **LA RAGAZZA DI TRIESTE** (1983).

Girl Goes on Shore, A *see* **EIN MADCHEN GEHT AN LAND** (1938).

GIRL GUIDE 1995 d: Juliusz MacHulski. PLN., Michal Szczepanski, Story

GIRL HABIT, THE 1931 d: Eddie Cline. USA., *Thirty Days*, Clayton Hamilton, 1915, Play, *Thirty Days; a Farce in Three Acts*, A. E. Thomas, 1915, Play

Girl He Left Behind, The *see* **ELIZABETH OF LADYMEAD** (1949).

GIRL HE LEFT BEHIND, THE 1956 d: David Butler. USA., *Girl He Left Behind; Or All Quiet in the Third Platoon*, Marion Hargrove, Novel

GIRL HUNTERS, THE 1963 d: Roy Rowland. UKN., *The Girl Hunters*, Mickey Spillane, New York 1962, Novel

Girl I Abandoned, The *see* **WATASHI GA SUTETA ONNA** (1969).

GIRL I LEFT BEHIND ME, THE 1915 d: Lloyd B. Carleton. USA., *The Girl I Left Behind Me*, David Belasco, Franklin Fyles, New York 1893, Play

Girl, I Like Her *see* **SIE GEFALLT MIR JUNGFER** (1968).

GIRL I LOVED, THE 1923 d: Joseph de Grasse. USA., *The Girl I Loved*, James Whitcomb Riley, Indianapolis 1910, Novel

Girl in a Dress-Coat *see* **FLICKAN I FRACK** (1956).

Girl in a Swing, The *see* **THE GIRL ON THE SWING** (1989).

GIRL IN BLACK STOCKINGS, THE 1957 d: Howard W. Koch. USA., *Wanton Murder*, Peter Godfrey, Novel

GIRL IN BOHEMIA, A 1919 d: Howard M. Mitchell. USA., *A Girl in Bohemia*, H. B. Daniel, Play

Girl in Distress *see* **JEANNIE** (1941).

GIRL IN EVERY PORT, A 1952 d: Chester Erskine. USA., *They Sell Sailors Elephants*, Frederick Hazlitt Brennan, Story

GIRL IN HIS HOUSE, THE 1918 d: Thomas R. Mills. USA., *Girl in His House*, Harold MacGrath, New York 1918, Novel

Girl in His Pocket *see* **UN AMOUR DE POCHE** (1957).

GIRL IN HIS ROOM, THE 1922 d: Edward Jose. USA., *Locked Out*, J. Raleigh Davies, Story

GIRL IN NUMBER 29, THE 1920 d: John Ford. USA., *The Girl in the Mirror*, Elizabeth Jordan, New York 1919, Novel

Girl in Pawn, The *see* **LITTLE MISS MARKER** (1934).

Girl in Room 17, The *see* **VICE SQUAD** (1953).

GIRL IN THE DARK, THE 1918 d: Stuart Paton. USA., *The Green Seal*, Charles Edmonds Walk, Chicago 1914, Novel

GIRL IN THE FLAT, THE 1934 d: Redd Davis. UKN., *The Girl in the Flat*, Evelyn Winch, Story

GIRL IN THE GLASS CAGE, THE 1929 d: Ralph Dawson. USA., *The Girl in the Glass Cage*, George Kibbe Turner, New York 1927, Novel

Girl in the Golden Knickers, The *see* **LA MUCHACHA DE LAS BRAGAS DE ORO** (1979).

Girl in the Golden Panties, The *see* **LA MUCHACHA DE LAS BRAGAS DE ORO** (1979).

GIRL IN THE HEADLINES 1963 d: Michael Truman. UKN., *The Nose on My Face*, Laurence Payne, London 1961, Novel

GIRL IN THE HOUSE-BOAT, THE 1913 d: Ashley Miller. USA., *Mr. Leander*, James Francis Dwyer, Short Story

GIRL IN THE LIMOUSINE, THE 1924 d: Larry Semon. USA., *The Girl in the Limousine*, Wilson Collison, Avery Hopwood, New York 1919, Play

Girl in the Mirror, The *see* **THE GIRL IN NUMBER 29** (1920).

Girl in the Moon *see* **DIE FRAU IM MOND** (1929).

GIRL IN THE NEWS, THE 1940 d: Carol Reed. UKN., *The Girl in the News*, Roy Vickers, Novel

Girl in the Park *see* **SANCTUARY OF FEAR** (1979).

GIRL IN THE PULLMAN, THE 1927 d: Erle C. Kenton. USA., *The Girl in Upper C*, Wilson Collison, Play

GIRL IN THE RAIN, THE 1920 d: Rollin S. Sturgeon. USA., *The Girl By the Roadside*, Varick Vanardy, New York 1917, Novel

GIRL IN THE SHOW, THE 1929 d: Edgar Selwyn. USA., *Eva the Fifth; the Odyssey of a Tom Show*, John Golden, Kenyon Nicholson, New York 1928, Play

GIRL IN THE TAXI, THE 1921 d: Lloyd Ingraham. USA., *The Girl in the Taxi*, Stanislaus Strange, New York 1910, Play

GIRL IN THE TAXI, THE 1937 d: Andre Berthomieu. UKN., Georg Okonowski, Play

GIRL IN THE WEB, THE 1920 d: Robert T. Thornby. USA., *Private Secretary Miss Maitland*, Geraldine Bonner, New York 1918, Novel

GIRL IN THE WOODS 1958 d: Tom Gries. USA., *Blood on the Branches*, Oliver Crawford, Novel

GIRL IN WHITE, THE 1952 d: John Sturges. USA., *Bowery to Bellevue*, Emily Dunning Barringer, 1950, Autobiography

GIRL MOST LIKELY TO., THE 1973 d: Lee Philips. USA., *The Girl Most Likely to*, Joan Rivers, Novel

GIRL MUST LIVE, A 1939 d: Carol Reed. UKN., *A Girl Must Live*, Emery Bonet, Novel

Girl Named Julius, A *see* **LA RAGAZZA DI NOME GIULIO** (1970).

GIRL NAMED MARY, A 1920 d: Walter Edwards. USA., *A Girl Named Mary*, Juliet Wilbor Tompkins, Indianapolis 1918, Novel

GIRL NAMED SOONER, A 1975 d: Delbert Mann. USA., *A Girl Named Sooner*, Suzanne Clauser, Novel

GIRL NAMED TAMIKO, A 1962 d: John Sturges. USA., *A Girl Named Tamiko*, Ronald de Levington Kirkbride, New York 1959, Novel

Girl Next Door, The *see* **THE WOMAN NEXT DOOR** (1919).

Girl Next Door, The *see* **PAKKAINTI AMMAYI** (1953).

Girl of Flanders, A *see* **EIN MADCHEN AUS FLANDERN** (1956).

GIRL OF GOLD, THE 1925 d: John Ince. USA., *The Girl of Gold*, Anna Alice Chapin, Cleveland Moffett, 1920, Short Story

GIRL OF LONDON, A 1925 d: Henry Edwards. UKN., *A Girl of London*, Douglas Walshe, Novel

GIRL OF MY DREAMS, THE 1918 d: Louis W. Chaudet. USA., *The Girl of My Dreams*, Otto Harbach, K. Hoschna, W. D. Nesbit, New York 1911, Musical Play

GIRL OF MY HEART, THE 1915 d: Leedham Bantock. UKN., *The Girl of My Heart*, Herbert Leonard, Play

GIRL OF MY HEART, THE 1920 d: Edward J. Le Saint. USA., *Joan of Rainbow Springs*, Frances Marian Mitchell, Boston 1911, Novel

Girl of Solbakken *see* **SYNNOVE SOLBAKKEN** (1957).

GIRL OF THE GOLDEN WEST, THE 1914 d: Cecil B. de Mille. USA., *Girl of the Golden West*, David Belasco, New York 1905, Play

GIRL OF THE GOLDEN WEST, THE 1923 d: Edwin Carewe. USA., *Girl of the Golden West*, David Belasco, New York 1905, Play

GIRL OF THE GOLDEN WEST, THE 1930 d: John Francis Dillon. USA., *Girl of the Golden West*, David Belasco, New York 1905, Play

GIRL OF THE GOLDEN WEST, THE 1938 d: Robert Z. Leonard. USA., *Girl of the Golden West*, David Belasco, New York 1905, Play

GIRL OF THE LIMBERLOST, A 1924 d: James Leo Meehan. USA., *A Girl of the Limberlost*, Gene Stratton-Porter, New York 1909, Novel

GIRL OF THE LIMBERLOST, A 1934 d: W. Christy Cabanne. USA., *A Girl of the Limberlost*, Gene Stratton-Porter, New York 1909, Novel

GIRL OF THE LIMBERLOST, A 1945 d: Mel Ferrer. USA., *A Girl of the Limberlost*, Gene Stratton-Porter, New York 1909, Novel

GIRL OF THE LIMBERLOST, A 1990 d: Burt Brinckerhoff. USA., *A Girl of the Limberlost*, Gene Stratton-Porter, New York 1909, Novel

Girl of the Moors, The *see* **DAS MADCHEN VOM MOORHOF** (1958).

GIRL OF THE NIGHT 1960 d: Joseph Cates. USA., *Girl of the Night*, Harold Greenwald, Novel

GIRL OF THE RIO 1932 d: Herbert Brenon. USA., *The Dove*, Willard Mack, New York 1925, Play

Girl of the Year *see* **THE PETTY GIRL** (1950).

Girl of Today, A *see* **LOVE'S OPTION** (1928).

GIRL OF YESTERDAY, A 1915 d: Allan Dwan. USA., *A Girl of Yesterday*, Wesley C. MacDermott, Story

GIRL ON A MOTORCYCLE 1968 d: Jack Cardiff. UKN./FRN., *La Motocyclette*, Andre Pieyre de Mandiarguew, Paris 1963, Novel

GIRL ON THE BARGE, THE 1929 d: Edward Sloman. USA., *The Girl on the Barge*, Rupert Hughes, 1927, Short Story

GIRL ON THE BOAT, THE 1961 d: Henry Kaplan. UKN., *The Girl on the Boat*, P. G. Wodehouse, 1922, Novel

GIRL ON THE STAIRS, THE 1924 d: William Worthington. USA., *The Girl on the Stairs*, Winston Bouve, 1924, Short Story

GIRL ON THE SWING, THE 1989 d: Gordon Hessler. USA./UKN., *Girl in a Swing*, Richard Adams, Novel

Girl on the Train, The *see* **THE GIRL IN THE PULLMAN** (1927).

GIRL PHILIPPA, THE 1917 d: S. Rankin Drew. USA., *My Girl Philippa*, Robert W. Chambers, New York 1916, Novel

GIRL STROKE BOY 1971 d: Bob Kellett. UKN., *Girlfriend*, David Percival, Play

Girl, The *see* **LA CHAVALA** (1925).

GIRL, THE GOLD WATCH & EVERYTHING, THE 1980 d: William Wiard. USA., *The Girl, the Gold Watch and Everything*, John D. MacDonald, Novel

Girl Was Young, The *see* **YOUNG AND INNOCENT** (1937).

GIRL WHO CAME BACK, THE 1918 d: Robert G. VignolA. USA., *Leah Kleschna*, C. M. S. McLellan, New York 1904, Play

GIRL WHO CAME BACK, THE 1923 d: Tom Forman. USA., *The Girl Who Came Back*, Charles E. Blaney, Samuel Ruskin Golding, Hoboken 1920, Play

GIRL WHO COULDN'T QUITE, THE 1950 d: Norman Lee. UKN., *The Girl Who Couldn't Quite*, Leo Marks, London 1947, Play

Girl Who Dared, The *see* **PAID IN ADVANCE** (1919).

Girl Who Dared, The *see* **THE LOVE FLOWER** (1920).

GIRL WHO DARED, THE 1944 d: Howard Bretherton. USA., *Blood on Her Shoe*, Medora Field, 1942, Novel

GIRL WHO FORGOT, THE 1939 d: Adrian Brunel. UKN., *The Young Person in Pink*, Gertrude E. Jennings, London 1920, Play

Girl Who Gave in, The *see* **UNDERTOW** (1930).

GIRL WHO HAD EVERYTHING, THE 1953 d: Richard Thorpe. USA., *A Free Soul*, Adela Rogers St. Johns, New York 1927, Novel

Girl Who Liked Purple Flowers, The *see* **LILA AKAC** (1934).

Girl Who Liked Purple Flowers, The *see* **LILA AKAC** (1973).

Girl Who Lived in the Woods, The *see* **THE LITTLE 'FRAID LADY** (1920).

GIRL WHO RAN WILD, THE 1922 d: Rupert Julian. USA., *M'liss: an Idyll of Red Mountain*, Bret Harte, Boston 1869, Novel

Girl Who Rode in the Palio, The *see* **LA RAGAZZA DEL PALIO** (1957).

Girl Who Saved His Honour, The *see* **MADAME PINKETTE & CO.** (1917).

GIRL WHO TOOK THE WRONG TURNING, THE 1915 d: Leedham Bantock. UKN., *The Girl Who Took the Wrong Turning*, Walter Melville, London 1906, Play

GIRL WHO WOULDN'T QUIT, THE 1918 d: Edgar Jones. USA., *The Quest of Joan*, James Oliver Curwood, Short Story

GIRL WHO WOULDN'T WORK, THE 1925 d: Marcel de Sano. USA., *The Girl Who Wouldn't Work*, Gertie Wentworth-James, London 1913, Novel

GIRL WHO WRECKED HIS HOME, THE 1916 d: Albert Ward. UKN., *The Girl Who Wrecked His Home*, Walter Melville, Play

Girl With a Jazz Heart, The *see* **THE GIRL WITH THE JAZZ HEART** (1920).

GIRL WITH AN ITCH 1958 d: Ronnie Ashcroft. USA., *Girl With an Itch*, Ralph S. Whitting, Novel

GIRL WITH GREEN EYES 1964 d: Desmond Davis. UKN., *The Lonely Girl*, Edna O'Brien, London 1962, Novel

Girl With Green Eyes, The *see* **THE GIRL WITH THE GREEN EYES** (1916).

Girl With the Golden Eyes, The *see* **LA FILLE AUX YEUX D'OR** (1961).

Girl With the Good Reputation, The *see* **DAS MADCHEN MIT DEM GUTEN RUF** (1938).

GIRL WITH THE GREEN EYES, THE 1916 d: Herbert Blache. USA., *The Girl With the Green Eyes*, Clyde Fitch, New York 1902, Play

Girl With the Green Eyes, The *see* **GIRL WITH GREEN EYES** (1964).

GIRL WITH THE JAZZ HEART, THE 1920 d: Lawrence C. Windom. USA., *The Girl With the Jazz Heart*, Robert Terry Shannon, 1920, Short Story

Girl With the Lucky Legs, The *see* **THE CASE OF THE LUCKY LEGS** (1935).

Girl With the Pitcher, The *see* **LA MOZA DEL CANTARO** (1953).

Girl With the Red Hair, The *see* **HET MEISJE MET HET RODE HAAR** (1981).

GIRL WITHOUT A ROOM 1933 d: Ralph Murphy. USA., *Girl Without a Room*, Jack Lait, Short Story, *I Can't Go Home*, Jack Lait, Short Story

Girl Without Pajamas, The *see* **DAS MADCHEN OHNE PYJAMA** (1957).

Girl/Boy *see* **GIRL STROKE BOY** (1971).

GIRLS 1919 d: Walter Edwards. USA., *Girls*, Clyde Fitch, New York 1908, Play

Girl's Abduction, A *see* **DER GEHEIMNISVOLLE KLUB** (1913).

GIRLS AT SEA 1958 d: Gilbert Gunn. UKN., *The Middle Watch*, Ian Hay, Stephen King-Hall, London 1929, Play

Girls at War *see* **DER MADCHENKRIEG** (1977).

Girl's Best Friend Is Wall Street, A *see* **SHE KNEW ALL THE ANSWERS** (1941).

Girls Disappear *see* **DES FEMMES DISPARAISSENT** (1959).

GIRLS DON'T GAMBLE 1920 d: Fred J. Butler. USA., *Girls Don't Gamble Anymore*, George Weston, 1920, Short Story

GIRLS' DORMITORY 1936 d: Irving Cummings. USA., *Matura*, Ladislaus Fodor, Budapest 1935, Play

Girls' Dormitory *see* **DORTOIR DES GRANDES** (1953).

Girls for Pleasure *see* **DOSSIER PROSTITUTION** (1969).

Girls for the Summer *see* **UNE FILLE POUR L'ETE** (1960).

Girls from Immen Farm, The *see* **DIE MADELS VOM IMMENHOF** (1955).

Girls from Nowolipki Street, The *see* **DZIEWCZETA Z NOWOLIPEK** (1985).

Girls from Wilko, The *see* **PANNY Z WILKO** (1979).

GIRLS IN THEIR SUMMER DRESSES, THE 1982 d: Nick HavingA. UKN./USA., *The Girls in Their Summer Dresses*, Irwin Shaw, Story

Girls in Uniform *see* **MADCHEN IN UNIFORM** (1931).

GIRLS MEN FORGET 1924 d: Maurice Campbell. USA., *The Girl Who Was the Life of the Party*, Fanny Kilbourne, 1923, Short Story

Girls Never Tell *see* **HER FIRST ROMANCE** (1951).

GIRLS OF HUNTINGTON HOUSE, THE 1973 d: Alf Kjellin. USA., *The Girls of Huntington House*, Blossom Elfman, Novel

Girls of Nowlipki, The *see* **DZIEWCZETA Z NOWOLIPEK** (1985).

Girls of Nowolipek *see* **DZIEWCZETA Z NOWOLIPEK** (1938).

GIRLS OF PLEASURE ISLAND, THE 1953 d: F. Hugh Herbert, Alvin Ganzer. USA., *Pleasure Island*, William Maier, 1949, Novel

Girls of San Frediano, The *see* **LE RAGAZZE DI SAN FREDIANO** (1955).

GIRLS' SCHOOL 1938 d: John Brahm. USA., *The Answer in the Magnolias*, Tess Slesinger, New York 1935, Novel

Girls Together *see* **THIS MODERN AGE** (1931).

Girl's War *see* **DER MADCHENKRIEG** (1977).

Girls' War, The *see* **DER MADCHENKRIEG** (1977).

GIRLS WILL BE BOYS 1934 d: Marcel Varnel. UKN., *The Last Lord*, Curt Siodmak, Play

Girlw With the Golden Panties, The *see* **LA MUCHACHA DE LAS BRAGAS DE ORO** (1979).

Girly *see* **NANNY, SONNY AND GIRLY MUMSY** (1969).

GIRO DEL MONDO DEGLI INNAMORATI DI PEYNET, IL 1974 d: Cesare Perfetto. ITL., *Il Giro Del Mondo Degli Innamorati Di Peynet*, Raymond Peynet, Book

GIRO DEL MONDO DI UN BIRICCHINO DI PARIGI, IL 1921 d: Luigi Maggi, Dante Cappelli. ITL., *Il Giro Del Mondo Di un Biricchino Di Parigi*, Luigi Boussenard, Novel

GIROVAGHI, I 1956 d: Hugo Fregonese. ITL., *Cardello*, Luigi Capuana, Short Story

Gismonda *see* **LOVE'S CONQUEST** (1918).

Gita Premio Ne Ticino *see* **JEUNES FILLES D'AUJOURD'HUI** (1942).

779

GITAN, LE 1975 d: Jose Giovanni. FRN/ITL., *Le Gitan*, Jose Giovanni, Novel

GITANILLA, LA 1940 d: Fernando Delgado. SPN., *La Gitanilla*, Miguel de Cervantes Saavedra, 1613, Short Story

Gitta Vom Rattenschloss see GRITTA VOM RATTENSCHLOSS (1985).

GIU IL SIPARIO 1940 d: Raffaello Matarazzo. ITL., Francesco Augusto Bon, Play

Giudice E I Suo Boia, Il see DER RICHTER UND SEIN HENKER (1976).

Giudice Haller, Il see IL CASO HALLER (1933).

GIULIA DI TRECOEUR 1921 d: Camillo de Riso. ITL., *Julie*, Octave Feuillet, 1869

GIULIETTA E ROMEO 1908 d: Mario Caserini?. ITL., *Romeo and Juliet*, William Shakespeare, c1596, Play

Giulietta E Romeo see ROMEO E GIULIETTA (1912).

Giulietta E Romeo see ROMEO AND JULIET (1954).

GIULIETTA E ROMEO 1964 d: Riccardo FredA. ITL/SPN., *Romeo and Juliet*, William Shakespeare, c1596, Play

GIULIO CESARE 1909 d: Giovanni Pastrone?. ITL., *Julius Caesar*, William Shakespeare, c1596, Play

Giulio Cesare E Bruto see GIULIO CESARE (1909).

Giumenta Verde, La see LA JUMENT VERTE (1959).

GIUNGLA 1942 d: Nunzio MalasommA. ITL., *Vom Schicksal Verweht*, Joseph Maria Franck, Play

GIUSEPPE VERDI 1953 d: Raffaello Matarazzo. ITL., *Verdi. Roman Der Oper*, Franz Werfel, 1924, Novel

Giustizia Di Scimmia see IL SOTTERRANEO FATALE (1920).

GIUSTIZIERE DEI MARI, IL 1962 d: Domenico PaolellA. ITL/FRN., *Cronache Del 1787-1790 a Botany Bay in Australia*, James Price, Book

GIUSTIZIERE INVISIBILE, IL 1916 d: Mario Roncoroni. ITL., *The Invisible Man*, H. G. Wells, London 1897, Novel

Giva 24 Aina Onah see HAGIVA (1955).

GIVE A DOG A BONE 1967 d: Henry Cass. UKN., *Give a Dog a Bone*, Peter Howard, Play

GIVE AND TAKE 1928 d: William Beaudine. USA., *Give and Take*, Aaron Hoffman, New York 1926, Novel

GIVE HER A RING 1934 d: Arthur Woods. UKN., *Fraulein Falsch Verbunden*, Herbert Rosenfeld, Play

Give Me a Child see LIFE BEGINS (1932).

Give Me a Child see A CHILD IS BORN (1940).

GIVE ME A SAILOR 1938 d: Elliott Nugent. USA., *Linger Longer Letty*, Anne Nichols, New York 1919, Play

Give Me the Simple Life see WAKE UP AND DREAM (1946).

Give Me This Woman see THE CONSPIRATORS (1944).

GIVE ME YOUR HEART 1936 d: Archie Mayo. USA., *Sweet Aloes*, Jay Mallory, London 1934, Play

GIVE US THE MOON 1944 d: Val Guest. UKN., *The Elephant Is White*, Caryl Brahms, S. J. Simon, Novel

Give Us the Night see WHEN TOMORROW COMES (1939).

GIVE US THIS DAY 1949 d: Edward Dmytryk. UKN., *Christ in Concrete*, Pietro Di Donato, Novel

Given Word, The see O PAGADOR DE PROMESSAS (1961).

Giving You the Stars see GIVE HER A RING (1934).

GLACE A TROIS FACES, LA 1927 d: Jean Epstein. FRN., *L' Europe Galante*, Paul Morand, Short Story

Glace Bay Miner's Museum, The see MARGARET'S MUSEUM (1995).

GLAD DIG I DIN UNGDOM 1939 d: Per Lindberg. SWD., *Sankt Sedebetyg*, Vilhelm Moberg, 1935, Novel

GLAD EYE, THE 1920 d: Kenelm Foss. UKN., *Le Zebre*, Paul Armont, Jose G. Levy, Nicolas Nancey, Play

GLAD EYE, THE 1927 d: Maurice Elvey, Victor Saville. UKN., *Le Zebre*, Paul Armont, Jose G. Levy, Nicolas Nancey, Play

GLAD GUTT, EN 1932 d: John W. Brunius. NRW., *En Glad Gutt*, Bjornstjerne Bjornson, 1859, Short Story

GLAD TIDINGS 1953 d: Wolf RillA. UKN., *Glad Tidings*, R. F. Delderfield, Play

GLADIATOR, THE 1938 d: Edward Sedgwick. USA., *The Gladiator*, Philip Wylie, New York 1930, Novel

GLAMOROUS NIGHT 1937 d: Brian Desmond Hurst. UKN., *Glamorous Night*, Ivor Novello, London 1935, Musical Play

GLAMOUR 1934 d: William Wyler. USA., *Glamour*, Edna Ferber, 1932, Short Story

Glanz Und Ende Eines Konigs see LUDWIG II (1955).

GLAS WASSER, DAS 1960 d: Helmut Kautner. GRM., *Le Verre d'Eau Ou Les Effets Et Les Causes*, Eugene Scribe, Paris 1840, Play

GLASAM ZA LJUBAV 1965 d: Toma Janic. YGS., *Glasam Za Ljubav*, Grozdana Olujic, 1953, Novel

GLASBLASARNS BARN 1998 d: Anders Gronros. SWD/NRW/DNM., *Glasblasarns Barn*, Maria Gripe, 1964, Novel

GLASERNE HIMMEL, DER 1987 d: Nina Grosse. GRM., Julio Cortazar, Story

GLASERNE ZELLE, DIE 1978 d: Hans W. Geissendorfer. GRM., *The Glass Cell*, Patricia Highsmith, 1964, Novel

GLASS CAGE, THE 1955 d: Montgomery Tully. UKN., *The Outsiders*, A. E. Martin, Novel

Glass Cell, The see DIE GLASERNE ZELLE (1978).

Glass Heaven, The see DER GLASERNE HIMMEL (1987).

GLASS HOUSE, THE 1972 d: Tom Gries. USA., *The Glass House*, Truman Capote, Story

GLASS KEY, THE 1935 d: Frank Tuttle. USA., *The Glass Key*, Dashiell Hammett, New York 1931, Novel

GLASS KEY, THE 1942 d: Stuart Heisler. USA., *The Glass Key*, Dashiell Hammett, New York 1931, Novel

Glass Madonna, The see LA VIRGEN DE CRISTAL (1925).

GLASS MENAGERIE, THE 1950 d: Irving Rapper. USA., *The Glass Menagerie*, Tennessee Williams, New York 1945, Play

GLASS MENAGERIE, THE 1973 d: Anthony Harvey. USA., *The Glass Menagerie*, Tennessee Williams, New York 1945, Play

GLASS MENAGERIE, THE 1987 d: Paul Newman. USA., *The Glass Menagerie*, Tennessee Williams, New York 1945, Play

Glass of Water, A see DAS GLAS WASSER (1960).

Glass Rabbit see GARASU NO USAGI (1979).

Glass Sky, The see DER GLASERNE HIMMEL (1987).

GLASS SLIPPER, THE 1954 d: Charles Walters. USA., *Cendrillon*, Charles Perrault, 1697, Short Story

Glass Slipper, The see KHRUSTALNYY BASHMACHOK (1961).

Glass Tomb, The see THE GLASS CAGE (1955).

GLASS WEB, THE 1953 d: Jack Arnold. USA., *Spin the Glass Web*, Max Simon Ehrlich, 1952, Novel

Glass With Three Faces, The see LA GLACE A TROIS FACES (1927).

Glass-Bead Rosary, A see PACIORKI JEDNEGO ROZANCA (1979).

Glassblower's Children, The see GLASBLASARNS BARN (1998).

Glavnye Svidetel see GLAVNYJ SVIDETEL (1969).

GLAVNYJ SVIDETEL 1969 d: Aida ManasarovA. USS., *Baby*, Anton Chekhov, 1891, Short Story

GLEAM O'DAWN 1922 d: John Francis Dillon. USA., *Gleam O'Dawn*, Arthur Frederick Goodrich, New York 1908, Novel

GLEISDREIECK 1936 d: R. A. Stemmle. GRM., *Gleisdreieck*, Rolf E. Vanloo, Novel

GLENGARRY SCHOOL DAYS 1923 d: Henry McRae. CND., *Glengarry School Days*, Ralph Connor, Novel

GLIMPSES OF THE MOON, THE 1923 d: Allan Dwan. USA., *The Glimpses of the Moon*, Edith Wharton, New York 1922, Novel

GLISSANDO 1985 d: Mircea Daneliuc. RMN., *Omul Din Vis*, Cezar Petrescu, 1926, Short Story

Glitter see I LIVE MY LIFE (1935).

GLITTER DOME, THE 1985 d: Stuart Margolin. USA/CND., *The Glitter Dome*, Joseph Wambaugh, Novel

GLITZ 1989 d: Sandor Stern. USA., *Glitz*, Elmore Leonard, Novel

GLOBAL AFFAIR, A 1963 d: Jack Arnold. USA., *A Global Affair*, Eugene Vale, Novel

Glocke von St. Marein, Die see PETRONELLA (1927).

GLOCKLEIN UNTERM HIMMELBETT, DAS 1970 d: Hans Heinrich. GRM., *Das Bayrische Dekameron*, Oskar Maria Graf, 1928, Novel

GLOIRE DE MON PERE, LE 1989 d: Yves Robert. FRN., *Souvenirs d'Enfance*, Marcel Pagnol, 1957, Autobiography

GLOIRE ROUGE, LA 1917 d: Albert Dieudonne. FRN., *Un Lache*, Albert Dieudonne, Play

Gloomy Morning, A see KHUROYE UTRO (1959).

GLORIA 1977 d: Claude Autant-LarA. FRN., *Gloria*, Solange Bellegarde, Novel

GLORIA SCOTT, THE 1923 d: George Ridgwell. UKN., *The Gloria Scott*, Arthur Conan Doyle, Short Story

GLORIOUS ADVENTURE, THE 1918 d: Hobart Henley. USA., *When Carey Came to Town*, Edith Barnard Delano, 1915, Serial Story

GLORIOUS BETSY 1928 d: Alan Crosland. USA., *Glorious Betsy*, Rida Johnson Young, New York 1908, Play

Glorious Dust, The see DIVOTA PRASINE (1976).

GLORIOUS FOOL, THE 1922 d: E. Mason Hopper. USA., *In the Pavilion*, Mary Roberts Rinehart, 1919, Short Story, *Twenty-Two*, Mary Roberts Rinehart, 1919, Short Story

Glorious Youth see EILEEN OF THE TREES (1928).

Glory see LAUGHING AT TROUBLE (1937).

GLORY 1989 d: Edward Zwick. USA., *One Gallant Rush*, Peter Burchard, Book, *Lay This Laurel*, Lincoln Kirstein, Book

Glory and Misery of Human Life, The see IHMISELON IHANUUS JA KURJUUS (1988).

GLORY BOYS, THE 1982 d: Michael Ferguson. USA/UKN., *The Glory Boys*, Gerald Seymour, Novel

Glory for Me see THE BEST YEARS OF OUR LIVES (1946).

GLORY GUYS, THE 1965 d: Arnold Laven. USA., *The Dice of God*, Hoffman Birney, New York 1956, Novel

GLORY OF CLEMENTINA, THE 1915 d: Ashley Miller. USA., *The Glory of Clementina*, William J. Locke, New York 1911, Novel

GLORY OF CLEMENTINA, THE 1922 d: Emile Chautard. USA., *The Glory of Clementina*, William J. Locke, New York 1911, Novel

Glory of Love, The see WHILE PARIS SLEEPS (1923).

Glove, The see IL GUANTO (1910).

Gloves see K'FAFOT (1986).

GLU, LA 1913 d: Albert Capellani. FRN., *La Glu*, Jean Richepin, Play

GLU, LA 1927 d: Henri Fescourt. FRN., *La Glu*, Jean Richepin, Play

GLU, LA 1938 d: Jean Choux. FRN., *La Glu*, Jean Richepin, Play

Gluck Auf Der Alm, Das see KINDER DER BERGE (1958).

GLUCK AUS OHIO 1951 d: Heinz Paul. GRM., *Spatzen in Gottes Hand*, L. Bender, Edgar Kahn, Play

GLUCK IM HINTERHAUS 1979 d: Hermann Zschoche. GDR., *Gluck Im Hinterhaus*, Gunter de Bruyn, Novel

GLUCK IM WINKEL 1937 d: Alfred Stoger. GRM., *Hinuber - Herbuer*, Johann Nestroy, 1844, Play

Gluck Ins Haus see EIN HAUS VOLL LIEBE (1954).

GLUCK LIEGT AUF DER STRASSE, DAS 1957 d: Franz Antel. GRM., *Dvenadtsat Stulyev*, Ilya Ilf, Evgeny Petrov, Moscow 1928, Novel

GLUCK MUSS MAN HABEN 1953 d: Axel von Ambesser. AUS., *Hau-Ruck*, Ladislaus Fodor, Play

GLUCK UNTERWEGS 1944 d: Friedrich Zittau. GRM., *Die Reise Nach Paris*, E. W. Schafer, Play

GLUCK VON GRINZING, DAS 1939 d: Otto Kanturek. AUS/CZC., *Das Hauschen in Grinzing*, Joseph Lanner, Opera

GLUCK WOHNT NEBENAN, DAS 1939 d: Hubert MarischkA. GRM/AUS., *Das Gluck Wohnt Nebenan*, F. Griebitz, Play

GLUCKLICHE REISE 1933 d: Alfred Abel. GRM., *Gluckliche Reise*, Max Bertuch, Eduard Kunneke, Kurt Schwabach, Opera

GLUCKLICHE REISE 1954 d: Thomas Engel. GRM., *Gluckliche Reise*, Max Bertuch, Eduard Kunneke, Kurt Schwabach, Opera

GLUCKLICHEN JAHRE DER THORWALDS, DIE 1962 d: Wolfgang Staudte, John Olden. GRM., *Time and the Conways*, J. B. Priestley, 1937, Play

GLUCKLICHER MENSCH, EIN 1943 d: Paul Verhoeven. GRM., *Swedenhielms*, Hjalmar Bergman, 1925, Play

GLUCKSHOGER, DER 1942 d: Richard Brewing. SWT., *D'glogge Vo Wallere Schwarzenburger Gschichte*, Emil Balmer, Berne 1924, Short Story

GLUHENDE GASSE, DIE 1927 d: Paul Sugar. GRM., *Die Gluhende Gasse*, Paul Rosenhayn, Novel

GLYKIA PATRIDA 1986 d: Michael Cacoyannis. GRC/PNM., Caroline Richards, Novel

G-MEN 1935 d: William Keighley. USA., *Public Enemy No. 1*, Gregory Rogers, Novel

GNANAMBIKA 1940 d: S. Nottani. IND., *Gnanambika*, C. Madhavan Pillai, Novel

GNESELLA 1918 d: Elvira Notari. ITL., *Gnesella*, Francesco Gabriello Starace, 1899, Play

GNOME-MOBILE, THE 1967 d: Robert Stevenson. USA., *The Gnomobile: a Gnice Gnew Gnarrative With Gnonsense.*, Upton Sinclair, 1962, Novel

Go and Get It see **BUTTSUKE HONBAN** (1958).

GO DOWN, DEATH! 1944 d: Spencer Williams. USA., *Go Down Death - a Funeral Sermon*, James Weldon Johnson, 1927, Poem

GO GETTER, THE 1937 d: Busby Berkeley. USA., *The Go-Getter*, Peter B. Kyne, Short Story

GO INTO YOUR DANCE 1935 d: Archie Mayo, Robert Florey (Uncredited). USA., *Go Into Your Dance*, Bradford Ropes, New York 1934, Novel

GO NAKED IN THE WORLD 1960 d: Ranald MacDougall. USA., *Go Naked in the World*, Tom T. Chamales, New York 1959, Novel

GO TELL IT ON THE MOUNTAIN 1985 d: Stan Lathan. USA., *Go Tell It on the Mountain*, James Baldwin, 1953, Novel

GO TELL THE SPARTANS 1978 d: Ted Post. USA., *Go Tell the Spartans*, Daniel Ford, Novel

GO WEST YOUNG MAN 1936 d: Henry Hathaway. USA., *Personal Appearance*, Lawrence Riley, New York 1934, Play

Goal in the Clouds see **ZIEL IN DEN WOLKEN** (1938).

Goalie's Anxiety at the Penalty Kick, The see **DIE ANGST DES TORMANNS BIEN ELFMETER** (1971).

Goalkeeper's Fear of the Penalty, The see **DIE ANGST DES TORMANNS BIEN ELFMETER** (1971).

Goat Horn, The see **KOZUU POS** (1972).

Goat in the Garden, A see **BOCK I ORTAGARD** (1958).

Gobbo Di Parigi, Il see **LES AVENTURES DE LAGARDERE** (1967).

GOBEN NO TSUBAKI 1964 d: Yoshitaro NomurA. JPN., *Goben No Tsubaki*, Shugoro Yamamoto, Tokyo 1959, Novel

GO-BETWEEN, THE 1970 d: Joseph Losey. UKN., *The Go-Between*, L. P. Hartley, 1953, Novel

Gobi Outpost see **DESTINATION GOBI** (1953).

GOBSEC 1987 d: Alexandr Orlov. USS., *Gobseck*, Honore de Balzac, 1830, Short Story

Gobseck see **GOBSEK** (1936).

GOBSEK 1936 d: Konstantin V. Eggert. USS., *Gobseck*, Honore de Balzac, 1830, Short Story

Gobsek see **GOBSEC** (1987).

God and His Servants, A see **HERREN OG HANS TJENERE** (1959).

GOD AND THE MAN 1918 d: Edwin J. Collins. UKN., *God and the Man*, Robert Buchanan, Novel

God Calls Dorian see **IL DIO CHIAMATO DORIAN** (1970).

God Game, The see **THE MAGUS** (1968).

God Gave Him a Dog see **THE BISCUIT EATER** (1940).

GOD GAVE ME TWENTY CENTS 1926 d: Herbert Brenon. USA., *God Gave Me Twenty Cents*, Dixie Willson, Short Story

GOD IN THE GARDEN, THE 1921 d: Edwin J. Collins. UKN., *The God in the Garden*, Keble Howard, Novel

GOD IS MY CO-PILOT 1945 d: Robert Florey. USA., *God Is My Co-Pilot*, Colonel Robert Lee Scott Jr., Book

God Needs Man see **DIEU A BESOIN DES HOMMES** (1950).

God Never Walked the West see **C'ERA UNA VOLTA DIO ANCHE NEL WEST** (1968).

God of the Masses, The see **GANADEVATA** (1978).

GOD ON THE ROCKS 1992 d: Ross Cramer. UKN., *God on the Rocks*, Jane Gardam, Novel

God Protects Lovers see **GOTT SCHUTZT DIE LIEBENDEN** (1973).

God Was in the West, Too, at One Time see **C'ERA UNA VOLTA DIO ANCHE NEL WEST** (1968).

God Will Pay You see **DIOS SE LO PAGUE** (1947).

Godaan see **GODAN** (1962).

GODAN 1962 d: Trilok Jetley. IND., *Godan*, Premchand, 1936, Novel

GODCHILD, THE 1974 d: John Badham. USA., *Three Godfathers*, Peter B. Kyne, New York 1913, Novel

GODDESS OF SAGEBRUSH GULCH, THE 1912 d: D. W. Griffith. USA., *The Goddess of Sagebrush Gulch*, Bret Harte, Short Story

GODELUREAUX, LES 1960 d: Claude Chabrol. FRN/ITL., *Les Godelureaux*, Eric Ollivier, Novel

GODFATHER, THE 1972 d: Francis Ford CoppolA. USA., *The Godfather*, Mario Puzo, Novel

GODLESS MEN 1921 d: Reginald Barker. USA., *Black Pawl*, Ben Ames Williams, Short Story

Godman, The see **DHARMAVEER** (1937).

GODS AND MONSTERS 1998 d: Bill Condon. USA., *Father of Frankenstein*, Christopher Bram, Novel

GOD'S CLAY 1919 d: Arthur Rooke. UKN., *God's Clay*, Alice Askew, Claude Askew, Novel

GOD'S CLAY 1928 d: Graham Cutts. UKN., *God's Clay*, Alice Askew, Claude Askew, Novel

GOD'S COUNTRY 1946 d: Robert Tansey. USA., *God's Country - and the Woman*, James Oliver Curwood, New York 1915, Novel

GOD'S COUNTRY AND THE LAW 1921 d: Sidney Olcott. USA., *God's Country - and the Woman*, James Oliver Curwood, New York 1915, Novel

GOD'S COUNTRY AND THE WOMAN 1916 d: Rollin S. Sturgeon. USA., *God's Country - and the Woman*, James Oliver Curwood, New York 1915, Novel

GOD'S COUNTRY AND THE WOMAN 1937 d: William Keighley. USA., *God's Country - and the Woman*, James Oliver Curwood, New York 1915, Novel

GOD'S CRUCIBLE 1921 d: Henry McRae. CND/USA., *The Foreigner; a Tale of Saskatchewan*, Ralph Connor, New York 1909, Novel

GOD'S GIFT TO WOMEN 1931 d: Michael Curtiz. USA., *The Devil Was Sick*, Jane Hinton, Play

GOD'S GOOD MAN 1919 d: Maurice Elvey. UKN., *God's Good Man*, Marie Corelli, Novel

GOD'S LAW AND MAN'S 1917 d: John H. Collins. USA., *A Wife By Purchase*, Paul Trent, London 1909, Novel

GOD'S LITTLE ACRE 1958 d: Anthony Mann. USA., *God's Little Acre*, Erskine Caldwell, 1933, Novel

GOD'S MAN 1917 d: George Irving. USA., *God's Man*, George Bronson Howard, New York 1915, Novel

God's Message see **REVELATION** (1918).

God's Mills see **BOZI MLYNY** (1929).

God's Mills see **BOZI MLYNY** (1938).

Gods Must Be Dancing, The see **LA DIVINE POURSUITE** (1997).

Gods of the Streets see **GATEGUTTER** (1949).

GOD'S PRODIGAL 1923 d: Bert Wynne, Edward Jose. UKN., *God's Prodigal*, Edward Jose, Novel

GODS REDEEM, THE 1915 d: Van Dyke Brooke. USA., *The Gods Redeem*, James Oliver Curwood, Story

God's Thunder see **LE TONNERRE DE DIEU** (1965).

GOD'S WITNESS 1915 d: Eugene W. Moore. USA., *At the Mercy of Tiberius*, Augusta Jane Evans Wilson, New York 1887, Novel

GODSEND, THE 1979 d: Gabrielle Beaumont. UKN., *The Godsend*, Bernard Taylor, Novel

Godson, The see **LE SAMOURAI** (1967).

GODSPELL 1973 d: David Greene. USA., *Godspell*, Stephen Schwartz, John-Michael Tebelak, Musical Play

GODVAKKER MAREN 1940 d: Knut Hergel. NRW., *Bak Hokerens Disk*, Oskar Braaten, 1918, Novel, *Godvakker - Maren*, Oskar Braaten, 1927, Play

GOETHE LEBT.! 1932 d: Eberhard Frowein. GRM., *Aus Meinem Leben. Dichtung Und Wahrheit*, Johann Wolfgang von Goethe, 1811-33, Autobiography

Goethe's Jugendgeliebte see **DIE JUGENDGELIEBTE** (1930).

Goforth see **BOOM!** (1968).

GO-GETTER, THE 1923 d: Edward H. Griffith. USA., *The Go-Getter*, Peter B. Kyne, Short Story

Go-Getter, The see **THE GO GETTER** (1937).

GOHA 1958 d: Jacques Baratier. FRN/TNS., *Le Livre de Goha le Simple*, Georges Ades, Josipovici, Novel

GOING ALL THE WAY 1997 d: Mark Pellington. USA., *Going All the Way*, Dan Wakefield, Novel

Going Ape see **WHERE'S POPPA?** (1970).

GOING BANANAS 1987 d: Boaz Davidson. USA., *Kofiko*, Tamar Borenstein, Novel

GOING CROOKED 1926 d: George Melford. USA., *Going Crooked*, William Collier, Winchell Smith, New York 1926, Play

Going Down see **ABWARTS: DAS DUELL UBER DER TIEFE** (1984).

GOING GENTLY 1981 d: Stephen Frears. UKN., *Going Gently*, Robert C. S. Downs, Novel

GOING OF THE WHITE SWAN, THE 1914 d: Colin Campbell. USA., *The Going of the White Swan*, Gilbert Parker, Story

GOING PLACES 1939 d: Ray Enright. USA., *The Hottentot*, William Collier Sr., Victor Mapes, New York 1920, Play

GOING SOME 1920 d: Harry Beaumont. USA., *Going Some*, Paul Armstrong, Rex Beach, New York 1909, Play

Going Straight see **DICE OF DESTINY** (1920).

Going Straight see **TAKE A BOW BABY** (1934).

GOING THE LIMIT 1926 d: Chet Withey. USA., *He Stopped at Murder*, Arthur Ebenhack, Story

GOING UP 1923 d: Lloyd Ingraham. USA., *Going Up*, Otto Harbach, Louis A. Hirch, New York 1917, Play

GOING WILD 1930 d: William A. Seiter. USA., *The Aviator*, James Montgomery, New York 1910, Play

Gojja, Ili Tjazkij Put Poznanija see **GOYA** (1971).

GOLA DEL LUPO, LA 1923 d: Torello Rolli. ITL., *La Gueule du Loup*, Pierre Bilhaud, Maurice Hennequin, 1904, Play

GOLD 1974 d: Peter Hunt. UKN., *Goldmine*, Wilbur Smith, Novel

Gold and Lead see **L' OR ET LE PLOMB** (1966).

Gold and Silver World see **JIN YIN SHI JIE** (1939).

GOLD CURE, THE 1919 d: John H. Collins. USA., *Annice! Oh*, Alexine Heyland, 1918, Short Story

GOLD CURE, THE 1925 d: W. P. Kellino. UKN., *The Gold Cure*, Sara J. Duncan, Novel

Gold Diggers in Las Vegas see **PAINTING THE CLOUDS WITH SUNSHINE** (1951).

GOLD DIGGERS OF 1933 1933 d: Mervyn Leroy. USA., *The Gold Diggers of Broadway*, Avery Hopwood, New York 1919, Play

GOLD DIGGERS OF 1937 1936 d: Lloyd Bacon. USA., *Sweet Mystery of Life*, George Haight, Richard Maibaum, Michael Wallace, New York 1935, Play

GOLD DIGGERS OF BROADWAY 1929 d: Roy Del Ruth. USA., *The Gold Diggers of Broadway*, Avery Hopwood, New York 1919, Play

GOLD DIGGERS, THE 1923 d: Harry Beaumont. USA., *The Gold Diggers of Broadway*, Avery Hopwood, New York 1919, Play

Gold Dredgers, The see **THE HELL DIGGERS** (1921).

GOLD DUST GERTIE 1931 d: Lloyd Bacon. USA., *The Life of the Party*, Len D. Hollister, Play

Gold Dust Girl see **GOLD DUST GERTIE** (1931).

Gold Fever see **DUHUL AURULUI** (1974).

Gold Fish, A see **RYBAR Z ZLATA RYBKA** (1951).

GOLD HEELS 1924 d: W. S. Van Dyke. USA., *Checkers: a Hard Luck Story*, Henry Martyn Blossom, Chicago 1896, Novel

GOLD HUNTERS, THE 1925 d: Paul C. Hurst. USA., *The Gold Hunters*, James Oliver Curwood, Indianapolis 1909, Novel

GOLD IN NEW FRISCO 1939 d: Paul Verhoeven. GRM., *Gold in New Frisco*, R. Arden, Novel

GOLD IN THE STREETS 1997 d: Elizabeth Gill. UKN/IRL., *Away Alone*, Janet Noble, Play

GOLD IS WHERE YOU FIND IT 1938 d: Michael Curtiz. USA., *Gold Is Where You Find It*, Clements Ripley, East Norwalk, Ct. 1936, Novel

Gold Lure, The see **THE LONE STAR RUSH** (1915).

GOLD MADNESS 1923 d: Robert T. Thornby. USA., *The Man from Ten Strike*, James Oliver Curwood, Story

Gold of Naples see **L' ORO DI NAPOLI** (1954).

GOLD OF THE SEVEN SAINTS 1961 d: Gordon Douglas. USA., *Desert Guns*, Steve Frazee, New York 1957, Novel

Gold Robbers see **ESTOUFFADE A LA CARAIBE** (1966).

GOLD THAT GLITTERED, THE 1917 d: Thomas R. Mills. USA., *The Gold That Glittered*, O. Henry, Short Story

Gold Watch, The *see* AZ ARANYORA (1945).

GOLDEN ARROW, THE 1936 d: Alfred E. Green. USA., *The Golden Arrow*, Michael Arlen, 1935, Short Story

GOLDEN BED, THE 1925 d: Cecil B. de Mille. USA., *Tomorrow's Bread*, Wallace Irwin, 1924, Short Story

Golden Bird, The *see* LITTLE MISS HOOVER (1918).

GOLDEN BOY 1939 d: Rouben Mamoulian. USA., *Golden Boy*, Clifford Odets, New York 1937, Play

GOLDEN BRAID 1991 d: Paul Cox. ASL., *La Chevelure*, Guy de Maupassant, 1885, Short Story

GOLDEN CAGE, THE 1933 d: Ivar Campbell. UKN., *The Golden Cage*, Lady Trowbridge, Play

Golden Cage, The *see* ARANYSARKANY (1966).

GOLDEN CALF, THE 1930 d: Millard Webb. USA., *The Golden Calf*, Aaron Davis, 1926, Short Story

Golden Calf, The *see* ZOLOTOY TELYONOK (1968).

Golden Carriage, The *see* LE CARROSSE D'OR (1952).

Golden Catherine *see* ZLATA KATERINA (1934).

Golden Chains *see* GOUDEN KETENEN (1917).

GOLDEN CHANCE, THE 1913 d: Percy Nash. UKN., *The Golden Chance*, St. Aubin Miller, Play

Golden Child *see* BANGARU PAPA (1954).

Golden Coach, The *see* LE CARROSSE D'OR (1952).

GOLDEN COCOON, THE 1926 d: Millard Webb. USA., *The Golden Cocoon*, Ruth Cross, New York 1924, Novel

GOLDEN DAWN 1930 d: Ray Enright. USA., *Golden Dawn*, Oscar Hammerstein II, Otto Harbach, Emmerich Kalman, New York 1927, Musical Play

Golden Demon *see* KONJIKI YASHA (1954).

GOLDEN EARRINGS 1947 d: Mitchell Leisen. USA., *Golden Earrings*, Yolanda Foldes, Novel

GOLDEN FETTER, THE 1917 d: Edward J. Le Saint. USA., *The Golden Fetter*, Charles Tenney Jackson, Short Story

Golden Fish, The *see* RYBAR A ZLATA RYBKA (1951).

GOLDEN FLEECE, THE 1918 d: G. P. Hamilton. USA., *Golden Fleece*, Frederick Irving Anderson, 1918, Short Story

GOLDEN GALLOWS, THE 1922 d: Paul Scardon. USA., *The Golden Gallows*, Victoria Galland, 1921, Short Story

Golden Gate, The *see* FOG OVER FRISCO (1934).

Golden Gift, The *see* THE DANGEROUS TALENT (1920).

Golden Girl *see* GOLDENGIRL (1979).

Golden Glasses, The *see* GLI OCCHIALI D'ORO (1987).

Golden Goat, The *see* LA CHEVRE D'OR (1942).

Golden Goddess, The *see* THE SUNSET PRINCESS (1918).

Golden Goose, The *see* DIE GOLDENE GANS (1953).

Golden Goose, The *see* DIE GOLDENE GANS (1964).

GOLDEN HAWK, THE 1952 d: Sidney Salkow. USA., *The Golden Hawk*, Frank Yerby, 1948, Novel

GOLDEN HONEYMOON, THE 1977 d: Noel Black. USA., *The Golden Honeymoon*, Ring Lardner, 1929, Short Story

GOLDEN IDIOT, THE 1917 d: Arthur Berthelet. USA., *The Golden Idiot*, Robert Rudd Whiting, 1916, Novel

Golden Katherine *see* ZLATA KATERINA (1934).

Golden Key *see* ZOLOTOI KLYUCHIK (1939).

Golden Kite, The *see* ARANYSARKANY (1966).

Golden Legends *see* CHASING YESTERDAY (1935).

Golden Man *see* ARANYEMBER (1917).

Golden Man, The *see* ZLATY CLOVEK (1939).

GOLDEN PINCE-NEZ, THE 1922 d: George Ridgwell. UKN., *The Golden Pince-Nez*, Arthur Conan Doyle, Short Story

GOLDEN POMEGRANATES, THE 1924 d: Fred Paul. UKN., *The Golden Pomegranates*, Sax Rohmer, Short Story

GOLDEN PRINCESS, THE 1925 d: Clarence Badger. USA., *Tennessee's Partner*, Bret Harte, 1869, Short Story

GOLDEN SALAMANDER, THE 1950 d: Ronald Neame. UKN., *Golden Salamander*, Victor Canning, Novel

GOLDEN SEAL, THE 1983 d: Frank ZunigA. USA., *A River Ran Out of Eden*, James Vance Marshall, Novel

GOLDEN SNARE, THE 1921 d: David M. Hartford. USA., *The Golden Snare*, James Oliver Curwood, New York 1921, Novel

GOLDEN STRAIN, THE 1925 d: Victor Schertzinger. USA., *Thoroughbreds*, Peter B. Kyne, 1925, Short Story

GOLDEN SUPPER, THE 1910 d: D. W. Griffith. USA., *Lover's Tale*, Alfred Tennyson, Poem

Golden Trail, The *see* THE RIDERS OF THE WHISTLING SKULL (1937).

Golden Virgin, The *see* THE STORY OF ESTHER COSTELLO (1957).

GOLDEN WEB, THE 1920 d: Geoffrey H. Malins. UKN., *The Golden Web*, E. Phillips Oppenheim, Boston 1910, Novel

GOLDEN WEB, THE 1926 d: Walter Lang. USA., *The Golden Web*, E. Phillips Oppenheim, Boston 1910, Novel

GOLDEN WEST, THE 1932 d: David Howard. USA., *The Last Trail*, Zane Grey, New York 1909, Novel

GOLDEN YEARS, THE 1992 d: Paul Bryers. UKN., *The Golden Years*, Arthur Miller, Play

Golden Youth *see* JUST SUPPOSE (1926).

GOLDENE ABGRUND, DER 1927 d: Mario Bonnard. GRM/FRN., *Rapa-Nui*, Andre Armandy, Novel

GOLDENE BETT, DAS 1913 d: Walter Schmidthassler. GRM., *Das Goldene Bett*, Olga Wohlbruck, Novel

GOLDENE FESSEL, DIE 1944 d: Hans Thimig. GRM., *Der Zerrissene*, Johann Nestroy, 1845, Play

GOLDENE GANS, DIE 1953 d: Walter Oehmichen. GRM., *Die Goldene Gans*, Jacob Grimm, Wilhelm Grimm, 1812, Short Story

GOLDENE GANS, DIE 1964 d: Siegfried Hartmann. GDR., *Die Goldene Gans*, Jacob Grimm, Wilhelm Grimm, 1812, Short Story

GOLDENE STADT, DIE 1942 d: Veit Harlan. GRM., *Der Gigant*, Richard Billinger, Play

GOLDENGIRL 1979 d: Joseph Sargent. USA., *Goldengirl*, Peter Lear, Novel

GOLDENROD 1977 d: Harvey Hart. CND/USA., *Goldenrod*, Herbert Harker, Novel

GOLDFINGER 1964 d: Guy Hamilton. UKN., *Goldfinger*, Ian Fleming, London 1959, Novel

GOLDFISH, THE 1924 d: Jerome Storm. USA., *The Goldfish*, Gladys Unger, New York 1922, Play

Goldie *see* GOLDIE GETS ALONG (1933).

GOLDIE GETS ALONG 1933 d: Malcolm St. Clair. USA., *Goldie Gets Along*, Hawthorne Hurst, New York 1931, Novel

Gold-Rimmed Glasses, The *see* GLI OCCHIALI D'ORO (1987).

Gold's Ghost *see* DUHUL AURULUI (1974).

Goldseekers of Arkansas *see* DIE GOLDSUCHER VON ARKANSAS (1964).

GOLDSTEIN 1965 d: Philip Kaufman, Benjamin Manaster. USA., Martin Buber, Short Story

GOLDSUCHER VON ARKANSAS, DIE 1964 d: Paul Martin, Alberto Cardone. GRM/ITL/FRN., *Regulatoren von Arkansas*, Friedrich Gerstackers, Novel

Golem *see* LE GOLEM (1935).

GOLEM 1979 d: Piotr Szulkin. PLN., *Der Golem*, Gustav Meyrink, 1915, Novel

GOLEM BEMA'AGAL 1993 d: Aner Preminger. ISR., Lily Perry Amitai, Book

GOLEM, LE 1935 d: Julien Duvivier. FRN/CZC., *Der Golem*, Gustav Meyrink, 1915, Novel

Golem, The *see* LE GOLEM (1935).

GOLEMANOV 1958 d: Kiril Ilinchev. BUL., *Golemanov*, Stefan Kostov, 1928, Play

Golondrinas Y Gaviotas *see* POR UN MILAGRO DE AMOR (1928).

GOLOWIN GEHT DURCH DIE STADT 1940 d: R. A. Stemmle. GRM., *Golowin Geht Durch Die Stadt*, Hugo Maria Kritz, Novel

GOLVEN 1982 d: Annette Apon. NTH., *The Waves*, Virginia Woolf, 1931, Novel

GOMMES, LES 1969 d: Lucien Deroisy. BLG/FRN., *Les Gommes*, Alain Robbe-Grillet, 1953, Novel

GONDOLA DELLE CHIMERE, LA 1936 d: Augusto GeninA. ITL/FRN., *La Gondole aux Chimeres*, Maurice Dekobra, Novel

Gondole aux Chimeres, La *see* LA GONDOLA DELLE CHIMERE (1936).

GONE ARE THE DAYS! 1963 d: Nicholas Webster. USA., *Purlie Victorious*, Ossie Davis, New York 1961, Play

GONE DU CHAABA, LE 1998 d: Christophe RuggiA. FRN., *Le Gone du Chaaba*, Azouz Begag, Novel

GONE IN THE NIGHT 1996 d: B. W. L. Norton. USA., *Gone in the Night*, David Protess, Rob Warden, Book

GONE TO EARTH 1950 d: Michael Powell, Emeric Pressburger. UKN., *Gone to Earth*, Mary Webb, 1917, Novel

Gone to the Dogs *see* THE GYPSY TRAIL (1915).

GONE WITH THE WIND 1939 d: Victor Fleming, Sam Wood (Uncredited). USA., *Gone With the Wind*, Margaret Mitchell, New York 1936, Novel

GONG CRIED MURDER, THE 1946 d: Ronald Haines. UKN., *The Gong Cried Murder*, John Dickson Carr, Short Story

Gonza, the Spearman *see* YARI NO GONZA (1985).

GONZAGUE 1916. FRN., *Gonzague*, Pierre Veber, Play

Good Age, The *see* LE BEL AGE (1958).

GOOD AND NAUGHTY 1926 d: Malcolm St. Clair. USA., *Pouche*, Henri Falk, Rene Peter, Paris 1923, Play

GOOD AS GOLD 1927 d: Scott R. Dunlap. USA., *The Owner of the Aztec*, Murray Leinster, 1926, Short Story

Good Bad Girl, The *see* INEZ FROM HOLLYWOOD (1924).

GOOD BAD GIRL, THE 1931 d: R. William Neill. USA., *The Good Bad Girl*, Winifred Van Duzer, New York 1926, Novel

Good Bad Man, A *see* DANGEROUS LOVE (1920).

Good Bad Man, The *see* PLOKHOY KHOROSHYI CHELOVEK (1974).

GOOD COMPANIONS, THE 1933 d: Victor Saville. UKN., *The Good Companions*, J. B. Priestley, 1929, Novel

GOOD COMPANIONS, THE 1957 d: J. Lee Thompson. UKN., *The Good Companions*, J. B. Priestley, 1929, Novel

GOOD COMPANIONS, THE 1980 d: Bill Hays. UKN., *The Good Companions*, J. B. Priestley, 1929, Novel

GOOD COUNTRY PEOPLE 1955 d: Flannery O'Connor. USA., *Good Country People*, Flannery O'Connor, 1955, Short Story

GOOD DAY FOR A HANGING 1958 d: Nathan Juran. USA., *The Reluctant Hangman*, Jo Carpenter, Story

Good Days Lost, The *see* LOS BUENOS DIAS PERDIDOS (1975).

Good Demon, The *see* ZENMA (1951).

GOOD DIE YOUNG, THE 1954 d: Lewis Gilbert. UKN., *The Good Die Young*, Richard Macauley, Novel

GOOD EARTH, THE 1937 d: Sidney A. Franklin, Victor (#u/C#) Fleming. USA., *The Good Earth*, Pearl Buck, New York 1931, Novel

GOOD FAIRY, THE 1935 d: William Wyler. USA., *A Jo Tunder*, Ferenc Molnar, Budapest 1931, Play

Good Fairy, The *see* ZENMA (1951).

GOOD FAIRY, THE 1956 d: George Schaefer. USA., *A Jo Tunder*, Ferenc Molnar, Budapest 1931, Play

GOOD FATHER, THE 1986 d: Mike Newell. UKN., *The Good Father*, Peter Prince, Novel

GOOD FELLOWS, THE 1943 d: Jo Graham. USA., *The Good Fellow*, George S. Kaufman, Herman J. Mankiewicz, New York 1926, Play

Good Fer Nothin', The *see* GLENGARRY SCHOOL DAYS (1923).

Good Fortune from Ohio *see* GLUCK AUS OHIO (1951).

Good Gracious Annabelle! *see* ANNABELLE GOOD GRACIOUS (1919).

Good Gracious Annabelle *see* ANNABELLE'S AFFAIRS (1931).

GOOD GRACIOUS, ANNABELLE 1919 d: George Melford. USA., *Good Gracious Annabelle*, Clare Kummer, New York 1916, Play

Good Guys Always Win, The *see* THE OUTFIT (1973).

GOOD GUYS WEAR BLACK 1978 d: Ted Post. USA., Joseph Fraley, Story

Good Hope, The *see* OP HOOP VAN ZEGEN (1918).

Good Hope, The *see* DIE FAHRT INS VERDERBEN (1924).

Good Hope, The *see* OP HOOP VAN ZEGEN (1934).

Good Hope, The *see* OP HOOP VAN ZEGEN (1986).

GOOD HUMOR MAN, THE 1950 d: Lloyd Bacon. USA., *Appointment With Fear*, Roy Huggins, Story

Good Intentions see HOLD THAT BLONDE! (1945).

GOOD LITTLE DEVIL, A 1914 d: Edwin S. Porter, J. Searle Dawley. USA., *Un Bon Petit Diable*, Rosemond Gerard, Maurice Rostand, Paris 1911, Play

Good Looking and Rich see EASY MILLIONS (1933).

Good Luck see THE SPORTING LOVER (1926).

GOOD LUCK, MISS WYCKOFF 1979 d: Marvin J. Chomsky. USA., *Good Luck Miss Wyckoff*, William Inge, 1970, Novel

GOOD MORNING, MISS DOVE 1955 d: Henry Koster. USA., *Good Morning Miss Dove*, Frances Gray Patton, 1954, Novel

GOOD MOTHER, THE 1988 d: Leonard Nimoy. USA., *The Good Mother*, Sue Miller, Novel

GOOD NEIGHBOR SAM 1964 d: David Swift. USA., *Good Neighbor Sam*, Jack Finney, New York 1963, Novel

GOOD NEWS 1930 d: Nick Grinde, Edgar J. MacGregor. USA., *Good News*, Lew Brown, Frank Mandel, Lawrence Schwab, New York 1927, Musical Play

GOOD NEWS 1947 d: Charles Walters. USA., *Good News*, Lew Brown, Frank Mandel, Lawrence Schwab, New York 1927, Musical Play

Good Night, Mary see DIE GESTORTE HOCHZEITSNACHT (1950).

Good Old School Days see THOSE WERE THE DAYS! (1940).

Good Old Siwash see THOSE WERE THE DAYS! (1940).

GOOD OLD SOAK, THE 1937 d: J. Walter Ruben. USA., *The Old Soak*, Don Marquis, New York 1922, Play

Good People's Sunday see LA DOMENICA DELLA BUONA GENTE (1954).

GOOD PROVIDER, THE 1922 d: Frank Borzage. USA., *The Good Provider*, Fannie Hurst, 1914, Short Story

GOOD REFERENCES 1920 d: R. William Neill. USA., *Good References*, E. J. Rath, London 1920, Novel

Good Soldier Schweik see DOBRY VOJAK SVEJK (1926).

Good Soldier Schweik, The see DOBRY VOJAK SVEJK (1931).

Good Soldier Schweik, The see NOVIYE POKHOZDENIYA SHVEIKA (1943).

Good Soldier Schweik, The see DER BRAVE SOLDAT SCHWEJK (1960).

Good Soldier Svejk, The see DOBRY VOJAK SVEJK (1926).

Good Thief, The see IL LADRONE (1979).

Good Thing, A see FROM HELL TO HEAVEN (1933).

GOOD TIME GIRL 1948 d: David MacDonald. UKN., *Night Darkens the Street*, Arthur la Bern, Novel

Good Will and Almond Shells see THE SHELL GAME (1918).

GOOD-BAD WIFE, THE 1920 d: Vera McCord. USA., *The Wild Fawn*, Mary Imlay Taylor, 1920, Short Story

GOOD-BY GIRLS! 1923 d: Jerome Storm. USA., *McPhee's Sensational Rest*, George Foxhall, 1917, Short Story

GOODBYE 1918 d: Maurice Elvey. UKN., *Goodbye*, John Strange Winter, Novel

GOODBYE & AMEN 1978 d: Damiano Damiani. ITL., *The Grosvenor Square Goodbye*, Francis Clifford, 1974, Novel

GOODBYE AGAIN 1933 d: Michael Curtiz. USA., *Goodbye Again*, George Haight, Allan Scott, New York 1932, Play

GOODBYE AGAIN 1961 d: Anatole Litvak. USA/FRN., *Aimez-Vous Brahms?*, Francoise Sagan, Paris 1959, Novel

Goodbye and Amen see GOODBYE & AMEN (1978).

GOODBYE BROADWAY 1938 d: Ray McCarey. USA., *The Shannons of Broadway*, James Gleason, New York 1927, Play

GOODBYE CHARLIE 1964 d: Vincente Minnelli. USA., *Goodbye Charlie*, George Axelrod, New York 1960, Play

GOODBYE, COLUMBUS 1969 d: Larry Peerce. USA., *Goodbye Columbus*, Philip Roth, Boston 1959, Novel

GOODBYE GEMINI 1970 d: Alan Gibson. UKN., *Ask Agamemnon*, Jenni Hall, London 1964, Novel

Goodbye, Lamb see CORDERA ADIOS (1966).

Goodbye Moscow see SARABA MOSUKUWA GURENTAI (1968).

GOODBYE, MR. CHIPS 1939 d: Sam Wood. UKN/USA., *Goodbye Mr. Chips*, James Hilton, 1934, Novel

GOODBYE, MR. CHIPS 1969 d: Herbert Ross. UKN., *Goodbye Mr. Chips*, James Hilton, 1934, Novel

GOODBYE, MR. CHIPS 1984 d: Gareth Davies. UKN., *Goodbye Mr. Chips*, James Hilton, 1934, Novel

GOODBYE, MY FANCY 1951 d: Vincent Sherman. USA., *Goodbye My Fancy*, Fay Kanin, New York 1949, Play

GOODBYE, MY LADY 1956 d: William A. Wellman. USA., *Goodbye My Lady*, James H. Street, 1954, Novel

GOODBYE PEOPLE, THE 1984 d: Herb Gardner. USA., *The Goodbye People*, Herb Gardner, Play

Goodbye to the Hill see PADDY (1969).

GOODFELLAS 1990 d: Martin Scorsese. USA., *Wiseguy*, Nicholas Pileggi, Novel

Good-for-Nothin', The see GLENGARRY SCHOOL DAYS (1923).

Good-for-Nothing, The see TAUGENICHTS (1978).

Good-for-Nothings, The see TAUGENICHTS (1978).

Goodheart see THE FAITH HEALER (1921).

GOODNIGHT MISTER TOM 1998 d: Jack Gold. UKN., *Goodnight Mister Tom*, Michelle Magorian, Novel

GOODNIGHT VIENNA 1932 d: Herbert Wilcox. UKN., Holt Marvel, George Posford, Radio Play

GOONIES, THE 1985 d: Richard Donner. USA., Steven Spielberg, Story

Goose Boy, The see LUDAS MATYI (1949).

GOOSE GIRL, THE 1915 d: Frederick A. Thompson. USA., *The Goose Girl*, Harold MacGrath, New York 1909, Novel

Goose Girl, The see DIE GANSEMAGD (1958).

GOOSE HANGS HIGH, THE 1925 d: James Cruze. USA., *The Goose Hangs High*, Lewis Beach, New York 1924, Play

Goose Hangs High, The see THIS RECKLESS AGE (1932).

Goose of Sedan, The see DIE GANS VON SEDAN (1959).

GOOSE WOMAN, THE 1925 d: Clarence Brown. USA., *The Goose Woman*, Rex Beach, 1925, Short Story

Goose Woman, The see THE PAST OF MARY HOLMES (1933).

GOR 1987 d: Fritz Kiersch. ITL/USA., *Tarnsman of Gor*, John Norman, Novel

GORACZKA 1980 d: Agnieszka Holland. PLN., *Dzieje Jednogo Pocisku*, Andrzej Strug, 1910, Novel

GORBALS STORY, THE 1950 d: David MacKane. UKN., *The Gorbals Story*, Robert McLeish, Play

Gordeyev Family, The see FOMA GORDEEV (1959).

GORDIAN, DER TYRANN 1937 d: Fred Sauer. GRM., *Der Tyrann Gordian*, Rudolf Greinz, Novel

GORECHTO PLADNE 1965 d: Zako HeskiyA. BUL., *Goreshto Pladne*, Yordan Radichkov, 1965, Short Story

Gorescho Pladne see GORECHTO PLADNE (1965).

Goreshto Pladne see GORECHTO PLADNE (1965).

Gorgeous Bird Like Me, A see UNE BELLE FILLE COMME MOI (1972).

GORGEOUS HUSSY, THE 1936 d: Clarence Brown. USA., *The Gorgeous Hussy*, Samuel Hopkins Adams, Boston 1934, Novel

GORGONA, LA 1915 d: Mario Caserini. ITL., *La Gorgona*, Sem Benelli, 1913, Play

GORGONA, LA 1942 d: Guido Brignone. ITL., *La Gorgona*, Sem Benelli, 1913, Play

GORIACHEE SERDTSE 1953 d: Gennadi Kazansky. USS., *Goriachee Serdtse*, Alexander Ostrovsky, 1869, Play

Gorilla Greets You, The see LE GORILLE VOUS SALUE BIEN (1957).

Gorilla of Soho, The see DER GORILLA VON SOHO (1968).

Gorilla Salutes You, The see LE GORILLE VOUS SALUE BIEN (1957).

Gorilla Strikes, The see THE APE MAN (1943).

GORILLA, THE 1927 d: Alfred Santell. USA., *The Gorilla*, Ralph Spence, New York 1925, Play

GORILLA, THE 1930 d: Bryan Foy. USA., *The Gorilla*, Ralph Spence, New York 1925, Play

GORILLA, THE 1939 d: Allan Dwan. USA., *The Gorilla*, Ralph Spence, New York 1925, Play

GORILLA VON SOHO, DER 1968 d: Alfred Vohrer. GRM., Edgar Wallace, Novel

GORILLAS IN THE MIST 1988 d: Michael Apted. USA., Dian Fossey, Harold T. P. Hayes, Article

GORILLE A MORDU L'ARCHEVEQUE, LE 1962 d: Maurice Labro. FRN., *Le Gorille a Mordu l'Archeveque*, Antoine Dominique, Novel

GORILLE VOUS SALUE BIEN, LE 1957 d: Bernard Borderie. FRN., *Le Gorille Vous Salue Bien*, Antoine Dominique, Novel

GORKY PARK 1983 d: Michael Apted. USA., *Gorky Park*, Martin Cruz Smith, Novel

Gorky's Childhood see DETSTVO GORKOVO (1938).

GORODA I GODY 1930 d: Yevgeni Chervyakov. USS., *Goroda I Gody*, Konstantin Fedin, 1924, Novel

GORODA I GODY 1973 d: Alexander Zarkhi. USS/GDR., *Goroda I Gody*, Konstantin Fedin, 1924, Novel

Gory Creatures, The see TERROR IS A MAN (1959).

GOSPODA MINISTARKA 1958 d: Zorz Skrigin. YGS., *Gospoda Ministarka*, Branislav Nusic, 1929, Play

Gospodica see GOSPODJICA (1980).

GOSPODJICA 1980 d: Vojtech Jasny. YGS/GRM., *Gospodica*, Ivo Andric, 1945, Novel

GOSSE DE LA BUTTE, UN 1964 d: Maurice Delbez. FRN., *Alain Et le Negre*, Robert Sabatier, Novel

GOSSES DANS LES RUINES, LES 1918 d: George Pearson. FRN., *Les Gosses Dans Les Ruines*, Paul Grex, Paul Gsell, M. Poulbot, Play

Gosses de Misere see BAGNES D'ENFANTS (1933).

GOSSES MENENT L'ENQUETE, LES 1946 d: Maurice Labro. FRN., *Les Gosses Menent l'Enquete*, Francis Didelot, Novel

GOSSETTE 1922 d: Germaine Dulac. FRN., *Gossette*, Charles Vayre, Novel

GOSSIP 1923 d: King Baggot. USA., *Gossip*, Edith Barnard Delano, Story

GOSSIP FROM THE FOREST 1979 d: Brian Gibson. UKN., *Gossip from the Forest*, Thomas Keneally, Novel

Gossip from the Front see GOSSIP FROM THE FOREST (1979).

GOSTA BERLINGS SAGA 1924 d: Mauritz Stiller. SWD., *Gosta Berlings Saga*, Selma Lagerlof, Novel

GOTT SCHUTZT DIE LIEBENDEN 1973 d: Alfred Vohrer. GRM/SPN/ITL., *Gott Schutzt Die Liebenden*, Johannes Mario Simmel, Novel

GOTTES ENGEL SIND UBERBALL 1948 d: Hans Thimig. AUS., *Anderthalb Weidinger*, Peter Francke, Novel

GOTTES MUHLEN, DIE 1938 d: Josef Medeotti-Bohac. GRM/CZC., *Bozi Mlyny*, Jan Vrba, Novel

Gottes Muhlen Mahlen Langsam see DIE GOTTES MUHLEN (1938).

Gottesmuhlen see STEIBRUCH (1942).

GOTZ VON BERLICHINGEN 1955 d: Alfred Stoger, Josef Gielen. GRM., *Gotz von Berlichingen Mit Der Eisernen Hand*, Johann Wolfgang von Goethe, 1773, Play

Gotz von Berlichingen see GOTZ VON BERLICHINGEN MIT DER EISERNEN HAND (1978).

GOTZ VON BERLICHINGEN MIT DER EISERNEN HAND 1978 d: Wolfgang Liebeneiner. GRM/YGS., *Gotz von Berlichingen Mit Der Eisernen Hand*, Johann Wolfgang von Goethe, 1773, Play

GOTZ VON BERLICHINGEN ZUBENANNT MIT DER EISERNEN HAND 1925 d: Hubert Moest. GRM., *Gotz von Berlichingen Mit Der Eisernen Hand*, Johann Wolfgang von Goethe, 1773, Play

GOUALEUSE, LA 1914 d: Georges Monca, Alexandre Devarennes. FRN., *La Goualeuse*, Ludovic Halevy, Georges Maret, Play

GOUALEUSE, LA 1938 d: Fernand Rivers. FRN., *La Goualeuse*, Ludovic Halevy, Georges Maret, Play

Goubbiah see GOUBBIAH MON AMOUR (1956).

GOUBBIAH MON AMOUR 1956 d: Robert Darene. FRN/ITL., *Goubbiah*, Jean Martet, Novel

GOUDEN KETENEN 1917 d: Maurits H. Binger. NTH., *Gouden Ketenen*, Princess Elsa, Novel

GOUDVISCHJE, HET 1919 d: Maurits H. Binger. NTH., *Het Goudvischje*, Willem Gerard Van Nouhuys, 1893, Play

GOUPI MAINS-ROUGES 1942 d: Jacques Becker. FRN., *Goupi Mains-Rouges*, Pierre Very, Novel

Gout du Massacre, Le see MADEMOISELLE ET SON GANG (1956).

GOUVERNEUR, DER 1939 d: Victor Tourjansky. GRM., *Die Fahne*, Otto Emmerich Groh, Play

Government Inspector see REVIZOR (1933).

GOVERNOR'S BOSS, THE 1915 d: Charles E. Davenport. USA., *The Governor's Boss*, James S. Barcus, New York 1914, Novel

GOVERNOR'S LADY, THE 1915 d: George Melford. USA., *The Governor's Lady*, Alice Bradley, New York 1912, Play

GOVERNOR'S LADY, THE 1923 d: Harry Millarde. USA., *The Governor's Lady*, Alice Bradley, New York 1912, Novel

Governor's Wife, The *see* **THE NOOSE** (1928).

GOWN OF DESTINY, THE 1918 d: Lynn Reynolds. USA., *Each According to His Gifts*, Earl Derr Biggers, Short Story

GOYA 1971 d: Konrad Wolf. GDR/USS/BUL., *Goya; Oder Der Arge Weg Der Erkenntnis*, Lion Feuchtwanger, 1951, Novel

Goya Oder Der Arge Weg Zur Erkenntnis *see* **GOYA** (1971).

Goya, Or the Road to Awareness *see* **GOYA** (1971).

GOYA QUE VUELVE 1927 d: Modesto Alonso. SPN., *Goya Que Vuelve*, Antonio Garcia Guzman, Novel

Grabmal Einer Groszen Liebe, Das *see* **SHIRAZ** (1928).

Grace, La *see* **LA GUEULE DE L'AUTRE** (1979).

Grace Moore Story, The *see* **SO THIS IS LOVE** (1953).

GRACIE ALLEN MURDER CASE, THE 1939 d: Alfred E. Green. USA., *The Gracie Allen Murder Case*, S. S. Van Dine, New York 1938, Novel

GRACIELA 1956 d: Leopoldo Torre-Nilsson. ARG., *Nada*, Carmen Laforet Diaz, 1945, Novel

GRADIVA 1970 d: Giorgio Albertazzi. ITL., Wilhelm Jensen, Story

GRADUATE, THE 1967 d: Mike Nichols. USA., *The Graduate*, Charles Webb, New York 1963, Novel

Graf Kostja *see* **LE COMTE KOSTIA** (1924).

GRAF VON LUXEMBURG, DER 1957 d: Werner Jacobs. GRM., *Der Graf von Luxembourg*, Franz Lehar, Vienna 1909, Operetta

GRAFIN MARIZA 1925 d: Hans Steinhoff. GRM., *Grafin Maritza*, Julius Brammer, Emmerich Kalman, Vienna 1924, Operetta

GRAFIN MARIZA 1932 d: Richard Oswald. GRM., *Grafin Maritza*, Julius Brammer, Emmerich Kalman, Vienna 1924, Operetta

GRAFIN MARIZA 1958 d: Rudolf Schundler. GRM., *Grafin Maritza*, Julius Brammer, Emmerich Kalman, Vienna 1924, Operetta

GRAFIN VON MONTE CHRISTO, DIE 1932 d: Karl Hartl. GRM., *Le Comte de Monte-Cristo*, Alexandre Dumas (pere), Paris 1845, Novel

Graham Murders, The *see* **BAD BLOOD** (1980).

GRAIL, THE 1923 d: Colin Campbell. USA., *The Grail*, George Scarborough, Play

GRAIN OF DUST, A 1915 d: Lloyd B. Carleton. USA., *The Grain of Dust*, David Graham Phillips, New York 1911, Novel

Grain of Dust, A *see* **THE GRAIN OF DUST** (1918).

GRAIN OF DUST, THE 1918 d: Harry Revier. USA., *The Grain of Dust*, David Graham Phillips, New York 1911, Novel

GRAIN OF DUST, THE 1928 d: George Archainbaud. USA., *The Grain of Dust*, David Graham Phillips, New York 1911, Novel

GRAINE AU VENT 1928 d: Maurice Keroul, Jacques Mills. FRN., *Graine Au Vent*, Lucie Delarue-Mardrus, Novel

GRAINE AU VENT 1943 d: Maurice Gleize. FRN., *Graine Au Vent*, Lucie Delarue-Mardrus, Novel

GRAMADA 1936 d: Alexander Vazov. BUL., *Gramada*, Ivan Vazov, 1880, Verse

GRAMBLING'S WHITE TIGER 1981 d: Georg Stanford Brown. USA., *My Little Brother Is Coming Tomorrow*, Bruce Behrenberg, Book

Gramigna's Lover *see* **L' AMANTE DI GRAMIGNA** (1968).

Gramina's Lover *see* **L' AMANTE DI GRAMIGNA** (1968).

GRAN GALEOTO, EL 1951 d: Rafael Gil. SPN., *El Gran Galeoto*, Jose Echegaray, Madrid 1881, Play

Gran Vita, La *see* **DAS KUNSTSEIDENE MADCHEN** (1960).

GRANATOVYY BRASLET 1965 d: Abram Room. USS., *Granatovyy Braslet*, Aleksander Ivanovich Kuprin, 1911, Short Story

GRAND BABYLON HOTEL, THE 1916 d: Frank Wilson. UKN., *The Grand Babylon Hotel*, Arnold Bennett, Novel

GRAND BLUFF, LE 1933 d: Maurice Champreux. FRN., *Le Grand Bluff*, Fred Heller, Adolf Schutz, Play

GRAND CANARY 1934 d: Irving Cummings. USA., *The Grand Canary*, A. J. Cronin, London 1933, Novel

GRAND CENTRAL MURDER 1942 d: S. Sylvan Simon. USA., *Grand Central Murder*, Sue McVeigh, Novel

GRAND CEREMONIAL, LE 1968 d: Pierre-Alain Jolivet. FRN., *Le Grand Ceremonial*, Fernando Arrabal, 1965, Play

GRAND CIRQUE, LE 1949 d: Georges Peclet. FRN., *Le Grand Cirque*, Pierre Clostermann

GRAND CRI D'AMOUR, UN 1998 d: Josiane Balasko. FRN., *Un Grand Cri d'Amour*, Josiane Balasko, Play

GRAND DADAIS, LE 1967 d: Pierre Granier-Deferre. FRN/GRM., *Le Grand Dadais*, Bertrand Poirot-Delpech, Novel

GRAND DUCHESS AND THE WAITER, THE 1926 d: Malcolm St. Clair. USA., *La Grande-Duchesse Et le Garcon d'Etage*, Alfred Savoir, Paris 1924, Play

Grand Duke and Mr. Pimm, The *see* **LOVE IS A BALL** (1962).

Grand Duke's Finances, The *see* **DIE FINANZEN DES GROSSHERZOGS** (1924).

Grand Duke's Finances, The *see* **DIE FINANZEN DES GROSSHERZOGS** (1934).

Grand Envolee, La *see* **CHIGNOLE** (1917).

GRAND ESCOGRIFFE, LE 1976 d: Claude Pinoteau. FRN/ITL., *Le Grand Escogriffe*, Rennie Airth, Novel

GRAND FRERE, LE 1982 d: Francis Girod. FRN., *Le Grand Frere*, Sam Ross, Novel

Grand Gosse *see* **BOY** (1925).

GRAND HOTEL 1932 d: Edmund Goulding. USA., *Menschen Im Hotel*, Vicki Baum, Berlin 1929, Novel

Grand Hotel *see* **MENSCHEN IM HOTEL** (1959).

GRAND HOTEL DES PALMES 1979 d: Meme Perlini. ITL., *Atti Relativi Alla Morte Di Raymond Roussel*, Leonardo Sciascia, Novel

Grand Illusion *see* **SUURI ILLUSIONI** (1986).

GRAND ISLE 1991 d: Mary Lambert. USA., *The Awakening*, Kate Chopin, 1899, Novel

GRAND LARCENY 1922 d: Wallace Worsley. USA., *Grand Larceny*, Albert Payson Terhune, 1920, Short Story

GRAND MEAULNES, LE 1967 d: Jean-Gabriel Albicocco. FRN., *Le Grand Meaulnes*, Alain Fournier, 1913, Novel

GRAND NATIONAL NIGHT 1953 d: Bob McNaught. UKN., *Grand National Night*, Campbell Christie, Dorothy Christie, London 1946, Play

GRAND PASSION, THE 1918 d: Ida May Park. USA., *The Boss of Powderville*, Thomas Addison, 1916, Short Story

Grand Reve, Le *see* **ALTITUDE 3200** (1938).

GRAND SABORDAGE, LE 1972 d: Alain Perisson. CND/FRN., *Le Nez Qui Vogue*, Rejean Ducharme, Novel

GRAND SLAM 1933 d: William Dieterle. USA., *Grand Slam; the Rise and Fall of a Bridge Wizard*, Benjamin Russell Herts, New York 1932, Novel

GRANDE AMIE, LA 1926 d: Max de Rieux. FRN., *La Grande Amie*, Pierre L'Ermite, Novel

Grande Angoisse, La *see* **LES VACANCES DE XAVIER** (1933).

GRANDE BRETECHE, LA 1909 d: Andre Calmettes. FRN., *La Grande Breteche Ou Les Trois Vengeances*, Honore de Balzac, 1837, Novel

GRANDE ENVOLEE, LA 1927 d: Rene Plaissetty. FRN., *Chignole*, Marcel Nadaud, Novel

GRANDE EPREUVE, LA 1927 d: Alexandre Ryder, A. Duges. FRN., *La Grande Epreuve*, Georges le Faure, Novel

Grande Fauche, La *see* **TRY THIS ONE FOR SIZE** (1989).

GRANDE FILLE TOUTE SIMPLE, UNE 1947 d: Jacques Manuel. FRN., *Une Grande Fille Toute Simple*, Andre Roussin, 1943, Play

GRANDE MAGUET, LA 1947 d: Roger Richebe. FRN., *Grande-Maguet*, Catulle Mendes, 1888, Novel

GRANDE MARE, LA 1930 d: Jacques Bataille-Henri, Hobart Henley. USA., *The Big Pond*, George Middleton, A. E. Thomas, New York 1928, Play

GRANDE MARNIERA, LA 1920 d: Gero Zambuto. ITL., *La Grande Marniere*, Georges Ohnet, 1888, Novel

GRANDE MARNIERE, LA 1913 d: Henri Pouctal. FRN., *La Grande Marniere*, Georges Ohnet, 1888, Novel

GRANDE MARNIERE, LA 1943 d: Jean de Marguenat. FRN., *La Grande Marniere*, Georges Ohnet, 1888, Novel

GRANDE MENTECAPTO, O 1989 d: Oswaldo CaldeirA. BRZ., *O Grande Mentecapto*, Fernando Tavares Sabino, 1979, Novel

GRANDE MEUTE, LA 1944 d: Jean de Limur. FRN., *La Grande Meute*, Paul Vialar, Novel

Grande Passion, La *see* **LIBERTE** (1937).

Grande Releve, La *see* **LA BANDERA** (1935).

Grande Ribelle, Il *see* **MATHIAS SANDORF** (1962).

GRANDE RINUNCIA, LA 1951 d: Aldo Vergano. ITL., *Suor Teresa*, Luigi Camoletti, Play

GRANDE SERTAO 1964 d: Geraldo Santos Pereira, Renato Santos PereirA. BRZ., *Grande Sertao: Veredas*, Guimaraes Rosa, 1956, Novel

GRANDE STRADA AZZURRA, LA 1957 d: Gillo Pontecorvo. ITL/YGS/GRM., *Squarcio*, Franco Solinas, Novel

GRANDE VEDETTE, LA 1917 d: Edouard-Emile Violet. FRN., *La Grande Vedette*, Rene Peter, M. Vaucaire, Play

Grande Vie, La *see* **DAS KUNSTSEIDENE MADCHEN** (1960).

GRANDES FAMILLES, LES 1959 d: Denys de La Patelliere. FRN., *Les Grandes Familles*, Maurice Druon, 1948, Novel

GRANDES GUEULES, LES 1965 d: Robert Enrico. FRN/ITL., *Le Haut Fer*, Jose Giovanni, Paris 1962, Novel

GRANDES PERSONNES, LES 1961 d: Jean Valere. FRN/ITL., *Histoire d'un Amour*, Roger Nimier, Paris 1953, Novel

Grandfather, The *see* **L' AVO** (1909).

Grandfather, The *see* **EL ABUELO** (1998).

GRANDHOTEL NEVADA 1934 d: Jan Svitak. CZC., *Grandhotel Nevada*, Frantisek Langer, Play

Grandmother *see* **BABICKA** (1921).

Grandmother *see* **BABICKA** (1940).

Grandmother Sabella *see* **LA NONNA SABELLA** (1957).

Grandpa Involuntarily *see* **DEDECKEM PROTI SVE VULI** (1939).

GRAND-PERE, LE 1911 d: Georges DenolA. FRN., *Le Grand-Pere*, Jules Mary, Play

GRANDS CHEMINS, LES 1963 d: Christian Marquand. FRN/ITL., *Les Grands Chemins*, Jean Giono, Paris 1951, Novel

GRANDS, LES 1916 d: Georges DenolA. FRN., *Les Grands*, Serge Basset, Pierre Veber, Play

GRANDS, LES 1924 d: Henri Fescourt. FRN., *Les Grands*, Serge Basset, Pierre Veber, Play

GRANDS, LES 1936 d: Felix Gandera, Robert Bibal. FRN., *Les Grands*, Serge Basset, Pierre Veber, Play

GRANDUCHESSA SI DIVERTE, LA 1940 d: Giacomo Gentilomo. ITL., *La Corona Di Strass*, Ugo Falena, Play

GRANICA 1938 d: Joseph Leytes. PLN., *Granica*, Zofia Nalkowska, 1936, Novel

GRANICA 1977 d: Jan Rybkowski. PLN., *Granica*, Zofia Nalkowska, 1936, Novel

GRANNY GET YOUR GUN 1940 d: George Amy. USA., *The Case of the Dangerous Dowager*, Erle Stanley Gardner, Novel

Granny, The *see* **BABICKA** (1940).

GRANUJAS, LOS 1924 d: Fernando Delgado, Manuel NoriegA. SPN., *Los Granujas*, Carlos Arniches, Jose Jackson Veyan, Play

Granzbsetzig 39 *see* **MOB 39** (1940).

Grapes are Ripe, The *see* **DER FROHLICHE WEINBERG** (1952).

GRAPES OF WRATH, THE 1940 d: John Ford. USA., *The Grapes of Wrath*, John Steinbeck, New York 1939, Novel

Graset Sjunger *see* **THE GRASS IS SINGING** (1981).

GRASP OF GREED, THE 1916 d: Joseph de Grasse. USA., *Mr. Meeson's Will*, H. Rider Haggard, New York 1888, Novel

GRASS ARENA, THE 1991 d: Gillies MacKinnon. UKN., *The Grass Arena*, John Healy, Novel

Grass Grows on the Kunlun Mountains *see* **KUN LUN SHAN SHANG YI KE CAO** (1962).

GRASS HARP, THE 1995 d: Charles Matthau. USA., *The Grass Harp*, Truman Capote, 1951, Novel

GRASS IS ALWAYS GREENER OVER THE SEPTIC TANK, THE 1978 d: Robert Day. USA., *The Grass Is Always Greener Over the Septic Tank*, Erma Bombeck, Book

GRASS IS GREENER, THE 1961 d: Stanley Donen. UKN., *The Grass Is Greener*, Hugh Williams, Margaret Williams, London 1958, Play

GRASS IS SINGING, THE 1981 d: Michael Raeburn. UKN/SWD., *The Grass Is Singing*, Doris Lessing, 1950, Novel

GRASS ORPHAN, THE 1922 d: Frank H. Crane. UKN., *The Paupers of Portman Square*, I. A. R. Wylie, Novel

Grasshopper, The see POPRYGUNYA (1955).

GRASSHOPPER, THE 1970 d: Jerry Paris. USA., *The Passing of Evil*, Mark McShane, London 1961, Novel

GRATTACIELI 1943 d: Guglielmo Giannini. ITL., *Grattacieli*, Guglielmo Giannini, Play

Grauen Kam Aus Dem Nebel, Das see LA MORTE RISALE A IERI SERA (1970).

Grausame Job, Der see PEAU D'ESPION (1967).

GRAUSTARK 1915 d: Fred E. Wright. USA., *Graustark*, George Barr McCutcheon, New York 1901, Novel

GRAUSTARK 1925 d: Dimitri Buchowetzki. USA., *Graustark*, George Barr McCutcheon, New York 1901, Novel

GRAVE ERREUR, UNE 1930 d: Joe Francys. FRN., *Une Grave Erreur*, Albert Willemetz, Play

Graveyard Shift see STEPHEN KING'S GRAVEYARD SHIFT (1990).

GRAY DAWN, THE 1922 d: Eliot (#?#) Howe. USA., *The Gray Dawn*, Stewart Edward White, Garden City, N.Y. 1915, Novel

GRAY LADY DOWN 1978 d: David Greene. USA., *Event 1000*, David Lavallee, Novel

GRAY MASK, THE 1915 d: Frank H. Crane. USA., *The Gray Mask*, Wadsworth Camp, 1915, Short Story

Gray Parasol, The see THE GREY PARASOL (1918).

GRAY TOWERS MYSTERY, THE 1919 d: John W. Noble. USA., *Fate in the Balance*, Seward W. Hopkins, Novel

GRAY WOLF'S GHOST, THE 1919 d: Park Frame. USA., *Maruja*, Bret Harte, Boston 1885, Novel

GRAZIA, LA 1929 d: Aldo de Benedetti. ITL., *La Notte*, Grazia Deledda, Short Story

GRAZIELLA 1917 d: Mario Gargiulo. ITL., *Graziella*, Alphonse de Lamartine, 1852, Poem

GRAZIELLA 1926 d: Marcel Vandal. FRN., *Graziella*, Alphonse de Lamartine, 1852, Poem

GRAZIELLA 1955 d: Giorgio Bianchi. ITL., *Graziella*, Alphonse de Lamartine, 1852, Poem

GREASE 1978 d: Randall Kleiser. USA., *Grease*, Warren Casey, Jim Jacobs, Musical Play

GREAT ACCIDENT, THE 1920 d: Harry Beaumont. USA., *The Great Accident*, Ben Ames Williams, New York 1920, Novel

GREAT ADVENTURE, THE 1915 d: Larry Trimble. UKN., *The Great Adventure*, Arnold Bennett, London 1913, Play

GREAT ADVENTURE, THE 1918 d: Alice Blache. USA., *The Painted Scene*, Henry Kitchell Webster, 1916, Short Story

GREAT ADVENTURE, THE 1921 d: Kenneth Webb. USA., *Buried Alive*, Arnold Bennett, London 1908, Novel

Great Adventure, The see DAS SCHONE ABENTEUER (1959).

Great Armored Car Swindle, The see THE BREAKING POINT (1961).

GREAT BALLS OF FIRE 1989 d: Jim McBride. USA., Myra Lewis, Murray Silver, Book

GREAT BANK ROBBERY, THE 1969 d: Hy Averback. USA., *The Great Bank Robbery*, Frank O'Rourke, New York 1969, Novel

GREAT BARRIER, THE 1937 d: Milton Rosmer. UKN., *The Great Divide*, Alan Sullivan, Novel

Great British Train Robbery, The see DIE GENTLEMEN BITTEN ZUR KASSE (1965).

GREAT CARUSO, THE 1951 d: Richard Thorpe. USA., *His Life and Death Enrico Caruso*, Dorothy Caruso, 1945, Biography

GREAT CATHERINE 1967 d: Gordon Flemyng. UKN., *Great Catherine*, George Bernard Shaw, London 1913, Play

GREAT COUP, A 1919 d: George Dewhurst. UKN., *A Great Coup*, Nat Gould, Novel

GREAT DAY 1945 d: Lance Comfort. UKN., *Great Day*, Lesley Storm, 1945, Play

GREAT DAY IN THE MORNING 1956 d: Jacques Tourneur. USA., *Great Day in the Morning*, Robert Hardy Andrews, 1950, Novel

GREAT DAY, THE 1920 d: Hugh Ford. UKN/USA., *The Great Day*, Louis N. Parker, George R. Sims, London 1919, Play

GREAT DECEPTION, THE 1926 d: Howard Higgin. USA., *The Yellow Door*, George Gibbs, New York 1915, Novel

Great Desire, The see CHRISTOPHER STRONG (1933).

GREAT DIAMOND ROBBERY, THE 1914 d: Edward A. Morange, Daniel V. Arthur (Spv). USA., *The Great Diamond Robbery*, Edward M. Alfriend, New York 1895, Play

GREAT DIAMOND ROBBERY, THE 1914 d: Edward A. Morange, Daniel V. Arthur. USA., *The Great Diamond Robbery*, A. C. Wheeler, New York 1895, Play

GREAT DIVIDE, THE 1916 d: Edgar Lewis. USA., *The Great Divide*, William Vaughn Moody, New York 1906, Play

GREAT DIVIDE, THE 1924 d: Reginald Barker. USA., *The Great Divide*, William Vaughn Moody, New York 1906, Play

GREAT DIVIDE, THE 1929 d: Reginald Barker. USA., *The Great Divide*, William Vaughn Moody, New York 1906, Play

GREAT ESCAPE, THE 1963 d: John Sturges. USA., *The Great Escape*, Paul Brickhill, 1950, Novel

GREAT EXPECTATIONS 1917 d: Robert G. Vignola, Joseph Kaufman. USA., *Great Expectations*, Charles Dickens, London 1861, Novel

GREAT EXPECTATIONS 1934 d: Stuart Walker. USA., *Great Expectations*, Charles Dickens, London 1861, Novel

GREAT EXPECTATIONS 1946 d: David Lean. UKN., *Great Expectations*, Charles Dickens, London 1861, Novel

GREAT EXPECTATIONS 1975 d: Joseph Hardy. UKN/USA., *Great Expectations*, Charles Dickens, London 1861, Novel

GREAT EXPECTATIONS 1982 d: Jean Tych. ASL., *Great Expectations*, Charles Dickens, London 1861, Novel

GREAT EXPECTATIONS 1982 d: Julian Amyes. UKN., *Great Expectations*, Charles Dickens, London 1861, Novel

GREAT EXPECTATIONS 1989 d: Kevin Connor. USA., *Great Expectations*, Charles Dickens, London 1861, Novel

GREAT EXPECTATIONS 1998 d: Alfonso Cuaron. USA., *Great Expectations*, Charles Dickens, London 1861, Novel

Great Galeoto, The see LOVERS? (1927).

GREAT GAME, THE 1918 d: A. E. Coleby. UKN., *The Straight Game*, Andrew Soutar, Novel

GREAT GAME, THE 1953 d: Maurice Elvey. UKN., *Shooting Star*, Basil Thomas, Play

GREAT GARRICK, THE 1937 d: James Whale. USA., *Ladies and Gentlemen*, Ernest Vajda, London 1937, Play

GREAT GATSBY, THE 1926 d: Herbert Brenon. USA., *The Great Gatsby*, F. Scott Fitzgerald, 1925, Novel

GREAT GATSBY, THE 1949 d: Elliott Nugent. USA., *The Great Gatsby*, F. Scott Fitzgerald, 1925, Novel

GREAT GATSBY, THE 1974 d: Jack Clayton. USA., *The Great Gatsby*, F. Scott Fitzgerald, 1925, Novel

GREAT GAY ROAD, THE 1920 d: Norman MacDonald. UKN., *The Great Gay Road*, Tom Gallon, Novel

GREAT GAY ROAD, THE 1931 d: Sinclair Hill. UKN., *The Great Gay Road*, Tom Gallon, Novel

Great Gilbert and Sullivan, The see THE STORY OF GILBERT AND SULLIVAN (1953).

GREAT GUY 1936 d: John G. Blystone. USA., *Full Measure*, James Edward Grant, 1934, Short Story, *Johnny Cave Goes Subtle*, James Edward Grant, 1934, Short Story, *Larceny on the Right*, James Edward Grant, 1934, Short Story

GREAT HOSPITAL MYSTERY, THE 1937 d: James Tinling. USA., *Dead Yesterday*, Mignon G. Eberhart, 1936, Short Story

GREAT HOTEL MURDER, THE 1935 d: Eugene J. Forde. USA., *Recipe for Murder*, Vincent Starrett, 1934, Short Story

Great Hotel Mystery, The see THE GREAT HOTEL MURDER (1935).

GREAT HUNGER DUEL, THE 1922 d: Kenneth Graeme. UKN., Derwent Nicol, Short Story

GREAT IMPERSONATION, THE 1921 d: George Melford. USA., *The Great Impersonation*, E. Phillips Oppenheim, Boston 1920, Novel

GREAT IMPERSONATION, THE 1935 d: Alan Crosland. USA., *The Great Impersonation*, E. Phillips Oppenheim, Boston 1920, Novel

GREAT IMPERSONATION, THE 1942 d: John Rawlins. USA., *The Great Impersonation*, E. Phillips Oppenheim, Boston 1920, Novel

GREAT IMPOSTOR, THE 1960 d: Robert Mulligan. USA., *The Great Impostor*, Robert Crichton, New York 1959, Novel

GREAT JASPER, THE 1933 d: J. Walter Ruben. USA., *The Great Jasper*, Fulton Oursler, New York 1930, Novel

GREAT JEWEL ROBBER, THE 1950 d: Peter Godfrey. USA., *Life of Gerard Graham Dennis*, Borden Chase, Gerard Graham Dennis, Story

GREAT K & A TRAIN ROBBERY, THE 1926 d: Lewis Seiler. USA., *The Great K & A Train Robbery*, Paul Leicester Ford, New York 1897, Novel

GREAT LIE, THE 1941 d: Edmund Goulding. USA., *January Heights*, Polan Banks, Novel

Great Life, A see BOLSHAYA ZHIZN (I SERIYA) (1940).

Great Life -Sequel, A see BOLSHAYA ZHIZN (II SERIYA) (1946).

GREAT LOVER, THE 1920 d: Frank Lloyd. USA., *The Great Lover*, Leo Ditrichstein, Fanny Hatton, Frederic Hatton, New York 1915, Play

GREAT LOVER, THE 1931 d: Harry Beaumont. USA., *The Great Lover*, Leo Ditrichstein, Fanny Hatton, Frederic Hatton, New York 1915, Play

GREAT MACARTHY, THE 1975 d: David Baker. ASL., *A Salute to the Great MacArthy*, Barry Oakley, 1970, Novel

Great Madman, The see O GRANDE MENTECAPTO (1989).

Great Magoo, The see SHOOT THE WORKS (1934).

GREAT MAN, THE 1956 d: Jose Ferrer. USA., *The Great Man*, Al Morgan, 1955, Novel

GREAT MAN VOTES, THE 1939 d: Garson Kanin. USA., *The Great Man Votes*, Gordon Malherbe Hillman, 1931, Short Story

Great Manhunt, The see STATE SECRET (1950).

Great Manhunt, The see LE SILENCIEUX (1972).

GREAT MAN'S LADY, THE 1942 d: William A. Wellman. USA., Vina Delmar, Story

GREAT MAN'S WHISKERS, THE 1971 d: Philip Leacock. USA., *The Great Man's Whiskers*, Adrian Scott, Play

Great McCarthy, The see THE GREAT MACARTHY (1975).

GREAT MEADOW, THE 1931 d: Charles J. Brabin. USA., *The Great Meadow*, Elizabeth Madox Roberts, New York 1930, Novel

GREAT MISSOURI RAID, THE 1950 d: Gordon Douglas. USA., *Broken Lance*, Frank Gruber, Novel

GREAT MOMENT, THE 1944 d: Preston Sturges. USA., *Triumph Over Pain*, Rene Fulop-Miller, Book

GREAT MOUSE DETECTIVE, THE 1986 d: John Musker, Ron Clements. USA., *Basil of Baker Street*, Eve Titus, Book

GREAT MR. HANDEL, THE 1942 d: Norman Walker. UKN., *The Great Mr. Handel*, L. Du Garde Peach, Radio Play

GREAT MR. NOBODY, THE 1941 d: Ben Stoloff. USA., *The Stuff of Heroes*, Harold Titus, 1924, Short Story

GREAT O'MALLEY, THE 1937 d: William Dieterle. USA., *The Making of O'Malley*, Gerald Beaumont, 1924, Short Story

Great Pimp, The see EL GRAN GALEOTO (1951).

GREAT POWER 1929 d: Joseph Rock. USA., *The Great Power*, Myron C. Fagan, New York 1928, Play

GREAT PRINCE SHAN, THE 1924 d: A. E. Coleby. UKN., *The Great Prince Shan*, E. Phillips Oppenheim, London 1922, Novel

Great Radio Mystery, The see TAKE THE STAND (1934).

Great Romance, The see FOREVER (1921).

Great Rothschilds, The see THE HOUSE OF ROTHSCHILD (1934).

GREAT RUBY, THE 1915 d: Barry O'Neil. USA., *The Great Ruby*, Henry Hamilton, Cecil Raleigh, London 1898, Play

Great Sacrifice, The *see* OPFERGANG (1944).

GREAT SANTINI, THE 1980 d: Lewis John Carlino. USA., *The Great Santini*, Pat Conroy, Novel

Great Shout of Love, A *see* UN GRAND CRI D'AMOUR (1998).

GREAT SILENCE, THE 1915. USA., *The Great Silence*, H. Tipton Steck, Novel

GREAT SINNER, THE 1949 d: Robert Siodmak, Mervyn Leroy. USA., *Igrok*, Fyodor Dostoyevsky, 1866, Novel

GREAT SNAKES 1920 d: Gerald James, Gaston Quiribet. UKN., *Great Snakes*, William Caine, Novel

Great Solitary, The *see* MARELE SINGURATIC (1976).

Great Temptation, The *see* DIE GROSSE VERSUCHUNG (1952).

Great Train Robbery, The *see* THE FIRST GREAT TRAIN ROBBERY (1979).

GREAT WELL, THE 1924 d: Henry Kolker. UKN., *The Great Well*, Alfred Sutro, Play

GREAT WHITE HOPE, THE 1970 d: Martin Ritt. USA., *The Great White Hope*, Howard Sackler, Washington D.C. 1967, Play

GREAT WHITE WAY, THE 1924 d: E. Mason Hopper. USA., *Cain and Mabel*, Harry Charles Witwer, Short Story

Great Without Glory *see* THE GREAT MOMENT (1944).

GREATER GLORY, THE 1926 d: Curt Rehfeld. USA., *The Viennese Medley*, Edith Louise O'Shaughnessy, New York 1924, Novel

GREATER LAW, THE 1917 d: Lynn Reynolds. USA., *The Code of the Klondyke*, Charles J. Wilson Jr., Short Story

Greater Law, The *see* THE LITTLE RED SCHOOLHOUSE (1923).

GREATER LOVE HATH NO MAN 1915 d: Herbert Blache. USA., *Greater Love Hath No Man*, Frank L. Packard, New York 1913, Novel

Greater Love, The *see* THE WEAKNESS OF MAN (1916).

GREATER THAN A CROWN 1925 d: R. William Neill. USA., *The Lady from Longacre*, Victor Bridges, New York 1919, Novel

GREATER THAN MARRIAGE 1924 d: Victor Hugo Halperin. USA., *Joan Thursday*, Louis Joseph Vance, Boston 1913, Novel

GREATER WAR, THE 1926 d: Jack Raymond. UKN., *The Greater War*, W. Townend, Short Story

GREATER WOMAN, THE 1917 d: Frank Powell. USA., *The Greater Woman*, Algernon Boyesen, Play

Greatest Attack, The *see* LE TOUBIB (1979).

Greatest Gift, The *see* IT'S A WONDERFUL LIFE (1946).

GREATEST GIFT, THE 1974 d: Boris Sagal. USA., *Ramey*, Jack Farris, Novel

Greatest Love, The *see* EL AMOR DE LOS AMORES (1960).

GREATEST STORY EVER TOLD, THE 1965 d: George Stevens. USA., *The Greatest Story Ever Told*, Fulton Oursler, New York 1949, Book

GREATEST, THE 1977 d: Tom Gries. USA/UKN., *Muhammad Ali*, Autobiography

GREATEST THING THAT ALMOST HAPPENED, THE 1977 d: Gilbert Moses. USA., *The Greatest Thing That Almost Happened*, Don Robertson, Novel

GREATEST WISH IN THE WORLD, THE 1918 d: Maurice Elvey. UKN., *The Greatest Wish in the World*, E. Temple Thurston, Novel

GREATHEART 1921 d: George Ridgwell. UKN., *Greatheart*, Ethel M. Dell, Novel

GREED 1924 d: Erich von Stroheim. USA., *McTeague; a Story of San Francisco*, Frank Norris, New York 1899, Novel

Greed *see* LUST FOR GOLD (1949).

Greed in the Sun *see* CENT MILLE DOLLARS AU SOLEIL (1963).

GREEK INTERPRETER, THE 1922 d: George Ridgwell. UKN., *The Greek Interpreter*, Arthur Conan Doyle, Short Story

Greek Interpreter, The *see* THE ADVENTURES OF SHERLOCK HOLMES: THE GREEK INTERPRETER (1985).

Greek Man Seeks Greek Woman *see* GRIECHE SUCHT GRIECHIN (1966).

GREEK TYCOON, THE 1978 d: J. Lee Thompson. USA., *The Greek Tycoon*, Nico Mastorakis, Novel

Greeks Bearing Gifts *see* INSPECTOR MORSE: GREEKS BEARING GIFTS (1989).

Greeks Had a Word for It, The *see* THE GREEKS HAD A WORD FOR THEM (1932).

GREEKS HAD A WORD FOR THEM, THE 1932 d: Lowell Sherman. USA., *The Greeks Had a Word for It*, Zoe Akins, New York 1930, Play

Green Archer, The *see* DER GRUNE BOGENSCHUTZE (1960).

GREEN BERETS, THE 1968 d: John Wayne, Ray Kellogg. USA., *The Green Berets*, Robin Moore, New York 1965, Novel

Green Car, The *see* ZELENY AUTOMOBIL (1921).

GREEN CARAVAN, THE 1922 d: Edwin J. Collins. UKN., *The Green Caravan*, Oliver Sandys, Novel

Green Carnation, The *see* THE TRIALS OF OSCAR WILDE (1960).

Green Chamber of Linnainen, The *see* LINNAISTEN VIHREA KAMARI (1945).

Green Cockatoo, The *see* FOUR DARK HOURS (1937).

Green Dice *see* MR. SKITCH (1933).

GREEN DOLPHIN STREET 1947 d: Victor Saville. USA., *Green Dolphin Street*, Elizabeth Goudge, Novel

GREEN DOOR, THE 1917 d: Thomas R. Mills. USA., *The Green Door*, O. Henry, Short Story

GREEN EYE OF THE YELLOW GOD 1913 d: Charles H. France. USA., *The Green Eye of the Yellow God*, J. Milton Hayes, Poem

GREEN EYES 1934 d: Richard Thorpe. USA., *The Murder of Steven Kester*, Harriette Ashbrook, New York 1931, Novel

Green Fields *see* GREENE FELDE (1937).

GREEN FINGERS 1947 d: John Harlow. UKN., *Persistent Warrior*, Edith Arundel, Novel

GREEN FIRE 1954 d: Andrew Marton. USA., *Green Fire*, Peter W. Rainier, 1942, Novel

GREEN FOR DANGER 1946 d: Sidney Gilliat. UKN., *Green for Danger*, Christianna Brand, Novel

Green Ghost, The *see* LE SPECTRE VERT (1930).

GREEN GOD, THE 1918 d: Paul Scardon. USA., *The Green God*, Frederic Arnold Kummer, New York 1911, Novel

GREEN GODDESS, THE 1923 d: Sidney Olcott. USA., *The Green Goddess*, William Archer, New York 1921, Play

GREEN GODDESS, THE 1930 d: Alfred E. Green. USA., *The Green Goddess*, William Archer, New York 1921, Play

GREEN GRASS OF WYOMING 1948 d: Louis King. USA., *Green Grass of Wyoming*, Mary O'Hara, Novel

GREEN GROW THE RUSHES 1951 d: Derek Twist. UKN., *Green Grow the Rushes*, Howard Clewes, Novel

Green Hat, The *see* OUTCAST LADY (1934).

GREEN HELMET, THE 1961 d: Michael Forlong. UKN., *The Green Helmet*, Jon Cleary, London 1957, Novel

GREEN ICE 1980 d: Ernest Day. USA/UKN., *Green Ice*, Gerald A. Browne, Novel

Green Journey, A *see* THE LOVE SHE SOUGHT (1990).

GREEN LIGHT 1937 d: Frank Borzage. USA., *Green Light*, Lloyd C. Douglas, Boston 1935, Novel

GREEN MAN, THE 1956 d: Robert Day. UKN., *Meet a Body*, Sidney Gilliat, Frank Launder, Play

GREEN MANSIONS 1959 d: Mel Ferrer. USA., *Green Mansions*, W. H. Hudson, 1904, Novel

Green Mare, The *see* LA JUMENT VERTE (1959).

Green Mare's Nest, The *see* LA JUMENT VERTE (1959).

GREEN MIST, THE 1924 d: Fred Paul. UKN., *The Green Mist*, Sax Rohmer, Short Story

Green Murder Case, The *see* NIGHT OF MYSTERY (1937).

GREEN ORCHARD, THE 1916 d: Harold Weston. UKN., *The Green Orchard*, Andrew Soutar, London 1916, Novel

GREEN PACK, THE 1934 d: T. Hayes Hunter. UKN., *The Green Pack*, Edgar Wallace, London 1933, Novel

GREEN PASTURES, THE 1936 d: William Keighley, Marc Connelly. USA., *The Green Pastures*, Marc Connelly, New York 1930, Play

Green Room of the Linnaeus Castle, The *see* LINNAISTEN VIHREA KAMARI (1945).

Green Room, The *see* LA CHAMBRE VERTE (1978).

GREEN SCARF, THE 1954 d: George M. O'Ferrall. UKN., *The Brute*, Guy Des Cars, Novel

Green Shadow, The *see* MUSS 'EM UP (1936).

GREEN STOCKINGS 1916 d: Wilfred North. USA., *Colonel Smith*, A. E. W. Mason, London 1909, Play

Green Stockings *see* THE FLIRTING WIDOW (1930).

GREEN TEMPTATION, THE 1922 d: William D. Taylor. USA., *The Noose*, Constance Lindsay Skinner, 1920, Short Story

GREEN TERROR, THE 1919 d: W. P. Kellino. UKN., *The Green Rust*, Edgar Wallace, London 1919, Novel

GREEN TREE, THE 1965 d: Joseph Roland, Ruth Zimmerman. USA/ITL., *General Mickey*, Peter Lappin, New Rochelle 1952, Novel

GREEN YEARS, THE 1946 d: Victor Saville. USA., *The Green Years*, A. J. Cronin, 1944, Novel

GREENE FELDE 1937 d: Edgar G. Ulmer, Jacob Ben-Ami. USA., *Grine Felder*, Peretz Hirshbein, New York 1918, Play

GREENE MURDER CASE, THE 1929 d: Frank Tuttle. USA., *The Greene Murder Case*, S. S. Van Dine, New York 1928, Novel

GREEN-EYED DEVIL, THE 1914 d: James Kirkwood. USA., *The Green-Eyed Devil*, Daniel Carson Goodwin, Story

GREENGAGE SUMMER, THE 1961 d: Lewis Gilbert. UKN., *The Greengage Summer*, Rumer Godden, London 1958, Novel

GREEP, DE 1909. NTH., *La Griffe*, Jean Sartene, Play

Gregorio Cortez *see* THE BALLAD OF GREGORIO CORTEZ (1982).

Greh *see* AM ANFANG WAR ES SUNDE (1954).

GRELL MYSTERY, THE 1917 d: Paul Scardon. USA., *The Grell Mystery*, Frank Froest, London 1913, Novel

GRELUCHON DELICAT, LE 1934 d: Jean Choux. FRN., *La Greluchon Delicat*, Jacques Natanson, Play

GRENDEL GRENDEL GRENDEL 1979 d: Alexander Stitt. ASL., *Grendel*, John Gardner, Novel

Grete Minde *see* GRETE MINDE - DER WALD IST VOLLER WOLFE (1977).

GRETE MINDE - DER WALD IST VOLLER WOLFE 1977 d: Heidi Genee. AUS/GRM., *Grete Minde*, Theodor Fontane, 1879, Novel

Grete Minde - the Woods are Full of Wolves *see* GRETE MINDE - DER WALD IST VOLLER WOLFE (1977).

GRETNA GREEN 1915 d: Thomas N. Heffron, Hugh Ford. USA., *Gretna Green*, Grace Livingston Furniss, New York 1903, Play

Greven Fra Liljenborg *see* ALT FOR KVINDEN (1964).

Grey Cart, The *see* KORKARLEN (1921).

GREY CONTRE X 1939 d: Pierre Maudru, Alfred Gragnon. FRN., *Grey Contre X*, Alfred Gragnon, Short Story

Grey Dawn *see* KHUROYE UTRO (1959).

Grey Dawn, The *see* THE GRAY DAWN (1922).

GREY GRANITE 1983 d: Tom Cotter. UKN., *Grey Granite*, Lewis Grassic Gibbon, Novel

Grey Lady Down *see* GRAY LADY DOWN (1978).

Grey Mask, The *see* THE GRAY MASK (1915).

GREY PARASOL, THE 1918 d: Lawrence C. Windom. USA., *The Gray Parasol*, Frederick Jackson, 1918, Short Story

Grey Towers Mystery, The *see* THE GRAY TOWERS MYSTERY (1919).

Grey Wolf's Ghost, The *see* THE GRAY WOLF'S GHOST (1919).

Grey-Eyed Demon, The *see* SIVOOKY DEMON (1919).

GREYFRIARS BOBBY 1961 d: Don Chaffey. UKN/USA., *Greyfriars Bobby*, Eleanor Atkinson, New York 1912, Novel

GREYHOUND, THE 1914 d: Lawrence McGill. USA., *The Greyhound*, Paul Armstrong, Wilson Mizner, New York 1912, Play

Greystoke *see* LORD OF THE APES GREYSTOKE: THE LEGEND OF TARZAN (1983).

GREYSTOKE: THE LEGEND OF TARZAN, LORD OF THE APES 1983 d: Hugh Hudson. UKN., *Tarzan of the Apes*, Edgar Rice Burroughs, Chicago 1914, Novel

GREYWATER PARK 1924 d: Fred Paul. UKN., *Greywater Park*, Sax Rohmer, Short Story

GRIBICHE 1925 d: Jacques Feyder. FRN., *Gribiche*, Frederic Boutet, Short Story

GRIBOUILLE 1937 d: Marc Allegret. FRN., Marcel Archard, Story

Gribouille see **THE LADY IN QUESTION** (1940).

GRIECHE SUCHT GRIECHIN 1966 d: Rolf Thiele. GRM., *Grieche Sucht Griechin*, Friedrich Durrenmatt, 1955, Short Story

Grief see **TOSKA** (1969).

Griffe, La see **DE GREEP** (1909).

Griffes du Destin, Les see **SINS** (1985).

Grigsby see **THE LAST GRENADE** (1970).

GRIJPSTRA & DE GIER 1979 d: Wim Verstappen. NTH., *Grijpstra & de Gier*, Janwillem Van de Wetering, Novel

GRILLON DU FOYER, LE 1922 d: Jean Manoussi. FRN., *Le Grillon du Foyer*, Charles Dickens, Short Story

GRILLON DU FOYER, LE 1933 d: Robert Boudrioz. FRN., *The Cricket on the Hearth*, Charles Dickens, London 1845, Novel

GRIM JUSTICE 1916 d: Larry Trimble. UKN., *Grim Justice*, Rita, Novel

GRIMALDI 1914 d: Charles Vernon. UKN., *Grimaldi*, Dion Boucicault, Play

Grine Felder see **GREENE FELDE** (1937).

GRINGALET 1946 d: Andre Berthomieu. FRN., *Gringalet*, Paul Vandenberghe, Play

GRIP 1915 d: Maurice Elvey. UKN., *Grip*, John Strange Winter, Novel

Grip of Fear, The see **EXPERIMENT IN TERROR** (1962).

GRIP OF IRON, THE 1913 d: Arthur Charrington. UKN., *Les Etrangleurs*, Adolphe Belot, Paris 1879, Novel

GRIP OF IRON, THE 1920 d: Bert Haldane. UKN., *Les Etrangleurs*, Adolphe Belot, Paris 1879, Novel

GRIP OF THE YUKON, THE 1928 d: Ernst Laemmle. USA., *The Yukon Trail; a Tale of the North*, William MacLeod Raine, Boston 1917, Novel

Grip, The see **DE GREEP** (1909).

GRIP, THE 1913 d: A. E. Coleby. UKN., *La Griffe*, Jean Sartene, Play

Gripsholm Castle see **SCHLOSS GRIPSHOLM** (1963).

Grisbi see **TOUCHEZ PAS AU GRISBI** (1953).

GRISOU 1938 d: Maurice de Canonge. FRN., *Grisou*, Pierre Brasseur, Marcel Dalio, Play

GRISSOM GANG, THE 1971 d: Robert Aldrich. USA., *The Grissom Gang*, James Hadley Chase, Novel

GRIT 1924 d: Frank Tuttle. USA., *Grit*, F. Scott Fitzgerald, Short Story

GRITOS EN LA NOCHE 1961 d: Jesus Franco. SPN/FRN., David Kuhne, Novel

Gritta of the Castle of Rats see **GRITTA VOM RATTENSCHLOSS** (1985).

GRITTA VOM RATTENSCHLOSS 1985 d: Jurgen Brauer. GDR., Bettina von Arnim, Gisela von Arnim, Story

Grona Kammarn Pa Linnais see **LINNAISTEN VIHREA KAMARI** (1945).

Gront Guld see **VIHREA KULTA** (1939).

GROS COUP, LE 1963 d: Jean Valere. FRN/ITL., *Avec un Elastique*, Charles Williams, Novel

GROSS UND KLEIN 1980 d: Peter Stein. GRM., *Gross Und Klein*, Botho Strauss, 1980, Play

GROSSALARM 1938 d: Georg Jacoby. GRM., *Funf Tage Und Eine Nacht*, H. O. Wuttig, Novel

GROSSE FALL, DER 1945 d: Karl Anton. GRM., *Holle Ahoi*, Georg Muhlen-Schulte, Novel

GROSSE FLATTER, DIE 1979 d: Marianne Ludcke. GRM., *Die Grosse Flatter*, Leonie Ossowski, Novel

Grosse Irrtum, Der see **IL CONFORMISTA** (1970).

Grosse Kaseverschworung, Die see **VELKA SYROVA SOUTEZ** (1987).

Grosse Liebe Um Das Welttheater see **MACHTRAUSCH - ABER DIE LIEBE SIEGT** (1942).

GROSSE LIEBESSPIEL, DAS 1963 d: Alfred Weidenmann. GRM/AUS., *Der Reigen*, Arthur Schnitzler, 1900, Play

Grosse Postraub, Der see **DIE GENTLEMEN BITTEN ZUR KASSE** (1965).

GROSSE PREIS, DER 1944 d: Karl Anton. GRM., *Werkmeister Berthold Kramp*, Rudolf Hoepner, Novel

GROSSE UNBEKANNTE, DER 1927 d: Manfred NoA. GRM., Edgar Wallace, Novel

GROSSE UND DIE KLEINE WELT, DIE 1921 d: Max Mack. GRM., *Die Grosse Und Die Kleine Welt*, Rudolf Eger, Play

GROSSE UND DIE KLEINE WELT, DIE 1936 d: Johannes Riemann. GRM., *Die Grosse Und Die Kleine Welt*, Hugo Maria Kritz, Novel

GROSSE VERSUCHUNG, DIE 1952 d: Rolf Hansen. GRM., *Der Erfolgreiche*, Hans Kades, Novel

Grosse Weltheater, Das see **MACHTRAUSCH - ABER DIE LIEBE SIEGT** (1942).

GROSSE ZAPFENSTREICH, DER 1952 d: Georg Hurdalek. GRM., *Der Zapfenstreich*, Franz Adam Beyerlein, Play

GROSSTADTNACHT 1950 d: Hans Wolff. AUS., *Der Zobelpelz*, Wilhelm Lichtenberg, Novel

GROSSTE GAUNER DES JAHRHUNDERTS, DER 1927 d: Max Obal. GRM., *Der Schwerverbrecher Jimmy*, Ludwig von Wohl, Novel

GROTESQUE, THE 1995 d: John-Paul Davidson. UKN., *The Grotesque*, Patrick McGrath, Book

GROUNDS FOR DIVORCE 1925 d: Paul Bern. USA., *Valoporos Holay*, Erno Vajda, Budapest 1923, Novel

Grounds for Divorce see **DUVOD K ROZVODU** (1937).

Grounds for Divorce: Love see **SCHEIDUNGSGRUND: LIEBE** (1960).

GROUNDSTAR CONSPIRACY, THE 1972 d: Lamont Johnson. USA/CND., *The Groundstar Conspiracy*, L. P. Davies, Novel

Group Portrait With a Lady see **GRUPPENBILD MIT DAME** (1977).

GROUP, THE 1966 d: Sidney Lumet. USA., *The Group*, Mary McCarthy, New York 1963, Novel

Growing Up see **TAKEKURABE** (1955).

Growing Up see **LITEN IDA** (1981).

GROZA 1934 d: Vladimir Petrov. USS., *Groza*, Alexander Ostrovsky, 1859, Play

GRUDGE, THE 1915 d: William S. Hart. USA., *The Haters*, J. G. Hawks, Story

GRUFT MIT DEM RATSELSCHLOSS, DIE 1964 d: Franz J. Gottlieb. GRM., *The Door With Seven Locks*, Edgar Wallace, London 1926, Novel

Grumbling White Tiger, The see **GRAMBLING'S WHITE TIGER** (1981).

GRUMPY 1923 d: William C. de Mille. USA., *Grumpy*, Horace Hodges, Thomas Wigney Percyval, New York 1921, Play

GRUMPY 1930 d: George Cukor, Cyril Gardner. USA., *Grumpy*, Horace Hodges, Thomas Wigney Percyval, New York 1921, Play

GRUNE BOGENSCHUTZE, DER 1960 d: Jurgen Roland. GRM., *The Green Archer*, Edgar Wallace, London 1923, Novel

GRUNE DOMINO, DER 1935 d: Herbert Selpin. GRM., *Der Fall Claasen*, Erich Ebermayer, Novel

GRUNE KAISER, DER 1939 d: Paul Mundorf. GRM., *Der Grune Kaiser*, Hans Medin, Novel

GRUNE MONOKEL, DAS 1929 d: Rudolf Meinert. GRM., *Das Grune Monokel*, Guido Kreutzer, Novel

GRUPPENBILD MIT DAME 1977 d: Aleksandar Petrovic. GRM/FRN/YGS., *Gruppenbild Mit Dame*, Heinrich Boll, 1971, Novel

Grustaini Bashmachok see **KHRUSTALNYY BASHMACHOK** (1961).

Grustalni Bashmachok see **KHRUSTALNYY BASHMACHOK** (1961).

GRZECHY DZIECINSTWA 1980 d: Krzysztof Nowak. PLN., *Grzechy Dziecinstwa*, Boleslaw Prus, 1883, Short Story

G-String Murders, The see **LADY OF BURLESQUE** (1943).

Gu Shu Yi Ren see **GUSHU YIREN** (1987).

GUA PENG NU JIE 1985 d: Wang Yi. CHN., *Gua Peng Nu Jie*, Liu Shaotang, Novel

GUADALCANAL DIARY 1943 d: Lewis Seiler. USA., *Guadalcanal Diary*, Richard W. Tregaskis, 1943, Novel

GUAI AI VINTI! 1955 d: Raffaello Matarazzo. ITL., *Vae Victis*, Annie Vivanti, Novel

GUAN BU ZHU 1956 d: Zhang XInshi, Liu Guoquan. CHN., *Guan Bu Zhu*, Zhao Yuxiang, Play

GUAN HANQING 1960 d: Xu Tao. CHN., *Guan Hanqing*, Tian Han, 1958, Play

Guanto Da Festa, Il see **IL GUANTO** (1910).

GUANTO, IL 1910 d: Luigi Maggi. ITL., *Der Handschuh*, Friedrich von Schiller, Poem

GUAPO DEL 1900, UN 1960 d: Leopoldo Torre-Nilsson. ARG., *Un Guapo Del 1900*, Samuel Eichelbaum, Play

GUAPOS O GENTE BRAVA, LOS 1923 d: Manuel NoriegA. SPN., *Los Guapos*, Carlos Arniches, Jose Jackson Veyan, Play

Guarani Indian, The see **O GUARANI** (1979).

GUARANI, O 1979 d: Fauze Mansur. BRZ., *O Guarani*, Jose Martiniano de Alencar, 1857, Novel

GUARANY, IL 1923 d: Salvatore Aversano. ITL., *O Guarani*, Jose Martiniano de Alencar, 1857, Novel

Guardian Deity, The see **KAVAL DAIVAM** (1969).

Guardian of Peace see **HE PING BAO WEI ZHE** (1950).

GUARDIAN OF THE ACCOLADE, THE 1919 d: Henry Houry. USA., *The Guardian of the Accolade*, O. Henry, Short Story

Guardian of the Fortress, The see **PAZACHAT NA KREPOSTA** (1974).

Guardians of Phare see **GARDIENS DE PHARE** (1928).

Guardians, The see **FORMYNDERNE** (1978).

GUARDSMAN, THE 1931 d: Sidney A. Franklin. USA., *A Testor*, Ferenc Molnar, Budapest 1910, Play

Guascone, Il see **LE CHEVALIER DE PARDAILLAN** (1962).

GUBIJINSO 1935 d: Kenji Mizoguchi. JPN., *Gubijinso*, Soseki Natsume, 1908, Novel

GUDRUN 1963 d: Anker Sorensen. DNM., *Gudrun*, Johannes Vilhelm Jensen, Copenhagen 1936, Novel

Guepard, Le see **IL GATTOPARDO** (1963).

Guerilla, The see **LA GUERRILLA** (1972).

Guerilleros, Les see **I BRIGANTI ITALIANI** (1961).

GUERNICA -JEDE STUNDE VERLETZT UND DIE LEUTE TOTET 1963 d: Peter Lilienthal. GRM., *Guernica*, Fernando Arrabal, 1961, Play

GUERRA DI TROIA, LA 1961 d: Giorgio Ferroni. ITL/FRN., *Iliad*, Homer, Verse

Guerra E Pace see **WAR AND PEACE** (1956).

GUERRA EMPIEZA EN CUBA, LA 1957 d: Mur Oti. SPN., *La Guerra Empieza En Cuba*, Victor Ruiz Iriarte, 1957, Play

GUERRA IN TEMPO DI PACE 1914 d: Camillo de Riso. ITL., *Krieg Im Frieden*, Gustav von Moser, Franz von Schonthan, 1880, Play

Guerra in Tempo Di Pace see **MANOVRE D'AMORE** (1941).

GUERRE DANS LE HAUT-PAYS, LA 1999 d: Francis Reusser. SWS/FRN/BLG., *La Guerre Dans le Haut-Pays*, Charles-Ferdinand Ramuz, 1915, Novel

Guerre de Troie, La see **LA GUERRA DI TROIA** (1961).

Guerre Des Boutons, La see **LA GUERRE DES GOSSES** (1936).

GUERRE DES BOUTONS, LA 1961 d: Yves Robert. FRN., *La Guerre Des Boutons*, Louis Pergaud, Paris 1912, Novel

GUERRE DES GOSSES, LA 1936 d: Jacques Daroy, Eugene Deslaw. FRN., *La Guerre Des Boutons*, Louis Pergaud, Paris 1912, Novel

GUERRE DU FEU, LA 1914 d: Georges DenolA. FRN., *La Guerre du Feu*, Joseph Henri Rosny, 1911, Novel

Guerre du Feu, La see **QUEST FOR FIRE** (1981).

GUERRILLA, LA 1972 d: Rafael Gil. SPN/FRN., *La Guerrilla*, Jose Martinez Ruiz, 1936, Play

Guerrillas on the Railway see **TIE DAO YOU JI DUI** (1956).

GUESA, O 1969 d: Sergio Santeiro. BRZ., *Guesa Errante*, Sousandrade, 1868-77, Verse

Guess Who's Coming for Breakfast see **DIE NICHTEN DER FRAU OBERST** (1968).

GUESS WHO'S SLEEPING IN MY BED? 1973 d: Theodore J. Flicker. USA., *Six Weeks in August*, Pamela Herbert Chais, Play

GUEST IN THE HOUSE, A 1944 d: John Brahm, Andre (#u/C#) de Toth. USA., *Dear Evelyn*, Dale M. Eunson, Hagar Wilde, Play

GUEST OF HONOUR 1934 d: George King. UKN., *The Man from Blankleys*, F. Anstey, 1893, Short Story

Guest, The *see* THE CARETAKER (1963).

Guest, The *see* ATITHI (1965).

Guests of Hercules, The *see* PASSION'S PLAYGROUND (1920).

GUESTS OF THE NATION 1936 d: Denis Johnston. IRL., *Guests of the Nation*, Frank O'Connor, 1931, Short Story

Gueule Cassee *see* LA MAISON AU SOLEIL (1929).

GUEULE D'AMOUR 1937 d: Jean Gremillon. FRN., *Gueule d'Amour*, Andre Beucler, Novel

GUEULE D'ANGE 1955 d: Marcel Blistene. FRN., *Gueule d'Ange*, Roger Normand, Play

GUEULE DE L'AUTRE, LA 1979 d: Pierre TcherniA. FRN., *La Grace*, Marcel Ayme, Novel

GUEUX AU PARADIS, LES 1945 d: Rene Le Henaff. FRN., *Les Gueux Au Paradis*, G. M. Martens, Play

GUGLIELMO TELL 1911 d: Ugo FalenA. ITL., *Wilhelm Tell*, Friedrich von Schiller, 1804, Play

GUGLIELMO TELL 1949 d: Giorgio PastinA. ITL., *Wilhelm Tell*, Friedrich von Schiller, 1804, Play

Guglielmo Tell - la Freccia Del Giustiziere *see* WILHELM TELL - BERGEN IN FLAMMEN (1960).

GUI HUA 1951 d: Wang Jiayi. CHN., Zhao Shuli, Story

GUI MEI 1985 d: Sun Yuanxun. CHN., *Liao Zhai Zhi Yi*, Pu Songling, Story

GUIDE FOR THE MARRIED MAN, A 1967 d: Gene Kelly. USA., *A Guide for the Married Man As Told to Frank Tarloff*, Frank Tarloff, Los Angeles 1967, Novel

GUIDE, THE 1965 d: Tad Danielewski, Vijay Anand. USA/IND., *The Guide*, R. K. Narayan, New York 1957, Novel

Guild of the Kutna Hora Virgins *see* CECH PANEN KUTNOHORSKYCH (1938).

Guild of the Maidens of Kutna Hora *see* CECH PANEN KUTNOHORSKYCH (1938).

Guild of the Virgins of Kutna *see* CECH PANEN KUTNOHORSKYCH (1938).

GUILLAUME TELL 1912 d: Georg Wackerlein. SWT., *Wilhelm Tell*, Friedrich von Schiller, 1804, Play

GUILLAUME TELL 1913 d: Friedrich Feher. SWT./GRM., *Wilhelm Tell*, Friedrich von Schiller, 1804, Play

GUILLAUME TELL 1914. SWT., *Wilhelm Tell*, Friedrich von Schiller, 1804, Play

Guillaume Tell *see* WILHELM TELL (1934).

Guillaume Tell *see* WILHELM TELL - BERGEN IN FLAMMEN (1960).

GUILT IS MY SHADOW 1950 d: Roy Kellino. UKN., *You're Best Alone*, Peter Curtis, Novel

GUILTY? 1930 d: George B. Seitz. USA., *The Black Sheep*, Dorothy Howell, Story

GUILTY? 1956 d: Edmond T. Greville. UKN/FRN., *Death Has Deep Roots*, Michael Gilbert, Novel

Guilty As Charged *see* GUILTY AS HELL (1932).

GUILTY AS HELL 1932 d: Erle C. Kenton. USA., *Riddle Me This*, Daniel N. Rubin, New York 1932, Play

Guilty By Suspicion *see* A CRY IN THE DARK (1988).

GUILTY BYSTANDER 1950 d: Joseph Lerner. USA., *Guilty Bystander*, Wade Miller, 1947, Novel

GUILTY GENERATION, THE 1931 d: Rowland V. Lee. USA., *The Guilty Generation*, J. Kirby Hawkes, Jo Milward, 1928, Play

GUILTY MAN, THE 1918 d: Irvin V. Willat. USA., *Le Coupable*, Francois Coppee, Paris 1896, Play

GUILTY MELODY 1936 d: Richard Pottier. UKN., *Guilty Melody*, Hans Rehfisch, Novel

GUILTY OF LOVE 1920 d: Harley Knoles. USA., *This Woman - This Man*, Avery Hopwood, New York 1909, Play

GUILTY OF TREASON 1949 d: Felix E. Feist. USA., *As We See Russia*, Overseas Press Club, 1948, Book

GUILTY ONE, THE 1924 d: Joseph Henabery. USA., *The Guilty One*, Michael Morton, Peter Traill, New York 1914, Play

GUILTY PARTY, THE 1917 d: Thomas R. Mills. USA., *The Guilty Party*, O. Henry, Short Story

Guilty Secret, The *see* THE INTIMATE STRANGER (1956).

GUILTY, THE 1947 d: John Reinhardt. USA., *He Looked Like Murder*, Cornell Woolrich, 1946, Short Story

Guilty Thing Surprised, A *see* INSPECTOR WEXFORD: A GUILTY THING SURPRISED (1988).

Guilty Though Guiltless *see* BEZ VINI VINOVATIYE (1945).

Guilty Though Innocent *see* BEZ VINI VINOVATIYE (1945).

GUINEA PIG, THE 1948 d: Roy Boulting. UKN., *The Guinea Pig*, Warren Chetham Strode, London 1946, Play

GUITAI 1965 d: Yin Zhi. CHN., *Guitai*, Gao Shiguo, Play

GUITARE ET LE JAZZ-BAND, LA 1923 d: Gaston Roudes. FRN., *La Guitare Et le Jazz-Band*, Robert Dieudonne, Henri Duvernois, Play

GULDREGN 1988 d: Soren Kragh-Jacobsen. DNM., *Guldregn*, Anders Bodelsen, Novel

GULLIVER'S TRAVELS 1939 d: Dave Fleischer. USA., *Gulliver's Travels*, Jonathan Swift, London 1726, Novel

GULLIVER'S TRAVELS 1977 d: Peter Hunt. UKN/BLG., *Gulliver's Travels*, Jonathan Swift, London 1726, Novel

GULLIVER'S TRAVELS 1979 d: Chris Cuddington. USA., *Gulliver's Travels*, Jonathan Swift, London 1726, Novel

GULLIVER'S TRAVELS 1996 d: Charles Sturridge. USA/UKN., *Gulliver's Travels*, Jonathan Swift, London 1726, Novel

Gulliver's Travels Part 2 *see* LOS VIAJES DE GULLIVER (1983).

GUMASTA 1953 d: R. M. Krishnaswamy. IND., *Ngo*, Acharya Athreya, Play

GUMASTAVIN PENN 1941 d: Balakrishna Narayan Rao. IND., *Gumastavin Penn*, Tks Brothers, Play

GUMMI TARZAN 1982 d: Soren Kragh-Jacobsen. DNM., *Gummi Tarzan*, Ole Lund Kierkegaard, Story

Gumshoes 4-B *see* BAB'S CANDIDATE (1920).

GUN AND THE PULPIT, THE 1974 d: Daniel Petrie. USA., *The Gun and the Pulpit*, Jack Erlich, Novel

Gun Before Butter *see* VAN DER VALK UND DAS MADCHEN (1972).

Gun Crazy *see* DEADLY IS THE FEMALE (1949).

GUN FURY 1953 d: Raoul Walsh. USA., *Ten Against Caesar*, Kathleen G. George, Robert A. Granger, 1952, Story

GUN GLORY 1957 d: Roy Rowland. USA., *Man of the West*, Philip Yordan, 1955, Novel

GUN GOSPEL 1927 d: Harry J. Brown. USA., *Gun Gospel*, William Dawson Hoffman, Chicago 1926, Novel

Gun Law *see* I GIORNI DELL'IRA (1967).

Gun Moll *see* LA MOME VERT-DE-GRIS (1952).

Gun of April Morning, The *see* CAPTAIN APACHE (1971).

GUN RUNNER, THE 1928 d: Edgar Lewis. USA., *The Gun Runner*, Arthur Stringer, New York 1909, Novel

GUN RUNNERS, THE 1958 d: Don Siegel. USA., *To Have and Have Not*, Ernest Hemingway, 1937, Novel

Gun Shy *see* HOUSE OF ERRORS (1942).

Gunfight at Abilene *see* GUNFIGHT IN ABILENE (1967).

GUNFIGHT AT THE O.K. CORRAL 1957 d: John Sturges. USA., *The Killer*, George Scullin, 1954, Article

GUNFIGHT IN ABILENE 1967 d: William Hale. USA., *Gun Shy*, Clarence Upson Young, Short Story

GUNFIGHTER, THE 1923 d: Lynn Reynolds. USA., *Hired Guns*, Max Brand, 1923, Short Story

GUNFIRE 1935 d: Harry L. Fraser. USA., *Pards in Paradise*, Eric Howard, Short Story

Gunfire at the Secret Bureau *see* BAO MI JU DE QIANG SHENG (1979).

GUNG HO 1985 d: Ron Howard. USA., *Gung Ho*, W. S. le Francois, Book

GUNGA DIN 1939 d: George Stevens. USA., *Gunga Din*, Rudyard Kipling, 1890, Poem

GUNMAN'S WALK 1958 d: Phil Karlson. USA., Ric Hardman, Short Story

Guns A'blazing *see* LAW AND ORDER (1932).

GUNS AT BATASI 1964 d: John Guillermin. UKN., *The Siege of Battersea*, Robert Holles, London 1962, Novel

Guns for San Sebastian *see* LOS CANONES DE SAN SEBASTIAN (1967).

Guns for the Dictator *see* L' ARME A GAUCHE (1965).

GUNS IN THE HEATHER 1969 d: Robert Butler. UKN., *Guns in the Heather*, Lockhart Amerman, Novel

GUNS OF AUGUST, THE 1964 d: Nathan Kroll. USA., *The Guns of August*, Barbara W. Tuchman, New York 1962, Book

GUNS OF DARKNESS 1962 d: Anthony Asquith. UKN., *Act of Mercy*, Francis Clifford, London 1959, Novel

GUNS OF DIABLO 1964 d: Boris Sagal. USA., *Guns of Diablo*, Robert Lewis Taylor, Novel

GUNS OF FORT PETTICOAT, THE 1957 d: George Marshall. USA., C. William Harrison, Story

GUNS OF NAVARONE, THE 1961 d: J. Lee Thompson. UKN/USA., *The Guns of Navarone*, Alistair MacLean, London 1957, Novel

Guns of the Revolution *see* RAIN FOR A DUSTY SUMMER (1971).

GUNS OF THE TIMBERLAND 1960 d: Robert D. Webb. USA., *Guns of the Timberland*, Louis L'Amour, Novel

Gunsmoke *see* HEART OF ARIZONA (1938).

GUNSMOKE 1953 d: Nathan Juran. USA., *Roughshod*, Norman A. Fox, Novel

GUNSMOKE IN TUCSON 1958 d: Thomas Carr. USA., *Tucson*, Paul Leslie Peil, Novel

GUNSUNDARI KATHA 1949 d: K. V. Reddy. IND., *King Lear*, William Shakespeare, c1605, Play

GUO QING SHI DIAN ZHONG 1956 d: Wu Tian. CHN., *Double Bell Watch*, Lu Shi, Wen Da, Novel

GUODAO FENGBI 1997 d: Ho Ping. TWN., *Kuo Cheng*, Short Stories

GURAMA-TO NO YUWAKU 1959 d: Yuzo KawashimA. JPN., *Gurama-to No Yuwaku*, Tadashi Iizawa, Play

GUSARSKAYA BALLADA 1962 d: Eldar Ryazanov. USS., *Davnym-Davno*, Aleksandr Gladkov, 1942, Play

GUSHU YIREN 1987 d: Tian Zhuangzhuang. CHN., *Gushu Yiren*, Shu Qingchun, 194-, Novel

GUSTAV ADOLFS PAGE 1960 d: Rolf Hansen. AUS./GRM., *Gustav Adolfs Page*, Conrad Ferdinand Meyer, 1882, Short Story

Gute Nacht, Mary *see* DIE GESTORTE HOCHZEITSNACHT (1950).

Gute Ruf, Der *see* LES MENSONGES (1927).

GUTEN TAG, SCHWIEGERMAMA 1928 d: Johannes Brandt. GRM., *Der Kernpunkt*, Eugene Labiche, Play

GUTTER MAGDALENE, THE 1916 d: George Melford. USA., *A Gutter Magdalen*, Willard Mack, Short Story

Gutter, The *see* THE VIRTUOUS MODEL (1919).

Guttersnipes *see* GATEGUTTER (1949).

GUV'NOR, THE 1935 d: Milton Rosmer. UKN., *Rothschild*, Paul Lafitte, Short Story

GUY FAWKES 1923 d: Maurice Elvey. UKN., *Guy Fawkes*, Harrison Ainsworth, Novel

GUY MANNERING 1912. USA., *Guy Mannering*, Sir Walter Scott, 1815, Novel

GUY WHO CAME BACK, THE 1951 d: Joseph M. Newman. USA., *The Man Who Sank the Navy*, William Fay, Short Story

Guy Who Sank the Navy, The *see* THE GUY WHO CAME BACK (1951).

Guy With a Grin *see* NO TIME FOR COMEDY (1940).

GUYS AND DOLLS 1955 d: Joseph L. Mankiewicz. USA., *The Idyll of Miss Sarah Brown*, Damon Runyon, 1944, Short Story

GWENDOLIN 1914 d: Travers Vale. USA., *Daniel Deronda*, George Eliot, 1876, Novel

GWYNETH OF THE WELSH HILLS 1921 d: F. Martin Thornton. UKN., *Gwyneth of the Welsh Hills*, Edith Nepean, Novel

GYERTEK EL A NEVNAPOMRA 1984 d: Zoltan Fabri. HNG., *Hazszentelo*, Ferenc Karinthy, 1977, Short Story

GYMKATA 1985 d: Robert Clouse. USA., *The Terrible Game*, Dan Tyler Moore, Novel

Gymkhana *see* CANNABIS (1969).

Gynecology Section *see* FRAUENSTATION (1975).

Gypsy *see* CIKANI (1921).

GYPSY 1937 d: R. William Neill. UKN., *Tzigane*, Lady Eleanor Smith, Novel

GYPSY 1962 d: Mervyn Leroy. USA., *Gypsy*, Arthur Laurents, New York 1959, Play

GYPSY AND THE GENTLEMAN, THE 1958 d: Joseph Losey. UKN., *Darkness I Leave You*, Nina Warner Hooke, Novel

Gypsy Baron *see* DER ZIGEUNERBARON (1954).

Gypsy Baron *see* DER ZIGEUNERBARON (1962).

Gypsy Baron, The *see* DER ZIGEUNERBARON (1927).

Gypsy Baron, The *see* DER ZIGEUNERBARON (1935).

GYPSY BLOOD 1931 d: Cecil Lewis. UKN., *Carmen*, Prosper Merimee, Paris 1846, Novel

GYPSY COLT 1953 d: Andrew Marton. USA., *Lassie Come Home*, Eric Knight, 1940, Novel

Gypsy Girl *see* SKY WEST AND CROOKED (1965).

GYPSY MELODY 1936 d: Edmond T. Greville. UKN., *Juanita*, Alfred Rode, Short Story

GYPSY MOTHS, THE 1969 d: John Frankenheimer. USA., *The Gypsy Moths*, James Drought, Norwalk, Ct. 1964, Novel

Gypsy Passion *see* LA FILLE A L'OURSE MIARKA (1920).

Gypsy, The *see* LE GITAN (1975).

GYPSY TRAIL, THE 1915 d: Harry Handworth. USA., *Gone to the Dogs*, Paul Kester, Story

GYPSY TRAIL, THE 1918 d: Walter Edwards. USA., *The Gipsy Trail*, Robert Housum, New York 1917, Play

Gyurkovics Girls *see* FLICKORNA GYURKOVICS (1926).

HA ENTRADO UN LADRON 1948 d: Jose Gascon. SPN., *Ha Entrado un Ladron*, Wenceslao Fernandez Florez, 1920, Novel

Haar Groote Dag *see* WAS SHE GUILTY? (1922).

Haar Vader *see* LA RENZONI (1916).

Haayo *see* EN BROLLOPSNATT (1959).

Haben Sie Interesse an Der Sache? *see* VOUS INTERESSEZ-VOUS A LA CHOSE? (1973).

HABIT 1921 d: Edwin Carewe. USA., Tom Barry, Play

HABIT VERT, L' 1937 d: Roger Richebe. FRN., *L' Habit Vert*, Gaston Arman de Caillavet, Robert de Flers, Play

HABITATION OF DRAGONS, THE 1992 d: Michael Lindsay-Hogg. USA., *The Habitation of Dragons*, Horton Foote, 1988, Play

HABITS NOIRS, LES 1914 d: Daniel Riche. FRN., *Les Habits Noirs*, Paul Feval, Novel

HACHIGATSU-NO-KYOSHIKYOKU 1991 d: Akira KurosawA. JPN/FRN/UKN., *Nabe-No-Kaka*, Kiyoko Murata, Novel

Hadimrsku Doesn't Know *see* TO NEZNATE HADIMRSKU (1931).

Hadisat an-Nusf Meter *see* HADITHA AL NASF METR (1983).

HADITHA AL NASF METR 1983 d: Samir ZikrA. SYR., Sobri Mosa, Story

HADYBBUK 1968 d: Ilan Eldad, Shraga Friedman. ISR/GRM., *Der Dibuk*, Solomon an-Ski, 1916, Play

HAENDELIGT UHELD 1971 d: Erik Balling. DNM., *Handeligt Uheld*, Anders Bodelsen, 1968, Novel

HAERVAERK 1977 d: Ole Roos. DNM., *Haervaerk*, Tom Kristensen, 1930, Novel

Hagbard and Signe *see* DEN RODA KAPPAN (1967).

HAGIVA 1955 d: Thorold Dickinson. ISR., Zvi Kolitz, Story

HAI XIA 1975 d: Qian Jiang, Chen Huaiai. CHN., *Island Militia Women*, Li Ruqin, Novel

HAI ZI WANG 1987 d: Chen Kaige. CHN., *Hai Zi Wang*, Zhong Ahcheng, 1982, Short Story

HAIE AN BORD 1970 d: Arthur M. Rabenalt. GRM., *Haie an Bord*, Becker-Riepen, Novel

HAIE UND KLEINE FISCHE 1957 d: Frank Wisbar. GRM., *Haie Und Kleine Fische*, Wolfgang Ott, Novel

HAIL, HERO! 1969 d: David Miller. USA., *Hero! Hail*, John Weston, New York 1968, Novel

Hail! Mafia *see* MAFIA JE VOUS SALUE (1965).

HAIR 1979 d: Milos Forman. USA., *Hair*, Galt MacDermot, Hames Rado, Gerome Ragni, Musical Play

Hair Trigger Casey *see* IMMEDIATE LEE (1916).

Hair Trigger Cassidy *see* IMMEDIATE LEE (1916).

HAIRY APE, THE 1944 d: Alfred Santell. USA., *The Hairy Ape*, Eugene O'Neill, 1922, Play

HAISHANG HUA 1998 d: Hou Hsiao-Hsien. TWN/JPN., *Haishang Hua Liezhuang*, Han Ziyun, Novel

HAITATSU SARENAI SANTSU NO TEGAMI 1979 d: Yoshitaro NomurA. JPN., *Calamity Town*, Ellery Queen, Novel

Haizi Wang *see* HAI ZI WANG (1987).

HAJKA 1977 d: Zivojin Pavlovic. YGS., *Hajka*, Mihailo Lalic, 1960, Novel

HAKAI 1948 d: Keisuke KinoshitA. JPN., *Hakai*, Toson Shimazaki, 1906, Novel

HAKAI 1961 d: Kon IchikawA. JPN., *Hakai*, Toson Shimazaki, 1906, Novel

Hakaitz Shel Avia *see* HAKAYITZ SHEL AVIYA (1988).

HAKAYITZ SHEL AVIYA 1988 d: Eli Cohen. ISR., Gila Almagor, Book

Hakim, El *see* EL HAKIM (1957).

HAKKARI'DE BIR MEVSIM 1987 d: Erden Kiral. TRK/GRM., *Hakkari'de Bir Mevsim*, Ferit Edgu, Novel

HAKOSEM MI-LUBLIN 1978 d: Menahem Golan. ISR/GRM/CND., *The Magician of Lublin*, Isaac Bashevis Singer, 1960, Novel

HAKUCHI 1951 d: Akira KurosawA. JPN., *Idiot*, Fyodor Dostoyevsky, 1868, Novel

HAKUCHU NO TORIMA 1966 d: Nagisa OshimA. JPN., *Hakuchu No Torima*, Taijun Takeda, 1960, Short Story

HAKUJITSUMU 1964 d: Tetsuji Takechi. JPN., *Hakujitsumu Yume*, Junichiro Tanizaki, 1926, Short Story

HALBSTARKEN, DIE 1956 d: Georg Tressler. GRM., Will Tremper, Story

HALF A BRIDE 1928 d: Gregory La CavA. USA., *White Hands*, Arthur Stringer, 1927, Short Story

HALF A CHANCE 1913 d: Oscar Apfel. USA., *Half a Chance*, Frederic Stewart Isham, Indianapolis 1909, Novel

HALF A CHANCE 1920 d: Robert T. Thornby. USA., *Half a Chance*, Frederic Stewart Isham, Indianapolis 1909, Novel

Half a Hero *see* MAKE ME A STAR! (1932).

HALF A ROGUE 1916 d: Henry Otto. USA., *Half a Rogue*, Harold MacGrath, Indianapolis 1906, Novel

HALF A SINNER 1934 d: Kurt Neumann. USA., *Alias the Deacon*, Leroy Clemens, John B. Hymer, New York 1925, Play

HALF A SIXPENCE 1967 d: George Sidney. UKN/USA., *Kipps*, H. G. Wells, London 1905, Novel

HALF A TRUTH 1922 d: Sinclair Hill. UKN., *Half a Truth*, Rita, Novel

HALF AN HOUR 1920 d: Harley Knoles. USA., *Half an Hour*, J. M. Barrie, New York 1913, Play

Half an Hour *see* THE DOCTOR'S SECRET (1930).

Half Angel *see* I TAKE THIS WOMAN (1931).

HALF BREED, THE 1922 d: Charles A. Taylor. USA., *Half Breed*, H. D. Cottrell, Oliver Morosco, 1906, Play

Half Flame, Half Brine *see* YI BAN HAI SHUI YI BAN HUO YAN (1989).

HALF MARRIAGE 1929 d: William J. Cowen. USA., *Half Marriage*, George Kibbe Turner, Story

Half Meter Incident, The *see* HADITHA AL NASF METR (1983).

HALF MILLION BRIBE, THE 1916 d: Edgar Jones. USA., *The Red Mouse; a Mystery Romance*, William Hamilton Osborne, New York 1909, Novel

HALF MOON STREET 1986 d: Bob Swaim. UKN/USA., *Dr. Slaughter*, Paul Theroux, 1984, Novel

HALF NAKED TRUTH, THE 1932 d: Gregory La CavA. USA., *Anatomy of Ballyhoo: Phantom Fame*, David Freedman, Reichenback Harry, New York 1931, Book

Half Way Decent *see* LITTLE MISS MARKER (1934).

Half-a-Minute Kendall *see* MILE-A-MINUTE KENDALL (1918).

Halfbreed, The *see* THE HALF-BREED (1916).

HALF-BREED, THE 1916 d: Allan Dwan. USA., *In the Carquinez Woods*, Bret Harte, London 1883, Novel

Half-Naked Truth, The *see* THE HALF NAKED TRUTH (1932).

Half-Truth *see* ARDH SATYA (1983).

HALFWAY HOUSE, THE 1944 d: Basil Dearden. UKN., *The Peaceful Inn*, Denis Ogden, Play

Halfway to Heaven *see* MAYBE IT'S LOVE (1935).

HALF-WAY TO HEAVEN 1929 d: George Abbott. USA., *Here Comes the Bandwagon*, Henry Leyford Gates, New York 1928, Novel

HALGATO 1995 d: Andrej Mlakar. SLO., Feri Lainscek, Novel

Hall of Mirrors *see* WUSA (1970).

HALLELUJAH TRAIL, THE 1965 d: John Sturges. USA., *Hallelujah Train*, Bill Gulick, New York 1963, Novel

Hallucination *see* LA RUPTURE (1970).

HALO FOR ATHUAN, A 1985 d: Alan Burke. ASL., *The Book of Athuan*, Julie Anne Ford, Radio Play

HAMACHTZAYYA 1990 d: Ron Ninio. ISR., Ehud Ben-Ezer, Story

HAMARTEF 1963 d: Natan Gross. ISR., Shimon Yisraeli, Story

HAME'AHEV 1985 d: Michal Bat-Adam. ISR., A. B. Yehoshua, Novel

Hameno Kormi *see* IL RELITTO (1961).

Hamile *see* GAMLET (1964).

HAMILTON 1998 d: Harald Zwart. SWD., *Den Enda Segern*, Jan Guillou, Novel, *Ingen Mans Land*, Jan Guillou, Novel

Hamlet *see* AMLETO (1908).

HAMLET 1910 d: August Blom. DNM., *Hamlet*, William Shakespeare, c1601, Play

HAMLET 1912 d: Charles Raymond. UKN., *Hamlet*, William Shakespeare, c1601, Play

HAMLET 1913 d: Hay Plumb. UKN., *Hamlet*, William Shakespeare, c1601, Play

HAMLET 1914. UKN., *Hamlet*, William Shakespeare, c1601, Play

HAMLET 1920 d: Svend Gade, Heinz Schall. GRM., *Hamlet*, William Shakespeare, c1601, Play

HAMLET 1948 d: Laurence Olivier. UKN., *Hamlet*, William Shakespeare, c1601, Play

HAMLET 1960 d: Franz Peter Wirth. GRM., *Hamlet*, William Shakespeare, c1601, Play

HAMLET 1964 d: Bill Colleran, John Gielgud. USA., *Hamlet*, William Shakespeare, c1601, Play

Hamlet *see* GAMLET (1964).

HAMLET 1969 d: Tony Richardson. UKN., *Hamlet*, William Shakespeare, c1601, Play

HAMLET 1970 d: Peter Wood. USA/UKN., *Hamlet*, William Shakespeare, c1601, Play

HAMLET 1971 d: Rene Bonniere. CND., *Hamlet*, William Shakespeare, c1601, Play

HAMLET 1976 d: Celestino Coronado. UKN., *Hamlet*, William Shakespeare, c1601, Play

Hamlet *see* PRINCE OF DENMARK HAMLET (1979).

HAMLET 1989 d: Pierre Cavassilas. FRN., *Hamlet*, William Shakespeare, c1601, Play

HAMLET 1990 d: Franco Zeffirelli. UKN/USA., *Hamlet*, William Shakespeare, c1601, Play

HAMLET 1996 d: Kenneth Branagh. UKN/USA., *Hamlet*, William Shakespeare, c1601, Play

HAMLET AT ELSINORE 1964 d: Philip Saville. UKN/DNM., *Hamlet*, William Shakespeare, c1601, Play

Hamlet Goes Business *see* HAMLET LIIKEMAALIMASSA (1987).

Hamlet Goes to Business *see* HAMLET LIIKEMAALIMASSA (1987).

HAMLET LIIKEMAALIMASSA 1987 d: Aki Kaurismaki. FNL., *Hamlet*, William Shakespeare, c1601, Play

HAMLET, PRINCE OF DENMARK 1979 d: Rodney Bennett. UKN., *Hamlet*, William Shakespeare, c1601, Play

HAMMARFORSENS BRUS 1948 d: Ragnar Frisk. SWD., *Die Vom Berghof*, Johannes Rohr, Novel

Hammer Against Witches, A *see* KLADIVO NA CARODEJNICE (1969).

Hammer for the Witches *see* KLADIVO NA CARODEJNICE (1969).

HAMMER THE TOFF 1952 d: MacLean Rogers. UKN., *Hammer the Toff*, John Creasey, Novel

HAMMERHEAD 1968 d: David Miller. UKN., *Hammerhead*, John Mayo, London 1964, Novel

HAMMERMORDER, DER 1990 d: Bernd Schadewald. GRM., *Der Hammermorder*, Fred Breinersdorfer, Book

HAMMERS OVER THE ANVIL 1991 d: Ann Turner. ASL., *Hammers Over the Anvil*, Alan Marshall, Book

HAMMETT 1982 d: Wim Wenders. USA., *Hammett*, Joe Gores, Novel

Hammond Mystery, The *see* THE UNDYING MONSTER (1942).

Hamp *see* KING AND COUNTRY (1964).

HAN YE 1984 d: Qiu Wen. CHN., *Han Ye*, Li Feigan, 1944, Novel

HANA HIRAKU 1948 d: Kon IchikawA. JPN., *MacHiko*, Yaeko Nogami, 1928, Novel

HANAOKA SEISHU NO TSUMA 1967 d: Yasuzo MasumurA. JPN., *Hanaoka Seishu No Tsuma*, Sawako Ariyoshi, 1966, Novel

789

HAND AT THE WINDOW, THE 1918 d: Raymond Wells. USA., *In the Spring*, John A. Moroso, 1918, Short Story

Hand in the Trap, The see **LA MANO EN LA TRAMPA** (1961).

HAND OF A CHILD, THE 1913 d: Wilfred Noy. UKN., *The Hand of a Child*, Alfred Berlyn, Poem

HAND OF PERIL, THE 1916 d: Maurice Tourneur. USA., *The Hand of Peril; a Novel of Adventure*, Arthur Stringer, New York 1915, Novel

Hand of the Gallows see **DIE BANDE DES SCHRECKENS** (1960).

HAND, THE 1981 d: Oliver Stone. USA., *The Lizard's Tail*, Marc Brandel, Novel

HANDCUFFS OR KISSES 1921 d: George Archainbaud. USA., *Handcuffs and Kisses*, Thomas Edgelow, 1920, Short Story

Handful of Clouds, A see **THE DOORWAY TO HELL** (1930).

HANDFUL OF DUST, A 1988 d: Charles Sturridge. UKN/USA., *A Handful of Dust*, Evelyn Waugh, 1934, Novel

HANDLE WITH CARE 1922 d: Phil Rosen. USA., *Handle With Care*, Charles Belmont Davis, Story

Handmaid's Tale, The see **DIE GESCHICHTE DER DIENERIN** (1989).

Hand-Me-Down Suit, A see **UBRANIE PRAWIE NOWE** (1963).

HANDS ACROSS THE ROCKIES 1941 d: Lambert Hillyer. USA., *A Gunsmoke Case for Major Cain*, Norbert Davis, Story

HANDS OF A STRANGER 1987 d: Larry Elikann. USA., *Hands of a Stranger*, Robert Daley, Novel

Hands of a Strangler see **LES MAINS D'ORLAC** (1959).

HANDS OF A STRANGLER 1962 d: Newt Arnold. USA., *Les Mains d'Orlac*, Maurice Renard, Paris 1920, Novel

HANDS OF NARA, THE 1922 d: Harry Garson. USA., *The Hands of Nara*, Richard Washburn Child, New York 1922, Novel

Hands of Orlac see **MAD LOVE** (1935).

Hands of Orlac, The see **ORLACS HANDE** (1925).

Hands of Orlac, The see **LES MAINS D'ORLAC** (1959).

Hands Off the Loot see **TOUCHEZ PAS AU GRISBI** (1953).

Handsome Antonio see **IL BELL'ANTONIO** (1960).

Handsome Tony see **IL BELL'ANTONIO** (1960).

HANDY ANDY 1921 d: Bert Wynne. UKN., *Handy Andy*, Samuel Lover, Novel

HANDY ANDY 1934 d: David Butler. USA., *Merry Andrew*, Lewis Beach, New York 1929, Play

HANGAR 18 1980 d: James L. Conway. USA., Tom Chapman, Story

HANGED MAN, THE 1965 d: Don Siegel. USA., *The Hanged Man*, Dorothy B. Hughes, Novel

Hanged Man's Farm see **LA FERME DU PENDU** (1945).

HANGING A PICTURE 1915. UKN., *Three Men in a Boat (to Say Nothing of the Dog)*, Jerome K. Jerome, London 1889, Novel

HANGING JUDGE, THE 1918 d: Henry Edwards. UKN., *The Hanging Judge*, Tom Gallon, Story

HANGING TREE, THE 1959 d: Delmer Daves. USA., *The Hanging Tree*, Dorothy M. Johnson, 1957, Novel

Hangman of London, The see **DER HENKER VON LONDON** (1963).

HANGMAN, THE 1959 d: Michael Curtiz. USA., Luke Short, Story

HANGMAN'S HOUSE 1928 d: John Ford. USA., *Hangman's House*, Brian Oswald Donn-Byrne, New York 1926, Novel

Hangman's Noose see **THE OCTOBER MAN** (1947).

Hangover Murders see **REMEMBER LAST NIGHT?** (1934).

HANGOVER SQUARE 1945 d: John Brahm. USA., *Hangover Square*, Patrick Hamilton, 1941, Novel

HANGYABOLY 1971 d: Zoltan Fabri. HNG., *Hangyaboly*, Margit Kaffka, 1917, Novel

Hank see **WILD HORSE HANK** (1978).

Hank O'Blue see **MAN'S CASTLE** (1933).

HANK WILLIAMS "THE SHOW HE NEVER GAVE" 1982 d: David AcombA. CND., *Hank Williams the Show He Never Gave*, Maynard Collins, Play

HANKA A JINDRA 1929 d: Oldrich Kminek. CZC., *Hanka a Jindra*, Vilem Neubauer, Novel

Hanka and Jindra see **HANKA A JINDRA** (1929).

Hannah Lee see **OUTLAW TERRITORY** (1953).

Hannah Senesh see **HANNA'S WAR** (1988).

HANNA'S WAR 1988 d: Menahem Golan. USA/ISR., *A Great Wind Cometh*, Yoel Palgi, Book, *The Diaries of Hannah Senesh*, Hanna Senesh, Book

HANNELE CHIGURIDAGA 1968 d: M. R. Vittal. IND., *Hannele Chigurdaga*, Triveni, Novel

HANNELES HIMMELFAHRT 1934 d: Thea von Harbou. GRM., *Hanneles Himmelfahrt*, Gerhart Hauptmann, 1893, Play

HANNERL UND IHRE LIEBHABER 1921 d: Felix Basch. GRM., *Hannerl Und Ihre Liebhaber*, Rudolf Hans Bartsch, Novel

HANNERL UND IHRE LIEBHABER 1935 d: Werner Hochbaum. AUS., *Hannerl Und Ihre Liebhaber*, Rudolf Hans Bartsch, Novel

HANNIBAL TANAR UR 1956 d: Zoltan Fabri. HNG., *Hannibal Foltamasztasa*, Ferenc Mora, 1949, Novel

Hans Christian Andersen see **MR. H. C. ANDERSEN** (1950).

Hans Forsta Sommar see **POIKA ELI KESAANSA** (1955).

HANS IM GLUCK 1949 d: Peter Hamel. GRM., *Hans Im Gluck*, Jacob Grimm, Wilhelm Grimm, 1812, Short Story

HANS LE MARIN 1948 d: Francois Villiers. FRN., *Hans le Marin*, Edouard Peisson, Novel

HANS NADS TESTAMENTE 1919 d: Victor Sjostrom. SWD., *Hans Nads Testamente*, Hjalmar Bergman, 1910, Novel

HANS NADS TESTAMENTE 1940 d: Per Lindberg. SWD., *Hans Nads Testamente*, Hjalmar Bergman, 1910, Novel

HANSEL AND GRETEL 1909 d: J. Searle Dawley. USA., *Hansel Und Gretel*, Jacob Grimm, Wilhelm Grimm, 1812, Short Story

HANSEL AND GRETEL 1954 d: John Paul. USA., *Hansel Und Gretel*, Jacob Grimm, Wilhelm Grimm, 1812, Short Story

Hansel and Gretel see **HANSEL UND GRETEL** (1954).

HANSEL AND GRETEL 1982 d: James Frawley. USA., *Hansel Und Gretel*, Jacob Grimm, Wilhelm Grimm, 1812, Short Story

HANSEL AND GRETEL 1987 d: Len Talan. UKN/ISR., *Hansel Und Gretel*, Jacob Grimm, Wilhelm Grimm, 1812, Short Story

HANSEL UND GRETEL 1954 d: Fritz Genschow. GRM., *Hansel Und Gretel*, Jacob Grimm, 1812, Short Story

HANSEL UND GRETEL 1954 d: Walter Janssen. GRM., *Hansel Und Gretel*, Jacob Grimm, 1812, Short Story

HANSEL UND GRETEL 1954 d: Fritz Genschow. GRM., *Hansel Und Gretel*, Wilhelm Grimm, 1812, Short Story

HANSEL UND GRETEL 1954 d: Walter Janssen. GRM., *Hansel Und Gretel*, Wilhelm Grimm, 1812, Short Story

HANTISE 1921 d: Jean Kemm. FRN., *Hantise*, Marcel Dupont, Novel

HANTISES 1997 d: Michel Ferry. FRN., *La Horla*, Guy de Maupassant, 1886, Short Story

HANUL DINTRE DEALURI 1988 d: Cristiana Nicolae. RMN., *La Hanul Lui Minjoala*, Ion Luca Caragiale, 1898, Short Story

HANY AZ ORA, VEKKER UR? 1985 d: Peter Bacso. HNG., *Hany Ora? Weiskopf Ur*, Geza Paskandi, 1968, Short Story

HAPPIEST DAYS OF YOUR LIFE, THE 1950 d: Frank Launder. UKN., *The Happiest Days of Your Life*, John Dighton, London 1947, Play

HAPPIEST MILLIONAIRE, THE 1967 d: Norman Tokar. USA., *The Happiest Millionaire*, Kyle Crichton, New York 1956, Play

HAPPINESS 1924 d: King Vidor. USA., *Happiness*, J. Hartley Manners, 1914, Play

Happiness see **KOFUKU** (1981).

HAPPINESS A LA MODE 1919 d: Walter Edwards. USA., *Happiness a la Mode*, Edwina Levin, 1919, Short Story

Happiness in the Outbuilding see **GLUCK IM HINTERHAUS** (1979).

Happiness Is a Small Corner see **GLUCK IM WINKEL** (1937).

Happiness of 3 Women, The see **THE HAPPINESS OF THREE WOMEN** (1954).

HAPPINESS OF THREE WOMEN, THE 1917 d: William D. Taylor. USA., *The Happiness of Three Women*, Albert Payson Terhune, 1914, Short Story

HAPPINESS OF THREE WOMEN, THE 1954 d: Maurice Elvey. UKN., *The Wishing Well*, E. Eynon Evans, Play

Happiness Preferred see **OUTCAST** (1936).

Happy Alexander see **ALEXANDRE LE BIENHEUREUX** (1968).

HAPPY ANNIVERSARY 1959 d: David Miller. USA., *Anniversary Waltz*, Jerome Chodorov, Joseph Fields, New York 1954, Play

HAPPY BIRTHDAY, GEMINI 1980 d: Richard Benner. USA., *Gemini*, Albert Innaurato, Play

HAPPY BIRTHDAY, WANDA JANE 1971 d: Mark Robson. USA., *Happy Birthday, Wanda June*, Kurt Vonnegut Jr., 1971, Play

HAPPY DEATHDAY 1969 d: Henry Cass. UKN., *Happy Deathday*, Peter Howard, Play

Happy Dollars see **THEY JUST HAD TO GET MARRIED** (1933).

HAPPY ENDING, THE 1925 d: George A. Cooper. UKN., *The Happy Ending*, Ian Hay, London 1922, Play

HAPPY ENDING, THE 1931 d: Millard Webb. UKN., *The Happy Ending*, Ian Hay, London 1922, Play

Happy Family see **SEMEJNOE SCASTE** (1969).

HAPPY FAMILY, THE 1936 d: MacLean Rogers. UKN., *French Salad*, Max Catto, 1934, Play

HAPPY FAMILY, THE 1952 d: Muriel Box. UKN., *The Happy Family*, Michael Clayton Hutton, Play

HAPPY IS THE BRIDE 1958 d: Roy Boulting. UKN., *Quiet Wedding*, Esther McCracken, London 1938, Play

HAPPY LAND 1943 d: Irving Pichel. USA., *Happy Land*, MacKinlay Kantor, 1943, Novel

Happy Landing see **FLYING HIGH** (1931).

Happy New Year see **SZCZESLIWEGO NOWEGO ROKU** (1997).

Happy Old Year see **FELIZ ANO VELHO** (1988).

Happy Pilgrimage, The see **DIE FROHLICHE WALLFAHRT** (1956).

Happy Prince, The see **PRINTUL FERICIT** (1968).

HAPPY PRISONER, THE 1924 d: Hugh Croise. UKN., *The Happy Prisoner*, W. Pett Ridge, Short Story

Happy Summer see **SOMMERGLAEDER** (1940).

HAPPY THIEVES, THE 1962 d: George Marshall. USA., *The Oldest Confession*, Richard Condon, New York 1958, Novel

HAPPY TIME, THE 1952 d: Richard Fleischer. USA., *Happy Time*, Robert L. Fontaine, Novel

Happy Times see **THE INSPECTOR GENERAL** (1949).

Happy Village, The see **DAS FROHLICHE DORF** (1955).

Happy Vineyard, The see **DER FROHLICHE WEINBERG** (1927).

Happy Vineyard, The see **DER FROHLICHE WEINBERG** (1952).

Happy Voyage see **GLUCKLICHE REISE** (1933).

Happy Voyage see **GLUCKLICHE REISE** (1954).

HAPPY WARRIOR, THE 1917 d: F. Martin Thornton. UKN., *The Happy Warrior*, A. S. M. Hutchinson, London 1912, Novel

HAPPY WARRIOR, THE 1925 d: J. Stuart Blackton. USA., *The Happy Warrior*, A. S. M. Hutchinson, London 1912, Novel

Happy Years of the Thorwalds, The see **DIE GLUCKLICHEN JAHRE DER THORWALDS** (1962).

HAPPY YEARS, THE 1950 d: William A. Wellman. USA., *Lawrenceville School Stories*, Owen Johnson, Short Stories

HAR HAR DU DITT LIV 1966 d: Jan Troell. SWD., *Romanen Om Olof*, Eyvind Johnson, Stockholm 1945, Novel

Harakiri see **SEPPUKU** (1962).

Hara-Kiri see **THE BATTLE** (1934).

Hara-Kiri see **SEPPUKU** (1962).

HARAM, AL- 1964 d: Henry Barakat. EGY., *Al- Haram*, Youssef Idris, Novel

Haram, El *see* **AL- HARAM** (1964).

Harap Alb *see* **DE-AS FI HARAP ALB** (1965).

HARASSED HERO, THE 1954 d: Maurice Elvey. UKN., *The Harassed Hero*, Ernest Dudley, Novel

HARBOUR LIGHTS, THE 1914 d: Percy Nash. UKN., *The Harbour Lights*, Henry Pettitt, George R. Sims, London 1885, Play

HARBOUR LIGHTS, THE 1923 d: Tom Terriss. UKN., *The Harbour Lights*, Henry Pettitt, George R. Sims, London 1885, Play

Hard Against Hard *see* **THE SKIN GAME** (1920).

Hard Bargain *see* **THIEVES' HIGHWAY** (1949).

HARD CASH 1913 d: Charles M. Seay. USA., *Hard Cash*, Charles Reade, 1864, Novel

HARD CASH 1921 d: Edwin J. Collins. UKN., *Hard Cash*, Charles Reade, 1864, Novel

HARD, FAST AND BEAUTIFUL 1951 d: Ida Lupino. USA., *American Girl*, John R. Tunis, 1930, Novel

HARD FEELINGS 1982 d: Daryl Duke. CND/USA., *Hard Feelings*, Don Bredes, Novel

HARD FISTS 1927 d: William Wyler. USA., *The Grappler*, Charles A. Logue, Story

Hard Luck Dame *see* **DANGEROUS** (1935).

Hard Luck Dame *see* **SATAN MET A LADY** (1936).

HARD MAN, THE 1957 d: George Sherman. USA., *The Hard Man*, Leo Katcher, 1957, Novel

Hard Ride Hank *see* **WILD HORSE HANK** (1978).

Hard Ride to Rantan *see* **WILD HORSE HANK** (1978).

HARD ROCK BREED, THE 1918 d: Raymond Wells. USA., *The Hard Rock Man*, Frederick R. Bechdolf, New York 1910, Novel

HARD STEEL 1942 d: Norman Walker. UKN., *Steel Saraband*, Roger Dataller, Novel

Hard Tegen Hard *see* **THE SKIN GAME** (1920).

HARD TIMES 1915 d: Thomas Bentley. UKN., *Hard Times*, Charles Dickens, London 1854, Novel

HARD TIMES 1977 d: John Irvin. UKN., *Hard Times*, Charles Dickens, London 1854, Novel

Hard Times *see* **TEMPOS DIFICEIS** (1988).

HARD TIMES 1995 d: Peter Barnes. UKN/USA., *Hard Times*, Charles Dickens, London 1854, Novel

Hard to Be a God *see* **EIN GOTT ZU SEIN ES IST NICHT LEICHT** (1988).

HARD TO GET 1929 d: William Beaudine. USA., *Mother Knows Best*, Edna Ferber, Garden City, N.Y. 1927, Novel

HARD TO GET 1938 d: Ray Enright. USA., *Stuffed Shirt*, Stephen Morehouse Avery, 1932, Short Story

HARD TRAVELING 1986 d: Dan Bessie. USA., *Bread and a Stone*, Alva Bessie, Novel

HARD WAY, THE 1916 d: Walter West. UKN., *The Hard Way*, a" "Peer, Novel

HARD-BOILED HAGGERTY 1927 d: Charles J. Brabin. USA., *Belated Evidence*, Elliott White Springs, 1926, Short Story

HARDER THEY FALL, THE 1956 d: Mark Robson. USA., *The Harder They Fall*, Budd Schulberg, 1947, Novel

HARLEM 1943 d: Carmine Gallone. ITL., Giuseppe Achille, Novel

Harlem Story *see* **THE COOL WORLD** (1964).

HARLOW 1965 d: Gordon Douglas. USA., *Harlow: an Intimate Biography*, Irving Shulman, New York 1964, Book

Harmonie *see* **LE TOUBIB** (1979).

HARMONY AT HOME 1930 d: Hamilton MacFadden. USA., *The Family Upstairs*, Harry Delf, Atlantic City 1925, Play

Harmony at Home *see* **LOOK AND LOVE STOP** (1939).

HARNESS FEVER 1976 d: Don Chaffey. ASL/USA., Walter D. Edmonds, Novel

HARNESS, THE 1971 d: Boris Sagal. USA., *The Harness*, John Steinbeck, Short Story

HARNESSING PEACOCKS 1992 d: James Cellan Jones. UKN., *Harnessing Peacocks*, Mary Wesley, Novel

HAROLD AND MAUDE 1971 d: Hal Ashby. USA., *Harold and Maude*, Colin Higgins, Novel

HAROLD ROBBINS' 79 PARK AVENUE 1977 d: Paul Wendkos. USA., *79 Park Avenue*, Harold Robbins, Novel

Harold Robbins' the Betsy *see* **THE BETSY** (1978).

Harold Robbins' the Pirate *see* **THE PIRATE** (1978).

HAROM TESTOR AFRIKABAN, A 1996 d: Istvan Bujtor. HNG., *A Harom Testor Afrikaban*, Jeno Rejto, Novel

HARP IN HOCK, A 1927 d: Renaud Hoffman. USA., *A Harp in Hock*, Evelyn Campbell, Story

Harp of Burma, The *see* **BIRUMA NO TATEGOTO** (1956).

HARPER 1966 d: Jack Smight. USA., *The Moving Target*, Ross MacDonald, New York 1949, Novel

Harper's Mystery, The *see* **BLOOD MONEY** (1921).

HARRIET AND THE PIPER 1920 d: Bertram Bracken. USA., *Harriet and the Piper*, Kathleen Norris, New York 1920, Novel

HARRIET CRAIG 1950 d: Vincent Sherman. USA., *Craig's Wife*, George Edward Kelly, New York 1925, Play

HARRIET THE SPY 1996 d: Bronwen Hughes. USA., *Harriet the Spy*, Louise Fitzhugh

Harry & Son *see* **HARRY AND SON** (1983).

HARRY AND SON 1983 d: Paul Newman. USA., *A Lost King*, Don Capite, Novel

HARRY BLACK 1958 d: Hugo Fregonese. UKN/USA., *Harry Black*, David Walker, Novel

Harry Black and the Tiger *see* **HARRY BLACK** (1958).

Harry Palmer Returns *see* **FUNERAL IN BERLIN** (1966).

Harry's Game *see* **BELFAST ASSASSIN** (1982).

Harry's Game: the Movie *see* **BELFAST ASSASSIN** (1982).

Harvest *see* **REGAIN** (1937).

Harvest Month *see* **ELOKUU** (1956).

HARVEST MOON, THE 1920 d: J. Searle Dawley. USA., *The Harvest Moon*, Augustus Thomas, New York 1909, Play

Harvest, The *see* **VOZVRASHCHENIE VASSILIYA BORTNIKOVA** (1953).

Harvest Thunder *see* **THE VINTAGE** (1957).

HARVESTER, THE 1927 d: James Leo Meehan. USA., *The Harvester*, Gene Stratton-Porter, Garden City, N.Y. 1911, Novel

HARVESTER, THE 1936 d: Joseph Santley. USA., *The Harvester*, Gene Stratton-Porter, Garden City, N.Y. 1911, Novel

HARVEY 1950 d: Henry Koster. USA., *Harvey*, Mary Coyle Chase, New York 1944, Play

HARVEY 1972 d: Fielder Cook. USA., *Harvey*, Mary Coyle Chase, New York 1944, Play

HARVEY 1996 d: George Schaefer. USA., *Harvey*, Mary Coyle Chase, New York 1944, Play

HARVEY GIRLS, THE 1945 d: George Sidney. USA., *The Harvey Girls*, Samuel Hopkins Adams, 1942, Novel

Hashachar *see* **L' AUBE** (1986).

HASHI NO NAI KAWA 1992 d: Yoichi Higashi. JPN., *Hashi No Nai Kawa*, Sue Sumi, Novel

HASHIMURA TOGO 1917 d: William C. de Mille. USA., *Hashimura Togo*, Wallace Irwin, New York 1914, Novel

HAST NOCH DER SOHNE JA? 1959 d: Lukas Ammann. SWT., *Hast Noch Der Sohne Ja?*, Erwin Heimann, Frauenfeld 1956, Novel

HASTHANDLARENS FLICKOR 1954 d: Egil Holmsen. SWD., *Hasthandlarens Flickor*, Nils Artur Lundkvist, 1935, Short Story

HASTY HEART, THE 1949 d: Vincent Sherman. UKN/USA., *The Hasty Heart*, John Patrick, London 1945, Play

HASTY HEART, THE 1983 d: Martin Speer. USA., *The Hasty Heart*, John Patrick, London 1945, Play

HAT CHECK GIRL 1932 d: Sidney Lanfield. USA., *Hat-Check Girl*, Rian James, New York 1932, Novel

HAT, COAT AND GLOVE 1934 d: Worthington Miner. USA., *A Hat a Coat a Glove*, Wilhelm Speyer, New York 1934, Play

HATARI! 1962 d: Howard Hawks. USA., Harry Kurnitz, Story

HATCHET MAN, THE 1932 d: William A. Wellman. USA., *The Honorable Mr. Wong*, Achmed Abdullah, David Belasco, Play

Hatchet, The *see* **BALTAGUL** (1969).

HATE 1922 d: Maxwell Karger. USA., *Hate*, Wadsworth Camp, Short Story

HATE SHIP, THE 1929 d: Norman Walker. UKN., *The Hate Ship*, Bruce Graeme, Novel

HATFUL OF RAIN, A 1957 d: Fred Zinnemann. USA., *A Hatful of Rain*, Michael V. Gazzo, New York 1955, Play

HATFUL OF RAIN, A 1968 d: John Llewellyn Moxey. USA., *A Hatful of Rain*, Michael V. Gazzo, New York 1955, Play

Hatmaker, The *see* **LES FANTOMES DU CHAPELIER** (1981).

Hatred *see* **MOLLENARD** (1937).

HATTER'S CASTLE 1941 d: Lance Comfort. UKN., *Hatters Castle*, A. J. Cronin, 1931, Novel

Hatter's Ghosts, The *see* **LES FANTOMES DU CHAPELIER** (1981).

Haubenlerche, Die *see* **WENN MENSCHEN REIF ZUR LIEBE WERDEN** (1927).

Haunted *see* **NIGHT OF THE DEMON** (1957).

HAUNTED 1995 d: Lewis Gilbert. UKN/USA., *Haunted*, James Herbert, Novel

Haunted Castle *see* **SCHLOSS VOGELOD** (1921).

Haunted City, The *see* **KISERTET LUBLON** (1976).

Haunted Honeymoon *see* **BUSMAN'S HONEYMOON** (1940).

HAUNTED HOUSE, THE 1928 d: Benjamin Christensen. USA., *The Haunted House*, Owen Davis, New York 1926, Play

HAUNTED PAJAMAS, THE 1917 d: Fred J. Balshofer. USA., *The Haunted Pajamas*, Francis Perry Elliott, Indianapolis 1911, Novel

HAUNTED PALACE, THE 1963 d: Roger Corman. USA., *The Haunted Palace*, Edgar Allan Poe, 1839, Short Story

HAUNTED SHIP, THE 1927 d: Forrest Sheldon. USA., *White and Yellow*, Jack London, 1905, Short Story

HAUNTED SUMMER 1989 d: Ivan Passer. USA., *Haunted Summer*, Anne Edwards, Novel

Haunting of Helen Walker, The *see* **THE TURN OF THE SCREW** (1995).

HAUNTING OF JULIA, THE 1976 d: Richard Loncraine. UKN/CND., *Julia*, Peter Straub, Novel

HAUNTING OF SARAH HARDY, THE 1989 d: Jerry London. USA., *The Haunting of Sarah Hardy*, Jim Flannagan, Novel

HAUNTING SHADOWS 1920 d: Henry King. USA., *The House of a Thousand Candles*, Meredith Nicholson, New York 1905, Novel

HAUNTING, THE 1963 d: Robert Wise. UKN., *The Haunting of Hill House*, Shirley Jackson, New York 1959, Novel

HAUNTING WINDS 1915 d: Carl M. Le Viness. USA., *Haunting Winds*, G. E. Jenks, Story

Hauntings *see* **HANTISES** (1997).

HAUNTS OF THE VERY RICH 1972 d: Paul Wendkos. USA., T. K. Brown, Story

HAUPTLEHRER HOFER 1974 d: Peter Lilienthal. GRM., *Hauptlehrer Hofer*, Gunter Herburger, 1975, Short Story

HAUPTMANN UND SEIN HELD, DER 1955 d: Max Nosseck. GRM., *Der Hauptmann Und Sein Held*, Claus Hubalek, Novel

HAUPTMANN VON KOPENICK, DER 1931 d: Richard Oswald. GRM., *Der Hauptmann von Kopenick*, Carl Zuckmayer, 1930, Play

HAUPTMANN VON KOPENICK, DER 1956 d: Helmut Kautner. GRM., *Der Hauptmann von Kopenick*, Carl Zuckmayer, 1930, Play

HAUS AM FLUSS, DAS 1985 d: Roland Graf. GDR., Friedrich Wolf, Story

HAUS AUF DEM HUGEL, DAS 1964 d: Werner Klinger. AUS., *Das Haus Auf Dem Hugel*, Jules Charpentier, Novel

HAUS DES LEBENS 1952 d: Karl Hartl. GRM., *Haus Des Lebens*, Kathe Lambert, Novel

Haus Im Wald *see* **LA MAISON DANS LA FORET** (1922).

HAUS IN DER KARPFENGASSE, DAS 1964 d: Kurt Hoffmann. GRM., *Das Haus in Der Karpfengasse*, M. Y. Ben-Gavriel, Novel

HAUS IN MONTEVIDEO, DAS 1951 d: Curt Goetz. GRM., Valerie von Maertens. GRM., *Das Haus in Montevideo*, Curt Goetz, Play

HAUS IN MONTEVIDEO, DAS 1963 d: Helmut Kautner. GRM., *Das Haus in Montevideo*, Curt Goetz, Play

HAUS NUMMER 17 1928 d: Geza von Bolvary. GRM., J. Jefferson Farjeon, Play

HAUS VOLL LIEBE, EIN 1954 d: Hans Schweikart. GRM/AUS., *Fraulein Fortuna*, Ladislaus Fodor, Play

Hauschen in Grinzing, Das see **DAS GLUCK VON GRINZING** (1933).

HAUSER'S MEMORY 1970 d: Boris Sagal. USA., *Hauser's Memory*, Curt Siodmak, Novel

HAUSTYRANN, DER 1959 d: Hans Deppe. GRM., *Der Haustyrann*, Hans Reimann, Novel

Haute Surveillance see **BLACK MIRROR** (1981).

HAVARIST, DER 1983 d: Wolf-Eckart Buhler. GRM., *Wanderer*, Sterling Hayden, Autobiography

Have No Fear, Jacob! see **JAKOB! FURCHTE DICH NICHT** (1981).

Have You Got It? see **IT PAYS TO ADVERTISE** (1931).

Have You Seen Bobik? see **NEVIDELI JSTE BOBIKA?** (1944).

HAVET OG MENNESKENE 1970 d: Sigfred Aagaard. DNM., *Havet Og Menneskene*, Kaj Munk, 1948, Play

HAVING OUR SAY: THE DELANY SISTERS' FIRST 100 YEARS 1999 d: Lynne Littman. USA., *Having Our Say*, A. Elizabeth Delany, Sarah L. Delany, Amy Hill Hearth, 1993, Book

HAVING WONDERFUL TIME 1938 d: Alfred Santell. USA., *Having Wonderful Time*, Arthur Kober, New York 1937, Play

HAVOC 1925 d: Rowland V. Lee. USA., *Havoc*, Henry Wall, Story

Havoc see **HAERVAERK** (1977).

HAVOC, THE 1916 d: Arthur Berthelet. USA., *The Havoc*, H. S. Sheldon, New York 1911, Play

HAWAII 1966 d: George Roy Hill. USA., *Hawaii*, James A. Michener, New York 1959, Novel

HAWAIIANS, THE 1970 d: Tom Gries. USA., *Hawaii*, James A. Michener, New York 1959, Novel

Hawk Island see **MIDNIGHT MYSTERY** (1930).

HAWK, THE 1917 d: Paul Scardon. USA., *L' Epervier*, Francis de Croisset, 1914, Play

Hawk, The see **COWBOY RIDE HIM** (1932).

HAWK, THE 1935 d: Edward Dmytryk. USA., *The Coyote*, James Oliver Curwood, Short Story

HAWK, THE 1992 d: David Hayman. UKN., *The Hawk*, Peter Ransley, Novel

Hawks, The see **NEAMUL SOIMARESTILOR** (1965).

HAWLEYS OF HIGH STREET 1933 d: Thomas Bentley. UKN., *Hawleys of the High Street*, Walter Ellis, 1922, Play

HAWTHORNE OF THE U.S.A. 1919 d: James Cruze. USA., *Hawthorne of the U.S.A.*, James B. Fagan, New York 1912, Play

Hawthorne the Adventurer see **HAWTHORNE OF THE U.S.A.** (1919).

HAXAN 1955 d: Andre Michel. SWD/FRN., *Oleissa*, Aleksander Ivanovich Kuprin, 1898, Short Story

HA'YERUSHA 1993 d: Amnon Rubinstein. ISR., Avi Toledano, Story

HAZARD OF HEARTS, A 1987 d: John Hough. UKN., *A Hazard of Hearts*, Barbara Cartland, Novel

HAZEL KIRKE 1912 d: Oscar Apfel. USA., *Hazel Kirke*, Steele MacKaye, New York 1880, Play

HAZEL KIRKE 1916 d: Leopold Wharton, Theodore Wharton. USA., *Hazel Kirke*, Steele MacKaye, New York 1880, Play

Hazy-Osterwald-Story, Die see **LA MUSIQUE EST MA PASSION** (1961).

HD LAPPLI 1959 d: Alfred Rasser. SWT., *Hd-Soldat Lappli. Volksstuck in 16 Bildern*, Alfred Rasser, Charles Vaucher, 1945, Play

Hd Lappli Wird Zivilist see **DEMOKRAT LAPPLI** (1961).

He see **EL** (1952).

He and His Sister see **ON A JEHO SESTRA** (1931).

He and She see **L' ASSOLUTO NATURALE** (1969).

HE COMES UP SMILING 1918 d: Allan Dwan. USA., *He Comes Up Smiling*, Charles Sherman, Indianapolis 1912, Novel

HE COULDN'T SAY NO 1938 d: Lewis Seiler. USA., *Larger Than Life*, Joseph Shrank, Springfield, MA. 1936, Play

He Died With His Eyes Open see **ON NE MEURT QUE DEUX FOIS** (1986).

HE FELL IN LOVE WITH HIS WIFE 1916 d: William D. Taylor. USA., *He Fell in Love With His Wife*, E. P. Roe, New York 1886, Novel

HE FOUND A STAR 1941 d: John Paddy Carstairs. UKN., *Ring O'Roses*, Monica Ewer, Novel

He Just Can't Stop It see **ER KANN'S NICHT LASSEN** (1962).

HE KNEW WOMEN 1930 d: F. Hugh Herbert, Lynn Shores. USA., *Second Man*, S. N. Behrman, New York 1927, Play

He Met a French Girl see **THIS IS THE NIGHT** (1932).

HE NEVER KNEW 1914 d: Ralph Ince. USA., *He Never Knew*, Bessie Boniel, Story

HE PING BAO WEI ZHE 1950 d: Shi Lan. CHN., *Six a.M.*, Liu Baiyu, Novel

HE RAN ALL THE WAY 1951 d: John Berry. USA., *He Ran All the Way*, Sam Ross, 1947, Novel

He, She Or It? see **LA POUPEE** (1962).

HE STAYED FOR BREAKFAST 1940 d: Alexander Hall. USA., *Liberte Provisoire*, Michel Duran, Paris 1934, Play, *Ode to Liberty*, Sidney Coe Howard, Washington, D.C. 1934, Play

He Walked Through the Fields see **HOU HALACH BASADOT** (1967).

He Walks Through the Fields see **HOU HALACH BASADOT** (1967).

He Wanted to Be King see **ITHELE NA YINI VASILIAS** (1967).

He Who Fears, Flees see **UTIKA KDO SE BOJI** (1986).

HE WHO GETS SLAPPED 1924 d: Victor Sjostrom. USA., *Kto Poluchaet Poshchechiny Tot*, Leonid Nikolaevich Andreyev, Play

He Who Must Die see **CELUI QUI DOIT MOURIR** (1956).

Head and Shoulders see **THE CHORUS GIRL'S ROMANCE** (1920).

Head Doctor Solm see **OBERARZT DR. SOLM** (1955).

Head for the Devil, A see **DIE NACKTE UND DER SATAN** (1959).

Head of the Family see **THE LAST GENTLEMAN** (1934).

HEAD OF THE FAMILY, THE 1922 d: Manning Haynes. UKN., *The Head of the Family*, W. W. Jacobs, Short Story

HEAD OF THE FAMILY, THE 1928 d: Joseph C. Boyle. USA., *The Head of the Family*, George Randolph Chester, 1912, Short Story

HEAD OFFICE 1936 d: Melville Brown. UKN., *Head Office*, Hugh Preston, Novel

HEAD ON 1998 d: Ana Kokkinos. ASL., *Loaded*, Christos Tsiolkas, Book

HEAD OVER HEELS 1937 d: Sonnie Hale. UKN., *Pierre Ou Jac*, Francis de Croisset, Play

Head Over Heels see **HARD TO GET** (1938).

HEAD OVER HEELS 1979 d: Joan Micklin Silver. USA., *Head Over Heals*, Ann Beattie, Novel

Head Over Heels in Love see **HEAD OVER HEELS** (1937).

Head Teacher Hofer see **HAUPTLEHRER HOFER** (1974).

Head, The see **DIE NACKTE UND DER SATAN** (1959).

Head Waiter, The see **SERVICE FOR LADIES** (1932).

HEAD WINDS 1925 d: Herbert Blache. USA., *Head Winds*, A. M. Sinclair Wilt, New York 1923, Novel

HEADING FOR HEAVEN 1947 d: Lewis D. Collins. USA., *Heading for Heaven*, Daniel Brown, Charles Webb, Play

HEADLEYS AT HOME, THE 1938 d: Chris Beute. USA., *Among Those Present*, William Miles, Carrington North, Play

HEADLINE 1943 d: John Harlow. UKN., *The Reporter*, Ken Attiwill, Novel

HEADLINE CRASHER 1937 d: Leslie Goodwins. USA., *A Motion to Adjourn*, Peter B. Kyne, 1914, Short Story

Headline Huntress see **CHANGE OF HEART** (1938).

HEADLINE SHOOTER 1933 d: Otto Brower. USA., *Muddy Waters*, Wallace West, Short Story

Headline Shooters see **HEADLINE SHOOTER** (1933).

Headlong see **KING RALPH** (1991).

HEADMASTER, THE 1921 d: Kenelm Foss. UKN., *The Headmaster*, Wilfred T. Coleby, Edward Knoblock, London 1913, Play

Headquarters State Secret see **SOLDATENSENDER CALAIS** (1960).

Heads Or Tails see **PILE OU FACE** (1980).

HEADS UP 1930 d: Victor Schertzinger. USA., *Heads Up*, John McGowan, Richard Rogers, P. G. Smith, New York 1929, Musical Play

HEALER, THE 1935 d: Reginald Barker. USA., *The Healer*, Robert Herrick, New York 1911, Novel

Heart and Hand see **A HOUSE DIVIDED** (1932).

HEART AND SOUL 1917 d: J. Gordon Edwards. USA., *Jess*, H. Rider Haggard, London 1887, Novel

Heart and Soul see **A NON-CONFORMIST PARSON** (1919).

Heart and Soul see **CUORE** (1948).

Heart at Dusk see **SRDCE V SOUMRAKU** (1936).

HEART BANDIT, THE 1924 d: Oscar Apfel. USA., *Angel-Face Molly*, Fred Kennedy Myton, Story

Heart Beat see **COL CUORE IN GOLA** (1967).

HEART BEAT 1979 d: John Byrum. USA., Carolyn Cassidy, Autobiography

Heart Beats for You, A see **EIN HERZ SCHLAGT FUR DICH** (1955).

Heart in Cellophane see **SRDCE V CELOFANU** (1939).

HEART IN PAWN, A 1919 d: William Worthington. USA., *Shadows*, Sessue Hayakawa, Play

HEART IS A LONELY HUNTER, THE 1968 d: Robert Ellis Miller. USA., *The Heart Is a Lonely Hunter*, Carson McCullers, Boston 1940, Novel

HEART LINE, THE 1921 d: Frederick A. Thompson. USA., *The Heart Line*, Gelett Burgess, Indianapolis 1907, Novel

HEART O' THE HILLS 1919 d: Sidney A. Franklin. USA., *The Heart of the Hills*, John Fox Jr., New York 1913, Novel

HEART OF A CHILD 1958 d: Clive Donner. UKN., *Heart of a Child*, Phyllis Bottome, Novel

HEART OF A CHILD, THE 1915 d: Harold Shaw. UKN., *The Heart of a Child*, Frank Danby, London 1908, Novel

HEART OF A CHILD, THE 1920 d: Ray C. Smallwood. USA., *The Heart of a Child*, Frank Danby, London 1908, Novel

Heart of a Fool see **IN THE HEART OF A FOOL** (1920).

Heart of a Gipsy, The see **THE HEART OF A GYPSY** (1919).

HEART OF A GYPSY, THE 1919 d: Charles Miller, Harry McRae Webster. USA., *The Romany Call*, Elizabeth Ethel Donoher, Short Story

HEART OF A HERO, THE 1916 d: Emile Chautard. USA., *Nathan Hale*, Clyde Fitch, New York 1899, Play

HEART OF A LION, THE 1918 d: Frank Lloyd. USA., *The Doctor: a Tale of the Rockies*, Ralph Connor, New York 1906, Novel

Heart of a Nation, The see **WE AMERICANS** (1928).

HEART OF A SIREN 1925 d: Phil Rosen. USA., *Hail and Farewell*, William Hurlbut, New York 1923, Play

Heart of a Temptress see **HEART OF A SIREN** (1925).

Heart of an Actress see **AME D'ARTISTE** (1924).

HEART OF ARIZONA 1938 d: Lesley Selander. USA., *The Heart of Arizona*, Clarence E. Mulford, Novel

HEART OF CERISE, THE 1915 d: Joseph de Grasse. USA., *The Spitfire*, Molly Elliot Seawell, Story

HEART OF DIXIE 1988 d: Martin Davidson. USA., *Heartbreak Hotel*, Anne Rivers Siddons, Novel

HEART OF MARYLAND, THE 1915 d: Herbert Brenon. USA., *The Heart of Maryland*, David Belasco, New York 1895, Play

HEART OF MARYLAND, THE 1921 d: Tom Terriss. USA., *The Heart of Maryland*, David Belasco, New York 1895, Play

HEART OF MARYLAND, THE 1927 d: Lloyd Bacon. USA., *The Heart of Maryland*, David Belasco, New York 1895, Play

HEART OF MIDLOTHIAN, THE 1914 d: Frank Wilson. UKN., *The Heart of Midlothian*, Sir Walter Scott, 1818, Novel

HEART OF NEW YORK, THE 1932 d: Mervyn Leroy. USA., *Inc. Mendel*, David Freedman, New York 1929, Play

Heart of Paris see **GRIBOUILLE** (1937).

HEART OF RACHAEL, THE 1918 d: Howard Hickman. USA., *The Heart of Rachael*, Kathleen Norris, Garden City N.Y. 1916, Novel

HEART OF SALOME, THE 1927 d: Victor Schertzinger. USA., *The Heart of Salome*, Allen Raymond, Boston 1925, Novel

HEART OF SISTER ANN, THE 1915 d: Harold Shaw. UKN., *The Heart of Sister Ann*, G. E. R. Mayne, Novel

Heart of Stone see **DAS KALTE HERZ** (1950).

HEART OF THE BLUE RIDGE, THE 1915 d: James Young. USA., *The Heart of the Blue Ridge*, Waldron Baily, New York 1915, Novel

HEART OF THE HILLS, THE 1916 d: Richard Ridgely. USA., *The Girl from the East*, David Whitelaw, Novel

HEART OF THE MATTER, THE 1953 d: George M. O'Ferrall. UKN., *The Heart of the Matter*, Graham Greene, 1948, Novel

HEART OF THE MATTER, THE 1983 d: Marco Leto. UKN/GRM., *The Heart of the Matter*, Graham Greene, 1948, Novel

HEART OF THE NORTH 1938 d: Lewis Seiler. USA., *Heart of the North*, William Byron Mowery, New York 1930, Novel

Heart of the Pirate see **DAS HERZ DES PIRATEN** (1987).

HEART OF THE SUN 1998 d: Francis Damberger. CND., *Jennie's Story*, Betty Lambert, Play

HEART OF THE SUNSET 1918 d: Frank Powell. USA., *Heart of the Sunset*, Rex Beach, New York 1913, Novel

HEART OF THE WEST 1936 d: Howard Bretherton. USA., *Tumbleweed Mesquite Jenkins*, Clarence E. Mulford, New York 1932, Novel

HEART OF THE WILDS 1918 d: Marshall Neilan. USA., *She of the Triple Chevron*, Gilbert Parker, 1892, Short Story, *Pierre of the Plains*, Edgar Selwyn, New York 1908, Play

Heart Plays Differently, The see **EIN HERZ SPIELT FALSCH** (1953).

Heart Royal see **SPORT OF KINGS** (1947).

Heart, The see **KOKORO** (1954).

HEART THIEF, THE 1927 d: Nils Chrisander. USA., *A Rabolovag*, Lajos Biro, Budapest 1912, Novel

HEART TO LET, A 1921 d: Eddie Dillon. USA., *Agatha's Aunt*, Harriet Lummis Smith, Indianapolis 1920, Novel

Heart Without Mercy see **HERZ OHNE GNADE** (1958).

Heartbeat see **ANGELE** (1934).

Heartbeat see **LA CHAMADE** (1968).

Heartbeat see **HEART BEAT** (1979).

HEARTBREAK 1931 d: Alfred L. Werker. USA., *Heartbreak*, Llewellyn Hughes, 1931, Short Story

HEARTBREAK KID, THE 1992 d: Michael Jenkins. ASL., *The Heartbreak Kid*, Richard Barrett, Play

HEARTBURN 1986 d: Mike Nichols. USA., *Heartburn*, Nora Ephron, Novel

Hearth Without a Fire, A see **KRB BEZ OHNE** (1937).

Heartless Grief see **SKORBNOE BESCUVSTVIE** (1986).

HEARTS ADRIFT 1914 d: Edwin S. Porter. USA., *As the Sparks Fly Upwards*, Cyrus Townsend Brady, Story

Hearts Afire see **HEARTS IN EXILE** (1915).

HEARTS AFLAME 1923 d: Reginald Barker. USA., *Timber*, Harold Titus, Boston 1922, Novel

Hearts and Armour see **LE ARMI E GLI AMORI** (1983).

Hearts and Diamonds see **HEARTS OR DIAMONDS?** (1918).

Hearts and Diamonds see **DER ORLOW** (1927).

HEARTS AND FISTS 1926 d: Lloyd Ingraham. USA., *Hearts and Fists*, Clarence Budington Kelland, 1924, Short Story

HEARTS AND MASKS 1914 d: Colin Campbell. USA., *Hearts and Masks*, Harold MacGrath, Indianapolis 1905, Novel

HEARTS AND MASKS 1921 d: William A. Seiter. USA., *Hearts and Masks*, Harold MacGrath, Indianapolis 1905, Novel

HEARTS AND SPURS 1925 d: W. S. Van Dyke. USA., *The Outlaw*, Jackson Gregory, New York 1914, Novel

HEARTS AND THE HIGHWAY 1915 d: Wilfred North. USA., *Hearts on the Highway*, Cyrus Townsend Brady, New York 1911, Novel

HEARTS ARE TRUMPS 1920 d: Rex Ingram. USA., *Hearts are Trumps*, Cecil Raleigh, New York 1900, Play

HEARTS DIVIDED 1936 d: Frank Borzage. USA., *Glorious Betsy*, Rida Johnson Young, New York 1908, Play

HEART'S HAVEN 1922 d: Benjamin B. Hampton. USA., *Heart's Haven*, Clara Louise Burnham, Boston 1918, Novel

HEARTS IN EXILE 1915 d: James Young. USA., *Hearts in Exile*, John Oxenham, New York 1904, Novel

HEARTS IN EXILE 1929 d: Michael Curtiz. USA., *Hearts in Exile*, John Oxenham, New York 1904, Novel

Hearts Link With Hearts see **XIN LIAN XIN** (1958).

HEARTS OF MEN 1915 d: Perry N. Vekroff. USA., *School Bells*, Charles K. Harris, New York 1915, Play

HEARTS OF MEN 1928 d: James P. Hogan. USA., *Hearts of Men*, James Oliver Curwood, Story

HEARTS OF OAK 1914 d: Wray Physioc. USA., *Hearts of Oak*, James A. Herne, New York 1880, Play

HEARTS OF OAK 1924 d: John Ford. USA., *Hearts of Oak*, James A. Herne, New York 1880, Play

HEARTS OF YOUTH 1921 d: Thomas N. Miranda, Millard Webb. USA., *In the Depths Ishmael; Or*, E. D. E. N. Southworth, New York 1904, Novel

HEARTS OR DIAMONDS? 1918 d: Henry King. USA., *Adrienne Gascoyne*, William Hamilton Osborne, 1915, Short Story

Hearts Without Destination see **HERZEN OHNE ZIEL** (1928).

HEARTSEASE 1919 d: Harry Beaumont. USA., *Heartease*, Joseph I. C. Clarke, Charles Klein, New York 1897, Play

HEARTSTRINGS 1923 d: Edwin Greenwood. UKN., *A Manchester Marriage*, Mrs. Gaskell, Novel

Heat see **ZNOI** (1963).

HEAT 1987 d: Dick Richards, Jerry Jameson. USA., *Heat*, William Goldman, 1985, Novel

HEAT AND DUST 1982 d: James Ivory. UKN., *Heat and Dust*, Ruth Prawer Jhabvala, 1975, Novel

Heat and Mud see **NETSUDEICHI** (1950).

HEAT LIGHTNING 1934 d: Mervyn Leroy. USA., *Heat Lightning*, George Abbott, Leon Abrams, New York 1933, Play

Heat Lightning on Maria see **WETTERLEUCHTEN UM MARIA** (1957).

Heat Wave, The see **ZNOI** (1963).

Heat-Haze Theatre see **KAGERO-ZA** (1981).

Heatwave see **THE HOUSE ACROSS THE LAKE** (1954).

HEAVEN 1998 d: Scott Reynolds. NZL., *Heaven*, Chad Taylor, Novel

Heaven and Hell see **TENGOKU TO JIGOKU** (1963).

Heaven and Hell see **HIMMEL OG HELVEDE** (1988).

HEAVEN CAN WAIT 1943 d: Ernst Lubitsch. USA., *Birthday*, Ladislaus Bus-Fekete, Play

HEAVEN CAN WAIT 1978 d: Warren Beatty, Buck Henry. USA., *Halfway to Heaven*, Harry Seagall, Play

Heaven Fell That Night see **LES BIJOUTIERS DU CLAIR DE LUNE** (1958).

HEAVEN KNOWS, MR. ALLISON 1957 d: John Huston. UKN/USA., *Heaven Knows Mr. Allison*, Charles Shaw, 1952, Novel

Heaven, Love, and Twine see **AMOR UND ZWIRN HIMMEL** (1960).

HEAVEN ON EARTH 1931 d: Russell MacK. USA., *Mississippi*, Ben Lucien Berman, New York 1929, Novel

Heaven Sent see **UN DROLE DE PAROISSIEN** (1963).

Heaven's Gate see **OUR LITTLE GIRL** (1935).

Heavy Trouble see **BARRA PESADA** (1977).

HEBIMUSUME TO HAKUHATSUKI 1968 d: Noriaki YuasA. JPN., *Hebisume to Hakuhatsuki*, Kazuo Kozu, Short Story

HECATE 1982 d: Daniel Schmid. SWT/FRN., *Hecate*, Paul Morand, Novel

Hecate, Maitresse de la Nuit see **HECATE** (1982).

Hector le Fortiche see **ETTORE LO FUSTO** (1972).

Hector Servadac's Ark see **NA KOMETE** (1970).

Hector the Mighty see **ETTORE LO FUSTO** (1972).

HEDDA 1975 d: Trevor Nunn. UKN., *Hedda Gabler*, Henrik Ibsen, 1890, Play

HEDDA GABLER 1917 d: Frank Powell. USA., *Hedda Gabler*, Henrik Ibsen, 1890, Play

HEDDA GABLER 1920 d: Gero Zambuto. ITL., *Hedda Gabler*, Henrik Ibsen, 1890, Play

HEDDA GABLER 1924 d: Franz Eckstein. GRM., *Hedda Gabler*, Henrik Ibsen, 1890, Play

HEDDA GABLER 1972 d: Waris Hussein. UKN., *Hedda Gabler*, Henrik Ibsen, 1890, Play

HEDDA GABLER 1979 d: Jan Decorte. BLG., *Hedda Gabler*, Henrik Ibsen, 1890, Play

HEEDLESS MOTHS 1921 d: Robert Z. Leonard. USA., Audrey Munson, Short Story

HEERA MOTI 1959 d: Krishan ChoprA. IND., *Do Bailon Ki Katha*, Munshi Premchand, 1936, Short Story

HEI JUN MA 1995 d: XIe Fei. CHN/HKG/MNG., *Hei Jun Ma*, Zhang Chengzhi, Novel

Hei Ma see **HEI JUN MA** (1995).

HEIDEMARIE 1956 d: Hermann Kugelstadt. SWT/FRN., *Wie Wieseli Seinen Weg Fand*, Johanna Spyri, Gotha 1878, Novel

HEIDESCHULMEISTER UWE KARSTEN 1933 d: Carl Heinz Wolff. GRM., *Heideschulmeister Uwe Karsten*, Felicitas Rose, Novel

HEIDESCHULMEISTER UWE KARSTEN 1954 d: Hans Deppe. GRM., *Heideschulmeister Uwe Karsten*, Felicitas Rose, Novel

HEIDI 1937 d: Allan Dwan. USA., *Heidi*, Johanna Spyri, Zurich 1880, Novel

Heidi see **SON TORNATA PER TE** (1953).

HEIDI 1965 d: Werner Jacobs. AUS., *Heidi*, Johanna Spyri, Zurich 1880, Novel

Heidi see **HEIDI KEHRT HEIM** (1967).

HEIDI 1974 d: June Wyndham-Davis. UKN., *Heidi*, Johanna Spyri, Zurich 1880, Novel

Heidi - Sehnsucht Nach Der Heimat see **SON TORNATA PER TE** (1953).

Heidi and Peter see **HEIDI UND PETER** (1954).

Heidi, Child of the Mountains see **SON TORNATA PER TE** (1953).

Heidi Et Pietro see **HEIDI UND PETER** (1954).

Heidi Goes Home see **HEIDI KEHRT HEIM** (1967).

Heidi Kann Brauchen, Was Es Gelernt Hat see **HEIDI UND PETER** (1954).

HEIDI KEHRT HEIM 1967 d: Delbert Mann. GRM/USA., *Heidi*, Johanna Spyri, Zurich 1880, Novel

Heidi Torna a Casa see **HEIDI UND PETER** (1954).

HEIDI UND PETER 1954 d: Franz Schnyder. SWT., *Was Es Gelernt Hat Heidi Kann Brauchen*, Johanna Spyri, Novel

HEIDI'S SONG 1982 d: Robert Taylor. USA., Johanna Spyri, Gotha 1880, Novel

HEIGHTS OF HAZARD, THE 1915 d: Harry Lambart. USA., *The Heights of Hazard*, Cyrus Townsend Brady, Story

Heil, Jennie see **JENNIE** (1940).

HEILIGE FLAMME, DIE 1931 d: Berthold Viertel, William Dieterle. GRM., *The Sacred Flame*, W. Somerset Maugham, New York 1928, Play

HEILIGE UND IHR NARR, DIE 1928 d: William Dieterle. GRM., *Die Heilige Und Ihr Narr*, Agnes Gunther, Novel

HEILIGE UND IHR NARR, DIE 1935 d: Hans Deppe. GRM., *Die Heilige Und Ihr Narr*, Agnes Gunther, Novel

HEILIGE UND IHR NARR, DIE 1957 d: Gustav Ucicky. AUS., *Die Heilige Und Ihr Narr*, Agnes Gunther, Novel

HEIMAT 1912 d: Adolf Gartner. GRM., *Heimat*, Hermann Sudermann, 1893, Play

HEIMAT 1938 d: Carl Froelich. GRM., *Heimat*, Hermann Sudermann, 1893, Play

HEIMAT, DEINE STERNE 1951 d: Hermann Kugelstadt. GRM., *Der Jagerloisl*, Ludwig Thoma, Novel

HEIMATLAND 1955 d: Franz Antel. AUS., *Krambambuli*, Maria von Ebner-Eschenbach, 1887, Short Story

HEIMKEHR 1928 d: Joe May. GRM., *Karl Und Anna*, Leonhard Frank, 1926, Short Story

HEIMLICHE GRAFIN, DIE 1942 d: Geza von Bolvary. GRM/HNG., *Die Heimliche Grafin*, Hugo Maria Kritz, Novel

HEINRICH PENTHESILEA VON KLEIST 1983 d: Max Neuenfel. GRM., *Penthesilea*, Heinrich von Kleist, 1808, Play

Heinrich von Kleist and Penthesilea see **HEINRICH PENTHESILEA VON KLEIST** (1983).

Heinrich von Kleist's the Prince of Homburg see **IL PRINCIPE DI HOMBURG** (1997).

HEINZ IM MOND 1934 d: R. A. Stemmle. GRM., *Heinz Im Mond*, M. Arnac, Novel

HEIPAO SHIJIAN 1985 d: Huang Jianxin. CHN., *Romance of the Black Cannon*, Zhang XIanliang, Novel

Heipao Shijian see HEIPAO SHIJIAN (1985).

HEIR TO THE HOORAH, THE 1916 d: William C. de Mille. USA., *The Heir to the Hoorah*, Paul Armstrong, New York 1905, Play

Heir to the Hoorah, The see EVER SINCE EVE (1934).

Heir to the Hurrah, The see THE HEIR TO THE HOORAH (1916).

HEIRATE MICH, CHERI 1964 d: Axel von Ambesser. GRM./AUS., *Heirate Mich Cheri*, Gabor von Vaszary, Novel

HEIRATEN - ABER WEN? 1938 d: Carl Boese. GRM./CZC., *Falesna Kocicka*, Josef Skruzny, Play

HEIRATSSCHWINDLER 1937 d: Herbert Selpin. GRM., *Heiratsschwindler*, Gertrud von Brockdorff, Novel

HEIRESS, THE 1949 d: William Wyler. USA., *Washington Square*, Henry James, 1881, Novel

Heisses Pflaster Fur Spione see DA BERLINO L'APOCALISSE (1967).

HEKSENLIED, HET 1928 d: Jan Van Dommelen. NTH., *Das Hexenlied*, Ernst von Wildenbruch, Poem

HELD BY THE ENEMY 1920 d: Donald Crisp. USA., *Held By the Enemy*, William Gillette, New York 1886, Play

HELD IN TRUST 1920 d: John Ince. USA., *Held in Trust*, George Kibbe Turner, 1920, Short Story

HELD TO ANSWER 1923 d: Harold Shaw. USA., *Held to Answer*, Peter Clark MacFarlane, Boston 1916, Novel

HELDEN 1958 d: Franz Peter Wirth. GRM., *Arms and the Man*, George Bernard Shaw, 1894, Play

Helden -Himmel Und Holle see SETTE CONTRO LA MORTE (1965).

Heldendaad Van Peter Wells, de see THE LITTLE HOUR OF PETER WELLS (1920).

HELDENTUM NACH LADENSCHLUSS 1955 d: Franz Seitz. GRM., *Heldentum Nach Ladenschluss*, John Forster, Book

HELDINNEN 1960 d: Dietrich Haugk. GRM., *Minna von Barnheim; Oder Das Soldatengluck*, Gotthold Ephraim Lessing, Hamburg 1767, Play

Helen Gardner in Cleopatra see CLEOPATRA (1912).

HELEN KELLER. THE MIRACLE CONTINUES 1983 d: Alan Gibson. UKN/USA., *Helen and Teacher*, Joseph P. Lash, Book

HELEN OF FOUR GATES 1920 d: Cecil M. Hepworth. UKN., *Helen of Four Gates*, Mrs. E. Holdsworth, Novel

Helen of Troy see THE PRIVATE LIFE OF HELEN OF TROY (1927).

HELEN OF TROY 1955 d: Robert Wise. USA., *Iliad*, Homer, Verse

Helen Willfuer, Student see STUDENTIN HELEN WILLFUER (1956).

Helene see L' ORDONNANCE (1933).

HELENE 1936 d: Jean Benoit-Levy, Marie Epstein. FRN., *Helene Wilfur*, Vicki Baum, Novel

HELEN'S BABIES 1915. USA., *Helen's Babies*, John Habberton, Boston 1876, Novel

HELEN'S BABIES 1924 d: William A. Seiter. USA., *Helen's Babies*, John Habberton, Boston 1876, Novel

HELIOTROPE 1920 d: George D. Baker. USA., *A Whiff of Heliotrope*, Richard Washburn Child, 1918, Short Story

Heliotrope see FORGOTTEN FACES (1936).

HELL AND HIGH WATER 1954 d: Samuel Fuller. USA., *Hell and High Water*, David Hempstead, Novel

HELL BELOW 1932 d: Jack Conway. USA., *Pigboats*, Edward Ellsberg, New York 1931, Novel

Hell Below, The see LES CAIDS (1972).

HELL BELOW ZERO 1954 d: Mark Robson. UKN., *The White South*, Hammond Innes, Novel

Hell Bent for Glory see LAFAYETTE ESCADRILLE (1958).

HELL BENT FOR LEATHER 1960 d: George Sherman. USA., Ray Hogan, Story

Hell Bent Kid, The see THE FIEND WHO WALKED THE WEST (1958).

HELL DIGGERS, THE 1921 d: Frank Urson. USA., *The Hell Diggers*, Byron Morgan, 1920, Short Story

HELL DRIVERS 1957 d: Cy Endfield. UKN., *Hell Drivers*, John Kruse, Short Story

HELL HARBOR 1930 d: Henry King. USA., *Out of the Night*, Rida Johnson Young, New York 1925, Novel

HELL HATH NO FURY 1991 d: Thomas J. Wright. USA., *Smithereens*, B. W. Battin, Novel

Hell! I'm Mature see ICH BIN ERWACHSEN..VERDAMMT (1974).

Hell in a Circus see THE CONSTANT WOMAN (1933).

Hell in Frauensee see DIE DREI FRAUEN VON URBAN HELL (1928).

Hell in Korea see A HILL IN KOREA (1956).

Hell in Manitoba see DIE HOLLE VON MANITOBA (1965).

HELL IN THE HEAVENS 1934 d: John G. Blystone. USA., *Flieger*, Hermann Rossman, 1931, Play

HELL IN THE PACIFIC 1968 d: John Boorman. USA/JPN., Reuben Bercovitch, Story

Hell in Town see NELLA CITTA L'INFERNO (1958).

HELL IS A CITY 1960 d: Val Guest. UKN., *Hell Is a City*, Maurice Proctor, Novel

HELL IS EMPTY 1967 d: John Ainsworth, Bernard Knowles. UKN/CZC., *Hell Is Empty*, J. F. Straker, Novel

HELL IS SOLD OUT 1951 d: Michael Anderson. UKN., *Hell Is Sold Out*, Maurice Dekobra, Novel

HELL ON FRISCO BAY 1955 d: Frank Tuttle. USA., *The Darkest Hour*, William P. McGivern, Serial Story

Hell Screen, The see JIGOKU-HEN (1969).

HELL-BENT FER HEAVEN 1926 d: J. Stuart Blackton. USA., *Hell-Bent Fer Heaven*, Hatcher Hughes, New York 1924, Play

Hell-Bent for Heaven see HELL-BENT FER HEAVEN (1926).

Hell-Bent Kid, The see FROM HELL TO TEXAS (1958).

Hellcab see CHICAGO CAB (1998).

HELLCAT, THE 1928 d: Harry Hughes. UKN., *Wilcat Hetty*, Florence Kilpatrick, Play

HELLCATS OF THE NAVY 1957 d: Nathan Juran. USA., *Hellcats of the Sea*, Hans C. Adamson, Charles A. Lockwood, 1955, Book

Hello! Beautiful see THE POWERS GIRL (1942).

Hello Bill see THE FIXER (1915).

Hello, Catherine see BONJOUR KATHRIN (1955).

HELLO, DOLLY! 1969 d: Gene Kelly. USA., *Hello, Dolly!*, Jerry Herman, Michael Stewart, New York 1964, Play

HELLO SISTER 1930 d: Walter Lang. USA., *Clipped Wings*, Rita Lambert, 1928, Short Story

HELLO, SISTER! 1933 d: Erich von Stroheim, Alfred L. Werker. USA., *Walking Down Broadway*, Dawn Powell, Play

HELLO SWEETHEART 1935 d: Monty Banks. UKN., *The Butter and Egg Man*, George S. Kaufman, New York 1925, Play

HELLRAISER 1987 d: Clive Barker. UKN/USA., *The Hellbound Heart*, Clive Barker, Novel

HELL'S 400 1926 d: John Griffith Wray. USA., *The Just and the Unjust*, Vaughan Kester, Indianapolis 1912, Novel

Hell's Cargo see MCGLUSKY THE SEA ROVER (1935).

Hell's Gate see JIGOKUMON (1953).

Hell's Gateway see THE GREAT BARRIER (1937).

HELL'S HEROES 1930 d: William Wyler. USA., *Three Godfathers*, Peter B. Kyne, New York 1913, Novel

HELL'S HIGHROAD 1925 d: Rupert Julian. USA., *Hell's Highroad*, Ernest Pascal, New York 1925, Novel

Hell's Highway see VIOLENT ROAD (1958).

Hell's Kitchen see TENTH AVENUE (1928).

Hell's Kitchen see THE DEVIL'S PARTY (1938).

HELL'S OASIS 1920 d: Neal Hart. USA., *The Fighting Parson*, William L. Roberts, New York 1908, Play

HELL'S OUTPOST 1954 d: Joseph Kane. USA., *Silver Rock*, Luke Short, 1953, Novel

Hell's River see THE MAN FROM HELL'S RIVER (1922).

Help see LEAVE IT TO ME (1933).

HELP, DE DOKTER VERZUIPT! 1974 d: Nikolai Van Der Heyde. NTH., *Help! de Dokter Verzuipt!*, Toon Kortooms, Novel

Help! the Doctor Is Drowning see DE DOKTER VERZUIPT! HELP (1974).

Help, the Doctor's Drowning! see DE DOKTER VERZUIPT! HELP (1974).

HELP WANTED 1915 d: Hobart Bosworth. USA., *Help Wanted*, Jack Lait, New York 1914, Play

Help Wanted Female see MORE THAN A SECRETARY (1936).

HELP YOURSELF 1920 d: Hugo Ballin. USA., *Trimmed With Red*, Wallace Irwin, New York 1920, Novel

HELP YOURSELF 1932 d: John Daumery. UKN., *Sinners All*, Jerome Kingston, Novel

HELTER SKELTER 1976 d: Tom Gries. USA., *Helter Skelter*, Vincent Bugliosi, Curt Gentry, Book

HEM FRAN BABYLON 1941 d: Alf Sjoberg. SWD., *Hem Fran Babylon*, Sigfrid Siwertz, 1923, Novel

HEMAREDDY MALAMAMMA 1945 d: S. Soundararajan, G. R. Rao. IND., *Hemareddy Mallamma*, Bellave Narahari Sastri, Play

Hemingway's Adventures of a Young Man see ADVENTURES OF A YOUNG MAN (1962).

HEMMELIGHETSFULLE LEILIGHETEN, DEN 1948 d: Tancred Ibsen. NRW., *Den Hemmelighetsfulde Leilighet*, Kristian, Jr. Elster, 1928, Short Story

Hemmungslose Manon see MANON 70 (1968).

HEMSOBORNA 1919 d: Carl Barcklind. SWD., *Hemsoborna*, August Strindberg, 1887, Novel

HEMSOBORNA 1944 d: Sigurd Wallen. SWD., *Hemsoborna*, August Strindberg, 1887, Novel

HEMSOBORNA 1955 d: Arne Mattsson. SWD., *Hemsoborna*, August Strindberg, 1887, Novel

HEN HAI 1931 d: Tan Zhiyuan, Gao Lihen. CHN., *Hen Hai*, Wu Jianren, Novel

HENKER VON LONDON, DER 1963 d: Edwin Zbonek. GRM., *White Carpet*, Bryan Edgar Wallace, Short Story

HENNESSY 1975 d: Don Sharp. UKN., Richard Johnson, Story

Henry & June see HENRY AND JUNE (1990).

HENRY AND JUNE 1990 d: Philip Kaufman. USA., *Henry and June: from the Unexpurgated Diary*, Anais Nin, 1986, Book

Henry III see ENRICO III (1909).

Henry IV see ENRICO IV (1984).

HENRY IV, PARTS 1 & 2 1979 d: David Giles. UKN., *Henry IV*, William Shakespeare, c1597-98, Play

HENRY, KING OF NAVARRE 1924 d: Maurice Elvey. UKN., Alexandre Dumas (pere), Novel

Henry Limpet see THE INCREDIBLE MR. LIMPET (1964).

Henry Stanley, the Lion Killer see THE LION KILLER RAINY (1914).

Henry the Third see ENRICO III (1909).

HENRY V 1945 d: Laurence Olivier. UKN., *Henry V*, William Shakespeare, c1598-99, Play

HENRY V 1979 d: David Giles. UKN., *Henry V*, William Shakespeare, c1598-99, Play

HENRY V 1989 d: Kenneth Branagh. UKN., *Henry V*, William Shakespeare, c1598-99, Play

HENRY VIII 1911 d: Louis N. Parker. UKN., *Henry VIIi*, William Shakespeare, 1613, Play

HENRY VIII 1978 d: Kevin Billington. UKN., *Henry VIIi*, William Shakespeare, 1613, Play

Hephaestus Plague, The see BUG (1975).

Her 106th Birthday see IHR 106 GEBURTSTAG (1958).

Her 12 Men see HER TWELVE MEN (1954).

HER AMERICAN PRINCE 1916 d: D. H. Turner. USA., *Her American Prince*, Carl Herbert, 1906, Play

HER BELOVED VILLAIN 1920 d: Sam Wood. USA., *La Veglione*, Alexandre Bisson, Albert Carre, Paris 1893, Play

HER BENNY 1920 d: A. V. Bramble. UKN., *Her Benny*, Silas K. Hocking, Novel

HER BIG NIGHT 1926 d: Melville Brown. USA., *Doubling for Lora*, Peggy Gaddis, Story

HER BITTER LESSON 1912 d: Hardee Kirkland. USA., *Aurora Floyd*, Mary Elizabeth Braddon, Novel

HER BOY 1918 d: George Irving. USA., *Conscription*, W. Carey Wonderly, 1917, Short Story

Her Brother see OTOTO (1960).

Her Cardboard Lover see THE CARDBOARD LOVER (1928).

HER CARDBOARD LOVER 1942 d: George Cukor. USA., *L' Amant Reve*, Jacques Deval, 1925, Play

Her Child *see* HER UNBORN CHILD (1930).

Her Condoned Sin *see* JUDITH OF BETHULIA (1914).

HER COUNTRY FIRST 1918 d: James Young. USA., *The G. A. C.*, Mary Roberts Rinehart, Short Story

Her Crime Was Love *see* DER POSTMEISTER (1940).

Her Crime Was Love *see* DER POSTMEISTER (1955).

HER DANCING PARTNER 1922 d: George A. Cooper. UKN., *Her Dancing Partner*, Mayell Bannister, Story

HER DECISION 1918 d: Jack Conway. USA., *Her Decision*, Lotta Gannet, Short Story

Her Doctor *see* JEJI LEKAR (1933).

HER ELEPHANT MAN 1920 d: Scott R. Dunlap. USA., *Her Elephant Man*, Pearl Doles Bell, New York 1919, Novel

HER FACE 1912. USA., *Her Face*, H. B. Marriott Watson, Story

HER FACE VALUE 1921 d: Thomas N. Heffron. USA., *The Girl Who Paid Dividends*, Earl Derr Biggers, 1921, Short Story

Her Father *see* LA RENZONI (1916).

Her Father's Daughter *see* HER FIRST ROMANCE (1940).

HER FAVOURITE HUSBAND 1950 d: Mario Soldati. UKN./ITL., *Quel Bandito Sono Io!*, Peppino de Filippo, Play

HER FINAL RECKONING 1918 d: Emile Chautard. USA., *Le Prince Zilah*, Jules Claretie, Paris 1885, Play

Her Finest Day *see* IHR SCHONSTER TAG (1962).

HER FIRST AFFAIRE 1932 d: Allan Dwan. UKN., *Her First Affaire*, Frederick Jackson, Merrill Rogers, London 1930, Play

HER FIRST APPEARANCE 1910 d: Edwin S. Porter. USA., *Her First Appearance*, Richard Harding Davis, Story

HER FIRST BEAU 1941 d: Theodore Reed. USA., *June Mad*, Colin Clements, Florence Ryerson, Play

Her First Consignment *see* UNDER COVER (1916).

HER FIRST ELOPEMENT 1920 d: Sam Wood. USA., *Her First Elopement*, Alice Duer Miller, New York 1915, Novel

Her First Experience *see* IHR ERSTES ERLEBNIS (1939).

Her First Love *see* THE COUNTRY FLAPPER (1922).

HER FIRST MATE 1933 d: William Wyler. USA., *Salt Water*, Frank Craven, John Golden, Daniel Jarrett, New York 1929, Play

HER FIRST ROMANCE 1940 d: Edward Dmytryk. USA., *Her Father's Daughter*, Gene Stratton-Porter, New York 1921, Novel

HER FIRST ROMANCE 1951 d: Seymour Friedman. USA., *The City Boy*, Herman Wouk, 1948, Novel

Her Fling *see* THE RISKY ROAD (1918).

HER GILDED CAGE 1922 d: Sam Wood. USA., *The Gilded Cage*, Anne Nichols, New York 1921, Play

Her Golden Calf *see* THE GOLDEN CALF (1930).

HER GREAT CHANCE 1918 d: Charles Maigne. USA., *Golden Fleece*, Fannie Hurst, 1917, Short Story

HER GREAT MATCH 1915 d: Rene Plaissetty. USA., *Her Great Match*, Clyde Fitch, New York 1905, Play

HER GREATEST LOVE 1917 d: J. Gordon Edwards. USA., *Moths*, Ouida, London 1880, Novel

Her Heart in Her Throat *see* THE UNSEEN (1945).

Her Honor *see* THE FINAL JUDGMENT (1915).

HER HONOR THE MAYOR 1920 d: Paul Cazeneuve. USA., *Her Honor the Mayor*, Arlin Van Ness Hines, New York 1918, Play

HER HOUR OF TRIUMPH 1912. USA., *A String of Pearls*, Guy de Maupassant, Short Story

HER HUSBAND'S FRIEND 1920 d: Fred Niblo. USA., *The Incubus*, Marjorie Benton Cooke, New York 1915, Novel

HER HUSBAND'S SECRET 1925 d: Frank Lloyd. USA., *Judgement*, May Edginton, 1924, Short Story

HER IDOL 1915 d: Joseph Smiley. USA., *A Phoenix of the Hills*, Vingie E. Roe, Story

HER IMAGINARY LOVER 1933 d: George King. UKN., *Green Stockings*, A. E. W. Mason, 1909, Play

HER KINGDOM OF DREAMS 1919 d: Marshall Neilan. USA., *Her Kingdom of Dreams*, Agnes Louise Provost, 1919, Short Story

HER LAST AFFAIRE 1935 d: Michael Powell. UKN., *S.O.S.*, Walter Ellis, London 1928, Play

Her Last Mile *see* LADY IN THE DEATH HOUSE (1944).

HER LIFE IN LONDON 1915 d: R. Harley West. UKN., *Her Life in London*, Arthur Shirley, Play

HER LIFE'S STORY 1914 d: Joseph de Grasse. USA., *The Cross*, Miriam Bode Rasmus, Poem

HER LORD AND MASTER 1921 d: Edward Jose. USA., *Her Lord and Master*, Martha Morton, New York 1912, Play

Her Love Cottage *see* MASKED ANGEL (1928).

HER LOVE STORY 1924 d: Allan Dwan. USA., *Her Majesty the Queen*, Mary Roberts Rinehart, 1924, Short Story

HER LUCK IN LONDON 1914 d: Maurice Elvey. UKN., *Her Luck in London*, Charles Darrell, Play

HER MAN 1918 d: Ralph Ince, John Ince. USA., *The Battle Cry*, Charles Neville Buck, New York 1914, Novel

HER MAN O' WAR 1926 d: Frank Urson. USA., *Black Marriage*, Frederick Jackson, Story

HER MARRIAGE VOW 1924 d: Millard Webb. USA., *At the Switch; Or Her Marriage Vow*, Owen Davis, Play

HER MARTYRDOM 1915. USA., *Her Martyrdom*, Frederick Jackson, Story

HER MASTER'S VOICE 1936 d: Joseph Santley. USA., *Her Master's Voice*, Clare Kummer, New York 1933, Play

HER NAMELESS(?) CHILD 1915 d: Maurice Elvey. UKN., *Her Nameless(?) Child*, Madge Duckworth, Play

HER NIGHT OF NIGHTS 1922 d: Hobart Henley. USA., *Her Night of Nights*, C. S. Montayne, 1921, Short Story

HER OWN FREE WILL 1924 d: Paul Scardon. USA., *Her Own Free Will*, Ethel M. Dell, 1922, Short Story

HER OWN MONEY 1922 d: Joseph Henabery. USA., *Her Own Money*, Mark Swan, New York 1915, Play

HER OWN WAY 1915 d: Herbert Blache. USA., *Her Own Way*, Clyde Fitch, New York 1903, Play

Her Panelled Door *see* THE WOMAN WITH NO NAME (1950).

Her Past *see* MY SIN (1931).

Her Primitive Mate *see* NO PLACE TO GO (1927).

HER PRIVATE AFFAIR 1929 d: Paul L. Stein. USA., *Her Private Affair*, Leo Urvantzov, Play

HER PRIVATE LIFE 1929 d: Alexander KordA. USA., *Declassee*, Zoe Akins, New York 1919, Play

HER REDEMPTION 1924 d: Bertram Phillips. UKN., *Her Redemption*, Arthur Shirley, Play

HER REPUTATION 1923 d: John Griffith Wray. USA., *Her Reputation*, Bradley King, Talbot Mundy, Indianapolis 1923, Novel

HER REPUTATION 1931 d: Sidney Morgan. UKN., *Passing Brompton Road*, Jevan Brandon-Thomas, London 1928, Play

HER ROSARY 1913 d: Oscar Apfel. USA., *The Rosary*, Edward E. Rose, New York 1910, Play

HER SACRIFICE 1926 d: Wilfred Lucas. USA., *El Pasado*, Manuel Acuna, 1890, Play

Her Sacrifice *see* BLIND DATE (1934).

HER SECOND CHANCE 1926 d: Lambert Hillyer. USA., *The Second Chance*, Mrs. Wilson Woodrow, New York 1924, Novel

HER SECRET 1933 d: Warren Millais. USA., Maude Fulton, Play

HER SHATTERED IDOL 1915 d: John B. O'Brien. USA., *Her Shattered Idol*, Ella Woods, Story

HER SILENT SACRIFICE 1917 d: Edward Jose. USA., *The Red Mouse*, Henry J. W. Dam, Philadelphia 1903, Play

Her Sin *see* JEJI HRICH (1939).

HER SISTER 1917 d: John B. O'Brien. USA., *Her Sister*, Clyde Fitch, Cosmo Gordon-Lennox, New York 1907, Play

Her Sister's Honour *see* THE KID SISTER (1927).

HER SISTER'S SECRET 1946 d: Edgar G. Ulmer. USA., *Dark Angel*, Gina Kaus, Novel

HER SON 1920 d: Walter West. UKN., *Her Son*, Horace Annesley Vachell, Play

HER SOUL'S INSPIRATION 1917 d: Jack Conway. USA., *Mary Keep Your Feet Still*, Harris Anson, Short Story

HER SPEEDY AFFAIR 1915 d: Horace Davey. USA., *Her Speedy Affair*, Irma Skinner, Story

HER SPLENDID FOLLY 1933 d: William A. O'Connor. USA., *Her Splendid Folly*, Beulah Poynter, Novel

Her Stepdaughter *see* JEJI PASTORKYNA (1929).

Her Stepdaughter *see* JEJI PASTORKYNE (1938).

Her Strange Desire *see* POTIPHAR'S WIFE (1931).

HER STRANGE WEDDING 1917 d: George Melford. USA., *Her Strange Wedding*, George Middleton, Short Story

Her Sweetheart *see* CHRISTOPHER BEAN (1933).

HER TEMPORARY HUSBAND 1923 d: John McDermott. USA., *Her Temporary Husband*, Edward A. Paulton, New York 1922, Play

HER TWELVE MEN 1954 d: Robert Z. Leonard. USA., *Snips and Snails*, Louise Baker, Novel

HER UNBORN CHILD 1930 d: Charles McGrath, Albert Ray. USA., *Her Unborn Child*, Howard McKent Barnes, New York 1928, Play

HER UNCLE 1915 d: George Loane Tucker. UKN., *Her Uncle*, W. W. Jacobs, Short Story

HER WEDDING NIGHT 1930 d: Frank Tuttle. USA., *Der Gatte Des Frauleins*, Gabor Dregely, Vienna 1916, Play

HER WINNING WAY 1921 d: Joseph Henabery. USA., *Ann Annington*, Edgar Jepson, Indianapolis 1918, Novel

Her Wonderful Lie *see* ADDIO MIMI! (1947).

HERANCA, A 1970 d: Ozualdo Candeias. BRZ., *Hamlet*, William Shakespeare, c1601, Play

HERBSTMILCH 1988 d: Joseph Vilsmaier. GRM., Anna Wimschneider, Autobiography

HERCEGNO ES A KOBOLD, A 1991 d: Jozsef Gemes. HNG./UKN., *The Princess and the Goblin*, George MacDonald, Novel

Hercules *see* LE FATICHE DI ERCOLE (1957).

Hercules' Pills *see* LE PILLOLE DI ERCOLE (1960).

Here, Beneath the North Star *see* TAALLA POHJANTAHDEN ALLA (1968).

HERE COME THE LITTLES 1985 d: Bernard Deyries. LXM., Jon Peterson, Novel

Here Comes a Policeman *see* STRICTLY ILLEGAL (1935).

HERE COMES HAPPINESS 1941 d: Noel Smith. USA., *Gentlemen are Born*, Harry Sauber, Story

HERE COMES MR. JORDAN 1941 d: Alexander Hall. USA., *Halfway to Heaven*, Harry Seagall, Play

Here Comes the Bandwagon *see* HALF-WAY TO HEAVEN (1929).

HERE COMES THE BRIDE 1919 d: John S. Robertson. USA., *Here Comes the Bride*, Roy Atwell, New York 1917, Play, **Are You My Wife?**, Max Marcin, New York 1910, Novel, *Here Comes the Bride*, Max Marcin, New York 1917, Play

HERE COMES THE GROOM 1934 d: Edward Sedgwick. USA., *Here Comes the Groom*, Richard F. Flournoy, Provincetown, MA. 1933, Play

Here Comes the Groom *see* BREAKFAST FOR TWO (1937).

Here Comes the Littles *see* HERE COME THE LITTLES (1985).

HERE I AM A STRANGER 1939 d: Roy Del Ruth. USA., *Here I Am a Stranger*, Gordon Malherbe Hillman, 1938, Novel

Here Is a Man *see* ALL THAT MONEY CAN BUY (1941).

HERE IS MY HEART 1934 d: Frank Tuttle. USA., *La Grande-Duchesse Et le Garcon d'Etage*, Alfred Savoir, Paris 1924, Play

Here Is Your Life *see* HAR HAR DU DITT LIV (1966).

Here Under the North Star *see* TAALLA POHJANTAHDEN ALLA (1968).

HERE WE GO ROUND THE MULBERRY BUSH 1967 d: Clive Donner. UKN., *Here We Go Round the Mulberry Bush*, Hunter Davies, London 1965, Novel

HERE WILL I NEST 1941 d: Melburn E. Turner. CND., *Here Will I Nest*, Hilda Hooke Smith, Play

HEREINSPAZIERT! 1953 d: Paul Verhoeven. AUS., *Hereinspaziert!*, Play

HERE'S FLASH CASEY 1938 d: Lynn Shores. USA., *Return Engagement*, George Harmon Coxe, 1934, Short Story

HERE'S GEORGE 1932 d: Redd Davis. UKN., *The Service Flat*, Marriott Edgar, Play

Here's Your Life *see* HAR HAR DU DITT LIV (1966).

HERIDA LUMINOSA, LA 1997 d: Jose Luis Garci. SPN., *La Herida Luminosa*, Josep Maria Sagarra, Novel

Heritage see **SLAEGTEN** (1978).

HERITAGE DE CABESTAN, L' 1913 d: Adrien Caillard. FRN., *Les Voleurs du Grand Monde*, Ponson Du Terrail

Heritage of Bjorndal, The see **DAS ERBE VON BJORNDAL** (1960).

HERITAGE OF THE DESERT 1933 d: Henry Hathaway. USA., *The Heritage of the Desert*, Zane Grey, New York 1910, Novel

HERITAGE OF THE DESERT 1939 d: Lesley Selander. USA., *The Heritage of the Desert*, Zane Grey, New York 1910, Novel

HERITAGE OF THE DESERT, THE 1924 d: Irvin V. Willat. USA., *The Heritage of the Desert*, Zane Grey, New York 1910, Novel

Heritage, The see **HA'YERUSHA** (1993).

HERITIER DU BAL TABARIN, L' 1933 d: Jean Kemm. FRN., *L' Heritier du Bal Tabarin*, Andre Mouezy-Eon, Nicolas Nancey, Play

Hermana de San Sulpicio, La see **LA HERMANA SAN SULPICIO** (1927).

HERMANA SAN SULPICIO, LA 1927 d: Florian Rey. SPN., *La Hermana San Sulpicio*, Armando Palacio Valdes, 1889, Novel

HERMANA SAN SULPICIO, LA 1934 d: Florian Rey. SPN., *La Hermana San Sulpicio*, Armando Palacio Valdes, 1889, Novel

HERMANA SAN SULPICIO, LA 1952 d: Luis LuciA. SPN., *La Hermana San Sulpicio*, Armando Palacio Valdes, 1889, Novel

HERMANAS, LAS 1962 d: Daniel Tinayre. ARG., *Las Hermanas*, Guy Des Cars, Novel

HERMANN 1920 d: Orlando Ricci. ITL., *Le Conte Hermann*, Alexandre Dumas (pere), 1849, Novel

Hermann Und Dorothea von Heute see **LIEBESLEUTE** (1935).

HERMANOS CORSOS, LOS 1954 d: Leo Fleider. ARG., *Les Freres Corses*, Alexandre Dumas (pere), 1845, Short Story

HERMIN UND DIE SIEBEN AUFRECTEN 1935 d: Frank Wisbar. GRM/SWT., *Das Fahnlein Der Sieben Aufrechten*, Gottfried Keller, Liepzig 1861, Short Story

Hermit Doctor of Gaya, The see **STRONGER THAN DEATH** (1920).

HERNANI 1910 d: Albert Capellani. FRN., *Hernani*, Victor Hugo, Play

Hernani see **ERNANI** (1911).

HERO AND THE TERROR 1982 d: William Tannen. USA., *Hero and the Terror*, Michael Blodgett, Novel

HERO ON HORSEBACK, A 1927 d: Del Andrews. USA., *Bread Upon the Waters*, Peter B. Kyne, 1923, Short Story

HERO, THE 1923 d: Louis J. Gasnier. USA., *The Hero*, Gilbert Emery, New York 1921, Play

Hero, The see **SATURDAY'S HERO** (1951).

Heroes see **HELDEN** (1958).

Heroes are Made see **KAK ZAKALYALAS STAL** (1942).

HEROES DE LA LEGION, LAS 1927 d: Rafael Lopez RiendA. SPN., *Juan Leon Legionario*, Rafael Lopez Rienda, Novel

Heroes Millonarios, Los see **GLI EROI** (1973).

Heroes of Luliang see **LU LIANG YING XIONG** (1950).

HEROES OF TELEMARK, THE 1965 d: Anthony Mann. UKN., *But for These Men*, John Drummond, London 1962, Book, *Skis Against the Atom*, Knut Haukelid, London 1954, Book

Heroes of the Marne see **LE HEROS DE LA MARNE** (1938).

HEROES OF THE STREET 1922 d: William Beaudine. USA., *Heroes of the Street*, Leon Parker, Play

Heroes, The see **THE INVINCIBLE SIX** (1970).

Heroes, The see **GLI EROI** (1973).

Heroic Deed of Peter Wells, The see **THE LITTLE HOUR OF PETER WELLS** (1920).

Heroic Son and Daughter, The see **YINGXIONG ERNU** (1964).

Heroic Sons and Daughters see **YINGXIONG ERNU** (1964).

Heroic Times see **DALIAS IDOK** (1983).

HEROIN GANG, THE 1968 d: Brian G. Hutton. USA., *Fruit of the Poppy*, Robert Wilder, New York 1965, Novel

Heroine of the Wild River (Part 1) see **HUANGJIANG NUXIA (PART 1)** (1930).

Heroines see **HELDINNEN** (1960).

HEROINES 1998 d: Gerard Krawczyk. FRN., *Playback*, Didier Daeninckx, Novel

Heroism see **EROICA** (1958).

Heroism After Shop Hours see **HELDENTUM NACH LADENSCHLUSS** (1955).

HEROS DE LA MARNE, LE 1938 d: Andre Hugon. FRN., *Le Heros de la Marne*, Andre Hugon, Novel

Hero's Wife, The see **ESHET HAGIBOR** (1963).

HERR ARNES PENNIGAR 1954 d: Gustaf Molander. SWD., *Herr Arnes Pengar*, Selma Lagerlof, 1903, Novel

Herr Auf Schloss Brassac see **LE TONNERRE DE DIEU** (1965).

Herr Bockerer see **DER BOCKERER** (1981).

HERR DES TODES, DER 1913 d: Max Obal. GRM., *Der Herr Des Todes*, Karl Rossner, Novel

HERR KANZLEIRAT, DER 1948 d: Hubert MarischkA. AUS., *Der Herr Kanzleirat*, J. Horst, W. Polaczek, Play

HERR MEISTER UND FRAU MEISTERIN 1928 d: Alfred Theodor Mann. GRM., *Herr Meister Und Frau Meisterin*, Alfred Theodor Mann, Short Story

HERR OHNE WOHNUNG, DER 1934 d: E. W. Emo. AUS., *Der Herr Ohne Wohnung*, B. Jenbach, Rudolf Osterreicher, Play

Herr Puntila and His Servant Matti see **HERR PUNTILA UND SEIN KNECHT MATTI** (1955).

Herr Puntila Och Hans Drang see **HERRA PUNTILA JA HANEN RENKINSA MATTI** (1979).

HERR PUNTILA UND SEIN KNECHT MATTI 1955 d: Alberto Cavalcanti. AUS., *Herr Puntila Und Sein Knecht Matti*, Bertolt Brecht, Hella Wuolijoki, 1948, Play

Herr Tartuff see **TARTUFF** (1925).

HERR UBER LEBEN UND TOD 1955 d: Victor Vicas. GRM., *Herr Uber Leben Und Tod*, Carl Zuckmayer, 1938, Novel

HERRA PUNTILA JA HANEN RENKINSA MATTI 1979 d: Ralf LangbackA. FNL/SWD., *Herr Puntila Und Sein Knecht Matti*, Bertolt Brecht, Hella Wuolijoki, 1948, Play

HERREN OG HANS TJENERE 1959 d: Arne Skouen. NRW., *Herren Og Hans Tjenere*, Axel Kielland, 1955, Play

HERRGOTTSSCHNITZER VON AMMERGAU, DER 1952 d: Harald Reinl. GRM., *Der Herrgottsschnitzer von Ammergau*, Ludwig Ganghofer, Novel

HERRIN UND IHR KNECHT, DIE 1929 d: Richard Oswald. GRM., *Die Herrin Und Ihr Knecht*, Georg Engel, Novel

Herrin Vom Salzerhof, Die see **WETTERLEUCHTEN AM DACHSTEIN** (1952).

HERRIN VON ATLANTIS, DIE 1932 d: G. W. Pabst. GRM., *L' Atlantide*, Pierre Benoit, Paris 1919, Novel

Herringbone Clouds see **IWASHIGUMO** (1958).

Herrschaft Des Ublen Geistes, Die see **LE REGNE DE L'ESPRIT MALIN** (1955).

HERRSCHER, DER 1937 d: Veit Harlan. GRM., *Vor Sonnenuntergang*, Gerhart Hauptmann, Berlin 1932, Play

HERRSCHER OHNE KRONE 1957 d: Harald Braun. GRM., *Der Favorit Der Konigin*, Robert Neumann, Frankfurt Am Main 1953, Novel

Herz Bleibt Allein, Ein see **MEIN LEOPOLD** (1955).

Herz Des Maharadscha, Das see **EMERALD OF THE EAST** (1928).

HERZ DES PIRATEN, DAS 1987 d: Jurgen Brauer. GDR., *Benno Pludra*, Story

Herz Geht Vor Anker see **FOUR DAYS LEAVE** (1950).

HERZ MODERN MOBLIERT 1940 d: Theo Lingen. GRM., *Herz Modern Mobliert*, Franz Gribitz, Play

HERZ OHNE GNADE 1958 d: Victor Tourjansky. GRM., *Herz Ohne Gnade*, Klaus Hellmer, Novel

HERZ OHNE HEIMAT 1940 d: Otto Linnekogel. GRM., *Die Beiden Diersbergs*, Renate Uhl, Novel

HERZ SCHLAGT FUR DICH, EIN 1955 d: Joe Stockel. GRM., *Reis Am Weg*, Wilhelmine von Hillern, Short Story

HERZ SPIELT FALSCH, EIN 1953 d: Rudolf Jugert. GRM., *Ein Herz Spielt Falsch*, Hans Ulrich Horster, Novel

HERZBUBE 1972 d: Jerzy Skolimowski. GRM/USA., *Dama, Valet Korol*, Vladimir Nabokov, 1928, Novel

HERZEN OHNE ZIEL 1928 d: Gustav Ucicky, Benito Perojo. GRM/SPN., Pedro Mata, Novel

Herzensdieb, Der see **WIE EIN DIEB IN DER NACHT** (1945).

HERZENSFREUD - HERZENSLIED 1940 d: Hubert MarischkA. GRM., *Junger Wein*, Raimund Martin, Play

HERZLICH WILLKOMMEN 1989 d: Hark Bohm. GRM., Walter Kempowski, Novel

HERZOG VON REICHSTADT, DER 1931 d: Victor Tourjansky. GRM., *L' Aiglon*, Edmond Rostand, 1900, Play

Herzogin von Langeais, Die see **LIEBE** (1927).

He's My Husband and I'll Kill Him When I Like see **IL MARITO E MIO E L'AMMAZZO QUANDO MI PARE** (1967).

He's My Man see **ES MI HOMBRE** (1928).

He's My Pal see **THE LONE COWBOY** (1933).

HESPER OF THE MOUNTAINS 1916 d: Wilfred North. USA., *Hesper: a Novel*, Hamlin Garland, New York 1903, Novel

Hesselbach Family, The see **DIE FAMILIE HESSELBACH** (1954).

HESTER STREET 1975 d: Joan Micklin Silver. USA., *Yekl*, Abraham Cahan, 1896, Novel

HET AR MIN LANGTAN 1956 d: Bengt Logardt. SWD., *Het Ar Min Langtan*, Ingrid Beije, Novel

Heta Fran Niskavuori see **NISKAVUOREN HETA** (1952).

Heta from Niskavuori see **NISKAVUOREN HETA** (1952).

Heta of Niskavuori Farm see **NISKAVUOREN HETA** (1952).

Heuchler, Die see **DIE GEJAGTEN** (1960).

Heure Exquise see **NUIT DE DECEMBRE** (1939).

HEURE PRES DE TOI, UNE 1932 d: Ernst Lubitsch. USA., *Nur Ein Traum*, Lothar Schmidt, Munchen 1909, Play

HEUREUX QUI COMME ULYSSE 1970 d: Henri Colpi. FRN/ITL., *The Homecoming*, Marlena Frick, Short Story

..HEUTE ABEND BEI MIR 1934 d: Carl Boese. GRM., *..Heute Abend Bei Mir*, Hans Jaray, Play

HEUTE HEIRATET MEIN MANN 1956 d: Kurt Hoffmann. GRM., *Heute Heiratet Mein Mann*, Annemarie Selinko, Novel

Heute macht Die Ganze Welt Musik Fur Mich see **MEINE FRAU TERESA** (1942).

HEXE, DIE 1954 d: Gustav Ucicky. GRM., *Die Hexe*, Fred Andreas, Novel

Hexen von Salem, Die see **LES SORCIERES DE SALEM** (1957).

HEXENSCHUSS 1987 d: Franz J. Gottlieb. GRM., John Graham, Play

HEXER, DER 1964 d: Alfred Vohrer. GRM., *The Gaunt Stranger*, Edgar Wallace, London 1925, Novel

HEY, I'M ALIVE! 1975 d: Lawrence Schiller. USA., *I'm Alive! Hey*, Beth Day, Book, *Hey I'm Alive!*, Helen Klaban, Book

HEY, ROOKIE 1944 d: Charles T. Barton. USA., *Rookie Hey*, Doris Culvan, K. E. B. Culvan, Play

H.G. Wells' the Shape of Things to Come see **THE SHAPE OF THINGS TO COME** (1979).

HI, BEAUTIFUL! 1944 d: Leslie Goodwins. USA., *Be It Ever So Humble*, Eleanore Griffin, William Rankin, Story

Hi in the Cellar see **UP IN THE CELLAR** (1970).

HI MO TSUKI MO 1969 d: Noboru NakamurA. JPN., *Hi Mo Tsuki Mo*, Yasunari Kawabata, Tokyo 1953, Novel

HI NELLIE! 1934 d: Mervyn Leroy. USA., *Hi Nellie*, Roy Chanslor, Story

HI NO ATARU SAKAMICHI 1958 d: Tomotaka TasakA. JPN., *Hi No Ataru Sakamichi*, Yojiro Ishizaka, 1958, Novel

HIAWATHA 1903 d: Joe Rosenthal. UKN/CND., *The Song of Hiawatha*, Henry Wadsworth Longfellow, Boston 1855, Poem

HIAWATHA 1909 d: William V. Ranous. USA., *The Song of Hiawatha*, Henry Wadsworth Longfellow, Boston 1855, Poem

HIAWATHA 1913. USA., *The Song of Hiawatha*, Henry Wadsworth Longfellow, Boston 1855, Poem

HIAWATHA 1952 d: Kurt Neumann. USA., *The Song of Hiawatha*, Henry Wadsworth Longfellow, Boston 1855, Poem

Hiawatha: the Indian Passion Play *see* HIAWATHA (1913).

Hiawatha, the Messiah of the Ojibway *see* HIAWATHA (1903).

HIBERNATUS 1969 d: Edouard Molinaro. FRN/ITL., *Hibernatus*, Jean-Bernard Luc, Novel

Hidden *see* FORBIDDEN (1986).

HIDDEN CHARMS 1920 d: Samuel Brodsky. USA., *Believe Me if All Those Endearing Young Charms*, Thomas Moore, 1807, Poem

HIDDEN CHILDREN, THE 1917 d: Oscar Apfel. USA., *The Hidden Children*, Robert W. Chambers, New York 1914, Novel

Hidden Corpse, The *see* STRANGERS OF THE EVENING (1932).

Hidden Dawn *see* MANHA SUBMERSA (1980).

HIDDEN HAND, THE 1942 d: Ben Stoloff. USA., *Invitation to a Murder*, Rufus King, Play

HIDDEN HOMICIDE 1959 d: Tony Young. UKN., *Murder at Shinglestrand*, Paul Capon, Novel

Hidden Life, The *see* HET VERBORGEN LEVEN (1920).

Hidden Menace *see* STAR OF THE CIRCUS (1938).

Hidden Path, The *see* THE DISCARDED WOMAN (1920).

Hidden Room of 1,000 Horrors, The *see* THE TELL-TALE HEART (1960).

Hidden Room, The *see* OBSESSION (1948).

HIDDEN SPRING, THE 1917 d: E. Mason Hopper. USA., *The Hidden Spring*, Clarence Budington Kelland, New York 1915, Novel

HIDE AND SEEK 1963 d: Cy Endfield. UKN., *Hide and Seek*, Harold Greene, Novel

Hide and Seek *see* THE HAUNTING OF JULIA (1976).

HIDE IN PLAIN SIGHT 1979 d: James Caan. USA., Leslie Waller, Book

HIDEAWAY 1937 d: Richard Rosson. USA., *A House in the Country*, Melvin Levy, New York 1937, Play

HIDEAWAY 1995 d: Brett Leonard. USA., *Hideaway*, Dean R. Koontz, Novel

HIDEAWAY GIRL 1937 d: George Archainbaud. USA., *Cabin Cruiser*, David Garth, 1936, Short Story

HIDEG NAPOK 1966 d: Andras Kovacs. HNG., *Hideg Napok*, Tibor Cseres, 1965, Novel

HIDEKO NO SHASHO-SAN 1941 d: Mikio Naruse. JPN., *Okomasan*, Masuji Ibuse, 1941, Novel

Hideko the Bus Conductor *see* HIDEKO NO SHASHO-SAN (1941).

HIDEOUS KINKY 1998 d: Gillies MacKinnon. UKN/FRN., *Hideous Kinky*, Esther Freud, Novel

HIDEOUT 1949 d: Philip Ford. USA., *Fourteen Hours from Chi*, William Porter, Serial Story

Hideout in the Alps *see* DUSTY ERMINE (1936).

Hideout, The *see* THE SMALL VOICE (1948).

HIDING OF BLACK BILL, THE 1918 d: David Smith. USA., *The Hiding of Black Bill*, O. Henry, Short Story

HIDING PLACE, THE 1975 d: James F. Collier. USA., *The Hiding Place*, Corrie Ten Boom, 1971, Book

Hier, Aujourd'hui Et Demain *see* OGGI, DOMANI IERI (1963).

HIER BIN ICH, HIER BLEIB ICH 1959 d: Werner Jacobs. GRM., *Hier Bleib Ich, Hier Bin Ich*, Jean Valmy, Play, *Hier Bin Ich, Hier Bleib Ich*, Raymond Vinci, Play

HIER ET AUJOURD'HUI 1918 d: Bernard-Deschamps. FRN., *La Belle Au Bois Dormant*, Charles Perrault, 1697, Short Story

HIGANBANA 1958 d: Yasujiro Ozu. JPN., *Higanbana*, Ton Santomi, 1958, Novel

High and Low *see* DU HAUT EN BAS (1933).

High and Low *see* TENGOKU TO JIGOKU (1963).

HIGH AND THE MIGHTY, THE 1954 d: William A. Wellman. USA., *The High and the Mighty*, Ernest K. Gann, 1953, Novel

High Ballin' *see* HIGH-BALLIN' (1978).

HIGH BARBAREE 1947 d: Jack Conway. USA., *High Barbaree*, James N. Hall, Charles Nordhoff, 1945, Novel

HIGH BRIGHT SUN, THE 1964 d: Ralph Thomas. UKN., *The High Bright Sun*, Ian Stuart Black, London 1962, Novel

High Class People *see* OONCHE LOG (1965).

HIGH COMMAND, THE 1937 d: Thorold Dickinson. UKN., *The General Goes Too Far*, Lewis Robinson, Novel

High Commissioner, The *see* NOBODY RUNS FOREVER (1968).

HIGH CONQUEST 1946 d: Irving Allen. USA., *High Conquest*, James Ramsey Ullman, Novel

High Explosive *see* THE SUNSET STRIP CASE (1938).

HIGH FLIGHT 1957 d: John Gilling. UKN., Jack Davies, Story

HIGH FLYER, THE 1926 d: Harry J. Brown. USA., *The Bird Man*, J. Frank Clark, Story

HIGH FLYERS 1937 d: Eddie Cline. USA., *The Kangaroos*, Victor Mapes, New York 1926, Play

HIGH HAND, THE 1915 d: William D. Taylor. USA., *The High Hand*, Jacques Futrelle, Indianapolis 1911, Novel

HIGH HAT 1937 d: Clifford Sanforth. USA., *High Hat a Radio Romance*, Alma Sioux Scarberry, New York 1930, Novel

HIGH HELL 1958 d: Burt Balaban. UKN., *High Hell*, Steve Frazee, Novel

High Life *see* GOLD DIGGERS OF 1933 (1933).

HIGH NOON 1952 d: Fred Zinnemann. USA., *The Tin Star*, John W. Cunningham, Short Story

High Noon *see* GORECHTO PLADNE (1965).

High Pavement *see* MY SISTER AND I (1948).

High Peril *see* THE KEY (1934).

HIGH POCKETS 1919 d: Ira M. Lowry. USA., *High Pockets*, William Patterson White, 1918, Novel

HIGH PRESSURE 1931 d: Mervyn Leroy. USA., *Hot Money*, Aben Kandel, New York 1931, Play

HIGH RISE DONKEY 1979 d: Michael Forlong. UKN., *High Rise Donkey*, Peter Buchanan, Novel

HIGH ROAD, THE 1915 d: John W. Noble. USA., *The High Road*, Edward Sheldon, New York 1912, Play

High Road, The *see* THE LADY OF SCANDAL (1930).

HIGH ROAD TO CHINA 1982 d: Brian G. Hutton. USA., *High Road to China*, Jon Cleary, Novel

High School Dream *see* IDEAL SEPTIMY (1938).

HIGH SEAS 1929 d: Denison Clift. UKN., *The Silver Rosary*, Monckton Hoffe, Short Story

High Season Tourist *see* DER HOCHTOURIST (1961).

HIGH SIERRA 1941 d: Raoul Walsh. USA., *High Sierra*, William Riley Burnett, 1940, Novel

High Society *see* SCANDAL (1929).

High Society *see* THE SOCIAL LION (1930).

HIGH SOCIETY 1956 d: Charles Walters. USA., *Philadelphia Story*, Philip Barry, New York 1939, Play

HIGH SOCIETY BLUES 1930 d: David Butler. USA., *Those High Society Blues*, Dana Burnet, 1925, Short Story

HIGH SPEED 1920 d: Charles Miller. USA., *High Speed*, Clinton H. Stagg, New York 1916, Novel

HIGH SPEED 1924 d: Herbert Blache. USA., *High Speed*, Frederick Jackson, 1918, Short Story

HIGH SPEED LEE 1923 d: Dudley Murphy. USA., *Only a Few of Us Left*, John Phillips Marquand, 1922, Short Story

HIGH STAKES 1918 d: Arthur Hoyt. USA., *High Stakes*, Andrew Soutar, 1917, Short Story

HIGH STEPPERS 1926 d: Edwin Carewe. USA., *Heirs Apparent*, Philip Hamilton Gibbs, London 1923, Novel

HIGH TIDE AT NOON 1957 d: Philip Leacock. UKN., *High Tide at Noon*, Elizabeth Oglivie, Novel

HIGH TREASON 1929 d: Maurice Elvey. UKN., *High Treason*, Noel Pemberton-Billing, Play

High Treason *see* HOCHVERRAT (1929).

High Treason *see* THE ROCKS OF VALPRE (1935).

High Vermilion *see* SILVER CITY (1951).

HIGH WALL 1947 d: Curtis Bernhardt. USA., *High Wall*, Alan R. Clark, Bradbury Foote, Play

HIGH WIND IN JAMAICA, A 1965 d: Alexander MacKendrick. UKN., *A High Wind in Jamaica*, Richard Hughes, London 1929, Novel

High Window, The *see* THE BRASHER DOUBLOON (1947).

HIGH YELLOW 1965 d: Larry Buchanan. USA., *Diary of a Negro Maid*, Erskine Williams

HIGH-BALLIN' 1978 d: Peter Carter. CND., Richard Robinson, Stephen Schneck, Short Story

HIGHER AND HIGHER 1943 d: Tim Whelan. USA., *Higher and Higher*, Gladys Hurlbut, Joshua Logan, Musical Play

HIGHER LAW, THE 1914 d: Charles Giblyn. USA., *The Higher Law*, George Bronson Howard, Story

Higher Law, The *see* THE NTH COMMANDMENT (1923).

Higher Principle, A *see* VYSSI PRINCIP (1960).

HIGHEST BIDDER, THE 1921 d: Wallace Worsley. USA., *The Trap*, Maximilian Foster, New York 1920, Novel

Highgrader, The *see* FIGHTING FOR GOLD (1919).

Highway Pickup *see* CHAIR DE POULE (1964).

Highway Racketeers *see* TIP-OFF GIRLS (1938).

Highway to Freedom *see* AMERICAN JOE SMITH (1942).

HIGHWAY WEST 1941 d: William McGann. USA., *Heat Lightning*, George Abbott, Leon Abrams, New York 1933, Play

Highwayman Rides, The *see* BILLY THE KID (1930).

HIGHWAYMAN, THE 1951 d: Lesley Selander. USA., *The Highwayman*, Alfred Noyes, 1907, Poem

Highwaymen of Chlum, The *see* LOUPEZNICI NA CHLUMU (1926).

HIGHWAYS BY NIGHT 1942 d: Peter Godfrey. USA., *Silver Spoon*, Clarence Budington Kelland, Serial Story

HIJA DEL MAR, LA 1928 d: Jose Maria Maristany. SPN., *La Hija Del Mar*, Angel Guimera

HIJA DEL MAR, LA 1953 d: Antonio Momplet. SPN., *La Filla Del Mar*, Angel Guimera, 1900, Play

HIJA DEL MESTRE, LA 1927 d: Carlos Luis Monzon, Francisco Gonzalez Gonzalez. SPN., *La Hija Del Mestre*, Santiago Tejera Ossavarry, Opera

Hi-Jack Highway *see* GAS-OIL (1955).

HIJO DE HOMBRE 1960 d: Lucas Demare. ARG., *Hijo de Hombre*, Augusto Roa Bastos, Novel

Hijo de Hombre -Choferes Del Chaco (la Sed) *see* HIJO DE HOMBRE (1960).

Hijos de la Noche, Los *see* I FIGLI DELLA NOTTE (1939).

Hijos de Sanchez, Los *see* THE CHILDREN OF SANCHEZ (1978).

HIJOS MANDAN, LOS 1939 d: Gabriel SoriA. USA., *El Caudal de Los Hijos*, Jose Lopez Pinillos, Madrid 1921, Play

HIKARIGOKE 1991 d: Kei Kumai. JPN., *Hikarigoke*, Taijun Takeda, Novel

Hilarity *see* HUAN TIAN XI DI (1949).

HILARY AND JACKIE 1998 d: Anand Tucker. UKN., *A Genius in the Family*, Hilary Du Pre, Piers Du Pre, Biography

HILDA CRANE 1956 d: Philip Dunne. USA., *Hilda Crane*, Samson Raphaelson, New York 1950, Play

HILITO DE SANGRE, UN 1995 d: Erwin Newmayer. MXC., *Un Hilito de Sangre*, Eusebio Ruvalcaba, Novel

HILJA, MAITOTYTTO 1953 d: Toivo SarkkA. FNL., *Maitotytto Hilja*, Johannes Linnankoski, 1913, Short Story

Hilja the Milkmaid *see* MAITOTYTTO HILJA (1953).

Hill 24 Doesn't Answer *see* HAGIVA (1955).

HILL IN KOREA, A 1956 d: Julian Amyes. UKN., *A Hill in Korea*, Max Catto, Novel

HILL, THE 1965 d: Sidney Lumet. UKN., *The Hill*, Ray Rigby, 1965, Novel

Hillman, The *see* IN THE BALANCE (1917).

Hill's Angels *see* THE NORTH AVENUE IRREGULARS (1979).

HILLS OF HOME 1948 d: Fred M. Wilcox. USA., *Doctor of the Old School*, John Watson, 1895, Novel

HILLS OF KENTUCKY 1927 d: Howard Bretherton. USA., *The Untamed Heart*, Dorothy Yost, Story

HILLS OF OLD WYOMING 1937 d: Nate Watt. USA., *The Round-Up*, Clarence E. Mulford, New York 1933, Novel

HILLS OF PERIL 1927 d: Lambert Hillyer. USA., *A Holy Terror*, George Abbott, Winchell Smith, New York 1925, Play

HILLS OF UTAH 1951 d: John English. USA., *The Doctor at Coffin Gap*, Les Savage Jr., Novel

HI-LO COUNTRY, THE 1998 d: Stephen Frears. USA., *The Hi-Lo Country*, Max Evans, 1961, Novel

Him and His Sister *see* ON A JEHO SESTRA (1931).

HIMMEL, AMOR UND ZWIRN 1960 d: Ulrich Erfurth. GRM., *Amor Und Zwirn Himmel*, Thomas Westa, Novel

HIMMEL AUF ERDEN, DER 1927 d: Alfred Schirokauer. GRM., *Der Doppelmensch*, Wilhelm Jacobi, Arthur Lippschutz, Play

HIMMEL OG HELVEDE 1988 d: Morten Arnfred. DNM., *Himmel Og Helvede*, Kirsten Thorup, 1982, Novel

HIMMEL, WIR ERBEN EIN SCHLOSS 1943 d: Peter P. Brauer. GRM., *Kleiner Mann Grosser Mann - Alles Vertauscht*, Hans Fallada, Novel

Himmo, King of Jerusalem *see* **MELECH YERUSHALAYAM HIMMO** (1987).

HIMMO, MELECH YERUSHALAYAM 1987 d: Amos Guttman. ISR., *Himmo Melech Yerushalayam*, Yoram Kaniuk, Novel

HIN UND HER 1950 d: Theo Lingen. AUS., *Hin Und Her*, Odon von Horvath, Play

HINDENBURG, THE 1975 d: Robert Wise. USA., *The Hindenburg*, Michael M. Mooney, Book

HINDLE WAKES 1918 d: Maurice Elvey. UKN., *Hindle Wakes*, Stanley Houghton, London 1912, Play

HINDLE WAKES 1927 d: Maurice Elvey. UKN., *Hindle Wakes*, Stanley Houghton, London 1912, Play

HINDLE WAKES 1931 d: Victor Saville. UKN., *Hindle Wakes*, Stanley Houghton, London 1912, Play

HINDLE WAKES 1952 d: Arthur Crabtree. UKN., *Hindle Wakes*, Stanley Houghton, London 1912, Play

HINTER KLOSTERMAUERN 1928 d: Franz Seitz. GRM., *Die Bruder von St. Bernhard*, Ohorn, Play

HINTER KLOSTERMAUERN 1952 d: Harald Reinl. GRM., *Hinter Klostermauern*, Hans Naderer, Play

Hippodrome *see* **GELIEBTE BESTIE** (1959).

Hippopotamus Parade, The *see* **WHAT'S YOUR HURRY?** (1920).

Hira Moti *see* **HEERA MOTI** (1959).

HIRED WIFE 1934 d: George Melford. USA., *The Flat Tire*, Alma Sioux Scarberry, New York 1930, Novel

HIRELING, THE 1973 d: Alan Bridges. UKN., *The Hireling*, L. P. Hartley, 1957, Novel

HIRTETTYJEN KETTUJEN METSA 1986 d: Jouko Suikkari. FNL., *Hirtettyjen Kettujen Metsa*, Arto Paasilinna, 1983, Novel

HIS APOLOGIES 1935 d: Widgey R. Newman. UKN., *His Apologies*, Rudyard Kipling, 1932, Poem

His Best Man *see* **TIMES SQUARE PLAYBOY** (1936).

HIS BRIDAL NIGHT 1919 d: Kenneth Webb. USA., *His Bridal Night*, Lawrence Irving Rising, New York 1916, Play

His Brother's Wife *see* **THE HERO** (1923).

HIS BUDDY'S WIFE 1925 d: Tom Terriss. USA., *His Buddy's Wife*, T. Howard Kelly, Story

HIS CAPTIVE WOMAN 1929 d: George Fitzmaurice. USA., *Changeling*, Brian Oswald Donn-Byrne, New York 1923, Short Story

HIS CHILDREN'S CHILDREN 1923 d: Sam Wood. USA., *His Children's Children*, Arthur Cheney Train, New York 1923, Novel

His Daily Bread *see* **USKI ROTI** (1969).

His Dark Chapter *see* **WHAT A MAN!** (1930).

His Daughter Is Peter *see* **SEINE TOCHTER IST DER PETER** (1936).

HIS DAUGHTER PAYS 1918 d: Paolo TrincherA. USA., *La Baccarat*, Frederick H. James, Play

HIS DIVORCED WIFE 1919 d: Douglas Gerrard. USA., *An Altar on Little Thunder*, Elmore Elliott Peake, 1912, Short Story

HIS DOG 1927 d: Karl Brown. USA., *His Dog*, Albert Payson Terhune, New York 1922, Novel

HIS DOUBLE LIFE 1933 d: Arthur Hopkins, William C. de Mille. USA., *Buried Alive*, Arnold Bennett, London 1908, Novel, *The Great Adventure*, Arnold Bennett, London 1913, Play

HIS DUTY 1909 d: D. W. Griffith, Frank Powell. USA., *His Duty*, O. Henry, Short Story

HIS EXCELLENCY 1952 d: Robert Hamer. UKN., *His Excellency*, Campbell Christie, Dorothy Christie, London 1950, Play

HIS EXCITING NIGHT 1938 d: Gus Meins. USA., *Adam's Evening*, Katharine Kavanaugh, Play

HIS FAMILY TREE 1935 d: Charles Vidor. USA., *Old Man Murphy*, Harry W. Gribble, Patrick Kearney, New York 1931, Play

HIS FIGHT 1914 d: Colin Campbell. USA., *His Fight*, James Oliver Curwood, Short Story

HIS FIGHTING BLOOD 1935 d: James W. English. USA., *His Fighting Blood*, James Oliver Curwood, Short Story

His Friend and His Wife *see* **MIDSUMMER MADNESS** (1920).

HIS GIRL FRIDAY 1940 d: Howard Hawks. USA., *The Front Page*, Ben Hecht, Charles MacArthur, New York 1928, Play

HIS GLORIOUS NIGHT 1929 d: Lionel Barrymore. USA., *Olympia*, Ferenc Molnar, Budapest 1928, Play

His Good Name *see* **TRIFLING WITH HONOR** (1923).

HIS GRACE GIVES NOTICE 1924 d: W. P. Kellino. UKN., *His Grace Gives Notice*, Lady Trowbridge, Novel

HIS GRACE GIVES NOTICE 1933 d: George A. Cooper. UKN., *His Grace Gives Notice*, Lady Trowbridge, Novel

His Grace's Last Testament *see* **HANS NADS TESTAMENTE** (1919).

His Grace's Will *see* **HANS NADS TESTAMENTE** (1919).

His Grace's Will *see* **HANS NADS TESTAMENTE** (1940).

His Great Moment *see* **THE SENTENCE OF DEATH** (1927).

His Harvest *see* **LOVE'S HARVEST** (1920).

HIS HEART, HIS HAND AND HIS SWORD 1914 d: Lorimer Johnston, G. P. Hamilton. USA., *His Heart His Hand and His Sword*, Louis Joseph Vance, Story

His, Hers and Theirs *see* **MINE AND OURS YOURS** (1968).

His Highness's Adjutant *see* **POBOCNIK JEHO VYSOSTI** (1933).

HIS HOUR 1924 d: King Vidor. USA., *His Hour*, Elinor Glyn, New York 1910, Novel

HIS HOUSE IN ORDER 1928 d: Randle Ayrton. UKN., *His House in Order*, Arthur Wing Pinero, London 1906, Play

HIS JAZZ BRIDE 1926 d: Herman C. Raymaker. USA., *The Flapper Wife*, Beatrice Burton, New York 1925, Novel

HIS KIND OF WOMAN 1951 d: John Farrow, Richard Fleischer (Uncredited). USA., *Star Sapphire*, Gerald Drayson Adams, Story

His Lady *see* **WHEN A MAN LOVES** (1927).

HIS LAST BOW 1923 d: George Ridgwell. UKN., *His Last Bow*, Arthur Conan Doyle, 1917, Short Story

HIS LAST DEFENCE 1919 d: Geoffrey Wilmer. UKN., *The K.C.*, Dion Titheradge, Play

HIS LAST DOLLAR 1914. USA., *His Last Dollar*, Baldwin G. Cooke, David Higgins, New York 1904, Play

HIS LORDSHIP 1915 d: George Loane Tucker. UKN., *His Lordship*, W. W. Jacobs, Short Story

HIS LORDSHIP 1932 d: Michael Powell. UKN., *The Right Honourable*, Oliver Heuffer, Play

HIS LORDSHIP 1936 d: Herbert Mason. UKN., *The Nelson Touch*, Neil Grant, London 1931, Play

HIS LORDSHIP REGRETS 1938 d: MacLean Rogers. UKN., *Bees and Honey*, H. F. Maltby, 1928, Play

His Majesty Bunker Bean *see* **BUNKER BEAN** (1936).

HIS MAJESTY, BUNKER BEAN 1918 d: William D. Taylor. USA., *Bunker Bean*, Harry Leon Wilson, New York 1913, Novel

HIS MAJESTY, BUNKER BEAN 1925 d: Harry Beaumont. USA., *Bunker Bean*, Harry Leon Wilson, New York 1913, Novel

HIS MAJESTY O'KEEFE 1954 d: Byron Haskin. UKN/USA., *His Majesty O'Keefe*, Gerald Green, Lawrence Kingman, 1950, Novel

His Majesty on the Wrong Path *see* **MAJESTAT AUF ABWEGEN** (1958).

His Majesty, the Scarecrow *see* **THE SCARECROW OF OZ HIS MAJESTY** (1914).

HIS MAJESTY, THE SCARECROW OF OZ 1914 d: L. Frank Baum. USA., *The New Wizard of Oz*, L. Frank Baum, Chicago 1903, Novel, *The Wizard of Oz*, L. Frank Baum, A. B. Sloane, Paul Tietjens, 1903, Play

His Majesty's Car *see* **MY LIPS BETRAY** (1933).

His Majesty's Dates *see* **MIT CSINALT FELSEGED 3-TOL 5-IG?** (1964).

His Majesty's Field Marshal *see* **C. A. K. POLNI MARSALEK** (1930).

HIS MASTERPIECE 1909 d: Bannister Merwin. USA., *His Masterpiece*, O. Henry, Short Story

HIS MISJUDGEMENT 1911. USA., *His Misjudgement*, Thomas W. Henshew, Story

HIS MOTHER'S BIRTHDAY 1913. USA., *His Mother's Birthday*, Henry Wadsworth Longfellow, Poem

His Night Out *see* **THEIR NIGHT OUT** (1933).

HIS OFFICIAL FIANCEE 1919 d: Robert G. VignolA. USA., *His Official Fiancee*, Berta Ruck, New York 1914, Novel

HIS OTHER WIFE 1921 d: Percy Nash. UKN., *His Other Wife*, George R. Sims, Play

His Other Woman *see* **THE DESK SET** (1957).

His Pal's Wife *see* **HIS BUDDY'S WIFE** (1925).

HIS PARISIAN WIFE 1919 d: Emile Chautard. USA., *The Green Orchard*, Andrew Soutar, London 1916, Novel

HIS PRICELESS TREASURE 1913 d: Allen Curtis. USA., *His Priceless Treasure*, Hy Mayer, Story

HIS REST DAY 1927 d: George A. Cooper. UKN., *His Rest Day*, Matthew Boulton, Play

HIS ROBE OF HONOR 1918 d: Rex Ingram. USA., *His Robe of Honor*, Ethel Dorrance, James Dorrance, New York 1916, Novel

His Secret Bride *see* **SECRET BRIDE** (1934).

His Sixteenth Wife *see* **THE SIXTEENTH WIFE** (1917).

HIS SUPREME MOMENT 1925 d: George Fitzmaurice. USA., *World Without End*, May Edginton, Story

His Supreme Moment *see* **THE SPORTING VENUS** (1925).

His Supreme Sacrifice *see* **THE CALL OF THE EAST** (1922).

His Temporary Affair *see* **EX-BAD BOY** (1931).

HIS TEMPORARY WIFE 1920 d: Joseph Levering. USA., *His Temporary Wife*, Robert Ames Bennet, 1917, Short Story

HIS TIGER LADY 1928 d: Hobart Henley. USA., *La Grande-Duchesse Et le Garcon d'Etage*, Alfred Savoir, Paris 1924, Play

His Vindication *see* **THE KING'S OUTCAST** (1915).

His Violin *see* **ZIJN VIOOL** (1914).

HIS WIFE 1915 d: George Foster Platt. USA., *My Poor Wife*, Bertha M. Clay, Novel

His Wife from Arizona *see* **HUNGRY EYES** (1918).

His Wife's Affair *see* **THE NIGHT WATCH** (1928).

HIS WIFE'S FRIEND 1919 d: Joseph de Grasse. USA., *The White Rook*, John Harris-Burland, New York 1918, Novel

HIS WIFE'S HUSBAND 1922 d: Kenneth Webb. USA., *The Mayor's Wife*, Anna Katharine Green, Indianapolis 1907, Novel

HIS WIFE'S MOTHER 1932 d: Harry Hughes. UKN., *The Queer Fish*, Will Scott, Play

HIS WOMAN 1931 d: Edward Sloman. USA., *The Sentimentalists*, Dale Collins, Boston 1927, Novel

His Young Wife *see* **LE MISERIE DEL SIGNOR TRAVET** (1946).

Hisbiscus Town *see* **FURONG ZHEN** (1985).

HISSHOKA 1945 d: Kenji Mizoguchi, Tomotaka TasakA. JPN., *Hisshoka*, Kei Moriyama, Novel

Hissyo Ka *see* **HISSHOKA** (1945).

Histoire Comique *see* **FELICIE NANTEUIL** (1942).

Histoire d'Amour, Une *see* **LIEBELEI** (1933).

Histoire de l'Oeil, L' *see* **SIMONA** (1974).

HISTOIRE DE RIRE 1941 d: Marcel L'Herbier. FRN., *Histoire de Rire*, Armand Salacrou, 1940, Play

Histoire Des Treize *see* **LIEBE** (1927).

HISTOIRE D'O, L' 1975 d: Just Jaeckin. FRN/GRM., *L' Histoire d'O*, Pauline Reage, Novel

HISTOIRE D'UN PIERROT 1914 d: Baldassarre Negroni. ITL., *Histoire d'un Pierrot*, Fernand Beissier, 1893

HISTOIRE IMMORTELLE 1968 d: Orson Welles. FRN., *Skibsdrengens Fortaelling*, Karen Blixen, Copenhagen 1942, Short Story

HISTOIRES D'HIVER 1999 d: Francois Bouvier. CND., *Des Histoires d'Hiver Avec Des Rues Des Ecoles Et du Hocke*, Marc Robitaille, Novel

HISTOIRES EXTRAORDINAIRES 1968 d: Roger Vadim, Louis Malle. FRN/ITL., *Metzengerstein*, Edgar Allan Poe, 1832, Short Story

HISTOIRES EXTRAORDINAIRES 1968 d: Federico Fellini. FRN/ITL., *Never Bet Your Head*, Edgar Allan Poe, 1841, Short Story

HISTOIRES EXTRAORDINAIRES 1968 d: Roger Vadim, Louis Malle. FRN/ITL., *William Wilson*, Edgar Allan Poe, 1839, Short Story

Histoirs de Cirque, Une *see* **CROQUETTE** (1927).

HISTORIA DA NUMISMATICA 1954 d: Wilson SilvA. BRZ., *Cristo No Lama*, Joao Felicio Dos Santos, 1964, Novel

Historia de un Joven Pobre see **IL ROMANZO DI UN GIOVANE POVERO** (1958).

HISTORIA DE UNA ESCALERA 1950 d: Ignacio F. Iquino. SPN., *Historia de Una Escalera*, Antonio Buero Vallejo, 1950, Play

HISTORIA DE UNA MALA MUJER 1948 d: Luis Saslavsky. ARG., *Lady Windermere's Fan*, Oscar Wilde, London 1892, Play

HISTORIEN OM EN MODER 1979 d: Claus Weeke. DNM., *Histoiren Om En Moder*, Hans Christian Andersen, 1848, Short Story

History see **LA STORIA** (1986).

History Instruction see **GESCHICHTSUNTERRICHT** (1972).

History Lessons see **GESCHICHTSUNTERRICHT** (1972).

HISTORY MAN, THE 1981 d: Robert Knights. UKN., *The History Man*, Malcolm Bradbury, Novel

HISTORY OF MR. POLLY, THE 1949 d: Anthony Pelissier. UKN., *The History of Mr. Polly*, H. G. Wells, London 1910, Novel

HIT AND RUN 1965 d: Paddy Russell. UKN., Jeffrey Ashford, Novel

HIT AND RUN 1982 d: Charles Braverman. USA., *80 Dollars to Stamford*, Lucille Fletcher, Novel

HIT AND RUN 1985 d: Claudio Cutry. USA., *Hit and Run*, James Hadley Chase, Novel

Hit and Run see **HITTING HOME** (1988).

Hit Man, The see **LA SCOUMOUNE** (1973).

HIT ME 1996 d: Steven Shainberg. USA., *A Swell-Looking Babe*, Jim Thompson, Novel

Hit Me Again see **SMARTY** (1934).

HIT OF THE SHOW 1928 d: Ralph Ince. USA., *Notices*, Viola Brothers Shore, Story

HIT THE DECK 1930 d: Luther Reed. USA., *Shore Leave*, Hubert Osborne, New York 1922, Play

HIT THE DECK 1955 d: Roy Rowland. USA., *Shore Leave*, Hubert Osborne, New York 1922, Play

Hitch-Hike see **AUTOSTOP** (1977).

Hitler: the Last Ten Days see **GLI ULTIMI DIECI GIORNI DI HITLER** (1973).

Hitlerjunge Salomon see **EUROPA EUROPA** (1991).

HITLER'S CHILDREN 1943 d: Edward Dmytryk. USA., *Education for Death*, Gregor Ziemer, Book

Hitler's Hangman see **HITLER'S MADMAN** (1943).

HITLER'S MADMAN 1943 d: Douglas Sirk. USA., *Hangman's Village*, Bart Lytton, Story

HIT-THE-TRAIL HOLLIDAY 1918 d: Marshall Neilan. USA., *Hit-the-Trail-Holliday*, George M. Cohan, New York 1915, Play

HITTING HOME 1988 d: Robin Spry. CND., *Hit and Run*, Tom Alderman, Novel

Hitting the Headlines see **YOKEL BOY** (1942).

HLIDAC C. 47 1937 d: Josef Rovensky. CZC., *Hlidac C. 47*, Josef Kopta, Novel

HLYAB - CHERTICHKATA 1972 d: Naum Shopov, Rashko Ouzunov. BUL., *Khlyab*, Yordan Radichkov, 1969, Short Story

H.M. PULMAN ESQ. 1941 d: King Vidor. USA., *Esquire H.M. Pulman*, John Phillips Marquand, 1941, Novel

H.M.S. DEFIANT 1962 d: Lewis Gilbert. UKN., *Mutiny*, Frank Tilsey, London 1958, Novel

H.M.S. PINAFORE 1950. USA., *H.M.S. Pinafore*, W. S. Gilbert, Arthur Sullivan, London 1878, Opera

Hmuroe Utro see **KHUROYE UTRO** (1959).

HO! 1968 d: Robert Enrico. FRN/ITL., *Ho*, Jose Giovanni, Novel

Ho! Criminal Face see **HO!** (1968).

HO PERDUTO MIO MARITO! 1937 d: Enrico Guazzoni. ITL., *Ho Perduto Mio Marito!*, Giovanni Cenzato, Play

HO SOGNATO IL PARADISO 1950 d: Giorgio PastinA. ITL., *Ho Sognato Il Paradiso*, Guido Cantini, Play

Ho Una Moglie Pazza, Pazza, Pazza see **CHERIE RELAXE-TOI** (1964).

HOA-BINH 1970 d: Raoul Coutard. FRN., *La Colonne de Cendres*, Francoise Lorrain, Novel

HOARDED ASSETS 1918 d: Paul Scardon. USA., *Hoarded Assets*, Raymond Smiley Spears, 1918, Short Story

Hoary Legends of the Caucasus, The see **ASHIK KERIB** (1988).

Hoboes in Paradise see **LES GUEUX AU PARADIS** (1945).

Hoboes, The see **DIE LANDSTREICHER** (1937).

HOBSON'S CHOICE 1920 d: Percy Nash. UKN., *Hobson's Choice*, Harold Brighouse, London 1916, Play

HOBSON'S CHOICE 1931 d: Thomas Bentley. UKN., *Hobson's Choice*, Harold Brighouse, London 1916, Play

HOBSON'S CHOICE 1954 d: David Lean. UKN., *Hobson's Choice*, Harold Brighouse, London 1916, Play

HOBSON'S CHOICE 1983 d: Gilbert Cates. USA., *Hobson's Choice*, Harold Brighouse, London 1916, Play

HOCHSTAPLERIN DER LIEBE 1954 d: Hans H. Konig. AUS., *Heiratsschwindlerin*, Kurt Joachim Fischer, H. H. Mantello, Book

HOCHSTAPLERIN, DIE 1927 d: Martin Berger. GRM., *Der Fall Gehrsdorf*, Hans Land, Novel

HOCHTOURIST, DER 1931 d: Alfred Zeisler. GRM., *Der Hochtourist*, Curt Kraatz, Max Neal, Play

HOCHTOURIST, DER 1942 d: Adolf Schlissleder. GRM., *Der Hochtourist*, Curt Kraatz, Max Neal, Play

HOCHTOURIST, DER 1961 d: Ulrich Erfurth. GRM., *Der Hochtourist*, Curt Kraatz, Max Neal, Play

HOCHVERRAT 1929 d: Johannes Meyer. GRM., *Hochverrat*, Wenzel Goldbaum, Play

HOCHZEIT AUF BARENHOF 1942 d: Carl Froelich. GRM., *Jolanthes Hochzeit*, Hermann Sudermann, 1892, Short Story

HOCHZEIT AUF REISEN 1953 d: Paul Verhoeven. GRM., *Die Hochzeitsreise*, Heinrich Spoerl, Play

HOCHZEIT DES FIGARO, DIE 1968 d: Joachim Hess. GRM., *Le Mariage de Figaro*, Pierre-Augustin Caron de Beaumarchais, Paris 1784, Play

HOCHZEIT IM HEU 1951 d: Arthur M. Rabenalt. GRM/AUS., *Doppelselbstmord*, Ludwig Anzengruber, 1876, Play

HOCHZEIT MIT ERIKA 1949 d: Eduard von Borsody. GRM., *Hochzeit Mit Erika*, Willi Webels, Play

HOCHZEITSNACHT 1941 d: Carl Boese. GRM., *Der Stier Geht Los*, O. C. A. Zur Nedden, Play

HOCHZEITSNACHT IM PARADIES 1950 d: Geza von Bolvary. GRM., *Hochzeitsnacht Im Paradies*, Heinz Hentschke, Opera

HOCHZEITSNACHT IM PARADIES 1962 d: Paul Martin. AUS., *Hochzeitsnacht Im Paradies*, Heinz Hentschke, Opera

HOCHZEITSREISE ZU DRITT 1939 d: Hubert MarischkA. GRM., *Hochzeitsreis Ohne Mann*, F. B. Cortan, Novel

HOCUSSING OF CIGARETTE, THE 1924 d: Hugh Croise. UKN., *The Hocussing of Cigarette*, Baroness Orczy, Short Story

HODJA FRA PJORT 1986 d: Brita WielopolskA. DNM., *Hodja Fra Pjort*, Ole Lund Kirkegaard, Novel

Hodja from Pjort see **HODJA FRA PJORT** (1986).

HOFFMAN 1970 d: Alvin Rakoff. UKN., *Shall I Eat You Now?*, Ernest Gebler, Novel

Hoffnung Auf Segen see **DIE FAHRT INS VERDERBEN** (1924).

Hofjagd in Ischl see **ZWEI HERZEN UND EIN THRON** (1955).

HOFKONZERT, DAS 1936 d: Douglas Sirk. GRM., *Das Kleine Hofkonzert*, Toni Impekoven, Paul Verhoeven, Play

H.O.G. see **THE HOUSE OF GOD** (1979).

HOGAN'S ALLEY 1925 d: Roy Del Ruth. USA., *Hogan's Alley*, Gregory Roger, Story

HOGY ALLUNK, FIATALEMBER? 1963 d: Gyorgy Revesz. HNG., *Gyerektukor*, Sandor Somogyi Toth, 1963, Novel

Hohe Lied Der Liebe, Das see **MANON LESCAUT** (1919).

HOHEIT TANZT WALZER 1935 d: Max Neufeld. AUS/CZC., *Hoheit Tanzt Walzer*, Julius Brammer, Alfred Grunwald, Operetta

HOHENFEUER 1985 d: Fredi M. Murer. SWT., *Hohenfeuer*, Fredi M. Murer, Novel

HOKUSPOKUS 1930 d: Gustav Ucicky. GRM., *Hokuspokus*, Curt Goetz, Play

HOKUSPOKUS 1953 d: Kurt Hoffmann. GRM., *Hokuspokus*, Curt Goetz, Play

HOKUSPOKUS - ODER WIE LASSE ICH MEINEN MANN VERSCHWINDEN? 1966 d: Kurt Hoffmann. GRM., *Hokuspokus*, Curt Goetz, Play

Hokuspokus Or, How Can I Get Rid of My Husband? see **HOKUSPOKUS - ODER WIE LASSE ICH MEINEN MANN VERSCHWINDEN?** (1966).

HOLCROFT COVENANT, THE 1985 d: John Frankenheimer. UKN/USA., *The Holcroft Covenant*, Robert Ludlum, Novel

Hold Autumn in Your Hand see **THE SOUTHERNER** (1945).

HOLD BACK THE NIGHT 1956 d: Allan Dwan. USA., *Hold Back the Night*, Pat Frank, 1952, Novel

HOLD 'EM YALE! 1928 d: Edward H. Griffith. USA., *Life at Yale*, Owen Davis, Play

HOLD 'EM, YALE 1935 d: Sidney Lanfield. USA., *Hold 'Em Yale!*, Damon Runyon, 1931, Short Story

HOLD EVERYTHING 1930 d: Roy Del Ruth. USA., *Hold Everything*, Lew Brown, Buddy De Sylva, John McGowan, New York 1928, Musical Play

HOLD MY HAND 1938 d: Thornton Freeland. UKN., *Hold My Hand*, Noel Gay, Stanley Lupino, London 1931, Musical Play

HOLD THAT BLONDE! 1945 d: George Marshall. USA., *The Heart of a Thief*, Paul Armstrong, New York 1914, Play

Hold That Dream see **HOLD THE DREAM** (1986).

Hold That Tiger see **SPRING TONIC** (1935).

HOLD THE DREAM 1986 d: Don Sharp. UKN/USA., *A Woman of Substance*, Barbara Taylor Bradford, Novel

HOLD YOUR HORSES 1921 d: E. Mason Hopper. USA., *Canavan the Man Who Had His Way*, Rupert Hughes, 1909, Short Story

Hold Your Horses see **STAGECOACH WAR** (1940).

Hold-Up see **LEUR DERNIERE NUIT** (1953).

HOLD-UP 1985 d: Alexandre Arcady. FRN/CND., *Quick Change*, Jay Cronley, Novel

HOLE IN THE HEAD, A 1959 d: Frank CaprA. USA., *The Heart's a Forgotten Hotel*, Arnold Shulman, 1955, Television Play

HOLE IN THE WALL, THE 1921 d: Maxwell Karger. USA., *The Hole in the Wall*, Frederick Jackson, New York 1920, Play

HOLE IN THE WALL, THE 1929 d: Robert Florey. USA., *The Hole in the Wall*, Frederick Jackson, New York 1920, Play

Hole, The see **LE TROU** (1960).

HOLI 1983 d: Ketan MehtA. IND., *Holi*, Mahesh Elkunchwar, Play

HOLIDAY 1930 d: Edward H. Griffith. USA., *Holiday*, Philip Barry, New York 1928, Play

HOLIDAY 1938 d: George Cukor. USA., *Holiday*, Philip Barry, New York 1928, Play

HOLIDAY AFFAIR 1949 d: Don Hartman. USA., *A Christmas Gift*, John D. Weaver, Story

HOLIDAY FOR LOVERS 1959 d: Henry Levin. USA., *Holiday for Lovers*, Ronald Alexander, New York 1957, Play

HOLIDAY FOR SINNERS 1952 d: Gerald Mayer. USA., *Days Before Lent*, Hamilton Basso, 1939, Novel

Holiday Hookers see **NATALE IN CASA D'APPUNTAMENTO** (1976).

HOLIDAY HUSBAND, THE 1920 d: A. C. Hunter. UKN., *The Holiday Husband*, Dolf Wyllarde, Novel

Holiday of St. Jorgen, The see **PRAZDNIK SVYATOVO IORGENE** (1930).

Holiday Song see **DER ZUG NACH MANHATTAN** (1981).

Holiday Week see **HINDLE WAKES** (1952).

HOLLE DER JUNGFRAUEN, DIE 1927 d: Robert Dinesen. GRM., *Die Holle Der Jungfrauen*, Gabriele Zapolska, Novel

HOLLE VON MANITOBA, DIE 1965 d: Sheldon Reynolds. GRM/SPN., Jerold Hayden Boyd, Story

HOLLISCHE LIEBE 1949 d: Geza von CziffrA. AUS., *Anita Und Der Teufel*, Geza von Cziffra, Play

Hollow of Her Hand, The see **IN THE HOLLOW OF HER HAND** (1918).

HOLLOW REED 1995 d: Angela Pope. UKN/GRM., *Hollow Reed*, Neville Bolt, Short Story

HOLLOW TRIUMPH 1948 d: Steve Sekely. USA., *Hollow Triumph*, Murray Forbes, Novel

HOLLOWAY'S TREASURE 1924 d: Sinclair Hill. UKN., *Holloway's Treasure*, Morley Roberts, Short Story

HOLLY AND THE IVY, THE 1952 d: George M. O'Ferrall. UKN., *The Holly and the Ivy*, Wynard Browne, London 1950, Play

Hollyhock *see* MALVALOCA (1926).

Hollyhocks *see* THINGS MEN DO (1920).

Hollywood Strangler, The *see* DON'T ANSWER THE PHONE! (1980).

HOLLYWOODISM: JEWS, MOVIES, AND THE AMERICAN DREAM 1998 d: Simcha Jacobovici. CND., *An Empire of Their Own: How the Jews Invented Hollywood*, Neal Gabler, Book

Holy Innocents, The *see* LOS SANTOS INOCENTES (1984).

Holy Lie, The *see* STAR FOR A NIGHT (1936).

Holy Man, The *see* MAHAPURUSH (1965).

Holy Martyr, The *see* YISKOR (1932).

HOLY MATRIMONY 1943 d: John M. Stahl. USA., *Buried Alive*, Arnold Bennett, London 1908, Novel

Holy Monkey Fights the White Boned Devil Three Times, The *see* SUN WUKONG SAN DA BAIGUJING (1960).

HOLY ORDERS 1917 d: A. E. Coleby, Arthur Rooke. UKN., *Holy Orders*, Marie Corelli, Novel

HOLY TERROR, A 1931 d: Irving Cummings. USA., *Trailin'*, Max Brand, New York 1920, Novel

Holy Terror, The *see* BEBERT ET L'OMNIBUS (1963).

HOMBRE 1967 d: Martin Ritt. USA., *Hombre*, Elmore Leonard, London 1961, Novel

Hombre de la Cruz Verde, El *see* EL SEGUNDO PODER (1976).

Hombre de Marrakech, El *see* L' HOMME DE MARRAKECH (1966).

HOMBRE DE MUNDO, EL 1948 d: Manuel Tamayo. SPN., *El Hombre de Mundo*, Ventura de La Vega, 1845, Play

Hombre Del Subsuelo, El *see* MEMORIAS DEL SUBSUELO (1981).

Hombre Desnudo, El *see* O HOMEM NU (1968).

Hombre Importante, El *see* EL HOMBRE IMPORTANTE ANIMAS TRUJANO (1961).

Hombre Llamado Noon, Un *see* THE MAN CALLED NOON (1973).

HOMBRE QUE SE QUISO MATAR, EL 1941 d: Rafael Gil. SPN., *El Hombre Que Se Quiso Matar*, Wenceslao Fernandez Florez, 1930, Short Story

HOMBRE QUE SE QUISO MATAR, EL 1970 d: Rafael Gil. SPN., *El Hombre Que Se Quiso Matar*, Wenceslao Fernandez Florez, 1930, Short Story

HOME 1915 d: Maurice Elvey. UKN., *Home Sweet Home*, Frank Lindo, Play

HOME 1972 d: Lindsay Anderson. UKN., *Home*, David Storey, 1970, Play

HOME AND AWAY 1956 d: Vernon Sewell. UKN., *Treble Trouble*, Heather McIntyre, Play

Home and the World, The *see* GHARE BHAIRE (1983).

HOME AT SEVEN 1952 d: Ralph Richardson. UKN., *Home at Seven*, R. C. Sherriff, London 1950, Play

HOME BEFORE DARK 1958 d: Mervyn Leroy. USA., *Home Before Dark*, Eileen Bassing, 1957, Novel

HOME FIRES BURNING 1992 d: L. A. Puopolo. USA., *Home Fires Burning*, Chris Cesaro, Play

Home from Babylon *see* HEM FRAN BABYLON (1941).

HOME FROM THE HILL 1960 d: Vincente Minnelli. USA., *Home from the Hill*, William Humphrey, 1958, Novel

HOME IN INDIANA 1944 d: Henry Hathaway. USA., *The Phantom Filly*, George Agnew Chamberlain, Novel

HOME IS THE HERO 1959 d: Fielder Cook. UKN., *Home Is the Hero*, Walter MacKen, New York 1954, Play

Home Is Where the Heart Is *see* SQUARE DANCE (1987).

HOME MAKER, THE 1925 d: King Baggot. USA., *The Home-Maker*, Dorothy Canfield, New York 1924, Novel

HOME OF THE BRAVE 1949 d: Mark Robson. USA., *Home of the Brave*, Arthur Laurents, New York 1945, Play

HOME ON THE RANGE 1935 d: Arthur Jacobson. USA., *Code of the West*, Zane Grey, New York 1924, Novel

Home Song *see* LAVYRLE SPENCER'S HOME SONG (1996).

HOME STRETCH, THE 1921 d: Jack Nelson. USA., *When Johnny Comes Marching Home*, Charles Belmont Davis, 1914, Short Story

HOME, SWEET HOME 1914 d: D. W. Griffith. USA., *Sweet Home Home*, Henry Bishop, John Howard Payne, 1823, Song

HOME, SWEET HOMICIDE 1946 d: Lloyd Bacon. USA., *Home Sweet Homicide*, Craig Rice, Novel

HOME TO STAY 1978 d: Delbert Mann. USA/CND., *Grandpa and Frank*, Janet Majerus, Novel

HOME TOWN GIRL, THE 1919 d: Robert G. VignolA. USA., *You Just Can't Wait*, Oscar Graeve, 1918, Short Story

HOME TOWNERS, THE 1928 d: Bryan Foy. USA., *The Hometowners*, George M. Cohan, New York 1926, Play

HOMEBOY 1989 d: Michael Seresin. USA., Mickey Rourke, Story

Homecoming *see* HEIMKEHR (1928).

HOMECOMING 1948 d: Mervyn Leroy. USA., *Homecoming*, Sidney Kingsley, Book

HOMECOMING: A CHRISTMAS STORY, THE 1971 d: Fielder Cook. USA., *The Homecoming*, Earl Hamner Jr., Novel

Homecoming, The *see* THE HOMECOMING: A CHRISTMAS STORY (1971).

HOMECOMING, THE 1973 d: Peter Hall. UKN/USA., *The Homecoming*, Harold Pinter, 1965, Play

Homeland *see* HEIMAT (1938).

HOMEM CELEBRE, O 1974 d: Miguel Faria Junior. BRZ., *Um Homem Celebre*, Joaquim Maria Machado de Assis, 1888, Short Story

HOMEM E SUA JAULA, UM 1969 d: Fernando Cony Campos, Paulo Gil Soares. BRZ., *Materia de Memoria*, Carlos Heitor Cony, 1962, Novel

HOMEM NU, O 1968 d: Roberto Santos. BRZ., *O Homem Nu*, Fernando Tavares Sabino, 1960, Short Story

Homero's Odyssey *see* L' ODISSEA (1911).

HOMESTEADER, THE 1919 d: Oscar Micheaux, Jerry Mills. USA., *The Homesteader*, Oscar Micheaux, Sioux City 1917, Novel

Homesteaders, The *see* ABILENE TOWN (1946).

Hometowners *see* LADIES MUST LIVE (1940).

HOMEWARD BOUND: THE INCREDIBLE JOURNEY 1993 d: Duwayne Dunham. USA., *The Incredible Journey*, Sheila Burnford, Novel

Homeward Trail, The *see* THE WALLOP (1921).

Homicide *see* LE REQUISITOIRE (1930).

HOMICIDE 1948 d: Felix Jacoves. USA., *Night Beat*, William Sackheim, Story

HOMICIDE FOR THREE 1948 d: George Blair. USA., *Puzzle for Puppets*, Patrick Quentin, Novel

HOMICIDE SQUAD, THE 1931 d: Edward L. Cahn, George Melford. USA., *The Mob*, Henry la Cossitt, 1928, Short Story

Hommage aux Femmes. d'un Certain Age *see* IN PRAISE OF OLDER WOMEN (1978).

HOMME A ABATTRE, L' 1936 d: Leon Mathot. FRN., *L' Homme a Abattre*, Charles-Robert Dumas, Novel

HOMME A FEMMES, L' 1960 d: Jacques-Gerard Cornu. FRN., *Shadow of Guilt*, Patrick Quentin, Novel

HOMME A LA BUICK, L' 1967 d: Gilles Grangier. FRN., *Cher Voyou*, Michel Lambesc, Novel

Homme a la Cagoule Noire, L' *see* LA BETE AUX SEPT MANTEAUX (1936).

HOMME A L'HISPANO, L' 1926 d: Julien Duvivier. FRN., *L' Homme a l'Hispano*, Pierre Frondaie, Novel

HOMME A L'HISPANO, L' 1932 d: Jean Epstein. FRN., *L' Homme a l'Hispano*, Pierre Frondaie, Novel

HOMME A L'IMPERMEABLE, L' 1957 d: Julien Duvivier. FRN/ITL., *L' Homme a l'Impermeable*, James Hadley Chase, Novel

HOMME A L'OREILLE CASSEE, L' 1934 d: Robert Boudrioz. FRN., *L' Homme a l'Oreille Cassee*, Edmond About, 1862, Short Story

Homme a Part Entiere, Un *see* LA SECONDE VERITE (1965).

Homme a Tout Faire, L' *see* DER GEHULFE (1976).

HOMME AU CHAPEAU ROND, L' 1946 d: Pierre Billon. FRN., *Vechnyi Muzh*, Fyodor Dostoyevsky, 1870, Short Story

HOMME AU COMPLET GRIS, L' 1914 d: Henry Houry. FRN., *L' Homme Au Complet Gris*, Arnould Galopin, Novel

Homme Au Crane Rase, L' *see* MAN DIE ZIJN HAAR KORT LIET KNIPPEN (1966).

Homme Au Sang Bleu, L' *see* NESTOR BURMA: L'HOMME AUS SANG BLEU (1994).

Homme aux Figures de Cire, L' *see* FIGURES DE CIRE (1912).

HOMME AUX YEUX D'ARGENT, L' 1985 d: Pierre Granier-Deferre. FRN., *L' Homme aux Yeux d'Argent*, Robert Rossner, Novel

HOMME BLEU, L' 1919 d: Jean Manoussi. FRN., *L' Homme Bleu*, Georges le Faure, Novel

HOMME DE JOIE, L' 1950 d: Gilles Grangier. FRN., *L' Homme de Joie*, Paul Geraldy, Robert Spitzer, Play

HOMME DE LA JAMAIQUE, L' 1950 d: Maurice de Canonge. FRN., *L' Homme de la Jamaique*, Robert Gaillard, Novel

HOMME DE LA NUIT, L' 1946 d: Rene Jayet. FRN., *L' Homme de la Nuit*, Jean-Louis Sanciaume, Novel

Homme de la Tour Eiffel, L' *see* THE MAN ON THE EIFFEL TOWER (1949).

HOMME DE LONDRES, L' 1943 d: Henri Decoin. FRN., *L' Homme de Londres*, Georges Simenon, 1934, Novel

HOMME DE MARRAKECH, L' 1966 d: Jacques Deray. FRN/ITL/SPN., *The Heisters*, Robert Page Jones, New York 1964, Novel

HOMME DE MYKONOS, L' 1965 d: Rene Gainville. FRN/ITL/BLG., *Un Soleil de Plomb*, Michel Lebrun, Novel

HOMME DE NULLE PART, L' 1936 d: Pierre Chenal. FRN., *Il Fu Mattia Pascal*, Luigi Pirandello, 1904, Novel

Homme de Prague, L' *see* THE AMATEUR (1982).

HOMME DE TROP A BORD, UN 1935 d: Roger Le Bon, Gerhard Lamprecht. FRN., *Un Homme de Trop a Bord*, Fred Andreas, Novel

HOMME DE TROP, UN 1967 d: Costa-Gavras. FRN/ITL., *Un Homme de Trop*, Jean-Pierre Chabrol, Paris 1958, Novel

Homme Des Baleares, L' *see* LA REPONSE DU DESTIN (1924).

HOMME DU LARGE, L' 1920 d: Marcel L'Herbier. FRN., *Un Drame Au Bord de la Mer*, Honore de Balzac

Homme du Sud, L' *see* THE SOUTHERNER (1945).

HOMME EN HABIT, UN 1931 d: Rene Guissart, Robert Bossis. FRN., *L' Homme En Habit*, Yves Mirande, Andre Picard, Paris 1922, Play

HOMME EN OR, UN 1934 d: Jean Dreville. FRN., *Un Homme En Or*, Roger Ferdinand, Play

HOMME MARCHE DANS LA VILLE, UN 1949 d: Marcello Pagliero. FRN., *Un Homme Marche Dans la Ville*, Jean Jausion, Novel

HOMME PRESSE, L' 1976 d: Edouard Molinaro. FRN/ITL., *L' Homme Presse*, Paul Morand, Novel

HOMME QUI ASSASSINA, L' 1912 d: Henri Andreani. FRN., *L' Homme Qui Assassina*, Claude Farrere, Paris 1908, Novel

HOMME QUI ASSASSINA, L' 1930 d: Jean Tarride, Curtis Bernhardt. FRN., *L' Homme Qui Assassina*, Claude Farrere, Paris 1908, Novel

Homme Qui Mourra Demain, L' *see* QUAND SONNERA MIDI (1957).

HOMME QUI NE SAIT PAS DIRE NON, L' 1932 d: Heinz Hilpert. FRN., *Herr Funf*, Alice Berend, Novel

Homme Qui Ne Savait Pas Dire Non, L' *see* DER NICHT NEIN SAGEN KONNTE, DER MANN (1958).

Homme Qui Nous Suit, L' *see* LES PASSAGERS (1976).

HOMME QUI REVIENT DE LOIN, L' 1917 d: Rene Navarre. FRN., *L' Homme Qui Revient de Loin*, Gaston Leroux, Novel

HOMME QUI REVIENT DE LOIN, L' 1949 d: Jean Castanier. FRN., *L' Homme Qui Revient de Loin*, Gaston Leroux, Novel

Homme Qui Rit, L' *see* L' UOMO CHE RIDE (1966).

HOMME QUI VALAIT DES MILLIARDS, L' 1967 d: Michel Boisrond. FRN/ITL., *L' Homme Qui Valait Des Milliards*, Jean Stuart, Novel

Homme Qui Vendait Son Ame Au Diable, L' *see* L' HOMME QUI VENDAIT SON AME (1943).

HOMME QUI VENDAIT SON AME, L' 1943 d: Jean-Paul Paulin. FRN., *L' Homme Qui Vendit Son Ame*, Pierre-Gilles Veber, Novel

HOMME SANS COEUR, L' 1936 d: Leo Joannon. FRN., *L' Homme Sans Coeur*, Alfred Machard, Novel

HOMME SANS NOM, UN 1932 d: Roger Le Bon, Gustav Ucicky. FRN., *Le Colonel Chabert*, Honore de Balzac, 1844, Novel

HOMME SE PENCHE SUR SON PASSE, UN 1957 d: Willy Rozier. FRN/GRM., *Un Homme Se Penche Sur Son Passe*, Maurice Constantin-Weyer, Novel

HOMME TRAQUE, L' 1946 d: Robert Bibal. FRN., *L' Homme Traque*, Francis Carco, 1922, Novel

HOMMES DE LA COTE, LES 1934 d: Andre Pellenc. FRN., *Les Hommes de la Cote*, Mme. Romilly, Short Story

Hommes de Las Vegas, Les see 500 MILLONES LAS VEGAS (1968).

HOMMES EN BLANC, L' 1955 d: Ralph Habib. FRN., *Les Hommes En Blanc*, Andre Soubiran, Novel

HOMMES NOUVEAUX, LES 1922 d: Edouard-Emile Violet, E. B. Donatien. FRN., *Les Hommes Nouveaux*, Claude Farrere, Novel

HOMMES NOUVEAUX, LES 1936 d: Marcel L'Herbier. FRN., *Les Hommes Nouveaux*, Claude Farrere, Novel

HOMMES SANS NOM, LES 1937 d: Jean Vallee. FRN., *Les Hommes Sans Nom*, Jean Desvallieres

Hommes Sans Soleil, Les see GRISOU (1938).

Homo Faber see PASSAGIER FABER (1990).

HON DANSADE EN SOMMAR 1951 d: Arne Mattsson. SWD., *Sommardansen*, Peter Olof Ekstrom, Novel

HONDO 1953 d: John Farrow. USA., *The Gift of Cochise*, Louis L'Amour, Short Story

Honest Courtesan, The see DANGEROUS BEAUTY (1998).

HONEST HUTCH 1920 d: Clarence Badger. USA., *Old Hutch Lives Up to It*, Garrett Smith, 1920, Short Story

HONEST MAN, AN 1918 d: Frank Borzage. USA., Henry Payson Dowst, Story

HONEY 1930 d: Wesley Ruggles. USA., *Come Out of the Kitchen!*, Alice Duer Miller, New York 1916, Novel

HONEY BEE, THE 1920 d: Rupert Julian. USA., *The Honey Bee*, Samuel Merwin, New York 1901, Novel

HONEY POT, THE 1967 d: Joseph L. Mankiewicz. UKN/USA/ITL., *Mr. Fox of Venice*, Frederick Knott, London 1959, Play

Honeymoon see HONIGMOND (1996).

HONEYMOON ADVENTURE, A 1931 d: Maurice Elvey. UKN., *A Honeymoon Adventure*, Cecily Fraser-Smith, Novel

HONEYMOON AHEAD 1945 d: Reginald Le Borg. USA., *Romance Incorporated*, Val Burton, Story

HONEYMOON EXPRESS, THE 1926 d: James Flood. USA., *The Doormat*, Ethel Clifton, Brenda Fowler, New York 1922, Play

HONEYMOON FLATS 1928 d: Millard Webb. USA., *Honeymoon Flats*, Earl Derr Biggers, 1927, Short Story

HONEYMOON FOR THREE 1941 d: Lloyd Bacon. USA., *Goodbye Again*, George Haight, Allan Scott, New York 1932, Play

Honeymoon for Three, A see LET'S ELOPE (1919).

HONEYMOON HATE 1927 d: Luther Reed. USA., *Honeymoon Hate*, Alice Muriel Williamson, 1927, Short Story

HONEYMOON IN BALI 1939 d: Edward H. Griffith. USA., *Free Woman*, Katharine Brush, 1936, Short Story, *Our Miss Keane*, Grace Sartwell Mason, 1923, Short Story

HONEYMOON LANE 1931 d: William James Craft. USA., *Honeymoon Lane*, Edward Dowling, James F. Hanley, New York 1926, Play

HONEYMOON LIMITED 1935 d: Arthur Lubin. USA., *Honeymoon Limited*, Vida Hurst, New York 1932, Novel

HONEYMOON LODGE 1943 d: Edward Lilley. USA., *Second Honeymoon*, Warren Wilson, Story

HONEYMOON MACHINE, THE 1961 d: Richard Thorpe. USA., *The Golden Fleecing*, Lorenzo Semple Jr., 1959, Play

Honeymoon Merry-Go-Round see OLYMPIC HONEYMOON (1936).

HONEYMOON WITH A STRANGER 1969 d: John Peyser. USA., *Piege Pour un Homme Seul*, Robert Thomas, Novel

HONEYMOON'S OVER, THE 1939 d: Eugene J. Forde. USA., *Six-Cylinder Love*, William Anthony McGuire, New York 1921, Play

HONEYPOT, THE 1920 d: Fred Leroy Granville. UKN., *The Honeypot*, Countess Barcynska, Novel

HONG CHEN 1994 d: Gu Rong. CHN., *Hong Chen*, Huo Da, Wang Weizhen, Novel

HONG GAOLIANG 1987 d: Zhang Yimou. CHN., *Hong Gao Liang*, Mo Yan, 1985, Novel

HONG LOU ER YOU 1951 d: Yang XIao-Zhong. CHN., *Hong Lou Meng*, Cao Zhan, c1750-92, Novel

HONG LOU MENG 1962 d: Chen Fan. CHN., *Hong Lou Meng*, Cao Zhan, c1750-92, Novel

HONG LOU MENG 1988-89 d: XIe Tieli. CHN., *Hong Lou Meng*, Cao Zhan, c1750-92, Novel

HONG QI GE 1950 d: Wu Zuguang. CHN., *Hong Qi Ge*, Liu Canglang, Lu Mei, Novel

HONG YANG HAOXIA ZHUAN 1935 d: Yang XIaozhong. CHN., *Hong Yang Haoxia Zhuan*, Shanghai Joint Stage, Opera

HONG YU 1975 d: Cui Wei. CHN., *Hong Yu*, Yang XIao, Novel

HONGFEN 1994 d: Li Shaohong. CHN/HKG., *Hongfen*, Su Tong, Novel

HONGQI PU 1960 d: Ling Zhifeng. CHN., *Hongqi Pu*, Liang Bin, 1958, Novel

HONIGMOND 1996 d: Gabriel Barylli. GRM., *Honigmond*, Gabriel Barylli, Play

Honky Tonk see SHE DONE HIM WRONG (1933).

HONKYTONK MAN 1983 d: Clint Eastwood. USA., *Honkytonk Man*, Clancy Carlile, Novel

HONNEUR D'ARTISTE 1917 d: Jean Kemm. FRN., *Honneur d'Artiste*, Octave Feuillet, Novel

Honor Among Men 1924 d: Denison Clift. USA., *The King's Jackal*, Richard Harding Davis, New York 1898, Novel

Honor Among Thieves see ADIEU L'AMI (1968).

HONOR BOUND 1928 d: Alfred E. Green. USA., *Honor Bound*, Jack Bethea, Boston 1927, Novel

HONOR BOUND 1989 d: Jeannot Szwarc. USA., *Recovery*, Steven L. Thompson, Book

Honor Bright see YOU BELONG TO ME (1934).

HONOR FIRST 1922 d: Jerome Storm. USA., *The Splendid Outcast*, George Gibbs, New York 1920, Novel

HONOR OF KENNETH MCGRATH, THE 1915 d: Sydney Ayres. USA., *The Honor of Kenneth McGrath*, Calder Johnstone, Story

HONOR OF THE FAMILY 1931 d: Lloyd Bacon. USA., *La Rabouilleuse*, Honore de Balzac, Paris 1842, Novel

Honor of the Family, The see THE CORSICAN BROTHERS (1920).

Honor, The see NAMIS (1996).

HONOR THY FATHER 1971 d: Paul Wendkos. USA., *Honor Thy Father*, Gay Talese, Novel

HONOR THY MOTHER 1992 d: David Greene. USA., *Blood Games*, Jerry Bledsoe, Novel

Honorable Ladies of Pardubice, The see POCESTNE PANI PARDUBICKE (1944).

Honorary Consul, The see BEYOND THE LIMIT (1983).

Honour Among Thieves see TOUCHEZ PAS AU GRISBI (1953).

Honour Among Thieves see WEEDS (1987).

HONOUR IN PAWN 1916 d: Harold Weston. UKN., *Honor in Pawn*, William Babington Maxwell, Novel

Honour Thy Father see LA GERLA DI PAPA MARTIN (1909).

Honour Thy Mother see HONOR THY MOTHER (1992).

Honourable Gentleman, The see PAGAN LOVE (1920).

HONOURABLE MEMBER FOR OUTSIDE LEFT, THE 1925 d: Sinclair Hill. UKN., *The Honourable Member for Outside Left*, Sidney Horler, Short Story

Honourable Mr. Wong, The see THE HATCHET MAN (1932).

HONOURABLE MURDER, AN 1960 d: Godfrey Grayson. UKN., *Julius Caesar*, William Shakespeare, c1599, Play

HONOURS EASY 1935 d: Herbert Brenon. UKN., *Honours Easy*, Roland Pertwee, London 1930, Play

HONRADEZ DE LA CERRADURA, LA 1950 d: Luis Escobar. SPN., *La Honradez de la Cerradura*, Jacinto Benavente y Martinez, 1943, Play

HONTE DE LA FAMILLE, LA 1969 d: Richard Balducci. FRN., *La Honte de la Famille*, Charles Exbrayat, Novel

HOODLUM, THE 1919 d: Sidney A. Franklin. USA., *Burkeses Amy*, Julie Mathilde Lippman, New York 1915, Novel

HOODMAN BLIND 1913 d: James Gordon. USA., *Hoodman Blind*, Wilson Barrett, Henry Arthur Jones, London 1885, Play

Hoodman Blind see A MAN OF SORROW (1916).

HOODMAN BLIND 1923 d: John Ford. USA., *Hoodman Blind*, Wilson Barrett, Henry Arthur Jones, London 1885, Play

HOOK 1991 d: Steven Spielberg. USA., *Peter Pan*, J. M. Barrie, London 1904, Play

HOOK, THE 1962 d: George Seaton. USA., *L' Hamecon*, Vahe Katcha, Paris 1957, Novel

Hooker Cult Murders, The see THE PYX (1973).

Hoopla see HOOP-LA (1933).

HOOP-LA 1933 d: Frank Lloyd. USA., *The Barker; a Play of Carnival Life*, Kenyon Nicholson, New York 1917, Play

Hooray - It's a Boy! see HURRA - EIN JUNGE! (1953).

Hooray - It's a Boy see HURRA - EIN JUNGE! (1931).

Hooray - the Company Has a Child see HURRA - DIE FIRMA HAT EINE KIND (1956).

Hooray, I'm Alive see THE GHOST COMES HOME (1940).

HOOSIER SCHOOLBOY, THE 1937 d: William Nigh. USA., *Hoosier Schoolboy*, Edward Eggleston, New York 1883, Novel

HOOSIER SCHOOLMASTER, THE 1914 d: Max Figman. USA., *The Hoosier Schoolmaster*, Edward Eggleston, New York 1871, Novel

HOOSIER SCHOOLMASTER, THE 1924 d: Oliver L. Sellers. USA., *The Hoosier Schoolmaster*, Edward Eggleston, New York 1871, Novel

HOOSIER SCHOOLMASTER, THE 1935 d: Lewis D. Collins. USA., *The Hoosier Schoolmaster*, Edward Eggleston, New York 1871, Novel

HOP, THE DEVIL'S BREW 1916 d: Phillips Smalley, Lois Weber. USA., Rufus Steele, Article

HOPALONG CASSIDY 1935 d: Howard Bretherton. USA., *Hopalong Cassidy*, Clarence E. Mulford, Chicago 1912, Novel

Hop-Along Cassidy see HOPALONG CASSIDY (1935).

Hop-a-Long Cassidy see HOPALONG CASSIDY (1935).

Hopalong Cassidy Enters see HOPALONG CASSIDY (1935).

HOPALONG RIDES AGAIN 1937 d: Lesley Selander. USA., *Black Buttes*, Clarence E. Mulford, New York 1923, Novel

HOPE 1919 d: Rex Wilson. UKN., *Hope*, W. S. Gilbert, Short Story

Hope and Pain see DAUNTAUN HIROZU (1988).

HOPE CHEST, THE 1918 d: Elmer Clifton. USA., *The Hope Chest*, Mark Lee Luther, Boston 1918, Novel

HOPE, THE 1920 d: Herbert Blache. USA., Henry Hamilton, London 1911, Play, *The Hope*, Cecil Raleigh, London 1911, Play

Hopeless, The see SOVSEM PROPASCIJ (1972).

Hopelessly Lost see SOVSEM PROPASCIJ (1972).

HOP-FROG 1912 d: Henri Desfontaines. FRN., *Hop-Frog*, Edgar Allan Poe, 1849, Short Story

HOPPER, THE 1918 d: Thomas N. Heffron. USA., *The Hopper*, Meredith Nicholson, 1916, Short Story

HOPSCOTCH 1980 d: Ronald Neame. UKN/USA., *Hopscotch*, Brian Garfield, Novel

HORA DA ESTRELA, A 1985 d: Suzana Amaral. BRZ., *A Hora Da Estrela*, Clarice Lispector, 1977, Novel

HORA E VEZ DE AUGUSTO MATRAGA, A 1965 d: Roberto Santos. BRZ., *A Hora E Vez de Augusto Matraga*, Guimaraes Rosa, 1946, Short Story

Hora Y El Momento de Augusto Matraga, La see A HORA E VEZ DE AUGUSTO MATRAGA (1965).

HORACE 62 1962 d: Andre Versini. FRN/ITL., *Horace*, Pierre Corneille, 1641, Play

Horatio Hornblower see CAPTAIN HORATIO HORNBLOWER R.N. (1951).

HORATIO SPARKINS 1913 d: Van Dyke Brooke. USA., *Sparkins*, Charles Dickens, Short Story

Hordubal Brothers, The see HORDUBALOVE (1937).

HORDUBALOVE 1937 d: Martin Fric. CZC., *Hordubal*, Karel Capek, 1933, Novel

Hordubals, The see HORDUBALOVE (1937).

HORIZON, L' 1967 d: Jacques Rouffio. FRN., *Les Honneurs de la Guerre*, Georges Conchon, Novel

HORIZONTAL LIEUTENANT, THE 1962 d: Richard Thorpe. USA., *The Bottletop Affair*, Gordon Cotler, New York 1959, Novel

Horla, The see DIARY OF A MADMAN (1963).

HORLOGER DE ST. PAUL, L' 1973 d: Bertrand Tavernier. FRN., *L' Horloger d'Everton*, Georges Simenon, 1954, Short Story

Horn see TOM HORN (1979).

HORNET'S NEST 1923 d: Walter West. UKN., *Hornet's Nest*, Andrew Soutar, Novel

HORNET'S NEST, THE 1919 d: James Young. USA., *The Hornet's Nest*, Nancy Mann Waddel Woodrow, Boston 1917, Novel

HOROKI 1962 d: Mikio Naruse. JPN., *Horoki*, Fumiko Hayashi, Tokyo 1928, Biography

Horrible Dr. Orloff, L' see GRITOS EN LA NOCHE (1961).

HORRIBLE HYDE 1915 d: Howell Hansel. USA., *The Strange Case of Dr. Jekyll and Mr. Hyde*, Robert Louis Stevenson, London 1886, Novel

Horror! see CHILDREN OF THE DAMNED (1963).

Horror Castle see LA VERGINE DI NORIMBERGA (1963).

Horror Castle (Where the Blood Flows) see LA VERGINE DI NORIMBERGA (1963).

Horror Chamber of Dr. Faustus, The see LES YEUX SANS VISAGE (1959).

Horror: l'Assassino Ha le Ore Contate see COPLAN SAUVE SA PEAU (1967).

Horror of a Deformed Man see KYOFU NIKEI NINGEN (1969).

Horror of an Ugly Woman see KAIDAN KASANE GA FUCHI (1970).

Horror of Dracula see DRACULA (1958).

HORROR OF FRANKENSTEIN, THE 1970 d: Jimmy Sangster. UKN., *Frankenstein; Or the Modern Prometheus*, Mary Wollstonecraft Shelley, London 1818, Novel

Horror of Malformed Men see KYOFU NIKEI NINGEN (1969).

Horror of the Stone Women see IL MULINO DELLE DONNE DI PIETRA (1960).

HORS LA VIE 1991 d: Maroun Bagdadi. FRN/ITL/BLG., *Hors la Vie*, Roger Auque, Patrick Forestier, Book

Horse Ate the Hat, The see UN CHAPEAU DE PAILLE D'ITALIE (1927).

Horse Called Comanche, A see TONKA (1958).

HORSE IN THE GRAY FLANNEL SUIT, THE 1968 d: Norman Tokar. USA., *The Year of the Horse*, Eric Hatch, New York 1965, Novel

HORSE, LA 1969 d: Pierre Granier-Deferre. FRN/ITL/GRM., *La Horse*, Michel Lambesc, Novel

Horse Named Comanche, A see TONKA (1958).

Horse of Pride, The see LE CHEVAL D'ORGEUIL (1980).

HORSE SOLDIERS, THE 1959 d: John Ford. USA., *The Horse Soldiers*, Harold Sinclair, Novel

HORSE WHISPERER, THE 1998 d: Robert Redford. USA., *The Horse Whisperer*, Nicholas Evans, Novel

HORSE WITHOUT A HEAD, THE 1963 d: Don Chaffey. UKN., *A Hundred Million Francs*, Paul Berna, Novel

Horseflesh see SPORTING BLOOD (1931).

HORSEMEN, THE 1971 d: John Frankenheimer. USA., *Les Cavaliers*, Joseph Kessel, 1967, Novel

Horses Fly Me see NESUT MENYA KONI (1997).

Horse's Mouth, The see THE ORACLE (1953).

HORSE'S MOUTH, THE 1959 d: Ronald Neame. UKN., *The Horse's Mouth*, Joyce Cary, 1944, Novel

Horses of My Father, The see MEINES VATERS PFERDE (1954).

Horsie see QUEEN FOR A DAY (1951).

HORVATOV IZBOR 1985 d: Eduard Galic. YGS., *Vucjak*, Miroslav Krieza, 1925, Play

Horvat's Choice see HORVATOV IZBOR (1985).

HOSE, DIE 1927 d: Hans Behrendt. GRM., *Skandal in Der Residenz*, Carl Sternheim, Play

HOSEKRAEMMEREN 1963 d: Max Hellner, Johannes Vaabensted. DNM., *Hosekraemmeren*, Steen Steensen Blicher, 1829, Short Story

HOSEKRAEMMEREN 1971 d: Knud Leif Thomsen. DNM., *Hosekraemmeren*, Steen Steensen Blicher, 1829, Short Story

HOSIANNA 1961 d: Peter Podehl. GRM., *Hosianna*, Eva Rechlin, Book

Hospital of Transfiguration, The see SZPITAL PRZEMIENIENIA (1978).

HOSSZU ALKONY 1997 d: Attila Janisch. HNG., *The Bus*, Shirley Jackson, Short Story

HOSTAGE 1992 d: Robert Young. UKN/ARG., *No Place to Hide*, Ted Allbeury, Novel

HOSTAGE HEART, THE 1977 d: Bernard McEveety. USA., *The Hostage Heart*, Gerald Green, Novel

HOSTAGE, THE 1967 d: Russell S. Doughton Jr. USA., *The Hostage*, Henry Farrell, New York 1959, Novel

HOSTAGES 1943 d: Frank Tuttle. USA., *Hostages*, Stefan Heym, 1942, Novel

HOSTILE WITNESS 1968 d: Ray Milland. UKN., *Hostile Witness*, Jack Roffey, Play

Hot Air see TWENTY MILLION SWEETHEARTS (1934).

Hot Blood see THE WILD ONE (1953).

Hot Blood see PETER UND SABINE (1968).

HOT CARGO 1946 d: Lew Landers. USA., *Redwood Highway*, Daniel Mainwaring, Story

HOT CARS 1956 d: Don McDougall. USA., *Sellout*, M. Haile Chace, Novel

HOT ENOUGH FOR JUNE 1963 d: Ralph Thomas. UKN., *Night of Wenceslas*, Lionel Davidson, London 1960, Novel

Hot Heiress see HARD TO GET (1938).

Hot Horse see ONCE UPON A HORSE (1958).

HOT ICE 1952 d: Kenneth Hume. UKN., *A Weekend at Thrackley*, Alan Melville, Play

Hot Marshland, The see NETSUDEICHI (1950).

HOT MONEY 1936 d: William McGann. USA., *Hot Money*, Aben Kandel, New York 1931, Play

Hot News see SCANDAL FOR SALE (1932).

Hot Nocturne see BLUES IN THE NIGHT (1941).

Hot Noon see GORECHTO PLADNE (1965).

HOT OFF THE PRESS 1935 d: Al Herman. USA., *The New Pardner*, Peter B. Kyne, Short Story

HOT ROCK, THE 1972 d: Peter Yates. USA., *The Hot Rock*, Donald E. Westlake, Novel

HOT RODS TO HELL 1967 d: John Brahm. USA., *Fifty-Two Miles to Terror*, Alex Gaby, 1956, Short Story

HOT SATURDAY 1932 d: William A. Seiter. USA., *Hot Saturday*, Harvey Fergusson, New York 1926, Novel

HOT SPELL 1958 d: Daniel Mann, George (#u/C#) Cukor. USA., *Next of Kin*, Lonnie Coleman, Play

Hot Spot see I WAKE UP SCREAMING (1941).

HOT SPUR 1968 d: R. L. Frost. USA., *Hot Spur*, R. W. Cresse, Novel

HOT SUMMER NIGHT 1956 d: David Friedkin. USA., *Capital Offense*, Edwin P. Hicks, Story

Hot Sweat see KEETJE TIPPEL (1975).

HOT TIP 1935 d: Ray McCarey, William Sistrom. USA., *Leander Clicks*, William Slavens McNutt, 1928, Short Story

Hot Wind see GARAM HAWA (1973).

Hot Winds see GARAM HAWA (1973).

HOTARUGAWA 1987 d: Eizo SugawA. JPN., *Hotarugawa*, Teru Miyamoto, Novel

HOTEL 1967 d: Richard Quine. USA., *Hotel*, Arthur Hailey, New York 1965, Novel

HOTEL BERLIN 1945 d: Peter Godfrey. USA., *Menschen Im Hotel*, Vicki Baum, Berlin 1929, Novel

HOTEL DE LIBRE ECHANGE, L' 1916 d: Marcel Simon. FRN., *L' Hotel du Libre-Echange*, Maurice Desvallieres, Georges Feydeau, Paris 1894, Play

HOTEL DER TOTEN GASTE 1965 d: Eberhard Itzenplitz. GRM/SPN., Heather Gardiner, Novel

HOTEL DU LAC 1985 d: Giles Foster. UKN., *Hotel du Lac*, Anita Brookner, Novel

HOTEL DU LIBRE ECHANGE, L' 1934 d: Marc Allegret. FRN., *L' Hotel du Libre-Echange*, Maurice Desvallieres, Georges Feydeau, Paris 1894, Play

HOTEL DU NORD 1938 d: Marcel Carne. FRN., *L' Hotel du Nord*, Eugene Dabit, 1929, Novel

HOTEL IMPERIAL 1927 d: Mauritz Stiller. USA., *Szinmu Negy Felvonasban*, Lajos Biro, Budapest 1917, Play

HOTEL IMPERIAL 1939 d: Robert Florey. USA., *Szinmu Negy Felvonasban*, Lajos Biro, Budapest 1917, Play

HOTEL MOUSE, THE 1923 d: Fred Paul. UKN., *The Hotel Mouse*, Armat, Gerbidon, Play

Hotel New Hampshire, L' see THE HOTEL NEW HAMPSHIRE (1983).

HOTEL NEW HAMPSHIRE, THE 1983 d: Tony Richardson. USA/CND., *The Hotel New Hampshire*, John Irving, 1981, Novel

Hotel of the Dead see HOTEL DER TOTEN GASTE (1965).

HOTEL PARADISO 1966 d: Peter Glenville. UKN/USA/FRN., *L' Hotel du Libre-Echange*, Maurice Desvallieres, Georges Feydeau, Paris 1894, Play

HOTEL RESERVE 1944 d: Lance Comfort, Max Greene. UKN., *Epitaph for a Spy*, Eric Ambler, 1938, Novel

HOTEL SAHARA 1951 d: Ken Annakin. UKN., *Szinmu Negy Felvonasban*, Lajos Biro, Budapest 1917, Play

HOTEL SHANGHAI 1997 d: Peter Patzak. GRM., Vicki Baum, Novel

HOTEL SORRENTO 1994 d: Richard Franklin. ASL., *Hotel Sorrento*, Hannie Rayson, Play

HOTEL ST. PAULI 1988 d: Petter Vennerod, Svend Wam. NRW., *Hotel St. Pauli*, Erland Kiosterod, Novel

Hotel, The see LA CIGARRA NO ES UN BICHO (1963).

Hothead see COUP DE TETE (1978).

HOTTENTOT, THE 1922 d: James W. Horne, Del Andrews. USA., *The Hottentot*, William Collier Sr., Victor Mapes, New York 1920, Play

HOTTENTOT, THE 1929 d: Roy Del Ruth. USA., *The Hottentot*, William Collier Sr., Victor Mapes, New York 1920, Play

HOU HALACH BASADOT 1967 d: Yoseph Millo. ISR., Moshe Shamir, Play

Hound Dog Man see HOUND-DOG MAN (1959).

Hound of Blackwood Castle, The see DER HUND VON BLACKWOOD CASTLE (1968).

Hound of the Baskervilles, The see DER HUND VON BASKERVILLE 3 (1915).

HOUND OF THE BASKERVILLES, THE 1921 d: Maurice Elvey. UKN., *The Hound of the Baskervilles*, Arthur Conan Doyle, London 1902, Novel

Hound of the Baskervilles, The see DER HUND VON BASKERVILLE (1929).

HOUND OF THE BASKERVILLES, THE 1931 d: V. Gareth Gundrey. UKN., *The Hound of the Baskervilles*, Arthur Conan Doyle, London 1902, Novel

Hound of the Baskervilles, The see DER HUND VON BASKERVILLE (1936).

HOUND OF THE BASKERVILLES, THE 1939 d: Sidney Lanfield. USA., *The Hound of the Baskervilles*, Arthur Conan Doyle, London 1902, Novel

HOUND OF THE BASKERVILLES, THE 1959 d: Terence Fisher. UKN., *The Hound of the Baskervilles*, Arthur Conan Doyle, London 1902, Novel

HOUND OF THE BASKERVILLES, THE 1972 d: Barry Crane. USA., *The Hound of the Baskervilles*, Arthur Conan Doyle, London 1902, Novel

HOUND OF THE BASKERVILLES, THE 1978 d: Paul Morrissey. UKN., *The Hound of the Baskervilles*, Arthur Conan Doyle, London 1902, Novel

HOUND OF THE BASKERVILLES, THE 1983 d: Douglas Hickox. UKN., *The Hound of the Baskervilles*, Arthur Conan Doyle, London 1902, Novel

Hound of the Baskervilles, The see THE RETURN OF SHERLOCK HOLMES: THE HOUND OF THE BASKERVILLES (1988).

HOUND-DOG MAN 1959 d: Don Siegel. USA., *Circles Round the Wagon*, Fred Gipson, 1949, Novel

Hounds of War see BROTHERS (1982).

Hounds of Zaroff, The see THE MOST DANGEROUS GAME (1932).

Hour and Turn of Augusto Matraga, The see A HORA E VEZ DE AUGUSTO MATRAGA (1965).

HOUR BEFORE THE DAWN, THE 1944 d: Frank Tuttle. USA., *The Hour Before the Dawn*, W. Somerset Maugham, 1942, Novel

HOUR OF 13, THE 1952 d: Harold French. UKN/USA., *X V Rex*, Philip MacDonald, London 1933, Novel

HOUR OF FREEDOM, AN 1915 d: Arthur Johnson. USA., *The Road to Thursday*, John Barton Oxford, Story

Hour of Glory see THE SMALL BACK ROOM (1948).

HOUR OF THE GUN 1967 d: John Sturges. USA., *The Tombstone Epitaph*, Douglas D. Martin, Albuquerque 1951, Novel

HOUR OF THE LYNX, THE 1990 d: Stuart Burge. UKN., *Per Olov Enquist*, Play

Hour of the Star, The see A HORA DA ESTRELA (1985).

Hour of Thirteen, The see **THE HOUR OF 13** (1952).

Hourglass Sanatorium, The see **SANATORIUM POD KLEPSYDRA** (1973).

Hours Between, The see **24 HOURS** (1931).

HOUSE ACROSS THE LAKE, THE 1954 d: Ken Hughes. UKN., *High Wray*, Ken Hughes, Novel

House Across the Street, The see **LA MAISON D'EN FACE** (1936).

HOUSE ACROSS THE STREET, THE 1949 d: Richard L. Bare. USA., *Hi Nellie*, Roy Chanslor, Story

House at the End of the World see **MONSTER OF TERROR** (1965).

House Behind the Hedge, The see **UNKNOWN TREASURES** (1926).

House By the River see **DAS HAUS AM FLUSS** (1985).

HOUSE BY THE RIVER, THE 1950 d: Fritz Lang. USA., *The House By the River*, A. P. Herbert, 1921, Novel

HOUSE DIVIDED, A 1919 d: J. Stuart Blackton. USA., *The Substance of His House*, Ruth Holt Boucicault, Boston 1914, Novel

HOUSE DIVIDED, A 1932 d: William Wyler. USA., *Heart and Hand*, Olive Edens, 1927, Short Story

House Full of Love, A see **EIN HAUS VOLL LIEBE** (1954).

HOUSE IN MARSH ROAD, THE 1960 d: Montgomery Tully. UKN., *The House in Marsh Road*, Laurence Meynell, Novel

House in Montevideo, The see **DAS HAUS IN MONTEVIDEO** (1951).

House in Montevideo, The see **DAS HAUS IN MONTEVIDEO** (1963).

HOUSE IN RUE RAPP, THE 1946 d: Ronald Haines. UKN., *The House in Rue Rapp*, John Dickson Carr, Short Story

House in the Country, A see **HIDEAWAY** (1937).

House in the Karpfengasse, The see **DAS HAUS IN DER KARPFENGASSE** (1964).

House in the Rain, The see **LA CASA DE LA LLUVIA** (1943).

HOUSE IN THE SQUARE, THE 1951 d: Roy Ward Baker. UKN/USA., *Berkeley Square*, John L. Balderston, London 1926, Play

House in the Suburbs, A see **DUM NA PREDMESTI** (1933).

HOUSE IN THE WOODS, THE 1957 d: Maxwell Munden. UKN., *Prelude to Murder*, Walter C. Brown, Short Story

HOUSE IS NOT A HOME, A 1964 d: Russell Rouse. USA., *A House Is Not a Home*, Polly Adler, New York 1953, Autobiography

HOUSE NEXT DOOR, THE 1914 d: Barry O'Neil. USA., *The House Next Door*, J. Hartley Manners, New York 1914, Play

HOUSE OF A THOUSAND CANDLES, THE 1915 d: Thomas N. Heffron. USA., *The House of a Thousand Candles*, Meredith Nicholson, New York 1905, Novel

House of a Thousand Candles, The see **HAUNTING SHADOWS** (1920).

HOUSE OF A THOUSAND CANDLES, THE 1936 d: Arthur Lubin. USA., *The House of a Thousand Candles*, Meredith Nicholson, New York 1905, Novel

HOUSE OF AMERICA 1997 d: Marc Evans. UKN., *House of America*, Edward Thomas, Play

House of Bernarda Alba, The see **LA CASA DE BERNARDA ALBA** (1987).

HOUSE OF BONDAGE, THE 1913 d: Raymond B. West. USA., *The House of Bondage*, Reginald Wright Kaufmann, New York 1910, Play

HOUSE OF BONDAGE, THE 1914 d: Pierce Kingsley. USA., *The House of Bondage*, Reginald Wright Kaufmann, New York 1910, Novel

HOUSE OF CARDS 1969 d: John Guillermin. USA., *House of Cards*, Stanley Ellin, New York 1967, Novel

HOUSE OF CARDS 1991 d: Paul Seed. UKN., *House of Cards*, Michael Dobbs, Novel

House of Chance see **CHEATING BLONDES** (1933).

House of Connelly, The see **CAROLINA** (1934).

HOUSE OF DARKNESS 1948 d: Oswald Mitchell. UKN., *Duet*, Batty Davies, Play

House of Doom see **THE BLACK CAT** (1934).

House of Dr. Edwardes, The see **SPELLBOUND** (1945).

HOUSE OF DREAMS 1933 d: Tony Frenguelli. UKN., *House of Dreams Come True*, Margaret Pedlar, Novel

HOUSE OF ERRORS 1942 d: Bernard B. Ray. USA., Harry Langdon, Story

House of Fate see **MUSS 'EM UP** (1936).

HOUSE OF FEAR, THE 1915 d: Arnold Daly, Ashley Miller. USA., *House of Fear*, John Thomas McIntyre, 1910, Short Story

HOUSE OF FEAR, THE 1939 d: Joe May. USA., *The House of Fear*, Wadsworth Camp, New York 1916, Novel, *The Last Warning*, Thomas F. Fallon, New York 1922, Play

HOUSE OF FEAR, THE 1945 d: R. William Neill. USA., *The Five Orange Pips*, Arthur Conan Doyle, 1892, Short Story

HOUSE OF FRANKENSTEIN 1944 d: Erle C. Kenton. USA., *The Devil's Brood*, Curt Siodmak, Story

House of Fright see **THE TWO FACES OF DR. JEKYLL** (1960).

House of Fright see **LA MASCHERA DEL DEMONIO** (1960).

HOUSE OF GLASS, THE 1918 d: Emile Chautard. USA., *The House of Glass*, Max Marcin, New York 1915, Play

HOUSE OF GOD, THE 1979 d: Donald Wrye. USA., *The House of God*, Samuel Shem, Novel

House of Ill Repute see **DAS FREUDENHAUS** (1971).

HOUSE OF INTRIGUE, THE 1919 d: Lloyd Ingraham. USA., *The House of Intrigue*, Arthur Stringer, Indianapolis 1918, Novel

House of Intrigue, The see **LONDRA CHIAMA POLO NORD** (1957).

House of Life see **HAUS DES LEBENS** (1952).

House of Long Shadows see **HOUSE OF THE LONG SHADOWS** (1983).

House of Lost Happiness, The see **DUM ZTRACENEHO STESTI** (1927).

House of Lovers see **POT-BOUILLE** (1957).

House of Madness see **LA MANSION DE LA LOCURA** (1971).

HOUSE OF MARNEY, THE 1926 d: Cecil M. Hepworth. UKN., *The House of Marney*, John Goodwin, Novel

House of Menace see **KIND LADY** (1935).

HOUSE OF MIRTH, THE 1918 d: Albert Capellani. USA., *The House of Mirth*, Edith Wharton, New York 1905, Novel

House of Mystery see **AT THE VILLA ROSE** (1939).

HOUSE OF MYSTERY 1961 d: Vernon Sewell. UKN., *L'Angoisse*, Celia de Vylars, Pierre Mills, Play

HOUSE OF MYSTERY, THE 1934 d: William Nigh. USA., *The Ape*, Adam Hull Shirk, Los Angeles 1927, Play

HOUSE OF NUMBERS 1957 d: Russell Rouse. USA., *House of Numbers*, Jack Finney, 1956, Novel

HOUSE OF PERIL, THE 1922 d: Kenelm Foss. UKN., *Chink in the Armour*, Mrs. Belloc Lowndes, Novel

House of Pleasure see **LE PLAISIR** (1951).

House of Pleasure see **MADAME UND IHRE NICHTE** (1969).

House of Refuge, The see **BONDAGE** (1933).

HOUSE OF ROTHSCHILD, THE 1934 d: Alfred L. Werker. USA., *Rothschild*, George Hembert Westley, 1932, Play

HOUSE OF SECRETS 1957 d: Guy Green. UKN., *House of Secrets*, Sterling Noel, Novel

HOUSE OF SECRETS, THE 1929 d: Edmund Lawrence. USA., *The House of Secrets*, Sidney Horler, London 1926, Novel

HOUSE OF SECRETS, THE 1936 d: Roland Reed. USA., *The House of Secrets*, Sidney Horler, London 1926, Novel

HOUSE OF SEVEN GABLES, THE 1940 d: Joe May. USA., *The House of the Seven Gables*, Nathaniel Hawthorne, Boston 1851, Novel

House of Seven Joys see **THE WRECKING CREW** (1968).

HOUSE OF SILENCE, THE 1918 d: Donald Crisp. USA., *Marcel Levignet*, Elwyn Alfred Barron, New York 1906, Novel

House of Sin see **LES MENTEURS** (1961).

House of Sleeping Virgins, The see **NEMURERU BIJO** (1968).

House of Spirits, The see **THE HOUSE OF THE SPIRITS** (1993).

HOUSE OF STRANGERS 1949 d: Joseph L. Mankiewicz. USA., *House of Strangers*, Jerome Weidman, Novel

HOUSE OF TEMPERLEY, THE 1913 d: Harold Shaw. UKN., *Rodney Stone*, Arthur Conan Doyle, 1896, Novel

HOUSE OF THE ARROW, THE 1930 d: Leslie Hiscott. UKN., *The House of the Arrow*, A. E. W. Mason, London 1924, Novel

HOUSE OF THE ARROW, THE 1940 d: Harold French. UKN., *The House of the Arrow*, A. E. W. Mason, London 1924, Novel

HOUSE OF THE ARROW, THE 1953 d: Michael Anderson. UKN., *The House of the Arrow*, A. E. W. Mason, London 1924, Novel

House of the Dead see **MYORTVYI DOM** (1932).

HOUSE OF THE LONG SHADOWS 1983 d: Pete Walker. UKN., *Seven Keys to Baldpate*, Earl Derr Biggers, Indianapolis 1913, Novel

HOUSE OF THE LOST COURT, THE 1915 d: Charles J. Brabin. USA., *The House of the Lost Court*, Alice Muriel Williamson, New York 1908, Novel

HOUSE OF THE SEVEN GABLES, THE 1910 d: J. Searle Dawley. USA., *The House of the Seven Gables*, Nathaniel Hawthorne, Boston 1851, Novel

House of the Seven Gables, The see **THE HOUSE OF SEVEN GABLES** (1940).

HOUSE OF THE SEVEN HAWKS, THE 1959 d: Richard Thorpe. UKN/USA., *The House of the Seven Flies*, Victor Canning, Novel

House of the Sleeping Virgins, The see **NEMURERU BIJO** (1968).

HOUSE OF THE SPANIARD, THE 1936 d: Reginald Denham. UKN., *The House of the Spaniard*, Arthur Behrend, Novel

HOUSE OF THE SPIRITS, THE 1993 d: Bille August. DNM/GRM/PRT., *The House of the Spirits*, Isabel Allende, Novel

House of the Three Girls, The see **DAS DREIMADERLHAUS** (1958).

HOUSE OF THE TOLLING BELL, THE 1920 d: J. Stuart Blackton. USA., *The House of the Tolling Bell*, Edith Sessions Tupper, Novel

HOUSE OF TOYS, THE 1920 d: George L. Cox. USA., *The House of Toys*, Henry Russell Miller, Indianapolis 1914, Novel

House of Troy, The see **IN GAY MADRID** (1930).

HOUSE OF UNREST, THE 1931 d: Leslie H. Gordon. UKN., *The House of Unrest*, Leslie Howard Gordon, Play

House of Usher, The see **THE FALL OF THE HOUSE OF USHER** (1960).

HOUSE OF USHER, THE 1988 d: Alan Birkinshaw. SAF/USA., *The Fall of the House of Usher*, Edgar Allan Poe, 1839, Short Story

House of Voices see **VOICES** (1973).

HOUSE OF WHISPERS, THE 1920 d: Ernest C. Warde. USA., *The House of Whispers*, William Andrew Johnston, Boston 1918, Novel

HOUSE OF YES, THE 1997 d: Mark Waters. USA., *The House of Yes*, Wendy MacLeod, Play

HOUSE OF YOUTH, THE 1924 d: Ralph Ince. USA., *The House of Youth*, Maude Radford Warren, Indianapolis 1923, Novel

House on Carp Lane, The see **DAS HAUS IN DER KARPFENGASSE** (1964).

HOUSE ON GARIBALDI STREET, THE 1979 d: Peter Collinson. USA., *The House on Garibaldi Street*, Isser Harel, Book

HOUSE ON GREENAPPLE ROAD, THE 1970 d: Robert Day. USA., *The House on Greenapple Road*, Harold R. Daniels, Novel

House on Marsh Road, The see **THE HOUSE IN MARSH ROAD** (1960).

HOUSE ON TELEGRAPH HILL 1951 d: Robert Wise. USA., *The Frightened Child*, Dana Lyon, 1948, Novel

House on the Dune, The see **LA MAISON DANS LA DUNE** (1934).

HOUSE ON THE MARSH, THE 1920 d: Fred Paul. UKN., *The House on the Marsh*, Florence Warden, Novel

House on the Square, The see **THE HOUSE IN THE SQUARE** (1951).

HOUSE OPPOSITE, THE 1917 d: Frank Wilson. UKN., *The House Opposite*, Percival Landon, London 1909, Play

HOUSE OPPOSITE, THE 1931 d: Walter Summers. UKN., *The House Opposite*, J. Jefferson Farjeon, Play

HOUSE THAT DRIPPED BLOOD, THE 1970 d: Peter Duffell. UKN., *Method for Murder*, Robert Bloch, Short Story, *Sweets to the Sweet*, Robert Bloch, Short Story, *Waxworks*, Robert Bloch, Short Story

HOUSE THAT JAZZ BUILT, THE 1921 d: Penrhyn Stanlaws. USA., *Sweetie Peach*, Sophie Kerr, Short Story

HOUSE THAT WOULD NOT DIE, THE 1970 d: John Llewellyn Moxey. USA., *Come Home Ammie*, Barbara Michaels, Novel

House That Wouldn't Die, The *see* THE HOUSE THAT WOULD NOT DIE (1970).

HOUSE WHERE EVIL DWELLS, THE 1982 d: Kevin Connor. USA/JPN., *The House Where Evil Dwells*, James W. Hardiman, Novel

House With an Attic *see* DOM S MEZONINOM (1961).

HOUSE WITHOUT CHILDREN, THE 1919 d: Samuel Brodsky. USA., *The House Without Children*, Robert H. McLaughlin, Cleveland 1917, Play

Householder, The *see* GHARBAR (1963).

Housekeeper, The *see* A JUDGEMENT IN STONE (1986).

HOUSEKEEPER'S DAUGHTER, THE 1939 d: Hal Roach. USA., *The Housekeeper's Daughter*, Donald Henderson Clarke, New York 1938, Novel

HOUSEKEEPING 1987 d: Bill Forsyth. USA., *Housekeeping*, Marilynne Robinson, Novel

HOUSEMASTER 1938 d: Herbert Brenon. UKN., *Housemaster*, Ian Hay, 1936, Novel

House-Warming, The *see* GYERTEK EL A NEVNAPOMRA (1984).

Housewives' Story, The *see* THE WEAKER SEX (1948).

HOW AWFUL ABOUT ALLAN 1970 d: Curtis Harrington. USA., *How Awful About Allan*, Henry Farrell, Novel

HOW BAXTER BUTTED IN 1925 d: William Beaudine. USA., *The Stuff of Heroes*, Harold Titus, 1924, Short Story

HOW COULD YOU, JEAN? 1918 d: William D. Taylor. USA., *Jean? How Could You*, Eleanor Hoyt Brainerd, Garden City N.Y.. 1917, Novel

How Do I Get to Be a Hero? *see* A LA GUERRE COMME A LA GUERRE (1971).

HOW DO I LOVE THEE? 1970 d: Michael Gordon. USA., *Let Me Count the Ways*, Peter de Vries, Boston 1965, Novel

HOW GREEN WAS MY VALLEY 1941 d: John Ford. USA., *How Green Was My Valley*, Richard Llewellyn, 1939, Novel

HOW GREEN WAS MY VALLEY 1976 d: Ronald Wilson. UKN., *How Green Was My Valley*, Richard Llewellyn, 1939, Novel

HOW HE LIED TO HER HUSBAND 1931 d: Cecil Lewis. UKN., *How He Lied to Her Husband*, George Bernard Shaw, London 1905, Play

How He Lied to Her Husband *see* KAK ON LGAL EIO MUZHU (1957).

How I Became a Negro *see* WIE ICH EIN NEGER WURDE (1970).

How I Became Black *see* WIE ICH EIN NEGER WURDE (1970).

HOW I WON THE WAR 1967 d: Richard Lester. UKN., *How I Won the War*, Patrick Ryan, London 1963, Novel

HOW IT HAPPENED 1925 d: Alexander Butler. UKN., *How It Happened*, Arthur Conan Doyle, Short Story

HOW MANY MILES TO BABYLON? 1982 d: Moira Armstrong. UKN., *How Many Miles to Babylon?*, Jennifer Johnston

How Many Roads *see* THE LOST MAN (1969).

How Much Space Does One Person Need *see* SCARABEA - WIEVIEL ERDE BRAUCHT DER MENSCH? (1968).

How Not to Rob a Department Store *see* CENT BRIQUES ET DES TUILES (1965).

HOW SIR ANDREW LOST HIS VOTE 1911. USA., *In the Fog*, Richard Harding Davis, Short Story

HOW STELLA GOT HER GROOVE BACK 1998 d: Kevin Rodney Sullivan. USA., *How Stella Got Her Groove Back*, Terry McMillan, Novel

HOW SWEET IT IS! 1968 d: Jerry Paris. USA., *The Girl in the Turquoise Bikini*, Muriel Resnik, New York 1961, Novel

How the Steel Was Tempered *see* KAK ZAKALYALAS STAL (1942).

How to Be Loved *see* JAK BYC KOCHANA (1962).

HOW TO BE VERY, VERY POPULAR 1955 d: Nunnally Johnson. USA., *She Loves Me Not*, Edward Hope, Indianapolis 1933, Novel

How to Make Love to a Negro Without Getting Tired *see* COMMENT FAIRE L'AMOUR AVEC UN NEGRE SANS SE FATIGUER (1988).

How to Marry a King *see* WIE HEIRATET MAN EINEN KONIG (1968).

HOW TO MARRY A MILLIONAIRE 1953 d: Jean Negulesco. USA., *The Greeks Had a Word for It*, Zoe Akins, New York 1930, Play, *Loco*, Kath Albert, Dale M. Eunson, New York 1946, Play

HOW TO MURDER A RICH UNCLE 1957 d: Nigel Patrick, Max Varnel. UKN., *Il Faut Tuer Julie*, Didier Daix, Play

How to Rob a Bank *see* A NICE LITTLE BANK THAT SHOULD BE ROBBED (1958).

How to Seduce a Playboy *see* BEL AMI 2000 ODER: WIE VERFUHRT MAN EINEN PLAYBOY? (1966).

How to Steal a Diamond in Four Uneasy Lessons *see* THE HOT ROCK (1972).

HOW TO STEAL A MILLION 1966 d: William Wyler. USA., *Venus Rising*, George Bradshaw, London 1962, Short Story

How to Steal a Million Dollars and Live Happily Ever After *see* HOW TO STEAL A MILLION (1966).

HOW TO SUCCEED IN BUSINESS WITHOUT REALLY TRYING 1967 d: David Swift. USA., *How to Succeed in Business Without Really Trying*, Shepherd Mead, New York 1952, Novel

How, When and With Whom *see* QUANDO, PERCHE COME (1968).

How, When, Why? *see* QUANDO, PERCHE COME (1968).

HOW WOMEN LOVE 1922 d: Kenneth Webb. USA., *The Dangerous Inheritance; Or Mystery of the Tittani Rubies*, Izola Forrester, Boston 1920, Novel

HOWARD CASE, THE 1936 d: Frank Richardson. UKN., *Fraud*, H. F. Maltby, Play

HOWARDS END 1992 d: James Ivory. UKN., *Howards End*, E. M. Forster, 1910, Novel

HOWARDS OF VIRGINIA, THE 1940 d: Frank Lloyd. USA., *The Tree of Liberty*, Elizabeth Page, New York 1939, Novel

Howdy Stranger *see* COWBOY FROM BROOKLYN (1938).

Howling 2, The *see* HOWLING II. YOUR SISTER IS A WEREWOLF (1984).

Howling 3: the Marsupials *see* THE HOWLING III (1987).

HOWLING II. YOUR SISTER IS A WEREWOLF 1984 d: Philippe MorA. USA/ITL/FRN., *The Howling II*, Gary Brandner, Novel

HOWLING III, THE 1987 d: Philippe MorA. ASL., *Howling III*, Gary Brandner, Novel

HOWLING IN THE WOODS, A 1971 d: Daniel Petrie. USA., *A Howling in the Woods*, Velda Johnson, Novel

Howling Miller, The *see* ULVOVA MYLLARI (1983).

HOWLING, THE 1981 d: Joe Dante. USA., *The Howling*, Gary Brandner, Novel

HOW'S CHANCES 1934 d: Anthony Kimmins. UKN., *Der Frauendiplomat*, Curt Johannes Braun, E. B. Leuthege, Play

HOYSOMMER 1958 d: Arild Brinchmann. NRW., *Nina*, Cora Sandel, 1949, Short Story

HRABENKA Z PODSKALI 1925 d: Carl Lamac. CZC., *Hrabenka Z Podskali*, Alois Koldinsky, Play

HRABINA COSEL 1968 d: Jerzy Antczak. PLN., *Hrabina Cosel*, Joszef Ignacy Kraszewski, 1874, Novel

HRST VODY 1969 d: Jan Kadar, Elmar Klos. CZC/USA., *Valamit Visz a Viz*, Lajos Zilahy, 1928, Novel

HUA HAO YUE YUAN 1958 d: Guo Wei. CHN., *Three Mile Bend*, Zhao Shuli, Novel

HUA HUN 1994 d: Huang Shuqin. CHN/TWN/FRN., *Hua Hun*, Shi Nan, Novel

HUA QIAO RONG JI 1998 d: Yang XIe. HKG/SRK., *Blossom Bridge*, Kenneth Pai, Novel

HUAI SHU ZHUANG 1962 d: Wang Ping. CHN., *Huai Shu Zhuang*, Hu Ke, Play

Huaishu Village *see* HUAI SHU ZHUANG (1962).

HUAN LE REN JIAN 1959 d: Wu Tian. CHN., *Two Marriages*, Ke Fu, Play

HUAN TIAN XI DI 1949 d: Zheng XIaoqiu. CHN., *La Poudre aux Yeux*, Eugene Labiche, Marc-Michel, 1861, Play

Huang le Ying XIong Part 2 *see* YINYANG JIE (1988).

HUANGHUA LING 1956 d: Jin Shan. CHN., *Huanghua Ling*, Shu Hui, Novel

Huanghua Mountain Ridge *see* HUANGHUA LING (1956).

HUANGJIANG NUXIA (PART 1) 1930 d: Cheng Kengran, Zheng Yisheng. CHN., *Huangjiang Nuxia*, Guo Mingdao, Novel

HUANLE YINGXIONG 1988 d: Wu Ziniu. CHN., *Stormy Tong River*, Sima Wensen, Novel

HUBERT AND ARTHUR 1914. UKN., *King John*, William Shakespeare, c1595, Play

Hubertus Castle *see* SCHLOSS HUBERTUS (1934).

Hubertus Castle *see* SCHLOSS HUBERTUS (1954).

Hubertus Castle *see* SCHLOSS HUBERTUS (1973).

Huck and Tom *see* HUCK AND TOM; OR THE FURTHER ADVENTURES OF TOM SAWYER (1918).

HUCK AND TOM; OR THE FURTHER ADVENTURES OF TOM SAWYER 1918 d: William D. Taylor. USA., *The Adventures of Huckleberry Finn*, Mark Twain, New York 1884, Novel, *Adventures of Tom Sawyer*, Mark Twain, San Francisco 1876, Novel

HUCKLEBERRY FINN 1920 d: William D. Taylor. USA., *The Adventures of Huckleberry Finn*, Mark Twain, New York 1884, Novel

HUCKLEBERRY FINN 1931 d: Norman Taurog. USA., *The Adventures of Huckleberry Finn*, Mark Twain, New York 1884, Novel

Huckleberry Finn *see* THE ADVENTURES OF HUCKLEBERRY FINN (1938).

Huckleberry Finn *see* THE ADVENTURES OF HUCKLEBERRY FINN (1960).

HUCKLEBERRY FINN 1974 d: J. Lee Thompson. USA., *The Adventures of Huckleberry Finn*, Mark Twain, New York 1884, Novel

HUCKLEBERRY FINN 1975 d: Robert Totten. USA., *The Adventures of Huckleberry Finn*, Mark Twain, New York 1884, Novel

HUCKLEBERRY FINN 1981 d: Bunker Jenkins. USA., *The Adventures of Huckleberry Finn*, Mark Twain, New York 1884, Novel

HUCKSTERS, THE 1947 d: Jack Conway. USA., *The Hucksters*, Frederic Wakeman, Novel

HUD 1963 d: Martin Ritt. USA., *Pass By Horseman*, Larry McMurtry, New York 1961, Novel

HUDDLE 1932 d: Sam Wood. USA., *Huddle*, Francis Wallace, New York 1931, Novel

HUELLA DE LUZ 1943 d: Rafael Gil. SPN., *Huella de Luz*, Wenceslao Fernandez Florez, 1925, Short Story

Hugh Black One-Eyed Man, The *see* LOVE IN A HURRY (1919).

Huis Clos *see* NO EXIT (1962).

HUIS-CLOS 1954 d: Jacqueline Audry. FRN., *Huis Clos*, Jean-Paul Sartre, Paris 1944, Play

HUIT HOMMES DANS LA CHATEAU 1942 d: Richard Pottier. FRN., *Huit Hommes Dans un Chateau*, Jean Kery, Novel

Huit Jeunes Filles a Marier *see* JEUNES FILLES A MARIER (1935).

HUK! 1956 d: John Barnwell. USA., *Huk!*, Stirling Silliphant, Novel

HULA 1927 d: Victor Fleming. USA., *Hula - a Romance of Hawaii*, Armine von Tempski, New York 1927, Novel

Hulda Fran Juurakko *see* JUURAKON HULDA (1937).

Hullabaloo *see* PEREPOLOH (1955).

Human Bait *see* THE BAIT (1921).

Human Beast, The *see* LA BETE HUMAINE (1938).

Human Beast, The *see* HUMAN DESIRE (1954).

Human Being and War *see* SENSO TO NINGEN (1970).

HUMAN CARGO 1936 d: Allan Dwan. USA., *I Will Be Faithful*, Kathleen Shepard, New York 1934, Novel

Human Chess Board, The *see* DANGEROUS BUSINESS (1920).

HUMAN COLLATERAL 1920 d: Lawrence C. Windom. USA., *The Last Woman*, Frederic Van Rensselaer Dey, Short Story

HUMAN COMEDY, THE 1943 d: Clarence Brown. USA., *The Human Comedy*, William Saroyan, 1943, Novel

Human Condition Part 2, The *see* NINGEN NO JOKEN II (1959).

Human Condition Part 3, The see NINGEN NO JOKEN III (1961).

Human Condition, The see NINGEN NO JOKEN I (1959).

HUMAN DESIRE 1919 d: Wilfred North. USA., *Human Desire*, Violet Irwin, Boston 1913, Novel

HUMAN DESIRE 1954 d: Fritz Lang. USA., *La Bete Humaine*, Emile Zola, 1890, Novel

Human Destinies see JOHAN ULFSTJERNA (1923).

HUMAN FACTOR, THE 1979 d: Otto Preminger. UKN., *The Human Factor*, Graham Greene, 1978, Novel

Human Ghost, The see AT THE VILLA ROSE (1939).

HUMAN HEARTS 1912 d: Otis Turner. USA., *Human Hearts*, Hal Reid, Play

HUMAN HEARTS 1914 d: King Baggot. USA., *Human Hearts*, Hal Reid, Play

HUMAN HEARTS 1922 d: King Baggot. USA., *Human Hearts*, Hal Reid, Play

Human Monster, The see THE DARK EYES OF LONDON (1939).

HUMAN SIDE, THE 1934 d: Edward Buzzell. USA., *The Human Side*, Christine Ames, Los Angeles 1933, Play

Human Woe see MENSCHENWEE (1921).

Humanity see WHOM THE GODS WOULD DESTROY (1919).

HUMANITY; OR, ONLY A JEW 1913 d: John Lawson, Bert Haldane. UKN., *Humanity*, John Lawson, Play

Humble One, The see KROTKAYA (1960).

Humbug, The see THE LOVE CAPTIVE (1934).

HUMMING BIRD, THE 1924 d: Sidney Olcott. USA., *The Humming Bird*, Maude Fulton, New York 1923, Play

HUMMINGBIRD TREE, THE 1992 d: Noella Smith. UKN., *The Hummingbird Tree*, Ian McDonald, Novel

HUMORESKA 1939 d: Otakar VavrA. CZC., *Humoreska*, Karel Matej Capek-Chod, Novel

HUMORESQUE 1920 d: Frank Borzage. USA., *Humoresque*, Fannie Hurst, 1919, Short Story

Humoresque see HUMORESKA (1939).

HUMORESQUE 1946 d: Jean Negulesco. USA., *Humoresque*, Fannie Hurst, 1919, Short Story

Humorismo Negro see UMORISMO NERO (1965).

Humorous Sketch see HUMORESKA (1939).

Humungus Hector see ETTORE LO FUSTO (1972).

Hunan Girl XIaoxiao see XIANGNU XIAOXIAO (1987).

HUNCH, THE 1921 d: George D. Baker. USA., *The Hunch*, Percival Wilde, 1921, Short Story

Hunchback see THE HUNCHBACK OF NOTRE DAME (1982).

Hunchback of Notre Dame see NOTRE DAME DE PARIS (1957).

Hunchback of Notre Dame, The see NOTRE DAME DE PARIS (1911).

HUNCHBACK OF NOTRE DAME, THE 1923 d: Wallace Worsley. USA., *Notre-Dame de Paris*, Victor Hugo, Paris 1831, Novel

HUNCHBACK OF NOTRE DAME, THE 1939 d: William Dieterle. USA., *Notre-Dame de Paris*, Victor Hugo, Paris 1831, Novel

HUNCHBACK OF NOTRE DAME, THE 1977 d: Alan Cooke. UKN., *Notre-Dame de Paris*, Victor Hugo, Paris 1831, Novel

HUNCHBACK OF NOTRE DAME, THE 1982 d: Michael Tuchner. UKN., *Notre-Dame de Paris*, Victor Hugo, Paris 1831, Novel

HUNCHBACK OF NOTRE DAME, THE 1996 d: Gary Trousdale, Kirk Wise. USA., *Notre-Dame de Paris*, Victor Hugo, Paris 1831, Novel

HUNCHBACK OF NOTRE DAME, THE 1997 d: Peter Medak. CND/USA., *Notre-Dame de Paris*, Victor Hugo, Paris 1831, Novel

HUNCHBACK'S ROMANCE, THE 1915 d: Sidney M. Goldin. USA., *An Interruption*, Bruno Lessing, Short Story

HUND VON BASKERVILLE 1, DER 1914 d: Rudolf Meinert. GRM., *The Hound of the Baskervilles*, Arthur Conan Doyle, London 1902, Novel

HUND VON BASKERVILLE 2, DER 1914 d: Rudolf Meinert. GRM., *The Hound of the Baskervilles*, Arthur Conan Doyle, London 1902, Novel

HUND VON BASKERVILLE 3, DER 1915 d: Richard Oswald. GRM., *The Hound of the Baskervilles*, Arthur Conan Doyle, London 1902, Novel

HUND VON BASKERVILLE, DER 1929 d: Richard Oswald. GRM., *The Hound of the Baskervilles*, Arthur Conan Doyle, London 1902, Novel

HUND VON BASKERVILLE, DER 1936 d: Carl Lamac. GRM., *The Hound of the Baskervilles*, Arthur Conan Doyle, London 1902, Novel

HUND VON BLACKWOOD CASTLE, DER 1968 d: Alfred Vohrer. GRM., Edgar Wallace, Novel

HUNDERT JAHRE ADOLF HITLER - DIE LETZTE STUNDE IM FUHRERBUNKER 1989 d: Christoph Schlingensief. GRM., *Hundert Jahre Adolf Hitler*, Christoph Schlingensief, Play

HUNDREDTH CHANCE, THE 1920 d: Maurice Elvey. UKN., *The Hundredth Chance*, Ethel M. Dell, Novel

HUNG LOU MENG 1966 d: Wang Ping. CHN., *Hung Lou Meng*, Ts'ao Chan, 1792

Hungarian Fragment see PANNON TOREDEK (1998).

Hungarian Nabob, A see EGY MAGYAR NABOB. KAPATHY ZOLTAN (1966).

HUNGARIAN NABOB, THE 1915 d: Travers Vale. USA., *Egy Magyar Nabob*, Mor Jokai, Budapest 1853, Novel

Hunger see SVALT (1966).

HUNGER ARTIST, THE 1976 d: Fred Smith. USA., *Ein Hungerkunstler*, Franz Kafka, 1924, Short Story

Hunger for Love see FOME DE AMOR (1968).

HUNGER, THE 1982 d: Anthony Scott. USA/UKN., *The Hunger*, Whitley Strieber, Novel

HUNGRY EYES 1918 d: Rupert Julian. USA., *His Wife in Arizona*, Elliott J. Clawson, Novel

Hungry for Love see FOME DE AMOR (1968).

HUNGRY HEART, A 1917 d: Emile Chautard. USA., *Frou-Frou*, Ludovic Halevy, Henri Meilhac, Paris 1869, Play

HUNGRY HEART, THE 1917 d: Robert G. VignolA. USA., *The Hungry Heart*, David Graham Phillips, New York 1909, Novel

HUNGRY HEARTS 1922 d: E. Mason Hopper. USA., *Hungry Hearts*, Anzia Yezierska, Boston 1920, Novel

HUNGRY HILL 1947 d: Brian Desmond Hurst. UKN., *Hungry Hill*, Daphne Du Maurier, 1943, Novel

Hungry Stones see KSHUDITA PASHAN (1960).

HUNT FOR RED OCTOBER, THE 1990 d: John McTiernan. USA., *The Hunt for Red October*, Tom Clancy, Novel

HUNT FOR THE UNICORN KILLER, THE 1999 d: William A. Graham. USA., *The Unicorn's Secret*, Steven Levy, Book

Hunt to Kill see THE WHITE BUFFALO (1976).

HUNTED MEN 1938 d: Louis King. USA., *Queen's Local*, Albert Duffy, Marian Grant, Play

Hunted People see GEHETZTE MENSCHEN (1932).

Hunted People see STVANI LIDE (1933).

Hunted, The see FIGURES IN A LANDSCAPE (1970).

HUNTED WOMAN, THE 1916 d: S. Rankin Drew. USA., *The Hunted Woman*, James Oliver Curwood, New York 1916, Novel

HUNTED WOMAN, THE 1925 d: Jack Conway. USA., *The Hunted Woman*, James Oliver Curwood, New York 1916, Novel

Hunter of Fall, The see DER JAGER VON FALL (1918).

Hunter of Fall, The see DER JAGER VON FALL (1926).

Hunter of Fall, The see DER JAGER VON FALL (1936).

Hunter of Fall, The see DER JAGER VON FALL (1957).

Hunter of Fall, The see DER JAGER VON FALL (1974).

Hunter of Roteck, The see DER JAGER VOM ROTECK (1955).

HUNTER, THE 1979 d: Buzz Kulik. USA., *The Hunter*, Christopher Keane, Book

Hunters are the Hunted, The see JAGDSZENEN AUS NIEDERBAYERN (1968).

HUNTER'S BLOOD 1986 d: Robert C. Hughes. USA., *Hunter's Blood*, Jere Cunningham, Novel

HUNTERS, THE 1958 d: Dick Powell. USA., *The Hunters*, James Salter, 1957, Novel

Hunting Accident, The see MOJ LASKOVYJ I NEZNYJ ZVER (1978).

Hunting Flies see POLOWANIE NA MUCHY (1969).

Hunting Scenes from Bavaria see JAGDSZENEN AUS NIEDERBAYERN (1968).

Hunting Scenes from Lower Bavaria see JAGDSZENEN AUS NIEDERBAYERN (1968).

HUNTINGTOWER 1927 d: George Pearson. UKN., *Huntingtower*, John Buchan, 1922, Novel

HUNTRESS, THE 1923 d: Lynn Reynolds. USA., *The Huntress*, Hubert Footner, New York 1922, Novel

HUOSHAO HONGLIANSI (PART 1) 1928 d: Zhang Shichuan. CHN., *Jiang Hu Qixia Zhuan*, XIang Kairan, Novel

HUOZHE 1994 d: Zhang Yimou. CHN/HKG., *Lifetimes*, Yu Hua, Novel

HURLEVENT 1986 d: Jacques Rivette. FRN., *Wuthering Heights*, Emily Jane Bronte, London 1847, Novel

HURLYBURLY 1998 d: Anthony Drazan. USA., *Hurlyburly*, David Rabe, 1984, Play

HURRA - DIE FIRMA HAT EINE KIND 1956 d: Hans Richter. GRM., *Bichon*, Jean de Letraz, Play

HURRA - EIN JUNGE! 1931 d: Georg Jacoby. GRM., *Hurra - Ein Junge!*, Franz Robert Arnold, Ernst Bach, Play

HURRA - EIN JUNGE! 1953 d: Ernst MarischkA. GRM., *Hurra - Ein Junge!*, Franz Robert Arnold, Ernst Bach, Play

Hurrah for Death see VIVA LA MUERTE (1970).

HURRAH! ICH LEBE! 1928 d: Wilhelm Thiele. GRM., *Der Mutige Seefahrer*, Georg Kaiser, 1926, Play

Hurrah! I'm Alive! see HURRAH! ICH LEBE! (1928).

Hurricane see BAOFENG-ZHOUYU (1961).

HURRICANE 1974 d: Jerry Jameson. USA., *Hurricane Hunters*, William C. Anderson, Novel

HURRICANE 1979 d: Jan Troell. USA., *The Hurricane*, James N. Hall, Charles Nordhoff, Boston 1936, Novel

Hurricane Rosie see TEMPORALE ROSY (1979).

Hurricane Rosy see TEMPORALE ROSY (1979).

HURRICANE SMITH 1952 d: Jerry Hopper. USA., *Hurricane Williams*, Gordon Young, Novel

HURRICANE, THE 1937 d: John Ford, Stuart Heisler (Uncredited). USA., *The Hurricane*, James N. Hall, Charles Nordhoff, Boston 1936, Novel

Hurricane, The see VOICE OF THE HURRICANE (1964).

Hurried Man, The see L' HOMME PRESSE (1976).

HURRY SUNDOWN 1967 d: Otto Preminger. USA., *Hurry Sundown*, K. B. Gilden, New York 1964, Novel

HUSBAND AND WIFE 1916 d: Barry O'Neil. USA., *Husband and Wife*, Charles Kenyon, New York 1915, Play

Husband and Wife see MARITO E MOGLIE (1952).

HUSBAND HUNTER 1920 d: Howard M. Mitchell. USA., *Myra Meets His Family*, F. Scott Fitzgerald, 1920, Short Story

HUSBAND HUNTER, THE 1920 d: Fred W. Durrant. UKN., *The Husband Hunter*, Olivia Roy, Novel

Husband, The see SWAMI (1977).

Husbands and Lovers see HONEYMOON IN BALI (1939).

HUSBANDS AND WIVES 1920 d: Joseph Levering. USA., *Making Her His Wife*, Corra Harris, New York 1918, Novel

Husbands Come and Go see THIS MAN IS MINE (1934).

HUSBAND'S HOLIDAY 1931 d: Robert Milton. USA., *The Marriage Bed*, Ernest Pascal, New York 1927, Novel

Husbands Or Lovers see HONEYMOON IN BALI (1939).

Huset I Fuglegaden see THE ISLAND ON BIRD STREET (1997).

HUSH. HUSH, SWEET CHARLOTTE 1964 d: Robert Aldrich. USA., *Hush Now, Sweet Charlotte*, Henry Farrell, Short Story

Hush-a-Bye Murder see MY SON MY LOVER (1970).

Husk see WE'RE ONLY HUMAN (1935).

HUSMANDSTOSEN 1952 d: Alice O'Fredericks. DNM., *Tosen Fran Stormyrtorpet*, Selma Lagerlof, Stockholm 1908, Short Story

Hussar Ballad, The see GUSARSKAYA BALLADA (1962).

HUSSARDS, LES 1955 d: Alex Joffe. FRN., *Les Hussards*, Pierre-Aristide Breal, Play

Hussar's Ballad see GUSARSKAYA BALLADA (1962).

HUSTLER, THE 1961 d: Robert Rossen. USA., *The Hustler*, Walter S. Tevis, New York 1959, Novel

HUSTLING 1975 d: Joseph Sargent. USA., *Hustling*, Gail Sheehy, Book

HUSZ ORA 1964 d: Zoltan Fabri. HNG., *Husz Ora*, Ferenc Santa, 1964, Novel

HUTCH STIRS 'EM UP 1923 d: Frank H. Crane. UKN., *The Hawk of Rede*, Harry Harding, Novel

HYDE PARK CORNER 1935 d: Sinclair Hill. UKN., *Hyde Park Corner*, Walter Hackett, London 1934, Play

HYGEIA AT THE SOLITO 1917 d: David Smith. USA., *Hygeia at the Solito*, O. Henry, Short Story

HYGIENE DE L'ASSASSIN 1999 d: Francois Ruggieri. FRN., *Hygiene de l'Assassin*, Amelie Nothomb, Novel

Hyinch Ha'gdi see CHI'UCH HAGDI (1985).

Hyiuch Hagdi see CHI'UCH HAGDI (1985).

HYMENEE 1946 d: Emile Couzinet. FRN., *Hymenee*, Edouard Bourdet, 1941, Play

Hymn to a Tired Man see NIHON NO SEISHUN (1968).

HYPNOTIC PORTRAIT, THE 1922 d: Kenneth Graeme. UKN., Derwent Nicol, Short Story

HYPNOTIST, THE 1957 d: Montgomery Tully. UKN., *The Hypnotist*, Falkland Cary, Philip Weathers, 1956, Play

Hypochondriac, The see DER EINGEBILDETE KRANKE (1952).

Hypocrieten, de see THE HYPOCRITES (1923).

Hypocrite, The see HELL-BENT FER HEAVEN (1926).

Hypocrites, Les see DIE GEJAGTEN (1960).

HYPOCRITES, THE 1915 d: Lois Weber. USA., *The Hypocrites*, Arthur Edmund Jones, Story

HYPOCRITES, THE 1916 d: George Loane Tucker. UKN., *The Hypocrites*, Henry Arthur Jones, 1906, Play

HYPOCRITES, THE 1923 d: Charles Giblyn. UKN/NTH., *The Hypocrites*, Henry Arthur Jones, 1906, Play

I - a Woman see JAG - EN KVINNA (I) (1965).

I - a Woman (Ii) see JAG - EN KVINNA (II) (1968).

I - a Woman Part Two: Marriage see JAG - EN KVINNA (II) (1968).

I, a Lover see JEG - EN ELSKER (1966).

I ACCUSE! 1958 d: Jose Ferrer. UKN., *I Accuse!*, Nicholas Halasz, Book

I Accuse see THE LIFE OF EMILE ZOLA (1937).

I AM A CAMERA 1955 d: Henry Cornelius. UKN., *The Berlin Stories*, Christopher Isherwood, 1945, Book, *I Am a Camera*, John Van Druten, 1952, Play

I Am a Cat see WAGAHAI WA NEKO DE ARU (1936).

I Am a Cat see WAGAHAI WA NEKO DEARU (1974).

I Am a Fugitive see I AM A FUGITIVE FROM A CHAIN GANG (1932).

I AM A FUGITIVE FROM A CHAIN GANG 1932 d: Mervyn Leroy. USA., *I Am a Fugitive from a Georgia Chain Gang!*, Robert E. Burns, 1932, Autobiography

I Am a Fugitive from a Georgia Chain Gang see I AM A FUGITIVE FROM A CHAIN GANG (1932).

I Am a Girl With the Devil in My Body see JSEM DEVCE S CERTEM V TELE (1933).

I Am Joaquin see ROBIN HOOD OF EL DORADO (1936).

I Am Legend see THE OMEGA MAN (1971).

I AM THE CHEESE 1983 d: Robert Jiras. USA., *I Am the Cheese*, Robert Cormier, Novel

I Am the Doctor see ANA AL DOCTOR (1968).

I AM THE LAW 1922 d: Edwin Carewe. USA., *The Poetic Justice of Uko San*, James Oliver Curwood, 1910, Short Story

I AM THE LAW 1938 d: Alexander Hall. USA., *Tracking New York's Crime Barons*, Fred Allhoff, 1936, Short Story

I Am the Law see IL PREFETTO DI FERRO (1977).

I Am Tien-Shan see YA-TYAN'-SHAN (1972).

I and My Love see GALIA (1966).

I, and My Lovers see GALIA (1966).

I Became a Criminal see THEY MADE ME A FUGITIVE (1947).

I BELIEVE IN YOU 1952 d: Basil Dearden, Michael Relph. UKN., *Court Circular*, Sewell Stokes, Book

I CAN EXPLAIN 1922 d: George D. Baker. USA., *Stay Home*, Edgar Franklin, 1921, Short Story

I CAN GET IT FOR YOU WHOLESALE 1951 d: Michael Gordon. USA., *I Can Get It for You Wholesale*, Jerome Weidman, 1937, Novel

I Can't Live Without Music see NEM ELHETEK MUZSIKASZO NELKUL (1979).

I Change My Life see SECOND SERVE (1986).

I, CLAUDIUS 1976 d: Herbert Wise. UKN., *Claudius the God*, Robert Graves, 1934, Novel, *I Claudius*, Robert Graves, 1934, Novel

I CONFESS 1953 d: Alfred Hitchcock. USA., *Nos Deux Consciences*, Paul Anthelme, 1902, Play

I Count My Woes Daily see ICH ZAHLE TAGLICH MEIN SORGEN (1960).

I COVER THE WATERFRONT 1933 d: James Cruze. USA., *I Cover the Waterfront*, Max Miller, New York 1932, Book

I DEMAND PAYMENT 1938 d: Clifford Sanforth. USA., *Second Choice*, Rob Eden, New York 1932, Novel

I Did It! see SONO STATO IO! (1937).

I Didn't Raise My Boy to Be a Soldier see I'M GLAD MY BOY GREW UP TO BE A SOLDIER (1915).

I DIED A THOUSAND TIMES 1955 d: Stuart Heisler. USA., *High Sierra*, William Riley Burnett, 1940, Novel

I Don't Give a Damn see LO SAM ZAYIN (1987).

I Don't.! I Don't! see NO QUIERO NO QUIERO (1938).

I Dream About Colours see SZINES TINTAKROL ALMODOM (1980).

I Found No Roses for My Mother see NO ENCONTRE ROSAS PARA MI MADRE (1972).

I Gave My Heart see GIVE ME YOUR HEART (1936).

I GIVE MY HEART 1935 d: Marcel Varnel. UKN., *The Dubarry*, Paul Knepler, J. M. Welleminsky, Opera

I Give My Heart see GIVE ME YOUR HEART (1936).

I Give My Life see PORT-ARTHUR (1936).

I Hate Actors see JE HAIS LES ACTEURS (1986).

I Hate Your Guts see THE INTRUDER (1961).

I Have a Stranger's Face see TANIN NO KAO (1966).

I Have Been Faithful see CYNARA (1932).

I Have No Mouth But I Must Scream see AND NOW THE SCREAMING STARTS! (1973).

I Have Two Mummies and Two Daddies see IMAM DVIJE MAME I DVA TATE (1968).

I HEARD THE OWL CALL MY NAME 1973 d: Daryl Duke. USA., *I Heard the Owl Call My Name*, Margaret Craven, Book

I, James Lewis see THIS WOMAN IS MINE (1941).

I Killed Rasputin see J'AI TUE RASPOUTINE (1967).

I KILLED THE COUNT 1938 d: Friedrich Zelnik. UKN., *I Killed the Count*, Alec Coppel, London 1937, Play

I Know What I'm Living for see WOFUR ICH LEBE ICH WEISS (1955).

I KNOW WHAT YOU DID LAST SUMMER 1997 d: Jim Gillespie. USA., *I Know What You Did Last Summer*, Lois Duncan, Novel

I KNOW WHY THE CAGED BIRD SINGS 1979 d: Fielder Cook. USA., *I Know Why the Caged Bird Sings*, Maya Angelou, 1969, Autobiography

I LIKE MIKE 1962 d: Peter Frye. ISR., Aharon Meged, Play

I Like Money see MR. TOPAZE (1961).

I Live for Your Death see VIVO PER LA TUA MORTE (1968).

I LIVE MY LIFE 1935 d: W. S. Van Dyke. USA., *Claustrophobia*, Abbie Carter Goodloe, 1926, Short Story

I LIVE WITH ME DAD 1987 d: Paul Moloney. ASL., *I Live With Me Dad*, Derry Moran, Short Story

I LIVED WITH YOU 1933 d: Maurice Elvey. UKN., *I Lived With You*, Ivor Novello, London 1932, Play

I Lost My Heart in Heidelberg see THE STUDENT'S ROMANCE (1935).

I LOVE A MYSTERY 1945 d: Henry Levin. USA., *I Love a Mystery*, Carleton E. Morse, Novel

I LOVE TROUBLE 1947 d: S. Sylvan Simon. USA., *Double Take*, Roy Huggins, Story

I LOVE YOU AGAIN 1940 d: W. S. Van Dyke. USA., *I Love You Again*, Octavus Roy Cohen, New York 1937, Novel

I LOVE YOU, I LOVE YOU NOT 1997 d: Billy Hopkins. FRN/GRM/USA., *I Love You I Love You Not*, Wendy Kesselman, Play

I Love You Madly see TE QUIERO CON LOCURA (1935).

I Loved a Soldier see HOTEL IMPERIAL (1939).

I LOVED A WOMAN 1933 d: Alfred E. Green. USA., *Red Meat*, David Karsner, Novel

I LOVED YOU WEDNESDAY 1933 d: Henry King, William Cameron Menzies. USA., *I Loved You Wednesday*, William Dubois, Molly Ricardel, New York 1932, Play

I Married a Dead Man see J'AI EPOUSE UNE OMBRE (1983).

I MARRIED A DOCTOR 1936 d: Archie Mayo. USA., *Main Street; the Story of Carol Kennicott*, Sinclair Lewis, New York 1920, Novel

I Married a Nazi see THE MAN I MARRIED (1940).

I Married a Shadow see J'AI EPOUSE UNE OMBRE (1983).

I Married a Spy see SECRET LIVES (1937).

I MARRIED A WITCH 1942 d: Rene Clair. USA., *The Passionate Witch*, Thorne Smith, 1941, Novel

I MARRIED ADVENTURE 1940. USA., *I Married Adventure*, Osa Johnson, New York 1940, Book

I MARRIED AN ANGEL 1942 d: W. S. Van Dyke. USA., Janos Vaszary, Play

I Married an Artist see SHE MARRIED AN ARTIST (1937).

I Married You for Fun see TI HO SPOSATO PER ALLEGRIA (1967).

I Married You for Gaiety see TI HO SPOSATO PER ALLEGRIA (1967).

I, MAUREEN 1980 d: Janine Manatis. CND., *I Maureen*, Elizabeth Spencer, Short Story

I MET MY LOVE AGAIN 1938 d: Joshua Logan, Arthur Ripley. USA., *Summer Lightning*, Allene Corliss, New York 1936, Novel

I, MONSTER 1972 d: Stephen Weeks. UKN., *The Strange Case of Dr. Jekyll and Mr. Hyde*, Robert Louis Stevenson, London 1886, Novel

I NEVER PROMISED YOU A ROSE GARDEN 1977 d: Anthony Page. USA., *I Never Promised You a Rose Garden*, Hannah Green, Novel

I NEVER SANG FOR MY FATHER 1970 d: Gilbert Cates. USA., *I Never Sang for My Father*, Robert Woodruff Anderson, New York 1968, Play

I Often Think of Piroschka see ICH DENKE OFT AN PIROSCHKA (1955).

I OUGHT TO BE IN PICTURES 1982 d: Herbert Ross. USA., *I Ought to Be in Pictures*, Neil Simon, 1981, Play

I Prefer My Wife see MI MUJER ME GUSTA MAS (1960).

I Promise to Pay see PAYROLL (1961).

I REMEMBER MAMA 1948 d: George Stevens. USA., *Mamma's Bank Account*, Kathryn Forbes, Book, *I Remember Mama*, John Van Druten, New York 1944, Play

I SAW WHAT YOU DID 1965 d: William Castle. USA., *Out of the Dark*, Ursula Curtiss, New York 1964, Novel

I SAW WHAT YOU DID 1987 d: Fred Walton. USA., *I Saw What You Did*, Ursula Curtiss, New York 1964, Novel

I See This Land from Afar see AUS DER FERNE SEHE ICH DIESES LAND (1978).

I Sent a Letter to My Love see CHERE INCONNUE (1980).

I Shall Return see AN AMERICAN GUERRILLA IN THE PHILIPPINES (1950).

I SHOT JESSE JAMES 1949 d: Samuel Fuller. USA., Homer Groy, Article

I SKRZYPCE PRZESTALY GRAC 1988 d: Alexander Ramati. PLN/USA., Alexander Ramati, Novel

I Spit on Your Grave see J'IRAI CRACHER SUR VOS TOMBES (1959).

I Stand Accused see AN ACT OF MURDER (1948).

I Stand Condemned see MOSCOW NIGHTS (1935).

I START COUNTING 1969 d: David Greene. UKN., *I Start Counting*, Audrey Erskine Lindop, Novel

I Surrender see SURRENDER (1931).

I TAKE THIS WOMAN 1931 d: Marion Gering, Slavko Vorkapich. USA., *Lost Ecstasy*, Mary Roberts Rinehart, New York 1927, Novel

I THANK A FOOL 1962 d: Robert Stevens. UKN/USA., *I Thank a Fool*, Audrey Erskine Lindop, London 1958, Novel

I, the Body see MORIANERNA (1965).

I. the Doctor see ANA AL DOCTOR (1968).

I the Doleful God see TRUCHLIVY BUH JA (1969).

I, THE JURY 1953 d: Harry Essex. USA., *I the Jury*, Mickey Spillane, Novel

I, THE JURY 1982 d: Richard T. Heffron. USA., *I the Jury*, Mickey Spillane, Novel

I the Sad God see TRUCHLIVY BUH JA (1969).

I, the Worst of Them All see LA PEOR DE TODAS YO (1990).

I. Thou. and She see TU Y ELLA YO (1933).

I TO CE PROCI 1985 d: Nenad Dizdarevic. YGS., *Zeko*, Ivo Andric, 1948, Short Story

I WAKE UP SCREAMING 1941 d: H. Bruce Humberstone. USA., *I Wake Up Screaming*, Steve Fisher, Novel

I WALK ALONE 1948 d: Byron Haskin. USA., *Beggars are Coming to Town*, Theodore Reeves, New York 1945, Play

I WALK THE LINE 1970 d: John Frankenheimer. USA., *An Exile*, Madison Jones, New York 1967, Novel

I WANT MY MAN 1925 d: Lambert Hillyer. USA., *The Interpreter's House*, Maxwell Struthers Burt, New York 1924, Novel

I WANT TO LIVE! 1958 d: Robert Wise. USA., Ed Montgomery, Article

I Want to Live see WO YAO HUO XIA CHU (1995).

I WANT YOU 1951 d: Mark Robson. USA., Edward Newhouse, Short Stories

I WAS A COMMUNIST FOR THE F.B.I. 1951 d: Gordon Douglas. USA., *I Posed As a Communist for the F.B.I.*, Matt Cvetic, Pete Martin, Book

I Was a Criminal see CAPTAIN OF KOEPENICK (1946).

I Was a Male Sex Bomb see UN MONSIEUR DE COMPAGNIE (1964).

I WAS A SPY 1933 d: Victor Saville. UKN., *I Was a Spy*, Marthe Cnockhaert McKenna, Book

I WAS AN AMERICAN SPY 1951 d: Lesley Selander. USA., *Manila Espionage*, Myron G. Goldsmith, Claire Phillips, Book

I Was an Ugly Girl see ICH WAR EIN HASSLICHES MADCHEN (1955).

I WAS FRAMED 1942 d: D. Ross Lederman. USA., Jerome Odlum, Story

I WAS HAPPY HERE 1965 d: Desmond Davis. UKN., *A Woman By the Seaside*, Edna O'Brien, Short Story

I WAS MONTY'S DOUBLE 1958 d: John Guillermin. UKN., *I Was Monty's Double*, M. E. Clifton-James, Book

I Was Seventeen see MES DIX-SEPT ANS (1996).

I Will Be Faithful see HUMAN CARGO (1936).

I WILL REPAY 1917 d: William P. S. Earle. USA., *A Municipal Report*, O. Henry, 1909, Short Story

I WILL REPAY 1923 d: Henry Kolker. UKN., *I Will Repay*, Baroness Orczy, Novel

I Will Repay see ANOTHER SCANDAL (1924).

I WONDER WHO'S KISSING YOU NOW 1999 d: Henning Carlsen. DNM., *The Silhouette*, Ib Lucas, Novel

I WOULDN'T BE IN YOUR SHOES 1948 d: William Nigh. USA., *I Wouldn't Be in Your Shoes*, Cornell Woolrich, 1943, Novel

IACOB 1988 d: Mircea Daneliuc. RMN., *Sfirsitul Lui Iacob Onisia*, Geo Bogza, 1949, Short Story

Ibanez' Torrent see THE TORRENT (1926).

IBIS BLEU, L' 1918 d: Camille de Morlhon. FRN., *L' Ibis Bleu*, Jean Aicard, Novel

IBO KYODAI 1957 d: Miyoji Ieki. JPN., *Ibo Kyodai*, Torahiko Tamiya, 1957, Short Story

Ice Age see DIE EISZEIT (1975).

ICE COLD IN ALEX 1958 d: J. Lee Thompson. UKN., *Ice Cold in Alex*, Christopher Landon, Novel

ICE FLOOD, THE 1926 d: George B. Seitz. USA., *The Brute Breaker*, Johnston McCulley, 1918, Novel

ICE HOUSE 1989 d: Eagle Pennell. USA., *Ice House*, Bo Brinkman, Play

ICE PALACE 1960 d: Vincent Sherman. USA., *Ice Palace*, Edna Ferber, 1958, Novel

Ice Palace, The see IS-SLOTTET (1987).

ICE STATION ZEBRA 1968 d: John Sturges. USA., *Ice Station Zebra*, Alistair MacLean, London 1963, Novel

ICE STORM, THE 1997 d: Ang Lee. USA., *The Ice Storm*, Rick Moody, 1994, Novel

ICEBOUND 1924 d: William C. de Mille. USA., *Icebound*, Owen Davis, Boston 1923, Novel

ICEMAN COMETH, THE 1973 d: John Frankenheimer. USA., *The Iceman Cometh*, Eugene O'Neill, 1946, Play

ICH BRAUCHE DICH 1944 d: Hans Schweikart. GRM., *Ich Brauche Dich*, Hans Schweikart, Play

ICH DENKE OFT AN PIROSCHKA 1955 d: Kurt Hoffmann. GRM., *Ich Denke Oft an Piroschka*, Hugo Hartung, Novel

ICH GLAUBE AN DICH 1945 d: Rolf Hansen. GRM., *Mathilde Mohring*, Theodor Fontane, 1907, Novel

ICH HAB MEIN HERZ IM AUTOBUS VERLOREN 1929 d: Domenico M. Gambino, Carlo Campogalliani. GRM., Mario Sarocchi, Short Story

ICH HAB MICH SO AN DICH GEWOHNT 1952 d: Eduard von Borsody. AUS., *Winterkuhle Hochzeitsreise*, Margot Daniger, Novel

ICH HEIRATE HERRN DIREKTOR 1960 d: Wolfgang Liebeneiner. AUS., *Ich Heirate Herrn Direktor*, H. Krackardt, Novel

ICH KLAGE AN 1941 d: Wolfgang Liebeneiner. GRM., *Sendung Und Gewissen*, Hellmuth Unger, Novel

ICH MACH' DICH GLUCKLICH 1949 d: Alexander von Szlatinay. GRM., *Ich MacH' Dich Glucklich*, Gabor von Vaszary, Play

Ich Mocht' Gern Dein Herz Klopfen Hor'n see JUNGGESELLENFALLE (1953).

ICH SCHWORE UND GELOBE 1960 d: Geza von Radvanyi. GRM., *Ich Schwore Und Gelobe*, Ernst Ludwig Ravius, Novel

ICH SUCHE DICH 1953 d: O. W. Fischer. GRM., *Jupiter Laughs*, A. J. Cronin, 1940, Play

ICH UND DU 1953 d: Alfred Weidenmann. GRM., *Ich Und Du*, Christian Bock, Play

ICH UND ER 1988 d: Doris Dorrie. GRM/USA., Alberto Moravia, Short Story

ICH VERTRAUE DIR MEINE FRAU AN 1943 d: Kurt Hoffmann. GRM., *Ich Vertraue Dir Meine Frau an*, Johann von Vaszary, Play

ICH WAR EIN HASSLICHES MADCHEN 1955 d: Wolfgang Liebeneiner. GRM., *Ich War Ein Hassliches Madchen*, Annemarie Selinko, Novel

ICH WAR JACK MORTIMER 1935 d: Carl Froelich. GRM., *Ich War Jack Mortimer*, Alexander Lernet-Holenia, Novel

ICH WEISS, WOFUR ICH LEBE 1955 d: Paul Verhoeven. GRM., *Ich Weiss Wofur Ich Lebe*, Ernst Neubach, Novel

ICH WERDE DICH AUF HANDEN TRAGEN 1958 d: Veit Harlan. GRM., *Viola Tricolor*, Theodor Storm, 1874, Novel

ICH ZAHLE TAGLICH MEIN SORGEN 1960 d: Paul Martin. GRM., *Ich Zahle Taglich Meine Sorgen*, H. B. Fredersdorf, Novel

ICHABOD AND MR. TOAD 1949 d: James Algar, Jack Kinney. USA., *The Wind in the Willows*, Kenneth Grahame, 1908, Novel, *The Legend of Sleepy Hollow*, Washington Irving, 1820, Short Story

Ichijoji No Ketto see MIYAMOTO MUSASHI: ICHIJOJI NO KETTO (1955).

Iconostasis see IKONOSTASAT (1968).

Icy Breasts see LES SEINS DE GLACE (1974).

I'D CLIMB THE HIGHEST MOUNTAIN 1951 d: Henry King. USA., *I'd Climb the Highest Mountain*, Corra Harris, Novel

I'D GIVE MY LIFE 1936 d: Edwin L. Marin. USA., *The Noose*, Willard Mack, H. H. Van Loan, New York 1926, Play

IDAHO KID, THE 1936 d: Robert F. Hill. USA., *Idaho*, Paul Evan Lehman, New York 1933, Novel

IDEAL HUSBAND, AN 1948 d: Alexander KordA. UKN., *An Ideal Husband*, Oscar Wilde, London 1895, Play

Ideal Husband, An see IDEALNY MUZH (1981).

IDEAL HUSBAND, AN 1999 d: Oliver Parker. UKN/USA., *An Ideal Husband*, Oscar Wilde, London 1895, Play

Ideal Schoolmaster, The see KANTOR IDEAL (1932).

IDEAL SEPTIMY 1938 d: Vaclav Kubasek. CZC., *Ideal Septimy*, Jaromira Huttlova, Novel

Ideal Woman, The see LA FEMME IDEALE (1933).

IDEALER GATTE, EIN 1935 d: Herbert Selpin. GRM., *An Ideal Husband*, Oscar Wilde, London 1895, Play

IDEALIST 1976 d: Igor Pretnar. YGS., *Martin Kacur*, Ivan Cankar, 1906, Novel

Idealist, The see IDEALIST (1976).

IDEALNY MUZH 1981 d: Viktor Georgiev. USS., *An Ideal Husband*, Oscar Wilde, London 1895, Play

IDEE DE FRANCOISE, L' 1923 d: Robert Saidreau. FRN., *L' Idee de Francoise*, Paul Gavault, Play

Idee de Genie, Une see UNE IDEE FOLLE (1932).

IDEE FOLLE, UNE 1932 d: Max de Vaucorbeil. FRN., *Une Idee Folle*, Carl Laufs, Play

IDENTIKIT 1974 d: Giuseppe Patroni Griffi. ITL., *The Driver's Seat*, Muriel Spark, 1970, Novel

IDENTITY UNKNOWN 1945 d: Walter Colmes. USA., *Johnny March*, Richard Newman, Story

IDI I SMOTRI 1986 d: Elem Klimov. USS., Alexei Adamovich, Books

Idillio 1848 see AMO TE SOLA (1935).

IDILLIO A BUDAPEST 1941 d: Giorgio Ansoldi, Gabriele Varriale. ITL., *Duca E Forse Una Duchessa*, Santiago Salvich, Play

IDILLIO TRAGICO 1922 d: Gaston Ravel. ITL., *Une Idylle Tragique*, Paul Bourget, 1896

IDIOT 1991 d: Mani Kaul. IND., *Idiot*, Fyodor Dostoyevsky, 1868, Novel

IDIOT A PARIS, UN 1967 d: Serge Korber. FRN., *Un Idiot a Paris*, Rene Fallet, Novel

Idiot in Love, An see CHIJIN NO AI (1967).

Idiot in Paris see UN IDIOT A PARIS (1967).

IDIOT, L' 1945 d: Georges Lampin. FRN., *Idiot*, Fyodor Dostoyevsky, 1868, Novel

Idiot: Part One, The see NASTASIA FILIPOVNA (1958).

Idiot, The see L' IDIOT (1945).

Idiot, The see HAKUCHI (1951).

Idiot, The see NASTASIA FILIPOVNA (1958).

Idiot, The see AHMAQ (1992).

IDIOTA, EL 1926 d: Juan Andreu Moragas. SPN., *El Idiota*, Emilio Gomez de Miguel, Play

IDIOTA, L' 1919 d: Salvatore Aversano. ITL., *Idiot*, Fyodor Dostoyevsky, 1868, Novel

IDIOT'S DELIGHT 1938 d: Clarence Brown. USA., *Idiot's Delight*, R. E. Sherwood, New York 1936, Play

IDLE RICH, THE 1921 d: Maxwell Karger. USA., *Junk*, Kenneth Harris, 1920, Short Story

IDLE RICH, THE 1929 d: William C. de Mille. USA., *White Collars*, Edith Ellis, New York 1923, Play

IDLE TONGUES 1924 d: Lambert Hillyer. USA., *Doctor Nye of North Ostable*, Joseph C. Lincoln, New York 1923, Novel

IDLE WIVES 1916 d: Lois Weber, Phillips Smalley. USA., *Idle Wives*, James Oppenheim, New York 1914, Novel

IDLER, THE 1915 d: Lloyd B. Carleton. USA., *The Idler*, C. Haddon Chambers, New York 1890, Play

IDOL OF PARIS 1948 d: Leslie Arliss. UKN., *Paiva Queen of Love*, Alfred Shirkauer, Novel

IDOL OF PARIS, THE 1914 d: Maurice Elvey. UKN., *The Idol of Paris*, Charles Darrell, Play

IDOL ON PARADE 1959 d: John Gilling. UKN., *Idol on Parade*, William Camp, Novel

IDOLES, LES 1968 d: Marc'o. FRN., Marc'o, Play

IDOLS 1916 d: Webster Cullison. USA., *Idols*, William J. Locke, London 1899, Novel

Idols in the Dust see SATURDAY'S HERO (1951).

IERI, OGGI, DOMANI 1963 d: Vittorio de SicA. ITL/FRN., *Troppa Rica*, Alberto Moravia, Short Story

Ieri, Oggi E Domani see OGGI, DOMANI IERI (1963).

IF A MAN ANSWERS 1962 d: Henry Levin. USA., *If a Man Answers*, Winifred Wolfe, New York 1961, Novel

If All the Women in the World see AN OLES I YINEKES TOU KOSMOU (1967).

If England Were Invaded see THE RAID OF 1915 (1914).

IF FOUR WALLS TOLD 1922 d: Fred Paul. UKN., *If Four Walls Told*, Edward Percy, London 1922, Play

IF I HAD A MILLION 1932 d: Stephen Roberts, James Cruze. USA., *Windfall*, Robert D. Andrews, New York 1931, Novel

IF I MARRY AGAIN 1925 d: John Francis Dillon. USA., *If I Marry Again*, Gilbert Frankau, Story

If I Was Rich see LET'S BE RITZY (1934).

IF I WERE FREE 1933 d: Elliott Nugent. USA., *Behold We Live!*, John Van Druten, London 1932, Play

If I Were Harap Alb see DE-AS FI HARAP ALB (1965).

IF I WERE KING 1920 d: J. Gordon Edwards. USA., *If I Were King*, Justin Huntly McCarthy, London 1901, Novel

IF I WERE KING 1938 d: Frank Lloyd. USA., **If I Were King**, Justin Huntly McCarthy, London 1901, Novel

IF I WERE QUEEN 1922 d: Wesley Ruggles. USA., *The Three Cornered Kingdom*, Du Vernet Rabell, Story

IF I WERE RICH 1936 d: Randall Faye. UKN., *Humpty Dumpty*, Horace Annesley Vachell, 1917, Play

IF MY COUNTRY SHOULD CALL 1916 d: Joseph de Grasse. USA., Virginia Terhune Van de Water, Story

"IF ONLY" JIM 1921 d: Jacques Jaccard. USA., *Bruvver Jim's Baby*, Philip Verrill Mighels, New York 1904, Novel

If Pigs Had Wings see **PORCI CON LE ALI** (1977).

If the Gods Laugh see **FIGHTING LOVE** (1927).

If They Tell You That I Fell see **SI TE DICEN QUE CAI** (1988).

If This Be Sin see **THAT DANGEROUS AGE** (1949).

If We All Were Angels see **WENN WIR ALLE ENGEL WAREN** (1936).

If We All Were Angels see **WENN WIR ALLE ENGEL WAREN** (1956).

IF WINTER COMES 1923 d: Harry Millarde. USA., **If Winter Comes**, A. S. M. Hutchinson, Boston 1921, Novel

IF WINTER COMES 1947 d: Victor Saville. USA., **If Winter Comes**, A. S. M. Hutchinson, Boston 1921, Novel

IF WOMEN ONLY KNEW 1921 d: Edward H. Griffith. USA., *La Physiologie du Mariage*, Honore de Balzac, Paris 1830, Novel

If You Can't Say It, Just See It see **WHORE** (1991).

IF YOU COULD SEE WHAT I HEAR 1981 d: Eric Till. CND., **If You Could See What I Hear**, Derek Gill, Tom Sullivan, Book

If You Love Me see **I LIVE MY LIFE** (1935).

If You Please: My Name Is Cox see **MEIN NAME IST COX GESTATTEN** (1955).

IF YOUTH BUT KNEW 1926 d: George A. Cooper. UKN., **If Youth But Knew**, K. C. Spiers, Play

I.F.1 NE REPOND PLUS 1932 d: Karl Hartl. FRN., *F.P.1 Antwortet Nicht*, Curt Siodmak, Novel

IFIGENIA 1977 d: Michael Cacoyannis. GRC., *Iphigenia in Aulia*, Euripides, c407 bc, Play

IGNACE 1937 d: Piere Colombier. FRN., *Ignace*, Jean Manse, Opera

IGROK 1972 d: Alexei Batalov. USS/CZC., *Igrok*, Fyodor Dostoyevsky, 1866, Novel

IGUANA DALLA LINGUA DI FUOCO, L' 1971 d: Riccardo FredA. ITL/FRN/GRM., *A Room Without a Door*, Richard Mann, Novel

IHMISELON IHANUUS JA KURJUUS 1988 d: Matti KassilA. FNL., *Ihmiselon Ihanuus Ja Kurjuus*, Frans E. Sillanpaa, 1945, Novel

IHMISET SUVIYOSSA 1949 d: Valentin VaalA. FNL., *Ihmiset Suviyossa*, Frans E. Sillanpaa, 1934, Novel

IHR 106 GEBURTSTAG 1958 d: Gunther Luders. GRM., *Mamouret*, Jean Sarment, 1943, Play

IHR DUNKLER PUNKT 1928 d: Johannes Guter. GRM., *Die Dame Mit Dem Schwarzen Herzen*, Frank Maraun, Short Story

IHR ERSTES ERLEBNIS 1939 d: Josef von Baky. GRM., *Tochter Aus Gutem Hause*, Susanne Kerckhoff, Novel

Ihr Grosser Fall see **DER GROSSE FALL** (1945).

IHR JUNGE 1931 d: Friedrich Feher. GRM/AUS/CZC., *Dabel*, Lev Nikolayevich Tolstoy, Short Story

IHR LEIBHUSAR 1937 d: Hubert MarischkA. GRM/AUS/HNG., *A Noszty Fiu Esete Toth Marival*, Kalman Mikszath, 1908, Novel

IHR PRIVATSEKRETAR 1940 d: Charles Klein. GRM., *Haus Kiepergass Und Seine Gaste*, Hannes Peter Stolp, Novel

IHR SCHONSTER TAG 1962 d: Paul Verhoeven. GRM., *Das Fenster Zum Flur*, Curt Flatow, Play

IKARI NO MACHI 1950 d: Mikio Naruse. JPN., *Ikari No MaCHi*, Fumio Niwa, 1949, Novel

Ike see **IKE: THE WAR YEARS** (1978).

IKE: THE WAR YEARS 1978 d: Melville Shavelson, Boris Sagal. USA., *Past Forgetting*, Kay Summersby Morgan, Autobiography

IKINAI 1998 d: Hiroshi Shimizu. JPN., *Ikinai*, Fumio Nakahara, Novel

IKONOSTASAT 1968 d: Hristo Hristov, Todor Dinov. BUL., *Zhelezniyat Svetilnik*, Dimitar Talev, 1952, Novel

IL EST CHARMANT 1931 d: Louis Mercanton. FRN., *Il Est Charmant*, Albert Willemetz, Opera

IL EST MINUIT, DR. SCHWEITZER 1952 d: Andre Haguet. FRN., *Il Est Minuit Dr. Schweitzer*, Gilbert Cesbron, Play

IL ETAIT UNE FOIS 1933 d: Leonce Perret. FRN., *Il Etait une Fois*, Francis de Croisset, Play

Il Etait une Fois Des Gens Heureux: Les Plouffe see **LES PLOUFFE** (1981).

IL FAUT QU'UNE PORTE SOIT OUVERTE OU FERME 1949 d: Louis Cuny. FRN., *Il Faut Qu'une Porte Soit Ouverte Ou Fermee*, Alfred de Musset, 1848, Play

IL FAUT VIVRE DANGEREUSEMENT 1975 d: Claude Makovski. FRN., *Il Faut Vivre Dangereusement*, R. Marlot, Novel

IL MAESTRO 1989 d: Marion Hansel. BLG/FRN., *I Due Maestri*, Mario Soldati, 1957, Short Story

Il Trovatore see **IL TROVATORE** (1914).

IL Y A DES PIEDS AU PLAFOND 1912 d: Abel Gance. FRN., *Balaoo*, Gaston Leroux, Paris 1912, Novel

Ile Au Tresor, L' see **TREASURE ISLAND** (1972).

Ile Au Tresor, L' see **L' ISOLA DEL TESORO** (1973).

ILE AU TRESOR, L' 1991 d: Raul Ruiz. FRN/USA., *Treasure Island*, Robert Louis Stevenson, London 1883, Novel

ILE D'AMOUR, L' 1927 d: Jean Durand, Berthe Dagmar. FRN., *Bicchi*, Saint-Sorny, Novel

ILE D'AMOUR, L' 1943 d: Maurice Cam. FRN., *L' Ile d'Amour*, Saint-Sorny, Novel

ILE DU BOUT DU MONDE, L' 1958 d: Edmond T. Greville. FRN., *L'Ile du Bout du Monde*, Henri Crouzat, Paris 1954, Novel

Ile du Tresor, L' see **L' ISOLA DEL TESORO** (1973).

ILE MYSTERIEUSE, L' 1973 d: Henri Colpi, Juan Antonio Bardem. FRN/ITL/SPN., *L' Ile Mysterieuse*, Jules Verne, Paris 1874, Novel

ILE SANS AMOUR, L' 1919 d: Andre Liabel. FRN., *L' Ile Sans Amour*, Andre Legrand, Novel

ILES ENCHANTEES, LES 1964 d: Carlos Vilardebo. FRN/PRT., *The Encantades*, Herman Melville, 1854, Short Story

Ilhas Encantadas, As see **LES ILES ENCHANTEES** (1964).

Iliac Passion, The see **PROMETHEUS BOUND -THE ILLIAC PASSION** (1966).

I'LL BE SEEING YOU 1944 d: William Dieterle, George Cukor (Uncredited). USA., *I'll Be Seeing You*, Charles Martin, Novel

I'LL BE YOURS 1947 d: William A. Seiter. USA., *A Jo Tunder*, Ferenc Molnar, Budapest 1931, Play

I'll Bet You see **BORN TO GAMBLE** (1935).

I'll Carry You in My Hands see **ICH WERDE DICH AUF HANDEN TRAGEN** (1958).

I'LL CRY TOMORROW 1955 d: Daniel Mann. USA., *I'll Cry Tomorrow*, Gerold Frank, Lillian Roth, Book

I'LL GET YOU FOR THIS 1951 d: Joseph M. Newman. UKN/USA., *High Stakes*, James Hadley Chase, Novel

I'll Give a Million see **DARO UN MILIONE** (1935).

I'll Give My Wife in Marriage see **PROVDAM SVOU ZENU** (1941).

I'll Make You Happy see **ICH MACH' DICH GLUCKLICH** (1949).

I'll Meet You in Heaven see **MAXIE** (1985).

ILL MET BY MOONLIGHT 1956 d: Michael Powell, Emeric Pressburger. UKN., *Ill Met By Moonlight*, W. Stanley Moss, Book

I'll Never Forget You see **THE HOUSE IN THE SQUARE** (1951).

I'LL REMEMBER APRIL 1945 d: Harold Young. USA., *Amateur Night*, Bob Dillon, Story, *Bob Goes to a Party*, Gene Lewis, Story

I'll Save My Love see **TWO LOVES** (1961).

I'll See You in Hell see **TI ASPETTERO ALL'INFERNO** (1960).

I'LL SHOW YOU THE TOWN 1925 d: Harry Pollard. USA., *I'll Show You the Town*, Elmer Holmes Davis, New York 1924, Novel

Ill Starred Babbie see **ILL-STARRED BABBIE** (1915).

I'LL TELL THE WORLD 1945 d: Leslie Goodwins. USA., *Miss Lonelyhearts*, Nathanael West, New York 1933, Novel

I'll Wait for You in Hell see **TI ASPETTERO ALL'INFERNO** (1960).

ILLEGAL 1955 d: Lewis Allen. USA., *The Mouthpiece*, Frank L. Collins, New York 1929, Play

Illegal Divorce, The see **SECOND HAND WIFE** (1933).

Ill-Fated Love see **AMOR DE PERDICAO** (1977).

Illiac Passion, The see **PROMETHEUS BOUND -THE ILLIAC PASSION** (1966).

ILLICIT 1931 d: Archie Mayo. USA., Edith Fitzgerald, Robert Riskin, 1930, Play

Ill-Loved, The see **LA MALQUERIDA** (1940).

ILL-STARRED BABBIE 1915 d: Sherwood MacDonald. USA., *Ill-Starred Babbie*, William Wilfred Whalen, Boston 1912, Novel

ILLTOWN 1996 d: Nick Gomez. USA., *The Cocaine Kids*, Terry Williams, Novel

ILLUMINATA 1998 d: John Turturro. USA., *Illuminata*, Brandon Cole, Play

ILLUSION 1929 d: Lothar Mendes. USA., *Illusion*, Arthur Cheney Train, New York 1929, Novel

Illusion of Blood see **YOTSUYA KAIDAN** (1949).

Illusion of Blood see **YOTSUYA KAIDAN** (1965).

ILLUSIONE, L' 1917 d: Guglielmo Zorzi. ITL., *L' Illusione*, Renato Simoni, 1916, Play

Illusory World see **MAYA MACHHINDRA** (1932).

ILLUSTRATED MAN, THE 1969 d: Jack Smight. USA., *The Last Night in the World*, Ray Bradbury, 1951, Short Story, *The Long Rain*, Ray Bradbury, 1950, Short Story, *The Veldt*, Ray Bradbury, 1951, Short Story

ILLUSTRE MAURIN, L' 1933 d: Andre Hugon. FRN., *L' Illustre Maurin*, Jean Aicard, 1908, Novel

Illustrious Corpses see **CADAVERI ECCELLENTI** (1976).

ILLUSTRIOUS PRINCE, THE 1919 d: William Worthington. USA., *The Illustrious Prince*, E. Phillips Oppenheim, Boston 1910, Novel

Ilona Comes With the Rain see **ILONA LLEGA CON LA LLUVA** (1996).

ILONA LLEGA CON LA LLUVA 1996 d: Sergio CabrerA. ITL/SPN., *Ilona Llega Con la Lluva*, Alvaro Mutis, Novel

ILS. 1970 d: Jean-Daniel Simon. FRN., *Ils*, Andre Hardellet, Novel

ILS ONT VINGT ANS 1950 d: Rene Delacroix. FRN., *Ils Ont Vingt Ans*, Roger Ferdinand, Play

ILS SONT DANS LES VIGNES 1951 d: Robert Vernay. FRN., *Le Plus Bel Ivrogne du Quartier*, Pierre Scize, Novel

ILUSTRE FREGONA, LA 1927 d: Armando Pou. SPN., *La Ilustre Fregona*, Miguel de Cervantes Saavedra

Im 6 Stock see **IM SECHSTEN STOCK** (1961).

I'M A FOOL 1977 d: Noel Black. USA., *I'm a Fool*, Sherwood Anderson, 1923, Short Story

I'm Accusing see **ICH KLAGE AN** (1941).

I'M ALL RIGHT, JACK 1959 d: John Boulting. UKN., *Private Life*, Alan Hackney, Novel

I'M AN EXPLOSIVE 1933 d: Adrian Brunel. UKN., *I'm an Explosive*, Gordon Phillips, Novel

IM BANNE DES UNHEIMLICHEN 1968 d: Alfred Vohrer. GRM., Edgar Wallace, Novel

I'm Crazy About You see **TE QUIERO CON LOCURA** (1935).

I'M DANCING AS FAST AS I CAN 1982 d: Jack Hofsiss. USA., *I'm Dancing As Fast As I Can*, Barbara Gordon, Book

I'M DANGEROUS TONIGHT 1990 d: Tobe Hooper. USA., *I'm Dangerous Tonight*, Cornell Woolrich, 1943, Short Story

I'M FROM MISSOURI 1939 d: Theodore Reed. USA., *Sixteen Hands*, Homer Croy, New York 1938, Novel, *Need of Change*, Julian Leonard Street, 1909, Novel

I'M GLAD MY BOY GREW UP TO BE A SOLDIER 1915 d: Frank Beal. USA., *I Didn't Raise My Boy to Be a Soldier*, Alfred Bryan, Al Piantadosi, 1915, Song

I'm Here and I'm Staying see **HIER BLEIB ICH HIER BIN ICH** (1959).

IM JAHR DER SCHILDKROTE 1988 d: Ute Wieland. GRM., *Im Jahr Der Schildkrote*, Hans Werner Kettenbach, Novel

I'm Jumping Over Puddles Again see **UZ ZASE SKACU PRES KALUZE** (1970).

Im Krug Zum Grunen Kranze see **DIE FUNF KARNICKEL** (1953).

I'M LOSING YOU 1998 d: Bruce Wagner. USA., *I'm Losing You*, Bruce Wagner, 1997, Novel

IM LUXUSZUG 1927 d: Erich Schonfelder. GRM., *Im Luxuszug*, Abel Hermant, Play

IM NAMEN DES TEUFELS 1962 d: John Paddy Carstairs. GRM/UKN., *In Namen Des Teufels*, Hans Habe, Novel

IM NAMEN EINER MUTTER 1960 d: Erich Engels. GRM., *Im Namen Einer Mutter*, Teda Bork, Novel

I'M NOBODY'S SWEETHEART NOW 1940 d: Arthur Lubin. USA., *The Bride Said No*, W. Scott Darling, Erna Lazarus, Story

I'M NOT RAPPAPORT 1996 d: Herb Gardner. USA., *I'm Not Rappaport*, Herb Gardner, Play

IM PARTERRE LINKS 1963 d: Kurt Fruh. SWT., *Das Fenster Xum Flur*, Curt Flatow, Horst Pillau, Play

IM PRATER BLUH'N WIEDER DIE BAUME 1958 d: Hans Wolff. AUS., *Die Sachertorte*, Siegfried Geyer, Rudolf Osterreicher, Play

IM REICHE DES SILBERNEN LOWEN 1965 d: Franz J. Gottlieb, Jose Antonio de La LomA. GRM/SPN., *Im Reiche Des Silbernen Lowen*, Karl Friedrich May, Novel

IM SECHSTEN STOCK 1961 d: John Olden. GRM., *Im Sechsten Stock*, Alfred Gehri, Play

Im Wirtshaus Zum "Goldenen Herzen" *see* DER SEELENBRAU (1950).

Imaginary Knight, The *see* IL CAVALIERE INESISTENTE (1970).

Imagine One Evening for Dinner *see* UNA SERA A CENA METTI (1969).

Imagine Robinson *see* TU IMAGINES ROBINSON (1968).

IMAM DVIJE MAME I DVA TATE 1968 d: Kreso Golik. YGS., *Imam Drije Mame I Dva Tate*, Miriam Tusek, Novel

IMAX NUTCRACKER, THE 1997 d: Christine Edzard. USA., *Nussknacker Und Mausekonig*, Ernst Theodor Amadeus Hoffmann, 1816, Short Story

IMBARCO A MEZZANOTTE 1952 d: Joseph Losey. ITL/USA., *La Bouteille de Lait*, Noel Calef, Story

Imi Hageneralit *see* EEMI HAGENERALIT (1979).

IMITATION GAME, THE 1980 d: Richard Eyre. UKN., *The Imitation Game*, Ian McEwan, 1981, Play

IMITATION OF LIFE 1934 d: John M. Stahl. USA., *Imitation of Life*, Fannie Hurst, New York 1933, Novel

IMITATION OF LIFE 1959 d: Douglas Sirk. USA., *Imitation of Life*, Fannie Hurst, New York 1933, Novel

IMMAGINI VIVE (CIO CHE DI ME HANNO LASCIATO) 1976 d: Ansano Giannarelli. ITL., *Quanto de Me Hanno Tagliato*, Ada Guareschi Verga, Autobiography

IMMEDIATE LEE 1916 d: Frank Borzage. USA., *Immediate Lee*, Kenneth B. Clarke, Short Story

IMMENSEE 1943 d: Veit Harlan. GRM., *Immensee*, Theodor Storm, 1852, Novel

IMMENSEE 1989 d: Klaus Gendries. GDR., *Immensee*, Theodor Storm, 1852, Novel

IMMIGRANTS, THE 1978 d: Alan J. Levi. USA., *The Immigrants*, Howard Fast, Novel

Immoral Charge *see* SERIOUS CHARGE (1959).

IMMORTAL SERGEANT, THE 1943 d: John M. Stahl. USA., *The Immortal Sergeant*, John Brophy, Novel

Immortal Story *see* HISTOIRE IMMORTELLE (1968).

IMMORTAL, THE 1969 d: Joseph Sargent. USA., *The Immortals*, James E. Gunn, Story

IMMORTALE, L' 1921 d: Guido Schamberg. ITL., *L' Immortale*, Giuliano Di Guida, Novel

Imp in the Bottle, The *see* TOD UND TEUFEL LIEBE (1934).

IMPASSIVE FOOTMAN, THE 1932 d: Basil Dean. UKN., *The Impassive Footman*, H. C. McNeile ("Sapper"), Play

IMPATIENT MAIDEN, THE 1932 d: James Whale. USA., *The Impatient Maiden*, Donald Henderson Clarke, New York 1931, Novel

Imperfect Lady, The *see* THE PERFECT GENTLEMAN (1935).

Imperial and Royal Field Marshal *see* C. A. K. POLNI MARSALEK (1930).

IMPERSONATOR, THE 1914 d: Charles H. France. USA., *The Impersonator*, Mary Imlay Taylor, Novel

Implacable Destiny *see* LOVE ME AND THE WORLD IS MINE (1928).

IMPORTANCE OF BEING EARNEST, THE 1952 d: Anthony Asquith. UKN., *The Importance of Being Earnest*, Oscar Wilde, London 1895, Play

IMPORTANCE OF BEING EARNEST, THE 1964 d: Bill Bain. UKN., *The Importance of Being Earnest*, Oscar Wilde, London 1895, Play

IMPORTANT, C'EST D'AIMER, L' 1974 d: Andrzej Zulawski. FRN/ITL/GRM., *C'est Daimer, L' Important*, Christopher Frank, Novel

Important Man, The *see* EL HOMBRE IMPORTANTE ANIMAS TRUJANO (1961).

IMPORTANT PEOPLE 1934 d: Adrian Brunel. UKN., *Important People*, F. Wyndham Mallock, Play

Importante E Amare, L' *see* C'EST D'AIMER, L' IMPORTANT (1974).

IMPORTUNO VINCE L'AVARO, L' 1916. ITL., *L' Importuno Vince l'Avaro*, O. Carlini, A. Consigli, 1887, Play

IMPOSIBILA IUBIRE 1984 d: Constantin Vaeni. RMN., *Intrusul*, Marin Preda, 1968, Novel

Impossible Love *see* IMPOSIBILA IUBIRE (1984).

Impossible Lover, The *see* HUDDLE (1932).

IMPOSSIBLE MRS. BELLEW, THE 1922 d: Sam Wood. USA., *The Impossible Mrs. Bellew*, David Lisle, New York 1916, Novel

Impossible Object *see* QUESTO IMPOSSIBILE OGGETTO (1973).

Impossible Objet, L' *see* QUESTO IMPOSSIBILE OGGETTO (1973).

IMPOSSIBLE WOMAN, THE 1919 d: Meyrick Milton. UKN., *Tante*, Anne Douglas Sedgwick, Novel

IMPOSSIBLE YEARS, THE 1968 d: Michael Gordon. USA., *The Impossible Years*, Bob Fisher, Arthur Marx, New York 1965, Play

Imposter *see* FOREIGN CORRESPONDENT (1940).

Imposter, The *see* THE IMPOSTOR (1918).

IMPOSTOR, EL 1931 d: Lewis Seiler. USA., *Scotland Yard*, Denison Clift, New York 1929, Play

IMPOSTOR, THE 1915 d: Albert Capellani. USA., *The Impostor*, Douglas Murray, Play

IMPOSTOR, THE 1918 d: Dell Henderson. USA., *The Imposter*, Leonard Merrick, Michael Morton, New York 1910, Play

Impostor, The *see* A TAILOR MADE MAN (1931).

Impostors, The *see* THE IMPOSTOR (1915).

Impotence *see* XALA (1974).

IMPRECATEUR, L' 1976 d: Jean-Louis Bertucelli. FRN/SWT., *L' Imprecateur*, Rene-Victor Pilhes, Novel

IMPREVU, L' 1916 d: Leonce Perret. FRN., *L' Imprevu*, Victor Margueritte, Play

IMPROPER DUCHESS, THE 1936 d: Harry Hughes. UKN., *The Improper Duchess*, James B. Fagan, London 1931, Play

Improper Ones, The *see* DE UANSTAENDIGE (1983).

Imprudent Lover, The *see* DEN UBETAENKSOMME ELSKER (1983).

Impudent Lover, The *see* DEN UBETAENKSOMME ELSKER (1983).

Impuissance Temporaire, L' *see* XALA (1974).

IMPULSE 1922 d: Norval MacGregor. USA., *Her Unknown Knight*, Maude Woodruff Newell, 1921, Short Story

Impulses *see* THE THIRTEENTH COMMANDMENT (1920).

IN A LONELY PLACE 1950 d: Nicholas Ray. USA., *In a Lonely Place*, Dorothy B. Hughes, Novel

In a Monastery Garden *see* REVELATION (1924).

IN A SHALLOW GRAVE 1988 d: Kenneth Bowser. USA., *In a Shallow Grave*, James Purdy, Novel

In a Village *see* DE SFASURAREA (1954).

In All Innocence *see* EN PLEIN COEUR (1998).

IN ANOTHER GIRL'S SHOES 1917 d: G. B. Samuelson, Alexander Butler. UKN., *In Another Girl's Shoes*, Berta Ruck, Novel

IN BARC A VELA CONTROMANO 1997 d: Stefano Reali. ITL., *Operations*, Stefano Reali, Play

IN BORROWED PLUMES 1926 d: Victor Hugo Halperin. USA., *In Borrowed Plumes*, Leroy Scott, Short Story

IN BORROWED PLUMES 1928 d: Geoffrey H. Malins. UKN., *In Borrowed Plumes*, W. W. Jacobs, Short Story

IN CAMERA 1964 d: Philip Saville. UKN., Jean-Paul Sartre, Play

IN CAMPAGNA E CADUTA UNA STELLA 1940 d: Eduardo de Filippo. ITL., *A Coperchia E Caduta Una Stella*, Peppino de Filippo, Play

IN CELEBRATION 1974 d: Lindsay Anderson. UKN/CND., *In Celebration*, David Storey, 1969, Novel

IN COLD BLOOD 1967 d: Richard Brooks. USA., *In Cold Blood*, Truman Capote, New York 1966, Book

IN COLD BLOOD 1996 d: Jonathan Kaplan. USA., *In Cold Blood*, Truman Capote, New York 1966, Book

In Country *see* CEASE FIRE (1985).

In de macht Van Het Noodlot *see* KITTY TAILLEUR (1921).

In Defense of Love *see* I TAKE THIS WOMAN (1931).

IN DEFIANCE OF THE LAW 1914 d: Colin Campbell. USA., *The Trail's End*, James Oliver Curwood, Novel

In Den Nacht *see* IN THE NIGHT (1921).

IN DER WUSTE 1986 d: Rafael Fuster-Pardo. GRM., Antonio Skarmeta, Story

In Desert and Jungle *see* W PUSTYNI I W PUSZCZY (1972).

In Desert and Wilderness *see* W PUSTYNI I W PUSZCZY (1972).

IN DREAMS 1999 d: Neil Jordan. USA., *Doll's Eyes*, Bari Wood, Novel

IN EVERY WOMAN'S LIFE 1924 d: Irving Cummings. USA., *Belonging*, Olive Wadsley, New York 1920, Novel

In Every Woman's Life *see* MY BILL (1938).

In Excess *see* LA VILLA DEL VENERDI (1992).

In Famiglia Si Spara *see* LES TONTONS FLINGEURS (1963).

In Fate's Power *see* KITTY TAILLEUR (1921).

IN FOLLY'S TRAIL 1920 d: Rollin S. Sturgeon. USA., *In Folly's Trail*, Katherine Leiser Robbins, 1920, Short Story

In Fondo Alla Piscina *see* LA ULTIMA SENORA ANDERSON (1970).

In for the Night *see* SIC-EM (1920?).

IN FULL CRY 1921 d: Einar J. Bruun. UKN., *In Full Cry*, Richard Marsh, Novel

IN GAY MADRID 1930 d: Robert Z. Leonard. USA., *La Casa de la Troya*, Alejandro Perez Lugin, Madrid 1915, Novel

IN HAMBURG SIND DIE NACHTE LANG 1955 d: Max Michel. GRM., *In Hamburg Sind Die Nachte Lang*, Peter Francke, Novel

IN HARM'S WAY 1965 d: Otto Preminger. USA., *Harm's Way*, James Bassett, Cleveland 1962, Novel

IN HIS GRIP 1921 d: Charles Calvert. UKN., *In His Grip*, David Christie Murray, Novel

IN HIS STEPS 1936 d: Karl Brown. USA., *In His Steps: "What Would Jesus Do?"*, Charles Monroe Sheldon, New York 1896, Novel

IN HOLLYWOOD WITH POTASH AND PERLMUTTER 1924 d: Alfred E. Green. USA., *Business Before Pleasure*, Montague Glass, Jules Eckert Goodman, New York 1917, Play

In Instalments *see* OP AFBETALING (1991).

IN LOVE AND WAR 1958 d: Philip Dunne. USA., *The Big War*, Anton Myrer, Novel

IN LOVE AND WAR 1987 d: Paul Aaron. USA., *In Love and War*, Jim Stockdale, Sybil Stockdale, Novel

IN LOVE AND WAR 1996 d: Richard Attenborough. USA., *Hemingway in Love and War*, James Nagel, Henry S. Villard, Book

IN LOVE WITH LOVE 1924 d: Rowland V. Lee. USA., *In Love With Love*, Vincent Lawrence, New York 1923, Play

IN MAREMMA 1924 d: Salvatore Aversano. ITL., *In Maremma*, Ouida, Novel

IN MIZZOURA 1914 d: Lawrence McGill. USA., *In Mizzoura*, Augustus Thomas, Chicago 1893, Play

IN MIZZOURA 1919 d: Hugh Ford. USA., *In Mizzoura*, Augustus Thomas, Chicago 1893, Play

In Name Der Menschlichkeit *see* DER PROZESS (1948).

IN NAME ONLY 1939 d: John Cromwell. USA., *Memory of Love*, Bessie Breuer, New York 1934, Novel

IN NAMEN DER UNSCHULD 1997 d: Andreas Kleinert. GRM., *In Namen Der Unschuld*, Dorothea Kleine, Novel

IN NOME DELLA LEGGE 1949 d: Pietro Germi. ITL., *Piccola Pretura*, G. G. Lo Schiavo, Novel

In Old California *see* ROBIN HOOD OF EL DORADO (1936).

In Old Heidelberg see OLD HEIDELBERG (1915).

IN OLD KENTUCKY 1919 d: Marshall Neilan, Alfred E. Green. USA., *In Old Kentucky*, Charles T. Dazey, Pittsburgh 1893, Play

IN OLD KENTUCKY 1927 d: John M. Stahl. USA., *In Old Kentucky*, Charles T. Dazey, Pittsburgh 1893, Play

IN OLD KENTUCKY 1935 d: George Marshall. USA., *In Old Kentucky*, Charles T. Dazey, Pittsburgh 1893, Play

In Old Louisiana see LAZY RIVER (1934).

In Old New York see LITTLE OLD NEW YORK (1940).

In Old Oklahoma see WAR OF THE WILDCATS (1943).

In Onion There Is Strength see PRODIGAL JACK SPURLOCK (1918).

In Pieno Sole see PLEIN SOLEIL (1960).

In Praise of James Carabine see BLARNEY (1926).

IN PRAISE OF OLDER WOMEN 1978 d: George Kaczender. CND., *In Praise of Older Women*, Stephen Vizinczey, Novel

In Praise of Older Women see EN BRAZOS DE LA MUJER MADURA (1997).

IN PRINCIPIO ERANO LE MUTANDE 1999 d: Anna Negri. ITL., *In Principio Erano le Mutande*, Rossana Campo, Novel

In Rechten Hersteld see ULBO GARVEEMA (1917).

In Rosie's Room see ROSIE THE RIVETER (1944).

IN SEARCH OF A HUSBAND 1915 d: Wilfred Noy. UKN., *Behind the Curtain*, Max Pemberton, Novel

IN SEARCH OF A SINNER 1920 d: David Kirkland. USA., *In Search of a Sinner*, Charlotte Thompson, Play

IN SEARCH OF A THRILL 1923 d: Oscar Apfel. USA., *The Spirit of the Road*, Kate Jordan, Story

IN SEARCH OF A WIFE 1915 d: William Worthington. USA., *In Search of a Wife*, Robert McGowan, Story

IN SEARCH OF ARCADY 1919 d: Bertram Bracken. USA., *In Search of Arcady*, Nina Wilcox Putnam, Garden City, N.Y. 1912, Novel

In Search of Famine see AKALER SANDHANEY (1980).

In Search of Happiness see V POISKACH RADOSTI (1939).

IN SEARCH OF HISTORIC JESUS 1979 d: Henning Schellerup. USA., *In Search of Historic Jesus*, Lee Roddy, Charles E. Sellier Jr., Book

IN SEARCH OF THE CASTAWAYS 1961 d: Robert Stevenson. UKN/USA., *Les Enfants du Capitaine Grant; Voyage Autour du Monde*, Jules Verne, Paris 1867-68, Novel

In Self Defense see PERILOUS WATERS (1948).

IN SILENZIO 1988 d: Luigi Filippo d'Amico. ITL., *In Silenzio*, Luigi Pirandello, 1905, Short Story

IN SLAVERY DAYS 1913 d: Otis Turner. USA., *In Slavery Days*, James Dayton, Story

IN SPITE OF ALL 1915 d: Ashley Miller. USA., *In Spite of All*, Steele MacKaye, Play

In Temptation see V POKUSENI (1938).

IN THE AFTERNOON OF WAR 1981 d: Karl Francis. UKN., *The Mouse and the Woman*, Dylan Thomas, 1936, Short Story

IN THE AISLES OF THE WILD 1912 d: D. W. Griffith. USA., *In the Aisles of the Wild*, Bret Harte, Short Story

IN THE BALANCE 1917 d: Paul Scardon. USA., *The Hillman*, E. Phillips Oppenheim, London 1917, Novel

In the Beginning There Was Underwear see IN PRINCIPIO ERANO LE MUTANDE (1999).

IN THE BISHOP'S CARRIAGE 1913 d: Edwin S. Porter, J. Searle Dawley. USA., *In the Bishop's Carriage*, Miriam Michelson, Indianapolis 1904, Novel

In the Bishop's Garden see SHE COULDN'T HELP IT (1920).

IN THE BLOOD 1923 d: Walter West. UKN., *In the Blood*, Andrew Soutar, Novel

In the Bottom of the Pool see LA ULTIMA SENORA ANDERSON (1970).

In the Carquinez Woods see THE HALF-BREED (1916).

In the Carquinez Woods see TONGUES OF FLAME (1919).

In the Clutches of a Sinful Woman see KAINOVO ZNAMENI (1928).

IN THE COOL OF THE DAY 1963 d: Robert Stevens. UKN/USA., *In the Cool of the Day*, Susan Ertz, New York 1960, Novel

IN THE DAYS OF FANNY 1915 d: Theodore Marston. USA., *In the Days of Fanny*, James Oliver Curwood, Story

IN THE DAYS OF THE SIX NATIONS 1911. USA., *The Last of the Mohicans*, James Fenimore Cooper, Boston 1826, Novel

In the Days of Trafalgar see BLACK-EYED SUSAN (1914).

In the Deep South see THEY WON'T FORGET (1937).

In the Desert see IN DER WUSTE (1986).

In the Desert and in a Wilderness see W PUSTYNI I W PUSZCZY (1972).

In the Devil's Bowl see THE DEVIL'S BOWL (1923).

In the Devil's Garden see ASSAULT (1971).

IN THE DOGHOUSE 1961 d: Darcy Conyers. UKN., *It's a Vet's Life*, Alex Duncan, London 1961, Novel

IN THE FIRELIGHT 1913 d: Thomas Ricketts. USA., *In the Firelight*, Marc Edmund Jones, Poem

IN THE FRENCH STYLE 1963 d: Robert Parrish. USA/FRN., *In the French Style*, Irwin Shaw, 1953, Short Story

IN THE GLOAMING 1997 d: Christopher Reeve. USA., *In the Gloaming*, Alice Elliott Dark, 1993, Short Story

IN THE GOOD OLD SUMMERTIME 1949 d: Robert Z. Leonard. USA., *Illatszertar*, Nikolaus Laszlo, 1936, Play

In the Gorge see NA KLANCU (1971).

In the Green Hills see PRINTRE COLINELE VERZI (1971).

In the Grip of the Sinister One see IM BANNE DES UNHEIMLICHEN (1968).

IN THE HANDS OF THE LAW 1917. USA., William O. H. Hurst, Novel

IN THE HANDS OF THE SPOILERS 1916 d: Leon Bary. UKN., *In the Hands of the Spoilers*, Sydney Paternoster, Novel

IN THE HEART OF A FOOL 1920 d: Allan Dwan. USA., *In the Heart of a Fool*, William Allen White, New York 1918, Novel

IN THE HEAT OF THE NIGHT 1967 d: Norman Jewison. USA., *In the Heat of the Night*, John Dudley Ball, New York 1965, Novel

IN THE HEAT OF THE NIGHT 1988 d: David Hemmings. USA., *In the Heat of the Night*, John Dudley Ball, New York 1965, Novel

In the Heat of the Sun see YANGGUANG CANLAN DE RIZI (1994).

IN THE HOLLOW OF HER HAND 1918 d: Charles Maigne. USA., *The Hollow of Her Hand*, George Barr McCutcheon, New York 1912, Novel

In the Line of Duty 3: Time to Kill see IN THE LINE OF DUTY: THE TWILIGHT MURDERS (1991).

In the Line of Duty: Manhunt in the Dakotas see IN THE LINE OF DUTY: THE TWILIGHT MURDERS (1991).

IN THE LINE OF DUTY: THE TWILIGHT MURDERS 1991 d: Dick Lowry. USA., *Bitter Harvest: Murder in the Heartland*, James Corcoran, Book

In the Little House Below Emauzy see V TOM DOMECKU POD EMAUZY (1933).

In the Little House Under Emauzy see V TOM DOMECKU POD EMAUZY (1933).

In the Mexican Quarter see BORDER CAFE (1937).

In the Name of a Mother see IM NAMEN EINER MUTTER (1960).

In the Name of His Majesty see JMENEM JEHO VELICENSTVA (1928).

IN THE NAME OF LOVE 1925 d: Howard Higgin. USA., *The Lady of Lyons*, Edward George Bulwer Lytton, London 1838, Play

In the Name of Our Motherland see VO IMYA RODINI (1943).

In the Name of the Fatherland see VO IMYA RODINI (1943).

In the Name of the Innocent see IN NAMEN DER UNSCHULD (1997).

In the Name of the Law see IN NOME DELLA LEGGE (1949).

IN THE NEXT ROOM 1930 d: Eddie Cline. USA., *The Mystery of the Boule Cabinet*, Burton Egbert Stevenson, New York 1911, Novel

IN THE NIGHT 1921 d: Frank Richardson. UKN/NTH., *In the Night*, Cyril Harcourt, London 1919, Play

In the Night Watch see VEILLE D'ARMES (1925).

IN THE PALACE OF THE KING 1915 d: Fred E. Wright. USA., *In the Palace of the King; a Love Story of Old Madrid*, F. Marion Crawford, New York 1900, Novel

IN THE PALACE OF THE KING 1923 d: Emmett J. Flynn. USA., *In the Palace of the King; a Love Story of Old Madrid*, F. Marion Crawford, New York 1900, Novel

IN THE RANKS 1914 d: Percy Nash. UKN., *In the Ranks*, Henry Pettitt, George R. Sims, London 1883, Play

In the Realm of the Silver Lion see IM REICHE DES SILBERNEN LOWEN (1965).

IN THE RED 1998 d: Marcus Mortimer. UKN., *In the Red*, Mark Tavener, Novel

In the Red of Morning see ZA RANNICH CERVANKU (1934).

IN THE SHADOW 1915 d: Harry Handworth. USA., *In the Shadow*, John B. Hymer, Novel

IN THE SHADOW OF DEATH 1915 d: Richard Ridgely. USA., *Fate and Pomegranate*, Mary Imlay Taylor, Story

In the Shadow of the Past see TINE ZABUTYKH PREDKIV (1965).

In the Shadows see IN THE SHADOW (1915).

IN THE SIGNAL BOX 1922 d: H. B. Parkinson. UKN., *In the Signal Box*, George R. Sims, Poem

IN THE SOUP 1936 d: Henry Edwards. UKN., *In the Soup*, Ralph R. Lumley, London 1900, Play

In the Summer Place see NA LETNIM BYTE (1926).

In the Toils of the Temptress see GEORGE BARNWELL THE LONDON APPRENTICE (1913).

In the Torrid Wind see CON EL VIENTO SOLANO (1968).

In the Town of "S" see V GORODE "S" (1966).

In the Ukrainian Steppes see V STEPJAH UKRAINY (1952).

In the Valley of the Giants see THE VALLEY OF THE GIANTS (1919).

IN THE WAKE OF A STRANGER 1959 d: David Eady. UKN., *In the Wake of a Stranger*, Ian Stuart Black, Novel

In the Wild Mountains see YE SHAN (1985).

IN THE WINTER DARK 1998 d: James Bogle. ASL., *In the Winter Dark*, Tim Winton, Novel

In the Woods see RASHOMON (1950).

IN THIS HOUSE OF BREDE 1975 d: George Schaefer. UKN/USA., *In This House of Brede*, Rumer Godden, Novel

IN THIS OUR LIFE 1942 d: John Huston. USA., *In This Our Life*, Ellen Glasgow, 1941, Novel

In Trouble With Eve see TROUBLE WITH EVE (1960).

In Two Minds see DUVIDHA (1973).

In Walked Eve see TROUBLE WITH EVE (1960).

IN WALKED MARY 1920 d: George Archainbaud. USA., *Liza Ann*, Oliver D. Bailey, Play

Ina Kahr's Confession see DAS BEKENNTNIS DER INA KAHR (1954).

INADMISSIBLE EVIDENCE 1968 d: Anthony Page. UKN., *Inadmissible Evidence*, John Osborne, London 1964, Play

INAINTE DE TACERE 1979 d: Alexa Visarion. RMN., *In Vreme de Razboi*, Ion Luca Caragiale, 1898-99, Short Story

Inassouvie, L' see UN AMORE A ROMA (1960).

INAZUMA 1952 d: Mikio Naruse. JPN., *Inazuma*, Fumiko Hayashi, 1935, Novel

INAZUMA 1967 d: Hideo ObA. JPN., *Inazuma*, Fumiko Hayashi, 1935, Novel

INCANTESIMO 1919 d: Ugo Gracci. ITL., *L' Enchantement*, Henry Bataille, 1900, Play

Incantesimo d'Amore see DULCINEA (1962).

Incendiary's Daughter, The see PALICOVA DCERA (1923).

Incendiary's Daughter, The see PALICOVA DCERA (1941).

INCENSE FOR THE DAMNED 1970 d: Robert Hartford-Davis. UKN., *Doctors Wear Scarlet*, Simon Raven, Novel

Inchiesta Su un Delitto Della Polizia see LES ASSASSINS DE L'ORDRE (1970).

INCIDENT AT MIDNIGHT 1963 d: Norman Harrison. UKN., Edgar Wallace, Short Story

INCIDENT IN SAN FRANCISCO 1970 d: Don Medford. USA., *Incident at 125th St.*, J. E. Brown, Story

INCIDENT, THE 1967 d: Larry Peerce. USA., *Ride With Terror*, Nicholas Baehr, 1963, Play

Incinerator of Cadavers *see* SPALOVAC MRTVOL (1968).

Incognito from St. Petersburg, The *see* INKOGNITO IZ PETERBURGA (1977).

INCOMPARABLE BELLAIRS, THE 1914 d: Harold Shaw. UKN., *The Bath Comedy*, Agnes Castle, Egerton Castle, 1900, Novel

Incomparable Mistress Bellairs, The *see* THE INCOMPARABLE BELLAIRS (1914).

INCOMPRESO 1966 d: Luigi Comencini. ITL., *Incompreso*, Florence Montgomery, Novel

INCONNUE, L' 1922 d: Charles Maudru. FRN., *L' Inconnue*, Jack Eden, Short Story

INCONNUS DANS LA MAISON, LES 1941 d: Henri Decoin. FRN., *Les Inconnus Dans la maison*, Georges Simenon, Paris 1940, Novel

INCONSTANTE, L' 1931 d: Andre Rigaud, Hans Behrendt. FRN., *L' Inconstante*, Wilhelm Speyer, Novel

INCORRIGIBLE DUKANE, THE 1915 d: James Durkin. USA., *The Incorrigible Dukane*, George Clifford Shedd, Play

INCORRIGIBLE, L' 1975 d: Philippe de BrocA. FRN., *L' Incorrigible*, Alex Vaoux, Novel

Incorrigible One, The *see* AKUTARO (1963).

INCREDIBLE JOURNEY, THE 1963 d: Fletcher Markle. USA., *The Incredible Journey*, Sheila Burnford, Boston 1961, Novel

INCREDIBLE MR. LIMPET, THE 1964 d: Arthur Lubin. USA., *Mr. Limpet*, Theodore Pratt, New York 1942, Novel

INCREDIBLE SHRINKING MAN, THE 1957 d: Jack Arnold. USA., *The Shrinking Man*, Richard Matheson, Novel

INCREDIBLE SHRINKING WOMAN, THE 1981 d: Joel Schumacher. USA., *The Shrinking Man*, Richard Matheson, Novel

INCREVABLE, L' 1959 d: Jean Boyer. FRN., *A la Belle Sirene*, Robert Goffin, Novel

Incubo *see* LA PAURA (1954).

INCUBUS 1981 d: John Hough. CND., *Incubus*, Ray Russell, Novel

Incubus, The *see* HER HUSBAND'S FRIEND (1920).

Incubus, The *see* INCUBUS (1981).

Indagine Su un Para Accusato Di Omicida *see* LE DERNIER SAUT (1969).

Indecent *see* UNHOLY LOVE (1932).

INDECENT OBSESSION, AN 1985 d: Lex Marinos. ASL., *An Indecent Obsession*, Colleen McCullough, Novel

INDECENT PROPOSAL 1993 d: Adrian Lyne. USA., *Indecent Proposal*, Jack Engelhard, Novel

INDEKS 1977 d: Janusz Kijowski. PLN., Andrzej Pastuszek, Story

INDES NOIRES, LES 1917. FRN., *Les Indes Noires*, Jules Verne, Novel

INDESTRUCTIBLE WIFE, THE 1919 d: Charles Maigne. USA., *The Indestructible Wife*, Fanny Hatton, Frederic Hatton, New York 1918, Play

Index *see* INDEKS (1977).

Indian Love Call *see* ROSE-MARIE (1936).

INDIAN LOVE LYRICS, THE 1923 d: Sinclair Hill. UKN., *The Garden of Karma*, Laurence Hope, Poem

Indian Nocturne *see* NOCTURNE INDIEN (1988).

INDIAN PAINT 1967 d: Norman Foster. USA., *Indian Paint*, Glenn Balch, New York 1942, Novel

INDIAN SUMMER OF DRY VALLEY JOHNSON, THE 1917 d: Martin Justice. USA., *The Indian Summer of Dry Valley Johnson*, O. Henry, 1907, Short Story

Indian Tomb, The *see* DAS INDISCHE GRABMAL (1938).

Indian Tomb, The *see* DAS INDISCHE GRABMAL (1959).

INDIANA 1920 d: Umberto FracchiA. ITL., *Indiana*, George Sand, 1831, Novel

INDIANI BA SHEMESH 1981 d: Ram Loevy. ISR., Adam Baruch, Story

Indiani in the Sun *see* INDIANI BA SHEMESH (1981).

INDIANS ARE COMING, THE 1930 d: Henry McRae. USA., *The Great West That Was*, William F. Cody, Book

Indian's Devotion, An *see* AN INDIAN'S DEVOTION ONAWANDA; OR (1909).

INDICT AND CONVICT 1974 d: Boris Sagal. USA., *Indict and Convict*, Bill Davidson, Book

INDIFFERENTI, GLI 1964 d: Francesco Maselli. ITL/FRN., *Gli Indifferenti*, Alberto Moravia, Milan 1929, Novel

INDIOS A NORD-OVEST 1964 d: Luigi de Marchi. ITL., *Odissea Verde*, Luigi de Marchi, Novel

INDISCHE GRABMAL, DAS 1938 d: Richard Eichberg. GRM., *Das Indische Grabmal*, Thea von Harbou, Novel

INDISCHE GRABMAL, DAS 1959 d: Fritz Lang. GRM/ITL/FRN., *Das Indische Grabmal*, Thea von Harbou, Novel

INDISCHE GRABMAL I, DAS 1921 d: Joe May. GRM., *Das Indische Grabmal*, Thea von Harbou, Novel

INDISCHE GRABMAL II, DAS 1921 d: Joe May. GRM., *Das Indische Grabmal*, Thea von Harbou, Novel

INDISCREET 1958 d: Stanley Donen. UKN/USA., *Kind Sir*, Norman Krasna, New York 1953, Play

INDISCRETION 1915 d: Edgar Jones. USA., *The Official Introducer*, Mary Rider Mechtold, Story

Indiscretion *see* STAZIONE TERMINI (1953).

Indiscretions of an American Wife *see* STAZIONE TERMINI (1953).

INDISKRETE FRAU, DIE 1927 d: Carl Boese. GRM., *Der Kopfpreis*, Friedrich Raff, Short Story

Indomabile Angelica, L' *see* INDOMPTABLE ANGELIQUE (1967).

INDOMPTABLE ANGELIQUE 1967 d: Bernard Borderie. FRN/ITL/GRM., *Indomptable Angelique*, Anne Golon, Serge Golon, Novel

INDOOR GAMES NEAR NEWBURY 1976 d: Chris Clough. UKN., *Indoor Games Near Newbury*, John Betjeman, 1948, Verse

INDRA SABHA 1932 d: J. J. Madan. IND., *Indrasabha*, Sayed Aga Hasan Amanat, 1853, Play

Indrasabha *see* INDRA SABHA (1932).

INDULTO, EL 1960 d: Jose Luis Saenz de HerediA. SPN., *El Indulto*, Emilia Pardo Bazan, 1885, Short Story

INEVITABLE MONSIEUR DUBOIS, L' 1943 d: Pierre Billon. FRN., *Metier de Femme*, Andre-Paul Antoine, Play

INEZ FROM HOLLYWOOD 1924 d: Alfred E. Green. USA., *The Worst Woman in Hollywood*, Adela Rogers St. Johns, 1924, Short Story

Infamous *see* THE CHILDREN'S HOUR (1961).

INFAMOUS MISS REVELL, THE 1921 d: Dallas M. Fitzgerald. USA., *The Infamous Miss Revell*, W. Carey Wonderly, Story

INFANTE A LA ROSE, L' 1921 d: Henry Houry. FRN., *L' Infante a la Rose*, Gabrielle Reval, Novel

INFANZIA, VOCAZIONE E PRIMA ESPERIENZE DI GIACOMO CASANOVA, VENEZIANO 1969 d: Luigi Comencini. ITL., *Memoires de Jacques Casanova de Seingalt*, Giacomo Casanova, 1826-38, Autobiography

INFATUATION 1915 d: Harry Pollard. USA., *Infatuation*, Lloyd Osbourne, Indianapolis 1909, Novel

INFATUATION 1925 d: Irving Cummings. USA., *Caesar's Wife*, W. Somerset Maugham, London 1919, Play

INFATUATION 1930 d: Sasha Geneen. UKN., *The Call*, Julian Frank, Play

INFELICE 1915 d: Fred Paul, L. C. MacBean. UKN., *Infelice*, Augusta Jane Evans, Novel

INFERIOR SEX, THE 1920 d: Joseph Henabery. USA., *The Inferior Sex*, Frank Slayton, New York 1910, Play

INFERMIERE DI TATA, L' 1916 d: Leopoldo Carlucci. ITL., *Cuore*, Edmondo de Amicis, 1886, Short Story

Infernal Idol, The *see* CRAZE (1973).

INFERNAL MACHINE 1933 d: Marcel Varnel. USA., *Die Hollen Maschine*, Carl Sloboda, 1928, Novel

Infernal Trio, The *see* TRIO INFERNAL (1974).

Inferno Dantesco, L' *see* L' INFERNO (1911).

INFERNO, L' 1911 d: Adolfo Padovan, Francesco Bertolini. ITL., *La Divina Commedia*, Dante Alighieri, 1310, Verse

INFERNO, L' 1911 d: Giuseppe Berardi, Arturo Busnengo. ITL., *La Divina Commedia*, Dante Alighieri, 1310, Verse

INFERNO, L' 1914. ITL., *L' Inferno*, Franco Liberati, Play

Infidelity *see* THE CLEMENCEAU CASE (1915).

Infidelity *see* DR. RAMEAU (1915).

Infidelity *see* L' AMANT DE CINQ JOURS (1960).

Infierno de Los Celos, El *see* CELOS (1946).

INFINITY 1996 d: Matthew Broderick. USA., *Surely You're Joking Mr. Feynman?*, Richard Feynman, Autobiography

INFORMANT, THE 1997 d: Jim McBride. IRL/USA., *Field of Blood*, Gerald Seymour, Novel

INFORMATION RECEIVED 1961 d: Robert Lynn. UKN., *Information Received*, Berkeley Mather, Novel

INFORMER, THE 1929 d: Arthur Robison. UKN., *The Informer*, Liam O'Flaherty, London 1925, Novel

INFORMER, THE 1935 d: John Ford. USA., *The Informer*, Liam O'Flaherty, London 1925, Novel

INFORMERS, THE 1963 d: Ken Annakin. UKN., *Death of a Snout*, Douglas Warner, London 1961, Novel

Infortunes de la Vertu, Les *see* MARQUIS DE SADE: JUSTINE (1968).

Inganno, L' *see* ROBERTO BURAT (1920).

Ingegerd Bremssen Case, The *see* FALLET INGEGERD BREMSSEN (1942).

INGEN MANS KVINNA 1953 d: Lars-Eric Kjellgren. SWD., *Ingen Mans Kvinna*, Bernhard Nordh, Novel

INGEN MORGONDAG 1957 d: Arne Mattsson. SWD., *Ek Koskaan Huomispaivaa*, Mika Waltari, 1942, Novel

INGENJOR ANDREES LUFTFARD 1982 d: Jan Troell. SWD/NRW/GRM., *Ingenjor Andrees Luftfard*, Olof Sundman, Novel

INGENU, L' 1971 d: Norbert Carbonnaux. FRN., *L' Ingenu*, Francois-Marie Arouet de Voltaire, 1767, Short Story

Ingenue Libertine, L' *see* MINNE L'INGENUE LIBERTINE (1950).

INGENUO, L' 1921 d: Giorgio Ricci. ITL., *Candide*, Francois-Marie Arouet de Voltaire, 1759, Short Story

INGHITITORUL DE SABIL 1982 d: Alexa Visarion. RMN., *Moartea Inghititorului de Sabii*, Alexandru Sahia, 1934, Short Story

INGLES DE LOS GUESOS, EL 1940 d: Carlos Hugo Christensen. ARG., *El Ingles de Los Guesos*, Benito Lynch, 1924, Novel

INHERIT THE WIND 1960 d: Stanley Kramer. USA., *Inherit the Wind*, Jerome Lawrence, Robert E. Lee, New York 1955, Play

INHERIT THE WIND 1988 d: David Greene. USA., *Inherit the Wind*, Jerome Lawrence, Robert E. Lee, New York 1955, Play

INHERIT THE WIND 1999 d: Daniel Petrie. USA., *Inherit the Wind*, Jerome Lawrence, Robert E. Lee, New York 1955, Play

Inheritance of the Prugger Estate, The *see* DAS ERBE VOM PRUGGERHOF (1956).

Inheritance, The *see* UNCLE SILAS (1947).

Inheritance, The *see* A HERANCA (1970).

Inheritance, The *see* L' EREDITA FERRAMONTI (1976).

INHERITED PASSIONS 1916 d: G. P. Hamilton. USA., *The Big Western Hat*, Jack Wolf, Story

Inheritors, The *see* THE GAIETY GIRL (1924).

Inheritors, The *see* L' EREDITA FERRAMONTI (1976).

Initiation a la Mort *see* LES MAGICIENS (1975).

INKOGNITO IZ PETERBURGA 1977 d: Leonid Gaidai. USS., *Revizor*, Nikolay Gogol, 1836, Play

Inn Among the Hills, The *see* HANUL DINTRE DEALURI (1988).

Inn at Spessart, The *see* DAS WIRTSHAUS IM SPESSART (1958).

Inn in the Hills, The *see* HANUL DINTRE DEALURI (1988).

Inn of Evil *see* INOCHI BONIFURO (1970).

INN OF THE SIXTH HAPPINESS 1958 d: Mark Robson. UKN/USA., *The Small Woman*, Alan Burgess, Book

Inn on Dartmoor, The *see* DAS WIRTSHAUS VON DARTMOOR (1964).

Inn on the Lahn, The *see* DIE WIRTIN AN DER LAHN (1955).

Inn on the River, The *see* DAS GASTHAUS AN DER THEMSE (1962).

INNAMORATA, L' 1920 d: Gennaro Righelli. ITL., *L' Orizzontale*, Augusto Genina, Novel

Innamorato Di un Giorno, L' *see* L' AMANTE DI UN GIORNO (1907).

INTERLUDE 1957 d: Douglas Sirk. USA., *Serenade*, James M. Cain, 1937, Novel

INTERLUDE 1967 d: Kevin Billington. UKN., *Serenade*, James M. Cain, 1937, Novel

International Ball see BALL DER NATIONEN (1954).

International Counterfeiters see DIE SPUR FUHRT NACH BERLIN (1952).

INTERNATIONAL CRIME 1938 d: Charles Lamont. USA., *The Fox Hound*, Maxwell Grant, Short Story

International Spy see THE SPY RING (1938).

INTERNATIONAL SQUADRON 1941 d: Lothar Mendes. USA., *Ceiling Zero*, Frank Wead, New York 1935, Play

INTERNATIONAL VELVET 1978 d: Bryan Forbes. UKN., *National Velvet*, Edith Bagnold, 1935, Novel

INTERNES CAN'T TAKE MONEY 1937 d: Alfred Santell. USA., *Internes Can't Take Money*, Max Brand, 1936, Story

INTERNO BERLINESE 1985 d: Liliana Cavani. ITL./GRM., *Manji*, Junichiro Tanizaki, 1930, Novel

INTERNO DI UN CONVENTO 1977 d: Walerian Borowczyk. ITL., *Promenades Dans Rome*, Stendhal, 1829, Novel

INTERNS, THE 1962 d: David Swift. USA., *The Interns*, Richard Frede, New York 1960, Novel

INTERPOL 1957 d: John Gilling. UKN., *Interpol*, A. J. Forrest, Book

Interpreter, The see BEFORE WINTER COMES (1969).

Interrupted Honeymoon, An see HOMICIDE FOR THREE (1948).

INTERRUPTED HONEYMOON, THE 1936 d: Leslie Hiscott. UKN., *Die Vertagte Hochzeitsnacht*, Franz Robert Arnold, Ernst Bach, Play

Interrupted Journey see THE UFO INCIDENT (1975).

INTERRUPTED MELODY 1955 d: Curtis Bernhardt. USA., *Interrupted Melody*, Marjorie Lawrence, Autobiography

Interrupted Wedding, The see THE LADY FROM HELL (1926).

Intimate see STRANGERS IN LOVE (1932).

Intimate Lightning see INTIMNI OSVETLENI (1965).

INTIMATE RELATIONS 1937 d: Clayton Hutton. UKN., *Intimate Relations*, C. Stafford Dickens, 1932, Play

INTIMATE RELATIONS 1953 d: Charles H. Frank. UKN., *Les Parents Terribles*, Jean Cocteau, 1938, Play

Intimate Story, An see SIPUR INTIMI (1981).

INTIMATE STRANGER, THE 1956 d: Joseph Losey. UKN., *Pay the Piper*, Peter Howard, Novel

Intimate Strangers see BETWEEN FRIENDS (1983).

Intimidation, The see BOCKSHORN (1983).

INTIMNI OSVETLENI 1965 d: Ivan Passer. CZC., Bohumil Hrabal, Story

INTINIREA DIN PAMINTURI 1983 d: Dumitru Dinulescu. RMN., *Intinirea Din Paminturi*, Marin Preda, 1948, Short Story

INTO HER KINGDOM 1926 d: Svend Gade. USA., *Into Her Kingdom*, Ruth Comfort Mitchell, 1925, Short Story

INTO NO MAN'S LAND 1928 d: Cliff Wheeler. USA., *You're in the Army Now*, Bennett Southard, Elsie Werner, Story

INTO THE BLUE 1998 d: Jack Gold. UKN., *Into the Blue*, Robert Goddard, Novel

Into the Crimson West see PRAIRIE SCHOONERS (1940).

Into the Darkness see SOTTO IL VESTITO NIENTE (1985).

Into the Genteel State of Life see DO PANSKEHO STAVU (1925).

Into the Light see THINGS MEN DO (1920).

INTO THE PRIMITIVE 1916 d: Thomas N. Heffron. USA., *Into the Primitive*, Robert Ames Bennet, Chicago 1908, Novel

INTO THE WEST 1992 d: Mike Newell. IRL., *Into the West*, Michael Pearce, Short Story

INTOARCEREA DIN IAD 1984 d: Nicolae Margineanu. RMN., *Jandarmul*, Ion Agarbiceanu, 1941, Short Story

INTOARCEREA VLASINILOR 1983 d: Mircea Dragan. RMN., *Intoarcerea Vlasinilor*, Ioana Postelnicu, 1979, Novel

INTOCCABILI, GLI 1969 d: Giuliano Montaldo. ITL./USA., *Candyleg*, Ovid Demaris, New York 1961, Novel

Intorbidotrice, L' see IL COLONNELLO BRIDEAU (1917).

INTRE OGLINZI PARALELE 1978 d: Mircea Veroiu. RMN., *Ultima Noapte de Dragoste Intiia Noapte de Razbol*, Camil Petrescu, 1930, Novel

Intrepid Fox, The see VUK (1982).

INTRIGANTE, L' 1939 d: Emile Couzinet. FRN., *Troches Et Cie*, Gaston Rullier, Play

Intrigo a Parigi see MONSIEUR (1964).

INTRIGO, L' 1964 d: Vittorio Sala, George Marshall. ITL./FRN., *Dark Purpose*, Doris Hume, New York 1960, Novel

Intrigue and Love see KABALE UND LIEBE (1959).

Intringer, Der see IN THE NIGHT (1921).

INTRUDER IN THE DUST 1949 d: Clarence Brown. USA., *Intruder in the Dust*, William Faulkner, 1948, Novel

Intruder, The see IN THE NIGHT (1921).

Intruder, The see GUILT IS MY SHADOW (1950).

INTRUDER, THE 1953 d: Guy Hamilton. UKN., *Line on Ginger*, Robin Maugham, 1949, Novel

INTRUDER, THE 1961 d: Roger Corman. USA., *The Intruder*, Charles Beaumont, New York 1959, Novel

Intruder, The see L' INNOCENTE (1976).

Intruder, The see A INTRUSA (1979).

Intruders, The see RALLARBLOD (1978).

INTRUSA, A 1979 d: Carlos Hugo Christensen. BRZ/ARG., *La Intrusa*, Jorge Luis Borges, 1952, Short Story

INTRUSA, L' 1955 d: Raffaello Matarazzo. ITL., *La Moglie Del Dottore*, Silvio Zambaldi, 1908, Play

Intrusion, The see A INTRUSA (1979).

INTUNECARE 1985 d: Alexandru Tatos. RMN., *Intunecare*, Cezar Petrescu, 1927-28, Novel

Inugami Family, The see INUGAMI-KE NO ICHIZOKU (1976).

INUGAMI-KE NO ICHIZOKU 1976 d: Kon IchikawA. JPN., *Inugamike No Ichizoku*, Seishi Yokomizo, Novel

INUTILE ATTESA 1919 d: Vittorio Tettoni. ITL., *Inutile Attesa*, Rina Maria Pierazzi, Novel

INVADERS, THE 1913 d: George Melford. USA., *The Invaders*, John Lloyd, Novel

INVANDRARNA 1970 d: Jan Troell. SWD., *Invandrarna*, Vilhelm Moberg, 1952, Novel, *Nybbgarna*, Vilhelm Moberg, 1956, Novel, *Sista Brevet Till Sverige*, Vilhelm Moberg, 1959, Novel

Invasion see NASHESTVIYE (1945).

Invasion 1700 see COL FERRO E COL FUOCO (1962).

Invasion Force see HANGAR 18 (1980).

INVASION OF THE BODY SNATCHERS 1956 d: Don Siegel. USA., *The Body Snatchers*, Jack Finney, 1954, Novel

INVASION OF THE BODY SNATCHERS 1978 d: Philip Kaufman. USA., *The Body Snatchers*, Jack Finney, 1954, Novel

INVASION QUARTET 1961 d: Jay Lewis. UKN., Norman Collins, Story

INVASORI, GLI 1918 d: Gian Paolo Rosmino. ITL., *L' Invasore*, Annie Vivanti, Novel

Inventeur, L' see DER ERFINDER (1981).

INVENTIAMO L'AMORE 1938 d: Camillo Mastrocinque. ITL., *Inventiamo l'Amore*, Giuseppe Achille, Bruno Corra, Play

INVENTING THE ABBOTTS 1997 d: Pat O'Connor. USA., *Inventing the Abbotts*, Sue Miller

Invention for Destruction see VYNALEZ ZKAZY (1958).

Invention of Destruction see VYNALEZ ZKAZY (1958).

Inventor, The see DER ERFINDER (1981).

INVENZIONE DI MOREL, L' 1974 d: Emidio Greco. ITL., *La Invencion Di Morel*, Adolfo Bioy Casares, 1940, Novel

Investigation of Murder, An see THE LAUGHING POLICEMAN (1973).

INVESTMENT, THE 1914 d: Lloyd B. Carleton. USA., *You Never Can Tell*, Clarence Budington Kelland, Story

INVINCIBLE SIX, THE 1970 d: Jean Negulesco. USA/IRN., *The Heroes of Yuka*, Michael Barrett, London 1968, Novel

INVIOLABILE, L' 1919 d: Mario Corte. ITL., *L' Inviolabile*, G. Ulcelli, Novel

INVISIBLE BOND, THE 1920 d: Charles Maigne. USA., *The See-Saw; a Story of Today*, Sophie Kerr, New York 1919, Novel

INVISIBLE BOY, THE 1957 d: Herman Hoffman. USA., Edmund Cooper, Story

Invisible Chain, The see THE CHAIN INVISIBLE (1916).

Invisible Claws of Dr. Mabuse, The see DIE UNSICHTBAREN KRALLEN DES DR. MABUSE (1962).

Invisible Creature see THE HOUSE IN MARSH ROAD (1960).

Invisible Dr. Mabuse, The see DIE UNSICHTBAREN KRALLEN DES DR. MABUSE (1962).

Invisible Horror, The see DIE UNSICHTBAREN KRALLEN DES DR. MABUSE (1962).

Invisible Man see TOMEI NINGEN (1954).

INVISIBLE MAN RETURNS, THE 1940 d: Joe May. USA., *The Invisible Man*, H. G. Wells, London 1897, Novel

INVISIBLE MAN, THE 1933 d: James Whale. USA., *The Invisible Man*, H. G. Wells, London 1897, Novel

INVISIBLE MAN, THE 1975 d: Robert Michael Lewis. USA., *The Invisible Man*, H. G. Wells, London 1897, Novel

INVISIBLE MENACE, THE 1938 d: John Farrow. USA., *Without Warning*, Ralph Spencer Zink, New York 1937, Play

Invisible Power see WASHINGTON MERRY-GO-ROUND (1932).

INVISIBLE STRIPES 1939 d: Lloyd Bacon. USA., *Invisible Stripes*, Lewis E. Lawes, New York 1938, Novel

INVITATION AND AN ATTACK, AN 1915 d: Charles J. Brabin. USA., *Young Lord Stranleigh*, Robert Barr, Story

Invitation to Death see THE WOMAN IN GREEN (1945).

Invitation to Happiness see HOTEL IMPERIAL (1939).

INVITATION TO THE WALTZ 1935 d: Paul Merzbach. UKN., *Invitation to the Waltz*, Holt Marvel, Eric Maschwitz, George Posford, Radio Play

INVITE DU MARDI, L' 1949 d: Jacques Deval. FRN., *La Femme de Ta Jeunesse*, Jacques Deval, Play

IO E LUI 1973 d: Luciano Salce. ITL., *Io E Lui*, Alberto Moravia, Short Story

IO SONO MIA 1978 d: Sofia ScandurrA. ITL/GRM/SPN., *Donna in Guerra*, Dacia Maraini, Novel

IO, SUO PADRE 1939 d: Mario Bonnard. ITL., *Suo Padre Io*, Alba de Cespedes, Novel

Io. Tu. Y. Ella see TU Y ELLA YO (1933).

Ioanide see BIETUL IOANIDE (1979).

IOLANDA, LA FIGLIA DEL CORSARO NERO 1921 d: Vitale de Stefano. ITL., *La Figlia Del Corsaro Nero Iolanda*, Emilio Salgari, Novel

IOLANTA 1963 d: Vladimir Gorikker. USS., *Iolanta*, Modest Tchaikovsky, Petr Tchaikovsky, St. Petersburg 1892, Opera

Ion - the Curse of Property, the Curse of Love see BLESTEMUL IUBIRII ION: BLESTEMUL PAMINTULUI (1979).

ION: BLESTEMUL PAMINTULUI, BLESTEMUL IUBIRII 1979 d: Mircea Muresan. RMN., *Ion*, Liviu Rebreanu, 1920, Novel

Ion: the Lust for the Land, the Lust for Love see BLESTEMUL IUBIRII ION: BLESTEMUL PAMINTULUI (1979).

IPCRESS FILE, THE 1965 d: Sidney J. Furie. UKN., *The Ipcress File*, Len Deighton, London 1962, Novel

Iphigenia see IFIGENIA (1977).

Ipocrita, L' see L' EREDE DI JAGO (1913).

IPPOCAMPO, L' 1943 d: Gian Paolo Rosmino. ITL., *L' Ippocampo*, Sergio Pugliese, Play

Ipu's Death see MOARTEA LUI IPU (1972).

IRACEMA, A VIRGEM DOS LABIOS DE MEL 1979 d: Carlos CoimbrA. BRZ., *Lenda Do Ceara Iracema*, Jose Martiniano de Alencar, 1865, Novel

Irca in a Boarding School see IRCIN ROMANEK II. (1921).

Irca in Her Little Nest see IRCA V HNIZDECKU (1926).

IRCA V HNIZDECKU 1926 d: Vaclav Binovec. CZC., *Irca V Hnizdecku*, Josef Roden, Novel

Irca V Pensionatu see **IRCIN ROMANEK II.** (1921).

Irca's Little Romance I. see **IRCIN ROMANEK I.** (1921).

Irca's Romance see **IRCIN ROMANEK** (1936).

Irca's Romance II. see **IRCIN ROMANEK II.** (1921).

IRCIN ROMANEK 1936 d: Karel Hasler. CZC., *Ircin Romanek*, Josef Roden, Novel

IRCIN ROMANEK I. 1921 d: Vaclav Binovec. CZC., *Ircin Romanek*, Josef Roden, Novel

IRCIN ROMANEK II. 1921 d: Vaclav Binovec. CZC., *Ircin V Pensionate*, Josef Roden, Novel

Irena V Stisci see **IRENE IN NOTEN** (1953).

IRENE 1926 d: Alfred E. Green. USA., *Irene*, James H. Montgomery, New York 1919, Musical Play

IRENE 1940 d: Herbert Wilcox. USA., *Irene*, James H. Montgomery, New York 1919, Musical Play

IRENE IN NOTEN 1953 d: E. W. Emo. AUS/YGS., *Verwirrung Um Inge*, Hans Nuchtern, Novel

Irezumi - Spirit of the Tattoo see **SEKATOMU RAI GISHI** (1982).

Irezumi (Spirit of Tattoo) see **SEKKA TOMURAI ZASHI IREZUMI** (1981).

Irezumi: the Spirit of Tattoo see **SEKKA TOMURAI ZASHI IREZUMI** (1981).

IRIS 1915 d: Cecil M. Hepworth. UKN., *Iris*, Arthur Wing Pinero, London 1901, Play

Iris see **A SLAVE OF VANITY** (1920).

Iris see **IRIS OCH LOJTNANTSHJARTA** (1946).

Iris and the Lieutenant see **IRIS OCH LOJTNANTSHJARTA** (1946).

Iris March see **OUTCAST LADY** (1934).

IRIS OCH LOJTNANTSHJARTA 1946 d: Alf Sjoberg. SWD., *Iris Och Lojtnantsjarta*, Olle Hedberg, 1934, Novel

IRIS PERDUE ET RETROUVEE 1933 d: Louis J. Gasnier. FRN., *Iris Perdue Et Retrouvee*, Pierre Frondaie, Novel

IRISH AND PROUD OF IT 1936 d: Donovan Pedelty. UKN., *Irish and Proud of It*, Dorothea Donn Byrne, Story

IRISH FOR LUCK 1936 d: Arthur Woods. UKN., *Irish for Luck*, L. A. G. Strong, Novel

IRISH HEARTS 1934 d: Brian Desmond Hurst. UKN., *Night Nurse*, Dr. Johnson Abrahams, Novel

IRISH LUCK 1925 d: Victor Heerman. USA., *The Imperfect Imposter*, Norman Venner, New York 1925, Novel

IRISH LUCK 1939 d: Howard Bretherton. USA., *Death Hops the Bells*, Charles Molyneaux Brown, 1938, Short Story

IRISHMAN, THE 1978 d: Donald Crombie. ASL., *The Irishman*, Elizabeth O'Conner, Novel

IRMA LA DOUCE 1963 d: Billy Wilder. USA., *Irma la Douce*, Alexandre Breffort, Paris 1956, Play

Iron Chalice, The see **THE BIG GAMBLE** (1931).

Iron Earth, Copper Sky see **GOK BAKIR YER DEMIR** (1987).

Iron Flood, The see **ZHELYEZNY POTOK** (1967).

Iron Gate, The see **I KANGELOPORTA** (1979).

Iron Heel of the Oligarchy, The see **ZHELEZNAYA PYATA OLIGARKHIJ** (1998).

IRON MAN 1931 d: Tod Browning. USA., *The Iron Man*, William Riley Burnett, New York 1930, Novel

IRON MAN 1951 d: Joseph Pevney. USA., *The Iron Man*, William Riley Burnett, New York 1930, Novel

IRON MASK, THE 1929 d: Allan Dwan. USA., *Le Vicomte de Bragelonne*, Alexandre Dumas (pere), Paris 1847, Novel

IRON MASTER, THE 1914 d: Travers Vale. USA., *Le Maitre de Forges*, Georges Ohnet, Paris 1882, Novel

IRON MASTER, THE 1933 d: Chester M. Franklin. USA., *Le Maitre de Forges*, Georges Ohnet, Paris 1882, Novel

IRON MAZE 1991 d: Hiroaki YoshidA. USA/JPN., *Yabu No Naka*, Ryunosuke Akutagawa, 1922, Short Story

IRON MISTRESS, THE 1952 d: Gordon Douglas. USA., *The Iron Mistress*, Paul I. Wellman, Novel

Iron Prefect, The see **IL PREFETTO DI FERRO** (1977).

Iron Road, The see **BUCKSKIN FRONTIER** (1943).

IRON STAIR, THE 1920 d: F. Martin Thornton. UKN., *The Iron Stair*, Rita, Novel

IRON STAIR, THE 1933 d: Leslie Hiscott. UKN., *The Iron Stair*, Rita, Novel

IRON TRAIL, THE 1921 d: R. William Neill. USA., *The Iron Trail*, Rex Beach, New York 1913, Novel

IRON WOMAN, THE 1916 d: Carl Harbaugh. USA., *The Iron Woman*, Margaret Deland, New York 1911, Novel

Iron Woman, The see **THAT'S MY UNCLE** (1935).

IRONSIDE 1967 d: James Goldstone. USA., Collier Young, Story

IRONWEED 1987 d: Hector Babenco. USA., *Ironweed*, William Kennedy, Novel

IROQUOIS TRAIL, THE 1950 d: Phil Karlson. USA., *The Pathfinder*, James Fenimore Cooper, 1840, Novel

IRRESISTIBLE CATHERINE, L' 1955 d: Andre Pergament. FRN., *L' Irresistible Catherine*, Jean de La Vallieres, Novel

Irrgarten Der Leidenschaft see **THE PLEASURE GARDEN** (1926).

Irrlichter see **DIE LIEBE DER BRUDER ROTT** (1929).

Is Constance Acting Right? see **DASS CONSTANZE SICH RICHTIG VERHALT? FINDEN SIE** (1962).

IS DIVORCE A FAILURE? 1923 d: Wallace Worsley. USA., *All Mine*, Dorian Neve, Play

Is Divorce the Only Answer? see **MUSS MAN SICH GLEICH SCHEIDEN LASSEN?** (1953).

IS LIFE WORTH LIVING? 1921 d: Alan Crosland. USA., *The Open Door*, George Weston, 1921, Short Story

Is Marriage a Failure? see **THE FOOLISH MATRONS** (1921).

IS MATRIMONY A FAILURE? 1922 d: James Cruze. USA., *Die Thur Ins Freis*, Leo Ditrichstein, Berlin 1908, Play

IS MY FACE RED? 1932 d: William A. Seiter. USA., Ben Markson, Allen Rivkin, Play

Is Paris Burning? see **PARIS BRULE-T-IL?** (1966).

IS YOUR HONEYMOON REALLY NECESSARY? 1953 d: Maurice Elvey. UKN., *Is Your Honeymoon Really Necessary?*, E. Vivian Tidmarsh, London 1944, Play

IS ZAT SO? 1927 d: Alfred E. Green. USA., *Is Zat So?*, James Gleason, Richard Taber, New York 1925, Play

ISAAC SINGER'S NIGHTMARE AND MRS. PUPKO'S BEARD 1973 d: Bruce Davidson. USA., *The Beard*, Isaac Bashevis Singer, 1973, Short Story

ISAAK, DER HANDELSJUDE 1912 d: Adolf Gartner. GRM., *Der Weihnachtsabend*, Henrik Wergeland, Poem

Isabelle and Lust see **ISABELLE DEVANT LE DESIR** (1974).

ISABELLE DEVANT LE DESIR 1974 d: Jean-Pierre Berckmans. FRN/BLG., *La Delice*, Maud Frere, Novel

ISADORA 1968 d: Karel Reisz. UKN., *My Life*, Isadora Duncan, New York 1927, Autobiography

ISHI, THE LAST OF HIS TRIBE 1978 d: Robert Ellis Miller. USA., *Ishi in Two Worlds*, Theodora Kroeber Quinn, Book

ISHINAKA SENSEI GYOJOKI 1950 d: Mikio Naruse. JPN., *Ishinaka-Sensei Gyojuki*, Yojiro Ishizaka, 1948-49, Novel

ISLA DEL DIABLO, LA 1995 d: Piquer Simon. SPN., *L' Isla Del Diablo*, Vincent Mulberry

Isla Del Tesoro, La see **TREASURE ISLAND** (1972).

Isla Del Tesoro, La see **L' ISOLA DEL TESORO** (1973).

Isla Misteriosa, La see **L' ILE MYSTERIEUSE** (1973).

ISLAND AT THE TOP OF THE WORLD, THE 1974 d: Robert Stevenson. USA., *The Island at the Top of the World*, Ian Cameron, Novel

ISLAND IN THE SKY 1953 d: William A. Wellman. USA., *Island in the Sky*, Ernest K. Gann, Novel

ISLAND IN THE SUN 1957 d: Robert Rossen. UKN/USA., *Island in the Sun*, Alec Waugh, 1955, Novel

Island of Adventure, The see **THE LIGHT OF VICTORY** (1919).

Island of Death see **QUIEN PUEDE MATAR A UN NINO?** (1975).

Island of Desire see **SATURDAY ISLAND** (1951).

ISLAND OF DESIRE, THE 1917 d: Otis Turner. USA., *Beyond the Rim*, J. Allen Dunn, 1916, Short Story

ISLAND OF DESPAIR, THE 1926 d: Henry Edwards. UKN., *The Island of Despair*, Margot Neville, Novel

Island of Dr. Moreau, The see **ISLAND OF LOST SOULS** (1933).

ISLAND OF DR. MOREAU, THE 1977 d: Don Taylor. USA., *The Island of Dr. Moreau*, H. G. Wells, London 1896, Novel

ISLAND OF DR. MOREAU, THE 1996 d: John Frankenheimer. USA., *The Island of Dr. Moreau*, H. G. Wells, London 1896, Novel

ISLAND OF INTRIGUE, THE 1919 d: Henry Otto. USA., *The Island of Intrigue*, Isabel Ostrander, New York 1918, Novel

ISLAND OF LOST MEN 1939 d: Kurt Neumann. USA., *Hangman's Whip*, Frank Butler, Norman Reilly Raine, New York 1933, Play

ISLAND OF LOST SOULS 1933 d: Erle C. Kenton. USA., *The Island of Dr. Moreau*, H. G. Wells, London 1896, Novel

ISLAND OF REGENERATION, THE 1915 d: Harry Davenport. USA., *The Island of Regeneration: a Story of What Ought to Be*, Cyrus Townsend Brady, New York 1909, Novel

Island of Shame see **THE YOUNG ONE** (1960).

ISLAND OF SURPRISE, THE 1916 d: Paul Scardon. USA., *The Island of Surprise*, Cyrus Townsend Brady, New York 1915, Novel

ISLAND OF THE BLUE DOLPHINS 1964 d: James B. Clark. USA., *Island of the Blue Dolphins*, Scott O'Dell, Boston 1960, Novel

Island of the Burning Damned see **NIGHT OF THE BIG HEAT** (1967).

Island of the Burning Doomed see **NIGHT OF THE BIG HEAT** (1967).

Island of the Damned see **QUIEN PUEDE MATAR A UN NINO?** (1975).

Island of the Dead see **DIE TOTENINSEL** (1955).

ISLAND ON BIRD STREET, THE 1997 d: Soren Kragh-Jacobsen. DNM/UKN/GRM., *The Island on Bird Street*, Uri Orlev, Book

Island Princess, The see **LA PRINCIPESSA DELLE CANARIE** (1956).

Island Rescue see **APPOINTMENT WITH VENUS** (1951).

ISLAND, THE 1977 d: Robert Fuest. USA., *The Island*, L. P. Hartley, 1948, Short Story

ISLAND, THE 1980 d: Michael Ritchie. USA., *The Island*, Peter Benchley, 1979, Novel

ISLANDS IN THE STREAM 1977 d: Franklin J. Schaffner. USA., *Islands in the Stream*, Ernest Hemingway, 1970, Novel

ISLE OF CONQUEST, THE 1919 d: Edward Jose. USA., *By Right of Conquest*, Arthur Hornblow, New York 1909, Novel

ISLE OF DESTINY, THE 1920 d: Tamar Lane. USA., *The Isle of Destiny*, MacK Arthur, Short Story

ISLE OF ESCAPE 1930 d: Howard Bretherton. USA., *Isle of Escape; a Story of the South Seas*, Jack McLaren, London 1926, Novel

ISLE OF FURY 1936 d: Frank McDonald. USA., *The Narrow Corner*, W. Somerset Maugham, London 1932, Novel

Isle of Fury see **ISLE OF MISSING MEN** (1942).

ISLE OF LIFE, THE 1916 d: Burton George. USA., *Isle of Life; a Romance*, Stephen French Whitman, New York 1913, Novel

ISLE OF LOST SHIPS, THE 1923 d: Maurice Tourneur. USA., *The Isle of Dead Ships*, Crittenden Marriott, Philadelphia 1909, Novel

ISLE OF LOST SHIPS, THE 1929 d: Irvin V. Willat. USA., *The Isle of Dead Ships*, Crittenden Marriott, Philadelphia 1909, Novel

ISLE OF MISSING MEN 1942 d: Richard Oswald. USA., *Isle of Terror*, Ladislaus Fodor, Gina Kaus, Play

ISLE OF RETRIBUTION, THE 1926 d: James P. Hogan. USA., *The Isle of Retribution*, Edison Marshall, Boston 1923, Novel

Isle of Sinners see **DIEU A BESOIN DES HOMMES** (1950).

Isle of Terror see **ISLE OF MISSING MEN** (1942).

ISN'T LIFE WONDERFUL! 1953 d: Harold French. UKN., *Uncle Willie and the Bicycle Shop*, Brock Williams, Novel

ISN'T LIFE WONDERFUL 1924 d: D. W. Griffith. USA., *Isn't Life Wonderful!*, Geoffrey Moss, 1924, Short Story

Isn't One Wife Enough? see **EINE FRAU GENUGT NICHT?** (1958).

ISOBEL 1920 d: Edwin Carewe. USA., *Isobel: a Romance of the Northern Trail*, James Oliver Curwood, Novel

Isobel; Or, the Trail's End *see* ISOBEL (1920).

Isola *see* LA PRINCIPESSA DELLE CANARIE (1956).

ISOLA DEL TESORO, L' 1973 d: Andrea Bianchi. ITL/FRN/SPN., *Treasure Island*, Robert Louis Stevenson, London 1883, Novel

Isola Del Tesoro, L' *see* SPACE ISLAND (1987).

Isola Del Tesoro, La *see* TREASURE ISLAND (1972).

Isola Delle Donne Sole, L' *see* LES POSSEDEES (1955).

Isola Dell'incanto, L' *see* SEI GRANDE! ALESSANDRO (1941).

ISOLA DI ARTURO, L' 1962 d: Damiano Damiani. ITL., *L'Isola Di Arturo*, Elsa Morante, 1957, Novel

Isola Misteriosa E Il Capitano Nemo, L' *see* L'ILE MYSTERIEUSE (1973).

ISPETTORE VARGAS, L' 1940 d: Gianni Franciolini. ITL., *La Sbarra*, Vincenzo Tieri, Play

ISRAEL 1919 d: Andre Antoine. ITL., *Israel*, Henri Bernstein, 1908, Play

IS-SLOTTET 1987 d: Per Blom. NRW., *Is-Slottet*, Tarjei Vesaas, 1963, Novel

ISTEN HOZTA, ORNAGY UR! 1969 d: Zoltan Fabri. HNG., *Totek*, Istvan Orkeny, 1964, Novel

Istid *see* DIE EISZEIT (1975).

Istituto Grimaldi *see* NESSUNO TORNA INDIETRO (1943).

ISTITUTRICE DI SEI BAMBINE, L' 1920 d: Mario Bonnard. ITL., *Histoire de Six Petites Filles*, Lucie Delorme Madrousse, Novel

ISTRUTTORIA E CHIUSA, DIMENTICHI, L' 1971 d: Damiano Damiani. ITL., *Tante Sbarre*, Leros Pittoni, Novel

ISTRUTTORIA, L' 1914 d: Enrico Guazzoni. ITL., *L'Istruttoria*, Paul Henriot, Play

ISZONY 1965 d: Gyorgy Hintsch. HNG., *Iszony*, Laszlo Nemeth, 1947, Novel

IT 1927 d: Clarence Badger, Josef von Sternberg. USA., *It*, Elinor Glyn, Novel

IT 1990 d: Tommy Lee Wallace. USA., *It*, Stephen King, 1986, Novel

IT AIN'T HAY 1943 d: Erle C. Kenton. USA., *Princess O'Hara*, Damon Runyon, 1934, Short Story

IT ALL CAME TRUE 1940 d: Lewis Seiler. USA., *Better Than Life*, Louis Bromfield, 1936, Short Story

IT ALWAYS RAINS ON SUNDAYS 1947 d: Robert Hamer. UKN., *It Always Rains on Sundays*, Arthur la Bern, Novel

IT CAME FROM OUTER SPACE 1953 d: Jack Arnold. USA., *The Meteor*, Ray Bradbury, Short Story

It Comes Up Murder *see* THE HONEY POT (1967).

It Couldn't Happen to a Dog *see* IT SHOULDN'T HAPPEN TO A DOG (1946).

IT HAD TO HAPPEN 1936 d: Roy Del Ruth. USA., *Canavan the Man Who Had His Way*, Rupert Hughes, 1909, Short Story

It Happened All Night *see* L'AFFAIRE D'UNE NUIT (1960).

It Happened at the Inn *see* GOUPI MAINS-ROUGES (1942).

It Happened in Aden *see* C'EST ARRIVE A ADEN (1956).

It Happened in Broad Daylight *see* ES GESCHAH AM HELLICHTEN TAG (1958).

IT HAPPENED IN PARIS 1932 d: M. J. Weisfeldt. USA., *Les Deux Orphelines*, Eugene Cormon, Adolphe-P. d'Ennery, 1874, Novel

IT HAPPENED IN PARIS 1935 d: Robert Wyler, Carol Reed. UKN., *L'Arpete*, Yves Mirande, Play

It Happened in Paris *see* THE LADY IN QUESTION (1940).

IT HAPPENED IN SPAIN 1935 d: Harry d'Abbadie d'Arrast. UKN/SPN., *El Sombrero de Tres Picos*, Pedro Antonio de Alarcon, 1874, Short Story

It Happened in Tokyo *see* TWENTY PLUS TWO (1961).

IT HAPPENED ONE CHRISTMAS 1977 d: Donald Wrye. USA., *The Greatest Gift*, Philip Van Doren Stern, Short Story

It Happened One Day *see* THIS SIDE OF HEAVEN (1932).

IT HAPPENED ONE NIGHT 1934 d: Frank CaprA. USA., *Night Bus*, Samuel Hopkins Adams, 1933, Short Story

It Happened One Night *see* YOU CAN'T RUN AWAY FROM IT (1956).

It Happened One Summer *see* STATE FAIR (1944).

IT HAPPENED ONE SUNDAY 1944 d: Carl Lamac. UKN., Victor Skutezky, Play

It Happened to One Man *see* GENTLEMAN OF VENTURE (1940).

IT HAPPENED WHILE HE FISHED 1915 d: Horace Davey. USA., *It Happened While He Fished*, Peter B. Kyne, Story

IT HAPPENS EVERY THURSDAY 1953 d: Joseph Pevney. USA., *It Happens Every Thursday*, Jane S. McIlvane, Novel

It Happens in Roma *see* GLI ULTIMI CINQUE MINUTI (1955).

It Hurts Only When I Laugh *see* ONLY WHEN I LAUGH (1981).

IT IS NEVER TOO LATE TO MEND 1913 d: Charles M. Seay. USA., *It Is Never Too Late to Mend*, Charles Reade, 1853, Novel

It Is Not Oranges -But Horses *see* DET ER IKKE APPELSINER -DET ER HESTE (1967).

IT IS THE LAW 1924 d: J. Gordon Edwards. USA., *It Is the Law*, Elmer Rice, Hayden Talbot, New York 1922, Play

IT ISN'T BEING DONE THIS SEASON 1921 d: George L. Sargent. USA., *It Isn't Being Done This Season*, Thomas Edgelow, 1918, Short Story

It Means That to Me *see* ME FAIRE CA A MOI. (1961).

IT MUST BE LOVE 1926 d: Alfred E. Green. USA., *Delicatessen*, Brooke Hanlon, 1925, Short Story

IT PAYS TO ADVERTISE 1919 d: Donald Crisp. USA., *It Pays to Advertise*, Walter Hackett, Roi Cooper Megrue, New York 1914, Play

IT PAYS TO ADVERTISE 1931 d: Frank Tuttle. USA., *It Pays to Advertise*, Walter Hackett, Roi Cooper Megrue, New York 1914, Play

It Rains on Our Love *see* DET REGNAR PA VAR KARLEK (1946).

IT SHOULDN'T HAPPEN TO A DOG 1946 d: Herbert I. Leeds. USA., Edwin Lanham, Serial Story

IT SHOULDN'T HAPPEN TO A VET 1976 d: Eric Till. UKN., James Herriot, Books

It Started at Midnight *see* SCHWEIK'S NEW ADVENTURES (1943).

It Started in Tokyo *see* TWENTY PLUS TWO (1961).

IT TAKES ALL KINDS 1969 d: Eddie Davis. ASL/USA., *A Girl Like Cathy*, Edward D. Hoch, Short Story

It Takes All Kinds, to Catch a Thief *see* IT TAKES ALL KINDS (1969).

It Was I *see* SONO STATO IO! (1937).

It Will Dawn Again *see* PHIR SUBAH HOGI (1958).

It Will Pass Also *see* I TO CE PROCI (1985).

It Won't Rub Off, Baby! *see* BITTER SWEET LOVE (1967).

Italian Gendarme, The *see* CARABINIERE (1913).

ITALIAN JOB, THE 1969 d: Peter Collinson. UKN., *The Italian Job*, Troy Kennedy Martin, Novel

Italian Straw Hat, The *see* UN CHAPEAU DE PAILLE D'ITALIE (1927).

Italian Women and Love *see* LE ITALIANE E L'AMORE (1961).

ITALIANE E L'AMORE, LE 1961 d: Florestano Vancini, Carlo Musso. ITL., *Le Italiane Si Confessano*, Gabriella Parca, Book

ITALIENREISE - LIEBE INBEGRIFFEN 1958 d: Wolfgang Becker. GRM., *Italienreise - Liebe Inbegriffen*, Barbara Noack, Novel

Itch, The *see* KUMPEL LASS JUCKEN (1972).

ITCHING PALMS 1923 d: James W. Horne. USA., *When Jerry Comes Home*, Roy Briant, Play

ITHELE NA YINI VASILIAS 1967 d: Angelos Theodoropoulos. GRC., *Hamlet*, William Shakespeare, c1601, Play

IT'S A 2'6" ABOVE THE GROUND WORLD 1972 d: Ralph Thomas. UKN., *It's a 2'6" Above the Ground World*, Kevin Laffan, Play

IT'S A BET 1935 d: Alexander Esway. UKN., *Hide and I'll Find You*, Marcus McGill, Novel

IT'S A BOY 1933 d: Tim Whelan. UKN., *It's a Boy*, Franz Robert Arnold, Ernst Bach, New York 1922, Play

IT'S A DOG'S LIFE 1955 d: Herman Hoffman. USA., *The Bar Sinister*, Richard Harding Davis, Novel

IT'S A GIFT 1934 d: Norman Z. McLeod. USA., *The Comic Supplement (of American Life)*, Joseph Patrick McEvoy, Washington D.C. 1925, Play

IT'S A GREAT LIFE 1920 d: E. Mason Hopper. USA., *Empire Builders*, Mary Roberts Rinehart, 1916, Short Story

It's a Great Life *see* TOLLER HECHT AUF KRUMMEN TOUREN (1961).

IT'S A SMALL WORLD 1935 d: Irving Cummings. USA., *Highway Robbery*, Albert Treynor, 1934, Short Story

IT'S A WISE CHILD 1931 d: Robert Z. Leonard. USA., *It's a Wise Child*, Laurence E. Johnson, New York 1929, Play

IT'S A WONDERFUL LIFE 1946 d: Frank CaprA. USA., *The Greatest Gift*, Philip Van Doren Stern, Short Story

It's Adam's Fault *see* C'EST LA FAUTE D'ADAM (1957).

It's All Adam's Fault *see* C'EST LA FAUTE D'ADAM (1957).

It's All Moonshine! *see* MESE HABBAL (1979).

It's All the Wine's Fault *see* SCHULD ALLEIN IST DER WEIN (1949).

It's All Up With Auntie *see* DET ER NAT MED FRU KNUDSEN (1971).

IT'S ALWAYS THE WOMAN 1916 d: Wilfred Noy. UKN., *It's Always the Woman*, Bryant Adair, Play

It's Dangerous to Lean Out of the Window *see* ES PELIGROSO ASOMARSE AL EXTERIOR (1945).

It's for a Good Cause *see* C'EST POUR LA BONNE CAUSE (1997).

IT'S GOOD TO BE ALIVE 1974 d: Michael Landon. USA., *It's Good to Be Alive*, Roy Campanella, Book

IT'S GREAT TO BE ALIVE 1933 d: Alfred L. Werker. USA., *The Last Man on Earth*, John D. Swain, 1923, Novel

It's Hard to Be a Father *see* VATER SEIN DAGEGEN SEHR (1957).

It's Hard to Be God *see* EIN GOTT ZU SEIN ES IST NICHT LEICHT (1988).

It's Hot in Hell *see* UN SINGE EN HIVER (1962).

IT'S IN THE BAG 1945 d: Richard Wallace. USA., *Dvenadtsat Stulyev*, Ilya Ilf, Evgeny Petrov, Moscow 1928, Novel

IT'S IN THE BLOOD 1938 d: Gene Gerrard. UKN., *The Big Picture*, David Whitelaw, Novel

It's Magic *see* ROMANCE ON THE HIGH SEAS (1948).

It's Me *see* JIUSHI WO (1928).

It's My Model *see* DET AR MIN MODELL (1946).

IT'S NEVER TOO LATE 1956 d: Michael McCarthy. UKN., *It's Never Too Late*, Felicity Douglas, London 1952, Play

IT'S NEVER TOO LATE TO MEND 1917 d: Dave Aylott. UKN., *It Is Never Too Late to Mend*, Charles Reade, 1853, Novel

IT'S NEVER TOO LATE TO MEND 1922 d: George Wynn. UKN., *It Is Never Too Late to Mend*, Charles Reade, 1853, Novel

IT'S NEVER TOO LATE TO MEND 1937 d: David MacDonald. UKN., *It Is Never Too Late to Mend*, Charles Reade, 1853, Novel

It's Not Easy to Get Married *see* POP CIRA I POP SPIRA (1965).

It's Now Or Never *see* POOR GIRL RICH MAN (1938).

It's Spring Again *see* ZENOBIA (1939).

IT'S THE OLD ARMY GAME 1926 d: A. Edward Sutherland. USA., *It's the Old Army Game*, Joseph Patrick McEvoy, Story

IT'S TOUGH TO BE FAMOUS 1932 d: Alfred E. Green. USA., *The Goldfish Bowl*, Mary McCall Jr., Boston 1932, Novel

IT'S YOU I WANT 1936 d: Ralph Ince. UKN., *It's You I Want*, Maurice Braddell, London 1933, Play

It's Your Turn, Laura *see* LAURA CADIEUX C'T'A TON TOUR (1998).

It's Your Turn, Laura Cadieux *see* LAURA CADIEUX C'T'A TON TOUR (1998).

IUBELEI 1944 d: Vladimir Petrov. USS., *Iubelei*, Anton Chekhov, 1891, Novel

IVAN KONDAREV 1973 d: Nicolai Korabov. BUL., *Ivan Kondarev*, Emilian Stanev, 1958-64, Novel

IVAN SHISHMAN 1969 d: Yuri Arnaudov. BUL., *Tsar Ivan Shishman*, Kamen Zidarov, 1962, Play

IVANHOE 1913 d: Leedham Bantock. UKN., *Ivanhoe*, Sir Walter Scott, Edinburgh 1819, Novel

IVANHOE 1913 d: Herbert Brenon. UKN/USA., *Ivanhoe*, Sir Walter Scott, Edinburgh 1819, Novel

IVANHOE 1952 d: Richard Thorpe. UKN/USA., *Ivanhoe*, Sir Walter Scott, Edinburgh 1819, Novel

IVANHOE 1982 d: Douglas Camfield. UKN., *Ivanhoe*, Sir Walter Scott, Edinburgh 1819, Novel

IVANHOE 1996 d: Stuart Orme. UKN., *Ivanhoe*, Sir Walter Scott, Edinburgh 1819, Novel

IVANOVO DETSTVO 1962 d: Andrei Tarkovsky. USS., *Ivan*, Vladimir Osipovich Bogomolov, Moscow 1959, Short Story

Ivan's Childhood see **IVANOVO DETSTVO** (1962).

I'VE ALWAYS LOVED YOU 1946 d: Frank Borzage. USA., *Concerto*, Borden Chase, Story

I've Got Two Mummies and Two Daddies see **IMAM DVIJE MAME I DVA TATE** (1968).

Ivo see **FLUCHTVERSUCH** (1976).

IVORY SNUFF BOX, THE 1915 d: Maurice Tourneur. USA., *The Ivory Snuff Box*, Frederic Arnold Kummer, New York 1912, Novel

IVY 1947 d: Sam Wood. USA., *Ivy*, Mrs. Belloc Lowndes, Novel

IWASHIGUMO 1958 d: Mikio Naruse. JPN., *Iwasigumo*, Den Wada, Novel

Ixe 13 see **IXE-13** (1971).

IXE-13 1971 d: Jacques Godbout. CND., *Ixe-13*, Pierre Saurel, Novel

IZBAVITELJ 1977 d: Krsto Papic. YGS., *Izbavitelj*, Aleksandr Grin, Short Story

Izu Dancer see **IZU NO ODORIKO** (1967).

Izu Dancer, The see **IZU NO ODORIKO** (1933).

IZU NO ODORIKO 1933 d: Heinosuke Gosho. JPN., *Izu No Odoriko*, Yasunari Kawabata, 1925, Short Story

IZU NO ODORIKO 1960 d: Yoshiro Kawazu. JPN., *Izu No Odoriko*, Yasunari Kawabata, 1925, Short Story

IZU NO ODORIKO 1967 d: Hideo Onchi. JPN., *Izu No Odoriko*, Yasunari Kawabata, 1925, Short Story

IZUMI 1956 d: Masaki Kobayashi. JPN., *Izumi*, Kunio Kishida, 1939, Novel

J 3, LES 1945 d: Roger Richebe. FRN., *Les J 3*, Roger Ferdinand, Play

Ja, Ja Die Liebe see **DIE VIER GESELLEN** (1938).

JA, JA, DIE LIEBE IN TIROL 1955 d: Geza von Bolvary. GRM., *Kohleisels Tochter*, Hans Kraly, Novel

Ja, So Ein Madchen Mit 16 see **EHESANATORIUM** (1955).

JA, TRUCHLIVY BUH 1969 d: Antonin Kachlik. CZC., *Truchlivy Buh Ja*, Milan Kundera, 1963, Short Story

JAAR VAN DE KREEFT, HET 1975 d: Herbert Curiel. NTH., *Het Jaar Van de Kreeft*, Hugo Claus, 1972, Novel

JABBERWOCKY 1977 d: Terry Gilliam. UKN., *Jabberwocky*, Lewis Carroll, 1872, Verse

JACA LUCERA, LA 1926 d: Luis Baleriola, Pedro Jara Carrillo. SPN., *La Yegua Lucera*, Pedro Jara Carrillo, Poem

JACHT DER SIEBEN SUNDEN, DIE 1928 d: Jacob Fleck, Luise Fleck. GRM., *Die Jacht Der Sieben Sunden*, Paul Rosenhayn, Novel

JACK 1913 d: Andre Liabel. FRN., *Jack*, Alphonse Daudet, Novel

JACK 1925 d: Robert Saidreau. FRN., *Jack*, Alphonse Daudet, Novel

JACK 1977 d: Jan Halldoff. SWD., *Jack*, Ulf Lundell, Novel

Jack and Jenny see **JACK UND JENNY** (1963).

JACK CHANTY 1915 d: Max Figman. USA., *Jack Chanty: a Story of Athabasca*, Hubert Footner, New York 1913, Novel

JACK FRUSCIANTE USCITO DAL GRUPPO 1996 d: Enza Negroni. ITL., *Jack Frusciante E Uscito Dal Gruppo*, Enrico Brizzi, Novel

Jack Frusciante Has Left the Band see **JACK FRUSCIANTE USCITO DAL GRUPPO** (1996).

Jack Frusicante Left the Band see **JACK FRUSCIANTE USCITO DAL GRUPPO** (1996).

Jack Knife Man, The see **THE JACK-KNIFE MAN** (1920).

JACK LONDON 1942 d: Alfred Santell. USA., *The Book of Jack London*, Charmian London, Biography

Jack London Story see **JACK LONDON'S KLONDIKE FEVER** (1979).

JACK LONDON'S KLONDIKE FEVER 1979 d: Peter Carter. CND., *Klondike Fever*, Jack London, Book

JACK O' CLUBS 1924 d: Robert F. Hill. USA., *Jack O' Clubs*, Gerald Beaumont, 1923, Short Story

JACK O' HEARTS 1926 d: David M. Hartford. USA., *Jack in the Pulpit*, Gordon Morris, New York 1925, Play

JACK OF ALL TRADES 1936 d: Jack Hulbert, Robert Stevenson. UKN., *Youth at the Helm*, Paul Vulpius, Play

Jack O'Lantern see **CONDEMNED TO DEATH** (1932).

JACK, SAM AND PETE 1919 d: Percy Moran. UKN., S. Clarke-Hook, Short Stories

JACK SHEPPARD 1912 d: Percy Nash. UKN., *Jack Sheppard*, Harrison Ainsworth, London 1839, Novel

JACK SHEPPARD 1923 d: Henry C. Taylor. UKN., *Jack Sheppard*, Harrison Ainsworth, London 1839, Novel

JACK SPURLOCK, PRODIGAL 1918 d: Carl Harbaugh. USA., *Jack Spurlock - Prodigal*, George Horace Lorimer, New York 1908, Novel

JACK STRAW 1920 d: William C. de Mille. USA., *Jack Straw*, W. Somerset Maugham, New York 1908, Play

JACK TAR 1915 d: Bert Haldane. UKN., *Jack Tar*, Ben Landeck, Arthur Shirley, Play

JACK UND JENNY 1963 d: Victor Vicas. GRM., *Jack Und Jenny*, Anne Piper, Novel

JACK WINTER'S DREAM 1980 d: David Sims. NZL., *Jack Winter's Dream*, James K. Baxter, 1959, Play

JACK-A-BOY 1980 d: Carl Colby. USA., *Jack-a-Boy*, Willa Cather, 1965, Short Story

JACKAL, THE 1997 d: Michael Caton-Jones. USA., *The Day of the Jackal*, Frederick Forsyth, 1971, Novel

JACKIE 1921 d: John Ford. USA., *Jackie*, Countess Barcynska, New York 1921, Novel

JACKIE BROWN 1997 d: Quentin Tarantino. USA., *Rum Punch*, Elmore Leonard, Novel

JACK-KNIFE MAN, THE 1920 d: King Vidor. USA., *The Jack-Knife Man*, Ellis Parker Butler, New York 1913, Novel

JACKNIFE 1988 d: David Jones. USA., *Strange Snow*, Stephen Metcalfe, Play

Jackpot in Bangkok for Oss 117 see **BANCO A BANGKOK** (1964).

Jack-Tars, The see **DE JANTJES** (1922).

Jacob see **TORRES SNORTEVOLD** (1940).

Jacob see **IACOB** (1988).

Jacob the Blacksmith see **YANKEL DER SCHMIDT** (1938).

Jacob the Liar see **JAKOB DER LUGNER** (1975).

JACOB TWO-TWO MEETS THE HOODED FANG 1978 d: Theodore J. Flicker. CND., *Jacob Two-Two Meets the Hooded Fang*, Mordecai Richler, 1975, Novel

Jacobo Timerman: Prisoner Without a Name, Cell Without a Number see **CELL WITHOUT A NUMBER PRISONER WITHOUT A NAME** (1983).

Jacob's Ladder see **JACOBS STEGE** (1942).

JACOBS STEGE 1942 d: Gustaf Molander. SWD., *Jacob*, Alexander Kielland, 1891, Novel

JACOPO ORTIS 1911. ITL., *Le Ultime Lettere Di Jacopo Ortis*, Ugo Foscolo, 1798, Novel

JACQUELINE 1959 d: Wolfgang Liebeneiner. GRM., Jochen Huth, Story

JACQUELINE, OR BLAZING BARRIERS 1923 d: Dell Henderson. USA., *Jacqueline*, James Oliver Curwood, 1918, Short Story

JACQUELINE SUSANN'S ONCE IS NOT ENOUGH 1975 d: Guy Green. USA., *Once Is Not Enough*, Jacqueline Susann, Novel

JACQUELINE SUSANN'S VALLEY OF THE DOLLS 1981 d: Walter Grauman. USA., *Valley of the Dolls*, Jacqueline Susann, New York 1966, Novel

JACQUES L'HONNEUR 1913 d: Henri Andreani. FRN., *Jacques l'Honneur*, Leon Sazie, Play

JAFFERY 1916 d: George Irving. USA., *Jaffery*, William J. Locke, New York 1915, Novel

JAG - EN KVINNA (I) 1965 d: Mac Ahlberg. SWD/DNM., *Jeg - En Kvinnde*, Siv Holm, Copenhagen 1961

JAG - EN KVINNA (II) 1968 d: Mac Ahlberg. SWD/DNM., *Jeg - En Kvinne II*, Siv Holm, Copenhagen 1968, Novel

Jag - En Kvinna Ii: Aktenskapet see **JAG - EN KVINNA (II)** (1968).

Jag -En Alskare see **JEG - EN ELSKER** (1966).

JAGD AUF BLAUE DIAMANTEN 1966 d: Paul Martin. SAF/GRM., *The Diamond Walkers*, Colin Burke, Novel

JAGD NACH DER MILLION, DIE 1930 d: Max Obal. GRM., *Lord Spleen*, Ludwig von Wohl, Novel

JAGDSZENEN AUS NIEDERBAYERN 1968 d: Peter Fleischmann. GRM., *Jagdszenen Aus Niederbayern*, Martin Sperr, Bremen 1966, Play

JAGER VOM ROTECK, DER 1955 d: Hermann Kugelstadt. GRM., *Der Jager Vom Roteck*, Andre Mairock, Novel

JAGER VON FALL, DER 1918 d: Ludwig Beck. GRM., *Der Jager von Fall*, Ludwig Ganghofer, Novel

JAGER VON FALL, DER 1926 d: Franz Seitz. GRM., *Der Jager von Fall*, Ludwig Ganghofer, Novel

JAGER VON FALL, DER 1936 d: Hans Deppe. GRM., *Der Jager von Fall*, Ludwig Ganghofer, Novel

JAGER VON FALL, DER 1957 d: Gustav Ucicky. GRM., *Der Jager von Fall*, Ludwig Ganghofer, Novel

JAGER VON FALL, DER 1974 d: Harald Reinl. GRM., *Der Jager von Fall*, Ludwig Ganghofer, Novel

Jagerloisl Vom Tegersee see **DEINE STERNE HEIMAT** (1951).

Jagged Edge see **I DIED A THOUSAND TIMES** (1955).

Jago's Inheritance see **L' EREDE DI JAGO** (1913).

JAGUAR 1967 d: Janos Domolky. HNG., *Jaguar*, Jeno Heltai, 1914, Novel

JAHR DES HERRN, DAS 1950 d: Alfred Stoger. AUS., *Das Jahr Des Herrn*, Karl Heinrich Waggerl, Novel

Jahre des Schweigens see **K - DAS HAUS DES SCHWEIGENS** (1951).

JAHRE VERGEHEN, DIE 1944 d: Gunther Rittau. GRM., *Romanze*, Erich Ebermayer, Play

JAHRMARKT DES LEBENS 1927 d: Bela Balogh. GRM., *Drei Wunsche*, Bela von Belogh, Novel

J'AI 17 ANS 1945 d: Andre Berthomieu. FRN., *J'ai Dix-Sept Ans*, Paul Vandenberghe, Play

J'ai Dix-Sept Ans see **J'AI 17 ANS** (1945).

J'AI EPOUSE UNE OMBRE 1983 d: Robin Davis. FRN., *I Married a Dead Man*, Cornell Woolrich, 1948, Novel

J'AI TUE RASPOUTINE 1967 d: Robert Hossein. FRN/ITL., *Avant l'Exil*, Prince Youssoupov, Book

J'AI UNE IDEE 1934 d: Roger Richebe. FRN., *Tons of Money*, Will Evans, Arthur Valentine, London 1922, Play

Jail Bait see **WILDWECHSEL** (1972).

Jail Birds see **JAILBIRDS** (1939).

Jail Breaker see **THE WHOLE TOWN'S TALKING** (1935).

JAIL HOUSE BLUES 1942 d: Albert S. Rogell. USA., *Rhapsody in Stripes*, Harold Tarshis, Story

JAILBIRDS 1939 d: Oswald Mitchell. UKN., *Jailbirds*, Fred Karno, Sketch

Jailbirds' Vacation see **LES GRANDES GUEULES** (1965).

Jailbreak see **NUMBERED MEN** (1930).

JAK BYC KOCHANA 1962 d: Wojciech J. Has. PLN., *Jak Byc Kochana*, Kazimierz Brandys, 1960, Short Story

JAK CHUTNA SMRT 1996 d: Milan Cieslar. CZE., Ladislav Mnacko, Story

JAKOB DER LUGNER 1975 d: Frank Beyer. GDR., *Jakob Der Lugner*, Jurek Becker, 1969, Novel

JAKOB VON GUNTEN 1971 d: Peter Lilienthal. GRM., *Jakob von Gunten*, Robert Walser, Novel

JALMA LA DOUBLE 1927 d: Roger Goupillieres. FRN., *Jalma la Double*, Paul d'Ivoi, Novel

JALNA 1935 d: John Cromwell. USA., *Jalna*, Mazo de la Roche, Boston 1927, Novel

JALNA 1994 d: Philippe Monnier. FRN/CND., *Jalna*, Mazo de la Roche, Boston 1927, Novel

JALSAGHAR 1958 d: Satyajit Ray. IND., *Jalsagar*, Tarashankar Banerjee, Calcutta 1937, Novel

Jamaica see **JAMAICA RUN** (1953).

JAMAICA INN 1939 d: Alfred Hitchcock. UKN., *Jamaica Inn*, Daphne Du Maurier, 1936, Novel

JAMAICA INN 1985 d: Lawrence Gordon Clark. UKN., *Jamaica Inn*, Daphne Du Maurier, 1936, Novel

JAMAICA RUN 1953 d: Lewis R. Foster. USA., *The Neat Little Corpse*, Max Murray, Novel

JAMES AND THE GIANT PEACH 1996 d: Henry Selick. USA., *James and the Giant Peach*, Roald Dahl, Book

James Clavell's Shogun see **SHOGUN** (1981).

James Clavell's Tai-Pan see **TAI-PAN** (1986).

James Joyce's Ulysses see **ULYSSES** (1967).

JAMES MICHENER'S DYNASTY 1976 d: Lee Philips. USA., *Dynasty*, James A. Michener, Novel

JAMES THURBER'S THE NIGHT THE GHOST GOT IN 1977 d: Robert Stitzel. USA., *The Night the Ghost Got in*, James Thurber, 1945, Short Story

JAMESTOWN 1923 d: Edwin L. Hollywood. USA., *Pioneers of the Old South*, Mary Johnston, New Haven 1918, Book

JAMILYA 1969 d: Irina PoplavskayA. USS., *Dzhamilia*, Chingiz Aitmatov, 1958, Short Story

JAN BARUJAN 1931 d: Tomu UchidA. JPN., *Les Miserables*, Victor Hugo, Paris 1862, Novel

JAN CIMBURA 1941 d: Frantisek Cap. CZC., *Jan Cimbura*, Jindrich Simon Baar, Novel

JAN OF THE BIG SNOWS 1922 d: Charles M. Seay. USA., *Honor of the Big Snows*, James Oliver Curwood, Indianapolis 1911, Novel

Jan Rohac of Duba see **JAN ROHAC Z DUBE** (1947).

JAN ROHAC Z DUBE 1947 d: Vladimir Borsky. CZC., *Jan Rohac*, Alois Jirasek, 1922, Play

JAN VYRAVA 1937 d: Vladimir Borsky. CZC., *Jan Vyrava*, Antonin Kubovy, Walter Schorsch, Play

JANA ARANYA 1975 d: Satyajit Ray. IND., *Jana Aranya*, Shankar, Novel

JANE 1915 d: Frank Lloyd. USA., *Jane*, W. H. Lestoq, Harry Nicholls, London 1890, Play

JANE AUSTEN'S PRIDE AND PREJUDICE 1995 d: Simon Langton. UKN., *Pride and Prejudice*, Jane Austen, London 1813, Novel

JANE EYRE 1910. ITL., *Jane Eyre*, Charlotte Bronte, London 1847, Novel

JANE EYRE 1910 d: Theodore Marston. USA., *Jane Eyre*, Charlotte Bronte, London 1847, Novel

JANE EYRE 1914 d: Frank H. Crane. USA., *Jane Eyre*, Charlotte Bronte, London 1847, Novel

JANE EYRE 1914 d: Martin J. Faust. USA., *Jane Eyre*, Charlotte Bronte, London 1847, Novel

JANE EYRE 1915 d: Travers Vale. USA., *Jane Eyre*, Charlotte Bronte, London 1847, Novel

Jane Eyre see **LE MEMORIE DI UNA ISTITUTRICE** (1917).

JANE EYRE 1921 d: Hugo Ballin. USA., *Jane Eyre*, Charlotte Bronte, London 1847, Novel

JANE EYRE 1934 d: W. Christy Cabanne. USA., *Jane Eyre*, Charlotte Bronte, London 1847, Novel

JANE EYRE 1944 d: Robert Stevenson. USA., *Jane Eyre*, Charlotte Bronte, London 1847, Novel

JANE EYRE 1968 d: Giorgos Lois. GRC., *Jane Eyre*, Charlotte Bronte, London 1847, Novel

JANE EYRE 1970 d: Delbert Mann. UKN/USA., *Jane Eyre*, Charlotte Bronte, London 1847, Novel

JANE EYRE 1983 d: Julian Amyes. UKN., *Jane Eyre*, Charlotte Bronte, London 1847, Novel

JANE EYRE 1996 d: Franco Zeffirelli. USA., *Jane Eyre*, Charlotte Bronte, London 1847, Novel

JANE SHORE 1908. UKN., *Jane Shore*, Nicholas Rowe, London 1714, Play

JANE SHORE 1911 d: Frank Powell. UKN., *Jane Shore*, Nicholas Rowe, London 1714, Play

JANE SHORE 1915 d: Bert Haldane, F. Martin Thornton. UKN., *Jane Shore*, Nicholas Rowe, London 1714, Play

JANE SHORE 1922 d: Edwin J. Collins. UKN., *Jane Shore*, Nicholas Rowe, London 1714, Play

JANE STEPS OUT 1938 d: Paul L. Stein. UKN., *Jane Steps Out*, Kenneth Horne, 1934, Play

JANE'S HOUSE 1993 d: Glenn Jordan. USA., *Jane's House*, Robert Kimmel Smith, Novel

JANET OF THE DUNES 1913 d: Richard Ridgely. USA., *Janet of the Dunes*, Harriet T. Comstock, Novel

Jangada, La see **OCHOCIENTAS MIL LEGUAS POR EL AMAZONAS** (1958).

JANICE MEREDITH 1924 d: E. Mason Hopper. USA., *Janice Meredith; a Story of the American Revolution*, Paul Leicester Ford, New York 1899, Novel

JANIE 1944 d: Michael Curtiz. USA., *Janie*, Josephine Bentham, Hershel V. Williams Jr., New York 1942, Play

JANIKSEN VUOSI 1977 d: Risto JarvA. FNL., *Janiksen Vuosi*, Arto Passilinna, 1975, Novel

JANKEN 1970 d: Lars Lennart Forsberg. SWD., *Janken*, Marta Weiss, Novel

JANKO MUZYKANT 1930 d: Ryszard Ordynski. PLN., *Janko Muzykant*, Henryk Sienkiewicz, 1879, Short Story

JANOS VITEZ 1973 d: Marcell Jankovics. HNG., *Janos Vitez*, Sandor Petofi, 1845, Verse

JANOSIK 1935 d: Martin Fric. CZC., *Janosik*, Jiri Mahen, Play

JANTJES, DE 1922 d: Maurits H. Binger, B. E. Doxat-Pratt. NTH., *De Jantjes*, Herman Bouber, 1920, Play

JAPANESE NIGHTINGALE, A 1918 d: George Fitzmaurice. USA., *A Japanese Nightingale*, Sir William Young, New York 1903, Novel

Japanese Youth see **NIHON NO SEISHUN** (1968).

JARDIN DES SUPPLICES, LE 1976 d: Christian Gion. FRN., *Le Jardin Des Supplices*, Octave Mirbeau, Paris 1899, Novel

JARDINIER D'ARGENTEUIL, LE 1966 d: Jean-Paul Le Chanois. FRN/GRM., *Le Jardinier d'Argenteuil*, Rene Jouglet, Novel

Jardins du Diable, Les see **COPLAN SAUVE SA PEAU** (1967).

JARKA A VERA 1938 d: Vaclav Binovec. CZC., *Jarka a Vera*, Eduard Kucera, Novel

Jarka and Vera see **JARKA A VERA** (1938).

Jarl the Widower see **ANKEMAN JARL** (1945).

JARNI VODY 1968 d: Vaclav KrskA. CZC., *Veshniye Vody*, Ivan Turgenev, 1872, Short Story

JAROSLAW MUDRYJ 1982 d: Grigori Kochan. USS., *Jaroslaw Mudryj*, Pawlo Sagrebelny, Novel

JARRAPELLEJOS 1987 d: Antonio Gimenez-Rico. SPN., *Jarrapellejos*, Felipe Trigo, 1914, Novel

JASSY 1947 d: Bernard Knowles. UKN., *Jassy*, Norah Lofts, Novel

Jatszani Kell see **LILY IN LOVE** (1985).

JAVA HEAD 1923 d: George Melford. USA., *Java Head*, Joseph Hergesheimer, New York 1919, Novel

JAVA HEAD 1934 d: J. Walter Ruben, Thorold Dickinson. UKN., *Java Head*, Joseph Hergesheimer, New York 1919, Novel

Java Seas see **EAST OF JAVA** (1935).

JAWS 1975 d: Steven Spielberg. USA., *Jaws*, Peter Benchley, 1974, Novel

Jaws of Hell see **BALACLAVA** (1928).

Jaws of Hell see **BALACLAVA** (1930).

JAZEERE 1989 d: Govind Nihalani. IND., *Lille Eyolf*, Henrik Ibsen, 1894, Play

Jazeerey see **JAZEERE** (1989).

Jazz All Around see **MIDT I EN JAZZTID** (1970).

Jazz Bride, The see **THE COMPANIONATE MARRIAGE** (1928).

Jazz King see **DANCERS IN THE DARK** (1932).

Jazz Parents see **THE MAD WHIRL** (1925).

JAZZ SINGER, THE 1927 d: Alan Crosland. USA., *The Day of Atonement*, Samson Raphaelson, 1922, Short Story

JAZZ SINGER, THE 1953 d: Michael Curtiz. USA., *The Day of Atonement*, Samson Raphaelson, 1922, Short Story

JAZZ SINGER, THE 1980 d: Richard Fleischer. USA., *The Day of Atonement*, Samson Raphaelson, 1922, Short Story

Jazz-Bank see **L' ARGENT** (1928).

Jderi Brothers, The see **FRATII JDERI** (1973).

JE HAIS LES ACTEURS 1986 d: Gerard Krawczyk. FRN., *I Hate Actors*, Ben Hecht, 1944, Novel

JE N'AIME QUE TOI 1949 d: Pierre Montazel. FRN., *Je N'aime Que Toi*, J. Montazel, Play

Je Plaide Non Coupable see **GUILTY?** (1956).

JE REVIENDRAI A KANDARA 1956 d: Victor Vicas. FRN., *Je Reviendrai a Kandara*, Jean Hougron, Novel

Je Sors Et Tu Restes la see **L' INCONSTANTE** (1931).

Je T'ai Ecrit une Lettre d'Amour see **CHERE INCONNUE** (1980).

Je T'attendrai see **MAQUILLAGE** (1932).

JE TE CONFIE MA FEMME 1933 d: Rene Guissart. FRN., *L' Ami de Ma Femme*, Henri Geroule, Yves Mirande, Play

JE VOUS SALUE, MAFIA 1965 d: Raoul J. Levy. FRN/ITL., *Je Vous Salue, Mafia!*, Pierre Vial-Lesou, Novel

Jealous Sex see **THE AWFUL TRUTH** (1925).

Jealousies see **CELOS** (1946).

JEALOUSY 1929 d: Jean de Limur. USA., *Monsieur Lamberthier*, Louis Verneuil, Play

JEALOUSY 1931 d: G. B. Samuelson. UKN., *The Green Eye*, John McNally, Play

JEALOUSY 1934 d: R. William Neill. USA., *Spring 3100*, Argyle Campbell, Willard Mack, New York 1928, Play

JEALOUSY 1945 d: Gustav Machaty. USA., Dalton Trumbo, Story

Jealousy see **GELOSIA** (1953).

Jealousy and Medicine see **ZAZDROSC I MEDYCYNA** (1973).

Jean see **THE BARONESS AND THE BUTLER** (1938).

JEAN D'AGREVE 1922 d: Rene Leprince. FRN., *Jean d'Agreve*, Melchior de Vogue, Novel

JEAN DE FLORETTE 1985 d: Claude Berri. FRN/ITL., *L' Eau Des Collines Vol. 1: Jean de Florette*, Marcel Pagnol, 1963, Novel

Jean de Florette 2E Partie see **MANON DES SOURCES** (1985).

JEAN DE LA LUNE 1931 d: Jean Choux. FRN., *Jean de la Lune*, Marcel Achard, 1929, Play

JEAN DE LA LUNE 1948 d: Marcel Achard. FRN., *Jean de la Lune*, Marcel Achard, 1929, Play

Jean Des Bandes Noires see **GIOVANNI DALLE BANDE NERE** (1957).

Jean Et Loulou see **LES EPOUX SCANDALEUX** (1935).

Jean Lefrancois, Heros de la Marne see **LE HEROS DE LA MARNE** (1938).

JEAN VALJEAN 1909. USA., *Les Miserables*, Victor Hugo, Paris 1862, Novel

Jean Valjean see **JAN BARUJAN** (1931).

JEANNE 1934 d: Georges Marret. FRN., *Jeanne*, Henri Duvernois, Play

Jeanne Au Bucher see **GIOVANNA D'ARCO AL ROGO** (1954).

Jeanne d'Arc Au Bucher see **GIOVANNA D'ARCO AL ROGO** (1954).

JEANNE DORE 1915 d: Louis Mercanton, Rene Hervil. FRN., *Jeanne Dore*, Tristan Bernard, Play

JEANNE DORE 1938 d: Mario Bonnard. ITL., *Jeanne Dore*, Tristan Bernard, Play

JEANNE LA MAUDITE 1913 d: Georges DenolA. FRN., *Jeanne la Maudite*, Delbes, Marquet, Play

Jeanne of the Marshes see **BEHIND MASKS** (1921).

JEANNIE 1941 d: Harold French. UKN., *Jeannie*, Aimee Stuart, London 1940, Play

JEDE MENGE SCHMIDT 1989 d: Franz J. Gottlieb. GRM., *Jede Menge Schmidt*, John Graham, Play

JEDE NACHT IN EINEM ANDERN BETT 1957 d: Paul Verhoeven. GRM., *Jede Nacht in Einem Anderen Bett*, Hans Gustl Kernmayr, Play

Jede Stunde Verletzt Und Die Letzte Totet see **GUERNICA -JEDE STUNDE VERLETZT UND DIE LEUTE TOTET** (1963).

JEDENACTE PRIKAZANI 1925 d: Vaclav Kubasek. CZC., *Jedenacte Prikazani*, Frantisek Ferdinand Samberk, Play

JEDER STIRBT FUR SICH ALLEIN 1962 d: Falk Harnack. GRM., *Jeder Stirbt Fur Sich Allein*, Hans Fallada, 1947, Novel

JEDER STIRBT FUR SICH ALLEIN 1976 d: Alfred Vohrer. GRM., *Jeder Stirbt Fur Sich Allein*, Hans Fallada, 1947, Novel

JEDERMANN 1961 d: Gottfried Reinhardt. AUS., *Jedermann: Das Spiel von Sterben Des Reichen Mannes*, Hugo von Hofmannsthal, 1911, Play

JEEVAN YATRA 1946 d: Winayak. IND., *Jeevan Yatra*, N. S. Phadke, Novel

JEEVANA NATAKA 1942 d: Wahab Kashmiri. IND., *Jeevana Nataka*, A. N. Krishnarao, Play

JEG - EN ELSKER 1966 d: Borje Nyberg. DNM/SWD., *Jeg - En Elsker*, Stiig Holm, Copenhagen 1965, Novel

Jeg - En Kvinde see **JAG - EN KVINNA (I)** (1965).

Jeg - En Kvinde II see **JAG - EN KVINNA (II)** (1968).

JEJI HRICH 1939 d: Oldrich Kminek. CZC., *Pitva*, Otakar Hanus, Short Story

JEJI LEKAR 1933 d: Vladimir Slavinsky. CZC., *Zazracny Lekar*, Bedrich Vrbsky, Play

JEJI PASTORKYNA 1929 d: Rudolf Mestak. CZC., *Jeji Pastorkyna*, Gabriela Preissova, Play

JEJI PASTORKYNE 1938 d: Miroslav Cikan. CZC., *Jeji Pastorkyna*, Gabriela Preissova, Play

JEKYLL AND HYDE. TOGETHER AGAIN 1982 d: Jerry Belson. USA., *The Strange Case of Dr. Jekyll and Mr. Hyde*, Robert Louis Stevenson, London 1886, Novel

Jekyll Junior see DOTTOR JEKYLL E GENTILE SIGNORA (1979).

Jekyll's Inferno see THE TWO FACES OF DR. JEKYLL (1960).

JELF'S 1915 d: George Loane Tucker. UKN., *Jelf's*, Horace Annesley Vachell, London 1912, Play

JENIFER HALE 1937 d: Bernerd Mainwaring. UKN., *Jenifer Hale*, Rob Eden, Novel

JENNIE 1940 d: David Burton. USA., *Jennie Heil*, Jane Eberle, 1939, Short Story

Jennie see PORTRAIT OF JENNIE (1948).

JENNIE GERHARDT 1933 d: Marion Gering. USA., *Jennie Gerhardt*, Theodore Dreiser, New York 1911, Novel

JENNY BE GOOD 1920 d: William D. Taylor. USA., *Jenny Be Good*, Wilbur Finley Fauley, New York 1919, Novel

Jenny Lamour see QUAI DES ORFEVRES (1947).

JENNY LIND 1931 d: Arthur Robison. USA., *Jenny Lind*, Dorothy Farnum, Novel

JENNY OMROYD OF OLDHAM 1920 d: Frank Etheridge. UKN., *Jenny Omroyd of Oldham*, T. G. Bailey, Play

JENNY UND DER HERR IM FRACK 1941 d: Paul Martin. GRM., *Jenny Und Der Herr Im Frack*, Georg Zoch, Play

JENNY'S WAR 1985 d: Steve Gethers. USA/UKN., Jack Stoneley, Novel

JENS LANGKNIV 1940 d: Peter Knutzon, Peter Lind. DNM., *Jens Langkniv*, Jeppe Aakjaer, 1915, Novel

JEOPARDY 1952 d: John Sturges. USA., *A Question of Time*, Maurice Zimm, Radio Play

Jeppe of the Hill see JEPPE PA BJERGET (1981).

JEPPE PA BJERGET 1981 d: Kaspar Rostrup. DNM., *Jeppe Paa Bjerget*, Ludvig Holberg, 1722, Play

JEPPE PASS BJERGET 1933 d: Harry Ivarsson, Per Aabel. NRW., *Jeppe Haa Bjerget*, Ludvig Holberg, 1722, Play

JEREMIAH JOHNSON 1972 d: Sydney Pollack. USA., *Mountain Man*, Vardis Fisher, 1965, Novel

JEROME PERREAU 1935 d: Abel Gance. FRN., *Jerome Perreau*, Henri Dupuy-Mazuel, Novel

Jerome Perreau, Heros Des Barricades see JEROME PERREAU (1935).

JEROMIN 1953 d: Luis LuciA. SPN., *Jeromin*, Luis Coloma, 1905-07, Novel

Jerry and Joan see MERRILY WE GO TO HELL (1932).

JERRY'S MOTHER-IN-LAW 1913 d: James Young. USA., *Jerry's Mother-in-Law*, V. D. Brown, H. Lidell, Play

JERUSALEM 1996 d: Bille August. SWD., *Jerusalem*, Selma Lagerlof, Novel

Jerusalem Delivered see LA GERUSALEMME LIBERATA (1911).

Jerusalem Set Free see LA GERUSALEMME LIBERATA (1957).

JES' CALL ME JIM 1920 d: Clarence Badger. USA., *Seven Oaks*, James G. Holland, New York 1875, Novel

JESS 1912. USA., *Jess*, H. Rider Haggard, London 1887, Novel

JESS 1914. USA., *Jess*, H. Rider Haggard, London 1887, Novel

Jess see HEART AND SOUL (1917).

JESSE JAMES VS. THE DALTONS 1954 d: William Castle. USA., E. Westrate, Story

JESSICA 1962 d: Jean Negulesco, Oreste PalellA. USA/FRN/ITL., *The Midwife of Pont Clery*, Flora Sandstrom, New York 1957, Novel

JESSICA'S FIRST PRAYER 1908 d: Dave Aylott?. UKN., *Jessica's First Prayer*, Hesba Stretton, Story

JESSICA'S FIRST PRAYER 1921 d: Bert Wynne. UKN., *Jessica's First Prayer*, Hesba Stretton, Story

Jest of God, A see RACHEL RACHEL (1968).

Jesus see THE GREATEST STORY EVER TOLD (1965).

JESUS CHRIST SUPERSTAR 1973 d: Norman Jewison. USA., *Jesus Christ Superstar*, Tim Rice, Andrew Lloyd Webber, Opera

Jesus la Caille see M'SIEUR LA CAILLE (1955).

Jesus of Ottakring see JESUS VON OTTAKRING (1976).

JESUS VON OTTAKRING 1976 d: Wilhelm Pellert. AUS., *Jesus von Ottakring*, Helmut Korherr, Wilhelm Pellert, Play

Jeu de la Puissance, Le see POWER PLAY (1978).

JEUNE COUPLE, UN 1968 d: Rene Gainville. FRN., *Un Jeune Couple*, Jean-Louis Curtis, 1967, Novel

Jeune de Les Cent Briques, La see CENT BRIQUES ET DES TUILES (1965).

Jeune Fille Effrayee, La see QUELQU'UN A TUE (1933).

Jeune Fille, La see THE YOUNG ONE (1960).

JEUNE FILLE SAVAIT, UNE 1947 d: Maurice Lehmann. FRN., *Une Jeune Fille Savait*, Andre Haguet, Play

Jeune Fille un Seul Amour, Une see KATJA (1959).

Jeune Filles En Uniforme see MADCHEN IN UNIFORM (1958).

Jeune Homme Honorable, Un see L' AINE DES FERCHAUX (1963).

Jeune Homme Qui Se Tue, Un see CHOURINETTE (1933).

Jeune Homme, Un see L' AINE DES FERCHAUX (1963).

JEUNES FILLES A MARIER 1935 d: Jean Vallee. FRN., *Dollars*, Raoul Praxy, Play

Jeunes Filles Aujourd'hui see DAS LEBEN BEGINNT (1942).

JEUNES FILLES D'AUJOURD'HUI 1942 d: Sigfrit Steiner, Jacques Feyder. SWT., *Matura-Reise*, Paul Matthias, Berne 1942, Novel

JEUNES FILLES EN DETRESSE 1939 d: G. W. Pabst. FRN., *Jeunes Filles En Detresse*, Peter Quinn, Novel

Jeunes Filles Sans Uniforme see JEUNES FILLES D'AUJOURD'HUI (1942).

JEUNES TIMIDES 1941 d: Yves Allegret. FRN., *Les Deux Timides*, Eugene Labiche, Marc-Michel, 1860, Play

Jeunesse de Nuit see GIOVENTU DI NOTTE (1962).

JEUNESSE, UNE 1983 d: Moshe Mizrahi. FRN., *Une Jeunesse*, Patrick Modiano, Novel

JEUX DANGEREUX 1958 d: Pierre Chenal. FRN/ITL., *Les Gamins du Roi de Sicile*, Rene Masson, Novel

JEW SUSS 1934 d: Lothar Mendes. UKN., *Jud Suss*, Lion Feuchtwanger, 1925, Novel

Jew Suss see JUD SUSS (1940).

Jew, The see YAHUDI (1958).

Jew-Boy Levi see VIEHJUD LEVI (1999).

JEWEL 1915 d: Phillips Smalley, Lois Weber. USA., *Jewel; a Chapter in Her Life*, Clara Louise Burnham, Boston 1903, Novel

Jewel see A CHAPTER IN HER LIFE (1923).

JEWEL IN THE CROWN, THE 1984 d: Jim O'Brien, Christopher Morahan. UKN., *Raj Quartet*, Paul Scott, Novel

JEWEL ROBBERY 1932 d: William Dieterle. USA., *Ekszerrablas a Vaci-Uccaban*, Ladislaus Fodor, 1931, Play

JEWEL, THE 1933 d: Reginald Denham. UKN., Edgar Wallace, Novel

Jewelled Lamp see RATNADEEP (1951).

Jewelled Lamp see RATNADEEP (1952).

Jewelled Lamp see RATNADEEPAM (1953).

Jewels see DANIELLE STEEL'S JEWELS (1992).

JEWELS OF DESIRE 1927 d: Paul Powell. USA., *Jewels of Desire*, Agnes Parsons, Story

Jewels, The see I GIOIELLI (1913).

JEZEBEL 1938 d: William Wyler. USA., *Jezebel*, Owen Davis Sr., New York 1933, Play

JEZIORO BODENSKIE 1985 d: Janusz Zaorski. PLN., *Jezioro Bodenskie*, Stanislaw Dygat, 1946, Novel, *Karnawal*, Stanislaw Dygat, 1968, Novel

JFK 1991 d: Oliver Stone. USA., *Trail of the Assassins*, Jim Garrison, Book, *Crossfire*, Jim Marrs, Book

JIA 1941 d: Bu Wancang, Hsu Hsin-Fu. CHN., *Jia*, Li Feigan, 1933, Novel

JIA 1957 d: Chen XIhe, Ye Ming. CHN., *Jia*, Li Feigan, 1933, Novel

JIA TING WEN TI 1964 d: Fu Chaowu. CHN., *Jia Ting Wen Ti*, Hu Wanchun, Novel

Jiating Shenshen see TINGYUAN SHENSHEN (1989).

JIE HUN 1953 d: Yan Gong. CHN., *Jie Hun*, Ma Feng, Novel

JIGOKU-HEN 1969 d: Shiro ToyodA. JPN., *Jigoku-Hen*, Ryunosuke Akutagawa, 1918, Novel

JIGOKUMON 1953 d: Teinosuke KinugasA. JPN., *Kesa's Husband*, Kan Kikuchi, Play

JIGSAW 1962 d: Val Guest. UKN., *Sleep Long My Love*, Hillary Waugh, New York 1959, Novel

JIGSAW 1968 d: James Goldstone. USA., *Fallen Angel*, Howard Fast, Boston 1952, Novel

JIGSAW MAN, THE 1984 d: Terence Young. UKN., *The Jigsaw Man*, Dorothea Bennett, Novel

JILLY COOPER'S RIDERS 1993 d: Gabrielle Beaumont. UKN., *Riders*, Jilly Cooper, Novel

JILTING OF GRANNY WEATHERALL, THE 1977 d: Randa Haines. USA., *The Jilting of Granny Weatherall*, Katherine Anne Porter, 1930, Short Story

JIM AND JOE 1911 d: Hal Reid. USA., *Jim and Joe*, Hal Reid, Poem

JIM BLACKWOOD JOCKEY 1909 d: Georges MoncA. FRN., *Jim Blackwood Jockey*, Valentin Mandelstamm, Novel

JIM BLUDSO 1912. USA., *Jim Bludso of the Prairie Belle*, John Hay, 1871, Poem

JIM BLUDSO 1917 d: Wilfred Lucas, Tod Browning. USA., *Jim Bludso of the Prairie Belle*, John Hay, 1871, Poem, *Little Breeches*, John Hay, 1871, Poem

JIM LA HOULETTE 1935 d: Andre Berthomieu. FRN., *Jim la Houlette*, Jean Guitton, Play

JIM LA HOULETTE ROI DES VOLEURS 1926 d: Nicolas Rimsky, Roger Lion. FRN., *Jim la Houlette*, Jean Guitton, Play

Jim la Houlette, Roi Des Voleurs see JIM LA HOULETTE (1935).

Jim Piersall Story, The see FEAR STRIKES OUT (1957).

JIM THE CONQUEROR 1927 d: George B. Seitz. USA., *Jim the Conqueror*, Peter B. Kyne, Short Story

JIM THE PENMAN 1915 d: Hugh Ford, Edwin S. Porter. USA., *Jim the Penman*, Sir Charles L. Young, New York 1886, Play

JIM THE PENMAN 1921 d: Kenneth Webb. USA., *Jim the Penman*, Charles Lawrence Young, New York 1886, Play

JIM THORPE - ALL AMERICAN 1951 d: Michael Curtiz. USA., *Jim Thorpe - All American*, Russell G. Birdwell, Jim Thorpe, Autobiography

Jim Vaus Story, The see WIRETAPPER (1956).

JIMMY 1916 d: A. V. Bramble, Eliot Stannard. UKN., *Jimmy*, John Strange Winter, Novel

JIMMY AND THE DESPERATE WOMAN 1967 d: Gerald Dynevor. UKN., *Jimmy and the Desperate Woman*, D. H. Lawrence, Short Story

JIMMY HAYES AND MURIEL 1914 d: Tom Mix. USA., *Jimmy Hayes and Muriel*, O. Henry, Short Story

Jimmy Reardon see A NIGHT IN THE LIFE OF JIMMY REARDON (1988).

JIMMY THE KID 1983 d: Gary Nelson. USA., *Jimmy the Kid*, Donald E. Westlake, Novel

JIM'S GIFT 1994 d: Bob Keen. UKN., *Jim's Gift*, Sylvia Wickham, Novel

JIN GUANG DA DAO 1975 d: Lin Nong, Sun Yu. CHN., *Jin Guang Da Dao*, Hao Ran, Novel

JIN GUANG DA DAO 2 1976 d: Sun Yu. CHN., *Part Three Bright Road*, Hao Ran, Novel

JIN YIN SHI JIE 1939 d: Li Pingqian. CHN., *Topaze*, Marcel Pagnol, Paris 1928, Play

JINDRA 1919 d: Oldrich Kminek. CZC., *Jindra - Hrabenka Ostrovinova*, Ivan Klicpera, Novel

Jindra, Countess of Ostrovin see HRABENKA OSTROVINOVA JINDRA (1924).

JINDRA, HRABENKA OSTROVINOVA 1924 d: Vaclav Kubasek. CZC., *Jindra - Hrabenka Ostrovinova*, Ivan Klicpera, Novel

JINDRA, HRABENKA OSTROVINOVA 1933 d: Carl Lamac. CZC., *Jindra - Hrabenka Ostrovinova*, Ivan Klicpera, Novel

Jindra, the Countess Ostrovin see HRABENKA OSTROVINOVA JINDRA (1933).

JING HUN TAO HUA DANG 1994 d: Zeng Jianfeng. CHN., *Jing Hun Tao Hua Dang*, Liu Zongdai, Novel

JINY VZDUCH 1939 d: Martin Fric. CZC., *Jiny Vzduch*, Matej Anastazia Simacek, Play

J'IRAI CRACHER SUR VOS TOMBES 1959 d: Michel Gast. FRN., *J'irai Cracher Sur Vos Tombes*, Boris Vian, Paris 1946, Novel

JIUSHI WO 1928 d: Zhu Shouju. CHN., *Huoli Zuiren*, Chen Lengxue, Novel

JIVARO 1954 d: Edward Ludwig. USA., *Lost Treasure of the Andes*, David Duncan, Story

JIZDNI HLIDKA 1936 d: Vaclav Binovec. CZC., *Jizdni Hlidka*, Frantisek Langer, Play

JMENEM JEHO VELICENSTVA 1928 d: Antonin Vojtechovsky. CZC., *Poprava Josefa Kudrny*, Antonin H. Rehor, Play

Jnanambika see GNANAMBIKA (1940).

Jo and Josette see JOSETTE (1938).

JO THE CROSSING SWEEPER 1910. UKN., *Bleak House*, Charles Dickens, London 1853, Novel

JO THE CROSSING SWEEPER 1918 d: Alexander Butler. UKN., *Bleak House*, Charles Dickens, London 1853, Novel

Joachim Murat, from the Tavern to the Throne see GIOACCHINO MURAT (DALLA LOCANDA AL TRONO) (1910).

Joan at the Stake see GIOVANNA D'ARCO AL ROGO (1954).

Joan Lowell, Adventure Girl see ADVENTURE GIRL (1934).

JOAN OF ARC 1948 d: Victor Fleming. USA., *Joan of Lorraine*, Maxwell Anderson, New York 1946, Play

Joan of Arc at the Stake see GIOVANNA D'ARCO AL ROGO (1954).

Joan of Flanders see WAR BRIDES (1916).

Joan of Rainbow Springs see THE GIRL OF MY HEART (1920).

Joan of the Angels see MATKA JOANNA OD ANIOLOW (1961).

JOANNA 1925 d: Edwin Carewe. USA., *Joanna of the Skirts Too Short and the Lips Too Red*, Henry Leyford Gates, New York 1926, Novel

Joao and the Knife see JOAO EN HET MES (1972).

JOAO EN HET MES 1972 d: George Sluizer. NTH/BRZ/BLG., *A Faca E O Rio*, Odylo Costa Filho, Novel

Joao, the Knife and the River see JOAO EN HET MES (1972).

JOCASTE 1924 d: Gaston Ravel. FRN., *Jocaste*, Anatole France

JOCELYN 1922 d: Leon Poirier. FRN., *Jocelyn*, Alphonse de Lamartine, 1836, Verse

JOCELYN 1933 d: Pierre Guerlais. FRN., *Jocelyn*, Alphonse de Lamartine, 1836, Verse

JOCELYN 1951 d: Jacques de Casembroot. FRN., *Jocelyn*, Alphonse de Lamartine, 1836, Verse

JOCK OF THE BUSHVELD 1988 d: Gray Hofmeyr. SAF., *Jock of the Bushveld*, Sir Percy Fitzpatrick, Book

JOE AND ETHEL TURP CALL ON THE PRESIDENT 1939 d: Robert B. Sinclair. USA., *A Call on the President*, Damon Runyon, 1937, Short Story

JOE BUTTERFLY 1957 d: Jesse Hibbs. USA., *Joe Butterfly*, Jack Ruge, Evan Wylie, Play

Joe Egg see A DAY IN THE DEATH OF JOE EGG (1972).

JOE IL ROSSO 1936 d: Raffaello Matarazzo. ITL., *Joe Il Rosso*, Dino Falconi, Play

JOE MACBETH 1955 d: Ken Hughes. UKN/USA., *MacBeth*, William Shakespeare, c1606, Play

JOE PANTHER 1976 d: Paul Krasny. USA., *Joe Panther*, Zachary Ball, Novel

JOE SMITH, AMERICAN 1942 d: Richard Thorpe. USA., *The Adventure of Joe Smith - American*, Paul Gallico, Story

Joe Valachi see COSA NOSTRA (1972).

Joe Valachi: a Segreti Di Cosa Nostra see COSA NOSTRA (1972).

JOEY BOY 1965 d: Frank Launder. UKN., *Joey Boy*, Eddie Chapman, Novel

JOFROI 1933 d: Marcel Pagnol. FRN., *Jofroi de la Maussan*, Jean Giono, 1930, Short Story

JOGO DA VIDA, O 1977 d: Maurice Capovilla. BRZ., *Perus E Bacanaco Malagueta*, Joao Antonio, 1963, Short Story

JOHAN ULFSTJERNA 1923 d: John W. Brunius. SWD., *Johan Ulfstjerna*, Tor Hedberg, Stockholm 1907, Play

JOHAN ULFSTJERNA 1936 d: Gustaf Edgren. SWD., *Johan Ulfstjerna*, Tor Hedberg, Stockholm 1907, Play

JOHANN 1943 d: R. A. Stemmle. GRM., *Johann*, Theo Lingen, Play

JOHANNA ENLISTS 1918 d: William D. Taylor. USA., *The Mobilization of Johanna*, Rupert Hughes, 1917, Short Story

JOHANNES FILS DE JOHANNES 1918 d: Andre Hugon. FRN., *Johannes Fils de Johannes*, Marcel Girette, Novel

JOHANNISFEUER 1939 d: Arthur M. Rabenalt. GRM., *Johannisfeuer*, Hermann Sudermann, 1900, Play

JOHANNISNACHT 1956 d: Harald Reinl. GRM., *Johannisnacht*, Werner Hill, Novel

JOHN AND MARY 1969 d: Peter Yates. USA., *John and Mary*, Mervyn Jones, London 1966, Novel

JOHN AND THE MISSUS 1986 d: Gordon Pinsent. CND., *John and the Missus*, Gordon Pinsent, Novel

JOHN BARLEYCORN 1914 d: Hobart Bosworth, J. Charles Haydon. USA., *John Barleycorn*, Jack London, New York 1913, Novel

John Braun's Body see MASTER DETECTIVE ELLERY QUEEN (1940).

JOHN BURNS OF GETTYSBURG 1913. USA., *John Burns of Gettysburg*, Bret Harte, Poem

JOHN CARPENTER'S VAMPIRES 1998 d: John Carpenter. USA., *Vampire$*, John Steakley, Novel

John Chilcote, M.P. see THE MASQUERADER (1922).

JOHN COLTER'S ESCAPE 1912. USA., *Astoria*, Washington Irving, Novel

John Doe, Dynamite see MEET JOHN DOE (1941).

JOHN ERMINE OF THE YELLOWSTONE 1917 d: Francis Ford. USA., *John Ermine of the Yellowstone*, Frederic Remington, New York 1902, Novel

John Ermine of Yellowstone see JOHN ERMINE OF THE YELLOWSTONE (1917).

JOHN GABRIEL BORKMAN 1958 d: Christopher Morahan. UKN., *John Gabriel Borkman*, Henrik Ibsen, 1896, Play

JOHN GILPIN 1908 d: Percy Stow. UKN., *John Gilpin*, William Cowper, 1782, Poem

JOHN GILPIN'S RIDE 1908 d: Lewin Fitzhamon. UKN., *John Gilpin*, William Cowper, 1782, Poem

JOHN GLAYDE'S HONOR 1915 d: George Irving. USA., *John Glayde's Honour*, Alfred Sutro, New York 1907, Play

John Glayde's Honour see JOHN GLAYDE'S HONOR (1915).

JOHN GLUCKSTADT 1975 d: Ulf Miehe. GRM., *Ein Doppelganger*, Theodor Storm, 1887, Short Story

JOHN GRISHAM'S THE RAINMAKER 1997 d: Francis Ford CoppolA. USA., *The Rainmaker*, John Grisham, Novel

JOHN HALIFAX, GENTLEMAN 1910 d: Theodore Marston. USA., *John Halifax - Gentleman*, Dinah Maria Craik, 1857, Novel

JOHN HALIFAX, GENTLEMAN 1915 d: George Pearson. UKN., *John Halifax - Gentleman*, Dinah Maria Craik, 1857, Novel

JOHN HALIFAX, GENTLEMAN 1938 d: George King. UKN., *John Halifax - Gentleman*, Dinah Maria Craik, 1857, Novel

John Heriot's Wife see DE VROUW VAN DEN MINISTER (1920).

JOHN LOVES MARY 1949 d: David Butler. USA., *John Loves Mary*, Norman Krasna, New York 1947, Play

JOHN NEEDHAM'S DOUBLE 1916 d: Lois Weber, Phillips Smalley. USA., *John Needham's Double; a Novel*, Joseph Hatton, New York 1885, Novel

JOHN OF THE FAIR 1952 d: Michael McCarthy. UKN., *John of the Fair*, Arthur William Groom, London 1950, Novel

John O'Hara's Gibbsville see THE TURNING POINT OF JIM MALLOY (1975).

JOHN PAUL JONES 1959 d: John Farrow. USA., *Nor'wester*, Clements Ripley, Story

John Steinbeck's East of Eden see EAST OF EDEN (1982).

JOHN TOM LITTLE BEAR 1917 d: David Smith. USA., *John Tom Little Bear*, O. Henry, 11short Story

Johnnie Corncob see JANOS VITEZ (1973).

JOHNNY ANGEL 1945 d: Edwin L. Marin. USA., *Mr. Angel Comes Aboard*, Charles Gordon Booth, Novel

JOHNNY BANCO 1967 d: Yves Allegret. FRN/ITL/GRM., *Le Flamenco Des Assassins*, Frederic Valmain, Paris 1961, Novel

JOHNNY BELINDA 1948 d: Jean Negulesco. USA., *Johnny Belinda*, Elmer Harris, New York 1940, Play

JOHNNY BELINDA 1967 d: Paul Bogart. USA., *Johnny Belinda*, Elmer Harris, New York 1940, Play

JOHNNY BELINDA 1982 d: Anthony Harvey. USA., *Johnny Belinda*, Elmer Harris, New York 1940, Play

JOHNNY COME LATELY 1943 d: William K. Howard. USA., *McLeod's Folly*, Louis Bromfield, 1939, Short Story

JOHNNY CONCHO 1956 d: Don McGuire. USA., David Harmon, Story

JOHNNY COOL 1963 d: William Asher. USA., *The Kingdom of Johnny Cool*, John McPartland, New York 1959, Novel

JOHNNY DOESN'T LIVE HERE ANY MORE 1944 d: Joe May. USA., *Alice Means Reeve*, Story

JOHNNY GET YOUR GUN 1919 d: Donald Crisp. USA., *Johnny Get Your Gun*, Edmund Lawrence Burke, New York 1917, Novel

Johnny Gets His Gun see STRAIGHT FROM THE SHOULDER (1936).

JOHNNY GOT HIS GUN 1971 d: Dalton Trumbo. USA., *Johnny Got His Gun*, Dalton Trumbo, Novel

JOHNNY GUITAR 1954 d: Nicholas Ray. USA., *Johnny Guitar*, Roy Chanslor, Novel

Johnny Hamlet see QUELLA SPORCA STORIA DEL WEST (1968).

JOHNNY HANDSOME 1989 d: Walter Hill. USA., *The Three Worlds of Johnny Handsome*, John Godey, Novel

JOHNNY NOBODY 1961 d: Nigel Patrick. UKN., *The Trial of Johnny Nobody*, Albert Z. Carr, 1950, Short Story

Johnny North see THE KILLERS (1964).

JOHNNY ON THE SPOT 1954 d: MacLean Rogers. UKN., *Paid in Full*, Michael Cronin, Novel

JOHNNY ONE-EYE 1950 d: Robert Florey. USA., *Johnny One-Eye*, Damon Runyon, 1944, Short Story

JOHNNY ROCCO 1958 d: Paul Landres. USA., Richard Carlson, Story

Johnny Saves Nebrador see JONNY RETTET NEBRADOR (1953).

JOHNNY TREMAIN 1957 d: Robert Stevenson. USA., *Johnny Tremain*, Esther Forbes, Novel

Johnny Vagabond see JOHNNY COME LATELY (1943).

JOHNNY, WE HARDLY KNEW YE 1977 d: Gilbert Cates. USA., *Johnny We Hardly Knew Ye*, Kenneth O'Donnell, David F. Powers, 1972, Book

JOIE FAIT PEUR, LA 1914 d: Jacques Roullet. FRN., *La Joie Fait Peur*, Mme de Girardin, Play

JOIE QUI TUE, LA 1912. FRN., *La Joie Fait Peur*, Mme de Girardin, Play

Joiner, The see ARE YOU A MASON? (1915).

Joi-Uchi see JOIUCHI - HAIRYOZUMA SHIMATSU (1967).

JOIUCHI - HAIRYOZUMA SHIMATSU 1967 d: Masaki Kobayashi. JPN., *Haiyo Zuma Shimatsu Yori*, Yasuhiko Takiguchi, Short Story

Joke, The see ZERT (1968).

Jokei see JOKYO (1960).

JOKER IS WILD, THE 1957 d: Charles Vidor. USA., *The Life of Joe E. Lewis*, Art Cohn, Biography

Jokers Banquet, The see LA CENA DELLE BEFFE (1941).

JOKIN IHMISESSA 1956 d: Aarne Tarkas. FNL., *Jokin Ihmisessa*, Mika Waltari, 1944, Novel

JOKYO 1960 d: Kon Ichikawa, Kozaburo YoshimurA. JPN., *Jokyo*, Shofu Muramatsu, Novel

Jolanda, la Figlia Del Corsaro Nero see LA FIGLIA DEL CORSARO NERO IOLANDA (1921).

JOLLY BAD FELLOW, A 1963 d: Don Chaffey. UKN., *Don Among the Dead Men*, C. E. Vulliamy, London 1952, Novel

JOLLY CORNER, THE 1977 d: Arthur Barron. USA., *The Jolly Corner*, Henry James, 1908, Short Story

Jolly, Der Wunderaffe see "JOLY" (1913).

"JOLY" 1913 d: Emil Albes. GRM., *Joly*, Arthur Zapp, Novel

819

Jonas Und Der Verschwundene Schatz see SZAFFI (1986).

Jonathan see VAMPIRE STERBEN NICHT JONATHAN (1969).

JONATHAN LIVINGSTONE SEAGULL 1973 d: Hall Bartlett. USA., *Jonathan Livingstone Seagull*, Richard Bach, Novel

JONATHAN, VAMPIRE STERBEN NICHT 1969 d: Hans W. Geissendorfer. GRM., *Dracula*, Bram Stoker, London 1897, Novel

Jone see GLI ULTIMI GIORNI DI POMPEI (1908).

JONE O GLI ULTIMI GIORNI DI POMPEI 1913 d: Enrico Vidali, Ubaldo Maria Del Colle. ITL., *The Last Days of Pompeii*, Edward George Bulwer Lytton, 1834, Novel

Jones Family in As Young As You Feel, The see YOUNG AS YOU FEEL (1940).

JONI 1980 d: James F. Collier. USA., *Joni*, Joni Eareckson, Book

Jonny Banco -Geliebter Taugenichts see JOHNNY BANCO (1967).

JONNY RETTET NEBRADOR 1953 d: Rudolf Jugert. GRM., *Manuel Erkennt Seine macht*, Karl Lerbs, Novel

JONS UND ERDME 1959 d: Victor Vicas. GRM/ITL., *Jons Und Erdme*, Hermann Sudermann, 1917, Short Story

JORDAN IS A HARD ROAD 1915 d: Allan Dwan. USA., *Jordan Is a Hard Road*, Gilbert Parker, Novel

JORDEN ER FLAD 1976 d: Henrik Stangerup. DNM., *Erasmus Montanus*, Ludvig Holberg, 1731, Play

Jorge, a Brazilian see UM BRASILEIRO JORGE (1988).

JORGE, UM BRASILEIRO 1988 d: Paulo Thiago. BRZ., *Um Brasileiro Jorge*, Oswaldo Franca Junior, 1967, Novel

JORINDE UND JORINGEL 1986 d: Wolfgang Hubner. GDR., Jacob Grimm, Wilhelm Grimm, Short Story

Jorio's Daughter see LA FIGLIA DI JORIO (1911).

Jorund Smed see DIT VINDARNA BAR (1948).

JOSE 1925 d: Manuel NoriegA. SPN., *Jose*, Armando Palacio Valdes, Novel

JOSEF KAJETAN TYL 1925 d: Svatopluk Innemann. CZC., *Zivot a Pusobeni J. K. Tyla*, Josef Ladislav Turnovsky

JOSEPH ANDREWS 1977 d: Tony Richardson. UKN., *Joseph Andrews*, Henry Fielding, 1742, Novel

Joseph Conrad's Nostromo see NOSTROMO (1996).

JOSEPH CONRAD'S THE SECRET AGENT 1996 d: Christopher Hampton. UKN/USA., *The Secret Agent*, Joseph Conrad, 1907, Novel

Joseph Greer and His Daughter see WHAT FOOLS MEN (1925).

Joseph the Pure see DER KEUSCHE JOSEF (1953).

Josephine see DIE ORTLIEBSCHEN FRAUEN (1980).

JOSEPHINE VENDUE PAR SES SOEURS 1913 d: Georges DenolA. FRN., *Josephine Vendue Par Ses Soeurs*, Fabrice Carre, Paul Ferrier, Play

JOSETTE 1938 d: Allan Dwan. USA., *Joe and Josette*, Paul Franck, Georg Fraser, Play

JOSHUA THEN AND NOW 1985 d: Ted Kotcheff. CND., *Joshua Then and Now*, Mordecai Richler, Novel

JOSSELYN'S WIFE 1919 d: Howard Hickman. USA., *Josselyn's Wife*, Kathleen Norris, New York 1918, Novel

JOSSELYN'S WIFE 1926 d: Richard Thorpe. USA., *Josselyn's Wife*, Kathleen Norris, New York 1918, Novel

JOSSER, K.C. 1929 d: Hugh Croise. UKN., *Josser K.C.*, Norman Lee, Play, *K.C. Josser*, Ernie Lotinga, Play

JOSSER ON THE FARM 1934 d: T. Hayes Hunter. UKN., *Josser on the Farm*, Herbert Sargent, Con West, Play

Josser P.C. see P.C. JOSSER (1931).

JOUEUR D'ECHECS, LE 1938 d: Jean Dreville. FRN., *Le Joueur d'Echecs*, Henri Dupuy-Mazuel, Novel

JOUEUR, LE 1938 d: Louis Daquin, Gerhard Lamprecht. FRN., *Igrok*, Fyodor Dostoyevsky, 1866, Novel

JOUEUR, LE 1958 d: Claude Autant-LarA. FRN/ITL., *Igrok*, Fyodor Dostoyevsky, 1866, Novel

JOUEUSE D'ORGUE, LA 1913 d: Georges DenolA. FRN., *La Joueuse d'Orgue*, Xavier de Montepin, Novel

JOUEUSE D'ORGUE, LA 1924 d: Charles Burguet. FRN., *La Joueuse d'Orgue*, Xavier de Montepin, Novel

JOUEUSE D'ORGUE, LA 1936 d: Gaston Roudes. FRN., *La Joueuse d'Orgue*, Xavier de Montepin, Novel

JOU-JOU 1916 d: Baldassarre Negroni. ITL., *Jou-Jou*, Henri Bernstein, 1902, Play

JOUR DE NOCES 1971 d: Claude GorettA. SWT., Guy de Maupassant, Short Story

Jour Des Parques, Le see LA RUPTURE (1970).

JOURNAL D'UN CURE DE CAMPAGNE, LE 1950 d: Robert Bresson. FRN., *Journal d'un Cure de Campagne*, Georges Bernanos, 1936, Novel

JOURNAL D'UN FOU, LE 1963 d: Roger Coggio. FRN., *Diary of a Madman*, Nikolay Gogol, 1836, Short Story

JOURNAL D'UN FOU, LE 1987 d: Roger Coggio. FRN., *Diary of a Madman*, Nikolay Gogol, 1836, Short Story

Journal d'une Femme de Chambre, Le see DIARY OF A CHAMBERMAID (1946).

JOURNAL D'UNE FEMME DE CHAMBRE, LE 1963 d: Luis Bunuel. FRN/ITL., *Le Journal d'une Femme de Chambre*, Octave Mirbeau, Paris 1900, Novel

JOURNAL D'UNE FEMME EN BLANC, LE 1964 d: Claude Autant-LarA. FRN/ITL., *Journal d'une Femme En Blanc*, Andre Soubiran, Novel

Journey see PUTESHESTVIYE (1967).

Journey Around My Skull see UTAZAS A KOPONYAM KORUL (1970).

Journey Beneath the Desert see L'AMANTE DELLA CITTA SEPOLTA ANTINEA (1961).

Journey Beyond the Stars see 2001: A SPACE ODYSSEY (1968).

JOURNEY FOR MARGARET 1942 d: W. S. Van Dyke. USA., *Journey for Margaret*, William L. White, Book

Journey Inside My Brain see UTAZAS A KOPONYAM KORUL (1970).

JOURNEY INTO FEAR 1942 d: Norman Foster, Orson Welles (Uncredited). USA., *Journey Into Fear*, Eric Ambler, Novel

JOURNEY INTO FEAR 1975 d: Daniel Mann. CND., *Journey Into Fear*, Eric Ambler, Novel

Journey Into the Depth of the Student's Soul see CESTA DO HUBLIN STUDAKOVY DUSE (1939).

JOURNEY OF AUGUST KING, THE 1995 d: John Duigan. USA., *The Journey of August King*, John Ehle, 1971, Novel

Journey of Life, The see JEEVAN YATRA (1946).

Journey of the Young Composer see PUTSCHESTWIE MOLODOGO KOMPOSITORA (1984).

Journey Round My Skull, A see UTAZAS A KOPONYAM KORUL (1970).

Journey That Shook the World, The see JULES VERNE'S ROCKET TO THE MOON (1967).

Journey, The see LASSIE'S GREAT ADVENTURE (1963).

Journey, The see IL VIAGGIO (1974).

Journey, The see ANTARJALI JATRA (1988).

Journey to Italy see VIAGGIO IN ITALIA (1953).

JOURNEY TO SHILOH 1968 d: William Hale. USA., *Journey to Shiloh*, Will Henry, New York 1960, Novel

JOURNEY TO THE CENTER OF THE EARTH 1959 d: Henry Levin. USA., *Voyage Au Centre de la Terre*, Jules Verne, 1864, Novel

JOURNEY TO THE CENTER OF THE EARTH 1988 d: Rusty Lemorande. USA., *Voyage Au Centre de la Terre*, Jules Verne, 1864, Novel

JOURNEY TO THE CENTRE OF THE EARTH 1976 d: Richard Slapczynski. ASL., *Voyage Au Centre de la Terre*, Jules Verne, 1864, Novel

Journey to the Centre of the Earth see VIAJE AL CENTRO DE LA TIERRA (1977).

Journey to the Depths of a Schoolboy's Soul, A see CESTA DO HUBLIN STUDAKOVY DUSE (1939).

Journey to the Lost City see DAS INDISCHE GRABMAL (1959).

Journey to the Past see THE HOUSE IN THE SQUARE (1951).

Journey to Tilsit, The see DIE REISE NACH TILSIT (1939).

Journeying West to Kill the Demon see XI XING PING YAO (1991).

JOURNEY'S END 1930 d: James Whale. UKN/USA., *Journey's End*, R. C. Sherriff, London 1929, Play

JOURNEY'S END 1988 d: Michael Simpson. UKN., *Journey's End*, R. C. Sherriff, London 1929, Play

JOURNEY'S END, THE 1921 d: Hugo Ballin. USA., *Ave Maria*, Sister Eileen, Story

JOURS HEUREUX, LES 1941 d: Jean de Marguenat. FRN., *Les Jours Heureux*, Claude-Andre Puget, Play

JOURS TRANQUILLES A CLICHY 1989 d: Claude Chabrol. FRN/GRM/ITL., *Quiet Days in Clichy*, Henry Miller, Paris 1956, Novel

Jovanka and the Others see JOVANKA E LE ALTRE (1960).

JOVANKA E LE ALTRE 1960 d: Martin Ritt. ITL/USA., *Jovanka E le Altre*, Ugo Pirro, Novel

Joven, La see THE YOUNG ONE (1960).

JOVEN SANCHEZ, EL 1963 d: Mario Camus. SPN., *Young Sanchez*, Ignacio Aldecoa, 1959, Short Story

Jovita see JOWITA (1967).

JOWITA 1967 d: Janusz Morgenstern. PLN., *Disneyland*, Stanislaw Dygat, Warsaw 1965, Novel

Joy see ZONNETJE (1920).

JOY 1983 d: Serge Bergon. FRN/CND., *Joy*, Joy Laurey, Novel

JOY GIRL, THE 1927 d: Allan Dwan. USA., *The Joy Girl*, May Edginton, 1926, Short Story

Joy Girls see SHUNPU-DEN (1965).

Joy House, The see LES FELINS (1964).

JOY IN THE MORNING 1965 d: Alex Segal. USA., *Joy in the Morning*, Betty Smith, New York 1963, Novel

JOY LUCK CLUB, THE 1993 d: Wayne Wang. USA., *The Joy Luck Club*, Amy Tan, Novel

Joy of Loving see FUTURES VEDETTES (1955).

JOY OF SEX, THE 1984 d: Martha Coolidge. USA., *The Joy of Sex*, Alex Comfort, Book

Joy Parade, The see LIFE BEGINS IN COLLEGE (1937).

JOYCE OF THE NORTH WOODS 1913 d: Ashley Miller. USA., *Joyce of the North Woods*, Harriet T. Comstock, Novel

Joyeux Noel see QUAI DES ORFEVRES (1947).

Joyful Wisdom, The see LE GAI SAVOIR (1967).

JOYMATI 1935 d: Jyoti Prasad Agarwal. IND., *Joymati Kunwari*, Lakhindranath Bezbaruah, Play

JOYOUS ADVENTURES OF ARISTIDE PUJOL, THE 1920 d: Frank Miller. UKN., *The Joyous Adventures of Aristiede Pujol*, William J. Locke, Novel

Joyous Heroes, The see HUANLE YINGXIONG (1988).

Joyous Trouble Maker, The see THE JOYOUS TROUBLEMAKER (1920).

JOYOUS TROUBLEMAKER, THE 1920 d: J. Gordon Edwards. USA., *The Joyous Troublemaker*, Jackson Gregory, New York 1918, Novel

Joyous Troublemakers, The see THE JOYOUS TROUBLEMAKER (1920).

JOYU SUMAKO NO KOI 1947 d: Kenji Mizoguchi. JPN., *Kurumen Yukinu*, Hideo Nagata, Play

JSEN DEVCE S CERTEM V TELE 1933 d: Karl Anton. CZC., *Une Petite Femme Dans le Train*, Leo Marches, Play

J'te Dis Qu'elle T'a Fait de l'Oeil see J'TE DIS QU'ELLE T'A FAIT DE L'OEIL ET MOI (1935).

Juan Jose see LIFE (1928).

JUAN MOREIRA 1936 d: Nelo Cosimi. ARG., *Juan Moreira*, Eduardo Gutierrez, 1879, Novel

JUAN MOREIRA 1948 d: Luis Barth-MogliA. ARG., *Juan Moreira*, Eduardo Gutierrez, 1879, Novel

JUAREZ 1939 d: William Dieterle. USA., *The Phantom Crown*, Bertita Harding, New York 1934, Play, *Juarez Und Maximilian*, Franz Werfel, Vienna 1924, Play

JUBAL 1956 d: Delmer Daves. USA., *Jubal Troop*, Paul I. Wellman, Novel

JUBIABA 1986 d: Nelson Pereira Dos Santos. BRZ/FRN., *Jubiaba*, Jorge Amado, 1935, Novel

Jubilee see IUBELEI (1944).

Jubilee see JUBILEUSZ (1995).

JUBILEE TRAIL 1954 d: Joseph Kane. USA., *Jubilee Trail*, Gwen Bristow, Novel

Jubilej see IUBELEI (1944).

JUBILEUSZ 1995 d: Zbigniew Kaminski. PLN/USA., *Germans*, Leon Kruczkowski, Novel

JUBILO 1919 d: Clarence Badger. USA., *Jubilo*, Ben Ames Williams, 1919, Short Story

Jubilo see TOO BUSY TO WORK (1932).

JUCKLINS, THE 1920 d: George Melford. USA., *The Jucklins*, Opie Read, Chicago 1896, Novel

JUD SUSS 1940 d: Veit Harlan. GRM., *Jud Suss*, Lion Feuchtwanger, 1925, Novel

Judah see THE CHEATER (1920).

Judas of Tyrol see DER JUDAS VON TIROL (1933).

JUDAS VON TIROL, DER 1933 d: Franz Osten. GRM., *Der Judas von Tirol*, Karl Schonherr, 1927, Play

Judas Was a Woman see LA BETE HUMAINE (1938).

JUDE 1996 d: Michael Winterbottom. UKN., *Jude the Obscure*, Thomas Hardy, Novel

Judge and His Hangman, The see DER RICHTER UND SEIN HENKER (1976).

Judge Dee see JUDGE DEE AND THE MONASTERY MURDERS (1974).

JUDGE DEE AND THE MONASTERY MURDERS 1974 d: Jeremy Paul Kagan. USA., *Judge Dee at the Haunted Monastery*, Robert Van Gulick, Novel

Judge Dee in the Monastery Murders see JUDGE DEE AND THE MONASTERY MURDERS (1974).

JUDGE HORTON AND THE SCOTTSBORO BOYS 1976 d: Fielder Cook. USA., *Scottsboro - a Tragedy of the American South*, Dan T. Carter, Book

JUDGE NOT; OR, THE WOMAN OF MONA DIGGINGS 1915 d: Robert Z. Leonard. USA., *Renunciation*, Peter B. Kyne, Story

Judge Not Thy Wife see THE WHITE DOVE (1920).

Judge of Instruction, The see L' ISTRUTTORIA (1914).

Judge of Zalamea, The see DER RICHTER VON ZALAMEA (1955).

Judge Roy Bean see ALL'OVEST DI SACRAMENTO (1971).

Judge, The see DOMAREN (1960).

Judge, The see SOSKENDE (1966).

JUDGEMENT BOOK, THE 1935 d: Charles Hutchison. USA., Homer King Gordon, Short Story

JUDGEMENT HOUSE, THE 1917 d: J. Stuart Blackton. USA., *The Judgement House*, Gilbert Parker, London 1913, Novel

JUDGEMENT IN STONE, A 1986 d: Ousama Rawi. CND., *A Judgement in Stone*, Ruth Rendell, 1977, Novel

Judgement in Stone, A see LA CEREMONIE (1995).

Judgment see HER HUSBAND'S SECRET (1925).

JUDGMENT AT NUREMBERG 1961 d: Stanley Kramer. USA., *Judgment at Nuremberg*, Abby Mann, 1959, Play

Judgment House, The see THE JUDGEMENT HOUSE (1917).

Judgment in the Sun see THE OUTRAGE (1964).

Judgment of God, The see LE JUGEMENT DE DIEU (1949).

JUDGMENT OF THE HILLS 1927 d: James Leo Meehan. USA., *Judgment of the Hills*, Larry Evans, Short Story

JUDITH 1922 d: Georges MoncA. FRN., *Judith*, Jean-Joseph Renaud, Novel

JUDITH 1966 d: Daniel Mann. USA/UKN/ISR., *Judith*, Lawrence Durrell, Novel

JUDITH OF BETHULIA 1914 d: D. W. Griffith. USA., *Judith of Bethulia*, Thomas Bailey Aldrich, 1904, Play

JUDITH OF THE CUMBERLANDS 1916 d: J. P. McGowan. USA., *Judith of the Cumberlands*, Alice MacGowan, New York 1908, Novel

JUDITH TRACHTENBERG 1920 d: Henrik Galeen. GRM., *Judith Trachtenberg*, Karl Emil Franzos, New York 1891, Novel

Judo Saga see SUGATA SANSHIRO (1943).

Judo Saga II see ZOKU SUGATA SANSHIRO (1945).

Judo Story see SUGATA SANSHIRO (1943).

JUDOKA, AGENT SECRET, LE 1966 d: Pierre Zimmer. FRN/ITL., *Le Judoka Dans la Ville*, Ernie Clerk, Novel

Judoka Dans l'Enfer, Le see CASSE-TETE CHINOIS POUR LE JUDOKA (1968).

JUDY FORGOT 1915 d: T. Hayes Hunter. USA., *Judy Forgot*, Avery Hopwood, New York 1910, Play

JUDY OF ROGUE'S HARBOR 1920 d: William D. Taylor. USA., *Judy of Rogue's Harbor*, Grace Miller White, New York 1918, Novel

JUE XIANG 1985 d: Zhang Zeming. CHN., *Jue Xiang*, Kong Jiesheng, Novel

JUEGO DE NINOS 1952 d: Enrique Cahen. SPN., *Juego de Ninos*, Victor Ruiz Iriarte, 1951, Play

Jugando En Los Campos de Senor see AT PLAY IN THE FIELDS OF THE LORD (1991).

JUGE D'INSTRUCTION, LE 1923 d: Marcel Dumont. FRN., *Le Juge d'Instruction*, Jules de Marthold, Play

JUGEMENT DE DIEU, LE 1949 d: Raymond Bernard. FRN., *Agnes Bernauer*, Christian Friedrich Hebbel, 1852, Play

JUGEMENT DE MINUIT, LE 1932 d: Alexander Esway, Andre Charlot. FRN., *The Gaunt Stranger*, Edgar Wallace, London 1925, Novel

JUGEND 1922 d: Fred Sauer. GRM., *Jugend*, Max Halbe, 1893, Play

JUGEND 1938 d: Veit Harlan. GRM., *Jugend*, Max Halbe, 1893, Play

Jugend von Heute see MANOUCHE - JEUNESSE D'AUJOURD'HUI (1942).

Jugend von Morgen see DER KAMPF DER TERTIA (1928).

JUGENDGELIEBTE, DIE 1930 d: Hans Tintner. GRM., *Aus Meinem Leben. Dichtung Und Wahrheit*, Johann Wolfgang von Goethe, 1811-33, Autobiography

JUGENDLIEBE 1944 d: Eduard von Borsody. GRM., *Romeo Und Julia Auf Dem Dorfe*, Gottfried Keller, Braunschweig 1865, Short Story

JUGENDSUNDE, DIE 1936 d: Franz Seitz. GRM., *Der G'wissenswurm*, Ludwig Anzengruber, 1905, Novel

JUGGERNAUT 1936 d: Henry Edwards. UKN., *Juggernaut*, Alice Campbell, Novel

JUGGLER, THE 1953 d: Edward Dmytryk. USA., *The Juggler*, Michael Blankfort, Novel

Jugglers, The see SALTIMBANCII (1981).

JUHA 1937 d: Nyrki TapiovaarA. FNL., *Juha*, Juhani Aho, 1911, Novel

JUHA 1956 d: Toivo SarkkA. FNL., *Juha*, Juhani Aho, 1911, Novel

JUHA 1999 d: Aki Kaurismaki. FNL., *Juha*, Juhani Aho, 1911, Novel

JUIF ERRANT, LE 1913. FRN., *Le Juif Errant*, Eugene Sue, 1845, Novel

JUIF ERRANT, LE 1926 d: Luitz-Morat. FRN., *Le Juif Errant*, Eugene Sue, 1845, Novel

JUIF POLONAIS, LE 1931 d: Jean Kemm. FRN., *Le Juif Polonais*, Alexandre Chatrian, Emile Erckmann, Paris 1869, Play

JUKE GIRL 1942 d: Curtis Bernhardt. USA., *Jook Girl*, Theodore Pratt, Novel

Jukusai No Chizu see JUKYUSAI NO CHIZU (1979).

JUKYUSAI NO CHIZU 1979 d: Mitsuo Yanagimachi. JPN., *Jukyusai No Chizu*, Kenji Nakagami, Novel

Jules and Jim see JULES ET JIM (1961).

JULES ET JIM 1961 d: Francois Truffaut. FRN., *Jules Et Jim*, Henri-Pierre Roche, Paris 1953, Novel

JULES OF THE STRONG HEART 1918 d: Donald Crisp. USA., *Jules of the Strong Heart*, William Merriam Rouse, 1915, Short Story

JULES VERNE'S ROCKET TO THE MOON 1967 d: Don Sharp. UKN., **De la Terre a la Lune; Trajet Direct En 97 Heures**, Jules Verne, 1865, Novel

JULIA 1977 d: Fred Zinnemann. USA., *Pentimento*, Lillian Hellman, 1973, Short Story

JULIA, DU BIST ZAUBERHAFT 1962 d: Alfred Weidenmann. AUS/FRN., *Theatre*, Guy Bolton, W. Somerset Maugham, 1941, Play

JULIA MISBEHAVES 1948 d: Jack Conway. USA., *The Nutmeg Tree*, Margery Sharp, Novel

JULIAN PO 1997 d: Alan Wade. USA., *La Mort de Monsieur Golouga*, Branimir Scepanovic, Novel

JULIE 1975 d: K. S. Sethumadhavan. IND., *Chattakari*, Pamman, Novel

JULIE DE CARNEILHAN 1949 d: Jacques Manuel. FRN., *Julie de Carneilhan*, Sidonie Gabrielle Colette, 1941, Novel

Julie Pot de Colle see JULIE POT-DE-COLLE (1977).

JULIE POT-DE-COLLE 1977 d: Philippe de BrocA. FRN., Peter de Polnay, Novel

Juliet Buys a Baby see JULIETA COMPRA UN HIJO (1935).

Juliet Buys a Son see JULIETA COMPRA UN HIJO (1935).

Juliet Or the Key of Dreams see JULIETTE OU LA CLE DES SONGES (1951).

JULIETA COMPRA UN HIJO 1935 d: Louis King. USA., *Julieta Compra un Hijo*, Gregorio Martinez Sierra, H. Maura, Madrid 1927, Play

Julieta Y Romeo see GIULIETTA E ROMEO (1964).

JULIETTA 1953 d: Marc Allegret. FRN., *Julietta*, Louise de Vilmorin, Novel

JULIETTE OU LA CLE DES SONGES 1951 d: Marcel Carne. FRN., *Juliette Ou la Cle des Songes*, Georges Neveux, 1930, Play

Julius Caesar see GIULIO CESARE (1909).

JULIUS CAESAR 1908 d: William V. Ranous. USA., *Julius Caesar*, William Shakespeare, c1599, Play

JULIUS CAESAR 1911. UKN., *Julius Caesar*, William Shakespeare, c1599, Play

JULIUS CAESAR 1926 d: George A. Cooper. UKN., *Julius Caesar*, William Shakespeare, c1599, Play

JULIUS CAESAR 1945 d: Compton Bennett. UKN., *Julius Caesar*, William Shakespeare, c1599, Play

JULIUS CAESAR 1950 d: David Bradley. USA., *Julius Caesar*, William Shakespeare, c1599, Play

JULIUS CAESAR 1953 d: Charles Deane. UKN., *Julius Caesar*, William Shakespeare, c1599, Play

JULIUS CAESAR 1953 d: Joseph L. Mankiewicz. USA., *Julius Caesar*, William Shakespeare, c1599, Play

JULIUS CAESAR 1970 d: Stuart Burge. UKN., *Julius Caesar*, William Shakespeare, c1599, Play

JULIUS CAESAR 1978 d: Herbert Wise. UKN., *Julius Caesar*, William Shakespeare, c1599, Play

JULORATORIET 1996 d: Kjelle-Ake Andersson. SWD., *Juloratoriet*, Goran Tunstrom, Novel

JULY GROUP, THE 1982 d: George McCowan. CND., *The July Group*, Stanley Ellin, Novel

Jumbo see BILLY ROSE'S JUMBO (1962).

JUMEAU, LE 1984 d: Yves Robert. FRN., *Two Much*, Donald E. Westlake, Novel

JUMENT VERTE, LA 1959 d: Claude Autant-LarA. FRN/ITL., *La Jument Verte*, Marcel Ayme, Paris 1933, Novel

JUMP FOR GLORY 1937 d: Raoul Walsh. UKN., *Jump for Glory*, Gordon MacDonnell, Novel

Jumping Over Puddles Again see UZ ZASE SKACU PRES KALUZE (1970).

Jumping the Puddles Again see UZ ZASE SKACU PRES KALUZE (1970).

JUMPING THE QUEUE 1989 d: Claude Whatham. UKN., *Jumping the Queue*, Mary Wesley, Novel

JUNE BRIDE 1948 d: Bretaigne Windust. USA., *Feature for June*, Graeme Lorimer, Eileen Tighe, Play

JUNE MOON 1931 d: A. Edward Sutherland. USA., *June Moon*, George S. Kaufman, Ring Lardner, New York 1929, Play

JUNGE ENGLANDER, DER 1958 d: Gottfried Kolditz. GDR., *Der Junge Englander*, Wilhelm Hauff, 1905, Short Story

JUNGE FRAU VON 1914 1969 d: Egon Gunther. GDR., *Junge Frau von 1914*, Arnold Zweig, Novel

JUNGE HERZEN 1944 d: Boleslav Barlog. GRM., *Ohne Sorge in Sanssouci*, E. W. Droge, Novel

Junge Jahre Der Liebe see ULI DER KNECHT (1954).

JUNGE LEUTE IN DER STADT 1985 d: Karl-Heinz Lotz. GDR., *Junge Leute in Der Stadt*, Rudolf Braune, Novel

JUNGE LORD, DER 1965 d: Gustav Rudolf Sellner. GRM., *Der Junge Lord: Komische Oper in Zwei Akten*, Ingeborg Bachmann, Berlin 1965, Opera, *Der Junge Lord; Komische Oper in Zwei Akten*, Hans Werner Henze, Berlin 1965, Opera

Junge Schrie Mord, Ein see THE BOY CRIED MURDER (1966).

JUNGE TORLESS, DER 1966 d: Volker Schlondorff. GRM/FRN., *Die Verwirrungen Des Zoglings Torless*, Robert Musil, Berlin 1906, Novel

JUNGER MANN, DER ALLES KANN 1957 d: Thomas Engel. GRM., *Der Alles Kann Junger Mann*, Ernst Rudolphi, Novel

JUNGFER, SIE GEFALLT MIR 1968 d: Gunter Reisch. GDR., *Der Zerbrochene Krug*, Heinrich von Kleist, 1811, Play

JUNGFERN VOM BISCHOFSBERG 1943 d: Peter P. Brauer. GRM., *Die Jungfern Vom Bischofsberg*, Gerhart Hauptmann, 1907, Play

JUNGFRAU AUF DEM DACH, DIE 1954 d: Otto Preminger. GRM., *The Moon Is Blue*, F. Hugh Herbert, New York 1951, Play

Jungfrau Mit Der Peitsche, Die see DAS GEHEIMNIS VOM BERGSEE (1951).

JUNGFRAUENKRIEG 1957 d: Hermann Kugelstadt. AUS., *Jungfrauenkrieg*, Hans Matschners, Novel

JUNGGESELLENFALLE 1953 d: Fritz Bottger. GRM., *Die Junggesellenfalle*, Albert Kalkus, Play

Jungle *see* **UNTAMED** (1929).

Jungle *see* **THE LAST OUTPOST** (1935).

Jungle Attack *see* **CROSSWINDS** (1951).

Jungle Book, The *see* **RUDYARD KIPLING'S JUNGLE BOOK** (1942).

Jungle Fighters *see* **THE LONG AND THE SHORT AND THE TALL** (1960).

Jungle Freaks *see* **MACUNAIMA** (1969).

Jungle Girl and the Slaver *see* **DIE WEISSE SKLAVIN LIANE** (1957).

JUNGLE HEAT 1984 d: Gus Trikonis. USA., *Dance of the Dwarfs*, Geoffrey Household, Novel

JUNGLE MASTER, THE 1914 d: Henry McRae. USA., *The Jungle Master*, Rex de Rosselli, Story

JUNGLE PATROL 1948 d: Joseph M. Newman. USA., *Jungle Patrol*, William Bowers, Play

JUNGLE PRINCESS, THE 1920. USA., *The Lost City*, Frederic Chapin, Short Story

Jungle Rampage *see* **RAMPAGE** (1963).

JUNGLE, THE 1914 d: Augustus Thomas, George Irving. USA., *The Jungle*, Upton Sinclair, New York 1906, Novel

JUNIOR MISS 1945 d: George Seaton. USA., *Junior Miss*, Sally Benson, Jerome Chodorov, Joseph Fields, New York 1941, Play

Junk *see* **THE IDLE RICH** (1921).

Junkerngasse 54 *see* **DAS GESPENSTERHAUS** (1942).

JUNO AND THE PAYCOCK 1929 d: Alfred Hitchcock. UKN., *Juno and the Peacock*, Sean O'Casey, London 1925, Play

JUNOON 1978 d: Shyam Benegal. IND., *A Flight of Pigeons*, Ruskin Bond, Short Story

JUNOST PETRA 1980 d: Sergei Gerasimov. USS/GDR., *Pyotr Pervy*, Alexsey Nikolayevich Tolstoy, 1929-45, Novel

JUPITER'S DARLING 1954 d: George Sidney. USA., *The Road to Rome*, R. E. Sherwood, 1927, Play

JURAMENTO DE LAGARDERE, EL 1954 d: Leon Klimovsky. ARG., Alexandre Dumas (pere), Novel

JUROR NUMBER SEVEN 1915 d: Ben Wilson. USA., *Juror Number Seven*, Joseph H. Trant, Story

JUROR, THE 1996 d: Brian Gibson. USA., *The Juror*, George Dawes Green, Book

Jury of One *see* **LE VERDICT** (1974).

JURY'S EVIDENCE 1936 d: Ralph Ince. UKN., *Jury's Evidence*, Jack Celestin, Jack de Leon, Play

JUSQU'AU BOUT DU MONDE 1962 d: Francois Villiers. FRN/ITL., Elio Vittorini, Novel

JUSQU'AU DERNIER 1956 d: Pierre Billon. FRN., *Jusqu'au Dernier*, A. Dusquesne, Novel

Just a Big Simple Girl *see* **UNE GRANDE FILLE TOUTE SIMPLE** (1947).

JUST A GIGOLO 1931 d: Jack Conway. USA., Alexander Engel, Alfred Grunwald, Play

JUST A GIRL 1916 d: Alexander Butler. UKN., *Just a Girl*, Charles Garvice, Novel

JUST A MOTHER 1923. USA., *Mrs. Thompson*, William Babington Maxwell, New York 1911, Novel

JUST A WIFE 1920 d: Howard Hickman. USA., *Just a Wife*, Eugene Walter, New York 1910, Play

JUST A WOMAN 1918 d: Julius Steger. USA., *Just a Woman*, Eugene Walter, New York 1916, Play

JUST A WOMAN 1925 d: Irving Cummings. USA., *Just a Woman*, Eugene Walter, New York 1916, Play

Just a Woman *see* **DOCTEUR FRANCOISE GAILLAND** (1975).

Just and Unjust *see* **HELL'S 400** (1926).

JUST ANOTHER BLONDE 1926 d: Alfred Santell. USA., *Even Stephen*, Gerald Beaumont, 1925, Short Story

Just Another War *see* **UOMINI CONTRO** (1970).

JUST AROUND THE CORNER 1921 d: Frances Marion. USA., *Just Around the Corner*, Fannie Hurst, 1914, Short Story

Just As I Am *see* **ZOOALS IK BEN.** (1920).

JUST ASK FOR DIAMOND 1988 d: Stephen Bayley. UKN., *The Falcon's Malteser*, Anthony Horowitz, Novel

Just Before Nightfall *see* **JUSTE AVANT LA NUIT** (1971).

JUST CAUSE 1995 d: Arne Glimcher. USA., *Just Cause*, John Katzenbach, Novel

JUST DECEPTION, A 1917 d: A. E. Coleby. UKN., *Aaron the Jew*, B. L. Farjeon, Novel

JUST FOR YOU 1952 d: Elliott Nugent. USA., *Famous*, Stephen Vincent Benet, 1946, Short Story

Just Forget That Case *see* **ZABRAVETE TOZI SLOUCHAI** (1984).

Just Half an Hour *see* **ARANAZHIKANERAM** (1970).

JUST LIKE A WOMAN 1992 d: Chris Monger. UKN., *Geraldine; for the Love of a Transvestite*, Monica Jay, Book

JUST MARRIED 1928 d: Frank Strayer. USA., *Just Married*, Adelaide Matthews, Anne Nichols, Play

JUST MY LUCK 1933 d: Jack Raymond. UKN., *Fifty-Fifty*, H. F. Maltby, London 1932, Play

Just Once More *see* **CHANS** (1962).

Just Once to Be Without a Care *see* **EINMAL KEINE SORGEN HABEN** (1953).

JUST OUT OF COLLEGE 1915 d: George Irving. USA., *Just Out of College*, George Ade, New York 1905, Play

JUST OUT OF COLLEGE 1920 d: Alfred E. Green. USA., *Just Out of College*, George Ade, New York 1905, Play

JUST OUTSIDE THE DOOR 1921 d: George Irving. USA., *Just Outside the Door*, Jules Eckert Goodman, New York 1915, Play

JUST SMITH 1933 d: Tom Walls. UKN., *Never Come Back*, Frederick Lonsdale, London 1932, Play

JUST SUPPOSE 1926 d: Kenneth Webb. USA., *Just Suppose*, A. E. Thomas, New York 1923, Play

JUST TELL ME WHAT YOU WANT 1979 d: Sidney Lumet. USA., *Just Tell Me What You Want*, Jay Presson Allen, Novel

JUST TONY 1922 d: Lynn Reynolds. USA., *Alcatraz*, Max Brand, New York 1923, Novel

JUST WILLIAM 1939 d: Graham Cutts. UKN., Richmal Crompton, Short Stories

JUST WILLIAM'S LUCK 1947 d: Val Guest. UKN., Richmal Crompton, Short Story

JUSTE AVANT LA NUIT 1971 d: Claude Chabrol. FRN/ITL., *The Thin Line*, Edward Atiyah, Novel

Justice *see* **NOT GUILTY** (1915).

JUSTICE 1917 d: Maurice Elvey. UKN., *Justice*, John Galsworthy, London 1910, Play

JUSTICE DE FEMME! 1917 d: Diana Karenne. ITL., *Justice de Femme!*, Daniel Lesuer, Novel

Justice for Sale *see* **NIGHT COURT** (1932).

Justice Rides Again *see* **DESTRY RIDES AGAIN** (1932).

JUSTICIERE, LA 1925 d: Maurice Gleize. FRN., *La Justiciere*, Jean Cassagne, Novel

JUSTIN MORGAN HAD A HORSE 1972 d: Hollingsworth Morse. USA., *Justin Morgan Had a Horse*, Marguerite Henry, Novel

Justine *see* **MARQUIS DE SADE: JUSTINE** (1968).

JUSTINE 1969 d: George Cukor, Joseph Strick (Uncredited). USA., *The Alexandria Quartet*, Lawrence Durrell, 1956-60, Novel

Justine *see* **JUSTINE DE SADE** (1970).

JUSTINE 1976 d: Stuart MacKinnon, Clive Myers. UKN., *Justine; Ou Les Malheurs de la Vertu*, Donatien Sade, 1791, Novel

Justine *see* **CRUEL PASSION** (1977).

Justine and Juliet *see* **MARQUIS DE SADE: JUSTINE** (1968).

JUSTINE DE SADE 1970 d: Claude Pierson. CND/FRN/ITL., *Justine; Ou Les Malheurs de la Vertu*, Donatien Sade, 1791, Novel

Justine Ovvero le Disavventure Della Vertu *see* **MARQUIS DE SADE: JUSTINE** (1968).

JUSTINIAN AND THEODORA 1911 d: Otis Turner. USA., *Justinian and Theodora*, Edward George Bulwer Lytton, Novel

JUURAKON HULDA 1937 d: Valentin VaalA. FNL., *Juurakon Hulda*, Hella Wuolijoki, 1937, Play

JUVE CONTRE FANTOMAS 1913 d: Louis Feuillade. FRN., *Juve Contre Fantomas*, Marcel Allain, Pierre Souvestre, Novel

Juve Vs. Fantomas *see* **JUVE CONTRE FANTOMAS** (1913).

Juvenile Toughs *see* **DIE HALBSTARKEN** (1956).

JUWELEN 1930 d: Hans Bruckner. AUS., *Das Fraulein von Scuderi*, Ernst Theodor Amadeus Hoffmann, 1819, Short Story

JUX WILL ER SICH MACHEN, EINEN 1928 d: Johannes Brandt. GRM., *Jux Will Er Sich machen*, Johann Nestroy, Play

J'Y SUIS, J'Y RESTE 1953 d: Maurice Labro. FRN., *J'y Suis. J'y Reste*, Jean Valmy, Raymond Vinci, Play

K 1997 d: Alexandre Arcady. FRN., *Pas de Kaddish Pour Sylberstein*, Guy Konopnicki, Novel

K - DAS HAUS DES SCHWEIGENS 1951 d: Hans Hinrich. GRM., *Abel*, Alfred Neumann, Play, *Viele Heissen Kain.*, Alfred Neumann, Novel

K - THE UNKNOWN 1924 d: Harry Pollard. USA., *K*, Mary Roberts Rinehart, Boston 1915, Novel

K. Und K. Feldmarschall, Der *see* **DER FALSCHE FELDMARSCHALL** (1930).

K2 *see* **K-2** (1991).

K-2 1991 d: Franc Roddam. USA., *K 2*, Patrick Meyers, Play

KAASUA, KOMISARIO PALMU 1961 d: Matti KassilA. FNL., *Kuka Murhasi Rouva Skrofin?*, Mika Waltari, 1939, Novel

KABALE UND LIEBE 1959 d: Martin Hellberg. GDR., *Kabale Und Liebe*, Friedrich von Schiller, 1784, Play

KABULIWALA 1956 d: Tapan SinhA. IND., *Kabulibala*, Rabindranath Tagore, 1892, Short Story

KADISBELLAN 1993 d: Ake Sandgren. SWD., *Kadisbellan*, Roland Schutt, Autobiography

Kaere Familie, Den *see* **DEN KARA FAMILJEN** (1962).

KAFUKU 1937 d: Mikio Naruse. JPN., *Kafuku*, Kan Kikuchi, 1936-37, Novel

KAGERO-ZA 1981 d: Seijun Suzuki. JPN., *Kagero-Za*, Kyoka Izumi, Novel

KAGI 1959 d: Kon IchikawA. JPN., *Kagi*, Junichiro Tanizaki, Tokyo 1956, Novel

KAGI 1998 d: Toshiharu IkedA. JPN., *Kagi*, Junichiro Tanizaki, Tokyo 1956, Novel

KAHN DER FROHLICHEN LEUTE, DER 1950 d: Hans Heinrich. GRM., *Der Kahn Der Frohlichen Leute*, Jochen Klepper, Novel

KAI AUS DER KISTE 1989 d: Gunther Meyer. GDR., Wolf Durian, Novel

Kai Out of the Box *see* **KAI AUS DER KISTE** (1989).

Kaidan *see* **KWAIDAN** (1964).

KAIDAN BANCHO SARAYASHIKI 1957 d: Juichi Kono. JPN., *Yotsuya Kaidan*, Nanboku Tsuruya, Play

KAIDAN KASANE GA FUCHI 1970 d: Kimiyoshi YasudA. JPN., *Shinkei Kasanegafuchi*, Encho Sanyutei, Short Story

KAIDAN KASANE-GA-FUCHI 1957 d: Nobuo NakagawA. JPN., *Shinkei Kasanegafuchi*, Encho Sanyutei, Short Story

KAIDAN KASANE-GA-FUCHI 1960 d: Kimiyoshi YasudA. JPN., *Shinkei Kasanegafuchi*, Encho Sanyutei, Short Story

KAIDAN OIWA NO BOREI 1961 d: Tai Kato. JPN., *Yotsuya Kaidan*, Nanboku Tsuruya, Play

KAIDAN YUKIJORO 1968 d: Tokuzo TanakA. JPN., *Yuki-Onna*, Lafcadio Hearn, Short Story

KAIDAN ZANKOKU MONOGATARI 1968 d: Kazuo Hase. JPN., *Kaidan Ruigafuchi*, Renzaburo Shibata, Novel

KAIN I ARTYOM 1930 d: Pavel Petrov-Bytov. USS., Maxim Gorky, Short Story

KAINOVO ZNAMENI 1928 d: Oldrich Kminek. CZC., *Vrah*, Zdenek Ron, Short Story

KAISER JOSEPH UND DIE BAHNWARTERTOCHTER 1962 d: Axel Corti. AUS., *Kaiser Joseph Und Die Bahnwartertochter*, Fritz von Herzmanovsky, Play

Kaiserhof Street 12 *see* **KAISERHOFSTRASSE 12** (1980).

KAISERHOFSTRASSE 12 1980 d: Rainer Wolffhardt. GRM., *Kaiserhofstrasse 12*, Valentin Senger, Novel

KAISERIN VON CHINA, DIE 1953 d: Steve Sekely. GRM., *Victoria Himmeldonnerwetter*, H. W. Loeb, Novel

Kaiser's Lackey, The *see* **DER UNTERTAN** (1951).

Kaiser's Shadow Or the Triple Cross, The *see* **THE KAISER'S SHADOW** (1918).

KAISER'S SHADOW, THE 1918 d: R. William Neill. USA., *The Triple Cross*, Octavus Roy Cohen, John U. Giesy, 1918, Serial Story

KAITEI GUNKAN 1963 d: Inoshiro HondA. JPN., *Kaitei Gunkan / Kaitei Okoku*, Shigeru Komatsuzaki, Shunro Oshikawa, Novel

Kaja, I'll Kill You *see* **UBIT CU TE! KAJA** (1967).

KAJA, UBIT CU TE! 1967 d: Vatroslav MimicA. YGS., *Unit Cu Te Kaja*, Kruno Quien

KAK ON LGAL EIO MUZHU 1957 d: Tatyana BerezantsevA. USS., *How He Lied to Her Husband*, George Bernard Shaw, London 1905, Play

KAK POSSORILIS IVAN IVANOVICH S IVANOM NIKIFOROVITCHEM 1941 d: Andrei Kustov. USS., *Kak Possorilis Ivan Ivanovich S Ivanom Nikiforovitchem*, Nikolay Gogol, 1835, Short Story

KAK POSSORILIS IVAN IVANOVICH S IVANOM NIKIFOROVITCHEM 1959 d: Vladimir Karasov. USS., *Kak Possorilis Ivan Ivanovich S Ivanom Nikiforovitchem*, Nikolay Gogol, 1835, Short Story

Kak Zakaljalas Stal see **KAK ZAKALYALAS STAL** (1942).

KAK ZAKALYALAS STAL 1942 d: Mark Donskoi. USS., *Kak Zakaljalas Stal*, Alexander Ostrovsky, 1932-34, Novel

KAKUK MARCI 1973 d: Gyorgy Revesz. HNG., *Kakuk Marci*, Jozsi Jeno Tersanszky, 1950, Novel

Kalahari see **A FAR OFF PLACE** (1993).

KALIYATTAM 1998 d: Jayaraj. IND., *Othello*, William Shakespeare, c1604, Play

KALLE BLOMKVIST - MASTERDETEKTIVEN LEVER FARLIGT 1997 d: Goran Carmback. SWD., *Kalle Blomkvist*, Astrid Lindgren, Novel

KALTE HERZ, DAS 1923 d: Fred Sauer. GRM., *Das Kalte Herz*, Wilhelm Hauff, 1828, Short Story

KALTE HERZ, DAS 1930. GRM., *Das Kalte Herz*, Wilhelm Hauff, 1828, Short Story

KALTE HERZ, DAS 1950 d: Paul Verhoeven. GDR., *Das Kalte Herz*, Wilhelm Hauff, 1828, Short Story

KAM S NIM? 1922 d: Vaclav Wasserman. CZC., *Kam S Nim?*, Jan Neruda

Kama Sutra see **KAMASUTRA - VOLLENDUNG DER LIEBE** (1969).

Kamasutra see **KAMASUTRA - VOLLENDUNG DER LIEBE** (1969).

Kamasutra - Perfection of Love see **KAMASUTRA - VOLLENDUNG DER LIEBE** (1969).

KAMASUTRA - VOLLENDUNG DER LIEBE 1969 d: Kobi Jaeger. GRM., *Kamasutra*, Mallanaga Vatsyayana, Book

Kamelien Dame, Die see **LA DAME AUX CAMELIAS** (1981).

KAMIKAZE 1982 d: Wolfgang Gremm. GRM., *Kamikaze*, Per Wahloo, Novel

Kamikaze '89 see **KAMIKAZE** (1982).

KAMIONAT 1980 d: Hristo Hristov. BUL., Emil Kaluchev, Kosta Strandjev, Short Story

KAMOURASKA 1973 d: Claude JutrA. CND/FRN., *Kamouraska*, Anne Hebert, Novel

Kamouraska Power of Passion see **KAMOURASKA** (1973).

KAMPF DER TERTIA, DER 1928 d: Max Mack. GRM., *Der Kampf Der Tertia*, Wilhelm Speyer, Novel

KAMPF DER TERTIA, DER 1953 d: Erik Ode. GRM., *Der Kampf Der Tertia*, Wilhelm Speyer, Novel

KAMPF DES DONALD WESTHOF, DER 1927 d: Fritz Wendhausen. GRM., *Der Kampf Des Donald Westhof*, Felix Hollaender, Novel

KAMPF UM DEN MANN, DER 1927 d: Hans Werckmeister. GRM., *Dre Kampf Um Den Mann*, Eugene Scribe, Play

Kampf Um Karthago, Der see **SALAMMBO** (1925).

KAMPF UM ROM, TEIL 1: KOMM NUR, MEIN LIEBSTES VOGELEIN 1968 d: Robert Siodmak. GRM/ITL/RMN., *Kampf Um Rom*, Felix Dahn, Novel

KAMPF UM ROM, TEIL 2: DER VERRAT 1969 d: Robert Siodmak. GRM/ITL/RMN., *Kampf Um Rom*, Felix Dahn, Novel

KAMPF UMS MATTERHORN, DER 1928 d: Mario Bonnard, Nunzio MalasommA. GRM/SWT., *Der Kampf Ums Matterhorn*, Carl Haensel, Novel

Kamrathustru see **LIVET GAR VIDARE** (1941).

KANAL 1957 d: Andrzej WajdA. PLN., *Kanal*, Jerzy Stefan Stawinski, Warsaw 1956, Novel

KANASHIMI NO BELLADONNA 1973 d: Eiichi Yamamoto. JPN., Jules Michelet, Story

KANDAM BACHA COAT 1961 d: T. R. Sundaram. IND., *Kandam Bacha Coat*, T. Mohammed Yusuf, Novel

Kandam Becha Kottu see **KANDAM BACHA COAT** (1961).

KANGAROO 1952 d: Lewis Milestone. ASL/USA., *Kangaroo*, Martin Berkeley, Novel

KANGAROO 1986 d: Tim Burstall. ASL., *Kangaroo*, D. H. Lawrence, 1923, Novel

KANGAROO, THE 1914. USA., *The Kangaroo*, Judge Harris Dickson, 1913, Short Story

Kangaroos, The see **HIGH FLYERS** (1937).

KANGELOPORTA, I 1979 d: Dimitris Makris. GRC., *I Kangeloporto*, Andreas Frangias, Novel

KANIKOSEN 1953 d: So YamamurA. JPN., *Kani-Kosen*, Takiji Kobayashi, 1929, Novel

KANINCHEN BIN ICH, DAS 1965 d: Kurt Maetzig. GDR., *Maria Morzeck Oder Das Kaninchen Bin Ich*, Manfred Bieler, 1965, Novel

KANSAN, THE 1943 d: George Archainbaud. USA., *The Kansan*, Frank Gruber, Novel

KANSKE EN DIKTARE 1933 d: Lorens Marmstedt. SWD., *Kanske En Diktare*, Ragnar Josephson, 1932, Play

KANTO MUSHUKU 1963 d: Seijun Suzuki. JPN., *Kanto Mushuku*, Taiko Hirabayashi, Novel

Kanto Wanderer see **KANTO MUSHUKU** (1963).

KANTOR IDEAL 1932 d: Martin Fric. CZC/GRM., *Kantor Ideal*, Adela Cervena, Novel

KANZO SENSEI 1998 d: Shohei ImamurA. JPN., *Doctor Liver*, Ango Sakaguchi, Book

Kaos see **XAOS** (1984).

KAPITAN KORDA 1979 d: Josef PinkavA. CZC., Marie Kubatova, Story

Kapitanleutnant Prien - Der Stier von Scapa Flow see **U 47 KAPITANLEUTNANT PRIEN** (1958).

KAPITANSKAIA DOCHKA 1928 d: Yuri Tarich. USS., *Kapitanskaya Dochka*, Alexander Pushkin, 1836, Short Story

KAPITANSKAIA DOTSHKA 1958 d: Vladimir Kaplunovsky. USS., *Kapitanskaya Dochka*, Alexander Pushkin, 1836, Short Story

Kapitanskaya Dochka see **KAPITANSKAIA DOTSHKA** (1958).

KAPURUSH 1965 d: Satyajit Ray. IND., *Janaiko Kapuruser Kahini*, Premendra Mitra

KARA FAMILJEN, DEN 1962 d: Erik Balling. SWD/DNM., *Den Kaere Familie*, Gustav Esmann, 1892, Play

KARAKTER 1997 d: Mike Van Diem. NTH., *Karakter*, F. Bordewijk, Novel

KARAMANEH 1924 d: Fred Paul. UKN., *Karamaneh*, Sax Rohmer, Short Story

Karamazof see **DER MORDER DIMITRI KARAMASOFF** (1931).

KARATE KILLERS, THE 1967 d: Barry Shear. USA., *The Karate Killers*, Boris Ingster, Novel

KARD, A 1976 d: Janos Domolky. HNG., *A 272. Tagy Leirasa*, Zoltan Jekely, 1975, Verse

KARE JOHN 1964 d: Lars-Magnus Lindgren. SWD., *Kare John*, Olle Lansberg, Stockholm 1959, Novel

KAREL HYNEK MACHA 1937 d: Zet Molas. CZC., *Mimo Proud*, Emil Synek, Play

KARIERA MATKY LIZALKY 1937 d: Ladislav Brom. CZC., Karel Anders, Novel

KARIERA PAVLA CAMRDY 1931 d: M. J. Krnansky. CZC., *Kariera Pavla Camrdy*, Ignat Herrmann, Novel

Karin Daughter of Man see **KARIN MANSDOTTER** (1954).

KARIN MANSDOTTER 1954 d: Alf Sjoberg. SWD., *Erik XIv*, August Strindberg, 1899, Play

Karina the Dancer see **LA MAISON DU MALTAIS** (1927).

KARIOSUTORO NO SHIRO 1991 d: Hayao Miyazaki. JPN., *Kariosutoro No Shiro*, Monkey Punch, Short Story

Karl Raumt Auf see **EIN GANZER KERL** (1935).

KARLEK 1952 d: Gustaf Molander. SWD., *Kaerlighed*, Kaj Munk, 1948, Play

KARLEK OCH KASSABRIST 1932 d: Gustaf Molander. SWD., *Kassabrit*, Vilhelm Moberg, Stockholm 1925, Play

KARLEK OCH VANSKAP 1941 d: Leif Sinding. NRW., *Kjaerlighet Og Vennskap*, Peter Egge, 1904, Play

KARLEKEN 1980 d: Theodor Kallifatides. SWD., *Karleken*, Theodor Kallifatides, Novel

KARLEKENS BROD 1953 d: Arne Mattsson. SWD., *Karlekens Brod*, Peder Sjogren, Novel

KARLEKS SOMMAR, EN 1979 d: Mats Arehn. SWD., *En Karleks Sommar*, Ivan Klima, Novel

KAROL LIR 1969 d: Grigori Kozintsev. USS., *King Lear*, William Shakespeare, c1605, Play

KARPATHY ZOLTAN 1966 d: Zoltan Varkonyi. HNG., *Karpathy Zoltan*, Mor Jokai, 1854, Novel

KARRIERE IN PARIS 1951 d: Georg C. Klaren. GDR., *Le Pere Goriot*, Honore de Balzac, Paris 1834, Novel

KARTKA Z PODROZY 1983 d: Waldemar Dziki. PLN., *Pan Theodor Mundstock*, Ladislav Fuks, 1963, Novel

KARTY 1965 d: Rollan Sergienko. USS., *Vint*, Anton Chekhov, 1884, Short Story

Karussell see **KORHINTA** (1955).

Karussell Des Lebens see **ROSAMUNDE PILCHER: KARUSSELL DES LEBENS** (1994).

KAR'YER 1990 d: Nikolai Skuibin. USS., *Kar'yer*, Valentin Bykov, Novel

KARYERA ARTURO UI: NOVAYA VYERSIYA 1996 d: Boris Blank. RSS., *Der Aufhaltsame Aufstieg Der Arturo Ui*, Bertolt Brecht, 1958, Play

KASAKI 1961 d: Vassily Pronin. USS., *Kazaki*, Lev Nikolayevich Tolstoy, 1863, Novel

KASBA 1990 d: Kumar Shahani. IND., *V Ovrage*, Anton Chekhov, 1900, Short Story

Kasbah see **KASBA** (1990).

KASEKI 1975 d: Masaki Kobayashi. JPN., *Kaseki*, Yasushi Inoue, 1967, Novel

KASEKI NO MORI 1973 d: Masahiro ShinodA. JPN., *Kaseki No Mori*, Shintaro Ishihara, 1970, Novel

KASEREI IN DER VEHFREUDE, DIE 1958 d: Franz Schnyder. SWT., *Die Kaserei in Der Vehfreude*, Jeremias Gotthelf, Berlin 1850, Novel

KASHI TO KODOMO 1962 d: Hiroshi TeshigaharA. JPN., *Otoshiana*, Ade Kobo, 1972, Play

KASHTANKA 1952 d: M. M. Tsekhanovsky. USS., *Kashtanka*, Anton Chekhov, 1887, Short Story

KASPER IN DE ONDERWERELD 1979 d: Jef Van Der Heyden. BLG., *Kasper in de Onderwereld*, Hubert Lampo, 1974, Novel

Kasr El Shawk see **QASR ASH-SHAWQ** (19—).

KASSBACH 1979 d: Peter Patzak. AUS., *Kassbach*, Helmut Zenker, Novel

KATA A KROKODYL 1965 d: Vera Plivova-SimkovA. CZC., *Kata a Krokodyl*, N. V. Gernet, G. B. Jagdfeld, Book

KATAKOMBY 1940 d: Martin Fric. CZC., *Musketyri Z Katakomb*, Gustav Davis, Play

Kate and the Crocodile see **KATA A KROKODYL** (1965).

Kate Plus Ten see **WANTED AT HEADQUARTERS** (1920).

KATE PLUS TEN 1938 d: Reginald Denham. UKN., *Kate Plus Ten*, Edgar Wallace, London 1919, Novel

Katerina Ismailova see **KATERINA ISMAYLOVA** (1966).

KATERINA ISMAYLOVA 1966 d: Mikhail Shapiro. USS., *Ledi Makbet Mtenskogo Uezda*, Nikolay Semyonovich Leskov, 1864, Short Story

Katerina Izmailova see **KATERINA ISMAYLOVA** (1966).

Katerina Izmaylova see **KATERINA ISMAYLOVA** (1966).

KATHARINA KNIE 1929 d: Karl Grune. GRM., *Katharina Knie*, Carl Zuckmayer, Berlin 1928, Play

Katherine the Last see **THE GIRL DOWNSTAIRS** (1938).

Kathleen see **KATHLEEN MAVOURNEEN** (1937).

KATHLEEN MAVOURNEEN 1913 d: Charles J. Brabin. USA., *Kathleen Mavourneen*, Dion Boucicault, Play

KATHLEEN MAVOURNEEN 1913 d: Herbert Brenon. USA., *Kathleen Mavourneen*, Dion Boucicault, Play

KATHLEEN MAVOURNEEN 1919 d: Charles J. Brabin. USA., *Kathleen Mavourneen*, Annie Crawford, Frederick Crouch, 1840, Song

KATHLEEN MAVOURNEEN 1930 d: Albert Ray. USA., *Kathleen Mavourneen*, Dion Boucicault, Play

KATHLEEN MAVOURNEEN 1937 d: Norman Lee. UKN., *Kathleen Mavourneen*, Clara Mulholland, Novel

KATHODOS TON ENEA, I 1984 d: Christos Shiopachas. GRC., *I Kathodos Ton Enea*, Thanassis Valtinos, Novel

Kathodos Ton Ennea see **I KATHODOS TON ENEA** (1984).

KATHY O' 1958 d: Jack Sher. USA., *Memo on Kathy O'Rourke*, Jack Sher, Short Story

823

Kathy's Love Affair see **THE COURTNEYS OF CURZON STREET** (1947).

KATIA 1938 d: Maurice Tourneur. FRN., *Katia*, Lucile Decaux, Novel

Katia see **KATJA** (1959).

Katia and the Crocodile see **KATA A KROKODYL** (1965).

Katia the Beauty see **KRASAVICE KATA** (1919).

Katie's Passion see **KEETJE TIPPEL** (1975).

Katinka see **VED VEJEN** (1988).

KATJA 1959 d: Robert Siodmak. GRM/FRN., *Katia le Demon Bleu du Tsar Alexandre*, Lucile Decaux, Paris 1938, Novel

KATRINA 1943 d: Gustaf Edgren. SWD., *Katrina*, Sally Salminen, 1936, Novel

Katrin's Seven Dresses see **DIE SIEBEN KLEIDER DER KATHRIN** (1954).

KATTORNA 1965 d: Henning Carlsen. SWD., *Kattorna*, Walentin Chorell, Helsinki 1963, Play

KATZ UND MAUS 1967 d: Hansjurgen Pohland. GRM/PLN., *Katz Und Maus*, Gunter Grass, Neuwid Am Rhein 1961, Short Story

KATZE, DIE 1987 d: Dominik Graf. GRM., *Die Katze*, Uwe Erichsen, Novel

KATZENSPIEL 1983 d: Istvan Szabo. GRM., *MacSkajatek*, Istvan Orkeny, 1963, Novel

KATZENSTEG, DER 1915 d: Max Mack. GRM., *Der Katzensteg*, Hermann Sudermann, 1889, Novel

KATZENSTEG, DER 1927 d: Gerhard Lamprecht. GRM., *Der Katzensteg*, Hermann Sudermann, 1889, Novel

KATZENSTEG, DER 1937 d: Fritz Peter Buch. GRM., *Der Katzensteg*, Hermann Sudermann, 1889, Novel

KAVAL DAIVAM 1969 d: K. Vijayan. IND., *Kai Vilangu*, Jayakanthan

KAVI 1949 d: Debaki Bose. IND., *Kavi*, Tarashankar Banerjee, 1942, Novel

Kavik, the Wolf Dog see **THE COURAGE OF KAVIK THE WOLF DOG** (1980).

Kavkazskij Plennik see **IL PRIGIONIERO DEL CAUCASO** (1911).

KAWACHI KARUMEN 1966 d: Seijun Suzuki. JPN., *Kawachi Karumen*, Toko Kon, Novel

KAWAITA HANA 1964 d: Masahiro ShinodA. JPN., *Kawaita Hana*, Shintaro Ishihara, 1958, Short Story

Kaya see **UBIT CU TE! KAJA** (1967).

Kaya, I'll Kill You see **UBIT CU TE! KAJA** (1967).

KAYLA 1998 d: Nicholas Kendall. CND., *Kayla*, Elizabeth Van Steenwik, Novel

KAZABLAN 1974 d: Menahem Golan. ISR., Yigal Mossensohn, Story

Kazaki see **KASAKI** (1961).

KAZAN 1921 d: Bertram Bracken. USA., *The Wolf Dog Kazan*, James Oliver Curwood, Indianapolis 1914, Novel

KAZAN 1949 d: Will Jason. USA., *The Wolf Dog Kazan*, James Oliver Curwood, Indianapolis 1914, Novel

Kazoku Gaimu see **KAZOKU GEEMU** (1983).

Kazoku Game see **KAZOKU GEEMU** (1983).

KAZOKU GEEMU 1983 d: Yoshimitsu MoritA. JPN., Yohei Homma, Novel

KDO SE BOJI, UTIKA 1986 d: Dusan Klein. CZC., *Utika Kdo Se Boji*, Josef Pohl, Novel

KDYZ STRUNY LKAJI 1930 d: Friedrich Feher. CZC., *Dabel*, Lev Nikolayevich Tolstoy, Short Story

KE SHAN HONG RI 1960 d: Dong Zhaoqi. CHN., *Ke Shan Hong Ri*, Chen Qitong, Opera

Kean see **OVVERO GENIO E SREGOLATEZZA KEAN** (1916).

KEAN 1922 d: Alexander Volkov. FRN., *Kean; Ou Desordre du Genie*, Alexandre Dumas (pere), 1836, Play

KEAN 1940 d: Guido Brignone. ITL., *Kean; Ou Desordre du Genie*, Alexandre Dumas (pere), 1836, Play

KEAN, GENIO E SREGOLATEZZA 1957 d: Vittorio Gassman, Francesco Rosi (Uncredited). ITL., *Kean; Ou Desordre de Genie*, Alexandre Dumas (pere), 1836, Play

Kean, Genius Or Scoundrel see **GENIO E SREGOLATEZZA KEAN** (1957).

Kean, Gli Amori Di un Artista see **KEAN** (1940).

KEAN, OVVERO GENIO E SREGOLATEZZA 1916 d: Armando Brunero. ITL., *Kean; Ou Desordre du Genie*, Alexandre Dumas (pere), 1836, Play

Keep an Eye on Amelia see **OCCUPE-TOI D'AMELIE** (1949).

Keep Cool see **YOU HUA HAO HAO SHUO** (1997).

KEEP 'EM ROLLING 1934 d: George Archainbaud. USA., *Rodney*, Leonard Nason, 1933, Short Story

Keep Off the Grass see **THE RIGHT THAT FAILED** (1922).

KEEP, THE 1983 d: Michael Mann. UKN/USA., *The Keep*, F. Paul Wilson, Novel

KEEP THE ASPIDISTRA FLYING 1997 d: Robert Bierman. UKN., *Keep the Aspidistra Flying*, George Orwell, 1936, Novel

KEEP THE CHANGE 1992 d: Andrew Tennant. USA., *Keep the Change*, Thomas McGuane, Novel

Keep Your Fingers Crossed see **CATCH ME A SPY** (1971).

KEEP YOUR SEATS PLEASE 1936 d: Monty Banks. UKN., *Dvenadtsat Stulyev*, Ilya Ilf, Evgeny Petrov, Moscow 1928, Novel

Keeper of Promises, The see **O PAGADOR DE PROMESSAS** (1961).

KEEPER OF THE BEES 1947 d: John Sturges. USA., *The Keeper of the Bees*, Gene Stratton-Porter, Garden City, N.Y. 1925, Novel

KEEPER OF THE BEES, THE 1925 d: James Leo Meehan. USA., *The Keeper of the Bees*, Gene Stratton-Porter, Garden City, N.Y. 1925, Novel

KEEPER OF THE BEES, THE 1935 d: W. Christy Cabanne. USA., *The Keeper of the Bees*, Gene Stratton-Porter, Garden City, N.Y. 1925, Novel

KEEPER OF THE CITY 1992 d: Bobby Roth. USA., *Keeper of the City*, Gerald Dipego, Novel

KEEPER OF THE DOOR 1919 d: Maurice Elvey. UKN., *Keeper of the Door*, Ethel M. Dell, Novel

KEEPER OF THE FLAME 1942 d: George Cukor. USA., *Keeper of the Flame*, I. A. R. Wylie, Novel

Keepers of the Earth, The see **THE BRAIN EATERS** (1958).

KEEPERS OF YOUTH 1931 d: Thomas Bentley. UKN., *Keepers of Youth*, Arnold Ridley, London 1929, Play

Keepers, The see **LA TETE CONTRE LES MURS** (1958).

Keepers, The see **THE BRAIN EATERS** (1958).

KEEPING IT DARK 1915 d: Horace Davey. USA., *Keeping It Dark*, Gertrude Hynes, Story

KEEPING MAN INTERESTED 1922 d: George A. Cooper. UKN., *Keeping Man Interested*, Mayell Bannister, Story

KEEPING UP WITH LIZZIE 1921 d: Lloyd Ingraham. USA., *Keeping Up with Lizzie*, Irving Addison Bacheller, New York 1911, Novel

KEETJE TIPPEL 1975 d: Paul Verhoeven. NTH., *Jours de Famine Et Detresse*, Neel Doff, Autobiography, *Keetje*, Neel Doff, Autobiography, *Keetje Trottin*, Neel Doff, Autobiography

KEIN HUSUNG 1954 d: Arthur Pohl. GDR., *Kein Husung*, Fritz Reuter, 1858, Verse

KEIN PLATZ FUR WILDE TIERE 1956 d: Bernard Grzimek, Michael Grzimek. GRM., *Kein Platz Fur Wilde Tiere*, Dr. Bernhard Grzimek, Book

KEIN REIHENHAUS FUR ROBIN HOOD 1980 d: Wolfgang Gremm. GRM., *Kein Reihenhaus Fur Robin Hood*, Horst Bosetzky, Novel

KEITH OF THE BORDER 1918 d: Cliff Smith. USA., *Keith of the Border*, Randall Parrish, Chicago 1910, Novel

KEJSARN AV PORTUGALLIEN 1944 d: Gustaf Molander. SWD., *Kejsarn Av Portugallien*, Selma Lagerlof, Stockholm 1914, Novel

KEJSARN AV PORTUGALLIEN 1992 d: Lars Molin. SWD., *Kejsarn Av Portugallien*, Selma Lagerlof, Stockholm 1914, Novel

Kek Alarc, A see **MASKE IN BLAU** (1942).

KELLY OF THE SECRET SERVICE 1936 d: Robert F. Hill. USA., *On Irish Hill*, Peter B. Kyne, Short Story

Kelvaney see **ROGUE COP** (1954).

Kempy see **WISE GIRLS** (1929).

KENILWORTH 1909 d: J. Stuart Blackton (Spv). USA., *Kenilworth*, Sir Walter Scott, 1821, Novel

Kenka Elegy see **KENKA SEREJII** (1966).

KENKA SEREJII 1966 d: Seijun Suzuki. JPN., *Kenka Ereji*, Seijun Suzuki, Novel

KENNEDY SQUARE 1916 d: S. Rankin Drew. USA., *Kennedy Square*, F. Hopkinson Smith, New York 1911, Novel

KENNEL MURDER CASE, THE 1933 d: Michael Curtiz. USA., *The Kennel Murder Case*, S. S. Van Dine, New York 1913, Novel

KENNWORT: MACHIN 1939 d: Erich Waschneck. GRM., *Herr Borb Besitzt Under Vertrauen*, C. V. Rock, Novel

KENNWORT: REIHER 1964 d: Rudolf Jugert. GRM., *The River Line*, Charles Morgan, 1949, Novel

KENSINGTON MYSTERY, THE 1924 d: Hugh Croise. UKN., *The Kensington Mystery*, Baroness Orczy, Short Story

Kent Chronicles, The see **THE BASTARD** (1978).

KENT THE FIGHTING MAN 1916 d: A. E. Coleby. UKN., *Kent the Fighting Man*, George Edgar, Novel

KENTUCKIAN, THE 1908 d: Wallace McCutcheon. USA., *The Kentuckian*, Augustus Thomas, Play

KENTUCKIAN, THE 1955 d: Burt Lancaster. USA., *The Gabriel Horn*, Felix Holt, Novel

KENTUCKIANS, THE 1921 d: Charles Maigne. USA., *The Kentuckians*, John Fox Jr., New York 1897, Novel

KENTUCKY 1938 d: David Butler. USA., *The Look of Eagles*, John Taintor Foote, New York 1916, Novel

KENTUCKY CINDERELLA, A 1917 d: Rupert Julian. USA., *A Kentucky Cinderella*, F. Hopkinson Smith, 1899, Short Story

KENTUCKY COLONEL, THE 1920 d: William A. Seiter. USA., *A Kentucky Colonel*, Opie Read, Chicago 1890, Novel

Kentucky Courage see **THE LITTLE SHEPHERD OF KINGDOM COME** (1928).

KENTUCKY DERBY, THE 1922 d: King Baggot. USA., *The Suburban*, Charles T. Dazey, 1902, Play

Kenya -Country of Treasure see **THE SYNDICATE** (1968).

KERRY GOW, THE 1912 d: Sidney Olcott. USA., *The Kerry Gow*, Joe Murphy, Play

KES 1969 d: Kenneth Loach. UKN., *A Kestrel for a Knave*, Barry Hines, London 1968, Novel

Kesher Hauranium see **A CHI TOCCA..TOCCA!** (1978).

KETTEN HALTAK MEG 1964 d: Gyorgy Palasthy, Antal Forgacs. HNG., *Ciklon*, Ivan Mandy, 1966, Short Story

Ketto Ganryujima see **MIYAMOTO MUSASHI: KETTO GANRYUJIMA** (1956).

KEUSCHE ADAM, DER 1950 d: Karl Sztollar, Paul Lowinger. AUS., *Der Keusche Adam*, Gretl Lowinger, Paul Lowinger, Play

KEUSCHE JOSEF, DER 1953 d: Carl Boese. GRM., *Unter Geschaftsaufsicht*, Franz Robert Arnold, Ernst Bach, Play

KEUSCHE LEBEMANN, DER 1952 d: Carl Boese. GRM., *Der Keusche Lebemann*, Franz Robert Arnold, Ernst Bach, Play

KEUSCHE SUNDERIN, DIE 1943 d: Joe Stockel. GRM., *Antiquitaten*, Friedrich Forster, Play

Kewi see **KAVI** (1949).

KEY LARGO 1948 d: John Huston. USA., *Key Largo*, Maxwell Anderson, 1939, Play

KEY MAN, THE 1957 d: Montgomery Tully. UKN., *The Key Man*, J. McLaren Ross, Play

KEY OF THE WORLD, THE 1918 d: J. L. V. Leigh. UKN., *The Key of the World*, Dorin Craig, Novel

KEY, THE 1934 d: Michael Curtiz. USA., *The Key*, Robert Gore-Browne, Joseph Lee Hardy, London 1933, Play

KEY, THE 1958 d: Carol Reed. UKN., *Stella*, Jan de Hartog, Novel

Key, The see **KAGI** (1959).

Key, The see **LA CHIAVE** (1984).

Key, The see **KAGI** (1998).

KEY TO HARMONY 1935 d: Norman Walker. UKN., *Suburban Retreat*, John B. Wilson, Novel

KEY TO REBECCA, THE 1985 d: David Hemmings. USA., *The Key to Rebecca*, Ken Follett, Novel

KEY TO YESTERDAY, THE 1914 d: John Francis Dillon. USA., *The Key to Yesterday*, Charles Neville Buck, New York 1910, Novel

KEYS OF THE KINGDOM, THE 1944 d: John M. Stahl. USA., *The Keys of the Kingdom*, A. J. Cronin, 1941, Novel

KEYS TO TULSA 1997 d: Leslie Greif. USA., *Keys to Tulsa*, Brian Fair Berkey, Novel

K'FAFOT 1986 d: Rafi Adar. ISR., Dan Tzelkah, Story

K'fafoth see **K'FAFOT** (1986).

KHARTOUM 1966 d: Basil Dearden. UKN., *Khartoum*, Alan Caillou, Book

Khavah see **BROKEN BARRIERS** (1919).

Khazakki see **KASAKI** (1961).

KHIRBET HIZA'A 1978 d: Ram Loevy. ISR., S. Izhar, Story

KHIRURGIA 1939 d: Jan Frid. USS., *Khirurgia*, Anton Chekhov, 1884, Short Story

Khlyab see **HLYAB - CHERTICHKATA** (1972).

KHORISTKA 1978 d: Alexander Muratov. USS., *Khorista*, Anton Chekhov, 1886, Short Story

KHRUSTALNYY BASHMACHOK 1961 d: Aleksandr Rou, Rostislav Zakharov. USS., *Cendrillon*, Charles Perrault, 1697, Short Story

KHU GAM 1996 d: Euthana Mukdasanit. THL., *Khu Gam*, Tomayantee, Novel

KHUDOZHESTVO 1960 d: Mark Kovalyov. USS., *Khudozhestvo*, Anton Chekhov, 1886, Short Story

KHUROYE UTRO 1959 d: Grigori Roshal, Marija Andjaparidze. USS., *Khozhdeniye Po Mukam*, Alexsey Nikolayevich Tolstoy, 1922-45, Novel

KHUTOROK V STEPI 1971 d: Boris Buneyev. USS., *Khutorok V Stepi*, Valentin Kataev, 1956, Novel

KIALTAS ES KIALTAS 1988 d: Zsolt Kezdi-Kovacs. HNG., *Kialtas Es Kialtas*, Gyula Hernadi, 1981, Novel

KIBITZER, THE 1930 d: Edward Sloman. USA., *The Kibitzer*, Edward G. Robinson, Joseph Swerling, New York 1929, Play

KICK IN 1917 d: George Fitzmaurice. USA., *Kick in*, Willard Mack, New York 1914, Play

KICK IN 1922 d: George Fitzmaurice. USA., *Kick in*, Willard Mack, New York 1914, Play

KICK IN 1931 d: Richard Wallace. USA., *Kick in*, Willard Mack, New York 1914, Play

KID BOOTS 1926 d: Frank Tuttle. USA., *Kid Boots*, Otto Harbach, J. P. McCarthy, William Anthony McGuire, New York 1923, Musical Play

KID DYNAMITE 1943 d: Wallace Fox. USA., *The Old Gang*, Paul Ernest, Story

KID FOR TWO FARTHINGS, A 1955 d: Carol Reed. UKN., *A Kid for Two Farthings*, Wolf Mankowitz, Novel

KID FROM BROOKLYN, THE 1946 d: Norman Z. McLeod. USA., *The Milky Way*, Harry Clork, Lynn Root, New York 1934, Play

Kid from Chaaba, The see **LE GONE DU CHAABA** (1998).

Kid from College see **THE BAND PLAYS ON** (1934).

KID FROM TEXAS, THE 1950 d: Kurt Neumann. USA., *Kid from Texas*, Robert Hardy Andrews, Novel

KID FROM THE KLONDYKE 1911 d: Harold Shaw. USA., *The Elusive Graft*, Rex Beach, Story

KID GALAHAD 1937 d: Michael Curtiz. USA., *Kid Galahad*, Francis Wallace, Boston 1936, Novel

KID GALAHAD 1962 d: Phil Karlson. USA., *Kid Galahad*, Francis Wallace, Boston 1936, Novel

KID RODELO 1966 d: Richard Carlson. USA/SPN., Louis L'Amour, Story

KID SISTER, THE 1927 d: Ralph Graves. USA., *The Lost House*, Dorothy Howell, Story

KIDDIES IN THE RUINS, THE 1918 d: George Pearson. UKN., *Les Gosses Dans Les Ruines*, Paul Grex, Paul Gsell, M. Poulbot, Play

KIDNAPPED 1917 d: Alan Crosland. USA., *Kidnapped*, Robert Louis Stevenson, London 1886, Novel

Kidnapped see **MISS FANE'S BABY IS STOLEN** (1934).

KIDNAPPED 1938 d: Alfred L. Werker, Otto Preminger (Uncredited). USA., *David Balfour*, Robert Louis Stevenson, New York 1893, Novel, *Kidnapped*, Robert Louis Stevenson, London 1886, Novel

KIDNAPPED 1948 d: William Beaudine. USA., *Kidnapped*, Robert Louis Stevenson, London 1886, Novel

KIDNAPPED 1960 d: Robert Stevenson. UKN., *Kidnapped*, Robert Louis Stevenson, London 1886, Novel

KIDNAPPED 1971 d: Delbert Mann. UKN/USA., *Kidnapped*, Robert Louis Stevenson, London 1886, Novel

Kidnapped - the Adventures of David Balfour see **KIDNAPPED** (1938).

KIDNAPPED KING, THE 1909. UKN., *The Kidnapped King*, C. Douglas Carlile, Play

KIDNAPPING OF THE PRESIDENT, THE 1980 d: George Menduluk. CND., *The Kidnapping of the President*, Charles Templeton, Novel

Kid's Last Fight, The see **THE LIFE OF JIMMY DOLAN** (1933).

KIEBICH UND DUTZ 1987 d: F. K. Wachter. GRM., *Kiebich Und Dutz*, F. K. Wachter, Play

Kiev Comedy, A see **ZA DVUMYA ZAYTSAMI** (1961).

Kiev Comedy: Or, Chasing Two Hares see **ZA DVUMYA ZAYTSAMI** (1961).

Kiez see **KIEZ - AUFSTIEG UND FALL EINES LUDEN** (1982).

KIEZ - AUFSTIEG UND FALL EINES LUDEN 1982 d: Walter Bockmayer, Rolf Buhrmann. GRM., *Kiez - Aufstieg Und Fall Eines Luden*, Peter Greiner, Play

Kiff Tebbi see **KIFF TEBBY** (1928).

KIFF TEBBY 1928 d: Mario Camerini. ITL., *Kiff Tebby*, Luciano Zuccoli, 1923, Novel

KIHLAUS 1922 d: Teuvo Puro. FNL., *Kihlaus*, Aleksis Kivi, 1866, Play

KIHLAUS 1955 d: Erik Blomberg. FNL., *Kihlaus*, Aleksis Kivi, 1866, Play

KIKI 1926 d: Clarence Brown. USA., *Kiki*, Andre Picard, Paris 1920, Play

KIKI 1931 d: Sam Taylor. USA., *Kiki*, Andre Picard, Paris 1920, Play

KIKI 1932 d: Carl Lamac. GRM., *Kiki*, Andre Picard, Paris 1920, Play

KIKI 1932 d: Pierre Billon, Carl Lamac. FRN., *Kiki*, Andre Picard, Paris 1920, Play

KIKI 1934 d: Raffaello Matarazzo. ITL., *Kiki*, Andre Picard, Paris 1920, Play

KIKLOP 1982 d: Antun Vrdoljak. YGS., *Kiklop*, Ranko Marinkovic, 1966, Novel

KILDARE OF STORM 1918 d: Harry L. Franklin. USA., *Kildares of Storm*, Eleanor Mercein Kelly, New York 1916, Novel

Kildares of Storm see **KILDARE OF STORM** (1918).

Kill! see **KIRU** (1968).

Kill Or Cure see **LA BONNE TISANE** (1957).

Kill Reflex, The see **SODA CRACKER** (1989).

KILLDOZER 1974 d: Jerry London. USA., *Killdozer*, Theodore Sturgeon, Novel

Killer! see **QUE LA BETE MEURE** (1969).

Killer 77 Alive Or Dead see **SICARIO 77 VIVO O MORTO** (1966).

KILLER: A JOURNAL OF MURDER 1995 d: Tim Metcalfe. USA., *Killer: a Journal of Murder*, Thomas E. Gaddis, James O. Long, Book

KILLER AT LARGE 1936 d: David Selman. USA., *Poker Face*, Carl Clausen, 1926, Short Story

Killer Bait see **TOO LATE FOR TEARS** (1949).

Killer Dino see **DINO** (1957).

KILLER ELITE, THE 1975 d: Sam Peckinpah. USA., *Monkey in the Middle*, Robert Rostand, Novel

KILLER INSIDE ME, THE 1976 d: Burt Kennedy. USA., *The Killer Inside Me*, Jim Thompson, Novel

Killer Lassen Bitten see **QUAND LA FEMME S'EN MELE** (1957).

Killer Likes Candy, The see **UN KILLER PER SUA MAESTA** (1968).

Killer Man see **LA SCOUMOUNE** (1973).

Killer of His Majesty, A see **UN KILLER PER SUA MAESTA** (1968).

Killer on a Horse see **WELCOME TO HARD TIMES** (1967).

KILLER PER SUA MAESTA, UN 1968 d: Federico Chentrens, Maurice Cloche. ITL/FRN/GRM., *A Coeur Ouvert Pour Face d'Ange*, Adam Saint-Moore, Novel

Killer Reflex, The see **SODA CRACKER** (1989).

KILLER THAT STALKED NEW YORK, THE 1950 d: Earl McEvoy. USA., Milton Lehman, Article

KILLER, THE 1921 d: Howard Hickman. USA., *The Killer*, Stewart Edward White, Garden City, N.Y. 1920, Novel

Killer, The see **MYSTERY RANCH** (1932).

KILLER WALKS, A 1952 d: Ronald Drake. UKN., *Envy My Simplicity*, Rayner Barton, Novel

Killer With the Third Eye, The see **IL TERZO OCCHIO** (1966).

KILLERS OF KILIMANJARO 1959 d: Richard Thorpe. UKN., *African Bush Adventures*, John A. Hunter, Daniel P. Mannix, Book

Killers of the East see **LA VENDETTA DEI TUGHS** (1955).

Killers on the Loose see **KILLER AT LARGE** (1936).

KILLERS, THE 1946 d: Robert Siodmak. USA., *The Killers*, Ernest Hemingway, New York 1927, Short Story

Killers, The see **QUAND LA FEMME S'EN MELE** (1957).

KILLERS, THE 1964 d: Don Siegel. USA., *The Killers*, Ernest Hemingway, New York 1927, Short Story

KILLERS, THE 1984 d: Patrick Roth. USA., *Short Story*, Charles Bukowski

Killers Who Wore Collars see **THE PACK** (1977).

KILLING AFFAIR, A 1988 d: David Saperstein. USA., *Monday Tuesday Wednesday*, Robert Houston, Novel

KILLING DAD 1989 d: Michael Austin. UKN., *Berg*, Ann Quinn, Novel

Killing Dad (Or How to Love Your Mother) see **KILLING DAD** (1989).

KILLING DRUGS 1988 d: Rolf von Sydow. GRM., *Killing Drugs*, Detlef Blettenberg, Novel

KILLING 'EM SOFTLY 1982 d: Max Fischer. CND., *The Neighbour*, Laird Koenig, Novel

Killin' Em Softly see **KILLING 'EM SOFTLY** (1982).

KILLING FIELDS, THE 1983 d: Roland Joffe. UKN., *The Death and Life of Dith Pran*, Sydney Schanberg, Article

Killing Games see **IDENTIKIT** (1974).

Killing Heat see **THE GRASS IS SINGING** (1981).

KILLING IN A SMALL TOWN, A 1990 d: Stephen Gyllenhaal. USA., *Evidence of Love*, John Bloom, Book

KILLING OF RANDY WEBSTER, THE 1981 d: Sam Wanamaker. USA., *The Throwdown*, Tom Curtis

KILLING OF SISTER GEORGE, THE 1968 d: Robert Aldrich. USA., *The Killing of Sister George*, Frank Marcus, Bristol 1965, Play

Killing of the Aunt, The see **ZABICIE CIOTKI** (1984).

KILLING, THE 1956 d: Stanley Kubrick. USA., *Clean Break*, Lionel White, 1955, Novel

Killing the Aunt see **ZABICIE CIOTKI** (1984).

KILL-OFF, THE 1990 d: Maggie Greenwald. USA., *The Kill-Off*, Jim Thompson, Novel

KIM 1950 d: Victor Saville. USA., *Kim*, Rudyard Kipling, 1901, Novel

KIM 1984 d: John Davies. USA/UKN., *Kim*, Rudyard Kipling, 1901, Novel

KIMEN 1973 d: Erik Solbakken. NRW., *Kimen*, Tarjei Vesaas, 1940, Novel

Kimiko see **TSUMA YO BARA NO YONI** (1935).

KIMURA-KE NO HITOBITO 1988 d: Yojiro TakitA. JPN., *The Kimura Family*, Toshihiko Tani, Short Story

KINCSKERESO KIS KODMON 1973 d: Mihaly Szemes. HNG., *Kincskereso Kiskodmon*, Ferenc Mora, 1918, Novel

KIND HEARTS AND CORONETS 1949 d: Robert Hamer. UKN., *Israel Rank*, Roy Horniman, Novel

KIND LADY 1935 d: George B. Seitz. USA., *Kind Lady*, Edward Chodorov, New York 1935, Play, *The Silver Mask*, Hugh Walpole, 1932, Short Story

KIND LADY 1951 d: John Sturges. USA., *The Silver Mask*, Hugh Walpole, 1932, Short Story

Kind Men Marry, The see **IN NAME ONLY** (1939).

KIND OF ALASKA, A 1975 d: Kenneth Ives. UKN., *Awakenings*, Dr. Oliver Sacks, Book

KIND OF HUSH, A 1998 d: Brian Stirner. UKN., *Getting Even*, Richard Johnson, Manuscript

KIND OF LOVING, A 1962 d: John Schlesinger. UKN., *A Kind of Loving*, Stan Barstow, London 1960, Novel

KINDER DER BERGE 1958 d: Georg Tressler. SWT/LCH., *LudmilA. a Legend of Liechtenstein*, Paul Gallico, London 1955, Short Story

KINDER DER LIEBE 1949 d: Walter Firner. AUS., *Kinder Der Liebe*, Irma Firner, Walter Firner, Play

KINDER, MUTTER UND EIN GENERAL 1955 d: Laslo Benedek. GRM., *Hauen Sie Ab Mit Heldentum*, Herbert Reinecker, Novel

KINDERSEELEN KLAGEN EUCH AN 1927 d: Curtis Bernhardt. GRM., *Die Drei Ringe*, Paul Keller, Short Story

KINDLING, THE 1915 d: Cecil B. de Mille. USA., *The Kindling*, Charles Kenyon, New York 1911, Play

KINDRED OF THE DUST 1922 d: Raoul Walsh. USA., *Kindred of the Dust*, Peter B. Kyne, New York 1920, Novel

KING AND COUNTRY 1964 d: Joseph Losey. UKN., *Return to the Wood*, James Hodson, London 1955, Novel

KING AND FOUR QUEENS, THE 1956 d: Raoul Walsh. USA., Margaret Fitts, Short Story

KING AND I, THE 1956 d: Walter Lang. USA., *Anna and the King of Siam*, Margaret Landon, Book

KING AND I, THE 1999 d: Richard Rich. USA., *The King and I*, Oscar Hammerstein II, Richard Rodgers, New York 1951, Musical Play

King and Mister Bird, The *see* LE ROI ET L'OISEAU (1979).

King and the Bird, The *see* LE ROI ET L'OISEAU (1979).

King Ape *see* KING KONG (1933).

KING CHARLES 1913 d: Wilfred Noy. UKN., *King Charles*, Harrison Ainsworth, Novel

KING CREOLE 1958 d: Michael Curtiz. USA., *A Stone for Danny Fisher*, Harold Robbins, Novel

King Drosselbart *see* KONIG DROSSELBART (1967).

King Had Rabies, The *see* EL REY QUE RABIO (1929).

King Henry V *see* HENRY V (1945).

King in Khaki, A *see* A MAN OF HONOR (1919).

King in Shadow *see* HERRSCHER OHNE KRONE (1957).

KING JOHN 1899. UKN., *King John*, William Shakespeare, c1595, Play

KING KONG 1933 d: Ernest B. Schoedsack, Merian C. Cooper. USA., Edgar Wallace, Story

KING LEAR 1909 d: William V. Ranous. USA., *King Lear*, William Shakespeare, c1605, Play

King Lear *see* RE LEAR (1910).

KING LEAR 1916 d: Ernest C. Warde. USA., *King Lear*, William Shakespeare, c1605, Play

King Lear *see* KAROL LIR (1969).

KING LEAR 1970 d: Peter Brook. UKN/DNM., *King Lear*, William Shakespeare, c1605, Play

KING LEAR 1982 d: Jonathan Miller. UKN., *King Lear*, William Shakespeare, c1605, Play

KING LEAR 1983 d: Michael Elliott. UKN., *King Lear*, William Shakespeare, c1605, Play

KING LEAR 1987 d: Jean-Luc Godard. SWT/USA., *King Lear*, William Shakespeare, c1605, Play

King Oedipus *see* EDIPO RE (1910).

King Oedipus *see* KONING OEDIPUS (1912).

King Oedipus *see* OEDIPUS REX (1957).

King of Camargue *see* ROI DE CAMARGUE (1934).

KING OF CHESS 1991 d: Yim Ho, Tsui Hark. HKG., *Qi Wang*, Chang Chang Hsi-Kuo, 1982, Novel

KING OF CRIME, THE 1914 d: Sidney Northcote. UKN., *The King of Crime*, Arthur Shirley, Play

KING OF HEARTS 1936 d: Oswald Mitchell, Walter Tennyson. UKN., *The Corduroy Diplomat*, Matthew Boulton, Play

KING OF PARIS, THE 1934 d: Jack Raymond. UKN., *La Voie Lactee*, Alfred Savoir, Play

King of Swing *see* MELODY FOR TWO (1937).

King of the Candle *see* O REI DA VELA (1982).

KING OF THE CASTLE 1925 d: Henry Edwards. UKN., *King of the Castle*, Keble Howard, Play

King of the Children *see* HAI ZI WANG (1987).

KING OF THE DAMNED 1936 d: Walter Forde. UKN., *King of the Damned*, John Chancellor, Play

King of the Edelweiss *see* DER EDELWEISSKONIG (1919).

King of the Edelweiss *see* DER EDELWEISSKONIG (1938).

King of the Edelweiss *see* DER EDELWEISSKONIG (1957).

King of the Edelweiss *see* DER EDELWEISSKONIG (1975).

KING OF THE GRIZZLIES 1970 d: Ron Kelly. USA/CND., *The Biography of a Grizzly*, Ernest Thompson Seton, New York 1903, Novel

KING OF THE JUNGLE 1933 d: H. Bruce Humberstone, Max Marcin. USA., *The Lion's Way; a Story of Men and Lions*, Charles Thurley Stoneham, London 1931, Novel

King of the Khyber Rifles *see* THE BLACK WATCH (1929).

KING OF THE KHYBER RIFLES 1953 d: Henry King. USA., *King - of the Khyber Rifles*, Talbot Mundy, New York 1916, Novel

KING OF THE LUMBERJACKS 1940 d: William Clemens. USA., *Timber*, Robert E. Kent, Story

KING OF THE MOUNTAIN 1981 d: Noel Nosseck. USA., *Thunder Road*, David Barry, Article

King of the Mountains *see* ETERNAL LOVE (1929).

KING OF THE RITZ 1932 d: Carmine Gallone. UKN., *Le Roi Des Palaces*, Henri Kistemaeckers, Play

King of the River *see* ISLAND OF LOST MEN (1939).

KING OF THE ROARING TWENTIES -THE STORY OF ARNOLD ROTHSTEIN 1961 d: Joseph M. Newman. USA., *The Big Bankroll; the Life and Times of Arnold Rothstein*, Leo Katcher, New York 1959, Biography

KING OF THE UNDERWORLD 1939 d: Lewis Seiler. USA., William Riley Burnett, Story

KING OF THE WIND 1989 d: Peter Duffell. UKN/USA., *King of the Wind*, Marguerite Henry, Novel

KING ON MAIN STREET, THE 1925 d: Monta Bell. USA., *Le Roi*, Gaston Arman de Caillavet, Robert de Flers, 1908, Play

King, Queen and Slave *see* SAHIB BIBI AUR GHULAM (1962).

King, Queen, Knave *see* SAHIB BIBI AUR GHULAM (1962).

King, Queen, Knave *see* HERZBUBE (1972).

King, Queen Or Knave *see* SAHIB BIBI AUR GHULAM (1962).

KING RALPH 1991 d: David S. Ward. USA., *Headlong*, Emlyn Williams, 1981, Novel

King Ralph I *see* KING RALPH (1991).

KING RAT 1965 d: Bryan Forbes. USA., *King Rat*, James Clavell, London 1963, Novel

KING RENE'S DAUGHTER 1913 d: USA., *King Rene's Daughter*, Henrik Heri, Play

KING RICHARD AND THE CRUSADERS 1954 d: David Butler. USA., *The Talisman*, Sir Walter Scott, 1825, Novel

KING ROBERT OF SICILY 1913 d: USA., *King Robert of Sicily*, Henry Wadsworth Longfellow, Poem

KING SOLOMON'S MINES 1937 d: Robert Stevenson. UKN., *King Solomon's Mines*, H. Rider Haggard, London 1885, Novel

KING SOLOMON'S MINES 1950 d: Compton Bennett, Andrew Marton. USA., *King Solomon's Mines*, H. Rider Haggard, London 1885, Novel

KING SOLOMON'S MINES 1984 d: J. Lee Thompson. USA., *King Solomon's Mines*, H. Rider Haggard, London 1885, Novel

KING SOLOMON'S TREASURE 1976 d: Alvin Rakoff. CND., *Allan Quartermain*, H. Rider Haggard, 1885, Novel

KING SPRUCE 1920 d: Roy Clements. USA., *King Spruce*, Holman Francis Day, New York 1908, Novel

KING STEPS OUT, THE 1936 d: Josef von Sternberg. USA., *Sissy's Brautfahrt*, Ernst Decsey, Gustav Holm, Play

King Thrushbeard *see* KONIG DROSSELBART (1954).

King Thrushbeard *see* KONIG DROSSELBART (1967).

King Thrushbeard *see* KRAL DROZDI BRADA (1984).

King Ubu *see* KRAL UBU (1996).

Kingdom of Ram, The *see* RAM RAJYA (1967).

King's Book, The *see* SIAVOSH DAR TAKHTE JAMSHID (1967).

KING'S BREAKFAST, THE 1963 d: Wendy Toye. UKN., *The King's Breakfast*, A. A. Milne, Poem

KING'S DAUGHTER, THE 1916 d: Maurice Elvey. UKN., *Une Fille du Regent*, Alexandre Dumas (pere), 1845, Play

KING'S GAME, THE 1916 d: Ashley Miller. USA., *The King's Game*, George B. Seitz, New York 1910, Play

KINGS GO FORTH 1958 d: Delmer Daves. USA., *Kings Go Forth*, Joe David Brown, Novel

KING'S HIGHWAY, THE 1927 d: Sinclair Hill. UKN., *Paul Clifford*, Edward George Bulwer Lytton, Novel

KINGS IN GRASS CASTLES 1998 d: John Woods. ASL/IRL., *Kings in Grass Castles*, Dame Mary Durack, Novel

King's Jester, The *see* O BOBO DO REI (1936).

King's Jester, The *see* IL RE SI DIVERTE (1941).

King's Knight, The *see* LE CAPITAN (1945).

KING'S MINISTER, THE 1914 d: Harold Shaw. UKN., *The King's Minister*, Cecil Raleigh, Play

KING'S OUTCAST, THE 1915 d: Ralph Dewsbury. UKN., *The King's Outcast*, W. Gayer MacKay, Robert Ord, Play

KING'S RHAPSODY 1955 d: Herbert Wilcox. UKN., *King's Rhapsody*, Ivor Novello, London 1949, Musical Play

KING'S ROMANCE, THE 1914 d: Ernest G. Batley. UKN., *The King's Romance*, May Austin, E. V. Edmonds, Play

KINGS ROW 1942 d: Sam Wood. USA., *King's Row*, Henry Bellamann, Novel

KING'S ROYAL 1982 d: Andrew Morgan, David Reynolds. UKN., *King's Royal*, John Quigley, Novel

King's Street *see* KUNGSGATAN (1943).

KING'S THIEF, THE 1955 d: Robert Z. Leonard. USA., Robert Hardy Andrews, Story

KING'S WHORE, THE 1990 d: Axel Corti. AUS/FRN/UKN., *Comtesse de Verue Jeanne de Luynes*, Jacques Tournier, Novel

Kinpeibei *see* CHIN-P'ING-MEI (1969).

Kinsey Report ,the *see* 1 + 1 (EXPLORING THE KINSEY REPORTS) (1961).

KINSMAN, THE 1919 d: Henry Edwards. UKN., *The Kinsman*, Mrs. Alfred Sedgwick, Novel

KIPPS 1921 d: Harold Shaw. UKN., *Kipps*, H. G. Wells, London 1905, Novel

KIPPS 1941 d: Carol Reed. UKN/USA., *Kipps*, H. G. Wells, London 1905, Novel

Kirchfeldpfarrer, Der *see* DAS MADCHEN VOM PFARRHOF (1955).

KIRKE OG ORGEL 1932 d: George Schneevoigt. DNM., *Kirk Og Orgel*, Holger Drachman, 1904, Short Story

KIRU 1968 d: Kihachi Okamoto. JPN., *Torideyama Non Jushichinichi*, Shugoro Yamamoto, Tokyo 1964, Short Story

KISERTET LUBLON 1976 d: Robert Ban. HNG., *Kisertet Lublon*, Kalman Mikszath, 1896, Novel

KISMASZAT ES A GEZENGUZOK 1985 d: Miklos Markos. HNG., *Kismaszat Es a Gezenguzok*, Miklos Ronaszegi, Novel

KISMET 1914 d: Leedham Bantock. UKN., *Kismet*, Edward Knoblock, London 1911, Play

KISMET 1920 d: Louis J. Gasnier. USA., *Kismet*, Edward Knoblock, London 1911, Play

KISMET 1930 d: John Francis Dillon. USA., *Kismet*, Edward Knoblock, London 1911, Play

KISMET 1931 d: William Dieterle. USA., *Kismet*, Edward Knoblock, London 1911, Play

KISMET 1944 d: William Dieterle. USA., *Kismet*, Edward Knoblock, London 1911, Play

KISMET 1955 d: Vincente Minnelli, Stanley Donen (Uncredited). USA., *Kismet*, Edward Knoblock, London 1911, Play

KISS AND MAKE UP 1934 d: Harlan Thompson. USA., *Kozmetika*, Istvan Bekeffy, 1933, Play

KISS AND TELL 1945 d: Richard Wallace. USA., *Kiss and Tell*, F. Hugh Herbert, New York 1943, Play

KISS BEFORE DYING, A 1956 d: Gerd Oswald. USA., *A Kiss Before Dying*, Ira Levin, 1953, Novel

KISS BEFORE DYING, A 1991 d: James Dearden. USA., *A Kiss Before Dying*, Ira Levin, 1953, Novel

KISS BEFORE THE MIRROR, THE 1933 d: James Whale. USA., *Der Kuss Vor Dem Spiegel*, Ladislaus Fodor, Vienna 1932, Play

KISS FOR CINDERELLA, A 1926 d: Herbert Brenon. USA., *A Kiss for Cinderella*, J. M. Barrie, New York 1920, Play

KISS IN A TAXI, A 1927 d: Clarence Badger. USA., *A Kiss in a Taxi*, Maurice Hennequin, Pierre Veber, Play

KISS IN THE DARK, A 1925 d: Frank Tuttle. USA., *Aren't We All?*, Frederick Lonsdale, London 1923, Play

KISS IN TIME, A 1921 d: Thomas N. Heffron. USA., *From Four to Eleven-Three*, Royal Brown, 1920, Short Story

Kiss Kiss, Kill Kill *see* KOMMISSAR X: JAGD AUF UNBEKANNT (1965).

KISS ME AGAIN 1925 d: Ernst Lubitsch. USA., *Cyprienne Or Divorcons*, Emile de Najac, Victorien Sardou, Paris 1883, Play

KISS ME AGAIN 1931 d: William A. Seiter. USA., *Mademoiselle Modiste; a Comic Opera*, Henry Martyn Blossom, Victor Herbert, New York 1905, Musical Play

KOENIGSMARK 1923 d: Leonce Perret. FRN., *Koenigsmark*, Pierre Benoit, Novel

KOENIGSMARK 1935 d: Maurice Tourneur. UKN., *Koenigsmark*, Pierre Benoit, Novel

KOENIGSMARK 1935 d: Maurice Tourneur. FRN., *Koenigsmark*, Pierre Benoit, Novel

KOENIGSMARK 1953 d: Solange Bussi, Christian-Jaque. FRN/ITL., *Koenigsmark*, Pierre Benoit, Novel

KOFUKU 1981 d: Kon IchikawA. JPN., *Lady Lady I Did It!*, Evan Hunter, 1961, Novel

KOGDA KAZAKI PLACHUT 1963 d: Eugene Morgunov. USS., *O Kolchake Krapive I Prochem*, Mikhail Sholokhov, 1926, Short Story

KOGE 1964 d: Keisuke KinoshitA. JPN., *Koge*, Sawako Ariyoshi, 1962, Novel

Kohana see YOSHIWARA (1937).

KOHRAA 1964 d: Biren Nag. IND., *Rebecca*, Daphne Du Maurier, London 1938, Novel

Kojak and the Marcus-Nelson Murders see THE MARCUS-NELSON MURDERS (1973).

KOJAK: THE PRICE OF JUSTICE 1987 d: Alan Metzger. USA., *The Price of Justice*, Dorothy Uhnak, Novel

Kokkina Farina, Ta see KOKKINA PHANARIA (1962).

KOKKINA PHANARIA 1962 d: Vassilis Georgiadis. GRC., *Ta Kokkina Phanaria*, Alekos Galanos, Play

KOKORO 1954 d: Kon IchikawA. JPN., *Kokoro*, Soseki Natsume, 1914, Novel

KOKOTSU NO HITO 1973 d: Shiro ToyodA. JPN., *Kokotsu No Hito*, Sawako Ariyoshi, Novel

KOLLEGE KOMMT GLEICH 1943 d: Karl Anton. GRM., *Kollege Kommt Gleich*, Wilhelm Utermann, Play

KOLYA 1996 d: Jan Sverak. CZE/UKN/FRN., Pavel Taussig, Story

KOMEDI I HAGERSKOG 1968 d: Torgny Anderberg. SWD., *Komedi I Hagerskog*, Nils Artur Lundkvist, 1959, Novel

KOMEDIANTKA 1987 d: Jerzy SztwiertniA. PLN., *Komediantka*, Wladyslaw Stanislaw Reymont, 1896, Novel

Komisar see KOMISSAR (1967).

KOMISARIO PLAMUN EREHDYS 1960 d: Matti KassilA. FNL., *Komisario Palmun Erehdys*, Mika Waltari, 1940, Novel

KOMISSAR 1967 d: Alexander Askoldov. USS., *V Gorode Berdicheve*, Vasily Grossman, 1934, Short Story

Komissar see KOMMISSAR (1987).

Komm in Die Gondel see EINE NACHT IN VENEDIG (1953).

Komm, Liebe Mald Und MacHe see DIE TOLLDREISTEN GESCHICHTEN - NACH HONORE DE BALZAC (1969).

KOMM NUR, MEIN LIEBSTES VOGELEIN 1968 d: Rolf Thiele. GRM/ITL., *Komm Nur Mein Liebstes Vogelein.*, Joachim Fernau, Novel

KOMMISSAR 1987 d: Alexander Askoldov. USS., *In the Town of Berdichev*, Vasily Grossman, Novel

Kommissar X - Hunter of the Unknown see KOMMISSAR X: JAGD AUF UNBEKANNT (1965).

KOMMISSAR X: DREI BLAUE PANTHER 1968 d: Gianfranco Parolini. GRM/ITL/CND., Robert F. Atkinson, Novel

KOMMISSAR X: DREI GELBE KATZEN 1966 d: Rudolf Zehetgruber. AUS/ITL/FRN., *Kommissar X: Drei Gelbe Katzen*, Bert F. Island, Novel

KOMMISSAR X: DREI GOLDENE SCHLANGEN 1968 d: Roberto Mauri. GRM/ITL., *Kommissar X: Drei Goldene Schlangen*, Bert F. Island, Novel

KOMMISSAR X: DREI GRUNE HUNDE 1967 d: Rudolf Zehetgruber, Gianfranco Parolini. GRM/FRN/ITL., *Kommissar X: Drei Grune Hunde*, Bert F. Island, Novel

KOMMISSAR X: IN DEN KLAUEN DES GOLDENEN DRACHEN 1966 d: Gianfranco Parolini. AUS/ITL/GRM., *Kommissar X: in Den Klauen Des Goldenen Drachen*, Bert F. Island, Novel

KOMMISSAR X: JAGD AUF UNBEKANNT 1965 d: Rudolf Zehetgruber, Gianfranco Parolini. GRM/ITL/YGS., *Kommissar X: Jagd Auf Unbekannt*, Bert F. Island, Novel

KOMMISSAR X: JAGT DIE ROTEN TIGER 1971 d: Harald Reinl, Giancarlo Romitelli. GRM/ITL/PKS., *Kommissar X Jagt Den Roten Tiger*, M. Wegener, Novel

KOMODIANTEN 1941 d: G. W. Pabst. GRM., *Philine*, Olly Boeheim, Novel

Komodianten Des Lebens see DIE VENUS VOM TIVOLI (1953).

KOMPLOTT AUF ERLENHOF 1950 d: Carl Froelich. GRM., *Drei Madchen Am Spinnrad*, Fedor von Zobeltitz, Novel

KOMPTOIRISTKA 1922 d: Svatopluk Innemann. CZC., *Komptoiristka Pana*, Josef Skruzny, Play

KONA COAST 1968 d: Lamont Johnson. USA., *Kona Coast*, John D. MacDonald, Short Story

KONCHU DAISENSO 1968 d: Kazui Nihonmatsu. JPN., *Konchu Dai Senso*, Kingen Amada, Short Story

Kondelik - Father-in-Law - Vejvara - Son-in-Law see TCHAN KONDELIK A ZET VEJVARA (1929).

Kondelik -Father, Vejvara -Bridegroom see OTEC KONDELIK A ZENICH VEJVARA I. (1926).

KONDURA 1977 d: Shyam Benegal. IND., *Kondura*, C. T. Khanolkar, 1966, Novel

KONEC STARYCH CASU 1989 d: Jiri Menzel. CZC., *Konec Starych Casu*, Vladislav Vancura, 1934, Novel

KONFERENZ DER TIERE, DIE 1969 d: Curt LindA. GRM., *Die Konferenz Der Tiere*, Erich Kastner, 1930, Short Story

Kong see KING KONG (1933).

Konge for En Dag see JEPPE PA BJERGET (1981).

KONGGU LAN 1925 d: Zhang Shichuan. CHN., *Flower in the Wilderness*, Ruika Kuroiwa, Novel

KONGI'S HARVEST 1971 d: Ossie Davis. USA/NGR/SWD., *Kongi's Harvest*, Wole Soyinka, 1967, Play

KONGO 1932 d: William J. Cowen. USA., *Kongo*, Chester de Vonde, Kilbourne Gordon, New York 1926, Play

KONIG DER BERNINA, DER 1957 d: Alfred Lehner. AUS/SWT., *Der Konig Der Bernina*, Jakob Christoph Heer, Stuttgart 1900, Novel

Konig Der Hochstapler, Der see MANOLESCU (1929).

Konig Des Mont-Blanc, Der see DER EWIGE TRAUM (1934).

KONIG DROSSELBART 1954 d: Herbert B. Fredersdorf. GRM., *Konig Drosselbart*, Jacob Grimm, Wilhelm Grimm, 1812, Short Story

KONIG DROSSELBART 1967 d: Walter Beck. GDR., *Konig Drosselbart*, Jacob Grimm, Wilhelm Grimm, 1812, Short Story

Konig Drosselbart see KRAL DROZDI BRADA (1984).

Konig Lachelt - Paris Lacht, Der see DER POSTILLON VON LONJUMEAU (1935).

KONIGIN DER ARENA 1952 d: Rolf Meyer. GRM., *Wanda*, Gerhart Hauptmann, 1928, Novel

KONIGIN EINER NACHT 1951 d: Kurt Hoffmann. GRM., *Konigin Einer Nacht*, Will Meisel, Opera

KONIGLICHE HOHEIT 1953 d: Harald Braun. GRM., *Konigsliche Hoheit*, Thomas Mann, 1909, Novel

KONING OEDIPUS 1912. NTH., *Oedipus Rex*, Sophocles, c420 bc, Play

Koniok Gorbunok see SKAZKA O KONKE-GORBUNKE (1961).

KONJIKI YASHA 1954 d: Koji ShimA. JPN., *Konjiki Yasha*, Koyo Ozaki, Novel

KONRAD AUS DER KONSERVENBUCHSE 1982 d: Claudia Schroder. GRM., *Konrad Aus Der Konservenbuchse*, Christine Nostlinger, Novel

KONSEQUENZ, DIE 1977 d: Wolfgang Petersen. GRM., *Die Konsequenz*, Wolfgang Ziegler, Novel

Konska Opera see LIMONADOVY JOE (1964).

KONYETS "SATURNA" 1968 d: Vilen Azarov. USS., W. Ardamatsij, Novel

KONZERT, DAS 1931 d: Leo Mittler. FRN., *Das Konzert*, Hermann Bahr, 1909, Play

KONZERT, DAS 1944 d: Paul Verhoeven. GRM., *Das Konzert*, Hermann Bahr, 1909, Play

KOPPANYI AGA TESTAMENTUMA, A 1967 d: Eva Zsurzs. HNG., *A Koppanyi Aga Testamentuma*, Istvan Fakete, Novel

KORA TERRY 1940 d: Georg Jacoby. GRM., *Kora Terry*, H. C. von Zobeltitz, Novel

Koral Lir see KAROL LIR (1969).

KORHINTA 1955 d: Zoltan Fabri. HNG., *Kutban*, Imre Sarkadi, 1971, Short Story

KORKARLEN 1921 d: Victor Sjostrom. SWD., *Korkarlen*, Selma Lagerlof, 1912, Novel

KORKARLEN 1958 d: Arne Mattsson. SWD., *Korkarlen*, Selma Lagerlof, 1912, Novel

Korol Lir see KAROL LIR (1969).

KORT AMERIKAANS 1979 d: Guido Pieters. NTH., *Kort Amerikaans*, Jan Hendrick Wolkers, 1964, Novel

KORT AR SOMMAREN 1962 d: Bjarne Henning-Jensen. SWD., *Pan*, Knut Hamsun, Kristiania 1894, Novel

Kosaken-Ende see TARAS BULBA 2 (1924).

Kosaken-Ende see TARAS BULBA (1924).

KOSHER KITTY KELLY 1926 d: James W. Horne. USA., *Kosher Kitty Kelly*, Leon de Costa, New York 1925, Play

Koshoku Ichidai Onna see SAIKAKU ICHIDAI ONNA (1952).

KOSZIVU EMBER FIAI, A 1964 d: Zoltan Varkonyi. HNG., *A Koszivu Ember Fiai*, Mor Jokai, 1869, Novel

Kot I Mysz see KATZ UND MAUS (1967).

KOTCH 1971 d: Jack Lemmon. USA., *Kotch*, Katherine Topkins, Novel

KOTO 1963 d: Noboru NakamurA. JPN., *Koto*, Yasunari Kawabata, Tokyo 1962, Novel

KOTO 1980 d: Kon IchikawA. JPN., *Koto*, Yasunari Kawabata, Tokyo 1962, Novel

KOUZELNY DUM 1939 d: Otakar VavrA. CZC., *Kouzelny Dum*, Karel J. Benes, Novel

KOYA 1993 d: Tetsutaro Murano. JPN., *Koya*, Yasushi Inoue, Novel

Koya: Memorial Notes of Choken see KOYA (1993).

Koziat Rog see KOZUU POS (1972).

Kozijat Rog see KOZUU POS (1972).

Koziyat Rog see KOZUU POS (1972).

KOZUU POS 1972 d: Metodi Andonov. BUL., *Koziyat Rog*, Nikolai Haitov, 1967, Play

Krabat see CARODEJUV UCEN (1977).

Krabat Carodejuv Ucen see CARODEJUV UCEN (1977).

KRACH IM HINTERHAUS 1935 d: Veit Harlan. GRM., *Krach Im Hinterhaus*, Maximilian Bottcher, Play

KRACH IM HINTERHAUS 1949 d: Erich Kobler. GRM., *Krach Im Hinterhaus*, Maximilian Bottcher, Play

KRACH IM VORDERHAUS 1941 d: Paul Heidemann. GRM., *Krach Im Vorderhaus*, Maximilian Bottcher, Play

KRACH UM JOLANTHE 1934 d: Carl Froelich. GRM., *Krach Um Jolanthe*, August Hinrichs, Play

Krach Um Jolanthe see DAS FROHLICHE DORF (1955).

Kradecat Na Praskovi see KRADETSAT NA PRASKOVI (1964).

KRADETSAT NA PRASKOVI 1964 d: Vulo Radev. BUL., *Kradetsat Na Praskovi*, Emilian Stanev, Sofia 1948, Novel

Kraft Der Liebe see DAS JAHR DES HERRN (1950).

Kraft-Mayr, Der see WENN DIE MUSIK NICHT WAR' (1935).

KRAFTPROBE 1982 d: Heidi Genee. GRM., *Kraftprobe*, Dagmar Kekule, Novel

KRAJOBRAZ PO BITWIE 1970 d: Andrzej WajdA. PLN., *Krajobraz Po Bitwie*, Tadeusz Borowski, Novel

KRAKATIT 1948 d: Otakar VavrA. CZC., *Krakatit*, Karel Capek, 1924, Novel

Krakatit see TEMNE SLUNCE (1980).

KRAL DROZDI BRADA 1984 d: Miroslav Luther. CZC/GRM., *Konig Drosselbart*, Jacob Grimm, Wilhelm Grimm, 1812, Short Story

KRAL UBU 1996 d: F. A. Brabec. CZC., *Ubu Roi*, Alfred Jarry, 1896, Play

Kralj Petroleja see DER OLPRINZ (1965).

KRALOVNA STRIBRNYCH HOR 1939 d: Karel SpelinA. CZC., Frantisek Poul, Short Story

Kralovska Polovacka see LA CHASSE ROYALE (1969).

KRAMBAMBULI 1940 d: Karl Kostlin. AUS., *Krambambuli*, Maria von Ebner-Eschenbach, 1887, Short Story

KRAMER VS. KRAMER 1979 d: Robert Benton. USA., *Kramer Vs. Kramer*, Avery Corman, Novel

Krane's Bakery Shop see KRANES KONDITORI (1950).

KRANES KONDITORI 1950 d: Astrid Henning-Jensen. NRW., *Kranes Konditori - Interior Med Figurer*, Cora Sandel, 1945, Novel

KRASAVICE KATA 1919 d: Vaclav Binovec. CZC., *Kat'a*, Alexander Pushkin, Short Story

KRASNA VYZVEDACKA 1927 d: M. J. Krnansky. CZC., *Krasna Vyzvedacka*, Josef Adler, Novel

Krasnoe Jabloko *see* KRASNOYE YABLOKO (1975).

KRASNOYE YABLOKO 1975 d: Tolomush Okeyev. USS., *Krasnoe Jabloko*, Chingiz Aitmatov, 1963, Short Story

KRATES 1913 d: Louis H. Chrispijn. NTH., *Krates*, Justus Van Maurik, 1885, Novel

Kratko Slantse *see* KRATKO SLUNTSE (1979).

Kratko Slunce *see* KRATKO SLUNTSE (1979).

KRATKO SLUNTSE 1979 d: Lyudmil Kirkov. BUL., *Kratko Slantse*, Stanislav Stratiev, 1978, Novel

KRB BEZ OHNE 1937 d: Karel SpelinA. CZC., *Krb Bez Ohne*, Maryna Radomerska, Novel

KREHKE VZTAHY 1979 d: Juraj Herz. CZC., *Krehke Vztahy*, Vaclav Dusek, Novel

Kreitzerova Sonata *see* KREJZEROWA SONATA (1987).

Krejcerova Sonata *see* KREJZEROWA SONATA (1987).

KREJZEROWA SONATA 1987 d: Mikhail Schweitzer, Sofiya MilkinA. USS., *Kreutserova Sonata*, Lev Nikolayevich Tolstoy, 1889, Short Story

Kremlevskie Kuranti *see* KREMLIEVSKIE KURANTY (1970).

KREMLEVSKIE TAJNY SHESTNADCATOGO VEKA 1991 d: Boris Blank. RSS., *The Death of Ivan the Terrible*, Alexey Konstantinovich Tolstoy, 1867, Play

KREMLIEVSKIE KURANTY 1970 d: Viktor Georgiev. USS., *Kremlyovskie Kuranty*, Nikolay Pogodin, 1941, Play

Kremlin Chimes, The *see* KREMLIEVSKIE KURANTY (1970).

KREMLIN LETTER, THE 1970 d: John Huston. USA., *The Kremlin Letter*, Noel Behn, New York 1966, Novel

Kremlin Mysteries of the Sixteen Century *see* KREMLEVSKIE TAJNY SHESTNADCATOGO VEKA (1991).

KREUTZER SONATA 1915 d: Herbert Brenon. USA., *The Kreutzer Sonata*, Jacob Gordin, New York 1906, Play

Kreutzer Sonata, The *see* KREUTZEROVA SONATA (1926).

Kreutzer Sonata, The *see* DIE KREUTZERSONATE (1937).

Kreutzer Sonata, The *see* KREJZEROWA SONATA (1987).

KREUTZEROVA SONATA 1926 d: Gustav Machaty. CZC., *Kreutserova Sonata*, Lev Nikolayevich Tolstoy, 1889, Short Story

Kreutzersonate *see* KREJZEROWA SONATA (1987).

KREUTZERSONATE, DIE 1937 d: Veit Harlan. GRM., *Kreutserova Sonata*, Lev Nikolayevich Tolstoy, 1889, Short Story

Kreuz Am Matterhorn, Das *see* LA CROIX DU CERVIN (1922).

KREUZLSCHREIBER, DER 1950 d: Eduard von Borsody. GRM., *Die Kreuzelschreiber*, Ludwig Anzengruber, 1892, Play

Kreytserova Sonata *see* KREJZEROWA SONATA (1987).

KRIEGSGERICHT 1959 d: Kurt Meisel. GRM., *Kriegsgericht*, Will Berthold, Munich 1959, Novel

KRIGERNES BORN 1979 d: Ernst Johansen. DNM., *Krigernes Born*, Hans Ovesen, Novel

KRIGSMANS ERINRAN 1947 d: Erik Faustman. SWD., *Krigsmans Erinran*, Herbert Grevenius, Goteberg 1946, Play

Kriminalfall Dr. Borstill *see* MATTO REGIERT (1947).

Kriminalkommissar Studer *see* WACHTMEISTER STUDER (1939).

KRIPPENDORF'S TRIBE 1998 d: Todd Holland. USA., *Krippendorff's Tribe*, Frank Parkin, Book

KRIS 1946 d: Ingmar Bergman. SWD., *Moderhjertet*, Leck Fischer, 1943, Play

KRISTNIHALD UNDIR JOKLI 1989 d: Gudny Halldorsdottir. ICL/GRM., *Kristnihald Undir Jokli*, Halldor Laxness, Novel

Krivi Put *see* THE CROOKED ROAD (1964).

KRIZ U POTOKA 1921 d: J. S. Kolar. CZC., *Kriz U Potoka*, Karolina Svetla, Novel

KRIZ U POTOKA 1937 d: Miloslav Jares. CZC., *Kriz U Potoka*, Karolina Svetla, Novel

Krol Olch *see* DER UNHOLD (1996).

KRONIKA WYPADKOW MILOSNYCH 1985 d: Andrzej WajdA. PLN., *Kronika Wypadkow Milosnych*, Tadeusz Konwicki, Autobiography

KRONISKE USKYLD, DEN 1985 d: Edward Fleming. DNM., *Den Kroniske Uskyld*, Klaus Rifbjerg, 1958, Novel

KRONVITTNET 1989 d: Jon Lindstrom. SWD., *De Kroongetuige*, Maarten 't Hart, Novel

KRONZEUGIN, DIE 1937 d: Georg Jacoby. GRM., *Die Kronzeugin*, G. C. Marivale, Play

KROON DER SCHANDE, DE 1918 d: Maurits H. Binger. NTH., *The Coronet of Shame*, Charles Garvice, 1900, Novel

KROTKAYA 1960 d: Alexander Borisov. USS., *Krotkaya*, Fyodor Dostoyevsky, 1876, Short Story

KRU BAN NOK 1978 d: Surasri Phatum. THL., *Kru Ban Nok*, Kamarn Khonkai, Novel

KRZYZACY 1960 d: Aleksander Ford. PLN., *Krzyzacy*, Henryk Sienkiewicz, 1900, Novel

KSHUDITA PASHAN 1960 d: Tapan SinhA. IND., *Kshudhita Pasan*, Rabindranath Tagore, 1910, Short Story

KU CAI HUA 1965 d: Li Ang. CHN., *Ku Cai Hua*, Feng Deying, Novel

KUARUP 1988 d: Ruy GuerrA. BRZ., *Quarup*, Antonio Callado, 1967, Novel

KUCHIZUKE III: ONNA DOSHI 1955 d: Mikio Naruse, Masanori Kakei. JPN., *Kiri No Naka No Shojo*, Yojiro Ishizaka, 1955, Short Story, *Kuchizuke*, Yojiro Ishizaka, 1954, Short Story

KUCHIZUKE III: ONNA DOSHI 1955 d: Hideo Suzuki. JPN., *Onna Doshi*, Yojiro Ishizaka, 1955, Short Story

Kuckucksei, Das *see* KINDER DER LIEBE (1949).

KUFSA SHECHORA 1993 d: Ye'ud Levanon. ISR., Amos Oz, Book

KULONC, A 1980 d: Laszlo Vamos. HNG., *A Kulonc*, Gyula Illyes, Play

KULONOS HAZASSAG 1951 d: Marton Keleti. HNG., *Kulonos Hazassag*, Kalman Mikszath, 1901, Novel

KUMONOSU-JO 1957 d: Akira KurosawA. JPN., *MacBeth*, William Shakespeare, c1606, Play

KUN LUN SHAN SHANG YI KE CAO 1962 d: Dong KenA. CHN., *Hui's Wife*, Wang Zongyuan, Novel

KUN SANDHEDEN 1975 d: Henning Ornbak. DNM., *Kun Sandheden*, Poul Orum, 1974, Novel

KUNGSGATAN 1943 d: Gosta Cederlund. SWD., *Kungsgatan*, Ivar Lo-Johansson, 1935, Novel

KUNGSLEDEN 1964 d: Gunnar Hoglund. SWD., *Kungsleden*, Bosse Gustafson, Stockholm 1963, Novel

KUNKU 1937 d: V. Shantaram. IND., *Na Patnari Goshta*, Narayan Hari Apte, 1923, Novel

KUNSTSEIDENE MADCHEN, DAS 1960 d: Julien Duvivier. GRM/FRN/ITL., *Das Kunstseidene Madchen*, Irmgard Keun, Novel

KUPFERNE HOCHZEIT, DIE 1948 d: Heinz Ruhmann. GRM., *Die Kupferne Hochzeit*, Svend Rindom, Play

Kuraishisu Nijugoju Nen *see* SOLAR CRISIS (1992).

KURIER DES ZAREN, DER 1935 d: Richard Eichberg. GRM., *Michel Strogoff*, Jules Verne, Paris 1876, Novel

Kurier Des Zaren, Der *see* MICHELE STROGOFF (1956).

Kurier Des Zaren, Der *see* STROGOFF (1970).

KURITON SUKUPOLVI 1937 d: Wilho Ilmari. FNL., *Kuriton Sukupolvi*, Mika Waltari, 1937, Play

KURITON SUKUPOLVI 1957 d: Matti KassilA. FNL., *Kuriton Sukupolvi*, Mika Waltari, 1937, Play

KUROBARA NO YAKATA 1969 d: Kinji Fukasaku. JPN., *Kurobara No Yakata*, Yukio Mishima, Play

KUROI AME 1988 d: Shohei ImamurA. JPN., *Kuroi Ame*, Masuji Ibuse, 1965-66, Novel

KUROTOKAGE 1968 d: Kinji Fukasaku. JPN., *Kuroktokage*, Yukio Mishima, 1962, Play

KURT VONNEGUT'S HARRISON BERGERON 1995 d: Bruce Pittman. CND/USA., *Harrison Bergeron*, Kurt Vonnegut Jr., Short Story

KURZE BRIEF ZUM LANGEN ABSCHIED, DER 1977 d: Herbert Vesely. GRM., *Der Kurze Brief Zum Langen Abschied*, Peter Handke, 1972

KURZER PROZESS 1967 d: Michael Kehlmann. GRM., *Kurzer Prozess*, J. Ashford, Novel

KUSS DES TIGERS, DER 1989 d: Petra Haffter. GRM/FRN., *Der Kuss Des Tigers*, Francis Ryck, Novel

Kuss Nach Ladenschluss, Ein *see* ANNETTE IM PARADIES (1934).

KUSSEN IST KEINE SUND 1950 d: Hubert MarischkA. AUS., *Bruder Straubinger*, Edmund Eysler, Opera

KUU ON VAARALLINEN 1961 d: Toivo SarkkA. FNL., *Besaettelse*, Hans Severinsen, Copenhagen 1942, Novel

KVARTETTEN SOM SPRANGDES 1936 d: Arne Bornebusch. SWD., *Kvartetten Som Sprangdes*, Birger Sjoberg, 1924, Novel

KVARTETTEN SOM SPRANGDES 1950 d: Gustaf Molander. SWD., *Kvartetten Som Sprangdes*, Birger Sjoberg, 1924, Novel

KVINDE ER OVERFLODIG, EN 1958 d: Gabriel Axel. DNM., *En Kvinde Er Overflodig*, Knud Sonderby, 1935, Novel

KVINNA OMBORD, EN 1941 d: Gunnar Skoglund. SWD., *Rymlingen Fast*, Dagmar Ingeborg Edqvist, 1933, Novel

KVINNAS ANSIKTE, EN 1938 d: Gustaf Molander. SWD., *Il Etait une Fois*, Francis de Croisset, Play

Kvinnorna Pa Niskavuori *see* NISKAVUOREN NAISET (1938).

Kvinnorna Pa Niskavuori *see* NISKAVUOREN NAISET (1958).

KVOCNA 1937 d: Hugo Haas. CZC., *Kvocna*, Edmond Konrad, Short Story

KWAIDAN 1964 d: Masaki Kobayashi. JPN., *Kwaidan*, Yakumo Koizumi, Novel

KYOFU NIKEI NINGEN 1969 d: Teruo Ishii. JPN., *Kyofo Nikei Ningen*, Rampo Edogawa, Short Story

L.A. CONFIDENTIAL 1997 d: Curtis Hanson. USA., *L.A. Confidential*, James Ellroy, Novel

La Dove Scende Il Sole *see* UNTER GEIERN (1964).

LA LA LUCILLE 1920 d: Eddie Lyons, Lee Moran. USA., *La la Lucille*, George Gershwin, Frederick Jackson, New York 1919, Musical Play

L.A. Medical Center - the Critical List *see* THE CRITICAL LIST (1978).

La Poupee *see* LA POUPEE (1920).

L.A. WITHOUT A MAP 1998 d: Mika Kaurismaki. UKN/FRN/FNL., *Los Angeles With a Map*, Richard Rayner, Novel

LAATSTE DAGEN VAN EEN EILAND, DE 1938 d: Ernest Winar. NTH., *Aan Dood Water*, Karel Norels, Novel

LAB KUSH 1967 d: Ashoke Chatterjee. IND., *Ramayana*, Valmiki, Verse

LABAKAN 1956 d: Vaclav KrskA. CZC/BUL., *Das Marchen Vom Falschen Prinzen*, Wilhelm Hauff, 1826, Short Story

LABURNUM GROVE 1936 d: Carol Reed. UKN., *Laburnum Grove*, J. B. Priestley, London 1933, Play

LABYRINTH 1959 d: Rolf Thiele. GRM/ITL., *Labyrinth*, Gladys Baker, Novel

Labyrinth Der Leidenschaften *see* LABYRINTH (1959).

Labyrinth of Dreams *see* YUME NO GINGA (1997).

LABYRINTH, THE 1915 d: E. Mason Hopper. USA., *The Labyrinth*, Harry Chandlee, Story

LAC AUX DAMES 1934 d: Marc Allegret. FRN., *Lac aux Dames*, Vicki Baum, Novel

Lac aux Desirs, Le *see* I LIMNI TON POTHON (1958).

Lac de la Liberte, Le *see* DIE FLUCHT INS PARADIES (1923).

LACE 1984 d: William Hale. USA/UKN., *Lace*, Shirley Conran, Novel

Lacemaker, The *see* LA PUNTAIRE (1928).

Lacemaker, The *see* LA DENTELLIERE (1977).

Lach En Een Traan, Een *see* LAUGHTER AND TEARS (1921).

LACHATZ 1984 d: Michele Ohayon. ISR., Natan Zehavi, Story

LACHE BAJAZZO! 1917 d: Richard Oswald. GRM., *Lache Bajazzo!*, Arthur Landsberger, Novel

LACHE BAJAZZO 1943 d: Leopold Hainisch. GRM., *Der Bajazzo*, Ruggero Leoncavallo, Opera

Lacheln Im Sturm, Ein *see* UN SOURIRE DANS LA TEMPETE (1950).

LACHENDE DRITTE, DER 1936 d: Georg Zoch. GRM., *Der Lachende Dritte*, Hans Naderer, Play

LACKEY AND THE LADY, THE 1919 d: Thomas Bentley. UKN., *The Lackey and the Lady*, Tom Gallon, Novel

LAD: A DOG 1962 d: Aram Avakian, Leslie H. Martinson. USA., *Lad: a Dog*, Albert Payson Terhune, New York 1919, Novel

LAD AND THE LION, THE 1917 d: Alfred E. Green. USA., *The Lad and the Lion*, Edgar Rice Burroughs, 1917, Short Story

Lad from Our Town see PAREN IZ NASHEGO GORODA (1942).

LAD, THE 1935 d: Henry Edwards. UKN., Edgar Wallace, Novel

LADDER OF LIES, THE 1920 d: Tom Forman. USA., *The Ladder*, Harold Vickers, 1918, Novel

Ladder, The see THE LADDER OF LIES (1920).

LADDIE 1926 d: James Leo Meehan. USA., *Laddie; a True Blue Story*, Gene Stratton-Porter, Garden City, N.Y. 1913, Novel

LADDIE 1934 d: George Stevens. USA., *Laddie; a True Blue Story*, Gene Stratton-Porter, Garden City, N.Y. 1913, Novel

LADDIE 1940 d: Jack Hively. USA., *Laddie; a True Blue Story*, Gene Stratton-Porter, Garden City, N.Y. 1913, Novel

LADENPRINZ, DER 1928 d: Erich Schonfelder. GRM., *Der Ladenprinz*, Karl Munzer, Novel

Ladies see DAMY (1954).

LADIES AT PLAY 1926 d: Alfred E. Green. USA., *Loose Ankles*, Sam Janney, New York 1926, Play

LADIES BEWARE 1927 d: Charles Giblyn. USA., *Jack of Diamonds*, Frederick Jackson, Story

LADIES CLUB, THE 1986 d: Janet Greek. USA., *Sisterhood*, Casey Bishop, Betty Black, Novel

LADIES COURAGEOUS 1944 d: John Rawlins. USA., *Looking for Trouble*, Virginia Spencer Cowles, Book

LADIES' DAY 1943 d: Leslie Goodwins. USA., *Ladies' Day*, Robert Considine, Edward Clark Lilley, Bertrand Robinson, Play

Ladies First see ELMER AND ELSIE (1934).

Ladies First see LES FEMMES D'ABORD (1962).

LADIES IN LOVE 1936 d: Edward H. Griffith. USA., *Three Girls*, Ladislaus Bus-Fekete, Play

LADIES IN RETIREMENT 1941 d: Charles Vidor. USA., *Ladies in Retirement*, Reginald Denham, Edward Percy, London 1939, Play

Ladies in the Green Hats, The see CES DAMES AUX CHAPEAUX VERTS (1937).

LADIES' MAN 1931 d: Lothar Mendes. USA., *Ladies' Man*, Rupert Hughes, New York 1930, Novel

Ladies' Man see LEMMY POUR LES DAMES (1961).

LADIES MUST LIVE 1921 d: George Loane Tucker. USA., *Ladies Must Live*, Alice Duer Miller, New York 1917, Novel

LADIES MUST LIVE 1940 d: Noel Smith. USA., *The Hometowners*, George M. Cohan, New York 1926, Play

Ladies' Night see LADIES' NIGHT IN A TURKISH BATH (1928).

LADIES' NIGHT IN A TURKISH BATH 1928 d: Eddie Cline. USA., *Ladies' Night in a Turkish Bath*, Charlton Andrews, Avery Hopwood, Play

LADIES OF LEISURE 1930 d: Frank CaprA. USA., *Ladies of the Evening*, Milton Herbert Gropper, New York 1924, Play

LADIES OF THE BIG HOUSE 1932 d: Marion Gering. USA., *Ladies of the Big House*, Ernest Booth, 1931, Play

Ladies of the Bois de Boulogne, The see LES DAMES DU BOIS DE BOULOGNE (1945).

LADIES OF THE JURY 1932 d: Lowell Sherman. USA., *Ladies of the Jury*, John Frederick Ballard, New York 1929, Play

LADIES OF THE MOB 1928 d: William A. Wellman. USA., *Ladies of the Mob*, Ernest Booth, 1927, Short Story

Ladies of the Park see LES DAMES DU BOIS DE BOULOGNE (1945).

Ladies Only see COMPARTIMENT DE DAMES SEULES (1934).

LADIES SHOULD LISTEN 1934 d: Frank Tuttle. USA., *Le Demoiselle de Passy*, Alfred Savoir, Play

LADIES THEY TALK ABOUT 1933 d: William Keighley, Howard Bretherton. USA., *Ladies They Talk About*, Dorothy MacKaye, Carlton Miles, Play

LADRAO EM NOITE DE CHUVA 1960 d: Armando Couto. BRZ., *Do Tamanho de Um Defunto*, Millor Fernandes, 1957, Play

LADRI DI BICICLETTE 1948 d: Vittorio de SicA. ITL., *Ladri Di Biciclette*, Luigi Bartolini, 1948, Novel

LADRO DI DONNE 1936 d: Abel Gance. ITL., *Le Voleur de Femmes*, Pierre Frondaie, Novel

LADRO, IL 1940 d: Anton Germano Rossi. ITL., *Il Ladro*, Anton Germano Rossi, Short Story

LADRO SONO IO!, IL 1940 d: Flavio CalzavarA. ITL., *Il Ladro Sono Io!*, Giovanni Cenzato, Play

LADRONE, IL 1979 d: Pasquale Festa Campanile. ITL./FRN., *Il Ladrone*, Pasquale Festa Campanile, Novel

LADRONES SOMOS GENTE HONRADA, LOS 1942 d: Ignacio F. Iquino. SPN., *Los Ladrones Somos Gente Honrada*, Enrique Jardiel Poncela, 1941, Play

LADRONES SOMOS GENTE HONRADA, LOS 1956 d: Pedro L. Ramirez. SPN., *Los Ladrones Somos Gente Honrada*, Enrique Jardiel Poncela, 1941, Play

Lady see THE LADY (1925).

LADY AND THE BANDIT, THE 1951 d: Ralph Murphy. USA., *The Highwayman*, Alfred Noyes, 1907, Poem

Lady and the Chauffeur, The see DIE DAME UND IHR CHAUFFEUR (1928).

Lady and the Doctor, The see THE LADY AND THE MONSTER (1944).

Lady and the Dragon, The see BIJO TO KAIRYU (1955).

LADY AND THE HIGHWAYMAN, THE 1988 d: John Hough. UKN., *Cupid Rides Pillion*, Barbara Cartland, Novel

LADY AND THE MOB, THE 1939 d: Ben Stoloff. USA., *Old Mrs. Leonard and the machine Guns*, George Bradshaw, Price Day, 1937, Short Story

LADY AND THE MONSTER, THE 1944 d: George Sherman. USA., *Donovan's Brain*, Curt Siodmak, New York 1943, Novel

LADY AND THE TRAMP 1955 d: Hamilton Luske, Clyde Geronimi. USA., *The Lady and the Tramp*, Ward Greene, 1953, Story

Lady and the Watchdog, The see DAMA S BARZOJEM (1912).

LADY AUDLEY'S SECRET 1906. UKN., *Lady Audley's Secret*, Mary Elizabeth Braddon, London 1862, Novel

LADY AUDLEY'S SECRET 1912 d: Otis Turner. USA., *Lady Audley's Secret*, Mary Elizabeth Braddon, London 1862, Novel

LADY AUDLEY'S SECRET 1915 d: Marshall Farnum. USA., *Lady Audley's Secret*, Mary Elizabeth Braddon, London 1862, Novel

LADY AUDLEY'S SECRET 1920 d: Jack Denton. UKN., *Lady Audley's Secret*, Mary Elizabeth Braddon, London 1862, Novel

LADY BARNACLE 1917 d: John H. Collins. USA., *Lady Barnacle*, Edgar Franklin, 1917, Short Story

LADY BE CAREFUL 1936 d: Theodore Reed. USA., *Sailor Beware*, Kenyon Nicholson, Charles Robinson, New York 1933, Play

LADY BE GOOD 1928 d: Richard Wallace. USA., *Lady Be Good*, Guy Bolton, George Gershwin, Fred Thompson, New York 1924, Musical Play

Lady Beware see THE THIRTEENTH GUEST (1932).

Lady Caliph, The see LA CALIFFA (1970).

LADY CHATTERLEY 1992 d: Ken Russell. UKN., *Lady Chatterley's Lover*, D. H. Lawrence, 1928, Novel

Lady Chatterley's Lover see L' AMANT DE LADY CHATTERLEY (1955).

LADY CHATTERLEY'S LOVER 1981 d: Just Jaeckin. UKN./FRN., *Lady Chatterley's Lover*, D. H. Lawrence, 1928, Novel

LADY CLARE 1911. USA., *The Lady Clare*, Alfred Tennyson, Poem

LADY CLARE, THE 1912 d: Ashley Miller. UKN/USA., *The Lady Clare*, Alfred Tennyson, Poem

LADY CLARE, THE 1919. UKN., *The Lady Clare*, Alfred Tennyson, Poem

Lady Dances, The see THE MERRY WIDOW (1934).

Lady Detective, The see PRIVATE DETECTIVE (1939).

Lady Dick see PRIVATE DETECTIVE (1939).

Lady Doctors see ARZTINNEN (1983).

LADY ESCAPES, THE 1937 d: Eugene J. Forde. USA., *Az En Masodik Felesegem*, Eugene Heltai, 1907, Novel

LADY EVE, THE 1941 d: Preston Sturges. USA., *The Lady Eve*, Monckton Hoffe, Play

Lady Eve, The see THE BIRDS AND THE BEES (1956).

LADY FIGHTS BACK, THE 1939 d: Milton Carruth. USA., *Heather of the High Hand*, Arthur Stringer, New York 1937, Novel

LADY FOR A DAY 1933 d: Frank CaprA. USA., *Madame la Gimp*, Damon Runyon, 1929, Short Story

Lady Frederick see THE DIVORCEE (1919).

LADY FROM HELL, THE 1926 d: Stuart Paton. USA., *My Lord of the Double B*, Norton S. Parker, Story

LADY FROM LONGACRE, THE 1921 d: George Marshall. USA., *The Lady from Longacre*, Victor Bridges, New York 1919, Novel

Lady from Musahino, The see MUSASHINO FUJIN (1951).

LADY FROM SHANGHAI, THE 1948 d: Orson Welles. USA., *If I Die Before I Wake*, Sherwood King, Novel

LADY FROM THE SEA, THE 1911 d: Theodore Marston. USA., *The Lady from the Sea*, Henrik Ibsen, 1888, Play

LADY GANGSTER 1942 d: Robert Florey. USA., *Lady Gangster*, Dorothy MacKaye, Carlton Miles, Play

LADY HARRINGTON 1926 d: Fred Leroy Granville, H. C. Grantham-Hayes. FRN., *Lady Harrington*, Maurice Level, Novel

Lady in Black, The see DIE DAME IN SCHWARZ (1928).

LADY IN CEMENT 1968 d: Gordon Douglas. USA., *Lady in Cement*, Anthony Rome, New York 1960, Novel

LADY IN DANGER 1934 d: Tom Walls. UKN., *O Mistress Mine*, Ben Travers, 1934, Play

LADY IN ERMINE, THE 1927 d: James Flood. USA., *Die Frau Im Hermelin*, Rudolph Schanzer, Ernst Welisch, Play

Lady in Flight see THE LADY ESCAPES (1937).

LADY IN LOVE, A 1920 d: Walter Edwards. USA., *A Lady in Love*, Caroline Duer, Harriet Ford, Play

LADY IN QUESTION, THE 1940 d: Charles Vidor. USA., Marcel Archard, Story

Lady in the Car With Glasses and a Gun, The see LA DAME DANS L'AUTO AVEC DES LUNETTES ET UN FUSIL (1970).

LADY IN THE DARK 1944 d: Mitchell Leisen. USA., *Lady in the Dark*, Moss Hart, New York 1941, Play

LADY IN THE DEATH HOUSE 1944 d: Steve Sekely. USA., *Meet the Executioner*, Frederick C. Davis, Story

LADY IN THE LAKE 1946 d: Robert Montgomery. USA., *The Lady in the Lake*, Raymond Chandler, 1943, Novel

LADY IN THE LIBRARY, THE 1917 d: Edgar Jones. USA., *The Lady in the Library*, Frederick Orin Bartlett, Short Story

LADY IN THE MORGUE, THE 1938 d: Otis Garrett. USA., *The Lady in the Morgue*, Jonathan Latimer, New York 1936, Novel

Lady in White, The see LA DAMA BIANCA (1938).

Lady Inger of Ostrat see FRU INGER TOL OSTRAT (1975).

Lady Is Waiting, The see FULL OF LIFE (1956).

LADY IS WILLING, THE 1934 d: Gilbert Miller. UKN., *The Lady Is Willing*, Louis Verneuil, Play

LADY JENNIFER 1915 d: James W. Vickers. UKN., *Lady Jennifer*, John Strange Winter, Novel

LADY L 1965 d: Peter Ustinov. USA/ITL/FRN., *Lady L*, Romain Gary, Paris 1963, Novel

LADY LIES, THE 1929 d: Hobart Henley. USA., *The Lady Lies*, John Meehan, New York 1928, Play

Lady Lou see SHE DONE HIM WRONG (1933).

Lady Luck see WOMEN AND HORSES WINE (1937).

Lady MacBeth of Mtsensk see SIBIRSKA LEDI MAGBET (1962).

Lady MacBeth of Mtsensk see KATERINA ISMAYLOVA (1966).

LADY MISLAID, A 1958 d: David MacDonald. UKN., *A Lady Mislaid*, Kenneth Horne, 1948, Play

Lady Musashino see MUSASHINO FUJIN (1951).

LADY NOGGS - PEERESS 1920 d: Sidney Morgan. UKN., *Lady Noggs - Peeress*, Selwyn Jepson, Novel

LADY OF BURLESQUE 1943 d: William A. Wellman. USA., *The G-String Murders*, Gypsy Rose Lee, Novel

LADY OF CHANCE, A 1928 d: Robert Z. Leonard. USA., *Little Angel*, Leroy Scott, Story

Lady of Deceit see BORN TO KILL (1947).

Lady of Lebanon see LA CHATELAINE DU LIBAN (1956).

LADY OF LYONS, THE 1913 d: Leon Bary. UKN., *The Lady of Lyons*, Edward George Bulwer Lytton, London 1838, Play

Lady of Monsoreau, The see LA SIGNORA DI MONSERAU (1909).

Lady of Monza, The see LA MONACA DI MONZA (1968).

Lady of Musashino, The see MUSASHINO FUJIN (1951).

LADY OF QUALITY, A 1913 d: J. Searle Dawley. USA., *A Lady of Quality*, Frances Hodgson Burnett, New York 1896, Novel

LADY OF QUALITY, A 1924 d: Hobart Henley. USA., *A Lady of Quality*, Frances Hodgson Burnett, New York 1896, Novel

LADY OF SCANDAL, THE 1930 d: Sidney A. Franklin. USA., *The High Road*, Frederick Lonsdale, London 1927, Play

LADY OF SECRETS 1936 d: Marion Gering. USA., *Maid of Honor*, Katharine Brush, 1932, Short Story

LADY OF SHALLOTT, THE 1912 d: Elwin Neame. UKN., *The Lady of Shallott*, Alfred Tennyson, 1833, Poem

LADY OF SHALLOTT, THE 1915 d: C. Jay Williams. USA., *The Lady of Shallott*, Alfred Tennyson, 1833, Poem

Lady of the Boulevards see NANA (1934).

LADY OF THE CAMELIAS, THE 1922 d: Edwin J. Collins. UKN., *La Dame aux Camelias*, Alexandre Dumas (fils), Paris 1848, Novel

LADY OF THE CAMELIAS, THE 1958 d: George M. O'Ferrall. UKN., *La Dame aux Camelias*, Alexandre Dumas (fils), Paris 1848, Novel

Lady of the Camelias, The see LA DAME AUX CAMELIAS (1981).

Lady of the Dawn, The see LA DAMA DEL ALBA (1965).

Lady of the Evening see LA PUPA DEL GANGSTER (1975).

LADY OF THE HAREM, THE 1926 d: Raoul Walsh. USA., *Hassan*, James Elroy Flecker, London 1922, Play

LADY OF THE LAKE, THE 1912 d: J. Stuart Blackton. USA., *The Lady of the Lake*, Sir Walter Scott, Poem

LADY OF THE LAKE, THE 1928 d: James A. Fitzpatrick. UKN/USA., *The Lady of the Lake*, Sir Walter Scott, Poem

Lady of the Lake, The see LA DONNA DEL LAGO (1965).

LADY OF THE LIGHTHOUSE, THE 1915 d: Harry Lambart, George Ridgwell. USA., *The Lady of the Lighthouse*, Helen S. Woodruff, Book

Lady of the Night see LADY OF THE PAVEMENTS (1929).

LADY OF THE PAVEMENTS 1929 d: D. W. Griffith. USA., *La Paiva*, Karl Vollmoller, Story

Lady of the Rose see BRIDE OF THE REGIMENT (1930).

LADY OF THE SNOWS, THE 1915. USA., *The Lady of the Snows*, Edith Ogden Harrison, Novel

LADY ON A TRAIN 1945 d: Charles David. USA., *Lady on a Train*, Leslie Charteris, Novel

Lady Oscar see BERUSAIYU NO BARA (1978).

Lady Peasant, The see BARYSHNYA-KRESTYANKA (1995).

LADY POSSESSED 1952 d: William Spier, Roy Kellino. USA., *Del Palma*, Pamela Kellino, 1948, Novel

Lady President, The see LA PRESIDENTESSA (1952).

LADY ROSE'S DAUGHTER 1920 d: Hugh Ford. USA., *Lady Rose's Daughter*, Mrs. Humphrey Ward, London 1903, Novel

LADY SINGS THE BLUES 1972 d: Sidney J. Furie. USA., *Lady Sings the Blues*, William Dufty, Billie Holiday, Autobiography

LADY SURRENDERS, A 1930 d: John M. Stahl. USA., *Sincerity*, John Erskine, Indianapolis 1929, Novel

Lady Surrenders, A see LOVE STORY (1944).

LADY TETLEY'S DECREE 1920 d: Fred Paul. UKN., *Lady Tetley's Decree*, Sybil Downing, W. F. Downing, Play

LADY, THE 1925 d: Frank Borzage. USA., *The Lady*, Martin Brown, New York 1923, Play

Lady, The see THE SECRET OF MADAME BLANCHE (1933).

Lady, The see LA SENORA (1987).

LADY TO LOVE, A 1929 d: Victor Sjostrom. USA., *They Knew What They Wanted*, Sidney Coe Howard, New York 1924, Play

LADY TUBBS 1935 d: Alan Crosland. USA., *Lady Tubbs*, Homer Croy, Novel

LADY VANISHES, THE 1938 d: Alfred Hitchcock. UKN., *The Wheel Spins*, Ethel Lina White, Novel

LADY VANISHES, THE 1979 d: Anthony Page. UKN., *The Wheel Spins*, Ethel Lina White, Novel

Lady Wang Xifeng Makes Trouble in the Mansion House see WANG XIFENG DANAO NING-KUOFU (1939).

LADY WHO DARED, THE 1931 d: William Beaudine. USA., *The Whisper Market*, W. E. Scutt, 1918, Short Story

LADY WHO LIED, THE 1925 d: Edwin Carewe. USA., *Snake-Bite*, Robert Hichens, 1919, Short Story

Lady Who Wades in the Sea, The see LA VIEILLE QUI MARCHAIT DANS LA MER (1991).

LADY WINDERMERES FACHER 1935 d: Heinz Hilpert. GRM., *Lady Windermere's Fan*, Oscar Wilde, London 1892, Play

LADY WINDERMERE'S FAN 1916 d: Fred Paul. UKN., *Lady Windermere's Fan*, Oscar Wilde, London 1892, Play

LADY WINDERMERE'S FAN 1925 d: Ernst Lubitsch. USA., *Lady Windermere's Fan*, Oscar Wilde, London 1892, Play

Lady Windermere's Fan see HISTORIA DE UNA MALA MUJER (1948).

Lady Windermere's Fan see THE FAN (1949).

LADY WINDERMERE'S FAN 1967 d: Joan Kemp-Welch. UKN., *Lady Windermere's Fan*, Oscar Wilde, London 1892, Play

LADY WITH A LAMP, THE 1951 d: Herbert Wilcox. UKN., *The Lady With a Lamp*, Reginald Berkeley, London 1929, Play

Lady With a Little Dog see DAMA S SOBACHKOI (1960).

LADY WITH A PAST 1932 d: Edward H. Griffith. USA., *Lady With a Past*, Harriet Henry, New York 1931, Novel

Lady With Camellias, The see CHA HUA NU (1938).

LADY WITH RED HAIR 1940 d: Curtis Bernhardt. USA., *Portrait of a Lady With Red Hair*, Norbert Faulkner, H. Brewster Morse, Story

Lady With the Borzoi, The see DAMA S BARZOJEM (1912).

Lady With the Camelias, The see LA SIGNORA DALLE CAMELIE (1909).

Lady With the Dog, The see DAMA S SOBACHKOI (1960).

Lady With the Lamp, The see THE LADY WITH A LAMP (1951).

Lady With the Little Dog, The see DAMA S SOBACHKOI (1960).

LADYFINGERS 1921 d: Bayard Veiller. USA., *Ladyfingers*, Jackson Gregory, New York 1920, Novel

Lady'o see BERUSAIYU NO BARA (1978).

LADY'S NAME, A 1918 d: Walter Edwards. USA., *A Lady's Name*, Cyril Harcourt, New York 1916, Play

LAFAYETTE ESCADRILLE 1958 d: William A. Wellman. USA., *C'est la Guerre*, William A. Wellman, Story

LAGARTERANOS, LOS 1928 d: Armando Pou. SPN., *Los Lagarteranos*, Luis de Vargas, Opera

LAGNA PAHAVA KARUN 1940 d: Winayak. IND., *Lagna Pahave Karun*, C. V. Joshi, Short Story

LAGUNA HEAT 1987 d: Simon Langton. USA., *Laguna Heat*, T. Jefferson Parker, Novel

LAGUNA NEGRA, LA 1952 d: Arturo Ruiz-Castillo. SPN., *La Tierra de Alvar Gonzalez*, Antonio Machado Y Ruiz, 1939, Verse

LAHOMA 1920 d: Edgar Lewis. USA., *Lahoma*, John Breckenridge Ellis, Indianapolis 1913, Novel

LAILA 1958 d: Rolf Husberg. SWD/GRM., *Fra Finmarken: Skildringer*, Jens Andreas Friis, Kristiania 1881, Novel

Laila - Liebe Unter Der Mitternachtssonne see LAILA (1958).

LAIR OF THE WHITE WORM, THE 1988 d: Ken Russell. UKN., *The Lair of the White Worm*, Bram Stoker, 1911, Novel

Lake, The see ONNA NO MISUMI (1966).

LAL AGHNIHAT ELMOUTAKASRA 1964 d: Yusuf Malouf. LBN., *The Broken Wings*, Kahlil Gibran, New York 1957, Novel

LALKA 1968 d: Wojciech J. Has. PLN., *Lalka*, Boleslaw Prus, 1890, Novel

LAMA NEL CORPO, LA 1966 d: Elio Scardamaglia, Domenico de Felice. ITL/FRN., *The Knife in the Body*, Robert Williams, Novel

Lamadel Giustiziere, La see DON CESARE DI BAZAN (1942).

LAMB 1986 d: Colin Gregg. UKN., *Lamb*, Bernard MacLaverty, Novel

Lamb, The see DAS LAMM (1964).

LAMBETH WALK, THE 1939 d: Albert de Courville. UKN., *Me and My Girl*, Douglas Furber, Noel Gay, Louis Rose, London 1937, Musical Play

Lame Devil, The see EL DIABLO COJUELO (1970).

Lament of the Path, The see PATHER PANCHALI (1955).

LAMIEL 1967 d: Jean Aurel. FRN/ITL., *La Fin de Lamiel*, Cecil Saint-Laurent, 1966, Novel, *Lamiel*, Stendhal, 1889, Novel

LAMM, DAS 1964 d: Wolfgang Staudte. GRM., Willy Kramp, Story

LAMP IN THE DESERT 1922 d: F. Martin Thornton. UKN., *Lamp in the Desert*, Ethel M. Dell, Novel

LAMP STILL BURNS, THE 1943 d: Maurice Elvey. UKN., *One Pair of Feet*, Monica Dickens, Novel

LAMPADA ALLA FINESTRA, UNA 1940 d: Gino Talamo. ITL., *Una Lampada Alla Finestra*, Gino Caprioli, Play

Lampelgasse, Die see VETERAN VOTRUBA (1928).

LAMPLIGHTER, THE 1921 d: Howard M. Mitchell. USA., *The Lamplighter*, Marie Susanna Cummins, Boston 1854, Novel

LANCELOT AND GUINEVERE 1962 d: Cornel Wilde. UKN., *Le Morte d'Arthur*, Sir Thomas Malory, 1485, Verse

LANCER SPY 1937 d: Gregory Ratoff. USA., *Lancer Spy*, Marthe Cnockhaert McKenna, London 1937, Novel

Land see ZEMYA (1957).

Land and Sons see LAND OG SYNIR (1978).

LAND DES LACHELNS, DAS 1930 d: Max Reichmann. GRM., *Das Land Des Lachelns*, Franz Lehar, Berlin 1929, Operetta

LAND DES LACHELNS, DAS 1952 d: Hans Deppe. GRM., *Das Land Des Lachelns*, Franz Lehar, Berlin 1929, Operetta

LAND GIRLS, THE 1998 d: David Leland. UKN/FRN., *The Land Girls*, Angela Huth, Novel

Land Is a Sinful Song, The see MAA ON SYNTINEN LAULAU (1973).

LAND JUST OVER YONDER, THE 1916 d: Julius Frankenburg. USA., *The Land Just Over Yonder*, Peter B. Kyne, 1915, Short Story

Land of Angels, The see ANGYALOK FOLDJE (1962).

Land of Desire, The see SKEPP TILL INDIALAND (1947).

Land of Fate, The see PRAESTEN I VEJLBY (1920).

Land of Fury see THE SEEKERS (1954).

Land of Heart's Desire see THE ARCADIANS (1927).

Land of Mirages, The see DELIBABOK ORSZAGA (1983).

Land of Oz, The see THE WONDERFUL LAND OF OZ (1969).

Land of Promise see ZIEMIA OBIECANA (1974).

LAND OF PROMISE, THE 1917 d: Joseph Kaufman. USA., *The Land of Promise*, W. Somerset Maugham, London 1913, Play

Land of Smiles see DAS LAND DES LACHELNS (1930).

Land of Smiles see DAS LAND DES LACHELNS (1952).

Land of the Deaf, The see STRANA GLUCHICH (1998).

Land of the Free, The see ONE MORE AMERICAN (1918).

Land of the Giants: Gulliver's Travels Part 2 see LOS VIAJES DE GULLIVER (1983).

Land of the Six-Shooter see THE CHEYENNE KID (1933).

LAND OG SYNIR 1978 d: Agust Gudmundsson. ICL., *Land Og Synir*, Indridi G. Thorsteinsson, Novel

LAND OHNE FRAUEN, DAS 1929 d: Carmine Gallone. GRM., *Die Braut Nr. 68*, Peter Bolt, Novel

Land Rush see NOT EXACTLY GENTLEMEN (1931).

LAND THAT TIME FORGOT, THE 1974 d: Kevin Connor. UKN/USA., *The Land That Time Forgot*, Edgar Rice Burroughs, 1924, Novel

LANDFALL 1949 d: Ken Annakin. UKN., *Landfall*, Nevil Shute, 1940, Novel

LANDLOPER, THE 1918 d: George Irving. USA., *The Landloper; the Romance of a Man on Foot*, Holman Francis Day, New York 1915, Novel

LANDLORD, THE 1970 d: Hal Ashby. USA., *The Landlord*, Kristin Hunter, New York 1966, Novel

Landscape After Battle see KRAJOBRAZ PO BITWIE (1970).

Landscape After the Battle see KRAJOBRAZ PO BITWIE (1970).

LANDSTREICHER, DIE 1937 d: Carl Lamac. GRM., *Die Landstreicher*, C. M. Ziehrer, Opera

LANDSTRYKERE 1988 d: Ola Solum. NRW., *Landstrykere*, Knut Hamsun, 1927, Novel

LANDVOGT VON GREIFENSEE, DER 1979 d: Wilfried Bolliger. SWT., *Der Landvogt von Griefensee*, Gottfried Keller, 1877, Short Story

LANE THAT HAD NO TURNING, THE 1922 d: Victor Fleming. USA., *The Lane That Had No Turning*, Gilbert Parker, 1900, Short Story

LANG TAO GUN GUN 1965 d: Cheng Yin. CHN., *Lang Tao Gun Gun*, Shao Hua, Novel

Lange Schatten Eines Morgens, Der see SCHNELLES GELD (1981).

Langes Radieux see FLEUR D'OSEILLE (1967).

LANGRISHE, GO DOWN 1978 d: David Jones. UKN., *Go Down Langrishe*, Aidan Higgins, Novel

Langtan see NATTLEK (1966).

LANGTAN TILL HAVET 1931 d: John W. Brunius. SWD., *Marius*, Marcel Pagnol, Paris 1931, Play

LANIGAN'S RABBI 1976 d: Lou Antonio. USA., *Friday the Rabbi Slept Late*, Harry Kemelman, Novel

LANSKY 1999 d: John McNaughton. USA., *Meyer Lansky: Mogul of the Mob*, Uri Dan, Dennis Eisenberg, Eli Landau, Book

Lantern, The see LUCERNA (1925).

Lantern, The see LUCERNA (1938).

Lantern, The see UTA ANDON (1960).

LANTUL SLABICIUNILOR 1952 d: Jean Georgescu. RMN., *Lantul Slabiciunilor*, Ion Luca Caragiale, 1901, Short Story

LANYARCOK TUKORBEN 1973 d: Robert Ban. HNG., *Borika Vendegei*, Ivan Mandy, 1965, Short Story

LAO JING 1987 d: Wu Tianming. CHN., *Lao Jing*, Zheng Yi, Novel

LAOREN HE GOU 1993 d: XIe Jin. CHN., *Laoren He Gou*, Zhang XIanliang, Novel

Laoren Yu Gou see LAOREN HE GOU (1993).

Lappli, Der Etappenheld see HD LAPPLI (1959).

LARAMIE TRAIL, THE 1944 d: John English. USA., *Mystery at Spanish Hacienda*, Jackson Gregory, Novel

LARCENY 1948 d: George Sherman. USA., *The Velvet Fleece*, Lois Eby, John Fleming, Novel

LARCENY IN HER HEART 1946 d: Sam Newfield. USA., *Brett Halliday*, Story

LARCENY INC. 1942 d: Lloyd Bacon. USA., *The Night Before Christmas*, Laura Perelman, S. J. Perelman, 1942, Novel

Large and Small see GROSS UND KLEIN (1980).

Larger Than Life see HE COULDN'T SAY NO (1938).

LARGO ALLE DONNE! 1924 d: Guido Brignone. ITL., *Place aux Femmes!*, Maurice Hennequin, 1898, Play

Lark, The see PACSIRTA (1964).

Lark's Song, The see SKRIVANCI PISEN (1933).

Larron, Le see IL LADRONE (1979).

LARS HARD 1948 d: Erik Faustman. SWD., *Lars Hard Jag*, Jan Fridegard, 1935, Novel

Larsen, Wolf of the Seven Seas see IL LUPO DEI MARI (1975).

LAS VEGAS, 500 MILLONES 1968 d: Antonio Isasi. SPN/FRN/GRM., *Les Hommes de Las Vegas*, Andre Lay, Paris 1969, Novel

LAS VEGAS STORY, THE 1952 d: Robert Stevenson. USA., Jay Dratler, Story

LASCA 1919 d: Norman Dawn. USA., *Lasca*, Frank Desprez, Poem

LASCA OF THE RIO GRANDE 1931 d: Edward Laemmle. USA., *Lasca*, Frank Desprez, Poem

LASCIA CANTARE IL CUORE 1943 d: Roberto Savarese. ITL., *Saison in Salzburg*, Kurt Feltz, Max Wallner, Opera

LASCIATE OGNI SPERANZA 1937 d: Gennaro Righelli. ITL., *L' Agonia Di Schizzo*, Athos Setti, Play

Lasciatemi Cantare! see CANTATE CON ME! (1940).

LASH, THE 1930 d: Frank Lloyd. USA., *Adios!*, Lanier Bartlett, Virginia S. Bartlett, New York 1929, Novel

LASH, THE 1934 d: Henry Edwards. UKN., *The Lash*, Cyril Campion, London 1926, Play

LASKA SLECNY VERY 1922 d: Vaclav Binovec. CZC., *Laska Slecny Very*, Otakar Hanus, Novel

Lasky - Vasne - Zrady see DAR SVATEBNI NOCI (1926).

LASKY KACENKY STRNADOVE 1926 d: Svatopluk Innemann. CZC., *Denik Kacenky Strnadove*, Josef Skruzny, Novel

Lass from the Stormy Croft, The see TOSEN FRAN STORMYRTORPET (1918).

LASS JUCKEN, KUMPEL 1972 d: Franz MarischkA. GRM., *Kumpel Lass Jucken*, Hans Henning Claer, Novel

LASS JUCKEN, KUMPEL (2): DAS BULLENKLOSTER 1972 d: Franz MarischkA. GRM., *Das Bullenkloster*, Hans Henning Claer, Novel

LASS JUCKEN, KUMPEL (6): LASS LAUFEN, KUMPEL! 1981 d: Franz MarischkA. GRM., *Kumpel! Lass Laufen*, Hans Henning Claer, Novel

Lass Laufen, Kumpel! see KUMPEL (6): LASS LAUFEN, KUMPEL! LASS JUCKEN (1981).

Lassie see LASSIE'S GREAT ADVENTURE (1963).

LASSIE COME HOME 1943 d: Fred M. Wilcox. USA., *Lassie Come Home*, Eric Knight, 1940, Novel

Lassie, The see TRNY A KVETY (1921).

LASSIE'S GREAT ADVENTURE 1963 d: William Beaudine. USA., Sumner Arthur Long, Story

Lassie's Greatest Adventure see LASSIE'S GREAT ADVENTURE (1963).

Last Act, The see DER LETZTE AKT (1955).

Last Adam, The see DOCTOR BULL (1933).

Last Adventure, The see LES AVENTURIERS (1966).

LAST ANGRY MAN, THE 1959 d: Daniel Mann. USA., *The Last Angry Man*, Gerald Green, 1956, Novel

LAST ANGRY MAN, THE 1974 d: Jerrold Freedman. USA., *The Last Angry Man*, Gerald Green, 1956, Novel

Last Aristocrats, The see ZUIHOUDE GUIZU (1989).

Last Assignment, The see FIGHTING COWARD (1935).

Last Ball in November, The see ULTIMUL BAL NOIEMBRIE (1989).

Last Bend, The see LE DERNIER TOURNANT (1939).

Last Blood see MURDER IN COWETA COUNTY (1982).

Last Bus to Woodstock see INSPECTOR MORSE: LAST BUS TO WOODSTOCK (1991).

Last Butterfly, The see POSLEDNI MOTYL (1989).

Last Call see ULTIMA LAMADA (1997).

LAST CARD, THE 1921 d: Bayard Veiller. USA., *Dated*, Maxwell Smith, 1920, Short Story

LAST CHALLENGE, THE 1967 d: Richard Thorpe. USA., *Pistolero's Progress*, John Sherry, New York 1966, Novel

LAST CHANCE, THE 1937 d: Thomas Bentley. UKN., *The Last Chance*, Frank Stayton, Play

Last Chance, The see L' ULTIMA CHANCE (1973).

Last Chapter see UN AIR SI PUR (1997).

LAST CHAPTER, THE 1915 d: William D. Taylor. USA., *The Unfinished Story*, Richard Harding Davis, Novel

Last Chapter, The see DAS LETZTE KAPITEL (1961).

LAST COUPON, THE 1932 d: Thomas Bentley. UKN., *The Last Coupon*, Ernest E. Bryan, Play

LAST CROOKED MILE, THE 1946 d: Philip Ford. USA., *The Last Crooked Mile*, Robert L. Richards, Radio Play

LAST CROP, THE 1990 d: Susan Clayton. ASL., *The Last Crop*, Elizabeth Jolley, 1983, Short Story

Last Days of Man on Earth see THE FINAL PROGRAMME (1973).

Last Days of Pompeii, The see GLI ULTIMI GIORNI DI POMPEI (1908).

Last Days of Pompeii see JONE O GLI ULTIMI GIORNI DI POMPEI (1913).

Last Days of Pompeii see GLI ULTIMI GIORNI DI POMPEI (1913).

Last Days of Pompeii, The see GLI ULTIMI GIORNI DI POMPEI (1908).

LAST DAYS OF POMPEII, THE 1935 d: Ernest B. Schoedsack. USA., *The Last Days of Pompeii*, Edward George Bulwer Lytton, 1834, Novel

Last Days of Pompeii, The see LES DERNIERS JOURS DE POMPEI (1948).

Last Days of Pompeii, The see DIE LETZTEN TAGE VON POMPEI (1959).

LAST DETAIL, THE 1973 d: Hal Ashby. USA., *The Last Detail*, Darryl Ponicsan, Novel

LAST DROP OF WATER, THE 1911 d: D. W. Griffith. USA., *The Last Drop of Water*, Bret Harte, Short Story

LAST EGYPTIAN, THE 1914 d: L. Frank Baum. USA., *The Last Egyptian*, L. Frank Baum, Philadelphia 1908, Novel

LAST EMBRACE 1979 d: Jonathan Demme. USA., *The 13th Man*, Murray Teigh Bloom, Novel

LAST EXIT TO BROOKLYN 1989 d: Ulrich Edel. USA/GRM., *Last Exit to Brooklyn*, Hubert Selby, 1964, Novel

LAST EXPRESS, THE 1938 d: Otis Garrett. USA., *The Last Express*, Baynard H. Kendrick, New York 1937, Novel

LAST FLIGHT OF NOAH'S ARK, THE 1980 d: Charles Jarrott. USA., *The Gremlin's Castle*, Ernest K. Gann, Short Story

Last Flight, The see L' EQUIPAGE (1927).

LAST FRONTIER, THE 1926 d: George B. Seitz. USA., *The Last Frontier*, Courtney Ryley Cooper, Boston 1923, Novel

Last Frontier, The see THE REAL GLORY (1939).

Last Frontier, The see SAVAGE WILDERNESS (1955).

Last Game, The see TRETIY TAYM (1963).

LAST GENTLEMAN, THE 1934 d: Sidney Lanfield. USA., *The Head of the Family*, Katharine Clugston, 1924, Play

LAST GIRAFFE, THE 1979 d: Jack Couffer. USA., *Raising Daisy Rothschild*, Betty Lesley-Manville, Jock Lesley-Manville, Book

Last Glory of Troy, The see LA LEGGENDA DI ENEA (1962).

LAST GRENADE, THE 1970 d: Gordon Flemyng. UKN., *The Ordeal of Major Grigsby*, John Sherlock, London 1964, Novel

Last Gunfighter, The see DEATH OF A GUNFIGHTER (1969).

LAST HARD MEN, THE 1976 d: Andrew V. McLaglen. USA., *The Last Hard Men*, Brian Garfield, Novel

Last Harvest, The see LA ULTIMA SIEMBRA (1991).

Last Hero, The see LONELY ARE THE BRAVE (1962).

LAST HOUR, THE 1923 d: Edward Sloman. USA., *Blind Justice*, Frank R. Adams, Short Story

LAST HOUR, THE 1930 d: Walter Forde. UKN., *The Last Hour*, Charles Bennett, Play

LAST HUNT, THE 1955 d: Richard Brooks. USA., *The Last Hunt*, Milton Lott, Novel

LAST HURRAH, THE 1958 d: John Ford. USA., *The Last Hurrah*, Edwin O'Connor, 1956, Novel

LAST HURRAH, THE 1978 d: Vincent Sherman. USA., *The Last Hurrah*, Edwin O'Connor, 1956, Novel

LAST INNOCENT MAN, THE 1987 d: Roger Spottiswoode. USA., *The Last Innocent Man*, Philip M. Margolin, Novel

Last Joy, The see POSLEDNI RADOST (1921).

Last King of the Incas, The see VIVA GRINGO (1966).

LAST LEAF, THE 1917 d: Ashley Miller. USA., *The Last Leaf*, O. Henry, Short Story

LAST LESSON, THE 1942 d: Allan Kenward. USA., *Le Petit Chose*, Alphonse Daudet, 1868, Novel

LAST MAN ON EARTH, THE 1924 d: John G. Blystone. USA., *The Last Man on Earth*, John D. Swain, 1923, Novel

Last Man on Earth, The see L' ULTIMO UOMO DELLA TERRA (1964).

Last Man, The see POSLEDNI MUZ (1934).

LAST MAN TO HANG, THE 1956 d: Terence Fisher. UKN., *The Jury*, Gerald Bullett, Novel

Last Manuscript, The *see* AZ UTOLSO KEZIRAT (1986).

LAST MILE, THE 1932 d: Sam Bischoff. USA., *The Last Mile*, John Wexley, New York 1930, Play

LAST MILE, THE 1959 d: Howard W. Koch. USA., *The Last Mile*, John Wexley, New York 1930, Play

Last Monsoon, The *see* SESHA SHRABANA (1976).

Last Mrs. Anderson, The *see* LA ULTIMA SENORA ANDERSON (1970).

Last Musketeer, The *see* LE VICOMTE DE BRAGELONNE (1954).

Last Nabob Part I, The *see* EGY MAGYAR NABOB. KAPATHY ZOLTAN (1966).

Last Nabob Part Ii: Zoltan Karpathy *see* KARPATHY ZOLTAN (1966).

Last New Year's Eve, The *see* L' ULTIMO CAPODANNO (1998).

Last Night of Love, The *see* LA PUERTA ABIERTA (1957).

Last Night of Love, The *see* ULTIMA NOAPTE DE DRAGOSTE (1979).

Last Night, The *see* DIE LETZTE NACHT (1927).

Last Night, The *see* DIE LETZTE NACHT (1949).

Last of His Race, The *see* L' ULTIMO DEGLI ABENCERAGI (1911).

LAST OF MRS. CHEYNEY, THE 1929 d: Sidney A. Franklin, Dorothy Arzner (Uncredited). USA., *The Last of Mrs. Cheyney*, Frederick Lonsdale, London 1925, Play

LAST OF MRS. CHEYNEY, THE 1937 d: Richard Boleslawski, George Fitzmaurice. USA., *The Last of Mrs. Cheyney*, Frederick Lonsdale, London 1925, Play

LAST OF PHILIP BANTER, THE 1986 d: Herve Hachuel. SPN/SWT., *The Last of Philip Banter*, John Franklin Bardin, Novel

LAST OF THE CLINTONS 1935 d: Harry L. Fraser. USA., *Last of the Clintons*, Monroe Talbot, Short Story

LAST OF THE DUANES, THE 1919 d: J. Gordon Edwards. USA., *The Last of the Duanes*, Zane Grey, 1914, Short Story

LAST OF THE DUANES, THE 1924 d: Lynn Reynolds. USA., *The Last of the Duanes*, Zane Grey, 1914, Short Story

LAST OF THE DUANES, THE 1930 d: Alfred L. Werker. USA., *The Last of the Duanes*, Zane Grey, 1914, Short Story

LAST OF THE DUANES, THE 1941 d: James Tinling. USA., *The Last of the Duanes*, Zane Grey, 1914, Short Story

Last of the Frontignacs, The *see* L' ULTIMO DEI FRONTIGNAC (1911).

LAST OF THE GOOD GUYS, THE 1978 d: Theodore J. Flicker. USA., Clark Howard, Short Story

LAST OF THE HIGH KINGS, THE 1996 d: David Keating. IRL/UKN/DNM., *The Last of the High Kings*, Ferdia MacAnna, Novel

LAST OF THE KNUCKLEMEN, THE 1979 d: Tim Burstall. ASL., *The Last of the Knucklemen*, John Powers, Play

LAST OF THE LONE WOLF, THE 1930 d: Richard Boleslawski. USA., *The Last of the Lone Wolf*, Louis Joseph Vance, Story

LAST OF THE MOBILE HOT-SHOTS, THE 1970 d: Sidney Lumet. USA., *The Seven Descents of Myrtle*, Tennessee Williams, New York 1968, Play

LAST OF THE MOHICANS 1932 d: Ford Beebe, B. Reeves Eason. USA., *The Last of the Mohicans*, James Fenimore Cooper, Boston 1826, Novel

LAST OF THE MOHICANS, THE 1911 d: Theodore Marston. USA., *The Last of the Mohicans*, James Fenimore Cooper, Boston 1826, Novel

LAST OF THE MOHICANS, THE 1911. USA., *The Last of the Mohicans*, James Fenimore Cooper, Boston 1826, Novel

LAST OF THE MOHICANS, THE 1920 d: Maurice Tourneur, Clarence Brown. USA., *The Last of the Mohicans*, James Fenimore Cooper, Boston 1826, Novel

LAST OF THE MOHICANS, THE 1936 d: George B. Seitz, Wallace Fox. USA., *The Last of the Mohicans*, James Fenimore Cooper, Boston 1826, Novel

Last of the Mohicans, The *see* EL FIN DE UNA RAZA UNCAS (1964).

Last of the Mohicans, The *see* DER LETZTE MOHIKANER (1965).

Last of the Mohicans, The *see* LE DERNIER DES MOHICANS (1968).

LAST OF THE MOHICANS, THE 1977 d: James L. Conway. USA., *The Last of the Mohicans*, James Fenimore Cooper, Boston 1826, Novel

LAST OF THE MOHICANS, THE 1992 d: Michael Mann. USA., *The Last of the Mohicans*, James Fenimore Cooper, Boston 1826, Novel

Last of the Nabobs, The *see* EGY MAGYAR NABOB. KAPATHY ZOLTAN (1966).

Last of the Nabobs, The *see* KARPATHY ZOLTAN (1966).

LAST OF THE RED HOT LOVERS 1972 d: Gene Saks. USA., *Last of the Red Hot Lovers*, Neil Simon, 1970, Play

LAST OF THE REDMEN 1947 d: George Sherman. USA., *The Last of the Mohicans*, James Fenimore Cooper, Boston 1826, Novel

Last of the Redskins *see* LAST OF THE REDMEN (1947).

Last of the Renegades *see* WINNETOU II (1964).

LAST OF THE TROUBADOURS, THE 1917 d: David Smith. USA., *The Last of the Troubadours*, O. Henry, Short Story

LAST OUTPOST, THE 1935 d: Charles T. Barton, Louis J. Gasnier. USA., *The Drum*, F. Britten Austin, 1923, Short Story

LAST OUTPOST, THE 1951 d: Lewis R. Foster. USA., David Lang, Story

LAST PAGE, THE 1952 d: Terence Fisher. UKN., *The Last Page*, James Hadley Chase, Play

Last Pedestrian, The *see* DER LETZTE FUSSGANGER (1960).

LAST PICTURE SHOW, THE 1971 d: Peter Bogdanovich. USA., *The Last Picture Show*, Larry McMurtry, 1966, Novel

Last Plantation, The *see* FOGO MORTO (1976).

Last Prescription, The *see* DAS LETZTE REZEPT (1952).

Last Rites *see* SAMSKARA (1970).

Last Rites *see* ANTARJALI JATRA (1988).

LAST ROSE OF SUMMER, THE 1920 d: Albert Ward. UKN., *The Last Rose of Summer*, Hugh Conway, Novel

LAST ROUND-UP, THE 1934 d: Henry Hathaway. USA., *The Border Legion*, Zane Grey, New York 1916, Novel

Last Sacrifice, The *see* POSLEDNJAJA SHERTWA (1975).

LAST SAFARI, THE 1967 d: Henry Hathaway. UKN., *Gilligan's Last Elephant*, Gerald Hanley, Cleveland 1962, Novel

LAST SENTENCE, THE 1917 d: Ben Turbett. USA., *The Last Sentence*, Maxwell Gray, London 1893, Novel

LAST SHOT YOU HEAR, THE 1969 d: Gordon Hessler. UKN., *The Sound of Murder*, William Fairchild, London 1959, Play

Last Slaver, The *see* SLAVE SHIP (1937).

Last Song, The *see* CANTICO FINAL (1976).

Last Sowing, The *see* LA ULTIMA SIEMBRA (1991).

LAST STAND AT SABER RIVER 1997 d: Dick Lowry. USA., *Last Stand at Saber River*, Elmore Leonard, Novel

LAST STRAW, THE 1920 d: Denison Clift, Charles Swickard. USA., *The Last Straw*, Harold Titus, 1920, Serial Story

LAST SUMMER 1969 d: Frank Perry. USA., *Last Summer*, Evan Hunter, New York 1968, Novel

Last Summer, The *see* DER LETZTE SOMMER (1954).

LAST SUNSET, THE 1961 d: Robert Aldrich. USA., *Sundown at Crazy Horse*, Howard Rigsby, New York 1957, Novel

LAST SUPPER, THE 1995 d: Cynthia Roberts. CND., *The Last Supper*, Hillar Liitoja, Play

Last Tale of Konigswald Castle *see* SCHLOSS KONIGSWALD (1987).

Last Taps *see* DER GROSSE ZAPFENSTREICH (1952).

LAST TEMPTATION OF CHRIST, THE 1988 d: Martin Scorsese. USA/CND., *O Teleftaios Peirasmos*, Nikos Kazantzakis, 1955, Novel

Last Ten Days of Adolf Hitler, The *see* DER LETZTE AKT (1955).

Last Ten Days of Hitler, The *see* DER LETZTE AKT (1955).

Last Ten Days, The *see* DER LETZTE AKT (1955).

LAST TIME I SAW PARIS, THE 1954 d: Richard Brooks. USA., *Babylon Revisited*, F. Scott Fitzgerald, 1931, Short Story

Last Tomahawk, The *see* DER LETZTE MOHIKANER (1965).

Last Tomb of Ligeia *see* THE TOMB OF LIGEIA (1964).

LAST TRAIL, THE 1921 d: Emmett J. Flynn. USA., *The Last Trail*, Zane Grey, New York 1909, Novel

LAST TRAIL, THE 1927 d: Lewis Seiler. USA., *The Last Trail*, Zane Grey, New York 1909, Novel

LAST TRAIL, THE 1933 d: James Tinling. USA., *The Last Trail*, Zane Grey, New York 1909, Novel

LAST TRAIN FROM GUN HILL 1959 d: John Sturges. USA., *Showdown*, Les Crutchfield, Story

Last Train, The *see* LE TRAIN (1973).

Last Trap, The *see* THE DARK HOUR (1936).

LAST TYCOON, THE 1976 d: Elia Kazan. USA., *The Last Tycoon*, F. Scott Fitzgerald, 1941, Novel

LAST UNICORN, THE 1982 d: Arthur Rankin Jr., Jules Bass. USA., *The Last Unicorn*, Peter S. Beagle, Novel

LAST VALLEY, THE 1970 d: James Clavell. UKN., *The Last Valley*, James Clavell, Novel

Last Waltz, The *see* DER LETZTE WALZER (1927).

Last Waltz, The *see* DER LETZTE WALZER (1934).

LAST WALTZ, THE 1936 d: Gerald Barry, Leo Mittler. UKN., *Der Letzte Walzer*, Oscar Straus, Max Wallner, G. Weber, Berlin 1920, Operetta

Last Waltz, The *see* DER LETZTE WALZER (1953).

LAST WARNING, THE 1929 d: Paul Leni. USA., *The Last Warning*, Thomas F. Fallon, New York 1922, Play

LAST WARNING, THE 1938 d: Albert S. Rogell. USA., *The Dead Don't Care*, Jonathan Latimer, New York 1938, Novel

Last Warrior, The *see* FLAP (1969).

Last Werewolf, The *see* VYZNAVACI SLUNCE (1925).

Last Will Be the First, The *see* DIE LETZTEN WERDEN DIE ERSTEN SEIN (1957).

Last Will of Dr. Mabuse, The *see* DAS TESTAMENT DES DR. MABUSE (1933).

Last Will of Dr. Mabuse, The *see* DAS TESTAMENT DES DR. MABUSE (1962).

LAST WITNESS, THE 1925 d: Fred Paul. UKN., *The Last Witness*, F. Britten Austin, Novel

Last Witness, The *see* DER LETZTE ZEUGE (1960).

LAST WORD, THE 1979 d: Roy Boulting. USA., Horatius Haeberle, Story

Last Year of Berkut *see* POSLEDNY GOD BERKOETA (1978).

Late Afternoon of a Faun, The *see* FAUNOVO VELMI POZDNI ODPOLEDNE (1984).

Late Autumn *see* AKIBIYORI (1960).

Late Christopher Bean, The *see* CHRISTOPHER BEAN (1933).

Late Chrysanthemums *see* BANGIKU (1954).

LATE EDWINA BLACK, THE 1951 d: Maurice Elvey. UKN., *The Late Edwina Black*, William Dinner, William Morum, London 1949, Play

LATE FLOWERING 1981 d: Charles Wallace. UKN., *Agricultural Caress*, John Betjeman, 1966, Poem, *Myfanwy*, John Betjeman, 1940, Poems, *Subaltern's Love Song*, John Betjeman, 1940, Poem

LATE GEORGE APLEY, THE 1947 d: Joseph L. Mankiewicz. USA., *The Late George Apley*, John Phillips Marquand, 1937, Novel

Late Mathias Pascal, The *see* L' HOMME DE NULLE PART (1936).

Late Matthew Pascal, The *see* FEU MATHIAS PASCAL (1925).

Late Spring *see* BANSHUN (1949).

Latest Episodes of the Ringer *see* NEUES VOM HEXER (1965).

LATHE OF HEAVEN, THE 1980 d: David Loxton, Fred Barzyk. USA., *The Lathe of Heaven*, Ursula K. Leguin, Novel

LATIN BOYS GO TO HELL 1997 d: Ela Troyano. USA/GRM/SPN., *Latin Boys Go to Hell*, Andre Salas, Novel

Latin Lovers *see* LE ITALIANE E L'AMORE (1961).

Latin Quarter *see* QUARTIER LATIN (1929).

LATIN QUARTER 1945 d: Vernon Sewell. UKN., *L' Angoisse*, Celia de Vylars, Pierre Mills, Play

LATINO BAR 1991 d: Paul Leduc. SPN/VNZ/CUB., *Santo*, Jose J. Blanco, Book

LATTIVENDOLE, LE 1914 d: Ernesto Vaser. ITL., *Marghere Di Cavouret*, L. D. Beccari, Play

Laugh and a Tear, A see LAUGHTER AND TEARS (1921).

Laugh Bajazzo! see LACHE BAJAZZO! (1917).

LAUGH, CLOWN, LAUGH 1928 d: Herbert Brenon. USA., *Clown, Laugh! Laugh*, David Belasco, New York 1923, Play, *Laugh Clown Laugh!*, Tom Cushing, New York 1923, Play

LAUGHING ANNE 1953 d: Herbert Wilcox. UKN., *Between the Tides*, Joseph Conrad, Short Story

Laughing at Death see LAUGHING AT TROUBLE (1937).

LAUGHING AT TROUBLE 1937 d: Frank Strayer. USA., *Glory*, Adelyn Bushnell, Play

LAUGHING BILL HYDE 1918 d: Hobart Henley. USA., *Laughing Bill Hyde*, Rex Beach, 1917, Short Story

LAUGHING BOY 1934 d: W. S. Van Dyke. USA., *Laughing Boy*, Oliver la Farge, Boston 1929, Novel

LAUGHING CAVALIER, THE 1917 d: A. V. Bramble, Eliot Stannard. UKN., *The Laughing Cavalier*, Baroness Orczy, Novel

LAUGHING LADY, THE 1929 d: Victor Schertzinger. USA., *The Laughing Lady*, Alfred Sutro, London 1922, Play

LAUGHING LADY, THE 1946 d: Paul L. Stein. UKN., *The Laughing Lady*, Ingram d'Abbes, Musical Play

LAUGHING POLICEMAN, THE 1973 d: Stuart Rosenberg. USA., *Maj Sjowall*, Per Wahloo, Novel

LAUGHING SINNERS 1931 d: Harry Beaumont. USA., *Torch Song*, Kenyon Nicholson, New York 1930, Play

Laughing Woman, The see KTERA SE SMEJE ZENA (1931).

LAUGHTER AND TEARS 1921 d: B. E. Doxat-Pratt. UKN/NTH., *Carnaval Tragique*, Adelqui Millar, Play

LAUGHTER IN HELL 1933 d: Edward L. Cahn. USA., *Laughter in Hell*, Jim Tully, New York 1932, Novel

LAUGHTER IN THE DARK 1969 d: Tony Richardson. UKN/FRN/ITL., *Kamera Obscura*, Vladimir Nabokov, 1932, Novel

LAUGHTER OF FOOLS, THE 1933 d: Adrian Brunel. UKN., *The Laughter of Fools*, H. F. Maltby, 1909, Play

LAULU TULIPUNAISESTA KUKASTA 1938 d: Teuvo Tulio. FNL., *Laulu Tulipunaisesta Kukasta*, Johannes Linnankoski, 1905, Novel

LAULU TULIPUNAISESTA KUKASTA 1971 d: Mikko Niskanen. FNL., *Laulu Tulipunaisesta Kukasta*, Johannes Linnankoski, 1905, Novel

LAUNCELOT AND ELAINE 1909. USA., *Launcelot and Elaine*, Alfred Tennyson, Poem

LAUNDRY GIRL, THE 1919 d: Albert G. Frenguelli, Edith Mellor. UKN., *The Laundry Girl*, Edward Waltyre, Opera

LAURA 1944 d: Otto Preminger. USA., *Laura*, Vera Caspary, Novel

LAURA 1955 d: John Brahm. USA., *Laura*, Vera Caspary, Novel

Laurel and Hardy in Toyland see BABES IN TOYLAND (1934).

LAURETTE OU LE CACHET ROUGE 1931 d: Jacques de Casembroot. FRN., *Servitude Et Grandeur Militaires*, Alfred de Vigny, Short Story

LAURIE LEE'S CIDER WITH ROSIE 1998 d: Charles Beeson. UKN., *Cider With Rosie*, Laurie Lee, 1959, Autobiography

LAUSBUBENGESCHICHTEN 1964 d: Helmut Kautner. GRM., Ludwig Thoma, Story

LAUTER LUGEN 1938 d: Heinz Ruhmann. GRM., *Lauter Lugen*, Hans Schweikart, Play

Lautlose Waffen see L' ESPION (1966).

LAVENDEL 1953 d: Arthur M. Rabenalt. GRM/AUS., *Lavendel*, Bruno Schuppler, Play

Lavendel, Eine Ganz Unmoralische Geschichte see LAVENDEL (1953).

LAVENDER AND OLD LACE 1921 d: Lloyd Ingraham. USA., *Lavender and Old Lace*, Myrtle Reed, New York 1902, Play

LAVINA 1981 d: Hristo Piskov, Irina AktashevA. BUL., *Lavina*, Blaga Dimitrova, 1971, Novel

Lavirint Smrti see OLD SUREHAND I (1965).

LAVYRLE SPENCER'S HOME SONG 1996 d: Nancy Malone. USA., *Home Song*, Lavyrle Spencer, Novel

LAW AND DISORDER 1958 d: Charles Crichton, Henry Cornelius. UKN., *Smugglers' Circuit*, Denys Roberts, Novel

LAW AND JAKE WADE, THE 1958 d: John Sturges. USA., *The Law and Jake Wade*, Marvin H. Albert, 1956, Novel

Law and Lady Loverly, The see THE LAW AND THE LADY (1951).

Law and Martin Rome, The see CRY OF THE CITY (1948).

LAW AND ORDER 1917 d: David Smith. USA., *Law and Order*, O. Henry, Short Story

LAW AND ORDER 1932 d: Edward L. Cahn. USA., *Saint Johnson*, William Riley Burnett, New York 1930, Novel

LAW AND ORDER 1940 d: Ray Taylor. USA., *Saint Johnson*, William Riley Burnett, New York 1930, Novel

LAW AND ORDER 1953 d: Nathan Juran. USA., *Saint Johnson*, William Riley Burnett, New York 1930, Novel

LAW AND ORDER 1976 d: Marvin J. Chomsky. USA., *Law and Order*, Dorothy Uhnak, Novel

LAW AND THE LADY, THE 1951 d: Edwin H. Knopf. USA., *The Last of Mrs. Cheyney*, Frederick Lonsdale, London 1925, Play

LAW AND THE MAN 1928 d: Scott Pembroke. USA., *False Fires*, Octavus Roy Cohen, Story

LAW AND THE WOMAN, THE 1922 d: Penrhyn Stanlaws. USA., *The Woman in the Case*, Clyde Fitch, New York 1905, Play

Law and Tombstone, The see HOUR OF THE GUN (1967).

Law at Randado see BORDER SHOOTOUT (1990).

LAW DIVINE, THE 1920 d: Challis Sanderson, H. B. Parkinson. UKN., *The Law Divine*, H. V. Esmond, Novel

Law Enforcer see AMMALDAR (1953).

Law Hustlers, The see THE LAW RUSTLERS (1923).

LAW OF 45'S, THE 1935 d: John P. McCarthy. USA., *Law of the Forty-Fives*, William Colt MacDonald, New York 1933, Novel

Law of Love see DAS GESETZ DER LIEBE (1945).

Law of the 45'S, The see THE LAW OF 45'S (1935).

LAW OF THE LAND, THE 1917 d: Maurice Tourneur. USA., *The Law of the Land*, George Broadhurst, New York 1914, Play

LAW OF THE LAWLESS, THE 1923 d: Victor Fleming. USA., *The Law of the Lawless*, Konrad Bercovici, 1921, Short Story

LAW OF THE RANGE, THE 1914 d: Henry McRae. USA., *The Law of the Range*, Wayne Groves Barrows, Novel

Law of the Sierras, The see SALOMY JANE (1923).

Law of the Streets see LA LOI DES RUES (1956).

LAW OF THE TIMBER 1941 d: Bernard B. Ray. USA., *The Speck on the Wall*, James Oliver Curwood, Novel

LAW OF THE TROPICS 1941 d: Ray Enright. USA., *Oil for the Lamps of China*, Alice Tisdale Hobart, New York 1933, Novel

LAW OF THE UNDERWORLD 1938 d: Lew Landers. USA., *Crime*, John B. Hymer, New York 1927, Play, *The Lost Game*, John B. Hymer, Short Story, *Crime*, Samuel Shipman, New York 1927, Play, *The Lost Game*, Samuel Shipman, Short Story

LAW OF THE YUKON, THE 1920 d: Charles Miller. USA., *The Law of the Yukon*, Robert W. Service, 1907, Poem

Law of Vengeance see TO THE LAST MAN (1933).

Law Rides West, The see THE SANTA FE TRAIL (1930).

LAW RUSTLERS, THE 1923 d: Louis King. USA., *The Law Rustlers*, W. C. Tuttle, 1921, Short Story

Law, The see LAW AND ORDER (1940).

Law, The see LA LOI (1958).

Law, The see TIAN WANG (1994).

Law Without Mercy see GESETZ OHNE GNADE (1951).

LAWFUL LARCENY 1923 d: Allan Dwan. USA., *Lawful Larceny*, Samuel Shipman, New York 1922, Play

LAWFUL LARCENY 1930 d: Lowell Sherman. USA., *Lawful Larceny*, Samuel Shipman, New York 1922, Play

LAWLESS BREED, THE 1952 d: Raoul Walsh. USA., *They Died With Their Boots on*, Thomas Ripley, 1937, Book

LAWLESS EIGHTIES, THE 1957 d: Joseph Kane. USA., *Brother Van*, Alson Jesse Smith, 1948, Novel

LAWLESS LOVE 1918 d: Robert T. Thornby. USA., *Above the Law*, Max Brand, 1918, Short Story

LAWLESS STREET, A 1955 d: Joseph H. Lewis. USA., *Marshal of Medicine Bend*, Brad Ward, 1933, Novel

LAWLESS VALLEY 1938 d: David Howard. USA., *No Law in Shadow Valley*, W. C. Tuttle, 1936, Short Story

LAWNMOWER MAN, THE 1992 d: Brett Leonard. UKN/USA., *The Lawnmower Man*, Stephen King, Short Story

LAWRENCE OF ARABIA 1962 d: David Lean. UKN/USA., *Seven Pillars of Wisdom*, T. E. Lawrence, 1926, Book

Law's the Law, The see CHEATING CHEATERS (1927).

LAWYER MAN 1932 d: William Dieterle. USA., *Lawyer Man*, Max Trell, New York 1932, Novel

Lawyer of the Poor see ADVOKAT CHUDYCH (1941).

LAWYER QUINCE 1914 d: Harold Shaw. UKN., *Lawyer Quince*, W. W. Jacobs, Short Story

LAWYER QUINCE 1924 d: Manning Haynes. UKN., *Lawyer Quince*, W. W. Jacobs, Short Story

Lawyer Vera see ADVOKATKA VERA (1937).

LAXDALE HALL 1952 d: John Eldridge. UKN., *Laxdale Hall*, Eric Linklater, 1951, Novel

LAY OF THE LAND, THE 1997 d: Larry Arrick. USA., *The Lay of the Land*, Mel Shapiro, Play

Laying of the Glourie Ghost, The see THE GHOST GOES WEST (1935).

Layla see LAYLA MA RAISON (1989).

LAYLA MA RAISON 1989 d: Taieb Louhichi. TNS., *Layla*, Andre Miquel, Novel

Layton. Bambole E Karate see CARRE DE DAMES POUR UN AS (1966).

Lazarillo see EL LAZARILLO DE TORMES (1959).

LAZARILLO DE TORMES, EL 1925 d: Florian Rey. SPN., *Lazarillo de Tormes*, Anon, 1554, Novel

LAZARILLO DE TORMES, EL 1959 d: Cesar Ardavin. SPN., *Lazarillo de Tormes*, Anon, 1554, Novel

Lazaro see WHERE THE RIVER RUNS BLACK (1986).

LAZY RIVER 1934 d: George B. Seitz. USA., *Ruby*, Lea David Freeman, Play

LAZYBONES 1925 d: Frank Borzage. USA., *Lazybones*, Owen Davis, New York 1924, Play

LAZYBONES 1935 d: Michael Powell. UKN., *Lazybones*, Ernest Denny, 1930, Play

Lazzarillo de Tomes see EL LAZARILLO DE TORMES (1959).

LEA 1910 d: Giuseppe de Liguoro?. ITL., *Lea*, Felice Cavallotti, 1888, Play

LEA 1916 d: Diana Karenne, Salvatore Aversano (Uncredited). ITL., *Lea*, Felice Cavallotti, 1888, Play

LEAGUE OF FRIGHTENED MEN, THE 1937 d: Alfred E. Green. USA., *The League of Frightened Men*, Rex Stout, New York 1935, Novel

LEAGUE OF GENTLEMEN, THE 1960 d: Basil Dearden. UKN., *The League of Gentlemen*, John Boland, London 1958, Novel

LEAH KLESCHNA 1913 d: J. Searle Dawley. USA., *Leah Kleschna*, C. M. S. McLellan, New York 1904, Play

LEAH THE FORSAKEN 1908 d: Van Dyke Brooke. USA., *Leah the Forsaken*, Ritter von Mosenthal, Short Story

Leander Clicks see HOT TIP (1935).

Leanyintezet see MADCHENPENSIONAT (1936).

Learn, Baby, Learn see THE LEARNING TREE (1969).

Learn from Experience see KAFUKU (1937).

LEARNING TO BE A FATHER 1915 d: Jacques Jaccard. USA., *Learning to Be a Father*, J. Fleming Wilson, Story

LEARNING TREE, THE 1969 d: Gordon Parks. USA., *The Learning Tree*, Gordon Parks, New York 1963, Novel

LEAT YOTER 1967 d: Avram Heffner. ISR., Simone de Beauvoir, Story

Leather and Nylon see LE SOLEIL DES VOYOUS (1967).

LEATHER BOYS, THE 1963 d: Sidney J. Furie. UKN., *The Leather Boys*, Eliot George, London 1961, Novel

LEATHER STOCKING 1909 d: D. W. Griffith. USA., *The Leather Stocking Tales*, James Fenimore Cooper, Novel

LEATHERNECKING 1930 d: Eddie Cline. USA., *Present Arms*, Herbert Fields, Lorenz Hart, Richard Rogers, New York 1928, Musical Play

Leave All Hope see **LASCIATE OGNI SPERANZA** (1937).

LEAVE HER TO HEAVEN 1945 d: John M. Stahl. USA., *Leave Her to Heaven*, Ben Ames Williams, Novel

LEAVE IT TO ME 1933 d: Monty Banks. UKN., *Leave It to Psmith*, Ian Hay, P. G. Wodehouse, London 1930, Play

Leave It to Smith see **JUST SMITH** (1933).

Leave It to the Irish see **THE LUCK OF THE IRISH** (1948).

Leave on Word of Honor see **URLAUB AUF EHRENWORT** (1937).

LEAVENWORTH CASE, THE 1923 d: Charles Giblyn. USA., *The Leavenworth Case*, Anna Katharine Green, New York 1878, Novel

LEAVENWORTH CASE, THE 1936 d: Lewis D. Collins. USA., *The Leavenworth Case*, Anna Katharine Green, New York 1878, Novel

LEAVES FROM MY LIFE 1921 d: Edward R. Gordon. UKN., *Secrets of Scotland Yard*, Ernest Haigh, Book

Lebanese Mission, The see **LA CHATELAINE DU LIBAN** (1956).

Lebediker Yusem, Der see **MY SON** (1939).

LEBEDINAYA PESNYA 1966 d: Juri Mogilevtzev. USS., *Kalkhas*, Anton Chekhov, 1896, Short Story

Leben Auf Dem Mississippi see **LIFE ON THE MISSISSIPPI** (1987).

LEBEN BEGINNT, DAS 1942 d: Sigfrit Steiner. SWT., *Matura-Reise*, Paul Mathies, Berne 1942, Novel

Leben Beginnt, Das see **JEUNES FILLES D'AUJOURD'HUI** (1942).

LEBEN BEGINNT UM ACHT, DAS 1962 d: Michael Kehlmann. GRM., Emlyn Williams, Play

LEBEN FUR DO, EIN 1954 d: Gustav Ucicky. GRM., *Daddy Und Do*, Robert Pilchowsky, Novel

Leben Ist Starker, Das see **HEREINSPAZIERT!** (1953).

LEBEN KANN SO SCHON SEIN, DAS 1938 d: Rolf Hansen. GRM., *Ultimo*, Jochen Huth, Play

LEBEN RUFT, DAS 1944 d: Arthur M. Rabenalt. GRM., *Mutter Erde*, Max Halbe, 1898, Play

LEBEN UM LEBEN 1913 d: Rudolf Meinert. GRM., *Sergius Panin*, Lev Nikolayevich Tolstoy

Lebende Leichham, Der see **ZHIVOI TRUP** (1929).

LEBENDE LEICHNAM, DER 1918 d: Richard Oswald. GRM., *Zhivoi Trup*, Lev Nikolayevich Tolstoy, Moscow 1911, Play

Lebende Ware see **GEHETZTE FRAUEN** (1927).

LEBENS UBERFLUSS, DES 1950 d: Wolfgang Liebeneiner. GRM., *Des Lebens Uberfluss*, Ludwig Tieck, 1871, Short Story

LEBENSZEICHEN 1967 d: Werner Herzog. GRM., *Der Tolle Invalide Auf Dem Fort Ratonneau*, Ludwig Achim von Arnim, 1818, Short Story

LECCIONES DE BUEN AMOR 1943 d: Rafael Gil. SPN., *Lecciones de Buen Amor*, Jacinto Benavente y Martinez, 1924, Play

LECTRICE, LA 1988 d: Michel Deville. FRN., *La Letrice*, Raymond Jean, Novel

Leda see **A DOUBLE TOUR** (1959).

LEDA SENZA CIGNO 1918 d: Giulio Antamoro. ITL., *Leda Senza Cigno*, Gabriele D'Annunzio, Novel

Lederstrumpf -Der Letzte Mohaniker see **EL FIN DE UNA RAZA UNCAS** (1964).

LEER OM LEER 1983 d: Juul Claes. BLG., *Leer Om Leer*, Jacques Post, Novel

Leeuw En de Muis, de see **THE LION'S MOUSE** (1923).

LEFT HAND OF GOD, THE 1955 d: Edward Dmytryk. USA., *The Left Hand of God*, William E. Barrett, 1951, Novel

Left Handed Law see **LEFT-HANDED LAW** (1937).

LEFT IN THE TRAIN 1914. USA., *Left in the Train*, Evelyn Van Buren, Story

LEFT LUGGAGE 1998 d: Jeroen Krabbe. NTH/BLG/USA., *The Shovel and the Loom*, Carl Friedman, Novel

LEFT-HANDED GUN, THE 1958 d: Arthur Penn. USA., *The Death of Billy the Kid*, Gore Vidal, 1955, Television Play

LEFT-HANDED LAW 1937 d: Lesley Selander. USA., *Left Handed Law*, Charles M. Martin, New York 1936, Novel

Left-Handed Woman, The see **DIE LINKSHANDIGE FRAU** (1978).

Lefty Farrell see **TWO OF A KIND** (1951).

Leg, The see **NOGA** (1991).

Legacy see **ADAM HAD FOUR SONS** (1941).

Legacy of a Spy see **THE DOUBLE MAN** (1967).

LEGACY OF SIN - THE WILLIAM COIT STORY 1995 d: Steven Schachter. USA., *Legacy of Sin*, Stephen Singular, Book

Legend About the Stewed Hare see **LEGENDA A NYULPAPRIKASROL** (1975).

Legend of Doom House, The see **MALPERTUIS** (1972).

Legend of Eight Samurai see **SATOMI HAKKEN DEN** (1984).

Legend of Gosta Berling, The see **GOSTA BERLINGS SAGA** (1924).

LEGEND OF HELL HOUSE, THE 1973 d: John Hough. UKN/USA., *Hell House*, Richard Matheson, Novel

LEGEND OF HOLLYWOOD, THE 1924 d: Renaud Hoffman. USA., *The Legend of Hollywood*, Frank Condon, 1924, Short Story

Legend of Judo, The see **SUGATA SANSHIRO** (1943).

LEGEND OF LOBO, THE 1962 d: James Algar. USA., *The King of the Currampaw Lobo*, Ernest Thompson-Seton, Novel

LEGEND OF LYLAH CLARE, THE 1968 d: Robert Aldrich. USA., *The Legend of Lylah Clare*, Edward Deblasio, Robert Thom, 1963, Play

Legend of Musashi, The see **MIYAMOTO MUSASHI** (1954).

Legend of Prague, The see **LE GOLEM** (1935).

LEGEND OF PROVENCE, THE 1913. USA., *The Legend of Provence*, Adelaide Anne Procter, London 1858-61, Poem

LEGEND OF SLEEPY HOLLOW 1908. USA., *The Legend of Sleepy Hollow*, Washington Irving, 1820, Short Story

LEGEND OF SLEEPY HOLLOW, THE 1949 d: Clyde Geronimi. USA., *The Legend of Sleepy Hollow*, Washington Irving, 1820, Short Story

LEGEND OF SLEEPY HOLLOW, THE 1980 d: Henning Schellerup. USA., *The Legend of Sleepy Hollow*, Washington Irving, 1820, Short Story

Legend of the Dogs of Satomi see **SATOMI HAKKEN DEN** (1984).

Legend of the Eight Samurai see **SATOMI HAKKEN DEN** (1984).

Legend of the Fool Killer, The see **THE FOOL KILLER** (1963).

Legend of the Fortress of Suram see **LEGENDA SURAMSKOI KREPOSTI** (1986).

Legend of the Holy Drinker, The see **LA LEGGENDA DEL SANTO BEVITORE** (1988).

Legend of the Incas, The see **VIVA GRINGO** (1966).

Legend of the Narayama see **NARAYAMA BUSHI-KO** (1958).

Legend of the Pianist on the Ocean, The see **LA LEGGENDA DEL PIANISTA SULL'OCEANO** (1998).

Legend of the Sea Wolf see **IL LUPO DEI MARI** (1975).

Legend of the Suram Fortress see **LEGENDA SURAMSKOI KREPOSTI** (1986).

Legend of Ubirajara, The see **A LENDA DE UBIRAJARA** (1975).

Legend of William Tell, The see **WILHELM TELL** (1934).

LEGENDA A NYULPAPRIKASROL 1975 d: Barna Kabay. HNG., *Legenda a Nyulpaprikasrol*, Jozsi Jeno Tersanszky, 1936, Novel

LEGENDA O SALIERI 1986 d: Vadim Kurtchevsky. USS., *Motsart I Saleri*, Alexander Pushkin, 1830, Short Story

Legenda O Suramskoj Kreposti see **LEGENDA SURAMSKOI KREPOSTI** (1986).

LEGENDA SURAMSKOI KREPOSTI 1986 d: Sergei Paradjanov, Dodo Abachidze. USS., *Legenda Suramskoi Kreposti*, D. Tchonghadze, Book

LEGENDE DE SOEUR BEATRIX, LA 1923 d: Jacques de Baroncelli. FRN., *La Legende de Soeur Beatrice*, Charles Nodier

LEGENDE VOM HEILIGEN TRINKER, DIE 1963 d: Franz J. Wild. GRM., *Die Legende Vom Heiligen Trinker*, Joseph Roth, 1939, Novel

Legends About Anika see **ANIKINA VREMENA** (1954).

LEGERE ET COURT VETUE 1952 d: Jean Laviron. FRN., *Legere Et Court-Vetue*, Jean Guitton, Play

Legge, La see **LA LOI** (1958).

LEGGENDA AZZURRA 1941 d: Joseph Guarino. ITL., Talia Volpiana, Story

LEGGENDA DEL PIANISTA SULL'OCEANO, LA 1998 d: Giuseppe Tornatore. ITL., *Novecento*, Alessandro Baricco, Play

LEGGENDA DEL SANTO BEVITORE, LA 1988 d: Ermanno Olmi. ITL/FRN., *Die Legende Vom Heiligen Trinker*, Joseph Roth, 1939, Novel

LEGGENDA DI ENEA, LA 1962 d: Giorgio RivaltA. ITL/FRN., *Aeneid*, Virgil, c20 bc, Verse

LEGGENDA DI FAUST, LA 1949 d: Carmine Gallone. ITL., *Faust*, Johann Wolfgang von Goethe, 1808-32, Play

Leggenda Di Una Voce see **ENRICO CARUSO** (1951).

Leghorn Hat, The see **DER FLORENTINER HUT** (1939).

LEGIONS D'HONNEUR 1938 d: Maurice Gleize. FRN., *La Griffe*, Jean Makis, Short Story

LEGY JO MINDHALALIG 1960 d: Laszlo Ranody. HNG., *Legy Jo Mindhalalig*, Zsigmond Moricz, 1921, Novel

Lehrer Hofer see **HAUPTLEHRER HOFER** (1974).

LEI YU 1938 d: Fang Peilin. CHN., *Lei Yu*, Wan Jiabao, 1934, Play

LEIBA ZIBAL 1930 d: Alexandru Stefanescu, Ion BrunA. RMN., *O Faclie de Paste*, Ion Luca Caragiale, 1890, Short Story

LEIBEIGENEN, DIE 1927 d: Richard Eichberg. GRM., *Die Danischeffs*, Pierre Newsky, Play

LEICHTE ISABELL, DIE 1927 d: Eddy Busch, Arthur Wellin. GRM., *Die Leichte Isabell*, Jean Gilbert, Opera

LEICHTE KAVALLERIE 1935 d: Werner Hochbaum. GRM., *Umwege Zur Heimat*, Heinz Lorenz-Lambrecht, Novel

LEICHTE MUSE 1941 d: Arthur M. Rabenalt. GRM., *Viva la Musica*, H. F. Kollner, Novel

LEIDEN DES JUNGEN WERTHERS, DIE 1976 d: Egon Gunther. GDR., *Die Leiden Des Jungen Werthers*, Johann Wolfgang von Goethe, 1774, Novel

Leidenschaften see **INTERNO BERLINESE** (1985).

LEIDENSCHAFTLICHE BLUMCHEN 1978 d: Andre Farwagi. GRM., *Leidenschaftliche Blumchen*, Rosalind Erskine, Novel

LEIDENSCHAFTLICHEN, DIE 1981 d: Thomas Koerfer. SWT/GRM/AUS., *Die Leiden Des Jungen Werthers*, Johann Wolfgang von Goethe, 1774, Novel

LEILA 1998 d: Dariush Mehrjui. IRN., Mahnaz Ansarian, Story

LEISE GIFT, DAS 1984 d: Erwin Keusch. GRM., *Das Leise Gift*, Marcus P. Nester, Book

LEIYU 1984 d: Sun Daolin. CHN., *Lei Yu*, Wan Jiabao, 1934, Play

LELEJSKA GORA 1968 d: Zdravko Velimirovic. YGS., *Lelejska Gora*, Mihailo Lalic, 1957, Novel

Lelicek in the Services of Sherlock Holmes see **LELICEK VE SLUZBACH SHERLOCKA HOLMESA** (1932).

LELICEK VE SLUZBACH SHERLOCKA HOLMESA 1932 d: Carl Lamac. CZC., *Frantisek Lelicek Ve Sluzbach Sherlocka Holmesa*, Hugo Vavris, Novel

Lelichek in Sherlock Holmes's Service see **LELICEK VE SLUZBACH SHERLOCKA HOLMESA** (1932).

Lemke's Blessed Widow see **LEMKES SEL. WITWE** (1928).

LEMKES SEL. WITWE 1928 d: Carl Boese. GRM., *Lemkes Sel. Witwe*, Erdmann Graeser, Novel

Lemmy for the Women see **LEMMY POUR LES DAMES** (1961).

LEMMY POUR LES DAMES 1961 d: Bernard Borderie. FRN., Peter Cheyney, Novel

LEMON DROP KID, THE 1934 d: Marshall Neilan. USA., *The Lemon Drop Kid*, Damon Runyon, 1934, Short Story

LEMON DROP KID, THE 1951 d: Sidney Lanfield, Frank Tashlin (Uncredited). USA., *The Lemon Drop Kid*, Damon Runyon, 1934, Short Story

Lemonade Joe *see* **LIMONADOVY JOE** (1964).

LEN DEIGHTON'S BULLET TO BEIJING 1995 d: George MihalkA. UKN/CND/RSS., *Bullet to Beijing*, Len Deighton, Novel

Lena: My 100 Children *see* **LENA: MY HUNDRED CHILDREN** (1988).

LENA: MY HUNDRED CHILDREN 1988 d: Edwin Sherin. USA., *My Hundred Children*, Lena Kuchler-Silberman, Book

LENA RIVERS 1910. USA., *Lena Rivers*, Mary Jane Holmes, New York 1856, Novel

LENA RIVERS 1914. USA., *Lena Rivers*, Mary Jane Holmes, New York 1856, Novel

LENA RIVERS 1925 d: Whitman Bennett. USA., *Lena Rivers*, Mary Jane Holmes, New York 1856, Novel

LENA RIVERS 1932 d: Phil Rosen. USA., *Lena Rivers*, Mary Jane Holmes, New York 1856, Novel

LEND ME YOUR NAME 1918 d: Fred J. Balshofer. USA., *Lend Me Your Name!*, Francis Perry Elliott, Chicago 1917, Novel

LEND ME YOUR WIFE 1935 d: W. P. Kellino. UKN., *Lend Me Your Wife*, Edmund Dalby, Fred Duprez, Play

LENDA DE UBIRAJARA, A 1975 d: Andre Luiz de OliveirA. BRZ., *Lenda Tupi Ubirajara*, Jose Martiniano de Alencar, 1875, Novel

Lenin, the Sealed Train *see* **DER ZUG** (1989).

LENNY 1974 d: Bob Fosse. USA., *Lenny*, Julian Barry, Play

LENORE 1913. GRM., *Lenore*, Gottfried August Burger, Poem

LENTE 1983 d: Dre Poppe. BLG., *Lente*, Cyriel Buysse, Book

Lenten Confession *see* **DIE FASTNACHTSBEICHTE** (1960).

LENZ 1971 d: Georg Moorse. GRM., *Lenz*, Georg Buchner, 1839, Short Story

LENZ 1981 d: Alexandre Rockwell. USA., *Lenz*, Georg Buchner, 1839, Short Story

LENZ 1987 d: Andras Szirtes. HNG., *Lenz*, Georg Buchner, 1839, Short Story

LEO THE LAST 1970 d: John Boorman. UKN., *The Prince*, George Tabori, Play

LEO TOLSTOY'S ANNA KARENINA 1997 d: Bernard Rose. USA., *Anna Karenina*, Lev Nikolayevich Tolstoy, Moscow 1876, Novel

Leon Morin, Prete *see* **PRETRE LEON MORIN** (1961).

LEON MORIN, PRETRE 1961 d: Jean-Pierre Melville. FRN/ITL., *Leon Morin - Pretre*, Beatrix Beck, 1952, Novel

Leon Morin, Priest *see* **PRETRE LEON MORIN** (1961).

LEONA HELMSLEY: THE QUEEN OF MEAN 1990 d: Richard Michaels. USA., *The Queen of Mean*, Randell Pierson, Book

LEONARDO'S LAST SUPPER 1976 d: Peter Barnes. UKN., *Leonardo's Last Supper*, Peter Barnes, 1970, Play

LEONE DI DAMASCO, IL 1942 d: Corrado d'Errico. ITL., *Il Leone Di Damasco*, Emilio Salgari, Novel

Leoni Scatterrati, I *see* **LES LIONS SONT LACHES** (1961).

LEONIE EST EN AVANCE 1935 d: Jean-Pierre Feydeau. FRN., *Leonie Est En Avance*, Georges Feydeau, Play

LEONTINES EHEMANNER 1928 d: Robert Wiene. GRM., *Leontines Ehemanner*, Alfred Capus, Play

LEOPARD IN THE SNOW 1977 d: Gerry O'HarA. UKN/CND., *Leopard in the Snow*, Ann Mather, Novel

LEOPARD LADY, THE 1928 d: Rupert Julian. USA., *The Leopard Lady*, Edward Childs Carpenter, Play

LEOPARD MAN, THE 1943 d: Jacques Tourneur. USA., *Black Alibi*, Cornell Woolrich, 1942, Novel

Leopard, The *see* **IL GATTOPARDO** (1963).

LEOPARD WOMAN, THE 1920 d: Wesley Ruggles. USA., *The Leopard Woman*, Stewart Edward White, New York 1916, Novel

LEOPARDESS, THE 1923 d: Henry Kolker. USA., *The Leopardess*, Katharine Newlin Burt, Story

LEOPOLD LE BIEN-AIME 1933 d: Arno-Charles Brun. FRN., *Leopold le Bien-aime*, Jean Sarment, 1927, Play

LEOS JANACEK: INTIMATE EXCURSIONS 1983 d: Brothers Quay, Keith Griffiths. UKN., *Leos Janacek; a Biography*, Jaroslav Vogel, Biography

Leper *see* **TREDOWATA** (1976).

LES 1953 d: Vladimir Vengerov, S. Timoshenko. USS., *Les*, Alexander Ostrovsky, 1871, Play

LES 1980 d: Vladimir Motyl. USS., *Les*, Alexander Ostrovsky, 1871, Play

LES GIRLS 1957 d: George Cukor. USA., *Les Girls*, Vera Caspary, Novel

LES MISERABLES 1918 d: Frank Lloyd. USA., *Les Miserables*, Victor Hugo, Paris 1862, Novel

LES MISERABLES 1922. UKN., *Les Miserables*, Victor Hugo, Paris 1862, Novel

LES MISERABLES 1935 d: Richard Boleslawski. USA., *Les Miserables*, Victor Hugo, Paris 1862, Novel

Les Miserables *see* **I MISERABILI** (1947).

Les Miserables *see* **RE MIZERABURU** (1950).

LES MISERABLES 1952 d: Lewis Milestone. USA., *Les Miserables*, Victor Hugo, Paris 1862, Novel

LES MISERABLES 1978 d: Glenn Jordan. UKN/USA., *Les Miserables*, Victor Hugo, Paris 1862, Novel

LES MISERABLES 1998 d: Bille August. USA., *Les Miserables*, Victor Hugo, Paris 1862, Novel

Lesbian Twins *see* **VIRGIN WITCH** (1970).

LESETINSKY KOVAR 1924 d: Ferry Seidl, Rudolf Mestak. CZC., *Lesetinsky Kovar*, Svatopluk Cech, Poem

LESNAYA PESNYA 1961 d: Viktor IVchenko. USS., *Lisova Pisnya: Drama-Feeriya*, Lesya Ukrainka, 1911

LESS THAN KIN 1918 d: Donald Crisp. USA., *Less Than Kin*, Alice Duer Miller, New York 1909, Novel

LESS THAN ZERO 1987 d: Marek KanievskA. USA., *Less Than Zero*, Bret Easton Ellis, Novel

Lesson in Love *see* **LICAO DE AMOR** (1975).

LESSONS IN LOVE 1921 d: Chet Withey. USA., *Perkins*, Douglas Murray, New York 1918, Play

Lessons in Love *see* **L' EDUCATION SENTIMENTALE** (1961).

Lessons of Good Love *see* **LECCIONES DE BUEN AMOR** (1943).

Let 'Em Run, Buddy *see* **KUMPEL (6): LASS LAUFEN, KUMPEL! LASS JUCKEN** (1981).

LET IT RIDE 1989 d: Joe PytkA. USA., *Good Vibes*, Jay Cronley, Novel

LET ME EXPLAIN DEAR 1932 d: Gene Gerrard, Frank Miller. UKN., *A Little Bit of Fluff*, Walter Ellis, London 1915, Play

LET NO MAN WRITE MY EPITAPH 1960 d: Philip Leacock. USA., *Let No Man Write My Epitaph*, Willard Motley, 1958, Novel

LET NOT MAN PUT ASUNDER 1924 d: J. Stuart Blackton. USA., *Let Not Man Put Asunder*, Basil King, New York 1901, Novel

Let Sleeping Dogs Lie *see* **BOGNOR: LET SLEEPING DOGS LIE** (1981).

LET THE PEOPLE SING 1942 d: John Baxter. UKN., *Let the People Sing*, J. B. Priestley, 1939, Novel

LET US BE GAY 1930 d: Robert Z. Leonard. USA., *Let Us Be Gay*, Rachel Crothers, New York 1929, Play

LET WOMEN ALONE 1925 d: Paul Powell. USA., *On the Shelf*, Viola Brothers Shore, 1922, Short Story

Lethal Lolita *see* **AMY FISHER: MY STORY** (1992).

Lethal Lolita - Amy Fisher: My Own Story *see* **AMY FISHER: MY STORY** (1992).

Letiat Jouravly *see* **LETYAT ZHURAVLI** (1957).

Letjat Zuravli *see* **LETYAT ZHURAVLI** (1957).

LETNIYE LYUDI 1995 d: Sergei Ursulyak. RSS., *The Vacationers*, Maxim Gorky, Play

Letra Escarlata, La *see* **DER SCHARLACHROTE BUCHSTABE** (1973).

LET'S BE HAPPY 1957 d: Henry Levin. UKN., *Jeannie*, Aimee Stuart, London 1940, Play

LET'S BE RITZY 1934 d: Edward Ludwig. USA., *If I Was Rich*, William Anthony McGuire, New York 1926, Play

LET'S DANCE 1950 d: Norman Z. McLeod. USA., *Little Boy Blue*, Maurice Zolotow, Story

LET'S DO IT AGAIN 1953 d: Alexander Hall. USA., *The Awful Truth*, Arthur Richman, New York 1922, Play

LET'S DO IT AGAIN 1976 d: Sidney Poitier. USA., *Let's Do It Again*, Timothy March, Novel

LET'S ELOPE 1919 d: John S. Robertson. USA., *The Naughty Wife*, Frederick Jackson, New York 1917, Play

LET'S FACE IT 1943 d: Sidney Lanfield. USA., *Let's Face It*, Dorothy Fields, Herbert Fields, Cole Porter, Musical Play

LET'S GET A DIVORCE 1918 d: Charles Giblyn. USA., *Cyprienne Or Divorcons*, Emile de Najac, Victorien Sardou, Paris 1883, Play

LET'S GET MARRIED 1926 d: Gregory La CavA. USA., *The Man from Mexico*, Henry A. Du Souchet, New York 1897, Play

LET'S GET MARRIED 1960 d: Peter Graham Scott. UKN., *Confessions of a Kept Woman*, Gina Klausen, Novel

Let's Go *see* **ACTION** (1921).

LET'S KILL UNCLE 1966 d: William Castle. USA/UKN., *Let's Kill Uncle*, Rohan O'Grady, New York 1963, Novel

LET'S LOVE AND LAUGH 1931 d: Richard Eichberg. UKN., *A Welcome Wife*, Ernest Paulton, Fred Thompson, Play

LET'S MAKE A NIGHT OF IT 1937 d: Graham Cutts. UKN., *The Silver Spoon*, Henrik N. Ege, Radio Play

Let's Make Paradise *see* **FACCIAMO PARADISO** (1995).

Let's Make the Impossible! *see* **VIVA LO IMPOSIBLE!** (1957).

Let's Make Up *see* **LILACS IN THE SPRING** (1954).

Let's Play King *see* **NEWLY RICH** (1931).

Let's Say One Night for Dinner *see* **UNA SERA A CENA METTI** (1969).

LET'S TRY AGAIN 1934 d: Worthington Miner. USA., *Sour Grapes*, Vincent Lawrence, New York 1926, Play

LETTER FOR EVIE, A 1945 d: Jules Dassin. USA., *The Adventure of a Ready Letter Writer*, Blanche Brace, 1920, Short Story

Letter from a Novice *see* **LETTERE DI UNA NOVIZIA** (1960).

LETTER FROM AN UNKNOWN WOMAN 1948 d: Max Ophuls. USA., *Brief Einer Unbekannten*, Stefan Zweig, 1922, Short Story

Letter from the Wife *see* **STREER PATRA** (1972).

LETTER OF WARNING, A 1932 d: John Daumery. UKN., *A Letter of Warning*, John Hastings Turner, Play

LETTER, THE 1929 d: Monta Bell, Jean de Limur. USA., *The Letter*, W. Somerset Maugham, 1925, Short Story

LETTER, THE 1940 d: William Wyler. USA., *The Letter*, W. Somerset Maugham, 1925, Short Story

LETTER, THE 1982 d: John Erman. USA., *The Letter*, W. Somerset Maugham, 1925, Short Story

LETTERE DAL FRONTE 1975 d: Vittorio Schiraldi. ITL., *Cenomila Lettere Di Guerra - Censura Militare*, Bino Bellomo, Book

Lettere d'Amore Smarrite, Le *see* **DIE MISSBRAUCHTEN LIEBESBRIEFE** (1940).

LETTERE DI UNA NOVIZIA 1960 d: Alberto LattuadA. ITL/FRN., *Lettere Di Una Novizia*, Guido Piovene, Verona 1941, Novel

Letters *see* **STANLEY AND IRIS** (1989).

Letters from My Windmill *see* **LES LETTRES DE MON MOULIN** (1954).

LETTERS, THE 1922 d: George A. Cooper. UKN., *The Letters*, Maurice Level, Story

LETTERS TO AN UNKNOWN LOVER 1985 d: Peter Duffell. UKN/FRN., *Les Louves*, Pierre Boileau, Thomas Narcejac, Novel

Letto, Fortuna E Femmine *see* **LE BATEAU D'EMILE** (1962).

LETTO IN PIAZZA, IL 1976 d: Bruno Alberto Gaburro. ITL., *Il Letto in Piazza*, Nantas Salvalaggio, Novel

Lettre Brulante, Une *see* **LES PATTES DE MOUCHE** (1936).

LETTRE, LA 1930 d: Louis Mercanton. FRN., *The Letter*, W. Somerset Maugham, 1925, Short Story

Lettres d'Amour *see* **DIE MISSBRAUCHTEN LIEBESBRIEFE** (1940).

LETTRES D'AMOUR 1942 d: Claude Autant-LarA. FRN., *Lettres d'Amour*, Jean Aurenche, Short Story

Lettres d'Amour d'une Nonne Portugaise *see* **DIE LIEBESBRIEFE EINER PORTUGIESISCHEN NONNE** (1977).

Lettres d'Amour Mal Employees, Les *see* **DIE MISSBRAUCHTEN LIEBESBRIEFE** (1940).

LETTRES DE MON MOULIN, LES 1954 d: Marcel Pagnol. FRN., *L' Elixir du Pere Gaucher*, Alphonse Daudet, 1869, Short Story, *Les Trois Messes Basses*, Alphonse Daudet, 1869, Short Story

LETTY LYNTON 1932 d: Clarence Brown. USA., *Letty Lynton*, Mrs. Belloc Lowndes, New York 1931, Novel

LETYAT ZHURAVLI 1957 d: Mikhail Kalatozov. USS., *Vechno Zhivye*, Victor S. Rozov, 1956, Play

LETZTE AKT, DER 1955 d: G. W. Pabst. AUS., *Ten Days to Die*, M. A. Musmano, Novel

Letzte Ausfahrt Brooklyn *see* LAST EXIT TO BROOKLYN (1989).

LETZTE FUSSGANGER, DER 1960 d: Wilhelm Thiele. GRM., Eckart Hachfeld, Story

Letzte Geschichte von Schloss Konigswald, Die *see* SCHLOSS KONIGSWALD (1987).

Letzte Harem, Der *see* L' ULTIMO HAREM (1981).

LETZTE KAPITEL, DAS 1961 d: Wolfgang Liebeneiner. GRM., *Siste Kapitel*, Knut Hamsun, 1923, Novel

LETZTE MOHIKANER, DER 1965 d: Harald Reinl. GRM/ITL/SPN., *The Last of the Mohicans*, James Fenimore Cooper, Boston 1826, Novel

LETZTE NACHT, DIE 1927 d: Graham Cutts. GRM., *Hochzeitsnacht*, Noel Coward, Play

LETZTE NACHT, DIE 1949 d: Eugen York. GRM., *Die Letzte Nacht*, Friedrich Hartau, Play

LETZTE REZEPT, DAS 1952 d: Rolf Hansen. GRM., *Das Letzte Rezept*, Thomas B. Foster, Play

Letzte Rose *see* MARTHA (1935).

LETZTE SOMMER, DER 1954 d: Harald Braun. GRM., *Der Letzte Sommer*, Ricarda Huch, 1902, Novel

LETZTE SOUPER, DAS 1928 d: Mario Bonnard. GRM., *Kapellmeister Stroganoff*, Otto Rung, Short Story

LETZTE WALZER, DER 1927 d: Arthur Robison. GRM., *Der Letzte Walzer*, Oscar Straus, Berlin 1920, Operetta

LETZTE WALZER, DER 1934 d: Georg Jacoby. GRM., *Der Letzte Walzer*, Oscar Straus, Berlin 1920, Operetta

LETZTE WALZER, DER 1953 d: Arthur M. Rabenalt. GRM., *Der Letzte Walzer*, Oscar Straus, Berlin 1920, Operetta

LETZTE ZEUGE, DER 1960 d: Wolfgang Staudte. GRM., Maximilian Vernberg, Article

Letzten Nachte Der Mrs. Orchard, Die *see* DER ANWALT DES HERZENS (1927).

LETZTEN TAGE VON POMPEI, DIE 1959 d: Mario Bonnard, Sergio Leone. GRM/ITL/SPN., *The Last Days of Pompeii*, Edward George Bulwer Lytton, 1834, Novel

LETZTEN WERDEN DIE ERSTEN SEIN, DIE 1957 d: Rolf Hansen. GRM., *The First and the Last*, John Galsworthy, 1918, Short Story

LEUR DERNIERE NUIT 1953 d: Georges Lacombe. FRN., *Leur Derniere Nuit*, Jacques Constant, Novel

LEVIATHAN 1966 d: Leonard Keigel. FRN., *Leviathan*, Julien Green, 1929, Novel

Levin's Mill *see* LEVINS MUHLE (1980).

LEVINS MUHLE 1980 d: Horst Seemann. GDR., *Levins Muhle*, Johannes Bobrowski, 1964, Novel

LEVKAS MAN 1980 d: Carl Schultz. UKN/GRM/ASL., *Levkas Man*, Hammond Innes, Novel

LEW TYLER'S WIVES 1926 d: Harley Knoles. USA., *Lew Taylor's Wives*, Wallace Irwin, New York 1923, Novel

LEWIS & CLARK - THE JOURNEY OF THE CORPS OF DISCOVERY 1997 d: Ken Burns. USA., *Lewis & Clark*, Ken Burns, Dayton Duncan, Book

L'HA FATTO UNA SIGNORA 1938 d: Mario Mattoli. ITL., *L'ha Fatto Una Signora*, Pio de Flaviis, Maria Ermolli, Play

LI MING DE HE BIAN 1958 d: Chen Ge. CHN., *Li Ming de He Bian*, Jun Qing, Novel

LI REN XIN 1948 d: Chen Liting. CHN., *Liren XIng*, Tian Han, 1945, Play

LI SHUANGSHUANG 1962 d: Lu Ren. CHN., *The Story of Li Shuangshuang*, Li Zhun, Novel

LI TING LANG 1920 d: Charles Swickard. USA., *Chinese Gentleman Li Ting Lang*, Howard P. Rockey, 1916, Short Story

LI XIANGJUN 1940 d: Wu Cun. CHN., *Tao Hua Shan*, Kong Shangren, c1690, Play

Liaisons Dangereuses 1960, Les *see* LES LIAISONS DANGEREUSES (1959).

LIAISONS DANGEREUSES, LES 1959 d: Roger Vadim. FRN/ITL., *Les Liaisons Dangereuses*, Pierre Ambrose Choderlos de Laclos, 1782, Novel

Liaisons Dangereuses, Les *see* DANGEROUS LIAISONS (1988).

Liana, la Schiava Bianca *see* DIE WEISSE SKLAVIN LIANE (1957).

LIAN'AI YU YIWU 1931 d: Bu Wancang. CHN., *La Symphonie Des Ombres*, Mme. S. Rosen Hoa, Novel

LIANBRON 1965 d: Sven Nykvist. SWD., *Musik I Morker*, Dagmar Ingeborg Edqvist, 1937, Novel

LIANE, DAS MADCHEN AUS DEM URWALD 1956 d: Eduard von Borsody. GRM., *Liane Das Madchen Aus Dem Urwald*, Anne Day-Helveg, Novel

LIANE, DIE WEISSE SKLAVIN 1957 d: Hermann Leitner, Gino Talamo. GRM/ITL., *Liane Die Weisse Sklavin*, Anne Day-Helveg, Novel

Liane, Girl of the Jungle *see* DAS MADCHEN AUS DEM URWALD LIANE (1956).

Liane, Jungle Goddess *see* DAS MADCHEN AUS DEM URWALD LIANE (1956).

Liane, the White Slave *see* DIE WEISSE SKLAVIN LIANE (1957).

LIANG JIA CHUN 1951 d: Ju Baiyin, XIu Bingduo. CHN., *Forced Bonding Cannot Be Sweet*, Gu Yu, Novel

LIANG JIA REN 1963 d: Yuan Naicheng. CHN., *The Bridge*, Liu Pengde, Novel

Liar and the Nun, The *see* DER LUGNER UND DIE NONNE (1967).

Liar, The *see* DER LUGNER (1961).

Liar, The *see* LOGNEREN (1970).

Liars, The *see* LES MENTEURS (1961).

LIBEL 1959 d: Anthony Asquith. UKN., *Libel*, Edward Wooll, Play

LIBERATION OF L.B. JONES, THE 1970 d: William Wyler. USA., *The Liberation of Lord Byron Jones*, Jesse Hill Ford, Boston 1965, Novel

Liberation of Lord Byron Jones, The *see* THE LIBERATION OF L.B. JONES (1970).

LIBERATION OF SKOPJE, THE 1981 d: William Fitzwater. ASL., *The Liberation of Skopje*, Dusan Jovanovic, Play

LIBERI ARMATI PERICOLOSI 1976 d: Romolo Guerrieri. ITL., *Liberi Armati Pericolosi*, Giorgio Scerbanenco, Short Story

LIBERTAD PROVISIONAL 1976 d: Roberto Bodegas. SPN., *Libertad Provisional*, Juan Marse, 1976, Short Story

LIBERTE 1937 d: Jean Kemm. FRN., *Bartholdi Et Son Vigneron*, Leopold Netter, Play

LIBERTY HALL 1914 d: Harold Shaw. UKN., *Liberty Hall*, R. C. Carton, London 1892, Play

LIBERTY MAN, THE 1958 d: Lionel Brett. UKN., Gillian Freeman, Novel

LIBRO DEL BUEN AMOR I, EL 1974 d: Tomas Aznar. SPN., *Libro de Buen Amor*, Juan Ruiz, 1330, Verse

LICAO DE AMOR 1975 d: Eduardo Escorel. BRZ., *Verbo Intransitivo Amor*, Mario de Andrade, 1927, Novel

LICHT AUF DEM GALGEN, DAS 1976 d: Helmut Nitzschke. GDR., *Das Licht Auf Dem Galgen*, Anna Seghers, 1960, Short Story

LICHT DER BERGEN, HET 1955 d: Gust Geens, Hugo Van Den Hoegaerde. BLG., *Das Licht Der Berge*, Franz Weiser

LICKING HITLER 1978 d: David Hare. UKN., *Licking Hitler*, David Hare, 1978, Play

LIDE NA KRE 1937 d: Martin Fric. CZC., *Lide Na Kre*, Vilem Werner, Novel

Lido Mystery, The *see* ENEMY AGENTS MEET ELLERY QUEEN (1942).

LIDOIRE 1913 d: Andre Liabel. FRN., *Lidoire*, Georges Courteline, 1892, Play

LIDOIRE 1933 d: Maurice Tourneur. FRN., *Lidoire*, Georges Courteline, 1892, Play

Liduska and Her Musician *see* MUSIKANTSKA LIDUSKA (1940).

Liduska of the Stage *see* MUSIKANTSKA LIDUSKA (1940).

LIE HUO JIN GANG 1991 d: He Qun, Jiang Hao. CHN., *Brave Hero*, Liu Liu, Novel, *Marvelous Hero*, Liu Liu, Novel

LIE HUOZHONG YONGSHENG 1965 d: Shui HuA. CHN., *Red Rock*, Luo Guangbing, Yang Yiyan, Novel

Lie of Nina Petrovna, The *see* LA MENSONGE DE NINA PETROVNA (1937).

LIE, THE 1918 d: J. Searle Dawley. USA., *The Lie*, Henry Arthur Jones, New York 1914, Play

Lie, The *see* DIE LUGE (1950).

Lie, The *see* NO MAN OF HER OWN (1950).

LIEB VATERLAND, MAGST RUHIG SEIN 1976 d: Roland Klick. GRM., *Lieb Vaterland Magst Ruhig Sein*, Johannes Mario Simmel, Novel

LIEBE 1927 d: Paul Czinner. GRM., Honore de Balzac, Short Story

LIEBE 1956 d: Horst Haechler. GRM/ITL., *Vor Rehen Wird Gewarnt*, Vicki Baum, Novel

LIEBE 47 1949 d: Wolfgang Liebeneiner. GRM., *Draussen von Der Tur*, Wolfgang Borchert, 1947, Play

Liebe Am Scheideweg *see* DAS GEHEIMNIS EINER AERZTIN (1955).

LIEBE AUGUSTIN, DER 1940 d: E. W. Emo. GRM., *Der Liebe Augustin*, Horst Wolfram Geissler, Novel

LIEBE DER BRUDER ROTT, DIE 1929 d: Erich Waschneck. GRM., *Kreuz Im Moor*, Fritz Gantzer, Novel

LIEBE DER JEANNE NEY, DIE 1927 d: G. W. Pabst. GRM., *Die Liebe Der Jeanne Ney*, Ilja Ehrenberg, Novel

LIEBE DES MAHARADSCHA, DIE 1936 d: Arthur M. Rabenalt. GRM., *Die Weisse Frau Des Maharadscha*, Ludwig von Wohl, Novel

Liebe Einer Frau, Die *see* CLAIR DE FEMME (1979).

LIEBE FAMILIE, DIE 1957 d: Helmut Weiss. AUS., *It's Never Too Late*, Felicity Douglas, London 1952, Play

LIEBE GEHT SELTSAME WEGE 1927 d: Fritz Kaufmann, Jean Rosen. GRM/FRN., *La Girl aux Mains Fines*, Maurice Dekobra, Short Story

LIEBE IM FINANZAMT 1952 d: Kurt Hoffmann. GRM., *Weekend Im Paradies*, Franz Robert Arnold, Ernst Bach, Play

Liebe in Deutschland, Eine *see* UN AMOUR EN ALLEMAGNE (1983).

Liebe in St. Moritz *see* DER SPRINGER VON PONTRESINA (1934).

Liebe Ist Etwas Zartliches *see* IO SONO MIA (1978).

LIEBE IST NUR EIN WORT 1971 d: Alfred Vohrer. GRM., *Liebe Ist Nur Ein Wort*, Johannes Mario Simmel, Novel

LIEBE IST STARKER ALS DER TOD 1988 d: Juraj Herz. GRM., Heinz G. Konsalik, Novel

LIEBE IST ZOLLFREI 1941 d: E. W. Emo. GRM/AUS., *Liebe Ist Zollfrei*, Fritz Gottwald, Play

Liebe Lasst Sich Nicht Erzwingen *see* ZWISCHEN HIMMEL UND HOLLE (1934).

LIEBE, LUFT UND LAUTER LUGEN 1959 d: Peter Beauvais. GRM., Karl Zumbro, Story

LIEBE OHNE ILLUSION 1955 d: Erich Engel. GRM., *Arztliches Geheimnis*, Ladislaus Fodor, Play

LIEBE, SCHERZ UND ERNST 1932 d: Franz Wenzler. GRM., *The Importance of Being Earnest*, Oscar Wilde, London 1895, Play

LIEBE, TANZ UND 1000 SCHLAGER 1955 d: Paul Martin. GRM., Frederick Kohner, Story

LIEBE, TOD UND TEUFEL 1934 d: Heinz Hilpert, Reinhart Steinbicker. GRM., *The Bottle Imp*, Robert Louis Stevenson, London 1891, Novel

Liebe Und Leidenschaft *see* LOVE AND SACRIFICE (1936).

LIEBE UND TROMPETENBLASEN 1925 d: Richard Eichberg. GRM., *Liebe Und Trompetenblasen*, Hans Bachwitz, Hans Sturm, Play

LIEBE UND TROMPETENBLASEN 1954 d: Helmut Weiss. GRM., *Liebe Und Trompetenblasen*, Hans Bachwitz, Hans Sturm, Play

LIEBE VERBOTEN - HEIRATEN ERLAUBT 1959 d: Kurt Meisel. GRM., Hans Nicklisch, Story

Liebe von Swann, Eine *see* UN AMOUR DE SWANN (1983).

LIEBE WILL GELERNT SEIN 1963 d: Kurt Hoffmann. GRM., *Liebe Will Gelernt Sein*, Erich Kastner, Play

LIEBELEI 1927 d: Jacob Fleck, Luise Fleck. GRM., *Liebelei*, Arthur Schnitzler, 1895, Play

LIEBELEI 1932 d: Max Ophuls. GRM/AUS., *Liebelei*, Arthur Schnitzler, 1895, Play

LIEBELEI 1933 d: Max Ophuls. FRN., *Liebelei*, Arthur Schnitzler, 1895, Play

LIEBESBRIEFE 1943 d: Hans H. Zerlett. GRM., *Liebesbriefe*, Felix Lutzkendorf, Play

LIEBESBRIEFE EINER PORTUGIESISCHEN NONNE, DIE 1977 d: Jesus Franco. SWT/GRM., *Liebesbriefe Einer Portugiesischen Nonne*, Maria Alcoforado, Novel

LIEBESGESCHICHTE, EINE 1954 d: Rudolf Jugert. GRM., *Eine Liebesgeschichte*, Carl Zuckmayer, 1934, Short Story

LIEBESKARNEVAL 1928 d: Augusto GeninA. GRM., *Liebeskarneval*, Augusto Genina, Short Story

LIEBESKOMODIE 1942 d: Theo Lingen. GRM., *Liebeskomodie*, Franz Gribitz, Play

LIEBESKONZIL, DAS 1981 d: Werner Schroeter. GRM., Oskar Panizza, Story

LIEBESLEUTE 1935 d: Erich Waschneck. GRM., *Herman Und Dorothea*, Johann Wolfgang von Goethe, 1774, Verse

LIEBESNACHTE IN DER TAIGA 1967 d: Harald Philipp. GRM., *Liebesnachte in Der Taiga*, Heinz G. Konsalik, Novel

Liebesnachte in Rom see **UN AMORE A ROMA** (1960).

LIEBESREIGEN 1927 d: Rudolf Walther-Fein. GRM., *Kampfer*, Ernst Klein, Novel

LIEBESTRAUM 1951 d: Paul Martin. GRM., *Cardillac*, Ernst Theodor Amadeus Hoffmann, Short Story, *Das Fraulein von Scuderi*, Ernst Theodor Amadeus Hoffmann, 1819, Short Story, *Der Spieler*, Ernst Theodor Amadeus Hoffmann, Short Story

LIEBLING, ICH MUSS DICH ERSCHIESSEN 1962 d: Jurgen Goslar. GRM., John O'Hara, Play

Liebling Schoner Frauen, Der see **BEL AMI** (1939).

Lied Der Liebe, Das see **WENN DIE MUSIK NICHT WAR'** (1935).

LIED DER NACHTIGALL, DAS 1943 d: Theo Lingen. GRM., *Die Gelbe Nachtigall*, Hermann Bahr, Berlin 1907, Play

LIED DER WUSTE, DAS 1939 d: Paul Martin. GRM., Werner Illig, Story

LIENS DE SANG, LES 1978 d: Claude Chabrol. FRN/CND., *Blood Relatives*, Evan Hunter, 1975, Novel

Lies see **GUI HUA** (1951).

LIES MY FATHER TOLD ME 1960 d: Don Chaffey. UKN., *Lies My Father Told Me*, Ted Allan, Short Story

LIES MY FATHER TOLD ME 1975 d: Jan Kadar. CND., *Lies My Father Told Me*, Ted Allan, Short Story

LIES OF THE TWINS 1991 d: Tim Hunter. USA., *Lies of the Twins*, Rosamund Smith, Novel

LIEVE JONGENS 1979 d: Paul de Lussanets. NTH., *Lieve Jongens*, Gerard Kornelius Van Het Reve, 1972, Novel, *Het Lieve Leven*, Gerard Kornelius Van Het Reve, 1974, Novel, **De Taal Der Liefde**, Gerard Kornelius Van Het Reve, 1971, Novel

LIEYAN 1933. CHN., *Huozhi Taowu*, Tian Han, Play

Life see **COSMOPOLIS** (1919).

LIFE 1920 d: Travers Vale. USA., *Life*, Thompson Buchanan, New York 1914, Play

LIFE 1928 d: Adelqui Millar. UKN., *Juan Jose*, Joaquin Dicenta, Novel

Life and Adventures of Nicholas Nickleby, The see **NICHOLAS NICKLEBY** (1948).

LIFE AND ADVENTURES OF NICHOLAS NICKLEBY, THE 1982 d: Jim Goddard. UKN., *Nicholas Nickleby*, Charles Dickens, London 1870, Novel

Life and Amazing Adventures of Robinson Crusoe see **ZHIZN I UDIVITELNIE PRIKLUCHENIA ROBINZONA CRUZO** (1973).

LIFE AND DEATH OF RICHARD III, THE 1912 d: James Keane. USA., *Richard III*, William Shakespeare, c1594, Play

Life and Death of Severina see **MORTE E VIDA SEVERINA** (1976).

Life and Incredible Adventures of Robinson Crusoe, the Sailor from York, The see **NAMORNIKA Z YORKU ZIVOT A PODIVUHODNA DOBRODRUZSTVI ROBINSONA CRUSOE** (1982).

Life and Loves of a She-Devil, The see **SHE-DEVIL** (1989).

Life and Loves of Mozart, The see **MEIN LEBEN REICH MIR DIE HAND** (1955).

Life and Music of Giuseppe Verdi, The see **GIUSEPPE VERDI** (1953).

Life and Opinion of Masseur Ichi, The see **ZATO ICHI MONOGATARI** (1962).

Life and Remarkable Adventures of Robinson Crusoe, The see **ZHIZN I UDIVITELNIE PRIKLUCHENIA ROBINZONA CRUZO** (1973).

LIFE AT THE TOP 1965 d: Ted Kotcheff. UKN., *Life at the Top*, John Braine, London 1962, Novel

LIFE BEGINS 1932 d: James Flood, Elliott Nugent. USA., *Life Begins*, Mary McDougal Axelson, New York 1932, Play

Life Begins Anew see **ZU NEUEN UFERN** (1937).

LIFE BEGINS AT 40 1935 d: George Marshall. USA., *Life Begins at 40*, Walter B. Pitkin, New York 1932, Novel

LIFE BEGINS AT 8.30 1942 d: Irving Pichel. USA., *The Light of Heart*, Emlyn Williams, 1940, Play

Life Begins at College see **LIFE BEGINS IN COLLEGE** (1937).

Life Begins at Eight see **DAS LEBEN BEGINNT UM ACHT** (1962).

Life Begins at Forty see **LIFE BEGINS AT 40** (1935).

LIFE BEGINS IN COLLEGE 1937 d: William A. Seiter. USA., Darrell Ware, Short Stories

Life Can Be So Beautiful see **DAS LEBEN KANN SO SCHON SEIN** (1938).

Life Doesn't Spare see **VIATA NU IARTA** (1957).

LIFE DURING WARTIME 1997 d: Evan Dunsky. USA., *Life During Wartime*, Keith Reddin, Play

Life for Do, A see **EIN LEBEN FUR DO** (1954).

Life Force see **LIFEFORCE** (1985).

Life Goes on see **SORRY YOU'VE BEEN TROUBLED** (1932).

Life Goes on see **LIVET GAR VIDARE** (1941).

Life Goes on see **EL MUNDO SIGUE** (1963).

Life in the Country see **LIVET PA LANDET** (1943).

LIFE IN THE RAW 1933 d: Louis King. USA., *From Missouri*, Zane Grey, 1926, Short Story

Life Is a Dream see **MEMOIRE DES APPARENCES** (1986).

Life Is Strange see **STRANA LA VITA** (1988).

LIFE LINE, THE 1919 d: Maurice Tourneur. USA., *The Romany Rye*, George R. Sims, London 1882, Play

Life of a Lancer Spy see **LANCER SPY** (1937).

Life of a Woman see **ONNA NO ISSHO** (1967).

Life of a Woman By Saikaku see **SAIKAKU ICHIDAI ONNA** (1952).

LIFE OF AN ACTRESS 1927 d: Jack Nelson. USA., *The Life of an Actress*, Langdon McCormick, 1907, Play

LIFE OF EMILE ZOLA, THE 1937 d: William Dieterle. USA., *Zola and His Time*, Matthew Josephson, New York 1928, Book

LIFE OF HER OWN, A 1950 d: George Cukor. USA., *Abiding Vision*, Rebecca West, 1935, Short Story

Life of Jack London, The see **JACK LONDON** (1942).

LIFE OF JIMMY DOLAN, THE 1933 d: Archie Mayo. USA., *Sucker*, Beulah Marie Dix, Bertram Millhauser, New York 1933, Play

Life of John Bunyan, The see **IL PELLEGRINO** (1912).

Life of Matthew, The see **ZYWOT MATEUSZA** (1968).

Life of Oharu, The see **SAIKAKU ICHIDAI ONNA** (1952).

Life of Surgeon Sauerbruch, The see **SAUERBRUCH** (1954).

LIFE OF THE PARTY, THE 1920 d: Joseph Henabery. USA., *The Life of the Party*, Irvin S. Cobb, 1919, Short Story

LIFE OF THE PARTY, THE 1934 d: Ralph Dawson. UKN., *Twin Beds*, Edward Salisbury Field, Margaret Mayo, New York 1914, Play

LIFE OF VERGIE WINTERS, THE 1934 d: Alfred Santell. USA., *A Scarlet Woman*, Louis Bromfield, 1929, Short Story

Life of Vernon and Irene Castle, The see **THE STORY OF VERNON AND IRENE CASTLE** (1939).

Life on a String see **BIAN ZOU BIAN CHANG** (1991).

Life on the Hegn Farm see **LIVET PAA HEGNSGAARD** (1939).

LIFE ON THE MISSISSIPPI 1987 d: Peter H. Hunt. UKN/GRM., Mark Twain, Story

Life on the Waterfront see **PORT OF SEVEN SEAS** (1938).

LIFE STORY OF BAAL ,THE 1978 d: Edward Bennett. UKN., *Baal*, Bertolt Brecht, 1922, Play

Life, The see **LA DEROBADE** (1979).

Life Together see **LA VIE A DEUX** (1958).

Life Triumphs see **VIATA INVINGE** (1951).

LIFE WITH FATHER 1947 d: Michael Curtiz. USA., *Life With Father*, Russel Crouse, Play, Clarence Day Jr., Memoirs, *Life With Father*, Howard Lindsay, Play

LIFE WITHOUT SOUL 1916 d: Joseph Smiley. USA., *Frankenstein; Or the Modern Prometheus*, Mary Wollstonecraft Shelley, London 1818, Novel

LIFEBOAT 1944 d: Alfred Hitchcock. USA., John Steinbeck, Story

LIFEBOAT, THE 1914. UKN., *The Lifeboat*, George R. Sims, Poem

LIFEFORCE 1985 d: Tobe Hooper. UKN., *The Space Vampires*, Colin Wilson, Novel

LIFEFORCE EXPERIMENT, THE 1993 d: Piers Haggard. CND/USA., *The Breakthrough*, Daphne Du Maurier, Short Story

LIFEGUARDSMAN, THE 1916 d: Frank G. Bayley. UKN., *The Lifeguardsman*, Walter Howard, Play

LIFEPOD 1993 d: Ron Silver. USA., John Steinbeck, Story

LIFE'S DARN FUNNY 1921 d: Dallas M. Fitzgerald. USA., *Caretakers Within*, Christine Jope Slade, 1921, Short Story

LIFE'S SHOP WINDOW 1914 d: Herbert Brenon, Henry Belmar. USA., *Life's Shop Window*, Victoria Cross, New York 1907, Novel

LIFE'S TWIST 1920 d: W. Christy Cabanne. USA., *Life's Twist*, Thomas Edgelow, Short Story

LIFE'S WHIRLPOOL 1916 d: Barry O'Neil. USA., *McTeague; a Story of San Francisco*, Frank Norris, New York 1899, Novel

Life's Worth Living see **DOCTOR BULL** (1933).

Lift to the Scaffold see **L' ASCENSEUR POUR L'ECHAFAUD** (1957).

Lifted Cross, The see **WOMAN AND WIFE** (1918).

LIFTED VEIL, THE 1917 d: George D. Baker. USA., *The Lifted Veil*, Basil King, New York 1917, Novel

LIGABUE 1978 d: Salvatore NocitA. ITL., *Ligabue*, Cesare Zavattini, Poem

Ligeia see **THE TOMB OF LIGEIA** (1964).

Light Ahead, The see **DIE KLATSCHE** (1939).

Light at the Edge of the World, The see **LA LUZ DEL FIN DEL MUNDO** (1971).

LIGHT IN DARKNESS 1917 d: Alan Crosland. USA., *Light in Darkness*, Peter B. Kyne, 1916, Short Story

LIGHT IN THE CLEARING, THE 1921 d: T. Hayes Hunter. USA., *The Light in the Clearing*, Irving Addison Bacheller, Indianapolis 1917, Novel

LIGHT IN THE DARK, THE 1922 d: Clarence Brown. USA., *The Light in the Dark*, William Dudley Pelley, Story

Light in the Darkness see **POKOLENIE** (1954).

LIGHT IN THE FOREST, THE 1958 d: Herschel Daugherty. USA., *The Light in the Forest*, Conrad Richter, 1953, Novel

LIGHT IN THE PIAZZA 1961 d: Guy Green. UKN/USA., *The Light in the Piazza*, Elizabeth Spencer, New York 1960, Novel

Light Love see **LIEBELEI** (1932).

Light of Day, The see **TOPKAPI** (1964).

Light of Heart, The see **LIFE BEGINS AT 8.30** (1942).

Light of His Eyes, The see **SVETLO JEHO OCI** (1936).

LIGHT OF VICTORY, THE 1919 d: William Wolbert. USA., *Breathes There the Man*, George Charles Hull, 1917, Short Story

LIGHT OF WESTERN STARS, THE 1918 d: Charles Swickard. USA., *The Light of Western Stars*, Zane Grey, New York 1914, Novel

LIGHT OF WESTERN STARS, THE 1925 d: William K. Howard. USA., *The Light of Western Stars*, Zane Grey, New York 1914, Novel

LIGHT OF WESTERN STARS, THE 1930 d: Otto Brower, Edwin H. Knopf. USA., *The Light of Western Stars*, Zane Grey, New York 1914, Novel

LIGHT OF WESTERN STARS, THE 1940 d: Lesley Selander. USA., *The Light of Western Stars*, Zane Grey, New York 1914, Novel

LIGHT THAT FAILED, THE 1916 d: Edward Jose. USA., *The Light That Failed*, Rudyard Kipling, New York 1890, Novel

LIGHT THAT FAILED, THE 1923 d: George Melford. USA., *The Light That Failed*, Rudyard Kipling, New York 1890, Novel

LIGHT THAT FAILED, THE 1939 d: William A. Wellman. USA., *The Light That Failed*, Rudyard Kipling, New York 1890, Novel

LIGHT UP THE SKY 1960 d: Lewis Gilbert. UKN., *Touch It Light*, Robert Sharrow, London 1958, Novel

LIGHT WOMAN, A 1920 d: George L. Cox. USA., *A Light Woman*, Robert Browning, 1855, Short Story

LIGHT YEARS AWAY 1981 d: Alain Tanner. IRL/FRN/SWT., *Les Annees Lumiere*, Daniel Odier, Novel

Lighthorse Harry *see* THE COWBOY QUARTERBACK (1939).

LIGHTHOUSE BY THE SEA, THE 1924 d: Malcolm St. Clair. USA., *The Lighthouse By the Sea*, Owen Davis, 1920, Play

LIGHTNIN' 1925 d: John Ford. USA., *Lightnin'*, Frank Bacon, Winchell Smith, New York 1918, Play

LIGHTNIN' 1930 d: Henry King. USA., *Lightnin'*, Frank Bacon, Winchell Smith, New York 1918, Play

LIGHTNING 1927 d: James C. McKay. USA., *Lightning*, Zane Grey, Short Story

Lightning *see* INAZUMA (1952).

LIGHTNING CONDUCTOR, THE 1914 d: Walter Hale. USA/ITL., *The Lighting Conductor*, Charles Norris Williamson, New York 1903, Novel

Lightning Lover, The *see* THE FAST WORKER (1924).

LIGHTNING STRIKES TWICE 1951 d: King Vidor. USA., *A Man Without Friends*, Margaret Echard, 1940, Novel

LIGHTNING-ROD MAN, THE 1975 d: John de Chancie. USA., *The Lightning-Rod Man*, Herman Melville, 1854, Short Story

Lights and Shadows *see* THE WOMAN RACKET (1929).

LIGHTS O' LONDON, THE 1914 d: Bert Haldane?. UKN., *The Lights O' London*, George R. Sims, London 1881, Play

LIGHTS O' LONDON, THE 1922 d: Edwin J. Collins. UKN., *The Lights O' London*, George R. Sims, London 1881, Play

LIGHTS OF HOME, THE 1920 d: Fred Paul. UKN., *The Lights of Home*, Robert Buchanan, George R. Sims, London 1892, Play

LIGHTS OF LONDON 1923 d: Charles Calvert. UKN., *The Lights O' London*, George R. Sims, London 1881, Play

LIGHTS OF OLD BROADWAY 1925 d: Monta Bell. USA., *Merry Wives of Gotham; Or Two and Sixpence*, Laurence Eyre, New York 1924, Play

LIGHTS OUT 1923 d: Alfred Santell. USA., *Lights Out*, Paul Dickey, Mann Page, New York 1922, Play

Lights Out *see* CRASHING HOLLYWOOD (1938).

Lights Out *see* BRIGHT VICTORY (1951).

Lightship, The *see* DAS FEUERSCHIFF (1963).

LIGHTSHIP, THE 1985 d: Jerzy Skolimowski. USA., *Das Feuerschiff*, Siegfried Lenz, 1960, Novel

LIGNE DROITE, LA 1961 d: Jacques Gaillard. FRN., *La Ligne Droite*, Yves Gibeau, Novel

Like a Storm Wind *see* WIE EIN STURMWIND (1957).

Like Father and Son *see* MARVIN AND TIGE (1982).

Like Father Like Son *see* MARVIN AND TIGE (1982).

Like Kelly Can *see* LOVE IN THE ROUGH (1930).

LIKE MOM, LIKE ME 1978 d: Michael Pressman. USA., *Like Me Like Mom*, Sheila Schwartz, Novel

LIKE NORMAL PEOPLE 1979 d: Harvey Hart. USA., *Like Normal People*, Robert Meyers, Book

Like the Birds of Heaven *see* VOGELVRIJ (1916).

Like the Leaves *see* COME LE FOGLIE (1934).

Like Two Drops of Water *see* ALS TWEE DRUPPELS WATER (1963).

Like Water for Chocolate *see* COMO AGUA PARA CHOCOLATE (1991).

LIKE WILDFIRE 1917 d: Stuart Paton. USA., *Ten Cent Lady*, Louis Weltzenkorn, Short Story

LIKENESS OF THE NIGHT, THE 1921 d: Percy Nash. UKN., *The Likeness of the Night*, Mrs. W. K. Clifford, London 1908, Play

Lila *see* LAILA (1958).

LILA AKAC 1934 d: Steve Sekely. HNG., *Lila Akac*, Erno Szep, 1919, Short Story

LILA AKAC 1973 d: Steve Sekely. HNG., *Lila Akac*, Erno Szep, 1919, Short Story

LILAC DOMINO, THE 1937 d: Friedrich Zelnik. UKN., *The Lilac Domino*, Rudolf Bernauer, E. Gatti, B. Jenbach, Play

LILAC SUNBONNET, THE 1922 d: Sidney Morgan. UKN., *The Lilac Sunbonnet*, S. R. Crockett, Novel

LILAC TIME 1928 d: George Fitzmaurice. USA., *Lilac Time*, Jane Cowl, Jane Murfin, New York 1917, Play

LILACS IN THE SPRING 1954 d: Herbert Wilcox. UKN., *The Glorious Days*, Harry Parr Davies, Robert Nesbitt, London 1953, Musical Play

Lilas Blanc *see* LA CINQUIEME EMPREINTE (1934).

LILEIA 1960 d: Vasil Lapoknysh, Vakhtong Vronsky. USS., *Lileya*, Taras Shevchenko, 1888, Verse

Lileya *see* LILEIA (1960).

LILI 1953 d: Charles Walters. USA., *The Man Who Hated People*, Paul Gallico, Short Story

LILIES 1996 d: John Greyson. CND., *Les Feluettes; Ou la Repetition d'un Drame Romantique*, Michel Marc Bouchard, 1987, Play

LILIES OF THE FIELD 1924 d: John Francis Dillon. USA., *Lilies of the Field*, William Hurlbut, New York 1921, Play

LILIES OF THE FIELD 1930 d: Alexander KordA. USA., *Lilies of the Field*, William Hurlbut, New York 1921, Play

LILIES OF THE FIELD 1934 d: Norman Walker. UKN., *Lilies of the Field*, John Hastings Turner, London 1923, Play

LILIES OF THE FIELD 1963 d: Ralph Nelson. USA., *The Lilies of the Field*, William E. Barrett, New York 1962, Novel

LILIKA 1971 d: Branko PlesA. YGS., *Lilika*, Dragoslav Mihailovic, 1967, Short Story

LILIOM 1930 d: Frank Borzage. USA., *Liliom*, Ferenc Molnar, 1910, Play

LILIOM 1934 d: Fritz Lang. FRN., *Liliom*, Ferenc Molnar, 1910, Play

LILIOMFI 1954 d: Karoly Makk. HNG., *Liliomfi*, Ede Szigligeti, 1849, Play

LILITH 1964 d: Robert Rossen. USA., *Lilith*, J. R. Salamanca, New York 1961, Novel

LILLE PIGE MED SVOVLSTIKKERNE, DEN 1953 d: Johan Jacobsen. DNM., *Den Lille Pige Med Svovlstikkerne*, Hans Christian Andersen, 1846, Short Story

LILLY TURNER 1933 d: William A. Wellman. USA., *Lilly Turner*, George Abbott, Philip Dunning, New York 1932, Play

LILY CHRISTINE 1932 d: Paul L. Stein. UKN., *Lily Christine*, Michael Arlen, Novel

LILY IN LOVE 1985 d: Karoly Makk. USA/HNG., *A Testor*, Ferenc Molnar, Budapest 1910, Play

LILY OF KILLARNEY 1927 d: H. B. Parkinson. UKN., *The Lily of Killarney*, Charles Benedict, Opera

LILY OF KILLARNEY 1929 d: George Ridgwell. UKN., *The Colleen Bawn*, Dion Boucicault, London 1860, Play

LILY OF KILLARNEY 1934 d: Maurice Elvey. UKN., *The Colleen Bawn*, Dion Boucicault, London 1860, Play

LILY OF KILLARNEY, THE 1922 d: Challis Sanderson. UKN., *The Lily of Killarney*, Charles Benedict, Opera

Lily of Life, The *see* LE LYS DE LA VIE (1921).

LILY OF POVERTY FLAT, THE 1915 d: George E. Middleton. USA., *Her Last Letter*, Bret Harte, Boston 1905, Poem, *Her Letter*, Bret Harte, Boston 1905, Poem, *His Answer*, Bret Harte, Boston 1905, Poem

LILY OF THE DUST 1924 d: Dimitri Buchowetzki. USA., *Das Hohe Lied*, Hermann Sudermann, Berlin 1908, Novel

LILY, THE 1926 d: Victor Schertzinger. USA., *Le Lys*, Gaston Leroux, Pierre Wolff, Play

LIMBO LINE, THE 1968 d: Samuel Gallu. UKN., *The Limbo Line*, Victor Canning, Novel

Limit, The *see* GRANICA (1977).

Limited Edition *see* TIRE A PART (1996).

LIMITED MAIL, THE 1925 d: George W. Hill. USA., *The Limited Mail*, Elmer E. Vance, 1889, Play

LIMNI TON POTHON, I 1958 d: Georges Zervos. GRC., *I Limni Ton Pothon*, Nicos Tsekuras, Play

LIMONADOVY JOE 1964 d: Oldrich Lipsky. CZC., *Limonadovy Joe*, Jiri Brdecka, Prague 1958, Novel

LIMOUSINE LIFE 1918 d: John Francis Dillon. USA., *Limousine Life*, Ida M. Evans, 1917, Story

Limping Man, The *see* CREEPING SHADOWS (1931).

LIMPING MAN, THE 1936 d: Walter Summers. UKN., *The Limping Man*, Will Scott, Croydon 1930, Play

Limpy *see* WHEN A FELLER NEEDS A FRIEND (1932).

Lin Chia P'tzu *see* LINJIA PUZHI (1959).

LIN CHONG 1958 d: Su Shi, Wu Yonggang. CHN., *Shuihu Zhuan*, Luo Guanzhong, Shi Naian, c1500, Novel

Lin Family Shop, The *see* LINJIA PUZHI (1959).

LIN HAI XUE YUAN 1960 d: Liu Peiran. CHN., *Lin Hai Xue Yuan*, Qu Bo, Novel

LINCEUL N'A PAS DE POCHES, UN 1975 d: Jean-Pierre Mocky. FRN., *No Pockets in a Shroud*, Horace McCoy, Novel

LINCOLN HIGHWAYMAN, THE 1920 d: Emmett J. Flynn. USA., *The Lincoln Highwayman*, Paul Dickey, New York 1917, Play

LINCOLN, THE LOVER 1914 d: Ralph Ince. USA., *Lincoln the Lover*, Catherine Van Dyke, Story

LINDA 1929 d: Dorothy Reid. USA., *Linda*, Margaret Prescott Montague, Boston 1912, Novel

LINDA DI CHAMOUNIX 1921 d: Luigi Ferraro. ITL., *Linda Di Chamounix*, Gaetano Donizetti, 1842, Opera

LINE 1961 d: Nils Reinhardt Christensen. NRW., *Line*, Axel Jensen, Oslo 1959, Novel

LINE ENGAGED 1935 d: Bernerd Mainwaring. UKN., *Line Engaged*, Jack Celestin, Jack de Leon, 1934, Play

Line of the Horizon *see* LE FIL DE L'HORIZON (1993).

Linea Del Horizonte, La *see* LE FIL DE L'HORIZON (1993).

LINJIA PUZHI 1959 d: Shui HuA. CHN., *Linjia Puzi*, Shen Yanbing, 1932, Short Story

Link, The *see* THE HAUNTING OF JULIA (1976).

LINKED BY FATE 1919 d: Albert Ward. UKN., *Linked By Fate*, Charles Garvice, Novel

Links *see* SCHAKELS (1920).

LINKSHANDIGE FRAU, DIE 1978 d: Peter Handke. GRM., *Die Linkshandige Frau*, Peter Handke, 1976, Novel

LINNA 1986 d: Jaakko PakkasvirtA. FNL., *Das Schloss*, Franz Kafka, Munich 1926, Novel

LINNAISTEN VIHREA KAMARI 1945 d: Valentin VaalA. FNL., *Grona Kammarn Pa Linnais Gard*, Zachris Topelius, 1859, Novel

LIOLA 1964 d: Alessandro Blasetti. ITL/FRN., *Liola*, Luigi Pirandello, Rome 1916, Play

Lion and the Hawk, The *see* MEMED (1983).

LION AND THE LAMB, THE 1931 d: George B. Seitz. USA., *The Lion and the Lamb*, E. Phillips Oppenheim, New York 1930, Novel

LION AND THE MOUSE, THE 1914 d: Barry O'Neil. USA., *The Lion and the Mouse*, Charles Klein, New York 1905, Play

LION AND THE MOUSE, THE 1919 d: Tom Terriss. USA., *The Lion and the Mouse*, Charles Klein, New York 1905, Play

Lion and the Mouse, The *see* THE LION'S MOUSE (1923).

Lion Girl, The *see* THE LOVE HUNGER (1919).

LION IN WINTER, THE 1968 d: Anthony Harvey. UKN., *The Lion in Winter*, James Goldman, New York 1966, Play

LION IS IN THE STREETS, A 1953 d: Raoul Walsh. USA., *A Lion Is in the Streets*, Adria Locke Langley, 1945, Novel

Lion of Babylon, The *see* LAS RUINAS DE BABILONIA (1959).

LION, THE 1962 d: Jack Cardiff. UKN/USA., *Le Lion*, Joseph Kessel, Paris 1958, Novel

LION, THE WITCH AND THE WARDROBE, THE 1972. UKN., *The Lion the Witch and the Wardrobe*, C. S. Lewis, 1950, Novel

LION, THE WITCH AND THE WARDROBE, THE 1978 d: Bill Melendez. USA/UKN., *The Lion the Witch and the Wardrobe*, C. S. Lewis, 1950, Novel

LIONCEAUX, LES 1959 d: Jacques Bourdon. FRN., *A Malin Et Demi*, Michel Lebrun, Novel

LIONHEART 1968 d: Michael Forlong. UKN., *Lionheart*, Alexander Fullerton, Novel

Lions are Loose, The *see* LES LIONS SONT LACHES (1961).

LION'S DEN, THE 1919 d: George D. Baker. USA., *The Lion's Den*, Frederick Orin Bartlett, 1919, Short Story

Lion's Den, The *see* EUROPA EUROPA (1991).

LION'S MOUSE, THE 1923 d: Oscar Apfel. UKN/NTH., *The Lion's Mouse (Vrouwenlist)*, Alice Muriel Williamson, Charles Norris Williamson, 1919, Novel

Lion's Share, The *see* THE BACHELOR FATHER (1931).

LIONS SONT LACHES, LES 1961 d: Henri Verneuil. FRN/ITL., *Les Lions Sont Laches*, Nicole, Novel

Lion's Way, The *see* KING OF THE JUNGLE (1933).

LIQUID DYNAMITE 1915 d: Cleo Madison. USA., *Liquid Dynamite*, Joe King, Story

Liquid Treasure *see* WHISKY GALORE! (1948).

LIQUIDATOR, THE 1966 d: Jack Cardiff. UKN/USA., *The Liquidator*, John Gardner, New York 1964, Novel

Liren XIng *see* LI REN XIN (1948).

LIS DE MER, LE 1970 d: Jacqueline Audry. FRN., *Vanina*, Andre Pieyre de Mandiargues, Novel

Lisa *see* THE INSPECTOR (1962).

Lisa and Lottie *see* DAS DOPPELTE LOTTCHEN (1950).

LISA, BRIGHT AND DARK 1973 d: Jeannot Szwarc. USA., *Bright and Dark Lisa*, John Neufeld, Novel

LISA FLEURON 1920 d: Roberto Leone Roberti. ITL., *Le Due Rivali*, Georges Ohnet, Novel

LISBON 1956 d: Ray Milland. USA., *Lisbon*, Martin Rackin, Novel

LISBON STORY 1946 d: Paul L. Stein. UKN., *Lisbon Story*, Harry Parr Davies, Harold Purcell, London 1943, Play

LISCA 1984 d: Ioan Carmazan. RMN., *Lisca*, Fanus Neagu, 1960, Short Story

LISETTA 1933 d: Carl Boese. ITL., *La Ragazza E Il Diamante*, Eberhard Frowein, Novel

LISISTRATI 1972 d: Giorgos Zervoulakos. GRC., *Lysistrata*, Aristophanes, 411 bc, Play

LISSY 1957 d: Konrad Wolf. GDR., *Lissy*, F. C. Weiskopf, Novel

LIST OF ADRIAN MESSENGER, THE 1963 d: John Huston. USA., *The List of Adrian Messenger*, Philip MacDonald, New York 1959, Novel

LISTEN LESTER 1924 d: William A. Seiter. USA., *Listen Lester*, H. L. Cort, H. Orlog, G. E. Stoddard, Play

LISTEN TO MY STORY 1974 d: Jurgen Goslar. SAF/GRM., *Und Die Nacht Kennt Kein Erbarmen*, Heinz G. Konsalik, Novel

Listige Vrouw, Een *see* THE LION'S MOUSE (1923).

Liszt Rhapsody *see* WENN DIE MUSIK NICHT WAR' (1935).

LIT A COLONNES, LE 1942 d: Roland Tual. FRN., *Le Lit a Colonnes*, Louise de Vilmorin, Novel

Lit a Deux Places, Le *see* RENDEZ-VOUS AVEC LA CHANCE (1949).

LIT, LE 1982 d: Marion Hansel. BLG/SWT., *Le Lit*, Dominique Rolin, Novel

LITEN IDA 1981 d: Laila Mikkelsen. NRW/SWD., *Liten Ida*, Laila Mikkelsen, Margit Paulsen, Novel

LITTLE ACCIDENT 1939 d: Charles Lamont. USA., *An Unmarried Father*, Floyd Dell, New York 1927, Novel

LITTLE ACCIDENT, THE 1930 d: William James Craft. USA., *An Unmarried Father*, Floyd Dell, New York 1927, Novel

LITTLE ADVENTURESS, THE 1927 d: William C. de Mille. USA., *The Dover Road*, A. A. Milne, New York 1921, Play

Little Angel *see* ANGELINA O EL HONOR DE UN BRIGADIER (1935).

LITTLE ANGEL OF CANYON CREEK, THE 1914 d: Rollin S. Sturgeon. USA., *The Little Angel of Canyon Creek*, Cyrus Townsend Brady, New York 1914, Novel

Little Angel, The *see* A LADY OF CHANCE (1928).

LITTLE ANNIE ROONEY 1925 d: William Beaudine. USA., Katherine Hennessey, Story

Little Apartment, The *see* EL PISITO (1957).

LITTLE ARK, THE 1972 d: James B. Clark. USA., *The Little Ark*, Jan de Hartog, Novel

LITTLE BIG MAN 1970 d: Arthur Penn. USA., *Little Big Man*, Thomas Berger, New York 1964, Novel

LITTLE BIG SHOT 1952 d: Jack Raymond. UKN., *Little Big Shot*, Janet Allan, Play

Little Bit of Broadway, A *see* BRIGHT LIGHTS (1925).

LITTLE BIT OF FLUFF, A 1919 d: Kenelm Foss. UKN., *A Little Bit of Fluff*, Walter Ellis, London 1915, Play

LITTLE BIT OF FLUFF, A 1928 d: Jess Robbins, Wheeler Dryden. UKN., *A Little Bit of Fluff*, Walter Ellis, London 1915, Play

LITTLE BLONDE IN BLACK 1915 d: Robert Z. Leonard. USA., *Little Blonde in Black*, Julius G. Furthmann, Story

Little Bobes in the City *see* MALY BOBES VE MESTE (1962).

LITTLE BOY LOST 1953 d: George Seaton. USA., *Little Boy Lost*, Marghanita Laski, 1949, Novel

LITTLE BREADWINNER, THE 1916 d: Wilfred Noy. UKN., *The Little Breadwinner*, James A. Campbell, Play

LITTLE BREECHES 1914. USA., *Little Breeches*, John Hay, 1871, Poem

Little Brother, Little Sister *see* BRUDERCHEN UND SCHWESTERCHEN (1953).

LITTLE BROTHER OF GOD 1922 d: F. Martin Thornton. UKN., *Little Brother of God*, Leslie Howard Gordon, Novel

LITTLE BROTHER OF THE RICH, A 1915 d: Hobart Bosworth, Otis Turner. USA., *A Little Brother of the Rich*, Joseph Medill Patterson, New York 1908, Novel

LITTLE BROTHER OF THE RICH, A 1919 d: Lynn Reynolds. USA., *A Little Brother of the Rich*, Joseph Medill Patterson, New York 1908, Novel

Little Brunette, The *see* A MORENINHA (1970).

Little Buckaroo, The *see* THE CHEROKEE STRIP (1937).

LITTLE CAESAR 1931 d: Mervyn Leroy. USA., *Little Caesar*, William Riley Burnett, New York 1929, Novel

LITTLE CHEVALIER, THE 1917 d: Alan Crosland. USA., *The Little Chevalier*, Mary Evelyn Moore Davis, New York 1903, Novel

Little Child Shall Lead Them, A *see* WHO ARE MY PARENTS? (1922).

LITTLE CHURCH AROUND THE CORNER 1923 d: William A. Seiter. USA., *Little Church Around the Corner*, Marion Russell, 1902, Play

LITTLE CHURCH AROUND THE CORNER, THE 1915 d: E. Mason Hopper. USA., *Little Church Around the Corner*, Marion Russell, 1902, Play

LITTLE CLOWN, THE 1921 d: Thomas N. Heffron. USA., *The Little Clown*, Avery Hopwood, Play

LITTLE COLONEL, THE 1935 d: David Butler. USA., *The Little Colonel*, Annie Fellows Johnston, New York 1895, Novel

Little Comrade *see* ON DANGEROUS GROUND (1917).

LITTLE COMRADE 1919 d: Chet Withey. USA., *The Two Benjamins*, Juliet Wilbor Tompkins, 1918, Serial Story

Little Courtly Concert, A *see* DAS KLEINE HOFKONZERT (1945).

Little Czar, The *see* DER ZAREWITSCH (1954).

LITTLE DAMOZEL, THE 1916 d: Wilfred Noy. UKN., *The Little Damozel*, Monckton Hoffe, London 1909, Play

LITTLE DAMOZEL, THE 1933 d: Herbert Wilcox. UKN., *The Little Damozel*, Monckton Hoffe, London 1909, Play

LITTLE DARLINGS 1980 d: Ronald F. Maxwell. USA., Kim Peck, Story

Little Devil-May-Care *see* LE DIABLE AU COEUR (1927).

LITTLE DORRIT 1913 d: James Kirkwood. USA., *Little Dorrit*, Charles Dickens, London 1857, Novel

LITTLE DORRIT 1920 d: Sidney Morgan. UKN., *Little Dorrit*, Charles Dickens, London 1857, Novel

LITTLE DORRIT 1987 d: Christine Edzard. UKN., *Little Dorrit*, Charles Dickens, London 1857, Novel

Little Dream King *see* DIE VOM SCHICKSAL VERFOLGTEN (1927).

LITTLE DRUMMER GIRL, THE 1985 d: George Roy Hill. USA., *The Little Drummer Girl*, John le Carre, 1983, Novel

LITTLE DUTCH GIRL, THE 1915 d: Emile Chautard. USA., *Bebee; Or Two Little Wooden Shoes*, Ouida, Philadelphia 1874, Novel

LITTLE EMILY 1911 d: Frank Powell. UKN., *David Copperfield*, Charles Dickens, London 1850, Novel

LITTLE EVA ASCENDS 1922 d: George D. Baker. USA., *Little Eva Ascends*, Thomas Beer, 1921, Short Story

Little Eva Egerton *see* LITTLE EVE EDGARTON (1916).

LITTLE EVE EDGARTON 1916 d: Robert Z. Leonard. USA., *Little Eva Egerton*, Eleanor Hallowell Abbott, New York 1914, Novel

Little Eyolf *see* JAZEERE (1989).

Little Flat in the Temple, A *see* DEVOTION (1931).

LITTLE FOXES, THE 1941 d: William Wyler. USA., *The Little Foxes*, Lillian Hellman, New York 1939, Play

LITTLE 'FRAID LADY, THE 1920 d: John G. Adolfi. USA., *The Girl Who Lived in the Woods*, Marjorie Benton Cooke, Chicago 1910, Novel

LITTLE FRENCH GIRL, THE 1925 d: Herbert Brenon. USA., *The Little French Girl*, Anne Douglas Sedgwick, New York 1924, Novel

LITTLE FRIEND 1934 d: Berthold Viertel. UKN., *Little Friend*, Ernst Lothar, Novel

LITTLE GAME, A 1971 d: Paul Wendkos. USA., *A Little Game*, Fielden Farrington, Novel

LITTLE GIANT, THE 1926 d: William Nigh. USA., *Once a Peddler*, Hugh MacNair Kahler, 1921, Short Story

LITTLE GIRL IN A BIG CITY 1925 d: Burton L. King. USA., *A Little Girl in a Big City*, James Kyrtle MacCurdy, 1909, Play

LITTLE GIRL NEXT DOOR, THE 1912 d: J. Searle Dawley. USA., *The Little Girl Next Door*, Nina Rhoades, Story

LITTLE GIRL THAT HE FORGOT, THE 1914. USA., *The Little Girl That He Forgot*, Beulah Poynter, Play

Little Girl Who Conquered Time, The *see* TOKI O KAKERU SHOJO (1983).

LITTLE GIRL WHO LIVES DOWN THE LANE, THE 1977 d: Nicolas Gessner. CND/FRN., *The Little Girl Who Lives Down the Lane*, Laird Koenig, Novel

LITTLE GLORIA. HAPPY AT LAST 1982 d: Waris Hussein. USA., *Little GloriA. Happy at Last*, Barbara Goldsmith, Novel

Little Gold Key, The *see* ZOLOTOI KLYUCHIK (1939).

Little Golden Key, The *see* ZOLOTOI KLYUCHIK (1939).

Little Goldfish, The *see* HET GOUDVISCHJE (1919).

LITTLE GRAY LADY, THE 1914 d: Francis Powers. USA., *The Little Gray Lady*, Channing Pollock, New York 1906, Play

LITTLE GYPSY, THE 1915 d: Oscar Apfel. USA., *The Little Minister*, J. M. Barrie, 1891, Novel

Little Gypsy, The *see* LA GITANILLA (1940).

LITTLE HOUR OF PETER WELLS, THE 1920 d: B. E. Doxat-Pratt, Maurits H. Binger. UKN/NTH., *The Little Hour of Peter Wells*, David Whitelaw, 1913, Novel

LITTLE HOUSE ON THE PRAIRIE, THE 1974 d: Michael Landon. USA., *Little House on the Prairie*, Laura Ingalls Wilder, Novel

Little Humpbacked Horse, The *see* SKAZKA O KONKE-GORBUNKE (1961).

LITTLE HUT, THE 1957 d: Mark Robson. USA., *La Petite Hutte*, Andre Roussin, 1948, Play

Little Ida *see* LITEN IDA (1981).

LITTLE IRISH GIRL, THE 1926 d: Roy Del Ruth. USA., *The Grifters*, C. D. Lancaster, Story

LITTLE JOHNNY JONES 1923 d: Arthur Rosson, Johnny Hines. USA., *Little Johnny Jones*, George M. Cohan, New York 1904, Play

LITTLE JOHNNY JONES 1929 d: Mervyn Leroy. USA., *Little Johnny Jones*, George M. Cohan, New York 1904, Play

LITTLE JOURNEY, A 1926 d: Robert Z. Leonard. USA., *A Little Journey*, Rachel Crothers, New York 1923, Play

Little Knight, The *see* PAN WOLODYJOWSKI (1969).

LITTLE LORD FAUNTLEROY 1914 d: F. Martin Thornton. UKN., *Little Lord Fauntleroy*, Frances Hodgson Burnett, New York 1886, Novel

LITTLE LORD FAUNTLEROY 1921 d: Alfred E. Green, Jack Pickford. USA., *Little Lord Fauntleroy*, Frances Hodgson Burnett, New York 1886, Novel

LITTLE LORD FAUNTLEROY 1936 d: John Cromwell. USA., *Little Lord Fauntleroy*, Frances Hodgson Burnett, New York 1886, Novel

LITTLE LORD FAUNTLEROY 1976 d: Paul Annett. UKN., *Little Lord Fauntleroy*, Frances Hodgson Burnett, New York 1886, Novel

LITTLE LORD FAUNTLEROY 1980 d: Jack Gold. UKN., *Little Lord Fauntleroy*, Frances Hodgson Burnett, New York 1886, Novel

LITTLE LORD FAUNTLEROY 1994 d: Andrew Morgan. UKN., *Little Lord Fauntleroy*, Frances Hodgson Burnett, New York 1886, Novel

LITTLE LOST SISTER 1917 d: Alfred E. Green. USA., *Little Lost Sister*, Virginia Brooks, Chicago 1914, Novel

Little Man, The *see* ANNI DIFFICILI (1948).

LITTLE MAN, WHAT NOW? 1934 d: Frank Borzage. USA., *Kleiner Mann - Was Nun?*, Hans Fallada, Berlin 1932, Novel

LITTLE MATCH GIRL, THE 1914 d: Percy Nash?. UKN., *Den Lille Pige Med Svovlstikkerne*, Hans Christian Andersen, 1846, Short Story

Little Match Girl, The *see* LA PETITE MARCHANDE D'ALLUMETTES (1928).

Little Match Girl, The *see* DEN LILLE PIGE MED SVOVLSTIKKERNE (1953).

Little Match Girl, The *see* FETITA CU CHIBRITURI (1967).

LITTLE MATCH GIRL, THE 1983 d: Wally Broodbent, Mark Hoeger. USA., *Den Lille Pige Med Svovlstikkerne*, Hans Christian Andersen, 1846, Short Story

LITTLE MATCH GIRL, THE 1987 d: Michael Constance. UKN., *Den Lille Pige Med Svovlstikkerne*, Hans Christian Andersen, 1846, Short Story

LITTLE MATCH GIRL, THE 1987 d: Michael Lindsay-Hogg. USA., *Den Lille Pige Med Svovlstikkerne*, Hans Christian Andersen, 1846, Short Story

LITTLE MEG AND I 1914. USA., *Little Meg and I*, G. C. T. Murphy, Poem

LITTLE MEG'S CHILDREN 1921 d: Bert Wynne. UKN., *Little Meg's Children*, Hesba Stretton, Novel

LITTLE MEN 1934 d: Phil Rosen. USA., *Little Men*, Louisa May Alcott, Boston 1871, Novel

LITTLE MEN 1940 d: Norman Z. McLeod. USA., *Little Men*, Louisa May Alcott, Boston 1871, Novel

Little Mermaid, The *see* MALA MORSKA VILA (1975).

Little Mermaid, The *see* RUSALOCHKA (1976).

LITTLE MERMAID, THE 1989 d: John Musker, Ron Clements. USA., *Den Lille Haufrue*, Hans Christian Andersen, 1837, Short Story

LITTLE MINISTER, THE 1913 d: James Young. USA., *The Little Minister*, J. M. Barrie, 1891, Novel

LITTLE MINISTER, THE 1915 d: Percy Nash. UKN., *The Little Minister*, J. M. Barrie, 1891, Novel

LITTLE MINISTER, THE 1921 d: Penrhyn Stanlaws. USA., *The Little Minister*, J. M. Barrie, 1891, Novel

LITTLE MINISTER, THE 1922 d: David Smith. USA., *The Little Minister*, J. M. Barrie, 1891, Novel

LITTLE MINISTER, THE 1934 d: Richard Wallace. USA., *The Little Minister*, J. M. Barrie, 1891, Novel

LITTLE MISS BROWN 1915 d: James Young. USA., *Little Miss Brown*, Philip Bartholomae, New York 1912, Play

LITTLE MISS HOOVER 1918 d: John S. Robertson. USA., *The Golden Bird*, Maria Thompson Davies, New York 1918, Novel

LITTLE MISS MARKER 1934 d: Alexander Hall. USA., *Little Miss Marker*, Damon Runyon, 1932, Short Story

LITTLE MISS MARKER 1980 d: Walter Bernstein. USA., *Little Miss Marker*, Damon Runyon, 1932, Short Story

LITTLE MISS NOBODY 1923 d: Wilfred Noy. UKN., *Little Miss Nobody*, A. E. Godfrey, H. Graham, Landon Ronald, London 1898, Musical Play

LITTLE MISS NOBODY 1936 d: John G. Blystone. USA., *The Matron's Report*, Frederick Hazlitt Brennan, 1928, Short Story

LITTLE MISS SMILES 1922 d: John Ford. USA., *Little Aliens*, Myra Kelly, New York 1910, Novel

Little Miss Somebody *see* NOBODY'S KID (1921).

Little Mobsters *see* KID DYNAMITE (1943).

Little Mook *see* DIE GESCHICHTE VOM KLEINEN MUCK (1953).

Little Mother Hubbard *see* IN WALKED MARY (1920).

LITTLE MOTHER, THE 1922 d: A. V. Bramble. UKN., *The Little Mother*, May Wynn, Novel

LITTLE MR. FIXER 1915 d: Frank Lloyd. USA., *Little Mr. Fixer*, Maurice de La Parelle, Story

LITTLE MR. JIM 1946 d: Fred Zinnemann. USA., *Army Brat*, Thomas D. Naddleton Jr., Novel

Little Muck's Treasure *see* DIE GESCHICHTE VOM KLEINEN MUCK (1953).

LITTLE MURDERS 1971 d: Alan Arkin. USA., *Little Murders*, Jules Feiffer, New York 1967, Play

LITTLE NELLIE KELLY 1940 d: Norman Taurog. USA., *Little Nellie Kelly*, George M. Cohan, New York 1922, Musical Play

LITTLE OLD MEN OF THE WOODS, THE 1910. USA., *Schneewittchen*, Jacob Grimm, Wilhelm Grimm, 1812, Short Story

LITTLE OLD NEW YORK 1923 d: Sidney Olcott. USA., *Little Old New York*, Rida Johnson Young, New York 1920, Play

Little Old New York *see* LIGHTS OF OLD BROADWAY (1925).

LITTLE OLD NEW YORK 1940 d: Henry King. USA., *Little Old New York*, Rida Johnson Young, New York 1920, Play

Little Old-Fashioned World *see* PICCOLO MONDO ANTICO (1940).

LITTLE ORPHAN ANNIE 1919 d: Colin Campbell. USA., *Little Orphan Annie*, James Whitcomb Riley, 1908, Poem

LITTLE ORVIE 1940 d: Ray McCarey. USA., *Little Orvie*, Booth Tarkington, New York 1934, Novel

LITTLE OUTCAST, THE 1920 d: Paul Price. USA., *Silas Marner*, George Eliot, London 1861, Novel

Little Pal *see* THE HEALER (1935).

Little Parade, The *see* LA PETITE PARADE (1930).

Little Peter's Diary *see* DRUZBA PERE KVRZICE (1971).

Little Playmates *see* XIAO HUO BAN (1956).

Little Prince, The *see* MALENKI PRINTS (1966).

LITTLE PRINCE, THE 1973 d: Stanley Donen. USA/UKN., *Le Petit Prince*, Antoine de Saint-Exupery, 1943, Novel

LITTLE PRINCESS, A 1986 d: Carol Wiseman. UKN., *Sara Crewe*, Frances Hodgson Burnett, New York 1888, Novel

LITTLE PRINCESS, A 1995 d: Alfonso Cuaron. USA., *Sara Crewe*, Frances Hodgson Burnett, New York 1888, Novel

LITTLE PRINCESS, THE 1917 d: Marshall Neilan, Howard Hawks (Uncredited). USA., *Sara Crewe*, Frances Hodgson Burnett, New York 1888, Novel

LITTLE PRINCESS, THE 1939 d: Walter Lang. USA., *Sara Crewe*, Frances Hodgson Burnett, New York 1888, Novel

LITTLE RED DECIDES 1918 d: Jack Conway. USA., *Little Red Decides*, William M. McCoy, 1917, Short Story

LITTLE RED MONKEY 1953 d: Ken Hughes. UKN., Eric Maschwitz, Short Story

LITTLE RED RIDING HOOD 1911. USA., *Le Petit Chaperon Rouge*, Charles Perrault, Paris 1697, Short Story

LITTLE RED RIDING HOOD 1911 d: George Loane Tucker, James Kirkwood. USA., *Le Petit Chaperon Rouge*, Charles Perrault, Paris 1697, Short Story

LITTLE RED RIDING HOOD 1917 d: Otis B. Thayer. USA., *Le Petit Chaperon Rouge*, Charles Perrault, Paris 1697, Short Story

Little Red Riding Hood *see* LE PETIT CHAPERON ROUGE (1929).

Little Red Riding Hood *see* LA CAPERUCITA ROJA (1960).

LITTLE RED SCHOOLHOUSE, THE 1923 d: John G. Adolfi. USA., *The Little Red Schoolhouse*, Hal Reid, Play

LITTLE ROMANCE, A 1979 d: George Roy Hill. USA/FRN., *A Little Romance*, Patrick Cauvin, Novel

LITTLE SAVAGE, THE 1959 d: Byron Haskin. USA., *The Little Savage*, Frederick Marryat, 1848-49, Novel

Little School Mistress, The *see* LA MAESTRINA (1933).

Little Schoolgirl, The *see* ZABEC (1939).

Little Sea Nymph, The *see* MALA MORSKA VILA (1975).

LITTLE SHEPHERD OF BARGAIN ROW, THE 1916 d: Fred E. Wright. USA., *The Little Shepherd of Bargain Row*, Howard McKent Barnes, Chicago 1915, Novel

LITTLE SHEPHERD OF KINGDOM COME, THE 1920 d: Wallace Worsley. USA., *The Little Shepherd of Kingdom Come*, John Fox Jr., New York 1903, Novel

LITTLE SHEPHERD OF KINGDOM COME, THE 1928 d: Alfred Santell. USA., *The Little Shepherd of Kingdom Come*, John Fox Jr., New York 1903, Novel

LITTLE SHEPHERD OF KINGDOM COME, THE 1961 d: Andrew V. McLaglen. USA., *The Little Shepherd of Kingdom Come*, John Fox Jr., New York 1903, Novel

LITTLE SHOES, THE 1917 d: Arthur Berthelet. USA., *The House of the Little Shoes*, Eleanor M. Ingram, Novel

Little Sister, The *see* MARLOWE (1969).

Little Soldier, The *see* LE PETIT SOLDAT (1947).

LITTLE SPECK IN GARNERED FRUIT, A 1917 d: Martin Justice. USA., *A Little Speck in Garnered Fruit*, O. Henry, Short Story

LITTLE SUNSET 1915. USA., *Little Sunset*, Charles E. Van Loan, 1912, Short Story

Little Theater, The *see* TOO BUSY TO WORK (1939).

LITTLE TURNCOAT, THE 1913 d: Fred J. Balshofer. USA., *The Little Turncoat*, Mary O'Connor, Story

LITTLE VOICE 1998 d: Mark Herman. UKN., *The Rise and Fall of Little Voice*, Jim Cartwright, Play

LITTLE VULGAR BOY, THE 1913 d: Wilfred Noy. UKN., *The Little Vulgar Boy*, Thomas Ingoldsby, Poem

Little White Cloud Caroline *see* WEISSE WOLKE CAROLIN (1984).

Little White Flag Dispute, The *see* XIAO BAI QI DE FENG BO (1956).

LITTLE WHITE LIES 1998 d: Philip Saville. UKN., *Little White Lies*, Elizabeth McGregor, Book

Little Window, The *see* OKENKO (1933).

LITTLE WOMEN 1917 d: G. B. Samuelson, Alexander Butler. UKN., *Little Women*, Louisa May Alcott, Boston 1868, Novel

LITTLE WOMEN 1919 d: Harley Knoles. USA., *Little Women*, Louisa May Alcott, Boston 1868, Novel

LITTLE WOMEN 1933 d: George Cukor. USA., *Little Women*, Louisa May Alcott, Boston 1868, Novel

LITTLE WOMEN 1948 d: Mervyn Leroy. USA., *Little Women*, Louisa May Alcott, Boston 1868, Novel

LITTLE WOMEN 1978 d: David Lowell Rich. USA., *Little Women*, Louisa May Alcott, Boston 1868, Novel

LITTLE WOMEN 1994 d: Gillian Armstrong. USA., *Little Women*, Louisa May Alcott, Boston 1868, Novel

Little World of Don Camillo, The *see* LE PETIT MONDE DE DON CAMILLO (1951).

LITTLE YELLOW HOUSE, THE 1928 d: James Leo Meehan. USA., *The Little Yellow House*, Beatrice Burton Morgan, Garden City, N.Y. 1928, Novel

LITTLEST OUTLAW, THE 1955 d: Roberto Gavaldon. USA., Larry Lansburgh, Story

LITTLEST REBEL, THE 1914 d: Edgar Lewis. USA., *The Littlest Rebel*, Edward Peple, New York 1911, Play

LITTLEST REBEL, THE 1935 d: David Butler. USA., *The Littlest Colonel*, Edward Peple, New York 1911, Play

LIU HAO MEN 1952 d: Lu Ban. CHN., *Liu Hao Men*, Wang Xuebao, Play

LIU ZHI QIN MO 1993 d: Wu Mianqin. CHN/HKG., *Liu Zhi Qin Mo*, Ni Kang, Novel

LIV 1934 d: Rasmus Breistein. NRW., *Liv*, Kristofer Janson, 1866, Short Story

LIVE A LITTLE, LOVE A LITTLE 1968 d: Norman Taurog. USA., *Kiss My Firm But Pliant Lips*, Dan Greenburg, New York 1965, Novel

LIVE AGAIN, DIE AGAIN 1974 d: Richard A. CollA. USA., *Come to Mother*, David Sale, Novel

LIVE AND LET DIE 1973 d: Guy Hamilton. UKN., *Live and Let Die*, Ian Fleming, Novel

Live and Let Live *see* SPY FOR A DAY (1940).

Live and Let Live *see* THE HAPPY FAMILY (1952).

LIVE FAST, DIE YOUNG 1958 d: Paul Henreid. USA., *Seed of Destruction*, Ib Melchior, Edwin B. Watson, Story

Live Flesh *see* CARNE TREMULA (1997).

LIVE NOW - PAY LATER 1962 d: Jay Lewis. UKN., *All on the Never-Never*, Jack Lindsay, Novel

Live the Impossible *see* VIVA LO IMPOSIBLE! (1957).

Live Today for Tomorrow *see* AN ACT OF MURDER (1948).

LIVE WIRE, THE 1925 d: Charles Hines. USA., *The Game of Light*, Richard Washburn Child, 1914, Short Story

LIVE WIRE, THE 1937 d: Herbert Brenon. UKN., *Plunder in the Air*, C. Stafford Dickens, Play

LIVELY AFFAIR, A 1912 d: James Young. USA., *A Lively Affair*, Alice M. Moore, Story

LIVES OF A BENGAL LANCER, THE 1935 d: Henry Hathaway. USA., *The Lives of a Bengal Lancer*, Francis Yeats-Brown, New York 1936, Novel

Lives of a Cat *see* DIE KATZE (1987).

LIVET GAR VIDARE 1941 d: Anders Henrikson. SWD., *Kamrathustru*, Dagmar Ingeborg Edqvist, 1932, Novel

LIVET PA LANDET 1943 d: Bror Bugler. SWD., *Ut Mine Stromtid*, Fritz Reuter, 1862-64, Novel

LIVET PAA HEGNSGAARD 1939 d: Arne Weel. DNM., *Livet Paa Hegnsgaard*, Jeppe Aakjaer, 1907, Play

Living and the Dead, The see ZHIVYE I MERTVYE (1964).

Living Corpse, The see DER LEBENDE LEICHNAM (1918).

Living Corpse, The see ZHIVOI TRUP (1929).

Living Corpse, The see NUITS DE FEU (1937).

Living Corpse, The see ZHIVOI TRUP (1953).

LIVING DANGEROUSLY 1936 d: Herbert Brenon. UKN., *Living Dangerously*, Frank Gregory, Reginald Simpson, London 1934, Play

Living Dead Man, The see FEU MATHIAS PASCAL (1925).

Living Dead, The see DER LEBENDE LEICHNAM (1918).

Living Dead, The see THE SCOTLAND YARD MYSTERY (1934).

Living Dust see POUSSIERES DE VIE (1996).

Living for Love see MAN TROUBLE (1930).

Living Forever in Burning Flames see LIE HUOZHONG YONGSHENG (1965).

LIVING FREE 1972 d: Jack Couffer. UKN., *Living Free*, Joy Adamson, Book

Living in Paradise see VIVRE AU PARADIS (1998).

LIVING IT UP 1954 d: Norman Taurog. USA., *Letter to the Editor*, James H. Street, 1937, Short Story

LIVING LIES 1922 d: Emile Chautard. USA., *Plunder*, Arthur Somers Roche, Indianapolis 1917, Novel

LIVING ON LOVE 1937 d: Lew Landers. USA., *Rafter Romance*, John Wells, New York 1932, Novel

Living Orphan, The see MY SON (1939).

Living Up to Lizzie see PERSONAL MAID'S SECRET (1935).

Livre de San Michele, Le see DER ARZT VON SAN MICHELE AXEL MUNTHE (1962).

LIZZIE 1957 d: Hugo Haas. USA., *The Bird's Nest*, Shirley Jackson, 1954, Novel

Ljubov Jarovaja see LYUBOV YAROAYA (1953).

Ljubov Jarovaja see LYUBOV YAROAYA (1970).

Ljudi Protiv see UOMINI CONTRO (1970).

Llama Blanca, La see NADA MAS QUE UNA MUJER (1934).

LLAMA SAGRADA, LA 1931 d: William McGann. USA., *The Sacred Flame*, W. Somerset Maugham, New York 1928, Play

LLANO KID, THE 1939 d: Edward D. Venturini. USA., *A Double-Dyed Deceiver*, O. Henry, 1905, Short Story

Llona Llega Con la Lluvia see ILONA LLEGA CON LA LLUVA (1996).

Lo Bayom Ve'lo Balayla see NEITHER BY DAY NOR BY NIGHT (1974).

LO SAM ZAYIN 1987 d: Shmuel Imberman. ISR., Dan Ben-Amotz, Novel

LOADED DICE 1918 d: Herbert Blache. USA., *Loaded Dice*, Ellery Harding Clark, Indianapolis 1909, Novel

LOADED DOOR, THE 1922 d: Harry Pollard. USA., *Cherub of Seven Bar*, Ralph Cummins, 1921, Short Story

Lobas, Las see LES LOUVES (1956).

LOBO, EL 1928 d: Joaquin DicentA. SPN., *El Lobo*, Joaquin Dicenta, Play

LOCA DE LA CASA, LA 1926 d: Luis R. Alonso. SPN., *La Loca de la Casa*, Benito Perez Galdos, Play

LOCAL BAD MAN, THE 1932 d: Otto Brower. USA., *All for Love*, Peter B. Kyne, 1928, Short Story

LOCAL BOY MAKES GOOD 1931 d: Mervyn Leroy. USA., *The Poor Nut*, Elliott Nugent, J. C. Nugent, New York 1925, Play

LOCANDIERA, LA 1912 d: Alfredo Robert. ITL., *La Locandiera*, Carlo Goldoni, 1753, Play

LOCANDIERA, LA 1912 d: Alberto Nepoti. ITL., *La Locandiera*, Carlo Goldoni, 1753, Play

LOCANDIERA, LA 1929 d: Telemaco Ruggeri. ITL., *La Locandiera*, Carlo Goldoni, 1753, Play

LOCANDIERA, LA 1944 d: Luigi Chiarini. ITL., *La Locandiera*, Carlo Goldoni, 1753, Play

LOCANDIERA, LA 1981 d: Paolo CavarA. ITL., *La Locandiera*, Carlo Goldoni, 1753, Play

Locataire, Le see THE TENANT (1976).

LOCHINVAR 1909 d: J. Searle Dawley. USA., *Marmion a Tale of Flodden Field*, Sir Walter Scott, 1808, Poem

LOCHINVAR 1915 d: Leslie Seldon-Truss. UKN., *Marmion a Tale of Flodden Field*, Sir Walter Scott, 1808, Poem

Lock Up see WALLS (1984).

LOCK UP YOUR DAUGHTERS! 1969 d: Peter Coe. UKN., *Lock Up Your Daughters*, Lionel Bart, Laurie Johnson, Bernard Miles, London 1959, Play

Lock Up Your Daughters see THE APE MAN (1943).

Lock Your Doors see THE APE MAN (1943).

LOCKED DOOR, THE 1929 d: George Fitzmaurice. USA., *The Sign on the Door*, Channing Pollock, New York 1924, Play

LOCKED LIPS 1920 d: William C. Dowlan. USA., *Blossom*, Clifford Howard, Short Story

Locked Out see THE GIRL IN HIS ROOM (1922).

LOCKENDE GEFAHR 1950 d: Eugen York. GRM., *Kleiner Fisch Im Grossen Netz*, Arthur A. Kuhnert, Story

LOCKENDES GIFT 1928 d: Fred Sauer. GRM., *Sweet Pepper*, Geoffrey Moss, Novel

LOCKER 69 1962 d: Norman Harrison. UKN., Edgar Wallace, Story

LOCO DE AMOR 1996 d: Fernando TruebA. SPN/USA., *Two Much*, Donald E. Westlake, Novel

LOCO LUCK 1927 d: Cliff Smith. USA., *The Eyes Win*, Alvin J. Neitz, Story

LOCSOLOKOCSI, A 1974 d: Zsolt Kezdi-Kovacs. HNG., *A Locsolokocsi*, Ivan Mandy, 1965, Novel

LOCURA DE AMOR 1948 d: Juan de OrdunA. SPN., *La Locura de Amor*, Manuel Tamayo Y Baus, 1855, Play

Locust Tree Village see HUAI SHU ZHUANG (1962).

LODGE IN THE WILDERNESS, THE 1926 d: Henry McCarty. USA., *The Lodge in the Wilderness*, Gilbert Parker, 1909, Short Story

LODGER: A STORY OF THE LONDON FOG, THE 1926 d: Alfred Hitchcock. UKN., *The Lodger*, Mrs. Belloc Lowndes, London 1913, Novel

Lodger, The see THE LODGER: A STORY OF THE LONDON FOG (1926).

LODGER, THE 1932 d: Maurice Elvey. UKN., *The Lodger*, Mrs. Belloc Lowndes, London 1913, Novel

LODGER, THE 1944 d: John Brahm. USA., *The Lodger*, Mrs. Belloc Lowndes, London 1913, Novel

Loffe As a Millionaire see LOFFE SOM MILJONAR (1948).

LOFFE SOM MILJONAR 1948 d: Gosta Bernhard. SWD., *Jeppe Haa Bjerget*, Ludvig Holberg, 1722, Play

LOGAN'S RUN 1976 d: Michael Anderson. USA., *Logan's Run*, William F. Nolan, Novel

LOGAN'S RUN 1977 d: Robert Day. USA., *Logan's Run*, William F. Nolan, Novel

LOGNEREN 1970 d: Knud Leif Thomsen. DNM., *Logneren*, Martin A. Hansen, 1950, Novel

LOHENGRIN 1936 d: Nunzio MalasommA. ITL., *Lohengrin*, Aldo de Benedetti, Play

LOHENGRIN 1947 d: Max Calandri. ITL., *Lohengrin*, Richard Wagner, Weimar 1850, Opera

Loi a l'Ouest de Pecos, La see ALL'OVEST DI SACRAMENTO (1971).

LOI DES RUES, LA 1956 d: Ralph Habib. FRN., *La Loi Des Rues*, Auguste le Breton, Novel

Loi du Nord, La see LA PISTE DU NORD (1939).

LOI DU PRINTEMPS, LA 1942 d: Jacques Daniel-Norman. FRN., *Les Petits*, Lucien Nepoty, Play

LOI DU SURVIVANT, LA 1966 d: Jose Giovanni. FRN., *La Loi du Survivant*, Jose Giovanni, Novel

LOI, LA 1958 d: Jules Dassin. FRN/ITL., *La Loi*, Roger Vailland, 1957, Novel

Loi Sacree, La see JEUNES FILLES EN DETRESSE (1939).

LOIN DES YEUX, PRES DU COEUR 1915 d: Louis Le Forestier. FRN., *Loin Des Yeux Pres du Coeur*, Pierre Mael, Novel

LOIN DU FOYER 1917 d: Pierre Bressol. FRN., *The Open House*, William Bates

LOJZICKA 1936 d: Miroslav Cikan. CZC., *Lojzicka*, Jiri Balda, Jara Kohout, Opera

LOKIS 1969 d: Janusz Majewski. PLN., *Lokis*, Prosper Merimee, 1869, Short Story

LOLA 1914 d: James Young. USA., *Lola*, Owen Davis, New York 1911, Play

Lola Goes Abroad see LA LOLA SE VA A LOS PUERTOS (1947).

LOLA MONTES 1955 d: Max Ophuls. FRN/GRM., *Lola Montes*, Cecil Saint-Laurent, Novel

Lola Montez see LOLA MONTES (1955).

LOLA SE VA A LOS PUERTOS, LA 1947 d: Juan de OrdunA. SPN., *Lola Se Va a Los Puertos*, Antonio Machado Y Ruiz, Manuel Machado Y Ruiz, 1929, Play

LOLITA 1962 d: Stanley Kubrick. UKN/USA., *Lolita*, Vladimir Nabokov, Paris 1955, Novel

LOLITA 1997 d: Adrian Lyne. USA/FRN., *Lolita*, Vladimir Nabokov, Paris 1955, Novel

Lollipop see ASFALTO SELVAGEM (1964).

LOMBARDI, LTD. 1919 d: Jack Conway. USA., *Lombardi, Ltd.*, Fanny Hatton, Frederic Hatton, New York 1917, Play

Lon Manach Rebels, The see LES REVOLTES DE LOMANACH (1953).

LONDON ASSURANCE 1913 d: Lawrence McGill. USA., *London Assurance*, Dion Boucicault, London 1841, Play

LONDON BELONGS TO ME 1948 d: Sidney Gilliat. UKN., *London Belongs to Me*, Norman Collins, Novel

LONDON BY NIGHT 1913 d: Alexander Butler?. UKN., *London By Night*, Charles Selby, Play

LONDON BY NIGHT 1937 d: Wilhelm Thiele. USA., *The Umbrella*, Will Scott, Play

London Counterfeiter, The see DER FALSCHER VON LONDON (1961).

LONDON LOVE 1926 d: Manning Haynes. UKN., *The Whirlpool*, Arthur Applin, Novel

LONDON NOBODY KNOWS, THE 1968 d: Norman Cohen. UKN., *The London Nobody Knows*, Geoffrey Fletcher, Book

LONDON PRIDE 1920 d: Harold Shaw. UKN., *London Pride*, A. Neil Lyons, Gladys Unger, London 1916, Play

LONDONDERRY AIR, THE 1938 d: Alex Bryce. UKN., *The Londonderry Air*, Rachel Field, Play

LONDRA CHIAMA POLO NORD 1957 d: Duilio Coletti. ITL., *London Calling North Pole*, H. J. Giskes, Novel

LONE COWBOY, THE 1933 d: Paul Sloane. USA., *Lone Cowboy*, Will James, New York 1930, Autobiography

Lone Duck at Sunset see LUOXIA GUWU (1932).

Lone Eagle, The see THE EAGLE (1925).

LONE FIGHTER 1923 d: Albert Russell. USA., *Certain Lee*, Keene Thompson, Story

LONE GUN, THE 1954 d: Ray Nazarro. USA., *Adios My Texas*, L. L. Foreman, Story

LONE HAND, THE 1922 d: B. Reeves Eason, Nat Ross. USA., *Laramie Ladd*, Ralph Cummins, Story

LONE STAR RANGER, THE 1919 d: J. Gordon Edwards. USA., *The Lone Star Ranger*, Zane Grey, New York 1915, Novel

LONE STAR RANGER, THE 1923 d: Lambert Hillyer. USA., *The Lone Star Ranger*, Zane Grey, New York 1915, Novel

LONE STAR RANGER, THE 1930 d: A. F. Erickson. USA., *The Lone Star Ranger*, Zane Grey, New York 1915, Novel

LONE STAR RANGER, THE 1941 d: James Tinling. USA., *The Lone Star Ranger*, Zane Grey, New York 1915, Novel

LONE STAR RUSH, THE 1915 d: Edmund Mitchell. USA., *The Lone Star Rush*, Edmund Mitchell, London 1902, Novel

LONE TEXAN, THE 1959 d: Paul Landres. USA., *The Lone Texan*, James Landis, Novel

Lone White Sail, The see BYELEYET PARUS ODINOKY (1937).

LONE WOLF IN PARIS, THE 1938 d: Albert S. Rogell. USA., *The Lone Wolf Returns*, Louis Joseph Vance, New York 1923, Novel

LONE WOLF RETURNS, THE 1926 d: Ralph Ince. USA., *The Lone Wolf Returns*, Louis Joseph Vance, New York 1923, Novel

LONE WOLF RETURNS, THE 1935 d: R. William Neill. USA., *The Lone Wolf Returns*, Louis Joseph Vance, New York 1923, Novel

LONE WOLF, THE 1917 d: Herbert Brenon. USA., *The Lone Wolf*, Louis Joseph Vance, London 1914, Novel

Lone Wolf, The see THE FALSE FACES (1919).

LONE WOLF, THE 1924 d: Stanner E. V. Taylor. USA., *The Lone Wolf*, Louis Joseph Vance, London 1914, Novel

Lone Wolf, The see THE LONE WOLF IN PARIS (1938).

Lone Wolf, The see BIRYUK (1979).

Lone Wolf's Last Adventure see THE LONE WOLF (1924).

Lone Wolf's Son, The see **CHEATERS AT PLAY** (1932).

LONELINESS OF THE LONG DISTANCE RUNNER, THE 1962 d: Tony Richardson. UKN., *The Loneliness of the Long-Distance Runner*, Alan Sillitoe, London 1959, Short Story

LONELY ARE THE BRAVE 1962 d: David Miller. USA., *Brave Cowboy*, Edward Abbey, New York 1956, Novel

Lonely Bachelor, The see **THE NOBLE BACHELOR** (1921).

LONELY GUY, THE 1984 d: Arthur Hiller. USA., *The Lonely Guy's Book of Life*, Bruce Jay Friedman, Novel

Lonely Heart, The see **THE MUSIC LOVERS** (1970).

Lonely Hearts see **KOFUKU** (1981).

LONELY LADY OF GROSVENOR SQUARE, THE 1922 d: Sinclair Hill. UKN., *The Lonely Lady of Grosvenor Square*, Mrs. Henry de La Pasture, Novel

LONELY LADY, THE 1983 d: Peter Sasdy. USA., *The Lonely Lady*, Harold Robbins, Novel

Lonely Lane see **HOROKI** (1962).

LONELY PASSION OF JUDITH HEARNE, THE 1987 d: Jack Clayton. UKN., *The Lonely Passion of Judith Hearne*, Brian Moore, 1955, Novel

LONELY PROFESSION, THE 1969 d: Douglas Heyes. USA., *The Twelfth of Never*, Douglas Heyes, Novel

LONELY ROAD, THE 1936 d: James Flood. UKN., *The Lonely Road*, Nevil Shute, 1932, Novel

LONELY VILLA, THE 1909 d: D. W. Griffith. USA., *Au Telephone*, Andre de Lorde, Play

Lonely White Sail see **BYELEYET PARUS ODINOKY** (1937).

Lonely Wife, The see **CHARULATA** (1964).

LONELY WIVES 1931 d: Russell MacK. USA., *Tanzanwaltz*, Pordes Milo, Walter Schutt, E. Urban, Berlin 1912, Play

Lonely Woman, The see **VIAGGIO IN ITALIA** (1953).

Lonely Woman, The see **CHARULATA** (1964).

Lonely Woman, The see **NO ENCONTRE ROSAS PARA MI MADRE** (1972).

LONELYHEARTS 1958 d: Vincent J. Donehue. USA., *Miss Lonelyhearts*, Nathanael West, New York 1933, Novel

LONESOME DOVE 1988 d: Simon Wincer. USA., *Lonesome Dove*, Larry McMurtry, Novel

LONESOME ROAD, THE 1917 d: David Smith. USA., *The Lonesome Road*, O. Henry, Short Story

LONESOME TRAIL, THE 1914 d: Colin Campbell. USA., *The Lonesome Trail*, B. M. Bower, Book

LONESOME TRAIL, THE 1955 d: Richard Bartlett. USA., *Silent Reckoning*, Gordon D. Shirreffs, Story

Long Ago Ladies see **CHATTERBOX** (1936).

Long Ago Tomorrow see **THE RAGING MOON** (1970).

LONG AND THE SHORT AND THE TALL, THE 1960 d: Leslie Norman. UKN., *The Long and the Short and the Tall*, Willis Hall, London 1959, Play

LONG ARM OF MANNISTER, THE 1919 d: Bertram Bracken. USA., *The Long Arm of Mannister*, E. Phillips Oppenheim, Boston 1908, Novel

Long Blue Road, The see **LA GRANDE STRADA AZZURRA** (1957).

LONG CHANCE, THE 1915 d: Edward J. Le Saint. USA., *The Long Chance*, Peter B. Kyne, New York 1914, Novel

LONG CHANCE, THE 1922 d: Jack Conway. USA., *The Long Chance*, Peter B. Kyne, New York 1914, Novel

Long Dark Night, The see **THE PACK** (1977).

LONG DAY'S DYING, THE 1968 d: Peter Collinson. UKN., *The Long Day's Dying*, Alan White, London 1965, Novel

LONG DAY'S JOURNEY INTO NIGHT 1962 d: Sidney Lumet. USA., *Long Day's Journey Into Night*, Eugene O'Neill, New York 1956, Play

LONG DAY'S JOURNEY INTO NIGHT 1996 d: David Wellington. CND., *Long Day's Journey Into Night*, Eugene O'Neill, New York 1956, Play

Long Fight, The see **THE CAPTAIN OF THE GRAY HORSE TROOP** (1917).

LONG GOODBYE, THE 1973 d: Robert Altman. USA., *The Long Goodbye*, Raymond Chandler, 1953, Novel

LONG GRAY LINE, THE 1955 d: John Ford. USA., *Bringing Up the Brass*, Nardi Reeder Campion, Martin Maher, 1951, Book

Long Hard Night, The see **THE PACK** (1977).

LONG HAUL, THE 1957 d: Ken Hughes. UKN., *The Long Haul*, Mervyn Mills, Novel

LONG HOLE, THE 1924 d: Andrew P. Wilson. UKN., *The Long Hole*, P. G. Wodehouse, Short Story

LONG HOT SUMMER, THE 1958 d: Martin Ritt. USA., *Barn Burning*, William Faulkner, 1939, Short Story, *The Hamlet*, William Faulkner, 1940, Novel, *The Spotted Horses*, William Faulkner, 1933, Short Story

LONG JOHN SILVER 1954 d: Byron Haskin. ASL., *Treasure Island*, Robert Louis Stevenson, London 1883, Novel

Long John Silver Returns to Treasure Island see **LONG JOHN SILVER** (1954).

LONG JOURNEY BACK 1978 d: Mel Damski. USA., Judith Ramsey, Article

LONG KNIFE, THE 1958 d: Montgomery Tully. UKN., *The Long Night*, Seldon Truss, Novel

LONG LANE'S TURNING, THE 1919 d: Louis W. Chaudet. USA., *The Long Lane's Turning*, Hallie Erminie Rives, New York 1917, Novel

LONG LIVE THE KING 1923 d: Victor Schertzinger. USA., *Long Live the King*, Mary Roberts Rinehart, Boston 1917, Novel

Long, Long Trail, The see **THE RAMBLIN' KID** (1923).

LONG, LONG TRAIL, THE 1929 d: Arthur Rosson. USA., *The Ramblin' Kid*, Earl Wayland Bowman, Indianapolis 1920, Novel

LONG, LONG TRAILER, THE 1953 d: Vincente Minnelli. USA., *The Long Long Trailer*, Clinton Twiss, 1951, Novel

LONG LOST FATHER 1934 d: Ernest B. Schoedsack. USA., *Long Lost Father*, Gladys Bronwyn Stern, New York 1933, Novel

LONG MEMORY, THE 1953 d: Robert Hamer. UKN., *The Long Memory*, Howard Clewes, Novel

Long Night of '43, The see **LA LUNGA NOTTE DEL '43** (1960).

LONG NIGHT, THE 1947 d: Anatole Litvak. USA., Jacques Viot, Story

Long Ride from Hell, A see **VIVO PER LA TUA MORTE** (1968).

Long Ride Home, The see **A TIME FOR KILLING** (1967).

Long Saturday Night, The see **VIVEMENT DIMANCHE** (1983).

LONG SHIFT, THE 1915. USA., *The Long Shift*, Eugene Manlove Rhodes, Short Story

LONG SHIPS, THE 1964 d: Jack Cardiff. UKN/YGS., *Rode Orm Sjofarara I Vasterled*, Frans Gunnar Bengtsson, Stockholm 1941, Novel

Long Shot see **WILD HORSE HANK** (1978).

Long Shot, The see **TIGERS DON'T CRY** (1976).

LONG STRIKE, THE 1912 d: Herbert Brenon. USA., *The Long Strike*, Dion Boucicault, Story

Long Twilight see **HOSSZU ALKONY** (1997).

LONG VOYAGE HOME, THE 1940 d: John Ford. USA., *S.S. Glencairn*, Eugene O'Neill, 1919, Plays

LONG WAIT, THE 1954 d: Victor Saville. USA., *The Long Wait*, Mickey Spillane, 1951, Novel

Long Way Round, The see **TOLLER HECHT AUF KRUMMEN TOUREN** (1961).

LONG WAY, THE 1914 d: Charles J. Brabin. USA., *The Long Way*, Mary Imlay Taylor, Novel

Long Weekend, The see **EL PUENTE** (1977).

LONGEST DAY, THE 1962 d: Andrew Marton, Gerd Oswald. USA., *The Longest Day: June 6 1944*, Cornelius Ryan, New York 1959, Novel

LONGEST HUNDRED MILES, THE 1967 d: Don Weis. USA., Hennie Leon, Story

LONGEST NIGHT, THE 1936 d: Errol Taggart. USA., *The Whispering Window*, Cortland Fitzsimmons, New York 1936, Novel

Longest Spur, The see **HOT SPUR** (1968).

Longhelder Fur Pittsville see **PITTSVILLE - EINE SAFE VOLL BLUT** (1974).

Longing for Love see **AI NO KAWAKI** (1967).

Longing for the Sea see **LANGTAN TILL HAVET** (1931).

LONGS MANTEAUX, LES 1985 d: Gilles Behat. FRN/ARG., *Les Longs Manteaux*, G.-J. Arnaud, Novel

LONGXU GOU 1952 d: XIan Qun. CHN., *Longxu Gou*, Shu Qingchun, 1950, Play

Look After Amelia see **OCCUPE-TOI D'AMELIE** (1949).

LOOK BACK IN ANGER 1959 d: Tony Richardson. UKN., *Look Back in Anger*, John Osborne, London 1956, Play

LOOK BACK IN ANGER 1989 d: David Jones. UKN., *Look Back in Anger*, John Osborne, London 1956, Play

Look Before You Leap see **ALL'S FAIR IN LOVE** (1921).

LOOK FOR THE SILVER LINING 1949 d: David Butler. USA., *The Life of Marilyn Miller*, Bert Kalmar, Harry Ruby, Book

Look Out, the Doctor's About! see **VIZITA! POZOR** (1981).

Looking After Sandy see **BAD LITTLE ANGEL** (1939).

Looking for a Live One see **THE CEMETERY CLUB** (1993).

Looking for Eileen see **ZOEKEN NAAR EILEEN** (1987).

LOOKING FOR MIRACLES 1991 d: Kevin Sullivan. CND., *Looking for Miracles*, A. E. Hochner, Novel

LOOKING FOR MR. GOODBAR 1977 d: Richard Brooks. USA., *Looking for Mr. Goodbar*, Judith Rossner, Novel

Looking for Paradise see **FACCIAMO PARADISO** (1995).

LOOKING FORWARD 1910 d: Theodore Marston. USA., *Looking Forward*, James Oliver Curwood, Short Story

LOOKING FORWARD 1933 d: Clarence Brown. USA., *Service*, C. L. Anthony, London 1932, Play

LOOKING GLASS WAR, THE 1969 d: Frank R. Pierson. UKN., *The Looking Glass War*, John le Carre, London 1965, Novel

LOONEY LOVE AFFAIR, A 1915 d: Horace Davey. USA., *A Looney Love Affair*, Neal Burns, Story

LOOPHOLE 1981 d: John Quested. UKN., *Loophole*, Robert Pollock, Novel

LOOSE ANKLES 1930 d: Ted Wilde. USA., *Loose Ankles*, Sam Janney, New York 1926, Play

LOOSE CHANGE 1978 d: Jules Irving. USA., *Loose Change*, Sara Davidson, Novel

LOOSE ENDS 1930 d: Norman Walker, Miles Mander. UKN., *Loose Ends*, Dion Titheradge, London 1926, Play

Loosening and Tightening see **OLDAS ES KOTES** (1963).

LOOT 1919 d: William C. Dowlan. USA., *Loot*, Arthur Somers Roche, Indianapolis 1916, Novel

LOOT 1970 d: Silvio Narizzano. UKN., *Loot*, Joe Orton, 1967, Play

Loot. Give Me Money, Honey! see **LOOT** (1970).

Looters, The see **ESTOUFFADE A LA CARAIBE** (1966).

Looting Looters see **THE LOCAL BAD MAN** (1932).

LOPEZ, LE BANDIT 1930 d: John Daumery. FRN., *The Bad Man*, Porter Emerson Browne, New York 1920, Play

LORD AND LADY ALGY 1919 d: Harry Beaumont. USA., *Lord and Lady Algy*, R. C. Carton, New York 1903, Play

Lord and Master see **SWAMI** (1977).

Lord Arthur Savile's Crime see **LE CRIME DE LORD ARTHUR SAVILE** (1921).

LORD ARTHUR SAVILE'S CRIME 1960 d: Alan Cooke. UKN., *Lord Arthur Savile's Crime*, Oscar Wilde, 1891, Short Story

LORD BABS 1932 d: Walter Forde. UKN., *Lord Babs*, Keble Howard, London 1928, Play

LORD BARRINGTON'S ESTATE 1915 d: William C. Dowlan. USA., *Lord Barrington's Estate*, Leonora Dowlan, Story

LORD BYRON OF BROADWAY 1930 d: William Nigh, Harry Beaumont. USA., *Lord Byron of Broadway*, Nell Martin, New York 1928, Novel

LORD CAMBER'S LADIES 1932 d: Benn W. Levy. UKN., *The Case of Lady Camber*, Horace Annesley Vachell, London 1915, Play

LORD CHUMLEY 1914 d: James Kirkwood. USA., *Lord Chumley*, David Belasco, Cecil B. de Mille, New York 1888, Play

LORD EDGWARE DIES 1934 d: Henry Edwards. UKN., *Lord Edgware Dies*, Agatha Christie, Novel

LORD JIM 1925 d: Victor Fleming. USA., *Lord Jim*, Joseph Conrad, London 1900, Novel

LORD JIM 1965 d: Richard Brooks. UKN/USA., *Lord Jim*, Joseph Conrad, London 1900, Novel

LORD JOHN IN NEW YORK 1915 d: Edward J. Le Saint. USA., *Lord John in New York*, Alice Muriel Williamson, Charles Norris Williamson, 1915, Short Story

LORD LOVE A DUCK 1966 d: George Axelrod. USA., *Lord Love a Duck*, Al Hine, New York 1961, Novel

LORD LOVELAND DISCOVERS AMERICA 1916 d: Arthur Maude. USA., *Lord Loveland Discovers America*, Alice Muriel Williamson, Charles Norris Williamson, New York 1910, Novel

Lord of Love and Power, The see **PRITHVI VALLABH** (1924).

LORD OF THE FLIES 1963 d: Peter Brook. UKN., *Lord of the Flies*, William Golding, London 1954, Novel

LORD OF THE FLIES 1990 d: Harry Hook. USA., *Lord of the Flies*, William Golding, London 1954, Novel

LORD OF THE FLIES 1990 d: Vladimir Tulkin. KZK., *Lord of the Flies*, William Golding, London 1954, Novel

LORD OF THE MANOR 1933 d: Henry Edwards. UKN., *Lord of the Manor*, John Hastings Turner, 1928, Play

LORD OF THE RINGS 1978 d: Ralph Bakshi. USA., *Lord of the Rings*, J. R. R. Tolkien, 1954-55, Novel

LORD RICHARD IN THE PANTRY 1930 d: Walter Forde. UKN., *Lord Richard in the Pantry*, Martin Swayne, Novel

Lordly Estate, A see **V PANSKEM STAVU** (1927).

LORDS OF DISCIPLINE, THE 1983 d: Franc Roddam. UKN/USA., *The Lords of Discipline*, Pat Conroy, Novel

LORDS OF HIGH DECISION, THE 1916 d: John Harvey. USA., *Lords of High Decision*, Meredith Nicholson, New York 1909, Novel

Lords of Treason see **SECRET HONOR** (1984).

Lord's Referee, The see **SILK HAT KID** (1935).

LORENZACCIO 1911. ITL/FRN., *Lorenzaccio*, Alfred de Musset, 1834, Novel

LORENZACCIO 1918 d: Giuseppe de Liguoro. ITL., *Lorenzaccio*, Alfred de Musset, 1834, Novel

LORENZACCIO 1989 d: Jean-Paul Carrere. FRN., *Lorenzaccio*, Alfred de Musset, 1834, Novel

LORENZACCIO 1989 d: Alexandre TartA. FRN., *Lorenzaccio*, Alfred de Musset, 1834, Novel

LORENZACCIO 1991 d: Georges Lavaudant. FRN., *Lorenzaccio*, Alfred de Musset, 1834, Novel

Lorenzo see **LORENZACCIO** (1911).

Lorenzo Il Magnifico see **LORENZACCIO** (1911).

LORETANSKE ZVONKY 1929 d: M. J. Krnansky. CZC., *Zlocin V Lorete*, Karel Ladislav Kukla, Novel

LORNA DOONE 1911 d: Theodore Marston. USA., *Lorna Doone*, R. D. Blackmore, 1869, Novel

LORNA DOONE 1912 d: Wilfred Noy. UKN., *Lorna Doone*, R. D. Blackmore, 1869, Novel

LORNA DOONE 1915 d: J. Farrell MacDonald. USA., *Lorna Doone*, R. D. Blackmore, 1869, Novel

LORNA DOONE 1920 d: H. Lisle Lucoque. UKN., *Lorna Doone*, R. D. Blackmore, 1869, Novel

LORNA DOONE 1922 d: Maurice Tourneur. USA., *Lorna Doone*, R. D. Blackmore, 1869, Novel

LORNA DOONE 1935 d: Basil Dean. UKN., *Lorna Doone*, R. D. Blackmore, 1869, Novel

LORNA DOONE 1951 d: Phil Karlson. USA., *Lorna Doone*, R. D. Blackmore, 1869, Novel

LORNA DOONE 1990 d: Andrew Grieve. UKN., *Lorna Doone*, R. D. Blackmore, 1869, Novel

Lorry, The see **KAMIONAT** (1980).

LORSQUE L'ENFANT PARAIT 1956 d: Michel Boisrond. FRN., *Lorsque l'Enfant Parait*, Andre Roussin, 1952, Play

LORSQU'UNE FEMME VEUT 1918 d: Georges MoncA. FRN., *Lorsqu'une Femme Veut*, Octave Pradels, Play

Los Angeles Without Maps see **L.A. WITHOUT A MAP** (1998).

LOS QUE NO FUIMOS A LA GUERRA 1961 d: Julio Diamante. SPN., *Los Que No Fuimos a la Guerre*, Wenceslao Fernandez Florez, 1930, Novel

LOSER TAKES ALL 1956 d: Ken Annakin. UKN., *Loser Takes All*, Graham Greene, 1955, Novel

LOSER TAKES ALL 1989 d: James Scott. UKN., *Loser Takes All*, Graham Greene, 1955, Novel

Losing Eloise see **LET'S ELOPE** (1919).

Loss of Innocence see **THE GREENGAGE SUMMER** (1961).

LOST - A WIFE 1925 d: William C. de Mille. USA., *Banco!*, Alfred Savoir, Paris 1920, Play

Lost and Won see **WHEN DREAMS COME TRUE** (1929).

Lost Army, The see **POPIOLY** (1966).

LOST AT SEA 1926 d: Louis J. Gasnier. USA., *Mainstream*, Louis Joseph Vance, Story

Lost Atlantis see **L' ATLANTIDE** (1921).

Lost Atlantis see **DIE HERRIN VON ATLANTIS** (1932).

LOST BATTALION, THE 1921. USA., *The Lost Chord*, Arthur Sullivan, Song

LOST BOUNDARIES 1949 d: Alfred L. Werker. USA., W. L. White, Article

Lost Child No. 312 see **SUCHKIND 312** (1955).

LOST CHORD, THE 1918. USA., *The Lost Chord*, Adelaide Anne Procter, 1877, Poem

LOST COMMAND 1966 d: Mark Robson. USA., *Les Centurions*, Jean Larteguy, Paris 1960, Novel

LOST CONTINENT, THE 1968 d: Michael Carreras, Leslie Norman (Uncredited). UKN., *Uncharted Seas*, Dennis Wheatley, London 1938, Novel

Lost Ecstasy see **I TAKE THIS WOMAN** (1931).

Lost Eyes see **LOS OJOS PERDIDOS** (1966).

LOST FOR WORDS 1998 d: Alan J. W. Bell. UKN., *Lost for Words*, Deric Longden, Book

Lost Forest, The see **PADUREA SPINZURATILOR** (1965).

Lost Honor of Katherina Blum, The see **DIE VERLORENE EHRE DER KATHERINA BLUM** (1975).

Lost Honor of Kathryn Beck, The see **ACT OF PASSION** (1984).

LOST HORIZON 1937 d: Frank CaprA. USA., *Lost Horizon*, James Hilton, New York 1933, Novel

LOST HORIZON 1973 d: Charles Jarrott. USA., *Lost Horizon*, James Hilton, New York 1933, Novel

Lost Horizon of Shangri-la see **LOST HORIZON** (1937).

LOST HOUSE, THE 1915 d: W. Christy Cabanne. USA., *The Lost House*, Richard Harding Davis, 1911, Short Story

Lost Illusion, The see **THE FALLEN IDOL** (1948).

Lost Illusions see **ELVESZETT ILLUZIOK** (1983).

LOST IN THE STARS 1974 d: Daniel Mann. USA., *Cry the Beloved Country*, Alan Paton, 1948, Novel

Lost in the Wilderness see **UEMURA NAOMI MONOGATARI** (1985).

Lost Kingdom, The see **L'AMANTE DELLA CITTA SEPOLTA ANTINEA** (1961).

Lost Lady see **THE LADY VANISHES** (1938).

LOST LADY, A 1924 d: Harry Beaumont. USA., *A Lost Lady*, Willa Cather, New York 1923, Novel

LOST LADY, A 1934 d: Alfred E. Green. USA., *A Lost Lady*, Willa Cather, New York 1923, Novel

LOST LANGUAGE OF CRANES, THE 1991 d: Nigel Finch. UKN., *The Lost Language of Cranes*, David Leavitt, Novel

LOST LEADER, A 1922 d: George Ridgwell. UKN., *A Lost Leader*, E. Phillips Oppenheim, London 1906, Novel

Lost Letter, A see **O SCRISOARE PIERDUTA** (1956).

Lost Man, The see **DER VERLORENE** (1951).

LOST MAN, THE 1969 d: Robert Alan Aurthur. USA., *Odd Man Out*, Frederick Lawrence Green, London 1945, Novel

Lost Men see **THE HOMICIDE SQUAD** (1931).

LOST MILLIONAIRE, THE 1913 d: Ralph Ince. USA., *The Lost Millionaire*, James Oliver Curwood, Story

LOST MOMENT, THE 1947 d: Martin Gabel. USA., *The Aspern Papers*, Henry James, 1888, Short Story

Lost My Love see **YONG SHI WO AI** (1994).

Lost Nancy Steele, The see **NANCY STEELE IS MISSING!** (1937).

LOST ON DRESS PARADE 1918 d: Martin Justice. USA., *Lost on Dress Parade*, O. Henry, Short Story

Lost on the Ice see **LIDE NA KRE** (1937).

Lost on the Western Front see **A ROMANCE IN FLANDERS** (1937).

Lost One, The see **DER VERLORENE** (1951).

Lost One, The see **TRAVIATA '53** (1953).

Lost Paradise see **SHITSURAKUEN** (1997).

LOST PARADISE, THE 1914 d: J. Searle Dawley, Oscar Apfel. USA., *Das Verlorene Paradies*, Ludwig Fulda, Berlin 1890, Play

Lost Paradise, The see **AZ ELVESZETT PARADICSOM** (1962).

LOST PATROL, THE 1929 d: Walter Summers. UKN., *Patrol*, Philip MacDonald, New York 1928, Novel

LOST PATROL, THE 1934 d: John Ford. USA., *Patrol*, Philip MacDonald, New York 1928, Novel

LOST PEOPLE, THE 1949 d: Bernard Knowles, Muriel Box. UKN., *Cockpit*, Bridget Boland, 1948, Play

LOST PHOEBE, THE 1983 d: Mel Damski. USA., *The Lost Phoebe*, Theodore Dreiser, 1916, Short Story

Lost Princess, The see **O PRINCEZNE JULINCE** (1987).

Lost Soul see **ANIMA PERSA** (1976).

Lost Soul, The see **BLUDNE DUSE** (1926).

LOST SOULS 1916. USA., *La Terribula*, George L. Knapp, Short Story

LOST SQUADRON, THE 1932 d: George Archainbaud. USA., *The Lost Squadron*, Dick Grace, New York 1932, Novel

Lost Talisman, The see **EGRI CSILLAGOK** (1968).

Lost Treasure of the Amazon see **JIVARO** (1954).

LOST WEEKEND, THE 1945 d: Billy Wilder. USA., *The Lost Weekend*, Charles Reginald Jackson, 1944, Novel

LOST WORLD: JURASSIC PARK, THE 1997 d: Steven Spielberg. USA., *The Lost World*, Michael Crichton, Novel

LOST WORLD, THE 1925 d: Harry O. Hoyt. USA., *The Lost World*, Arthur Conan Doyle, London 1912, Novel

LOST WORLD, THE 1960 d: Irwin Allen. USA., *The Lost World*, Arthur Conan Doyle, London 1912, Novel

LOST WORLD, THE 1992 d: Timothy Bond. USA., *The Lost World*, Arthur Conan Doyle, London 1912, Novel

LOTELING, DE 1974 d: Roland Verhavert. BLG., *De Loteling*, Hendrik Conscience, 1850, Novel

LOTNA 1959 d: Andrzej WajdA. PLN., *Lotna*, Wojciech Zukrowski, 1945, Short Story

LOTOSBLUTEN FUR MISS QUON 1966 d: Jurgen Roland. GRM/FRN/ITL., James Hadley Chase, Novel

LOTTA PER LA VITA, LA 1921 d: Guido Brignone. ITL., *La Lutte Pour la Vie*, Alphonse Daudet, 1889, Novel

LOTTE IN WEIMAR 1975 d: Egon Gunther. GDR., *Lotte in Weimar*, Thomas Mann, 1939, Novel

LOTTERIESCHWEDE, DER 1958 d: Joachim Kunert. GDR., *Lotterisvenken*, Martin Andersen Nexo, 1919, Short Story

LOTTERY MAN, THE 1916. USA., *The Lottery Man*, Rida Johnson Young, New York 1909, Play

LOTTERY MAN, THE 1919 d: James Cruze. USA., *The Lottery Man*, Rida Johnson Young, New York 1909, Play

Lottery Swede, The see **DER LOTTERIESCHWEDE** (1958).

Lotus Blossoms for Miss Quon see **LOTOSBLUTEN FUR MISS QUON** (1966).

LOTUS D'OR, LE 1916 d: Louis Mercanton. FRN., *Heath Hooken*, Coralie Stanton, Novel

Lotus for Miss Quon, A see **LOTOSBLUTEN FUR MISS QUON** (1966).

Loudest Whisper, The see **THE CHILDREN'S HOUR** (1961).

LOUDWATER MYSTERY, THE 1921 d: Norman MacDonald. UKN., *The Loudwater Mystery*, Edgar Jepson, Novel

Louis de Funes E Il Nonno Surgelato see **HIBERNATUS** (1969).

Louis l'Amour's the Sacketts see **THE SACKETTS** (1979).

LOUISA MAY ALCOTT'S LITTLE MEN 1998 d: Rodney Gibbons. CND., *Little Men*, Louisa May Alcott, Boston 1871, Novel

Louisa Miller see **LUISA MILLER** (1910).

LOUISE 1939 d: Abel Gance. FRN., *Louise*, Gustave Charpentier, Paris 1900, Opera

Louise see **CHERE LOUISE** (1971).

LOUISIANA 1919 d: Robert G. VignolA. USA., *Louisiana*, Frances Hodgson Burnett, New York 1919, Novel

Louisiana see **THE LOVE MART** (1927).

Louisiana see **LAZY RIVER** (1934).

Louisiana see **DRUMS O' VOODOO** (1934).

Louisiana see **LOUISIANE** (1984).

LOUISIANA PURCHASE 1941 d: Irving Cummings. USA., *Louisiana Purchase*, Morrie Ryskind, New York 1940, Musical Play

LOUISIANE 1984 d: Philippe de Broca, Jacques Demy (Uncredited). FRN/CND/ITL., *Fausse Riviere*, Maurice Denuziere, Book, *Louisiana*, Maurice Denuziere, Book

Loup Garon, Le *see* GEHETZTE MENSCHEN (1932).

LOUPEZNICI NA CHLUMU 1926 d: Milos Hajsky. CZC., *Loupeznici Na Chlumu*, Karel Leger, Short Story

LOUPEZNIK 1931 d: Josef Kodicek. CZC., *Loupeznik*, Karel Capek, Play

LOUP-GAROU, LE 1923 d: Jacques Roullet, Pierre Bressol. FRN., *Le Loup-Garou*, Alfred Machard, Novel

LOUPIOTE, LA 1908-18. FRN., *La Loupiote*, Arthur Bernede, Aristide Bruant, Novel

LOUPIOTE, LA 1922 d: Georges Hatot. FRN., *La Loupiote*, Arthur Bernede, Aristide Bruant, Novel

LOUPIOTE, LA 1936 d: Jean Kemm, Jean-Louis Bouquet. FRN., *La Loupiote*, Arthur Bernede, Aristide Bruant, Novel

LOUPS DANS LA BERGERIE, LES 1959 d: Herve Bromberger. FRN., *La Loups Dans la Bergerie*, John Amila, Novel

LOUPS ENTRE EUX, LES 1936 d: Leon Mathot. FRN., *Ceux du Deuxieme Bureau*, Charles-Robert Dumas, Novel

LOUVE SOLITAIRE, LA 1968 d: Edouard Logereau. FRN/ITL., *La Louvre Solitaire*, Albert Sainte Aube, Novel

LOUVES, LES 1956 d: Luis Saslavsky. FRN., *Les Louves*, Pierre Boileau, Thomas Narcejac, Novel

Louves, Les *see* LETTERS TO AN UNKNOWN LOVER (1985).

LOVABLE CHEAT, THE 1949 d: Richard Oswald. USA., *Mercadet*, Honore de Balzac, 1851, Play

Love *see* EVE'S DAUGHTER (1916).

LOVE 1927 d: Edmund Goulding. USA., *Anna Karenina*, Lev Nikolayevich Tolstoy, Moscow 1876, Novel

Love *see* LIEBE (1927).

Love *see* KARLEK (1952).

Love *see* LIEBE (1956).

Love *see* SZERELEM (1970).

Love *see* KARLEKEN (1980).

Love & Crime *see* RIKOS & RAKKAUS (1999).

Love 47 *see* LIEBE 47 (1949).

LOVE AFFAIR 1932 d: Thornton Freeland. USA., *Love Affair*, Ursula Parrott, 1930, Short Story

LOVE AFFAIR: THE ELEANOR & LOU GEHRIG STORY, A 1977 d: Fielder Cook. USA., *My Luke and I*, Joseph Durso, Eleanor Gehrig, Book

Love Affairs Chronicle, The *see* KRONIKA WYPADKOW MILOSNYCH (1985).

Love, Air and a Lot of Lies *see* LUFT UND LAUTER LUGEN LIEBE (1959).

LOVE ALWAYS 1996 d: Jude Pauline Eberhard. USA., *Finding Signs*, Sharlene Baker, Novel

LOVE AMONG THE ARTISTS 1979 d: Howard Baker, Marc Miller. UKN., *Love Among the Artists*, George Bernard Shaw, Novel

LOVE AND A WHIRLWIND 1922 d: Duncan MacRae, Harold Shaw. UKN., *Love and a Whirlwind*, Helen Prothero Lewis, Novel

LOVE AND DEATH ON LONG ISLAND 1997 d: Richard Kwietniowski. UKN/CND., *Love and Death on Long Island*, Gilbert Adair, Novel

Love and Deficit *see* KARLEK OCH KASSABRIST (1932).

Love and Duty *see* LIAN'AI YU YIWU (1931).

Love and Fear *see* PAURA E AMORE (1987).

LOVE AND GLORY 1924 d: Rupert Julian. USA., *We are French!*, Robert Hobart Davis, Perley Poore Sheehan, New York 1914, Novel

LOVE AND HATE 1924 d: Thomas Bentley. UKN., *Love and Hate*, W. Pett Ridge, Short Story

LOVE AND HATRED 1911. USA., *The Greater Hate*, Roy Norton, Story

Love and Kisses *see* BETWEEN US GIRLS (1942).

LOVE AND KISSES 1965 d: Ozzie Nelson. USA., *Love and Kisses*, Anita Rowe Block, New York 1963, Play

Love and Lies in the Air *see* LUFT UND LAUTER LUGEN LIEBE (1959).

Love and Loneliness *see* DEN ALLVARSAMMA LEKEN (1977).

Love and Loyalty *see* TERESA CONFALONIERI (1934).

Love and Money *see* A NOSZTY FIU ESETE TOTH MARIVAL (1960).

Love and Other Crimes *see* ALEX AND THE GYPSY (1976).

Love and Revenge in the Black Forest *see* SHENLIN ENCHOU JI (1941).

LOVE AND SACRIFICE 1936 d: Joseph Seiden. USA., *Liebe Und Leidenschaft*, Isidore Zolotarefsky, Poland 1936, Novel

Love and Sex in Rome *see* ROMA BENE (1971).

LOVE AND THE LAW 1910 d: Edwin S. Porter. USA., *David Copperfield*, Charles Dickens, London 1850, Novel

LOVE AND THE LAW 1919 d: Edgar Lewis. USA., *The Troop Train*, William Hamilton Osborne, 1918, Story

Love and Trumpets *see* LIEBE UND TROMPETENBLASEN (1925).

Love and Trumpets *see* LIEBE UND TROMPETENBLASEN (1954).

Love and War *see* HEARTBREAK (1931).

Love and War *see* WAR AND LOVE (1985).

Love and War *see* IN LOVE AND WAR (1987).

Love at Last *see* NICE GIRL? (1941).

Love at the Top *see* LE MOUTON ENRAGE (1974).

Love Ban, The *see* IT'S A 2'6" ABOVE THE GROUND WORLD (1972).

LOVE BANDIT, THE 1924 d: Dell Henderson. USA., *The Love Bandit*, Charles E. Blaney, Norman Houston, 1921, Play

LOVE BEFORE BREAKFAST 1936 d: Walter Lang. USA., *Spinster Dinner*, Faith Baldwin, 1934, Short Story

Love Begins *see* THAT MAN'S HERE AGAIN (1937).

LOVE BEGINS AT 20 1936 d: Frank McDonald. USA., *Broken Dishes*, Martin Flavin, New York 1929, Play

LOVE BURGLAR, THE 1919 d: James Cruze. USA., *One of Us*, Jack Lait, Joseph Swerling, New York 1918, Play

Love By Appointment *see* NATALE IN CASA D'APPUNTAMENTO (1976).

Love Cage, The *see* LES FELINS (1964).

LOVE CALL, THE 1919 d: Louis W. Chaudet. USA., *The Love Call*, Marjorie Benton Cooke, Short Story

Love Can't Wait *see* TWO HEADS ON A PILLOW (1934).

LOVE CAPTIVE, THE 1934 d: Max Marcin. USA., *The Humbug*, Max Marcin, New York 1929, Play

LOVE CHEAT, THE 1919 d: George Archainbaud. USA., *Le Danseur Inconnu*, Tristan Bernard, France 1909, Play

Love Circle, The *see* UNA SERA A CENA METTI (1969).

LOVE COMES ALONG 1930 d: Rupert Julian. USA., *Conchita*, Edward Knoblock, Play

LOVE CONTRACT, THE 1932 d: Herbert Selpin. UKN., *Chauffeur Antoinette*, Blum, Suzette Desty, Jean de Letraz, Play

Love, Dancing, and a Thousand Hits *see* TANZ UND 1000 SCHLAGER LIEBE (1955).

Love, Death and the Devil *see* TOD UND TEUFEL LIEBE (1934).

LOVE DOCTOR, THE 1929 d: Melville Brown. USA., *The Boomerang*, Victor Mapes, Winchell Smith, New York 1915, Play

Love Duet, The *see* BRAND IN DER OPER (1930).

LOVE 'EM AND LEAVE 'EM 1926 d: Frank Tuttle. USA., *Love 'Em and Leave 'Em*, George Abbott, John V. A. Weaver, New York 1926, Play

LOVE ETC. 1996 d: Marion Vernoux. FRN., *Talking It Over*, Julian Barnes, Novel

Love Finds a Way *see* ALIAS FRENCH GERTIE (1930).

LOVE FLOWER, THE 1920 d: D. W. Griffith. USA., *Black Beach*, Ralph Stock, 1919, Short Story

LOVE FOR LYDIA 1977 d: Tony Wharmby. UKN., *Love for Lydia*, H. E. Bates, Novel

Love Forbidden - Marriage Permitted *see* LIEBE VERBOTEN - HEIRATEN ERLAUBT (1959).

LOVE FROM A STRANGER 1937 d: Rowland V. Lee. UKN., *Philomel Cottage*, Agatha Christie, Story

LOVE FROM A STRANGER 1947 d: Richard Whorf. USA., *Philomel Cottage*, Agatha Christie, Story

Love from Paris *see* MONTPI (1957).

LOVE GAMBLE, THE 1925 d: Edward J. Le Saint. USA., *Peggy of Beacon Hill*, Maysie Greig, Boston 1924, Novel

LOVE GAMBLER, THE 1922 d: Joseph J. Franz. USA., *Where the Heat Lies*, Lillian Bennett-Thompson, George Hubbard, 1922, Short Story

LOVE HABIT, THE 1930 d: Harry Lachman. UKN., *The Love Habit*, Louis Verneuil, Play

LOVE, HONOR AND BEHAVE 1938 d: Stanley Logan. USA., *Everybody Was Very Nice*, Stephen Vincent Benet, 1936, Short Story

Love, Honor and Goodbye *see* ISADORA (1968).

LOVE, HONOR AND OBEY 1920 d: Leander de CordovA. USA., *The Tyranny of Weakness*, Charles Neville Buck, 1917, Novel

LOVE, HONOR AND OH, BABY! 1933 d: Edward Buzzell. USA., *Oh Promise Me*, Howard Lindsay, Bertrand Robinson, New York 1930, Play

LOVE, HONOR AND OH-BABY! 1940 d: Charles Lamont. USA., *No Exit*, Elizabeth Troy, Story

LOVE HUNGER, THE 1919 d: William P. S. Earle. USA., *Fran*, John Breckenridge Ellis, Indianapolis 1912, Novel

Love Image, The *see* THE FACE ON THE BARROOM FLOOR (1923).

Love in 47 *see* LIEBE 47 (1949).

Love in a Basement *see* LIVING ON LOVE (1937).

LOVE IN A COLD CLIMATE 1980 d: Donald McWhinnie. UKN., *Nancy Mitford*, Novel

Love in a Fallen City *see* QINGCHENGZHI LIAN (1984).

Love in a Hot Climate *see* SANG ET LUMIERE (1954).

LOVE IN A HURRY 1919 d: Dell Henderson. USA., *Black One-Eyed Man, a Huge*, Kenyon Gambier, 1917, Short Story

LOVE IN A WOOD 1915 d: Maurice Elvey. UKN., *As You Like It*, William Shakespeare, c1600, Play

LOVE IN AN ATTIC 1923 d: Edwin Greenwood. UKN., *The Little Milliner*, Robert Buchanan, Poem

LOVE IN EXILE 1936 d: Alfred L. Werker. UKN., *His Majesty's Pyjamas*, Gene Markey, Novel

Love in Germany, A *see* UN AMOUR EN ALLEMAGNE (1983).

Love in Rome *see* UN AMORE A ROMA (1960).

Love in Tears *see* LAUGHTER AND TEARS (1921).

LOVE IN THE AFTERNOON 1957 d: Billy Wilder. USA., *Ariane*, Claude Anet, 1933, Novel

Love in the Afternoon *see* L' AMOUR L'APRES-MIDI (1972).

LOVE IN THE DARK 1922 d: Harry Beaumont. USA., *Page Tim O'Brien*, John A. Moroso, 1922, Short Story

LOVE IN THE ROUGH 1930 d: Charles F. Reisner. USA., *Spring Fever*, Vincent Lawrence, New York 1925, Musical Play

Love in the Snow *see* YUKIGUNI (1965).

Love in the Tax Office *see* LIEBE IM FINANZAMT (1952).

Love in the Vineyard *see* ILS SONT DANS LES VIGNES (1951).

LOVE IN THE WILDERNESS 1920 d: Alexander Butler. UKN., *Love in the Wilderness*, Gertrude Page, Novel

Love Inc. *see* AMOR & CIA (1999).

LOVE INSURANCE 1920 d: Donald Crisp. USA., *Love Insurance*, Earl Derr Biggers, Indianapolis 1914, Novel

LOVE IS A BALL 1962 d: David Swift. USA., *The Grand Duke and Mr. Pimm*, Lindsay Hardy, New York 1959, Novel

Love Is a Day's Work *see* LA GIORNATA BALORDA (1960).

Love Is a Dog from Hell *see* CRAZY LOVE (1986).

LOVE IS A MANY-SPLENDORED THING 1955 d: Henry King. USA., *A Many Splendored Thing*, Han Suyin, 1952, Novel

LOVE IS A RACKET 1932 d: William A. Wellman. USA., *Love Is a Racket*, Rian James, New York 1931, Novel

Love Is a Racket *see* L' ATHLETE INCOMPLET (1932).

Love Is My Profession *see* EN CAS DE MALHEUR (1958).

LOVE IS NEVER SILENT 1985 d: Joseph Sargent. USA., *In This Sign*, Joanne Greenberg, Novel

LOVE IS ON THE AIR 1937 d: Nick Grinde. USA., *Hi Nellie*, Roy Chanslor, Story

Love Is Only a Word *see* LIEBE IST NUR EIN WORT (1971).

Love Is Red *see* ROT IST DIE LIEBE (1957).

Love Is Something Tender *see* IO SONO MIA (1978).

Love Is When You Make It *see* LE BEL AGE (1958).

Love Lead Them Through Life *see* ZIVOTEM VEDLA JE LASKA (1928).

Love Led Them Through Life *see* ZIVOTEM VEDLA JE LASKA (1928).

Love Letter *see* RABU RETA (1959).

LOVE LETTERS 1924 d: David Soloman. USA., *Morocco Box*, Frederick Jackson, 1923, Short Story

LOVE LETTERS 1945 d: William Dieterle. USA., *Pity My Simplicity*, Chris Massie, Novel

Love Letters from a Portuguese Nun *see* DIE LIEBESBRIEFE EINER PORTUGIESISCHEN NONNE (1977).

Love Letters of a Portuguese Nun *see* DIE LIEBESBRIEFE EINER PORTUGIESISCHEN NONNE (1977).

LOVE LETTERS OF A STAR 1936 d: Lewis R. Foster, Milton Carruth. USA., *The Case of the Constant God*, Rufus King, 1936, Short Story

LOVE LIES 1931 d: Lupino Lane. UKN., *Love Lies*, Stanley Lupino, Arthur Rigby, Musical Play

Love Lies Bleeding *see* THE STRANGE LOVE OF MARTHA IVERS (1946).

Love Like That, A *see* BREAKFAST FOR TWO (1937).

LOVE, LIVE AND LAUGH 1929 d: William K. Howard. USA., *The Hurdy-Gurdy Man*, Leroy Clemens, John B. Hymer, 1922, Play

LOVE MACHINE, THE 1971 d: Jack Haley Jr. USA., *The Love machine*, Jacqueline Susann, Novel

LOVE MAGGY 1921 d: Fred Leroy Granville. UKN., *Love Maggy*, Countess Barcynska, Novel

Love Makers, The *see* LA VIACCIA (1961).

LOVE MAKES 'EM WILD 1927 d: Albert Ray. USA., *Willie the Worm*, Florence Ryerson, 1926, Short Story

Love, Marriage and Divorce *see* A HOUSE DIVIDED (1919).

LOVE MART, THE 1927 d: George Fitzmaurice. USA., *The Code of Victor Jallot*, Edward Childs Carpenter, Philadelphia 1907, Novel

LOVE MATCH, THE 1955 d: David Paltenghi. UKN., *The Love Match*, Glenn Melvyn, London 1953, Play

Love Mates *see* FINNS DOM? ANGLAR (1961).

LOVE ME AND THE WORLD IS MINE 1928 d: E. A. Dupont. USA., *Die Geschichte von Der Hannerl Und Ihren Liebhabern*, Rudolf Hans Bartsch, Leipzig 1913, Novel

Love Me for Myself Alone *see* THE SQUARE DECEIVER (1917).

Love Me Or Love My Cow *see* YUAN NU HE NIU CHI NAN (1994).

Love Me, Take Me, Pay Me *see* NANA (1970).

LOVE ME TONIGHT 1932 d: Rouben Mamoulian. USA., *Le Tailleur Au Chateau*, Paul Armont, Leopold Marchand, Paris 1924, Play

LOVE NEST 1951 d: Joseph M. Newman. USA., *The Reluctant Landlord*, Scott Corbett, 1950, Novel

LOVE NEVER DIES 1921 d: King Vidor. USA., *The Cottage of Delight*, William Nathaniel Harben, New York 1919, Novel

Love Never Dies *see* LILAC TIME (1928).

Love of a Clown (Pagliacci) *see* I PAGLIACCI (1949).

Love of a Patriot *see* BARBARA FRIETCHIE (1924).

Love of a Woman, The *see* CLAIR DE FEMME (1979).

Love of Jeanne Ney, The *see* DIE LIEBE DER JEANNE NEY (1927).

Love of Madame Sand, The *see* A SONG TO REMEMBER (1945).

Love of Miss Vera, The *see* LASKA SLECNY VERY (1922).

Love of Perdition *see* AMOR DE PERDICAO (1977).

LOVE OF PIERRE LAROSSE, THE 1914 d: Theodore Marston. USA., *The Love of Pierre Larosse*, J. Herbert Chestnut, Story

Love of Sumako the Actress, The *see* JOYU SUMAKO NO KOI (1947).

LOVE OF SUNYA, THE 1927 d: Albert Parker. USA., *Eyes of Youth*, Charles Guernon, Max Marcin, New York 1917, Play

Love of Women *see* SINGED (1927).

Love on a Budget *see* PLAY GIRL (1932).

Love on a Pillow *see* LE REPOS DU GUERRIER (1962).

LOVE ON THE DOLE 1941 d: John Baxter. UKN., *Love on the Dole*, Walter Greenwood, Novel

LOVE ON THE RUN 1936 d: W. S. Van Dyke. USA., *Beauty and the Beat*, Julian Brodie, Alan Green, 1936, Short Story

LOVE ON THE SPOT 1932 d: Graham Cutts. UKN., *Three of a Kind*, H. C. McNeile ("Sapper"), Novel

Love Or Limelight *see* THE SKYROCKET (1926).

LOVE PARADE, THE 1929 d: Ernst Lubitsch. USA., *Le Prince Consort*, Jules Chancel, Leon Xanrof, 1919, Play

LOVE PAST THIRTY 1934 d: Vin Moore. USA., *Love Past Thirty*, Priscilla Wayne, New York 1932, Novel

LOVE PHILTRE OF IKEY SCHOENSTEIN, THE 1917 d: Thomas R. Mills. USA., *The Love Philtre of Ikey Schoenstein*, O. Henry, Short Story

Love Play *see* LA RECREATION (1961).

Love Problems *see* L' ETA DEL MALESSERE (1968).

LOVE RACE, THE 1931 d: Lupino Lane, Pat Morton. UKN., *The Love Race*, Stanley Lupino, London 1930, Musical Play

LOVE RACKET, THE 1929 d: William A. Seiter. USA., *The Woman on the Jury*, Bernard K. Burns, New York 1923, Play

Love Re-Conquered *see* LA GIOCONDA (1912).

Love Root, The *see* LA MANDRAGOLA (1965).

LOVE ROUTE, THE 1915 d: Allan Dwan. USA., *The Love Route*, Edward Peple, New York 1906, Play

LOVE SHE SOUGHT, THE 1990 d: Joseph Sargent. USA., *A Green Journey*, John Hassler, Book

Love Should Be Guarded *see* ASYA (1977).

Love Song *see* LET'S DO IT AGAIN (1953).

LOVE SPECIAL, THE 1921 d: Frank Urson. USA., *The Daughter of a Magnate*, Frank Hamilton Spearman, New York 1903, Novel

Love Specialist, The *see* LA RAGAZZA DEL PALIO (1957).

Love Spray *see* QING HAI LANG HUA (1991).

Love Starved *see* YOUNG BRIDE (1932).

Love Storm, The *see* CAPE FORLORN (1930).

Love Storms *see* CAPE FORLORN (1930).

Love Story *see* DOUCE (1943).

LOVE STORY 1944 d: Leslie Arliss. UKN., *Love Story*, J. W. Drawbell, Novel

LOVE STORY 1970 d: Arthur Hiller. USA., *Love Story*, Erich Segal, 1970, Novel

Love Story, A *see* EINE LIEBESGESCHICHTE (1954).

LOVE STORY OF ALIETTE BRUNTON, THE 1924 d: Maurice Elvey. UKN., *The Love Story of Aliette Brunton*, Gilbert Frankau, Novel

Love Story of Mr. Gilfil *see* MR. GILFIL'S LOVE STORY (1920).

LOVE STREAMS 1983 d: John Cassavetes. USA., *Love Streams*, Ted Allan, Play

LOVE SUBLIME, A 1917 d: Tod Browning, Wilfred Lucas. USA., *Orpheus*, Samuel Hopkins Adams, 1916, Short Story

Love Synod, The *see* DAS LIEBESKONZIL (1981).

Love Test, The *see* TWO CAN PLAY (1926).

Love Trail, The *see* THE DOP DOCTOR (1915).

LOVE UNDER FIRE 1937 d: George Marshall. USA., *The Fugitives*, Walter Hackett, London 1936, Play

Love Under the Crucifix *see* OGHIN-SAMA (1960).

LOVE UP THE POLE 1936 d: Clifford Gulliver. UKN., *Love Up the Pole*, Herbert Sargent, Con West, 1935, Play

LOVE! VALOUR! COMPASSION! 1997 d: Joe Mantello. USA., *Love! Valour! Compassion!*, Terrence McNally, Play

Love Walked in *see* THE BITTER END (1997).

LOVE WATCHES 1918 d: Henry Houry. USA., *L'Amour Veille*, Gaston Arman de Caillavet, Robert de Flers, Paris 1907, Play

LOVE WITH A PERFECT STRANGER 1986 d: Desmond Davis. UKN., *Love With a Perfect Stranger*, Pamela Wallace, Novel

Love With a Spirit *see* CHI NAN KUANG NU LIANG SHI QING (1993).

Love Without Illusions *see* LIEBE OHNE ILLUSION (1955).

LOVE WITHOUT QUESTION 1920 d: B. A. Rolfe. USA., *The Abandoned Room*, Wadsworth Camp, New York 1917, Novel

Love Without Reason *see* MERRILY WE LIVE (1938).

LOVED ONE, THE 1965 d: Tony Richardson. USA., *The Loved One*, Evelyn Waugh, Boston 1948, Novel

Loveless Woman, A *see* UNA MUJER SIN AMOR (1951).

Lovelorn Minstrel, The *see* ASHIK KERIB (1988).

Lovely Lola *see* LA BELLA LOLA (1962).

Lovely to Look at *see* THIN ICE (1937).

LOVELY TO LOOK AT 1952 d: Mervyn Leroy, Vincente Minnelli (Uncredited). USA., *Gowns By Roberta*, Alice Duer Miller, New York 1933, Novel

Love-Nights in the Taiga *see* LIEBESNACHTE IN DER TAIGA (1967).

Lover Boy *see* KNAVE OF HEARTS (1954).

Lover Boy *see* L' AMANT DE POCHE (1977).

Lover Come Back *see* NEW MOON (1940).

Lover for the Summer, A *see* UNE FILLE POUR L'ETE (1960).

LOVER OF CAMILLE, THE 1924 d: Harry Beaumont. USA., *Deburau*, Sacha Guitry, Play

Lover of the Great Bear, The *see* L' AMANTE DELL'ORSA MAGGIORE (1971).

Lover, The *see* HAME'AHEV (1985).

Lover, The *see* L' AMANT (1992).

LOVERS? 1927 d: John M. Stahl. USA., *El Gran Galeoto*, Jose Echegaray, Madrid 1881, Play

Lovers *see* AMANTI (1968).

LOVERS AND OTHER STRANGERS 1970 d: Cy Howard. USA., *Lovers and Other Strangers*, Joseph Bologna, Renee Taylor, New York 1968, Play

LOVER'S EXILE, THE 1980 d: Marty Gross. CND., *Meido No Hikyaku (the Courier to Hell)*, Monzaemon Chikamatsu, Play

Lovers, Happy Lovers *see* KNAVE OF HEARTS (1954).

Lovers in Paris *see* POT-BOUILLE (1957).

LOVERS IN QUARANTINE 1925 d: Frank Tuttle. USA., *Quarantine*, F. Tennyson Jesse, New York 1924, Play

LOVER'S ISLAND 1925 d: Henri Diamant-Berger. USA., *Lover's Island*, T. Howard Kelly, Short Story

LOVERS' LANE 1924 d: Phil Rosen, William Beaudine (Uncredited). USA., *Lovers' Lane*, Clyde Fitch, Boston 1915, Play

Lovers Must Learn *see* ROME ADVENTURE (1962).

Lover's Net *see* LES AMANTS DU TAGE (1955).

LOVER'S OATH, A 1925 d: Ferdinand P. Earle. USA., *The Rubaiyat of Omar Khayyam*, Edward Fitzgerald, London 1899, Book

Lovers of Lisbon, The *see* LES AMANTS DU TAGE (1955).

Lovers of Marona, The *see* KOCHANKOWIE Z MARONY (1966).

Lovers of Montparnasse, The *see* MONTPARNASSE 19 (1957).

Lovers of Paris *see* POT-BOUILLE (1957).

Lovers of Toledo, The *see* LES AMANTS DE TOLEDE (1953).

Lovers on a Tightrope *see* LA CORDE RAIDE (1959).

Lovers' Suicide in Sonezaki *see* SONEZAKI SHINJU (1978).

Lovers, The *see* LES AMANTS (1958).

Loves - Passions - Betrayals *see* DAR SVATEBNI NOCI (1926).

LOVE'S A LUXURY 1952 d: Francis Searle. UKN., *Love's a Luxury*, Edward V. Hole, Guy Paxton, Play

LOVE'S BLINDNESS 1926 d: John Francis Dillon. USA., *Love's Blindness*, Elinor Glyn, New York 1925, Novel

LOVE'S BOOMERANG 1916 d: P. C. Hartigan. USA., *Perpetua; Or the Way to Treat a Woman*, Dion Clayton Calthrop, New York 1911, Novel

Love's Boomerang *see* PERPETUA (1922).

LOVE'S CONQUEST 1918 d: Edward Jose. USA., *Gismonda*, Victorien Sardou, Paris 1894, Play

LOVE'S CRUCIBLE 1916 d: Emile Chautard. USA., *The Point of View*, Jules Eckert Goodman, New York 1912, Play

Love's Crucifixion *see* MARTER DER LIEBE (1928).

LOVE'S GREATEST MISTAKE 1927 d: A. Edward Sutherland. USA., *Love's Greatest Mistake*, Frederic Arnold Kummer, New York 1927, Novel

LOVE'S HARVEST 1920 d: Howard M. Mitchell. USA., *His Harvest*, Pearl Doles Bell, New York 1915, Novel

Love's Legacy *see* **THE YOKE** (1915).

LOVES OF A MUGHAL PRINCE, THE 1928 d: Charu Chandra Roy, Prafulla Roy. IND., *Anarkali*, Imtiaz Ali Taj, Play

Loves of Actress Sumako, The *see* **JOYU SUMAKO NO KOI** (1947).

Loves of Ariane, The *see* **ARIANE** (1931).

LOVES OF CARMEN, THE 1927 d: Raoul Walsh. USA., *Carmen*, Prosper Merimee, Paris 1846, Novel

LOVES OF CARMEN, THE 1948 d: Charles Vidor. USA., *Carmen*, Prosper Merimee, Paris 1846, Novel

Loves of Colleen Bawn, The *see* **THE COLLEEN BAWN** (1924).

Loves of Isadora, The *see* **ISADORA** (1968).

Loves of Jeanne Ney, The *see* **DIE LIEBE DER JEANNE NEY** (1927).

LOVES OF JOANNA GODDEN, THE 1947 d: Charles Frend, Robert Hamer. UKN., *Joanna Godden*, Sheila Kaye-Smith, Novel

Loves of Kacenka Strnadova, The *see* **LASKY KACENKY STRNADOVE** (1926).

LOVES OF LETTY, THE 1920 d: Frank Lloyd. USA., *Letty*, Arthur Wing Pinero, London 1903, Play

Loves of Madame Dubarry, The *see* **I GIVE MY HEART** (1935).

Loves of Salammbo, The *see* **SALAMBO** (1961).

Loves of Sumako the Actress, The *see* **JOYU SUMAKO NO KOI** (1947).

Loves of the Angels, The *see* **GLI AMORI DEGLI ANGELI** (1910).

LOVE'S OPTION 1928 d: George Pearson. UKN., *Love's Option*, Douglas Newton, Novel

LOVE'S REDEMPTION 1921 d: Albert Parker. USA., *On Principal*, Andrew Soutar, 1918, Short Story

Love's Sacrifice *see* **DIE DURCHGANGERIN** (1928).

Love's Story *see* **POVESTEA DRAGOSTEI** (1976).

Love's Western Flight *see* **CHILDREN OF FATE** (1914).

LOVE'S WILDERNESS 1924 d: Robert Z. Leonard. USA., *Wilderness*, Helen Campbell, Story

Lovesick on the Moselle *see* **MOSELFAHRT AUS LIEBESKUMMER** (1953).

LOVEY: A CIRCLE OF CHILDREN, PART II 1978 d: Jud Taylor. USA., *Lovey a Very Special Child*, Mary MacCracken, Book

LOVEY MARY 1926 d: King Baggot. USA., *Lovey Mary*, Alice Hegan Rice, New York 1903, Novel

Loviisa *see* **NISKAVUOREN NUORIEMANTA LOVIISA** (1946).

Loviisa - Unga Vardinnan Pa Niskavuori *see* **NISKAVUOREN NUORIEMANTA LOVIISA** (1946).

LOVIISA, NISKAVUOREN NUORIEMANTA 1946 d: Valentin VaalA. FNL., *Niskavuoren Nuori Emanta*, Hella Wuolijoki, 1940, Play

LOVIN' MOLLY 1973 d: Sidney Lumet. USA., *Leaving Cheyenne*, Larry McMurtry, 1963, Novel

LOVIN' THE LADIES 1930 d: Melville Brown. USA., *I Love You*, William le Baron, New York 1919, Play

LOVING 1970 d: Irvin Kershner. USA., *Ltd. Brooks Wilson*, J. M. Ryan, New York 1966, Novel

Loving Couples *see* **ALSKANDE PAR** (1964).

LOVING LIES 1924 d: W. S. Van Dyke. USA., *The Harbor Bar*, Peter B. Kyne, 1914, Short Story

Loving Servant, The *see* **LA SERVANTE AIMANTE** (1996).

Loving Walter *see* **WALTER** (1982).

LOVING YOU 1957 d: Hal Kanter. USA., *A Call from Mitch Miller*, Mary Agnes Thompson, Short Story

Lowe von Babylon, Der *see* **LAS RUINAS DE BABILONIA** (1959).

Lower Depths, The *see* **LES BAS-FONDS** (1936).

Lower Depths, The *see* **DONZOKO** (1957).

Lowland *see* **TIEFLAND** (1954).

LOWLAND CINDERELLA, A 1921 d: Sidney Morgan. UKN., *A Lowland Cinderella*, S. R. Crockett, Novel

Lowly City *see* **NEECHA NAGAR** (1946).

Loyal 47 of the Genroku Era, The *see* **GENROKU CHUSHINGURA PART I** (1941).

Loyal 47, The *see* **GENROKU CHUSHINGURA PART I** (1941).

Loyal Forty-Seven Ronin, The *see* **CHUSHINGURA** (1962).

LOYAL HEART 1946 d: Oswald Mitchell. UKN., *Beth the Sheepdog*, Ernest Lewis, Novel

Loyal Infantry, The *see* **LA FIEL INFANTERIA** (1959).

LOYALTIES 1933 d: Basil Dean. UKN., *Loyalties*, John Galsworthy, London 1922, Play

LOYALTY 1918 d: Jack Pratt. USA., Ray Lewis, Novel

LOZANA ANDALUZA, LA 1976 d: Vicente EscrivA. SPN., *El Retrato de la Lozana Andaluza*, Francisco Delicado, 1528, Novel

L-SHAPED ROOM, THE 1962 d: Bryan Forbes. UKN., *The L-Shaped Room*, Lynne Reid Banks, London 1960, Novel

Lu *see* **DIE TOTE VON BEVERLY HILLS** (1964).

LU 1983 d: Chen Lizhou. CHN., *Gold*, Tian Fen, Novel

LU LIANG YING XIONG 1950 d: Lu Ban, Yi Ling. CHN., *Lu Liang Ying XIong*, Ma Feng, Novel

Lubov Yarovaya *see* **LYUBOV YAROVAYA** (1970).

LUCE CHE SI SPEGNE, LA 1915 d: Umberto Paradisi. ITL., *The Light That Failed*, Rudyard Kipling, New York 1890, Novel

LUCE DEL MONDO, LA 1935 d: Gennaro Righelli. ITL., *Mater Admirabilis*, Lucio d'Ambra, Novel

LUCERNA 1925 d: Carl Lamac. CZC., *Lucerna*, Alois Jirasek, Play

LUCERNA 1938 d: Carl Lamac. CZC., *Lucerna*, Alois Jirasek, Play

LUCIA 1998 d: Don Boyd. UKN., *The Bride of Lammermoor*, Sir Walter Scott, 1819, Novel

LUCIA DI LAMMERMOOR 1908 d. ITL., *The Bride of Lammermoor*, Sir Walter Scott, 1819, Novel

LUCIA DI LAMMERMOOR 1910 d: Mario Caserini. ITL., *The Bride of Lammermoor*, Sir Walter Scott, 1819, Novel

LUCIA DI LAMMERMOOR 1948 d: Piero Ballerini. ITL., *Lucia Di Lammermoor*, Salvatore Cammarano, Gaetano Donizetti, 1835, Opera

LUCIA MCCARTNEY, UMA GAROTA DE PROGRAMA 1971 d: David Neves. BRZ., *O Caso de F.a.*, Rubem Fonseca, 1969, Short Story, *Lucia McCartney*, Rubem Fonseca, 1969, Short Story

LUCIE 1979 d: Jan Erik During. NRW., *Lucie*, Amalie Skram, 1888, Novel

LUCIE AUBRAC 1997 d: Claude Berri. FRN., *Ils Partiront Dans l'Ivresse*, Lucie Aubrac, Book

LUCILE 1912 d: Theodore Marston. USA., *Lucile*, Owen Meredith, Poem

LUCILE 1923 d: Georges MoncA. FRN., *Lucile*, Cyril Berger, Short Story

Lucio Flavio *see* **O PASSAGEIRO DA AGONIA LUCIO FLAVIO** (1978).

LUCIO FLAVIO, O PASSAGEIRO DA AGONIA 1978 d: Hector Babenco. BRZ., *O Passageiro Da Agonia Lucio Flavio*, Jose Louzeiro, 1975, Novel

LUCIOLA, O ANJO PECADOR 1975 d: Alfredo Sternheim. BRZ., *Luciola*, Jose Martiniano de Alencar, 1862, Short Story

LUCK 1923 d: C. C. Burr. USA., *Luck*, Jackson Gregory, Short Story

Luck Comes Out of the Clouds *see* **AMPHITRYON** (1935).

LUCK IN PAWN 1919 d: Walter Edwards. USA., *Luck in Pawn*, Marvin Taylor, New York 1919, Play

LUCK OF A SAILOR, THE 1934 d: Robert Milton. UKN., *Contraband*, Horton Giddy, Play

Luck of Barry Lyndon, The *see* **BARRY LYNDON** (1975).

LUCK OF GERALDINE LAIRD, THE 1920 d: Edward Sloman. USA., *The Luck of Geraldine Laird*, Kathleen Norris, 1919, Novel

LUCK OF GINGER COFFEY, THE 1959 d: Harvey Hart. CND., *The Luck of Ginger Coffey*, Brian Moore, Boston 1960, Novel

LUCK OF GINGER COFFEY, THE 1964 d: Irvin Kershner. CND/USA., *The Luck of Ginger Coffey*, Brian Moore, Boston 1960, Novel

LUCK OF ROARING CAMP, THE 1910 d: Edwin S. Porter. USA., *The Luck of Roaring Camp*, Bret Harte, 1868, Short Story

LUCK OF ROARING CAMP, THE 1937 d: Irvin V. Willat. USA., *The Luck of Roaring Camp*, Bret Harte, 1868, Short Story

LUCK OF THE IRISH, THE 1920 d: Allan Dwan. USA., *The Luck of the Irish*, Harold MacGrath, New York 1917, Novel

LUCK OF THE IRISH, THE 1935 d: Donovan Pedelty. UKN., *The Luck of the Irish*, Victor Haddick, Novel

LUCK OF THE IRISH, THE 1948 d: Henry Koster. USA., *There Was a Little Man*, Constance Jones, Guy Jones, Novel

LUCK OF THE NAVY 1938 d: Norman Lee. UKN., *The Luck of the Navy*, Clifford Mills, London 1918, Play

LUCK OF THE NAVY, THE 1927 d: Fred Paul. UKN., *The Luck of the Navy*, Clifford Mills, London 1918, Play

LUCKIEST GIRL IN THE WORLD, THE 1936 d: Edward Buzzell. USA., *Kitchen Privileges*, Anne Jordan, 1935, Short Story

Lucky 13 *see* **UNA SU TREDICI** (1969).

LUCKY CARSON 1921 d: Wilfred North. USA., *Salvage*, Aquila Kempster, New York 1906, Novel

LUCKY GIRL 1932 d: Gene Gerrard, Frank Miller. UKN., *Mr. Abdulla*, Reginald Berkeley, Douglas Furber, Play

LUCKY JIM 1957 d: John Boulting. UKN., *Lucky Jim*, Kingsley Amis, 1953, Novel

LUCKY JO 1964 d: Michel Deville. FRN., *Main Pleine*, Pierre Lesou, Novel

LUCKY LOSER 1934 d: Reginald Denham. UKN., *The Big Sweep*, Matthew Brennan, Play

Lucky Nicky Cain *see* **I'LL GET YOU FOR THIS** (1951).

LUCKY NIGHT 1939 d: Norman Taurog. USA., *Lucky Night*, Oliver Claxton, 1935, Short Story

LUCKY PARTNERS 1940 d: Lewis Milestone. USA., *Bonne Chance*, Sacha Guitry, Short Story

Lucky Ralston *see* **LAW AND ORDER** (1940).

LUCKY STAR 1929 d: Frank Borzage. USA., *Three Episodes in the Life of Timothy Osborn*, Tristram Tupper, 1927, Short Story

LUCKY STIFF, THE 1949 d: Lewis R. Foster. USA., *The Lucky Stiff*, Craig Rice, Novel

LUCRECE BORGIA 1935 d: Abel Gance. FRN., *Lucrece Borgia*, Victor Hugo, Paris 1833, Play

LUCRECIA BORGIA 1947 d: Luis Bayon HerrerA. ARG., *Lucrece Borgia*, Victor Hugo, Paris 1833, Play

Lucretia Borgia *see* **THE ETERNAL SIN** (1917).

Lucretia Borgia *see* **LUCRECE BORGIA** (1935).

LUCRETIA LOMBARD 1923 d: Jack Conway. USA., *Lucretia Lombard*, Kathleen Norris, New York 1922, Novel

Lucrezia *see* **L'AMANTE DEL DIAVOLO LUCREZIA BORGIA** (1968).

LUCREZIA BORGIA 1940 d: Hans Hinrich. ITL., *Lucrece Borgia*, Victor Hugo, Paris 1833, Play

Lucrezia Borgia -Die Tochter Des Papstes *see* **L'AMANTE DEL DIAVOLO LUCREZIA BORGIA** (1968).

LUCREZIA BORGIA, L'AMANTE DEL DIAVOLO 1968 d: Osvaldo Civirani. ITL/AUS., *Lucrece Borgia*, Victor Hugo, Paris 1833, Play

Lucrezia Borgia -the Devil's Lover *see* **L'AMANTE DEL DIAVOLO LUCREZIA BORGIA** (1968).

LUCY GALLANT 1955 d: Robert Parrish. USA., *The Life of Lucy Gallant*, Margaret Cousins, Novel

Lucy of Lammermoor *see* **LUCIA DI LAMMERMOOR** (1908).

LUDAS MATYI 1949 d: Laszlo Ranody, Kalman Nadasdy. HNG., *Ludas Matyi*, Mihaly Fazekas, 1815, Verse

LUDAS MATYI 1977 d: Attila Dargay. HNG., *Ludas Matyi*, Mihaly Fazekas, 1815, Verse

Ludmila Die Kuh *see* **KINDER DER BERGE** (1958).

Ludo *see* **MESSIEURS LUDOVIC** (1945).

LUDWIG AUF FREIERSFUSZEN 1969 d: Franz Seitz. GRM., Ludwig Thoma, Story

Ludwig Ganghofer: Der Edelweiskonig *see* **DER EDELWEISSKONIG** (1975).

LUDWIG II 1955 d: Helmut Kautner. GRM/AUS., Kadidja Wedekind, Story

Ludwig the Courter *see* **LUDWIG AUF FREIERSFUSZEN** (1969).

Ludwig Thomas Lausbubengeschichten *see* **LAUSBUBENGESCHICHTEN** (1964).

LUELLA'S LOVE STORY 1913 d: L. Rogers Lytton, James Young. USA., *Luella's Love Story*, Winnifred A. Kirkland, Story

LUFFAREN OCH RASMUS 1955 d: Rolf Husberg. SWD., Astrid Lindgren, Story

Lugar Llamada "Glory", Un see **DIE HOLLE VON MANITOBA** (1965).

LUGE, DIE 1950 d: Gustav Frohlich. GRM., *Morder Ohne Mord*, Martha Maria Gehrke, Hans Schweikart, Novel

LUGNER, DER 1961 d: Ladislao VajdA. GRM., *Der Lugner*, Hermann Shiffrin, Play

LUGNER UND DIE NONNE, DER 1967 d: Rolf Thiele, Joseph Czech. AUS., *Der Lugner Und Die Nonne*, Curt Goetz, Play

LUISA MILLER 1910. ITL., *Kabale Und Liebe*, Friedrich von Schiller, 1784, Play

LUISA MILLER 1911 d: Ugo FalenA. ITL., *Kabale Und Liebe*, Friedrich von Schiller, 1784, Play

LUISE, KONIGIN VON PREUSSEN 1931 d: Carl Froelich. GRM., *Luise*, Walter von Molo, Novel

Luise, Queen of Prussia see **KONIGIN VON PREUSSEN LUISE** (1931).

Lullaby see **THE SIN OF MADELON CLAUDET** (1931).

LULLABY OF BROADWAY 1951 d: David Butler. USA., *My Irish Molly*, Earl Baldwin, Story

Lullaby, The see **THE SIN OF MADELON CLAUDET** (1931).

Lulu see **LULU O UN RENDEZ-VOUS A MONTMARTRE** (1914).

Lulu see **DIE BUCHSE DER PANDORA** (1929).

LULU 1962 d: Rolf Thiele. AUS., *Die Buchse Der Pandora*, Frank Wedekind, 1904, Play, *Der Erdgeist*, Frank Wedekind, 1895, Play

LULU 1977 d: Ronald Chase. USA., *Die Buchse Der Pandora*, Frank Wedekind, 1904, Play

LULU 1980 d: Walerian Borowczyk. ITL/GRM/FRN., *Die Buchse Der Pandora*, Frank Wedekind, 1904, Play, *Der Erdgeist*, Frank Wedekind, 1895, Play

LULU BELLE 1948 d: Leslie Fenton. USA., *My Lulu Belle*, Charles MacArthur, Edward Sheldon, 1925, Play

LULU O UN RENDEZ-VOUS A MONTMARTRE 1914 d: Augusto GeninA. ITL., *Montmartre*, C. Delorbe, Play

LUME DELL'ALTRA CASA, IL 1920 d: Ugo Gracci. ITL., Luigi Pirandello, Short Story

Lumie Di Sicilia see **IL CROLLO** (1920).

LUMIERE QUI S'ETEINT, LA 1917 d: Louis J. Gasnier. FRN., *The Light That Failed*, Rudyard Kipling, New York 1890, Novel

LUMIKUNINGATAR 1986 d: Paivi Hartzell. FNL., *Snedronningen*, Hans Christian Andersen, 1845, Short Story

LUMINOUS MOTION 1998 d: Bette Gordon. USA., *The History of Luminous Motion*, Scott Bradfield, Novel

LUMMEL VON DER ERSTEN BANK 1. ZUR HOLLE MIT DEN PAUKERN, DIE 1968 d: Werner Jacobs. GRM., *Zur Holle Mit Den Paukern*, Alexander Wolf, Novel

LUMMOX 1930 d: Herbert Brenon. USA., *Lummox*, Fannie Hurst, New York 1923, Novel

Lumpaci the Vagabond see **LUMPAZIVAGABUNDUS** (1937).

Lumpaci Vagabundus see **LUMPAZIVAGABUNDUS** (1937).

Lumpacivagabundus see **LUMPAZIVAGABUNDUS** (1937).

LUMPAZIVAGABUNDUS 1937 d: Geza von Bolvary. AUS., *Der Bose Geist Lumpazivagabundus*, Johann Nestroy, 1835, Play

LUMPAZIVAGABUNDUS 1956 d: Franz Antel. GRM., *Der Bose Geist Lumpazivagabundus*, Johann Nestroy, 1835, Play

LUNA DE SANGRE 1950 d: Francisco Rovira BeletA. SPN., *La Familia Alvareda*, Fernan Caballero, 1856, Novel

LUNATIC AT LARGE, THE 1921 d: Henry Edwards. UKN., *The Lunatic at Large*, J. Storer Clouston, Novel

LUNATIC AT LARGE, THE 1927 d: Fred Newmeyer. USA., J. Storer Clouston, Short Stories

LUNATIC, THE 1990 d: Lol Creme. UKN/JMC., *The Lunatic*, Anthony C. Winkler, Novel

LUNCH HOUR 1962 d: James Hill. UKN., *Lunch Hour*, John Mortimer, London 1961, Play

Lunchbreak Cafe, The see **CAFE LUNCHRASTEN** (1954).

LUNE DANS LE CANIVEAU, LA 1983 d: Jean-Jacques Beineix. FRN/ITL., *The Moon in the Gutter*, David Goodis, 1954, Novel

LUNE DE FIEL 1992 d: Roman Polanski. FRN/UKN., *Lune de Fiel*, Pascal Bruckner, Novel

LUNEGARDE 1944 d: Marc Allegret. FRN., *Lunegarde*, Pierre Benoit, Novel

Lunettes d'Or, Les see **GLI OCCHIALI D'ORO** (1987).

LUNGA NOTTE DEL '43, LA 1960 d: Florestano Vancini. ITL., *Una Notte Del '43*, Giorgio Bassani, 1960, Novel

Lunga Notte Del Terrore, La see **DANZA MACABRA** (1964).

Lunga Notte Di Louise, La see **CHERE LOUISE** (1971).

Lunga Notte, La see **L' EBREO FASCISTA** (1980).

LUNGHE NOTTI DELLA GESTAPO, LE 1977 d: Fabio de Agostini. ITL., *Solstizio Di Tenebre*, Berthe von Uhland, Book

LUNGO VIAGGIO, IL 1974 d: Franco Giraldi. ITL., *Memorie Del Sottosuolo*, Fyodor Dostoyevsky, Short Story, *Il Sosia*, Fyodor Dostoyevsky, Short Story

LUNHUI 1988 d: Huang Jianxin. CHN., *Emerging from the Sea*, Wang Shuo, Novel

Lunule, La see **THE PYX** (1973).

LUO TOU XIANGZI 1982 d: Ling Zhifeng. CHN., *Luo Tou XIangzi*, Shu Qingchun, 1944, Novel

LUO XIAO LIN DE JUE XIN 1955 d: Yan Gong. CHN., *The Story of Luo XIaolin*, Zhang Tianyi, Novel

Luo XIaolin's Resolution see **LUO XIAO LIN DE JUE XIN** (1955).

Luotuo XIangzi see **LUO TOU XIANGZI** (1982).

LUOXIA GUWU 1932 d: Cheng Bugao. CHN., *Luoxia Guwu*, Zhang Henshui, Novel

LUPA, LA 1953 d: Alberto LattuadA. ITL., *La Lupa*, Giovanni Verga, 1880, Short Story

LUPA, LA 1996 d: Gabriele LaviA. ITL., *La Lupa*, Giovanni Verga, 1880, Short Story

LUPO DEI MARI, IL 1975 d: Giuseppe Vari. ITL., *The Sea Wolf*, Jack London, New York 1904, Novel

LUPO E LA SIRENETTA, IL 1918 d: Emilio Graziani-Walter. ITL., *L' Olmo E l'Edera*, Giuseppe Adami, Novel

Lupul Marilor see **DER SEEWOLF** (1971).

LURE OF CROONING WATER, THE 1920 d: Arthur Rooke. UKN., *The Lure of Crooning Water*, Marion Hill, Novel

LURE OF EGYPT, THE 1921 d: Howard Hickman. USA., *There Was a King in Egypt*, Norma Lorimer, New York 1918, Novel

LURE OF HEART'S DESIRE, THE 1916 d: Francis J. Grandon. USA., *The Spell of the Yukon*, Robert W. Service, 1907, Poem

LURE OF JADE, THE 1921 d: Colin Campbell. USA., *The House of Glass*, George M. Cohan, Max Marcin, New York 1915, Play

LURE OF LONDON, THE 1914 d: Bert Haldane?. UKN., *The Lure of London*, Arthur Applin, Play

Lure of Love, The see **LA NOTTE DELL'ALTA MAREA** (1977).

LURE OF LUXURY, THE 1918 d: Elsie Jane Wilson. USA., *The Bargain True*, Mrs. Nalbro Isadorah Bartley, Boston 1918, Novel

Lure of the Jungle, The see **PAW** (1959).

LURE OF THE MASK, THE 1915 d: Thomas Ricketts. USA., *The Lure of the Mask*, Harold MacGrath, Indianapolis 1908, Novel

LURE OF THE SWAMP, THE 1957 d: Hubert Cornfield. USA., *Hell's Our Destination*, Gil Brewer, Novel

LURE OF THE WILDERNESS 1952 d: Jean Negulesco. USA., *Swamp Water*, Vereen Bell, Novel

LURE OF WOMAN, THE 1915 d: Travers Vale. USA., *The Renegade*, Paul Armstrong, New York C.1910, Play

Lure of Women, The see **THE LURE OF WOMAN** (1915).

LURE, THE 1914 d: Alice Blache. USA., *The Lure*, George Scarborough, New York 1913, Play

LURE, THE 1933 d: Arthur Maude. UKN., *The Lure*, J. W. Sabben-Clare, Play

LURING LIGHTS, THE 1915 d: Robert G. VignolA. USA., *Anna Malleen*, George Hugh Brennan, New York 1911, Novel

LURING LIPS 1921 d: King Baggot. USA., *The Gossamer Web*, John A. Moroso, Story

LUST FOR A VAMPIRE 1970 d: Jimmy Sangster. UKN., *Carmilla*, Sheridan le Fanu, London 1872, Short Story

Lust for Evil see **PLEIN SOLEIL** (1960).

LUST FOR GOLD 1949 d: S. Sylvan Simon. USA., *Thunder God's Gold*, Barry Storm, Novel

Lust for Gold see **DUHUL AURULUI** (1974).

LUST FOR LIFE 1956 d: Vincente Minnelli. USA., *Lust for Life*, Irving Stone, 1934, Novel

LUSTIGEN WEIBER, DIE 1935 d: Carl Hoffmann. GRM., *The Merry Wives of Windsor*, William Shakespeare, c1598, Play

LUSTIGEN WEIBER VON WINDSOR, DIE 1950 d: Georg Wildhagen. GDR., *The Merry Wives of Windsor*, William Shakespeare, c1598, Play

LUSTIGEN WEIBER VON WINDSOR, DIE 1965 d: Georg Tressler. AUS/UKN., *The Merry Wives of Windsor*, William Shakespeare, c1598, Play

Lusts of the Flesh see **DIE LIEBE DER JEANNE NEY** (1927).

LUTHER 1974 d: Guy Green. UKN/USA/CND., *Luther*, John Osborne, 1961, Play

LUTHIER DE CREMONE, LE 1909 d: Andre Calmettes. FRN., *Le Luthier de Cremone*, Francois Coppee, Play

LUV 1967 d: Clive Donner. USA., *Luv*, Murray Schisgal, New York 1964, Play

Luxury Cabin see **CAMAROTE DE LUJO** (1957).

LUXURY LINER 1933 d: Lothar Mendes. USA., *Die Uberfahrt*, Gina Kaus, New York 1932, Novel

LUZ DEL FIN DEL MUNDO, LA 1971 d: Kevin Billington. SPN/USA/LCH., *Le Phare du Bout du Monde*, Jules Verne, 1905, Novel

LYDIA 1964 d: Diederik d'Ailly. CND., *Our Lady the Siren*, Stratis Myrivilis, Book

Lydia Ate the Apple see **POZEGNANIA** (1958).

LYDIA BAILEY 1952 d: Jean Negulesco. USA., *Lydia Bailey*, Kenneth Lewis Roberts, 1947, Novel

LYDIA GILMORE 1916 d: Edwin S. Porter, Hugh Ford. USA., *Lydia Gilmore*, Henry Arthur Jones, New York 1912, Play

Lynx see **RYS** (1981).

LYNX, LE 1914 d: Bernard-Deschamps. FRN., *Le Lynx*, Michel Corday, Andre Couvreur, Novel

LYONS MAIL, THE 1916 d: Fred Paul. UKN., *The Lyons Mail*, Charles Reade, London 1877, Play

LYONS MAIL, THE 1931 d: Arthur Maude. UKN., *The Lyons Mail*, Charles Reade, London 1877, Play

LYS DE LA VIE, LE 1921 d: Loie Fuller, Georgette Sorrere. FRN., *Lily of Life*, la Reine Marie de Roumanie, Novel

LYS DU MONT SAINT-MICHEL, LE 1920 d: Henry Houry, J. Sheffer. FRN., *Reve d'Amour*, Trilby, Novel

LYS ROUGE, LE 1920 d: Charles Maudru. FRN., *Le Lys Rouge*, Anatole France, Novel

Lysistrata see **LISISTRATI** (1972).

LYUBOV YAROVAYA 1953 d: Jan Frid. USS., *Lyubov Yarovaya*, Konstantin Trenyov, 1926, Play

LYUBOV YAROVAYA 1970 d: Vladimir Fetin. USS., *Lyubov Yarovaya*, Konstantin Trenyov, 1926, Play

Lyubovnitsata Na Graminya see **L' AMANTE DI GRAMIGNA** (1968).

LYUBOVYU ZA LYUBOV 1983 d: Tatyana BerezantsevA. USS., *Much Ado About Nothing*, William Shakespeare, c1598, Play

M 1931 d: Fritz Lang. GRM., Egon Jacobson, Article

M 1951 d: Joseph Losey. USA., Egon Jacobson, Article

M - Eine Stadt Sucht Einen Morder see **M** (1931).

MA CHI TE LO FARE? 1948 d: Ignazio Ferronetti. ITL., *Se Quell'Idiota Ci Pensasse.*, Silvio Benedetti, Play

MA COUSINE DE VARSOVIE 1931 d: Carmine Gallone. FRN., *Ma Cousine de Varsovie*, Louis Verneuil, Play

Ma Femme Est une Sorciere see **I MARRIED A WITCH** (1942).

Ma Femme, Ma Gosse Et Moi see **L' AMOUR EST UN JEU** (1957).

MA MAISON DE SAINT-CLOUD 1926 d: Jean Manoussi. FRN., *Anomalies*, Paul Bourget, Short Story

MA NON E UNA COSA SERIA 1936 d: Mario Camerini. ITL., *Ma Non E Una Cosa Seria*, Luigi Pirandello, 1910, Short Story

MA NUIT CHEZ MAUD 1969 d: Eric Rohmer. FRN., *Ma Nuit Chez Maud*, Eric Rohmer, 1974, Short Story

MA TANTE D'HONFLEUR 1923 d: Robert Saidreau. FRN., *Ma Tante d'Honfleur*, Paul Gavault, Play

MA TANTE D'HONFLEUR 1931 d: D. B. Maurice. FRN., *Ma Tante d'Honfleur*, Paul Gavault, Play

MA TANTE D'HONFLEUR 1948 d: Rene Jayet. FRN., *Ma Tante d'Honfleur*, Paul Gavault, Play

MA TANTE DICTATEUR 1939 d: Rene Pujol. FRN., *Maman Sabouleux*, Eugene Labiche, Marc-Michel, Play

MA ZHENHUA 1928 d: Wang Yuanlong, Zhu Shouju. CHN., *Ma Zhenhua*, Zheng Zhenqiu, Play

Maa Bhoomi *see* MAABHOOMI (1979).

MAA ON SYNTINEN LAULAU 1973 d: Rauni Mollberg. FNL., *Maa on Syntinen Laulu*, Timo K Mukka, 1964, Novel

MAABHOOMI 1979 d: Gautam Ghose. IND., *Jab Khet Jaage*, Krishnan Chander, 1948, Novel

Ma'am Chiritza *see* CUCOANA CHIRITA (1987).

Ma'am Chiritza Goes to Jassy *see* CHIRITA LA LASI (1988).

MACABRE 1958 d: William Castle. USA., *The Marble Forest*, Theo Durrant, 1951, Novel

MACAO 1952 d: Josef von Sternberg, Nicholas Ray (Uncredited). USA., Bob Williams, Story

MACAO, L'ENFER DU JEU 1939 d: Jean Delannoy. FRN., *MacAo - l'Enfer du Jeu*, Maurice Dekobra, Novel

MACARIO 1959 d: Roberto Gavaldon. MXC., *MacArio*, Ben Traven, Zurich 1950, Novel

MacArthur's Children *see* SETOUCHI SHONEN YAKYUDAN (1984).

MacArthur's Children - Part II *see* SETOUCHI SHONEN YAKYU DAN SEISHUNHEN SAIGO NO RAKUEN (1987).

MACBETH 1908 d: J. Stuart Blackton. USA., *MacBeth*, William Shakespeare, c1606, Play

MACBETH 1909 d: Mario Caserini. ITL., *MacBeth*, William Shakespeare, c1606, Play

MACBETH 1909 d: Andre Calmettes. FRN., *MacBeth*, William Shakespeare, c1606, Play

MACBETH 1911. UKN., *MacBeth*, William Shakespeare, c1606, Play

MACBETH 1916 d: John Emerson. USA., *MacBeth*, William Shakespeare, c1606, Play

MACBETH 1916 d: Gustave Labruyere. FRN., *MacBeth*, William Shakespeare, c1606, Play

MACBETH 1922 d: H. B. Parkinson. UKN., *MacBeth*, William Shakespeare, c1606, Play

MACBETH 1945 d: Henry Cass. UKN., *MacBeth*, William Shakespeare, c1606, Play

MACBETH 1946 d: David Bradley. USA., *MacBeth*, William Shakespeare, c1606, Play

MACBETH 1948 d: Orson Welles. USA., *MacBeth*, William Shakespeare, c1606, Play

MACBETH 1953 d: Charles Deane. UKN., *MacBeth*, William Shakespeare, c1606, Play

MACBETH 1954 d: George Schaefer. USA., *MacBeth*, William Shakespeare, c1606, Play

MACBETH 1961 d: George Schaefer. UKN/USA., *MacBeth*, William Shakespeare, c1606, Play

MACBETH 1966 d: Michael Simpson. UKN., *MacBeth*, William Shakespeare, c1606, Play

MACBETH 1970 d: John Gorrie. UKN., *MacBeth*, William Shakespeare, c1606, Play

MACBETH 1971 d: Roman Polanski. UKN., *MacBeth*, William Shakespeare, c1606, Play

MACBETH 1978 d: Philip Casson. UKN., *MacBeth*, William Shakespeare, c1606, Play

MACBETH 1983 d: Jack Gold. UKN., *MacBeth*, William Shakespeare, c1606, Play

MACBETH 1987 d: Pauli Pentti. FNL., *MacBeth*, William Shakespeare, c1606, Play

MACBETH 1988 d: Charles Warren. UKN., *MacBeth*, William Shakespeare, c1606, Play

MACBETH 1997 d: Jeremy Freeston. UKN., *MacBeth*, William Shakespeare, c1606, Play

MacBeth, Shakespeare's Sublime Tragedy *see* MACBETH (1908).

MacChie Di Belletto *see* UN DETECTIVE (1969).

MacDonald of the Canadian Mounties *see* PONY SOLDIER (1952).

MacHine Gun McCain *see* GLI INTOCCABILI (1969).

MACHO CALLAHAN 1970 d: Bernard L. Kowalski. USA., *MacHo Callahan*, Richard Carr, Novel

MACHORKA-MUFF 1962 d: Jean-Marie Straub, Daniele Huillet. GRM., *Hauptstadtisches Journal*, Heinrich Boll, 1957, Short Story

MACHTRAUSCH - ABER DIE LIEBE SIEGT 1942 d: Ernst Biller. SWT., *El Gran Teatro Del Mundo*, Pedro Calderon de La Barca, 1645

MACKENNA'S GOLD 1968 d: J. Lee Thompson. USA., *MacKenna's Gold*, Will Henry, New York 1963, Novel

MacKenzie Break, The *see* THE MCKENZIE BREAK (1970).

MACKINTOSH MAN, THE 1973 d: John Huston. UKN/USA., *The Freedom Trap*, Desmond Bagley, Novel

MACOMBER AFFAIR, THE 1947 d: Zoltan KordA. USA., *The Short Happy Life of Francis MacOmber*, Ernest Hemingway, 1938, Short Story

MACSKAJATEK 1974 d: Karoly Makk. HNG., *MacSkajatek*, Istvan Orkeny, 1963, Novel

MACUNAIMA 1969 d: Joaquim Pedro de Andrade. BRZ., *O Heroi Sem Nenhum Carater MacUnaima*, Mario de Andrade, 1928, Novel

MAD DANCER, THE 1925 d: Burton L. King. USA., *The Mad Dancer*, Louise Winter, 1924, Short Story

MAD DEATH, THE 1983 d: Robert Young. UKN., *The Mad Death*, Nigel Slater, Novel

MAD DOG 1976 d: Philippe MorA. ASL., *Mad Dog*, Margaret Carnegie, Novel

Mad Dog Morgan *see* MAD DOG (1976).

Mad Emperor, The *see* LE PATRIOTE (1938).

Mad Executioners, The *see* DER HENKER VON LONDON (1963).

MAD GENIUS, THE 1931 d: Michael Curtiz. USA., *The Idol*, Martin Brown, Great Neck, N.Y. 1929, Play

MAD HATTERS, THE 1935 d: Ivar Campbell. UKN., *The Only Son*, James Stewart, Short Story

MAD HOLIDAY 1936 d: George B. Seitz. USA., *Murder in a Chinese Theatre*, Joseph Stanley, Novel

Mad Honeymoon *see* ONCE TO EVERY BACHELOR (1934).

MAD HOUR 1928 d: Joseph C. Boyle. USA., *The Man and the Moment*, Elinor Glyn, New York 1914, Novel

Mad Lady of Chester, The *see* JANE EYRE (1910).

Mad Little Island *see* ROCKETS GALORE (1958).

MAD LOVE 1935 d: Karl Freund. USA., *Les Mains d'Orlac*, Maurice Renard, Paris 1920, Novel

MAD MARRIAGE, THE 1921 d: Rollin S. Sturgeon. USA., *Cinderella Jane*, Marjorie Benton Cooke, Garden City, N.Y. 1917, Novel

Mad Marriage, The *see* BAD COMPANY (1931).

MAD MARTINDALES, THE 1942 d: Alfred L. Werker. USA., Ludwig Hirschfeld, Play, *Not for Children*, Wesley Towner, Play, Dr. Edmund Wolf, Play

Mad Masquerade *see* THE WASHINGTON MASQUERADE (1932).

Mad Men of Europe *see* AN ENGLISHMAN'S HOME (1939).

Mad Queen, The *see* LOCURA DE AMOR (1948).

MAD ROOM, THE 1969 d: Bernard Girard. USA., *Ladies in Retirement*, Reginald Denham, Edward Percy, London 1939, Play

MAD WHIRL, THE 1925 d: William A. Seiter. USA., *Here's How*, Richard Washburn Child, 1924, Short Story

Madam Chirita *see* CUCOANA CHIRITA (1987).

Madam Chirita in Jassy *see* CHIRITA LA LASI (1988).

Madam la Gimp *see* LADY FOR A DAY (1933).

MADAMA BUTTERFLY 1955 d: Carmine Gallone. ITL/JPN., *Madame Butterfly*, John Luther Long, New York 1898, Play

MADAMA, LA 1976 d: Duccio Tessari. ITL., *La Madama*, Massimo Felisatti, Fabio Pittoru, Novel

Madama Musashino *see* MUSASHINO FUJIN (1951).

Madame *see* MADAME SANS-GENE (1961).

Madame and Her Niece *see* MADAME UND IHRE NICHTE (1969).

MADAME BEHAVE 1925 d: Scott Sidney. USA., Jean Arlette, Play

MADAME BO-PEEP 1917 d: Chet Withey. USA., *Madame Bo-Peep of the Ranches*, O. Henry, New York 1910, Short Story

Madame Bovary *see* UNHOLY LOVE (1932).

MADAME BOVARY 1933 d: Jean Renoir. FRN., *Madame Bovary*, Gustave Flaubert, Paris 1857, Novel

MADAME BOVARY 1937 d: Gerhard Lamprecht. GRM., *Madame Bovary*, Gustave Flaubert, Paris 1857, Novel

MADAME BOVARY 1947 d: Carlos Schlieper. ARG., *Madame Bovary*, Gustave Flaubert, Paris 1857, Novel

MADAME BOVARY 1949 d: Vincente Minnelli. USA., *Madame Bovary*, Gustave Flaubert, Paris 1857, Novel

Madame Bovary *see* DIE NACKTE BOVARY (1969).

MADAME BOVARY 1975 d: Rodney Bennett. UKN., *Madame Bovary*, Gustave Flaubert, Paris 1857, Novel

MADAME BOVARY 1979 d: Daniele d'AnzA. ITL., *Madame Bovary*, Gustave Flaubert, Paris 1857, Novel

MADAME BOVARY 1991 d: Claude Chabrol. FRN., *Madame Bovary*, Gustave Flaubert, Paris 1857, Novel

MADAME BUTTERFLY 1915 d: Sidney Olcott. USA., *Madame Butterfly*, John Luther Long, New York 1898, Novel

MADAME BUTTERFLY 1932 d: Marion Gering. USA., *Madame Butterfly*, John Luther Long, New York 1898, Novel

Madame Butterfly *see* MADAMA BUTTERFLY (1955).

MADAME BUTTERFLY 1995 d: Frederic Mitterand. FRN/JPN/GRM., *Madame Butterfly*, John Luther Long, New York 1898, Novel

Madame Coralie E C. *see* CORALIE & C. (1914).

MADAME CORENTINE 1914 d: Maurice Mariaud. FRN., *Madame Corentine*, Rene Bazin, Novel

MADAME CURIE 1943 d: Mervyn Leroy. USA., *Madame Curie*, Eve Curie, 1937, Biography

MADAME DE. 1953 d: Max Ophuls. FRN/ITL., *Madame de.*, Louise de Vilmorin, Novel

Madame du Barry *see* DU BARRY (1918).

MADAME ET LE MORT 1942 d: Louis Daquin. FRN., *Madame Et le Mort*, Pierre Very, Novel

MADAME ET SON AUTO 1958 d: Robert Vernay. FRN., *Madame Et Son Auto*, Guy Verdot, Novel

MADAME ET SON FLIRT 1945 d: Jean de Marguenat. FRN., *Cousine Lea*, Henri Falk, Novel

Madame Fifi *see* BOULE-DE-SUIF (1945).

Madame Julie *see* THE WOMAN BETWEEN (1931).

Madame Julie *see* LE FILS DE L'AUTRE (1931).

MADAME LA PRESIDENTE 1916 d: Frank Lloyd. USA., *Madame la Presidente*, Maurice Hennequin, Jose G. Levy, Pierre Veber, Paris C.1898, Play

MADAME L'AMBASSADRICE 1921 d: Ermanno Geymonat. ITL., *Madame l'Ambassadrice*, Daniel le Sueur, Novel

MADAME LOUISE 1951 d: MacLean Rogers. UKN., *Madame Louise*, Vernon Sylvaine, London 1945, Play

Madame Lucy *see* MADAME BEHAVE (1925).

MADAME NE VEUT PAS D'ENFANTS 1932 d: Constantin Landau, Hans Steinhoff. FRN., *Madame Ne Veut Pas d'Enfants*, Clement Vautel, Novel

MADAME PEACOCK 1920 d: Ray C. Smallwood. USA., *Madame Peacock*, Rita Weiman, 1919, Short Story

Madame Pimpernel *see* PARIS UNDERGROUND (1945).

MADAME PINKETTE & CO. 1917 d: Maurits H. Binger. NTH., *The Girl Who Saved His Honour*, Arthur Applin, 1913, Novel

MADAME POMPADOUR 1927 d: Herbert Wilcox. UKN., *Madame Pompadour*, Rudolph Schanzer, Ernst Welisch, Play

Madame Presidente *see* MADAME LA PRESIDENTE (1916).

MADAME RECAMIER 1920 d: Joseph Delmont. GRM., *Mme Recamier Et Ses Amis*, Edouard Herriot

Madame Rosa *see* LA VIE DEVANT SOI (1977).

MADAME SANS-GENE 1911 d: Andre Calmettes, Henri Desfontaines. FRN., *Madame Sans-Gene*, Emile Moreau, Victorien Sardou, Paris 1893, Play

MADAME SANS-GENE 1925 d: Leonce Perret. USA., *Madame Sans-Gene*, Emile Moreau, Victorien Sardou, Paris 1893, Play

MADAME SANS-GENE 1941 d: Roger Richebe. FRN., *Madame Sans-Gene*, Emile Moreau, Victorien Sardou, Paris 1893, Play

MADAME SANS-GENE 1961 d: Christian-Jaque. FRN/ITL/SPN., *Madame Sans-Gene*, Emile Moreau, Victorien Sardou, Paris 1893, Play

MADAME SHERRY 1917 d: Ralph Dean. USA., *Madame Sherry*, Otto Hauerbach, Karl Hoschna, New York 1910, Musical Play

MADAME SOUSATZKA 1989 d: John Schlesinger. UKN., *Madame Sousatzka*, Bernice Rubens, Novel

MADAME SPY 1934 d: Karl Freund. USA., *Unter Falsche Flagge*, Max W. Kimmich, Novel

MADAME TALLIEN 1911 d: Camille de Morlhon. FRN., *Madame Tallien*, Victorien Sardou, Play

MADAME TALLIEN 1916 d: Enrico Guazzoni. ITL., *Madame Tallien*, Victorien Sardou, Play

MADAME UND IHRE NICHTE 1969 d: Eberhard Schroeder. GRM., Guy de Maupassant, Novel

Madame Waleska *see* CONQUEST (1937).

MADAME X 1916 d: George F. Marion. USA., *La Femme X*, Alexandre Bisson, Paris 1908, Play

MADAME X 1920 d: Frank Lloyd. USA., *La Femme X*, Alexandre Bisson, Paris 1908, Play

MADAME X 1929 d: Lionel Barrymore. USA., *La Femme X*, Alexandre Bisson, Paris 1908, Play

MADAME X 1937 d: Sam Wood, Gustav Machaty (Uncredited). USA., *La Femme X*, Alexandre Bisson, Paris 1908, Play

MADAME X 1966 d: David Lowell Rich. USA., *La Femme X*, Alexandre Bisson, Paris 1908, Play

MADAME X 1981 d: Robert Ellis Miller. USA., *La Femme X*, Alexandre Bisson, Paris 1908, Play

MADAMIGELLA DI MAUPIN 1966 d: Mauro Bolognini. ITL/FRN/SPN., *Madamoiselle de Maupin*, Theophile Gautier, 1835-36, Play

Madcap *see* TAMING THE WILD (1936).

Madchen Aus Dem Wald, Das *see* HAXAN (1955).

MADCHEN AUS FLANDERN, EIN 1956 d: Helmut Kautner. GRM., *Engele von Loewen*, Carl Zuckmayer, 1952, Novel

MADCHEN AUS FRISCO, DAS 1927 d: Wolfgang Neff. GRM., *Das Madchen Aus Frisco*, Karl Figdor, Short Story

MADCHEN DER STRASSE, DAS 1928 d: Augusto GeninA. GRM., *Scampolo*, Dario Niccodemi, 1915, Play

MADCHEN FUR ALLES 1937 d: Carl Boese. GRM., *Madchen Fur Alles*, Hans Adler, Play

MADCHEN GEHT AN LAND, EIN 1938 d: Werner Hochbaum. GRM., *Ein Madchen Geht an Land*, Eva Leidmann, Novel

MADCHEN, HUTET EUCH! 1928 d: Valy Arnheim. GRM., *Die Kindermorderin*, H. L. Wagner, Play

Madchen Im Tigerfell, Das *see* GELIEBTE BESTIE (1959).

MADCHEN IN UNIFORM 1931 d: Leontine Sagan. GRM., *Gestern Und Heute*, Christa Winsloe, Play

MADCHEN IN UNIFORM 1958 d: Geza von Radvanyi. GRM/FRN., *Gestern Und Heute*, Christa Winsloe, Play

MADCHEN IRENE, DAS 1936 d: Reinhold Schunzel. GRM., *Das Madchen Irene*, Eva Leidmann, Play

MADCHEN MIT DEM GUTEN RUF, DAS 1938 d: Hans Schweikart. GRM., *La Locandiera*, Carlo Goldoni, 1753, Play

MADCHEN MIT DEN SCHWEFELHOLZERN, DAS 1953 d: Fritz Genschow. GRM., *Den Lille Pige Med Svovlstikkerne*, Hans Christian Andersen, 1846, Short Story

Madchen Mit Der Peitsche, Das *see* DAS GEHEIMNIS VOM BERGSEE (1951).

MADCHEN OHNE PYJAMA, DAS 1957 d: Hans Quest. GRM., *Das Madchen Ohne Pyjama*, Christian Bock, Play

Madchen Scampolo, Das *see* SCAMPOLO (1958).

MADCHEN VOM MOORHOF, DAS 1935 d: Douglas Sirk. GRM., *Tosen Fran Stormyrtorpet*, Selma Lagerlof, Stockholm 1908, Short Story

MADCHEN VOM MOORHOF, DAS 1958 d: Gustav Ucicky. GRM., *Tosen Fran Stormyrtorpet*, Selma Lagerlof, Stockholm 1908, Short Story

MADCHEN VOM PFARRHOF, DAS 1955 d: Alfred Lehner. AUS., *Der Pfarrer von Kirchfeld*, Ludwig Anzengruber, 1897, Play

Madchen von Der Strass, Das *see* DAS MADCHEN DER STRASSE (1928).

MADCHEN VON FANO, DAS 1940 d: Hans Schweikart. GRM., *Das Madchen von Fano*, Gunter Weisenborn, 1935, Novel

MADCHENJAHRE EINER KONIGIN 1954 d: Ernst MarischkA. AUS/GRM., *Madchenjahre Einer Konigin*, Sil Vara, Play

MADCHENKRIEG, DER 1977 d: Bernhard Sinkel, Alf Brustellin. GRM., *Madchenkrieg*, Manfred Bieler, 1975, Novel

MADCHENPENSIONAT 1936 d: Geza von Bolvary. AUS/HNG., *Prinzessin Dagmar*, Rudolf Brettschneider, Play

MADDALENA 1954 d: Augusto GeninA. ITL., *Servant of God*, Madeleine Masson de Belavalle, Play

MADDALENA FERAT 1920 d: Febo Mari. ITL., *Madeleine*, Emile Zola, 1865, Novel

MADDALENA. ZERO IN CONDOTTA 1940 d: Vittorio de SicA. ITL., *Magdat Kicsapja*, Laszlo Kadar, Play

MADE 1972 d: John MacKenzie. UKN., *No One Was Saved*, Howard Barker, 1970, Play

MADE IN BRITAIN 1982 d: Alan Clarke. UKN., *Made in Britain*, David Leland, Play

MADE IN U.S.A. 1966 d: Jean-Luc Godard. FRN., *Rien Dans le Coffre*, Donald E. Westlake, Novel

MADEJA DE LANA AZUL CELESTE, UNA 1964 d: Jose Luis Madrid. SPN., *Una Madeja de Lana Azul Celeste*, Jose Lopez Rubio, 1952, Play

Madel Fur Frohe Stunden, Ein *see* PHILINE (1945).

MADEL MIT DER PEITSCHE, DAS 1929 d: Carl Lamac. GRM., *Das Madel Mit Der Peitsche*, Hans H. Zerlett, Play

MADEL MIT TEMPERAMENT, EIN 1928 d: Victor Janson. GRM., *Lillebil Aus U.S.A.*, Ludwig von Wohl, Novel

MADEL WIRBELT DURCH DIE WELT, EIN 1934 d: Georg Jacoby. GRM., *Ein Madel Wirbelt Durch Die Welt*, Hans Holm, Novel

MADELEINE 1916 d: Jean Kemm. FRN., *Madeleine*, Jules Sandeau, Novel

MADELEINE DE VERCHERES 1922 d: J.-Arthur Homier. CND., *Marie-Madeleine de Vercheres Et Les Siens*, F. A. Baillarge, Novel

MADELEINE'S CHRISTMAS 1912 d: Joseph Smiley. USA., *Madeleine's Christmas*, Hugh Antoine d'Arcy, Story

MADELINE 1998 d: Daisy von Scherler Mayer. USA/GRM., *Madeline*, Ludwig Bemelmans, Book

Madelon *see* PORT OF SEVEN SEAS (1938).

Madelon of the Redwoods *see* FALSE EVIDENCE (1919).

MADELS VOM IMMENHOF, DIE 1955 d: Wolfgang Schleif. GRM., *Dick Und Dalli Und Die Ponies*, Ursula Bruns, Novel

MADEMOISELLE DE LA FERTE 1949 d: Roger Dallier. FRN., *Mademoiselle de la Ferte*, Pierre Benoit, Novel

MADEMOISELLE DE LA SEIGLIERE 1920 d: Andre Antoine, Georges DenolA. FRN., *Mademoiselle de la Seigliere*, Jules Sandeau, Novel

Mademoiselle de Maupin (Spn) *see* MADAMIGELLA DI MAUPIN (1966).

Mademoiselle Di Montecristo *see* MADEMOISELLE MONTECRISTO (1918).

MADEMOISELLE ET SON GANG 1956 d: Jean Boyer. FRN., *Mademoiselle Et Son Gang*, Rodolphe-Marie Arlaud, Novel

MADEMOISELLE FIFI 1944 d: Robert Wise. USA., *Boule de Suif*, Guy de Maupassant, 1880, Short Story, *Mademoiselle Fifi*, Guy de Maupassant, 1881, Short Story

Mademoiselle Gobette *see* LA PRESIDENTESSA (1952).

Mademoiselle Hauser *see* FRAULEIN HUSER (1940).

MADEMOISELLE JOSETTE, MA FEMME 1914 d: Andre Liabel. FRN., *Mademoiselle Josette, Ma Femme*, Robert Charvay, Paul Gavault, Play

MADEMOISELLE JOSETTE, MA FEMME 1926 d: Gaston Ravel. FRN., *Mademoiselle Josette, Ma Femme*, Robert Charvay, Paul Gavault, Play

MADEMOISELLE JOSETTE, MA FEMME 1932 d: Andre Berthomieu. FRN., *Mademoiselle Josette, Ma Femme*, Robert Charvay, Paul Gavault, Play

MADEMOISELLE JOSETTE, MA FEMME 1950 d: Andre Berthomieu. FRN., *Mademoiselle Josette, Ma Femme*, Robert Charvay, Paul Gavault, Play

Mademoiselle la Presidente *see* LA PRESIDENTESSA (1952).

MADEMOISELLE MODISTE 1926 d: Robert Z. Leonard. USA., *Mademoiselle Modiste; a Comic Opera*, Henry Martyn Blossom, Victor Herbert, New York 1905, Musical Play

Mademoiselle Modiste *see* KISS ME AGAIN (1931).

MADEMOISELLE MONTECRISTO 1918 d: Camillo de Riso. ITL., *Mademoiselle Montecristo*, Paul Mahalin, Novel

MADHOUSE 1974 d: Jim Clark. UKN/USA., *Devilday*, Angus Hall, Novel

Madicken *see* MADICKEN PA JUNIBACKEN (1979).

MADICKEN PA JUNIBACKEN 1979 d: Goran Graffman. SWD., Astrid Lindgren, Story

MADIGAN 1968 d: Don Siegel. USA., *The Commissioner*, Richard Dougherty, New York 1962, Novel

MADISON AVENUE 1962 d: H. Bruce Humberstone. USA., *The Build-Up Boys*, Jeremy Kirk, New York 1951, Novel

MADISON SQUARE ARABIAN NIGHT, A 1918 d: Ashley Miller. USA., *A Madison Square Arabian Night*, O. Henry, Short Story

Madla from the Brick-Kiln *see* MADLA Z CIHELNY (1933).

Madla from the Brickworks *see* MADLA Z CIHELNY (1933).

Madla Sings to Europe *see* MADLA ZPIVA EVROPE (1940).

MADLA Z CIHELNY 1933 d: Vladimir Slavinsky. CZC., *Madla Z Cihelny*, Olga Scheinpflugova, Play

MADLA ZPIVA EVROPE 1940 d: Vaclav Binovec. CZC., *Madla Zpiva Evrope*, Jan Wenig, Novel

Madman at War *see* SCEMO DI GUERRA (1985).

Madman of Lab 4, The *see* LE FOU DU LABO 4 (1967).

Madmen of Europe *see* AN ENGLISHMAN'S HOME (1939).

MADNESS OF KING GEORGE, THE 1994 d: Nicholas Hytner. UKN/USA., *The Madness of George III*, Alan Bennett, Play

Madness of Love *see* LOCURA DE AMOR (1948).

MADNESS OF THE HEART 1949 d: Charles Bennett. UKN., *Madness of the Heart*, Flora Sandstrom, Novel

MADNESS OF YOUTH 1923 d: Jerome Storm. USA., *Red Darkness*, George Frank Worts, 1922, Short Story

MADONA DE CEDRO, A 1968 d: Carlos CoimbrA. BRZ., *Madona de Cedro*, Antonio Callado, 1957, Novel

MADONE DES SLEEPINGS, LA 1928 d: Maurice Gleize, Marco de Gastyne. FRN., *La Madone Des Sleepings*, Maurice Dekobra, Novel

MADONE DES SLEEPINGS, LA 1955 d: Henri Diamant-Berger. FRN., *La Madone Des Sleepings*, Maurice Dekobra, Novel

MADONNA DI NEVE 1919 d: Alfredo de Antoni. ITL., *Mater Dolorosa*, Gerolamo Rovetta, 1882, Novel

MADONNA: INNOCENCE LOST 1994 d: Bradford May. USA., *Madonna: Unauthorized*, Christopher Andersen, Book

MADONNA OF THE CELLS, A 1925 d: Fred Paul. UKN., *A Madonna of the Cells*, Morley Roberts, Short Story

MADONNA OF THE SEVEN MOONS 1944 d: Arthur Crabtree. UKN., *Madonna of the Seven Moons*, Margery Lawrence, Novel

MADONNA OF THE STREETS 1924 d: Edwin Carewe. USA., *The Ragged Messenger*, William Babington Maxwell, London 1904, Novel

MADONNA OF THE STREETS 1930 d: John S. Robertson. USA., *The Ragged Messenger*, William Babington Maxwell, London 1904, Novel

MADRE, LA 1917 d: Giuseppe Sterni. ITL., *La Mere*, Santiago Rusinol I Prats, 1907, Play

Madre, La *see* PROIBITO (1955).

Madrid Front *see* CARMEN FRA I ROSSI (1939).

MADRUGADA 1957 d: Antonio Roman. SPN., *Madrugada*, Antonio Buero Vallejo, 1954, Play

MADWOMAN OF CHAILLOT, THE 1969 d: Bryan Forbes, John Huston. UKN/USA., *La Folle de Chaillot*, Jean Giraudoux, Paris 1945, Play

MAELSTROM, THE 1917 d: Paul Scardon. USA., *The Maelstrom*, Frank Froest, New York 1917, Novel

MAESTRA NORMAL, LA 1997 d: Carlos Orgambide. ARG., *La Maestra Normal*, Manuel Galvez, Novel

MAESTRINA, LA 1919 d: Eleuterio Rodolfi. ITL., *La Maestrina*, Dario Niccodemi, 1917, Play

MAESTRINA, LA 1933 d: Guido Brignone. ITL., *La Maestrina*, Dario Niccodemi, 1917, Play

MAESTRINA, LA 1942 d: Giorgio Bianchi. ITL., *La Maestrina*, Dario Niccodemi, 1917, Play

Maestro *see* IL MAESTRO (1989).

MAESTRO DI VIGEVANO, IL 1963 d: Elio Petri. ITL., *Il Maestro Di Vigevano*, Lucio Mastronardi, Novel

Maestro E Margherita, Il *see* MAJSTOR I MARGARITA (1973).

MAESTRO LANDI 1935 d: Giovacchino Forzano. ITL., *Maestro Landi*, Giovacchino Forzano, Ferdinando Paolieri, Play

Maffia Fait la Loi, La see **IL GIORNO DELLA CIVETTA** (1967).

Mafia see **IN NOME DELLA LEGGE** (1949).

Mafia see **IL GIORNO DELLA CIVETTA** (1967).

Mafia Fait la Loi, La see **IL GIORNO DELLA CIVETTA** (1967).

MAFIA PRINCESS 1986 d: Robert Collins. USA., *Mafia Princess*, Antoinette Giancana, Book

Mafia Warfare see **LA SCOUMOUNE** (1973).

MAGASISKOLA 1970 d: Istvan Gaal. HNG., *Magasiskola*, Miklos Meszoly, 1967, Short Story

MAGDA 1917 d: Emile Chautard. USA., *Heimat*, Hermann Sudermann, 1893, Play

Magda see **HEIMAT** (1938).

MAGDALENA 1920 d: Vladimir Majer. CZC., *Magdalena*, Josef Svatopluk MacHar, Novel

MAGGIE PEPPER 1919 d: Chet Withey. USA., *Maggie Pepper*, Charles Klein, New York 1911, Play

Maggiorato Fisico, Il see **VOUS PIGEZ?** (1955).

MAGIC 1978 d: Richard Attenborough. USA., *Magic*, William Goldman, 1976, Novel

Magic Bird, The see **PUTIFERIO VA ALLA GUERRA** (1968).

MAGIC BOW, THE 1946 d: Bernard Knowles. UKN., *The Magic Bow*, Manuel Komroff, Novel

MAGIC BOX, THE 1951 d: John Boulting. UKN., *Friese-Greene*, Ray Allister, Book

MAGIC CHRISTIAN, THE 1969 d: Joseph McGrath. UKN., *The Magic Christian*, Terry Southern, New York 1960, Novel

MAGIC CLOAK OF OZ, THE 1914 d: L. Frank Baum. USA., *Queen Zixi of Oz*, L. Frank Baum, Novel

Magic Donkey, The see **PEAU D'ANE** (1970).

MAGIC FIRE 1956 d: William Dieterle. USA., *Magic Fire*, Bertita Harding, 1953, Biography

MAGIC FLAME, THE 1927 d: Henry King. USA., *Konig Harlekin*, Rudolph Lothar, Munich 1904, Play

MAGIC FOUNTAIN, THE 1961 d: Allan David. USA., *Das Wasser Des Lebens*, Jacob Grimm, Wilhelm Grimm, Short Story

MAGIC GARDEN OF STANLEY SWEETHEART, THE 1970 d: Leonard Horn. USA., *The Magic Garden of Stanley Sweetheart*, Robert T. Westbrook, New York 1969, Novel

MAGIC GARDEN, THE 1927 d: James Leo Meehan. USA., *The Magic Garden*, Gene Stratton-Porter, Novel

Magic House, The see **KOUZELNY DUM** (1939).

Magic Jacket, The see **KINCSKERESO KIS KODMON** (1973).

Magic Lighter see **FYRTOJET** (1946).

MAGIC MOMENTS 1989 d: Lawrence Gordon Clark. UKN., *Magic Moments*, Nora Roberts, Novel

Magic Mountain, The see **DER ZAUBERBERG** (1981).

Magic Night see **GOODNIGHT VIENNA** (1932).

Magic Sampo, The see **SAMPO** (1959).

MAGIC SHOP, THE 1982 d: Ian Emes. UKN., *The Magic Shop*, H. G. Wells, 1905, Short Story

MAGIC SKIN, THE 1915 d: Richard Ridgely. USA., *La Peau de Chagrin*, Honore de Balzac, Paris 1831, Novel

Magic Skin, The see **DESIRE** (1920).

Magic Skin, The see **SLAVE OF DESIRE** (1923).

Magic Sword Quest for Camelot, The see **QUEST FOR CAMELOT** (1998).

MAGIC TOYSHOP, THE 1986 d: David Wheatley. UKN., *The Magic Toyshop*, Angela Carter, 1967, Novel

MAGIC WAND, THE 1922 d: George Wynn. UKN., *The Magic Wand*, George R. Sims, Poem

MAGICIAN FISHERMAN, THE 1913 d: Charles H. France. USA., *The Magician Fisherman*, A. F. Zamloch, Story

Magician of Lublin, The see **HAKOSEM MI-LUBLIN** (1978).

MAGICIAN, THE 1926 d: Rex Ingram. USA., *The Magician*, W. Somerset Maugham, London 1908, Novel

Magician, The see **DER HEXER** (1964).

Magician's Apprentice, The see **CARODEJUV UCEN** (1977).

Magicians, The see **LES MAGICIENNES** (1960).

MAGICIENNES, LES 1960 d: Serge Friedman. FRN., *Les Magiciennes*, Pierre Boileau, Thomas Narcejac, Novel

MAGICIENS, LES 1975 d: Claude Chabrol. FRN/GRM/ITL., *Les Magiciens*, Frederic Dard, Novel

MAGIE MODERNE 1931 d: Dimitri Buchowetzki. FRN., Howard Irving Young, Play

Magier, Der see **HAKOSEM MI-LUBLIN** (1978).

MAGISTRATE, THE 1921 d: Bannister Merwin. UKN., *The Magistrate*, Arthur Wing Pinero, London 1885, Play

Magistrate, The see **THOSE WERE THE DAYS** (1934).

MAGNATE OF PARADISE, THE 1915 d: Charles J. Brabin. USA., *The Magnate of Paradise*, Mary Imlay Taylor, Novel

Magnet of Doom see **L' AINE DES FERCHAUX** (1963).

MAGNETISORENS FEMTE VINTER 1999 d: Morten Henriksen. DNM/NRW/SWD., *Magnetisorens Femte Vinter*, Per Olov Enquist, Novel

Magnetist's Fifth Winter, The see **MAGNETISORENS FEMTE VINTER** (1999).

Magnificent Ambersons, The see **PAMPERED YOUTH** (1925).

MAGNIFICENT AMBERSONS, THE 1942 d: Orson Welles. USA., *The Magnificent Ambersons*, Booth Tarkington, Garden City, N.Y. 1918, Novel

MAGNIFICENT BRUTE, THE 1936 d: John G. Blystone. USA., *Big*, Owen Francis, 1934, Short Story

Magnificent Cuckold, The see **IL MAGNIFICO CORNUTO** (1964).

MAGNIFICENT FLIRT, THE 1928 d: Harry d'Abbadie d'Arrast. USA., *Maman*, Jose Germain Drouilly, Paris 1924, Play

Magnificent Jacala, The see **THE BRAZEN BEAUTY** (1918).

MAGNIFICENT LIE, THE 1931 d: Berthold Viertel. USA., *Laurels and the Lady*, Leonard Merrick, 1908, Short Story

MAGNIFICENT OBSESSION 1935 d: John M. Stahl. USA., *Magnificent Obsession*, Lloyd C. Douglas, New York 1933, Novel

MAGNIFICENT OBSESSION 1954 d: Douglas Sirk. USA., *Magnificent Obsession*, Lloyd C. Douglas, New York 1933, Novel

Magnificent Sinner see **KATJA** (1959).

MAGNIFICENT YANKEE, THE 1950 d: John Sturges. USA., *Mr. Justice Holmes*, Francis Biddle, Book

MAGNIFICO CORNUTO, IL 1964 d: Antonio Pietrangeli. ITL/FRN., *Le Cocu Magnifique*, Fernand Crommelynck, Paris 1920, Play

Magnolia see **RIVER OF ROMANCE** (1929).

MAGOKORO 1939 d: Mikio Naruse. JPN., *Magokoro*, Yojiro Ishizaka, 1939, Short Story

MAGOT DE JOSEFA, LE 1963 d: Claude Autant-LarA. FRN/ITL., *Le Magot de Josefa*, Catherine Claude, Novel

MAGUS, THE 1968 d: Guy Green. UKN., *The Magus*, John Fowles, 1965, Novel

Magyar Nabob, Egy see **EGY MAGYAR NABOB. KAPATHY ZOLTAN** (1966).

MAGYAR NABOB. KAPATHY ZOLTAN, EGY 1966 d: Zoltan Varkonyi. HNG., *Egy Magyar Nabob*, Mor Jokai, Budapest 1853, Novel

Maha Prasthaner Pathey see **MAHAPRASTHANER PATHEY** (1952).

MAHABHARATA 1989 d: Peter Brook. FRN/UKN., *Mahabharata*, Vyasa, Poem

MAHANAGAR 1963 d: Satyajit Ray. IND., *Mahanagar*, Naredranath Mitra, 1949, Short Story

MAHAPRASTHANER PATHEY 1952 d: Kartick Chattopadhyay. IND., *Mahaprasthaner Pathey*, Prabodh Kumar Sanyal, Novel

MAHAPURUSH 1965 d: Satyajit Ray. IND., *Birinchi Baba*, Rajasekhar Bose

Maharaja's Love, The see **DIE LIEBE DES MAHARADSCHA** (1936).

Mahayatra see **ANTARJALI JATRA** (1988).

MAHLIA LA METISSE 1942 d: Walter Kapps. FRN., *Mahlia la Metisse*, Jean Francoux, Novel

Maid for Murder see **SHE'LL HAVE TO GO** (1962).

MAID OF CEFN YDFA, THE 1914 d: William Haggar Jr. UKN., *The Maid of Cefn Ydfa*, James Haggar, Play

Maid of Honor see **LADY OF SECRETS** (1936).

MAID OF THE MOUNTAINS, THE 1932 d: Lupino Lane. UKN., *The Maid of the Mountains*, Frederick Lonsdale, London 1917, Musical Play

MAID OF THE SILVER SEA, A 1922 d: Guy Newall. UKN., *A Maid of the Silver Sea*, John Oxenham, Novel

Maid Pleases Me, The see **SIE GEFALLT MIR JUNGFER** (1968).

Maid Servant see **VELAIKKARI** (1949).

Maid Tine see **TINE** (1964).

Maiden and the Beast, The see **PANNA A NETVOR** (1978).

Maiden of Bezkydy, The see **DEVCICA Z BESKYD** (1944).

Maiden, The see **PANNA** (1940).

Maiden, The see **GOSPODJICA** (1980).

Maidenhood see **PANENSTVI** (1937).

Maids in Uniform see **MADCHEN IN UNIFORM** (1931).

Maids of Wilko, The see **PANNY Z WILKO** (1979).

MAIDS, THE 1975 d: Christopher Miles. UKN/CND., *Les Bonnes*, Jean Genet, 1948, Play

MAIFU 1997 d: Huang Jianxin, Yang Yazhou. CHN., *Maifu*, Fang Fang, Novel

MAIGRET A PIGALLE 1966 d: Mario Landi. ITL/FRN., *Maigret Au "Picratt's"*, Georges Simenon, 1951, Novel

Maigret E I Gangsters see **MAIGRET VOIT ROUGE** (1963).

MAIGRET ET L'AFFAIRE SAINT-FIACRE 1959 d: Jean Delannoy. FRN/ITL., *L' Affaire Saint-Fiacre*, Georges Simenon, 1932, Novel

Maigret Fait Mouche see **MAIGRET UND SEIN GROSSTER FALL** (1966).

Maigret Sets a Trap see **MAIGRET TEND UN PIEGE** (1957).

MAIGRET TEND UN PIEGE 1957 d: Jean Delannoy. FRN/ITL., *Maigret Tend un Piege*, Georges Simenon, 1955, Novel

MAIGRET UND SEIN GROSSTER FALL 1966 d: Alfred Weidenmann. AUS/ITL/FRN., *La Danseuse du Gai-Moulin*, Georges Simenon, 1931, Novel

MAIGRET VOIT ROUGE 1963 d: Gilles Grangier. FRN/ITL., *Lognon Et Les Gangsters Maigret*, Georges Simenon, 1952, Novel

MAIHIME 1951 d: Mikio Naruse. JPN., *Maihime*, Yasunari Kawabata, 1951, Short Story

MAIL ORDER BRIDE 1963 d: Burt Kennedy. USA., *Mail-Order Bride*, Van Cort, 1951, Short Story

MAIN A COUPER, LA 1974 d: Etienne Perier. FRN/ITL., *La Main a Couper*, Pierre Salva, Novel

MAIN CHANCE, THE 1964 d: John Knight. UKN., Edgar Wallace, Novel

MAIN DU DIABLE, LA 1942 d: Maurice Tourneur. FRN., *La Main de Gloire*, Gerard de Nerval, 1832, Short Story

Main Enchantee, La see **LA MAIN DU DIABLE** (1942).

MAIN STREET 1923 d: Harry Beaumont. USA., *Main Street; the Story of Carol Kennicott*, Sinclair Lewis, New York 1920, Novel

Main Street see **I MARRIED A DOCTOR** (1936).

MAIN STREET KID, THE 1948 d: R. G. Springsteen. USA., *The Main Street Kid*, Caryl Coleman, Radio Play

Main Witness, The see **GLAVNYJ SVIDETEL** (1969).

Mains d'Orlac, Les see **MAD LOVE** (1935).

MAINS D'ORLAC, LES 1959 d: Edmond T. Greville. FRN/UKN., *Les Mains d'Orlac*, Maurice Renard, Paris 1920, Novel

MAINS LIEES, LES 1955 d: Roland-Jean Quignon, Aloysius Vachet. FRN., *Mon Petit Pretre*, Pierre Lhande, Novel

MAINS SALES, LES 1951 d: Fernand Rivers. FRN., *Les Mains Sales*, Jean-Paul Sartre, 1948, Play

MAINS VENGERESSES, LES 1911 d: Georges MoncA. FRN., *Les Yeux Qui Changent*, Cyril, Froyez, Play

MAINSPRING, THE 1917 d: Henry King. USA., *The Mainspring*, Louis Joseph Vance, Short Story

MAIS N'TE PROMENE DONC PAS TOUTE NUE! 1936 d: Leo Joannon. FRN., *Mais N'te Promene Donc Pas Toute Nue!*, Georges Feydeau, Play

Mais Qu'est-Ce Qui Se Passe Dans Mon Harem? see **WAS ISCH DENN I MYM HAREM LOS?** (1937).

Mais Qui a Vu le Vent see **WHO HAS SEEN THE WIND** (1977).

MAISIE 1939 d: Edwin L. Marin. USA., *Dark Dame*, Wilson Collison, New York 1935, Novel

Maisie Was a Lady see **MAISIE** (1939).

MAISON ASSASSINEE, LA 1989 d: Georges Lautner. FRN., *La Maison Assassinee*, Pierre Magnan, Novel

MAISON AU SOLEIL, LA 1929 d: Gaston Roudes. FRN., *La Maison Au Soleil*, Raymond Clauzel, Novel

MAISON DANS LA DUNE, LA 1934 d: Pierre Billon. FRN., *La Maison Dans la Dune*, Maxence Van Der Meersch, Novel

MAISON DANS LA DUNE, LA 1952 d: Georges Lampin. FRN., *La Maison Dans la Dune*, Maxence Van Der Meersch, Novel

MAISON DANS LA FORET, LA 1922 d: Jean Legrand. FRN/GRM., *Within the Maze*, Henry Wood, Novel

MAISON D'ARGILE, LA 1918 d: Gaston Ravel. FRN., *La Maison d'Argile*, Emile Fabre, Play

MAISON DE DANSES 1930 d: Maurice Tourneur. FRN., *Maison de Danses*, Paul Reboux, Novel

MAISON DE LA FLECHE, LA 1930 d: Henri Fescourt. FRN., *The House of the Arrow*, A. E. W. Mason, London 1924, Novel

MAISON DE L'ESPION, LA 1915 d: Jacques de Baroncelli. FRN., *La Maison de l'Espion*, Jacques de Baroncelli, Novel

Maison de Poupee see **A DOLL'S HOUSE** (1972).

MAISON D'EN FACE, LA 1936 d: Christian-Jaque. FRN., *La Maison d'En Face*, Paul Nivoix, Play

MAISON DES BORIES, LA 1969 d: Jacques Doniol-Valcroze. FRN., *La Maison Des Bories*, Simone Ratel, Novel

MAISON DES HOMMES VIVANTS, LA 1929 d: Marcel Dumont, Gaston Roudes. FRN., *La Maison Des Hommes Vivants*, Claude Farrere, Novel

MAISON DES SEPT JEUNES FILLES, LA 1941 d: Albert Valentin. FRN., *La Maison Des Sept Jeunes Filles*, Georges Simenon, 1941, Novel

MAISON DU BAIGNEUR, LA 1914 d: Adrien Caillard, Georges MoncA. FRN., *La Maison du Baigneur*, Auguste Maquet, Play

Maison du Crime, La see **MINUIT QUAI DE BERCY** (1952).

MAISON DU MALTAIS, LA 1927 d: Henri Fescourt. FRN., *La Maison du Maltais*, Jean Vignaud, Novel

MAISON DU MALTAIS, LA 1938 d: Pierre Chenal. FRN., *La Maison du Maltais*, Jean Vignaud, Novel

MAISON DU MYSTERE, LA 1922 d: Alexander Volkov. FRN., *La Maison du Mystere*, Jules Mary, Novel

MAISON DU PRINTEMPS, LA 1949 d: Jacques Daroy. FRN., *La Maison du Printemps*, Fernand Millau, Play

Maison Hantee, La see **DAS GESPENSTERHAUS** (1942).

MAISON JAUNE DE RIO, LA 1930 d: Robert Peguy, Karl Grune. FRN., *Das Gelbe Haus von Rio*, Jos M. Velter, Play

MAISON SANS AMOUR, L' 1927 d: Emilien Champetier. FRN., *La Maison Des Deux Barbeaux*, Andre Theuriet, Novel

MAISON SOUS LA MER, LA 1946 d: Henri Calef. FRN., *La Maison Sous le Mer*, Paul Vialar, Novel

MAISON SOUS LES ARBRES, LA 1971 d: Rene Clement. FRN/ITL., *The Deadly Trap*, Arthur Cavanaugh, Novel

MAISON VIDE, LA 1991 d: Denys Granier-Deferre. FRN., *La Maison Vide*, Claude Gutman, Novel

MAITRE APRES DIEU 1950 d: Louis Daquin. FRN., *Maitre Apres Dieu*, Jan de Hartog, Play

MAITRE BOLBEC ET SON MARI 1934 d: Jacques Natanson. FRN., *Maitre Bolbec Et Son Mari*, Georges Berr, Louis Verneuil, Play

MAITRE DE FORGES, LE 1913 d: Henri Pouctal. FRN., *Le Maitre de Forges*, Georges Ohnet, Paris 1882, Novel

MAITRE DE FORGES, LE 1933 d: Fernand Rivers, Abel Gance. FRN., *Le Maitre de Forges*, Georges Ohnet, Paris 1882, Novel

MAITRE DE FORGES, LE 1947 d: Fernand Rivers. FRN., *Le Maitre de Forges*, Georges Ohnet, Paris 1882, Novel

Maitre du Canton, Le see **SANGO MALO** (1990).

Maja the Student of Philosophy see **FILOSOFKA MAJA** (1928).

MAJESTAT AUF ABWEGEN 1958 d: R. A. Stemmle. GRM., *Let's Play King*, Sinclair Lewis, 1931, Short Story

Majhli Didi see **MANJHLI DIDI** (1968).

MAJKA TARAKJA 1979 d: Peter Solan. CZC., *Majka Tarakja*, Maria Durickova, Novel

MAJOOR FRANS 1916 d: Maurits H. Binger. NTH., *Majoor Frans*, Anna L. G. Bosboom-Toussaint, 1874, Novel

Major and the Bulls, The see **DER MAJOR UND DIE STIERE** (1955).

MAJOR AND THE MINOR, THE 1942 d: Billy Wilder. USA., *Connie Goes Home*, Edward Childs Carpenter, Play, *Sunny Goes Home*, Fanny Kilbourne, Short Story

MAJOR BARBARA 1941 d: Gabriel Pascal, Harold French. UKN., *Major Barbara*, George Bernard Shaw, London 1905, Play

Major Frans see **MAJOOR FRANS** (1916).

MAJOR UND DIE STIERE, DER 1955 d: Eduard von Borsody. GRM., *Der Major Und Die Stiere*, Hans Venatier, Novel

MAJORATSHERR, DER 1944 d: Hans Deppe. GRM., *Der Majoratsherr*, Alfred von Hedenstjerna, Novel

Majorettes, The see **ONE BY ONE** (1986).

MAJORITY OF ONE, A 1961 d: Mervyn Leroy. USA., *A Majority of One*, Leonard Spigelgass, New York 1959, Play

MAJSTOR I MARGARITA 1973 d: Aleksandar Petrovic. YGS/ITL., *Master I Margarita*, Mikhail Bulgakov, 1967, Novel

MAKAI TENSHO 1981 d: Kinji Fukasaku. JPN., *Makai Tensho*, Hutaro Yamada, Novel

Make and Break see **TELL ME LIES** (1968).

MAKE HASTE TO LIVE 1954 d: William A. Seiter. USA., *Make Haste to Live*, Gordon Gordon, Mildred Gordon, 1950, Novel

MAKE LOVE NOT WAR - DIE LIEBESGESCHICHTE UNSERER ZEIT 1968 d: Werner Klett. GRM., *Make Love Not War - Die Liebesgeschichte Unserer Zeit*, Gunter Adrian, Novel

Make Love Not War - the Love Story of Our Time see **MAKE LOVE NOT WAR - DIE LIEBESGESCHICHTE UNSERER ZEIT** (1968).

MAKE ME A STAR! 1932 d: William Beaudine. USA., *Merton of the Movies*, Harry Leon Wilson, New York 1922, Novel

MAKE ME AN OFFER 1954 d: Cyril Frankel. UKN., *Make Me an Offer*, Wolf Mankowitz, Novel

MAKE MINE MINK 1960 d: Robert Asher. UKN., *Breath of Spring*, Peter Coke, London 1958, Play

MAKE UP 1937 d: Alfred Zeisler. UKN., *Bux*, Hans Passendorf, Novel

MAKE WAY FOR A LADY 1936 d: David Burton. USA., *Daddy and I*, Elizabeth Jordon, New York 1935, Novel

Make Way for Lila see **LAILA** (1958).

MAKE WAY FOR TOMORROW 1937 d: Leo McCarey. USA., *Years are So Long*, Josephine Lawrence, New York 1934, Novel

MAKE YOUR OWN BED 1944 d: Peter Godfrey. USA., *Make Your Own Bed*, Harriet Ford, Harvey J. O'Higgins, Play

MAKING A MAN 1922 d: Joseph Henabery. USA., *Humanizing Mr. Winsby*, Peter B. Kyne, 1915, Short Story

MAKING IT 1971 d: John Erman. USA., *Making It*, James Leigh, Novel

MAKING OF BOBBY BURNIT, THE 1914 d: Oscar Apfel. USA., *The Making of Bobby Burnit*, George Randolph Chester, New York 1909, Novel

MAKING OF MADDALENA, THE 1916 d: Frank Lloyd. USA., *The Making of Maddalena; Or the Compromise*, Mary E. Lewis, Samuel G. Lewis, Play

MAKING OF O'MALLEY, THE 1925 d: Lambert Hillyer. USA., *The Making of O'Malley*, Gerald Beaumont, 1924, Short Story

Making of O'Malley, The see **THE GREAT O'MALLEY** (1937).

Making of the World, The see **FACEREA LUMII** (1971).

MAKING THE GRADE 1921 d: Fred J. Butler. USA., *Sophie Semenoff*, Wallace Irwin, 1920, Short Story

MAKING THE GRADE 1929 d: Alfred E. Green. USA., *Making the Grade*, George Ade, 1928, Short Story

Makioka Sisters, The see **SASAMEYUKI** (1983).

MAKRA 1974 d: Tamas Renyi. HNG., *Makra*, Akos Kertesz, 1971, Novel

Mal Del Mico, La see **LA GARRA DEL MONO** (1925).

Mal Morska Vila see **MALA MORSKA VILA** (1975).

MALA CARODEJNICE 1983 d: Zdenek SmetanA. CZC/GRM., *Mala Carodejnice*, Otfried Preussler, Novel

MALA LEY, LA 1924 d: Manuel NoriegA. SPN., *La Mala Ley*, Manuel Linares Rivas, Play

MALA MORSKA VILA 1975 d: Karel KachynA. CZC., *Den Lille Haufrue*, Hans Christian Andersen, 1837, Short Story

MALA NOCHE 1987 d: Gus Van Sant Jr. USA., *Mala Noche*, Walt Curtis, Story

MALA NOVA, 'A 1920 d: Eduardo Notari, Elvira Notari. ITL., *'A Mala Nova*, Libero Bavio, 1902

MALA PASQUA 1919 d: Ignazio Lupi. ITL., *Dodici Anni Dopo*, Giovanni Grasso Sr., 1917, Play

Mala the Magnificent see **ESKIMO** (1933).

MALA YERBA 1940 d: Gabriel SoriA. MXC., *Mala Yerba*, Mariano Azuela, 1909, Novel

Malachias see **DAS WUNDER DES MALACHIAS** (1961).

MALACHI'S COVE 1974 d: Henry Herbert. UKN/CND., *The Seaweed Children*, Anthony Trollope, 1864, Short Story

MALADE IMAGINAIRE, LE 1934 d: Jaquelux, Marc MerendA. FRN., *Le Malade Imaginaire*, Moliere, 1673, Play

MALADE IMAGINAIRE, LE 1966 d: Jean Pignol. FRN., *Le Malade Imaginaire*, Moliere, 1673, Play

MALADE IMAGINAIRE, LE 1990 d: Jean-Laurent Cochet. FRN., *Le Malade Imaginaire*, Moliere, 1673, Play

MALADE IMAGINAIRE, LE 1990 d: Jacques Deschamps. FRN., *Le Malade Imaginaire*, Moliere, 1673, Play

Malaga see **MOMENT OF DANGER** (1960).

MALAJANHA 1965 d: Nitai Palit. IND., *Malajanha*, Upendra Kishore Dash, Novel

Malandro see **OPERA DO MALANDRO** (1985).

MALARPIRATER 1923 d: Gustaf Molander. SWD., *Malarpirater*, Sigfrid Siwertz, 1911, Novel

MALARPIRATER 1959 d: Per Gosta Holmgren. SWD., *Malarpirater*, Sigfrid Siwertz, 1911, Novel

MALATESTA 1964 d: Christopher Morahan. UKN., *Malatesta*, Henry de Montherlant, Play

MALATO IMMAGINARIO, IL 1979 d: Tonino Cervi. ITL., *Le Malade Imaginaire*, Moliere, 1673, Play

Malaya see **BEYOND THE BLUE HORIZON** (1942).

MALAYADAAN 1971 d: Ajay Kar. IND., *Malyadaan*, Rabindranath Tagore, 1903, Short Story

MALCASADA, LA 1926 d: Francisco Gomez Hidalgo. SPN., *La Malcasada*, Jose Luis de Lucio, F. Gomez Hidalgo, Play

Malchanceuse, La see **LA SIN VENTURA** (1923).

MALCOLM X 1992 d: Spike Lee. USA., *The Autobiography of Malcolm X*, Alex Haley, Malcolm X, Autobiography

Maldicion de Los Karnstein, La see **LA CRIPTA E L'INCUBO** (1964).

MALDONNE 1968 d: Sergio Gobbi. ITL/FRN., *Maldonne*, Pierre Boileau, Thomas Narcejac, Novel

MALE AND FEMALE 1919 d: Cecil B. de Mille. USA., *The Admirable Crichton*, J. M. Barrie, London 1902, Play

MALE ANIMAL, THE 1942 d: Elliott Nugent. USA., *The Male Animal*, Elliott Nugent, James Thurber, New York 1940, Play

Male Companion see **UN MONSIEUR DE COMPAGNIE** (1964).

Male Stesti see **VCERA NEDELE BYLA** (1938).

MALEDETTO IMBROGLIO, UN 1959 d: Pietro Germi. ITL., *Quer Pasticciaccio Brutto de Via Merulana*, Carlo Emilio Gadda, Milan 1957, Novel

Malefactor, The see **THE TEST OF HONOR** (1919).

MALEFICES 1961 d: Henri Decoin. FRN., *Malefices*, Pierre Boileau, Thomas Narcejac, Paris 1961, Novel

MALEFICES 1990 d: Carlo RolA. FRN., *Malefices*, Pierre Boileau, Thomas Narcejac, Paris 1961, Novel

MALEFICO ANELLO, IL 1916 d: Ugo FalenA. ITL., *Il Malefico Anello*, Vincenzo Morello, 1909, Play

MALENA ES UN NOMBRE DE TANGO 1996 d: Gerardo Herrero. SPN/FRN/GRM., *Malena Es un Nombre de Tango*, Almudena Grandes, Novel

Malena Is a Name from a Tango see **MALENA ES UN NOMBRE DE TANGO** (1996).

MALENCONTRE 1920 d: Germaine Dulac. FRN., *Malencontre*, Guy de Chantepleure, Novel

MALENKI PRINTS 1966 d: Arunas Zhebriunas. USS., *Le Petit Prince*, Antoine de Saint-Exupery, 1943, Novel

Malenkij Princ see **MALENKI PRINTS** (1966).

Malenky Prince see **MALENKI PRINTS** (1966).

MALEVIL 1981 d: Christian de Chalonge. FRN/GRM., *Malevil*, Robert Merle, Novel

Malgudi Days *see* SWAMI (1987).

MALHEURS DE SOPHIE, LES 1945 d: Jacqueline Audry. FRN., *Les Malheurs de Sophie*, la Comtesse de Segur, Novel

MALHEURS DE SOPHIE, LES 1979 d: Jean-Claude Brialy. FRN., *Les Malheurs de Sophie*, la Comtesse de Segur, Novel

MALIA 1912. ITL., *Malia*, Luigi Capuana, 1895, Play

MALIA 1946 d: Giuseppe Amato. ITL., Luigi Capuana, Short Story

Malibu *see* SEQUOIA (1934).

MALICE AFORETHOUGHT 1979 d: Cyril Coke. UKN., *Malice Aforethought*, Francis Iles, Novel

MALICE IN WONDERLAND 1985 d: Gus Trikonis. USA., *Hedda and Louella*, George Eels, Book

MALIZIE DI VENERE, LE 1969 d: Massimo Dallamano. ITL/GRM., *Venus Im Pelz*, Lepold Sacher-Masoch, Novel

Malkata Roussalka *see* RUSALOCHKA (1976).

Malko Otklonenie *see* OTKLONENIE (1967).

MALLENS: PART 1 - THE MALLEN STREAK, THE 1978 d: Richard (5) Martin, Ronald Wilson. UKN., *The Mallen Trilogy*, Catherine Cookson, Novel

MALLENS: PART 2 - THE MALLEN GIRLS, THE 1978 d: Richard (5) Martin, Ronald Wilson. UKN., *The Mallen Trilogy*, Catherine Cookson, Novel

MALLENS: PART 3 - THE MALLEN SECRET, THE 1980 d: Roy Roberts, Mary McMurray. UKN., *The Mallen Trilogy*, Catherine Cookson, Novel

MALLENS: PART 4 - THE MALLEN CURSE, THE 1980 d: Mary McMurray, Brian Mills. UKN., *The Mallen Trilogy*, Catherine Cookson, Novel

MALOM A POKOLBAN 1987 d: Gyula Maar. HNG., *Malom a Pokolban*, Gyorgy Moldova, 1968, Novel

MALOMBRA 1917 d: Carmine Gallone. ITL., *Malombra*, Antonio Fogazzaro, 1881, Novel

MALOMBRA 1942 d: Mario Soldati. ITL., *Malombra*, Antonio Fogazzaro, 1881, Novel

Malombra *see* MALOMBRA: LE PERVERSIONI SESSUALI DI UNA ADOLESCENTE (1983).

MALOMBRA: LE PERVERSIONI SESSUALI DI UNA ADOLESCENTE 1983 d: Bruno Alberto Gaburro. ITL., *Malombra*, Antonio Fogazzaro, 1881, Novel

Malombra, the Sexual Perversions of an Adolescent *see* MALOMBRA: LE PERVERSIONI SESSUALI DI UNA ADOLESCENTE (1983).

MALONE 1987 d: Harley Cokliss. USA., *Shotgun*, William Wingate, Novel

MALPAS MYSTERY, THE 1960 d: Sidney Hayers. UKN., *The Face in the Night*, Edgar Wallace, London 1924, Novel

MALPERTUIS 1972 d: Harry Kumel. FRN/BLG/GRM., *Malpertuis*, Jean Ray, Novel

Malpertuis: Histoire d'une Maison Maudite *see* MALPERTUIS (1972).

MALQUERIDA, LA 1940 d: Jose Luis Lopez Rubio. SPN., *La Malquerida*, Jacinto Benavente y Martinez, 1913, Play

MALQUERIDA, LA 1949 d: Emilio Fernandez. MXC., *La Malquerida*, Jacinto Benavente y Martinez, 1913, Play

MALTCHIKI 1990 d: Yuri Grigoriev, Renita GrigorievA. USS., *Bratya Karamazovy*, Fyodor Dostoyevsky, 1880, Novel

MALTESE FALCON, THE 1931 d: Roy Del Ruth. USA., *The Maltese Falcon*, Dashiell Hammett, New York 1930, Novel

MALTESE FALCON, THE 1941 d: John Huston. USA., *The Maltese Falcon*, Dashiell Hammett, New York 1930, Novel

Maltschik-S-Paltschik *see* POHADKA O MALICKOVI (1985).

MALVA 1957 d: Vladimir Braun. USS., *Malva*, Maxim Gorky, 1897, Short Story

MALVADO CARABEL, EL 1934 d: Edgar Neville. SPN., *El Malvado Carabel*, Wenceslao Fernandez Florez, 1931, Novel

MALVADO CARABEL, EL 1955 d: Fernando Fernan Gomez. SPN., *El Malvado Carabel*, Wenceslao Fernandez Florez, 1931, Novel

MALVALOCA 1926 d: Benito Perojo. SPN., *Malvaloca*, Joaquin Alvarez Quintero, Serafin Alvarez Quintero, Play

MALY BOBES VE MESTE 1962 d: Jan Valasek. CZC., *Maly Bobes Ve Meste*, J. V. Plevas, Book

Malyadaan *see* MALAYADAAN (1971).

Malyadan *see* MALAYADAAN (1971).

MAMA 1931 d: Gregorio Martinez Sierra, Benito Perojo. USA., *Mama*, Gregorio Martinez Sierra, Spain 1913, Play

Mama *see* MA-MA (1977).

MA-MA 1977 d: Elisabeta Bostan. RMN/USS/FRN., *Capra Cu Trei Iezi*, Ion Creanga, 1875, Short Story

MAMA STEPS OUT 1937 d: George B. Seitz. USA., *Ada Beats the Drum*, John Alexander Kirkpatrick, New York 1930, Play

MAMA YAO WO CHU JIA 1956 d: Huang Shu. CHN., *Sister Chun*, Liu Zhen, Novel

MAMAN COLIBRI 1918 d: Alfredo de Antoni. ITL., *Maman Colibri*, Henry Bataille, 1904, Play

MAMAN COLIBRI 1929 d: Julien Duvivier. FRN., *Maman Colibri*, Henry Bataille, 1904, Play

MAMAN COLIBRI 1937 d: Jean Dreville. FRN., *Maman Colibri*, Henry Bataille, 1904, Play

MAMA'S AFFAIR 1921 d: Victor Fleming. USA., *Mama's Affair*, Rachel Burton Butler, New York 1920, Play

MAMBO KINGS, THE 1992 d: Arne Glimcher. USA., *The Mambo Kings Play Songs of Love*, Oscar Hijuelos, Novel

MAME 1974 d: Gene Saks. USA., *Auntie Mame*, Patrick Dennis, Novel

MAMITSCHKA 1955 d: Rolf Thiele. GRM., *Das Gluck Am Sonntagabend*, Viktor Schuller, Novel

MAMMON AND THE ARCHER 1918 d: Kenneth Webb. USA., *Mammon and the Archer*, O. Henry, Short Story

MAMMY 1930 d: Michael Curtiz. USA., *Mr. Bones*, Irving Berlin, James Gleason, Musical Play

Mamouret *see* LE BRISEUR DE CHAINES (1941).

Ma'mselle Jo *see* SILENT YEARS (1921).

Mam'selle Nitouche *see* SANTARELLINA (1912).

Ma'mselle Nitouche *see* SANTARELLINA (1912).

MAM'ZELLE BONAPARTE 1941 d: Maurice Tourneur. FRN., *Mam'zelle Bonaparte*, Gerard Bourgeois, Pierre Chanlaine, Novel

MAM'ZELLE NITOUCHE 1931 d: Marc Allegret. FRN., *Mam'zelle Nitouche*, Herve, Henri Meilhac, Albert Milhaud, Paris 1882, Operetta

MAM'ZELLE NITOUCHE 1954 d: Yves Allegret. FRN/ITL., *Mam'zelle Nitouche*, Herve, Henri Meilhac, Albert Milhaud, Paris 1882, Operetta

MAM'ZELLE SPAHI 1934 d: Max de Vaucorbeil. FRN., *Manoeuvres de Nuit*, Etienne Arnaud, Andre Heuze, Play

Man, a Woman and a Child, A *see* WOMAN AND CHILD MAN (1983).

MAN ABOUT THE HOUSE, A 1947 d: Leslie Arliss. UKN., *A Man About the House*, Francis Brett Young, Novel

MAN ABOUT TOWN 1932 d: John Francis Dillon. USA., *Man About Town*, Denison Clift, New York 1932, Novel

Man Afraid, A *see* THE KILLERS (1946).

Man Alive *see* LE REVOLVER AUX CHEVEUX ROUGES (1973).

MAN ALONE, A 1955 d: Ray Milland. USA., Mort Briskin, Story

Man and a Woman, A *see* A MAN AND THE WOMAN (1917).

MAN AND HIS KINGDOM 1922 d: Maurice Elvey. UKN., *Man and His Kingdom*, A. E. W. Mason, Novel

MAN AND HIS MATE, A 1915 d: John G. Adolfi. USA., *A Man and His Mate*, Harold Riggs Durant, Springfield, MA. 1908, Play

MAN AND HIS MONEY, A 1919 d: Harry Beaumont. USA., *A Man and His Money*, Frederic Stewart Isham, Indianapolis 1912, Novel

Man and His Prison, A *see* UM HOMEM E SUA JAULA (1969).

Man and His Woman, A *see* UN HOMME EN OR (1934).

MAN AND MAID 1925 d: Victor Schertzinger. USA., *Man and Maid*, Elinor Glyn, Philadelphia 1922, Novel

MAN AND THE MOMENT, THE 1918 d: Arrigo Bocchi. UKN., *The Man and the Moment*, Elinor Glyn, New York 1914, Novel

MAN AND THE SNAKE, THE 1972 d: Sture Rydman. UKN., *The Man and the Snake*, Ambrose Bierce, 1891, Short Story

MAN AND THE WOMAN, A 1917 d: Alice Blache. USA., *Nana*, Emile Zola, Paris 1880, Novel

Man and War *see* SENSO TO NINGEN (1970).

MAN AT SIX, THE 1931 d: Harry Hughes. UKN., *The Man at Six*, Jack Celestin, Jack de Leon, London 1928, Play

Man at the Best Age, A *see* EIN MANN IM SCHONSTEN ALTER (1963).

MAN AT THE CARLTON TOWER 1961 d: Robert Tronson. UKN., *The Man at the Carlton*, Edgar Wallace, London 1931, Novel

MAN AT THE GATE, THE 1941 d: Norman Walker. UKN., *The Man at the Gate*, Louise Haskin, Poem

MAN BAIT 1926 d: Donald Crisp. USA., *Man Bait*, Norman Houston, Story

Man, Beast and Virtue *see* LA BESTIA, LA VIRTU, L' UOMO (1953).

MAN BEHIND THE DOOR, THE 1914 d: Wally Van. USA., *The Man Behind the Door*, Archibald Clavering Gunter, New York 1907, Novel

MAN BEHIND THE GUN, THE 1952 d: Felix E. Feist. USA., *The Man Behind the Mask*, Robert Buckner, Short Story

MAN BEHIND THE MASK, THE 1936 d: Michael Powell. UKN., *The Chase of the Golden Plate*, Jacques Futrelle, Novel

MAN BENEATH, THE 1919 d: William Worthington. USA., *Only a Nigger*, Edmund Mitchell, London 1901, Novel

MAN BETWEEN, THE 1953 d: Carol Reed. UKN., *Susanne in Berlin*, Walter Ebert, Novel

MAN BRAUCHT KEIN GELD 1931 d: Carl Boese. GRM., *Man Braucht Kein Geld*, Ferdinand Altenkirch, Play

MAN CALLED BACK, THE 1932 d: Robert Florey. USA., *Silent Thunder*, Andrew Soutar, London 1932, Novel

MAN CALLED GANNON, A 1969 d: James Goldstone. USA., *Man Without a Star*, Dee Linford, New York 1952, Novel

MAN CALLED HORSE, A 1970 d: Elliot Silverstein. USA., *A Man Called Horse*, Dorothy M. Johnson, 1950, Short Story

MAN CALLED INTREPID, A 1979 d: Peter Carter. UKN/CND/USA., *A Man Called Intrepid*, William Stevenson, Book

MAN CALLED NOON, THE 1973 d: Peter Collinson. UKN/SPN/ITL., *The Man Called Noon*, Louis L'Amour, Novel

MAN CALLED PETER, A 1955 d: Henry Koster. USA., *A Man Called Peter*, Catherine Marshall, Biography

Man Cannot Be Raped *see* MANRAPE (1978).

MAN COULD GET KILLED, A 1966 d: Ronald Neame, Cliff Owen. USA., *Diamonds for Danger*, David Esdaile Walker, New York 1954, Novel

MAN CRAZY 1927 d: John Francis Dillon. USA., *Clarissa and the Post Road*, Grace Sartwell Mason, 1923, Short Story

MAN DETAINED 1961 d: Robert Tronson. UKN., *A Debt Discharged*, Edgar Wallace, London 1916, Novel

MAN DIE ZIJN HAAR KORT LIET KNIPPEN 1966 d: Andre Delvaux. BLG., **De Man Die Zijn Haar Liet Knippen**, Johan Daisne, 1947, Novel

MAN FOR ALL SEASONS, A 1966 d: Fred Zinnemann. UKN., *A Man for All Seasons*, Robert Bolt, London 1960, Play

MAN FOR ALL SEASONS, A 1988 d: Charlton Heston. USA., *A Man for All Seasons*, Robert Bolt, London 1960, Play

MAN FOUR-SQUARE, A 1926 d: R. William Neill. USA., *A Man Four-Square*, William MacLeod Raine, Boston 1919, Novel

MAN FRIDAY 1975 d: Jack Gold. UKN/MXC., *Man Friday*, Adrian Mitchell, 1974, Play

MAN FROM BITTER ROOTS, THE 1916 d: Oscar Apfel. USA., *The Man from the Bitter Roots*, Caroline Lockhart, New York 1915, Novel

MAN FROM BLANKLEYS, THE 1930 d: Alfred E. Green. USA., *The Man from Blankleys*, F. Anstey, 1893, Short Story

MAN FROM BRODNEY'S, THE 1923 d: David Smith. USA., *The Man from Brodney's*, George Barr McCutcheon, New York 1908, Novel

Man from Cheyenne, The *see* **LAW AND ORDER** (1940).

MAN FROM CHICAGO, THE 1930 d: Walter Summers. UKN., *Speed*, Reginald Berkeley, Play

MAN FROM COLORADO, THE 1949 d: Henry Levin. USA., *The Man from Colorado*, Borden Chase, Novel

Man from C.O.T.T.O.N. Or How I Stopped Worrying and Learned to Love the Boll Weevil, The *see* **GONE ARE THE DAYS!** (1963).

Man from C.O.T.T.O.N., The *see* **GONE ARE THE DAYS!** (1963).

MAN FROM DAKOTA, THE 1940 d: Leslie Fenton. USA., *Arouse and Beware*, MacKinlay Kantor, New York 1936, Novel

MAN FROM FUNERAL RANGE, THE 1918 d: Walter Edwards. USA., *Broken Threads*, W. Ernest Wilkes, New York 1917, Play

MAN FROM GLENGARRY, THE 1922 d: Henry McRae. CND/USA., *Man from Glengarry*, Ralph Connor, Chicago 1901, Novel

MAN FROM HEADQUARTERS, THE 1928 d: Duke Worne. USA., *The Black Book*, George Bronson Howard, New York 1920, Novel

MAN FROM HELL'S RIVER, THE 1922 d: Irving Cummings. USA., *God of Her People*, James Oliver Curwood, Story

MAN FROM HOME, THE 1914 d: Cecil B. de Mille, Oscar Apfel. USA., *The Man from Home*, Booth Tarkington, Harry Leon Wilson, Louisville, Ky. 1907, Play

MAN FROM HOME, THE 1922 d: George Fitzmaurice. UKN., *The Man from Home*, Booth Tarkington, Harry Leon Wilson, Louisville, Ky. 1907, Play

Man from Kabul, The *see* **KABULIWALA** (1956).

MAN FROM LARAMIE, THE 1955 d: Anthony Mann. USA., Thomas T. Flynn, Story

Man from Majorca, The *see* **MANNEN FRAN MALLORCA** (1984).

Man from Make Believe, The *see* **A BROADWAY COWBOY** (1920).

Man from Mallorca, The *see* **MANNEN FRAN MALLORCA** (1984).

Man from Medicine Hat, The *see* **THE MANAGER OF THE B. & A.** (1916).

MAN FROM MEXICO, THE 1914 d: Thomas N. Heffron. USA., *The Man from Mexico*, Henry A. Du Souchet, New York 1897, Play

Man from Montana, The *see* **DESTRY RIDES AGAIN** (1939).

MAN FROM MOROCCO, THE 1945 d: Max Greene. UKN., Rudolph Cartier, Story

Man from Nowhere, The *see* **L' HOMME DE NULLE PART** (1936).

MAN FROM O.R.G.Y., THE 1970 d: James A. Hill. USA., *The Man from O.R.G.Y.*, Ted Mark, New York 1965, Novel

MAN FROM PAINTED POST, THE 1917 d: Joseph Henabery. USA., *Silver Slippers*, Jackson Gregory, 1916, Short Story

Man from Podskali, The *see* **PODSKALAK** (1928).

MAN FROM RED GULCH, THE 1925 d: Edmund Mortimer. USA., *The Idyll of Red Gulch*, Bret Harte, Story

MAN FROM SNOWY RIVER, THE 1920 d: Beaumont Smith, John Wells. ASL., *The Man from Snowy River*, Andrew Barton Paterson, 1895, Poem

MAN FROM SNOWY RIVER, THE 1982 d: George Miller. ASL., *The Man from Snowy River*, Andrew Barton Paterson, 1895, Poem

Man from Ten Strike, The *see* **GOLD MADNESS** (1923).

MAN FROM TEXAS, THE 1948 d: Leigh Jason. USA., *The Man from Texas*, E. B. Ginty, Play

Man from the Folies Bergere, The *see* **FOLIES BERGERE DE PARIS** (1935).

Man from the Subsoil, The *see* **MEMORIAS DEL SUBSUELO** (1981).

Man from Tokyo, The *see* **TOKYO NAGARE MONO** (1966).

MAN FROM TORONTO, THE 1933 d: Sinclair Hill. UKN., *The Man from Toronto*, Douglas Murray, London 1918, Play

MAN FROM WYOMING, THE 1924 d: Robert North Bradbury. USA., *A Story of the Outdoor West Wyoming*, William MacLeod Raine, New York 1908, Novel

MAN FROM YESTERDAY, THE 1932 d: Berthold Viertel. USA., *The Wound Stripe*, Nell Blackwell, Rowland G. Edwards, 1925, Play

Man Goes Through the Wall, A *see* **EIN MANN GEHT DURCH DIE WAND** (1959).

MAN HATER, THE 1917 d: Albert Parker. USA., *The Man Hater*, Mary Brecht Pulver, 1917, Short Story

Man, His Pride and Vengeance *see* **L'ORGOGLIO, LA VENDETTA, L' UOMO** (1967).

MAN HUNT 1941 d: Fritz Lang. USA., *Rogue Male*, Geoffrey Household, 1939, Novel

MAN HUNTER, THE 1969 d: Don Taylor. USA., *The Man Hunter*, Wade Miller, Novel

Man I Killed, The *see* **BROKEN LULLABY** (1932).

MAN I LOVE, THE 1947 d: Raoul Walsh. USA., *The Man I Love*, Maritta Martin Wolff, Novel

MAN I MARRIED, THE 1940 d: Irving Pichel. USA., *Swastika*, Oscar Schisgall, Novel

Man in 5a, The *see* **KILLING 'EM SOFTLY** (1982).

Man in a Hurry *see* **L' HOMME PRESSE** (1976).

MAN IN BLUE, THE 1925 d: Edward Laemmle. USA., *The Flower of Napoli*, Gerald Beaumont, 1924, Short Story

Man in Demand on All Sides *see* **PAN NA ROZTRHANI** (1934).

MAN IN GREY, THE 1943 d: Leslie Arliss. UKN., *The Man in Grey*, Lady Eleanor Smith, Novel

MAN IN HALF MOON STREET, THE 1944 d: Ralph Murphy. USA., *The Man in Half Moon Street*, Barre Lyndon, London 1939, Play

Man in Her House *see* **PERSONAL PROPERTY** (1937).

Man in Hiding *see* **MANTRAP** (1953).

MAN IN HOBBLES, THE 1928 d: George Archainbaud. USA., *The Man in Hobbles*, Peter B. Kyne, 1913, Short Story

MAN IN MOTLEY, THE 1916 d: Ralph Dewsbury. UKN., *The Man in Motley*, Tom Gallon, Novel

MAN IN POSSESSION, THE 1931 d: Sam Wood. USA., *The Man in Possession*, H. M. Harwood, London 1930, Play

Man in Possession, The *see* **PERSONAL PROPERTY** (1937).

Man in Rapture *see* **KOKOTSU NO HITO** (1973).

Man in Rue Noir, The *see* **THE MAN WHO COULD CHEAT DEATH** (1959).

MAN IN THE ATTIC 1954 d: Hugo Fregonese. USA., *The Lodger*, Mrs. Belloc Lowndes, London 1913, Novel

MAN IN THE ATTIC, THE 1915 d: Ralph Dewsbury. UKN., *The Man in the Attic*, Charles McEvoy, Play

Man in the Background, The *see* **DE MAN OP DEN ACHTERGROND** (1923).

Man in the Black Hat, The *see* **SATAN MET A LADY** (1936).

Man in the Current *see* **DER MANN IM STROM** (1958).

MAN IN THE GRAY FLANNEL SUIT, THE 1956 d: Nunnally Johnson. USA., *The Man in the Gray Flannel Suit*, Sloan Wilson, 1955, Novel

Man in the Hispano-Suiza, The *see* **L' HOMME A L'HISPANO** (1932).

MAN IN THE IRON MASK, THE 1939 d: James Whale. USA., *Le Vicomte de Bragelonne*, Alexandre Dumas (pere), Paris 1847, Novel

MAN IN THE IRON MASK, THE 1977 d: Mike Newell. USA/UKN., *Le Vicomte de Bragelonne*, Alexandre Dumas (pere), Paris 1847, Novel

MAN IN THE IRON MASK, THE 1998 d: William Richert. USA., *Le Vicomte de Bragelonne*, Alexandre Dumas (pere), Paris 1847, Novel

MAN IN THE IRON MASK, THE 1998 d: Randall Wallace. USA., *Le Vicomte de Bragelonne*, Alexandre Dumas (pere), Paris 1847, Novel

MAN IN THE MIDDLE 1963 d: Guy Hamilton. UKN/USA., *The Winston Affair*, Howard Fast, New York 1959, Novel

MAN IN THE MIRROR, THE 1936 d: Maurice Elvey. UKN., *The Man in the Mirror*, William Garrett, Novel

MAN IN THE NET, THE 1959 d: Michael Curtiz. USA., *Man in the Net; a Novel of Suspense*, Patrick Quentin, 1956, Novel

MAN IN THE OPEN, A 1919 d: Ernest C. Warde. USA., *A Man in the Open*, Roger S. Pocock, Indianapolis 1912, Novel

Man in the Raincoat, The *see* **L' HOMME A L'IMPERMEABLE** (1957).

MAN IN THE ROAD, THE 1956 d: Lance Comfort. UKN., *He Was Found in the Road*, Anthony Armstrong, Novel

MAN IN THE ROUGH 1928 d: Wallace Fox. USA., *Sir Piegan Passes*, W. C. Tuttle, New York 1923, Short Story

Man in the Rushes, The *see* **DER MANN IM SCHILF** (1978).

MAN IN THE SADDLE 1951 d: Andre de Toth. USA., *The Man in the Saddle*, Ernest Haycox, 1938, Novel

Man in the Shade, The *see* **CHOVEKAT V SYANKA** (1967).

MAN IN THE SHADOW 1956 d: Jack Arnold. USA., *Man in the Shadow*, Harry Whittington, Novel

Man in the Shadow, The *see* **CHOVEKAT V SYANKA** (1967).

MAN IN THE SHADOWS, THE 1915 d: Charles McEvoy. UKN., *Village Wedding*, Charles McEvoy, Play

Man in the Skull Mask, The *see* **WHO?** (1974).

Man in the Steel Mask, The *see* **WHO?** (1974).

MAN IN THE STREET, THE 1914 d: Charles J. Brabin. USA., *The Man in the Street*, Mary Imlay Taylor, Novel

Man in the Street, The *see* **SOKAKTAKI ADAM** (1995).

MAN IN THE VAULT 1956 d: Andrew V. McLaglen. USA., *The Lock and the Key*, Frank Gruber, 1948, Novel

MAN IN THE WATER, THE 1963 d: Mark Stevens. USA., *The Man in the Water*, Robert Sheckley, New York 1962, Novel

MAN INSIDE, THE 1916 d: John G. Adolfi. USA., *The Man Inside*, Natalie Sumner Lincoln, New York 1914, Novel

MAN INSIDE, THE 1958 d: John Gilling. UKN., *The Man Inside*, M. E. Chaber, Novel

Man Is Ten Feet Tall, A *see* **EDGE OF THE CITY** (1956).

MAN IST NUR ZWEIMAL JUNG 1958 d: Helmut Weiss. AUS., *Man Ist Nur Zweim Jung*, Otto F. Beer, Peter Preses, Play

Man Kan Inte Valdtas *see* **MANRAPE** (1978).

MAN LEBT NUR EINMAL 1952 d: Ernst Neubach. GRM., *Der Mann Der Seinen Morder Sucht*, Ernst Neubach, Play

Man Lock *see* **UNDER PRESSURE** (1935).

MAN MADE MONSTER 1941 d: George Waggner. USA., *The Electric Man*, Len Colos, Harry J. Essex, Sid Schwartz, Story

Man Maker, The *see* **TWENTY DOLLARS A WEEK** (1924).

Man Maker, The *see* **$20 A WEEK** (1935).

MAN MUST LIVE, A 1925 d: Paul Sloane. USA., *Jungle Law*, I. A. R. Wylie, Short Story

Man Named John, A *see* **E VENNE UN UOMO** (1964).

Man Named Rocca, A *see* **UN NOMME LA ROCCA** (1962).

MAN NEXT DOOR, THE 1923 d: Victor Schertzinger, David Smith. USA., *The Man Next Door*, Emerson Hough, New York 1917, Novel

Man Next Door, The *see* **KILLING 'EM SOFTLY** (1982).

MAN NOBODY KNOWS, THE 1925 d: Errett Leroy Kenepp. USA., *The Man Nobody Knows; a Discovery of Jesus*, Bruce Barton, Indianapolis 1925, Book

MAN O' WARSMAN, THE 1914 d: Thomas E. SheA. USA., *The Man O' Warsman*, Eugene Thomas, New York 1898, Play

Man of Affaires *see* **HIS LORDSHIP** (1936).

Man of Affairs *see* **HIS LORDSHIP** (1936).

Man of Bronze *see* **JIM THORPE - ALL AMERICAN** (1951).

Man of Evil *see* **FANNY BY GASLIGHT** (1944).

Man of His Word, A *see* **JELF'S** (1915).

MAN OF HONOR, A 1919 d: Fred J. Balshofer. USA., *A King in Khaki*, Henry Kitchell Webster, New York 1909, Novel

MAN OF IRON 1935 d: William McGann. USA., *Story of a Country Boy*, Dawn Powell, New York 1934, Novel

MAN OF LA MANCHA 1972 d: Arthur Hiller. USA/ITL., *El Ingenioso Hidalgo Don Quijote de la Mancha*, Miguel de Cervantes Saavedra, 1605-15, Novel

MAN OF LETTERS 1984 d: Chris Thomson. ASL., *Man of Letters*, Glen Tomasetti, Novel

MAN OF MAYFAIR 1931 d: Louis Mercanton. UKN., *A Child in Their Midst*, May Edginton, Novel

MAN OF MYSTERY, THE 1917 d: Frederick A. Thompson. USA., *Archibald Clavering Gunter*, Novel

MAN OF SHAME, THE 1915 d: Harry Myers. USA., *The Shadow of Roger Laroque*, Jules Mary, Novel

MAN OF SORROW, A 1916 d: Oscar Apfel. USA., *Hoodman Blind*, Wilson Barrett, Henry Arthur Jones, London 1885, Play

Man of Stone, The *see* LE GOLEM (1935).

MAN OF THE FOREST 1926 d: John Waters. USA., *The Man of the Forest*, Zane Grey, New York 1920, Novel

MAN OF THE FOREST 1933 d: Henry Hathaway. USA., *The Man of the Forest*, Zane Grey, New York 1920, Novel

MAN OF THE FOREST, THE 1921 d: Benjamin B. Hampton. USA., *The Man of the Forest*, Zane Grey, New York 1920, Novel

Man of the Hour *see* COLONEL EFFINGHAM'S RAID (1945).

MAN OF THE HOUR, THE 1914 d: Maurice Tourneur. USA., *The Man of the Hour*, George Broadhurst, New York 1906, Play

Man of the Moment *see* TOKI NO UJIGAMI (1932).

MAN OF THE MOMENT 1935 d: Monty Banks. UKN., *Water Nymph*, Yves Mirande, Play

MAN OF THE MOMENT 1955 d: John Paddy Carstairs. UKN., Maurice Gowan, Story

Man of the North *see* TOHOKU NO ZUNMUTACHI (1957).

Man of the Open Seas *see* L' HOMME DU LARGE (1920).

Man of the Right Moment, The *see* TOKI NO UJIGAMI (1932).

Man of the Soil *see* MATIR MANISHA (1966).

Man of the Trail *see* END OF THE TRAIL (1936).

Man of the Waterfront *see* PORT OF SEVEN SEAS (1938).

MAN OF THE WEST 1958 d: Anthony Mann. USA., *The Border Jumpers*, Will C. Brown, 1955, Novel

Man of the Wide-Open Spaces, The *see* L' HOMME DU LARGE (1920).

MAN OF TWO WORLDS 1934 d: J. Walter Ruben. USA., *Man of Two Worlds; the Novel of a Stranger*, Ainsworth Morgan, New York 1933, Novel

Man of Two Worlds *see* THE HOUSE IN THE SQUARE (1951).

MAN ON A STRING 1960 d: Andre de Toth. USA., *Ten Years a Counterspy*, Boris Morros, Book

MAN ON A TIGHTROPE 1953 d: Elia Kazan. USA., *International Incident*, Neil Paterson, Story

MAN ON FIRE 1957 d: Ranald MacDougall. USA., *Man of Fire*, Jack Jacobs, Malvin Wald, Television Play

MAN ON FIRE 1987 d: Elie Chouraqui. FRN/ITL., *Man on Fire*, A. J. Quinell, Novel

Man on the Balcony, The *see* MANNEN PA BALKONGEN (1993).

MAN ON THE BEACH, A 1956 d: Joseph Losey. UKN., *Chance at the Wheel*, Victor Canning, Short Story

MAN ON THE BOX, THE 1914 d: Cecil B. de Mille, Oscar Apfel. USA., *The Man on the Box*, Harold MacGrath, Indianapolis 1904, Novel

MAN ON THE BOX, THE 1925 d: Charles F. Reisner. USA., *The Man on the Box*, Harold MacGrath, Indianapolis 1904, Novel

MAN ON THE EIFFEL TOWER, THE 1949 d: Burgess Meredith. USA/FRN., *La Tete d'un Homme*, Georges Simenon, 1931, Novel

Man on the Roof, The *see* MANNEN PA TAKET (1977).

Man on the Wall, The *see* DER MANN AUF DER MAUER (1982).

MAN OP DEN ACHTERGROND, DE 1923 d: Ernest Winar. NTH/GRM., **De Man Op Den Achtergrond**, Ivans, 1918, Novel

Man Or a Monkey, A *see* REN HOU DA LIE BIAN (1992).

Man Or Mouse *see* THERE'S ONE BORN EVERY MINUTE (1942).

MAN OUTSIDE, THE 1967 d: Samuel Gallu. UKN., *Double Agent*, Gene Stackleborg, New York 1959, Novel

MAN POWER 1927 d: Clarence Badger. USA., *Man Power*, Byron Morgan, Story

Man, Pride and Vengeance *see* L'ORGOGLIO, LA VENDETTA, L' UOMO (1967).

MAN REDE MIR NICHT VON LIEBE 1943 d: Erich Engel. GRM., *Man Rede Mir Nicht von Liebe*, Hugo Maria Kritz, Novel

Man Saves the Queen *see* LADY IN DANGER (1934).

MAN SPIELT NICHT MIT DER LIEBE 1949 d: Hans Deppe. GRM., *Die Glucklichste Ehe Der Welt*, Karl Georg Kulb, Play

MAN SPRICHT UBER JACQUELINE 1937 d: Werner Hochbaum. GRM., *Man Spricht Uber Jacqueline*, Katrin Holland, Novel

MAN STEIGT NACH 1928 d: Erno Metzner. GRM., *Man Steigt Nach*, Jeno Heltai, Play

MAN TAMER, THE 1921 d: Harry B. Harris. USA., *The Man-Tamer*, John Barton Oxford, 1918, Short Story

MAN THAT CORRUPTED HADLEYBURG, THE 1980 d: Ralph Rosenblum. USA., *The Man That Corrupted Hadleyburg*, Mark Twain, 1900, Short Story

MAN, THE MISSION AND THE MAID, THE 1915 d: Theodore Marston. USA., *The Mission and the Maid, the Man*, George Randolph Chester, Story

MAN THEY COULD NOT ARREST, THE 1931 d: T. Hayes Hunter. UKN., Edgar Wallace, Novel

Man They Couldn't Arrest, The *see* THE MAN THEY COULD NOT ARREST (1931).

Man Thou Gavest Me, The *see* THE ETERNAL STRUGGLE (1923).

MAN TO MAN 1922 d: Stuart Paton. USA., *Man to Man*, Jackson Gregory, New York 1920, Novel

MAN TO MAN 1930 d: Allan Dwan. USA., *Barber John's Boy*, Ben Ames Williams, Story

MAN TO REMEMBER, A 1938 d: Garson Kanin. USA., *Failure*, Katharine Haviland-Taylor, 1932, Short Story

MAN TRAIL, THE 1915 d: E. H. Calvert. USA., *The Man Trail*, Henry Oyen, New York 1915, Novel

MAN TROUBLE 1930 d: Berthold Viertel. USA., *A Very Practical Joke*, Ben Ames Williams, 1925, Short Story

MAN UPSTAIRS, THE 1926 d: Roy Del Ruth. USA., *The Man Upstairs*, Earl Derr Biggers, Indianapolis 1916, Novel

MAN WHO BOUGHT LONDON, THE 1916 d: F. Martin Thornton. UKN., *The Man Who Bought London*, Edgar Wallace, London 1915, Novel

MAN WHO BROKE 1,000 CHAINS, THE 1987 d: Daniel Mann. USA., Vincent Godfrey Burns, Book

Man Who Broke His Heart, The *see* WHARF ANGEL (1934).

MAN WHO BROKE THE BANK AT MONTE CARLO, THE 1935 d: Stephen Roberts. USA., *Igra*, Ilya Surgutchoff, Play, *Monsieur Andre*, Frederick A. Swann, Play

MAN WHO CAME BACK, THE 1924 d: Emmett J. Flynn. USA., *The Man Who Came Back*, John Fleming Wilson, New York 1912, Novel

MAN WHO CAME BACK, THE 1931 d: Raoul Walsh. USA., *The Man Who Came Back*, John Fleming Wilson, New York 1912, Novel

Man Who Came Back, The *see* SWAMP WATER (1941).

Man Who Came for Coffee, The *see* VENGA A PRENDERE IL CAFFE DA NOI (1970).

MAN WHO CAME TO DINNER, THE 1941 d: William Keighley. USA., *The Man Who Came to Dinner*, Moss Hart, George S. Kaufman, New York 1939, Play

MAN WHO CAME TO DINNER, THE 1972 d: Buzz Kulik. USA., *The Man Who Came to Dinner*, Moss Hart, George S. Kaufman, New York 1939, Play

MAN WHO CAPTURED EICHMANN, THE 1996 d: William A. Graham. USA., *Eichmann in My Hands*, Peter Z. Malkin, Harry Stein, Book

MAN WHO CHANGED HIS NAME, THE 1928 d: A. V. Bramble. UKN., *The Man Who Changed His Name*, Edgar Wallace, London 1928, Play

MAN WHO CHANGED HIS NAME, THE 1934 d: Henry Edwards. UKN., *The Man Who Changed His Name*, Edgar Wallace, London 1928, Play

Man Who Cheated Life, The *see* DER STUDENT VON PRAG (1926).

MAN WHO COULD CHEAT DEATH, THE 1959 d: Terence Fisher. UKN., *The Man in Half Moon Street*, Barre Lyndon, London 1939, Play

Man Who Could Not Forget, The *see* DEBT OF HONOUR (1936).

MAN WHO COULD NOT LOSE, THE 1914 d: Carlyle Blackwell. USA., *The Man Who Could Not Lose*, Richard Harding Davis, New York 1911, Novel

Man Who Could Walk Through Walls, The *see* EIN MANN GEHT DURCH DIE WAND (1959).

MAN WHO COULD WORK MIRACLES, THE 1936 d: Lothar Mendes. UKN., *The Man Who Could Work Miracles*, H. G. Wells, 1899, Short Story

Man Who Died Twice, The *see* LE SILENCIEUX (1972).

MAN WHO DISAPPEARED, THE 1914 d: Charles J. Brabin. USA., *The Man Who Disappeared*, Richard Washburn Child, Story

MAN WHO FELL TO EARTH, THE 1976 d: Nicolas Roeg. UKN., *The Man Who Fell to Earth*, Walter S. Tevis, 1963, Novel

MAN WHO FELL TO EARTH, THE 1987 d: Robert J. Roth. USA., *The Man Who Fell to Earth*, Walter S. Tevis, 1963, Novel

MAN WHO FIGHTS ALONE, THE 1924 d: Wallace Worsley. USA., *The Miracle of Hate*, William Blacke, James Shelley Hamilton, Story

MAN WHO FORGOT, THE 1917 d: Emile Chautard. USA., *The Man Who Forgot*, James Hay Jr., New York 1915, Novel

MAN WHO FOUND HIMSELF, THE 1915 d: Frank H. Crane. USA., *The Mills of the Gods*, George Broadhurst, New York 1907, Play

MAN WHO HAD EVERYTHING, THE 1920 d: Alfred E. Green. USA., *The Man Who Had Everything*, Ben Ames Williams, Short Story

Man Who Had His Hair Cut Short, The *see* MAN DIE ZIJN HAAR KORT LIET KNIPPEN (1966).

MAN WHO HAD POWER OVER WOMEN, THE 1970 d: John Krish. UKN., *The Man Who Had Power Over Women*, Gordon M. Williams, London 1967, Novel

MAN WHO HAUNTED HIMSELF, THE 1970 d: Basil Dearden. UKN., *The Case of Mr. Pelham*, Anthony Armstrong, Story

MAN WHO KNEW TOO LITTLE, THE 1997 d: Jon Amiel. USA/GRM., *Watch That Man*, Robert Farrar, Novel

MAN WHO KNEW TOO MUCH, THE 1934 d: Alfred Hitchcock. UKN., *The Man Who Knew Too Much*, G. K. Chesterton, 1922, Short Story

MAN WHO KNEW TOO MUCH, THE 1956 d: Alfred Hitchcock. USA., *The Man Who Knew Too Much*, G. K. Chesterton, 1922, Short Story

MAN WHO LAUGHS, THE 1927 d: Paul Leni. USA., *L' Homme Qui Rit*, Victor Hugo, 1869, Novel

Man Who Laughs, The *see* L' UOMO CHE RIDE (1966).

MAN WHO LIKED LEMONS, THE 1923 d: George A. Cooper. UKN., *Untold Gold*, Will Scott, Short Story

MAN WHO LIVED AT THE RITZ, THE 1988 d: Desmond Davis. UKN/USA/FRN., A. E. Hotchner, Novel

MAN WHO LOST HIMSELF, THE 1920 d: George D. Baker. USA., *The Man Who Lost Himself*, Henry de Vere Stacpoole, New York 1918, Novel

MAN WHO LOST HIMSELF, THE 1941 d: Edward Ludwig. USA., *The Man Who Lost Himself*, Henry de Vere Stacpoole, New York 1918, Novel

MAN WHO LOVED CAT DANCING, THE 1973 d: Richard C. Sarafian. USA., *The Man Who Loved Cat Dancing*, Marilyn Durham, Novel

MAN WHO LOVED REDHEADS, THE 1955 d: Harold French. UKN., *Who Is Sylvia?*, Terence Rattigan, London 1950, Play

MAN WHO MARRIED A FRENCH WIFE, THE 1982 d: John Glenister. UKN/USA., *The Man Who Married a French Wife*, Irwin Shaw, Story

MAN WHO MARRIED HIS OWN WIFE, THE 1922 d: Stuart Paton. USA., *The Man Who Married His Own Wife*, Mary Ashe Miller, John Fleming Wilson, 1922, Short Story

Man Who Murdered, The *see* DER DEN MORD BEGING, DER MANN (1930).

MAN WHO NEVER WAS, THE 1956 d: Ronald Neame. UKN., *The Man Who Never Was*, Ewen Montagu, Book

Man Who Pawned His Soul, The *see* UNKNOWN BLONDE (1934).

MAN WHO PLAYED GOD, THE 1922 d: F. Harmon Weight. USA., *The Silent Voice*, Jules Eckert Goodman, New York 1914, Play

MAN WHO PLAYED GOD, THE 1932 d: John G. Adolfi. USA., *The Silent Voice*, Jules Eckert Goodman, New York 1914, Play

MAN WHO RECLAIMED HIS HEAD, THE 1934 d: Edward Ludwig. USA., *The Man Who Reclaimed His Head*, Jean Bart, New York 1932, Play

Man Who Returned from Afar, The *see* L' HOMME QUI REVIENT DE LOIN (1949).

MAN WHO RETURNED TO LIFE, THE 1942 d: Lew Landers. USA., *The Man Who Came to Life*, Samuel W. Taylor, Story

MAN WHO SHOT LIBERTY VALANCE, THE 1962 d: John Ford. USA., *The Man Who Shot Liberty Valance*, Dorothy M. Johnson, New York 1953, Short Story

Man Who Sold His Soul, The *see* L' HOMME QUI VENDAIT SON AME (1943).

MAN WHO STAYED AT HOME, THE 1915 d: Cecil M. Hepworth. UKN., *The Man Who Stayed at Home*, J. E. Harold Terry, Lechmere Worrall, London 1914, Play

MAN WHO STAYED AT HOME, THE 1919 d: Herbert Blache. USA., *The Man Who Stayed at Home*, J. E. Harold Terry, Lechmere Worrall, London 1914, Play

Man Who Stayed at the Ritz, The *see* THE MAN WHO LIVED AT THE RITZ (1988).

Man Who Stole a Dream, A *see* MANHANDLED (1949).

MAN WHO STOOD STILL, THE 1916 d: Frank H. Crane. USA., *The Man Who Stood Still*, Jules Eckert Goodman, New York 1908, Play

MAN WHO TALKED TOO MUCH, THE 1940 d: Vincent Sherman. USA., *The Mouthpiece*, Frank L. Collins, New York 1929, Play

MAN WHO, THE 1921 d: Maxwell Karger. USA., *The Man Who*, Lloyd Osbourne, 1921, Short Story

MAN WHO TURNED WHITE, THE 1919 d: Park Frame. USA., *The Man Who Turned White*, F. McGrew Willis, Short Story

MAN WHO UNDERSTOOD WOMEN, THE 1959 d: Nunnally Johnson. USA., *The Colors of the Day*, Romain Gary, 1953, Novel

Man Who Walked Through the Wall, The *see* EIN MANN GEHT DURCH DIE WAND (1959).

Man Who Wanted to Kill Himself, The *see* EL HOMBRE QUE SE QUISO MATAR (1941).

Man Who Wanted to Kill Himself, The *see* EL HOMBRE QUE SE QUISO MATAR (1970).

MAN WHO WAS AFRAID, THE 1917 d: Fred E. Wright. USA., Mary Brecht Pulver, Story

MAN WHO WAS NOBODY, THE 1960 d: Montgomery Tully. UKN., *The Man Who Was Nobody*, Edgar Wallace, London 1927, Novel

Man Who Watched the Trains Go By, The *see* THE MAN WHO WATCHED TRAINS GO BY (1952).

MAN WHO WATCHED TRAINS GO BY, THE 1952 d: Harold French. UKN., *L' Homme Qui Regardait Passer Les Trains*, Georges Simenon, 1938, Novel

Man Who Went Out of Fashion, The *see* NEMODLENEC (1927).

Man Who Went Up in Smoke, The *see* A SVED AKINEK NYOMA VESZETT (1980).

MAN WHO WON, THE 1918 d: Rex Wilson. UKN., *The Man Who Won*, Mrs. Baillie Reynolds, Novel

MAN WHO WON, THE 1919 d: Paul Scardon. USA., *The Man Who Won*, Cyrus Townsend Brady, Chicago 1919, Novel

MAN WHO WON, THE 1923 d: William A. Wellman. USA., *Twins of Suffering Creek*, Ridgwell Cullum, London 1912, Novel

MAN WHO WOULD BE KING, THE 1975 d: John Huston. USA., *The Man Who Would Be King*, Rudyard Kipling, 1888, Short Story

MAN WHO WOULDN'T DIE, THE 1942 d: Herbert I. Leeds. USA., *No Coffin for the Corpse*, Clayton Rawson, Novel

MAN WHO WOULDN'T TALK, THE 1940 d: David Burton. USA., *The Valiant*, Holworthy Hall, Robert M. Middlemass, 1920, Play

MAN WHO WOULDN'T TALK, THE 1958 d: Herbert Wilcox. UKN., *The Man Who Wouldn't Talk*, Stanley Jackson, Novel

Man With 100 Faces *see* CRACKERJACK (1938).

MAN WITH A CLOAK, THE 1951 d: Fletcher Markle. USA., *Gentleman from Paris*, John Dickson Carr, Novel

Man With a Gun, The *see* CHELOVEK S RUZHYOM (1938).

Man With a Hundred Faces, The *see* CRACKERJACK (1938).

Man With a Million *see* THE MILLION POUND NOTE (1953).

Man With a Rifle, The *see* CHELOVEK S RUZHYOM (1938).

Man With a Shaven Head, The *see* MAN DIE ZIJN HAAR KORT LIET KNIPPEN (1966).

Man With an Umbrella *see* DET REGNAR PA VAR KARLEK (1946).

MAN WITH BOGART'S FACE, THE 1980 d: Robert Day. USA., *The Man With Bogart's Face*, Andrew J. Fenady, Novel

MAN WITH MY FACE, THE 1951 d: Edward J. Montagne. USA., *The Man With My Face*, Samuel W. Taylor, 1948, Novel

Man With the Black Hat, The *see* SATAN MET A LADY (1936).

Man With the Deadly Lens, The *see* WRONG IS RIGHT (1982).

Man With the Glass Eye, The *see* DER MANN MIT DEM GLASAUGE (1968).

MAN WITH THE GOLDEN ARM, THE 1955 d: Otto Preminger. USA., *The Man With the Golden Arm*, Nelson Algren, 1949, Novel

MAN WITH THE GOLDEN GUN, THE 1974 d: Guy Hamilton. UKN., *The Man With the Golden Gun*, Ian Fleming, Novel

Man With the Golden Mask, The *see* L' UOMO CHE RIDE (1966).

Man With the Golden Touch, The *see* ARANYEMBER (1917).

Man With the Golden Touch, The *see* AZ ARANYEMBER (1962).

Man With the Green Carnation, The *see* THE TRIALS OF OSCAR WILDE (1960).

Man With the Gun, The *see* CHELOVEK S RUZHYOM (1938).

Man With the Iron Fist *see* GOTZ VON BERLICHINGEN MIT DER EISERNEN HAND (1978).

MAN WITH THE LIMP, THE 1923 d: A. E. Coleby. UKN., *The Man With the Limp*, Sax Rohmer, Short Story

MAN WITH THE MAGNETIC EYES, THE 1945 d: Ronald Haines. UKN., *The Man With the Magnetic Eyes*, Roland Daniel, Novel

MAN WITH THE TWISTED LIP, THE 1921 d: Maurice Elvey. UKN., *The Man With the Twisted Lip*, Arthur Conan Doyle, 1892, Short Story

MAN WITH THE TWISTED LIP, THE 1951 d: Richard M. Grey. UKN., *The Man With the Twisted Lip*, Arthur Conan Doyle, 1892, Short Story

Man With the Twisted Lip, The *see* THE RETURN OF SHERLOCK HOLMES: THE MAN WITH THE TWISTED LIP (1986).

Man With the Umbrella, The *see* FROM NINE TO NINE (1936).

Man With the Whistling Nose, The *see* IL FISCHIO AL NASO (1967).

Man With Thirty Sons, The *see* THE MAGNIFICENT YANKEE (1950).

MAN WITH TWO FACES, THE 1934 d: Archie Mayo. USA., *The Dark Tower*, George S. Kaufman, Alexander Woollcott, New York 1933, Play

Man With Wax Faces, The *see* FIGURES DE CIRE (1912).

Man Within, The *see* DER ANDERE (1930).

MAN WITHIN, THE 1947 d: Bernard Knowles. UKN., *The Man Within*, Graham Greene, 1929, Novel

MAN WITHOUT A COUNTRY, THE 1909 d: Bannister Merwin. USA., *The Man Without a Country*, Edward Everett Hale, 1863, Short Story

MAN WITHOUT A COUNTRY, THE 1917 d: Ernest C. Warde. USA., *The Man Without a Country*, Edward Everett Hale, 1863, Short Story

MAN WITHOUT A COUNTRY, THE 1925 d: Rowland V. Lee. USA., *The Man Without a Country*, Edward Everett Hale, 1863, Short Story

MAN WITHOUT A COUNTRY, THE 1973 d: Delbert Mann. USA., *The Man Without a Country*, Edward Everett Hale, 1863, Short Story

Man Without a Face *see* WHO? (1974).

Man Without a Heart *see* DER MANN OHNE HERZ (1923).

MAN WITHOUT A HEART, THE 1924 d: Burton L. King. USA., *The Man Without a Heart*, Ruby M. Ayres, New York 1924, Novel

Man Without a Map, The *see* MOETSUKITA CHIZU (1968).

Man Without a Name *see* MENSCH OHNE NAMEN (1932).

MAN WITHOUT A STAR 1955 d: King Vidor. USA., *Man Without a Star*, Dee Linford, New York 1952, Novel

Man Without Fear, A *see* END OF THE TRAIL (1936).

Man Without Mercy *see* LA HORSE (1969).

MAN, WOMAN AND CHILD 1983 d: Dick Richards. USA., *Man Woman and Child*, Erich Segal, Novel

MAN, WOMAN AND WIFE 1929 d: Edward Laemmle. USA., *Fallen Angels*, Arthur Somers Roche, 1927, Short Story

MAN WORTH WHILE, THE 1921 d: Romaine Fielding. USA., Ella Wheeler Wilcox, Poem

MANAGER OF THE B. & A., THE 1916 d: J. P. McGowan. USA., *The Manager of the B and A*, Vaughan Kester, New York 1901, Novel

Manbait *see* THE LAST PAGE (1952).

MANCHA QUE LIMPIA 1924 d: Jose Buchs. SPN., *Mancha Que Limpia*, Jose Echegaray, Play

MANCHE ET LA BELLE, UNE 1957 d: Henri Verneuil. FRN., *Une Manche Et la Belle*, James Hadley Chase, Novel

MANCHESTER MAN, THE 1920 d: Bert Wynne. UKN., *The Manchester Man*, Mrs. Linnaeus Banks, Novel

MANCHURIAN CANDIDATE, THE 1962 d: John Frankenheimer. USA., *The Manchurian Candidate*, Richard Condon, New York 1959, Novel

Mandabi *see* LE MANDAT (1968).

MANDAGARNA MED FANNY 1977 d: Lars Lennart Forsberg. SWD., *Mandagarna Med Fanny*, Gunnar Evander, Novel

MANDALA 1981 d: Im Kwon-Taek. SKR., *Mandala*, Kim Song Dong, Novel

MANDARIN MYSTERY, THE 1936 d: Ralph Staub. USA., *The Chinese Orange Mystery*, Ellery Queen, New York 1934, Novel

MANDARINO PER TEO, UN 1960 d: Mario Mattoli. ITL., *Un Mandarino Per Teo*, Pietro Garinei, Sandro Giovannini, Musical Play

MANDAT, LE 1968 d: Ousmane Sembene. SNL/FRN., *Le Mandat*, Ousmane Sembene, 1965, Short Story

Manden, Der Ikki Kunne Sige Nej *see* DER NICHT NEIN SAGEN KONNTE, DER MANN (1958).

MANDINGO 1975 d: Richard Fleischer. USA., *Mandingo*, Kyle Onstott, Novel

MANDRAGOLA, LA 1965 d: Alberto LattuadA. ITL/FRN., *La Mandragola*, Niccolo MacHiavelli, 1514, Play

Mandragola -the Love Root *see* LA MANDRAGOLA (1965).

Mandragore *see* ALRAUNE (1928).

Mandragore *see* ALRAUNE (1952).

Mandragore, La *see* LA MANDRAGOLA (1965).

Mandrake *see* ALRAUNE (1928).

Mandrake *see* ALRAUNE (1952).

Mandrake, The *see* LA MANDRAGOLA (1965).

MANDY 1952 d: Alexander MacKendrick. UKN., *The Day Is Ours*, Hilda Lewis, Novel

Maneater *see* SHARK! (1969).

MAN-EATER OF KUMAON 1948 d: Byron Haskin. USA., *Man-Eaters of Kumaon*, James Corbett, Story

MANEATERS ARE LOOSE! 1978 d: Timothy Galfas. USA., *Maneater*, Ted Willis, Book

Man-Eating Tiger *see* SPRING TONIC (1935).

MANEGE 1927 d: Max Reichmann. GRM., *Manege*, Walter Angel, Novel

MANFISH 1955 d: W. Lee Wilder. USA., *Gold Bug*, Edgar Allan Poe, 1843, Short Story, *The Tell-Tale Heart*, Edgar Allan Poe, 1843, Short Story

Mangalsutram *see* VANDE MATARAM (1939).

MANGANINNIE 1980 d: John Honey. ASL., *Manganinnie*, Beth Roberts, Novel

MANGGAO ZHI GE 1976 d: Chang Yan, Zhang Puren. CHN., *Overture*, Gu Yu, Short Story

MANGO TREE, THE 1977 d: Kevin Dobson. ASL., *The Mango Tree*, Ronald McKie, Novel

MANHA SUBMERSA 1980 d: Lauro Antonio. PRT., *Manha Submersa*, Vergilio Ferreira, 1954, Novel

MANHANDLED 1924 d: Allan Dwan. USA., *Manhandled*, Arthur Stringer, 1924, Short Story

MANHANDLED 1949 d: Lewis R. Foster. USA., *The Man Who Stole a Dream*, L. S. Goldsmith, Novel

MANHATTAN 1924 d: R. H. Burnside. USA., *The Definite Object*, Jeffrey Farnol, Boston 1917, Novel

MANHATTAN BUTTERFLY 1935 d: Lewis D. Collins. USA., *Broadway Virgin*, Lois Bull, New York 1931, Novel

MANHATTAN HEARTBEAT 1940 d: David Burton. USA., *Bad Girl*, Vina Delmar, New York 1928, Novel

MANHATTAN KNIGHT, A 1920 d: George A. Beranger. USA., *Find the Woman*, Gelett Burgess, Indianapolis 1911, Novel

MANHATTAN LOVE SONG 1934 d: Leonard Fields. USA., *Manhattan Love Song*, Cornell Woolrich, New York 1932, Novel

Manhattan Love Song *see* CHANGE OF HEART (1934).

Manhattan Madness *see* WOMAN WANTED (1935).

Manhattan Madness *see* ADVENTURE IN MANHATTAN (1936).

Manhattan Mary *see* FOLLOW THE LEADER (1930).

MANHATTAN MERRY-GO-ROUND 1937 d: Charles F. Reisner. USA., *Manhattan Merry-Go-Round*, Frank Hummert, Musical Play

Manhattan Music Box *see* MANHATTAN MERRY-GO-ROUND (1937).

MANHATTAN PARADE 1932 d: Lloyd Bacon. USA., *She Means Business*, Samuel Shipman, New York 1931, Play

MANHATTAN SHAKEDOWN 1939 d: Leon BarshA. CND., Theodore A. Tinsley, Story

Manhattan Whirlwind *see* MANHATTAN SHAKEDOWN (1939).

Manhunt *see* FROM HELL TO TEXAS (1958).

MANHUNT FOR CLAUDE DALLAS 1986 d: Jerry London. USA., *Outlaw*, Jeff Long, Book

MANHUNT IN THE JUNGLE 1958 d: Tom McGowan. USA., *Man Hunting in the Jungle*, George M. Dyott, 1930, Book

Manhunt, The *see* HAJKA (1977).

MANHUNTER 1986 d: Michael Mann. USA., *Red Dragon*, Thomas Harris, Novel

Manhunter, The *see* THE MAN HUNTER (1969).

Maniacs on Wheels *see* ONCE A JOLLY SWAGMAN (1948).

MANIFESTO 1989 d: Dusan Makavejev. USA/YGS., *Pour une Nuit d'Amour*, Emile Zola, 1882, Short Story

Manila *see* SA MGA KUKO NG LIWANAG MAYNILA (1975).

Manila: in the Claws of Darkness *see* SA MGA KUKO NG LIWANAG MAYNILA (1975).

Manila in the Claws of Light *see* SA MGA KUKO NG LIWANAG MAYNILA (1975).

Manila: in the Claws of Neon *see* SA MGA KUKO NG LIWANAG MAYNILA (1975).

MANITOU, THE 1978 d: William Girdler. USA., *The Manitou*, Graham Masterton, Novel

MANJHLI DIDI 1968 d: Hrishikesh Mukherjee. IND., *Mej-Didi*, Sarat Candra Cattopadhyay, 1915, Short Story

MANJI 1964 d: Yasuzo MasumurA. JPN., *Manji*, Junichiro Tanizaki, 1930, Novel

MANJIANG HONG 1933 d: Cheng Bugao. CHN., *Manjiang Hong*, Zhang Henshui, Novel

Manly Times *see* MUZHKI VREMENA (1977).

Man-Made Monster *see* MAN MADE MONSTER (1941).

MANMOYEE GIRLS' SCHOOL 1935 d: Jyotish Bannerji. IND., *Manmoyee Girls' School*, Rabindranath Maitra, Play

MANMOYEE GIRLS' SCHOOL 1958 d: Hemchandra Chunder. IND., *Manmoyee Girls' School*, Rabindranath Maitra, Play

MANN AUF ABWEGEN, EIN 1940 d: Herbert Selpin. GRM., *Percy Auf Abwegen*, Hans Thomas, Novel

MANN AUF DER MAUER, DER 1982 d: Reinhard Hauff. GRM., *Der Mann Auf Der Mauer*, Peter Schneider, Novel

MANN, DER DEN MORD BEGING, DER 1930 d: Curtis Bernhardt. GRM., Claude Farrere, Novel

MANN, DER NICHT LIEBT, DER 1929 d: Guido Brignone. GRM., *Kean; Ou Desordre du Genie*, Alexandre Dumas (pere), 1836, Play

MANN, DER NICHT NEIN SAGEN KONNTE, DER 1958 d: Kurt Fruh, Hans Mehringer (Uncredited). SWT/DNM/GRM., *Der Unmoralische Herr Thomas Traumer*, Hans Jacoby, Short Story

Mann, Der Sich in Luft Aufloste, Der *see* A SVED AKINEK NYOMA VESZETT (1980).

MANN, DER SICH VERDACHTIG MACHTE, DER 1989 d: Yves Boisset. GRM/FRN., Georges Simenon, Novel

Mann, Der Stolze, Die Rache, Der *see* L'ORGOGLIO, LA VENDETTA, L' UOMO (1967).

MANN GEHT DURCH DIE WAND, EIN 1959 d: Ladislao VajdA. GRM., *Le Passe-Muraille*, Marcel Ayme, Paris 1943, Short Story

Mann Im Hintergrund, Der *see* DE MAN OP DEN ACHTERGROND (1923).

MANN IM SCHILF, DER 1978 d: Manfred Purzer. GRM., *Der Mann Im Schilf*, George Emmanuel Saiko, 1955, Novel

MANN IM SCHONSTEN ALTER, EIN 1963 d: Franz Peter Wirth. GRM., *Ein Mann Im Schonsten Alter*, Rudolf Schnider-Schelde, Novel

MANN IM STROM, DER 1958 d: Eugen York. GRM., *Der Mann Im Strom*, Siegfried Lenz, 1957, Novel

MANN IN DER WANNE, DER 1952 d: Franz Antel. AUS., *Der Mann in Der Wanne*, Karl Fellmar, Ernst Friese, Play

MANN MIT DEM GLASAUGE, DER 1968 d: Alfred Vohrer. GRM., Edgar Wallace, Novel

MANN MIT DEN BAUMEN, DER 1990 d: Werner Kubny. GRM., Jean Giono, Story

Mann Mit Der Torpedohaut, Der *see* LA PEAU DE TORPEDO (1970).

MANN NEBENAN, DER 1991 d: Petra Haffter. GRM., Ruth Rendell, Novel

MANN OHNE HERZ, DER 1923 d: Franz W. Koebner, Josef Hornak. GRM/CZC., *Muz Bez Srdce*, Ernst Klein, Novel

Mann Will in Die Heimat, Ein *see* EIN MANN WILL NACH DEUTSCHLAND (1934).

MANN WILL NACH DEUTSCHLAND, EIN 1934 d: Paul Wegener. GRM., *Ein Mann Will Nach Deutschland*, Fred Andreas, Novel

MANNEN FRAN MALLORCA 1984 d: Bo Widerberg. SWD/DNM., *Mannen Fran Mallorca*, Leif G. W. Persson, Novel

MANNEN I SKUGAN 1978 d: Arne Mattsson. SWD/YGS., *De Vrachtwagen*, Per Wahloo, Novel

MANNEN PA BALKONGEN 1993 d: Daniel Alfredson. SWD/DNM., *De Man Op Het Balkon*, Maj Sjowall, Per Wahloo, Novel

MANNEN PA TAKET 1977 d: Bo Widerberg. SWD., *Mannen Pa Taket*, Maj Sjowall, Per Wahloo, Novel

Mannen Som Gick Upp I Rok *see* A SVED AKINEK NYOMA VESZETT (1980).

MANNEN UTAN ANSIKTE 1959 d: Albert Band. SWD/USA., *The Monster*, Stephen Crane, 1899, Short Story

MANNEQUIN 1926 d: James Cruze. USA., *Mannequin*, Fannie Hurst, New York 1926, Novel

MANNEQUIN ASSASSINE, LE 1947 d: Pierre de Herain. FRN., *Le Mannequin Assassine*, Stanislas-Andre Steeman, Novel

MANNEQUINS 1933 d: Rene Hervil. FRN., *Mannequins*, Jacques Bousquet, Henri Falk, Opera

Manner Mussen Es Sein *see* MANNER MUSSEN SO SEIN (1939).

MANNER MUSSEN SO SEIN 1939 d: Arthur M. Rabenalt. GRM., *Manner Mussen So Sein*, Heinrich Seiler, Ebendorf 1938, Novel

Manner Mussen So Sein *see* GELIEBTE BESTIE (1959).

Manner of Behaving, A *see* SPOSOB BYCIA (1966).

Manners Make Man *see* SATY DELAJI CLOVECKA (1912).

Manniskor Mots Och Ljuv Music Uppstar I Hjartet *see* MENNESKER MODES OG SOD MUSIK OPSTAR I HJERTET (1968).

MANO DELLA MORTA, LA 1949 d: Carlo Campogalliani. ITL., *La Mano Della Morta*, Carolina Invernizio, Novel

MANO DELLO STRANIERO, LA 1954 d: Mario Soldati. ITL/UKN., *The Stranger's Hand*, Graham Greene, Novel

MANO EN LA TRAMPA, LA 1961 d: Leopoldo Torre-Nilsson. ARG/SPN., *La Mano En la Trampa*, Beatriz Guido, Buenos Aires 1961, Novel

MANO TAGLIATA, LA 1919 d: Alberto Degli Abbati. ITL., *La Mano Tagliata*, Matilde Serao, Novel

MANOLESCU 1929 d: Victor Tourjansky. GRM., *Manolescu*, Hans Szekely, Short Story

MANON 1948 d: Henri-Georges Clouzot. FRN., *L' Histoire du Chevalier Des Grieux Et de Manon Lescaut*, Antoine-Francois Prevost d'Exiles, la haye 1731, Novel

Manon 326 *see* LA ROUTE DU BAGNE (1945).

MANON 70 1968 d: Jean Aurel. FRN/GRM/ITL., *L' Histoire du Chevalier Des Grieux Et de Manon Lescaut*, Antoine-Francois Prevost d'Exiles, la haye 1731, Novel

Manon '70 *see* MANON 70 (1968).

MANON DES SOURCES 1985 d: Claude Berri. FRN/ITL/SWT., *L' Eau Des Collines Vol. 2: Manon Des Sources*, Marcel Pagnol, 1963, Novel

MANON LESCAUT 1908. ITL., *L' Histoire du Chevalier Des Grieux Et de Manon Lescaut*, Antoine-Francois Prevost d'Exiles, la haye 1731, Novel

MANON LESCAUT 1912 d: Albert Capellani. FRN., *L' Histoire du Chevalier Des Grieux Et de Manon Lescaut*, Antoine-Francois Prevost d'Exiles, la haye 1731, Novel

MANON LESCAUT 1914 d: Herbert Hall Winslow. USA., *L' Histoire du Chevalier Des Grieux Et de Manon Lescaut*, Antoine-Francois Prevost d'Exiles, la Haye 1731, Novel

MANON LESCAUT 1918 d: Mario Gargiulo. ITL., *L' Histoire du Chevalier Des Grieux Et de Manon Lescaut*, Antoine-Francois Prevost d'Exiles, la haye 1731, Novel

MANON LESCAUT 1919 d: Friedrich Zelnik. GRM., *L' Histoire du Chevalier Des Grieux Et de Manon Lescaut*, Antoine-Francois Prevost d'Exiles, la haye 1731, Novel

MANON LESCAUT 1926 d: Arthur Robison. GRM., *L' Histoire du Chevalier Des Grieux Et de Manon Lescaut*, Antoine-Francois Prevost d'Exiles, la haye 1731, Novel

MANON LESCAUT 1940 d: Carmine Gallone. ITL., *L' Histoire du Chevalier Des Grieux Et de Manon Lescaut*, Antoine-Francois Prevost d'Exiles, la haye 1731, Novel

Manon of the Spring *see* MANON DES SOURCES (1985).

Manon, Woman Without Scruples *see* MANON 70 (1968).

MANOUCHE - JEUNESSE D'AUJOURD'HUI 1942 d: Fred Surville. SWT., *Printemps*, Mme M. L. de Wyttenbach, Short Story

Manouche, Das Madchen, Das Den Weg Verlor *see* MANOUCHE - JEUNESSE D'AUJOURD'HUI (1942).

Manoverzwilling *see* WENN POLDI INS MANOVER ZIEHT (1956).

MANOVRE D'AMORE 1941 d: Gennaro Righelli. ITL., *Krieg Im Frieden*, Gustav von Moser, Franz von Schonthan, 1880, Play

Manpower *see* MAN POWER (1927).

MAN-PROOF 1937 d: Richard Thorpe. USA., *The Four Marys*, Fanny Heaslip Lea, New York 1937, Novel

MANRAPE 1978 d: Jorn Donner. SWD/FNL., Marta Tikkanen, Novel

MAN'S CASTLE 1933 d: Frank Borzage. USA., *Man's Castle*, Lawrence Hazard, 1932, Play

Man's Castle, A *see* MAN'S CASTLE (1933).

MAN'S FAVORITE SPORT? 1964 d: Howard Hawks. USA., *The Girl Who Almost Got Away*, Pat Frank, Short Story

MAN'S HOME, A 1921 d: Ralph Ince. USA., *A Man's Home*, Edmund Breese, Anna Steese Richardson, Albany, N.Y. 1917, Play

Man's Honor, The *see* JOHN GLAYDE'S HONOR (1915).

Man's Hope *see* ESPOIR (1939).

MANS KVINNA 1945 d: Gunnar Skoglund. SWD., *Mans Kvinna*, Vilhelm Moberg, 1933, Novel

MAN'S LAW 1915 d: Colin Campbell. USA., *Man's Law*, James Oliver Curwood, Story

MAN'S MAN, A 1917 d: Oscar Apfel. USA., *A Man's Man*, Peter B. Kyne, 1917, Serial Story

MAN'S MAN, A 1923 d: Oscar Apfel. USA., *A Man's Man*, Peter B. Kyne, 1917, Serial Story

MAN'S MAN, A 1929 d: James Cruze. USA., *A Man's Man*, Patrick Kearney, New York 1925, Novel

MAN'S PAST, A 1927 d: George Melford. USA., *Diploma*, Emric Foldes, Play

MAN'S SHADOW, A 1920 d: Sidney Morgan. UKN., *A Man's Shadow*, Robert Buchanan, London 1889, Play

MAN'S SIZE 1923 d: Howard M. Mitchell. USA., *Man Size*, William MacLeod Raine, New York 1922, Novel

Mans Vag, En *see* MIEHEN TIE (1940).

MAN'S WORLD, A 1918 d: Herbert Blache. USA., *A Man's World*, Rachel Crothers, New York 1910, Play

Man's World, A *see* DADDY'S GONE A-HUNTING (1925).

MANSFIELD PARK 1986 d: David Giles. UKN., *Mansfield Park*, Jane Austen, 1814, Novel

857

MANSION DE LA LOCURA, LA 1971 d: Juan Lopez MoctezumA. MXC., *The System of Doctor Tarr and Professor Feather*, Edgar Allan Poe, 1845, Short Story

MANSION OF ACHING HEARTS, THE 1925 d: James P. Hogan. USA., *The Mansion of Aching Hearts*, Arthur J. Lamb, Harry von Tilzer, 1902, Song

Mansion of Madness, The *see* LA MANSION DE LA LOCURA (1971).

MANSLAUGHTER 1922 d: Cecil B. de Mille. USA., *Manslaughter*, Alice Duer Miller, New York 1921, Novel

MANSLAUGHTER 1930 d: George Abbott. USA., *Manslaughter*, Alice Duer Miller, New York 1921, Novel

Manster -Half Man, Half Monster, The *see* THE MANSTER (1962).

MANSTER, THE 1962 d: George Breakston, Kenneth L. Crane. USA/JPN., *Nightmare*, George P. Breakston

MANTRAP 1926 d: Victor Fleming. USA., *Mantrap*, Sinclair Lewis, New York 1926, Novel

MANTRAP 1953 d: Terence Fisher. UKN., *Queen in Danger*, Elleston Trevor, Novel

MAN-TRAP 1961 d: Edmond O'Brien. USA., *Taint of the Tiger*, John D. MacDonald, 1958, Short Story

MANU 1987 d: Alfredo Giannetti. FRN/ITL., Luigi Pirandello, Short Story

MANUELA 1957 d: Guy Hamilton. UKN., *Manuela*, William Woods, Play

Manuscript Found in Saragossa *see* REKOPIS ZNALEZIONY W SARAGOSSIE (1965).

MANUSCRITO DE UNA MADRE, EL 1928 d: Reinhardt Blothner. SPN., *El Manuscrito de Una Madre*, Enrique Perez Escrich, Story

MANXMAN, THE 1916 d: George Loane Tucker. UKN., *The Manxman*, Hall Caine, 1894, Novel

MANXMAN, THE 1929 d: Alfred Hitchcock. UKN., *The Manxman*, Hall Caine, 1894, Novel

MANY A SLIP 1931 d: Vin Moore. USA., *Many a Slip*, Edith Fitzgerald, Robert Riskin, New York 1930, Play

MANY HAPPY RETURNS 1934 d: Norman Z. McLeod. USA., *Often a Bridegroom*, Lady Mary Cameron, Short Story

Many Loves of Hilda Crane, The *see* HILDA CRANE (1956).

MANY RIVERS TO CROSS 1954 d: Roy Rowland. USA., *Many Rivers to Cross*, Steve Frazee, Short Story

Many Wars Ago *see* UOMINI CONTRO (1970).

MANY WATERS 1931 d: Milton Rosmer. UKN., *Many Waters (the Unnamed Play)*, Monckton Hoffe, London 1926, Play

Many-Splendored Thing, A *see* LOVE IS A MANY-SPLENDORED THING (1955).

MANZELKA NECO TUSI 1938 d: Karel SpelinA. CZC., *Manzelka Neco Tusi*, Mana Dubska, Novel

MANZELSTVI NA UVER 1936 d: Oldrich Kminek. CZC., *Spodni Tony*, Marie Blazkova, Novel

MAOS VAZIAS 1971 d: Luiz Carlos LacerdA. BRZ., *Maos Vazias*, Lucio Cardoso, 1938, Short Story

Map for 19 Years Old, A *see* JUKYUSAI NO CHIZU (1979).

MAPP AND LUCIA 1985 d: Donald McWhinnie. UKN., E. F. Benson, Novel

Maquillage *see* DA HALT DIE WELT DEN ATEM AN (1927).

MAQUILLAGE 1932 d: Karl Anton. FRN., *The Feeder*, Mildred Cram, 1926, Short Story

MAR DEL TIEMPO PERDIDO, EL 1978 d: Solveig Hoogesteijn. VNZ/GRM., *Cien Anos de Soledad*, Gabriel Garcia Marquez, 1967, Novel

MARACAIBO 1958 d: Cornel Wilde. USA., *Maracaibo*, Stirling Silliphant, 1955, Novel

MARARIA 1998 d: Antonio Jose Betancor. SPN., *Mararia*, Rafael Arozarena, Novel

Marat/de Sade *see* PERSECUTION AND ASSASSINATION OF JEAN-PAUL MARAT AS PERFORMED BY THE INMATES OF THE ASYLUM. (1966).

Marathon *see* SWEET REVENGE (1987).

MARATHON MAN 1976 d: John Schlesinger. USA., *Marathon Man*, William Goldman, 1974, Novel

MARATRE, LA 1918 d: Jacques Gretillat. FRN., *La Maratre*, Honore de Balzac

MARATTAM 1989 d: G. Aravindan. IND., *Marattam*, Kavalam Narayana Panicker, Play

MARAUDERS, THE 1955 d: Gerald Mayer. USA., *The Marauders*, Alan Marcus, Novel

Marauders, The *see* MERRILL'S MARAUDERS (1962).

MARBLE HEART, THE 1913. USA., *The Marble Heart*, Charles Selby, New York 1864, Play

MARBLE HEART, THE 1915 d: George A. Lessey. USA., *The Marble Heart*, Charles Selby, New York 1864, Play

MARBLE HEART, THE 1916 d: Kenean Buel. USA., *Therese Raquin*, Emile Zola, 1867, Novel

MARCELLA 1915 d: Baldassarre Negroni. ITL., *Marcella*, Victorien Sardou, 1895, Play

MARCELLA 1937 d: Guido Brignone. ITL., *Marcella*, Victorien Sardou, 1895, Play

MARCH HARE, THE 1956 d: George M. O'Ferrall. UKN., *Gamblers Sometimes Win*, T. H. Bird, Novel

March of the Toys *see* BABES IN TOYLAND (1934).

March of the Wooden Soldiers *see* BABES IN TOYLAND (1934).

March to the Gallows *see* STRAFBATAILLON 999 (1960).

MARCHAND DE BONHEUR, LE 1918 d: Georges-Andre Lacroix. FRN., *Le Marchand de Bonheur*, Henri Kistemaeckers, Play

MARCHAND DE BONHEUR, LE 1927 d: Joseph Guarino. FRN., *Le Marchand de Bonheur*, Henri Kistemaeckers, Play

MARCHAND DE SABLE, LE 1931 d: Andre Hugon. FRN., *Le Marchand de Sable*, Georges-Andre Cuel, Novel

MARCHAND DE VENISE, LE 1952 d: Pierre Billon. FRN/ITL., *The Merchant of Venice*, William Shakespeare, c1595, Play

MARCHE NUPTIALE, LA 1928 d: Andre Hugon. FRN., *La Marche Nuptiale*, Henry Bataille, 1905, Play

MARCHE NUPTIALE, LA 1934 d: Mario Bonnard. FRN., *La Marche Nuptiale*, Henry Bataille, 1905, Play

MARCHE OU CREVE 1960 d: Georges Lautner. FRN/BLG., *Otages*, Jack Murray, Novel

MARCHESE DI LANTENAC, LA 1911. ITL., *Quatrevingt-Treize*, Victor Hugo, 1874, Novel

MARCHESE DI RUVOLITO, IL 1939 d: Raffaello Matarazzo. ITL., *Il Marchese Di Ruvolito*, Nino Martoglio, Play

Marcheurs de la Nuit, Les *see* CAIN (1965).

Marching Along *see* STARS AND STRIPES FOREVER (1952).

MARCIA NUZIALE, LA 1915 d: Carmine Gallone. ITL., *La Marche Nuptiale*, Henry Bataille, 1905, Play

MARCIA NUZIALE, LA 1934 d: Mario Bonnard. ITL., *La Marche Nuptiale*, Henry Bataille, 1905, Play

Marco Antonio Y Cleopatra *see* ANTONY AND CLEOPATRA (1973).

MARCO VISCONTI 1909 d: Mario Caserini. ITL., *Marco Visconti*, Tommaso Grossi, 1834, Novel

MARCO VISCONTI 1911 d: Ugo FalenA. ITL., *Marco Visconti*, Tommaso Grossi, 1834, Novel

MARCO VISCONTI 1925 d: Aldo de Benedetti. ITL., *Marco Visconti*, Tommaso Grossi, 1834, Novel

MARCO VISCONTI 1941 d: Mario Bonnard. ITL., *Marco Visconti*, Tommaso Grossi, 1834, Novel

Marcus, the Venetian Tribune *see* LA NAVE (1912).

MARCUS-NELSON MURDERS, THE 1973 d: Joseph Sargent. USA., *Justice in the Back Room*, Selwyn Rabb, Novel

MARE AU DIABLE, LA 1923 d: Pierre Caron. FRN., *La Mare Au Diable*, George Sand, Novel

MARE DI GUAI, UN 1940 d: Carlo Ludovico BragagliA. ITL., *Theodore Et Cie*, Robert Armont, Nicolas Nancey, 1909, Play

MARE NOSTRUM 1925 d: Rex Ingram. USA., *Mare Nostrum*, Vicente Blasco Ibanez, 1916, Novel

MARE NOSTRUM 1948 d: Rafael Gil. SPN/ITL., *Mare Nostrum*, Vicente Blasco Ibanez, 1916, Novel

MARELE SINGURATIC 1976 d: Iulian Mihu. RMN., *Marele Singuratic*, Marin Preda, 1972, Novel

Maremma *see* IN MAREMMA (1924).

MARESI 1948 d: Hans Thimig. AUS., *Maresi*, Alexander Lernet-Holenia, Novel

MARGARET BOURKE-WHITE: THE TRUE STORY 1989 d: Lawrence Schiller. USA., Vicki Goldberg, Biography

MARGARET'S MUSEUM 1995 d: Mort Ransen. CND/UKN., *The Glace Bay Miner's Museum*, Sheldon Currie, Short Story

MARGARITA, ARMANDO Y SU PADRE 1939 d: Francisco MujicA. ARG., *Armando Y Su Padre Margarita*, Enrique Jardiel Poncela, 1931, Play

Margayya the Banker *see* BANKER MARGAYYA (1983).

Marghere Di Cavouret, Le *see* LE LATTIVENDOLE (1914).

Margherita Della Notte *see* MARGUERITE DE LA NUIT (1955).

MARGHERITA FRA I TRE 1942 d: Ivo Perilli. ITL., *Margherita Fra I Tre*, Fritz Schwiefert, Play

MARGHERITA PUSTERLA 1910 d: Mario Caserini. ITL., *Margherita Pusterla*, Cesare Cantu, 1838, Novel

MARGIE 1946 d: Henry King. USA., Richard Bransten, Ruth McKenney, Short Stories

MARGIN FOR ERROR 1943 d: Otto Preminger. USA., *Margin for Error*, Clare Boothe, New York 1939, Play

MARGOT 1914 d: Ubaldo Maria Del Colle. ITL., *Margot*, Alfred de Musset, 1838, Short Story

MARGUERITE DE LA NUIT 1955 d: Claude Autant-LarA. FRN/ITL., *Marguerite de la Nuit*, Pierre Mac Orlan, 1925, Short Story

Marguerite of the Night *see* MARGUERITE DE LA NUIT (1955).

MARI A PRIX FIXE, UN 1965 d: Claude de Givray. FRN., *Un Mari a Prix Fixe*, Maria-Luisa Linares, Novel

Mari de la Reine, La *see* ECHEC AU ROI (1931).

Mari de la Reine, Le *see* LE PLUS BEAU GOSSE DE FRANCE (1937).

MARI GARCON, LE 1933 d: Alberto Cavalcanti. FRN., *Le Mari Garcon*, Paul Armont, Marcel Gerbidon, Play

Mari Modele, Le *see* DER MUSTERGATTE (1959).

Mari Quadrupede, Le *see* UNE VIE DE CHIEN (1941).

MARIA 1947 d: Gosta Folke. SWD., *Maria*, Gustav Sandgren, 1942, Novel

MARIA 1975 d: Mats Arehn. SWD., *I Stallet for En Pappa*, Kerstin Thorvall, 1971, Novel

Maria Antonia *see* LA LOTTA PER LA VITA (1921).

MARIA BONITA 1936 d: Julien Mandel. BRZ., *Maria Bonita*, Julio Afranio Peixoto, 1914, Novel

MARIA CHAPDELAINE 1934 d: Julien Duvivier. FRN., *Maria Chapdelaine; Recit du Canada Francais*, Louis Hemon, 1916, Novel

Maria Chapdelaine *see* THE NAKED HEART (1950).

MARIA CHAPDELAINE 1983 d: Gilles Carle. CND/FRN., *Maria Chapdelaine; Recit du Canada Francais*, Louis Hemon, 1916, Novel

MARIA DU BOUT DU MONDE 1950 d: Jean Stelli. FRN., *Chasse a l'Homme*, Jean Martet, Novel

MARIA ILONA 1939 d: Geza von Bolvary. GRM., *Ilona Beck*, Oswald Richter-Tersik, Novel

MARIA MARTEN 1928 d: Walter West. UKN., *Maria Marten*, Anon, London 1840, Play

Maria Marten *see* THE MURDER IN THE RED BARN MARIA MARTEN; OR (1935).

MARIA MARTEN; OR, THE MURDER AT THE RED BARN 1902 d: Dicky Winslow. UKN., *Maria Marten*, Anon, London 1840, Play

MARIA MARTEN; OR, THE MURDER AT THE RED BARN 1913 d: Maurice Elvey. UKN., *Maria Marten*, Anon, London 1840, Play

MARIA MARTEN; OR, THE MURDER IN THE RED BARN 1935 d: Milton Rosmer. UKN., *Maria Marten*, Anon, London 1840, Play

MARIA MONTECRISTO 1950 d: Luis Cesar Amadori. MXC., Grisha Malinin, Novel

MARIA MORZEK 1976 d: Horst Flick. GRM., *Maria Morzeck Oder Das Kaninchen Bin Ich*, Manfred Bieler, 1965, Novel

MARIA NO OYUKI 1935 d: Kenji Mizoguchi. JPN., *Boule de Suif*, Guy de Maupassant, 1880, Short Story

MARIA ROSA 1916 d: Cecil B. de Mille. USA., *Maria Rosa*, Angel Guimera, Spain 1890, Play

MARIA ROSA 1964 d: Armando Moreno. SPN., *Maria Rosa*, Angel Guimera, Spain 1890, Play

MARIA STUART 1959 d: Alfred Stoger, Leopold Lindtberg. AUS., *Maria Stuart*, Friedrich von Schiller, 1801, Play

MARIA VANDAMME 1988 d: Jacques Ertaud. FRN., *Maria Vandamme*, Jacques Duquesne, Novel

Maria Zef *see* CONDANNATA SENZA COLPA (1954).

Mariage a l'Italienne *see* MATRIMONIO ALL'ITALIANA (1964).

MARIAGE A RESPONSABILITE LIMITEE 1933 d: Jean de Limur. FRN., *Causa Kaiser*, Eisler, Stark, Play

MARIAGE DE CHIFFON, LE 1917 d: Alberto Carlo Lolli. ITL., *Le Mariage de Chiffon*, Gyp, 1894, Novel

MARIAGE DE CHIFFON, LE 1941 d: Claude Autant-LarA. FRN., *Le Mariage de Chiffon*, Gyp, 1894, Novel

MARIAGE DE FIGARO, LE 1959 d: Jean Meyer. FRN., *Le Mariage de Figaro*, Pierre-Augustin Caron de Beaumarchais, Paris 1784, Play

MARIAGE DE MADEMOISELLE BEULEMANS, LE 1926 d: Julien Duvivier. FRN., *Le Mariage de Mademoiselle Beulemans*, Franz Fonson, Fernand Wicheler, Play

MARIAGE DE MADEMOISELLE BEULEMANS, LE 1950 d: Andre Cerf. FRN/BLG., *Le Mariage de Mademoiselle Beulemans*, Franz Fonson, Fernand Wicheler, Play

MARIAGE DE MADEMOISELLE BEULEMANS, LE 1983 d: Michel Rochat. BLG., *Le Mariage de Mademoiselle Beulemans*, Franz Fonson, Fernand Wicheler, Play

MARIAGE DE MLLE BEULEMANS, LE 1932 d: Jean Choux. FRN., *Le Mariage de Mademoiselle Beulemans*, Franz Fonson, Fernand Wicheler, Play

Mariage de Monsieur Mississippi, Le *see* DIE EHE DES HERRN MISSISSIPPI (1961).

MARIAGE DE RAMUNTCHO, LE 1946 d: Max de Vaucorbeil. FRN., *Ramuntcho*, Pierre Loti, 1896, Novel

MARIAGE DE VERENA, LE 1938 d: Jacques Daroy. FRN/SWT., *Verenas Hochzeit*, Lisa Wenger, Novel

MARIAGES 1977 d: Teff Erhat. BLG., *Mariages*, Charles Plisnier, 1936, Novel

MARIANDL 1961 d: Werner Jacobs. AUS., *Mariandl*, Martin Costa, Play

MARIANELA 1940 d: Benito Perojo. SPN., *Marianela*, Benito Perez Galdos, 1878, Novel

MARIANELA 1972 d: Angelino Fons. SPN/FRN., *Marianela*, Benito Perez Galdos, 1878, Novel

Marianna Sirca *see* AMORE ROSSO (1953).

MARIANNA UCRIA 1997 d: Roberto FaenzA. ITL/FRN., *The Long Life of Marianna Ucria*, Dacia Maraini, Novel

Marianne *see* MARIANNE DE MA JEUNESSE (1954).

MARIANNE DE MA JEUNESSE 1954 d: Julien Duvivier. FRN/GRM., *Douloureuse Arcadie*, Peter Mendelssohn, Novel

Marianne of My Youth *see* MARIANNE DE MA JEUNESSE (1954).

Maria-Pilar *see* AU COEUR DE LA CASBAH (1951).

Maribel and the Estranged Family *see* MARIBEL Y LA EXTRANA FAMILIA (1960).

Maribel and the Strange Family *see* MARIBEL Y LA EXTRANA FAMILIA (1960).

MARIBEL Y LA EXTRANA FAMILIA 1960 d: Jose Maria Forque. SPN., *Maribel Y la Extrana Familia*, Miguel Mihura Santos, 1960, Play

MARIDO DE IDA Y VUELTA, UN 1957 d: Luis LuciA. SPN., *Un Marido de Ida Y Vuelta*, Enrique Jardiel Poncela, 1939, Play

MARIE 1986 d: Roger Donaldson. USA., *Marie: a True Story*, Peter Maas, Book

Marie: a True Story *see* MARIE (1986).

MARIE ANTOINETTE 1938 d: W. S. Van Dyke, Julien Duvivier. USA., *Marie Antoinette; Bildnis Eines Mittleren Charakters*, Stefan Zweig, Leipzig 1932, Biography

Marie Baschkirtzeff *see* DAS TAGEBUCH DER GELIEBTEN (1936).

Marie Claire *see* DEVIL IN THE FLESH (1986).

MARIE DES ANGOISSES 1935 d: Michel Bernheim. FRN., *Marie Des Angoisses*, Marcel Prevost, Novel

MARIE DES ISLES 1959 d: Georges Combret. FRN/ITL., *Marie Des Isles*, Robert Gaillard, Novel

MARIE DU PORT, LA 1949 d: Marcel Carne. FRN., *La Marie du Port*, Georges Simenon, 1938, Novel

MARIE GALANTE 1934 d: Henry King. USA., *Marie Galante*, Jacques Deval, Paris 1931, Novel

MARIE, LTD. 1919 d: Kenneth Webb. USA., *Marie Ltd.*, Louise Winter, Short Story

Marie Octobre *see* MARIE-OCTOBRE (1958).

Marie of the Isles *see* MARIE DES ISLES (1959).

Marie Tout Court *see* LE GARCON SAUVAGE (1951).

MARIE TUDOR 1913 d: Albert Capellani. FRN., *Marie Tudor*, Victor Hugo, Play

Marie Walewska *see* CONQUEST (1937).

MARIEE DU REGIMENT, LA 1935 d: Maurice Cammage. FRN., *La Mariee du Regiment*, Etienne Arnaud, Andre Heuze, Play

MARIEE EST TROP BELLE, LA 1956 d: Pierre Gaspard-Huit. FRN., *La Mariee Est Trop Belle*, Odette Joyeux, Novel

MARIEE ETAIT EN NOIR, LA 1968 d: Francois Truffaut. FRN/ITL., *The Bride Wore Black*, Cornell Woolrich, New York 1940, Novel

Mariee Etait Trop Belle, La *see* LA MARIEE EST TROP BELLE (1956).

MARIEE RECALCITRANTE, LA 1916 d: Georges MoncA. FRN., *La Mariee Recalcitrante*, Leon Gandillot, Play

MARIE-OCTOBRE 1958 d: Julien Duvivier. FRN., *Marie-Octobre*, Jacques Robert, Novel

Marie's Millions *see* TILLIE'S PUNCTURED ROMANCE (1914).

Marigaya *see* MRIGAYA (1976).

MARIGOLD 1938 d: Thomas Bentley. UKN., *Marigold*, L. Allen Harker, F. R. Pryor, London 1936, Play

Marika *see* MASKE IN BLAU (1953).

Mariken from Nijmegen *see* MARIKEN VAN NIEUMEGHEN (1974).

MARIKEN VAN NIEUMEGHEN 1974 d: Jos Stelling. NTH., *Mariken Van Nieumeghen*, Anon, c1485-1510, Play

MARILI 1959 d: Josef von Baky. GRM., *Marili*, Stefan Zagon, Play

MARILIA E MARINA 1976 d: Luis Fernando Goulart. BRZ., *Balada Das Duas Mocinhas de Botafogo*, Vinicius de Moraes, 1959, Verse

MARILYN 1953 d: Wolf RillA. UKN., *Marian*, Peter Jones, Play

Marines Have a Word for It, The *see* SOUTH SEA WOMAN (1953).

MARIO 1984 d: Jean Beaudin. CND., *La Sabliere*, Claude Jasmin, Novel

MARIO PUZO'S THE LAST DON 1997 d: Graeme Clifford. USA., *The Last Don*, Mario Puzo, Novel

Mario S'en Va-T-En Guerre *see* MARIO (1984).

Mariolles, Les *see* LA MENACE (1960).

Marion *see* MARILYN (1953).

MARION DELORME 1912 d: Albert Capellani. FRN., *Marion Delorme*, Victor Hugo, 1831, Play

MARION DELORME 1918 d: Henry Krauss. FRN., *Marion Delorme*, Victor Hugo, 1831, Play

MARIONA REBULL 1947 d: Jose Luis Saenz de HerediA. SPN., *Mariona Rebull*, Ignacio Agusti, 1944, Novel, *El Viudo Rius*, Ignacio Agusti, 1945, Novel

MARIONETTES, THE 1917 d: Thomas R. Mills. USA., *The Marionettes*, O. Henry, Short Story

MARIONETTES, THE 1918 d: Emile Chautard. USA., *Les Marionettes*, Pierre Wolff, Play

MARIONS-NOUS 1931 d: Louis Mercanton. FRN., *Little Miss Bluebeard*, Avery Hopwood, Henry Meyers, Play

MARIPOSA QUE VOLO SOBRE EL MAR, LA 1951 d: Antonio Obregon. SPN., *La Mariposa Que Volo Sobre El Mar*, Jacinto Benavente y Martinez, 1926, Play

MARIQUITA, LA 1913 d: Henri Fescourt. FRN., *La Mariquita*, Pierre Sales, Novel

MARIS DE LEONTINE, LES 1947 d: Rene Le Henaff. FRN., *Les Maris de Leontine*, Alfred Capus, Play

MARIS DE MA FEMME, LES 1936 d: Maurice Cammage. FRN., *Fallait Pas M'ecraser*, Jean Guitton, Play

MARITANA 1922 d: George Wynn. UKN., *Maritana*, Vincent Wallace, London 1845, Opera

MARITANA 1927 d: H. B. Parkinson. UKN., *Maritana*, Vincent Wallace, London 1845, Opera

MARITI - TEMPESTA D'AMORE, I 1941 d: Camillo Mastrocinque. ITL., *I Mariti*, Achille Torelli, Play

MARITI ALLEGRI, I 1914 d: Camillo de Riso. ITL., *Le Mari Sans Femme*, Albert Carre, Antony Mars, Play

Mariti, I *see* I MARITI - TEMPESTA D'AMORE (1941).

MARITO DELL'AMICA, IL 1919 d: Ugo de Simone. ITL., *Il Marito Dell'Amica*, Neera, 1885, Novel

MARITO DI ELENA, IL 1921 d: Riccardo Cassano. ITL., *Il Marito Di Elena*, Giovanni Verga, 1881, Novel

MARITO E MIO E L'AMMAZZO QUANDO MI PARE, IL 1967 d: Pasquale Festa Campanile. ITL., Aldo de Benedetti, Story

MARITO E MOGLIE 1952 d: Eduardo de Filippo. ITL., *Gennariello*, Eduardo de Filippo, Play, *Tonio*, Guy de Maupassant, Short Story

MARITO IN CAMPAGNA, IL 1912. ITL., *Le Mari a la Campagne*, Bayard, de Vally, 1844, Play

MARITO IN CAMPAGNA, IL 1920 d: Mario Almirante. ITL., *Le Mari a la Campagne*, Bayard, de Vally, 1844, Play

MARITO IN COLLEGIO, IL 1977 d: Maurizio Lucidi. ITL., *Il Marito in Collegio*, Giovanni Guareschi, Novel

MARIUS 1931 d: Alexander Korda, Marcel Pagnol. FRN., *Marius*, Marcel Pagnol, Paris 1931, Play

MARJORIE MORNINGSTAR 1958 d: Irving Rapper. USA., *Marjorie Morningstar*, Herman Wouk, 1955, Novel

MARK I LOVE YOU 1980 d: Gunnar Hellstrom. USA., *Mark I Love You*, Hal W. Painter, Book

Mark of Cain, The *see* KAINOVO ZNAMENI (1928).

MARK OF CAIN, THE 1948 d: Brian Desmond Hurst. UKN., *Airing in a Closed Carriage*, Gabrielle Margaret Vere Long, Novel

Mark of Terror *see* DRUMS OF JEOPARDY (1931).

Mark of the Avenger *see* THE MYSTERIOUS RIDER (1938).

MARK OF ZORRO, THE 1920 d: Fred Niblo. USA., *The Curse of Capistrano*, Johnston McCulley, 1919, Novel

MARK OF ZORRO, THE 1940 d: Rouben Mamoulian. USA., *The Curse of Capistrano*, Johnston McCulley, 1919, Novel

MARK OF ZORRO, THE 1974 d: Don McDougall. USA., *The Curse of Capistrano*, Johnston McCulley, 1919, Novel

Mark, The *see* NISHAN (1949).

MARK, THE 1961 d: Guy Green. UKN., *The Mark*, Charles Israel, New York 1958, Novel

MARK TWAIN AND ME 1991 d: Daniel Petrie. CND., *Enchantment; a Little Girl's Friendship With Mark Twain*, Dorothy Quick, Novel

MARKED MAN, A 1916 d: Frank Miller. UKN., *A Marked Man*, W. W. Jacobs, Short Story

Marked Man, The *see* L' HOMME A ABATTRE (1936).

MARKED MEN 1920 d: John Ford. USA., *Three Godfathers*, Peter B. Kyne, New York 1913, Novel

Marked Woman, The *see* THE WOMAN FROM MONTE CARLO (1932).

MARKETA LAZAROVA 1967 d: Frantisek Vlacil. CZC., *Marketa Lazarova*, Vladislav Vancura, 1931, Novel

MARKISCHE FORSCHUNGEN 1982 d: Roland Graf. GRM., *Markische Forschungen*, Gunter de Bruyn, Novel

Markopoulos Passion, The *see* PROMETHEUS BOUND -THE ILLIAC PASSION (1966).

Marksman, The *see* DER FREISCHUTZ (1968).

MARKURELLS I WADKOPING 1930 d: Victor Sjostrom. SWD/GRM., *Markurells I Wadkoping*, Hjalmar Bergman, 1919, Novel

Markurells of Wadkoping, The *see* MARKURELLS I WADKOPING (1930).

Markus and Diana *see* MARKUS OG DIANA (1997).

MARKUS OG DIANA 1997 d: Svein Scharffenberg. NRW., *Markus Og Diana*, Klaus Hagerup, Novel

MARLOWE 1969 d: Paul Bogart. USA., *The Little Sister*, Raymond Chandler, Boston 1949, Novel

MARMA YOGI 1951 d: K. Ramnoth. IND., *Vendetta*, Marie Corelli, 1886, Novel

MARMAILLE, LA 1935 d: Bernard-Deschamps. FRN., *La Marmaille*, Alfred Machard, Novel

Marmayogi *see* MARMA YOGI (1951).

MARNIE 1964 d: Alfred Hitchcock. USA., *Marnie*, Winston Graham, London 1961, Novel

MAROONED 1969 d: John Sturges. USA., *Marooned*, Martin Caidin, New York 1964, Novel

MARQUIS AND MISS SALLY, THE 1918 d: Allen Watt. USA/THE MARQUIS AND MISS SALLY., O. Henry, Short Story

MARQUIS DE SADE: JUSTINE 1968 d: Jesus Franco. GRM/ITL/FRN., *Juliette*, Donatien Sade, 1797, Novel, *Justine; Ou Les Malheurs de la Vertu*, Donatien Sade, 1791, Novel

Marquis de Sade's Justine *see* CRUEL PASSION (1977).

Marquis of Lantenac, The see **LA MARCHESE DI LANTENAC** (1911).

MARQUISE D'O, LA 1976 d: Eric Rohmer. FRN/GRM., *Die Marquise von O.*, Heinrich von Kleist, 1810, Short Story

Marquise of O., The see **LA MARQUISE D'O** (1976).

Marquise von O., Die see **LA MARQUISE D'O** (1976).

MARQUISE VON O., DIE 1989 d: Hans-Jurgen Syberberg. GRM., *Die Marquise von O.*, Heinrich von Kleist, 1810, Short Story

MARRAINE DE CHARLEY, LA 1935 d: Piere Colombier. FRN., *Charley's Aunt*, Brandon Thomas, London 1892, Play

MARRAINE DE CHARLEY, LA 1959 d: Pierre Chevalier. FRN., *Charley's Aunt*, Brandon Thomas, London 1892, Play

Marratom see **MARATTAM** (1989).

MARRIAGE 1927 d: R. William Neill. USA., *Marriage*, H. G. Wells, London 1912, Novel

Marriage a la Carte see **MARRYING MONEY** (1915).

Marriage Bargain, The see **WITHIN THE ROCK** (1935).

MARRIAGE BOND, THE 1916 d: Lawrence Marston. USA., Rida Johnson Young, Play

Marriage Broker, The see **ASCHENBROEDEL** (1916).

Marriage Business, The see **SECOND WIFE** (1936).

Marriage Came Tumbling Down, The see **CE SACRE GRAND-PERE** (1968).

MARRIAGE CIRCLE, THE 1924 d: Ernst Lubitsch. USA., *Nur Ein Traum*, Lothar Schmidt, Munchen 1909, Play

MARRIAGE CLAUSE, THE 1926 d: Lois Weber. USA., *Technic*, Dana Burnet, 1925, Short Story

Marriage for a Night see **EHE FUR EINE NACHT** (1953).

MARRIAGE FORBIDDEN 1936 d: Phil Goldstone. USA., *Les Avaries*, Eugene Brieux, Liege 1902, Play, *Damaged Goods*, Upton Sinclair, 1913, Novel

Marriage in Tears and Laughter see **TIXIAO YINYUAN** (1932).

Marriage in the Shadow see **EHE IM SCHATTEN** (1947).

Marriage in Transit see **MANHATTAN HEARTBEAT** (1940).

MARRIAGE IS A PRIVATE AFFAIR 1944 d: Robert Z. Leonard. USA., *Marriage Is a Private Affair*, Judith Kelley, Novel

Marriage Italian Style see **MATRIMONIO ALL'ITALIANA** (1964).

"MARRIAGE LICENSE?" 1926 d: Frank Borzage. USA., *The Pelican*, H. M. Harwood, F. Tennyson Jesse, London 1924, Play

MARRIAGE LIE, THE 1918 d: Stuart Paton. USA., *The Other Thing*, Blair Hall, 1917, Short Story

MARRIAGE LINES, THE 1921 d: Wilfred Noy. UKN., *The Marriage Lines*, J. S. Fletcher, Novel

MARRIAGE MAKER, THE 1923 d: William C. de Mille. USA., *The Faun; Or Thereby Hangs a Tale*, Edward Knoblock, New York 1911, Play

MARRIAGE OF A YOUNG STOCKBROKER, THE 1971 d: Lawrence Turman. USA., *The Marriage of a Young Stockbroker*, Charles Webb, 1970, Novel

Marriage of Balzaminov, The see **ZHENITBA BALZAMINOVA** (1965).

Marriage of Convenience see **HIRED WIFE** (1934).

MARRIAGE OF CONVENIENCE 1960 d: Clive Donner. UKN., *The Three Oak Mystery*, Edgar Wallace, London 1924, Novel

MARRIAGE OF CORBAL, THE 1936 d: Karl Grune. UKN., *The Nuptials of Corbal*, Rafael Sabatini, Novel

Marriage of Figaro, The see **LE NOZZE DI FIGARO** (1911).

Marriage of Figaro, The see **LE NOZZE DI FIGARO** (1913).

Marriage of Figaro, The see **LE MARIAGE DE FIGARO** (1959).

Marriage of Figaro, The see **DIE HOCHZEIT DES FIGARO** (1968).

MARRIAGE OF KITTY, THE 1915 d: George Melford. USA., *La Passerelle*, Francis de Croisset, Fred de Gresac, Paris 1902, Play

Marriage of Little Jeanne Sterling, The see **THE MIDNIGHT BRIDE** (1920).

Marriage of Mayfair, The see **THE FATAL HOUR** (1920).

MARRIAGE OF WILLIAM ASHE, THE 1916 d: Cecil M. Hepworth. UKN., *The Marriage of William Ashe*, Mrs. Humphrey Ward, New York 1905, Novel

MARRIAGE OF WILLIAM ASHE, THE 1921 d: Edward Sloman, Bayard Veiller (Spv). USA., *The Marriage of William Ashe*, Mrs. Humphrey Ward, New York 1905, Novel

MARRIAGE ON APPROVAL 1933 d: Howard Higgin. USA., *Marriage on Approval*, Priscilla Wayne, New York 1930, Novel

Marriage on Credit see **MANZELSTVI NA UVER** (1936).

MARRIAGE PLAYGROUND, THE 1929 d: Lothar Mendes. USA., *The Children*, Edith Wharton, New York 1928, Novel

MARRIAGE PRICE, THE 1919 d: Emile Chautard. USA., *For Sale*, Griswold Wheeler, 1918, Short Story

Marriage Strike see **DER EHESTREIK** (1953).

Marriage Symphony, The see **LET'S TRY AGAIN** (1934).

Marriage, The see **SVADBA** (1944).

Marriage Wrestler, The see **AKTENSKAPSBROTTAREN** (1964).

MARRIAGE-GO-ROUND 1961 d: Walter Lang. USA., *Marriage-Go-Round*, Leslie Stevens, New York 1958, Play

MARRIED ALIVE 1927 d: Emmett J. Flynn. USA., *Married Alive*, Ralph Strauss, New York 1925, Novel

MARRIED AND IN LOVE 1940 d: John Farrow. USA., *Distant Fields*, S. K. Lauren, London 1937, Play

Married Bliss see **TILL OUR SHIP COMES IN** (1919).

Married But Single see **THIS THING CALLED LOVE** (1940).

Married for Murder see **TILL DEATH US DO PART** (1991).

Married for the First Time see **VPERVYE ZAMUZEM** (1979).

Married in Haste see **MARRIAGE ON APPROVAL** (1933).

MARRIED IN HOLLYWOOD 1929 d: Marcel Silver. USA., *Married in Hollywood*, Bruno Hardt-Warden, Leopold Jacobson, Vienna 1928, Play

MARRIED LIFE 1921 d: Georges Treville. UKN., *Married Life*, J. B. Buckstone, London 1834, Play

Married Life see **GIFTAS** (1957).

Married Life see **LA VIDA CONYUGAL** (1992).

Married Life, A see **MESHI** (1951).

MARRIED MAN, A 1983 d: Charles Jarrott. UKN., *A Married Man*, Piers Paul Read, Novel

Married, Pretty and Poor see **SATURDAY'S CHILDREN** (1940).

Married to a Child see **XIANGNU XIAOXIAO** (1987).

Married Woman Needs a Husband, A see **SENORA CASADA NECESITA MARIDO** (1935).

MARRY ME 1925 d: James Cruze. USA., *The Nest Egg*, Anne Caldwell, New York 1910, Play

Marry Me, Cheri see **CHERI HEIRATE MICH** (1964).

MARRY THE BOSS'S DAUGHTER 1941 d: Thornton Freeland. USA., *The Boy the Girl and the Dog*, Sandor Farago, Alexander Kenedi, Story

MARRY THE GIRL 1935 d: MacLean Rogers. UKN., *Marry the Girl*, George Arthurs, Arthur Miller, London 1930, Play

MARRY THE GIRL 1937 d: William McGann. USA., *Marry the Girl*, Edward Hope, 1935, Short Story

MARRY THE POOR GIRL 1921 d: Lloyd Ingraham. USA., *Marry the Poor Girl*, Owen Davis, New York 1920, Play

MARRYING MONEY 1915 d: James Young. USA., *Marrying Money*, Bertram Marburgh, Washington Pezet, New York 1914, Play

Mars En Careme see **NE JOUEZ PAS AVEC LES MARTIANS** (1967).

MARSE COVINGTON 1915 d: Edwin Carewe. USA., *Marse Covington*, George Ade, 1906, Play

MARSEILLE MES AMOURS 1939 d: Jacques Daniel-Norman. FRN., *Marseille Mes Amours*, Audiffred, Marco Cab, Charles Tutelier, Opera

Marshmallow Moon see **AARON SLICK FROM PUNKIN CRICK** (1951).

Marsupials: the Howling 3, The see **THE HOWLING III** (1987).

MARTA 1971 d: Jose Antonio Nieves Conde. SPN/ITL., *Estado Civile: Marta*, Juan Jose Alonso Millan, Novel

MARTA OF THE LOWLANDS 1914 d: J. Searle Dawley. USA., *Terra Baixa*, Angel Guimera, Madrid 1896, Play

Martanda Varma see **MARTHANDA VARMA** (1931).

MARTER DER LIEBE 1928 d: Carmine Gallone. GRM., *Marter Der Liebe*, Carmine Gallone, Short Story

MARTHA 1922 d: George Wynn. UKN., *Martha*, Friedrich von Flotow, Vienna 1847, Opera

MARTHA 1927 d: H. B. Parkinson. UKN., *Martha*, Friedrich von Flotow, Vienna 1847, Opera

MARTHA 1935 d: Karl Anton. GRM., *Martha*, Friedrich von Flotow, Vienna 1847, Opera

MARTHA 1935 d: Karl Anton. FRN., *Martha*, Friedrich von Flotow, Vienna 1847, Opera

MARTHA DUBRONSKY 1984 d: Beat Kuert. SWT., *Martha Dubronsky*, Ingrid Puganigg, Novel

MARTHA, RUTH AND EDIE 1988 d: Norma Bailey, Daniele J. SuissA. CND., *The Californian Aunts*, Cynthia Flood, Short Story, *How I Met My Husband*, Alice Munro, Short Story

MARTHA, RUTH AND EDIE 1988 d: Deepa Mehta Saltzman. CND., *Guilt*, B. Lambert, Short Story

MARTHANDA VARMA 1931 d: P. V. Rao. IND., *Martanda Varma*, C. V. Raman Pillai, 1891, Novel

MARTHE 1919 d: Gaston Roudes. FRN., *Marthe*, Henri Kistemaeckers, Play

MARTIAN CHRONICLES, THE 1979 d: Michael Anderson. USA., *The Silver Locusts*, Ray Bradbury, Short Story

MARTIN CHUZZLEWIT 1912 d: Oscar Apfel, J. Searle Dawley. USA., *The Life and Adventures of Martin Chuzzlewit*, Charles Dickens, London 1844, Novel

MARTIN CHUZZLEWIT 1914 d: Travers Vale. USA., *The Life and Adventures of Martin Chuzzlewit*, Charles Dickens, London 1844, Novel

MARTIN CHUZZLEWIT 1995 d: Pedr James. UKN/USA., *The Life and Adventures of Martin Chuzzlewit*, Charles Dickens, London 1844, Novel

Martin Cuckoo see **KAKUK MARCI** (1973).

MARTIN EDEN 1914 d: Hobart Bosworth. USA., *Martin Eden*, Jack London, 1906, Novel

Martin Eden see **THE ADVENTURES OF MARTIN EDEN** (1942).

MARTIN EDEN 1979 d: Giacomo Battiato. ITL., *Martin Eden*, Jack London, 1906, Novel

MARTIN FIERRO 1968 d: Leopoldo Torre-Nilsson. ARG., *Martin Fierro*, Jose Herandez, 1872-79, Verse

MARTIN LUTHER, HIS LIFE AND TIME 1924. USA., *Martin Luther His Life and Times*, P. Kurz, Book

Martin Rome see **CRY OF THE CITY** (1948).

MARTIN ROUMAGNAC 1946 d: Georges Lacombe. FRN., *Martin Roumagnac*, Pierre Wolff, Novel

MARTIN TOCCAFERRO 1954 d: Leonardo de Mitri. ITL., *Martin Toccaferro*, Enzo la Rosa, Play

MARTINO IL TROVATELLO 1919 d: Alberto A. Capozzi, Ubaldo Maria Del Colle. ITL., *Martin Et Bambouche; Ou Les Amis d'Enfance*, Eugene Sue, 1847, Novel

MARTINSKLAUSE, DIE 1951 d: Richard Haussler. GRM., *Die Martinsklause*, Ludwig Ganghofer, Novel

MARTIR, LA 1921 d: Francesc Xandri. SPN., Leonel Yanez, Play

MARTIRE! 1917 d: Camillo de Riso. ITL., *Martyre!*, Adolphe-P. d'Ennery, Novel

Martire Dello Spielberg, Il see **SILVIO PELLICO** (1915).

MARTIRES DEL ARROYO, LOS 1924 d: Enrique Santos. SPN., *Los Martires Del Arroyo*, Luis de Val, Novel

MARTY 1953 d: Delbert Mann. USA., *Marty*, Paddy Chayefsky, 1953, Television Play

MARTY 1955 d: Delbert Mann. USA., *Marty*, Paddy Chayefsky, 1953, Television Play

MARTYR DE BOUGIVAL, LE 1949 d: Jean Loubignac. FRN., *Et la Police N'en Savait Rien*, Jean Guitton, Play

MARTYRDOM OF PHILIP STRONG, THE 1916 d: Richard Ridgely. USA., *The Crucifixion of Philip Strong*, Charles Monroe Sheldon, Chicago 1894, Novel, *In His Steps: "What Would Jesus Do?"*, Charles Monroe Sheldon, New York 1896, Novel

Martyrdom of Phillip Strong, The see **THE MARTYRDOM OF PHILIP STRONG** (1916).

MARTYRE DE L'OBESE, LE 1932 d: Pierre Chenal. FRN., *Le Martyre de l'Obese*, Henri Beraud, Novel

MARTYRE DE SAINTE MAXENCE, LE 1927 d: E. B. Donatien. FRN., *La Legende de la Primitive Eglise*, Eugene Barbier, Novel

MARTYRS OF THE ALAMO, THE 1915 d: W. Christy Cabanne. USA., *Martyrs of the Alamo*, Theodosia Harris, Novel

Maruja *see* THE GRAY WOLF'S GHOST (1919).

MARUSIA 1938 d: Leo Bulgakov. USA., *Marusia*, Mikhaylo Petrovich Staritsky, 1872, Play

MARUXA 1923 d: Henri Vorins. SPN., *Maruxa*, Luis Pascual Frutos, Amadeo Vives, Opera

Marvelous Journey of Nils Holgersson, The *see* NILS HOLGERSSONS UNDERBARA RESA (1962).

MARVIN AND TIGE 1982 d: Eric Weston. USA., Frankcina Glass, Novel

MARVIN'S ROOM 1996 d: Jerry Zaks. USA., *Marvin's Room*, Scott McPherson, Play

Mary *see* MURDER (1930).

Mary and the Goblins *see* MARYSIA I KRASNOLUDKI (1961).

Mary Cary *see* NOBODY'S KID (1921).

Mary Forever *see* MERY PER SEMPRE (1988).

MARY GIRL 1917 d: Maurice Elvey. UKN., *Mary Girl*, Hope Merrick, Play

Mary 'Gusta *see* A PETTICOAT PILOT (1918).

MARY HAD A LITTLE. 1961 d: Edward Buzzell. UKN., *Mary Had a Little.*, Muriel Herman, Arthur Herzog Jr., London 1951, Play

MARY JANE'S PA 1917 d: William P. S. Earle. USA., *Mary Jane's Pa*, Edith Ellis Furness, New York 1908, Play

MARY JANE'S PA 1935 d: William Keighley. USA., *Mary Jane's Pa*, Edith Ellis Furness, New York 1908, Play

Mary Keep Your Feet Still *see* HER SOUL'S INSPIRATION (1917).

MARY LATIMER, NUN 1920 d: Bert Haldane. UKN., *Nun Mary Latimer*, Eva Elwen, Novel

MARY, MARY 1963 d: Mervyn Leroy. USA., *Mary Mary*, Jean Kerr, New York 1961, Play

MARY MORELAND 1917 d: Frank Powell. USA., *Mary Moreland*, Marie Van Vorst, Boston 1915, Novel

MARY OF SCOTLAND 1936 d: John Ford. USA., *Mary of Scotland*, Maxwell Anderson, New York 1933, Play

MARY POPPINS 1964 d: Robert Stevenson. USA., *Mary Poppins*, P. L. Travers, Book

MARY REGAN 1919 d: Lois Weber. USA., *Mary Regan*, Leroy Scott, Boston 1918, Novel

MARY REILLY 1996 d: Stephen Frears. USA., *Mary Reilly*, Valerie Martin, Novel

MARY SHELLEY'S FRANKENSTEIN 1994 d: Kenneth Branagh. UKN/USA., *Frankenstein; Or the Modern Prometheus*, Mary Wollstonecraft Shelley, London 1818, Novel

MARY STUART 1913 d: J. Searle Dawley. USA., *Mary Stuart*, Friedrich Schiller, Play

Mary Was Love *see* THOSE WHO LOVE (1929).

MARY WHITE 1977 d: Jud Taylor. USA., William Allen White, Book

MARYS GROSSES GEHEIMNIS 1928 d: Guido Brignone. GRM., *Eine Dumme Geschichte*, Paul Langenscheidt, Novel

MARY'S LAMB 1915 d: Donald MacKenzie. USA., *Mary's Lamb*, Richard Carle, New York 1908, Play

MARYSA 1935 d: Josef Rovensky. CZC., *Marysa*, Alois Mrstikove, Vilem Mrstikove, Play

MARYSIA I KRASNOLUDKI 1961 d: Jerzy Szeski, Konrad Paradowski. PLN., *O Krasnoludkach I O Sierotce Marysi*, Maria Konopnicka, 1896, Short Story

MAS ALLA DE LA MUERTE 1924 d: Benito Perojo, Jacinto Benavente. SPN/FRN., *Mas Alla de la Muerte*, Jacinto Benavente y Martinez, Novel

MAS ALLA DE LAS MONTANAS 1967 d: Alexander Ramati. SPN/USA., *Beyond the Mountains*, Alexander Ramati, London 1958, Novel

MAS ALLA DEL JARDIN 1996 d: Pedro OleA. SPN., *Turkish Passion*, Antonio Gala, Novel

MASADA 1980 d: Boris Sagal. USA., *Masada*, Ernest K. Gann, Novel

Masaniello *see* THE DUMB GIRL OF PORTICI (1916).

Mascara de Scaramouche, La *see* SCARAMOUCHE (1963).

MASCHENKA 1987 d: John Goldschmidt. UKN/GRM/FNL., *Maschenka*, Vladimir Nabokov, Novel

MASCHERA DEL DEMONIO, LA 1960 d: Mario BavA. ITL/GRM., *Viy*, Nikolay Gogol, 1835, Short Story

Maschera Di Ferro, La *see* IL PRIGIONIERO DEL RE (1954).

MASCHERA E IL VOLTO, LA 1919 d: Augusto GeninA. ITL., *La Maschera E Il Volto*, Luigi Chiarelli, 1916, Play

MASCHERA E IL VOLTO, LA 1942 d: Camillo Mastrocinque. ITL., *La Maschera E Il Volto*, Luigi Chiarelli, 1916, Play

MASCHERA, LA 1921 d: Ivo Illuminati. ITL., *La Masque*, Henry Bataille, 1908, Play

MASCHERA SUL CUORE, LA 1942 d: Abel Gance. ITL., *Le Capitaine Fracasse*, Theophile Gautier, 1863, Novel

MASCHERA TRAGICA, LA 1911. ITL., *The Masque of the Red Death*, Edgar Allan Poe, 1842, Short Story

MASCOTTE DES POILUS, LA 1918. FRN., *La Mascotte Des Poilus*, Arnould Galopin, Novel

MASCOTTE, LA 1935 d: Leon Mathot. FRN., *La Mascotte*, Edmond Audran, Chivot, Duru, Opera

MASCULINE ENDING, A 1992 d: Antonia Bird. UKN., *A Masculine Ending*, Joan Smith, Novel

Masculine-Feminine *see* MASCULIN-FEMININ (1966).

MASCULIN-FEMININ 1966 d: Jean-Luc Godard. FRN/SWD., *La Femme de Paul*, Guy de Maupassant, 1881, Short Story, *Le Signe*, Guy de Maupassant, 1887, Short Story

Masculin-Feminin 15 Faits Precis *see* MASCULIN-FEMININ (1966).

Mash *see* M*A*S*H (1970).

M*A*S*H 1970 d: Robert Altman. USA., *Mash*, Richard Hooker, New York 1968, Novel

Masjki Vremena *see* MUZHKI VREMENA (1977).

Mask and Destiny, The *see* SHUZENJI MONOGATARI (1955).

Mask in Blue *see* MASKE IN BLAU (1942).

Mask in Blue *see* MASKE IN BLAU (1953).

Mask of Death, The *see* LA MASCHERA TRAGICA (1911).

Mask of Destiny, The *see* SHUZENJI MONOGATARI (1955).

MASK OF DIMITRIOS, THE 1944 d: Jean Negulesco. USA., *The Mask of Dimitrios*, Eric Ambler, 1939, Novel

MASK OF DUST 1954 d: Terence Fisher. UKN., *Mask of Dust*, Jon Manchip White, Novel

MASK OF FU MANCHU, THE 1932 d: Charles J. Brabin, Charles Vidor (Uncredited). USA., *The Mask of Fu Manchu*, Sax Rohmer, New York 1932, Novel

Mask of Fu Manchu, The *see* THE FACE OF FU MANCHU (1965).

Mask of Korea *see* L'ENFER DU JEU MACAO (1939).

MASK OF THE AVENGER 1951 d: Phil Karlson. USA., George Bruce, Story

Mask of the Red Death, The *see* LA MASCHERA TRAGICA (1911).

MASK, THE 1921 d: Bertram Bracken. USA., *The Mask*, Arthur Hornblow, New York 1913, Novel

MASKARAD 1941 d: Sergei Gerasimov. USS., *Maskarad*, Mikhail Lermontov, 1836, Play

MASKE FALLT, DIE 1930 d: William Dieterle. USA., *Syndafloden*, Henning Berger, Play

MASKE IN BLAU 1942 d: Paul Martin. GRM/HNG., *Maske in Blau*, Heinz Hentschke, Fred Raymond, Opera

MASKE IN BLAU 1953 d: Georg Jacoby. GRM., *Maske in Blau*, Heinz Hentschke, Fred Raymond, Opera

MASKED ANGEL 1928 d: Frank O'Connor. USA., Evelyn Campbell, Short Story

MASKED DANCER, THE 1924 d: Burton L. King. USA., *Die Frau Mit Der Maske*, Rudolph Lothar, Berlin 1922, Novel

MASKED EMOTIONS 1929 d: David Butler, Kenneth Hawks. USA., *A Son of Anak*, Ben Ames Williams, 1928, Short Story

Masked Lover, The *see* MASKOVANA MILENKA (1940).

MASKED WOMAN, THE 1927 d: Silvano Balboni. USA., *La Femme Masquee*, Charles Mere, Paris 1923, Play

MASKOVANA MILENKA 1940 d: Otakar VavrA. CZC., *L'Amour Masque*, Honore de Balzac, Short Story

MASKS AND FACES 1914 d: Lawrence Marston. USA., *Peg Woffington*, Charles Reade, 1852, Novel

MASKS AND FACES 1917 d: Fred Paul. UKN., *Peg Woffington*, Charles Reade, 1852, Novel

MASKS OF THE DEVIL, THE 1928 d: Victor Sjostrom. USA., *Die Masken Erwin Reiners*, Jakob Wassermann, Berlin 1910, Novel

Maskulinum-Femininum *see* MASCULIN-FEMININ (1966).

Maslova *see* FUKKATSU (1950).

MASNADIERI, I 1911 d: Mario Caserini. ITL., *Die Rauber*, Friedrich von Schiller, 1782, Play

Masque de Fer, La *see* IL PRIGIONIERO DEL RE (1954).

MASQUE DE FER, LE 1962 d: Henri Decoin. FRN/ITL., *Le Vicomte de Bragelonne*, Alexandre Dumas (pere), Paris 1847, Novel

MASQUE D'HOLLYWOOD, LE 1931 d: John Daumery, Clarence Badger. USA., *Hollywood Girl*, Joseph Patrick McEvoy, New York 1929, Novel

MASQUE OF THE RED DEATH 1988 d: Alan Birkinshaw. USA., *The Masque of the Red Death*, Edgar Allan Poe, 1842, Short Story

MASQUE OF THE RED DEATH, THE 1964 d: Roger Corman. UKN/USA., *Hop-Frog*, Edgar Allan Poe, 1849, Short Story, *The Masque of the Red Death*, Edgar Allan Poe, 1842, Short Story

MASQUE OF THE RED DEATH, THE 1989 d: Larry Brand. USA., *The Masque of the Red Death*, Edgar Allan Poe, 1842, Short Story

MASQUE QUI TOMBE, LE 1933 d: Mario Bonnard. FRN., *Il Trattato Scomparso*, Artu (Riccardo Artuffo), Galar (Leo Galetto), Play

MASQUERADE 1929 d: Russell J. Birdwell. USA., *The Brass Bowl*, Louis Joseph Vance, Indianapolis 1907, Novel

Masquerade *see* PLEASURE CRAZED (1929).

Masquerade *see* MASKARAD (1941).

MASQUERADE 1964 d: Basil Dearden. UKN., *Castle Minerva*, Victor Canning, London 1955, Novel

Masquerade *see* MARATTAM (1989).

MASQUERADER, THE 1922 d: James Young. USA., *John Chilcote M.P.*, Katherine Cecil Thurston, 1904, Novel

MASQUERADER, THE 1933 d: Richard Wallace. USA., *The Masquerader*, John Hunter Booth, Katherine Cecil Thurston, London 1904, Novel

MASQUERADERS, THE 1915 d: James Kirkwood. USA., *The Masqueraders*, Henry Arthur Jones, London 1894, Play

MASS APPEAL 1984 d: Glenn Jordan. USA., *Mass Appeal*, Bill C. Davis, Play

Massacre at Fort Grant *see* FUERTE PERDIDO (1965).

Massacre at Fort Perdition *see* FUERTE PERDIDO (1965).

Massacre at Marble City *see* DIE GOLDSUCHER VON ARKANSAS (1964).

Massacre in Hollywood *see* HELTER SKELTER (1976).

Massacre in Rome *see* RAPPRESAGLIA (1973).

MASSACRE RIVER 1949 d: John Rawlins. USA., *Massacre River*, Harold Bell Wright, Novel

Masses' Music, The *see* JANA ARANYA (1975).

Masseur's Curse *see* KAIDAN KASANE GA FUCHI (1970).

MASSINELLI IN VACANZA 1914 d: Arnaldo Giacomelli. ITL., *Massinelli in Vacanza*, Eduardo Ferravilla, Play

Master and His Servants, The *see* HERREN OG HANS TJENERE (1959).

MASTER AND MAN 1915 d: Percy Nash. UKN., *Master and Man*, Henry Pettitt, George R. Sims, London 1889, Play

Master and Margarita, The *see* MAJSTOR I MARGARITA (1973).

Master Blackmailer, The *see* THE ADVENTURES OF SHERLOCK HOLMES: THE MASTER BLACKMAILER (1991).

MASTER BOB, GAGNANT DU PRIX DE L'AVENIR 1913. FRN., *Master Bob Gagnant du Prix de l'Avenir*, Henri de Brisay, Play

MASTER CRACKSMAN, THE 1913 d: Oscar Apfel. USA., *The Master Cracksman*, Stephen Allen Reynolds, Story

Master Detective and Rasmus *see* MASTERDETEKTIVEN OCH RASMUS (1953).

Master Detective Lives Dangerously, The *see* KALLE BLOMKVIST - MASTERDETEKTIVEN LEVER FARLIGT (1997).

MASTER HAND, THE 1915 d: Harley Knoles. USA., *The Master Hand*, Carroll Fleming, New York 1907, Play

Master Ideal *see* KANTOR IDEAL (1932).

MASTER KEY, THE 1915 d: Robert Z. Leonard. USA., *The Master Key*, John Fleming Wilson, Story

MASTER MIND, THE 1914 d: Oscar Apfel, Cecil B. de Mille. USA., *The Master Mind*, Daniel D. Carter, New York 1913, Play

MASTER MIND, THE 1920 d: Kenneth Webb. USA., *The Master Mind*, Daniel D. Carter, New York 1913, Play

Master, Mistress, Servant *see* SAHIB BIBI AUR GHULAM (1962).

MASTER MUMMER, THE 1915 d: Walter Edwin. USA., *The Master Mummer*, E. Phillips Oppenheim, London 1905, Novel

MASTER OF BALLANTRAE, THE 1953 d: William Keighley. UKN/USA., *The Master of Ballantrae*, Robert Louis Stevenson, 1888, Novel

MASTER OF BALLANTRAE, THE 1984 d: Douglas Hickox. USA/UKN., *The Master of Ballantrae*, Robert Louis Stevenson, 1888, Novel

MASTER OF BANKDAM, THE 1947 d: Walter Forde. UKN., *The Crowthers of Bankdam*, Thomas Armstrong, Novel

MASTER OF CRAFT, A 1922 d: Thomas Bentley. UKN., *A Master of Craft*, W. W. Jacobs, Short Story

Master of Death, The *see* DER HERR DES TODES (1913).

MASTER OF DRAGONARD HILL 1989 d: Gerard Kikoine. USA., *Master of Dragonard Hill*, Rupert Galchrist, Novel

Master of Horror *see* OBRAS MAESTRAS DEL TERROR (1960).

Master of Lassie *see* HILLS OF HOME (1948).

Master of Life and Death *see* HERR UBER LEBEN UND TOD (1955).

MASTER OF MEN, A 1917 d: Wilfred Noy. UKN., *A Master of Men*, E. Phillips Oppenheim, 1901, Novel

MASTER OF MERRIPIT, THE 1915 d: Wilfred Noy. UKN., E. Phillips Oppenheim, Novel

Master of One's Own Body *see* SVOGA TJELA GOSPODAR (1957).

Master of the District, The *see* SANGO MALO (1990).

MASTER OF THE GAME 1984 d: Harvey Hart, Kevin Connor. USA/UKN., *Master of the Game*, Sidney Sheldon, Novel

MASTER OF THE HOUSE, THE 1915 d: Joseph A. Golden. USA., *The Master of the House*, Edgar James, New York 1912, Play

Master of the Islands *see* THE HAWAIIANS (1970).

MASTER OF THE WORLD 1961 d: William Witney. USA., *Maitre du Monde*, Jules Verne, Paris 1904, Novel, *Robur le Conquerant*, Jules Verne, Paris 1886, Novel

Master of Woman, The *see* THE ETERNAL STRUGGLE (1923).

Master Over Life and Death *see* HERR UBER LEBEN UND TOD (1955).

MASTER PLAN, THE 1954 d: Cy Endfield. UKN., *Operation North Star*, Harald Bratt, Television Play

MASTER SPY 1963 d: Montgomery Tully. UKN., *They Also Serve*, Gerald Anstruther, Paul White, Short Story

MASTER STROKE, A 1920 d: Chester Bennett. USA., *The Three Keys*, Frederic Van Rensselaer Dey, New York 1909, Novel

Master Swordsman, The *see* MIYAMOTO MUSASHI (1954).

MASTERDETEKTIVEN OCH RASMUS 1953 d: Rolf Husberg. SWD., *Masterdetektiven Och Rasmus*, Astrid Lindgren, Novel

MASTERFUL HIRELING, THE 1915. USA., *The Masterful Hireling*, Roy Norton, Story

Mastermind, The *see* THE MASTER MIND (1920).

Mastermind, The *see* THE ITALIAN JOB (1969).

MASTERS OF MEN 1923 d: David Smith. USA., *Masters of Men; a Romance of the New Navy*, Morgan Robertson, New York 1901, Novel

Masterworks of Terror *see* OBRAS MAESTRAS DEL TERROR (1960).

Masuccio Salernitano *see* FUGGENDO CON LE BRACHE IN MANO, RIUSCI A CONSERVALO SANO COME FU CHE MASUCCIO SALERNITANO (1973).

MAT 1926 d: V. I. Pudovkin. USS., *Mat*, Maxim Gorky, 1906, Novel

MAT 1956 d: Mark Donskoi. USS., *Mat*, Maxim Gorky, 1906, Novel

MATA AU HI MADE 1950 d: Tadashi Imai. JPN., *Pierre Et Luce*, Romain Rolland, 1920, Novel

MATADORES, OS 1997 d: Beto Brant. BRZ., Marcal Aquino, Novel

MATANGO 1963 d: Inoshiro Honda, Eiji TsuburayA. JPN., *The Voice of the Night*, W. H. Hodgson, Short Story

Matango -Fungus of Terror *see* MATANGO (1963).

Match Girl *see* FETITA CU CHIBRITURI (1967).

MATCH KING, THE 1932 d: Howard Bretherton, William Keighley. USA., *The Match King*, Einar Thorvaldson, New York 1932, Novel

Match, The *see* LA PARTITA (1991).

MATCH-BREAKER, THE 1921 d: Dallas M. Fitzgerald. USA., *The Match Breaker*, Meta White, Story

Matchmaker, The *see* IL PARANINFO (1934).

MATCHMAKER, THE 1958 d: Joseph Anthony. USA., *The Merchant of Yonkers*, Thornton Wilder, New York 1938, Play

MATCINA ZPOVED 1937 d: Karel SpelinA. CZC., *Sumrak Nad Detvou*, Josef Hobl, Play

MATELOT 512, LE 1984 d: Rene Allio. FRN., *Le Matelot 512*, Emile Guinde, Novel

MATER DOLOROSA 1913 d: Mario Caserini. ITL., *Mater Dolorosa*, Gerolamo Rovetta, 1882, Novel

MATER DOLOROSA 1943 d: Giacomo Gentilomo. ITL., *Mater Dolorosa*, Gerolamo Rovetta, 1882, Novel

Materassi Sisters, The *see* SORELLE MATERASSI (1943).

Materinskaya Polye *see* MATERINSKOYE POLYE (1968).

Materinskoe Pole *see* MATERINSKOYE POLYE (1968).

MATERINSKOYE POLYE 1968 d: Gennadi Bazarov. USS., *Materinskoe Pole*, Chingiz Aitmatov, 1963, Short Story

MATERNELLE, LA 1925 d: Gaston Roudes. FRN., *La Maternelle*, Leon Frapie, Novel

MATERNELLE, LA 1933 d: Jean Benoit-Levy, Marie Epstein. FRN., *La Maternelle*, Leon Frapie, Novel

MATERNELLE, LA 1948 d: Henri Diamant-Berger. FRN., *La Maternelle*, Leon Frapie, Novel

MATERNITA 1917 d: Ugo de Simone. ITL., *Maternita*, Roberto Bracco, 1903, Play

MATHIAS SANDORF 1921 d: Henri Fescourt. FRN., *Mathias Sandorf*, Jules Verne, 1885, Novel

MATHIAS SANDORF 1962 d: Georges Lampin. FRN/ITL/SPN., *Mathias Sandorf*, Jules Verne, 1885, Novel

Mathias Sandorf *see* MATHIAS SANDORF (1962).

Mathilde Mohring *see* ICH GLAUBE AN DICH (1945).

MATHRU BHOOMI 1939 d: H. M. Reddy. IND., *Chandragupta*, Dwijendralal Roy, 1911, Play

Mathrubhoomi *see* MATHRU BHOOMI (1939).

MATILDA 1978 d: Daniel Mann. USA., *Matilda*, Paul Gallico, Novel

MATILDA 1996 d: Danny Devito. USA., *Matilda*, Roald Dahl, Novel

MATINEE IDOL, THE 1928 d: Frank CaprA. USA., *Come Back to Aaron*, Robert Lord, Story

MATING CALL, THE 1928 d: James Cruze. USA., *The Mating Call*, Rex Beach, New York 1927, Novel

MATING GAME, THE 1958 d: George Marshall. USA., *The Darling Buds of May*, H. E. Bates, 1958, Novel

MATING OF MARCUS, THE 1924 d: W. P. Kellino. UKN., *The Mating of Marcus*, Mabel Barnes Grundy, Novel

MATING OF MILLIE, THE 1948 d: Henry Levin. USA., *The Mating of Millie*, Adele Comandini, Novel

MATING, THE 1915 d: Raymond B. West. USA., *The Winning of Denise*, Charles T. Dazey, Story

MATIR MANISHA 1966 d: Mrinal Sen. IND., *Matir Manisha*, Kalindi Charan Panigrahi, 1930, Novel

Matira Manisha *see* MATIR MANISHA (1966).

MATKA JOANNA OD ANIOLOW 1961 d: Jerzy Kawalerowicz. PLN., *Matka Joanna Od Aniolow*, Jaroslaw Iwaszkiewicz, 1946, Short Story

MATKA KRACMERKA 1934 d: Vladimir Slavinsky. CZC., *Do Panskeho Stavu*, Popelka Bilianova, Novel, *V Panskem Stavu*, Popelka Bilianova, Novel

Matka Kracmerka I. *see* DO PANSKEHO STAVU (1925).

Matka Kracmerka II *see* V PANSKEM STAVU (1927).

MATKA KROLOW 1982 d: Janusz Zaorski. PLN., *Matka Krolow*, Kazimierz Brandys, 1957, Novel

Matkina Spoved *see* MATCINA ZPOVED (1937).

MATOU, LE 1985 d: Jean Beaudin. CND/FRN/ITL., *Le Matou*, Yves Beauchemin, Novel

Matraga *see* A HORA E VEZ DE AUGUSTO MATRAGA (1965).

Matriarchate *see* MATRIARHAT (1977).

Matriarchy *see* MATRIARHAT (1977).

MATRIARHAT 1977 d: Lyudmil Kirkov. BUL., *Matriarkhat*, Georgi Mishev, 1967, Novel

Matriarkhat *see* MATRIARHAT (1977).

MATRICULE 33 1933 d: Karl Anton. FRN., *Matricule 33*, Robert Bouchard, Alex Madis, Play

MATRIMONIAL BED, THE 1930 d: Michael Curtiz. USA., *The Matrimonial Bed*, Seymour Hicks, Yves Mirande, Andre Mouezy-Eon, New York 1927, Play

Matrimonial Holidays *see* EHEFERIEN (1927).

Matrimonial Problem, A *see* THE MATRIMONIAL BED (1930).

Matrimonio Alla Francese *see* LE TONNERRE DE DIEU (1965).

MATRIMONIO ALL'ITALIANA 1964 d: Vittorio de SicA. ITL/FRN., *Filumena Marturano*, Eduardo de Filippo, Naples 1946, Play

Matrimonio Del Signore Mississippi, Il *see* DIE EHE DES HERRN MISSISSIPPI (1961).

Matrimonio Di Figaro, Il *see* LE NOZZE DI FIGARO (1913).

MATRIMONIO DI OLIMPIA, IL 1918 d: Gero Zambuto. ITL., *Le Mariage d'Olympe*, Emile Paul Augier, 1885, Play

MATRIMONIO, IL 1954 d: Antonio Petrucci. ITL., *Una Domanda Dim Matrimonio*, Anton Chekhov, Play, *L' Orso*, Anton Chekhov, Play, *Il Pranzo Di Nozze*, Anton Chekhov, Play

MATRIMONIO SEGRETO, IL 1943 d: Camillo Mastrocinque. ITL., *Il Matrimonio Segreto*, Giovanni Bertati, Domenico Cimarosa, Opera

Matrimony in the Shadows *see* EHE IM SCHATTEN (1947).

Matron's Report, The *see* LITTLE MISS NOBODY (1936).

MATS-PETER 1972 d: Jarl Kulle. SWD., *Mats-Peter*, John Einar Aberg, Novel

MATT 1918 d: A. E. Coleby. UKN., *Matt*, Robert Buchanan, Novel

Matt the Gooseboy *see* LUDAS MATYI (1977).

Matter of Conviction, A *see* THE YOUNG SAVAGES (1961).

Matter of Innocence, A *see* PRETTY POLLY (1967).

Matter of Pride, A *see* BORROW OR STEAL BEG (1937).

MATTER OF TIME, A 1976 d: Vincente Minnelli. USA/UKN/ITL., *La Volupte d'Etre*, Maurice Druon, 1954, Novel

MATTERS OF THE HEART 1990 d: Michael Ray Rhodes. USA., *The Country of the Heart*, Barbara Wersby, Book

Mattie, the Goose Boy *see* LUDAS MATYI (1949).

Mattie the Gooseboy *see* LUDAS MATYI (1977).

Mattig the Gooseboy *see* LUDAS MATYI (1977).

MATTO REGIERT 1947 d: Leopold Lindtberg. SWT., *Meutre a l'Asile*, Friedrich Glauser, Zurich 1936, Novel

Maturareise *see* DAS LEBEN BEGINNT (1942).

Matura-Reise *see* JEUNES FILLES D'AUJOURD'HUI (1942).

MAUD 1911 d: Wilfred Noy. UKN., *Maud*, Alfred Tennyson, Poem

MAUD MULLER 1911. USA., *Maud Muller*, John Greenleaf Whittier, 1854, Poem

MAUD MULLER 1912 d: Thomas Ricketts. USA., *Maud Muller*, John Greenleaf Whittier, 1854, Poem

MAUDE MULLER 1909. USA., *Maud Muller*, John Greenleaf Whittier, 1854, Poem

Maudite: Legend of Doom House *see* **MALPERTUIS** (1972).

MAULKORB, DER 1938 d: Erich Engel. GRM., *Der Maulkorb*, Heinrich Spoerl, Novel

MAULKORB, DER 1958 d: Wolfgang Staudte. GRM., *Der Maulkorb*, Heinrich Spoerl, Novel

MAUPRAT 1926 d: Jean Epstein. FRN., *Mauprat*, George Sand, Novel

MAURICE 1987 d: James Ivory. UKN., *Maurice*, E. M. Forster, 1971, Novel

Maurice from the Advertising Pillar *see* **MORITZ IN DER LITFASSAULE** (1983).

MAURIN DES MAURES 1932 d: Andre Hugon. FRN., *Maurin Des Maures*, Jean Aicard, 1905, Novel

Maurin the Illustrious *see* **L' ILLUSTRE MAURIN** (1933).

Maurizius Case, The *see* **L' AFFAIRE MAURIZIUS** (1953).

MAUVAIS COUPS, LES 1961 d: Francois Leterrier. FRN., *Les Mauvais Corps*, Roger Vailland, Paris 1948, Novel

MAUVAIS GARCON, LE 1921 d: Henri Diamant-Berger. FRN., *Le Mauvais Garcon*, Jacques Deval, Play

MAUVAISES RENCONTRES, LES 1955 d: Alexandre Astruc. FRN., *Les Mauvaises Rencontres*, Cecil Saint-Laurent, Novel

MAVERICK QUEEN, THE 1956 d: Joseph Kane. USA., *The Maverick Queen*, Romer Grey, Zane Grey, 1953, Novel

Max *see* **MAX ET LES FERRAILLEURS** (1970).

MAX ET LES FERRAILLEURS 1970 d: Claude Sautet. FRN./ITL., *Max Et Les Ferrailleurs*, Claude Neron, Novel

MAX HAVELAAR 1976 d: Fons Rademakers. NTH/INN., *Max Havelaar*, Eduard Douwes Dekker, 1859, Novel

Max Havelaar of de Koffieveilingen Der Nederlandse Handelsmaatschappij *see* **MAX HAVELAAR** (1976).

MAX UND MORITZ 1956 d: Norbert Schultze. GRM., *Max Und Moritz: Eine Bubengeschichte in Sieben Streichen*, Wilhelm Busch, 1865, Short Story

MAXIE 1985 d: Paul Aaron. USA., *Marion's Wall*, Jack Finney, Novel

MAXIM MAXIMYCH TAMAN 1967 d: Stanislav Rostotsky. USS., *Geroi Nashego Vremeni*, Mikhail Lermontov, 1840, Novel

MAXIME 1958 d: Henri Verneuil. FRN., *Maxime*, Henri Duvernois, Paris 1929, Novel

Maximilian and Carlotta *see* **JUAREZ** (1939).

Maxwell Archer, Detective *see* **MEET MAXWELL ARCHER** (1939).

MAY BLOSSOM 1915 d: Allan Dwan. USA., *May Blossom*, David Belasco, New York 1884, Play

May Fairy Tale *see* **POHADKA MAJE** (1940).

MAY QUEEN, THE 1914. UKN., *The May Queen*, Alfred Tennyson, Poem

May Storms *see* **GEWITTER IM MAI** (1988).

May Story, The *see* **POHADKA MAJE** (1940).

MAY WE BORROW YOUR HUSBAND? 1986 d: Bob Mahoney. UKN., Graham Greene, Short Story

MAYA 1949 d: Raymond Bernard. FRN., *Maya*, Simon Gantillon, Play

MAYA 1966 d: John Berry. USA., *The Wild Elephant*, Jalal Din, Lois Roth, Short Story

Maya and Breuda *see* **A DREAM OF PASSION** (1978).

MAYA MACHHINDRA 1932 d: V. Shantaram. IND., *Siddhasansar*, Shankar Trivedi, Play

Maya MacHhindra *see* **MAYA MACHHINDRA** (1932).

MAYBE IT'S LOVE 1935 d: William McGann. USA., *Saturday's Children*, Maxwell Anderson, New York 1927, Play

Mayday: 40,000 Feet! *see* **000 FEET MAYDAY AT 40** (1976).

MAYDAY AT 40,000 FEET 1976 d: Robert Butler. USA., *Jet Stream*, Austin Ferguson, Novel

MAYERLING 1936 d: Anatole Litvak. FRN., *La Fin d'une Idylle*, Claude Anet, Novel

MAYERLING 1968 d: Terence Young. UKN/FRN., *Mayerling*, Claude Anet, Paris 1931, Book, *The Archduke*, Michael Arnold, New York 1967, Book

Mayn Zundele *see* **MY SON** (1939).

MAYNILA, SA MGA KUKO NG LIWANAG 1975 d: Lino BrockA. PHL., *Sa Mga Kuko Ng Liwanag Maynila*, Edgardo Reyes, Novel

MAYOR OF 44TH STREET 1942 d: Alfred E. Green. USA., Robert D. Andrews, John Cleveland, Luther Davis, Article

MAYOR OF CASTERBRIDGE, THE 1921 d: Sidney Morgan. UKN., *The Mayor of Casterbridge*, Thomas Hardy, 1886, Novel

MAYOR OF CASTERBRIDGE, THE 1978 d: David Giles. UKN., *The Mayor of Casterbridge*, Thomas Hardy, 1886, Novel

MAYOR OF FILBERT, THE 1919 d: W. Christy Cabanne. USA., *The Mayor of Filbert*, Charles Francis Stocking, Chicago 1916, Novel

Mayor, The *see* **IL SINDACO** (1997).

MAYORAZGO DE BASTERRETXE, EL 1928 d: Mauro AzconA. SPN., *Mirentxu*, Pierre Lhande, Novel

Mayordomo, El *see* **EL HOMBRE IMPORTANTE ANIMAS TRUJANO** (1961).

MAYSKAYA NOCH 1940 d: Nikolay Sadkovitch. USS., *Mayskaya Noch*, Nikolay Gogol, 1831, Short Story

MAYTIME 1923 d: Louis J. Gasnier. USA., *Maytime*, Cyrus Wood, Rida Johnson Young, New York 1917, Play

MAYTIME 1937 d: Robert Z. Leonard. USA., *Maytime*, Rida Johnson Young, New York 1917, Play

Mazarin Stone, The *see* **THE STONE OF MAZARIN** (1923).

Mazazis Princas *see* **MALENKI PRINTS** (1966).

MAZEPA 1975 d: Gustaw Holoubek. PLN., *Mazepa*, Juliusz Slowacki, 1840, Play

MAZEPPA 1908 d: Frank Dudley. UKN., *Mazeppa*, Lord Byron, Poem

Mazeppa *see* **MAZEPA** (1975).

Mazes and Monsters *see* **RONA JAFFE'S MAZES & MONSTERS** (1982).

Mazhki Vremena *see* **MUZHKI VREMENA** (1977).

MAZURKA DER LIEBE 1957 d: Hans Muller. GDR., *Fernande*, Victorien Sardou, 1870, Play

Mazza, La *see* **BALTAGUL** (1969).

MAZZETTA, LA 1978 d: Sergio Corbucci. ITL., *La Mazzetta*, Attilio Veraldi, Novel

MCCABE AND MRS. MILLER 1971 d: Robert Altman. USA., *McCabe*, Edmund Naughton, Novel

MCFADDEN'S FLATS 1927 d: Richard Wallace. USA., *McFadden's Row of Flats*, Gus Hill, London 1896, Play

MCFADDEN'S FLATS 1935 d: Ralph Murphy. USA., *McFadden's Row of Flats*, Gus Hill, London 1896, Play

MCGLUSKY THE SEA ROVER 1935 d: Walter Summers. UKN., *McGlusky the Sea Rover*, A. G. Hales, Novel

McGuire Go Home *see* **THE HIGH BRIGHT SUN** (1964).

McKenna's Gold *see* **MACKENNA'S GOLD** (1968).

MCKENZIE BREAK, THE 1970 d: Lamont Johnson. UKN., *The Bowmanville Break*, Sidney Shelley, New York 1968, Novel

MCVICAR 1980 d: Tom Clegg. UKN., *McVicar By Himself*, John McVicar, Autobiography

ME 1976 d: John Palmer. CND., *Me*, Martin Kinch, Play

ME & DAD'S NEW WIFE 1976 d: Larry Elikann. USA., *A Smart Kid Like You*, Stella Pevsner, Novel

Me and Him *see* **ICH UND ER** (1988).

Me and My Girl *see* **MORD EM'LY** (1922).

ME AND THE COLONEL 1958 d: Peter Glenville. USA., *Jacobowsky Und Der Oberst*, Franz Werfel, 1944, Play

ME AND THE GIRLS 1985 d: Jack Gold. UKN., *Me and the Girls*, Noel Coward, 1965, Short Story

ME FAIRE CA A MOI. 1961 d: Pierre Grimblat. FRN., *Me Faire Ca a Moi*, Jean-Michel Sorel, Novel

ME, GANGSTER 1928 d: Raoul Walsh. USA., *Gangster Me*, Charles Francis Coe, New York 1927, Novel

ME, NATALIE 1969 d: Fred Coe. USA., *Natalie Me*, Stanley Shapiro, Novel

Meadow on the Border, The *see* **DIE ALM AN DER GRENZE** (1951).

ME'AL HACHURAVOT 1936 d: Natan Axelrod, Alfred Wolf. ISR., Tzvi Lieberman-Livne, Story

Me'al Hekhoravot *see* **ME'AL HACHURAVOT** (1936).

MEAN SEASON, THE 1985 d: Philip Borsos. USA., *In the Heat of Summer*, John Katzenbach, Novel

MEANEST MAN IN THE WORLD, THE 1923 d: Eddie Cline. USA., *The Meanest Man in the World*, George M. Cohan, Everett S. Ruskay, 1915, Play

MEANEST MAN IN THE WORLD, THE 1943 d: Sidney Lanfield. USA., *The Meanest Man in the World*, George M. Cohan, Augustin MacHugh, New York 1920, Play

Means of Evil *see* **INSPECTOR WEXFORD: MEANS OF EVIL** (1991).

MEASURE FOR MEASURE 1978 d: Desmond Davis. UKN., *Measure for Measure*, William Shakespeare, c1604, Play

MEASURE OF A MAN, THE 1924 d: Arthur Rosson. USA., *The Measure of a Man*, Norman Duncan, New York 1911, Novel

MEASURE OF LEON DUBRAY, THE 1915 d: Henry Otto. USA., *The Measure of Leon Dubray*, Harvey Gates, Story

Mechanical Man *see* **AJANTRIK** (1958).

Mechanical Piano, The *see* **NEOKONTCHENNIA PIESSA DLIA MEKANITCHESKOVO PIANINA** (1977).

MECHTY IDIOTA 1993 d: Vasily Pichul. RSS/FRN., *Zolotoy Telyonok*, Ilya Ilf, Evgeny Petrov, 1931, Novel

MEDAL FOR BENNY, A 1945 d: Irving Pichel. USA., John Steinbeck, Jack Wagner, Story

MEDAL FOR THE GENERAL 1944 d: Maurice Elvey. UKN., *Medal for the General*, James Ronald, Novel

Medals *see* **SEVEN DAYS LEAVE** (1930).

MEDEA 1970 d: Pier Paolo Pasolini. ITL/GRM/FRN., *Medea*, Euripides, 431 bc, Play

Medea *see* **A DREAM OF PASSION** (1978).

MEDEA DI PORTAMEDINA 1919 d: Elvira Notari. ITL., *Medea Di Portamedina*, Francesco Mastriani, 1882, Novel

Medea's Return *see* **I EPISTROFI TIS MIDIAS** (1968).

MEDECIN DES ENFANTS, LE 1916 d: Georges DenolA. FRN., *Le Medecin Des Enfants*, Anicet Bourgeois, Adolphe-P. d'Ennery, Play

MEDECIN MALGRE LUI, LE 1910 d: Emile Chautard. FRN., *Le Medecin Malgre Lui*, Moliere, 1666, Play

MEDECIN MALGRE LUI, LE 1934 d: Pierre Weill. FRN., *Le Medecin Malgre Lui*, Moliere, 1666, Play

Medee *see* **MEDEA** (1970).

MEDIATOR, THE 1916 d: Otis Turner. USA., *The Mediator*, Roy Norton, New York 1913, Novel

Medic, The *see* **LE TOUBIB** (1979).

Medicine *see* **YAO** (1981).

MEDICINE BEND 1916 d: J. P. McGowan. USA., *Whispering Smith*, Frank Hamilton Spearman, New York 1906, Novel

MEDICINE MAN, THE 1930 d: Scott Pembroke. USA., *The Medicine Man*, Elliott Lester, Play

MEDICO A PALOS, EL 1926 d: Sabino A. Micon. SPN., *El Medico a Palos*, Leandro Fernandez de Moratin, Play

MEDICO DEI PAZZI, IL 1954 d: Mario Mattoli. ITL., *O' Miedeco d'E Pazze*, Eduardo Scarpetta, Play

MEDICO DELLA MUTUA, IL 1968 d: Luigi ZampA. ITL., *Il Medico Della Mutua*, Giuseppe d'Agata, Novel

MEDICO DELLE PAZZE, IL 1919 d: Mario Roncoroni. ITL., *Le Medecin Des Folles*, Xavier de Montepin, 1891, Novel

MEDICO PER FORZA, IL 1931 d: Carlo Campogalliani. ITL., *Le Medecin Malgre Lui*, Moliere, 1666, Play

MEDIUM COOL 1969 d: Haskell Wexler. USA., *The Concrete Wilderness*, Jack Couffer, New York 1967, Novel

MEDIUM, THE 1934 d: Vernon Sewell. UKN., *L' Angoisse*, Celia de Vylars, Pierre Mills, Play

Medju Jastrebovima *see* **UNTER GEIERN** (1964).

Medor *see* **UNE VIE DE CHIEN** (1941).

MEDUSA TOUCH, THE 1977 d: Jack Gold. UKN., *The Medusa Touch*, Peter Van Greenway, Novel

MEDVED 1938 d: Isider Annensky. USS., *Medved*, Anton Chekhov, 1888, Play

MEER, DAS 1927 d: Peter Paul Felner. GRM., *Das Meer*, Bernhard Kellermann, Novel

Men and War see **SENSO TO NINGEN** (1970).

MEN AND WOMEN 1914 d: James Kirkwood. USA., *Men and Women*, Henry C. de Mille, Play

MEN AND WOMEN 1925 d: William C. de Mille. USA., *Men and Women*, David Belasco, Henry C. de Mille, Play

Men are Children Twice see **VALLEY OF SONG** (1953).

MEN ARE LIKE THAT 1930 d: Frank Tuttle. USA., *The Show-Off*, George Edward Kelly, New York 1924, Play

Men are Like That see **ARIZONA** (1931).

Men are Not Men see **UOMINI E NO** (1979).

MEN ARE SUCH FOOLS 1938 d: Busby Berkeley. USA., *Men are Such Fools*, Faith Baldwin, New York 1936, Novel

Men are That Way see **MANNER MUSSEN SO SEIN** (1939).

Men Behind Bars see **DUFFY OF SAN QUENTIN** (1954).

MEN CALL IT LOVE 1931 d: Edgar Selwyn. USA., *Among the Married*, Vincent Lawrence, New York 1929, Play

Men Can't Be Raped see **MANRAPE** (1978).

Men Don't Age see **MUZI NESTARNOU** (1942).

MEN IN HER LIFE, THE 1941 d: Gregory Ratoff. USA., *Ballerina*, Lady Eleanor Smith, Novel

Men in Offside, The see **MUZI V OFFSIDU** (1931).

Men in the Offside see **MUZI V OFFSIDU** (1931).

MEN IN THE RAW 1923 d: George Marshall. USA., *Men in the Raw*, W. Bert Foster, Short Story

MEN IN WAR 1957 d: Anthony Mann. USA., *Combat*, Van Van Praag, 1945, Novel

MEN IN WHITE 1934 d: Richard Boleslawski. USA., *Men in White*, Sidney Kingsley, New York 1933, Play

Men in White see **L' HOMMES EN BLANC** (1955).

MEN IN WHITE 1960 d: Don Richardson. USA., *Men in White*, Sidney Kingsley, New York 1933, Play

MEN MUST FIGHT 1932 d: Edgar Selwyn. USA., *Men Must Fight*, S. K. Lauren, Reginald Lawrence, New York 1932, Play

Men Must Fight see **PARTNERS OF THE PLAINS** (1938).

Men Never Cry see **CHLAPI PRECE NEPLACOU** (1980).

MEN OF ACTION 1935 d: Alan James. USA., *The New Freedom*, Peter B. Kyne, Short Story

MEN OF RESPECT 1991 d: William Reilly. USA., *MacBeth*, William Shakespeare, c1606, Play

MEN OF STEEL 1926 d: George Archainbaud. USA., *United States Flavor*, Ralph G. Kirk, 1914, Short Story

MEN OF STEEL 1932 d: George King. UKN., *Men of Steel*, Douglas Newton, Novel

Men of the Dawn see **THE SILENT LOVER** (1926).

MEN OF THE FIGHTING LADY 1954 d: Andrew Marton. USA., *Case of the Blind Pilot*, Com. Harry A. Burns, Short Story, *The Forgotten Heroes of Korea*, James A. Michener, Short Story

Men of the Sea see **MIDSHIPMAN EASY** (1935).

Men of the Sea see **THE MAN AT THE GATE** (1941).

Men of Tohoku, The see **TOHOKU NO ZUNMUTACHI** (1957).

MEN OF TOMORROW 1932 d: Zoltan Korda, Leontine Sagan. UKN., *Young Apollo*, Anthony Gibbs, Novel

Men of Tomorrow see **NO GREATER GLORY** (1934).

MEN OF ZANZIBAR, THE 1922 d: Rowland V. Lee. USA., *The Men of Zanzibar*, Richard Harding Davis, 1913, Short Story

Men Off-Side see **MUZI V OFFSIDU** (1931).

Men on Her Mind see **THE GIRL FROM 10TH AVENUE** (1935).

Men on Her Mind see **SATAN MET A LADY** (1936).

MEN SHE MARRIED, THE 1916 d: Travers Vale. USA., *The Men She Married*, Harold Vickers, 1916, Novel

MEN WHO HAVE MADE LOVE TO ME 1918 d: Arthur Berthelet. USA., *I Mary MacLane*, Mary MacLane, New York 1917, Autobiography

Men Who Tread on the Tiger's Tail, The see **TORA NO OO FUMA OTOKOTACHI** (1945).

Men Without Morals see **LA NUIT DES TRAQUES** (1959).

Men Without Women see **UOMINI SENZA DONNE** (1996).

MEN, WOMEN AND MONEY 1919 d: George Melford. USA., *Men, Women and Money*, Cosmo Hamilton, 1918, Short Story

Men Women Love see **SALVATION NELL** (1931).

MENACE 1934 d: Ralph Murphy. USA., *Menace*, Philip MacDonald, New York 1933, Novel

Menace in the Night see **FACE IN THE NIGHT** (1957).

MENACE, LA 1927 d: Jean Bertin. FRN., *La Menace*, Pierre Frondaie, Play

MENACE, LA 1960 d: Gerard Oury. FRN/ITL., *Les Mariolles*, Frederic Dard, Novel

MENACE OF THE MUTE, THE 1915 d: Ashley Miller, Arnold Daly. USA., *The Menace of the Mute*, John Thomas McIntyre, 1910, Short Story

MENACE, THE 1932 d: R. William Neill. USA., *The Feathered Serpent*, Edgar Wallace, London 1927, Novel

Menace, The see **LA MENACE** (1960).

MENDIANTE DE SAINT-SUPLICE, LA 1923 d: Charles Burguet. FRN., *La Mendiante de Saint-Sulpice*, Xavier de Montepin, Novel

MENDICANTE DI SASSONIA, IL 1921 d: Giovanni PezzingA. ITL., *La Mendicante Di Sassonia*, Bourgeois, Novel

MENESGAZDA, A 1978 d: Andras Kovacs. HNG., *A Menesgazda*, Istvan Gall, Novel

MENEUR DE JOIES, LE 1929 d: Charles Burguet. FRN/GRM., *Le Meneur de Joies*, Georges-Andre Cuel, Novel

MENILMONTANT 1936 d: Rene Guissart. FRN., *Menilmontant*, Roger Devigne, Novel

MENINO DE ENGENHO 1966 d: Walter Lima Jr. BRZ., *Fogo Morto*, Jose Lins Do Rego, 1943, Novel, *Menino de Engenho*, Jose Lins Do Rego, 1932, Novel

MENINO E O VENTO, O 1967 d: Carlos Hugo Christensen. BRZ., *O Iniciado Do Vento*, Anibal Machado, 1959, Short Story

MENNESKER MODES OG SOD MUSIK OPSTAR I HJERTET 1968 d: Henning Carlsen. DNM/SWD., *Mennesker Modes Og Sod Musik Opstar I Hjertet*, Jens August Schade, Copenhagen 1945, Novel

Meno En la Trampa, La see **LA CAIDA** (1959).

MEN'S CLUB, THE 1986 d: Peter Medak. USA., *The Men's Club*, Leonard Michaels, Novel

Mensaka see **PAGINAS DE UNA HISTORIA: MENSAKA** (1998).

MENSCH OHNE NAMEN 1932 d: Gustav Ucicky. GRM., *Le Colonel Chabert*, Honore de Balzac, 1844, Novel

Menschen Der Berge see **GELD UND GEIST** (1964).

MENSCHEN DIE VORUBERZIEHN 1942 d: Max Haufler. SWT., *Katharina Knie*, Carl Zuckmayer, Berlin 1928, Play

MENSCHEN IM HOTEL 1959 d: Gottfried Reinhardt. GRM/FRN., *Menschen Im Hotel*, Vicki Baum, Berlin 1929, Novel

MENSCHEN IM NETZ 1959 d: Franz Peter Wirth. GRM., *Menschen Im Netz*, Erich Kern, Munich 1957, Book

MENSCHENWEE 1921 d: Theo Frenkel Sr. NTH., *Menschenwee*, Israel Querido, 1903, Novel

Menschlein Matthias, Das see **LE BATARD** (1941).

MENSONGE DE NINA PETROVNA, LA 1937 d: Victor Tourjansky. FRN., *Le Mensonge de Nina Petrovna*, Hans Szekely, Novel

MENSONGES, LES 1927 d: Pierre Marodon. FRN/GRM., *La Bonne Reputation*, Hermann Sudermann, Play

Mensonges Que Mon Pere Me Contait, Les see **LIES MY FATHER TOLD ME** (1975).

MENTEURS, LES 1961 d: Edmond T. Greville. FRN., *Cette Mort Dont Tu Parlais*, Frederic Dard, Paris 1957, Novel

Menteuse, La see **LA BUGIARDA** (1965).

MENTIONED IN CONFIDENCE 1917 d: Edgar Jones. USA., *Mentioned in Confidence*, Howard Fielding, Short Story

Mentirosa, La see **LA BUGIARDA** (1965).

MENUET 1982 d: Lili Rademakers. NTH/BLG., *Menuet*, Louis Paul Boon, Book

MEO PATACCA 1972 d: Marcello Ciorciolini. ITL., *Meo Patacca*, Giuseppe Berneri, Poem

MEPHISTO 1981 d: Istvan Szabo. AUS/HNG/GRM., *Mephisto*, Klaus Mann, 1936, Novel

MEPHISTO WALTZ, THE 1971 d: Paul Wendkos. USA., *The Mephisto Waltz*, Fred Mustard Stewart, Novel

MEPRIS, LE 1963 d: Jean-Luc Godard. FRN/ITL., *Il Disprezzo*, Alberto Moravia, Milan 1954, Novel

MER DE CHINE: LE PAYS POUR MEMOIRE 1990 d: Jacques Perrin. FRN., *Les Remparts du Silence*, Pierre Fyot, Book

MER OM OSS BARN I BULLERBYN 1988 d: Lasse Hallstrom. SWD., Astrid Lindgren, Story

Meraviglia Di Damasco, La see **ACCADDE A DAMASCO E FEBBRE** (1943).

Meravigliosa Angelica, La see **MERVEILLEUSE ANGELIQUE** (1964).

Meravigliosa Notte, Una see **NON E MAI TROPPO TADRI** (1953).

MERCANTE DI SCHIAVE, IL 1942 d: Duilio Coletti. ITL., *I Fuggiaschi*, Ferdinando Paolieri, Novel

MERCANTE DI VENEZIA, IL 1910 d: Gerolamo Lo Savio?. ITL., *The Merchant of Venice*, William Shakespeare, c1595, Play

Mercante Di Venezia, Il see **LE MARCHAND DE VENISE** (1952).

MERCENAIRE, LE 1962 d: Etienne Perier, Baccio Bandini. FRN/ITL., *Swordsman of Siena*, Anthony Marshall, Novel

Mercenaires du Rio Grande, Les see **DER SCHATZ DER AZTEKEN** (1965).

MERCENARIES, THE 1967 d: Jack Cardiff. UKN/SAF., *The Dark of the Sun*, Wilbur Smith, London 1965, Novel

Mercenario, Il see **LE MERCENAIRE** (1962).

Mercenarios Del Aire see **LE CANARD EN FER BLANC** (1967).

Merchant from Kabul, The see **KABULIWALA** (1956).

Merchant of Slaves see **IL MERCANTE DI SCHIAVE** (1942).

MERCHANT OF VENICE, THE 1908 d: William V. Ranous, J. Stuart Blackton (Spv). USA., *The Merchant of Venice*, William Shakespeare, c1595, Play

Merchant of Venice, The see **IL MERCANTE DI VENEZIA** (1910).

MERCHANT OF VENICE, THE 1912 d: Theodore Marston. USA., *The Merchant of Venice*, William Shakespeare, c1595, Play

MERCHANT OF VENICE, THE 1914 d: Phillips Smalley, Lois Weber. USA., *The Merchant of Venice*, William Shakespeare, c1595, Play

MERCHANT OF VENICE, THE 1916 d: Walter West. UKN., *The Merchant of Venice*, William Shakespeare, c1595, Play

MERCHANT OF VENICE, THE 1922 d: Challis Sanderson. UKN., *The Merchant of Venice*, William Shakespeare, c1595, Play

MERCHANT OF VENICE, THE 1927 d: Widgey R. Newman. UKN., *The Merchant of Venice*, William Shakespeare, c1595, Play

Merchant of Venice, The see **SHEJLOK** (1993).

MERCURY RISING 1998 d: Harold Becker. USA., *Simple Simon*, Ryne Douglas Peardon, Novel

MERCY ISLAND 1941 d: William Morgan. USA., *Mercy Island*, Theodore Pratt, Novel

MERELY MARY ANN 1916 d: John G. Adolfi. USA., *Merely Mary Ann*, Israel Zangwill, London 1893, Novel

MERELY MARY ANN 1920 d: Edward J. Le Saint. USA., *Merely Mary Ann*, Israel Zangwill, London 1893, Novel

MERELY MARY ANN 1931 d: Henry King. USA., *Merely Mary Ann*, Israel Zangwill, London 1893, Novel

MERETTE 1982 d: Jean-Jacques Lagrange. SWT., Gottfried Keller, Story

Merlin and the Knights of King Arthur see **EXCALIBUR** (1981).

MERLO MASCHIO, IL 1971 d: Pasquale Festa Campanile. ITL., *Il Complesso Di Loth*, Luciano Bianciardi, Novel

Mermaid, The see **MORSKA PANNA** (1926).

Mermaid, The see **MORSKA PANNA** (1939).

MERMAIDS 1990 d: Richard Benjamin. USA., *Mermaids*, Patty Dann, Novel

MERRILL'S MARAUDERS 1962 d: Samuel Fuller. USA., *The Marauders*, Charlton Ogburn Jr., New York 1959, Novel

Merrily We Go to... see **MERRILY WE GO TO HELL** (1932).

MERRILY WE GO TO HELL 1932 d: Dorothy Arzner. USA., *I Jerry Take Thee Joan*, Cleo Lucas, New York 1911, Novel

MERRILY WE LIVE 1938 d: Norman Z. McLeod. USA., *The Dark Chapter*, E. J. Rath, New York 1924, Novel, *They All Want Something*, Courtenay Savage, New York 1926, Play

Merry Andrew *see* HANDY ANDY (1934).

MERRY ANDREW 1958 d: Michael Kidd. USA., *The Romance of Henry Menafee*, Paul Gallico, Book

Merry Christmas and a Happy New York *see* SZCZESLIWEGO NOWEGO ROKU (1997).

MERRY CHRISTMAS, MR. LAWRENCE 1982 d: Nagisa OshimA. UKN/JPN/NZL., *The Seed and the Sower*, Laurens Van Der Post, 1951, Novel

Merry Go Round *see* KORHINTA (1955).

Merry Go Round *see* REIGEN (1974).

Merry Rasplyuev Days *see* VESYOLYYE RASPLYUYEVSKIYE DNI (1966).

MERRY WIDOW, THE 1925 d: Erich von Stroheim. USA., *Die Lustige Witwe*, Viktor Leon, Leo Stein, Vienna 1905, Operetta

MERRY WIDOW, THE 1934 d: Ernst Lubitsch. USA., *Die Lustige Witwe*, Franz Lehar, Viktor Leon, Leo Stein, Vienna 1905, Operetta

MERRY WIDOW, THE 1952 d: Curtis Bernhardt. USA., *Die Lustige Witwe*, Franz Lehar, Viktor Leon, Leo Stein, Vienna 1905, Operetta

Merry Wives of Gotham *see* LIGHTS OF OLD BROADWAY (1925).

MERRY WIVES OF WINDSOR, THE 1910 d: Frank Boggs. USA., *The Merry Wives of Windsor*, William Shakespeare, c1598, Play

Merry Wives of Windsor, The *see* DIE LUSTIGEN WEIBER VON WINDSOR (1950).

Merry Wives of Windsor, The *see* DIE LUSTIGEN WEIBER VON WINDSOR (1965).

MERRY WIVES OF WINDSOR, THE 1983 d: David Jones. UKN., *The Merry Wives of Windsor*, William Shakespeare, c1598, Play

Merry Wives, The *see* CECH PANEN KUTNOHORSKYCH (1938).

Merry-Go-Round *see* ONCE IN A LIFETIME (1932).

Merry-Go-Round *see* AFRAID TO TALK (1932).

MERTON OF THE MOVIES 1924 d: James Cruze. USA., *Merton of the Movies*, Harry Leon Wilson, New York 1922, Novel

MERTON OF THE MOVIES 1947 d: Robert Alton. USA., *Merton of the Movies*, Harry Leon Wilson, New York 1922, Novel

MERTVIYE DUSHI 1960 d: Leonid Trauberg. USS., *Myortvye Dushi*, Nikolay Gogol, 1842, Novel

Mertvye Dusi *see* MERTVIYE DUSHI (1960).

MERVEILLEUSE ANGELIQUE 1964 d: Bernard Borderie. FRN/ITL/GRM., *Marveilleuse Angelique*, Anne Golon, Serge Golon, Novel

MERVEILLEUSE JOURNEE, LA 1928 d: Rene Barberis. FRN., *La Merveilleuse Journee*, Yves Mirande, Gustave Quinson, Play

MERVEILLEUSE JOURNEE, LA 1932 d: Robert Wyler, Yves Mirande. FRN., *La Merveilleuse Journee*, Yves Mirande, Gustave Quinson, Play

MERVEILLEUSE VISITE, LA 1973 d: Marcel Carne. FRN/ITL., *The Wonderful Visit*, H. G. Wells, 1895, Novel

Merveilleux Automne, Un *see* UN BELLISSIMO NOVEMBRE (1968).

Mery for Ever *see* MERY PER SEMPRE (1988).

MERY PER SEMPRE 1988 d: Marco Risi. ITL., *Mery Per Sempere*, Aurelio Grimaldi, Novel

MES DIX-SEPT ANS 1996 d: Philippe Faucon. FRN., *You're Not Serious When You're Seventeen*, Barbara Samson, Novel

MES, HET 1960 d: Fons Rademakers. NTH., *Het Mes*, Hugo Claus, Novel

MES NUITS SONT PLUS BELLES QUE VOS JOURS 1988 d: Andrzej Zulawski. FRN., *Mes Nuits Sont Plus Belles Que Vos Jours*, Raphaelle Billetdoux, Novel

MESAVENTURE DU CAPITAINE CLAVAROCHE, LA 1910. FRN., *Le Chandelier*, Alfred de Musset, Play

MESE HABBAL 1979 d: Istvan Bacskai-Lauro. HNG., *Mese Habbal*, Zsigmond Remenyik, 1934, Novel

MESE MARIANO 1929 d: Ubaldo Pittei. ITL., *Mese Mariano*, Salvatore Di Giacomo, 1898, Play

MESHI 1951 d: Mikio Naruse. JPN., *Meshi*, Fumiko Hayashi, 1951, Novel

MESSAGE FROM MARS, A 1913 d: Wallett Waller. UKN., *A Message from Mars*, Richard Ganthony, London 1899, Play

MESSAGE FROM MARS, A 1921 d: Maxwell Karger. USA., *A Message from Mars*, Richard Ganthony, London 1899, Play

MESSAGE IN A BOTTLE 1999 d: Luis Mandoki. USA., *Message in a Bottle*, Nicholas Sparks, Novel

MESSAGE, THE 1930 d: Sewell Collins. UKN., *The Message*, Brandon Fleming, Story

MESSAGE TO GARCIA, A 1916 d: Richard Ridgely. USA., *A Message to Garcia*, Elbert Hubbard, 1899, Essay

MESSAGE TO GARCIA, A 1936 d: George Marshall. USA., *A Message to Garcia*, Elbert Hubbard, 1899, Essay, *How I Carried the Message to Garcia*, Andrew Summers Rowan, San Francisco 1922, Book

MESSAGER, LE 1937 d: Raymond Rouleau. FRN., *Le Messager*, Henri Bernstein, Play

MESSENGER OF DEATH 1988 d: J. Lee Thompson. USA., *The Avenging Angel*, Rex Burns, Novel

MESSIEURS LES RONDS DE CUIR 1914 d: Andre Liabel. FRN., *Messieurs Les Ronds-de-Cuir*, Georges Courteline, 1893, Novel

MESSIEURS LES RONDS DE CUIR 1936 d: Yves Mirande. FRN., *Messieurs Les Ronds-de-Cuir*, Georges Courteline, 1893, Novel

MESSIEURS LES RONDS-DE-CUIR 1959 d: Henri Diamant-Berger. FRN., *Messieurs Les Ronds-de-Cuir*, Georges Courteline, 1893, Novel

MESSIEURS LUDOVIC 1945 d: Jean-Paul Le Chanois. FRN., *Ludo*, Pierre Scize, Novel

MESTECKO NA DLANI 1942 d: Vaclav Binovec. CZC., *Mestecko Na Dlani*, Jan Drda, Novel

METAL MESSIAH 1977 d: Tibor Takacs. CND., *Metal Messiah*, Stephen Zoller, Play

METAMORPHOSE DES CLOPORTES 1965 d: Pierre Granier-Deferre. FRN/ITL., *La Metamorphose Des Cloportes*, Alphonse Boudard, Paris 1962, Novel

METAMORPHOSES 1978 d: Takashi. JPN/USA., *Metamorphoses*, Ovid, c2-8, Verse

Metamorphosis *see* FORVANDLINGEN (1975).

Metel' *see* METELJ (1964).

METELJ 1964 d: Vladimir Basov. USS., *Metel'*, Alexander Pushkin, 1831, Short Story

METELLO 1970 d: Mauro Bolognini. ITL., *Metello*, Vasco Pratolini, 1955, Novel

METROLAND 1997 d: Philip Saville. UKN/FRN/SPN., *Metroland*, Julian Barnes, 1980, Novel

Metschti W Kibritena Kutijka *see* MIGOVE V KIBRITENA KOUTIYKA (1979).

METTI, UNA SERA A CENA 1969 d: Giuseppe Patroni Griffi. ITL., *Metti - Una Sera a Cena*, Giuseppe Patroni Griffi, Play

Meu Caso, O *see* MON CAS (1986).

Meu Caso: Repeticoes, O *see* MON CAS (1986).

MEU DESTINO E PECAR 1952 d: Manuel Peluffo. BRZ., *Meu Destino E Pecar*, Nelson Rodrigues, 1944, Novel

Meurtre a l'Asile *see* MATTO REGIERT (1947).

MEURTRE EN 45 TOURS 1960 d: Etienne Perier. FRN., *A Coeur Perdu*, Pierre Boileau, Thomas Narcejac, Paris 1959, Novel

MEURTRE EST UN MEURTRE, UN 1972 d: Etienne Perier. FRN/ITL., *Un Meurtre Est un Meurtre*, Dominique Fabre, Novel

Meurtre Par Decret *see* MURDER BY DECREE (1979).

MEURTRES 1950 d: Richard Pottier. FRN., *Meurtres*, Charles Plisnier, Novel

MEURTRIER DE THEODORE, LE 1908-18 d: Georges MoncA. FRN., *Le Meurtrier de Theodore*, Bernard, Brot, Clairville, Play

MEURTRIER, LE 1962 d: Claude Autant-LarA. FRN/ITL/GRM., *The Blunderer*, Patricia Highsmith, New York 1954, Novel

Meutre a Montmartre *see* REPRODUCTION INTERDITE (1956).

MEUTRE EN DOUCE 1990 d: Patrick Dromgoole. FRN/CND/SWT., *Murder on Side*, Day Keene

Mexican Affair, A *see* FLOR DE MAYO (1957).

MEXICAN HAYRIDE 1948 d: Charles T. Barton. USA., *Mexican Hayride*, Dorothy Fields, Herbert Fields, Cole Porter, Musical Play

Mexican Quarter *see* BORDER CAFE (1937).

Mexican, The *see* MEKSIKANETS (1957).

MEXICANO, EL 1944 d: Agustin P. Delgado. MXC., *The Mexican*, Jack London, 1913, Short Story

MEXICAN'S GRATITUDE, THE 1914 d: Richard Ridgely. USA., *A Chaparral Christmas Gift*, O. Henry, Short Story

MEZEI PROFETA 1947 d: Frigyes Ban. HNG., *Tundoklo Jeromos*, Aron Tamasi, 1941, Play

MHARI PYARI CHANANA 1983 d: Jatin Kumar. IND., *Ramu Chanana*, Bharat Vyas, Play

Mi Boda Contigo *see* NOTRE MARIAGE (1984).

MI KLALAH LE BRACHAH 1950 d: Joseph Krumgold. ISR., *Yehuda Ya'ari*, Novel

MI MUJER ME GUSTA MAS 1960 d: Antonio Roman. SPN/ITL., *Mia Moglie Mi Piace Di Piu*, Luis Alfayate, Luis Tejador, Play

Mi Segunda Mujer *see* SENORA CASADA NECESITA MARIDO (1935).

MI ULTIMO AMOR 1931 d: Lewis Seiler. USA., *Basquerie*, Eleanor Mercein, New York 1927, Book

Mia Droga Si Chiama Julie, La *see* LA SIRENE DU MISSISSIPPI (1969).

MIA FIA 1928 d: Orlando Vassallo. ITL., *Mia Fia*, Giacinto Gallina, 1878, Play

MIA MOGLIE SI DIVERTE 1939 d: Paul Verhoeven. ITL., *Our Little Wife*, Avery Hopwood, New York 1916, Play

MIA MOGLIE SI E FIDANZATA 1921 d: Gero Zambuto. ITL., *Mia Moglie Si E Fidanzata*, Gino Calza-Bini, 1914, Play

MIA VITA PER LA TUA!, LA 1914 d: Emilio Ghione. ITL., *Tentativo Di Romanzo Cinematografico*, Matilde Serao

Miami *see* MOON OVER MIAMI (1941).

MIAMI BLUES 1990 d: George Armitage. USA., *Miami Blues*, Charles Willeford, Novel

Miarka, Daughter of the Bear *see* LA FILLE A L'OURSE MIARKA (1920).

MIARKA, LA FILLE A L'OURSE 1914 d: Georges-Andre Lacroix. FRN., *La Fille a l'Ourse Miarka*, Jean Richepin, Novel

MIARKA, LA FILLE A L'OURSE 1920 d: Louis Mercanton. FRN., *La Fille a l'Ourse Miarka*, Jean Richepin, Novel

MIARKA, LA FILLE A L'OURSE 1937 d: Jean Choux. FRN., *La Fille a l'Ourse Miarka*, Jean Richepin, Novel

MICA INTIMPLARE, O 1957 d: Gheorghe Turcu. RMN., *Felrjaro Salamon*, Andras Suto, 1955, Short Story

MICE AND MEN 1916 d: J. Searle Dawley. USA., *Mice and Men*, Madeleine Lucette Ryley, Manchester 1901, Play

Michael and His Lost Angel *see* WHISPERING DEVILS (1920).

MICHAEL AND MARY 1931 d: Victor Saville. UKN., *Michael and Mary*, A. A. Milne, London 1930, Play

Michael Kohlhaas *see* MICHAEL KOHLHAAS - DER REBELL (1969).

MICHAEL KOHLHAAS - DER REBELL 1969 d: Volker Schlondorff. GRM., *Michel Kohlhaas*, Heinrich von Kleist, 1810, Short Story

Michael Kohlhaas - the Rebel *see* MICHAEL KOHLHAAS - DER REBELL (1969).

MICHAEL O'HALLORAN 1923 d: James Leo Meehan. USA., *Michael O'Halloran*, Gene Stratton-Porter, New York 1915, Novel

MICHAEL O'HALLORAN 1937 d: Karl Brown. USA., *Michael O'Halloran*, Gene Stratton-Porter, New York 1915, Novel

MICHAEL O'HALLORAN 1948 d: John Rawlins. USA., *Michael O'Halloran*, Gene Stratton-Porter, New York 1915, Novel

Michael Perrine *see* MICHELE PERRIN (1913).

MICHAEL SHAYNE, PRIVATE DETECTIVE 1940 d: Eugene J. Forde. USA., *The Private Practice of Michael Shayne*, Brett Halliday, New York 1940, Novel

MICHAEL SHELI 1975 d: Dan Wolman. ISR., *Michael Sheli*, Amos Oz, 1968, Novel

MICHAEL STROGOFF 1910 d: J. Searle Dawley. USA., *Michel Strogoff*, Jules Verne, Paris 1876, Novel

MICHAEL STROGOFF 1914 d: Lloyd B. Carleton. USA., *Michel Strogoff*, Jules Verne, Paris 1876, Novel

Michael Strogoff see **MICHEL STROGOFF** (1926).

Michael Strogoff see **THE SOLDIER AND THE LADY** (1937).

Michael Strogoff see **MICHELE STROGOFF** (1956).

MICHE 1931 d: Jean de Marguenat. FRN., *Miche*, Etienne Rey, Play

Michel Ezra Safra and Sons see **MICHEL EZRA SAFRA VE'BANAV** (1983).

MICHEL EZRA SAFRA VE'BANAV 1983 d: Nissim Dayan. ISR., Amnon Shamosh, Novel

MICHEL STROGOFF 1926 d: Victor Tourjansky. FRN., *Michel Strogoff*, Jules Verne, Paris 1876, Novel

MICHEL STROGOFF 1935 d: Jacques de Baroncelli, Richard Eichberg. FRN., *Michel Strogoff*, Jules Verne, Paris 1876, Novel

Michel Strogoff see **MICHELE STROGOFF** (1956).

Michel Strogoff see **LE TRIOMPHE DE MICHEL STROGOFF** (1961).

MICHEL STROGOFF 1975 d: Jean-Pierre Decourt. FRN., *Michel Strogoff*, Jules Verne, Paris 1876, Novel

MICHELE PERRIN 1913 d: Eleuterio Rodolfi. ITL., *Michele Perrin*, C. Duveyrier, Melesville, 1834, Play

MICHELE STROGOFF 1956 d: Carmine Gallone. ITL/FRN/GRM., *Michel Strogoff*, Jules Verne, Paris 1876, Novel

Michele Strogoff see **STROGOFF** (1970).

MICHELINE 1921 d: Jean Kemm. FRN., *Micheline*, Andre Theuriet, Novel

MICHIGAN KID, THE 1928 d: Irvin V. Willat. USA., *The Michigan Kid*, Rex Beach, 1925, Short Story

MICHIGAN KID, THE 1947 d: Ray Taylor. USA., *The Michigan Kid*, Rex Beach, 1925, Short Story

MICKEY 1948 d: Ralph Murphy. USA., *Clementine*, Peggy Goodin, Novel

MICROBE, THE 1919 d: Henry Otto. USA., *The Microbe*, Henry Altimus, 1919, Short Story

MIDAS TOUCH, THE 1939 d: David MacDonald. UKN., *The Midas Touch*, Margaret Kennedy, Novel

MID-CHANNEL 1920 d: Harry Garson. USA., *Mid-Channel*, Arthur Wing Pinero, New York 1910, Play

Middle Man, The see **JANA ARANYA** (1975).

MIDDLE OF THE NIGHT 1959 d: Delbert Mann. USA., *Middle of the Night*, Paddy Chayefsky, 1954, Television Play

Middle Sister see **MANJHLI DIDI** (1968).

MIDDLE WATCH, THE 1930 d: Norman Walker. UKN., *The Middle Watch*, Ian Hay, Stephen King-Hall, London 1929, Play

MIDDLE WATCH, THE 1939 d: Thomas Bentley. UKN., *The Middle Watch*, Ian Hay, Stephen King-Hall, London 1929, Play

MIDDLE-AGE SPREAD 1979 d: John Reid. NZL., *Middle Age Spread*, Roger Hall, Play

MIDDLEMAN, THE 1915 d: George Loane Tucker. UKN., *The Middleman*, Henry Arthur Jones, London 1889, Play

Middleman, The see **JANA ARANYA** (1975).

MIDDLEMARCH 1994 d: Anthony Page. UKN/USA., *Middlemarch*, George Eliot, 1872, Novel

MIDDLETON'S CHANGELING 1997 d: Marcus Thompson. UKN., *The Changeling*, Thomas Middleton, William Rowley, Play

MIDLANDERS, THE 1920 d: Ida May Park, Joseph de Grasse. USA., *The Midlanders*, Charles Tenney Jackson, Indianapolis 1912, Novel

Midnight see **MIDNIGHT LIFE** (1928).

MIDNIGHT 1931 d: George King. UKN., *After Midnight*, Charles Bennett, 1929, Play

MIDNIGHT 1934 d: Chester Erskine. USA., *Midnight*, Claire Sifton, Paul Sifton, New York 1930, Play

Midnight see **ZI YE** (1981).

MIDNIGHT ALARM, THE 1923 d: David Smith. USA., *The Midnight Alarm*, James W. Harkins Jr., Play

MIDNIGHT ALIBI 1934 d: Alan Crosland. USA., *The Old Doll's House*, Damon Runyon, 1933, Short Story

MIDNIGHT BELL, A 1913 d: Charles H. France. USA., *A Midnight Bell*, Charles Hale Hoyt, Play

MIDNIGHT BELL, A 1921 d: Charles Ray. USA., *A Midnight Bell*, Charles Hale Hoyt, Play

MIDNIGHT BRIDE, THE 1920 d: William J. Humphrey. USA., *The Marriage of Little Jeanne Sterling*, Charles Stokes Wayne, 1918, Short Story

Midnight Butterfly see **MANHATTAN BUTTERFLY** (1935).

MIDNIGHT CALL, THE 1914 d: Fred W. Huntley. USA., *The Midnight Call*, James Oliver Curwood, Story

MIDNIGHT CLEAR, A 1992 d: Keith Gordon. USA., *A Midnight Clear*, William Wharton, Novel

MIDNIGHT CLUB 1933 d: Alexander Hall, George Somnes. USA., *Gangster's Glory*, E. Phillips Oppenheim, Boston 1931, Novel

MIDNIGHT COWBOY 1969 d: John Schlesinger. USA., *Midnight Cowboy*, James Leo Herlihy, New York 1965, Novel

Midnight Cruise, The see **THE SPIDER** (1931).

MIDNIGHT EPISODE 1950 d: Gordon Parry. UKN., *Monsieur la Souris*, Georges Simenon, 1938, Novel

MIDNIGHT EXPRESS 1978 d: Alan Parker. UKN/USA., *Midnight Express*, Billy Hayes, William Hoffer, Book

Midnight in Paris see **MONSIEUR LA SOURIS** (1942).

MIDNIGHT IN ST. PETERSBURG 1995 d: Douglas Jackson. UKN/CND/RSS., *Midnight in St. Petersburg*, Len Deighton, Novel

MIDNIGHT IN THE GARDEN OF GOOD AND EVIL 1997 d: Clint Eastwood. USA., *Midnight in the Garden of Good and Evil*, John Berendt, Book

MIDNIGHT INTRUDER 1937 d: Arthur Lubin. USA., *Synthetic Gentleman*, Channing Pollock, New York 1934, Novel

MIDNIGHT KISS, THE 1926 d: Irving Cummings. USA., *Pigs*, Patterson McNutt, Anne Morrison, New York 1924, Play

MIDNIGHT LACE 1960 d: David Miller. USA., *Matilda Shouted Fire*, Janet Green, Play

MIDNIGHT LIFE 1928 d: Scott R. Dunlap. USA., *The Spider's Web*, Reginald Wright Kauffman, New York 1913, Novel

MIDNIGHT LOVERS 1926 d: John Francis Dillon. USA., *Collusion*, J. E. Harold Terry, Play

MIDNIGHT MADNESS 1928 d: F. Harmon Weight. USA., *The Lion Trap*, Daniel N. Rubin, Play

MIDNIGHT MYSTERY 1930 d: George B. Seitz. USA., *Hawk Island*, Howard Irving Young, New York 1929, Play

Midnight Raiders see **TROUBLE AT MIDNIGHT** (1938).

MIDNIGHT J. RIDE OF PAUL REVERE, THE 1914 d: Charles J. Brabin. USA., *The Midnight Ride of Paul Revere*, Henry Wadsworth Longfellow, Poem

MIDNIGHT ROMANCE, A 1919 d: Lois Weber. USA., *A Midnight Romance*, Marion Orth, Short Story

MIDNIGHT STAGE, THE 1919 d: Ernest C. Warde. USA., *Le Courrier de Lyon*, A. Delacour, Giraoudin Delacour, Emile Moureau, London 1877, Play

Midnight Sting see **DIGGSTOWN** (1992).

MIDNIGHT SUMMONS 1924 d: Fred Paul. UKN., *The Midnight Summons*, Sax Rohmer, Short Story

MIDNIGHT SUN, THE 1926 d: Dimitri Buchowetzki. USA., *The Midnight Sun*, Lauridas Brunn, Story

Midshipmaid Gob see **THE MIDSHIPMAID** (1932).

MIDSHIPMAID, THE 1932 d: Albert de Courville. UKN., *The Midshipmaid*, Ian Hay, Stephen King-Hall, London 1931, Play

MIDSHIPMAN EASY 1915 d: Maurice Elvey. UKN., *Mr. Midshipman Easy*, Frederick Marryat, 1836, Novel

MIDSHIPMAN EASY 1935 d: Carol Reed. UKN., *Mr. Midshipman Easy*, Frederick Marryat, 1836, Novel

MIDSOMER MURDERS: THE KILLINGS AT BADGERS DRIFT 1998 d: Jeremy Silberston. UKN., *The Killings at Badgers Drift*, Caroline Graham, Novel

Midsummer Day's Smile, A see **UN SURIS IN PLINA VARA** (1963).

MIDSUMMER MADNESS 1920 d: William C. de Mille. USA., *His Friend and His Wife*, Cosmo Hamilton, Boston 1920, Novel

Midsummer Night see **JOHANNISNACHT** (1956).

MIDSUMMER NIGHT'S DREAM, A 1909 d: Charles Kent, J. Stuart Blackton (Spv). USA., *A Midsummer Night's Dream*, William Shakespeare, c1594, Play

MIDSUMMER NIGHT'S DREAM, A 1935 d: Max Reinhardt, William Dieterle. USA., *A Midsummer Night's Dream*, William Shakespeare, c1594, Play

MIDSUMMER NIGHT'S DREAM, A 1953 d: Charles Deane. UKN., *A Midsummer Night's Dream*, William Shakespeare, c1594, Play

MIDSUMMER NIGHT'S DREAM, A 1958 d: Rudolph Cartier. UKN., *A Midsummer Night's Dream*, William Shakespeare, c1594, Play

Midsummer Night's Dream, A see **SEN NOCI SVATOJANSKE** (1959).

MIDSUMMER NIGHT'S DREAM, A 1964 d: Joan Kemp-Welch. UKN., *A Midsummer Night's Dream*, William Shakespeare, c1594, Play

MIDSUMMER NIGHT'S DREAM, A 1966 d: Dan Eriksen, George Balachine. USA., *A Midsummer Night's Dream*, William Shakespeare, c1594, Play

MIDSUMMER NIGHT'S DREAM, A 1968 d: Peter Hall. UKN., *A Midsummer Night's Dream*, William Shakespeare, c1594, Play

MIDSUMMER NIGHT'S DREAM, A 1981 d: Elijah Moshinsky. UKN., *A Midsummer Night's Dream*, William Shakespeare, c1594, Play

MIDSUMMER NIGHT'S DREAM, A 1984 d: Celestino Coronado. SPN/UKN., *A Midsummer Night's Dream*, William Shakespeare, c1594, Play

MIDSUMMER NIGHT'S DREAM, A 1996 d: Adrian Noble. UKN., *A Midsummer Night's Dream*, William Shakespeare, c1594, Play

MIDT I EN JAZZTID 1970 d: Knud Leif Thomsen. DNM., *Midt I En Jazztid*, Knud Sonderby, 1931, Novel

MIDWIVE'S TALE, A 1997 d: Richard P. Rogers. USA., Laurel Thatcher Ulrich, Book

Mie Prigioni, Le see **SILVIO PELLICO** (1915).

MIEHEN TIE 1940 d: Nyrki Tapiovaara, Erik Blomberg. FNL., *Miehen Tie*, Frans E. Sillanpaa, 1932, Novel

MIEI PRIMI QUARANT'ANNI, I 1988 d: Carlo VanzinA. ITL., *I Miei Primi Quarant'anni*, Marina Ripa Di Meana, Novel

Miesta Ei Voi Raiskata see **MANRAPE** (1978).

Mighty Crusaders, The see **LA GERUSALEMME LIBERATA** (1957).

Mighty Invaders, The see **LA GERUSALEMME LIBERATA** (1957).

MIGHTY QUINN, THE 1989 d: Carl Schenkel. USA., *Finding Maubee*, A. H. Z. Carr, Novel

MIGHTY, THE 1998 d: Peter Chelsom. USA., *Freak the Mighty*, Rodman Philbrick, Novel

MIGHTY TREVE, THE 1937 d: Lewis D. Collins. USA., *Treve*, Albert Payson Terhune, New York 1925, Novel

Miglior Sindico, Il Re, Il see **EL REY, EL MEJOR ALCALDE** (1973).

MIGNON 1915 d: William Nigh. USA., *Mignon*, Ambroise Thomas, Paris 1866, Opera

MIGNON 1919 d: Mario Gargiulo. ITL., *Mignon*, Ambroise Thomas, Paris 1866, Opera

MIGOVE V KIBRITENA KOUTIYKA 1979 d: Marianna EvstatievA. BUL., Lev Nikolayevich Tolstoy, Short Story

MIGRANTS, THE 1974 d: Tom Gries. USA., Tennessee Williams, Story

Miguel Pro see **RAIN FOR A DUSTY SUMMER** (1971).

Mihail Strogov see **STROGOFF** (1970).

MIJNHEER HAT LAUTER TOCHTER 1967 d: Volker Vogeler. GRM., *Mijnheer Hat Lauter Tochter*, Maria Becker, Book

Mikado, The see **FAN FAN** (1918).

MIKADO, THE 1939 d: Victor Schertzinger. UKN., *The Mikado*, W. S. Gilbert, Arthur Sullivan, London 1885, Opera

MIKADO, THE 1967 d: Stuart Burge. UKN., *The Mikado*, W. S. Gilbert, Arthur Sullivan, London 1885, Opera

Miklos Akli see **AKLI MIKLOS** (1986).

MIKRES APHRODITES 1962 d: Nikos Koundouros. GRC., *Daphnis and Chloe*, Longus, c200, Novel

Milady and the Musketeers see **IL BOIA DI LILLA** (1953).

Milady Et Les Mousquetaires see **IL BOIA DI LILLA** (1953).

MILAGRO BEANFIELD WAR, THE 1987 d: Robert Redford. USA., *The Milagro Beanfield War*, John Nichols, Novel

MILAGRO DEL CRISTO DE LA VEGA, EL 1940 d: Adolfo Aznar. SPN., *A Buen Juez Mejor Testigo*, Jose Zorrilla Y Moral, 1837, Verse

MILAN 1946 d: Nitin Bose. IND., *Nauka Dubi*, Rabindranath Tagore, 1916, Novel

MILANO CALIBRO 9 1972 d: Fernando Di Leo. ITL., *Milano Calibro 9*, Giorgio Scerbanenco, Novel

Milczaca Gwiazda *see* DER SCHWEIGENDE STERN (1960).

MILCZENIE 1963 d: Kazimierz Kutz. PLN., *Milczenie*, Jerzy Szczygiel, Novel

MILDRED PIERCE 1945 d: Michael Curtiz. USA., *Mildred Pierce*, James M. Cain, 1941, Novel

MILE-A-MINUTE KENDALL 1918 d: William D. Taylor. USA., *Mile-a-Minute Kendall*, Owen Davis, New York 1916, Play

MILE-A-MINUTE ROMEO 1923 d: Lambert Hillyer. USA., *Gun Gentlemen*, Max Brand, Short Story

MILES AGAINST MINUTES 1924 d: Lee Morrison. UKN., *Pixie at the Wheel*, Dudley Sturrock, Short Story

MILESTONES 1916 d: Thomas Bentley. UKN., *Milestones*, Arnold Bennett, Edward Knoblock, London 1912, Play

MILESTONES 1920 d: Paul Scardon. USA., *Milestones*, Arnold Bennett, Edward Knoblock, London 1912, Play

MILIARDI, CHE FOLLIA! 1942 d: Guido Brignone. ITL., *Un Milionario Si Ribella*, Raffaele Carrieri, Novel

MILIONE, IL 1920 d: Wladimiro Apolloni. ITL., *Le Million*, Georges Berr, Marcel Guillemaud, Paris 1910, Play

Military Court *see* KRIEGSGERICHT (1959).

Military Secrets of Prague *see* VALECNE TAJNOSTI PRAZSKE (1926).

MILITONA O LA TRAGEDIA DE UN TORERO 1922 d: Henri Vorins. SPN/FRN., *La Militona*, Theophile Gautier, Novel

MILIZIA TERRITORIALE 1935 d: Mario Bonnard. ITL., *Militizia Territoriale*, Aldo de Benedetti, Play

Milk Girl, The *see* LE LATTIVENDOLE (1914).

Milky Way, The *see* THE INNOCENTS OF CHICAGO (1932).

MILKY WAY, THE 1936 d: Leo McCarey. USA., *The Milky Way*, Harry Clork, Lynn Root, New York 1934, Play

Mill of Good Luck, The *see* MOARA CU NOROC (1956).

Mill of Luck and Plenty, The *see* MOARA CU NOROC (1956).

Mill of the Stone Maidens *see* IL MULINO DELLE DONNE DI PIETRA (1960).

Mill of the Stone Women *see* IL MULINO DELLE DONNE DI PIETRA (1960).

MILL ON THE FLOSS, THE 1915 d: W. Eugene Moore. USA., *The Mill on the Floss*, George Eliot, London 1860, Novel

MILL ON THE FLOSS, THE 1937 d: Tim Whelan. UKN., *The Mill on the Floss*, George Eliot, London 1860, Novel

MILL ON THE FLOSS, THE 1997 d: Graham Theakston. UKN., *The Mill on the Floss*, George Eliot, London 1860, Novel

Mill on the Po, The *see* IL MULINO DEL PO (1949).

Mill on the River *see* IL MULINO DEL PO (1949).

MILLE DI GARIBALDI, I 1933 d: Alessandro Blasetti. ITL., Gino Mazzucchi, Story

Millenial Bee, The *see* TISICROCNA VCELA (1983).

MILLENIUM 1989 d: Michael Anderson. CND/USA., *Air Raid*, John Varley, Short Story

Miller and His Child, The *see* MLYNAR A JEHO DITE (1928).

Miller and His Son, The *see* MLYNAR A JEHO DITE (1928).

Miller Karafiat, The *see* PAN OTEC KARAFIAT (1935).

Miller's Beautiful Wife, The *see* LA BELLA MUGNAIA (1955).

Miller's Wife, The *see* LA BELLA MUGNAIA (1955).

Milles Et Chateaugue *see* LE GRAND SABORDAGE (1972).

MILLIE 1931 d: John Francis Dillon. USA., *Millie*, Donald Henderson Clarke, New York 1930, Novel

MILLIE'S DAUGHTER 1947 d: Sidney Salkow. USA., *Millie's Daughter*, Donald Henderson Clarke, Novel

MILLION A MINUTE, A 1916 d: John W. Noble. USA., *A Million a Minute: a Romance of Modern New York and Paris*, Robert Aitken, New York 1908, Novel

MILLION BID, A 1914 d: Ralph Ince. USA., *Agnes*, George Cameron, New York 1908, Play

MILLION BID, A 1927 d: Michael Curtiz. USA., *Agnes*, George Cameron, New York 1908, Play

MILLION DE DOT, UN 1916. FRN., *Un Million de Dot*, Daniel Riche, Novel

MILLION DOLLAR BABY 1941 d: Curtis Bernhardt. USA., *Miss Wheelwright Discovers America*, Leonhard Spiegelgass, Story

Million Dollar Diamond *see* THE DIAMOND (1954).

Million Dollar Ghost *see* THE MAN WHO WOULDN'T DIE (1942).

MILLION DOLLAR HANDICAP, THE 1925 d: Scott Sidney. USA., *Thoroughbreds*, William Alexander Fraser, New York 1902, Novel

Million Dollar Man *see* L' HOMME QUI VALAIT DES MILLIARDS (1967).

Million Dollar Manhunt *see* ASSIGNMENT REDHEAD (1956).

MILLION DOLLAR MYSTERY, THE 1914 d: Howell Hansel. USA., *The Million Dollar Mystery*, Harold MacGrath, Story

MILLION DOLLAR RANSOM 1934 d: Murray Roth. USA., *One Million Dollars Ransom*, Damon Runyon, Short Story

Million Dollar Swindle, The *see* PUBLIC DEFENDER (1931).

Million Dollar Tattoo *see* LE TATOUE (1968).

Million Eyes of Su-Muru, The *see* SUMURU (1967).

MILLION, LE 1931 d: Rene Clair. FRN., *Le Million*, Georges Berr, Marcel Guillemaud, Paris 1910, Play

MILLION POUND NOTE, THE 1953 d: Ronald Neame. UKN., *The £1.000.000 Bank-Note*, Mark Twain, 1893, Short Story

MILLION, THE 1915 d: Thomas N. Heffron. USA., *Le Million*, Georges Berr, Marcel Guillemaud, Paris 1910, Play

MILLION TO JUAN, A 1994 d: Paul Rodriguez. USA., *The £1.000.000 Bank-Note*, Mark Twain, 1893, Short Story

Million to One, A *see* A MILLION TO JUAN (1994).

MILLIONAIRE BABY, THE 1915 d: Lawrence Marston. USA., *The Millionaire Baby*, Anna Katharine Green Rohlfs, Indianapolis 1905, Novel

Millionaire for a Day *see* LET'S BE RITZY (1934).

MILLIONAIRE FOR CHRISTY, A 1951 d: George Marshall. USA., *The Golden Goose*, Robert Harari, Story

MILLIONAIRE PIRATE, THE 1919 d: Rupert Julian. USA., Emil Nyitray, Story

Millionaire Playboy *see* PARK AVENUE LOGGER (1937).

MILLIONAIRE POLICEMAN, THE 1926 d: Edward J. Le Saint. USA., *The Millionaire Policeman*, Samuel J. Briskin, Story

MILLIONAIRE, THE 1931 d: John G. Adolfi. USA., *Idle Hands*, Earl Derr Biggers, 1921, Short Story

MILLIONAIRES 1926 d: Herman C. Raymaker. USA., *The Inevitable Millionaires*, E. Phillips Oppenheim, London 1923, Novel

MILLIONAIRESS, THE 1960 d: Anthony Asquith. UKN., *The Millionairess*, George Bernard Shaw, New York 1936, Play

MILLIONENRAUB IM RIVIERAEXPRESS, DER 1927 d: Joseph Delmont. GRM., Louis Delluc, Novel

Mills of Hell *see* MALOM A POKOLBAN (1987).

Mills of the Gods, The *see* DIE GOTTES MUHLEN (1938).

Millstone, The *see* A TOUCH OF LOVE (1969).

MILOVANI ZAKAZANO 1938 d: Miroslav Cikan, Carl Lamac. CZC., *Milovani Zakazano*, Jan Sedlak, Novel

Mimi *see* LA VIE DE BOHEME (1916).

MIMI 1935 d: Paul L. Stein. UKN., *La Vie de Boheme*, Henri Murger, Paris 1848, Play

MIMI BLUETTE FIORE DEL MIO GIARDINO 1976 d: Carlo Di PalmA. ITL., *Mimi Bluette Fiore Del Mio Giardino*, Guido Da Verona, Novel

MIMI PINSON 1957 d: Robert Darene. FRN., *Mademoiselle Mimi Pinson*, Alfred de Musset, 1853, Short Story

MIMIC 1997 d: Guillermo Del Toro. USA., *Mimic*, Donald A. Wolheim, Short Story

MIMI-TROTTIN 1921 d: Henri Andreani. FRN., *Mimi Trottin*, Marcel Nadaud, Novel

MIN AND BILL 1930 d: George W. Hill. USA., *Dark Star*, Lorna Moon, Indianapolis 1929, Novel

MIN BING DE ER ZI 1958 d: Huang Can. CHN., *Changing Heaven*, Jun Qing, Novel

MIN MARION 1975 d: Nils R. Muller. NRW., *Min Marion*, Terje Stigen, 1972, Novel

Min Van Oscar *see* MON PHOQUE ET ELLES (1951).

MINA DROMMARS STAD 1976 d: Ingvar Skogsberg. SWD., *Mina Drommars Stad*, Per Anders Fogelstrom, Novel

Minaccia, La *see* LA MENACE (1960).

MINAMI NO SHIMA NI YUKI GA FURA 1961 d: Seiji Hisamatsu. JPN., Daisuke Kato, Autobiography

Mind Games *see* AGENCY (1979).

MIND OF MR. REEDER, THE 1939 d: Jack Raymond. UKN., *The Mind of Mr. Reeder*, Edgar Wallace, London 1925, Novel

MIND OF MR. SOAMES, THE 1969 d: Alan Cooke. UKN., *The Mind of Mr. Soames*, Charles Eric Maine, London 1961, Novel

MIND OVER MOTOR 1923 d: Ward Lascelle. USA., *Mind Over Motor*, Mary Roberts Rinehart, 1912, Short Story

MIND THE PAINT GIRL 1919 d: Wilfred North. USA., *The "Mind-the-Paint" Girl*, Arthur Wing Pinero, London 1912, Play

Mind-the-Paint Girl, The *see* MIND THE PAINT GIRL (1919).

MINE ON THE YUKON, THE 1912. USA., *The Thaw at Sliscos*, Rex Beach, Story

MINE OWN EXECUTIONER 1947 d: Anthony Kimmins. UKN., *Mine Own Executioner*, Nigel Balchin, 1945, Novel

MINE WITH THE IRON DOOR, THE 1924 d: Sam Wood. USA., *The Mine With the Iron Door*, Harold Bell Wright, New York 1923, Novel

MINE WITH THE IRON DOOR, THE 1936 d: David Howard. USA., *The Mine With the Iron Door*, Harold Bell Wright, New York 1923, Novel

Minister's Wife, The *see* DE VROUW VAN DEN MINISTER (1920).

MINISTRY OF FEAR 1944 d: Fritz Lang. USA., *Ministry of Fear*, Graham Greene, 1943, Novel

MINISZTER FELRELEP, A 1998 d: Andras Kern, Robert Koltai. HNG., *Out of Order*, Ray Cooney, Play

MINNA VON BARNHEIM 1966 d: Ludwig Cremer. GRM., *Minna von Barnheim; Oder Das Soldatengluck*, Gotthold Ephraim Lessing, Hamburg 1767, Play

MINNA VON BARNHEIM 1976 d: Franz Peter Wirth. GRM., *Minna von Barnheim; Oder Das Soldatengluck*, Gotthold Ephraim Lessing, Hamburg 1767, Play

MINNA VON BARNHELM 1962 d: Martin Hellberg. GDR., *Minna von Barnheim; Oder Das Soldatengluck*, Gotthold Ephraim Lessing, Hamburg 1767, Play

MINNE 1916 d: Andre Hugon. FRN., *L' Ingenue Libertine*, Sidonie Gabrielle Colette, 1909, Novel

Minne *see* MINNE L'INGENUE LIBERTINE (1950).

MINNE L'INGENUE LIBERTINE 1950 d: Jacqueline Audry. FRN., *L' Ingenue Libertine*, Sidonie Gabrielle Colette, 1909, Novel

MINTS OF HELL, THE 1919 d: Park Frame. USA., *Flat Gold*, James B. Hendryx, Short Story

Minty's Triumph *see* A PHYLLIS OF THE SIERRAS (1915).

Minuet *see* MENUET (1982).

MINUIT, PLACE PIGALLE 1928 d: Rene Hervil. FRN., *Minuit Place Pigalle*, Maurice Dekobra, Novel

MINUIT, PLACE PIGALLE 1934 d: Roger Richebe. FRN., *Minuit Place Pigalle*, Maurice Dekobra, Novel

MINUIT QUAI DE BERCY 1952 d: Christian Stengel. FRN., *Minuit Quai de Bercy*, Pierre Lambin, Novel

MINUS MAN, THE 1999 d: Hampton Fancher. USA., *The Minus Man*, Lew McCreary, 1990, Novel

Minute Man, The *see* SIX CYLINDER LOVE (1931).

Minx *see* ULICNICE (1936).

MINYA ZAVUT ARLEKIN 1988 d: Valeri Rybarev. USS., *Minya Zavur Arlekin*, Juri Schtschekotschichin, Play

MIO CADAVERE, IL 1917 d: Anton Giulio Bragaglia, Riccardo Cassano (Uncredited). ITL., *Francesco Lannois*, Francesco Mastriani, 1851, Novel

MIO CARO DOTTOR GRASLER 1989 d: Roberto FaenzA. ITL/HNG., *Doktor Grasler*, Arthur Schnitzler, 1917, Short Story

Mio Figlio *see* RUE DES PRAIRIES (1959).

Mio in the Land of Faraway *see* MIN MIO! MIO (1987).

MIO, MIN MIO! 1987 d: Vladimir Grammatikov. SWD/USS/NRW., *Mio, Min Mio!*, Astrid Lindgren, Novel

Mio, Moj Mio *see* MIO. MIN MIO! (1987).

Mio, My Mio! *see* MIN MIO! MIO (1987).

MIO PADRE MONSIGNORE 1971 d: Antonio Racioppi. ITL., *Roma Baffuta*, Antonio Racioppi, Play

MIO WEST, IL 1998 d: Giovanni Veronesi. ITL., *Jodo Cartamigli*, Vincenzo Pardini, Novel

MIO ZIO BARBASSOUS 1921 d: Riccardo Cassano. ITL., *Mio Zio Barbassous*, E. Blavet, Fabrice Carre, 1891, Play

Mio Zio Beniamino *see* MON ONCLE BENJAMIN (1969).

MIQUETTE 1940 d: Jean Boyer. FRN., *Miquette Et Sa Mere*, Gaston Arman de Caillavet, Robert de Flers, Play

Miquette *see* MIQUETTE ET SA MERE (1949).

MIQUETTE ET SA MERE 1914 d: Henri Pouctal. FRN., *Miquette Et Sa Mere*, Gaston Arman de Caillavet, Robert de Flers, Play

MIQUETTE ET SA MERE 1933 d: Henri Diamant-Berger, D. B. Maurice. FRN., *Miquette Et Sa Mere*, Gaston Arman de Caillavet, Robert de Flers, Play

Miquette Et Sa Mere *see* MIQUETTE (1940).

MIQUETTE ET SA MERE 1949 d: Henri-Georges Clouzot. FRN., *Miquette Et Sa Mere*, Gaston Arman de Caillavet, Robert de Flers, Play

MIR LOND NOD LUGG 1940 d: Hermann Haller. SWT., *Mir Lond Nod Lugg*, Rudolf Eger, Play

MIRA 1971 d: Fons Rademakers. BLG/NTH., **De Teleurgang Van de Waterhoek**, Stijn Streuvels, 1927, Novel

Miracle *see* A WOMAN'S FAITH (1925).

Miracle *see* AMORE (1948).

MIRACLE BABY, THE 1923 d: Val Paul. USA., *The Miracle Baby*, Frank Richardson Pierce, 1921, Short Story

MIRACLE DES LOUPS, LE 1924 d: Raymond Bernard. FRN., *Le Miracle Des Loups*, Henri Dupuy-Mazuel, Novel

MIRACLE DES LOUPS, LE 1930 d: Raymond Bernard. FRN., *Le Miracle Des Loups*, Henri Dupuy-Mazuel, Novel

MIRACLE DES LOUPS, LE 1961 d: Andre Hunebelle. FRN/ITL., *Le Miracle Des Loups*, Henri Dupuy-Mazuel, Novel

Miracle from Mars *see* RED PLANET MARS (1952).

Miracle in Milan *see* MIRACOLO A MILANO (1951).

MIRACLE IN THE RAIN 1956 d: Rudolph Mate. USA., *Miracle in the Rain*, Ben Hecht, 1943, Novel

Miracle in the Sand *see* THREE GODFATHERS (1936).

MIRACLE IN THE WILDERNESS 1991 d: Kevin Dobson. USA., Paul Gallico, Short Story

MIRACLE MAN, THE 1919 d: George Loane Tucker. USA., *The Miracle Man*, Frank L. Packard, New York 1914, Novel

Miracle of Father Malachias, The *see* DAS WUNDER DES MALACHIAS (1961).

Miracle of Love *see* SON RISE: A MIRACLE OF LOVE (1979).

MIRACLE OF LOVE, THE 1920 d: Robert Z. Leonard. USA., *The Miracle of Love*, Cosmo Hamilton, New York 1915, Novel

Miracle of Love, The *see* OSWALT KOLLE: DAS WUNDER DER LIEBE -SEXUALITAT IN DER EHE (1968).

Miracle of Malachias, The *see* DAS WUNDER DES MALACHIAS (1961).

MIRACLE OF MONEY, THE 1920 d: Hobart Henley. USA., *The Marrying of Emmy*, Beulah Poynter, 1919, Short Story

MIRACLE OF THE BELLS, THE 1948 d: Irving Pichel. USA., *The Miracle of the Bells*, Richard Janney, Novel

Miracle of the Christ at la Vega *see* EL MILAGRO DEL CRISTO DE LA VEGA (1940).

MIRACLE OF THE WHITE STALLIONS, THE 1962 d: Arthur Hiller. USA., *Ein Leben Fur Die Lipizzaner*, Alois Podhajsky, Munich 1960, Book

Miracle of the Wolves, The *see* LE MIRACLE DES LOUPS (1924).

Miracle of the Wolves, The *see* LE MIRACLE DES LOUPS (1930).

Miracle of the Wolves, The *see* LE MIRACLE DES LOUPS (1961).

MIRACLE ON 34TH STREET 1947 d: George Seaton. USA., Valentine Davies, Story

MIRACLE ON 34TH STREET 1973 d: Fielder Cook. USA., Valentine Davies, Story

MIRACLE ON 34TH STREET 1994 d: Les Mayfield. USA., Valentine Davies, Story

Miracle, The *see* DAS MIRAKEL (1913).

MIRACLE, THE 1923 d: A. E. Coleby. UKN., *The Miracle*, Sax Rohmer, Short Story

MIRACLE, THE 1959 d: Irving Rapper. USA., *Das Mirakel*, Karl Vollmoller, 1911, Play

MIRACLE WOMAN 1931 d: Frank CaprA. USA., *Bless You Sister*, John Meehan, Robert Riskin, New York 1927, Play

MIRACLE WORKER, THE 1962 d: Arthur Penn. USA., *The Miracle Worker*, William Gibson, New York 1959, Play

MIRACLE WORKER, THE 1979 d: Paul Aaron. USA., *The Miracle Worker*, William Gibson, New York 1959, Play

MIRACLES FOR SALE 1939 d: Tod Browning. USA., *Death from a Top Hat*, Clayton Rawson, New York 1938, Novel

MIRACOLO A MILANO 1951 d: Vittorio de SicA. ITL., *Toto Il Buono*, Cesare Zavattini, Story

MIRAD LOS LIRIOS DEL CAMPO 1947 d: Ernesto ArancibiA. ARG., *Olhai Os Lirios Do Campo*, Erico Verissimo, 1937, Novel

MIRADA DEL OTRO, LA 1998 d: Vicente ArandA. SPN., *La Mirada Del Otro*, Fernando G. Delgado, Novel

MIRAGE 1965 d: Edward Dmytryk. USA., *Fallen Angel*, Howard Fast, Boston 1952, Novel

MIRAGE DU COEUR, LE 1916 d: Georges Treville. FRN., *Le Mirage du Coeur*, Georges Dolley, Short Story

MIRAGE, THE 1920 d: Arthur Rooke. UKN., *The Mirage*, E. Temple Thurston, Novel

MIRAGE, THE 1924 d: George Archainbaud. USA., *The Mirage*, Edgar Selwyn, New York 1920, Play

Mirage, The *see* POSSESSED (1931).

MIRAKEL, DAS 1913 d: Max Reinhardt. GRM/AUS., *Das Mirakel*, Karl Vollmoller, 1911, Play

MIRANDA 1948 d: Ken Annakin. UKN., *Miranda*, Peter Blackmore, Play

Miranda of the Balcony *see* SLAVES OF DESTINY (1924).

Mirandolina, Das Madchen Mit Dem Schlecten Ruf *see* DAS MADCHEN MIT DEM GUTEN RUF (1938).

MIRANDY SMILES 1918 d: William C. de Mille. USA., *The Littlest Scrub Lady*, Belle K. Maniates, Short Story

Mire of Prague, The *see* BAHNO PRAHY (1927).

MIREILLE 1909 d: Henri Cain. FRN., *Mireille*, Frederic Mistral, Poem

MIREILLE 1922 d: Ernest Servaes. FRN., *Mireille*, Frederic Mistral, Poem

MIREILLE 1933 d: Rene Gaveau, Ernest Servaes. FRN., *Mireille*, Frederic Mistral, Poem

MIRELE EFROS 1939 d: Josef Berne. USA., *Mirele Efros*, Jacob Gordin, 1898, Play

MIRIAM 1957 d: William Markus. FNL., *Miriam*, Walentin Chorell, 1954, Novel

MIRIAM ROZELLA 1924 d: Sidney Morgan. UKN., *Miriam Rozella*, B. J. Farjeon, Novel

MIRJAMS MUTTER 1992 d: Vera Loebner. GRM., *Anna Im Goldenen Tor*, Erika Wisselinck, Novel

MIRROR AND MARKHEIM, THE 1954 d: John Lemont. UKN., *The Mirror and Markheim*, Robert Louis Stevenson, Short Story

MIRROR CRACK'D, THE 1980 d: Guy Hamilton. UKN/USA., *The Mirror Crack'd from Side to Side*, Agatha Christie, Novel

Mirror Death Ray of Dr. Mabuse, The *see* DIE TODESSTRAHLEN DES DR. MABUSE (1964).

Mirror, The *see* AYNA (1984).

Mirror With Three Faces *see* LA GLACE A TROIS FACES (1927).

Misadventures of Don Quixote and Sancho Panza, The *see* AS TRAPALHADAS DE DOM QUIXOTE & SANCHO PANCA (1980).

MISADVENTURES OF MARGARET, THE 1998 d: Brian Skeet. UKN/FRN., *Rameau's Niece*, Cathleen Schine, Novel

Misadventures of Mr. Wilt, The *see* WILT (1989).

MISANTHROPE, LE 1966 d: Louis-Georges Carrier. CND., *Le Misanthrope*, Moliere, 1666, Play

MISBEHAVING LADIES 1931 d: William Beaudine. USA., *Once There Was a Princess*, Juliet Wilbor Tompkins, 1926, Short Story

MISCHIEF 1931 d: Jack Raymond. UKN., *Mischief*, Ben Travers, London 1928, Play

Mischievous Meg *see* MADICKEN PA JUNIBACKEN (1979).

Mischievous One, The *see* LA REVOLTOSA (1924).

Miscreant, The *see* NEMODLENEC (1927).

MISE A SAC 1967 d: Alain Cavalier. FRN/ITL., *Mise a Sac*, Donald E. Westlake, Novel

MISERABILI, I 1947 d: Riccardo FredA. ITL., *Les Miserables*, Victor Hugo, Paris 1862, Novel

Miserables du Vingtieme Siecle, Les *see* LES MISERABLES (1995).

Miserables du XXe Siecle, Les *see* LES MISERABLES (1995).

MISERABLES, LES 19— d: Marcel Bluwal. FRN., *Les Miserables*, Victor Hugo, Paris 1862, Novel

MISERABLES, LES 1912 d: Albert Capellani. FRN., *Les Miserables*, Victor Hugo, Paris 1862, Novel

MISERABLES, LES 1925 d: Henri Fescourt. FRN., *Les Miserables*, Victor Hugo, Paris 1862, Novel

MISERABLES, LES 1933 d: Raymond Bernard. FRN., *Les Miserables*, Victor Hugo, Paris 1862, Novel

Miserables, Les *see* LES MISERABLES (1935).

Miserables, Les *see* LOS MISERABLES (1943).

Miserables, Les *see* EL BOUASSA (1944).

Miserables, Les *see* EZAI PADUM PADU (1950).

MISERABLES, LES 1957 d: Jean-Paul Le Chanois. FRN/GRM/ITL., *Les Miserables*, Victor Hugo, Paris 1862, Novel

MISERABLES, LES 1982 d: Robert Hossein. FRN., *Les Miserables*, Victor Hugo, Paris 1862, Novel

MISERABLES, LES 1995 d: Claude Lelouch. FRN., *Les Miserables*, Victor Hugo, Paris 1862, Novel

MISERABLES, LOS 1943 d: Fernando A. Rivero. MXC., *Les Miserables*, Victor Hugo, Paris 1862, Novel

MISERIA E NOBILTA 1914 d: Enrico Guazzoni?. ITL., *Miseria e Nobilta*, Eduardo Scarpetta, 1888, Play

MISERIA E NOBILTA 1941 d: Corrado d'Errico. ITL., *Miseria e Nobilta*, Eduardo Scarpetta, 1888, Play

MISERIA E NOBILTA 1954 d: Mario Mattoli. ITL., *Miseria e Nobilta*, Eduardo Scarpetta, 1888, Play

MISERICORDE 1917 d: Camille de Morlhon. FRN., *Misericorde*, Octave Pradels, Short Story

Miserie Dei Trovatelli, Le *see* MARTINO IL TROVATELLO (1919).

MISERIE DEL SIGNOR TRAVET, LE 1946 d: Mario Soldati. ITL., *Le Miserie Di Monsu Travet*, Vittorio Bersezio, 1871, Play

MISERY 1990 d: Rob Reiner. USA., *Misery*, Stephen King, Novel

Misfit Brigade, The *see* WHEELS OF TERROR (1987).

MISFIT WIFE, THE 1920 d: Edmund Mortimer. USA., *The Outsider*, Julie Herne, New Britain, Ct. 1916, Play

MISFITS, THE 1961 d: John Huston. USA., *The Misfits*, Arthur Miller, 1961, Short Story

Mishima *see* MISHIMA: A LIFE IN FOUR CHAPTERS (1985).

MISHIMA: A LIFE IN FOUR CHAPTERS 1985 d: Paul Schrader. USA/JPN., *Homba*, Yukio Mishima, 1969, Novel, *Kinkaku-Ji*, Yukio Mishima, 1956, Novel, *Kyoko No Ie*, Yukio Mishima, 1959, Novel

MISI MOKUS KALANDJAI 1984 d: Otto Foky. HNG., *Misi Mokus Kalandjai*, Jozsi Jeno Tersanszky, 1953, Novel

Mision Especial En Caracas *see* MISSION SPECIALE A CARACAS (1965).

MISLEADING LADY, THE 1916 d: Arthur Berthelet. USA., *The Misleading Lady*, Paul Dickey, Charles W. Goddard, New York 1913, Play

MISLEADING LADY, THE 1920 d: George Irving, George W. Terwilliger. USA., *The Misleading Lady*, Paul Dickey, Charles W. Goddard, New York 1913, Play

MISLEADING LADY, THE 1932 d: Stuart Walker. USA., *The Misleading Lady*, Paul Dickey, Charles W. Goddard, New York 1913, Play

MISLEADING WIDOW, THE 1919 d: John S. Robertson. USA., *Billeted*, H. M. Harwood, F. Tennyson Jesse, London 1917, Play

MISMATES 1926 d: Charles J. Brabin. USA., *Mismates*, Myron C. Fagan, New York 1925, Play

MISS BLUEBEARD 1925 d: Frank Tuttle. USA., *Der Gatte Des Frauleins*, Gabor Dregely, Vienna 1916, Play

MISS BRACEGIRDLE DOES HER DUTY 1926 d: Edwin Greenwood. UKN., *Miss Bracegirdle Does Her Duty*, Stacy Aumonier, Short Story

MISS BRACEGIRDLE DOES HER DUTY 1936 d: Lee Garmes. UKN., *Miss Bracegirdle Does Her Duty*, Stacy Aumonier, Short Story

MISS BREWSTER'S MILLIONS 1926 d: Clarence Badger. USA., *Brewster's Millions*, George Barr McCutcheon, New York 1902, Novel

MISS CHARITY 1921 d: Edwin J. Collins. UKN., *Miss Charity*, Keble Howard, Novel

MISS DULCIE FROM DIXIE 1919 d: Joseph Gleason. USA., *Miss Dulcie from Dixie*, Lulah Ragsdale, 1917, Novel

MISS EVERS' BOYS 1997 d: Joseph Sargent. USA., *Miss Evers' Boys*, David Feldshuh, Play

MISS FANE'S BABY IS STOLEN 1934 d: Alexander Hall. USA., *Kidnapt*, Rupert Hughes, 1933, Short Story

MISS FIRECRACKER 1989 d: Thomas Schlamme. USA., *The Miss Firecracker Contest*, Beth Henley, 1985, Play

MISS HELYETT 1927 d: Georges Monca, Maurice Keroul. FRN., *Miss Helyett*, Edmond Audran, Maxime Boucheron, Opera

MISS HELYETT 1933 d: Hubert Bourlon, Jean Kemm. FRN., *Miss Helyett*, Edmond Audran, Maxime Boucheron, Opera

MISS HOBBS 1920 d: Donald Crisp. USA., *Miss Hobbs*, Jerome K. Jerome, New York 1899, Play

Miss Jude see **THE TRUTH ABOUT SPRING** (1964).

Miss Julie see **FROKEN JULIE** (1951).

MISS JULIE 1972 d: Robin Philips, John Glenister. UKN., *Froken Julie*, August Strindberg, 1888, Play

Miss Lohengrin see **MON BEGUIN** (1929).

Miss Lonelyhearts see **LONELYHEARTS** (1958).

MISS LULU BETT 1921 d: William C. de Mille. USA., *Miss Lulu Bett*, Zona Gale, New York 1920, Novel

Miss Maitland, Private Secretary see **THE GIRL IN THE WEB** (1920).

MISS MARPLE: A CARIBBEAN MYSTERY 1989 d: Christopher Petit. UKN., *A Caribbean Mystery*, Agatha Christie, Novel

MISS MARPLE: A MURDER IS ANNOUNCED 1984 d: David Giles. UKN., *A Murder Is Announced*, Agatha Christie, Novel

MISS MARPLE: A POCKETFUL OF RYE 1985 d: Guy Slater. UKN., *A Pocketful of Rye*, Agatha Christie, Story

MISS MARPLE: THE BODY IN THE LIBRARY 1985 d: Silvio Narizzano. UKN., *The Body in the Library*, Agatha Christie, Novel

MISS MORRISON'S GHOSTS 1981 d: John Bruce. UKN., *An Adventure*, Frances Lamont, Elizabeth Morrison, Book

Miss Mother see **SLECNA MATINKA** (1938).

MISS NOBODY 1926 d: Lambert Hillyer. USA., *Shebo*, Tiffany Wells, Story

Miss Nobody see **PANNA NIKT** (1997).

Miss Oyu see **OYU-SAMA** (1951).

MISS PACIFIC FLEET 1935 d: Ray Enright. USA., *Miss Pacific Fleet*, Frederick Hazlitt Brennan, 1934, Short Story

MISS PETTICOATS 1916 d: Harley Knoles. USA., *Miss Petticoats*, Dwight Tilton, Boston 1902, Novel

MISS PINKERTON 1932 d: Lloyd Bacon. USA., *Miss Pinkerton: Adventures of a Nurse Detective*, Mary Roberts Rinehart, New York 1932, Novel

MISS RAFFLES 1914 d: Theodore Marston. USA., *Miss Raffles*, C. S. Morton, Story

MISS ROSE WHITE 1992 d: Joseph Sargent. USA., *A Shayna Maidel*, Barbara Lebow, Play

MISS ROVEL 1921 d: Jean Kemm. FRN., *Miss Rovel*, Victor Cherbuliez, Novel

MISS SADIE THOMPSON 1953 d: Curtis Bernhardt. USA., *Rain*, W. Somerset Maugham, 1921, Short Story

Miss Shumway Casts a Spell see **MISS SHUMWAY JETTE UN SORT** (1962).

MISS SHUMWAY JETTE UN SORT 1962 d: Jean Jabely. FRN/ARG., *Miss Shumway Waves a Wand*, James Hadley Chase, Novel

Miss Shumway Jette un Sort see **ROUGH MAGIC** (1995).

MISS SUSIE SLAGLE'S 1945 d: John Berry. USA., *Miss Susie Slagle's*, Augusta Tucker, Novel

MISS TATLOCK'S MILLIONS 1948 d: Richard Haydn. USA., *Oh! Brother*, Jacques Deval, Play

Miss Wheelwright Discovers America see **MILLION DOLLAR BABY** (1941).

MISSBRAUCHTEN LIEBESBRIEFE, DIE 1940 d: Leopold Lindtberg. SWT., *Die Missbrauchten Liebesbriefe*, Gottfried Keller, Stuttgart 1865, Short Story

MISSBRAUCHTEN LIEBESBRIEFE, DIE 1969 d: Hans D. Schwarze. GRM., *Die Missbrauchten Liebesbriefe*, Gottfried Keller, Stuttgart 1865, Short Story

Missiles from Hell see **BATTLE OF THE V 1** (1958).

MISSING 1918 d: James Young. USA., *Missing*, Mrs. Humphrey Ward, New York 1917, Novel

MISSING 1982 d: Costa-Gavras. USA., *The Execution of Charles Horman*, Thomas Hauser, Book

MISSING GUEST, THE 1938 d: John Rawlins. USA., Eric Philippi, Story

Missing Husbands see **L' ATLANTIDE** (1921).

MISSING MILLION, THE 1942 d: Phil Brandon. UKN., *The Missing Million*, Edgar Wallace, London 1923, Novel

MISSING MILLIONS 1922 d: Joseph Henabery. USA., *An Answer in Grand Larceny*, Jack Boyle, 1919, Short Story, *A Problem in Grand Larceny*, Jack Boyle, 1919, Short Story

Missing Miniature, The see **DIE VERSCHWUNDENE MINIATUR** (1954).

MISSING PEOPLE, THE 1939 d: Jack Raymond. UKN., *The Mind of Mr. Reeder*, Edgar Wallace, London 1925, Novel

Missing Persons see **BUREAU OF MISSING PERSONS** (1933).

MISSING PIECES 1983 d: Mike Hodges. USA., *A Private Investigation*, Karl Alexander, Novel

Missing Principal, The see **DEN FORSVUNDNE FULDMAEGTIG** (1972).

MISSING REMBRANDT, THE 1932 d: Leslie Hiscott. UKN., *Charles Augustus Milverton*, Arthur Conan Doyle, 1904, Short Story

Missing Ten Days see **TEN DAYS IN PARIS** (1939).

MISSING THE TIDE 1918 d: Walter West. UKN., *Missing the Tide*, Alfred Turner, Novel

MISSING THREE QUARTER, THE 1923 d: George Ridgwell. UKN., *The Missing Three Quarter*, Arthur Conan Doyle, Short Story

Mission for a Killer see **FURIA A BAHIA POUR OSS 117** (1965).

Mission of Lysistrata, The see **DIE SENDUNG DER LYSISTRATA** (1961).

MISSION SPECIALE A CARACAS 1965 d: Raoul Andre. FRN/SPN.ITL., *Mission Speciale a Caracas*, Claude Rank, Novel

Mission to Hong Kong see **DAS GEHEIMNIS DER DREI DSCHUNKEN** (1965).

MISSION TO MOSCOW 1943 d: Michael Curtiz. USA., *Mission to Moscow*, Joseph E. Davis, Book

Missione Caracas see **MISSION SPECIALE A CARACAS** (1965).

MISSIONER, THE 1922 d: George Ridgwell. UKN., *The Missioner*, E. Phillips Oppenheim, London 1908, Novel

Missionnaire, Le see **TAM TAM MAYUMBE** (1955).

Mississippi see **HEAVEN ON EARTH** (1931).

MISSISSIPPI 1935 d: A. Edward Sutherland. USA., *Magnolia*, Booth Tarkington, New York 1923, Play

Mississippi Mermaid see **LA SIRENE DU MISSISSIPPI** (1969).

Missouri Story, The see **THE ROMANCE OF ROSY RIDGE** (1947).

MISSOURI TRAVELER, THE 1958 d: Jerry Hopper. USA., *The Missouri Traveler*, John Burress, 1955, Novel

Mist in the Moorland see **MLHY NA BLATECH** (1943).

MIST IN THE VALLEY 1923 d: Cecil M. Hepworth. UKN., *Mist in the Valley*, Dorin Craig, Novel

Mist Over the Swamps see **MLHY NA BLATECH** (1943).

Mistaken Identity see **DEATH FLIES EAST** (1935).

MISTER 44 1916 d: Henry Otto. USA., *Mister 44*, E. J. Rath, New York 1916, Novel

MISTER 880 1950 d: Edmund Goulding. USA., *Old Eight Eighty*, St. Clair McKelway, Article

Mister and Mistress see **BUT THE FLESH IS WEAK** (1932).

MISTER AND MRS. EDGEHILL 1985 d: Gavin Millar. UKN., *Mister and Mrs. Edgehill*, Noel Coward, 1951, Short Story

MISTER ANTONIO 1929 d: James Flood, Frank Reicher. USA., *Mister Antonio*, Booth Tarkington, Play

Mister Bird to the Rescue see **LE ROI ET L'OISEAU** (1979).

MISTER BUDDWING 1965 d: Delbert Mann. USA., *Buddwing*, Evan Hunter, New York 1964, Novel

MISTER CINDERS 1934 d: Friedrich Zelnik. UKN., *Mister Cinders*, Clifford Grey, Greatrex Newman, London 1929, Musical Play

MISTER DYNAMIT - MORGEN KUSST EUCH DER TOD 1967 d: Franz J. Gottlieb. AUS/GRM/ITL., *Mister Dynamit - Morgen Kusst Euch Der Tod*, C. H. Guenter, Novel

Mister Esteve see **EL SENOR ESTEVE** (1948).

MISTER FLOW 1936 d: Robert Siodmak. FRN., *Mister Flow*, Gaston Leroux, Novel

Mister Hawarden see **MONSIEUR HAWARDEN** (1968).

MISTER JOHNSON 1990 d: Bruce Beresford. USA., *Mister Johnson*, Joyce Cary, 1939, Novel

MISTER MOSES 1964 d: Ronald Neame. UKN., *Mister Moses*, Max Catto, London 1961, Novel

MISTER QUILP 1974 d: Michael Tuchner. UKN., *The Old Curiosity Shop*, Charles Dickens, London 1841, Novel

MISTER ROBERTS 1955 d: John Ford, Mervyn Leroy. USA., *Mister Roberts*, Thomas Heggen, 1946, Novel

MISTER SCOUTMASTER 1953 d: Henry Levin. USA., *Be Prepared*, Rice E. Cochran, 1952, Novel

MISTER WU 1920. ITL., *Mr. Wu*, Harold Owen, Harry M. Vernon, London 1913, Play

MISTERI DELLA GIUNGLA NERA, I 1964 d: Luigi Capuano. ITL/GRM., *I Misteri Della Jungla Nera*, Emilio Salgari, Genoa 1895, Novel

Misteri Delle Catacombe, I see **FABIOLA** (1918).

Misteri Di Parigi, I see **IL VENTRE DI PARIGI** (1917).

MISTERI DI PARIGI, I 1958 d: Fernando Cerchio, Giorgio RivaltA. ITL/FRN., *Les Mysteres de Paris*, Eugene Sue, 1842-43, Novel

Misteri Di Parigi, I see **LES MYSTERES DE PARIS** (1962).

MISTERIO EN LA ISLA DE LOS MONSTRUOS 1981 d: Piquer Simon. SPN/USA., *L'ile Mysterieuse*, Jules Verne, Paris 1874, Novel

Misterios de Tanger, Los see **AGUILAS DE ACERO** (1927).

MISTERO DEI BERNARDO BROWN, IL 1922 d: Ermanno Geymonat. ITL., *The Mystery of Mr. Bernard Brown*, E. Phillips Oppenheim, 1896, Novel

MISTERO DI JACK HILTON, IL 1913 d: Ubaldo Maria Del Colle. ITL., *The Mystery of Jack Hilton*, Charles Darlington, Novel

MISTERO DI OBERWALD, IL 1979 d: Michelangelo Antonioni. ITL/GRM., *L' Aigle a Deux Tetes*, Jean Cocteau, 1946, Play

Mistic, El see **EL MISTICO** (1926).

MISTICO, EL 1926 d: Juan Andreu Moragas. SPN., *El Mistic*, Santiago Rusinol, Play

MISTIGRI 1931 d: Harry Lachman. FRN., *Mistigri*, Marcel Achard, 1931, Play

MISTLETOE BOUGH, THE 1904 d: Percy Stow. UKN., *The Mistletoe Bough*, E. T. Bayley, Poem

MISTLETOE BOUGH, THE 1923 d: Edwin J. Collins. UKN., *The Mistletoe Bough*, Charles Somerset, Play

MISTRAL, LE 1942 d: Jacques Houssin. FRN., *Le Mistral*, Jacques Carton, Novel

Mistress for the Summer, A see **UNE FILLE POUR L'ETE** (1960).

Mistress Holle see **FRAU HOLLE** (1964).

MISTRESS NELL 1915 d: James Kirkwood. USA., *Mistress Nell*, George Cochrane Hazelton, New York 1900, Play

Mistress of Atlantis, The see **DIE HERRIN VON ATLANTIS** (1932).

MISTRESS OF SHENSTONE, THE 1921 d: Henry King. USA., *The Mistress of Shenstone*, Florence L. Barclay, New York 1910, Novel

Mistress of the Inn see **LA LOCANDIERA** (1981).

MISTRESS PAMELA 1973 d: Jim O'Connolly. UKN., *Pamela*, Samuel Richardson, 1740, Novel

Mistress, The see **VASSA ZHELEZNOVA** (1953).

Mistress, The see **GAN** (1953).

MISTY 1961 d: James B. Clark. USA., *Misty of Chincoteague*, Marguerite Henry, Chicago 1947, Novel

Misunderstood see **INCOMPRESO** (1966).

MISUNDERSTOOD 1983 d: Jerry Schatzberg. USA., *Misunderstood*, Florence Montgomery, Novel

MIT BESTEN EMPFEHLUNGEN 1963 d: Kurt Nachmann. AUS., *Mit Besten Empfehlungen*, Hans Schubert, Play

MIT CSINALT FELSEGED 3-TOL 5-IG? 1964 d: Karoly Makk. HNG., *A Szelistyei Asszonyok*, Kalman Mikszath, 1901, Novel

Mit Django Kam Der Tod see **L'ORGOGLIO, LA VENDETTA, L' UOMO** (1967).

Mit Gift Jager see **LE ROMAN D'UN JEUNE HOMME PAUVRE** (1927).

MIT HIMBEERGEIST GEHT ALLES BESSER 1960 d: Georg MarischkA. AUS., *Mit Himbeergeist Geht Alles Besser*, Johannes Mario Simmel, Novel

Mit Teuflischen Grussen see **DIABOLIQUEMENT VOTRE** (1967).

MIT VERSIEGELTER ORDER 1938 d: Karl Anton. GRM., *Vertrag Um Karakat*, Fritz Peter Buch, Play

MITASARETA SEIKATSU 1962 d: Susumu Hani. JPN., *Mitasareta Seikatsu*, Tatsuzo Ishikawa, Novel

MITICA POPESCU 1984 d: Manole Marcus. RMN., *Mitica Popescu*, Camil Petrescu, 1928, Play

MITREA COCOR 1952 d: Victor Iliu, Marietta SadovA. RMN., *Mitrea Cocor*, Mihail Sadoveanu, 1949, Novel

MITSOU 1956 d: Jacqueline Audry. FRN., *Comment l'Esprit Vient aux Filles Mitsou; Ou*, Sidonie Gabrielle Colette, 1919, Novel

Mitsou Ou Comment l'Esprit Vient aux Filles see **MITSOU** (1956).

MITT LIV SOM HUND 1985 d: Lasse Hallstrom. SWD., *Mitt Liv Som Hund*, Reidar Jonsson, Autobiography

MIX ME A PERSON 1962 d: Leslie Norman. UKN., *Mix Me a Person*, Jack Trevor Story, Novel

Mixed Doubles see **EX-FLAME** (1930).

MIXED DOUBLES 1933 d: Sidney Morgan. UKN., *Mixed Doubles*, Frank Stayton, London 1925, Play

MIXED FACES 1922 d: Rowland V. Lee. USA., *Mixed Faces*, Roy Norton, New York 1921, Novel

Mixed Feelings see **SUZANNE** (1930).

MIXED RELATIONS 1916 d: George Loane Tucker. UKN., *Mixed Relations*, W. W. Jacobs, Short Story

MIYAMOTO MUSASHI 1954 d: Hiroshi Inagaki. JPN., *Miyamoto Musashi*, Eiji Yoshikawa, 1937-39, Novel

MIYAMOTO MUSASHI: ICHIJOJI NO KETTO 1955 d: Hiroshi Inagaki. JPN., *Miyamoto Musashi*, Eiji Yoshikawa, 1937-39, Novel

MIYAMOTO MUSASHI: KETTO GANRYUJIMA 1956 d: Hiroshi Inagaki. JPN., *Miyamoto Musashi*, Eiji Yoshikawa, 1937-39, Novel

MIZPAH; OR, LOVE'S SACRIFICE 1915 d: Stuart Kinder. UKN., *Mizpah; Or Love's Sacrifice*, Wood Lawrence, Play

Mjortvaje Duschy see **MERTVIYE DUSHI** (1960).

MLHY NA BLATECH 1943 d: Frantisek Cap. CZC., *Mlhy Na Blatech*, Karel Klostermann, Novel

M'LISS 1915 d: O. A. C. Lund. USA., *M'liss: an Idyll of Red Mountain*, Bret Harte, Boston 1869, Novel

M'LISS 1918 d: Marshall Neilan. USA., *M'liss: an Idyll of Red Mountain*, Bret Harte, Boston 1869, Novel

M'LISS 1936 d: George Nicholls Jr. USA., *M'liss: an Idyll of Red Mountain*, Bret Harte, Boston 1869, Novel

Mlle. Froufrou see **THE TOY WIFE** (1938).

M'LORD OF THE WHITE ROAD 1923 d: Arthur Rooke. UKN., *M'lord of the White Road*, Cedric D. Fraser, Novel

MLYNAR A JEHO DITE 1928 d: Zet Molas. CZC., *Mlynar a Jeho Dite*, Ernst Raupach, Play

MNOGO SHUMA IZ NICHEVO 1956 d: L. Zamkovoy. USS., *Much Ado About Nothing*, William Shakespeare, c1598, Play

Mnogo Shuma Iz Nichevo see **MNOGO SUMA IZ NICEGO** (1973).

MNOGO SUMA IZ NICEGO 1973 d: Samson Samsonov. USS., *Much Ado About Nothing*, William Shakespeare, c1598, Play

Moaning Mountain see **LELEJSKA GORA** (1968).

MOARA CU NOROC 1956 d: Victor Iliu. RMN., *Moara Cu Noroc*, Ioan Slavici, 1881, Short Story

MOARA LUI CALIFAR 1984 d: Serban Marinescu. RMN., *Moara Lui Califar*, Gala Galaction, 1902, Short Story

MOARTEA LUI IPU 1972 d: Sergiu Nicolaescu. RMN., *Moartea Lui Ipu*, Titus Popovici, 1970, Short Story

MOARTEA LUI JOE INDIANUL 1968 d: Mihai Iacob, Wolfgang Liebeneiner. RMN/FRN., *Adventures of Tom Sawyer*, Mark Twain, San Francisco 1876, Novel

MOARTEA UNUI ARTIST 1991 d: Horea Popescu. RMN., *Moartea Unui Artist*, Horia Lovinescu, 1965, Play

MOB 39 1940 d: Arthur Porchet. SWT., Yves Louys, Short Story

MOB, THE 1951 d: Robert Parrish. USA., *Waterfront*, Ferguson Findley, Novel

Mobilisation 39 see **MOB 39** (1940).

Mobilizing of Johanna see **JOHANNA ENLISTS** (1918).

MOBY DICK 1930 d: Lloyd Bacon. USA., *Moby Dick Or the Whale*, Herman Melville, New York 1851, Novel

Moby Dick see **DAMON DES MEERES** (1931).

MOBY DICK 1954 d: Albert McCleery. USA., *Moby Dick Or the Whale*, Herman Melville, New York 1851, Novel

MOBY DICK 1956 d: John Huston. UKN/USA., *Moby Dick Or the Whale*, Herman Melville, New York 1851, Novel

MOBY DICK 1998 d: Franc Roddam. USA/ASL/UKN., *Moby Dick Or the Whale*, Herman Melville, New York 1851, Novel

MOCKERY 1927 d: Benjamin Christensen. USA., Stig Esbern, Story

MODCHE A REZI 1926 d: Premysl Prazsky. CZC., *Modche a Rezi*, Vojtech Rakous, Short Story

Modche and Rezi see **MODCHE A REZI** (1926).

Model from Montmartre, The see **LA FEMME NUE** (1926).

Model from Paris see **THAT MODEL FROM PARIS** (1926).

Model Husband see **DER MUSTERGATTE** (1937).

Model Love see **LA RAGAZZA DI NOME GIULIO** (1970).

Model Murder Case, The see **GIRL IN THE HEADLINES** (1963).

MODEL, THE 1915 d: Frederick A. Thompson. USA., *Women and Wine*, Ben Landeck, Arthur Shirley, New York 1900, Play

MODEL YOUNG MAN, A 1914 d: James Young. USA., *A Model Young Man*, Jacques Futrelle, Story

MODELLA, LA 1920 d: Mario Caserini. ITL., *La Modella*, Alfredo Testoni, 1907, Play

MODEL'S CONFESSION, THE 1918 d: Ida May Park. USA., *Ruby M. Ayres*, Short Story

MODERATO CANTABILE 1960 d: Peter Brook. FRN/ITL., *Moderato Cantabile*, Marguerite Duras, Paris 1958, Novel

Modern Camille, A see **CAMILLE** (1915).

Modern Cinderella, The see **WHEN TOMORROW COMES** (1939).

MODERN HERO, A 1934 d: G. W. Pabst. USA., *A Modern Hero*, Louis Bromfield, New York 1932, Novel

MODERN MAGDALEN, A 1915 d: Will S. Davis. USA., *A Modern Magdalen*, C. Haddon Chambers, New York 1902, Play

Modern Magdalene see **MODERNI MAGDALENA** (1921).

MODERN MARRIAGE 1923 d: Lawrence C. Windom. USA., *Lady Varley*, Derek Vane, Story

MODERN MUSKETEER, A 1917 d: Allan Dwan. USA., *D'artagnan of Kansas*, Eugene P. Lyle Jr., 1912, Short Story

MODERN PRODIGAL, THE 1910 d: D. W. Griffith. USA., *The Southerner*, Bess Meredyth, Story

MODERN SALOME, A 1920 d: Leonce Perret. USA., *Salome*, Oscar Wilde, 1893, Play

MODERN THELMA, A 1916 d: John G. Adolfi. USA., *Thelma - a Norwegian Princess*, Marie Corelli, London 1887, Novel

Modern Wife, The see **FREE LOVE** (1931).

MODERNI MAGDALENA 1921 d: Boris Orlicky. CZC., *Moderni Magdalena*, Jakub Arbes, Play

MODESTA 1956 d: Benji Doniger. PRC., *Modesta*, Domingo Silas Ortiz, Short Story

MODIFICATION, LA 1970 d: Michel Worms. FRN/ITL., *La Modification*, Michel Butor, 1957, Novel

Modigliani of Montparnasse see **MONTPARNASSE 19** (1957).

MOERU TAIRIKU 1968 d: Shogoro NishimurA. JPN., Haruo Ikushima, Short Story

MOETSUKITA CHIZU 1968 d: Hiroshi TeshigaharA. JPN., *Moetsukita Chizu*, Abe Kobo, 1967, Novel

MOFTURI 1900 1965 d: Jean Georgescu. RMN., C.F.R., Ion Luca Caragiale, 1899-1909, Short Story, *O Conferenta*, Ion Luca Caragiale, 1899-1909, Short Story, *Diplomatie*, Ion Luca Caragiale, 1899-1909, Short Story

MOG 1985 d: Nic Phillips. UKN., Peter Tinniswood, Novel

MOGAMBO 1953 d: John Ford. USA., *Red Dust*, Wilson Collison, New York 1928, Play

MOGG MEGONE 1909 d: J. Stuart Blackton (Spv). USA., *Mogg Megone*, John Greenleaf Whittier, Poem

Moghreb see **BOURRASQUE** (1935).

MOGLIE CHE SI GETTO DALLA FINESTRA, LA 1920 d: Gian Bistolfi. ITL., *Une Femme Qui Se Jette Par la Fenetre*, G. Lemoine, Eugene Scribe, 1847

MOGLIE DEL DOTTORE, LA 1916 d: Giovanni Zannini. ITL., *La Moglie Del Dottore*, Silvio Zambaldi, 1908, Play

MOGLIE DI CLAUDIO, LA 1918 d: Gero Zambuto. ITL., *La Femme de Claude*, Alexandre Dumas (fils), 1873, Play

Moglie Di Mio Marito, La see **MI MUJER ME GUSTA MAS** (1960).

MOGLIE DI SUA ECCELLENZA, LA 1921 d: Eduardo BencivengA. ITL., *Remigia*, Gerolamo Rovetta, Novel

Moglie Nuova, La see **LA MODIFICATION** (1970).

MOGLIE PER UNA NOTTE 1950 d: Mario Camerini. ITL., *L' Ora Della Fantasia*, Anna Bonacci, Rome 1944, Play

MOHAMMED-BIN-TUGHLAQ 1971 d: Cho Ramaswamy. IND., *Mohammed-Bin-Tughlaq*, Cho Ramaswamy, Play

MOHICANI DI PARIGI, I 1917 d: Leopoldo Carlucci. ITL., *Les Mohicans de Paris*, Alexandre Dumas (pere), 1864, Novel

MOHICAN'S DAUGHTER, THE 1922 d: Stanner E. V. Taylor. USA., *The Story of Jees Uck*, Jack London, 1904, Short Story

MOI DRUG IVAN LAPSHIN 1986 d: Alexei Gherman. USS., Yuri Gherman, Short Stories

Moi Laskovei I Nezhnei Zver see **MOJ LASKOVYJ I NEZNYJ ZVER** (1978).

MOI MLADSHII BRAT 1962 d: Alexander Zarkhi. USS., *Zvyozdnv Bilet*, Vasili Aksyonov, 1961, Novel

MOI UNIVERSITETI 1940 d: Mark Donskoi. USS., *Moi Universiteti*, Maxim Gorky, 1921-22, Autobiography

MOINE, LE 1972 d: Ado Kyrou. FRN/ITL/GRM., *Le Moine*, Matthew Gregory Lewis, Novel

Moine Noir, Le see **TCHIORNI MONAK** (1988).

MOIS D'AVRIL SONT MEURTRIERS, LES 1986 d: Laurent Heynemann. FRN., *Les Mois d'Avril Sont Meurtriers*, Derek Raymond, Novel

Moj Droeg Ivan Lapsjin see **MOI DRUG IVAN LAPSHIN** (1986).

MOJ LASKOVYJ I NEZNYJ ZVER 1978 d: Emil Lotyanu. USS., *Drama Na Okhote*, Anton Chekhov, 1884, Short Story

Moj Mladsij Brat see **MOI MLADSHII BRAT** (1962).

MOJU 1969 d: Yasuzo MasumurA. JPN., *Moju*, Rampo Edogawa, Short Story

Molester, The see **NEVER TAKE SWEETS FROM A STRANGER** (1960).

MOLL FLANDERS 1996 d: David Attwood. USA/UKN., *Moll Flanders*, Daniel Defoe, 1722, Novel

MOLLENARD 1937 d: Robert Siodmak. FRN., *Mollenard*, Oscar-Paul Gilbert, Novel

Mollie O' Pigtail Alley see **SALLY IN OUR ALLEY** (1916).

Molly see **SEX IN SWEDEN** (1977).

Molly and I see **MY UNMARRIED WIFE** (1918).

MOLLY AND I 1920 d: Howard M. Mitchell. USA., *Molly and I and the Silver Ring*, Frank R. Adams, Boston 1915, Novel

MOLLY BAWN 1916 d: Cecil M. Hepworth. UKN., *Molly Bawn*, Margaret Wolfe Hungerford, 1878, Novel

Molly, Gid and Johnny see **LOVIN' MOLLY** (1973).

Molly l'Ingenue Perverse see **SEX IN SWEDEN** (1977).

MOLLY MAGUIRES, THE 1970 d: Martin Ritt. USA., *Lament for the Molly Maguires*, Arthur H. Lewis, New York 1964, Novel

MOLLY MAKE-BELIEVE 1916 d: J. Searle Dawley. USA., *Molly Make-Believe*, Eleanor Hallowell Abbott, New York 1910, Novel

MOLLY OF THE FOLLIES 1919 d: Edward Sloman. USA., *The Side-Show Girl*, Peter Clark MacFarlane, 1918, Short Story

MOLLY, THE DRUMMER BOY 1914 d: George A. Lessey. USA., *The Drummer Boy Molly*, Harriet T. Comstock, Novel

Molly-Familjeflickan *see* SEX IN SWEDEN (1977).

Molodaja Gvardija *see* MOLODAYA GVARDIYA (1948).

MOLODAYA GVARDIYA 1948 d: Sergei Gerasimov. USS., *Molodaya Gvardiya*, Alexander Fadeev, 1945, Novel

Mom *see* LADY TUBBS (1935).

Mom By Magic, A *see* A MOM FOR CHRISTMAS (1990).

MOM FOR CHRISTMAS, A 1990 d: George Miller. USA., *A Mom for Christmas*, Barbara Dillon, Novel

Mom Has to Get Married *see* KOMPLOTT AUF ERLENHOF (1950).

MOM, THE WOLFMAN AND ME 1980 d: Edmond Levy. USA., Norma Klein, Novel

Mome du Cirque, La *see* CROQUETTE (1927).

Mome Piaf, La *see* PIAF (1973).

MOME VERT-DE-GRIS, LA 1952 d: Bernard Borderie. FRN., *La Mome Vert-de-Gris*, Peter Cheyney, Novel

MOMENT BEFORE, THE 1916 d: Robert G. VignolA. USA., *The Moment of Death*, Israel Zangwill, New York 1900, Play

MOMENT OF DANGER 1960 d: Laslo Benedek. UKN., *The Scent of Danger*, Donald MacKenzie, Boston 1958, Novel

MOMENT OF VICTORY, THE 1918SMITH, Usa./THE MOMENT OF VICTORY., O. Henry, Short Story

MOMENT TO MOMENT 1966 d: Mervyn Leroy. USA., *Laughs With a Stranger*, Alec Coppel, Short Story

Moments in a Matchbox *see* MIGOVE V KIBRITENA KOUTIYKA (1979).

Moments of Love *see* IL FRULLO DEL PASSERO (1988).

MOMMIE DEAREST 1981 d: Frank Perry. USA., *Mommie Dearest*, Christina Crawford, Book

MOMO 1986 d: Johannes Schaaf. GRM/ITL., *Momo*, Michael Ende, Novel

MON AMI LE CAMBRIOLEUR 1950 d: Henri Lepage. FRN., *Mon Ami le Cambrioleur*, Andre Haguet, Play

MON AMI SAINFOIN 1949 d: Marc-Gilbert Sauvajon. FRN., *Mon Ami Sainfoin*, Paul-Adrien Schaye, Novel

Mon Amour *see* GOUBBIAH MON AMOUR (1956).

MON BEGUIN 1929 d: Hans Behrendt. FRN., *Mon Beguin*, Paul Forro, Novel

MON CAS 1986 d: Manoel de OliveirA. FRN/PRT., Jose Regio, Play

MON COEUR AU RALENTI 1927 d: Marco de Gastyne. FRN., *Mon Coeur Au Ralenti*, Maurice Dekobra, Novel

MON COEUR BALANCE 1932 d: Rene Guissart. FRN., *Une Petite Femme Dans le Lit*, Yves Mirande, Play

Mon Crime *see* TRUE CONFESSION (1937).

MON CURE CHEZ LES PAUVRES 1925 d: E. B. Donatien. FRN., *Mon Cure Chez Les Pauvres*, Clement Vautel, Novel

MON CURE CHEZ LES RICHES 1926 d: E. B. Donatien. FRN., *Mon Cure Chez Les Riches*, Clement Vautel, Novel

MON CURE CHEZ LES RICHES 1932 d: E. B. Donatien. FRN., *Mon Cure Chez Les Riches*, Clement Vautel, Novel

MON CURE CHEZ LES RICHES 1938 d: Jean Boyer. FRN., *Mon Cure Chez Les Riches*, Clement Vautel, Novel

MON CURE CHEZ LES RICHES 1952 d: Henri Diamant-Berger. FRN., *Mon Cure Chez Les Riches*, Clement Vautel, Novel

MON DEPUTE ET SA FEMME 1937 d: Maurice Cammage. FRN., *Mon Depute Et Sa Femme*, Robert Bodet, Play

MON GOSSE DE PERE 1930 d: Jean de Limur. FRN., *Mon Gosse de Pere*, Leopold Marchand, Play

MON GOSSE DE PERE 1952 d: Leon Mathot. FRN., *Mon Gosse de Pere*, Leopold Marchand, Play

Mon Oncle Barbassous *see* MIO ZIO BARBASSOUS (1921).

MON ONCLE BENJAMIN 1923 d: Rene Leprince. FRN., *Mon Oncle Benjamin*, Claude Tillier, Novel

MON ONCLE BENJAMIN 1969 d: Edouard Molinaro. FRN/ITL., *Mon Oncle Benjamin*, Claude Tillier, Novel

Mon Oncle d'Arles *see* UN COUP DE MISTRAL (1933).

MON PERE AVAIT RAISON 1936 d: Sacha Guitry. FRN., *Mon Pere Avait Raison*, Sacha Guitry, Play

Mon Petit *see* MONTPI (1957).

Mon Phoque *see* MON PHOQUE ET ELLES (1951).

MON PHOQUE ET ELLES 1951 d: Pierre Billon. FRN/SWD., *Mon Phoque Et Elles*, Charles de Richter, Novel

MON POTE LE GITAN 1959 d: Francois Gir. FRN., *Les Pittuiti's*, Michel Duran, Play

MON PREMIER AMOUR 1978 d: Elie Chouraqui. FRN., *Mon Premier Amour*, Jack-Alain Leger, Novel

MON VILLAGE 1920 d: J.-P. Pinchon. FRN., *Mon Village*, Hansi

MONA, L'ETOILE SANS NOM 1966 d: Henri Colpi. FRN/RMN., *Steaua Fara Nume*, Mihail Sebastian, 1946, Play

Mona Lisa *see* SMARTY (1934).

MONACA DI MONZA, LA 1947 d: Raffaello Pacini. ITL., *La Monaca Di Monza*, Giovanni Rosini, Novel

MONACA DI MONZA, LA 1968 d: Eriprando Visconti. ITL., *La Monaca Di Monza*, Mario Mazzucchelli, Milan 1961, Novel

MONACHE DI SANT'ARCANGELO, LE 1973 d: Domenico PaolellA. ITL/FRN., Stendhal, Short Story

Monaco, Il *see* LE MOINE (1972).

MONASTERY 1938 d: Robert Alexander. USA., *Les Moines*, Emile Verhaeren, Belgium 1886, Poem

MONCH MIT DER PEITSCHE, DER 1967 d: Alfred Vohrer. GRM., Edgar Wallace, Novel

MONCHE, MADCHEN UND PANDUREN 1952 d: Ferdinand Dorfler. GRM., *Salvator*, Max Ferner, Philip Weichand, Play

MONDE OU L'ON S'ENNUIE, LE 1934 d: Jean de Marguenat. FRN., *Le Monde Ou l'On S'ennuie*, Edouard Pailleron, Play

MONDE TREMBLERA, LE 1939 d: Richard Pottier. FRN., *La machine a Predire la Mort*, Roger-F. Didelot, Robert-Claude Dumas, Novel

MONDJAGER 1989 d: Jens-Peter Behrend. GRM., *Mondjager*, Sigrid Heuck, Novel

MONDO 1997 d: Tony Gatlif. FRN., *Mondo*, Jean-Marie le Clezio, Novel

MONDO CANDIDO 1975 d: Gualtiero Jacopetti, Franco Prosperi. ITL., *Candide*, Francois-Marie Arouet de Voltaire, 1759, Short Story

Mondo Nella Mia Tasca, Il *see* AN EINEM FREITAG UM HALB ZWOLF (1961).

MONDO VUOLE COSI, IL 1946 d: Giorgio Bianchi. ITL., *Il Mondo Vuole Cosi*, Aldo de Benedetti, Mario Luciani, Play

MONDSCHEINGASSE, DIE 1988 d: Edouard Molinaro. GRM/FRN/ITL., *Die Mondscheingasse*, Stefan Zweig, Short Story

MONELLA, LA 1914 d: Nino OxiliA. ITL., *La Gamine*, Henri de Gorsse, Pierre Veber, 1911, Play

Moneta Spezzata, La *see* F.B.I. OPERAZIONE BAALBECK (1964).

MONEY 1915 d: A. C. Marston, Lawrence Marston. USA., *Money*, Edward George Bulwer Lytton, London 1840, Play

MONEY 1921 d: Duncan MacRae. UKN., *Money*, Edward George Bulwer Lytton, London 1840, Play

Money *see* L' ARGENT (1928).

Money *see* L' ARGENT (1983).

MONEY AND THE WOMAN 1940 d: William K. Howard. USA., *The Embezzler*, James M. Cain, 1940, Short Story

Money Box, The *see* OUR RELATIONS (1936).

Money Changers, The *see* THE MONEY-CHANGERS (1920).

Money Corporal, The *see* THE MONEY CORRAL (1919).

MONEY CORRAL, THE 1919 d: William S. Hart, Lambert Hillyer. USA., Charles Alden Seltzer, Short Story

Money for Jam *see* IT AIN'T HAY (1943).

MONEY FOR NOTHING 1916 d: Maurice Elvey. UKN., *Money for Nothing*, Arthur Eckersley, Guy Newall, Play

MONEY FROM HOME 1953 d: George Marshall. USA., *Money from Home*, Damon Runyon, 1935, Short Story

MONEY HABIT, THE 1924 d: Walter Niebuhr. UKN., *The Money Habit*, Paul M. Potter, Novel

MONEY ISN'T EVERYTHING 1918 d: Edward Sloman. USA., *Beauty to Let*, Frederick Jackson, Short Story

MONEY ISN'T EVERYTHING 1925 d: Thomas Bentley. UKN., *Money Isn't Everything*, Sophie Cole, Novel

MONEY MADNESS 1917 d: Henry McRae. USA., *Whispering Smith*, Frank Hamilton Spearman, New York 1906, Novel

MONEY, MADNESS & MURDER 1987 d: Paul Bogart. USA., *Madness & Murder Money*, Shana Alexander, Novel

MONEY MAGIC 1917 d: William Wolbert. USA., *Money Magic*, Hamlin Garland, New York 1907, Novel

Money Maniac, The *see* LE DEMON DE LA HAINE (1921).

MONEY MASTER, THE 1915 d: George Fitzmaurice. USA., *The Battle*, Cleveland Moffett, New York 1908, Play

Money Master, The *see* A WISE FOOL (1921).

MONEY MEANS NOTHING 1934 d: W. Christy Cabanne. USA., *The Cost of Living*, William Anthony McGuire, Cincinnati, Oh. 1913, Play

Money, Money, Money *see* LE PRESIDENT (1960).

Money, Money, Money *see* LE CAVE SE REBIFFE (1961).

MONEY MOON, THE 1920 d: Fred Paul. UKN., *The Money Moon*, Jeffrey Farnol, Novel

MONEY MOVERS, THE 1979 d: Bruce Beresford. ASL., *The Money Movers*, Devon Minchin, Book

Money Order, The *see* LE MANDAT (1968).

MONEY, POWER, MURDER 1989 d: Lee Philips. USA., *Power, Murder Money*, Mike Lupica, Novel

Money Talks *see* LOSER TAKES ALL (1989).

MONEY TO BURN 1922 d: Rowland V. Lee. USA., *Cherub Divine*, Sewell Ford, New York 1909, Novel

MONEY TO BURN 1926 d: Walter Lang. USA., *Money to Burn*, Reginald Wright Kauffman, New York 1924, Novel

MONEY TRAP, THE 1965 d: Burt Kennedy. USA., *The Money Trap*, Lionel White, New York 1963, Novel

MONEYCHANGERS, THE 1976 d: Boris Sagal. USA., *The Moneychangers*, Arthur Hailey, Novel

MONEY-CHANGERS, THE 1920 d: Jack Conway. USA., *The Money Changers*, Upton Sinclair, London 1908, Novel

Mongolian Tale, A *see* HEI JUN MA (1995).

MONGO'S BACK IN TOWN 1971 d: Marvin J. Chomsky. USA., *Mongo's Back in Town*, E. Richard Johnson, Novel

MONIQUE 1921 d: Lucio d'AmbrA. ITL., *Monique*, Paul Bourget, 1920, Novel

Monique, Poupee Francaise *see* LA FAUTE DE MONIQUE (1928).

MONITORS, THE 1969 d: Jack SheA. USA., *The Monitors*, Keith Laumer, New York 1966, Novel

MONK DAWSON 1997 d: Tom Waller. UKN., *Monk Dawson*, Piers Paul Read, Novel

Monk, The *see* LE MOINE (1972).

MONK, THE 1990 d: Francisco Lara Polop. UKN/SPN., *The Monk*, M. G. Lewis, Novel

Monk With the Whip, The *see* DER MONCH MIT DER PEITSCHE (1967).

MONKEY BUSINESS 1952 d: Howard Hawks. USA., Harry Segall, Story

MONKEY GRIP 1982 d: Ken Cameron. ASL., *Monkey Grip*, Helen Garner, Novel

Monkey in Winter, A *see* UN SINGE EN HIVER (1962).

Monkey Pete *see* PEDRO MICO (1985).

Monkey Shines *see* MONKEY SHINES: AN EXPERIMENT IN FEAR (1988).

MONKEY SHINES: AN EXPERIMENT IN FEAR 1988 d: George A. Romero. USA., *Ella*, Michael Stewart, Novel

MONKEY TALKS, THE 1927 d: Raoul Walsh. USA., *Le Singe Qui Parle*, Rene Fauchois, Paris 1925, Novel

Monkeynuts *see* CROQUETTE (1927).

MONKEYS, GO HOME 1967 d: Andrew V. McLaglen. USA., *The Monkeys*, G. K. Wilkinson, London 1962, Novel

MONKEY'S PAW, THE 1915 d: Sidney Northcote. UKN., *The Monkey's Paw*, W. W. Jacobs, 1902, Short Story

MONKEY'S PAW, THE 1923 d: Manning Haynes. UKN., *The Monkey's Paw*, W. W. Jacobs, 1902, Short Story

MONKEY'S PAW, THE 1933 d: Wesley Ruggles. USA., *The Monkey's Paw*, W. W. Jacobs, 1902, Short Story

MONKEY'S PAW, THE 1948 d: Norman Lee. UKN., *The Monkey's Paw*, W. W. Jacobs, 1902, Short Story

Monks, Girls, and Hungarian Soldiers see MADCHEN UND PANDUREN MONCHE (1952).

MONNA VANNA 1916 d: Mario Caserini. ITL., *Monna Vanna*, Maurice Maeterlinck, 1902, Play

MONOCLE NOIR, LE 1961 d: Georges Lautner. FRN., *Le Monocle Noir*, Remy, Novel

MONSEIGNEUR 1949 d: Roger Richebe. FRN., *Monseigneur*, Jean Martet, Novel

MONSIEUR 1964 d: Jean-Paul Le Chanois. FRN/ITL/GRM., *Monsieur*, Claude Gevel, Play

MONSIEUR ABEL 1983 d: Jacques Doillon. FRN/SWT., *Monsieur Abel*, Alain Demouzon, Novel

MONSIEUR ALBERT 1932 d: Karl Anton. FRN., *The Head Waiter*, Erno Vajda, Novel

Monsieur Arkadin see CONFIDENTIAL REPORT (1955).

MONSIEUR BADIN 1912. FRN., *Monsieur Badin*, Georges Courteline, Play

MONSIEUR BADIN 1947 d: Georges Regnier. FRN., *Monsieur Badin*, Georges Courteline, Play

MONSIEUR BEAUCAIRE 1924 d: Sidney Olcott. USA., *Monsieur Beaucaire*, Booth Tarkington, New York 1900, Short Story

MONSIEUR BEAUCAIRE 1946 d: George Marshall. USA., *Monsieur Beaucaire*, Booth Tarkington, New York 1900, Short Story

MONSIEUR BEGONIA 1937 d: Andre Hugon. FRN., *Monsieur Begonia*, Georges Fagot, Novel

MONSIEUR BRELOQUE A DISPARU 1937 d: Robert Peguy. FRN., *Dicky*, Paul Armont, Marcel Gerbidon, Play

MONSIEUR BROTONNEAU 1939 d: Alexander Esway. FRN., *Monsieur Brotonneau*, Gaston Arman de Caillavet, Robert de Flers, Play

MONSIEUR CHASSE 1946 d: Willy Rozier. FRN., *Monsieur Chasse*, Georges Feydeau, 1896, Play

Monsieur Cognac see WILD AND WONDERFUL (1964).

MONSIEUR DE 5 HEURES, LE 1938 d: Pierre Caron. FRN., *Le Monsieur de 5 Heures*, Maurice Hennequin, Pierre Veber, Play

MONSIEUR DE COMPAGNIE, UN 1964 d: Philippe de BrocA. FRN/ITL., *Un Monsieur de Compagnie*, Andre Couteaux, Paris 1961, Novel

MONSIEUR DE FALINDOR 1946 d: Rene Le Henaff. FRN., *Monsieur de Falindor*, Georges Manoir, Armand Verhylle, Play

MONSIEUR DE MINUIT, LE 1931 d: Harry Lachman. FRN., *Almost a Honeymoon*, Walter Ellis, London 1930, Play

MONSIEUR DE POURCEAUGNAC 1932 d: Gaston Ravel, Tony Lekain. FRN., *Monsieur de Pourceaugnac*, Moliere, 1670, Play

MONSIEUR DES LOURDINES 1942 d: Pierre de Herain. FRN., *Monsieur Des Lourdines*, Alphonse de Chateaubriant, 1911, Novel

Monsieur Gangster see LES TONTONS FLINGUEURS (1963).

MONSIEUR HAWARDEN 1968 d: Harry Kumel. NTH/BLG., *Monsieur Hawarden*, Filip de Pillecyn, 1935, Short Story

MONSIEUR HIRE 1988 d: Patrice Leconte. FRN., *Les Fiancailles de Mr. Hire*, Georges Simenon, 1933, Novel

Monsieur Hire's Engagement see MONSIEUR HIRE (1988).

Monsieur la Caille see M'SIEUR LA CAILLE (1955).

MONSIEUR LA SOURIS 1942 d: Georges Lacombe. FRN., *Monsieur la Souris*, Georges Simenon, 1938, Novel

MONSIEUR LE DIRECTEUR 1913 d: Georges MoncA. FRN., *Monsieur le Directeur*, Alexandre Bisson, Fabrice Carre, Play

MONSIEUR LE DIRECTEUR 1924 d: Robert Saidreau. FRN., *Monsieur le Directeur*, Alexandre Bisson, Fabrice Carre, Play

MONSIEUR LE MAIRE 1939 d: Jacques Severac. FRN., *Monsieur le Maire*, Gustave Stoskopf, Play

MONSIEUR LE MARECHAL 1931 d: Carl Lamac. FRN/CZC., *Der K. Und K. Feldmarschall*, Emil Artur Longen, Play

MONSIEUR LE PRESIDENT-DIRECTEUR GENERAL 1966 d: Jean Girault. FRN., *Appelez-Moi Maitre*, Jacques Vilfred, Play

MONSIEUR LECOQ 1914 d: Maurice Tourneur. FRN., *Monsieur Lecoq*, Emile Gaboriau, Paris 1869, Novel

MONSIEUR LECOQ 1915. USA., *Monsieur Lecoq*, Emile Gaboriau, Paris 1869, Novel

MONSIEUR, MADAME ET BIBI 1932 d: Jean Boyer, Max Neufeld. FRN., *Geschaft Mit Amerika*, Paul Franck, Ludwig Hirschfeld, Play

Monsieur Nicolas, Nourrice see MA TANTE DICTATEUR (1939).

MONSIEUR PERSONNE 1936 d: Christian-Jaque. FRN., *Monsieur Personne*, Marcel Allain, Novel

Monsieur Petrus see PETRUS (1946).

MONSIEUR PINSON, POLICIER 1915 d: Jacques Feyder, Gaston Ravel. FRN., *Policier Monsieur Pinson*, H. R. Woestyn, Novel

Monsieur Ripois see KNAVE OF HEARTS (1954).

MONSIEUR SUZUKI 1959 d: Robert Vernay. FRN., *Monsieur Suzuki*, Pierre Conty, Novel

MONSIEUR VERNET 1916. FRN., *Monsieur Vernet*, Georges Courteline, Play

MONSIEUR VERNET 1988 d: Pierre Sabbagh. FRN., *L' Ecornifleur*, Jules Renard, Novel

MONSIGNOR 1983 d: Frank Perry. USA., *Monsignor*, Jack-Alain Leger, Novel

MONSIGNOR QUIXOTE 1985 d: Rodney Bennett. UKN., *Monsignor Quixote*, Graham Greene, 1982, Novel

MONSOON 1953 d: Rod Amateau. USA/IND., *Romeo Et Jeannette*, Jean Anouilh, 1946, Play

Monsoon Day, A see ASHAD KA EK DIN (1971).

Monster and the Lady, The see THE LADY AND THE MONSTER (1944).

MONSTER CLUB, THE 1980 d: Roy Ward Baker. UKN., Ronald Chetwynd-Hayes, Story

Monster Island see MISTERIO EN LA ISLA DE LOS MONSTRUOS (1981).

Monster of Santa Tereza, The see O MONSTRO DE SANTA TEREZA (1980).

MONSTER OF TERROR 1965 d: Daniel Haller. UKN., *The Colour Out of Space*, H. P. Lovecraft, 1927, Short Story

Monster Show, The see FREAKS (1932).

MONSTER THAT CHALLENGED THE WORLD, THE 1957 d: Arnold Laven. USA., David Duncan, Story

MONSTER, THE 1925 d: Roland West. USA., *The Monster*, Crane Wilbur, New York 1922, Play

Monster, The see THE LADY AND THE MONSTER (1944).

Monsters of the Night see THE NAVY VS. THE NIGHT MONSTERS (1966).

MONSTRO DE SANTA TEREZA, O 1980 d: William Cobbett. BRZ., *O Monstro*, Josue Montello, 1966, Short Story

Monstruo de la Montana Hueca, El see THE BEAST OF HOLLOW MOUNTAIN (1956).

MONT MAUDIT, LE 1920 d: Paul Garbagny. FRN., *Le Mont Maudit*, Georges de Buysieulx, Play

MONTAGNA DI LUCE, LA 1965 d: Umberto Lenzi. ITL., *La Montagna Di Luce*, Emilio Salgari, Novel

MONT-DRAGON 1971 d: Jean Valere. BLG/FRN., *Mont-Dragon*, Robert Margerit, Novel

MONTE CARLO 1930 d: Ernst Lubitsch. USA., *Monsieur Beaucaire*, Booth Tarkington, New York 1900, Short Story

Monte Carlo, Jr. see THE MASQUERADER (1922).

MONTE CARLO MADNESS 1931 d: Hanns Schwarz. UKN., *Monte Carlo Madness*, Reck-Malleczewen, Novel

MONTE CARLO NIGHTS 1934 d: William Nigh. USA., *Number of Deaths*, E. Phillips Oppenheim, Short Story

Monte Cristo see IL CONTE DI MONTECRISTO (1908).

MONTE CRISTO 1911. USA., *Le Comte de Monte-Cristo*, Alexandre Dumas (pere), Paris 1845, Novel

MONTE CRISTO 1912 d: Colin Campbell. USA., *Le Comte de Monte-Cristo*, Alexandre Dumas (pere), Paris 1845, Novel

MONTE CRISTO 1922 d: Emmett J. Flynn. USA., *Le Comte de Monte-Cristo*, Alexandre Dumas (pere), Paris 1845, Novel

MONTE WALSH 1970 d: William A. Fraker. USA., *Monte Walsh*, Jack Schaefer, Boston 1963, Novel

MONTE-CARLO 1925 d: Louis Mercanton. FRN., *Monte-Carlo*, E. Phillips Oppenheim, Novel

MONTECASSINO 1946 d: Arturo Gemmiti. ITL., *Montecassino*, Tommaso Leccisotti, Book

Montecassino Nel Cerchio Di Fuoco see MONTECASSINO (1946).

MONTE-CHARGE, LE 1961 d: Marcel Bluwal. FRN/ITL., *La Monte-Charge*, Frederic Dard, Paris 1961, Novel

Monte-Cristo see LE COMTE DE MONTE-CRISTO (1917).

MONTE-CRISTO 1928 d: Henri Fescourt. FRN., *Le Comte de Monte-Cristo*, Alexandre Dumas (pere), Paris 1845, Novel

Montecristo '70 see SOUS LE SIGNE DE MONTE-CRISTO (1968).

MONTH BY THE LAKE, A 1994 d: John Irvin. USA/UKN., *A Month By the Lake*, H. E. Bates, Novel

MONTH IN THE COUNTRY, A 1955 d: Robert Hamer. UKN., *Mesyats V Derevne*, Ivan Turgenev, 1855, Play

MONTH IN THE COUNTRY, A 1985 d: Quentin Lawrence. UKN/USA., *Mesyats V Derevne*, Ivan Turgenev, 1855, Play

MONTH IN THE COUNTRY, A 1985 d: Bill Hays. UKN., *Mesyats V Derevne*, Ivan Turgenev, 1855, Play

MONTH IN THE COUNTRY, A 1987 d: Pat O'Connor. UKN., *A Month in the Country*, J. L. Carr, Novel

Montiel's Widow see LA VIUDA DE MONTIEL (1979).

MONTMARTRE 1914 d: Rene Leprince. FRN., *Montmartre*, Pierre Frondaie, Play

Montone Infuriato, Il see LE MOUTON ENRAGE (1974).

Montparnasse see MONTPARNASSE 19 (1957).

MONTPARNASSE 19 1957 d: Jacques Becker. FRN/ITL., *Les Montparnos*, Georges Michel, Paris 1924, Book

MONTPI 1957 d: Helmut Kautner. GRM., *Monpti*, Gabor von Vaszary, Novel

Monty's Double see I WAS MONTY'S DOUBLE (1958).

MONUMENT, THE 1982 d: Nick HavingA. UKN/USA., *The Monument*, Irwin Shaw, Story

MOODS OF LOVE, THE 1972 d: David Wickes. UKN., *Sonnets*, William Shakespeare, 1609, Verse

MOOI JUULTJE VAN VOLDENDAM 1924 d: Alex Benno. NTH/BLG., *Mooi Juultje Van Volendam*, Johan Lemaire, 1920, Play

Moolu Manek see MULU MANEK (1955).

MOON AND SIXPENCE, THE 1942 d: Albert Lewin. USA., *The Moon and Sixpence*, W. Somerset Maugham, 1919, Novel

Moon in the Gutter see LA LUNE DANS LE CANIVEAU (1983).

MOON IS BLUE, THE 1953 d: Otto Preminger. USA., *The Moon Is Blue*, F. Hugh Herbert, New York 1951, Play

MOON IS DOWN, THE 1943 d: Irving Pichel. USA., *The Moon Is Down*, John Steinbeck, 1942, Novel

Moon Mask Rider, The see GEKKO KAMEN (1981).

MOON OF THE WOLF 1972 d: Daniel Petrie. USA., *Moon of the Wolf*, Leslie H. Whitten, Novel

MOON OVER MIAMI 1941 d: Walter Lang. USA., *Three Blind Mice*, Stephen Powys, London 1938, Play

MOON OVER PARADOR 1988 d: Paul Mazursky. USA., Charles G. Booth, Story

MOON PILOT 1962 d: James Neilson. USA., *Moon Pilot*, Robert Buckner, 1960, Short Story

Moon Stalkers, The see TICKET TO HEAVEN (1981).

Moon Walk see A TICKLISH AFFAIR (1963).

MOONDIAL 1990 d: Colin Grant. UKN., *Moondial*, Helen Cresswell, Novel

MOONFLEET 1955 d: Fritz Lang. USA., *Moonfleet*, J. Meade Falkner, Novel

MOONLIGHT AND HONEYSUCKLE 1921 d: Joseph Henabery. USA., *Moonlight and Honeysuckle*, George Scarborough, New York 1919, Play

MORTE A VENEZIA 1971 d: Luchino Visconti. ITL/FRN., *Der Tod in Venedig*, Thomas Mann, 1912, Short Story

MORTE AL LAVORO, LA 1978 d: Gianni Amelio. ITL., *Il Ragno*, Hans H. Hewers, Short Story

MORTE CIVILE, LA 1910 d: Gerolamo Lo Savio?. ITL/FRN., *La Morte Civile*, Paolo Giacometti, 1861, Play

MORTE CIVILE, LA 1913 d: Ubaldo Maria Del Colle. ITL., *La Morte Civile*, Paolo Giacometti, 1861, Play

MORTE CIVILE, LA 1919 d: Eduardo BencivengA. ITL., *La Morte Civile*, Paolo Giacometti, 1861, Play

MORTE CIVILE, LA 1942 d: Ferdinando M. Poggioli. ITL., *La Morte Civile*, Paolo Giacometti, 1861, Play

Morte Civile, La *see* LA FIGLIA DEL FORZATO (1955).

MORTE E VIDA SEVERINA 1976 d: Zelito VianA. BRZ., *Morte E Vida Severina*, Joao Cabral de Melo Neto, 1955, Verse, *O Rio*, Joao Cabral de Melo Neto, 1954, Verse

MORTE NEGLI OCCHI DEL GATTO, LA 1973 d: Antonio Margheriti. ITL/FRN/GRM., Peter Bryan, Short Story

MORTE RISALE A IERI SERA, LA 1970 d: Duccio Tessari. ITL/GRM., *I Milanesi Ammazzano Al Sabato*, Giorgio Scerbanenco, Novel

Morte Sale in Ascensore, La *see* LE MONTE-CHARGE (1961).

Morte Vestita Di Dollari, La *see* EINER FRISST DEN ANDEREN (1964).

MORTELLE RANDONNEE 1983 d: Claude Miller. FRN., *Mortelle Randonnee*, Marc Behm, Novel

MORTI NON PAGANO TASSE, I 1953 d: Sergio Grieco. ITL., *I Morti Non Pagano Tasse*, Nicola Manzari, Play

MORTMAIN 1915 d: Theodore Marston. USA., *Mortmain*, Arthur Cheney Train, New York 1907, Novel

MOSCOW NIGHTS 1935 d: Anthony Asquith. UKN., *Les Nuits de Moscou*, Pierre Benoit, Novel

MOSELFAHRT AUS LIEBESKUMMER 1953 d: Kurt Hoffmann. GRM., *Moselfahrt Aus Liebeskummer*, Rudolf Georg Binding, 1932, Short Story

MOSQUITO COAST, THE 1986 d: Peter Weir. USA., *The Mosquito Coast*, Paul Theroux, 1981, Novel

Moss on the Stones *see* MOOS AUF DEN STEINEN (1968).

MOSS ROSE 1947 d: Gregory Ratoff. USA., *Moss Rose*, Joseph Shearing, Novel

MOST DANGEROUS GAME, THE 1932 d: Ernest B. Schoedsack, Irving Pichel. USA., *The Most Dangerous Game*, Richard Connell, 1930, Short Story

Most Dangerous Game, The *see* A GAME OF DEATH (1946).

Most Dangerous Game, The *see* DROLE DE JEU (1968).

MOST DANGEROUS MAN ALIVE, THE 1961 d: Allan Dwan. USA., *The Steel Monster*, Michael Pate, Philip Rock, Short Story

Most Dangerous Man in the World, The *see* THE CHAIRMAN (1969).

MOST DANGEROUS MAN IN THE WORLD, THE 1988 d: Gavin Millar. UKN., Paul Henze, Novel

Most Dangerous Sin, The *see* CRIME ET CHATIMENT (1956).

MOST IMMORAL LADY, A 1929 d: John Griffith Wray. USA., *A Most Immoral Lady*, Townsend Martin, New York 1928, Play

Most Important Thing: Love, The *see* C'EST D'AIMER, L' IMPORTANT (1974).

MOST PEREYTI NELIEYA 1960 d: Teodor Vulfovich, Nikita Kurikhin. USS., *Death of a Salesman*, Arthur Miller, New York 1949, Play

MOST PRECIOUS THING IN LIFE 1934 d: Lambert Hillyer. USA., *Biddy*, Travis Ingham, 1933, Short Story

Most Wonderful Evening of My Life, The *see* LA PIU BELLA SERATA DELLA MIA VITA (1972).

MOSTRO DI FRANKENSTEIN, IL 1920 d: Eugenio TestA. ITL., *Frankenstein; Or the Modern Prometheus*, Mary Wollstonecraft Shelley, London 1818, Novel

MOTEL THE OPERATOR 1939 d: Joseph Seiden. USA., *Motel the Operator*, Chaim Tauber, New York 1936, Play

Motel Vacancy *see* TALKING WALLS (1984).

MOTH AND RUST 1921 d: Sidney Morgan. UKN., *Moth and Rust*, Mary Cholmondeley, Novel

MOTH AND THE FLAME, THE 1915 d: Sidney Olcott. USA., *The Moth and the Flame*, Clyde Fitch, New York 1898, Play

MOTH, THE 1917 d: Edward Jose. USA., *The Moth*, William Dana Orcutt, New York 1912, Novel

MOTH, THE 1996 d: Roy Battersby. UKN., *The Moth*, Catherine Cookson, Novel

MOTHER 1914 d: Maurice Tourneur. USA., *Mother*, Jules Eckert Goodman, New York 1910, Play

Mother *see* MAT (1926).

MOTHER 1927 d: James Leo Meehan. USA., *Mother*, Kathleen Norris, New York 1911, Novel

Mother *see* MAT (1956).

Mother Alone, A *see* DUWATA MAWAKA MISA (1997).

Mother and Child *see* MUTTER UND KIND (1924).

Mother and Child *see* MUTTER UND KIND (1933).

MOTHER AND DAUGHTER 1967 d: Richard Everitt. UKN., *Mother and Daughter*, D. H. Lawrence, Short Story

Mother and the Law, The *see* CORRUPTION (1917).

Mother Carey *see* FRAU HOLLE (1985).

MOTHER CAREY'S CHICKENS 1938 d: Rowland V. Lee. USA., *Mother Carey's Chickens*, Kate Douglas Wiggin, Boston 1911, Novel

Mother Courage and Her Children *see* MUTTER COURAGE UND IHRE KINDER (1960).

MOTHER DIDN'T TELL ME 1950 d: Claude Binyon. USA., *The Doctor Wears Three Faces*, Mary Bard, 1949, Book

MOTHER INSTINCT, THE 1915 d: Wilfred Lucas. USA., *The Mother Instinct*, Mrs. Haines W. Reed, Story

Mother Joan and Angels *see* MATKA JOANNA OD ANIOLOW (1961).

Mother Joan of the Angels *see* MATKA JOANNA OD ANIOLOW (1961).

MOTHER KNOWS BEST 1928 d: John G. Blystone. USA., *Mother Knows Best*, Edna Ferber, Garden City, N.Y. 1927, Story

Mother Kracmerka *see* MATKA KRACMERKA (1934).

Mother Kracmerka I, The *see* DO PANSKEHO STAVU (1925).

Mother Kracmerka II *see* V PANSKEM STAVU (1927).

Mother Lode *see* YELLOW DUST (1936).

MOTHER LOVE 1989 d: Simon Langton. UKN/USA., *Mother Love*, Domini Taylor, Novel

MOTHER MACHREE 1928 d: John Ford. USA., *The Story of Mother MacHree*, Rida Johnson Young, 1924, Short Story

MOTHER NIGHT 1996 d: Keith Gordon. USA., *Mother Night*, Kurt Vonnegut Jr., Novel

MOTHER O' MINE 1921 d: Fred Niblo. USA., *The Octopus*, Charles Belmont Davis, 1917, Short Story

MOTHER OF DARTMOOR, THE 1916 d: George Loane Tucker. UKN., *The Mother of Dartmoor*, Eden Philpotts, Novel

Mother of Kings, The *see* MATKA KROLOW (1982).

Mother of Krols *see* MATKA KROLOW (1982).

Mother of Mine *see* GRIBICHE (1925).

Mother of Shyam *see* SHYAMCHI AAI (1953).

Mother of the Krol Family *see* MATKA KROLOW (1982).

Mother Ought to Marry *see* THE SECOND TIME AROUND (1961).

Mother Superior *see* THE TROUBLE WITH ANGELS (1966).

Mother Wants Me to Marry *see* MAMA YAO WO CHU JIA (1956).

MOTHER WORE TIGHTS 1947 d: Walter Lang. USA., *Mother Wore Tights*, Miriam Young, Novel

Mother-Hen *see* KVOCNA (1937).

Motherland *see* MATHRU BHOOMI (1939).

Motherland, The *see* MAABHOOMI (1979).

Mother's Boy *see* PERCY (1925).

Mother's Confession, A *see* MATCINA ZPOVED (1937).

MOTHER'S CRY 1930 d: Hobart Henley. USA., *Mother's Cry*, Helen Grace Carlisle, New York 1930, Novel

Mother's Field, The *see* MATERINSKOYE POLYE (1968).

MOTHER'S INFLUENCE, A 1916 d: George Loane Tucker. UKN., *The Mother*, Eden Philpotts, Novel

Mother's Love, A *see* A MOTHER'S LOVE FANTINE; OR (1909).

MOTHER'S MILLIONS 1931 d: James Flood. USA., *Mother's Millions*, Howard McKent Barnes, Novel

MOTHERS OF MEN 1920 d: Edward Jose. USA., *Mothers of Men*, de Witte Kaplan, William H. Warnert, New York 1919, Novel

MOTHER'S SIN, A 1918 d: Thomas R. Mills. USA., *The Stars in Their Courses*, Hilda Mary Sharp, New York 1917, Novel

MOTHER'S TALE, A 1977 d: Rex Goff. USA., *A Mother's Tale*, James Agee, 1952, Short Story

MOTHERTIME 1997 d: Matthew Jacobs. UKN., *Mothertime*, Gillian White, Novel

MOTHS 1913 d: W. Christy Cabanne. USA., *Moths*, Ouida, London 1880, Novel

MOTHS 1922. UKN., *Moths*, Ouida, London 1880, Novel

MOTION TO ADJOURN, A 1921 d: Roy Clements. USA., *A Motion to Adjourn*, Peter B. Kyne, 1914, Short Story

Moto Shel Yehudi *see* SABRA (1970).

Motocyclette, La *see* GIRL ON A MOTORCYCLE (1968).

MOTS POUR LE DIRE, LES 1983 d: Jose Pinheiro. FRN., *Les Mots Pour le Dire*, Marie Cardinal, Novel

MOTSART I SALYERI 1962 d: Vladimir Gorikker. USS., *Motsart I Saleri*, Alexander Pushkin, 1830, Short Story

MOTTIGE JANUS 1922 d: Maurits H. Binger. NTH., *Mottige Janus*, Arnold Werumeus Buning, Play

MOUCHARDE, LA 1958 d: Guy Lefranc. FRN., *La Fille de Proie*, Christian Coffinet, Paris 1953, Novel

MOUCHETTE 1966 d: Robert Bresson. FRN., *Novelle Histoire de Mouchette*, Georges Bernanos, Paris 1937, Novel

MOUCHOIR DE JOSEPH, LE 1988 d: Jacques Fansten. FRN., *Chez Krull*, Georges Simenon, Novel

MOUETTES, LES 1916 d: Maurice Mariaud. FRN., *Le Serpent Noir*, Paul Adam, Play

MOULIN DANS LE SOLEIL, LE 1938 d: Marc Didier. FRN., *Chantecaille*, Gaston Rullier, Novel

Moulin Des Amours, Le *see* LA PICARA MOLINERA (1955).

Moulin Des Supplices, Le *see* IL MULINO DELLE DONNE DI PIETRA (1960).

MOULIN ROUGE 1952 d: John Huston. UKN/USA., *Moulin Rouge*, Pierre la Mure, Novel

Mount Lelej *see* LELEJSKA GORA (1968).

Mountain Europa, A *see* A CUMBERLAND ROMANCE (1920).

Mountain Flowers *see* FLORADAS NA SERRA (1954).

MOUNTAIN GIRL, THE 1915 d: James Kirkwood. USA., *The Mountain Girl*, Mary Rider Mechtold, Story

MOUNTAIN JUSTICE 1915 d: Joseph de Grasse. USA., *Mountain Justice*, Julius G. Furthmann, Story

MOUNTAIN MADNESS 1920 d: Lloyd B. Carleton. USA., *Mountain Madness*, Anna Alice Chapin, New York 1917, Novel

MOUNTAIN MUSIC 1937 d: Robert Florey. USA., MacKinlay Kantor, 1935, Short Story

Mountain of Horror *see* LELEJSKA GORA (1968).

Mountain of Lament *see* LELEJSKA GORA (1968).

MOUNTAIN RAT, THE 1914 d: James Kirkwood. USA., *The Mountain Rat*, Mary Rider Mechtold, Story

MOUNTAIN ROAD, THE 1960 d: Daniel Mann. USA., *The Mountain Road*, Theodore H. White, Novel

MOUNTAIN, THE 1956 d: Edward Dmytryk. USA., *La Neige En Deuil*, Henri Troyat, 1952, Novel

Mountain Village, The *see* POHORSKA VESNICE (1928).

Mountains are My Kingdom *see* FORBIDDEN VALLEY (1938).

MOUNTAINS OF THE MOON 1990 d: Bob Rafelson. USA., *Burton and Speke*, William Harrison, Novel

Mounted Patrol, The *see* JIZDNI HLIDKA (1936).

MOUNTED STRANGER, THE 1930 d: Arthur Rosson. USA., *The Ridin' Kid from Powder River*, Henry Herbert Knibbs, Story

MOURIR D'AMOUR 1960 d: Dany Fog. FRN., *Ma Mort a Des Yeux Bleus*, Andre Lay, Novel

Mournful Unconcern *see* **SKORBNOE BESCUVSTVIE** (1986).

MOURNING BECOMES ELECTRA 1947 d: Dudley Nichols. USA., *Oresteia*, Agamemnon, Play, *Mourning Becomes Electra*, Eugene O'Neill, New York 1931, Play

Mouse and the Woman, The *see* **IN THE AFTERNOON OF WAR** (1981).

Mouse in the Corner, The *see* **INSPECTOR WEXFORD: THE MOUSE IN THE CORNER** (1992).

MOUSE ON THE MOON, THE 1963 d: Richard Lester. UKN., *The Mouse on the Moon*, Leonard Wibberley, New York 1962, Novel

MOUSE THAT ROARED, THE 1959 d: Jack Arnold. UKN., *The Wrath of the Grapes*, Leonard Wibberley, Novel

MOUSSAILLON, LE 1941 d: Jean Gourguet. FRN., *Le Moussaillon*, Jean Rouix, Novel

MOUTHPIECE, THE 1932 d: James Flood, Elliott Nugent. USA., *The Mouthpiece*, Frank L. Collins, New York 1929, Play

MOUTON ENRAGE, LE 1974 d: Michel Deville. FRN/ITL., *Mouton Enrage le*, Roger Blondel, Novel

MOVE 1970 d: Stuart Rosenberg. USA., *Move!*, Joel Lieber, New York 1968, Novel

Moving Forward Shoulder to Shoulder *see* **BING JIAN QIAN JIN** (1958).

Moving Hazard, The *see* **THE LONG HOLE** (1924).

Moving Target, The *see* **HARPER** (1966).

Moving Targets *see* **CHRISSIE, RUN RUN** (1984).

MOZA DEL CANTARO, LA 1953 d: Florian Rey. SPN., *La Moza Del Cantaro*, Lope de Vega, 1646, Play

Mozart *see* **WEN DIE GOTTER LIEBEN** (1942).

Mozart and Salieri *see* **MOTSART I SALYERI** (1962).

Mozart Story, The *see* **WEN DIE GOTTER LIEBEN** (1942).

MR. & MRS. BRIDGE 1990 d: James Ivory. USA., *Mr. Bridge*, Evan S. Connell, 1969, Novel, *Mrs. Bridge*, Evan S. Connell, 1959, Novel

MR. AND MRS. BO JO JONES 1971 d: Robert Day. USA., Ann Head, Novel

Mr. and Mrs. Bridge *see* **MR. & MRS. BRIDGE** (1990).

Mr. and Mrs. Bulldog Drummond *see* **BULLDOG DRUMMOND'S BRIDE** (1939).

Mr. and Mrs. Cugat *see* **ARE HUSBANDS NECESSARY?** (1942).

MR. AND MRS. NORTH 1941 d: Robert B. Sinclair. USA., *Mrs. and Mrs. North*, Owen Davis, New York 1941, Play

Mr. Arkadin *see* **CONFIDENTIAL REPORT** (1955).

Mr. Ashton Was Indiscreet *see* **THE SENATOR WAS INDISCREET** (1947).

MR. BARNES OF NEW YORK 1914 d: Maurice Costello, Robert Gaillord. USA., *Mr. Barnes of New York*, Archibald Clavering Gunter, New York 1887, Novel

MR. BARNES OF NEW YORK 1922 d: Victor Schertzinger. USA., *Mr. Barnes of New York*, Archibald Clavering Gunter, New York 1887, Novel

MR. BELVEDERE RINGS THE BELL 1951 d: Henry Koster. USA., *The Silver Whistle*, Robert C. McEnroe, New York 1948, Play

Mr. Billings Puts Things Right *see* **MR. BILLINGS SPENDS HIS DIME** (1923).

MR. BILLINGS SPENDS HIS DIME 1923 d: Wesley Ruggles. USA., *Mr. Billings Spends His Dime*, Dana Burnet, 1920, Short Story

MR. BLANDINGS BUILDS HIS DREAM HOUSE 1948 d: H. C. Potter. USA., *Mr. Blanding Builds His Dream House*, Eric Hodgins, Novel

Mr. Boggs Buys a Barrel *see* **MR. BOGGS STEPS OUT** (1938).

MR. BOGGS STEPS OUT 1938 d: Gordon Wiles. USA., *Face the Facts*, Clarence Budington Kelland, 1936, Short Story

Mr. Broucek's Excursion to Mars *see* **VYLET PANA BROUCKA NA MARS** (1921).

MR. BROWN COMES DOWN THE HILL 1966 d: Henry Cass. UKN., *Mr. Brown Comes Down the Hill*, Peter Howard, Play

Mr. Bruggs' Strange Life *see* **DAS SELTSAME LEBEN DES HERRN BRUGGS** (1951).

MR. BUTTLES 1915 d: Joseph Byron Totten. USA., *Mr. Buttles*, Frederic Arnold Kummer, Short Story

MR. COHEN TAKES A WALK 1935 d: William Beaudine. UKN., *Mr. Cohen Takes a Walk*, Mary Roberts Rinehart, Novel

MR. DEEDS GOES TO TOWN 1936 d: Frank CaprA. USA., *Opera Hat*, Clarence Budington Kelland, 1935, Short Story

MR. DENNING DRIVES NORTH 1951 d: Anthony Kimmins. UKN., *Mr. Denning Drives North*, Alec Coppel, Novel

MR. DODD TAKES THE AIR 1937 d: Alfred E. Green. USA., *The Great Crooner*, Clarence Budington Kelland, New York 1933, Novel

MR. DRAKE'S DUCK 1951 d: Val Guest. UKN., *Mr. Drake's Duck*, Ian Messiter, Radio Play

Mr. Dynamite - Death Will Kiss You Tomorrow *see* **MISTER DYNAMIT - MORGEN KUSST EUCH DER TOD** (1967).

MR. EMMANUEL 1944 d: Harold French. UKN., *Mr. Emmanuel*, Louis Golding, Novel

Mr. Faintheart *see* **$10 RAISE** (1935).

Mr. Frederick Warde in Shakespeare's Masterpiece, "the Life and Death of King Richard III *see* **THE LIFE AND DEATH OF RICHARD III** (1912).

Mr. Gilbert and Mr. Sullivan *see* **THE STORY OF GILBERT AND SULLIVAN** (1953).

MR. GILFIL'S LOVE STORY 1920 d: A. V. Bramble. UKN., *Mr. Gilfil's Love Story*, George Eliot, 1857, Short Story

MR. GREX OF MONTE CARLO 1915 d: Frank Reicher. USA., *Mr. Grex of Monte Carlo*, E. Phillips Oppenheim, Boston 1915, Novel

Mr. Griggs Returns *see* **THE COCKEYED MIRACLE** (1946).

MR. H. C. ANDERSEN 1950 d: Ronald Haines. UKN., Hans Christian Andersen, Autobiography

MR. HOBBS TAKES A VACATION 1962 d: Henry Koster. USA., *Mr. Hobbs's Vacation*, Edward Streeter, New York 1954, Novel

Mr. Hobo *see* **THE GUV'NOR** (1935).

MR. HORATIO KNIBBLES 1971 d: Robert Hird. UKN., Wally Bosco, Story

Mr. Jericho *see* **FAIR WARNING** (1937).

Mr. Jordan Comes to Town *see* **HERE COMES MR. JORDAN** (1941).

MR. JUSTICE RAFFLES 1921 d: Gerald Ames, Gaston Quiribet. UKN., *Mr. Justice Raffles*, E. W. Hornung, 1909, Novel

MR. LEMON OF ORANGE 1931 d: John G. Blystone. USA., *Mr. Lemon of Orange*, Jack Hays, 1930, Play

Mr. Limpet *see* **THE INCREDIBLE MR. LIMPET** (1964).

Mr. Logan *see* **FAME AND FORTUNE** (1918).

Mr. Lord Says No *see* **THE HAPPY FAMILY** (1952).

MR. LYNDON AT LIBERTY 1915 d: Harold Shaw. UKN., *Mr. Lyndon at Liberty*, Victor Bridges, Novel

MR. MEESON'S WILL 1915 d: Frederick Sullivan. USA., *Mr. Meeson's Will*, H. Rider Haggard, New York 1888, Novel

Mr. Meeson's Will *see* **THE GRASP OF GREED** (1916).

MR. MOTO IN DANGER ISLAND 1939 d: Herbert I. Leeds. USA., *Murder in Trinidad*, John W. Vandercook, New York 1933, Novel

Mr. Moto in Puerto Rico *see* **MR. MOTO IN DANGER ISLAND** (1939).

Mr. Moto in Trinidad *see* **MR. MOTO IN DANGER ISLAND** (1939).

Mr. Moto on Danger Island *see* **MR. MOTO IN DANGER ISLAND** (1939).

Mr. Mouse *see* **MONSIEUR LA SOURIS** (1942).

MR. MUSIC 1950 d: Richard Haydn. USA., *Accent on Youth*, Samson Raphaelson, New York 1934, Play

Mr. Nobody *see* **MONSIEUR PERSONNE** (1936).

MR. NORTH 1988 d: Danny Huston. USA., *Theophilus North*, Thornton Wilder, 1973, Novel

MR. OPP 1917 d: Lynn Reynolds. USA., *Mr. Opp*, Alice Hegan Rice, New York 1909, Novel

MR. PEABODY AND THE MERMAID 1948 d: Irving Pichel. USA., *Peabody's Mermaid*, Constance Jones, Guy Jones, Novel

Mr. Peek-a-Boo *see* **GAROU-GAROU LE PASSE-MURAILLE** (1950).

MR. PERRIN AND MR. TRAILL 1948 d: Lawrence Huntington. UKN., *Mr. Perrin and Mr. Traill*, Hugh Walpole, 1911, Novel

MR. PICKWICK IN A DOUBLE BEDDED ROOM 1913 d: Wilfred Noy. UKN., *The Pickwick Papers*, Charles Dickens, London 1836, Novel

MR. PICKWICK'S PREDICAMENT 1912 d: J. Searle Dawley. UKN., *The Pickwick Papers*, Charles Dickens, London 1836, Novel

MR. PIM PASSES BY 1921 d: Albert Ward. UKN., *Mr. Pim Passes By*, A. A. Milne, London 1920, Play

MR. POTTER OF TEXAS 1922 d: Leopold Wharton. USA., *Mr. Potter of Texas*, Archibald Clavering Gunter

MR. PREEDY AND THE COUNTESS 1925 d: George Pearson. UKN., *Mr. Preedy and the Countess*, R. C. Carton, London 1909, Play

Mr. President *see* **EL SR. PRESIDENTE** (1983).

Mr. Prohack *see* **DEAR MR. PROHACK** (1949).

Mr. Pulver and the Captain *see* **ENSIGN PULVER** (1964).

Mr. Puntila and His Servant Matti *see* **HERRA PUNTILA JA HANEN RENKINSA MATTI** (1979).

Mr. Puntila and His Valet Matti *see* **HERR PUNTILA UND SEIN KNECHT MATTI** (1955).

MR. REEDER IN ROOM 13 1938 d: Norman Lee. UKN., *Room 13*, Edgar Wallace, London 1924, Novel

MR. SAMPAT 1952 d: S. S. Vasan. IND., *Mr. Sampat*, R. K. Narayan, 1949, Novel

MR. SARDONICUS 1961 d: William Castle. USA., *Sardonicus*, Ray Russell, 1961, Short Story

Mr. Scoutmaster *see* **MISTER SCOUTMASTER** (1953).

Mr. Servadac's Ark *see* **NA KOMETE** (1970).

Mr. Shadow *see* **THE SHADOW STRIKES** (1937).

MR. SKEFFINGTON 1944 d: Vincent Sherman. USA., *Mr. Skeffington*, Elizabeth, Novel

MR. SKITCH 1933 d: James Cruze. USA., *Green Dice*, Anne Cameron, 1926, Short Story

Mr. Steve *see* **L' ETRANGE MONSIEUR STEVE** (1957).

MR. TOPAZE 1961 d: Peter Sellers. UKN., *Topaze*, Marcel Pagnol, Paris 1928, Play

MR. WHAT'S-HIS-NAME 1935 d: Ralph Ince. UKN., Yves Mirande, Play

MR. WINKLE GOES TO WAR 1944 d: Alfred E. Green. USA., *Mr. Winkle Goes to War*, Theodore Pratt, Novel

MR. WRONG 1986 d: Gaylene Preston. NZL., Elizabeth Jane Howard, Story

MR. WU 1919 d: Maurice Elvey. UKN., *Mr. Wu*, Harold Owen, Harry M. Vernon, London 1913, Play

MR. WU 1927 d: William Nigh. USA., *Mr. Wu*, Harold Owen, Harry M. Vernon, London 1913, Play

MRIGAYA 1976 d: Mrinal Sen. IND., *Mrigaya*, Bhagbati Charan Panigrahi, Short Story

Mrigayaa *see* **MRIGAYA** (1976).

MRITYUDAND 1997 d: Prakash JhA. IND., Sahiwal, Novel

MRS. 'ARRIS GOES TO PARIS 1991 d: Anthony Shaw. USA., *Mrs. 'Arris Goes to Paris*, Paul Gallico, Short Story

MRS. BALFAME 1917 d: Frank Powell. USA., *Mrs. Balfame*, Gertrude Franklin Atherton, New York 1906, Novel

MRS. BLACK IS BACK 1914 d: Thomas N. Heffron. USA., *Mrs. Black Is Back*, George V. Hobart, New York 1904, Play

Mrs. Brown from Chicago *see* **MARYS GROSSES GEHEIMNIS** (1928).

MRS. CAPPER'S BIRTHDAY 1985 d: Mike Ockrent. UKN., *Mrs. Capper's Birthday*, Noel Coward, 1965, Short Story

Mrs. Cassell's Profession *see* **THE STRIPED STOCKING GANG** (1915).

Mrs. Cheney's Demise *see* **FRAU CHENEYS ENDE** (1961).

Mrs. Christopher *see* **BLACKMAILED** (1951).

MRS. CORNEY MAKES TEA 1913 d: Wilfred Noy. UKN., *Oliver Twist*, Charles Dickens, London 1838, Novel

MRS. DALLOWAY 1997 d: Marleen Gorris. USA/UKN/NTH., *Mrs. Dalloway*, Virginia Woolf, Novel

MRS. DANE'S DEFENCE 1933 d: A. V. Bramble. UKN., *Mrs. Dane's Defence*, Henry Arthur Jones, London 1900, Play

MRS. DANE'S DEFENSE 1918 d: Hugh Ford. USA., *Mrs. Dane's Defence*, Henry Arthur Jones, London 1900, Play

Mrs. Drake's Duck see MR. DRAKE'S DUCK (1951).

MRS. ERRICKER'S REPUTATION 1920 d: Cecil M. Hepworth. UKN., *Mrs. Erricker's Reputation*, Thomas Cobb, Novel

MRS. FITZHERBERT 1947 d: Montgomery Tully. UKN., *Princess Fitz*, Winifred Carter, Novel

MRS. GIBBONS' BOYS 1962 d: Max Varnel. UKN., *Mrs. Gibbons' Boys*, Will Glickman, Joseph Stein, Play

Mrs. Holle see FRAU HOLLE (1964).

Mrs. Kacka Intervenes. see PANI KACKA ZASAHUJE. (1939).

Mrs. Knudsen, Down and Out see DET ER NAT MED FRU KNUDSEN (1971).

Mrs. Latter's Boarding School see PENSJA PANI LATTER (1982).

Mrs. Leffingwell's Boot see MRS. LEFFINGWELL'S BOOTS (1919).

MRS. LEFFINGWELL'S BOOTS 1919 d: Walter Edwards. USA., *Mrs. Leffingwell's Boots*, Augustus Thomas, 1905, Play

Mrs. Leonard Misbehaves see THE LADY AND THE MOB (1939).

MRS. MIKE 1949 d: Louis King. USA., *Mrs. Mike*, Benedict Freedman, Nancy Freedman, Book

MRS. MINIVER 1942 d: William Wyler. USA., *Mrs. Miniver*, Jan Struther, Novel

MRS. PARKINGTON 1944 d: Tay Garnett. USA., *Mrs. Parkington*, Louis Bromfield, 1943, Novel

MRS. PYM OF SCOTLAND YARD 1939 d: Fred Elles. UKN., *Mrs. Pym of Scotland Yard*, Nigel Morland, Novel

Mrs. Rettich, Czerny and Me see DIE CZERNI UND ICH FRAU RETTICH (1998).

MRS. TEMPLE'S TELEGRAM 1920 d: James Cruze. USA., *Mrs. Temple's Telegram*, William Morris, Frank Wyatt, New York 1905, Play

MRS. THOMPSON 1919 d: Rex Wilson. UKN., *Mrs. Thompson*, William Babington Maxwell, New York 1911, Novel

Mrs. Warren's Profession see FRAU WARRENS GEWERBE (1960).

MRS. WARREN'S PROFESSION 1991 d: Mike Newman. UKN., *Mrs. Warren's Profession*, George Bernard Shaw, 1898, Play

Mrs. Warren's Trade see FRAU WARRENS GEWERBE (1960).

MRS. WIGGS OF THE CABBAGE PATCH 1914 d: Harold Entwhistle. USA., *Lovey Mary*, Alice Hegan Rice, New York 1903, Novel, *Mrs. Wiggs of the Cabbage Patch*, Alice Hegan Rice, New York 1901, Novel

MRS. WIGGS OF THE CABBAGE PATCH 1919 d: Hugh Ford. USA., *Mrs. Wiggs of the Cabbage Patch*, Alice Hegan Rice, New York 1901, Novel

MRS. WIGGS OF THE CABBAGE PATCH 1934 d: Norman Taurog. USA., *Mrs. Wiggs of the Cabbage Patch*, Alice Hegan Rice, New York 1901, Novel

MRS. WIGGS OF THE CABBAGE PATCH 1942 d: Ralph Murphy. USA., *Mrs. Wiggs of the Cabbage Patch*, Alice Hegan Rice, New York 1901, Novel

Mrs. Winter see FRAU HOLLE (1985).

MRS. WINTERBOURNE 1996 d: Richard Benjamin. USA., *I Married a Dead Man*, Cornell Woolrich, 1948, Novel

MRTVI ZIJI 1922 d: J. S. Kolar. CZC., *Mrtvi Ziji*, Karel Dewetter, Novel

MRTVY MEZI ZIVYMI 1947 d: Borivoj Zeman. CZC., *To Levende Og En Dod*, Sigurd Wesley Christiansen, Oslo 1925, Novel

MS. SCROOGE 1997 d: John Korty. USA., *A Christmas Carol*, Charles Dickens, London 1843, Novel

M'SIEUR LA CAILLE 1955 d: Andre Pergament. FRN., *Jesus la Caille*, Francis Carco, 1914, Novel

Much Ado About Nothing see MNOGO SHUMA IZ NICHEVO (1956).

Much Ado About Nothing see VIEL LARM UM NICHTS (1964).

Much Ado About Nothing see MNOGO SUMA IZ NICEGO (1973).

MUCH ADO ABOUT NOTHING 1978 d: A. J. Anton, Nick HavingA. USA., *Much Ado About Nothing*, William Shakespeare, c1598, Play

MUCH ADO ABOUT NOTHING 1984 d: Stuart Burge. UKN., *Much Ado About Nothing*, William Shakespeare, c1598, Play

MUCH ADO ABOUT NOTHING 1993 d: Kenneth Branagh. UKN., *Much Ado About Nothing*, William Shakespeare, c1598, Play

Much Noise from Nothing see MNOGO SUMA IZ NICEGO (1973).

MUCHACHA DE LAS BRAGAS DE ORO, LA 1979 d: Vicente ArandA. SPN/VNZ., *La Muchacha de Las Brages de Oro*, Juan Marse, 1978, Novel

Muchacha de Moscu, La see SANCTA MARIA (1941).

MUCHACHAS DE UNIFORME 1950 d: Alfredo B. CrevennA. MXC., *Gestern Und Heute*, Christa Winsloe, Play

MUCHACHITA DE VALLADOLID, UNA 1958 d: Luis Cesar Amadori. SPN., *Una Muchachita de Valladolid*, Joaquin Calvo Sotelo, 1957, Play

Mud and Reeds see PALUDE TRAGICA (1953).

Mud Honey see ROPE OF FLESH (1965).

Mud Lark see THE PURCHASE PRICE (1932).

Mud River see DORO NO KAWA (1981).

Muddy River see DORO NO KAWA (1981).

MUDE THEODOR, DER 1936 d: Veit Harlan. GRM., *Der Mude Theodor*, Max Ferner, Max Neal, Play

Mudhoney! see ROPE OF FLESH (1965).

MUDLARK, THE 1950 d: Jean Negulesco. UKN., *The Mudlark*, Theodore Bonnet, Novel

MUEDA, MEMORIA E MASSACRE 1980 d: Ruy GuerrA. MZM., *Memoria E Massacre Mueda*, Calisto Dos Lagos, Play

Mueda, Memory and Massacre see MEMORIA E MASSACRE MUEDA (1980).

Muerte Del Che Guevara, La see EL CHE GUEVARA (1968).

Muerte En Este Jardin, La see LA MORT EN CE JARDIN (1956).

MUERTE EN LAS CALLES, LA 1952 d: Leo Fleider. ARG., *La Muerte En Las Calles*, Manuel Galvez, 1949, Novel

Muerte Viaja Demasiado, La see UMORISMO NERO (1965).

Muerte Viscosa see THE MOVIE SLUGS (1988).

MUERTO HACE LAS MALETAS, EL 1970 d: Jesus Franco. SPN/GRM., Bryan Edgar Wallace, Novel

MUFLES, LES 1929 d: Robert Peguy. FRN., *Les Mufles*, Eugene Barbier, Novel

MUGGABLE MARY, STREET COP 1982 d: Sandor Stern. USA., *Muggable Mary*, Mary Glatzle, Book

MUGGER, THE 1958 d: William Berke. USA., *The Mugger*, Evan Hunter, 1956, Novel

MUHOMATSU NO ISSHO 1958 d: Hiroshi Inagaki. JPN., *Muhomatsu No Issho*, Shunsaku Iwashita, Novel

MUJER, EL TORERO Y EL TORO, LA 1950 d: Fernando Butragueno. SPN., *La Mujer El Torero Y El Toro*, Alberto Insua, 1926, Novel

MUJER SIN AMOR, UNA 1951 d: Luis Bunuel. MXC., *Pierre Et Jean*, Guy de Maupassant, 1888, Novel

MUJER X, LA 1931 d: Carlos Borcosque. USA., *La Femme X*, Alexandre Bisson, Paris 1908, Play

MUKHTI 1970 d: N. Lakshminarayan. IND., *Shapa*, V. M. Inamdar, Novel

Mukti see MUKHTI (1970).

MULINO DEL PO, IL 1949 d: Alberto LattuadA. ITL., *Il Mulino Del Po*, Riccardo Bacchelli, 1938-46, Novel

MULINO DELLE DONNE DI PIETRA, IL 1960 d: Giorgio Ferroni. ITL/FRN., *I Racconti Fiamminghi*, Peter Van Weigen, Short Story

MULL 1988 d: Don McLennan. ASL., *Mullaway*, Bron Nicholls, Novel

Mullaway see MULL (1988).

MULLER UND SEIN KIND, DER 1911 d: Adolf Gartner. GRM., *Der Muller Und Sein Kind*, Ernst Raupach, Play

MULTIPLICITY 1996 d: Harold Ramis. USA., *Multiplicity*, Chris Miller, Short Story

MULU MANEK 1955 d: Manhar Rangildas Raskapur. IND., *Allabeli*, Gunwantrai Acharya, Play

Mummers, The see MY OLD DUCHESS (1933).

Mummy see MA-MA (1977).

MUMMY AND THE HUMMING BIRD, THE 1915 d: James Durkin. USA., *The Mummy and the Humming Bird*, Isaac Henderson, New York 1902, Play

MUMSIE 1927 d: Herbert Wilcox. UKN., *Mumsie*, Edward Knoblock, Play

MUMSY, NANNY, SONNY AND GIRLY 1969 d: Freddie Francis. UKN., *The Happy Family*, Maisie Mosco, London 1966, Play

MUMU 1959 d: Anatoli Bobrovsky, Yevgeniy Teterin. USS., *Mumu*, Ivan Turgenev, 1854, Short Story

MUMU 1987 d: V. Karavaev. USS., *Mumu*, Ivan Turgenev, 1854, Short Story

MUMU 1998 d: Yuri Grymov. RSS., *Mumu*, Ivan Turgenev, 1854, Short Story

MUNAKATA SHIMAI 1950 d: Yasujiro Ozu. JPN., *Munakata Shimai*, Jiro Osaragi, 1949, Novel

Munakata Sisters, The see MUNAKATA SHIMAI (1950).

Munchen Strike, The see THE SWORD OF GIDEON (1986).

Munchhausen see BARON PRASIL (1940).

MUNCHHAUSEN IN AFRIKA 1958 d: Werner Jacobs. GRM., Paul H. Rameau, Story

MUNCHNERINNEN 1944 d: Philipp L. Mayring. GRM., *Muncherinnen*, Ludwig Thoma, Novel

MUNDO SIGUE, EL 1963 d: Fernando Fernan Gomez. SPN., *El Mundo Sigue*, Juan Antonio de Zunzunegui, 1960, Novel

Munekata Shimai see MUNAKATA SHIMAI (1950).

Municipal Report, A see I WILL REPAY (1917).

MUNKBROGREVEN 1935 d: Edvin Adolphson, Sigurd Wallen. SWD., *Greven Av Gamla Sta'n*, Arthur Fischer, Siegfried Fischer, Play

Muori Lentamente. Ta la Godi Di Piu see MISTER DYNAMIT - MORGEN KUSST EUCH DER TOD (1967).

MUPPET CHRISTMAS CAROL, THE 1992 d: Brian Henson. USA., *A Christmas Carol*, Charles Dickens, London 1843, Novel

MUR, LE 1968 d: Serge Roullet. FRN., *Le Mur*, Jean-Paul Sartre, 1939, Short Story

MURAILLES DU SILENCE, LES 1925 d: Louis de Carbonnat. FRN., *Les Murailles du Silence*, Charles Vayre, Novel

MURALLA, LA 1958 d: Luis LuciA. SPN., *La Muralla*, Joaquin Calvo Sotelo, 1955, Play

MURDER 1930 d: Alfred Hitchcock. UKN., *Enter Sir John*, Clemence Dane, Helen Simpson, London 1928, Play

Murder at 45 Rpm see MEURTRE EN 45 TOURS (1960).

MURDER AT COVENT GARDEN 1932 d: Leslie Hiscott, Michael Barringer. UKN., *Murder at Covent Garden*, W. J. Makin, Novel

MURDER AT GLEN ATHOL 1936 d: Frank Strayer. USA., *Murder at Glen Athol*, Norman Lippincott, Garden City, N.Y. 1935, Novel

MURDER AT MONTE CARLO 1935 d: Ralph Ince. UKN., *Murder at Monte Carlo*, Tom Van Dyke, Novel

MURDER AT SITE THREE 1959 d: Francis Searle. UKN., *Crime Is My Business*, W. Howard Baker, Novel

Murder at the Baskervilles see SILVER BLAZE (1937).

MURDER AT THE GALLOP 1963 d: George Pollock. UKN., *After the Funeral*, Agatha Christie, London 1953, Novel

MURDER AT THE VANITIES 1934 d: Mitchell Leisen. USA., *Murder at the Vanities*, Earl Carroll, Rufus King, New York 1933, Play

Murder Being Once Done see INSPECTOR WEXFORD: MURDER BEING ONCE DONE (1991).

MURDER BY AN ARISTOCRAT 1936 d: Frank McDonald. USA., *Murder By an Aristocrat*, Mignon G. Eberhart, New York 1932, Novel

MURDER BY DECREE 1979 d: Bob Clark. UKN/CND., *The Ripper File*, Elwyn Jones, John Lloyd, Book

Murder By Demand see MURDER ON DEMAND (1991).

MURDER BY PROXY 1955 d: Terence Fisher. UKN., *Murder By Proxy*, Helen Neilson, Novel

MURDER: BY REASON OF INSANITY 1985 d: Anthony Page. USA., *Always a Victim*, Marilyn Goldstein

MURDER BY THE BOOK 1987 d: Mel Damski. USA., *Alter Ego*, Mel Arrighi, Novel

MURDER BY THE CLOCK 1931 d: Edward Sloman. USA., *Dangerously Yours*, Charles Behan, 1929, Play, *Murder By the Clock*, Rufus King, New York 1929, Novel

Murder Case see A CASA ASSASSINADA (1971).

Murder Clinic, The see LA LAMA NEL CORPO (1966).

Murder C.O.D. see MURDER ON DEMAND (1991).

MURDER ELITE 1985 d: Claude Whatham. UKN., Edward Abraham, Valerie Abraham, Story

Murder Go Round see UN CONDE (1970).

MURDER GOES TO COLLEGE 1937 d: Charles F. Reisner. USA., Murder Goes to College, Kurt Steel, Indianapolis 1936, Novel

Murder Goes to Jail see PARTNERS IN CRIME (1937).

MURDER IN COWETA COUNTY 1982 d: Gary Nelson. USA., Murder in Coweta County, Margaret Anne Barnes, Book

Murder in Diamond Row see THE SQUEAKER (1937).

Murder in Island Street see VRAZDA V OSTROVNI ULICI (1933).

MURDER IN MIND 1997 d: Andy Morahan. USA/UKN., Murder in Mind, Michael Cooney, Play

MURDER IN REVERSE 1945 d: Montgomery Tully. UKN., Query, Seamark, Novel

MURDER IN TEXAS 1981 d: William Hale. USA., Prescription: Murder, John McGreevey, Book

MURDER IN THE AIR 1940 d: Lewis Seiler. USA., Uncle Sam Awakens, Raymond L. Schrock, Story

MURDER IN THE BLUE ROOM 1944 d: Leslie Goodwins. USA., Eric Philippi, Story

MURDER IN THE CATHEDRAL 1952 d: George Hoellering. UKN., Murder in the Cathedral, T. S. Eliot, London 1935, Play

MURDER IN THE CATHEDRAL 1964 d: George R. FoA. UKN., Murder in the Cathedral, T. S. Eliot, London 1935, Play

Murder in the Dark see SENOR JIM (1936).

MURDER IN THE FAMILY 1938 d: Albert Parker. UKN., Murder in the Family, James Ronald, Novel

Murder in the Family see LE CRIME D'OVIDE PLOUFFE (1984).

Murder in the Footlights see THE TROJAN BROTHERS (1946).

Murder in the Hotel Diplomat see ONE NEW YORK NIGHT (1935).

Murder in the Library see PLAYTHINGS OF DESIRE (1934).

Murder in the Old Red Barn see THE MURDER IN THE RED BARN MARIA MARTEN; OR (1935).

MURDER IN THE PRIVATE CAR 1934 d: Harry Beaumont. USA., The Rear Car, Edward E. Rose, Los Angeles 1922, Play

Murder in the Stalls see NOT WANTED ON VOYAGE (1936).

Murder in the Surgery see MYSTERY OF THE WHITE ROOM (1939).

Murder in Thorton Square, The see GASLIGHT (1944).

Murder in Three Acts see AGATHA CHRISTIE'S MURDER IN THREE ACTS (1986).

MURDER IN TRINIDAD 1934 d: Louis King. USA., Murder in Trinidad, John W. Vandercook, New York 1933, Novel

Murder Is a Murder, A see UN MEURTRE EST UN MEURTRE (1972).

Murder Is a Murder. Is a Murder, A see UN MEURTRE EST UN MEURTRE (1972).

Murder Is Announced, A see MISS MARPLE: A MURDER IS ANNOUNCED (1984).

MURDER IS EASY 1982 d: Claude Whatham. USA., Agatha Christie, Novel

MURDER IS MY BUSINESS 1946 d: Sam Newfield. USA., The Uncomplaining Corpse, Brett Halliday, Novel

MURDER IS NEWS 1939 d: Leon BarshA. CND., Theodore A. Tinsley, Story

Murder Is News see THE DELAVINE AFFAIR (1954).

MURDER MOST FOUL 1964 d: George Pollock. UKN., Mrs. McGinty's Dead, Agatha Christie, London 1952, Novel

MURDER, MY SWEET 1945 d: Edward Dmytryk. USA., Farewell My Lovely, Raymond Chandler, 1940, Novel

Murder of Dimitri Karamazov, The see BRATYA KARAMAZOVY (1968).

MURDER OF DR. HARRIGAN, THE 1936 d: Frank McDonald. USA., From This Dark Stairway, Mignon G. Eberhart, New York 1931, Novel

MURDER OF QUALITY, A 1991 d: Gavin Millar. USA., A Murder of Quality, John le Carre, Novel

Murder of the Brothers Johan and Cornelius de Witt see THE BLACK TULIP (1921).

MURDER ON A BRIDLE PATH 1936 d: Edward Killy, William Hamilton. USA., The Puzzle of the Red Stallion, Stuart Palmer, New York 1936, Novel

MURDER ON A HONEYMOON 1935 d: Lloyd Corrigan. USA., The Puzzle of the Pepper Tree, Susan Palmer, New York 1933, Novel

MURDER ON DEMAND 1991 d: Alan Metzger. USA., Kill Free, Barbara Paul, Novel

Murder on Monday see HOME AT SEVEN (1952).

Murder on Ostrovni Street see VRAZDA V OSTROVNI ULICI (1933).

Murder on Sunset Blvd see THE SUNSET STRIP CASE (1938).

Murder on Sunset Boulevard see THE SUNSET STRIP CASE (1938).

Murder on the Bayou see A GATHERING OF OLD MEN (1987).

MURDER ON THE BLACKBOARD 1934 d: George Archainbaud. USA., Murder on the Blackboard, Stuart Palmer, New York 1932, Novel

MURDER ON THE CAMPUS 1934 d: Richard Thorpe. USA., The Campanile Murders, Whitman Chambers, New York 1933, Novel

Murder on the Grand Canal see VOIR VENISE ET CREVER (1966).

MURDER ON THE ORIENT EXPRESS 1974 d: Sidney Lumet. UKN., Murder on the Orient Express, Agatha Christie, Novel

Murder on the Runaway Car see MURDER IN THE PRIVATE CAR (1934).

Murder on the Runaway Train see MURDER IN THE PRIVATE CAR (1934).

MURDER ON THE SECOND FLOOR 1932 d: William McGann. USA., Murder on the Second Floor, Frank Vosper, London 1929, Play

Murder on the Set see DEATH ON THE SET (1935).

MURDER ON THE WATERFRONT 1943 d: B. Reeves Eason. USA., Without Warning, Robert Spencer Zink, New York 1937, Play

MURDER ON THE YUKON 1940 d: Louis J. Gasnier. USA., Renfrew Rides North, Laurie York Erskine, New York 1931, Novel

Murder Party, The see THE NIGHT OF THE PARTY (1934).

MURDER REPORTED 1957 d: Charles Saunders. UKN., Murder for the Millions, Robert Chapman, Novel

Murder Ring, The see ELLERY QUEEN AND THE MURDER RING (1941).

MURDER SHE SAID 1961 d: George Pollock. UKN/USA., 4.50 from Paddington, Agatha Christie, London 1957, Novel

Murder Society, The see LA LAMA NEL CORPO (1966).

MURDER TOMORROW 1938 d: Donovan Pedelty. UKN., Murder Tomorrow?, Frank Harvey, London 1938, Play

MURDER WILL OUT 1930 d: Clarence Badger. USA., The Purple Hieroglyph, Will F. Jenkins, 1920, Short Story

MURDER WITH MIRRORS 1985 d: Dick Lowry. USA., Murder With Mirrors, Agatha Christie, Novel

MURDER WITHOUT CRIME 1950 d: J. Lee Thompson. UKN., Double Error, J. Lee Thompson, 1935, Play

Murdered House, The see LA MAISON ASSASSINEE (1989).

Murderer Dimitri Karamasoff, The see DER MORDER DIMITRI KARAMASOFF (1931).

Murderer Lives at Number 21, The see L' ASSASSIN HABITE AU 21 (1942).

Murderer, The see LE MEURTRIER (1962).

MURDERER, THE 1976 d: Andrew Silver. USA., The Murderer, Ray Bradbury, 1953, Short Story

Murderer, The see DER MORDER (1978).

Murderer With the Silk Scarf, The see DER MORDER MIT DEM SEIDENSCHAL (1965).

Murderers are Coming, The see UBITZI VYKHODYAT NA DOROGU (1942).

Murderers are on Their Way see UBITZI VYKHODYAT NA DOROGU (1942).

Murderer's Conscience, The see THE AVENGING CONSCIENCE OR THOU SHALT NOT KILL (1914).

MURDERERS' ROW 1966 d: Henry Levin. USA., Murderers' Row, Donald Hamilton, New York 1962, Novel

Murderers Welcome see UNDER SUSPICION (1937).

MURDERS IN THE RUE MORGUE 1932 d: Robert Florey. USA., Murders in the Rue Morgue, Edgar Allan Poe, 1841, Short Story

MURDERS IN THE RUE MORGUE 1971 d: Gordon Hessler. USA., Murders in the Rue Morgue, Edgar Allan Poe, 1841, Short Story

MURDERS IN THE RUE MORGUE, THE 1914 d: Robert Goodman. USA., Murders in the Rue Morgue, Edgar Allan Poe, 1841, Short Story

MURDERS IN THE RUE MORGUE, THE 1986 d: Jeannot Szwarc. USA., Murders in the Rue Morgue, Edgar Allan Poe, 1841, Short Story

Murietta see ROBIN HOOD OF EL DORADO (1936).

MURPHY'S ROMANCE 1985 d: Martin Ritt. USA., Murphy's Romance, Max Schott, Novel

MURPHY'S WAKE 1906. UKN., Conn the Shaugraun, Dion Boucicault, Play

MURPHY'S WAR 1970 d: Peter Yates. UKN., Murphy's War, Max Catto, Novel

Musashi and Kojiro see MIYAMOTO MUSASHI: KETTO GANRYUJIMA (1956).

MUSASHINO FUJIN 1951 d: Kenji Mizoguchi. JPN., Musashino Fujin, Shohei Oka, 1951, Novel

Musette Fra le Spire Del Destino see MUSOTTE (1920).

MUSGRAVE RITUAL, THE 1912 d: Georges Treville. UKN., The Musgrave Ritual, Arthur Conan Doyle, Short Story

MUSGRAVE RITUAL, THE 1922 d: George Ridgwell. UKN., The Musgrave Ritual, Arthur Conan Doyle, Short Story

Musgrave Ritual, The see THE RETURN OF SHERLOCK HOLMES: THE MUSGRAVE RITUAL (1986).

Music By Night see MUSIK BEI NACHT (1953).

Music in Darkness see MUSIK I MORKER (1947).

MUSIC IN THE AIR 1934 d: Joe May. USA., Music in the Air, Oscar Hammerstein II, Jerome Kern, New York 1932, Operetta

Music in the Dark see MUSIK I MORKER (1947).

MUSIC IS MAGIC 1935 d: George Marshall. USA., Private Beach, Jesse Lasky Jr., Gladys Unger, Beverly Hills 1934, Play

MUSIC LOVERS, THE 1970 d: Ken Russell. UKN., Beloved Friend, Catherine D. Bowen, Barbara von Meck, Book

MUSIC MAN, THE 1962 d: Morton Da CostA. USA., The Music Man, Franklin Lacey, Meredith Willson, New York 1957, Musical Play

MUSIC MASTER, THE 1927 d: Allan Dwan. USA., The Music Master, Charles Klein, Novel

Music, Music, Only Music see MUSIK - UND NUR MUSIK MUSIK (1955).

MUSIC OF CHANCE, THE 1993 d: Philip Haas. USA., The Music of Chance, Paul Auster, Novel

Music Room, The see JALSAGHAR (1958).

MUSIC SCHOOL, THE 1977 d: John Korty. USA., The Music School, John Updike, 1966, Short Story

MUSICA, LA 1966 d: Paul Seban, Marguerite Duras. FRN., La Musica, Marguerite Duras, Play

Musical Score see BANDISH (1955).

Musician, The see THE CLOWN AND THE KIDS (1968).

Musician's Girl, The see MUSIKANTSKA LIDUSKA (1940).

Musician's Liduska, The see MUSIKANTSKA LIDUSKA (1940).

MUSICIENS DU CIEL, LES 1939 d: Georges Lacombe. FRN., Les Musiciens du Ciel, Rene Lefevre, Novel

Music's the Thing, The see NEM ELHETEK MUZSIKASZO NELKUL (1979).

MUSIK BEI NACHT 1953 d: Kurt Hoffmann. GRM., Die Grosse Kurve, Curt Johannes Braun, Play

MUSIK I MORKER 1947 d: Ingmar Bergman. SWD., Musik I Morker, Dagmar Ingeborg Edqvist, 1937, Novel

Musik Ist Trumpf *see* **LA MUSIQUE EST MA PASSION** (1961).

MUSIK, MUSIK - UND NUR MUSIK 1955 d: Ernst Matray. GRM., *Karl III Und Anna von Osterreich*, Manfred Rossner, Play

MUSIKANTSKA LIDUSKA 1940 d: Martin Fric. CZC., *Muzikantska Liduska*, Vitezslav Halek, Short Story

MUSIQUE EST MA PASSION, LA 1961 d: Franz J. Gottlieb. SWT/GRM., *Die Hazy Osterwald Story*, Walter Grieder, Zurich 1961, Book

MUSODURO 1954 d: Giuseppe Bennati. ITL., *Memorie Di un Bracconiere Musoduro*, Luigi Ugolini, Novel

MUSOTTE 1920 d: Mario Corsi. ITL., *Musotte*, Guy de Maupassant, 1891

MUSS 'EM UP 1936 d: Charles Vidor. USA., *The Green Shadow*, James Edward Grant, New York 1935, Novel

MUSS MAN SICH GLEICH SCHEIDEN LASSEN? 1953 d: Hans Schweikart. GRM., *Lauter Lugen*, Hans Schweikart, Play

MUSTA RAKKAUS 1957 d: Edvin Laine. FNL., *Musta Rakkaus*, Vaino Linna, 1948, Novel

MUSTERGATTE, DER 1937 d: Wolfgang Liebeneiner. GRM., Avery Hopwood, Play

MUSTERGATTE, DER 1959 d: Karl Suter. SWT., *Fair and Warmer*, Avery Hopwood, New York 1915, Play

MUSUKO 1991 d: Yoji YamadA. JPN., *Musuko*, Makoto Shiina, Book

MUSUME TO WATASHI 1962 d: Hiromichi HorikawA. JPN., *Musume to Watashi*, Bunroku Shishi, 1953-56, Serial

MUTA DI PORTICI, LA 1911. ITL., *La Muette de Portici*, Daniel Francois Auber, Eugene Scribe, Casimir Delavigne, Paris 1828, Opera

MUTA DI PORTICI, LA 1924 d: Telemaco Ruggeri. ITL., *La Muette de Portici*, Auber, Daniel Francois, Eugene Scribe, Casimir Delavigne, Paris 1828, Opera

MUTIGE SEEFAHRER, THE 1935 d: Hans Deppe. GRM., *Der Mutige Seefahrer*, Georg Kaiser, 1926, Play

Mutineers, The *see* **H.M.S. DEFIANT** (1962).

MUTINES DE L'ELSENEUR, LES 1936 d: Pierre Chenal. FRN., *The Mutiny of the Elsinore*, Jack London, New York 1914, Novel

MUTINY 1925 d: F. Martin Thornton. UKN., *Diana of the Islands*, Ben Bolt, Novel

MUTINY 1952 d: Edward Dmytryk. USA., *The Golden Anchor*, Hollister Noble, Novel

MUTINY OF THE ELSINORE, THE 1920 d: Edward Sloman. USA., *The Mutiny of the Elsinore*, Jack London, New York 1914, Novel

MUTINY OF THE ELSINORE, THE 1937 d: Roy Lockwood. UKN., *The Mutiny of the Elsinore*, Jack London, New York 1914, Novel

MUTINY ON THE BOUNTY 1935 d: Frank Lloyd. USA., *Men Against the Sea*, James N. Hall, Charles Nordhoff, 1934, Novel, *Mutiny on the Bounty*, James N. Hall, Charles Nordhoff, Boston 1932, Novel

MUTINY ON THE BOUNTY 1962 d: Lewis Milestone, Carol Reed. USA., *Mutiny on the Bounty*, James N. Hall, Charles Nordhoff, Boston 1932, Novel

MUTINY ON THE BOUNTY 1983 d: Roger Donaldson. USA/UKN., *Captain Bligh and Mr. Christian*, Richard Hough, Book

Mutiny, The *see* **THE MUTINY OF THE ELSINORE** (1920).

MUTTER COURAGE UND IHRE KINDER 1960 d: Peter Palitzsch, Manfred Wekwerth. GDR., *Mutter Courage Und Ihre Kinder*, Bertolt Brecht, 1949, Play

MUTTER UND KIND 1924 d: Carl Froelich. GRM., *Mutter Und Kind*, Christian Friedrich Hebbel, 1859, Poem

MUTTER UND KIND 1933 d: Hans Steinhoff. GRM., *Mutter Und Kind*, Christian Friedrich Hebbel, 1859, Poem

Mutters Courage *see* **MY MOTHER'S COURAGE** (1995).

Mutti Muss Heiraten *see* **KOMPLOTT AUF ERLENHOF** (1950).

MUURMANNIN PAKOLAISET 1926 d: Erkki Karu. FNL., *Kivelion Karkurit*, Kaarlo Hanninen, 1923, Novel

Muz Bez Srdce *see* **DER MANN OHNE HERZ** (1923).

MUZHKI VREMENA 1977 d: Edward Zahariev. BUL., *Mazhki Vremena*, Nikolai Haitov, 1967, Short Story

MUZI NESTARNOU 1942 d: Vladimir Slavinsky. CZC., *Muzi Nestarnou*, Jan Patrny, Play

MUZI V OFFSIDU 1931 d: Svatopluk Innemann. CZC., *Muzi V Offsidu*, Karel Polacek, Novel

Muzki Vremena *see* **MUZHKI VREMENA** (1977).

Muzzle, The *see* **DER MAULKORB** (1958).

My 99 Brides *see* **MEINE 99 BRAUTE** (1958).

My African Adventure *see* **GOING BANANAS** (1987).

MY AMERICAN WIFE 1922 d: Sam Wood. USA., *My American Wife*, Hector Turnbull, Story

MY AMERICAN WIFE 1936 d: Harold Young. USA., *Old-Timer*, Elmer Holmes Davis, 1935, Short Story

MY ANTONIA 1995 d: Joseph Sargent. USA., *My Antonia*, Willa Cather, 1918, Novel

My Apprenticeship *see* **V LYUDKYAKH** (1939).

My Aunt, Your Aunt *see* **MEINE TANTE - DEINE TANTE** (1927).

My Aunt, Your Aunt *see* **MEINE TANTE - DEINE TANTE** (1939).

My Baby Loves Music *see* **MY GAL LOVES MUSIC** (1944).

MY BEST GIRL 1915. USA., *My Best Girl*, Clifton Crawford, Channing Pollock, Rennold Wolf, New York 1912, Musical Play

MY BEST GIRL 1927 d: Sam Taylor. USA., *My Best Girl*, Kathleen Norris, New York 1927, Novel

MY BILL 1938 d: John Farrow. USA., *Courage*, Tom Barry, New York 1928, Play

MY BLUE HEAVEN 1950 d: Henry Koster. USA., *Storks Don't Bring Babies*, S. K. Lauren, Story

MY BREAST 1994 d: Betty Thomas. USA., *My Breast*, Joyce Wadler, Autobiography

MY BRILLIANT CAREER 1979 d: Gillian Armstrong. ASL., *My Brilliant Career*, Miles Franklin, 1901, Novel

MY BROTHER JONATHAN 1948 d: Harold French. UKN., *My Brother Jonathan*, Francis Brett Young, Novel

MY BROTHER TALKS TO HORSES 1946 d: Fred Zinnemann. USA., *Joe the Wounded Tennis Player*, Morton Thompson, Novel

My Brother, the Outlaw *see* **MY OUTLAW BROTHER** (1951).

My Brother's Gun *see* **LA PISTOLA DE MI HERMANO** (1997).

MY BROTHER'S KEEPER 1948 d: Alfred Roome, Roy Rich. UKN., Maurice Wiltshire, Story

My Case *see* **MON CAS** (1986).

MY CHAMPION 1981 d: Gwen Arner. USA/JPN., Michiko Tsuwa-Gorman, Autobiography

MY COUSIN RACHEL 1952 d: Henry Koster. USA., *My Cousin Rachel*, Daphne Du Maurier, 1951, Novel

MY COUSIN RACHEL 198- d: Brian Farnham. UKN., *My Cousin Rachel*, Daphne Du Maurier, 1951, Novel

My Darling *see* **TESORO MIO** (1979).

MY DARLING CLEMENTINE 1946 d: John Ford. USA., *Wyatt Earp - Frontier Marshal*, Stuart N. Lake, New York 1931, Book

My Darlings *see* **AMORI MIEI** (1978).

My Daughter and I *see* **MUSUME TO WATASHI** (1962).

MY DAUGHTER JOY 1950 d: Gregory Ratoff. UKN., *David Golder*, Irene Nemirovsky, Novel

My Dear Doctor Grasler *see* **MIO CARO DOTTOR GRASLER** (1989).

My Dearest Treasure *see* **TESORO MIO** (1979).

MY DEATH IS A MOCKERY 1952 d: Tony Young. UKN., *My Death Is a Mockery*, Douglas Baber, Novel

MY DOG, THE THIEF 1969 d: Robert Stevenson. USA., Gordon Buford, Story

My Dream City *see* **MINA DROMMARS STAD** (1976).

MY DREAM IS YOURS 1949 d: Michael Curtiz. USA., *Hot Air*, Paul Finder Moss, Jerry Wald, Story

My Enemy the Sea *see* **TAIHEIYO HITORIBOTCHI** (1963).

MY FAIR LADY 1964 d: George Cukor. USA., *Pygmalion*, George Bernard Shaw, London 1913, Play

MY FAMILY AND OTHER ANIMALS 1987 d: Peter Barber-Fleming. UKN/ASL/USA., *My Family and Other Animals*, Gerald Durrell, Book

My Father's Dragon *see* **ELMER NO BOKEN** (1999).

My Father's Glory *see* **LE GLOIRE DE MON PERE** (1989).

My Father's House *see* **BEIT AVI** (1947).

MY FATHER'S HOUSE 1975 d: Alex Segal. USA., *My Father's House*, Philip Kunhardt Jr., Novel

My First Forty Years *see* **I MIEI PRIMI QUARANT'ANNI** (1988).

My First Love *see* **J'AI 17 ANS** (1945).

MY FOOLISH HEART 1949 d: Mark Robson. USA., *Uncle Wiggily in Connecticut*, J. D. Salinger, 1948, Short Story

MY FORBIDDEN PAST 1951 d: Robert Stevenson. USA., *Carriage Entrance*, Polan Banks, 1947, Novel

MY FOUR YEARS IN GERMANY 1918 d: William Nigh. USA., *My Four Years in Germany*, James W. Gerard, New York 1917, Book

My Friend Barbara *see* **MEINE FREUNDIN BARBARA** (1937).

MY FRIEND FLICKA 1943 d: Harold Schuster. USA., *My Friend Flicka*, Mary O'Hara, 1941, Novel

MY FRIEND FROM INDIA 1914 d: Ashley Miller, Harry Beaumont. USA., *My Friend from India*, Henry A. Du Souchet, New York 1912, Play

MY FRIEND FROM INDIA 1927 d: E. Mason Hopper. USA., *My Friend from India*, Henry A. Du Souchet, New York 1912, Play

My Friend Ivan Lapshin *see* **MOI DRUG IVAN LAPSHIN** (1986).

MY FRIEND, THE DEVIL 1922 d: Harry Millarde. USA., *Le Docteur Rameau*, Georges Ohnet, Paris 1889, Novel

MY GAL LOVES MUSIC 1944 d: Edward Lilley. USA., *My Baby Loves Music*, Patricia Harper, Story

MY GAL SAL 1942 d: Irving Cummings. USA., *My Brother Paul*, Theodore Dreiser, 1919, Short Story

MY GIRL TISA 1948 d: Elliott Nugent. USA., *Ever the Beginning*, Lucille S. Prumbs, Sara B. Smith, Play

MY GUN IS QUICK 1957 d: George A. White, Phil Victor. USA., *My Gun Is Quick*, Mickey Spillane, 1950, Novel

My Heart Belongs to You *see* **ICH GLAUBE AN DICH** (1945).

My Heart Hesitates *see* **MON COEUR BALANCE** (1932).

My Heart Wavers *see* **MON COEUR BALANCE** (1932).

My Hot Desire *see* **HET AR MIN LANGTAN** (1956).

My Husband's Getting Married Today *see* **HEUTE HEIRATET MEIN MANN** (1956).

My Husband's Wife *see* **MI MUJER ME GUSTA MAS** (1960).

MY KIDNAPPER, MY LOVE 1980 d: Sam Wanamaker. USA., *The Dark Side of Love*, Oscar Saul, Novel

MY LADY FRIENDS 1921 d: Lloyd Ingraham. USA., *My Lady Friends*, Frank Mandel, Emil Nyitray, New York 1919, Play

MY LADY OF WHIMS 1925 d: Dallas M. Fitzgerald. USA., *Protecting Prue*, Edgar Franklin, 1924, Short Story

MY LADY'S DRESS 1917 d: Alexander Butler. UKN., *My Lady's Dress*, Edward Knoblock, London 1914, Play

My Lady's Dress *see* **BLIND WIVES** (1920).

MY LADY'S GARTER 1920 d: Maurice Tourneur. USA., *My Lady's Garter*, Jacques Futrelle, Chicago 1912, Novel

MY LADY'S LATCHKEY 1921 d: Edwin Carewe. USA., *The Second Latchkey*, Charles N. Williams, Alice Muriel Williamson, Garden City, N.Y. 1920, Novel

My Last Duchess *see* **DARLING DROP DEAD** (1966).

MY LEFT FOOT 1989 d: Jim Sheridan. UKN/IRL., *My Left Foot*, Christy Brown, Book

My Leopold *see* **MEIN LEOPOLD** (1955).

My Life As a Dog *see* **MITT LIV SOM HUND** (1985).

MY LIFE WITH CAROLINE 1941 d: Lewis Milestone. USA., *Le Train Pour Venise*, Georges Berr, Louis Verneuil, Play

MY LIPS BETRAY 1933 d: John G. Blystone. USA., *A Tuenemeny*, Attila Orbok, Budapest 1922, Play

MY LITTLE SISTER 1919 d: Kenean Buel. USA., *My Little Sister*, Elizabeth Robins, New York 1913, Novel

MY LORD CONCEIT 1921 d: F. Martin Thornton. UKN., *My Lord Conceit*, Rita, Novel

My Love and I *see* **KUNGSLEDEN** (1964).

My Love Burns *see* **WAGA KOI WA MOENU** (1949).

MY LOVE CAME BACK 1940 d: Curtis Bernhardt. USA., *Episode*, Walter Reisch, Story

My Love Comes Back *see* **MY LOVE CAME BACK** (1940).

My Love Electra *see* **SZERELMEM ELEKTRA** (1974).

My Love for Yours see HONEYMOON IN BALI (1939).

My Love Has Been Burning see WAGA KOI WA MOENU (1949).

MY LOVER, MY SON 1970 d: John Newland. UKN/USA., *Second Level*, Wilbur Stark, Short Story

My Loves see AMORI MIEI (1978).

MY MADONNA 1915 d: Alice Blache. USA., *My Madonna*, Robert W. Service, 1907, Poem

MY MAN 1924 d: David Smith. USA., *A Tale of Red Roses*, George Randolph Chester, Indianapolis 1914, Novel

MY MAN GODFREY 1936 d: Gregory La CavA. USA., *My Man Godfrey*, Eric Hatch, Boston 1935, Novel

MY MAN GODFREY 1957 d: Henry Koster. USA., *My Man Godfrey*, Eric Hatch, Boston 1935, Novel

My Memories of Old Beijing see CHENG NAN JIU SHI (1982).

My Michael see MICHAEL SHELI (1975).

My Mother see SELF-DEFENSE (1932).

My Mother, the General see EEMI HAGENERALIT (1979).

My Mother's Castle see LA CHATEAU DE MA MERE (1990).

MY MOTHER'S COURAGE 1995 d: Michael Verhoeven. UKN/GRM., *My Mother's Courage*, George Tabori, Novel

My Name Is Ivan see IVANOVO DETSTVO (1962).

MY NAME IS JULIA ROSS 1945 d: Joseph H. Lewis. USA., *The Woman in Red*, Anthony Gilbert, Novel

MY NEIGHBOR'S WIFE 1925 d: Clarence Geldert. USA., *The Other Man's Wife*, James Oliver Curwood, 1920, Short Story

My Niece Susanne see MEINE NICHTE SUSANNE (1950).

My Night at Maud's see MA NUIT CHEZ MAUD (1969).

My Night With Maud see MA NUIT CHEZ MAUD (1969).

My Nights are More Beautiful Than Your Days see MES NUITS SONT PLUS BELLES QUE VOS JOURS (1988).

MY OFFICIAL WIFE 1914 d: James Young. USA., *My Official Wife*, Richard Henry Savage, New York 1891, Novel

MY OFFICIAL WIFE 1926 d: Paul L. Stein. USA., *My Official Wife*, Archibald Clavering Gunter, Play

MY OLD DUCHESS 1933 d: Lupino Lane. UKN., *Mumming Birds*, Fred Karno, Sketch

MY OLD DUTCH 1911 d: George D. Baker. USA., *My Old Dutch*, Albert Chevalier, Poem

MY OLD DUTCH 1926 d: Larry Trimble. USA., *My Old Dutch*, Albert Chevalier, Arthur Shirley, London 1919, Play

My Old Man see UNDER MY SKIN (1950).

MY OUTLAW BROTHER 1951 d: Elliott Nugent. USA., *South of the Rio Grande*, Max Brand, 1936, Novel

My Own Master see SVOGA TJELA GOSPODAR (1957).

MY OWN PAL 1926 d: John G. Blystone. USA., *My Own Pal*, Gerald Beaumont, Story

MY OWN TRUE LOVE 1948 d: Compton Bennett. USA., *Make You a Good Wife*, Yolanda Foldes, Novel

MY PALIKARI 1982 d: Dezso Magyar, Charles S. Dubin. USA., Leon Capetanos, Novel

MY PARTNER 1916 d: Mr. Sanger. USA., *My Partner*, Bartley Campbell, New York 1879, Play

MY PARTNER MR. DAVIS 1936 d: Claude Autant-LarA. UKN., *Il Mio Socio Davis*, Gennaro Prieto, Novel

MY PAST 1931 d: Roy Del Ruth. USA., *Ex-Mistress*, Dora Macy, New York 1930, Novel

My Pretty Mama see MEINE SCHONE MAMA (1958).

MY REPUTATION 1946 d: Curtis Bernhardt. USA., *Instruct My Sorrows*, Clare Jaynes, Novel

My Rice Noodle Soup see HUA QIAO RONG JI (1998).

My Second Wife see SENORA CASADA NECESITA MARIDO (1935).

My Second Wife see THE LADY ESCAPES (1937).

MY SIDE OF THE MOUNTAIN 1969 d: James B. Clark. USA/CND., *My Side of the Mountain*, Jean Craighead George, New York 1969, Novel

MY SIN 1931 d: George Abbott. USA., *Her Past*, Frederick Jackson, London 1929, Play

My Sister and I see MEINE SCHWESTER UND ICH (1929).

MY SISTER AND I 1948 d: Harold Huth. UKN., *High Pavement*, Emery Bonnet, Novel

My Sister and I see MEINE SCHWESTER UND ICH (1954).

MY SISTER EILEEN 1942 d: Alexander Hall. USA., *My Sister Eileen*, Ruth McKinney, Book

MY SISTER EILEEN 1955 d: Richard Quine. USA., *My Sister Eileen*, Ruth McKinney, Book

My Sister's Keeper see A KILLING AFFAIR (1988).

MY SIX CONVICTS 1952 d: Hugo Fregonese. USA., *My Six Convicts*, Donald Powell Wilson, Book

MY SIX LOVES 1963 d: Gower Champion. USA., *My Six Loves*, Peter V. K. Funk, New York 1963, Novel

MY SON 1925 d: Edwin Carewe. USA., *My Son*, Martha M. Stanley, New York 1924, Play

MY SON 1939 d: Joseph Seiden. USA., *My Sonny*, Sholem Secunda, Play

MY SON, MY SON! 1940 d: Charles Vidor. USA., *My Son - My Son!*, Howard Spring, London 1938, Novel

MY SON THE FANATIC 1997 d: Udayan Prasad. UKN., *My Son the Fanatic*, Hanif Kureishi, Short Story

My Sons see MUSUKO (1991).

My Sweet and Tender Animal see MOJ LASKOVYJ I NEZNYJ ZVER (1978).

MY SWEET CHARLIE 1970 d: Lamont Johnson. USA., *My Sweet Charlie*, David Westheimer, New York 1965, Novel

My Sweet Victim see MURDER: BY REASON OF INSANITY (1985).

MY SWEETHEART 1918 d: Meyrick Milton. UKN., *My Sweetheart*, Minnie Palmer, Play

My True Swedish Friend see L' AMICO DEL CUORE (1999).

My Two Husbands see TOO MANY HUSBANDS (1940).

My Uncle, the Gangster see LES TONTONS FLINGUEURS (1963).

My Uncle Theodore see MEIN ONKEL THEODOR (1975).

My Undercover Years With the Ku Klux Klan see UNDERCOVER WITH THE KKK (1979).

My Universities see MOI UNIVERSITETI (1940).

MY UNMARRIED WIFE 1918 d: George Siegmann. USA., *Molly and I and the Silver Ring*, Frank R. Adams, Boston 1915, Novel

My West see IL MIO WEST (1998).

MY WICKED, WICKED WAYS. THE LEGEND OF ERROL FLYNN, THE 1985 d: Don Taylor. USA., *My Wicked, Wicked Ways*, Errol Flynn, Autobiography

My Widow and I see LO SBAGLIO DI ESSERE VIVO (1945).

My Wife see HIS WIFE (1915).

MY WIFE 1918 d: Dell Henderson. USA., *My Wife*, Michael Morton, New York 1907, Play

My Wife Teresa see MEINE FRAU TERESA (1942).

MY WIFE'S FAMILY 1931 d: Monty Banks. UKN., *My Wife's Family*, Harry B. Linton, Hal Stephens, Play

MY WIFE'S FAMILY 1941 d: Walter C. Mycroft. UKN., *My Wife's Family*, Harry B. Linton, Hal Stephens, Play

MY WIFE'S FAMILY 1956 d: Gilbert Gunn. UKN., *My Wife's Family*, Harry B. Linton, Hal Stephens, Play

MY WIFE'S LODGER 1952 d: Maurice Elvey. UKN., *My Wife's Lodger*, Dominic Roche, London 1951, Play

MY WILD IRISH ROSE 1922 d: David Smith. USA., *The Shaughraun*, Dion Boucicault, London 1875, Play

MY WILD IRISH ROSE 1947 d: David Butler. USA., *Song in His Heart*, Rita Olcott, Book

My Younger Brother see MOI MLADSHII BRAT (1962).

Myortvye Dushi see MERTVIYE DUSHI (1960).

MYORTVYI DOM 1932 d: Vasiliy Fyodorov. USS., *Zapiski Iz Myortvogo Doma*, Fyodor Dostoyevsky, 1864, Short Story

MYRA BRECKENRIDGE 1970 d: Mike Sarne. USA., *Myra Breckenridge*, Gore Vidal, Boston 1968, Novel

Myra Meets His Family see HUSBAND HUNTER (1920).

MYSTERE 1919 d: Serrador. FRN., *Slings and Arrows*, Hugh Conway, Novel

MYSTERE A SHANGAI 1950 d: Roger Blanc. FRN., *La Nuit du 13*, Stanislas-Andre Steeman, Novel

MYSTERE BARTON, LE 1948 d: Charles Spaak. FRN., *Le Mystere Barton*, William Hackett, Play

MYSTERE DE LA CHAMBRE JAUNE, LE 1913 d: Emile Chautard. FRN., *Le Mystere de la Chambre Jaune*, Gaston Leroux, Paris 1908, Novel

MYSTERE DE LA CHAMBRE JAUNE, LE 1930 d: Marcel L'Herbier. FRN., *Le Mystere de la Chambre Jaune*, Gaston Leroux, Paris 1908, Novel

MYSTERE DE LA CHAMBRE JAUNE, LE 1948 d: Henri Aisner. FRN., *Le Mystere de la Chambre Jaune*, Gaston Leroux, Paris 1908, Novel

Mystere de la Dame Blonde, Le see LE JUGEMENT DE MINUIT (1932).

Mystere de la Pension Edelweiss, Le see SURSIS POUR UN VIVANT (1958).

MYSTERE DE LA VILLA ROSE, LE 1929 d: Louis Mercanton, Rene Hervil. FRN., *At the Villa Rose*, A. E. W. Mason, 1910, Novel

MYSTERE DU 421, LE 1937 d: Leopold Simons. FRN., *Le Mystere du 421*, Leopold Simons, Play

Mystere du Bois Belleau, Le see LE COLLIER DE CHANVRE (1940).

MYSTERE IMBERGER, LE 1935 d: Jacques Severac. FRN., *Le Spectre de Monsieur Imberger*, Frederic Boutet, Henri Clerc, Henri Gorsse, Play

MYSTERES DE PARIS, LES 1909 d: Victorin Jasset. FRN., *Les Mysteres de Paris*, Eugene Sue, 1842-43, Novel

MYSTERES DE PARIS, LES 1912 d: Albert Capellani, Georges DenolA. FRN., *Les Mysteres de Paris*, Eugene Sue, 1842-43, Novel

MYSTERES DE PARIS, LES 1922 d: Charles Burguet. FRN., *Les Mysteres de Paris*, Eugene Sue, 1842-43, Novel

MYSTERES DE PARIS, LES 1935 d: Felix GanderA. FRN., *Les Mysteres de Paris*, Eugene Sue, 1842-43, Novel

MYSTERES DE PARIS, LES 1943 d: Jacques de Baroncelli. FRN., *Les Mysteres de Paris*, Eugene Sue, 1842-43, Novel

Mysteres de Paris, Les see I MISTERI DI PARIGI (1958).

MYSTERES DE PARIS, LES 1962 d: Andre Hunebelle. FRN/ITL., *Les Mysteres de Paris*, Eugene Sue, 1842-43, Novel

MYSTERES DES BOIS, LES 1908-18. FRN., *Les Mysteres Des Bois*, Ponson Du Terrail

MYSTERIE VAN DE MONDSCHEIN SONATE, HET 1935 d: Kurt Gerron. NTH., *Het Mysterie Van de Monscheinsonate*, Willi Corsari, Novel

MYSTERIES 1977 d: Paul de Lussanets, Fons Rademakers. NTH., *Mysterier*, Knut Hamsun, 1892, Novel

Mysteries of Paris see LES MYSTERES DE PARIS (1962).

Mysteries of Paris, The see LES MYSTERES DE PARIS (1912).

MYSTERIES OF PARIS, THE 1920? d: Ed Cornell. USA., *Les Mysteres de Paris*, Eugene Sue, 1842-43, Novel

Mysteries of Paris, The see LES MYSTERES DE PARIS (1922).

Mysteries of Paris, The see LES MYSTERES DE PARIS (1935).

Mysteries of Paris, The see LES MYSTERES DE PARIS (1943).

Mysteries of Tangier, The see AGUILAS DE ACERO (1927).

Mysteries of the French Secret Police see SECRETS OF THE FRENCH POLICE (1932).

Mysteriet Rygseck see KOMISARIO PLAMUN EREHDYS (1960).

MYSTERIOUS AFFAIR AT STYLES, THE 1990 d: Ross Devenish. UKN., *The Mysterious Affair at Styles*, Agatha Christie, Novel

Mysterious Castle in the Carpathians, The see TAJEMSTVI HRADU V KARPATECH (1981).

Mysterious Doctor of Prague, The see MRTVI ZIJI (1922).

MYSTERIOUS DR. FU MANCHU, THE 1929 d: Rowland V. Lee. USA., Sax Rohmer, Story

Mysterious Dr. R. see MAN MADE MONSTER (1941).

Mysterious Island see TAINSTVENNI OSTROV (1941).

MYSTERIOUS ISLAND 1960 d: Cy Endfield. UKN/USA., *L' Ile Mysterieuse*, Jules Verne, Paris 1874, Novel

Mysterious Island of Captain Nemo, The *see* L' ILE MYSTERIEUSE (1973).

MYSTERIOUS ISLAND, THE 1929 d: Lucien Hubbard, Maurice Tourneur. USA., *L' Ile Mysterieuse*, Jules Verne, Paris 1874, Novel

Mysterious Island, The *see* L' ILE MYSTERIEUSE (1973).

MYSTERIOUS LADY, THE 1928 d: Fred Niblo. USA., *Der Krieg Im Dunkel*, Ludwig Wolff, Berlin 1915, Novel

Mysterious Magician, The *see* DER HEXER (1964).

Mysterious Monk, The *see* DER UNHEIMLICHE MONCH (1965).

Mysterious Mr. Chautard, The *see* THE MAN WITH TWO FACES (1934).

Mysterious Mr. Davis, The *see* MY PARTNER MR. DAVIS (1936).

Mysterious Mr. Reeder, The *see* THE MIND OF MR. REEDER (1939).

Mysterious Mr. Sheffield *see* THE LAW OF 45'S (1935).

MYSTERIOUS MR. WONG, THE 1935 d: William Nigh. USA., *The Twelve Coins of Confucius*, Harry Stephen Keeler, Short Story

MYSTERIOUS MRS. M., THE 1917 d: Lois Weber. USA., Thomas Edgelow, Short Story

Mysterious Mrs. Musslewhite, The *see* THE MYSTERIOUS MRS. M. (1917).

MYSTERIOUS RIDER 1921 d: Benjamin B. Hampton. USA., *The Mysterious Rider*, Zane Grey, New York 1921, Novel

MYSTERIOUS RIDER, THE 1927 d: John Waters. USA., *The Mysterious Rider*, Zane Grey, New York 1921, Novel

MYSTERIOUS RIDER, THE 1933 d: Fred Allen. USA., *The Mysterious Rider*, Zane Grey, New York 1921, Novel

MYSTERIOUS RIDER, THE 1938 d: Lesley Selander. USA., *The Mysterious Stranger*, Zane Grey, New York 1921, Novel

Mysterious Sanatorium, The *see* BULLDOG DRUMMOND (1923).

Mysterious Satellite *see* UCHUJIN TOKYO NI ARAWARU (1956).

MYSTERIOUS SHOT, THE 1914 d: Donald Crisp, James Kirkwood. USA., *The Higher Law*, George Patullo, Story

Mysterious Stranger, The *see* WESTERN GOLD (1937).

MYSTERIOUS STRANGER, THE 1982 d: Peter H. Hunt. UKN/GRM., Mark Twain, Story

Mysterious Traveling Companion *see* SHEN MI DE LU BAN (1955).

MYSTERIOUS WITNESS, THE 1923 d: Seymour Zeliff. USA., *The Stepsons of Light*, Eugene Manlove Rhodes, Boston 1921, Novel

Mystery at the Villa Rose *see* AT THE VILLA ROSE (1929).

Mystery Castle in the Carpathians *see* TAJEMSTVI HRADU V KARPATECH (1981).

MYSTERY CLUB, THE 1926 d: Herbert Blache. USA., *The Crimes of the Armchair Club*, Arthur Somers Roche, 1920, Short Story

MYSTERY GIRL, THE 1918 d: William C. de Mille. USA., *Green Fancy*, George Barr McCutcheon, New York 1917, Novel

MYSTERY HOUSE 1938 d: Noel Smith. USA., *Mystery of Hunting's End*, Mignon G. Eberhart, New York 1930, Novel

Mystery in Room 309 *see* ONE NEW YORK NIGHT (1935).

MYSTERY LINER 1934 d: William Nigh. USA., *The Ghost of John Holling*, Edgar Wallace, 1924, Short Story

MYSTERY OF A HANSOM CAB, THE 1915 d: Harold Weston. UKN., *The Mystery of a Hansom Cab*, Fergus Hume, Novel

MYSTERY OF BOSCOMBE VALE, THE 1912 d: Georges Treville. UKN., *The Mystery of Boscombe Vale*, Arthur Conan Doyle, Short Story

MYSTERY OF BRUDENELL COURT, THE 1924 d: Hugh Croise. UKN., *The Mystery of Brudenell Court*, Baroness Orczy, Short Story

MYSTERY OF DOGSTOOTH CLIFF, THE 1924 d: Hugh Croise. UKN., *The Mystery of Dogstooth Cliff*, Baroness Orczy, Short Story

MYSTERY OF EDWIN DROOD 1935 d: Stuart Walker. USA., *The Mystery of Edwin Drood*, Charles Dickens, London 1870, Novel

MYSTERY OF EDWIN DROOD, THE 1909 d: Arthur Gilbert. UKN., *The Mystery of Edwin Drood*, Charles Dickens, London 1870, Novel

MYSTERY OF EDWIN DROOD, THE 1914 d: Tom Terriss, Herbert Blache. USA., *The Mystery of Edwin Drood*, Charles Dickens, London 1870, Novel

MYSTERY OF EDWIN DROOD, THE 1993 d: Timothy Forder. UKN., *The Mystery of Edwin Drood*, Charles Dickens, London 1870, Novel

MYSTERY OF GREEN PARK, THE 1914. USA., *The Mystery of Green Park*, Arnould Galopin, Novel

Mystery of Hunting's End, The *see* MYSTERY HOUSE (1938).

Mystery of Jack Hilton, The *see* IL MISTERO DI JACK HILTON (1913).

MYSTERY OF MARIE ROGET, THE 1942 d: Phil Rosen. USA., *The Mystery of Marie Roget*, Edgar Allan Poe, 1842, Short Story

MYSTERY OF MR. BERNARD BROWN, THE 1921 d: Sinclair Hill. UKN., *The Mystery of Mr. Bernard Brown*, E. Phillips Oppenheim, 1896, Novel

MYSTERY OF MR. X, THE 1934 d: Edgar Selwyn. USA., *X V Rex*, Philip MacDonald, London 1933, Novel

MYSTERY OF NUMBER 47, THE 1917 d: Otis B. Thayer. USA., *The Mystery of Number 47*, J. Storer Clouston, New York 1911, Novel

Mystery of Oberwald, The *see* IL MISTERO DI OBERWALD (1979).

Mystery of Room 13 *see* MR. REEDER IN ROOM 13 (1938).

MYSTERY OF THE 13TH GUEST, THE 1943 d: William Beaudine. USA., *The Thirteenth Guest*, Armitage Trail, New York 1929, Novel

MYSTERY OF THE DANCING MEN, THE 1923 d: George Ridgwell. UKN., *The Dancing Men*, Arthur Conan Doyle, Short Story

Mystery of the Dead Police, The *see* THE MYSTERY OF MR. X (1934).

MYSTERY OF THE KHAKI TUNIC, THE 1924 d: Hugh Croise. UKN., *The Mystery of the Khaki Tunic*, Baroness Orczy, Short Story

Mystery of the Moonlight Sonata, The *see* HET MYSTERIE VAN DE MONDSCHEIN SONATE (1935).

MYSTERY OF THE TAPESTRY ROOM, THE 1915 d: Murdock MacQuarrie. USA., *The Mystery of the Tapestry Room*, George Edwardes Hall, Story

Mystery of the Villa Rose, The *see* LE MYSTERE DE LA VILLA ROSE (1929).

MYSTERY OF THE WHITE ROOM 1939 d: Otis Garrett. USA., *Murder in the Surgery*, James G. Edwards, New York 1935, Novel

Mystery of the Yellow Room, The *see* LE MYSTERE DE LA CHAMBRE JAUNE (1913).

MYSTERY OF THE YELLOW ROOM, THE 1919 d: Emile Chautard. USA., *Le Mystere de la Chambre Jaune*, Gaston Leroux, Paris 1908, Novel

Mystery of the Yellow Room, The *see* LE MYSTERE DE LA CHAMBRE JAUNE (1930).

Mystery of the Yellow Room, The *see* LE MYSTERE DE LA CHAMBRE JAUNE (1948).

MYSTERY OF THOR BRIDGE, THE 1923 d: George Ridgwell. UKN., *Thor Bridge*, Arthur Conan Doyle, Short Story

Mystery of Thug Island, The *see* I MISTERI DELLA GIUNGLA NERA (1964).

MYSTERY OF WEST SEDGWICK, THE 1913. USA., *The Gold Bag*, Carolyn Wells, Story

Mystery on Monster Island *see* MISTERIO EN LA ISLA DE LOS MONSTRUOS (1981).

MYSTERY RANCH 1932 d: David Howard. USA., *The Killer*, Stewart Edward White, 1919, Short Story

MYSTERY ROAD, THE 1921 d: Paul Powell. USA/UKN., *The Mystery Road*, E. Phillips Oppenheim, Boston 1923, Novel

Mystery Ship *see* SUICIDE FLEET (1931).

MYSTERY STREET 1950 d: John Sturges. USA., Leonhard Spiegelgass, Story

MYSTERY SUBMARINE 1963 d: C. M. Pennington-Richards. UKN., *Mystery Submarine*, Jon Manchip White, Play

Mystery Submarines *see* MYSTERY SUBMARINE (1963).

MYSTERY VALLEY 1928 d: J. P. McGowan. USA., *Snow Dust*, Howard E. Morgan, Story

Mystic Mountain, The *see* RAPT (1934).

Mystifiers, The *see* SYMPHONIE POUR UN MASSACRE (1963).

Mystifies, Les *see* SYMPHONIE POUR UN MASSACRE (1963).

Mystique *see* BRAINWASH (1981).

NA BOIKOM MESTE 1955 d: Vladimir Sukhobokov, Elena Skatchko. USS., *Na Boikom Meste*, Alexander Ostrovsky, 1865, Play

Na Comete *see* NA KOMETE (1970).

NA DACHE 1954 d: Georgy Lomidze. USS., *Na Dache*, Anton Chekhov, 1886, Short Story

NA DIKOM BEREGYE 1967 d: Anatoli Granik. USS., *Na Dikom Beregye*, Boris Nikolaevich Polevoy, 1962, Novel

NA KLANCU 1971 d: Vojko Duletic. YGS., *Na Klancu*, Ivan Cankar, 1902, Novel

NA KOMETE 1970 d: Karel Zeman. CZC., *Hector Servadac*, Jules Verne, 1878, Novel

NA LETNIM BYTE 1926 d: Vladimir Slavinsky. CZC., *Na Letnim Byte*, Josef Stolba, Play

NA RUZICH USTLANO 1934 d: Miroslav Cikan. CZC., *Na Ruzich Ustlano*, Bohumir Polach, Opera

NA SREBRNYM GLOBIE 1977 d: Andrzej Zulawski. PLN., Jerzy Zulawski, Novel

NA SVATEM KOPECKU 1934 d: Miroslav Cikan. CZC., *Na Svatem Kopecku*, Jiri Balda, Rudolf Nizkovsky, Opera

NA TY LOUCE ZELENY 1936 d: Carl Lamac. CZC., *Na Ty Louce Zeleny*, Vaclav Mirovsky, Vladimir Rohan, Karel Tobis, Opera

NA VSYAKOGO MUDRETSA DOVOLNO PROSTOTY 1952 d: A. Dormenko. USS., *Na Vsyakogo Mudretsa Dovolno Prostoty*, Alexander Ostrovsky, 1868, Play

Naaede Faergen, de *see* DE NAEDE FARGEN (1948).

NAAR BONDER ELSKER 1942 d: Arne Weel. DNM., *Naar Bender Elsker*, Jeppe Aakjaer, 1911, Play

NABAB, LE 1913 d: Albert Capellani. FRN., *Le Nabab*, Alphonse Daudet, Novel

NACH DEM STURM 1948 d: Gustav Ucicky. AUS/SWT., *Nach Dem Sturm*, Carl Zuckmayer, Short Story

NACH LANGER ZEIT 1993 d: Robert Mazoyer. GRM/FRN/CND., Jean-Pierre Jaubert, Novel

NACH MITTERNACHT 1981 d: Wolfgang Gremm. GRM., *Nach Mitternacht*, Irmgard Keun, Novel

NACHA REGULES 1950 d: Luis Cesar Amadori. ARG., *Nacha Regules*, Manuel Galvez, 1919, Novel

Nacht Der 1000 Sensationen, Die *see* DER UNMOGLICHE HERR PITT (1938).

Nacht Der 12, Die *see* DIE NACHT DER ZWOLF (1945).

NACHT DER ENTSCHEIDUNG 1956 d: Falk Harnack. GRM., Charles Cordier, Story

NACHT DER ENTSCHEIDUNG, DIE 1931 d: Dimitri Buchowetzki. GRM., *A Tabornok*, Lajos Zilahy, Budapest 1928, Play

NACHT DER ZWOLF, DIE 1945 d: Hans Schweikart. GRM., *Shiva Und Die Nacht Der Zwolf*, Felicitas von Reznicek, Novel

NACHT IM SEPAREE, EINE 1950 d: Hans Deppe. GRM., *Der Wahre Jakob*, Franz Robert Arnold, Ernst Bach, Play

NACHT IN VENEDIG, EINE 1934 d: Robert Wiene, Carmine Gallone. GRM/ITL., *Eine Nacht in Venedig*, Johann Strauss, Berlin 1883, Operetta

NACHT IN VENEDIG, EINE 1953 d: Georg Wildhagen. AUS., *Eine Nacht in Venedig*, Johann Strauss, Berlin 1883, Operetta

NACHT OHNE ABSCHIED 1943 d: Erich Waschneck. GRM., *Nacht Ohne Abschied*, Max W. Kimmich, Short Story

Nachtblende *see* C'EST D'AIMER, L' IMPORTANT (1974).

Nachte Am Bosporus *see* DER DEN MORD BEGING, DER MANN (1930).

NACHTE AM NIL 1949 d: Arthur M. Rabenalt. GRM., *Darf Man? Darf Man Nicht?*, Bobby E. Luthge, Play

NACHTGESTALTEN 1929 d: Hans Steinhoff. GRM., *The Alley Cat*, Anthony Carlyle, Novel

Nachtronde, de *see* TUSSCHEN LIEFDE EN PLICHT (1912).

Nachts, Wenn Dracula Erwacht *see* **EL CONDE DRACULA** (1970).

Nachtsonne *see* **IL SOLE ANCHE DI NOTTE** (1990).

Nacimiento de Salome, El *see* **LA NASCITA DI SALOME** (1940).

NACKT UNTER WOLFEN 1962 d: Frank Beyer. GDR., *Nackt Unter Wolfen*, Bruno Apitz, Halle 1958, Novel

NACKTE BOVARY, DIE 1969 d: Hans Schott-Schobinger. GRM/ITL., *Madame Bovary*, Gustave Flaubert, Paris 1857, Novel

NACKTE UND DER SATAN, DIE 1959 d: Victor Trivas. GRM., Jacques Mage, Story

NAD NIEMNEM 1986 d: Zbigniew Kuzminski, Zbigniew Kaminski. PLN., *Nad Niemnem*, Eliza Orzeszkowa, 1888, Novel

NADA! 1973 d: Claude Chabrol. FRN/ITL., *Nada!*, Jean-Patrick Manchette, Novel

NADA 1947 d: Edgar Neville. SPN., *Nada*, Carmen Laforet Diaz, 1945, Novel

Nada Gang, The *see* **NADA!** (1973).

NADA MAS QUE UNA MUJER 1934 d: Harry Lachman. USA., *The Painted Lady*, Larry Evans, 1912, Short Story

NADA MENOS QUE TODO UN HOMBRE 1971 d: Rafael Gil. SPN/USA., *Nada Menos Que Todo un Hombre*, Miguel de Unamuno, 1916, Short Story

NADARE 1937 d: Mikio Naruse. JPN., *Nadare*, Jiro Osaragi, 1937, Novel

NADIA 1986 d: Amnon Rubinstein. ISR., *Nadia*, Galila Ron-Feder, Book

NADIA, LA FEMME TRAQUEE 1939 d: Claude Orval. FRN., *La Femme Traquee Nadia*, Claude Orval, Short Story

Nadia, la Lutte Secrete *see* **LA FEMME TRAQUEE NADIA** (1939).

NAEDE FARGEN, DE 1948 d: Carl T. Dreyer. DNM., **De Naaede Forgen**, Johannes Vilhelm Jensen, 1925, Short Story

Nagot I Manniskan *see* **JOKIN IHMISESSA** (1956).

NAGRA SOMMARKVALLAR PA JORDEN 1987 d: Gunnel Lindblom. SWD., *Nagra Sommarkvallar Pa Jorden*, Agneta Pleijel, Play

NAIF AUX QUARANTE ENFANTS, LE 1957 d: Philippe Agostini. FRN., *Le Naif aux Quarante Enfants*, Paul Guth, Novel

Nail of Brightness, The *see* **SA MGA KUKO NG LIWANAG MAYNILA** (1975).

Nail, The *see* **EL CLAVO** (1944).

NAIN ROUGE, LE 1998 d: Yvan Le Moine. BLG/FRN/ITL., Michel Tournier, Short Story

NAIS 1945 d: Raymond Leboursier, Marcel Pagnol. FRN., *Nais Micoulin*, Emile Zola, 1884, Short Story

NAIS MICOULIN 1910. FRN., *Nais Micoulin*, Emile Zola, 1884, Short Story

NAISKOHTALOITA 1948 d: Toivo SaakkA. FNL., *Une Vie: l'Humble Verite*, Guy de Maupassant, Paris 1883, Novel

Naissance de Salome, La *see* **LA NASCITA DI SALOME** (1940).

NAJA 1998 d: Angelo Longoni. ITL., *Naja*, Angelo Longoni, Massimo Sgorbani, Play

Nakanune *see* **NAKANUNYE** (1959).

NAKANUNYE 1959 d: Vladimir Petrov. USS/BUL., *Nakanune*, Ivan Turgenev, 1860, Novel

NAKED ALIBI 1954 d: Jerry Hopper. USA., *Cry Copper*, Gladys Atwater, J. Robert Bren, Story

Naked Among the Wolves *see* **NACKT UNTER WOLFEN** (1962).

Naked Among Wolves *see* **NACKT UNTER WOLFEN** (1962).

Naked and Satan, The *see* **DIE NACKTE UND DER SATAN** (1959).

NAKED AND THE DEAD, THE 1958 d: Raoul Walsh. USA., *The Naked and the Dead*, Norman Mailer, 1948, Novel

Naked Angel, The *see* **EL ANGEL DESNUDO** (1946).

Naked As the Wind from the Sea *see* **SOM HAVETS NAKNA VIND** (1968).

Naked Autumn *see* **LES MAUVAIS COUPS** (1961).

NAKED CIVIL SERVANT, THE 1975 d: Jack Gold. UKN., *The Naked Civil Servant*, Quentin Crisp, Autobiography

Naked Country, The *see* **MORRIS WEST'S THE NAKED COUNTRY** (1985).

NAKED EDGE, THE 1961 d: Michael Anderson. UKN., *First Train to Babylon*, Max Simon Ehrlich, New York 1955, Novel

NAKED EVIL 1966 d: Stanley Goulder. UKN., *The Obi*, Jon Manchip White, Play

Naked Eye, The *see* **LA MIRADA DEL OTRO** (1998).

NAKED FACE, THE 1984 d: Bryan Forbes. USA., *The Naked Face*, Sidney Sheldon, Novel

NAKED HEART, THE 1950 d: Marc Allegret. UKN/CND/FRN., *Maria Chapdelaine; Recit du Canada Francais*, Louis Hemon, 1916, Novel

Naked Hours, The *see* **LE ORE NUDE** (1964).

NAKED IN THE SUN 1957 d: R. John Hugh. USA., *The Warrior*, Frank G. Slaughter, 1956, Novel

NAKED JUNGLE, THE 1954 d: Byron Haskin. USA., *Leiningen Vs. the Ants*, Carl Stephenson, 1940, Short Story

Naked Lady Bovary *see* **DIE NACKTE BOVARY** (1969).

NAKED LUNCH, THE 1991 d: David Cronenberg. CND/UKN., *The Naked Lunch*, William S. Burroughs, Novel

NAKED MAN, THE 1923 d: Henry Edwards. UKN., *Felix Gets a Month*, Tom Gallon, Leon M. Lion, Play

Naked Man, The *see* **O HOMEM NU** (1968).

NAKED RUNNER, THE 1967 d: Sidney J. Furie. UKN., *The Naked Runner*, Francis Clifford, London 1966, Novel

Naked Spur, The *see* **HOT SPUR** (1968).

NAKED TANGO 1990 d: Leonard Schrader. USA/ARG., Manuel Puig, Story

Naked Truth, The *see* **LA DONNA NUDA** (1914).

Naked Truth, The *see* **THE PERFECT LOVER** (1919).

Naked Under Leather *see* **GIRL ON A MOTORCYCLE** (1968).

Naked Weekend, The *see* **BRAINWASH** (1981).

Naked Winds of the Sea, The *see* **SOM HAVETS NAKNA VIND** (1968).

Naked Woman, The *see* **LA FEMME NUE** (1949).

NAKHALENOK 1961 d: Yevgyeni Karelov. USS., *Nakhalenok*, Mikhail Sholokhov, 1926, Short Story

NAKHLEBNIK 1953 d: Vladimir Basov, M. Korchagin. USS., *Nakhlebnik*, Ivan Turgenev, 1869, Play

Nakoz Alenky *see* **NECO Z ALENKY** (1987).

NALIM 1938 d: Sergei Sploshnov. USS., *Nalim*, Anton Chekhov, 1885, Short Story

NALIM 1953 d: Alexei Zolotnitzkie. USS., *Nalim*, Anton Chekhov, 1885, Short Story

NAM IRUVAR 1947 d: A. V. Meiyappan. IND., *Nam Iruvar*, P. Neelakantan, Play

Name Der Rose, Der *see* **THE NAME OF THE ROSE** (1986).

NAME OF THE ROSE, THE 1986 d: Jean-Jacques Annaud. ITL/GRM/FRN., *Il Nome Della Rosa*, Umberto Eco, 1980, Novel

NAME THE WOMAN 1928 d: Erle C. Kenton. USA., *Bridge*, Erle C. Kenton, Story

Nameless Castle, The *see* **NEVTELEN VAR** (1982).

Nameless Heroes *see* **WU MING YING XIONG** (1958).

NAMIS 1996 d: Ulzhan KoldauovA. KZK., *The Ordinary Life*, Dulat Isabekov

NAN OF MUSIC MOUNTAIN 1917 d: George Melford. USA., *Nan of Music Mountain*, Frank Hamilton Spearman, New York 1916, Novel

NANA 1912. DNM., *Nana*, Emile Zola, Paris 1880, Novel

NANA 1914 d: Ugo Pittei. ITL., *Nana*, Emile Zola, Paris 1880, Novel

NANA 1917 d: Camillo de Riso. ITL., *Nana*, Emile Zola, Paris 1880, Novel

Nana *see* **UNA DONNA FUNESTA** (1919).

NANA 1926 d: Jean Renoir. FRN/GRM., *Nana*, Emile Zola, Paris 1880, Novel

NANA 1934 d: Dorothy Arzner. USA., *Nana*, Emile Zola, Paris 1880, Novel

NANA 1944 d: Celestino Gorostiza, Roberto Gavaldon. MXC., *Nana*, Emile Zola, Paris 1880, Novel

NANA 1955 d: Christian-Jaque. FRN/ITL., *Nana*, Emile Zola, Paris 1880, Novel

NANA 1968. UKN., *Nana*, Emile Zola, Paris 1880, Novel

NANA 1970 d: Mac Ahlberg. SWD/FRN., *Nana*, Emile Zola, Paris 1880, Novel

NANA 1982 d: Dan Wolman. GRM/FRN., *Nana*, Emile Zola, Paris 1880, Novel

NANBANJI NO SEMUSHI-OTOKO 1957 d: Torajiro Saito. JPN., *Notre-Dame de Paris*, Victor Hugo, Paris 1831, Novel

NANCE 1920 d: Albert Ward. UKN., *Nance*, Charles Garvice, Novel

NANCY 1922 d: H. B. Parkinson. UKN., *Oliver Twist*, Charles Dickens, London 1838, Novel

NANCY DREW AND THE HIDDEN STAIRCASE 1939 d: William Clemens. USA., *The Hidden Staircase*, Carolyn Keene, New York 1930, Novel

NANCY DREW -DETECTIVE 1938 d: William Clemens. USA., *The Password to Larkspur Lane*, Carolyn Keene, New York 1933, Novel

Nancy from Naples *see* **BEHAVE! OH! SAILOR** (1930).

NANCY FROM NOWHERE 1922 d: Chester M. Franklin. USA., *Spring Fever*, Grace Drew Brown, Katherine Pinkerton, Story

Nancy Lee *see* **THE WAY OF A WOMAN** (1919).

NANCY STEELE IS MISSING! 1937 d: George Marshall. USA., *Ransom*, Charles Francis Coe, Philadelphia 1934, Novel

Nancy's Affair *see* **SMART WOMAN** (1931).

Nancy's Private Affair *see* **SMART WOMAN** (1931).

Naniwa Elegy *see* **NANIWA EREJI** (1936).

NANIWA EREJI 1936 d: Kenji Mizoguchi. JPN., *Mieko*, Saburo Okada, Serial

Naniwa Hika *see* **NANIWA EREJI** (1936).

NANNY, THE 1965 d: Seth Holt. UKN., *The Nanny*, Evelyn Piper, New York 1964, Novel

NANO ROSSO, IL 1917 d: Elvira Notari. ITL., *Raffaella O I Misteri Del Vecchio Mercato*, Carolina Invernizio, Novel

NANON 1924 d: Hanns Schwarz. GRM., *Nanon*, Richard Genee, F. von Zell, Play

NANON 1938 d: Herbert Maisch. GRM., *Nanon*, Richard Genee, F. von Zell, Play

Nanynka Kulichova's Marriage *see* **VDAVKY NANYNKY KULICHOVY** (1925).

Nanynka Kulichova's Wedding *see* **VDAVKY NANYNKY KULICHOVY** (1941).

NAOMI & WYNONNA: LOVE CAN BUILD A BRIDGE 1995 d: Bobby Roth. USA., *Love Can Build a Bridge*, Naomi Judd, Bud Schaetzle, Autobiography

NAPASTA 1982 d: Alexa Visarion. RMN., *Napasta*, Ion Luca Caragiale, 1890, Play

NAPLES AU BAISER DE FEU 1925 d: Serge Nadejdine, Jacques Robert. FRN., *Naples Au Baiser de Feu*, Auguste Bailly, Novel

NAPLES AU BAISER DE FEU 1937 d: Augusto GeninA. FRN., *Naples Au Baiser de Feu*, Auguste Bailly, Novel

NAPOLEON II L'AIGLON 1961 d: Claude Boissol. FRN., *Napoleon II l'Aiglon*, Andre Castelot, Novel

NAPOLI, MILIONARIA 1950 d: Eduardo de Filippo. ITL., *Napoli Milionaria!*, Eduardo de Filippo, 1945, Play

NAPPALI SOTETSEG 1963 d: Zoltan Fabri. HNG., *Nappali Sotetseg*, Boris Palotai, Novel

NAR ANGARNA BLOMMAR 1946 d: Erik Faustman. SWD., *En Natt I Juli*, Jan Fridegard, 1933, Novel

NARA LIVET 1958 d: Ingmar Bergman. SWD., *Det Vangila Vardiga*, Ulla Isaksson, Story

NARAYAMA BUSHI-KO 1958 d: Keisuke KinoshitA. JPN., *Narayamabushi-Ko*, Shichiro Fukazawa, 1956, Short Story

NARAYAMA BUSHI-KO 1983 d: Shohei ImamurA. JPN., *Narayamabushi-Ko*, Shichiro Fukazawa, 1956, Short Story

NARAYANA 1920 d: Leon Poirier. FRN., *La Peau de Chagrin*, Honore de Balzac, Paris 1831, Novel

Narcissus and Psyche *see* **NARCISZ ES PSYCHE** (1980).

NARCISZ ES PSYCHE 1980 d: Gabor Body. HNG., *Psyche: Egy Hajdani Koltono Irasai*, Sandor Weores, 1972, Novel

Narcosis *see* **NARKOSE** (1929).

NARKOSE 1929 d: Alfred Abel. GRM., *Brief Einer Unbekannten*, Stefan Zweig, 1922, Short Story

NARR SEINER LIEBE, DER 1929 d: Olga TschechowA. GRM., *Poliche*, Henry Bataille, 1906, Play

NARREN IM SCHNEE 1938 d: Hans Deppe. GRM., *Narren Im Schnee*, Roland Betsch, Novel

NARROW CORNER, THE 1933 d: Alfred E. Green. USA., *The Narrow Corner*, W. Somerset Maugham, London 1932, Novel

NARROW PATH, THE 1918 d: George Fitzmaurice. USA., *The Narrow Path*, John Montague, New York 1909, Play

NARROW STREET, THE 1924 d: William Beaudine. USA., *The Narrow Street*, Edwin Bateman Morris, Philadelphia 1924, Novel

NARROWING CIRCLE, THE 1956 d: Charles Saunders. UKN., *The Narrowing Circle*, Julian Symons, Novel

NASANU NAKA 1932 d: Mikio Naruse. JPN., *Nasanu Naka*, Yanagawa Shunyo, 1912-13, Novel

NASCITA DI SALOME, LA 1940 d: Jean Choux. ITL/SPN/FRN., *La Nascita Di Salome*, Cesare Meano, Play

NASE XI. 1936 d: Vaclav Binovec. CZC., *Ta Nase Jedenactka*, H. G. Rubell, Novel

NASHESTVIYE 1945 d: Abram Room, Oleg Zhakov. USS., *Nashestviye*, Leonid Maksimovich Leonov, 1942, Play

NASHORNER, DIE 1963 d: Jan LenicA. PLN/GRM., *Le Rhinoceros*, Eugene Ionesco, 1959, Play

Nashta Neerh *see* CHARULATA (1964).

Nashville Lady *see* THE COAL MINER'S DAUGHTER (1980).

NASI FURIANTI 1937 d: Vladislav Vancura, Vaclav Kubasek. CZC., *Nasi Furianti*, Ladislav Stroupeznicky, Play

Naso Di Cuoio *see* NEZ-DE-CUIR (1952).

NASTASIA FILIPOVNA 1958 d: Ivan Pyriev. USS., *Idiot*, Fyodor Dostoyevsky, 1868, Novel

Nastro d'Argento *see* LA FIGLIA DEL CAPITANO (1947).

NASTY HABITS 1976 d: Michael Lindsay-Hogg. UKN/USA., *The Abbess of Crewe; a Modern Morality Tale*, Muriel Spark, 1974, Novel

Nasty Love *see* L' AMORE MOLESTO (1995).

Natacha *see* MOSCOW NIGHTS (1935).

NATALE IN CASA D'APPUNTAMENTO 1976 d: Armando Nannuzzi. ITL., *Natale in Casa d'Appuntamento*, Ugo Moretti, Novel

NATALKA POLTAVKA 1937 d: Edgar G. Ulmer, Vasile Avramenko. USA., *Natalka Poltavka*, Iwan Kotlyarevsky, 1818, Opera

NATHALIE 1957 d: Christian-Jaque. FRN/ITL., *Nathalie Princesse*, Frank Marchal, Novel

NATHALIE AGENT SECRET 1959 d: Henri Decoin. FRN/ITL., *Nathalie Agent Secret*, Frank Marchal, Novel

NATHAN DER WEISE 1967 d: Franz Peter Wirth. GRM., *Nathan Der Weise*, Gotthold Ephraim Lessing, 1779, Play

Nathan Hale *see* THE HEART OF A HERO (1916).

Nathaniel Hawthorne's "Twice-Told Tales" *see* TWICE-TOLD TALES (1963).

National Health, Or Nurse Norton's Affair, The *see* THE NATIONAL HEALTH (1973).

NATIONAL HEALTH, THE 1973 d: Jack Gold. UKN., *Nurse Norton's Affair, the National Health; Or*, Peter Nichols, 1970, Play

National Lampoon's Joy of Sex *see* THE JOY OF SEX (1984).

NATIONAL VELVET 1944 d: Clarence Brown. USA., *National Velvet*, Edith Bagnold, 1935, Novel

Native Drums *see* TAM TAM MAYUMBE (1955).

Native Son *see* SANGRE NEGRA (1948).

NATIVE SON 1986 d: Jerrold Freedman. USA., *Native Son*, Richard Wright, 1940, Novel

NATIVITY, THE 1978 d: Bernard L. Kowalski. USA., *The Nativity*, Marjorie Holmes, Novel

NATT PA GLIMMINGEHUS, EN 1954 d: Torgny Wickman. SWD., *Brollopsbesvar*, Stig Dagerman, Stockholm 1949, Novel

NATTLEK 1966 d: Mai Zetterling. SWD., *Night Games*, Mai Zetterling, London 1966, Novel

NATTMARA 1965 d: Arne Mattsson. SWD., Patrick Hamilton, Play

NATUN YAHUDI 1953 d: Salil Sen. IND., *Natun Yahudi*, Salil Sen, Play

Natural Born Salesman, A *see* EARTHWORM TRACTORS (1936).

NATURAL LAW, THE 1917 d: Charles H. France. USA., *The Natural Law*, Howall Hall, New York 1915, Play

NATURAL, THE 1984 d: Barry Levinson. USA., *The Natural*, Bernard Malamud, 1952, Novel

NATURE OF THE BEAST, THE 1988 d: Franco Rosso. UKN., *The Nature of the Beast*, Janni Howker, Novel

Nature's Mistakes *see* FREAKS (1932).

NATZIV HAMELACH 1979 d: Haim Shiran. ISR., *Natziv Hamelach*, Albert Memmi, Book

Naufrage du Pacifique, Le *see* ROBINSON CRUSOE (1950).

NAUFRAGIO 1916 d: Umberto Paradisi. ITL., *Cuore*, Edmondo de Amicis, 1886, Short Story

NAUFRAGIO 1977 d: Jaime Humberto Hermosillo. MXC., *Tomorrow*, Joseph Conrad, 1903, Short Story

Naufrago Del Pacifico, Il *see* ROBINSON CRUSOE (1950).

NAUFRAGO, IL 1909. ITL., *Robinson Crusoe*, Daniel Defoe, 1719, Novel

Naughty Arlette *see* THE ROMANTIC AGE (1949).

Naughty Blue Knickers *see* LES FOLIES D'ELODIE (1981).

NAUGHTY BUT NICE 1927 d: Millard Webb. USA., *The Bigamists*, Lewis Allen Browne, Story

NAUGHTY DUCHESS, THE 1928 d: Tom Terriss. USA., *The Indiscretion of the Duchess*, Anthony Hope, New York 1894, Novel

NAUGHTY MARIETTA 1935 d: W. S. Van Dyke. USA., *Naughty Marietta*, Victor Herbert, Rida Johnson Young, London 1910, Operetta

Naughty Nun *see* BELLA ANTONIA PRIMA MONICA E POI DIMONIA (1972).

Naughty Wife, The *see* LET'S ELOPE (1919).

NAUKA DUBI 1946 d: Nitin Bose. IND., *Nauka Dubi*, Rabindranath Tagore, 1916, Novel

Naukadubi *see* NAUKA DUBI (1946).

NAUKAR KI KAMEEZ 1999 d: Mani Kaul. IND/NTH., *Naukar Ki Kameez*, Kumar Shukla, Novel

NAULAHKA, THE 1918 d: George Fitzmaurice. USA., *Naulahka: a Story of West and East*, Charles W. Balestier, London 1892, Novel, *Naulahka; a Story of West and East*, Rudyard Kipling, London 1892, Novel

NAVAL TREATY, THE 1922 d: George Ridgwell. UKN., *The Naval Treaty*, Arthur Conan Doyle, Short Story

Naval Treaty, The *see* THE ADVENTURES OF SHERLOCK HOLMES: THE NAVAL TREATY (1984).

NAVALHA NA CARNE, A 1970 d: Braz Chediak. BRZ., *Navalha Na Carne*, Plinio Marcos, 1968, Play

NAVE DELLE DONNE MALEDETTE, LA 1953 d: Raffaello Matarazzo. ITL., *Histoire de 130 Femmes*, Leon Gozlan, Novel

NAVE, LA 1912 d: Eduardo BencivengA. ITL., *La Nave*, Gabriele D'Annunzio, 1908, Play

NAVE, LA 1921 d: Gabriellino d'Annunzio, Mario Roncoroni. ITL., *La Nave*, Gabriele D'Annunzio, 1908, Play

NAVIRE AVEUGLE, LE 1927 d: Joseph Guarino, Adelqui Millar. FRN., *Le Navire Aveugle*, Jean Barreyre, Novel

Navire Des Filles Perdues, Le *see* LA NAVE DELLE DONNE MALEDETTE (1953).

Navire Des Hommes Perdus, Le *see* DAS SCHIFF DER VERLORENEN MENSCHEN (1929).

NAVY BLUE AND GOLD 1937 d: Sam Wood. USA., *Navy Blue and Gold*, George Bruce, New York 1937, Novel

NAVY BOUND 1951 d: Paul Landres. USA., *Navy Bound*, Talbot Josselyn, 1935, Short Story

NAVY COMES THROUGH, THE 1942 d: A. Edward Sutherland. USA., *Pay to Learn*, Borden Chase, Story

Navy Girl *see* NAVY SECRETS (1939).

NAVY SECRETS 1939 d: Howard Bretherton. USA., *Shore Leave*, Steve Fisher, 1938, Short Story

NAVY VS. THE NIGHT MONSTERS, THE 1966 d: Michael Hoey. USA., *Monster from the Earth's End*, Murray Leinster, Greenwich CT. 1959, Novel

NAVY WIFE 1935 d: Allan Dwan. USA., *Beauty's Daughter*, Kathleen Norris, New York 1935, Novel

Nazacat Na Krepostta *see* PAZACHAT NA KREPOSTTA (1974).

NAZAR 1990 d: Mani Kaul. IND., *The Meek Creature*, Fyodor Dostoyevsky, Story

NAZARIN 1958 d: Luis Bunuel. MXC., *Nazarin*, Benito Perez Galdos, Madrid 1895, Novel

NE JOUEZ PAS AVEC LES MARTIANS 1967 d: Henri Lanoe. FRN., *Les Sextuples de Locmaria*, Michel Labry, Novel

NE REVEILLEZ PAS UN FLIC QUI DORT 1988 d: Jose Pinheiro. FRN., *Ne Reveillez Pas un Flic Qui Dort*, Catherine Storr, Novel

Neak Sre *see* NEAK SRI (1992).

NEAK SRI 1992 d: Rithy Panh. CMB/FRN., *Ranju Sepanjang Jalan*, Shahnon Ahmad, Novel

NEAL OF THE NAVY 1915 d: William M. Harvey, William Bertram. USA., *Neal of the Navy*, William Hamilton Osborne, Story

NEAMUL SOIMARESTILOR 1965 d: Mircea Dragan. RMN., *Neamul Soimarestilor*, Mihail Sadoveanu, 1915, Novel

Near-Honest Adultery, A *see* UN ADULTERIO CASI DECENTE (1969).

NEARLY A NASTY ACCIDENT 1961 d: Don Chaffey. UKN., *Touch Wood*, David Carr, David Stringer, Play

NEARLY MARRIED 1917 d: Chet Withey. USA., *Nearly Married*, Edgar Selwyn, New York 1913, Play

Neat Lola *see* DIE TOLLE LOLA (1954).

NECESSARY EVIL, THE 1925 d: George Archainbaud. USA., *Uriah's Son*, Stephen Vincent Benet, 1924, Short Story

NECESSITY 1988 d: Michael Miller. USA., *Necessity*, Brian Garfield, Novel

Necklace for My Beloved, A *see* OZERELE DLJA MOEJ LJUBIMOJ (1972).

NECKLACE, THE 1909 d: D. W. Griffith. USA., *Le Collier*, Guy de Maupassant, Short Story

Neco Nese Voda *see* HRST VODY (1969).

NECO Z ALENKY 1987 d: Jan Svankmajer. SWT/GRM/UKN., *Alice's Adventures in Wonderland*, Lewis Carroll, London 1865, Book

N'ecrivez Jamais *see* CAPITAINE BLOMET (1947).

NED MCCOBB'S DAUGHTER 1929 d: William J. Cowen. USA., *Ned McCobb's Daughter*, Sidney Coe Howard, Play

NEDRA 1915 d: Edward Jose. USA., *Nedra*, George Barr McCutcheon, New York 1905, Novel

NEECHA NAGAR 1946 d: Chetan Anand. IND., *The Lower Depths*, Maxim Gorky, 1902, Play

NEEDFUL THINGS 1994 d: Fraser C. Heston. USA., *Needful Things*, Stephen King, Novel

Ne'er Do Well, The *see* THE NE'ER-DO-WELL (1915).

NE'ER-DO-WELL, THE 1915 d: Colin Campbell. USA., *The Ne'er-Do-Well*, Rex Beach, New York 1911, Novel

NE'ER-DO-WELL, THE 1923 d: Alfred E. Green. USA., *The Ne'er-Do-Well*, Rex Beach, New York 1911, Novel

NEGATIVES 1968 d: Peter Medak. UKN., *Negatives*, Peter Everett, London 1964, Novel

Neglected Wives *see* WHY WOMEN SIN (1920).

Neglected Women *see* THE GREAT WELL (1924).

NEGRO QUE TENIA EL ALMA BLANCA, EL 1926 d: Benito Perojo. SPN/FRN., *El Negro Que Tenia El Aima Blanca*, Alberto Insua, 1922, Novel

NEGRO QUE TENIA EL ALMA BLANCA, EL 1933 d: Benito Perojo. SPN., *El Negro Que Tenia El Alma Blanca*, Alberto Insua, 1922, Novel

NEGRO QUE TENIA EL ALMA BLANCA, EL 1951 d: Hugo Del Carril. ARG/SPN., *El Negro Que Tenia El Alma Blanca*, Alberto Insua, 1922, Novel

Neider Nicht Gezahlt, Die *see* JESUS VON OTTAKRING (1976).

NEIGE ETAIT SALE, LA 1952 d: Luis Saslavsky. FRN., *La Neige Etait Sale*, Georges Simenon, 1948, Novel

NEIGE SUR LES PAS, LA 1923 d: Henri Etievant. FRN., *La Neige Sur Les Pas*, Henri Bordeaux, Novel

NEIGE SUR LES PAS, LA 1941 d: Andre Berthomieu. FRN., *La Neige Sur Les Pas*, Henri Bordeaux, Novel

NEIGHBORS 1981 d: John G. Avildsen. USA., *Neighbors*, Thomas Berger, 1980, Novel

Neighbour, The *see* KILLING 'EM SOFTLY (1982).

NEIGUNGSEHE 1944 d: Carl Froelich. GRM., *Neigungsehe*, Jochen Kuhlmey, Play, *Familie Buchholz*, Julius Stinde, Novel

NEIL SIMON'S BROADWAY BOUND 1991 d: Paul Bogart. USA., *Broadway Bound*, Neil Simon, 1987, Play

NEIL SIMON'S LONDON SUITE 1996 d: Jay Sandrich. USA., *London Suite*, Neil Simon, Play

NEITHER BY DAY NOR BY NIGHT 1974 d: Steven Hilliard Stern. USA/ISR., Abraham Raz, Play

NEW ADVENTURES OF GET RICH QUICK WALLINGFORD, THE 1931 d: Sam Wood. USA., George Randolph Chester, Short Stories

NEW ADVENTURES OF PIPPI LONGSTOCKING, THE 1988 d: Ken Annakin. USA/SWD., Astrid Lindgren, Story

New Adventures of Schweik, The see NOVIYE POKHOZDENIYA SHVEIKA (1943).

New Adventures of the Robber Hotzenplotz, The see NEUES VOM RAUBER HOTZENPLOTZ (1978).

New Angels, The see I NUOVI ANGELI (1962).

New Bordertown see BORDERTOWN (1935).

NEW BROOMS 1925 d: William C. de Mille. USA., *New Brooms*, Frank Craven, New York 1925, Play

NEW CENTURIONS, THE 1972 d: Richard Fleischer. USA., *The New Centurions*, Joseph Wambaugh, 1971, Novel

New Clothes see UBRANIE PRAWIE NOWE (1963).

NEW CLOWN, THE 1916 d: Fred Paul. UKN., *The New Clown*, H. M. Paull, London 1902, Play

NEW COMMANDMENT, THE 1925 d: Howard Higgin. USA., *Invisible Wounds*, Frederick Palmer, New York 1925, Novel

New Deal, The see LOOKING FORWARD (1933).

New Drama, A see UN DRAMA NUEVO (1946).

NEW EVE AND OLD ADAM 1967 d: Gerald Dynevor. UKN., *New Eve and Old Adam*, Gerald Dynevor, Short Story

NEW FACES OF 1937 1937 d: Leigh Jason. USA., *Shoestring*, George Bradshaw, 1933, Short Story, *Day at the Brokers*, David Freedman, 1936, Play

New Gentlemen, The see LES NOUVEAUX MESSIEURS (1928).

New Governor, The see THE NIGGER (1915).

New Gulliver, A see NOVYI GULLIVER (1935).

New Heroes and Heroines see XIN ER NU YING XIONG ZHUAN (1951).

New Land, The see INVANDRARNA (1970).

New Lease of Death, A see INSPECTOR WEXFORD: A NEW LEASE OF DEATH (1991).

NEW LIFE, A 1909. USA., *Les Miserables*, Victor Hugo, Paris 1862, Novel

NEW MAGDALEN, THE 1910 d: Joseph A. Golden. USA., *The New Magdalen*, Wilkie Collins, 1873, Novel

NEW MAGDALEN, THE 1912 d: Herbert Brenon. USA., *The New Magdalen*, Wilkie Collins, 1873, Novel

NEW MAGDALEN, THE 1914 d: Travers Vale. USA., *The New Magdalen*, Wilkie Collins, 1873, Novel

New Mexico see FOUR FACES WEST (1948).

NEW MOON 1931 d: Jack Conway. USA., *New Moon*, Oscar Hammerstein II, Sigmund Romberg, New York 1928, Musical Play

NEW MOON 1940 d: Robert Z. Leonard. USA., *New Moon*, Oscar Hammerstein II, Sigmund Romberg, New York 1928, Musical Play

NEW MORALS FOR OLD 1932 d: Charles J. Brabin. USA., *After All*, John Van Druten, London 1930, Play

New Orleans Blues see BLUES IN THE NIGHT (1941).

NEW ROSE HOTEL 1998 d: Abel FerrarA. USA., William Gibson, Short Story

NEW SCHOOL TEACHER, THE 1924 d: Gregory La CavA. USA., *The Young Nuts of America*, Irvin S. Cobb, 1923, Short Story

New Tales of the Taira Clan see SHIN HEIKE MONOGATARI (1955).

NEW TEACHER, THE 1922 d: Joseph J. Franz. USA., *The Island of Faith*, Margaret Elizabeth Sangster, New York 1921, Novel

NEW TENANT, THE 1964 d: George Brandt. UKN., *Le Nouveau Locataire*, Eugene Ionesco, 1958, Play

NEW TOYS 1925 d: John S. Robertson. USA., *New Toys*, Milton Herbert Gropper, Arthur Hammerstein, New York 1924, Play

New Vidas, The see VEDHAM PUDITHU (1987).

New Wallingford, The see THE NEW ADVENTURES OF GET RICH QUICK WALLINGFORD (1931).

New Wizard of Oz, The see THE SCARECROW OF OZ HIS MAJESTY (1914).

New Year Sacrifice see ZHUFU (1956).

NEW YEAR'S EVE 1929 d: Henry Lehrman. USA., *$100.00*, Richard Connell, 1928, Short Story

New Year's Sacrifice see ZHUFU (1956).

NEW YORK 1916 d: George Fitzmaurice. USA., *New York*, William Hurlbut, New York 1910, Play

NEW YORK CONFIDENTIAL 1955 d: Russell Rouse. USA., *New York Confidential*, Jack Lait, Lee Mortimer, 1948, Book

NEW YORK NIGHTS 1929 d: Lewis Milestone. USA., *Tin Pan Alley*, Hugh Stange, New York 1928, Play

NEW YORK NIGHTS 1984 d: Simon Nuchtern, Romano Vanderbes. USA., *Der Reigen*, Arthur Schnitzler, 1900, Play

New York-Parigi Per Una Condanna a Morte see CANNABIS (1969).

NEWLY RICH 1931 d: Norman Taurog. USA., *Let's Play King*, Sinclair Lewis, 1931, Short Story

Newspaper Story see FRONT PAGE STORY (1954).

NEWTON BOYS, THE 1998 d: Richard Linklater. USA., *The Newton Boys*, Claude Stanush, Book

NEXT CORNER, THE 1924 d: Sam Wood. USA., *The Next Corner*, Kate Jordan, Boston 1921, Novel

Next Corner, The see TRANSGRESSION (1931).

NEXT DOOR 1975 d: Andrew Silver. USA., *Next Door*, Kurt Vonnegut Jr., 1968, Short Story

Next Door Neighbor, The see TALK ABOUT A STRANGER (1952).

Next Time We Live see NEXT TIME WE LOVE (1936).

NEXT TIME WE LOVE 1936 d: Edward H. Griffith. USA., *Next Time We Live*, Ursula Parrott, New York 1935, Novel

NEXT TO NO TIME 1958 d: Henry Cornelius. UKN., *The Enchanted Hour*, Paul Gallico, Novel

Nez de Cuir see NEZ-DE-CUIR (1952).

Nez de Cuir, Gentilhomme d'Amour see NEZ-DE-CUIR (1952).

NEZABYVAYEMI 1919-J GOD 1951 d: Mikhail Chiaureli. USS., *Nezabyvayemyi 1919 God*, Vsevolod Vishnevsky, 1949, Play

NEZ-DE-CUIR 1952 d: Yves Allegret, Jacques Sigurd. FRN/ITL., *Nez de Cuir*, Jean de La Varende, Novel

NEZLOBTE DEDECKA 1934 d: Carl Lamac. CZC., *V Tlame Velryby*, Emil Artur Longen, Play

Ngo Oi Chuifong see WO AI CHUFANG (1997).

NI HONG DENG XIA DE SHAO BING 1964 d: Wang Ping, Ko Hsin. CHN., *Ni Hong Deng XIa de Shao Bing*, Shen XImeng, Play

NI LIV 1957 d: Arne Skouen. NRW., David Howarth, Novel

Ni Saints Ni Saufs see LES FELINS (1964).

NI VU, NI CONNU. 1958 d: Yves Robert. FRN., *L' Affaire Blaireau*, Alphonse Allais, 1899, Novel

NIAN QING DE YI DAI 1965 d: Zhao Ming. CHN., *Nian Qing de Yi Dai*, Chen Yun, Play

NIAN QING DE YI DAI 1976 d: Ling Zhiao, Zhang Huijun. CHN., *Nian Qing de Yi Dai*, Chen Yun, Play

NICCOLO DE' LAPI 1909. ITL., *Niccolo De' Lapi*, Massimo d'Azeglio, 1841, Novel

NICE GIRL? 1941 d: William A. Seiter. USA., *Nice Girl?*, Phyllis Duganne, Play

NICE GIRL LIKE ME, A 1969 d: Desmond Davis. UKN., *Marry at Leisure*, Anne Piper, New York 1959, Novel

Nice Guys Finish Last see FOOTSTEPS (1972).

NICE LITTLE BANK THAT SHOULD BE ROBBED, A 1958 d: Henry Levin. USA., Evan Wylie, Story

NICE PEOPLE 1922 d: William C. de Mille. USA., *Nice People*, Rachel Crothers, New York 1921, Play

NICE WOMEN 1932 d: Edwin H. Knopf. USA., *Nice Women*, William A. Grew, New York 1929, Play

NICHIREN 1978 d: Noboru NakamurA. JPN., *Nichiren*, Matsutaro Kawaguchi, Novel

NICHOLAS AND ALEXANDRA 1971 d: Franklin J. Schaffner. UKN., *Nicholas and Alexandria*, Robert K. Massie, Book

NICHOLAS NICKLEBY 1912 d: George Nicholls. USA., *Nicholas Nickleby*, Charles Dickens, London 1870, Novel

NICHOLAS NICKLEBY 1948 d: Alberto Cavalcanti. UKN., *Nicholas Nickleby*, Charles Dickens, London 1870, Novel

Nicht Versohnt see WO GEWALT HERRSCHT' NICHT VERSOHNT ODER "ES HILFT NUR GEWALT" (1965).

NICHT VERSOHNT ODER "ES HILFT NUR GEWALT, WO GEWALT HERRSCHT" 1965 d: Jean-Marie Straub, Daniele Huillet. GRM., *Billard Um Halb Zehn*, Heinrich Boll, Cologne 1959, Novel

NICHTEN DER FRAU OBERST, DIE 1968 d: Erwin C. Dietrich, Edoardo MulargiA. GRM/ITL., *Die Nichten Der Frau Oberst*, Guy de Maupassant, Short Story

NICHTEN DER FRAU OBERST, DIE 1980 d: Erwin C. Dietrich. SWT., *Die Nichten Der Frau Oberst*, Guy de Maupassant, Short Story

NICHTS ALS ARGER MIT DER LIEBE 1956 d: Thomas Engel. AUS., *Das Konzert*, Hermann Bahr, 1909, Play

NICHTS ALS SUNDE 1965 d: Hanus Burger. GDR., *Twelfth Night*, William Shakespeare, c1600, Play

Nick Carter and the Red Club see NICK CARTER ET LE TREFLE ROUGE (1965).

Nick Carter E Il Trifoglio Rosso see NICK CARTER ET LE TREFLE ROUGE (1965).

NICK CARTER ET LE TREFLE ROUGE 1965 d: Jean-Paul Savignac. FRN/ITL., *Nick Carter Et le Trefle Rouge*, Claude Rank, Novel

NICKEL MOUNTAIN 1984 d: Drew Denbaum. USA., *Nickel Mountain*, John Gardner, Novel

Nicolas de Flue - Paix Sur Terre see NIKLAUS VON FLUE - PACEM IN TERRIS (1963).

NICOLE ET SA VERTU 1931 d: Rene Hervil. FRN., *Nicole E Sa Vertu*, Felix Gandera, Play

NIDO DI FALASCO, IL 1950 d: Guido Brignone. ITL., *Il Nido Di Falasco*, Luigi Ugolini, Novel

NIE WIEDER LIEBE 1931 d: Anatole Litvak. GRM., *Nie Wieder Liebe*, Julius Berstel, Play

NIEBEZPIECZNY ROMANS 1930 d: Michael Waszynski. PLN., *Fortuna Kasjera Spiewankiewicza*, Andrzej Strug, 1928, Novel

NIEBLA 1975 d: Jose JarA. SPN., *Niebla*, Miguel de Unamuno, 1914, Novel

NIECE D'AMERIQUE, LA 1913. FRN., *La Niece d'Amerique*, E. Ravet, Play

Nieces of Frau Oberst, The see DIE NICHTEN DER FRAU OBERST (1968).

Nieces of the Colonel's Wife, The see DIE NICHTEN DER FRAU OBERST (1968).

NIENTE ROSE PER OSS 117 1968 d: Jean-Pierre Desagnat, Renzo Cerrato. FRN/ITL., *Pas de Roses a Ispahan Pour O.S.S. 117*, Jean Bruce, Novel

Nieve Estaba Sucia, La see LA NEIGE ETAIT SALE (1952).

NIGGER, THE 1915 d: Edgar Lewis. USA., *The Nigger*, Edward Sheldon, New York 1909, Play

Night see NOITE (1985).

Night. a Train, A see UN TRAIN, UN SOIR (1968).

Night Affair see LE DESORDRE ET LA NUIT (1958).

NIGHT AFTER NIGHT 1932 d: Archie Mayo. USA., *Single Night*, Louis Bromfield, 1932, Story

NIGHT ALONE 1938 d: Thomas Bentley. UKN., *Night Alone*, Jeffrey Dell, London 1937, Play

Night Ambush see ILL MET BY MOONLIGHT (1956).

Night and Day see NOCE I DNIE (1975).

NIGHT AND MORNING 1915 d: Wilfred Noy. UKN., *Night and Morning*, Edward George Bulwer Lytton, Novel

NIGHT AND THE CITY 1950 d: Jules Dassin. UKN/USA., *Night and the City*, Gerald Kersh, 1938, Novel

NIGHT AND THE CITY 1992 d: Irwin Winkler. USA., *Night and the City*, Gerald Kersh, 1938, Novel

Night at Glimminge Castle see EN NATT PA GLIMMINGEHUS (1954).

Night at the Crossroads see LA NUIT DU CARREFOUR (1932).

Night Before Christmas, A see VECHERA NA KHUTORE BLIZ DIKANKI (1961).

NIGHT BEFORE THE DIVORCE, THE 1942 d: Robert Siodmak. USA., Ladislaus Fodor, Gina Kaus, Play

Night Breed see NIGHTBREED (1989).

Night Bus see IT HAPPENED ONE NIGHT (1934).

Night Caller from Outer Space see THE NIGHT CALLER (1966).

NIGHT CALLER, THE 1966 d: John Gilling. UKN., *The Night Callers*, Frank Crisp, London 1960, Novel

Night Child see NIGHT HAIR CHILD (1971).

Night Club see NIGHT CLUB GIRL (1944).

NIGHT CLUB GIRL 1944 d: Eddie Cline. USA., *Night Life*, Adele Commandini, Story

Night-Round, The see TUSSCHEN LIEFDE EN PLICHT (1912).

Nights and Days see NOCE I DNIE (1975).

Nights are Long in Hamburg, The see IN HAMBURG SIND DIE NACHTE LANG (1955).

Nights in Andalusia see ANDALUSISCHE NACHTE (1938).

Nights of Fire see NUITS DE FEU (1937).

Nights of Love in the Taiga see LIEBESNACHTE IN DER TAIGA (1967).

Nights of Lucretia Borgia, The see LE NOTTI DI LUCREZIA BORGIA (1959).

Nights of Temptation see LE NOTTI DI LUCREZIA BORGIA (1959).

Nights of Terror see TWICE-TOLD TALES (1963).

Nights on the Nile see NACHTE AM NIL (1949).

Nightstick see ALIBI (1929).

NIGHTWING 1979 d: Arthur Hiller. USA/NTH., *Nightwing*, Martin Cruz Smith, Novel

NIHON CHINBOTSU 1973 d: Shiro Moritani, Andrew Meyer. JPN., *Nihon Chinbotsu*, Shinobu Hashimoto, Novel

NIHON NO ICHIBAN NAGAI HI 1967 d: Kihachi Okamoto. JPN., *Nippon No Ichiban Nagai Hi*, Soichi Oya, Tokyo 1965, Short Story

NIHON NO SEISHUN 1968 d: Masaki Kobayashi. JPN., *Dokkoisho*, Shusaku Endo, 1967, Novel

NIHONBASHI 1956 d: Kon IchikawA. JPN., *Nihonbashi*, Kyoka Izumi, 1914, Novel

NIJI NO HASHI 1993 d: Zenzo MatsuyamA. JPN., *Niji No Hashi*, Fujiko Sawada, Novel

NIJINSKY 1980 d: Herbert Ross. USA/UKN., *Nijinsky*, Romola Nijinsky, Book, *The Diary of Vaslav Nijinsky*, Vaslav Nijinsky, Book

NIJUSHI NO HITOMI 1954 d: Keisuke KinoshitA. JPN., *Nijushi No Hitomi*, Sakae Tsuboi, 1952, Novel

NIJUSHI NO HITOMI 1988 d: Yoshitaka AsamA. JPN., *Nijushi No Hitomi*, Sakae Tsuboi, 1952, Novel

NIKDO SE NEBUDE SMAT 1965 d: Hynek Bocan. CZC., *Nikdo Se Nebude Smat*, Milan Kundera, 1963, Short Story

NIKKI, WILD DOG OF THE NORTH 1961 d: Jack Couffer, Don Haldane. USA/CND., *Nomads of the North*, James Oliver Curwood, New York 1919, Novel

NIKLAUS VON FLUE - PACEM IN TERRIS 1963 d: Michel Dickoff. SWT., *Niklaus von Flue*, Heinrich Federer, Leipzig 1928, Book

NIKOLETINA BURSAC 1964 d: Branko Bauer. YGS., *Dozivljaji Nikoletine Bursaca*, Branko Copic, 1956, Short Story

NIKUTAI NO GAKKO 1965 d: Ryo KinoshitA. JPN., *Nikutai No Gakko*, Yukio Mishima, Tokyo 1964, Novel

NIKUTAI NO MON 1948 d: Masahiro Makino. JPN., *Nikutai No Mon*, Tajiro Tamura, 1947, Novel

NIKUTAI NO MON 1964 d: Seijun Suzuki. JPN., *Nikutai No Mon*, Tajiro Tamura, 1947, Novel

NILS HOLGERSSONS UNDERBARA RESA 1962 d: Kenne Fant. SWD., *Nils Holgerssons Underbara Resa*, Selma Lagerlof, 1906-07, Novel

NINA 1956 d: Rudolf Jugert. GRM., *Romeo Und Julia in Wien*, Milo Dor, Reinhard Federmann, Novel

NINA 1958 d: Jean Boyer. FRN., *Nina*, Andre Roussin, 1951, Play

Nina see A MATTER OF TIME (1976).

Nina B Affair, The see AFFAIRE NINA B (1961).

NINA DE LUZMELA, LA 1949 d: Jose Gascon. SPN., *La Nina de Luzmela*, Concha Espina de Serna, 1909, Novel

NINA, NON FAR LA STUPIDA 1937 d: Nunzio MalasommA. ITL., *Nina Non Far la Stupida*, Gian Capo, Play

NINA OF THE THEATRE 1914 d: George Melford. USA., *Nina of the Theatre*, Rupert Hughes, Story

Nina Petrovna see LA MENSONGE DE NINA PETROVNA (1937).

Nine and a Half Weeks see 9½ WEEKS (1984).

NINE FORTY-FIVE 1934 d: George King. UKN., *Nine Forty-Five*, Sewell Collins, Owen Davis, Play

NINE GIRLS 1944 d: Leigh Jason. USA., *Nine Girls*, William H. Pettit, Play

Nine Hours to Live see NINE HOURS TO RAMA (1963).

NINE HOURS TO RAMA 1963 d: Mark Robson. UKN/USA., *Nine Hours to Rama*, Stanley Wolpert, New York 1962, Novel

Nine Lives see NI LIV (1957).

NINE TILL SIX 1932 d: Basil Dean. UKN., *Nine Till Six*, Aimee Stuart, Philip Stuart, London 1930, Play

NINETEEN EIGHTY-FOUR 1954 d: Rudolph Cartier. UKN., *Nineteen Eighty-Four*, George Orwell, 1949, Novel

Nineteen Year Old's Plan, A see JUKYUSAI NO CHIZU (1979).

NINETY AND NINE, THE 1916 d: Ralph Ince. USA., *The Ninety and Nine*, Ramsay Morris, New York 1902, Play

NINETY AND NINE, THE 1922 d: David Smith. USA., *The Ninety and Nine*, Ramsay Morris, New York 1902, Play

Ninety Nights and One Day see SETTE CONTRO LA MORTE (1965).

Ninety-Two in the Shade see 92° IN THE SHADE (1975).

NINFA PLEBEA 1996 d: Lina Wertmuller. ITL., *Ninfa Plebea*, Domenico Rea, Novel

NINGEN NO JOKEN I 1959 d: Masaki Kobayashi. JPN., *Ningen No Joken Vol. 1 & 2*, Jumpei Gomikawa, Kyoto 1958, Novel

NINGEN NO JOKEN II 1959 d: Masaki Kobayashi. JPN., *Ningen No Joken Vol. 3 & 4*, Jumpei Gomikawa, Novel

NINGEN NO JOKEN III 1961 d: Masaki Kobayashi. JPN., *Ningen No Joken Vol. 5 & 6*, Jumpei Gomikawa, Novel

NINGEN NO SHOMEI 1977 d: Junya Sato. JPN., *Ningen No Shomei*, Seiichi Morimura, Novel

NINI 1962 d: Shlomo Suryano. ISR., *Nini*, Meir Zarchi, Book

NINI FALPALA 1933 d: Amleto Palermi. ITL., *Il Coraggio*, Augusto Novelli, Play

NINI VERBENA 1913 d: Baldassarre Negroni. ITL., *L' Anima Del Demi-Monde*, Augusto Genina, Short Story

NINICHE 1918 d: Camillo de Riso. ITL., *Niniche*, A. N. Hennequin, Albert Milhaud, 1878, Play

Ninjitsu see YAGYU BUGEICHO (1957).

Ninjutsu see YAGYU BUGEICHO -SORYU HIKEN (1958).

NINNA NANNA 1914 d: Guglielmo Zorzi. ITL., *Le Petit Jacques*, Jules Claretie, 1881, Novel

NINNOLA 1920 d: Orlando Vassallo. ITL., *L' Amica Del Cuore*, Alfredo Testoni, 1914, Play

NINO DE LAS MONJAS, EL 1925 d: Antonio Calvache. SPN., *El Nino de Las Monjas*, Juan Lopez Nunez, Novel

NINO DE ORO, EL 1925 d: Jose Maria GranadA. SPN., *El Nino de Oro*, Jose Maria Granada, Play

NINOS DEL HOSPICIO, LOS 1926 d: Jose Fernandez. SPN., *Los Ninos Del Hospicio*, Jover Y Valenti, Play

NINTH CONFIGURATION, THE 1980 d: William Peter Blatty. USA., *The Ninth Configuration*, William Peter Blatty, Novel

NINTH GUEST, THE 1934 d: R. William Neill. USA., *The Ninth Guest*, Gwen Bristow, Bruce Manning, New Orleans 1930, Novel

NIOBE 1915 d: Hugh Ford, Edwin S. Porter. USA., *Niobe*, Edward A. Paulton, Harry Paulton, London 1892, Play

NIPOTI D'AMERICA, LE 1921 d: Camillo de Riso. ITL., *L' Ajo Nell'Imbarazzo*, Giovanni Giraud, 1807, Play

Nipoti Della Colonnella, Le see DIE NICHTEN DER FRAU OBERST (1968).

NIPPER, THE 1930 d: Louis Mercanton. UKN., *La Mome*, A. Acremont, Michel Carre, Play

Nippon Chinbotsu see NIHON CHINBOTSU (1973).

Nippon No Ichiban Nagai Hi see NIHON NO ICHIBAN NAGAI HI (1967).

Nippon No Seishun see NIHON NO SEISHUN (1968).

NISHAN 1949 d: S. S. Vasan. IND., *Les Freres Corses*, Alexandre Dumas (pere), 1845, Short Story

NISKAVUOREN AARNE 1954 d: Edvin Laine. FNL., *Niskavuoren Leipa*, Hella Wuolijoki, 1938, Play

NISKAVUOREN HETA 1952 d: Edvin Laine. FNL., *Niskavuoren Heta*, Hella Wuolijoki, 1950, Play

NISKAVUOREN NAISET 1938 d: Valentin VaalA. FNL., *Niskavuoren Naiset*, Hella Wuolijoki, 1936, Play

NISKAVUOREN NAISET 1958 d: Valentin VaalA. FNL., *Niskavuoren Naiset*, Hella Wuolijoki, 1936, Play

NISKAVUORI 1984 d: Matti KassilA. FNL., *Niskavuoren Leipa*, Hella Wuolijoki, 1938, Play, *Niskavuoren Naiset*, Hella Wuolijoki, 1936, Play

Niskavuori Fights see NISKAVUORI TAISTELEE (1957).

NISKAVUORI TAISTELEE 1957 d: Edvin Laine. FNL., *Entas Nyt Niskavuori?*, Hella Wuolijoki, 1953, Play

Niskavuoris Kamp see NISKAVUORI TAISTELEE (1957).

NO 1998 d: Robert Lepage. CND., *Les Sept Branches de la Riviere Ota*, Robert Lepage, Play

NO. 5 JOHN STREET 1921 d: Kenelm Foss. UKN., *No. 5 John Street*, Richard Whiteing, Novel

NO. 7 BRICK ROW 1922 d: Fred W. Durrant. UKN., *Brick Row No.7*, William Riley, Novel

No Answer from F.P.1 see F.P.1 ANTWORTET NICHT (1932).

No Beast So Fierce see STRAIGHT TIME (1978).

No Bed of Her Own see GIRL WITHOUT A ROOM (1933).

NO BLADE OF GRASS 1970 d: Cornel Wilde. UKN., *The Death of Grass*, John Christopher, London 1956, Novel

No Brakes see YEAH! OH (1929).

No Burials on Sunday see ON N'ENTERRE PAS LE DIMANCHE (1959).

No Cannons Roar see NO GREATER GLORY (1934).

NO CONTROL 1927 d: Scott Sidney, E. J. Babille. USA., *Speed But No Control*, Frank Condon, 1924, Short Story

No Crossing the Bridge see MOST PEREYTI NELIEYA (1960).

No Crying He Makes see INSPECTOR WEXFORD: NO CRYING HE MAKES (1988).

NO DEFENSE 1921 d: William Duncan. USA., *The Comeback*, J. Raleigh Davies, Story

NO DEJES LA PUERTA ABIERTA 1933 d: Lewis Seiler. USA., *Pleasure Cruise*, Austen Allen, London 1932, Play

NO DOWN PAYMENT 1957 d: Martin Ritt. USA., *No Down Payment*, John McPartland, 1957, Novel

NO ENCONTRE ROSAS PARA MI MADRE 1972 d: Francisco Rovira BeletA. SPN/FRN/ITL., *Non Ho Trovato Rose Per Mia Madre*, Jose Antonio Garcia Blasquez, Short Story

NO ESCAPE 1936 d: Norman Lee. UKN., *No Exit*, George Goodchild, Frank Witty, London 1936, Play

No Exit see NO ESCAPE (1936).

No Exit see HONOR AND OH-BABY! LOVE (1940).

No Exit see HUIS-CLOS (1954).

NO EXIT 1962 d: Tad Danielewski. USA/ARG., *Huis Clos*, Jean-Paul Sartre, Paris 1944, Play

No Experience Required see THE POINTING FINGER (1919).

No Gold for a Dead Diver see EIN TOTER TAUCHER NIMMT KEIN GELD (1975).

NO GREATER GLORY 1934 d: Frank Borzage. USA., *A Pal-Utcai Fiuk*, Ferenc Molnar, 1907, Novel

No Greater Love see NINGEN NO JOKEN I (1959).

NO HABRA MAS PENA NI OLVIDO 1985 d: Hector OliverA. ARG., *No Habra Mas Pena Ni Olvido*, Osvaldo Soriano, Novel

NO HANDS ON THE CLOCK 1941 d: Frank McDonald. USA., *No Hands on the Clock*, Daniel Mainwaring, Novel

NO HIGHWAY 1951 d: Henry Koster. UKN/USA., *No Highway*, Nevil Shute, 1948, Novel

No Highway in the Sky see NO HIGHWAY (1951).

NO KIDDING 1960 d: Gerald Thomas. UKN., *Beware of Children*, Verily Anderson, London 1958, Novel

No Laughing Matter see NIKDO SE NEBUDE SMAT (1965).

No Les Digas Que Cai see SI TE DICEN QUE CAI (1988).

No Less Than a Real Man see NADA MENOS QUE TODO UN HOMBRE (1971).

NO LIMIT 1935 d: Monty Banks. UKN., Walter Greenwood, Story

No Linha Do Horizonte see LE FIL DE L'HORIZON (1993).

NO LOVE FOR JOHNNIE 1961 d: Ralph Thomas. UKN., *No Love for Johnnie*, Wilfred Fienburgh, London 1959, Novel

NO MAN OF HER OWN 1950 d: Mitchell Leisen. USA., *I Married a Dead Man*, Cornell Woolrich, 1948, Novel

No Man Walks Alone see BLACK LIKE ME (1964).

No Man's Daughter see ARVACSKA (1976).

NO MAN'S GOLD 1926 d: Lewis Seiler. USA., *Dead Man's Gold*, J. Allen Dunn, New York 1920, Novel

NO MAN'S LAND 1918 d: Will S. Davis. USA., *No Man's Land*, Louis Joseph Vance, New York 1910, Novel

No Man's Woman *see* INGEN MANS KVINNA (1953).

NO MARRIAGE TIES 1933 d: J. Walter Ruben. USA., *Ad-Man*, Charles Curran, Arch A. Gaffney, 1932, Play

No Medals for Martha *see* THE WEAKER SEX (1948).

No Mercy *see* SIN COMPASION (1994).

No More Dying Then *see* INSPECTOR WEXFORD: NO MORE DYING THEN (1989).

NO MORE LADIES 1935 d: Edward H. Griffith, George Cukor (Uncredited). USA., *No More Ladies*, A. E. Thomas, New York 1934, Play

No More Love *see* NIE WIEDER LIEBE (1931).

NO MORE ORCHIDS 1933 d: Walter Lang. USA., *No More Orchids*, Grace Perkins, New York 1932, Novel

No More Yesterdays *see* LADY OF SECRETS (1936).

NO MOTHER TO GUIDE HER 1923 d: Charles Horan. USA., *No Mother to Guide Her*, Lillian Mortimer, Play

NO, MY DARLING DAUGHTER! 1961 d: Ralph Thomas. UKN., *Handful of Tansy (Don't Tell Father)*, Kay Bannerman, Harold Brooke, 1959, Play

NO NAME ON THE BULLET 1959 d: Jack Arnold. USA., *The Death Rider*, Harold Amacker, Story

NO, NO NANETTE 1930 d: Clarence Badger. USA., *No No Nanette*, Otto Harbach, Frank Mandel, New York 1925, Musical Play

NO, NO NANETTE 1940 d: Herbert Wilcox. USA., *No No Nanette*, Otto Harbach, Frank Mandel, New York 1925, Musical Play

No One Cheers *see* WUREN HECAI (1993).

NO ONE MAN 1932 d: Lloyd Corrigan. USA., *No One Man*, Rupert Hughes, New York 1931, Novel

No Orchids for Lulu *see* LULU (1962).

NO ORCHIDS FOR MISS BLANDISH 1948 d: St. John L. Clowes. UKN., *No Orchids for Miss Blandish*, James Hadley Chase, Novel

NO PLACE FOR JENNIFER 1950 d: Henry Cass. UKN., *No Difference to Me*, Phyllis Hambledon, Novel

No Place Like Homicide *see* WHAT A CARVE UP! (1961).

NO PLACE TO GO 1927 d: Mervyn Leroy. USA., *Isles of Romance*, Richard Connell, 1924, Short Story

NO PLACE TO GO 1939 d: Terry O. Morse. USA., *Old Man Minick*, Edna Ferber, 1922, Short Story

No Power on Earth *see* THE BIG GUY (1940).

No Questions Asked *see* BEWARE OF BACHELORS (1928).

NO QUIERO, NO QUIERO 1938 d: Francisco Elias. SPN., *No Quiero No Quiero!*, Jacinto Benavente y Martinez, 1928, Play

NO RANSOM 1934 d: Fred Newmeyer. USA., *The Big Mitten*, Damon Runyon, Short Story

No Relations *see* SANS FAMILLE (1925).

NO RESTING PLACE 1951 d: Paul RothA. UKN., *No Resting Place*, Ian Niall, Novel

NO ROAD BACK 1957 d: Montgomery Tully. UKN., *Madame Tictac*, Falkland Cary, Philip Weathers, 1950, Play

NO ROOM AT THE INN 1948 d: Daniel Birt. UKN., *No Room at the Inn*, Joan Temple, London 1945, Play

No Room for the Groom *see* A MILLIONAIRE FOR CHRISTY (1951).

NO ROOM FOR THE GROOM 1952 d: Douglas Sirk. USA., *My True Love*, Darwin L. Teilhet, Novel

No Room for Wild Animals *see* KEIN PLATZ FUR WILDE TIERE (1956).

No Roses for Oss 117 *see* NIENTE ROSE PER OSS 117 (1968).

NO SAD SONGS FOR ME 1950 d: Rudolph Mate. USA., *No Sad Songs for Me*, Ruth Southard, Novel

NO SE LO DIGAS A NADIE 1998 d: Francisco Lombardi. SPN/PRU., *No Se Lo Digas a Nadie*, Jaime Bayly, Novel

NO SEX PLEASE - WE'RE BRITISH 1973 d: Cliff Owen. UKN., *No Sex Please - We're British*, Alistair Foot, Anthony Marriott, Play

NO SMOKING 1955 d: Henry Cass. UKN., *No Smoking*, George Moresby-White, Rex Rienits, Television Play

NO STORY 1917 d: Thomas R. Mills. USA., *No Story*, O. Henry, Short Story

No Time for Breakfast *see* DOCTEUR FRANCOISE GAILLAND (1975).

NO TIME FOR COMEDY 1940 d: William Keighley. USA., *No Time for Comedy*, S. N. Behrman, Indianapolis 1939, Play

No Time for Ecstasy *see* LA FETE ESPAGNOLE (1961).

No Time for Pity *see* TIME WITHOUT PITY (1957).

NO TIME FOR SERGEANTS 1958 d: Mervyn Leroy. USA., *No Time for Sergeants*, Mac Hyman, Novel

No Time for Tears *see* PURPLE HEART DIARY (1951).

NO TIME TO MARRY 1938 d: Harry Lachman. USA., *'Twas the Night Before Christmas*, Paul Gallico, 1937, Short Story

No Tomorrow *see* INGEN MORGONDAG (1957).

No Townhouse for Robin Hood *see* KEIN REIHENHAUS FUR ROBIN HOOD (1980).

No Toys for Christmas *see* ONCE BEFORE I DIE (1965).

NO TRAINS NO PLANES 1999 d: Jos Stelling. NTH., *Broederweelde*, Jean Paul Franssens, Novel

No Tree in the Street *see* NO TREES IN THE STREET (1959).

NO TREES IN THE STREET 1959 d: J. Lee Thompson. UKN., *No Trees in the Street*, Ted Willis, Liverpool 1948, Play

NO TRESPASSING 1922 d: Edwin L. Hollywood. USA., *The Rise of Roscoe Paine*, Joseph C. Lincoln, New York 1912, Novel

NO WAY BACK 1949 d: Stefan Osiecki. UKN., *Beryl and the Croucher*, Thomas Burke, Short Story

NO WAY OUT 1987 d: Roger Donaldson. USA., *The Big Clock*, Kenneth Fearing, 1946, Novel

NO WAY TO TREAT A LADY 1968 d: Jack Smight. USA., *No Way to Treat a Lady*, William Goldman, New York 1964, Novel

NO WOMAN KNOWS 1921 d: Tod Browning. USA., *Fanny Herself*, Edna Ferber, New York 1917, Novel

No.99 *see* NUMBER 99 (1920).

Noah's Ark *see* L' ARCHE DE NOE (1946).

NOAPTE FURTUNOASA, O 1943 d: Jean Georgescu. RMN., *O Noapte Furtunoasa*, Ion Luca Caragiale, 1879, Play

NOBI 1959 d: Kon IchikawA. JPN., *Nobi*, Shohei Ooka, Tokyo 1952, Novel

NOBLE BACHELOR, THE 1921 d: Maurice Elvey. UKN., *The Noble Bachelor*, Arthur Conan Doyle, Short Story

Noblemen from Casa Mourisca, The *see* OS FIDALGOS DA CASA MOURISCA (1938).

NOBLESSE OBLIGE 1918 d: Marcello Dudovich?. ITL., *Noblesse Oblige!*, Maurice Hennequin, Pierre Veber, 1910, Play

Nobody Applauds *see* WUREN HECAI (1993).

Nobody Gets the Last Laugh *see* NIKDO SE NEBUDE SMAT (1965).

Nobody Likes to Die Under Palms *see* WER STIRBT SCHON GERNE UNTER PALMEN? (1974).

NOBODY LIVES FOREVER 1946 d: Jean Negulesco. USA., *Nobody Lives Forever*, William Riley Burnett, 1943, Novel

Nobody Loves a Drunken Indian *see* FLAP (1969).

Nobody Loves Flapping Eagle *see* FLAP (1969).

Nobody Makes Me Cry *see* BETWEEN FRIENDS (1983).

NOBODY RUNS FOREVER 1968 d: Ralph Thomas. UKN., *The High Commissioner*, Jon Cleary, London 1966, Novel

Nobody Shall Be Laughing *see* NIKDO SE NEBUDE SMAT (1965).

Nobody Will Laugh *see* NIKDO SE NEBUDE SMAT (1965).

Nobody's Bride *see* WHICH WOMAN? (1918).

NOBODY'S CHILD 1919 d: George Edwardes Hall. UKN., *The Whirlpool*, George Edwardes Hall, Play

NOBODY'S KID 1921 d: Howard Hickman. USA., *"Frequently Martha" Mary Cary*, Kate Langley Bosher, New York 1910, Novel

Nobody's Land *see* TERRA DI NESSUNO (1939).

NOBODY'S MONEY 1923 d: Wallace Worsley. USA., *Nobody's Money*, William le Baron, New York 1921, Play

NOBODY'S PERFECT 1968 d: Alan Rafkin. USA., *The Crows of Edwina Hill*, Allan R. Bosworth, New York 1961, Novel

NOBODY'S PERFEKT 1981 d: Peter Bonerz. USA., *Two for the Price of One*, Tony Kenrick, Novel

NOBODY'S WIDOW 1927 d: Donald Crisp. USA., *Nobody's Widow*, Avery Hopwood, New York 1910, Play

Noc Poslubna *see* EN BROLLOPSNATT (1959).

Nocciolo Della Questione, Il *see* THE HEART OF THE MATTER (1983).

NOCE I DNIE 1975 d: Jerzy Antczak. PLN., *Noce I Dnie*, Maria Dabrowska, 1934-35, Novel

NOCES BARBARES, LES 1987 d: Marion Hansel. BLG/FRN., *Les Noces Barbares*, Yann Queffelec, Novel

NOCES CORINTHIENNES, LES 1908-18. FRN., *Les Noces Corinthiennes*, Anatole France, Play

Noces de Sang *see* ORS AL-DAM (1977).

Noces de Sang *see* BODAS DE SANGRE (1980).

NOCES VENITIENNES, LES 1958 d: Alberto Cavalcanti. FRN/ITL., *Les Noces Venitiennes*, Abel Hermant, Novel

Noces Venitiennes, Les *see* LA PRIMA NOTTE (1959).

Noch Pered Rozhdestvom *see* VECHERA NA KHUTORE BLIZ DIKANKI (1961).

NOCHE DEL SABADO, LA 1950 d: Rafael Gil. SPN., *La Noche Del Sabado*, Jacinto Benavente y Martinez, 1903, Play

NOCHE TERRIBLE 1967 d: Rodolfo Kuhn. ARG., *Noche Terrible*, Roberto Arlt, 1933, Short Story

Noches de Monsieur Max, Las *see* LA TETE DU CLIENT (1964).

NOCNI MOTYL 1941 d: Frantisek Cap. CZC., *Medvedi a Tanecnice*, Karel Novak, Novel

Nocturnal Butterfly *see* NOCNI MOTYL (1941).

NOCTURNE INDIEN 1988 d: Alain Corneau. FRN., *Nocturne Indienne*, Antonio Tabucchi, Novel

NOEUD DE VIPERES, LE 1990 d: Jacques TreboutA. FRN., *Le Noeud de Viperes*, Francois Mauriac, Novel

NOGA 1991 d: Nikita Tjagunov. RSS., *The Leg*, W. Faulkner, Story

NOGIKU NO GOTOKI KIMI NARIKI 1955 d: Keisuke KinoshitA. JPN., *Nogiku No Haka*, Sachio Ito, 1906, Novel

Noh Mask Murders, The *see* TENKAWA DENSETSU SATSUJIN JIKEN (1991).

Noi Due Senza Domani *see* LE TRAIN (1973).

Noi Tre Soltanto *see* THREE (1969).

NOI VIVI 1942 d: Goffredo Alessandrini. ITL., *We the Living*, Ayn Rand, 1936, Novel

NOIA, LA 1964 d: Damiano Damiani. ITL/FRN., *La Noia*, Alberto Moravia, Milan 1960, Novel

NOIEMBRIE, ULTIMUL BAL 1989 d: Dan PitA. RMN., *Locul Unde Nu S-a Intimplat Nimic*, Mihail Sadoveanu, 1933, Novel

NOIRE DE., LA 1967 d: Ousmane Sembene. SNL/FRN., *Voltaique*, Ousmane Sembene, 1962, Short Story

NOISES OFF 1992 d: Peter Bogdanovich. USA., *Noises Off*, Michael Frayn, Play

NOITA PALAA ELAMAAN 1952 d: Roland Hallstrom. FNL., *Noita Palaa Elamaan*, Mika Waltari, 1947, Play

NOITE 1985 d: Gilberto Loureiro. BRZ., *Noite*, Erico Verissimo, 1954, Novel

NOITE E A MADRUGADA, A 1983 d: Artur Ramos. PRT., *A Noite E a Madrugada*, Fernando Namora, 1950, Novel

NOIX DE COCO 1938 d: Jean Boyer. FRN., *Noix de Coco*, Marcel Achard, 1936, Play

Nom de la Rose, Le *see* THE NAME OF THE ROSE (1986).

Nomades du Nord *see* WILD DOG OF THE NORTH NIKKI (1961).

NOMADS OF THE NORTH 1920 d: David M. Hartford. USA., *Nomads of the North*, James Oliver Curwood, New York 1919, Novel

Nomads of the North *see* WILD DOG OF THE NORTH NIKKI (1961).

Nome Della Rosa, Il *see* THE NAME OF THE ROSE (1986).

NOMME LA ROCCA, UN 1962 d: Jean Becker. FRN/ITL., *L' Excommunie*, Jose Giovanni, Novel

Non Credo Piu All'amore *see* LA PAURA (1954).

NON E MAI TROPPO TADRI 1953 d: Filippo Walter Ratti. ITL., *A Christmas Carol*, Charles Dickens, London 1843, Novel

NON E VERO. MA CI CREDO 1952 d: Sergio Grieco. ITL., *Non E Vero. Ma Ci Credo*, Peppino de Filippo, Play

NON MI MUOVO! 1943 d: Giorgio C. Simonelli. ITL., '*O Quatto 'E Maggio*, Diego Petriccione, Play

Non Plus Ultra Della Disperazione, Il *see* **UN ANTICO CAFFE NAPOLETANO** (1914).

NON TI CONOSCO PIU 1936 d: Nunzio MalasommA. ITL., *Non Ti Conosco Piu*, Aldo de Benedetti, Play

NON TI PAGO! 1942 d: Carlo Ludovico BragagliA. ITL., *Non Ti Pago!*, Eduardo de Filippo, Play

NON TI PAGO! 1954 d: Eduardo de Filippo. ITL., *Non Ti Pago!*, Eduardo de Filippo, Play

NON VENDO MIA FIGLIA! 1920 d: Nicola Fausto Neroni. ITL., *Vecchi Sofismi*, Guillaume Vuillermot, Play

NONA 1973 d: Grisha Ostrovski. BUL., *Chiflikat Kray Granitsata*, Yordan Yovkov, 1933-34, Novel

NON-CONFORMIST PARSON, A 1919 d: A. V. Bramble. UKN., *A Non-Conformist Parson*, Roy Horniman, Novel

None are Born Soldiers *see* **SOLDATAMI NYE ROZHDAYUTSYA** (1968).

NONE BUT THE BRAVE 1965 d: Frank SinatrA. USA/JPN., *Yusha Nomi*, Kikumaru Okuda, Novel

NONE BUT THE LONELY HEART 1944 d: Clifford Odets. USA., *None But the Lonely Heart*, Richard Llewellyn, 1943, Novel

Non-Existent Knight, The *see* **IL CAVALIERE INESISTENTE** (1970).

Non-Matrimonial Story *see* **DULSCY** (1975).

NONNA FELICITA 1938 d: Mario Mattoli. ITL., *Nonna Felicita*, Giuseppe Adami, Play

NONNA SABELLA, LA 1957 d: Dino Risi. ITL., *La Nonna Sabella*, Pasquale Festa Campanile, Novel

NON-STOP NEW YORK 1937 d: Robert Stevenson. UKN., *Sky Steward*, Ken Attiwill, Novel

NOON WINE 1985 d: Michael Fields. USA., Katherine Anne Porter, Short Story

NOOSE 1948 d: Edmond T. Greville. UKN., *Noose*, Richard Llewellyn, London 1947, Play

NOOSE FOR A GUNMAN 1960 d: Edward L. Cahn. USA., Steve Fisher, Story

NOOSE FOR A LADY 1953 d: Wolf RillA. UKN., *Whispering Woman*, Gerald Verner, Novel

NOOSE, THE 1928 d: John Francis Dillon. USA., *The Noose*, Willard Mack, H. H. Van Loan, New York 1926, Play

Noose, The *see* **I'D GIVE MY LIFE** (1936).

Noose, The *see* **PETLA** (1957).

NOR THE MOON BY NIGHT 1958 d: Ken Annakin. UKN/SAF., *Nor the Moon By Night*, Joy Packer, Novel

Nora *see* **LA BARAONDA** (1923).

NORA 1944 d: Harald Braun. GRM., *Et Dukkehjem*, Henrik Ibsen, Copenhagen 1879, Play

NORA PRENTISS 1947 d: Vincent Sherman. USA., Jack Sobell, Paul Webster, Story

Norah O'Neale *see* **IRISH HEARTS** (1934).

NORD ATLANTIQUE 1939 d: Maurice Cloche. FRN., *Nord Atlantique*, Oscar-Paul Gilbert, Novel

Norma *see* **LA NORMA** (1911).

NORMA (EPISODIO DELLA GALLIA SOTTO IL DOMINIO DI ROMA IMPERIALE) 1911 d: Romolo Bacchini. ITL., *Norma*, Vincenzo Bellini, Felice Romani, 1831, Opera

NORMA, LA 1911. ITL., *Norma*, Vincenzo Bellini, Felice Romani, 1831, Opera

Normal Young Man, The *see* **IL GIOVANE NORMALE** (1969).

Norman Conquest *see* **PARK PLAZA 605** (1953).

NORMAN CONQUESTS, THE 1977 d: Herbert Wise. UKN., *The Norman Conquests*, Alan Ayckbourn, 1974, Play

Norman Vincent Peale Story, The *see* **ONE MAN'S WAY** (1964).

NORTH 1994 d: Rob Reiner. USA., *North*, Alan Zweibel, Novel

NORTH AND SOUTH 1985 d: Richard T. Heffron. USA., *Love and War*, John Jakes, Novel

NORTH AND SOUTH: BOOK 2 1986 d: Kevin Connor. USA., *Love and War*, John Jakes, Novel

NORTH AVENUE IRREGULARS, THE 1979 d: Bruce Bilson. USA., *The North Avenue Irregulars*, Albert Fay Hill, Novel

NORTH OF 36 1924 d: Irvin V. Willat. USA., *North of 36*, Emerson Hough, New York 1923, Novel

North of Rio Grande *see* **NORTH OF THE RIO GRANDE** (1937).

North of Singapore *see* **ISLAND OF LOST MEN** (1939).

NORTH OF THE RIO GRANDE 1922 d: Rollin S. Sturgeon, Joseph Henabery. USA., *Val of Paradise*, Vingie E. Roe, New York 1921, Novel

NORTH OF THE RIO GRANDE 1937 d: Nate Watt. USA., *Cottonwood Gulch*, Clarence E. Mulford, 1924, Short Story

NORTH SEA HIJACK 1980 d: Andrew V. McLaglen. UKN., *Esther, Ruth and Jennifer*, Jack Davies, Novel

North Sea Patrol *see* **LUCK OF THE NAVY** (1938).

North Shore *see* **THE WOMAN IN RED** (1935).

NORTH STAR 1925 d: Paul Powell. USA., *North Star; a Dog Story of the Canadian Northwest*, Rufus King, New York 1925, Novel

North Star *see* **TASHUNGA** (1996).

NORTH TO THE KLONDIKE 1942 d: Erle C. Kenton. USA., *Gold Raiders of the North*, Jack London, Novel

North Wind *see* **VIENTO DEL NORTE** (1954).

NORTH WIND'S MALICE, THE 1920 d: Paul Bern, Carl Harbaugh. USA., *The North Wind's Malice*, Rex Beach, 1917, Short Story

NORTHANGER ABBEY 1987 d: Giles Foster. UKN., *Northanger Abbey*, Jane Austen, 1818, Novel

NORTHERN FRONTIER 1935 d: Sam Newfield. USA., *Four Minutes Late*, James Oliver Curwood, Short Story

NORTHERN LIGHTS 1914 d: Edgar Lewis. USA., *Northern Lights*, Edwin Barbour, James W. Harkins Jr., New York 1895, Play

NORTHERN LIGHTS 1997 d: Linda Yellen. USA., *Northern Lights*, John Hoffmann, Play

NORTHERN MYSTERY, THE 1924 d: Hugh Croise. UKN., *The Northern Mystery*, Baroness Orczy, Short Story

NORTHERN PURSUIT 1943 d: Raoul Walsh. USA., *Five Thousand Trojan Soldiers*, Leslie T. White, Story

Northern Star, The *see* **L' ETOILE DU NORD** (1982).

Northing Tramp, The *see* **STRANGERS ON A HONEYMOON** (1936).

NORTHWEST OUTPOST 1947 d: Allan Dwan. USA., Angela Stuart, Story

Northwest Passage *see* **NORTHWEST PASSAGE (BOOK I -ROGERS' RANGERS)** (1939).

NORTHWEST PASSAGE (BOOK I -ROGERS' RANGERS) 1939 d: King Vidor. USA., *Northwest Passage*, Kenneth Lewis Roberts, New York 1937, Novel

NORTHWEST TERRITORY 1951 d: Frank McDonald. USA., James Oliver Curwood, Novel

NORWOOD 1970 d: Jack Haley Jr. USA., *Norwood*, Charles Portis, New York 1966, Novel

NORWOOD BUILDER, THE 1922 d: George Ridgwell. UKN., *The Norwood Builder*, Arthur Conan Doyle, Short Story

Norwood Builder, The *see* **THE ADVENTURES OF SHERLOCK HOLMES: THE NORWOOD BUILDER** (1985).

Nose Dwarf *see* **ZWERG NASE** (1952).

Nose on My Face, The *see* **GIRL IN THE HEADLINES** (1963).

NOSFERATU - EINE SYMPHONIE DES GRAUENS 1921 d: F. W. Murnau. GRM., *Dracula*, Bram Stoker, London 1897, Novel

NOSFERATU - PHANTOM DER NACHT 1979 d: Werner Herzog. GRM/FRN/USA., *Dracula*, Bram Stoker, London 1897, Novel

Nosferatu, a Symphony of Horror *see* **NOSFERATU - EINE SYMPHONIE DES GRAUENS** (1921).

Nosferatu, the Vampire *see* **NOSFERATU - EINE SYMPHONIE DES GRAUENS** (1921).

Nosferatu, the Vampyre *see* **NOSFERATU - PHANTOM DER NACHT** (1979).

NOSTALGIE 1937 d: Victor Tourjansky. FRN., *Stantsionny Smotritel*, Alexander Pushkin, 1831, Short Story

NOSTRA SIGNORA DEI TURCHI 1968 d: Carmelo Bene. ITL., *Nostra Signora Dei Turchi*, Carmelo Bene, Novel

NOSTRI BUONI VILLICI, I 1918 d: Camillo de Riso. ITL., *Nos Bons Villageois*, Victorien Sardou, 1866, Play

NOSTRI FIGLI, I 1914 d: Ugo FalenA. ITL., *Le Jeu de l'Amour Et du Hasard*, Pierre Carlet de Marivaux, 1730, Play

NOSTRI SOGNI, I 1943 d: Vittorio Cottafavi. ITL., *I Nostri Sogni*, Ugo Betti, Play

NOSTRO PROSSIMO, IL 1943 d: Gherardo Gherardi, Antonio Rossi. ITL., *Il Nostro Prossimo*, Tino Santoni, Play

Nostromo *see* **THE SILVER TREASURE** (1926).

NOSTROMO 1996 d: Alastair Reid. UKN., *Nostromo*, Joseph Conrad, 1904, Novel

NOSZTY FIU ESETE TOTH MARIVAL, A 1960 d: Viktor Gertler. HNG., *A Noszty Fiu Esete Toth Marival*, Kalman Mikszath, 1908, Novel

NOT A PENNY MORE, NOT A PENNY LESS 1990 d: Clive Donner. UKN/USA., *Not a Penny More Not a Penny Less*, Jeffrey Archer, London 1975, Novel

NOT AS A STRANGER 1955 d: Stanley Kramer. USA., *Not As a Stranger*, Morton Thompson, 1954, Novel

Not Blood Relations *see* **NASANU NAKA** (1932).

NOT DAMAGED 1930 d: Chandler Sprague. USA., *The Solid Gold Article*, Richard Connell, 1929, Short Story

NOT EXACTLY GENTLEMEN 1931 d: Ben Stoloff. USA., *Over the Border*, Herman Whitaker, New York 1917, Novel

Not for Children *see* **THE MAD MARTINDALES** (1942).

Not for Each Other *see* **A BILL OF DIVORCEMENT** (1940).

Not for Honor and Glory *see* **LOST COMMAND** (1966).

NOT FOR PUBLICATION 1927 d: Ralph Ince. USA., *The Temple of the Giants*, Robert Welles Ritchie, Story

NOT FOR SALE 1924 d: W. P. Kellino. UKN., *Not for Sale*, Monica Ewer, Novel

NOT GUILTY 1915 d: Joseph A. Golden. USA., *Justice*, Edgar James, New York 1915, Play

NOT GUILTY 1921 d: Sidney A. Franklin. USA., *Parrot and Company*, Harold MacGrath, Indianapolis 1913, Novel

NOT NOW, COMRADE 1976 d: Harold Snoad, Ray Cooney. UKN., *Comrade Chase Me*, Ray Cooney, Play

NOT NOW, DARLING 1972 d: Ray Cooney, David Croft. UKN., *Darling Not Now*, Ray Cooney, Play

Not One to Spare *see* **WHICH SHALL IT BE?** (1924).

NOT QUITE A LADY 1928 d: Thomas Bentley. UKN., *The Cassilis Engagement*, St. John Hankin, Play

NOT QUITE DECENT 1929 d: Irving Cummings. USA., *The Grouch Bag*, Wallace Smith, Short Story

NOT QUITE JERUSALEM 1984 d: Lewis Gilbert. UKN., *Not Quite Jerusalem*, Paul Kember, 1982, Play

Not Quite Paradise *see* **NOT QUITE JERUSALEM** (1984).

Not Reconciled, Or "Only Violence Helps Where It Rules" *see* **WO GEWALT HERRSCHT" NICHT VERSOHNT ODER "ES HILFT NUR GEWALT** (1965).

NOT SO DUMB 1930 d: King Vidor. USA., *Dulcy*, Marc Connelly, George S. Kaufman, New York 1921, Play

NOT SO LONG AGO 1925 d: Sidney Olcott. USA., *Not So Long Ago*, Arthur Richman, New York 1924, Play

Not So Quiet Days *see* **STILLE DAGE I CLICHY** (1970).

Not Too Narrow, Not Too Deep *see* **STRANGE CARGO** (1940).

Not Wanted *see* **NO PLACE TO GO** (1939).

NOT WANTED ON VOYAGE 1936 d: Emile Edwin Reinert. UKN., *Murder in the Stalls*, Maurice Messenger, Play

NOT WANTED ON VOYAGE 1957 d: MacLean Rogers. UKN., *Wanted on Voyage*, Ken Attiwill, Evadne Price, Novel

NOT WITHOUT MY DAUGHTER 1991 d: Brian Gilbert. USA., *Not Without My Daughter*, William Hoffer, Betty Mahmoody, Book

Nothing *see* **NADA** (1947).

Nothing a Year *see* **A WOMAN'S BUSINESS** (1920).

NOTHING BUT LIES 1920 d: Lawrence C. Windom. USA., *Nothing But Lies*, Aaron Hoffman, New York 1918, Play

NOTHING BUT THE BEST 1963 d: Clive Donner. UKN., *The Best of Everything*, Stanley Ellin, 1952, Short Story

NOTHING BUT THE NIGHT 1972 d: Peter Sasdy. UKN., *Nothing But the Night*, John Blackburn, Novel

NOTHING BUT THE TRUTH 1920 d: David Kirkland. USA., *Nothing But the Truth*, Frederic Stewart Isham, Indianapolis 1914, Novel

NOTHING BUT THE TRUTH 1929 d: Victor Schertzinger. USA., *Nothing But the Truth*, Frederic Stewart Isham, Indianapolis 1914, Novel

NOTHING BUT THE TRUTH 1941 d: Elliott Nugent. USA., *Nothing But the Truth*, Frederic Stewart Isham, Indianapolis 1914, Novel

Nothing But the Truth see KUN SANDHEDEN (1975).

NOTHING EVER HAPPENS RIGHT 1915 d: Roy McCray. USA., *Nothing Ever Happens Right*, L. V. Jefferson, Story

Nothing Less Than a Man see NADA MENOS QUE TODO UN HOMBRE (1971).

NOTHING PERSONAL 1995 d: Thaddeus O'Sullivan. UKN/IRL., *All Our Fault*, Daniel Mornin, Novel

NOTHING SACRED 1937 d: William A. Wellman. USA., *Letter to the Editor*, James H. Street, 1937, Short Story

Nothing to Lose see GENTLEMEN, PLEASE TIME (1952).

Nothing Under the Dress see SOTTO IL VESTITO NIENTE (1985).

Nothing Underneath see SOTTO IL VESTITO NIENTE (1985).

Nothing Works Without Mom see OHNE MUTTER GEHT ES NICHT (1958).

NOTORIOUS AFFAIR, A 1930 d: Lloyd Bacon. USA., *Fame*, Audrey Carter, Waverly Carter, London 1929, Play

Notorious Concubines, The see CHIN-P'ING-MEI (1969).

Notorious Gentleman see SMOOTH AS SILK (1946).

Notorious Gentleman, The see THE RAKE'S PROGRESS (1945).

NOTORIOUS LADY, THE 1927 d: King Baggot. USA., *The River*, Patrick Hastings, Play

NOTORIOUS LANDLADY, THE 1962 d: Richard Quine. USA., *The Notorious Tenant*, Margery Sharp, 1956, Short Story

NOTORIOUS MISS LISLE, THE 1920 d: James Young. USA., *The Notorious Miss Lisle*, Mrs. Baillie Reynolds, New York 1911, Novel

NOTORIOUS MRS. CARRICK, THE 1924 d: George Ridgwell. UKN., *Pools of the Past*, Charles Proctor, Novel

NOTORIOUS SOPHIE LANG, THE 1934 d: Ralph Murphy. USA., *The Notorious Sophie Lang*, Frederick Irving Anderson, London 1925, Novel

NOTRE DAME DE PARIS 1911 d: Albert Capellani. FRN., *Notre-Dame de Paris*, Victor Hugo, Paris 1831, Novel

NOTRE DAME DE PARIS 1957 d: Jean Delannoy. FRN/ITL., *Notre-Dame de Paris*, Victor Hugo, Paris 1831, Novel

NOTRE MARIAGE 1984 d: Valeria Sarmiento. FRN/SWT/PRT., *Mi Boda Contigo*, Corin Tellado, Novel

NOTRE-DAME D'AMOUR 1922 d: Andre Hugon. FRN., *Notre-Dame d'Amour*, Jean Aicard, 1896, Novel

NOTRE-DAME D'AMOUR 1936 d: Pierre Caron. FRN., *Notre-Dame d'Amour*, Jean Aicard, 1896, Novel

NOTRE-DAME DE LA MOUISE 1941 d: Robert Peguy. Rene Delacroix. CND/FRN., *Le Christ Dans la Banlieue*, Pierre Lhande, Book

Notre-Dame de Paris see NOTRE DAME DE PARIS (1957).

Notte a Venezia, Una see EINE NACHT IN VENEDIG (1934).

NOTTE BRAVA, LA 1959 d: Mauro Bolognini. ITL/FRN., *Ragazza Di Vita*, Pier Paolo Pasolini, 1955, Novel

NOTTE DELL'ALTA MAREA, LA 1977 d: Luigi Scattini. ITL/CND., *Il Corpo*, Alfredo Todisco, Novel

NOTTE DELLE BEFFE, LA 1940 d: Carlo Campogalliani. ITL., *Il Passatore*, Alberto Donini, Guglielmo Zorzi, Play

NOTTE DI NEVE 1921 d: Giulio Tanfani-Moroni. ITL., *Notte Di Neve*, Roberto Bracco, 1906, Play

Notte Di Pioggia, Una see L' UOMO DELLA GUERRA POSSIBILE (1979).

NOTTE DI TEMPESTA 1946 d: Gianni Franciolini. ITL., *I Pescatori*, Raffaele Viviani, Play

NOTTE DI TENTAZIONE 1919 d: Giuseppe Pinto. ITL., Victoria Cross, Novel

Notte Erotique see LA DROGUE DU VICE (1963).

Notte Per 5 Rapine, Una see MISE A SAC (1967).

NOTTI BIANCHE, LE 1957 d: Luchino Visconti. ITL/FRN., *Belye Nochi*, Fyodor Dostoyevsky, St. Petersburg 1848, Short Story

NOTTI DI LUCREZIA BORGIA, LE 1959 d: Sergio Grieco. ITL/FRN., *Lucrece Borgia*, Victor Hugo, Paris 1833, Play

NOTTI PECCAMINOSE DE PIETRO L'ARETINO 1972 d: Manlio Scarpelli. ITL., *Capricciosi Ragionamenti*, Pietro L'Arentino, Short Story, *Lettere*, Pietro L'Arentino, Short Story, *Piacevoli Ragionamenti*, Pietro L'Arentino, Short Story

NOTTURNI 1919 d: Guido Di Sandro. ITL., *Le Quattro Stagioni*, Washington Borg

NOUS AVONS TOUT FAIT LA MEME CHOSE 1949 d: Rene Sti. FRN., *Nous Avons Tout Fait la Meme Chose*, Jean de Letraz, Play

Nous, Les Gosses see LA GUERRE DES GOSSES (1936).

Nous Les Jeunes see ALTITUDE 3200 (1938).

NOUS NE SOMMES PLUS DES ENFANTS 1934 d: Augusto GeninA. FRN., *Nous Ne Sommes Plus Des Enfants*, Leopold Marchand, Play

NOUVEAU JOURNAL D'UNE FEMME EN BLANC, LE 1966 d: Claude Autant-LarA. FRN., *Une Femme En Blanc Se Revolte*, Andre Soubiran, Novel

NOUVEAU TESTAMENT, LE 1936 d: Sacha Guitry. Alexandre Ryder. FRN., *Le Nouveau Testament*, Sacha Guitry, Play

NOUVEAUX ARISTOCRATES, LES 1961 d: Francis Rigaud. FRN., *Les Nouveaux Aristocrates*, Michel de Saint-Pierre, Novel

NOUVEAUX MESSIEURS, LES 1928 d: Jacques Feyder. FRN., *Les Nouveaux Messieurs*, Francis de Croisset, Robert de Flers, Play

NOUVEAUX RICHES, LES 1938 d: Andre Berthomieu. FRN., *Les Nouveaux Riches*, Charles d'Abadie, Robert de Cesse, Play

NOVACEK: LE CROISE DE L'ORDRE 1994 d: Marco Pico. BLG/FRN/PRT., *Le Croise de l'Ordre*, Didier Daeninckx, Novel

Novel of a Gynecologist see ROMAN EINES FRAUENARZTES (1954).

NOVELA DE UN JOVEN POBRE, LA 1942 d: Luis Bayon HerrerA. ARG., *Le Roman d'un Jeune Homme Pauvre*, Octave Feuillet, 1858, Novel

NOVELA DE UN JOVEN POBRE, LA 1968 d: Enrique Cahen. ARG., *Le Roman d'un Jeune Homme Pauvre*, Octave Feuillet, 1858, Novel

Novela de un Torero, La see EL RELICARIO (1926).

Novella Di Shakespeare, Una see RACCONTO D'INVERNO (1913).

Novella d'Inverno see RACCONTO D'INVERNO (1913).

November Cats see NOVEMBERKATZEN (1985).

November, the Last Ball see ULTIMUL BAL NOIEMBRIE (1989).

NOVEMBERKATZEN 1985 d: Sigrun Koeppe. GRM., *Novemberkatzen*, Mirjam Pressler, Novel

NOVIA ENSANGRENTADA, LA 1972 d: Vicente ArandA. SPN., *Carmilla*, Sheridan le Fanu, London 1872, Short Story

Novice, La see LETTERE DI UNA NOVIZIA (1960).

Novice, The see LETTERE DI UNA NOVIZIA (1960).

NOVICIA REBELDE, LA 1971 d: Luis LuciA. SPN., *La Hermana San Sulpicio*, Armando Palacio Valdes, 1889, Novel

NOVIYE POKHOZDENIYA SHVEIKA 1943 d: Sergei Yutkevich. USS., *Osudy Dobreho Vojaka Svejka Za Svetove Valky*, Jaroslav Hasek, Prague 1920-23, Novel

NOVYE PRIKLUCHENIA JANKE PRI DVORE KOVOLA ARTURA 1989 d: Victor Gres. USS., *A Connecticut Yankee in King Arthur's Court*, Mark Twain, New York 1889, Novel

NOVYI GULLIVER 1935 d: Alexander Ptushko. USS., *Gulliver's Travels*, Jonathan Swift, London 1726, Novel

NOW AND FOREVER 1956 d: Mario Zampi. UKN., *The Orchard Walls*, R. F. Delderfield, 1953, Play

NOW AND FOREVER 1982 d: Adrian Carr, Richard Cassidy. ASL., *Now and Forever*, Danielle Steel, Novel

NOW BARABBAS WAS A ROBBER. 1949 d: Gordon Parry. UKN., *Now Barabbas.*, William Douglas Home, London 1947, Play

Now I Lay Me Down see RACHEL RACHEL (1968).

Now It Can Be Told see THE SECRET DOOR (1962).

NOW LET HIM GO 1957 d: Dennis Vance. UKN., *Now Let Him Go*, J. B. Priestley, Play

NOW THAT APRIL'S HERE 1958 d: William Davidson. CND., Morley Callaghan, Short Stories

NOW, VOYAGER 1942 d: Irving Rapper. USA., *Voyager Now*, Olive Higgins Prouty, Novel

NOWHERE TO GO 1958 d: Seth Holt. UKN/USA., *Nowhere to Go*, Donald MacKenzie, Novel

NOWHERE TO RUN 1978 d: Richard Lang. USA., *Nowhere to Run*, Charles Einstein, Novel

NOYADE INTERDITE 1987 d: Pierre Granier-Deferre. FRN., *Widow's Walk*, Andrew Coburn, Novel

NOZZE DI FIGARO, LE 1911. ITL., *Le Mariage de Figaro*, Pierre-Augustin Caron de Beaumarchais, Paris 1784, Play

NOZZE DI FIGARO, LE 1913 d: Luigi Maggi. ITL., *Le Mariage de Figaro*, Pierre-Augustin Caron de Beaumarchais, Paris 1784, Play

NOZZE DI SANGUE 1941 d: Goffredo Alessandrini. ITL., *Immacolata*, Lina Pietravalle, Short Story

NTH COMMANDMENT, THE 1923 d: Frank Borzage. USA., *The Nth Commandment*, Fannie Hurst, 1916, Short Story

NU HOU BA, HUANG HE 1979 d: Shen Dan, Jia Shihong. CHN., *Huang He Nu Hou Ba*, Wang XIngpu, Play

Nuclear Countdown see TWILIGHT'S LAST GLEAMING (1977).

Nude in a White Car see TOI LE VENIN (1958).

Nude in His Pocket see UN AMOUR DE POCHE (1957).

NUESTRA NATACHA 1936 d: Benito Perojo. SPN., *Nuestra Natacha*, Alejandro Casona, 1936, Play

NUEVAS AMISTADES 1964 d: Ramon Comas. SPN., *Nuevas Amistades*, Juan Garcia Hortelano, 1959, Novel

NUIT A L'HOTEL, LA 1931 d: Leo Mittler. FRN., *Une Nuit a l'Hotel*, Eliot Crawshay-Williams, Novel

NUIT A MEGEVE, UNE 1953 d: Raoul Andre. FRN., *Une Nuit a Megeve*, Jean de Letraz, Play

NUIT AUX BALEARES, UNE 1956 d: Paul Mesnier. FRN., *Une Nuit aux Baleares*, Louis Gaste, Jean Guitton, Opera

NUIT DE DECEMBRE 1939 d: Curtis Bernhardt. FRN., *Les Aventures de Schwedenklees*, Bernhard Kellermann, Novel

NUIT DE FOLIES, UNE 1934 d: Maurice Cammage. FRN., *Le Gars du Milieu*, Paul Chartrettes, Henri Hubert, Play

Nuit de la Saint-Jean, La see DAS SCHWEIGEN IM WALDE (1929).

NUIT DE MAI 1934 d: Henri Chomette, Gustav Ucicky. FRN., *Nuit de Mai*, Stephan Kamare, Play

NUIT DE NOCES 1935 d: Georges Monca, Maurice Keroul. FRN., *Une Nuit de Noces*, Albert Barre, Henri Keroul, Play

NUIT DE NOCES 1949 d: Rene Jayet. FRN., *Une Nuit de Noces*, Albert Barre, Henri Keroul, Play

NUIT DE NOCES, UNE 1920 d: Marcel Simon. FRN., *Une Nuit de Noces*, Albert Barre, Henri Keroul, Play

Nuit de Serail, La see THE FAVORITE (1989).

Nuit Des Generaux, La see THE NIGHT OF THE GENERALS (1966).

NUIT DES TRAQUES, LA 1959 d: Bernard-Roland. FRN/BLG., *La Nuit Des Traques*, Benoit Becker, Novel

NUIT D'ESPAGNE 1931 d: Henri de La Falaise. USA., *The Next Corner*, Kate Jordan, Boston 1921, Novel

NUIT DU 11 SEPTEMBRE, LA 1923 d: Bernard-Deschamps. FRN., *Le Crime de Jean Malory*, Ernest Daudet, Novel

Nuit du 3, La see LES DEVOYES (1925).

NUIT DU CARREFOUR, LA 1932 d: Jean Renoir. FRN., *La Nuit du Carrefour*, Georges Simenon, 1931, Novel

NUIT DU COUCOU, LA 1987 d: Michel Favart. FRN., *Le Coucou*, G. V. Arnaud, Novel

Nuit du Treize, La see MYSTERE A SHANGAI (1950).

NUIT EST A NOUS, LA 1929 d: Henry Roussell, Carl Froelich. FRN., *La Nuit Est a Nous*, Henri Kistemaeckers, Play

NUIT EST A NOUS, LA 1953 d: Jean Stelli. FRN., *La Nuit Est a Nous*, Henri Kistemaeckers, Play

NUIT SANS PERMISSION, LA 1943 d: Franz Schnyder. SWT., *La Nuit Sans Permission*, Kurt Guggenheim, Zurich 1941, Novel

Nuits Blanches see LE NOTTI BIANCHE (1957).

NUITS BLANCHES DE SAINT-PETERSBOURG, LES 1937 d: Jean Dreville. FRN., *Kreutserova Sonata*, Lev Nikolayevich Tolstoy, 1889, Short Story

Nuits Blanches, Les *see* PEPE LE MOKO (1936).

NUITS DE FEU 1937 d: Marcel L'Herbier. FRN., *Zhivoi Trup*, Lev Nikolayevich Tolstoy, Moscow 1911, Play

Nuits de l'Epouvante, Les *see* LA LAMA NEL CORPO (1966).

Nuits de Lucrece Borgia, Les *see* LE NOTTI DI LUCREZIA BORGIA (1959).

NUITS DE MONTMARTRE, LES 1955 d: Pierre Franchi. FRN., *Les Nuits de Montmartre*, Claude Orval, Novel

Nuits de Papa, Les *see* SERVICE DE NUIT (1931).

NUITS DE PIGALLE 1958 d: Georges Jaffe. FRN., *Sa Majeste Arsene*, Zadoc Monteil, Short Story

NUITS DE PRINCES 1929 d: Marcel L'Herbier. FRN., *Nuits de Princes*, Joseph Kessel, 1927, Novel

NUITS DE PRINCES 1937 d: Wladimir von Strischewski. FRN., *Nuits de Princes*, Joseph Kessel, 1927, Novel

Nuits de Tziganes *see* NUITS DE PRINCES (1929).

NUITS MOSCOVITES, LES 1934 d: Alexis Granowsky. FRN., *Les Nuits de Moscou*, Pierre Benoit, Novel

Null-Acht-Fuffzehn *see* 08/15 I (1954).

Number 44, the Mysterious Stranger *see* THE MYSTERIOUS STRANGER (1982).

NUMBER 99 1920 d: Ernest C. Warde. USA., *One Week-End*, Wyndham Martyn, New York 1919, Novel

Number One Killer in the East *see* DONG FANG DI YI CHI KE (1993).

NUMBER SEVENTEEN 1928 d: Geza von Bolvary. UKN., *Number Seventeen*, J. Jefferson Farjeon, Play

NUMBER SEVENTEEN 1932 d: Alfred Hitchcock. UKN., *Number Seventeen*, J. Jefferson Farjeon, Play

NUMBER SIX 1962 d: Robert Tronson. UKN., *Number Six*, Edgar Wallace, London 1927, Novel

NUMBERED MEN 1930 d: Mervyn Leroy. USA., *Jailbreak*, Dwight Taylor, Story

Numbers of Monte Carlo *see* MONTE CARLO NIGHTS (1934).

NUMMISUUTARIT 1923 d: Erkki Karu. FNL., *Nummisuutarit*, Aleksis Kivi, 1864, Play

NUMMISUUTARIT 1938 d: Wilho Ilmari. FNL., *Nummisuutarit*, Aleksis Kivi, 1864, Play

NUMMISUUTARIT 1957 d: Valentin Vaala. FNL., *Nummisuutarit*, Aleksis Kivi, 1864, Play

NUN AND THE BANDIT, THE 1992 d: Paul Cox. ASL., *The Nun and the Bandit*, E. L. Grant Watson, Novel

Nun and the Devil, The *see* LE MONACHE DI SANT'ARCANGELO (1973).

Nun of Monza, The *see* LA MONACA DI MONZA (1968).

Nun, The *see* LA RELIGIEUSE DE DIDEROT SUZANNE SIMONIN (1965).

NUN'S STORY, THE 1959 d: Fred Zinnemann. USA., *The Nun's Story*, Kathryn C. Hulme, Book

NUNTA DE PIATRA 1972 d: Mircea Veroiu, Dan Pita. RMN., *Fefeleaga*, Ion Agarbiceanu, 1908, Short Story, *La O Nunta*, Ion Agarbiceanu, 1909, Short Story

NUORENA NUKKUNUT 1937 d: Teuvo Tulio. FNL., *Nuorena Nukkunut*, Frans E. Sillanpaa, 1931, Novel

NUOVI ANGELI, I 1962 d: Ugo Gregoretti. ITL., *I Ventenni Non Sono Deliquneti*, Mino Guerrini, Book

Nur Der Himmel Uber Uns *see* BERGWIND (1963).

Nur Ein Gassenmadel *see* NACHTGESTALTEN (1929).

Nur Eine Frage Der Zeit *see* PAS FOLLE LA GUEPE (1972).

NUREN HUA 1994 d: Wang Jin. CHN., *Story of Adopted Sisters*, Su Fanggui, Novel

NURSE 1980 d: David Lowell Rich. USA., *Nurse*, Peggy Anderson, Book

NURSE EDITH CAVELL 1939 d: Herbert Wilcox. USA., *Dawn*, Reginald Berkeley, New York 1928, Novel

NURSE FROM BROOKLYN 1938 d: S. Sylvan Simon. USA., *If You Break My Heart*, Steve Fisher, 1937, Short Story

NURSE MARJORIE 1920 d: William D. Taylor. USA., *Nurse Marjorie*, Israel Zangwill, New York 1906, Play

NURSE ON WHEELS 1963 d: Gerald Thomas. UKN., *Nurse Is a Neighbour*, Joanna Jones, London 1958, Novel

Nurse, The *see* ADELE (1919).

NURSEMAID WHO DISAPPEARED, THE 1939 d: Arthur Woods. UKN., *The Nursemaid Who Disappeared*, Philip MacDonald, Novel

Nursery School *see* LA MATERNELLE (1933).

NURSE'S SECRET, THE 1941 d: Noel Smith. USA., *Miss Pinkerton: Adventures of a Nurse Detective*, Mary Roberts Rinehart, New York 1932, Novel

NUSUMARETA KOI 1951 d: Kon Ichikawa. JPN., Jiro Kagami, Novel

NUSUMARETA YOKUJO 1958 d: Shohei Imamura. JPN., *Tento Gekijo*, Toko Kon, 1957, Novel

NUT FARM, THE 1935 d: Melville Brown. USA., *The Nut Farm*, John C. Brownell, New York 1929, Play

Nutcracker *see* NUTCRACKER FANTASY (1979).

Nutcracker Fantasies *see* NUTCRACKER FANTASY (1979).

NUTCRACKER FANTASY 1979 d: Takeo Nakamura. JPN., *Nussknacker Und Mausekonig*, Ernst Theodor Amadeus Hoffmann, 1816, Short Story

Nutcracker: Money, Madness and Murder *see* MADNESS & MURDER MONEY (1987).

NUTCRACKER, THE 1926 d: Lloyd Ingraham. USA., *The Nut-Cracker*, Frederic Stewart Isham, Indianapolis 1920, Novel

NUTCRACKER, THE 1986 d: Carroll Ballard. USA., *Nussknacker Und Mausekonig*, Ernst Theodor Amadeus Hoffmann, 1816, Story

Nutcracker, the Motion Picture *see* THE NUTCRACKER (1986).

Nutidsungdom *see* KURITON SUKUPOLVI (1957).

NUTRICE, LA 1914 d: Alessandro Boutet. ITL., *A' Nutriccia*, Eduardo Scarpetta, 1882, Play

NUTS 1987 d: Martin Ritt. USA., *Nuts*, Tom Topor, Play

Nutty, Naughty Chateau *see* CHATEAU EN SUEDE (1963).

Nybyggarna *see* INVANDRARNA (1970).

O ADRIENU 1919 d: Max Urban. CZC., *O Adrienu*, Louis Verneuil, Play

O CZYM SIE NIE MOWI 1939 d: Mecislas Krawicz. PLN., *O Czym Sie Nie Mowi*, Gabriela Zapolska, 1909, Novel

O DIESE BAYERN 1960 d: Arnulf Schroeder. GRM., *Die Medaille*, Ludwig Thoma, Play

O GIOVANNINO O. LA MORTE! 1914 d: Gino Rossetti. ITL., *O Giovannino O la Morte!*, Matilde Serao, 1912, Novel

O. HENRY'S FULL HOUSE 1952 d: Henry Koster, Henry King, Henry Hathaway, Howard Hawks, Jean Negulesco. USA., *The Clarion Call, The Cop and the Anthem, The Gift of the Magi, The Last Leaf, Ransom of Red Chief*, O. Henry, Short Stories

O LA BORSA O LA VITA 1933 d: Carlo Ludovico Bragaglia. ITL., *La Dinamo Dell'Eroismo*, Alessandro de Stefani, Radio Play

O PIONEERS! 1992 d: Glenn Jordan. USA., *O Pioneers!*, Willa Cather, 1913, Novel

O QUE E ISSO, COMPANHEIRO? 1997 d: Bruno Barreto. BRZ., *O Que E Isso, Companheiro?*, Fernando Gabeira, Book

O Serafina! *see* SERAFINA! OH (1976).

O SNEHURCE 1972 d: Vera Plivova-Simkova. CZC., *Schneewittchen*, Jacob Grimm, Wilhelm Grimm, 1812, Short Story

O Velike Vasni *see* CERNI MYSLIVCI (1921).

O! XIANG XUE 1989 d: Wang Haowei. CHN., Tie Ning, Story

O Zlate Rybce *see* RYBAR A ZLATA RYBKA (1951).

OAKDALE AFFAIR, THE 1919 d: Oscar Apfel. USA., *The Oakdale Affair*, Edgar Rice Burroughs, 1918, Novel

Oar of Orlac, The *see* MAD LOVE (1935).

OATH, THE 1921 d: Raoul Walsh. USA., *Idols*, William J. Locke, London 1899, Novel

Oats and the Woman *see* THE DAY SHE PAID (1919).

OBCAN BRYCH 1958 d: Otakar Vavra. CZC., *Obcan Brych*, Jan Otcenasek, 1955, Novel

OBCHOD NA KORSE 1965 d: Jan Kadar, Elmar Klos. CZC., *Obchod Na Korze*, Ladislav Grosman, Prague 1965, Novel

OBERARZT DR. SOLM 1955 d: Paul May. GRM., *Oberarzt Dr. Solm*, Harald Baumgarten, Novel

Oberleutnant Franzl *see* IHR LEIBHUSAR (1937).

OBERST CHABERT 1914 d: Rudolf Meinert. GRM., *Le Colonel Chabert*, Honore de Balzac, 1844, Novel

OBERSTEIGER, DER 1952 d: Franz Antel. AUS., *Der Obersteiger*, Carl Zeller, Operetta

OBERWACHTMEISTER BORCK 1955 d: Gerhard Lamprecht. GRM., *Oberwachtmeister Schwenke*, Hans Joachim Freiherr von Reitzenstein, Novel

OBERWACHTMEISTER SCHWENKE 1935 d: Carl Froelich. GRM., *Oberwachsmeister Schwenke*, Hans Joachim Freiherr von Reitzenstein, Novel

Oberwald Mystery, The *see* IL MISTERO DI OBERWALD (1979).

OBEY THE LAW 1926 d: Alfred Raboch. USA., *Obey the Law*, Max Marcin, Play

OBJECT OF MY AFFECTION, THE 1998 d: Nicholas Hytner. USA., *The Object of My Affection*, Stephen McCauley, Novel

Oblomov *see* NESKOLKO DNEI IZ ZHIZNI I.I. OBLOMOV (1980).

OBLONG BOX, THE 1969 d: Gordon Hessler. UKN/USA., *The Oblong Box*, Edgar Allan Poe, 1844, Short Story

OBRACENI FERDYSE PISTORY 1931 d: Josef Kodicek. CZC., *Obraceni Ferdyse Pistory*, Frantisek Langer, Play

OBRAS MAESTRAS DEL TERROR 1960 d: Enrique Carreras. ARG., *The Cask of Amontillado*, Edgar Allan Poe, 1846, Short Story, *The Facts in the Case of M. Valdemar*, Edgar Allan Poe, 1845, Short Story

Obsessed *see* THE LATE EDWINA BLACK (1951).

Obsessed *see* HITTING HOME (1988).

OBSESSION 1948 d: Edward Dmytryk. UKN., *A Man About a Dog*, Alec Coppel, Novel

OBSESSION 1954 d: Jean Delannoy. FRN/ITL., *Silent As the Grave*, Cornell Woolrich, Novel

Obsession *see* KUNGSLEDEN (1964).

Obsession *see* JUNOON (1978).

Obsessions *see* FLESH AND FANTASY (1943).

Obstinate Man, The *see* DER BOCKERER (1981).

OBZALOVANY 1964 d: Jan Kadar, Elmar Klos. CZC., *Obzalovany*, Lenka Haskova, Short Story

OCCHI CONSACRATI 1918 d: Luigi Mele. ITL., *Uocchie Cunzacrate*, Roberto Bracco, 1916, Play

OCCHI CONSACRATI 1919 d: Luigi Mele. ITL., *Ouchie Cunzacrate*, Roberto Bracco, 1916, Play

Occhi Senza Volto *see* LES YEUX SANS VISAGE (1959).

OCCHIALI D'ORO, GLI 1987 d: Giuliano Montaldo. ITL/FRN/YGS., *Gli Occhiali d'Oro*, Giorgio Bassani, 1956, Novel

OCCIDENT, L' 1928 d: Henri Fescourt. FRN., *L'Occident*, Henri Kistemaeckers, Paris 1913, Play

OCCIDENT, L' 1937 d: Henri Fescourt. FRN., *L'Occident*, Henri Kistemaeckers, Paris 1913, Play

OCCUPATI D'AMELIA 1925 d: Telemaco Ruggeri. ITL., *Occupe-Toi d'Amelie*, Georges Feydeau, 1911, Play

Occupati d'Amelia *see* OCCUPE-TOI D'AMELIE (1949).

OCCUPE-TOI D'AMELIE 1912 d: Emile Chautard. FRN., *Occupe-Toi d'Amelie*, Georges Feydeau, 1911, Play

OCCUPE-TOI D'AMELIE 1932 d: Richard Weisbach, Marguerite Viel. FRN., *Occupe-Toi d'Amelie*, Georges Feydeau, 1911, Play

OCCUPE-TOI D'AMELIE 1949 d: Claude Autant-Lara. FRN/ITL., *Occupe-Toi d'Amelie*, Georges Feydeau, 1911, Play

Ocean Gold *see* PHANTOM SUBMARINE (1940).

Ocean Odyssey *see* OCEANO (1971).

OCEANO 1971 d: Folco Quilici. ITL., *Oceano*, Folco Quilici, Book

OCHI DE URS 1983 d: Stere Gulea. RMN., *Ochi de Urs*, Mihail Sadoveanu, 1938, Short Story

OCHOCIENTAS MIL LEGUAS POR EL AMAZONAS 1958 d: Emilio Gomez Muriel. MXC., *La Jangada*, Jules Verne, 1881, Novel

OCHSENKRIEG, DER 1920 d: Franz Osten. GRM., *Der Ochsenkrieg*, Ludwig Ganghofer, Novel

OCHSENKRIEG, DER 1942 d: Hans Deppe. GRM., *Der Ochsenkrieg*, Ludwig Ganghofer, Novel

OCHSENKRIEG, DER 1986 d: Sigi Rothemund. GRM/AUS/CZC., *Der Ochsenkrieg*, Ludwig Ganghofer, Novel

OCI CIORNIE 1987 d: Nikita Mikhalkov. ITL., *Dama S Sobachkoy*, Anton Chekhov, 1899, Short Story

OCTAVE 1909. FRN., *Octave*, Henri Geroule, Yves Mirande, Play

Octave of Claudius, The *see* A BLIND BARGAIN (1922).

OCTOBER MAN, THE 1947 d: Roy Ward Baker. UKN., *The October Man*, Eric Ambler, Novel

OCTOBER SKY 1999 d: Joe Johnston. USA., *Rocket Boys*, Homer H. Hickam Jr., Book

OCTOPUS, THE 1915 d: Thomas Santschi. USA., *The Octopus*, Frank Norris, 1901, Novel

Octopus, The *see* FIFTH AVENUE (1926).

OCTOPUSSY 1983 d: John Glen. UKN., *Octopussy*, Ian Fleming, Short Story, *The Property of a Lady*, Ian Fleming, Short Story

OCTOROON, THE 1913 d: Kenean Buel. USA., *The Quadroon*, Mayne Reid, 1856, Novel

ODALISQUE, THE 1914 d: W. Christy Cabanne. USA., *The Odalisque*, Leroy Scott, Story

ODD ANGRY SHOT, THE 1979 d: Tom Jeffrey. ASL., *The Odd Angry Shot*, William Nagle, Novel

ODD CHARGES 1916 d: Frank Miller. UKN., *Odd Charges*, W. W. Jacobs, Short Story

ODD COUPLE, THE 1968 d: Gene Saks. USA., *The Odd Couple*, Neil Simon, New York 1965, Play

ODD FREAK, AN 1916 d: George Loane Tucker. UKN., *Light Freights*, W. W. Jacobs, Short Story

ODD FREAK, AN 1923 d: Manning Haynes. UKN., *Light Freights*, W. W. Jacobs, Short Story

Odd Lovers *see* KOMEDI I HAGERSKOG (1968).

ODD MAN OUT 1947 d: Carol Reed. UKN., *Odd Man Out*, Frederick Lawrence Green, London 1945, Novel

Odd Obsession *see* KAGI (1959).

Odd Obsessions *see* KAGI (1959).

ODDS AGAINST TOMORROW 1959 d: Robert Wise. USA., *Odds Against Tomorrow*, William P. McGivern, 1957, Novel

ODED HANODED 1932 d: Haim Halachmi. ISR., Tzvi Lieberman-Livne, Story

Oded the Wanderer *see* ODED HANODED (1932).

Odeon 36.72 *see* ENTRE ONZE HEURES ET MINUIT (1948).

ODESSA FILE, THE 1974 d: Ronald Neame. UKN/GRM., *The Odessa File*, Frederick Forsyth, 1972, Novel

ODETTE 1916 d: Giuseppe de Liguoro. ITL., *Odette*, Victorien Sardou, 1881, Play

Odette *see* MEIN LEBEN FUR DAS DEINE (1927).

ODETTE 1934 d: Jacques Houssin, Giorgio Zambon. FRN/ITL., *Odette*, Victorien Sardou, 1881, Play

Odette *see* DESARROI (1946).

ODETTE 1950 d: Herbert Wilcox. UKN., *Odette*, Jerrard Tickell, Book

ODISSEA, L' 1911 d: Francesco Bertolini, Adolfo Padovan. ITL., *The Odyssey*, Homer, Verse

ODORE DELLA NOTTE, L' 1999 d: Claudio Caligari. ITL., *Le Notti Di Arancia Meccanica*, Dido Sacchettoni, Book

ODORIKO 1957 d: Hiroshi Shimizu. JPN., *Odoriko*, Kafu Nagai, 1944, Novel

Odyssee *see* ULISSE (1954).

Odyssey *see* L' ODISSEA (1911).

ODYSSEY OF THE NORTH, AN 1914 d: Hobart Bosworth. USA., *An Odyssey of the North*, Jack London, 1900, Short Story

ODYSSEY, THE 1997 d: Andrei Konchalovsky. USA., *The Odyssey*, Homer, Verse

Oedipus *see* KONING OEDIPUS (1912).

Oedipus King *see* EDIPO RE (1910).

OEDIPUS REX 1957 d: Tyrone Guthrie. CND., *Oedipus Rex*, Sophocles, c420 bc, Play

Oedipus Rex *see* EDIPO RE (1967).

OEDIPUS THE KING 1967 d: Philip Saville. UKN., *Oedipus Rex*, Sophocles, c420 bc, Play

Oedipus the King *see* EDIPO RE (1967).

Oeil de l'Ombre, L' *see* PEEP (1974).

OEIL DE LYNX DETECTIVE 1936 d: Pierre-Jean Ducis. FRN., *Oeil de Lynx Detective*, Andre Cuel, Play

OEIL DE LYNX, DETECTIVE 1936 d: Pierre-Jean Ducis. FRN., *Oeil de Lynx Detective*, Abel Deval, Daniel Poire, Play

OEUF, L' 1971 d: Jean Herman. FRN., *L' Oeuf*, Felicien Marceau, 1957, Play

OEUFS DE L'AUTRUCHE, LES 1957 d: Denys de La Patelliere. FRN., *Les Oeufs de l'Autruche*, Andre Roussin, 1955, Play

Of Flesh and Blood *see* LES GRANDS CHEMINS (1963).

OF HUMAN BONDAGE 1934 d: John Cromwell. USA., *Of Human Bondage*, W. Somerset Maugham, London 1915, Novel

OF HUMAN BONDAGE 1946 d: Edmund Goulding. USA., *Of Human Bondage*, W. Somerset Maugham, London 1915, Novel

OF HUMAN BONDAGE 1964 d: Ken Hughes, Henry Hathaway (Uncredited). UKN/USA., *Of Human Bondage*, W. Somerset Maugham, London 1915, Novel

OF HUMAN HEARTS 1938 d: Clarence Brown. USA., *Benefits Forgot*, Honore Morrow, New York 1917, Novel

Of Love and Lust *see* GIFTAS (1957).

OF MICE AND MEN 1939 d: Lewis Milestone. USA., *Of Mice and Men*, John Steinbeck, New York 1937, Novel

OF MICE AND MEN 1981 d: Reza Badiyi. USA., *Of Mice and Men*, John Steinbeck, New York 1937, Novel

OF MICE AND MEN 1992 d: Gary Sinise. USA., *Of Mice and Men*, John Steinbeck, New York 1937, Novel

OF STARS AND MEN 1964 d: John Hubley. USA., *Of Stars and Men*, Harlow Shapley, Boston 1958, Book

OF UNKNOWN ORIGIN 1983 d: George Pan Cosmatos. USA/CND., *The Visitor*, Chauncey G. Parker III, Novel

OFF THE HIGHWAY 1925 d: Tom Forman. USA., *Tatterly - the Story of a Dead Man*, Tom Gallon, New York 1897, Novel

OFFENCE, THE 1973 d: Sidney Lumet. UKN., *This Story of Yours*, John Hopkins, 1969, Play

Offence, The *see* DA CHONGZHUANG (1993).

Office Girl, The *see* SUNSHINE SUSIE (1932).

OFFICE WIFE, THE 1930 d: Lloyd Bacon. USA., *The Office Wife*, Faith Baldwin, New York 1930, Novel

OFFICE WIFE, THE 1934 d: George King. USA., *The Office Wife*, Faith Baldwin, New York 1930, Novel

OFFICER 666 1914 d: Frank Powell. USA., *Officer 666*, Augustin MacHugh, New York 1912, Play

OFFICER 666 1920 d: Harry Beaumont. USA., *Officer 666*, Augustin MacHugh, New York 1912, Play

Officer Factory, The *see* FABRIK DER OFFIZIERE (1960).

OFFICER'S MESS, THE 1931 d: Manning Haynes. UKN., *The Officer's Mess*, Sidney Blow, Douglas Hoare, London 1918, Play

Official Secret *see* SPIES OF THE AIR (1939).

Offizierstragodie, Eine *see* ROSENMONTAG (1924).

OFF-SHORE PIRATE, THE 1921 d: Dallas M. Fitzgerald. USA., *Offshore Pirate*, F. Scott Fitzgerald, 1920, Short Story

OGHIN-SAMA 1960 d: Kinuyo TanakA. JPN., *O-Gin Sama*, Toko Kon, Tokyo 1927, Short Story

Ogin Sama *see* OGHIN-SAMA (1960).

O-Gin Sama *see* OGHIN-SAMA (1960).

Ogre, The *see* DER UNHOLD (1996).

OGRO 1979 d: Gillo Pontecorvo. ITL/SPN/FRN., *Operazione Ogro*, Julien Aguirre, Book

Oh Amelia *see* OCCUPE-TOI D'AMELIE (1949).

Oh, Annice! *see* THE GOLD CURE (1919).

OH, BOY! 1919 d: Albert Capellani. USA., *Oh Boy!*, Guy Bolton, Jerome Kern, P. G. Wodehouse, New York 1917, Musical Play

OH DAD, POOR DAD, MAMA'S HUNG YOU IN THE CLOSET AND I'M FEELING SO SAD 1967 d: Richard Quine, Alexander MacKendrick. USA., *Oh Dad, Poor Dad, Mamma's Hung You in the Closet and I'm Feeling So Sad*, Arthur Kopit, 1960, Play

OH DADDY! 1935 d: Graham Cutts, Austin Melford. UKN., *Oh Daddy!*, Austin Melford, London 1930, Play

OH DEAR UNCLE! 1939 d: Richard Llewellyn. UKN., *Peter's Pence*, W. W. Jacobs, Short Story

OH DIESE MANNER 1941 d: Hubert MarischkA. GRM., *Drei Blaue Augen*, Geza von Cziffra, Play

Oh, Diese Weiber *see* DIE KASEREI IN DER VEHFREUDE (1958).

OH, DOCTOR! 1925 d: Harry Pollard. USA., *Oh Doctor!*, Harry Leon Wilson, New York 1923, Novel

OH, DOCTOR! 1937 d: Ray McCarey. USA., *Doctor! Oh, Harry Leon Wilson, New York 1923, Novel

Oh, Egon *see* EGON ACH (1961).

OH, FOR A MAN! 1930 d: Hamilton MacFadden. USA., *Stolen Thunder*, Mary T. Watkins, 1930, Short Story

Oh! for a Man! *see* WILL SUCCESS SPOIL ROCK HUNTER? (1957).

OH, GOD! 1977 d: Carl Reiner. USA., *Oh God!*, Avery Corman, Novel

Oh, Jo! *see* THE COUNTRY FLAPPER (1922).

OH, KAY! 1928 d: Mervyn Leroy. USA., *Oh Kay!*, Guy Bolton, P. G. Wodehouse, New York 1926, Play

Oh, Lady, Lady *see* LADY! LADY! OH (1920).

OH, LADY! LADY! 1920 d: Maurice Campbell. USA., *Oh Lady Lady!*, Guy Bolton, Jerome Kern, P. G. Wodehouse, New York 1918, Musical Play

Oh, Mein Papa *see* FEUERWERK (1956).

OH, MEN! OH, WOMEN! 1957 d: Nunnally Johnson. USA., *Oh Men! Oh Women!*, Edward Chodorov, Play

Oh! My Papa *see* FEUERWERK (1956).

Oh No, Mam'zelle *see* MAM'ZELLE NITOUCHE (1954).

OH ROSALINDA! 1955 d: Michael Powell, Emeric Pressburger. UKN/GRM., *Die Fledermaus*, Henri Meilhac, Johann Strauss, Vienna 1874, Operetta

Oh! Sabella *see* LA NONNA SABELLA (1957).

OH! SAILOR, BEHAVE! 1930 d: Archie Mayo. USA., *See Naples and Die*, Elmer Rice, New York 1929, Play

OH, SERAFINA! 1976 d: Alberto LattuadA. ITL., *Oh Serafina!*, Giuseppe Berto, 1973, Novel

Oh! Sweet Snow *see* O! XIANG XUE (1989).

Oh That Tyrolean Love *see* JA, DIE LIEBE IN TIROL JA (1955).

Oh These Bavarians *see* O DIESE BAYERN (1960).

Oh What a Duchess! *see* MY OLD DUCHESS (1933).

OH! WHAT A LOVELY WAR 1969 d: Richard Attenborough. UKN., *Oh! What a Lovely War*, Joan Littlewood, 1965, Play, *Long Trail, the Long*, Charles Chilton, Play

OH, WHAT A NIGHT! 1935 d: Frank Richardson. UKN., *The Irresistible Marmaduke*, Ernest Denny, London 1918, Play

OH, WHAT A NURSE! 1926 d: Charles F. Reisner. USA., *Oh, What a Nurse!*, Bert Bloch, R. E. Sherwood, Play

OH, YEAH! 1929 d: Tay Garnett. USA., *No Brakes*, Andrew W. Somerville, 1928, Short Story

OHAN 1984 d: Kon IchikawA. JPN., *Ohan*, Chiyo Uno, Novel

Oharu *see* SAIKAKU ICHIDAI ONNA (1952).

Ohne Datenschutz *see* LE DOSSIER 51 (1978).

OHNE MUTTER GEHT ES NICHT 1958 d: Erik Ode. GRM., *Ohne Mutter Geht Es Nicht*, Hans Nicklisch, Novel

OHNIVE LETO 1939 d: Frantisek Cap, Vaclav KrskA. CZC., *Odchazeti S Podzimem*, Vaclav Krska, Novel

OIL FOR THE LAMPS OF CHINA 1935 d: Mervyn Leroy. USA., *Oil for the Lamps of China*, Alice Tisdale Hobart, New York 1933, Novel

Oil Lamps *see* PETROLEJOVE LAMPY (1972).

Oil Prince, The *see* DER OLPRINZ (1965).

Oil Town *see* LUCY GALLANT (1955).

OISEAU BLESSE, L' 1914 d: Leonce Perret?, Maurice Mariaud?. FRN., *L' Oiseau Blesse*, Alfred Capus, Play

OISEAU MOQUEUR, L' 1962 d: Robert Enrico. FRN., Ambrose Bierce, Short Story

OISEAUX DE PASSAGE 1925 d: Gaston Roudes. FRN., *Oiseaux de Passage*, Lucien Descaves, Maurice Donnay, Novel

OISEAUX VONT MOURIR AU PEROU, LES 1968 d: Romain Gary. FRN., *Les Oiseaux Vont Mourir Au Perou*, Romain Gary, 1962, Short Story

Oiwa No Borei *see* YOTSUYA KAIDAN -OIWA NO BOREI (1969).

OJOS PERDIDOS, LOS 1966 d: Rafael Garcia Serrano. SPN., *Los Ojos Perdidos*, Rafael Garcia Serrano, 1958, Novel

OKA OORIE KATHA 1977 d: Mrinal Sen. IND., *Do Bailon Ki Katha*, Munshi Premchand, 1936, Short Story

OKENKO 1933 d: Vladimir Slavinsky. CZC., *Okenko*, Olga Scheinpflugova, Play

OKLAHOMA! 1955 d: Fred Zinnemann. USA., *Green Grow the Lilacs*, Lynn Riggs, New York 1930, Play

OKOVY 1925 d: Vaclav Kubasek. CZC., *Okovy*, Jan Kobr, Novel

OKTOBERFEST 1987 d: Dragan KresojA. YGS., *Oktoberfest*, Branko Dimitrijevic, Novel

Okuni and Gohei *see* OKUNI TO GOHEI (1952).

OKUNI TO GOHEI 1952 d: Mikio Naruse. JPN., *Okuni to Gohei*, Junichiro Tanizaki, 1922, Play

OLD ACQUAINTANCE 1943 d: Vincent Sherman. USA., *Old Acquaintance*, John Van Druten, New York 1940, Play

OLD ACTOR'S STORY, THE 1922 d: H. B. Parkinson. UKN., *The Old Actor's Story*, George R. Sims, Poem

OLD ARM CHAIR, THE 1920 d: Percy Nash. UKN., *The Old Arm Chair*, Mrs. O. F. Walton, Novel

OLD BONES OF THE RIVER 1938 d: Marcel Varnel. UKN., *Bones*, Edgar Wallace, London 1915, Novel, *Lieutenant Bones*, Edgar Wallace, London 1918, Novel

Old Capital, The see **KOTO** (1963).

Old Clergyman, The see **DEN GAMLE PRAEST** (1939).

OLD CODE, THE 1915. USA., *The Old Code*, James Oliver Curwood, Story

OLD COUNTRY, THE 1921 d: A. V. Bramble. UKN., *The Old Country*, Dion Clayton Calthrop, Play

OLD CURIOSITY SHOP, THE 1909. USA., *The Old Curiosity Shop*, Charles Dickens, London 1841, Novel

OLD CURIOSITY SHOP, THE 1911 d: Theodore Marston. USA., *The Old Curiosity Shop*, Charles Dickens, London 1841, Novel

OLD CURIOSITY SHOP, THE 1912 d: Frank Powell. UKN., *The Old Curiosity Shop*, Charles Dickens, London 1841, Novel

OLD CURIOSITY SHOP, THE 1913 d: Thomas Bentley. UKN., *The Old Curiosity Shop*, Charles Dickens, London 1841, Novel

OLD CURIOSITY SHOP, THE 1921 d: Thomas Bentley. UKN., *The Old Curiosity Shop*, Charles Dickens, London 1841, Novel

OLD CURIOSITY SHOP, THE 1934 d: Thomas Bentley. UKN., *The Old Curiosity Shop*, Charles Dickens, London 1841, Novel

Old Curiosity Shop, The see **MISTER QUILP** (1974).

OLD CURIOSITY SHOP, THE 1989 d: Warwick Gilbert. ASL., *The Old Curiosity Shop*, Charles Dickens, London 1841, Novel

OLD CURIOSITY SHOP, THE 1995 d: Kevin Connor. USA/UKN., *The Old Curiosity Shop*, Charles Dickens, London 1841, Novel

OLD DAD 1920 d: Lloyd Ingraham. USA., *Old Dad*, Eleanor Hallowell Abbott, New York 1919, Novel

OLD DARK HOUSE, THE 1932 d: James Whale. USA., *Benighted*, J. B. Priestley, London 1927, Novel

OLD DARK HOUSE, THE 1963 d: William Castle. UKN/USA., *Benighted*, J. B. Priestley, London 1927, Novel

OLD DEVILS, THE 1991 d: Tristram Powell. UKN., *The Old Devils*, Kingsley Amis, 1986, Novel

Old Doll's House, The see **MIDNIGHT ALIBI** (1934).

OLD DUTCH 1915 d: Frank H. Crane. USA., *Old Dutch*, Victor Herbert, George V. Hobart, Edgar Smith, New York 1909, Musical Play

OLD ENGLISH 1930 d: Alfred E. Green. USA., *Old English*, John Galsworthy, 1924, Play

OLD GRINGO 1989 d: Luis Puenzo. USA., *The Old Gringo*, Carlos Fuentes, 1985, Novel

Old Guard see **LES VIEUX DE LA VIEILLE** (1960).

OLD HEIDELBERG 1915 d: John Emerson. USA., *Karl Heinrich*, Wilhelm Meyer-Forster, 1899, Novel

Old Heidelberg see **THE STUDENT PRINCE IN OLD HEIDELBERG** (1927).

Old Heidelberg see **THE STUDENT'S ROMANCE** (1935).

Old Heidelberg see **ALT-HEIDELBERG** (1959).

OLD HOMESTEAD, THE 1916 d: James Kirkwood. USA., *The Old Homestead*, Denman Thompson, Boston 1886, Play

OLD HOMESTEAD, THE 1922 d: James Cruze. USA., *Denman Thompson's the Old Homestead*, John Russell Coryell, New York 1889, Novel

OLD HOMESTEAD, THE 1935 d: William Nigh. USA., *Denman Thompson's the Old Homestead*, John Russell Coryell, New York 1889, Novel

Old Hutch see **HONEST HUTCH** (1920).

OLD HUTCH 1936 d: J. Walter Ruben. USA., *Old Hutch Lives Up to It*, Garrett Smith, 1920, Short Story

Old Jo see **THE COUNTRY FLAPPER** (1922).

OLD LADY 31 1920 d: John Ince. USA., *Old Lady 31*, Rachel Crothers, New York 1916, Play

Old Lady 31 see **THE CAPTAIN IS A LADY** (1940).

Old Lady Thirty-One see **THE CAPTAIN IS A LADY** (1940).

Old Lady Who Walked in the Sea, The see **LA VIEILLE QUI MARCHAIT DANS LA MER** (1991).

Old Lantern, The see **UTA ANDON** (1960).

OLD LOVES AND NEW 1926 d: Maurice Tourneur. USA., *The Desert Healer*, Edith Maude Hull, Boston 1923, Novel

Old Madrid see **A WIFE'S ROMANCE** (1923).

OLD MAID, THE 1914 d: John B. O'Brien. USA., *Dorothy in the Garret*, John Townsend Trowbridge, Poem

OLD MAID, THE 1939 d: Edmund Goulding. USA., *The Old Maid*, Edith Wharton, New York 1924, Novel

Old Maid, The see **DOMNISOARA AURICA** (1986).

Old Man and His Dog, An see **LAOREN HE GOU** (1993).

OLD MAN AND JIM, THE 1911 d: Ulysses Davis. USA., *The Old Man and Jim*, James Whitcomb Riley, Poem

OLD MAN AND THE SEA, THE 1958 d: John Sturges, Henry King (Uncredited). USA., *The Old Man and the Sea*, Ernest Hemingway, 1952, Novel

OLD MAN AND THE SEA, THE 1990 d: Jud Taylor. USA., *The Old Man and the Sea*, Ernest Hemingway, 1952, Novel

Old Man Bezousek, The see **PANTATA BEZOUSEK** (1941).

Old Man Minick see **THE EXPERT** (1932).

Old Man Minick see **NO PLACE TO GO** (1939).

Old Man Murphy see **HIS FAMILY TREE** (1935).

OLD MAN, THE 1931 d: Manning Haynes. UKN., *The Old Man*, Edgar Wallace, Play

OLD MEN AT THE ZOO, THE 1982 d: Stuart Burge. UKN., *The Old Men at the Zoo*, Angus Wilson, Novel

Old Mrs. Leonard and Her machine Guns see **THE LADY AND THE MOB** (1939).

Old Mrs. Leonard and the machine Guns see **THE LADY AND THE MOB** (1939).

OLD NEST, THE 1921 d: Reginald Barker. USA., *The Old Nest*, Rupert Hughes, 1911, Short Story

Old School Chum see **MEIN SCHULFREUND** (1960).

Old Seterhand see **OLD SHATTERHAND** (1964).

OLD SHATTERHAND 1964 d: Hugo Fregonese. GRM/FRN/ITL., *Old Shatterhand*, Karl Friedrich May, Novel

OLD SOAK, THE 1926 d: Edward Sloman. USA., *The Old Soak*, Don Marquis, New York 1922, Play

Old Soak, The see **THE GOOD OLD SOAK** (1937).

Old Soldiers Never Die see **FIXED BAYONETS** (1951).

OLD ST. PAUL'S 1914 d: Wilfred Noy. UKN., *Old St. Paul's*, Harrison Ainsworth, Novel

OLD SUREHAND I 1965 d: Alfred Vohrer. GRM/YGS., *Old Surehand*, Karl Friedrich May, Freiberg Im Breisgau 1894, Novel

OLD SWEETHEART OF MINE, AN 1911 d: Bannister Merwin. USA., *An Old Sweetheart of Mine*, James Whitcomb Riley, Poem

OLD SWEETHEART OF MINE, AN 1923 d: Harry Garson. USA., *An Old Sweetheart of Mine*, James Whitcomb Riley, Poem

OLD SWIMMIN' HOLE, THE 1921 d: Joseph de Grasse. USA., *Teh Old Swimmin' Hole*, James Whitcomb Riley, 1883, Poem

Old Tin Can, The see **LE CANARD EN FER BLANC** (1967).

Old Well, The see **LAO JING** (1987).

Old West Per Contract, The see **'49 - '17** (1917).

OLD WIVES FOR NEW 1918 d: Cecil B. de Mille. USA., *Old Wives for New*, David Graham Phillips, New York 1908, Novel

OLD WIVES' TALE, THE 1921 d: Denison Clift. UKN., *The Old Wives' Tale*, Arnold Bennett, 1908, Novel

Old Woman Ghost, The see **YOBA** (1976).

OLD YELLER 1957 d: Robert Stevenson. USA., *Old Yeller*, Fred Gipson, Novel

OLDAS ES KOTES 1963 d: Miklos Jancso. HNG., *Oldas Es Kotes*, Jozsef Lengyel, 1964, Short Story

Older Sister, The see **STARSHAYA SESTRA** (1967).

Oldest Confession, The see **THE HAPPY THIEVES** (1962).

Old-Fashioned Education see **L' AJO NELL'IMBARAZZO** (1911).

OLD-FASHIONED GIRL, AN 1949 d: Arthur Dreifuss. USA., *An Old Fashioned Girl*, Louisa May Alcott, 1870, Novel

Old-Timer, The see **MY AMERICAN WIFE** (1936).

OLE OPFINDERS OFFER 1924 d: Lau Lauritzen. DNM., *Ole Opfinders Offer*, Palle Rosencrantz, Novel

Olette the Elusive see **THE SIXTEENTH WIFE** (1917).

OLIMPIA 1930 d: Miguel de ZarragA. USA., *Olympia*, Ferenc Molnar, Budapest 1928, Play

Olive Trees of Justice, The see **LES OLIVIERS DE LA JUSTICE** (1962).

OLIVER! 1968 d: Carol Reed. UKN., *Oliver Twist*, Charles Dickens, London 1838, Novel

OLIVER & COMPANY 1989 d: George Scribner. USA., *Oliver Twist*, Charles Dickens, London 1838, Novel

OLIVER AND THE ARTFUL DODGER 1972 d: William Hanna, Joseph BarberA. USA., *Oliver Twist*, Charles Dickens, London 1838, Novel

OLIVER TWIST 1909 d: J. Stuart Blackton. USA., *Oliver Twist*, Charles Dickens, London 1838, Novel

Oliver Twist see **STORIA DI UN ORFANO** (1911).

OLIVER TWIST 1912 d: Thomas Bentley. UKN., *Oliver Twist*, Charles Dickens, London 1838, Novel

OLIVER TWIST 1912. USA., *Oliver Twist*, Charles Dickens, London 1838, Novel

OLIVER TWIST 1916 d: James Young. USA., *Oliver Twist*, Charles Dickens, London 1838, Novel

OLIVER TWIST 1922 d: Frank Lloyd. USA., *Oliver Twist*, Charles Dickens, London 1838, Novel

OLIVER TWIST 1933 d: William J. Cowen. USA., *Oliver Twist*, Charles Dickens, London 1838, Novel

OLIVER TWIST 1940 d: David Bradley. USA., *Oliver Twist*, Charles Dickens, London 1838, Novel

OLIVER TWIST 1948 d: David Lean. UKN., *Oliver Twist*, Charles Dickens, London 1838, Novel

OLIVER TWIST 1974 d: Hal Sutherland. USA., *Oliver Twist*, Charles Dickens, London 1838, Novel

OLIVER TWIST 1982 d: Richard Slapczynski. ASL., *Oliver Twist*, Charles Dickens, London 1838, Novel

OLIVER TWIST 1982 d: Clive Donner. USA., *Oliver Twist*, Charles Dickens, London 1838, Novel

OLIVER TWIST 1985 d: Gareth Davies. UKN., *Oliver Twist*, Charles Dickens, London 1838, Novel

OLIVER TWIST, JR. 1921 d: Millard Webb. USA., *Oliver Twist*, Charles Dickens, London 1838, Novel

OLIVER'S STORY 1978 d: John Korty. USA., *Oliver's Story*, Erich Segal, 1977, Novel

OLIVIER TWIST 1908-10 d: Camille de Morlhon. FRN., *Oliver Twist*, Charles Dickens, London 1838, Novel

OLIVIER TWIST 1910 d: Andre Calmettes. FRN., *Oliver Twist*, Charles Dickens, London 1838, Novel

OLIVIERS DE LA JUSTICE, LES 1962 d: James Blue. FRN., *Les Oliviers de la Justice*, Jean Pelegri, Paris 1959, Novel

OLPRINZ, DER 1965 d: Harald Philipp. GRM/YGS., *Der Olprinz*, Karl Friedrich May, Stuttgart 1893, Novel

Olprinz, Der see **DER OLPRINZ** (1965).

OLTRE L'AMORE 1940 d: Carmine Gallone. ITL., *Vanina Vanini*, Stendhal, 1855, Short Story

Olvova Myllari see **ULVOVA MYLLARI** (1983).

OLYMPE DE NOS AMOURS 1989 d: Serge Moati. FRN., *Les Chapellieres*, Pierre Pean, Novel

OLYMPIA 1930 d: Jacques Feyder, Lionel Barrymore. USA., *Olympia*, Ferenc Molnar, Budapest 1928, Play

Olympia see **SI L'EMPEREUR SAVAIT CA** (1930).

Olympia see **A BREATH OF SCANDAL** (1960).

OLYMPIA 1998 d: Robert Byington. USA., *Javelkemeiche*, Robert Byington, Story

Olympic 13 Gagnant see **L' ATHLETE INCOMPLET** (1932).

OLYMPIC HONEYMOON 1936 d: Alf Goulding. UKN., *He and Ski*, F. Dawson Gratix, Novel

Om Zijn Eer see **MADAME PINKETTE & CO.** (1917).

OMAR THE TENTMAKER 1922 d: James Young. USA., *Omar the Tentmaker*, Richard Walton Tully, New York 1914, Play

Ombra Della Montagna, L' see **LA DONNA DELLA MONTAGNA** (1943).

OMBRA, L' 1917 d: Mario Caserini. ITL., *L' Ombra*, Dario Niccodemi, 1915, Play

OMBRA, L' 1923 d: Mario Almirante. ITL., *L' Ombra*, Dario Niccodemi, 1915, Play

OMBRA, L' 1955 d: Giorgio Bianchi. ITL., *L' Ombra*, Dario Niccodemi, 1915, Play

OMBRA NELL'OMBRA, UN' 1979 d: Pier Carpi. ITL., *Un' Ombra Nell'Ombra*, Piero Carpi, Novel

Ombre Bianche see **THE SAVAGE INNOCENTS** (1959).

Ombre du Deuxieme Bureau, L' see **LA FEMME TRAQUEE NADIA** (1939).

OMBRE, L' 1948 d: Andre Berthomieu. FRN., *L' Ombre*, Francis Carco, 1933, Novel

OMBRE, LE 1918 d: Oreste Gherardini. ITL., *Le Ombre*, Francesco Mastriani, 1883, Play

OMBYTE AV TAG 1943 d: Hasse Ekman. SWD., *Ombye Av Tag*, Walter Ljungquist, 1933, Novel

OMEGA MAN, THE 1971 d: Boris Sagal. USA., *I Am Legend*, Richard Matheson, New York 1954, Novel

Omicida, L' see **LE MEURTRIER** (1962).

OMICIDIO PER APPUNTAMENTO 1967 d: Mino Guerrini. ITL/GRM., *Tempo Di Massacro*, Franco Enna, Novel

OMOO OMOO 1949 d: Leon Leonard. USA., *Omoo*, Herman Melville, 1851, Novel

ON A CLEAR DAY YOU CAN SEE FOREVER 1970 d: Vincente Minnelli. USA., *On a Clear Day You Can See Forever*, Burton Lane, Alan Jay Lerner, New York 1965, Play

On a Comet see **NA KOMETE** (1970).

On a Friday in Las Vegas see **500 MILLONES LAS VEGAS** (1968).

ON A JEHO SESTRA 1931 d: Martin Fric, Carl Lamac. CZC., *On a Jeho Sestra*, Bernhard Buchbinder, Play

On a Narrow Bridge see **GESHER TZAR ME'OD** (1985).

On a Perdu une Femme Nue see **ON A TROUVE UNE FEMME NUE** (1934).

On a Quiet Evening see **V TIHATA VECHER** (1959).

On a Steep Bank see **U KRUTOGO YARA** (1962).

ON A TROUVE UNE FEMME NUE 1934 d: Leo Joannon. FRN., *On a Trouve une Femme Nue*, Andre Birabeau, Jean Guitton, Play

ON AGAIN -OFF AGAIN 1937 d: Eddie Cline. USA., *A Pair of Sixes*, Edward Peple, New York 1914, Play

On Any Street see **LA NOTTE BRAVA** (1959).

ON APPROVAL 1930 d: Tom Walls. UKN., *On Approval*, Frederick Lonsdale, London 1927, Play

ON APPROVAL 1944 d: Clive Brook. UKN., *On Approval*, Frederick Lonsdale, London 1927, Play

ON BORROWED TIME 1939 d: Harold S. Bucquet. USA., *On Borrowed Time*, Lawrence Edward Watkin, New York 1937, Novel

ON DANGEROUS GROUND 1917 d: Robert T. Thornby. USA., *Little Comrade: a Tale of the Great War*, Burton Egbert Stevenson, New York 1915, Novel

ON DANGEROUS GROUND 1951 d: Nicholas Ray. USA., *Mad With Much Heart*, Gerald Butler, 1945, Novel

ON DEMANDE UN ASSASSIN 1949 d: Ernst Neubach. FRN., *On Demande un Assassin*, Ernest Neubach, Andre Tabet, Play

ON DEMANDE UN MENAGE 1945 d: Maurice Cam. FRN., *On Demande un Menage*, Jean de Letraz, Play

ON DONOVAN'S DIVISION 1912 d: Walter Edwin. USA., *On Donovan's Division*, W. Hanson Durham, Story

ON EST TOUJOURS TROP BON AVEC LES FEMMES 1970 d: Michel Boisrond. FRN., *On Est Toujours Trop Bon Avec Les Femmes*, Raymond Queneau, 1947, Novel

On Fertile Lands see **BEREKETLI TOPRAKLAR UZERINDE** (1980).

ON GIANT'S SHOULDERS 1979 d: Anthony Simmons. UKN., *On Giant's Shoulders*, Michael Robson, Marjorie Wallace, Book

ON GOLDEN POND 1981 d: Mark Rydell. USA., *On Golden Pond*, Ernest Thompson, Play

On Guard! see **LE BOSSU** (1997).

ON HER BED OF ROSES 1966 d: Albert Zugsmith. USA., *Psychopathia Sexualis: Klinischfornsische Studie*, Richard von Krafft-Ebing, Stuttgart 1886, Book

On Her Honor see **THE DAZZLING MISS DAVISON** (1917).

ON HER MAJESTY'S SECRET SERVICE 1969 d: Peter Hunt. UKN., *On Her Majesty's Secret Service*, Ian Fleming, London 1963, Novel

On His Own see **V LYUDKYAKH** (1939).

On Holy Hill see **NA SVATEM KOPECKU** (1934).

On Monday Next see **CURTAIN UP** (1952).

ON MOONLIGHT BAY 1951 d: Roy Del Ruth. USA., *Penrod - His Complete Story*, Booth Tarkington, 1931, Novel

On My Honor see **ICH SCHWORE UND GELOBE** (1960).

On My Own see **EL ATZMI** (1988).

ON N'AIME QU'UNE FOIS 1949 d: Jean Stelli. FRN., *La Caille*, Paul Vialar, Novel

ON NE BADINE PAS AVEC L'AMOUR 1909. FRN., *On Ne Badine Pas Avec l'Amour*, Alfred de Musset, 1834, Play

ON NE BADINE PAS AVEC L'AMOUR 1961 d: Jean Dessailly. FRN., *On Ne Badine Pas Avec l'Amour*, Alfred de Musset, 1834, Play

On Ne Cede Pas see **MIR LOND NOD LUGG** (1940).

ON NE MEURT QUE DEUX FOIS 1986 d: Jacques Deray. FRN., *He Died With His Eyes Open*, Derek Raymond, Novel

ON NE ROULE PAS ANTOINETTE 1936 d: Paul Madeux, Christian-Jaque (Spv) FRN., *On Ne Roule Pas Antoinette*, Maurice Hennequin, Pierre Veber, Play

ON N'ENTERRE PAS LE DIMANCHE 1959 d: Michel Drach. FRN., *On N'enterre Pas le Dimanche*, Fred Kassak, Novel

On Parole see **THE WESTERN WALLOP** (1924).

On Pentagon Business see **S.A.S. A SAN SALVADOR** (1982).

ON PURGE BEBE 1908-15. FRN., *On Purge Bebe*, Georges Feydeau, 1910, Play

ON PURGE BEBE 1931 d: Jean Renoir. FRN., *On Purge Bebe*, Georges Feydeau, 1910, Play

ON SECRET SERVICE 1933 d: Arthur Woods. UKN., *Spione Am Werk*, Robert Baberske, Georg Kloren, Novel

On the Air see **TWENTY MILLION SWEETHEARTS** (1934).

On the Air see **AUNT JULIA AND THE SCRIPTWRITER** (1990).

ON THE BANKS OF THE WABASH 1923 d: J. Stuart Blackton. USA., *On the Banks of the Wabash*, Paul Dresser, Song

ON THE BEACH 1959 d: Stanley Kramer. USA., *On the Beach*, Nevil Shute, 1957, Novel

ON THE BLACK HILL 1987 d: Andrew Grieve. UKN., *On the Black Hill*, Bruce Chatwin, 1982, Novel

On the Black Sea see **THE WORLD AND THE FLESH** (1932).

On the Brink see **THE DAMNED** (1962).

On the Dotted Line see **LET WOMEN ALONE** (1925).

On the Eve see **NAKANUNYE** (1959).

ON THE FIDDLE 1961 d: Cyril Frankel. UKN., *Stop at a Winner*, R. F. Delderfield, London 1961, Novel

On the Fringe see **BOUBA** (1987).

On the Gallows Hangs Their Love see **AM GALGEN HANGT DIE LIEBE** (1960).

On the Great White Trail see **RENFREW ON THE GREAT WHITE TRAIL** (1938).

On the Green Meadow see **NA TY LOUCE ZELENY** (1936).

ON THE ISLE OF SARNE 1914 d: Richard Ridgely. USA., *The Picaroon*, H. B. Marriott Watson, Novel

On the Lookout for Trains see **OSTRE SLEDOVANE VLAKY** (1966).

On the Make see **A DEVIL WITH WOMEN** (1930).

On the Niemen River see **NAD NIEMNEM** (1986).

ON THE NIGHT OF THE FIRE 1939 d: Brian Desmond Hurst. UKN., *On the Night of the Fire*, Frederick Lawrence Green, Novel

ON THE QUIET 1918 d: Chet Withey. USA., *On the Quiet*, Augustus Thomas, New York 1901, Play

ON THE RIVIERA 1951 d: Walter Lang. USA., *The Red Cat*, Hans Adler, Rudolph Lothar, New York 1934, Play

ON THE RUN 1963 d: Ernest Tronson. UKN., *Edgar Wallace*, Short Story

ON THE RUN 1969 d: Pat Jackson. UKN., *On the Run*, Nina Bawden, Novel

On the Shelf see **LET WOMEN ALONE** (1925).

On the Steep Cliff see **U KRUTOGO YARA** (1962).

On the Stroke of Nine see **MURDER ON THE CAMPUS** (1934).

ON THE STROKE OF THREE 1924 d: F. Harmon Weight. USA., *The Man from Ashaluna*, Henry Payson Dowst, Boston 1920, Novel

ON THE STROKE OF TWELVE 1927 d: Charles J. Hunt. USA., *On the Stroke of Twelve*, Joseph le Brandt, 1898, Play

ON THE SUNNY SIDE 1942 d: Harold Schuster. USA., *Fraternity*, Mary McCall Jr., Short Story

ON THE THRESHOLD 1925 d: Renaud Hoffman. USA., *On the Threshold*, Wilbur Hall, Short Story

ON THE TOWN 1949 d: Gene Kelly, Stanley Donen. USA., *On the Town*, Leonard Bernstein, Betty Comden, Adolph Green, Musical Play

ON THE WATERFRONT 1954 d: Elia Kazan. USA., *Waterfront*, Budd Schulberg, 1955, Novel

On the Wild Shore see **NA DIKOM BEREGYE** (1967).

ON THE YARD 1978 d: Raphael D. Silver. USA., *On the Yard*, Malcolm Braly, Novel

ON THIN ICE 1925 d: Malcolm St. Clair. USA., *The Dear Pretender*, Alice Ross Colver, Philadelphia 1924, Novel

On Tour see **LITTLE EVA ASCENDS** (1922).

ON TRIAL 1917 d: James Young. USA., *On Trial*, Elmer Rice, New York 1914, Play

ON TRIAL 1928 d: Archie Mayo. USA., *On Trial*, Elmer Rice, New York 1914, Play

ON TRIAL 1939 d: Terry O. Morse. USA., *On Trial*, Elmer Rice, New York 1914, Play

On Trial see **L' AFFAIRE MAURIZIUS** (1953).

ON VALENTINE'S DAY 1986 d: Ken Harrison. USA., *Valentine's Day*, Horton Foote, Play

ON WITH THE DANCE 1920 d: George Fitzmaurice. USA., *On With the Dance*, Michael Morton, New York 1917, Play

ON WITH THE SHOW 1929 d: Alan Crosland. USA., *On With the Show*, Humphrey Pearson, Play

ON YOUR BACK 1930 d: Guthrie McClintic. USA., *On Your Back*, Rita Weiman, 1930, Short Story

ON YOUR TOES 1939 d: Ray Enright. USA., *On Your Toes*, George Abbott, Lorenz Hart, Richard Rodgers, New York 1936, Musical Play

Onassis: the Richest Man in the World see **RICHEST MAN IN THE WORLD: THE STORY OF ARISTOTLE ONASSIS** (1988).

ONAWANDA; OR, AN INDIAN'S DEVOTION 1909 d: J. Stuart Blackton (Spv). USA., *Onawanda*, Dion Boucicault, Play

ONCE A CROOK 1941 d: Herbert Mason. UKN., *Once a Crook*, Ken Attiwill, Evadne Price, Play

ONCE A JOLLY SWAGMAN 1948 d: Jack Lee. UKN., *Once a Jolly Swagman*, Montague Slater, Novel

ONCE A LADY 1931 d: Guthrie McClintic. USA., *Das Zweite Leben*, Rudolf Bernauer, Rudolf Osterreicher, 1927, Play

ONCE A SINNER 1950 d: Lewis Gilbert. UKN., *Irene*, Ronald Marsh, Novel

Once a Thief see **THE HAPPY THIEVES** (1962).

ONCE A THIEF 1965 d: Ralph Nelson. USA/FRN., *Scratch a Thief*, Zekial Marko, New York 1961, Novel

ONCE ABOARD THE LUGGER 1920 d: Gerald Ames, Gaston Quiribet. UKN., *Once Aboard the Lugger*, A. S. M. Hutchinson, Novel

ONCE AN EAGLE 1976 d: E. W. Swackhamer, Richard Michaels. USA., *Once an Eagle*, Anton Myrer, Novel

ONCE BEFORE I DIE 1965 d: John Derek. USA/PHL., *Quit for the Next*, Anthony March, New York 1945, Novel

ONCE IN A LIFETIME 1932 d: Russell MacK. USA., *Once in a Lifetime*, Moss Hart, George S. Kaufman, New York 1930, Play

ONCE IN A LIFETIME 1988 d: Robin Midgley. UKN/USA., *Once in a Lifetime*, Moss Hart, George S. Kaufman, New York 1930, Play

ONCE IN A NEW MOON 1935 d: Anthony Kimmins. UKN., *Lucky Star*, Owen Rutter, Novel

Once Is Not Enough see **JACQUELINE SUSANN'S ONCE IS NOT ENOUGH** (1975).

ONCE MORE MY DARLING 1949 d: Robert Montgomery. USA., *Come Be My Love*, Robert Carson, Short Story

ONCE MORE, WITH FEELING 1960 d: Stanley Donen. USA., *Once More With Feeling*, Harry Kurnitz, Play

Once Over Lightly see **DON'T TELL THE WIFE** (1937).

Once There Was a Lady see **THE BRIDE WORE RED** (1937).

Once There Was a Princess *see* MISBEHAVING LADIES (1931).

ONCE TO EVERY BACHELOR 1934 d: William Nigh. USA., *Search for the Spring*, Eleanor Gates, Short Story

ONCE TO EVERY MAN 1919 d: T. Hayes Hunter. USA., *Once to Every Man*, Larry Evans, New York 1913, Novel

Once to Every Man *see* THE FIGHTING HEART (1925).

Once to Every Man *see* ONCE TO EVERY BACHELOR (1934).

ONCE TO EVERY WOMAN 1934 d: Lambert Hillyer. USA., *Kaleidoscope in K*, A.J. Cronin, 1933, Short Story

ONCE UPON A FOREST 1992 d: Charles Grosvenor. USA., *Once Upon a Forest*, Rae Lambert, Short Story

ONCE UPON A HORSE 1958 d: Hal Kanter. USA., *Why Rustlers Never Win*, Henry Gregor Felsen, Novel

Once Upon a Murder *see* CHIEFS (1985).

Once Upon a Summer *see* GIRL WITH GREEN EYES (1964).

Once Upon a Time *see* DER VAR ENGANG (1922).

ONCE UPON A TIME 1944 d: Alexander Hall. USA., *My Client Curly*, Norman Corwin, Radio Play

ONCE UPON A TIME IN AMERICA 1983 d: Sergio Leone. USA/ITL., *The Hoods*, Harry Grey, Novel

Once Were Heroes *see* ONCE WERE WARRIORS (1994).

ONCE WERE WARRIORS 1994 d: Lee Tamahori. NZL., *Once Were Warriors*, Alan Duff, Novel

ONCE YOU KISS A STRANGER 1969 d: Robert Sparr. USA., *Strangers on a Train*, Patricia Highsmith, 1950, Novel

Onder Spiritistischen Dwang *see* THE OTHER PERSON (1921).

ONDINA, L' 1917 d: A. Albertoni. ITL., *L'Ondina*, Marco Praga, 1903, Play

ONE A MINUTE 1921 d: Jack Nelson. USA., *One a Minute*, Frederick Jackson, Play

One Against Seven *see* COUNTER-ATTACK (1945).

ONE AND ONLY, GENUINE, ORIGINAL FAMILY BAND, THE 1968 d: Michael O'Herlihy. USA., *The Family Band*, Laura Bower Van Nuys, Lincoln, Nb. 1961, Novel

One Born Every Minute *see* THE FLIM-FLAM MAN (1967).

ONE BRIEF SUMMER 1970 d: John MacKenzie. UKN., *Valkyrie's Armour*, Harry Tierney, Play

One Bright Idea *see* ALL NIGHT (1918).

ONE BY ONE 1986 d: Bill Hinzman. USA., *The Majorettes*, John Russo, Novel

One Clear Call *see* THE WIFE HE BOUGHT (1918).

ONE CLEAR CALL 1922 d: John M. Stahl. USA., *One Clear Call*, Frances Nimmo Greene, New York 1914, Novel

ONE COLOMBO NIGHT 1926 d: Henry Edwards. UKN., *One Colombo Night*, Austin Phillips, Novel

ONE DAY 1916 d: Hal Clarendon. USA., *One Day; a Sequel to "Three Weeks"*, Elinor Glyn, New York 1909, Novel

One Day, Every Day *see* EK DIN PRATIDIN (1979).

ONE DAY IN THE LIFE OF IVAN DENISOVICH 1971 d: Caspar Wrede. UKN/NRW/USA., *Odin Den Ivana Denisovicha*, Alexander Solzhenitsyn, 1962, Novel

One Day More, One Day Less *see* PLUSZ MINUSZ EGY NAP (1972).

One Day More Or Less *see* PLUSZ MINUSZ EGY NAP (1972).

One Deadly Summer *see* UN ETE MEURTRIER (1983).

ONE DESIRE 1955 d: Jerry Hopper. USA., *Tacey Cromwell*, Conrad Richter, 1942, Novel

ONE DOLLAR BID 1918 d: Ernest C. Warde. USA., *Toby*, Credo Fitch Harris, Boston 1912, Novel

ONE DOLLAR'S WORTH 1917 d: David Smith. USA.,6., *One Dollar's Worth*, O. Henry, Short Story

ONE EIGHTH APACHE 1922 d: Ben Wilson. USA., *One Eighth Apache*, Peter B. Kyne, Short Story

One Embarrassing Night *see* ROOKERY NOOK (1930).

One Evening on a Train *see* UN TRAIN, UN SOIR (1968).

ONE EXCITING ADVENTURE 1934 d: Ernst L. Frank. USA., *Was Frauen Traumen*, Emil Hosler, Novel

One Exciting Kiss *see* NORTHWEST OUTPOST (1947).

One Exciting Night *see* A NIGHT OF ADVENTURE (1944).

One Fatal Hour *see* FIVE STAR FINAL (1931).

One Fatal Hour *see* TWO AGAINST THE WORLD (1936).

ONE FLEW OVER THE CUCKOO'S NEST 1975 d: Milos Forman. USA., *One Flew Over the Cuckoo's Nest*, Ken Kesey, 1962, Novel

ONE FOOT IN HEAVEN 1941 d: Irving Rapper. USA., Hartzell Spence, Biography

One for All *see* THE PRESIDENT'S MYSTERY (1936).

One for the Book *see* THE VOICE OF THE TURTLE (1947).

One Full Moon *see* UN NOS OLA LEUAD (1991).

One Horse Town *see* SMALL TOWN GIRL (1936).

ONE HOUR 1917 d: Paul McAllister, Edwin L. Hollywood. USA., *One Hour*, Elinor Glyn, Novel

ONE HOUR BEFORE DAWN 1920 d: Henry King. USA., *Behind Red Curtains*, Mansfield Scott, Boston 1919, Novel

ONE HOUR OF LOVE 1927 d: Robert Florey. USA., *The Broken Gate*, Emerson Hough, New York 1917, Novel

ONE HOUR WITH YOU 1932 d: Ernst Lubitsch, George Cukor (Uncredited). USA., *Nur Ein Traum*, Lothar Schmidt, Munchen 1909, Play

ONE HUNDRED AND ONE DALMATIANS 1961 d: Wolfgang Reitherman, Hamilton Luske. USA., *The One Hundred and One Dalmatians*, Dodie Smith, New York 1957, Novel

One in a Million *see* BIGGER THAN LIFE (1956).

ONE IN A MILLION: THE RON LEFLORE STORY 1978 d: William A. Graham. USA., *Breakout*, Jim Hawkins, Ron Leflore, Book

ONE INCREASING PURPOSE 1927 d: Harry Beaumont. USA., *One Increasing Purpose*, A. S. M. Hutchinson, Boston 1925, Novel

One Is Not Born a Soldier *see* SOLDATAMI NYE ROZHDAYUTSYA (1968).

ONE JUMP AHEAD 1955 d: Charles Saunders. UKN., *One Jump Ahead*, Robert Chapman, Novel

One Life *see* UNE VIE (1958).

One Life *see* ONNA NO ISSHO (1967).

One Man Came Back *see* WE WHO ARE ABOUT TO DIE (1936).

One Man Too Many *see* UN HOMME DE TROP (1967).

One Man's Fate *see* MIEHEN TIE (1940).

ONE MAN'S JOURNEY 1933 d: John S. Robertson. USA., *Failure*, Katharine Haviland-Taylor, 1932, Short Story

One Man's Secret *see* POSSESSED (1947).

ONE MAN'S WAY 1964 d: Denis Sanders. USA., *Norman Vincent Peale: Minister to Millions*, Arthur Gordon, Englewood Cliffs NJ. 1958, Biography

ONE MILE FROM HEAVEN 1937 d: Allan Dwan. USA., *The Koudenhoffen Case*, Wainwright Evans, Benjamin B. Lindsey, New York 1925, Book

ONE MILLION DOLLARS 1915 d: John W. Noble. USA., *One Million Francs*, Arnold Fredericks, New York 1912, Novel

One Monsoon Day *see* ASHAD KA EK DIN (1971).

ONE MORE AMERICAN 1918 d: William C. de Mille. USA., *The Land of the Free*, William C. de Mille, New York 1917, Play

ONE MORE RIVER 1934 d: James Whale. USA., *Over the River*, John Galsworthy, London 1933, Novel

ONE MORE SPRING 1935 d: Henry King. USA., *One More Spring*, Robert Nathan, New York 1933, Novel

One More Time, One More Chance *see* TSUKI TO KYABETSU (1998).

ONE MORE TOMORROW 1946 d: Peter Godfrey. USA., *The Animal Kingdom*, Philip Barry, New York 1932, Play

ONE NEW YORK NIGHT 1935 d: Jack Conway. USA., *Sorry You've Been Troubled*, Walter Hackett, London 1929, Play

One Night. a Train *see* UN TRAIN, UN SOIR (1968).

One Night at Dinner *see* UNA SERA A CENA METTI (1969).

ONE NIGHT AT SUSIE'S 1930 d: John Francis Dillon. USA., *One Night at Susie's*, Frederick Hazlitt Brennan, Story

One Night. By Accident *see* UN SOIR. PAR HASARD (1964).

ONE NIGHT IN LISBON 1941 d: Edward H. Griffith. USA., *There's Always Juliet*, John Van Druten, New York 1931, Play

ONE NIGHT IN THE TROPICS 1940 d: A. Edward Sutherland. USA., *Love Insurance*, Earl Derr Biggers, Indianapolis 1914, Novel

ONE NIGHT OF LOVE 1934 d: Victor Schertzinger. USA., *Don't Fall in Love*, Charles Beahan, Dorothy Speare, 1931, Play

ONE NIGHT STAND 1978 d: Allan King. CND., *One Night Stand*, Carol Bolt, Play

One Night's Intoxication *see* RAUSCH EINER NACHT (1951).

ONE OF MY WIVES IS MISSING 1976 d: Glenn Jordan. USA., *Piege Pour un Homme Seul*, Robert Thomas, Play

ONE OF OUR DINOSAURS IS MISSING 1975 d: Robert Stevenson. USA., *The Great Dinosaur Robbery*, David Forrest, Novel

ONE OF OUR GIRLS 1914 d: Thomas N. Heffron. USA., *One of Our Girls*, Bronson Howard, New York 1885, Play

ONE OF THE BEST 1927 d: T. Hayes Hunter. UKN., *One of the Best*, George Edwardes Hall, Seymour Hicks, London 1895, Play

One of the Boston Bullertons *see* PRIVATE AFFAIRS (1940).

One of Those Things *see* HAENDELIGT UHELD (1971).

One Parisian Knight *see* OPEN ALL NIGHT (1924).

ONE PRECIOUS YEAR 1933 d: Henry Edwards. UKN., *Driven*, E. Temple Thurston, London 1914, Play

ONE ROMANTIC NIGHT 1930 d: Paul L. Stein. USA., *A Hattyu*, Ferenc Molnar, Budapest 1921, Play

One Russian Summer *see* IL GIORNO DEL FURORE (1973).

ONE SHOE MAKES IT MURDER 1982 d: William Hale. USA., *So Little Cause for Caroline*, Eric Bercovici, Novel

One Spy Too Many *see* WHERE THE SPIES ARE (1966).

One Step to Eternity *see* BONNES A TUER (1954).

ONE STOLEN NIGHT 1923 d: Robert Ensminger. USA., *The Arab*, D. D. Calhoun, Story

ONE STOLEN NIGHT 1929 d: Scott R. Dunlap. USA., *The Arab*, D. D. Calhoun, Story

One Summer of Happiness *see* HON DANSADE EN SOMMAR (1951).

ONE SUMMER'S DAY 1917 d: Frank G. Bayley. UKN., *One Summer's Day*, H. V. Esmond, London 1897, Play

ONE SUNDAY AFTERNOON 1933 d: Stephen Roberts. USA., *One Sunday Afternoon*, James Hagan, New York 1933, Play

ONE SUNDAY AFTERNOON 1948 d: Raoul Walsh. USA., *One Sunday Afternoon*, James Hagan, New York 1933, Play

One Swedish Summer *see* SOM HAVETS NAKNA VIND (1968).

ONE THAT GOT AWAY, THE 1957 d: Roy Ward Baker. UKN., *The One That Got Away*, Kendall Burt, James Leasor, Book

..ONE THIRD OF A NATION.. 1939 d: Dudley Murphy. USA., *..One Third of a Nation.*, Arthur Arent, New York 1937, Play

ONE THOUSAND DOLLARS 1918 d: Kenneth Webb. USA., *One Thousand Dollars*, O. Henry, 1908, Short Story

ONE TOUCH OF NATURE 1917 d: Edward H. Griffith. USA., *One Touch of Nature*, Peter B. Kyne, 1913, Short Story

ONE TOUCH OF VENUS 1948 d: William A. Seiter. USA., *The Tinted Venus*, F. Anstey, 1885, Novel, *One Touch of Venus*, Ogden Nash, S. J. Perelman, Kurt Weill, 1944, Musical Play

ONE TRUE THING 1998 d: Carl Franklin. USA., *One True Thing*, Anna Quindlen, Novel

ONE, TWO, THREE 1961 d: Billy Wilder. USA., *Egy - Ketto - Harom*, Ferenc Molnar, Budapest 1929, Play

ONE WAY PENDULUM 1964 d: Peter Yates. UKN., *One Way Pendulum*, N. F. Simpson, London 1959, Play

ONE WAY STREET 1925 d: John Francis Dillon. USA., *One Way Street*, Beale Davis, New York 1924, Novel

ONE WAY TICKET 1935 d: Herbert J. Biberman. USA., *One Way Ticket*, Ethel Turner, New York 1934, Novel

ONE WILD OAT 1951 d: Charles Saunders. UKN., *One Wild Oat*, Vernon Sylvaine, London 1948, Play

ONE WOMAN IDEA, THE 1929 d: Berthold Viertel. USA., *The One-Woman Idea*, Alan Williams, 1927, Short Story

ONE WOMAN, THE 1918 d: Reginald Barker. USA., *The One Woman*, Thomas Dixon, New York 1903, Novel

ONE WOMAN TO ANOTHER 1927 d: Frank Tuttle. USA., *The Ruined Lady*, Frances Nordstrom, New York 1920, Play

One Woman's Answer see **WOMAN AGAINST WOMAN** (1938).

One Woman's Revenge see **REVENGE** (1971).

One Woman's Story see **THE PASSIONATE FRIENDS** (1948).

ONE WONDERFUL NIGHT 1914 d: E. H. Calvert. USA., *One Wonderful Night*, Louis Tracy, New York 1912, Novel

ONE WONDERFUL NIGHT 1922 d: Stuart Paton. USA., *One Wonderful Night*, Louis Tracy, New York 1912, Novel

ONE-EYED JACKS 1961 d: Marlon Brando. USA., *The Authentic Death of Hendry Jones*, Charles Neider, New York 1956, Novel

O'NEIL OF THE GLEN 1916 d: J. M. Kerrigan. IRL/UKN., *O'Neil of the Glen*, M. T. Pender, Play

O'NEIL, THE 1911 d: Sidney Olcott. IRL/USA., *Erin's Isle*, Dion Boucicault, Play

O'Neill, The see **THE O'NEIL** (1911).

One-Night Stand see **ONE NIGHT STAND** (1978).

ONE-THING-AT-A-TIME O'DAY 1919 d: John Ince. USA., *One-Thing-at-a-Time O'Day*, William Dudley Pelley, 1917, Short Story

ONE-WAY STREET 1950 d: Hugo Fregonese. USA., *Death on a Side Street*, Lawrence Kimble, Story

ONI SRAJALIS ZA RODINOU 1974 d: Sergei Bondarchuk. USS., *Oni Srazhalis Za Rodinu*, Mikhail Sholokhov, 1943-44, Novel

Oni Srazhalis Za Rodinu see **ONI SRAJALIS ZA RODINOU** (1974).

ONIBI 1997 d: Rokuro Mochizuki. JPN., Yukio Yamanouchi, Novel

Onibi: the Fire Within see **ONIBI** (1997).

ONION FIELD, THE 1979 d: Harold Becker. USA., *The Onion Field*, Joseph Wambaugh, Novel

ONIONHEAD 1958 d: Norman Taurog. USA., *Onionhead*, Weldon Hill, Novel

ONKEL AUS AMERIKA, DER 1953 d: Carl Boese. GRM., *Man Braucht Kein Geld*, Ferdinand Altenkirch, Play

ONKEL BRASIG 1936 d: Erich Waschneck. GRM., *Ut Mine Stromtid*, Fritz Reuter, 1862-64, Novel

Onkel Brasig see **LIVET PA LANDET** (1943).

ONKEL FILSER - ALLERNEUESTE LAUSBUBENGESCHICHTEN 1966 d: Werner Jacobs. GRM., Ludwig Thoma, Story

ONKEL TOMS HUTTE 1965 d: Geza von Radvanyi. GRM/FRN/ITL., *Uncle Tom's Cabin*, Harriet Beecher Stowe, Boston 1852, Novel

ONLY 38 1923 d: William C. de Mille. USA., *Only 38*, A. E. Thomas, New York 1921, Play

ONLY A MILL GIRL 1919 d: Lewis Willoughby. UKN., *Only a Mill Girl*, Sheila Walsh, Play

Only a Mother see **BARA EN MOR** (1949).

ONLY A SHOP GIRL 1922 d: Edward J. Le Saint. USA., *Only a Shopgirl*, Charles E. Blaney, Play

Only a Woman see **NADA MAS QUE UNA MUJER** (1934).

Only Clouds Move the Stars see **BARE SKYER BEVEGER STJERNENE** (1998).

ONLY EIGHT HOURS 1934 d: George B. Seitz. USA., *The Harbor*, Theodore Reeves, Play

ONLY GAME IN TOWN, THE 1970 d: George Stevens. USA., *The Only Game in Town*, Frank D. Gilroy, New York 1968, Play

ONLY JEALOUSY OF EMER, THE 1980 d: John McCormick, Alan Stamford. IRL., *The Only Jealousy of Emer*, William Butler Yeats, 1919, Play

ONLY SAPS WORK 1930 d: Cyril Gardner, Edwin H. Knopf. USA., *Easy Come Easy Go*, Owen Davis, New York 1925, Play

ONLY SON, THE 1914 d: Thomas N. Heffron, Cecil B. de Mille. USA., *The Only Son*, Winchell Smith, New York 1911, Play

Only the Best see **I CAN GET IT FOR YOU WHOLESALE** (1951).

Only the Cool see **LA PEAU DE TORPEDO** (1970).

ONLY THE VALIANT 1951 d: Gordon Douglas. USA., *Only the Valiant*, Charles Marquis Warren, 1943, Novel

Only the Wind Knows the Answer see **DIE ANTWORT KENNT NUR DER WIND** (1975).

ONLY THRILL, THE 1997 d: Peter Masterson. USA., *The Trading Post*, Larry Ketron, Play

ONLY TWO CAN PLAY 1962 d: Sidney Gilliat. UKN., *That Uncertain Feeling*, Kingsley Amis, London 1955, Novel

ONLY WAY, THE 1925 d: Herbert Wilcox. UKN., *A Tale of Two Cities*, Charles Dickens, London 1859, Novel

ONLY WHEN I LARF 1968 d: Basil Dearden. UKN., *Only When I Larf*, Len Deighton, London 1968, Novel

ONLY WHEN I LAUGH 1981 d: Glenn Jordan. USA., *The Gingerbread Lady*, Neil Simon, 1970, Play

ONNA GOROSHI ABURA JIGOKU 1958 d: Hiromichi HorikawA. JPN., *Onna Goroshi Abura No Jigoku*, Monzaemon Chikamatsu, 1721, Play

ONNA KEIJI RIKO 2: SEIBO NO SHINKI-EN 1998 d: Satoshi IsakA. JPN., Yoshiki Shibata, Story

ONNA NO ISSHO 1967 d: Yoshitaro NomurA. JPN., *Une Vie: l'Humble Verite*, Guy de Maupassant, Paris 1883, Novel

ONNA NO MISUMI 1966 d: Yoshishige YoshidA. JPN., *Mizumi*, Yasunari Kawabata, 1954, Short Story

Onna No Mizuumi see **ONNA NO MISUMI** (1966).

ONNA NO SONO 1954 d: Keisuke KinoshitA. JPN., *Jinko Teien*, Abe Tomoji, 1954, Short Story

ONOKO'S VOW 1910 d: Edwin S. Porter. USA., *Onoko's Vow*, Bret Harte, Short Story

Onoko's Vow see **ONOKO'S VOW** (1910).

ONOREVOLE CAMPODARSEGO, L' 1915 d: Camillo de Riso. ITL., *L' Onorevole Campodarsego*, Libero Pilotto, 1889, Play

Ont-Ils Des Jambes? see **L' ARME A GAUCHE** (1965).

Oomo Omoo, the Shark God see **OMOO OMOO** (1949).

OONCHE LOG 1965 d: Phani Majumdar. IND., *Major Chandrakant*, K. Balachander, Play

OP AFBETALING 1991 d: Frans Weisz. NTH., *Op Afbetaling*, Simon Vestdijk, 1952, Novel

Op Center see **TOM CLANCY'S OP CENTER** (1995).

OP HOOP VAN ZEGEN 1918 d: Maurits H. Binger. NTH., *Op Hoop Van Zegen*, Herman Heijermans, 1900, Play

Op Hoop Van Zegen see **DIE FAHRT INS VERDERBEN** (1924).

OP HOOP VAN ZEGEN 1934 d: Alex Benno, Louis Saalborn. NTH., *Op Hoop Van Zegen*, Herman Heijermans, 1900, Play

OP HOOP VAN ZEGEN 1986 d: Guido Pieters. NTH., *Op Hoop Van Zegen*, Herman Heijermans, 1900, Play

Op O' Me Thumb see **SUDS** (1920).

OPEN ALL NIGHT 1924 d: Paul Bern. USA., Paul Morand, Short Stories

OPEN ALL NIGHT 1934 d: George Pearson. UKN., *Open All Night*, John Chancellor, Play

OPEN COUNTRY 1922 d: Sinclair Hill. UKN., *Open Country*, Maurice Hewlett, Novel

Open Door, The see **LA PUERTA ABIERTA** (1957).

Open Doors see **PORTE APERTE** (1989).

OPEN RANGE 1927 d: Cliff Smith. USA., *Open Range*, Zane Grey, Story

Open Road, The see **LE CHEMINEAU** (1935).

Open Switch, The see **WHISPERING SMITH** (1926).

OPENED SHUTTERS, THE 1914 d: Otis Turner. USA., *The Opened Shutters*, Clara Louise Burnham, New York 1906, Novel

Opera Ball see **OPERNBALL** (1939).

OPERA DE QUAT' SOUS, L' 1930 d: G. W. Pabst. GRM., *Die Dreigroschenoper*, Bertolt Brecht, Berlin 1928, Play

Opera de Quat'sous, L' see **DIE DREIGROSCHENOPER** (1963).

OPERA DO MALANDRO 1985 d: Ruy GuerrA. FRN/BRZ/MZM., *Opera Do Malandro*, Chico Buarque, Play

Opera Hat see **MR. DEEDS GOES TO TOWN** (1936).

OPERACION EMBAJADA 1964 d: Fernando Palacios. SPN., *Cartas Credenciales*, Joaquin Calvo Sotelo, 1961, Play, *Operacion Embajada*, Joaquin Calvo Sotelo, 1962, Play

Operacion Ogro see **OGRO** (1979).

Operacion Silencio see **BARAKA SUR X 13** (1965).

OPERATION AMSTERDAM 1959 d: Michael McCarthy. UKN., *Adventure in Diamonds*, David E. Walker, Novel

Operation Disaster see **MORNING DEPARTURE** (1949).

Operation Double Cross see **TRAIN D'ENFER** (1965).

Operation Edelweiss see **UNTERNEHMEN EDELWEISS** (1954).

Operation Embassy see **OPERACION EMBAJADA** (1964).

Operation Gold Ingot see **EN PLEIN CIRAGE** (1961).

OPERATION MAD BALL 1957 d: Richard Quine. USA., *The Mad Ball*, Arthur Carter, Play

Operation Masquerade see **MASQUERADE** (1964).

Operation Ogre see **OGRO** (1979).

Operation Overthrow see **POWER PLAY** (1978).

Operation Sleeping Bag see **UNTERNEHMEN SCHLAFSACK** (1955).

Operation Snafu see **ON THE FIDDLE** (1961).

Operation Terrorist see **THE GLORY BOYS** (1982).

Operation Undercover see **REPORT TO THE COMMISSIONER** (1975).

Operation War Head see **ON THE FIDDLE** (1961).

Operation X see **MY DAUGHTER JOY** (1950).

OPERATOR 13 1934 d: Richard Boleslawski. USA., *Secret Service Operator*, Robert W. Chambers, New York 1934, Novel

Operazione Gold Ingot see **EN PLEIN CIRAGE** (1961).

OPERAZIONE RICCHEZZA 1968 d: Vittorio Musy Glori. ITL., *Il Materasso Di Maria Ricchezza*, Michele d'Avino, Novel

OPERENE STINY 1930 d: Leo Marten. CZC., *The System of Doctor Tarr and Professor Feather*, Edgar Allan Poe, 1845, Short Story

OPERNBALL 1939 d: Geza von Bolvary. GRM., *Opernball*, Richard Heuberger, Vienna 1898, Operetta

OPERNBALL 1956 d: Ernst MarischkA. AUS., *Opernball*, Richard Heuberger, Vienna 1898, Operetta

Opfer Aus Liebe see **NACH DEM STURM** (1948).

Opfer Der Leidenschaft see **UNE FEMME FATALE** (1976).

OPFERGANG 1944 d: Veit Harlan. GRM., *Der Opfergang*, Rudolf Georg Binding, 1911, Short Story

OPHELIA 1961 d: Claude Chabrol. FRN/ITL., *Hamlet*, William Shakespeare, c1601, Play

Opinions of a Clown see **ANSICHTEN EINES CLOWNS** (1975).

Oppenheim Family, The see **SEMJA OPPENHEIM** (1939).

OPPORTUNITY 1918 d: John H. Collins. USA., *Opportunity*, Edgar Franklin, 1917, Short Story

OPPOSITE SEX, THE 1956 d: David Miller. USA., *The Women*, Clare Boothe Luce, New York 1936, Play

OPRAH WINFREY PRESENTS: THE WEDDING 1998 d: Charles Burnett. USA., *The Wedding*, Dorothy West, Novel

OPTIMIST, DER 1938 d: E. W. Emo. AUS., *Der Optimist*, J. Larric, Play

Optimistic Tragedy, The see **OPTIMISTICHESKAYA TRAGEDIYA** (1963).

Optimisticeskaja Tragedija see **OPTIMISTICHESKAYA TRAGEDIYA** (1963).

OPTIMISTICHESKAYA TRAGEDIYA 1963 d: Samson Samsonov. USS., *Optimisticheskaya Tragediya*, Vsevolod Vishnevsky, Moscow 1934, Play

OR DANS LA MONTAGNE, L' 1938 d: Max Haufler. FRN/SWT., *Farinet*, Charles-Ferdinand Ramuz, Paris 1932, Novel

Or de Naples, L' see **L' ORO DI NAPOLI** (1954).

Or Des Cesars, L' see **ORO PER I CESARI** (1963).

OR DU CRISTOBAL, L' 1939 d: Jean Stelli, Jacques Becker (Uncredited). FRN., *L' Or du Cristobel*, A. 't Serstevens, Novel

OR ET LE PLOMB, L' 1966 d: Alain Cuniot. FRN., *Ou le Monde Comme Il Va Babouc*, Francois-Marie Arouet de Voltaire, 1750, Short Story

Or Pour Les Cesars see ORO PER I CESARI (1963).

Ora Di Uccidere, L' see EINER FRISST DEN ANDEREN (1964).

ORACLE, THE 1953 d: C. M. Pennington-Richards. UKN., *To Tell You the Truth*, Robert Barr, Radio Play

ORAGE 1937 d: Marc Allegret. FRN., *Le Venin*, Henri Bernstein, Play

Orange Hein see ORANJE HEIN (1925).

Orange Watering Truck, The see A LOCSOLOKOCSI (1974).

ORANGES ARE NOT THE ONLY FRUIT 1989 d: Beeban Kidron. UKN., *Oranges are Not the Only Fruit*, Jeanette Winterson, Novel

Oranges d'Israel, Les see VALSE A TROIS (1974).

ORANJE HEIN 1925 d: Alex Benno. NTH., *Oranje Hein*, Herman Bouber, 1918, Play

ORANJE HEIN 1936 d: Max Nosseck. NTH., *Oranje Hein*, Herman Bouber, 1918, Play

Orchestra D-2 see CASTLES IN THE AIR (1919).

Orchid Dancer, The see LA DANSEUSE ORCHIDEE (1928).

Orchid in the Empty Valley see KONGGU LAN (1925).

ORDEAL BY GOLF 1924 d: Andrew P. Wilson. UKN., *Ordeal By Golf*, P. G. Wodehouse, Short Story

ORDEAL BY INNOCENCE 1984 d: Desmond Davis. UKN., *Ordeal By Innocence*, Agatha Christie, Novel

ORDEAL IN THE ARCTIC 1993 d: Mark Sobel. CND/USA., *Death and Deliverance*, Robert Mason Lee, Book

ORDEAL, THE 1909. USA., *Les Miserables*, Victor Hugo, Paris 1862, Novel

Orden Interpol: Sin un Moment de Tregua see GOTT SCHUTZT DIE LIEBENDEN (1973).

ORDER OF DEATH 1983 d: Roberto FaenzA. ITL., *The Order of Death*, Hugh Fleetwood, Novel

Order Please see ONE NEW YORK NIGHT (1935).

ORDERLY ROOM, THE 1928 d: Hugh Croise. UKN., *The Orderly Room*, Ernie Lotinga, Play

Orderly, The see L' ORDONNANCE (1933).

ORDERS ARE ORDERS 1954 d: David Paltenghi. UKN., *Orders are Orders*, Anthony Armstrong, Ian Hay, London 1932, Play

ORDERS IS ORDERS 1933 d: Walter Forde. UKN., *Orders are Orders*, Anthony Armstrong, Ian Hay, London 1932, Play

ORDET 1943 d: Gustaf Molander. SWD., *Ordet*, Kaj Munk, 1932, Play

ORDET 1954 d: Carl T. Dreyer. DNM., *Ordet*, Kaj Munk, 1932, Play

ORDINARY PEOPLE 1980 d: Robert Redford. USA., *Ordinary People*, Judith Guest, Novel

ORDINATEUR DES POMPES FUNEBRES, L' 1976 d: Gerard Pires. FRN/ITL., *L' Ordinateur Des Pompes Funebres*, Walter Kempley, Novel

Ordine Interpol: Senza un Attimo Di Tregua see GOTT SCHUTZT DIE LIEBENDEN (1973).

ORDINI SONO ORDINI, GLI 1972 d: Franco Giraldi. ITL., *Gli Ordini Sono Ordini*, Alberto Moravia, 1970, Short Story

ORDONNANCE, L' 1921 d: Victor Tourjansky. FRN., *L' Ordonnance*, Guy de Maupassant, 1889, Short Story

ORDONNANCE, L' 1933 d: Victor Tourjansky. FRN., *L' Ordonnance*, Guy de Maupassant, 1889, Short Story

ORE NUDE, LE 1964 d: Marco Vicario. ITL., *Appuntamento Al Mare*, Alberto Moravia, 1962, Short Story

Ore Violente see CASSE-TETE CHINOIS POUR LE JUDOKA (1968).

OREGON PASSAGE 1957 d: Paul Landres. USA., *Oregon Passage*, Gordon D. Shirreffs, Novel

OREGON TRAIL, THE 1945 d: Thomas Carr. USA., *The Oregon Trail*, Frank Gruber, Novel

ORENO CHI WA TANIN NO CHI 1974 d: Toshio SendA. JPN., *Oreno Chi Wa Tanin No Chi*, Yasutaka Tsutsui, Novel

ORFANA DEL GHETTO, L' 1955 d: Carlo Campogalliani. ITL., *L' Orfana Del Ghetto*, Carolina Invernizio, Novel

Orfanella di Londra, L' see LE MEMORIE DI UNA ISTITUTRICE (1917).

Orfeo Negro see ORFEU NEGRO (1958).

ORFEU NEGRO 1958 d: Marcel Camus. FRN/ITL., *Orfeu Dea Conceicao*, Vinicius de Moraes, 1956, Play

Organillos, Los see LOS PIANOS MECANICOS (1965).

Orgia Di Sole see SIGNORA! AI VOSTRI ORDINI (1939).

ORGOLII 1981 d: Manole Marcus. RMN., *Orgolii*, Augustin Buzura, 1977, Novel

ORGULLO DE ALBACETE, EL 1928 d: Luis R. Alonso. SPN., *El Orgullo de Albacete*, Joaquin Abati, Antonio Paso, Play

ORGY OF THE DEAD 1965 d: A. C. Stephen. USA., *Orgy of the Dead*, Edward Davis Wood Jr., Novel

Orgy of the Vampires see ORGY OF THE DEAD (1965).

ORIANA 1986 d: Fina Torres. VNZ/FRN/VNZ., *Oriana*, Marvel Moreno, Novel

Oriane see ORIANA (1986).

ORIAS, AZ 1984 d: Erika Szanto. HNG., *Az Orias*, Tibor Dery, 1948, Short Story

Oribe's Crime see EL CRIMEN DE ORIBE (1950).

ORIENT EXPRESS 1934 d: Paul Martin. USA., *Stamboul Train*, Graham Greene, London 1932, Novel

Oriental Dreams see KISMET (1944).

Origin of Man, The see THE LOST WORLD (1960).

O'Riley's Luck see ROSE BOWL (1936).

Orion's Belt see ORIONS BELTE (1984).

ORIONS BELTE 1984 d: Ola Solum. NRW., *Orions Belte*, Jan Michelet, Novel

ORIZURU OSEN 1934 d: Kenji Mizoguchi. JPN., *Baishoku Kamonanban*, Kyoka Izumi, 1920, Novel

ORIZZONTE DI SANGUE 1942 d: Gennaro Righelli. ITL., *I Senza Dio*, Federico Sinibaldi, Novel

Orizzonte in Fiamme see ORIZZONTE DI SANGUE (1942).

ORLACS HANDE 1925 d: Robert Wiene. AUS., *Les Mains d'Orlac*, Maurice Renard, Paris 1920, Novel

ORLANDO 1992 d: Sally Potter. UKN/USS/FRN., *Orlando*, Virginia Woolf, Novel

ORLOVI RANO LETE 1966 d: Soja Jovanovic. YGS., *Orlovi Rano Lete*, Branko Copic, 1957, Novel

ORLOW, DER 1927 d: Jacob Fleck, Luise Fleck. GRM., *Der Orlow*, Bruno Granichstaedten, Ernst Marischka, Operetta

Orlow, Der see DER DIAMANT DES ZAREN (1932).

ORME, LE 1975 d: Luigi Bazzoni. ITL., *Las Huellas*, Mario Fenelli, Novel

ORMEN 1966 d: Hans Abramson. SWD., *Ormen*, Stig Dagerman, 1945, Novel

ORNIFLE ODER ERZURNTE HIMMEL 1972 d: Helmut Kautner. GRM., *Ornifle; Ou le Courant d'Air*, Jean Anouilh, 1956, Play

ORO DI NAPOLI, L' 1954 d: Vittorio de SicA. ITL., *L' Oro Di Napoli*, Giuseppe Marotta, Book

ORO MALEDETTO, L' 1911. ITL., *L'Or Maudit*, Xavier de Montepin

ORO PER I CESARI 1963 d: Andre de Toth, Sabatino Ciuffini. ITL/FRN., *Gold for the Caesars*, Florence A. Seward, Englewood Cliffs NJ 1961, Novel

OROLOGIO A CUCU, L' 1938 d: Camillo Mastrocinque. ITL., *L' Orologio a Cucu*, Alberto Donini, Play

Orphan Mary and the Dwarfs see MARYSIA I KRASNOLUDKI (1961).

Orphan of the Streets, An see BIAO (1949).

ORPHAN, THE 1920 d: J. Gordon Edwards. USA., *The Orphan*, Clarence E. Mulford, New York 1908, Novel

ORPHANS 1988 d: Alan J. PakulA. USA., *Orphans*, Lyle Kessler, Play

ORPHANS OF THE STORM 1921 d: D. W. Griffith. USA., *Les Deux Orphelines*, Eugene Cormon, Adolphe-P. d'Ennery, 1874, Novel

ORPHEE 1950 d: Jean Cocteau. FRN., *Orphee*, Jean Cocteau, 1927, Play

ORPHELIN DU CIRQUE, L' 1926 d: Georges Lannes. FRN., *L' Orphelin du Cirque*, Pierre Mariel, Novel

Orpheus see A LOVE SUBLIME (1917).

Orpheus see ORPHEE (1950).

ORS AL-DAM 1977 d: Sohail Ben BarakA. MRC., *Bodas de Sangre*, Federico Garcia Lorca, 1936, Play

ORSOLA MIROUET 1914. ITL., *Ursula Mirouet*, Honore de Balzac, 1843, Novel

Ortlieb Family Women, The see DIE ORTLIEBSCHEN FRAUEN (1980).

Ortlieb Women, The see DIE ORTLIEBSCHEN FRAUEN (1980).

ORTLIEBSCHEN FRAUEN, DIE 1980 d: Luc Bondy. GRM., *Das Grab Des Lebendigen*, Franz Nabl, 1917, Novel

ORVOS HALALA, AZ 1966 d: Frigyes Mamcserov. HNG., *Az Orvos Halala*, Gyula Fekete, 1963, Novel

ORZOWEI 1975 d: Yves Allegret. GRM/ITL., *Orzowei*, Alberto Manzi, Novel

Orzowei, la Figlia Della Savana see ORZOWEI (1975).

OSADA MLADYCH SNU 1931 d: Oldrich Kminek. CZC., *Osada Mladych Snu*, Vilem Neubauer, Novel

OSADENI DUSHI 1975 d: Vulo Radev. BUL., *Osadeni Dushi*, Dimitar Dimov, 1945, Novel

Osaka Elegy see NANIWA EREJI (1936).

OSCAR 1967 d: Edouard Molinaro. FRN., *Oscar*, Claude Magnier, Play

OSCAR 1991 d: John Landis. USA., *Oscar*, Claude Magnier, Play

OSCAR AND LUCINDA 1997 d: Gillian Armstrong. USA/ASL., *Oscar and Lucinda*, Peter Carey, Novel

OSCAR, THE 1966 d: Russell Rouse. USA., *The Oscar*, Richard Sale, New York 1963, Novel

Oskar Bider see BIDER DER FLIEGER (1941).

OSMNACTILETA 1939 d: Miroslav Cikan. CZC., *Kdo Jsi Bez Viny*, Marie Dolezalova, Novel

OSMY DZIEN TYGODNIA 1958 d: Aleksander Ford. PLN/GRM., *Osmy Dzien Tygodnia*, Marek Hlasko, 1957, Novel

Oss 117 see O.S.S. 117 SE DECHAINE (1963).

Oss 117 -Double Agent see NIENTE ROSE PER OSS 117 (1968).

Oss 117 Furia a Bahia see FURIA A BAHIA POUR OSS 117 (1965).

O.S.S. 117 Is Not Dead see O.S.S. 117 N'EST PAS MORT (1956).

Oss 117 Minaccia Bangkok see BANCO A BANGKOK (1964).

Oss 117 -Mission for a Killer see FURIA A BAHIA POUR OSS 117 (1965).

Oss 117 Murder for Sale see NIENTE ROSE PER OSS 117 (1968).

Oss 117 N'est Pas Mort see O.S.S. 117 N'EST PAS MORT (1956).

O.S.S. 117 N'EST PAS MORT 1956 d: Jean SachA. FRN., *O.S.S. 117 N'est Pas Mort*, Jean Bruce, Novel

O.S.S. 117 PREND DES VACANCES 1969 d: Pierre Kalfon. FRN/BRZ., *Vacances Pour O.S.S. 117*, Jean Bruce, Novel

O.S.S. 117 SE DECHAINE 1963 d: Andre Hunebelle. FRN/ITL., *O.S.S. 117 Prend le Maquis*, Jean Bruce, Novel

Oss 117 Segretissimo see O.S.S. 117 SE DECHAINE (1963).

Oss 117 Takes a Vacation see O.S.S. 117 PREND DES VACANCES (1969).

OSSEGG ODER DIE WAHRHEIT UBER HANSEL UND GRETEL 1987 d: Thees Klahn. GRM., Hans Traxler, Book

OSSESSIONE 1943 d: Luchino Visconti. ITL., *The Postman Always Rings Twice*, James M. Cain, 1934, Novel

Ossessione Nuda see LE CHANT DU MONDE (1965).

OSSI HAT DIE HOSEN AN 1928 d: Carl Boese. GRM., *Sir Or Madam*, Berta Ruck, Novel

OSSO, AMOR E PAPAGAIOS 1957 d: Carlos Alberto de Souza Barros. BRZ., *A Nova California*, Afonso Henriques de Lima Barreto, 1948, Short Story

Ossudeni Dushu see OSADENI DUSHI (1975).

Ostatni Rozdzial see UN AIR SI PUR (1997).

OSTERMAN WEEKEND, THE 1983 d: Sam Peckinpah. USA., *The Osterman Weekend*, Robert Ludlum, Novel

'OSTLER JOE 1908 d: Wallace McCutcheon. USA., *'Ostler Joe*, James Brown Potter, Short Story

'OSTLER JOE 1912 d: J. Searle Dawley. USA., *'Ostler Joe*, George R. Sims, Poem

OSTRA E O VENTO, O 1997 d: Walter Lima Jr. BRZ., Moacir C. Lopes, Novel

OSTRE SLEDOVANE VLAKY 1966 d: Jiri Menzel. CZC., *Ostre Sledovane Vlaky*, Bohumil Hrabal, Prague 1965, Novel

Ostrich Has Two Eggs, The see LES OEUFS DE L'AUTRUCHE (1957).

OSTROV SOKROVISC 1971 d: Yevgeni Friedman. USS., *Treasure Island*, Robert Louis Stevenson, London 1883, Novel

OSTROV SOKROVISHCH 1937 d: Vladimir Vainshtok. USS., *Treasure Island*, Robert Louis Stevenson, London 1883, Novel

Ostrov Sokrovishch *see* **OSTROV SOKROVISC** (1971).

OSUDNE NOCI 1928 d: Josef Medeotti-Bohac. CZC., *Vrazda Primadony*, Walter Hauff, Novel

OSWALT KOLLE: DAS WUNDER DER LIEBE -SEXUALITAT IN DER EHE 1968 d: Franz J. Gottlieb. GRM., *Das Wunder Der Liebe*, Oswald Kolle, Bielefeld 1969, Book

Oswalt Kolle: the Wonder of Love -Sexuality in Marriage *see* **OSWALT KOLLE: DAS WUNDER DER LIEBE -SEXUALITAT IN DER EHE** (1968).

OTEC KONDELIK A ZENICH VEJVARA 1937 d: M. J. Krnansky. CZC., *Otec Kondelik a Zenich Vejvara*, Ignat Herrmann, Novel

OTEC KONDELIK A ZENICH VEJVARA I. 1926 d: Karl Anton. CZC., *Otec Kondelik a Zenich Vejvara*, Ignat Herrmann, Novel

OTEC KONDELIK A ZENICH VEJVARA II. 1926 d: Karl Anton. CZC., *Otec Kondelik a Zenich Vejvara*, Ignat Herrmann, Novel

OTELLO 1906 d: Mario Caserini, Gaston Velle. ITL., *Othello*, William Shakespeare, c1604, Play

OTELLO 1909 d: Gerolamo Lo Savio. ITL., *Othello*, William Shakespeare, c1604, Play

OTELLO 1914 d: Luigi Maggi. ITL., *Othello*, William Shakespeare, c1604, Play

OTELLO 1951 d: Orson Welles. ITL/USA/FRN., *Othello*, William Shakespeare, c1604, Play

OTELLO 1955 d: Sergei Yutkevich. USS., *Othello*, William Shakespeare, c1604, Play

OTELLO 1986 d: Franco Zeffirelli. ITL/USA., *Othello*, William Shakespeare, c1604, Play

Otets Sergii *see* **OTYETS SERGII** (1978).

Othello *see* **OTELLO** (1906).

Othello *see* **OTELLO** (1909).

Othello *see* **OTELLO** (1914).

OTHELLO 1946 d: David MacKane. UKN., *Othello*, William Shakespeare, c1604, Play

Othello *see* **OTELLO** (1951).

OTHELLO 1953 d: Charles Deane. UKN., *Othello*, William Shakespeare, c1604, Play

Othello *see* **OTELLO** (1955).

Othello *see* **VENETSIANSKIY MAVR** (1961).

OTHELLO 1965 d: Stuart Burge. UKN., *Othello*, William Shakespeare, c1604, Play

OTHELLO 1981 d: Jonathan Miller. UKN., *Othello*, William Shakespeare, c1604, Play

OTHELLO 1982 d: Frank Melton. USA., *Othello*, William Shakespeare, c1604, Play

Othello *see* **OTELLO** (1986).

OTHELLO 1989 d: Trevor Nunn. UKN., *Othello*, William Shakespeare, c1604, Play

OTHELLO 1990 d: Ted Lange. USA., *Othello*, William Shakespeare, c1604, Play

OTHELLO 1995 d: Oliver Parker. UKN/USA., *Othello*, William Shakespeare, c1604, Play

Othello the Moor *see* **OTELLO** (1914).

Other Cinderella, The *see* **CINDERELLA** (1977).

Other Francisco, The *see* **EL OTRO FRANCISCO** (1974).

OTHER GIRL, THE 1915 d: Percy Winter. USA., *The Other Girl*, Augustus Thomas, New York 1903, Play

OTHER HALVES 1985 d: John Laing. NZL., *Other Halves*, Sue McCanley, Novel

OTHER KIND OF LOVE, THE 1924 d: Duke Worne. USA., *Thicker Than Water*, Buckleigh Fritz Oxford, Story

Other Life of Lynn Stuart, The *see* **THE TRUE STORY OF LYNN STUART** (1958).

OTHER LOVE, THE 1947 d: Andre de Toth. USA., *Beyond*, Erich Maria Remarque, Novel

Other Man, The *see* **THE ROAD TO SINGAPORE** (1931).

OTHER MAN, THE 1970 d: Richard A. CollA. USA., *The Other Man*, Margaret Lynn, Novel

Other Man's Look, The *see* **LA MIRADA DEL OTRO** (1998).

Other Men *see* **ALTRI UOMINI** (1997).

OTHER MEN'S SHOES 1920 d: Edgar Lewis. USA., Andrew Soutar, Novel

OTHER PEOPLE'S MONEY 1991 d: Norman Jewison. USA., *Other People's Money*, Jerry Sterner, Play

OTHER PERSON, THE 1921 d: B. E. Doxat-Pratt, Maurits H. Binger. UKN/NTH., *The Other Man*, Fergus Hume, 1920, Novel

Other Shore, The *see* **LA OTRA ORILLA** (1966).

OTHER SIDE OF MIDNIGHT, THE 1977 d: Charles Jarrott. USA., *The Other Side of Midnight*, Sidney Sheldon, Novel

OTHER SIDE OF PARADISE, THE 1991 d: Renny Rye. UKN/ASL/NZL., *The Other Side of Paradise*, Noel Barber, Novel

Other Side of Sunday, The *see* **SONDAGSENGLER** (1996).

Other Side of the Bridge, The *see* **DINCOLO DE POD** (1975).

OTHER SIDE OF THE DOOR, THE 1916 d: Thomas Ricketts. USA., *The Other Side of the Door*, Lucia Chamberlain, Indianapolis 1909, Novel

OTHER SIDE OF THE MOUNTAIN, THE 1975 d: Larry Peerce. USA., *The Other Side of the Mountain*, E. G. Valens, Novel

Other, The *see* **DER ANDERE** (1913).

Other, The *see* **DER ANDERE** (1930).

Other, The *see* **DIE ANDERE** (1949).

OTHER, THE 1972 d: Robert Mulligan. USA., *The Other*, Thomas Tryon, Novel

OTHER WOMAN, THE 1918 d: Albert Parker. USA., *The Other Woman*, Frederic Arnold Kummer, 1910, Play

OTHER WOMAN, THE 1921 d: Edward Sloman. USA., *The Other Woman*, Norah Davis, New York 1920, Novel

OTHER WOMAN, THE 1931 d: G. B. Samuelson. UKN., *The Slave Bracelet*, Olga Hall Brown, Story

Other Woman, The *see* **DIE ANDERE** (1949).

OTHER WOMEN'S CLOTHES 1922 d: Hugo Ballin. USA., *The Luxury Tax*, Ethel Donoher, Story

Othon *see* **YEUX NE VEULENT PAS EN TOUT TEMPS SE FERMER OU PEUT-ETRE QU'UN JOUR ROME SE PERMETTRA DE CHOISIR A.** (1970).

OTKLONENIE 1967 d: Grisha Ostrovski, Todor Stoyanov. BUL., *Patuvane Kam Sebe Si*, Blaga Dimitrova, 1965, Novel

OTLEY 1968 d: Dick Clement. UKN., *Otley*, Martin Waddell, London 1966, Novel

OTODIK PECSET, AZ 1977 d: Zoltan Fabri. HNG., *Az Otodik Pecset*, Ferenc Santa, 1963, Novel

OTOME-GOKORO SANNIN SHIMAI 1935 d: Mikio Naruse. JPN., *Asakusa No Shimai*, Yasunari Kawabata, 1932, Short Story

Otoshi Ana *see* **KASHI TO KODOMO** (1962).

OTOTO 1960 d: Kon IchikawA. JPN., Aya Koda, Novel

OTRA ESPERANZA 1991 d: Mercedes Frutos. ARG., *Otra Esperanza*, Adolfo Bioy Casares, 1978, Short Story

OTRA ESPERANZA 1996 d: Mercedes Frutos. ARG., Adolfo Bioy Casares, Short Story

Otra Mujer, La *see* **L' AUTRE FEMME** (1963).

OTRA ORILLA, LA 1966 d: Jose Luis Madrid. SPN., *La Otra Orilla*, Jose Lopez Rubio, 1955, Play

OTRO FRANCISCO, EL 1974 d: Sergio Giral, Julio Garcia EspinosA. CUB., *Francisco*, Anselmo Suarez Y Romero, 1880, Novel

OTTO ER ET NAESEHORN 1982 d: Rumle Hammerich. DNM., Ole Lund Kirkegaard, Short Story

Otto Is a Rhino *see* **OTTO ER ET NAESEHORN** (1982).

Otto the Rhino *see* **OTTO ER ET NAESEHORN** (1982).

OTTSY I DETI 1958 d: Natalya Rashevskaya, Adolf Bergunkev. USS., *Ottsy I Deti*, Ivan Turgenev, 1862, Novel

OTYETS SERGII 1978 d: Igor Talankin. USS., *Otets Sergei*, Lev Nikolayevich Tolstoy, 1898, Short Story

OU EST PASSE TOM? 1971 d: Jose Giovanni. FRN/ITL., Bill Reade, Novel

Oublie, L' *see* **PRINCESSE MANDANE** (1927).

Oublier Palermo *see* **DIMENTICARE PALERMO** (1990).

OUBLIETTE, THE 1914 d: Charles Giblyn. USA., *The Oubliette*, George Bronson Howard, Story

OUR BETTERS 1933 d: George Cukor. USA., *Our Betters*, W. Somerset Maugham, New York 1917, Play

OUR BOYS 1915 d: Sidney Morgan. UKN., *Our Boys*, H. J. Byron, London 1875, Play

Our Daily Bread *see* **CITY GIRL** (1930).

Our Daily Bread *see* **USKI ROTI** (1969).

Our Defiant Ones *see* **NASI FURIANTI** (1937).

Our Dreams *see* **TERE MERE SAPNE** (1971).

Our Eleven *see* **NASE XI.** (1936).

OUR EXPLOITS AT WEST POLEY 1987 d: Diarmuid Lawrence. UKN., *Our Exploits at West Poley*, Thomas Hardy, 1892-93, Short Story

OUR GIRL FRIDAY 1953 d: Noel Langley. UKN., *The Cautious Amorist*, Norman Lindsay, Novel

OUR GOD'S BROTHER 1997 d: Krzysztof Zanussi. ITL/PLN/GRM., *Brat Naszego Boga*, Karol Wojtyla, 1949, Play

OUR HEARTS WERE YOUNG AND GAY 1944 d: Lewis Allen. USA., *Our Hearts Were Young and Gay*, Emily Kimbrough, Cornelia Otis Skinner, Book

Our Lady of Compassion *see* **A COMPADECIDA** (1969).

Our Lady of the Big Snows *see* **BACK TO GOD'S COUNTRY** (1919).

Our Lady of the Turks *see* **NOSTRA SIGNORA DEI TURCHI** (1968).

Our Land *see* **MAABHOOMI** (1979).

OUR LITTLE GIRL 1935 d: John S. Robertson. USA., *Heaven's Gate*, Florence Leighton Pfalzgraf, 1934, Short Story

Our Little Town *see* **MESTECKO NA DLANI** (1942).

OUR LITTLE WIFE 1918 d: Eddie Dillon. USA., *Our Little Wife*, Avery Hopwood, New York 1916, Play

OUR MAN IN HAVANA 1960 d: Carol Reed. UKN., *Our Man in Havana*, Graham Greene, 1958, Novel

Our Man in Marrakesh *see* **L' HOMME DE MARRAKECH** (1966).

OUR MOTHER'S HOUSE 1967 d: Jack Clayton. UKN/USA., *Our Mother's House*, Julian Gloag, New York 1963, Novel

OUR MRS. MCCHESNEY 1918 d: Ralph Ince. USA., *Our Mrs. McChesney*, Edna Ferber, George V. Hobart, New York 1915, Play

Our Natacha *see* **NUESTRA NATACHA** (1936).

OUR NEW MINISTER 1913. USA., *Our New Minister*, George W. Ryer, Denman Thompson, Play

OUR RELATIONS 1936 d: Harry Lachman. USA., *The Money Box*, W. W. Jacobs, 1931, Short Story

Our Sea *see* **MARE NOSTRUM** (1925).

Our Short Life *see* **UNSER KURZES LEBEN** (1980).

Our Swaggerers *see* **NASI FURIANTI** (1937).

OUR TOWN 1940 d: Sam Wood. USA., *Our Town*, Thornton Wilder, New York 1938, Play

OUR TOWN 1977 d: George Schaefer. USA., *Our Town*, Thornton Wilder, New York 1938, Play

OUR VINES HAVE TENDER GRAPES 1945 d: Roy Rowland. USA., *Our Vines Have Tender Grapes*, George Victor Martin, Novel

Our Virgin Island *see* **VIRGIN ISLAND** (1958).

OUR WIFE 1941 d: John M. Stahl. USA., *Lillian Day*, Lloyd Mearson, Play

OURS EN PELUCHE, L' 1988 d: Edouard Logereau. FRN., Georges Simenon, Novel

OURS, L' 1988 d: Jean-Jacques Annaud. FRN/CND., *The Grizzly King*, James Oliver Curwood, Novel

OURSELVES ALONE 1936 d: Walter Summers, Brian Desmond Hurst. UKN., *The Trouble*, Noel Scott, Dudley Sturrock, Play

OUT 1982 d: Eli Hollander. USA., *Out*, Ronald Sukenick, Novel

Out in the World *see* **V LYUDKYAKH** (1939).

OUT OF A CLEAR SKY 1918 d: Marshall Neilan. USA., *Out of a Clear Sky*, Maria Thompson Davies, New York 1917, Novel

OUT OF AFRICA 1985 d: Sydney Pollack. USA/UKN., *Afrikanske Farm*, Karen Blixen, 1937, Short Story, *Breve Fra Africa*, Karen Blixen, 1960, Short Story, *Skygger Paa Graesset*, Karen Blixen, 1978, Short Story

Out of Contention *see* **THE VICTIM** (1972).

Out of Evil *see* **MI KLALAH LE BRACHAH** (1950).

Out of My Control *see* **SHEN BU YOU JI** (1993).

Out of Order *see* **ABWARTS: DAS DUELL UBER DER TIEFE** (1984).

Out of Order see A MINISZTER FELRELEP (1998).

OUT OF SIGHT 1998 d: Steven Soderbergh. USA., *Out of Sight*, Elmore Leonard, Novel

OUT OF THE BLUE 1931 d: Gene Gerrard, John Orton. UKN., *Little Tommy Tucker*, Desmond Carter, Caswell Garth, Play

OUT OF THE CLOUDS 1955 d: Basil Dearden, Michael Relph. UKN., *The Springboard*, John Fores, Novel

Out of the Dark see THE SAGEBRUSHER (1920).

Out of the Dark see A VOICE IN THE DARK (1921).

OUT OF THE DARKNESS 1985 d: John Krish. UKN., *The Ivy Garland*, John Hoyland, Novel

OUT OF THE FOG 1919 d: Albert Capellani. USA., *'Ception Shoals*, H. Austin Adams, New York 1917, Play

OUT OF THE FOG 1941 d: Anatole Litvak. USA., *The Gentle People; a Brooklyn Fable*, Irwin Shaw, New York 1939, Play

Out of the Frying Pan see YOUNG AND WILLING (1942).

Out of the Mist see DER SOHN DER HAGAR (1926).

OUT OF THE NIGHT 1918 d: James Kirkwood. USA., *Out of the Night*, E. Lloyd Sheldon, Play

Out of the Night see FOOTLIGHTS AND SHADOWS (1920).

OUT OF THE PAST 1947 d: Jacques Tourneur. USA., *Build My Gallows High*, Daniel Mainwaring, Novel

OUT OF THE RUINS 1915 d: Ashley Miller. USA., *Miss 318 and Mr. 37*, Rupert Hughes, Story

OUT OF THE RUINS 1928 d: John Francis Dillon. USA., *Out of the Ruins*, Philip Hamilton Gibbs, London 1927, Novel

OUT OF THE SHADOW 1919 d: Emile Chautard. USA., *The Shadow of the Rope*, E. W. Hornung, New York 1902, Novel

OUT OF THE SHADOWS 1988 d: Willi Patterson. USA., *Out of the Shadows*, Andrea Davidson, Novel

OUT OF THE STORM 1920 d: William Parke. USA., *Tower of Ivory*, Gertrude Franklin Atherton, New York 1910, Novel

OUT OF THE STORM 1926 d: Louis J. Gasnier. USA., *The Travis Coup*, Arthur Stringer, Story

OUT TO WIN 1923 d: Denison Clift. UKN., *Out to Win*, Dion Clayton Calthrop, Roland Pertwee, London 1921, Play

OUT WEST WITH THE PEPPERS 1940 d: Charles T. Barton. USA., *Five Little Peppers Abroad*, Margaret Sidney, Boston 1902, Novel

OUT YONDER 1920 d: Ralph Ince. USA., *The Girl from Out Yonder*, Pauline Phelps, Marion Short, Baltimore 1914, Play

OUTBACK 1971 d: Ted Kotcheff. ASL., *Wake in Fright*, Kenneth Cook, Novel

OUTCAST 1917 d: Dell Henderson. USA., *Outcast*, Hubert Henry Davies, New York 1914, Play

OUTCAST 1922 d: Chet Withey. USA., *Outcast*, Hubert Henry Davies, New York 1914, Play

OUTCAST 1928 d: William A. Seiter. USA., *Outcast*, Hubert Henry Davies, New York 1914, Play

OUTCAST 1936 d: Robert Florey. USA., *Happiness Preferred*, Frank R. Adams, 1936, Short Story

OUTCAST LADY 1934 d: Robert Z. Leonard. USA., *The Green Hat*, Michael Arlen, New York 1924, Novel

OUTCAST OF THE ISLANDS 1951 d: Carol Reed. UKN., *An Outcast of the Islands*, Joseph Conrad, 1896, Novel

OUTCAST SOULS 1928 d: Louis W. Chaudet. USA., *On the Back Seat*, John Peter Toohey, 1925, Short Story

OUTCAST, THE 1915 d: John B. O'Brien. USA., *The Outcast*, Thomas Nelson Page, Short Story

Outcast, The see MAN IN THE SADDLE (1951).

OUTCAST, THE 1954 d: William Witney. USA., *Two-Edged Vengeance*, Todhunter Ballard, Novel

Outcast, The see HAKAI (1961).

Outcasts see STVANI LIDE (1933).

Outcasts see HAKAI (1961).

OUTCASTS OF POKER FLAT, THE 1919 d: John Ford. USA., *The Outcasts of Poker Flat*, Bret Harte, 1868, Short Story

OUTCASTS OF POKER FLAT, THE 1937 d: W. Christy Cabanne. USA., *The Outcasts of Poker Flat*, Bret Harte, 1868, Short Story

OUTCASTS OF POKER FLAT, THE 1952 d: Joseph M. Newman. USA., *The Luck of Roaring Camp*, Bret Harte, 1868, Short Story, *The Outcasts of Poker Flat*, Bret Harte, 1868, Short Story

OUTER GATE, THE 1937 d: Raymond Cannon. USA., *The Outer Gate*, Octavus Roy Cohen, Boston 1927, Novel

OUTFIT, THE 1973 d: John Flynn. USA., *The Outfit*, Donald E. Westlake, Novel

OUTLAW 1987 d: John Bud Cardos. ITL., John Norman, Novel

OUTLAW DEPUTY, THE 1935 d: Otto Brower. USA., *King of Cactusville*, Johnston McCulley, 1923, Short Story

OUTLAW JOSEY WALES, THE 1976 d: Clint Eastwood. USA., *Gone to Texas*, Forrest Carter, Novel

Outlaw Law see THE OUTLAW DEPUTY (1935).

Outlaw of Gor see OUTLAW (1987).

OUTLAW TERRITORY 1953 d: John Ireland, Lee Garmes. USA., *Wicked Waster*, MacKinlay Kantor, Novel

OUTLAW, THE 1943 d: Howard Hughes, Howard Hawks (Uncredited). USA., Ben Hecht, Story

Outlawed see VOGELVRIJ (1916).

OUTLAWED GUNS 1935 d: Ray Taylor. USA., *Outlawed Guns*, Cliff Farrell, 1934, Short Story

Outlaws see BURAIKAN (1970).

Outlaws of Palouse see END OF THE TRAIL (1936).

OUTLAWS OF THE PRAIRIE 1937 d: Sam Nelson. USA., *Trigger Fingers*, Harry F. Olmstead, Short Story

OUTLAW'S SON, THE 1957 d: Lesley Selander. USA., *Gambling Man*, Clifton Adams, Novel

OUTPUT 1974 d: Michael Fengler. GRM., Ulf Miehe, Novel

OUTRAGE, THE 1964 d: Martin Ritt. USA., *Rashomon*, Ryunosuke Akutagawa, 1915, Short Story, *Yabu No Naka*, Ryunosuke Akutagawa, 1922, Short Story

OUTRAGEOUS! 1977 d: Richard Benner. CND., *Making It*, Margaret Gibson Gilboord, Short Story

OUTSIDE EDGE 1982 d: Kevin Billington. UKN., *Outside Edge*, Richard Harris, Play

Outside the Law see I AM THE LAW (1938).

OUTSIDE THE WALL 1950 d: Crane Wilbur. USA., Henry Edward Helseth, Story

OUTSIDE WOMAN, THE 1921. USA., *All Night Long*, Philip Bartholomae, Paul B. Sipe, Play

Outsider in Amsterdam see GRIJPSTRA & DE GIER (1979).

OUTSIDER, THE 1917 d: William C. Dowlan. USA., *Nobody*, Louis Joseph Vance, New York 1915, Novel

OUTSIDER, THE 1926 d: Rowland V. Lee. USA., *The Outsider*, Dorothy Brandon, London 1923, Play

OUTSIDER, THE 1931 d: Harry Lachman. UKN., *The Outsider*, Dorothy Brandon, London 1923, Play

OUTSIDER, THE 1939 d: Paul L. Stein. UKN., *The Outsider*, Dorothy Brandon, London 1923, Play

Outsider, The see THE GUINEA PIG (1948).

OUTSIDER, THE 1961 d: Delbert Mann. USA., *Torture Execution of a Hero Marine*, William Bradford Huie, 1958, Story

Outsider, The see LO STRANIERO (1967).

OUTSIDER, THE 1979 d: Tony Luraschi. NTH/USA., *The Heritage of Michael Flaherty*, Colin Leinster, Novel

Outsiders, The see BANDE A PART (1964).

Outsiders, The see OKA OORIE KATHA (1977).

OUTSIDERS, THE 1983 d: Francis Ford CoppolA. USA., *The Outsiders*, S. E. Hinton, 1967, Novel

OUTWARD BOUND 1930 d: Robert Milton. USA., *Outward Bound*, Sutton Vane, New York 1924, Play

Outward Bound see BETWEEN TWO WORLDS (1944).

OVAL DIAMOND, THE 1916 d: W. Eugene Moore. USA., *The Oval Diamond*, David S. Foster, 1915, Novel

OVER 21 1945 d: Charles Vidor. USA., *Over Twenty-One*, Ruth Gordon, New York 1944, Play

Over Grensen see FELDMANN-SAKEN (1986).

OVER MY DEAD BODY 1942 d: Malcolm St. Clair. USA., *Over My Dead Body*, James O'Hanlon, Novel

Over My Dead Body see VENGEANCE (1962).

OVER NIGHT 1915 d: James Young. USA., *Over Night*, Philip Bartholomae, New York 1911, Play

OVER SHE GOES 1937 d: Graham Cutts. UKN., *Over She Goes*, Stanley Lupino, 1936, Play

OVER THE BORDER 1922 d: Penrhyn Stanlaws. USA., *She of the Triple Chevron*, Gilbert Parker, 1892, Short Story

OVER THE GARDEN WALL 1934 d: John Daumery. UKN., *The Youngest of Three*, H. F. Maltby, 1905, Play

Over the Hill see OVER THE HILL TO THE POORHOUSE (1920).

OVER THE HILL 1931 d: Henry King. USA., *Over the Hill from the Poorhouse*, Will Carleton, 1873, Poem, *Over the Hill to the Poorhouse*, Will Carleton, 1873, Poem

OVER THE HILL 1992 d: George Miller. ASL., *Alone in the Australian Outback*, Gladys Taylor, Book

OVER THE HILL TO THE POORHOUSE 1920 d: Harry Millarde. USA., *Over the Hill from the Poorhouse*, Will Carleton, 1873, Poem, *Over the Hill to the Poorhouse*, Will Carleton, 1873, Poem

OVER THE HILLS 1911 d: Joseph Smiley, George Loane Tucker. USA., *Over the Hill to the Poorhouse*, Will Carleton, 1873, Poem

OVER THE HILLS TO THE POORHOUSE 1908 d: Wallace McCutcheon. USA., *Over the Hills to the Poorhouse*, E. M. Hutchinson, Novel

OVER THE ODDS 1961 d: Michael Forlong. UKN., *Over the Odds*, Rex Howard Arundel, Play

Over the River see ONE MORE RIVER (1934).

Over the Ruins see ME'AL HACHURAVOT (1936).

OVER THE TOP 1918 d: Wilfred North. USA., *Over the Top*, Arthur Guy Empey, New York 1917, Book

Overboard see HEAD WINDS (1925).

OVERBOARD 1978 d: John Newland. USA., *Overboard*, Henry Searls, Novel

OVERCOAT SAM 1937 d: Wallace Orton. UKN., *Overcoat Sam*, W. J. Makin, Short Story

Overcoat, The see SHINEL (1926).

Overcoat, The see IL CAPPOTTO (1952).

Overcoat, The see SHINEL (1960).

OVERLAND RED 1920 d: Lynn Reynolds. USA., *Overland Red*, Henry Herbert Knibbs, Boston 1914, Novel

OWD BOB 1924 d: Henry Edwards. UKN., *Bob, Son of Battle*, Alfred Ollivant, New York 1898, Novel

OWD BOB 1938 d: Robert Stevenson. UKN., *Bob, Son of Battle*, Alfred Ollivant, New York 1898, Novel

OWL AND THE PUSSYCAT, THE 1970 d: Herbert Ross. USA., *The Owl and the Pussycat*, Bill Manhoff, New York 1964, Play

OX-BOW INCIDENT, THE 1943 d: William A. Wellman. USA., *The Ox-Bow Incident*, Walter Van Tilburg Clark, 1940, Novel

OX-BOW INCIDENT, THE 1956 d: Gerd Oswald. USA., *The Ox-Bow Incident*, Walter Van Tilburg Clark, 1940, Novel

OXBRIDGE BLUES 1984 d: James Cellan Jones. UKN., *Oxbridge Blues*, Frederic Raphael, Novel, *Sleeps Six*, Frederic Raphael, Novel

Oy Di Shviger! see WHAT A MOTHER-IN-LAW! (1934).

OYAYUBIME 19— d: Yugo SerikawA. JPN., *Tommelise*, Hans Christian Andersen, 1835, Short Story

Oyster and the Wind, The see O OSTRA E O VENTO (1997).

Oyuki the Madonna see MARIA NO OYUKI (1935).

Oyuki the Virgin see MARIA NO OYUKI (1935).

OYU-SAMA 1951 d: Kenji Mizoguchi. JPN., *Ashikari*, Junichiro Tanizaki, 1932, Novel

OZERELE DLJA MOEJ LJUBIMOJ 1972 d: Tengiz Abuladze. USS., A. Abu-Bakar, Novel

OZORA NO SAMURAI 1976 d: Seiji MaruyamA. JPN., *Ozora No Samurai*, Saburo Sakai, Novel

P. RESPECTUEUSE, LA 1952 d: Marcello Pagliero, Charles Brabant. FRN., *La Putain Respectueuse*, Jean-Paul Sartre, 1946, Play

PA SOLSIDEN 1956 d: Edith Carlmar. NRW., *Pa Solsiden*, Helge Krog, 1927, Play

PAAR 1984 d: Gautam Ghose. IND., *Paar*, Samaresh Bose, Short Story

PAARUNGEN 1967 d: Michael Verhoeven. GRM., *Dodsdansen*, August Strindberg, 1901, Play

PABO SUNON 1983 d: Chang-Ho Lee. KOR., *Pabo Sunon*, Dong-Chul Lee, Novel

PACE, MIO DIO!. 1914 d: Carlo Simoneschi. ITL., *Mio Dio!. Pace*, Luigi Clumez, Novel

PACHA, LE 1968 d: Georges Lautner. FRN/ITL., *Pouce*, Jean Delion, Novel

PACIENTKA DR. HEGLA 1940 d: Otakar VavrA. CZC., *Pacientka Dr. Hegla*, Marie Pujmanova, Novel

PACIFIC DESTINY 1956 d: Wolf RillA. UKN., *A Pattern of Islands*, Sir Arthur Grimble, Book

PACIFIC RENDEZVOUS 1942 d: George Sidney. USA., *The American Black Chamber*, Major Herbert O. Yardley, Book

Pacific War *see* HELL IN THE PACIFIC (1968).

PACIORKI JEDNEGO ROZANCA 1979 d: Kazimierz Kutz. PLN., *Paciorki Jednego Rozanca*, A. Siekierski, Short Story

PACK OF LIES 1987 d: Anthony Page. UKN/USA., *Pack of Lies*, Hugh Whitemore, Play

Pack, The *see* BEHIND THE MASK (1958).

PACK, THE 1977 d: Robert Clouse. USA., *The Pack*, David Fisher, Novel

PACKING UP 1927 d: Miles Mander. UKN., *Packing Up*, Roland Pertwee, Play

Pacsirta *see* WO DIE LERCHE SINGT (1936).

PACSIRTA 1964 d: Laszlo Ranody. HNG., *Pacsirta*, Dezso Kosztolanyi, 1924, Novel

PAD (AND HOW TO USE IT), THE 1966 d: Brian G. Hutton. USA., *The Private Ear*, Peter Shaffer, London 1962, Play

PADDY 1969 d: Daniel Haller. UKN/IRL., *Goodbye to the Hill*, Lee Dunne, London 1965, Novel

PADDY THE NEXT BEST THING 1923 d: Graham Cutts. UKN., *Paddy the Next Best Thing*, Gertrude Page, London 1916, Novel

PADDY THE NEXT BEST THING 1933 d: Harry Lachman. USA., *Paddy the Next Best Thing*, Gertrude Page, London 1916, Novel

PADLOCKED 1926 d: Allan Dwan. USA., *Padlocked*, Rex Beach, New York 1926, Novel

Padma Nadir Majhi *see* PADMA NADIR MANJHI (1992).

PADMA NADIR MANJHI 1992 d: Gautam Ghose. IND., *Padma Nadir Majhi*, Manik Bandyyopadhyay, Novel

PADRE E A MOCA, O 1966 d: Joaquim Pedro de Andrade. BRZ., *A Moca, O Padre*, Carlos Drummond de Andrade, 1959-62, Verse

PADRE JUANICO, EL 1923. SPN., *Mosen Janot*, Angel Guimera

PADRE PADRONE 1977 d: Paolo Taviani, Vittorio Taviani. ITL., *L'educazione Di un Pastore Padre Padrone*, Gavino Ledda, Novel

Padrone Del Mondo, Il *see* LA LUCE DEL MONDO (1935).

PADRONE DELLE FERRIERE, IL 1919 d: Eugenio Perego. ITL., *Le Maitre de Forges*, Georges Ohnet, Paris 1882, Novel

PADRONE DELLE FERRIERE, IL 1959 d: Anton Giulio Majano. ITL/SPN., *Le Maitre de Forges*, Georges Ohnet, Paris 1882, Novel

PADRONE SONO ME, IL 1956 d: Franco Brusati. ITL., *Il Padrone Sono Me*, Alfredo Panzini, 1925, Novel

PADUREA NEBUNA 1982 d: Nicolae Corjos. RMN., *Padurea Nebuna*, Zaharia Stancu, 1963, Novel

PADUREA SPINZURATILOR 1965 d: Liviu Ciulei. RMN., *Padurea Spinzuratilor*, Liviu Rebreanu, 1922, Novel

PADUREANCA 1988 d: Nicolae Margineanu. RMN., *Padureanca*, Ioan Slavici, 1884, Short Story

PAESE SENZA PACE, IL 1943 d: Leo Menardi. ITL., *Le Baruffe Chiozzotte*, Carlo Goldoni, Play

PAGADOR DE PROMESSAS, O 1961 d: Anselmo Duarte. BRZ., *O Pagador de Promessas*, Alfredo Dias Gomes, Sao Paolo 1960, Play

PAGAN LADY, THE 1931 d: John Francis Dillon. USA., *The Pagan Lady*, William Du Bois, New York 1930, Play

PAGAN LOVE 1920 d: Hugo Ballin. USA., *The Honourable Gentleman*, Achmed Abdullah, 1919, Short Story

PAGAN LOVE SONG 1950 d: Robert Alton. USA., *Tahiti Landfall*, William S. Stone, 1946, Novel

PAGAN PASSIONS 1924 d: Colin Campbell. USA., *Pagan Passions*, Grace Sanderson Michie, Story

Pagati Per Morire *see* ESTOUFFADE A LA CARAIBE (1966).

PAGE MISS GLORY 1935 d: Mervyn Leroy. USA., *Page Miss Glory*, Philip Dunning, Joseph Shrank, New York 1934, Play

Page Tim O'Brien *see* LOVE IN THE DARK (1922).

PAGE VOM DALMASSE-HOTEL, DER 1933 d: Victor Janson. GRM., *Der Page Vom Dalmasse-Hotel*, Maria Peteani, Novel

PAGE VOM PALAST-HOTEL, DER 1957 d: Thomas Engel. AUS., *Der Page Vom Dalmasse-Hotel*, Maria Peteani, Novel

PAGINA D'AMORE, UNA 1923 d: Telemaco Ruggeri. ITL., *Une Page d'Amour*, Emile Zola, 1878

PAGINAS DE UNA HISTORIA: MENSAKA 1998 d: Salvador Garcia Ruiz. SPN., *Paginas de Una Historia: Mensaka*, Jose Angel Manas, Novel

PAGLIACCI 1931 d: Joe W. Coffman. USA., *I Pagliacci*, Ruggero Leoncavallo, Milan 1892, Opera

PAGLIACCI 1936 d: Karl Grune. UKN., *I Pagliacci*, Ruggero Leoncavallo, Milan 1892, Opera

PAGLIACCI 1982 d: Franco Zeffirelli. ITL., *I Pagliacci*, Ruggero Leoncavallo, Milan 1892, Opera

PAGLIACCI, I 1915 d: Francesco Bertolini. ITL., *I Pagliacci*, Ruggero Leoncavallo, Milan 1892, Opera

PAGLIACCI, I 1923 d: G. B. Samuelson, Walter Summers. UKN., *I Pagliacci*, Ruggero Leoncavallo, Milan 1892, Opera

PAGLIACCI, I 1943 d: Giuseppe Fatigati. ITL/GRM., *I Pagliacci*, Ruggero Leoncavallo, Milan 1892, Opera

PAGLIACCI, I 1949 d: Mario CostA. ITL., *I Pagliacci*, Ruggero Leoncavallo, Milan 1892, Opera

PAGLIACCI, I 1970 d: Herbert von Karajan. GRM/AUS/SWT., *I Pagliacci*, Ruggero Leoncavallo, Milan 1892, Opera

Pahala Adhyay *see* PEHLA ADHYAY (1981).

PAID 1930 d: Sam Wood. USA., *Within the Law*, Bayard Veiller, New York 1912, Play

PAID IN ADVANCE 1919 d: Allen Holubar. USA., James Oliver Curwood, Story

PAID IN FULL 1914 d: Augustus Thomas. USA., *Paid in Full*, Eugene Walter, New York 1908, Play

PAID IN FULL 1919 d: Emile Chautard. USA., *Paid in Full*, Eugene Walter, New York 1908, Play

PAID IN FULL 1950 d: William Dieterle. USA., Frederic M. Loomis, Article

PAIN DES JULES, LE 1959 d: Jacques Severac. FRN., *Le Pain Des Jules*, Ange Bastiani, Play

Pain Des Pauvres, Le *see* VERTIGINE D'AMORE (1951).

Pain Et Pierres *see* BROT UND STEINE (1979).

Pain in the a., A *see* L' EMMERDEUR (1973).

PAINT YOUR WAGON 1969 d: Joshua Logan. USA., *Paint Your Wagon*, Alan Jay Lerner, Frederick Loewe, New York 1951, Musical Play

PAINTED ANGEL, THE 1929 d: Millard Webb. USA., *Give the Little Girl a Hand*, Fannie Hurst, 1929, Short Story

PAINTED FLAPPER, THE 1924 d: John Gorman. USA., *The Painted Flapper*, Alan Pearl, Novel

PAINTED HILLS, THE 1951 d: Harold F. Kress. USA., *Shep of the Painted Hills*, Alexander Hull, 1930, Novel

PAINTED LADY, THE 1914 d: Frederick Sullivan. USA., *The Cavalier*, Charles S. Thompson, Short Story

PAINTED LADY, THE 1924 d: Chester Bennett. USA., *The Painted Lady*, Larry Evans, 1912, Short Story

PAINTED PEOPLE 1924 d: Clarence Badger. USA., *The Swamp Angel*, Richard Connell, 1923, Short Story

PAINTED PONIES 1927 d: B. Reeves Eason. USA., *Painted Ponies*, John Harold Hamlin, Short Story

PAINTED VEIL, THE 1934 d: Richard Boleslawski, W. S. Van Dyke (Uncredited). USA., *The Painted Veil*, W. Somerset Maugham, New York 1925, Novel

PAINTED WOMAN, THE 1932 d: John G. Blystone. USA., *After the Rain*, Alfred C. Kennedy, 1931, Play

PAINTED WORLD, THE 1914 d: Ralph Ince. USA., *The Painted World*, Jacques Futrelle, Story

PAINTED WORLD, THE 1919 d: Ralph Ince. USA., Jacques Futrelle, Story

PAINTING THE CLOUDS WITH SUNSHINE 1951 d: David Butler. USA., *The Gold Diggers of Broadway*, Avery Hopwood, New York 1919, Play

PAIR OF BRIEFS, A 1962 d: Ralph Thomas. UKN., *How Say You?*, Kay Bannerman, Harold Brooke, London 1959, Play

PAIR OF SILK STOCKINGS, A 1918 d: Walter Edwards. USA., *A Pair of Silk Stockings*, Cyril Harcourt, New York 1914, Play

PAIR OF SIXES, A 1918 d: Lawrence C. Windom. USA., *A Pair of Sixes*, Edward Peple, New York 1914, Play

PAIR OF SPECTACLES, A 1916 d: Alexander Butler. UKN., *A Pair of Spectacles*, Sidney Grundy, London 1890, Play

PAIX CHEZ SOI, LA 1929. FRN., *La Paix Chez Soi*, Georges Courteline, 1903, Play

PAIX SUR LE RHIN 1938 d: Jean Choux. FRN., *Paix Sur le Rhin*, Pierre Claude, Novel

PAIX SUR LES CHAMPS 1970 d: Jacques Boigelot. BLG., *Paix Sur Les Champs*, Marie Gevers, Novel

PAIXAO DE GAUCHO 1958 d: Walter George Durst. BRZ., *O Gaucho*, Jose Martiniano de Alencar, 1870, Novel

PAJAMA GAME, THE 1957 d: George Abbott, Stanley Donen. USA., *7½ Cents*, Richard Bissell, Novel

PAJAROS DE BADEN-BADEN, LOS 1974 d: Mario Camus. SPN., *Los Pajaros de Baden-Baden*, Ignacio Aldecoa, 1965, Short Story

Pakka Inti Ammayi *see* PAKKAINTI AMMAYI (1953).

PAKKAINTI AMMAYI 1953 d: Chittajalu PullayyA. IND., *Pasher Bari*, Arun Choudhury

PAKLIC 1944 d: Miroslav Cikan. CZC., *Paklic*, Eduard Fiker, Novel

Pako Pohjoiseen *see* FLUCHT IN DEN NORDEN (1986).

Pakt Mit Dem Satan, Der *see* DAS KALTE HERZ (1923).

PAL JOEY 1957 d: George Sidney. USA., *Pal Joey*, John O'Hara, 1939, Short Story

PAL UTCAI FIUK, A 1968 d: Zoltan Fabri. HNG/USA., *A Pal-Utcai Fiuk*, Ferenc Molnar, 1907, Novel

PALACE OF DARKENED WINDOWS, THE 1920 d: Henry Kolker. USA., *The Palace of Darkened Windows*, Mary Hastings Bradley, New York 1914, Novel

PALACE OF PLEASURE, THE 1926 d: Emmett J. Flynn. USA., *Lola Montez*, Adolf Paul, Story

Palace of the Darkened Windows, The *see* THE PALACE OF DARKENED WINDOWS (1920).

PALACES 1927 d: Jean Durand. FRN., *Palaces*, Saint-Sorny, Novel

Paladini, I *see* LE ARMI E GLI AMORI (1983).

Paladini, Storia d'Armi E d'Amori, I *see* LE ARMI E GLI AMORI (1983).

Palais Des Passions, Le *see* QASR ASH-SHAWQ (19—).

Pale Bet *see* BLEEKE BET (1923).

Pale Betty *see* BLEEKE BET (1934).

Pale Flower *see* KAWAITA HANA (1964).

PALICOVA DCERA 1923 d: Thea CervenkovA. CZC., *Palicova Dcera*, Josef Kajetan Tyl, Play

PALICOVA DCERA 1941 d: Vladimir Borsky. CZC., *Palicova Dcera*, Josef Kajetan Tyl, Play

PALIO 1932 d: Alessandro Blasetti. ITL., *Palio*, Luigi Bonelli, Play

PALLA DI NEVE 1996 d: Maurizio Nichetti. ITL., *Palla Di Neve*, Emilio Nessi, Novel

PALLARD THE PUNTER 1919 d: J. L. V. Leigh. UKN., *Grey Timothy*, Edgar Wallace, London 1913, Novel

PALLET ON THE FLOOR 1984 d: Lynton Butler. NZL., *Pallet on the Floor*, Ronald Hugh Morrieson, Novel

PALLIETER 1975 d: Roland Verhavert. NTH/BLG., *Pallieter*, Felix Timmermans, 1916, Novel

PALM BEACH GIRL, THE 1926 d: Erle C. Kenton. USA., *Please Help Emily*, H. M. Harwood, London 1916, Play

PALM SPRINGS 1936 d: Aubrey Scotto. USA., *Lady Smith*, Myles Connolly, 1936, Short Story

Palm Springs Affair *see* PALM SPRINGS (1936).

PALMES DE M. SCHUTZ, LES 1997 d: Claude Pinoteau. FRN., *Les Palmes de M. Schutz*, Jean-Noel Fenwick, Play

PALMETTO 1998 d: Volker Schlondorff. USA/GRM., *Just Another Sucker*, James Hadley Chase, Novel

Paloma Fair, The *see* LA VERBENA DE LA PALOMA (1921).

PALOOKAVILLE 1995 d: Alan Taylor. USA., *Ultimo Viene Il Corvo*, Italo Calvino, Short Stories

PALS 1925 d: John P. McCarthy. USA., Perry O'Neill, Story

PALS FIRST 1918 d: Edwin Carewe. USA., *Pals First*, Francis Perry Elliott, New York 1915, Novel

PALS FIRST 1926 d: Edwin Carewe. USA., *Pals First*, Francis Perry Elliott, New York 1915, Novel

PALS IN PARADISE 1926 d: George B. Seitz. USA., *Pals in Paradise*, Peter B. Kyne, Story

PALTOQUET, LE 1986 d: Michel Deville. FRN., *On a Tue Pendant l'Escale*, Franz-Rudolf Falk, Novel

Palude Del Peccato, La *see* PALUDE TRAGICA (1953).

PALUDE TRAGICA 1953 d: Juan de OrdunA. SPN/ITL., *Canas Y Barro*, Vicente Blasco Ibanez, 1902, Novel

PAMELA 1944 d: Pierre de Herain. FRN., *Pamela Marchande de Frivolites*, Victorien Sardou, 1936, Play

Pamela Ou l'Enigma du Temple *see* **PAMELA** (1944).

PAMPA SALVAJE 1966 d: Hugo Fregonese. SPN/USA/ARG., *Pampa Barbara*, Homero Manzi, Ulises Petit de Murat

PAMPERED YOUTH 1925 d: David Smith. USA., *The Magnificent Ambersons*, Booth Tarkington, Garden City, N.Y. 1918, Novel

PAN 1937 d: Olaf Fjord. GRM., *Pan*, Knut Hamsun, Kristiania 1894, Novel

Pan *see* **KORT AR SOMMAREN** (1962).

PAN 1995 d: Henning Carlsen. DNM/NRW/GRM., *Pan*, Knut Hamsun, Kristiania 1894, Novel

Pan Michael *see* **PAN WOLODYJOWSKI** (1969).

PAN NA ROZTRHANI 1934 d: Miroslav Cikan. CZC., Hans Jaray, Play

PAN OTEC KARAFIAT 1935 d: Jan Svitak. CZC., *Slecna Konvalinka*, Otomar Schafer, Play

PAN WOLODYJOWSKI 1969 d: Jerzy Hoffman. PLN., *Pan Wolodyjowski*, Henryk Sienkiewicz, 1887, Novel

Pan Yu Liang, a Woman Painter *see* **HUA HUN** (1994).

PANAMA HATTIE 1942 d: Norman Z. McLeod, Vincente Minnelli (Uncredited). USA., *Panama Hattie*, Buddy De Sylva, Herbert Fields, Cole Porter, New York 1940, Musical Play

Paname *see* **DIE APACHEN VON PARIS** (1927).

Paname N'est Pas Paris *see* **DIE APACHEN VON PARIS** (1927).

Pandemonium *see* **SHURA** (1970).

Pandora's Box *see* **DIE BUCHSE DER PANDORA** (1929).

PANDORA'S CLOCK 1996 d: Eric Laneuville. USA., *Pandora's Clock*, John J. Nance, Novel

PANE ALTRUI, IL 1913 d: Ubaldo Maria Del Colle. ITL., *Cuzoj Chleb*, S. Turgenev, 1848, Novel

PANE ALTRUI, IL 1924 d: Telemaco Ruggeri. ITL., *Cuzoj Chleb*, S. Turgenev, 1848, Novel

PANE, BURRO E MARMELLATA 1977 d: Giorgio Capitani. ITL., *Les Bonshommes*, Francois Dorin, Play

Panel Doctor, The *see* **IL MEDICO DELLA MUTUA** (1968).

PANENSTVI 1937 d: Otakar VavrA. CZC., *Panenstvi*, Marie Majerova, Novel

PANI KACKA ZASAHUJE. 1939 d: Karel SpelinA. CZC., *Kacka Vomacena*, Antonin Jenne, Novel

PANI KLUCI 1975 d: Vera Plivova-SimkovA. CZC., *Adventures of Tom Sawyer*, Mark Twain, San Francisco 1876, Novel

Panic *see* **PANIQUE** (1946).

PANIC IN NEEDLE PARK 1971 d: Jerry Schatzberg. USA., *Panic in Needle Park*, James Mills, Novel

Panic in the Parlor *see* **SAILOR BEWARE!** (1956).

PANIC IN THE STREETS 1950 d: Elia Kazan. USA., *Quarantine*, Edna Anhalt, Short Story, *Some Like 'Em Cold*, Edna Anhalt, Short Story, *Quarantine*, Edward Anhalt, Short Story, *Some Like 'Em Cold*, Edward Anhalt, Short Story

PANIC ON THE AIR 1936 d: D. Ross Lederman. USA., *Five Spot*, Theodore A. Tinsley, 1935, Short Story

Panico En la Mafia *see* **PAS DE PANIQUE** (1965).

PANIQUE 1946 d: Julien Duvivier. FRN., *Les Fiancailles de Mr. Hire*, Georges Simenon, 1933, Novel

PANNA 1940 d: Frantisek Cap. CZC., *Panna*, Frantisek Zavrel, Play

PANNA A NETVOR 1978 d: Juraj Herz. CZC., *La Belle Et la Bete*, Marie Leprince de Beaumont, 1785-89, Short Story

PANNA NIKT 1997 d: Andrzej WajdA. PLN., *Panna Nikt*, Tomek Tryzna, Novel

PANNON TOREDEK 1998 d: Andras Solyom. HNG., *Pannon Toredek*, Miklos Meszoly, Novel

PANNY Z WILKO 1979 d: Andrzej WajdA. PLN/FRN., *Panny Z Wilko*, Jaroslaw Iwaszkiewicz, 1933, Short Story

PANTALASKAS 1959 d: Paul Paviot. FRN., *Pantalaskas*, Rene Masson, Novel

PANTATA BEZOUSEK 1941 d: Jiri Slavicek. CZC., *Pantata Bezousek*, Karel Vaclav Rais, Novel

PANTERA NERA, LA 1942 d: Domenico M. Gambino. ITL., *La Pantera Nera*, Luis Velter, Novel

PANTERAS SE COMEN A LOS RICOS, LAS 1969 d: Ramon Fernandez. SPN., *Las Entretenidas*, Miguel Mihura Santos, 1963, Play

PANTHEA 1917 d: Allan Dwan. USA., *Panthea*, Monckton Hoffe, London 1913, Play

PANTHER 1995 d: Mario Van Peebles. USA., *Panther*, Melvin Van Peebles, Novel

PANTHER WOMAN, THE 1919 d: Ralph Ince. USA., *Patience Sparhawk and Her Times*, Gertrude Franklin Atherton, New York 1897, Novel

Panthers Eat Rich Men *see* **LAS PANTERAS SE COMEN A LOS RICOS** (1969).

Panthers Eat the Rich, The *see* **LAS PANTERAS SE COMEN A LOS RICOS** (1969).

Panther's Moon *see* **SPY HUNT** (1950).

Panzerkreuzer Sebastopol *see* **WEISSE SKLAVEN** (1936).

Pao Feng Tsou Yu *see* **BAOFENG-ZHOUYU** (1961).

PAODA SHUANG DENG 1993 d: He Ping. CHN/HKG., *Paoda Shuang Deng*, Feng Jicai, Novel

PAOLINA 1915 d: Vitale de Stefano. ITL., *Paoline*, Xavier de Montepin, Alexandre Dumas (pere), 1850

PAOLO E FRANCESCA 1950 d: Raffaello Matarazzo. ITL., *La Divina Commedia*, Dante Alighieri, 1310, Verse

PAOLO IL CALDO 1973 d: Marco Vicario. ITL., *Paolo Il Caldo*, Vitaliano Brancati, 1955, Novel

PAPA 1915 d: Nino OxiliA. ITL., *Papa*, Gaston Arman de Caillavet, Robert de Flers, 1911, Play

PAPA ECCELLENZA 1919 d: Ivo Illuminati. ITL., *Papa Eccellenza*, Gerolamo Rovetta, 1906, Play

PAPA LEBONNARD 1920 d: Mario Bonnard. ITL., *Le Pere Lebonnard*, Jean Aicard, 1889, Play

Papa Lebonnard *see* **LE PERE LEBONNARD** (1938).

Papa Paga *see* **UN CATTIVO SOGGETTO** (1933).

PAPA PER UNA NOTTE 1939 d: Mario Bonnard. ITL., *Bichon*, Jean de Letraz, Play

PAPA SANS LE SAVOIR 1931 d: Robert Wyler. FRN., *An Unmarried Father*, Floyd Dell, New York 1927, Novel

PAPA'S DELICATE CONDITION 1963 d: George Marshall. USA., *Papa's Delicate Condition*, Corinne Griffith, Boston 1952, Biography

PAPER CHASE, THE 1973 d: James Bridges. USA., *The Paper Chase*, John Jay Osborn Jr., Novel

Paper Cranes from Osen *see* **ORIZURU OSEN** (1934).

PAPER LION 1968 d: Alex March. USA., *Paper Lion*, George Plimpton, New York 1966, Biography

PAPER MASK 1989 d: Christopher Morahan. UKN., *Paper Mask*, John Collee, Novel

PAPER MOON 1973 d: Peter Bogdanovich. USA., *Addie Pray*, Joe David Brown, Novel

PAPER ORCHID 1949 d: Roy Ward Baker. UKN., *Paper Orchid*, Arthur la Bern, Novel

PAPERHOUSE 1989 d: Bernard Rose. UKN., *Marianne Dreams*, Catherine Storr, Novel

Papiers d'Aspern, Les *see* **ASPERN** (1981).

PAPILLON 1973 d: Franklin J. Schaffner. USA., *Papillon*, Henri Charriere, Book

Papillon Dit Lyonnais le Juste *see* **BACH MILLIONNAIRE** (1933).

PAPILLON SUR L'EPAULE, UN 1978 d: Jacques Deray. FRN., *Un Papillon Sur l'Epaule*, John Gearon, Novel

PAPOUL 1929 d: Marc Allegret. FRN., *L' Agadadza*, Louis d'Hee, Short Story

Pappa Reale, La *see* **LA BONNE SOUPE** (1964).

PAPRIKA 1932 d: Carl Boese. GRM., *Der Sprung in Die Ehe*, Max Reimann, Otto Schwartz, Play

PAPRIKA 1933 d: Jean de Limur. FRN., *Der Sprung in Die Ehe*, Max Reimann, Play

PAPRIKA 1933 d: Carl Boese. ITL., *Der Sprung in Die Ehe*, Max Reimann, Play

PAPRIKA 1933 d: Jean de Limur. FRN., *Der Sprung in Die Ehe*, Otto Schwartz, Play

PAPRIKA 1933 d: Carl Boese. ITL., *Der Sprung in Die Ehe*, Otto Schwartz, Play

PAPRIKA 1957 d: Kurt Wilhelm. GRM., *Der Sprung in Die Ehe*, Max Reimann, Otto Schwartz, Play

PAQUEBOT TENACITY, LE 1934 d: Julien Duvivier. FRN., *Le Paquebot Tenacity*, Charles Vildrac, Play

PAR HABITUDE 1932 d: Maurice Cammage. FRN., *Par Habitude*, Abel Tarride, Vernayre, Play

Par le Fer Et Par le Feu *see* **COL FERRO E COL FUOCO** (1962).

PAR UN BEAU MATIN D'ETE 1964 d: Jacques Deray. FRN/ITL/SPN., *Par un Beat Matin d'Ete*, James Hadley Chase, Novel

Para Toda la Vida *see* **POUR TOUTE LA VIE** (1924).

Parabola Dei Mariti, La *see* **I MARITI - TEMPESTA D'AMORE** (1941).

Parade d'Amour *see* **THE LOVE PARADE** (1929).

Paradies Am See, Das *see* **DIE FLUCHT INS PARADIES** (1923).

PARADIES DER JUNGGESELLEN 1939 d: Kurt Hoffmann. GRM., *Paradies Der Junggesellen*, Johannes Boldt, Novel

PARADIES DER MATROSEN 1959 d: Harald Reinl. GRM., Vineta Bastian-Klinger, Novel

PARADIES IM SCHNEE, DAS 1923 d: Georg Jacoby. GRM/SWT., *Das Paradies Im Schnee*, Rudolf Stratz, Novel

Paradies von Heute, Das *see* **EVAS TOCHTER** (1928).

PARADINE CASE, THE 1947 d: Alfred Hitchcock. USA., *The Paradine Case*, Robert Hichens, Novel

Paradis Dans la Neige, La *see* **DAS PARADIES IM SCHNEE** (1923).

PARADIS DE SATAN, LE 1938 d: Felix Gandera, Jean Delannoy. FRN., *Le Paradis de Satan*, Andre Armandy, Novel

PARADIS, LE 1914 d: Gaston Leprieur. FRN., *Le Paradis*, Paul Bilhaud, Maurice Hennequin, Play

PARADISE 1926 d: Irvin V. Willat. USA., *Paradise*, Cosmo Hamilton, John Russell, Boston 1925, Play

PARADISE 1928 d: Denison Clift. UKN., *The Crossword Puzzle*, Philip Hamilton Gibbs, Novel

Paradise and Purgatory *see* **IL PURGATORIO** (1911).

Paradise and Purgatory *see* **IL PARADISO (VISIONI DANTESCHE)** (1912).

PARADISE FOR THREE 1938 d: Edward Buzzell. USA., *Drei Manner Im Schnee*, Erich Kastner, Zurich 1934, Novel

PARADISE GARDEN 1917 d: Fred J. Balshofer. USA., *Paradise Garden*, George Gibbs, New York 1916, Novel

PARADISE ISLE 1937 d: Arthur G. Collins. USA., *The Belled Palm*, Allan Vaughan Elston, Short Story

Paradise Lagoon *see* **THE ADMIRABLE CRICHTON** (1957).

Paradise Lost *see* **AZ ELVESZETT PARADICSOM** (1962).

Paradise Place *see* **PARADISTORG** (1977).

PARADISE ROAD 1997 d: Bruce Beresford. ASL/USA., *White Coolies*, Betty Jeffrey, Diary

Paradise Square *see* **PARADISTORG** (1977).

Paradiso E Il Purgatorio, Il *see* **IL PARADISO (VISIONI DANTESCHE)** (1912).

Paradiso, Hotel du Libre-Exchange *see* **HOTEL PARADISO** (1966).

PARADISO (VISIONI DANTESCHE), IL 1912. ITL., *La Divina Commedia*, Dante Alighieri, 1310, Verse

PARADISTORG 1977 d: Gunnel Lindblom. SWD., *Paradistorg*, Ulla Isaksson, Novel

PARAITRE 1917 d: Maurice Challiot. FRN., *Paraitre*, Maurice Donnay, 1906, Play

PARALLAX VIEW, THE 1974 d: Alan J. PakulA. USA., *The Parallax View*, Loren Singer, Novel

Parallel Corpse, The *see* **DET PARALLELE LIG** (1982).

Parallel Faces *see* **LANYARCOK TUKORBEN** (1973).

PARALLELE LIG, DET 1982 d: Soren Melson, Hans-Erik Philip. DNM., *Det Parallele Lig*, Frits Remar, Novel

Paramatta *see* **ZU NEUEN UFERN** (1937).

PARANINFO, IL 1934 d: Amleto Palermi. ITL., *Lu Paraninfu*, Luigi Capuana, Play

PARANOIA 1967 d: Adriaan Ditvoorst. NTH., *Paranoia*, Willem Frederik Hermans, 1953, Short Story

PARASITE, THE 1925 d: Louis J. Gasnier. USA., *The Parasite*, Helen Reimensnyder Martin, Philadelphia 1913, Novel

Parasites *see* **DRAG** (1929).

Parasites, The *see* **M'SIEUR LA CAILLE** (1955).

Paratrooper *see* **THE RED BERET** (1953).

PARCE QUE JE T'AIME 1929 d: H. C. Grantham-Hayes. FRN., *Parce Que Je T'aime*, Charles Lafaurie, Play

PARDNERS 1910 d: Edwin S. Porter. USA., *Pardners*, Rex Beach, New York 1905, Novel

PARDNERS 1917. USA., *Pardners*, Rex Beach, New York 1905, Novel

Pardners see **THE LONE COWBOY** (1933).

PARDON MY FRENCH 1921 d: Sidney Olcott. USA., *Polly in the Pantry*, Edward Childs Carpenter, Story

PARDON MY NERVE! 1922 d: B. Reeves Eason. USA., *The Heart of the Range*, William Patterson White, Garden City, N.Y. 1921, Novel

PARDON MY RHYTHM 1944 d: Felix E. Feist. USA., *Miss I.Q.*, Hurd Barrett, Story

Pardon, The see **EL INDULTO** (1960).

PARDONNEE 1927 d: Jean Cassagne. FRN., *Pardonnee*, Eugene Barbier, Short Story

PAREN IZ NASHEGO GORODA 1942 d: Alexander Stolper, Boris Ivanov. USS., *Paren Iz Nashego Goroda*, Konstantin Simonov, 1941, Play

PARENT TRAP, THE 1961 d: David Swift. USA., *Das Doppelte Lottchen*, Erich Kastner, Vienna 1949, Novel

PARENT TRAP, THE 1998 d: Nancy Meyers. USA., *Das Doppelte Lottchen*, Erich Kastner, Vienna 1949, Novel

PARENTS TERRIBLES, LES 1948 d: Jean Cocteau. FRN., *Les Parents Terribles*, Jean Cocteau, 1938, Play

PARFUM DE LA DAME EN NOIR, LE 1914 d: Maurice Tourneur. FRN., *Le Parfum de la Dame En Noir*, Gaston Leroux, Novel

PARFUM DE LA DAME EN NOIR, LE 1930 d: Marcel L'Herbier. FRN., *Le Parfum de la Dame En Noir*, Gaston Leroux, Novel

PARFUM DE LA DAME EN NOIR, LE 1949 d: Louis Daquin. FRN., *Le Parfum de la Dame En Noir*, Gaston Leroux, Novel

PARFUM D'YVONNE, LE 1994 d: Patrice Leconte. FRN., *Villa Triste*, Patrick Modiano, Novel

Pariahs of Glory see **PARIAS DE LA GLOIRE** (1963).

PARIAS DE LA GLOIRE 1963 d: Henri Decoin. FRN/ITL/SPN., *Parias de la Gloire*, Roger Delpey, Novel

Parias de la Gloria see **PARIAS DE LA GLOIRE** (1963).

Parigi Di Notte see **LES GODELUREAUX** (1960).

PARIGI MISTERIOSA 1917 d: Gustavo SerenA. ITL., *Les Mysteres de Paris*, Eugene Sue, 1842-43, Novel

Parigina, Una see **UNE PARISIENNE** (1957).

PARINEETA 1952 d: Bimal Roy. IND., *Parinita*, Sarat Candra Cattopadhyay, 1914, Short Story

PARIS 1929 d: Clarence Badger. USA., *Paris*, Martin Brown, New York 1928, Musical Play

PARIS AT MIDNIGHT 1926 d: E. Mason Hopper. USA., *Le Pere Goriot*, Honore de Balzac, Paris 1834, Novel

PARIS AU MOIS D'AOUT 1966 d: Pierre Granier-Deferre. FRN., *Paris Au Mois d'Aout*, Rene Fallet, Paris 1964, Novel

PARIS BLUES 1961 d: Martin Ritt. USA., *Paris Blues*, Harold Flender, New York 1957, Novel

PARIS BOUND 1929 d: Edward H. Griffith. USA., *Paris Bound*, Philip Barry, New York 1927, Play

PARIS BRULE-T-IL? 1966 d: Rene Clement. FRN., *Is Paris Burning?*, Larry Collins, Dominique Lapierre, New York 1965, Novel

Paris Comme Il Va see **L' OR ET LE PLOMB** (1966).

Paris Express see **THE MAN WHO WATCHED TRAINS GO BY** (1952).

PARIS, FRANCE 1993 d: Gerard Ciccoritti. CND., *Paris France*, Tom Walmsley, Novel

Paris in August see **PARIS AU MOIS D'AOUT** (1966).

PARIS IN SPRING 1935 d: Lewis Milestone. USA., *Two on a Tower*, Dwight Taylor, 1934, Play

Paris in Spring see **CHASING YESTERDAY** (1935).

Paris in the Month of August see **PARIS AU MOIS D'AOUT** (1966).

Paris in the Spring see **PARIS IN SPRING** (1935).

PARIS INTERLUDE 1934 d: Edwin L. Marin. USA., *All Good Americans*, Laura Perelman, S. J. Perelman, New York 1933, Play

Paris, Je T'aime see **IL EST CHARMANT** (1931).

Paris Love Song see **PARIS IN SPRING** (1935).

PARIS MYSTERIEUX 1921 d: Louis Paglieri. FRN., *Paris Mysterieux*, Georges Spitzmuller, Novel

Paris Pick-Up see **LE MONTE-CHARGE** (1961).

PARIS, TEXAS 1984 d: Wim Wenders. FRN/GRM/USA., *Paris, Texas Motel Chronicles*, Sam Shepard, 1985, Play

PARIS TROUT 1991 d: Stephen Gyllenhaal. USA., *Paris Trout*, Peter Dexter, Novel

PARIS UNDERGROUND 1945 d: Gregory Ratoff. USA., *Paris Underground*, Etta Shiber, Book

Paris Underground see **TOUCHEZ PAS AU GRISBI** (1953).

Pariser Leben see **LA VIE PARISIENNE** (1977).

PARISH PRIEST, THE 1920 d: Joseph J. Franz. USA., *The Parish Priest*, Daniel L. Hart, New York 1900, Play

Parisian Belle see **NEW MOON** (1940).

Parisian Life see **LA VIE PARISIENNE** (1977).

PARISIAN ROMANCE, A 1916 d: Frederick A. Thompson. USA., *Un Roman Parisien*, Octave Feuillet, Paris 1882, Play

PARISIAN ROMANCE, A 1932 d: Chester M. Franklin. USA., *Le Roman d'un Jeune Homme Pauvre*, Octave Feuillet, 1858, Novel

Parisienne, La see **UNE PARISIENNE** (1957).

PARISIENNE, UNE 1957 d: Michel Boisrond. FRN/ITL., *La Parisienne*, Henri Becque, 1885, Play

PARISINA (UN AMORE ALLA CORTE DI FERRARA NEL XV SECOLO) 1909 d: Giuseppe de Liguoro. ITL., *Parisina*, Domenico Tumiati, 1903, Poem

PARK AVENUE LOGGER 1937 d: David Howard. USA., *Park Avenue Logger*, Bruce Hutchison, 1935, Short Story

PARK IS MINE, THE 1985 d: Steven Hilliard Stern. CND., *The Park Is Mine*, Stephen Peters, Novel

PARK LANE SCANDAL, A 1915 d: Warwick Buckland. UKN., *Park Lane Scandal*, Rita, Novel

PARK PLAZA 605 1953 d: Bernard Knowles. UKN., *Daredevil Conquest*, Berkeley Gray, Novel

PARKER ADDERSON, PHILOSOPHER 1977 d: Arthur Barron. USA., *Parker Adderson, Philosopher*, Ambrose Bierce, 1891, Short Story

PARKETTSESSEL 47 1926 d: Gaston Ravel. GRM/FRN., *Le Fauteuil 47*, Louis Verneuil, Play

PARKSTRASSE 13 1939 d: Jurgen von Alten. GRM., *Parkstrasse 13*, Axel Ivers, Play

PARLEZ-MOI D'AMOUR 1935 d: Rene Guissart. FRN., *Parlez-Moi d'Amour*, Georges Berr, Louis Verneuil, Play

PARLOR, BEDROOM AND BATH 1920 d: Eddie Dillon. USA., *Parlor, Bedroom and Bath*, Charles W. Bell, Mark Swan, New York 1917, Play

PARLOR, BEDROOM AND BATH 1931 d: Edward Sedgwick. USA., *Parlor, Bedroom and Bath*, Charles W. Bell, Mark Swan, New York 1917, Play

PARMI LES PIERRES 1912 d: Adrien Caillard. FRN., *Parmi Les Pierres*, Hermann Sudermann, Play

Parmi Les Vautours see **UNTER GEIERN** (1964).

PARMIGIANA, LA 1963 d: Antonio Pietrangeli. ITL., *La Parmigiana*, Bruno Piatti, Novel

PARNASIE 1925 d: Josef Kokeisl. CZC., *Parnasie*, Alois Vojtech Smilovsky, Novel

PARNELL 1937 d: John M. Stahl. USA., *Parnell*, Elsie T. Schauffler, New York 1935, Play

PAROLE A VENIRE, LE 1970 d: Peter Del Monte. ITL., *Les Muets*, Albert Camus, 1957, Short Story

Parole Fixer see **UNDERCOVER DOCTOR** (1939).

PAROLE FIXER 1940 d: Robert Florey. USA., *Persons in Hiding*, J. Edgar Hoover, Boston 1938, Book

PARPAILLON 1992 d: Luc Moullet. FRN., *Parpaillon; Ou a la Recherche de l'Homme a la Pompe d'Ursus*, Alfred Jarry

PARRISH 1961 d: Delmer Daves. USA., *Parrish*, Mildred Savage, New York 1958, Novel

Parrot and Co. see **NOT GUILTY** (1921).

PARSIFAL 1981 d: Hans-Jurgen Syberberg. GRM/FRN., *Parsifal*, Richard Wagner, Bayreuth 1882, Opera

Parson Cira and Parson Spira see **POP CIRA I POP SPIRA** (1965).

PARSON OF PANAMINT, THE 1916 d: William D. Taylor. USA., *The Parson of Panamint*, Peter B. Kyne, 1915, Short Story

PARSON OF PANAMINT, THE 1941 d: William McGann. USA., *The Parson of Panamint*, Peter B. Kyne, 1915, Short Story

Parsonage Comedy see **DIE PFARRHAUSKOMODIE** (1971).

Parson's End, The see **FARARUV KONEC** (1968).

PARSON'S FIGHT, THE 1922 d: Edwin J. Collins. UKN., *The Parson's Fight*, George R. Sims, Poem

PART 2 SOUNDER 1976 d: William A. Graham. USA., *Sounder*, William Armstrong, 1969, Novel

PART TIME WIFE 1930 d: Leo McCarey. USA., *The Shepper-Newfounder*, Stewart Edward White, 1930, Short Story

PART TIME WIFE, THE 1925 d: Henry McCarty. USA., *The Part-Time Wife*, Peggy Gaddis, 1925, Short Story

Partage de Catherine, Le see **LA BUGIARDA** (1965).

PARTED CURTAINS 1920 d: Bertram Bracken. USA., *Parted Curtains*, Franklyn Hall, Short Story

PARTHENOS, O 1967 d: Dimis Dadiras. GRC., *Dyscolus*, Menander, 316 bc, Play

PARTIE DE CAMPAGNE, UNE 1936 d: Jean Renoir. FRN., *Une Partie de Campagne*, Guy de Maupassant, 1881, Short Story

Partie Fine see **L' HOMME A L'IMPERMEABLE** (1957).

Partings see **POZEGNANIA** (1958).

PARTIR. 1931 d: Maurice Tourneur. FRN., *Partir*, Roland Dorgeles, Novel

Partir! see **PARTIR.** (1931).

PARTIRE 1938 d: Amleto Palermi. ITL., *Partire*, Gherardo Gherardi, Play

Partisans in the Plains of Ukraine see **PARTIZANI V STEPYAKH UKRAINY** (1943).

Partisans in the Ukrainian Steppes, The see **PARTIZANI V STEPYAKH UKRAINY** (1943).

PARTITA, LA 1991 d: Carlo VanzinA. ITL., *La Partita*, Alberto Ongaro, Novel

PARTIZANI V STEPYAKH UKRAINY 1943 d: Igor Savchenko. USS., *Partizany V Stepnakh Ukrayiny*, Aleksander Korniychuk, 1941, Play

Partizany V Stepyakh Ukrayiny see **PARTIZANI V STEPYAKH UKRAINY** (1943).

Partly Confidential see **THANKS FOR LISTENING** (1937).

PARTNER 1968 d: Bernardo Bertolucci. ITL., *Dvoynik*, Fyodor Dostoyevsky, 1846, Novel

PARTNER, THE 1963 d: Gerald Glaister. UKN., *The Million Dollar Story*, Edgar Wallace, London 1926, Novel

PARTNERS AGAIN 1926 d: Henry King. USA., *Partners Again*, Montague Glass, Jules Eckert Goodman, New York 1922, Play

PARTNERS IN CRIME 1937 d: Ralph Murphy. USA., *Murder Goes to College*, Kurt Steel, Indianapolis 1936, Novel

PARTNERS IN CRIME 1961 d: Peter Duffell. UKN., *The Man Who Knew*, Edgar Wallace, London 1919, Novel

PARTNERS OF THE NIGHT 1920 d: Paul Scardon. USA., *Partners of the Night*, Leroy Scott, 1916, Short Story

PARTNERS OF THE PLAINS 1938 d: Lesley Selander. USA., *The Man from Bar-20; a Story of the Cow Country*, Clarence E. Mulford, Chicago 1918, Novel

PARTNERS OF THE TIDE 1915 d: George A. Lessey. USA., *Partners of the Tide*, Joseph C. Lincoln, New York 1905, Novel

PARTNERS OF THE TIDE 1921 d: L. V. Jefferson. USA., *Partners of the Tide*, Joseph C. Lincoln, New York 1905, Novel

PARTY 1984 d: Govind Nihalani. IND., *Party*, Mahesh Elkunchwar, Play

PARTY GIRL 1930 d: Victor Hugo Halperin. USA., *Dangerous Business*, Edwin Balmer, New York 1927, Novel

PARTY GIRL 1958 d: Nicholas Ray. USA., *Party Girl*, Leo Katcher, Novel

PARTY HUSBAND 1931 d: Clarence Badger. USA., *Party Husband*, Geoffrey Barnes, New York 1930, Novel

PARTY, THE 1987 d: Sebastian Graham-Jones. UKN., *The Party*, Trevor Griffiths, 1973, Play

PARTY WIRE 1935 d: Erle C. Kenton. USA., *Party Wire*, Bruce Manning, New York 1934, Novel

PARTY'S OVER, THE 1934 d: Walter Lang. USA., *The Party's Over*, Daniel Kusell, New York 1933, Play

PAS BESOIN D'ARGENT 1933 d: Jean-Paul Paulin. FRN., *Pas Besoin d'Argent*, Ferdinand Altenkirch, Play

PAS DE CAVIAR POUR TANTE OLGA 1965 d: Jean Becker. FRN., *Espion Ou Est-Tu M'entends-Tu?*, Charles Exbrayat, Novel

PAS DE FEMMES 1932 d: Mario Bonnard. FRN., *Pas de Femmes*, Georgius, Play

Pas de Mentalite *see* AN EINEM FREITAG UM HALB ZWOLF (1961).

PAS DE PANIQUE 1965 d: Sergio Gobbi. FRN/SPN., *Pas de Panique*, Yvan Audouard, Novel

PAS DE PITIE POUR LES FEMMES 1950 d: Christian Stengel. FRN., *Pas de Pitie Pour Les Femmes*, Jean Giltene, Novel

Pas de Roses Pour Oss 117 *see* NIENTE ROSE PER OSS 117 (1968).

PAS FOLLE LA GUEPE 1972 d: Jean Delannoy. FRN/GRM/ITL., James Hadley Chase, Novel

PAS LA VERITE 1917 d: Gaston Leprieur?, Maurice de Feraudy?. FRN., *Par la Verite*, Ernest Daudet, Short Story

PAS PERDUS, LES 1964 d: Jacques Robin. FRN., *Les Pas Perdus*, Rene Fallet, Novel

PAS SUR LA BOUCHE 1931 d: Nicolas Rimsky, Nicolas Evreinoff. FRN., *Pas Sur la Bouche*, Andre Barde, Maurice Yvain, Opera

PAS UN MOT A LA REINE-MERE 1946 d: Maurice Cloche. FRN., *Pas un Mot a la Reine-Mere*, Maurice Goudeket, Yves Mirande, Play

PASAK HOLEK 1929 d: Hans Tintner. CZC., *Pasak Holek*, Egon Erwin Kisch, Novel

PASAZERKA 1963 d: Andrzej Munk, Witold Lesiewicz. PLN., *Pasazerka*, Zofia Posmysz-Piasecka, Novel

PASCALI'S ISLAND 1989 d: James Dearden. UKN/USA., *Pascali's Island*, Barry Unsworth, Novel

PASCUAL DUARTE 1975 d: Ricardo Franco. SPN., *La Familia de Pascual Duarte*, Camilo Jose Cela, 1945, Novel

Paso Al Marino! *see* EN CADA PUERTO UN AMOR (1931).

PASOS DE MUJER, UNOS 1941 d: Eusebio F. Ardavin. SPN., *Unos Pasos de Mujer*, Wenceslao Fernandez Florez, 1934, Short Story

Pass to Romance *see* BEAUTIFUL! HI (1944).

PASSADO E O PRESENTE, O 1970 d: Manoel de OliveirA. PRT., *O Passado E O Presente*, Vicente Sanchez, Play

PASSAGE 1997 d: Juraj Herz. CZC/FRN/BLG., *Passage*, Karel Pecka, Novel

PASSAGE A L'ACTE 1996 d: Francis Girod. FRN., *Neutralite Malveillante*, Jean-Pierre Gattegno, Novel

Passage Cloute *see* D'AMOUR ET D'EAU FRAICHE (1933).

PASSAGE FROM HONG KONG 1941 d: D. Ross Lederman. USA., *The Agony Column*, Earl Derr Biggers, Indianapolis 1916, Novel

PASSAGE HOME 1955 d: Roy Ward Baker. UKN., *Passage Home*, Richard Armstrong, Novel

Passage of Love *see* I WAS HAPPY HERE (1965).

PASSAGE, THE 1979 d: J. Lee Thompson. UKN., *The Perilous Passage*, Bruce Micolaysen, Novel

PASSAGE TO INDIA, A 1965 d: Waris Hussein. UKN., *A Passage to India*, E. M. Forster, 1924, Novel

PASSAGE TO INDIA, A 1984 d: David Lean. UKN., *A Passage to India*, E. M. Forster, 1924, Novel

PASSAGE TO MARSEILLE 1944 d: Michael Curtiz. USA., *Men Without Country*, James N. Hall, Charles Nordhoff, 1944, Novel

Passage to Marseilles *see* PASSAGE TO MARSEILLE (1944).

PASSAGER CLANDESTIN, LE 1960 d: Ralph Habib. FRN/ASL., *Le Passager Clandestin*, Georges Simenon, 1947, Novel

Passager, Le *see* CARAVAN TO VACCARES (1974).

PASSAGERE, LA 1948 d: Jacques Daroy. FRN., *La Passagere*, Guy Chantepleure, Novel

Passagere, La *see* PASAZERKA (1963).

PASSAGERS, LES 1976 d: Serge Leroy. FRN/ITL., *Shattered*, K. R. Dwyer, Book

PASSAGES FROM "FINNEGAN'S WAKE" 1967 d: Mary Ellen Bute. USA., *Finnegan's Wake*, James Joyce, 1939, Novel

Passages from James Joyce's "Finnegan's Wake" *see* PASSAGES FROM "FINNEGAN'S WAKE" (1967).

PASSAGIER FABER 1990 d: Volker Schlondorff. GRM., *Homo Faber*, Max Frisch, 1957, Novel

Passagierin, Die *see* PASAZERKA (1963).

PASSANTE DU SANS-SOUCI, LA 1982 d: Jacques Rouffio. FRN/GRM., *La Passante du San-Souci*, Joseph Kessel, Novel

Passante, La *see* LA PASSANTE DU SANS-SOUCI (1982).

Passatore, Il *see* LA NOTTE DELLE BEFFE (1940).

PASSATORE, IL 1947 d: Duilio Coletti. ITL., *Il Passatore*, Bruno Corra, Novel

PASSE SIMPLE, LE 1977 d: Michel Drach. FRN., *Le Passe Simple*, Dominique Saint-Alban, Novel

PASSEGGERA, LA 1918 d: Gero Zambuto. ITL., *La Passegere*, Madame Guy de Chantepleure, Novel

PASSEGGIATA, LA 1953 d: Renato Rascel. ITL., *La Prospettiva*, Nikolay Gogol, Short Story

Passe-Muraille, Le *see* GAROU-GAROU LE PASSE-MURAILLE (1950).

Passenger *see* PASAZERKA (1963).

Passenger Faber *see* PASSAGIER FABER (1990).

Passengers, The *see* LES PASSAGERS (1976).

PASSEPORT DIPLOMATIQUE, AGENT K8 1965 d: Robert Vernay. FRN/ITL., *Agent K8 Passeport Diplomatique*, Maurice Dekobra, Novel

PASSERELLE, LA 1987 d: Jean-Claude Sussfeld. FRN., *Savage Holiday*, Richard Wright, Novel

PASSERS BY 1916 d: Stanner E. V. Taylor. USA., *Passers-By*, C. Haddon Chambers, London 1911, Play

Passers By *see* PASSERS-BY (1920).

Passers-By *see* PASSERS BY (1916).

PASSERS-BY 1920 d: J. Stuart Blackton. USA., *Passers-By*, C. Haddon Chambers, London 1911, Play

PASSEURS D'HOMMES 1937 d: Rene Jayet. FRN., *Passeurs d'Hommes*, Martial Lekeux, Novel

PASSI FURTIVI IN UNA NOTTE BOIA 1976 d: Vincenzo Rigo. ITL., *Zelmaide; un Colpo in Tre Atti*, Giorgio Santi, Novel

Passing Clouds *see* SPELLBOUND (1941).

Passing Fancy *see* FELHOJATEK! (1984).

PASSING OF BLACK EAGLE, THE 1920 d: Joe Ryan. USA., *The Passing of Black Eagle*, O. Henry, Short Story

Passing of Evil, The *see* THE GRASSHOPPER (1970).

PASSING OF MR. QUIN, THE 1928 d: Leslie Hiscott. UKN., *The Passing of Mr. Quin*, Agatha Christie, Novel

PASSING OF THE THIRD FLOOR BACK, THE 1918 d: Herbert Brenon. USA., *The Passing of the Third Floor Back*, Jerome K. Jerome, London 1908, Play

PASSING OF THE THIRD FLOOR BACK, THE 1935 d: Berthold Viertel. UKN., *The Passing of the Third Floor Back*, Jerome K. Jerome, London 1908, Play

Passion *see* MANJI (1964).

Passion *see* SZENVEDELY (1998).

Passion d'Amour *see* PASSIONE D'AMORE (1981).

PASSION FLOWER 1930 d: William C. de Mille. USA., *Passion Flower*, Kathleen Norris, 1929, Short Story

Passion Flower Hotel *see* LEIDENSCHAFTLICHE BLUMCHEN (1978).

PASSION FLOWER, THE 1921 d: Herbert Brenon. USA., *La Malquerida*, Jacinto Benevente Y Martinez, 1913, Play

PASSION IN THE DESERT 1997 d: Lavinia Currier. USA., Honore de Balzac, Novel

PASSION ISLAND 1927 d: Manning Haynes. UKN., *Passion Island*, W. W. Jacobs, Novel

PASSION OF ANY RAND, THE 1999 d: Christopher Menaul. USA., *The Passion of Any Rand*, Barbara Branden, Book

Passion of Jesus, The *see* ACTO DA PRIMAVERA (1963).

Passion of Love *see* PASSIONE D'AMORE (1981).

Passion of Slow Fire, The *see* LA MORT DE BELLE (1961).

Passion Sauvage *see* CAMELIA (1953).

Passion Sin Barreras *see* WHITE PALACE (1990).

PASSION SONG, THE 1928 d: Harry O. Hoyt. USA., *Paid With Tears*, Francis Fenton, Story

PASSIONATE ADVENTURE, THE 1924 d: Graham Cutts. UKN., *The Passionate Adventure*, Frank Stayton, Novel

Passionate Adventure, The *see* TWO LOVERS (1928).

Passionate Affair *see* TENDRE ET VIOLENTE ELISABETH (1960).

Passionate Demons, The *see* LINE (1961).

PASSIONATE FRIENDS, THE 1922 d: Maurice Elvey. UKN., *The Passionate Friends*, H. G. Wells, 1913, Novel

PASSIONATE FRIENDS, THE 1948 d: David Lean. UKN., *The Passionate Friends*, H. G. Wells, 1913, Novel

Passionate Little Flowers *see* LEIDENSCHAFTLICHE BLUMCHEN (1978).

Passionate Ones, The *see* DIE LEIDENSCHAFTLICHEN (1981).

PASSIONATE PILGRIM, THE 1921 d: Robert G. VignolA. USA., *The Passionate Pilgrim*, Samuel Merwin, Indianapolis 1919, Novel

PASSIONATE PLUMBER, THE 1932 d: Edward Sedgwick. USA., *Her Cardboard Lover*, P. G. Wodehouse, Valerie Wyngate, New York 1927, Play

PASSIONATE QUEST, THE 1926 d: J. Stuart Blackton. USA., *The Passionate Quest*, E. Phillips Oppenheim, Boston 1924, Novel

Passionate Sentry, The *see* WHO GOES THERE! (1952).

Passionate Summer *see* LES POSSEDEES (1955).

PASSIONATE SUMMER 1958 d: Rudolph Cartier. UKN., *The Shadow and the Peak*, Richard Mason, Novel

Passionate Thief, The *see* RISATE DI GIOIA (1960).

Passione *see* OLTRE L'AMORE (1940).

PASSIONE D'AMORE 1981 d: Ettore ScolA. ITL/FRN., *Fosca*, Ignio Ugo Tarchetti, Novel

Passionnelle *see* POUR UNE NUIT D'AMOUR (1946).

PASSIONNEMENT 1932 d: Rene Guissart, Louis Mercanton (Uncredited). FRN., *Passionnement*, Maurice Hennequin, Albert Willemetz, Opera

Passion's Fool *see* LIEBELEI (1927).

Passions of Love *see* PASSIONE D'AMORE (1981).

PASSION'S PLAYGROUND 1920 d: J. A. Barry. USA., *The Guests of Hercules*, Alice Muriel Williamson, Charles Norris Williamson, New York 1912, Novel

Passport to Fame *see* THE WHOLE TOWN'S TALKING (1935).

Passport to Larkspur Lane *see* NANCY DREW -DETECTIVE (1938).

Passport to Oblivion *see* WHERE THE SPIES ARE (1966).

PASSPORT TO TERROR 1989 d: Lou Antonio. USA., *Never Pass This Way Again*, Naar Lepere, Book

PASSPORT TO TREASON 1956 d: Robert S. Baker. UKN., *Passport to Treason*, Manning O'Brine, Novel

Password: Heron *see* KENNWORT: REIHER (1964).

PASSWORD IS COURAGE, THE 1962 d: Andrew L. Stone. UKN., *The Password Is Courage*, John Castle, 1955, Biography

Past and Present *see* O PASSADO E O PRESENTE (1970).

PAST OF MARY HOLMES, THE 1933 d: Harlan Thompson, Slavko Vorkapich. USA., *The Goose Woman*, Rex Beach, 1925, Short Story

PAST ONE AT ROONEY'S 1917 d: Thomas R. Mills. USA., *Past One at Rooney's*, O. Henry, Short Story

Pasteboard Lover, The *see* THE FAITHLESS LOVER (1928).

Pasto Delle Belve, Il *see* LE REPAS DES FAUVES (1964).

PASTOR FIDO, IL 1918 d: Telemaco Ruggeri. ITL., *Il Pastor Fido*, Giovan Battista Guarini, 1590, Poem

PASTOR HALL 1940 d: Roy Boulting. UKN., *Pastor Hall*, Ernst Toller, 1937, Play

Pastor of Kirchfeld, The *see* DER PFARRER VON KIRCHFELD (1926).

Pastor of Kirchfeld, The *see* DER PFARRER VON KIRCHFELD (1937).

Pastor of Kirchfeld, The *see* DER PFARRER VON KIRCHFELD (1955).

Pastoral Symphony *see* LA SYMPHONIE PASTORALE (1946).

Pastorale *see* PASTORALE 1943 (1977).

PASTORALE 1943 1977 d: Wim Verstappen. NTH., *Pastorale 1943*, Simon Vestdijk, Novel

Pastor's End *see* FARARUV KONEC (1968).

PAT CLANCY'S ADVENTURE 1911. USA., *The Shamrock and the Palm*, O. Henry, Short Story

PAT UND PATACHON IM PARADIES 1937 d: Carl Lamac. AUS., *Eine Insel Entdeckt*, Karl von Stigler, Play

PATATE 1964 d: Robert Thomas. FRN/ITL., *Patate*, Marcel Achard, Paris 1957, Play

PATATES, LES 1969 d: Claude Autant-LarA. FRN., *Les Patates*, Jacques Vacherot, Novel

Patch *see* **DEATH OF A GUNFIGHTER** (1969).

PATCH ADAMS 1998 d: Tom Shadyac. USA., *Gesundheit: Good Health Is a Laughing Matter*, Hunter Doherty Adams, Maureen Mylander, 1993, Book

PATCH OF BLUE, A 1965 d: Guy Green. USA., *Be Ready With Bells and Drums*, Elizabeth Kata, New York 1961, Novel

Patched Coat *see* **KANDAM BACHA COAT** (1961).

Patched-Up Coat, The *see* **KANDAM BACHA COAT** (1961).

PATENT LEATHER KID, THE 1927 d: Alfred Santell. USA., *Patent Leather Kid*, Rupert Hughes, 1927, Short Story

Pater Brown: Er Kann's Nicht Lassen *see* **ER KANN'S NICHT LASSEN** (1962).

PATER VOJTECH 1928 d: Martin Fric. CZC., *Pater Vojtech*, Jan Klecanda, Novel

PATER VOJTECH 1936 d: Martin Fric. CZC., *Pater Vojtech*, Jan Klecanda, Novel

PATERNAL LOVE 1915 d: Frank Lloyd. USA., *Paternal Love*, William Wolbert, Story

PATH FORBIDDEN, THE 1914 d: Harry Handworth. USA., *The Path Forbidden*, John B. Hymer, Novel

PATH OF GLORY, THE 1934 d: Dallas Bower. UKN., *The Path of Glory*, L. Du Garde Peach, Radio Play

Path of Hope, The *see* **IL CAMMINO DELLA SPERANZA** (1950).

Path of Salvation *see* **VEREDA DA SALVACAO** (1965).

PATH SHE CHOSE, THE 1920 d: Phil Rosen. USA., *Virginia*, Ida M. Evans, Short Story

Path Under the Plane-Trees, The *see* **SUZUKAKE NO SANPOMICHI** (1959).

Path Under the Platanes, The *see* **SUZUKAKE NO SANPOMICHI** (1959).

PATHER PANCHALI 1955 d: Satyajit Ray. IND., *Pather Pancali*, Bibhutibhushan Bannerjee, 1929, Novel

Pathetic Fallacy, The *see* **AJANTRIK** (1958).

Pathetic Folly *see* **AJANTRIK** (1958).

PATHFINDER, THE 1952 d: Sidney Salkow. USA., *The Pathfinder*, James Fenimore Cooper, 1840, Novel

Pathfinder, The *see* **AVENTURE EN ONTARIO** (1968).

PATHFINDER, THE 1994 d: Donald Shebib. CND., *The Pathfinder*, James Fenimore Cooper, 1840, Novel

PATHLAAG 1964 d: Raja Paranjape. IND., *Asha Parat Yete*, Jayant Devkule, Novel

Pathlag *see* **PATHLAAG** (1964).

PATHS OF FLAME 1926. USA., *The Heart of a Thief*, Paul Armstrong, New York 1914, Play

PATHS OF GLORY 1957 d: Stanley Kubrick. USA., *Paths of Glory*, Humphrey Cobb, 1935, Novel

Paths of Life, The *see* **SMERY ZIVOTA** (1940).

PATHS TO PARADISE 1925 d: Clarence Badger. USA., *The Heart of a Thief*, Paul Armstrong, New York 1914, Play

Patience Sparhawk *see* **THE PANTHER WOMAN** (1919).

PATIENT IN ROOM 18, THE 1938 d: Crane Wilbur, Bobby Connolly. USA., *The Patient in Room 18*, Mignon G. Eberhart, Garden City, N.Y. 1929, Novel

Patient Vanishes, The *see* **THIS MAN IS DANGEROUS** (1941).

PATIO DE LOS NARANJOS, EL 1926 d: Guillermo Hernandez Mir. SPN., *El Patio de Los Naranjos*, Guillermo Hernandez Mir, Novel

PATRICIA BRENT, SPINSTER 1919 d: Geoffrey H. Malins. UKN., *Patricia Brent - Spinster*, Herbert Jenkins, Novel

PATRICIA NEAL STORY, THE 1981 d: Anthony Harvey, Anthony Page. USA., *Pat and Roald*, Barry Farrell, Book

PATRICK WHITE'S THE NIGHT THE PROWLER 1978 d: Jim Sharman. ASL., *The Night the Prowler*, Patrick White, 1974, Short Story

PATRIE 1914 d: Albert Capellani. FRN., *Patrie*, Louis Gallet, Victorien Sardou, 1869, Play

PATRIE 1945 d: Louis Daquin. FRN., *Patrie*, Louis Gallet, Victorien Sardou, 1869, Play

Patrie, Te Reste-T-Il Des Fils? *see* **HAST NOCH DER SOHNE JA?** (1959).

PATRIOT GAMES 1992 d: Phil Noyce. USA., *Patriot Games*, Tom Clancy, Novel

PATRIOT, THE 1928 d: Ernst Lubitsch. USA., *Der Patriot*, Alfred Neumann, 1925, Short Story

PATRIOTE, LE 1938 d: Maurice Tourneur. FRN., *Der Patriot*, Alfred Neumann, 1925, Short Story

Patrol *see* **THE LOST PATROL** (1934).

PATRONNE, LA 1949 d: Robert Dhery. FRN., *La Patronne*, Andre Luguet, Play

PATSY 1921 d: John McDermott. USA., *Patsy*, Er Lawshe, c1914, Play

Patsy *see* **BAD LITTLE ANGEL** (1939).

PATSY, THE 1928 d: King Vidor. USA., *The Patsy*, Barry Connors, New York 1925, Play

PATTERN OF ROSES, A 1983 d: Lawrence Gordon Clark. UKN/GRM., *A Pattern of Roses*, K. M. Peyton, Novel

PATTERNS 1956 d: Fielder Cook. USA., *Patterns*, Rod Serling, 1956, Television Play

Patterns of Power *see* **PATTERNS** (1956).

PATTES DE MOUCHE, LES 1936 d: Jean Gremillon. FRN., *Les Pattes de Mouche*, Victorien Sardou, Paris 1860, Play

PATTON 1970 d: Franklin J. Schaffner. USA., *Patton: Ordeal and Triumph*, Ladislas Farago, New York 1964, Biography

Patton: a Salute to a Rebel *see* **PATTON** (1970).

Patton: Lust for Glory *see* **PATTON** (1970).

Patton: Salute to a Rebel *see* **PATTON** (1970).

Pattuglia Anti-Gang *see* **BRIGADE ANTI-GANGS** (1966).

Patty *see* **PATTY HEARST** (1988).

PATTY HEARST 1988 d: Paul Schrader. USA/UKN., *Every Secret Thing*, Patricia Campbell Hearst, Alvin Moscow, Autobiography

Patty Hearst: Her Own Story *see* **PATTY HEARST** (1988).

PAUL ET VIRGINIE 1926 d: Robert Peguy. FRN., *Paul Et Virginie*, Bernardin de Saint-Pierre, Novel

Paul Street Boys, The *see* **NO GREATER GLORY** (1934).

PAUL TEMPLE'S TRIUMPH 1950 d: MacLean Rogers. UKN., Francis Durbridge, Radio Play

PAULA 1915 d: Cecil Birch. UKN., *Paula*, Victoria Cross, Novel

PAULA 1952 d: Rudolph Mate. USA., Lawrence B. Marcus, Short Story

PAULINA 1880 1972 d: Jean-Louis Bertucelli. FRN/GRM., *Paulina 1880*, Pierre-Jean Jouve, 1925, Novel

PAUL'S CASE 1977 d: Lamont Johnson. USA., *Paul's Case*, Willa Cather, 1905, Short Story

Paume, Le *see* **LE SOIR, AU-DESSUS DES JONGES, LE CRI DU CORMORAN** (1970).

PAUPER MILLIONAIRE, THE 1922 d: Frank H. Crane. UKN., *The Pauper Millionaire*, Austin Fryer, Novel

Pauper Student, The *see* **DER BETTELSTUDENT** (1956).

PAURA E AMORE 1987 d: Margarethe von TrottA. ITL/GRM/FRN., *Tri Sestry*, Anton Chekhov, Moscow 1901, Play

PAURA, LA 1954 d: Roberto Rossellini. ITL/GRM., *Die Angst*, Stefan Zweig, 1920, Short Story

PAUVRES DE PARIS, LES 1913 d: Georges DenolA. FRN., *Les Pauvres de Paris*, Brisbarre, Nus, Play

PAUVRES GENS, LES 1937 d: Antoine Mourre. FRN., *Les Pauvres Gens*, Victor Hugo, 1859, Verse

Pavane Des Poisons, La *see* **SOUPCONS** (1956).

PAVE DU GORILLE, LE 1990 d: Roger Hanin. FRN/GRM/ITL., *Le Pave du Gorille*, Antoine Dominique, Novel

Pavel Camrda's Career *see* **KARIERA PAVLA CAMRDY** (1931).

Pavel Korcagin *see* **PAVEL KORCHAGIN** (1957).

PAVEL KORCHAGIN 1957 d: Alexander Alov, Vladimir Naumov. USS., *Kak Zakalyalas Stal*, Alexander Ostrovsky, 1932-34, Novel

Pavilion on the Links, The *see* **THE WHITE CIRCLE** (1920).

Pavilion Vi *see* **PAVILJON VI** (1979).

PAVILJON VI 1979 d: Lucian Pintilie. YGS., *Palata No.6*, Anton Chekhov, 1892, Short Story

PAVILLON BRULE, LE 1941 d: Jacques de Baroncelli. FRN., *Le Pavillon Brule*, Steve Passeur, Play

PAW 1959 d: Astrid Henning-Jensen. DNM., *Der Indianerjunge Paw*, Torry Gredsted, Cologne 1931, Novel

PAWN TICKET 210 1922 d: Scott R. Dunlap. USA., *Pawn Ticket No. 210*, David Belasco, Clay M. Greene, Play

PAWNBROKER, THE 1965 d: Sidney Lumet. USA., *The Pawnbroker*, Edward Lewis Wallant, New York 1961, Novel

PAWNED 1922 d: Irvin V. Willat. USA., *Pawned*, Frank L. Packard, New York 1921, Novel

PAX DOMINE 1924 d: Rene Leprince. FRN., *L' Homme Que J'ai Tue*, Maurice Rostand, Novel

PAY DAY 1918 d: Sidney Drew, Mrs. Sidney Drew. USA., *Pay-Day*, Oliver D. Bailey, Lottie M. Meaney, New York 1916, Play

Pay Off *see* **PAYOFF** (1991).

Pay the Devil *see* **MAN IN THE SHADOW** (1956).

PAYBACK 1999 d: Brian Helgeland. USA., *The Hunter*, Donald E. Westlake, New York 1963, Novel

Paying the Piper *see* **THE FALLEN ANGEL** (1918).

PAYMENT DEFERRED 1932 d: Lothar Mendes. USA., *Payment Deferred*, C. S. Forester, 1926, Novel

PAYOFF 1991 d: Stuart Cooper. USA., *The Payoff*, Ronald T. Owen, Novel

Payoff, The *see* **LA MAZZETTA** (1978).

PAYROLL 1961 d: Sidney Hayers. UKN., *Payroll*, Derek Bickerton, London 1959, Novel

PAYS SANS ETOILES, LE 1945 d: Georges Lacombe. FRN., *Le Pays Sans Etoiles*, Pierre Very, Novel

PAYSANS, LES 1909 d: Charles Decroix. FRN., *Les Paysans*, Honore de Balzac, Novel

PAYSANS NOIRS 1947 d: Georges Regnier. FRN., *Paysans Noirs*, Roger Delavignette, Novel

PAZACHAT NA KREPOSTA 1974 d: Milen Nikolov. BUL., *Diva Patitsa Mezhdu Darvetata*, Stanislav Stratiev, 1972, Novel

P.C. JOSSER 1931 d: Milton Rosmer. UKN., *The Police Force*, Ernie Lotinga, Play

Peace *see* **HOA-BINH** (1970).

PEACE AND QUIET 1929 d: Sinclair Hill. UKN., *Peace and Quiet*, Ronald Jeans, Play

PEACEFUL PETERS 1922 d: Louis King. USA., *Peaceful*, W. C. Tuttle, Short Story

PEACEFUL VALLEY 1920 d: Jerome Storm. USA., *Peaceful Valley*, Edward E. Kidder, New York 1893, Play

PEACEMAKER, THE 1956 d: Ted Post. USA., *The Peacemaker*, Richard Poole, 1954, Novel

Peacemaker, The *see* **THE AMBASSADOR** (1984).

PEACETIME SPIES 1924 d: Lee Morrison. UKN., *Peacetime Spies*, Dudley Sturrock, Short Story

Peach Blossom Party *see* **JING HUN TAO HUA DANG** (1994).

Peach Flower Fan *see* **TAO HUA SHAN** (1963).

Peach Thief, The *see* **KRADETSAT NA PRASKOVI** (1964).

Peaches in Syrup *see* **MELOCOTON EN ALMIBAR** (1960).

PEACOCK FEATHERS 1925 d: Svend Gade. USA., *Peacock Feathers*, Temple Bailey, Novel

PEARL FOR PEARL 1922 d: George A. Cooper. UKN., *Pearl for Pearl*, Atreus Van Schraeder, Story

PEARL OF DEATH, THE 1944 d: R. William Neill. USA., *Adventure of the Six Napoleons*, Arthur Conan Doyle, 1904, Short Story

PEARL OF THE ANTILLES, THE 1915 d: Tom Terriss. USA., *The Sword of Honor*, William Terriss, Play

PEARL OF THE SOUTH PACIFIC 1955 d: Allan Dwan. USA., Anna Hunger, Story

Pearl of Tlayucan, The *see* **TLAYUCAN** (1961).

PEARL, THE 1946 d: Emilio Fernandez. USA/MXC., *The Pearl*, John Steinbeck, 1945, Novel

Pearls of St. Lucia, The *see* **TLAYUCAN** (1961).

Peasants *see* **CHLOPI** (1973).

PEAU D'ANE 1970 d: Jacques Demy. FRN., *Peau d'Ane*, Charles Perrault, 1697, Short Story

PEAU DE BANANE 1964 d: Marcel Ophuls. FRN/ITL., *Nothing in Her Way*, Charles Williams, 1953, Novel

PEAU DE CHAGRIN, LA 1911 d: Georges Denola ?, Albert Capellani ?. FRN., *La Peau de Chagrin*, Honore de Balzac, Paris 1831, Novel

Peau de Chagrin, La see SAGRENSKA KOZA (1960).

PEAU DE L'OURS, LA 1957 d: Claude Boissol. FRN., *Monsieur Bon Appetit*, Gilbert Laporte, Novel

PEAU DE PECHE 1926 d: Jean Benoit-Levy, Marie Epstein. FRN., *Peau de Peche*, Gabriel Mauriere, Novel

PEAU DE TORPEDO, LA 1970 d: Jean Delannoy. FRN/ITL/GRM., *La Peau de Torpedo*, Francis Ryck, Novel

PEAU D'ESPION 1967 d: Edouard Molinaro. FRN/ITL/GRM., *Peau d'Espion*, Jacques Robert, Paris 1966, Novel

Peau, La see LA PELLE (1981).

Peau Noire, Ame Blanche see EL NEGRO QUE TENIA EL ALMA BLANCA (1926).

Peau-de-Peche see PEAU DE PECHE (1926).

PECADO DE JULIA, EL 1947 d: Mario Soffici. ARG., *Froken Julie*, August Strindberg, 1888, Play

Peccati Di Madame Bovary, I see DIE NACKTE BOVARY (1969).

PECCATO CHE SIA UNA CANAGLIA 1955 d: Alessandro Blasetti. ITL., *Faccia Di Mascalzone*, Alberto Moravia, 1954, Short Story

PECCATO DI ROGELIA SANCHEZ, IL 1939 d: Carlo Borghesio, Edgar Neville. ITL/SPN., *Santa Rogelia*, Armando Palacio Valdes, 1926, Novel

Peccato Mortale see NO ENCONTRE ROSAS PARA MI MADRE (1972).

Peccatori Della Foresta Nera, I see LA CHAMBRE ARDENTE (1961).

PECCATRICE, UNA 1918 d: Giulio Antamoro. ITL., *Una Peccatrice*, Giovanni Verga, 1866, Novel

Peche, Le see AL- HARAM (1964).

PECHEUR D'ISLANDE 1915 d: Henri Pouctal. FRN., *Pecheur d'Islande*, Pierre Loti, 1886, Novel

PECHEUR D'ISLANDE 1924 d: Jacques de Baroncelli. FRN., *Pecheur d'Islande*, Pierre Loti, 1886, Novel

PECHEUR D'ISLANDE 1933 d: Pierre Guerlais. FRN., *Pecheur d'Islande*, Pierre Loti, 1886, Novel

PECHEUR D'ISLANDE 1959 d: Pierre Schoendoerffer. FRN., *Pecheur d'Islande*, Pierre Loti, 1886, Novel

Pechvogel, Der see DE WINZIG SIMULIERT (1942).

PECK'S BAD BOY 1921 d: Sam Wood. USA., *Peck's Bad Boy and His Pa*, George Wilbur Peck, Story

PEDAZO DE NOCHE, UN 1995 d: Roberto Rochin. MXC., Juan Rulfo, Short Story

Peddler Lover, The see ARSHIN MAL ALAN (1937).

PEDDLER OF LIES, THE 1920 d: William C. Dowlan. USA., *The Peddler*, Henry C. Rowland, 1919, Novel

PEDDLER, THE 1917 d: Herbert Blache. USA., *The Peddler*, Hal Reid, New York 1902, Play

PEDRO MICO 1985 d: Ipojuca Fontes. BRZ., *Zumbi Do Catacumba Pedro Mico*, Antonio Callado, 1957, Play

PEDRO PARAMO 1966 d: Carlos Velo. MXC., *Pedro Paramo*, Juan Rulfo, 1955, Novel

PEDRO PARAMO 1976 d: Jose Bolanos. MXC., *Pedro Paramo*, Juan Rulfo, 1955, Novel

PEEP 1974 d: Jack Cunningham. CND., *See No Evil*, Jack Cunningham, Play

PEEP BEHIND THE SCENES, A 1918 d: Geoffrey H. Malins, Kenelm Foss. UKN., *A Peep Behind the Scenes*, Mrs. O. F. Walton, Novel

PEEP BEHIND THE SCENES, A 1929 d: Jack Raymond. UKN., *A Peep Behind the Scenes*, Mrs. O. F. Walton, Novel

PEER GYNT 1915 d: Oscar Apfel. USA., *Peer Gynt*, Henrik Ibsen, Copenhagen 1867, Play

PEER GYNT 1934 d: Fritz Wendhausen. GRM., *Peer Gynt*, Henrik Ibsen, Copenhagen 1867, Play

PEER GYNT 1941 d: David Bradley. USA., *Peer Gynt*, Henrik Ibsen, Copenhagen 1867, Play

Peers, The see LE ARMI E GLI AMORI (1983).

PEG O' MY HEART 1919 d: William C. de Mille. USA., *Peg O' My Heart*, J. Hartley Manners, New York 1912, Play

PEG O' MY HEART 1922 d: King Vidor. USA., *Peg O' My Heart*, J. Hartley Manners, New York 1912, Play

PEG O' MY HEART 1933 d: Robert Z. Leonard. USA., *Peg O' My Heart*, J. Hartley Manners, New York 1912, Play

PEG OF OLD DRURY 1935 d: Herbert Wilcox. UKN., *Peg Woffington*, Charles Reade, 1852, Novel

PEG WOFFINGTON 1910 d: Edwin S. Porter. USA., *Peg Woffington*, Charles Reade, 1852, Novel

PEG WOFFINGTON 1912 d: A. E. Coleby. UKN., *Peg Woffington*, Charles Reade, 1852, Novel

PEGEEN 1920 d: David Smith. USA., *Pegeen*, Eleanor Hoyt Brainerd, New York 1915, Novel

PEGGIO OFFESA, 'A 1924 d: Goffredo d'AndreA. ITL., *O Schiaffo*, Pasquale Ponzillo, Play

PEGGY DOES HER DARNDEST 1919 d: George D. Baker. USA., *Peggy Does Her Darndest*, Royal Brown, 1918, Short Story

PEHLA ADHYAY 1981 d: Vishnu Mathur. IND., *Milechan*, Ambai, Short Story

PEINE D'AMOUR 1914 d: Henri Fescourt. FRN., *Peine d'Amour*, Pierre Sales, Novel

PEINTRE EXIGEANT, LE 1929 d: Maurice Champreux, Robert Beaudoin. FRN., *Le Peintre Exigeant*, Tristan Bernard, Play

Peking Blonde see LA BLONDE DE PEKIN (1968).

Pelegrin Method, The see EL SISTEMA PELEGRIN (1951).

PELICAN BRIEF, THE 1993 d: Alan J. PakulA. USA., *The Pelican Brief*, John Grisham, Novel

Pelican, The see "MARRIAGE LICENSE?" (1926).

Pelle Di Donna see LE JOURNAL D'UNE FEMME EN BLANC (1964).

Pelle d'Oca see CHAIR DE POULE (1964).

PELLE EROBREREN 1987 d: Bille August. DNM/SWD., *Pelle Erobreren*, Martin Andersen Nexo, 1906-10, Novel

PELLE, LA 1981 d: Liliana Cavani. ITL/FRN., *La Pelle*, Curzio Malaparte, Novel

Pelle the Conqueror see PELLE EROBREREN (1987).

PELLEAS AND MELISANDE 1913 d: Mr. MacDonald. USA., *Pelleas Et Melisande*, Maurice Maeterlinck, 1892, Play

PELLEAS ET MELISANDE 1973 d: Joseph Benedek. BLG., *Pelleas Et Melisande*, Maurice Maeterlinck, 1892, Play

PELLEGRINO, IL 1912 d: Mario Caserini. ITL., *The Pilgrim's Progress*, John Bunyan, 1684, Allegory

PELOTON D'EXECUTION 1945 d: Andre Berthomieu. FRN., *Peloton d'Execution*, Pierre Nord, Novel

Penal Camp see LA COLONIA PENAL (1971).

Penal Colony, The see LA COLONIA PENAL (1971).

PENALTY, THE 1920 d: Wallace Worsley. USA., *The Penalty*, Gouverneur Morris, New York 1913, Novel

Penalty, The see THE TATTLERS (1920).

PENALTY, THE 1941 d: Harold S. Bucquet. USA., *The Penalty*, Martin Berkeley, Play

Pendragon Legend, The see A PENDRAGON LEGENDA (1974).

PENDRAGON LEGENDA, A 1974 d: Gyorgy Revesz. HNG., *A Pendragon Legenda*, Antal Szerb, 1934, Novel

PENELOPE 1966 d: Arthur Hiller. USA., *Penelope*, Howard Fast, New York 1965, Novel

PENGUIN POOL MURDER 1932 d: George Archainbaud. USA., *The Penguin Pool Murder*, Stuart Palmer, New York 1931, Novel

Penguin Pool Mystery, The see PENGUIN POOL MURDER (1932).

Penitent, The see THE PENITENTES (1915).

PENITENTES, THE 1915 d: Jack Conway. USA., *The Penitentes*, Robert Ellis Wales, Novel

PENITENTIARY 1938 d: John Brahm. USA., *The Criminal Code*, Martin Flavin, New York 1929, Play

Penitents, The see THE PENITENTES (1915).

PENMARIC 1979 d: Tina Wakerell, Derek Martinus. UKN., *Penmaric*, Susan Howatch, Novel

PENN OF PENNSYLVANIA 1941 d: Lance Comfort. UKN., *William Penn*, C. E. Vulliamy, Book

PENNIES FROM HEAVEN 1936 d: Norman Z. McLeod. USA., *The Peacock Feather*, Katharine Leslie Moore, London 1913, Novel

PENNIES FROM HEAVEN 1981 d: Herbert Ross. USA., *Pennies from Heaven*, Dennis Potter, 1981, Play

PENNILESS MILLIONAIRE, THE 1921 d: Einar J. Bruun. UKN., *The Penniless Millionaire*, David Christie Murray, Novel

PENNIN PERUMAI 1956 d: P. Pullaiah. IND., *Swayamsiddha*, Manilal Gangopadhyay, Novel

Pennsylvania Uprising see ALLEGHENY UPRISING (1939).

PENNY OF TOP HILL TRAIL 1921 d: Arthur Berthelet. USA., *Penny of Top Hill Trail*, Belle K. Maniates, Novel

PENNY PHILANTHROPIST, THE 1917 d: Guy W. McConnell. USA., *The Penny Philanthropist; a Story That Could Be True*, Clara E. Laughlin, New York 1912, Novel

PENROD 1922 d: Marshall Neilan. USA., *Penrod*, Booth Tarkington, New York 1914, Novel

PENROD AND HIS TWIN BROTHER 1938 d: William McGann. USA., *Penrod*, Booth Tarkington, New York 1914, Novel, *Penrod and Sam*, Booth Tarkington, New York 1916, Novel

PENROD AND SAM 1923 d: William Beaudine. USA., *Penrod and Sam*, Booth Tarkington, New York 1916, Novel

PENROD AND SAM 1931 d: William Beaudine. USA., *Penrod and Sam*, Booth Tarkington, New York 1916, Novel

PENROD AND SAM 1937 d: William McGann. USA., *Penrod and Sam*, Booth Tarkington, New York 1916, Novel

PENROD'S DOUBLE TROUBLE 1938 d: Lewis Seiler. USA., *Penrod*, Booth Tarkington, New York 1914, Novel, *Penrod and Sam*, Booth Tarkington, New York 1916, Novel

PENSACI, GIACOMINO! 1936 d: Gennaro Righelli. ITL., *Pensaci Giacomino!*, Luigi Pirandello, 1910, Short Story

Pension de Famille see UNE VIE DE CHIEN (1941).

Pension Filoda see FREMDENHEIM FILODA (1937).

PENSION JONAS 1941 d: Pierre Caron. FRN., *Barnabe Tignol Et San Baleine*, Thevenin, Novel

PENSION PRO SVOBODNE PANY 1967 d: Jiri Krejcik. CZC., *Bedtime Story*, Sean O'Casey, 1951, Play

PENSION SCHOLLER 1930 d: Georg Jacoby. GRM., *Pension Scholler*, Wilhelm Jacoby, Carl Laufs, Play

PENSION SCHOLLER 1952 d: Georg Jacoby. GRM., *Pension Scholler*, Wilhelm Jacoby, Carl Laufs, Play

PENSION SCHOLLER 1960 d: Georg Jacoby. GRM., *Pension Scholler*, Wilhelm Jacoby, Carl Laufs, Play

Pensione Edelweiss see SURSIS POUR UN VIVANT (1958).

PENSJA PANI LATTER 1982 d: Stanislaw Rozewicz. PLN., *Emancypantki*, Boleslaw Prus, 1894, Novel

PENTHESILEA 1988 d: Hans-Jurgen Syberberg. GRM., *Penthesilea*, Heinrich von Kleist, 1808, Play

PENTHOUSE 1933 d: W. S. Van Dyke. USA., *Penthouse*, Arthur Somers Roche, New York 1935, Novel

Penthouse see SOCIETY LAWYER (1939).

Penthouse Legend see PENTHOUSE (1933).

Penthouse Party see WITHOUT CHILDREN (1935).

PENTHOUSE, THE 1967 d: Peter Collinson. UKN., *The Meter Man*, C. Scott Forbes, London 1964, Play

PEOPLE AGAINST O'HARA, THE 1951 d: John Sturges. USA., *The People Against O'Hara*, Eleazar Lipsky, 1950, Novel

People in the Hotel see MENSCHEN IM HOTEL (1959).

People in the Net see MENSCHEN IM NETZ (1959).

People Meet see MENNESKER MODES OG SOD MUSIK OPSTAR I HJERTET (1968).

People Meet and Sweet Music Fills the Heart see MENNESKER MODES OG SOD MUSIK OPSTAR I HJERTET (1968).

PEOPLE NEXT DOOR, THE 1970 d: David Greene. USA., *The People Next Door*, J. P. Miller, 1968, Play

People of Abrimes, The see THE LOST CONTINENT (1968).

People of Hemso see HEMSOBORNA (1919).

People of Hemso, The see HEMSOBORNA (1944).

People of Hemso, The see HEMSOBORNA (1955).

People of the Grasslands see CAO YUAN SHANG DE REN MEN (1953).

People of the Rice Fields see NEAK SRI (1992).

People of the Summer Night see IHMISET SUVIYOSSA (1949).

People on a Glacier see LIDE NA KRE (1937).

People on an Iceberg see LIDE NA KRE (1937).

People on the Iceberg see LIDE NA KRE (1937).

People Still Ask see MEG KER A NEP (1971).

PEOPLE, THE 1971 d: John Korty. USA., *Pilgrimage*, Zenna Henderson, Novel

People, The see GANADEVATA (1978).

PET SEMATARY 1989 d: Mary Lambert. USA., *Pet Sematary*, Stephen King, Novel

PETE 'N' TILLIE 1972 d: Martin Ritt. USA., *The Cat's Pajamas*, Peter de Vries, 1968, Novel, *Witches Milk*, Peter de Vries, 1968, Novel

Peter and Sabine see **PETER UND SABINE** (1968).

PETER BENCHLEY'S CREATURE 1998 d: Stuart Gillard. USA., *Creature*, Peter Benchley, Novel

Peter Ibbetson see **FOREVER** (1921).

PETER IBBETSON 1935 d: Henry Hathaway. USA., *Peter Ibbetson*, George Du Maurier, New York 1891, Novel

PETER LUNDY AND THE MEDICINE HAT STALLION 1977 d: Michael O'Herlihy. USA., *San Domingo the Medicine Hat Stallion*, Marguerite Henry, Novel

Peter Monkey see **PEDRO MICO** (1985).

PETER PAN 1924 d: Herbert Brenon. USA., *Peter Pan*, J. M. Barrie, London 1904, Play

PETER PAN 1953 d: Hamilton Luske, Clyde Geronimi. USA., *Peter Pan*, J. M. Barrie, London 1904, Play

PETER PAN 1960 d: Vincent J. Donehue. USA., *Peter Pan*, J. M. Barrie, London 1904, Play

PETER PAN 1976 d: Dwight Hemion. UKN., *Peter Pan*, J. M. Barrie, London 1904, Play

PETER PAN 1988. ASL., *Peter Pan*, J. M. Barrie, London 1904, Play

Peter Rabbit and Tales of Beatrix Potter see **TALES OF BEATRIX POTTER** (1971).

Peter the First see **PYOTR PERVY** (1937-39).

Peter the Great see **PYOTR PERVY** (1937-39).

PETER THE GREAT 1985 d: Marvin J. Chomsky, Lawrence Schiller. USA., *Peter the Great*, Robert K. Massie, Book

PETER UND SABINE 1968 d: August Rieger. GRM., *Peter Und Sabine*, Marie Louise Fischer, Book

PETER VOSS, DER MILLIONENDIEB 1945 d: Karl Anton. GRM., *Peter Voss Der Millionendieb*, Ewald G. Seeliger, Book

PETER VOSS, DER MILLIONENDIEB 1958 d: Wolfgang Becker. GRM., *Peter Voss Der Millionendieb*, Ewald G. Seeliger, Book

Peterburgskaja Noc see **PETERBURGSKAYA NOCH** (1934).

PETERBURGSKAYA NOCH 1934 d: Grigori Roshal, Vera StroyevA. USS., *Belye Nochi*, Fyodor Dostoyevsky, St. Petersburg 1848, Short Story, *Netochka Nezvanova*, Fyodor Dostoyevsky, 1849, Short Story

PETERCHENS MONDFAHRT 1990 d: Wolfgang Urchs. GRM., *Peterchens Mondfahrt*, Gerd von Basewitz, Book

Peters Jugend see **JUNOST PETRA** (1980).

Petersburg Nights see **PETERBURGSKAYA NOCH** (1934).

PETERVILLE DIAMOND, THE 1942 d: Walter Forde. UKN., *Ekszerrablas a Vaci-Uccaban*, Ladislaus Fodor, 1931, Play

PETICION, LA 1976 d: Pilar Miro. SPN., *Pour une Nuit d'Amour*, Emile Zola, 1882, Short Story

PETIT CAFE, LE 1919 d: Max Linder, Raymond Bernard. FRN., *Le Petit Cafe*, Tristan Bernard, Paris 1912, Play

PETIT CAFE, LE 1931 d: Ludwig Berger. USA., *Le Petit Cafe*, Tristan Bernard, Paris 1912, Play

Petit Carambouilleur, Le see **TOUT POUR RIEN** (1933).

PETIT CHAPERON ROUGE, LE 1929 d: Alberto Cavalcanti. FRN., *Le Petit Chaperon Rouge*, Charles Perrault, Paris 1697, Short Story

PETIT CHOSE, LE 1912 d: Rene Leprince. FRN., *Le Petit Chose*, Alphonse Daudet, 1868, Novel

PETIT CHOSE, LE 1923 d: Andre Hugon. FRN., *Le Petit Chose*, Alphonse Daudet, 1868, Novel

PETIT CHOSE, LE 1938 d: Maurice Cloche. FRN., *Le Petit Chose*, Alphonse Daudet, 1868, Novel

Petit Fille Au Bout du Chemin, La see **THE LITTLE GIRL WHO LIVES DOWN THE LANE** (1977).

PETIT GARCON DE L'ENSCENSEUR, LE 1961 d: Pierre Granier-Deferre. FRN., *Le Petit Garcon de l'Ascenseur*, Paul Vialar, Play

PETIT JACQUES, LE 1912 d: Georges MoncA. FRN., *Le Petit Jacques*, Jules Claretie, 1881, Novel

PETIT JACQUES, LE 1923 d: Georges Lannes, Georges Raulet. FRN., *Le Petit Jacques*, Jules Claretie, 1881, Novel

PETIT JACQUES, LE 1934 d: Gaston Roudes. FRN., *Le Petit Jacques*, Jules Claretie, 1881, Novel

PETIT MATIN, LE 1971 d: Jean-Gabriel Albicocco. FRN., *Le Petit Matin*, Christine de Rivoyre, Novel

Petit Millionaire, Le see **TROIS POUR CENT** (1933).

PETIT MONDE DE DON CAMILLO, LE 1951 d: Julien Duvivier. FRN/ITL., *Le Petit Monde de Don Camillo*, Giovanni Guareschi, Novel

PETIT PARADIS, UN 1981 d: Michel Wyn. FRN., *Un Petit Paradis*, G. J. Arnaud, Novel

PETIT POUCET, LE 1908 d: Albert Capellani. FRN., *Le Petit Poucet*, Charles Perrault, 1697, Short Story

PETIT POUCET, LE 1912 d: Georges-Andre Lacroix. FRN., *Le Petit Poucet*, Charles Perrault, 1697, Short Story

PETIT POUCET, LE 1972 d: Michel Boisrond. FRN., *Le Petit Poucet*, Charles Perrault, 1697, Short Story

PETIT PROF', LE 1958 d: Carlo-Rim. FRN., *La Question du Latin*, Guy de Maupassant, 1900, Short Story

PETIT RADJAH, LE 1918 d: Paul Barlatier. FRN., *Le Petite Radjah*, Maurice de Marsan, Short Story

PETIT ROI, LE 1933 d: Julien Duvivier. FRN., *Le Petit Roi*, Anton Lichtenberger, Novel

PETIT SOLDAT, LE 1947 d: Paul Grimault. FRN., *Den Standhaftige Tinsoldat*, Hans Christian Andersen, 1838, Short Story

PETIT TROU PAS CHER, UN 1934 d: Pierre-Jean Ducis. FRN., *Un Petit Trou Pas Cher*, Henri Caen, Yves Mirande, Play

PETITE AMIE, LA 1916 d: Marcel Simon. FRN., *La Petite Amie*, Eugene Brieux, Play

PETITE APOCALYPSE, LA 1992 d: Costa-Gavras. FRN/ITL/PLN., *La Petite Apocalypse*, Tadeusz Konwicki, Novel

PETITE CHOCOLATIERE, LA 1913 d: Andre Liabel. FRN., *La Petite Chocolatiere*, Paul Gavault, Play

PETITE CHOCOLATIERE, LA 1927 d: Rene Hervil. FRN., *La Petite Chocolatiere*, Paul Gavault, Play

PETITE CHOCOLATIERE, LA 1931 d: Marc Allegret. FRN., *La Petite Chocolatiere*, Paul Gavault, Play

PETITE CHOCOLATIERE, LA 1949 d: Andre Berthomieu. FRN., *La Petite Chocolatiere*, Paul Gavault, Play

PETITE DE MONTPARNASSE, LA 1931 d: Max de Vaucorbeil, Hanns Schwarz. FRN., *Pile Ou Face*, Louis Verneuil, Play

PETITE FADETTE, LA 1921 d: Raphael Adams. FRN., *La Petite Fadette*, George Sand, Paris 1849, Novel

PETITE FEMME EN OR, UNE 1933 d: Andre Pellenc. FRN., *Une Petite Femme En Or*, Lebreton, Saint-Paul, Play

PETITE FIFI, LA 1913 d: Henri Pouctal. FRN., *La Petite Fifi*, Henri Demesse, Novel

Petite Fille aux Allumettes, La see **LA PETITE MARCHANDE D'ALLUMETTES** (1928).

PETITE FONCTIONNAIRE, LA 1912 d: Rene Leprince. FRN., *La Petite Fonctionnaire*, Alfred Capus, Play

PETITE FONCTIONNAIRE, LA 1926 d: Roger Goupillieres. FRN., *La Petite Fonctionnaire*, Alfred Capus, Play

PETITE MARCHANDE D'ALLUMETTES, LA 1928 d: Jean Renoir, Jean Tedesco. FRN., *Den Lille Pige Med Svovlstikkerne*, Hans Christian Andersen, 1846, Short Story

Petite Mere see **LA MATERNELLE** (1925).

PETITE MOBILISEE, LA 1917 d: Gaston Leprieur. FRN., *La Petite Mobilisee*, Marcel Priollet, Novel

PETITE PARADE, LA 1930 d: Ladislas Starevitch. FRN., *Den Standhaftige Tinsoldat*, Hans Christian Andersen, 1838, Short Story

PETITE PESTE 1938 d: Jean de Limur. FRN., *Petite Peste*, Romain Coolus, Play

PETITE SIRENE, LA 1980 d: Roger Andrieux. FRN., *La Petite Sirene*, Yves Dangerfield, Novel

PETITE VERTU, LA 1968 d: Serge Korber. FRN., *La Petite Vertu*, James Hadley Chase, Novel

PETITES ALLIEES, LES 1936 d: Jean Dreville. FRN., *Les Petites Alliees*, Claude Farrere, Novel

Petites Aphrodites see **MIKRES APHRODITES** (1962).

PETITES CARDINAL, LES 1950 d: Gilles Grangier. FRN., *Les Petites Cardinald*, Ludovic Halevy, Novel

PETITES FILLES MODELES, LES 1972 d: Jean-Claude Roy. FRN., *Les Petites Filles Modeles*, la Comtesse de Segur, Novel

PETITS, LES 1925 d: Gaston Roudes, Marcel Dumont. FRN., *Les Petits*, Lucien Nepoty, Play

PETLA 1957 d: Wojciech J. Has. PLN., *Petla*, Marek Hlasko, 1956, Short Story

Petr Pervyj see **PYOTR PERVY** (1937-39).

Petria's Wreath see **PETRIJIN VENAC** (1980).

PETRIFIED FOREST, THE 1936 d: Archie Mayo. USA., *The Petrified Forest*, R. E. Sherwood, New York 1935, Play

Petrified Forest, The see **KASEKI NO MORI** (1973).

Petrija's Wreath see **PETRIJIN VENAC** (1980).

PETRIJIN VENAC 1980 d: Srdjan Karanovic. YGS., *Petrijin Venac*, Dragoslav Mihailovic, 1975, Novel

Petrin Hillside, The see **TY PETRINSKE STRANE** (1922).

Petroff, the Vassal (a Russian Romance) see **IL PANE ALTRUI** (1913).

PETROLEJOVE LAMPY 1972 d: Juraj Herz. CZC., *Petrolejove Lampy*, Jaroslav Havlicek, Novel

PETRONELLA 1927 d: Hanns Schwarz. GRM/SWT., *Petronella*, Johannes Jegerlehner, 1912, Novel

PETRUS 1946 d: Marc Allegret. FRN/SWT., *Petrus*, Marcel Achard, 1934, Play

PETTICOAT FEVER 1936 d: George Fitzmaurice. USA., *Petticoat Fever*, Mark Reed, New York 1935, Play

PETTICOAT LOOSE 1922 d: George Ridgwell. UKN., *Petticoat Loose*, Rita, Novel

PETTICOAT PILOT, A 1918 d: Rollin S. Sturgeon. USA., *Mary-'Gusta*, Joseph C. Lincoln, New York 1916, Novel

Petticoats and Bluejeans see **THE PARENT TRAP** (1961).

PETTIGREW'S GIRL 1919 d: George Melford. USA., *Pettigrew's Girl*, Dana Burnet, 1918, Short Story

PETTY GIRL, THE 1950 d: Henry Levin. USA., Mary McCarthy, Story

PETULIA 1968 d: Richard Lester. UKN/USA., *Me and the Arch Kook Petulia*, John Haase, New York 1966, Novel

PEU D'AMOUR, UN 1933 d: Hans Steinhoff. FRN., *Scampolo*, Dario Niccodemi, 1915, Play

PEU DE SOLEIL DANS L'EAU FROIDE, UN 1971 d: Jacques Deray. FRN/ITL., *Un Peu de Soleil Dans l'Eau Froide*, Francoise Sagan, 1969, Novel

PEUR DES COUPS, LA 1932 d: Claude Autant-LarA. FRN., *La Peur Des Coups*, Georges Courteline, 1895, Play

Peur Et Amour see **PAURA E AMORE** (1987).

PEUR, LA 1936 d: Victor Tourjansky. FRN., *Die Angst*, Stefan Zweig, 1920, Short Story

PEYTON PLACE 1957 d: Mark Robson. USA., *Peyton Place*, Grace Metalious, 1956, Novel

P.F. Flyer see **HIGH-BALLIN'** (1978).

PFARRER VON KIRCHFELD, DER 1926 d: Jacob Fleck, Luise Fleck. GRM., *Der Pfarrer von Kirchfeld*, Ludwig Anzengruber, 1897, Play

PFARRER VON KIRCHFELD, DER 1937 d: Jacob Fleck, Luise Fleck. AUS., *Der Pfarrer von Kirchfeld*, Ludwig Anzengruber, 1897, Play

PFARRER VON KIRCHFELD, DER 1955 d: Hans Deppe. GRM., *Der Pfarrer von Kirchfeld*, Ludwig Anzengruber, 1897, Play

PFARRHAUSKOMODIE, DIE 1971 d: Veit Relin. GRM., *Die Pfarrhauskomodie*, Heinrich Lautensack, Play

Pfeifen see **DYMKY** (1966).

Pfeifen, Betten, Turteltauben see **DYMKY** (1966).

PFERDEMADCHEN, DER 1978 d: Egon Schlegel. GDR., Alfred Wellm, Short Story

PFINGSTORGEL, DIE 1938 d: Franz Seitz. GRM., *Die Pfingstorgel*, Alois Johannes Lippl, Play

PFLICHT ZU SCHWEIGEN, DIE 1927 d: Carl Wilhelm. GRM., *Die Pflicht Zu Schweigen*, F. W. von Oesteren, Novel

Phaedra see **FEDRA (DRAMMA MITOLOGICO DELL'ANTICA GRECIA)** (1909).

Phaedra see **FEDRA** (1956).

PHAEDRA 1962 d: Jules Dassin. USA/FRN/GRC., *Hippolytus*, Euripides, 428 bc, Play

Phantom Bride, The see **THE FACE BETWEEN** (1922).

PHANTOM BUCCANEER, THE 1916 d: J. Charles Haydon. USA., *Another Man's Shoes*, Victor Bridges, New York 1913, Novel

PHANTOM BULLET, THE 1926 d: Cliff Smith. USA., *Click of the Triangle T*, Oscar J. Friend, Chicago 1925, Novel

Phantom Carriage, The see **KORKARLEN** (1958).

Phantom Chariot, The see **KORKARLEN** (1958).

Phantom Crown, The see **JUAREZ** (1939).

Phantom Fame see **THE HALF NAKED TRUTH** (1932).

Phantom Fiend, The see **THE LODGER** (1932).

PHANTOM FORTUNE, THE 1915 d: Henry Otto. USA., *The Phantom Fortune*, L. V. Jefferson, Story

Phantom Horse, The see **KORKARLEN** (1921).

PHANTOM IN THE HOUSE, THE 1929 d: Phil Rosen. USA., *The Phantom in the House*, Andrew Soutar, London 1928, Novel

Phantom Killer see **HAKUCHU NO TORIMA** (1966).

PHANTOM LADY 1944 d: Robert Siodmak. USA., *Phantom Lady*, Cornell Woolrich, 1942, Novel

Phantom Lady, The see **LA DAMA DUENDE** (1945).

PHANTOM LIGHT, THE 1935 d: Michael Powell. UKN., *The Haunted Light*, Joan Byford, Evadne Price, 1928, Play

Phantom Love see **AI NO BOREI** (1977).

PHANTOM OF 42ND STREET, THE 1945 d: Al Herman. USA., *The Phantom of 42nd Street*, Jack Harvey, Milton Raison, Novel

Phantom of Love, The see **AI NO BOREI** (1977).

Phantom of Paris see **THE MYSTERY OF MARIE ROGET** (1942).

PHANTOM OF PARIS, THE 1931 d: John S. Robertson. USA., *Cheri-Bibi Et Cecily*, Gaston Leroux, Paris 1916, Novel

Phantom of Soho, The see **DAS PHANTOM VON SOHO** (1964).

Phantom of Terror see **L' UCCELLO DALLE PIUME DE CRISTALLO** (1970).

PHANTOM OF THE FOREST, THE 1926 d: Henry McCarty. USA., *The Phantom of the Forest*, Frank Foster Davis, Story

PHANTOM OF THE OPERA, THE 1925 d: Rupert Julian, Edward Sedgwick. USA., *Le Fantome de l'Opera*, Gaston Leroux, Paris 1910, Novel

PHANTOM OF THE OPERA, THE 1929 d: Rupert Julian, Ernst Laemmle. USA., *Le Fantome de l'Opera*, Gaston Leroux, Paris 1910, Novel

PHANTOM OF THE OPERA, THE 1943 d: Arthur Lubin. USA., *Le Fantome de l'Opera*, Gaston Leroux, Paris 1910, Novel

PHANTOM OF THE OPERA, THE 1962 d: Terence Fisher. UKN., *Le Fantome de l'Opera*, Gaston Leroux, Paris 1910, Novel

PHANTOM OF THE OPERA, THE 1982 d: Robert Markowitz. USA., *Le Fantome de l'Opera*, Gaston Leroux, Paris 1910, Novel

PHANTOM OF THE OPERA, THE 1987. USA., *Le Fantome de l'Opera*, Gaston Leroux, Paris 1910, Novel

PHANTOM OF THE OPERA, THE 1989 d: Dwight H. Little. USA., *Le Fantome de l'Opera*, Gaston Leroux, Paris 1910, Novel

PHANTOM OF THE OPERA, THE 1990 d: Tony Richardson. UKN/USA., *Le Fantome de l'Opera*, Gaston Leroux, Paris 1910, Novel

Phantom of the Opera, The see **IL FANTASMA DELL'OPERA** (1997).

PHANTOM OF THE RUE MORGUE 1954 d: Roy Del Ruth. USA., *Murders in the Rue Morgue*, Edgar Allan Poe, 1841, Short Story

Phantom on Horseback, The see **KISERTET LUBLON** (1976).

PHANTOM PATROL 1936 d: Charles Hutchison. USA., *The Fatal Noise*, James Oliver Curwood, Short Story

PHANTOM PICTURE, THE 1916 d: Albert Ward. UKN., *The Phantom Picture*, Harold Simpson, Play

PHANTOM PRESIDENT, THE 1932 d: Norman Taurog. USA., *The Phantom President*, George Frank Worts, New York 1932, Novel

Phantom Strikes, The see **THE GAUNT STRANGER** (1938).

PHANTOM SUBMARINE 1940 d: Charles T. Barton. USA., *Ocean Gold*, Augustus Muir, 1938, Short Story

PHANTOM TOLLBOOTH, THE 1969 d: David Monahan, Charles M. Jones. USA., *The Phantom Tollbooth*, Norman Juster, New York 1961, Novel

PHANTOM VON SOHO, DAS 1964 d: Franz J. Gottlieb. GRM., *Murder By Proxy*, Bryan Edgar Wallace, Novel

Phantom Wagon, The see **LA CHARRETTE FANTOME** (1939).

PHANTOMS 1998 d: Joe Chappelle. USA., *Phantoms*, Dean R. Koontz, Novel

PHAR LAP 1983 d: Simon Wincer. ASL., *The Phar Lap Story*, Michael Wilkinson, Book

Phar Lap: Heart of a Nation see **PHAR LAP** (1983).

Pharaoh, The see **FARAON** (1965).

Phare du Bout du Monde, Le see **LA LUZ DEL FIN DEL MUNDO** (1971).

Pharisees, The see **THE HYPOCRITES** (1923).

Pharmacist, The see **DIE APOTHEKERIN** (1998).

Pharmicien, Le see **UNE CLIENTE PAS SERIEUSE** (1934).

PHEDRE 1968 d: Pierre Jourdan. FRN., *Phedre*, Jean Racine, 1677, Play

PHFFFT! 1954 d: Mark Robson. USA., *Phffft*, George Axelrod, Unproduced, Play

PHIL BLOOD'S LEAP 1913 d: Wilfred Noy. UKN., *Phil Blood's Leap*, Robert Buchanan, Poem

PHILADELPHIA STORY, THE 1940 d: George Cukor. USA., *Philadelphia Story*, Philip Barry, New York 1939, Play

PHILINE 1945 d: Theo Lingen. GRM., *Philine*, Jo Hanns Rosler, Play

Philip see **RUN FREE RUN WILD** (1969).

PHILISTINE IN BOHEMIA, A 1920 d: Edward H. Griffith. USA., *A Philistine in Bohemia*, O. Henry, Short Story

Philly see **PRIVATE LESSONS** (1981).

Philo Vance Comes Back see **CALLING PHILO VANCE** (1940).

Philo Vance Returns see **CALLING PHILO VANCE** (1940).

Philosophical History see **FILOSOFSKA HISTORIE** (1937).

Philosophical Story, A see **FILOSOFSKA HISTORIE** (1937).

Philosophy in the Boudoir see **EUGENIE. THE STORY OF HER JOURNEY INTO PERVERSION** (1970).

PHI-PHI 1926 d: Georges Pallu. FRN., *Phi-Phi*, Henri Christine, Opera

PHIR SUBAH HOGI 1958 d: Ramesh Saigal. IND., *Prestupleniye I Nakazaniye*, Fyodor Dostoyevsky, 1867, Novel

Phir Subha Hogi see **PHIR SUBAH HOGI** (1958).

PHONE CALL FROM A STRANGER, A 1952 d: Jean Negulesco. USA., *Phone Call from a Stranger*, I. A. R. Wylie, Novel

Phony Adam, The see **DER FALSCHE ADAM** (1955).

Phony American, The see **TOLLER HECHT AUF KRUMMEN TOUREN** (1961).

PHOTOGRAPHING FAIRIES 1997 d: Nick Willing. UKN., *Photographing Fairies*, Steve Szilagyi, Book

PHROSO 1921 d: Louis Mercanton. FRN., *Phroso*, Anthony Hope, Novel

PHYLLIS OF THE SIERRAS, A 1915 d: George E. Middleton. USA., *A Phyllis of the Sierras*, Bret Harte, Boston 1888, Novel

Physical Jerks see **IN BARC A VELA CONTROMANO** (1997).

PHYSICIAN, THE 1928 d: Georg Jacoby. UKN., *The Physician*, Henry Arthur Jones, London 1897, Play

PI BAO 1956 d: Wang Lan. CHN., *Father Liu Shihai's Wallet*, Bai XIaowen, Novel

Piacere E l'Amore, Il see **LA RONDE** (1964).

PIACERE, IL 1918 d: Amleto Palermi. ITL., *Il Piacere*, Gabriele D'Annunzio, 1889, Novel

Piaceri Coniugali, I see **LA DIFFICULTE D'ETRE INFIDELE** (1963).

Piaceri Della Contessa Gamiani, I see **POURVU QU'ON AIT L'IVRESSE** (1974).

PIAF 1973 d: Guy Casaril. FRN/USA., Simone Bertaut, Book

Piaf - the Early Years see **PIAF** (1973).

Piano Tuner Has Arrived, The see **E ARRIVATO L'ACCORDATORE** (1952).

PIANOS MECANICOS, LOS 1965 d: Juan Antonio Bardem. SPN/ITL/FRN., *Les Pianos Mecaniques*, Henri-Francois Rey, Paris 1962, Novel

Pianos Mecaniques, Les see **LOS PIANOS MECANICOS** (1965).

PIATTO PIANGE, IL 1974 d: Paolo Nuzzi. ITL., *Il Piatto Piange*, Piero Chiara, Novel

PICADOR, LE 1932 d: Jaquelux. FRN., *Le Picador*, Tony Blas, Henri d'Astier, Novel

PICAPAU AMARELO, O 1974 d: Geraldo Sarno. BRZ., *O Sitio Do Picapau Amarelo*, Monteiro Lobato, 1939, Short Story

PICARA MOLINERA, LA 1955 d: Leon Klimovsky. SPN/FRN., *El Sombrero de Tres Picos*, Pedro Antonio de Alarcon, 1874, Short Story

PICCADILLY JIM 1920 d: Wesley Ruggles. USA., *Piccadilly Jim*, P. G. Wodehouse, London 1917, Novel

PICCADILLY JIM 1936 d: Robert Z. Leonard. USA., *Piccadilly Jim*, P. G. Wodehouse, London 1917, Novel

PICCOLA FONTE, LA 1917 d: Roberto Leone Roberti. ITL., *La Piccola Fonte*, Roberto Bracco, 1905, Play

PICCOLA MOGLIE, UNA 1944 d: Giorgio Bianchi. ITL., *Una Piccola Moglie*, Zoltan Nagyivanyi Szitnyai, Novel

PICCOLA PARROCCHIA, LA 1923 d: Mario Almirante. ITL., *La Petite Paroisse*, Alphonse Daudet, 1901, Novel

PICCOLA VEDETTA LOMBARDA, LA 1915 d: Vittorio Rossi Pianelli. ITL., *Cuore*, Edmondo de Amicis, 1886, Short Story

PICCOLO ALPINO 1940 d: Oreste Biancoli. ITL., *Piccolo Alpino*, Salvator Gotta, Novel

PICCOLO ARCHIMEDE, IL 1979 d: Gianni Amelio. ITL., Aldous Huxley, Short Story

PICCOLO MARTIRI 1917 d: Enrico Vidali. ITL., *Piccoli Martiri*, Carolina Invernizio, Novel

Piccolo Matthias II see **LE BATARD** (1941).

PICCOLO MONDO ANTICO 1940 d: Mario Soldati. ITL., *Piccolo Mondo Antico*, Antonio Fogazzaro, 1896, Novel

Piccolo Mondo Di Don Camillo, Il see **LE PETIT MONDE DE DON CAMILLO** (1951).

PICCOLO PATRIOTA PADOVANO, IL 1915 d: Leopoldo Carlucci. ITL., *Cuore*, Edmondo de Amicis, 1886, Short Story

PICCOLO RE, IL 1940 d: Redo Romagnoli. ITL., *Il Piccole Re*, Giuseppe Romualdi, Play

PICCOLO SCRIVANO FIORENTINO, IL 1915 d: Leopoldo Carlucci. ITL., *Cuore*, Edmondo de Amicis, 1886, Short Story

PICCOLO VETRAIO, IL 1955 d: Giorgio Capitani. ITL/FRN., *Il Racconto Del Piccolo Vetraio*, Olimpia de Gasperi, Novel

Pichler's Books are Not in Order see **BEI PICHLER STIMMT DIE KASSE NICHT** (1961).

Pick Up see **PICK-UP** (1933).

PICKET GUARD, THE 1913 d: Allan Dwan. USA., *The Picket Guard*, Ethelin Elliot Beers, Poem

PICKPOCKET 1959 d: Robert Bresson. FRN., *Prestupleniye I Nakazaniye*, Fyodor Dostoyevsky, 1867, Novel

PICKUP 1951 d: Hugo Haas, Edgar E. Walden. USA., *Watchman 47*, Joseph Kopta, Novel

PICK-UP 1933 d: Marion Gering. USA., *Pick-Up*, Vina Delmar, 1928, Short Story

Pickup Alley see **INTERPOL** (1957).

PICKUP ON SOUTH STREET 1953 d: Samuel Fuller. USA., Dwight Taylor, Story

PICKWICK PAPERS PARTS 1 & 2, THE 1912 d: Larry Trimble. UKN/USA., *The Pickwick Papers*, Charles Dickens, London 1836, Novel

PICKWICK PAPERS, THE 1952 d: Noel Langley. UKN., *The Pickwick Papers*, Charles Dickens, London 1836, Novel

PICKWICK PAPERS, THE 1985 d: Brian Lighthill. UKN., *The Pickwick Papers*, Charles Dickens, London 1836, Novel

PICKWICK PAPERS, THE 1985 d: Warwick Gilbert. ASL., *The Pickwick Papers*, Charles Dickens, London 1836, Novel

PICKWICK VERSUS BARDELL 1913 d: Wilfred Noy. UKN., *The Pickwick Papers*, Charles Dickens, London 1836, Novel

PICNIC 1955 d: Joshua Logan. USA., *Picnic*, William Inge, New York 1953, Play

PICNIC AT HANGING ROCK 1975 d: Peter Weir. ASL., *Picnic at Hanging Rock*, Joan Lindsay, 1967, Novel

PICPUS 1942 d: Richard Pottier. FRN., *Signe Picpus*, Georges Simenon, 1944, Short Story

PICTURE BRIDES 1934 d: Phil Rosen. USA., *Red Kisses*, Charles E. Blaney, Harry Clay Blaney, Play

PICTURE OF DORIAN GRAY, THE 1915 d: Mr. Moore. USA., *The Picture of Dorian Gray*, Oscar Wilde, London 1891, Novel

PICTURE OF DORIAN GRAY, THE 1916 d: Fred W. Durrant. UKN., *The Picture of Dorian Gray*, Oscar Wilde, London 1891, Novel

Picture of Dorian Gray, The *see* **DAS BILDNIS DES DORIAN GRAY** (1917).

PICTURE OF DORIAN GRAY, THE 1944 d: Albert Lewin. USA., *The Picture of Dorian Gray*, Oscar Wilde, London 1891, Novel

PICTURE OF DORIAN GRAY, THE 1973 d: Glenn Jordan. USA., *The Picture of Dorian Gray*, Oscar Wilde, London 1891, Novel

PICTURE OF DORIAN GRAY, THE 1976 d: John Gorrie. UKN., *The Picture of Dorian Gray*, Oscar Wilde, London 1891, Novel

Picture of Madame Yuki, The *see* **YUKI FUJIN EZU** (1950).

PICTURE SHOW MAN, THE 1977 d: John Power. ASL., *The Picture Show Man*, Lyle Penn, Novel

PIDGIN ISLAND 1916 d: Fred J. Balshofer. USA., *Pidgin Island*, Harold MacGrath, Indianapolis 1914, Novel

PIECE OF STRING, THE 1911 d: Joseph Smiley, George Loane Tucker. USA., *The Piece of String*, Guy de Maupassant, Novel

PIECES OF DREAMS 1970 d: Daniel Haller. USA., *The Wine and the Music*, William E. Barrett, New York 1968, Novel

Pied Piper *see* **CROSSING TO FREEDOM** (1990).

PIED PIPER OF HAMELIN, THE 1911 d: Theodore Marston. USA., *The Pied Piper of Hamelin*, Robert Browning, 1842, Poem

PIED PIPER OF HAMELIN, THE 1911. FRN., *The Pied Piper of Hamelin*, Robert Browning, 1842, Poem

PIED PIPER OF HAMELIN, THE 1913 d: George A. Lessey. USA., *The Pied Piper of Hamelin*, Robert Browning, 1842, Poem

PIED PIPER OF HAMELIN, THE 1916. USA., *The Pied Piper of Hamelin*, Robert Browning, 1842, Poem

PIED PIPER OF HAMELIN, THE 1926 d: Frank Tilley. UKN., *The Pied Piper of Hamelin*, Robert Browning, 1842, Poem

PIED PIPER OF HAMELIN, THE 1957 d: Bretaigne Windust. USA., *The Pied Piper of Hamelin*, Robert Browning, 1842, Poem

PIED PIPER OF HAMELIN, THE 1960 d: Lotte Reiniger. UKN., *The Pied Piper of Hamelin*, Robert Browning, 1842, Poem

Pied Piper of Hamelin, The *see* **THE PIED PIPER** (1972).

PIED PIPER OF HAMELIN, THE 1982 d: Brian Cosgrove, Mark Hall. UKN., *The Pied Piper of Hamelin*, Robert Browning, 1842, Poem

PIED PIPER OF HAMELIN, THE 1985 d: Nicholas Meyer. USA., *The Pied Piper of Hamelin*, Robert Browning, 1842, Poem

PIED PIPER, THE 1907 d: Percy Stow. UKN., *The Pied Piper of Hamelin*, Robert Browning, 1842, Poem

PIED PIPER, THE 1942 d: Irving Pichel. USA., *The Pied Piper*, Nevil Shute, 1942, Novel

Pied Piper, The *see* **THE CLOWN AND THE KIDS** (1968).

PIED PIPER, THE 1972 d: Jacques Demy. UKN/GRM., *The Pied Piper of Hamelin*, Robert Browning, 1842, Poem

Pied Piper, The *see* **THE PIED PIPER OF HAMELIN** (1985).

PIEL DE VERANO 1961 d: Leopoldo Torre-Nilsson. ARG., *Convalecencia*, Beatriz Guido, Story

PIER 23 1951 d: William Berke. USA., Herbert Margolis, Louis Morhei, Radio Play

PIERO E TERESA 1920 d: Mario Caserini. ITL., *Pierre Et Therese*, Marcel Prevost, 1909, Novel

Pierre and Marie *see* **LES PALMES DE M. SCHUTZ** (1997).

PIERRE DE LUNE, LA 1911. FRN., *The Moonstone*, Wilkie Collins, London 1868, Novel

PIERRE ET JEAN 1924 d: E. B. Donatien. FRN., *Pierre Et Jean*, Guy de Maupassant, 1888, Novel

PIERRE ET JEAN 1943 d: Andre Cayatte. FRN., *Pierre Et Jean*, Guy de Maupassant, 1888, Novel

PIERRE OF THE PLAINS 1914 d: Lawrence McGill. USA., *Pierre and His People*, Gilbert Parker, London 1892, Novel, *Pierre of the Plains*, Edgar Selwyn, New York 1908, Play

PIERRE OF THE PLAINS 1942 d: George B. Seitz. USA., *Pierre of the Plains*, Edgar Selwyn, New York 1908, Play

PIERROT LE FOU 1965 d: Jean-Luc Godard. FRN/ITL., *Obsession*, Lionel White, New York 1962, Novel

Pierrot the Prodigal *see* **HISTOIRE D'UN PIERROT** (1914).

PIERSCIEN I ROZA 1987 d: Jerzy GruzA. PLN., *The Rose and the Ring*, William Makepeace Thackeray, 1855, Short Story

PIERWSZY DZIEN WOLNOSCI 1964 d: Aleksander Ford. PLN., *Pierwszy Dzien Wolnosci*, Leon Kruczkowski, Play

PIETA PER CHI CADE 1954 d: Mario CostA. ITL., *La Barriera*, Anton Giulio Majano, Domenico Meccoli, Novel

Pietro Angelina *see* **DAS GEHEIMNIS VOM BERGSEE** (1951).

PIETRO MICCA 1938 d: Aldo Vergano, Pietro Scharoff. ITL., *I Dragoni Azzurri*, L. Gramegna, Novel

Pieuvre, La *see* **LES SUSPECTS** (1974).

Pig Across Paris *see* **LA TRAVERSEE DE PARIS** (1956).

Pigboats *see* **HELL BELOW** (1932).

PIGEON THAT TOOK ROME, THE 1962 d: Melville Shavelson. USA., *The Easter Dinner*, Donald C. Downes, New York 1960, Novel

PIGEON, THE 1969 d: Earl Bellamy. USA., Stanley Andrews, Story

Pigeons *see* **SIDELONG GLANCES OF A PIGEON FANCIER** (1971).

PIGMALION 1957 d: Sergei Alexeyev. USS., *Pygmalion*, George Bernard Shaw, London 1913, Play

Pigs *see* **THE MIDNIGHT KISS** (1926).

PIGS IS PIGS 1914 d: George D. Baker. USA., *Pigs Is Pigs*, Ellis Parker Butler, Book

Pigskin Parade of 1937 *see* **LIFE BEGINS IN COLLEGE** (1937).

Pigskin Parade of 1938 *see* **LIFE BEGINS IN COLLEGE** (1937).

PIKANTERIE 1951 d: Alfred Braun. GRM., *Eine Jener Seltenen Frauen*, Franz Gribitz, Play

PIKOVAYA DAMA 1960 d: Roman Tikhomirov. USS., *Pikovaya Dama*, Alexander Pushkin, 1834, Short Story

Pila Della Peppa, La *see* **LE MAGOT DE JOSEFA** (1963).

PILAR GUERRA 1926 d: Jose Buchs. SPN., *Pilar Guerra*, Guillermo Diaz Caneja, Novel

Pile Ou Face *see* **LA PETITE DE MONTPARNASSE** (1931).

PILE OU FACE 1980 d: Robert Enrico. FRN., *Suivez le Veuf*, Alfred Harris, Novel

Pilebuck *see* **THE SECRET COMMAND** (1944).

Pilgrim, The *see* **IL PELLEGRINO** (1912).

PILGRIMAGE 1933 d: John Ford. USA., *Pilgrimage*, I. A. R. Wylie, 1932, Short Story

Pilgrimage at Night *see* **ANYA KORO** (1959).

PILGRIMAGE, THE 1912. USA., *The Pilgrimage*, Heinrich Heine, Poem

PILGRIMS OF THE NIGHT 1921 d: Edward Sloman. USA., *Passers-By*, E. Phillips Oppenheim, Boston 1910, Novel

Pilgrim's Progress, The *see* **IL PELLEGRINO** (1912).

Pill of Death *see* **LA PEAU DE TORPEDO** (1970).

Pillar of Salt *see* **NATZIV HAMELACH** (1979).

PILLARS OF SOCIETY, THE 1911. USA., *Samfundets Stotter*, Henrik Ibsen, Odense 1877, Play

PILLARS OF SOCIETY 1916 d: Raoul Walsh. USA., *Samfundets Stotter*, Henrik Ibsen, Odense 1877, Play

PILLARS OF SOCIETY 1920 d: Rex Wilson. UKN., *Samfundets Stotter*, Henrik Ibsen, Odense 1877, Play

Pillars of Society *see* **STUTZEN DER GESELLSCHAFT** (1935).

PILLARS OF THE SKY 1956 d: George Marshall. USA., *Frontier Fury*, Will Henry, Novel

Pillole d'Ercole, Le *see* **LE PILLOLE DI ERCOLE** (1960).

PILLOLE DI ERCOLE, LE 1960 d: Luciano Salce. ITL., *Le Pillole Di Ercole*, Paul Bilhaud, Maurice Hennequin, Play

PILLOW TO POST 1945 d: Vincent Sherman. USA., *Pillar to Post*, Rose Simon Kohn, New York 1943, Play

PILOT, THE 1979 d: Cliff Robertson. USA., *The Pilot*, Robert P. Davis, Novel

Pimp, The *see* **PASAK HOLEK** (1929).

PINES OF LORY, THE 1914 d: Ashley Miller. USA., *The Pines of Lory*, J. A. Mitchell, Novel

PINE'S REVENGE, THE 1915 d: Joseph de Grasse. USA., *The King's Keeper*, Nell Shipman, Story

PINK GODS 1922 d: Penrhyn Stanlaws. USA., *Pink Gods and Blue Demons*, Cynthia Stockley, Story

PINK JUNGLE, THE 1968 d: Delbert Mann. USA., *Snake Water*, Alan Williams, London 1965, Novel

PINK STRING AND SEALING WAX 1945 d: Robert Hamer. UKN., *Pink String and Sealing Wax*, Roland Pertwee, London 1943, Play

PINKY 1949 d: Elia Kazan, John Ford (Uncredited). USA., *Quality*, Cid Ricketts, Novel

Pinnacle *see* **BLIND HUSBANDS** (1918).

PINOCCHIO 1911 d: Giulio Antamoro. ITL., *Le Avventure Di Pinocchio*, Carlo Collodi, 1883, Short Story

PINOCCHIO 1940 d: Hamilton Luske, Ben Sharpsteen. USA., *Le Avventure Di Pinocchio*, Carlo Collodi, 1883, Short Story

Pinocchio *see* **TURLIS ABENTEUER** (1967).

PINOCCHIO 1968 d: Sidney Smith. USA., *Le Avventure Di Pinocchio*, Carlo Collodi, 1883, Short Story

Pinocchio *see* **LE AVVENTURE DI PINOCCHIO** (1968).

Pinocchio *see* **LE AVVENTURE DI PINOCCHIO** (1972).

PINOCCHIO 1976 d: Ron Field, Sidney Smith. USA., *Le Avventure Di Pinocchio*, Carlo Collodi, 1883, Short Story

PINOCCHIO 1983 d: Peter Medak. USA., *Le Avventure Di Pinocchio*, Carlo Collodi, 1883, Short Story

PINOCCHIO 1985 d: Barry Letts. UKN., *Le Avventure Di Pinocchio*, Carlo Collodi, 1883, Short Story

PINOCCHIO 1991 d: Hiroshi Saito. JPN., *Le Avventure Di Pinocchio*, Carlo Collodi, 1883, Short Story

PINOCCHIO E LE SUE AVVENTURE 1958 d: Attilio Giovannini. ITL., *Le Avventure Di Pinocchio*, Carlo Collodi, 1883, Short Story

PINTO BEN 1915 d: William S. Hart. USA., *Pinto Ben*, William S. Hart, Poem

Pioneer, Go Home! *see* **FOLLOW THAT DREAM** (1962).

Pioneers in Ingolstadt *see* **PIONIERE IN INGOLSTADT** (1971).

PIONEERS, THE 1941 d: Al Herman. USA., *The Pioneers*, James Fenimore Cooper, 1823, Novel

PIONIERE IN INGOLSTADT 1971 d: R. W. Fassbinder. GRM., *Pionere in Ingolstadt*, Marieluise Fleisser, 1970, Play

Piotr Pervyi *see* **PYOTR PERVY** (1937-39).

Pious Helen *see* **DIE FROMME HELENE** (1965).

PIPER'S PRICE, THE 1917 d: Joseph de Grasse. USA., *The Piper's Price*, Mrs. Wilson Woodrow, Short Story

Pipes *see* **DYMKY** (1966).

PIPPA PASSES OR THE SONG OF CONSCIENCE 1909 d: D. W. Griffith. USA., *Pippa Passes*, Robert Browning, London 1841, Poem

PIPPI LANGSTRUMP 1949 d: Per Gunwall. SWD., *Pippi Langstrump*, Astrid Lindgren, 1945, Novel

PIPPI LANGSTRUMP 1969 d: Olle Hellbom. SWD/GRM., *Pippi Langstrump*, Astrid Lindgren, 1945, Novel

Pippi Langstrumpf *see* **PIPPI LANGSTRUMP** (1969).

Pippi Long Stocking *see* **PIPPI LANGSTRUMP** (1949).

Pippi Longstocking *see* **PIPPI LANGSTRUMP** (1969).

PIPPI LONGSTOCKING 1997 d: Clive A. Smith. CND/GRM/SWD., *Pippi Langstrump*, Astrid Lindgren, 1945, Novel

PIQUE DAME 1918 d: Arthur Wellin. GRM., *Pikovaya Dama*, Alexander Pushkin, 1834, Short Story

PIQUE DAME 1927 d: Alexander Rasumny. GRM., *Pikovaya Dama*, Alexander Pushkin, 1834, Short Story

PIQUE DAME 1937 d: Fedor Ozep. FRN., *Pikovaya Dama*, Alexander Pushkin, 1834, Short Story

PIRATE MOVIE, THE 1982 d: Ken Annakin. ASL/USA., *The Pirates of Penzance*, W. S. Gilbert, Arthur Sullivan, London 1880, Opera

PIRATE, THE 1948 d: Vincente Minnelli. USA., *The Pirate*, S. N. Behrman, New York 1942, Play

PIRATE, THE 1978 d: Ken Annakin. USA., *The Pirate*, Harold Robbins, Novel

Pirates de la Malasia, Los *see* I PIRATI DELLA MALESIA (1941).

Pirates de Malaisia, Les *see* I PIRATI DELLA MALESIA (1941).

Pirates de Malaisie, Les *see* I PIRATI DELLA MALESIA (1964).

Pirates de Malasia, Los *see* I PIRATI DELLA MALESIA (1964).

Pirates du Mississippi, The *see* DIE FLUSSPIRATEN VOM MISSISSIPPI (1963).

PIRATES DU RAIL, LES 1937 d: Christian-Jaque. FRN., *Les Pirates du Rail*, Oscar-Paul Gilbert, Novel

Pirate's Heart, The *see* DAS HERZ DES PIRATEN (1987).

PIRATES OF PENZANCE, THE 1983 d: Wilford Leach. UKN., *The Pirates of Penzance*, W. S. Gilbert, Arthur Sullivan, London 1880, Opera

Pirates of Spring Cove, The *see* THE TRUTH ABOUT SPRING (1964).

Pirates of the Mississippi, The *see* DIE FLUSSPIRATEN VOM MISSISSIPPI (1963).

Pirates of the Seven Seas *see* QUEER CARGO (1938).

Pirates on Lake Malar *see* MALARPIRATER (1923).

Pirates on Lake Malar *see* MALARPIRATER (1959).

PIRATI DEL GOLFO, I 1940 d: Romolo Marcellini. ITL., *Guardafui*, Marcello Orano, Novel

PIRATI DELLA MALESIA, I 1941 d: Enrico Guazzoni. ITL/SPN/FRN., *I Pirati Della Malesia*, Emilio Salgari, Novel

PIRATI DELLA MALESIA, I 1964 d: Umberto Lenzi. ITL/SPN/FRN., *I Pirati Della Malesia*, Emilio Salgari, Novel

Piratti Din Pacific *see* DEUX ANS DE VACANCES (1973).

Pirx Test-Flight *see* TEST PILOTA PIRXA (1978).

PISITO, EL 1957 d: Marco Ferreri, Isidoro Martinez Ferry. SPN., *El Pisito*, Rafael Azcona, Novel

PISTE DU NORD, LA 1939 d: Jacques Feyder. FRN., *Telle Qu'elle Etait En Son Vivant*, Maurice Constantin-Weyer, Novel

Pistol Shot, A *see* VYSTREL (1967).

PISTOLA DE MI HERMANO, LA 1997 d: Ray LorigA. SPN., *La Pistola de Mi Hermano*, Ray Loriga, Novel

Pistolero *see* THE LAST CHALLENGE (1967).

Pistolero Cherche Son Nom, Le *see* THE MAN CALLED NOON (1973).

Pistolero of Red River *see* THE LAST CHALLENGE (1967).

Pit and the Pendulum, The *see* LE PUITS ET LE PENDULE (1912).

PIT AND THE PENDULUM, THE 1913 d: Alice Blache. USA., *The Pit and the Pendulum*, Edgar Allan Poe, 1845, Short Story

PIT AND THE PENDULUM, THE 1961 d: Roger Corman. USA., *The Pit and the Pendulum*, Edgar Allan Poe, 1845, Short Story

Pit and the Pendulum, The *see* DIE SCHLANGENGRUBE UND DAS PENDEL (1967).

PIT AND THE PENDULUM, THE 1990 d: Stuart Gordon. USA., *The Pit and the Pendulum*, Edgar Allan Poe, 1845, Short Story

PIT OF DARKNESS 1961 d: Lance Comfort. UKN., *To Dusty Death*, Hugh McCutcheon, Novel

PIT, THE 1915 d: Maurice Tourneur. USA., *The Pit*, Frank Norris, New York 1903, Novel

PIT, THE 1962 d: Edward Abrahams. UKN., *The Pit and the Pendulum*, Edgar Allan Poe, 1845, Short Story

PITFALL 1948 d: Andre de Toth. USA., *The Pitfall*, Jay Dratler, Novel

Pitfall, The *see* KASHI TO KODOMO (1962).

PITIE DANGEREUSE, LA 1979 d: Edouard Molinaro. FRN., *La Pitie Dangereuse*, Stefan Zweig, Novel

Pitie Pour le Prof! *see* WHY SHOOT THE TEACHER? (1976).

Pitiless Gendarme *see* LE GENDARME EST SANS PITIE, LE COMMISSAIRE EST BON ENFANT (1934).

Pitiless Life *see* VIATA NU IARTA (1957).

PITTSBURGH KID, THE 1942 d: Jack Townley. USA., *Kid Tinsel*, Octavus Roy Cohen, Novel

Pittsville *see* PITTSVILLE - EINE SAFE VOLL BLUT (1974).

PITTSVILLE - EINE SAFE VOLL BLUT 1974 d: Krzysztof Zanussi. GRM/USA., James Hadley Chase, Novel

Pity the Chorus Girl *see* TROUPING WITH ELLEN (1924).

PIU BELLA DONNA DEL MONDO, LA 1920 d: Luigi Mele. ITL., *La Piu Bella Donna Del Mondo*, Salvator Gotta, 1919, Novel

PIU BELLA SERATA DELLA MIA VITA, LA 1972 d: Ettore ScolA. ITL/FRN., *Die Panne*, Friedrich Durrenmatt, 1956, Short Story

Piu Grande Colpo Del Secolo, Il *see* LE SOLEIL DES VOYOUS (1967).

Piu Piccola Guerra Del Mondo, La *see* PUTIFERIO VA ALLA GUERRA (1968).

Pixote *see* A LEI DO MAIS FRACO PIXOTE (1981).

PIXOTE, A LEI DO MAIS FRACO 1981 d: Hector Babenco. BRZ., *Infancia Dos Mortos*, Jose Louzeiro, 1977, Novel

Pixote: la Ley Del Mas Debil *see* A LEI DO MAIS FRACO PIXOTE (1981).

Pixote, the Law of the Weaker *see* A LEI DO MAIS FRACO PIXOTE (1981).

Pjat Vecerov *see* PYAT VECHEROV (1979).

Pjat Vetsjerov *see* PYAT VECHEROV (1979).

PLACE AT THE COAST, THE 1987 d: George Ogilvie. ASL., *The Place at the Coast*, Jane Hyde, Novel

PLACE BEYOND THE WINDS, THE 1916 d: Joseph de Grasse. USA., *The Place Beyond the Winds*, Harriet T. Comstock, Garden City, N.Y. 1914, Novel

Place Called Glory, A *see* DIE HOLLE VON MANITOBA (1965).

Place Called Glory City *see* DIE HOLLE VON MANITOBA (1965).

Place for Lovers, A *see* AMANTI (1968).

PLACE IN THE SUN, A 1916 d: Larry Trimble. UKN., *A Place in the Sun*, Cyril Harcourt, Play

PLACE IN THE SUN, A 1951 d: George Stevens. USA., *An American Tragedy*, Theodore Dreiser, New York 1925, Novel

PLACE OF HONEYMOONS, THE 1920 d: Kenean Buel. USA., *The Place of Honeymoons*, Harold MacGrath, Indianapolis 1912, Novel

PLACE OF HONOUR, THE 1921 d: Sinclair Hill. UKN., *The Place of Honour*, Ethel M. Dell, Novel

PLACE OF ONE'S OWN, A 1945 d: Bernard Knowles. UKN., *A Place of One's Own*, Osbert Sitwell, 1916, Short Story

PLACE TO GO, A 1963 d: Basil Dearden. UKN., *Bethnal Green*, Michael Fisher, Novel

PLAGUE DOGS, THE 1984 d: Martin Rosen. UKN/USA., *The Plague Dogs*, Richard Adams, Novel

Plague, The *see* LA PESTE (1991).

Plainlands *see* POHJANMAA (1988).

PLAINSMAN, THE 1936 d: Cecil B. de Mille. USA., *Wild Bill Hickok the Prince of the Pistoleros*, Frank J. Wilstach, Garden City, N.Y. 1934, Novel

PLAISIR, LE 1951 d: Max Ophuls. FRN., *La Maison Tellier*, Guy de Maupassant, 1881, Short Story, *Le Masque*, Guy de Maupassant, 1890, Short Story, *La Modele*, Guy de Maupassant, 1888, Short Story

Plaisirs de l'Amour, Les *see* ET LA FEMME CREA L'AMOUR (1964).

Planet of Blood *see* TERRORE NELLO SPAZIO (1965).

PLANET OF JUNIOR BROWN, THE 1997 d: Clement Virgo. CND., *The Planet of Junior Brown*, Virginia Hamilton, Novel

Planet of Terror *see* TERRORE NELLO SPAZIO (1965).

PLANET OF THE APES 1968 d: Franklin J. Schaffner. USA., *La Planete Des Singes*, Pierre Boulle, Paris 1963, Novel

Planet of the Vampires *see* TERRORE NELLO SPAZIO (1965).

PLANETE SAUVAGE, LA 1973 d: Rene Laloux. FRN/CZC., *Oms En Serie*, Stephen Wul, Novel

Plans of Men *see* SOONER OR LATER (1920).

Plantation Boy *see* MENINO DE ENGENHO (1966).

PLANTER, THE 1917 d: Thomas N. Heffron. USA., *The Planter*, Herman Whitaker, New York 1909, Novel

PLASTIC AGE, THE 1925 d: Wesley Ruggles. USA., *The Plastic Age*, Percy Marks, New York 1924, Novel

Plastic Age, The *see* RED LIPS (1928).

Plastic Nightmare *see* SHATTERED (1990).

Platero and I *see* PLATERO Y YO (1968).

PLATERO Y YO 1968 d: Alfredo Castellon. SPN., *Platero Y Yo*, Juan Ramon Jimenez, 1914, Autobiography

PLATINUM HIGH SCHOOL 1960 d: Charles Haas. USA., Howard Breslin, Story

Platoon 317 *see* LA 317EME SECTION (1965).

PLATOON LEADER 1988 d: Aaron Norris. USA., *Platoon Leader*, James R. McDonough, Book

PLAY DIRTY 1968 d: Andre de Toth. UKN., *Play Dirty*, George Marton, Novel

PLAY GIRL 1932 d: Ray Enright. USA., *God's Gift to Women*, Frederick Hazlitt Brennan, 1930, Short Story

PLAY IT AGAIN SAM 1972 d: Herbert Ross. USA., *Play It Again Sam*, Woody Allen, Play

PLAY IT AS IT LAYS 1972 d: Frank Perry. USA., *Play It As It Lays*, Joan Didion, 1970, Novel

Play Italy *see* TOGLI LE GAMBE DAL PARABREZZA (1969).

PLAY ME SOMETHING 1989 d: Timothy Neat. UKN., *Play Me Something*, John Berger, 1987, Short Story

Play of God, The *see* KALIYATTAM (1998).

Play the Game Or Leave the Bed *see* DIE NACKTE BOVARY (1969).

PLAY THINGS 1976 d: Stephen Frears. UKN., *Play Things*, Peter Prince, Novel

PLAYBACK 1962 d: Quentin Lawrence. UKN., Edgar Wallace, Story

PLAYBOY OF PARIS 1930 d: Ludwig Berger. USA., *Le Petit Cafe*, Tristan Bernard, Paris 1912, Play

PLAYBOY OF THE WESTERN WORLD, THE 1962 d: Brian Desmond Hurst. UKN., *The Playboy of the Western World*, John Millington Synge, Dublin 1907, Play

Player Pianos, The *see* LOS PIANOS MECANICOS (1965).

PLAYER, THE 1992 d: Robert Altman. USA., *The Player*, Michael Tolkin, Novel

Players *see* DAVID WILLIAMSON'S THE CLUB (1980).

Players *see* LILY IN LOVE (1985).

Players, The *see* KOMODIANTEN (1941).

Playful Kind, The *see* LES LIONCEAUX (1959).

Playgirl *see* PLAY GIRL (1932).

Playgirl and the Minister, The *see* THE AMOROUS PRAWN (1962).

PLAYING AROUND 1930 d: Mervyn Leroy. USA., *Sheba*, Vina Delmar, Story

PLAYING BEATIE BOW 1986 d: Donald Crombie. ASL., *Playing Beatie Bow*, Ruth Park, Novel

PLAYING DEAD 1915 d: Sidney Drew. USA., *Playing Dead*, Richard Harding Davis, 1915, Short Story

Playing for Keeps *see* LILY IN LOVE (1985).

Playing the Game *see* LOVE'S REDEMPTION (1921).

Playing the Game *see* TOUCHDOWN (1931).

PLAYING THE SAME GAME 1915 d: Edwin McKim. USA., *Playing the Same Game*, Cornelia Bleakney, Story

PLAYING WITH SOULS 1925 d: Ralph Ince. USA., *Play With Souls*, Clara Longworth, New York 1922, Novel

PLAYTHING OF BROADWAY, THE 1921 d: John Francis Dillon. USA., *Emergency House*, Sidney Morgan, Story

PLAYTHING, THE 1929 d: Castleton Knight. UKN., *Life Is Pretty Much the Same*, Arthur Black, Play

PLAYTHINGS 1918 d: Douglas Gerrard. USA., *Playthings*, Sidney Toler, Play

PLAYTHINGS OF DESIRE 1924 d: Burton L. King. USA., *Playthings of Desire*, Wesley J. Putnam, Story

PLAYTHINGS OF DESIRE 1934 d: George Melford. USA., *Playthings of Desire*, Harry Sinclair Drago, New York 1934, Novel

Playtime *see* LA RECREATION (1961).

PLAZA DE ORIENTE 1962 d: Mateo Cano. SPN., *Plaza de Oriente*, Joaquin Calvo Sotelo, 1947, Play

PLAZA SUITE 1971 d: Arthur Hiller. USA., *Plaza Suite*, Neil Simon, 1969, Play

PLEASE DON'T EAT THE DAISIES 1960 d: Charles Walters. USA., *Please Don't Eat the Daisies*, Jean Kerr, Play

Please Don't Go *see* SEN DE GITME (1997).

PLEASE GET MARRIED 1919 d: John Ince. USA., *Please Get Married*, Lewis Allen Browne, James Cullen, New York 1919, Play

PLEASE HELP EMILY 1917 d: Dell Henderson. USA., *Please Help Emily*, H. M. Harwood, London 1916, Play

Please, Let the Flowers Live *see* BITTE LASST DIE BLUMEN LEBEN (1986).

Please, Sir! *see* PROSIM PANE PROFESORE! (1940).

PLEASE TEACHER 1937 d: Stafford Dickens. UKN., *Please Teacher*, K. R. G. Browne, Bert Lee, R. P. Weston, London 1935, Play

PLEASE TURN OVER 1959 d: Gerald Thomas. UKN., *Book of the Month*, Basil Thomas, London 1954, Play

Please Write, Danny *see* BITTE SCHREIBEN SIE! DANY (1956).

PLEASURE BUYERS, THE 1925 d: Chet Withey. USA., *The Pleasure Buyers*, Arthur Somers Roche, New York 1925, Novel

PLEASURE CRAZED 1929 d: Donald Gallaher, Charles Klein (Spv). USA., *The Scent of Sweet Almonds*, Monckton Hoffe, Play

PLEASURE CRUISE 1933 d: Frank Tuttle. USA., *Pleasure Cruise*, Austen Allen, London 1928, Play

PLEASURE GARDEN, THE 1926 d: Alfred Hitchcock. UKN/GRM., *The Pleasure Garden*, Oliver Sandys, Novel

PLEASURE MAD 1923 d: Reginald Barker. USA., *The Valley of Content*, Blanche Upright, New York 1922, Novel

PLEASURE OF HIS COMPANY, THE 1961 d: George Seaton. USA., *The Pleasure of His Company*, Cornelia Otis Skinner, Samuel Taylor, New York 1958, Play

PLEASURE SEEKERS, THE 1964 d: Jean Negulesco. USA., *Coins in a Fountain*, John H. Secondari, Philadelphia 1952, Novel

Pleasures and Vices *see* GUEULE D'ANGE (1955).

PLEASURES OF THE RICH 1926 d: Louis J. Gasnier. USA., *The Wrong Coat*, Harold MacGrath, Story

PLECAREA VLASINILOR 1982 d: Mircea Dragan. RMN., *Plecarea Vlasinilor*, Ioana Postelnicu, 1964, Novel

PLEIN AUX AS 1933 d: Jacques Houssin. FRN., *Plein aux As*, Henri Kistemaeckers, Short Story

PLEIN SOLEIL 1960 d: Rene Clement. FRN/ITL., *The Talented Mr. Ripley*, Patricia Highsmith, New York 1955, Novel

PLENENO YATO 1962 d: Dutcho Mundrov. BUL., *Pleneno Yato*, Emil Manov, 1947, Novel

PLENTY 1985 d: Fred Schepisi. USA., *Plenty*, David Hare, 1978, Play

PLEYDELL MYSTERY, THE 1916 d: Albert Ward. UKN., *Poison*, Alice Askew, Claude Askew, Novel

Plicht En Liefde *see* TUSSCHEN LIEFDE EN PLICHT (1912).

Plight of the Poor *see* EZAI PADUM PADU (1950).

PLOD 1972 d: Michael Cort. UKN., *After the Merrymaking*, Roger McGough, 1971, Verse

Plohoj Horosij Celovek *see* PLOKHOY KHOROSHYI CHELOVEK (1974).

PLOKHOY KHOROSHYI CHELOVEK 1974 d: Josif Heifitz. USS., *Duel*, Anton Chekhov, 1891, Short Story

PLOMBIER AMOREUX, LE 1932 d: Claude Autant-LarA. USA., *Her Cardboard Lover*, P. G. Wodehouse, Valerie Wyngate, New York 1927, Play

PLOT THICKENS, THE 1936 d: Ben Holmes. USA., *The Riddle of the Dangling Pearl*, Stuart Palmer, 1933, Short Story

Plotone Di Esecuzione *see* QUAND SONNERA MIDI (1957).

PLOUF A EU PEUR 1918 d: Fernand Rivers. FRN., *Plouf a eu Peur*, Fred Argel, Short Story

Plouffe Family, The *see* LES PLOUFFE (1981).

Plouffe II, Les *see* LE CRIME D'OVIDE PLOUFFE (1984).

PLOUFFE, LES 1981 d: Gilles Carle. CND., *Les Plouffe*, Roger Lemelin, Novel

PLOUGH AND THE STARS, THE 1936 d: John Ford. USA., *The Plough and the Stars*, Sean O'Casey, Dublin 1926, Play

PLOW WOMAN, THE 1917 d: Charles Swickard. USA., *The Plow Woman*, Eleanor Gates, New York 1906, Novel

Pluck *see* AMERICAN PLUCK (1925).

Pluck of the Irish *see* GREAT GUY (1936).

PLUFT, O FANTASMINHA 1962 d: Romain Lesage. BRZ., *O Fantasminha Pluft*, Maria Clara Machado, 1957, Play

PLUKOVNIK SVEC 1929 d: Svatopluk Innemann. CZC., *Plukovnik Svec*, Rudolf Medek, Play

Pluma Al Viento *see* PLUME AU VENT (1952).

PLUME AU VENT 1952 d: Louis Cuny, Ramon Torrado. FRN/SPN., *Plume Au Vent*, Jean Nohain, Opera

PLUNDER 1931 d: Tom Walls. UKN., *Plunder*, Ben Travers, London 1928, Play

PLUNDER OF THE SUN 1953 d: John Farrow. USA., *Plunder of the Sun*, David Dodge, 1949, Novel

PLUNDER ROAD 1957 d: Hubert Cornfield. USA., *Plunder Road*, Jack Carney, Steven Ritch, Novel

PLUNDERER, THE 1915 d: Edgar Lewis. USA., *The Plunderer*, Roy Norton, New York 1912, Novel

PLUNDERER, THE 1924 d: George Archainbaud. USA., *The Plunderer*, Roy Norton, New York 1912, Novel

Plunge, The *see* DER STURZ (1979).

PLUS BEAU GOSSE DE FRANCE, LE 1937 d: Rene Pujol. FRN., *Le Plus Beau Gosse de France*, Andre Mouezy-Eon, Play

Plus Belle Soiree de Ma Vie, La *see* LA PIU BELLA SERATA DELLA MIA VITA (1972).

PLUS DE WHISKY POUR CALLAGHAN 1955 d: Willy Rozier. FRN., *Plus de Whisky Pour Callaghan*, Peter Cheyney, Novel

Plus Grand Amour, Le *see* FELICIE NANTEUIL (1942).

Plus Haut, Plus Loin *see* CROSSBAR (1979).

PLUS HEUREUX DES HOMMES, LE 1952 d: Yves Ciampi. FRN., *Le Plus Heureux Des Hommes*, Jean Guitton, Play

Plus Mort Que Vif *see* L' ETRANGE MONSIEUR STEVE (1957).

PLUS QUE REINE 1915 d: Rene Leprince. FRN., *Plus Que Reine*, Pierre Decourcelle, Novel

Plusch Und Plumowski *see* DAS FRAUENHAUS VON RIO (1927).

PLUSZ MINUSZ EGY NAP 1972 d: Zoltan Fabri. HNG., Adam Boder, Novel

Plutocrat, The *see* BUSINESS AND PLEASURE (1931).

PLYMOUTH ADVENTURE 1952 d: Clarence Brown. USA., *Plymouth Adventure*, Ernest Gebler, 1950, Novel

PO CHU MI XING 1958 d: Wang Bing. CHN., *24 Nights*, Zhang Yang, Short Story

Po' Di Sole Nell'aqua Gelida, Un *see* UN PEU DE SOLEIL DANS L'EAU FROIDE (1971).

Po Zakonoe *see* PO ZAKONU (1926).

PO ZAKONU 1926 d: Lev Kuleshov. USS., Jack London, Story

Poacher of Tyrol, The *see* BERGKRISTALL (1949).

Poacher's Daughter, The *see* SALLY'S IRISH ROGUE (1958).

POBOCNIK JEHO VYSOSTI 1933 d: Martin Fric. CZC., *Kasta Pro Sebe*, Emil Artur Longen, Play

POBRE VALBUENA, EL 1923 d: Jose Buchs. SPN., *El Pobre Valbuena*, Carlos Arniches, E. Garcia Alvarez, Opera

POCESTNE PANI PARDUBICKE 1944 d: Martin Fric. CZC., *Mistr Ostreho Mece*, Karel Krpata, Play

POCHARDE, LA 1921 d: Henri Etievant. FRN., *La Pocharde*, Jules Mary, Novel

POCHARDE, LA 1936 d: Jean Kemm, Jean-Louis Bouquet. FRN., *La Pocharde*, Jules Mary, Novel

POCHARDE, LA 1952 d: Georges Combret. FRN., *La Pocharde*, Jules Mary, Novel

Pocket Love, A *see* UN AMOUR DE POCHE (1957).

POCKET MONEY 1972 d: Stuart Rosenberg. USA., *Pocket Money*, J. P. S. Brown, Novel

POCKETFUL OF MIRACLES, A 1961 d: Frank CaprA. USA., *Madame la Gimp*, Damon Runyon, 1929, Short Story

Pocketful of Rye, A *see* MISS MARPLE: A POCKETFUL OF RYE (1985).

Pock-Marked Janus *see* MOTTIGE JANUS (1922).

POD IGOTO 1952 d: Dako Dakovski. BUL., *Pod Igoto*, Ivan Vazov, 1889-90, Novel

POD JEDNOU STRECHOU 1938 d: M. J. Krnansky. CZC., *Pod Jednou Strechou*, Ignat Herrmann, Short Story

Podnjataja Celina *see* PODNYATAYA TZELINA (1940).

Podnyataya Tselina *see* PODNYATAYA TZELINA (1940).

PODNYATAYA TSELINA 1959-61 d: Alexander Ivanov. USS., *Podnyataya Tselina*, Mikhail Sholokhov, 1932, Novel

PODNYATAYA TZELINA 1940 d: Yuli Raizman. USS., *Podnyataya Tselina*, Mikhail Sholokhov, 1932, Novel

PODSKALAK 1928 d: Premysl Prazsky. CZC., *Podskalak*, Frantisek Ferdinand Samberk, Play

POEDINOK 1957 d: Vladimir Petrov. USS., Aleksander Ivanovich Kuprin, Short Story

Poe's Tales of Terror *see* TALES OF TERROR (1962).

POET AND THE SOLDIER, THE 1913. USA., *Apollo and the Seaman*, Herbert Trench, Poem

Poet Maybe, A *see* KANSKE EN DIKTARE (1933).

Poet, The *see* KAVI (1949).

POETIC LICENSE 1922 d: George A. Cooper. UKN., *Poetic License*, F. K. Junior, Story

Poetry of Adalen *see* ADALENS POESI (1928).

POET'S PUB 1949 d: Frederick Wilson. UKN., *Poet's Pub*, Eric Linklater, 1929, Novel

POEZDKA V VISBADEN 1989 d: Evgenij Gerasimov. USS/AUS/CZC., *Veshniye Vody*, Ivan Turgenev, 1872, Short Story

POHADKA MAJE 1940 d: Otakar VavrA. CZC., *Pohadka Maje*, Vilem Mrstik, Novel

POHADKA O MALICKOVI 1985 d: Gunar Piesis. CZC/USS., Anna Brigadere, Story

POHISHTENIE V ZHALTO 1980 d: Marianna EvstatievA. BUL., *Proizshestvie Na Tikhata Ulitsa*, Pavel Vezhinov, 1960, Novel

POHJANMAA 1988 d: Pekka ParikkA. FNL., *Pohjanmaa*, Antti Tuuri, 1982, Novel

POHORSKA VESNICE 1928 d: M. J. Krnansky. CZC., *Pohorska Vesnice*, Bozena Nemcova, Novel

Poi Ti Sposero *see* UN MONSIEUR DE COMPAGNIE (1964).

POIGNARD MALAIS, LE 1930 d: Roger Goupillieres. FRN., Tristan Bernard, Short Story

POIKA ELI KESAANSA 1955 d: Roland Hallstrom. FNL., *Elama Ja Aurinko*, Frans E. Sillanpaa, 1916, Novel

POIL DE CAROTTE 1926 d: Julien Duvivier. FRN., *Poil de Carotte*, Jules Renard, 1894, Novel

POIL DE CAROTTE 1932 d: Julien Duvivier. FRN., *La Bigote*, Jules Renard, 1900, Play, *Poil de Carotte*, Jules Renard, 1894, Novel

POIL DE CAROTTE 1951 d: Paul Mesnier. FRN., *Poil de Carotte*, Jules Renard, 1894, Novel

POILU DE LA VICTOIRE, LE 1915 d: Roger Lion (Spv). FRN., *Le Poilu de la Victoire*, Francois Mair, Play

POILUS DE LA 9E, LES 1915 d: G. Remond. FRN., *Les Poilus de la 9E*, Arnould Galopin, Novel

Point Blank *see* PRESSURE POINT (1962).

POINT BLANK 1967 d: John Boorman. USA., *The Hunter*, Donald E. Westlake, New York 1963, Novel

POINT OF VIEW, THE 1920 d: Alan Crosland. USA., *The Point of View*, Edith Ellis, New York 1912, Play

Point of View, The *see* WHITE AND UNMARRIED (1921).

Point Two Two *see* STONE COLD DEAD (1979).

POINTED HEELS 1929 d: A. Edward Sutherland. USA., *Pointed Heels*, Charles William Brackett, 1929, Short Story

POINTING FINGER, THE 1919 d: Edward Kull, Edward Morrisey. USA., *No Experience Required*, Frank R. Adams, 1917, Short Story

POINTING FINGER, THE 1922 d: George Ridgwell. UKN., *The Pointing Finger*, Rita, Novel

POINTING FINGER, THE 1933 d: George Pearson. UKN., *The Pointing Finger*, Rita, Novel

POINTS WEST 1929 d: Arthur Rosson. USA., *Points West*, B. M. Bower, Boston 1928, Novel

Pointsman, The *see* DE WISSELWACHTER (1986).

Poison Affair, The *see* L' AFFAIRE DES POISONS (1955).

911

POISON D'AMOUR 1990 d: Hugues de Laugardiere. FRN., *Le Dejeuner Interrompu*, Julien Vartet, Novel

Poison Ivy *see* LA MOME VERT-DE-GRIS (1952).

POISON PEN 1939 d: Paul L. Stein. UKN., *Poison Pen*, Richard Llewellyn, London 1937, Play

POISONED PARADISE: THE FORBIDDEN STORY OF MONTE CARLO 1924 d: Louis J. Gasnier. USA., *Poisoned Paradise; a Romance of Monte Carlo*, Robert W. Service, New York 1922, Novel

Poisonous Snake *see* ZEHARI SAAP (1933).

Poisson Chinois, Le *see* LA BATAILLE SILENCIEUSE (1937).

POKER D'AS 1928 d: Henri Desfontaines. FRN., *Poker d'As*, Arthur Bernede, Novel

Poker Face *see* KILLER AT LARGE (1936).

POKER FACES 1926 d: Harry Pollard. USA., *Poker Faces*, Edgar Franklin, 1923, Short Story

POKHALO 1936 d: Maria Balazs. HNG., *Pokhalo*, Kalman Csatho, Novel

POKHALO 1974 d: Imre Mihalyfi. HNG., *Pokhalo*, Erzsebet Galgoczi, 1972, Novel

POKHOZDENYA GRAFA NEVZOROVA 1982 d: Aleksandr Pankratov. USS., *Pokhozdenya Grafa Nevzorova Ili Ybikus*, Alexsey Nikolayevich Tolstoy, 1925, Short Story

POKKERS UNGER, DE 1947 d: Astrid Henning-Jensen, Bjarne Henning-Jensen. DNM., **De Pokkers Unger**, Estrid Ott, Play

POKOLENIE 1954 d: Andrzej WajdA. PLN., *Pokolenie*, Bohdan Czeszko, 1951, Novel

POLAR 1984 d: Jacques Bral. FRN., *Polar*, Jean-Patrick Manchette, Novel

POLDARK 1996 d: Richard Laxton. UKN., *Poldark*, Winston Graham, Novel

POLDARK: SERIES 1 AND 2 1975 d: Paul Annett, Christopher Barry. UKN., *Poldark*, Winston Graham, Novel

POLE POPPENSPALER 1935 d: Curt Oertel. GRM., *Pole Poppenspaler*, Theodor Storm, 1874, Short Story

POLE POPPENSPALER 1955 d: Arthur Pohl. GDR., *Pole Poppenspaler*, Theodor Storm, 1874, Short Story

POLENBLUT 1934 d: Carl Lamac. GRM/CZC., *Polska Krev*, Oskar Nedbal, Leo Stein, Opera

Policarpo, Maitre Calligraphe *see* UFFICIALE DI SCITTURA POLICARPO (1959).

Policarpo, Master Writer *see* UFFICIALE DI SCITTURA POLICARPO (1959).

Policarpo, Oficial Diplomado *see* UFFICIALE DI SCITTURA POLICARPO (1959).

POLICARPO, UFFICIALE DI SCITTURA 1959 d: Mario Soldati. ITL/FRN/SPN., *La Famiglia De'tappeti*, Arnaldo Luigi Vassallo, Novel

POLICE DES MOEURS 1987 d: Jean Rougeron. FRN., *Police Des Moeurs*, Pierre Lucas, Novel

Police Lieutenant Borck *see* OBERWACHTMEISTER BORCK (1955).

POLICE PATROL, THE 1925 d: Burton L. King. USA., *The Police Patrol*, A. Y. Pearson, Story

POLICHE 1934 d: Abel Gance. FRN., *Poliche*, Henry Bataille, 1906, Play

POLICING THE PLAINS 1927 d: A. D. Kean. CND., *Policing the Plains*, R. G. MacBeth, Novel

Polijuschka *see* POLIKUSKA (1958).

Polikuschka *see* POLIKUSKA (1958).

POLIKUSKA 1958 d: Carmine Gallone. ITL/FRN/GRM., *Polikushka*, Lev Nikolayevich Tolstoy, 1863, Short Story

POLIS POLIS POTATISMOS 1993 d: Pelle Berglund. SWD/GRM., Maj Sjowall, Per Wahloo, Novel

Polish Blood *see* POLENBLUT (1934).

Polish Blood *see* POLSKA KREV (1934).

Polish Blood *see* POLENBLUT (1934).

Polish Blood *see* POLSKA KREV (1934).

POLISHING UP 1914 d: George D. Baker. USA., *Polishing Up*, James Oliver Curwood, Story

POLISMORDAREN 1993 d: Peter Keglevic. SWD/GRM., Maj Sjowall, Per Wahloo, Novel

Politic Flapper, The *see* THE PATSY (1928).

POLIZEIFUNK MELDET, DER 1939 d: Rudolf Van Der Noss. GRM., *Aktenbundel M 2-1706/35*, Axel Rudolph, Novel

POLIZEISPIONIN 77 1929 d: Willi Wolff. GRM., *Der Ruf Der Tiefe*, Max Uebelhoer, Novel

Polizia Indaga: Siamo Tutti Sospettati, La *see* LES SUSPECTS (1974).

Polly Fulton *see* B.F.'S DAUGHTER (1948).

POLLY OF THE CIRCUS 1917 d: Charles Horan, Edwin L. Hollywood. USA., *Polly of the Circus*, Margaret Mayo, New York 1907, Play

POLLY OF THE CIRCUS 1932 d: Alfred Santell. USA., *Polly of the Circus*, Margaret Mayo, New York 1907, Play

POLLY REDHEAD 1917 d: Jack Conway. USA., *Pollyooly*, Edgar Jepson, Indianapolis 1912, Novel

POLLY WITH A PAST 1920 d: Leander de CordovA. USA., *Polly With a Past*, Guy Bolton, George Middleton, New York 1917, Play

POLLYANNA 1920 d: Paul Powell. USA., *Pollyanna*, Eleanor H. Porter, Boston 1913, Novel

POLLYANNA 1960 d: David Swift. USA., *Pollyanna*, Eleanor H. Porter, Boston 1913, Novel

POLLYANNA 1973 d: June Wyndham-Davis. UKN., *Pollyanna*, Eleanor H. Porter, Boston 1913, Novel

POLNISCHE WIRTSCHAFT 1928 d: E. W. Emo. GRM., *Polnische Wirtschaft*, Kurt Kraatz, Georg Okonowski, Play

POLOWANIE NA MUCHY 1969 d: Andrzej WajdA. PLN., *Polowanie Na Muchy*, Janusz Glowacki, Short Story

POLSKA KREV 1934 d: Carl Lamac. CZC., *Polska Krev*, Oskar Nedbal, Leo Stein, Opera

POLTERABEND 1940 d: Carl Boese. GRM., *Polterabend*, Waldemar Frank, Leo Lenz, Play

Polvere Di Eroi *see* QUATTRO NOTTI CON ALBA (1962).

POMME D'AMOUR 1932 d: Jean Dreville. FRN., *Pomme d'Amour*, Charles d'Abadie, Raymond de Cesse, Play

POMSTA MORE 1921 d: Vladimir Pospisil-Born. CZC., *Pomsta More*, Grigorij MacTeta, Short Story

PONJOLA 1923 d: Donald Crisp, James Young. USA., *Ponjola*, Cynthia Stockley, London 1923, Novel

Pont Des Soupirs, Le *see* IL PONTE DEI SOSPIRI (1964).

PONT ENTRE DEUX RIVES, UN 1999 d: Gerard Depardieu, Frederic Auburtin. FRN., *Un Pont Entre Deux Rives*, Alain Leblanc, Novel

Pont Vers le Soleil, Le *see* BRIDGE TO THE SUN (1961).

PONTCARRAL, COLONEL D'EMPIRE 1942 d: Jean Delannoy. FRN., *Colonel d'Empire Pontcarral*, Alberic Cahuet, Novel

PONTE DEI SOSPIRI, IL 1921 d: Domenico Gaido. ITL., *Le Pont Des Soupirs*, Michel Zevaco, Novel

PONTE DEI SOSPIRI, IL 1940 d: Mario Bonnard. ITL., *Le Pont Des Soupirs*, Michel Zevaco, Novel

PONTE DEI SOSPIRI, IL 1964 d: Piero Pierotti. ITL/SPN/FRN., *Le Pont Des Soupirs*, Michel Zevaco, Novel

Ponte Della Concordia, Il *see* NESSUNO HA TRADITO (1954).

PONY EXPRESS, THE 1925 d: James Cruze. USA., *The Pony Express*, Henry James Forman, Walter Woods, New York 1925, Novel

PONY SOLDIER 1952 d: Joseph M. Newman. USA., *Mounted Patrol*, Garnett Weston, Serial Story

POODLE SPRINGS 1998 d: Bob Rafelson. USA., *Poodle Springs*, Raymond Chandler, Robert B. Parker, Novel

POOJAPALAM 1964 d: B. N. Reddi. IND., *Pujari*, Munipalle Raju, Novel

Pookie *see* THE STERILE CUCKOO (1969).

POOL OF FLAME, THE 1916 d: Otis Turner. USA., *The Pool of Flame*, Louis Joseph Vance, New York 1909, Novel

Pools of the Past *see* THE NOTORIOUS MRS. CARRICK (1924).

Poopsie and Company *see* LA PUPA DEL GANGSTER (1975).

POOR BOOB, THE 1919 d: Donald Crisp. USA., *Poor Boob*, Margaret Mayo, Play

POOR COW 1967 d: Kenneth Loach. UKN., *Poor Cow*, Nell Dunn, London 1967, Novel

POOR, DEAR MARGARET KIRBY 1921 d: William P. S. Earle. USA., *Poor Dear Margaret Kirby*, Kathleen Norris, 1913, Short Story

Poor Erendira *see* ERENDIRA (1982).

Poor Girl *see* CHUDA HOLKA (1929).

Poor Little Rich Girl *see* POOR LITTLE RICH GIRL: THE BARBARA HUTTON STORY (1987).

POOR LITTLE RICH GIRL, THE 1917 d: Maurice Tourneur. USA., *Poor Little Rich Girl*, Eleanor Gates, New York 1913, Play

POOR LITTLE RICH GIRL: THE BARBARA HUTTON STORY 1987 d: Charles Jarrott. USA., *Poor Little Rich Girl*, C. David Heymann, Book

Poor Millionaire, The *see* DER ARME MILLIONAR (1939).

Poor Millionaires *see* STACKARS MILJONARER (1936).

POOR NUT, THE 1927 d: Richard Wallace. USA., *The Poor Nut*, Elliott Nugent, J. C. Nugent, New York 1925, Play

Poor Nut, The *see* LOCAL BOY MAKES GOOD (1931).

POOR RELATION, A 1915. USA., *A Poor Relation*, Sol Smith Russell, Play

POOR RELATION, A 1921 d: Clarence Badger. USA., *A Poor Relation*, Edward E. Kidder, 1911, Play

Poor Rich *see* SZEGENY GAZDAGOK (1959).

Poor Sister *see* THE KING STEPS OUT (1936).

Poor Valbueno *see* EL POBRE VALBUENA (1923).

POP CIRA I POP SPIRA 1965 d: Soja Jovanovic. YGS., *Pop Cira I Pop Spira*, Steven Sremac, 1898, Novel

POPAUL ET VIRGINIE 1919 d: Adrien Caillard. FRN., *Popaul Et Virginie*, Alfred Machard, Novel

POPIOL I DIAMENT 1958 d: Andrzej WajdA. PLN., *Popiol I Diament*, Jerzy Andrzejewski, 1948, Novel

POPIOLY 1966 d: Andrzej WajdA. PLN., *Popioly*, Stefan Zeromski, 1904, Novel

POPP UND MINGEL 1975 d: Ula Stockl. GRM., *Popp Und Mingel*, Frigyes Karinthy, 1937, Novel

POPPIES 1914 d: Stuart Kinder. UKN., *Garden of Sleep*, de Lana, Poem, *Poppyland*, Clement Scott, Poem

Poppies *see* GUBIJINSO (1935).

Poppies in Flanders *see* POPPIES OF FLANDERS (1927).

POPPIES OF FLANDERS 1927 d: Arthur Maude. UKN., *The Hopeless Case*, H. C. McNeile ("Sapper"), Short Story

POPPY 1917 d: Edward Jose. USA., *Poppy*, Cynthia Stockley, London 1911, Novel

Poppy *see* GUBIJINSO (1935).

POPPY 1936 d: A. Edward Sutherland, Stuart Heisler (Uncredited). USA., *Poppy Comes to Town*, Dorothy Donnelly, S. Jones, A. Samuel, New York 1923, Musical Play

Poppy Girl *see* THE POPPY GIRL'S HUSBAND (1919).

POPPY GIRL'S HUSBAND, THE 1919 d: William S. Hart, Lambert Hillyer. USA., *The Poppy Girl's Husband*, Jack Boyle, 1918, Short Story

Poprava Pesaka Kudrny *see* JMENEM JEHO VELICENSTVA (1928).

Poprigunya *see* POPRYGUNYA (1955).

POPRYGUNYA 1955 d: Samson Samsonov. USS., *Poprygunya*, Anton Chekhov, 1892, Short Story

POR QUE TE ENGANA TU MARIDO? 1968 d: Manuel Summers. SPN., *Por Que Te Engana Tu Marido?*, Wenceslao Fernandez Florez, 1940, Short Story

POR UN MILAGRO DE AMOR 1928 d: Luis R. Alonso. SPN., *Por un Milagro de Amor*, Leopoldo Lopez de Saa, Poem

Porc-Epic, Le *see* TOUTE LA FAMILLE ETAIT LA (1948).

PORCI CON LE ALI 1977 d: Paolo Pietrangeli. ITL., *Porci Con Le Ali*, Antonia (Lidia Ravera), Rocco, Book

PORGI L'ALTRA GUANCIA 1974 d: Franco Rossi. ITL/FRN., Rodolfo Sonego, Short Story

Porgi l'AltrA. Sberla *see* L' EREDITA DELLO ZIO BUONANIMA (1975).

PORGY AND BESS 1959 d: Otto Preminger. USA., *Porgy*, Dubose Heyward, 1925, Novel

PORION, LE 1921 d: Georges Champavert. FRN., *Le Porion*, Marcel Gerbidon, Play

Pork Butcher, The *see* SOUVENIR (1988).

PORT AFRIQUE 1956 d: Rudolph Mate. UKN., *Port Afrique*, Bernard Victor Dyer, Novel

PORT ARTHUR 1936 d: Nicolas Farkas. GRM/CZC., *Port-Arthur*, Pierre Frondaie, Novel

PORT OF ESCAPE 1956 d: Tony Young. UKN., *Safe Harbour*, Barbara Harper, Short Story

Port of Lost Souls, The see WHITE SLIPPERS (1924).

PORT OF MISSING MEN, THE 1914 d: Francis Powers. USA., *The Port of Missing Men*, Meredith Nicholson, Indianapolis 1907, Novel

PORT OF SEVEN SEAS 1938 d: James Whale. USA., *Fanny*, Marcel Pagnol, Paris 1931, Play, *Marius*, Marcel Pagnol, Paris 1931, Play

Port of Shadows see QUAI DES BRUMES (1938).

Port of Shame see LES AMANTS DU TAGE (1955).

PORTA DEL CANNONE, LA 1969 d: Leopoldo SavonA. ITL./YGS., *La Porta Del Cannone*, Giuliano Friz, Novel

PORT-ARTHUR 1936 d: Nicolas Farkas. FRN/CZC., *Port-Arthur*, Pierre Frondaie, Novel

PORTATRICE DI PANE, LA 1911 d: Romolo Bacchini. ITL., *La Porteuse de Pain*, Xavier de Montepin, 1884, Novel

PORTATRICE DI PANE, LA 1916 d: Enrico Vidali. ITL., *La Porteuse de Pain*, Xavier de Montepin, 1884, Novel

Portatrice Di Pane, La see LA PORTEUSE DE PAIN (1949).

Portatrice Di Pane, La see LA PORTEUSE DE PAIN (1963).

PORTE APERTE 1989 d: Gianni Amelio. ITL., *Porte Aperte*, Leonardo Sciasia, 1987, Novel

PORTE DES LILAS 1957 d: Rene Clair. FRN/ITL., *Portes Des Lilas*, Rene Fallet, Novel

PORTE D'ORIENT 1950 d: Jacques Daroy. FRN., *Porte d'Orient*, Rene Roques, Novel

PORTERHOUSE BLUE 1987 d: Robert Knights. UKN., *Porterhouse Blue*, Tom Sharpe, Novel

PORTES CLAQUENT, LES 1960 d: Jacques Poitrenaud, Michel Fermaud. FRN., *Les Portes Claquent*, Michel Fermaud, Play

PORTES TOURNANTES, LES 1988 d: Francis Mankiewicz. CND/FRN., *Les Portes Tournantes*, Jacques Savoie, Novel

PORTEUSE DE PAIN, LA 1912 d: Georges DenolA. FRN., *La Porteuse de Pain*, Xavier de Montepin, 1884, Novel

PORTEUSE DE PAIN, LA 1923 d: Rene Le Somptier. FRN., *La Porteuse de Pain*, Xavier de Montepin, 1884, Novel

PORTEUSE DE PAIN, LA 1934 d: Rene Sti. FRN., *La Porteuse de Pain*, Xavier de Montepin, 1884, Novel

PORTEUSE DE PAIN, LA 1949 d: Maurice Cloche. FRN/ITL., *La Porteuse de Pain*, Xavier de Montepin, 1884, Novel

PORTEUSE DE PAIN, LA 1963 d: Maurice Cloche. FRN/ITL., *La Porteuse de Pain*, Xavier de Montepin, 1884, Novel

PORTILE ALBASTRE ALE ORASULUI 1973 d: Mircea Muresan. RMN., *Albastra Zare a Mortii*, Marin Preda, 1948, Short Story

PORTNOY'S COMPLAINT 1972 d: Ernest Lehman. USA., *Portnoy's Complaint*, Philip Roth, 1969, Novel

PORTO-FRANCO 1961 d: Paul Calinescu. RMN., *Europolis*, Jean Bart, 1933, Novel

Portrait d'Aieule, Visage de Jeune Fille see VISAGE D'AIEULE (1926).

PORTRAIT DE DORIAN GRAY, LE 1977 d: Pierre Boutron. FRN., *The Picture of Dorian Gray*, Oscar Wilde, London 1891, Novel

Portrait de Groupe Avec Dame see GRUPPENBILD MIT DAME (1977).

Portrait de Province En Rouge see AL PIACERE DI RIVEDERLA (1976).

PORTRAIT IN BLACK 1960 d: Michael Gordon. USA., *Portrait in Black*, Ivan Goff, Ben Roberts, Play

Portrait in Smoke see WICKED AS THEY COME (1956).

Portrait of a Bourgeois in Black see RITRATTO DI BORGHESIA IN NERO (1978).

PORTRAIT OF A LADY 1967 d: James Cellan Jones. UKN/USA., *Portrait of a Lady*, Henry James, 1881, Novel

PORTRAIT OF A LADY 1996 d: Jane Campion. UKN/USA., *Portrait of a Lady*, Henry James, 1881, Novel

PORTRAIT OF A MARRIAGE 1990 d: Stephen Whittaker. UKN/USA/NZL., *Portrait of a Marriage*, Nigel Nicholson, Book

PORTRAIT OF A MOBSTER 1961 d: Joseph Pevney. USA., *Portrait of a Mobster*, Harry Grey, New York 1958, Novel

Portrait of a Rebel see A WOMAN REBELS (1936).

Portrait of a Sinner see THE ROUGH AND THE SMOOTH (1959).

Portrait of a Woman see UNE FEMME DISPARAIT (1942).

Portrait of Chieko see CHIEKO-SHO (1967).

PORTRAIT OF CLARE 1950 d: Lance Comfort. UKN., *Portrait of Clare*, Francis Brett Young, Novel

Portrait of Hell see JIGOKU-HEN (1969).

PORTRAIT OF JENNIE 1948 d: William Dieterle. USA., *Portrait of Jennie*, Robert Nathan, 1940, Novel

Portrait of Madame Yuki see YUKI FUJIN EZU (1950).

PORTRAIT OF THE ARTIST AS A YOUNG MAN 1977 d: Joseph Strick. UKN., *A Portrait of the Artist As a Young Man*, James Joyce, 1916, Novel

PORTRAIT OF THE ARTIST AS FILIPINO 1965 d: Lamberto V. AvellanA. PHL., Nick Joaquin, Play

PORTRAIT ROBOT 1960 d: Paul Paviot. FRN., *Portrait-Robot*, Michel Lebrun, Novel

Portrait Robot, Ou Echec a l'Assassin see PORTRAIT ROBOT (1960).

PORTRAIT, THE 1993 d: Arthur Penn. USA., *Painting Churches*, Tina Howe, Play

POSAUNIST, DER 1945 d: Carl Boese. GRM., *Der Posaunist*, Heinz Schwitzke, Short Story

POSEIDON ADVENTURE, THE 1972 d: Ronald Neame. USA., *The Poseidon Adventure*, Paul Gallico, Novel

Poslednaya Zhertva see POSLEDNJAJA SHERTWA (1975).

POSLEDNI MOTYL 1989 d: Karel KachynA. CZC/FRN/UKN., *Le Cri du Papillon*, Michel Jacot, Novel

POSLEDNI MUZ 1934 d: Martin Fric. CZC., *Posledni Muz*, F. X. Svoboda, Play

POSLEDNI RADOST 1921 d: Vaclav Binovec. CZC., *Posledni Radost*, Knut Hamsun, Novel

Posledni Vlkodlak see VYZNAVACI SLUNCE (1925).

POSLEDNJAJA SHERTWA 1975 d: Petr Todorovsky. USS., *Poslednaya Zhertva*, Alexander Ostrovsky, 1878, Play

Poslednjaja Zertva see POSLEDNJAJA SHERTWA (1975).

POSLEDNY GOD BERKOETA 1978 d: Vadim Lisenko. USS., *In a Remote Village*, Nikolai Domojakov, Novel

POSSE FROM HELL 1961 d: Herbert Coleman. USA., *Posse from Hell*, Clair Huffaker, New York 1958, Novel

POSSEDEES, LES 1955 d: Charles Brabant. FRN/ITL., *Delitto All'isola Della Capre*, Ugo Betti, 1946, Play

POSSEDES, LES 1988 d: Andrzej WajdA. FRN., *Besy*, Fyodor Dostoyevsky, 1872, Novel

POSSESSED 1931 d: Clarence Brown. USA., *The Mirage*, Edgar Selwyn, New York 1920, Play

POSSESSED 1947 d: Curtis Bernhardt. USA., *One Man's Secret*, Rita Weiman, Novel

Possessed see JUNOON (1978).

Possessed, The see LES POSSEDEES (1955).

Possessed, The see LA DONNA DEL LAGO (1965).

Possessed, The see YOBA (1976).

Possessed, The see LES POSSEDES (1988).

POSSESSION 1919 d: Henry Edwards. UKN., *Possession*, Olive Wadsley, Novel

POSSESSION DU CONDAMNE 1967 d: Albert Andre L'Heureux. BLG., *Le Condamne a Mort*, Jean Genet, 1942, Verse

POSSESSION, LA 1929 d: Leonce Perret. FRN., *La Possession*, Henry Bataille, Play

Possessors, The see LES GRANDES FAMILLES (1959).

POSTAL ORDERS 1932 d: John Daumery. UKN., *Postal Orders*, Roland Pertwee, 1916, Play

Postcard from a Journey see KARTKA Z PODROZY (1983).

Postcard from the Trip, A see KARTKA Z PODROZY (1983).

POSTCARDS FROM THE EDGE 1990 d: Mike Nichols. USA., *Postcards from the Edge*, Carrie Fisher, Novel

Poste Sud see FORT DE LA SOLITUDE (1947).

Postillon de Lonjumeau, Le see DER POSTILLON VON LONJUMEAU (1935).

Postillon Im Hochzeitsrock see DER POSTILLON VON LONJUMEAU (1935).

POSTILLON VON LONJUMEAU, DER 1935 d: Carl Lamac. AUS/SWT., *Le Postillon de Lonjumeau*, Adolphe Adam, Leon Brunswick, Leuwen, Paris 1836, Opera

POSTINO, IL 1995 d: Michael Radford. ITL/FRN/BLG., *Ardiente Pacienca*, Antonio Skarmeta, Novel

Postman Always Rings Twice, The see LE DERNIER TOURNANT (1939).

Postman Always Rings Twice, The see OSSESSIONE (1943).

POSTMAN ALWAYS RINGS TWICE, THE 1946 d: Tay Garnett. USA., *The Postman Always Rings Twice*, James M. Cain, 1934, Novel

POSTMAN ALWAYS RINGS TWICE, THE 1981 d: Bob Rafelson. USA., *The Postman Always Rings Twice*, James M. Cain, 1934, Novel

Postman Goes to War, The see LE FACTEUR S'EN VA-T-EN GUERRE (1966).

Postman, The see IL POSTINO (1995).

POSTMAN, THE 1997 d: Kevin Costner. USA., *The Postman*, David Brin, Novel

Postmaster's Daughter, The see NOSTALGIE (1937).

POSTMEISTER, DER 1940 d: Gustav Ucicky. AUS., *Stantsionny Smotritel*, Alexander Pushkin, 1831, Short Story

POSTMEISTER, DER 1955 d: Josef von Baky. GRM., *Stantsionny Smotritel*, Alexander Pushkin, 1831, Short Story

Postponed Wedding Night, The see DIE VERTAGTE HOCHZEITSNACHT (1953).

POSTRIZINY 1980 d: Jiri Menzel. CZC., *Postriziny*, Bohumil Hrabal, 1976, Short Story

Postzug-Uberfall, Der see DIE GENTLEMEN BITTEN ZUR KASSE (1965).

POT CARRIERS, THE 1962 d: Peter Graham Scott. UKN., *The Pot Carriers*, Mike Watts, Television Play

POTASH AND PERLMUTTER 1923 d: Clarence Badger. USA., *Potash and Perlmutter*, Montague Glass, New York 1921, Play

POT-BOUILLE 1957 d: Julien Duvivier. FRN/ITL., *Pot-Bouille*, Emile Zola, 1882, Novel

POTERE SOVRANO, IL 1916 d: Baldassarre Negroni, Percy Nash. ITL., *Temporal Power*, Marie Corelli, Novel

POTIPHAR'S WIFE 1931 d: Maurice Elvey. UKN., *Potiphar's Wife*, Edgar C. Middleton, London 1927, Play

POTOP 1974 d: Jerzy Hoffman. PLN., *Potop*, Henryk Sienkiewicz, 1886, Novel

POTTERS, THE 1927 d: Fred Newmeyer. USA., *The Potters*, Joseph Patrick McEvoy, Chicago 1923, Novel

POTTING SHED, THE 1981 d: David Cunliffe. UKN., *The Potting Shed*, Graham Greene, 1957, Play

POUCETTE OU LE PLUS JEUNE DETECTIVE DU MONDE 1919 d: Adrien Caillard. FRN., *Poucette; Ou le Plus Jeune Detective du Monde*, Alfred Machard, Novel

Pouche see THIS IS THE NIGHT (1932).

POULE, LA 1932 d: Rene Guissart. FRN., *La Poule*, Henri Duvernois, Novel

POULE SUR UN MUR, UNE 1936 d: Maurice Gleize. FRN., *Une Poule Sur un Mur*, Leopold Marchand, Play

POULET AU VINAIGRE 1984 d: Claude Chabrol. FRN., *Une Mort En Trop*, Dominique Roulet, Novel

POUND 1970 d: Robert Downey. USA., *The Comeuppance*, Robert Downey, Play

POUPEE, LA 1920 d: Meyrick Milton. UKN., *La Poupee*, Edmond Audran, Arthur Sturgess, London 1897, Opera

POUPEE, LA 1962 d: Jacques Baratier. FRN/ITL., *La Poupee*, Jacques Audiberti, Paris 1958, Novel

POUPONNIERE, LA 1932 d: Jean Boyer. FRN., *La Pouponniere*, Charles Pothier, Rene Pujol, Opera

Pour Avoir Adrienne see VOUS SEREZ MA FEMME (1932).

POUR DON CARLOS 1921 d: Musidora, Jacques Lasseyne. FRN., *Pour Don Carlos*, Pierre Benoit, Novel

POUR LA COURONNE 1912 d: Henri Pouctal. FRN., *Pour la Couronne*, Francois Coppee, Play

POUR LA PEAU D'UN FLIC 1981 d: Alain Delon. FRN., *Pour la Peau d'un Flic*, Jean-Patrick Manchette, Novel

POUR MAMAN 1910 d: Emile Chautard. FRN., *Pour Maman*, Rene Marquis, Short Story

Pour Service de Nuit see SERVICE DE NUIT (1931).

POUR TOUTE LA VIE 1924 d: Benito Perojo. FRN/SPN., *Pour Toute la Vie*, Jacinto Benavente y Martinez, Novel

Pour un Si Doux Regard see **LA SECONDE VERITE** (1965).

POUR UN SOURIRE 1969 d: Francois Dupont-Midy. FRN., *Saute Barbara*, Anna Langfus, Novel

Pour une Etoile Sans Nom see **L'ETOILE SANS NOM MONA** (1966).

POUR UNE NUIT D'AMOUR 1921 d: Yakov Protazanov. FRN., *Pour une Nuit d'Amour*, Emile Zola, 1882, Short Story

POUR UNE NUIT D'AMOUR 1946 d: Edmond T. Greville. FRN., *Pour une Nuit d'Amour*, Emile Zola, 1882, Short Story

POUR VIVRE HEUREUX 1932 d: Claudio de La Torre. FRN., *Un Homme Heureux*, Yves Mirande, Andre Rivoire, Play

Poursuite, La see **UN ROI SANS DIVERTISSEMENT** (1962).

POURVU QU'ON AIT L'IVRESSE 1974 d: Rinaldo Bassi. FRN/ITL., *Gamiani*, Alfred de Musset, Novel

POUSSIERE SUR LA VILLE 1965 d: Arthur Lamothe. CND., *Poussiere Sur la Ville*, Andre Langevin, Novel

POUSSIERES DE VIE 1996 d: Rachid Bouchareb. ALG., *La Coline de Fanta*, Duyen Ahn, Novel

POVERE BIMBE! 1923 d: Gero Zambuto. ITL., *Les Deux Orphelines*, Eugene Cormon, Adolphe-P. d'Ennery, 1874, Novel

Povero Fornaretto Di Venezia, Il see **IL FORNARETTO DI VENEZIA** (1923).

POVERO PIERO, IL 1921 d: Umberto Mozzato. ITL., *Il Povero Piero*, Felice Cavallotti, 1884, Play

Poverty and Nobility see **MISERIA E NOBILTA** (1954).

POVERTY OF RICHES, THE 1921 d: Reginald Barker. USA., *The Mother*, Leroy Scott, 1914, Short Story

POVEST NEPOGASHENOI LUNY 1991 d: Yevgeny Tsymbal. RSS., *Povest Nepogashenoi Luny*, Boris Pilnyak, 1926, Short Story

POVESTE SENTIMENTALA 1961 d: Iulian Mihu. RMN., *Febre*, Horia Lovinescu, 1963, Play

POVESTEA DRAGOSTEI 1976 d: Ion Popescu-Gopo. RMN., *Povestea Porcului*, Ion Creanga, 1876, Short Story

POWDER RIVER 1953 d: Louis King. USA., *Wyatt Earp - Frontier Marshal*, Stuart N. Lake, New York 1931, Book

POWDER TOWN 1942 d: Rowland V. Lee. USA., *Powder Town*, Max Brand, Novel

POWDERSMOKE RANGE 1935 d: Wallace Fox. USA., *Powdersmoke Range*, William Colt MacDonald, New York 1934, Novel

Power see **JEW SUSS** (1934).

POWER AND THE GLORY, THE 1918 d: Lawrence C. Windom. USA., *The Power and the Glory*, Mrs. Grace MacGowan, New York 1910, Novel

POWER AND THE GLORY, THE 1961 d: Marc Daniels. USA., *The Power and the Glory*, Graham Greene, 1940, Novel

POWER AND THE PRIZE, THE 1956 d: Henry Koster. USA., *The Power and the Prize*, Harold Swiggett, 1954, Novel

POWER OF A LIE, THE 1922 d: George Archainbaud. USA., *The Power of a Lie*, Johan Bojer, London 1908, Novel

POWER OF LIFE, THE 1938 d: Henry Lynn. USA., *The Power of Life*, Isidore Zolotarefsky, Play

POWER OF ONE, THE 1992 d: John G. Avildsen. USA., *The Power of One*, Bryce Courtenay, Novel

POWER PLAY 1978 d: Martyn Burke. CND/UKN., *Coup d'Etat*, Edward N. Luttwak, Novel

POWER PLAY 1992 d: Alastair Reid. USA., *Mobbed Up*, James Neff, Book

POWER, THE 1967 d: Byron Haskin. USA., *The Power*, Frank M. Robinson, Philadelphia 1956, Novel

Power to Burn see **ROMANCE OF THE REDWOODS** (1939).

POWERS GIRL, THE 1942 d: Norman Z. McLeod. USA., *John Robert Powers*, John R. Powers, Book

Powers of Evil see **HISTOIRES EXTRAORDINAIRES** (1968).

Powers That Pray see **BLACKIE'S REDEMPTION** (1919).

Powiatowa Lady Makbet see **SIBIRSKA LEDI MAGBET** (1962).

POWWOW HIGHWAY 1988 d: Jonathan Wacks. UKN/USA., *Powwow Highway*, David Seals, Novel

Poyezdka V Visbaden see **POEZDKA V VISBADEN** (1989).

POZDNI LASKA 1935 d: Vaclav Kubasek. CZC., *Pozdni Laska*, Karel Klostermann, Novel

POZEGNANIA 1958 d: Wojciech J. Has. PLN., *Pozegnania*, Stanislaw Dygat, Warsaw 1948, Novel

POZOR, VIZITA! 1981 d: Karel KachynA. CZC., *Vizita*, Adolf Branald, Novel

POZZO DEI MIRACOLI, IL 1941 d: Gennaro Righelli. ITL., *Il Pozzo Dei Miracoli*, Giuseppe Achille, Bruno Corra, Play

Pozzo Delle Tre Verita, Il see **LE PUITS AUX TROIS VERITES** (1961).

PRACTICAL MAGIC 1998 d: Griffin Dunne. USA., *Practical Magic*, Alice Hoffman, Novel

Practice of a Crime see **ENSAYO DE UN CRIMEN** (1955).

PRAESTEN I VEJLBY 1920 d: August Blom. DNM., *Praesten I Veljby*, Steen Steensen Blicher, 1829, Novel

PRAESTEN I VEJLBY 1931 d: George Schneevoigt. DNM., *Praesten I Vejlby*, Steen Steensen Blicher, 1829, Novel

PRAESTEN I VEJLBY 1972 d: Claus Orsted. DNM., *Praesten I Vejlby*, Steen Steensen Blicher, 1829, Novel

Prague Boozer, The see **PRAZSKY FLAMENDR** (1926).

Prague Boozer, The see **PRAZSKY FLAMENDR** (1941).

Prague Executioner, The see **PRAZSKY KAT** (1927).

Prague Gallivanter, The see **PRAZSKY FLAMENDR** (1941).

Prague Seamstresses see **PRAZSKE SVADLENKY** (1929).

Prague War Secrecy see **VALECNE TAJNOSTI PRAZSKE** (1926).

PRAIRIE, LA 1968 d: Pierre Gaspard-Huit, Sergiu Nicolaescu. FRN/RMN., *The Prairie*, James Fenimore Cooper, 1827, Novel

PRAIRIE PIRATE, THE 1925 d: Edmund Mortimer. USA., *The Yellow Seal*, W. C. Tuttle, 1925, Short Story

PRAIRIE SCHOONERS 1940 d: Sam Nelson. USA., *Into the Crimson West*, George Cory Franklin, 1930, Short Story

PRAIRIE, THE 1947 d: Frank Wisbar. USA., *The Prairie*, James Fenimore Cooper, 1827, Novel

Prairie, The see **LA PRAIRIE** (1968).

PRAISE 1998 d: John Curran. ASL., *Praise*, Andrew McGahan, Novel

PRAPANCHA PASH 1929 d: Franz Osten. IND/GRM., *Prapancha Pash*, Niranjan Pal, Short Story

PRASHNAI GULSARA 1969 d: Sergei Urusevsky. USS., *Gul'sary Proshchay*, Chingiz Aitmatov, 1966, Short Story

PRASIDENT, DER 1928 d: Gennaro Righelli. GRM., *Der Prasident von Costa Nuova*, Ludwig von Wohl, Novel

Praterherzen see **HEREINSPAZIERT!** (1953).

PRATIBHA 1937 d: Baburao Painter. IND., *Hridayachi Shrimanti*, Narayan Hari Apte, Novel

PRATIDWANDI 1970 d: Satyajit Ray. IND., *Pratidwandi*, Sunil Ganguly, Novel

PRAVDA KHOROSHO, A SCHASTE LUCHSHE 1951 d: Sergei Alexeyev. USS., *A Schaste Luchshe Pravda Khorosho*, Alexander Ostrovsky, 1877, Play

PRAVO NA HRICH 1932 d: Vladimir Slavinsky. CZC., *Pravo Na Hrich*, Vilem Werner, Play

PRAWDZIWY KONIEC WIELKIEJ WOJNY 1957 d: Jerzy Kawalerowicz. PLN., *Prawdziwy Koniec Wielkiej Wojny*, Jerzy Zawiejski, Novel

PRAYER FOR THE DYING, A 1987 d: Mike Hodges. UKN., *A Prayer for the Dying*, Jack Higgins, Novel

Prazdnik Sviatogo Yorgena see **PRAZDNIK SVYATOVO IORGENE** (1930).

PRAZDNIK SVYATOVO IORGENE 1930 d: Yakov Protazanov. USS., G. Bergstaedt, Novel

PRAZSKE SVADLENKY 1929 d: Premysl Prazsky. CZC., *Prazske Svadlenky*, Otto Faster, Play

PRAZSKY FLAMENDR 1926 d: Premysl Prazsky. CZC., *Prazsky Flamendr*, Josef Kajetan Tyl, Play

PRAZSKY FLAMENDR 1941 d: Karel SpelinA. CZC., *Prazsky Flamendr*, Josef Kajetan Tyl, Play

PRAZSKY KAT 1927 d: Rudolf Mestak. CZC., *Prazsky Kat*, Josef Svatek, Novel

PRECIEUSES RIDICULES, LES 1934 d: Leonce Perret. FRN., *Less Precieuses Ridicules*, Moliere, 1660, Play

Precinct 45 - Los Angeles Police see **THE NEW CENTURIONS** (1972).

PRECIO DE UN HOMBRE, EL 1966 d: Eugenio Martin. SPN/ITL., *The Bounty Killer*, Marvin H. Albert, Greenwich, Ct. 1958, Novel

Precious see **BACHELOR'S AFFAIRS** (1932).

PRECIOUS BANE 1988 d: Christopher Menaul. UKN/USA., *Precious Bane*, Mary Webb, 1924, Novel

PRECIOUS PACKET, THE 1916 d: Donald MacKenzie. USA., Frederick Jackson, Novel

PREDILETO, O 1975 d: Roberto Palmari. BRZ., *Totonia Pacheco*, Joao Alphonsus, 1935, Novel

Predoni Del Deserto, I see **I CAVALIERI DEL DESERTO** (1942).

Predoni Del Sahara, I see **I CAVALIERI DEL DESERTO** (1942).

PREDONI DEL SAHARA, I 1966 d: Guido MalatestA. ITL., *I Predoni Del Sahara*, Emilio Salgari, Novel

PREDTUCHA 1944 d: Miroslav Cikan. CZC., *Predtucha*, Marie Pujmanova, Novel

PREDTUCHA 1947 d: Otakar VavrA. CZC., *Predtucha*, Marie Pujmanova, Novel

PREFETTO DI FERRO, IL 1977 d: Pasquale Squitieri. ITL., *Il Prefetto Di Ferro*, Arrigo Petacco, Novel

Prehistoric Valley see **VALLEY OF THE DRAGONS** (1961).

PREJUDICE OF PIERRE MARIE 1911 d: Larry Trimble. USA., *Prejudice of Pierre Marie*, James Oliver Curwood, Story

Preliminary Investigation see **VORUNTERSUCHUNG** (1931).

PRELUDE 1927 d: Castleton Knight. UKN., *The Premature Burial*, Edgar Allan Poe, 1844, Short Story

Prelude to Apocalypse see **LE TOUBIB** (1979).

Prelude to Ecstasy see **KUU ON VAARALLINEN** (1961).

PRELUDE TO FAME 1950 d: Fergus McDonnell. UKN., *Young Archimedes*, Aldous Huxley, 1924, Novel

Premature Burial, The see **THE CRIME OF DR. CRESPI** (1935).

Premature Burial, The see **THRILLER: THE PREMATURE BURIAL** (1960-61).

PREMATURE BURIAL, THE 1962 d: Roger Corman. USA., *The Premature Burial*, Edgar Allan Poe, 1844, Short Story

PREMATURE COMPROMISE, THE 1914 d: Charles J. Brabin. USA., *The Premature Compromise*, Robert Barr, Short Story

Premeditated see **PREMEDITATION** (1959).

PREMEDITATION 1959 d: Andre Berthomieu. FRN., *Toi Qui Vivais*, Frederic Dard, Novel

PREMIER DE CORDEE 1943 d: Louis Daquin. FRN., *Premier de Cordee*, Roger Frison-Roche, Novel

PREMIERA 1976 d: Mihai Constantinescu. RMN., *Travesti*, Aurel Baranga, 1971, Play

Premiere see **PREMIERA** (1976).

PREMIERE DER BUTTERFLY 1939 d: Carmine Gallone. GRM., *Madame Chrysantheme*, Pierre Loti, 1888, Novel

PREMIERES ARMES DE ROCAMBOLE, LES 1924 d: Charles Maudru. FRN., *Les Premieres Armes de Rocambole*, Ponson Du Terrail, Novel

Premonition see **PREDTUCHA** (1944).

Premonition see **PREDTUCHA** (1947).

PRENEZ GARDE A LA PEINTURE 1932 d: Henri Chomette. FRN., *Prenez Garde a la Peinture*, Rene Fauchois, 1932, Play

Preria see **LA PRAIRIE** (1968).

Presbyterian Church Wager, The see **MCCABE AND MRS. MILLER** (1971).

PRESCOTT KID, THE 1934 d: David Selman. USA., *Wolves of Catclaw*, Claude Rister, 1933, Short Story

PRESCRIPTION: MURDER 1967 d: Richard Irving. USA., *Prescription: Murder*, Richard Levinson, William Link, Play

Present Arms see **LEATHERNECKING** (1930).

Presentiment see **PREDTUCHA** (1947).

PRESENTING LILY MARS 1943 d: Norman Taurog. USA., *Presenting Lily Mars*, Booth Tarkington, 1933, Novel

PRESIDENT HAUDECOEUR, LE 1939 d: Jean Dreville. FRN., *Le President Haudecoeur*, Roger Ferdinand, Play

PRESIDENT, LE 1960 d: Henri Verneuil. FRN/ITL., *Le President*, Georges Simenon, 1958, Novel

PRESIDENT PANCHATCHARAM 1959 d: A. Bhimsingh. IND., *The Government Inspector*, Nikolay Gogol, 1836, Play

President, The *see* SURRENDER (1927).

President, The *see* DER PRASIDENT (1928).

President, The *see* LE PRESIDENT (1960).

PRESIDENT VANISHES, THE 1934 d: William A. Wellman. USA., *The President Vanishes*, Rex Stout, New York 1934, Novel

Presidente, Il *see* LE PRESIDENT (1960).

PRESIDENTE, LA 1938 d: Fernand Rivers. FRN., *La Presidente*, Maurice Hennequin, Pierre Veber, Play

PRESIDENTESSA, LA 1952 d: Pietro Germi. ITL., *La Presidentessa*, Maurice Hennequin, Pierre Veber, Play

PRESIDENTESSA, LA 1976 d: Luciano Salce. ITL., *La Presidentessa*, Maurice Hennequin, Pierre Veber, Play

PRESIDENT'S CHILD, THE 1992 d: Sam Pillsbury. USA., Fay Weldon, Novel

PRESIDENT'S LADY, THE 1953 d: Henry Levin. USA., *The President's Lady*, Irving Stone, 1951, Novel

PRESIDENT'S MISTRESS, THE 1978 d: John Llewellyn Moxey. USA., *The President's Mistress*, Patrick Anderson, Novel

PRESIDENT'S MYSTERY, THE 1936 d: Phil Rosen. USA., *The President's Mystery Sotyr*, Rupert Hughes, S. S. & Others Van Dine, 1935, Novel

PRESIDENT'S PLANE IS MISSING, THE 1971 d: Daryl Duke. USA., *The President's Plane Is Missing*, Robert J. Serling, Novel

President's Wife, The *see* ASSASSINATION (1987).

PRESS FOR TIME 1966 d: Robert Asher. UKN., *Yea Yea Yea*, Angus McGill, Novel

Pressure *see* LACHATZ (1984).

PRESSURE POINT 1962 d: Hubert Cornfield. USA., *Destiny's Tot*, Robert Mitchell Lindner, New York 1955, Short Story

PRESTIGE 1932 d: Tay Garnett. USA., *Lips of Steel*, Harry Hervey, Novel

PRESTUPLENIE I NAKAZANIE 1970 d: Lev Kulidjanov. USS., *Prestupleniye I Nakazaniye*, Fyodor Dostoyevsky, 1867, Novel

PRESUMED INNOCENT 1990 d: Alan J. PakulA. USA., *Presumed Innocent*, Scott Turow, 1990, Novel

PRESUMPTION OF STANLEY HAY, M.P., THE 1925 d: Sinclair Hill. UKN., *The Presumption of Stanley Hay M.P.*, Nowell Kaye, Novel

PRETE-MOI TA FEMME 1914 d: Jacques Roullet. FRN., *Prete-Moi Ta Femme*, Maurice Desvallieres, Play

PRETE-MOI TA FEMME 1936 d: Maurice Cammage. FRN., *Prete-Moi Ta Femme*, Maurice Desvallieres, Play

PRETE-MOI TON HABIT 1917 d: Georges MoncA. FRN., *Prete-Moi Ton Habit*, Mme d'Herbeville, Play

Pretty As Sin *see* CAROLINE CHERIE (1967).

PRETTY BABY 1950 d: Bretaigne Windust. USA., *Gay Deception*, Jules Furthman, John D. Klorer, Story

Pretty But Wicked *see* MAS ORDINARIA BONITINHA (1963).

PRETTY LADIES 1925 d: Monta Bell. USA., *Pretty Ladies*, Adela Rogers St. Johns, Short Story

PRETTY MAIDS ALL IN A ROW 1971 d: Roger Vadim. USA., *Pretty Maids All in a Row*, Francis Pollini, Novel

PRETTY MRS. SMITH 1915 d: Hobart Bosworth. USA., *Pretty Mrs. Smith*, Elmer Harris, Oliver Morosco, New York 1914, Play

PRETTY POISON 1968 d: Noel Black. USA., *She Let Him Continue*, Stephen Geller, New York 1966, Novel

PRETTY POLLY 1966 d: Bill Bain. UKN., *Pretty Polly Barlow*, Noel Coward, London 1964, Short Story

PRETTY POLLY 1967 d: Guy Green. UKN., *Pretty Polly Barlow*, Noel Coward, London 1964, Short Story

PRETTY SISTER OF JOSE, THE 1915 d: Allan Dwan. USA., *The Pretty Sister of Jose*, Frances Hodgson Burnett, New York 1889, Novel

PREY OF THE DRAGON, THE 1921 d: F. Martin Thornton. UKN., *The Prey of the Dragon*, Ethel M. Dell, Novel

Prey of the Wind, The *see* LA PROIE DU VENT (1926).

Prey, The *see* DE PROOI (1984).

PRIBEH JEDNOHO DNE 1926 d: M. J. Krnansky. CZC., *Pribeh Jednoho Dne*, Ignat Herrmann, Novel

PRICE HE PAID, THE 1914 d: Lawrence McGill. USA., *The Price He Paid*, Ella Wheeler Wilcox, Poem

Price of a Man, The *see* EL PRECIO DE UN HOMBRE (1966).

PRICE OF A PARTY, THE 1924 d: Charles Giblyn. USA., *The Price of a Party*, William Briggs MacHarg, Short Story

PRICE OF A SOUL, THE 1909 d: Edwin S. Porter. USA., *Les Miserables*, Victor Hugo, Paris 1862, Novel

PRICE OF APPLAUSE, THE 1918 d: Thomas N. Heffron. USA., *The Price of Applause*, Norman Jacobsen, Nina Wilcox Putnam, Short Story

Price of Doubt, The *see* THREE GREEN EYES (1919).

PRICE OF FOLLY, THE 1937 d: Walter Summers. UKN., *Double Error*, J. Lee Thompson, 1935, Play

PRICE OF HUMAN LIVES, THE 1913 d: Charles H. France. USA., *The Red Cross Seal Story*, E. W. Sargent, Story

Price of Justice, The *see* BEAUTIFUL JIM (1914).

Price of Justice, The *see* KOJAK: THE PRICE OF JUSTICE (1987).

Price of Love, The *see* I TIMI TIS AGAPIS (1984).

Price of Passion, The *see* THE GOOD MOTHER (1988).

PRICE OF REDEMPTION, THE 1920 d: Dallas M. Fitzgerald. USA., *The Temple of Dawn*, I. A. R. Wylie, London 1915, Novel

PRICE OF SILENCE, THE 1916 d: Joseph de Grasse. USA., W. Carey Wonderly, Short Story

Price of Silence, The *see* AT THE MERCY OF TIBERIUS (1920).

PRICE OF SILENCE, THE 1921 d: Fred Leroy Granville. USA., *At the Mercy of Tiberius*, Augusta Jane Evans Wilson, New York 1887, Novel

PRICE OF SILENCE, THE 1960 d: Montgomery Tully. UKN., *One Step from Murder*, Laurence Meynell, Novel

PRICE OF THINGS, THE 1930 d: Elinor Glyn. UKN., *The Price of Things*, Elinor Glyn, Novel

PRICE OF WISDOM, THE 1935 d: Reginald Denham. UKN., *The Price of Wisdom*, Lionel Brown, 1932, Play

PRICE SHE PAID, THE 1917 d: Charles Giblyn. USA., *The Price She Paid*, David Graham Phillips, New York 1912, Novel

PRICE SHE PAID, THE 1924 d: Henry McRae. USA., *The Price She Paid*, David Graham Phillips, New York 1912, Novel

PRICE, THE 1915 d: Joseph A. Golden. USA., *The Price*, George Broadhurst, New York 1911, Play

PRICK UP YOUR EARS 1987 d: Stephen Frears. UKN., *Prick Up Your Ears*, John Lahr, Biography

Pride *see* ORGOLII (1981).

PRIDE AND PREJUDICE 1940 d: Robert Z. Leonard. USA., *Pride and Prejudice*, Jane Austen, London 1813, Novel

PRIDE AND PREJUDICE 1980 d: Cyril Coke. UKN/ASL., *Pride and Prejudice*, Jane Austen, London 1813, Novel

Pride and Prejudice *see* JANE AUSTEN'S PRIDE AND PREJUDICE (1995).

PRIDE AND THE PASSION, THE 1957 d: Stanley Kramer. USA., *The Gun*, C. S. Forester, 1933, Novel

Pride and Vengeance *see* L'ORGOGLIO, LA VENDETTA, L' UOMO (1967).

Pride, Love and Suspicion *see* LA FIAMMATA (1952).

PRIDE OF JENNICO, THE 1914 d: J. Searle Dawley. USA., *The Pride of Jennico*, Grace Livingston Furniss, Abby Richardson, New York 1900, Play

PRIDE OF PALOMAR, THE 1922 d: Frank Borzage. USA., *The Pride of Palomar*, Peter B. Kyne, New York 1921, Novel

PRIDE OF THE FANCY, THE 1920 d: Albert Ward. UKN., *The Pride of the Fancy*, George Edgar, Novel

PRIDE OF THE LEGION, THE 1932 d: Ford Beebe. USA., *A Film Star's Holiday*, Peter B. Kyne, Short Story

PRIDE OF THE MARINES 1936 d: D. Ross Lederman. USA., *Pride of the Marines*, Gerald Beaumont, 1921, Story

PRIDE OF THE MARINES 1945 d: Delmer Daves. USA., Roger Butterfield, Story

Pride of the Paddock, The *see* THE MILLION DOLLAR HANDICAP (1925).

Pride of the Triple X *see* THE HAWK (1935).

PRIDE OF THE YANKEES, THE 1942 d: Sam Wood. USA., Paul Gallico, Story

Priest and the Girl, The *see* O PADRE E A MOCA (1966).

PRIEST AND THE MAN, THE 1913 d: J. Searle Dawley. USA., *The Going of the White Swan*, Gilbert Parker, Story

Priest Nichiren, The *see* NICHIREN (1978).

PRIEST OF LOVE 1980 d: Christopher Miles. UKN., *The Priest of Love*, Harry T. Moore, Book

Priest's End, The *see* FARARUV KONEC (1968).

PRIGIONE, LA 1942 d: Ferruccio Cerio. ITL., *La Prigione*, Mario Puccini, Novel

Prigioniera Dell'isola, La *see* LA DANSE DE MORT (1946).

PRIGIONIERI DEL MALE 1956 d: Mario CostA. ITL/SPN., *Sancta Maria*, Guido Milanesi, Novel

PRIGIONIERI DELLE TENEBRE 1953 d: Enrico BombA. ITL., *La Cieca Di Sorrento*, Francesco Mastriani, 1826, Novel

PRIGIONIERO DEL CAUCASO, IL 1911 d: Giovanni Vitrotti. ITL/USS., *Kavkazskij Plennik*, Alexander Pushkin, 1821, Poem

PRIGIONIERO DEL RE, IL 1954 d: Giorgio Rivalta, Richard Pottier. ITL., *Le Vicomte de Bragelonne*, Alexandre Dumas (pere), Paris 1847, Novel

PRIKLADY TAHNOU 1939 d: Miroslav Cikan. CZC., *Priklady Tahnou*, Jan Snizek, Play

PRIKLJUCENIJA BURATINO 1959 d: Ivan Ivanov-Vano. USS., *Zolotoy Klyuchik; Ili Priklyuchenya Buratino*, Alexsey Nikolayevich Tolstoy, 1936, Play

Prikloeutstsjenija Boeratino *see* PRIKLJUCENIJA BURATINO (1959).

PRIMA DELLA RIVOLUZIONE 1964 d: Bernardo Bertolucci. ITL., *La Chartreuse de Parme*, Stendhal, 1839, Novel

Prima Notte Del Dottere Danieli, La *see* INDUSTRIALE COL COMPLESSO DEL GIOCATTOLO PRIMA NOTTE DEL DR. DANIELI (1970).

PRIMA NOTTE DEL DR. DANIELI, INDUSTRIALE COL COMPLESSO DEL GIOCATTOLO 1970 d: Gianni Grimaldi. ITL/FRN., *Aragoste Di Sicilia*, Bruno Corbucci, Gianni Grimaldi, Play

PRIMA NOTTE, LA 1959 d: Alberto Cavalcanti. ITL/FRN., *Les Noces Venitiennes*, Abel Hermant, Novel

PRIMADONNA, LA 1943 d: Ivo Perilli. ITL., *La Primadonna*, Filippo Sacchi, Novel

Primal Law, The *see* THE PRIMAL LURE (1916).

PRIMAL LURE, THE 1916 d: William S. Hart. USA., *The Primal Lure; a Romance of Fort Lu Cerne*, Vingie E. Roe, New York 1914, Novel

PRIMANERINNEN 1951 d: Rolf Thiele. GRM., *Ursula*, Klaus Erich Boerner, Short Story

PRIMARY COLORS 1998 d: Mike Nichols. USA., *Primary Colors*, Joe Klein, Novel

Primavera a Pianabianco *see* ROSALBA (1945).

PRIMAVERA EN OTONO 1932 d: Eugene J. Forde. USA., *Primavera En Otono*, Gregorio Martinez Sierra, Madrid 1911, Play

PRIME OF MISS JEAN BRODIE, THE 1969 d: Ronald Neame. UKN., *The Prime of Miss Jean Brodie*, Muriel Spark, London 1961, Novel

Primel Drives the Family Crazy *see* PRIMEL MACHT IHR HAUS VERRUCKT (1979).

PRIMEL MACHT IHR HAUS VERRUCKT 1979 d: Monica Teuber. GRM., *Primel macht Ihr Haus Verruckt*, Kathe Jaenicke, Novel

PRIMER AMOR 1942 d: Claudio de La Torre. SPN., *Pervaya Lyubov*, Ivan Turgenev, 1860, Short Story

PRIMEROSE 1919 d: Mario Caserini. ITL., *Primerose*, Gaston Arman de Caillavet, Robert de Flers, 1911, Play

PRIMEROSE 1933 d: Rene Guissart. FRN., *Primerose*, Gaston Arman de Caillavet, Robert de Flers, 1911, Play

PRIMITIVE LOVER, THE 1922 d: Sidney A. Franklin. USA., *The Divorcee*, Edgar Selwyn, Play

PRIMO BASILIO, O 1959 d: Antonio Lopes Ribeiro. PRT., *O Primo Basilio*, Jose Maria de Eca de Queiros, 1878, Novel

PRIMROSE PATH 1940 d: Gregory La CavA. USA., *February Hill*, Victoria Lincoln, New York 1934, Novel

PRIMROSE PATH, THE 1915 d: Theodore Marston, Lawrence Marston. USA., *The Primrose Path*, Bayard Veiller, New York 1907, Play

Primrose Path, The *see* BURNT WINGS (1920).

PRIMROSE PATH, THE 1925 d: Harry O. Hoyt. USA., *The Primrose Path*, E. Lanning Masters, Story

PRIMROSE PATH, THE 1934 d: Reginald Denham. UKN., *The Primrose Path*, Joan Temple, Story

PRIMROSE RING, THE 1917 d: Robert Z. Leonard. USA., *The Primrose Ring*, Ruth Sawyer, New York 1915, Novel

PRIN CENUSA IMPERIULUI 1975 d: Andrei Blaier. RMN., *Jocul Cu Moartea*, Zaharia Stancu, 1962, Novel

PRINC BAJAJA 1950 d: Jiri TrnkA. CZC., *Princ Bajaja*, Bozena Nemcova, Short Story

PRINC BAJAJA 1971 d: Antonin Kachlik. CZC., *Princ Bajaja*, Bozena Nemcova, Short Story

Princ Z Ulice *see* EVAS TOCHTER (1928).

PRINCE AND BETTY, THE 1919 d: Robert T. Thornby. USA., *The Prince and Betty*, P. G. Wodehouse, New York 1912, Novel

PRINCE AND THE BEGGAR MAID, THE 1921 d: A. V. Bramble. UKN., *The Prince and the Beggarmaid*, Walter Howard, London 1908, Play

PRINCE AND THE PAUPER, THE 1909 d: J. Searle Dawley. USA., *The Prince and the Pauper*, Mark Twain, New York 1881, Novel

PRINCE AND THE PAUPER, THE 1915 d: Edwin S. Porter, Hugh Ford. USA., *The Prince and the Pauper*, Mark Twain, New York 1881, Novel

Prince and the Pauper, The *see* DAS BETTLEKIND SEINE MAJESTAT (1920).

Prince and the Pauper, The *see* YISKOR (1932).

PRINCE AND THE PAUPER, THE 1937 d: William Keighley. USA., *The Prince and the Pauper*, Mark Twain, New York 1881, Novel

PRINCE AND THE PAUPER, THE 1962 d: Don Chaffey. UKN., *The Prince and the Pauper*, Mark Twain, New York 1881, Novel

PRINCE AND THE PAUPER, THE 1969 d: Elliot Geisinger. USA., *The Prince and the Pauper*, Mark Twain, New York 1881, Novel

PRINCE AND THE PAUPER, THE 1971. ASL., *The Prince and the Pauper*, Mark Twain, New York 1881, Novel

PRINCE AND THE PAUPER, THE 1978 d: Richard Fleischer. UKN/PNM., *The Prince and the Pauper*, Mark Twain, New York 1881, Novel

PRINCE AND THE SHOWGIRL, THE 1957 d: Laurence Olivier, Anthony Bushell. UKN/USA., *The Sleeping Prince*, Terence Rattigan, London 1953, Play

Prince Bajaja *see* PRINC BAJAJA (1971).

Prince Bayaya *see* PRINC BAJAJA (1950).

Prince Chap *see* THE BELOVED BACHELOR (1931).

PRINCE CHAP, THE 1916 d: Marshall Neilan. USA., *The Prince Chap*, Edward Peple, New York 1905, Play

PRINCE CHAP, THE 1920 d: William C. de Mille. USA., *The Prince Chap*, Edward Peple, New York 1905, Play

PRINCE CHARMING 1912 d: James Kirkwood, George Loane Tucker. USA., *Contes Des Fees*, Marie Catherine Aulnoy, 1698, Short Stories

Prince Charming *see* CHASING YESTERDAY (1935).

Prince Dimitri *see* RESURRECTION (1927).

Prince from the Street *see* EVAS TOCHTER (1928).

Prince in Bondage, The *see* EL PRINCIPE ENCADENADO (1960).

Prince in Chains, The *see* EL PRINCIPE ENCADENADO (1960).

PRINCE JEAN, LE 1928 d: Rene Hervil. FRN., *Le Prince Jean*, Charles Mere, Play

PRINCE JEAN, LE 1934 d: Jean de Marguenat. FRN., *Le Prince Jean*, Charles Mere, Play

PRINCE OF A KING, A 1923 d: Albert Austin. USA., *John of the Woods*, Alice Farwell Brown, Story

PRINCE OF ARCADIA 1933 d: Hanns Schwarz. UKN., *Der Prinz von Arkadien*, Walter Reisch, Play

PRINCE OF BROADWAY, THE 1926 d: John Gorman. USA., John Gorman, Play

PRINCE OF CENTRAL PARK, THE 1977 d: Harvey Hart. USA., *The Prince of Central Park*, Evan H. Rhodes, Novel

Prince of Darkness *see* BELTENEBROS (1991).

PRINCE OF FOXES 1949 d: Henry King. USA., *Prince of Foxes*, Samuel Shellabarger, Novel

PRINCE OF GRAUSTARK, THE 1916 d: Fred E. Wright. USA., *The Prince of Graustark*, George Barr McCutcheon, New York 1914, Novel

PRINCE OF HEADWAITERS, THE 1927 d: John Francis Dillon. USA., *The Prince of Head Waiters*, Garrett Fort, Viola Brothers Shore, 1927, Short Story

PRINCE OF INDIA, A 1914 d: Leopold Wharton. USA., *The Prince of India*, Lew Wallace, New York 1893, Novel

Prince of Jutland *see* PRINSEN AF JYLLAND (1994).

PRINCE OF LOVERS, A 1922 d: Charles Calvert. UKN., *Byron*, Alicia Ramsey, Play

Prince of Pappenheim, The *see* DER FURST VON PAPPENHEIM (1927).

PRINCE OF PILSEN, THE 1926 d: Paul Powell. USA., *The Prince of Pilsen*, Gustav Luders, Frank Pixley, New York 1902, Musical Play

PRINCE OF PLAYERS 1955 d: Philip Dunne. USA., *Prince of Players*, Eleanor Ruggles, 1953, Book

Prince of Rogues, The *see* SCHINDERHANNES (1928).

Prince of Shadows *see* BELTENEBROS (1991).

PRINCE OF TEMPTERS, THE 1926 d: Lothar Mendes. USA., *The Ex-Duke*, E. Phillips Oppenheim, London 1927, Novel

PRINCE OF THE CITY 1981 d: Sidney Lumet. USA., *Prince of the City*, Robert Daley, Book

PRINCE OF THIEVES, THE 1948 d: Howard Bretherton. USA., *Credits*, Alexandre Dumas (pere), Story

PRINCE OF TIDES, THE 1991 d: Barbra Streisand. USA., *The Prince of Tides*, Pat Conroy, Novel

Prince Or Clown *see* FURST ODER CLOWN (1927).

Prince the the Ass's Ears, The *see* O PRINCIPE COM ORELHAS DE BURRO (1980).

PRINCE THERE WAS, A 1921 d: Tom Forman. USA., *Enchanted Hearts*, Darragh Aldrich, Garden City, N.Y. 1917, Novel

PRINCE WHO WAS A THIEF, THE 1951 d: Rudolph Mate. USA., *The Prince Who Was a Thief*, Theodore Dreiser, 1927, Short Story

Prince With a Donkey's Ear, The *see* O PRINCIPE COM ORELHAS DE BURRO (1980).

PRINCE ZILAH, LE 1926 d: Gaston Roudes. FRN., *Le Prince Zilah*, Jules Claretie, Paris 1885, Play

Princess and the Dancer, The *see* JUST A GIGOLO (1931).

Princess and the Goblin, The *see* A HERCEGNO ES A KOBOLD (1991).

PRINCESS AND THE PEA, THE 1979 d: Keith Goddard. UKN., *Prinsessen Pa Aerten*, Hans Christian Andersen, 1835, Short Story

PRINCESS AND THE PEA, THE 1983 d: Tony Bill. USA., *Prinsessen Pa Aerten*, Hans Christian Andersen, 1835, Short Story

PRINCESS AND THE PIRATE, THE 1944 d: David Butler. USA., Sy Bartlett, Story

PRINCESS AND THE PLUMBER, THE 1930 d: Alexander KordA. USA., *The Princess and the Plumber*, Alice Duer Miller, 1929, Short Story

Princess and the Swineherd, The *see* DIE PRINZESSIN UND DER SCHWEINEHIRT (1953).

PRINCESS BRIDE, THE 1987 d: Rob Reiner. USA., *The Princess Bride*, William Goldman, Novel

PRINCESS CHARMING 1934 d: Maurice Elvey. UKN., *Alexandra*, Franz Martos, Play

PRINCESS CLEMENTINA 1911 d: Will Barker. UKN., *The Princess Clementina*, A. E. W. Mason, Novel

PRINCESS COMES ACROSS 1936 d: William K. Howard. USA., *A Halalkabin*, Louis Lucien Rogger, Budapest 1934, Novel

PRINCESS DAISY 1983 d: Waris Hussein. USA., *Daisy*, Judith Krantz, Novel

Princess from the Poorhouse, The *see* THE ROYAL PAUPER (1917).

PRINCESS IN LOVE 1996 d: David Greene. UKN., *Princess in Love*, Anna Pasternak, Book

Princess Jasna and the Flying Cobbler *see* PRINCEZNE JASNENCE A LETAJICIM SEVCI (1987).

Princess Mary, The *see* KNJAZHNA MARY (1955).

PRINCESS OF HAPPY CHANCE, THE 1916 d: Maurice Elvey. UKN., *The Princess of Happy Chance*, Tom Gallon, Novel

PRINCESS OF NEW YORK, THE 1921 d: Donald Crisp. USA/UKN., *The Princess of New York*, Cosmo Hamilton, New York 1911, Novel

PRINCESS OF PATCHES, THE 1917 d: Alfred E. Green. USA., *The Princess of Patches*, Mark Swan, 1901, Play

Princess of St. Wolfgang, The *see* DIE PRINZESSIN VON ST. WOLFGANG (1957).

Princess of the Canary Islands *see* LA PRINCIPESSA DELLE CANARIE (1956).

PRINCESS O'HARA 1935 d: David Burton. USA., *Princess O'Hara*, Damon Runyon, 1934, Short Story

PRINCESS ON BROADWAY, THE 1927 d: Dallas M. Fitzgerald. USA., *Silver Lanterns*, Ethel Donoher, Story

Princess Priscilla's Fortnight *see* THE RUNAWAY PRINCESS (1929).

PRINCESS ROMANOFF 1915 d: Frank Powell. USA., *Fedora*, Victorien Sardou, Paris 1882, Play

Princess, The *see* PRINSESSAN (1966).

PRINCESS VIRTUE 1917 d: Robert Z. Leonard. USA., *Princess Virtue*, Louise Winter, Story

Princesse Alexandra *see* ALEXANDRA (1991).

PRINCESSE AUX CLOWNS, LA 1925 d: Andre Hugon. FRN., *La Princesse aux Clowns*, Jean-Jose Frappa, Novel

PRINCESSE CZARDAS 1934 d: Andre Beucler, Georg Jacoby. FRN., *Die Czardasfurstin*, B. Jenbach, Emmerich Kalman, Leo Stein, Vienna 1915, Operetta

PRINCESSE DE CLEVES, LA 1960 d: Jean Delannoy. FRN/ITL., *La Princesse de Cleves*, Marie-Madeleine la Fayette, 1678, Novel

PRINCESSE MANDANE 1927 d: Germaine Dulac. FRN., *L' Oublie*, Pierre Benoit, Short Story

Princesse Tzigane *see* DER ZIGEUNERBARON (1962).

PRINCESSEN SOM INGEN KUNNE MALBINDE 1932 d: Walter Fyrst. NRW., *Prinsessen Som Ingen Kunde Malbinde Felgesvenden*, Peder Christen Asbjornsen, 1910, Short Story

PRINCEZNE JASNENCE A LETAJICIM SEVCI 1987 d: Zdenek TroskA. CZC., Jan Drda, Short Story

PRINCEZNE JULINCE, O 1987 d: Antonin Kachlik. CZC., Josef Lada, Short Stories

PRINCIPE COM ORELHAS DE BURRO, O 1980 d: Antonio de Macedo. PRT., *O Principe Come Orelhas de Burro*, Jose Regio, 1942, Novel

PRINCIPE DI HOMBURG, IL 1997 d: Marco Bellocchio. ITL., *Prinz Friedrich von Homburg*, Heinrich von Kleist, 1811, Play

PRINCIPE ENCADENADO, EL 1960 d: Luis LuciA. SPN., *La Vida Es Sueno*, Pedro Calderon de La Barca, 1647, Play

PRINCIPE FUSTO, IL 1960 d: Maurizio ArenA. ITL., *Er Piu de Roma*, Marco Guglielmo, Lucio Mandara, Novel

PRINCIPE GONDOLERO, EL 1933 d: Edward D. Venturini. USA., *Honeymoon Hate*, Alice Muriel Williamson, 1927, Short Story

PRINCIPE IDIOTA, IL 1919 d: Eugenio Perego. ITL., *Idiot*, Fyodor Dostoyevsky, 1868, Novel

Principe Y la Aldeana, El *see* RESURRECCION (1931).

PRINCIPE ZILAH, IL 1919 d: Ugo de Simone. ITL., *Le Prince Zilah*, Jules Claretie, Paris 1885, Play

PRINCIPESSA DEL SOGNO, LA 1942 d: Roberto Savarese, Maria Teresa Ricci. ITL., Luciana Peverelli, Story

PRINCIPESSA DELLE CANARIE, LA 1956 d: Paolo Moffa, Carlos Serrano de OsmA. ITL/SPN., *Tyrma*, Juan Del Rio Ayala, Novel

PRINCIPESSA DI BAGDAD, LA 1918 d: Baldassarre Negroni. ITL., *La Princesse de Bagdad*, Alexandre Dumas (fils), 1881, Play

Principessa Di Cleves, La *see* LA PRINCESSE DE CLEVES (1960).

PRINCIPESSA GIORGIO, LA 1920 d: Roberto Leone Roberti. ITL., *La Principessa Georges*, Alexandre Dumas (fils), 1871, Novel

PRINCIPESSA, LA 1917 d: Camillo de Riso. ITL., *La Principessa*, Roberto Bracco

PRINCIPESSINA 1943 d: Tulio Gramantieri. ITL., *Sara Crewe*, Frances Hodgson Burnett, New York 1888, Novel

PRINSEN AF JYLLAND 1994 d: Gabriel Axel. DNM/FRN/UKN., Saxo Grammaticus, Book

PRINSESSA RUUSUNEN 1949 d: Edvin Laine. FNL., *Prinsessan Tornrosa*, Zachris Topelius, 1870, Play

PRINSESSAN 1966 d: Ake Falck. SWD., *Prinsessan*, Gunnar Mattsson, Stockholm 1960, Novel

Prinsessan Tornrosa see **PRINSESSA RUUSUNEN** (1949).

Printemps see **MANOUCHE - JEUNESSE D'AUJOURD'HUI** (1942).

PRINTRE COLINELE VERZI 1971 d: Nicolae Breban. RMN., *Animale Bolnave*, Nicolae Breban, 1968, Novel

PRINTUL FERICIT 1968 d: Aurel Miheles. RMN., *The Happy Prince*, Oscar Wilde, 1888, Short Story

PRINTZESSA NA GOROSHINE 1976 d: Boris Rytsarev. USS., *Prinsessen Pa Aerten*, Hans Christian Andersen, 1835, Short Story

Prinz Und Bettelknabe see **DAS BETTLEKIND SEINE MAJESTAT** (1920).

PRINZESSA NA GOROSCHINE 1976 d: Boris Ryazarev. USS., *Prinsessen Pa Aerten*, Hans Christian Andersen, 1835, Short Story

Prinzessin Dagmar see **MADCHENPENSIONAT** (1936).

PRINZESSIN OLALA 1928 d: Robert Land. GRM., *Prinzessin Olala*, Jean Gilbert, Opera

PRINZESSIN UND DER SCHWEINEHIRT, DIE 1953 d: Herbert B. Fredersdorf. GRM., *Svinedrengen*, Hans Christian Andersen, 1842, Short Story

PRINZESSIN VON ST. WOLFGANG, DIE 1957 d: Harald Reinl. GRM., *Die Prinzessin von St. Wolfgang*, Ernst Neubach, Short Story

PRIORY SCHOOL, THE 1921 d: Maurice Elvey. UKN., *The Priory School*, Arthur Conan Doyle, Short Story

Priory School, The see **THE RETURN OF SHERLOCK HOLMES: THE PRIORY SCHOOL** (1986).

Pripad Plukovnika Svarce see **VZDUSNE TORPEDO 48** (1936).

PRIPAD PRO ZACINAJICIHO KATA 1969 d: Pavel Juracek. CZC., *Gulliver's Travels*, Jonathan Swift, London 1726, Novel

Priscilla the Rake see **SHE WAS ONLY A VILLAGE MAIDEN** (1933).

PRISCILLAS FAHRT INS GLUCK 1928 d: Anthony Asquith. GRM., *Princess Priscilla's Fortnight*, Elizabeth Russell, Novel

PRISIONEROS DE LA TIERRA 1939 d: Mario Soffici. ARG., *Una Bofetada*, Horacio Quiroga, 1916, Short Story, *Los Destiladores de Naranja*, Horacio Quiroga, 1923, Short Story

PRISON BREAKER 1936 d: Adrian Brunel. UKN., Edgar Wallace, Novel

PRISON EN FOLIE, LA 1930 d: Henry Wulschleger. FRN., *Le Soleil a l'Ombre*, Georges Dolley, Novel

PRISON SANS BARREAUX 1937 d: Leonide Moguy. FRN., *Prison Sans Barreaux*, Thomas B. Forster, Play

Prison, The see **UN CONDE** (1970).

PRISON, THE 1975 d: David Wickes. UKN., Georges Simenon, Novel

Prison Without Bars see **PRISON SANS BARREAUX** (1937).

PRISON WITHOUT BARS 1938 d: Brian Desmond Hurst. UKN., *Prison Sans Barreaux*, Egon Eis, Otto Eis, Hilde Koveloff, Play

Prisoner of Corbal see **THE MARRIAGE OF CORBAL** (1936).

PRISONER OF SECOND AVENUE, THE 1975 d: Melvin Frank. USA., *The Prisoner of Second Avenue*, Neil Simon, 1972, Play

Prisoner of the Andamans, The see **ANDAMAN KAITHI** (1952).

Prisoner of the Caucaso, The see **IL PRIGIONIERO DEL CAUCASO** (1911).

Prisoner of the Caucasus, A see **IL PRIGIONIERO DEL CAUCASO** (1911).

Prisoner of the Iron Mask see **VENGEANCE DU MASQUE DE FER** (1962).

Prisoner of the Skull see **WHO?** (1974).

PRISONER OF ZENDA, THE 1913 d: Edwin S. Porter, Hugh Ford. USA., *The Prisoner of Zenda*, Anthony Hope, London 1894, Novel

PRISONER OF ZENDA, THE 1915 d: George Loane Tucker. UKN., *The Prisoner of Zenda*, Anthony Hope, London 1894, Novel

PRISONER OF ZENDA, THE 1922 d: Rex Ingram. USA., *The Prisoner of Zenda*, Anthony Hope, London 1894, Novel

PRISONER OF ZENDA, THE 1937 d: John Cromwell, W. S. Van Dyke (Uncredited). USA., *The Prisoner of Zenda*, Anthony Hope, London 1894, Novel

PRISONER OF ZENDA, THE 1952 d: Richard Thorpe. USA., *The Prisoner of Zenda*, Anthony Hope, London 1894, Novel

PRISONER OF ZENDA, THE 1979 d: Richard Quine. USA., *The Prisoner of Zenda*, Anthony Hope, London 1894, Novel

PRISONER, THE 1923 d: Jack Conway. USA., *Castle Craneycrow*, George Barr McCutcheon, Chicago 1902, Novel

Prisoner, The see **DER BAGNOSTRAFLING** (1949).

PRISONER, THE 1955 d: Peter Glenville. UKN., *The Prisoner*, Bridget Boland, London 1954, Play

PRISONER WITHOUT A NAME, CELL WITHOUT A NUMBER 1983 d: David Greene, Linda Yellen. USA., *Cell Without a Number Prisoner Without a Name*, Jacobo Timerman, 1981, Book

PRISONERS 1929 d: William A. Seiter. USA., *Prisoners*, Ferenc Molnar, Play

Prisoners of Altona, The see **I SEQUESTRATI DI ALTONA** (1962).

Prisoners of Earth see **PRISIONEROS DE LA TIERRA** (1939).

Prisoners of the Earth see **PRISIONEROS DE LA TIERRA** (1939).

PRISONERS OF THE STORM 1926 d: Lynn Reynolds. USA., *The Quest of Joan*, James Oliver Curwood, Short Story

PRISONNIER DE MON COEUR 1931 d: Jean Tarride. FRN., *Guignol*, Marcel Espiau, Paul Gordeaux, Play

PRISONS DE FEMMES 1938 d: Roger Richebe. FRN., *Prisons de Femmes*, Francis Carco, 1930, Novel

PRISONS DE FEMMES 1958 d: Maurice Cloche. FRN., *Prisons de Femmes*, Francis Carco, 1930, Novel

PRITHVI VALLABH 1924 d: Manilal Joshi. IND., *Prithvi Vallabh*, V. B. Joshi, Novel

PRITHVI VALLABH 1943 d: Sohrab Modi. IND., *Prithvi Vallabh*, K. M. Munshi, 1920, Novel

PRIVARZANIAT BALON 1967 d: Binka ZheljazkovA. BUL., *Privarzaniyat Balon*, Yordan Radichkov, 1965, Short Story

Privarzaniyat Balon see **PRIVARZANIAT BALON** (1967).

PRIVATE AFFAIRS 1925 d: Renaud Hoffman. USA., *The Ledger of Life*, George Patullo, 1922, Short Story

PRIVATE AFFAIRS 1940 d: Albert S. Rogell. USA., *One of the Boston Bullertons*, Walton Atwater Green, Short Story

PRIVATE AFFAIRS OF BEL AMI, THE 1947 d: Albert Lewin. USA., *Bel-Ami*, Guy de Maupassant, 1885, Novel

PRIVATE ANGELO 1949 d: Peter Ustinov, Michael Anderson. UKN., *Private Angelo*, Eric Linklater, 1946, Novel

Private Beach see **MUSIC IS MAGIC** (1935).

Private Conversation, A see **BEZ SVIDETELEI** (1983).

PRIVATE DETECTIVE 1939 d: Noel Smith. USA., *Invitation to Murder*, Kay Krausse, 1937, Short Story

Private Entrance see **EGEN INGANG** (1956).

Private Eye see **THE DAIN CURSE** (1978).

Private Gale, A see **SOUKROMA VICHRICE** (1967).

PRIVATE HISTORY OF A CAMPAIGN THAT FAILED, THE 1982 d: Peter H. Hunt. UKN/GRM., Mark Twain, Story

Private Hurricane see **SOUKROMA VICHRICE** (1967).

PRIVATE INFORMATION 1952 d: Fergus McDonnell. UKN., *Garden City*, Gordon Glennon, Play

Private Investigation, A see **MISSING PIECES** (1983).

PRIVATE LESSONS 1981 d: Alan Myerson. USA., *Philly*, Dan Greenberg, Novel

PRIVATE LIFE OF DON JUAN, THE 1934 d: Alexander KordA. UKN., *L' Homme a la Rose*, Henry Bataille, 1921, Play

PRIVATE LIFE OF HELEN OF TROY, THE 1927 d: Alexander KordA. USA., *The Private Life of Helen of Troy*, John Erskine, Indianapolis 1925, Novel

Private Life of the Gods see **NIGHT LIFE OF THE GODS** (1935).

PRIVATE LIVES 1931 d: Sidney A. Franklin. USA., *Private Lives*, Noel Coward, London 1930, Play

PRIVATE LIVES OF ELIZABETH AND ESSEX, THE 1939 d: Michael Curtiz. USA., *Elizabeth the Queen*, Maxwell Anderson, New York 1930, Play

PRIVATE NUMBER 1936 d: Roy Del Ruth. USA., *Common Clay*, Cleves Kinkead, Boston 1915, Play

PRIVATE PARTS 1997 d: Betty Thomas. USA., *Private Parts*, Howard Stern, Book

PRIVATE PEAT 1918 d: Edward Jose. USA., *Private Peat*, Harold Reginald Peat, Indianpolis 1917, Book

Private Pettigrew's Girl see **PETTIGREW'S GIRL** (1919).

PRIVATE POTTER 1962 d: Caspar Wrede. UKN., *Private Potter*, Ronald Harwood, 1961, Television Play

Private Practice of Michael Shayne, The see **PRIVATE DETECTIVE MICHAEL SHAYNE** (1940).

Private Secretary see **BEHIND OFFICE DOORS** (1931).

Private Secretary see **DIE PRIVATSEKRETARIN** (1953).

Private Secretary, The see **DIE PRIVATSEKRETARIN** (1931).

PRIVATE SECRETARY, THE 1935 d: Henry Edwards. UKN., *Der Bibliothekar*, Gustav von Moser, Play

Private Windstorm see **SOUKROMA VICHRICE** (1967).

PRIVATE WORLDS 1935 d: Gregory La CavA. USA., *Private Worlds*, Phyllis Bottome, Boston 1934, Novel

PRIVATE'S AFFAIR, A 1959 d: Raoul Walsh. USA., Ray Livingston Murphy, Story

PRIVATES ON PARADE 1983 d: Michael Blakemore. UKN., *Privates on Parade*, Peter Nichols, 1977, Play

PRIVATE'S PROGRESS 1956 d: John Boulting. UKN., *Private's Progress*, Alan Hackney, Novel

PRIVATSEKRETARIN, DIE 1931 d: Wilhelm Thiele. GRM., *Die Privatsekretarin*, Stefan Szomahazy, Novel

PRIVATSEKRETARIN, DIE 1953 d: Paul Martin. GRM., *Die Privatsekretarin*, Stefan Szomahazy, Novel

PRIX DU DANGER, LE 1983 d: Yves Boisset. FRN/YGS., *The Prize of Peril*, Robert Sheckley, Short Story

PRIZE OF GOLD, A 1955 d: Mark Robson. UKN., *A Prize of Gold*, Max Catto, Novel

Prize of Peril, The see **LE PRIX DU DANGER** (1983).

Prize, The see **LE ROSIER DE MADAME HUSSON** (1950).

PRIZE, THE 1963 d: Mark Robson. USA., *The Prize*, Irving Wallace, New York 1962, Novel

PRIZZI'S HONOR 1985 d: John Huston. USA., *Prizzi's Honor*, Richard Condon, 1982, Novel

PRO DOMO 1918 d: Theo Frenkel Sr. NTH., *Pro Domo*, Jonkheer A. W. G. Van Riemsdijk, 1914, Play

PRO KAMARADA 1940 d: Miroslav Cikan. CZC., *Pro Kamarada*, Ladislav Jilek, Radio Play

PROCES DE MARY DUGAN, LE 1931 d: Marcel de Sano. USA., *The Trial of Mary Dugan*, Bayard Veiller, New York 1927, Play

Proces Des Doges, Les see **IL FORNARETTO DI VENEZIA** (1963).

Proces, Le see **DER PROZESS** (1962).

PROCESO DE MARY DUGAN, EL 1931 d: Marcel de Sano. SPN., *The Trial of Mary Dugan*, Bayard Veiller, New York 1927, Play

PROCESSO CLEMENCEAU, IL 1917 d: Alfredo de Antoni. ITL., *L' Affaire Clemenceau*, Alexandre Dumas (fils), Paris 1866, Novel

Processo Dei Veleni, Il see **L' AFFAIRE DES POISONS** (1955).

PROCESSO E MORTE DI SOCRATE 1940 d: Corrado d'Errico. ITL., *I Dialoghi*, Plato, Dialogues

Processo, Il see **DER PROZESS** (1962).

PROCESUL ALB 1966 d: Iulian Mihu. RMN., *Soseaua Nordului*, Eugen Barbu, 1959, Novel

PROCUREUR HALLERS, LE 1930 d: Robert Wiene. FRN., *Der Andere*, Paul Lindau, 1893, Play

PRODANA NEVESTA 1933 d: Svatopluk Innemann, Jaroslav Kvapil. CZC., *Prodana Nevesta*, Bedrich Smetana, Prague 1866, Opera

PRODANA NEVESTA 1913 d: Max Urban. CZC., *Prodana Nevesta*, Karel Sabina, Bedrich Smetana, Prague 1866, Opera

PRODANA NEVESTA 1922 d: Oldrich Kminek. CZC., *Prodana Nevesta*, Karel Sabina, Prague 1866, Opera

PRODANA NEVESTA 1933 d: Svatopluk Innemann, Jaroslav Kvapil. CZC., *Prodana Nevesta*, Karel Sabina, Prague 1866, Opera

Prodezze Di Dicky, Le see **TRAPPOLA D'AMORE** (1940).

917

PRODIGA, LA 1946 d: Rafael Gil. SPN., *La Prodiga*, Pedro Antonio de Alarcon, 1882, Novel

PRODIGAL DAUGHTERS 1923 d: Sam Wood. USA., *Prodigal Daughters*, Joseph Hocking, New York 1921, Novel

Prodigal Father, The *see* TATAL RISIPITOR (1974).

PRODIGAL JUDGE, THE 1922 d: Edward Jose. USA., *The Prodigal Judge*, Vaughan Kester, Indianapolis 1911, Novel

Prodigal Knight, A *see* THE AFFAIRS OF ANATOL (1921).

PRODIGAL SON, THE 1923 d: A. E. Coleby. UKN., *The Prodigal Son*, Hall Caine, 1904, Novel

Prodigal Son, The *see* ONNA GOROSHI ABURA JIGOKU (1958).

Prodigal, The *see* LA PRODIGA (1946).

PRODIGAL WIFE, THE 1918 d: Frank Reicher. USA., *The Flaming Ramparts*, Edith Barnard Delano, 1914, Short Story

Prodigal Woman, The *see* LA PRODIGA (1946).

PROFESOR DE MI MUJER, EL 1930 d: Robert Florey. SPN., *L' Amour Chante*, Jacques Bousquet, Henri Falk, Novel

Profession - Orderly *see* SLOUZHEBNO -ORDINARETS (1979).

Professional Blonde *see* LA BLONDE DE PEKIN (1968).

PROFESSIONAL GUEST, THE 1931 d: George King. UKN., *The Professional Guest*, William Garrett, Novel

PROFESSIONAL SOLDIER 1935 d: Tay Garnett. USA., *Gentlemen the King*, Damon Runyon, 1931, Short Story

Professional, The *see* LE PROFESSIONNEL (1981).

PROFESSIONALS, THE 1966 d: Richard Brooks. USA., *A Mule for the Marquesa*, Frank O'Rourke, New York 1964, Novel

PROFESSIONNEL, LE 1981 d: Georges Lautner. FRN., *Death of a Thin-Skinned Animal*, Patrick Alexander, Novel

Professor Di Mi Senora, El *see* EL PROFESOR DE MI MUJER (1930).

Professor Hannibal *see* HANNIBAL TANAR UR (1956).

PROFESSOR MAMLOCK 1961 d: Konrad Wolf. GDR., *Professor Mamlock*, Friedrich Wolf, Play

Professor, Please. *see* KEREM! TANAR UR (1956).

Professor, The *see* IL CAMORRISTA (1986).

PROFESSOR TIM 1957 d: Henry Cass. UKN., *Professor Tim*, George Shiels, Play

Professoren *see* FORMYNDERNE (1978).

PROFETA VELATO, IL 1912. ITL., *Lalla Rooks*, Thomas Moore, 1917, Poem

PROFETA VOLTAL, SZIVEM 1968 d: Pal Zolnay. HNG., *Szivem Profeta Voltal*, Sandor Somogyi Toth, 1965, Novel

Profezia Di un Delitto *see* LES MAGICIENS (1975).

PROFIT AND THE LOSS 1917 d: A. V. Bramble, Eliot Stannard. UKN., *Profit - and the Loss*, H. F. Maltby, Play

PROFLIGATE, THE 1915. USA., *The Profligate*, Arthur Hornblow, Novel

PROFLIGATE, THE 1917 d: Meyrick Milton. UKN., *The Profligate*, Arthur Wing Pinero, London 1889, Play

PROFUMO DI DONNA 1974 d: Dino Risi. ITL., *Il Buio E Il Miele*, Giovanni Arpino, Novel

PROGNOZA POGODY 1982 d: Antoni Krauze. PLN., Marek Nowakowski, Story

PROIBITO 1955 d: Mario Monicelli. ITL/FRN., *La Madre*, Grazia Deledda, 1920, Novel

PROIE DU VENT, LA 1926 d: Rene Clair. FRN., *L' Aventure Amoureuse*, A. Mercier, Pierre Vignal, Novel

PROIE, LA 1917 d: Georges MoncA. FRN., *La Proie*, Victor Cyril, Play

PROIZVEDENIYE ISKUSSTVA 1959 d: Mark Kovalyov. USS., *Proizvedeniye Iskusstva*, Anton Chekhov, 1886, Short Story

Project M 7 *see* THE NET (1953).

PROJECT X 1968 d: William Castle. USA., *The Artificial Man*, L. P. Davies, London 1965, Novel, *Pyschogeist*, L. P. Davies, London 1966, Novel

PROJECTED MAN, THE 1966 d: Ian Curteis. UKN., *The Projected Man*, Frank Quattrocchi, Novel

Promesa Sagrada *see* I PROMESSI SPOSI (1964).

PROMESSA, A 1973 d: Antonio de Macedo. PRT., *A Promessa*, Bernardo Santareno, 1957, Play

PROMESSA, LA 1979 d: Alberto Negrin. ITL., *La Promessa*, Friedrich Durrenmatt, Novel

PROMESSE DE L'AUBE, LA 1970 d: Jules Dassin. FRN/USA., *La Promesse de l'Aube*, Romain Gary, Paris 1960, Book

PROMESSES 1935 d: Rene Delacroix. FRN., *Une Idylle Dans la Zone Rouge*, Pierre Gourdon, Play

PROMESSI SPOSI, I 1908 d: Mario Morais. ITL., *I Promessi Sposi*, Alessandro Manzoni, 1827, Novel

PROMESSI SPOSI, I 1911 d: Ugo FalenA. ITL., *I Promessi Sposi*, Alessandro Manzoni, 1827, Novel

PROMESSI SPOSI, I 1913 d: Ubaldo Maria Del Colle, Ernesto Maria Pasquali. ITL., *I Promessi Sposi*, Alessandro Manzoni, 1827, Novel

PROMESSI SPOSI, I 1913 d: Eleuterio Rodolfi. ITL., *I Promessi Sposi*, Alessandro Manzoni, 1827, Novel

PROMESSI SPOSI, I 1922 d: Mario Bonnard. ITL., *I Promessi Sposi*, Alessandro Manzoni, 1827, Novel

PROMESSI SPOSI, I 1941 d: Mario Camerini. ITL., *I Promessi Sposi*, Alessandro Manzoni, 1827, Novel

PROMESSI SPOSI, I 1964 d: Mario Maffei. ITL/SPN., *I Promessi Sposi*, Alessandro Manzoni, 1827, Novel

Prometheas Se Deftero Prosopo *see* PROMITHEAS SE DEFTERO PROSOPO (1975).

Prometheas Se Theftero Prosopo *see* PROMITHEAS SE DEFTERO PROSOPO (1975).

PROMETHEUS BOUND -THE ILLIAC PASSION 1966 d: Gregory J. Markopoulos. USA., *Prometheus Vinctus*, Aeschylus, c468 bc, Play

Prometheus Second Person Singular *see* PROMITHEAS SE DEFTERO PROSOPO (1975).

Promise at Dawn *see* LA PROMESSE DE L'AUBE (1970).

Promise Her Anything *see* PROMISES! PROMISES! (1963).

Promise Made, A *see* THE THANKSGIVING PROMISE (1986).

Promise Me Nothing *see* VERSPRICH MIR NICHTS (1937).

PROMISE, THE 1917 d: Fred J. Balshofer. USA., *The Promise; a Tale of the Great Northwest*, James B. Hendryx, New York 1915, Novel

Promise, The *see* O PAGADOR DE PROMESSAS (1961).

PROMISE, THE 1969 d: Michael Hayes. UKN., *Moy Bednyy Marat*, Aleksei Nikolaevich Arbuzov, 1965, Play

Promise, The *see* A PROMESSA (1973).

PROMISED A MIRACLE 1988 d: Stephen Gyllenhaal. USA., *We Let Our Son Die*, Larry Parker, Book

Promised Land *see* ZIEMIA OBIECANA (1974).

Promised Land *see* INSPECTOR MORSE: PROMISED LAND (1989).

Promised Land, The *see* LES BRULES (1958).

PROMISES! PROMISES! 1963 d: King Donovan. USA., *The Plant*, Edna Sheklow, Play

PROMITHEAS SE DEFTERO PROSOPO 1975 d: Kostas Ferris. GRC., *Prometheus Vinctus*, Aeschylus, c468 bc, Play

Promoter, The *see* THE CARD (1952).

PROMOZIONE PER. MERITI PERSONALI 1914 d: Oreste Gherardini. ITL., *Il Signor Direttore*, Guglielmo Torelli, Play

Proof of the Man *see* NINGEN NO SHOMEI (1977).

PROOI, DE 1984 d: Vivian Pieters. NTH., Catherine Aird, Novel

PROPAVSHAYA GRAMOTA 1972 d: Boris IVchenko. USS., *Propavshaya Gramota*, Nikolay Gogol, 1831, Short Story

Prophet of the Field, The *see* MEZEI PROFETA (1947).

Proposal *see* YI JIAN TIAN (1954).

PROSCANIE 1981 d: Elem Klimov, Larissa Shepitko. USS., *Proscanie*, Valentin Rasputin, Novel

Proshchanie *see* PROSCANIE (1981).

PROSIM PANE PROFESORE! 1940 d: Karel Hasler. CZC., *Prosim Pane Profesore!*, Otto Jun, Novel

PROSPERO'S BOOKS 1990 d: Peter Greenaway. NTH/FRN/ITL., *The Tempest*, William Shakespeare, c1611, Play

PROSTAYA SMERT 1985 d: Alexander Kaidanovski. USS., *Smert Ivana Ilicha*, Lev Nikolayevich Tolstoy, 1886, Short Story

Protar Affair *see* AFACEREA PROTAR (1956).

PROTEUS 1995 d: Bob Keen. UKN., *Slimmer*, John Brosnan, Novel

Proteus Generation *see* DEMON SEED (1977).

PROUD AND THE PROFANE, THE 1956 d: George Seaton. USA., *The Magnificent Bastards*, Lucy Herndon Crockett, 1954, Novel

PROUD FLESH 1925 d: King Vidor. USA., *Proud Flesh*, Lawrence Irving Rising, New York 1924, Novel

Proud of This Girl *see* PENNIN PERUMAI (1956).

PROUD ONES, THE 1956 d: Robert D. Webb. USA., *The Proud Ones*, Verne Athanas, 1952, Novel

Proud Ones, The *see* LE CHEVAL D'ORGEUIL (1980).

PROUD REBEL, THE 1958 d: Michael Curtiz. USA., James Edward Grant, Story

PROVDAM SVOU ZENU 1941 d: Miroslav Cikan. CZC., *Provdam Svou Zenu*, Jindrich Horejsi, Julius Lebl, Play

Provincial Correspondent, The *see* SELCOR (1975).

PROVINCIALE, LA 1953 d: Mario Soldati. ITL., *La Provinciale*, Alberto Moravia, 1952, Novel

Provisional Freedom *see* LIBERTAD PROVISIONAL (1976).

PROWLERS OF THE SEA 1928 d: John G. Adolfi. USA., *The Siege of the Lancashire Queen*, Jack London, 1905, Short Story

Proxenetes, The *see* ETTORE LO FUSTO (1972).

PROXIES 1921 d: George D. Baker. USA., *Proxies*, Frank R. Adams, 1920, Short Story

PROZESS, DER 1948 d: G. W. Pabst. AUS., *Prozess Auf Leben Und Tod*, Rudolf Brunngraber, Novel

PROZESS, DER 1962 d: Orson Welles. GRM/ITL/FRN., *Der Prozess*, Franz Kafka, Berlin 1925, Novel

Prude, The *see* THE DANGEROUS FLIRT (1924).

PRUDENCE AND THE PILL 1968 d: Fielder Cook, Ronald Neame. UKN/USA., *Prudence and the Pill*, Hugh Mills, London 1965, Novel

PRUDE'S FALL, THE 1924 d: Graham Cutts. UKN., *The Prude's Fall*, Rudolf Besier, May Edginton, London 1920, Play

PRUNELLA 1918 d: Maurice Tourneur. USA., *Prunella Or Love in a Dutch Garden*, Harley Granville-Barker, London 1904, Play, *Prunella; Or Love in a Dutch Garden*, L. Housman, London 1904, Play

Pruning Knife, The *see* WAS SHE JUSTIFIED? (1922).

PRVNI PARTA 1959 d: Otakar VavrA. CZC., *Prvni Parta*, Karel Capek, 1937, Novel

PRVNI POLIBENI 1935 d: Vladimir Slavinsky. CZC., Kurt Juhn, Novel

PSOHLAVCI 1931 d: Svatopluk Innemann. CZC., *Psohlavci*, Alois Jirasek, Novel

Psyche 59 *see* PSYCHE 63 (1963).

PSYCHE 63 1963 d: Alexander Singer. UKN., *Psyche 58*, Francoise Des Ligneris, Paris 1958, Novel

Psychka *see* PYSHKA (1934).

PSYCHO 1960 d: Alfred Hitchcock. USA., *Psycho*, Robert Bloch, 1959, Novel

PSYCHO 1998 d: Gus Van Sant. USA., *Pyscho*, Robert Bloch, Novel

Psycho-Circus *see* CIRCUS OF FEAR (1966).

Psychotic *see* IDENTIKIT (1974).

PT 109 1963 d: Leslie H. Martinson. USA., *John F. Kennedy in World War II Pt 109*, Robert J. Donovan, New York 1961, Biography

P.T. Barnum's Rocket to the Moon *see* JULES VERNE'S ROCKET TO THE MOON (1967).

Pt Raiders *see* THE SHIP THAT DIED OF SHAME (1955).

P'TIT VIENT VITE, LE 1972 d: Louis-Georges Carrier. CND., *Leonie Est En Avance*, Georges Feydeau, Play

PUBERTY BLUES 1982 d: Bruce Beresford. ASL., *Puberty Blues*, Gabrielle Carey, Kathy Lette, Novel

Public Be Sold, The *see* NO MARRIAGE TIES (1933).

PUBLIC DEFENDER 1931 d: J. Walter Ruben. USA., *The Splendid Crime*, George Goodchild, London 1930, Novel

PUBLIC DEFENDER, THE 1917 d: Burton L. King. USA., *The Public Defender*, Mayer C. Goldman, New York 1917, Book

PUBLIC EYE, THE 1972 d: Carol Reed. USA/UKN., *The Public Eye*, Peter Shaffer, 1962, Play

Public Life *see* THE WASHINGTON MASQUERADE (1932).

Public Nuisance No.1 see **LITTLE MISS NOBODY** (1936).

PUBLIC PIGEON NO. 1 1957 d: Norman Z. McLeod. USA., *Public Pigeon No. 1*, Devery Freeman, 1956, Television Play

Public Woman, The see **LA FEMME PUBLIQUE** (1984).

PUCE A L'OREILLE, LA 1914 d: Marcel Simon. FRN., *La Puce a l'Oreille*, Georges Feydeau, Paris 1907, Play

Puce a l'Oreille, La see **A FLEA IN HER EAR** (1968).

PUCHINA 1958 d: Antonin Dawson, Yu. Muzykant. USS., *Puchina*, Alexander Ostrovsky, 1866, Play

Puddin' Head Wilson see **PUDD'NHEAD WILSON** (1916).

Pudding Tarzan see **GUMMI TARZAN** (1982).

PUDD'NHEAD WILSON 1916 d: Frank Reicher. USA., *Pudd'nhead Wilson*, Mark Twain, Hartford 1894, Novel

PUDD'NHEAD WILSON 1984 d: Alan Bridges. USA., *Pudd'nhead Wilson*, Mark Twain, Hartford 1894, Novel

PUDELNACKT IN OBERBAYERN 1968 d: Hans Albin. GRM., *Pudelnackt in Oberbayern*, Peter Ammer, Novel

Puente de Los Suspiros, El see **IL PONTE DEI SOSPIRI** (1964).

PUENTE, EL 1977 d: Juan Antonio Bardem. SPN., *Solo de Moto*, Daniel Sueiro, 1967, Novel

PUERTA ABIERTA, LA 1957 d: Cesar Ardavin. SPN/ITL., *Tuzmadar*, Lajos Zilahy, Budapest 1932, Play

Puerta Cerrada, La see **UN ALLER SIMPLE** (1970).

Puishka see **PYSHKA** (1934).

PUITS AUX TROIS VERITES, LE 1961 d: Francois Villiers. FRN/ITL., *Le Puits aux Trois Verites*, Jean Jacques Gautier, Paris 1949, Novel

PUITS DE JACOB, LES 1925 d: Edward Jose. FRN., *Le Puits de Jacobs*, Pierre Benoit, Novel

PUITS ET LE PENDULE, LE 1912 d: Henri Desfontaines. FRN., *The Pit and the Pendulum*, Edgar Allan Poe, 1845, Short Story

Puja Phalamu see **POOJAPALAM** (1964).

PUJARIN 1936 d: Prafulla Roy. IND., *Dena Paona*, Saratchandra Chatterjee, Novel

PULGARCITO 1958 d: Rene CardonA. MXC., *Le Petit Poucet*, Charles Perrault, 1697, Short Story

PULL FOR THE SHORE, SAILOR 1911. USA., *The Madonna of the Tubs*, Elizabeth Stuart Phelps, Story

PULL-OVER ROUGE, LE 1979 d: Michel Drach. FRN., *Le Pull-Over Rouge*, Gilles Perrault, Book

Pulse of the Earth, The see **BACK TO GOD'S COUNTRY** (1919).

PUMPING IRON II: THE WOMEN 1985 d: George Butler. USA., *Pumping Iron II: the Unprecedented Woman*, George Butler, Charles Gaines, Book

PUMPKIN EATER, THE 1964 d: Jack Clayton. UKN., *The Pumpkin Eater*, Penelope Mortimer, London 1962, Novel

PUNAO DE ROSAS, EL 1923 d: Rafael Salvador. SPN., *El Punao de Rosas*, Carlos Arniches, Ruperto Chapi, A. Mas, Opera

Punishment Battalion see **STRAFBATAILLON 999** (1960).

Punishment Island see **SHOKEI NO SHIMA** (1966).

Punishment Room see **SHOKEI NO HEYA** (1956).

PUNK AND THE PRINCESS, THE 1993 d: Mike Sarne. UKN., *The Punk*, Gideon Sams, Novel

Punk Lawyer see **ADVOCAAT VAN DE HANEN** (1996).

Punk, The see **THE PUNK AND THE PRINCESS** (1993).

PUNKS KOMMT AUS AMERIKA 1935 d: Karl Heinz Martin. GRM., *Punks Kommt Aus Amerika*, Ludwig von Wohl, Novel

PUNKTCHEN UND ANTON 1953 d: Thomas Engel, Erich Engel. AUS/GRM., *Punktchen Und Anton*, Erich Kastner, 1930, Novel

PUNKTCHEN UND ANTON 1999 d: Caroline Link. GRM., *Punktchen Und Anton*, Erich Kastner, 1930, Novel

PUNKTUR, PUNKTUR, COMMA, STRIK 1980 d: Thorsteinn Jonsson. ICL., *Punktur, Komma, Strik Punktur*, Petur Gunnarsson, Novel

PUNTAIRE, LA 1928 d: Jose Claramunt, Fructuoso Gelabert. SPN., *Manuel Ribot I Serra*, Poem

Puntila see **HERR PUNTILA UND SEIN KNECHT MATTI** (1955).

PUPA DEL GANGSTER, LA 1975 d: Giorgio Capitani. ITL/FRN., *Collared*, Cornell Woolrich, Story

Pupil Gerber, The see **DER SCHULER GERBER** (1981).

Pupil of the Sixth Grade see **SEXTANKA** (1927).

Pupil, The see **L' ELEVE** (1996).

PUPILAS DO SENHOR REITOR, AS 1935 d: Jose Leitao de Barros. PRT., *As Pupilas Do Senhor Reitor*, Julio Dinis, 1867, Novel

PUPILAS DO SENHOR REITOR, AS 1960 d: Perdigao QueirogA. PRT., *As Pupilas Do Senhor Reitor*, Julio Dinis, 1867, Novel

Pupils of the Dean, The see **AS PUPILAS DO SENHOR REITOR** (1935).

Pupils of the Dean, The see **AS PUPILAS DO SENHOR REITOR** (1960).

PUPPET CROWN, THE 1915 d: George Melford. USA., *The Puppet Crown*, Harold MacGrath, Indianapolis 1901, Novel

PUPPET MAN, THE 1921 d: Frank H. Crane. UKN., *The Puppet Man*, Cosmo Gordon Lennox, Novel

PUPPET ON A CHAIN 1970 d: Geoffrey Reeve, Don Sharp. UKN., *Puppet on a Chain*, Alistair MacLean, 1969, Novel

PUPPETS 1926 d: George Archainbaud. USA., *Puppets*, Frances Lightner, Play

Puppets of Fate see **THE PUPPET MAN** (1921).

PURCHASE PRICE, THE 1932 d: William A. Wellman. USA., *The Mud Lark*, Arthur Stringer, New York 1932, Novel

PURE GRIT 1923 d: Nat Ross. USA., *A Texas Ranger*, William MacLeod Raine, New York 1911, Novel

PUREZA 1940 d: Eduardo Chianca de GarciA. BRZ., *Pureza*, Jose Lins Do Rego, 1937, Novel

Purgatorio see **SKARSELD** (1975).

PURGATORIO, IL 1911. ITL., *La Divina Commedia*, Dante Alighieri, 1310, Verse

PURGATORIO, IL 1911 d: Giuseppe Berardi, Arturo Busnengo. ITL., *La Divina Commedia*, Dante Alighieri, 1310, Verse

Purgatory see **SKARSELD** (1975).

Purgatory and Paradise see **IL PURGATORIO** (1911).

Purge, The see **PURUSHARTHAM** (1987).

PURITAIN, LE 1937 d: Jeff Musso. FRN., *The Puritan*, Liam O'Flaherty, 1931, Novel

PURITAN PASSIONS 1923 d: Frank Tuttle. USA., *The Scarecrow; Or the Glass of Truth*, Percy MacKaye, New York 1908, Novel

Puritan, The see **LE PURITAIN** (1937).

Purity see **PUREZA** (1940).

Purlie Victorious see **GONE ARE THE DAYS!** (1963).

Purple and Fine Linen see **THREE HOURS** (1927).

PURPLE CIPHER, THE 1920 d: Chester Bennett. USA., *The Purple Hieroglyph*, Will F. Jenkins, 1920, Short Story

PURPLE DRESS, THE 1918 d: Martin Justice. USA., *The Purple Dress*, O. Henry, Short Story

Purple Harvest, The see **THE VINTAGE** (1957).

PURPLE HEART DIARY 1951 d: Richard Quine. USA., Frances Langford, Article

Purple Hieroglyph, The see **THE PURPLE CIPHER** (1920).

PURPLE HIGHWAY, THE 1923 d: Henry Kolker. USA., *Dear Me Or April Changes*, Hamilton Hale, New York 1921, Play, *Or April Changes Dear Me*, Luther Reed, New York 1921, Play

PURPLE LADY, THE 1916 d: George A. Lessey. USA., *The Purple Lady*, Sydney Rosenfeld, New York 1899, Play

PURPLE MASK, THE 1955 d: H. Bruce Humberstone. USA., *Le Chevalier Au Masques*, Paul Armont, Jean Manoussi, Play

Purple Noon see **PLEIN SOLEIL** (1960).

Purple Phial, The see **THE ELEVENTH HOUR** (1922).

PURPLE PLAIN, THE 1954 d: Robert Parrish. UKN., *The Purple Plain*, H. E. Bates, 1947, Novel

Purple Pride see **ASHES OF VENGEANCE** (1923).

Purple Taxi see **UN TAXI MAUVE** (1977).

PURSE STRINGS 1933 d: Henry Edwards. UKN., *The Purse Strings*, Bernard Parry, Play

PURSUED 1934 d: Louis King. USA., *The Painted Lady*, Larry Evans, 1912, Short Story

PURSUING VENGEANCE, THE 1916 d: Martin Sabine. USA., *The Mystery of the Boule Cabinet*, Burton Egbert Stevenson, New York 1911, Novel

PURSUIT 1935 d: Edwin L. Marin. USA., *Golden Goose Wild Goose*, Lawrence G. Blochman, Story

PURSUIT 1972 d: Michael Crichton. USA., *Binary*, Michael Crichton, Novel

Pursuit see **HAJKA** (1977).

Pursuit and Loves of Queen Victoria, The see **MADCHENJAHRE EINER KONIGIN** (1954).

PURSUIT OF HAPPINESS, THE 1934 d: Alexander Hall. USA., *The Pursuit of Happiness*, Lawrence Langner, Armina Marshall, New York 1933, Play

PURSUIT OF HAPPINESS, THE 1971 d: Robert Mulligan. USA., *The Pursuit of Happiness*, Thomas Rogers, Novel

PURSUIT OF PAMELA, THE 1920 d: Harold Shaw. UKN., *The Pursuit of Pamela*, C. B. Fernald, London 1913, Play

Pursuit of the Graf Spree see **BATTLE OF THE RIVER PLATE** (1956).

Pursuit, The see **UN ROI SANS DIVERTISSEMENT** (1962).

PURUSHARTHAM 1987 d: K. R. Mohanan. IND., *Irikkapindam*, C. V. Sriraman

PUSHER, THE 1959 d: Gene Milford. USA., *The Pusher*, Evan Hunter, 1956, Novel

PUSHING TIN 1999 d: Mike Newell. USA., *Something's Got to Give*, Darcy Frey, Article

Pushka see **PYSHKA** (1934).

PUSHOVER 1954 d: Richard Quine. USA., *Rafferty*, William S. Ballinger, Novel, *The Night Watch*, Thomas Walsh, Novel

PUSS IN BOOTS 1931. USA., *Le Maitre Chat Ou le Chat Botte*, Charles Perrault, Paris 1697, Short Story

PUSS IN BOOTS 1987 d: Eugene Marner. USA., *Le Maitre Chat Ou le Chat Botte*, Charles Perrault, Paris 1697, Short Story

Puss 'N Boots see **DER GESTIEFELTE KATER** (1955).

Puss 'N Boots see **EL GATO CON BOTAS** (1961).

Puss 'N Boots see **PUSS IN BOOTS** (1987).

Pusztaliebe see **ZWISCHEN STROM UND STEPPE** (1938).

Put on By Cunning see **INSPECTOR WEXFORD: PUT ON BY CUNNING** (1991).

Put on the Spot see **RIO GRANDE ROMANCE** (1936).

PUT U RAJ 1971 d: Mario Fanelli. YGS., *Cvrcak Pod Vodopadom*, Miroslav Krieza, 1937, Short Story

PUT YOURSELF IN HIS PLACE 1912 d: Theodore Marston. USA., *Put Yourself in His Place*, Charles Reade, Novel

Putain du Roi, La see **THE KING'S WHORE** (1990).

Putain Respectueuse, La see **LA P. RESPECTUEUSE** (1952).

Putesestvie Molodogo Kompozitora see **PUTSCHESTWIE MOLODOGO KOMPOSITORA** (1984).

PUTESHESTVIYE 1967 d: Inessa Selezneva, Inna Tumanyan. USS., *Papa Slozhi!*, Vasili Aksyonov, 1962, Short Story, *Zavtraki Sorok Tret'ego Godo*, Vasili Aksyonov, 1962, Short Story

Putiferio Goes to War see **PUTIFERIO VA ALLA GUERRA** (1968).

PUTIFERIO VA ALLA GUERRA 1968 d: Roberto Gavioli. ITL., *La Guerriera Nera*, Mario Piereghin, Short Story

PUTSCHESTWIE MOLODOGO KOMPOSITORA 1984 d: Georgi ShengelayA. USS., *Putchestwie Molodogo Kompozitora*, Otar Tschcheidse, Novel

PUTTING ONE OVER 1919 d: Eddie Dillon. USA., *The Man Who Awoke*, Mary Imlay Taylor, Short Story

Puzzle Man see **RENDEZVOUS** (1935).

Puzzle of Horror see **A DOPPIA FACCIA** (1969).

Puzzle of the Briar Pipe, The see **MURDER ON A BRIDLE PATH** (1936).

Puzzle of the Pepper Tree, The see **MURDER ON A HONEYMOON** (1935).

Puzzle of the Red Orchid, The see **DAS RATSEL DER ROTEN ORCHIDEE** (1961).

PYAT VECHEROV 1979 d: Nikita Mikhalkov. USS., *Pyat Vecherov*, Alexander Volodin, 1959, Play

PYATNADTZATILETNY KAPITAN 1945 d: Vasili Zhuravlyov. USS., *Un Capitaine de Quinze Ans*, Jules Verne, 1878, Novel

PYGMALION 1935 d: Erich Engel. GRM., *Pygmalion*, George Bernard Shaw, London 1913, Play

PYGMALION 1937 d: Ludwig Berger. NTH., *Pygmalion*, George Bernard Shaw, London 1913, Play

PYGMALION 1938 d: Anthony Asquith, Leslie Howard. UKN., *Pygmalion*, George Bernard Shaw, London 1913, Play

PYGMALION 1981 d: John Glenister. UKN., *Pygmalion*, George Bernard Shaw, London 1913, Play

PYJAMAS PREFERRED 1932 d: Val Valentine. UKN., *The Red Dog*, J. O. Twiss, Play

Pylon *see* **THE TARNISHED ANGELS** (1957).

PYOTR PERVY 1937-39 d: Vladimir Petrov. USS., *Pyotr Pervy*, Alexsey Nikolayevich Tolstoy, 1929-45, Novel

Pyramid of the Sun God *see* **DIE PYRAMIDE DES SONNENGOTTES** (1965).

PYRAMIDE DES SONNENGOTTES, DIE 1965 d: Robert Siodmak. GRM/FRN/ITL., *Die Pyramide Des Sonnengottes*, Karl Friedrich May, Novel

PYSHKA 1934 d: Mikhail Romm. USS., *Boule de Suif*, Guy de Maupassant, 1880, Short Story

PYX, THE 1973 d: Harvey Hart. CND., *The Pyx*, John Buell, Novel

Q & A 1990 d: Sidney Lumet. USA., *Q & A*, Edwin Torres, Novel

Qasr Al-Shauq *see* **QASR ASH-SHAWQ** (19—).

QASR ASH-SHAWQ 19— d: Hassan Al Imam. EGY., *Quasr Al-Shauq*, Najib Mahfuz, 1957, Novel

QB VII 1974 d: Tom Gries. USA., *QB VII*, Leon Uris, Novel

QI SHI ER JIA FANG KE 1963 d: Wang Weiyi. CHN., *Qi Shi Er Jia Fang Ke*, Shanghai Public Comedy Troupe, Play

QI WANG 1988 d: Teng Wenji. CHN., *Qi Wang*, Zhong Ahcheng, 1982, Short Story

QIAN WAN BUY YAO WANG JI 1964 d: XIe Tieli, Cong Shen. CHN., *Qian Wan Buy Yao Wang Ji*, Cong Shen, Play

QING HAI LANG HUA 1991 d: Pao Zhifang. CHN., *Spray*, Qiong Yao, Novel

QING XUMENG 1922 d: Ren Pengnian. CHN., *Laoshan Daoshi*, Pu Songling, Short Story

QINGCHENGZHI LIAN 1984 d: Hsu An-HuA. HKG., *Qingchengzhi Lian*, Eileen Chang, Novel

QINGSONG LING 1965 d: Liu Guoquan. CHN., *Qingsong Ling*, Zhang Zhongpeng, Play

Qingsong Mountain Range *see* **QINGSONG LING** (1965).

Qiu Ju Goes to Court *see* **QIUJU DA GUANSI** (1992).

QIU MI 1963 d: Xu Changlin. CHN., *Outside the Soccer Field*, Jin Zhengjia, Play

QIUJU DA GUANSI 1992 d: Zhang Yimou. HKG/CHN., *Quiju Da Guanshi*, Chen Yuanbin, Novel

Quadrante Della Fortuna, Il *see* **LA DANZA DEI MILIONI** (1940).

QUADRILLE 1937 d: Sacha Guitry. FRN., *Quadrille*, Sacha Guitry, Play

QUADRILLE D'AMOUR 1934 d: Germain Fried, Richard Eichberg. FRN., *Die Katz' Im Sack*, Michael Eisemann, Ladislaus Szilagyi, Play

QUAI DE GRENELLE 1950 d: Emile Edwin Reinert. FRN., *Quai de Grenelle*, Jacques Laurent, Novel

QUAI DES BRUMES 1938 d: Marcel Carne. FRN., *Le Quai Des Brumes*, Pierre Mac Orlan, 1927, Novel

QUAI DES ORFEVRES 1947 d: Henri-Georges Clouzot. FRN., *Quai Des Orfevres*, Stanislas-Andre Steeman, Novel

QUAI NOTRE-DAME 1960 d: Jacques Berthier. FRN., *Quai Notre-Dame*, Dominique Rolin, Novel

QUALCUNO DIETRO LA PORTA 1971 d: Nicolas Gessner. ITL/FRN., *Quelqu'un Derriere la Porte*, Jacques Robert, Novel

QUALIFIED ADVENTURER, THE 1925 d: Sinclair Hill. UKN., *The Qualified Adventurer*, Selwyn Jepson, Novel

QUALITY STREET 1927 d: Sidney A. Franklin. USA., *Quality Street*, J. M. Barrie, New York 1901, Play

QUALITY STREET 1937 d: George Stevens. USA., *Quality Street*, J. M. Barrie, New York 1901, Play

Quand la Chair Succombe *see* **SENILITA** (1962).

QUAND LA FEMME S'EN MELE 1957 d: Yves Allegret. FRN/ITL/GRM., *Sans Attendre Godot*, John Amila, Novel

QUAND MINUIT SONNERA 1936 d: Leo Joannon. FRN., *Qu'as-Tu Fait de Mon Coeur?*, Alfred Machard, Novel

QUAND NOUS ETIONS DEUX 1929 d: Leonce Perret. FRN., *Quand Nous Etions Deux*, Huguette Garnier, Novel

QUAND ON EST BELLE 1931 d: Arthur Robison. USA., *The Easiest Way*, Eugene Walter, Hartford, Ct. 1908, Play

QUAND SONNERA MIDI 1957 d: Edmond T. Greville. FRN/ITL., *L' Homme Qui Mourra Demain*, Henri Champly, Novel

QUAND TE TUES-TU? 1931 d: Roger Capellani. FRN., *Quand Te Tues-Tu?*, Andre Dahl, Novel

QUANDO GLI UOMINI ARMARONO LA CLAVA. E CON LE DONNE FECERO DIN DON 1971 d: Bruno Corbucci. ITL., *La Donne Alla Festa Di Demetra*, Aristophanes, Play, *Lysistrata*, Aristophanes, 411 bc, Play

Quando Il Sole Scotta *see* **SUR LA ROUTE DE SALINA** (1969).

QUANDO LA PRIMAVERA RITORNO 1916 d: Ivo Illuminati. ITL., *Jeanne la Pale*, Honore de Balzac, Novel

QUARANTINED RIVALS 1927 d: Archie Mayo. USA., *Quarantined Rivals*, George Randolph Chester, 1906, Short Story

QUARE FELLOW, THE 1962 d: Arthur Dreifuss. UKN/IRL., *The Quare Fellow*, Brendan Behan, 1956, Play

QUARE FELLOW, THE 1967 d: Harvey Hart. CND., *The Quare Fellow*, Brendan Behan, 1956, Play

QUARREL, THE 1990 d: Ellis Cohen. CND., *My Quarrel With Hersh Rasseyner*, Chaim Grade, Autobiography

QUARRY, THE 1915 d: Lawrence Marston. USA., *The Quarry*, Gilson Willets, Novel

Quarry, The *see* **HAMACHTZAYYA** (1990).

QUARRY, THE 1998 d: Marion Hansel. BLG/FRN/NTH., *The Quarry*, Damon Galgut, Novel

Quarrymen *see* **TRHANI** (1936).

QUARTET 1948 d: Arthur Crabtree, Ralph Smart. UKN., *The Alien Corn*, W. Somerset Maugham, 1940, Short Story

QUARTET 1948 d: Ken Annakin, Harold French. UKN., *Colonel's Lady*, W. Somerset Maugham, 1947, Short Story

QUARTET 1948 d: Arthur Crabtree, Ralph Smart. UKN., *The Facts of Life*, W. Somerset Maugham, 1940, Short Story

QUARTET 1948 d: Ken Annakin, Harold French. UKN., *The Kite*, W. Somerset Maugham, 1931, Short Story

QUARTET 1980 d: James Ivory. UKN/FRN., *Quartet*, Jean Rhys, 1929, Novel

Quartet That Split Up, The *see* **KVARTETTEN SOM SPRANGDES** (1950).

QUARTETTO PAZZO 1947 d: Guido Salvini. ITL., *Quartetto Pazzo*, Ernst Eklund, Play

QUARTIER LATIN 1929 d: Augusto GeninA. GRM., *Quartier Latin*, Maurice Dekobra, Novel

Quartiere Dei Lilla *see* **PORTE DES LILAS** (1957).

QUARTIERI ALTI 1944 d: Mario Soldati. ITL., *Le Rendez-Vous de Senlis*, Jean Anouilh, Play, *Quartieri Alti*, Ercole Patti, Novel

QUATRE NUITS D'UN REVEUR 1971 d: Robert Bresson. FRN/ITL., *Belye Nochi*, Fyodor Dostoyevsky, St. Petersburg 1848, Short Story

Quattrini a Palate *see* **VENTO DI MILIONI** (1940).

Quattro Donne Nella Notte *see* **BONNES A TUER** (1954).

Quattro Ladroni a Caccia Di Milioni *see* **LA TROMBATA** (1979).

QUATTRO MOSCHETTIERI, I 1936 d: Carlo Campogalliani. ITL., *I Quattro Moschettieri*, Riccardo Morbelli, Angelo Nizza, Radio Play

QUATTRO NOTTI CON ALBA 1962 d: Luigi Filippo d'Amico. ITL., *Un Viaggio Di Piacere*, Enzo Gicca Palli, Novel

QUAX, DER BRUCHPILOT 1941 d: Kurt Hoffmann. GRM., *Quax Der Bruchpilot*, Hermann Grote, Short Story

Quax in Africa *see* **QUAX IN FAHRT** (1945).

QUAX IN FAHRT 1945 d: Helmut Weiss. GRM., *Quax Auf Abwegen*, Hermann Grote, Short Story

Que Esperen Los Cuervos *see* **LES ETRANGERS** (1968).

QUE LA BETE MEURE 1969 d: Claude Chabrol. FRN/ITL., *The Beast Must Die*, Nicholas Blake, London 1938, Novel

QUE PERSONNE NE SORTE 1963 d: Yvan Govar. FRN/BLG., *Six Hommes a Tuer*, Stanislas-Andre Steeman, Novel

Queen and the Cardinal, The *see* **JEROME PERREAU** (1935).

Queen Anne's Secret Or Musketeers Thirty Years Later *see* **TAJNA KOROLEVY ANNY ILI MUSHKETERY TRIDCAT LET SPUSTJA** (1993).

QUEEN BEE 1955 d: Ranald MacDougall. USA., *Queen Bee*, Edna Lee, 1949, Novel

Queen Bess -Her Love Story *see* **LES AMOURS DE LA REINE ELISABETH** (1912).

Queen Elisabeth *see* **LES AMOURS DE LA REINE ELISABETH** (1912).

QUEEN FOR A DAY 1951 d: Arthur Lubin. USA., *Horsie*, Dorothy Parker, 1933, Short Story

Queen for a Night *see* **KONIGIN EINER NACHT** (1951).

QUEEN HIGH 1930 d: Fred Newmeyer. USA., *A Pair of Sixes*, Edward Peple, New York 1914, Play

QUEEN MOTHER, THE 1916 d: Wilfred Noy. UKN., *The Queen Mother*, James A. Campbell, Play

Queen Mother, The *see* **THE ETERNAL SIN** (1917).

Queen of Atlantis *see* **SIREN OF ATLANTIS** (1948).

Queen of Broadway *see* **KID DYNAMITE** (1943).

Queen of Crime *see* **KATE PLUS TEN** (1938).

QUEEN OF HEARTS, THE 1923 d: A. E. Coleby. UKN., *The Queen of Hearts*, Sax Rohmer, Short Story

QUEEN OF JUNGLE LAND, THE 1915 d: Joseph J. Franz. USA., *The Queen of Jungle Land*, James Oliver Curwood, Story

Queen of Main Street *see* **MISBEHAVING LADIES** (1931).

Queen of Mean, The *see* **LEONA HELMSLEY: THE QUEEN OF MEAN** (1990).

Queen of Sierra Morena *see* **LA DUQUESA DE BENAMEJI** (1949).

Queen of Spades *see* **PIQUE DAME** (1918).

Queen of Spades *see* **PIQUE DAME** (1927).

Queen of Spades *see* **PIQUE DAME** (1937).

QUEEN OF SPADES, THE 1949 d: Thorold Dickinson. UKN., *Pikovaya Dama*, Alexander Pushkin, 1834, Short Story

Queen of Spades, The *see* **PIKOVAYA DAMA** (1960).

Queen of Spades, The *see* **LA DAME DE PIQUE** (1965).

Queen of the Big Top *see* **KONIGIN DER ARENA** (1952).

QUEEN OF THE MOB 1940 d: James P. Hogan. USA., *Persons in Hiding*, J. Edgar Hoover, Boston 1938, Book

QUEEN OF THE MOULIN ROUGE 1922 d: Ray C. Smallwood. USA., *Queen of the Moulin Rouge*, John T. Hall, Paul M. Potter, New York 1908, Play

Queen of the Silver Mountains *see* **KRALOVNA STRIBRNYCH HOR** (1939).

QUEEN OF THE WICKED 1916 d: Albert Ward. UKN., *Queen of the Wicked*, Ronald Grahame, Play

Queen of Turnovo, The *see* **TURNOVSKATA TSARITSA** (1981).

Queen, The *see* **THE QUEEN'S AFFAIR** (1934).

Queen Was in the Parlor, The *see* **TONIGHT IS OURS** (1933).

QUEEN WAS IN THE PARLOUR, THE 1927 d: Graham Cutts. UKN., *The Queen Was in the Parlour*, Noel Coward, London 1926, Play

QUEENIE 1921 d: Howard M. Mitchell. USA., *The Adventures of a Nice Young Lady Queenie*, Wilbur Finley Fauley, New York 1921, Novel

QUEENIE 1987 d: Larry Peerce. USA., *Queenie*, Michael Korda, Novel

QUEEN'S AFFAIR, THE 1934 d: Herbert Wilcox. UKN., *Die Konigin*, Bruno Granichstaedten, Ernst Marischka, Play

Queen's Diamonds, The *see* **THE THREE MUSKETEERS** (1974).

QUEEN'S EVIDENCE 1919 d: James McKay. UKN., *Adam and Eve*, C. E. Munro, Louisa Parr, Play

Queen's Husband, The *see* **THE ROYAL BED** (1931).

Queen's Necklace, The *see* **L' AFFAIRE DU COLLIER DE LA REINE** (1945).

QUEER CARGO 1938 d: Harold Schuster. UKN., *Queer Cargo*, Noel Langley, London 1934, Play

QUEI DUE 1935 d: Gennaro Righelli. ITL., *Sik Sik l'Artifice Magico*, Eduardo de Filippo, Play

Quel Bandito Sono Io! *see* **HER FAVOURITE HUSBAND** (1950).

Quel Giorno Il Mondo Tremera *see* **ARMAGUEDON** (1977).

Quel Nostro Impossibile Amore *see* **LA BELLA LOLA** (1962).

QUELLA SPORCA STORIA DEL WEST 1968 d: Enzo G. Castellari. ITL., *Hamlet*, William Shakespeare, c1601, Play

QUELLA VECCHIA CANAGLIA 1934 d: Carlo Ludovico BragagliA. ITL., *Cette Vieille Canaille*, Fernand Noziere, Play

Quelle Terribile Notte *see* **L' AUTRE FEMME** (1963).

Quelli Che Sanno Uccidere *see* **LES ETRANGERS** (1968).

Quello Che M'e Costato Amare *see* **PETRUS** (1946).

Quello Che Non T'aspetti *see* **LA FABBRICA DELL'IMPREVISTO** (1943).

Quello Che Spara Per Primo *see* **UN NOMME LA ROCCA** (1962).

Quelque Part Dans le Monde *see* **UN ACTE D'AMOUR** (1953).

QUELQUES JOURS AVEC MOI 1987 d: Claude Sautet. FRN., *Quelques Jours Avec Moi*, Jean-Francois Josselin, Novel

QUELQU'UN A TUE 1933 d: Jack Forrester. FRN., *The Case of the Frightened Lady*, Edgar Wallace, London 1931, Play

Quelqu'un Derriere la Porte *see* **QUALCUNO DIETRO LA PORTA** (1971).

QUEM MATOU PACIFICO 1977 d: Renato Santos PereirA. BRZ., *Quem Matou Pacifico*, Maria Alice Barroso, 1969, Novel

QUEM MATOU PIXOTE? 1996 d: Jose Joffily. BRZ., *Who Killed Pixote?*, Jose Loureiro, Book, *Pixote, the Law of the Strongest*, Cida Venancio Da Silva, Book

Quenched Thirst *see* **UTOLYENIYE ZHAZHDY** (1968).

Quenching of the Thirst *see* **UTOLYENIYE ZHAZHDY** (1968).

Quenching Thirst *see* **UTOLYENIYE ZHAZHDY** (1968).

Quenouille de Barberine, La *see* **BARBERINE** (1910).

QUENTIN DURWARD 1912 d: Adrien Caillard. FRN., *Quentin Durward*, Sir Walter Scott, 1823, Novel

Quentin Durward *see* **THE ADVENTURES OF QUENTIN DURWARD** (1956).

Querelle *see* **QUERELLE DE BREST** (1982).

Querelle - Ein Pakt Mit Dem Teufel *see* **QUERELLE DE BREST** (1982).

QUERELLE DE BREST 1982 d: R. W. Fassbinder. GRM/FRN., *Querelle de Brest*, Jean Genet, 1952, Novel

Query *see* **MURDER IN REVERSE** (1945).

QUEST FOR CAMELOT 1998 d: Frederick Du Chan. USA., *The King's Damosel*, Vera Chapman, Novel

QUEST FOR FIRE 1981 d: Jean-Jacques Annaud. CND/FRN., *La Guerre du Feu*, Joseph Henri Rosny, 1911, Novel

Quest for King Solomon's Mines, The *see* **WATUSI** (1959).

QUEST FOR LOVE 1971 d: Ralph Thomas. UKN., *Random Quest*, John Wyndham, 1961, Short Story

QUEST FOR LOVE 1987 d: Helena NogueirA. SAF., *Things As They are*, Gertrude Stein, 1950, Novel

Quest of Happiness, The *see* **DUNUNGEN** (1919).

QUEST OF LIFE, THE 1916 d: Ashley Miller. USA., *Ellen Young*, Gabriel Enthoven, Edmund Goulding, Play

Quest of Truth *see* **QUEST FOR LOVE** (1987).

Quest, The *see* **TSUMA YO BARA NO YONI** (1935).

QUESTI FANTASMI 1954 d: Eduardo de Filippo. ITL., *Questi Fantasmi!*, Eduardo de Filippo, 1946, Play

QUESTI FANTASMI 1967 d: Renato Castellani. ITL/FRN., *Questi Fantasmi!*, Eduardo de Filippo, 1946, Play

QUESTI RAGAZZI 1937 d: Mario Mattoli. ITL., *Questi Ragazzi*, Gherardo Gherardi, Play

QUESTION OF ADULTERY, A 1958 d: Don Chaffey. UKN., *A Breach of Marriage*, Dan Sutherland, London 1948, Play

QUESTION OF ATTRIBUTION, A 1991 d: John Schlesinger. UKN., *A Question of Attribution*, Alan Bennett, Play

QUESTION OF HATS AND GOWNS, A 1914 d: Ashley Miller. USA., *Town Pumps and Gold Leaf*, Ida M. Evans, Story

QUESTION OF HONOR, A 1922 d: Edwin Carewe. USA., *A Question of Honor*, Ruth Cross, 1920, Short Story

QUESTION OF HONOR, A 1982 d: Jud Taylor. USA., *A Question of Honor*, Sonny Grosso, Philip Rosenberg, Book

QUESTION OF IDENTITY, A 1914 d: Charles J. Brabin. USA., *The Window That Monsieur Forgot*, Mary Imlay Taylor, Story

QUESTION OF PRINCIPLE, A 1922 d: George A. Cooper. UKN., *A Question of Principle*, Mayell Bannister, Story

QUESTION OF SUSPENSE, A 1961 d: Max Varnel. UKN., *A Question of Suspense*, Roy Vickers, Novel

QUESTION OF TRUST, A 1920 d: Maurice Elvey. UKN., *A Question of Trust*, Ethel M. Dell, Novel

QUESTIONE PRIVATA, UNA 1966 d: Giorgio Trentin. ITL., *Una Questione Privata*, Beppe Fenoglio, Novel

Questions and Answers *see* **Q & A** (1990).

QUESTO IMPOSSIBILE OGGETTO 1973 d: John Frankenheimer. ITL/FRN., *Impossible Object*, Nicholas Mosley, 1968, Novel

Qui Ju Da Guanshi *see* **QIUJU DA GUANSI** (1992).

Qui Veut Tuer Carlos? *see* **GEHEIMNISSE IN GOLDENEN NYLONS** (1966).

QUICK 1932 d: Robert Siodmak. FRN., *Quick*, Felix Gandera, Play

QUICK AND THE DEAD, THE 1987 d: Robert Day. USA., *The Quick and the Dead*, Louis L'Amour, Novel

QUICK, BEFORE IT MELTS 1965 d: Delbert Mann. USA., *Quick Before It Melts*, Philip Benjamin, New York 1964, Novel

QUICK CHANGE 1925 d: Dell Henderson. USA., *Quick Change*, E. A. Ullman, Short Story

Quick Change *see* **HOLD-UP** (1985).

QUICK CHANGE 1990 d: Howard Franklin, Bill Murray. USA., *Quick Change*, Jay Cronley, Novel

QUICK GUN, THE 1964 d: Sidney Salkow. USA., *The Fastest Gun*, Steve Fisher, Short Story

QUICKER THAN THE EYE 1988 d: Nicolas Gessner. SWT/AUS/GRM., *Quicker Than the Eye*, Claude Cueni, Novel

Quicksands *see* **BROKEN BARRIER** (1917).

QUIEN PUEDE MATAR A UN NINO? 1975 d: Narciso Ibanez Serrador. SPN., *Quien Puede Matar a un Nino?*, Juan Jose Plans, Novel

QUIET AMERICAN, THE 1958 d: Joseph L. Mankiewicz. USA., *The Quiet American*, Graham Greene, 1955, Novel

Quiet American, The *see* **THE UGLY AMERICAN** (1963).

Quiet Business, A *see* **UN COMMERCE TRANQUILLE** (1964).

QUIET DAY IN BELFAST, A 1974 d: Milad BessadA. CND., *A Quiet Day in Belfast*, Andrew Angus Dalrymple, Play

Quiet Days in Clichy *see* **STILLE DAGE I CLICHY** (1970).

Quiet Days in Clichy *see* **JOURS TRANQUILLES A CLICHY** (1989).

Quiet Don, The *see* **TIKHU DON** (1931).

Quiet Duel, The *see* **SHIZUKANARU KETTO** (1949).

QUIET EARTH, THE 1985 d: Geoff Murphy. NZL., *The Quiet Earth*, Craig Harrison, Novel

Quiet Fight, The *see* **SHIZUKANARU KETTO** (1949).

Quiet Flows the Don *see* **TIKHII DON** (1958).

QUIET GUN, THE 1957 d: William F. Claxton. USA., *Lawman*, Lauran Paine, 1955, Novel

Quiet Is the Night *see* **WSROD NOCNEJ CISZY** (1978).

QUIET MAN, THE 1952 d: John Ford. USA., Maurice Walsh, Story

Quiet Rolls the Day *see* **EK DIN PRATIDIN** (1979).

QUIET WEDDING 1941 d: Anthony Asquith. UKN., *Quiet Wedding*, Esther McCracken, London 1938, Play

QUIET WEEKEND 1946 d: Harold French. UKN., *Quiet Weekend*, Esther McCracken, London 1941, Play

Quijote, Ayer Y Hoy, El *see* **DON QUIJOTE AYER Y HOY** (1964).

QUILLER MEMORANDUM, THE 1966 d: Michael Anderson. UKN/USA., *The Berlin Memorandum*, Elleston Trevor, London 1965, Novel

Quilp *see* **MISTER QUILP** (1974).

Qu'importe le Flacon Pourvu Qu'on Ait l'Ivresse *see* **POURVU QU'ON AIT L'IVRESSE** (1974).

QUINCANNON, FRONTIER SCOUT 1956 d: Lesley Selander. USA., *Frontier Feud*, Will Cook, Novel

Quincy Adams Sawyer *see* **QUINCY ADAMS SAWYER AND MASON'S CORNER FOLKS** (1912).

QUINCY ADAMS SAWYER 1922 d: Clarence Badger. USA., *Quincy Adams Sawyer and Mason's Corner Folks*, Charles Felton Pidgin, Boston 1900, Novel

QUINCY ADAMS SAWYER AND MASON'S CORNER FOLKS 1912. USA., *Quincy Adams Sawyer*, Justin Adams, New York 1902, Play

QUINNEYS 1919 d: Rex Wilson. UKN., *Quinneys*, Horace Annesley Vachell, London 1915, Play

QUINNEYS 1927 d: Maurice Elvey. UKN., *Quinneys*, Horace Annesley Vachell, London 1915, Play

Quite a Complicated Girl *see* **UNA RAGAZZA PIUTTOSTA COMPLICATA** (1968).

QUITS 1915 d: Joseph de Grasse. USA., *The Sheriff of Long Butte*, Julius G. Furthmann, Story

QUITTER, THE 1929 d: Joseph Henabery. USA., *The Spice of Life*, Dorothy Howell, Story

Quitter, The *see* **NO RANSOM** (1934).

QUN MO 1948 d: Xu Changlin. CHN., *Qun Mo*, Chen Baichen, 1947, Play

QUO VADIS? 1913 d: Enrico Guazzoni. ITL., *Quo Vadis?*, Henryk Sienkiewicz, 1896, Novel

QUO VADIS? 1924 d: Gabriellino d'Annunzio, Georg Jacoby. ITL., *Quo Vadis?*, Henryk Sienkiewicz, 1896, Novel

QUO VADIS? 1951 d: Mervyn Leroy. USA., *Quo Vadis?*, Henryk Sienkiewicz, 1896, Novel

QUO VADIS? 1985 d: Franco Rossi. ITL., *Quo Vadis?*, Henryk Sienkiewicz, 1896, Novel

RAB RABY 1965 d: Gyorgy Hintsch. HNG., *Rab Raby*, Mor Jokai, 1879, Novel

RABAGAS 1922 d: Gaston Ravel. ITL., *Rabagas*, Victorien Sardou, 1872

Rabanser Case, The *see* **DER FALL RABANSER** (1950).

Rabbia Dentro, La *see* **DELITTO AL CIRCOLO DEL TENNIS** (1969).

Rabbit Is Me, The *see* **DAS KANINCHEN BIN ICH** (1965).

RABBIT, RUN 1970 d: Jack Smight. USA., *Rabbit, Run*, John Updike, New York 1960, Novel

Rabbit Stew, The *see* **LEGENDA A NYULPAPRIKASROL** (1975).

RABBIT TRAP, THE 1959 d: Philip Leacock. USA., *The Rabbit Trap*, J. P. Miller, 1955, Television Play

Rabbits *see* **NIGHT OF THE LEPUS** (1972).

RABOLIOT 1945 d: Jacques Daroy. FRN., *Raboliot*, Maurice Genevoix, Novel

RABOUILLEUSE, LA 1943 d: Fernand Rivers. FRN., *La Rabouilleuse*, Honore de Balzac, Paris 1842, Novel

Rabouilleuse, La *see* **LES ARRIVISTES** (1960).

RABU RETA 1959 d: Seijun Suzuki. JPN., *Rabu Reta*, Takeo Matsuura, Novel

RACCONTI DI CANTERBURY, I 1972 d: Pier Paolo Pasolini. ITL/FRN., *The Canterbury Tales*, Geoffrey Chaucer, c1400, Verse

RACCONTI D'INVERNO 1910. ITL., *The Winter's Tale*, William Shakespeare, c1611, Play

RACCONTI ROMANI 1955 d: Gianni Franciolini. ITL., *Racconti Romani*, Alberto Moravia, Milan 1954, Short Stories

RACCONTO DELLA GIUNGLA, IL 1973 d: GibbA. ITL., *Robinson Crusoe*, Daniel Defoe, 1719, Novel

Racconto d'Inverno *see* **RACCONTI D'INVERNO** (1910).

RACCONTO D'INVERNO 1913. ITL., *The Winter's Tale*, William Shakespeare, c1611, Play

RACE DES SEIGNEURS, LA 1974 d: Pierre Granier-Deferre. FRN/ITL., *La Race Des Seigneurs*, Felicien Marceau, Novel

Race for Life *see* **MASK OF DUST** (1954).

Race for Life, A see ROZE KATE (1912).

Race for Millions, A see LE DEMON DE LA HAINE (1921).

Race Gang see FOUR DARK HOURS (1937).

RACERS, THE 1955 d: Henry Hathaway. USA., *The Racers*, Hans Ruesch, 1953, Novel

Races see RAPT (1934).

Rache Ist Mein, Die see ALEXANDRA (1914).

RACHEL AND THE STRANGER 1948 d: Norman Foster. USA., *Rachel*, Howard Fast, 1945, Short Story

RACHEL CADE 1961 d: Gordon Douglas. USA., *Rachel Cade*, Charles E. Mercer, New York 1956, Novel

RACHEL PAPERS, THE 1989 d: Damian Harris. UKN., *The Rachel Papers*, Martin Amis, 1973, Novel

RACHEL, RACHEL 1968 d: Paul Newman. USA., *A Jest of God*, Margaret Laurence, New York 1966, Novel

RACHEL RIVER 1987 d: Sandy Smolan. USA., Carol Bly, Short Stories

RACHER, DER 1960 d: Karl Anton. GRM., *The Avenger*, Edgar Wallace, London 1926, Novel

RACINES DU MAL, LES 1967 d: Maurice Cam. FRN., *Les Mauvaises Frequentations*, Louis Thomas, Novel

RACK, THE 1916 d: Emile Chautard. USA., *The Rack*, Thompson Buchanan, New York 1911, Play

RACK, THE 1956 d: Arnold Laven. USA., *The Rack*, Rod Serling, Television Play

RACKET, THE 1928 d: Lewis Milestone. USA., *The Racket*, Bartlett Cormack, New York 1927, Play

RACKET, THE 1951 d: John Cromwell, Nicholas Ray (Uncredited). USA., *The Racket*, Bartlett Cormack, New York 1927, Play

Racketeer, The see RICH PEOPLE (1929).

RACKETY RAX 1932 d: Alfred L. Werker. USA., *Rackety Rax*, Joel Sayre, 1932, Short Story

RADFAHRER VOM SAN CHRISTOBAL, DER 1987 d: Peter Lilienthal. GRM., Antonio Skarmeta, Story

RADIO FRECCIA 1998 d: Luciano Ligabue. ITL., *Fuori E Dentro Il Borgo*, Luciano Ligabue, Short Stories

Radio Jamboree see STARS OVER BROADWAY (1935).

Radio Murder Mystery, The see LOVE IS ON THE AIR (1937).

RADIO NO JIKAN 1998 d: Koki Mitani. JPN., *Radio No Jikan*, Koki Mitani, Tokyo Sunshine Boys, Play

Radio Revels see THE CUCKOOS (1930).

Radio Revue of 1937 see LET'S MAKE A NIGHT OF IT (1937).

Radiografia d'un Colpo d'Oro see 500 MILLONES LAS VEGAS (1968).

RAFALE, LA 1920 d: Jacques de Baroncelli. FRN., *La Rafale*, Henri Bernstein, 1905, Play

RAFFERTY'S RISE 1918 d: J. M. Kerrigan. IRL/UKN., *The Rise of Constable Rafferty*, Nicholas Hayes, Play

RAFFICHE 1920 d: Enrico RomA. ITL., *La Rafale*, Henri Bernstein, 1905, Play

RAFFINIERTESTE FRAU BERLINS, DIE 1927 d: Franz Osten. GRM., *Die Raffinierteste Frau Berlins*, Garai-Arvay, Novel

RAFFLES 1930 d: Harry d'Abbadie d'Arrast (Uncredited), George Fitzmaurice. USA., *The Amateur Cracksman*, E. W. Hornung, London 1899, Novel

RAFFLES 1940 d: Sam Wood. USA., *The Amateur Cracksman*, E. W. Hornung, London 1899, Novel

RAFFLES, THE AMATEUR CRACKSMAN 1917 d: George Irving. USA., *The Amateur Cracksman*, E. W. Hornung, London 1899, Novel

RAFFLES, THE AMATEUR CRACKSMAN 1925 d: King Baggot. USA., *The Amateur Cracksman*, E. W. Hornung, London 1899, Novel

RAFLES SUR LA VILLE 1957 d: Pierre Chenal. FRN., *Rafles Sur la Ville*, Auguste le Breton, Novel

RAFTER ROMANCE 1934 d: William A. Seiter. USA., *Rafter Romance*, John Wells, New York 1932, Novel

Raga Leela see GNANAMBIKA (1940).

Ragamuffin, The see THE HOODLUM (1919).

Ragamuffins, The see TRHANI (1936).

RAGAZZA DAL LIVIDO AZZURRO, LA 1933 d: E. W. Emo. ITL., *..Und Wer Kusst Mich?*, F. D. Andam, Herbert Rosenfeld, Novel

RAGAZZA DEL BERSAGLIERE, LA 1967 d: Alessandro Blasetti. ITL., *La Fidanzata Del Bersagliere*, Edoardo Anton, Play

RAGAZZA DEL PALIO, LA 1957 d: Luigi ZampA. ITL., *La Ragazza Del Palio*, Raffaello Giannelli, Novel

Ragazza Del Peccato, La see EN CAS DE MALHEUR (1958).

RAGAZZA DI BUBE, LA 1963 d: Luigi Comencini. ITL/FRN., *La Ragazza Di Bube*, Carlo Cassola, 1960, Novel

RAGAZZA DI MILLE MESI, LA 1961 d: Steno. ITL., *Le Rayon Des Jouets*, Jacques Deval, 1951, Play

RAGAZZA DI NOME GIULIO, LA 1970 d: Tonino Valerii. ITL., *La Ragazza Di Nome Giulio*, Milena Milani, Novel

RAGAZZA DI TRIESTE, LA 1983 d: Pasquale Festa Campanile. ITL., *La Ragazza Di Trieste*, Pasquale Festa Campanile, Novel

Ragazza, La see LA RAGAZZA DI BUBE (1963).

Ragazza Per l'Estate, Una see UNE FILLE POUR L'ETE (1960).

Ragazza Perduta, La see SPERDUTI NEL BUIO (1947).

RAGAZZA PIUTTOSTA COMPLICATA, UNA 1968 d: Damiano Damiani. ITL., *La Marcia Indietro*, Alberto Moravia, Short Story

RAGAZZE DI SAN FREDIANO, LE 1955 d: Valerio Zurlini. ITL., *Le Ragazze Di Sanfrediano*, Vasco Pratolini, 1949, Novel

RAGAZZI DEI PARIOLI, I 1959 d: Sergio Corbucci. ITL., *Ai Galli Piacciono le Stelle*, Luciano Martino, Play

RAGAZZI DEL MASSACRO, I 1969 d: Fernando Di Leo. ITL., Giorgio Scerbanenco, Novel

RAGE IN HARLEM, A 1991 d: Bill Duke. UKN/USA., *For Love of Imabelle (a Rage in Harlem)*, Chester Himes, 1957, Novel

RAGE IN HEAVEN 1941 d: W. S. Van Dyke. USA., *Dawn of Reckoning*, James Hilton, 1925, Novel

RAGE OF ANGELS 1982 d: Buzz Kulik. USA., *Rage of Angels*, Sidney Sheldon, Novel

Rage of Angels - Part Two see RAGE OF ANGELS: THE STORY CONTINUES (1986).

RAGE OF ANGELS: THE STORY CONTINUES 1986 d: Paul Wendkos. USA., *Rage of Angels*, Sidney Sheldon, Novel

RAGE OF PARIS, THE 1921 d: Jack Conway. USA., *The White Peacock Feathers*, Du Vernet Rabell, Story

RAGE TO LIVE, A 1965 d: Walter Grauman. USA., *A Rage to Live*, John O'Hara, New York 1949, Novel

Rage Within, The see DELITTO AL CIRCOLO DEL TENNIS (1969).

RAGGED EARL, THE 1914 d: Lloyd B. Carleton. USA., *The Ragged Earl*, Joseph Humphries, Ernest Lacy, New York 1899, Play

RAGGED EDGE, THE 1923 d: F. Harmon Weight. USA., *The Ragged Edge*, Harold MacGrath, New York 1922, Novel

Ragged Lover, The see THE BELOVED ROGUE (1927).

Ragged Men see TRHANI (1936).

RAGGED MESSENGER, THE 1917 d: Frank Wilson. UKN., *The Ragged Messenger*, William Babington Maxwell, London 1904, Novel

RAGGED TROUSERED PHILANTHROPISTS, THE 1967 d: Christopher Morahan. UKN., *The Ragged Trousered Philanthropists*, Robert Tressell, Book

Raggedy Ann see THE EXQUISITE THIEF (1919).

Raggi Mortali Del Dr. Mabuse, I see DIE TODESSTRAHLEN DES DR. MABUSE (1964).

Raging Flames see LIEYAN (1933).

RAGING MOON, THE 1970 d: Bryan Forbes. UKN., *The Raging Moon*, Peter Marshall, Novel

RAGING TIDE, THE 1951 d: George Sherman. USA., *Fiddler's Green*, Ernest K. Gann, 1950, Novel

RAGMAN'S DAUGHTER, THE 1972 d: Harold Becker. UKN., *The Ragman's Daughter*, Alan Sillitoe, 1963, Short Story

RAGS 1915 d: James Kirkwood. USA., *Rags*, Edith Barnard Delano, Story

RAGTIME 1981 d: Milos Forman. USA., *Ragtime*, E. L. Doctorow, 1971, Novel

RAHI 1953 d: Khwaya Ahmad Abbas. IND., *Two Leaves and a Bud*, Mulk Raj Anand, 1937, Novel

RAICES 1953 d: Benito Alazraki. MXC., Francisco Rojas Gonzalez, Story

Raid see RAZZIA (1958).

RAID OF 1915, THE 1914 d: Fred W. Durrant. UKN., *The Invasion of 1910*, William le Queux, Novel

RAID, THE 1954 d: Hugo Fregonese. USA., *Affair at St. Albans*, Herbert Ravenal Sass, 1947, Article

RAIDERS OF THE GOLDEN TRIANGLE 1985 d: Tom Saichur. HKG., *Raiders of the Golden Triangle*, Norman Carrigan, Novel

RAIDERS OF THE LOST ARK 1981 d: Steven Spielberg. USA., Philip Kaufman, George Lucas, Story

RAIDERS, THE 1921 d: Nate Watt. USA., *The Whiskey Runners*, Bertrand W. Sinclair, Story

RAIL RIDER, THE 1916 d: Maurice Tourneur. USA., *B*, Edgar Franklin, 1916, Short Story

RAILROADED 1923 d: Edmund Mortimer. USA., *Richard*, Marguerite Bryant, New York 1922, Novel

RAILROADER, THE 1919 d: Colin Campbell. USA., *Caleb Conover - Railroader*, Albert Payson Terhune, New York 1907, Novel

Railroaders, The see THE RAILROADER (1919).

RAILWAY CHILDREN, THE 1970 d: Lionel Jeffries. UKN., *The Railway Children*, E. Nesbit, 1906, Novel

RAILWAY STATION MAN, THE 1993 d: Michael Whyte. UKN/USA., *The Railway Station Man*, Jennifer Johnston, Novel

RAIN 1932 d: Lewis Milestone. USA., *Rain*, W. Somerset Maugham, 1921, Short Story

RAIN FOR A DUSTY SUMMER 1971 d: Arthur Lubin. USA/SPN., Franklyn Lacey, Story

RAIN OR SHINE 1930 d: Frank CaprA. USA., *Rain Or Shine*, James Gleason, New York 1928, Play

Rain Or Shine see MANHATTAN HEARTBEAT (1940).

Rain, Rain, Go Away see SHADOW IN THE SKY (1951).

RAINBOW 1978 d: Jackie Cooper. USA., *Rainbow*, Christopher Finch, Book

Rainbow Bridge see NIJI NO HASHI (1993).

RAINBOW DRIVE 1990 d: Bobby Roth. USA., *Rainbow Drive*, Roderick Thorp, Novel

Rainbow for Rimbaud see RAINBOW POUR RIMBAUD (1996).

RAINBOW POUR RIMBAUD 1996 d: Jean Teule. FRN., *Rainbow Pour Rimbaud*, Jean Teule, 1991, Novel

RAINBOW RILEY 1926 d: Charles Hines. USA., *The Cub*, Thompson Buchanan, New York 1910, Play

RAINBOW, THE 1917 d: Ralph Dean. USA., *The Rainbow*, A. E. Thomas, New York 1912, Play

RAINBOW, THE 1989 d: Ken Russell. UKN., *The Rainbow*, D. H. Lawrence, 1915, Novel

RAINBOW TRAIL, THE 1918 d: Frank Lloyd. USA., *The Rainbow Trail*, Zane Grey, New York 1915, Novel

RAINBOW TRAIL, THE 1925 d: Lynn Reynolds. USA., *The Rainbow Trail*, Zane Grey, New York 1915, Novel

RAINBOW TRAIL, THE 1932 d: David Howard. USA., *The Rainbow Trail*, Zane Grey, New York 1915, Novel

RAINMAKER, THE 1926 d: Clarence Badger. USA., *Heavenbent*, Gerald Beaumont, Short Story

RAINMAKER, THE 1956 d: Joseph Anthony. USA., *The Rainmaker*, N. Richard Nash, 1955, Television Play

Rainmaker, The see JOHN GRISHAM'S THE RAINMAKER (1997).

RAINS CAME, THE 1939 d: Clarence Brown. USA., *The Rains Came*, Louis Bromfield, New York 1937, Novel

RAINS OF RANCHIPUR, THE 1955 d: Jean Negulesco. USA., *The Rains Came*, Louis Bromfield, New York 1937, Novel

RAINTREE COUNTY, THE 1957 d: Edward Dmytryk. USA., *Raintree County*, Ross Lockridge, 1948, Novel

RAINY, THE LION KILLER 1914 d: Sidney Drew. USA., *Rainy the Lion Killer*, Leonard Grover, Story

Raise the Red Lantern see DAHONG DENGLONG GAOGAO GUA (1991).

RAISE THE TITANIC 1980 d: Jerry Jameson. USA/UKN., *Raise the Titanic!*, Clive Cussler, Novel

RAISIN IN THE SUN, A 1961 d: Daniel Petrie. USA., *A Raisin in the Sun*, Lorraine Hansberry, New York 1959, Play

RAISING A RIOT 1955 d: Wendy Toye. UKN., *Raising a Riot*, Alfred Toombs, Novel

Raising Daisy Rothschild see THE LAST GIRAFFE (1979).

RAJANIGANDHA 1974 d: Basu Chatterjee. IND., *Yeh Sach Hai*, Manu Bhandari, Short Story

Rajnigandha see RAJANIGANDHA (1974).

RAJSKA JABLON 1985 d: Barbara Sass. PLN., *Rajska Jablon*, Pola Gojawiczynska, 1937, Novel

Rajska Jablon see DZIEWCZETA Z NOWOLIPEK (1985).

RAKE'S PROGRESS, THE 1945 d: Sidney Gilliat. UKN., Val Valentine, Story

RAKKA SURU YUGATA 1998 d: Naoe Gozu. JPN., *Rakka Suru Yugata*, Kaori Ekuni, Novel

RAKKAUDEN RISTI 1946 d: Teuvo Tulio. FNL., *Stantsionny Smotritel*, Alexander Pushkin, 1831, Short Story

RAKOCZY-MARSCH 1933 d: Gustav Frohlich. GRM/AUS., *A Dolovai Nabob Leanya*, Ferenc Herczeg, 1894, Play

Rakoszy-Marsch see **RAKOCZY-MARSCH** (1933).

RALLARBLOD 1978 d: Erik Solbakken. NRW., *Dansen Gjenom Skuggeheim*, Kristofer Uppdal, 1911-24, Novel

RALLY 'ROUND THE FLAG, BOYS! 1958 d: Leo McCarey. USA., *Rally 'Round the Flag Boys!*, Max Shulman, 1957, Novel

RAM RAJYA 1967 d: Vijay Bhatt. IND., *Ramayana*, Valmiki, Verse

RAMASAGUL 1985 d: Ion Popescu-Gopo. RMN., *Punguta Cu Doi Bani*, Ion Creanga, 1876, Short Story

RAMBLE IN APHASIA, A 1918 d: Kenneth Webb. USA., *A Ramble in Aphasia*, O. Henry, Short Story

RAMBLIN' KID, THE 1923 d: Edward Sedgwick. USA., *The Ramblin' Kid*, Earl Wayland Bowman, Indianapolis 1920, Novel

RAMBLING ROSE 1991 d: Martha Coolidge. USA., *Rambling Rose*, Calder Willingham, 1972, Novel

RAMO PARA LUIZA, UM 1965 d: J. B. Tanko. BRZ., *Um Ramo Para Luisa*, Jose Conde, 1959, Short Story

RAMONA 1910 d: D. W. Griffith. USA., *Ramona*, Helen Hunt Jackson, Boston 1884, Novel

RAMONA 1916 d: Donald Crisp. USA., *Ramona*, Helen Hunt Jackson, Boston 1884, Novel

RAMONA 1928 d: Edwin Carewe. USA., *Ramona*, Helen Hunt Jackson, Boston 1884, Novel

RAMONA 1936 d: Henry King. USA., *Ramona*, Helen Hunt Jackson, Boston 1884, Novel

RAMPAGE 1963 d: Phil Karlson, Henry Hathaway (Uncredited). USA., *Rampage*, Alan Caillou, New York 1961, Novel

RAMPAGE 1987 d: William Friedkin. USA., *Rampage*, William P. Wood, Novel

Rampage at Apache Wells see **DER OLPRINZ** (1965).

RAMPER, DER TIERMENSCH 1927 d: Max Reichmann. GRM., *Der Kampfer*, Max Mohr, Play

Ramper the Beastman see **DER TIERMENSCH RAMPER** (1927).

Ramrajya see **RAM RAJYA** (1967).

RAMROD 1947 d: Andre de Toth. USA., *Ramrod*, Luke Short, Short Story

RAMSBOTTOM RIDES AGAIN 1956 d: John Baxter. UKN., *Ramsbottom Rides Again*, Harold G. Robert, Play

RAMSHACKLE HOUSE 1924 d: F. Harmon Weight. USA., *Ramshackle House*, Hubert Footner, New York 1922, Novel

RAMUNTCHO 1919 d: Jacques de Baroncelli. FRN., *Ramuntcho*, Pierre Loti, 1896, Novel

RAMUNTCHO 1937 d: Rene Barberis. FRN., *Ramuntcho*, Pierre Loti, 1896, Novel

RAMUNTCHO 1958 d: Pierre Schoendoerffer. FRN., *Ramuntcho*, Pierre Loti, 1896, Novel

RAN 1985 d: Akira KurosawA. JPN/FRN., *King Lear*, William Shakespeare, c1605, Play

RANCHEADOR 1977 d: Sergio Giral. CUB., *Palenques de Negros Cimarrones*, Cirilo Villaverde, 1890, Short Story

Rancher, The see **RANCHEADOR** (1977).

RANCHO NOTORIOUS 1952 d: Fritz Lang. USA., *Gunsight Whitman*, Silvia Richards, Story

Rancune, La see **DER BESUCH** (1964).

RANDIDANGAZHI 1958 d: P. Subramanyam. IND., *Randidangazhi*, Thakazhy Shivashankar Pillai, Novel

Randolph '64 see **ROSE OF THE SOUTH** (1916).

Randolph Family, The see **DEAR OCTOPUS** (1943).

RANDOM HARVEST 1942 d: Mervyn Leroy. USA., *Random Harvest*, James Hilton, 1941, Novel

RANGE BOSS, THE 1917 d: W. S. Van Dyke. USA., *The Range Boss*, Charles Alden Seltzer, Chicago 1916, Novel

RANGE COURAGE 1927 d: Ernst Laemmle. USA., *Blinky*, Gene Markey, 1923, Short Story

Range Riders of the Great Wild West see **WALLOPING WALLACE** (1924).

RANGE WARFARE 1935 d: S. Roy Luby. USA., *The Death Whistler*, E. B. Mann, Story

Rangeen Zamana see **AJIT** (1948).

RANGER OF THE BIG PINES 1925 d: W. S. Van Dyke. USA., *Cavanaugh - Forest Ranger; a Romance of the Mountain West*, Hamlin Garland, New York 1910, Novel

RANK OUTSIDER, A 1920 d: Richard Garrick. UKN., *A Rank Outsider*, Nat Gould, Novel

RANNIE ZHURAVLI 1979 d: Bolotbek Shamshiev. USS., *Rannie Zhuravli*, Chingiz Aitmatov, 1975, Short Story

Rannie Zuravli see **RANNIE ZHURAVLI** (1979).

Ransacked Shop, The see **U SNEDENEHO KRAMU** (1933).

RANSOM OF MACK, THE 1920 d: Kenneth Webb. USA., *The Ransom of MacK*, O. Henry, Short Story

Ransom One Million Dollars see **MILLION DOLLAR RANSOM** (1934).

RANSOM, THE 1916 d: Edmund Lawrence. USA., *The Marionettes*, Oliver W. Geoffreys, Play

Ransom, The see **TENGOKU TO JIGOKU** (1963).

RANSON'S FOLLY 1910 d: Edwin S. Porter. USA., *Ranson's Folly*, Richard Harding Davis, New York 1902, Novel

RANSON'S FOLLY 1915 d: Richard Ridgely. USA., *Ranson's Folly*, Richard Harding Davis, New York 1902, Novel

RANSON'S FOLLY 1926 d: Sidney Olcott. USA., *Ranson's Folly*, Richard Harding Davis, New York 1902, Novel

RANTZAU, LES 1924 d: Gaston Roudes. FRN., *Les Rantzau*, Erckmann-Chatrian, Play

Rapace, Il see **LE RAPACE** (1968).

RAPACE, LE 1968 d: Jose Giovanni. FRN/ITL/MXC., *Le Vautour*, John Garrick, Novel

RAPACITE 1929 d: Andre Berthomieu. FRN., *Rapacite*, Eugene Barbier, Novel

Rapa-Nui see **DER GOLDENE ABGRUND** (1927).

Rape of Malaya, The see **A TOWN LIKE ALICE** (1956).

Rape of the Third Reich, The see **ENGLAND MADE ME** (1972).

RAPIDS, THE 1922 d: David M. Hartford. CND., *The Rapids*, Alan Sullivan, Novel

Rapids, The see **PEREJE** (1940).

Rapina Al Sole see **PAR UN BEAU MATIN D'ETE** (1964).

Rapports de Classes see **KLASSENVERHALTNISSE** (1984).

RAPPRESAGLIA 1973 d: George Pan Cosmatos. ITL/FRN., *Morte a Roma*, Robert Katz, Book

RAPT 1934 d: Dimitri Kirsanoff. FRN/GRM/SWT., *La Separation Des Races*, Charles-Ferdinand Ramuz, 1923, Novel

RAPT, LE 1984 d: Pierre Koralnik. FRN/SWT., *Le Rapt*, Charles-Ferdinand Ramuz, Novel

Rapto de Elena, la Decente Italiana, El see **ETTORE LO FUSTO** (1972).

RAPTURE 1965 d: John Guillermin. USA/FRN., *Rapture in My Rags*, Phyllis Hastings, London 1964, Novel

Rare Book Murder, The see **FAST COMPANY** (1938).

RARIN' TO GO 1924 d: Richard Thorpe. USA., *Rattler Rock*, Ralph Cummins, 1923, Short Story

Ras El Gua see **FORT DE LA SOLITUDE** (1947).

RASCAL 1969 d: Norman Tokar. USA., *Rascal; a Memoir of a Better Era*, Sterling North, New York 1963, Novel

Rascals of the Front Bench I. to Hell With Teachers, The see **DIE LUMMEL VON DER ERSTEN BANK 1. ZUR HOLLE MIT DEN PAUKERN** (1968).

Rascals' Tales see **LAUSBUBENGESCHICHTEN** (1964).

RASCOALA 1965 d: Mircea Muresan. RMN., *Rascoala*, Liviu Rebreanu, 1932, Novel

RASHOMON 1950 d: Akira KurosawA. JPN., *Rashomon*, Ryunosuke Akutagawa, 1915, Short Story, *Yabu No Naka*, Ryunosuke Akutagawa, 1922, Short Story

RASKOLNIKOW 1923 d: Robert Wiene. GRM., *Prestuplenije I Nakazanije*, Fyodor Dostoyevsky, 1867, Novel

Rasmus and the Tramp see **LUFFAREN OCH RASMUS** (1955).

RASMUS PAA LUFFEN 1982 d: Olle Hellbom. SWD., Astrid Lindgren, Story

RASP, THE 1931 d: Michael Powell. UKN., *The Rasp*, Philip MacDonald, Novel

Rasplyuyev's Gay Days see **VESYOLYYE RASPLYUYEVSKIYE DNI** (1966).

Raspoutine see **LA TRAGEDIE IMPERIALE** (1937).

Rasputin see **LA TRAGEDIE IMPERIALE** (1937).

Rasputin see **J'AI TUE RASPOUTINE** (1967).

RASSKAZ NEIZVESTNOGO CELOVEKA 1980 d: Vitautus Zalakevicius. USS., *Rasskaz Neizvestnogo Cheloveka*, Anton Chekhov, 1893, Short Story

Rasumoff see **SOUS LES YEUX D'OCCIDENT** (1936).

Rasumov see **SOUS LES YEUX D'OCCIDENT** (1936).

RAT D'AMERIQUE, LE 1962 d: Jean-Gabriel Albicocco. FRN/ITL., *Le Rat d'Amerique*, Jacques Lanzmann, Novel

Rat Saviour, The see **IZBAVITELJ** (1977).

RAT, THE 1925 d: Graham Cutts. UKN., *The Rat*, Constance Collier, Ivor Novello, London 1924, Play

RAT, THE 1937 d: Jack Raymond. UKN., *The Rat*, Constance Collier, Ivor Novello, London 1924, Play

RATAI 1962 d: Masashige NarusawA. JPN., *Ratai*, Kafu Nagai, Tokyo 1954, Novel

RATAS, LAS 1997 d: Antonio Gimenez-Rico. SPN., *Las Ratas*, Miguel Delibes, Novel

RATELRAT, DE 1987 d: Wim Verstappen. NTH., *De Ratelrat*, Janwillem Van Der Wetering, Novel

RATHER ENGLISH MARRIAGE, A 1998 d: Paul Seed. UKN., *A Rather English Marriage*, Angela Carter, Novel

RATHSKELLER AND THE ROSE, THE 1918 d: George Ridgwell. USA., *The Rathskeller and the Rose*, O. Henry, Short Story

RATNADEEP 1951 d: Debaki Bose. IND., *Ratnadeep*, Prabhat Kumar Mukherjee, Novel

RATNADEEP 1952 d: Debaki Bose. IND., *Ratnadeep*, Prabhat Kumar Mukherjee, Novel

RATNADEEPAM 1953 d: Debaki Bose. IND., *Ratnadeep*, Prabhat Kumar Mukherjee, Novel

RATON PASS 1951 d: Edwin L. Marin. USA., *Raton Pass*, Thomas W. Blackburn, 1950, Novel

Rats Awake, The see **BUDENJE PACOVA** (1967).

Rat's Tale, A see **DIE STORY VON MONTY SPINNERRATZ** (1998).

Rats, The see **DIE RATTEN** (1955).

Rats, The see **DEADLY EYES** (1982).

Rats, The see **LAS RATAS** (1997).

Rats Wake Up, The see **BUDENJE PACOVA** (1967).

RATSEL DER ROTEN ORCHIDEE, DAS 1961 d: Helmut Ashley. GRM., Edgar Wallace, Novel

RATSEL UM BEATE 1938 d: Johannes Meyer. GRM., *Ratsel Um Beate*, Hanz Lorenz, Alfred Moller, Play

RATTEN DER GROSSTADT 1930 d: Wolfgang Neff. GRM., *Ratten Der Grosstadt*, Fr. Glaser, Novel

RATTEN, DIE 1921 d: Hanns Kobe. GRM., *Die Ratten*, Gerhart Hauptmann, 1911, Play

RATTEN, DIE 1955 d: Robert Siodmak. GRM., *Die Ratten*, Gerhart Hauptmann, 1911, Play

RATTLE OF A SIMPLE MAN 1964 d: Muriel Box. UKN., *Rattle of a Simple Man*, Charles Dyer, London 1962, Play

Rattle Rat, The see **DE RATELRAT** (1987).

RAUB DER SABINERINNEN, DER 1919 d: Heinrich Bolten-Baeckers. GRM., *Der Raub Der Sabinerinnen*, Franz von Schonthan, Paul von Schonthan, Play

RAUB DER SABINERINNEN, DER 1928 d: Robert Land. GRM., *Der Raub Der Sabinerinnen*, Franz von Schonthan, Paul von Schonthan, Play

RAUB DER SABINERINNEN, DER 1936 d: R. A. Stemmle. GRM., *Der Raub Der Sabinerinnen*, Franz von Schonthan, Paul von Schonthan, Play

RAUB DER SABINERINNEN, DER 1954 d: Kurt Hoffmann. GRM., *Der Raub Der Sabinerinnen*, Franz von Schonthan, Paul von Schonthan, Play

RAUBER HOTZENPLOTZ, DER 1973 d: Gustav Ehmck. GRM., *Der Rauber Hotzenplotz*, Otfried Preussler, Book

RAUBERBANDE, DIE 1928 d: Hans Behrendt. GRM., *Die Rauberbande*, Leonhard Frank, Novel

RAUBFISCHER IN HELLAS 1959 d: Horst Haechler. GRM/USA/YGS., *Raubfischer in Hellas*, Werner Helwig, Novel

RAUSCH EINER NACHT 1951 d: Eduard von Borsody. GRM., *Alexa*, Harald Bratt, Play

Rauschende Melodien see **DIE FLEDERMAUS** (1955).

Rautha Skikkjan see **DEN RODA KAPPAN** (1967).

RAVEN, THE 1915 d: Charles J. Brabin. USA., *The Raven; the Love Story of Edgar Allan Poe*, George Cochrane Hazelton, New York 1909, Novel

RAVEN, THE 1935 d: Lew Landers. USA., *The Pit and the Pendulum*, Edgar Allan Poe, 1845, Short Story, *The Raven*, Edgar Allan Poe, 1845, Poem

RAVEN, THE 1963 d: Roger Corman. USA., *The Raven*, Edgar Allan Poe, 1845, Poem

Ravished Armenia see **AUCTION OF SOULS** (1919).

Ravishing Barmaid, The see **SENKYRKA "U DIVOKE KRASY"** (1932).

Ravishing Idiot, A see **UNE RAVISSANTE IDIOTE** (1964).

Ravishing Idiots, The see **UNE RAVISSANTE IDIOTE** (1964).

RAVISSANTE IDIOTE, UNE 1964 d: Edouard Molinaro. FRN/ITL., *Une Ravissante Idiote*, Charles Exbrayat, Paris 1962, Novel

RAVNOVESSIE 1983 d: Lyudmil Kirkov. BUL., *Divi Pcheli*, Stanislav Stratiev, 1978, Novel

RAWHEAD 1987 d: George Pavlou. UKN/IRL., *Rawhead Rex*, Clive Barker, Short Story

Rawhead Rex see **RAWHEAD** (1987).

RAWHIDE HALO, THE 1960 d: Roger Kay. USA., *Barb Wire*, Walter J. Coburn, New York 1931, Novel

RAWHIDE YEARS, THE 1956 d: Rudolph Mate. USA., *The Rawhide Years*, Norman A. Fox, 1953, Novel

RAY BRADBURY'S NIGHTMARES VOLUME 1 1985 d: Bruce Pittman, William Fruet. USA., *The Playground*, Ray Bradbury, 1953, Short Story, *The Screaming Woman*, Ray Bradbury, 1951, Short Story

RAY BRADBURY'S NIGHTMARES VOLUME 2 1985 d: Douglas Jackson, Ralph L. Thomas. USA., *Banshee*, Ray Bradbury, 1988, Short Story, *The Crowd*, Ray Bradbury, 1943, Short Story

RAY BRADBURY'S THE ELECTRIC GRANDMOTHER 1981 d: Noel Black. USA., *I Sing the Body Electric!*, Ray Bradbury, Short Story

Rayon Lady see **DAS KUNSTSEIDENE MADCHEN** (1960).

Rayons Mortels du Docteur Mabuse, Les see **DIE TODESSTRAHLEN DES DR. MABUSE** (1964).

RAZORBACK 1983 d: Russell Mulcahy. ASL., *Razorback*, Peter Brennan, Novel

RAZOR'S EDGE, THE 1946 d: Edmund Goulding. USA., *The Razor's Edge*, W. Somerset Maugham, 1944, Novel

RAZOR'S EDGE, THE 1984 d: John Byrum. USA., *The Razor's Edge*, W. Somerset Maugham, 1944, Novel

Razzia see **RAZZIA SUR LA CHNOUF** (1955).

RAZZIA 1958 d: Laszlo Nadasy. HNG., *Razzia*, Lajos Nagy, 1929, Short Story

RAZZIA SUR LA CHNOUF 1955 d: Henri Decoin. FRN., *Razzia Sur la Chnouf*, Auguste le Breton, Novel

RAZZIA SUR LE PLAISIR 1976 d: Marius Lesoeur, Jesus Franco. FRN., *Greetings from Hong Kong*, A. L. Malraux

RE BURLONE 1935 d: Enrico Guazzoni. ITL., *Re Burlone*, Gerolamo Rovetta, Play

Re Dei Falsari, Il see **LE CAVE SE REBIFFE** (1961).

RE DELLA MASCHERA D'ORO, IL 1920 d: Alfredo Robert. ITL., *Le Roi a la Masque d'Or*, Marcel Schwob, 1893, Novel

Re Di Danari see **RE DI DENARI** (1936).

RE DI DENARI 1936 d: Enrico Guazzoni. ITL., *I Don*, Pippo Marchese, Play

Re in Esilio, I see **FEDERICA D'ILLIRIA** (1919).

RE LEAR 1910 d: Giuseppe de Liguoro. ITL., *King Lear*, William Shakespeare, c1605, Play

RE LEAR 1910 d: Gerolamo Lo Savio. ITL., *King Lear*, William Shakespeare, c1605, Play

RE MIZERABURU 1950 d: Daisuke Ito, Masahiro Makino. JPN., *Les Miserables*, Victor Hugo, Paris 1862, Novel

RE SI DIVERTE, IL 1941 d: Mario Bonnard. ITL., *Le Roi S'amuse*, Victor Hugo, 1832, Play

REACH FOR GLORY 1962 d: Philip Leacock. UKN., *The Custard Boys*, John Rae, London 1960, Novel

REACH FOR THE SKY 1956 d: Lewis Gilbert. UKN., *Reach for the Sky*, Paul Brickhill, 1954, Novel

Reach for Tomorrow see **LET NO MAN WRITE MY EPITAPH** (1960).

REACHING FOR THE SUN 1941 d: William A. Wellman. USA., *F.O.B. Detroit*, Wessel Smitter, Novel

REACTOR, THE 1989 d: David Heavener. USA., Thomas Baldwin, Story

READY FOR LOVE 1934 d: Marion Gering. USA., *The Whipping*, Roy Flannagan, New York 1930, Novel

READY FOR THE PEOPLE 1964 d: Buzz Kulik. USA., Eleazar Lipsky, Short Story

READY MONEY 1914 d: Oscar Apfel. USA., *Ready Money*, James Montgomery, New York 1912, Play

READY, WILLING AND ABLE 1937 d: Ray Enright. USA., *Ready Willing and Able*, Richard Macauley, Short Story

REAL ADVENTURE, THE 1922 d: King Vidor. USA., *The Real Adventure*, Henry Kitchell Webster, New York 1915, Novel

REAL AGATHA, THE 1914 d: Richard C. Travers. USA., *The Real Agatha*, Edith Huntington Mason, Novel

Real End of the Great War, The see **PRAWDZIWY KONIEC WIELKIEJ WOJNY** (1957).

REAL GLORY, THE 1939 d: Henry Hathaway. USA., *The Real Glory*, Charles L. Clifford, London 1938, Novel

Real Gone Girls, The see **THE MAN FROM O.R.G.Y.** (1970).

Real Jacob, The see **DER WAHRE JAKOB** (1960).

Real Schlemiel, The see **AARON'S MAGIC VILLAGE** (1997).

REALITIES 1930 d: Bernerd Mainwaring. UKN., *The Love Doctor*, Eric D. Brand, Play

Realm Between the Living and the Dead, The see **YINYANG JIE** (1988).

RE-ANIMATOR 1985 d: Stuart Gordon. USA., *Herbert West: the Re-Animator*, H. P. Lovecraft, Story

REAP THE WILD WIND 1942 d: Cecil B. de Mille. USA., Thelma Strabel, Story

Rear Car, The see **MURDER IN THE PRIVATE CAR** (1934).

Rear Echelon Man see **DER ETAPPENHASE** (1956).

Rear Guard see **THE COMMAND** (1953).

REAR WINDOW 1954 d: Alfred Hitchcock. USA., *Rear Window*, Cornell Woolrich, 1944, Short Story

REAR WINDOW 1998 d: Jeff Bleckner. USA., *Rear Window*, Cornell Woolrich, 1944, Short Story

REARVIEW MIRROR 1984 d: Lou Antonio. USA., *Rearview Mirror*, Caroline B. Cooney, Novel

REASON WHY, THE 1918 d: Robert G. VignolA. USA., *The Reason Why*, Elinor Glyn, London 1911, Novel

Reasons of State see **EL RECURSO DEL METODO** (1978).

REBECCA 1940 d: Alfred Hitchcock. USA., *Rebecca*, Daphne Du Maurier, London 1938, Novel

REBECCA 1979 d: Simon Langton. UKN., *Rebecca*, Daphne Du Maurier, London 1938, Novel

REBECCA 1995. UKN., *Rebecca*, Daphne Du Maurier, London 1938, Novel

REBECCA OF SUNNYBROOK FARM 1917 d: Marshall Neilan. USA., *Rebecca of Sunnybrook Farm*, Kate Douglas Wiggin, New York 1903, Novel

REBECCA OF SUNNYBROOK FARM 1932 d: Alfred Santell. USA., *Rebecca of Sunnybrook Farm*, Kate Douglas Wiggin, New York 1903, Novel

REBECCA OF SUNNYBROOK FARM 1938 d: Allan Dwan. USA., *Rebecca of Sunnybrook Farm*, Kate Douglas Wiggin, New York 1903, Novel

Rebecca the Jewess see **IVANHOE** (1913).

REBEL 1985 d: Michael Jenkins. ASL., *No Names. No Packdrill*, Bob Herbert, Play

Rebel Against the Light see **SANDS OF BEERSHEBA** (1965).

REBEL HIGH 1987 d: Harry Jakobs. USA., *Rebel High*, Evan Keliher, Novel

Rebel Nun, The see **LA NOVICIA REBELDE** (1971).

REBEL SON, THE 1938 d: Adrian Brunel, Alex Granowsky. UKN., Nikolay Gogol, Story

Rebel With a Cause see **THE LONELINESS OF THE LONG DISTANCE RUNNER** (1962).

Rebel With a Cause see **EL CHE GUEVARA** (1968).

REBELION DE LOS COLGADOS, LA 1953 d: Alfredo B. Crevenna, Emilio Fernandez. MXC., *Die Rebellion Der Gehenkten*, Ben Traven, 1936, Novel

Rebelion de Los Esclavos, La see **LA RIVOLTA DEGLI SCHIAVI** (1961).

REBELLE, LE 1930 d: Adelqui Millar. FRN., *A Tabornok*, Lajos Zilahy, Budapest 1928, Play

Rebellion see **JOIUCHI - HAIRYOZUMA SHIMATSU** (1967).

REBELLION, DIE 1962 d: Wolfgang Staudte. GRM., *Die Rebellion*, Joseph Roth, 1924, Short Story

Rebellion of the Hanged, The see **LA REBELION DE LOS COLGADOS** (1953).

Rebellious Girl, The see **DON'T** (1925).

REBELS, THE 1979 d: Russ Mayberry. USA., *The Rebels*, John Jakes, Novel

REBOZO DE SOLEDAD, EL 1952 d: Roberto Gavaldon. MXC., *El Rebozo de Soledad*, Dr. Ferrer, Novel

RECAPTURED LOVE 1930 d: John G. Adolfi. USA., *Misdeal*, Basil Dillon Woon, Play

RECHTER THOMAS 1953 d: Walter Smith. NTH., *Rechter Thomas*, Francois Pauwels, Novel

Recipe for Murder see **THE GREAT HOTEL MURDER** (1935).

RECKLESS AGE 1944 d: Felix E. Feist. USA., *Make Way for Love*, Al Martin, Story

RECKLESS AGE, THE 1924 d: Harry Pollard. USA., *Love Insurance*, Earl Derr Biggers, Indianapolis 1914, Novel

Reckless Age, The see **THIS RECKLESS AGE** (1932).

RECKLESS HOUR, THE 1931 d: John Francis Dillon. USA., *Ambush*, Arthur Richman, New York 1921, Play

RECKLESS LADY, THE 1926 d: Howard Higgin. USA., *The Reckless Lady*, Philip Hamilton Gibbs, London 1924, Novel

RECKLESS LIVING 1931 d: Cyril Gardner. USA., *The Up and Up*, Eva Kay Flint, Martha Madison, New York 1930, Play

RECKLESS LIVING 1938 d: Frank McDonald. USA., *Riders Up*, Gerald Beaumont, New York 1922, Novel

RECKLESS MOMENT, THE 1949 d: Max Ophuls. USA., *The Blank Wall*, Elisabeth Sanxay Holding, Novel

RECKLESS ROMANCE 1924 d: Scott Sidney. USA., *What's Your Wife Doing?*, Emil Nyitray, Herbert Hall Winslow, New York 1923, Play

RECKLESS YOUTH 1922 d: Ralph Ince. USA., *Reckless Youth*, Cosmo Hamilton, Story

Reckoner, The see **PUBLIC DEFENDER** (1931).

RECKONING, THE 1908 d: D. W. Griffith. USA., *The Reckoning*, Dwight Cummings, Story

RECKONING, THE 1970 d: Jack Gold. UKN., *The Harp That Once*, Patrick Hall, Novel

Recluse, The see **BIRYUK** (1979).

RECOIL, THE 1922 d: Geoffrey H. Malins. UKN., *The Dream*, Rafael Sabatini, Novel

RECOIL, THE 1924 d: T. Hayes Hunter. USA., *Recoil*, Rex Beach, 1922, Short Story

Recollections from Childhood see **AMINTIRI DIN COPILARIE** (1964).

RECOMPENSE 1925 d: Harry Beaumont. USA., *Recompense*, Robert Keable, London 1924, Novel

Recompense, La see **THE REWARD** (1965).

Reconciliation, La see **GELD UND GEIST** (1964).

Recording of Wandering, A see **HOROKI** (1962).

RECOURS EN GRACE 1960 d: Laslo Benedek. FRN/ITL., *Recours En Grace*, Noel Calef, Novel

Recourse to the Method, The see **EL RECURSO DEL METODO** (1978).

RECREATION, LA 1961 d: Francois Moreuil, Fabien Collin. FRN., *La Recreation*, Francoise Sagan, Short Story

RE-CREATION OF BRIAN KENT, THE 1925 d: Sam Wood. USA., *The Re-Creation of Brian Kent*, Harold Bell Wright, Chicago 1919, Novel

Recreation, The see **LA RECREATION** (1961).

Recruits in Ingolstadt see **PIONIERE IN INGOLSTADT** (1971).

RECTOR'S WIFE, THE 1993 d: Giles Foster. UKN., *The Rector's Wife*, Joanna Trollope, Novel

RECURSO DEL METODO, EL 1978 d: Miguel Littin. MXC/CUB/FRN., *El Recurso Del Metodo*, Alejo Carpentier, 1974, Novel

RED ACES 1929 d: Edgar Wallace. UKN., *Red Aces*, Edgar Wallace, London 1929, Novel

RED ALERT 1977 d: William Hale. USA., *Paradigm Red*, Harold King

Red Apple, The see **KRASNOYE YABLOKO** (1975).

Red Apples see **BRIDES ARE LIKE THAT** (1936).

RED BADGE OF COURAGE, THE 1951 d: John Huston. USA., *The Red Badge of Courage*, Stephen Crane, 1895, Novel

RED BADGE OF COURAGE, THE 1974 d: Lee Philips. USA., *The Red Badge of Courage*, Stephen Crane, 1895, Novel

Red Beard see AKAHIGE (1965).

RED BERET, THE 1953 d: Terence Young. UKN., *The Red Beret*, Hilary St. George Sanders, Book

RED BLOOD OF COURAGE 1935 d: John English. USA., *Red Blood of Courage*, James Oliver Curwood, Short Story

RED CANYON 1949 d: George Sherman. USA., *Wildfire*, Zane Grey, New York 1916, Novel

RED CIRCLE, THE 1922 d: George Ridgwell. UKN., *The Red Circle*, Arthur Conan Doyle, Short Story

Red Circle, The see DER ROTE KREIS (1959).

RED COURAGE 1921 d: B. Reeves Eason. USA., *The Sheriff of Cinnabar*, Peter B. Kyne, Story

Red Crag see LIE HUOZHONG YONGSHENG (1965).

RED DANCE, THE 1928 d: Raoul Walsh. USA., *The Red Dancer of Moscow*, Henry Leyford Gates, New York 1928, Novel

Red Dancer of Moscow, The see THE RED DANCE (1928).

RED DANUBE, THE 1949 d: George Sidney. USA., *Vespers in Vienna*, Bruce Marshall, Novel

RED DICE 1926 d: William K. Howard. USA., *The Iron Chalice*, Octavus Roy Cohen, Boston 1925, Novel

Red Dragon see DAS GEHEIMNIS DER DREI DSCHUNKEN (1965).

Red Dragon see MANHUNTER (1986).

RED DUST 1932 d: Victor Fleming. USA., *Red Dust*, Wilson Collison, New York 1928, Play

Red Dwarf, The see LE NAIN ROUGE (1998).

RED EARTH, WHITE EARTH 1989 d: David Greene. USA., *Red Earth - White Earth*, Will Weaver, Book

Red Firecracker, Green Firecracker see PAODA SHUANG DENG (1993).

RED FOX 1991 d: Ian Toynton. UKN., *Red Fox*, Gerald Seymour, Novel

RED HAIR 1928 d: Clarence Badger. USA., *The Vicissitudes of Evangeline*, Elinor Glyn, New York 1905, Novel

RED HAIRED ALIBI 1932 d: W. Christy Cabanne. USA., *Red-Haired Alibi*, Wilson Collison, New York 1932, Novel

Red Harvest see THE WORLD AND THE FLESH (1932).

RED HEADED WOMAN 1932 d: Jack Conway. USA., *Red-Headed Woman*, Katharine Brush, New York 1931, Novel

Red Herrings see CHEMMEEN (1965).

Red Horse Hill see THE ETERNAL MOTHER (1917).

Red Hot Sinners see GOLD DUST GERTIE (1931).

Red Inn, The see L' AUBERGE ROUGE (1923).

Red Inn, The see L' AUBERGE ROUGE (1951).

RED LANE, THE 1920 d: Lynn Reynolds. USA., *The Red Lane; a Romance of the Border*, Holman Francis Day, New York 1912, Novel

RED LANTERN, THE 1919 d: Albert Capellani. USA., *The Red Lantern*, Edith Wherry, New York 1911, Novel

Red Lanterns see KOKKINA PHANARIA (1962).

RED LIGHT 1949 d: Roy Del Ruth. USA., *This Guy Gideon*, Donald Barry, Story

RED LIGHT STING, THE 1984 d: Rod Holcomb. USA., Henry Post, Article

RED LIGHTS 1923 d: Clarence Badger. USA., *The Rear Car*, Edward E. Rose, Los Angeles 1922, Play

RED LIPS 1928 d: Melville Brown. USA., *The Plastic Age*, Percy Marks, New York 1924, Novel

Red Mantle, The see DEN RODA KAPPAN (1967).

Red Meat see I LOVED A WOMAN (1933).

RED MILL, THE 1926 d: Roscoe Arbuckle. USA., *The Red Mill*, Henry Martyn Blossom, Victor Herbert, New York 1906, Musical Play

Red Mirage, The see THE FOREIGN LEGION (1928).

RED MONARCH 1982 d: Jack Gold. UKN., Juri Krotkow, Short Story

Red Mouse, The see HER SILENT SACRIFICE (1917).

Red Nights of the Gestapo, The see LE LUNGHE NOTTI DELLA GESTAPO (1977).

RED PEARLS 1930 d: Walter Forde. UKN., *Nearer! Nearer!*, J. Randolph James, Novel

RED PLANET MARS 1952 d: Harry Horner. USA., *Red Planet*, John L. Balderston, John Hoare, 1933, Play

RED PONY, THE 1949 d: Lewis Milestone. USA., *The Long Valley*, John Steinbeck, 1939, Novel

RED PONY, THE 1973 d: Robert Totten. USA., *The Long Valley*, John Steinbeck, 1939, Novel

Red Poppy see GUBIJINSO (1935).

RED POTTAGE 1918 d: Meyrick Milton. UKN., *Red Pottage*, Mary Cholmondeley, Novel

Red Psalm see MEG KER A NEP (1971).

Red Rage see DER ROTE RAUSCH (1962).

RED, RED HEART, THE 1918 d: Wilfred Lucas. USA., *The Heart of the Desert*, Honore Morrow, New York 1913, Novel

Red Republic see BOLSHEVISM ON TRIAL (1919).

RED RIVER 1948 d: Howard Hawks. USA., *The Chisholm Trail*, Borden Chase, Short Story

RED RIVER 1988 d: Richard Michaels. USA., *The Chisholm Trail*, Borden Chase, Short Story

Red Roan see STRAWBERRY ROAN (1933).

Red Rose, The see LA ROSA ROSSA (1973).

RED SHOES, THE 1948 d: Michael Powell, Emeric Pressburger. UKN., **De Rode Skoe**, Hans Christian Andersen, 1845, Short Story

RED SKY AT MORNING 1944 d: Hartney Arthur. ASL., *Red Sky at Morning*, Dymphna Cusack, 1942, Play

Red Song see MEG KER A NEP (1971).

Red Sorghum see HONG GAOLIANG (1987).

Red Stocking, The see DER ROTE STRUMPF (1980).

Red Sun see SOLEIL ROUGE (1971).

Red Sun Over the Ke Mountains, The see KE SHAN HONG RI (1960).

RED SUNDOWN 1956 d: Jack Arnold. USA., *Back Trail*, Lewis B. Patten, Novel

Red Sweater, The see LE PULL-OVER ROUGE (1979).

RED WAGON 1934 d: Paul L. Stein. UKN., *Red Wagon*, Lady Eleanor Smith, Novel

RED WIDOW, THE 1916 d: James Durkin. USA., *The Red Widow*, Charles J. Gebest, Channing Pollock, Rennold Wolf, New York 1911, Musical Play

Redeemer, The see IZBAVITELJ (1977).

REDEEMING SIN, THE 1925 d: J. Stuart Blackton. USA., *The Redeeming Sin*, L. V. Jefferson, Story

REDEMPTA 1917 d: Servaes. FRN., *Redempta*, M. de Mylio, Short Story

REDEMPTION 1930 d: Fred Niblo. USA., *Zhivoi Trup*, Lev Nikolayevich Tolstoy, Moscow 1911, Play

REDEMPTION OF DAVID CORSON, THE 1914. USA., *The Redemption of David Corson*, Charles Frederick Goss, New York 1900, Novel

REDENZIONE 1942 d: Marcello Albani. ITL., *Redenzione*, Roberto Farinacci, Play

Red-Haired Alibi see RED HAIRED ALIBI (1932).

RED-HAIRED CUPID, THE 1918 d: Cliff Smith. USA., *Red-Haired Cupid*, Henry Wallace Phillips, 1901, Short Story

Red-Haired Kate see ROZE KATE (1912).

Redhead see POIL DE CAROTTE (1932).

REDHEAD 1934 d: Melville Brown. USA., *Redhead*, Vera Brown, New York 1933, Novel

REDHEAD 1941 d: Edward L. Cahn. USA., *Redhead*, Vera Brown, New York 1933, Novel

REDHEAD AND THE COWBOY, THE 1950 d: Leslie Fenton. USA., *The Redhead and the Cowboy*, Charles Marquis Warren, Novel

Redhead, The see DIE ROTE (1962).

Red-Headed Cupid, The see THE RED-HAIRED CUPID (1918).

RED-HEADED LEAGUE, THE 1921 d: Maurice Elvey. UKN., *The Red-Headed League*, Arthur Conan Doyle, 1891, Short Story

Red-Headed League, The see THE ADVENTURES OF SHERLOCK HOLMES: THE RED-HEADED LEAGUE (1985).

Red-Headed Woman see RED HEADED WOMAN (1932).

Reditel Sklarny see ROMAN HLOUPEHO HONZY (1926).

Red-Light District see SPERRBEZIRK (1966).

Red-Light Sting, The see THE RED LIGHT STING (1984).

REDMAN AND THE CHILD, THE 1908 d: D. W. Griffith. USA., *The Redman and the Child*, Bret Harte, Short Story

Re-Examination, The see FU SHI (1957).

REFEREE, THE 1922 d: Ralph Ince. USA., *Referee John McArdle*, Gerald Beaumont, 1921, Short Story

REFLECTIONS 1984 d: Kevin Billington. UKN., *The Newton Letter*, John Banville, 1982, Novel

REFLECTIONS IN A GOLDEN EYE 1967 d: John Huston. USA., *Reflections in a Golden Eye*, Carson McCullers, Boston 1941, Novel

REFLECTIONS OF MURDER 1974 d: John Badham. USA., *Celle Qui N'etait Plus*, Pierre Boileau, Thomas Narcejac, Novel

REFLET DE CLAUDE MERCOEUR, LE 1923 d: Julien Duvivier. FRN., *Le Reflet de Claude Mercoeur*, Frederic Boutet, Novel

REFLUX, LE 1961 d: Paul Gegauff. FRN., Robert Louis Stevenson, Novel

REGAIN 1937 d: Marcel Pagnol. FRN., *Regain*, Jean Giono, 1930, Novel

Regalo, Il see LE CADEAU (1982).

REGARD LES HOMMES TOMBER 1994 d: Jacques Audiard. FRN., *Triangle*, Teri White, Novel

REGATES DE SAN FRANCISCO, LES 1959 d: Claude Autant-LarA. FRN/ITL., *Les Regates de San Francisco*, Quarantotti Gambini, Story

REGENERATION 1915 d: Raoul Walsh. USA., *My Mamie Rose; the Story of My Regeneration*, Owen Frawley Kildare, New York 1903, Book

REGENERATION 1997 d: Gillies MacKinnon. UKN/CND., *Regeneration*, Pat Barker, 1991, Novel

Regeneration Isle see LOVE'S REDEMPTION (1921).

Regent, The see LA REGENTA (1974).

REGENTA, LA 1974 d: Gonzalo Suarez. SPN., *La Regenta*, Leopoldo Alas, 1884, Novel

REGENT'S PARK MYSTERY, THE 1924 d: Hugh Croise. UKN., *The Regent's Park Mystery*, Baroness Orczy, Short Story

Regent's Wife, The see LA REGENTA (1974).

REGI IDOK FOCIJA 1973 d: Pal Sandor. HNG., *A Palya Szelen*, Ivan Mandy, 1963, Novel, *Regi Idok Mozija*, Ivan Mandy, 1967, Short Story

Regimentsmusik see DIE SCHULD DER GABRIELE ROTTWEIL (1944).

REGIMENTSTOCHTER, DIE 1928 d: Hans Behrendt. GRM., *La Fille du Regiment*, Gaetano Donizetti, Paris 1840, Opera

REGIMENTSTOCHTER, DIE 1953 d: Georg C. Klaren, Gunther Haenel. AUS., *La Fille du Regiment*, Gaetano Donizetti, Paris 1840, Opera

REGINA AMSTETTEN 1954 d: Kurt Neumann. GRM., *Regina Amstetten*, Ernst Weichert, 1936, Short Story

REGINA DEL MERCATO, LA 1921 d: Giovanni PezzingA. ITL., *La Regina Del Mercato*, Carolina Invernizio, Novel

Regina Di Marechiaro, La see GLI SPETTRI (1918).

REGINA DI NAVARRA, LA 1942 d: Carmine Gallone. ITL., *La Regina Di Navarra*, Eugene Scribe, Play

Regina Margot, La see LA REINE MARGOT (1954).

REGINE 1934 d: Erich Waschneck. GRM., *Regine*, Gottfried Keller, 1872, Short Story

REGINE 1956 d: Harald Braun. GRM., *Regine*, Gottfried Keller, 1872, Short Story

REGINETTA DELLE ROSE, LA 1914 d: Luigi CarambA. ITL., *La Reginetta Delle Rose*, Giovacchino Forzano, 1912, Opera

REGINETTA ISOTTA 1918. ITL., *Le Bal Des Sceaux*, Honore de Balzac

REGISTERED NURSE 1934 d: Robert Florey. USA., *Miss Benton R.N.*, Florence Johns, William Lackaye Jr., 1930, Play

Registered Woman see A WOMAN OF EXPERIENCE (1931).

REGLE DU JEU, LA 1939 d: Jean Renoir. FRN., *Les Caprices de Marianne*, Alfred de Musset, 1834, Play

REGNE DE L'ESPRIT MALIN, LE 1955 d: Guido Wurth. SWT., *Le Regne de l'Esprit Malin*, Charles-Ferdinand Ramuz, Lausanne 1917, Novel

Regne de Matto, Le see MATTO REGIERT (1947).

Regret for the Past see SHANG SHI (1981).

Regular As Clockwork see NE JOUEZ PAS AVEC LES MARTIANS (1967).

Rehabilitated see ULBO GARVEEMA (1917).

REHABILITIERT 1910. GRM., *Stein Unter Steinen*, Hermann Sudermann, Play

Rehearsal for a Crime see ENSAYO DE UN CRIMEN (1955).

REI DA VELA, O 1982 d: Jose Celso Martinez Correa, Noilton Nunes. BRZ., *O Rei Da Vela*, Oswald de Andrade, Play

Rei Pasmado, O see EL REY PASMADO (1991).

REICH MIR DIE HAND, MEIN LEBEN 1955 d: Karl Hartl. AUS., *Mein Leben Reich Mir Die Hand*, Fritz Habeck, Short Story

REIFENDE JUGEND 1933 d: Carl Froelich. GRM., *Die Reifeprufung*, Max Dreyer, Play

REIFENDE JUGEND 1955 d: Ulrich Erfurth. GRM., *Die Reifeprufung*, Max Dreyer, Play

REIGATE SQUIRES, THE 1912 d: Georges Treville. UKN., *The Reigate Squires*, Arthur Conan Doyle, Short Story

REIGATE SQUIRES, THE 1922 d: George Ridgwell. UKN., *The Reigate Squires*, Arthur Conan Doyle, Short Story

REIGEN 1974 d: Otto Schenk. GRM/AUS., *Der Reigen*, Arthur Schnitzler, 1900, Play

Reign of Lord Ram, The see RAM RAJYA (1967).

REIGN OF TERROR 1914. USA., *Le Chevalier de Maison Rouge*, Alexandre Dumas (pere), 1846, Novel

REILLY: ACE OF SPIES 1983 d: Jim Goddard. UKN., *Ace of Spies*, Robin Bruce Lockhart, Book

Reilly: the Ace of Spies see REILLY: ACE OF SPIES (1983).

Reina de Sierra Morena, La see LA DUQUESA DE BENAMEJI (1949).

REINA MORA, LA 1922 d: Jose Buchs. SPN., *La Reina Mora*, Hermanos Alvarez Quintero, J. Serrano, Opera

REINCARNATION OF PETER PROUD, THE 1974 d: J. Lee Thompson. USA., *The Reincarnation of Peter Proud*, Max Simon Ehrlich, Novel

REINE DE BIARRITZ, LA 1934 d: Jean Toulout. FRN., *La Reine de Biarritz*, Romain Coolus, Maurice Hennequin, Play

Reine Elisabeth, La see LES AMOURS DE LA REINE ELISABETH (1912).

REINE MARGOT, LA 1910 d: Camille de Morlhon. FRN., *La Reine Margot*, Alexandre Dumas (pere), 1845, Novel

REINE MARGOT, LA 1914 d: Henri Desfontaines. FRN., *La Reine Margot*, Alexandre Dumas (pere), 1845, Novel

REINE MARGOT, LA 1954 d: Jean Dreville. FRN/ITL., *La Reine Margot*, Alexandre Dumas (pere), 1845, Novel

REINE MARGOT, LA 1961 d: Rene Lucot. FRN., *La Reine Margot*, Alexandre Dumas (pere), 1845, Novel

REINE MARGOT, LA 1994 d: Patrice Chereau. FRN/GRM/ITL., *La Reine Margot*, Alexandre Dumas (pere), 1845, Novel

REISE NACH TILSIT, DIE 1939 d: Veit Harlan. GRM., *Die Reise Nach Tilsit*, Hermann Sudermann, Berlin 1917, Novel

REITER VON DEUTSCH-OSTAFRIKA, DIE 1934 d: Herbert Selpin. GRM., *Kwa Heri*, Marie-Luise Droop, Novel

REIVERS, THE 1969 d: Mark Rydell. USA., *The Reivers; a Reminiscence*, William Faulkner, New York 1962, Novel

REJAS Y VOTOS 1925 d: Rafael Salvador. SPN., *Rejas Y Votos*, Vicente Diez Peydro, Opera

Rejoice While You are Young see GLAD DIG I DIN UNGDOM (1939).

REJUVENATION OF AUNT MARY, THE 1914 d: Eddie Dillon. USA., *The Rejuvenation of Aunt Mary*, Anne Warner, New York 1907, Play

REJUVENATION OF AUNT MARY, THE 1916 d: Dell Henderson. USA., *The Rejuvenation of Aunt Mary*, Anne Warner, New York 1907, Play

REJUVENATION OF AUNT MARY, THE 1927 d: Erle C. Kenton. USA., *The Rejuvenation of Aunt Mary*, Anne Warner, New York 1907, Play

REKOPIS ZNALEZIONY W SARAGOSSIE 1965 d: Wojciech J. Has. PLN., *Le Manuscrit Trouve a Saragosse*, Jan Potocki, 1815, Novel

Relations see AN AMATEUR WIDOW (1919).

Relations see TUMULT (1969).

Relatives see ROKONOK (1954).

Relativity see YOUNG IDEAS (1924).

RELAXE-TOI, CHERIE 1964 d: Jean Boyer. FRN/ITL., *Le Complexe de Philemon*, Jean-Bernard Luc, Play

Relazioni Pericolose see LES LIAISONS DANGEREUSES (1959).

RELENTLESS 1948 d: George Sherman. USA., *Three Were Thoroughbreds*, Kenneth Perkins, Story

RELENTLESS 1977 d: Lee H. Katzin. USA., *Relentless*, Brian Garfield, 1972, Novel

RELIC, THE 1997 d: Peter Hyams. USA., *The Relic*, Lincoln Child, Douglas Preston, Novel

Relicario de Joseito, El see EL RELICARIO (1926).

RELICARIO, EL 1926 d: Miguel Contreras Torres. SPN., *El Relicario*, Castellvi Y Oliveras, Jose Padilla, Song

Religieuse de Diderot, La see LA RELIGIEUSE DE DIDEROT SUZANNE SIMONIN (1965).

Religieuse, La see LA RELIGIEUSE DE DIDEROT SUZANNE SIMONIN (1965).

Religieuses du Saint Archange, Les see LE MONACHE DI SANT'ARCANGELO (1973).

RELITTO, IL 1961 d: Giovanni Paolucci, Michael Cacoyannis. ITL., *The Wastrel*, Frederic Wakeman, New York 1949, Novel

RELUCTANT DEBUTANTE, THE 1958 d: Vincente Minnelli. USA., *The Reluctant Debutante*, William Douglas Home, London 1956, Play

Reluctant Grandfather, The see DEDECKEM PROTI SVE VULI (1939).

RELUCTANT HEROES 1951 d: Jack Raymond. UKN., *Reluctant Heroes*, Colin Morris, London 1950, Play

RELUCTANT WIDOW, THE 1950 d: Bernard Knowles. UKN., *The Reluctant Widow*, Georgette Heyer, Novel

REMAINS OF THE DAY, THE 1993 d: James Ivory. UKN/USA., *The Remains of the Day*, Kazuo Ishiguro, Novel

REMAINS TO BE SEEN 1953 d: Don Weis. USA., *Remains to Be Seen*, Russel Crouse, Howard Lindsay, New York 1951, Play

REMARKABLE ANDREW, THE 1942 d: Stuart Heisler. USA., *The Remarkable Andrew*, Dalton Trumbo, Novel

Remarkable Mr. Kipps, The see KIPPS (1941).

REMARKABLE MR. PENNYPACKER, THE 1959 d: Henry Levin. USA., *The Remarkable Mr. Pennypacker*, Liam O'Brien, New York 1953, Play

Remedy see DERMAN (1983).

REMEMBER 1993 d: John Herzfeld. USA., *Remember*, Barbara Taylor Bradford, Novel

REMEMBER LAST NIGHT? 1934 d: James Whale. USA., *Hangover Murders*, Adam Hobhouse, New York 1935, Novel

Remember That Face see THE MOB (1951).

REMEMBER THE DAY 1941 d: Henry King. USA., *Remember the Day*, Philip Dunning, Philo Higley, Play

Remember Tomorrow see DANGEROUSLY THEY LIVE (1942).

Reminiscences see SMRITICHITRE (1982).

REMITTANCE WOMAN, THE 1923 d: Wesley Ruggles. USA., *The Remittance Woman*, Achmed Abdullah, Garden City, Ny. 1924, Novel

Remo: Unarmed and Dangerous see REMO WILLIAMS: THE ADVENTURE BEGINS (1985).

REMO WILLIAMS: THE ADVENTURE BEGINS 1985 d: Guy Hamilton. USA., Warren Murphy, Richard Sapir, Novel

Remo Williams: the Adventure Continues see REMO WILLIAMS: THE ADVENTURE BEGINS (1985).

Remo Williams .Unarmed and Dangerous see REMO WILLIAMS: THE ADVENTURE BEGINS (1985).

REMORQUES 1940 d: Jean Gremillon. FRN., *Remorques*, Roger Vercel, Novel

REMOTE CONTROL 1930 d: Nick Grinde, Malcolm St. Clair. USA., *Remote Control*, A. C. Fuller, J. Nelson, Clyde North, New York 1929, Play

REMOUS 1934 d: Edmond T. Greville. FRN., *A Kiss in the Dark*, Peggy Thompson, Novel

REMOVALISTS, THE 1975 d: Tom Jeffrey. ASL., *The Removalists*, David Williamson, 1972, Play

REMPART DES BEGUINES, LE 1972 d: Guy Casaril. FRN/ITL., *Le Rempart Des Beguines*, Francoise Mallet-Joris, 1951, Novel

RENAISSANCE AT CHARLEROI, THE 1917 d: Thomas R. Mills. USA., *The Renaissance at Charleroi*, O. Henry, Short Story

REN DAO ZHONGNIAN 1982 d: Wang Qimin, Sun Yu. CHN., *Ren Dao Zhong Nian*, Shen Rong, Novel

REN HOU DA LIE BIAN 1992 d: Pan Peicheng. CHN., Zhou Daxin, Story

RENAISSANCE AT CHARLEROI, THE 1917 d: Thomas R. Mills. USA., *The Renaissance at Charleroi*, O. Henry, 1903, Short Story

REND MIG I TRADIONERNE 1979 d: Edward Fleming. DNM., *Rend Mig I Traditionerne*, Leif Panduro, 1958, Novel

RENDEZVOUS 1935 d: William K. Howard. USA., *The American Black Chamber*, Major Herbert O. Yardley, Book

Rendezvous see HOW COULD YOU? DARLING (1951).

RENDEZ-VOUS A BRAY 1971 d: Andre Delvaux. FRN/GRM/BLG., *Le Roi Cophetua*, Julien Gracq, 1970, Short Story

Rendezvous at Bray see RENDEZ-VOUS A BRAY (1971).

RENDEZVOUS AT MIDNIGHT 1935 d: W. Christy Cabanne. USA., *The Silver Fox*, Gaetano Sazio, New York 1921, Play

Rendez-Vous aux Champs-Elysees see RENDEZ-VOUS CHAMPS-ELYSEES (1937).

RENDEZ-VOUS AVEC LA CHANCE 1949 d: Emile Edwin Reinert. FRN., *Rendez-Vous Avec la Chance*, Gilbert Dupe, Novel

RENDEZ-VOUS CHAMPS-ELYSEES 1937 d: Jacques Houssin. FRN., *Rendez-Vous Champs-Elysees*, Frank Arnold, Short Story

Rendezvous in Bray see RENDEZ-VOUS A BRAY (1971).

Rendezvous in the Alps see DUSTY ERMINE (1936).

RENDEZ-VOUS IN WIEN 1959 d: Helmut Weiss. AUS., *Rendez-Vous in Wien*, Fritz Eckhardt, Play

RENDEZ-VOUS, LE 1961 d: Jean Delannoy. FRN/ITL., *The Man With Two Wives*, Patrick Quentin, Novel

Rendezvous With Forgotten Years see STEVNEMOTE MED GLEMTE AR (1957).

RENE LA CANNE 1976 d: Francis Girod. FRN/ITL., *L' Ultima Invasione*, Roger Borniche, Novel

Renee Richards Story, The see SECOND SERVE (1986).

Renegade Posse see BULLET FOR A BADMAN (1964).

Renegade, The see THE LIGHT OF VICTORY (1919).

RENEGADES 1930 d: Victor Fleming. USA., *Le Renegat*, Andre Armandy, Paris 1929, Novel

Renegades of Fort Grant see FUERTE PERDIDO (1965).

RENEGADES OF THE WEST 1932 d: Casey Robinson. USA., *The Miracle Baby*, Frank Richardson Pierce, 1921, Short Story

Renewal Trilogy see TRILOGIE DES WIEDERSEHENS (1978).

Renfrew Crashes Through see CRASHING THRU (1939).

Renfrew of the Great White Trail see RENFREW ON THE GREAT WHITE TRAIL (1938).

Renfrew of the Mounted in Sky Bandits see SKY BANDITS (1940).

RENFREW OF THE ROYAL MOUNTED 1937 d: Al Herman. USA., *Renfrew of the Royal Mounted*, Laurie York Erskine, New York 1922, Novel

Renfrew of the Royal Mounted in Crashin' Thru see CRASHING THRU (1939).

Renfrew of the Royal Mounted in Fighting Mad see FIGHTING MAD (1939).

Renfrew of the Royal Mounted in Yukon Flight see YUKON FLIGHT (1940).

RENFREW ON THE GREAT WHITE TRAIL 1938 d: Al Herman. USA., *Renfrew Rides North*, Laurie York Erskine, New York 1931, Novel

Renfrew Rides North see RENFREW ON THE GREAT WHITE TRAIL (1938).

RENO 1930 d: George J. Crone. USA., *Reno*, Cornelius Vanderbilt Jr., New York 1929, Novel

Renunciation see THE WOMAN OF MONA DIGGINGS JUDGE NOT; OR (1915).

RENZONI, LA 1916 d: Maurits H. Binger. NTH., *La Renzoni*, Melati Van Java, Novel

REPAS DES FAUVES, LE 1964 d: Christian-Jaque. FRN./ITL./SPN., Vahe Katcha, Short Story

Repast see **MESHI** (1951).

Repeal see **THE GAY BRIDE** (1934).

Repeat Dive see **TZLILA CHOZERET** (1982).

Replay see **LE PASSE SIMPLE** (1977).

REPONSE DU DESTIN, LA 1924 d: Andre Hugon. FRN., *El Jefe Politico*, Jose-Maria Carretero, Novel

REPORT TO THE COMMISSIONER 1975 d: Milton Katselas. USA., *Report to the Commissioner*, James Mills, Novel

REPOS DU GUERRIER, LE 1962 d: Roger Vadim. FRN./ITL., *Le Repos du Guerrier*, Christiane Rochefort, Paris 1958, Novel

Reprieve see **CONVICTS FOUR** (1962).

REPRISAL! 1956 d: George Sherman. USA., *Reprisal!*, Arthur Gordon, 1950, Novel

REPROACH OF ANNESLEY, THE 1915. USA., *The Reproach of Annesley*, Maxwell Gray, Novel

REPRODUCTION INTERDITE 1956 d: Gilles Grangier. FRN., *Reproduction Interdite*, Michel Lenoir, Novel

REPROUVES, LES 1936 d: Jacques Severac. FRN., *Les Reprouves*, Andre Armandy, Novel

Republic of Sin see **LA FIEVRE MONTE A EL PAO** (1959).

REPUBLICA DOS ASSASSINOS 1979 d: Miguel Faria Junior. BRZ., *Republica Dos Assassinos*, Aguinaldo Silva, 1976, Novel

REPUTATION 1921 d: Stuart Paton. USA., *False Colors*, Edwina Levin, Story

Reputation see **LADY WITH A PAST** (1932).

Request, The see **LA PETICION** (1976).

REQUIEM 1981 d: Zoltan Fabri. HNG., *Rekviem*, Istvan Orkeny, 1957-58, Short Story

REQUIEM 1998 d: Alain Tanner. SWT/FRN/PRT., *Requiem*, Antonio Tabucchi, Novel

REQUIEM FOR A HEAVYWEIGHT 1962 d: Ralph Nelson. USA., *Requiem for a Heavyweight*, Rod Serling, 1956, Play

Requiem for Mozart see **MOTSART I SALYERI** (1962).

REQUIEM PER VOCE E PIANOFORTE 1993 d: Tomaso Sherman. ITL., *What's Better Than Money*, James Hadley Chase

REQUISITOIRE, LE 1930 d: Dimitri Buchowetzki. FRN., *Manslaughter*, Alice Duer Miller, New York 1921, Novel

RESA DI TITI, LA 1946 d: Giorgio Bianchi. ITL., *La Resa Di Titi*, Aldo de Benedetti, Guglielmo Zorzi, Play

RESCUE, THE 1929 d: Herbert Brenon. USA., *The Rescue*, Joseph Conrad, London 1920, Novel

RESCUING ANGEL, THE 1919 d: Walter Edwards. USA., *The Rescuing Angel*, Clare Kummer, New York 1917, Play

Reserved for Ladies see **SERVICE FOR LADIES** (1932).

RESIDENT PATIENT, THE 1921 d: Maurice Elvey. UKN., *The Resident Patient*, Arthur Conan Doyle, Short Story

Resident Patient, The see **THE ADVENTURES OF SHERLOCK HOLMES: THE RESIDENT PATIENT** (1985).

Resistance see **PELOTON D'EXECUTION** (1945).

Resort of the Method, The see **EL RECURSO DEL METODO** (1978).

Respectable Ladies of Pardubicke, The see **POCESTNE PANI PARDUBICKE** (1944).

Respectable Prostitute, The see **LA P. RESPECTUEUSE** (1952).

Respectable Women of Pardubice, The see **POCESTNE PANI PARDUBICKE** (1944).

Respectful Prostitute, The see **LA P. RESPECTUEUSE** (1952).

Respondent, The see **THE SPENDERS** (1921).

Responsabilite Limitee? see **I COLPEVOLI** (1957).

REST CURE, THE 1923 d: A. E. Coleby. UKN., *The Rest Cure*, George Robey, Novel

Rest Is Silence, The see **DER REST IST SCHWEIGEN** (1959).

REST IST SCHWEIGEN, DER 1959 d: Helmut Kautner. GRM., *Hamlet*, William Shakespeare, c1601, Play

Restless see **MAN-TRAP** (1961).

Restless and the Damned, The see **L' AMBITIEUSE** (1958).

Restless Daughters see **UNRUHIGE TOCHTER** (1967).

Restless Night, The see **UNRUHIGE NACHT** (1958).

RESTLESS SEX, THE 1920 d: Robert Z. Leonard. USA., *The Restless Sex*, Robert W. Chambers, New York 1918, Novel

RESTLESS SOULS 1919 d: William C. Dowlan. USA., *Restless Souls*, Cosmo Hamilton, Short Story

RESTLESS SOULS 1922 d: Robert Ensminger. USA., *Playing Dead*, Richard Harding Davis, 1915, Short Story

RESTLESS SPIRIT, THE 1913 d: Allan Dwan. USA., *Elegy Written in a Country Churchyard*, Thomas Gray, 1751, Poem

RESTLESS WIVES 1924 d: Gregory La CavA. USA., *Restless Wives*, Izola Forrester, Short Story

RESTLESS YEARS, THE 1958 d: Helmut Kautner. USA., *Teach Me How to Cry*, Patricia Joudry-Steele, Play

RESTLESS YOUTH 1928 d: W. Christy Cabanne. USA., *Restless Youth*, Cosmo Hamilton, Story

RESTORATION 1995 d: Michael Hoffman. USA., *Restoration*, Rose Tremain, Novel

RESURRECCION 1931 d: Edwin Carewe. USA., *Voskreseniye*, Lev Nikolayevich Tolstoy, Moscow 1899, Novel

RESURRECCION 1943 d: Gilberto Martinez Solares. MXC., *Voskreseniye*, Lev Nikolayevich Tolstoy, Moscow 1899, Novel

RESURRECTED, THE 1991 d: Dan O'Bannon. USA., *The Strange Case of Charles Dexter Ward*, H. P. Lovecraft

RESURRECTION 1909 d: D. W. Griffith. USA., *Voskreseniye*, Lev Nikolayevich Tolstoy, Moscow 1899, Novel

RESURRECTION 1909 d: Andre Calmettes, Henri Desfontaines. FRN., *Voskreseniye*, Lev Nikolayevich Tolstoy, Moscow 1899, Novel

RESURRECTION 1918 d: Edward Jose. USA., *Voskreseniye*, Lev Nikolayevich Tolstoy, Moscow 1899, Novel

RESURRECTION 1927 d: Edwin Carewe. USA., *Voskreseniye*, Lev Nikolayevich Tolstoy, Moscow 1899, Novel

RESURRECTION 1931 d: Edwin Carewe. USA., *Voskreseniye*, Lev Nikolayevich Tolstoy, Moscow 1899, Novel

Resurrection see **WE LIVE AGAIN** (1934).

Resurrection see **DUNIYA KYA HAI** (1938).

Resurrection see **FU HUO** (1941).

Resurrection see **FUKKATSU** (1950).

Resurrection see **AUFERSTEHUNG** (1958).

Resurrection see **VOSKRESENIE** (1961).

Resurrection Day see **FUKKATSU NO HI** (1979).

RESURRECTION MAN 1997 d: Marc Evans. UKN., *Resurrection Man*, Eoin McNamee, Novel

Resurrection Syndicate, The see **NOTHING BUT THE NIGHT** (1972).

RESURREZIONE 1917 d: Mario Caserini. ITL., *Voskreseniye*, Lev Nikolayevich Tolstoy, Moscow 1899, Novel

RESURREZIONE 1944 d: Flavio CalzavarA. ITL., *Voskreseniye*, Lev Nikolayevich Tolstoy, Moscow 1899, Novel

Resurrezione see **AUFERSTEHUNG** (1958).

RETAGGIO DI SANGUE 1956 d: Max Calandri. ITL., *Retaggio Di Sangue*, Anna Luce, Novel

RETALHOS DA VIDA DE UM MEDICO 1962 d: Jorge Brum Do Canto. PRT., *Retalhos Da Vida de Um Medico*, Fernando Namora, 1949, Short Story

RETOUR A L'AUBE 1938 d: Henri Decoin. FRN., *Six a Six*, Vicki Baum, Short Story

RETOUR DE CASANOVA, LE 1991 d: Edouard Niermans. FRN., *Casanovas Heimfahrt*, Arthur Schnitzler, Novel

RETOUR DE DON CAMILLO, LE 1953 d: Julien Duvivier. FRN./ITL., Giovanni Guareschi, Short Stories

RETOUR DE FLAMME 1942 d: Henri Fescourt. FRN., *Retour de Flamme*, Herve Lauwick, Novel

RETOUR DE MANIVELLE 1957 d: Denys de La Patelliere. FRN./ITL., *Retour de Manivelle*, James Hadley Chase, Novel

RETOUR, LE 1990 d: Michel Boisrond. FRN., *Le Retour*, Daniele Thompson, Novel

RETRAITE, LA 1910 d: Andre Calmettes, Henri Pouctal. FRN., *Le Retraite*, Beyerlein, Play

RETRATO DE FAMILIA 1976 d: Antonio Gimenez-Rico. SPN., *Mi Idolatrado Hijo Sisi*, Miguel Delibes, 1953, Novel

RETROSCENA 1939 d: Alessandro Blasetti. ITL., Carlo Duse, Story

RETTENDE ENGEL, DER 1940 d: Ferdinand Dorfler. GRM., *St. Pauli in St. Peter*, Maximilian Vitus, Play

Return from Hell see **INTOARCEREA DIN IAD** (1984).

Return from Limbo see **WOMEN ARE LIKE THAT** (1938).

RETURN FROM THE ASHES 1965 d: J. Lee Thompson. UKN/USA., *Le Retour Des Cendres*, Hubert Monteilhet, Paris 1961, Novel

RETURN FROM THE RIVER KWAI 1989 d: Andrew V. McLaglen. UKN/USA., *Return from the River Kwai*, Joan Blair, Clay Blair Jr., Book

RETURN FROM THE SEA 1954 d: Lesley Selander. USA., *No Home of His Own*, Jacland Marmur, Short Story

RETURN OF A STRANGER 1937 d: Victor Hanbury. UKN., *Return of a Stranger*, Rudolph Lothar, Play

RETURN OF BULLDOG DRUMMOND, THE 1934 d: Walter Summers. UKN., *The Black Gang*, H. C. McNeile ("Sapper"), Novel

RETURN OF CAROL DEANE, THE 1938 d: Arthur Woods. UKN., *The House on 56th Street*, Joseph Santley, Story

Return of Casanova, The see **LE RETOUR DE CASANOVA** (1991).

RETURN OF CASEY JONES, THE 1933 d: John P. McCarthy. USA., *The Return of Casey Jones*, John Johns, 1933, Short Story

Return of Custer, The see **SEVENTH CAVALRY** (1956).

Return of Don Camillo, The see **LE RETOUR DE DON CAMILLO** (1953).

RETURN OF DR. FU MANCHU, THE 1930 d: Rowland V. Lee. USA., *The Return of Dr. Fu Manchu*, Sax Rohmer, New York 1916, Novel

RETURN OF DR. X, THE 1939 d: Vincent Sherman. USA., *The Doctor's Secret*, W. J. Makin, 1938, Short Story

RETURN OF EVE, THE 1916 d: Arthur Berthelet. USA., *The Return of Eve*, Lee Wilson Dodd, New York 1909, Play

Return of Frankenstein, The see **BRIDE OF FRANKENSTEIN** (1935).

RETURN OF JIMMY VALENTINE, THE 1936 d: Lewis D. Collins. USA., *Alias Jimmy Valentine*, Paul Armstrong, New York 1910, Play

RETURN OF MARY, THE 1918 d: Wilfred Lucas. USA., *The Return of Mary*, Hale Hamilton, Play

RETURN OF PETER GRIMM, THE 1926 d: Victor Schertzinger. USA., *The Return of Peter Grimm*, David Belasco, New York 1911, Play

RETURN OF PETER GRIMM, THE 1935 d: George Nicholls Jr. USA., *The Return of Peter Grimm*, David Belasco, New York 1911, Play

RETURN OF RAFFLES, THE 1932 d: Mansfield Markham. UKN., E. W. Hornung, Story

Return of Sandokan see **SANDOKAN CONTRO IL LEOPARDO DI SARAWAK** (1965).

RETURN OF SHERLOCK HOLMES: SILVER BLAZE, THE 1986 d: Brian Mills. UKN., *Silver Blaze*, Arthur Conan Doyle, 1894, Short Story

RETURN OF SHERLOCK HOLMES: THE ABBEY GRANGE, THE 1986 d: Peter Hammond. UKN., *The Abbey Grange*, Arthur Conan Doyle, Short Story

RETURN OF SHERLOCK HOLMES: THE BRUCE PARTINGTON PLANS, THE 1986 d: John Gorrie. UKN., *The Bruce Partington Plans*, Arthur Conan Doyle, Short Story

RETURN OF SHERLOCK HOLMES: THE DEVIL'S FOOT, THE 1986 d: Ken Hannam. UKN., *The Devil's Foot*, Arthur Conan Doyle, Short Story

RETURN OF SHERLOCK HOLMES: THE EMPTY HOUSE, THE 1986 d: Howard Baker. UKN., *The Empty House*, Arthur Conan Doyle, 1903, Short Story

RETURN OF SHERLOCK HOLMES: THE HOUND OF THE BASKERVILLES, THE 1988 d: Brian Mills. UKN., *The Hound of the Baskervilles*, Arthur Conan Doyle, London 1902, Novel

RETURN OF SHERLOCK HOLMES: THE MAN WITH THE TWISTED LIP, THE 1986 d: Patrick Lau. UKN., *The Man With the Twisted Lip*, Arthur Conan Doyle, 1892, Short Story

RETURN OF SHERLOCK HOLMES: THE MUSGRAVE RITUAL, THE 1986 d: David Carson. UKN., *The Musgrave Ritual*, Arthur Conan Doyle, Short Story

RETURN OF SHERLOCK HOLMES: THE PRIORY SCHOOL, THE 1986 d: John Madden. UKN., *The Priory School*, Arthur Conan Doyle, Short Story

RETURN OF SHERLOCK HOLMES: THE SECOND STAIN, THE 1986 d: John Bruce. UKN., *The Second Stain*, Arthur Conan Doyle, Short Story

RETURN OF SHERLOCK HOLMES: THE SIX NAPOLEONS, THE 1986 d: David Carson. UKN., *The Six Napoleons*, Arthur Conan Doyle, Short Story

RETURN OF SHERLOCK HOLMES: WISTERIA LODGE, THE 1986 d: Peter Hammond. UKN., *Wisteria Lodge*, Arthur Conan Doyle, Short Story

RETURN OF SOPHIE LANG, THE 1936 d: George Archainbaud. USA., Frederick Irving Anderson, Short Stories

RETURN OF TARZAN, THE 1920 d: Harry Revier. USA., *The Revenge of Tarzan*, Edgar Rice Burroughs, New York 1915, Novel

RETURN OF THE CISCO KID, THE 1939 d: Herbert I. Leeds. USA., *Caballero's Way*, O. Henry, 1904, Short Story

RETURN OF THE FROG, THE 1938 d: Maurice Elvey. UKN., *The India Rubber Men*, Edgar Wallace, London 1929, Novel

Return of the Hero see **THE ROAD BACK** (1937).

Return of the Lone Wolf see **THE LONE WOLF RETURNS** (1926).

RETURN OF THE MUSKETEERS, THE 1989 d: Richard Lester. UKN/FRN/SPN., *Vingt Ans Apres; Suite de Trois Mousquetaires*, Alexandre Dumas (pere), 1845, Novel

RETURN OF THE SCARLET PIMPERNEL, THE 1937 d: Hanns Schwarz. UKN., *The Return of the Scarlet Pimpernel*, Baroness Orczy, Novel

RETURN OF THE SOLDIER 1982 d: Alan Bridges. UKN., *The Return of the Soldier*, Rebecca West, 1918, Novel

Return of the Stranger see **RETURN OF A STRANGER** (1937).

RETURN OF THE TERROR 1934 d: Howard Bretherton. USA., *The Terror*, Edgar Wallace, London 1927, Play

RETURN OF THE TEXAN 1952 d: Delmer Daves. USA., *The Home Place*, Fred Gipson, 1950, Novel

Return of Vassili Bortnikov, The see **VOZVRASHCHENIE VASSILIYA BORTNIKOVA** (1953).

RETURN TO EARTH 1976 d: Jud Taylor. USA., *Return to Earth*, Edwin E. "Buzz" Aldrin, Wayne Warga, Book

Return to King Solomon's Mines see **WATUSI** (1959).

Return to Manhood see **NANBANJI NO SEMUSHI-OTOKO** (1957).

RETURN TO OZ 1964 d: Arthur Rankin Jr. USA., *The Land of Oz*, L. Frank Baum, 1904, Novel, *Ozma of Oz*, L. Frank Baum, 1907, Novel

RETURN TO OZ 1985 d: Walter Murch. USA., *The Land of Oz*, L. Frank Baum, 1904, Novel, *Ozma of Oz*, L. Frank Baum, 1907, Novel

RETURN TO PARADISE 1953 d: Mark Robson. USA., *Mr. Morgan*, James A. Michener, 1951, Short Story

RETURN TO PEYTON PLACE 1961 d: Jose Ferrer. USA., *Return to Peyton Place*, Grace Metalious, New York 1959, Novel

RETURN TO SENDER 1963 d: Gordon Hales. UKN., Edgar Wallace, Short Story

RETURN TO THE BLUE LAGOON 1991 d: William A. Graham. USA., *The Garden of God*, Henry de Vere Stacpoole, Novel

RETURN TO WARBOW 1958 d: Ray Nazarro. USA., *Return to Warbow*, Les Savage Jr., 1955, Novel

RETURN TO YESTERDAY 1940 d: Robert Stevenson. UKN., *Goodness How Sad*, Robert Morley, London 1938, Play

REUBEN, REUBEN 1983 d: Robert Ellis Miller. USA., *Reuben Reuben*, Peter de Vries, 1964, Novel

REUNION 1932 d: Ivar Campbell. UKN., Reginald Hargreaves, Article

Reunion see **TILL WE MEET AGAIN** (1936).

Reunion see **CHRISSIE, RUN RUN** (1984).

REUNION 1989 d: Jerry Schatzberg. UKN/FRN/GRM., *Reunion*, Fred Uhlman, Novel

REUNION 1994 d: Lee Grant. USA., *Points of Light*, Linda Gray Sexton, Novel

REUNION IN VIENNA 1932 d: Sidney A. Franklin. USA., *Reunion in Vienna*, R. E. Sherwood, New York 1931, Play

Reunited in Victory see **SHENG LI CHONG FENG** (1951).

REVANCHE DE ROGER-LA-HONTE, LA 1946 d: Andre Cayatte. FRN., *Le Revanche de Roger la Honte*, Jules Mary, Novel

Revanche d'Ivanhoe, Le see **LA RIVINCITA DI IVANHOE** (1965).

Reve Et Realite see **AME D'ARTISTE** (1924).

REVE ETERNEL 1934 d: Henri Chomette, Arnold Fanck. FRN., *Paccard Wider Balmat*, Karl Ziak, Novel

REVE, LE 1922 d: Jacques de Baroncelli. FRN., *Le Reve*, Emile Zola, 1888, Novel

REVE, LE 1930 d: Jacques de Baroncelli. FRN., *Le Reve*, Emile Zola, 1888, Novel

REVEIL, LE 1914. FRN., *Le Reveil*, Paul Hervieu, Play

REVEILLE-TOI, CHERIE 1960 d: Claude Magnier. FRN., *Monsieur Masure*, Claude Magnier, Paris 1956, Play

Revelacion see **PRIGIONIERI DEL MALE** (1956).

REVELACION, LA 1997 d: Mario David. ARG., Oscar Yedaide, Short Story

Revelation see **REVELATIONS** (1916).

REVELATION 1918 d: George D. Baker. USA., *The Rose-Bush of a Thousand Years*, Mabel Wagnalls, 1916, Short Story

REVELATION 1924 d: George D. Baker. USA., *The Rose-Bush of a Thousand Years*, Mabel Wagnalls, 1916, Short Story

Revelation, The see **LA REVELACION** (1997).

REVELATIONS 1916 d: Arthur Maude. USA., *Magda*, Hermann Sudermann, Berlin 1893, Play

REVENANT, LE 1979 d: Mahama Johnson Traore. CND/SNL., *Le Revenant*, Aminal Snowfall, Book

Revenge! see **END OF THE TRAIL** (1936).

REVENGE 1918 d: Tod Browning. USA., *Hearts Steadfast*, Edward Stewart Moffat, New York 1915, Novel

REVENGE 1928 d: Edwin Carewe. USA., *The Bear Tamer's Daughter*, Konrad Bercovici, 1921, Short Story

Revenge see **ZEMSTA** (1957).

REVENGE 1960 d: Irina Poplavskay A. USS., *Mest*, Anton Chekhov, 1886, Short Story

REVENGE 1971 d: Jud Taylor. USA., *Revenge*, Elizabeth Davis, Novel

REVENGE 1990 d: Anthony Scott. USA., *Revenge*, Jim Harrison, Novel

Revenge Is Sweet see **BABES IN TOYLAND** (1934).

Revenge of Dr. Death, The see **MADHOUSE** (1974).

Revenge of Dracula see **DRACULA - PRINCE OF DARKNESS** (1965).

Revenge of Ivanhoe, The see **LA RIVINCITA DI IVANHOE** (1965).

Revenge of Milady, The see **THE FOUR MUSKETEERS** (1975).

Revenge of Tarzan, The see **THE RETURN OF TARZAN** (1920).

Revenge of the Sea, The see **POMSTA MORE** (1921).

Revenge of the Vampire see **LA MASCHERA DEL DEMONIO** (1960).

Revenge Squad see **HIT AND RUN** (1982).

REVENGERS' COMEDIES, THE 1998 d: Malcolm Mowbray. UKN/FRN., *The Revengers' Comedies*, Alan Ayckbourn, Play

REVERSE BE MY LOT, THE 1938 d: Raymond Stross. UKN., *The Reverse Be My Lot*, Margaret Morrison, Novel

REVERSE OF THE MEDAL, THE 1923 d: George A. Cooper. UKN., *The Reverse of the Medal*, Lionel James, Short Story

REVES D'AMOUR 1946 d: Christian Stengel. FRN., *Reves d'Amour*, Rene Fauchois, 1944, Play

Revisor see **REVIZOR** (1933).

REVIZOR 1933 d: Martin Fric. CZC., *Revizor*, Nikolay Gogol, 1836, Play

REVIZOR 1952 d: Vladimir Petrov. USS., *Revizor*, Nikolay Gogol, 1836, Play

REVIZOR 1996 d: Sergei Gazarov. RSS., *Revizor*, Nikolay Gogol, 1836, Play

Revolt see **SCARLET DAWN** (1932).

Revolt in the Reformatory see **REVOLTE IM ERZIEHUNGSHAUS** (1929).

REVOLT OF MAMIE STOVER, THE 1956 d: Raoul Walsh. USA., *The Revolt of Mamie Stover*, William Bradford Huie, 1951, Novel

Revolt of the Fishermen, The see **VOSTANIYE RYBAKOV** (1934).

Revolt of the Hanged see **LA REBELION DE LOS COLGADOS** (1953).

Revolt of the Holy Monkey in the Heavenly Palace see **DA NAO TIAN GONG** (1964).

Revolt of the Living, The see **LE MONDE TREMBLERA** (1939).

Revolt of the Lost Children, The see **UTBOROPPRORET** (1997).

Revolt of the Slaves, The see **LA RIVOLTA DEGLI SCHIAVI** (1961).

Revolt of the Tartars see **MICHELE STROGOFF** (1956).

Revolt of the Volga see **IL VENDICATORE** (1959).

REVOLT, THE 1916 d: Barry O'Neil. USA., *The Revolt*, Edward Locke, New York 1915, Novel

Revolte Des Indiens Apaches, La see **WINNETOU I** (1963).

Revolte Des Vivants, Les see **LE MONDE TREMBLERA** (1939).

REVOLTE IM ERZIEHUNGDHAUS 1929 d: Georg Asagaroff. GRM., *Revolt Im Erziehungshaus*, Peter Martin Lampel, Play

REVOLTE, LE 1938 d: Leon Mathot, Robert Bibal. FRN., *Le Revolte*, Maurice Larrouy, Novel

Revolte Sur la Volga see **IL VENDICATORE** (1959).

REVOLTEE, LA 1947 d: Marcel L'Herbier. FRN., *La Revoltee*, Pierre Sabatier, Novel

REVOLTES DE LOMANACH, LES 1953 d: Richard Pottier. FRN/ITL., *Les Chouans*, Honore de Balzac, 1834, Novel

Revoltes de Lon Manach, Les see **LES REVOLTES DE LOMANACH** (1953).

REVOLTOSA, LA 1924 d: Florian Rey. SPN., *La Revoltosa*, Ruperto Chapi, Carlos Fernandez Shaw, J. Lopez Silva, Opera

Revolution see **THE KING'S ROMANCE** (1914).

Revolutionary Family, A see **GEMING JIAYING** (1960).

Revolutionary Road, The see **ZHENG TU** (1976).

REVOLUTIONARY, THE 1970 d: Paul Williams. UKN/USA., *The Revolutionary*, Hans Koningsberger, New York 1967, Novel

Revolutionist, The see **THE KING'S ROMANCE** (1914).

Revolutionsbryllup see **REVOLUTIONSHOCHZEIT** (1928).

REVOLUTIONSHOCHZEIT 1928 d: Anders W. Sandberg. GRM/DNM., *Revolutionshochzeit*, Sophus Michaelis, Play

REVOLVER AUX CHEVEUX ROUGES, LE 1973 d: Frederic Geilfus. BLG/FRN., *Man Alive*, G. K. Chesterton, 1912, Novel

Revolver Met Het Rode Haar, de see **LE REVOLVER AUX CHEVEUX ROUGES** (1973).

Revolving Doors, The see **LES PORTES TOURNANTES** (1988).

Revue of Artistes, The see **DE ARTISTEN-REVUE** (1926).

Revue-Artistek, de see **DE ARTISTEN-REVUE** (1926).

REWARD, THE 1965 d: Serge Bourguignon. USA/FRN., *The Reward*, Michael Barrett, London 1955, Novel

Rex Stout's Nero Wolfe see **NERO WOLFE** (1977).

REY PASMADO, EL 1991 d: Imanol Uribe. SPN/FRN/PRT., *Cronica de un Rey Pasmado*, Gonzalo Torrente Ballester, Novel

REY QUE RABIO, EL 1929 d: Jose Buchs. SPN., *El Rey Que Rabio*, V. Aza, Ruperto Chapi, Miguel Ramos Carrion, Opera

Rez-de-Chaussee Gauche see **IM PARTERRE LINKS** (1963).

Rhapsodie Des Sens see **BEL AMI** (1975).

Rhapsodie En Aout see **HACHIGATSU-NO-KYOSHIKYOKU** (1991).

RHAPSODY 1954 d: Charles Vidor. USA., *Maurice Guest*, Ethel Florence Richardson, 1908, Novel

Rhapsody in August *see* HACHIGATSU-NO-KYOSHIKYOKU (1991).

Rhapsody in Stripes *see* JAIL HOUSE BLUES (1942).

RHEINSBERG 1967 d: Kurt Hoffmann. GRM., *Rheinsberg; Ein Bilderbuch Fur Verliebte*, Kurt Tucholsky, 1912, Short Story

RHINEMANN EXCHANGE, THE 1977 d: Burt Kennedy. USA., *The Rhinemann Exchange*, Robert Ludlum, Novel

RHINO! 1964 d: Ivan Tors. USA/SAF., *Rhino!*, Art Arthur, Novel

Rhinoceros *see* DIE NASHORNER (1963).

RHINOCEROS 1973 d: Tom O'Horgan. USA., *Le Rhinoceros*, Eugene Ionesco, 1959, Play

Rhinoceroses *see* DIE NASHORNER (1963).

Rhodes *see* RHODES OF AFRICA (1936).

RHODES OF AFRICA 1936 d: Berthold Viertel. UKN/SAF., *Rhodes*, Sarah Millin, Book

Rhodes, the Empire Builder *see* RHODES OF AFRICA (1936).

RHUBARB 1951 d: Arthur Lubin. USA., *Rhubarb*, H. Allen Smith, 1946, Novel

Rhythm in the Air *see* TWENTY MILLION SWEETHEARTS (1934).

Rhythm on the River *see* FRESHMAN LOVE (1936).

Rhythm Romance *see* SOME LIKE IT HOT (1939).

RI CHU 1938 d: Yueh Feng. CHN., *Ri Chu*, Wan Jiabao, 1936, Play

RIBALTA, LA 1912 d: Mario Caserini. ITL., *La Rampe*, Henri de Rotschild, 1909, Play

Riccardo Cuor Di Leone *see* IL TALISMANO (1911).

RICCHEZZA SENZA DOMANI 1939 d: Ferdinando M. Poggioli. ITL., *Rosso E Nero Verde*, Fabrizio Sarazani, Play

Rice People *see* NEAK SRI (1992).

Rice, The *see* MESHI (1951).

RICH AND FAMOUS 1981 d: George Cukor. USA., *Old Acquaintance*, John Van Druten, New York 1940, Play

RICH AND STRANGE 1931 d: Alfred Hitchcock. UKN., *Rich and Strange*, Dale Collins, Novel

RICH ARE ALWAYS WITH US, THE 1932 d: Alfred E. Green. USA., *The Rich are Always With Us*, Ethel Pettit, New York 1931, Novel

RICH BUT HONEST 1927 d: Albert Ray. USA., *Rich But Honest*, Arthur Somers Roche, 1926, Short Story

Rich Full Life, The *see* CYNTHIA (1947).

RICH IN LOVE 1992 d: Bruce Beresford. USA., *Rich in Love*, Josephine Humphreys, Novel

RICH MAN, POOR GIRL 1938 d: Reinhold Schunzel. USA., *White Collars*, Edith Ellis, New York 1923, Play

RICH MAN, POOR MAN 1918 d: J. Searle Dawley. USA., *Poor Man Rich Man*, Maximilian Foster, New York 1916, Novel

RICH MAN, POOR MAN 1975 d: David Greene, Boris Sagal. USA., *Poor Man Rich Man*, Irwin Shaw, Novel

RICH MAN'S FOLLY 1931 d: John Cromwell. USA., *Dombey and Son*, Charles Dickens, London 1848, Novel

RICH MEN'S SONS 1927 d: Ralph Graves. USA., *The Lightning Express*, Dorothy Howell, Story

RICH PEOPLE 1929 d: Edward H. Griffith. USA., *Rich People*, Jay Gelzer, 1928, Short Story

RICH RELATIONS 1937 d: Clifford Sanforth. USA., *Rich Relations*, Priscilla Wayne, Chicago 1934, Novel

Rich, Young and Deadly *see* PLATINUM HIGH SCHOOL (1960).

RICHARD CARVEL 1915?. USA., *Richard Carvel*, Winston Churchill, New York 1899, Novel

RICHARD II 1978 d: David Giles. UKN., *Richard II*, William Shakespeare, c1595, Play

RICHARD III 1908 d: William V. Ranous, J. Stuart Blackton (Spv). USA., *Richard III*, William Shakespeare, c1594, Play

RICHARD III 1911 d: F. R. Benson. UKN., *Richard III*, William Shakespeare, c1594, Play

RICHARD III 1912 d: James Keene. USA., *Richard III*, William Shakespeare, c1594, Play

Richard III *see* THE LIFE AND DEATH OF RICHARD III (1912).

RICHARD III 1955 d: Laurence Olivier, Anthony Bushell. UKN., *Richard III*, William Shakespeare, c1594, Play

RICHARD III 1995 d: Richard Loncraine. USA/UKN., *Richard III*, William Shakespeare, c1594, Play

RICHARD LVINOE SERDCE 1992 d: Evgenij Gerasimov. RSS., *The Talisman*, Sir Walter Scott, 1825, Novel

RICHARD THE BRAZEN 1917 d: Perry N. Vekroff. USA., *Richard the Brazen*, Cyrus Townsend Brady, Edward Peple, New York 1906, Novel

Richard, the Lion Heart *see* RICHARD LVINOE SERDCE (1992).

Richard, the Lion-Hearted *see* IL TALISMANO (1911).

RICHARD, THE LION-HEARTED 1923 d: Chet Withey. USA., *The Talisman*, Sir Walter Scott, 1825, Novel

RICHARD'S THINGS 1980 d: Anthony Harvey. UKN., *Richard's Things*, Frederic Raphael, Novel

RICHELIEU 1914 d: Allan Dwan. USA., *Richelieu; Or the Conspiracy*, Edward George Bulwer Lytton, London 1839, Play

RICHELIEU OR THE CONSPIRACY 1909 d: J. Stuart Blackton. USA., *Richelieu; Or the Conspiracy*, Edward George Bulwer Lytton, London 1839, Play

Riches and Romance *see* THE AMAZING QUEST OF ERNEST BLISS (1936).

RICHEST GIRL, THE 1918 d: Albert Capellani. USA., *The Richest Girl*, Paul Gabault, Michael Morton, New York 1909, Play

RICHEST MAN IN THE WORLD, THE 1930 d: Sam Wood. USA., *Father's Day*, Elliott Nugent, J. C. Nugent, Story

RICHEST MAN IN THE WORLD: THE STORY OF ARISTOTLE ONASSIS 1988 d: Waris Hussein. USA., Peter Evans, Biography

RICHIAMO DEL CUORE, IL 1930 d: Jack Salvatori. FRN., *Sarah and Son*, Timothy Shea, New York 1929, Novel

Richiamo Del Sangue, Il *see* CALL OF THE BLOOD (1948).

Richiamo Della Foresta, Il *see* CALL OF THE WILD (1972).

RICHIAMO DELLA FORESTA, IL 1992 d: Alan Smithee. ITL/CND., *Call of the Wild*, Jack London, New York 1903, Novel

Richie *see* THE DEATH OF RICHIE (1977).

RICHTER UND SEIN HENKER, DER 1976 d: Maximilian Schell. GRM/ITL., *Die Richter Und Sein Henker*, Friedrich Durrenmatt, 1950-51, Novel

RICHTER VON ZALAMEA, DER 1920 d: Ludwig Berger. GRM., *El Alcalde de Zalamea*, Pedro Calderon de La Barca, 1651, Play

RICHTER VON ZALAMEA, DER 1955 d: Martin Hellberg. GDR., *El Alcalde de Zalamea*, Pedro Calderon de La Barca, 1651, Play

RICHU 1985 d: Yu Bengzheng. CHN., *Ri Chu*, Wan Jiabao, 1936, Play

Rickshaw Boy *see* LUO TOU XIANGZI (1982).

Rickshaw Man, The *see* MUHOMATSU NO ISSHO (1958).

RICOCHET 1963 d: John Llewellyn Moxey. UKN., *The Angel of Terror*, Edgar Wallace, London 1922, Novel

RID I NATT! 1942 d: Gustaf Molander. SWD., *Rid I Natt!*, Vilhelm Moberg, 1941, Novel

RIDDLE GAWNE 1918 d: William S. Hart, Lambert Hillyer. USA., *The Vengeance of Jefferson Gawne*, Charles Alden Seltzer, Chicago 1917, Novel

Riddle Me This *see* GUILTY AS HELL (1932).

Riddle of the 40 Naughty Girls, The *see* FORTY NAUGHTY GIRLS (1937).

Riddle of the Dangling Pearl, The *see* THE PLOT THICKENS (1936).

RIDDLE OF THE SANDS, THE 1978 d: Tony Maylam. UKN/GAL., *The Riddle of the Sands*, Erskine Childers, 1903, Novel

RIDDLE: WOMAN, THE 1920 d: Edward Jose. USA., *The Riddle: Woman*, Carl Jacobi, Play

RIDE BEYOND VENGEANCE 1966 d: Bernard McEveety. USA., *The Night of the Tiger*, Al Dewlen, New York 1956, Novel

RIDE HARD, RIDE WILD 1970 d: Elov Petterssons. DNM., *Krosor 500*, Lennart Nielsen

RIDE HIM, COWBOY 1932 d: Fred Allen. USA., *Ride Him Cowboy*, Kenneth Perkins, New York 1923, Novel

RIDE, KELLY, RIDE 1941 d: Norman Foster. USA., Peter B. Kyne, Story

RIDE OUT FOR REVENGE 1957 d: Bernard Girard. USA., *Ride Out for Revenge*, Burt Arthur, Novel

RIDE THE HIGH WIND 1965 d: David Millin. SAF., *North to Bushman's Rock*, George Harding, London 1965, Novel

RIDE THE PINK HORSE 1947 d: Robert Montgomery. USA., *Ride the Pink Horse*, Dorothy B. Hughes, Novel

Ride Tonight! *see* RID I NATT! (1942).

RIDEAU CRAMOISI, LE 1952 d: Alexandre Astruc. FRN., *Le Rideau Cramosi*, Barbey d'Aurevilly, Short Story

RIDEAU ROUGE, LE 1952 d: Andre Barsacq. FRN., *MacBeth*, William Shakespeare, c1606, Play

Rider in Blue *see* RYTTARE I BLATT (1959).

Rider in the Night, The *see* DIE RUITER IN DIE NAG (1963).

RIDER OF THE KING LOG, THE 1921 d: Harry O. Hoyt. USA., *The Rider of the King Log*, Holman Francis Day, New York 1919, Novel

Rider of the White Horse, The *see* DER SCHIMMELREITER (1934).

Rider of the White Horse, The *see* DER SCHIMMELREITER (1978).

Rider on the White Horse, The *see* DER SCHIMMELREITER (1934).

Riders *see* JILLY COOPER'S RIDERS (1993).

RIDERS IN THE SKY 1949 d: John English. USA., Herbert A. Woodbury, Story

RIDERS OF THE DAWN 1920 d: Jack Conway. USA., *The Desert of Wheat*, Zane Grey, New York 1919, Novel

RIDERS OF THE NEW FOREST 1946 d: Philip Leacock. UKN., *Bonny the Pony*, Ruth Clark, Novel

RIDERS OF THE PURPLE SAGE 1918 d: Frank Lloyd. USA., *Riders of the Purple Sage*, Zane Grey, New York 1912, Novel

RIDERS OF THE PURPLE SAGE 1925 d: Lynn Reynolds. USA., *Riders of the Purple Sage*, Zane Grey, New York 1912, Novel

RIDERS OF THE PURPLE SAGE 1931 d: Hamilton MacFadden. USA., *Riders of the Purple Sage*, Zane Grey, New York 1912, Novel

RIDERS OF THE PURPLE SAGE 1941 d: James Tinling. USA., *Riders of the Purple Sage*, Zane Grey, New York 1912, Novel

RIDERS OF THE PURPLE SAGE 1996 d: Charles Haid. USA., *Riders of the Purple Sage*, Zane Grey, New York 1912, Novel

RIDERS OF THE WHISTLING SKULL, THE 1937 d: MacK V. Wright. USA., *Riders of the Whistling Skull*, William Colt MacDonald, New York 1934, Novel

RIDERS TO THE SEA 1935 d: Brian Desmond Hurst. UKN., *Riders to the Sea*, John Millington Synge, London 1904, Play

RIDERS TO THE SEA 1987 d: Ronan O'Leary. IRL., *Riders to the Sea*, John Millington Synge, London 1904, Play

RIDERS UP 1924 d: Irving Cummings. USA., *Riders Up*, Gerald Beaumont, New York 1922, Novel

RIDGEWAY OF MONTANA 1924 d: Cliff Smith. USA., *A Sacrifice to Mammon*, William MacLeod Raine, New York 1906, Novel

RIDICOLO, IL 1916 d: Eduardo BencivengA. ITL., *Il Ridicolo*, Paolo Ferrari, 1859, Play

RIDIN' KID FROM POWDER RIVER, THE 1924 d: Edward Sedgwick. USA., *The Ridin' Kid from Powder River*, Henry Herbert Knibbs, Story

RIDIN' RASCAL, THE 1926 d: Cliff Smith. USA., *Mavericks*, William MacLeod Raine, New York 1912, Novel

RIDIN' THUNDER 1925 d: Cliff Smith. USA., *Jean of the Lazy a*, B. M. Bower, Boston 1915, Novel

RIDING AVENGER, THE 1936 d: Harry L. Fraser. USA., *Big Bend Buckaroo*, Walter West, Short Story

Riding for a Fall *see* SIX CYLINDER LOVE (1931).

RIDING HIGH 1943 d: George Marshall. USA., *Ready Money*, James Montgomery, New York 1912, Play

RIDING ON AIR 1937 d: Edward Sedgwick. USA., *All Is Confusion*, Richard Macauley, 1934, Short Story

RIDING SHOTGUN 1954 d: Andre de Toth. USA., *Riding Solo*, Kenneth Perkins, Short Story

Riding Thunder *see* RIDIN' THUNDER (1925).

RIEN QUE DES MENSONGES 1932 d: Karl Anton. FRN., *Les Francs-MacOns*, G. Leprince, Claude Rolland, Play

RIEN QUE LA VERITE 1931 d: Rene Guissart. FRN., *Nothing But the Truth*, James Montgomery, Play

Rienzi *see* COLA DI RIENZI (1910).

RIESENRAD, DAS 1961 d: Geza von Radvanyi. GRM., *Das Riesenrad*, Jan de Hartog, Play

Riff Raff Girls *see* DU RIFIFI CHEZ LES FEMMES (1959).

Riff-Raff *see* LES CANAILLES (1959).

Rififi *see* DU RIFIFI CHEZ LES HOMMES (1955).

Rififi and the Women *see* DU RIFIFI CHEZ LES FEMMES (1959).

Rififi for Girls *see* DU RIFIFI CHEZ LES FEMMES (1959).

Rififi Fra le Donne *see* DU RIFIFI CHEZ LES FEMMES (1959).

Rififi in Paris *see* DU RIFIFI A PANAMA (1966).

Rififi Internazionale *see* DU RIFIFI A PANAMA (1966).

Riflemen, The *see* LES CARABINIERS (1962).

RIFUGIO, IL 1918 d: Giulio Antamoro. ITL., *Le Refuge*, Dario Niccodemi, 1909, Play

Rigadoon *see* ZANZIBAR (1940).

Rigged *see* HIT AND RUN (1985).

RIGHT AGE TO MARRY, THE 1935 d: MacLean Rogers. UKN., *The Right Age to Marry*, H. F. Maltby, 1925, Play

RIGHT APPROACH, THE 1961 d: David Butler. USA., *The Live Wire*, Garson Kanin, New York 1950, Play

Right Guy *see* THE FRAME-UP (1937).

RIGHT HAND MAN, THE 1986 d: Di Drew. ASL., *The Right Hand Man*, Kathleen Peyton, Novel

Right Man, The *see* HER FIRST ROMANCE (1940).

RIGHT OF WAY 1983 d: George Schaefer. USA., *Right of Way*, Richard Lees, Play

RIGHT OF WAY, THE 1915 d: John W. Noble. USA., *The Right of Way*, Gilbert Parker, London 1901, Novel

RIGHT OF WAY, THE 1920 d: John Francis Dillon. USA., *The Right of Way*, Gilbert Parker, London 1901, Novel

RIGHT OF WAY, THE 1931 d: Frank Lloyd. USA., *The Right of Way*, Gilbert Parker, London 1901, Novel

RIGHT STUFF, THE 1983 d: Philip Kaufman. USA., *The Right Stuff*, Tom Wolfe, 1979, Novel

RIGHT THAT FAILED, THE 1922 d: Bayard Veiller. USA., *The Right That Failed*, John Phillips Marquand, Short Story

RIGHT TO BE HAPPY, THE 1916 d: Rupert Julian. USA., *A Christmas Carol*, Charles Dickens, London 1843, Novel

RIGHT TO LIVE, THE 1935 d: William Keighley. USA., *The Sacred Flame*, W. Somerset Maugham, New York 1928, Play

RIGHT TO LOVE, THE 1920 d: George Fitzmaurice. USA., *L' Homme Qui Assassina*, Claude Farrere, Paris 1908, Novel

RIGHT TO LOVE, THE 1930 d: Richard Wallace. USA., *Brook Evans*, Susan Glaspell, London 1928, Novel

Right to Sin, The *see* PRAVO NA HRICH (1932).

RIGHT TO STRIKE, THE 1923 d: Fred Paul. UKN., *The Right to Strike*, Ernest Hutchinson, London 1920, Play

RIGHT TO THE HEART 1942 d: Eugene J. Forde. USA., *You Can't Always Tell*, Harold MacGrath, Short Story

RIGHTFUL HEIR, THE 1913 d: J. Searle Dawley. USA., *The Lane That Had No Turning*, Gilbert Parker, 1900, Short Story

Right-Hand Man, The *see* THE RIGHT HAND MAN (1986).

RIGOLETTO 1922 d: George Wynn. UKN., *Le Roi S'amuse*, Victor Hugo, 1832, Play

RIGOLETTO 1927 d: H. B. Parkinson. UKN., *Le Roi S'amuse*, Victor Hugo, 1832, Play

Rigoletto *see* IL RE SI DIVERTE (1941).

RIGOLETTO 1947 d: Carmine Gallone. ITL., *Rigoletto*, Francesco M. Piave, Giuseppe Verdi, Venice 1851, Opera

Rigoletto *see* RIGOLETTO E LA SUA TRAGEDIA (1956).

RIGOLETTO E LA SUA TRAGEDIA 1956 d: Flavio CalzavarA. ITL., *Rigoletto*, Francesco M. Piave, Giuseppe Verdi, Venice 1851, Opera

RIGUANG XIAGU 1995 d: He Ping. CHN., *Riguang Xiagu*, Zhang Rui, Novel

Rikisha Man, The *see* MUHOMATSU NO ISSHO (1958).

RIKKI-TIKKI-TAVI 1975 d: Alexander Zguridi. USS., *Rikki-Tikki-Tavi*, Rudyard Kipling, Novel

RIKOS & RAKKAUS 1999 d: Pekka Milonoff. FNL., *Rikos & Rakkaus*, Jari Tervo, Novel

RIKOS JA RANGAISTUS 1983 d: Aki Kaurismaki. FNL., *Prestupleniye I Nakazaniye*, Fyodor Dostoyevsky, 1867, Novel

Riky-Tiky-Tavy *see* RIKKI-TIKKI-TAVI (1975).

RIKYU 1989 d: Hiroshi TeshigaharA. JPN., *Rikyu*, Yaeko Nogami, Novel

RIMEDIO PER LE DONNE, IL 1914 d: Ernesto Vaser. ITL., *L' Rimedi Par le Done*, Fulberto Alarini, Play

RIMROCK JONES 1918 d: Donald Crisp. USA., *Rimrock Jones*, Dane Coolidge, New York 1917, Novel

RINA 1926 d: J. S. Kolar. CZC., *Rina*, Rudolf Jaroslav Kronbauer, Novel

RINA, L'ANGELO DELLE ALPI 1917 d: Enrico Vidali. ITL., *Rina l'Angelo Delle Alpe*, Carolina Invernizio, 1877, Novel

RING AND THE BOOK, THE 1914. USA., *The Ring and the Book*, Robert Browning, Poem

RING AND THE MAN, THE 1914 d: Francis Powers. USA., *The Ring and the Man*, Cyrus Townsend Brady, New York 1909, Novel

Ring and the Rose, The *see* PIERSCIEN I ROZA (1987).

RING AROUND THE MOON 1936 d: Charles Lamont. USA., *Ring Around the Moon*, Vere Hobart, New York 1935, Novel

RING OF BRIGHT WATER 1969 d: Jack Couffer. UKN., *Ring of Bright Water*, Gavin Maxwell, London 1960, Novel

Ring of Death *see* UN DETECTIVE (1969).

RING OF DESTINY, THE 1915 d: Cleo Madison. USA., *Ring of Destiny*, Marshall Stedman, Story

RING, THE 1927 d: H. B. Parkinson. UKN., *Der Ring Des Nibelungen*, Richard Wagner, Bayreuth 1876, Opera

RINGER, THE 1928 d: Arthur Maude. UKN., *The Gaunt Stranger*, Edgar Wallace, London 1925, Novel

RINGER, THE 1931 d: Walter Forde. UKN., *The Gaunt Stranger*, Edgar Wallace, London 1925, Novel

RINGER, THE 1952 d: Guy Hamilton. UKN., *The Gaunt Stranger*, Edgar Wallace, London 1925, Novel

Ringer, The *see* DER HEXER (1964).

RINGING THE CHANGES 1929 d: Leslie Hiscott. UKN., *Jix*, Raleigh King, Novel

Ringmaster, The *see* THE CIRCUS MAN (1914).

RIO CONCHOS 1964 d: Gordon Douglas. USA., *Guns of Rio Conchos*, Clair Huffaker, Greenwich CT. 1964, Novel

RIO GRANDE 1920 d: Edwin Carewe. USA., *Rio Grande*, Augustus Thomas, New York 1916, Play

RIO GRANDE 1950 d: John Ford. USA., *Mission Without a Record*, James Warner Bellah, Story

RIO GRANDE ROMANCE 1936 d: Robert F. Hill. USA., *One Day's Work*, Peter B. Kyne, Short Story

RIO RITA 1929 d: Luther Reed. USA., *Rio Rita*, Guy Bolton, Fred Thompson, New York 1927, Musical Play

RIO RITA 1942 d: S. Sylvan Simon. USA., *Rio Rita*, Guy Bolton, Fred Thompson, New York 1927, Musical Play

RIO Y LA MUERTE, EL 1954 d: Luis Bunuel. MXC., *El Rio Y la Muerte*, Miguel Alvarez Acosta, Novel

RIOT 1969 d: Buzz Kulik. USA., *The Riot*, Frank Elli, New York 1967, Novel

Riot Patrol *see* THE DEVIL'S PARTY (1938).

Riotous Girl, The *see* LA REVOLTOSA (1924).

RIP ROARIN' ROBERTS 1924 d: Richard Thorpe. USA., *A Man of Action*, Robert J. Horton, Short Story

RIP VAN WINKLE 1903 d: Alf Collins. UKN., *Rip Van Winkle*, Washington Irving, 1820, Short Story

RIP VAN WINKLE 1908 d: Otis Turner. USA., *Rip Van Winkle*, Washington Irving, 1820, Short Story

RIP VAN WINKLE 1910 d: Theodore Marston. USA., *Rip Van Winkle*, Washington Irving, 1820, Short Story

RIP VAN WINKLE 1912 d: Charles Kent. USA., *Rip Van Winkle*, Washington Irving, 1820, Short Story

RIP VAN WINKLE 1912. USA., *Rip Van Winkle*, Washington Irving, 1820, Short Story

RIP VAN WINKLE 1914 d: Stuart Kinder. UKN., *Rip Van Winkle*, Washington Irving, 1820, Short Story

RIP VAN WINKLE 1914. USA., *Rip Van Winkle*, Washington Irving, 1820, Short Story

RIP VAN WINKLE 1921 d: Ward Lascelle. USA., *Rip Van Winkle*, Washington Irving, 1820, Short Story

Ripening Seed, The *see* LE BLE EN HERBE (1953).

Ripening Youth *see* REIFENDE JUGEND (1933).

Riposo Del Guerriero, Il *see* LE REPOS DU GUERRIER (1962).

RISATE DI GIOIA 1960 d: Mario Monicelli. ITL., *Ladri in Chiesa*, Alberto Moravia, 1954, Short Story, *Risate Di Gioia*, Alberto Moravia, 1954, Short Story

RISE AND FALL OF OFFICER 13, THE 1915 d: Horace Davey. USA., *The Rise and Fall of Officer 13*, Smith Addison, Story

RISE AND SHINE 1941 d: Allan Dwan. USA., *My Life and Hard Times*, James Thurber, 1933, Short Story

Rise of Catherine the Great, The *see* CATHERINE THE GREAT (1934).

Rise of Helga, The *see* SUSAN LENOX (HER FALL AND RISE) (1931).

RISE OF JENNIE CUSHING, THE 1917 d: Maurice Tourneur. USA., *The Rise of Jennie Cushing*, Mary S. Watts, New York 1914, Novel

Rise of Jenny Cushing, The *see* THE RISE OF JENNIE CUSHING (1917).

Rise of Roscoe Payne, The *see* NO TRESPASSING (1922).

RISING GENERATION, THE 1928 d: Harley Knoles, George Dewhurst. UKN., *The Rising Generation*, Laura Leycester, Wyn Weaver, London 1923, Play

RISING OF THE MOON, THE 1957 d: John Ford. UKN/IRL., *A Minute's Wait*, Martin McHugh, Play

RISING OF THE MOON, THE 1957. UKN/IRL., *1921*, Lady Gregory, Play

RISING OF THE MOON, THE 1957 d: John Ford. UKN/IRL., *The Majesty of the Law*, Frank O'Connor, Play

RISING SUN 1993 d: Philip Kaufman. USA., *Rising Sun*, Michael Crichton, Novel

Rising to Fame *see* SUSAN LENOX (HER FALL AND RISE) (1931).

Risk, The *see* SUSPECT (1960).

Risking Witness *see* TESTIMONE A RISCHIO (1997).

RISKY BUSINESS 1926 d: Alan Hale. USA., *Pearls Before Cecily*, Charles William Brackett, 1923, Short Story

RISKY ROAD, THE 1918 d: Ida May Park. USA., *Her Fling*, Katherine Leiser Robbins, Short Story

Risveglio Dell'istinto, Il *see* LES REGATES DE SAN FRANCISCO (1959).

Rita *see* LETTERE DI UNA NOVIZIA (1960).

RITA HAYWORTH: THE LOVE GODDESS 1983 d: James Goldstone. USA., *Rita Hayworth*, John Kobal, Book

RITA, SUE AND BOB TOO 1987 d: Alan Clarke. UKN., *The Arbour*, Andrea Dunbar, Play, *Rita, Sue and Bob Too!*, Andrea Dunbar, Play

Rites of Passage *see* BERNICE BOBS HER HAIR (1976).

RITORNO AL NIDO 1944 d: Giorgio Ferroni. ITL., *Sans Famille*, Hector Malot, Novel

RITORNO D'ANIMA 1917 d: Mario Ceccatelli. ITL., *Il Ritorno Di Un'anima*, Vittorio Mariani, Novel

RITORNO DI CASANOVA, IL 1978 d: Pasquale Festa Campanile. ITL., *Casanovas Heimfahrt*, Arthur Schnitzler, Novel

Ritorno Di Don Camillo, Il *see* LE RETOUR DE DON CAMILLO (1953).

Ritoru Champion *see* MY CHAMPION (1981).

RITRATTO DI BORGHESIA IN NERO 1978 d: Tonino Cervi. ITL., *La Maitresse de Piano*, Roger Peyrefitte, 1949, Short Story

RIVA DEI BRUTI, LA 1930 d: Mario Camerini. FRN., *Victory*, Joseph Conrad, London 1915, Novel

RIVAL DE SON PERE 1909 d: Andre Calmettes. FRN., *Don Carlos*, Friedrich von Schiller, 1787, Play

Rival, The *see* PRATIDWANDI (1970).

Rivalinnen *see* WEEP NO MORE MY LADY (1994).

RIVALS (DUEL SCENE), THE 1914. UKN., *The Rivals*, Richard Brinsley Sheridan, London 1775, Play

RIVALS, THE 1913 d: Theodore Marston. USA., *The Rivals*, Richard Brinsley Sheridan, London 1775, Play

RIVALS, THE 1963 d: Max Varnel. UKN., *Elegant Edward*, Edgar Wallace, London 1928, Novel

RIVAUX DE LA PISTE 1932 d: Serge de Poligny. FRN., *Strich Durch Die Rechnung*, Fred A. Angermayer, Play

River and Death, The *see* EL RIO Y LA MUERTE (1954).

River Flows Back, The see LAS AGUAS BAJAN NEGRAS (1948).

River for Death see RIVER OF DEATH (1988).

River Fuefuki, The see FUEFUKI-GAWA (1960).

River Inn, The see ROADHOUSE NIGHTS (1930).

RIVER LADY 1948 d: George Sherman. USA., River Lady, Houston Branch, Frank Waters, Novel

River Niemen, The see NAD NIEMNEM (1986).

River Niger: Ghetto Warriors, The see THE RIVER NIGER (1976).

RIVER NIGER, THE 1976 d: Krishna Shah. USA., The River Niger, Joseph A. Walker, Play

RIVER OF DEATH 1988 d: Steve Carver. USA., River of Death, Alistair MacLean, Novel

River of Destiny see FORLORN RIVER (1926).

River of Fireflies see HOTARUGAWA (1987).

RIVER OF NO RETURN 1954 d: Otto Preminger. USA., Louis Lantz, Story

RIVER OF ROMANCE 1929 d: Richard Wallace. USA., Magnolia, Booth Tarkington, New York 1923, Play

RIVER OF STARS, THE 1921 d: F. Martin Thornton. UKN., The River of Stars, Edgar Wallace, London 1913, Novel

River of Three Junks, The see LA RIVIERE DES TROIS JONQUES (1956).

River of Unrest see OURSELVES ALONE (1936).

RIVER PIRATE, THE 1928 d: William K. Howard. USA., The River Pirate, Charles Francis Coe, New York 1928, Novel

River Pirates of the Mississippi see DIE FLUSSPIRATEN VOM MISSISSIPPI (1963).

RIVER RED 1998 d: Eric Drilling. USA., River Red, Eric Drilling, Play

RIVER, THE 1928 d: Frank Borzage. USA., The River, Tristram Tupper, Philadelphia 1928, Novel

RIVER, THE 1951 d: Jean Renoir. UKN/FRN/IND., The River, Rumer Godden, Novel

RIVER, THE 1978 d: Barbara Noble. USA., The River, Flannery O'Connor, 1955, Short Story

River With No Bridge, The see HASHI NO NAI KAWA (1992).

RIVER WOLVES, THE 1934 d: George Pearson. UKN., The Lion and the Lamb, Edward Dignon, Geoffrey Swaffer, Play

Riverbank at Dawn, The see LI MING DE HE BIAN (1958).

RIVER'S EDGE, THE 1957 d: Allan Dwan. USA., The Highest Mountain, Harold Jacob Smith, Story

RIVER'S END 1930 d: Michael Curtiz. USA., The River's End: a New Story of God's Country, James Oliver Curwood, New York 1919, Novel

RIVER'S END 1940 d: Ray Enright. USA., The River's End: a New Story of God's Country, James Oliver Curwood, New York 1919, Novel

RIVER'S END, THE 1920 d: Marshall Neilan, Victor Heerman. USA., The River's End: a New Story of God's Country, James Oliver Curwood, New York 1919, Novel

RIVERSIDE MURDER, THE 1935 d: Albert Parker. UKN., Six Dead Men, Andre Steedman, Novel

Rivets see FAST WORKERS (1933).

RIVIERA-STORY 1961 d: Wolfgang Becker. GRM., Hans Nicklisch, Wolfgang Steinhardt, Story

RIVIERE DES TROIS JONQUES, LA 1956 d: Andre Pergament. FRN., Le Gentleman de Hong-Kong, Georges Godefroy, Novel

RIVINCITA DI IVANHOE, LA 1965 d: Tanio BocciA. ITL/FRN., Ivanhoe, Sir Walter Scott, Edinburgh 1819, Novel

Rivincita Di Montecristo, La see LE COMTE DE MONTE-CRISTO (1942).

RIVOLTA DEGLI SCHIAVI, LA 1961 d: Nunzio MalasommA. ITL/SPN/GRM., Fabiola Or the Church of the Catacombs, Nicholas Patrick Wiseman, London 1854, Novel

Rivolta Dei Cosacchi, La see IL FABBRO DEL CONVENTO (1949).

RIVOLUZIONE SESSUALE, LA 1968 d: Riccardo Ghione. ITL., La Rivoluzione Sessuale, Wilhelm Reich, Book

ROAD 1987 d: Alan Clarke. UKN., Road, Jim Cartwright, Play

ROAD BACK, THE 1937 d: James Whale. USA., Der Weg Zuruck, Erich Maria Remarque, 1931, Novel

Road Builder, The see THE NIGHT DIGGER (1971).

ROAD HOUSE 1934 d: Maurice Elvey. UKN., Road House, Walter Hackett, London 1932, Play

ROAD HOUSE 1948 d: Jean Negulesco. USA., Road House, M. Gruen, Oscar Saul, Novel

Road House Girl see WHEEL OF FATE (1953).

ROAD SHOW 1941 d: Hal Roach, Gordon Douglas. USA., Road Show, Eric Hatch, Novel

Road, The see EL CAMINO (1963).

Road, The see LU (1983).

ROAD THROUGH THE DARK, THE 1918 d: Edmund Mortimer. USA., The Road Through the Dark, Maude Radford Warren, 1918, Short Story

ROAD TO ALCATRAZ 1945 d: Nick Grinde. USA., Murder Stole My Missing Hours, Francis K. Allen, Short Story

Road to Corinth, The see LA ROUTE DE CORINTHE (1967).

ROAD TO DENVER, THE 1955 d: Joseph Kane. USA., Man from Texas, Bill Gulick, 1950, Serial Story

Road to Eternity see NINGEN NO JOKEN II (1959).

ROAD TO FORTUNE, THE 1930 d: Arthur Varney-Serrao. UKN., Moorland Terror, Hugh Broadbridge, Novel

Road to 'Frisco, The see THEY DRIVE BY NIGHT (1940).

ROAD TO HAPPINESS 1941 d: Phil Rosen. USA., First Performance, Matt Taylor, Short Story

ROAD TO HEAVEN, THE 1922 d: Challis Sanderson. UKN., The Road to Heaven, George R. Sims, Poem

Road to Hope, The see IL CAMMINO DELLA SPERANZA (1950).

Road to Klockrike see VAGEN TILL KLOCKRIKE (1953).

ROAD TO LONDON, THE 1921 d: Eugene Mullin. UKN/USA., The Road to London, David S. Foster, New York 1914, Novel

Road to Nowhere see END OF THE TRAIL (1936).

Road to Nowhere, The see YOU CAN'T GET AWAY WITH IT (1923).

ROAD TO PARADISE 1930 d: William Beaudine. USA., Cornered, Dodson Mitchell, Zelda Sears, New York 1920, Play

ROAD TO RENO, THE 1938 d: S. Sylvan Simon. USA., The Road to Reno, I. A. R. Wylie, 1937, Story

Road to Rio see THAT NIGHT IN RIO (1941).

ROAD TO ROMANCE, THE 1927 d: John S. Robertson. USA., Romance, Joseph Conrad, Ford Madox Ford, 1903, Novel

ROAD TO RUIN, THE 1913 d: George Gray, Bert Haldane. UKN., The Road to Ruin, Thomas Holcroft, London 1792, Play

Road to Salina see SUR LA ROUTE DE SALINA (1969).

Road to Shame, The see DES FEMMES DISPARAISSENT (1959).

ROAD TO SINGAPORE, THE 1931 d: Alfred E. Green. USA., Heat Wave, Roland Pertwee, Cardiff 1929, Play

ROAD TO WELLVILLE, THE 1994 d: Alan Parker. USA., The Road to Wellville, G. Cograghessan Boyle, Novel

ROAD TO YESTERDAY, THE 1925 d: Cecil B. de Mille. USA., The Road to Yesterday, Beulah Marie Dix, Evelyn Sutherland, New York 1906, Play

Roadhouse see WILD COMPANY (1930).

Roadhouse Girl see MARILYN (1953).

ROADHOUSE MURDER, THE 1932 d: J. Walter Ruben. USA., L' Epouvante, Maurice Level, Paris 1908, Novel

ROADHOUSE NIGHTS 1930 d: Hobart Henley. USA., Roadhouse Nights, Dashiell Hammett, 1929, Novel

ROADS OF DESTINY 1921 d: Frank Lloyd. USA., Roads of Destiny, Channing Pollock, New York 1918, Novel

ROADS WE TAKE, THE 1920 d: David Smith. USA., The Roads We Take, O. Henry, Short Story

Roald Dahl's Danny the Champion of the World see CHAMPION OF THE WORLD DANNY (1989).

Roald Dahl's Matilda see MATILDA (1996).

ROAMING LADY 1936 d: Albert S. Rogell. USA., Roaming Lady, Diana Bourbon, 1933, Short Story

Roar of Hammer Rapids, The see HAMMARFORSENS BRUS (1948).

ROAR OF THE DRAGON 1932 d: Wesley Ruggles. USA., A Passage to Hong Kong, George Kibbe Turner, Novel

Roar, Yellow River! see HUANG HE NU HOU BA (1979).

ROARING ADVENTURE, A 1925 d: Cliff Smith. USA., The Tenderfoot, Jack Rollens, Story

Roaring Mountain see THUNDER MOUNTAIN (1935).

Roaring Nineties, The see IT ALL CAME TRUE (1940).

ROARING ROAD, THE 1919 d: James Cruze. USA., Junkpile Sweepstakes, Byron Morgan, 1918, Short Story, The Roaring Road, Byron Morgan, 1918, Short Story, Undertaker's Handicap, Byron Morgan, 1918, Short Story

ROARING SIX GUNS 1937 d: J. P. McGowan. USA., His Fight, James Oliver Curwood, Short Story

Roaring Timber see COME AND GET IT! (1936).

ROB ROY 1911 d: Arthur Vivian. UKN., Rob Roy, Sir Walter Scott, Novel

Robber Band, The see DIE RAUBERBANDE (1928).

Robber Barons, The see THE TOAST OF NEW YORK (1937).

Robber Hotzenplotz, The see DER RAUBER HOTZENPLOTZ (1973).

Robber, The see LOUPEZNIK (1931).

ROBBERS' ROOST 1933 d: Louis King. USA., Robbers' Roost, Zane Grey, New York 1932, Novel

ROBBERS' ROOST 1955 d: Sidney Salkow. USA., Robbers' Roost, Zane Grey, New York 1932, Novel

Robbers, The see I MASNADIERI (1911).

ROBBERS, THE 1913 d: Walter Edwin, J. Searle Dawley. USA., Die Rauber, Friedrich von Schiller, 1782, Play

Robbery En Route see CHEZHONG DAO (1920).

ROBBERY UNDER ARMS 1957 d: Jack Lee. UKN/ASL., Robbery Under Arms, Rolf Boldrewood, 1888, Novel

ROBBERY UNDER ARMS 1985 d: Ken Hannam, Donald Crombie. ASL., Robbery Under Arms, Rolf Boldrewood, 1888, Novel

ROBE ROUGE, LA 1912 d: Henri Pouctal. FRN., La Robe Rouge, Eugene Brieux, 1900, Play

ROBE ROUGE, LA 1933 d: Jean de Marguenat. FRN., La Robe Rouge, Eugene Brieux, 1900, Play

ROBE, THE 1953 d: Henry Koster. USA., The Robe, Lloyd C. Douglas, 1946, Novel

Robert and Fanny see MANDAGARNA MED FANNY (1977).

ROBERT RYLAND'S LAST JOURNEY 1996 d: Gracia QuerejetA. SPN., All Souls, Javier Marias, Novel

ROBERT UND BERTRAM 1939 d: Hans H. Zerlett. GRM., Robert Und Bertram, Gustav Raeder, Play

ROBERTA 1935 d: William A. Seiter. USA., Gowns By Roberta, Alice Duer Miller, New York 1933, Novel

ROBERTO BURAT 1920 d: Mario Almirante. ITL., Un Assassin, Jules Claretie, 1866, Novel

ROBIN COOK'S FORMULA FOR DEATH 1995 d: Robin Cook. USA., Outbreak, Robin Cook, Novel

ROBIN COOK'S "INVASION" 1997 d: Armand Mastroianni. USA., Invasion, Robin Cook, Novel

Robin Cook's Mortal Fear see MORTAL FEAR (1994).

ROBIN HOOD OF EL DORADO 1936 d: William A. Wellman. USA., The Robin Hood of El Dorado, Walter Noble Burns, New York 1932, Book

ROBINSON CRUSOE 1910 d: August Blom. DNM., Robinson Crusoe, Daniel Defoe, 1719, Novel

ROBINSON CRUSOE 1913 d: Otis Turner. USA., Robinson Crusoe, Daniel Defoe, 1719, Novel

ROBINSON CRUSOE 1916 d: George F. Marion. USA., Robinson Crusoe, Daniel Defoe, 1719, Novel

Robinson Crusoe see LES AVENTURES DE ROBINSON CRUSOE (1921).

ROBINSON CRUSOE 1927 d: M. A. Wetherell. UKN., Robinson Crusoe, Daniel Defoe, 1719, Novel

ROBINSON CRUSOE 1946 d: Alexander Andrievski. USS., Robinson Crusoe, Daniel Defoe, 1719, Novel

ROBINSON CRUSOE 1950 d: Jeff Musso, Amasi Damiani. FRN/ITL., Robinson Crusoe, Daniel Defoe, 1719, Novel

Robinson Crusoe see LAS AVENTURAS DE ROBINSON CRUSOE (1952).

Robinson Crusoe *see* **ROBINSON Y VIERNES EN LA ISLA ENCANTADA** (1969).

ROBINSON CRUSOE 1972 d: GibbA. ASL., *Robinson Crusoe*, Daniel Defoe, 1719, Novel

Robinson Crusoe *see* **ZHIZN I UDIVITELNIE PRIKLUCHENIA ROBINZONA CRUZO** (1973).

ROBINSON CRUSOE 1974 d: James MacTaggart. UKN., *Robinson Crusoe*, Daniel Defoe, 1719, Novel

Robinson Crusoe *see* **NAMORNIKA Z YORKU ZIVOT A PODIVUHODNA DOBRODRUZSTVI ROBINSONA CRUSOE** (1982).

Robinson Crusoe and the Tiger *see* **ROBINSON Y VIERNES EN LA ISLA ENCANTADA** (1969).

ROBINSON CRUSOE ON MARS 1964 d: Byron Haskin. USA., *Robinson Crusoe*, Daniel Defoe, 1719, Novel

Robinson Shall Not Die *see* **ROBINSON SOLL NICHT STERBEN** (1957).

ROBINSON SOLL NICHT STERBEN 1957 d: Josef von Baky. GRM., *Robinson Soll Nicht Sterben*, Friedrich Forster, Berlin 1932, Play

ROBINSON Y VIERNES EN LA ISLA ENCANTADA 1969 d: Rene Cardona Jr. MXC., *Robinson Crusoe*, Daniel Defoe, 1719, Novel

Robo Man *see* **WHO?** (1974).

ROCAMBOLE 1919 d: Giuseppe ZaccariA. ITL., *Les Aventures de Rocambole*, Pierre-Alexis Ponson Du Terrail

ROCAMBOLE 1932 d: Gabriel RoscA. FRN., *Le Feuilleton*, Pierre-Alexis Ponson Du Terrail

ROCAMBOLE 1947 d: Jacques de Baroncelli. FRN/ITL., *Rocambole*, Pierre-Alexis Ponson Du Terrail, Novel

ROCCA: MORTELS RENDEZ-VOUS 1994 d: Paul Planchon. FRN., *Rocca: Mortels Rendez-Vous*, Claude Brami, Marcel Jullian, Novel

Rocco and His Brothers *see* **ROCCO E I SUOI FRATELLI** (1960).

ROCCO E I SUOI FRATELLI 1960 d: Luchino Visconti. ITL/FRN., *I Segretti Di Milano: Il Ponte Della Ghisolfa*, Giovanni Testori, Milan 1958, Novel

Rocco Et Ses Freres *see* **ROCCO E I SUOI FRATELLI** (1960).

ROCHE AUX MOUETTES, LA 1932 d: Georges MoncA. FRN., *La Roche aux Mouettes*, Jules Sandeau, Novel

Rock Crystal *see* **BERGKRISTALL** (1949).

ROCK ISLAND TRAIL 1950 d: Joseph Kane. USA., *A Yankee Dared*, Frank J. Nevins, 1933, Novel

Rock 'N' Roll Wolf *see* **MA-MA** (1977).

ROCKABYE 1932 d: George Cukor. USA., *Rockabye*, Lucia Bronder, 1924, Play

Rocket Bus, The *see* **ALF'S CARPET** (1929).

Rocket from Fenwick, A *see* **THE MOUSE ON THE MOON** (1963).

Rocket to the Moon *see* **JULES VERNE'S ROCKET TO THE MOON** (1967).

ROCKETS GALORE 1958 d: Michael Relph. UKN., *Rockets Galore*, Compton Mackenzie, 1957, Novel

ROCKETS IN THE DUNES 1960 d: William C. Hammond. UKN., *Rockets in the Dunes*, Lois Lamplugh, Novel

ROCKING HORSE WINNER, THE 1949 d: Anthony Pelissier. UKN., *The Rocking Horse Winner*, D. H. Lawrence, 1932, Short Story

ROCKING HORSE WINNER, THE 1977 d: Peter Medak. UKN., *The Rocking Horse Winner*, D. H. Lawrence, 1932, Short Story

ROCKING HORSE WINNER, THE 1983 d: Robert Bierman. UKN., *The Rocking Horse Winner*, D. H. Lawrence, 1932, Short Story

ROCKING MOON 1926 d: George Melford. USA., *Rocking Moon*, Barrett Willoughby, New York 1925, Novel

Rockinghorse *see* **SUSETZ** (1977).

Rockpeople, The *see* **SKALNI PLEMENO** (1944).

ROCKS OF VALPRE, THE 1919 d: Maurice Elvey. UKN., *The Rocks of Valpre*, Ethel M. Dell, Novel

ROCKS OF VALPRE, THE 1935 d: Henry Edwards. UKN., *The Rocks of Valpre*, Ethel M. Dell, Novel

ROCKY HORROR PICTURE SHOW, THE 1975 d: Jim Sharman. USA/UKN., *The Rocky Horror Show*, Richard O'Brien, Play

ROCKY MOUNTAIN 1950 d: William Keighley. USA., *Ghost Mountain*, Alan Lemay, Story

RODA KAPPAN, DEN 1967 d: Gabriel Axel. SWD/DNM/ICL., *Gesta Danorum*, Saxo Grammaticus, c1195, Books

Rode Kappe, Den *see* **DEN RODA KAPPAN** (1967).

Rode Rubin, Den *see* **SANGEN OM DEN RODE RUBIN** (1970).

Rodeo Romance *see* **I TAKE THIS WOMAN** (1931).

Rodney *see* **KEEP 'EM ROLLING** (1934).

RODNEY FAILS TO QUALIFY 1924 d: Andrew P. Wilson. UKN., *Rodney Fails to Qualify*, P. G. Wodehouse, Short Story

RODNEY STONE 1920 d: Percy Nash. UKN., *Rodney Stone*, Arthur Conan Doyle, 1896, Novel

Roedin *see* **RUDIN** (1976).

ROGELIA 1962 d: Rafael Gil. SPN., *Santa Rogelia*, Armando Palacio Valdes, 1926, Novel

ROGER LA HONTE 1913 d: Adrien Caillard. FRN., *Roger-la-Honte*, Jules Mary, Novel

ROGER LA HONTE 1932 d: Gaston Roudes. FRN., *Roger-la-Honte*, Jules Mary, Novel

ROGER LA HONTE 1966 d: Riccardo FredA. FRN/ITL., *Roger-la-Honte*, Jules Mary, Novel

ROGER-LA-HONTE 1922 d: Jacques de Baroncelli. FRN., *Roger-la-Honte*, Jules Mary, Novel

ROGER-LA-HONTE 1945 d: Andre Cayatte. FRN., *Roger-la-Honte*, Jules Mary, Novel

Rogue and Riches *see* **ROUGE AND RICHES** (1920).

ROGUE COP 1954 d: Roy Rowland. USA., *Rogue Cop*, William P. McGivern, 1954, Novel

ROGUE IN LOVE, A 1916 d: Bannister Merwin. UKN., *A Rogue in Love*, Tom Gallon, Novel

ROGUE IN LOVE, A 1922 d: Albert Brouett. UKN., *A Rogue in Love*, Tom Gallon, Novel

ROGUE MALE 1976 d: Clive Donner. UKN., *Rogue Male*, Geoffrey Household, 1939, Novel

ROGUE SONG, THE 1929 d: Lionel Barrymore. USA., *Gipsy Love*, Robert Bodansky, Franz Lehar, A. M. Willner, London 1912, Operetta

ROGUES AND ROMANCE 1920 d: George B. Seitz. USA., *The Golden Senorita*, George B. Seitz, Play

Rogues' Gallery *see* **THE DEVIL'S TRAIL** (1942).

ROGUES OF THE TURF 1923 d: Wilfred Noy. UKN., *Rogues of the Turf*, John F. Preston, Play

Rogue's Opera, The *see* **OPERA DO MALANDRO** (1985).

Rogues, The *see* **LOS GRANUJAS** (1924).

Rogue's Trial, The *see* **A COMPADECIDA** (1969).

ROI BIS, LE 1932 d: Robert Beaudoin. FRN., *Frantisek Lelicek Ve Sluzbach Sherlocka Holmesa*, Hugo Vavris, Novel

ROI DE CAMARGUE 1934 d: Jacques de Baroncelli. FRN., *Le Roi de Camargue*, Jean Aicard, 1890, Novel

ROI DE CAMARGUE, LE 1921 d: Andre Hugon. FRN., *Le Roi de Camargue*, Jean Aicard, 1890, Novel

Roi de la Bernina, Le *see* **DER KONIG DER BERNINA** (1957).

ROI DE LA PEDALE, LE 1925 d: Maurice Champreux. FRN., *Le Roi de la Pedale*, Paul Cartoux, Henri Decoin, Novel

ROI DE PARIS, LE 1923 d: Charles Maudru, Maurice de Marsan. FRN., *Le Roi de Paris*, Georges Ohnet, Novel

ROI DE PARIS, LE 1930 d: Leo Mittler, Maurice de Marsan. FRN., *Le Roi de Paris*, Georges Ohnet, Novel

ROI DES AULNES, LE 1930 d: Marie-Louise Iribe. FRN., *Der Erlkonig*, Johann Wolfgang von Goethe, 1782, Verse

ROI DES CONS, LE 1981 d: Claude Confortes. FRN., *Le Roi Des Cons*, Claude Confortes, Georges Wolinski, Play

Roi Des Montagnes, Le *see* **LE VOLEUR DE FEMMES** (1963).

ROI DES PALACES ,LE 1932 d: Carmine Gallone. FRN., *Le Roi Des Palaces*, Henri Kistemaeckers, Play

Roi du Mont Blanc, Le *see* **REVE ETERNEL** (1934).

Roi Ebahi, Le *see* **EL REY PASMADO** (1991).

ROI ET L'OISEAU, LE 1979 d: Paul Grimault. FRN., Hans Christian Andersen, Short Story

ROI KOKO, LE 1913 d: Georges MoncA. FRN., *Le Roi Koko*, Alexandre Bisson, Play

ROI, LE 1936 d: Piere Colombier. FRN., *Le Roi*, Gaston Arman de Caillavet, Robert de Flers, 1908, Play

ROI, LE 1949 d: Marc-Gilbert Sauvajon. FRN., *Le Roi*, Gaston Arman de Caillavet, Robert de Flers, 1908, Play

ROI PANDORE, LE 1949 d: Andre Berthomieu. FRN., *Le Roi Pandore*, Corriem, Novel

ROI S'AMUSE, LE 1909 d: Albert Capellani. FRN., *Le Roi S'amuse*, Victor Hugo, 1832, Play

Roi S'amuse, Le *see* **LE ROI** (1936).

ROI SANS DIVERTISSEMENT, UN 1962 d: Francois Leterrier. FRN., *Un Roi Sans Divertissement*, Jean Giono, 1947, Novel

Roi S'ennuie, Le *see* **ECHEC AU ROI** (1931).

Rois d'une Nuit, Les *see* **LE RIDEAU ROUGE** (1952).

ROJIN TO UMI 1990 d: John Junkerman. JPN., *The Old Man and the Sea*, Ernest Hemingway, 1952, Novel

ROJO NO REIKAN 1921 d: Minoru MuratA. JPN., *Children of the Night*, Wilhelm Schmidtbonn, Novel

ROKONOK 1954 d: Felix Mariassy. PLN., *Rokonok*, Zsigmond Moricz, 1930, Novel

Roland Or Chronicle of Passion *see* **ROLANDE MET DE BLES** (1970).

ROLANDE MET DE BLES 1970 d: Roland Verhavert. BLG., *Rolande Met de Bles*, Herman Teirlinck, 1944, Novel

Role, The *see* **BHUMIKA** (1977).

ROLLING HOME 1926 d: William A. Seiter. USA., *Rolling Home*, John Hunter Booth, Play

ROLLING IN MONEY 1934 d: Albert Parker. UKN., *Mr. Hopkinson*, R. C. Carton, London 1905, Play

ROLLING STONES 1916 d: Dell Henderson. USA., *Rolling Stones*, Edgar Selwyn, New York 1915, Play

Rolling Waves *see* **LANG TAO GUN GUN** (1965).

ROLLTREPPE ABWARTS 1987 d: Martin Ruffert. GRM., *Rolltreppe Abwarts*, Hans-Georg Noack, Novel

ROMA BENE 1971 d: Carlo Lizzani. ITL/GRM/FRN., *Mani Aperte Sull'acqua*, Luigi Bruno Di Belmonte, Play

Roma Bene -Liebe Und Sex in Rom *see* **ROMA BENE** (1971).

ROMAIN KALBRIS 1911 d: Georges DenolA. FRN., *Romain Kalbris*, Hector Malot, Novel

ROMAIN KALBRIS 1923 d: Georges MoncA. FRN., *Romain Kalbris*, Hector Malot, Novel

Roman Aus Den Bergen, Ein *see* **DIE GEIER-WALLY** (1921).

ROMAN BE'HEMSHACHIM 1985 d: Oded Kotler. ISR., *Roman Be'hemshachim*, Yitzhak Ben-Nir, Novel

ROMAN BOXERA 1921 d: Vaclav Binovec. CZC., *Cashel Byron's Profession*, George Bernard Shaw, Novel

ROMAN DE CARPENTIER, LE 1913. FRN., *Le Roman de Carpentier*, Ed de Perrodil

ROMAN DE LA MOMIE, LA 1911 d: Albert Capellani, Henri Pouctal. FRN., *Le Roman de la Momie*, Theophile Gautier, Novel

ROMAN DE WERTHER, LE 1938 d: Max Ophuls. FRN., *Die Leiden Des Jungen Werthers*, Johann Wolfgang von Goethe, 1774, Novel

ROMAN D'UN JEUNE HOMME PAUVRE, LE 1913 d: Albert Capellani, Georges DenolA. FRN., *Le Roman d'un Jeune Homme Pauvre*, Octave Feuillet, 1858, Novel

ROMAN D'UN JEUNE HOMME PAUVRE, LE 1927 d: Gaston Ravel. FRN/GRM., *Le Roman d'un Jeune Homme Pauvre*, Octave Feuillet, 1858, Novel

ROMAN D'UN JEUNE HOMME PAUVRE, LE 1935 d: Abel Gance. FRN., *Le Roman d'un Jeune Homme Pauvre*, Octave Feuillet, 1858, Novel

ROMAN D'UN SPAHI, LE 1914 d: Henri Pouctal. FRN., *Le Roman d'un Spahi*, Pierre Loti, 1881, Novel

ROMAN D'UN SPAHI, LE 1936 d: Michel Bernheim. FRN., *Le Roman d'un Spahi*, Pierre Loti, 1881, Novel

Roman d'un Voleur de Chevaux, Le *see* **ROMANCE OF A HORSETHIEF** (1972).

ROMAN EINES ARZTES 1939 d: Jurgen von Alten. GRM., *Heimkehr Ins Leben*, Curt Reinhard Dietz, Novel

ROMAN EINES FRAUENARZTES 1954 d: Falk Harnack. GRM., *Roman Eines Frauenarztes*, Curt Riess, Novel

Roman Eines Spielers *see* **DER SPIELER** (1938).

Roman Grey *see* **THE ART OF CRIME** (1975).

ROMAN HLOUPEHO HONZY 1926 d: Frantisek Hlavaty. CZC., *Roman Hloupeho Honzy*, Jan Barta, Novel

ROMAN HOLIDAY 1987 d: Noel Nosseck. USA., Ian McLellan Hunter, Story

Roman Nights of Love *see* **UN AMORE A ROMA** (1960).

ROMAN SPRING OF MRS. STONE, THE 1961 d: Jose Quintero. UKN/USA., *The Roman Spring of Mrs. Stone*, Tennessee Williams, New York 1950, Novel

ROMAN, THE 1910 d: Otis Turner. USA., *The Roman*, Edward George Bulwer Lytton, Novel

ROMANA, LA 1954 d: Luigi ZampA. ITL/FRN., *La Romana*, Alberto Moravia, 1947, Novel

ROMANA, LA 1988 d: Giuseppe Patroni Griffi. ITL., *La Romana*, Alberto Moravia, 1947, Novel

ROMANCE 1920 d: Chet Withey. USA., *Romance*, Edward Sheldon, New York 1913, Play

Romance see THE ROAD TO ROMANCE (1927).

Romance see POHADKA MAJE (1940).

ROMANCE A TROIS 1942 d: Roger Richebe. FRN., *Trois Et une*, Denys Amiel, Play

ROMANCE AND ARABELLA 1919 d: Walter Edwards. USA., *Romance and Arabella*, William Hurlbut, New York 1917, Play

Romance and Bright Lights see ROMANCE OF THE UNDERWORLD (1928).

ROMANCE AND REALITY 1921 d: Harry Lambart. UKN., *The Cradle of the Washingtons*, Arthur Branscombe, Book

Romance and Rhythm see COWBOY FROM BROOKLYN (1938).

Romance and Riches see THE AMAZING QUEST OF ERNEST BLISS (1936).

Romance for Three see PARADISE FOR THREE (1938).

Romance in a Minor Key see ROMANZE IN MOLL (1943).

ROMANCE IN FLANDERS, A 1937 d: Maurice Elvey. UKN., *Widow's Island*, Mario Fort, Ralph Vanio, Novel

ROMANCE IN THE DARK 1938 d: H. C. Potter. USA., *Die Gelbe Nachtigall*, Hermann Bahr, Berlin 1907, Play

Romance, Incorporated see HONEYMOON AHEAD (1945).

ROMANCE LAND 1923 d: Edward Sedgwick. USA., *The Gun Fanner*, Kenneth Perkins, New York 1922, Novel

Romance of a Boxer, The see ROMAN BOXERA (1921).

ROMANCE OF A HORSETHIEF 1972 d: Abraham Polonsky, Fedor Hanzekovic. USA/FRN/YGS., *Romance of a Horsethief*, Joseph Opatoshu, Novel

ROMANCE OF A MILLION DOLLARS, THE 1926 d: Tom Terriss. USA., *Romance of a Million Dollars*, Elizabeth Dejeans, Indianapolis 1922, Novel

ROMANCE OF A MOVIE STAR, THE 1920 d: Richard Garrick. UKN., *The World's Best Girl*, E. Hoskin, Coralie Stanton, Novel

ROMANCE OF A POOR YOUNG MAN, THE 1914. USA., *Le Roman d'un Jeune Homme Pauvre*, Octave Feuillet, 1858, Novel

Romance of a Queen, The see THREE WEEKS (1924).

Romance of an Actress see LIFE OF AN ACTRESS (1927).

ROMANCE OF ANNIE LAURIE, THE 1920 d: Gerald Somers. UKN., *The Romance of Annie Laurie*, Alfred Denville, Play

ROMANCE OF BILLY GOAT HILL, A 1916 d: Lynn Reynolds. USA., *A Romance of Billy-Goat Hill*, Alice Hegan Rice, New York 1912, Novel

Romance of Book & Sword, The see SHU JIAN EN CHOU LU (1987).

ROMANCE OF MAYFAIR, A 1925 d: Thomas Bentley. UKN., *The Crime of Constable Kelly*, J. C. Snaith, Novel

ROMANCE OF OLD BAGDAD, A 1922 d: Kenelm Foss. UKN., *A Romance of Old Bagdad*, Jessie Douglas Kerruish, Novel

Romance of Riches, A see THE SQUIRE OF LONG HADLEY (1925).

Romance of Rio Grande see ROMANCE OF THE RIO GRANDE (1929).

ROMANCE OF ROSY RIDGE, THE 1947 d: Roy Rowland. USA., *The Romance of Rosy Ridge*, MacKinlay Kantor, 1937, Novel

ROMANCE OF SEVILLE, A 1929 d: Norman Walker. UKN., *The Majo*, Arline Lord, Short Story

ROMANCE OF SUNSHINE ALLEY 1914 d: Charles Miller. USA., *A Kentucky Romance*, Mary O'Connor, Story

ROMANCE OF TARZAN, THE 1918 d: Wilfred Lucas. USA., *Tarzan of the Apes*, Edgar Rice Burroughs, Chicago 1914, Novel

Romance of Teresa Hennert, The see ROMANS TERESY HENNERT (1978).

ROMANCE OF THE AIR, A 1919 d: Harry Revier, Franklin B. Coates. USA., *En l'Air! (in the Air)*, Bert Hall, New York 1918, Book

ROMANCE OF THE LIMBERLOST 1938 d: William Nigh. USA., *A Girl of the Limberlost*, Gene Stratton-Porter, New York 1909, Novel

Romance of the Mummy, The see LA ROMAN DE LA MOMIE (1911).

ROMANCE OF THE REDWOODS 1939 d: Charles Vidor. USA., *White Silence*, Jack London, 1900, Short Story

ROMANCE OF THE RIO GRANDE 1929 d: Alfred Santell. USA., *Conquistador*, Katharine Fullerton Gerould, New York 1923, Novel

ROMANCE OF THE RIO GRANDE 1940 d: Herbert I. Leeds. USA., *Conquistador*, Katharine Fullerton Gerould, New York 1923, Novel

Romance of the Rosary, The see THE ROSARY (1922).

ROMANCE OF THE UNDERWORLD 1928 d: Irving Cummings. USA., *A Romance of the Underworld*, Paul Armstrong, New York 1911, Play

ROMANCE OF THE UNDERWORLD, A 1918 d: James Kirkwood. USA., *A Romance of the Underworld*, Paul Armstrong, New York 1911, Play

ROMANCE OF WASTDALE, A 1921 d: Maurice Elvey. UKN., *A Romance of Wastdale*, A. E. W. Mason, Novel

Romance on the Beach see LE CRI DE LA CHAIR (1963).

ROMANCE ON THE HIGH SEAS 1948 d: Michael Curtiz. USA., *Romance in High C*, Carlos A. Olivari, S. Pondal Rios, Story

ROMANCE WITH A DOUBLE BASS 1976 d: Robert Young. UKN., *Roman I Kontrabasom*, Anton Chekhov, 1886, Short Story

ROMANCES OF THE PRIZE RING 1926 d: H. B. Parkinson, Geoffrey H. Malins. UKN., Andrew Soutar, Short Stories

Romanian Farmer, The see ARENDASUL ROMAN (1952).

ROMANOFF AND JULIET 1961 d: Peter Ustinov. USA., *Romanoff and Juliet*, Peter Ustinov, New York 1957, Play

ROMANS TERESY HENNERT 1978 d: Ignacy Gogolewski. PLN., *Romans Teresy Hennert*, Zofia Nalkowska, 1927, Novel

Romansa Konjokradice see ROMANCE OF A HORSETHIEF (1972).

Romantic Age, The see GIRLS' SCHOOL (1938).

ROMANTIC AGE, THE 1949 d: Edmond T. Greville. UKN., *Lycee Des Jeunes Filles*, Serge Weber, Novel

Romantic Age, The see HER FIRST ROMANCE (1951).

ROMANTIC COMEDY 1983 d: Arthur Hiller. USA., *Romantic Comedy*, Bernard Slade, Play

ROMANTIC ENGLISHWOMAN, THE 1974 d: Joseph Losey. UKN/FRN., *The Romantic Englishwoman*, Thomas Wiseman, Novel

Romantic Mr. Hinklin, The see YOU CAN'T FOOL YOUR WIFE (1940).

Romantic Rosa see WHAT HAPPENED TO ROSA (1920).

Romantic Vernon Castles, The see THE STORY OF VERNON AND IRENE CASTLE (1939).

Romantic Widow, The see UNA VIUDA ROMANTICA (1933).

ROMANTICA AVVENTURA, UNA 1940 d: Mario Camerini. ITL., *The Loves of Margery*, Thomas Hardy, Short Story

ROMANTICISMO 1915 d: Carlo Campogalliani. ITL., *Romanticismo*, Gerolamo Rovetta, 1901, Play

ROMANTICISMO 1951 d: Clemente Fracassi. ITL., *Romanticismo*, Gerolamo Rovetta, 1901, Play

Romany Rye see THE LIFE LINE (1919).

ROMANY RYE, THE 1915 d: Percy Nash. UKN., *The Romany Rye*, George R. Sims, London 1882, Play

ROMANZE IN MOLL 1943 d: Helmut Kautner. GRM., *Les Bijoux*, Guy de Maupassant, 1884, Short Story

ROMANZE MIT AMELIE 1981 d: Ulrich Thein. GDR., *Romanze Mit Amelie*, Benito Wogatzki, Novel

ROMANZO DI MAUD, IL 1917 d: Diana Karenne. ITL., *Les Demi-Vierges*, Marcel Prevost, 1895, Novel

Romanzo Di un Giovane Povero, Il see L' ULTIMO DEI FRONTIGNAC (1911).

ROMANZO DI UN GIOVANE POVERO, IL 1920 d: Amleto Palermi. ITL., *Le Roman d'un Jeune Homme Pauvre*, Octave Feuillet, 1858, Novel

ROMANZO DI UN GIOVANE POVERO, IL 1943 d: Guido Brignone. ITL., *Le Roman d'un Jeune Homme Pauvre*, Octave Feuillet, 1858, Novel

ROMANZO DI UN GIOVANE POVERO, IL 1958 d: Marino Girolami, Luis MarquinA. ITL/SPN., *Le Roman d'un Jeune Homme Pauvre*, Octave Feuillet, 1858, Novel

ROMANZO DI UN GIOVANE POVERO, IL 1974 d: Cesare Canevari. ITL., *Le Roman d'un Jeune Homme Pauvre*, Octave Feuillet, 1858, Novel

Romanzo Di un Ladro Di Cavallo, Il see ROMANCE OF A HORSETHIEF (1972).

ROMANZO DI UNA GIOVANE POVERA, IL 1920 d: Enrico Vidali. ITL., *Il Romanzo Di Una Giovane Povera*, H. Townbridge, Novel

ROME ADVENTURE 1962 d: Delmer Daves. USA., *Lovers Must Learn*, Irving Fineman, New York 1932, Novel

ROMEO AND JULIET 1908. UKN., *Romeo and Juliet*, William Shakespeare, c1596, Play

ROMEO AND JULIET 1908 d: J. Stuart Blackton. USA., *Romeo and Juliet*, William Shakespeare, c1596, Play

Romeo and Juliet see GIULIETTA E ROMEO (1908).

ROMEO AND JULIET 1911 d: Theodore Marston. USA., *Romeo and Juliet*, William Shakespeare, c1596, Play

Romeo and Juliet see ROMEO E GIULIETTA (1912).

ROMEO AND JULIET 1914 d: Travers Vale. USA., *Romeo and Juliet*, William Shakespeare, c1596, Play

ROMEO AND JULIET 1916 d: J. Gordon Edwards. USA., *Romeo and Juliet*, William Shakespeare, c1596, Play

ROMEO AND JULIET 1916 d: John W. Noble. USA., *Romeo and Juliet*, William Shakespeare, c1596, Play

ROMEO AND JULIET 1936 d: George Cukor. USA., *Romeo and Juliet*, William Shakespeare, c1596, Play

ROMEO AND JULIET 1954 d: Renato Castellani. UKN/ITL., *Romeo and Juliet*, William Shakespeare, c1596, Play

Romeo and Juliet see ROMEO I DZULETTA (1955).

Romeo and Juliet see GIULIETTA E ROMEO (1964).

ROMEO AND JULIET 1966 d: Paul Czinner. UKN., *Romeo and Juliet*, William Shakespeare, c1596, Play

ROMEO AND JULIET 1968 d: Franco Zeffirelli. UKN/ITL., *Romeo and Juliet*, William Shakespeare, c1596, Play

ROMEO AND JULIET 1979 d: Alvin Rakoff. UKN., *Romeo and Juliet*, William Shakespeare, c1596, Play

ROMEO AND JULIET 1988 d: Joan Kemp-Welch. UKN., *Romeo and Juliet*, William Shakespeare, c1596, Play

Romeo and Juliet see WILLIAM SHAKESPEARE'S ROMEO & JULIET (1996).

Romeo and Juliet - 1971 see WHAT BECAME OF JACK AND JILL? (1971).

Romeo and Juliette see ROMEO AND JULIET (1908).

Romeo E Giulietta see GIULIETTA E ROMEO (1908).

ROMEO E GIULIETTA 1912 d: Ugo FalenA. ITL/FRN., *Romeo and Juliet*, William Shakespeare, c1596, Play

Romeo E Giulietta see ROMEO AND JULIET (1968).

Romeo E Giulietta Al Villaggio see ROMEO UND JULIA AUF DEM DORFE (1941).

ROMEO ET JULIETTE 1912. FRN., *Romeo and Juliet*, William Shakespeare, c1596, Play

Romeo Et Juliette see ROMEO E GIULIETTA (1912).

Romeo Et Juliette Au Village see ROMEO UND JULIA AUF DEM DORFE (1941).

ROMEO I DZULETTA 1955 d: Leo Arnstam, Leonid Lavrovskiy. USS., *Romeo and Juliet*, William Shakespeare, c1596, Play

Romeo in Pyjamas, A see BEDROOM AND BATH PARLOR (1931).

ROMEO, JULIE A TMA 1960 d: Jiri Weiss. CZC., *Romeo Julie a Tma*, Jan Otcenasek, Prague 1960, Novel

Romeo, Juliet and Darkness see JULIA A TMA ROMEO (1960).

Romeo, Juliet and the Darkness see JULIE A TMA ROMEO (1960).

ROMEO UND JULIA AUF DEM DORFE 1941 d: Hans Trommer, Valerien Schmidely. SWT., *Romeo Und Julia Auf Dem Dorfe*, Gottfried Keller, Braunschweig 1865, Short Story

ROMEO UND JULIA AUF DEM DORFE 1983 d: Siegfried Kuhn. GDR., *Romeo Und Julia Auf Dem Dorfe*, Gottfried Keller, Braunschweig 1865, Short Story

Romeo Und Julia in Wien *see* NINA (1956).

ROMEO Y JULIETA 1943 d: Miguel M. Delgado. MXC., *Romeo and Juliet*, William Shakespeare, c1596, Play

Rommel - Desert Fox *see* THE DESERT FOX (1951).

ROMOLA 1911 d: Mario Caserini. ITL., *Romola*, George Eliot, London 1862, Novel

ROMOLA 1925 d: Henry King. USA., *Romola*, George Eliot, London 1862, Novel

Romp of Fanny Hill *see* FANNY HILL (1964).

Rompiballe, Il *see* L' EMMERDEUR (1973).

Rompiballe. Rompe Ancora, Il *see* FANTASIA CHEZ LES PLOUCS (1970).

ROMULUS DER GROSSE 1965 d: Helmut Kautner. GRM., *Romulus Der Grosse*, Friedrich Durrenmatt, 1956, Play

RONA JAFFE'S MAZES & MONSTERS 1982 d: Steven Hilliard Stern. USA/CND., *Mazes & Monsters*, Rona Jaffe, Novel

RONDE, LA 1950 d: Max Ophuls. FRN., *Der Reigen*, Arthur Schnitzler, 1900, Play

RONDE, LA 1964 d: Roger Vadim. FRN/ITL., *Der Reigen*, Arthur Schnitzler, 1900, Play

Ronde, La *see* REIGEN (1974).

RONJA ROVARDOTTER 1984 d: Tage Danielsson. NRW/SWD., *Ronja de Roversdochter*, Astrid Lindgren, Novel

Ronja Roverdatter *see* RONJA ROVARDOTTER (1984).

Ronja, the Robber's Daughter *see* RONJA ROVARDOTTER (1984).

ROOF, THE 1933 d: George A. Cooper. UKN., *The Roof*, David Whitelaw, Novel

ROOF TREE, THE 1921 d: John Francis Dillon. USA., *The Roof Tree*, Charles Neville Buck, New York 1921, Novel

ROOKERY NOOK 1930 d: Tom Walls, Byron Haskin. UKN., *Rookery Nook*, Ben Travers, London 1926, Play

ROOKIE OF THE YEAR 1973 d: Larry Elikann. USA., *Not Bad for a Girl*, Isabella Taves, Book

ROOKSPOREN 1992 d: Frans Van de Staak. NTH., *Vrouw Die Een Rookspoor Achterliet*, Lidy Van Marissing, Story

Room 13 *see* ZIMMER 13 (1964).

ROOM AT THE TOP 1959 d: Jack Clayton. UKN., *Room at the Top*, John Braine, 1957, Novel

ROOM FOR ONE MORE 1952 d: Norman Taurog. USA., *Room for One More*, Anna Perrott Rose, 1950, Novel

ROOM FOR TWO 1940 d: Maurice Elvey. UKN., *Room for Two*, Gilbert Wakefield, London 1938, Play

ROOM IN THE HOUSE 1955 d: Maurice Elvey. UKN., *Bless This House*, E. Eynon Evans, Play

ROOM OF WORDS, THE 1989 d: Joe d'Amato. ITL., *The Room of Words*, Franco Mole, Play

ROOM, THE 1987 d: Robert Altman. USA., *The Room*, Harold Pinter, Play

ROOM TO LET 1950 d: Godfrey Grayson. UKN., *Room to Let*, Margery Allingham, Radio Play

Room Upstairs, The *see* MARTIN ROUMAGNAC (1946).

ROOM WITH A VIEW, A 1986 d: James Ivory. UKN., *A Room With a View*, E. M. Forster, 1908, Novel

ROONEY 1958 d: George Pollock. UKN., *Rooney*, Catherine Cookson, Novel

Roosty *see* THE PENALTY (1941).

ROOT OF ALL EVIL, THE 1947 d: Brock Williams. UKN., *The Root of All Evil*, J. S. Fletcher, Novel

ROOTED 1985 d: Ron Way. ASL., *Rooted*, Alexander Buzo, Play

Roots *see* RAICES (1953).

ROOTS 1977 d: David Greene, Marvin J. Chomsky. USA., *Roots*, Alex Haley, Book

ROOTS OF HEAVEN, THE 1958 d: John Huston. USA., *The Roots of Heaven*, Romain Gary, 1956, Novel

ROOTS: THE NEXT GENERATIONS 1978 d: John Erman, Lloyd Richards. USA., *Roots*, Alex Haley, Book, *Search*, Alex Haley, Book

ROPE 1948 d: Alfred Hitchcock. USA., *Rope*, Patrick Hamilton, 1929, Play

Rope *see* ROPE OF FLESH (1965).

Rope Around the Neck *see* LA CORDE AU COU (1964).

ROPE OF FLESH 1965 d: Russ Meyer. USA., *Streets Paved With Gold*, Raymond Friday Locke, Novel

Ropes *see* FALSE KISSES (1921).

ROQUEVILLARD, LES 1922 d: Julien Duvivier. FRN., *Les Roquevillard*, Henri Bourdeaux, Novel

ROQUEVILLARD, LES 1943 d: Jean Dreville. FRN., *Les Roquevilard*, Henri Bordeaux, Novel

Rory O'Moore *see* RORY O'MORE (1911).

RORY O'MORE 1911 d: Sidney Olcott. USA., *Rory O'More*, Samuel Lover, 1839, Novel

Rosa Alvaro *see* WHAT HAPPENED TO ROSA (1920).

ROSA BLANCA 1961 d: Roberto Gavaldon. MXC., *Die Weisse Rose*, Ben Traven, 1929, Novel

Rosa de Levante *see* TIERRA VALENCIANA (1926).

ROSA DE MADRID 1927 d: Eusebio F. Ardavin. SPN., Luis Fernandez Ardavin, Play

Rosa Di Sangue *see* ANGELICA (1939).

Rosa la Pazza *see* GABRIELE IL LAMPIONARO DI PORTO (1919).

Rosa Moline *see* BEYOND THE FOREST (1949).

ROSA PER TUTTI, UNA 1967 d: Franco Rossi. ITL., *Procura-Se Uma Rosa*, Glaucio Gill, Play

ROSA ROSSA, LA 1973 d: Franco Giraldi. ITL., *La Rosa Rossa*, Pier Antonio Quarantotti Gambini, Novel

ROSAIRE, LE 1934 d: Gaston Ravel, Tony Lekain. FRN., *Le Rosaire*, Florence L. Barclay, Novel

ROSALBA 1945 d: Ferruccio Cerio, Max Calandri. ITL., *Primavera a Pianabianco*, Luigi Volpicelli, Novel

ROSALEEN DHU 1920 d: William Powers. UKN., *Rosaleen Dhu*, Joseph Denver, Play

ROSALIE 1929 d: Maurice Champreux, Robert Beaudoin. FRN., *Rosalie*, Max Maurey, Play

Rosalie *see* NOT SO DUMB (1930).

ROSALIE 1937 d: W. S. Van Dyke. USA., *Rosalie*, Guy Bolton, William Anthony McGuire, 1928, Musical Play

Rosalie Byrnes *see* THE SHADOW OF ROSALIE BYRNES (1920).

ROSAMUNDE PILCHER: KARUSSELL DES LEBENS 1994 d: Rolf von Sydow. GRM., Rosamunde Pilcher, Novel

Rosanne Ozanne *see* THE SINS OF ROSANNE (1920).

ROSARIO LA CORTIJERA 1923 d: Jose Buchs. SPN., *Rosario la Cortijera*, Ruperto Chapi, Joaquin Dicenta, Manuel Paso, Opera

Rosario, the Girl of the Farm *see* ROSARIO LA CORTIJERA (1923).

ROSARY MURDERS, THE 1987 d: Fred Walton. USA., *The Rosary Murders*, William X. Kienzle, Novel

ROSARY, THE 1915 d: Colin Campbell. USA., *The Rosary*, Edward E. Rose, New York 1910, Play

ROSARY, THE 1922 d: Jerome Storm. USA., *The Rosary*, Edward E. Rose, New York 1910, Play

ROSAS DE OTONO 1943 d: Juan de OrdunA. SPN., *Rosas de Otono*, Jacinto Benavente y Martinez, 1914, Play

ROSAURA A LAS DIEZ 1958 d: Mario Soffici. ARG., *Rosaura a Las Diez*, Marco Denevi, 1955, Novel

Rosaura at 10:00 *see* ROSAURA A LAS DIEZ (1958).

ROSE BERND 1919 d: Alfred Halm. GRM., *Rose Bernd*, Gerhart Hauptmann, 1903, Play

ROSE BERND 1957 d: Wolfgang Staudte. GRM., *Rose Bernd*, Gerhart Hauptmann, 1903, Play

ROSE BOWL 1936 d: Charles T. Barton. USA., *O'Reilly of Notre Dame*, Francis Wallace, New York 1931, Novel

ROSE DE LA MER, LA 1946 d: Jacques de Baroncelli. FRN., *La Rose de la Mer*, Paul Vialar, Novel

ROSE DE NICE 1921 d: Maurice Challiot, Alexandre Ryder. FRN., *Rose de Nice*, Gaston Dumestre, Play

Rose de Sang, La *see* ANGELICA (1939).

ROSE DI DANZICA, LE 1979 d: Alberto BevilacquA. ITL., *Il Pugno Del Potere*, Erich von Lehner, Diary

ROSE FOR EMILY, A 1983 d: John Carradine. USA., *A Rose for Emily*, William Faulkner, 1930, Short Story

Rose for Everyone, A *see* UNA ROSA PER TUTTI (1967).

Rose from Madrid *see* ROSA DE MADRID (1927).

Rose Garden, The *see* DER ROSENGARTEN (1989).

Rose Marie *see* ROSE-MARIE (1936).

ROSE MARIE 1954 d: Mervyn Leroy. USA., *Rose-Marie*, Oscar Hammerstein II, Otto Harbach, New York 1924, Operetta

Rose Monday *see* ROSENMONTAG (1924).

Rose Monday *see* ROSENMONTAG (1955).

ROSE O' PARADISE 1918 d: James Young. USA., *Rose O' Paradise*, Grace Miller White, New York 1915, Novel

ROSE O' THE RIVER 1919 d: Robert T. Thornby. USA., *Rose O' the River*, Kate Douglas Wiggin, Boston 1905, Novel

ROSE O' THE SEA 1922 d: Fred Niblo. USA., *Rose O' the Sea*, Countess Barcynska, New York 1920, Novel

ROSE OF KILDARE, THE 1927 d: Dallas M. Fitzgerald. USA., *The Rose of Kildare*, Gerald Beaumont, 1922, Short Story

Rose of Monterey *see* ROSE OF THE GOLDEN WEST (1927).

ROSE OF PARIS, THE 1924 d: Irving Cummings. USA., *Mitsi*, Delly, Paris 1922, Novel

Rose of Stamboul, The *see* DIE ROSE VON STAMBUL (1953).

ROSE OF THE GOLDEN WEST 1927 d: George Fitzmaurice. USA., *Rose of the Golden West*, Minna Caroline Smith, Eugene Woodward, Story

ROSE OF THE RANCHO 1914 d: Cecil B. de Mille, Wilfred Buckland. USA., *Rose of the Rancho*, David Belasco, Richard Walton Tully, New York 1906, Play

ROSE OF THE RANCHO 1936 d: Marion Gering, Robert Florey (Uncredited). USA., *Rose of the Rancho*, David Belasco, Richard Walton Tully, New York 1906, Play

Rose of the River *see* ROSE O' THE RIVER (1919).

ROSE OF THE SOUTH 1916 d: Paul Scardon. USA., *Randolph '64*, Arthur Cheney Train, 1905, Short Story

ROSE OF THE TENDERLOIN, A 1909 d: J. Searle Dawley. USA., *A Rose of the Tenderloin*, Edward Waterman Townsend, Story

ROSE OF THE TENEMENTS 1926 d: Phil Rosen. USA., *The Stumbling Herd*, John A. Moroso, New York 1923, Novel

ROSE OF THE WORLD 1925 d: Harry Beaumont. USA., *Rose of the World*, Kathleen Norris, New York 1926, Novel

ROSE OF THE WORLD, THE 1918 d: Maurice Tourneur. USA., *Rose of the World*, Agnes Castle, Egerton Castle, New York 1905, Novel

Rose of Thistle Island *see* ROSEN PA TISTELON (1945).

Rose of Versailles, The *see* BERUSAIYU NO BARA (1978).

ROSE ROSSE PER ANGELICA 1966 d: Steno. ITL/SPN/FRN., Alexandre Dumas (pere), Story

ROSE SCARLATTE 1940 d: Vittorio de SicA. ITL., *Due Dozzine Di Rose Scarlatte*, Aldo de Benedetti, Play

ROSE TATTOO, THE 1955 d: Daniel Mann. USA., *The Rose Tattoo*, Tennessee Williams, New York 1951, Play

Rose, The *see* ROZA (1936).

ROSE VON STAMBUL, DIE 1953 d: Karl Anton. GRM., *Die Rose von Stambul*, Leo Fall, Vienna 1916, Operetta

ROSEBUD 1974 d: Otto Preminger. USA., *Rosebud*, Paul Bonnecarrere, Joan Hemingway, Novel

Rose-Girl Resli *see* ROSEN-RESLI (1954).

ROSE-MARIE 1927 d: Lucien Hubbard. USA., *Rose-Marie*, Oscar Hammerstein II, Otto Harbach, New York 1924, Operetta

ROSE-MARIE 1936 d: W. S. Van Dyke. USA., *Rose-Marie*, Oscar Hammerstein II, Otto Harbach, New York 1924, Operetta

ROSEMARY 1915 d: William J. Bowman, Fred J. Balshofer. USA., *Rosemary*, Murray Carson, Louis N. Parker, London 1896, Play

ROSEMARY'S BABY 1968 d: Roman Polanski. USA., *Rosemary's Baby*, Ira Levin, New York 1967, Novel

ROSEN BLUH'N AUF DEM HEIDEGRAB 1929 d: Curt Blachnitzky. GRM., *Rosen Bluh'n Auf Dem Heidegrab*, Fritz Mischke, Short Story

ROSEN IM HERBST 1955 d: Rudolf Jugert. GRM., *Effi Briest*, Theodor Fontane, 1894-95, Novel

ROSEN IN TIROL 1940 d: Geza von Bolvary. GRM., *Der Vogelhandler*, Carl Zeller, Vienna 1891, Operetta

ROSEN PA TISTELON 1945 d: Ake Ohberg. SWD., *Rosen Pa Tistelon*, Emilie Flygare-Carlen, 1842, Novel

Rosencrantz and Guildenstern *see* ROSENCRANTZ AND GUILDENSTERN ARE DEAD (1990).

ROSENCRANTZ AND GUILDENSTERN ARE DEAD 1990 d: Tom Stoppard. USA., *Rosencrantz and Guildenstern are Dead*, Tom Stoppard, 1968, Play

ROSENDA 1948 d: Julio Bracho. MXC., *Rosenda*, Jose Ruben Romero, 1946, Novel

ROSENGARTEN, DER 1989 d: Fons Rademakers. GRM/USA., *Der Rosengarten*, Paul Hengge, Novel

ROSENKAVALIER, DER 1926 d: Robert Wiene. AUS., *Der Rosenkavalier*, Richard Strauss, Hugo von Hofmannsthal, Dresden 1911, Opera

ROSENKAVALIER, DER 1962 d: Paul Czinner. UKN., *Der Rosenkavalier*, Richard Strauss, Hugo von Hofmannsthal, Dresden 1911, Opera

ROSENMONTAG 1924 d: Rudolf Meinert. GRM., *Rosenmontag*, O. E. Hartleben, Play

ROSENMONTAG 1955 d: Willy Birgel. GRM., *Rosenmontag*, O. E. Hartleben, Play

ROSEN-RESLI 1954 d: Harald Reinl. GRM., *Rosen-Resli*, Johanna Spyri, Novel

ROSES ARE FOR THE RICH 1987 d: Michael Miller. USA., *Roses are for the Rich*, Jonell Lawson, Novel

Roses in Autumn *see* ROSEN IM HERBST (1955).

Roses of Danzica, The *see* LE ROSE DI DANZICA (1979).

ROSES OF PICARDY 1927 d: Maurice Elvey. UKN., *The Spanish Farm*, R. H. Mottram, Short Story

Roses Rouges Et Piments Verts *see* NO ENCONTRE ROSAS PARA MI MADRE (1972).

ROSIE! 1968 d: David Lowell Rich. USA., *Les Joies de la Famille*, Philippe Heriat, Paris 1960, Play

ROSIE DIXON: NIGHT NURSE 1977 d: Justin Cartwright. UKN., *Confessions of a Night Nurse*, Rosie Dixon, Novel

ROSIE THE RIVETER 1944 d: Joseph Santley. USA., *Room for Two*, Dorothy Curnor Handley, Story

ROSIE: THE ROSEMARY CLOONEY STORY 1982 d: Jackie Cooper. USA., *This for Remembrance*, Rosemary Clooney, Raymond Strait, Autobiography

ROSIER DE MADAME HUSSON, LE 1931 d: Bernard-Deschamps. FRN., *Le Rosier de Madame Husson*, Guy de Maupassant, 1888, Short Story

ROSIER DE MADAME HUSSON, LE 1950 d: Jean Boyer. FRN., *Le Rosier de Madame Husson*, Guy de Maupassant, 1888, Short Story

ROSITA 1923 d: Ernst Lubitsch. USA., *Don Cesar de Bazan*, Adolphe-P. d'Ennery, Philippe F. Pinel, 1844, Play

Rossa, La *see* DIE ROTE (1962).

ROSSITER CASE, THE 1951 d: Francis Searle. UKN., *The Rossiters*, Kenneth Hyde, Play

ROSSO VENEZIANO 1975 d: Marco Leto. ITL., *Rosso Veneziano*, Pier Maria Pasinetti, Novel

ROSWELL 1994 d: Jeremy Paul Kagan. USA., *Ufo Crash at Roswell*, Kevin D. Randle, Donald K. Schmitt, Book

Roswell: the Ufo Cover-Up *see* ROSWELL (1994).

Rosy Dawn, The *see* ZA RANNICH CERVANKU (1934).

Rosy la Bourrasque *see* TEMPORALE ROSY (1979).

ROT IST DIE LIEBE 1957 d: Karl Hartl. GRM., *Das Zweite Gesicht*, Hermann Lons, Novel

ROTE, DIE 1962 d: Helmut Kautner. GRM/ITL., *Die Rote*, Alfred Andersch, 1960, Novel

ROTE KREIS, DER 1928 d: Friedrich Zelnik. GRM/UKN., *The Crimson Circle*, Edgar Wallace, London 1922, Novel

ROTE KREIS, DER 1959 d: Jurgen Roland. GRM., *The Crimson Circle*, Edgar Wallace, London 1922, Novel

ROTE MUHLE, DIE 1940 d: Jurgen von Alten. GRM., *Die Rote Muhle*, Jurgen von Alten, Play

Rote Mutze, Die *see* HEIRATSSCHWINDLER (1937).

ROTE RAUSCH, DER 1962 d: Wolfgang Schleif. GRM., *Der Rote Rausch*, Hans Ulrich Horster, Novel

Rote Rosen - Blaue Adria *see* DER WILDFANG (1936).

ROTE STRUMPF, DER 1980 d: Wolfgang Tumler. GRM., *Der Rote Strumpf*, Elfie Donnelly, Book

ROTHAUSGASSE, DIE 1928 d: Richard Oswald. GRM., *Der Heilige Skarabaus*, Else Jerusalem, Novel

ROTHCHILD 1933 d: Marco de Gastyne. FRN., *Rothschild*, Paul Laffite, Short Story

Rothschild *see* THE HOUSE OF ROTHSCHILD (1934).

ROTKAPPCHEN 1953 d: Fritz Genschow. GRM., *Rotkappchen*, Jacob Grimm, Wilhelm Grimm, Short Story

ROTKAPPCHEN 1954 d: Walter Janssen. GRM., *Rotkappchen*, Jacob Grimm, Wilhelm Grimm, Short Story

Rotten Blood *see* ZKAZENA KREV (1913).

ROTTERS, THE 1921 d: A. V. Bramble. UKN., *The Rotters*, H. F. Maltby, Play

Rouge *see* YANZHI (1925).

Rouge *see* YANZHI KOU (1987).

Rouge *see* HONGFEN (1994).

ROUGE AND RICHES 1920 d: Harry L. Franklin. USA., *Myself Becky*, W. Carey Wonderly, Short Story

ROUGE EST MIS, LE 1957 d: Gilles Grangier. FRN., *Le Rouge Est Mis*, Auguste le Breton, Novel

ROUGE ET LE NOIR, LE 1920 d: Mario Bonnard. ITL., *Le Rouge Et le Noir*, Stendhal, 1830, Novel

Rouge Et le Noir, Le *see* IL CORRIERE DEL RE (1948).

ROUGE ET LE NOIR, LE 1954 d: Claude Autant-LarA. FRN/ITL., *Le Rouge Et le Noir*, Stendhal, 1830, Novel

Rouge Et Noir *see* DER GEHEIME KURIER (1928).

Rouge Et Noir *see* LE ROUGE ET LE NOIR (1954).

ROUGED LIPS 1923 d: Harold Shaw. USA., *Upstage*, Rita Weiman, 1922, Short Story

ROUGH AND THE SMOOTH, THE 1959 d: Robert Siodmak. UKN., *The Rough and the Smooth*, Robin Maugham, London 1951, Novel

Rough Company *see* THE VIOLENT MEN (1954).

ROUGH CUT 1980 d: Don Siegel. USA/UKN., *Touch the Lion's Paw*, Derek Lambert, Novel

Rough Diamond *see* DIAMANTE BRUTO (1977).

ROUGH HOUSE ROSIE 1927 d: Frank Strayer. USA., *Rough House Rosie*, Nunnally Johnson, 1926, Short Story

ROUGH MAGIC 1995 d: Clare Peploe. UKN/FRN., *Miss Shumway Waves a Wand*, James Hadley Chase, Novel

ROUGH NIGHT IN JERICHO 1967 d: Arnold Laven. USA., *The Man in Black*, Marvin H. Albert, Story

Rough Ridin' Rhythm *see* ROUGH RIDING RHYTHM (1937).

ROUGH RIDING RHYTHM 1937 d: J. P. McGowan. USA., *Getting a Start in Life*, James Oliver Curwood, Short Story

Rough Riding Romeo *see* FLAMING GUNS (1932).

ROUGH ROMANCE 1930 d: A. F. Erickson. USA., *The Girl Who Wasn't Wanted*, Kenneth B. Clarke, 1928, Short Story

ROUGH SHOD 1922 d: B. Reeves Eason. USA., *West!*, Charles Alden Seltzer, New York 1922, Novel

ROUGH SHOOT 1952 d: Robert Parrish. UKN., *A Rough Shoot*, Geoffrey Household, Novel

Rough Sketch *see* WE WERE STRANGERS (1949).

ROUGH STUFF 1925 d: Dell Henderson. USA., *Rough Stuff*, A. E. Ullman, Short Story

Roughcut *see* ROUGH CUT (1980).

Rough-House Rosie *see* ROUGH HOUSE ROSIE (1927).

ROUGHLY SPEAKING 1945 d: Michael Curtiz. USA., *Roughly Speaking*, Louise Randall Pierson, Book

Roughneck Lover *see* LOVIN' THE LADIES (1930).

ROUGHNECK, THE 1924 d: Jack Conway. USA., *The Roughneck*, Robert W. Service, New York 1923, Novel

ROULETABILLE AVIATEUR 1932 d: Steve Sekely. FRN., *Rouletabille Aviateur*, Gaston Leroux, Novel

ROULETABILLE CHEZ LES BOHEMIENS 1922 d: Henri Fescourt. FRN., *Rouletabille Chez Les Bohemiens*, Gaston Leroux, Novel

Rouletabille II -la Derniere Incarnation de Larsan *see* LE PARFUM DE LA DAME EN NOIR (1914).

Roulette *see* WHEEL OF CHANCE (1928).

Round the Bend *see* OVER THE HILL (1992).

'ROUND THE WORLD IN 80 DAYS 1914. USA., *Le Tour du Monde En Quatre-Vingt Jours*, Jules Verne, France 1873, Novel

Round Up, The *see* THE ROUND-UP (1920).

ROUNDERS, THE 1964 d: Burt Kennedy. USA., *The Rounders*, Max Evans, New York 1960, Novel

ROUND-UP, THE 1920 d: George Melford. USA., *The Round Up*, Edmund Day, New York 1907, Play

ROUSSEAUISM AND THE YOUNG GOETHE 1972 d: Alasdair Clayre. UKN., *Satyos*, Johann Wolfgang von Goethe, 1840, Play

ROUTE DE CORINTHE, LA 1967 d: Claude Chabrol. FRN/ITL/GRC., *La Route de Corinthe*, Claude Rank, Paris 1966, Novel

ROUTE DE DEVOIR, LA 1915 d: Georges MoncA. FRN., *La Route du Devoir*, J. Berr de Turique, Novel

Route de Noumea, La *see* LA ROUTE DU BAGNE (1945).

Route de Salina, La *see* SUR LA ROUTE DE SALINA (1969).

ROUTE DU BAGNE, LA 1945 d: Leon Mathot. FRN., *Manon 326*, Pierre-Gilles Veber, Novel

ROUTE IMPERIALE, LA 1935 d: Marcel L'Herbier. FRN., *La Maison Cernee*, Pierre Frondaie, Novel

Rover, The *see* L' AVVENTURIERO (1967).

ROWDY, THE 1921 d: David Kirkland. USA., *The Ark Angel*, Hamilton Thompson, Short Story

ROXANNE 1987 d: Fred Schepisi. USA., *Cyrano de Bergerac*, Edmond Rostand, 1897, Play

ROXIE HART 1942 d: William A. Wellman. USA., *Chicago*, Maurine Dallas Watkins, New York 1926, Play

Royal Affair, A *see* LE ROI (1949).

ROYAL BED, THE 1931 d: Lowell Sherman. USA., *The Queen's Husband*, R. E. Sherwood, New York 1928, Play

ROYAL BOX, THE 1914 d: Oscar Eagle. USA., *The Royal Box*, Charles Coghlan, New York 1897, Play

ROYAL BOX, THE 1930 d: Bryan Foy. USA., *The Royal Box*, Charles Coghlan, New York 1897, Play

ROYAL DIVORCE, A 1923 d: Alexander Butler. UKN., *A Royal Divorce*, G. C. Collingham, W. G. Wills, London 1891, Play

ROYAL DIVORCE, A 1938 d: Jack Raymond. UKN., *Josephine*, Jacques Thery, Novel

ROYAL FAMILY OF BROADWAY, THE 1930 d: George Cukor, Cyril Gardner. USA., *The Royal Family*, Edna Ferber, George S. Kaufman, New York 1927, Play

ROYAL FLASH 1975 d: Richard Lester. UKN., *Royal Flash*, George MacDonald Fraser, Novel

Royal Game, The *see* DIE SCHACHNOVELLE (1960).

Royal Highness *see* KONIGLICHE HOHEIT (1953).

ROYAL HUNT OF THE SUN, THE 1969 d: Irving Lerner. UKN/USA., *The Royal Hunt of the Sun*, Peter Shaffer, London 1964, Play

Royal Hunt, The *see* MRIGAYA (1976).

Royal Hunting, The *see* LA CHASSE ROYALE (1969).

Royal Mercy *see* TSARSKA MILOST (1962).

ROYAL OAK, THE 1923 d: Maurice Elvey. UKN., *The Royal Oak*, Henry Hamilton, Augustus Harris, London 1889, Play

ROYAL PAUPER, THE 1917 d: Ben Turbett. USA., *The Princess from the Poorhouse*, Henry Albert Phillips, Short Story

Royal Scandal *see* DIE HOSE (1927).

ROYAL SCANDAL, A 1945 d: Otto Preminger, Ernst Lubitsch. USA., *A Carno Szinmu: Harom Felvonasban*, Lajos Biro, Budapest 1913, Play, *A Carno Szinmu; Harom Felvonasban*, Menyhert Lengyel, Budapest 1913, Play

Royal Track, The *see* KUNGSLEDEN (1964).

ROZA 1936 d: Joseph Leytes. PLN., *Roza*, Stefan Zeromski, 1909, Play

ROZE KATE 1912 d: Oscar Tourniaire. NTH., *Of Het Treurspel de Smeden Roze Kate*, Nestor de Tiere, 1893, Play

ROZKOSNY PRIBEH 1936 d: Vladimir Slavinsky. CZC., *Podej Stesti Ruku*, Karel Melisek, Jaroslav Mottl, Opera

ROZMARNE LETO 1967 d: Jiri Menzel. CZC., *Rozmarne Leto*, Vladislav Vancura, Prague 1926, Novel

ROZTOMILY CLOVEK 1941 d: Martin Fric. CZC., *Kasparek*, F. X. Svoboda, Novel

RU CHI DUO QING 1956 d: Fang Ying. CHN., *Love the Man, Not His Position*, Li Li, Story

RUBAIYAT OF A SCOTCH HIGH BALL, THE 1918 d: Martin Justice. USA., *The Rubaiyat of a Scotch High Ball*, O. Henry, Short Story

RUBBER 1936 d: Gerard Rutten, Johan de Meester. NTH., *Rubber*, M. H. Szekely-Lulofs, Novel

Rubber Tarzan *see* GUMMI TARZAN (1982).

Ruby *see* LAZY RIVER (1934).

RUBY 1992 d: John MacKenzie. USA., *Love Field*, Stephen Davis, Play

Ruby Red see SHE DONE HIM WRONG (1933).

RUBY RIDGE: AN AMERICAN TRAGEDY 1996 d: Roger Young. USA., *Every Knee Shall Bow*, Jess Walter, Book

RUCKFAHRT IN DEN TOD 199- d: Hans-Jurgen Togel. GRM., *Terminus*, Pierre Boileau, Thomas Narcejac, Novel

RUDIN 1976 d: Konstantin Voinov. USS., *Rudin*, Ivan Turgenev, 1856, Novel

RUDYARD KIPLING'S JUNGLE BOOK 1942 d: Zoltan KordA. USA., *The King's Ankus*, Rudyard Kipling, 1895, Short Story

RUDYARD KIPLING'S THE SECOND JUNGLE BOOK: MOWGLI AND BALOO 1997 d: Duncan McLachlan. USA., *The Second Jungle Book*, Rudyard Kipling, Book

RUE BARBARE 1983 d: Gilles Behat. FRN., *Epaves*, David Goodis, Novel

RUE CASES-NEGRES 1983 d: Euzhan Palcy. FRN., *Ruse Cases Negres*, Joseph Zobel, Novel

RUE DE LA PAIX 1926 d: Henri Diamant-Berger. FRN., *Rue de la Paix*, Marc de Toledo, Abel Hermant, Play

Rue de Paris see RUE DES PRAIRIES (1959).

Rue Des Amours Faciles, La see VIA MARGUTTA (1960).

RUE DES BOUCHES PEINTES, LA 1955 d: Robert Vernay. FRN., *La Rue Des Bouches Peintes*, Maurice Dekobra, Novel

Rue Des Cascades see UN GOSSE DE LA BUTTE (1964).

RUE DES PRAIRIES 1959 d: Denys de La Patelliere. FRN/ITL., *Rue Des Prairies*, Rene Lefevre, Novel

RUE DU PAVE D'AMOUR, LA 1923 d: Andre Hugon. FRN., *La Rue du Pave d'Amour*, Jean Aicard, Novel

Rue, La see THE STREET (1976).

Rue Saint-Sulpice see THE WATCH AND THE VERY BIG FISH, THE FAVOUR (1991).

RUE SANS JOIE, LA 1938 d: Andre Hugon. FRN., *La Rue Sans Joie*, Hugo Bettauer, Novel

RUE SANS NOM, LA 1934 d: Pierre Chenal. FRN., *La Rue Sans Nom*, Marcel Ayme, Novel

RUELLE AU CLAIR DE LUNE, LA 1990 d: Edouard Molinaro. FRN., *La Ruelle Au Clair de Lune*, Stefan Zweig, Novel

RUF DER WILDGANSE, DER 1961 d: Hans Heinrich. AUS., *Ruf Der Wildganse*, Martha Ostenso, Novel

Ruf Der Wildnis see TUMULTO DE PAIXOES (1958).

Ruf Der Wildnis see CALL OF THE WILD (1972).

RUFFIAN, LE 1983 d: Jose Giovanni. FRN/CND., *Le Ruffian*, Jose Giovanni, Novel

Ruffian, The see LE RUFFIAN (1983).

Ruffians, The see LES CANAILLES (1959).

RUGANTINO 1973 d: Pasquale Festa Campanile. ITL/SPN., *Rugantino*, Pietro Garinei, Sandro Giovannini, Play

Rugged O'Riordans, The see SONS OF MATTHEW (1949).

RUGGED PATH, THE 1918. UKN., *The Rugged Path*, Charles Garvice, Novel

RUGGED WATER 1925 d: Irvin V. Willat. USA., *Rugged Water*, Joseph C. Lincoln, London 1924, Novel

RUGGLES OF RED GAP 1918 d: Lawrence C. Windom. USA., *Ruggles of Red Gap*, Harry Leon Wilson, New York 1915, Novel

RUGGLES OF RED GAP 1923 d: James Cruze. USA., *Ruggles of Red Gap*, Harry Leon Wilson, New York 1915, Novel

RUGGLES OF RED GAP 1935 d: Leo McCarey. USA., *Ruggles of Red Gap*, Harry Leon Wilson, New York 1915, Novel

RUINAS DE BABILONIA, LAS 1959 d: Ramon Torrado, Johannes Kai. SPN/GRM., *Der Lowe von Babylon*, Karl Friedrich May, Novel

Ruined Map, The see MOETSUKITA CHIZU (1968).

Ruined Shopkeeper, The see U SNEDENEHO KRAMU (1933).

Ruins of Babylon, The see LAS RUINAS DE BABILONIA (1959).

RUISSEAU, LE 1912 d: Georges DenolA. FRN., *Le Ruisseau*, Pierre Wolff, Paris 1907, Play

RUISSEAU, LE 1929 d: Rene Hervil. FRN., *Le Ruisseau*, Pierre Wolff, Paris 1907, Play

RUISSEAU, LE 1938 d: Maurice Lehmann, Claude Autant-LarA. FRN., *Le Ruisseau*, Pierre Wolff, Paris 1907, Play

RUITER IN DIE NAG, DIE 1963 d: Jan Perold. SAF., *Die Ruiter in Die Nag*, Mikro, Bloemfontein 1936, Novel

RUKAJARVEN TIE 1999 d: Olli SaarelA. FNL., *Rukajarven Tie*, Antti Tuuri, Novel

RULE G 1915 d: George W. Lawrence, G. M. Noble. USA., *Keeping John Barleycorn Off the Tracks*, Rufus Steele, 1914, Short Story

RULER OF MEN, A 1920 d: David Smith. USA., *A Ruler of Men*, O. Henry, Short Story

RULER OF THE ROAD 1918 d: Ernest C. Warde. USA., *Simeon Tetlow's Shadow*, Jennette Barbour Perry Lee, New York 1909, Novel

Ruler, The see DER HERRSCHER (1937).

Ruler Without a Crown see HERRSCHER OHNE KRONE (1957).

Rules of the Game, The see LA REGLE DU JEU (1939).

RULING CLASS, THE 1972 d: Peter Medak. UKN., *The Ruling Class*, Peter Barnes, 1969, Play

RULING PASSION, THE 1922 d: F. Harmon Weight. USA., *The Ruling Passion*, Earl Derr Biggers, 1922, Short Story

Ruling Passion, The see THE MILLIONAIRE (1931).

Rum Runner see BOULEVARD DU RHUM (1971).

RUMBLE FISH 1983 d: Francis Ford CoppolA. USA., *Rumble Fish*, S. E. Hinton, Novel

RUMBLE ON THE DOCKS 1956 d: Fred F. Sears. USA., *Rumble on the Docks*, Frank Paley, 1953, Novel

Rumor Mill, The see MALICE IN WONDERLAND (1985).

RUMPELSTILTSKIN 1915 d: Raymond B. West. USA., *Rumpelstilzchen*, Jacob Grimm, Wilhelm Grimm, 1812, Short Story

RUMPELSTILTSKIN 1987 d: David Irving. USA., *Rumpelstilzchen*, Jacob Grimm, Wilhelm Grimm, 1812, Short Story

RUMPELSTILZCHEN 1955 d: Herbert B. Fredersdorf. GRM., *Rumpelstilzchen*, Jacob Grimm, Wilhelm Grimm, 1812, Short Story

Rumpelstilzchen see DAS ZAUBERMANNCHEN (1960).

Rumpestiltskin see RUMPELSTILZCHEN (1955).

Rumplestiltskin see RUMPELSTILTSKIN (1987).

RUN, CHRISSIE, RUN 1984 d: Chris Langman. ASL., *When We Ran*, Keith Leopold, Novel

RUN, COUGAR, RUN 1972 d: Jerome Courtland. USA., *Run Cougar Run*, Robert Murphy, Novel

RUN FOR THE SUN 1956 d: Roy Boulting. USA., *The Most Dangerous Game*, Richard Connell, 1930, Short Story

Run for Your Life see SWEET REVENGE (1987).

Run, Miki, Run see MY CHAMPION (1981).

RUN OF THE COUNTRY, THE 1995 d: Peter Yates. UKN/IRL., *The Run of the Country*, Shane Connaughton, Novel

RUN SILENT, RUN DEEP 1958 d: Robert Wise. USA., *Run Deep Run Silent*, Com. Edward L. Beach, 1955, Novel

RUN WILD, RUN FREE 1969 d: Richard C. Sarafian. UKN., *The White Colt*, David Rook, New York 1967, Novel

Run With the Devil see VIA MARGUTTA (1960).

Runaway Angel see BAD LITTLE ANGEL (1939).

Runaway Enchantress, The see THE SEA TIGER (1927).

RUNAWAY EXPRESS, THE 1926 d: Edward Sedgwick. USA., *The Nerve of Foley*, Frank Hamilton Spearman, 1900, Short Story

RUNAWAY LADIES 1935 d: Jean de Limur. UKN., *Le Voyage Imprevu*, Tristan Bernard, Novel

RUNAWAY PRINCESS, THE 1929 d: Anthony Asquith, Frederick Wendhausen. UKN/GRM., *Princess Priscilla's Fortnight*, Elizabeth Russell, Novel

Runaway Queen see THE QUEEN'S AFFAIR (1934).

RUNAWAY, THE 1917 d: Dell Henderson. USA., *The Runaway*, Michael Morton, New York 1911, Play

RUNAWAY, THE 1926 d: William C. de Mille. USA., *The Flight to the Hills*, Charles Neville Buck, Garden City, Ny. 1926, Novel

Runaway, The see ATITHI (1965).

RUNAWAY WIFE, THE 1915 d: Kenean Buel. USA., *The Runaway Wife*, McKee Rankin, Play

RUNAWAYS, THE 1975 d: Harry Harris. USA., *The Runaways*, Victor Canning, Novel

RUNNING AGAINST TIME 1990 d: Bruce Seth Green. USA., *Time to Remember*, Stanley Shapiro

Running Bear see ROMANCE OF A HORSETHIEF (1972).

RUNNING FIGHT, THE 1915 d: James Durkin. USA., *The Running Fight*, William Hamilton Osborne, New York 1910, Novel

RUNNING MAN, THE 1963 d: Carol Reed. UKN/USA., *The Ballad of the Running Man*, Shelley Smith, London 1961, Novel

Running Man, The see THE CITY'S EDGE (1983).

RUNNING MAN, THE 1987 d: Paul Michael Glaser. USA., *The Running Man*, Stephen King, Novel

RUNNING TARGET 1956 d: Marvin R. Weinstein. USA., *My Brother Down There*, Steve Frazee, Story

RUNNING WATER 1922 d: Maurice Elvey. UKN., *Running Water*, A. E. W. Mason, Novel

RUPERT OF HENTZAU 1915 d: George Loane Tucker. UKN., *Rupert of Hentzau*, Anthony Hope, 1898, Novel

RUPERT OF HENTZAU 1923 d: Victor Heerman. USA., *Rupert of Hentzau*, Anthony Hope, 1898, Novel

RUPTURE, LA 1970 d: Claude Chabrol. FRN/ITL/BLG., *Le Jour Des Parques*, Charlotte Armstrong, Novel

Rural Teachers see KRU BAN NOK (1978).

RUSALOCHKA 1976 d: Vladimir Bychkov. USS/BUL., *Den Lille Haufrue*, Hans Christian Andersen, 1837, Short Story

Rusalotchka see RUSALOCHKA (1976).

RUSAR I HANS FAMN 1996 d: Lennart Hjulstrom. SWD., *Karleks Pris*, Yvonne Gronin, Novel

RUSE, LA 1921 d: Edouard-Emile Violet. FRN., *La Ruse*, Hersent, Claude Rolland, Play

RUSH 1991 d: Lili Fini Zanuck. USA., *Rush*, Kim Wozencraft, Book

RUSH HOUR, THE 1927 d: E. Mason Hopper. USA., *The Azure Shore*, Fanny Hatton, Frederic Hatton, 1923, Short Story

RUSH TO JUDGMENT 1967 d: Emile de Antonio. USA., *Rush to Judgment*, Mark Lane, New York 1966, Book

Rushing Into His Arms see RUSAR I HANS FAMN (1996).

RUSHYA SHRINGA 1976 d: V. R. K. Prasad. IND., *Rushya Shringa*, Chandrasekhar Kambhar, Play

Ruskij Vopros see RUSSKI VOPROZ (1947).

RUSLAN I LJUDMILA 1970 d: Alexander Ptushko. USS., *Ruslan I Lyudmila*, Alexander Pushkin, 1820, Verse

RUSLAN I LYUDMILA 1938 d: Ivan Nikitchenko, Viktor Nevezhin. USS., *Ruslan I Lyudmila*, Alexander Pushkin, 1820, Verse

Rusland I Liudmila see RUSLAN I LJUDMILA (1970).

RUSSEN KOMMEN, DIE 1970 d: Heiner Carow. GDR., Egon Richter, Story

RUSSIA HOUSE, THE 1990 d: Fred Schepisi. USA/UKN., *The Russia House*, John le Carre, 1989, Novel

Russian Forest, The see RUSSKIJ LES (1964).

Russian Question, The see RUSSKI VOPROZ (1947).

RUSSIAN ROULETTE 1975 d: Lou Lombardo. USA., *Russian Roulette*, Tom Ardies, Novel

Russians are Coming, The see DIE RUSSEN KOMMEN (1970).

RUSSIANS ARE COMING, THE RUSSIANS ARE COMING, THE 1966 d: Norman Jewison. USA., *The Off-Islanders*, Nathaniel Benchley, New York 1961, Novel

RUSSICUM 1989 d: Pasquale Squitieri. ITL., *I Mertedi Del Diavolo*, Enzo Russo, Novel

Russicum - I Giorni Del Diavolo see RUSSICUM (1989).

RUSSKI VOPROZ 1947 d: Mikhail Romm. USS., *Russkiy Vopros*, Konstantin Simonov, 1946, Play

RUSSKIJ LES 1964 d: Vladimir Petrov. USS., *Russkiy Les*, Leonid Maksimovich Leonov, 1953, Novel

Russkiy Les see RUSSKIJ LES (1964).

Russkiy Voproz see RUSSKI VOPROZ (1947).

RUSTLE OF SILK, THE 1923 d: Herbert Brenon. USA., *The Rustle of Silk*, Cosmo Hamilton, Boston 1922, Novel

Rustler of Wind River, The see WINNER TAKES ALL (1918).

RUSTLER'S VALLEY 1937 d: Nate Watt. USA., *Rustler's Valley*, Clarence E. Mulford, New York 1924, Novel

RUSTLING FOR CUPID 1926 d: Irving Cummings. USA., *Rustling for Cupid*, Peter B. Kyne, 1926, Short Story

Rustling of Wind River, The *see* WINNER TAKES ALL (1918).

Ruta Del Marino, La *see* EN CADA PUERTO UN AMOR (1931).

RUTH 1983 d: Jerzy Hoffman. PLN/GRM., Art Bernd, Story

Ruth Rendell Mysteries: an Unwanted Woman *see* INSPECTOR WEXFORD: AN UNWANTED WOMAN (1992).

Ruth Rendell Mysteries: from Doon With Death *see* INSPECTOR WEXFORD: FROM DOON WITH DEATH (1991).

Ruth Rendell Mysteries: Kissing the Gunner's Daughter *see* INSPECTOR WEXFORD: KISSING THE GUNNER'S DAUGHTER (1992).

Ruth Rendell Mysteries: the Mouse in the Corner *see* INSPECTOR WEXFORD: THE MOUSE IN THE CORNER (1992).

Ruth Rendell Mysteries: the Speaker of Mandarin *see* INSPECTOR WEXFORD: THE SPEAKER OF MANDARIN (1992).

RUTHLESS 1948 d: Edgar G. Ulmer. USA., *Prelude to Night*, Dayton Stoddert, Novel

Ruthless Romance *see* ZESTOKIJ ROMANS (1984).

RUTSCHBAHN 1928 d: Richard Eichberg. GRM., *Das Bekenntnis*, Clara Ratzka, Novel

RUY BLAS 1909 d: J. Stuart Blackton (Spv). USA., *Ruy Blas*, Victor Hugo, 1838, Play

RUY BLAS 1914 d: Lucius Henderson. USA., *Ruy Blas*, Victor Hugo, 1838, Play

RUY BLAS 1916. FRN., *Ruy Blas*, Victor Hugo, 1838, Play

RUY BLAS 1947 d: Pierre Billon. FRN/ITL., *Ruy Blas*, Victor Hugo, 1838, Play

RUY-BLAS 1912. ITL., *Ruy Blas*, Victor Hugo, 1838, Play

Rx Murder *see* FAMILY DOCTOR (1958).

RYBA NA SUCHU 1942 d: Vladimir Slavinsky. CZC., *Ryba Na Suchu*, Karel Konstantin, Play

RYBAR A ZLATA RYBKA 1951 d: Jiri TrnkA. CZC., *Skazka O Rybake I Rybke*, Alexander Pushkin, 1833, Poem

RYNOX 1931 d: Michael Powell. UKN., *Rynox*, Philip MacDonald, Novel

RYS 1981 d: Stanislaw Rozewicz. PLN., *Kosciot W Skaryszewie*, Jaroslaw Iwaszkiewicz, 1967, Short Story

RYTTARE I BLATT 1959 d: Arne Mattsson. SWD., *Ryttare I Blatt*, Folke Mellwig, Novel

S. A. S. Malko - Im Auftrag Des Pentagon *see* S.A.S. A SAN SALVADOR (1982).

S Bernardo *see* SAO BERNARDO (1972).

S. Ilario *see* SANT'ILARIO (1923).

SA CONSCIENCE 1919 d: Daniel Riche. FRN., *Sa Conscience*, Daniel Riche, Novel

Sa Nuit de Noces *see* MARIONS-NOUS (1931).

SAADIA 1953 d: Albert Lewin. USA., *Echee Au Destin*, Francis d'Autheville, 1950, Novel

Saahil *see* PAAR (1984).

SABATO, DOMENICA E LUNEDI 1990 d: Lina Wertmuller. ITL., *Sabato Domenica E Lunedi*, Eduardo de Filippo, 1959, Play

Sabine Und Der Zufall *see* MEIN MANN DARF ES NICHT WISSEN (1940).

SABINE WULFF 1978 d: Erwin StrankA. GDR., *Sabine Wulff*, Karl-Heinz Kruschel, Novel

Sable and the Maiden, The *see* SOBOL I PANNA (1983).

SABLE LORCHA, THE 1915 d: Lloyd Ingraham. USA., *The Sable Lorcha*, Horace Hazeltine, Chicago 1912, Novel

SABOTAGE 1936 d: Alfred Hitchcock. UKN., *The Secret Agent*, Joseph Conrad, 1907, Novel

Saboteur, Code Name Morituri *see* MORITURI (1965).

Saboteur, The *see* MORITURI (1965).

SABRA 1970 d: Denys de La Patelliere. FRN/ITL/ISR., *La Mort d'un Juif*, Vahe Katcha, Novel

SABRINA 1954 d: Billy Wilder. USA., *Sabrina Fair*, Samuel Taylor, New York 1953, Play

SABRINA 1995 d: Sydney Pollack. USA., *Sabrina Fair*, Samuel Taylor, New York 1953, Play

Sabrina Fair *see* SABRINA (1954).

SACHE MIT SCHORRSIEGEL, DIE 1928 d: Jaap Speyer. GRM., *Die Sache Mit Schorrsiegel*, Fred Andreas, Novel

SACHE MIT STYX, DIE 1942 d: Karl Anton. GRM., *Rittmeister Styx*, Georg Muhlen-Schulte, Novel

SACI, O 1952 d: Rodolfo Nanni. BRZ., *O Saci*, Monteiro Lobato, 1921, Short Story

SACKCLOTH AND SCARLET 1925 d: Henry King. USA., *Sackcloth and Scarlet*, George Gibbs, London 1924, Novel

SACKETTS, THE 1979 d: Robert Totten. USA., *The Daybreakers*, Louis L'Amour, Novel, *Sackett*, Louis L'Amour, Novel

SACRAMENT, HET 1989 d: Hugo Claus. BLG., *Omtrent Deedee*, Hugo Claus, Novel

Sacrament, The *see* HET SACRAMENT (1989).

SACRE LEONCE 1935 d: Christian-Jaque. FRN., *Sacre Leonce*, Pierre Wolff, Play

SACRED AND PROFANE LOVE 1921 d: William D. Taylor. USA., *Sacred and Profane Love*, Arnold Bennett, London 1919, Play

SACRED FLAME, THE 1929 d: Archie Mayo. USA., *The Sacred Flame*, W. Somerset Maugham, New York 1928, Play

Sacred Flame, The *see* THE RIGHT TO LIVE (1935).

SACRED ORDER, THE 1923 d: A. E. Coleby. UKN., *The Sacred Order*, Sax Rohmer, Short Story

SACRED SILENCE 1919 d: Harry Millarde. USA., *The Deserters*, Robert P. Carter, Anna Alice Chapin, New York 1910, Play

Sacree Balade Pour Les Gros Bras *see* HIGH-BALLIN' (1978).

SACREE JEUNESSE 1958 d: Andre Berthomieu. FRN., *Sacree Jeunesse*, Andre Mouezy-Eon, Play

Sacrifice *see* BALIDAN (1927).

SACRIFICE 1929 d: Victor Peers. UKN., *The Pelican*, H. M. Harwood, F. Tennyson Jesse, London 1924, Play

Sacrifice d'Honneur *see* VEILLE D'ARMES (1935).

SACRIFICE, THE 1909 d: D. W. Griffith. USA., *The Gift of the Magi*, O. Henry, 1906, Short Story

Sacrilegious Hero, The *see* SHIN HEIKE MONOGATARI (1955).

Sacro Testamento, Il *see* IL CRISANTEMO MACCHIATO DI SANGUE (1921).

SAD HORSE, THE 1959 d: James B. Clark. USA., *The Sad Horse*, Zoe Akins, Unpublished, Novel

Sad Sack, The *see* TIRE-AU-FLANC (1961).

SADDLE ACES 1935 d: Harry L. Fraser. USA., *Deuces Wild*, Jay J. Kaley, Story

Saddle Hawk, The *see* THE RIDIN' KID FROM POWDER RIVER (1924).

SADDLE MATES 1928 d: Richard Thorpe. USA., *Saddle Mates*, Harrington Strong, 1924, Short Story

Sade Ou Les Malheurs de Justine *see* JUSTINE DE SADE (1970).

Sade's Justine *see* JUSTINE DE SADE (1970).

SADGATI 1981 d: Satyajit Ray. IND., *Sadgati*, Premchand, 1931, Short Story

Sadie *see* CHASING RAINBOWS (1919).

SADIE 1980 d: Robert C. Chinn. USA., *Rain*, W. Somerset Maugham, 1921, Short Story

SADIE GOES TO HEAVEN 1917 d: W. S. Van Dyke. USA., *Sadie Goes to Heaven*, Dana Burnet, 1917, Short Story

SADIE LOVE 1919 d: John S. Robertson. USA., *Sadie Love*, Avery Hopwood, New York 1915, Play

SADIE MCKEE 1934 d: Clarence Brown. USA., *Pretty Sadie McKee*, Vina Delmar, 1933, Short Story

SADIE THOMPSON 1928 d: Raoul Walsh. USA., *Rain*, W. Somerset Maugham, 1921, Short Story

Sadist, The *see* TRAFRACKEN (1966).

SADOUNAH 1915 d: Louis Mercanton. FRN., *Sadounah*, William le Queux, Novel

SAENGGWABU WIJARYO CHYEONGGUSOSONG 1998 d: Kang Woo-Suk. SKR., *Saenggwabu Wijaryo Chyeonggusosong*, Um in-Hee, Play

SAFARI 1956 d: Terence Young. UKN., *Safari*, Robert Buckner, Novel

Safari in Paradise *see* MORE THAN A SECRETARY (1936).

Safe Bet, A *see* IT'S A BET (1935).

Safe Home *see* POD JEDNOU STRECHOU (1938).

SAFE PASSAGE 1994 d: Robert Allan Ackerman. USA., *Safe Passage*, Ellen Bache, Novel

SAFE, THE 1932. UKN., *The Safe*, W. P. Lipscomb, Play

SAFECRACKER, THE 1957 d: Ray Milland. UKN/USA., *The Safecracker*, Rhys Davis, Bruce Thomas, Book

SAFETY CURTAIN, THE 1918 d: Sidney A. Franklin. USA., *The Safety Curtain*, Ethel M. Dell, 1917, Short Story

SAFETY FIRST 1926 d: Fred Paul. UKN., *Safety First*, Margot Neville, Novel

Safety Match, The *see* SVEDSKAYA SPICKA (1954).

SAFO, HISTORIA DE UNA PASION 1943 d: Carlos Hugo Christensen. ARG., *Sapho*, Alphonse Daudet, Paris 1884, Novel

SAG' DIE WAHRHEIT 1946 d: Helmut Weiss. GRM., *Sag Die Wahrheit*, Johann von Vaszary, Play

Saga of Anatahan, The *see* ANATAHAN (1954).

Saga of Gosta Berling, The *see* GOSTA BERLINGS SAGA (1924).

Saga of H.M.S. Bounty, The *see* MUTINY ON THE BOUNTY (1983).

Saga of Jeremiah Johnson, The *see* JEREMIAH JOHNSON (1972).

Saga of the Road, The *see* PATHER PANCHALI (1955).

Saga of the West *see* WHEN A MAN'S A MAN (1935).

Sage from the Sea, The *see* KONDURA (1977).

SAGEBRUSHER, THE 1920 d: Edward Sloman. USA., *The Sagebrusher*, Emerson Hough, New York 1919, Novel

Sage-Femme, le Cure Et le Bon Dieu, La *see* JESSICA (1962).

SAGGI DELL'INFERNO DANTESCO 1909 d: Adolfo Padovan, Francesco Bertolini. ITL., *La Divina Commedia*, Dante Alighieri, 1310, Verse

SAGRENSKA KOZA 1960 d: Vlado Kristl, Ivo Vrbanic. YGS., *La Peau de Chagrin*, Honore de Balzac, Paris 1831, Novel

SAHARA BRULE, LE 1960 d: Michel Gast. FRN., *La Sahara Brule*, Gilles Perrault, Novel

SAHARA LOVE 1926 d: Sinclair Hill. UKN., *Sahara Love*, A. L. Vincent, Novel

SAHIB BIBI AUR GHULAM 1962 d: Abrar Alvi. IND., *Saheb Bibi Golam*, Bimal Mitra, 1952, Novel

SAIGON 1948 d: Leslie Fenton. USA., Julian Zimet, Story

SAIGON COMMANDOS 1987 d: Clark Henderson. USA., *Saigon Commandos - Mad Minute*, Jonathan Cain, Novel

SAIKAKU ICHIDAI ONNA 1952 d: Kenji Mizoguchi. JPN., *Koshoku Ichidai Onna*, Saikaku Ihara, 1686, Novel

SAIL A CROOKED SHIP 1961 d: Irving S. Brecher. USA., *Sail a Crooked Ship*, Nathaniel Benchley, New York 1960, Novel

SAILOR BEWARE! 1956 d: Gordon Parry. UKN., *Sailor Beware*, Philip King, London 1955, Play

SAILOR BEWARE 1951 d: Hal Walker. USA., *Sailor Beware*, Kenyon Nicholson, Charles Robinson, New York 1933, Play

SAILOR FROM GIBRALTAR, THE 1967 d: Tony Richardson. UKN., *Le Marin de Gibraltar*, Marguerite Duras, Paris 1952, Novel

Sailor of the King *see* SINGLE-HANDED (1953).

Sailor of the Sea *see* SINGLE-HANDED (1953).

SAILOR TRAMP, A 1922 d: F. Martin Thornton. UKN., *A Sailor Tramp*, Bart Kennedy, Novel

SAILOR WHO FELL FROM GRACE WITH THE SEA, THE 1976 d: Lewis John Carlino. UKN., *Gogo No Eiko*, Yukio Mishima, 1963, Novel

Sailor's Broken Vow, The *see* IL NAUFRAGO (1909).

SAILORS DON'T CARE 1928 d: W. P. Kellino. UKN., *Sailors Don't Care*, Seamark, Novel

Sailor's Paradise *see* PARADIES DER MATROSEN (1959).

SAILOR'S RETURN, THE 1977 d: Jack Gold. UKN., *The Sailor's Return*, David Garnett, Novel

SAILORS' WIVES 1928 d: Joseph Henabery. USA., *Sailors' Wives*, Warner Fabian, New York 1924, Novel

Saint and Her Fool, The *see* DIE HEILIGE UND IHR NARR (1928).

Saint Bernard *see* SAO BERNARDO (1972).

Saint Conduit le Bal, Le *see* LE SAINT MENE LA DANSE (1960).

SAINT IN LONDON, THE 1939 d: John Paddy Carstairs. UKN., *The Million Pound Day*, Leslie Charteris, Short Story

SAINT IN NEW YORK, THE 1938 d: Ben Holmes. USA., *The Saint in New York*, Leslie Charteris, London 1935, Novel

SAINT JACK 1979 d: Peter Bogdanovich. USA., *Saint Jack*, Paul Theroux, 1973, Novel

SAINT JOAN 1927 d: Widgey R. Newman. UKN., *Saint Joan*, George Bernard Shaw, New York 1923, Play

SAINT JOAN 1957 d: Otto Preminger. UKN/USA., *Saint Joan*, George Bernard Shaw, New York 1923, Play

SAINT JOAN 1977 d: Steven Rumbelow. UKN., *Saint Joan*, George Bernard Shaw, New York 1923, Play

Saint Johnson *see* LAW AND ORDER (1932).

SAINT MEETS THE TIGER, THE 1941 d: Paul L. Stein. UKN., *Meet the Tiger*, Leslie Charteris, Novel

SAINT MENE LA DANSE, LE 1960 d: Jacques Nahum. FRN., *Le Saint a Palm Springs*, Leslie Charteris, Novel

Saint Petersburg *see* PETERBURGSKAYA NOCH (1934).

SAINT PREND L'AFFUT, LE 1966 d: Christian-Jaque. FRN/ITL., Leslie Charteris, Novel

Saint Rogela *see* IL PECCATO DI ROGELIA SANCHEZ (1939).

SAINT STRIKES BACK, THE 1939 d: John Farrow. USA., *Angels of Doom*, Leslie Charteris, New York 1931, Novel

Saint Strikes Twice, The *see* THE SAINT STRIKES BACK (1939).

Saint Tropez Vice *see* POLICE DES MOEURS (1987).

Saint Versus., The *see* LE SAINT PREND L'AFFUT (1966).

Sainte Et le Fou, La *see* DIE HEILIGE UND IHR NARR (1928).

SAINTED DEVIL, A 1924 d: Joseph Henabery. USA., *Rope's End*, Rex Beach, 1913, Short Story

SAINTED SISTERS, THE 1948 d: William D. Russell. USA., *The Sainted Sisters of Sandy Creek*, Elisa Bialk, Story

SAINTS AND SINNERS 1916 d: James Kirkwood. USA., *Saints and Sinners*, Henry Arthur Jones, London 1884, Play

SAINT'S VACATION, THE 1941 d: Leslie Fenton. UKN., *Getaway*, Leslie Charteris, Short Story

SAISIE, LA 1932 d: Jean Margueritte. FRN., *La Saisie*, Albert Dieudonne, Play

Saison in Salzburg *see* ..UND DIE MUSIK SPIELT DAZU (1943).

SAISON IN SALZBURG 1952 d: Ernst MarischkA. AUS., *Saison in Salzburg*, Kurt Feltz, Fred Raymond, Max Wallner, Opera

SAISON IN SALZBURG 1961 d: Franz J. Gottlieb. AUS., *Saison in Salzburg*, Kurt Feltz, Fred Raymond, Max Wallner, Opera

SAL GROGAN'S FACE 1922 d: Edwin J. Collins. UKN., *Sal Grogan's Face*, George R. Sims, Poem

SAL OF SINGAPORE 1929 d: Howard Higgin. USA., *The Sentimentalists*, Dale Collins, Boston 1927, Novel

Sal of Singapore *see* HIS WOMAN (1931).

SALAIRE DE LA PEUR, LE 1953 d: Henri-Georges Clouzot. FRN/ITL., *Le Salaire de la Peur*, Georges Arnaud, 1950, Novel

SALAIRE DU PECHE, LE 1956 d: Denys de La Patelliere. FRN., *Le Salaire du Peche*, Nancy Rutledge, Novel

SALAMANDER, THE 1915 d: Arthur Donaldson. USA., *The Salamander*, Owen Johnson, New York 1913, Novel

SALAMANDER, THE 1981 d: Peter Zinner. USA/UKN/ITL., *The Salamander*, Morris West, Novel

SALAMBO 1911 d: Arturo Ambrosio. ITL., *Salammbo*, Gustave Flaubert, 1862, Novel

SALAMBO 1914 d: Domenico Gaido. ITL., *Salammbo*, Gustave Flaubert, 1862, Novel

Salambo *see* SALAMMBO (1925).

SALAMBO 1961 d: Sergio Grieco. ITL/FRN., *Salammbo*, Gustave Flaubert, 1862, Novel

Salammbo *see* SALAMBO (1911).

SALAMMBO 1925 d: Pierre Marodon. FRN., *Salammbo*, Gustave Flaubert, 1862, Novel

Salammbo *see* SALAMBO (1961).

Salario Della Paura, Il *see* LE SALAIRE DE LA PEUR (1953).

SALAUDS VONT EN ENFER, LES 1955 d: Robert Hossein. FRN., *Les Salauds Vont En Enfer*, Frederic Dard, Play

SALEM'S LOT 1979 d: Tobe Hooper. USA., *Salem's Lot*, Stephen King, 1974, Novel

Salem's Lot: the Movie *see* SALEM'S LOT (1979).

Salerno Beachhead *see* A WALK IN THE SUN (1946).

Salesman, The *see* SEEMABADHA (1971).

SALKA VALKA 1954 d: Arne Mattsson. SWD/ICL., *Fuglinn I Fjorunni*, Halldor Laxness, 1931-32, Novel, *Pu Vinvidur Hreini*, Halldor Laxness, 1931-32, Novel

SALLY 1925 d: Alfred E. Green. USA., *Sally*, Guy Bolton, Clifford Grey, P. G. Wodehouse, New York 1920, Musical Play

SALLY 1929 d: John Francis Dillon. USA., *Sally*, Guy Bolton, Clifford Grey, P. G. Wodehouse, New York 1920, Musical Play

SALLY ANN'S STRATEGY 1912 d: Walter Edwin. USA., *Sally Ann's Strategy*, Louise Alvord, Story

SALLY BISHOP 1916 d: George Pearson. UKN., *Sally Bishop*, E. Temple Thurston, Novel

SALLY BISHOP 1923 d: Maurice Elvey. UKN., *Sally Bishop*, E. Temple Thurston, Novel

SALLY BISHOP 1932 d: T. Hayes Hunter. UKN., *Sally Bishop*, E. Temple Thurston, Novel

SALLY IN OUR ALLEY 1913 d: Colin Campbell. USA., *Sally in Our Alley*, Henry Carey, c1715, Song

SALLY IN OUR ALLEY 1916 d: Travers Vale. USA., *Sally in Our Alley*, Henry Carey, c1715, Song

SALLY IN OUR ALLEY 1931 d: Maurice Elvey. UKN., *The Likes of Her*, Charles McEvoy, London 1923, Play

SALLY, IRENE AND MARY 1925 d: Edmund Goulding. USA., *Sally Irene and Mary*, Edward Dowling, Cyrus Wood, New York 1922, Play

SALLY, IRENE AND MARY 1938 d: William A. Seiter. USA., *Sally Irene and Mary*, Edward Dowling, Cyrus Wood, New York 1922, Play

SALLY OF THE SAWDUST 1925 d: D. W. Griffith. USA., *Poppy*, Dorothy Donnelly, New York 1923, Play

Sally Shows the Way *see* ANNIE-FOR-SPITE (1917).

SALLY'S IRISH ROGUE 1958 d: George Pollock. UKN., *The New Gossoon*, George Shiels, Novel

SALLY'S SHOULDERS 1928 d: Lynn Shores. USA., *Sally's Shoulders*, Beatrice Burton, New York 1927, Novel

SALO O LE CENTOVENTI GIORNATE DI SODOMA 1975 d: Pier Paolo Pasolini. ITL/FRN., *Les 120 Journees de Sodome Ou l'Ecole du Libertinage*, Donatien Sade, 1904, Novel

Salo Or the 120 Days of Sodom *see* SALO O LE CENTOVENTI GIORNATE DI SODOMA (1975).

Salo Ou Les 120 Journees de Sodome *see* SALO O LE CENTOVENTI GIORNATE DI SODOMA (1975).

Salo -the 120 Days of Sodom *see* SALO O LE CENTOVENTI GIORNATE DI SODOMA (1975).

SALOME 1908 d: Albert Capellani?. FRN., *Salome*, Oscar Wilde, 1893, Play

Salome *see* THE DANCE OF THE SEVEN VEILS SALOME; OR (1908).

SALOME 1910 d: Ugo FalenA. ITL., *Salome*, Oscar Wilde, 1893, Play

SALOME 1918 d: J. Gordon Edwards. USA., *The Jewish Antiquities*, Flavius Josephus, 93-94 a.D., Book

SALOME 1922 d: Charles Bryant. USA., *Salome*, Oscar Wilde, 1893, Play

SALOME 1971 d: Werner Schroeter. GRM., *Salome*, Oscar Wilde, 1893, Play

SALOME 1972 d: Carmelo Bene. ITL., *Salome*, Oscar Wilde, 1893, Play

SALOME 1986 d: Claude d'AnnA. FRN/ITL., *Salome*, Oscar Wilde, 1893, Play

SALOME OF THE TENEMENTS 1925 d: Sidney Olcott. USA., *Salome of the Tenements*, Anzia Yezierska, New York 1923, Novel

SALOME; OR, THE DANCE OF THE SEVEN VEILS 1908 d: J. Stuart Blackton. USA., *Salome*, Oscar Wilde, 1893, Play

SALOME'S LAST DANCE 1988 d: Ken Russell. UKN., *Salome*, Oscar Wilde, 1893, Play

SALOMY JANE 1914 d: Lucius Henderson, William Nigh. USA., *Salomy Jane's Kiss*, Bret Harte, 1900, Short Story

SALOMY JANE 1923 d: George Melford. USA., *Salomy Jane's Kiss*, Bret Harte, 1900, Short Story

Salomy Jane *see* WILD GIRL (1932).

SALON MEXICO 1996 d: Jose Luis Garcia Agraz. MXC., *Salon Mexico*, Rafael Ramirez Heredia, Short Story

SALOON BAR 1940 d: Walter Forde. UKN., *Saloon Bar*, Frank Harvey Jr., London 1939, Play

SALT OF THE EARTH 1917 d: Saul Harrison. USA., *Salt of the Earth*, Peter B. Kyne, 1917, Short Story

SALT ON OUR SKIN 1992 d: Andrew Birkin. GRM/CND/FRN., *Les Vaisseaux du Coeur*, Benoit Groult, Novel

Salt to the Devil *see* GIVE US THIS DAY (1949).

Saltimbanchi, I *see* LES SALTIMBANQUES (1930).

SALTIMBANCII 1981 d: Elisabeta Bostan. RMN/USS., *Fram Ursul Polar*, Cezar Petrescu, 1932, Novel

SALTIMBANQUES, LES 1930 d: Jaquelux, Robert Land. FRN/GRM/ITL., *Les Saltimbanques*, Louis Ganne, Maurice Ordonneau, Opera

SALTO MORTALE 1931 d: E. A. Dupont. FRN., *Salto Mortale*, Alfred Machard, Novel

SALUTE JOHN CITIZEN 1942 d: Maurice Elvey. UKN., *Mr. Bunting*, Robert Greenwood, Novel, *Mr. Bunting at War*, Robert Greenwood, Novel

Salute the Motherland *see* VANDE MATARAM (1939).

SALUTE THE TOFF 1952 d: MacLean Rogers. UKN., *Salute the Toff*, John Creasey, Novel

Salute to the Great MacArthy, A *see* THE GREAT MACARTHY (1975).

Salvaje Kurdistan *see* DURCHS WILDE KURDISTAN (1965).

SALVAJES EN PUENTE SAN GIL, LOS 1967 d: Antoni Ribas. SPN., *Las Salvajes En Puente San Gil*, Jose Martin Recuerda, 1963, Play

SALVATION ARMY LASS, THE 1909 d: D. W. Griffith. USA., *Salvation Nell*, Edward Sheldon, New York 1908, Play

SALVATION NELL 1915 d: George E. Middleton. USA., *Salvation Nell*, Edward Sheldon, New York 1908, Play

SALVATION NELL 1921 d: Kenneth Webb. USA., *Salvation Nell*, Edward Sheldon, New York 1908, Play

SALVATION NELL 1931 d: James Cruze. USA., *Salvation Nell*, Edward Sheldon, New York 1908, Play

SALVATION OF NANCE O'SHAUGNESSY, THE 1914 d: Colin Campbell. USA., *The Salvation of Nance O'Shaughnessy*, Honore Wilsie, Story

Salvation Road *see* VEREDA DA SALVACAO (1965).

SALZBURG CONNECTION, THE 1972 d: Lee H. Katzin. USA., *The Salburg Connection*, Helen MacInnes, Novel

Salzburg Everyman, The *see* JEDERMANN (1961).

Salzburg Stories *see* SALZBURGER GESCHICHTEN (1957).

SALZBURGER GESCHICHTEN 1957 d: Kurt Hoffmann. GRM., *Georg Und Die Zwischenfalle*, Erich Kastner, 1938, Novel

Sam Marlowe, Private Eye *see* THE MAN WITH BOGART'S FACE (1980).

Samapti *see* TEEN KANYA (1961).

Samaritan, The *see* A HARP IN HOCK (1927).

SAMBIZANGA 1972 d: Sarah Maldoror. CNG/FRN., Luandino Vieira, Short Story

Same Skin, The *see* COUNTRY DANCE (1969).

SAME TIME, NEXT YEAR 1978 d: Robert Mulligan. USA., *Same Time Next Year*, Bernard Slade, Play

Samkauli Satr Posatvis *see* OZERELE DLJA MOEJ LJUBIMOJ (1972).

SAMMY GOING SOUTH 1963 d: Alexander MacKendrick. UKN., *Sammy Going South*, W. H. Canway, London 1961, Novel

SAMOURAI, LE 1967 d: Jean-Pierre Melville. FRN/ITL., *The Ronin*, Goan McLeod, Story

SAMPO 1959 d: Alexander Ptushko, Gregg Sebelious. USS/FNL., *Kalevala*, Elias Lonnrot, 1835, Verse

SAM'S BOY 1922 d: Manning Haynes. UKN., *Sam's Boy*, W. W. Jacobs, Novel

Samsara *see* LUNHUI (1988).

SAMSKARA 1970 d: Pattabhi Rama Reddy. IND., *Samskara*, U. R. Ananthamurthy, 1966, Novel

SAMSON 1915 d: Edgar Lewis. USA., *Samson*, Henri Bernstein, New York 1908, Play

SAMSON 1936 d: Maurice Tourneur. FRN., *Samson*, Henri Bernstein, New York 1908, Play

SAMSON 1961 d: Andrzej WajdA. PLN., *Samson*, Kazimierz Brandys, 1948, Novel

SAMSON AND DELILAH 1922 d: Edwin J. Collins. UKN., *Samson Et Dalila*, Charles Saint-Saens, Weimar 1877, Opera

SAMSON AND DELILAH 1927 d: H. B. Parkinson. UKN., *Samson Et Dalila*, Charles Saint-Saens, Weimar 1877, Opera

SAMSON AND DELILAH 1967 d: Peter Plummer. UKN., *Samson and Delilah*, D. H. Lawrence, Short Story

Samurai see MIYAMOTO MUSASHI (1954).

SAMURAI 1965 d: Kihachi Okamoto. JPN., *Samurai Nippon*, Jiromasa Gunji, Novel

Samurai Assassin see SAMURAI (1965).

Samurai Banners see FURIN KAZAN (1969).

Samurai Ii: Duel at Ichijoji Temple see MIYAMOTO MUSASHI: ICHIJOJI NO KETTO (1955).

Samurai III: Duel on Ganryu Island see MIYAMOTO MUSASHI: KETTO GANRYUJIMA (1956).

Samurai (Part Ii) see MIYAMOTO MUSASHI: ICHIJOJI NO KETTO (1955).

Samurai (Part III) see MIYAMOTO MUSASHI: KETTO GANRYUJIMA (1956).

Samurai Rebellion see JOIUCHI - HAIRYOZUMA SHIMATSU (1967).

Samurai Reincarnation see MAKAI TENSHO (1981).

Samurai, The see LE SAMOURAI (1967).

SAN ANTONE 1952 d: Joseph Kane. USA., *San Antone*, Curt Carroll, Short Story

SAN ANTONIO NE PENSE QU'A CA 1981 d: Joel SeriA. FRN., *San Antonio Ne Pense Qu'a Ca*, Frederic Dard, Novel

SAN DOMINGO 1970 d: Hans-Jurgen Syberberg. GRM., *Die Verlobung von San Domingo*, Heinrich von Kleist, 1811, Short Story

SAN FRANCISCO STORY, THE 1952 d: Robert Parrish. USA., *Vigilante*, Richard Aldrich Summers, 1949, Novel

SAN GIOVANNI DECOLLATO 1917 d: Telemaco Ruggeri. ITL., *San Giuvanni Decullatu*, Nino Martoglio, 1908, Play

SAN GIOVANNI DECOLLATO 1940 d: Amleto Palermi. ITL., *San Giuvanni Decullatu*, Nino Martoglio, 1908, Play

SAN KAN HU DIE MENG 1958 d: Cai ZhenyA. CHN., *San Kan Hu Die Meng*, Guan Hanqing, c1230, Play

SAN MICHELE AVEVA UN GALLO 1972 d: Paolo Taviani, Vittorio Taviani. ITL., *Il Divino E l'Umano*, Lev Nikolayevich Tolstoy, Short Story

SAN SALVATORE 1956 d: Werner Jacobs. GRM., *San Salvatore*, Hans Kades, Novel

SAN SEBASTIANO 1911 d: Enrique Santos. ITL., *Fabiola Or the Church of the Catacombs*, Nicholas Patrick Wiseman, London 1854, Novel

SAN TOY 1900. UKN., *San Toy*, Edward Morton, London 1899, Play

SAN ZIMEI 1934 d: Li Pingqian. CHN., *Green Pearl*, Kan Kikuchi, Novel

Sanatorium see SANATORIUM POD KLEPSYDRA (1973).

Sanatorium Beneath the Obituary, A see SANATORIUM POD KLEPSYDRA (1973).

SANATORIUM POD KLEPSYDRA 1973 d: Wojciech J. Has. PLN., *Sanatorium Pod Klepsydra*, Bruno Schulz, 1937, Short Story

SANATORIUM POUR MAIGRIR 1909. FRN., *Sanatorium Pour Maigrir*, Ch. Esquier, Play

SANCTA MARIA 1941 d: Edgar Neville, Pier Luigi Faraldo. ITL/SPN., *Sancta Maria*, Guido Milanesi, Novel

SANCTUARY 1916 d: Claude Harris. UKN., *Sanctuary*, Malcolm Watson, Play

SANCTUARY 1961 d: Tony Richardson. USA., *Sanctuary*, William Faulkner, New York 1931, Novel

SANCTUARY OF FEAR 1979 d: John Llewellyn Moxey. USA., *Detective Father Brown*, G. K. Chesterton, Novel

SAND! 1920 d: Lambert Hillyer. USA., *Dan Kurrie's Inning*, Russell A. Boggs, Short Story

Sand see WILL JAMES' SAND (1949).

Sand Cliffs see FALEZE DE NISIP (1983).

SAND PEBBLES, THE 1966 d: Robert Wise. USA., *The Sand Pebbles*, Richard McKenna, New York 1962, Novel

SANDBURG'S LINCOLN 1974-76 d: George Schaefer. USA., *Abraham Lincoln*, Carl Sandburg, 1926-1939, Biography

Sanders see COAST OF SKELETONS (1964).

SANDERS OF THE RIVER 1935 d: Zoltan KordA. UKN., *Sanders of the River*, Edgar Wallace, London 1911, Novel

SANDFLOW 1936 d: Lesley Selander. USA., *Starr of the Southwest*, Cherry Wilson, 1936, Short Story

Sandglass, The see SANATORIUM POD KLEPSYDRA (1973).

SANDGRAFIN, DIE 1927 d: Hans Steinhoff. GRM., *Die Sandgrafin*, Gustav Frenssen, Novel

Sandman, The see DAS SANDMANNCHEN (1955).

SANDMANNCHEN, DAS 1955 d: Emil Surmann. GRM., *The Canterville Ghost*, Oscar Wilde, 1891, Short Story

SANDOK, IL MACISTE DELLA GIUNGLA 1964 d: Umberto Lenzi. ITL/FRN., *Sandok Il MacIste Della Giungla*, Fulvia Giacca, Novel

Sandok, the Giant of the Jungle see IL MACISTE DELLA GIUNGLA SANDOK (1964).

SANDOKAN 1964 d: Umberto Lenzi. SPN/FRN/ITL., *Le Tigri Di Mompracem*, Emilio Salgari, Genoa 1900, Novel

Sandokan Against the Leopard of Sarawak see SANDOKAN CONTRO IL LEOPARDO DI SARAWAK (1965).

SANDOKAN ALLA RISCOSSA 1964 d: Luigi Capuano. ITL., Emilio Salgari, Novel

SANDOKAN CONTRO IL LEOPARDO DI SARAWAK 1965 d: Luigi Capuano. ITL/GRM., Emilio Salgari, Novel

Sandokan Fights Back see SANDOKAN ALLA RISCOSSA (1964).

Sandokan, la Tigre Di Mompracem see SANDOKAN (1964).

Sandokan, le Tigre de Borneo see SANDOKAN (1964).

Sandokan Strikes Back see SANDOKAN ALLA RISCOSSA (1964).

Sandokan the Great see SANDOKAN (1964).

Sandokan Und Der Leopard see SANDOKAN CONTRO IL LEOPARDO DI SARAWAK (1965).

Sandpit Generals, The see THE WILD PACK (1971).

SANDRA 1924 d: Arthur H. Sawyer. USA., *Sandra*, Pearl Doles Bell, New York 1924, Novel

SANDS OF BEERSHEBA 1965 d: Alexander Ramati. USA/ISR., *Rebel Against the Light*, Alexander Ramati, New York 1960, Novel

SANDS OF DEE, THE 1912 d: D. W. Griffith. USA., *The Sands of Dee*, Charles Kingsley, Poem

SANDS OF THE KALAHARI 1965 d: Cy Endfield. UKN/SAF., *Sands of the Kalahari*, William Mulvihill, New York 1960, Novel

SANDS OF TIME, THE 1992 d: Gary Nelson. USA., *The Sands of Time*, Sidney Sheldon, Novel

Sand-Woman see SUNA NO ONNA (1964).

SANDY 1918 d: George Melford. USA., *Sandy*, Alice Hegan Rice, New York 1905, Novel

SANDY 1926 d: Harry Beaumont. USA., *Sandy*, Elenore Meherin, Story

SANDY GETS HER MAN 1940 d: Otis Garrett, Paul Gerard Smith. USA., *Save My Child Fireman*, Sy Bartlett, Story, *Fireman Save My Child*, Paul Girard Smith, Story

SANG A LA TETE, LE 1956 d: Gilles Grangier. FRN., *Le Fils Cardinaud*, Georges Simenon, 1942, Novel

SANG DES AUTRES, LE 1983 d: Claude Chabrol. FRN/CND., *Le Sang Des Autres*, Simone de Beauvoir, Novel

SANG DES FINOELS, LE 1922 d: Georges Monca, Rose Pansini. FRN., *Le Sang Des Finoel*, Andre Theuriet, Novel

Sang Et la Rose, Le see ET MOURIR DE PLAISIR (1960).

SANG ET LUMIERE 1954 d: Georges Rouquier, Ricardo Munoz Suay. FRN/SPN., *Sang Et Lumiere*, Joseph Peyre, Novel

SANGAREE 1953 d: Edward Ludwig. USA., *Sangaree*, Frank G. Slaughter, 1948, Novel

SANGEN OM DEN ELDRODA BLOMMAN 1918 d: Mauritz Stiller. SWD., *Laulu Tulipunaisesta Kukasta*, Johannes Linnankoski, 1905, Novel

SANGEN OM DEN ELDRODA BLOMMAN 1934 d: Per-Axel Branner. SWD., *Laulu Tulipunaisesta Kukasta*, Johannes Linnankoski, 1905, Novel

Sangen Om Den Eldroda Blomman see LAULU TULIPUNAISESTA KUKASTA (1938).

SANGEN OM DEN ELDRODA BLOMMAN 1956 d: Gustaf Molander. SWD., *Laulu Tulipunaisesta Kukasta*, Johannes Linnankoski, 1905, Novel

Sangen Om Den Eldroda Blomman see LAULU TULIPUNAISESTA KUKASTA (1971).

SANGEN OM DEN RODE RUBIN 1970 d: Annelise Meineche. DNM., Agnar Mykle, Story

SANGEN TILL LIVET 1943 d: Leif Sinding. NRW., Sigurd Braa, Johan Bojer, 1916, Play

SANGHARSH 1968 d: H. S. Rawail. IND., *Sangharsh*, Mahashweta Devi, Story

SANGO MALO 1990 d: Bassek Ba Kobhio. CMR/BRK., *Sango Malo - le Maitre du Canton*, Bassek Ba Kobhio, Novel

Sangre En Indochina see LA 317EME SECTION (1965).

SANGRE NEGRA 1948 d: Pierre Chenal. ARG/USA., *Native Son*, Richard Wright, 1940, Novel

Sangre Y Luces see SANG ET LUMIERE (1954).

Sangue E la Rosa, Il see ET MOURIR DE PLAISIR (1960).

SANGUE ROMAGNOLO 1916 d: Leopoldo Carlucci. ITL., *Cuore*, Edmondo de Amicis, 1886, Short Story

Sangue Sull'asfalto see DELIT DE FUITE (1958).

Sanjuro see TSUBAKI SANJURO (1962).

SANKT HANS FEST 1947 d: Toralf Sando. NRW., *Sankt Hans Fest*, Alexander Kielland, 1887, Short Story

SANNIAN ZAO ZHIDAO 1958 d: Wang Yan. CHN., *Sannian Zao Zhidao*, Ma Feng, Novel

SANS ESPOIR DE RETOUR 1989 d: Samuel Fuller. FRN/PRT., *Street of No Return*, David Goodis, Novel

SANS FAMILLE 1913 d: Georges MoncA. FRN., *Sans Famille*, Hector Malot, Novel

SANS FAMILLE 1925 d: Georges Monca, Maurice Keroul. FRN., *Sans Famille*, Hector Malot, Novel

SANS FAMILLE 1934 d: Marc Allegret. FRN., *Sans Famille*, Hector Malot, Novel

SANS FAMILLE 1957 d: Andre Michel. FRN/ITL., *Sans Famille*, Hector Malot, Novel

SANS FORTUNE 1922 d: Geo Kessler. FRN., *Sans Fortune*, Ludovic Morin, Novel

SANS MOBILE APPARENT 1971 d: Philippe Labro. FRN/ITL., *Ten Plus One*, Evan Hunter, 1963, Novel

SANS PITIE 1916. FRN., *Sans Pitie*, Pierre Maldagne, Novel

Sans Pitie see SIN COMPASION (1994).

Sans Tambour Ni Trompette see DIE GANS VON SEDAN (1959).

SANS TAMBOUR, NI TROMPETTE 1949 d: Roger Blanc. FRN., *Un Dimanche Au Champ d'Honneur*, Jean L'Hote, Paris 1958, Novel

Sanshiro Sugata see SUGATA SANSHIRO (1943).

Sanshiro Sugata Part II see ZOKU SUGATA SANSHIRO (1945).

Sanshiro Sugata Zoku see ZOKU SUGATA SANSHIRO (1945).

Sansho Daiyu see SANSHO DAYU (1954).

SANSHO DAYU 1954 d: Kenji Mizoguchi. JPN., *Chuo Koron*, Mori Ogai, 1915, Short Story

Sansho the Bailiff see SANSHO DAYU (1954).

SANSIBAR ODER DER LETZTE GRUND 1986 d: Bernhard Wicki. GRM/GDR., *Zanzibar*, Alfred Andersch, Novel

SANSONE 1922 d: Torello Rolli. ITL., *Samson*, Henri Bernstein, New York 1908, Play

SANTA CECILIA 1919 d: Vasco Salvini. ITL., *Santa Cecilia*, Anton Giulio Barrili, 1866, Novel

SANTA FE 1951 d: Irving Pichel. USA., *Santa Fe; the Railroad That Built an Empire*, James Leslie Marshall, 1945, Book

SANTA FE PASSAGE 1955 d: William Witney. USA., *Santa Fe Passage*, Clay Fisher, Short Story

Santa Fe Satan see CATCH MY SOUL (1974).

SANTA FE TRAIL, THE 1930 d: Otto Brower, Edwin H. Knopf. USA., *Spanish Acres*, Hal G. Evarts, Boston 1925, Novel

SANTA ISABEL DE CERES 1923 d: Jose Sobrado de OnegA. SPN., Alfonso Vidal Y Planas, Play

Santa Rogelia see **IL PECCATO DI ROGELIA SANCHEZ** (1939).

SANTARELLINA 1912 d: Mario Caserini. ITL., *Mam'zelle Nitouche*, Herve, Henri Meilhac, Albert Milhaud, Paris 1882, Operetta

SANTARELLINA 1923 d: Eugenio Perego. ITL., *Mam'zelle Nitouche*, Herve, Henri Meilhac, Albert Milhaud, Paris 1882, Operetta

Santarellina see **IL DIAVOLO VA IN COLLEGIO** (1944).

Santarellina see **MAM'ZELLE NITOUCHE** (1954).

SANT'ILARIO 1923 d: Henry Kolker. ITL., *Sant'Ilario*, F. Marion Crawford, Novel

SANTITOS 1999 d: Alejandro Springall. MXC., *Santitos*, Maria Amparo Escandon, Novel

SANTO DISONORE 1949 d: Guido Brignone. ITL., *Santo Disonore*, Leone Ciprelli, Play

SANTO MILAGROSO, O 1965 d: Carlos CoimbrA. BRZ., *O Santo Milagroso*, Lauro Cesar Muniz, 1967, Play

Santo Prende la Mira, Il see **LE SAINT PREND L'AFFUT** (1966).

SANTOS INOCENTES, LOS 1984 d: Mario Camus. SPN., *Los Santos Inocentes*, Miguel Delibes, 1981, Novel

SAO BERNARDO 1972 d: Leon Hirszman. BRZ., *Sao Bernardo*, Graciliano Ramos, 1934, Novel

Sap Abroad, The see **THE SAP FROM SYRACUSE** (1930).

SAP FROM SYRACUSE, THE 1930 d: A. Edward Sutherland. USA., *A Sap from Syracuse*, John Hayden, J. O'Donnell, John Wray, Play

SAP, THE 1926 d: Erle C. Kenton. USA., *The Sap*, William A. Grew, New York 1924, Play

SAP, THE 1929 d: Archie Mayo. USA., *The Sap*, William A. Grew, New York 1924, Play

SAPHEAD, THE 1920 d: Herbert Blache. USA., *The Henrietta*, Bronson Howard, New York 1887, Play, *The New Henrietta*, Victor Mapes, Winchell Smith, New York 1913, Play

SAPHO 1913 d: W. Christy Cabanne. USA., *Sapho*, Alphonse Daudet, Paris 1884, Novel

SAPHO 1917 d: Hugh Ford. USA., *Sapho*, Alphonse Daudet, Paris 1884, Novel

SAPHO 1934 d: Leonce Perret. FRN., *Sapho*, Alphonse Daudet, Paris 1884, Novel

Sapho see **SAPHO OU LA FUREUR D'AIMER** (1970).

SAPHO OU LA FUREUR D'AIMER 1970 d: Georges Farrel. FRN/ITL., *Sapho*, Alphonse Daudet, Paris 1884, Novel

SAPOGI 1957 d: Vladimir Niemoliaiev. USS., *Sapogi*, Anton Chekhov, 1884-85, Short Story

Sapore Della Paura, Il see **LA TRAQUE** (1975).

SAPPHO 1913. USA., *Sapho*, Alphonse Daudet, Paris 1884, Novel

Sappho see **SAPHO** (1913).

SAPPHO 1922. UKN., *Sapho*, Alphonse Daudet, Paris 1884, Novel

Sappho, Story of a Passion see **HISTORIA DE UNA PASION SAFO** (1943).

Saqueadores Del Domingo, Los see **L' HOMME DE MARRAKECH** (1966).

SARA AKASH 1969 d: Basu Chatterjee. IND., *Sara Akas*, Rajendra Yadagv, 1960, Novel

Sara Crewe see **THE LITTLE PRINCESS** (1939).

SARA DANE 1982 d: Rod Hardy, Gary Conway. ASL., *Sara Dane*, Catherine Gaskin, Novel

SARABA MOSUKUWA GURENTAI 1968 d: Hiromichi HorikawA. JPN., *Saraba Mosukuwa Gurentai*, Hirosuki Itsuki, Tokyo 1967, Short Story

Saraband see **SARABAND FOR DEAD LOVERS** (1948).

SARABAND FOR DEAD LOVERS 1948 d: Basil Dearden, Michael Relph. UKN., *Saraband for Dead Lovers*, Helen Simpson, 1935, Novel

SARACEN BLADE, THE 1954 d: William Castle. USA., *The Saracen Blade*, Frank Yerby, 1952, Novel

Saragossa Manuscript, The see **REKOPIS ZNALEZIONY W SARAGOSSIE** (1965).

SARAH AND SON 1930 d: Dorothy Arzner. USA., *Sarah and Son*, Timothy Shea, New York 1929, Novel

SARAH, PLAIN AND TALL 1991 d: Glenn Jordan. USA., *Plain and Tall Sarah*, Patricia MacLachlan, Novel

SARAKA BO 1977 d: Denis Amar. FRN., *Sarako Bo*, Tobie Nathan, Novel

Saraswati Chandra see **SARASWATICHANDRA** (1968).

SARASWATICHANDRA 1968 d: Govind SaraiyA. IND., *Saraswatichandra*, Govardhanram Tripathi, Novel

SARATI LE TERRIBLE 1923 d: Louis Mercanton, Rene Hervil. FRN., *Sarati le Terrible*, Jean Vignaud, Novel

SARATI LE TERRIBLE 1937 d: Andre Hugon. FRN., *Sarati le Terrible*, Jean Vignaud, Novel

SARATOGA TRUNK 1945 d: Sam Wood. USA., *Saratoga Trunk*, Edna Ferber, 1941, Novel

Sardinian Drummer Boy see **IL TAMBURINO SARDO** (1911).

Sardonicus see **MR. SARDONICUS** (1961).

SARG AUS HONGKONG, EIN 1964 d: Manfred R. Kohler. GRM/FRN., James Hadley Chase, Novel

SARRAOUNIA 1986 d: Abid Med Hondo. BRK., *Sarraounia*, Abdoulaye Mamani, Book

Sas a San Salvador see **S.A.S. A SAN SALVADOR** (1982).

S.A.S. A SAN SALVADOR 1982 d: Raoul Coutard. FRN/GRM., *S.a.S. a San Salvador*, Gerald de Villiers, Novel

Sasa Meyuki see **SASAMEYUKI** (1983).

SASAMEYUKI 1983 d: Kon IchikawA. JPN., *Sasame Yuki*, Junichiro Tanizaki, 1948, Novel

Satan see **SATANA** (1912).

Satan and the Naked Woman see **DIE NACKTE UND DER SATAN** (1959).

SATAN AND THE WOMAN 1928 d: Burton L. King. USA., *Courage*, Mary Lanier Magruder, Short Story

SATAN BUG, THE 1965 d: John Sturges. USA., *The Satan Bug*, Ian Stuart, New York 1963, Novel

SATAN JUNIOR 1919 d: Herbert Blache, John H. Collins. USA., *Diana Ardway*, Van Zo Post, Philadelphia 1913, Novel

SATAN MET A LADY 1936 d: William Dieterle. USA., *The Maltese Falcon*, Dashiell Hammett, New York 1930, Novel

SATAN NEVER SLEEPS 1962 d: Leo McCarey. USA/UKN., *Satan Never Sleeps*, Pearl Buck, New York 1952, Novel

SATAN SANDERSON 1915 d: John W. Noble. USA., *Satan Sanderson*, Hallie Erminie Rives, Indianapolis 1907, Novel

SATANA 1912 d: Luigi Maggi. ITL., *Paradise Lost*, John Milton, 1667

SATANELLA 1919 d: Joseph Guarino, A. G. CaldierA. ITL., *Satanella*, Carolina Invernizio, 1897, Novel

Satanic Games see **PAARUNGEN** (1967).

Satan's Bride see **TO THE DEVIL A DAUGHTER** (1976).

Satan's Five Warnings see **LAS CINCO ADVERTENCIAS DE SATANAS** (1938).

Satan's Five Warnings see **LAS CINCO ADVERTENCIAS DE SATANAS** (1969).

SATAN'S SISTER 1925 d: George Pearson. UKN., *Satan; a Romance of the Bahamas*, Henry de Vere Stacpoole, New York 1921, Novel

SATOGASHI GA KOWARERU TOKI 1967 d: Tadashi Imai. JPN., *Satogashi Ga Kowareru Toki*, Ayako Sono, 1965, Novel

SATOMI HAKKEN DEN 1984 d: Kinji Fukasaku. JPN., *Satomi Hakkenden*, Hutaro Yamada, Novel

Satoshi Ga Kowareru Toki see **SATOGASHI GA KOWARERU TOKI** (1967).

SATSUJIN KYO JIDAI 1967 d: Kihachi Okamoto. JPN., *Ueta Isan*, Michio Tsuzuki, Novel

SATURDAY ISLAND 1951 d: Stuart Heisler. UKN., *Saturday Island*, Hugh Brooke, Novel

Saturday Night see **LA NOCHE DEL SABADO** (1950).

SATURDAY NIGHT AND SUNDAY MORNING 1960 d: Karel Reisz. UKN., *Saturday Night and Sunday Morning*, Alan Sillitoe, London 1958, Novel

SATURDAY NIGHT FEVER 1977 d: John Badham. USA., Nik Cohn, Story

Saturday, Sunday and Monday see **DOMENICA E LUNEDI SABATO** (1990).

Saturday to Monday see **EXPERIMENTAL MARRIAGE** (1919).

SATURDAY'S CHILDREN 1929 d: Gregory La CavA. USA., *Saturday's Children*, Maxwell Anderson, New York 1927, Play

SATURDAY'S CHILDREN 1940 d: Vincent Sherman. USA., *Saturday's Children*, Maxwell Anderson, New York 1927, Play

SATURDAY'S CHILDREN 1950. USA., *Saturday's Children*, Maxwell Anderson, New York 1927, Play

SATURDAY'S CHILDREN 1952. USA., *Saturday's Children*, Maxwell Anderson, New York 1927, Play

SATURDAY'S CHILDREN 1962 d: Leland Hayward. USA., *Saturday's Children*, Maxwell Anderson, New York 1927, Play

SATURDAY'S HERO 1951 d: David Miller. USA., *The Hero*, Millard Lampell, 1949, Book

SATURN 3 1980 d: Stanley Donen. UKN., *Saturn 3*, John Barry, Short Story

SATY DELAJI CLOVECKA 1912 d: Max Urban, Jara Sedlacek. CZC., *Much Ado About Nothing*, William Shakespeare, c1598, Play

SATYAKAM 1969 d: Hrishikesh Mukherjee. IND., *Satyakam*, Narayan Sanyal, Novel

SATYRICON 1968 d: Gian Luigi Polidoro. ITL., *Satyricon*, Petronius Arbiter, c50-66 a.D., Manuscript

Satyricon see **FELLINI-SATYRICON** (1969).

SAUCE FOR THE GOOSE 1918 d: Walter Edwards. USA., *Sauce for the Goose*, Geraldine Bonner, Hutcheson Boyd, New York 1911, Play

SAUERBRUCH 1954 d: Rolf Hansen. GRM., *Sauerbruch - Das War Mein Leben*, Ernst Ferdinand Sauerbruch, Autobiography

Sauerbruch - Das War Mein Leben see **SAUERBRUCH** (1954).

Sauf Votre Respect see **TRY THIS ONE FOR SIZE** (1989).

SAUT DE L'ANGE, LE 1971 d: Yves Boisset. FRN/ITL., *Le Saut de l'Ange*, Bernard-Paul Lallier, Novel

SAUTELA BHAI 1962 d: Mahesh Kaul. IND., *Boikunther Will*, Saratchandra Chatterjee, 1916, Novel

SAVAGE INNOCENTS, THE 1959 d: Nicholas Ray, Baccio Bandini. UKN/FRN/ITL., *Top of the World*, Hans Ruesch, New York 1950, Novel

Savage Instinct, The see **THE HEART OF THE BLUE RIDGE** (1915).

Savage Land see **YUAN YE** (1988).

Savage Pampas see **PAMPA SALVAJE** (1966).

Savage Planet, The see **LA PLANETE SAUVAGE** (1973).

SAVAGE SAM 1963 d: Norman Tokar. USA., *Savage Sam*, Fred Gipson, New York 1962, Novel

SAVAGE, THE 1926 d: Fred Newmeyer. USA., *The Savage*, Ernest Pascal, Story

SAVAGE, THE 1952 d: George Marshall. USA., *The Renegade*, L. L. Foreman, 1942, Novel

Savage Triangle see **LE GARCON SAUVAGE** (1951).

SAVAGE WILDERNESS 1955 d: Anthony Mann. USA., *The Gilded Rooster*, Richard Emery Roberts, 1947, Novel

SAVAGE WOMAN, THE 1918 d: Edmund Mortimer, Robert G. VignolA. USA., *La Fille Sauvage*, Francois de Curel, Paris 1902, Play

SAVAGES 1974 d: Lee H. Katzin. USA., *Death Watch*, Robb White, Story

Savages of St. Gil's Bridge see **LOS SALVAJES EN PUENTE SAN GIL** (1967).

Savarona Syndrome, The see **THE LONELY PROFESSION** (1969).

SAVE A LITTLE SUNSHINE 1938 d: Norman Lee. UKN., *Lights Out at Eleven*, W. Armitage Owen, Play

SAVE THE LADY 1982 d: Leon Thau. ASL., *Save the Lady*, Yoram Gross, Novel

SAVED BY A SKIRT 1915 d: Horace Davey. USA., *Saved By a Skirt*, Neal Burns, Story

SAVED FROM THE SEA 1908. UKN., *Saved from the Sea*, Ben Landeck, Arthur Shirley, London 1895, Play

SAVED FROM THE SEA 1920 d: W. P. Kellino. UKN., *Saved from the Sea*, Ben Landeck, Arthur Shirley, London 1895, Play

Savelli, La see **FANATISME** (1934).

SAVING GRACE 1986 d: Robert M. Young. USA., *Saving Grace*, Celia Gittelson, Novel

SAVING GRACE 1998 d: Costa Bodes. NZL., *Saving Grace*, Duncan Sarkies, Play

SAVING OF YOUNG ANDERSON, THE 1914. USA., *The Saving of Young Anderson*, O. Henry, Short Story

SAXO 1987 d: Ariel Zeitoun. FRN., *Saxo*, Gilbert Tanugi, Novel

SAXON CHARM, THE 1948 d: Claude Binyon. USA., *The Saxon Charm*, Frederic Wakeman, Novel

SAXOPHON-SUSI 1928 d: Carl Lamac. GRM., *Saxophon-Susi*, Hans H. Zerlett, Play

SAY IT IN FRENCH 1938 d: Andrew L. Stone. USA., *Soubrette*, Jacques Deval, Vienna 1938, Play

SAYONARA 1957 d: Joshua Logan. USA., *Sayonara*, James A. Michener, 1954, Novel

SAYONARA JIYUPETA 1983 d: Koji Hashimoto. JPN., *Sayonara Jiyupeta*, Sakyo Komatsu, Novel

SBAGLIO DI ESSERE VIVO, LO 1945 d: Carlo Ludovico BragagliA. ITL., *Lo Sbaglio Di Essere Vivo*, Aldo de Benedetti, Play

SBANDATA, LA 1974 d: Alfredo Malfatti. ITL., *Il Volantino*, Pietro Buttitta, Novel

SBARCO DI ANZIO, LO 1968 d: Edward Dmytryk, Duilio Coletti. ITL., *Anzio*, Wynford Vaughan-Thomas, New York 1961, Book

Sbarra, La *see* **L' ISPETTORE VARGAS** (1940).

SCACCO ALLA REGINA 1969 d: Pasquale Festa Campanile. ITL/GRM., *Scacco Alla Regina*, Renato Ghiotto, Novel

SCALA DI SETA, LA 1920 d: Arnaldo Frateili. ITL., *La Scala Di Seta*, Luigi Chiarelli, 1917, Play

SCALA, LA 1931 d: Gennaro Righelli. ITL., *La Scala*, Pier Maria Rosso Di San Secondo, Play

SCALDALETTO, LO 1915 d: Gino Rossetti. ITL., *O Scarfalietto*, Eduardo Scarpetta, 1881, Play

SCALDINO, LO 1920 d: Augusto GeninA. ITL., *Lo Scaldino*, Luigi Pirandello, Short Story

SCALES OF JUSTICE, THE 1914 d: Thomas N. Heffron. USA., *The Scales of Justice*, John Rinehardt, Play

SCALLYWAG, THE 1921 d: Challis Sanderson. UKN., *The Scallywag*, Grant Allen, Novel

Scalpel *see* **BAD FOR EACH OTHER** (1953).

Scalpel, Please *see* **PROSIM SKALPEL** (1986).

SCAM 1993 d: John Flynn. USA., *Ladystinger*, Craig Smith, Novel

Scambio Della Anime, Lo *see* **AVATAR** (1916).

SCAMP, THE 1957 d: Wolf RillA. UKN., *Uncertain Joy*, Charlotte Hastings, London 1953, Play

SCAMPOLO 1917 d: Giuseppe Sterni. ITL., *Scampolo*, Dario Niccodemi, 1915, Play

Scampolo *see* **DAS MADCHEN DER STRASSE** (1928).

Scampolo *see* **UN PEU D'AMOUR** (1933).

SCAMPOLO 1941 d: Nunzio MalasommA. ITL., *Scampolo*, Dario Niccodemi, 1915, Play

SCAMPOLO 1958 d: Alfred Weidenmann. GRM., *Scampolo*, Dario Niccodemi, 1915, Play

SCAMPOLO '53 1954 d: Giorgio Bianchi. ITL/FRN., *Scampolo*, Dario Niccodemi, 1915, Play

SCAMPOLO, EIN KIND DER STRASSE 1932 d: Hans Steinhoff. AUS/GRM., *Scampolo*, Dario Niccodemi, 1915, Play

SCANDAL 1929 d: Wesley Ruggles. USA., *The Haunted Lady*, Adela Rogers St. Johns, 1925, Short Story

SCANDAL AT SCOURIE 1953 d: Jean Negulesco. USA., *Good Boy*, Mary McSherry, Short Story

Scandal at the Embassy *see* **SKANDAL IN DER BOTSCHAFT** (1950).

SCANDAL FOR SALE 1932 d: Russell MacK. USA., *Hot News*, Emile Gauvreau, New York 1931, Novel

Scandal House *see* **SLANDER HOUSE** (1938).

SCANDAL IN BOHEMIA, A 1921 d: Maurice Elvey. UKN., *A Scandal in Bohemia*, Arthur Conan Doyle, Short Story

Scandal in Bohemia, A *see* **THE ADVENTURES OF SHERLOCK HOLMES: A SCANDAL IN BOHEMIA** (1984).

Scandal in Denmark *see* **DER KOM EN SOLDAT** (1969).

Scandal in Paris, A *see* **DIE FRAU AUF DER FOLTER** (1928).

Scandal Market *see* **SCANDAL FOR SALE** (1932).

Scandal Sheet *see* **SCANDAL FOR SALE** (1932).

SCANDAL SHEET 1952 d: Phil Karlson. USA., *The Dark Page*, Samuel Fuller, 1944, Novel

SCANDAL, THE 1923 d: Arthur Rooke. UKN/FRN., *Le Scandale*, Henry Bataille, 1909, Play

Scandal, The *see* **EL ESCANDALO** (1943).

Scandale a Rome *see* **ROMA BENE** (1971).

SCANDALE, LE 1916 d: Jacques de Baroncelli. FRN., *Le Scandale*, Henry Bataille, 1909, Play

Scandale, Le *see* **THE SCANDAL** (1923).

SCANDALE, LE 1934 d: Marcel L'Herbier. FRN., *Le Scandale*, Henry Bataille, 1909, Play

SCANDALO PER BENE 1940 d: Esodo Pratelli. ITL., *Dui Gentiluomini Veneziani Onoratamente Da le Moglie Sono.*, Matteo Maria Bandello, Novel

Scandalous Adventures of Buraikan, The *see* **BURAIKAN** (1970).

Scandals of Clochemerle, The *see* **CLOCHEMERLE** (1947).

SCANO BOA 1961 d: Renato Dall'arA. ITL/SPN., *Scano Boa*, G. A. Cibotto, Novel

SCAPEGOAT, THE 1959 d: Robert Hamer. UKN/USA., *The Scapegoat*, Daphne Du Maurier, 1957, Novel

Scapegoat, The *see* **IL FORNARETTO DI VENEZIA** (1963).

Scapegoat, The *see* **TARNAGOL KAPAROT** (1991).

Scappamento Aperto *see* **ECHAPPEMENT LIBRE** (1964).

Scar, A *see* **BLIZNA** (1976).

Scar, The *see* **HOLLOW TRIUMPH** (1948).

SCARAB MURDER CASE, THE 1936 d: Michael Hankinson. UKN., *The Scarab Murder Case*, S. S. Van Dine, Novel

SCARAB RING, THE 1921 d: Edward Jose. USA., *The Desperate Heritage*, Harriet Gaylord, Story

Scarabea *see* **SCARABEA - WIEVIEL ERDE BRAUCHT DER MENSCH?** (1968).

SCARABEA - WIEVIEL ERDE BRAUCHT DER MENSCH? 1968 d: Hans-Jurgen Syberberg. GRM., *Mnogo Il Chelovka Zemli Nuzno?*, Lev Nikolayevich Tolstoy, 1885, Short Story

Scarabea -How Much Land Does a Man Need? *see* **SCARABEA - WIEVIEL ERDE BRAUCHT DER MENSCH?** (1968).

SCARABEE D'OR, LE 1910 d: Henri Desfontaines. FRN., *Gold Bug*, Edgar Allan Poe, 1843, Short Story

SCARAMOUCHE 1923 d: Rex Ingram. USA., *Scaramouche; a Romance of the French Revolution*, Rafael Sabatini, Boston 1921, Novel

SCARAMOUCHE 1952 d: George Sidney. USA., *Scaramouche; a Romance of the French Revolution*, Rafael Sabatini, Boston 1921, Novel

SCARAMOUCHE 1963 d: Antonio Isasi. FRN/SPN/ITL., *Scaramouche; a Romance of the French Revolution*, Rafael Sabatini, Boston 1921, Novel

Scarecrow of Oz, The *see* **THE SCARECROW OF OZ HIS MAJESTY** (1914).

Scarecrow of Romney Marsh, The *see* **DR. SYN - ALIAS THE SCARECROW** (1963).

Scarecrow, The *see* **PURITAN PASSIONS** (1923).

SCARECROW, THE 1981 d: Sam Pillsbury. NZL., *The Scarecrow*, Ronald Hugh Morrieson, Novel

Scarecrow, The *see* **TSCHUTSCHELO** (1986).

Scared! *see* **WHISTLING IN THE DARK** (1932).

SCARED STIFF 1953 d: George Marshall. USA., *The Ghost Breaker*, Paul Dickey, Charles W. Goddard, New York 1909, Play

SCARF JACK 1981 d: Chris McMaster. UKN., *Scarf Jack*, P. J. Kavanagh, Novel

SCARFACE 1932 d: Howard Hawks. USA., *Scarface*, Armitage Trail, New York 1930, Novel

SCARFACE MOB, THE 1962 d: Phil Karlson. USA., *The Untouchables*, Oscar Fraley, New York 1957, Book, *The Untouchables*, Eliot Ness, New York 1957, Book

Scarface, Shame of a Nation *see* **SCARFACE** (1932).

Scarlet and Black *see* **LE ROUGE ET LE NOIR** (1954).

SCARLET AND THE BLACK, THE 1982 d: Jerry London. USA/ITL., *The Scarlet Pimpernel of the Vatican*, J. P. Gallagher, Book

Scarlet Camellia, The *see* **GOBEN NO TSUBAKI** (1964).

SCARLET CAR, THE 1918 d: Joseph de Grasse. USA., *The Scarlet Car*, Richard Harding Davis, New York 1907, Novel

SCARLET CAR, THE 1923 d: Stuart Paton. USA., *Adventures of the Scarlet Car*, Richard Harding Davis, New York 1907, Novel

Scarlet Daredevil, The *see* **THE TRIUMPH OF THE SCARLET PIMPERNEL** (1928).

SCARLET DAWN 1932 d: William Dieterle. USA., *Revolt*, Mary McCall Jr., Novel

Scarlet Jungle, The *see* **SCOTLAND YARD JAGT DOKTOR MABUSE** (1963).

SCARLET KISS, THE 1920 d: Fred Goodwins. UKN., *The Scarlet Kiss*, Gertrude de S. Wentworth James, Novel

SCARLET LETTER, THE 1911 d: Joseph Smiley, George Loane Tucker. USA., *The Scarlet Letter*, Nathaniel Hawthorne, New York 1850, Novel

SCARLET LETTER, THE 1913 d: David Miles. USA., *The Scarlet Letter*, Nathaniel Hawthorne, New York 1850, Novel

SCARLET LETTER, THE 1917 d: Carl Harbaugh. USA., *The Scarlet Letter*, Nathaniel Hawthorne, New York 1850, Novel

SCARLET LETTER, THE 1922 d: Challis Sanderson. UKN., *The Scarlet Letter*, Nathaniel Hawthorne, New York 1850, Novel

SCARLET LETTER, THE 1926 d: Victor Sjostrom. USA., *The Scarlet Letter*, Nathaniel Hawthorne, New York 1850, Novel

SCARLET LETTER, THE 1934 d: Robert G. VignolA. USA., *The Scarlet Letter*, Nathaniel Hawthorne, New York 1850, Novel

Scarlet Letter, The *see* **DER SCHARLACHROTE BUCHSTABE** (1973).

SCARLET LETTER, THE 1979 d: Rick Hauser. USA., *The Scarlet Letter*, Nathaniel Hawthorne, New York 1850, Novel

SCARLET LETTER, THE 1995 d: Roland Joffe. USA., *The Scarlet Letter*, Nathaniel Hawthorne, New York 1850, Novel

SCARLET PAGES 1930 d: Ray Enright. USA., *Scarlet Pages*, John B. Hymer, Samuel Shipman, New York 1929, Play

SCARLET PIMPERNEL, THE 1917 d: Richard Stanton. USA., *The Scarlet Pimpernel*, Baroness Orczy, 1905, Novel

SCARLET PIMPERNEL, THE 1935 d: Harold Young. UKN., *The Scarlet Pimpernel*, Baroness Orczy, 1905, Novel

Scarlet Pimpernel, The *see* **THE ELUSIVE PIMPERNEL** (1950).

SCARLET PIMPERNEL, THE 1982 d: Clive Donner. USA/UKN., *The Scarlet Pimpernel*, Baroness Orczy, 1905, Novel

Scarlet Ring, The *see* **A STUDY IN SCARLET** (1933).

SCARLET SAINT, THE 1925 d: George Archainbaud. USA., *The Lady Who Played Fidele*, Gerald Beaumont, 1925, Short Story

SCARLET SHADOW, THE 1919 d: Robert Z. Leonard. USA., *The Scarlet Strain*, Lorne H. Fontaine, Katherine Leiser Robbins, Novel

SCARLET SIN, THE 1915 d: Otis Turner, Hobart Bosworth. USA., *The Scarlet Sin*, Olga Printzlau Clark, Story

Scarlet Strain, The *see* **THE SCARLET SHADOW** (1919).

SCARLET STREET 1945 d: Fritz Lang. USA., *La Chienne*, Georges de La Fouchardiere, Play

SCARLET THREAD 1951 d: Lewis Gilbert. UKN., *Scarlet Thread*, Moie Charles, A. R. Rawlinson, 1949, Play

SCARLET TRAIL, THE 1919 d: John S. Lawrence. USA., *Don't Take a Chance*, Charles Larned Robinson, 1918, Pamphlet

SCARLET TUNIC, THE 1997 d: Stuart St. Paul. UKN., *The Melancholy Hussar of the German Legion*, Thomas Hardy, Short Story

SCARLET WEEK-END, A 1932 d: George Melford. USA., *The Woman in Purple Pajamas*, Wilson Collison, New York 1931, Novel

SCARLET WEST, THE 1925 d: John G. Adolfi. USA., *The Scarlet West*, A. B. Heath, Story

SCARLETT 1994 d: John Erman. USA/UKN., *Scarlett*, Alexandra Ripley, Novel

SCARPE AL SOLE, LE 1935 d: Marco Elter. ITL., *Le Scarpe Al Sole*, Paolo Monelli, Diary

SCARPE GROSSE 1940 d: Dino Falconi. ITL., *Bors Istvan*, Sandor Hunyady, Play

Scassinatori, Gli *see* **LE CASSE** (1971).

SCATTERGOOD BAINES 1941 d: W. Christy Cabanne. USA., Clarence Budington Kelland, Short Story

SCATTERGOOD MEETS BROADWAY 1941 d: W. Christy Cabanne. USA., Clarence Budington Kelland, Story

SCATTERGOOD PULLS THE STRINGS 1941 d: W. Christy Cabanne. USA., Clarence Budington Kelland, Short Story

SCATTERGOOD RIDES HIGH 1942 d: W. Christy Cabanne. USA., Clarence Budington Kelland, Short Story

SCATTERGOOD SURVIVES A MURDER 1942 d: W. Christy Cabanne. USA., Clarence Budington Kelland, Short Story

SCEMO DI GUERRA 1985 d: Dino Risi. ITL., *Il Deserto de la Libra*, Mario Tobino, Book

SCENA A SOGGETTO MUSICALE 1914 d: Arnaldo Giacomelli. ITL., *Dal Tecc Alla Cantina*, Cletto Arrighi, Play

SCENE OF THE CRIME 1949 d: Roy Rowland. USA., *Smashing the Bookie Gang Marauders*, John Bartlow Martin, Novel

SCENES DE MENAGE 1954 d: Andre Berthomieu. FRN., *Les Boulingrin*, Georges Courteline, 1914, Play, *La Paix Chez Soi*, Georges Courteline, 1903, Play, *La Peur Des Coups*, Georges Courteline, 1895, Play

Scenes from a German Life see **AUS EINEM DEUTSCHEN LEBEN** (1978).

Scent of a Woman see **PROFUMO DI DONNA** (1974).

SCENT OF A WOMAN 1992 d: Martin Brest. USA., *Il Buio E Il Miele*, Giovanni Arpino, Novel

Scent of Incense, The see **KOGE** (1964).

Scent of the Night, The see **L' ODORE DELLA NOTTE** (1999).

Scent of Woman see **PROFUMO DI DONNA** (1974).

SCENTED ENVELOPES, THE 1923 d: A. E. Coleby. UKN., *The Scented Envelopes*, Sax Rohmer, Short Story

SCHACHNOVELLE, DIE 1960 d: Gerd Oswald. GRM., *Schachnovelle*, Stefan Zweig, Buenos Aires 1942, Novel

SCHAFER VOM TRUTZBERG, DER 1959 d: Eduard von Borsody. GRM., *Die Trutze Auf Trutzberg*, Ludwig Ganghofer, Novel

SCHAKELS 1920 d: Maurits H. Binger. NTH., *Schakels*, Herman Heijermans, 1903, Play

Schaking Van Een Meisje see **DER GEHEIMNISVOLLE KLUB** (1913).

Scham Dich, Brigitte see **WIR WERDEN DAS KIND SCHON SCHAUKELN** (1952).

SCHANDFLECK, DER 1956 d: Herbert B. Fredersdorf. AUS/GRM., *Der Schandfleck*, Ludwig Anzengruber, 1904, Novel

SCHARLACHROTE BUCHSTABE, DER 1973 d: Wim Wenders. GRM/SPN., *The Scarlet Letter*, Nathaniel Hawthorne, New York 1850, Novel

Scharlachrote Dschunke, Die see **SCOTLAND YARD JAGT DOKTOR MABUSE** (1963).

Schatten, Der see **VIOLANTHA** (1927).

SCHATTEN DER ENGEL 1976 d: Daniel Schmid. SWT/GRM., *Schatten Der Engel*, Rainer Werner Fassbinder, Play

SCHATTENGRENZE, DIE 1978 d: Wolfgang Gremm. GRM., *Die Schattengrenze*, Dieter Wellershoff, Novel

SCHATZ DER AZTEKEN, DER 1965 d: Robert Siodmak. GRM/FRN/ITL., *Der Schatz Der Azteken*, Karl Friedrich May, Novel

SCHATZ IM SILBERSEE, DER 1962 d: Harald Reinl. GRM/FRN/YGS., *Der Schatz Im Silbersee*, Karl Friedrich May, Stuttgart 1890, Novel

Schatze Des Teufels, Die see **DAS FRAULEIN VON SCUDERI** (1955).

Schatzinsel, Die see **TREASURE ISLAND** (1972).

Schatzinsel, Die see **L' ISOLA DEL TESORO** (1973).

SCHAUKEL, DIE 1983 d: Percy Adlon. GRM., *Die Schaukel*, Annette Kolb, Novel

SCHEIDUNGSGRUND, DER 1937 d: Carl Lamac. GRM/CZC., *Der Spieler*, Karel Bachmann, Play

SCHEIDUNGSGRUND: LIEBE 1960 d: Cyril Frankel. GRM., *Scheidungsgrund: Liebe*, Ellinor Hartung, Novel

SCHEINHEILIGE FLORIAN, DER 1941 d: Joe Stockel. GRM., *Der Scheinheilige Florian*, Max Neal, Philipp Weichand, Play

Schellen-Ursli see **UN CLOCHE POUR URSLI** (1964).

Schemer, The see **REPRODUCTION INTERDITE** (1956).

Scheusal, Das see **DUVAD** (1959).

Schiave Bianche, Le see **LE BAL DES ESPIONS** (1960).

SCHIAVE ESISTONO ANCORA, LE 1964 d: Roberto Malenotti, Folco Quilici. ITL/FRN., *The Slaves of Timbuktu*, Robin Maugham, Book, *The Slave Trade*, Sean O'Callaghan, London 1961, Book

Schicksal Am Matterhorn see **VON DER LIEBE BESIEGT** (1956).

Schicksal Des Leutnant Thomas Glahn, Das see **PAN** (1937).

Schicksal Einer Arztin, Das see **DIE FRAU AM SCHEIDEWEGE** (1938).

SCHICKSAL EINER NACHT, DAS 1927 d: Erich Schonfelder. GRM., *Vierundzwanzig Stunden Aus Dem Leben Einer Frau*, Stefan Zweig, Short Story

SCHICKSAL IN KETTEN 1946 d: Eduard Hoesch. AUS., Karl Jantsch, Story

Schicksalswurfel see **PRAPANCHA PASH** (1929).

Schielende Gluck, Das see **ZEZOWATE SZCZESCIE** (1960).

SCHIFF DER VERLORENEN MENSCHEN, DAS 1929 d: Maurice Tourneur. GRM., *Das Schiff Der Verlorenen Menschen*, Franzos Keremen, Novel

Schilder En Zijn Pierrette, de see **LAUGHTER AND TEARS** (1921).

SCHILTEN 1980 d: Beat Kuert. SWT., *Schilten*, Hermann Burger, Novel

Schilten - "Mit Dem Nebel Davongekommen" see **SCHILTEN** (1980).

SCHIMMELREITER, DER 1934 d: Curt Oertel, Hans Deppe. GRM., *Der Schimmelreiter*, Theodor Storm, 1888, Short Story

SCHIMMELREITER, DER 1978 d: Alfred Weidenmann. GRM., *Der Schimmelreiter*, Theodor Storm, 1888, Short Story

SCHINDERHANNES 1928 d: Curtis Bernhardt. GRM., *Schinderhannes*, Carl Zuckmayer, 1927, Play

SCHINDERHANNES 1958 d: Helmut Kautner. GRM., *Schinderhannes*, Carl Zuckmayer, 1927, Play

Schizo see **ALL WOMAN** (1967).

SCHLAFWAGENKONTROLLEUR, DER 1935 d: Richard Eichberg. GRM/FRN., *Le Controleur Des Wagons-Lits*, Alexandre Bisson, 1898, Play

Schlange, Der see **LE SERPENT** (1973).

SCHLANGENGRUBE UND DAS PENDEL, DIE 1967 d: Harald Reinl. GRM., *The Pit and the Pendulum*, Edgar Allan Poe, 1845, Short Story

Schleiertanzerin, Die see **LE MENEUR DE JOIES** (1929).

Schlemmer-Orgie, Die see **WHO IS KILLING THE GREAT CHEFS OF EUROPE?** (1978).

SCHLOSS, DAS 1968 d: Rudolf Noelte. GRM/SWT., *Das Schloss*, Franz Kafka, Munich 1926, Novel

Schloss Des Schreckens, Das see **DAS GEHEIMNIS DER SCHWARZEN KOFFER** (1962).

SCHLOSS GRIPSHOLM 1963 d: Kurt Hoffmann. GRM., *Schloss Gripsholm*, Kurt Tucholsky, 1931, Novel

SCHLOSS HUBERTUS 1934 d: Hans Deppe. GRM., *Schloss Hubertus*, Ludwig Ganghofer, Novel

SCHLOSS HUBERTUS 1954 d: Helmut Weiss. GRM., *Schloss Hubertus*, Ludwig Ganghofer, Novel

SCHLOSS HUBERTUS 1973 d: Harald Reinl. GRM., *Schloss Hubertus*, Ludwig Ganghofer, Novel

SCHLOSS KONIGSWALD 1987 d: Peter Schamoni. GRM., *Schloss Konigswald*, Horst Bienek, Novel

SCHLOSS VOGELOD 1921 d: F. W. Murnau. GRM., *Schloss Vogelod*, Rudolf Stratz, Novel

SCHLOSS VOGELOD 1936 d: Max Obal. GRM., *Schloss Vogelod*, Rudolf Stratz, Novel

SCHMETTERLINGE 1987 d: Wolfgang Becker. GRM., Ian McEwan, Story

SCHMETTERLINGE WEINEN NICHT 1970 d: Klaus Uberall. SWT/GRM., *Schmetterlinge Weinen Nicht*, Willi Heinrich, Novel

Schmutziges Geld see **SONG** (1928).

SCHNEEMANN, DER 1984 d: Peter F. Bringmann. GRM., *Der Schneemann*, Jorg Fauser, Novel

SCHNEESCHUHBANDITEN 1928 d: Uwe Jens Krafft. GRM., *Schneeschuhbanditen*, Jonathan Jew, Novel

SCHNEEWEISSCHEN UND ROSENROT 1955 d: Erich Kobler. GRM., *Schneeweisschen Und Rosenrot*, Jacob Grimm, Wilhelm Grimm, 1812, Short Story

SCHNEEWEISSCHEN UND ROSENROT 1978 d: Siegfried Hartmann. GDR., *Schneeweisschen Und Rosenrot*, Jacob Grimm, Wilhelm Grimm, 1812, Short Story

SCHNEEWITTCHEN 1928 d: Aloys Alfons Zengerling. GRM., *Schneewittchen*, Jacob Grimm, Wilhelm Grimm, 1812, Short Story

SCHNEEWITTCHEN UND DIE SIEBEN ZWERGE 1956 d: Erich Kobler. GRM., *Schneewittchen*, Jacob Grimm, Wilhelm Grimm, 1812, Short Story

SCHNEEWITTCHEN UND DIE SIEBEN ZWERGE 1961 d: Gottfried Kolditz. GDR., *Schneewittchen*, Jacob Grimm, Wilhelm Grimm, 1812, Short Story

SCHNEIDER WIBBEL 1920 d: Manfred NoA. GRM., *Schneider Wibbel*, Hans Muller-Schlosser, Play

SCHNEIDER WIBBEL 1939 d: Viktor de KowA. GRM., *Schneider Wibbel*, Hans Muller-Schlosser, Play

Schneller Als Das Auge see **QUICKER THAN THE EYE** (1988).

SCHNELLES GELD 1981 d: Raimund Koplin, Renate Stegmuller. GRM., *Schnelles Geld*, Frank Gohre, Novel

Scholler's Inn see **PENSION SCHOLLER** (1952).

Schon Wie Die Sunde see **CAROLINE CHERIE** (1967).

SCHONE ABENTEUER, DAS 1959 d: Kurt Hoffmann. GRM., *Das Schone Abenteuer*, Antonia Ridge, Novel

SCHONE FRAULEIN SCHRAGG, DAS 1937 d: Hans Deppe. GRM., *Das Schone Fraulein Schragg*, Fred Andreas, Novel

SCHONE LUGNERIN, DIE 1959 d: Axel von Ambesser. GRM/FRN., *Die Schone Lugnerin*, Ernst Nebhut, Just Scheu, Opera

Schone Meisje Van Volendam, Het see **MOOI JUULTJE VAN VOLENDAM** (1924).

SCHONE TOLZERIN, DIE 1952 d: Richard Haussler. GRM., *Die Schone Tolzerin*, Karl Weinberger, Short Story

SCHONEN TAGE VON ARANJUEZ, DIE 1933 d: Johannes Meyer. GRM., *Die Schonen Tage von Aranjuez*, Robert A. Stemmle, Hans Szekely, Play

SCHONHEITSFLECKCHEN, DAS 1936 d: Rolf Hansen. GRM., *La Mouche*, Alfred de Musset, 1854, Short Story

SCHONSTE FRAU VON PARIS, DIE 1928 d: Jacob Fleck, Luise Fleck. GRM., *Madame Circe*, Ernst Klein, Novel

SCHONZEIT FUR FUCHSE 1966 d: Peter Schamoni. GRM., *Das Gatter*, Gunter Seuren, Novel

School Bells see **HEARTS OF MEN** (1915).

SCHOOL FOR GIRLS 1934 d: William Nigh. USA., *Our Undisciplined Daughters*, Reginald Wright Kauffman, Short Story

SCHOOL FOR HUSBANDS 1937 d: Andrew Marton. UKN., *School for Husbands*, Frederick Jackson, 1932, Play

School for Husbands see **IL MARITO IN COLLEGIO** (1977).

School for Love see **FUTURES VEDETTES** (1955).

SCHOOL FOR SCANDAL, THE 1914 d: Kenean Buel. USA., *The School for Scandal*, Richard Brinsley Sheridan, London 1777, Play

SCHOOL FOR SCANDAL, THE 1923 d: Bertram Phillips. UKN., *The School for Scandal*, Richard Brinsley Sheridan, London 1777, Play

SCHOOL FOR SCANDAL, THE 1923 d: Edwin Greenwood. UKN., *The School for Scandal*, Richard Brinsley Sheridan, London 1777, Play

SCHOOL FOR SCANDAL, THE 1930 d: Maurice Elvey. UKN., *The School for Scandal*, Richard Brinsley Sheridan, London 1777, Play

SCHOOL FOR SCANDAL, THE 1975 d: Stuart Burge. UKN., *The School for Scandal*, Richard Brinsley Sheridan, London 1777, Play

School for Scoundrels see **SCHOOL FOR SCOUNDRELS OR HOW TO WIN WITHOUT ACTUALLY CHEATING** (1960).

SCHOOL FOR SCOUNDRELS OR HOW TO WIN WITHOUT ACTUALLY CHEATING 1960 d: Robert Hamer. UKN., *Gamesmanship / Oneupmanship / Lifemanship*, Stephen Potter, Books

School for Sex see **NIKUTAI NO GAKKO** (1965).

SCHOOL FOR WIVES 1925 d: Victor Hugo Halperin. USA., *The House of Lynch*, Leonard Merrick, London 1907, Novel

School Ghost, The see **DAS SCHULGESPENST** (1986).

School Is the Foundation of Life see **SKOLA ZAKLAD ZIVOTA** (1938).

School of Flesh, The see **L' ECOLE DE LA CHAIR** (1998).

School of Love *see* NIKUTAI NO GAKKO (1965).

School of Sex *see* NIKUTAI NO GAKKO (1965).

School Teacher from Vigevano, The *see* IL MAESTRO DI VIGEVANO (1963).

School Teacher, The *see* LA MAESTRA NORMAL (1997).

School, the Basis of Life *see* SKOLA ZAKLAD ZIVOTA (1938).

School, the Beginning of Life *see* SKOLA ZAKLAD ZIVOTA (1938).

School Where Life Begins *see* SKOLA ZAKLAD ZIVOTA (1938).

Schoolboys, The *see* LOS CHICOS DE LA ESCUELA (1925).

Schoolmaster Hofer *see* HAUPTLEHRER HOFER (1974).

Schoolmaster Karsten *see* HEIDESCHULMEISTER UWE KARSTEN (1933).

Schoolmaster Karsten *see* HEIDESCHULMEISTER UWE KARSTEN (1954).

Schoolmaster, The *see* THE HOOSIER SCHOOLMASTER (1935).

Schoolmistress, The *see* A TANITONO (1945).

SCHOOLS AND SCHOOLS 1918 d: Martin Justice. USA., *Schools and Schools*, O. Henry, Short Story

SCHOONER, THE 1983 d: Bill Miskelly. IRL., *The Schooner*, Michael McLaverty, 1978, Short Story

SCHOPFER, DER 1928 d: Robert Boudrioz. GRM., *Der Schopfer*, Hans Muller, Play

Schopfer Zwischen Liebe Und Pflicht, Der *see* VIVRE (1928).

SCHREI DER EULE, DER 1987 d: Tom Toelle. GRM., *The Cry of the Owl*, Patricia Highsmith, 1964, Novel

SCHREI DER SCHWARZEN WOLFE, DER 1972 d: Harald Reinl. GRM., *Cry of the Black Wolves*, Jack London, Novel

SCHRITT VOM WEGE, DER 1939 d: Gustaf Grundgens. GRM., *Effi Briest*, Theodor Fontane, 1894-95, Novel

SCHULD ALLEIN IST DER WEIN 1949 d: Fritz Kirchhoff. GRM., *Schweinefleisch in Dosen*, Paul Neuhaus, Walter Thier, Play

SCHULD DER GABRIELE ROTTWEIL, DIE 1944 d: Arthur M. Rabenalt. GRM., *Die Schuld Der Gabriele Rottweil*, Hans Gustl, Novel

Schuld Und Suhne *see* RASKOLNIKOW (1923).

Schuldig? *see* EDES ANNA (1958).

SCHULDIG 1927 d: Johannes Meyer. GRM., *Schuldig*, Richard Voss, Play

Schule Der Liebe, Die *see* LE VOYAGE IMPREVU (1934).

Schule Des Lebens *see* EIN GLUCKLICHER MENSCH (1943).

SCHULE FUR EHEGLUCK 1954 d: Toni Schelkopf, Rainer Geis. GRM., *Schule Fur Ehegluck*, Andre Maurois, Book

SCHULER GERBER, DER 1981 d: Wolfgang Gluck. AUS/GRM., *Der Schuler Gerber Hat Absolviert*, Friedrich Torberg, 1930, Novel

Schulfreund, Der *see* MEIN SCHULFREUND (1960).

SCHULGESPENST, DAS 1986 d: Rolf Losansky. GDR., *Das Schulgespenst*, Peter Abraham, Novel

SCHULMADCHEN-REPORT 1. TEIL - WAS ELTERN NICHT FUR MOGLICH HALTEN 1970 d: Ernst Hofbauer. GRM., Gunther Hunold, Book

SCHUSS VON DER KANZEL, DER 1942 d: Leopold Lindtberg. SWT., *Der Schuss von Der Kanzel*, Conrad Ferdinand Meyer, Zurich 1877, Short Story

SCHUSSE UNTERM GALGEN 1968 d: Horst Seemann. GDR., *Catriona*, Robert Louis Stevenson, 1892, Novel, *Kidnapped*, Robert Louis Stevenson, London 1886, Novel

SCHUT, DER 1964 d: Robert Siodmak. GRM/ITL/FRN., *Der Schut*, Karl Friedrich May, Novel

Schutt Die Sorgen in Glaschen Wein *see* DAS VERLEGENHEITSKIND (1938).

SCHUTZENLIESEL 1954 d: Rudolf Schundler. GRM., *Schutzenliesel*, Edmund Eysler, Carl Lindau, Leo Stein, Opera

SCHWARMER, DIE 1984 d: Hans Neuenfels. GRM., *Die Schwarmer*, Robert Musil, 1921, Play

Schwarzbrot Und Kipferl *see* ..UND DIE LIEBE LACHT DAZU (1957).

SCHWARZE ABT, DER 1963 d: Franz J. Gottlieb. GRM., *The Black Abbot*, Edgar Wallace, London 1926, Novel

SCHWARZE DOMINO, DER 1929 d: Victor Janson. GRM., *Le Domino Noir*, Daniel Francois Auber, Paris 1837, Opera

SCHWARZE GALEERE, DIE 1962 d: Martin Hellberg. GDR., *Die Schwarze Galeere*, Wilhelm Raabe, 1902, Novel

Schwarze Geiger, Der *see* ROMEO UND JULIA AUF DEM DORFE (1941).

SCHWARZE MUHLE, DIE 1975 d: Celino Bleiweiss. GDR., Jurij Brezan, Story

SCHWARZE SCHAF, DAS 1943 d: Friedrich Zittau, Walter Janssen. GRM., *Schutzenfest*, Harald Bratt, Play

SCHWARZE SCHAF, DAS 1960 d: Helmut Ashley. GRM., G. K. Chesterton, Story

SCHWARZE TANNER, DER 1986 d: Xavier Koller. SWT., *Der Schwarze Tanner*, Meinrad Inglin, Short Story

SCHWARZE WALFISCH, DER 1934 d: Fritz Wendhausen. GRM., *Fanny*, Marcel Pagnol, Paris 1931, Play

SCHWARZER JAGER JOHANNA 1934 d: Johannes Meyer. GRM., *Schwarzer Jager Johanna*, George von Der Vring, Novel

SCHWARZER NERZ AUF ZARTER HAUT 1969 d: Erwin C. Dietrich. GRM/SWT., *Schwarzer Nerz Auf Zarter Haut*, Henry Pahlen, Novel

Schwarzer Stern in Weissen Nacht *see* UN HOMME SE PENCHE SUR SON PASSE (1957).

Schwarzes Wochenende *see* TATORT - SCHIMANSKI: SCHWARZES WOCHENENDE (1985).

SCHWARZWALDMADEL 1920 d: Arthur Wellin. GRM., *Schwarzwaldmadel*, Leon Jessel, August Neidhardt, Opera

SCHWARZWALDMADEL 1929 d: Victor Janson. GRM., *Schwarzwaldmadel*, Leon Jessel, August Neidhardt, Opera

SCHWARZWALDMADEL 1933 d: Georg Zoch. GRM., *Schwarzwaldmadel*, Leon Jessel, August Neidhardt, Opera

SCHWARZWALDMADEL 1950 d: Hans Deppe. GRM., *Schwarzwaldmadel*, Leon Jessel, August Neidhardt, Opera

SCHWARZ-WEISS-ROTE HIMMELBETT, DAS 1962 d: Rolf Thiele. GRM., *Das Schwarz-Weiss-Rote Himmelbett*, Hans Rudolf Berndorff, Novel

SCHWEDISCHE NACHTIGALL, DIE 1941 d: Peter P. Brauer. GRM., *Gastspiel in Kopenhagen*, Friedrich Forster-Burggraf, Play

SCHWEIGEN DES DICHTERS, DAS 1986 d: Peter Lilienthal. GRM., Abraham B. Jehoschua, Story

SCHWEIGEN IM WALDE 1 1918 d: Paul von Woringen. GRM., *Das Schweigen Im Walde*, Richard Skowronnek, Novel

SCHWEIGEN IM WALDE 2 1918 d: Paul von Woringen. GRM., *Das Schweigen Im Walde*, Richard Skowronnek, Novel

SCHWEIGEN IM WALDE, DAS 1929 d: William Dieterle. GRM., *Das Schweigen Im Walde*, Ludwig Ganghofer, Novel

SCHWEIGEN IM WALDE, DAS 1937 d: Hans Deppe. GRM., *Das Schweigen Im Walde*, Ludwig Ganghofer, Novel

SCHWEIGEN IM WALDE, DAS 1955 d: Helmut Weiss. GRM., *Das Schweigen Im Walde*, Ludwig Ganghofer, Novel

SCHWEIGEN IM WALDE, DAS 1976 d: Alfred Vohrer. GRM., *Das Schweigen Im Walde*, Ludwig Ganghofer, Novel

SCHWEIGENDE MUND, DER 1951 d: Karl Hartl. AUS., Hugo Maria Kritz, Story

SCHWEIGENDE STERN, DER 1960 d: Kurt Maetzig. GDR/PLN., *Astronauci*, Stanislaw Lem, Warsaw 1951, Novel

Schweigepflicht *see* DU MEIN STILLES TAL (1955).

Schweik As a Civilian *see* SVEJK V CIVILU (1927).

Schweik at the Front *see* SVEJK NA FRONTE (1926).

Schweik in Civilian Life *see* SVEJK V CIVILU (1927).

Schweik in Russian Captivity *see* SVEJK V RUSKEM ZAJETI (1926).

SCHWEIK'S NEW ADVENTURES 1943 d: Carl Lamac. UKN., Jaroslav Hasek, Novel

Schwejk in Zivil *see* SVEJK V CIVILU (1927).

SCHWEJKS FLEGELJAHRE 1964 d: Wolfgang Liebeneiner. AUS., Jaroslav Hasek, Story

SCHWERE JUNGENS - LEICHTE MADCHEN 1927 d: Carl Boese. GRM., *Martin Overbeck*, Felix Salten, Novel

SCHWUR DES SOLDATEN POOLEY, DER 1962 d: Kurt Jung-Alsen. GRM/UKN., *The Vengeance of Private Pooley*, Cyrill Jolly, Novel

Sciacalllo, Lo *see* L' AINE DES FERCHAUX (1963).

Sciarada Per Quattro Spie *see* AVEC LA PEAU DES AUTRES (1966).

SCIENCE 1911. USA., *A Dog's Tale*, Mark Twain, Short Story

SCINTILLA, LA 1915 d: Eleuterio Rodolfi. ITL., *La Scintilla*, Alfredo Testoni, 1906, Play

Scintillating Sin *see* VIOLATED PARADISE (1963).

Scirocco *see* LA STANZA DELLO SCIROCCO (1998).

Scomunicato, Lo *see* LA SCOUMOUNE (1973).

SCOOP 1987 d: Gavin Millar. UKN., *Scoop*, Evelyn Waugh, 1938, Novel

SCOOP, THE 1934 d: MacLean Rogers. UKN., *The Scoop*, Jack Heming, Play

Scorbnoye Beschuvstvie *see* SKORBNOE BESCUVSTVIE (1986).

SCORCHERS 1991 d: David Beaird. USA., *Scorchers*, David Beaird, Play

SCORPIO LETTERS, THE 1968 d: Richard Thorpe. USA., *The Scorpio Letters*, Victor Canning, Novel

Scotch on the Rocks *see* LAXDALE HALL (1952).

Scotch Valley *see* AMATEUR DADDY (1932).

SCOTLAND YARD 1930 d: William K. Howard. USA., *Scotland Yard*, Denison Clift, New York 1929, Play

SCOTLAND YARD 1941 d: Norman Foster. USA., *Scotland Yard*, Denison Clift, New York 1929, Play

Scotland Yard Commands *see* THE LONELY ROAD (1936).

Scotland Yard Dragnet *see* THE HYPNOTIST (1957).

Scotland Yard Hunts Dr. Mabuse *see* SCOTLAND YARD JAGT DOKTOR MABUSE (1963).

SCOTLAND YARD JAGT DOKTOR MABUSE 1963 d: Paul May. GRM., Bryan Edgar Wallace, Novel

SCOTLAND YARD MYSTERY, THE 1934 d: Thomas Bentley. UKN., *The Scotland Yard Mystery*, Wallace Geoffrey, Play

Scotland Yard Vs. Bulldog Drummond *see* ARREST BULLDOG DRUMMOND (1939).

Scotland Yard Vs. Dr. Mabuse *see* SCOTLAND YARD JAGT DOKTOR MABUSE (1963).

SCOUMOUNE, LA 1973 d: Jose Giovanni. FRN/ITL., *La Scoumoune*, Jose Giovanni, Novel

Scourge of the Little C, The *see* TUMBLING RIVER (1927).

SCOURGE, THE 1922 d: Geoffrey H. Malins. UKN., *The Scourge*, Rafael Sabatini, Novel

SCRAMBLED WIVES 1921 d: Edward H. Griffith. USA., *The First Mrs. Chiverick*, Adelaide Matthews, Martha M. Stanley, Play

SCRAP IRON 1921 d: Charles Ray. USA., *Scrap Iron*, Charles E. Van Loan, Short Story

Scrap of Paper, A *see* THREE GREEN EYES (1919).

SCRAPPER, THE 1922 d: Hobart Henley. USA., *Malloy Campeador*, Ralph G. Kirk, 1921, Short Story

SCRAPPLE 1998 d: Christopher Hanson. USA., *Spam*, Sean McNamara, Story

SCREAM AND SCREAM AGAIN 1969 d: Gordon Hessler. UKN/USA., *The Disoriented Man*, Peter Saxon, London 1966, Novel

SCREAM IN THE DARK, A 1943 d: George Sherman. USA., *The Morgue Is Always Open*, Jerome Odlum, Novel

SCREAM OF THE WOLF 1974 d: Dan Curtis. USA., *The Hunter*, David Chase, Story

Screamer *see* SCREAM AND SCREAM AGAIN (1969).

SCREAMERS 1995 d: Christian Duguay. USA/CND/JPN., *Second Variety*, Philip K. Dick, Short Story

SCREAMING EAGLES 1956 d: Charles Haas. USA., Virginia Kellogg, Story

Screaming Head, The *see* DIE NACKTE UND DER SATAN (1959).

SCREAMING MIMI 1958 d: Gerd Oswald. USA., *Screaming Mimi*, Frederick Brown, 1949, Novel

Screaming Target *see* SITTING TARGET (1971).

SCREAMING WOMAN, THE 1972 d: Jack Smight. USA., *The Screaming Woman*, Ray Bradbury, 1951, Short Story

SCRISOARE PIERDUTA, O 1956 d: Victor Iliu, Sica Alexandrescu. RMN., *O Scrisoare Pierduta*, Ion Luca Caragiale, 1885, Play

SCROLLINA 1920 d: Gero Zambuto. ITL., *Scrollina*, Achille Torelli, 1885, Play

SCROOGE 1913 d: Leedham Bantock. UKN., *A Christmas Carol*, Charles Dickens, London 1843, Novel

SCROOGE 1922 d: George Wynn. UKN., *A Christmas Carol*, Charles Dickens, London 1843, Novel

SCROOGE 1923 d: Edwin Greenwood. UKN., *A Christmas Carol*, Charles Dickens, London 1843, Novel

SCROOGE 1928 d: Hugh Croise. UKN., *A Christmas Carol*, Charles Dickens, London 1843, Novel

SCROOGE 1935 d: Henry Edwards. UKN., *A Christmas Carol*, Charles Dickens, London 1843, Novel

SCROOGE 1951 d: Brian Desmond Hurst. UKN., *A Christmas Carol*, Charles Dickens, London 1843, Novel

SCROOGE 1970 d: Ronald Neame. UKN., *A Christmas Carol*, Charles Dickens, London 1843, Novel

SCROOGE; OR, MARLEY'S GHOST 1901 d: W. R. Booth. UKN., *A Christmas Carol*, Charles Dickens, London 1843, Novel

Scrooge the Skinflint *see* THE RIGHT TO BE HAPPY (1916).

SCROOGED 1988 d: Richard Donner. USA., *A Christmas Carol*, Charles Dickens, London 1843, Novel

SCRUPLES 1980 d: Alan J. Levi. USA., *Scruples*, Judith Krantz, Novel

Scudda Hoo Scudda Hay *see* SCUDDA-HOO! SCUDDA HAY! (1948).

SCUDDA-HOO! SCUDDA HAY! 1948 d: F. Hugh Herbert. USA., *Scudda Hoo Scudda Hay*, George Agnew Chamberlain, Novel

Scuffle Elegy *see* KENKA SEREJII (1966).

SCULACCIATA, LA 1974 d: Pasquale Festa Campanile. ITL., *Neurotandem*, Silvano Ambrogi, Novel

SCULPTEUR DE MASQUES, LE 1910. FRN., *Le Sculpteur de Masques*, Fernand Crommelynck, Play

Sculptor of Ammergau, the *see* DER HERRGOTTSSCHNITZER VON AMMERGAU (1952).

SCULPTRESS, THE 1996. UKN., *The Sculptress*, Minette Walters, Novel

SCUTTLERS, THE 1920 d: J. Gordon Edwards. USA., *The Scuttlers*, Clyde C. Westover, New York 1914, Novel

SE NON SON MATTI NO LI VOGLIAMO 1941 d: Esodo Pratelli. ITL., *Se No I Xe Mati No Li Volemo*, Gino Rocca, 1926, Play

SE QUELL'IDIOTA CI PENSASSE. 1939 d: Nino Giannini. ITL., *Se Quell'Idiota Ci Pensasse.*, Silvio Benedetti, Play

SEA AROUND US, THE 1952 d: Irwin Allen. USA., *The Sea Around Us*, Rachel Carson, 1951, Book

SEA BEAST, THE 1926 d: Millard Webb. USA., *Moby Dick Or the Whale*, Herman Melville, New York 1851, Novel

SEA CHASE, THE 1955 d: John Farrow. USA., *The Sea Chase*, Andrew Geer, 1948, Novel

SEA DEVILS 1953 d: Raoul Walsh. UKN., *Les Travailleurs de la Mer*, Victor Hugo, 1866, Novel

Sea Eagle, The *see* THE EAGLE OF THE SEA (1926).

SEA FLOWER, THE 1918 d: Colin Campbell. USA., *The Sea Flower*, George Charles Hull, Short Story

SEA GOD, THE 1930 d: George Abbott. USA., *The Lost God*, John Russell, 1921, Short Story

SEA GULL, THE 1969 d: Sidney Lumet. UKN/USA., *Chayka*, Anton Chekhov, St. Petersburg 1896, Play

Sea Gull, The *see* IL GABBIANO (1977).

SEA HAWK, THE 1924 d: Frank Lloyd. USA., *The Sea Hawk*, Rafael Sabatini, London 1915, Novel

SEA HAWK, THE 1940 d: Michael Curtiz. USA., *The Sea Hawk*, Rafael Sabatini, London 1915, Novel

SEA HORSES 1926 d: Allan Dwan. USA., *Sea Horses*, Francis Brett Young, London 1925, Novel

Sea Killer *see* BEYOND THE REEF (1981).

Sea Lily, The *see* LE LIS DE MER (1970).

Sea Nymphs *see* VIOLATED PARADISE (1963).

Sea of Forests and Plains of Snow *see* LIN HAI XUE YUAN (1960).

SEA OF GRASS, THE 1946 d: Elia Kazan. USA., *The Sea of Grass*, Conrad Richter, 1936, Novel

Sea of Hate *see* HEN HAI (1931).

Sea of the Lost Time, The *see* EL MAR DEL TIEMPO PERDIDO (1978).

SEA PANTHER, THE 1918 d: Thomas N. Heffron. USA., *The Sea Panther*, Kenneth B. Clarke, Short Story

Sea Prowlers *see* PROWLERS OF THE SEA (1928).

Sea Quest *see* BLUE FIN (1978).

Sea Raiders *see* THE SEA RIDERS (1922).

SEA RIDERS, THE 1922 d: Edward H. Griffith. CND., Wallace MacDonald, Story

SEA SHALL NOT HAVE THEM, THE 1954 d: Lewis Gilbert. UKN., *The Sea Shall Not Have Them*, John Harris, Novel

SEA TIGER, THE 1927 d: John Francis Dillon. USA., *A Runaway Enchantress*, Mary Heaton Vorse, Story

SEA TIGER, THE 1952 d: Frank McDonald. USA., *Island Freighter*, Charles Yerkow, Short Story

SEA URCHIN, THE 1926 d: Graham Cutts. UKN., *The Sea Urchin*, John Hastings Turner, 1925, Play

Sea Wall, The *see* BARRAGE CONTRE LE PACIFIQUE (1958).

SEA WIFE 1957 d: Bob McNaught. UKN., *Seawyf and Biscuit*, J. D. Scott, Novel

SEA WOLF, THE 1913 d: Hobart Bosworth. USA., *The Sea Wolf*, Jack London, New York 1904, Novel

SEA WOLF, THE 1920 d: George Melford. USA., *The Sea Wolf*, Jack London, New York 1904, Novel

SEA WOLF, THE 1926 d: Ralph Ince. USA., *The Sea Wolf*, Jack London, New York 1904, Novel

SEA WOLF, THE 1930 d: Alfred Santell. USA., *The Sea Wolf*, Jack London, New York 1904, Novel

SEA WOLF, THE 1941 d: Michael Curtiz. USA., *The Sea Wolf*, Jack London, New York 1904, Novel

Sea Wolf, The *see* DER SEEWOLF (1971).

SEA WOLF, THE 1993 d: Michael Anderson. USA., *The Sea Wolf*, Jack London, New York 1904, Novel

SEA WOLVES, THE 1980 d: Andrew V. McLaglen. UKN/USA/SWT., *Boarding Party*, James Leasor, Novel

Sea Woman, The *see* WHY WOMEN LOVE (1925).

Sea Wyf and Biscuit *see* SEA WIFE (1957).

Seagull, The *see* CHAIKA (1971).

Seagull, The *see* IL GABBIANO (1977).

SEAGULLS OVER SORRENTO 1954 d: John Boulting, Roy Boulting. UKN., *Seagulls Over Sorrento*, Hugh Hastings, London 1949, Play

SEAL OF SILENCE, THE 1913 d: Thomas H. Ince. USA., *The Seal of Silence*, William Hamilton Osborne, Story

Seal, The *see* MON PHOQUE ET ELLES (1951).

SEALED CARGO 1951 d: Alfred L. Werker. USA., *The Gaunt Woman*, Edmund Gilligan, 1943, Novel

SEALED LIPS 1915 d: John Ince. USA., *The Silence of Dean Maitland*, Maxwell Gray, New York 1886, Novel

SEALED ROOM 1909 d: D. W. Griffith. USA., *The Cask of Amontillado*, Edgar Allan Poe, 1846, Short Story

Sealed Train, The *see* DER ZUG (1989).

SEALED VALLEY 1915 d: Lawrence McGill. USA., *The Sealed Valley*, Hubert Footner, New York 1914, Novel

SEALED VERDICT 1948 d: Lewis Allen. USA., *Sealed Verdict*, Lionel Shapiro, Novel

Seamen's Wives *see* ZEEMANSVROUWEN (1930).

SEANCE ON A WET AFTERNOON 1964 d: Bryan Forbes. UKN., *Seance on a Wet Afternoon*, Mark McShane, 1964, Novel

SEARA VERMELHA 1963 d: Alberto d'AversA. BRZ., *Seara Vermelha*, Jorge Amado, 1946, Novel

SEARCH FOR BEAUTY 1934 d: Erle C. Kenton. USA., *Love Your Body*, Schuyler E. Grey, Paul R. Milton, Play

SEARCH FOR BRIDIE MURPHY, THE 1956 d: Noel Langley. USA., *The Search for Bridey Murphy*, Morey Bernstein, Book

Search, The *see* LA BUSCA (1967).

SEARCHERS, THE 1956 d: John Ford. USA., *The Searchers*, Alan Lemay, 1954, Novel

SEARCHING FOR BOBBY FISCHER 1993 d: Steven Zaillian. USA., *Searching for Bobby Fischer*, Fred Waitzkin, Book

Searching for Eileen *see* ZOEKEN NAAR EILEEN (1987).

Searching for Joy *see* V POISKACH RADOSTI (1939).

Searching the Hearts of Students *see* CESTA DO HUBLIN STUDAKOVY DUSE (1939).

Searching the Ship Plant *see* CHUAN CHANG ZHUI ZONG (1959).

SEARCHING WIND, THE 1946 d: William Dieterle. USA., *The Searching Wind*, Lillian Hellman, New York 1944, Play

Season in Hakkari, A *see* HAKKARI'DE BIR MEVSIM (1987).

SEASON IN PURGATORY, A 1996 d: David Greene. USA., *A Season in Purgatory*, Dominick Dunne, Novel

Season of Passion *see* SUMMER OF THE 17TH DOLL (1959).

SEATS OF THE MIGHTY, THE 1914 d: T. Hayes Hunter. USA., *The Seats of the Mighty*, Gilbert Parker, New York 1894, Novel

Seaweed Children, The *see* MALACHI'S COVE (1974).

Seawife *see* SEA WIFE (1957).

Secheresse *see* VIDAS SECAS (1963).

SECHS MADCHEN SUCHEN NACHT QUARTIER 1928 d: Hans Behrendt. GRM., *Gretchen*, Davis, Lipschutz, Play

SECOND BEST 1994 d: Chris Menges. USA/UKN., *Second Best*, David Cook, Novel

Second Breath *see* LE DEUXIEME SOUFFLE (1966).

SECOND BUREAU 1936 d: Victor Hanbury. UKN., *Deuxieme Bureau*, Robert-Claude Dumas, Novel

SECOND CHANCE 1950 d: William Beaudine. USA., *Second Chance*, Faith Baldwin, Short Story

Second Chances *see* THIS RECKLESS AGE (1932).

SECOND CHOICE 1930 d: Howard Bretherton. USA., *Second Choice*, Elizabeth Alexander, New York 1928, Novel

SECOND FLOOR MYSTERY, THE 1930 d: Roy Del Ruth. USA., *The Agony Column*, Earl Derr Biggers, Indianapolis 1916, Novel

Second Floor, The *see* O SOBRADO (1956).

SECOND HAND ROSE 1922 d: Lloyd Ingraham. USA., *Second Hand Rose*, Grant Clarke, James F. Hanley, 1921, Song

SECOND HAND WIFE 1933 d: Hamilton MacFadden. USA., *Second Hand Wife*, Kathleen Norris, New York 1932, Novel

SECOND HONEYMOON 1930 d: Phil Rosen. USA., *The Second Honeymoon*, Ruby M. Ayres, New York 1921, Novel

SECOND HONEYMOON 1937 d: Walter Lang. USA., *Second Honeymoon*, Philip Wylie, Story

SECOND IN COMMAND, THE 1915 d: William J. Bowman. USA., *The Second in Command*, Robert Marshall, London 1900, Play

Second Life, The *see* DAS ZWEITE LEBEN (1954).

Second Marriage *see* SECOND WIFE (1936).

SECOND MATE, THE 1929 d: J. Steven Edwards. UKN., *The Second Mate*, R. W. Rees, Novel

SECOND MR. BUSH, THE 1940 d: John Paddy Carstairs. UKN., *The Second Mr. Bush*, C. Stafford Dickens, London 1938, Play

SECOND MRS. ROEBUCK, THE 1914 d: Jack O'Brien, W. Christy Cabanne. USA., *Smart Set*, W. Carey Wonderly, Story

SECOND MRS. TANQUERAY, THE 1914. USA., *The Second Mrs. Tanqueray*, Arthur Wing Pinero, London 1893, Play

SECOND MRS. TANQUERAY, THE 1916 d: Fred Paul. UKN., *The Second Mrs. Tanqueray*, Arthur Wing Pinero, London 1893, Play

SECOND MRS. TANQUERAY, THE 1952 d: Dallas Bower. UKN., *The Second Mrs. Tanqueray*, Arthur Wing Pinero, London 1893, Play

Second Power, The *see* EL SEGUNDO PODER (1976).

SECOND SERVE 1986 d: Anthony Page. USA., John Ames, Renee Richards, Book

SECOND SIGHT: A LOVE STORY 1984 d: John Korty. USA., *Emma and I*, Sheila Hockens, Book

Second Sister *see* MANJHLI DIDI (1968).

SECOND STAIN, THE 1922 d: George Ridgwell. UKN., *The Second Stain*, Arthur Conan Doyle, Short Story

Second Stain, The *see* THE RETURN OF SHERLOCK HOLMES: THE SECOND STAIN (1986).

Second Story Murder, The *see* THE SECOND FLOOR MYSTERY (1930).

Second Story Mystery, The *see* THE SECOND FLOOR MYSTERY (1930).

SECOND TIME AROUND, THE 1961 d: Vincent Sherman. USA., *Star in the West*, Richard Emery Roberts, New York 1951, Novel

Second Touch *see* TWEE VROUWEN (1978).

SECOND VICTORY, THE 1987 d: Gerald Thomas. UKN/ASL., *The Second Victory*, Morris West, Novel

SECOND WIFE 1930 d: Russell MacK. USA., *Stepchild of the Moon*, Fulton Oursler, New York 1926, Novel

SECOND WIFE 1936 d: Edward Killy. USA., *Stepchild of the Moon*, Fulton Oursler, New York 1926, Novel

Second Wind *see* LE DEUXIEME SOUFFLE (1966).

SECOND YOUTH 1924 d: Albert Parker. USA., *Second Youth*, Allan Eugene Updegraff, New York 1917, Novel

Second Youth *see* DRUHE MLADI (1938).

SECONDA MOGLIE, LA 1922 d: Amleto Palermi. ITL., *The Second Mrs. Tanqueray*, Arthur Wing Pinero, London 1893, Play

SECONDE VERITE, LA 1965 d: Christian-Jaque. FRN/ITL., *La Second Verite*, Jean Laborde, Novel

SECONDO TRAGICO FANTOZZI, IL 1976 d: Luciano Salce. ITL., *Fantozzi*, Paolo Villaggio, Novel, *Il Secondo Tragico Fantozzi*, Paolo Villaggio, Book

SECONDS 1966 d: John Frankenheimer. USA., *Seconds*, David Ely, New York 1963, Novel

Secret Agent *see* ON SECRET SERVICE (1933).

SECRET AGENT, THE 1936 d: Alfred Hitchcock. UKN., *The Hairless Mexican*, W. Somerset Maugham, 1928, Short Story, *Triton*, W. Somerset Maugham, 1928, Short Story

SECRET BEYOND THE DOOR 1947 d: Fritz Lang. USA., *Museum Piece No. 13*, Rufus King, Story

SECRET BRIDE 1934 d: William Dieterle. USA., *Concealment*, Leonard Ide, 1930, Play

SECRET CALL, THE 1931 d: Stuart Walker. USA., *The Woman*, William C. de Mille, New York 1911, Play

SECRET CAVE, THE 1953 d: John Durst. UKN., *Our Exploits at West Poley*, Thomas Hardy, 1892-93, Short Story

SECRET CEREMONY 1968 d: Joseph Losey. UKN., *Ceremonia Secreta*, Marco Denevi, 1955, Short Story

Secret Club, The *see* DER GEHEIMNISVOLLE KLUB (1913).

SECRET COMMAND, THE 1944 d: A. Edward Sutherland. USA., *The Saboteurs*, John Hawkins, Ward Hawkins, Story

Secret Courier, The *see* DER GEHEIME KURIER (1928).

Secret de Delia, Le *see* L' EVADEE (1928).

Secret de la Banquise, Le *see* BEAR ISLAND (1979).

SECRET DE L'EMERALDE, LE 1936 d: Maurice de Canonge. FRN., *L' Enigmatique Gentleman*, Alfred Gragnon, Play

SECRET DE MADAME CLAPAIN, LE 1943 d: Andre Berthomieu. FRN., *Madame Clapain*, Edouard Estaunie, Novel

SECRET DE MONTE-CRISTO, LE 1948 d: Albert Valentin. FRN., *Le Comte de Monte-Cristo*, Alexandre Dumas (pere), Paris 1845, Novel

SECRET DE POLICHINELLE, LE 1913 d: Henri Desfontaines. FRN., *Le Secret de Polichinelle*, Pierre Wolff, Play

SECRET DE POLICHINELLE, LE 1923 d: Rene Hervil. FRN., *Le Secret de Polichinelle*, Pierre Wolff, Play

SECRET DE POLICHINELLE, LE 1936 d: Andre Berthomieu. FRN., *Le Secret de Polichinelle*, Pierre Wolff, Play

SECRET DES WORONZEFF, LE 1934 d: Andre Beucler, Arthur Robison. FRN., *Le Secret Des Woronzeff*, Margot von Simpson, Novel

SECRET D'HELENE MARIMON, LE 1953 d: Henri Calef. FRN/ITL., *Le Secret d'Helene Marimon*, J.-B. Cherrier, Novel

Secret Document -Vienna *see* FUSILLE A L'AUBE (1950).

SECRET DOOR, THE 1962 d: Gilbert L. Kay. UKN/USA., *Paper Door*, Stephen Longstreet, Short Story

SECRET DU CHEVALIER D'EON, LE 1960 d: Jacqueline Audry. FRN/ITL., Cecil Saint-Laurent, Story

SECRET DU DOCTEUR, LE 1930 d: Charles de Rochefort. FRN/USA., *Half an Hour*, J. M. Barrie, New York 1913, Play

Secret du Vieux Prieure, Le *see* QUELQU'UN A TUE (1933).

SECRET D'UNE MERE, LE 1926 d: Georges Pallu. FRN., *L' Abandonne*, Eugene Barbier, Novel

Secret d'une Vie, Le *see* UNE FEMME SANS IMPORTANCE (1937).

Secret Four, The *see* THE FOUR JUST MEN (1939).

Secret French Prostitution Report *see* DOSSIER PROSTITUTION (1969).

SECRET FRIENDS 1991 d: Dennis Potter. UKN., *Ticket to Ride*, Dennis Potter, Novel

SECRET GARDEN, THE 1919 d: Gustav von Seyffertitz. USA., *The Secret Garden*, Frances Hodgson Burnett, New York 1909, Novel

SECRET GARDEN, THE 1949 d: Fred M. Wilcox. USA., *The Secret Garden*, Frances Hodgson Burnett, New York 1909, Novel

SECRET GARDEN, THE 1975 d: Dorothea Brooking. UKN., *The Secret Garden*, Frances Hodgson Burnett, New York 1909, Novel

SECRET GARDEN, THE 1984 d: Katrina Murray. UKN., *The Secret Garden*, Frances Hodgson Burnett, New York 1909, Novel

SECRET GARDEN, THE 1987 d: Alan Grint. UKN., *The Secret Garden*, Frances Hodgson Burnett, New York 1909, Novel

SECRET GARDEN, THE 1993 d: Agnieszka Holland. USA., *The Secret Garden*, Frances Hodgson Burnett, New York 1909, Novel

SECRET HONOR 1984 d: Robert Altman. USA., *Secret Honor*, Donald Freed, Arnold M. Stone, Play

Secret Honor: a Political Myth *see* SECRET HONOR (1984).

Secret Honor: the Last Testament of Richard M. Nixon *see* SECRET HONOR (1984).

SECRET HOUR, THE 1928 d: Rowland V. Lee. USA., *They Knew What They Wanted*, Sidney Coe Howard, New York 1924, Play

Secret Interlude *see* PRIVATE NUMBER (1936).

Secret Interlude *see* THE VIEW FROM POMPEY'S HEAD (1955).

SECRET JOURNEY, THE 1939 d: John Baxter. UKN., *Lone Wolves*, Charles Dumas, Novel

SECRET KINGDOM, THE 1925 d: Sinclair Hill. UKN., *Hidden Fires*, Bertram Atkey, Novel

SECRET, LE 1974 d: Robert Enrico. FRN/ITL., *Le Secret*, Francis Rick, Novel

Secret Lie, The *see* INTO NO MAN'S LAND (1928).

SECRET LIFE OF ALGERNON, THE 1997 d: Charles Jarrott. CND., *The Secret Life of Algernon Pendleton*, Russell H. Greenan, Novel

SECRET LIFE OF JOHN CHAPMAN, THE 1976 d: David Lowell Rich. USA., *Blue Collar Journal*, John R. Coleman, Book

SECRET LIFE OF T. K. DEARING, THE 1975 d: Harry Harris. USA., *The Secret Life of T. K. Dearing*, Jean Robinson, Book

SECRET LIFE OF WALTER MITTY, THE 1947 d: Norman Z. McLeod. USA., *The Secret Life of Walter Mitty*, James Thurber, 1945, Short Story

SECRET LIVES 1937 d: Edmond T. Greville. UKN., *Secret Lives*, Paul de Saint-Colombe, Novel

SECRET LOVE 1916 d: Robert Z. Leonard. USA., *That Lass O' Lowrie's*, Frances Hodgson Burnett, New York 1877, Novel

Secret Mating, The *see* SOUL MATES (1916).

Secret Meeting *see* MARIE-OCTOBRE (1958).

Secret of a Marriage *see* DAS GEHEIMNIS EINER EHE (1951).

Secret of a Woman Doctor *see* DAS GEHEIMNIS EINER AERZTIN (1955).

SECRET OF BLACK MOUNTAIN, THE 1917 d: Otto Hoffman. USA., *The Secret of Black Mountain*, Jackson Gregory, Short Story

Secret of Boyne Castle, The *see* GUNS IN THE HEATHER (1969).

SECRET OF DEEP HARBOR 1961 d: Edward L. Cahn. USA., *I Cover the Waterfront*, Max Miller, New York 1932, Book

Secret of Dorian Gray, The *see* IL DIO CHIAMATO DORIAN (1970).

SECRET OF DR. KILDARE, THE 1939 d: Harold S. Bucquet. USA., *The Secret of Dr. Kildare*, Max Brand, 1939, Story

Secret of Fylfot, The *see* SHINOBI NO MANJI (1968).

SECRET OF MADAME BLANCHE, THE 1933 d: Charles J. Brabin. USA., *The Lady*, Martin Brown, New York 1923, Play

Secret of Monte Cristo, The *see* THE TREASURE OF MONTE CRISTO (1961).

SECRET OF NIMH, THE 1982 d: Don Bluth. USA., *Mrs. Frisby and the Rats of N.I.M.H.*, Robert C. O'Brien, Novel

Secret of N.I.M.H., The *see* THE SECRET OF NIMH (1982).

Secret of Oberwald, The *see* IL MISTERO DI OBERWALD (1979).

SECRET OF ROAN INISH, THE 1993 d: John Sayles. USA/IRL., *Secret of the Ron Mor Skerry*, Rosalie K. Fry, Novel

SECRET OF SANTA VITTORIA, THE 1969 d: Stanley Kramer. USA., *The Secret of Santa Vittoria*, Robert Crichton, New York 1966, Novel

SECRET OF ST. IVES, THE 1949 d: Phil Rosen. USA., *St. Ives*, Arthur Quiller-Couch, Robert Louis Stevenson, 1898, Novel

SECRET OF STAMBOUL, THE 1936 d: Andrew Marton. UKN., *Eunuch of Stamboul*, Dennis Wheatley, Novel

Secret of the Black Suitcases *see* DAS GEHEIMNIS DER SCHWARZEN KOFFER (1962).

Secret of the Black Trunk, The *see* DAS GEHEIMNIS DER SCHWARZEN KOFFER (1962).

Secret of the Black Widow, The *see* DAS GEHEIMNIS DER SCHWARZEN WITWE (1963).

SECRET OF THE BLUE ROOM 1933 d: Kurt Neumann. USA., Eric Philippi, Story

Secret of the Chevalier d'Eon, The *see* LE SECRET DU CHEVALIER D'EON (1960).

Secret of the Chinese Carnation, The *see* DAS GEHEIMNIS DER CHINESISCHEN NELKE (1964).

SECRET OF THE HILLS, THE 1921 d: Chester Bennett. USA., *The Secret of the Hills*, William Garrett, London 1920, Novel

SECRET OF THE INCAS 1954 d: Jerry Hopper. USA., *Legend of the Incas*, Sydney Boehm, Story

Secret of the Leather Strap *see* I MISTERI DELLA GIUNGLA NERA (1964).

SECRET OF THE MOOR, THE 1919 d: Lewis Willoughby. UKN., *The Secret of the Moor*, Maurice Gerard, Novel

Secret of the Ninja *see* SHINOBI NO MANJI (1968).

Secret of the Red Orchid, The *see* DAS RATSEL DER ROTEN ORCHIDEE (1961).

Secret of the Steel Town, The *see* TAJEMSTVI OCELOVEHO MESTA (1978).

SECRET OF THE STORM COUNTRY, THE 1917 d: Charles Miller. USA., *The Secret of the Storm Country*, Grace Miller White, New York 1917, Novel

Secret of the Three Junks, The *see* DAS GEHEIMNIS DER DREI DSCHUNKEN (1965).

Secret Operator *see* PACIFIC RENDEZVOUS (1942).

SECRET ORCHARD, THE 1915 d: Frank Reicher. USA., *The Secret Orchard*, Channing Pollock, New York 1907, Play

SECRET PLACES 1985 d: Zelda Barron. UKN., *Secret Places*, Janice Elliott, Novel

SECRET RAPTURE, THE 1993 d: Howard Davies. UKN., *The Secret Rapture*, David Hare, Play

Secret Scrolls (Part I) *see* YAGYU BUGEICHO (1957).

Secret Scrolls (Part Ii) *see* YAGYU BUGEICHO -SORYU HIKEN (1958).

SECRET SERVANT, THE 1984. UKN., Gavin Lyall, Novel

SECRET SERVICE 1919 d: Hugh Ford. USA., *Secret Service*, William Gillette, New York 1896, Play

SECRET SERVICE 1932 d: J. Walter Ruben. USA., *Secret Service*, William Gillette, New York 1896, Play

Secret Spring, The *see* THE HIDDEN SPRING (1917).

SECRET STRINGS 1918 d: John Ince. USA., *Secret Strings*, Kate Jordan, New York 1914, Play

SECRET STUDIO, THE 1927 d: Victor Schertzinger. USA., *Rosemary*, Hazel Livingston, 1926, Novel

SECRET TENT, THE 1956 d: Don Chaffey. UKN., *The Secret Tent*, Elizabeth Addeyman, Play

Secret, The *see* POSSESSED (1947).

SECRET, THE 1955 d: Cy Endfield. UKN., *The Secret*, Robert Brenon, Play

Secret, The see **LE SECRET** (1974).

SECRET TUNNEL, THE 1947 d: William C. Hammond. UKN., *The House With the Blue Door*, Mary Cathcart Borer, Novel

SECRET WAYS, THE 1961 d: Phil Karlson. USA., *The Secret Ways*, Alistair MacLean, New York 1959, Novel

Secret Weapon see **SHERLOCK HOLMES AND THE SECRET WEAPON** (1942).

SECRET WITNESS, THE 1931 d: Thornton Freeland. USA., *Murder in the Gilded Cage*, Samuel Spewack, New York 1929, Novel

SECRET WOMAN, THE 1918 d: A. E. Coleby. UKN., *The Secret Woman*, Eden Philpotts, Novel

Secret Women see **LES CLANDESTINES** (1954).

Secret Yearnings see **MISS WYCKOFF GOOD LUCK** (1979).

SECRETARY OF FRIVOLOUS AFFAIRS, THE 1915 d: Thomas Ricketts. USA., *Secretary of Frivolous Affairs*, May Peel Futrelle, Indianapolis 1911, Novel

SECRETS 1924 d: Frank Borzage. USA., *Secrets*, Rudolf Besier, May Edginton, London 1922, Play

SECRETS 1933 d: Frank Borzage, Marshall Neilan (Uncredited). USA., *Secrets*, Rudolf Besier, May Edginton, London 1922, Play

SECRETS 1942 d: Pierre Blanchar. FRN., *Mesyats V Derevne*, Ivan Turgenev, 1855, Play

Secrets de Famille see **COUP DE FEU DANS LA NUIT** (1942).

SECRETS OF A NURSE 1938 d: Arthur Lubin. USA., *West Side Romance*, Quentin Reynolds, 1936, Short Story

Secrets of a Sexy Game see **CONFESSIONS FROM THE DAVID GALAXY AFFAIR** (1979).

Secrets of a Soul see **CONFESSIONS OF AN OPIUM EATER** (1962).

SECRETS OF CHINATOWN 1934 d: Fred Newmeyer. CND., *The Black Robe*, Guy Morton, Novel

Secrets of Dr. Mabuse see **DIE TODESSTRAHLEN DES DR. MABUSE** (1964).

Secrets of F.P.1 see **F.P.1** (1932).

SECRETS OF PARIS, THE 1922 d: Kenneth Webb. USA., *Les Mysteres de Paris*, Eugene Sue, 1842-43, Novel

SECRETS OF SCOTLAND YARD 1944 d: George Blair. USA., *Room 40 O. B.*, Denison Clift, Novel

Secrets of Society, The see **LADY AUDLEY'S SECRET** (1915).

Secrets of the Blue Room see **SECRET OF THE BLUE ROOM** (1933).

Secrets of the City see **DIE STADT IST VOLLER GEHEIMNISSE** (1955).

SECRETS OF THE FRENCH POLICE 1932 d: A. Edward Sutherland. USA., *Secrets of the Surete*, H. Ashton Wolfe, 1931, Article

SECRETS OF THE NIGHT 1925 d: Herbert Blache. USA., *The Nightcap*, Guy Bolton, Max Marcin, New York 1921, Play

Secrets of the Satin Blues see **LES FOLIES D'ELODIE** (1981).

SECTION DES DISPARUS 1956 d: Pierre Chenal. FRN/ARG., *Of Missing Persons*, David Goodis, Novel

SECTION SPECIALE 1975 d: Costa-Gavras. GRM/ITL/FRN., *Section Speciale*, Herve Villere, Book

Secuestro Bajo El Sol see **PAR UN BEAU MATIN D'ETE** (1964).

Sed, La see **HIJO DE HOMBRE** (1960).

SEDEM JEDNOU RANOU 1988 d: Dusan Trancik. CZC/GRM/FRN., *Das Tapfere Schneiderlein*, Jacob Grimm, Wilhelm Grimm, Short Story

Sedia a Rotelle, La see **UN MEURTRE EST UN MEURTRE** (1972).

SEDUCCION, LA 1980 d: Arturo Ripstein. MXC., *Die Verlobung von San Domingo*, Heinrich von Kleist, 1811, Short Story

Seduced in Sodom see **LA FILLE DE LA MER MORTE** (1966).

Seducer, The see **LE MOUTON ENRAGE** (1974).

Seducteur Ingenu, Le see **TOUTE LA FAMILLE ETAIT LA** (1948).

Seduction see **LA SEDUZIONE** (1973).

Seduction of a Priest see **THE MONK** (1990).

Seduction of Julia, The see **DU BIST ZAUBERHAFT JULIA** (1962).

Seduction of the South see **I BRIGANTI ITALIANI** (1961).

Seduction, The see **LA SEDUCCION** (1980).

Seduction: the Cruel Woman see **VERFUHRUNG: DIE GRAUSAME FRAU** (1984).

SEDUZIONE, LA 1973 d: Fernando Di Leo. ITL., *Graziella*, Ercole Patti, Novel

See How They Fall see **REGARD LES HOMMES TOMBER** (1994).

See How They Run see **BRIGHT ROAD** (1953).

SEE HOW THEY RUN 1955 d: Leslie Arliss. UKN., *See How They Run*, Philip King, London 1945, Play

SEE HOW THEY RUN 1965 d: David Lowell Rich. USA., *The Widow Makers*, Michael Blankfort, Novel

SEE JANE RUN 1994 d: John Patterson. USA., *See Jane Run*, Joy Fielding, Book

SEE MY LAWYER 1921 d: Al Christie. USA., *See My Lawyer*, Max Marcin, New York 1915, Play

See No Evil see **LAW OF THE UNDERWORLD** (1938).

SEE YOU IN JAIL 1927 d: Joseph Henabery. USA., *See You in Jail*, William H. Clifford, Story

See You Monday see **A LUNDI AU REVOIR** (1980).

SEED 1931 d: John M. Stahl. USA., *Seed; a Novel of Birth Control*, Charles Gilman Norris, New York 1930, Novel

Seed, The see **KIMEN** (1973).

SEEDS OF VENGEANCE 1920 d: Oliver L. Sellers. USA., *The Sowing of Alderson Cree*, Margaret Prescott Montague, New York 1907, Novel

SEEING RED 1991 d: Virginia Rouse. ASL., *Red Herring*, Virginia Rouse, Short Story

SEEKERS, THE 1954 d: Ken Annakin. UKN., *The Seekers*, John Guthrie, Novel

SEELENBRAU, DER 1950 d: Gustav Ucicky. AUS., *Der Seelenbrau*, Carl Zuckmayer, 1945, Novel

Seemabaddha see **SEEMABADHA** (1971).

SEEMABADHA 1971 d: Satyajit Ray. IND., *Seemabaddha*, Shankar, Novel

Seemann Ist Kein Schneemann, Ein see **FOUR DAYS LEAVE** (1950).

See-Saw, The see **THE INVISIBLE BOND** (1920).

SEEWOLF, DER 1971 d: Wolfgang Staudte. GRM/RMN., *The Sea Wolf*, Jack London, New York 1904, Novel

SEGRETARIA PRIVATA, LA 1931 d: Goffredo Alessandrini. ITL., *Die Privatsekretarin*, Stefan Szomahazy, Novel

Segreti Che Scottano see **GEHEIMNISSE IN GOLDENEN NYLONS** (1966).

SEGRETO DEL DOTTORE, IL 1930 d: Jack Salvatori. FRN., *Half an Hour*, J. M. Barrie, New York 1913, Play

Segreto Del Garofano Cinese, Il see **DAS GEHEIMNIS DER CHINESISCHEN NELKE** (1964).

Segreto, Il see **LE SECRET** (1974).

SEGRETO INVIOLABILE, IL 1939 d: Julio Fleischner. ITL/SPN., *Successo a Paganigua*, Ernesto Lucente, P. Tellini, Story

SEGUNDO PODER, EL 1976 d: Jose Maria Forque. SPN., *El Hombre de la Cruz Verde*, Segundo Serrano Poncela, 1969, Novel

SEHNSUCHT 1989 d: Jurgen Brauer. GDR., *Sehnsucht*, Jirij Koch, Novel

SEHNSUCHT DES HERZENS 1951 d: Paul Martin. GRM., *D-Zug 517*, Maria von Peteani, Novel

Sei Anni Dopo see **MALA PASQUA** (1919).

Seine Hoheit Der Dienstmann see **DIE BEIDEN SEEHUNDE** (1934).

SEINE MAJESTAT, DAS BETTLEKIND 1920 d: Alexander KordA. AUS., *The Prince and the Pauper*, Mark Twain, New York 1881, Novel

Seine Offizielle Frau see **ESKAPADE** (1936).

SEINE TOCHTER IST DER PETER 1936 d: Heinz Helbig. AUS., *Und Seine Tochter Ist Der Peter*, Edith Zellwecker, Novel

SEINE TOCHTER IST DER PETER 1955 d: Gustav Frohlich. AUS., *Und Seine Tochter Ist Der Peter*, Edith Zellwecker, Novel

SEINS DE GLACE, LES 1974 d: Georges Lautner. FRN/ITL., *Someone Is Bleeding*, Richard Matheson, Novel

Seishu Hanaoka's Wife see **HANAOKA SEISHU NO TSUMA** (1967).

SEISHUN KAIDAN 1955 d: Kon IchikawA. JPN., *Bunroku Shishi*, Short Story

SEITENSPRUNGE 1940 d: Alfred Stoger. GRM., *Seitensprunge*, Hellmut Lange, Novel

SEITSEMAN VELJESTA 1939 d: Wilho Ilmari. FNL., *Seitseman Veljesta*, Aleksis Kivi, 1870, Novel

SEIZE THE DAY 1986 d: Fielder Cook. USA., *Seize the Day*, Saul Bellow, 1956, Short Story

SEKATOMU RAI GISHI 1982 d: Yoichi Takabayashi. JPN., *Sekatomu Rai Gishi*, Baku Akae, Novel

SEKKA TOMURAI ZASHI IREZUMI 1981 d: Yoichi Takabayashi. JPN., *Sekka Tomurai Zashi Irezumi*, Baku Akae, Novel

SELCOR 1975 d: Atanas Traikov. BUL., *Selkor*, Georgi Karaslavov, 1933, Novel

Self Defense see **SELF-DEFENSE** (1932).

SELF-DEFENSE 1932 d: Phil Rosen. USA., *The Just Judge*, Peter B. Kyne, Short Story

SELF-MADE LADY 1932 d: George King. UKN., *Sookey*, Douglas Newton, Novel

SELF-MADE MAN, A 1922 d: Rowland V. Lee. USA., *Jack Spurlock - Prodigal*, George Horace Lorimer, New York 1908, Novel

SELF-MADE WIFE, THE 1923 d: John Francis Dillon. USA., *The Self-Made Wife*, Elizabeth Alexander, 1922, Short Story

Self-Portrait see **SMARTY** (1934).

Self-Willed Girl, A see **SVEHLAVICKA** (1926).

Selkor see **SELCOR** (1975).

SELTSAME GESCHICHTE DES BRANDNER KASPER, DIE 1949 d: Josef von Baky. GRM., Franz Kobell, Short Story, *Der Brandner Kaspar Schaut Ins Paradies*, Joseeph Maria Lutz, Play

SELTSAME GRAFIN, DIE 1961 d: Josef von Baky. GRM., *The Strange Countess*, Edgar Wallace, London 1925, Novel

SELTSAME LEBEN DES HERRN BRUGGS, DAS 1951 d: Erich Engel. GRM., *Das Verschlossene Haus*, Curt Johannes Braun, Book

SELTSAME NACHT DER HELGA WANGEN, DIE 1928 d: Holger-Madsen. GRM., *Eine Seltsame Nacht*, Laurids Bruun, Novel

SELTSAME VERGANGENHEIT DER THEA CARTER, DIE 1929 d: Josef Levigard. GRM., *The House of Glass*, George M. Cohan, Max Marcin, New York 1915, Play

SELTSAMER FALL, EIN 1914 d: Max Mack. GRM., *The Strange Case of Dr. Jekyll and Mr. Hyde*, Robert Louis Stevenson, London 1886, Novel

SELVA TRAGICA 1964 d: Roberto Farias. BRZ., *Selva Tragica*, Hermani Donati, 1959, Novel

Sembazuru see **SENBAZURU** (1969).

Semeinoe Schaste see **SEMEJNOE SCASTE** (1969).

SEMEJNOE SCASTE 1969 d: Sergei Soloviev, Alexander Shein. USS., *Nervy*, Anton Chekhov, Short Story, *Ot Nechego Delat*, Anton Chekhov, 1885-1888, Short Story

SEMEJNOE SCASTE 1969 d: Andrei Ladynin. USS., *Mstitel*, Anton Chekhov, Short Story, *Preloyheniye*, Anton Chekhov, Short Story

Seminarist, The see **O SEMINARISTA** (1976).

SEMINARISTA, O 1976 d: Geraldo Santos PereirA. BRZ., *O Seminarista*, Bernardo Guimaraes, 1895, Novel

SEMINOLE UPRISING 1955 d: Earl Bellamy. USA., *Bugle's Wake*, Curt Brandon, 1952, Novel

SEMI-TOUGH 1977 d: Michael Ritchie. USA., *Semi-Tough*, Dan Jenkins, Book

SEMJA OPPENHEIM 1939 d: Grigori Roshal. USS., *Die Geschwister Oppenheim*, Lion Feuchtwanger, 1933, Novel

Semla Oppenheim see **SEMJA OPPENHEIM** (1939).

SEMPRE PIU DIFFICILE 1943 d: Renato Angiolillo, Piero Ballerini. ITL., *Sua Eccellenza Di Falconmarzano*, Nino Martoglio, Play

Semya Oppengeim see **SEMJA OPPENHEIM** (1939).

SEN DE GITME 1997 d: Tunc Basaran. TRK., Ayla Kutlu, Novel

SEN NO RIKYU - HONGAKUBO IBUN 1989 d: Kei Kumai. JPN., *Hongakubo Ibun*, Yasushi Inoue, Novel

SEN NOCI SVATOJANSKE 1959 d: Jiri TrnkA. CZC., *A Midsummer Night's Dream*, William Shakespeare, c1594, Play

Senator, Der see **DIE JAHRE VERGEHEN** (1944).

SENATOR WAS INDISCREET, THE 1947 d: George S. Kaufman. USA., Edwin Lanham, Story

SENATOR'S BROTHER, THE 1914 d: William Humphrey. USA., *The Senator's Brother*, Gouverneur Morris, Story

SENATOR'S LADY, THE 1914. USA., *Hannah Jane*, D. R. Locke, Poem

SENBAZURU 1969 d: Yasuzo MasumurA. JPN., *Senbazuru*, Yasunari Kawabata, Tokyo 1958, Novel

Send Another Coffin see **SLIGHTLY HONORABLE** (1939).

Send in Another Coffin see **SLIGHTLY HONORABLE** (1939).

SEND ME NO FLOWERS 1964 d: Norman Jewison. USA., *Send Me No Flowers*, Norman Barasch, Carroll Moore, New York 1960, Play

SENDUNG DER LYSISTRATA, DIE 1961 d: Fritz Kortner. GRM., Aristophanes, Story

Sendung Des Joghi, Die see **DAS INDISCHE GRABMAL I** (1921).

SENGOKU JIEITAI 1980 d: Kosei Saito. JPN., *Sengoku Jieitai*, Ryo Hanmura, Novel

SENILITA 1962 d: Mauro Bolognini. ITL/FRN., *Senilita*, Italo Svevo, 1898, Novel

SENIORCHEF, DER 1942 d: Peter P. Brauer. GRM., *Seine Majestat Gustav Krause*, Eberhard Foerster, Play

SENKYRKA "U DIVOKE KRASY" 1932 d: Svatopluk Innemann. CZC., *Romanek Na Horach*, Josef Skruzny, Play

SENOR DE OSANTO, EL 1972 d: Jaime Humberto Hermosillo. MXC., *The Master of Ballantrae*, Robert Louis Stevenson, 1888, Novel

SENOR ESTEVE, EL 1929 d: Lucas Argiles. SPN., *L'Auca Del Senyor Esteve*, Santiago Rusinol, 1907, Play

SENOR ESTEVE, EL 1948 d: Edgar Neville. SPN., *L'Auca Del Senyor Esteve*, Santiago Rusinol, 1907, Play

SENOR FEUDAL, EL 1925 d: Agustin Carrasco. SPN., *El Senor Feudal*, Joaquin Dicenta, Play

SENOR JIM 1936 d: Jacques Jaccard. USA., *I.O.U.'S of Death*, Ciela Jaccard, Story

SENOR MUY VIEJO CON UNAS ALAS ENORMES, UN 1988 d: Fernando Birri. CUB/ITL/SPN., Gabriel Garcia Marquez, Story

Senor Presidente, El see **EL SR. PRESIDENTE** (1983).

SENORA AMA 1954 d: Julio Bracho. MXC/SPN., *Senora Ama*, Jacinto Benavente y Martinez, 1908, Play

SENORA CASADA NECESITA MARIDO 1935 d: James Tinling. USA., *Az En Masodik Felesegem*, Eugene Heltai, 1907, Novel

SENORA, LA 1987 d: Jordi CadenA. SPN., *La Senora*, Antoni Mus, Novel

SENORITO OCTAVIO, EL 1950 d: Jeronimo MihurA. SPN., *El Senorito Octavio*, Armando Palacio Valdes, 1881, Novel

SENS DE LA MORT, LE 1922 d: Yakov Protazanov. FRN., *Le Sens de la Mort*, Paul Bourget, Novel

Sensation see **THE MISLEADING LADY** (1932).

SENSATION 1937 d: Brian Desmond Hurst. UKN., *Murder Gang*, Basil Dean, George Munro, London 1935, Play

Sensation at the Savoy Hotel see **SENSATION IM SAVOY** (1950).

SENSATION HUNTERS 1933 d: Charles Vidor. USA., *Cabaret*, Whitman Chambers, Short Story

SENSATION IM SAVOY 1950 d: Eduard von Borsody. GRM., *Sensation in Budapest*, Karl Georg Kulb, Play

SENSATION SEEKERS 1927 d: Lois Weber. USA., *Egypt*, Ernest Pascal, Story

Sensations see **SENSATIONS OF 1945** (1944).

SENSATIONS OF 1945 1944 d: Andrew L. Stone. USA., Frederick Jackson, Story

SENSATIONS-PROZESS 1928 d: Friedrich Feher. GRM., *Prozess Bunterbart*, Max Brod, Play

SENSATIONSPROZESS CASSILLA 1939 d: Eduard von Borsody. GRM., *Sensationsprozess Casilla*, Hans Possendorff, Novel

SENSE AND SENSIBILITY 1980 d: Rodney Bennett. UKN., *Sense and Sensibility*, Jane Austen, 1811, Novel

SENSE AND SENSIBILITY 1995 d: Ang Lee. UKN/USA., *Sense and Sensibility*, Jane Austen, 1811, Novel

SENSE OF FREEDOM, A 1979 d: John MacKenzie. UKN., *A Sense of Freedom*, Jimmy Boyle, Autobiography

SENSITIVE, PASSIONATE MAN, A 1977 d: John Newland. USA., *Passionate Man, a Sensitive*, Barbara Mahoney, Novel

SENSO 1954 d: Luchino Visconti. ITL., *Senso*, Camillo Boito, Milan 1883, Novel

SENSO TO NINGEN 1970 d: Satsuo Yamamoto. JPN., *Senso to Ningen*, Jumpei Gomikawa, Novel

Sensual Man, The see **PAOLO IL CALDO** (1973).

Sensualist, The see **TURKS FRUITS** (1973).

SENSUALIST, THE 1992 d: Yukio Abe. JPN., *The Sensualist*, Saikaku Ihara, Novel

Sensuous Sicilian, The see **PAOLO IL CALDO** (1973).

SENTENCE OF DEATH, THE 1927 d: Miles Mander. UKN., *The Sentence of Death*, Cyril Campion, Edward Dignon, Play

Sentence, The see **THE MAN WHO TALKED TOO MUCH** (1940).

Sentenced to Soft Labor see **THE BREATHLESS MOMENT** (1924).

Sentiero Dei Disperati, Il see **LE RAT D'AMERIQUE** (1962).

Sentiment see **SENSO** (1954).

SENTIMENTAL JOURNEY 1946 d: Walter Lang. USA., *The Little Horse*, Nelia Gardner White, Short Story

SENTIMENTAL JOURNEY 1984 d: James Goldstone. USA., *The Little Horse*, Nelia Gardner White, Short Story

SENTIMENTAL LADY, THE 1915 d: Walter Edwin, Sidney Olcott. USA., *The Sentimental Lady*, Owen Davis, Play

Sentimental Romance see **SENTIMENTALNYI ROMAN** (1976).

Sentimental Story, A see **POVESTE SENTIMENTALA** (1961).

Sentimental Story, A see **SENTIMENTALNYI ROMAN** (1976).

SENTIMENTAL TOMMY 1921 d: John S. Robertson. USA., *Sentimental Tommy*, J. M. Barrie, 1895, Novel

SENTIMENTALNYI ROMAN 1976 d: Igor Maslennikov. USS., *Sentimentalnyi Roman*, Vera Fyodorovna Panova, 1958, Novel

SENTINEL, THE 1977 d: Michael Winner. USA., *The Sentinel*, Jeffrey Konvitz, Novel

SENTINELLE DI BRONZO 1937 d: Romolo Marcellini. ITL., *Marrabo*, Marcello Orano, Sandro Sandri, Short Story

Sentinels Under the Neon Lights see **NI HONG DENG XIA DE SHAO BING** (1964).

Sentries Under Neon Lights see **NI HONG DENG XIA DE SHAO BING** (1964).

Senyora, La see **LA SENORA** (1987).

Senza Dio, I see **ORIZZONTE DI SANGUE** (1942).

SENZA FAMIGLIA 1945 d: Giorgio Ferroni. ITL., *Sans Famille*, Hector Malot, Novel

Senza Famiglia see **SANS FAMILLE** (1957).

Senza Movente see **SANS MOBILE APPARENT** (1971).

Separate Beds see **THE WHEELER DEALERS** (1963).

SEPARATE TABLES 1958 d: Delbert Mann. USA., *Separate Tables*, Terence Rattigan, London 1955, Play

SEPARATE TABLES 1983 d: John Schlesinger. UKN/USA., *Separate Tables*, Terence Rattigan, London 1955, Play

SEPARATE VACATIONS 1986 d: Michael Anderson. CND., *Separate Vacations*, Eric Webber, Novel

SEPARATION 1990 d: Barry Davis. UKN/USA., *Separation*, Tom Kempinski, Play

Separation Des Races, La see **RAPT** (1934).

SEPARATION 1994 d: Christian Vincent. FRN., *La Separation*, Dan Franck, Novel

Separation, The see **LA SEPARATION** (1994).

Sepolcro Indiano, Il see **DAS INDISCHE GRABMAL** (1959).

SEPOLTA VIVA, LA 1916 d: Enrico Vidali. ITL., *La Sepolta Viva*, Carolina Invernizio, 1900, Novel

SEPOLTA VIVA, LA 1949 d: Guido Brignone. ITL., *La Sepolta Viva*, Francesco Mastriani, Novel

SEPOLTA VIVA, LA 1973 d: Aldo Lado. ITL/FRN., *Sepolta Viva*, Marie Eugenie Saffray, Novel

SEPPUKU 1962 d: Masaki Kobayashi. JPN., *Ibunronin Ki*, Yasuhiko Takiguchi, 1958, Short Story

SEPT FOIS PAR JOUR. 1971 d: Denis Heroux. CND/ISR., *The Woman Luli Sent Me*, Ted Allan, Novel

SEPTEMBER 1994 d: Colin Bucksey. UKN/GRM., *September*, Rosamunde Pilcher, Novel

SEPTEMBER AFFAIR 1950 d: William Dieterle. USA., Fritz Rotter, Story

SEPTEMBER STORM 1960 d: Byron Haskin. USA., *The Girl in the Red Bikini*, Steve Fisher, Novel

SEPTIEME CIEL, LE 1957 d: Raymond Bernard. FRN/ITL., *Le Septieme Ciel*, Andre Lang, Novel

SEPTIEME JURE, LE 1962 d: Georges Lautner. FRN., *Le Septieme Jure*, Francis Didelot, Paris 1958, Novel

Septima's Ideal see **IDEAL SEPTIMY** (1938).

Septimo de Caballeria, El see **SEVENTH CAVALRY** (1956).

SEQUESTRATI DI ALTONA, I 1962 d: Vittorio de SicA. ITL/FRN., *Les Sequestres d'Altona*, Jean-Paul Sartre, 1959, Play

Sequestres d'Altona, Les see **I SEQUESTRATI DI ALTONA** (1962).

SEQUOIA 1934 d: Chester M. Franklin. USA., *Malibu*, Vance Joseph Hoyt, Boston 1931, Novel

SERA C'INCONTRAMMO, UNA 1976 d: Piero SchivazappA. ITL., *Amare Significa.*, Italo Terzoli, Enrico Vaime, Novel

Serata Di Gala see **LA FORZA BRUTA** (1941).

Serbian Lady MacBeth see **SIBIRSKA LEDI MAGBET** (1962).

SERENADE 1921 d: Raoul Walsh. USA., *Maria Del Carmen*, Jose Felin Y Codina, Novel

Serenade see **PRINCESSE CZARDAS** (1934).

SERENADE 1937 d: Willi Forst. GRM., *Viola Tricolor*, Theodor Storm, 1874, Novel

SERENADE 1956 d: Anthony Mann. USA., *Serenade*, James M. Cain, 1937, Novel

Serenade for Two Spies see **SERENADE FUR ZWEI SPIONE** (1965).

SERENADE FUR ZWEI SPIONE 1965 d: Michael Pfleghar, Alberto Cardone. GRM/ITL., K. H. Gunther, Novel

SERENATA AL VENTO 1956 d: Luigi de Marchi. ITL., *Serenata Al Vento*, Carlo Veneziani, Play

Serenata d'Amore see **LA PRIGIONE** (1942).

Sereza see **SEREZHA** (1960).

SEREZHA 1960 d: Georgi Daneliya, Igor Talankin. USS., *Seryozha*, Vera Fyodorovna Panova, Leningrad 1955, Novel

SERGE PANINE 1913 d: Henri Pouctal. FRN., *Serge Panine*, Georges Ohnet, Novel

SERGE PANINE 1915 d: Wray Physioc. USA., *Serge Panine*, Georges Ohnet, Novel

SERGE PANINE 1922 d: Charles Maudru, Maurice de Marsan. FRN/AUS., *Serge Panine*, Georges Ohnet, Novel

SERGE PANINE 1938 d: Charles Mere, Paul Schiller. FRN., *Serge Panine*, Georges Ohnet, Novel

SERGEANT BERRY 1938 d: Herbert Selpin. GRM., *Sergeant Berry*, Robert Arden, Novel

SERGEANT MUSGRAVE'S DANCE 1961 d: Stuart Burge. UKN., *Sergeant Musgrave's Dance*, John Arden, 1959, Play

SERGEANT, THE 1968 d: John Flynn. USA., *The Sergeant*, Dennis Murphy, New York 1958, Novel

SERGEANT YORK 1941 d: Howard Hawks. USA., *War Diary of Sergeant York*, Sam K. Cowan, Book, *Sergeant York - Last of the Long Hunters*, Tom Skeyhill, Article

Sergente Studer, Il see **WACHTMEISTER STUDER** (1939).

SERIAL 1980 d: Bill Persky. USA., *Serial*, Cyra McFadden, Novel

SERIOUS CHARGE 1959 d: Terence Young. UKN., *Serious Charge*, Philip King, London 1955, Play

Serious Game see **DEN ALLVARSAMMA LEKEN** (1945).

SERPENT, LE 1973 d: Henri Verneuil. FRN/ITL/GRM., *Le Serpent*, Pierre Nord, Novel

Serpent, The see **ORMEN** (1966).

Serpent, The see **LE SERPENT** (1973).

SERPENTE A SONAGLI, IL 1935 d: Raffaello Matarazzo. ITL., *Il Serpente a Sonagli*, Edoardo Anton, Play

Serpente, Il see **LE SERPENT** (1973).

SERPICO 1973 d: Sidney Lumet. USA/ITL., *Serpico*, Peter Maas, Book

SERPICO: THE DEADLY GAME 1976 d: Robert Collins. USA., *Serpico*, Peter Maas, Book

SERVA PADRONA, LA 1934 d: Giorgio Mannini. ITL., *La Serva Padrona*, G. A. Federico, Giovanni Battista Pergolesi, Napoli 1733, Opera

SERVANT IN THE HOUSE, THE 1915. USA., *The Servant in the House*, Charles Ryan Kennedy, New York 1908, Play

SERVANT IN THE HOUSE, THE 1920 d: Jack Conway. USA., *The Servant in the House*, Charles Ryan Kennedy, New York 1908, Play

SERVANT, THE 1963 d: Joseph Losey. UKN., *The Servant*, Robin Maugham, London 1948, Novel

SERVANTE AIMANTE, LA 1996 d: Jean Douchet. FRN., *La Serva Amorosa*, Carlo Goldoni, 1752, Play

SERVANTS' ENTRANCE 1934 d: Frank Lloyd. USA., *Vi Som Gar Kjokkenveien*, Sigrid Boo, Oslo 1930, Novel

SERVANTS OF TWILIGHT 1991 d: Jeffrey Obrow. USA., *Twilight*, Dean R. Koontz, Novel

Servant's Shirt, The see **NAUKAR KI KAMEEZ** (1999).

Servar Sundaram see **SERVER SUNDARAM** (1964).

SERVER SUNDARAM 1964 d: R. Krishnan, S. Panju. IND., *Server Sundaram*, K. Balachander, Play

Service see **LOOKING FORWARD** (1933).

SERVICE DE NUIT 1931 d: Henri Fescourt. FRN., *Der Mude Theodor*, Max Ferner, Max Neal, Play

SERVICE FOR LADIES 1932 d: Alexander KordA. UKN/USA., *The Head Waiter*, Erno Vajda, Novel

SERVICE OF LOVE, A 1917 d: John S. Robertson. USA., *A Service of Love*, O. Henry, Short Story

SERVING TWO MASTERS 1921. USA., *Break the Walls Down*, Mrs. Alexander Gross, 1914, Play

Seryozha see **SEREZHA** (1960).

Seryozha (the Splendid Days) see **SEREZHA** (1960).

SESHA SHRABANA 1976 d: Prashanta NandA. IND., *Shesha Shrabana*, Basant Mahapatra, Play

SESSO IN CONFESSIONALE 1974 d: Vittorio de Sisti. ITL., C. Di Meglio, N. Valentini, Book

SEST MUSKETYRU 1925 d: Premysl Prazsky. CZC., *Sest Musketyru*, Jan Klecanda, Novel

SESTRY 1957 d: Grigori Roshal. USS., *Khozhdeniye Po Mukam*, Alexsey Nikolayevich Tolstoy, 1922-45, Novel

SETE GATINHOS, OS 1979 d: Neville d'AlmeidA. BRZ., *Os Sete Gatinhos*, Nelson Rodrigues, 1958, Play

SETEA 1960 d: Mircea Dragan. RMN., *Setea*, Titus Popovici, 1958, Novel

SETENTA VECES SIETE 1962 d: Leopoldo Torre-Nilsson. ARG., *Setenta Veces Siete*, Dalmiro A. Saenz, Buenos Aires 1957, Short Story

SETOUCHI MOONLIGHT SERENADE 1997 d: Masahiro ShinodA. JPN., *Setouchi Moonlight Serenade*, Yu Aku, Novel

SETOUCHI SHONEN YAKYU DAN SEISHUNHEN SAIGO NO RAKUEN 1987 d: Haruhiko MimurA. JPN., *Setouchi Shonen Yakyu Dan*, Yu Aku, Novel

SETOUCHI SHONEN YAKYUDAN 1984 d: Masahiro ShinodA. JPN., *Setouchi Shonen Yakyu Dan*, Yu Aku, Novel

SETTE BASCHI ROSSI 1968 d: Mario Siciliano. ITL/GRM., *Rebellion*, Piero Regnoli, Novel

SETTE CONTRO LA MORTE 1965 d: Edgar G. Ulmer, Paolo Bianchini. ITL/GRM/YGS., Leon Uris, Novel

SETTE GIORNI ALL'ALTRO MONDO 1936 d: Mario Mattoli. ITL., *Sette Giorni All'altro Mondo*, Aldo de Benedetti, Play

SETTE NANI ALLA RISCOSSA, I 1952 d: Paolo William TamburellA. ITL., *Wanda Petrini*, Short Story

SETTE ORE DI GUAI 1951 d: Vittorio Metz, Marcello Marchesi. ITL., *'Na Creatura Sperduta*, Eduardo Scarpetta, 1899, Play

SETTE PECCATI, I 1942 d: Ladislao Kish. ITL., Zoltan Magyivanyi, Short Story

Settlers, The see **INVANDRARNA** (1970).

SET-UP, THE 1926 d: Cliff Smith. USA., *Horse Sense*, L. V. Jefferson, Story

SET-UP, THE 1949 d: Robert Wise. USA., *The Set-Up*, Joseph Moncure March, 1928, Poem

SET-UP, THE 1963 d: Gerald Glaister. UKN., Edgar Wallace, Short Story

SEUL AMOUR, UN 1943 d: Pierre Blanchar. FRN., *La Grande Breteche Ou Les Trois Vengeances*, Honore de Balzac, 1837, Novel

SEUL BANDIT DU VILLAGE, LE 1931 d: Robert Bossis. FRN., *Le Seul Bandit du Village*, Tristan Bernard, Play

Seul le Vent Connait la Response see **DIE ANTWORT KENNT NUR DER WIND** (1975).

SEULEMENT PAR AMOUR: CLARA 1991 d: Andrea Frazzi, Antonio Frazzi. FRN/ITL., *Una Storia Spezzata*, Maria Venturi, Novel

SEVA SADAN 1938 d: K. Subrahmanyam. IND., *Bazaar-E-Husn*, Premchand, 1919, Novel

Seva Sadanam see **SEVA SADAN** (1938).

SEVEN AGES OF MAN, THE 1914 d: Charles Vernon. UKN., *The Seven Ages of Man*, William Shakespeare, Poem

SEVEN ALONE 1974 d: Earl Bellamy. USA., *Seven Alone*, Honore Morrow, Novel

SEVEN BRIDES FOR SEVEN BROTHERS 1954 d: Stanley Donen. USA., *The Sobbin' Women*, Stephen Vincent Benet, 1937, Short Story

Seven Brothers see **SEITSEMAN VELJESTA** (1939).

SEVEN CHANCES 1925 d: Buster Keaton. USA., *Seven Chances*, Roi Cooper Megrue, 1924, Play

SEVEN CITIES OF GOLD 1955 d: Robert D. Webb. USA., *The Nine Days of Father Sierra*, Isabelle Gibson Zeigler, 1951, Novel

SEVEN DAYS 1925 d: Scott Sidney. USA., *Seven Days*, Mary Roberts Rinehart, 1908, Short Story

SEVEN DAYS IN MAY 1964 d: John Frankenheimer. USA., *Seven Days in May*, Charles Waldo Bailey, Fletcher Knebel, New York 1962, Novel

SEVEN DAYS LEAVE 1930 d: Richard Wallace, John Cromwell. USA., *The Old Lady Shows Her Medals*, J. M. Barrie, New York 1918, Play

SEVEN DAYS LEAVE 1942 d: Tim Whelan. USA., *The Old Lady Shows Her Medals*, J. M. Barrie, New York 1918, Play

Seven Days. Seven Nights see **MODERATO CANTABILE** (1960).

Seven Days Time see **SIEBEN TAGE FRIST** (1969).

Seven Dead in the Cat's Eye see **LA MORTE NEGLI OCCHI DEL GATTO** (1973).

Seven Deaths in the Cat's Eye see **LA MORTE NEGLI OCCHI DEL GATTO** (1973).

SEVEN DIALS MYSTERY, THE 1980 d: Tony Wharmby. UKN., *The Seven Dials Mystery*, Agatha Christie, Novel

Seven Dirty Devils see **SETTE BASCHI ROSSI** (1968).

Seven Dwarfs to the Rescue, The see **I SETTE NANI ALLA RISCOSSA** (1952).

SEVEN FACES 1929 d: Berthold Viertel. USA., *A Friend of Napoleon*, Richard Connell, 1923, Short Story

SEVEN FACES OF DR. LAO, THE 1964 d: George Pal. USA., *The Circus of Dr. Lao*, Charles G. Finney, New York 1961, Novel

SEVEN FOOTPRINTS TO SATAN 1929 d: Benjamin Christensen. USA., *7 Footprints to Satan*, Abraham Merritt, New York 1928, Novel

Seven Girls see **SEVEN SWEETHEARTS** (1942).

SEVEN HILLS OF ROME, THE 1957 d: Roy Rowland, Mario Russo. USA/ITL., *Sera Di Pioggia*, Peppino Amato, Story

SEVEN IN DARKNESS 1969 d: Michael Caffey. USA., *Against Heaven's Hand*, Leonard Bishop, Novel

SEVEN KEYS TO BALDPATE 1917 d: Hugh Ford. USA., *Seven Keys to Baldpate*, Earl Derr Biggers, Indianapolis 1913, Novel

SEVEN KEYS TO BALDPATE 1925 d: Fred Newmeyer. USA., *Seven Keys to Baldpate*, Earl Derr Biggers, Indianapolis 1913, Novel

SEVEN KEYS TO BALDPATE 1929 d: Reginald Barker. USA., *Seven Keys to Baldpate*, Earl Derr Biggers, Indianapolis 1913, Novel

SEVEN KEYS TO BALDPATE 1935 d: William Hamilton, Edward Killy. USA., *Seven Keys to Baldpate*, Earl Derr Biggers, Indianapolis 1913, Novel

SEVEN KEYS TO BALDPATE 1947 d: Lew Landers. USA., *Seven Keys to Baldpate*, Earl Derr Biggers, Indianapolis 1913, Novel

Seven Lives Were Changed see **ORIENT EXPRESS** (1934).

Seven Mad Men see **LOS SIETE LOCOS** (1973).

Seven Madmen, The see **LOS SIETE LOCOS** (1973).

SEVEN MILES FROM ALCATRAZ 1942 d: Edward Dmytryk. USA., *Southwest Pass*, John D. Klorer, Story

Seven Minutes see **GEORG ELSER - EINER AUS DEUTSCHLAND** (1989).

Seven Red Berets see **SETTE BASCHI ROSSI** (1968).

SEVEN SINNERS 1936 d: Albert de Courville. UKN., *The Wrecker*, Bernard Merivale, Arnold Ridley, London 1927, Play

SEVEN SISTERS 1915 d: Sidney Olcott. USA., *Seven Sisters*, Ferenc Herczeg, Play

Seven Sisters, The see **SEVEN SISTERS** (1915).

SEVEN SWANS, THE 1918 d: J. Searle Dawley. USA., *The Seven Swans*, Hans Christian Andersen, Short Story

SEVEN SWEETHEARTS 1942 d: Frank Borzage. USA., *La Maison Des Sept Jeunes Filles*, Georges Simenon, 1941, Novel

SEVEN THIEVES 1960 d: Henry Hathaway. USA., *Seven Thieves*, Max Catto, Novel

SEVEN THUNDERS 1957 d: Hugo Fregonese. UKN., *Seven Thunders*, Rupert Croft-Cooke, Novel

Seven Times a Day see **SEPT FOIS PAR JOUR.** (1971).

SEVEN WAYS FROM SUNDOWN 1960 d: Harry Keller. USA., *Seven Ways from Sundown*, Clair Huffaker, Novel

SEVEN WOMEN 1965 d: John Ford. USA., *Chinese Finale*, Norah Lofts, London 1935, Short Story

SEVEN YEAR ITCH, THE 1955 d: Billy Wilder. USA., *The Seven Year Itch*, George Axelrod, New York 1952, Play

SEVEN YEARS IN TIBET 1997 d: Jean-Jacques Annaud. USA/UKN., *Seven Years in Tibet*, Heinrich Harrer, Book

SEVEN-PER-CENT SOLUTION, THE 1976 d: Herbert Ross. USA., *The Seven-Per-Cent Solution*, Nicholas Meyer, Novel

SEVENTEEN 1916 d: Robert G. VignolA. USA., *Seventeen*, Booth Tarkington, New York 1913, Novel

SEVENTEEN 1940 d: Louis King. USA., *Seventeen*, Booth Tarkington, New York 1913, Novel

Seventeen see **SYTTEN** (1965).

SEVENTH AVENUE 1977 d: Richard Irving. USA., *Seventh Avenue*, Norman Bogner, Novel

SEVENTH CAVALRY 1956 d: Joseph H. Lewis, Raphael J. SevillA. USA., *A Horse for Mrs. Custer*, Glendon Swarthout, Story

SEVENTH CROSS, THE 1944 d: Fred Zinnemann. USA., *Das Siebte Kreuz*, Anna Seghers, 1939, Novel

SEVENTH DAWN, THE 1964 d: Lewis Gilbert. UKN/USA., *The Durian Tree*, Michael Keon, New York 1960, Novel

Seventh Floor, The see **IL FISCHIO AL NASO** (1967).

Seventh Heaven see **7TH HEAVEN** (1927).

SEVENTH HEAVEN 1937 d: Henry King. USA., *Seventh Heaven*, Austin Strong, New York 1922, Play

Seventh Horse of the Sun, The see **SURAJ KA SATWAN GHODA** (1992).

Seventh Horse of the Sun's Chariot see **SURAJ KA SATWAN GHODA** (1992).

Seventh Juror, The see **LE SEPTIEME JURE** (1962).

SEVENTH NOON, THE 1915. USA., *The Seventh Noon*, Frederick Orin Bartlett, New York 1910, Novel

SEVENTH SIN, THE 1957 d: Ronald Neame, Vincente Minnelli (Uncredited). USA., *The Painted Veil*, W. Somerset Maugham, New York 1925, Novel

Seventh Victim, The see **DAS SIEBENTE OPFER** (1964).

Seventy Times Seven see **SETENTA VECES SIETE** (1962).

SEVENTY-SEVEN, PARK LANE 1931 d: Albert de Courville. UKN., *77 Park Lane*, Walter Hackett, London 1928, Play

Seventy-Two Tenants see **QI SHI ER JIA FANG KE** (1963).

Several Days in the Life of I.I. Oblomov see **NESKOLKO DNEI IZ ZHIZNI I.I. OBLOMOV** (1980).

SEVERED HEAD, A 1970 d: Dick Clement. UKN., *A Severed Head*, Iris Murdoch, 1961, Novel

SEVERINO 1977 d: Claus Dobberke. GDR., *Severino*, Eduard Klein, Novel

SEVERO TORELLI 1914 d: Louis Feuillade. FRN., *Severo Torelli*, Francois Coppee, Play

Sewer see **KANAL** (1957).

Sewers of Paris, The see **LES EGOUTS DU PARADIS** (1978).

SEX AND THE SINGLE GIRL 1964 d: Richard Quine. USA., *Sex and the Single Girl*, Helen Gurley Brown, New York 1962, Novel

Sex Demons, The *see* LES DEMONS (1973).

Sex Diary *see* IL LETTO IN PIAZZA (1976).

SEX IN SWEDEN 1977 d: Mac Ahlberg. SWD., *Moll Flanders*, Daniel Defoe, 1722, Novel

Sex in the Classroom *see* I RAGAZZI DEL MASSACRO (1969).

Sex Is a Pleasure *see* DIE TOLLDREISTEN GESCHICHTEN - NACH HONORE DE BALZAC (1969).

Sex Is My Game *see* SAPHO OU LA FUREUR D'AIMER (1970).

Sex Life in a Convent *see* INTERNO DI UN CONVENTO (1977).

Sex, Love, Murder *see* HERZBUBE (1972).

Sex machine, The *see* CONVIENE FAR BENE L'AMORE (1975).

Sex, Shame and Tears *see* PUDOR Y LAGRIMAS SEXO (1999).

SEX SYMBOL, THE 1974 d: David Lowell Rich. USA., *The Symbol*, Alva Bessie, 1966, Novel

SEXE FAIBLE, LE 1934 d: Robert Siodmak. FRN., *Le Sexe Faible*, Edouard Bourdet, 1931, Play

SEXO, PUDOR Y LAGRIMAS 1999 d: Antonio Serrano. MXC., *Sexo Pudor y Lagrimas*, Antonio Serrano, Play

SEXTANERIN, DIE 1936 d: Svatopluk Innemann. GRM/CZC., *Sextanka*, Vilem Neubauer, Novel

SEXTANKA 1927 d: Josef Medeotti-Bohac. CZC., *Sextanka*, Vilem Neubauer, Novel

SEXTANKA 1936 d: Svatopluk Innemann. CZC., *Sextanka*, Vilem Neubauer, Novel

SEXTON BLAKE 1909 d: C. Douglas Carlile. UKN., *Sexton Blake*, C. Douglas Carlile, Play

SEXTON BLAKE AND THE BEARDED DOCTOR 1935 d: George A. Cooper. UKN., *The Blazing Launch Murder*, Rex Hardinge, Novel

SEXTON BLAKE AND THE HOODED TERROR 1938 d: George King. UKN., *Sexton Blake and the Hooded Terror*, Pierre Quiroule, Novel

SEXTON BLAKE AND THE MADEMOISELLE 1935 d: Alex Bryce. UKN., *They Shall Repay*, G. H. Teed, Novel

Sexual Perversity in Chicago *see* ABOUT LAST NIGHT (1986).

Sexual Revolution, The *see* LA RIVOLUZIONE SESSUALE (1968).

Sexy Girl *see* VOULEZ-VOUS DANSER AVEC MOI? (1960).

Sfinge Dello Jonio, La *see* CHRISTUS (1914).

SFINGE, LA 1920 d: Roberto Leone Roberti. ITL., *Le Sphinx*, Octave Feuillet, 1874, Novel

Sguardo Dal Ponte, Uno *see* VU DU PONT (1962).

SH! THE OCTOPUS 1937 d: William McGann. USA., *Sh! the Octopus*, Donald Gallaher, Ralph Murphy, Ralph Spence, New York 1928, Play

Shabby Tiger, The *see* MASQUERADE (1964).

SHACKLES OF GOLD 1922 d: Herbert Brenon. USA., *Samson*, Henri Bernstein, New York 1908, Play

Shadow Army *see* L' ARMEE DES OMBRES (1969).

SHADOW BETWEEN, THE 1920 d: George Dewhurst. UKN., *The Shadow Between*, Silas K. Hocking, Novel

SHADOW BOX, THE 1980 d: Paul Newman. USA., *The Shadow Box*, Michael Christopher, Play

SHADOW IN THE SKY 1951 d: Fred M. Wilcox. USA., *Come Another Day*, Edward Newhouse, Story

Shadow Line, The *see* SMUGA CIENIA (1976).

Shadow Man *see* STREET OF SHADOWS (1953).

Shadow Murder Case, The *see* INTERNATIONAL CRIME (1938).

SHADOW OF A DOUBT 1943 d: Alfred Hitchcock. USA., *Uncle Charlie*, Gordon McDonell, Story

SHADOW OF A DOUBT 1991 d: Karen Arthur. USA., *Uncle Charlie*, Gordon McDonell, Story

SHADOW OF A MAN 1955 d: Michael McCarthy. UKN., *Shadow of a Man*, Paul Erickson, Play

Shadow of a Rope, The *see* OUT OF THE SHADOW (1919).

SHADOW OF A WOMAN 1946 d: Joseph Santley. USA., *He Fell Down Dead*, Virginia Purdue, Novel

SHADOW OF DEATH 1939 d: Harry S. Marks. UKN., *Shadow of Death*, John Quin, Play

SHADOW OF DOUBT 1935 d: George B. Seitz. USA., *Shadow of Doubt*, Arthur Somers Roche, New York 1935, Novel

SHADOW OF EGYPT, THE 1924 d: Sidney Morgan. UKN., *The Shadow of Egypt*, Norma Lorimer, Novel

SHADOW OF EVIL 1921 d: James Reardon. UKN., *Shadow of Evil*, Carlton Dawe, Novel

Shadow of Evil *see* BANCO A BANGKOK (1964).

Shadow of Fear *see* BEFORE I WAKE (1954).

SHADOW OF FEAR 1963 d: Ernest Morris. UKN., *Decoy Be Damned*, T. F. Fotherby, Novel

SHADOW OF FEAR 1979 d: Noel Nosseck. USA., *The Healer*, Daniel P. Mannix, Book

SHADOW OF ROSALIE BYRNES, THE 1920 d: George Archainbaud. USA., *The Shadow of Rosalie Byrnes*, Grace Sartwell Mason, New York 1919, Novel

Shadow of the Desert *see* THE SHADOW OF THE EAST (1924).

SHADOW OF THE EAST, THE 1924 d: George Archainbaud. USA., *The Shadow of the East*, Edith Maude Hull, Boston 1921, Novel

SHADOW OF THE LAW 1930 d: Louis J. Gasnier, Max Marcin. USA., *The Quarry*, John A. Moroso, Boston 1913, Novel

SHADOW OF THE LAW, THE 1926 d: Wallace Worsley. USA., *Two Gates*, Harry Chapman Ford, Story

Shadow of the Mosque, The *see* THE SHADOW OF EGYPT (1924).

SHADOW OF THE WOLF 1992 d: Jacques Dorfmann. CND/FRN., *Shadow of the Wolf*, Yves Theriault, Novel

Shadow of Their Wings *see* WINGS FOR THE EAGLE (1942).

SHADOW ON THE WALL 1949 d: Pat Jackson. USA., *Death in the Doll's House*, Hannah Lees, 1943, Short Story

SHADOW ON THE WALL, THE 1925 d: B. Reeves Eason. USA., *The Picture on the Wall*, John Breckenridge Ellis, Kansas City 1920, Novel

SHADOW ON THE WINDOW 1957 d: William Asher. USA., *The Missing Witness*, John Hawkins, Ward Hawkins, Short Story

SHADOW OVER ELVERON 1968 d: James Goldstone. USA., *Shadow Over Alveron*, Michael Kingsley, Novel

SHADOW RANCH 1930 d: Louis King. USA., George M. Johnson, Short Story

Shadow Speaks, The *see* INTERNATIONAL CRIME (1938).

SHADOW STRIKES, THE 1937 d: Lynn Shores. USA., *The Ghost of the Manor*, Maxwell Grant, 1933, Short Story

SHADOW, THE 1933 d: George A. Cooper. UKN., *The Shadow*, Donald Stuart, Play

Shadow, The *see* THE SHADOW STRIKES (1937).

SHADOW, THE 1976 d: Don Ham. USA., *Skyggen*, Hans Christian Andersen, 1847, Short Story

Shadowed *see* THE GIRL IN THE WEB (1920).

SHADOWLANDS 1985 d: Norman Stone. UKN/USA/NTH., *Shadowlands*, William Nicholson, Play

SHADOWLANDS 1993 d: Richard Attenborough. UKN., *Shadowlands*, William Nicholson, Play

Shadows *see* A HEART IN PAWN (1919).

SHADOWS 1922 d: Tom Forman. USA., *Ching,Ching, Chinaman*, Wilbur Daniel Steele, 1917, Short Story

Shadow's Edge *see* DIE SCHATTENGRENZE (1978).

SHADOWS OF A GREAT CITY 1913 d: Frank Wilson. UKN., *The Shadows of a Great City*, Joseph Jefferson, L. R. Shewell, New York 1884, Play

SHADOWS OF A GREAT CITY, THE 1915. USA., *The Shadows of a Great City*, Joseph Jefferson, L. R. Shewell, New York 1884, Play

Shadows of Angels *see* SCHATTEN DER ENGEL (1976).

Shadows of Fear *see* THERESE RAQUIN (1928).

Shadows of Forgotten Ancestors *see* TINE ZABUTYKH PREDKIV (1965).

Shadows of Our Forgotten Ancestors *see* TINE ZABUTYKH PREDKIV (1965).

SHADOWS OF PARIS 1924 d: Herbert Brenon. USA., *Mon Homme*, Francis Carco, Andre Picard, Paris 1921, Play

SHADOWS OF SUSPICION 1919 d: Edwin Carewe. USA., *The Yellow Dove*, George Gibbs, New York 1915, Novel

SHADOWS OF THE NORTH 1923 d: Robert F. Hill. USA., *The Skyline of Spruce*, Edison Marshall, Boston 1922, Novel

SHADOWS OF THE PAST 1914 d: Ralph Ince. USA., *Shadows of the Past*, George Randolph Chester, Story

SHADOWS ON OUR SKIN 1980 d: Jim O'Brien. UKN., *Shadows on Our Skin*, Jennifer Johnston, Novel

SHADOWS ON THE STAIRS 1941 d: D. Ross Lederman. USA., *Murder on the Second Floor*, Frank Vosper, London 1929, Play

SHADRACH 1998 d: Susanna Styron. USA., William Styron, Short Story

SHAFT 1971 d: Gordon Parks. USA., *Shaft*, Ernest Tidyman, Novel

SHAGGY DOG, THE 1959 d: Charles T. Barton. USA., *The Hound of Florence*, Felix Salten, 1923, Novel

SHAGGY DOG, THE 1994 d: Dennis Dugan. USA., *The Hound of Florence*, Felix Salten, 1923, Novel

Shaitan, Il Diavolo Del Deserto *see* FORTUNE CARREE (1954).

Shake Hands Forever *see* INSPECTOR WEXFORD: SHAKE HANDS FOREVER (1988).

SHAKE HANDS WITH THE DEVIL 1959 d: Michael Anderson. UKN/IRL., *Shake Hands With the Devil*, Reardon Connor, Novel

Shakespeare's Tragedy, King Lear *see* KING LEAR (1909).

SHALAKO! 1968 d: Edward Dmytryk. UKN/GRM., *Shalako*, Louis L'Amour, New York 1962, Novel

SHALL WE FORGIVE HER? 1917 d: Arthur Ashley. USA., *Shall We Forgive Her?*, Frank Harvey, London 1894, Play

Shalom *see* SABRA (1970).

SHAM 1921 d: Thomas N. Heffron. USA., *Sham*, Geraldine Bonner, Elmer Harris, New York 1909, Play

SHAME 1921 d: Emmett J. Flynn. USA., *Clung*, Max Brand, 1920, Serial Story

Shame *see* THE INTRUDER (1961).

Shame Child, The *see* NAKHALENOK (1961).

Shame of a Nation, The *see* SCARFACE (1932).

Shame of Mary Boyle, The *see* JUNO AND THE PAYCOCK (1929).

Shame of Temple Drake, The *see* THE STORY OF TEMPLE DRAKE (1933).

SHAMEFUL BEHAVIOR? 1926 d: Albert Kelley. USA., *Shameful Behavior?*, Mrs. Belloc Lowndes, New York 1910, Short Story

Shameless Old Lady, The *see* LA VIEILLE DAME INDIGNE (1964).

Shaming, The *see* MISS WYCKOFF GOOD LUCK (1979).

SHAMROCK AND THE ROSE, THE 1927 d: Jack Nelson. USA., *The Shamrock and the Rose*, Owen Davis, Play

Shamrock Touch, The *see* THE LUCK OF THE IRISH (1948).

SHAMS OF SOCIETY 1921 d: Thomas B. Walsh. USA., *Shams*, Walter McNamara, Story

SHAMUS O'BRIEN 1912 d: Otis Turner. USA., *Shamus O'Brien*, Sheridan le Fanu, Poem

SHAN NIANG 1994 d: Xu Tongjun. CHN., Zhao Tingguang, Poem

SHAN SHAN DE HONG XING 1974 d: Li Jun, Li Ang. CHN., *Shan Shan de Hong XIng*, Li XIntian, Novel

SHANE 1953 d: George Stevens. USA., *Shane*, Jack Schaefer, 1949, Novel

SHANG SHI 1981 d: Shui HuA. CHN., *Shang Shi*, Zhou Shuren, 1925, Short Story

SHANG YI DANG 1992 d: He Qun, Liu Baolin. CHN., *Our Recollections of Youth*, Liang Man, Novel

Shanghai Drama, The *see* LE DRAME DE SHANGHAI (1938).

SHANGHAI GESTURE, THE 1941 d: Josef von Sternberg. USA., *The Shanghai Gesture*, John Colton, New York 1929, Play

SHANGHAI LADY 1929 d: John S. Robertson. USA., *Drifting*, Daisy H. Andrews, John Colton, New York 1910, Play

Shanghai Love *see* SHANGHAIED LOVE (1931).

SHANGHAI MADNESS 1933 d: John G. Blystone. USA., *Shanghai Madness*, Frederick Hazlitt Brennan, 1932, Short Story

SHANGHAI STORY, THE 1954 d: Frank Lloyd. USA., *The Shanghai Story*, Lester Yard, Novel

949

SHEPHERD OF THE HILLS, THE 1928 d: Albert S. Rogell. USA., *The Shepherd of the Hills*, Harold Bell Wright, New York 1907, Novel

SHEPHERD OF THE HILLS, THE 1964 d: Ben Parker. USA., *The Shepherd of the Hills*, Harold Bell Wright, New York 1907, Novel

Shepherd of the Mines, The see THE SCARLET SIN (1915).

Shepherd of Trutzberg, The see DER SCHAFER VOM TRUTZBERG (1959).

SHERIFF OF FRACTURED JAW, THE 1958 d: Raoul Walsh. UKN., *The Sheriff of Fractured Jaw*, Jacob Hay, Short Story

SHERIFF OF SUN-DOG, THE 1922 d: Ben Wilson, Louis King. USA., *The Sheriff of Sun-Dog*, W. C. Tuttle, 1921, Short Story

SHERIFF'S SON, THE 1919 d: Victor Schertzinger. USA., *The Sheriff's Son*, William MacLeod Raine, Boston 1918, Novel

SHERLOCK HOLMES 1916 d: Arthur Berthelet. USA., *Sherlock Holmes*, William Gillette, Buffalo 1899, Play

SHERLOCK HOLMES 1922 d: Albert Parker. USA., *Sherlock Holmes*, William Gillette, Buffalo 1899, Play

SHERLOCK HOLMES 1932 d: William K. Howard. USA., *The Red-Headed League*, Arthur Conan Doyle, 1891, Short Story, *Sherlock Holmes*, William Gillette, Buffalo 1899, Play

Sherlock Holmes see THE ADVENTURES OF SHERLOCK HOLMES (1939).

Sherlock Holmes and Saucy Jack see MURDER BY DECREE (1979).

Sherlock Holmes and the Baskerville Curse see SHERLOCK HOLMES: THE BASKERVILLE CURSE (1983).

Sherlock Holmes and the Missing Rembrandt see THE MISSING REMBRANDT (1932).

Sherlock Holmes and the Pearl of Death see THE PEARL OF DEATH (1944).

SHERLOCK HOLMES AND THE SECRET WEAPON 1942 d: R. William Neill. USA., *Adventure of the Dancing Man*, Arthur Conan Doyle, 1903, Short Story

SHERLOCK HOLMES AND THE VOICE OF TERROR 1942 d: John Rawlins. USA., *His Last Bow*, Arthur Conan Doyle, 1917, Short Story

Sherlock Holmes and the Woman in Green see THE WOMAN IN GREEN (1945).

SHERLOCK HOLMES FACES DEATH 1943 d: R. William Neill. USA., *Adventure of the Musgrave Ritual*, Arthur Conan Doyle, 1893, Short Story

Sherlock Holmes' Fatal Hour see THE SLEEPING CARDINAL (1931).

Sherlock Holmes Fights Back see SHERLOCK HOLMES AND THE SECRET WEAPON (1942).

Sherlock Holmes' Final Hour see THE SLEEPING CARDINAL (1931).

Sherlock Holmes Grosster Fall see A STUDY IN TERROR (1965).

Sherlock Holmes: Hound of the Baskervilles see THE HOUND OF THE BASKERVILLES (1972).

Sherlock Holmes in Terror By Night see TERROR BY NIGHT (1946).

Sherlock Holmes: Murder By Decree see MURDER BY DECREE (1979).

Sherlock Holmes Saves London see SHERLOCK HOLMES AND THE VOICE OF TERROR (1942).

SHERLOCK HOLMES SOLVES "THE SIGN OF THE FOUR" 1913. USA., *The Sign of Four*, Arthur Conan Doyle, London 1890, Novel

SHERLOCK HOLMES: THE BASKERVILLE CURSE 1983 d: Alex Nicholas. UKN., *The Hound of the Baskervilles*, Arthur Conan Doyle, London 1902, Novel

SHERLOCK HOLMES: THE LAST VAMPYRE 1993 d: Tim Sullivan. UKN., *The Sussex Vampire*, Arthur Conan Doyle, Novel

Sherlock Holmes: the Master Blackmailer see THE ADVENTURES OF SHERLOCK HOLMES: THE MASTER BLACKMAILER (1991).

SHERLOCK HOLMES' THE SIGN OF FOUR 1983 d: Desmond Davis. UKN., *The Sign of Four*, Arthur Conan Doyle, London 1890, Novel

Sherlock Holmes: Vampire of Lamberley see SHERLOCK HOLMES: THE LAST VAMPYRE (1993).

SHERRY 1920 d: Edgar Lewis. USA., *Sherry*, George Barr McCutcheon, New York 1919, Novel

She's a Good Girl see DER SPRUNG INS GLUCK (1927).

SHE'S MY WEAKNESS 1930 d: Melville Brown. USA., *Tommy*, Howard Lindsay, Bertrand Robinson, New York 1928, Play

SHE'S WORKING HER WAY THROUGH COLLEGE 1952 d: H. Bruce Humberstone. USA., *The Male Animal*, Elliott Nugent, James Thurber, New York 1940, Play

Shesha Sravana see SESHA SHRABANA (1976).

She-Wolf see LA LUPA (1996).

She-Wolf of Wall Street, The see MOTHER'S MILLIONS (1931).

She-Wolf, The see MOTHER'S MILLIONS (1931).

She-Wolf, The see LA LUPA (1953).

She-Wolf, The see U KRUTOGO YARA (1962).

She-Wolf, The see THE WHISTLE BLOWER (1987).

She-Wolves, The see LES LOUVES (1956).

SHI LIAN ZHE 1987 d: Qin Zhiyu. CHN., *Geng Er in Beijing*, Chen Ruoxi, Novel

SHIBIL 1967 d: Zahari Zhandov. BUL., *Shibil*, Yordan Yovkov, 1925, Short Story

SHIELD FOR MURDER 1954 d: Edmond O'Brien, Howard W. Koch. USA., *Shield for Murder*, William P. McGivern, 1951, Novel

SHIIKU 1961 d: Nagisa OshimA. JPN., *Shiiku*, Kenzaburo Oe, 1958, Short Story

Shilling for Candles, A see YOUNG AND INNOCENT (1937).

SHILOH 1996 d: Dale Rosenbloom. USA., *Shiloh*, Phyllis Reynolds Naylor, Novel

SHILOH 2: SHILOH SEASON 1999 d: Sandy Tung. USA., *Shiloh*, Phyllis Reynolds Naylor, Novel

SHIN HEIKE MONOGATARI 1955 d: Kenji Mizoguchi. JPN., *Shin Heike Monogatari*, Eiji Yoshikawa, Novel

SHIN SANTO JUYAKU: TEISHU KYO IKU NO MAKI 1961 d: Shue Matsubayashi. JPN., *Zuiko-San*, Keita Genji, Novel

SHINA NINGYO 1981 d: Shuji TerayamA. JPN/FRN., *Retour a Roissy*, Pauline Reage, Novel

SHINEL 1926 d: Grigori Kozintsev, Leonid Trauberg. USS., *Shinel*, Nikolay Gogol, 1842, Short Story

SHINEL 1960 d: Alexei Batalov. USS., *Shinel*, Nikolay Gogol, 1842, Short Story

Shin-Heike Monogatari see SHIN HEIKE MONOGATARI (1955).

SHINING ADVENTURE, THE 1925 d: Hugo Ballin. USA., *The Shining Adventure*, Dana Burnet, New York 1916, Novel

Shining Band, The see EVEN AS EVE (1920).

SHINING HOUR, THE 1938 d: Frank Borzage. USA., *The Shining Hour*, Keith Winter, New York 1934, Play

SHINING, THE 1980 d: Stanley Kubrick. UKN., *The Shining*, Stephen King, 1976, Novel

SHINING VICTORY 1941 d: Irving Rapper. USA., *Jupiter Laughs*, A. J. Cronin, 1940, Play

Shinjel see SHINEL (1926).

Shinjel see SHINEL (1960).

SHINJU TEN NO AMIJIMA 1969 d: Masahiro ShinodA. JPN., *Shinju Ten No Amijima*, Monzaemon Chikamatsu, 1720, Play

SHINKU CHITAI 1952 d: Satsuo Yamamoto. JPN., *Shinku Chitai*, Hiroshi Noma, 1952, Novel

SHINOBI NO MANJI 1968 d: Noribumi Suzuki. JPN., *Shinobi No Manji*, Futaro Yamada, Short Story

Shinshaku Yotsuya Kaidan see YOTSUYA KAIDAN (1949).

Shiny Moss see HIKARIGOKE (1991).

SHIOSAI 1954 d: Senkichi Taniguchi. JPN., *Shiosai*, Yukio Mishima, 1954, Novel

Ship Bound for India, A see SKEPP TILL INDIALAND (1947).

SHIP FROM SHANGHAI, THE 1929 d: Charles J. Brabin. USA., *Ordeal*, Dale Collins, New York 1924, Novel

Ship of Condemned Women, The see LA NAVE DELLE DONNE MALEDETTE (1953).

SHIP OF FOOLS 1965 d: Stanley Kramer. USA., *Ship of Fools*, Katherine Anne Porter, Boston 1962, Novel

Ship of Lost Men, The see DAS SCHIFF DER VERLORENEN MENSCHEN (1929).

SHIP OF SOULS 1925 d: Charles Miller. USA., *Ship of Souls*, Emerson Hough, New York 1925, Novel

Ship of the Dead see DAS TOTENSCHIFF (1959).

SHIP THAT DIED OF SHAME, THE 1955 d: Basil Dearden, Michael Relph. UKN., *The Ship That Died of Shame*, Nicholas Monsarrat, 1952, Novel

Ship, The see LA NAVE (1912).

Ship to India, A see SKEPP TILL INDIALAND (1947).

Ship Was Loaded, The see CARRY ON ADMIRAL (1957).

SHIPBUILDERS, THE 1943 d: John Baxter. UKN., *The Shipbuilders*, George Blake, 1935, Novel

SHIPMATES 1931 d: Harry Pollard. USA., *Maskee*, Ernest Paynter, 1926, Short Story

SHIPS THAT PASS IN THE NIGHT 1921 d: Percy Nash. UKN., *Ships That Pass in the Night*, Beatrice Marraden, Novel

Shipwreck see NAUFRAGIO (1977).

SHIPWRECKED 1913. USA., *The Admirable Crichton*, J. M. Barrie, London 1902, Play

SHIPWRECKED 1926 d: Joseph Henabery. USA., *Shipwrecked*, Langdon McCormick, New York 1924, Play

Shipwrecked see NAUFRAGIO (1977).

Shipwrecked Man, The see IL NAUFRAGO (1909).

SHIR HASHIRIM 1935 d: Henry Lynn. USA., *Shir Hashirim*, Anshel Shorr, Play

SHIRALEE, THE 1957 d: Leslie Norman. UKN/ASL., *The Shiralee*, Darcy Niland, Novel

SHIRALEE, THE 1987 d: George Ogilvie. ASL., *The Shiralee*, Darcy Niland, Novel

SHIRASAGI 1958 d: Teinosuke KinugasA. JPN., *Shirasagi*, Kyoka Izumi, 1909, Novel

SHIRAZ 1928 d: Franz Osten. GRM/IND., *Shiraz*, Niranjan Pal, Play

SHIRLEY 1922 d: A. V. Bramble. UKN., *Shirley*, Charlotte Bronte, 1849, Novel

SHIRLEY KAYE 1917 d: Joseph Kaufman. USA., *Shirley Kaye*, Hubert Footner, New York 1916, Play

SHIRLEY VALENTINE 1989 d: Lewis Gilbert. UKN/USA., *Shirley Valentine*, Willy Russell, 1988, Play

Shirley Yorke see THE STORY OF SHIRLEY YORKE (1948).

SHITSURAKUEN 1997 d: Yoshimitsu MoritA. JPN., *Shitsurakuen*, Watanabe Junichi, Novel

SHIZUKANARU KETTO 1949 d: Akira KurosawA. JPN., *Shizukanaru Ketto*, Kazuo Kikuta, Play

SHNEI KUNI LEMEL 1965 d: Israel Becker. ISR., *Der Fanatik Oder Id Tsvey Kuni Lemels*, Abraham Goldfaden, 1880, Play

SHOCK PUNCH, THE 1925 d: Paul Sloane. USA., *The Shock Punch*, John Monk Saunders, Story

SHOCK TO THE SYSTEM, A 1990 d: Jan Egleson. USA., *A Shock to the System*, Simon Brett, Novel

SHOCK TREATMENT 1964 d: Denis Sanders. USA., *Shock Treatment*, Winfred Van Atta, New York 1961, Novel

Shock Troops see UN HOMME DE TROP (1967).

Shocker see STADT OHNE MITLEID (1961).

SHOCKING ACCIDENT, A 1983 d: James Scott. UKN., *A Shocking Accident*, Graham Greene, 1967, Short Story

SHOCKS OF DOOM 1919 d: Henry Houry. USA., *Shocks of Doom*, O. Henry, Short Story

SHOD WITH FIRE 1920 d: Emmett J. Flynn. USA., *Bruce of Circle a*, Harold Titus, Boston 1918, Novel

SHOE FROM YOUR HOMELAND, A 1980 d: Peter Bernardos. ASL., *A Shoe from Your Homeland*, N. Tsiforos, P. Vassilliadis, Play

Shoeless Joe see FIELD OF DREAMS (1989).

SHOES 1916 d: Lois Weber. USA., *Shoes*, Stella Wynne Herron, 1916, Short Story

SHOES OF THE FISHERMAN, THE 1968 d: Michael Anderson. USA/ITL., *The Shoes of the Fisherman*, Morris West, New York 1963, Novel

SHOES THAT DANCED, THE 1918 d: Frank Borzage. USA., *The Shoes That Danced*, John A. Moroso, 1917, Short Story

SHOGUN 1981 d: Jerry London. USA/JPN., *Shogun*, James Clavell, Novel

SHOKEI NO HEYA 1956 d: Kon IchikawA. JPN., *Shokei No Heya*, Shintaro Ishihara, 1956, Short Story

SHOKEI NO SHIMA 1966 d: Masahiro ShinodA. JPN., *Runinto Nite*, Taijun Takeda, 1953, Short Story

SHOOT 1976 d: Harvey Hart. CND/USA., *Shoot*, Douglas Fairbairn, Novel

Shoot First see ROUGH SHOOT (1952).

Shoot Loud, Louder. I Don't Understand see PIU FORTE. NON CAPISCO SPARA FORTE (1966).

Shoot Out at Big Sag see THE RAWHIDE HALO (1960).

Shoot, The see DER SCHUT (1964).

Shoot the Chutes see STRIKE ME PINK (1936).

Shoot the Pianist see TIREZ SUR LE PIANISTE (1960).

Shoot the Piano Player see TIREZ SUR LE PIANISTE (1960).

SHOOT THE WORKS 1934 d: Wesley Ruggles. USA., *The Great Magoo*, Gene Fowler, Ben Hecht, New York 1932, Play

SHOOTER 1988 d: Gary Nelson. USA., *Shooter*, David Hume Kennerly, Book

SHOOTIN' IRONS 1927 d: Richard Rosson. USA., *Shootin' Irons*, Richard Allen Gates, Story

SHOOTING OF DAN MCGREW, THE 1915 d: Herbert Blache. USA., *The Shooting of Dan McGrew*, Robert W. Service, 1907, Poem

SHOOTING OF DAN MCGREW, THE 1924 d: Clarence Badger. USA., *The Shooting of Dan McGrew*, Robert W. Service, 1907, Poem

SHOOTING OF DAN MCGREW, THE 1966 d: Ed Graham. USA., *The Shooting of Dan McGrew*, Robert W. Service, 1907, Poem

Shooting Party, The see MOJ LASKOVYJ I NEZNYJ ZVER (1978).

SHOOTING PARTY, THE 1984 d: Alan Bridges. UKN., *The Shooting Party*, Isabel Colegate, Novel

Shooting, The see BAD BLOOD (1980).

SHOOTIST, THE 1976 d: Don Siegel. USA., *The Shootist*, Glendon Swarthout, Novel

SHOP AROUND THE CORNER, THE 1939 d: Ernst Lubitsch. USA., *Illatszertar*, Nikolaus Laszlo, 1936, Play

SHOP AT SLY CORNER, THE 1947 d: George King. UKN., *The Shop at Sly Corner*, Edward Percy, London 1945, Play

Shop Girl, The see WINIFRED THE SHOP GIRL (1916).

Shop on Main Street see OBCHOD NA KORSE (1965).

Shop on the High Street, The see OBCHOD NA KORSE (1965).

Shop-Girls of Paris see AU BONHEUR DES DAMES (1943).

SHOPSOILED GIRL, THE 1915 d: Leedham Bantock. UKN., *The Shopsoiled Girl*, Walter Melville, Play

SHOPWORN ANGEL, THE 1928 d: Richard Wallace. USA., *Pettigrew's Girl*, Dana Burnet, 1918, Short Story

SHOPWORN ANGEL, THE 1938 d: H. C. Potter. USA., *Pettigrew's Girl*, Dana Burnet, 1918, Short Story

SHORE ACRES 1914 d: Jack Pratt. USA., *Shore Acres*, James A. Herne, Boston 1892, Play

SHORE ACRES 1920 d: Rex Ingram. USA., *Shore Acres*, James A. Herne, Boston 1892, Play

SHORE LEAVE 1925 d: John S. Robertson. USA., *Shore Leave*, Hubert Osborne, New York 1922, Play

Shores of Twilight see TA RODINA AKROYIALIA (1998).

Short Cut see POSTRIZINY (1980).

SHORT CUT TO HELL 1957 d: James Cagney. USA., *A Gun for Sale*, Graham Greene, 1936, Novel

SHORT GRASS 1950 d: Lesley Selander. USA., *Range War*, Thomas W. Blackburn, 1949, Novel

Short Is the Summer see KORT AR SOMMAREN (1962).

Short Letter to the Long Goodbye, The see DER KURZE BRIEF ZUM LANGEN ABSCHIED (1977).

SHORT SKIRTS 1921 d: Harry B. Harris. USA., *What Can You Expect?*, Alice L. Tildesley, Short Story

Short Sun see KRATKO SLUNTSE (1979).

Short Trial see KURZER PROZESS (1967).

Short Weights see DAS FALSCHE GEWICHT (1970).

Short Work see KURZER PROZESS (1967).

SHOT IN THE DARK, A 1933 d: George Pearson. UKN., *A Shot in the Dark*, Gerard Fairlie, Novel

SHOT IN THE DARK, A 1935 d: Charles Lamont. USA., *The Dartmouth Murders*, Clifford Orr, New York 1929, Novel

SHOT IN THE DARK, A 1941 d: William McGann. USA., *No Hard Feelings*, Frederick Nebel, Story

SHOT IN THE DARK, A 1964 d: Blake Edwards. UKN/USA., *L' Idiot*, Marcel Achard, Paris 1960, Play

Shot, The see VYSTREL (1967).

SHOT THROUGH THE HEART 1998 d: David Attwood. UKN/CND/HNG., *Anti-Sniper*, John Falk, Article

Shots Under the Gallows see SCHUSSE UNTERM GALGEN (1968).

Should a Wife Forgive? see THE INVISIBLE BOND (1920).

SHOULD LADIES BEHAVE? 1933 d: Harry Beaumont. USA., *The Vinegar Tree*, Paul Osborn, New York 1930, Play

SHOUT AT THE DEVIL 1976 d: Peter Hunt. UKN., *Shout at the Devil*, Wilbur Smith, Novel

Shout It from the House Tops see CRIEZ-LE SUR LES TOITS (1932).

SHOUT, THE 1978 d: Jerzy Skolimowski. UKN., *The Shout*, Robert Graves, 1929, Short Story

SHOW BOAT 1929 d: Harry Pollard. USA., *Showboat*, Edna Ferber, New York 1926, Novel

SHOW BOAT 1936 d: James Whale. USA., *Showboat*, Edna Ferber, New York 1926, Novel

SHOW BOAT 1951 d: George Sidney. USA., *Showboat*, Edna Ferber, New York 1926, Novel

SHOW FLAT 1936 d: Bernerd Mainwaring. UKN., *Show Flat*, Cecil Maiden, Martha Robinson, Play

SHOW GIRL 1928 d: Alfred Santell. USA., *Show Girl*, Joseph Patrick McEvoy, New York 1928, Novel

SHOW GIRL IN HOLLYWOOD 1930 d: Mervyn Leroy. USA., *Hollywood Girl*, Joseph Patrick McEvoy, New York 1929, Novel

Show Life see SONG (1928).

SHOW OF FORCE 1989 d: Bruno Barreto. USA., *Murder Under Two Flags*, Anne Nelson, Book

SHOW OFF, THE 1926 d: Malcolm St. Clair. USA., *The Show-Off*, George Edward Kelly, New York 1924, Play

SHOW, THE 1926 d: Tod Browning. USA., *The Day of Souls*, Charles Tenney Jackson, Indianapolis 1910, Novel

Showdown see LE PACHA (1968).

SHOWDOWN AT ABILENE 1956 d: Charles Haas. USA., *Gun Shy*, Clarence Upson Young, Short Story

SHOWDOWN, THE 1928 d: Victor Schertzinger. USA., *Wildcat*, Houston Branch, New York 1921, Play

Showdown, The see CONFLICT (1936).

SHOWDOWN, THE 1950 d: Dorrell McGowan, Stuart E. McGowan. USA., *Sleep All Winter*, Dan Gordon, Richard Wormser, Short Story

Shower of Gold see GULDREGN (1988).

Show-Off, The see THE SHOW OFF (1926).

Show-Off, The see MEN ARE LIKE THAT (1930).

SHOW-OFF, THE 1934 d: Charles F. Reisner. USA., *The Show-Off*, George Edward Kelly, New York 1924, Play

SHOW-OFF, THE 1946 d: Harry Beaumont. USA., *The Show-Off*, George Edward Kelly, New York 1924, Play

Shozo, a Cat and Two Women see NEKO TO SHOZO TO FUTARI NO ONNA (1956).

SHRIKE, THE 1955 d: Jose Ferrer. USA., *The Shrike*, Joseph Kramm, New York 1952, Play

Shrimp, The see CHEMMEEN (1965).

SHRINE OF THE SEVEN LAMPS, THE 1923 d: A. E. Coleby. UKN., *The Shrine of the Seven Lamps*, Sax Rohmer, Short Story

Shroud for a Nightingale see DALGLIESH: SHROUD FOR A NIGHTINGALE (1984).

SHU JIAN EN CHOU LU 1987 d: Hsu An-HuA. HKG/CHN., *Shu Jian En Chou Lu*, Kam Yung, Novel

SHUI KU SHANG GE DE GE SHENG 1958 d: Yu Yanfu. CHN., *The Best News*, Liu Dawei, Story

SHUI SHOU ZHANG DE GU SHI 1963 d: Qiang Ming. CHN., *Shui Shou Zhang de Gus Hi*, Guo Yuan, Novel

SHULAMITE, THE 1915 d: George Loane Tucker. UKN., *The Shulamite*, Claude Askew, Edward Knoblock, London 1906, Play

Shulamite, The see UNDER THE LASH (1921).

Shumpuden see SHUNPU-DEN (1965).

SHUNKIN MONOGATARI 1954 d: Daisuke Ito. JPN., *Shunkin-Sho*, Junichiro Tanizaki, 1933, Novel

SHUNPU-DEN 1965 d: Seijun Suzuki. JPN., *Shumpu-Den*, Tamura Taijiro, Novel

SHURA 1970 d: Toshio Matsumoto. JPN., *Shura*, Nanboku Tsuruya, Play

Shurochka see SUROCKA (1982).

SHUTO SHOSHITSU 1987 d: Toshio MasudA. JPN., *Shuto Shoshitsu*, Sakyo Komatsu, Book

SHUTTERED ROOM, THE 1967 d: David Greene. UKN., *The Shuttered Room*, August Deleth, H. P. Lovecraft, 1959, Short Story

SHUTTLE OF LIFE, THE 1920 d: D. J. Williams. UKN., *The Shuttle of Life*, Isobel Bray, Novel

SHUTTLE, THE 1918 d: Rollin S. Sturgeon. USA., *The Shuttle*, Frances Hodgson Burnett, New York 1906, Novel

SHUU 1956 d: Mikio Naruse. JPN., *Shu-U*, Kunio Kishida, 1926, Play

Shu-U see SHUU (1956).

SHUZENJI MONOGATARI 1955 d: Noboru NakamurA. JPN., *Shuzenji Monogatari*, Kido Okamoto, Play

SHYAMCHI AAI 1953 d: Pralhad Keshav Atre. IND., *Shyamchi Aai*, Sane Guruji, Novel

Shyam's Mother see SHYAMCHI AAI (1953).

Shylock see SHEJLOK (1993).

SHYLOCK, LE MARCHAND DE VENISE 1913 d: Henri Desfontaines, Louis Mercanton. FRN., *The Merchant of Venice*, William Shakespeare, c1595, Play

SI JAMAIS JE TE PINCE 1917 d: Georges MoncA. FRN., *Si Jamais Je Te Pince.*, Eugene Labiche, Marc-Michel, Play

SI LE ROI SAVAIT CA 1956 d: Caro Canaille, Edoardo Anton. FRN/ITL., *Le Trompette de la Beresina*, Ponson Du Terrail, Novel

SI L'EMPEREUR SAVAIT CA 1930 d: Jacques Feyder. FRN/USA., *Olympia*, Ferenc Molnar, Budapest 1928, Play

Si Signora see SISSIGNORA (1942).

SI TE DICEN QUE CAI 1988 d: Vicente ArandA. SPN., *Si Te Dican Que Cai*, Juan Marse, 1973, Novel

SIAMO TUTTI MILANESI 1954 d: Mario Landi. ITL., *Siamo Tutti Milanesi*, Arnaldo Fraccaroli, 1952, Play

Siavacch a Persepolis see SIAVOSH DAR TAKHTE JAMSHID (1967).

Siavash in Persepolis see SIAVOSH DAR TAKHTE JAMSHID (1967).

SIAVOSH DAR TAKHTE JAMSHID 1967 d: Ferydoun RahnemA. IRN., *Shahnameh*, Ferdowsi, c1010

Siavosh in Persepolis see SIAVOSH DAR TAKHTE JAMSHID (1967).

SIBERIA 1926 d: Victor Schertzinger. USA., *Siberia*, Bartley Campbell, New York 1911, Play

Siberian Lady MacBeth see SIBIRSKA LEDI MAGBET (1962).

Siberian Patrol see TOMMY (1931).

Sibil see SHIBIL (1967).

SIBIRSKA LEDI MAGBET 1962 d: Andrzej WajdA. YGS/PLN., *Ledi Makbet Mtenskogo Uezda*, Nikolay Semyonovich Leskov, 1864, Short Story

Sibirsky Patrol see TOMMY (1931).

SICARIO 77 VIVO O MORTO 1966 d: Mino Guerrini. ITL/SPN., Henry Vaughan, Story

SIC-EM 1920? d: Frederick Sullivan. USA., *In for the Night*, James Savery, New York 1917, Play

Sicilian Checkmate see LA VIOLENZA: QUINTO POTERE (1972).

Sicilian Clan, The see LE CLAN DES SICILIENS (1969).

SICILIAN, THE 1987 d: Michael Cimino. USA., *The Sicilian*, Mario Puzo, Novel

Sick Animals see PRINTRE COLINELE VERZI (1971).

SIDDHARTHA 1972 d: Conrad Rooks. USA/IND., *Siddhartha; Eine Indische Dichtung*, Hermann Hesse, 1922, Novel

Siddhartha and the City see PRATIDWANDI (1970).

SIDE SHOW OF LIFE, THE 1924 d: Herbert Brenon. USA., *The Mountebank*, William J. Locke, London 1921, Novel

Side Street Story see MILIONARIA NAPOLI (1950).

Side Track see OTKLONENIE (1967).

SIDELONG GLANCES OF A PIGEON FANCIER 1971 d: John Dexter. USA., *The Sidelong Glances of a Pigeon Kicker*, David Boyer, New York 1968, Novel

Sideshow of Life, The see THE SIDE SHOW OF LIFE (1924).

Sidetrack see OTKLONENIE (1967).

SIDEWALKS OF NEW YORK 1923 d: Lester Park. USA., *Sidewalks of New York*, James W. Blake, Charles B. Lawlor, Song

SIDNEY SHELDON'S BLOODLINE 1979 d: Terence Young. USA., *Bloodline*, Sidney Sheldon, Novel

Sidney Sheldon's Memories of Midnight see MEMORIES OF MIDNIGHT (1991).

Sidney Sheldon's the Sands of Time see THE SANDS OF TIME (1992).

Sidney Sheldon's Windmills of the Gods see WINDMILLS OF THE GODS (1988).

SIDONIE PANACHE 1934 d: Henry Wulschleger. FRN/ALG., *Sidonie Panache*, Andre Mouezy-Eon, Albert Willemetz, Opera

SIDSTE AKT 1987 d: Edward Fleming. DNM., *Waiting in the Wings*, Noel Coward, Play

SIE 1954 d: Rolf Thiele. GRM., *Sie*, Gabor von Vaszary, Novel

SIE NANNTEN IHN KRAMBAMBULI 1972 d: Franz Antel. GRM/AUS., *Krambambuli*, Maria von Ebner-Eschenbach, 1887, Short Story

Sieben Dreckige Teufel see SETTE BASCHI ROSSI (1968).

SIEBEN KLEIDER DER KATHRIN, DIE 1954 d: Hans Deppe. GRM., *Die Sieben Kleider Der Katrin*, Gisi Gruber, Book

Sieben Masken Des Judoka, Die see CASSE-TETE CHINOIS POUR LE JUDOKA (1968).

SIEBEN TAGE FRIST 1969 d: Alfred Vohrer. GRM., *Sieben Tage Frist*, Paul Henricks, Novel

Sieben Tochter Der Frau Gyurkovics, Die see FLICKORNA GYURKOVICS (1926).

Sieben Tote in Den Augen Der Katze see LA MORTE NEGLI OCCHI DEL GATTO (1973).

SIEBENTE OPFER, DAS 1964 d: Franz J. Gottlieb. GRM., Bryan Edgar Wallace, Novel

SIEBZEHNJAHRIGEN, DIE 1919 d: Hanna Henning. GRM., *Die Siebzehnjahrigen*, Max Dreyer, 1904, Play

SIEBZEHNJAHRIGEN, DIE 1928 d: Georg Asagaroff. GRM., *Die Siebzehnjahrigen*, Max Dreyer, 1904, Play

Sieg Der Liebe see AN HEILIGEN WASSERN (1932).

SIEGE 1925 d: Svend Gade. USA., *Siege*, Samuel Hopkins Adams, New York 1924, Novel

Siege of Besztercze, The see BESZTERCE OSTROMA (1948).

Siege of Ruby Ridge, The see RUBY RIDGE: AN AMERICAN TRAGEDY (1996).

Siempre Carmen see CARMEN PROIBITA (1953).

SIERRA 1950 d: Alfred E. Green. USA., *Forbidden Valley*, Stuart Hardy, Novel

SIERRA BARON 1958 d: James B. Clark, Raphael J. SevillA. USA., *Sierra Baron*, Thomas W. Blackburn, 1955, Novel

Sierra de Teruel see ESPOIR (1939).

Siervos see DIE LEIBEIGENEN (1927).

SIESTA 1988 d: Mary Lambert. USA/UKN., *Siesta*, Patrice Chaplin, Novel

SIETE LOCOS, LOS 1973 d: Leopoldo Torre-Nilsson. ARG., *Los Siete Locos*, Roberto Arlt, 1929, Novel

Sif, Das Weib, Das Den Mord Beging see ARME KLEINE SIF (1927).

SIGN OF FOUR, THE 1923 d: Maurice Elvey. UKN., *The Sign of Four*, Arthur Conan Doyle, London 1890, Novel

SIGN OF FOUR, THE 1932 d: Rowland V. Lee, Graham Cutts. UKN., *The Sign of Four*, Arthur Conan Doyle, London 1890, Novel

Sign of Four, The see SHERLOCK HOLMES' THE SIGN OF FOUR (1983).

Sign of Four, The see THE ADVENTURES OF SHERLOCK HOLMES: THE SIGN OF FOUR (1987).

SIGN OF THE CROSS, THE 1904 d: William Haggar. UKN., *The Sign of the Cross*, Wilson Barrett, London 1895, Play

SIGN OF THE CROSS, THE 1914 d: Frederick A. Thompson. USA., *The Sign of the Cross*, Wilson Barrett, London 1895, Play

SIGN OF THE CROSS, THE 1932 d: Cecil B. de Mille. USA., *The Sign of the Cross*, Wilson Barrett, London 1895, Play

SIGN OF THE RAM 1948 d: John Sturges. USA., *Sign of the Ram*, Margaret Ferguson, Book

SIGN OF THE ROSE, THE 1915 d: Thomas H. Ince. USA., *The Sign of the Rose*, George Beban, Charles T. Dazey, New York 1911, Play

Sign of the Rose, The see THE ALIEN (1915).

SIGN OF THE WOLF 1941 d: Howard Bretherton. USA., *That Spot*, Jack London, 1910, Short Story

SIGN ON THE DOOR, THE 1921 d: Herbert Brenon. USA., *The Sign on the Door*, Channing Pollock, New York 1924, Play

SIGNAL ROUGE, LE 1948 d: Ernst Neubach. FRN., *Le Signal Rouge*, Bandisch, Schutz, Novel

SIGNAL TOWER, THE 1924 d: Clarence Brown. USA., *The Signal Tower*, Wadsworth Camp, 1920, Short Story

SIGNALET 1966 d: Ole Gammeltoft. DNM., *Signalet*, Anders Bodelsen, 1965, Short Story

Signe Picpus see PICPUS (1942).

SIGNORA DALLE CAMELIE, LA 1909 d: Ugo FalenA. ITL., *La Dame aux Camelias*, Alexandre Dumas (fils), Paris 1848, Novel

SIGNORA DALLE CAMELIE, LA 1915 d: Baldassarre Negroni. ITL., *La Dame aux Camelias*, Alexandre Dumas (fils), Paris 1848, Novel

SIGNORA DALLE CAMELIE, LA 1915 d: Gustavo SerenA. ITL., *La Dame aux Camelias*, Alexandre Dumas (fils), Paris 1848, Novel

Signora Dalle Camelie, La see LA DAME AUX CAMELIAS (1953).

Signora Dalle Camilie, La see LA DAME AUX CAMELIAS (1981).

Signora Delle Camelie, La see LA SIGNORA DALLE CAMELIE (1909).

SIGNORA DELLE PERLE, LA 1918 d: Gennaro Righelli. ITL., *La Dame aux Perles*, Alexandre Dumas (fils), Novel

SIGNORA DELL'OVEST, UNA 1942 d: Carl Koch. ITL., Pierre Benoit, Novel

SIGNORA DI MONSERAU, LA 1909 d: Mario Caserini. ITL., *La Dame de Monsoreau*, Alexandre Dumas (pere), 1856, Novel

SIGNORA DI TUTTI, LA 1934 d: Max Ophuls. ITL., *La Signora Di Tutti*, Salvator Gotta, Novel

SIGNORA IN NERO, LA 1943 d: Nunzio MalasommA. ITL., *La Petite Chocolatiere*, Paul Gavault, Play

SIGNORA PARADISO, LA 1934 d: Enrico Guazzoni. ITL., *La Signora Paradiso*, Guido Cantini, Play

Signorina Dal Livido Azzurro, La see LA RAGAZZA DAL LIVIDO AZZURRO (1933).

SIGNORINA, LA 1920 d: Gian Bistolfi. ITL., *La Signorina*, Gerolamo Rovetta, 1900, Novel

SIGNORINA, LA 1942 d: Ladislao Kish. ITL., *La Signorina*, Gerolamo Rovetta, 1900, Novel

SIGNORINE DELLA VILLA ACCANTO, LE 1942 d: Gian Paolo Rosmino. ITL., *Le Signorine Della Villa Accanto*, Ugo Farulli, Play

SIGNORINETTE 1943 d: Luigi ZampA. ITL., *Signorinette*, Wanda Bonta, Novel

SIGNPOST TO MURDER 1964 d: George Englund. USA., *Signpost to Murder*, Monte Doyle, London 1962, Play

Signs of Life see LEBENSZEICHEN (1967).

SIKATOR 1966 d: Tamas Renyi. HNG., *Sikator*, Akos Kertesz, 1965, Novel

SILA NERANGALIL SILA MANITHARGAL 1975 d: A. Bhimsingh. IND., *Sila Neragalil Sila Manithargal*, Jayakanthan, Novel

SILAS MARNER 1911 d: Theodore Marston. USA., *Silas Marner*, George Eliot, London 1861, Novel

SILAS MARNER 1913 d: Charles J. Brabin. USA., *Silas Marner*, George Eliot, London 1861, Novel

SILAS MARNER 1916 d: Ernest C. Warde. USA., *Silas Marner*, George Eliot, London 1861, Novel

SILAS MARNER 1985 d: Giles Foster. UKN., *Silas Marner*, George Eliot, London 1861, Novel

SILENCE 1926 d: Rupert Julian. USA., *Silence*, Max Marcin, New York 1924, Play

Silence see LA DERNIERE BERCEUSE (1930).

SILENCE 1931 d: Louis J. Gasnier, Max Marcin. USA., *Silence*, Max Marcin, New York 1924, Play

Silence see CHINMOKU (1972).

Silence and Cry see CSEND ES KIALTAS (1968).

Silence and the Cry see CSEND ES KIALTAS (1968).

Silence Dans la Foret, Le see DAS SCHWEIGEN IM WALDE (1929).

SILENCE DE LA MER, LE 1947 d: Jean-Pierre Melville. FRN., *Le Silence de la Mer*, Vercors, 1942, Novel

Silence de Mort, Un see CETTE NUIT-LA (1958).

Silence in the North see SILENCE OF THE NORTH (1981).

Silence of Dean Maitland, The see SEALED LIPS (1915).

SILENCE OF THE LAMBS, THE 1991 d: Jonathan Demme. USA., *The Silence of the Lambs*, Thomas Harris, Novel

SILENCE OF THE NORTH 1981 d: Allan King. CND., *Silence of the North*, Ben East, Olive Fredrickson, Book

Silence of the Poet, The see DAS SCHWEIGEN DES DICHTERS (1986).

SILENCE SELLERS, THE 1917 d: Burton L. King. USA., Blair Hall, Short Story

Silence, The see MILCZENIE (1963).

Silence! the Court Is in Session see COURT CHALU AAHE SHANTATA (1970).

SILENCERS, THE 1966 d: Phil Karlson. USA., *Death of a Citizen*, Donald Hamilton, New York 1960, Novel, *The Silencers*, Donald Hamilton, New York 1961, Novel

SILENCIEUX, LE 1972 d: Claude Pinoteau. FRN/ITL., *Drole de Pistolet*, Francis Ryck, Novel

SILENT BARRIER, THE 1920 d: William Worthington. USA., *The Silent Barrier*, Louis Tracy, London 1909, Novel

Silent Barriers see THE GREAT BARRIER (1937).

SILENT BATTLE, THE 1916 d: Jack Conway. USA., *The Silent Battle*, George Gibbs, New York 1913, Novel

SILENT BATTLE, THE 1939 d: Herbert Mason. UKN., *Le Poisson Chinois*, Jean Bommart, Novel

Silent Bell, The see MADEMOISELLE FIFI (1944).

SILENT CALL, THE 1921 d: Larry Trimble. USA., *The Cross Pull*, Hal G. Evarts, New York 1920, Novel

Silent Duel, The see SHIZUKANARU KETTO (1949).

SILENT DUST 1949 d: Lance Comfort. UKN., *The Paragon*, Michael Pertwee, Roland Pertwee, London 1948, Play

SILENT ENEMY, THE 1958 d: William Fairchild. UKN., *Commander Crabb*, Marshall Pugh, Book

Silent Fear see EEN ZAAK VAN LEVEN OF DOOD (1983).

Silent Guest, The see DER STUMME GAST (1945).

SILENT HOUSE, THE 1929 d: Walter Forde. UKN., *The Silent House*, John G. Brandon, George Pickett, London 1927, Play

SILENT LIE, THE 1917 d: Raoul Walsh. USA., Conahan, Larry Evans, Short Story

SILENT LOVER, THE 1926 d: George Archainbaud. USA., *Der Legioner*, Lajos Biro, Play

SILENT MASTER, THE 1917 d: Leonce Perret. USA., *The Court of St. Simon*, E. Phillips Oppenheim, Boston 1912, Novel

Silent Night see WSROD NOCNEJ CISZY (1978).

SILENT NIGHT, LONELY NIGHT 1969 d: Daniel Petrie. USA., *Silent Night Lonely Night*, Robert Anderson, Play

Silent One, The see LE SILENCIEUX (1972).

SILENT ONE, THE 1984 d: Yvonne MacKay. NZL., *The Silent One*, Joy Cowley, Novel

SILENT PAL 1925 d: Henry McCarty. USA., *The Silent Pal*, Frank Foster Davis, Story

SILENT PARTNER, THE 1923 d: Charles Maigne. USA., *The Silent Partner*, Maximilian Foster, 1908, Short Story

SILENT PARTNER, THE 1978 d: Daryl Duke. CND., *Taenk Pa Et Tal (Think of a Number)*, Anders Bodelsen, 1968, Novel

SILENT PASSENGER, THE 1935 d: Reginald Denham. UKN., *The Silent Passenger*, Dorothy L. Sayers, Novel

Silent Planet, The see DER SCHWEIGENDE STERN (1960).

SILENT PLEA, THE 1915 d: Lionel Belmore. USA., *The Silent Plea*, Mae Koch, Story

Silent Rebellion see MY PALIKARI (1982).

SILENT RIDER, THE 1927 d: Lynn Reynolds. USA., *The Red-Headed Husband*, Katharine Newlin Burt, 1926, Short Story

SILENT SNOW, SECRET SNOW 1966 d: Gene Kearney. USA., *Secret Snow Silent Snow*, Conrad Aiken, 1934, Short Story

Silent Stranger, The *see* STEP DOWN TO TERROR (1958).

Silent Thunder *see* THE MAN CALLED BACK (1932).

SILENT VOICE, THE 1915 d: William J. Bowman. USA., *The Silent Voice*, Jules Eckert Goodman, New York 1914, Play

Silent Voice, The *see* THE MAN WHO PLAYED GOD (1922).

Silent Voice, The *see* THE MAN WHO PLAYED GOD (1932).

Silent Voice, The *see* PAULA (1952).

SILENT WITNESS, THE 1917 d: Harry Lambart. USA., *The Silent Witness*, Otto Harbach, New York 1916, Play

SILENT WITNESS, THE 1932 d: Marcel Varnel, R. Lee Hough. USA., *The Silent Witness*, Jack Celestin, Jack de Leon, New York 1931, Play

Silent World of Nicholas Quinn, The *see* INSPECTOR MORSE: THE SILENT WORLD OF NICHOLAS QUINN (1987).

SILENT YEARS 1921 d: Louis J. Gasnier. USA., *Mam'selle Jo*, Harriet T. Comstock, Garden City, N.Y. 1918, Novel

Silenzio *see* LA CANZONE DELL'AMORE (1930).

SILENZIO, IL 1921 d: Luciano DoriA. ITL., *Suona la Ritirata*, Beyerlein, Play

Silja *see* NUORENA NUKKUNUT (1937).

Silja *see* SILJA - NUORENA NUKKUNUT (1956).

Silja - Fallen Asleep When Young *see* NUORENA NUKKUNUT (1937).

Silja - Fallen Asleep When Young *see* SILJA - NUORENA NUKKUNUT (1956).

SILJA - NUORENA NUKKUNUT 1956 d: Jack WitikkA. FNL., *Nuorena Nukkunut*, Frans E. Sillanpaa, 1931, Novel

SILK HAT KID 1935 d: H. Bruce Humberstone. USA., *The Lord's Referee*, Gerald Beaumont, 1923, Short Story

SILK LINED BURGLAR, THE 1919 d: John Francis Dillon. USA., *Miss Doris - Safe-Cracker*, Jack Boyle, 1918, Short Story

Silk Noose, The *see* NOOSE (1948).

SILK STOCKINGS 1927 d: Wesley Ruggles. USA., *A Pair of Silk Stockings*, Cyril Harcourt, New York 1914, Play

Silnice Bila Prede Mnou *see* TULAK (1925).

SILVER BEARS 1977 d: Ivan Passer. UKN/USA., *Silver Bears*, Paul Erdman, Novel

SILVER BLAZE 1912 d: Georges Treville. UKN., *Silver Blaze*, Arthur Conan Doyle, 1894, Short Story

SILVER BLAZE 1923 d: George Ridgwell. UKN., *Silver Blaze*, Arthur Conan Doyle, 1894, Short Story

SILVER BLAZE 1937 d: Thomas Bentley. UKN., *Silver Blaze*, Arthur Conan Doyle, 1894, Short Story

Silver Blaze *see* THE RETURN OF SHERLOCK HOLMES: SILVER BLAZE (1986).

SILVER BRIDGE, THE 1920 d: Dallas Cairns. UKN., *The Silver Bridge*, Helen Prothero Lewis, Novel

SILVER BUDDHA, THE 1923 d: A. E. Coleby. UKN., *The Silver Buddha*, Sax Rohmer, Short Story

SILVER BULLET 1985 d: Daniel Attias. USA., *Cycle of the Werewolf*, Stephen King, Novel

SILVER CHALICE, THE 1954 d: Victor Saville. USA., *The Silver Chalice*, Thomas B. Costain, 1952, Novel

Silver City *see* ALBUQUERQUE (1948).

SILVER CITY 1951 d: Byron Haskin. USA., *High Vermilion*, Luke Short, 1948, Novel

SILVER CORD, THE 1933 d: John Cromwell. USA., *The Silver Cord*, Sidney Coe Howard, New York 1926, Play

SILVER DARLINGS, THE 1947 d: Clarence Elder, Clifford Evans. UKN., *The Silver Darlings*, Neil Gunn, Novel

Silver Devil *see* WILD HORSE (1930).

SILVER DOLLAR 1932 d: Alfred E. Green. USA., *Silver Dollar*, David Karsner, New York 1932, Book

SILVER GIRL, THE 1919 d: Frank Keenan, Eliot Howe. USA., *The Silver Girl*, Edward Peple, New York 1907, Play

Silver Globe, The *see* NA SREBRNYM GLOBIE (1977).

SILVER HORDE, THE 1920 d: Frank Lloyd. USA., *The Silver Horde*, Rex Beach, New York 1909, Novel

SILVER HORDE, THE 1930 d: George Archainbaud. USA., *The Silver Horde*, Rex Beach, New York 1909, Novel

SILVER KING, THE 1919 d: George Irving. USA., *The Silver King*, Henry Herman, Henry Arthur Jones, London 1882, Play

SILVER KING, THE 1929 d: T. Hayes Hunter. UKN., *The Silver King*, Henry Herman, Henry Arthur Jones, London 1882, Play

Silver Lining *see* LOOK FOR THE SILVER LINING (1949).

SILVER RIVER 1948 d: Raoul Walsh. USA., *Silver River*, Stephen Longstreet, Novel

Silver Skies *see* STRIBRNA OBLAKA (1938).

SILVER THREADS AMONG THE GOLD 1911 d: Edwin S. Porter. USA., *Silver Threads Among the Gold*, Pierce Kingsley, Story

SILVER TREASURE, THE 1926 d: Rowland V. Lee. USA., *Nostromo*, Joseph Conrad, 1904, Novel

SILVER WHIP, THE 1953 d: Harmon Jones. USA., *The Big Range*, Jack Schaefer, 1953, Short Story

Silversmith and I, The *see* PLATERO Y YO (1968).

SILVIO PELLICO 1915 d: Livio Pavanelli. ITL., *Le Mie Prigioni*, Silvio Pellico, 1832, Novel

Silvio Pellico Il Martire Dello Spielberg *see* SILVIO PELLICO (1915).

SIMBA 1955 d: Brian Desmond Hurst. UKN., *Simba*, Anthony Perry, Novel

Simhasan *see* SINHASAN (1979).

SIMON AND LAURA 1955 d: Muriel Box. UKN., *Simon and Laura*, Alan Melville, London 1954, Play

SIMON BIRCH 1998 d: Mark Steven Johnson. USA., *A Prayer for Owen Meany*, John Irving, Novel

SIMON TANNER 1993 d: Joel Jouanneau. FRN/SWT., *Les Enfants Tanner*, Robert Walser, Novel

SIMON THE JESTER 1925 d: George Melford. USA., *Simon the Jester*, William J. Locke, New York 1909, Novel

SIMON, THE JESTER 1915 d: Edward Jose. USA., *Simon the Jester*, William J. Locke, New York 1909, Novel

SIMONA 1974 d: Patrick Longchamps. ITL/BLG., *Histoire de l'Oeil*, Georges Bataille, 1928, Novel

SIMONE 1918 d: Camille de Morlhon. FRN., *Simone*, Eugene Brieux, Novel

SIMONE 1926 d: E. B. Donatien. FRN., *Simone*, Eugene Brieux, Novel

SIMOUN, LE 1933 d: Firmin Gemier. FRN., *Le Simoun*, Henri-Rene Lenormand, 1921, Play

SIMPATYA BISHVIEL KELEV 1981 d: Sam Firstenberg. ISR., *Yigael Lev*, Story

SIMPLE ERREUR 1922 d: Maurice Challiot. FRN., *Simple Erreur*, Gaston Dumestre, Play

Simple Heart, A *see* UN CUORE SEMPLICE (1976).

Simple Life, The *see* THE HONEYMOON'S OVER (1939).

Simple Past, The *see* LE PASSE SIMPLE (1977).

SIMPLE PLAN, A 1998 d: Sam Raimi. USA., *A Simple Plan*, Scott B. Smith, Novel

SIMPLE SOULS 1920 d: Robert T. Thornby. USA., *Simple Souls*, John Hastings Turner, New York 1918, Novel

SIMPLE TWIST OF FATE, A 1994 d: Gillies MacKinnon. USA., *Silas Marner*, George Eliot, London 1861, Novel

Simulant, Der *see* DE WINZIG SIMULIERT (1942).

SIN CARGO 1926 d: Louis J. Gasnier. USA., *Sin Cargo*, Lee Renick Brown, Story

SIN COMPASION 1994 d: Francisco Lombardi. PRU/MXC/FRN., *Prestupleniye I Nakazaniye*, Fyodor Dostoyevsky, 1867, Novel

Sin Flood *see* THE WAY OF ALL MEN (1930).

SIN FLOOD, THE 1922 d: Frank Lloyd. USA., *Syndafloden*, Henning Berger, Play

Sin of Esther Waters, The *see* ESTHER WATERS (1948).

Sin of Father Mouret, The *see* LA FAUTE DE L'ABBE MOURET (1970).

Sin of Lena Rivers, The *see* LENA RIVERS (1932).

SIN OF MADELON CLAUDET, THE 1931 d: Edgar Selwyn. USA., *The Lullaby*, Edward Knoblock, New York 1923, Play

SIN OF NORA MORAN, THE 1933 d: Phil Goldstone. USA., *Willis Maxwell Goodhue*, Play

Sin of Rogelia Sanchez, The *see* IL PECCATO DI ROGELIA SANCHEZ (1939).

Sin of St. Anthony, The *see* THE SINS OF ST. ANTHONY (1920).

Sin of the Past, The *see* STARY HRICH (1929).

Sin on the Beach *see* LE CRI DE LA CHAIR (1963).

Sin Sniper, The *see* STONE COLD DEAD (1979).

SIN THAT WAS HIS, THE 1920 d: Hobart Henley. USA., *The Sin That Was His*, Frank L. Packard, New York 1917, Novel

Sin, The *see* HAKAI (1961).

Sin, The *see* MISS WYCKOFF GOOD LUCK (1979).

SIN VENTURA, LA 1923 d: Benito Perojo, E. B. Donatien. SPN/FRN., *El Caballero Audaz*, Jose-Maria Carretero, Novel

Sinbad *see* SZINDBAD (1971).

Sinbad *see* SINBAD OF THE SEVEN SEAS (1986).

SINBAD OF THE SEVEN SEAS 1986 d: Enzo G. Castellari. ITL/USA., Edgar Allan Poe, Short Story

SINCE YOU WENT AWAY 1944 d: John Cromwell, Andre de Toth (Uncredited). USA., *Since You Went Away*, Margaret Buell Wilder, Book

SINCERELY YOURS 1955 d: Gordon Douglas. USA., *The Silent Voice*, Jules Eckert Goodman, New York 1914, Play

Sincerity *see* MAGOKORO (1939).

SINDACO, IL 1997 d: Ugo Fabrizio Giordani. ITL., *Il Sindaco Del Rione Sanita*, Eduardo de Filippo, 1960, Play

Sindbad *see* SZINDBAD (1971).

Sindbad of the Seven Seas *see* SINBAD OF THE SEVEN SEAS (1986).

SINDROME DI STENDHAL, LA 1996 d: Dario Argento. ITL., *La Sindrome Di Stendhal*, Graziella Magherini, Novel

Sinel *see* SHINEL (1926).

Sinfonia Per Due Spie *see* SERENADE FUR ZWEI SPIONE (1965).

Sinfonia Per un Massacro *see* SYMPHONIE POUR UN MASSACRE (1963).

Sinful Adventures of Davey Haggart, The *see* SINFUL DAVEY (1969).

SINFUL DAVEY 1969 d: John Huston. UKN., *The Life of David Haggart*, David Haggart, 1821, Novel

Sinful Village *see* DAS SUNDIGE DORF (1954).

Sinful Village *see* DAS SUNDIGE DORF (1966).

SING, BOY, SING 1957 d: Henry Ephron. USA., *The Singing Idol*, Paul Monash, Television Play

Singapore, Singapore *see* CINQ GARS POUR SINGAPOUR (1967).

SINGAPORE WOMAN 1941 d: Jean Negulesco. USA., *Hard Luck Dame*, Laird Doyle, Story

SINGE EN HIVER, UN 1962 d: Henri Verneuil. FRN., *Un Singe En Hiver*, Antoine Blondin, Paris 1959, Novel

SINGED 1927 d: John Griffith Wray. USA., *Love O' Women*, Adela Rogers St. Johns, 1926, Short Story

SINGED WINGS 1922 d: Penrhyn Stanlaws. USA., *Singed Wings*, Katharine Newlin Burt, Story

SINGER NOT THE SONG, THE 1961 d: Roy Ward Baker. UKN., *The Singer Not the Song*, Audrey Erskine Lindop, London 1953, Novel

Singer of Naples, The *see* EL CANTANTE DE NAPOLES (1935).

Singin' Idol, The *see* BOY, SING SING (1957).

Singing Blacksmith, The *see* YANKEL DER SCHMIDT (1938).

SINGING FOOL, THE 1928 d: Lloyd Bacon. USA., *The Singing Fool*, Leslie S. Barrows, Story

SINGING GUNS 1950 d: R. G. Springsteen. USA., *Singing Guns*, Max Brand, Novel

Singing Musketeer, The *see* THE THREE MUSKETEERS (1939).

Singing Rangers, The *see* OUTLAWS OF THE PRAIRIE (1937).

SINGLE LIFE 1921 d: Edwin J. Collins. UKN., *Single Life*, J. B. Buckstone, London 1839, Play

SINGLE MAN, A 1928 d: Harry Beaumont. USA., *A Single Man*, Hubert Henry Davies, London 1910, Play

SINGLE MAN, THE 1919 d: A. V. Bramble. UKN., *A Single Man*, Hubert Henry Davies, London 1910, Play

SINGLE ROOM FURNISHED 1968 d: Matt Cimber. USA., Gerald Sanford, Play

Single Standard, The *see* THE BATTLE OF THE SEXES (1914).

SINGLE STANDARD, THE 1929 d: John S. Robertson. USA., *The Single Standard*, Adela Rogers St. Johns, New York 1928, Novel

SINGLE WHITE FEMALE 1992 d: Barbet Schroeder. USA., *Swf Seeks Same*, John Lutz, Novel

SINGLE-HANDED 1953 d: Roy Boulting. UKN., *Brown on Resolution*, C. S. Forester, 1929, Novel

SINHAGAD 1923 d: Baburao Painter. IND., *Gad Aala Pan Sinha Gela*, Hari Narayan Apte, Novel

SINHAGAD 1933 d: V. Shantaram. IND., *Gad Aala Pan Sinha Gela*, Hari Narayan Apte, Novel

SINHASAN 1979 d: Jabbar Patel. IND., *Mumbai Dinank*, Arun Sadhu, Novel, *Simhasan*, Arun Sadhu, Novel

SININEN VIIKKO 1954 d: Matti KassilA. FNL., *Den Bla Veckan*, Jarl Hemmer, 1928, Short Story

SINISTER HANDS 1932 d: Armand Schaefer. USA., *Seance Mystery*, Norton S. Parker, Novel

Sinister Hands of Dr. Orlak, The see ORLACS HANDE (1925).

Sinister House see MUSS 'EM UP (1936).

SINISTER MAN, THE 1961 d: Clive Donner. UKN., *The Sinister Man*, Edgar Wallace, London 1924, Novel

Sinister Monk, The see DER UNHEIMLICHE MONCH (1965).

SINISTER STREET 1922 d: George A. Beranger. UKN., *Sinister Street*, Compton Mackenzie, 1914, Novel

Sinister Wish, The see DIE UNHEIMLICHEN WUNSCHE (1939).

SINK THE BISMARCK! 1960 d: Lewis Gilbert. UKN., *Sink the Bismarck!*, C. S. Forester, Book

SINNER OR SAINT 1923 d: Lawrence C. Windom. USA., *The Man Who Wouldn't Love*, Dorothy Farnum, Story

SINNER TAKE ALL 1936 d: Errol Taggart. USA., *Murder of a Wanton*, Whitman Chambers, New York 1934, Novel

Sinner, The see THE SIREN'S SONG (1915).

SINNERS 1920 d: Kenneth Webb. USA., *Sinners*, Owen Davis, New York 1915, Play

Sinners Go to Hell see NO EXIT (1962).

SINNER'S HOLIDAY 1930 d: John G. Adolfi. USA., *Penny Arcade*, Marie Baumer, New York 1930, Play

Sinners I Summertime see SYNDERE I SOMMERSOL (1934).

SINNERS IN HEAVEN 1924 d: Alan Crosland. USA., *Sinners in Heaven*, Clive Arden, Indianapolis 1923, Novel

Sinners of Paris see RAFLES SUR LA VILLE (1957).

Sinners Three see THE MASTER MIND (1920).

Sinning Urge, The see BRANT BARN (1967).

SINS 1985 d: Douglas Hickox. USA/FRN., *Sins*, Judith Gould, Novel

SINS OF A FATHER, THE 1923 d: Edwin Greenwood. UKN., *The Sins of a Father*, Mrs. Gaskell, Novel

Sins of Childhood see GRZECHY DZIECINSTWA (1980).

Sins of Children see IN HIS STEPS (1936).

Sins of Desire see ANDRE CORNELIS (1927).

Sins of Fashion see RUE DE LA PAIX (1926).

Sins of Lola Montes, The see LOLA MONTES (1955).

Sins of Madame Bovary, The see DIE NACKTE BOVARY (1969).

SINS OF MAN 1936 d: Gregory Ratoff, Otto Brower. USA., *Hiob Roman Eines Ein Fachen Mannes*, Joseph Roth, Berlin 1930, Novel

Sins of Pompei see LES DERNIERS JOURS DE POMPEI (1948).

Sins of Rachel Cade, The see RACHEL CADE (1961).

SINS OF ROSANNE, THE 1920 d: Tom Forman. USA., *Rosanne Ozanne*, Cynthia Stockley, Short Story

Sins of Rose Bernd, The see ROSE BERND (1957).

Sins of Rozanne, The see THE SINS OF ROSANNE (1920).

SINS OF SOCIETY, THE 1915 d: Oscar Eagle. USA., *The Sins of Society*, Henry Hamilton, Cecil Raleigh, London 1907, Play

SINS OF ST. ANTHONY, THE 1920 d: James Cruze. USA., *The Sins of St. Anthony*, Charles Collins, Short Story

Sins of the Children see THE RICHEST MAN IN THE WORLD (1930).

Sins of the Children see IN HIS STEPS (1936).

SINS OF THE CHILDREN, THE 1918 d: John S. Lopez. USA., *The Sins of the Children*, Cosmo Hamilton, Boston 1916, Novel

Sins of the Father see HOME IS THE HERO (1959).

SINS YE DO, THE 1924 d: Fred Leroy Granville. UKN., *The Sins Ye Do*, Emmeline Morrison, Novel

SINYAYA PTITSA 1975 d: George Cukor. USS/USA., *L' Oiseau Bleu*, Maurice Maeterlinck, Moscow 1908, Play

Sipor Sh'matchil Be'halvayah Shel Nachash see SIPUR SHEMATCHIL BELEVAYA SHEL NACHASH (1993).

SIPUR INTIMI 1981 d: Nadav Levithan. ISR., Nadav Levithan, Story

SIPUR SHEMATCHIL BELEVAYA SHEL NACHASH 1993 d: Dina Zvi-Riklis. ISR., Ronit Matalon, Book

Sir Arne's Treasure see HERR ARNES PENNIGAR (1954).

SIR OR MADAM 1928 d: Carl Boese. UKN., *Sir Or Madam*, Berta Ruck, Novel

SIR RUPERT'S WIFE 1922 d: Challis Sanderson. UKN., *Sir Rupert's Wife*, George R. Sims, Poem

SIREN OF ATLANTIS 1948 d: Gregg R. Tallas. USA., *L' Atlantide*, Pierre Benoit, Paris 1919, Novel

Siren of the South Seas see PARADISE ISLE (1937).

SIRENA 1947 d: Karel Stekly. CZC., *Sirena*, Marie Majerova, 1935, Novel

Sirena Del Golfo, La see MA CHI TE LO FARE? (1948).

SIRENA NEGRA, LA 1947 d: Carlos Serrano de OsmA. SPN., *La Sirena Negra*, Emilia Pardo Bazan, 1908, Novel

SIRENE DE PIERRE 1922 d: Roger Lion, Virginia de Castro. FRN/PRT., *Obra Do Domonio*, Virginia de Castro, Novel

SIRENE DU MISSISSIPPI, LA 1969 d: Francois Truffaut. FRN/ITL., *Waltz Into Darkness*, Cornell Woolrich, New York 1947, Novel

SIREN'S SONG, THE 1915 d: George W. Lederer. USA., *The Siren's Song*, George Middleton, Leonidas Westervelt, Play

Sirocco see LA MAISON DU MALTAIS (1938).

SIROCCO 1951 d: Curtis Bernhardt. USA., *Le Coup de Grace*, Joseph Kessel, 1931, Novel

Sirocco see SIROKKO (1969).

Sirocco d'Hiver see SIROKKO (1969).

SIROKKO 1969 d: Miklos Jancso. HNG/FRN., *Sirokko*, Gyula Hernadi, Budapest 1969, Novel

SIS HOPKINS 1919 d: Clarence Badger. USA., *Sis Hopkins*, Carroll Fleming, George A. Nichols, Buffalo, N.Y. 1899, Play

SIS HOPKINS 1941 d: Joseph Santley. USA., *Sis Hopkins*, Carroll Fleming, George A. Nichols, Buffalo, N.Y. 1899, Play

SISSI 1956 d: Ernst MarischkA. AUS., *Sissi*, Marie Blank-Eismann, Novel

SISSIGNORA 1942 d: Ferdinando M. Poggioli. ITL., *Sissignora*, Flavia Steno, Novel

Siste Karolen, Den see ELI SJURSDOTTER (1938).

SISTEMA PELEGRIN, EL 1951 d: Ignacio F. Iquino. SPN., *El Sistema Pelegrin*, Wenceslao Fernandez Florez, 1949, Novel

Sister Act see FOUR DAUGHTERS (1938).

Sister Act see FOUR WIVES (1939).

SISTER DORA 1977 d: Marc Miller. UKN., *Sister Dora*, Jo Manton, Book

SISTER KENNY 1946 d: Dudley Nichols. USA., *And They Shall Walk*, Mary Kenny, Autobiography

SISTER MY SISTER 1994 d: Nancy Meckler. UKN., *My Sister in This House*, Wendy Kesselman, Play

Sister of Six, A see FLICKORNA GYURKOVICS (1926).

Sister Saint Sulpice see LA HERMANA SAN SULPICIO (1927).

Sister Saint Sulpice see LA HERMANA SAN SULPICIO (1934).

Sister Saint Sulpice see LA HERMANA SAN SULPICIO (1952).

SISTER TO ASSIST 'ER, A 1922 d: George Dewhurst. UKN., *A Sister to Assist 'Er*, John le Breton, Play

SISTER TO ASSIST 'ER, A 1927 d: George Dewhurst. UKN., *A Sister to Assist 'Er*, John le Breton, Play

SISTER TO ASSIST 'ER, A 1930 d: George Dewhurst. UKN., *A Sister to Assist 'Er*, John le Breton, Play

SISTER TO ASSIST 'ER, A 1938 d: Widgey R. Newman, George Dewhurst. UKN., *A Sister to Assist 'Er*, John le Breton, Play

SISTER TO ASSIST 'ER, A 1948 d: George Dewhurst. UKN., *A Sister to Assist 'Er*, John le Breton, Play

Sisterhood, The see THE LADIES CLUB (1986).

Sisters see SESTRY (1957).

Sisters' Flowers see ZIMEI HUA (1933).

Sister's Keeper see A KILLING AFFAIR (1988).

SISTERS OF EVE 1928 d: Scott Pembroke. USA., *The Tempting of Tavarnake*, E. Phillips Oppenheim, Boston 1911, Novel

Sisters of the Gion see GION NO SHIMAI (1936).

SISTERS OF THE GOLDEN CIRCLE 1918 d: Kenneth Webb. USA., *Sisters of the Golden Circle*, O. Henry, Short Story

SISTERS, THE 1938 d: Anatole Litvak. USA., *The Sisters*, Myron Brinig, New York 1937, Novel

Sisters, The see SURORILE (1984).

SITTER, THE 1991 d: Rick Berger. USA., *Mischief*, Charlotte Armstrong, 1950, Novel

SITTING ON THE MOON 1936 d: Ralph Staub. USA., *Tempermental Lady*, Julian Field, 1936, Short Story

Sitting on the World see FICKLE WOMEN (1920).

SITTING PRETTY 1948 d: Walter Lang. USA., *Belvedere*, Gwen Davenport, Novel

SITTING TARGET 1971 d: Douglas Hickox. UKN., *Sitting Target*, Lawrence Henderson, Novel

SITUATION HOPELESS - BUT NOT SERIOUS 1965 d: Gottfried Reinhardt. USA., *The Hiding Place*, Robert Shaw, London 1959, Novel

SIVOOKY DEMON 1919 d: Vaclav Binovec. CZC., *Sivooky Demon*, Jakub Arbes, Novel

SIX BEST CELLARS, THE 1920 d: Donald Crisp. USA., *The Six Best Cellars*, Holworthy Hall, Hugh MacNair Kahler, 1919, Short Story

SIX BRIDGES TO CROSS 1955 d: Joseph Pevney. USA., *500,000 - and Got Away With It They Stole $2*, Joseph F. Dinneen, Story

SIX CENT MILLE FRANCS PAR MOIS 1925 d: Robert Peguy, Nicolas Koline. FRN., *600.000 Francs Par Mois*, Jean Drault, Novel

SIX CENT MILLE FRANCS PAR MOIS 1933 d: Leo Joannon. FRN., *Six Cent Mille Francs Par Mois*, Albert-Jean, Andre Mouezy-Eon, Play

SIX CHARACTERS IN SEARCH OF AN AUTHOR 1992 d: Bill Bryden. UKN., *Sei Personaggi in Cerca d'Autore*, Luigi Pirandello, Play

SIX CHEVAUX BLEUS 1967 d: Philippe JouliA. FRN., *Six Chevaux Bleus*, Yvonne Esconda, Novel

SIX CYLINDER LOVE 1923 d: Elmer Clifton. USA., *Six-Cylinder Love*, William Anthony McGuire, New York 1921, Play

SIX CYLINDER LOVE 1931 d: Thornton Freeland. USA., *Six-Cylinder Love*, William Anthony McGuire, New York 1921, Play

Six Cylinder Love see THE HONEYMOON'S OVER (1939).

SIX DAYS 1923 d: Charles J. Brabin. USA., *Six Days*, Elinor Glyn, Philadelphia 1923, Novel

Six Days a Week see LA BUGIARDA (1965).

SIX DEGREES OF SEPARATION 1994 d: Fred Schepisi. USA., *Six Degrees of Separation*, John Guare, Play

SIX FEET FOUR 1919 d: Henry King. USA., *Six Feet Four*, Jackson Gregory, New York 1918, Novel

SIX MILLION DOLLAR MAN, THE 1973 d: Richard Irving. USA., *Cyborg*, Martin Caidin, Novel

Six Musketeers, The see SEST MUSKETYRU (1925).

SIX NAPOLEONS, THE 1922 d: George Ridgwell. UKN., *The Six Napoleons*, Arthur Conan Doyle, Short Story

Six Napoleons, The see THE RETURN OF SHERLOCK HOLMES: THE SIX NAPOLEONS (1986).

SIX SHOOTIN' ROMANCE, A 1926 d: Cliff Smith. USA., *Dashing*, Ruth Comfort Mitchell, Story

SIX WAYS TO SUNDAY 1997 d: Adam Bernstein. USA., *Portrait of a Young Man Drowning*, Charles Perry, Novel

SIX WEEKS 1982 d: Tony Bill. USA., *Six Weeks*, Fred Mustard Stewart, Novel

SIX-FIFTY, THE 1923 d: Nat Ross. USA., *The Six-Fifty*, Kate L. McLaurin, New York 1921, Play

SIXIEME ETAGE 1939 d: Maurice Cloche. FRN., *Sixieme Etage*, Alfred Gehri, Play

SIXTEEN FATHOMS DEEP 1934 d: Armand Schaefer. USA., *Sixteen Fathoms Under*, Eustace L. Adams, 1932, Short Story

Sixteen Fathoms Under *see* **SIXTEEN FATHOMS DEEP** (1934).

SIXTEENTH WIFE, THE 1917 d: Charles J. Brabin. USA., Molly Elliot Seawell, Story

Sixth Floor *see* **IM SECHSTEN STOCK** (1961).

SIXTH HAPPINESS 1997 d: Waris Hussein. UKN., *Trying to Grow*, Firdaus Kanga, Novel

Sixth Man, The *see* **THE OUTSIDER** (1961).

Sixty Saddles for Gobi *see* **DESTINATION GOBI** (1953).

Size 36 Girls *see* **36 FILLETTE** (1987).

Sjalvsvaldiga Slaktet, Det *see* **KURITON SUKUPOLVI** (1937).

Sju Broder *see* **SEITSEMAN VELJESTA** (1939).

SKABENGA 1953 d: George Michael. SAF., *African Fury*, George Michaels, Book

Skabenka *see* **SKABENGA** (1953).

SKALNI PLEMENO 1944 d: Ladislav Brom. CZC., *Skalni Plemeno*, Jan Moravek, Novel

SKALPEL, PROSIM 1986 d: Jiri SvobodA. CZC., *Prosim Skalpel*, Valja Styblova, Novel

SKANDAL IN BADEN-BADEN 1928 d: Erich Waschneck. GRM., *Die Geliebte Roswolskys*, Georg Froschel, Novel

SKANDAL IN DER BOTSCHAFT 1950 d: Erik Ode. GRM., *Ein Anstandiger Mensch*, Georg Fraser, Play

Skandal in Einer Kleinen Residenz *see* **DIE HOSE** (1927).

SKANDAL IN ISCHL 1957 d: Rolf Thiele. AUS., *Der Meister*, Hermann Bahr, 1909, Play

SKANDAL UM DR. VLIMMEN 1956 d: Arthur M. Rabenalt. GRM., *Doctor Vlimmen*, A. Roothaert, Novel

Skandal Um Dr. Vlimmen *see* **TIERARZT DR. VLIMMEN** (1956).

SKAREDA DEDINA 1975 d: Karel KachynA. CZC., *Skareda Dedina*, Petr Jilemnicky, Novel

SKARSELD 1975 d: Michael Meschke. SWD., *La Divina Commedia*, Dante Alighieri, 1310, Verse

SKAZKA O KONKE-GORBUNKE 1961 d: Aleksandr Radunskiy, Zoya TulubyevA. USS., Pavel Erchow, Story

SKAZKA O MERTVOY TSAREVNE I O SEMI BOGATYRYAKH 1951 d: Ivan Ivanov-Vano. USS., *Skazka O Mertvoy Tsarevne I O Semi Bogatyryakh*, Alexander Pushkin, 1833, Poem

SKAZKA O POPE I O RABOT EGO BALDE 1939 d: Piotr Sazonov. USS., *Skazka O Pope I O Rabotnike Ego Balde*, Alexander Pushkin, 1831, Short Story

SKAZKA O POPE I O RABOTNIKE EGO BALDE 1956 d: Anatoli Karanovich. USS., *Skazka O Pope I O Rabotnike Ego Balde*, Alexander Pushkin, 1831, Short Story

SKAZKA O RYBAKE I RYBKE 1937 d: Alexander Ptushko. USS., *Skazka O Rybake I Rybke*, Alexander Pushkin, 1833, Poem

SKAZKA O TSARE SALTANE 1943 d: Valentina Brumberg, Zinaida Brumberg. USS., *Skazka O Tsare Saltane*, Alexander Pushkin, 1831, Poem

SKAZKA O TSARE SALTANE 1967 d: Alexander Ptushko. USS., *Skazka O Tsare Saltane*, Alexander Pushkin, 1831, Poem

SKAZKA O TSARE SALTANE 1984 d: Ivan Ivanov-Vano, L. Milchin. USS., *Skazka O Tsare Saltane*, Alexander Pushkin, 1831, Poem

SKAZKA O ZOLOTOM PETUKHE 1967 d: Alexander Snezhko-BlotskayA. USS., *Skazka O Zolotom Petukhe*, Alexander Pushkin, 1834, Short Story

SKEEZER 1982 d: Peter H. Hunt. USA., *Skeezer - Dog With a Mission*, Elizabeth Yates, Novel

SKEIN OF LIFE, THE 1915 d: Donald MacDonald. USA., *The Skein of Life*, Will M. Ritchey, Story

Skeleton Key, The *see* **PAKLIC** (1944).

Skeleton on Horseback *see* **BILA NEMOC** (1937).

SKEPP TILL INDIALAND 1947 d: Ingmar Bergman. SWD., *Skepp Till Indialand*, Martin Soederhjelm, Play

Sketch of Madame Yuki *see* **YUKI FUJIN EZU** (1950).

Sketches in Charcoal *see* **SZKICE WEGLEM** (1957).

Skidding *see* **A FAMILY AFFAIR** (1937).

Skids *see* **BURN 'EM UP O'CONNOR** (1938).

SKIN DEEP 1922 d: Lambert Hillyer. USA., *Lucky Damage*, Marc Edmund Jones, Story

SKIN DEEP 1929 d: Ray Enright. USA., *Lucky Damage*, Marc Edmund Jones, Story

SKIN GAME, THE 1920 d: B. E. Doxat-Pratt. UKN/NTH., *The Skin Game*, John Galsworthy, London 1920, Play

SKIN GAME, THE 1931 d: Alfred Hitchcock. UKN., *The Skin Game*, John Galsworthy, London 1920, Play

Skin of Sorrow, The *see* **SAGRENSKA KOZA** (1960).

Skin, The *see* **LA PELLE** (1981).

SKINNER STEPS OUT 1929 d: William James Craft. USA., *Skinner's Dress Suit*, Henry Irving Dodge, 1916, Short Story

SKINNER'S BABY 1917 d: Harry Beaumont. USA., *Skinner's Baby*, Henry Irving Dodge, New York 1917, Novel

SKINNER'S BIG IDEA 1928 d: Lynn Shores. USA., *Skinner's Big Idea*, Henry Irving Dodge, New York 1918, Novel

SKINNER'S DRESS SUIT 1917 d: Harry Beaumont. USA., *Skinner's Dress Suit*, Henry Irving Dodge, 1916, Short Story

SKINNER'S DRESS SUIT 1926 d: William A. Seiter. USA., *Skinner's Dress Suit*, Henry Irving Dodge, 1916, Short Story

Skipper Next to God *see* **MAITRE APRES DIEU** (1950).

SKIPPER OF THE OSPREY 1933 d: Norman Walker. UKN., *The Skipper of the Osprey*, W. W. Jacobs, Short Story

SKIPPER OF THE OSPREY, THE 1916 d: Frank Miller. UKN., *The Skipper of the Osprey*, W. W. Jacobs, Short Story

SKIPPER SURPRISED HIS WIFE, THE 1950 d: Elliott Nugent. USA., *The Skipper Surprised His Wife*, Com. W. J. Lederer, Article

SKIPPER'S WOOING, THE 1922 d: Manning Haynes. UKN., *The Skipper's Wooing*, W. W. Jacobs, Novel

SKIPPY 1931 d: Norman Taurog. USA., *Skippy*, Percy Lee Crosby, New York 1929, Novel

Skirts *see* **A LITTLE BIT OF FLUFF** (1928).

SKJAERGARDSFLIRT 1932 d: Rasmus Breistein. NRW., *Skjaergardsflirt*, Gideon Wahlberg, Play

Sklaven Roms, Die *see* **LA RIVOLTA DEGLI SCHIAVI** (1961).

SKOLA ZAKLAD ZIVOTA 1938 d: Martin Fric. CZC., *Skola Zaklad Zivota*, Jaroslav Zak, Book

SKORBNOE BESCUVSTVIE 1986 d: Alexander Sokurov. USS., *Heartbreak House*, George Bernard Shaw, 1919, Play

SKRIVANCI PISEN 1933 d: Svatopluk Innemann. CZC., *Oblaka*, Jaroslav Kvapil, Play

Skull Island *see* **THE MOST DANGEROUS GAME** (1932).

SKULL, THE 1965 d: Freddie Francis. UKN., *The Skull of the Marquis de Sade*, Robert Bloch, New York 1965, Short Story

SKULLDUGGERY 1970 d: Gordon Douglas, Richard Wilson (Uncredited). USA., *Les Animaux Denatures*, Vercors, Paris 1952, Novel

SKULLDUGGERY 1989 d: Philip Davis. UKN., *Skullduggery*, Philip Davis, Play

SKVENEI ANEKDOT 1965 d: Alexander Alov, Vladimir Naumov. USS., *Skverny Anekdot*, Fyodor Dostoyevsky, 1862, Short Story

Skvernyj Anekdot *see* **SKVENEI ANEKDOT** (1965).

Skwernyj Anekdot *see* **SKVENEI ANEKDOT** (1965).

SKY BANDITS 1940 d: Ralph Staub. USA., *Renfrew Rides the Sky*, Laurie York Erskine, New York 1928, Novel

Sky Full of Stars *see* **UM CEU DE ESTRELAS** (1996).

SKY HAWK, THE 1929 d: John G. Blystone. USA., *Chap Called Barwell*, Llewellyn Hughes, 1929, Short Story

Sky High *see* **RIDING ON AIR** (1937).

SKY IS GRAY, THE 1977 d: Stan Lathan. USA., *The Sky Is Gray*, Ernest J. Gaines, 1966, Short Story

SKY PILOT, THE 1921 d: King Vidor. USA., *The Sky Pilot*, Ralph Connor, Chicago 1899, Novel

SKY RAIDER, THE 1925 d: T. Hayes Hunter. USA., *The Great Air Mail Robbery*, Jack Lait, Story

Sky Terror *see* **SKYJACKED** (1972).

SKY WEST AND CROOKED 1965 d: John Mills. UKN., *Bats With Baby Faces*, John Prebble, Novel

SKYJACKED 1972 d: John Guillermin. USA., *Skyjacked*, David Harper, Novel

SKYLARK 1941 d: Mark Sandrich. USA., *Skylark*, Samson Raphaelson, New York 1939, Play

Skylark *see* **PACSIRTA** (1964).

Skylark *see* **PLAIN AND TALL SARAH** (1991).

SKYLIGHT ROOM, THE 1917 d: Martin Justice. USA., *The Skylight Room*, O. Henry, 1906, Short Story

SKYLINE 1931 d: Sam Taylor. USA., *East Side - West Side*, Felix Riesenberg, New York 1927, Novel

Skyline of Spruce, The *see* **SHADOWS OF THE NORTH** (1923).

SKYROCKET, THE 1926 d: Marshall Neilan. USA., *The Skyrocket*, Adela Rogers St. Johns, New York 1925, Novel

SKYSCRAPER 1928 d: Howard Higgin. USA., *The White Frontier*, Jeffrey Deprend, Story

Skyscraper *see* **SKYSCRAPER SOULS** (1932).

SKYSCRAPER SOULS 1932 d: Edgar Selwyn. USA., *Skyscraper*, Faith Baldwin, New York 1931, Novel

Skywatch *see* **LIGHT UP THE SKY** (1960).

SLAB BOYS, THE 1997 d: John Byrne. UKN., *Cuttin' a Rug*, John Byrne, Play, *The Slab Boys*, John Byrne, Play

Sladky Cas Kalimagdory *see* **DIE SUSSE ZEIT MIT KALIMAGDORA** (1968).

SLAEGTEN 1978 d: Anders Refn. DNM., *Slaegten*, Gustav Weid, 1898, Novel

SLAMENY KLOBOUK 1972 d: Oldrich Lipsky. CZC., *Un Chapeau de Paille d'Italie*, Eugene Labiche, Marc-Michel, 1847, Play

SLANDER 1956 d: Roy Rowland. USA., *A Public Figure*, Harry W. Junkin, Television Play

SLANDER HOUSE 1938 d: Charles Lamont. USA., *Scandal House*, Madeline Woods, New York 1933, Novel

SLANDER THE WOMAN 1923 d: Allen Holubar. USA., *Judgement of the West*, Valma Clark, Story

Slapstick *see* **SLAPSTICK (OF ANOTHER KIND)** (1984).

SLAPSTICK (OF ANOTHER KIND) 1984 d: Steven Paul. USA., *Slapstick Or Lonesome No More!*, Kurt Vonnegut Jr., 1976, Novel

Slasher, The *see* **COSH BOY** (1952).

Slate & Wyn and Blanche McBride *see* **SLATE WYN AND ME** (1986).

Slate, Wyn and McBride *see* **SLATE WYN AND ME** (1986).

SLATE WYN AND ME 1986 d: Don McLennan. ASL., *Slate and Wyn and Blanche McBride*, Georgia Savage, Novel

SLATTERY'S HURRICANE 1949 d: Andre de Toth. USA., *Slattery's Hurricane*, Herman Wouk, Novel

SLAUGHTER ON TENTH AVENUE 1957 d: Arnold Laven. USA., *The Man Who Rocked the Boat*, Richard Carter, William J. Keating, 1956, Novel

SLAUGHTERHOUSE FIVE 1972 d: George Roy Hill. USA., *Slaughterhouse Five*, Kurt Vonnegut Jr., 1969, Novel

SLAVE MARKET, THE 1917 d: Hugh Ford. USA., *The Painted Woman*, Frederic Arnold Kummer, New York 1913, Play

SLAVE OF DESIRE 1923 d: George D. Baker. USA., *La Peau de Chagrin*, Honore de Balzac, Paris 1831, Novel

SLAVE OF VANITY, A 1920 d: Henry Otto. USA., *Iris*, Arthur Wing Pinero, London 1901, Play

SLAVE SHIP 1937 d: Tay Garnett. USA., *The Last Slaver*, George S. King, New York 1933, Novel

SLAVE, THE 1918 d: Arrigo Bocchi. UKN., *The Slave*, Robert Hichens, Novel

Slave Trade in the World Today *see* **LE SCHIAVE ESISTONO ANCORA** (1964).

Slavedriver *see* **RANCHEADOR** (1977).

Slave-Hunter *see* **RANCHEADOR** (1977).

SLAVES OF BEAUTY 1927 d: John G. Blystone. USA., *The Grandflapper*, Nina Wilcox Putnam, 1926, Short Story

SLAVES OF DESTINY 1924 d: Maurice Elvey. UKN., *Miranda of the Balcony*, A. E. W. Mason, Novel

SLAVES OF NEW YORK 1989 d: James Ivory. USA., Tama Janowitz, Short Stories

Slaves of Rome *see* **LA RIVOLTA DEGLI SCHIAVI** (1961).

SLAVNOSTI SNEZENEK 1983 d: Jiri Menzel. CZC., Bohumil Hrabal, Story

SLAWA I CHWALA 1997 d: Kazimierz Kuc. PLN., *Slawa I Chwala*, Jaroslaw Iwaszkiewicz, Novel

SLAYGROUND 1983 d: Terry Bedford. UKN., *Slayground*, Donald E. Westlake, Novel

SLECNA MATINKA 1938 d: Vladimir Slavinsky. CZC., *Parizanka*, Jara Benes, Vaclav Mirovsky, Vladimir Rohan, Opera

SLEDITE OSTAVAT 1956 d: Peter Vassilev. BUL., *Sledite Ostavat*, Pavel Vezhinov, 1954, Novel

SLEDOPYT 1987 d: Pavel Lyubimov. USS., *The Pathfinder*, James Fenimore Cooper, 1840, Novel

Sleep Is Lovely *see* NEGATIVES (1968).

SLEEP MY LOVE 1948 d: Douglas Sirk. USA., *Sleep My Love*, Leo Rosten, 1946, Novel

Sleep No More *see* INVASION OF THE BODY SNATCHERS (1956).

SLEEPERS 1996 d: Barry Levinson. USA., *Sleepers*, Lorenzo Carcaterra, Book

SLEEPERS EAST 1934 d: Kenneth MacKennA. USA., *Sleepers East*, Frederick Nebel, Boston 1933, Novel

SLEEPERS WEST 1941 d: Eugene J. Forde. USA., *Sleepers East*, Frederick Nebel, Boston 1933, Novel

Sleeping Beauty *see* LA BELLA ADDORMENTATA (1942).

Sleeping Beauty *see* PRINSESSA RUUSUNEN (1949).

Sleeping Beauty *see* DORNROSCHEN (1955).

SLEEPING BEAUTY 1959 d: Clyde Geronimi. USA., *La Belle Au Bois Dormant*, Charles Perrault, 1697, Short Story

Sleeping Beauty *see* NEMURERU BIJO (1968).

SLEEPING BEAUTY 1983 d: Jeremy Paul Kagan. USA., *La Belle Au Bois Dormant*, Charles Perrault, 1697, Short Story

SLEEPING BEAUTY 1987 d: David Irving. USA/ISR., *La Belle Au Bois Dormant*, Charles Perrault, 1697, Short Story

Sleeping Beauty, The *see* SPYASHCHAYA KRASAVITSA (1964).

Sleeping Car Murders, The *see* COMPARTIMENT TUEURS (1965).

SLEEPING CARDINAL, THE 1931 d: Leslie Hiscott. UKN., *Adventure of the Final Problem*, Arthur Conan Doyle, 1894, Short Story, *The Empty House*, Arthur Conan Doyle, 1903, Short Story

SLEEPING DOGS 1977 d: Roger Donaldson. NZL., *Smith's Dream*, Karl Stead, Novel

Sleeping Life, A *see* INSPECTOR WEXFORD: A SLEEPING LIFE (1989).

SLEEPING MEMORY, A 1917 d: George D. Baker. USA., *A Sleeping Memory (the Great Awakening)*, E. Phillips Oppenheim, New York 1902, Novel

SLEEPING PARTNERS 1930 d: Seymour Hicks. UKN., *Faison un Reve*, Sacha Guitry, 1917, Play

Sleeping Partners *see* CARNIVAL OF CRIME (1961).

SLEEPING SENTINEL, THE 1914. USA., *The Sleeping Sentinel*, F. H. de Janvier, Poem

SLEEPING TIGER, THE 1954 d: Joseph Losey. UKN., *The Sleeping Tiger*, Maurice Moiseiwitch, Novel

SLEEPING WITH THE ENEMY 1991 d: Joseph Ruben. USA., *Sleeping With the Enemy*, Nancy Price, Novel

Sleepless Nights *see* LE NOTTI BIANCHE (1957).

SLENDER THREAD, THE 1965 d: Sydney Pollack. USA., *Decision to Die*, Shana Alexander, 1964, Short Story

SLEPOY MUZYKANT 1961 d: Tatyana Lukashevich. USS., *Slepoy Musykant*, Vladimir Galaktionovich Korolenko, Moscow 1888, Novel

SLEUTH 1972 d: Joseph L. Mankiewicz. UKN/USA., *Sleuth*, Anthony Shaffer, 1971, Play

SLIGHT CASE OF MURDER, A 1938 d: Lloyd Bacon. USA., *A Slight Case of Murder*, Howard Lindsay, Damon Runyon, New York 1935, Play

SLIGHTLY HONORABLE 1939 d: Tay Garnett. USA., *Send Another Coffin*, Frank G. Presnell, New York 1939, Novel

SLIGHTLY SCARLET 1956 d: Allan Dwan. USA., *Love's Lovely Counterfeit*, James M. Cain, 1942, Novel

SLIM 1937 d: Ray Enright. USA., *Slim*, William Wister Haines, Boston 1934, Novel

SLIM PRINCESS, THE 1915 d: E. H. Calvert. USA., *The Slim Princess*, George Ade, 1906, Short Story

SLIM PRINCESS, THE 1920 d: Victor Schertzinger. USA., *The Slim Princess*, George Ade, 1906, Short Story

Slingshot, The *see* KADISBELLAN (1993).

Slip of the Battlefield, The *see* SENGOKU JIEITAI (1980).

Slip Slide Adventures *see* THE WATER BABIES (1979).

SLIPPER AND THE ROSE, THE 1976 d: Bryan Forbes. UKN., *Cendrillon*, Charles Perrault, 1697, Short Story

Slipper and the Rose -the Story of Cinderella, The *see* THE SLIPPER AND THE ROSE (1976).

Slippery McGee *see* SLIPPY MCGEE (1948).

SLIPPING-DOWN LIFE, A 1999 d: Toni Kalem. USA., *A Slipping-Down Life*, Anne Tyler, 1970, Novel

SLIPPY MCGEE 1948 d: Albert Kelley. USA., *Slippy McGee: Sometimes Known As the Butterfly Man*, Marie Conway Oemler, Novel

SLIVER 1993 d: Phil Noyce. USA., *Sliver*, Ira Levin, Novel

Sliver of Night, A *see* UN PEDAZO DE NOCHE (1995).

SLOTH 1917 d: Theodore Marston. USA., Florence Morse Kingsley, Short Story

SLOUZHEBNO -ORDINARETS 1979 d: Keran Kolarov. BUL., *Vestovoi Dimo*, Georgi Stamatov, 1929, Novel

SLOW BURN 1986 d: Matthew Chapman. USA., *Castles Burning*, Arthur Lyon, Novel

Slow Descent Into Hell, A *see* YOUR TICKET IS NO LONGER VALID (1980).

Slow Down *see* LEAT YOTER (1967).

Sluchai S Polynnym *see* CHTO SLUCHILOS S POLINIM? (1971).

Slugs *see* THE MOVIE SLUGS (1988).

Slugs, Muerte Viscosa *see* THE MOVIE SLUGS (1988).

SLUGS, THE MOVIE 1988 d: Piquer Simon. USA/SPN., *Slugs*, Shaun Hutson, Novel

Slzhebno Polozhenie - Ordinarets *see* SLOUZHEBNO -ORDINARETS (1979).

SMALL BACHELOR, THE 1927 d: William A. Seiter. USA., *The Small Bachelor*, P. G. Wodehouse, 1926, Short Story

SMALL BACK ROOM, THE 1948 d: Michael Powell, Emeric Pressburger. UKN., *The Small Back Room*, Nigel Balchin, 1943, Novel

Small Border Traffic *see* KLEINE GRENZVERKEHR (1943).

Small Farm in the Steppe, The *see* KHUTOROK V STEPI (1971).

SMALL HOTEL 1957 d: David MacDonald. UKN., *Small Hotel*, Rex Frost, Play

SMALL KILLING, A 1981 d: Steven Hilliard Stern. USA., *The Rag Bay Clan*, Richard Barth, Novel

Small Miracle *see* FOUR HOURS TO KILL! (1935).

Small Revenge *see* PEQUENA REVANCHA (1986).

SMALL TOWN BOY 1937 d: Glenn Tryon. USA., *The $1000 Bill*, Manuel Komroff, 1935, Short Story

Small Town Called Hisbiscus, A *see* FURONG ZHEN (1985).

SMALL TOWN GIRL 1936 d: William A. Wellman. USA., *Small Town Girl*, Ben Ames Williams, New York 1935, Novel

SMALL TOWN GIRL 1952 d: Leslie Kardos. USA., *Small Town Girl*, Ben Ames Williams, New York 1935, Novel

SMALL TOWN GUY, THE 1917 d: Lawrence C. Windom. USA., *A Picture of Innocence*, Freeman Tilden, 1917, Novel

Small Town Sinners *see* KLEINSTADTSUNDER (1927).

SMALL VOICE, THE 1948 d: Fergus McDonnell. UKN., *The Small Voice*, Robert Westerby, Novel

SMALL WORLD OF SAMMY LEE, THE 1963 d: Ken Hughes. UKN., *Sammy*, Ken Hughes, 1958, Television Play

SMART GIRLS DON'T TALK 1948 d: Richard L. Bare. USA., *Dames Don't Talk*, William Sackheim, Story

SMART WOMAN 1931 d: Gregory La CavA. USA., *Nancy's Private Affair*, Myron C. Fagan, New York 1930, Play

SMARTY 1934 d: Robert Florey. USA., *Smarty*, F. Hugh Herbert, Philadelphia 1927, Play

SMASHING THE RACKETS 1938 d: Lew Landers. USA., *Smashing the Rackets*, Forest Davis, 1937-38, Article

SMASH-UP ON INTERSTATE FIVE 1973 d: John Llewellyn Moxey. USA., *Expressway*, Elleston Trevor, Novel

SMEMORATO, LO 1936 d: Gennaro Righelli. ITL., *Lo Smemorato*, Emilio Caglieri, Novel

SMERTELNI VRAG 1971 d: Yevgeni Matveyev. USS., *Donskie Rasskazy*, Mikhail Sholokhov, 1926, Short Story

Smertnyi Vrag *see* SMERTELNI VRAG (1971).

Smertnyj Vrag *see* SMERTELNI VRAG (1971).

SMERY ZIVOTA 1940 d: Jiri Slavicek. CZC., *Smery Zivota*, F. X. Svoboda, Play

Smile of a Child, The *see* NINNA NANNA (1914).

Smile of the Evil Eye, The *see* RYS (1981).

Smile of the Lamb, The *see* CHI'UCH HAGDI (1985).

SMILES ARE TRUMPS 1922 d: George Marshall. USA., *The Iron Rider*, Frank L. Packard, 1916, Short Story

SMILEY 1956 d: Anthony Kimmins. UKN/ASL., *Smiley*, Moore Raymond, Novel

SMILEY GETS A GUN 1958 d: Anthony Kimmins. UKN/ASL., *Smiley Gets a Gun*, Moore Raymond, Novel

SMILEY'S PEOPLE 1982 d: Simon Langton. UKN/USA., *Smiley's People*, John le Carre, Novel

SMILIN' THROUGH 1922 d: Sidney A. Franklin. USA., *Smilin' Through*, Jane Cowl, Jane Murfin, New York 1919, Play

SMILIN' THROUGH 1932 d: Sidney A. Franklin. USA., *Smilin' Through*, Jane Cowl, Jane Murfin, New York 1919, Play

SMILIN' THROUGH 1941 d: Frank Borzage. USA., *Smilin' Through*, Jane Cowl, Jane Murfin, New York 1919, Play

SMILING ALL THE WAY 1920 d: Fred J. Butler, Hugh McClung. USA., *Alice in Wonderland*, Henry Payson Dowst, Short Story

Smiling Land, The *see* DAS LAND DES LACHELNS (1952).

SMILING LIEUTENANT, THE 1931 d: Ernst Lubitsch. USA., *Ein Waltzertraum*, Felix Dormann, Leopold Jacobson, Leipzig 1907, Opera

Smiling Through *see* SMILIN' THROUGH (1922).

Smillas Feeling for Snow *see* SMILLA'S SENSE OF SNOW (1997).

SMILLA'S SENSE OF SNOW 1997 d: Bille August. GRM/DNM/SWD., *Smilla's Sense of Snow*, Peter Hoeg, Novel

SMITH! 1969 d: Michael O'Herlihy. USA., *Breaking Smith's Quarter Horse*, Paul St. Pierre, Chicago 1966, Novel

SMITH 1917 d: Maurice Elvey. UKN., *Smith*, W. Somerset Maugham, London 1909, Play

SMITH'S WIVES 1935 d: Manning Haynes. UKN., *Facing the Music*, James H. Darnley, London 1899, Play

SMOKE 1995 d: Wayne Wang. USA., *Auggie Wren's Christmas Story*, Paul Auster, Short Story

SMOKE BELLEW 1929 d: Scott R. Dunlap. USA., *Smoke Bellew*, Jack London, New York 1912, Novel

SMOKE LIGHTNING 1933 d: David Howard. USA., *Canon Walls*, Zane Grey, 1930, Story

SMOKE SIGNALS 1998 d: Chris Eyre. USA., *The Lone Ranger and Tonto Fistfight in Heaven*, Sherman Alexie, Book

SMOKING/NO SMOKING 1993 d: Alain Resnais. FRN., *Intimate Exchanges*, Alan Ayckbourn, Play

SMOKY 1933 d: Eugene J. Forde. USA., *Smoky the Cowhorse*, Will James, New York 1926, Novel

SMOKY 1946 d: Louis King. USA., *Smoky the Cowhorse*, Will James, New York 1926, Novel

SMOKY 1966 d: George Sherman. USA., *Smoky the Cowhorse*, Will James, New York 1926, Novel

SMOOTH AS SATIN 1925 d: Ralph Ince. USA., *The Chatterbox*, Bayard Veiller, Play

SMOOTH AS SILK 1946 d: Charles T. Barton. USA., *Notorious Gentleman*, Colin Clements, Florence Ryerson, Story

SMOOTH TALK 1985 d: Joyce ChoprA. USA., *Where Have You Been? Where are You Going*, Joyce Carol Oates, 1967, Short Story

Smriti Chitre *see* SMRITICHITRE (1982).

SMRITICHITRE 1982 d: Vijaya MehtA. IND., *Smritichitre*, Laxmibai Tilak, Autobiography

SMRT KRASNYCH SRNCU 1987 d: Karel KachynA. CZC., *Smrt Krasnych Srncu*, Ota Pavel, Novel

957

SMRT SI RIKA ENGELCHEN 1963 d: Jan Kadar, Elmar Klos. CZC., *Smrt' Sa Vola Engelchen*, Ladislav Mnacko, 1959, Novel

SMUGA CIENIA 1976 d: Andrzej WajdA. PLN/UKN., *The Shadow Line*, Joseph Conrad, 1916, Novel

Smugglers *see* L' AMANTE DELL'ORSA MAGGIORE (1971).

SMUGGLERS' COVE 1948 d: William Beaudine. USA., *Smugglers' Cove*, Talbert Josselyn, Short Story

Smugglers, The *see* THE MAN WITHIN (1947).

SMUGGLERS, THE 1968 d: Alfred Hayes. USA., *The Smugglers*, Elizabeth Hely, Novel

Smugglers, The *see* SMUGLERE (1968).

SMUGLERE 1968 d: Rolf Clemens. NRW., *Smuglere*, Arthur Omre, 1935, Novel

SNACK BAR BUDAPEST 1988 d: Tinto Brass. ITL., *Snack Bar Budapest*, Silvia Bre, Marco Lodoli, Novel

SNAFU 1945 d: Jack Moss. USA., *Snafu*, Harold Buchman, Louis Solomon, New York 1944, Play

SNAHA 1954 d: Anton Marinovich, Krastyo Mirski. BUL., *Snakha*, Georgi Karaslavov, 1942, Novel

Snake Girl and the Silver-Haired Witch, The *see* HEBIMUSUME TO HAKUHATSUKI (1968).

Snake of Death *see* QUAI DE GRENELLE (1950).

Snake Pit and the Pendulum, The *see* DIE SCHLANGENGRUBE UND DAS PENDEL (1967).

SNAKE PIT, THE 1948 d: Anatole Litvak. USA., *The Snake Pit*, Mary Jane Ward, Novel

Snakha *see* SNAHA (1954).

SNAPPER, THE 1993 d: Stephen Frears. UKN., *The Snapper*, Roddy Doyle, Novel

Sneakers *see* HARD FEELINGS (1982).

SNEGUROTCHKA 1969 d: Pavel Kadochnikov. USS., *Snegurochka*, Alexander Ostrovsky, 1873, Play

Snejnaia Koroleva *see* SNYEZHNAYA KOROLYEVA (1967).

Snezhnaya Koroleva *see* SNYEZHNAYA KOROLYEVA (1967).

SNOB, THE 1921 d: Sam Wood. USA., *The Snob*, William J. Neidig, 1918, Short Story

SNOB, THE 1924 d: Monta Bell. USA., *The Snob; the Story of a Marriage*, Helen Reimensnyder Martin, New York 1924, Novel

SNOBS 1915 d: Oscar Apfel. USA., *Snobs*, George Bronson Howard, New York 1911, Play

SNORKEL, THE 1958 d: Guy Green. UKN., *The Snorkel*, Anthony Dawson, Novel

Snout, The *see* THE INFORMERS (1963).

Snow Beauty *see* SNEGUROTCHKA (1969).

Snow Blindness *see* SNOWBLIND (1921).

Snow Country *see* YUKIGUNI (1957).

Snow Country *see* YUKIGUNI (1965).

SNOW DOG 1950 d: Frank McDonald. USA., *Tentacles of the North*, James Oliver Curwood, 1915, Short Story

Snow Ghost *see* KAIDAN YUKIJORO (1968).

SNOW GOOSE, THE 1971 d: Patrick Garland. UKN., *The Snow Goose*, Paul Gallico

SNOW IN THE DESERT 1919 d: Walter West. UKN., *Snow in the Desert*, Andrew Soutar, Novel

Snow in the South Seas *see* MINAMI NO SHIMA NI YUKI GA FURA (1961).

Snow Lark *see* SUZANNE (1980).

Snow Queen, The *see* SNYEZHNAYA KOROLYEVA (1967).

Snow Queen, The *see* LUMIKUNINGATAR (1986).

SNOW TREASURE 1968 d: Irving Jacoby. USA., *Snow Treasure*, Marie McSwigan, New York 1942, Novel

Snow Was Black, The *see* LA NEIGE ETAIT SALE (1952).

SNOW WHITE 1916 d: J. Searle Dawley. USA., *Schneeweisschen Und Rosenrot*, Jacob Grimm, Wilhelm Grimm, 1812, Short Story

Snow White *see* SCHNEEWITTCHEN UND DIE SIEBEN ZWERGE (1956).

SNOW WHITE 1987 d: Michael Berz. USA., *Schneewittchen*, Jacob Grimm, Wilhelm Grimm, 1812, Short Story

Snow White and Rose Red *see* SCHNEEWEISSCHEN UND ROSENROT (1955).

SNOW WHITE AND THE SEVEN DWARFS 1937 d: David Hand. USA., *Schneewittchen*, Jacob Grimm, Wilhelm Grimm, 1812, Short Story

Snow White and the Seven Dwarfs *see* SCHNEEWITTCHEN UND DIE SIEBEN ZWERGE (1956).

Snow White and the Seven Dwarfs *see* SCHNEEWITTCHEN UND DIE SIEBEN ZWERGE (1961).

SNOW WHITE AND THE SEVEN DWARFS 1983 d: Peter Medak. USA., *Schneewittchen*, Jacob Grimm, Wilhelm Grimm, 1812, Short Story

Snow White and the Seven Dwarfs *see* SNOW WHITE (1987).

SNOWBALL 1960 d: Pat Jackson. UKN., *Snowball*, James Lake, Novel

Snowball *see* PALLA DI NEVE (1996).

SNOWBLIND 1921 d: Reginald Barker. USA., *Snowblind*, Katharine Newlin Burt, 1921, Short Story

SNOWBOUND 1948 d: David MacDonald. UKN., *The Lonely Skier*, Hammond Innes, Novel

SNOW-BURNER, THE 1915 d: E. H. Calvert. USA., *The Snow-Burner*, Henry Oyen, Story

SNOWDRIFT 1923 d: Scott R. Dunlap. USA., *Snowdrift*, James B. Hendryx, New York 1922, Novel

Snowdrop Festival *see* SLAVNOSTI SNEZENEK (1983).

Snowdrop Festivities, The *see* SLAVNOSTI SNEZENEK (1983).

SNOWED UNDER 1936 d: Ray Enright. USA., *Snowed Under*, Lawrence Saunders, Story

SNOWMAN, THE 1983 d: Dianne Jackson. UKN., *The Snowman*, Raymond Briggs, Book

Snowman, The *see* DER SCHNEEMANN (1984).

SNOWS OF KILIMANJARO, THE 1952 d: Henry King. USA., *The Snows of Kilimanjaro*, Ernest Hemingway, 1938, Short Story

SNOWSHOE TRAIL, THE 1922 d: Chester Bennett. USA., *The Snowshoe Trail*, Edison Marshall, Boston 1921, Novel

Snow-White *see* O SNEHURCE (1972).

Snowy Heron *see* SHIRASAGI (1958).

SNYEZHNAYA KOROLYEVA 1967 d: Gennadi Kazansky. USS., *Snedronningen*, Hans Christian Andersen, 1845, Short Story

SO BIG 1924 d: Charles J. Brabin. USA., *So Big!*, Edna Ferber, Garden City, N.Y. 1924, Novel

SO BIG 1932 d: William A. Wellman. USA., *So Big!*, Edna Ferber, Garden City, N.Y. 1924, Novel

SO BIG 1953 d: Robert Wise. USA., *So Big!*, Edna Ferber, Garden City, N.Y. 1924, Novel

So Bright the Flame *see* THE GIRL IN WHITE (1952).

So Close to Life *see* NARA LIVET (1958).

SO DEAR TO MY HEART 1948 d: Harold Schuster, Hamilton Luske. USA., *Midnight and Jeremiah*, Sterling North, Novel

So Ein Flegel! *see* DIE FEUERZANGENBOWLE (1944).

SO EIN FLEGEL 1934 d: R. A. Stemmle. GRM., *So Ein Flegel*, Heinrich Spoerl, Novel

SO EIN FRUCHTCHEN 1942 d: Alfred Stoger. GRM., *So Ein Fruchtchen*, Franz Gribitz, Play

So Ein Mustergatte *see* DER MUSTERGATTE (1959).

SO ENDS OUR NIGHT 1941 d: John Cromwell. USA., *Strandgut*, Erich Maria Remarque, 1940, Novel

SO EVIL MY LOVE 1948 d: Lewis Allen. UKN., *For Her to See*, Joseph Shearing, Novel

So Great a Man *see* ABE LINCOLN IN ILLINOIS (1940).

SO LITTLE TIME 1952 d: Compton Bennett. UKN., *Je Ne Suis Pas une Heroine*, Noelle Henry, Novel

SO LONG AT THE FAIR 1950 d: Anthony Darnborough, Terence Fisher. UKN., *So Long at the Fair*, Anthony Thorne, Novel

So Long Friend *see* ADIEU L'AMI (1968).

SO LONG LETTY 1920 d: Al Christie. USA., *So Long Letty*, Carroll, Elmer Harris, Oliver Morosco, New York 1916, Musical Play

SO LONG LETTY 1929 d: Lloyd Bacon. USA., *So Long Letty*, Earl Carroll, Elmer Harris, Oliver Morosco, New York 1916, Musical Play

SO RED THE ROSE 1935 d: King Vidor. USA., *So Red the Rose*, Stark Young, New York 1934, Novel

SO THIS IS ARIZONA 1922 d: Francis Ford. USA., *So This Is Arizona*, Marie Schrader, C. C. Wadde, 1921, Serial Story

So This Is Hollywood *see* IN HOLLYWOOD WITH POTASH AND PERLMUTTER (1924).

SO THIS IS LONDON 1930 d: John G. Blystone. USA., *So This Is London*, Arthur Frederick Goodrich, London 1923, Play

SO THIS IS LONDON 1939 d: Thornton Freeland. UKN., *So This Is London*, Arthur Frederick Goodrich, London 1923, Play

SO THIS IS LOVE 1953 d: Gordon Douglas. USA., *You're Only Human Once*, Grace Moore, 1944, Autobiography

SO THIS IS NEW YORK 1948 d: Richard Fleischer. USA., *The Big Town*, Ring Lardner, 1938, Novel

SO THIS IS PARIS 1926 d: Ernst Lubitsch. USA., *Le Reveillon*, Ludovic Halevy, Henri Meilhac, 1872, Play

SO WELL REMEMBERED 1947 d: Edward Dmytryk. UKN., *So Well Remembered*, James Hilton, 1947, Novel

So What Is Papa Doing in Italy? *see* WAS MACHT PAPA DENN IN ITALIEN? (1961).

SOB SISTER 1931 d: Alfred Santell. USA., *Sob Sister*, Mildred Gilman, New York 1931, Novel

SOB SISTER, THE 1914 d: Otis Turner. USA., *The Sob Sister*, Harry Care, Story

Sob Sisters *see* SOB SISTER (1931).

SOBOL I PANNA 1983 d: Hubert DrapellA. PLN., *Sobol I Panna*, Jozef Weyssenhoff, 1912, Novel

SOBRADO, O 1956 d: Cassiano G. Mendes, Walter George Durst. BRZ., *O Sobrado*, Erico Verissimo, 1949, Short Story

Sobre Su Espalda *see* ESCLAVAS DE LA MODA (1931).

SOBRENATURAL 1996 d: Daniel Gruener. MXC., *Sobrenatural*, Gabriel Gonzalez Melendez, Novel

Soccer Fans *see* QIU MI (1963).

SOCIAL BUCCANEER, THE 1916 d: Jack Conway. USA., *The Social Buccaneer*, Frederic Stewart Isham, Indianapolis 1910, Novel

Social Buccaneers *see* THE SOCIAL BUCCANEER (1916).

SOCIAL CODE, THE 1923 d: Oscar Apfel. USA., *To Whom It May Concern*, Rita Weiman, 1922, Short Story

Social Errors *see* ONLY SAPS WORK (1930).

Social Exile, The *see* DECLASSEE (1925).

SOCIAL HIGHWAYMAN, THE 1916 d: Edwin August. USA., *A Social Highwayman*, Mary Stone, New York 1895, Play

SOCIAL HYPOCRITES 1918 d: Albert Capellani. USA., *Bridge*, Alice Ramsey, 1917, Play

SOCIAL LION, THE 1930 d: A. Edward Sutherland. USA., *Marco Himself*, Octavus Roy Cohen, 1929, Short Story

SOCIAL REGISTER 1934 d: Marshall Neilan. USA., *The Social Register*, John Emerson, Anita Loos, New York 1931, Play

Societa Del Malessere, La *see* BARBAGIA (1969).

Society *see* THE TWO MRS. GRENVILLES (1987).

Society Doctor *see* ONLY EIGHT HOURS (1934).

SOCIETY EXILE, A 1919 d: George Fitzmaurice. USA., *We Can't Be As Bad As That*, Henry Arthur Jones, New York 1910, Play

SOCIETY GIRL 1932 d: Sidney Lanfield. USA., *Society Girl*, Charles Beahan, John Larkin Jr., New York 1931, Play

SOCIETY LAWYER 1939 d: Edwin L. Marin. USA., *Penthouse*, Arthur Somers Roche, New York 1935, Novel

SOCIETY SCANDAL, A 1924 d: Allan Dwan. USA., *The Laughing Lady*, Alfred Sutro, London 1922, Play

SOCIETY SENSATION, A 1918 d: Paul Powell. USA., *The Borrowed Duchess*, Perley Poore Sheehan, Short Story

Socio, Il *see* IL SOCIO INVISIBILE (1939).

SOCIO INVISIBILE, IL 1939 d: Roberto Leone Roberti. ITL., *Il Mio Socio Davis*, Gennaro Prieto, Novel

Sockenskomakarna *see* NUMMISUUTARIT (1938).

Sockenskomakarna *see* NUMMISUUTARIT (1957).

Sockenskomakarne *see* NUMMISUUTARIT (1923).

SODA CRACKER 1989 d: Fred Williamson. USA., *Soda Cracker*, Jaron Summers, Novel

Soedba Tsjeloveka *see* SUDBA CHELOVEKA (1959).

SOEURETTE 1913 d: Maurice Tourneur. FRN., *Soeurette*, Gyp, Novel

SOEURS D'ARMES 1937 d: Leon Poirier. FRN., *La Guerre Des Femmes*, Antoine Redier, Poem

Soeurs Garnier, Les see CONFLIT (1938).

SOEURS HORTENSIAS, LES 1935 d: Rene Guissart. FRN., *Les Soeurs Hortensias*, Henri Duvernois, Novel

SOFI 1967 d: Robert Carlisle. USA., *Zapiski Sumasshedshego*, Nikolay Gogol, 1835, Short Story

SOFIE 1992 d: Liv Ullmann. DNM/NRW/SWD., *Mendel Philipsen and Son*, Henri Nathensen, Novel

SOFKA 1948 d: Rados Novakovic. YGS., *Necista Krv*, Borislav Stankovic, 1911, Novel

Soft Touch of Night see YORU NO HADA (1960).

SOGEKI 1968 d: Hiromichi HorikawA. JPN., *Sogeki*, Hidekazu Nagahara, Play

SOGNI MUOIONO ALL'ALBA, I 1961 d: Indro Montanelli, Mario Craveri. ITL., *I Sogni Muoiono All'alba*, Indro Montanelli, Play

SOGNI NEL CASSETTO, I 1957 d: Renato Castellani. ITL., *I Sogni Nel Cassetto*, Adriana Chiaromonte, Novel

SOGNO D'AMORE 1922 d: Gennaro Righelli. ITL., *Mecta Ljubvi*, Aleksandr Kosotorov, 1911, Play

SOGNO DELL'USURAIO, IL 1910. ITL., *Christmas Books*, Charles Dickens, 1848

SOGNO DI BUTTERFLY, IL 1939 d: Carmine Gallone. ITL., *Madame Chrysantheme*, Pierre Loti, 1888, Novel

SOGNO DI GIACOBBE, IL 1914 d: Ugo FalenA. ITL., *Il Sogno Di Giacobbe*, Ugo Falena, 1900, Play

SOGNO DI UN TRAMONTO D'AUTUNNO 1911 d: Luigi Maggi. ITL., *Sogno Di un Tramonto d'Autunno*, Gabriele D'Annunzio, 1898

SOGNO DI UNA NOTTE DI MEZZA SBORNIA 1959 d: Eduardo de Filippo. ITL., *L'Agonia Di Schizzo*, Athos Setti, Play

SOHN DER HAGAR, DER 1926 d: Fritz Wendhausen. GRM., *Der Sohn Der Hagar*, Paul Keller, Novel

SOHN OHNE HEIMAT 1955 d: Hans Deppe. GRM., *Der Sohn Der Hagar*, Paul Keller, Novel

SOHNE DER GROSSEN BARIN, DIE 1966 d: Josef MacH. GDR., *Die Sohne Der Grossen Barin*, Lieselotte Welskopf-Henrich, Novel

SOHO INCIDENT 1956 d: Vernon Sewell. UKN., *Wide Boys Never Work*, Robert Westerby, Novel

Soif d'Amour see FOME DE AMOR (1968).

SOIF DES HOMMES, LA 1949 d: Serge de Poligny. FRN., *Le Sang Des Bou Okba*, Suzanne Pairault, Novel

Soil Under Your Feet, The see TALPALATNYI FOLD (1948).

Soil Upturned, The see PODNYATAYA TZELINA (1940).

SOILED 1924 d: Fred Windermere. USA., *Debt of Dishonor*, Jack Boyle, Short Story

SOIR AU FRONT, UN 1931 d: Alexandre Ryder. FRN., *Un Soir Au Front*, Henri Kistemaeckers, Play

SOIR DE REVEILLON, UN 1933 d: Karl Anton. FRN., *Un Soir de Reveillon*, Marcel Gerbidon, Albert Willemetz, Opera

SOIR DES ROIS, LE 1932 d: John Daumery. FRN., *Sinners All*, Jerome Kingston, Novel

SOIR. PAR HASARD, UN 1964 d: Yvan Govar. FRN/BLG., *L'Aventure Commencera Ce Soir*, Robert Collard, Novel

SOIR, UN TRAIN, UN 1968 d: Andre Delvaux. BLG/FRN., Johan Daisne, Short Story

SOIXANTE-DIX-SEPT RUE CHALGRIN 1931 d: Albert de Courville. FRN., *77 Park Lane*, Walter Hackett, London 1928, Play

SOKAKTAKI ADAM 1995 d: Biket Ilhan. TRK., Attila Ilhan, Novel

Sol Madrid see THE HEROIN GANG (1968).

Sol Y Sombra see SOLEIL ET OMBRE (1922).

SOLANG' ES HUBSCHE MADCHEN GIBT 1955 d: Arthur M. Rabenalt. GRM., *Okay Mama*, Artinger Annemarie, Novel

SOLAR CRISIS 1992 d: Richard C. Sarafian. USA/JPN., *Kuraishisu Nijugoju Nen*, Takeshi Kawata, Novel

Solaris see SOLYARIS (1972).

SOLD 1915 d: Edwin S. Porter, Hugh Ford. USA., *Sold*, George Erastov, 1910, Play

Sold for Cash see ON THE STROKE OF THREE (1924).

Sold Life, A see UNA VITA VENDUTA (1977).

SOLDAAT VAN ORANJE 1977 d: Paul Verhoeven. NTH., *Soldaat Van Oranje*, Erik Hazelhoff Roelfzema, Autobiography

Soldat Auxiliaire Lappli, Le see HD LAPPLI (1959).

SOLDATAMI NYE ROZHDAYUTSYA 1968 d: Alexander Stolper. USS., *Soldatami Ne Rozhdaivtsia*, Konstantin Simonov, 1964, Novel

Soldatendochter, de see MAJOOR FRANS (1916).

SOLDATENSENDER CALAIS 1960 d: Paul May. GRM., *Soldatensender Calais*, Michael Mohr, Novel

SOLDATESSE, LE 1965 d: Valerio Zurlini. ITL/FRN/GRM., *Le Soldatesse*, Ugo Pirro, Novel

Soldi E Spirito see GELD UND GEIST (1964).

SOLDIER AND A MAN, A 1916 d: Dave Aylott. UKN., *A Soldier and a Man*, Ben Landeck, Play

SOLDIER AND THE LADY, THE 1937 d: George Nicholls Jr. USA., *Michel Strogoff*, Jules Verne, Paris 1876, Novel

SOLDIER BLUE 1970 d: Ralph Nelson. USA., *Arrow in the Sun*, Theodore V. Olsen, New York 1969, Novel

SOLDIER IN THE RAIN 1963 d: Ralph Nelson. USA., *Soldier in the Rain*, William Goldman, New York 1960, Novel

Soldier of Orange see SOLDAAT VAN ORANJE (1977).

Soldier Who Declared Peace, The see TRIBES (1970).

SOLDIERS AND WOMEN 1930 d: Edward Sloman. USA., *The Soul Kiss*, Paul Hervey Fox, George Tilton, New York 1908, Play

Soldiers Aren't Born see SOLDATAMI NYE ROZHDAYUTSYA (1968).

SOLDIER'S DAUGHTER NEVER CRIES, A 1998 d: James Ivory. UKN., *A Soldier's Daughter Never Cries*, Kaylie Jones, Novel

Soldier's Duties, A see KRIGSMANS ERINRAN (1947).

SOLDIER'S HOME 1977 d: Robert Malcolm Young. USA., *Soldier's Home*, Ernest Hemingway, 1930, Short Story

Soldiers in Skirts see THE TRIPLE ECHO (1972).

SOLDIERS OF FORTUNE 1914 d: William F. Haddock, Augustus Thomas. USA., *Soldiers of Fortune*, Richard Harding Davis, New York 1897, Novel

SOLDIERS OF FORTUNE 1919 d: Allan Dwan. USA., *Soldiers of Fortune*, Richard Harding Davis, New York 1897, Novel

Soldier's Prayer, A see NINGEN NO JOKEN III (1961).

SOLDIER'S STORY, A 1984 d: Norman Jewison. USA., *A Soldier's Play*, Charles Fuller, 1982, Play

SOLDIER'S SWEETHEART, A 1998 d: Thomas Michael Donnelly. USA., *Sweetheart of the Song Tra Bong*, Tim O'Brien, Short Story

SOLDIER'S TALE, A 1988 d: Larry Parr. NZL., *A Soldier's Tale*, M. K. Joseph, Novel

SOLDIER'S TALE, THE 1964 d: Michael Birkett. UKN., *Histoire du Soldat*, Charles-Ferdinand Ramuz, Igor Stravinsky, Lausanne 1918, Opera

Soldiers, The see LES CARABINIERS (1962).

SOLDIERS THREE 1911 d: George D. Baker. USA., *Soldiers Three*, Rudyard Kipling, 1888, Short Story

SOLDIERS THREE 1951 d: Tay Garnett. USA., *Soldiers Three*, Rudyard Kipling, 1888, Short Story

SOLE ANCHE DI NOTTE, IL 1990 d: Paolo Taviani, Vittorio Taviani. ITL/FRN/GRM., *Otets Sergei*, Lev Nikolayevich Tolstoy, 1898, Short Story

Sole Rosso see SOLEIL ROUGE (1971).

Soledad see EL REBOZO DE SOLEDAD (1952).

Soledad see FRUITS AMERS (1967).

SOLEDADE 1976 d: Paulo Thiago. BRZ., *A Bagaceira*, Jose Americo de Almeida, 1928, Novel

Soleil a l'Ombre, Le see LA PRISON EN FOLIE (1930).

SOLEIL DANS L'OEIL, LE 1961 d: Jacques Bourdon. FRN., *Le Soleil Dans l'Oeil*, Michele Perrein, Novel

SOLEIL D'AUTOMNE 1992 d: Jacques Ertaud. FRN/SWT., *Soleil d'Automne*, Christian Signol

SOLEIL DE MINUIT, LE 1943 d: Bernard-Roland. FRN., *Le Soleil de Minuit*, Pierre Benoit, Novel

SOLEIL DES VOYOUS, LE 1967 d: Jean Delannoy. FRN/ITL., *The Action Man*, J. M. Flynn, New York 1961, Novel

SOLEIL ET OMBRE 1922 d: Musidora, Jacques Lasseyne. FRN/SPN., *L'Espagnole*, Maria Star, Novel

Soleil Meme la Nuit, Le see IL SOLE ANCHE DI NOTTE (1990).

SOLEIL ROUGE 1971 d: Terence Young. FRN/ITL/SPN., *Soleil Rouge*, Laird Koenig, Novel

SOLID GOLD CADILLAC, THE 1956 d: Richard Quine. USA., *The Sold Gold Cadillac*, George S. Kaufman, New York 1953, Play, *The Solid Gold Cadillac*, Howard Teichmann, New York 1953, Play

SOLITAIRE MAN, THE 1933 d: Jack Conway. USA., *The Solitaire Man*, Bella Spewack, Samuel Spewack, Boston 1927, Play

SOLITARY CHILD, THE 1958 d: Gerald Thomas. UKN., *The Solitary Child*, Nina Bawden, Novel

SOLITARY CYCLIST, THE 1921 d: Maurice Elvey. UKN., *The Solitary Cyclist*, Arthur Conan Doyle, Short Story

Solitary Cyclist, The see THE ADVENTURES OF SHERLOCK HOLMES: THE SOLITARY CYCLIST (1984).

Soljaris see SOLYARIS (1972).

SOLO 1996 d: Norberto BarbA. USA., *Weapon*, Robert Mason, Novel

Solo Andata see UN ALLER SIMPLE (1970).

Solo for Clarinet see SOLO FUR KLARINETTE (1998).

SOLO FOR SPARROW 1962 d: Gordon Flemyng. UKN., *The Gunner*, Edgar Wallace, London 1928, Novel

SOLO FUR KLARINETTE 1998 d: Nico Hofmann. GRM., *I Anna*, Elsa Lewin, Novel

SOLO PARA HOMBRES 1960 d: Fernando Fernan Gomez. SPN., *Sublime Decision!*, Miguel Mihura Santos, 1960, Play

Solo Sailor, The see DIE ALLEINSEGLERIN (1987).

SOLOMON AND SHEBA 1959 d: King Vidor. USA., Crane Wilbur, Story

SOLYARIS 1972 d: Andrei Tarkovsky. USS., *Solaris*, Stanislaw Lem, 1961, Novel

SOM HAVETS NAKNA VIND 1968 d: Gunnar Hoglund. SWD., *..Som Havets Nakna Vind*, Gustav Sandgren, Stockholm 1965, Novel

SOMBRAS DE GLORIA 1930 d: Andrew L. Stone. USA., *The Long Shot*, Thomas Alexander Boyd, New York 1925, Short Story

SOMBRERO 1952 d: Norman Foster. USA., *A Mexican Village*, Josefina Niggli, 1945, Novel

Sombrero de Tres Picos, El see LA TRAVIESA MOLINERA (1935).

SOME BLONDES ARE DANGEROUS 1937 d: Milton Carruth. USA., *The Iron Man*, William Riley Burnett, New York 1930, Novel

SOME CAME RUNNING 1958 d: Vincente Minnelli. USA., *Some Came Running*, James Jones, 1957, Novel

SOME DAY 1935 d: Michael Powell. UKN., *Young Nowheres*, I. A. R. Wylie, 1927, Short Story

SOME FIXER 1915 d: Al Christie. USA., *Some Fixer*, Marjorie Jones, Story

SOME KIND OF HERO 1982 d: Michael Pressman. USA., *Some Kind of Hero*, James Kirkwood, Novel

SOME KIND OF MIRACLE 1979 d: Jerrold Freedman. USA., *But There are Always Miracles*, Jack Wills, Mary Wills, Book

SOME LIAR 1919 d: Henry King. USA., *Some Liar*, James Oliver Curwood, 1918, Short Story

Some Lie and Some Die see INSPECTOR WEXFORD: SOME LIE AND SOME DIE (1990).

SOME LIKE IT HOT 1939 d: George Archainbaud. USA., *The Great Magoo*, Gene Fowler, Ben Hecht, New York 1932, Play

Some People Sometimes see SILA NERANGALIL SILA MANITHARGAL (1975).

Some Soul of Goodness see MOTHER (1914).

SOMEBODY HAS TO SHOOT THE PICTURE 1990 d: Frank R. Pierson. USA., *Slow Coming Dark*, Doug Magee, Book

SOMEBODY UP THERE LIKES ME 1956 d: Robert Wise. USA., Rocky Graziano, 1955, Autobiography

SOMEBODY'S DARLING 1992 d: George A. Cooper. UKN., *Somebody's Darling*, Sidney Morgan, Novel

Someday see SOME DAY (1935).

SOMEHOW GOOD 1927 d: Jack Raymond. UKN., *Somehow Good*, William de Morgan, Novel

SOMEONE AT THE DOOR 1936 d: Herbert Brenon. UKN., *Someone at the Door*, Campbell Christie, Dorothy Christie, London 1935, Play

SOMEONE AT THE DOOR 1950 d: Francis Searle. UKN., *Someone at the Door*, Campbell Christie, Dorothy Christie, London 1935, Play

959

Someone Behind the Door *see* QUALCUNO DIETRO LA PORTA (1971).

SOMEONE IN THE HOUSE 1920 d: John Ince. USA., *Someone in the House*, Larry Evans, George S. Kaufman, W. Percival, New York 1918, Play

Someone Is Bleeding *see* LES SEINS DE GLACE (1974).

SOMEONE TO LOVE 1928 d: F. Richard Jones. USA., *The Charm School*, Alice Duer Miller, 1919, Short Story

Somerset Maugham's Quartet *see* QUARTET (1948).

SOMETHING DIFFERENT 1920 d: R. William Neill. USA., *Calderon's Prisoner*, Alice Duer Miller, New York 1903, Novel

Something Else Again *see* IF YOU COULD SEE WHAT I HEAR (1981).

Something for Alice *see* NECO Z ALENKY (1987).

SOMETHING FOR EVERYONE 1970 d: Harold Prince. USA., *The Cook*, Harry Kressing, New York 1965, Novel

SOMETHING FOR THE BOYS 1944 d: Lewis Seiler. USA., *Something for the Boys*, Dorothy Fields, Herbert Fields, Cole Porter, New York 1943, Musical Play

SOMETHING IN DISGUISE 1982 d: Moira Armstrong. UKN., *Something in Disguise*, Elizabeth Jane Howard, Novel

Something Is Drifting on the Water *see* HRST VODY (1969).

Something Like the Truth *see* THE OFFENCE (1973).

SOMETHING OF VALUE 1957 d: Richard Brooks. USA., *Something of Value*, Robert Ruark, 1955, Novel

SOMETHING TO HIDE 1971 d: Alastair Reid. UKN., *Something to Hide*, Nicholas Monsarrat, 1966, Novel

Something to Live for *see* FORGOTTEN FACES (1936).

SOMETHING WICKED THIS WAY COMES 1983 d: Jack Clayton. USA., *Something Wicked This Way Comes*, Ray Bradbury, 1962, Novel

SOMETHING WILD 1961 d: Jack Garfein. USA., *Mary Ann*, Alex Karmel, New York 1958, Novel

SOMETIMES A GREAT NOTION 1971 d: Paul Newman. USA., *Sometimes a Great Notion*, Ken Kesey, 1966, Novel

Sometimes Some People *see* SILA NERANGALIL SILA MANITHARGAL (1975).

Sometimes They Come Back *see* STEPHEN KING'S SOMETIMES THEY COME BACK (1991).

Somewhere I'll Find Him *see* THESE WILDER YEARS (1956).

SOMEWHERE IN FRANCE 1915 d: Tom Watts. UKN., *None But the Brave*, Ruby M. Ayres, Novel

SOMEWHERE IN FRANCE 1916 d: Charles Giblyn. USA., *Somewhere in France*, Richard Harding Davis, New York 1915, Novel

Somewhere in France *see* THE FOREMAN WENT TO FRANCE (1942).

SOMEWHERE IN SONORA 1927 d: Albert S. Rogell. USA., *Somewhere in Sonora*, Will Levington Comfort, Boston 1925, Novel

SOMEWHERE IN SONORA 1933 d: MacK V. Wright. USA., *Somewhere in Sonora*, Will Levington Comfort, Boston 1925, Novel

SOMEWHERE IN THE NIGHT 1946 d: Joseph L. Mankiewicz. USA., *The Long Journey*, Marvin Borowsky, Story

SOMEWHERE IN TIME 1980 d: Jeannot Szwarc. USA., *Bid Time Return*, Richard Matheson, Novel

SOMMAR OCH SYNDARE 1960 d: Arne Mattsson. SWD/DNM., *Sommar Och Syndare*, Willy Breinholst, Erik Pouplier, Novel

Sommardansen *see* HON DANSADE EN SOMMAR (1951).

Sommarkvallar Pa Jorden *see* NAGRA SOMMARKVALLAR PA JORDEN (1987).

SOMMERGASTE 1976 d: Peter Stein. GRM., *Dachniki*, Maxim Gorky, 1904, Play

SOMMERGLAEDER 1940 d: Sven Methling. DNM., *Sommerglaeder*, Herman Bang, 1902, Novel

SOMMERLIEBE 1942 d: Erich Engel. GRM., *Sommerliebe*, O. E. Hartleben, Novel

Son *see* MUSUKO (1991).

SON ALTESSE 1922 d: Henri Desfontaines. FRN., *Le Prince Curacao*, Delphi-Fabrice, Oscar Metenier, Novel

SON ALTESSE IMPERIALE 1933 d: Jean Bernard-Derosne, Victor Janson. FRN., *Le Tzarewitch*, Franz Lehar, Berlin 1927, Operetta

Son Commands, The *see* LOS HIJOS MANDAN (1939).

SON CRIME 1922 d: Albert Dieudonne. FRN., *Un Lache*, Albert Dieudonne, Play

Son of a Buccaneer, The *see* LE FILS DU FLIBUSTIER (1922).

Son of Bakunin, The *see* IL FIGLIO DI BAKUNIN (1998).

Son of Dear Caroline, The *see* LE FILS DE CAROLINE CHERIE (1954).

SON OF FRANKENSTEIN 1939 d: Rowland V. Lee. USA., *Frankenstein; Or the Modern Prometheus*, Mary Wollstonecraft Shelley, London 1818, Novel

SON OF FURY 1942 d: John Cromwell. USA., *Son of Fury*, Edison Marshall, Novel

Son of Fury - the Story of Benjamin Blake *see* SON OF FURY (1942).

SON OF HIS FATHER, A 1925 d: Victor Fleming. USA., *A Son of His Father*, Harold Bell Wright, New York 1925, Novel

SON OF HIS FATHER, THE 1917 d: Victor Schertzinger. USA., *The Son of His Father*, Ridgwell Cullum, London 1915, Novel

SON OF INDIA 1931 d: Jacques Feyder. USA., *Mr. Isaacs*, F. Marion Crawford, New York 1882, Novel

Son of Man (Thirst) *see* HIJO DE HOMBRE (1960).

Son of Russia *see* THE GUARDSMAN (1931).

SON OF THE GODS 1930 d: Frank Lloyd. USA., *Son of the Gods*, Rex Beach, 1929, Serial Story

SON OF THE HILLS, A 1917 d: Harry Davenport. USA., *A Son of the Hills*, Harriet T. Comstock, New York 1913, Novel

Son of the Lone Wolf *see* CHEATERS AT PLAY (1932).

Son of the Militia *see* MIN BING DE ER ZI (1958).

SON OF THE MORNING STAR 1991 d: Mike Robe. USA., *Son of the Morning Star*, Evan S. Cornell

Son of the Rajah, The *see* SON OF INDIA (1931).

Son of the Red Corsair *see* IL FIGLIO DEL CORSARO ROSSO (1960).

Son of the Red Pirate *see* IL FIGLIO DEL CORSARO ROSSO (1960).

SON OF THE SAHARA 1967 d: Frederic Goode. UKN., *Son of the Sahara*, Kelman D. Frost, Novel

SON OF THE SAHARA, A 1924 d: Edwin Carewe. USA., *A Son of the Sahara*, Louise Gerard, New York 1922, Novel

SON OF THE SHEIK, THE 1926 d: George Fitzmaurice. USA., *The Sons of the Sheik*, Edith Maude Hull, Novel

SON OF THE WOLF, THE 1922 d: Norman Dawn. USA., *Son of the Wolf*, Jack London, 1900, Short Story

SON RISE: A MIRACLE OF LOVE 1979 d: Glenn Jordan. USA., *Son Rise: a Miracle of Love*, Barry Neil Kaufman, Book

Son, The *see* BONCHI (1960).

SON TORNATA PER TE 1953 d: Luigi Comencini. ITL/SWT., *Heidi's Lehr- Und Wanderjahre*, Johanna Spyri, Gotha 1881, Novel

Son Without a Home *see* SOHN OHNE HEIMAT (1955).

SONATA A KREUTZER, LA 1920 d: Umberto FracchiA. ITL., *Kreutserova Sonata*, Lev Nikolayevich Tolstoy, 1889, Short Story

SONBAINI CHUNDADI 1976 d: Girish Manukant. IND., *Sonbaini Chundadi*, Jagjivan Mehta, Play

SONDAGSENGLER 1996 d: Berit Nesheim. NRW., *Sundays*, Reidun Nortvedt, Novel

SON-DAUGHTER, THE 1932 d: Clarence Brown. USA., *The Son-Daughter*, David Belasco, George Scarborough, New York 1919, Play

SONEZAKI SHINJU 1978 d: Yasuzo MasumurA. JPN., *Sonezaki Shinju*, Monzaemon Chikamatsu, 1703, Play

SONG 1928 d: Richard Eichberg. GRM., *Schmutziges Geld*, Karl Vollmoller, Short Story

SONG AND DANCE MAN 1936 d: Allan Dwan. USA., *The Song and Dance Man*, George M. Cohan, New York 1923, Play

SONG AND DANCE MAN, THE 1926 d: Herbert Brenon. USA., *The Song and Dance Man*, George M. Cohan, New York 1923, Play

SONG AND THE SERGEANT, THE 1918 d: George Ridgwell. USA., *The Song and the Sergeant*, O. Henry, Short Story

SONG FOR MISS JULIE, A 1945 d: William Rowland. USA., Michael Foster, Story

Song Lantern, The *see* UTA ANDON (1943).

SONG OF BERNADETTE, THE 1943 d: Henry King. USA., *Das Lied von Bernadette*, Franz Werfel, 1941, Novel

Song of Bwana Toshi, The *see* BUWANA TOSHI NO UTA (1965).

SONG OF HATE, THE 1915 d: J. Gordon Edwards. USA., *La Tosca*, Victorien Sardou, Paris 1887, Play

SONG OF LOVE 1947 d: Clarence Brown. USA., *Song of Love*, Bernard Schubert, Mario Silva, Play

SONG OF LOVE, THE 1923 d: Chester M. Franklin, Frances Marion. USA., *Dust of Desire*, Margaret Peterson, New York 1922, Novel

Song of Mangguo *see* MANGGAO ZHI GE (1976).

SONG OF NORWAY 1970 d: Andrew L. Stone. USA., *Song of Norway*, George Forrest, Milton Lazarus, Robert Wright, New York 1944, Play

Song of Remembrance *see* LA CHANSON DU SOUVENIR (1936).

SONG OF SIXPENCE, A 1917 d: Ralph Dean. USA., *A Song of Sixpence*, Frederic Arnold Kummer, New York 1913, Novel

Song of Songs *see* SHIR HASHIRIM (1935).

SONG OF SONGS, THE 1918 d: Joseph Kaufman. USA., *Das Hohe Lied*, Hermann Sudermann, Berlin 1908, Novel

SONG OF SONGS, THE 1933 d: Rouben Mamoulian. USA., *Das Hohe Lied*, Hermann Sudermann, Berlin 1908, Novel

Song of the Blood-Red Flower *see* LAULU TULIPUNAISESTA KUKASTA (1971).

Song of the Blood-Red Flower, The *see* LAULU TULIPUNAISESTA KUKASTA (1938).

Song of the Cornfields *see* ENEK A BUZAMEZOKROL (1947).

SONG OF THE FLAME 1930 d: Alan Crosland. USA., *Song of the Flame*, George Gershwin, Otto Harbach, H. Stothart, New York 1925, Musical Play

Song of the Forest *see* LESNAYA PESNYA (1961).

Song of the Lantern *see* UTA ANDON (1943).

Song of the Lark *see* SKRIVANCI PISEN (1933).

Song of the Little Road *see* PATHER PANCHALI (1955).

SONG OF THE LOON 1970 d: Andrew Herbert. USA., *Song of the Loon*, Richard Amory, New York 1966, Novel

Song of the Narayama *see* NARAYAMA BUSHI-KO (1958).

Song of the Red Flag *see* HONG QI GE (1950).

Song of the Red Flag *see* HONGQI PU (1960).

Song of the Red Ruby, The *see* SANGEN OM DEN RODE RUBIN (1970).

Song of the Road, The *see* PATHER PANCHALI (1955).

Song of the Scarlet Flower *see* SANGEN OM DEN ELDRODA BLOMMAN (1918).

Song of the Scarlet Flower *see* SANGEN OM DEN ELDRODA BLOMMAN (1934).

Song of the Scarlet Flower, The *see* LAULU TULIPUNAISESTA KUKASTA (1938).

Song of the Scarlet Flower, The *see* SANGEN OM DEN ELDRODA BLOMMAN (1956).

Song of the Scarlet Flower, The *see* LAULU TULIPUNAISESTA KUKASTA (1971).

SONG OF THE SHIRT, THE 1908 d: D. W. Griffith. USA., *The Song of the Shirt*, Thomas Hood, 1843, Poem

Song of the Siren, The *see* THE SIREN'S SONG (1915).

SONG OF THE SOUL, THE 1920 d: John W. Noble. USA., *An Old World Romance*, William J. Locke, 1909, Novel

SONG OF THE TRAIL 1936 d: Russell Hopton. USA., *Playing With Fire*, James Oliver Curwood, Story

SONG OF THE WAGE SLAVE, THE 1915 d: Herbert Blache. USA., *Song of the Wage Slave*, Robert W. Service, 1907, Poem

SONG OF THE WEST 1930 d: Ray Enright. USA., *Rainbow*, Oscar Hammerstein II, Laurence Stallings, New York 1928, Play

Song of the Witch, The see HET HEKSENLIED (1928).

Song of Vengeance see FUKUSHU NO UTA GA KIKOERU (1968).

Song of Victory see HISSHOKA (1945).

Song Over Moscow see CHERYOMUSHKI (1963).

Song Over the Reservoir see SHUI KU SHANG DE GE SHENG (1958).

Song That Lived Forever, The see A SONG TO REMEMBER (1945).

SONG TO REMEMBER, A 1945 d: Charles Vidor. USA., Ernst Marischka, Story

Song Writer, The see CHILDREN OF PLEASURE (1930).

SONG YOU GAVE ME, THE 1933 d: Paul L. Stein. UKN., The Song Is Ended, Walter Reisch, Play

SONIA 1921 d: Denison Clift. UKN., Sonia, Stephen McKenna, Novel

Sonia Scharrt Die Wirklichkeit Ab Oder. Ein Unheimlich Starker Abgang see EIN UNHEIMLICH STARKER ABGANG (1973).

SONJA 1943 d: Erik Faustman. SWD., Sonja, Herbert Grevenius, Stockholm 1927, Play

Sonja - 16 Ar see TUMULT (1969).

SONNAMBULA, LA 1952 d: Cesare Barlacchi. ITL., La Sonnambula, Vincenzo Bellini, Milan 1831, Opera

SONNBLICK RUFT, DER 1952 d: Eberhard Frowein. GRM/AUS., Der Sonnblick Ruft, Edmund Josef Bendl, Novel

SONNE ANGREIFEN, DIE 1970 d: Peter Lilienthal. GRM., Die Sonne Angreifen, Witold Gombrowicz, Novel

SONNENSCHEIN UN WOLKENBRUCH 1955 d: Rudolf Nussgruber. AUS., Abenteuer in Budapest, Fritz Knechtl-Ostenburg, Novel

SONNETTE D'ALARME, LA 1935 d: Christian-Jaque. FRN., La Sonnette d'Alarme, Romain Coolus, Maurice Hennequin, Play

SONNTAGSKIND, DAS 1956 d: Kurt Meisel. GRM., Schneider Wibbel, Hans Muller-Schlosser, Play

SONNY 1922 d: Henry King. USA., Sonny, George V. Hobart, Raymond Hubbell, New York 1921, Play

Sono Lo Sposo Di Teresina see IL CROLLO (1920).

SONO STATO IO! 1937 d: Raffaello Matarazzo. ITL., Sara Stato Giovannino, Paola Riccora, Play

SONORA KID, THE 1927 d: Robert de Lacy. USA., A Knight of the Range, William Wallace Cook, Story

Son-Rise: a Miracle of Love see SON RISE: A MIRACLE OF LOVE (1979).

SONS AND LOVERS 1960 d: Jack Cardiff. UKN., Sons and Lovers, D. H. Lawrence, 1913, Novel

Sons, Mothers and the General see MUTTER UND EIN GENERAL KINDER (1955).

SONS OF MATTHEW 1949 d: Charles Chauvel. ASL., Cullenbenbong, Bernard O'Reilly, Novel, Green Mountains, Bernard O'Reilly, Novel

SONS OF SATAN, THE 1915 d: George Loane Tucker. UKN., The Sons of Satan, William le Queux, Novel

Sons of the Great Bear see DIE SOHNE DER GROSSEN BARIN (1966).

Sons of the Musketeers see AT SWORD'S POINT (1951).

SON'S RETURN, THE 1909 d: D. W. Griffith. USA., The Son's Return, Guy de Maupassant, Short Story

Sookha see BARA (1981).

SOOKY 1931 d: Norman Taurog. USA., Dear Sooky, Percy Lee Crosby, New York 1929, Novel

SOONER OR LATER 1920 d: Wesley Ruggles. USA., The Woman Hater, Lewis Allen Browne, Short Story

SOPHIA'S IMAGINARY VISITORS 1914 d: Walter Edwin. USA., Beasley's Christmas Party, Booth Tarkington, Story

SOPHIE ET LE CRIME 1955 d: Pierre Gaspard-Huit. FRN., Sophie Et le Crime, Cecil Saint-Laurent, Novel

Sophie of Kravonia see THE VIRGIN OF PARIS SOPHY OF KRAVONIA; OR (1920).

Sophie Semenoff see MAKING THE GRADE (1921).

SOPHIENLUND 1943 d: Heinz Ruhmann. GRM., Sophienlund, Fritz von Woedtke, Helmut Weiss, Play

SOPHIE'S CHOICE 1982 d: Alan J. Pakula. USA., Sophie's Choice, William Styron, 1979, Novel

Sophie's Ways see LES STANCES A SOPHIE (1970).

SOPHISTICATED GENTS, THE 1981 d: Harry Falk. USA., The Junior Bachelor Society, John A. Williams, 1976, Book

SOPHY OF KRAVONIA; OR, THE VIRGIN OF PARIS 1920 d: Gerard Fontaine. USA., Sophy of Kravonia, Anthony Hope, London 1905, Novel

SORCERER 1977 d: William Friedkin. USA., Le Salaire de la Peur, Georges Arnaud, 1950, Novel

Sorcerer, The see SORTILEGES (1944).

Sorcerer's Love see EL AMOR BRUJO (1967).

SORCERER'S VILLAGE, THE 1958 d: Hassoldt Davis. USA., The Sorcerer's Village, Hassoldt Davis, Book

Sorceress, The see THE WITCH (1916).

Sorceress, The see HAXAN (1955).

Sorcery see MALEFICES (1961).

SORCIER, LE 1919 d: Maurice Challiot. FRN., Le Sorcier, Henri Germain, Novel

Sorciere, La see HAXAN (1955).

SORCIERES DE SALEM, LES 1957 d: Raymond Rouleau. FRN/GDR., The Crucible, Arthur Miller, 1953, Play

Sordid Affair, A see UN MALEDETTO IMBROGLIO (1959).

SOREKARA 1985 d: Yoshimitsu MoritA. JPN., Sore Kara, Natsume Soseki, 1910, Novel

SORELLE MATERASSI 1943 d: Ferdinando M. Poggioli. ITL., Sorelle Materassi, Aldo Palazzeschi, 1934, Novel

Sorochinskaya Jamarka see SOROCHINSKY YARMAROK (1939).

Sorochinskaya Yamarka see SOROCHINSKY YARMAROK (1939).

Sorochinski Fair, The see SOROCHINSKY YARMAROK (1939).

SOROCHINSKY YARMAROK 1939 d: Nikolai Ekk. USS., Sorochinskaya Jamarka, Nikolay Gogol, 1831, Short Story

Sorority House see SPRING MADNESS (1938).

SORORITY HOUSE 1939 d: John Farrow. USA., Chi House, Mary Coyle Chase, 1939, Play

SORPRESE DEL DIVORZIO, LE 1923 d: Guido Brignone. ITL., Les Surprises du Divorce, Alexandre Bisson, Antony Mars, 1888, Play

SORPRESE DEL DIVORZIO, LE 1939 d: Guido Brignone. ITL., Les Surprises du Divorce, Alexandre Bisson, Antony Mars, 1888, Play

SORRELL AND SON 1927 d: Herbert Brenon. USA., Sorrell and Son, Warwick Deeping, 1925, Novel

SORRELL AND SON 1933 d: Jack Raymond. UKN., Sorrell and Son, Warwick Deeping, 1925, Novel

SORRELL AND SON 1984 d: Derek Bennett. UKN., Sorrell and Son, Warwick Deeping, 1925, Novel

Sorriso Dell'inncenza, Il see NINNA NANNA (1914).

SORROWFUL JONES 1949 d: Sidney Lanfield. USA., Little Miss Marker, Damon Runyon, 1932, Short Story

SORROWS OF SATAN, THE 1917 d: Alexander Butler. UKN., The Sorrows of Satan, Marie Corelli, New York 1895, Novel

SORROWS OF SATAN, THE 1926 d: D. W. Griffith. USA., The Sorrows of Satan, Marie Corelli, New York 1895, Novel

Sorrows of Youn Werther, The see DIE LEIDEN DES JUNGEN WERTHERS (1976).

SORRY, WRONG NUMBER 1948 d: Anatole Litvak. USA., Sorry Wrong Number, Lucille Fletcher, Radio Play

SORRY, WRONG NUMBER 1989 d: Tony Wharmby. USA., Sorry Wrong Number, Lucille Fletcher, Radio Play

SORRY YOU'VE BEEN TROUBLED 1932 d: Jack Raymond. UKN., Sorry You've Been Troubled, Walter Hackett, London 1929, Play

SORTEZ DES RANGS 1996 d: Jean-Denis Robert. FRN., Le Boucher Des Hurlus, Jean Amila, Novel

SORTILEGES 1944 d: Christian-Jaque. FRN., Sortileges, Claude Boncompain, Novel

Soryu Hiken see YAGYU BUGEICHO (1957).

S.O.S. 1928 d: Leslie Hiscott. UKN., S.O.S., Walter Ellis, London 1928, Play

S.O.S. NORONHA 1956 d: Georges Rouquier. FRN/ITL/GRM., S.O.S. Noronha, Pierre Vire, Novel

SO'S YOUR AUNT EMMA! 1942 d: Jean Yarbrough. USA., Aunt Emma Paints the Town, Harry Hervey, Story

SO'S YOUR OLD MAN 1926 d: Gregory La CavA. USA., So's Your Old Man, Julian Leonard Street, 1925, Short Story

SOSKENDE 1966 d: Johan Jacobsen. DNM., Soskende, Hans Christian Branner, 1952, Play

SOSTITUZIONE, LA 1971 d: Franco B. Taviani. ITL., Alcesti, Euripides, Play

SOTTERRANEO FATALE, IL 1920 d: Domenico M. Gambino. ITL., Justice de Singe, Paul de Rochefort, Novel

SOTTO DIECI BANDIERE 1960 d: Duilio Coletti, Silvio Narizzano. ITL/UKN/USA., Schiff 16, Wolfgang Frank, Bernhard Rogge, Book

Sotto Il Tallone see METAMORPHOSE DES CLOPORTES (1965).

SOTTO IL VESTITO NIENTE 1985 d: Carlo VanzinA. ITL., Sotto Il Vestito Niente, Marco Parma, Novel

SOTTO VOCE 1996 d: Mario Levin. ARG., Tennessee, Louis Gusman, Short Story

SOUBOJ S BOHEM 1921 d: Boris Orlicky. CZC., Souboj S Bohem, Mor Jokai, Short Story

SOUD BOZI 1938 d: Jiri Slavicek. CZC., Bartova Pomsta, Jiri Hora, Play

Souffle de la Liberte, Le see ANDREA CHENIER (1955).

SOUFFLE DU DESIR, LE 1957 d: Henri Lepage. FRN., Le Souffle du Desir, Gaston Montho, Novel

SOUKROMA VICHRICE 1967 d: Hynek Bocan. CZC., V. Paral, Short Story

SOUL FOR SALE, A 1918 d: Allen Holubar. USA., Barter, Evelyn Campbell, 1917, Novel

SOUL MATES 1916 d: William Russell, John Prescott. USA., The Secret Mating, Edward A. Kaufman, Short Story

SOUL MATES 1925 d: Jack Conway. USA., The Reason Why, Elinor Glyn, London 1911, Novel

Soul of a Painter see HUA HUN (1994).

SOUL OF BRONZE, THE 1921. USA., The Soul of Bronze, Georges le Faure, Story

SOUL OF GUILDA LOIS, THE 1919 d: Frank Wilson. UKN., Crucifixion, Newman Flower, Novel

Soul of Jade and Pear see YU LI HUN (1924).

SOUL OF PIERRE, THE 1915 d: Travers Vale. USA., The Soul of Pierre, Georges Ohnet, Novel

SOUL-FIRE 1925 d: John S. Robertson. USA., Great Music, Martin Brown, New York 1924, Play

Soul's Crucifixion, A see THE SOUL OF GUILDA LOIS (1919).

SOULS FOR SABLES 1925 d: James C. McKay. USA., Garlan & Co., David Graham Phillips, Story

SOULS FOR SALE 1923 d: Rupert Hughes. USA., Souls for Sale, Rupert Hughes, New York 1922, Novel

Souls for Sale see CONFESSIONS OF AN OPIUM EATER (1962).

Souls in Exile see BROKEN HEARTS (1926).

Souls of the Road see ROJO NO REIKAN (1921).

Souls on the Road see ROJO NO REIKAN (1921).

SOULS TRIUMPHANT 1917 d: Jack O'Brien. USA., The Little Savior, Mary O'Connor, Short Story

SOUND AND THE FURY, THE 1959 d: Martin Ritt. USA., The Sound and the Fury, William Faulkner, 1929, Novel

SOUND OF FURY, THE 1950 d: Cy Endfield. USA., The Condemned, Jo Pagano, Novel

Sound of Life see SLEPOY MUZYKANT (1961).

SOUND OF MUSIC, THE 1965 d: Robert Wise. USA., The Sound of Music, Oscar Hammerstein II, Richard Rodgers, New York 1959, Musical Play

SOUND OF ONE HAND CLAPPING, THE 1998 d: Richard Flanagan. ASL., The Sound of One Hand Clapping, Richard Flanagan, Novel

Sound of the Mountain see YAMA NO OTO (1954).

Sound of Waves, The see SHIOSAI (1954).

SOUNDER 1972 d: Martin Ritt. USA., Sounder, William Armstrong, 1969, Novel

Sounder II see PART 2 SOUNDER (1976).

Sounds from the Mountains see YAMA NO OTO (1954).

Sounds of Street Cars see DODESKA DEN (1970).

Sounds of the Mountain see YAMA NO OTO (1954).

SOUPCONS 1956 d: Pierre Billon. FRN., Soupcons, Maurice Dekobra, Novel

SOUPE A LA GRIMACE, LA 1954 d: Jean SachA. FRN., La Soupe a la Grimace, Terry Stewart, Novel

SOUPE AUX CHOUX, LA 1981 d: Jean Girault. FRN., La Soupe aux Choux, Rene Fallet, Novel

SOUPE AUX POULETS, LA 1963 d: Philippe Agostini. FRN., *Killer's Wedge*, Evan Hunter, 1959, Novel

Sour Grapes *see* **LET'S TRY AGAIN** (1934).

SOUR SWEET 1989 d: Mike Newell. UKN., *Sour Sweet*, Timothy Mo, 1982, Novel

SOURCE, THE 1918 d: George Melford. USA., *The Source*, Clarence Budington Kelland, New York 1918, Novel

SOURD DANS LA VILLE, LE 1986 d: Mireille Dansereau. CND., *Le Sourd Dans la Ville*, Marie-Claire Blais, Novel

SOURIRE DANS LA TEMPETE, UN 1950 d: Rene Chanas. FRN/GRM/AUS., *Un Sourire Dans la Tempete*, Maurice Constantin-Weyer, Novel

Souris Blonde, La *see* **BLANC COMME NEIGE** (1931).

SOURIS CHEZ LES HOMMES, UNE 1964 d: Jacques Poitrenaud. FRN., *Les Jours Ouvrables*, Francis Rick, Novel

SOURIS D'HOTEL 1927 d: Adelqui Millar. FRN., *Souris d'Hotel*, Paul Armont, Marcel Gerbidon, Play

Soursweet *see* **SOUR SWEET** (1989).

Sous la Rafale *see* **FOHN** (1950).

Sous le Casque! *see* **MOB 39** (1940).

SOUS LE CASQUE DE CUIR 1931 d: Albert de Courville, Francisco Elias. FRN., *Sous le Casque de Cuir*, Rene Chambe, Novel

SOUS LE CIEL D'ORIENT 1927 d: Fred Leroy Granville, H. C. Grantham-Hayes. FRN., *Sous Les Cieux d'Arabie*, C. R. Wells, Novel

SOUS LE SIGNE DE MONTE-CRISTO 1968 d: Andre Hunebelle, Jean-Pierre Desagnat. FRN/ITL., *Le Comte de Monte-Cristo*, Alexandre Dumas (pere), Paris 1845, Novel

SOUS LE SIGNE DU TAUREAU 1968 d: Gilles Grangier. FRN., *Fin de Journee*, Roger Vrigny, Novel

SOUS LE SOLEIL DE SATAN 1987 d: Maurice Pialat. FRN., *Sous le Soleil de Satan*, Georges Bernanos, 1926, Novel

SOUS L'EPAULETTE 1908-18. FRN., *Sous l'Epaulette*, Arthur Bernede, Play

SOUS LES YEUX D'OCCIDENT 1936 d: Marc Allegret. FRN., *Under Western Eyes*, Joseph Conrad, 1911, Novel

SOUTH CENTRAL 1992 d: Steve Anderson. USA., *Crips*, Donald Bakeer, Novel

South Central L.a. *see* **SOUTH CENTRAL** (1992).

SOUTH PACIFIC 1958 d: Joshua Logan. USA., *Tales of the South Pacific*, James A. Michener, 1947, Short Story

SOUTH RIDING 1938 d: Victor Saville. UKN., *South Riding*, Winifred Holtby, 1935, Novel

SOUTH SEA BUBBLE, A 1928 d: T. Hayes Hunter. UKN., *A South Sea Bubble*, Roland Pertwee, Novel

SOUTH SEA LOVE 1923 d: David Soloman. USA., *With the Tide*, Fanny Hatton, Frederic Hatton, 1923, Short Story

SOUTH SEA LOVE 1927 d: Ralph Ince. USA., *A Game in the Bush*, Georges Arthur Surdez, Short Story

SOUTH SEA ROSE 1929 d: Allan Dwan. USA., *La Gringa*, Tom Cushing, New York 1928, Play

SOUTH SEA WOMAN 1953 d: Arthur Lubin. USA., *General Court-Martial*, William Rankin, Play

South, The *see* **EL SUR** (1983).

Southern Blade *see* **A TIME FOR KILLING** (1967).

SOUTHERN LOVE 1924 d: Herbert Wilcox. UKN., *The Spanish Student*, Henry Wadsworth Longfellow, Poem

SOUTHERN MAID, A 1933 d: Harry Hughes. UKN., *A Southern Maid*, Dion Clayton Calthrop, Harold Fraser-Simson, London 1920, Musical Play

SOUTHERN ROSES 1936 d: Friedrich Zelnik. UKN., *Southern Roses*, Rudolf Bernauer, Play

Southern Skies *see* **WHITE SHADOWS IN THE SOUTH SEAS** (1928).

SOUTHERN STAR, THE 1969 d: Sidney Hayers. UKN/FRN/USA., *L' Etoile du Sud le Pays de Diamants*, Jules Verne, Paris 1884, Novel

SOUTHERNER, THE 1945 d: Jean Renoir. USA., *Hold Autumn in Your Hand*, George Sessions Perry, Novel

SOUTHERNERS, THE 1914 d: Richard Ridgely, John H. Collins. USA., *The Southerners*, Cyrus Townsend Brady, Novel

Southwest to Sonora *see* **THE APPALOOSA** (1966).

SOUVENIR 1988 d: Geoffrey Reeve. UKN., *The Pork Butcher*, David Hughes, Novel

SOVRANETTA 1923 d: Enrico Roma, Mario Gargiulo. ITL., *Suzeraine*, Dario Niccodemi, 1906, Play

SOVSEM PROPASCIJ 1972 d: Georgi DaneliyA. USS., *The Adventures of Huckleberry Finn*, Mark Twain, New York 1884, Novel

Sovsem Propashtshiy *see* **SOVSEM PROPASCIJ** (1972).

SOWERS, THE 1916 d: William C. de Mille. USA., *The Sowers*, Henry Seton Merriman, New York 1895, Novel

Sowing of Alderson Cree, The *see* **SEEDS OF VENGEANCE** (1920).

SOWING THE WIND 1916 d: Cecil M. Hepworth. UKN., *Sowing the Wind*, Sidney Grundy, London 1893, Play

SOWING THE WIND 1921 d: John M. Stahl. USA., *Sowing the Wind*, Sidney Grundy, London 1893, Play

Soyas En Tagsten I Hovedet *see* **SOYAS TAGSTEN** (1966).

SOYAS TAGSTEN 1966 d: Annelise Meineche. DNM., *Bare En Tagsten*, Carl Erik Soya, 1959, Play

Soyez Les Bienvenus *see* **LE SOIR DES ROIS** (1932).

SOYLENT GREEN 1973 d: Richard Fleischer. USA., *Make Room! Make Room!*, Harry Harrison, 1966, Novel

SOYONS GAIS 1931 d: Arthur Robison, Andre Luguet. USA., *Let Us Be Gay*, Rachel Crothers, New York 1929, Play

Soyons Serieux *see* **TOUCHONS DU BOIS** (1933).

SPACE ISLAND 1987 d: Antonio Margheriti. ITL/GRM., *Treasure Island*, Robert Louis Stevenson, London 1883, Novel

Space Men Appear in Tokyo *see* **UCHUJIN TOKYO NI ARAWARU** (1956).

Space Monster Dogora *see* **UCHU DAIKAIJU DOGORA** (1964).

Space Pirates *see* **SPACE ISLAND** (1987).

Space Vampires *see* **LIFEFORCE** (1985).

SPACEMAN AND KING ARTHUR, THE 1979 d: Russ Mayberry. UKN/USA., *A Connecticut Yankee in King Arthur's Court*, Mark Twain, New York 1889, Novel

Spaceship to Venus *see* **DER SCHWEIGENDE STERN** (1960).

SPACEWAYS 1953 d: Terence Fisher. UKN., *Spaceways*, Charles Eric Maine, Radio Play

Spacious Courtyard, The *see* **TINGYUAN SHENSHEN** (1989).

SPADA IMBATTIBILE, LA 1957 d: Hugo Fregonese. ITL., *Les Trois Mousquetaires*, Alexandre Dumas (pere), Paris 1844, Novel

Spadaccini Della Serenissima, Gli *see* **BLACK MAGIC** (1949).

Spadaccino Di Siena, Lo *see* **LE MERCENAIRE** (1962).

SPAGHETTI HOUSE 1983 d: Giulio Paradisi. ITL., *Spaghetti House*, Peter Barnes, Play

SPALOVAC MRTVOL 1968 d: Juraj Herz. CZC., *Spalovac Mrtvol*, Ladislav Fuks, 1967, Novel

SPAN OF LIFE, THE 1914 d: Edward MacKey. USA., *The Span of Life*, Sutton Vane, New York 1893, Play

SPANIARD, THE 1925 d: Raoul Walsh. USA., *The Spaniard*, Juanita Savage, New York 1924, Novel

SPANIARD'S CURSE, THE 1958 d: Ralph Kemplen. UKN., *The Assize of the Dying*, Edith Pargiter, Novel

SPANISCHE FLIEGE, DIE 1955 d: Carl Boese. GRM., *Die Spanische Fliege*, Franz Robert Arnold, Ernst Bach, Play

Spanish Acres *see* **THE SANTA FE TRAIL** (1930).

SPANISH CAPE MYSTERY, THE 1935 d: Lewis D. Collins. USA., *The Spanish Cape Mystery*, Ellery Queen, New York 1935, Novel

SPANISH DANCER, THE 1923 d: Herbert Brenon. USA., *Don Cesar de Bazan*, Adolphe-P. d'Ennery, Philippe F. Pinel, 1844, Play

Spanish Fandango *see* **LOVE UNDER FIRE** (1937).

SPANISH FARM TRILOGY, THE 1968. UKN., *The Spanish Farm Trilogy*, R. H. Mottram, Novel

Spanish Fly, The *see* **DIE SPANISCHE FLIEGE** (1955).

SPANISH GARDENER, THE 1956 d: Philip Leacock. UKN., *The Spanish Gardener*, A. J. Cronin, 1950, Novel

Spanish Jade *see* **THE SPANISH JADE** (1922).

SPANISH JADE, THE 1915 d: Wilfred Lucas. USA., *The Spanish Jade*, Maurice Hewlett, New York 1908, Novel

SPANISH JADE, THE 1922 d: John S. Robertson, Tom Geraghty. UKN/USA., *The Spanish Jade*, Maurice Hewlett, New York 1908, Novel

Spanish Love *see* **THE SPANIARD** (1925).

SPARA FORTE, PIU FORTE. NON CAPISCO 1966 d: Eduardo de Filippo. ITL., *Le Voci Di Dentro*, Eduardo de Filippo, Milan 1948, Play

Spare Man *see* **ALBERT R.N.** (1953).

SPARE THE ROD 1961 d: Leslie Norman. UKN., *Spare the Rod*, Michael Croft, Novel

SPARKLING CYANIDE 1983 d: Robert Lewis. USA., *Sparkling Cyanide*, Agatha Christie, Novel

Sparkling Red Star, A *see* **SHAN SHAN DE HONG XING** (1974).

Sparrow *see* **STORIA DI UNA CAPINERA** (1993).

Sparrow of Pigalle, The *see* **PIAF** (1973).

Sparrows *see* **VOGELVRIJ** (1916).

SPARROWS CAN'T SING 1963 d: Joan Littlewood. UKN., *Sparrers Can't Sing*, Stephen Lewis, Stratford 1960, Play

SPARTACUS 1960 d: Stanley Kubrick. USA., *Spartacus*, Howard Fast, 1951, Novel

SPARVIERI DEL RE, GLI 1954 d: Joseph Lerner. ITL., *Les Trois Mousquetaires*, Alexandre Dumas (pere), Paris 1844, Novel

Spate Suhne *see* **STEIBRUCH** (1942).

Spatzen in Gottes Hand *see* **GLUCK AUS OHIO** (1951).

SPAWN OF THE DESERT 1923 d: Ben Wilson, Louis King. USA., *Spawn of the Desert*, W. C. Tuttle, 1922, Short Story

SPAWN OF THE NORTH 1938 d: Henry Hathaway. USA., *Spawn of the North*, Florence Barrett Willoughby, Boston 1932, Novel

Spaziergangerin von Sans-Souci, Die *see* **LA PASSANTE DU SANS-SOUCI** (1982).

SPAZZACAMINI DELLA VAL D'AOSTA, GLI 1914 d: Umberto Paradisi. ITL., *I Spaciafornej d'La Val d'Aosta*, Giovanni Sabbatini, 1848, Novel

SPEAK EASILY 1932 d: Edward Sedgwick. USA., *Speak Easily*, Clarence Budington Kelland, New York 1932, Novel

SPEAKEASY 1929 d: Ben Stoloff. USA., *Speakeasy*, Edward Knoblock, George Rosener, Story

Speaker of Mandarin, The *see* **INSPECTOR WEXFORD: THE SPEAKER OF MANDARIN** (1992).

Speaking of Murder *see* **LE ROUGE EST MIS** (1957).

Special Arrangements *see* **MELODY FOR TWO** (1937).

SPECIAL INVESTIGATOR 1936 d: Louis King. USA., *Fugitive Road*, Erle Stanley Gardner, 1935, Story

Special Kommando Wildganse *see* **APPUNTAMENTO COL DISONORE** (1970).

Special Mission to Caracas *see* **MISSION SPECIALE A CARACAS** (1965).

Special Priority Trains *see* **OSTRE SLEDOVANE VLAKY** (1966).

Special Section *see* **SECTION SPECIALE** (1975).

SPECIALIST, THE 1966 d: James Hill. UKN., *The Specialist*, Charles Sale, Novel

SPECIALIST, THE 1975 d: Howard Avedis. USA., *Come Now the Lawyers*, Ralph B. Potts, Novel

SPECIALIST, THE 1994 d: Luis LlosA. USA., John Shirley, Novel

SPECK ON THE WALL, THE 1914 d: Colin Campbell. USA., *The Speck on the Wall*, James Oliver Curwood, Novel

SPECKLED BAND, THE 1912 d: Georges Treville. UKN., *The Speckled Band*, Arthur Conan Doyle, 1892, Short Story

SPECKLED BAND, THE 1923 d: George Ridgwell. UKN., *The Speckled Band*, Arthur Conan Doyle, 1892, Short Story

SPECKLED BAND, THE 1931 d: Jack Raymond. UKN., *The Speckled Band*, Arthur Conan Doyle, 1892, Short Story

Speckled Band, The *see* **THE ADVENTURES OF SHERLOCK HOLMES: THE SPECKLED BAND** (1984).

SPECTER OF THE ROSE 1946 d: Ben Hecht. USA., *Specter of the Rose*, Ben Hecht, 1945, Short Story

SPECTRE BRIDEGROOM, THE 1913. USA., *The Spectre Bridegroom*, Washington Irving, Story

Spectre de M. Imberger, Le *see* **LE MYSTERE IMBERGER** (1935).

Spectre of the Rose *see* **SPECTER OF THE ROSE** (1946).

SPECTRE VERT, LE 1930 d: Jacques Feyder, Lionel Barrymore. USA/FRN., *The Unholy Night*, Ben Hecht, Novel

SPEED CLASSIC, THE 1928 d: Bruce Mitchell. USA., *They're Off*, Arthur Hoerl, Story

SPEEDING INTO TROUBLE 1924 d: Lee Morrison. UKN., *Speeding Into Trouble*, Dudley Sturrock, Short Story

SPEEDING VENUS, THE 1926 d: Robert T. Thornby. USA., *Behind the Wheel*, Welford Beaton, Story

Spell of Amy Nugent, The see **SPELLBOUND** (1941).

Spell of the Uncanny, The see **IM BANNE DES UNHEIMLICHEN** (1968).

SPELL OF THE YUKON, THE 1916 d: Burton L. King. USA., *The Spell of the Yukon*, Robert W. Service, 1907, Poem

SPELLBOUND 1941 d: John Harlow. UKN., *The Necromancers*, Robert Benson, Novel

SPELLBOUND 1945 d: Alfred Hitchcock. USA., *The House of Dr. Edwardes*, Francis Beeding, Novel

SPENCER'S MOUNTAIN 1963 d: Delmer Daves. USA., *Spencer's Mountain*, Earl Hammer Jr., New York 1961, Novel

SPEND, SPEND, SPEND 1977 d: John Goldschmidt. UKN., *Spend - Spend - Spend*, Vivian Nicholson, Book

SPENDER, THE 1919 d: Charles Swickard. USA., *The Spender*, Frederick Orin Bartlett, 1916, Short Story

SPENDERS, THE 1921 d: Jack Conway. USA., *The Spenders; a Tale of the Third Generation*, Harry Leon Wilson, Boston 1902, Novel

SPENDTHRIFT 1936 d: Raoul Walsh. USA., *Spendthrift*, Eric Hatch, 1936, Novel

SPENDTHRIFT, THE 1915 d: Walter Edwin. USA., *The Spendthrift*, Porter Emerson Browne, New York 1910, Play

SPERDUTI NEL BUIO 1914 d: Nino Martoglio, Roberto Danesi. ITL., *Sperduti Nel Buio*, Roberto Bracco, 1901, Play

SPERDUTI NEL BUIO 1947 d: Camillo Mastrocinque. ITL., *Sperduti Nel Buio*, Roberto Bracco, 1901, Play

SPERGIURA! 1909 d: Luigi Maggi, Arturo Ambrosio. ITL., *La Grande Breteche Ou Les Trois Vengeances*, Honore de Balzac, 1837, Novel

SPERRBEZIRK 1966 d: Will Tremper. GRM., *Sperrbezirk*, Ernst Neubach, Novel

Spessart Inn, The see **DAS WIRTSHAUS IM SPESSART** (1958).

SPETTRI, GLI 1918 d: A. G. CaldierA. ITL., *Gengangere*, Henrik Ibsen, 1881, Play

SPHERE 1998 d: Barry Levinson. USA., *Sphere*, Michael Crichton, Novel

SPHINX 1981 d: Franklin J. Schaffner. USA., *Sphinx*, Robin Cook, Novel

Sphinx Has Spoken, The see **FRIENDS AND LOVERS** (1931).

Spia Che Venne Dall'Ovest, La see **VOIR VENISE ET CREVER** (1966).

Spicy Story see **PIKANTERIE** (1951).

Spider in the Rain, A see **UMA ABELHA NA CHUVA** (1971).

SPIDER, THE 1931 d: William Cameron Menzies, Kenneth MacKennA. USA., *The Spider*, Lowell Brentano, Fulton Oursler, New York 1927, Play

SPIDER, THE 1939 d: Maurice Elvey. UKN., *Night Mail*, Henry Holt, Novel

SPIDER WEBS 1927 d: Wilfred Noy. USA., *The Fast Pace*, H. G. Logalton, Story

Spider's Stratagem, The see **LA STRATEGIA DEL RAGNO** (1969).

Spider's Strategy, The see **LA STRATEGIA DEL RAGNO** (1969).

SPIDER'S WEB, THE 1960 d: Godfrey Grayson. UKN., *The Spider's Web*, Agatha Christie, London 1954, Play

Spider's Web, The see **DAS SPINNENNETZ** (1989).

Spiegel, Der see **AYNA** (1984).

Spiegel Der Helena, Der see **DIE UNHEIMLICHE WANDLUNG DES ALEX ROSCHER** (1943).

SPIEL AUF DER TENNE 1937 d: Georg Jacoby. GRM., *Spiel Auf Der Tenne*, Hans Matscher, Novel

SPIELER, DER 1938 d: Gerhard Lamprecht. GRM., *Igrok*, Fyodor Dostoyevsky, 1866, Novel

SPIELEREIEN EINER KAISERIN 1929 d: Wladimir von Strischewski. GRM., *Spielereien Einer Kaiserin*, Max Dauthendey, Play

SPIELERIN, DIE 1927 d: Graham Cutts. GRM., *Chance the Idol*, Henry Arthur Jones, London 1902, Play

Spies see **SPIONE** (1928).

SPIES OF THE AIR 1939 d: David MacDonald. UKN., *Official Secret*, Jeffrey Dell, London 1938, Play

SPIKES GANG, THE 1974 d: Richard Fleischer. USA., *The Spikes Gang*, Giles Tippette, Novel

Spin a Dark Web see **SOHO INCIDENT** (1956).

SPINDLE OF LIFE, THE 1917 d: George Cochrane. USA., *Gladstone*, Sidney Robinson, Novel

SPINNENNETZ, DAS 1989 d: Bernhard Wicki. GRM., *Das Spinnennetz*, Joseph Roth, Novel

SPINNER O' DREAMS 1918 d: Wilfred Noy. UKN., *Spinner O' Dreams*, W. Strange Hall, Leon M. Lion, Play

Spinster see **TWO LOVES** (1961).

Spinster Dinner see **LOVE BEFORE BREAKFAST** (1936).

SPION FUR DEUTSCHLAND 1956 d: Werner Klinger. GRM., *Munchner Illustrierten*, Will Berthold, Book

SPIONE 1928 d: Fritz Lang. GRM., *Spione*, Thea von Harbou, Novel

Spione Des Kaisers, Der see **SCHWARZER JAGER JOHANNA** (1934).

Spione, Lo see **LE DOULOS** (1962).

SPIRAL ROAD, THE 1962 d: Robert Mulligan. USA., *The Spiral Road*, Jan de Hartog, New York 1957, Novel

SPIRAL STAIRCASE, THE 1946 d: Robert Siodmak. USA., *Some Must Watch*, Ethel Lina White, Novel

SPIRAL STAIRCASE, THE 1975 d: Peter Collinson. UKN., *Some Must Watch*, Ethel Lina White, Novel

SPIRALE DI NEBBIA, UNA 1977 d: Eriprando Visconti. ITL/FRN., *Una Spirale Di Nebbia*, Michele Prisco, Novel

Spirit and the Flesh, The see **I PROMESSI SPOSI** (1941).

SPIRIT IS WILLING, THE 1967 d: William Castle. USA., *The Visitors*, Nathaniel Benchley, New York 1964, Novel

SPIRIT OF LAFAYETTE, THE 1919 d: James Vincent. USA., *The Spirit of Lafayette*, James Mott Hallowell, Garden City, N.Y. 1918, Book

SPIRIT OF ST. LOUIS, THE 1957 d: Billy Wilder. USA., *The Spirit of St. Louis*, Charles A. Lindbergh, 1953, Book

Spirit of the People see **ABE LINCOLN IN ILLINOIS** (1940).

Spiritism see **ESPIRITISMO** (1961).

SPIRITISMO 1919 d: Camillo de Riso. ITL., *Spiritisme*, Victorien Sardou, 1897, Play

Spirits of the Dead see **HISTOIRES EXTRAORDINAIRES** (1968).

SPITE BRIDE, THE 1919 d: Charles Giblyn. USA., *The Spite Bride*, Louise Winter, Novel

SPITFIRE 1934 d: John Cromwell. USA., *Trigger*, Lula Vollmer, New York 1927, Play

SPITFIRE, THE 1914 d: Edwin S. Porter, Frederick A. Thompson. USA., *The Spitfire*, Edward Peple, New York 1910, Play

SPITFIRE, THE 1924 d: W. Christy Cabanne. USA., *Plaster Saints*, Frederic Arnold Kummer, New York 1922, Novel

Spitting Image, The see **ALS TWEE DRUPPELS WATER** (1963).

Spitzenhoschen Und Schusterpech see **VETERAN VOTRUBA** (1928).

Spitzenklopplerin, Die see **LA DENTELLIERE** (1977).

SPLENDID COWARD, THE 1918 d: F. Martin Thornton. UKN., *The Splendid Coward*, Houghton Townley, Novel

Splendid Days, The see **SEREZHA** (1960).

SPLENDID FOLLY 1919 d: Arrigo Bocchi. UKN., *Splendid Folly*, Margaret Pedlar, Novel

Splendid Folly see **HER SPLENDID FOLLY** (1933).

SPLENDID HAZARD, A 1920 d: Arthur Rosson, Allan Dwan. USA., *The Splendid Hazard*, Harold MacGrath, New York 1910, Novel

SPLENDID ROAD, THE 1925 d: Frank Lloyd. USA., *The Splendid Road*, Vingie E. Roe, New York 1925, Novel

SPLENDID SCAPEGRACE, A 1913 d: Charles J. Brabin. USA., *A Blackjack Bargainer*, O. Henry, Short Story

Splinter Fleet, The see **SUBMARINE PATROL** (1938).

Split, The see **THE MANSTER** (1962).

SPLIT, THE 1968 d: Gordon Flemyng. USA., *The Seventh*, Donald E. Westlake, New York 1966, Novel

Spoiled Blood see **ZKAZENA KREV** (1913).

Spoilers of the Sea see **FLOR DE MAYO** (1957).

SPOILERS, THE 1914 d: Colin Campbell. USA., *The Spoilers*, Rex Beach, New York 1906, Novel

SPOILERS, THE 1923 d: Lambert Hillyer. USA., *The Spoilers*, Rex Beach, New York 1906, Novel

SPOILERS, THE 1930 d: Edwin Carewe. USA., *The Spoilers*, Rex Beach, New York 1906, Novel

SPOILERS, THE 1942 d: Ray Enright. USA., *The Spoilers*, Rex Beach, New York 1906, Novel

SPOILERS, THE 1955 d: Jesse Hibbs. USA., *The Spoilers*, Rex Beach, New York 1906, Novel

SPOILS OF WAR 1994 d: David Greene. USA., *Spoils of War*, Michael Wellers, 1988, Play

SPOOK VAN MONNIKSVEER, HET 1989 d: Eddy Asselbergs, Frank Van Mechelen. BLG., *Het Spook Van Monniksveer*, Aster Berkhofs, Novel

SPORT OF KINGS 1947 d: Robert Gordon. USA., *Major Denning's Trust Estate*, Gordon Grand, Story

SPORT OF KINGS, THE 1919 d: Frederick A. Thompson. USA., *The Sport of Kings*, Arthur Somers Roche, Indianapolis 1917, Novel

SPORT OF KINGS, THE 1931 d: Victor Saville, T. Hayes Hunter. UKN., *The Sport of Kings*, Ian Hay, London 1924, Play

SPORT OF THE GODS, THE 1921 d: Henry J. Vernot. USA., *The Sport of the Gods*, Paul Laurence Dunbar, New York 1902, Novel

SPORTING BLOOD 1931 d: Charles J. Brabin. USA., *Horse Flesh*, Frederick Hazlitt Brennan, 1930, Short Story

SPORTING CHANCE, A 1919 d: George Melford. USA., *Impulses*, Roger Hartman, 1919, Short Story

SPORTING CLUB, THE 1971 d: Larry Peerce. USA., *The Sporting Club*, Thomas McGuane, 1968, Novel

SPORTING DUCHESS, THE 1915 d: Barry O'Neil. USA., *The Sporting Duchess*, Hamilton Hamilton, Augustus Harris, Cecil Raleigh, New York 1895, Play

SPORTING DUCHESS, THE 1920 d: George W. Terwilliger. USA., *The Sporting Duchess*, Henry Hamilton, Augustus Harris, Cecil Raleigh, New York 1895, Play

SPORTING LIFE 1918 d: Maurice Tourneur. USA., *Sporting Life*, Seymour Hicks, Cecil Raleigh, London 1897, Play

SPORTING LIFE 1925 d: Maurice Tourneur. USA., *Sporting Life*, Seymour Hicks, Cecil Raleigh, London 1897, Play

Sporting Life see **NIGHT PARADE** (1929).

SPORTING LOVE 1936 d: J. Elder Wills. UKN., *Sporting Love*, Stanley Lupino, Billy Mayerl, London 1934, Musical Play

SPORTING LOVER, THE 1926 d: Alan Hale. USA., *Good Luck*, Ian Hay, Seymour Hicks, London 1923, Play

SPORTING VENUS, THE 1925 d: Marshall Neilan. USA., *The Sporting Venus*, Gerald Beaumont, 1924, Short Story

SPOSA DEI RE, LA 1939 d: Duilio Coletti. ITL., *La Sposa Dei Re*, Ugo Falena, Play

Sposa in Nero, La see **LA MARIEE ETAIT EN NOIR** (1968).

SPOSOB BYCIA 1966 d: Jan Rybkowski. PLN., *Sposob Bycia*, Kazimierz Brandys, 1963, Novel

Spot and Tony see **PUNKTCHEN UND ANTON** (1953).

SPOT OF BOTHER, A 1938 d: David MacDonald. UKN., *A Spot of Bother*, Vernon Sylvaine, London 1937, Play

SPOTLIGHT, THE 1927 d: Frank Tuttle. USA., *Footlights*, Rita Weiman, 1919, Short Story

SPOWIEDZ DZIECIECIA WIEKU 1985 d: Marek Nowicki. PLN., *La Confession d'un Enfant du Siecle*, Alfred de Musset, 1836, Novel

Spray of Plum Blossoms, A see **YIJIAN MEI** (1931).

Spread Eagle see **THE EAGLE AND THE HAWK** (1950).

SPREADING DAWN, THE 1916 d: Larry Trimble. USA., *The Spreading Dawn*, Basil King, 1916, Short Story

Spring 3100 see **JEALOUSY** (1934).

SPRING AND PORT WINE 1970 d: Peter Hammond. UKN., *Spring and Port Wine*, Bill Naughton, London 1964, Play

Spring Cleaning see **WOMEN WHO PLAY** (1932).

Spring Dance see **SPRING MADNESS** (1938).

SPRING FEVER 1927 d: Edward Sedgwick. USA., *Spring Fever*, Vincent Lawrence, New York 1925, Musical Play

Spring Floods see **JARNI VODY** (1968).

SPRING HANDICAP 1937 d: Herbert Brenon. UKN., *The Last Coupon*, Ernest E. Bryan, Play

Spring in Budapest see **BUDAPESTI TAVASZ** (1955).

SPRING IN PARK LANE 1948 d: Herbert Wilcox. UKN., *Come Out of the Kitchen!*, Alice Duer Miller, New York 1916, Novel

SPRING IS HERE 1930 d: John Francis Dillon. USA., *Spring Is Here*, Owen Davis, Lorenz Hart, Richard Rodgers, New York 1929, Musical Play

SPRING MADNESS 1938 d: S. Sylvan Simon. USA., *Spring Dance*, Philip Barry, New York 1936, Play

Spring Magic see **THE MARRIAGE MAKER** (1923).

SPRING MEETING 1941 d: Walter C. Mycroft. UKN., *Spring Meeting*, M. J. Farrell, John Perry, London 1938, Play

Spring of the Year see **THE GREAT ADVENTURE** (1918).

Spring on the Oder see **VESNA NA ODERYE** (1968).

Spring Play, The see **ACTO DA PRIMAVERA** (1963).

Spring Silkworms see **CHUNCAN** (1933).

Spring, The see **IZUMI** (1956).

Spring Three Thousand One Hundred see **JEALOUSY** (1934).

SPRING TONIC 1935 d: Clyde Bruckman. USA., *Man-Eating Tiger*, Rose Caylor, Ben Hecht, Allentown, PA. 1927, Play

Spring Waters see **JARNI VODY** (1968).

Spring Wind Blows Over the Nuoming River, The see **CHUN FENG CUI DAO NUOMING HE** (1954).

SPRINGER VON PONTRESINA, DER 1934 d: Herbert Selpin. GRM/SWT., *Der Springer von Pontresina*, Hans Richter, Berlin 1930, Novel

SPRINGTIME 1915 d: Will S. Davis. USA., *Springtime*, Booth Tarkington, Harry Leon Wilson, New York 1909, Play

SPRINGTIME A LA CARTE 1918 d: Kenneth Webb. USA., *Springtime a la Carte*, O. Henry, Short Story

SPRINGTIME FOR HENRY 1934 d: Frank Tuttle. USA., *Springtime for Henry*, Benn W. Levy, New York 1931, Play

Springtime in Budapest see **BUDAPESTI TAVASZ** (1955).

Sprung Ins Gluck see **FLUCHT AN DIE ADRIA** (1936).

SPRUNG INS GLUCK, DER 1927 d: Augusto GeninA. GRM/FRN/ITL., *Totte Et Sa Chance*, Pierre Soulaine, Novel

SPUK MIT MAX UND MORITZ 1951 d: Ferdinand Diehl. GRM., *Max Und Moritz: Eine Bubengeschichte in Sieben Streichen*, Wilhelm Busch, 1865, Short Story

SPUR DER STEINE 1966 d: Frank Beyer. GDR., *Spur Der Steine*, Erik Neutsch, Novel

Spur Eines Steinem see **SPUR DER STEINE** (1966).

SPUR FUHRT NACH BERLIN, DIE 1952 d: Frantisek Cap. GRM/USA., Artur Brauner, Story

Spurs see **FREAKS** (1932).

Spy 13 see **OPERATOR 13** (1934).

Spy 77 see **ON SECRET SERVICE** (1933).

Spy Busters see **GUNS IN THE HEATHER** (1969).

Spy for a Day see **MICHELE PERRIN** (1913).

SPY FOR A DAY 1940 d: Mario Zampi. UKN., *Source of Irritation*, Stacy Aumonier, Short Story

Spy for Germany see **SPION FUR DEUTSCHLAND** (1956).

Spy Games see **DIRTY TRICKS** (1980).

SPY HUNT 1950 d: George Sherman. USA., *Panther's Moon*, Victor Canning, 1948, Novel

Spy I Love, The see **COPLAN PREND DES RISQUES** (1963).

SPY IN BLACK, THE 1939 d: Michael Powell. UKN., *The Spy in Black*, J. Storer Clouston, Novel

Spy in the Pantry see **TEN DAYS IN PARIS** (1939).

SPY IN THE SKY 1958 d: W. Lee Wilder. USA., *Counterspy Express*, Albert Sidney Fleischman, 1954, Novel

Spy in White, The see **THE SECRET OF STAMBOUL** (1936).

SPY KILLER, THE 1969 d: Roy Ward Baker. UKN., *Private I*, Jimmy Sangster, Novel

SPY OF NAPOLEON 1936 d: Maurice Elvey. UKN., *Spy of Napoleon*, Baroness Orczy, Novel

Spy Pit, The see **DA BERLINO L'APOCALISSE** (1967).

Spy Ring see **SPY HUNT** (1950).

SPY RING, THE 1938 d: Joseph H. Lewis. USA., *International Team*, Frank Van Wyck Mason, 1935, Short Story

SPY SHIP 1942 d: B. Reeves Eason. USA., *The Five Fragments*, George Dyer, Boston 1932, Novel

SPY, THE 1914 d: Otis Turner. USA., *The Spy*, James Fenimore Cooper, New York 1821, Novel

Spy, The see **SPIONE** (1928).

SPY WHO CAME IN FROM THE COLD, THE 1965 d: Martin Ritt. UKN., *The Spy Who Came in from the Cold*, John le Carre, London 1963, Novel

SPY WHO LOVED ME, THE 1977 d: Lewis Gilbert. UKN., *The Spy Who Loved Me*, Ian Fleming, Novel

SPYASHCHAYA KRASAVITSA 1964 d: Apollinari Dudko, Konstantin Sergeyev. USS., *La Belle Au Bois Dormant*, Charles Perrault, 1697, Short Story

SPYSHIP 1983 d: Michael Custance. UKN., *Spyship*, Brian Haynes, Tom Keene, Book

SQUADRONE BIANCO 1936 d: Augusto GeninA. ITL., *L' Escadron Blanc*, Joseph Peyre, Novel

SQUALL, THE 1929 d: Alexander KordA. USA., *The Squall*, Jean Bart, New York 1926, Play

Squandered Lives see **DUKE'S SON** (1920).

Squarcia see **LA GRANDE STRADA AZZURRA** (1957).

SQUARE CROOKS 1928 d: Lewis Seiler. USA., *Square Crooks*, James P. Judge, New York 1926, Play

SQUARE DANCE 1987 d: Daniel Petrie. USA., *Square Dance*, Alan Hines, Novel

SQUARE DEAL SANDERSON 1919 d: William S. Hart, Lambert Hillyer. USA., *Square Del Sanderson*, Charles Alden Seltzer, 1918, Novel

SQUARE DEAL, THE 1918 d: Lloyd Ingraham. USA., *A Square Deal*, Albert Payson Terhune, 1917, Short Story

SQUARE DECEIVER, THE 1917 d: Fred J. Balshofer. USA., *Love Me for Myself*, Francis Perry Elliott, Novel

Square Peg in a Round Hole, A see **BOCK I ORTAGARD** (1958).

Square Peg, The see **THE DENIAL** (1925).

SQUARE RING, THE 1953 d: Basil Dearden, Michael Relph. UKN., *The Square Ring*, Ralph Peterson, Play

SQUAW MAN, THE 1914 d: Cecil B. de Mille, Oscar Apfel. USA., *The Squaw Man*, Edwin Milton Royle, New York 1905, Play

SQUAW MAN, THE 1918 d: Cecil B. de Mille. USA., *The Squaw Man*, Edwin Milton Royle, New York 1905, Play

SQUAW MAN, THE 1931 d: Cecil B. de Mille. USA., *The Squaw Man*, Edwin Milton Royle, New York 1905, Play

SQUAW MAN'S SON, THE 1917 d: Edward J. Le Saint. USA., *The Silent Call*, Edwin Milton Royle, New York 1910, Novel

SQUEAKER, THE 1930 d: Edgar Wallace. UKN., *The Squeaker*, Edgar Wallace, London 1927, Novel

SQUEAKER, THE 1937 d: William K. Howard. UKN., *The Squeaker*, Edgar Wallace, London 1927, Novel

Squeaker, The see **DER ZINKER** (1965).

SQUEALER, THE 1930 d: Harry J. Brown. USA., *The Squealer*, Mark Linder, New York 1928, Play

SQUEEZE, THE 1977 d: Michael Apted. UKN., *The Squeeze*, David Craig, Novel

SQUIBS 1935 d: Henry Edwards. UKN., *Squibs*, George Pearson, Clifford Seyler, Play

SQUIRE OF LONG HADLEY, THE 1925 d: Sinclair Hill. UKN., *The Squire of Long Hadley*, E. Newton Bungey, Novel

SR. PRESIDENTE, EL 1983 d: Manuel Octavio Gomez. CUB/NCR/FRN., *El Senor Presidente*, Miguel Angel Asturias, 1946, Novel

SRDCE V CELOFANU 1939 d: Jan Svitak. CZC., E. F. Saman, Novel

SRDCE V SOUMRAKU 1936 d: Vladimir Slavinsky. CZC., *Srdce V Soumraku*, Maryna Radomerska, Novel

S.S. Represailles see **RAPPRESAGLIA** (1973).

ST. ELMO 1910. USA., *St. Elmo*, Augusta Jane Evans Wilson, New York 1867, Novel

ST. ELMO 1914 d: J. Gordon Edwards. USA., *St. Elmo*, Augusta Jane Evans, New York 1867, Novel

ST. ELMO 1923 d: Jerome Storm. USA., *St. Elmo*, Augusta Jane Evans, New York 1867, Novel

ST. ELMO 1923 d: Rex Wilson. UKN., *St. Elmo*, Augusta Jane Evans, New York 1867, Novel

St. Elmo Murray see **ST. ELMO** (1923).

ST. IVES 1976 d: J. Lee Thompson. USA., *The Procane Chronicle*, Oliver Bleeck, Novel

St. John's Fire see **JOHANNISFEUER** (1939).

ST. LOUIS KID, THE 1934 d: Ray Enright. USA., *A Perfect Weekend*, Frederick Hazlitt Brennan, 1934, Short Story

St. Martin's Pass see **DIE MARTINSKLAUSE** (1951).

St. Michael Had a Rooster see **SAN MICHELE AVEVA UN GALLO** (1972).

St. Peter's Umbrella see **SZENT PETER ESERNYOJE** (1958).

St. Sebastian see **SAN SEBASTIANO** (1911).

STACKARS MILJONARER 1936 d: Tancred Ibsen, Ragnar Arvedson. SWD., *Drei Manner Im Schnee*, Erich Kastner, Zurich 1934, Novel

STADT DER TAUSEND FREUDEN, DIE 1927 d: Carmine Gallone. GRM/FRN., *La Ville Des Milles Joies*, Arnold Bennett, Novel

STADT IST VOLLER GEHEIMNISSE, DIE 1955 d: Fritz Kortner. GRM., *Die Stadt Ist Voller Geheimnisse*, Curt Johannes Braun, Play

STADT OHNE MITLEID 1961 d: Gottfried Reinhardt. GRM/SWT/USA., *Das Urteil*, Manfred Gregor, Vienna 1960, Novel

STADT STEHT KOPF, EINE 1932 d: Gustaf Grundgens. GRM., *Revizor*, Nikolay Gogol, 1836, Play

STAG 1997 d: Gavin Wilding. CND., Jason Schombing, Story

STAGE DOOR 1937 d: Gregory La CavA. USA., *Stage Door*, Edna Ferber, George S. Kaufman, New York 1936, Play

STAGE FRIGHT 1950 d: Alfred Hitchcock. UKN/USA., *Man Running*, Selwyn Jepson, Novel

STAGE MOTHER 1933 d: Charles J. Brabin. USA., *Stage Mother*, Bradford Ropes, New York 1933, Novel

STAGE ROMANCE, A 1922 d: Herbert Brenon. USA., *Kean; Ou Desordre du Genie*, Alexandre Dumas (pere), 1836, Play

STAGE STRUCK 1958 d: Sidney Lumet. USA., *Morning Glory*, Zoe Akins, Los Angeles 1939, Play

Stage, The see **LA RIBALTA** (1912).

STAGECOACH 1939 d: John Ford. USA., *Stage to Lordsburg*, Ernest Haycox, 1937, Short Story

STAGECOACH 1966 d: Gordon Douglas. USA., *Stage to Lordsburg*, Ernest Haycox, 1937, Short Story

STAGECOACH 1986 d: Ted Post. USA., *Stage to Lordsburg*, Ernest Haycox, 1937, Short Story

STAGECOACH BUCKAROO 1942 d: Ray Taylor. USA., *Shotgun Messenger*, Arthur St. Claire, Story

STAGECOACH TO FURY 1956 d: William F. Claxton. USA., *Stagecoach to Fury*, Earle Lyon, Eric Norden, Novel

STAGECOACH WAR 1940 d: Lesley Selander. USA., *War Along the Stage Trails*, Harry F. Olmstead, Story

Stain on the Snow, The see **LA NEIGE ETAIT SALE** (1952).

Stain That Cleans, The see **MANCHA QUE LIMPIA** (1924).

STAIN, THE 1914 d: Frank Powell. USA., *The Stain*, Robert Hobart Davis, Forrest Halsey, Novel

STAIRCASE 1969 d: Stanley Donen. USA., *Staircase*, Charles Dyer, London 1966, Play

Staircase C see **ESCALIER C** (1984).

STAIRS OF SAND 1929 d: Otto Brower. USA., *Stairs of Sand*, Zane Grey, 1928, Novel

STALAG 17 1953 d: Billy Wilder. USA., *Stalag 17*, Donald Bevan, Edmund Trzcinski, New York 1951, Play

STALKER 1979 d: Andrei Tarkovsky. USS., *Piknik Na Obochine*, Arkadi Strugatsky, Boris Strugatsky, 1972, Short Story

STALKER'S APPRENTICE, THE 1998 d: Marcus D. F. White. UKN., *The Stalker's Apprentice*, M. S. Power, Novel

STALKING MOON, THE 1969 d: Robert Mulligan. USA., *The Stalking Moon*, Theodore V. Olsen, New York 1965, Novel

STALLION ROAD 1947 d: James V. Kern, Raoul Walsh (Uncredited). USA., *Stallion Road*, Stephen Longstreet, Novel

STAMBOUL 1931 d: Reginald Denham, Dimitri Buchowetzki. UKN., *L' Homme Qui Assassina*, Pierre Frondaie, Play

Stamboul Train see ORIENT EXPRESS (1934).

Stampede see THE CONQUERING HORDE (1931).

STAMPEDE 1949 d: Lesley Selander. USA., *Stampede*, E. B. Mann, New York 1934, Novel

Stampeded see THE BIG LAND (1956).

STANCES A SOPHIE, LES 1970 d: Moshe Mizrahi. FRN/CND., *Les Stances a Sophie*, Christiane Rochefort, 1964, Novel

Stand Accused see A FAMILY AFFAIR (1937).

STAND AT APACHE RIVER, THE 1953 d: Lee Sholem. USA., *Apache Landing*, Robert J. Hogan, 1951, Novel

STAND BY ME 1986 d: Rob Reiner. USA., *The Body*, Stephen King, Short Story

STAND UP VIRGIN SOLDIERS 1977 d: Norman Cohen. UKN., *Stand Up Virgin Soldiers*, Leslie Thomas, Novel

Standard, The see DIE STANDARTE (1977).

STANDARTE, DIE 1977 d: Ottokar Runze. AUS/GRM/SPN., *Die Standarte*, Alexander Lernet-Holenia, Novel

STAND-IN 1937 d: Tay Garnett. USA., *Stand-in*, Clarence Budington Kelland, 1937, Story

STAND-INS 1997 d: Harvey Keith. USA., *Stand-Ins*, Ed Kelleher, Play

STANLEY AND IRIS 1989 d: Martin Ritt. USA., *Union Street*, Pat Barker, Novel

STANLEY AND THE WOMEN 1991 d: David Tucker. UKN., *Stanley and the Women*, Kingsley Amis, 1984, Novel

Stanley, the Lion-Killer see THE LION KILLER RAINY (1914).

STANTON'S LAST FLING 1913 d: Charles M. Seay. USA., *The Interlude*, H. B. Marriott Watson, Story

STANZA DEL VESCOVO, LA 1977 d: Dino Risi. ITL/FRN., *La Stanza Del Vescovo*, Piero Chiara, Novel

STANZA DELLO SCIROCCO, LA 1998 d: Maurizio SciarrA. ITL., *Domenico Campana*, Novel

STAR FOR A NIGHT 1936 d: Lewis Seiler. USA., *Die Heilige Luge*, Karin Michaelis, 1915, Play

Star from Heaven see GALLANT BESS (1946).

STAR IN THE DUST 1956 d: Charles Haas. USA., *Lawman*, Lee Leighton, Novel

Star in the West see THE SECOND TIME AROUND (1961).

Star Maker, The see THE MARRIAGE CLAUSE (1926).

STAR OF MIDNIGHT 1935 d: Stephen Roberts. USA., *Star of Midnight*, Arthur Somers Roche, New York 1936, Novel

STAR OF THE CIRCUS 1938 d: Albert de Courville. UKN., *December With Truxa*, Heinrich Zeiler, Novel

STAR REPORTER, THE 1921 d: Duke Worne. USA., *The Mysterious Mr. Garland*, Wyndham Martin, London 1922, Novel

STAR ROVER, THE 1920 d: Edward Sloman. USA., *The Star Rover*, Jack London, New York 1915, Novel

Star Sex see CONFESSIONS FROM THE DAVID GALAXY AFFAIR (1979).

STAR SPANGLED GIRL 1971 d: Jerry Paris. USA., *The Star Spangled Girl*, Neil Simon, 1967, Play

Star Without a Sky, A see STERN OHNE HIMMEL (1981).

Star Without Sky see STERN OHNE HIMMEL (1981).

STARBUCKS, THE 1912 d: William J. Bowman. USA., *The Tennessee Judge*, Opie Read, Play

STARDUST 1921 d: Hobart Henley. USA., *Stardust*, Fannie Hurst, New York 1919, Novel

Starfall, The see SVESDOPAD (1981).

Starfire see SOLAR CRISIS (1992).

Stark Naked in Upper Bavaria see PUDELNACKT IN OBERBAYERN (1968).

STARKARE AN LAGEN 1951 d: Arnold Sjostrand, Bengt Logardt. SWD., *Starkare an Lagen*, Bernhard Nordhs, Novel

STARKER ALS DIE LIEBE 1938 d: Joe Stockel. GRM., *Die Beiden Wildtauben*, Richard Skowronnek, Novel

STARKERE, DIE 1953 d: Wolfgang Liebeneiner. GRM., *Die Starkere*, Christa Linden, Novel

STARLIGHT HOTEL 1987 d: Sam Pillsbury. NZL., *The Dream Monger*, Grant Hinden Miller, Novel

STARLIT GARDEN, THE 1923 d: Guy Newall. UKN., *The Starlit Garden*, Henry de Vere Stacpoole, Novel

Starry Sky, A see UM CEU DE ESTRELAS (1996).

Starry-Eye see A CSILLAGSZEMU (1977).

STARS AND BARS 1988 d: Pat O'Connor. USA., *Stars and Bars*, William Boyd, Novel

STARS AND STRIPES FOREVER 1952 d: Henry Koster. USA., *Marching Along*, John Philip Sousa, 1928, Autobiography

STARS ARE SINGING, THE 1953 d: Norman Taurog. USA., Paul Hervey Fox, Story

STARS IN MY CROWN 1950 d: Jacques Tourneur. USA., *Stars in My Crown*, Joe David Brown, 1947, Novel

STARS LOOK DOWN, THE 1939 d: Carol Reed. UKN., *The Stars Look Down*, A. J. Cronin, 1935, Novel

Stars of Eger see EGRI CSILLAGOK (1968).

Stars of the Homeland see DEINE STERNE HEIMAT (1951).

STARS OVER BROADWAY 1935 d: William Keighley. USA., *Thin Air*, Mildred Cram, 1934, Short Story

STARSHAYA SESTRA 1967 d: Georgi Natanson. USS., *Moya Starshaya Sestra*, Alexander Volodin, 1961, Play

STARSHIP TROOPERS 1997 d: Paul Verhoeven. USA., *Starship Troopers*, Robert A. Heinlein, Novel

Star-Spangled Girl see STAR SPANGLED GIRL (1971).

STARY HRICH 1929 d: M. J. Krnansky. CZC., *Stary Hrich*, Jan Klecanda, Novel

STATE FAIR 1933 d: Henry King. USA., *State Fair*, Philip Duffield Stong, New York 1932, Novel

STATE FAIR 1944 d: Walter Lang. USA., *State Fair*, Philip Duffield Stong, New York 1932, Novel

STATE FAIR 1962 d: Jose Ferrer. USA., *State Fair*, Philip Duffield Stong, New York 1932, Novel

STATE FAIR 1976 d: David Lowell Rich. USA., *State Fair*, Philip Duffield Stong, New York 1932, Novel

State of Shock see POWER PLAY (1978).

STATE OF SIEGE, A 1979 d: Vincent Ward. NZL., *A State of Siege*, Janet Frame, 1966, Novel

STATE OF THE UNION 1948 d: Frank CaprA. USA., *State of the Union*, Russel Crouse, Howard Lindsay, New York 1945, Play

STATE SECRET 1950 d: Sidney Gilliat. UKN., *Appointment With Fear*, Ross Huggins, Novel

State Trooper see YOUNG DYNAMITE (1937).

State Versus Elinor Norton, The see ELINOR NORTON (1935).

Stateless see NO EXIT (1962).

Stateline Motel see L' ULTIMA CHANCE (1973).

STATION SIX SAHARA 1962 d: Seth Holt. UKN/GRM., *Men Without a Past*, Jacques Maret, Play

STATION WEST 1948 d: Sidney Lanfield. USA., *Station West*, Luke Short, Novel

Stato Civile: Marta see MARTA (1971).

STATUA DI CARNE, LA 1912 d: Giuseppe de Liguoro. ITL., *La Statua Di Carne*, Teobaldo Ciconi, 1862, Play

STATUA DI CARNE, LA 1912 d: Attilio Fabbri. ITL., *La Statua Di Carne*, Teobaldo Ciconi, 1862, Play

STATUA DI CARNE, LA 1921 d: Mario Almirante. ITL., *La Statua Di Carne*, Teobaldo Ciconi, 1862, Play

Statua Di Carne, La see LA STATUA VIVENTE (1943).

STATUA VIVENTE, LA 1943 d: Camillo Mastrocinque. ITL., *La Statua Di Carne*, Teobaldo Ciconi, 1862, Play

STATUE, THE 1970 d: Rod Amateau. UKN., *Chip, Chip Chip*, Alec Coppel, Play

Status - Orderly see SLOUZHEBNO -ORDINARETS (1979).

STAY AWAY, JOE 1968 d: Peter Tewkesbury. USA., *Joe Stay Away*, Dan Cushman, New York 1953, Novel

Stay Home see I CAN EXPLAIN (1922).

STAY HUNGRY 1976 d: Bob Rafelson. USA., *Stay Hungry*, Charles Gaines, Novel

Stay, The see DER AUFENTHALT (1983).

STAYING ON 1980 d: Silvio Narizzano, Waris Hussein. UKN., *Staying on*, Paul Scott, Novel

STAZIONE TERMINI 1953 d: Vittorio de SicA. ITL/USA., *Stazione Termini*, Cesare Zavattini, Novel

STEADFAST HEART, THE 1923 d: Sheridan Hall. USA., *The Steadfast Heart*, Clarence Budington Kelland, New York 1924, Novel

STEADY COMPANY 1915 d: Joseph de Grasse. USA., *Steady Company*, Julius G. Furthmann, Story

STEALING HEAVEN 1988 d: Clive Donner. UKN/YGS., *Stealing Heaven*, Marion Meade, Novel

Steamboat Bill see STEAMBOAT ROUND THE BEND (1935).

STEAMBOAT ROUND THE BEND 1935 d: John Ford. USA., *Steamboat 'Round the Bend*, Ben Lucien Burman, New York 1933, Novel

STEAMIE, THE 1989 d: Haldane Duncan. UKN., *The Steamie*, Tony Roper, Play

STEAMING 1984 d: Joseph Losey. UKN., *Steaming*, Nell Dunn, 1981, Play

Steaua Fara Nume see L'ETOILE SANS NOM MONA (1966).

Steckbrief Z 48 see GEHETZTE MENSCHEN (1932).

Steel see ACCIAIO (1933).

STEEL AGAINST THE SKY 1942 d: A. Edward Sutherland. USA., *Bridge Built at Night*, Maurice Hanline, Jesse Lasky Jr., Story

STEEL CAGE, THE 1954 d: Walter Doniger. USA., *The San Quentin Story*, Clinton T. Duffy, Dean Jennings, 1950, Book

Steel Eagles see AGUILAS DE ACERO (1927).

STEEL FIST, THE 1952 d: Wesley E. Barry. USA., *Flight Into Freedom*, Phyllis Parker, Story

Steel Giant see GANG TIE JU REN (1974).

Steel Jungle, The see VIOLENT ROAD (1958).

STEEL MAGNOLIAS 1989 d: Herbert Ross. USA., *Steel Magnolias*, Robert Harling, Play

Steel Meets Fire see LIE HUO JIN GANG (1991).

Steel Monster, The see THE MOST DANGEROUS MAN ALIVE (1961).

STEEL PREFERRED 1926 d: James P. Hogan. USA., *Steel Preferred*, Herschel S. Hall, New York 1920, Novel

Steel Wreath see MONGO'S BACK IN TOWN (1971).

STEELE OF THE ROYAL MOUNTED 1925 d: David Smith. USA., *Steele of the Royal Mounted*, James Oliver Curwood, New York 1911, Novel

Stefania see STEPHANIA (1967).

STEFANIE 1958 d: Josef von Baky. GRM., *Stefanie*, Gitta von Cetto, Novel

STEIBRUCH 1942 d: Sigfrit Steiner. SWT., *Steibruch*, A. J. Welti, Elgg 1939, Play

Steiner -Das Eiserne Kreuz see CROSS OF IRON (1977).

STELLA 1921 d: Edwin J. Collins. UKN., *Stella Fregelius*, H. Rider Haggard, Novel

STELLA 1950 d: Claude Binyon. USA., *Family Skeleton*, Doris Miles Disney, 1949, Novel

STELLA 1989 d: John Erman. USA., *Stella Dallas*, Olive Higgins Prouty, Boston 1923, Novel

STELLA DALLAS 1925 d: Henry King. USA., *Stella Dallas*, Olive Higgins Prouty, Boston 1923, Novel

STELLA DALLAS 1937 d: King Vidor. USA., *Stella Dallas*, Olive Higgins Prouty, Boston 1923, Novel

STELLA LUCENTE 1922 d: Raoul d'Auchy. FRN., *Stella Lucente*, A. Erlande, Novel

STELLA MARIS 1918 d: Marshall Neilan. USA., *Stella Maris*, William J. Locke, New York 1913, Novel

STELLA MARIS 1925 d: Charles J. Brabin. USA., *Stella Maris*, William J. Locke, New York 1913, Novel

Stendhal Syndrome, The see LA SINDROME DI STENDHAL (1996).

STEP 1978 d: Sergei Bondarchuk. USS., *Step*, Anton Chekhov, 1888, Short Story

STEP DOWN TO TERROR 1958 d: Harry Keller. USA., *Uncle Charlie*, Gordon McDonell, Story

STEP LIVELY 1944 d: Tim Whelan. USA., *Room Service*, Allan Boretz, John Murray, Play

STEP ON IT! 1922 d: Jack Conway. USA., *The Land of the Lost*, Courtney Ryley Cooper, Story

Step on It, Inspector Palmu see KOMISARIO PALMU KAASUA (1961).

Step on the Gas, Inspector Palmu see KOMISARIO PALMU KAASUA (1961).

Stepbrother, The see SAUTELA BHAI (1962).

Stepbrothers see IBO KYODAI (1957).

Stepchild see NASANU NAKA (1932).

Stepfather see BEAU-PERE (1981).

STEPFORD WIVES, THE 1975 d: Bryan Forbes. USA., *The Stepford Wives*, Ira Levin, Novel

STEPHANIA 1967 d: Ioannis Dalianidis. GRC., *He Stephania Sto Anamorphoterio*, Nelle Theodorou, Athens 1960, Novel

Stephen King's Cat's Eye see CAT'S EYE (1985).

STEPHEN KING'S GRAVEYARD SHIFT 1990 d: Ralph S. Singleton. USA., *Graveyard Shift*, Stephen King, Short Story

Stephen King's It see IT (1990).

Stephen King's Silver Bullet see SILVER BULLET (1985).

STEPHEN KING'S SOMETIMES THEY COME BACK 1991 d: Tom McLoughlin. USA., *Sometimes They Come Back*, Stephen King, Short Story

STEPHEN KING'S THE NIGHT FLYER 1997 d: Mark PaviA. USA., *The Night Flier*, Stephen King, Story

STEPHEN KING'S THE STAND 1994 d: Mick Garris. USA., *The Stand*, Stephen King, 1978, Novel

Stephen King's the Tommyknockers see THE TOMMYKNOCKERS (1993).

STEPHEN KING'S THINNER 1996 d: Tom Holland. USA., *Thinner*, Stephen King, 1984, Novel

STEPHEN STEPS OUT 1923 d: Joseph Henabery. USA., *The Grand Cross of the Desert*, Richard Harding Davis, 1927, Short Story

Stepmother, The see FEDRA (1956).

STEPPA, LA 1962 d: Alberto LattuadA. ITL/FRN., *Istoriya Odnoy Poyezdki*, Anton Chekhov, 1888, Novel

Steppe, La see LA STEPPA (1962).

STEPPE, LA 1989 d: Jean-Jacques Goron. FRN., *The Steppe*, Anton Chekhov, Short Story

Steppe, The see LA STEPPA (1962).

Steppe, The see STEP (1978).

STEPPENWOLF 1974 d: Fred Haines. USA/SWT/FRN., *Der Steppenwolf*, Hermann Hesse, 1927, Novel

Steppes, The see STEP (1978).

STEPPIN' IN SOCIETY 1945 d: Alexander Esway. USA., Marcel Arnac, Novel

STEPPING ALONG 1926 d: Charles Hines. USA., *The Knickerbocker Kid*, Matt Taylor, Story

STEPPING OUT 1991 d: Lewis Gilbert. USA/CND., *Stepping Out*, Richard Harris, 1984, Play

STEPPING SISTERS 1932 d: Seymour Felix. USA., *Stepping Sisters*, Howard Warren Comstock, New York 1930, Play

Steps of Women see UNOS PASOS DE MUJER (1941).

Stepsister, The see CINDERELLA (1914).

STERILE CUCKOO, THE 1969 d: Alan J. PakulA. USA., *The Sterile Cuckoo*, John Treadwell Nichols, New York 1965, Novel

Sterminate "Gruppo Zero" see NADA! (1973).

STERN OHNE HIMMEL 1981 d: Ottokar Runze. GRM., *Stern Ohne Himmel*, Leonie Ossowski, Novel

Sternstein Estate see STERNSTEINHOF (1976).

Sternstein Manor, The see STERNSTEINHOF (1976).

STERNSTEINHOF 1976 d: Hans W. Geissendorfer. GRM., *Der Sternsteinhof*, Ludwig Anzengruber, 195-, Novel

STESTI MA IMENO JONAS 1986 d: Libuse KoutnA. CZC., *Stesti Ma Imeno Jonas*, Elisky Horelove, Novel

STEVNEMOTE MED GLEMTE AR 1957 d: Jon Lennart Mjoen. NRW., *Stevnemote Med Glemte Ar*, Sigurd Hoel, 1954, Novel

STICK 1985 d: Burt Reynolds. USA., *Stick*, Elmore Leonard, Novel

STILETTO 1969 d: Bernard L. Kowalski. USA., *Stiletto*, Harold Robbins, New York 1969, Novel

STILL ALARM, THE 1918 d: Colin Campbell. USA., *The Still Alarm*, Joseph Arthur, New York 1887, Play

STILL ALARM, THE 1926 d: Edward Laemmle. USA., *The Still Alarm*, Joseph Arthur, A. C. Wheeler, New York 1887, Play

STILL WATERS RUN DEEP 1916 d: Fred Paul. UKN., *Still Waters Run Deep*, Tom Taylor, London 1855, Play

STILLE DAGE I CLICHY 1970 d: Jens Jorgen Thorsen. DNM., *Quiet Days in Clichy*, Henry Miller, Paris 1956, Novel

Stille Tage in Clichy see JOURS TRANQUILLES A CLICHY (1989).

STILLWATCH 1987 d: Rod Holcomb. USA., *Stillwatch*, Mary Higgins Clark, Novel

Stimme Des Anderen, Die see UNTER DEN TAUSAND LATERNEN (1952).

Stimme Des Blutes see STEIBRUCH (1942).

STINGAREE 1915 d: James W. Horne. USA., *Stingaree*, E. W. Hornung, New York 1905, Novel

STINGAREE 1916. ASL., *Stingaree*, E. W. Hornung, New York 1905, Novel

STINGAREE 1934 d: William A. Wellman. USA., *Stingaree*, E. W. Hornung, New York 1905, Novel

STINGIEST MAN IN TOWN, THE 1956 d: Jules Bass, Arthur Rankin Jr. USA., *A Christmas Carol*, Charles Dickens, London 1843, Novel

Stirb Fur Zapata see TRINI (1976).

STIRRUP BROTHER, THE 1914. USA., *The Stirrup Brother*, O. Henry, Short Story

STITCH IN TIME, A 1919 d: Ralph Ince. USA., *A Stitch in Time*, Oliver D. Bailey, Lottie M. Meaney, New York 1918, Play

STOCKBROKER'S CLERK, THE 1922 d: George Ridgwell. UKN., *The Stockbroker's Clerk*, Arthur Conan Doyle, Short Story

STOFF AUS DEM DIE TRAUME SIND, DER 1972 d: Alfred Vohrer. GRM., *Aus Dem Die Traum Sind, Der Stoff*, Johannes Mario Simmel, Novel

Stolen Affections see LA REVOLTEE (1947).

STOLEN AIRLINER, THE 1955 d: Don Sharp. UKN., *Thursday Adventure*, John Pudney, London 1955, Novel

STOLEN CLAIM, THE 1910 d: Edwin S. Porter. USA., *The Stolen Claim*, Bret Harte, Short Story

Stolen Desire, The see NUSUMARETA YOKUJO (1958).

STOLEN HOURS 1918 d: Travers Vale. USA., Olive Wadsley, Short Story

STOLEN HOURS 1963 d: Daniel Petrie. UKN/USA., *Dark Victory*, Bert Bloch, George Emerson Brewer Jr., New York 1934, Play

STOLEN IDENTITY 1953 d: Gunther V. Fritsch. USA/AUS., *Ich War Jack Mortimer*, Alexander Lernet-Holenia, Novel

STOLEN KISS, THE 1920 d: Kenneth Webb. USA., *Little Miss By-the-Day*, Lucille Van Slyke, New York 1919, Novel

STOLEN LIFE 1939 d: Paul Czinner. UKN., *Stolen Life*, Karel J. Benes, Novel

Stolen Life see VOLEUR DE VIE (1998).

STOLEN LIFE, A 1946 d: Curtis Bernhardt. USA., *Stolen Life*, Karel J. Benes, Novel

Stolen Love see NUSUMARETA KOI (1951).

STOLEN ORDERS 1918 d: Harley Knoles, George Kelson. USA., *Sealed Orders*, Henry Hamilton, Cecil Raleigh, London 1913, Play

STOLEN PAPERS, THE 1912 d: Georges Treville. UKN., *The Stolen Papers*, Arthur Conan Doyle, Short Story

STOLEN VOICE, THE 1915. USA., *The Stolen Voice*, Paul McAllister, Story

Stolen Year, The see DAS GESTOHLENE JAHR (1951).

STONE COLD DEAD 1979 d: George Mendeluk. CND., *The Sin Sniper*, Hugh Garner, Novel

STONE FOX 1987 d: Harvey Hart. USA., *Stone Fox*, John Reynolds Gardiner, Novel

STONE KILLER, THE 1973 d: Michael Winner. USA/ITL., *A Complete State of Death*, John Gardner, Novel

STONE OF MAZARIN, THE 1923 d: George Ridgwell. UKN., *The Stone of Mazarin*, Arthur Conan Doyle, Short Story

Stone Wedding, The see NUNTA DE PIATRA (1972).

STONES FOR IBARRA 1988 d: Jack Gold. USA., *Stones for Ibarra*, Harriet Doerr, Novel

STONEWALL 1995 d: Nigel Finch. UKN/USA., *Stonewall*, Martin Duberman, Book

STONING, THE 1915 d: Charles J. Brabin. USA., *The Stoning*, James Oppenheim, Story

STOP FLIRTING 1925 d: Scott Sidney. USA., *Stop Flirting*, Frederick Jackson, London 1923, Play

Stop It see AT DERE TOR! (1980).

STOP, LOOK AND LISTEN 1926 d: Larry Semon. USA., *Stop Look and Listen*, Irving Berlin, Harry B. Smith, Play

STOP, LOOK AND LOVE 1939 d: Otto Brower. USA., *The Family Upstairs*, Harry Delf, Atlantic City 1925, Play

Stop Me Before I Kill! see THE FULL TREATMENT (1961).

STOP THE WORLD - I WANT TO GET OFF 1966 d: Philip Saville. UKN., *Stop the World - I Want to Get Off*, Leslie Bricusse, Anthony Newley, London 1961, Play

STOP THIEF! 1915 d: George Fitzmaurice. USA., *Stop Thief*, Carlyle Moore, New York 1912, Play

STOP THIEF 1920 d: Harry Beaumont. USA., *Stop Thief*, Carlyle Moore, New York 1912, Play

Stop! Think of Something Else see STOPP! TANK PA NAGOT ANNAT (1944).

STOP, YOU'RE KILLING ME 1952 d: Roy Del Ruth. USA., *A Slight Case of Murder*, Howard Lindsay, Damon Runyon, New York 1935, Play

Stopover in Paris see ESCALE A ORLY (1955).

STOPOVER TOKYO 1957 d: Richard L. Breen. USA., *Stopover Tokyo*, John Phillips Marquand, 1957, Novel

STOPP! TANK PA NAGOT ANNAT 1944 d: Ake Ohberg. SWD., *Stopp! Tank Pa Nagot Annat*, Olle Hedberg, 1939, Novel

Stora Illusionen, Den see SUURI ILLUSIONI (1986).

STORE BARNEDAPEN, DEN 1931 d: Einer Sissener, Tancred Ibsen. NRW., *Den Store Barnedapen*, Oskar Braaten, 1926, Play

STORFOLK OG SMAFOLK 1951 d: Tancred Ibsen. NRW., Hans Aanrud, Short Stories

STORIA D'AMORE E D'AMICIZIA 1982 d: Franco Rossi. ITL., *Ballad of a Champion*, Guglielmo Spoletini, Novel

STORIA D'AMORE, UNA 1942 d: Mario Camerini. ITL., *Life Begins*, Mary McDougal Axelson, New York 1932, Play

STORIA DEI TREDICI, LA 1917 d: Carmine Gallone. ITL., *La Duchesse de Langeais*, Honore de Balzac, 1839, Novel

Storia Di Francesca Da Rimini, La see PAOLO E FRANCESCA (1950).

Storia Di San Michele, La see DER ARZT VON SAN MICHELE AXEL MUNTHE (1962).

Storia Di un Criminale see HO! (1968).

STORIA DI UN ORFANO 1911. ITL., *Oliver Twist*, Charles Dickens, London 1838, Novel

STORIA DI UNA CAPINERA 1943 d: Gennaro Righelli. ITL., *La Storia Di Una Capinera*, Giovanni Verga, 1870, Novel

STORIA DI UNA CAPINERA 1993 d: Franco Zeffirelli. ITL., *La Storia Di Una Capinera*, Giovanni Verga, 1870, Novel

STORIA DI UNA CAPINERA, LA 1917 d: Giuseppe Sterni. ITL., *La Storia Di Una Capinera*, Giovanni Verga, 1870, Novel

Storia Di Una Strano Amore see MODERATO CANTABILE (1960).

STORIA, LA 1986 d: Luigi Comencini. ITL., *La Storia*, Elsa Morante, 1974, Novel

Storia Lombarda, Una see LA MONACA DI MONZA (1968).

Storie d'Amore Proibite see LE SECRET DU CHEVALIER D'EON (1960).

STORIE DI ORDINARIA FOLLIA 1981 d: Marco Ferreri. ITL/FRN., *Erections, Ejaculations, Exhibitions and Tales of Ordinary.*, Charles Bukowski, Book

Storie Straordinarie see HISTOIRES EXTRAORDINAIRES (1968).

Storiella Di Montagna see IL TORRENTE (1938).

STORIES FROM A FLYING TRUNK 1980 d: Christine Edzard. UKN., Hans Christian Andersen, Short Stories

Stories of Poor Lovers see CRONACHE DI POVERI AMANTI (1954).

Stories of the Vienna Woods see GESCHICHTEN AUS DEM WIENERWALD (1979).

STORK 1971 d: Tim Burstall. ASL., *The Coming of Stork*, David Williamson, 1974, Play

STORK TALK 1962 d: Michael Forlong. UKN., *The Night Life of a Virile Potato*, Gloria Russell, London 1960, Play

Stork's Nest, The see EMMY OF STORK'S NEST (1915).

STORM AT DAYBREAK 1932 d: Richard Boleslawski. USA., *Fekete Szaru Csereszyne*, Sandor Hunyady, 1931, Play

STORM BOY 1976 d: Henri Safran. ASL., *Storm Boy*, Colin Thiele, 1963, Novel

STORM BREAKER, THE 1925 d: Edward Sloman. USA., *Titans*, Charles Guernon, New York 1922, Novel

STORM FEAR 1956 d: Cornel Wilde. USA., *Storm Fear*, Clinton Seeley, Novel

STORM IN A TEACUP 1937 d: Victor Saville, Ian Dalrymple. UKN., *Sturm Im Wasserglas*, Bruno Frank, 1930, Play

Storm in Jamaica see **PASSIONATE SUMMER** (1958).

STORM OVER THE NILE 1955 d: Zoltan Korda, Terence Young. UKN., *The Four Feathers*, A. E. W. Mason, London 1902, Novel

STORM OVER TJURO 1954 d: Arne Mattsson. SWD., *Storm Over Tjuro*, Gustav Hellstrom, 1942, Novel

STORM RIDER, THE 1957 d: Edward Bernds. USA., *The Storm Rider*, L. L. Foreman, Novel

STORM, THE 1922 d: Reginald Barker. USA., *The Storm*, Langdon McCormick, New York 1919, Play

STORM, THE 1930 d: William Wyler. USA., *The Storm*, Langdon McCormick, New York 1919, Play

Storm, The see **GROZA** (1934).

Storm, The see **AANDHI** (1975).

Storm Within, The see **LES PARENTS TERRIBLES** (1948).

STORMY 1935 d: Lew Landers. USA., *Stormy*, Cherry Wilson, New York 1929, Novel

Stormy Night see **O NOAPTE FURTUNOASA** (1943).

STORMY TRAILS 1936 d: Sam Newfield. USA., *Stampede*, E. B. Mann, New York 1934, Novel

STORMY WATERS 1928 d: Edgar Lewis. USA., *Yellow Handkerchief*, Jack London, Short Story

Stormy Waters see **REMORQUES** (1940).

Story from Chikamatsu, A see **CHIKAMATSU MONOGATARI** (1954).

Story of a Blackcap see **STORIA DI UNA CAPINERA** (1993).

Story of a Knife see **DA DAO JI** (1977).

Story of a Love Story, The see **QUESTO IMPOSSIBILE OGGETTO** (1973).

Story of a Marriage see **ON VALENTINE'S DAY** (1986).

Story of a Mother see **HISTORIEN OM EN MODER** (1979).

Story of a Poor Young Man see **LA NOVELA DE UN JOVEN POBRE** (1942).

Story of a Poor Young Man, The see **LA NOVELA DE UN JOVEN POBRE** (1968).

Story of a Prostitute see **SHUNPU-DEN** (1965).

Story of a Sin, The see **DZIEJE GRZECHU** (1975).

Story of a Staircase, The see **HISTORIA DE UNA ESCALERA** (1950).

Story of a Stranger, The see **RASSKAZ NEIZVESTNOGO CELOVEKA** (1980).

Story of a Three Day Pass, The see **LA PERMISSION** (1968).

Story of a Village see **OKA OORIE KATHA** (1977).

Story of Ah Q, The see **AH Q ZHEN ZHUAN** (1982).

Story of an Adventurer, Naomi Uemura see **UEMURA NAOMI MONOGATARI** (1985).

Story of an Unfaithful Woman, The see **HISTORIA DE UNA MALA MUJER** (1948).

Story of an Unknown Man see **RASSKAZ NEIZVESTNOGO CELOVEKA** (1980).

Story of Cinderella, The see **THE SLIPPER AND THE ROSE** (1976).

Story of Doctor Schweitzer, The see **DR. SCHWEITZER IL EST MINUIT** (1952).

STORY OF DR. WASSELL, THE 1944 d: Cecil B. de Mille. USA., *The Story of Dr. Wassell*, James Hilton, 1943, Book

STORY OF ESTHER COSTELLO, THE 1957 d: David Miller. UKN., *The Story of Esther Costello*, Nicholas Monsarrat, 1953, Novel

Story of Folsom, The see **INSIDE THE WALLS OF FOLSOM PRISON** (1951).

STORY OF G.I. JOE, THE 1945 d: William A. Wellman. USA., *The Story of G.I. Joe*, Ernie Pyle, Book

STORY OF GILBERT AND SULLIVAN, THE 1953 d: Sidney Gilliat. UKN., *The Gilbert and Sullivan Book*, Leslie Bailey, Book

Story of Gosta Berling, The see **GOSTA BERLINGS SAGA** (1924).

Story of Gunsundari, The see **GUNSUNDARI KATHA** (1949).

Story of Hell, A see **JIGOKU-HEN** (1969).

Story of Little Mook, The see **DIE GESCHICHTE VOM KLEINEN MUCK** (1953).

Story of Love, The see **POVESTEA DRAGOSTEI** (1976).

Story of Mandy, The see **MANDY** (1952).

STORY OF MANKIND, THE 1957 d: Irwin Allen. USA., *The Story of Mankind*, Hendrik Willem Van Loon, 1921, Book

Story of Monte Cristo, The see **LE COMTE DE MONTE-CRISTO** (1961).

Story of O, The see **L' HISTOIRE D'O** (1975).

Story of One Day, The see **PRIBEH JEDNOHO DNE** (1926).

Story of Private Pooley, The see **DER SCHWUR DES SOLDATEN POOLEY** (1962).

Story of Qiu Ju, The see **QIUJU DA GUANSI** (1992).

Story of Roan Inish, The see **THE SECRET OF ROAN INISH** (1993).

STORY OF SHIRLEY YORKE, THE 1948 d: MacLean Rogers. UKN., *The Case of Lady Camber*, Horace Annesley Vachell, London 1915, Play

Story of Shunkin see **SHUNKIN MONOGATARI** (1954).

Story of Simple Simon, The see **ROMAN HLOUPEHO HONZY** (1926).

Story of Sin, The see **DZIEJE GRZECHU** (1933).

Story of Sin, The see **DZIEJE GRZECHU** (1975).

Story of Tabara, The see **TABARANA KATHE** (1986).

Story of Tabarana, The see **TABARANA KATHE** (1986).

STORY OF TEMPLE DRAKE, THE 1933 d: Stephen Roberts. USA., *Sanctuary*, William Faulkner, New York 1931, Novel

STORY OF THE BLOOD-RED ROSE, THE 1914 d: Colin Campbell. USA., *The Story of the Blood-Red Rose*, James Oliver Curwood, Story

Story of the Count of Monte Cristo, The see **LE COMTE DE MONTE-CRISTO** (1961).

Story of the Eye, The see **SIMONA** (1974).

Story of the Red Sheep Hero see **HONG YANG HAOXIA ZHUAN** (1935).

STORY OF THE ROSARY, THE 1920 d: Percy Nash. UKN., *The Story of the Rosary*, Walter Howard, London 1913, Play

Story of Tosca, The see **TOSCA** (1941).

STORY OF VERNON AND IRENE CASTLE, THE 1939 d: H. C. Potter. USA., *My Husband*, Irene Castle, New York 1919, Book, *My Memories of Vernon Castle*, Irene Castle, 1919, Short Story

Story of Vickie, The see **MADCHENJAHRE EINER KONIGIN** (1954).

STORY OF WILL ROGERS, THE 1952 d: Michael Curtiz. USA., *Uncle Clem's Boy*, Betty Blake Rogers, 1941, Book

Story of Women, A see **UNE AFFAIRE DE FEMMES** (1988).

Story of Xiangyang Compound, The see **XIANGYANG YUAN DE GUSHI** (1974).

STORY VON MONTY SPINNERRATZ, DIE 1998 d: Michael F. Huse. GRM., *Die Story von Monty Spinnerratz*, Tor Seidler, Book

STORY WITHOUT A NAME, THE 1924 d: Irvin V. Willat. USA., *The Story Without a Name*, Arthur Stringer, New York 1924, Novel

STORYVILLE 1992 d: Mark Frost. USA., *Juryman*, Frank Galbally, Robert MacKlin, Novel

Stowaway Girl see **MANUELA** (1957).

Stowaway, The see **LE PASSAGER CLANDESTIN** (1960).

STOWAWAY TO THE MOON 1975 d: Andrew V. McLaglen. USA., *Stowaway to the Moon: the Camelot Odyssey*, William R. Shelton, Novel

STRADA BUIA, LA 1949 d: Sidney Salkow, Marino Girolami. ITL/USA., *Fugitive Lady*, Doris Miles Disney, Novel

Stradivarius, de see **ZIJN VIOOL** (1914).

Stradivarius, The see **ZIJN VIOOL** (1914).

STRAFBATAILLON 999 1960 d: Harald Philipp. GRM., *Strafbataillon 999*, H. G. Konsalik, Novel

STRAFLING AUS STAMBUL, DER 1929 d: Gustav Ucicky. GRM., *Das Fraulein Und Der Levantiner*, Fedor von Zobeltitz, Novel

STRAIGHT FROM THE SHOULDER 1936 d: Stuart Heisler. USA., *Johnny Gets His Gun*, Lucian Cary, 1934, Short Story

STRAIGHT IS THE WAY 1921 d: Robert G. VignolA. USA., *The Manifestations of Henry Ort*, Ethel Watts Mumford, Story

STRAIGHT IS THE WAY 1934 d: Paul Sloane. USA., *Four Walls*, George Abbott, Dana Burnet, New York 1927, Play

STRAIGHT PLACE AND SHOW 1938 d: David Butler. USA., *Saratoga Chips*, Irving Caesar, Damon Runyon, Play

STRAIGHT ROAD, THE 1914 d: Allan Dwan. USA., *The Straight Road*, Clyde Fitch, New York 1907, Play

STRAIGHT TIME 1978 d: Ulu Grosbard. USA., *Straight Time*, Edward Bunker, Novel

STRAINUL 1964 d: Mihai Iacob. RMN., *Strainul*, Titus Popovici, 1955, Novel

STRANA 1917 d: Alfredo Robert. ITL., *Strana*, Vincenzo Bucci, Play

STRANA GLUCHICH 1998 d: Valeri Todorovsky. RSS., *To Possess and to Belong*, Renata Litvinova, Novel

STRANA LA VITA 1988 d: Giuseppe Bertolucci. ITL., *Strana la Vita*, Giovanni Pascuto, Novel

Strana Voglia Di Una Vedova see **DU GRABUGE CHEZ LES VEUVES** (1963).

STRANDED IN ARCADY 1917 d: Frank H. Crane. USA., *Stranded in Arcady*, Francis Lynde, New York 1917, Novel

Stranded in Paradise see **HIS CAPTIVE WOMAN** (1929).

STRANDED IN PARIS 1926 d: Arthur Rosson. USA., *Jennys Bummel*, Hans Bachwitz, Fritz Jakobstetter, Berlin 1926, Play

Strange Adventure of David Gray, The see **VAMPYR** (1931).

STRANGE AFFAIR 1944 d: Alfred E. Green. USA., *Stalk the Hunter*, Oscar Saul, Story

STRANGE AFFAIR OF UNCLE HARRY, THE 1945 d: Robert Siodmak. USA., *Uncle Henry*, Thomas Job, Play

STRANGE AFFAIR, THE 1968 d: David Greene. UKN., *The Strange Affair*, Bernard Toms, London 1966, Novel

Strange Affection see **THE SCAMP** (1957).

Strange Appointment see **STRANO APPUNTAMENTO** (1951).

STRANGE AWAKENING 1958 d: Montgomery Tully. UKN., *Puzzle for Fiends*, Patrick Quentin, Novel

STRANGE BOARDERS 1938 d: Herbert Mason. UKN., *Strange Boarders of Paradise Crescent*, E. Phillips Oppenheim, London 1935, Novel

Strange Brothers see **APOORVA SAHODARARGAL** (1949).

Strange Brothers see **APOORVA SAHODHARALU** (1949).

STRANGE CARGO 1940 d: Frank Borzage. USA., *Not Too Narrow - Not Too Deep*, Richard Sale, London 1936, Novel

Strange Case of Captain Ramper, The see **DER TIERMENSCH RAMPER** (1927).

STRANGE CASE OF CLARA DEANE, THE 1932 d: Louis J. Gasnier, Max Marcin. USA., Arthur M. Brilant, Play

Strange Case of District Attorney M., The see **DER FALL DES STAATSANWALTS M..** (1928).

STRANGE CASE OF DR. JEKYLL AND MR. HYDE, THE 1967 d: Charles Jarrott. USA/CND., *The Strange Case of Dr. Jekyll and Mr. Hyde*, Robert Louis Stevenson, London 1886, Novel

STRANGE CASE OF DR. JEKYLL AND MR. HYDE, THE 1989 d: Michael Lindsay-Hogg. USA., *The Strange Case of Dr. Jekyll and Mr. Hyde*, Robert Louis Stevenson, London 1886, Novel

Strange Case of Mr. Chautard, The see **THE MAN WITH TWO FACES** (1934).

Strange Case of the Missing Rembrandt, The see **THE MISSING REMBRANDT** (1932).

Strange Conspiracy see **THE PRESIDENT VANISHES** (1934).

Strange Countess, The see **DIE SELTSAME GRAFIN** (1961).

Strange Deception see **IL CRISTO PROIBITO** (1951).

967

Strange Deception, The *see* THE ACCUSED (1948).

STRANGE DISAPPEARANCE, A 1915 d: George A. Lessey. USA., *A Strange Disappearance*, Anna Katharine Green, Novel

STRANGE DOOR, THE 1951 d: Joseph Pevney. USA., *The Sire of Maletroit's Door*, Robert Louis Stevenson, 1878, Short Story

STRANGE EXPERIMENT 1937 d: Albert Parker. UKN., *Two Worlds*, John Golden, Hubert Osborne, Play

Strange Girl, The *see* CUDNA DEVOJKA (1961).

Strange Holiday *see* DEATH TAKES A HOLIDAY (1934).

STRANGE HOLIDAY 1945 d: Arch Oboler. USA., *Strange Holiday*, Arch Oboler, Radio Play

STRANGE HOLIDAY 1970 d: Mende Brown. ASL., *Deux Ans de Vacances*, Jules Verne, Paris 1888, Novel

Strange Incident *see* THE OX-BOW INCIDENT (1943).

STRANGE INTERLUDE 1932 d: Robert Z. Leonard. USA., *Strange Interlude*, Eugene O'Neill, New York 1928, Play

Strange Interval *see* STRANGE INTERLUDE (1932).

STRANGE INTRUDER 1956 d: Irving Rapper. USA., *The Intruder*, Helen Fowler, 1952, Novel

Strange Laws *see* THE CHEROKEE STRIP (1937).

Strange Love *see* THE STRANGE LOVE OF MARTHA IVERS (1946).

Strange Love Affair, A *see* IL BEL MOSTRO (1971).

STRANGE LOVE OF MARTHA IVERS, THE 1946 d: Lewis Milestone. USA., *Love Lies Bleeding*, John Patrick, Story

STRANGE LOVE OF MOLLY LOUVAIN, THE 1932 d: Michael Curtiz. USA., *Tinsel Girl*, Maurine Dallas Watkins, 1931, Play

Strange Marriage *see* KULONOS HAZASSAG (1951).

Strange Money *see* WOMEN WITHOUT NAMES (1940).

Strange Obsession, The *see* LA STREGA IN AMORE (1966).

STRANGE ONE, THE 1957 d: Jack Garfein. USA., *End As a Man*, Calder Willingham, 1947, Novel

Strange Ones, The *see* LES ENFANTS TERRIBLES (1949).

Strange Rhapsody *see* STORM AT DAYBREAK (1932).

Strange Skirts *see* WHEN LADIES MEET (1933).

Strange Skirts *see* WHEN LADIES MEET (1941).

Strange Story of Brandner Kasper, The *see* DIE SELTSAME GESCHICHTE DES BRANDNER KASPER (1949).

Strange Story of East of the River Sumida, A *see* BOKUTO KIDAN (1960).

Strange Tales *see* HISTOIRES EXTRAORDINAIRES (1968).

STRANGE WIVES 1935 d: Richard Thorpe. USA., *Bread Upon the Waters*, Edith Wharton, 1934, Short Story

STRANGE WOMAN, THE 1918 d: Edward J. Le Saint. USA., *The Strange Woman*, William Hurlbut, New York 1913, Play

STRANGE WOMAN, THE 1946 d: Edgar G. Ulmer. USA., *The Strange Woman*, Ben Ames Williams, Novel

STRANGE WORLD OF PLANET X, THE 1958 d: Gilbert Gunn. UKN., *Strange World of Planet X*, Rene Ray, Novel

Strange World, The *see* THE STRANGE WORLD OF PLANET X (1958).

Strangely Powerful Exit, A *see* EIN UNHEIMLICH STARKER ABGANG (1973).

Stranger Came Home, A *see* VIERAS MIES (1958).

STRANGER CAME HOME, THE 1954 d: Terence Fisher. UKN., *Stranger at Home*, George Sanders, Novel

Stranger Case of Murder, A *see* GASLIGHT (1940).

Stranger from St. Petersburg *see* INKOGNITO IZ PETERBURGA (1977).

STRANGER IN MY ARMS 1959 d: Helmut Kautner. USA., *And Ride a Tiger*, Robert Wilder, 1951, Novel

STRANGER IN OUR HOUSE 1978 d: Wes Craven. USA., *Summer of Fear*, Lois Duncan, Novel

Stranger in Sacramento, A *see* UNO STRANIERO A SACRAMENTO (1965).

STRANGER IN THE HOUSE 1967 d: Pierre Rouve. UKN., *Les Inconnus Dans la Maison*, Georges Simenon, Paris 1940, Novel

STRANGER IN THE KINGDOM, A 1998 d: Jay Craven. USA., *A Stranger in the Kingdom*, Howard Frank Mosher, Novel

Stranger in the Night *see* HANK WILLIAMS "THE SHOW HE NEVER GAVE" (1982).

STRANGER IN TOWN 1957 d: George Pollock. UKN., *The Uninvited*, Frank Chittenden, Novel

STRANGER IS WATCHING, A 1982 d: Sean S. Cunningham. USA., *A Stranger Is Watching*, Mary Higgins Clark, Novel

Stranger of the North *see* BIG TIMBER (1921).

STRANGER ON HORSEBACK 1955 d: Jacques Tourneur. USA., *Louis L'Amour*, Story

Stranger on the Prowl *see* IMBARCO A MEZZANOTTE (1952).

STRANGER ON THE RUN 1967 d: Don Siegel. USA., Reginald Rose, Story

STRANGER, THE 1924 d: Joseph Henabery. USA., *The First and the Last*, John Galsworthy, 1918, Short Story

Stranger, The *see* UKJENT MANN (1951).

Stranger, The *see* THE STRANGER CAME HOME (1954).

Stranger, The *see* THE INTRUDER (1961).

Stranger, The *see* STRAINUL (1964).

Stranger, The *see* LO STRANIERO (1967).

Stranger Walked in, A *see* LOVE FROM A STRANGER (1947).

STRANGER WITHIN, THE 1974 d: Lee Philips. USA., *The Stranger Within*, Richard Matheson, Short Story

STRANGER WORE A GUN, THE 1953 d: Andre de Toth. USA., *Yankee Gold*, John M. Cunningham, Novel

Strangers *see* I NEVER SANG FOR MY FATHER (1970).

STRANGERS ALL 1935 d: Charles Vidor. USA., *Strangers All; Or Separate Lives*, Marie M. Bercovici, 1934, Play

STRANGER'S BANQUET, THE 1922 d: Marshall Neilan. USA., *The Stranger's Banquet*, Brian Oswald Donn-Byrne, New York 1919, Novel

Stranger's Hand, The *see* LA MANO DELLO STRANIERO (1954).

STRANGERS IN 7A, THE 1972 d: Paul Wendkos. USA., *The Strangers in 7a*, Fielden Farrington, Novel

STRANGERS IN LOVE 1932 d: Lothar Mendes. USA., *The Shorn Lamb*, William J. Locke, 1930, Novel

Strangers in Our Midst *see* ESCAPE IN THE DESERT (1945).

Strangers in the House *see* LES INCONNUS DANS LA MAISON (1941).

STRANGERS MAY KISS 1931 d: George Fitzmaurice. USA., *Strangers May Kiss*, Ursula Parrott, New York 1930, Novel

STRANGERS OF THE EVENING 1932 d: H. Bruce Humberstone. USA., *The Illustrious Corpse*, Tiffany Thayer, New York 1930, Novel

STRANGERS OF THE NIGHT 1923 d: Fred Niblo. USA., *Captain Applejack*, Walter Hackett, New York 1921, Play

STRANGERS ON A HONEYMOON 1936 d: Albert de Courville. UKN., *The Northing Tramp*, Edgar Wallace, London 1926, Novel

STRANGERS ON A TRAIN 1951 d: Alfred Hitchcock. USA., *Strangers on a Train*, Patricia Highsmith, 1950, Novel

STRANGER'S RETURN, THE 1933 d: King Vidor. USA., *Stranger's Return*, Philip Duffield Stong, New York 1933, Novel

Strangers, The *see* VIAGGIO IN ITALIA (1953).

STRANGERS WHEN WE MEET 1960 d: Richard Quine. USA., *Strangers When We Meet*, Evan Hunter, 1958, Novel

Strangler of Blackmoor Castle, The *see* DER WURGER VON SCHLOSS BLACKMOOR (1963).

Strangler of Rillington Place, The *see* RILLINGTON PLACE 10 (1971).

Strangler, The *see* EAST OF PICCADILLY (1939).

STRANGLERS OF PARIS, THE 1913 d: James Gordon. USA., *Les Etrangleurs*, Adolphe Belot, Paris 1879, Novel

STRANGLING THREADS 1923 d: Cecil M. Hepworth. UKN., *The Cobweb*, Naunton Davies, Leon M. Lion, Play

STRANIERA, LA 1930 d: Amleto Palermi, Gaston Ravel. FRN., *L'Etrangere*, Alexandre Dumas (fils), 1877, Play

STRANIERO A SACRAMENTO, UNO 1965 d: Sergio Bergonzelli. ITL., *I Will Kill You*, Jim Murphy, Novel

STRANIERO, LO 1967 d: Luchino Visconti. ITL/FRN/ALG., *L'Etranger*, Albert Camus, Paris 1942, Novel

STRANITZY RASSKAZA 1957 d: Boris Kryzhanovsky, Mikhail Tereshchenko. USS., *Sudba Cheloveka*, Mikhail Sholokhov, Moscow 1957, Novel

STRANNAYA ISTORIA DOCTORA DZHEKILA I MISTERA KHAYDA 1985 d: Alexandr Orlov. USS., *The Strange Case of Dr. Jekyll and Mr. Hyde*, Robert Louis Stevenson, London 1886, Novel

STRANO APPUNTAMENTO 1951 d: D. Akos HamzA. ITL., *La Torre Sul Pollaio*, Vittorio Calvino, Play

Strasse Des Bosen, Die *see* VIA MALA (1944).

STRASSENMUSIK 1936 d: Hans Deppe. GRM., *Strassenmusik*, Paul Schurek, Play

STRASSENSERENADE 1953 d: Georg Jacoby. GRM., Max Neufeld, Story

STRATEGIA DEL RAGNO, LA 1969 d: Bernardo Bertolucci. ITL., *Tema Del Traidor Y Del Heroe*, Jorge Luis Borges, 1944, Short Story

Strategic Command Chiama Jo Walker *see* KOMMISSAR X: DREI GRUNE HUNDE (1967).

STRATHMORE 1915 d: Francis J. Grandon. USA., *Strathmore; Or Wrought By His Own Hand*, Ouida, Philadelphia 1866, Novel

Strauss' Great Waltz *see* WALTZES FROM VIENNA (1933).

STRAW DOGS 1971 d: Sam Peckinpah. UKN., *The Siege of Trencher's Farm*, Gordon M. Williams, Novel

Straw Hat, The *see* SLAMENY KLOBOUK (1972).

STRAW MAN, THE 1953 d: Donald Taylor. UKN., *The Straw Man*, Doris Miles Disney, Novel

Strawberry and Chocolate *see* FRESA Y CHOCOLATE (1993).

STRAWBERRY BLONDE, THE 1941 d: Raoul Walsh. USA., *One Sunday Afternoon*, James Hagan, New York 1933, Play

Strawberry Road *see* SUTOROBERI ROAD (1991).

STRAWBERRY ROAN 1933 d: Alan James. USA., *The Strawberry Roan*, Curly Fletcher, Los Angeles 1931, Poem

STRAWBERRY ROAN 1945 d: Maurice Elvey. UKN., *Strawberry Roan*, A. G. Street, Novel

STRAWBERRY STATEMENT, THE 1970 d: Stuart Hagmann. USA., *The Strawberry Statement: Notes of a College Revolutionary*, James Simon Kunen, New York 1969, Novel

STREAM OF LIFE, THE 1919 d: Horace G. Plympton. USA., *Philip Maynard*, James K. Shields, Pamphlet

STREAMERS 1983 d: Robert Altman. USA., *Streamers*, David Rabe, Play

STREER PATRA 1972 d: Purnendu PattreA. IND., *Strir Patra*, Rabindranath Tagore, c1916, Short Story

STREET ANGEL 1928 d: Frank Borzage. USA., *Cristilinda*, Monckton Hoffe, New York 1926, Novel

STREET CALLED STRAIGHT, THE 1920 d: Wallace Worsley. USA., *The Street Called Straight*, Basil King, 1912, Short Story

Street Cop *see* STREET COP MUGGABLE MARY (1982).

STREET GIRL 1929 d: Wesley Ruggles. USA., *The Viennese Charmer*, W. Carey Wonderly, Story

Street Girl *see* THAT GIRL FROM PARIS (1936).

Street in the Sun *see* HI NO ATARU SAKAMICHI (1958).

STREET OF ADVENTURE, THE 1921 d: Kenelm Foss. UKN., *The Street of Adventure*, Philip Hamilton Gibbs, Novel

STREET OF CHANCE 1942 d: Jack Hively. USA., *The Black Curtain*, Cornell Woolrich, 1941, Novel

Street of Childhood *see* BARNDOMMENS GADE (1986).

STREET OF DREAMS 1988 d: William A. Graham. USA., *Good Night and Good Bye*, Timothy Harris, Novel

STREET OF FORGOTTEN MEN, THE 1925 d: Herbert Brenon. USA., *Street of the Forgotten Men*, George Kibbe Turner, 1925, Short Story

STREET OF ILLUSION, THE 1928 d: Erle C. Kenton. USA., *The Street of Illusion*, Channing Pollock, Story

Street of My Childhood *see* BARNDOMMENS GADE (1986).

Street of No Return *see* SANS ESPOIR DE RETOUR (1989).

STREET OF SEVEN STARS, THE 1918 d: John B. O'Brien. USA., *The Street of Seven Stars*, Mary Roberts Rinehart, Boston 1914, Novel

STREET OF SHADOWS 1953 d: Richard Vernon. UKN., *The Creaking Chair*, Laurence Meynell, Novel

STREET OF SINNERS 1957 d: William Berke. USA., Philip Yordan, Story

Street of the Damned see RUE BARBARE (1983).

Street of the Flying Dragon, The see FIVE DAYS TO LIVE (1922).

Street of the Lost see RUE BARBARE (1983).

STREET OF WOMEN 1932 d: Archie Mayo. USA., *The Street of Women*, Polan Banks, New York 1931, Novel

STREET SCENE 1931 d: King Vidor. USA., *Street Scene*, Elmer Rice, New York 1929, Play

Street Serenade see STRASSENSERENADE (1953).

Street Sings, The see ULICE ZPIVA (1939).

STREET, THE 1976 d: Caroline Leaf. CND., *The Summer My Grandma Was Supposed to Die*, Mordecai Richler, 1969, Short Story

STREET TUMBLERS, THE 1922 d: George Wynn. UKN., *The Street Tumblers*, George R. Sims, Poem

STREETCAR NAMED DESIRE, A 1951 d: Elia Kazan. USA., *A Streetcar Named Desire*, Tennessee Williams, New York 1947, Play

STREETCAR NAMED DESIRE, A 1984 d: John Erman. USA., *A Streetcar Named Desire*, Tennessee Williams, New York 1947, Play

STREETCAR NAMED DESIRE, A 1995 d: Glenn Jordan. USA., *A Streetcar Named Desire*, Tennessee Williams, New York 1947, Play

Streetcar to Malvarrosa see TRAM A LA MALVARROSA (1997).

Streets of Eternity see CORRUZIONE AL PALAZZO DI GIUSTIZIA (1975).

STREETS OF LONDON, THE 1929 d: Norman Lee. UKN., *The Streets of London*, Dion Boucicault, London 1864, Play

STREETS OF NEW YORK, THE 1913 d: Travers Vale. USA., *The Streets of New York*, Dion Boucicault, Play

STREETS OF NEW YORK, THE 1922 d: Burton L. King. USA., *The Streets of New York*, Leota Morgan, Play

Streets of Paris see RUE DES PRAIRIES (1959).

STREETS OF SAN FRANCISCO, THE 1972 d: Walter Grauman. USA., *Poor Ophelia Poor*, Carolyn Weston, Novel

Streets of Sorrow see HO SOGNATO IL PARADISO (1950).

STREETWISE 1984 d: Martin Bell, Mary Ellen Mark. USA., *Streets of the Lost*, Cheryl McCall, Article

STREGA IN AMORE, LA 1966 d: Damiano Damiani. ITL., *Aura*, Carlos Fuentes, Mexico City 1962, Novel

STREIT UM DEN KNABEN JO 1937 d: Erich Waschneck. GRM., *Streit Um Den Knaben Jo*, Hedda Westenberger, Novel

STRENGTH OF MEN, THE 1913. USA., *The Strength of Men*, James Oliver Curwood, Story

STRENGTH OF THE PINES 1922 d: Edgar Lewis. USA., *The Strength of the Pines*, Edison Marshall, Boston 1921, Novel

STRENGTH OF THE WEAK, THE 1916 d: Lucius Henderson. USA., *The Strength of the Weak*, Alice M. Smith, Charlotte Thompson, New York 1906, Play

Strength of the Weak, The see THE TRIUMPH OF THE WEAK (1918).

STRIBRNA OBLAKA 1938 d: Cenek Slegl. CZC., *Stribrna Oblaka*, Jan Drda, Novel

Strickland Case, The see ON TRIAL (1939).

STRICTLY BUSINESS 1917 d: Thomas R. Mills. USA., *Strictly Business*, O. Henry, Short Story

STRICTLY CONFIDENTIAL 1919 d: Clarence Badger. USA., *The New Lady Bantock*, Jerome K. Jerome, 1909, Play

STRICTLY DISHONORABLE 1931 d: John M. Stahl. USA., *Strictly Dishonorable*, Preston Sturges, New York 1929, Play

STRICTLY DISHONORABLE 1951 d: Norman Panama, Melvin Frank. USA., *Strictly Dishonorable*, Preston Sturges, New York 1929, Play

STRICTLY ILLEGAL 1935 d: Ralph Ceder. UKN., *The Naughty Age*, Herbert Sargent, Con West, Play

STRICTLY MODERN 1930 d: William A. Seiter. USA., *Cousin Kate*, Hubert Henry Davies, Boston 1910, Play

STRICTLY UNCONVENTIONAL 1930 d: David Burton. USA., *The Circle*, W. Somerset Maugham, London 1921, Play

Strife Eternal, The see JANE SHORE (1915).

Strife Over the Boy Jo see STREIT UM DEN KNABEN JO (1937).

Strike It Rich see LOSER TAKES ALL (1989).

STRIKE ME PINK 1936 d: Norman Taurog. USA., *Dreamland*, Clarence Budington Kelland, New York 1935, Novel

STRIKE PAY AND HER TURN 1967 d: Richard Everitt. UKN., *Strike Pay and Her Turn*, D. H. Lawrence, Short Story

Strike, The see SIRENA (1947).

STRIKEBOUND 1984 d: Richard Lowenstein. ASL., *Dead Men Don't Dig Coal*, Wendy Lowenstein, Book

STRIPED STOCKING GANG, THE 1915 d: Fred W. Durrant. UKN., *The Striped Stocking Gang*, Irene Miller, Novel

STRIPPED FOR A MILLION 1919 d: M. de La Parelle. USA., *Stripped for a Million*, Parker Fischer, Short Story

STRIPPER, THE 1963 d: Franklin J. Schaffner. USA., *A Loss of Roses*, William Inge, New York 1959, Play

STRIPTEASE 1996 d: Andrew Bergman. USA., *Strip Tease*, Carl Hiaasen, Novel

Striptease Lady see LADY OF BURLESQUE (1943).

Strir Patra see STREER PATRA (1972).

STROGOFF 1970 d: Eriprando Visconti. ITL/FRN/BUL., *Michel Strogoff*, Jules Verne, Paris 1876, Novel

Stroke of Midnight, The see KORKARLEN (1921).

STROKER ACE 1983 d: Hal Needham. USA., *Stand on It*, William Neely, Robert K. Ottum, Novel

Strolling Woman, The see LA PASSANTE DU SANS-SOUCI (1982).

STROM, DER 1942 d: Gunther Rittau. GRM., *Der Strom*, Max Halbe, 1903, Play

STRONG MEDICINE 1986 d: Guy Green. USA/UKN., *Strong Medicine*, Arthur Hailey, Novel

Stronger Party, The see DIE STARKERE (1953).

STRONGER SEX, THE 1931 d: V. Gareth Gundrey. UKN., *The Stronger Sex*, John Valentine, London 1907, Play

STRONGER THAN DEATH 1920 d: Herbert Blache, Charles Bryant. USA., *The Hermit Doctor of Gaya*, I. A. R. Wylie, New York 1916, Novel

STRONGER THAN DESIRE 1939 d: Leslie Fenton. USA., *Evelyn Prentice*, W. E. Woodward, New York 1933, Novel

Stronger Than Fear see EDGE OF DOOM (1950).

Stronger Than the Law see STARKARE AN LAGEN (1951).

STRONGER, THE 1980 d: Ian Knox. UKN., *Den Starkare*, August Strindberg, 1890, Play

STRONGEST, THE 1920 d: Raoul Walsh. USA., *Les Plus Forts*, Georges Clemenceau, Paris 1898, Novel

STRONGHEART 1914 d: James Kirkwood. USA., *Strongheart*, William C. de Mille, Play

Stronghold see WILDSCHUT (1986).

Stronghold, The see WHISPERING CITY (1947).

Structure of a Crystal see STRUKTURA KRYSZTALU (1970).

Structure of Crystals, The see STRUKTURA KRYSZTALU (1970).

STRUGGLE EVERLASTING, THE 1918 d: James Kirkwood. USA., *The Struggle Everlasting*, Edwin Milton Royle, New York 1917, Play

Struggle for Rome, The see TEIL 1: KOMM NUR, MEIN LIEBSTES VOGELEIN KAMPF UM ROM (1968).

Struggle for the Matterhorn see DER KAMPF UMS MATTERHORN (1928).

Struggle in an Ancient City With Wild Fire and Spring Wind see YEHUO CHUNFENG DOU GU CHENG (1963).

Struggle of the Ninth Graders, The see DER KAMPF DER TERTIA (1953).

STRUGGLE, THE 1915 d: Joseph de Grasse. USA., *The Struggle*, L. V. Jefferson, Story

STRUKTURA KRYSZTALU 1970 d: Krzysztof Zanussi. PLN., *Struktura Krysztalu*, Edward Zebrowski, Novel

STRUWWELPETER, DER 1954 d: Fritz Genschow. GRM., *Der Struwwelpeter*, Heinrich Hoffmann, Book

STUBBORNNESS OF GERALDINE, THE 1915 d: Gaston Mervale. USA., *The Stubbornness of Geraldine*, Clyde Fitch, New York 1902, Play

STUBBY PRINGLE'S CHRISTMAS 1978 d: Burt Brinckerhoff. USA., *Stubby Pringle's Christmas*, Jack Schaefer, Short Story

STUD. CHEM. HELENE WILLFUER 1929 d: Fred Sauer. GRM., *Stud. Chem. Helene Willfuer*, Vicki Baum, Novel

STUD, THE 1978 d: Quentin Masters. UKN., *The Stud*, Jackie Collins, Novel

Student Gerber see DER SCHULER GERBER (1981).

STUDENT GING VORBEI, EIN 1960 d: Werner Klinger. GRM., *Ein Student Ging Vorbei*, Hans Ulrich Horster, Novel

Student Just Went Past, A see EIN STUDENT GING VORBEI (1960).

Student of Prague, The see DER STUDENT VON PRAG (1913).

Student of Prague, The see DER STUDENT VON PRAG (1926).

Student of Prague, The see DER STUDENT VON PRAG (1935).

STUDENT PRINCE IN OLD HEIDELBERG, THE 1927 d: Ernst Lubitsch. USA., *Alt Heidelberg*, Wilhelm Meyer-Forster, New York 1902, Play

Student Prince, The see THE STUDENT PRINCE IN OLD HEIDELBERG (1927).

STUDENT PRINCE, THE 1954 d: Richard Thorpe. USA., *Karl Heinrich*, Wilhelm Meyer-Forster, 1899, Novel

STUDENT VON PRAG, DER 1913 d: Stellan Rye. GRM., *Der Student von Prag*, Hanns Heinz Ewers, Novel

STUDENT VON PRAG, DER 1926 d: Henrik Galeen. GRM., *Der Student von Prag*, Hanns Heinz Ewers, Novel

STUDENT VON PRAG, DER 1935 d: Arthur Robison. GRM., *Der Student von Prag*, Hanns Heinz Ewers, Novel

STUDENTIN HELEN WILLFUER 1956 d: Rudolf Jugert. GRM., *Stud. Chem. Helene Willfuer*, Vicki Baum, Novel

Students of Mr. Reitor, The see AS PUPILAS DO SENHOR REITOR (1935).

STUDENT'S ROMANCE, THE 1935 d: Otto Kanturek. UKN., *I Lost My Heart in Heidelberg*, Beda Neumann, Ernst Neumann, Play

Stud-Farm, The see A MENESGAZDA (1978).

STUDIO ESCAPADE, A 1915 d: Lloyd B. Carleton. USA., *The Escape*, Charles Belmont Davis, Story

STUDIO GIRL, THE 1918 d: Charles Giblyn. USA., *La Gamine*, Henri de Gorsse, Pierre Veber, 1911, Play

STUDIO MURDER MYSTERY, THE 1929 d: Frank Tuttle. USA., *The Studio Murder Mystery*, A. Channing Edington, Carmen Edington, Chicago 1929, Novel

STUDS LONIGAN 1960 d: Irving Lerner. USA., *Studs Lonigan*, James Thomas Farrell, 1934, Novel

STUDS LONIGAN 1979 d: James Goldstone. USA., *Studs Lonigan*, James Thomas Farrell, 1934, Novel

STUDY IN SCARLET, A 1914 d: George Pearson. UKN., *A Study in Scarlet*, Arthur Conan Doyle, London 1887, Novel

STUDY IN SCARLET, A 1914. USA., *A Study in Scarlet*, Arthur Conan Doyle, London 1887, Novel

STUDY IN SCARLET, A 1933 d: Edwin L. Marin. USA., *A Study in Scarlet*, Arthur Conan Doyle, London 1887, Novel

STUDY IN TERROR, A 1965 d: James Hill. UKN/GRM/USA., *A Study in Terror*, Ellery Queen, Novel

Stuff of Dreams, The see DER STOFF AUS DEM DIE TRAUME SIND (1972).

Stuff of Heroes see THE GREAT MR. NOBODY (1941).

STUMME GAST, DER 1945 d: Harald Braun. GRM., *Unterm Birnbaum*, Theodor Fontane, 1885, Short Story

Stunde Wenn Drakula Kommt, Die see LA MASCHERA DEL DEMONIO (1960).

Sturdy As a Rock see SKALNI PLEMENO (1944).

Sturm Im Wasserglas see DIE BLUMENFRAU VON LINDENAU (1931).

STURM IM WASSERGLAS 1960 d: Josef von Baky. GRM., *Sturm Im Wasserglas*, Bruno Frank, 1930, Play

STURMFLUT DER LIEBE 1929 d: Martin Berger. GRM., *Sturmflut Der Liebe*, Sadovean, Novel

STURZ, DER 1979 d: Alf Brustellin. GRM., *Der Sturz*, Martin Walser, 1973, Novel

Sturzende Wasser *see* AN HEILIGEN WASSERN (1932).

STUTZEN DER GESELLSCHAFT 1935 d: Douglas Sirk. GRM., *Samfundets Stotter*, Henrik Ibsen, Odense 1877, Play

STVANI LIDE 1933 d: Friedrich Feher, Jan Svitak. CZC/GRM., *Cerny Muz*, Alfred Machard, Novel

Styep *see* STEP (1978).

Su Mayor Aventura *see* IL SEGRETO INVIOLABILE (1939).

SU ULTIMA NOCHE 1931 d: Chester M. Franklin. USA., *Patachon*, Felix Duquesnel, Maurice Hennequin, Paris 1907, Play

Subah *see* UMBARTHA (1982).

SUBJECT WAS ROSES, THE 1968 d: Ulu Grosbard. USA., *The Subject Was Roses*, Frank D. Gilroy, New York 1964, Play

SUBMARINE PATROL 1938 d: John Ford. USA., *The Splinter Fleet of the Otranto Barrage*, Ray Millholland, Indianapolis 1936, Book

Submersion of Japan, The *see* NIHON CHINBOTSU (1973).

Submissive, The *see* DER UNTERTAN (1951).

SUBSTANCE OF FIRE, THE 1996 d: Daniel Sullivan. USA., *The Substance of Fire*, Jon Robin Baitz, Play

SUBTERRANEANS, THE 1960 d: Ranald MacDougall. USA., *The Subterraneans*, Jack Kerouac, 1958, Novel

Suburb Crocodiles *see* VORSTADTKROKODILE (1978).

Suburban Girl Or Everything Comes to Light *see* DEVCE Z PREDMESTI ANEBO VSECKO PRIJDE NA JEVO (1939).

Suburban Handicap, The *see* THE KENTUCKY DERBY (1922).

Suburban House, The *see* DUM NA PREDMESTI (1933).

SUBURBAN, THE 1915 d: George A. Lessey. USA., *The Suburban*, Charles T. Dazey, 1902, Play

SUBURBIA 1996 d: Richard Linklater. USA., *Suburbia*, Eric Bogosian, Play

SUBWAY EXPRESS 1931 d: Fred Newmeyer. USA., *Subway Express*, Eva Kay Flint, Martha Madison, New York 1929, Play

SUBWAY IN THE SKY 1959 d: Muriel Box. UKN., *Subway in the Sky*, Ian Main, London 1957, Play

SUBWAY SADIE 1926 d: Alfred Santell. USA., *Sadie of the Desert*, Mildred Cram, 1925, Short Story

SUCCESS 1923 d: Ralph Ince. USA., *Success*, Adeline Leitzbach, Theodore Liebler, New York 1918, Play

SUCCESS AT ANY PRICE 1934 d: J. Walter Ruben. USA., *Success Story*, John Howard Lawson, New York 1932, Play

Success Story *see* SUCCESS AT ANY PRICE (1934).

SUCCESSFUL CALAMITY, A 1932 d: John G. Adolfi. USA., *A Successful Calamity*, Clare Kummer, New York 1917, Play

SUCCESSFUL FAILURE 1934 d: Arthur Lubin. USA., *Your Uncle William*, Michael Kane, Short Story

Sucedio En Damasco *see* ACCADDE A DAMASCO E FEBBRE (1943).

Such a Gorgeous Kid Like Me *see* UNE BELLE FILLE COMME MOI (1972).

SUCH A LITTLE QUEEN 1914 d: Edwin S. Porter, Hugh Ford. USA., *Such a Little Queen*, Channing Pollock, New York 1909, Play

SUCH A LITTLE QUEEN 1921 d: George Fawcett. USA., *Such a Little Queen*, Channing Pollock, New York 1909, Play

SUCH A LONG JOURNEY 1998 d: Sturla Gunnarsson. CND/UKN., *Such a Long Journey*, Rohinton Mistry, Novel

Such Affection *see* RU CHI DUO QING (1956).

SUCH GOOD FRIENDS 1971 d: Otto Preminger. USA., *Such Good Friends*, Lois Gould, Novel

Such Men are Dangerous *see* THE RACERS (1955).

Such Things Happen *see* THE LOVE RACKET (1929).

Such Things Happen *see* LOVE IS A RACKET (1932).

SUCHKIND 312 1955 d: Gustav Machaty. GRM., *Suchkind 312*, Hans Ulrich Horster, Novel

Sucker *see* THE LIFE OF JIMMY DOLAN (1933).

SUD 1967 d: David Kocharyan. USS., *V Sude*, Anton Chekhov, 1886, Short Story

Sudba Celoveka *see* SUDBA CHELOVEKA (1959).

SUDBA CHELOVEKA 1959 d: Sergei Bondarchuk. USS., *Sudba Cheloveka*, Mikhail Sholokhov, Moscow 1957, Novel

Sudden Death *see* ONCE YOU KISS A STRANGER (1969).

Sudden Departure *see* EIN UNHEIMLICH STARKER ABGANG (1973).

SUDDEN FEAR 1952 d: David Miller. USA., *Sudden Fear*, Edna Sherry, 1948, Novel

SUDDEN FURY 1993 d: Craig R. Baxley. USA., *Sudden Fury*, Leslie Walker, Book

Sudden Fury: a Family Torn Apart *see* SUDDEN FURY (1993).

SUDDEN JIM 1917 d: Victor Schertzinger. USA., *Sudden Jim*, Clarence Budington Kelland, New York 1917, Novel

Sudden Love *see* XAFNIKOS EROTAS (1984).

SUDDEN MONEY 1939 d: Nick Grinde. USA., *Whatever Goes Up*, Milton Lazarus, New York 1935, Play

Sudden Rain *see* SHUU (1956).

Sudden Terror *see* EYEWITNESS (1970).

Suddenly, a Woman! *see* GUDRUN (1963).

SUDDENLY, LAST SUMMER 1959 d: Joseph L. Mankiewicz. UKN/USA., *Suddenly Last Summer*, Tennessee Williams, New York 1958, Play

SUDDENLY, LAST SUMMER 1992 d: Richard Eyre. UKN., *Suddenly Last Summer*, Tennessee Williams, New York 1958, Play

SUDIE AND SIMPSON 1990 d: Joan Tewkesbury. USA., *Sudie and Simpson*, Sara Flanigan Carter, Novel

SUDS 1920 d: John Francis Dillon. USA., *Op O' Me Thumb*, Frederick Fenn, Richard Pryce, New York 1905, Play

SUE 1912. USA., *Sue*, Hal Reid, Play

Sue of Fury *see* THE KEY (1934).

SUE OF THE SOUTH 1919 d: W. Eugene Moore. USA., *Sue of the South*, Maud Reeves White, Novel

Sueno de Andalucia, El *see* ANDALOUSIE (1950).

SUENO DE LOS HEROES, EL 1997 d: Sergio Renan. ARG., Adolfo Bioy Casares, Novel

Sueno de Una Noche de Verano *see* A MIDSUMMER NIGHT'S DREAM (1984).

Sufferings of Young W., The *see* DIE NEUEN LEIDEN DES JUNGEN W. (1975).

Sufferings of Young Werther *see* DIE LEIDEN DES JUNGEN WERTHERS (1976).

Sugar Cane Alley *see* RUE CASES-NEGRES (1983).

SUGAR FACTORY, THE 1998 d: Robert Carter. ASL., *The Sugar Factory*, Robert Carter, Play

Sugar for the Murderer *see* UN KILLER PER SUA MAESTA (1968).

SUGATA SANSHIRO 1943 d: Akira KurosawA. JPN., *Sugata Sanshiro*, Tsuneo Tomita, Novel

Sugata Sanshiro Part II *see* ZOKU SUGATA SANSHIRO (1945).

SUICIDE CLUB, THE 1909 d: D. W. Griffith. USA., *The Suicide Club*, Robert Louis Stevenson, London 1882, Short Stories

SUICIDE CLUB, THE 1914 d: Maurice Elvey. UKN., *The Suicide Club*, Robert Louis Stevenson, London 1882, Short Stories

Suicide Club, The *see* TROUBLE FOR TWO (1936).

SUICIDE CLUB, THE 1973 d: Bill Glenn. USA., *The Suicide Club*, Robert Louis Stevenson, London 1882, Short Stories

SUICIDE CLUB, THE 1988 d: James Bruce. USA., *The Suicide Club*, Robert Louis Stevenson, London 1882, Short Stories

Suicide Commando *see* COMMANDO SUICIDA (1968).

Suicide Commandos *see* COMMANDO SUICIDA (1968).

SUICIDE FLEET 1931 d: Albert S. Rogell. USA., *Mystery Ship*, Commander Herbert A. Jones, Short Story

Suicide Fleet *see* SUBMARINE PATROL (1938).

SUICIDIO, IL 1916 d: Alberto Carlo Lolli. ITL., *Il Suicidio*, Paolo Ferrari, 1875, Play

Suit Almost New, The *see* UBRANIE PRAWIE NOWE (1963).

Suitable Case for Treatment, A *see* MORGAN - A SUITABLE CASE FOR TREATMENT (1966).

SUIVEZ-MOI, JEUNE HOMME! 1958 d: Guy Lefranc. FRN., Roland Moronval, Story

Sult *see* SVALT (1966).

SULTANA, THE 1916 d: Sherwood MacDonald. USA., *The Sultana*, Henry C. Rowland, New York 1914, Novel

SULTANS, LES 1966 d: Jean Delannoy. FRN/ITL., *Les Sultans*, Christine de Rivoyre, Novel

Sultan's Slave, The *see* A SON OF THE SAHARA (1924).

Sultry Weather *see* BOCHORNO (1962).

Summer Afternoon, A *see* DOMINGO A TARDE (1965).

Summer and Sinners *see* SOMMAR OCH SYNDARE (1960).

SUMMER AND SMOKE 1961 d: Peter Glenville. USA., *Summer and Smoke*, Tennessee Williams, New York 1948, Play

SUMMER BACHELORS 1926 d: Allan Dwan. USA., *Summer Widowers*, Warner Fabian, New York 1926, Novel

Summer Before, The *see* O VERAO ANTES (1968).

Summer Camp Massacre *see* BUTTERFLY REVOLUTION (1985).

Summer Camp Nightmare *see* BUTTERFLY REVOLUTION (1985).

SUMMER CAMP NIGHTMARE 1987 d: Bert L. Dragin. USA., *The Butterfly Revolution*, William Butler, Novel

Summer Camp of Young Dreams, The *see* OSADA MLADYCH SNU (1931).

Summer Clouds *see* BOLOND APRILIS (1957).

Summer Clouds *see* IWASHIGUMO (1958).

Summer Flight *see* STOLEN HOURS (1963).

Summer Guests *see* SOMMERGASTE (1976).

SUMMER HEAT 1987 d: Michie Gleason. USA., *Here to Get My Baby Out of Jail*, Louise Shivers, Novel

SUMMER HOLIDAY 1948 d: Rouben Mamoulian. USA., *Ah Wilderness!*, Eugene O'Neill, New York 1933, Play

Summer House, The *see* CLOTHES IN THE WARDROBE (1992).

Summer Lightning *see* TROUBLESOME WIVES (1928).

SUMMER LIGHTNING 1933 d: MacLean Rogers. UKN., *Summer Lightning*, P. G. Wodehouse, 1929, Novel

Summer Lightning *see* I MET MY LOVE AGAIN (1938).

Summer Lightning *see* SCUDDA-HOO! SCUDDA HAY! (1948).

SUMMER LIGHTNING 1984 d: Paul Joyce. UKN., Ivan Turgenev, Novel

Summer Madness *see* SUMMERTIME (1955).

SUMMER MAGIC 1963 d: James Neilson. USA., *Mother Carey's Chickens*, Kate Douglas Wiggin, Boston 1911, Novel

Summer Nights on the Planet Earth *see* NAGRA SOMMARKVALLAR PA JORDEN (1987).

Summer of Aviya, The *see* HAKAYITZ SHEL AVIYA (1988).

Summer of Fear *see* STRANGER IN OUR HOUSE (1978).

SUMMER OF MY GERMAN SOLDIER 1978 d: Michael Tuchner. USA., *Summer of My German Soldier*, Bette Greene, Novel

SUMMER OF THE 17TH DOLL 1959 d: Leslie Norman. UKN/ASL., *The Summer of the Seventeenth Doll*, Ray Lawler, Melbourne 1954, Play

SUMMER OF THE MONKEY 1998 d: Michael Anderson. CND., *Summer of the Monkey*, Wilson Rawls, Book

Summer Paradise *see* PARADISTORG (1977).

Summer People *see* LETNIYE LYUDI (1995).

SUMMER PLACE, A 1959 d: Delmer Daves. USA., *A Summer Place*, Sloan Wilson, 1958, Novel

Summer Residents *see* DACHNIKI (1967).

Summer Residents in the Countryside *see* DACHNIKI (1967).

Summer Skin *see* PIEL DE VERANO (1961).

SUMMER STORM 1944 d: Douglas Sirk. USA., *Drama Na Okhote*, Anton Chekhov, 1884, Short Story

SUMMER STORY, A 1988 d: Piers Haggard. UKN., *The Apple Tree*, John Galsworthy, 1918, Short Story

Summer Tale, A *see* TANASE SCATIU (1976).

Summer to Remember, A *see* SEREZHA (1960).

Summer's Love, A *see* EN KARLEKS SOMMAR (1979).

Summerskin *see* PIEL DE VERANO (1961).

SUMMERTIME 1955 d: David Lean. USA/UKN., *The Time of the Cuckoo*, Arthur Laurents, New York 1952, Play

SUMNER LOCKE ELLIOTT'S CAREFUL, HE MIGHT HEAR YOU 1983 d: Carl Schultz. ASL., *Careful, He Might Hear You*, Sumner Locke Elliott, 1963, Novel

SUMNJIVO LICE 1954 d: Soja Jovanovic, Predrag Dinulovic. YGS., *Sumnjivo Lice*, Branislav Nusic, 1887, Play

SUMURU 1967 d: Lindsay Shonteff. UKN., *Sumuru*, Sax Rohmer, Novel

Sun Above, Death Below *see* SOGEKI (1968).

SUN ALSO RISES, THE 1957 d: Henry King. USA., *The Sun Also Rises*, Ernest Hemingway, 1926, Novel

SUN ALSO RISES, THE 1984 d: James Goldstone. USA., *The Sun Also Rises*, Ernest Hemingway, 1926, Novel

Sun and Shadow *see* SOLEIL ET OMBRE (1922).

SUN COMES UP, THE 1948 d: Richard Thorpe. USA., Marjorie K. Rawlings, Short Stories

Sun Disciples, The *see* VYZNAVACI SLUNCE (1925).

Sun in the Morning *see* THE SUN COMES UP (1948).

Sun Is Far Away, The *see* DALEKO JE SUNCE (1953).

Sun Is Rising, The *see* DIE REISE NACH TILSIT (1939).

Sun Just Came Over the Mountains, The *see* TAI YANG GANG GANG CHU SHAN (1960).

SUN SHINES BRIGHT, THE 1953 d: John Ford. USA., *The Lord Provides*, Irvin S. Cobb, Short Story, *The Mob from Massac*, Irvin S. Cobb, Short Story, *The Sun Shines Bright*, Irvin S. Cobb, Short Story

SUN THE MOON AND THE STARS, THE 1996 d: Geraldine Creed. IRL., *The Sun the Moon and the Stars*, Geraldine Creed, Short Story

Sun Valley *see* RIGUANG XIAGU (1995).

SUN WUKONG SAN DA BAIGUJING 1960 d: Yang XIao-Zhong, Yu Zhongying. CHN., *Xi You Ji*, Wu Chengen, 1592, Novel

SUNA NO KAORI 1968 d: Katsumi Iwauchi. JPN., *Mermaid*, Matsutaro Kawaguchi, Novel

SUNA NO ONNA 1964 d: Hiroshi TeshigaharA. JPN., *Suna No Onna*, Abe Kobo, Tokyo 1952, Novel

Sunbeam Shaft *see* STRIKEBOUND (1984).

SUNBURN 1979 d: Richard C. Sarafian. UKN/USA., *The Bind*, Stanley Ellin, Novel

Sunburst *see* BOOM! (1968).

SUNDAY 1915 d: George W. Lederer. USA., *Sunday*, Thomas Raceward, New York 1904, Play

Sunday Afternoon *see* DOMINGO A TARDE (1965).

Sunday Child *see* DAS SONNTAGSKIND (1956).

SUNDAY IN NEW YORK 1963 d: Peter Tewkesbury. USA., *Sunday in New York*, Norman Krasna, New York 1961, Play

Sunday in the Afternoon *see* DOMINGO A TARDE (1965).

Sunday in the Country *see* UN DIMANCHE A LA COMPAGNE (1984).

Sunday of Life, The *see* LE DIMANCHE DE LA VIE (1967).

Sunday Romance, A *see* BAKARUHABAN (1957).

Sunday Woman, The *see* LA DONNA DELLA DOMENICA (1976).

Sundays and Cybele *see* LES DIMANCHES DE VILLE D'AVRAY (1962).

Sundays of Frances, The *see* FRANCISKA VASARNAPJAI (1997).

Sunderin Vom Fernerhof, Die *see* DER MEINEIDBAUER (1956).

SUNDIGE DORF, DAS 1940 d: Joe Stockel. GRM., *Das Sundige Dorf*, Max Neal, Play

SUNDIGE DORF, DAS 1954 d: Ferdinand Dorfler. GRM., *Das Sundige Dorf*, Max Neal, Play

SUNDIGE DORF, DAS 1966 d: Werner Jacobs. GRM., *Das Sundige Dorf*, Max Neal, Play

SUNDOWN 1941 d: Henry Hathaway. USA., *Sundown*, Barre Lyndon, Short Story

SUNDOWN JIM 1942 d: James Tinling. USA., *Sundown Jim*, Ernest Haycox, 1940, Novel

SUNDOWN SLIM 1920 d: Val Paul. USA., *Sundown Slim*, Henry Herbert Knibbs, Boston 1915, Novel

SUNDOWNERS, THE 1950 d: George Templeton. USA., *Thunder in the Dust*, Alan Lemay, 1934, Novel

SUNDOWNERS, THE 1960 d: Fred Zinnemann. UKN/USA/ASL., *The Sundowners*, Jon Cleary, Novel

Sunghursh *see* SANGHARSH (1968).

Sunken Boat *see* NAUKA DUBI (1946).

Sunkissed *see* A LADY TO LOVE (1929).

Sunlight on Cold Water *see* UN PEU DE SOLEIL DANS L'EAU FROIDE (1971).

Sunny *see* ZONNETJE (1920).

SUNNY 1930 d: William A. Seiter. USA., *Sunny*, Oscar Hammerstein II, Otto Harbach, Jerome Kern, New York 1925, Musical Play

SUNNY 1941 d: Herbert Wilcox. USA., *Sunny*, Oscar Hammerstein II, Otto Harbach, Jerome Kern, New York 1925, Musical Play

SUNNY SIDE UP 1926 d: Donald Crisp. USA., *Sunny Ducrow*, Henry St. John Cooper, New York 1920, Novel

Sunrise *see* SUNRISE - A SONG OF TWO HUMANS (1927).

Sunrise *see* RI CHU (1938).

Sunrise *see* RICHU (1985).

SUNRISE 1986 d: Yu Bun Ching. TWN., Tsao Yu, Novel

SUNRISE - A SONG OF TWO HUMANS 1927 d: F. W. Murnau. USA., *Die Reise Nach Tilsit*, Hermann Sudermann, Berlin 1917, Novel

Sunrise -a Story of Two Humans *see* SUNRISE - A SONG OF TWO HUMANS (1927).

Sunset *see* RICHU (1985).

Sunset at Chaopraya *see* KHU GAM (1996).

SUNSET DERBY, THE 1927 d: Albert S. Rogell. USA., *The Sunset Derby*, William Dudley Pelley, 1926, Short Story

Sunset Murder Case, The *see* THE SUNSET STRIP CASE (1938).

SUNSET PASS 1929 d: Otto Brower. USA., *Sunset Pass*, Zane Grey, Novel

SUNSET PASS 1933 d: Henry Hathaway. USA., *Sunset Pass*, Zane Grey, Novel

SUNSET PASS 1946 d: William Berke. USA., *Sunset Pass*, Zane Grey, Novel

SUNSET PRINCESS, THE 1918. USA., *Yellowstone Pete's Only Daughter*, Wallace G. Coburn, Poem

SUNSET SONG 1971. UKN., *Sunset Song*, Lewis Grassic Gibbon, Novel

SUNSET STRIP CASE, THE 1938 d: Louis J. Gasnier. USA., *Murder on Sunset Boulevard*, Harold Joyce, Short Story

SUNSET TRAIL, THE 1924 d: Ernst Laemmle. USA., *Overland Red*, Henry Herbert Knibbs, Boston 1914, Novel

SUNSHINE 1973 d: Joseph Sargent. USA., Jacqueline Helton, Journal

SUNSHINE BOYS, THE 1975 d: Herbert Ross. USA., *The Sunshine Boys*, Neil Simon, 1972, Play

SUNSHINE BOYS, THE 1997 d: John Erman. USA., *The Sunshine Boys*, Neil Simon, 1972, Play

Sunshine Even By Night *see* IL SOLE ANCHE DI NOTTE (1990).

SUNSHINE NAN 1918 d: Charles Giblyn. USA., *Calvary Alley*, Alice Hegan Rice, New York 1917, Novel

SUNSHINE OF PARADISE ALLEY 1926 d: Jack Nelson. USA., *The Sunshine of Paradise Alley*, George W. Ryer, Denman Thompson, 1895, Play

SUNSHINE SUSIE 1932 d: Victor Saville. UKN., *Die Privatsekretarin*, Franz Schulz, Stefan Szomahazy, Novel

SUN-UP 1925 d: Edmund Goulding. USA., *Sun-Up*, Lula Vollmer, New York 1925, Play

SUONATRICE D'ARPA, LA 1917 d: Mario Ceccatelli. ITL., *La Suonatrice d'Arpa*, Davide Chiossone, 1848, Novel

Suor Teresa *see* LA GRANDE RINUNCIA (1951).

SUOTORPAN TYTTO 1940 d: Toivo SarkkA. FNL., *Tosen Fran Stormyrtorpet*, Selma Lagerlof, Stockholm 1908, Short Story

SUPER, EL 1979 d: Leon Ichaso, Orlando Jimenez Leal. USA/CUB., *El Super*, Ivan Acosta, Play

Superfluous People *see* UBERFLUSSIGE MENSCHEN (1926).

Superintendent Sansho, The *see* SANSHO DAYU (1954).

SUPERIOR LAW, THE 1913. USA., *The Right of Way*, Gilbert Parker, London 1901, Novel

Supernatural *see* SOBRENATURAL (1996).

SUPER-SEX, THE 1922 d: Lambert Hillyer. USA., *Miles Brewster and the Super Sex*, Frank R. Adams, 1921, Short Story

Superstition *see* LA VENENOSA (1928).

SUPERSTITION 1982 d: James W. Roberson. USA., *The Witch*, Michael Sajbel, Novel

SUPREME SACRIFICE, THE 1916 d: Lionel Belmore, Harley Knoles. USA., *To Him That Hath*, Leroy Scott, New York 1907, Novel

SUPREME TEST, THE 1915 d: Edward J. Le Saint. USA., *The Supreme Test*, L. V. Jefferson, Short Story

SUR, EL 1983 d: Victor Erice. SPN/FRN., Adelaide Garcia Morales, Story

SUR LA ROUTE DE SALINA 1969 d: Georges Lautner. FRN/ITL., *La Route de Salina*, Maurice Curry, Novel

Sur Les Hautes Cimes (L'ascension du Mont Cervin) *see* LA CROIX DU CERVIN (1922).

SUR LES TRACES DE BALINT 1977 d: Eric Duvivier. FRN., *La Formation Psychologique du Medecin*, Michael Sapir, Book

Suraj Ka Satva Ghoda *see* SURAJ KA SATWAN GHODA (1992).

SURAJ KA SATWAN GHODA 1992 d: Shyam Benegal. IND., *Suraj Ka Satwan Ghoda*, Dharamvir Bharati, Novel

SURE FIRE FLINT 1922 d: Dell Henderson. USA., *Sure Fire Flint*, Gerald C. Duffy, 1922, Short Story

Sure-Shot Lisa *see* SCHUTZENLIESEL (1954).

Surf *see* SHIOSAI (1954).

SURFACING 1980 d: Claude JutrA. CND., *Surfacing*, Margaret Atwood, Novel

SURGEON'S CHILD, THE 1912 d: Harry T. Harris. UKN., *The Surgeon's Child*, Fred Weatherley, Poem

SURGEON'S KNIFE, THE 1957 d: Gordon Parry. UKN., *The Wicked Flee*, Anne Hocking, Novel

SUROCKA 1982 d: Josif Heifitz. USS., *Poyedinok*, Aleksander Ivanovich Kuprin, 1905, Short Story

SURORILE 1984 d: Iulian Mihu. RMN., *Surorile Boga*, Horia Lovinescu, 1959, Play

Surprise By Joy *see* SHADOWLANDS (1985).

SURPRISE PACKAGE 1960 d: Stanley Donen. UKN., *A Gift from the Boys*, Art Buchwald, Novel

SURPRISES DU DIVORCE, LES 1912 d: Georges MoncA. FRN., *Les Surprises du Divorce*, Alexandre Bisson, Antony Mars, 1888, Play

SURPRISES DU DIVORCE, LES 1933 d: Jean Kemm. FRN., *Les Surprises du Divorce*, Alexandre Bisson, Antony Mars, 1888, Play

SURPRISES DU SLEEPING, LES 1933 d: Karl Anton. FRN., *Couchette No.3*, Alex Madis, Albert Willemetz, Opera

SURPRISES D'UNE NUIT DE NOCES, LES 1951 d: Jean Vallee. FRN., *Les Surprises d'une Nuit de Noces*, Paul Van Stalle, Play

SURPRISES OF AN EMPTY HOTEL, THE 1916 d: Theodore Marston. USA., *The Princess of Copper*, Archibald Clavering Gunter, New York 1900, Novel

SURRENDER 1927 d: Edward Sloman. USA., *Lea Lyon*, Alexander Brody, Play

SURRENDER 1931 d: William K. Howard. USA., *Axelle*, Pierre Benoit, Paris 1928, Novel

SURRENDER - HELL! 1959 d: John Barnwell. USA., *Blackburn's Headhunters*, Philip Harkins, 1955, Book

Surrender, The *see* SURRENDER (1931).

SURSIS POUR UN VIVANT 1958 d: Victor Merenda, Ottorino Franco Bertolini. FRN/ITL., *Thanatos Palace Hotel*, Andre Maurois, 1951, Short Story

Surveillance *see* MAIFU (1997).

Survival *see* THE GUIDE (1965).

Survival Run *see* SOLDAAT VAN ORANJE (1977).

Survival Run *see* DAMNATION ALLEY (1977).

SURVIVE THE SAVAGE SEA 1992 d: Kevin Dobson. USA/ASL., *Survive the Savage Sea*, Dougal Robertson, Book

SURVIVING PICASSO 1996 d: James Ivory. USA/UKN., *Picasso: Creator and Destroyer*, Arianna Stassinopoulos Huffington, Book

Survivor, The *see* DER SCHWUR DES SOLDATEN POOLEY (1962).

SURVIVOR, THE 1980 d: David Hemmings. ASL/UKN., *The Survivor*, James Herbert, Novel

SUSAN AND GOD 1940 d: George Cukor. USA., *Susan and God*, Rachel Crothers, Princeton N.J. 1937, Play

SUSAN AND GOD 1951 d: Alex Segal. USA., *Susan and God*, Rachel Crothers, Princeton N.J. 1937, Play

Susan Lenox *see* SUSAN LENOX (HER FALL AND RISE) (1931).

SUSAN LENOX (HER FALL AND RISE) 1931 d: Robert Z. Leonard. USA., *Susan Lennox - Her Fall and Rise*, David Graham Phillips, New York 1917, Novel

SUSAN SLADE 1961 d: Delmer Daves. USA., *The Sin of Susan Slade*, Doris Hume, New York 1961, Novel

SUSAN SLEPT HERE 1954 d: Frank Tashlin. USA., *Susan*, Steve Fisher, Alex Gottlieb, 1952, Play

Susannah *see* SUSANNAH OF THE MOUNTIES (1939).

SUSANNAH OF THE MOUNTIES 1939 d: William A. Seiter. USA., *Susannah a Little Girl of the Mounties*, Muriel Denison, New York 1936, Novel

SUSANNE 1950 d: Torben Anton Svendsen. DNM., *Susanne*, Johannes Buchholtz, 1931, Novel

SUSETZ 1977 d: Yaki YoshA. ISR., *Susetz*, Yoram Kaniuk, Book

SUSPECT 1960 d: Roy Boulting, John Boulting. UKN., *Sort of Traitors*, Nigel Balchin, London 1949, Novel

SUSPECT, THE 1916 d: S. Rankin Drew. USA., *The Silver Shell*, Henry J. W. Dam, Novel

SUSPECT, THE 1944 d: Robert Siodmak. USA., *The Suspect*, James Ronald, Novel

SUSPECTS, LES 1974 d: Michel Wyn. FRN./ITL., *Les Suspects*, Paul Andreota, Novel

Suspence *see* SUSPENSE (1919).

SUSPENSE 1919 d: Frank Reicher. USA., *Suspense*, Isabel Ostrander, New York 1918, Novel

SUSPENSE 1930 d: Walter Summers. UKN., *Suspense*, Patrick MacGill, Play

Suspicion *see* WIVES UNDER SUSPICION (1938).

SUSPICION 1941 d: Alfred Hitchcock. USA., *Before the Fact*, Francis Iles, Novel

Suspicious Character, A *see* SUMNJIVO LICE (1954).

SUSSE ZEIT MIT KALIMAGDORA, DIE 1968 d: Leopold LaholA. GRM/CZC., Jan Weiss, Story

SUTOROBERI ROAD 1991 d: Koreyoshi KuraharA. JPN., *Sutoroberi Road*, Yoshimi Ishikawa, Novel

SUTTER'S GOLD 1936 d: James Cruze. USA., *Or. la Merveilleuse Histoire du General Johann August Suter*, Blaise Cendrars, Paris 1925, Novel

SUURI ILLUSIONI 1986 d: Tuija-Maija Niskanen. FNL., *Suuri Illusioni*, Mika Waltari, 1928, Novel

SUZANNA 1922 d: F. Richard Jones. USA., *Suzanna*, Linton Wells, Story

SUZANNE 1932 d: Raymond Rouleau, Leo Joannon. FRN., *Suzanne*, Steve Passeur

SUZANNE 1980 d: Robin Spry. CND., *Snow Lark*, Ronald Sutherland, Book

Suzanne Lenox *see* SUSAN LENOX (HER FALL AND RISE) (1931).

SUZANNE SIMONIN, LA RELIGIEUSE DE DIDEROT 1965 d: Jacques Rivette. FRN., *La Religieuse*, Denis Diderot, 1796, Novel

Suzanne's Profession *see* LA CARRIERE DE SUZANNE (1963).

SUZUKAKE NO SANPOMICHI 1959 d: Hiromichi HorikawA. JPN., *Suzukake No Sanpomichi*, Yojiro Ishizaka, Play

SUZY 1936 d: George Fitzmaurice. USA., *Suzy*, Herbert Gorman, New York 1934, Novel

Suzy Saxophone *see* SAXOPHON-SUSI (1928).

SVADBA 1944 d: Isider Annensky. USS., *Svadba*, Anton Chekhov, 1889, Play

SVADBA 1973 d: Radomir Saranovic. YGS/USS., *Svadba*, Mihailo Lalic, 1962, Novel

SVALT 1966 d: Henning Carlsen. SWD/DNM/NRW., *Sult*, Knut Hamsun, Kristiania 1890, Novel

SVANDA DUDAK 1937 d: Svatopluk Innemann. CZC., *Strakonicky Dudak Aneb Hody Divych Zen*, Josef Kajetan Tyl, 1847, Play

Svanda, the Bagpiper *see* SVANDA DUDAK (1937).

SVARA PROVNINGEN, DEN 1969 d: Torgny Wickman. SWD., Bengt Anderberg, Story

SVATEBNI KOSILE 1925 d: Theodor Pistek. CZC., *Svatebni Kosile Ze Sbirky Kytice*, Karel Jaromir Erben, Poem

SVATEK VERITELU 1939 d: Gina Hasler. CZC., *Svatek Veritelu*, Karel Piskor, Play

SVED AKINEK NYOMA VESZETT, A 1980 d: Peter Bacso. HNG/SWD/GRM., *Mannen Som Gick Upp I Rok*, Maj Sjowall, Per Wahloo, Novel

Svedskaya Spichka *see* SVEDSKAYA SPICKA (1954).

SVEDSKAYA SPICKA 1954 d: Konstantin Yudin. USS., *Shvedskaya Spichka*, Anton Chekhov, 1883, Short Story

SVEHLAVICKA 1926 d: Rudolf Mestak. CZC., *Svehlavicka*, Emmy von Rhoden, Novel

Svejk As a Civilian *see* SVEJK V CIVILU (1927).

Svejk at the Front *see* SVEJK NA FRONTE (1926).

SVEJK NA FRONTE 1926 d: Carl Lamac. CZC., *Osudy Dobreho Vojaka Svejka Za Svetove Valky*, Jaroslav Hasek, Prague 1920-23, Novel

SVEJK V CIVILU 1927 d: Gustav Machaty. CZC/GRM., *Osudy Dobreho Vojaka Svejka Za Svetove Valky*, Jaroslav Hasek, Prague 1920-23, Novel

SVEJK V RUSKEM ZAJETI 1926 d: Svatopluk Innemann. CZC., *Osudy Dobreho Vojaka Svejka Za Svetove Valky*, Jaroslav Hasek, Prague 1920-23, Novel

SVENGALI 1927 d: Gennaro Righelli. GRM., *Trilby*, George Du Maurier, London 1894, Novel

SVENGALI 1931 d: Archie Mayo. USA., *Trilby*, George Du Maurier, London 1894, Novel

SVENGALI 1954 d: Noel Langley. UKN., *Trilby*, George Du Maurier, London 1894, Novel

SVENGALI 1982 d: Anthony Harvey. USA., *Trilby*, George Du Maurier, London 1894, Novel

SVENSKA HJALTAR 1997 d: Daniel Bergman. SWD., *Swedish Heroes*, Reidar Jonsson, Book

SVESDOPAD 1981 d: Igor Talankin. USS., Viktor Astafjew, Story

SVET BEZ HRANIC 1931 d: Julius Lebl. CZC., *Television*, Howard Irving Young, Play

SVET KDE SE ZEBRA 1938 d: Miroslav Cikan. CZC., *Kde Se Zebra*, Edmond Konrad, Play

SVET PATRI NAM 1937 d: Martin Fric. CZC., *Rub a Lic*, Jiri Voskovec, Jan Werich, Play

SVETLO JEHO OCI 1936 d: Vaclav Kubasek. CZC., *Svetlo Jeho Oci*, Maryna Radomerska, Novel

SVINEDRENGEN OG PRINSESSEN PA AERTEN 1962 d: Poul Ilsoe. DNM., *Prinsessen Pa Aerten*, Hans Christian Andersen, 1835, Short Story

SVINOPAS 1941 d: Alexander MacHeret. USS., *Svinedrengen*, Hans Christian Andersen, 1842, Short Story

Svirachut *see* THE CLOWN AND THE KIDS (1968).

Svoga Tela Gospodar *see* SVOGA TJELA GOSPODAR (1957).

SVOGA TJELA GOSPODAR 1957 d: Fedor Hanzekovic. YGS., *Svoga Tela Gospodar*, Slavko Kolar, 1942, Play

S'VRENELI AM THUNERSEE 1936 d: Paul Schmid. SWT., *S'vreneli Am Thunersee*, Karl Grunder, Berne 1925, Musical Play

Swaggerers, The *see* NASI FURIANTI (1937).

S'waisechind Vo Engelberg *see* HEIDEMARIE (1956).

SWALLOWS AND AMAZONS 1974 d: Claude Whatham. UKN., *Swallows and Amazons*, Arthur Ransome, Novel

SWALLOWS AND AMAZONS FOREVER! 1982 d: Andrew Morgan. UKN., Arthur Ransome, Book

SWAMI 1977 d: Basu Chatterjee. IND., *Swami*, Saratchandra Chatterjee, 1918, Novel

SWAMI 1987 d: Shankar Nag. IND., *Swamy and Friends*, R. K. Narayan, 1935, Novel

SWAMP WATER 1941 d: Jean Renoir. USA., *Swamp Water*, Vereen Bell, Novel

Swamy *see* SWAMI (1987).

Swan Song *see* JUE XIANG (1985).

SWAN, THE 1925 d: Dimitri Buchowetzki. USA., *A Hattyu*, Ferenc Molnar, Budapest 1921, Play

Swan, The *see* ONE ROMANTIC NIGHT (1930).

SWAN, THE 1956 d: Charles Vidor. USA., *A Hattyu*, Ferenc Molnar, Budapest 1921, Play

SWANN 1996 d: Anna Benson Gyles. UKN/CND., *Swann*, Carol Shields, Novel

Swann in Love *see* UN AMOUR DE SWANN (1983).

SWARM, THE 1978 d: Irwin Allen. USA., *The Swarm*, Arthur Herzog, Novel

SWEDENHIELMS 1935 d: Gustaf Molander. SWD., *Swedenhielms*, Hjalmar Bergman, 1925, Play

Swedish Fanny Hill, The *see* FANNY HILL (1968).

Swedish Heroes *see* SVENSKA HJALTAR (1997).

Swedish Match, The *see* SVEDSKAYA SPICKA (1954).

Swedish Wedding Night *see* BROLLOPSBESVAR (1964).

SWEENEY TODD 1928 d: Walter West. UKN., *Sweeney Todd; Or the Fiend of Fleet Street*, George Dibdin Pitt, London 1847, Play

SWEENEY TODD, THE DEMON BARBER OF FLEET STREET 1936 d: George King. UKN., *Sweeney Todd; Or the Fiend of Fleet Street*, George Dibdin-Pitt, London 1847, Play

SWEEPINGS 1933 d: John Cromwell. USA., *Sweepings*, Lester Cohen, New York 1926, Novel

Sweepstakes Millionaire *see* SUDDEN MONEY (1939).

SWEET ADELINE 1926 d: Jerome Storm. USA., *Sweet Adeline*, Harry Armstrong, Richard H. Gerrard, 1903, Song

SWEET ADELINE 1935 d: Mervyn Leroy. USA., *Sweet Adeline*, Oscar Hammerstein II, Jerome Kern, New York 1929, Musical Play

Sweet Aloes *see* GIVE ME YOUR HEART (1936).

SWEET ALYSSUM 1915 d: Colin Campbell. USA., *Sweet Alyssum; a Story of the Indiana Oilfields*, Charles Major, 1911, Short Story

SWEET AND TWENTY 1919 d: Sidney Morgan. UKN., *Sweet and Twenty*, Basil Hood, London 1901, Play

SWEET ANGEL MINE 1996 d: Curtis Radclyffe. UKN/CND., *Love's Executioners*, Tim Willocks

SWEET BIRD OF YOUTH 1962 d: Richard Brooks. USA., *Sweet Bird of Youth*, Tennessee Williams, New York 1959, Play

SWEET BIRD OF YOUTH 1989 d: Nicolas Roeg. USA., *Sweet Bird of Youth*, Tennessee Williams, New York 1959, Play

Sweet Bird of Youth *see* THE WITCHES (1989).

SWEET CHARITY 1969 d: Bob Fosse. USA., *Sweet Charity*, Cy Coleman, Dorothy Fields, Neil Simon, New York 1966, Play

Sweet Country *see* GLYKIA PATRIDA (1986).

SWEET HEREAFTER, THE 1997 d: Atom Egoyan. CND., *The Sweet Hereafter*, Russell Banks, Novel

SWEET HOSTAGE 1975 d: Lee Philips. USA., *Welcome to Xanadu*, Nathaniel Benchley, Novel

SWEET KITTY BELLAIRS 1916 d: James Young. USA., *Sweet Kitty Bellairs*, David Belasco, New York 1903, Play

SWEET KITTY BELLAIRS 1930 d: Alfred E. Green. USA., *Sweet Kitty Bellairs*, David Belasco, New York 1903, Play

SWEET LAVENDER 1915 d: Cecil M. Hepworth. UKN., *Sweet Lavender*, Arthur Wing Pinero, London 1888, Play

SWEET LAVENDER 1920 d: Paul Powell. USA., *Sweet Lavender*, Arthur Wing Pinero, London 1888, Play

Sweet Light in a Dark Room *see* JULIE A TMA ROMEO (1960).

Sweet Light in the Dark Window *see* JULIE A TMA ROMEO (1960).

SWEET LOVE, BITTER 1967 d: Herbert DanskA. USA., *Night Song*, John A. Williams, New York 1961, Novel

Sweet Person *see* ROZTOMILY CLOVEK (1941).

SWEET REVENGE 1987 d: Terence Young. USA/ITL., Tommy Iwering, Novel

SWEET RIDE, THE 1968 d: Harvey Hart. USA., *The Sweet Ride*, William Murray, New York 1967, Novel

SWEET ROSIE O'GRADY 1926 d: Frank Strayer. USA., *Sweet Rosie O'Grady*, Maude Nugent, 1896, Song

Sweet Scent of Death, A *see* UN DULCE OLOR A MUERTE (1999).

Sweet Sixteen *see* SEXTANKA (1936).

Sweet Sixteen *see* FUTURES VEDETTES (1955).

SWEET SMELL OF SUCCESS, THE 1957 d: Alexander MacKendrick. USA., *Tell Me About It Tomorrow*, Ernest Lehman, Novel

Sweet Time of Kalimagdora, The *see* DIE SUSSE ZEIT MIT KALIMAGDORA (1968).

SWEET WILLIAM 1980 d: Claude Whatham. UKN., *Sweet William*, Beryl Bainbridge, 1975, Novel

Sweetheart in Mask see **MASKOVANA MILENKA** (1940).

Sweethearts see **HOPE** (1919).

SWEETHEARTS 1938 d: W. S. Van Dyke. USA., *Sweethearts*, Fred de Gresac, Harry & Robert Smith, New York 1913, Opera

SWEETHEARTS AND WIVES 1930 d: Clarence Badger. USA., *Other Men's Wives*, Walter Hackett, Play 1929, Play

Sweetness of Sin, The see **DER TURM DER VERBOTENEN LIEBE** (1968).

SWELLHEAD, THE 1930 d: James Flood. USA., *Cyclone Hickey*, A. P. Younger, Story

SWEPT FROM THE SEA 1997 d: Beeban Kidron. UKN., *Amy Foster*, Joseph Conrad, Short Story

Swept from the Sea - the Story of Amy Foster see **SWEPT FROM THE SEA** (1997).

Swift Lightning see **CALL OF THE YUKON** (1938).

SWIFTY 1935 d: Alan James. USA., *Tracks*, Stephen Payne, 1928, Short Story

SWIMMER, THE 1968 d: Frank Perry, Sydney Pollack (Uncredited). USA., *The Swimmer*, John Cheever, 1964, Short Story

SWINDLER, THE 1919 d: Maurice Elvey. UKN., *The Swindler*, Ethel M. Dell, Novel

SWING HIGH, SWING LOW 1937 d: Mitchell Leisen. USA., *Burlesque*, Arthur Hopkins, George Manker Watters, New York 1927, Play

Swing, The see **DIE SCHAUKEL** (1983).

SWING YOUR LADY 1938 d: Ray Enright. USA., *Swing Your Lady*, Kenyon Nicholson, Charles Robinson, New York 1936, Play

SWINGING DOORS, THE 1915 d: Murdock MacQuarrie. USA., *The Swinging Doors*, Virginia Whitmore, Story

Swinging Pearl Mystery, The see **THE PLOT THICKENS** (1936).

SWISS FAMILY ROBINSON 1940 d: Edward Ludwig. USA., *Der Schweizerische Robinson*, Johann David Wyss, 1812-27, Novel

SWISS FAMILY ROBINSON 1961 d: Ken Annakin. UKN/USA., *Der Schweizerische Robinson*, Johann David Wyss, 1812-27, Novel

SWISS FAMILY ROBINSON 1971 d: Leif Gram. ASL., *Der Schweizerische Robinson*, Johann David Wyss, 1812-27, Novel

SWISS FAMILY ROBINSON 1975 d: Harry Harris. USA., *Der Schweizerische Robinson*, Johann David Wyss, 1812-27, Novel

Swiss Tour see **FOUR DAYS LEAVE** (1950).

Swiss Tour - Suzanne Et Son Marin see **FOUR DAYS LEAVE** (1950).

Swiss Tour B Xv see **FOUR DAYS LEAVE** (1950).

SWITCHING CHANNELS 1988 d: Ted Kotcheff. USA., *The Front Page*, Ben Hecht, Charles MacArthur, New York 1928, Play

SWORD AND THE ROSE, THE 1953 d: Ken Annakin. UKN/USA., *When Knighthood Was in Flower*, Charles Major, Indianapolis 1898, Novel

SWORD IN THE STONE, THE 1963 d: Wolfgang Reitherman. USA., *The Sword in the Stone*, T. H. White, London 1938, Novel

SWORD OF DAMOCLES, THE 1920 d: George Ridgwell. UKN., *Leonie*, H. V. Esmond, Play

Sword of Doom, The see **DAIBOSATSU TOGE** (1966).

SWORD OF FATE, THE 1921 d: Frances E. Grant. UKN., *The Sword of Fate*, Henry Herman, Novel

SWORD OF GIDEON, THE 1986 d: Michael Anderson. UKN/CND., *Vengeance*, George Jonas, Book

SWORD OF HONOUR 1967 d: Donald McWhinnie. UKN., *Sword of Honour*, Evelyn Waugh, Novel

Sword of Lancelot see **LANCELOT AND GUINEVERE** (1962).

Sword Stained With Royal Blood, The see **BI XUE JIAN** (1993).

Sword, The see **A KARD** (1976).

Swords and the Woman see **I WILL REPAY** (1923).

Swordsman of Siena see **LE MERCENAIRE** (1962).

Sworn Enemies see **SMERTELNI VRAG** (1971).

SWORN ENEMY 1936 d: Edwin L. Marin. USA., *It's All in the Racket*, Richard Wormser, Short Story

SWORN TO SILENCE 1987 d: Peter Levin. USA., *Privileged Information*, Tom Alibrandi, Frank H. Armani, Book

S/Y GLADJEN 1989 d: Goran Du Rees. SWD., *S/Y Gladjen*, Inger Alfven, Novel

S/Y Joy see **S/Y GLADJEN** (1989).

SYBIL 1921 d: Jack Denton. UKN., *Sybil*, Benjamin Disraeli, 1846, Novel

Sybil see **THE DUCHESS OF BUFFALO** (1926).

SYBIL 1976 d: Daniel Petrie. USA., *Sybil*, Flora Rheta Schreiber, Book

Sylvestre Bonnard see **CHASING YESTERDAY** (1935).

SYLVIA 1965 d: Gordon Douglas. USA., *Sylvia*, Howard Fast, New York 1960, Novel

SYLVIA 1985 d: Michael Firth. NZL., *I Passed This Way*, Sylvia Ashton-Warner, Book, *Teacher*, Sylvia Ashton-Warner, Book

Sylvia and the Ghost see **SYLVIE ET LE FANTOME** (1946).

SYLVIA SCARLETT 1936 d: George Cukor. USA., *The Early Life and Adventures of Sylvia Scarlett*, Compton Mackenzie, New York 1918, Novel

Sylvie and the Phantom see **SYLVIE ET LE FANTOME** (1946).

SYLVIE ET LE FANTOME 1946 d: Claude Autant-LarA. FRN., *Sylvie Et le Fantome*, Alfred Adam, Play

Sylvie's Ark see **HOUSEKEEPING** (1987).

Symphonie d'Amour see **LE DISQUE 413** (1936).

Symphonie Des Grauens, Eine see **NOSFERATU - EINE SYMPHONIE DES GRAUENS** (1921).

Symphonie Pastorale, La see **DENEN KOKYOGAKU** (1938).

SYMPHONIE PASTORALE, LA 1946 d: Jean Delannoy. FRN., *La Symphonie Pastorale*, Andre Gide, 1919, Novel

SYMPHONIE POUR UN MASSACRE 1963 d: Jacques Deray. FRN/ITL., *Les Mystifies*, Alain Reynaud-Fourton, Paris 1962, Novel

Symphony for a Massacre see **SYMPHONIE POUR UN MASSACRE** (1963).

SYMPHONY IN TWO FLATS 1930 d: V. Gareth Gundrey. UKN., *Symphony in Two Flats*, Ivor Novello, London 1929, Play

SYNCOPATING SUE 1926 d: Richard Wallace. USA., *Syncopating Sue*, Reginald Butler Goode, Play

SYNCOPATION 1929 d: Bert Glennon. USA., *Stepping High*, Gene Markey, Garden City, N.Y. 1929, Novel

SYNDERE I SOMMERSOL 1934 d: Einer Sissener. NRW., *Syndere I Sommersol*, Sigurd Hoel, 1928, Novel

SYNDICATE, THE 1968 d: Frederic Goode. UKN., *The Syndicate*, Denys Rhodes, New York 1960, Novel

SYNNOVE SOLBAKKEN 1934 d: Tancred Ibsen. SWD., *Synnove Solbakken*, Bjornstjerne Bjornson, 1857, Novel

SYNNOVE SOLBAKKEN 1957 d: Gunnar Hellstrom. SWD., *Synnove Solbakken*, Bjornstjerne Bjornson, 1857, Novel

SYNTHETIC SIN 1929 d: William A. Seiter. USA., *Synthetic Sin*, Fanny Hatton, Frederic Hatton, New York 1927, Play

SYSTEM 1971 d: Janusz Majewski. PLN., *The System of Doctor Tarr and Professor Feather*, Edgar Allan Poe, 1845, Short Story

System of Dr. Tarr and Professor Fether, The see **LA MANSION DE LA LOCURA** (1971).

SYSTEM, THE 1953 d: Lewis Seiler. USA., *Investigation*, Edith Grafton, Samuel Grafton, Story

SYSTEME DU DOCTEUR GOUDRON ET DU PROFESSEUR PLUME, LE 1980 d: Claude Chabrol. FRN., *The System of Doctor Tarr and Professor Feather*, Edgar Allan Poe, 1845, Short Story

SYTTEN 1965 d: Annelise Meineche. DNM., *Sytten: Erindringer Og Refleksioner*, Carl Erik Soya, Copenhagen 1953, Novel

SZAFFI 1986 d: Attila Dargay. HNG/GRM/CND., Mor Jokai, Novel

Szczesliwego Nowego Jorku see **SZCZESLIWEGO NOWEGO ROKU** (1997).

SZCZESLIWEGO NOWEGO ROKU 1997 d: Janusz Zaorski. PLN., *Miracle on Greenpoint*, Edward Redlinski, Novel, *Rat-Poles*, Edward Redlinski, Novel

SZEGENY GAZDAGOK 1959 d: Frigyes Ban. HNG., *Szegeny Gazdagok*, Mor Jokai, 1860, Novel

SZENT PETER ESERNYOJE 1958 d: Frigyes Ban. HNG/CZC., *Szent Peter Esernyoje*, Kalman Mikszath, 1895, Novel

SZENVEDELY 1998 d: Gyorgy Feher. HNG., *The Postman Always Rings Twice*, James M. Cain, 1934, Novel

SZERELEM 1970 d: Karoly Makk. HNG., *Ket Asszony*, Tibor Dery, 1962, Short Story, *Szerelem*, Tibor Dery, 1956, Short Story

SZERELEM HATARAI, A 1973 d: Janos Szucs. HNG., *A Szerelem Hatarai*, Judit Fenakel, Novel

SZERELMEM ELEKTRA 1974 d: Miklos Jancso. HNG., *Elektra Szerelmem*, Laszlo Gyurko, 1968, Play

SZINDBAD 1971 d: Zoltan Huszarik. HNG., *Szindbad Ifjusaga*, Gyula Krudy, 1911, Novel, *Szindbad Utazasai*, Gyula Krudy, 1912, Novel

SZINES TINTAKROL ALMODOM 1980 d: Laszlo Ranody. HNG., *Furdes*, Dezso Kosztolanyi, 1943, Short Story, *Kinai Kancso*, Dezso Kosztolanyi, 1943, Short Story, *A Kulcs*, Dezso Kosztolanyi, 1943, Short Story

SZKICE WEGLEM 1957 d: Antoni Bohdziewicz. PLN., *Szkice Weglem*, Henryk Sienkiewicz, 1877, Short Story

SZPITAL PRZEMIENIENIA 1978 d: Edward Zebrowski. PLN., *Szpital Przemienienia*, Stanislaw Lem, 1975, Novel

TA AI SHANG LE GU XIANG 1958 d: Huang Shu, Zhang Qi. CHN., *Plant in Spring - Harvest in Fall*, Kang Qu, Novel

TA RODINA AKROYIALIA 1998 d: Efthimios Hatzis. GRC., *Ta Rodina Akroyialia*, Alexandros Papadiamantis, Novel

TAAFE FANGA 1997 d: Adama Drabo. MLI/GRM., *Taafe Fanga*, Adama Drabo, Play

TAALLA POHJANTAHDEN ALLA 1968 d: Edvin Laine. FNL., *Taalla Pohjantahden Alla*, Vaino Linna, 1962, Novel

TABARANA KATHE 1986 d: Girish Kasaravalli. IND., *Tabarana Kathe*, Poornachandra Tejaswi, Short Story

Tabaranakathe see **TABARANA KATHE** (1986).

Tabara's Tale see **TABARANA KATHE** (1986).

TABLE AUX CREVES, LA 1951 d: Henri Verneuil. FRN., *La Table-aux-Creves*, Marcel Ayme, 1929, Novel

TABOR PADLYCH ZIEN 1998 d: Laco HalamA. SVK/GRM/CZE., *Tabor Padlych Zien*, Anton Balaz, Novel

TABULA RASA 1979 d: Bert Struys. BLG., *Tabula Rasa*, Roger Van de Velde, Novel

Tabula Rasa-Funf, Die Toten see **AN EINEM FREITAG UM HALB ZWOLF** (1961).

TABUSSE 1948 d: Jean Gehret. FRN., *Tabusse*, Andre Chamson, 1928, Novel

TACCHINO, IL 1925 d: Mario Bonnard. ITL., *Le Dindon*, Georges Feydeau, 1896, Play

TACKNAMEN: COQ ROUGE 1989 d: Pelle Berglund. SWD., *Tacknamen: Coq Rouge*, Jan Guillon, Novel

TAENK PA ET TAL 1969 d: Palle Kjaerulff-Schmidt. DNM., *Taenk Pa Et Tal (Think of a Number)*, Anders Bodelsen, 1968, Novel

TAFFIN 1988 d: Francis Megahy. UKN/IRL., *Taffin*, Lyndon Megahy, Novel

Taffin: a Different Kind of Hero see **TAFFIN** (1988).

Tag Mej - Alska Mej see **NANA** (1970).

TAGEBUCH 1975 d: Rudolf Thome. GRM., *Die Wahlverwandtschaften*, Johann Wolfgang von Goethe, 1809, Novel

TAGEBUCH DER GELIEBTEN, DAS 1936 d: Henry Koster. GRM/AUS., *Journal*, Maria Baschkirtzeff, 1885, Book

TAGEBUCH EINER VERLIEBTEN 1953 d: Josef von Baky. GRM., *Ich an Mich*, Dinah Nelken, Novel

TAGEBUCH EINER VERLORENEN 1929 d: G. W. Pabst. GRM., *Tagebuch Einer Verlorenen*, Margarethe Boehme, Novel

TAGGART 1964 d: R. G. Springsteen. USA., *Taggart*, Louis L'Amour, New York 1959, Novel

TAGGET 1991 d: Richard T. Heffron. USA., *Tagget*, Irving A. Greenfield, Novel

Tagget: Dragonfire see **TAGGET** (1991).

TAI YANG GANG GANG CHU SHAN 1960 d: Wang Yi. CHN., Ma Feng, Novel

Taifun see **IL CICLONE** (1916).

Taiheiyo Hitori Bochi see **TAIHEIYO HITORIBOTCHI** (1963).

TAIHEIYO HITORIBOTCHI 1963 d: Kon IchikawA. JPN., *Taiheiyo Hitoribotchi*, Kenichi Horie, Book

Taiheiyo No Jigoku *see* **HELL IN THE PACIFIC** (1968).

TAILOR MADE MAN, A 1922 d: Joseph de Grasse. USA., *A Szerencse Fia*, Gabor Dregely, Budapest 1908, Play

TAILOR MADE MAN, A 1931 d: Sam Wood. USA., *A Szerencse Fia*, Gabor Dregely, Budapest 1908, Play

TAILOR OF GLOUCESTER, THE 1990 d: John Michael Philips. UKN., *The Tailor of Gloucester*, Beatrix Potter, Story

Tailor-Made Man, A *see* **A TAILOR MADE MAN** (1931).

TAINATA NA APOLONIA 1984 d: Ivo Toman. BUL/CZC., *The Wrecker*, Lloyd Osbourne, Robert Louis Stevenson, 1892, Novel

TAINSTVENNI OSTROV 1941 d: E. Pentzlin, B. M. Chelintsev. USS., *L' Ile Mysterieuse*, Jules Verne, Paris 1874, Novel

TAINTED MONEY 1915 d: Ulysses Davis. USA., *Tainted Money*, George Edwardes Hall, Story

TAI-PAN 1986 d: Daryl Duke. USA., *Tai-Pan*, James Clavell, Novel

Taira Clan, The *see* **SHIN HEIKE MONOGATARI** (1955).

Tajemny Hrad V Karpatech *see* **TAJEMSTVI HRADU V KARPATECH** (1981).

Tajemny Prazsky Doktor *see* **MRTVI ZIJI** (1922).

TAJEMSTVI HRADU V KARPATECH 1981 d: Oldrich Lipsky. CZC., *Le Chateau Des Carpathes*, Jules Verne, 1892, Novel

Tajemstvi Hradu V Karpatech *see* **TAJEMSTVI HRADU V KARPATECH** (1981).

TAJEMSTVI LEKAROVO 1930 d: Julius Lebl. CZC., *Half an Hour*, J. M. Barrie, New York 1913, Play

TAJEMSTVI OCELOVEHO MESTA 1978 d: Ludvik RazA. CZC., Jules Verne, Novel

TAJNA KOROLEVY ANNY ILI MUSHKETERY TRIDCAT LET SPUSTJA 1993 d: Georgij Jungvald-Khilkevich. RSS., Alexandre Dumas (pere), Novel

TAKE A CHANCE 1933 d: Monte Brice, Laurence Schwab. USA., *Take a Chance*, Buddy De Sylva, Lawrence Schwab, New York 1932, Musical Play

TAKE A CHANCE 1937 d: Sinclair Hill. UKN., *Take a Chance*, Walter Hackett, 1931, Play

TAKE A GIANT STEP 1959 d: Philip Leacock. USA., *Take a Giant Step*, Louis S. Peterson, 1954, Play

TAKE A GIRL LIKE YOU 1969 d: Jonathan Miller. UKN., *Take a Girl Like You*, Kingsley Amis, London 1960, Novel

TAKE CARE OF MY LITTLE GIRL 1951 d: Jean Negulesco. USA., *Take Care of My Little Girl*, Peggy Goodin, 1950, Novel

Take Care, Red Riding Hood *see* **AKAZUKINCHAN KIOTSUKETE** (1970).

TAKE HER, SHE'S MINE 1963 d: Henry Koster. USA., *Take Her, She's Mine*, Henry Ephron, Phoebe Ephron, New York 1961, Play

Take It Easy *see* **MERRILY WE LIVE** (1938).

TAKE IT FROM ME 1926 d: William A. Seiter. USA., *Take It from Me*, Will Anderson, William B. Johnstone, Play

Take Me As I Am *see* **LES CANAILLES** (1959).

Take Me, Love Me *see* **NANA** (1970).

TAKE ME TO TOWN 1953 d: Douglas Sirk. USA., *Flame of the Timberline*, Richard Morris, Story

TAKE ONE FALSE STEP 1949 d: Chester Erskine. USA., *Night Call*, David Shaw, Irwin Shaw, Novel

TAKE, THE 1974 d: Robert Hartford-Davis. USA., *The Take*, G. F. Newman, Novel

TAKE THE STAND 1934 d: Phil Rosen. USA., *The Deuce of Hearts*, Earl Derr Biggers, Short Story

TAKEKURABE 1955 d: Heinosuke Gosho. JPN., *Takekurabe*, Ichiyo Higuchi, 1896, Novel

Taken for a Ride *see* **BOCKSHORN** (1983).

Takers, The *see* **MOMENT OF DANGER** (1960).

TAKI NO SHIRAITO 1933 d: Kenji Mizoguchi. JPN., *Taki No Shiraito*, Kyoka Izumi, Novel

TAKING A CHANCE 1928 d: Norman Z. McLeod. USA., *The Saint of Calamity Gulch*, Bret Harte, Short Story

TAKING OF PELHAM ONE-TWO-THREE, THE 1974 d: Joseph Sargent. USA., *The Taking of Pelham One-Two-Three*, John Godey, Novel

Tal Des Lebens, Das *see* **DER AMMENKONIG** (1935).

TALANTY I POKLONNIKI 1955 d: Andrey Apsolon, Boris Dmokhovski. USS., *Talanty I Poklonniki*, Alexander Ostrovsky, 1882, Play

TALANTY I POKLONNIKI 1973 d: Isider Annensky. USS., *Talanty I Poklonniki*, Alexander Ostrovsky, 1882, Play

Talbot of Canada *see* **HERE WILL I NEST** (1941).

Tale from Genji, A *see* **GENJI MONOGATARI** (1951).

Tale of a Dead Princess, The *see* **SKAZKA O MERTVOY TSAREVNE I O SEMI BOGATYRYAKH** (1951).

TALE OF BEATRIX POTTER, THE 1983 d: Bill Hays. UKN., *The Tale of Beatrix Potter*, Margaret Lane, Biography

Tale of Czar Saltan, The *see* **SKAZKA O TSARE SALTANE** (1967).

Tale of Genji, A *see* **GENJI MONOGATARI** (1951).

Tale of the Don, A *see* **DONSKAYA POVEST** (1964).

Tale of the Fisherman and the Little Fish *see* **SKAZKA O RYBAKE I RYBKE** (1937).

TALE OF THE FROG PRINCE 1982 d: Eric Idle. USA., *Der Froschkonig Oder Der Eiserne Heinrich*, Jacob Grimm, Wilhelm Grimm, 1812, Short Story

Tale of the Gallant Hong Yang, The *see* **HONG YANG HAOXIA ZHUAN** (1935).

Tale of the Unextinguished Moon, A *see* **POVEST NEPOGASHENOI LUNY** (1991).

Tale of Tsar Saltan, The *see* **SKAZKA O TSARE SALTANE** (1967).

TALE OF TWO CITIES, A 19— d: Michael E. Briant. UKN., *A Tale of Two Cities*, Charles Dickens, London 1859, Novel

TALE OF TWO CITIES, A 1911 d: William Humphrey. USA., *A Tale of Two Cities*, Charles Dickens, London 1859, Novel

TALE OF TWO CITIES, A 1917 d: Frank Lloyd. USA., *A Tale of Two Cities*, Charles Dickens, London 1859, Novel

TALE OF TWO CITIES, A 1922 d: W. C. Rowden. UKN., *A Tale of Two Cities*, Charles Dickens, London 1859, Novel

Tale of Two Cities, A *see* **THE ONLY WAY** (1925).

TALE OF TWO CITIES, A 1936 d: Jack Conway, W. S. Van Dyke (Uncredited). USA., *A Tale of Two Cities*, Charles Dickens, London 1859, Novel

TALE OF TWO CITIES, A 1958 d: Ralph Thomas. UKN., *A Tale of Two Cities*, Charles Dickens, London 1859, Novel

TALE OF TWO CITIES, A 1980 d: Jim Goddard. USA., *A Tale of Two Cities*, Charles Dickens, London 1859, Novel

TALE OF TWO CITIES, A 1984 d: Warwick Gilbert, Di Rudder. ASL., *A Tale of Two Cities*, Charles Dickens, London 1859, Novel

TALE OF TWO CITIES, A 1989 d: Philippe Monnier. UKN/FRN., *A Tale of Two Cities*, Charles Dickens, London 1859, Novel

Tales After the Rain *see* **UGETSU MONOGATARI** (1953).

TALES FROM THE DARKSIDE: THE MOVIE 1990 d: John Harrison. USA., *Lot 29*, Arthur Conan Doyle, Story, *Cat from Hell*, Stephen King, Story

Tales from the Vienna Woods *see* **GESCHICHTEN AUS DEM WIENERWALD** (1979).

TALES OF BEATRIX POTTER 1971 d: Reginald Mills. UKN., Beatrix Potter, Short Stories

Tales of Czar Tsaltan *see* **SKAZKA O TSARE SALTANE** (1967).

Tales of Erotica *see* **I GIOCHI PROIBITI DELL'ARETINO PIETRO** (1972).

Tales of Mystery *see* **HISTOIRES EXTRAORDINAIRES** (1968).

Tales of Ordinary Madness *see* **STORIE DI ORDINARIA FOLLIA** (1981).

TALES OF TERROR 1962 d: Roger Corman. USA., *The Black Cat*, Edgar Allan Poe, 1843, Short Story, *The Facts in the Case of M. Valdemar*, Edgar Allan Poe, 1845, Short Story, *Morella*, Edgar Allan Poe, 1835, Short Story

TALES OF THE CITY 1993 d: Alastair Reid. USA., Armistead Maupin, Novel

Tales of the Pale and Silvery Moon After the Rain *see* **UGETSU MONOGATARI** (1953).

Tales of the Taira Clan *see* **SHIN HEIKE MONOGATARI** (1955).

Tales of the Uncanny *see* **UNHEIMLICHE GESCHICHTEN** (1932).

TALE-TELLER PHONE, THE 1928 d: Arthur Stanley. UKN., *The Tale-Teller Phone*, Arthur Stanley, Play

Talgo *see* **XAFNIKOS EROTAS** (1984).

TALION, LE 1921 d: Charles Maudru. FRN., *Le Talion*, Pierre Maudru, Play

Talisman, The *see* **IL TALISMANO** (1911).

TALISMANO, IL 1911. ITL., *The Talisman*, Sir Walter Scott, 1825, Novel

TALK ABOUT A STRANGER 1952 d: David Bradley. USA., *The Enemy*, Charlotte Armstrong, Short Story

Talk About Jacqueline *see* **MAN SPRICHT UBER JACQUELINE** (1937).

TALK ABOUT JACQUELINE 1942 d: Paul L. Stein. UKN., *Talk About Jacqueline*, Katherine Holland, Novel

TALK OF A MILLION 1951 d: John Paddy Carstairs. UKN., *They Got What They Wanted*, Louis d'Alton, Play

TALK OF ANGELS 1998 d: Nick Hamm. USA., *Mary Lavelle*, Kate O'Brien, Novel

TALK OF THE TOWN, THE 1918 d: Allen Holubar. USA., *Discipline and Genevra*, Harold Vickers, 1917, Novel

TALK RADIO 1988 d: Oliver Stone. USA., *Talked to Death: the Life and Murder of Alan Berg*, Stephen Singular, Book

TALKER, THE 1925 d: Alfred E. Green. USA., *The Talker*, Marion Fairfax, New York 1912, Play

TALKIE OF TALKIES 1937 d: Sisir Kumar Bhaduri. IND., *Reetimata Natak*, Jaladhar Chattopadhyay, 1936, Play

Talking Caftan, The *see* **A BESZELO KONTOS** (1969).

TALKING WALLS 1984 d: Stephen F. VeronA. USA., *The Motel Tapes*, Mike McGrady, Novel

TALL HEADLINES, THE 1952 d: Terence Young. UKN., *The Tall Headlines*, Audrey Erskine Lindop, Novel

TALL MAN RIDING 1955 d: Lesley Selander. USA., *Tall Man Riding*, Norman A. Fox, 1951, Novel

TALL MEN, THE 1955 d: Raoul Walsh. USA., *The Tall Men*, Clay Fisher, 1954, Novel

TALL STORY 1960 d: Joshua Logan. USA., *Tall Story*, Russel Crouse, Howard Lindsay, New York 1959, Play

TALL STRANGER, THE 1957 d: Thomas Carr. USA., *Plunder*, Louis L'Amour, Story

TALL 'T', THE 1957 d: Budd Boetticher. USA., *The Captives*, Elmore Leonard, Story

Tall Timber *see* **PARK AVENUE LOGGER** (1937).

TALLY HO! 1901 d: Frank Parker. UKN., *Tally Ho!*, W. H. Risque, London 1901, Play

TALPALATNYI FOLD 1948 d: Frigyes Ban. HNG., *Bolcso*, Pal Szabo, Novel, *Keresztelo*, Pal Szabo, 1943, Novel, *Lakodalom*, Pal Szabo, 1942, Novel

TALVISOTA 1989 d: Pekka ParikkA. FNL., *Talvisota*, Antti Tuuri, 1984, Novel

TAM TAM MAYUMBE 1955 d: Gian Gaspare Napolitano, Folco Quilici. ITL/FRN., *La Mariposa*, G. G. Napolitano, Short Story

TAMAHINE 1963 d: Philip Leacock. UKN., *Tamahine*, Thelma Nicklaus, London 1957, Novel

TAMANGO 1957 d: John Berry. FRN/ITL., *Tamango*, Prosper Merimee, 1829, Short Story

TAMARA 1968 d: Hansjurgen Pohland. GRM., *Kein Schnaps Fur Tamara*, Hansjorg Martin, Novel

TAMARA LA COMPLAISANTE 1937 d: Felix Gandera, Jean Delannoy. FRN., *Tamara la Complaisante*, Georges-Andre Cuel, Novel

TAMARIND SEED, THE 1974 d: Blake Edwards. UKN., *The Tamarind Seed*, Evelyn Anthony, Novel

TAMAS 1986 d: Govind Nihalani. IND., *Tamas*, Bhishm Sahni, Novel

Tambour, Le *see* **DIE BLECHTROMMEL** (1979).

TAMBURINO SARDO, IL 1911. ITL., *Cuore*, Edmondo de Amicis, 1886, Short Story

TAMBURINO SARDO, IL 1915 d: Vittorio Rossi Pianelli. ITL., *Cuore*, Edmondo de Amicis, 1886, Short Story

TAME CAT, THE 1921 d: William Bradley. USA., *The Rajah's Diamond*, Robert Louis Stevenson, Short Story

Taming of Dorothy, The *see* **HER FAVOURITE HUSBAND** (1950).

TAMING OF THE SHREW 1908 d: D. W. Griffith. USA., *The Taming of the Shrew*, William Shakespeare, c1593, Play

TAMING OF THE SHREW, THE 1911. UKN., *The Taming of the Shrew*, William Shakespeare, c1593, Play

Taming of the Shrew, The see **LA BISBETICA DOMATA** (1913).

TAMING OF THE SHREW, THE 1915 d: Arthur Backner. UKN., *The Taming of the Shrew*, William Shakespeare, c1593, Play

TAMING OF THE SHREW, THE 1923 d: Edwin J. Collins. UKN., *The Taming of the Shrew*, William Shakespeare, c1593, Play

TAMING OF THE SHREW, THE 1929 d: Sam Taylor. USA., *The Taming of the Shrew*, William Shakespeare, c1593, Play

Taming of the Shrew, The see **LA FIERECILLA DOMADA** (1955).

TAMING OF THE SHREW, THE 1967 d: Franco Zeffirelli. USA/ITL., *The Taming of the Shrew*, William Shakespeare, c1593, Play

TAMING OF THE SHREW, THE 1976 d: William Ball, Kirk Browning. USA., *The Taming of the Shrew*, William Shakespeare, c1593, Play

TAMING OF THE SHREW, THE 1980 d: Jonathan Miller. UKN., *The Taming of the Shrew*, William Shakespeare, c1593, Play

TAMING OF THE SHREW, THE 1981 d: Peter Dews. USA., *The Taming of the Shrew*, William Shakespeare, c1593, Play

TAMING OF THE WEST, THE 1925 d: Arthur Rosson. USA., *The Range Dwellers*, Bertha Sinclair Muzzy, New York 1906, Novel

TAMING THE WILD 1936 d: Robert F. Hill. USA., *Shipmates*, Peter B. Kyne, Short Story

Tammy see **TAMMY AND THE BACHELOR** (1957).

TAMMY AND THE BACHELOR 1957 d: Joseph Pevney. USA., *Tammy Out of Time*, Cid Ricketts Sumner, Indianapolis 1948, Novel

TAMMY AND THE MILLIONAIRE 1967 d: Sidney Miller, Ezra C. Stone. USA., *Tammy Out of Time*, Cid Ricketts Sumner, Indianapolis 1948, Novel

TAMMY TELL ME TRUE 1961 d: Harry Keller. USA., *Tammy Tell Me True*, Cid Ricketts Sumner, Indianapolis 1959, Novel

Tampico see **THE WOMAN I STOLE** (1933).

TAMPON DU CAPISTON, LE 1930 d: Jean Toulout, Joe Francis. FRN., *Mam'zelle Culot*, Andre Mouezy-Eon, Alfred Vercourt, Opera

TAMPON DU CAPISTON, LE 1950 d: Maurice Labro. FRN., *Le Tampon du Capiston*, Andre Mouezy-Eon, Play

Tanacek Panny Marinky see **HOHEIT TANZT WALZER** (1935).

TANAMERA 1989 d: Kevin Dobson, John Power. ASL., *Tanamera*, Noel Barber, Novel

TANAR UR, KEREM! 1956 d: Frigyes Mamcserov. HNG., *Kerem! Tanar Ur*, Frigyes Karinthy, 1916, Short Story

TANASE SCATIU 1976 d: Dan PitA. RMN., *Tanase Scatiu*, Duiliu Zamfirescu, 1885-86, Novel

TANGE SAZEN 1963 d: Seiichiro UchikawA. JPN., *Tange Sazen*, Fubo Hayashi, Novel

TANGLED EVIDENCE 1934 d: George A. Cooper. UKN., *Tangled Evidence*, Mrs. Champion de Crespigny, Novel

Tangled Hearts see **THE WIFE WHOM GOD FORGOT** (1920).

TANGLED LIVES 1917 d: J. Gordon Edwards. USA., *The Woman in White*, Wilkie Collins, London 1860, Novel

TANGO 1936 d: Phil Rosen. USA., *Tango*, Vida Hurst, New York 1935, Novel

TANGO 1969 d: Vassil Mirchev. BUL., *Tango*, Georgi Karaslavov, 1948, Novel

TANIN NO KAO 1966 d: Hiroshi TeshigaharA. JPN., *Tanin No Kao*, Ade Kobo, 1964, Novel

TANITONO, A 1945 d: Marton Keleti. HNG., *A Tanitono*, Sandor Brody, 1908, Play

TANSSI YLI HAUTOJEN 1950 d: Toivo SaakkA. FNL., *Tanssi Yli Hautojen*, Mika Waltari, 1944, Novel

TANSY 1921 d: Cecil M. Hepworth. UKN., *Tansy*, Tickner Edwardes, Novel

TANT QU'IL Y AURA DES FEMMES 1955 d: Edmond T. Greville. FRN., *Tant Qu'il Y Aura Des Femmes*, Marcel Frank, Play

TANTE FRIEDA - NEUE LAUSBUBENGESCHICHTEN 1965 d: Werner Jacobs. GRM., *Tante Frieda*, Ludwig Thoma, Novel

TANTE JUTTA AUS KALKUTTA 1953 d: Karl G. Kulb. GRM., *Familie Hannemann*, Max Reimann, Otto Schwartz, Play

TANTE POSE 1940 d: Leif Sinding. NRW., *Tante Pose*, Gabriel Scott, 1904, Short Story

Tante Sbarre see **DIMENTICHI, L' ISTRUTTORIA E CHIUSA** (1971).

TANTEI JIMUSHO 2-3: KUTABARE AKUTODOMO 1963 d: Seijun Suzuki. JPN., *Tantei Jimusho 2-3: Kutabare Akutodomo*, Haruhiko Oyabu, Novel

TANTES 1984 d: Juul Claes. BLG., *Tantes*, Cyriel Buysse, 1924, Novel

TANZ GEHT WEITER, DER 1930 d: William Dieterle. USA., *Those Who Dance*, George Kibbe Turner, Story

TANZ INS GLUCK 1951 d: Alfred Stoger. AUS., *Tanz Ins Gluck*, Robert Bodansky, Bruno Hardt-Warden, Robert Stolz, Opera

TANZ MIT DEM KAISER, DER 1941 d: Georg Jacoby. GRM., *Die Nacht in Siebenburgen*, Nikolas Asztalos, Play

TANZENDE HERZ, DAS 1953 d: Wolfgang Liebeneiner. GRM., *Das Tanzende Herz*, W. F. Fichelscher, Novel

TAO 1923 d: Gaston Ravel. FRN., *Tao*, Arnould Galopin, Novel

TAO HUA SHAN 1963 d: Sun Jing. CHN., *Peach Flower Legend*, Kong Shangren, Play, *Peach Flower Fan*, Ouyang Yuqian, Play

TAP ROOTS 1948 d: George Marshall. USA., *Tap Roots*, James H. Street, Novel

TAPAGE NOCTURNE 1951 d: Marc-Gilbert Sauvajon. FRN., *Tapage Nocturne*, Marc-Gilbert Sauvajon, Play

Tapfere Heidemarie see **HEIDEMARIE** (1956).

TAPFERE SCHNEIDERLEIN, DAS 1956 d: Helmut Spiess. GDR., *Das Tapfere Schneiderlein*, Jacob Grimm, Wilhelm Grimm, Short Story

Tapfere Schneiderlein, Das see **SEDEM JEDNOU RANOU** (1988).

TAPS 1981 d: Harold Becker. USA., *Father Sky*, Devery Freeman, Novel

T.a.P.S. see **TAPS** (1981).

Tar Babies see **FANDO Y LIS** (1968).

TARAKANOVA 1930 d: Raymond Bernard. FRN., *Tarakanova*, Henri Dupuy-Mazuel, Novel

TARANTOS, LOS 1963 d: Francisco Rovira BeletA. SPN., *La Historia de Los Tarantos*, Alfredo Manas, Play

TARAS BULBA 1924 d: Wladimir von Strischewski. GRM., *Taras Bulba*, Nikolay Gogol, St. Petersburg 1835, Novel

Taras Bulba see **THE REBEL SON** (1938).

TARAS BULBA 1962 d: J. Lee Thompson. USA., *Taras Bulba*, Nikolay Gogol, St. Petersburg 1835, Novel

TARAS BULBA 2 1924 d: Wladimir von Strischewski. GRM., *Taras Bulba*, Nikolay Gogol, St. Petersburg 1835, Novel

TARAS BULBA, IL COSACCO 1963 d: Ferdinando Baldi. ITL., *Taras Bulba*, Nikolay Gogol, St. Petersburg 1835, Novel

TARASS BOULBA 1936 d: Alexis Granowsky. FRN., *Taras Bulba*, Nikolay Gogol, St. Petersburg 1835, Novel

TARDE OUTRA TARDE, UMA 1975 d: William Cobbett. BRZ., *Outra Tarde, Uma Tarde*, Josue Montello, 1968, Novel

Target see **ANNAPOLIS FAREWELL** (1935).

TARGET EARTH! 1954 d: Sherman A. Rose. USA., *The Deadly City*, Paul W. Fairman, Story

Target for an Assassin see **TIGERS DON'T CRY** (1976).

Target of an Assassin see **TIGERS DON'T CRY** (1976).

TARGET ZERO 1955 d: Harmon Jones. USA., *Bug Out*, James Warner Bellah, Story

TARKA THE OTTER 1978 d: David Cobham. UKN., *Tarka the Otto*, Henry Williamson, Novel

TARNAGOL KAPAROT 1991 d: Dan Wolman. ISR., Eli Amir, Book

TARNISH 1924 d: George Fitzmaurice. USA., *Tarnish*, Gilbert Emery, New York 1923, Play

TARNISHED 1950 d: Harry Keller. USA., *Turn Home*, Eleanor R. Mayo, 1945, Novel

TARNISHED ANGELS, THE 1957 d: Douglas Sirk. USA., *Pylon*, William Faulkner, 1935, Novel

Tarnovskata Tsaritsa see **TURNOVSKATA TSARITSA** (1981).

TAROT 1985 d: Rudolf Thome. GRM., *Die Wahlverwandtschaften*, Johann Wolfgang von Goethe, 1809, Novel

TARTARIN DE TARASCON 1934 d: Raymond Bernard. FRN., *Tartarin de Tarascon*, Alphonse Daudet, 1872, Novel

TARTARIN DE TARASCON 1962 d: Francis Blanche. FRN., *Tartarin de Tarascon*, Alphonse Daudet, 1872, Novel

TARTARIN SUR LES ALPES 1921 d: Henri Vorins, Paul Barlatier. FRN., *Tartarin Sur Les Alpes*, Alphonse Daudet, Novel

TARTUFF 1925 d: F. W. Murnau. GRM., *Tartuffe*, Moliere, 1669, Play

TARTUFFE 1908-18. FRN., *Tartuffe*, Moliere, 1669, Play

Tartuffe see **TARTUFF** (1925).

TARTUFFE 1963 d: Jean Meyer. FRN., *Tartuffe*, Moliere, 1669, Play

TARTUFFE DE MOLIERE, LE 1984 d: Jacques Lasalle, Gerard Depardieu. FRN., *Tartuffe*, Moliere, 1669, Play

Tartuffe the Hypocrite see **TARTUFF** (1925).

TARZAN AND THE GOLDEN LION 1927 d: J. P. McGowan. USA., *Tarzan and the Golden Lion*, Edgar Rice Burroughs, Chicago 1923, Novel

TARZAN OF THE APES 1918 d: Scott Sidney. USA., *Tarzan of the Apes*, Edgar Rice Burroughs, Chicago 1914, Novel

TARZAN THE APE MAN 1959 d: Joseph M. Newman. USA., *Tarzan of the Apes*, Edgar Rice Burroughs, Chicago 1914, Novel

TARZAN THE APE MAN 1981 d: John Derek. USA., *Tarzan of the Apes*, Edgar Rice Burroughs, Chicago 1914, Novel

TARZAN, THE APE MAN 1932 d: W. S. Van Dyke. USA., *Tarzan of the Apes*, Edgar Rice Burroughs, Chicago 1914, Novel

TASHUNGA 1996 d: Nils Gaup. NRW/FRN/UKN., *The North Star*, Will Henry, Novel

Taste for Death, A see **DALGLIESH: A TASTE FOR DEATH** (1988).

Taste for Women, A see **AIMEZ-VOUS LES FEMMES?** (1964).

TASTE OF EXCITEMENT 1969 d: Don Sharp. UKN., *Waiting for a Tiger*, Ben Healey, Novel

TASTE OF HEMLOCK, A 1988 d: Geoffrey Darwin. USA., *The Astrakhan Coat*, Pauline Macaulay, Play

TASTE OF HONEY, A 1961 d: Tony Richardson. UKN., *A Taste of Honey*, Shelagh Delaney, Stratford 1958, Play

Taste of Love, A see **LES GRANDES PERSONNES** (1961).

TAT DES ANDERN, DIE 1951 d: Helmut Weiss. GRM., *Die Unheimliche Schachpartie*, Paul Van Der Hurk, Novel

TATAL RISIPITOR 1974 d: Adrian Petringenaru. RMN., *Oaie Si Ai Sai*, Eugen Barbu, 1958, Short Story

Tatarenwuste, Die see **IL DESERTO DEI TARTARI** (1976).

TATI, A GAROTA 1973 d: Bruno Barreto. BRZ., *A Garota Tati*, Anibal Machado, 1959, Short Story

TATORT - SCHIMANSKI: SCHWARZES WOCHENENDE 1985 d: Dominik Graf. GRM., *Denunzianten*, Michael Hatry, Book

TATOUE, LE 1968 d: Denys de La Patelliere. FRN/ITL., *Gegene le Tatoue*, Alphonse Boudard, Novel

TATTERLY 1916 d: H. Lisle Lucoque. UKN., *Tatterly - the Story of a Dead Man*, Tom Gallon, New York 1897, Novel

TATTLERS, THE 1920 d: Howard M. Mitchell. USA., *The Penalty*, Henry Clifford Colwell, New York 1910, Play

TATUL 1972 d: Atanas Traikov. BUL., *Tatul*, Georgi Karaslavov, 1938, Novel

TAUGENICHTS 1978 d: Bernhard Sinkel. GRM., *Aus Dem Leben Eines Taugenichts*, Joseph von Eichendorff, 1826, Novel

TAUSEND FUR EINE NACHT 1932 d: Max Mack. GRM/CZC., *Stopsel*, Franz Robert Arnold, Ernst Bach, Play

Tausendjahrige Biene, Die see **TISICROCNA VCELA** (1983).

TAVERN KNIGHT, THE 1920 d: Maurice Elvey. UKN., *The Tavern Knight*, Rafael Sabatini, Novel

Taverne de Nouvelle-Orleans, La see **ADVENTURES OF CAPTAIN FABIAN** (1951).

TAVOLA DEI POVERI, LA 1932 d: Alessandro Blasetti. ITL., *La Tavola Dei Poveri*, Raffaele Viviani, Play

TAXI 1919 d: Lawrence C. Windom. USA., *Taxi!*, George Agnew Chamberlain, 1919, Short Story

Taxi see **HIT AND RUN** (1982).

TAXI 313 X 7, LE 1923 d: Piere Colombier. FRN., *Le Taxi 313 X 7*, Leonnec, Short Story

Taxi Colo Malva, Un see **UN TAXI MAUVE** (1977).

TAXI DANCER, THE 1926 d: Harry Millarde. USA., *The Taxi Dancer*, Robert Terry Shannon, Novel

TAXI MAUVE, UN 1977 d: Yves Boisset. FRN/IRL/ITL., *Un Taxi Mauve*, Michel Deon, 1973, Novel

TAXI! TAXI! 1927 d: Melville Brown. USA., *Taxi! Taxi!*, George Weston, 1925, Short Story

TAXI TO PARADISE 1933 d: Adrian Brunel. UKN., *Misconduct*, Graham Hope, Play

TAZZA DI THE, UNA 1923 d: Toddi. ITL., *Une Tasse de the*, N. Desarbres, Charles-Louis Nuitter, 1860

T-BONE 'N WEASEL 1992 d: Lewis Teague. USA., *T-Bone 'N Weasel*, John Klein, Novel

TCHAN KONDELIK A ZET VEJVARA 1929 d: Svatopluk Innemann. CZC., *Tchan Kondelik a Zet Vejvara*, Ignat Herrmann, Novel

TCHAO PANTIN 1983 d: Claude Berri. FRN., *Tchao Pantin*, Alain Page, Novel

TCHIORNI MONAK 1988 d: Ivan Dykhovichny. USS., *Chernyi Monakh*, Anton Chekhov, 1894, Short Story

Te Con Il Duce see **TEA WITH MUSSOLINI** (1999).

Te Nel Deserto, Il see **THE SHELTERING SKY** (1989).

TE QUIERO CON LOCURA 1935 d: John J. Boland. USA., *La Cura de Reposo*, Enrique Garcia Velloso, Madrid 1927, Play

TEA AND SYMPATHY 1956 d: Vincente Minnelli. USA., *Tea and Sympathy*, Robert Woodruff Anderson, New York 1953, Play

TEA AND TOAST 1913 d: C. Jay Williams, Charles H. France. USA., *The Postmaster*, Joseph C. Lincoln, Novel

TEA FOR THREE 1927 d: Robert Z. Leonard. USA., *Am Teetisch*, Carl Sloboda, Vienna 1915, Play

TEA FOR TWO 1950 d: David Butler. USA., *No No Nanette*, Otto Harbach, Frank Mandel, New York 1925, Musical Play

Tea in the Harem see **LE THE AU HAREM D'ARCHIMEDE** (1984).

TEA WITH MUSSOLINI 1999 d: Franco Zeffirelli. ITL/UKN., *The Autobiography of Franco Zeffirelli*, Franco Zeffirelli, Autobiography

Teahouse see **CHA GUAN** (1982).

TEAHOUSE OF THE AUGUST MOON, THE 1956 d: Daniel Mann. USA., *The Teahouse of the August Moon*, Vern J. Sneider, Novel

Tea-Leaf, The see **THE RAGMAN'S DAUGHTER** (1972).

Teamster Boss: the Jackie Presser Story see **POWER PLAY** (1992).

TEARS IN THE RAIN 1988 d: Don Sharp. UKN., *Tears in the Rain*, Pamela Wallace, Novel

TEASER, THE 1925 d: William A. Seiter. USA., *The Teaser*, Adelaide Matthews, Martha M. Stanley, New York 1921, Play

TED L'INVISIBILE 1922 d: Carlo Campogalliani. ITL., *La Canne*, Honore de Balzac

TEEN KANYA 1961 d: Satyajit Ray. IND., *Monihara*, Rabindranath Tagore, Short Story, *Postmastar*, Rabindranath Tagore, Short Story, *Samapti*, Rabindranath Tagore, Short Story

TEENAGE REBEL 1956 d: Edmund Goulding. USA., *A Roomful of Roses*, Edith Sommer, Play

Teenage Wolf Pack see **DIE HALBSTARKEN** (1956).

TEETH 1924 d: John G. Blystone. USA., *Teeth*, Clinton H. Stagg, 1917, Short Story

TELEFON 1977 d: Don Siegel. USA., *Telefon*, Walter Wager, Novel

TELEFONISTA, LA 1932 d: Nunzio MalasommA. ITL., Herbert Rosenfeld, Novel

TELEGRAME 1959 d: Gheorghe Naghi, Aurel Miheles. RMN., *Telegrame*, Ion Luca Caragiale, 1899, Short Story

Telegrams see **TELEGRAME** (1959).

TELEMACHUS, FRIEND 1920 d: David Smith. USA., *Telemachus, Friend*, O. Henry, Short Story

TELEPHONE GIRL, THE 1927 d: Herbert Brenon. USA., *The Woman*, William C. de Mille, New York 1911, Play

Teleurgang Van de Waterhoek, de see **MIRA** (1971).

Television see **MAGIE MODERNE** (1931).

TELEVISIONE 1931 d: Charles de Rochefort. FRN., Howard Irving Young, Play

Teli Sirokko see **SIROKKO** (1969).

TELL ENGLAND 1931 d: Anthony Asquith, Geoffrey Barkas. UKN., *Tell England*, Ernest Raymond, Novel

TELL IT TO THE JUDGE 1949 d: Norman Foster. USA., Devery Freeman, Story

TELL ME A RIDDLE 1980 d: Lee Grant. USA., *Tell Me a Riddle*, Tillie Olsen, Novel

TELL ME LIES 1968 d: Peter Brook. UKN., *Us*, Denis Cannan, Play

TELL ME MY NAME 1977 d: Delbert Mann. USA/CND., *Tell Me My Name*, Mary Carter, Book

Tell Me Nothing see **ERZAHL MIR NICHTS** (1964).

TELL ME THAT YOU LOVE ME, JUNIE MOON 1970 d: Otto Preminger. USA., *Tell Me That You Love Me Junie Moon*, Marjorie Kellogg, New York 1968, Novel

Tell the Truth see **SAG' DIE WAHRHEIT** (1946).

TELL THEM WILLIE BOY IS HERE 1969 d: Abraham Polonsky. USA., *Willie Boy; a Desert Manhunt*, Harry Lawton, Balboa Island, CA. 1960, Novel

TELL YOUR CHILDREN 1922 d: Donald Crisp. UKN., *Lark's Gate*, Rachel McNamara, Novel

TELL-TALE HEART, THE 1934 d: Brian Desmond Hurst. UKN., *The Tell-Tale Heart*, Edgar Allan Poe, 1843, Short Story

TELL-TALE HEART, THE 1953 d: J. B. Williams. UKN., *The Tell-Tale Heart*, Edgar Allan Poe, 1843, Short Story

TELL-TALE HEART, THE 1960 d: Ernest Morris. UKN., *The Tell-Tale Heart*, Edgar Allan Poe, 1843, Short Story

TELL-TALE HEART, THE 1973 d: Steve Carver. USA., *The Tell-Tale Heart*, Edgar Allan Poe, 1843, Short Story

TELO DIANA 1969 d: Jean-Louis Richard. CZC/FRN., *Le Corps de Diane*, Francois Nourissier, Novel

TEMNE SLUNCE 1980 d: Otakar VavrA. CZC., *Krakatit*, Karel Capek, 1924, Novel

TEMOIN, LE 1977 d: Jean-Pierre Mocky. FRN/ITL., *Shadow of a Doubt*, Harrison Judd, Novel

TEMPERAMENTAL WIFE, A 1919 d: David Kirkland. USA., *Information Please*, Jane Cowl, Jane Murfin, New York 1918, Play

TEMPERANCE FETE, THE 1931 d: Graham Cutts. UKN., *The Temperance Fete*, Herbert Jenkins, Story

TEMPEST 1983 d: Paul Mazursky. USA., *The Tempest*, William Shakespeare, c1611, Play

TEMPEST AND SUNSHINE 1914 d: Frank H. Crane. USA., *Tempest and Sunshine*, Mary Jane Holmes, New York 1844, Novel

TEMPEST AND SUNSHINE 1916 d: Carleton S. King, Warren Hughes. USA., *Tempest and Sunshine*, Mary Jane Holmes, New York 1844, Novel

Tempest (in a Teapot) see **TEMPETE DANS UN VERRE D'EAU** (1997).

Tempest in a Water Glass see **STURM IM WASSERGLAS** (1960).

Tempest in May see **GEWITTER IM MAI** (1988).

TEMPEST, THE 1905 d: Charles Urban. UKN., *The Tempest*, William Shakespeare, c1611, Play

TEMPEST, THE 1911. USA., *The Tempest*, William Shakespeare, c1611, Play

Tempest, The see **LA TEMPESTA** (1958).

TEMPEST, THE 1960 d: George Schaefer. USA., *The Tempest*, William Shakespeare, c1611, Play

Tempest, The see **BAOFENG-ZHOUYU** (1961).

TEMPEST, THE 1969 d: Nicholas Young, David Snasdell. UKN., *The Tempest*, William Shakespeare, c1611, Play

TEMPEST, THE 1972 d: Mats Lonnerblad. SWD., *The Tempest*, William Shakespeare, c1611, Play

TEMPEST, THE 1979 d: John Gorrie. UKN., *The Tempest*, William Shakespeare, c1611, Play

TEMPEST, THE 1979 d: Derek Jarman. UKN., *The Tempest*, William Shakespeare, c1611, Play

TEMPESTA, LA 1958 d: Alberto Lattuada, Michelangelo Antonioni (Uncredited). ITL/FRN/YGS., *Kapitanskaya Dochka*, Alexander Pushkin, 1836, Short Story

Tempestuous Love see **WIE EIN STURMWIND** (1957).

TEMPETE DANS UN VERRE D'EAU 1997 d: Arnold Barkus. FRN/USA., *Femme de Berroyer Est Plus Belle Que Toi - Connasse!*, Jackie Berroyer, Novel

Tempete, La see **LA TEMPESTA** (1958).

TEMPIO DEL SACRIFICIO, IL 1920 d: Luigi Mele. ITL., *Il Tempio Del Sacrificio*, Miriam Klington, Novel

Tempio Dell'elefante Bianco, Il see **IL MACISTE DELLA GIUNGLA SANDOK** (1964).

Temple de l'Elephant Blanc, Le see **IL MACISTE DELLA GIUNGLA SANDOK** (1964).

Temple of Dawn, The see **THE PRICE OF REDEMPTION** (1920).

Temple of Dusk, The see **WITHOUT LIMIT** (1921).

Temple of Shadows, The see **LA VESTALE DU GANGE** (1927).

Temple of the White Elephants see **IL MACISTE DELLA GIUNGLA SANDOK** (1964).

TEMPLE TOWER 1930 d: Donald Gallaher. USA., *Temple Tower*, H. C. McNeile ("Sapper"), Garden City, N.Y. 1929, Novel

Tempo Di Charleston see **FEBBRE DI VIVERE** (1953).

TEMPO DI ROMA 1964 d: Denys de La Patelliere. FRN/ITL., *La Ville Eternelle*, Alexis Curvers, Novel

Tempo Dificeis, Este Tempo see **TEMPOS DIFICEIS** (1988).

Temporal Power see **IL POTERE SOVRANO** (1916).

TEMPORALE ROSY 1979 d: Mario Monicelli. ITL/FRN/GRM., *Temporale Rosy*, Carlo Brizzolara, Novel

Temporary Fiancee see **THIS IS THE NIGHT** (1932).

TEMPORARY GENTLEMAN, A 1920 d: Fred W. Durrant. UKN., *A Temporary Gentleman*, H. F. Maltby, London 1919, Play

TEMPORARY WIDOW, THE 1930 d: Gustav Ucicky. UKN/GRM., *Hokuspokus*, Curt Goetz, Play

TEMPOS DIFICEIS 1988 d: Joao Botelho. PRT/UKN., *Hard Times*, Charles Dickens, London 1854, Novel

TEMPS DE VIVRE, LE 1969 d: Bernard Paul. FRN., *Le Temps de Vivre*, Andre Remacle, Novel

Temps Des Amants, Le see **AMANTI** (1968).

Temps d'un Reflet, Le see **QUAI NOTRE-DAME** (1960).

TEMPTATION 1934 d: Max Neufeld. UKN., *Antonia*, Melchior Lengyel, Play

TEMPTATION 1946 d: Irving Pichel. USA., *Bella Donna*, Robert Hichens, London 1909, Novel

Temptation see **L' ILE DU BOUT DU MONDE** (1958).

TEMPTATION HARBOUR 1947 d: Lance Comfort. UKN., *L' Homme de Londres*, Georges Simenon, 1934, Novel

Temptation in Glamour Island see **GURAMA-TO NO YUWAKU** (1959).

Temptation Island see **L' ILE DU BOUT DU MONDE** (1958).

TEMPTATION OF CARLTON EARLYE, THE 1923 d: Wilfred Noy. UKN., *The Temptation of Carlton Earlye*, Stella During, Novel

Tempting Luck see **THE HUNCH** (1921).

Temptress and the Monk, The see **BYAKUYA NO YOJO** (1958).

TEMPTRESS, THE 1920 d: George Edwardes Hall. UKN., *L' Aventuriere*, Emile Paul Augier, Play, *Home*, T. W. Robertson, London 1869, Play

TEMPTRESS, THE 1926 d: Fred Niblo, Mauritz Stiller. USA., *La Tierra de Todos*, Vicente Blasco Ibanez, Novel

TEMPTRESS, THE 1949 d: Oswald Mitchell. UKN., *Juggernaut*, Alice Campbell, Novel

Temptress, The see **BYAKUYA NO YOJO** (1958).

Ten Billion Dollar Vitagraph Mystery Serial, The see **THE FATES AND FLORA FOURFLUSH** (1914).

TEN DAYS IN PARIS 1939 d: Tim Whelan. UKN., *The Disappearance of Roger Tremayne*, Bruce Graeme, Novel

Ten Days to Die see **DER LETZTE AKT** (1955).

Ten Dollar Raise see **$10 RAISE** (1935).

TEN DOLLAR RAISE, THE 1921 d: Edward Sloman. USA., *The Ten Dollar Raise*, Peter B. Kyne, 1909, Short Story

TEN LITTLE INDIANS 1965 d: George Pollock. UKN., *Ten Little Niggers*, Agatha Christie, London 1939, Novel

Ten Little Indians *see* **AND THEN THERE WERE NONE** (1974).

Ten Little Negroes *see* **ZEHN KLEINE NEGERLEIN** (1954).

Ten Little Niggers *see* **AND THEN THERE WERE NONE** (1945).

Ten Little Niggers *see* **AND THEN THERE WERE NONE** (1974).

TEN MINUTE ALIBI 1935 d: Bernard Vorhaus. UKN., *Ten Minute Alibi*, Anthony Armstrong, London 1933, Play

TEN NIGHTS IN A BAR ROOM 1911 d: Frank Boggs. USA., *Ten Nights in a Bar Room and What I Saw There*, Timothy Shay Arthur, Philadelphia 1839, Novel

TEN NIGHTS IN A BAR ROOM 1921 d: Oscar Apfel. USA., *Ten Nights in a Bar-Room and What I Saw There*, Timothy Shay Arthur, Philadelphia 1839, Novel

TEN NIGHTS IN A BARROOM 1913 d: Lee Beggs. USA., *Ten Nights in a Bar-Room and What I Saw There*, Timothy Shay Arthur, Philadelphia 1839, Novel

TEN NIGHTS IN A BAR-ROOM 1926 d: Roy Calnek. USA., *Ten Nights in a Bar-Room and What I Saw There*, Timothy Shay Arthur, Philadelphia 1839, Novel

TEN NORTH FREDERICK 1958 d: Philip Dunne. USA., *Ten North Frederick*, John O'Hara, 1955, Novel

Ten Rillington Place *see* **RILLINGTON PLACE 10** (1971).

TEN SECONDS TO HELL 1959 d: Robert Aldrich. UKN/USA., *The Phoenix*, Lawrence P. Bachmann, 1955, Novel

T'en Souviens-Tu Mon Amour? *see* **LES MARIS DE LEONTINE** (1947).

Ten Years a Counterspy *see* **MAN ON A STRING** (1960).

TENANT OF WILDFELL HALL, THE 1996 d: Mike Barker. UKN., *The Tenant of Wildfell Hall*, Anne Bronte, 1848, Novel

TENANT, THE 1976 d: Roman Polanski. USA/FRN., *Le Locataire*, Roland Topor, 1934, Novel

TEN-CENT ADVENTURE, A 1915 d: Sidney A. Franklin, Chester M. Franklin. USA., *A Ten-Cent Adventure*, Anita Loos, Story

TENDA DOS MILAGRES 1977 d: Nelson Pereira Dos Santos. BRZ., *Tenda Dos Milagres*, Jorge Amado, 1969, Novel

Tender Age, The *see* **ADOLPHE OU L'AGE TENDRE** (1968).

Tender Enemy, The *see* **LA TENDRE ENNEMIE** (1935).

TENDER IS THE NIGHT 1962 d: Henry King. USA., *Tender Is the Night*, F. Scott Fitzgerald, New York 1934, Novel

TENDER IS THE NIGHT 1985 d: Robert Knights. UKN/USA., *Tender Is the Night*, F. Scott Fitzgerald, New York 1934, Novel

Tender Relationships *see* **KREHKE VZTAHY** (1979).

Tender Secret *see* **ZARTLICHES GEHEIMNIS** (1956).

Tender Skin in Black Silk *see* **ZARTE HAUT IN SCHWARZER SEIDE** (1961).

TENDER TRAP, THE 1955 d: Charles Walters. USA., *The Tender Trap*, Max Shulman, Robert Paul Smith, New York 1954, Play

TENDERFOOT, THE 1917 d: William Duncan. USA., *The Tenderfoot*, Alfred Henry Lewis, Short Story

TENDERFOOT, THE 1932 d: Ray Enright. USA., *The Tenderfoot*, Richard Carle, Chicago 1903, Play, *The Butter and Egg Man*, George S. Kaufman, New York 1925, Play

TENDERFOOT, THE 1966 d: Byron Paul. USA., *Arizona in the '50S*, James H. Tevis, Novel

TENDERFOOT'S TRIUMPH, THE 1910 d: Frank Powell, D. W. Griffith. USA., *The Butter and Egg Man*, Arthur Caesar, Novel

TENDRE ENNEMIE, LA 1935 d: Max Ophuls. FRN., *L' Ennemie*, Andre-Paul Antoine, Play

TENDRE ET VIOLENTE ELISABETH 1960 d: Henri Decoin. FRN., *Tendre Et Violente Elisabeth*, Henri Troyat, 1957, Novel

TENDRE POULET 1978 d: Philippe de BrocA. FRN., *Tendre Poulet*, Claude Olivier, J. P. Rouland, Novel

TENDRES COUSINES 1980 d: David Hamilton. FRN/GRM., *Tendres Cousins*, Pascal Laine, Novel

TENDRESSE, LA 1930 d: Andre Hugon. FRN., *La Tendresse*, Henry Bataille, 1921, Play

Tenement, The *see* **O CORTICO** (1945).

TENENTE GIORGIO, IL 1952 d: Raffaello Matarazzo. ITL., *Il Tenente Giorgio*, Nicola Misasi, Novel

TENGOKU TO JIGOKU 1963 d: Akira KurosawA. JPN., *King's Ransom*, Evan Hunter, 1959, Novel

Teni Zabytykh Predkov *see* **TINE ZABUTYKH PREDKIV** (1965).

TENKAWA DENSETSU SATSUJIN JIKEN 1991 d: Kon IchikawA. JPN., *Tenkawa Densetsu Satsujin Jiken*, Yasuo Uchida, Novel

TENNESSEE CHAMP 1953 d: Fred M. Wilcox. USA., *The World in His Corner*, Eustace Cockrell, Short Story

Tennessee Nights *see* **TENNESSEE WALTZ** (1989).

Tennessee Valley *see* **THE ONLY THRILL** (1997).

TENNESSEE WALTZ 1989 d: Nicolas Gessner. SWT/USA., *Minnie*, Hans Werner Kettenbach, Novel

TENNESSEE'S PARDNER 1916 d: George Melford. USA., *Tennessee's Partner*, Bret Harte, 1869, Short Story

TENNESSEE'S PARTNER 1955 d: Allan Dwan. USA., *Tennessee's Partner*, Bret Harte, 1869, Short Story

TENSION AT TABLE ROCK 1956 d: Charles Marquis Warren. USA., *Bitter Sage*, Frank Gruber, 1954, Novel

Tent of Miracles *see* **TENDA DOS MILAGRES** (1977).

TENTACLES OF THE NORTH 1926 d: Louis W. Chaudet. USA., *Tentacles of the North*, James Oliver Curwood, 1915, Short Story

TENTATION, LA 1929 d: Rene Barberis, Rene Leprince. FRN., *La Tentation*, Charles Mere, Play

TENTATION, LA 1936 d: Pierre Caron. FRN., *La Tentation*, Charles Mere, Play

TENTAZIONI DI SANT'ANTONIO, LE 1911. ITL., *La Tentation de Saint Antoine*, Gustave Flaubert, 1849

TENTH AVENUE 1928 d: William C. de Mille. USA., *Tenth Avenue*, Lloyd Griscom, John McGowan, New York 1927, Play

TENTH MAN, THE 1936 d: Brian Desmond Hurst. UKN., *The Tenth Man*, W. Somerset Maugham, 1913, Play

TENTH MAN, THE 1988 d: Jack Gold. UKN., *The Tenth Man*, Graham Greene, Novel

TENTH MONTH, THE 1979 d: Joan Tewkesbury. USA., *The Tenth Month*, Laura Z. Hobson, Novel

TENTH WOMAN, THE 1924 d: James Flood. USA., *The Tenth Woman*, Harriet T. Comstock, Garden City, N.Y. 1923, Novel

TEODORA 1922 d: Leopoldo Carlucci. ITL., *Theodora*, Victorien Sardou, 1884, Play

TEODORA, IMPERATRICE DI BISANZIO 1954 d: Riccardo FredA. ITL/FRN., *Theodora*, Victorien Sardou, 1884, Play

Teodora, l'Imperatrice Di Bisanzio *see* **IMPERATRICE DI BISANZIO TEODORA** (1954).

TEODORO E SOCIO 1925 d: Mario Bonnard. ITL., *Theodore Et Cie*, Robert Armont, Nicolas Nancey, 1909, Play

TEOREMA 1968 d: Pier Paolo Pasolini. ITL., *Teorema*, Pier Paolo Pasolini, Milan 1968, Novel

TEPPICH DES GRAUENS, DER 1962 d: Harald Reinl. GRM/ITL/SPN., *Der Teppich Des Grauens*, Louis Weinert-Wilton, Novel

TERE MERE SAPNE 1971 d: Vijay Anand. IND., *The Citadel*, A. J. Cronin, 1937, Novel

TERESA CONFALONIERI 1934 d: Guido Brignone. ITL., *Il Conte Aquila*, Rino Alessi, Play

Teresa Etienne *see* **THERESE ETIENNE** (1957).

Teresa Hennert's Love Affair *see* **ROMANS TERESY HENNERT** (1978).

Teresa Hennert's Romance *see* **ROMANS TERESY HENNERT** (1978).

TERESA LA LADRA 1973 d: Carlo Di PalmA. ITL., *Memorie Di Una Ladra*, Dacia Maraini, Novel

TERESA RAQUIN 1914 d: Nino Martoglio. ITL., *Therese Raquin*, Emile Zola, 1867, Novel

Teresa Raquin *see* **THERESE RAQUIN** (1953).

Teresa the Thief *see* **TERESA LA LADRA** (1973).

TERESA VENERDI 1941 d: Vittorio de SicA. ITL., *Teresa Venerdi*, Rudolf Torok, Novel

TERM OF TRIAL 1962 d: Peter Glenville. UKN., *Term of Trial*, James Barlow, London 1961, Novel

TERMINAL MAN, THE 1973 d: Mike Hodges. USA., *The Terminal Man*, Michael Crichton, Novel

Terminal Station *see* **STAZIONE TERMINI** (1953).

Terminate With Extreme Prejudice *see* **S.A.S. A SAN SALVADOR** (1982).

TERMS OF ENDEARMENT 1983 d: James L. Brooks. USA., *Terms of Endearment*, Larry McMurtry, 1975, Novel

TERRA DI NESSUNO 1939 d: Mario Baffico. ITL., *Requiem Aeternam Dona Eis Domine!*, Luigi Pirandello, 1913, Short Story

Terra Senza Donne *see* **DAS LAND OHNE FRAUEN** (1929).

TERRAIN VAGUE 1960 d: Marcel Carne. FRN/ITL., *Tomboy*, Hal Ellison, Novel

Terre d'Angoisse *see* **DEUXIEME BUREAU CONTRE KOMMANDANTUR** (1939).

Terre Etrangere *see* **DAS WEITE LAND** (1987).

TERRE, LA 1921 d: Andre Antoine. FRN., *La Terre*, Emile Zola, Novel

TERRE QUI MEURT, LA 1926 d: Jean Choux. FRN., *La Terre Qui Meurt*, Rene Bazin, 1899, Novel

TERRE QUI MEURT, LA 1936 d: Jean Vallee. FRN., *La Terre Qui Meurt*, Rene Bazin, 1899, Novel

TERREUR DES DAMES, LA 1956 d: Jean Boyer. FRN., *Ce Cochon de Morin*, Guy de Maupassant, 1883, Short Story

Terreur Des Gladiateurs, La *see* **EROE SENZA PATRIA CORIOLANO** (1965).

TERRIBLE BEAUTY, A 1960 d: Tay Garnett. UKN., *A Terrible Beauty*, Arthur Roth, Novel

Terrible Lola, La *see* **DIE TOLLE LOLA** (1927).

Terrible Night, The *see* **NOCHE TERRIBLE** (1967).

Terrible People, The *see* **DIE BANDE DES SCHRECKENS** (1960).

TERRIBLE TRUTH, THE 1915 d: Lynn Reynolds. USA., *The Terrible Truth*, Harvey Gates, Story

Terrier and the Child, The *see* **THE DOP DOCTOR** (1915).

TERRITORIO COMANCHE 1997 d: Gerardo Herrero. SPN/GRM/FRN., *Territorio Comanche*, Arturo Perez-Reverte, Novel

TERRONAUTS, THE 1967 d: Montgomery Tully. UKN., *The Waiting Asteroid*, Murray Leinster, New York 1961, Novel

Terror *see* **MOCKERY** (1927).

Terror After Midnight *see* **NEUNZIG MINUTEN NACH MITTERNACHT** (1962).

TERROR AT BLACK FALLS 1962 d: Richard C. Sarafian. USA., *Terror at Black Falls*, Charles Martin, Novel

Terror Band *see* **DIE BANDE DES SCHRECKENS** (1960).

Terror By Night *see* **THE SECRET WITNESS** (1931).

TERROR BY NIGHT 1946 d: R. William Neill. USA., *The Empty House*, Arthur Conan Doyle, 1903, Short Story

Terror Castle *see* **LA VERGINE DI NORIMBERGA** (1963).

TERROR E EXTASE 1980 d: Antonio Calmon. BRZ., *Terror E Extase*, Jose Carlos de Oliveira, 1978, Novel

Terror En El Espacio *see* **TERRORE NELLO SPAZIO** (1965).

Terror En la Noche *see* **DER TEPPICH DES GRAUENS** (1962).

Terror from Space *see* **TERRORE NELLO SPAZIO** (1965).

Terror House *see* **THE NIGHT HAS EYES** (1942).

TERROR IN BEVERLY HILLS 1988 d: John Myhers. USA., *Terror in Beverly Hills*, Simon Bibiyan, Novel

Terror in the Crypt *see* **LA CRIPTA E L'INCUBO** (1964).

TERROR IN THE SHADOWS 1995 d: William A. Graham. USA., *Night of Reunion*, Michael Allegretto, Book

TERROR IN THE SKY 1971 d: Bernard L. Kowalski. USA., *Runway Zero 8*, Arthur Hailey, Novel

TERROR IS A MAN 1959 d: Gerardo de Leon. USA., *The Island of Dr. Moreau*, H. G. Wells, London 1896, Novel

TERROR OF BAR X, THE 1927 d: Scott Pembroke. USA., *Cowboy Stan Willis*, George M. Johnson, Story

Terror of Dr. Frankenstein *see* **VICTOR FRANKENSTEIN** (1977).

Terror of Dr. Mabuse, The *see* **DAS TESTAMENT DES DR. MABUSE** (1962).

Terror of Dracula, The *see* **NOSFERATU - EINE SYMPHONIE DES GRAUENS** (1921).

Terror of Frankenstein *see* **VICTOR FRANKENSTEIN** (1977).

977

Terror of the Mad Doctor see DAS TESTAMENT DES DR. MABUSE (1962).

Terror on a Train see TIME BOMB (1952).

Terror on Half Moon Street see DER MANN MIT DEM GLASAUGE (1968).

TERROR ON TIPTOE 1936 d: Louis Renoir. UKN., *Shadow Man*, Ingram d'Abbes, Fenn Sherie, Play

TERROR, THE 1928 d: Roy Del Ruth. USA., *The Terror*, Edgar Wallace, London 1927, Play

TERROR, THE 1938 d: Richard Bird. UKN., *The Terror*, Edgar Wallace, London 1927, Play

TERROR TRAIL 1933 d: Armand Schaefer. USA., *Riders of Terror Trail*, Grant Taylor, 1926, Short Story

Terrore see DANZA MACABRA (1964).

Terrore Di Notte, Il see DER TEPPICH DES GRAUENS (1962).

TERRORE NELLO SPAZIO 1965 d: Mario BavA. ITL/SPN/USA., *Una Notte Di 21 Ore*, Renato Pestriniero, Short Story

Terrornauts, The see THE TERRONAUTS (1967).

TERRY ON THE FENCE 1987 d: Frank Godwin. UKN., *Terry on the Fence*, Bernard Ashley, Novel

TERZO OCCHIO, IL 1966 d: Mino Guerrini. ITL., Gilles de Reys, Story

TESHA 1928 d: Victor Saville. UKN., *Tesha*, Countess Barcynska, Novel

TESORO DEL BENGALA, IL 1954 d: Gianni Vernuccio. ITL., Emilio Salgari, Novel

Tesoro Dell'africa, Il see BEAT THE DEVIL (1953).

Tesoro Di Montecristo, Il see LE COMTE DE MONTE-CRISTO (1953).

TESORO MIO 1979 d: Giulio Paradisi. ITL., *Cherie Noire*, Francois Campaux, Play

Tesoromio see TESORO MIO (1979).

TESS 1980 d: Roman Polanski. UKN/FRN., *Tess of the d'Urbervilles*, Thomas Hardy, London 1891, Novel

TESS OF THE D'URBERVILLES 1913 d: J. Searle Dawley. USA., *Tess of the d'Urbervilles*, Thomas Hardy, London 1891, Novel

TESS OF THE D'URBERVILLES 1924 d: Marshall Neilan. USA., *Tess of the d'Urbervilles*, Thomas Hardy, London 1891, Novel

TESS OF THE D'URBERVILLES 1998 d: Ian Sharp. UKN., *Tess of the d'Urbervilles*, Thomas Hardy, London 1891, Novel

TESS OF THE STORM COUNTRY 1914 d: Edwin S. Porter. USA., *Tess of the Storm Country*, Grace Miller White, New York 1909, Novel

TESS OF THE STORM COUNTRY 1922 d: John S. Robertson. USA., *Tess of the Storm Country*, Grace Miller White, New York 1909, Novel

TESS OF THE STORM COUNTRY 1932 d: Alfred Santell. USA., *Tess of the Storm Country*, Grace Miller White, New York 1909, Novel

TESS OF THE STORM COUNTRY 1961 d: Paul Guilfoyle. USA., *Tess of the Storm Country*, Grace Miller White, New York 1909, Novel

TESSIE 1925 d: Dallas M. Fitzgerald. USA., *Tessie and the Little Sap*, Sewell Ford, 1925, Short Story

TEST OF DONALD NORTON, THE 1926 d: B. Reeves Eason. USA., *The Test of Donald Norton*, Robert E. Pinkerton, Chicago 1924, Novel

TEST OF HONOR, THE 1919 d: John S. Robertson. USA., *Mr. Wingrave - Millionaire (the Malefactor)*, E. Phillips Oppenheim, London 1904, Novel

Test of Love, A see ANNIE'S COMING OUT (1984).

Test of Pilot Pirx, The see TEST PILOTA PIRXA (1978).

Test of Strength see KRAFTPROBE (1982).

TEST OF WOMANHOOD, THE 1917. USA., *The Conquerors*, Paul M. Potter, New York 1898, Play

Test Pilot Pirx see TEST PILOTA PIRXA (1978).

TEST PILOTA PIRXA 1978 d: Marek Piestrak. PLN/USS., *Test Pilota Pirxa*, Stanislaw Lem, Short Story

TEST, THE 1916 d: George Fitzmaurice. USA., R. E. McGlinn, J. Quinlan, Play

TEST, THE 1923 d: Edwin Greenwood. UKN., *Madame Firmiani*, Honore de Balzac, Short Story

TESTAMENT 1983 d: Lynne Littman. USA., *The Last Testament*, Carol Amen, Story

TESTAMENT DES DR. MABUSE, DAS 1933 d: Fritz Lang. GRM., *Dr. Mabuse*, Norbert Jacques, Novel

TESTAMENT DES DR. MABUSE, DAS 1962 d: Werner Klinger. GRM., *Dr. Mabuse*, Norbert Jacques, Novel

TESTAMENT DU DR. CORDELIER, LE 1959 d: Jean Renoir. FRN., *The Strange Case of Dr. Jekyll and Mr. Hyde*, Robert Louis Stevenson, London 1886, Novel

TESTAMENT D'UN POETE JUIF ASSASSINE, LE 1987 d: Frank Cassenti. FRN., *Le Testament d'un Poete Juif Assassine*, Elie Wiesel, Novel

Testament, Le see LE VERDICT (1974).

Testament of Dr. Cordelier, The see LE TESTAMENT DU DR. CORDELIER (1959).

Testament of Dr. Mabuse, The see DAS TESTAMENT DES DR. MABUSE (1933).

Testament of Dr. Mabuse, The see DAS TESTAMENT DES DR. MABUSE (1962).

Testament of Koppany's Agha, The see A KOPPANYI AGA TESTAMENTUMA (1967).

TESTAMENT OF YOUTH 1979 d: Moira Armstrong. UKN., *Testament of Youth*, Vera Brittain, 1933, Autobiography

TESTAMENTO 1998 d: Francisco Manso. PRT/BRZ/CPV., *Mr. Napumoceno's Last Will and Testament*, Germano Almeida, Novel

TESTIMONE A RISCHIO 1997 d: Pasquale Pozzessere. ITL., *L' Avventura Di un Uomo Tranquillo*, Pietro Calderoni, Book

Testimone, Il see LE TEMOIN (1977).

TESTIMONY 1920 d: Guy Newall. UKN., *Testimony*, Alice Askew, Claude Askew, Novel

TESTIMONY 1988 d: Tony Palmer. UKN., Dimitri Schostakovich, Autobiography

TESTIMONY OF TWO MEN 1977 d: Larry Yust, Leo Penn. USA., *Testimony of Two Men*, Taylor Caldwell, Novel

TETE CONTRE LES MURS, LA 1958 d: Georges Franju. FRN., *La Tete Contre Les Murs*, Herve Bazin, 1949, Novel

TETE DU CLIENT, LA 1964 d: Jacques Poitrenaud. FRN/SPN., *La Tete du Client*, Michel Lebrun, Novel

TETE D'UN HOMME, LA 1932 d: Julien Duvivier. FRN., *La Tete d'un Homme*, Georges Simenon, 1931, Novel

TETES BRULEES, LES 1967 d: Willy Rozier. FRN/SPN., *La Longue Piste*, Jean-Louis Cotte, Novel

TETICKA 1941 d: Martin Fric. CZC., *Strasidelna Teticka*, Jaroslav Tumlir, Play

TEUFEL IN SEIDE 1956 d: Rolf Hansen. GRM., *Teufel in Seide*, Gina Kaus, Gutersloh 1956, Novel

TEUFEL KAM AUS AKASAWA, DER 1971 d: Jesus Franco. GRM/SPN., Edgar Wallace, Novel

Teufel Mit Den 3 Goldenen Haaren, Der see WER REISST DENN GLEICH VORM TEUFEL AUS? (1978).

TEUFEL MIT DEN DREI GOLDENEN HAAREN, DER 1955 d: Hans F. Wilhelm. GRM., *Der Teufel Mit Den Drei Goldenen Haaren*, Jacob Grimm, Wilhelm Grimm, Short Story

Teufelsschlucht Der Wilden Wolfe, Die see ZANNA BIANCA (1973).

Teutonic Knights see KRZYZACY (1960).

TEVYA 1939 d: Maurice Schwartz. USA., *Tevye Der Milkhiker*, Shalom Aleichem, New York 1919, Play

Tevya the Milkman see TEVYA (1939).

Tevye and His Seven Daughters see TUVIYAH VE SHEVA BENOTAIV (1968).

Tevye Und Seine Sieben Tochter see TUVIYAH VE SHEVA BENOTAIV (1968).

TEX 1982 d: Tim Hunter. USA., *Tex*, S. E. Hinton, Novel

TEXAN, THE 1920 d: Lynn Reynolds. USA., *The Texan*, James B. Hendryx, New York 1918, Novel

TEXAN, THE 1930 d: John Cromwell. USA., *A Double-Dyed Deceiver*, O. Henry, 1905, Short Story

Texas Desperadoes see DRIFT FENCE (1936).

Texas Kid, Outlaw see THE KID FROM TEXAS (1950).

Texas Ranger, A see PURE GRIT (1923).

TEXAS RANGERS, THE 1936 d: King Vidor. USA., *The Texas Rangers*, Walter Prescott Webb, Boston 1935, Book

TEXAS RANGERS, THE 1951 d: Phil Karlson. USA., Frank Gruber, Story

TEXAS STEER, A 1915 d: Giles R. Warren. USA., *A Texas Steer*, Charles Hale Hoyt, 1890, Play

TEXAS STEER, A 1927 d: Richard Wallace. USA., *A Texas Steer*, Charles Hale Hoyt, 1890, Play

TEXAS TRAIL 1937 d: David Selman. USA., *Tex*, Clarence E. Mulford, Chicago 1922, Novel

TEXAS TRAIL, THE 1925 d: Scott R. Dunlap. USA., *Rangy Pete*, Guy Morton, Boston 1922, Novel

TEXASVILLE 1990 d: Peter Bogdanovich. USA., *Texasville*, Larry McMurtry, 1990, Novel

THAIS 1914 d: Arthur Maude, Constance Crawley. USA., *Thais*, Anatole France, Paris 1890, Novel

THAIS 1917 d: Frank H. Crane, Hugo Ballin. USA., *Thais*, Anatole France, Paris 1890, Novel

THAIS 1983 d: Ryszard Ber. PLN., *Thais*, Anatole France, Paris 1890, Novel

THAKICHA LAGNA 1935 d: Vishram Bedekar, Vamanrao N. Bhat. IND., *Thakicha Lagna*, Ram Ganesh Gadkari, Play

Thakiche Lagna see THAKICHA LAGNA (1935).

Thaki's Marriage see THAKICHA LAGNA (1935).

THANK EVANS 1938 d: R. William Neill. UKN., *Good Evans*, Edgar Wallace, London 1927, Novel

Thank Heaven for Small Favors see UN DROLE DE PAROISSIEN (1963).

THANK YOU 1925 d: John Ford. USA., *Thank You*, Tom Cushing, Winchell Smith, New York 1921, Play

Thank You All Very Much see A TOUCH OF LOVE (1969).

THANK YOU, JEEVES! 1936 d: Arthur G. Collins. USA., *Thank You, Jeeves!*, P. G. Wodehouse, London 1934, Novel

THANK YOU, M'AM 1976 d: Andrew Sugerman. USA., *Thank You M'am*, Langston Hughes, 1963, Short Story

Thank You, Mr. Jeeves see JEEVES! THANK YOU (1936).

THANK YOU, MR. MOTO 1937 d: Norman Foster. USA., *Thank You Mr. Moto*, John Phillips Marquand, Boston 1936, Novel

Thank Your Stars see SHOOT THE WORKS (1934).

THANKS FOR LISTENING 1937 d: Marshall Neilan. USA., *Don't Fall in Love*, John B. Clymer, Short Story

THANKS FOR THE MEMORY 1938 d: George Archainbaud. USA., *Up Pops the Devil*, Frances Goodrich, Albert Hackett, New York 1930, Play

THANKSGIVING PROMISE, THE 1986 d: Beau Bridges. USA., *A Promise Made*, Blaine M. Yorgason, Brenton Yorgason, Novel

THARK 1932 d: Tom Walls. UKN., *Thark*, Ben Travers, London 1927, Play

Thark, the Haunted House see THARK (1932).

That Certain Captain Rodrigo see UM CERTO CAPITAO RODRIGO (1970).

THAT CERTAIN FEELING 1956 d: Norman Panama, Melvin Frank. USA., *The King of Hearts*, Eleanor Brooke, Jean Kerr, New York 1954, Play

THAT CERTAIN SUMMER 1972 d: Lamont Johnson. USA., *That Certain Summer*, Richard Levinson, William Link, Play

THAT CHAMPIONSHIP SEASON 1982 d: Jason Miller. USA., *That Championship Season*, Jason Miller, Play

THAT COLD DAY IN THE PARK 1969 d: Robert Altman. USA/CND., *That Cold Day in the Park*, Richard Miles, New York 1965, Novel

THAT DANGEROUS AGE 1949 d: Gregory Ratoff. UKN., *Autumn*, Ilya Surgutchoff, Play

THAT DARN CAT! 1965 d: Robert Stevenson. USA., *Undercover Cat*, Gordon Gordon, Mildred Gordon, New York 1963, Novel

THAT DARN CAT 1997 d: Bob Spiers. USA., *Undercover Cat*, Gordon Gordon, Mildred Gordon, New York 1963, Novel

That Dirty Story of the West see QUELLA SPORCA STORIA DEL WEST (1968).

That Female Scent see PROFUMO DI DONNA (1974).

THAT FORTSYTE WOMAN 1949 d: Compton Bennett. USA., *The Man of Property*, John Galsworthy, 1906, Novel

That Girl Elisa see LA FILLE ELISA (1956).

That Girl from Beverly Hills see DIE TOTE VON BEVERLY HILLS (1964).

That Girl from College see SORORITY HOUSE (1939).

THAT GIRL FROM PARIS 1936 d: Leigh Jason. USA., *The Viennese Charmer*, W. Carey Wonderly, Story

THAT GIRL MONTANA 1921 d: Robert T. Thornby. USA., *That Girl Montana*, Marah Ellis Ryan, New York 1901, Novel

That Is Called Dawn *see* CELA S'APPELLE L'AURORE (1955).

THAT KIND OF WOMAN 1959 d: Sidney Lumet. USA., *Pettigrew's Girl*, Dana Burnet, 1918, Short Story

THAT LADY 1955 d: Terence Young. UKN., *That Lady*, Kate O'Brien, Novel

THAT LADY IN ERMINE 1948 d: Ernst Lubitsch, Otto Preminger (Uncredited). USA., *Die Frau Im Hermelin*, Rudolph Schanzer, Ernst Welisch, Play

That Lass O' Lowrie's *see* SECRET LOVE (1916).

That Lassie O' Lowrie's *see* SECRET LOVE (1916).

That Luzmela Girl *see* LA NINA DE LUZMELA (1949).

That Man from Hong Kong *see* LES TRIBULATIONS D'UN CHINOIS EN CHINE (1965).

That Man George *see* L' HOMME DE MARRAKECH (1966).

THAT MAN'S HERE AGAIN 1937 d: Louis King. USA., *Young Nowheres*, I. A. R. Wylie, 1927, Short Story

THAT MODEL FROM PARIS 1926 d: Louis J. Gasnier, Robert Florey (Uncredited). USA., *The Right to Live*, Gouverneur Morris, Story

THAT NIGHT 1957 d: John Newland. USA., *The Long Way Home*, Burton J. Rowles, Robert Wallace, Television Play

THAT NIGHT IN RIO 1941 d: Irving Cummings. USA., *The Red Cat*, Hans Adler, Rudolph Lothar, New York 1934, Play

That Obscure Object of Desire *see* CET OBSCUR OBJET DU DESIR (1977).

THAT OLD GANG OF MINE 1925 d: May Tully. USA., *That Old Gang of Mine*, Mort Dixon, Ray Henderson, Billy Rose, 1923, Song

"THAT ROYLE GIRL" 1925 d: D. W. Griffith. USA., *That Royle Girl*, Edwin Balmer, New York 1925, Novel

That Shamrock Touch *see* THE LUCK OF THE IRISH (1948).

THAT SOMETHING 1921 d: Margery Wilson, Lawrence Underwood. USA., *That Something*, William Witherspoon Woodbridge, Tacoma, Wash. 1914, Short Story

THAT SORT 1916 d: Charles J. Brabin. USA., *That Sort*, Basil McDonald Hastings, New York 1914, Play

That Sort of Girl *see* THAT SORT (1916).

That Splendid November *see* UN BELLISSIMO NOVEMBRE (1968).

That Summer of White Roses *see* DJAVOLJI RAJ - ONO LJETO BIJELIH RUZA (1989).

That to Will Pass *see* I TO CE PROCI (1985).

THAT UNCERTAIN FEELING 1941 d: Ernst Lubitsch. USA., *Cyprienne Or Divorcons*, Emile de Najac, Victorien Sardou, Paris 1883, Play

That Uncertain Feeling *see* ONLY TWO CAN PLAY (1962).

That Was My Life *see* DAS WAR MEIN LEBEN (1944).

THAT WAS THEN. THIS IS NOW 1985 d: Christopher Cain. USA., *That Was Then - This Is Now*, S. E. Hinton, 1971, Novel

THAT WAY WITH WOMEN 1947 d: Frederick de CordovA. USA., *Idle Hands*, Earl Derr Biggers, 1921, Short Story

THAT WILD WEST 1924 d: Alvin J. Neitz. USA., *The Bar-T Mystery*, J. F. Natteford, Story

THAT WOMAN OPPOSITE 1957 d: Compton Bennett. UKN., *The Emperor's Snuffbox*, John Dickson Carr, Novel

THAT'S A GOOD GIRL 1933 d: Jack Buchanan. UKN., *That's a Good Girl*, Douglas Furber, London 1928, Musical Play

THAT'S GOOD 1919 d: Harry L. Franklin. USA., *That's Good*, Richard Washburn Child, 1915, Short Story

THAT'S GRATITUDE 1934 d: Frank Craven. USA., *That's Gratitude*, Frank Craven, New York 1930, Play

That's My Baby! *see* A SON TO DOROTHY (1954).

THAT'S MY BOY 1932 d: R. William Neill. USA., *That's My Boy*, Francis Wallace, New York 1932, Novel

THAT'S MY UNCLE 1935 d: George Pearson. USA., *The Iron Woman*, Frederick Jackson, 1932, Play

That's Not the Way to Go *see* BU NENG ZOU NEI TIAO LU (1954).

THE AU HAREM D'ARCHIMEDE, LE 1984 d: Mehdi Charef. FRN., *Le the Au Harem d'Archimede*, Mehdi Charef, Novel

The Viscount, Furto Alla Banca Mondiale *see* LE VICOMTE REGLE SES COMPTES (1967).

Theatre of Shimmering Light *see* KAGERO-ZA (1981).

Theatre Royal *see* THE ROYAL FAMILY OF BROADWAY (1930).

Theatre Troupe Kagero *see* KAGERO-ZA (1981).

Thee I Love *see* FRIENDLY PERSUASION (1956).

Theft of the Sabines *see* DER RAUB DER SABINERINNEN (1954).

THEIR BIG MOMENT 1934 d: James Cruze. USA., *Afterwards*, Walter Hackett, London 1933, Play

THEIR HERO 1912. USA., *At Good Old Siwash*, George Fitch, Boston 1911, Novel

Their Last Night *see* LEUR DERNIERE NUIT (1953).

THEIR MAD MOMENT 1931 d: Hamilton MacFadden, Chandler Sprague. USA., *Basquerie*, Eleanor Mercein, New York 1927, Book

THEIR MUTUAL CHILD 1920 d: George L. Cox. USA., *Their Mutual Child*, P. G. Wodehouse, New York 1919, Novel

THEIR NIGHT OUT 1933 d: Harry Hughes. UKN., *Their Night Out*, George Arthurs, Arthur Miller, Play

THEIR OWN DESIRE 1929 d: E. Mason Hopper. USA., *Their Own Desire*, Sarita Fuller, Story

Their Secret Affair *see* TOP SECRET AFFAIR (1956).

THELMA 1910 d: Theodore Marston. USA., *Thelma - a Norwegian Princess*, Marie Corelli, London 1887, Novel

THELMA 1911. USA., *Thelma - a Norwegian Princess*, Marie Corelli, London 1887, Novel

THELMA 1918 d: A. E. Coleby, Arthur Rooke. UKN., *Thelma - a Norwegian Princess*, Marie Corelli, London 1887, Novel

THELMA 1922 d: Chester Bennett. USA., *Thelma - a Norwegian Princess*, Marie Corelli, London 1887, Novel

Them *see* ILS. (1970).

THEN I'LL COME BACK TO YOU 1916 d: George Irving. USA., *Then I'll Come Back to You*, Larry Evans, New York 1915, Novel

Then We Condemned Them All to Death *see* MOARTEA LUI IPU (1972).

THEODORA 1912 d: Henri Pouctal. FRN., *Theodora*, Victorien Sardou, 1884, Play

Theodora, Queen of Byzantium *see* IMPERATRICE DI BISANZIO TEODORA (1954).

Theodora, Slave Empress *see* IMPERATRICE DI BISANZIO TEODORA (1954).

THEODORE CHERCHE DES ALLUMETTES 1923 d: Andrew F. Brunelle. FRN., *Theodore Cherche Des Allumettes*, Georges Courteline, Play

Theodore Est Fatigue *see* SERVICE DE NUIT (1931).

THEODORE ET CIE 1933 d: Piere Colombier. FRN., *Theodore Et Cie*, Robert Armont, Nicolas Nancey, 1909, Play

Theodore, Imperatrice Byzantine *see* IMPERATRICE DI BISANZIO TEODORA (1954).

Theodore, Imperatrice de Byzance *see* IMPERATRICE DI BISANZIO TEODORA (1954).

Theorem *see* TEOREMA (1968).

THERE AIN'T NO JUSTICE 1939 d: Pen Tennyson. UKN., *There Ain't No Justice*, James Curtis, Novel

There are Also People *see* TOZHE LYUDI (1960).

THERE ARE NO CHILDREN HERE 1993 d: Anita W. Addison. USA., *There are No Children Here*, Alex Kotlowitz, Book

THERE ARE NO VILLAINS 1921 d: Bayard Veiller. USA., *There are No Villains*, Frank R. Adams, Story

THERE GOES THE BRIDE 1980 d: Terry Marcel. UKN., *There Goes the Bride*, Ray Cooney, Play

THERE GOES THE GROOM 1937 d: Joseph Santley. USA., *Let Freedom Swing*, David Garth, 1937, Short Story

THERE, LITTLE GIRL, DON'T CRY 1910. USA., *A Life's Story*, James Whitcomb Riley, Poem

There Once Was a Woman *see* REVENGE (1971).

THERE WAS A CROOKED MAN 1960 d: Stuart Burge. UKN., *The Golden Legend of Shults*, James Bridie, 1939, Play

THERE WAS A LITTLE BOY 1993 d: Mimi Leder. USA., *There Was a Little Boy*, Claire R. Jacobs, Book

There Will Be No More Sadness Nor Oblivion *see* NO HABRA MAS PENA NI OLVIDO (1985).

There Will Come a Day *see* ES KOMMT EIN TAG (1950).

THERE YOU ARE! 1926 d: Edward Sedgwick. USA., *There You are*, F. Hugh Herbert, New York 1925, Play

THERE'S A GIRL IN MY SOUP 1970 d: Roy Boulting. UKN., *There's a Girl in My Soup*, Terence Frisby, London 1966, Play

There's Alway's a Price Tag *see* RETOUR DE MANIVELLE (1957).

THERE'S ALWAYS A WOMAN 1938 d: Alexander Hall. USA., *There's Always a Woman*, Wilson Collison, 1937, Short Story

There's Always Tomorrow *see* MR. SKITCH (1933).

THERE'S ALWAYS TOMORROW 1956 d: Douglas Sirk. USA., Ursula Parrott, Story

There's an Ace Up My Sleeve *see* CRIME AND PASSION (1975).

There's Millions in It *see* HOT MONEY (1936).

THERE'S NO BUSINESS LIKE SHOW BUSINESS 1954 d: Walter Lang. USA., Lamar Trotti, Story

THERE'S ONE BORN EVERY MINUTE 1942 d: Harold Young. USA., *Man Or Mouse*, Robert B. Hunt, Story

Therese *see* THERESE DESQUEYROUX (1962).

THERESE AND ISABELLE 1969 d: Radley H. Metzger. USA/GRM/FRN., *Therese Et Isabelle*, Violette Leduc, Paris 1966, Novel

THERESE DESQUEYROUX 1962 d: Georges Franju. FRN., *Therese Desqueyroux*, Francois Mauriac, Paris 1927, Novel

Therese Et Isabelle *see* THERESE AND ISABELLE (1969).

THERESE ETIENNE 1957 d: Denys de La Patelliere. FRN/ITL/SWT., *Therese Etienne*, John Knittel, 1927, Novel

THERESE RAQUIN 1928 d: Jacques Feyder. FRN/GRM., *Therese Raquin*, Emile Zola, 1867, Novel

THERESE RAQUIN 1953 d: Marcel Carne. FRN/ITL., *Therese Raquin*, Emile Zola, 1867, Novel

Therese Und Isabell *see* THERESE AND ISABELLE (1969).

These are the Damned *see* THE DAMNED (1962).

THESE CHARMING PEOPLE 1931 d: Louis Mercanton. UKN., *Dear Father (These Charming People)*, Michael Arlen, 1924, Play

These Ghosts *see* QUESTI FANTASMI (1954).

These Ghosts *see* QUESTI FANTASMI (1967).

THESE GLAMOUR GIRLS 1939 d: S. Sylvan Simon. USA., *These Glamour Girls*, Jane Hall, Short Story

These Things Happen *see* LES CHOSES DE LA VIE (1970).

THESE THOUSAND HILLS 1959 d: Richard Fleischer. USA., *These Thousand Hills*, A. B. Guthrie Jr., 1956, Novel

THESE THREE 1936 d: William Wyler. USA., *The Children's Hour*, Lillian Hellman, New York 1934, Play

THESE WILDER YEARS 1956 d: Roy Rowland. USA., Ralph Wheelwright, Story

They All Died Laughing *see* A JOLLY BAD FELLOW (1963).

They All Want Something *see* WHAT A MAN! (1930).

They are Also People *see* TOZHE LYUDI (1960).

THEY CALL IT MURDER 1971 d: Walter Grauman. USA., *The D.A. Draws a Circle*, Erle Stanley Gardner, Novel

THEY CALL IT SIN 1932 d: Thornton Freeland. USA., *They Call It Sin*, Alberta Stedman Eagan, New York 1933, Novel

They Called Him Krambambuli *see* SIE NANNTEN IHN KRAMBAMBULI (1972).

THEY CAME BY NIGHT 1940 d: Harry Lachman. UKN/USA., *They Came By Night*, Barre Lyndon, London 1937, Play

They Came from Another World *see* INVASION OF THE BODY SNATCHERS (1956).

THEY CAME FROM BEYOND SPACE 1967 d: Freddie Francis. UKN., *The Gods Hate Kansas*, Joseph Millard, 1941, Short Story

THEY CAME TO A CITY 1944 d: Basil Dearden. UKN., *They Came to a City*, J. B. Priestley, London 1943, Play

THEY CAME TO CORDURA 1959 d: Robert Rossen. USA., *They Came to Cordura*, Glendon Swarthout, 1958, Novel

They Came to Rob Las Vegas *see* 500 MILLONES LAS VEGAS (1968).

They Can't Hang Me *see* THE WITNESS VANISHES (1939).

THEY CAN'T HANG ME 1955 d: Val Guest. UKN., *They Can't Hang Me*, Leonard Moseley, Novel

They Caught the Ferry *see* DE NAEDE FARGEN (1948).

They Cracked Her Glass Slipper *see* THIRD TIME LUCKY (1949).

THEY DRIVE BY NIGHT 1938 d: Arthur Woods. UKN., *They Drive By Night*, James Curtis, Novel

THEY DRIVE BY NIGHT 1940 d: Raoul Walsh. USA., *Long Haul*, Albert Isaac Bezzerides, New York 1938, Novel

They Eat Each Other Up *see* EINER FRISST DEN ANDEREN (1964).

They Fought for the Motherland *see* ONI SRAJALIS ZA RODINOU (1974).

They Fought for Their Country *see* ONI SRAJALIS ZA RODINOU (1974).

They Fought for Their Motherland *see* ONI SRAJALIS ZA RODINOU (1974).

THEY GAVE HIM A GUN 1937 d: W. S. Van Dyke. USA., *They Gave Him a Gun*, William Joyce Cowen, New York 1936, Novel

They Had to Get Married *see* THEY JUST HAD TO GET MARRIED (1933).

THEY HAD TO SEE PARIS 1929 d: Frank Borzage. USA., *They Had to See Paris*, Homer Croy, New York 1926, Novel

THEY JUST HAD TO GET MARRIED 1933 d: Edward Ludwig. USA., *A Pair of Silk Stockings*, Cyril Harcourt, New York 1914, Play

THEY KNEW MR. KNIGHT 1945 d: Norman Walker. UKN., *They Knew Mr. Knight*, Dorothy Whipple, Novel

THEY KNEW WHAT THEY WANTED 1940 d: Garson Kanin. USA., *They Knew What They Wanted*, Sidney Coe Howard, New York 1924, Play

THEY LIVE 1988 d: John Carpenter. USA., *Eight O'Clock in the Morning*, Ray Nelson, Story

THEY LIVE BY NIGHT 1948 d: Nicholas Ray. USA., *Thieves Like Us*, Edward Anderson, 1937, Novel

They Loved Life *see* KANAL (1957).

THEY MADE ME A CRIMINAL 1939 d: Busby Berkeley. USA., *Sucker*, Beulah Marie Dix, Bertram Millhauser, New York 1933, Play

They Made Me a Criminal *see* THEY MADE ME A FUGITIVE (1947).

THEY MADE ME A FUGITIVE 1947 d: Alberto Cavalcanti. UKN., *A Convict Has Escaped*, Jackson Budd, Novel

THEY MET IN THE DARK 1943 d: Carl Lamac. UKN., *The Vanishing Corpse*, Anthony Gilbert, Novel

They Passed This Way *see* FOUR FACES WEST (1948).

THEY'RE SHOOT HORSES, DON'T THEY? 1969 d: Sydney Pollack. USA., *They Shoot Horses, Don't They?*, Horace McCoy, New York 1935, Novel

THEY WERE EXPENDABLE 1945 d: John Ford. USA., *They Were Expendable*, William L. White, Book

THEY WERE SISTERS 1945 d: Arthur Crabtree. UKN., *They Were Sisters*, Dorothy Whipple, Novel

They Who Step on the Tiger's Tail *see* TORA NO OO FUMA OTOKOTACHI (1945).

THEY WON'T FORGET 1937 d: Mervyn Leroy. USA., *Death in the Deep South*, Ward Greene, Harrisburg, PA. 1936, Novel

THEY'RE A WEIRD MOB 1966 d: Michael Powell. UKN/ASL., *They're a Weird Mob*, Nino Culotta, Book

They're Off *see* THE KENTUCKY DERBY (1922).

They're Off *see* STRAIGHT PLACE AND SHOW (1938).

They've Kidnapped Anne Benedict *see* THE ABDUCTION OF SAINT ANNE (1975).

Thicker Than Water *see* RAILROADED (1923).

THICKER THAN WATER 1994 d: Marc Evans. UKN., *Thicker Than Water*, Dylan Jones, Novel

THIEF 1981 d: Michael Mann. USA., *The Home Invaders*, Frank Hohimer, Novel

Thief Has Arrived, A *see* HA ENTRADO UN LADRON (1948).

THIEF IN PARADISE, A 1925 d: George Fitzmaurice. USA., *The Worldlings*, Leonard Merrick, New York 1900, Novel

Thief in the Car, The *see* CHEZHONG DAO (1920).

THIEF IN THE NIGHT, A 1915. USA., *A Thief in the Night*, Albert Payson Terhune, Story

Thief of Paris, The *see* LE VOLEUR (1967).

THIEF, THE 1914 d: Edgar Lewis. USA., *Le Voleur*, Henri Bernstein, Paris 1907, Play

THIEF, THE 1920 d: Charles Giblyn. USA., *Le Voleur*, Henri Bernstein, Paris 1907, Play

THIEF, THE 1922 d: George A. Cooper. UKN., *The Thief*, F. K. Junior, Story

Thief, The *see* LE VOLEUR (1967).

Thief Who Came in the Night, The *see* THE THIEF WHO CAME TO DINNER (1973).

THIEF WHO CAME TO DINNER, THE 1973 d: Bud Yorkin. USA., *The Thief Who Came to Dinner*, Terence L. Smith, Novel

Thieves are Honorable People *see* LOS LADRONES SOMOS GENTE HONRADA (1956).

Thieves are Honourable People *see* LOS LADRONES SOMOS GENTE HONRADA (1942).

THIEVES FALL OUT 1941 d: Ray Enright. USA., *30 Days Hath September*, Irving Gaumont, Jack Sobell, New York 1938, Play

THIEVES' GOLD 1918 d: John Ford. USA., *Back to the Right Trail*, Frederick R. Bechdolf, Short Story

THIEVES' HIGHWAY 1949 d: Jules Dassin. USA., *Thieves' Market*, Albert Isaac Bezzerides, Novel

THIEVES LIKE US 1973 d: Robert Altman. USA., *Thieves Like Us*, Edward Anderson, 1937, Novel

Thieves' Market *see* THIEVES' HIGHWAY (1949).

THIMBLE, THIMBLE 1920 d: Edward H. Griffith. USA., *Thimble, Thimble*, O.Henry, Short Story

THIN ICE 1937 d: Sidney Lanfield. USA., *Der Komet*, Attila Orbok, Budapest 1922, Play

THIN MAN, THE 1934 d: W. S. Van Dyke. USA., *The Thin Man*, Dashiell Hammett, New York 1932, Novel

THIN RED LINE, THE 1964 d: Andrew Marton. USA., *The Thin Red Line*, James Jones, New York 1962, Novel

THIN RED LINE, THE 1998 d: Terrence Malick. USA., *The Thin Red Line*, James Jones, New York 1962, Novel

Thing from Another World, The *see* THE THING (1951).

Thing Is the Play, The *see* GOODBYE BROADWAY (1938).

THING, THE 1951 d: Christian Nyby, Howard Hawks (Uncredited). USA., *Who Goes There?*, Don A. Stuart, Story

THING, THE 1982 d: John Carpenter. USA., *Who Goes There?*, Don A. Stuart, Story

Things Began to Happen *see* EXCLUSIVE (1937).

THINGS HAPPEN AT NIGHT 1948 d: Francis Searle. UKN., *The Poltergeist*, Frank Harvey Jr., London 1946, Play

THINGS MEN DO 1920 d: Robert North Bradbury. USA., *Into the Light*, Cyrus J. Williams, Story

Things of Life, The *see* LES CHOSES DE LA VIE (1970).

THING'S THE PLAY, THE 1918 d: George Ridgwell. USA., *The Thing's the Play*, O. Henry, Short Story

THINGS TO COME 1936 d: William Cameron Menzies. UKN., *The Shape of Things to Come*, H. G. Wells, 1933, Novel

THINK FAST, MR. MOTO 1937 d: Norman Foster. USA., *The Girl and Mr. Moto*, John Phillips Marquand, 1936, Short Story

Think of a Number *see* TAENK PA ET TAL (1969).

Third After the Sun *see* TRETA SLED SLANTSETO (1972).

THIRD ALIBI, THE 1961 d: Montgomery Tully. UKN., *Moment of Blindness*, Jane Baker, Pip Baker, Play

THIRD CLUE, THE 1934 d: Albert Parker. UKN., *The Shakespeare Murders*, Neil Gordon, Novel

Third Company, The *see* TRETI ROTA (1931).

THIRD DAY, THE 1965 d: Jack Smight. USA., *The Third Day*, Joseph Hayes, New York 1964, Novel

THIRD DEGREE, THE 1914 d: Barry O'Neil. USA., *The Third Degree*, Charles Klein, New York 1909, Play

THIRD DEGREE, THE 1919 d: Tom Terriss. USA., *The Third Degree*, Charles Klein, New York 1909, Play

THIRD DEGREE, THE 1926 d: Michael Curtiz. USA., *The Third Degree*, Charles Klein, New York 1909, Play

Third Eye, The *see* IL TERZO OCCHIO (1966).

Third from the Sun *see* TRETA SLED SLANTSETO (1972).

THIRD GENERATION, THE 1915 d: Harold Shaw. UKN., *The Third Generation*, Charles McEvoy, Novel

THIRD INGREDIENT, THE 1917 d: Thomas R. Mills. USA., *The Third Ingredient*, O. Henry, Short Story

THIRD KISS, THE 1919 d: Robert G. VignolA. USA., *The Third Kiss*, Heliodore Tenno, 1918, Short Story

Third Lady You, The *see* YOU SAN JIE (1963).

THIRD MAN ON THE MOUNTAIN 1959 d: Ken Annakin. UKN/USA., *Banner in the Sky*, James Ramsay Ullman, Novel

THIRD MAN, THE 1949 d: Carol Reed. UKN., *The Third Man*, Graham Greene, 1950, Novel

Third One, The *see* DER DRITTE (1972).

THIRD PARTY RISK 1955 d: Daniel Birt. UKN., *Third Party Risk*, Nicolas Bentley, Novel

Third Planet in the Solar System, The *see* TRETA SLED SLANTSETO (1972).

Third Ringing, The *see* TRETI ZVONENI (1938).

Third Road, The *see* THE SEVENTH DAWN (1964).

Third Round, The *see* BULLDOG DRUMMOND'S THIRD ROUND (1925).

Third Solution, The *see* RUSSICUM (1989).

Third Squad, The *see* TRETI ROTA (1931).

THIRD STRING, THE 1914 d: George Loane Tucker. UKN., *The Third String*, W. W. Jacobs, Short Story

THIRD STRING, THE 1932 d: George Pearson. UKN., *The Third String*, W. W. Jacobs, Short Story

Third, The *see* DER DRITTE (1972).

THIRD TIME LUCKY 1931 d: Walter Forde. UKN., *Third Time Lucky*, Arnold Ridley, London 1929, Play

THIRD TIME LUCKY 1949 d: Gordon Parry. UKN., *They Cracked Her Glass Slipper*, Gerald Butler, Novel

Third Time, The *see* TRETIY TAYM (1963).

Third Time Unlucky *see* CROWN V STEVENS (1936).

THIRD VISITOR, THE 1951 d: Maurice Elvey. UKN., *The Third Visitor*, Gerald Anstruther, London 1945, Play

THIRD VOICE, THE 1960 d: Hubert Cornfield. USA., *All the Way*, Charles Williams, Novel

Thirst *see* TORST (1949).

Thirst *see* SETEA (1960).

Thirst for Love, The *see* AI NO KAWAKI (1967).

Thirteen Chairs *see* DAS GLUCK LIEGT AUF DER STRASSE (1957).

THIRTEEN WOMEN 1932 d: George Archainbaud. USA., *Thirteen Women*, Tiffany Thayer, New York 1932, Novel

THIRTEENTH CHAIR, THE 1919 d: Leonce Perret. USA., *The Thirteenth Chair*, Bayard Veiller, New York 1916, Play

THIRTEENTH CHAIR, THE 1929 d: Tod Browning. USA., *The Thirteenth Chair*, Bayard Veiller, New York 1916, Play

THIRTEENTH CHAIR, THE 1937 d: George B. Seitz. USA., *The Thirteenth Chair*, Bayard Veiller, New York 1916, Play

THIRTEENTH COMMANDMENT, THE 1920 d: Robert G. VignolA. USA., *The Thirteenth Commandment*, Rupert Hughes, New York 1916, Novel

THIRTEENTH GIRL, THE 1915 d: Theodore Marston. USA., *Where Did Lottie Go?*, Frances Aymar Mathews, Short Story

THIRTEENTH GUEST, THE 1932 d: Albert Ray. USA., *The Thirteenth Guest*, Armitage Trail, New York 1929, Novel

THIRTEENTH JUROR, THE 1927 d: Edward Laemmle. USA., *Counsel for the Defense*, Henry Irving Dodge, Play

THIRTIETH PIECE OF SILVER, THE 1920 d: George L. Cox. USA., *The Thirtieth Piece of Silver*, Albert Payson Terhune, Novel

THIRTY A WEEK 1918 d: Harry Beaumont. USA., *Thirty a Week*, Thompson Buchanan, Play

THIRTY DAY PRINCESS 1934 d: Marion Gering. USA., *Thirty-Day Princess*, Clarence Budington Kelland, 1933, Story

THIRTY DAYS 1922 d: James Cruze. USA., *Thirty Days*, Clayton Hamilton, 1915, Play, *Thirty Days; a Farce in Three Acts*, A. E. Thomas, 1915, Play

THIRTY DAYS AT HARD LABOR 1912. USA., *The Halberdier of the Little Rheinschloss*, O. Henry, 1907, Short Story

Thirty Days Hath September *see* THIEVES FALL OUT (1941).

Thirty-Day Princess *see* **THIRTY DAY PRINCESS** (1934).

Thirty-Nine Steps, The *see* **THE 39 STEPS** (1935).

Thirty-Nine Steps, The *see* **THE 39 STEPS** (1959).

THIRTY-NINE STEPS, THE 1978 d: Don Sharp. UKN., *The Thirty-Nine Steps*, John Buchan, 1915, Novel

Thirty-Six Hours *see* **36 HOURS** (1964).

This Angry Age *see* **BARRAGE CONTRE LE PACIFIQUE** (1958).

THIS BOY'S LIFE 1993 d: Michael Caton-Jones. USA., *This Boy's Life*, Tobias Wolff, Book

THIS COULD BE THE NIGHT 1957 d: Robert Wise. USA., *It's Hard to Find Mecca*, Cordelia Baird Gross, Short Story, *Protection for a Tough Racket*, Cordelia Baird Gross, Short Story

This Crazy Urge *see* **LA VOGLIA MATTA** (1962).

THIS EARTH IS MINE 1959 d: Henry King. USA., *The Cup and the Sword*, Alice Tisdale Hobart, Novel

THIS FREEDOM 1923 d: Denison Clift. UKN., *This Freedom*, A. S. M. Hutchinson, Novel

THIS GUN FOR HIRE 1942 d: Frank Tuttle. USA., *A Gun for Sale*, Graham Greene, 1936, Novel

THIS HAPPY BREED 1944 d: David Lean. UKN., *This Happy Breed*, Noel Coward, London 1943, Play

THIS HAPPY FEELING 1958 d: Blake Edwards. USA., *For Love Or Money*, F. Hugh Herbert, New York 1947, Play

This Is Callan *see* **CALLAN** (1974).

This Is Dynamite *see* **THE TURNING POINT** (1952).

This Is My Affair *see* **I CAN GET IT FOR YOU WHOLESALE** (1951).

THIS IS MY LIFE 1992 d: Nora Ephron. USA., *This Is Your Life*, Meg Wolitzer, Novel

THIS IS MY LOVE 1954 d: Stuart Heisler. USA., *Fear Has Black Wings*, Hugh Brooke, Novel

THIS IS MY STREET 1963 d: Sidney Hayers. UKN., *This Is My Street*, Nan Maynard, Novel

THIS IS THE LIFE 1915 d: William Bertram. USA., *This Is the Life*, Charles E. Van Loan, Short Story

This Is the Life *see* **IT'S A GREAT LIFE** (1920).

THIS IS THE NIGHT 1932 d: Frank Tuttle. USA., *Pouche*, Henri Falk, Rene Peter, Paris 1923, Play

This Is the Night *see* **PER QUESTA NOTTE** (1977).

THIS ISLAND EARTH 1955 d: Joseph M. Newman, Jack Arnold. USA., *This Island Earth*, Raymond F. Jones, 1952, Novel

This Life of Mine *see* **WO ZHE YIBEIZI** (1950).

THIS LOVE OF OURS 1945 d: William Dieterle. USA., *Come Prima Meglio Di Prima*, Luigi Pirandello, 1921, Play

THIS MAD WORLD 1930 d: William C. de Mille. USA., *Terre Inhumaine*, Francois de Curel, Paris 1923, Play

This Madding Crowd *see* **AOBEKA MONOGATARI** (1962).

This Man Belongs to Me *see* **DIESER MANN GEHORT MIR** (1950).

THIS MAN IS DANGEROUS 1941 d: Lawrence Huntington. UKN., *They Called Him Death*, David Hume, Novel

This Man Is Dangerous *see* **CET HOMME EST DANGEREUX** (1953).

THIS MAN IS MINE 1934 d: John Cromwell. USA., *Love Flies in the Window*, Anne Morrison Chapin, Stockbridge, MA. 1933, Play

THIS MAN IS MINE 1946 d: Marcel Varnel. UKN., *A Soldier for Christmas*, Reginald Beckwith, London 1944, Play

This Man Must Die *see* **QUE LA BETE MEURE** (1969).

This Man -Vautrin *see* **VAUTRIN** (1943).

THIS MODERN AGE 1931 d: Nick Grinde, Clarence Brown (Uncredited). USA., *Girls Together*, Mildred Cram, 1931, Short Story

THIS OTHER EDEN 1959 d: Muriel Box. UKN., *This Other Eden*, Louis d'Alton, 1954, Play

THIS PROPERTY IS CONDEMNED 1966 d: Sydney Pollack. USA., *This Property Is Condemned*, Tennessee Williams, New York 1956, Play

THIS RECKLESS AGE 1932 d: Frank Tuttle. USA., *The Goose Hangs High*, Lewis Beach, New York 1924, Play

THIS SIDE OF HEAVEN 1932 d: William K. Howard. USA., *It Happened One Day*, Marjorie Bartholomew Paradis, New York 1932, Novel

THIS SIDE OF THE LAW 1950 d: Richard L. Bare. USA., *The Doctor Doubles in Death*, Richard Sale, Short Story

This Special Friendship *see* **LES AMITIES PARTICULIERES** (1964).

THIS SPORTING LIFE 1963 d: Lindsay Anderson. UKN., *This Sporting Life*, David Storey, 1960, Novel

This Strange Passion *see* **EL** (1952).

This Sweet Sickness *see* **DITES-LUI QUE JE L'AIME** (1977).

THIS THING CALLED LOVE 1929 d: Paul L. Stein. USA., *This Thing Called Love*, Edwin Burke, New York 1928, Play

THIS THING CALLED LOVE 1940 d: Alexander Hall. USA., *This Thing Called Love*, Edwin Burke, New York 1928, Play

This Time, Caviar *see* **DIESMAL MUSS ES KAVIAR SEIN** (1961).

THIS WAS A WOMAN 1948 d: Tim Whelan. UKN., *This Was a Woman*, Joan Morgan, London 1944, Play

This Way Out, Please *see* **YOU'VE GOT TO BE KIDDING DOCTOR** (1967).

This Wine of Love *see* **L' ELISIR D'AMORE** (1947).

THIS WOMAN 1924 d: Phil Rosen. USA., *This Woman*, Howard P. Rockey, New York 1924, Novel

This Woman Is Dangerous *see* **WOMEN ARE LIKE THAT** (1938).

THIS WOMAN IS DANGEROUS 1952 d: Felix E. Feist. USA., *Stab of Pain*, Bernard Girard, Story

THIS WOMAN IS MINE 1941 d: Frank Lloyd. USA., *James Lewis I*, Gilbert Wolff Gabriel, 1932, Novel

This Woman Is Trouble *see* **THE FLANAGAN BOY** (1953).

This Woman -This Man *see* **GUILTY OF LOVE** (1920).

THIS WORLD, THEN THE FIREWORKS 1997 d: Michael Oblowitz. USA., *This World Then the Fireworks*, Jim Thompson, Short Story

THIS'LL MAKE YOU WHISTLE 1936 d: Herbert Wilcox. UKN., *This'll Make You Whistle*, Guy Bolton, Fred Thompson, London 1935, Play

Thistles of Baragan, The *see* **CIULINII BARAGANULUI** (1957).

Thistles of the Baragan, The *see* **CIULINII BARAGANULUI** (1957).

THOMAS L'IMPOSTEUR 1964 d: Georges Franju. FRN., *Thomas l'Imposteur*, Jean Cocteau, 1923, Novel

Thomas the Imposter *see* **THOMAS L'IMPOSTEUR** (1964).

THOR, LORD OF THE JUNGLES 1913 d: Colin Campbell. USA., *Lord of the Jungles Thor*, James Oliver Curwood, Story

THORN BIRDS, THE 1982 d: Daryl Duke. USA., *The Thorn Birds*, Colleen McCullough, Novel

Thorn Rose *see* **DORNROSCHEN** (1955).

Thorn-Apple *see* **TATUL** (1972).

Thorns and Flowers *see* **TRNY A KVETY** (1921).

THORNS AND ORANGE BLOSSOMS 1922 d: Louis J. Gasnier. USA., *Thorns and Orange Blossoms*, Bertha M. Clay, New York 1883, Novel

Thorns of Passion *see* **THE ROUGHNECK** (1924).

Thorwalds' Happy Years, The *see* **DIE GLUCKLICHEN JAHRE DER THORWALDS** (1962).

Those Blasted Kids *see* **DE POKKERS UNGER** (1947).

THOSE CALLOWAYS 1965 d: Norman Tokar. USA., *Swiftwater*, Paul Annixter, New York 1950, Novel

Those Crazy Calloways *see* **THOSE CALLOWAYS** (1965).

Those Crazy Rasplyuyev Days *see* **VESYOLYYE RASPLYUYEVSKIYE DNI** (1966).

THOSE ENDEARING YOUNG CHARMS 1945 d: Lewis Allen. USA., *Those Endearing Young Charms*, Jerome Chodorov, Play

Those Fantastic Flying Fools *see* **JULES VERNE'S ROCKET TO THE MOON** (1967).

Those Glamorous Girls *see* **THESE GLAMOUR GIRLS** (1939).

THOSE KIDS AND CUPID 1915. USA., *Those Kids and Cupid*, Thomas Delmar, Story

THOSE KIDS FROM TOWN 1942 d: Lance Comfort. UKN., *These Our Strangers*, Adrian Arlington, Novel

Those of Us Who Didn't Go to War *see* **LOS QUE NO FUIMOS A LA GUERRA** (1961).

THOSE PEOPLE NEXT DOOR 1953 d: John Harlow. UKN., *Wearing the Pants*, Zelda Davees, Play

Those Pursued By Fate *see* **DIE VOM SCHICKSAL VERFOLGTEN** (1927).

Those Restless Years *see* **LOOSE CHANGE** (1978).

THOSE WE LOVE 1932 d: Robert Florey. USA., *Those We Love*, George Abbott, S. K. Lauren, New York 1930, Play

THOSE WERE THE DAYS! 1940 d: Theodore Reed. USA., *At Good Old Siwash*, George Fitch, Boston 1911, Novel

THOSE WERE THE DAYS 1934 d: Thomas Bentley. UKN., *The Magistrate*, Arthur Wing Pinero, London 1885, Play

Those Were the Days (at Good Old Siwash) *see* **THOSE WERE THE DAYS!** (1940).

THOSE WHO JUDGE 1924 d: Burton L. King. USA., *Such As Sit in Judgement*, Margery Land May, London 1923, Novel

THOSE WHO LOVE 1929 d: Manning Haynes. UKN., *Mary Was Love*, Guy Fletcher, Novel

Those Who Pay With Their Lives *see* **CEI CARE PLATESC CU VIATA** (1989).

Those Wonderful Years That Sucked *see* **BAJECNA LETA POD PSA** (1997).

THOU ART THE MAN 1920 d: Thomas N. Heffron. USA., *Myles Calthrope I.D.B.*, F. E. Mills Young, London 1913, Novel

THOU FOOL 1926 d: Fred Paul. UKN., *Thou Fool*, J. J. Bell, Novel

Thou Shalt Not *see* **WAS SHE GUILTY?** (1922).

Thou Shalt Not *see* **THERESE RAQUIN** (1928).

Thou Shalt Not Be Jealous *see* **YOTSUYA KAIDAN** (1959).

Thou Shalt Not Kill *see* **WAS SHE GUILTY?** (1922).

THOU SHALT NOT STEAL 1917 d: William Nigh. USA., *Le Dossier Nr. 113*, Emile Gaboriau, Paris 1867, Short Story

Thou, Which Art in Heaven *see* **KOITO SI NA NEBETO TI** (1990).

THOUSAND ACRES, A 1997 d: Jocelyn Moorhouse. USA., *A Thousand Acres*, Jane Smiley, Novel

THOUSAND CLOWNS, A 1965 d: Fred Coe. USA., *A Thousand Clowns*, Herb Gardner, New York 1962, Play

Thousand Cranes *see* **SENBAZURU** (1969).

Thousand Dollar Bill, The *see* **SMALL TOWN BOY** (1937).

Thousand for One Night, A *see* **TAUSEND FUR EINE NACHT** (1932).

Thousand for One Night, A *see* **TISIC ZA JEDNU NOC** (1932).

Thousand for One Night, A *see* **TAUSEND FUR EINE NACHT** (1932).

Thousand for One Night, A *see* **TISIC ZA JEDNU NOC** (1932).

Thousand Pieces of Gold *see* **000 PIECES OF GOLD 1** (1991).

THOUSAND PLANE RAID, THE 1969 d: Boris Sagal. USA., *The Thousand Plan*, Ralph Barker, London 1965, Novel

THOUSAND SKIES, A 1985 d: David Stevens. ASL., *A Thousand Skies*, Tasman Beattie, Novel

THOUSAND TO ONE, A 1920 d: Rowland V. Lee. USA., *Fate's Honeymoon*, Max Brand, 1917, Short Story

Thousand-Year-Old Bee, The *see* **TISICROCNA VCELA** (1983).

Thrane's Method *see* **THRANES METODE** (1999).

THRANES METODE 1999 d: Unni Straume. NRW., *Thranes Metode*, Oystein Lonn, Short Story

THREAD O' SCARLET 1930 d: Peter Godfrey. UKN., *Thread O' Scarlet*, J. J. Bell, Play

THREADS 1932 d: G. B. Samuelson. UKN., *Threads*, Frank Stayton, Play

Three *see* **TRI** (1965).

THREE 1969 d: James Salter. UKN/ITL., *Then We Were Three*, Irwin Shaw, 1961, Short Story

Three & One-Half Musketeers *see* **LOS TRES MOSQUETAROS. Y MEDIO** (1956).

Three and a Half Musketeers *see* **LOS TRES MOSQUETAROS. Y MEDIO** (1956).

THREE BAD MEN 1926 d: John Ford. USA., *Over the Border*, Herman Whitaker, New York 1917, Novel

Three Bad Men *see* **NOT EXACTLY GENTLEMEN** (1931).

THREE STRIPES IN THE SUN 1955 d: Richard Murphy. USA., *The Gentle Wolfhound*, E. J. Kahn Jr., Story

THREE STUDENTS, THE 1923 d: George Ridgwell. UKN., *The Three Students*, Arthur Conan Doyle, Short Story

Three Truths in the Well see LE PUITS AUX TROIS VERITES (1961).

Three Undelivered Letters, The see HAITATSU SARENAI SANTSU NO TEGAMI (1979).

THREE VIOLENT PEOPLE 1956 d: Rudolph Mate. USA., *The Maverick*, Leonard Praskins, Barney Slater, Short Story

Three Wagers, The see THE GAY CORINTHIAN (1924).

THREE WEEKS 1915 d: Perry N. Vekroff. USA., *Three Weeks*, Elinor Glyn, London 1907, Novel

THREE WEEKS 1924 d: Alan Crosland. USA., *Three Weeks*, Elinor Glyn, London 1907, Novel

THREE WEIRD SISTERS, THE 1948 d: Daniel Birt. UKN., *The Case of the Three Weird Sisters*, Charlotte Armstrong, Novel

Three Were Thoroughbreds see RELENTLESS (1948).

THREE WHO PAID 1923 d: Colin Campbell. USA., *Three Who Paid*, George Owen Baxter, 1922, Short Story

Three Wise Brides see SPRING MEETING (1941).

THREE WISE FOOLS 1923 d: King Vidor. USA., *Three Wise Fools*, Winchell Smith, Austin Strong, Ottawa 1919, Play

THREE WISE FOOLS 1946 d: Edward Buzzell. USA., *Three Wise Fools*, Winchell Smith, Austin Strong, Ottawa 1919, Play

THREE WISE GIRLS 1932 d: William Beaudine. USA., *Blonde Baby*, Wilson Collison, New York 1931, Book

THREE WISE GUYS 1936 d: George B. Seitz. USA., *Three Wise Guys*, Damon Runyon, 1933, Short Story

THREE WITNESSES 1935 d: Leslie Hiscott. UKN., *Three Witnesses*, S. Fowler Wright, Novel

THREE WOMEN 1924 d: Ernst Lubitsch. USA., Jolanteh Mares, Novel

Three Women see TEEN KANYA (1961).

THREE WORLDS OF GULLIVER, THE 1960 d: Jack Sher. UKN/USA/SPN., *Gulliver's Travels*, Jonathan Swift, London 1726, Novel

THREE YOUNG TEXANS 1954 d: Henry Levin. USA., *Three Young Texans*, William MacLeod Raine, Novel

Three-Cornered Hat, The see IT HAPPENED IN SPAIN (1935).

Three-Cornered Hat, The see IL CAPPELLO A TRE PUNTE (1935).

Three-Cornered Moon see THREE CORNERED MOON (1933).

Threepenny Opera, The see DIE DREIGROSCHENOPER (1930).

Threepenny Opera, The see L' OPERA DE QUAT' SOUS (1930).

Threepenny Opera, The see DIE DREIGROSCHENOPER (1963).

THREE-RING MARRIAGE 1928 d: Marshall Neilan. USA., *Help Yourself to Hay*, Dixie Willson, Short Story

THREE'S A CROWD 1945 d: Lesley Selander. USA., *Hasty Wedding*, Mignon G. Eberhart, Novel

Three's Company see DOUBLE WEDDING (1937).

Three-Thousand Mile Chase, The see 000 MILE CHASE, THE 3 (1977).

Three-Way Mirror, The see LA GLACE A TROIS FACES (1927).

Threshold see UMBARTHA (1982).

THRILLER: THE PREMATURE BURIAL 1960-61 d: Douglas Heyes. USA., *The Premature Burial*, Edgar Allan Poe, 1844, Short Story

Thron Fur Christine, Eine see TRONO PARA CRISTY (1959).

Throne for Christine, A see TRONO PARA CRISTY (1959).

Throne of Blood see KUMONOSU-JO (1957).

Throne, The see SINHASAN (1979).

Through Days and Months see HI MO TSUKI MO (1969).

THROUGH FIRE AND WATER 1923 d: Thomas Bentley. UKN., *Greensea Island*, Victor Bridges, Novel

Through the Ashes of the Empire see PRIN CENUSA IMPERIULUI (1975).

THROUGH THE BREAKERS 1928 d: Joseph C. Boyle. USA., *Through the Breakers*, Owen Davis, Play

THROUGH THE DARK 1924 d: George W. Hill. USA., *The Daughter of Mother McGinn*, Jack Boyle, Story

Through the Storm see PRAIRIE SCHOONERS (1940).

THROUGH THE WALL 1916 d: Rollin S. Sturgeon. USA., *Through the Wall*, Cleveland Moffett, New York 1909, Novel

THROUGH THE WRONG DOOR 1919 d: Clarence Badger. USA., *The Wrong Door*, Jesse Lynch Williams, 1917, Serial Story

THROUGH TROUBLED WATERS 1915 d: Ulysses Davis. USA., *Through Troubled Waters*, William MacLeod Raine, Story

Throw of Dice, A see PRAPANCHA PASH (1929).

Throw of the Dice see PRAPANCHA PASH (1929).

Thumbelina see OYAYUBIME (19—).

THUMBELINA 1970 d: Barry Mahon. USA., *Tommelise*, Hans Christian Andersen, 1835, Short Story

THUMMELUMSEN 1941 d: Emanuel Gregers. DNM., *Livsens Ondskab*, Gustav Wied, 1899, Novel, *Thummelumsen*, Gustav Wied, 1901, Novel

Thunder and Lightning see BLIXT OCH DUNDER (1938).

THUNDER BELOW 1932 d: Richard Wallace. USA., *Thunder Below*, Thomas Rourke, New York 1931, Novel

Thunder in Alaska see CALL OF THE YUKON (1938).

Thunder in the Dust see THE SUNDOWNERS (1950).

Thunder in the East see THE BATTLE (1934).

THUNDER IN THE EAST 1953 d: Charles Vidor. USA., *Rage of the Vulture*, Alan Moorehead, 1948, Novel

THUNDER IN THE NIGHT 1935 d: George Archainbaud. USA., *Eine Frau Lugt*, Ladislaus Fodor, 1934, Play

THUNDER IN THE VALLEY 1947 d: Louis King. USA., *Bob - Son of Battle*, Alfred Ollivant, 1898, Novel

THUNDER ISLAND 1921 d: Norman Dawn. USA., *My Lady of the Island*, Beatrice Grimshaw, Chicago 1916, Novel

THUNDER MOUNTAIN 1925 d: Victor Schertzinger. USA., *Thunder*, Elia W. Peattie, Short Story

THUNDER MOUNTAIN 1935 d: David Howard. USA., *Thunder Mountain*, Zane Grey, New York 1935, Novel

THUNDER MOUNTAIN 1947 d: Lew Landers. USA., *Thunder Mountain*, Zane Grey, New York 1935, Novel

Thunder Mountain see THE SHEPHERD OF THE HILLS (1964).

Thunder of Battle see EROE SENZA PATRIA CORIOLANO (1965).

Thunder of the Gods see SON OF THE GODS (1930).

THUNDER ON THE HILL 1951 d: Douglas Sirk. USA., *Bonaventure*, Charlotte Hastings, London 1949, Play

Thunder Over St. Petersburg see J'AI TUE RASPOUTINE (1967).

THUNDER ROAD 1958 d: Arthur Ripley. USA., Robert Mitchum, Story

THUNDER ROCK 1942 d: Roy Boulting. UKN., *Thunder Rock*, Robert Ardrey, London 1940, Play

THUNDER TRAIL 1937 d: Charles T. Barton. USA., *Arizona Ames*, Zane Grey, New York 1932, Novel

THUNDERBALL 1965 d: Terence Young. UKN., *Thunderball*, Ian Fleming, London 1961, Novel

THUNDERCLOUD, THE 1919 d: Alexander Butler. UKN., *Still Waters Run Deep*, Tom Taylor, London 1855, Play

THUNDERGOD 1928 d: Charles J. Hunt. USA., James Oliver Curwood, Story

Thunderhead see SON OF FLICKA THUNDERHEAD (1945).

THUNDERHEAD, SON OF FLICKA 1945 d: Louis King. USA., *Son of Flicka Thunderhead*, Mary O'Hara, Novel

Thundering Dawn see BAVU (1923).

THUNDERING HERD 1933 d: Henry Hathaway. USA., *The Thundering Herd*, Zane Grey, New York 1925, Novel

THUNDERING HERD, THE 1925 d: William K. Howard. USA., *The Thundering Herd*, Zane Grey, New York 1925, Novel

Thunderstorm see LEIYU (1984).

Thunderstorm, The see GROZA (1934).

THURSDAY'S CHILD 1943 d: Rodney Ackland. UKN., *Thursday's Child*, Donald MacArdle, Novel

THURSDAY'S CHILD 1982 d: David Lowell Rich. USA., *Thursday's Child*, Victoria Poole, Book

Thus Do They All see COSI FAN TUTTE (1991).

Thus Spake Bellavista see COSI PARLO BELLAVISTA (1984).

Thy Last Will Be the First see DIE LETZTEN WERDEN DIE ERSTEN SEIN (1957).

THY NAME IS WOMAN 1924 d: Fred Niblo. USA., *This Name Is Woman*, C. Schoner, Play

THY NEIGHBOR'S WIFE 1953 d: Hugo Haas. USA., *The Peasant Judge*, Oskar Jellinek, 1933, Novel

Thy Soul Shall Bear Witness see KORKARLEN (1921).

Thyl l'Espiegle see LES AVENTURES DE TILL L'ESPIEGLE (1956).

TI ASPETTERO ALL'INFERNO 1960 d: Piero Regnoli. ITL., *Ti Aspettero All'inferno*, Piero Regnoli, Novel

TI CONOSCO, MASCHERINA! 1944 d: Eduardo de Filippo. ITL., *Mascherina! Ti Conosco*, Eduardo Scarpetta, Play

TI HO SEMPRE AMATO! 1954 d: Mario CostA. ITL., Enrico Ragusa, Play

TI HO SPOSATO PER ALLEGRIA 1967 d: Luciano Salce. ITL., *Ti Ho Sposato Per Allegria*, Natalia Ginzburg, Turin 1966, Novel

TI, KOITO SI NA NEBETO 1990 d: Docho Bodzhakov. BUL., *Balada Za Georg Henig*, Viktor Paskov, 1987, Novel

TIA TULA, LA 1964 d: Miguel Picazo. SPN., *La Tia Tula*, Miguel de Unamuno, Madrid 1921, Novel

TIAN WANG 1994 d: XIe Tieli, Qiu Zhongyi. CHN., *Tian Wang*, Zhang Ping, Novel

Tian Yu see XIU XIU: THE SENT-DOWN GIRL (1998).

TIARA TAHITI 1962 d: Ted Kotcheff. UKN., *Tiari Tahiti*, Geoffrey Cotterell, London 1960, Novel

Tichi Don see TIKHU DON (1931).

TICKET O' LEAVE 1922 d: Edwin J. Collins. UKN., *Ticket O' Leave*, George R. Sims, Poem

TICKET OF LEAVE MAN, THE 1937 d: George King. UKN., *The Ticket-of-Leave Man*, Tom Taylor, London 1863, Play

TICKET TO HEAVEN 1981 d: Ralph L. Thomas. CND., *Moonwebs*, Josh Freed, Book

TICKET-OF-LEAVE MAN, THE 1914 d: Louis J. Gasnier, Donald MacKenzie. USA., *The Ticket-of-Leave Man*, Charles Reade, Story

TICKET-OF-LEAVE MAN, THE 1914 d: Travers Vale. USA., *The Ticket-of-Leave Man*, Tom Taylor, London 1863, Play

TICKET-OF-LEAVE MAN, THE 1918 d: Bert Haldane. UKN., *The Ticket-of-Leave Man*, Tom Taylor, London 1863, Play

TICKETS PLEASE AND MONKEY NUTS 1967 d: Claude Whatham. UKN., *Tickets Please and Monkey Nuts*, D. H. Lawrence, Short Story

TICKLISH AFFAIR, A 1963 d: George Sidney. USA., *Moon Walk*, Barbara Luther, 1962, Short Story

Tidal Wave see PORTRAIT OF JENNIE (1948).

Tidal Wave see NIHON CHINBOTSU (1973).

TIDAL WAVE, THE 1920 d: Sinclair Hill. UKN., *The Tidal Wave*, Ethel M. Dell, Novel

TIDE OF EMPIRE 1929 d: Allan Dwan. USA., *Tide of Empire*, Peter B. Kyne, New York 1928, Novel

TIDE OF LIFE, THE 1995 d: David Wheatley. UKN., *The Tide of Life*, Catherine Cookson, Novel

TIDES OF BARNEGAT, THE 1917 d: Marshall Neilan. USA., *The Tides of Barnegat*, F. Hopkinson Smith, New York 1906, Novel

TIDES OF FATE, THE 1917 d: Marshall Farnum. USA., *Creeping Tides*, Kate Jordan, Boston 1913, Novel

TIDES OF PASSION 1925 d: J. Stuart Blackton. USA., *In the Garden of Charity*, Basil King, New York 1903, Novel

TIDES OF TIME, THE 1915 d: Joseph Levering. USA., *The Conqueror Worm*, Edgar Allan Poe, Short Story

TIE DAO YOU JI DUI 1956 d: Zhao Ming. CHN., *Tie Dao You Ji Dui*, Liu Zhixia, Novel

TIE THAT BINDS, THE 1923 d: Joseph Levering. USA., *The Tie That Binds*, Peter B. Kyne, Story

TIE XUE KUN LUN GUAN 1994 d: Yang Guangyuan. CHN., *The Soul of Kunlun Pass*, Chen Dunde, Novel

TIEFLAND 1954 d: Leni Riefenstahl. GRM., *Tiefland*, Eugen d'Albert, Opera

Tiempos Dificiles *see* **TEMPOS DIFICEIS** (1988).

TIERARZT DR. VLIMMEN 1944 d: Boleslav Barlog. GRM., *Doctor Vlimmen*, A. Roothaert, Novel

TIERARZT DR. VLIMMEN 1956 d: Arthur M. Rabenalt. GRM., *Doctor Vlimmen*, A. Roothaert, Novel

Tierarzt Dr. Vlimmen *see* **SKANDAL UM DR. VLIMMEN** (1956).

Tierra Del Fuego, a Whole Night Long *see* **E NACHTLANG FUURLAND** (1982).

TIERRA VALENCIANA 1926 d: Mario Roncoroni. SPN., *Barca VellA. Dolora Del Mar Azul*, Federico Minana, Fernando Miranda, Poem

TIETA DO AGRESTE 1996 d: Carlos Diegues. BRZ./UKN., *Tieta Do Agreste*, Jorge Amado, Novel

Tieta of Agreste *see* **TIETA DO AGRESTE** (1996).

TIGER AKBAR, DER 1951 d: Harry Piel. GRM., *Der Tiger Akbar*, William Quindt, Novel

Tiger Akbar, The *see* **DER TIGER AKBAR** (1951).

Tiger Among Us, The *see* **13 WEST STREET** (1962).

TIGER BAY 1959 d: J. Lee Thompson. UKN., *Rodolphe Et le Revolveur*, Noel Calef, Novel

TIGER BY THE TAIL 1955 d: John Gilling. UKN., *Never Come Back*, John Mair, Novel

Tiger Cub, The *see* **THE TIGER'S CUB** (1920).

Tiger Doesn't Cry, The *see* **TIGERS DON'T CRY** (1976).

Tiger Gang *see* **KOMMISSAR X: JAGT DIE ROTEN TIGER** (1971).

TIGER IN THE SMOKE 1956 d: Roy Ward Baker. UKN., *Tiger in the Smoke*, Margery Allingham, 1952, Novel

TIGER LOVE 1924 d: George Melford. USA., *El Gato Montes*, Manuel Penella, Opera

TIGER, LOWE, PANTHER 1989 d: Dominik Graf. GRM., *Tiger Lowe Panther*, Sherry Hormann, Novel

TIGER MAKES OUT, THE 1968 d: Arthur Hiller. USA., *The Tiger*, Murray Schisgal, New York 1963, Play

Tiger Man *see* **THE LADY AND THE MONSTER** (1944).

Tiger of Bengal *see* **DER TIGER VON ESCHNAPUR** (1959).

TIGER OF SAN PEDRO, THE 1921 d: Maurice Elvey. UKN., Arthur Conan Doyle, Short Story

TIGER ROSE 1923 d: Sidney A. Franklin. USA., *Tiger Rose*, Willard Mack, New York 1917, Play

TIGER ROSE 1929 d: George Fitzmaurice. USA., *Tiger Rose*, Willard Mack, New York 1917, Play

Tiger, The *see* **THE TIGER MAKES OUT** (1968).

TIGER TRUE 1921 d: J. P. McGowan. USA., *Tiger*, Max Brand, 1921, Serial Story

Tiger von Eschnapur, Der *see* **DAS INDISCHE GRABMAL II** (1921).

TIGER VON ESCHNAPUR, DER 1937 d: Richard Eichberg. GRM., *Das Indische Grabmal*, Thea von Harbou, Novel

TIGER VON ESCHNAPUR, DER 1959 d: Fritz Lang. GRM/ITL/FRN., *Das Indische Grabmal*, Thea von Harbou, Novel

TIGER WALKS, A 1964 d: Norman Tokar. USA., *A Tiger Walks*, Ian Niall, London 1960, Novel

Tigerin, Die *see* **THE TIGRESS** (1992).

TIGER'S COAT, THE 1920 d: Roy Clements. USA., *The Tiger's Coat*, Elizabeth Dejeans, Indianapolis 1917, Novel

TIGER'S CUB, THE 1920 d: Charles Giblyn. USA., *The Tiger's Cub*, George Potter, London 1915, Play

TIGERS DON'T CRY 1976 d: Peter Collinson. SAF., *Tigers Don't Cry*, Jon Burmeister, Novel

TIGER'S TALE, A 1987 d: Peter Douglas. USA., *Love and Other Natural Disasters*, Allen Hannay III, Book

Tight Little Island *see* **WHISKY GALORE!** (1948).

TIGHT SHOES 1941 d: Albert S. Rogell. USA., *Tight Shoes*, Damon Runyon, 1938, Short Story

TIGHT SPOT 1955 d: Phil Karlson. USA., *Dead Pigeon*, Leonard Kantor, New York 1953, Play

Tigre Di Eschnapur, La *see* **DER TIGER VON ESCHNAPUR** (1959).

TIGRE DU BENGALE, LE 1937 d: Richard Eichberg. FRN., *Das Indische Grabmal*, Thea von Harbou, Novel

Tigre du Bengale, Le *see* **DER TIGER VON ESCHNAPUR** (1959).

Tigre du Ciel, Le *see* **ACES HIGH** (1976).

Tigre E Ancora Viva, La *see* **LA TIGRE E ANCORA VIVA: SANDOKAN ALLA RISCOSSA** (1977).

TIGRE E ANCORA VIVA: SANDOKAN ALLA RISCOSSA, LA 1977 d: Sergio SollimA. ITL., Emilio Salgari, Story

TIGRE REALE 1916 d: Giovanni Pastrone. ITL., *Tigre Reale*, Giovanni Verga, 1873

Tigre Sort Sans Sa Mere, Le *see* **DA BERLINO L'APOCALISSE** (1967).

Tigres de Mompracem, Los *see* **LE TIGRI DI MOMPRACEM** (1970).

Tigress of Bengal *see* **DER TIGER VON ESCHNAPUR** (1959).

TIGRESS, THE 1992 d: Karin Howard. USA/GRM., *Die Tigerin*, Walter Serner, Novel

TIGRI DI MOMPRACEM, LE 1970 d: Mario Sequi. ITL/SPN., *Le Tigri Di Mompracem*, Emilio Salgari, Genoa 1900, Story

Tihij Don *see* **TIKHII DON** (1958).

TIKHII DON 1958 d: Sergei Gerasimov. USS., *Tikhy Don*, Mikhail Sholokhov, 1929, Novel

TIKHU DON 1931 d: Olga Preobrazhenskaya, Ivan Pravov. USS., *Tikhy Don*, Mikhail Sholokhov, 1929, Novel

Tikhy Don *see* **TIKHU DON** (1931).

Tikhy Don *see* **TIKHII DON** (1958).

Tiko and the Shark *see* **TI-KOYO E IL SUO PESCECANE** (1962).

Ti-Koyo and His Shark *see* **TI-KOYO E IL SUO PESCECANE** (1962).

TI-KOYO E IL SUO PESCECANE 1962 d: Folco Quilici. ITL/FRN/USA., *Ti-Koyo Et Son Requin*, Clement Richer, Paris 1941, Novel

Ti-Koyo Et Son Requin *see* **TI-KOYO E IL SUO PESCECANE** (1962).

'Til Death Us Do Part *see* **TILL DEATH US DO PART** (1991).

'Til We Meet Again *see* **TILL WE MEET AGAIN** (1936).

Till Death Do Us Part *see* **LA NOVIA ENSANGRENTADA** (1972).

TILL DEATH US DO PART 1914 d: Colin Campbell. USA., *Till Death Us Do Part*, James Oliver Curwood, Story

TILL DEATH US DO PART 1991 d: Yves Simoneau. USA., *Till Death Us Do Part*, Vincent Bugliosi, Book

Till Eulenspiegel *see* **LES AVENTURES DE TILL L'ESPIEGLE** (1956).

Till Marriage Do Us Part *see* **ATE QUE O CASAMENTO NOS SEPARE** (1968).

Till Marriage Does Us Apart *see* **ATE QUE O CASAMENTO NOS SEPARE** (1968).

TILL OUR SHIP COMES IN 1919 d: Frank Miller. UKN., *Till Our Ship Comes in*, Kenelm Foss, Novel

TILL THE BELLS RING 1933 d: Graham Moffatt. UKN., *Till the Bells Ring*, Graham Moffatt, Glasgow 1908, Play

TILL THE END OF TIME 1946 d: Edward Dmytryk. USA., *They Dream of Home*, Niven Busch, Novel

TILL WE MEET AGAIN 1936 d: Robert Florey. USA., *Last Curtain*, Alfred Davis, 1933, Play

TILL WE MEET AGAIN 1944 d: Frank Borzage. USA., *Tomorrow's Harvest*, Alfred Maury, Play

TILLIE 1922 d: Frank Urson. USA., *A Mennonite Maid Tillie*, Helen Reimensnyder, New York 1904, Novel

Tillie, a Mennonite Maid *see* **TILLIE** (1922).

Tillie's Nightmare *see* **TILLIE'S PUNCTURED ROMANCE** (1914).

TILLIE'S PUNCTURED ROMANCE 1914 d: MacK Sennett. USA., *Tillie's Nightmare*, A. Baldwin Sloane, Edgar Sloane, New York 1910, Musical Play

TILLY OF BLOOMSBURY 1921 d: Rex Wilson. UKN., *Happy-Go-Lucky*, Ian Hay, 1913, Novel

TILLY OF BLOOMSBURY 1931 d: Jack Raymond. UKN., *Happy-Go-Lucky*, Ian Hay, 1913, Novel

TILLY OF BLOOMSBURY 1940 d: Leslie Hiscott. UKN., *Happy-Go-Lucky*, Ian Hay, 1913, Novel

TIM 1979 d: Michael Pate. ASL., *Tim*, Colleen McCullough, Novel

Timber *see* **KING OF THE LUMBERJACKS** (1940).

TIMBER FURY 1950 d: Bernard B. Ray. USA., *Retribution*, James Oliver Curwood, Short Story

TIMBER WAR 1936 d: Sam Newfield. USA., *Hell's Gulch*, James Oliver Curwood, Short Story

TIMBERJACK 1955 d: Joseph Kane. USA., *Timberjack*, Dan Cushman, Novel

TIME AFTER TIME 1985 d: Bill Hays. UKN., *Time After Time*, Molly Keane, Novel

Time and Hour of Augusto Matraga, The *see* **A HORA E VEZ DE AUGUSTO MATRAGA** (1965).

TIME BOMB 1952 d: Ted Tetzlaff. UKN., *Death at Attention*, Kem Bennett, Novel

Time for Action *see* **TIP ON A DEAD JOCKEY** (1957).

Time for Giving, A *see* **GENERATION** (1969).

Time for Indifference *see* **GLI INDIFFERENTI** (1964).

TIME FOR KILLING, A 1967 d: Phil Karlson, Roger Corman (Uncredited). USA., *The Southern Blade*, Nelson Wolford, Shirley Wolford, New York 1961, Novel

Time for Men, A *see* **MUZHKI VREMENA** (1977).

Time Games *see* **PLAYING BEATIE BOW** (1986).

TIME, GENTLEMEN, PLEASE 1952 d: Lewis Gilbert. UKN., *Nothing to Lose*, R. J. Minney, Novel

Time in the Sun, A *see* **PRINSESSAN** (1966).

TIME IS MY ENEMY 1954 d: Don Chaffey. UKN., *Second Chance*, Ella Adkins, Play

TIME LIMIT 1957 d: Karl Malden. USA., *Time Limit!*, Ralph Berkey, Henry Denker, New York 1956, Play

TIME LOCK 1957 d: Gerald Thomas. UKN., *Time Lock*, Arthur Hailey, Television Play

Time Lost and Time Remembered *see* **I WAS HAPPY HERE** (1965).

TIME MACHINE, THE 1960 d: George Pal. USA., *The Time machine*, H. G. Wells, 1895, Novel

TIME MACHINE, THE 1978 d: Henning Schellerup. USA., *The Time machine*, H. G. Wells, 1895, Novel

Time of Desire *see* **HASTHANDLARENS FLICKOR** (1954).

Time of Indifference *see* **GLI INDIFFERENTI** (1964).

Time of Losing Faith *see* **FUSHIN NO TOKI** (1968).

Time of Parting *see* **VREME NA NASILIE** (1988).

Time of Reckoning, The *see* **FUSHIN NO TOKI** (1968).

Time of the Innocent, The *see* **DIE ZEIT DER SCHULDLOSEN** (1964).

TIME OF THEIR LIVES, THE 1946 d: Charles T. Barton. USA., *Gramercy Ghost*, John Cecil Holm, Play

Time of Violence *see* **VREME NA NASILIE** (1988).

TIME OF YOUR LIFE, THE 1948 d: H. C. Potter. USA., *The Time of Your Life*, William Saroyan, New York 1939, Play

TIME OF YOUR LIFE, THE 1958 d: Philip Saville. UKN., *The Time of Your Life*, William Saroyan, New York 1939, Play

Time Out for Love *see* **LES GRANDES PERSONNES** (1961).

TIME OUT FOR RHYTHM 1941 d: Sidney Salkow. USA., *Show Business*, Alex Ruben, Play

TIME OUT FOR ROMANCE 1937 d: Malcolm St. Clair. USA., *Thanks for the Ride*, Eleanore Griffin, William Rankin, 1936, Short Story

TIME OUT OF MIND 1947 d: Robert Siodmak. USA., *Time Out of Mind*, Rachel Field, Novel

Time Slip *see* **SENGOKU JIEITAI** (1980).

Time Slip of the Battlefield *see* **SENGOKU JIEITAI** (1980).

TIME, THE COMEDIAN 1925 d: Robert Z. Leonard. USA., *Time, the Comedian*, Kate Jordan, New York 1905, Novel

TIME, THE PLACE AND THE GIRL, THE 1929 d: Howard Bretherton. USA., *The Time the Place and the Girl*, Frank Adams, New York 1907, Musical Play

TIME, THE PLACE AND THE GIRL, THE 1929 d: Howard Bretherton. USA., *The Time the Place and the Girl*, W. Hough, Joseph Howard, New York 1907, Musical Play

TIME TO DANCE, A 1991 d: Kevin Billington. UKN., *A Time to Dance*, Melvyn Bragg, Novel

Time to Die, A *see* **AMELIE OU LE TEMPS D'AIMER** (1961).

TIME TO KILL 1942 d: Herbert I. Leeds. USA., *The High Window*, Raymond Chandler, 1942, Novel

TIME TO KILL, A 1996 d: Joel Schumacher. USA., *A Time to Kill*, John Grisham, Novel

TO THE PUBLIC DANGER 1948 d: Terence Fisher. UKN., *To the Public Danger*, Patrick Hamilton, 1939, Radio Play

To the Starry Island *see* GESOM E KAKO SHIPTA (1993).

To the Victor *see* OWD BOB (1938).

TO WHAT RED HELL 1929 d: Edwin Greenwood. UKN., *To What Red Hell*, Percy Robinson, Play

To Whom It May Concern *see* THE SOCIAL CODE (1923).

TOA 1949 d: Sacha Guitry. FRN., *Toa*, Sacha Guitry, Play

TOAST OF NEW YORK, THE 1937 d: Rowland V. Lee. USA., *Robber Barons*, Matthew Josephson, New York 1934, Book, *Book of Daneile Drew*, Bouck White, New York 1910, Book

Toast of the Legion *see* KISS ME AGAIN (1931).

TOAST TO MELBA, A 1980 d: Alan Burke. ASL., *A Toast to Melba*, Jack Hibberd, Play

Tobacco *see* TYUTYUN (1962).

TOBACCO ROAD 1941 d: John Ford. USA., *Tobacco Road*, Erskine Caldwell, 1932, Novel

TOBIAS KNOPP, ABENTEUER EINES JUNGGESELLEN 1950 d: Walter Pentzlin. GRM., *Abenteuer Eines Junggesellen*, Wilhelm Busch, 1875, Short Story

TOBIN'S PALM 1918 d: Kenneth Webb. USA., *Tobin's Palm*, O. Henry, Short Story

Toby *see* ONE DOLLAR BID (1918).

TOBY TYLER 1960 d: Charles T. Barton. USA., *Toby Tyler; Or Ten Weeks With a Circus*, James Otis Kaler, New York 1881, Novel

Toby Tyler, Or Ten Weeks With a Circus *see* TOBY TYLER (1960).

TOBY'S BOW 1919 d: Harry Beaumont. USA., *Toby's Bow*, John Taintor Foote, New York 1919, Play

Tochter Des Woiwoden, Die *see* TARAS BULBA (1924).

Tochter Einer Kurtisane, Die *see* YVETTE (1938).

TOCHTER IHRER EXZELLENZ, DIE 1934 d: Reinhold Schunzel. GRM., *Die Kleine Trafik*, Emil Burri, Play

Tod Aus Der Themse, Die *see* DIE TOTE AUS DER THEMSE (1971).

TOD DES EMPEDOKLES, DER 1986 d: Jean-Marie Straub, Daniele Huillet. GRM/FRN., *Der Tod Des Empedockles*, Friedrich Holderlin, 1826, Play

Tod Eines Handlungsreisenden *see* DEATH OF A SALESMAN (1985).

Tod Im Spiegel *see* SHATTERED (1990).

Tod Ritt Dienstags, Der *see* I GIORNI DELL'IRA (1967).

TOD UND AUFERSTEHUNG DES WILHELM HAUSMANN 1977 d: Christa Muhl. GDR., *Arbeitsplatz Oder Im Schweisse Deines Angesichts Sollst Du.*, Bertolt Brecht, 1962, Short Story

TOD UND TEUFEL 1973 d: Stephen Dwoskin. GRM., *Tod Und Teufel*, Frank Wedekind, 1909, Play

Toda Desnudez Sera Castigada *see* TODA NUDEZ SERA CASTIGADA (1973).

TODA NUDEZ SERA CASTIGADA 1973 d: Arnaldo Jabor. BRZ., *Toda Nudez Sera Castigada*, Nelson Rodrigues, 1965-66, Play

Today *see* TO-DAY (1917).

TODAY 1930 d: William Nigh. USA., *Today*, George Broadhurst, Abraham S. Schomer, New York 1913, Play

TODAY 1917 d: Ralph Ince. USA., *Today*, George Broadhurst, Abraham S. Schomer, New York 1913, Play

TODAY WE LIVE 1932 d: Howard Hawks. USA., *Turn About*, William Faulkner, 1932, Short Story

Todesracher von Soho, Der *see* EL MUERTO HACE LAS MALETAS (1970).

TODESSTRAHLEN DES DR. MABUSE, DIE 1964 d: Hugo Fregonese. GRM/FRN/ITL., *Dr. Mabuse*, Norbert Jacques, Novel

Todlichen Traume, Die *see* LIEBESTRAUM (1951).

TODO MODO 1976 d: Elio Petri. ITL., *Todo Modo*, Leonardo Sciasia, 1974, Novel

TODO SEA PARA BIEN 1957 d: Carlos Rinaldi. ARG., *Tutto Per Bene*, Luigi Pirandello, 1906, Short Story

TODO UN HOMBRE 1943 d: Pierre Chenal. ARG., *Nada Menos Que Todo un Hombre*, Miguel de Unamuno, 1916, Short Story

TODO UN HOMBRE 1983 d: Rafael Villasenor. MXC/SPN., *Nada Menos Que Todo un Hombre*, Miguel de Unamuno, 1916, Short Story

TOEN 'T LICHT VERDWEEN 1918 d: Maurits H. Binger. NTH., **De Sphinx**, Jonkheer A. W. G. Van Riemsdijk, Play

TOGETHER 1918 d: O. A. C. Lund. USA., *The Lone Dit*, Louis R. Wolheim, Short Story

TOGLI LE GAMBE DAL PARABREZZA 1969 d: Massimo FranciosA. ITL., *La Ragazza Va in Calabria*, Giuseppe Berto, Short Story

Tognazzi E la Minorenne *see* LA RAGAZZA DI MILLE MESI (1961).

Tohoku No Jinmutachi *see* TOHOKU NO ZUNMUTACHI (1957).

TOHOKU NO ZUNMUTACHI 1957 d: Kon IchikawA. JPN., *Tohoku No Jinmutachi*, Shichiro Fukazawa, 1957, Short Story

TOI C'EST MOI 1936 d: Rene Guissart. FRN., *Toi C'est Moi*, Henri Duvernois, Albert Willemetz, Opera

TOI LE VENIN 1958 d: Robert Hossein. FRN., *C'est Toi le Venin.*, Frederic Dard, Novel

TOILERS OF THE SEA 1923 d: R. William Neill. USA/ITL., *Les Travailleurs de la Mer*, Victor Hugo, 1866, Novel

TOILERS OF THE SEA 1936 d: Selwyn Jepson, Ted Fox. UKN., *Les Travailleurs de la Mer*, Victor Hugo, 1866, Novel

TOINON LA RUINE 1913 d: Alexandre Devarennes. FRN., *Toinon la Ruine*, Georges G. Toudouze, Novel

TOISON D'OR, LA 1916. FRN., *La Toison d'Or*, Barre, Maurice Keroul, Play

TOKAIDO YOTSUYA KAIDAN 1959 d: Nobuo NakagawA. JPN., *Tokaido Yotsuya Kaidan*, Nanboku Tsuruya, 1825, Play

TOKI NO UJIGAMI 1932 d: Kenji Mizoguchi. JPN., *Toki No Ujigami*, Kan Kikuchi, 1924, Play

TOKI O KAKERU SHOJO 1983 d: Nobuhiko Obayashi. JPN., *Toki O Kakeru Shojo*, Yasutaka Tsutsui, Novel

TOKIO SIREN, A 1920 d: Norman Dawn. USA., *Sayonara*, Gwendolyn Logan, Short Story

Tokyo Blackout *see* SHUTO SHOSHITSU (1987).

Tokyo Bordello *see* YOSHIWARA ENJO (1987).

Tokyo Chorus *see* TOKYO NO GASSHO (1931).

Tokyo Drifter *see* TOKYO NAGARE MONO (1966).

TOKYO NAGARE MONO 1966 d: Seijun Suzuki. JPN., *Tokyo Nagare Mono*, Yasunori Kawauchi, Novel

TOKYO NO GASSHO 1931 d: Yasujiro Ozu. JPN., *Tokyo No Gassho*, Komatsu Kitamura, Novel

TOL'ABLE DAVID 1921 d: Henry King. USA., *Tol'able David*, Joseph Hergesheimer, 1919, Short Story

TOL'ABLE DAVID 1930 d: John G. Blystone. USA., *Tol'able David*, Joseph Hergesheimer, 1919, Short Story

TOLD IN THE HILLS 1919 d: George Melford. USA., *Told in the Hills*, Marah Ellis Ryan, Chicago 1891, Novel

TOLL OF YOUTH, THE 1915 d: Frank Lloyd. USA., *The Toll of Youth*, Donald Meaney, Story

TOLLDREISTEN GESCHICHTEN - NACH HONORE DE BALZAC, DIE 1969 d: Jozef Zachar. GRM., *Les Contes Drolatiques*, Honore de Balzac, 1832-37, Short Stories

TOLLE KOMTESS, DIE 1928 d: Richard Lowenbein. GRM., *Die Tolle Komtess*, Rudolf Bernauer, Walter Kollo, Rudolph Schanzer, Opera

TOLLE LOLA, DIE 1927 d: Richard Eichberg. GRM., *Der Weg Zur Holle*, Gustav Kadelburg, Play

TOLLE LOLA, DIE 1954 d: Hans Deppe. GRM., *Der Weg Zur Holle*, Gustav Kadelburg, Play

TOLLER EINFALL, EIN 1932 d: Kurt Gerron. GRM., *Ein Toller Einfall*, Carl Laufs, Play

Toller Fall, Ein *see* DER GROSSE FALL (1945).

TOLLER HECHT AUF KRUMMEN TOUREN 1961 d: Akos von Rathony. GRM., *Toller Hecht Auf Krummer Tour*, Heinz Gross, Egon G. Schleinitz, Bad Worishofen 1959, Novel

Toller Hecht Auf Krummer Tour *see* TOLLER HECHT AUF KRUMMEN TOUREN (1961).

TOLLER TAG, EIN 1945 d: Oscar F. Schuh. GRM., *Le Mariage de Figaro*, Pierre-Augustin Caron de Beaumarchais, Paris 1784, Play

TOM & VIV 1994 d: Brian Gilbert. UKN., *Tom & Viv*, Michael Hastings, Play

Tom and Viv *see* TOM & VIV (1994).

Tom Brown of Harvard *see* BROWN OF HARVARD (1918).

TOM BROWN'S SCHOOLDAYS 1916 d: Rex Wilson. UKN., *Tom Brown's Schooldays*, Thomas Hughes, London 1857, Novel

TOM BROWN'S SCHOOLDAYS 1940 d: Robert Stevenson. USA., *Tom Brown's Schooldays*, Thomas Hughes, London 1857, Novel

TOM BROWN'S SCHOOLDAYS 1951 d: Gordon Parry. UKN., *Tom Brown's Schooldays*, Thomas Hughes, London 1857, Novel

TOM CLANCY'S OP CENTER 1995 d: Lewis Teague. USA., *Op Center*, Tom Clancy, Novel

TOM CRINGLE IN JAMAICA 1913 d: Charles Raymond. UKN., *Tom Cringle's Log*, Michael Scott, 1836, Novel

TOM DOLLAR 1967 d: Marcello Ciorciolini. ITL/FRN., *Tom Dollar*, Al Petrie, Novel

Tom Dooley - Held Der Grunen Holle *see* TUMULTO DE PAIXOES (1958).

Tom Dooley - Hero of the Green Hell *see* TUMULTO DE PAIXOES (1958).

TOM HORN 1979 d: William Wiard. USA., *Life of Tom Horn Government Scout and Interpreter*, Tom Horn, Autobiography

TOM JONES 1917 d: Edwin J. Collins. UKN., *Tom Jones a Foundling*, Henry Fielding, 1749, Novel

TOM JONES 1963 d: Tony Richardson. UKN., *Tom Jones a Foundling*, Henry Fielding, 1749, Novel

TOM SAWYER 1917 d: William D. Taylor. USA., *Adventures of Tom Sawyer*, Mark Twain, San Francisco 1876, Novel

TOM SAWYER 1930 d: John Cromwell. USA., *Adventures of Tom Sawyer*, Mark Twain, San Francisco 1876, Novel

TOM SAWYER 1973 d: Don Taylor. USA., *Adventures of Tom Sawyer*, Mark Twain, San Francisco 1876, Novel

TOM SAWYER 1973 d: James Neilson. USA., *Adventures of Tom Sawyer*, Mark Twain, San Francisco 1876, Novel

TOM SAWYER 1983 d: Stanislav Govorukhin. USS., *Adventures of Tom Sawyer*, Mark Twain, San Francisco 1876, Novel

TOM SAWYER, DETECTIVE 1938 d: Louis King. USA., *Tom Sawyer, Detective*, Mark Twain, 1897, Short Story

Tom Thumb *see* LE PETIT POUCET (1912).

TOM THUMB 1958 d: George Pal. UKN/USA., *Daumesdick*, Jacob Grimm, Wilhelm Grimm, 1812, Short Story

Tom Thumb *see* PULGARCITO (1958).

Tom Thumb *see* LE PETIT POUCET (1972).

Tom Toms of Mayumba *see* TAM TAM MAYUMBE (1955).

Tomahawk and the Cross, The *see* PILLARS OF THE SKY (1956).

Tomahawk Trail, The *see* THE IROQUOIS TRAIL (1950).

TOMB OF LIGEIA, THE 1964 d: Roger Corman. UKN., *Ligeia*, Edgar Allan Poe, 1838, Short Story

Tomb of the Cat *see* THE TOMB OF LIGEIA (1964).

TOMB, THE 1986 d: Fred Olen Ray. USA., *The Jewel of the Seven Stars*, Bram Stoker, 1903, Novel

Tombeau Hindou, Le *see* DAS INDISCHE GRABMAL (1959).

TOMBEUR, LE 1957 d: Rene Delacroix. FRN., *Deux Paillassons un Coeur*, Marcel Arnac, Play

TOMEI NINGEN 1954 d: Motoyoshi OdA. JPN., *The Invisible Man*, H. G. Wells, London 1897, Novel

TOMMASO BLU 1986 d: Florian Furtwangler. GRM., *Tommaso Blu*, Tommaso Di Ciaula, Novel

TOMMY 1931 d: Yakov Protazanov. USS., *Bronepoezd No.14-69*, Vsevolod Ivanov, 1922, Play

TOMMY 1975 d: Ken Russell. UKN., *Tommy*, Peter Townshend, Opera

TOMMY ATKINS 1910. UKN., *Tommy Atkins*, Ben Landeck, Arthur Shirley, London 1895, Play

TOMMY ATKINS 1915 d: Bert Haldane. UKN., *Tommy Atkins*, Ben Landeck, Arthur Shirley, London 1895, Play

TOMMY ATKINS 1928 d: Norman Walker. UKN., *Tommy Atkins*, Ben Landeck, Arthur Shirley, London 1895, Play

TOMMYKNOCKERS, THE 1993 d: John Power. USA., *The Tommyknockers*, Stephen King, Novel

TOMORROW 1972 d: Joseph Anthony. USA., *Tomorrow*, William Faulkner, 1940, Short Story

TOMORROW AND TOMORROW 1932 d: Richard Wallace. USA., *Tomorrow and Tomorrow*, Philip Barry, New York 1931, Play

Tomorrow Is a Wonderful Day see ADAMAH (1947).

TOMORROW IS FOREVER 1946 d: Irving Pichel. USA., *Tomorrow Is Forever*, Gwen Bristow, Novel

Tomorrow Is Too Late see DOMANI E TROPPO TARDI (1950).

TOMORROW THE WORLD 1944 d: Leslie Fenton. USA., *Tomorrow the World*, Arnold d'Usseau, James Gow, New York 1943, Play

TOMORROW'S LOVE 1925 d: Paul Bern. USA., *Interlocutory*, Charles William Brackett, 1924, Short Story

TONG MAN, THE 1919 d: William Worthington. USA., *The Dragon's Daughter*, Clyde C. Westover, New York 1912, Novel

Tong War see CHINATOWN NIGHTS (1929).

TONGUES OF FLAME 1919 d: Colin Campbell. USA., *In the Carquinez Woods*, Bret Harte, London 1883, Novel

TONGUES OF FLAME 1924 d: Joseph Henabery. USA., *Tongues of Flame*, Peter Clark MacFarlane, New York 1924, Novel

TONGUES OF MEN 1916 d: Frank Lloyd. USA., *The Tongues of Men*, Edward Childs Carpenter, New York 1913, Play

Tongues of Men, The see TONGUES OF MEN (1916).

TONI 1928 d: Arthur Maude. UKN., *Toni*, Douglas Furber, Harry Graham, Hugo Hirsch, London 1924, Musical Play

TONIC, THE 1928 d: Ivor Montagu. UKN., *The Tonic*, H. G. Wells, Short Story

Tonight at 8.30 see MEET ME TONIGHT (1952).

TONIGHT AT TWELVE 1929 d: Harry Pollard. USA., *Tonight at 12*, Owen Davis, New York 1928, Play

Tonight Belongs to Us see THE MEN IN HER LIFE (1941).

TONIGHT IS OURS 1933 d: Stuart Walker, Mitchell Leisen (Uncredited). USA., *The Queen Was in the Parlour*, Noel Coward, London 1926, Play

TONIGHT OR NEVER 1931 d: Mervyn Leroy. USA., *Tonight Or Never*, Lili Hatvany, New York 1930, Play

TONIGHT WE SING 1953 d: Mitchell Leisen. USA., *Impresario*, Ruth Goode, Sol Horuk, Book

Tonight's Our Night see TOVARICH (1937).

TONIO KROGER 1964 d: Rolf Thiele. GRM/FRN., *Tonio Kroger*, Thomas Mann, Berlin 1903, Short Story

TONIO, SON OT THE SIERRAS 1925 d: Ben Wilson. USA., *Tonio Son of the Sierras; a Story of the Apache Wars*, Gen. Charles King, New York 1906, Novel

TONKA 1958 d: Lewis R. Foster. USA., *Comanche*, David Appel, 1951, Novel

Tonka of the Gallows see TONKA SIBENICE (1930).

TONKA SIBENICE 1930 d: Karl Anton. CZC., *Nanebevstoupeni Tonky Sibenice*, Egon Erwin Kisch, Short Story

Tonka, Tart of the Gallows Mob see TONKA SIBENICE (1930).

TONNERRE DE DIEU, LE 1965 d: Denys de La Patelliere. FRN/ITL/GRM., *Le Tonnerre de Dieu*, Bernard Clavel, Novel

Tonnerre Sur Saint-Petersburg see J'AI TUE RASPOUTINE (1967).

TONNY 1962 d: Nils R. Muller. NRW., *Den Onde Hyrde*, Jens Bjorneboe, 1960, Novel

TONS OF MONEY 1924 d: Frank H. Crane. UKN., *Tons of Money*, Will Evans, Arthur Valentine, London 1922, Play

TONS OF MONEY 1931 d: Tom Walls. UKN., *Tons of Money*, Will Evans, Arthur Valentine, London 1922, Play

TONTO KID, THE 1935 d: Harry L. Fraser. USA., *The Daughter of Diamond*, Christopher B. Booth, Novel

TONTONS FLINGEURS, LES 1963 d: Georges Lautner. FRN/GRM/ITL., *Les Tontons Flingueurs*, Albert Simonin, Novel

TONY DRAWS A HORSE 1950 d: John Paddy Carstairs. UKN., *Tony Draws a Horse*, Lesley Storm, London 1939, Play

TONY ROME 1967 d: Gordon Douglas. USA., *Miami Mayhem*, Anthony Rome, New York 1960, Novel

Too Bad She's Bad see PECCATO CHE SIA UNA CANAGLIA (1955).

TOO BUSY TO WORK 1932 d: John G. Blystone. USA., *Jubilo*, Ben Ames Williams, 1919, Short Story

TOO BUSY TO WORK 1939 d: Otto Brower. USA., *The Torchbearers*, George Edward Kelly, New York 1922, Play, *Your Uncle Dudley*, Howard Lindsay, Bertrand Robinson, New York 1929, Play

TOO DANGEROUS TO LIVE 1939 d: Leslie Norman, Anthony Hankey. UKN., *Crime Unlimited*, David Hume, Novel

Too Dangerous to Love see PERFECT STRANGERS (1949).

TOO FAR TO GO 1979 d: Fielder Cook. USA., John Updike, Short Stories

TOO FAT TO FIGHT 1918 d: Hobart Henley. USA., *Too Fat to Fight*, Rex Beach, Short Story

TOO GOOD TO BE TRUE 1988 d: Christian Nyby II. USA., *Too Good to Be True*, Ben Ames Williams, Novel

TOO LATE FOR TEARS 1949 d: Byron Haskin. USA., *Too Late for Tears*, Roy Huggins, 1947, Serial Story

Too Many Chefs see WHO IS KILLING THE GREAT CHEFS OF EUROPE? (1978).

TOO MANY COOKS 1931 d: William A. Seiter. USA., *Too Many Cooks*, Frank Craven, New York 1914, Play

TOO MANY CROOKS 1919 d: Ralph Ince. USA., *Too Many Crooks*, E. J. Rath, New York 1918, Novel

TOO MANY CROOKS 1927 d: Fred Newmeyer. USA., *Too Many Crooks*, E. J. Rath, New York 1918, Novel

TOO MANY GIRLS 1940 d: George Abbott. USA., *Too Many Girls*, Lorenz Hart, George Marion Jr., Richard Rodgers, New York 1939, Musical Play

TOO MANY HUSBANDS 1938 d: Ivar Campbell. UKN., *Mirabelle*, Guy Bolton, Play

TOO MANY HUSBANDS 1940 d: Wesley Ruggles. USA., *Too Many Husbands*, W. Somerset Maugham, Atlantic City, N.J. 1919, Play

TOO MANY KISSES 1925 d: Paul Sloane. USA., *A Maker of Gestures*, John Monk Saunders, 1923, Short Story

TOO MANY MILLIONS 1918 d: James Cruze. USA., *Someone and Somebody*, Porter Emerson Browne, New York 1917, Novel

TOO MANY PARENTS 1936 d: Robert F. McGowan. USA., *Too Many Parents*, George Templeton, Short Story, *Not Wanted*, Jesse Lynch Williams, 1923, Short Story

Too Many Parents see IMAM DVIJE MAME I DVA TATE (1968).

Too Many Women see GOD'S GIFT TO WOMEN (1931).

TOO MUCH BUSINESS 1922 d: Jess Robbins. USA., *John Henry and the Restless Sex*, Earl Derr Biggers, 1921, Short Story

TOO MUCH JOHNSON 1920 d: Donald Crisp. USA., *Too Much Johnson*, William Gillette, New York 1894, Play

TOO MUCH MONEY 1926 d: John Francis Dillon. USA., *Too Much Money*, Israel Zangwill, London 1924, Play

Too Much Speed see WHAT'S YOUR HURRY? (1920).

TOO MUCH SPEED 1921 d: Frank Urson. USA., *Too Much Speed*, Byron Morgan, 1921, Short Story

TOO MUCH, TOO SOON 1958 d: Art Napoleon. USA., *Too Soon Too Much*, Diana Barrymore, 1957, Autobiography

Too Much Woman see EN KVINDE ER OVERFLODIG (1958).

TOO YOUNG TO KNOW 1945 d: Frederick de CordovA. USA., *Too Young to Know*, Harlan Ware, Serial Story

TOO YOUNG TO LOVE 1960 d: Muriel Box. UKN., *Pickup Girl*, Elsa Shelley, London 1946, Play

TOO YOUNG TO MARRY 1931 d: Mervyn Leroy. USA., *Broken Dishes*, Martin Flavin, New York 1929, Play

TOP DOG, THE 1918 d: Arrigo Bocchi. UKN., *The Top Dog*, Fergus Hume, Novel

TOP HAT 1935 d: Mark Sandrich. USA., *The Girl Who Dared (Scandal in Budapest)*, Alexander Farago, Aladar Laszlo, 1911, Play

TOP O' THE MORNING, THE 1922 d: Edward Laemmle. USA., *Top O' the Mornin'*, Anne Caldwell, c1913, Play

TOP OF THE WORLD, THE 1925 d: George Melford. USA., *The Top of the World*, Ethel M. Dell, London 1920, Novel

TOP SECRET AFFAIR 1956 d: H. C. Potter. USA., *Melville Goodwin U.S.A.*, John Phillips Marquand, 1951, Novel

TOP SPEED 1930 d: Mervyn Leroy. USA., *Top Speed*, Guy Bolton, Bert Kalmar, Harry Ruby, New York 1929, Musical Play

TOPAZ 1969 d: Alfred Hitchcock. USA., *Topaz*, Leon Uris, New York 1967, Novel

TOPAZE 1932 d: Louis J. Gasnier. FRN., *Topaze*, Marcel Pagnol, Paris 1928, Play

TOPAZE 1933 d: Harry d'Abbadie d'Arrast. USA., *Topaze*, Marcel Pagnol, Paris 1928, Play

TOPAZE 1936 d: Marcel Pagnol. FRN., *Topaze*, Marcel Pagnol, Paris 1928, Play

TOPAZE 1950 d: Marcel Pagnol. FRN., *Topaze*, Marcel Pagnol, Paris 1928, Play

TOPKAPI 1964 d: Jules Dassin. USA/FRN., *The Light of Day*, Eric Ambler, London 1962, Novel

TOPPER 1937 d: Norman Z. McLeod. USA., *Topper*, Thorne Smith, New York 1926, Novel

TOPPER 1979 d: Charles S. Dubin. USA., *Topper*, Thorne Smith, New York 1926, Novel

TOPPER RETURNS 1941 d: Roy Del Ruth. USA., *Topper*, Thorne Smith, New York 1926, Novel

TOPPER TAKES A TRIP 1939 d: Norman Z. McLeod. USA., *Topper Takes a Trip*, Thorne Smith, New York 1932, Novel

Tops Is the Limit see ANYTHING GOES (1936).

TOPSY AND EVA 1927 d: Del Lord, D. W. Griffith (Uncredited). USA., *Topsy and Eva*, Catherine Chisholm Cushing, New York 1924, Play

Tor Zum Paradies, Das see DIE SELTSAME GESCHICHTE DES BRANDNER KASPER (1949).

TORA NO OO FUMA OTOKOTACHI 1945 d: Akira KurosawA. JPN., *Kanjincho*, Gohei III Namiki, 1840, Play

TORA! TORA! TORA! 1970 d: Richard Fleischer, Toshio MasudA. USA/JPN., *Tora! Tora! Tora!*, Gordon W. Prange, New York 1969, Book

TORA! TORA! TORA! 1970 d: Kinji Fukasaku. USA/JPN., *The Broken Seal*, Ladislas Farago, New York 1967, Book

Torch Bearers, The see DOUBTING THOMAS (1935).

TORCH SINGER 1933 d: Alexander Hall, George Somnes. USA., *Mike*, Grace Perkins, 1933, Short Story

TORCH SONG 1953 d: Charles Walters. USA., *Why Should I Cry?*, I. A. R. Wylie, Story

Torch Song, The see LAUGHING SINNERS (1931).

TORCH SONG TRILOGY 1988 d: Paul Bogart. USA., *Torch Song Trilogy*, Harvey Fierstein, Play

TORMENT 1924 d: Maurice Tourneur. USA., *Torment*, William Dudley Pelley, Story

Torment see TORMENTO (1974).

Torment of Young Love, The see WERTHER (1926).

TORMENTO 1974 d: Pedro OleA. SPN., *Tormento*, Benito Perez Galdos, 1884, Novel

TORN APART 1990 d: Jack Fisher. USA/ISR., Chayim Zeldis, Novel

TORN SAILS 1920 d: A. V. Bramble. UKN., *Torn Sails*, Allen Raine, Novel

Torn to Bits see MISE A SAC (1967).

TORNADO 1943 d: William Berke. USA., *Tornado*, John Guedel, Novel

TORNADO, THE 1924 d: King Baggot. USA., *The Tornado*, Lincoln J. Carter, 1891, Play

Torpedo Bay see FINCHE DURA LA TEMPESTA (1962).

Torpedo Raider see BROWN ON RESOLUTION (1935).

Torre Del Piacere, La see LA TOUR DE NESLE (1954).

TORRE DI PIETRA, LA 1914 d: Roberto Troncone. ITL., *La Torre Di Pietra*, Camillo Antona-Traversi, 1913, Play

TORRENT, THE 1921 d: Stuart Paton. USA., *Out of the Sunset*, George Rix, 1920, Short Story

TORRENT, THE 1924 d: A. P. Younger, William Doner. USA., *The Torrent*, Langdon McCormick, Story

TORRENT, THE 1926 d: Monta Bell. USA., *Entre Naranjos*, Vicente Blasco Ibanez, Novel

TORRENTE, IL 1938 d: Marco Elter. ITL., *Storiella Di Montagna*, Pier Maria Rosso Di San Secondo, Play

TORRENTS 1946 d: Serge de Poligny. FRN., *Torrents*, Anne-Marie Desmarets, Novel

Torrents of Spring see ACQUE DI PRIMAVERA (1989).

TORRES SNORTEVOLD 1940 d: Tancred Ibsen. NRW., *Jacob*, Alexander Kielland, 1891, Novel

Torrid Noon *see* **GORECHTO PLADNE** (1965).

Torso Murder Mystery, The *see* **TRAITOR SPY** (1939).

TORST 1949 d: Ingmar Bergman. SWD., *Torst*, Birgit Tengroth, Book

TORTILLA FLAT 1942 d: Victor Fleming. USA., *Tortilla Flat*, John Steinbeck, 1935, Novel

Torture *see* **TORMENTO** (1974).

Torture Chamber of Dr. Sadism, The *see* **DIE SCHLANGENGRUBE UND DAS PENDEL** (1967).

TORTURE GARDEN 1967 d: Freddie Francis. UKN., *Enoch*, Robert Bloch, 1965, Short Story, *Mr. Steinway*, Robert Bloch, 1954, Short Story, *Terror Over Hollywood*, Robert Bloch, 1957, Short Story

TORTURE SHIP 1939 d: Victor Hugo Halperin. USA., *A Thousand Deaths*, Jack London, 1899, Short Story

TOSCA 1918 d: Alfredo de Antoni. ITL., *La Tosca*, Victorien Sardou, Paris 1887, Play

TOSCA 1941 d: Carl Koch, Jean Renoir. ITL., *La Tosca*, Victorien Sardou, Paris 1877, Play

Tosca *see* **DAVANTI A LUI TREMAVA TUTTA ROMA** (1946).

TOSCA 1956 d: Carmine Gallone. ITL., *La Tosca*, Victorien Sardou, Paris 1877, Play

TOSCA, LA 1908 d: Andre Calmettes. FRN., *La Tosca*, Victorien Sardou, Paris 1887, Play

TOSCA, LA 1909 d: Charles Le Bargy. FRN., *La Tosca*, Victorien Sardou, Paris 1887, Play

TOSCA, LA 1918 d: Edward Jose. USA., *La Tosca*, Victorien Sardou, Paris 1887, Play

TOSCA, LA 1922. UKN., *La Tosca*, Victorien Sardou, Paris 1887, Play

TOSCA, LA 1973 d: Luigi Magni. ITL., *La Tosca*, Victorien Sardou, Paris 1887, Play

TOSEN FRAN STORMYRTORPET 1918 d: Victor Sjostrom. SWD., *Tosen Fran Stormyrtorpet*, Selma Lagerlof, Stockholm 1908, Short Story

Tosen Fran Stormyrtorpet *see* **SUOTORPAN TYTTO** (1940).

TOSEN FRAN STORMYRTORPET 1947 d: Gustaf Edgren. SWD., *Tosen Fran Stormyrtorpet*, Selma Lagerlof, Stockholm 1908, Short Story

TOSKA 1969 d: Aleksandr Blank. USS., *Toska*, Anton Chekhov, 1885, Short Story

TOSSEDE PARADIS, DET 1962 d: Gabriel Axel. DNM., *Det Tossede Paradis*, Ole Juul, Copenhagen 1953, Novel

TOT AUF HALDE 1995 d: Theodor KotullA. GRM., *Gluck Auf Kumpel Oder Der Grosse Beschiss*, Henry Jaeger, Novel

Tot Family, The *see* **ORNAGY UR! ISTEN HOZTA** (1969).

TOT NUT VAN 'T ALGEMEEN 1988 d: Lode Verstraete, Raf Verpooten. BLG., *Tot Nut Van 'T Algemeen*, Walter Van Den Broeck, Play

TOTAL RECALL 1990 d: Paul Verhoeven. USA., *We Can Remember It for You Wholesale*, Philip K. Dick, 1966, Short Story

TOTE AUS DER THEMSE, DIE 1971 d: Harald Philipp. GRM., Edgar Wallace, Novel

TOTE VON BEVERLY HILLS, DIE 1964 d: Michael Pfleghar. GRM., *Die Tote von Beverly Hills*, Kurt Gotz, Berlin 1951, Novel

TOTEN AUGEN VON LONDON, DIE 1960 d: Alfred Vohrer. GRM., *The Dark Eyes of London*, Edgar Wallace, London 1924, Novel

TOTEN BLEIBEN JUNG, DIE 1968 d: Joachim Kunert. GDR., *Die Toten Bleiben Jung*, Anna Seghers, 1949, Novel

TOTENINSEL, DIE 1955 d: Victor Tourjansky. GRM., *Die Toteninsel*, Hans Ulrich Horster, Novel

TOTENSCHIFF, DAS 1959 d: Georg Tressler. GRM/MXC., *Das Totenschiff*, Ben Traven, 1926, Novel

Toter Sucht Seinen Morder, Ein *see* **VENGEANCE** (1962).

TOTER TAUCHER NIMMT KEIN GELD, EIN 1975 d: Harald Reinl. GRM., *Ein Toter Taucher Nimmt Kein Gold*, Heinz G. Konsalik, Novel

Toth Family, The *see* **ORNAGY UR! ISTEN HOZTA** (1969).

Toto *see* **THE GAY DECEIVER** (1926).

Toto *see* **SU ULTIMA NOCHE** (1931).

TOTO CERCA CASA 1949 d: Steno, Mario Monicelli. ITL., *Il Custode*, M. Moscariello, Play

TOTO CERCA PACE 1954 d: Mario Mattoli. ITL., Emilio Caglieri, Play

TOTO E IL RE DI ROMA 1952 d: Steno, Mario Monicelli. ITL., Anton Chekhov, Short Stories

TOTO E MARCELLINO 1958 d: Antonio Musu. ITL/FRN., *Una Chitarra in Paradiso*, Massimo Franciosa, Short Story

Toto Nella Fossa Dei Leoni *see* **DUE CUORI FRA LE BELVE** (1943).

Toto Wants a Home *see* **TOTO CERCA CASA** (1949).

Totschlager, Der *see* **LOCKENDE GEFAHR** (1950).

Totte Et Sa Chance *see* **DER SPRUNG INS GLUCK** (1927).

Totte Et Sa Chance *see* **DEFENSE D'AIMER** (1942).

Toubib En Delire, La *see* **INDUSTRIALE COL COMPLESSO DEL GIOCATTOLO PRIMA NOTTE DEL DR. DANIELI** (1970).

TOUBIB, LE 1979 d: Pierre Granier-Deferre. FRN., *Le Toubib*, Jean Freustie, Novel

Toucas de Marseille *see* **FORTUNE DE MARSEILLE** (1951).

TOUCH 1997 d: Paul Schrader. USA/FRN., *Touch*, Elmore Leonard, Novel

TOUCH OF A CHILD, THE 1918 d: Cecil M. Hepworth. UKN., *The Touch of a Child*, Tom Gallon, Story

TOUCH OF EVIL 1958 d: Orson Welles. USA., *Badge of Evil*, Whit Masterson, 1955, Novel

TOUCH OF FROST: CARE AND PROTECTION, A 1992 d: Don Leaver. UKN., R. D. Wingfield, Novel

Touch of Hell, A *see* **SERIOUS CHARGE** (1959).

TOUCH OF LARCENY, A 1959 d: Guy Hamilton. UKN/USA., *The Megstone Plot*, Andrew Garve, Novel

TOUCH OF LOVE, A 1969 d: Waris Hussein. UKN., *The Millstone*, Margaret Drabble, London 1964, Novel

TOUCH OF THE MOON, A 1936 d: MacLean Rogers. UKN., *A Touch of the Moon*, Cyril Campion, Play

Touch of Treason, A *see* **LES ENNEMIS** (1961).

TOUCHDOWN 1931 d: Norman Z. McLeod. USA., *Stadium*, Francis Wallace, New York 1931, Novel

TOUCHE-A-TOUT 1935 d: Jean Dreville. FRN., *Touche-a-Tout*, Roger Ferdinand, Play

TOUCHEZ PAS AU GRISBI 1953 d: Jacques Becker. FRN/ITL., *Touchez Pas Au Grisbi*, Albert Simonin, Novel

TOUCHEZ PAS AUX BLONDES! 1960 d: Maurice Cloche. FRN., *A Palir la Nuit*, Carter Brown, Novel

TOUCHONS DU BOIS 1933 d: Maurice Champreux. FRN., *Bunbury*, Oscar Wilde, Play

Tough Guy *see* **COSH BOY** (1952).

Tough Guy of 1900 *see* **UN GUAPO DEL 1900** (1960).

TOUGH GUYS DON'T DANCE 1987 d: Norman Mailer. USA., *Tough Guys Don't Dance*, Norman Mailer, 1984, Novel

Tough to Be Famous *see* **IT'S TOUGH TO BE FAMOUS** (1932).

Touha Zvana Anada *see* **HRST VODY** (1969).

TOUR DE COCHON, UN 1934 d: Joseph Tzipine. FRN., *Un Tour de Cochon*, Raoul Prazy, Robert Tremois, Play

TOUR DE NESLE, LA 1912 d: Albert Capellani. FRN., *La Tour de Nesle*, Alexandre Dumas (pere), F. Gaillardet, Play

TOUR DE NESLE, LA 1937 d: Gaston Roudes. FRN., *La Tour de Nesle*, Alexandre Dumas (pere), F. Gaillardet, 1832, Play

TOUR DE NESLE, LA 1954 d: Abel Gance. FRN/ITL., *La Tour de Nesle*, Alexandre Dumas (pere), F. Gaillardet, 1832, Play

TOURBILLON DE PARIS, LE 1928 d: Julien Duvivier. FRN., *La Sarrazine*, Germaine Acremant, Novel

TOURMENTE, LA 1912 d: Victorin Jasset. FRN., *La Tourmente*, Pierre Salles, Novel

Tournament Tempo *see* **GAY BLADES** (1946).

TOUT EST DANS LA FIN 1986 d: Jean Delannoy. FRN., *Tout Est Dans la Fin*, Gilbert Prouteau, Novel

TOUT POUR RIEN 1933 d: Rene Pujol. FRN., *Tout Pour Rien*, Andre Mouezy-Eon, Play

TOUT SE PAIE 1920 d: Henry Houry. FRN., *L'Echeance*, Paul Bourget, Short Story

TOUTE LA FAMILLE ETAIT LA 1948 d: Jean de Marguenat. FRN., *Toute la Famille Etait la*, Henri Falk, Novel

TOUTE SA VIE 1930 d: Alberto Cavalcanti. FRN/USA., *Sarah and Son*, Timothy Shea, New York 1929, Novel

TOUTES PEINES CONFONDUES 1991 d: Michel Deville. FRN., *Sweetheart*, Andrew Coburn

TOVARICH 1937 d: Anatole Litvak. USA., *Tovarich*, Jacques Deval, Paris 1933, Play

TOVARITCH 1935 d: Jacques Deval, Jean Tarride. FRN., *Tovarich*, Jacques Deval, Paris 1933, Play

Tow *see* **DE WITTE VAN SICHEM** (1980).

Tower of Forbidden Love, The *see* **DER TURM DER VERBOTENEN LIEBE** (1968).

Tower of Ivory, The *see* **OUT OF THE STORM** (1920).

TOWER OF LIES, THE 1925 d: Victor Sjostrom. USA., *Kejsarn Av Portugallien*, Selma Lagerlof, Stockholm 1914, Novel

TOWER OF LONDON, THE 1909 d: James Williamson ?. UKN., *The Tower of London*, Harrison Ainsworth, Novel

Tower of Lust, The *see* **LA TOUR DE NESLE** (1954).

Tower of Screaming Virgins *see* **DER TURM DER VERBOTENEN LIEBE** (1968).

Tower of Terror *see* **ASSAULT** (1971).

TOWERING INFERNO, THE 1974 d: Irwin Allen, John Guillermin. USA., *The Glass Inferno*, Frank M. Robinson, Thomas M. Scortia, Novel, *The Tower*, Richard Martin Stern, Novel

Town in Mourning, A *see* **A FEKETE VAROS** (1971).

Town in the Palm of His Hand, The *see* **MESTECKO NA DLANI** (1942).

TOWN LIKE ALICE, A 1956 d: Jack Lee. UKN., *A Town Like Alice*, Nevil Shute, 1950, Novel

TOWN LIKE ALICE, A 1981 d: David Stevens. ASL., *A Town Like Alice*, Nevil Shute, 1950, Novel

Town of Anger *see* **IKARI NO MACHI** (1950).

TOWN OF CROOKED WAYS, THE 1920 d: Bert Wynne. UKN., *The Town of Crooked Ways*, J. S. Fletcher, Novel

TOWN SCANDAL, THE 1923 d: King Baggot. USA., *The Town Scandal*, Frederic Arnold Kummer, Story

TOWN TAMER 1965 d: Lesley Selander. USA., *Town Tamer*, Frank Gruber, New York 1958, Novel

Town Without Pity *see* **STADT OHNE MITLEID** (1961).

Towns and Years *see* **GORODA I GODY** (1973).

Township, The *see* **KASBA** (1990).

TOY SOLDIERS 1991 d: Daniel Petrie Jr. USA., *Toy Soldiers*, William P. Kennedy, Novel

TOY WIFE, THE 1938 d: Richard Thorpe. USA., *Frou-Frou*, Ludovic Halevy, Henri Meilhac, Paris 1869, Play

TOYS IN THE ATTIC 1963 d: George Roy Hill. USA., *Toys in the Attic*, Lillian Hellman, New York 1960, Play

Toys Which Saved Christmas, The *see* **LA FRECCIA AZZURRA** (1996).

Toze Ljudi *see* **TOZHE LYUDI** (1960).

TOZHE LYUDI 1960 d: Georgi Daneliya, Igor Talankin. USS., *Voyna I Mir*, Lev Nikolayevich Tolstoy, 1863-69, Novel

Tra Due Donne *see* **RECOURS EN GRACE** (1960).

Trabajo Tranquilo, Un *see* **RUGANTINO** (1973).

Trace of Blood, A *see* **UN HILITO DE SANGRE** (1995).

Traces of Light *see* **HUELLA DE LUZ** (1943).

Traces of the Stones *see* **SPUR DER STEINE** (1966).

Traces Remain, The *see* **SLEDITE OSTAVAT** (1956).

Track Leads to Berlin, The *see* **DIE SPUR FUHRT NACH BERLIN** (1952).

TRACK OF THE CAT 1954 d: William A. Wellman. USA., *The Track of the Cat*, Walter Van Tilburg Clark, 1949, Novel

TRACKED TO EARTH 1922 d: William Worthington. USA., *Tracked to Earth*, William J. Neidig, Short Story

Tracks of Stones *see* **SPUR DER STEINE** (1966).

TRACY THE OUTLAW 1928 d: Otis B. Thayer. USA., *Tracy the Outlaw*, Pierce Kingsley, Play

TRADE SECRET, A 1915 d: William F. Haddock. USA., *A Trade Secret*, Ernest M. Poate, 1915, Novel

Trade Winds *see* **THE PAINTED WOMAN** (1932).

TRADER HORN 1931 d: W. S. Van Dyke. USA., *Trader Horn*, Alfred Aloysius Horn, Ethelreda Lewis, New York 1927, Book

Tradimento Di Elena Marimon, Il *see* **LE SECRET D'HELENE MARIMON** (1953).

TRADITION DE MINUIT, LA 1939 d: Roger Richebe. FRN., *La Tradition de Minuit*, Pierre Mac Orlan, 1930, Novel

Traditions Altar *see* LI TING LANG (1920).

Traditions, Up Yours! *see* REND MIG I TRADIONERNE (1979).

TRAFFIC 1915 d: Charles Raymond. UKN., *Traffic*, E. Temple Thurston, Novel

TRAFRACKEN 1966 d: Lars-Magnus Lindgren. SWD., *Trafracken*, Jan Ekstrom, Novel

Tragedia Della Cerniera, La *see* UN CATTIVO SOGGETTO (1933).

Tragedias de la Vida Bohemia *see* LA VIDA BOHEMIA (1938).

TRAGEDIE DE CARMEN, LA 1983 d: Peter Brook. FRN/UKN/GRM., *Carmen*, Prosper Merimee, Paris 1846, Novel

TRAGEDIE IMPERIALE, LA 1937 d: Marcel L'Herbier. FRN., *La Tragedie Imperiale*, Alfred Neumann, Novel

Tragedy Burlesque *see* URNEBESNA TRAGEDIJA (1995).

TRAGEDY OF A COMIC SONG, THE 1921 d: Maurice Elvey. UKN., Leonard Merrick, Story

TRAGEDY OF BARNSDALE MANOR, THE 1924 d: Hugh Croise. UKN., *The Tragedy of Barnsdale Manor*, Baroness Orczy, Short Story

Tragedy of Carmen, The *see* LA TRAGEDIE DE CARMEN (1983).

Tragedy of Passion, A *see* TRAGODIE EINER LEIDENSCHAFT (1949).

Tragedy of Pudd'nhead Wilson, The *see* PUDD'NHEAD WILSON (1984).

Tragedy of the Blacksmiths, The *see* ROZE KATE (1912).

Tragedy of the Street *see* DIRNENTRAGODIE (1927).

TRAGEDY OF WHISPERING CREEK, THE 1914 d: Allan Dwan. USA., *The Tragedy of Whispering Creek*, Elliott J. Clawson, Story

TRAGEDY THAT LIVED, THE 1914 d: Colin Campbell. USA., *The Tragedy That Lived*, James Oliver Curwood, Short Story

Tragic Burlesque, The *see* URNEBESNA TRAGEDIJA (1995).

Tragic Dawn *see* MARE NOSTRUM (1948).

Tragic Holiday *see* VACANTA TRAGICA (1978).

TRAGICA NOTTE 1942 d: Mario Soldati. ITL., *La Trappola*, Delfino Cinelli, Novel

Tragicall Hiftorie of Hamlet Prince of Denmark, The *see* HAMLET (1971).

TRAGODIE EINER LEIDENSCHAFT 1949 d: Kurt Meisel. GRM., *Pavlin*, Nikolay Semyonovich Leskov, 1874, Novel

TRAIL BEYOND, THE 1934 d: Robert North Bradbury. USA., *The Wolf Hunters; a Tale of Adventure in the Wilderness*, James Oliver Curwood, Indianapolis 1908, Novel

TRAIL DUST 1936 d: Nate Watt. USA., *Trail Dust*, Clarence E. Mulford, New York 1934, Novel

Trail Leads to Berlin, The *see* DIE SPUR FUHRT NACH BERLIN (1952).

TRAIL OF '98, THE 1928 d: Clarence Brown. USA., *The Trail of '98*, Robert W. Service, New York 1911, Novel

TRAIL OF COURAGE, THE 1928 d: Wallace Fox. USA., *Better Than a Rodeo*, Kenneth Perkins, Story

Trail of the Hawk *see* THE HAWK (1935).

TRAIL OF THE HORSE THIEVES, THE 1929 d: Robert de Lacy. USA., *Desert Madness*, William E. Wing, Story

TRAIL OF THE LONESOME PINE, THE 1914 d: Frank L. Dear. USA., *The Trail of the Lonesome Pine*, John Fox Jr., New York 1908, Novel

TRAIL OF THE LONESOME PINE, THE 1916 d: Cecil B. de Mille. USA., *The Trail of the Lonesome Pine*, John Fox Jr., New York 1908, Novel

TRAIL OF THE LONESOME PINE, THE 1923 d: Charles Maigne. USA., *The Trail of the Lonesome Pine*, John Fox Jr., New York 1908, Novel

TRAIL OF THE LONESOME PINE, THE 1936 d: Henry Hathaway. USA., *The Trail of the Lonesome Pine*, John Fox Jr., New York 1908, Novel

TRAIL OF THE LOST CHORD, THE 1913 d: Thomas Ricketts. USA., *The Trail of the Lost Chord*, Adelaide Anne Procter, Poem

TRAIL OF THE YUKON 1949 d: William X. Crowley, William Beaudine. USA., *The Gold Hunters*, James Oliver Curwood, Indianapolis 1909, Novel

TRAIL RIDER, THE 1925 d: W. S. Van Dyke. USA., *The Trail Rider*, George Washington Ogden, New York 1924, Novel

TRAIL STREET 1947 d: Ray Enright. USA., *Trail Street*, William Corcoran, Novel

TRAIL TO YESTERDAY, THE 1918 d: Edwin Carewe. USA., *The Trail to Yesterday*, Charles Alden Seltzer, New York 1913, Novel

TRAILIN' 1921 d: Lynn Reynolds. USA., *Trailin'*, Max Brand, New York 1920, Novel

Trail's End, The *see* ISOBEL (1920).

TRAILS OF THE WILD 1935 d: Sam Newfield. USA., *Caryl of the Mountains*, James Oliver Curwood, Short Story

Train 2419 *see* THE RETURN OF CASEY JONES (1933).

TRAIN DANS LA NUIT, UN 1934 d: Rene Hervil. FRN., *The Ghost Train*, Arnold Ridley, London 1925, Play

TRAIN DE 8H.47, LE 1925 d: Georges Pallu. FRN., *Le Train de 8H.47*, Georges Courteline, 1891, Novel

TRAIN DE 8H.47, LE 1934 d: Henry Wulschleger. FRN., *Le Train de 8H.47*, Georges Courteline, 1891, Novel

TRAIN DE VIENNE, LE 1989 d: Caroline Huppert. GRM/FRN/SWT., *Le Train de Venise*, Georges Simenon, Novel

TRAIN D'ENFER 1965 d: Gilles Grangier. FRN/SPN/ITL., *Combat de Negres*, Rene Cambon, Novel

TRAIN, LE 1964 d: John Frankenheimer, Bernard Farrel. FRN/ITL., *Le Front de l'Art*, Rose Valland, Novel

TRAIN, LE 1973 d: Pierre Granier-Deferre. FRN/ITL., *Le Train*, Georges Simenon, 1961, Novel

TRAIN POUR VENISE, LE 1938 d: Andre Berthomieu. FRN., *Le Train Pour Venise*, Georges Berr, Louis Verneuil, Play

TRAIN SANS YEUX, LE 1926 d: Alberto Cavalcanti. FRN., *Le Train Sans Yeux*, Louis Delluc, Short Story

Train, The *see* LE TRAIN (1964).

Train, The *see* DER ZUG (1989).

TRAIN TO PAKISTAN 1998 d: Pamela Rooks. IND., *Train to Pakistan*, Khushwant Singh, Novel

TRAINSPOTTING 1996 d: Danny Boyle. UKN., *Trainspotting*, Irvine Welsh, Novel

TRAIT D'UNION, LE 1910 d: Emile Chautard. FRN., *Le Trait d'Union*, Alfred Bernier, Short Story

TRAITOR SPY 1939 d: Walter Summers. UKN., *Traitor Spy*, T. C. H. Jacobs, Novel

Traitor, The *see* FORRAEDERNE (1984).

TRAITOR'S GATE 1964 d: Freddie Francis. UKN/GRM., *The Traitor's Gate*, Edgar Wallace, London 1927, Novel

Traitors, The *see* FORRAEDERNE (1984).

TRAJET DE LA FOUDRE, LE 1994 d: Jacques Bourton. BLG/FRN., *Le Trajet de la Foudre*, Stanislas-Andre Steeman, Novel

TRAM A LA MALVARROSA 1997 d: Jose Luis Garcia Sanchez. SPN., *Tram a la Malvarrosa*, Manuel Vincent, Novel

TRAMONTANA, IL 1966 d: Adriano Barbano. ITL., *Tramontana*, Rina Durante, Short Story

TRAMP AT THE DOOR 1987 d: Allan Kroeker. CND., *Un Vagabond Frappe a Notre Porte*, Gabrielle Roy, Short Story

Tramp, The *see* TULAK (1925).

Tramp, The *see* VRAT SE! ANICKO (1926).

Trampa Bajo El Sol *see* TRAIN D'ENFER (1965).

Tramplers, The *see* GLI UOMINI DAL PASSO PESANTE (1966).

Tramway to Malvarrosa *see* TRAM A LA MALVARROSA (1997).

Transatlantic Tunnel *see* THE TUNNEL (1935).

TRANSATLANTIQUES, LES 1927 d: Piere Colombier. FRN., *Les Transatlantiques*, Abel Hermant, Novel

Transcontinent Express *see* ROCK ISLAND TRAIL (1950).

Transfiguration Hospital *see* SZPITAL PRZEMIENIENIA (1978).

TRANSFUGE, LE 1976 d: Yves Prigent. FRN., *L' Ile Sans Rivage*, Therese Doguet, Novel

TRANSGRESSION 1931 d: Herbert Brenon. USA., *The Next Corner*, Kate Jordan, Boston 1921, Novel

TRANSGRESSOR, THE 1913. USA., *The Scarlet Letter*, Nathaniel Hawthorne, New York 1850, Novel

TRANSIENT LADY 1935 d: Edward Buzzell. USA., *Transient Lady*, Octavus Roy Cohen, 1934, Short Story

Transient Love *see* THIS MAN IS MINE (1934).

TRANSIENTS IN ARCADIA 1918 d: Kenneth Webb. USA., *Transients in Arcadia*, O. Henry, Short Story

TRANSIENTS IN ARCADIA 1925 d: Daniel Keefe. USA., *Transients in Arcadia*, O. Henry, Short Story

TRANSIGEONS 1936 d: Hubert de Rouvres. FRN., *Transigeons*, Gabriel d'Hervilliez, Play

TRANSIT 1990 d: Rene Allio. FRN., *Transit*, Anna Seghers, 1944, Novel

TRANSLATION OF A SAVAGE, THE 1913 d: Walter Edwin. USA., *The Translation of a Savage*, Gilbert Parker, New York 1893, Novel

Translation of a Savage, The *see* BEHOLD MY WIFE! (1920).

TRANSPLANT 1979 d: William A. Graham. USA., *Transplant*, Philip Dossick, Book

TRANSPORT, DER 1961 d: Jurgen Roland. GRM., *Der Transport*, Wolfgang Altendorf, Novel

Transport from Paradise *see* TRANSPORT Z RAJE (1962).

Transport, The *see* DER TRANSPORT (1961).

TRANSPORT Z RAJE 1962 d: Zbynek Brynych. CZC., *Noc a Nadeje*, Arnost Lustig, Prague 1957, Novel

Trap for a Killer *see* RAFLES SUR LA VILLE (1957).

Trap for the Assassin *see* ROGER LA HONTE (1966).

TRAP THAT FAILED, THE 1915 d: Murdock MacQuarrie. USA., *The Trap That Failed*, Ben Cohn, Story

TRAP, THE 1919 d: Frank Reicher. USA., *The Trap*, Richard Harding Davis, Jules Eckert Goodman, New York 1915, Play

TRAPALHADAS DE DOM QUIXOTE & SANCHO PANCA, AS 1980 d: Ary Fernandes. BRZ., *El Ingenioso Hidalgo Don Quijote de la Mancha*, Miguel de Cervantes Saavedra, 1605-15, Novel

TRAPEZE 1956 d: Carol Reed. USA., *The Killing Frost*, Max Catto, Novel

Trapp Family, The *see* DIE TRAPP-FAMILIE (1956).

Trapped By Fear *see* LES DISTRACTIONS (1960).

TRAPPED BY THE MORMONS 1922 d: H. B. Parkinson. UKN., *The Love Story of a Mormon*, Winifred Graham, Novel

Trapped By Wireless *see* PANIC ON THE AIR (1936).

TRAPPED IN SPACE 1994 d: Arthur Allan Seidelman. USA., *Breaking Strain*, Arthur C. Clarke, Short Story

TRAPPER'S FIVE DOLLAR BILL, THE 1911. USA., *The Whirligig of Life*, O. Henry, Short Story

TRAPP-FAMILIE, DIE 1956 d: Wolfgang Liebeneiner. GRM., *The Story of the Trapp Family Singers*, Maria Augusta Trapp, Philadelphia 1949, Autobiography

TRAPPOLA D'AMORE 1940 d: Raffaello Matarazzo. ITL., *Dicky*, Paul Armont, Marcel Gerbidon, Play

Trappola, La *see* TRAGICA NOTTE (1942).

Trappola Per 4 *see* LOTOSBLUTEN FUR MISS QUON (1966).

Trappola Per l'Assassino *see* ROGER LA HONTE (1966).

TRAPS 1993 d: Pauline Chan. ASL., *Dreamhouse*, Kate Grenville, Novel

TRAQUE, LA 1975 d: Serge Leroy. FRN/ITL., *La Traque*, Serge Leroy, Novel

TRATTATO SCOMPARSO, IL 1933 d: Mario Bonnard. ITL., *Il Trattato Scomparso*, Artu (Riccardo Artuffo), Galar (Leo Galetto), Play

Traum Des Allan Gray, Der *see* VAMPYR (1931).

TRAUMENDE MUND, DER 1932 d: Paul Czinner. GRM., Henri Bernstein, Plays

TRAUMENDE MUND, DER 1953 d: Josef von Baky. GRM., *Melo*, Henri Bernstein, Play

Traumereien Uber Eine Inszenierung *see* HEINRICH PENTHESILEA VON KLEIST (1983).

TRAUMSTADT 1973 d: Johannes Schaaf. GRM., *Die Andere Seite*, Alfred Kubin, 1908, Novel

TRAUMULUS 1936 d: Carl Froelich. GRM., *Traumulus*, Arno Holz, Oskar Jerschke, 1904, Play

TRAVAIL 1919 d: Henri Pouctal. FRN., *Travail*, Emile Zola, Novel

TRAVAIL, C'EST LA LIBERTE, LE 1959 d: Louis Grospierre. FRN., *Les Poubelles*, Francoise Mallet-Joris, 1956, Short Story

TRAVAILLEURS DE LA MER, LES 1918 d: Andre Antoine. FRN., *Les Travailleurs de la Mer*, Victor Hugo, 1866, Novel

Traveling Lady *see* **THE RAIN MUST FALL BABY** (1965).

Traveling Saints *see* **SANTITOS** (1999).

TRAVELING SALESMAN, THE 1916 d: Joseph Kaufman. USA., *The Traveling Salesman*, James Grant Forbes, New York 1908, Play

TRAVELING SALESMAN, THE 1921 d: Joseph Henabery. USA., *The Traveling Salesman*, James Grant Forbes, New York 1908, Play

TRAVELLER'S JOY 1949 d: Ralph Thomas. UKN., *Traveller's Joy*, Arthur MacRae, London 1948, Play

TRAVELLING NORTH 1986 d: Carl Schultz. ASL., *Travelling North*, David Williamson, 1980, Play

Travelling Picture Show Man, The *see* **THE PICTURE SHOW MAN** (1977).

Travelling Players *see* **GUSHU YIREN** (1987).

TRAVELS WITH MY AUNT 1972 d: George Cukor. UKN/USA., *Travels With My Aunt*, Graham Greene, 1969, Novel

TRAVERSATA NERA 1939 d: Domenico M. Gambino. ITL., *Traversata Nera*, Giuseppe Achille, Bruno Corra, Play

TRAVERSEE DE PARIS, LA 1956 d: Claude Autant-LarA. FRN/ITL., *La Traversee de Paris*, Marcel Ayme, 1946, Short Story

TRAVIATA '53 1953 d: Vittorio Cottafavi. ITL/FRN., *La Dame aux Camelias*, Alexandre Dumas (fils), Paris 1848, Novel

Traviata, La *see* **LA SIGNORA DALLE CAMELIE** (1909).

TRAVIATA, LA 1922 d: Challis Sanderson. UKN., *La Traviata*, Francesco M. Piave, Giuseppe Verdi, Venice 1853, Opera

TRAVIATA, LA 1927 d: H. B. Parkinson. UKN., *La Traviata*, Francesco M. Piave, Giuseppe Verdi, Venice 1853, Opera

TRAVIATA, LA 1967 d: Mario Lanfranchi. ITL., *La Traviata*, Francesco M. Piave, Giuseppe Verdi, Venice 1853, Opera

TRAVIATA, LA 1982 d: Franco Zeffirelli. ITL., *La Traviata*, Francesco M. Piave, Giuseppe Verdi, Venice 1853, Opera

TRAVIESA MOLINERA, LA 1935 d: Harry d'Abbadie d'Arrast, Ricardo Soriano. SPN., *El Sombrero de Tres Picos*, Pedro Antonio de Alarcon, 1874, Short Story

TRE AAR EFTER 1948 d: Johan Jacobsen. DNM., *Efter*, Carl Erik Soya, 1947, Play

Tre Amici, le Moglie E (Affettuosamente) le Altre *see* **FRANCOIS, PAUL. ET LES AUTRES VINCENT** (1974).

Tre Avventurieri, I *see* **LES AVENTURIERS** (1966).

TRE CORSARI, I 1952 d: Mario Soldati. ITL., *Il Corsaro Verde*, Emilio Salgari, Novel

Tre Eccetera Del Colonello, Le *see* **LES TROIS ETC. DU COLONEL** (1960).

Tre Giorni in Paradiso *see* **CASTELLI IN ARIA** (1939).

TRE LADRI, I 1954 d: Lionello de Felice. ITL/FRN., *I Trei Ladri*, Umberto Notari, 1907, Novel

TRE MILIONI DI DOTE 1920 d: Camillo de Riso. ITL., *Trois Millions de Dot*, Xavier de Montepin

TRE MOSCHETTIERI, I 1909 d: Mario Caserini?. ITL., *Les Trois Mousquetaires*, Alexandre Dumas (pere), Paris 1844, Novel

TRE NOTTI VIOLENTE 1966 d: Nick Nostro. ITL/SPN., *L' Altra Faccia Della Luna*, Sergio Donati, Novel

Tre Passi Nel Delirio *see* **HISTOIRES EXTRAORDINAIRES** (1968).

TRE PECORE VIZIOSE 1915 d: Gino Rossetti. ITL., *Tre Pecore Viziose*, Eduardo Scarpetta, 1881, Play

TRE SENTIMENTALI, I 1921 d: Augusto GeninA. ITL., *I Tre Sentimentali*, Nino Berrini, Sandro Camasio, 1918, Play

TRE SERGENTI DEL BENGALA, I 1965 d: Umberto Lenzi. ITL/SPN., *Forte Madras*, Umberto Lenzi, Novel

Tre Simpathice Carogne *see* **RENE LA CANNE** (1976).

Tre Simpatiche Carogne. E Vissero Insieme Felici, Imbrogliando E Truffando *see* **RENE LA CANNE** (1976).

TRE SORELLE, LE 1918 d: Giuseppe Sterni. ITL., *Le Vergini*, Marco Praga, 1889, Play

TREACHEROUS CROSSING 1992 d: Tony Wharmby. USA., *Cabin B-16*, John Dickson Carr, Radio Play

Treachery on the High Seas *see* **NOT WANTED ON VOYAGE** (1936).

TREAD SOFTLY STRANGER 1958 d: Gordon Parry. UKN., *Blind Alley*, Jack Popplewell, 1953, Play

Treason *see* **GUILTY OF TREASON** (1949).

TREASURE AT THE MILL 1957 d: Max Anderson. UKN., Malcolm Saville, Story

TREASURE HUNT 1952 d: John Paddy Carstairs. UKN., *Treasure Hunt*, M. J. Farrell, John Perry, London 1949, Play

TREASURE IN MALTA 1963 d: Derek Williams. UKN., *By Jiminy*, David Scott Daniell, Novel

TREASURE ISLAND 1912 d: J. Searle Dawley. USA., *Treasure Island*, Robert Louis Stevenson, London 1883, Novel

TREASURE ISLAND 1917 d: Chester M. Franklin, Sidney A. Franklin. USA., *Treasure Island*, Robert Louis Stevenson, London 1883, Novel

TREASURE ISLAND 1920 d: Maurice Tourneur. USA., *Treasure Island*, Robert Louis Stevenson, London 1883, Novel

TREASURE ISLAND 1934 d: Victor Fleming. USA., *Treasure Island*, Robert Louis Stevenson, London 1883, Novel

TREASURE ISLAND 1950 d: Byron Haskin. UKN/USA., *Treasure Island*, Robert Louis Stevenson, London 1883, Novel

TREASURE ISLAND 1970 d: Leif Gram, Zoran Janzic. ASL., *Treasure Island*, Robert Louis Stevenson, London 1883, Novel

Treasure Island *see* **OSTROV SOKROVISC** (1971).

TREASURE ISLAND 1972 d: John Hough, Andrea Bianchi. UKN/ITL/SPN., *Treasure Island*, Robert Louis Stevenson, London 1883, Novel

Treasure Island *see* **DEUX ANS DE VACANCES** (1973).

TREASURE ISLAND 1977 d: Michael E. Briant. UKN., *Treasure Island*, Robert Louis Stevenson, London 1883, Novel

TREASURE ISLAND 1982 d: Dave Heather. UKN., *Treasure Island*, Robert Louis Stevenson, London 1883, Novel

TREASURE ISLAND 1987 d: Warwick Gilbert. ASL., *Treasure Island*, Robert Louis Stevenson, London 1883, Novel

TREASURE ISLAND 1988 d: Kei Ijima, Hiroshi IkedA. JPN., *Treasure Island*, Robert Louis Stevenson, London 1883, Novel

TREASURE ISLAND 1990 d: Fraser C. Heston. UKN/USA., *Treasure Island*, Robert Louis Stevenson, London 1883, Novel

Treasure Island *see* **L' ILE AU TRESOR** (1991).

Treasure Island in Outer Space *see* **SPACE ISLAND** (1987).

Treasure Island: the Musical *see* **TREASURE ISLAND** (1982).

TREASURE OF DESERT ISLE, THE 1913 d: Ralph Ince. USA., *The Treasure of Desert Isle*, James Oliver Curwood, Story

TREASURE OF HEAVEN, THE 1916 d: A. E. Coleby. UKN., *The Treasure of Heaven*, Marie Corelli, Novel

TREASURE OF LOST CANYON, THE 1952 d: Ted Tetzlaff. USA., *Treasure of Franchard*, Robert Louis Stevenson, 1887, Short Story

TREASURE OF MONTE CRISTO, THE 1961 d: Robert S. Baker. UKN., *Le Comte de Monte-Cristo*, Alexandre Dumas (pere), Paris 1845, Novel

Treasure of Sierra Madre, The *see* **THE TREASURE OF THE SIERRA MADRE** (1948).

Treasure of Silver Lake *see* **DER SCHATZ IM SILBERSEE** (1962).

Treasure of the Aztecs *see* **DER SCHATZ DER AZTEKEN** (1965).

TREASURE OF THE GOLDEN CONDOR 1953 d: Delmer Daves. USA., *Son of Fury*, Edison Marshall, Novel

TREASURE OF THE SIERRA MADRE, THE 1948 d: John Huston. USA., *Der Schatz Der Sierra Madre*, Ben Traven, 1927, Novel

Treasured Earth *see* **TALPALATNYI FOLD** (1948).

TREAT 'EM ROUGH 1919 d: Lynn Reynolds. USA., *The Two-Gun Man*, Charles Alden Seltzer, New York 1911, Novel

Treatment, The *see* **THE FULL TREATMENT** (1961).

TREDOWATA 1976 d: Jerzy Hoffman. PLN., *Tredowata*, Helena Mniszkowna, Novel

TREE GROWS IN BROOKLYN, A 1945 d: Elia Kazan. USA., *A Tree Grows in Brooklyn*, Betty Smith, 1943, Novel

TREE GROWS IN BROOKLYN, A 1974 d: Joseph Hardy. USA., *A Tree Grows in Brooklyn*, Betty Smith, 1943, Novel

TREE OF HANDS 1989 d: Giles Foster. UKN., *The Tree of Hands*, Ruth Rendell, Novel

TREE OF KNOWLEDGE, THE 1920 d: William C. de Mille. USA., *The Tree of Knowledge*, R. C. Carton, London 1897, Play

Tree of Liberty, The *see* **THE HOWARDS OF VIRGINIA** (1940).

TREGUA, LA 1974 d: Sergio Renan. ARG., *La Tregua*, Mario Benedetti, 1960, Novel

TREGUA, LA 1997 d: Francesco Rosi. ITL/FRN/GRM., *La Tregua*, Primo Levi, Book

TREI ZILE SI TREI NOPTI 1976 d: Dinu Tanase. RMN., *Apa*, Alexandru Ivasiuc, 1973, Novel

TREIBHAUS, DAS 1987 d: Peter Goedel. GRM., *Das Treibhaus*, Wolfgang Koeppen, Novel

TREIZE A TABLE 1955 d: Andre Hunebelle. FRN., *Treize a Table*, Marc-Gilbert Sauvajon, 1953, Play

TREIZE A TABLE 1990 d: Philippe Ducrest. FRN., *Treize a Table*, Marc-Gilbert Sauvajon, 1953, Play

Treizieme Caprice, Le *see* **LE 13E CAPRICE** (1967).

TREIZIEME ENQUETE DE GREY, LA 1937 d: Pierre Maudru. FRN., *La Triezieme Enquete de Grey*, Alfred Gragnon, Max Viterbo, Play

Treizieme Jure, Le *see* **GRIBOUILLE** (1937).

TRELAWNY OF THE WELLS 1916 d: Cecil M. Hepworth. UKN., *Trelawny of the Wells*, Arthur Wing Pinero, London 1898, Play

Trelawney of the Wells *see* **THE ACTRESS** (1928).

TREMARNE CASE, THE 1924 d: Hugh Croise. UKN., *The Tremarne Case*, Baroness Orczy, Short Story

TREN EXPRESO, EL 1954 d: Leon Klimovsky. SPN., *El Tren Expreso*, Ramon de Campoamor, 1872-74, Verse

TRENCK 1932 d: Ernst Neubach, Heinz Paul. GRM., *Der Roman Eines Gunstlings Trenck*, Bruno Frank, 1926, Novel

TRENCK DER PANDUR 1940 d: Herbert Selpin. GRM., *Trenck Der Pandur*, Otto Emmerich Groh, Play

Trenck, Der Roman Eines Gunstlings *see* **TRENCK** (1932).

Trenck, Roman Einer Grossen Liebe *see* **TRENCK** (1932).

TRENO DELLE 21.15, IL 1933 d: Amleto Palermi. ITL., *Il Treno Delle 21.15*, Alvus, Colin, Play

Treno Di Lenin, Il *see* **DER ZUG** (1989).

TRENO DI LUSSO 1917 d: Mario Bonnard. ITL., *Treno Di Lusso*, Umberto Notari, Novel

TRENO DORIA 1924 d: Luciano DoriA. ITL., *Train de Plaisir*, Maurice Hennequin, Mortier, Saint-Albin, 1884, Play

Treno, Il *see* **LE TRAIN** (1964).

TRENTA SECONDI D'AMORE 1936 d: Mario Bonnard. ITL., *Trenta Secondi d'Amore*, Aldo de Benedetti, Play

TRENT'ANNI DI SERVIZIO 1945 d: Mario Baffico. ITL., Ada Salvatore, Radio Play

TRENTE ET QUARANTE 1945 d: Gilles Grangier. FRN., *Trente Et Quarante*, Edmond About, 1859, Novel

TRENTE MILLIONS DE GLADIATOR, LES 1914 d: Georges MoncA. FRN., *Les Trente Millions de Gladiator*, Philippe Gilles, Eugene Labiche, Play

TRENT'S LAST CASE 1920 d: Richard Garrick. UKN., *Trent's Last Case*, E. C. Bentley, London 1913, Novel

TRENT'S LAST CASE 1929 d: Howard Hawks. USA., *Trent's Last Case*, E. C. Bentley, London 1913, Novel

TRENT'S LAST CASE 1952 d: Herbert Wilcox. UKN., *Trent's Last Case*, E. C. Bentley, London 1913, Novel

Tres Etceteras Del Coronel, Los *see* **LES TROIS ETC. DU COLONEL** (1960).

TRES HOMBRES MALOS 1948 d: Raul de AndA. MXC., *Three Godfathers*, Peter B. Kyne, New York 1913, Novel

Tres Invencibles Sargentos, Los *see* **I TRE SERGENTI DEL BENGALA** (1965).

TRES MOSQUETAROS. Y MEDIO, LOS 1956 d: Gilberto Martinez Solares. MXC., *Les Trois Mousquetaires*, Alexandre Dumas (pere), Paris 1844, Novel

TRES MOSQUETEROS, LOS 1942 d: Miguel M. Delgado. MXC., *Les Trois Mousquetaires*, Alexandre Dumas (pere), Paris 1844, Novel

Tres Noches Violentas see **TRE NOTTI VIOLENTE** (1966).

TRES PERFECTAS CASADAS, LAS 1972 d: Benito Alazraki. SPN/MXC., *Las Tres Perfectas Casadas*, Alejandro Casona, 1941, Play

Tres Sargentos Bengalies see **I TRE SERGENTI DEL BENGALA** (1965).

TRESOR DE KERIOLET, LE 1920 d: Felix Leonnec. FRN., *Le Tresor de Keriolet*, M. Pellerin, Novel

Tresor Des Montagnes Bleues, Le see **WINNETOU II** (1964).

Tresor du Lac d'Argent, Le see **DER SCHATZ IM SILBERSEE** (1962).

Trespass see **THE STRANGER WITHIN** (1974).

Trespasser, The see **NIGHT EDITOR** (1946).

TRESPASSER, THE 1982 d: Colin Gregg. UKN., *The Trespasser*, D. H. Lawrence, 1912, Novel

Treta Sled Slanceto see **TRETA SLED SLANTSETO** (1972).

TRETA SLED SLANTSETO 1972 d: Georgi Stoyanov. BUL., *Sinite Peperudi*, Pavel Vezhinov, 1968, Novel

TRETI ROTA 1931 d: Svatopluk Innemann. CZC., *Treti Rota*, Josef Kopta, Novel

TRETI ZVONENI 1938 d: Jan Svitak. CZC., *Treti Zvoneni*, Vaclav Stech, Play

TRETIY TAYM 1963 d: Yevgyeni Karelov. USS., *Trevoshnyye Oblaka*, A. Borshchagovskiy

TREUE JOHANNES, DER 1987 d: Slavo Luther. GRM/CZC/AUS., Jacob Grimm, Wilhelm Grimm, Short Story

Treurspel Der Smeden, Het see **ROZE KATE** (1912).

Treve see **THE MIGHTY TREVE** (1937).

TREY O'HEARTS, THE 1914 d: Wilfred Lucas, Henry McRae. USA., *The Trey O'Hearts*, Louis Joseph Vance, Story

TRHANI 1936 d: Vaclav Wasserman. CZC., *Trhani*, Jan Neruda, Novel

TRI 1965 d: Aleksandar Petrovic. YGS., *Paprat I Vatra*, Antonije Isakovic, Belgrade 1962, Novel

Tri Lasky Riny Sezimove see **RINA** (1926).

TRI MEDVEDYA 1958 d: Roman Davydov. USS., *Tri Medvedya*, Lev Nikolayevich Tolstoy, 1875, Short Story

TRI MUZI VE SNEHU 1936 d: Vladimir Slavinsky. CZC., *Tri Muzi Ve Snehu*, Erich Kastner, Novel

TRI SESTRY 1964 d: Samson Samsonov. USS., *Tri Sestry*, Anton Chekhov, Moscow 1901, Play

TRI SESTRY 1994 d: Sergei Soloviev. RSS/GRM., *Tri Sestry*, Anton Chekhov, Moscow 1901, Play

TRI TOLSTYAKA 1967 d: Alexei Batalov, Iosif Shapiro. USS., *Tri Tolstyaka*, Yury Karlovich Olesha, 1928, Short Story

TRIAL 1955 d: Mark Robson. USA., *Trial*, Don M. Mankiewicz, 1955, Novel

Trial and Error see **THE DOCK BRIEF** (1962).

TRIAL OF CHAPLAIN JENSEN, THE 1975 d: Robert Day. USA., *The Trial of Chaplain Jensen*, Martin Abrahamson, Andrew Jensen, Book

Trial of Donald Westhof, The see **DER KAMPF DES DONALD WESTHOF** (1927).

TRIAL OF MADAME X, THE 1948 d: Paul England. UKN., *La Femme X*, Alexandre Bisson, Paris 1908, Play

TRIAL OF MARY DUGAN, THE 1929 d: Bayard Veiller. USA., *The Trial of Mary Dugan*, Bayard Veiller, New York 1927, Play

TRIAL OF MARY DUGAN, THE 1940 d: Norman Z. McLeod. USA., *The Trial of Mary Dugan*, Bayard Veiller, New York 1927, Play

TRIAL OF VIVIENNE WARE, THE 1932 d: William K. Howard. USA., *The Trial of Vivienne Ware*, Kenneth M. Ellis, New York 1931, Play

Trial, The see **DER PROZESS** (1948).

Trial, The see **DER PROZESS** (1962).

TRIAL, THE 1992 d: David Jones. UKN., *Der Prozess*, Franz Kafka, Berlin 1925, Novel

TRIAL: THE PRICE OF PASSION 1992 d: Paul Wendkos. USA., *Trial*, Clifford Irving, Book

TRIALS OF OSCAR WILDE, THE 1960 d: Ken Hughes. UKN., *The Trials of Oscar Wilde*, Montgomery Hyde, Book

Trials of Private Schwejk, The see **SCHWEJKS FLEGELJAHRE** (1964).

Triangolo Del Delitto, Il see **LE GROS COUP** (1963).

Triangolo Magico, Il see **BRIVIDO** (1941).

TRIBES 1970 d: Joseph Sargent. USA., *The D.I.*, James Lee Barrett, Television Play

TRIBULATIONS D'UN CHINOIS EN CHINE, LES 1965 d: Philippe de BrocA. FRN/ITL., *Les Tribulations d'un Chinois En Chine*, Jules Verne, Paris 1879, Novel

TRIBULATIONS D'UNE MARRAINE, LES 1916. FRN., *Les Tribulations d'une Marraine*, Georges Hugot, Play

Tribuno Sebastiano, Il see **SAN SEBASTIANO** (1911).

TRIBUTE 1980 d: Bob Clark. CND., *Tribute*, Bernard Slade, Play

TRIBUTE TO A BAD MAN 1956 d: Robert Wise. USA., *Jeremy Rodock (Hanging's for the Lucky)*, Jack Schaefer, Short Story

TRIBUTE TO MOTHER, A 1915 d: Raymond L. Schrock. USA., *A Tribute to Mother*, James Elliott, Story

TRICK FOR TRICK 1933 d: Hamilton MacFadden. USA., *Trick for Trick*, V. Cosby, Harry W. Gribble, S. Warde, New York 1932, Play

TRICOCHE ET CACOLET 1938 d: Piere Colombier. FRN., *Tricoche Et Cacolet*, Ludovic Halevy, Henri Meilhac, Play

TRIFLERS, THE 1924 d: Louis J. Gasnier. USA., *The Triflers*, Frederick Orin Bartlett, Boston 1917, Novel

Trifles see **PEQUENECES** (1949).

Trifles 1900 see **MOFTURI 1900** (1965).

TRIFLING WITH HONOR 1923 d: Harry Pollard. USA., *His Good Name*, William Slavens McNutt, 1922, Short Story

Trigger see **SPITFIRE** (1934).

Trigger see **TO KILL THE KING** (1974).

Trigger Happy see **THE DEADLY COMPANIONS** (1961).

TRILBY 1914 d: Harold Shaw. UKN., *Trilby*, George Du Maurier, London 1894, Novel

TRILBY 1915 d: Maurice Tourneur. USA., *Trilby*, George Du Maurier, London 1894, Novel

TRILBY 1922. UKN., *Trilby*, George Du Maurier, London 1894, Novel

TRILBY 1923 d: James Young. USA., *Trilby*, George Du Maurier, London 1894, Novel

TRILOGIA DI DORINA, LA 1917 d: Gero Zambuto. ITL., *La Trilogia Di Dorina*, Gerolamo Rovetta, 1889, Play

TRILOGIE DES WIEDERSEHENS 1978 d: Peter Stein. GRM., *Trilogie Des Wiedersehens*, Botho Strauss, 1976, Play

TRILOGIE Z PRAVEKU: OSADA HAVRANU 1977 d: Jan Schmidt. CZC., Eduard Storch, Novel

TRILOGIE Z PRAVEKU: VOLANI RODU 1977 d: Jan Schmidt. CZC., *Volani Rodu*, Eduard Storch, Novel

TRILOGY 1969 d: Frank Perry. USA., *Among the Paths to Eden*, Truman Capote, 1960, Short Story, *A Christmas Memory*, Truman Capote, 1946, Short Story, *Miriam*, Truman Capote, 1944, Short Story

Trilogy from the Primeval Ages see **TRILOGIE Z PRAVEKU: OSADA HAVRANU** (1977).

TRILOGY OF TERROR 1975 d: Dan Curtis. USA., *Julie*, Richard Matheson, Short Story, *Millicent and Therese*, Richard Matheson, Short Story, *Prey*, Richard Matheson, Short Story

TRIMMED 1922 d: Harry Pollard. USA., *Trimmed and Burning*, Hapsburg Liebe, 1921, Short Story

TRIMMED IN SCARLET 1923 d: Jack Conway. USA., *Trimmed in Scarlet*, William Hurlbut, New York 1920, Play

TRIMMED LAMP, THE 1918 d: George Ridgwell. USA., *The Trimmed Lamp*, O. Henry, Short Story

Trimmed With Red see **HELP YOURSELF** (1920).

TRINE 1952 d: Toralf Sando. NRW., *Trine!*, Hans Geelmuyden, 1940, Novel

TRINI 1976 d: Walter Beck. GDR., *Trini*, Ludwig Renn, Novel

TRIO 1950 d: Ken Annakin, Harold French. UKN., *Mr. Knowall*, W. Somerset Maugham, 1947, Short Story, *Sanatorium*, W. Somerset Maugham, 1947, Short Story, *The Verger*, W. Somerset Maugham, 1947, Short Story

Trio see **TRI** (1965).

TRIO INFERNAL 1974 d: Francis Girod. FRN/ITL/GRM., *Le Trio Infernal*, Solange Fasquelle, Novel

Trio Infernale see **TRIO INFERNAL** (1974).

TRIOMPHE DE MICHEL STROGOFF, LE 1961 d: Victor Tourjansky. FRN/ITL., *Michel Strogoff*, Jules Verne, Paris 1876, Novel

Triomphe du Coeur, Le see **L' ESPRIT DU MAL** (1954).

Trionfo Di Masaniello, Il see **LA MUTA DI PORTICI** (1911).

Trionfo Di Michele Strogoff, Il see **LE TRIOMPHE DE MICHEL STROGOFF** (1961).

Trip Around My Cranium, A see **UTAZAS A KOPONYAM KORUL** (1970).

TRIP NACH TUNIS 1993 d: Peter Goedel. GRM., *The Tremor of Forgery*, Patricia Highsmith, Novel

Trip, The see **IL VIAGGIO** (1974).

TRIP TO BOUNTIFUL, THE 1986 d: Peter Masterson. USA., *The Trip to Bountiful*, Horton Foote, Play

TRIP TO CHINATOWN, A 1926 d: Robert Kerr, George Marshall (Spv). USA., *A Trip to Chinatown*, Charles Hale Hoyt, Short Story

Trip to Italy, A see **VIAGGIO IN ITALIA** (1953).

Trip to Nowhere see **NO DEJES LA PUERTA ABIERTA** (1933).

TRIP TO PARADISE, A 1921 d: Maxwell Karger. USA., *Liliom*, Ferenc Molnar, 1910, Play

Trip to Tilsit, The see **DIE REISE NACH TILSIT** (1939).

Trip to Visbaden, A see **POEZDKA V VISBADEN** (1989).

Trip to Wiesbaden, A see **POEZDKA V VISBADEN** (1989).

TRIPLE CROSS 1966 d: Terence Young. UKN/FRN., *The Eddie Chapman Story*, Frank Owen, London 1953, Biography

Triple Deception see **HOUSE OF SECRETS** (1957).

TRIPLE ECHO, THE 1972 d: Michael Apted. UKN., *The Triple Echo*, H. E. Bates, 1970, Novel

TRIPLEPATTE 1922 d: Raymond Bernard. FRN., *Triplepatte*, Tristan Bernard, Andre Godfernaux, Play

TRIPODS, THE 1986 d: Graham Theakston, Christopher Barry. UKN/ASL., John Christopher, Novel

TRIPOLI 1950 d: Will Price. USA., *The Barbarians*, Winston Miller, Will Price, Story

TRIPORTEUR, LE 1957 d: Jack Pinoteau. FRN., *Le Triporteur*, Rene Fallet, Novel

TRIQUE, GAMIN DE PARIS 1960 d: Marco de Gastyne. FRN., *Trique - Gamin de Paris*, Alfred Machard, Novel

TRISTANA 1970 d: Luis Bunuel. SPN/ITL/FRN., *Tristana*, Benito Perez Galdos, Madrid 1892, Novel

TRISTE REALTA 1917 d: Franco Dias. ITL., *Triste Realta*, Achille Torelli, 1871, Play

TRISTI AMORI 1917 d: Giuseppe Sterni. ITL., *Tristi Amori*, Giuseppe Giacosa, 1887, Play

TRISTI AMORI 1943 d: Carmine Gallone. ITL., *Tristi Amori*, Giuseppe Giacosa, 1887, Play

TRIUMPH 1917 d: Joseph de Grasse. USA., *Triumph*, Samuel Hopkins Adams, 1916, Short Story

TRIUMPH 1924 d: Cecil B. de Mille. USA., *Triumph*, May Edginton, New York 1924, Novel

TRIUMPH DER GERECHTEN 1987 d: Josef Bierbichler. GRM., Oskar Maria Graf, Story

TRIUMPH DER LIEBE 1947 d: Alfred Stoger. AUS., *Lysistrata*, Aristophanes, 411 bc, Play

Triumph of Michael Strogoff, The see **LE TRIOMPHE DE MICHEL STROGOFF** (1961).

TRIUMPH OF SHERLOCK HOLMES, THE 1935 d: Leslie Hiscott. UKN., *The Valley of Fear*, Arthur Conan Doyle, London 1914, Novel

TRIUMPH OF THE SCARLET PIMPERNEL, THE 1928 d: T. Hayes Hunter. UKN., *The Triumph of the Scarlet Pimpernel*, Baroness Orczy, Novel

TRIUMPH OF THE WEAK, THE 1918 d: Tom Terriss. USA., *My Man*, Edith Ellis, Forrest Halsey, New York 1910, Play

Triumph Over Pain see **THE GREAT MOMENT** (1944).

Triumphant Hero see **IL CID** (1910).

TRNY A KVETY 1921 d: Theodor Pistek. CZC., Anna Ziegloserova, Short Story

Trois Cent Dixseptieme see **LA 317EME SECTION** (1965).

TROIS CENTS A L'HEURE 1934 d: Willy Rozier. FRN., *Trois Cents a l'Heure*, Victor de Cottens, Pierre Veber, Play

TROIS CHAMBRES A MANHATTAN 1965 d: Marcel Carne. FRN., *Trois Chambres a Manhattan*, Georges Simenon, 1946, Novel

Trois Dans la Ville *see* LE BATARD (1941).

TROIS DE LA CANEBIERE 1955 d: Maurice de Canonge. FRN., *Trois de la Canebiere*, Henri Alibert, Rene Sarvil, Opera

TROIS DE LA MARINE 1934 d: Charles Barrois. FRN., *Trois de la Marine*, Henri Alibert, Rene Sarvil, Vincent Scotto, Opera

TROIS DE LA MARINE 1956 d: Maurice de Canonge. FRN., *Trois de la Marine*, Henri Alibert, Rene Sarvil, Vincent Scotto, Opera

TROIS ETC. DU COLONEL, LES 1960 d: Claude Boissol. FRN/ITL/SPN., *Les Trois Etc. du Colonel*, Jose-Maria Peman, Play

TROIS GARCONS, UNE FILLE 1948 d: Maurice Labro. FRN., *Une Fille Trois Garcons*, Roger Ferdinand, Play

Trois Histoires Extraordinaires d'Edgar Poe *see* HISTOIRES EXTRAORDINAIRES (1968).

TROIS HOMMES A ABATTRE 1980 d: Jacques Deray. FRN., *Trois Hommes a Abattre*, Jean-Patrick Manchette, Novel

TROIS JEUNES FILLES NUES 1928 d: Robert Boudrioz. FRN., *Trois Jeunes Filles Nues*, Yves Mirande, Albert Willemetz, Opera

TROIS JOURS A VIVRE 1957 d: Gilles Grangier. FRN., *Trois Jours a Vivre*, Peter Vanett

TROIS JOURS DE BRINGUE A PARIS 1953 d: Emile Couzinet. FRN., *La Cagnotte*, A. Delacour, Eugene Labiche, 1864, Play

Trois K *see* LES TROIS KK (1918).

TROIS KK, LES 1918 d: Jacques de Baroncelli. FRN., *La Guerre Des Momes*, Alfred Machard, Novel

TROIS LYS, LES 1921 d: Henri Desfontaines. FRN., *Les Trois Lys*, Lucie Delarue-Mardrus, Novel

TROIS MARINS DANS UN COUVENT 1949 d: Emile Couzinet. FRN., *Trois Marins Dans un Couvent*, Duport, Saint-Hilaire, Play

TROIS MASQUES, LES 1921 d: Henry Krauss. FRN., *Les Trois Masques*, Charles Mere, Play

TROIS MASQUES, LES 1929 d: Andre Hugon. FRN., *Les Trois Masques*, Charles Mere, Play

TROIS MOUSQUETAIRES, LES 1912 d: Andre Calmettes. FRN., *Les Trois Mousquetaires*, Alexandre Dumas (pere), Paris 1844, Novel

TROIS MOUSQUETAIRES, LES 1921 d: Henri Diamant-Berger. FRN., *Les Trois Mousquetaires*, Alexandre Dumas (pere), Paris 1844, Novel

TROIS MOUSQUETAIRES, LES 1932 d: Henri Diamant-Berger. FRN., *Les Trois Mousquetaires*, Alexandre Dumas (pere), Paris 1844, Novel

TROIS MOUSQUETAIRES, LES 1953 d: Andre Hunebelle. FRN/ITL., *Les Trois Mousquetaires*, Alexandre Dumas (pere), Paris 1844, Novel

TROIS MOUSQUETAIRES, LES 1961 d: Bernard Borderie. FRN/ITL., *Les Trois Mousquetaires*, Alexandre Dumas (pere), Paris 1844, Novel

Trois Passions, Les *see* THE THREE PASSIONS (1928).

Trois Points C'est Tout *see* RIEN QUE DES MENSONGES (1932).

TROIS POUR CENT 1933 d: Jean Dreville. FRN., *Trois Pour Cent*, Roger Ferdinand, Play

TROIS. SIX. NEUF 1936 d: Raymond Rouleau. FRN., *Trois. Six. Neuf*, Michel Duran, Play

Trois Soeurs *see* PAURA E AMORE (1987).

TROIS SULTANES, LES 1911 d: Adrien Caillard. FRN., *Les Trois Sultanes*, Favart, Play

Trois Verites *see* LE PUITS AUX TROIS VERITES (1961).

Trois Voleurs, Les *see* I TRE LADRI (1954).

TROJAN BROTHERS, THE 1946 d: MacLean Rogers. UKN., *The Trojan Brothers*, Pamela Hansford Johnson, Novel

Trojan Horse, The *see* LA GUERRA DI TROIA (1961).

Trojan War, The *see* LA GUERRA DI TROIA (1961).

TROJAN WOMEN, THE 1971 d: Michael Cacoyannis. USA/GRC., *The Trojan Women*, Euripides, 415 bc, Play

TROMBATA, LA 1979 d: Sergio Bergonzelli. ITL., *Il Sorriso Della Pithia*, Janis Maris

Trombone from Heaven *see* FOLLOW THE BAND (1943).

Trombonist, The *see* DER POSAUNIST (1945).

TROMEO & JULIET 1996 d: Lloyd Kaufman. USA., *Romeo and Juliet*, William Shakespeare, c1596, Play

TRONO PARA CRISTY 1959 d: Luis Cesar Amadori. SPN/GRM., *Un Trono Para Cristy*, Jose Lopez Rubio, 1957, Play

TROOP BEVERLY HILLS 1989 d: Jeff Kanew. USA., *Troop Beverly Hills*, Ava Ostern Fries

Troop Commander *see* DAI BING DE REN (1964).

Troop Train, The *see* LOVE AND THE LAW (1919).

TROOPER BILLY 1913. USA., *Trooper Billy*, Frederick Paulding, Play

TROOPER HOOK 1957 d: Charles Marquis Warren. USA., *Trooper Hook*, Jack Schaefer, Story

TROOPER O'NEILL 1922 d: Scott R. Dunlap, C. R. Wallace. USA., *Trooper O'Neil*, George Goodchild, London 1921, Novel

Trooper, The *see* THE FIGHTING TROOPER (1934).

TROP PETIT, MON AMI 1969 d: Eddy Matalon. FRN., *The Way the Cookie Crumbles*, James Hadley Chase, Novel

TROPENNACHTE 1930 d: Leo Mittler. FRN., *Victory*, Joseph Conrad, London 1915, Novel

TROPIC 1979 d: Matthew Robinson. UKN., *The Tropic of Ruislip*, Leslie Thomas, Novel

TROPIC OF CANCER 1970 d: Joseph Strick. USA., *Tropic of Cancer*, Henry Miller, Paris 1934, Novel

TROPIC OF DESIRE 1979 d: Cash Baxter. USA., *Tropic of Desire*, George Edwards, Novel

TROPIC ZONE 1953 d: Lewis R. Foster. USA., *Gentleman of the Jungle*, Tom Gill, 1940, Novel

Tropical Lady *see* THE PAINTED WOMAN (1932).

TROPICAL LOVE 1921 d: Ralph Ince. USA., *Peaks of Gold*, Guy M. McConnell, Story

TROPICAL NIGHTS 1928 d: Elmer Clifton. USA., *A Raid on the Oyster Pirates*, Jack London, 1905, Short Story

TROPICAL TROUBLE 1936 d: Harry Hughes. UKN., *Bunga-Bunga*, Stephen King-Hall, Novel

TROPPO TARDI T'HO CONOSCIUTA 1940 d: Emanuele Caracciolo. ITL., *Il Divo*, Nino Martoglio, Play

TROTTA 1972 d: Johannes Schaaf. GRM., *Die Kapuzinergruft*, Joseph Roth, 1938, Novel

Trotter's Gait, The *see* PRASHNAI GULSARA (1969).

TROTTIE TRUE 1948 d: Brian Desmond Hurst. UKN., *Trottie True*, Caryl Brahms, S. J. Simon, Novel

Trotzige Herzen *see* ERDE (1947).

TROU DANS LE MUR, UN 1931 d: Rene Barberis. FRN., *Un Trou Dans le Mur*, Yves Mirande, Play

TROU DANS LE MUR, UN 1949 d: Emile Couzinet. FRN., *Un Trou Dans le Mur*, Yves Mirande, Play

TROU, LE 1960 d: Jacques Becker. FRN/ITL., *Le Trou*, Jose Giovanni, Paris 1957, Novel

Troubadour, The *see* IL TROVATORE (1910).

Troubadour, The *see* IL TROVATORE (1949).

Trouble Agent *see* AGENT TROUBLE (1987).

Trouble at 16 *see* PLATINUM HIGH SCHOOL (1960).

TROUBLE AT MIDNIGHT 1938 d: Ford Beebe. USA., *Night Patrol*, Kimball Herrick, 1937, Short Story

Trouble Back Stairs *see* KRACH IM HINTERHAUS (1935).

TROUBLE FOR NOTHING 1916 d: Maurice Elvey. UKN., *Trouble for Nothing*, Arthur Eckersley, Guy Newall, Play

TROUBLE FOR TWO 1936 d: J. Walter Ruben. USA., *The Suicide Club*, Robert Louis Stevenson, London 1882, Short Stories

Trouble in Bahia for Oss 117 *see* FURIA A BAHIA POUR OSS 117 (1965).

TROUBLE IN MOROCCO 1937 d: Ernest B. Schoedsack. USA., *Sowing Glory*, J. D. Newsom, 1933, Short Story

Trouble in Sacramento *see* ALL'OVEST DI SACRAMENTO (1971).

Trouble in the Back House *see* KRACH IM HINTERHAUS (1949).

TROUBLE IN THE GLEN 1954 d: Herbert Wilcox. UKN., *Maurice Walsh*, Story

Trouble in the Sky *see* CONE OF SILENCE (1960).

Trouble Makers, The *see* THE JOYOUS TROUBLEMAKER (1920).

TROUBLE WITH ANGELS, THE 1966 d: Ida Lupino. USA., *Life With Mother Superior*, Jane Trahey, New York 1962, Novel

TROUBLE WITH EVE 1960 d: Francis Searle. UKN., *Widows are Dangerous*, June Garland, London 1953, Play

TROUBLE WITH GIRLS, THE 1969 d: Peter Tewkesbury. USA., *Chautauqua*, Dwight Babcock, Day Keene, New York 1960, Novel

TROUBLE WITH HARRY, THE 1955 d: Alfred Hitchcock. USA., *The Trouble With Harry*, Jack Trevor Story, 1950, Novel

TROUBLE WITH SPIES, THE 1984 d: Burt Kennedy. USA., *Apple Pie in the Sky*, Marc Lovell, Novel

Troubles *see* SHATTERED (1990).

TROUBLESOME WIVES 1928 d: Harry Hughes. UKN., *Summer Lightning*, Ernest Denny, Play

TROUPING WITH ELLEN 1924 d: T. Hayes Hunter. USA., *Trouping With Ellen*, Earl Derr Biggers, 1922, Short Story

Trousers, The *see* DIE HOSE (1927).

Trout, The *see* LA TRUITE (1982).

Trouvere, Le *see* IL TROVATORE (1910).

TROVATELLA DI MILANO, LA 1956 d: Giorgio Capitani. ITL., *La Trovatella Di Milano*, Carolina Invernizio, Novel

TROVATELLA DI POMPEI, LA 1958 d: Giacomo Gentilomo. ITL., *Alfredo Polacci*, Short Story

TROVATORE, IL 1910 d: Louis J. Gasnier. ITL/FRN., *El Trovador*, Antonio Garcia Gutierrez, Madrid 1836, Play

TROVATORE, IL 1914 d: Charles Simone. USA., *El Trovador*, Antonio Garcia Gutierrez, Madrid 1836, Play

TROVATORE, IL 1922 d: Edwin J. Collins. UKN., *El Trovador*, Antonio Garcia Gutierrez, Madrid 1836, Play

TROVATORE, IL 1927 d: A. E. Coleby. UKN., *El Trovador*, Antonio Garcia Gutierrez, Madrid 1836, Play

TROVATORE, IL 1949 d: Carmine Gallone. ITL., *El Trovador*, Antonio Garcia Gutierrez, Madrid 1836, Play

TRUANTS, THE 1922 d: Sinclair Hill. UKN., *The Truants*, A. E. W. Mason, Novel

Trube Wasser *see* LES ARRIVISTES (1960).

TRUBKA KUMMUNARA 1929 d: Konstantin Mardzhanov. USS., *The Communard's Pipe*, Ilja Erenburg

TRUC DU BRESILIEN, LE 1932 d: Alberto Cavalcanti. FRN., *Le Truc du Bresilien*, Paul Armont, Nicolas Nancey, Play

Truce, The *see* LA TREGUA (1974).

Truce, The *see* LA TREGUA (1997).

TRUCK BUSTERS 1943 d: B. Reeves Eason. USA., *Night Freight*, Robert E. Kent, Raymond L. Schrock, Story

Truck, The *see* KAMIONAT (1980).

Trudno Byt Bogom *see* EIN GOTT ZU SEIN ES IST NICHT LEICHT (1988).

True and the False, The *see* DEN UNDERBARA LOGNEN (1955).

TRUE AS A TURTLE 1957 d: Wendy Toye. UKN., *True As a Turtle*, John Coates, Novel

TRUE AS STEEL 1924 d: Rupert Hughes. USA., *True As Steel*, Rupert Hughes, 1923, Short Story

TRUE BLUE 1996 d: Ferdinand Fairfax. UKN., *True Blue*, Patrick Robinson, Daniel Topolski, Book

True Colors of a Hero *see* YINGXIONG BENSE (1993).

TRUE CONFESSION 1937 d: Wesley Ruggles. USA., *Mon Crime*, Georges Berr, Louis Verneuil, Paris 1934, Play

TRUE CONFESSIONS 1981 d: Ulu Grosbard. USA., *True Confessions*, John Gregory Dunne, 1977, Novel

TRUE CRIME 1999 d: Clint Eastwood. USA., *True Crime*, Andrew Klavan, Novel

True End of the Great War, The *see* PRAWDZIWY KONIEC WIELKIEJ WOJNY (1957).

TRUE GRIT 1969 d: Henry Hathaway. USA., *True Grit*, Charles Portis, New York 1968, Novel

TRUE HEAVEN 1929 d: James Tinling. USA., *Judith*, Charles Edward Montague, Short Story

True Stories of Poor Lovers *see* CRONACHE DI POVERI AMANTI (1954).

True Story of a Q, The *see* A Q ZHENGZHUAN (1981).

True Story of Ah Q, The *see* AH Q ZHENG ZHUAN (1958).

True Story of Ah Q, The see AH Q ZHEN ZHUAN (1982).

True Story of Camille, The see LA DAME AUX CAMELIAS (1981).

TRUE STORY OF LYNN STUART, THE 1958 d: Lewis Seiler. USA., Pat Michaels, Article

TRUE STORY OF THE LYONS MAIL, THE 1915 d: George Pearson. UKN., *The Lyons Mail*, Charles Reade, London 1877, Play

TRUE TILDA 1920 d: Harold Shaw. UKN., *True Tilda*, Arthur Quiller-Couch, Novel

TRUE TO THE ARMY 1942 d: Albert S. Rogell. USA., *She Loves Me Not*, Edward Hope, Indianapolis 1933, Novel

TRUE WEST 1983 d: Gary Sinise. USA., *True West*, Sam Shepard, 1980, Play

TRUE WOMEN 1997 d: Karen Arthur. USA., *True Women*, Janice Woods Windle, Book

TRUFFLERS, THE 1917 d: Fred E. Wright. USA., *The Trufflers*, Samuel Merwin, Indianapolis 1916, Novel

TRUITE, LA 1982 d: Joseph Losey. FRN., *La Truite*, Roger Vailland, 1964, Novel

Truman Capote's the Glass House see THE GLASS HOUSE (1972).

Truman Capote's Trilogy see TRILOGY (1969).

TRUMPET CALL, THE 1915 d: Percy Nash. UKN., *The Trumpet Call*, Robert Buchanan, George R. Sims, London 1891, Play

Trumps see ENORMOUS CHANGES AT THE LAST MINUTE (1983).

TRUNK CRIME 1939 d: Roy Boulting. UKN., *Trunk Crime*, Reginald Denham, Edward Percy, Play

Trunk Mystery, The see ONE NEW YORK NIGHT (1935).

TRUST DER DIEBE 1929 d: Erich Schonfelder. GRM., *Trust Der Diebe*, Ernst Klein, Novel

TRUST YOUR WIFE 1921 d: J. A. Barry. USA., *Conscience*, H. S. Sheldon, Play

Trust Your Wife see THE FALL GUY (1930).

TRUTH ABOUT HUSBANDS, THE 1920 d: Kenneth Webb. USA., *The Profligate*, Arthur Wing Pinero, London 1889, Play

Truth About Our Marriage, The see LA VERITE SUR LE BEBE DONGE (1951).

TRUTH ABOUT SPRING, THE 1964 d: Richard Thorpe. UKN/USA., *Satan; a Romance of the Bahamas*, Henry de Vere Stacpoole, New York 1921, Novel

TRUTH ABOUT YOUTH, THE 1930 d: William A. Seiter. USA., *When We Were Twenty-One*, H. V. Esmond, New York 1900, Play

Truth Game, The see BUT THE FLESH IS WEAK (1932).

Truth Is Stranger see WHEN LADIES MEET (1933).

TRUTH, THE 1920 d: Lawrence C. Windom. USA., *The Truth*, Clyde Fitch, Cleveland 1906, Play

TRUTH WAGON, THE 1914 d: Max Figman. USA., *The Truth Wagon*, Hayden Talbot, New York 1912, Play

TRUTHFUL SEX, THE 1926 d: Richard Thomas. USA., *Husbands Preferred*, Albert Shelby le Vino, Story

TRUXA 1936 d: Hans H. Zerlett. GRM., *Truxa*, Heinrich Seiler, Novel

TRUXTON KING 1923 d: Jerome Storm. USA., *Truxton King; a Story of Graustark*, George Barr McCutcheon, New York 1909, Novel

Truxtonia see TRUXTON KING (1923).

TRY AND GET IT 1924 d: Cullen Tate. USA., *The Ringtailed Galliwampus*, Eugene P. Lyle Jr., 1922, Short Story

Try and Get Me see THE SOUND OF FURY (1950).

TRY THIS ONE FOR SIZE 1989 d: Guy Hamilton. USA/FRN/ITL., *Try This One for Size*, James Hadley Chase, Novel

TRYGON FACTOR, THE 1967 d: Cyril Frankel. UKN., Edgar Wallace, Novel

TRYING TO GET ARRESTED 1909 d: D. W. Griffith. USA., *Trying to Get Arrested*, O. Henry, Short Story

Tsar Ivan Shishman see IVAN SHISHMAN (1969).

Tsar Peter's Youth see JUNOST PETRA (1980).

Tsar's Bride, The see TSARSKAYA NEVESTA (1965).

Tsar's Courier, The see DER KURIER DES ZAREN (1935).

Tsar's Pardon, The see TSARSKA MILOST (1962).

TSARSKA MILOST 1962 d: Stefan Surchadgiev. BUL., *Tsarka Milost*, Kamen Zidarov, 1949, Play

TSARSKAYA NEVESTA 1965 d: Vladimir Gorikker. USS., *Tsarskaya Nevesta*, Lev Aleksandrovich Mey, 1849, Play

TSCHUTSCHELO 1986 d: Rolan Bykov. USS., Wladimir Schelesnikow, Story

Tsebrokhene Hertser, Di see BROKEN HEARTS (1926).

TSUBAKI SANJURO 1962 d: Akira KurosawA. JPN., *Tsubaki Sanjuro*, Shugoro Yamamoto, Novel

TSUCHI 1939 d: Tomu UchidA. JPN., *Tsuchi*, Takashi Nagatsuka, 1910, Novel

TSUKI TO KYABETSU 1998 d: Tetsuo ShinoharA. JPN., *End of Sleepless Nights*, Kaoru Tsuruma, Story

TSUMA 1953 d: Mikio Naruse. JPN., *Chairo No Me*, Fumiko Hayashi, 1950, Novel

TSUMA TO ONNA NO AIDA 1976 d: Kon Ichikawa, Shiro ToyodA. JPN., Harumi Setouchi, Novel

TSUMA YO BARA NO YONI 1935 d: Mikio Naruse. JPN., *Tsuma No Bara No Yoni*, Minoru Nakano, Play

TU ERES LA PAZ 1942 d: Gregorio Martinez SierrA. ARG., *Tu Eres la Paz*, Gregorio Martinez Sierra, 1906, Novel

Tu Es un Imbecile see FOYER PERDU (1952).

TU IMAGINES ROBINSON 1968 d: Jean-Daniel Pollet. FRN., *Robinson Crusoe*, Daniel Defoe, 1719, Novel

TU NOMBRE ENVENENA MIS SUENOS 1996 d: Pilar Miro. SPN., *Tu Nombre Envenena Mis Suenos*, Joaquin Leguina, Novel

TU RIDI 1998 d: Paolo Taviani, Vittorio Taviani. ITL., Luigi Pirandello, Novel

TU TAN YU QIAO NIU 1994 d: Lei XIanhe, Li Jun. CHN., *Tu Tan Yu Qiao Niu*, Huang Huizhong, Novel

TU Y YO SOMOS TRES 1961 d: Rafael Gil. SPN/ARG., *Tu Y Yo Somos Tres*, Enrique Jardiel Poncela, 1946, Play

Tua Presenza Nuda, La see NIGHT HAIR CHILD (1971).

Tube Rose see RAJANIGANDHA (1974).

Tuberoses see RAJANIGANDHA (1974).

TUCK EVERLASTING 1980 d: Frederick King Keller. USA., *Tuck Everlasting*, Natalie Babbitt, Novel

Tueur Aime Les Bonbons, Le see UN KILLER PER SUA MAESTA (1968).

Tueurs de San Francisco, Les see ONCE A THIEF (1965).

Tug of Home: the Famous Niskavuori Saga see NISKAVUORI (1984).

TUGBOAT ANNIE 1933 d: Mervyn Leroy. USA., Norman Reilly Raine, Short Stories

TUGBOAT ANNIE SAILS AGAIN 1940 d: Lewis Seiler. USA., Norman Reilly Raine, 1938, Serial Story

TUGBOAT PRINCESS 1936 d: David Selman. CND., *Tugboat Princess*, Isadore Bernstein, Dalton Trumbo, Story

TULAK 1925 d: Josef Kokeisl. CZC., *Tulak*, Karel Hasler, Poem

Tulak see VRAT SE! ANICKO (1926).

Tulipan Negro, El see LA TULIPE NOIRE (1963).

Tulipano Nero, Il see LA TULIPE NOIRE (1963).

TULIPE NOIRE, LA 1963 d: Christian-Jaque. FRN/ITL/SPN., *La Tulipe Noire*, Alexandre Dumas (pere), 1846, Novel

TUMBA DES VAMPIRO, LA 1974 d: Leon Klimovsky. SPN/ITL., *La Tumba Des Vampiro*, David Chase, Novel

TUMBLEWEED 1953 d: Nathan Juran. USA., *Three Were Renegades*, Kenneth Parker, Novel

TUMBLING RIVER 1927 d: Lewis Seiler. USA., *The Scourge of the Little C*, Jesse Edward Grinstead, New York 1925, Novel

TUMULT 1969 d: Hans Abramson. DNM., *Nu*, Johannes Allen, Copenhagen 1967, Novel

Tumult -Sonja, Age 16 see TUMULT (1969).

TUMULTO DE PAIXOES 1958 d: Zygmunt Sulistrowski. BRZ/GRM., Anita Manville, Story

Tune in Tomorrow. see AUNT JULIA AND THE SCRIPTWRITER (1990).

Tunel see OGRO (1979).

TUNEL, EL 1952 d: Leon Klimovsky. ARG., *El Tunel*, Ernesto Sabato, 1948, Novel

TUNEL, EL 1988 d: Antonio Drove. SPN., *El Tunel*, Ernesto Sabato, 1948, Novel

TUNES OF GLORY 1960 d: Ronald Neame. UKN., *Tunes of Glory*, James Kennaway, 1956, Novel

Tunnel see OGRO (1979).

TUNNEL, DER 1933 d: Curtis Bernhardt. GRM., *Der Tunnel*, Bernhard Kellermann, Novel

TUNNEL, LE 1933 d: Curtis Bernhardt. FRN., *Der Tunnel*, Bernhard Kellermann, Novel

TUNNEL OF LOVE, THE 1958 d: Gene Kelly. USA., *Tunnel of Love*, Peter de Vries, 1954, Novel

TUNNEL SOTTO IL MONDO, IL 1968 d: Luigi Cozzi. ITL., *Tunnel Under the World*, Frederik Pohl, Novel

Tunnel, The see DER TUNNEL (1933).

TUNNEL, THE 1935 d: Maurice Elvey. UKN., *Der Tunnel*, Bernhard Kellermann, Novel

Tunnel, The see EL TUNEL (1988).

Tunnel Under the World, The see IL TUNNEL SOTTO IL MONDO (1968).

TUNNYNG OF ELINOUR RUMMYNG 1976 d: Julien Temple. UKN., *The Tunnyng of Elynoure Rummyng*, John Skelton, c1520, Verse

TUNTEMATON SOTILAS 1955 d: Edvin Laine. FNL., *Tuntematon Sotilas*, Vaino Linna, 1954, Novel

TUNTEMATON SOTILAS 1985 d: Rauni Mollberg. FNL., *Tuntematon Sotilas*, Vaino Linna, 1954, Novel

TUO PIACERE E IL MIO, IL 1973 d: Claudio RaccA. ITL., *I Racconti Licenziosi*, Honore de Balzac, Book

TUO VIZIO E UNA STANZA CHIUSA E SOLO IO NE HO LE CHIAVI, IL 1972 d: Sergio Martino. ITL., *The Black Cat*, Edgar Allan Poe, Short Story

TUR MIT DEN SIEBEN SCHLOSSERN, DIE 1962 d: Alfred Vohrer. GRM., *The Door With Seven Locks*, Edgar Wallace, London 1926, Novel

TURANDOT, PRINCESSE DE CHINE 1934 d: Serge Veber, Gerhard Lamprecht. FRN., *Turandot*, Carlo Gozzi, Friedrich Schiller, Play

TURBAMENTO 1942 d: Guido Brignone. ITL., *Turbamento*, Arturo Cantini, Play

TURBINA 1941 d: Otakar VavrA. CZC., *Turbina*, Karel Matej Capek-Chod, Novel

Turbine Fatale see CIRCE MODERNA (1914).

Turbine, The see TURBINA (1941).

TURCO NAPOLETANO, UN 1953 d: Mario Mattoli. ITL., *Un Turco Napoletano*, Eduardo Scarpetta, Play

TURF CONSPIRACY, A 1918 d: Frank Wilson. UKN., *A Turf Conspiracy*, Nat Gould, Novel

TURKEY TIME 1933 d: Tom Walls. UKN., *Turkey Time*, Ben Travers, London 1931, Play

Turkish Delight see TURKS FRUITS (1973).

TURKS FRUITS 1973 d: Paul Verhoeven. NTH., *Turks Fruit*, Jan Hendrick Wolkers, 1970, Novel

TURLIS ABENTEUER 1967 d: Walter Beck, Ron Merk. GDR., *Le Avventure Di Pinocchio*, Carlo Collodi, 1883, Short Story

Turli's Adventure see TURLIS ABENTEUER (1967).

TURM DER VERBOTENEN LIEBE, DER 1968 d: Franz Antel. GRM/ITL/FRN., *La Tour de Nesle*, Alexandre Dumas (pere), F. Gaillardet, 1832, Play

Turmoil see SINS OF MAN (1936).

TURMOIL, THE 1916 d: Edgar Jones. USA., *The Turmoil*, Booth Tarkington, New York 1915, Novel

TURMOIL, THE 1924 d: Hobart Henley. USA., *The Turmoil*, Booth Tarkington, New York 1915, Novel

TURN BACK THE HOURS 1928 d: Howard Bretherton. USA., *Turn Back the Hours*, Edward E. Rose, Hoboken, N.J. 1917, Play

TURN HIM OUT 1913. USA., *Turn Him Out*, Thomas J. Williams, Play

TURN OF THE SCREW 1974 d: Dan Curtis. USA/UKN., *The Turn of the Screw*, Henry James, New York 1898, Short Story

TURN OF THE SCREW, THE 1989 d: Graeme Clifford. USA., *The Turn of the Screw*, Henry James, New York 1898, Short Story

TURN OF THE SCREW, THE 1992 d: Rusty Lemorande. UKN/FRN., *The Turn of the Screw*, Henry James, New York 1898, Short Story

TURN OF THE SCREW, THE 1995 d: Tom McLoughlin. USA., *The Turn of the Screw*, Henry James, New York 1898, Short Story

TURN OF THE TIDE 1935 d: Norman Walker. UKN., *Three Fevers*, Leo Walmsley, Novel

TURN THE KEY SOFTLY 1953 d: Jack Lee. UKN., *Turn the Key Softly*, John Brophy, Novel

Turn the Other Cheek see PORGI L'ALTRA GUANCIA (1974).

TURN TO THE RIGHT 1922 d: Rex Ingram. USA., *Turn to the Right*, Jack E. Hazzard, Winchell Smith, New York 1916, Play

TWO FOR TEXAS 1997 d: Rod Hardy. USA., *Two for Texas*, James Lee Burke, Novel

TWO FOR THE SEESAW 1962 d: Robert Wise. USA., *Two for the Seesaw*, William Gibson, New York 1958, Play

TWO FOR TONIGHT 1935 d: Frank Tuttle. USA., *Two for Tonight*, J. O. Lief, Max Lief, Play

TWO GENTLEMEN SHARING 1970 d: Ted Kotcheff. UKN., *Two Gentlemen Sharing*, David Stuart Leslie, London 1963, Novel

Two Girls from the Red Star *see* ZWEI GIRLS VOM ROTEN STERN (1966).

TWO GLASSES, THE 1913. USA., *The Two Glasses*, Ella Wheeler Wilcox, Poem

Two Green Feathers *see* PAN (1995).

Two Have Died *see* KETTEN HALTAK MEG (1964).

TWO HEADS ON A PILLOW 1934 d: William Nigh. USA., *The Eternal Masculine*, Dorothy Canfield, Short Story

Two Hearts, One Throne *see* ZWEI HERZEN UND EIN THRON (1955).

Two Heavenly Blockheads *see* ZWEI HIMMLISCHE DICKSCHADEL (1974).

Two Humans *see* ZWEI MENSCHEN (1930).

TWO IN THE DARK 1936 d: Ben Stoloff. USA., *Two O'Clock Courage*, Gelett Burgess, Indianapolis 1934, Novel

TWO KINDS OF LOVE 1983 d: Jack Bender. USA., *There are Two Kinds of Terrible*, Peggy Mann, Novel

TWO KINDS OF WOMEN 1922 d: Colin Campbell. USA., *Judith of Blue Lake Ranch*, Jackson Gregory, New York 1919, Novel

TWO KINDS OF WOMEN 1932 d: William C. de Mille. USA., *This Is New York*, R. E. Sherwood, New York 1930, Play

Two Kuni Lemel *see* SHNEI KUNI LEMEL (1965).

TWO LANCASHIRE LASSIES IN LONDON 1916 d: Dave Aylott. UKN., *Two Lancashire Lassies in London*, Arthur Shirley, Sutton Vane, Play

TWO LEAVES AND A BUD 1952 d: Khwaya Ahmad Abbas. IND., *Two Leaves and a Bud*, Mulk Raj Anand, 1937, Novel

TWO LEFT FEET 1963 d: Roy Ward Baker. UKN., *In My Solitude*, David Stuart Leslie, Novel

TWO LETTER ALIBI 1962 d: Robert Lynn. UKN., *Death and the Sky Above*, Andrew Garve, Novel

TWO LITTLE DRUMMER BOYS 1928 d: G. B. Samuelson. UKN., *Two Little Drummer Boys*, Walter Howard, Play

TWO LITTLE WOODEN SHOES 1920 d: Sidney Morgan. UKN., *Two Little Wooden Shoes*, Ouida, Novel

Two Lives *see* DVOJI ZIVOT (1924).

Two Lives *see* ZWEI MENSCHEN (1930).

Two Living and One Dead *see* TO LEVENDE OG EN DOD (1937).

Two Living and One Dead *see* TVA LEVANDE OCH EN DOD (1961).

Two Living, One Dead *see* TVA LEVANDE OCH EN DOD (1961).

Two Lottery Tickets *see* DOUA LOZURI (1957).

TWO LOVERS 1928 d: Fred Niblo. USA., *Leatherface; a Tale of Old Flanders*, Baroness Orczy, New York 1916, Novel

Two Lovers Around the World *see* IL GIRO DEL MONDO DEGLI INNAMORATI DI PEYNET (1974).

TWO LOVES 1961 d: Charles Walters. USA., *Spinster*, Sylvia Ashton-Warner, London 1958, Novel

Two Marriages, The *see* GIOVANNA LA PALLIDA (1911).

Two Measures of Paddy *see* RANDIDANGAZHI (1958).

Two Men and a Woman(?) *see* THE UNCHASTENED WOMAN (1918).

Two Men, and Two Women Among Them *see* DOS HOMBRES Y EN MEDIO DOS MUJERES (1977).

Two Men for One Death *see* DOI BARBATI PENTRU O MOARTE (1970).

TWO MEN OF SANDY BAR 1916 d: Lloyd B. Carleton. USA., *Two Men of Sandy Bar*, Bret Harte, New York 1876, Play

TWO MEN OF THE DESERT 1913 d: D. W. Griffith. USA., *Two Men of the Desert*, Jack London, Short Story

Two Minds for Murder *see* QUALCUNO DIETRO LA PORTA (1971).

Two Minute Alibi *see* ALIBI FOR MURDER (1936).

Two Monks *see* MANDALA (1981).

TWO MOONS 1920 d: Edward J. Le Saint. USA., *Trails to Two Moons*, Robert Welles Ritchie, Boston 1920, Novel

Two Mothers *see* DVE MATKY (1920).

Two Mothers, The *see* LE DUE MADRI (1909).

TWO MRS. CARROLLS, THE 1947 d: Peter Godfrey. USA., *The Two Mrs. Carrolls*, Martin Vale, Play

TWO MRS. GRENVILLES, THE 1987 d: John Erman. USA., *The Two Mrs. Grenvilles*, Dominick Dunne, Novel

Two Much *see* LOCO DE AMOR (1996).

Two Neckties *see* ZWEI KRAWATTEN (1930).

Two O'Clock Courage *see* TWO IN THE DARK (1936).

TWO O'CLOCK COURAGE 1945 d: Anthony Mann. USA., *Two O'Clock Courage*, Gelett Burgess, Indianapolis 1934, Novel

TWO OF A KIND 1951 d: Henry Levin. USA., *Lefty Farrell*, James Edward Grant, Novel

TWO OF A TRADE 1928 d: Geoffrey H. Malins. UKN., *Two of a Trade*, W. W. Jacobs, Short Story

Two of Gus, The *see* DON'T TELL HER IT'S ME (1990).

Two of Us, The *see* JACK OF ALL TRADES (1936).

Two on a Tower *see* PARIS IN SPRING (1935).

TWO ORPHANS, THE 1911 d: Otis Turner. USA., *Les Deux Orphelines*, Eugene Cormon, Adolphe-P. d'Ennery, 1874, Novel

TWO ORPHANS, THE 1915 d: Herbert Brenon. USA., *Les Deux Orphelines*, Eugene Cormon, Adolphe-P. d'Ennery, 1874, Novel

Two Orphans, The *see* ORPHANS OF THE STORM (1921).

Two Orphans, The *see* LES DEUX ORPHELINES (1932).

Two Orphans, The *see* LE DUE ORFANELLE (1942).

Two Orphans, The *see* LE DUE ORFANELLE (1966).

Two People *see* ZWEI MENSCHEN (1952).

Two Pros Call It Quits *see* UN DIMANCHE DE FLICS (1982).

TWO RENEGADES, THE 1917 d: David Smith. USA., *The Two Renegades*, O. Henry, Short Story

Two Roads *see* DO RAASTE (1969).

Two Roads *see* DUVIDHA (1973).

TWO ROADS, THE 1915 d: Harold Shaw. UKN., *The Two Roads*, Ben Landeck, Play

TWO RODE TOGETHER 1961 d: John Ford. USA., *Comanche Captives*, Will Cook, New York 1960, Novel

TWO SECONDS 1932 d: Mervyn Leroy. USA., *Two Seconds*, Elliott Lester, New York 1931, Play

Two Sergeants, The *see* I DUE SERGENTI (1909).

Two Sergeants, The *see* I DUE SERGENTI (1913).

TWO SHALL BE BORN 1924 d: Whitman Bennett. USA., *Two Shall Be Born*, Susan Marr Spaulding, Poem

TWO SINNERS 1935 d: Arthur Lubin. USA., *Two Black Sheep*, Warwick Deeping, New York 1933, Novel

TWO SISTERS 1929 d: Scott Pembroke. USA., *The Two Sisters*, Virginia Terhune Vandewater, New York 1914, Novel

Two Soldiers East and West *see* HELL IN THE PACIFIC (1968).

TWO SOLITUDES 1978 d: Lionel Chetwynd. CND., *Two Solitudes*, Hugh MacLennan, Novel

Two Souled Woman, The *see* THE UNTAMEABLE (1923).

Two Times Lotte *see* DAS DOPPELTE LOTTCHEN (1950).

Two Timid Ones, The *see* LES DEUX TIMIDES (1928).

TWO TO TANGO 1987 d: Robert McCallum. USA., *Two to Tango*, J. P. Feinmann, Novel

TWO VANREVELS, THE 1914 d: Richard Ridgely. USA., *The Two Vanrevels*, Booth Tarkington, Novel

Two Virtuous Women *see* ZHEN NU (1988).

TWO WEEKS 1920 d: Sidney A. Franklin. USA., *At the Barn*, Anthony Wharton, New York 1914, Play

TWO WEEKS IN ANOTHER TOWN 1962 d: Vincente Minnelli. USA., *Two Weeks in Another Town*, Irwin Shaw, New York 1960, Novel

TWO WEEKS OFF 1929 d: William Beaudine. USA., *Two Weeks Off*, Thomas Barrows, Kenyon Nicholson, New York 1927, Novel

TWO WEEKS WITH PAY 1921 d: Maurice Campbell. USA., *Two Weeks With Pay*, Nina Wilcox Putnam, 1920, Short Story

TWO WHITE ARMS 1932 d: Fred Niblo. UKN., *Two White Arms*, Harold Dearden, London 1928, Play

Two Wives *see* TSUMA YO BARA NO YONI (1935).

TWO WOMEN 1915 d: Ralph Ince. USA., *Two Women*, James Oliver Curwood, Story

Two Women *see* THE GHOSTS OF YESTERDAY (1918).

Two Women *see* SHE LOVES AND LIES (1920).

Two Women *see* TVA KVINNOR (1947).

Two Women *see* LA CIOCIARA (1961).

Two Worlds of Angelita, The *see* LOS DOS MUNDOS DE ANGELITA (1982).

TWO WORLDS OF JENNIE LOGAN, THE 1979 d: Frank de FelittA. USA., *Second Sight*, David Williams, Novel

Two Year Long Holidays *see* DEUX ANS DE VACANCES (1973).

TWO YEARS BEFORE THE MAST 1946 d: John Farrow. USA., *Two Years Before the Mast*, R. H. Dana, 1840, Novel

Two You Sisters in the Red Mansion, The *see* HONG LOU ER YOU (1951).

TWO-BIT SEATS 1917 d: Lawrence C. Windom. USA., *Two-Bit Seats*, Gladys E. Johnson, 1917, Short Story

Two-Edged Knife *see* FACA DE DOIS GUMES (1989).

TWO-FACED WOMAN 1941 d: George Cukor. USA., *The Twin Sister*, Ludwig Fulda, 1902, Play

Two-Fisted *see* TWO FISTED (1935).

Two-Gun Cupid *see* THE BAD MAN (1941).

Two-Gun Man, The *see* TREAT 'EM ROUGH (1919).

Two-Headed Monster, The *see* THE MANSTER (1962).

TWO-MINUTE WARNING 1976 d: Larry Peerce. USA., *Two-Minute Warning*, George la Fontaine, Novel

TWO'S COMPANY 1936 d: Tim Whelan. UKN., *Romeo and Julia*, Sidney Horler, Novel

TWO-SOUL WOMAN, THE 1918 d: Elmer Clifton. USA., *The White Cat*, Gelett Burgess, New York 1907, Novel

TY PETRINSKE STRANE 1922 d: Thea CervenkovA. CZC., *Bludicka*, Jaroslav Kvapil, Play

TYCOON 1947 d: Richard Wallace. USA., *Tycoon*, Charles E. Scoggins, Novel

Tyoma's Childhood *see* DETSTVO TEMY (1991).

TYPHOON, THE 1914 d: Reginald Barker. USA., *Taifun*, Menyhert Lengyel, Budapest 1909, Play

Tyrma *see* LA PRINCIPESSA DELLE CANARIE (1956).

Tyrnovskata Tzaritza *see* TURNOVSKATA TSARITSA (1981).

Tyson *see* TYSON: THE TRUE STORY (1994).

TYSON: THE TRUE STORY 1994 d: Ulrich Edel. USA., *Fire and Fear*, Jose Torres, Book

TYUTYUN 1962 d: Nicolai Korabov. BUL., *Tyutyun*, Dimitar Dimov, 1951, Novel

Tzarevitch, Le *see* DER ZAREWITSCH (1954).

Tzarewitch, Le *see* SON ALTESSE IMPERIALE (1933).

Tzigane *see* GYPSY (1937).

Tzila Khozereth *see* TZLILA CHOZERET (1982).

TZLILA CHOZERET 1982 d: Shimon Dotan. ISR., Yehudit Handel, Story

Tzvety Zapozdalye *see* CHVETI ZAPOZDALIE (1969).

U 47 - Lt. Prien *see* U 47 KAPITANLEUTNANT PRIEN (1958).

U 47 KAPITANLEUTNANT PRIEN 1958 d: Harald Reinl. GRM., Udo Wolter, Story

U Boat 55 *see* HAIE UND KLEINE FISCHE (1957).

U KRUTOGO YARA 1962 d: Kira Muratova, Alexander Muratov. USS., *U Krutogo Yara*, G. Troyepolskiy, Moscow 1956, Short Story

U SNEDENEHO KRAMU 1933 d: Martin Fric. CZC., *U Snedeneho Kramu*, Ignat Herrmann, Novel

U Sv. Mateje *see* KDYZ SE SLUNKO ZASMEJE U SVATEHO MATEJE (1928).

U SVATEHO MATEJE, KDYZ SE SLUNKO ZASMEJE 1928 d: Josef Kokeisl. CZC., *U Svateho Mateje*, Karel Hasler, Poem

U SVETEHO ANTONICKA 1933 d: Svatopluk Innemann. CZC., *U Svateho Antonicka*, J. Armand, Jiri Balda, Opera

U-47 Lt. Commander Prien see U 47 KAPITANLEUTNANT PRIEN (1958).

UANSTAENDIGE, DE 1983 d: Edward Fleming. DNM., *De Uanstaendige*, Leif Panduro, 1960, Novel

UBAT 39 1952 d: Erik Faustman. SWD., *U 39*, Rudolf Varnlund, 1939, Play

Uber Alles Die Liebe see MUNCHNERINNEN (1944).

UBERFLUSSIGE MENSCHEN 1926 d: Alexander Rasumny. GRM., Anton Chekhov, Novel

Ubers Jahr, Wenn Die Kornblumen Bluhen see JUGENDLIEBE (1944).

UBETAENKSOMME ELSKER, DEN 1983 d: Claus Ploug. DNM., *Den Ubetaeksomme Elsker*, Leif Panduro, 1973, Novel

UBITZI VYKHODYAT NA DOROGU 1942 d: V. I. Pudovkin, Yuri Tarich. USS., *Furchte Und Elend Des Dritten Reiches*, Bertolt Brecht, 1941, Play

U-Boat 29 see THE SPY IN BLACK (1939).

U-Boat 39 see UBAT 39 (1952).

U-BOAT PRISONER 1944 d: Lew Landers. USA., *U-Boat Prisoner; the Life of a Texas Sailor*, Archie Gibbs, Book

UBRANIE PRAWIE NOWE 1963 d: Wlodzimierz Haupe. PLN., *Roza*, Jaroslaw Iwaszkiewicz, 1936, Short Story

Ubu and the Great Gidouille see UBU ET LA GRANDE GIDOUILLE (1979).

UBU ET LA GRANDE GIDOUILLE 1979 d: Jan LenicA. FRN., *Ubu Roi*, Alfred Jarry, 1896, Play

UCCELLO DALLE PIUME DE CRISTALLO, L' 1970 d: Dario Argento. ITL/GRM., Bryan Edgar Wallace, Novel

Uccidero un Uomo see QUE LA BETE MEURE (1969).

Uccidete Agente Segreto 777-Stop see AGENT SECRET FX18 COPLAN (1964).

UCHU DAIKAIJU DOGORA 1964 d: Inoshiro HondA. JPN., *Space Moons*, Jojiro Okami, Short Story

Uchudai Dogora see UCHU DAIKAIJU DOGORA (1964).

UCHUJIN TOKYO NI ARAWARU 1956 d: Koji ShimA. JPN., *Uchujin Tokyo Ni Arawaru*, Gentaro Nakajima, Novel

UDEN EN TRAEVL 1968 d: Annelise Meineche. DNM., *Uten En Trad*, Jens Bjorneboe, Oslo 1966, Novel

Udivitel'naja Istozijz Pokhozhaja Na Skazhu see POCHOSHAJA NA SKASKU UDIWITJELNAJA ISTORIJA (1966).

UDIWITJELNAJA ISTORIJA, POCHOSHAJA NA SKASKU 1966 d: Boris Dolin. USS., *Der Grimme Aelling*, Hans Christian Andersen, 1844, Short Story

UEMURA NAOMI MONOGATARI 1985 d: Junya Sato. JPN., *Uemura Naomi Monogatari*, Naomi Uemura, Autobiography

UFO INCIDENT, THE 1975 d: Richard A. CollA. USA., *The Interrupted Journey*, John G. Fuller, Book

Ugetsu see UGETSU MONOGATARI (1953).

UGETSU MONOGATARI 1953 d: Kenji Mizoguchi. JPN., *Asaji Ga Yado*, Akinari Ueda, c1768, Short Story, *Jasei No in*, Akinari Ueda, c1768, Short Story

UGLER I MOSEN 1959 d: Ivo Caprino. NRW., *Marens Lille Ugle*, Finn Havrevold, 1957, Novel

UGLY AMERICAN, THE 1963 d: George Englund. USA., *The Ugly American*, Eugene Burdick, William J. Lederer, New York 1958, Novel

UGLY DACHSHUND, THE 1966 d: Norman Tokar. USA., *Dogs in an Omnibus*, Gladys Bronwyn Stern, London 1942, Novel

UGLY DUCKLING, THE 1959 d: Lance Comfort. UKN., *The Strange Case of Dr. Jekyll and Mr. Hyde*, Robert Louis Stevenson, London 1886, Novel

UGLY LITTLE BOY, THE 1978 d: Barry Morse. USA., *The Ugly Little Boy*, Isaac Asimov, 1966, Short Story

Ugly Ones, The see EL PRECIO DE UN HOMBRE (1966).

Ugly Story, An see SKVENEI ANEKDOT (1965).

Ugly Village, The see SKAREDA DEDINA (1975).

Ugo E la Parisina see PARISINA (UN AMORE ALLA CORTE DI FERRARA NEL XV SECOLO) (1909).

Ugo E Parisina see PARISINA (UN AMORE ALLA CORTE DI FERRARA NEL XV SECOLO) (1909).

UILENSPIEGEL LEEFT NOG 1935 d: Jan Vanderheyden. BLG., *Fanfare de Sint-Jansvrienden*, Ernest Claes, Novel

Uira, an Indian in Search of God see UM INDIO EM BUSCA DE DEUS UIRA (1973).

Uira, Um Indio a Procura de Dios see UM INDIO EM BUSCA DE DEUS UIRA (1973).

UIRA, UM INDIO EM BUSCA DE DEUS 1973 d: Gustavo Dahl. BRZ., Darcy Ribeiro, Story

UKIGUMO 1955 d: Mikio Naruse. JPN., *Ukigumo*, Fumiko Hayoshi, 1935, Novel

UKJENT MANN 1951 d: Astrid Henning-Jensen, Bjarne Henning-Jensen. NRW., *Flukten*, Arthur Omre, 1936, Novel

UKRIZOVANA 1921 d: Boris Orlicky. CZC., *Ukrizovana*, Jakub Arbes, Novel

UKROSHCHENIE STROPTIVOY 1961 d: Sergei Kolosov. USS., *The Taming of the Shrew*, William Shakespeare, c1593, Play

ULBO GARVEEMA 1917 d: Maurits H. Binger. NTH., *Ulbo Garvema*, Ernest Scheidius, Novel

ULI DER KNECHT 1954 d: Franz Schnyder. SWT., *Wie Uli Der Knecht Glucklich Wird*, Jeremias Gotthelf, Zurich 1841, Novel

ULI DER PACHTER 1955 d: Franz Schnyder. SWT., *Uli Der Pachter*, Jeremias Gotthelf, Berlin 1849, Novel

Uli Il Mezzadro see ULI DER PACHTER (1955).

Uli Il Servo see ULI DER KNECHT (1954).

Uli le Fermier see ULI DER PACHTER (1955).

Uli le Valet de Ferme see ULI DER KNECHT (1954).

ULICE ZPIVA 1939 d: Vlasta Burian, Cenek Slegl. CZC., Pavel Schuek, Play

ULICNICE 1936 d: Vladimir Slavinsky. CZC., *Ulicnice*, Vaclav Mirovsky, Vaclav Spilar, Karel Tobis, Opera

ULISSE 1954 d: Mario Camerini. ITL/USA., *The Odyssey*, Homer, Verse

Ulisse Non Deve Morire see HEUREUX QUI COMME ULYSSE (1970).

ULLA MIN ULLA 1930 d: Julius Jaenzon. SWD., *Bellman Vaudeville*, Edvin Ziedner, Stockholm 1922, Musical Play

Ulla My Ulla see ULLA MIN ULLA (1930).

ULTIMA CARTA, L' 1939 d: Piero Ballerini. ITL., *L' Ultima Carta*, Giuseppe Romualdi, Play

ULTIMA CHANCE, L' 1973 d: Maurizio Lucidi. ITL., *L' Ultima Chance*, Franco Enna, Novel

Ultima Giovinezza see DERNIERE JEUNESSE (1939).

ULTIMA LAMADA 1997 d: Carlos Garcia Agraz. MXC., *Bandera Negra*, Horacio Ruiz de La Fuente, Play

ULTIMA NOAPTE DE DRAGOSTE 1979 d: Sergiu Nicolaescu. RMN., *Ultima Noapte de Dragoste Intiia Noapte de Razbol*, Camil Petrescu, 1930, Novel

Ultima Notte d'Amore, L' see LA PUERTA ABIERTA (1957).

ULTIMA SENORA ANDERSON, LA 1970 d: Eugenio Martin. SPN/ITL., J. B. Gilford, Short Story

ULTIMA SIEMBRA, LA 1991 d: Miguel PereirA. ARG/UKN., *Los Humilides*, Miguel Angel Pereira, Novel

ULTIMA VOLTA, L' 1976 d: Aldo Lado. ITL., *Una Leggera Euforia*, S. Calanchi, Luigi Collo, Short Story

Ultimate Imposter, The see THE ULTIMATE IMPOSTOR (1979).

ULTIMATE IMPOSTOR, THE 1979 d: Paul Stanley. USA., *The Capricorn Man*, William Zacha Sr., Novel

ULTIMATUM 1938 d: Robert Wiene, Robert Siodmak (Uncredited). FRN., *Ultimatum*, Ewald Bertram, Novel

Ultimatum, Das see TWILIGHT'S LAST GLEAMING (1977).

ULTIME LETTERE DI JACOPO ORTIS 1973 d: Peter Del Monte. ITL., *Le Ultime Lettere Di Jacopo Ortis*, Ugo Foscolo, 1798, Novel

ULTIME LETTERE DI JACOPO ORTIS, LE 1921 d: Lucio d'AmbrA. ITL., *Le Ultime Lettere Di Jacopo Ortis*, Ugo Foscolo, 1798, Novel

Ultime Passion, L' see YOUR TICKET IS NO LONGER VALID (1980).

ULTIMI CINQUE MINUTI, GLI 1955 d: Giuseppe Amato. ITL/FRN., Aldo de Benedetto, Play

ULTIMI DIECI GIORNI DI HITLER, GLI 1973 d: Ennio de Concini. ITL/UKN., *The Last Days of the Chancellery*, Gerhardt Boldt, Book

ULTIMI FILIBUSTIERI, GLI 1921 d: Vitale de Stefano. ITL., *Gli Ultimi Filibustieri*, Emilio Salgari, Novel

ULTIMI FILIBUSTIERI, GLI 1943 d: Marco Elter. ITL., *Gli Ultimi Filibustieri*, Emilio Salgari, Novel

ULTIMI GIORNI DI POMPEI, GLI 1908 d: Luigi Maggi. ITL., *The Last Days of Pompeii*, Edward George Bulwer Lytton, 1834, Novel

ULTIMI GIORNI DI POMPEI, GLI 1913 d: Eleuterio Rodolfi. ITL., *The Last Days of Pompeii*, Edward George Bulwer Lytton, 1834, Novel

ULTIMI GIORNI DI POMPEI, GLI 1926 d: Amleto Palermi, Carmine Gallone. ITL., *The Last Days of Pompeii*, Edward George Bulwer Lytton, 1834, Novel

Ultimi Giorni Di Pompei, Gli see LES DERNIERS JOURS DE POMPEI (1948).

Ultimi Giorni Di Pompeii, Gli see DIE LETZTEN TAGE VON POMPEI (1959).

Ultimi Taureg, Gli see I CAVALIERI DEL DESERTO (1942).

Ultimo see DAS LEBEN KANN SO SCHON SEIN (1938).

ULTIMO ADDIO, L' 1942 d: Ferruccio Cerio. ITL., Janos Smolka, Play

ULTIMO BALLO, L' 1941 d: Camillo Mastrocinque. ITL., *Utolso Tanc*, Ferenc Herczeg, Play

ULTIMO CAPODANNO, L' 1998 d: Marco Risi. ITL., *L' Ultimo Capodanna Dell'Umanita*, Niccolo Ammaniti, Novel

ULTIMO DEGLI ABENCERAGI, L' 1911. ITL., *Aventures du Dernier Abencerage*, Francois Rene Chateaubriand, 1826

ULTIMO DEI BERGERAC, L' 1934 d: Gennaro Righelli. ITL., *La Signorina Di Bergerac*, Gaetano Campanile Mancini, Short Story

ULTIMO DEI FRONTIGNAC, L' 1911 d: Mario Caserini?. ITL., *Le Roman d'un Jeune Homme Pauvre*, Octave Feuillet, 1858, Novel

Ultimo Dei Mohicani, L' see EL FIN DE UNA RAZA UNCAS (1964).

Ultimo Dei Mohicani, L' see DER LETZTE MOHIKANER (1965).

Ultimo Domicilio Conosciuto see DERNIER DOMICILE CONNU (1970).

Ultimo Giorno d'Amore, L' see L' HOMME PRESSE (1976).

ULTIMO HAREM, L' 1981 d: Sergio Garrone. ITL/GRM/SPN., *El Ultimo Haren*, Alberto Vazquez Figueroa, Novel

Ultimo Haren, El see L' ULTIMO HAREM (1981).

ULTIMO INCONTRO 1952 d: Gianni Franciolini. ITL., *La Biondina*, Marco Praga, 1893, Novel

ULTIMO LORD, L' 1926 d: Augusto GeninA. ITL., *Little Lord Fauntleroy*, Frances Hodgson Burnett, New York 1886, Novel

Ultimo Mohicano, El see DER LETZTE MOHIKANER (1965).

Ultimo Rey de Los Incas, El see VIVA GRINGO (1966).

ULTIMO UOMO DELLA TERRA, L' 1964 d: Ubaldo Ragona, Sidney Salkow. ITL/USA., *I Am Legend*, Richard Matheson, New York 1954, Novel

Ultimos Dias de Pompeya, Los see DIE LETZTEN TAGE VON POMPEI (1959).

Ultimul Mohican see LE DERNIER DES MOHICANS (1968).

ULVOVA MYLLARI 1983 d: Jaakko PakkasvirtA. FNL., *Ulvova Myllari*, Arto Paasilinna, 1981, Novel

Ulysses see ULISSE (1954).

ULYSSES 1967 d: Joseph Strick. UKN/USA., *Ulysses*, James Joyce, 1922, Novel

Um Einen Groschen Liebe see EIN KIND DER STRASSE SCAMPOLO (1932).

UMANITA 1919 d: Elvira GiallanellA. ITL., *Umanita*, Vittorio Emanuele Bravetta, Poem

UMBARTHA 1982 d: Jabbar Patel. IND., *Beghar*, Shanta Nisal, Novel

Umbrella Man, The see LONDON BY NIGHT (1937).

Umbrella, The see LONDON BY NIGHT (1937).

Umgliklikhe Kale, Di see THE UNFORTUNATE BRIDE (1937).

Uminchu - the Old Man and the East China Sea see ROJIN TO UMI (1990).

UMORISMO NERO 1965 d: Giancarlo Zagni, Jose Maria Forque. ITL/SPN/FRN., *La Fourmi*, Guy de Maupassant, Short Story

UMRAO JAAN 1979 d: Muzaffar Ali. IND., *Umrao Jaan Ada*, Meer Hadi Hassan Rusva, 1899, Novel

UMWEGE DES SCHONEN KARL, DIE 1938 d: Carl Froelich. GRM., *Die Umwege Des Schonen Karl*, Paul Enderling, Novel

Un Coup de Feu Dans la Nuit *see* **COUP DE FEU DANS LA NUIT** (1942).

UN DE LA CANEBIERE 1938 d: Rene Pujol. FRN., *Un de la Canebiere*, Henri Alibert, Vincent Scotto, Opera

UN NOS OLA LEUAD 1991 d: Endaf Emlyn. UKN., *One Full Moon*, Caradog Prichard, Novel

UN SALTIMBANC LA POLUL NORD 1982 d: Elisabeta Bostan. RMN/USS., *Fram Ursul Polar*, Cezar Petrescu, 1932, Novel

UN SURIS IN PLINA VARA 1963 d: Geo Saizescu. RMN., *Padurea*, Dumitru Radu Popescu, 1962, Short Story

Una Su 13 *see* **UNA SU TREDICI** (1969).

UNA SU TREDICI 1969 d: Nicolas Gessner, Luciano Lucignani. ITL/FRN., *Dvenadtsat Stulyev*, Ilya Ilf, Evgeny Petrov, Moscow 1928, Novel

UNAFRAID, THE 1915 d: Cecil B. de Mille. USA., *The Unafraid*, Eleanor M. Ingram, Philadelphia 1913, Novel

Unafraid, The *see* **KISS THE BLOOD OFF MY HANDS** (1948).

UNAGI 1997 d: Shohei ImamurA. JPN., *Yami Ni Hirameku*, Akira Yoshimura, Story

UNBEARABLE LIGHTNESS OF BEING, THE 1987 d: Philip Kaufman. USA., *Wesnesitelna Lehkost Byti*, Milan Kundera, 1985, Novel

Unbecoming Habits *see* **BOGNOR: UNBECOMING HABITS** (1981).

Unbekannter Rechnet Ab, Ein *see* **AND THEN THERE WERE NONE** (1974).

UNBELIEVER, THE 1918 d: Alan Crosland. USA., *The Three Things*, Mary Raymond Shipman Andrews, Boston 1915, Novel

Unbezahmbare Angelique *see* **INDOMPTABLE ANGELIQUE** (1967).

UNBROKEN PROMISE, THE 1919 d: Frank Powell. USA., *Sundown Slim*, Henry Herbert Knibbs, Boston 1915, Novel

UNBROKEN ROAD, THE 1915. USA., *The Unbroken Road*, Thomas W. Dickinson, Providence, R.I. 1909, Play

UNCAS, EL FIN DE UNA RAZA 1964 d: Mateo Cano. SPN/ITL/GRM., *The Last of the Mohicans*, James Fenimore Cooper, Boston 1826, Novel

UNCENSORED 1942 d: Anthony Asquith. UKN., *Uncensored*, Oscar Millard, Novel

UNCERTAIN LADY 1934 d: Karl Freund. USA., *The Behavior of Mrs. Crane*, Harry Segall, New York 1928, Play

UNCHAINED 1955 d: Hall Bartlett. USA., *Prisoners are People*, Kenyon J. Scudder, 1952, Book

Unchained *see* **000 CHAINS, THE MAN WHO BROKE 1** (1987).

UNCHANGING SEA, THE 1910 d: D. W. Griffith. USA., *The Three Fishers*, Charles Kingsley, Poem

Uncharted Sea, The *see* **UNCHARTED SEAS** (1921).

UNCHARTED SEAS 1921 d: Wesley Ruggles. USA., *The Uncharted Sea*, John Fleming Wilson, 1920, Short Story

UNCHASTENED WOMAN, THE 1918 d: William Humphrey. USA., *The Unchastened Woman*, Louis K. Anspacher, New York 1915, Play

UNCHASTENED WOMAN, THE 1925 d: James Young. USA., *The Unchastened Woman*, Louis K. Anspacher, New York 1915, Play

UNCLAIMED GOODS 1918 d: Rollin S. Sturgeon. USA., *Unclaimed Goods*, Johnston McCulley, 1917, Short Story

UNCLE DICK'S DARLING 1920 d: Fred Paul. UKN., *Uncle Dick's Darling*, H. J. Byron, London 1869, Play

Uncle Filser *see* **ONKEL FILSER - ALLERNEUESTE LAUSBUBENGESCHICHTEN** (1966).

Uncle Harry *see* **THE STRANGE AFFAIR OF UNCLE HARRY** (1945).

UNCLE MOSES 1932 d: Sidney M. Goldin, Aubrey Scotto. USA., *Uncle Moses*, Sholom Asch, New York 1918, Novel

UNCLE MUN AND THE MINISTER 1912. USA., *Uncle Mun and the Minister*, Fred Nankivel, Story

UNCLE SAM OF FREEDOM RIDGE 1920 d: George A. Beranger. USA., *Uncle Sam of Freedom Ridge*, Margaret Prescott Montague, New York 1920, Novel

Uncle Sam of the Freedom Ridge *see* **UNCLE SAM OF FREEDOM RIDGE** (1920).

UNCLE SILAS 1947 d: Charles H. Frank. UKN., *Uncle Silas*, Sheridan le Fanu, 1864, Novel

UNCLE, THE 1964 d: Desmond Davis. UKN., *The Uncle*, Margaret Abrams, Boston 1962, Novel

UNCLE TOM'S CABIN 1903 d: Edwin S. Porter. USA., *Uncle Tom's Cabin*, Harriet Beecher Stowe, Boston 1852, Novel

UNCLE TOM'S CABIN 1903. USA., *Uncle Tom's Cabin*, Harriet Beecher Stowe, Boston 1852, Novel

UNCLE TOM'S CABIN 1910. USA., *Uncle Tom's Cabin*, Harriet Beecher Stowe, Boston 1852, Novel

UNCLE TOM'S CABIN 1910 d: J. Stuart Blackton. USA., *Uncle Tom's Cabin*, Harriet Beecher Stowe, Boston 1852, Novel

UNCLE TOM'S CABIN 1913 d: Otis Turner. USA., *Uncle Tom's Cabin*, Harriet Beecher Stowe, Boston 1852, Novel

UNCLE TOM'S CABIN 1913. USA., *Uncle Tom's Cabin*, Harriet Beecher Stowe, Boston 1852, Novel

UNCLE TOM'S CABIN 1913 d: Sidney Olcott. USA., *Uncle Tom's Cabin*, Harriet Beecher Stowe, Boston 1852, Novel

UNCLE TOM'S CABIN 1914 d: William Robert Daly. USA., *Uncle Tom's Cabin*, Harriet Beecher Stowe, Boston 1852, Novel

UNCLE TOM'S CABIN 1918 d: J. Searle Dawley. USA., *Uncle Tom's Cabin*, Harriet Beecher Stowe, Boston 1852, Novel

UNCLE TOM'S CABIN 1927 d: Harry Pollard. USA., *Uncle Tom's Cabin*, Harriet Beecher Stowe, Boston 1852, Novel

Uncle Tom's Cabin *see* **ONKEL TOMS HUTTE** (1965).

UNCLE TOM'S CABIN 1987 d: Stan Lathan. USA., *Uncle Tom's Cabin*, Harriet Beecher Stowe, Boston 1852, Novel

UNCLE VANYA 1958 d: John Goetz, Franchot Tone. USA., *Dyadya Vanya*, Anton Chekhov, 1899, Play

UNCLE VANYA 1963 d: Stuart Burge. UKN., *Dyadya Vanya*, Anton Chekhov, 1899, Play

Uncle Vanya *see* **DYADYA VANYA** (1971).

Uncle Willie's Bicycle Shop *see* **ISN'T LIFE WONDERFUL!** (1953).

Uncle's Dream, An *see* **DYADYUSHKIN SON** (1967).

UNCONQUERED 1947 d: Cecil B. de Mille. USA., *The Judas Tree*, Neil Harmon Swanson, Novel

Unconventional Linda *see* **HOLIDAY** (1938).

..UND DAS AM MONTAGMORGEN 1959 d: Luigi Comencini. GRM., *The Scandalous Affair of Mr. Kettle and Mrs. Moon*, J. B. Priestley, 1956, Play

UND DER HIMMEL LACHT DAZU 1954 d: Axel von Ambesser. AUS., *Bruder Martin*, Carl Costa, Play

..Und Der Himmel Steht Still *see* **THE INNOCENT** (1993).

UND DER REGEN VERWISCHT JEDE SPUR 1972 d: Alfred Vohrer. GRM/FRN., *Metel'*, Alexander Pushkin, 1831, Short Story

..UND DIE LIEBE LACHT DAZU 1957 d: R. A. Stemmle. GRM., *Und Die Liebe Lacht Dazu*, Werner von Der Schulenburg, Play

..UND DIE MUSIK SPIELT DAZU 1943 d: Carl Boese. GRM., *Saison in Salzburg*, Kurt Feltz, Fred Raymond, Max Wallner, Opera

..Und Die Nacht Kennt Kein Erbarmen *see* **LISTEN TO MY STORY** (1974).

..UND EWIG BLEIBT DIE LIEBE 1954 d: Wolfgang Liebeneiner. GRM., *Johannisfeuer*, Hermann Sudermann, 1900, Play

..UND EWIG KNALLEN DIE RAUBER 1962 d: Franz Antel. AUS., *Und Ewig Knallen Die Rauber*, J. F. Perkonig, Novel

..Und Ewig Ruft Die Heimat *see* **ULI DER PACHTER** (1955).

UND EWIG SINGEN DIE WALDER 1959 d: Paul May. AUS., *Trygve Gulbrannssen*, Novel

UND FINDEN DEREINST WIR UNS WIEDER 1947 d: Hans Muller. GRM., *Und Finden Dereinst Wir Uns Wieder*, Hertha von Gebhardt, Novel

UND JIMMY GING ZUM REGENBOGEN 1971 d: Alfred Vohrer. GRM/AUS., *Und Jimmy Ging Zum Regenbogen*, Johannes Mario Simmel, Novel

..UND KEINER SCHAMTE SICH 1960 d: Hans Schott-Schobinger. GRM., *Und Keiner Schamte Sich*, Rudi Mahr, Joe Tauppe, Novel

..UND NICHTS ALS DIE WAHRHEIT 1958 d: Franz Peter Wirth. GRM., *Der Fall Deruga*, Ricarda Huch, 1917, Novel

UNDER 18 1931 d: Archie Mayo. USA., *Sky Life*, Frank Dazey, Agnes Christine Johnston, 1929, Short Story

UNDER A SHADOW 1915 d: Joseph de Grasse. USA., *A Secret Service Affair*, F. McGrew Willis, Story

Under a Spell *see* **UN EMBRUJO** (1998).

UNDER A TEXAS MOON 1930 d: Michael Curtiz. USA., *Two-Gun Man*, Edward Stuart White, 1925, Short Story

UNDER CAPRICORN 1949 d: Alfred Hitchcock. USA/UKN., *Under Capricorn*, Helen Simpson, 1937, Novel

UNDER COVER 1916 d: Robert G. VignolA. USA., *Under Cover*, Roi Cooper Megrue, New York 1914, Play

Under Eighteen *see* **UNDER 18** (1931).

UNDER FIRE 1926 d: Clifford S. Elfelt. USA., *Under Fire*, Gen. Charles King, Philadelphia 1895, Novel

UNDER HANDICAP 1917 d: Fred J. Balshofer. USA., *Under Handicap*, Jackson Gregory, New York 1914, Novel

UNDER MILK WOOD 1972 d: Andrew Sinclair. UKN., *Under Milk Wood*, Dylan Thomas, 1954, Play

UNDER MILK WOOD 1992. UKN., *Under Milk Wood*, Dylan Thomas, 1954, Play

UNDER MY SKIN 1950 d: Jean Negulesco. USA., *My Old Man*, Ernest Hemingway, 1923, Short Story

Under One Roof *see* **POD JEDNOU STRECHOU** (1938).

UNDER PRESSURE 1935 d: Raoul Walsh. USA., *East River*, Borden Chase, Edward Doherty, New York 1935, Novel

UNDER PROOF 1936 d: Roland Gillett. UKN., *Dudley Does It*, Tod Waller, Play

Under Satan's Sun *see* **SOUS LE SOLEIL DE SATAN** (1987).

Under Sealed Orders *see* **MIT VERSIEGELTER ORDER** (1938).

UNDER SOLEN 1998 d: Colin Nutley. SWD., *The Little Farm*, H. E. Bates, Short Story

UNDER SOUTHERN SKIES 1915 d: Lucius Henderson. USA., *Under Southern Skies*, Lottie Blair Lathrop, New York 1901, Play

Under Spiritualistic Coercion *see* **THE OTHER PERSON** (1921).

Under Suspicion *see* **THE GAME OF LIBERTY** (1916).

UNDER SUSPICION 1918 d: Will S. Davis. USA., *The Woolworth Diamonds*, Hugh C. Weir, Short Story

UNDER SUSPICION 1919 d: Walter West. UKN., *Under Suspicion*, Horace Hunter, Play

UNDER SUSPICION 1937 d: Lewis D. Collins. USA., *Murderers Welcome*, Philip Wylie, 1936, Short Story

Under Ten Flags *see* **SOTTO DIECI BANDIERE** (1960).

Under the Banner of Samurai *see* **FURIN KAZAN** (1969).

UNDER THE FIDDLER'S ELM 1915 d: Edgar Jones. USA., *Under the Fiddler's Elm*, Elliot Balestier, Story

Under the Flag *see* **BAJO BANDERA** (1997).

UNDER THE FROZEN FALLS 1948 d: Darrell Catling. UKN., *Under the Frozen Falls*, J. H. Martin-Cross, Novel

UNDER THE GASLIGHT 1914 d: Lawrence Marston. USA., *Under the Gaslight; Or Life and Love in These Times*, Augustin Daly, New York 1867, Play

UNDER THE GREENWOOD TREE 1918 d: Emile Chautard. USA., *Under the Greenwood Tree*, H. V. Esmond, London 1907, Play

UNDER THE GREENWOOD TREE 1929 d: Harry Lachman. UKN., *Under the Greenwood Tree*, Thomas Hardy, 1873, Novel

UNDER THE LASH 1921 d: Sam Wood. USA., *The Shulamite*, Claude Askew, Edward Knoblock, London 1906, Play

Under the Pear Tree *see* **UNTERM BIRNBAUM** (1974).

UNDER THE RED ROBE 1915 d: Wilfred Noy. UKN., *Under the Red Robe*, Stanley Weyman, 1894, Novel

UNDER THE RED ROBE 1923 d: Alan Crosland. USA., *Under the Red Robe*, Stanley Weyman, 1894, Novel

UNDER THE RED ROBE 1937 d: Victor Sjostrom. UKN/USA., *Under the Red Robe*, Stanley Weyman, 1894, Novel

Under the Sun *see* UNDER SOLEN (1998).

Under the Sun of Satan *see* SOUS LE SOLEIL DE SATAN (1987).

UNDER THE TONTO RIM 1928 d: Herman C. Raymaker. USA., *Under the Tonto Rim*, Zane Grey, New York 1926, Novel

UNDER THE TONTO RIM 1933 d: Henry Hathaway. USA., *Under the Tonto Rim*, Zane Grey, New York 1926, Novel

UNDER THE TONTO RIM 1947 d: Lew Landers. USA., *Under the Tonto Rim*, Zane Grey, New York 1926, Novel

UNDER THE VOLCANO 1984 d: John Huston. USA., *Under the Volcano*, Malcolm Lowry, Novel

Under the Yoke *see* POD IGOTO (1952).

UNDER THE YUM YUM TREE 1963 d: David Swift. USA., *Under the Yum Yum Tree*, Lawrence Roman, New York 1960, Play

UNDER TWO FLAGS 1912 d: Theodore Marston. USA., *Under Two Flags*, Ouida, London 1867, Novel

UNDER TWO FLAGS 1912 d: George Nicholls. USA., *Under Two Flags*, Ouida, London 1867, Novel

UNDER TWO FLAGS 1915 d: Travers Vale. USA., *Under Two Flags*, Ouida, London 1867, Novel

UNDER TWO FLAGS 1916 d: J. Gordon Edwards. USA., *Under Two Flags*, Ouida, London 1867, Novel

UNDER TWO FLAGS 1922 d: Tod Browning. USA., *Under Two Flags*, Ouida, London 1867, Novel

UNDER TWO FLAGS 1936 d: Frank Lloyd. USA., *Under Two Flags*, Ouida, London 1867, Novel

Under Western Skies *see* WOMAN HUNGRY (1931).

UNDER YOUR HAT 1940 d: Maurice Elvey. UKN., *Under Your Hat*, Jack Hulbert, Arthur MacRae, Archie Menzies, London 1938, Play

UNDERBARA LOGNEN, DEN 1955 d: Michael Road. SWD/USA., Honore de Balzac, Guy de Maupassant, Short Stories

Undercover Agent *see* COUNTERSPY (1953).

UNDERCOVER DOCTOR 1939 d: Louis King. USA., *Persons in Hiding*, J. Edgar Hoover, Boston 1938, Book

Undercover Girl *see* ASSIGNMENT REDHEAD (1956).

UNDER-COVER MAN 1932 d: James Flood. USA., *Under Cover Man*, John Wilstach, New York 1931, Novel

UNDERCOVER MAN, THE 1949 d: Joseph H. Lewis. USA., *Undercover Man: He Trapped Capone*, Frank, J. Wilson, Book

UNDERCOVER WITH THE KKK 1979 d: Barry Shear. USA., *My Undercover Years With the Ku Klux Klan*, Gary Thomas Rowe Jr.

UNDERCURRENT 1946 d: Vincente Minnelli. USA., *You Were There*, Thelma Strabel, Book

Underdog, The *see* DER UNTERTAN (1951).

UNDERGROUND MAN, THE 1974 d: Paul Wendkos. USA., *The Underground Man*, Ross MacDonald, Novel

UNDERPUP, THE 1939 d: Richard Wallace. USA., *The Underpup*, I. A. R. Wylie, 1938, Short Story

Under-Pup, The *see* THE UNDERPUP (1939).

UNDERSTANDING HEART, THE 1927 d: Jack Conway. USA., *The Understanding Heart*, Peter B. Kyne, New York 1926, Novel

UNDERSTUDY, THE 1917 d: William Bertram. USA., *The Understudy*, Leigh Gordon Giltner, Short Story

Undertaker, The *see* FUNEBRAK (1932).

UNDERTOW 1930 d: Harry Pollard. USA., *Ropes*, Wilbur Daniel Steele, 1921, Short Story

UNDERTOW 1949 d: William Castle. USA., *The Big Frame*, Arthur T. Horman, Story

UNDERWATER! 1955 d: John Sturges. USA., *The Big Rainbow*, Robert B. Bailey, Hugh King, Story

Underwater Warship *see* KAITEI GUNKAN (1963).

Underworld *see* LES BAS-FONDS (1936).

UNDERWORLD 1937 d: Oscar Micheaux. USA., *Chicago After Midnight*, Edna Mae Baker, Short Story

Underworld Informers *see* THE INFORMERS (1963).

UNDERWORLD STORY, THE 1950 d: Cy Endfield. USA., *The Big Story*, Craig Rice, Novel

UNDINE 1912 d: Theodore Marston. USA., *Undine*, Friedrich de La Motte Fouque, 1811, Short Story

UNDINE 1916 d: Henry Otto. USA., *Undine*, Friedrich de La Motte Fouque, 1811, Short Story

UNDINE 74 1974 d: Rolf Thiele. AUS/GRM., *Undine*, Friedrich de La Motte Fouque, 1811, Short Story

Undisclosed *see* A LETTER OF WARNING (1932).

Undiscovered Country *see* DAS WEITE LAND (1987).

Undying Bum, The *see* DER UNSTERBLICHE LUMP (1953).

UNDYING MONSTER, THE 1942 d: John Brahm. USA., *The Undying Monster*, Jessie Douglas Kerruish, Novel

Une Nuit de Noces *see* NUIT DE NOCES (1949).

UNEASY MONEY 1918 d: Lawrence C. Windom. USA., *Uneasy Money*, P. G. Wodehouse, New York 1916, Novel

UNEASY TERMS 1948 d: Vernon Sewell. UKN., *Uneasy Terms*, Peter Cheyney, Novel

UNEASY VIRTUE 1931 d: Norman Walker. UKN., *The Happy Husband*, Harrison Owen, London 1927, Play

Unendliche Geschichte, Die *see* THE NEVERENDING STORY (1984).

Unendliche Geschichte II -Auf Der Suche Nach Phantasien, Die *see* THE NEVERENDING STORY II (1990).

UNENDLICHE WEG, DER 1943 d: Hans Schweikart. GRM., *Ein Deutscher Ohne Deutschland*, Walter von Molo, Novel

UNENTSCHULDIGTE STUNDE, DIE 1957 d: Willi Forst. AUS., *Die Unentschuldigte Stunde*, Stefan Bekeffi, Adorian Stella, Play

Unexpected Bride *see* WHIPSAW (1935).

Unexpected Father *see* THE LITTLE ACCIDENT (1930).

Unexpected Meeting *see* OMBYTE AV TAG (1943).

UNEXPECTED PLACES 1918 d: E. Mason Hopper. USA., *Unexpected Places*, Frank R. Adams, Novel

Unexpected, The *see* PO ZAKONU (1926).

Unexpected, The *see* KUNKU (1937).

Unexpected, The *see* DUNIYA NA MANE (1937).

Unexpected, The *see* ANKAHEE (1984).

UNEXPECTED UNCLE 1941 d: Peter Godfrey. USA., *Unexpected Uncle*, Eric Hatch, Novel

UNFAITHFUL 1992 d: Steven Schachter. USA., *Unfaithful*, Robert Anderson, Book

UNFAITHFUL, THE 1947 d: Vincent Sherman. USA., *The Letter*, W. Somerset Maugham, 1925, Short Story

UNFINISHED DANCE, THE 1947 d: Henry Koster. USA., *La Mort du Cygne*, Paul Morand, Story

Unfinished Piece for Player-Piano *see* NEOKONTCHENNIA PIESSA DLIA MEKANITCHESKOVO PIANINA (1977).

Unfinished Sentence in 148 Minutes, The *see* 148 PERC A BEFEJEZETLEN MONDATBOL (1974).

Unfinished Sentence, The *see* 148 PERC A BEFEJEZETLEN MONDATBOL (1974).

Unfinished Work for Mechanical Piano *see* NEOKONTCHENNIA PIESSA DLIA MEKANITCHESKOVO PIANINA (1977).

Unforgettable Year of 1919, The *see* NEZABYVAYEMI 1919-J GOD (1951).

UNFORGIVEN, THE 1960 d: John Huston. USA., *The Unforgiven*, Alan le May, Novel

UNFORSEEN, THE 1917 d: John B. O'Brien. USA., *The Unforseen*, Robert Marshall, London 1902, Play

UNFORTUNATE BRIDE, THE 1932 d: Henry Lynn. USA., *Di Gebrokhene Hertser Oder Libe un Flikht*, Zalmen Libin, New York 1903, Play

UNFUG DER LIEBE 1928 d: Robert Wiene. GRM., *Unfug Der Liebe*, Alexander Castell, Novel

UNG FLUKT 1959 d: Edith Kalmar. NRW., *Ettersokte Er Atten Ar*, Nils Johan Rud, 1958, Novel

UNG LEG 1956 d: Johannes Allen. DNM., *Ung Leg*, Johannes Allen, Novel

UNG SOMMAR 1954 d: Kenne Fant. SWD., *Ung Sommar*, Peter Ekstrom, Novel

UNGEN 1938 d: Rasmus Breistein. NRW., *Ungen*, Oskar Braaten, 1911, Play

UNGEN 1974 d: Barthold Halle. NRW., *Bak Hokerens Disk*, Oskar Braaten, 1918, Novel, *Ungen*, Oskar Braaten, 1911, Play

UNGETREUE ECKEHART, DER 1940 d: Hubert MarischkA. GRM., *Der Ungetreue Eckehart*, Hans Sturm, Play

Unglaubliche Und Traurige Geschichte von Der Unschulden Erendira Und Ihrer Herzlosen Grossmutter *see* ERENDIRA (1982).

UNGUARDED HOUR, THE 1936 d: Sam Wood. USA., *The Unguarded Hour*, Ladislaus Fodor, London 1935, Play

UNGUARDED MOMENT, THE 1956 d: Harry Keller. USA., *The Gentle Web*, Lawrence B. Marcus, Rosalind Russell, Story

UNGUARDED WOMEN 1924 d: Alan Crosland. USA., *Face*, Lucy Stone Terrill, 1924, Short Story

Unhappy Bride, The *see* VAIVAISUKON MORSIAN (1944).

UNHEIMLICH STARKER ABGANG, EIN 1973 d: Michael Verhoeven. GRM., *Ein Unheimlich Starker Abgang*, Harald Sommer, Play

Unheimliche, Der *see* DER GROSSE UNBEKANNTE (1927).

Unheimliche, Der *see* DIE TAT DES ANDERN (1951).

UNHEIMLICHE GESCHICHTEN 1932 d: Richard Oswald. GRM., *The Black Cat*, Edgar Allan Poe, Short Story, *The Suicide Club*, Robert Louis Stevenson, London 1882, Short Stories

UNHEIMLICHE MONCH, DER 1965 d: Harald Reinl. GRM., Edgar Wallace, Novel

UNHEIMLICHE WANDLUNG DES ALEX ROSCHER, DIE 1943 d: Paul May. GRM., *Die Unheimliche Wandlung Des Alex Roscher*, Curt Corinth, Novel

Unheimliche Zimmer, Das *see* DER HUND VON BASKERVILLE 3 (1915).

Unheimlichen Hande Des Dr. Orlak, Die *see* ORLACS HANDE (1925).

UNHEIMLICHEN WUNSCHE, DIE 1939 d: Heinz Hilpert. GRM., *La Peau de Chagrin*, Honore de Balzac, Paris 1831, Novel

UNHOLD, DER 1996 d: Volker Schlondorff. GRM/FRN/UKN., *The Erl King*, Michel Tournier, Novel

Unholy Four, The *see* THE STRANGER CAME HOME (1954).

Unholy Love *see* ALRAUNE (1928).

UNHOLY LOVE 1932 d: Albert Ray. USA., *Madame Bovary*, Gustave Flaubert, Paris 1857, Novel

UNHOLY THREE, THE 1925 d: Tod Browning. USA., *The Unholy Three*, Clarence Aaron Robbins, New York 1917, Novel

UNHOLY THREE, THE 1930 d: Jack Conway. USA., *The Unholy Three*, Clarence Aaron Robbins, New York 1917, Novel

Unholy Wish, The *see* DIE UNHEIMLICHEN WUNSCHE (1939).

Unico Indizio Una Sciarpa Gialla *see* LA MAISON SOUS LES ARBRES (1971).

Unicorn, The *see* ENHORNINGEN (1955).

Unicorn, The *see* DAS EINHORN (1978).

Unidentified Flying Oddball *see* THE SPACEMAN AND KING ARTHUR (1979).

Unidos Por El Destino *see* LE DUE ORFANELLE (1978).

Uniform Lovers *see* YALE HOLD 'EM (1935).

Unimportant Event, An *see* O MICA INTIMPLARE (1957).

Uninhibited, The *see* LOS PIANOS MECANICOS (1965).

Uninvited Love *see* NEPROSHENAYA LYUBOV (1964).

UNINVITED, THE 1944 d: Lewis Allen. USA., *Uneasy Freehold*, Dorothy MacArdle, Novel

Union *see* MILAN (1946).

UNION CITY 1980 d: Mark Reichert. USA., *The Corpse Next Door*, Cornell Woolrich, Short Story

UNION DEPOT 1932 d: Alfred E. Green. USA., *Union Depot*, D. Durkin, Gene Fowler, Joe Laurie Jr, 1929, Play

UNION PACIFIC 1939 d: Cecil B. de Mille. USA., *Trouble Shooter*, Ernest Haycox, Garden City, N.Y. 1937, Novel

UNION STATION 1950 d: Rudolph Mate. USA., *Nightmare in Manhattan*, Thomas Walsh, Novel

Union Street *see* STANLEY AND IRIS (1989).

UNITY 1981 d: James Cellan Jones. UKN., *Unity Mitford: a Quest*, David Pryce-Jones, Book

University of Life *see* MOI UNIVERSITETI (1940).

UNIZHENNIEI OSKORBLENNIE 1996 d: Andrei A. Eshpay. RSS/ITL., *Unizhenniei Oskorblennie*, Fyodor Dostoyevsky, Novel

Unkindness of Ravens, An *see* INSPECTOR WEXFORD: AN UNKINDNESS OF RAVENS (1991).

Unknown Battle, The *see* THE HEROES OF TELEMARK (1965).

UNKNOWN BLONDE 1934 d: Hobart Henley. USA., *Collusion*, Theodore D. Irwin, New York 1932, Novel

UNKNOWN CAVALIER, THE 1926 d: Albert S. Rogell. USA., *Ride Him Cowboy*, Kenneth Perkins, New York 1923, Novel

Unknown Dancer, The *see* THE LOVE CHEAT (1919).

Unknown Man *see* UKJENT MANN (1951).

Unknown Man's Story, The *see* RASSKAZ NEIZVESTNOGO CELOVEKA (1980).

UNKNOWN PURPLE, THE 1923 d: Roland West. USA., *The Unknown Purple*, Carlyle Moore, Roland West, New York 1918, Play

UNKNOWN QUANTITY, THE 1919 d: Thomas R. Mills. USA., *The Unknown Quantity*, O. Henry, 1910, Short Story

Unknown Satellite Over Tokyo *see* UCHUJIN TOKYO NI ARAWARU (1956).

Unknown Soldier, The *see* TUNTEMATON SOTILAS (1955).

Unknown Soldier, The *see* TUNTEMATON SOTILAS (1985).

UNKNOWN, THE 1915 d: George Melford. USA., *The Red Mirage*, I. A. R. Wylie, London 1913, Novel

Unknown, The *see* O DESCONHECIDO (1980).

UNKNOWN TREASURES 1926 d: Archie Mayo. USA., *The House Behind the Hedge*, Mary Spain Vigus, Story

Unlawful *see* KING OF THE UNDERWORLD (1939).

Unlucky Woman, The *see* LA SIN VENTURA (1923).

UNMAN, WITTERING AND ZIGO 1971 d: John MacKenzie. UKN., *Wittering and Zigo Unman*, Giles Cooper, Television Play

Unmechanical, The *see* AJANTRIK (1958).

UNMOGLICHE HERR PITT, DER 1938 d: Harry Piel. GRM., *Der Unmogliche Herr Pitt*, Georg Muhlen-Schulte, Novel

Unmoralische Novizzinnen *see* INTERNO DI UN CONVENTO (1977).

UNNAMEABLE 2, THE 1992 d: Jean-Paul Ouellette. USA., *The Unnameable*, H. P. Lovecraft, Short Story

UNNAMEABLE II, THE 1992 d: Jean-Paul Ouellette. USA., *The Statement of Randolph Carter*, H. P. Lovecraft, Short Story

Unnameable Returns, The *see* THE UNNAMEABLE II (1992).

Unnameable Returns, The *see* THE UNNAMEABLE 2 (1992).

UNNAMEABLE, THE 1988 d: Jean-Paul Ouellette. USA., *The Statement of Randolph Carter*, H. P. Lovecraft, Short Story, *The Unnameable*, H. P. Lovecraft, Short Story

Unnatural *see* ALRAUNE (1952).

UNORDNUNG UND FRUHES LEID 1975 d: Franz Seitz. GRM., *Unordnung Und Fruhes Leid*, Thomas Mann, 1925, Short Story

UNPAID RANSOM, AN 1915. USA., *The Under Secretary*, Scott Campbell, Story

UNPARDONABLE SIN, THE 1919 d: Marshall Neilan. USA., *The Unpardonable Sin*, Rupert Hughes, New York 1918, Novel

Unpeaceful Night *see* UNRUHIGE NACHT (1958).

Unreconciled *see* WO GEWALT HERRSCHT" NICHT VERSOHNT ODER "ES HILFT NUR GEWALT (1965).

UNREST 1920 d: Dallas Cairns. UKN., *Unrest*, Warwick Deeping, Novel

UNRUHIGE NACHT 1958 d: Falk Harnack. GRM., *Unruhige Nacht*, Albrecht Goes, Hamburg 1950, Novel

UNRUHIGE TOCHTER 1967 d: Hansjorg Amon. SWT/GRM., *Unruhige Tochter*, Ilse Collignon, Novel

Unruly Generation, The *see* KURITON SUKUPOLVI (1957).

Unschuldigen Mit Den Schmutzigen Handen, Die *see* LES INNOCENTS AUX MAINS SALES (1975).

UNSEEING EYES 1923 d: Edward H. Griffith. USA., *Snowblind*, Arthur Stringer, 1921, Short Story

UNSEEN ENEMY, AN 1912 d: D. W. Griffith. USA., *An Unseen Enemy*, Edward Acker, Play

UNSEEN FORCES 1920 d: Sidney A. Franklin. USA., *Athalie*, Robert W. Chambers, New York 1915, Novel

Unseen Heroes *see* BATTLE OF THE V 1 (1958).

UNSEEN, THE 1945 d: Lewis Allen. USA., *Her Heart in Her Throat*, Ethel Lina White, Novel

Unseen, The *see* HOUSE OF MYSTERY (1961).

Unspoken, The *see* ANKAHEE (1984).

UNSER KURZES LEBEN 1980 d: Lothar Warneke. GDR., *Unser Kurzes Leben*, Brigitte Reimann, Novel

UNSICHTBAREN KRALLEN DES DR. MABUSE, DIE 1962 d: Harald Reinl. GRM., *Dr. Mabuse*, Norbert Jacques, Novel

UNSINKABLE MOLLY BROWN, THE 1964 d: Charles Walters. USA., *The Unsinkable Molly Brown*, Richard Morris, Meredith Willson, New York 1960, Musical Play

Unspoken, The *see* ANKAHEE (1984).

UNSTERBLICHE GELIEBTE 1951 d: Veit Harlan. GRM., *Aquis Submersus*, Theodor Storm, 1877, Novel

UNSTERBLICHE HERZ, DAS 1939 d: Veit Harlan. GRM., *Das Nurnbergisch Ei*, Walter Harlan, Play

Unsterbliche Liebe *see* WAS DIE SCHWALBE SANG (1956).

UNSTERBLICHE LUMP, DER 1953 d: Arthur M. Rabenalt. GRM., *Der Unsterbliche Lump*, Felix Dormann, Edmund Eysler, Novel

UNSTOPPABLE MAN, THE 1960 d: Terry Bishop. UKN., *Amateur in Violence*, Michael Gilbert, Novel

UNSTRAP ME 1968 d: George Kuchar. USA., *The Trip to Chicago*, Walter Gutman

UNSTRUNG HEROES 1995 d: Diane Keaton. USA., *Unstrung Heroes*, Franz Lidz, Book

UNSUITABLE JOB FOR A WOMAN, AN 1981 d: Christopher Petit. UKN., *A Unsuitable Job for a Woman*, P. D. James, Novel

UNSUSPECTED, THE 1947 d: Michael Curtiz. USA., *The Unsuspected*, Charlotte Armstrong, Novel

Untameable Angelique *see* INDOMPTABLE ANGELIQUE (1967).

UNTAMEABLE, THE 1923 d: Herbert Blache. USA., *The White Cat*, Gelett Burgess, New York 1907, Novel

UNTAMED 1929 d: Jack Conway. USA., Charles E. Scoggins, Story

UNTAMED 1940 d: George Archainbaud. USA., *Mantrap*, Sinclair Lewis, New York 1926, Novel

UNTAMED 1955 d: Henry King. USA., *Untamed*, Helga Moray, 1950, Novel

Untamed *see* ARAKURE (1957).

UNTAMED FURY 1947 d: Ewing Scott. USA., *Gator Bait*, Ewing Scott, Story

UNTAMED LADY, THE 1926 d: Frank Tuttle. USA., *The Untamed Lady*, Fannie Hurst, Story

UNTAMED LOVE 1994 d: Paul Aaron. USA., *One Child*, Torey Hayden, Book

UNTAMED, THE 1920 d: Emmett J. Flynn. USA., *The Untamed*, Max Brand, New York 1919, Novel

Untamed West *see* THE FAR HORIZONS (1955).

Untamed Woman *see* ARAKURE (1957).

UNTAMED YOUTH 1924 d: Emile Chautard. USA., *Born of the Cyclone*, G. Marion Burton, Play

UNTER DEN TAUSAND LATERNEN 1952 d: Erich Engel. GRM., *Das Lies 1st Aus*, Robert Gilbert, Novel

UNTER FALSCHER FLAGGE 1932 d: Johannes Meyer. GRM., *Unter Falsche Flagge*, Max W. Kimmich, Novel

UNTER GEIERN 1964 d: Alfred Vohrer. GRM/ITL/YGS., *Unter Geiern*, Karl Friedrich May, Radebeul-Ober. 1914, Novel

Unter Geschaftsaufsicht *see* WENN ER LOSGELASSEN WEHE (1931).

UNTERM BIRNBAUM 1974 d: Ralf Kirsten. GDR., Theodor Fontane, Story

UNTERNEHMEN EDELWEISS 1954 d: Heinz Paul. GRM., *Der Glaserne Berg*, Hans Gustl Kernmayr, Novel

UNTERNEHMEN SCHLAFSACK 1955 d: Arthur M. Rabenalt. GRM., *Unternehmen Schlafsack*, Hans Nogly, Novel

UNTERTAN, DER 1951 d: Wolfgang Staudte. GDR., *Der Untertan*, Heinrich Mann, 1914-18, Novel

Until Marriage Separates Us *see* ATE QUE O CASAMENTO NOS SEPARE (1968).

Until the Bitter End *see* BIS ZUR BITTEREN NEIGE (1975).

Until the Day We Meet Again *see* MATA AU HI MADE (1950).

Until the End of All Time *see* BIS ZUM ENDE ALLER TAGE (1961).

UNTIL THEY SAIL 1957 d: Robert Wise. USA., *Until They Sail*, James A. Michener, 1951, Short Story

Until We Meet Again *see* MATA AU HI MADE (1950).

Until You Have Mamma *see* DOKUD MAS MAMINKU (1934).

Unto a Good Land *see* INVANDRARNA (1970).

Unto a New Land *see* INVANDRARNA (1970).

Untouchables, The *see* GLI INTOCCABILI (1969).

Untouchables: the Scarface Mob *see* THE SCARFACE MOB (1962).

Untrodden Road, The *see* AMADA BATA (1964).

Unvanquished, The *see* APARAJITO (1956).

Unwanted *see* THE DECEIVER (1931).

Unwanted Woman, An *see* INSPECTOR WEXFORD: AN UNWANTED WOMAN (1992).

Unwelcome Lady, An *see* HONG CHEN (1994).

UNWELCOME MRS. HATCH, THE 1914 d: Allan Dwan. USA., *The Unwelcome Mrs. Hatch*, Mrs. Burton Harrison, New York 1901, Play

Unwilling Agent *see* MENSCHEN IM NETZ (1959).

UNWILLING HERO, AN 1921 d: Clarence Badger. USA., *Whistling Dick's Christmas Stocking*, O. Henry, 1909, Short Story

Unwilling Love *see* NEPROSHENAYA LYUBOV (1964).

Unwilling Society *see* DUNIYA NA MANE (1937).

UNWRITTEN LAW, THE 1916 d: George E. Middleton. USA., *The Unwritten Law*, Edwin Milton Royle, New York 1913, Play

UNWRITTEN LAW, THE 1929 d: Sinclair Hill. UKN., *The Unwritten Law*, Violet Heckstall Smith, Play

UNWRITTEN PLAY, THE 1914 d: Theodore Marston. USA., *The Unwritten Play*, J. Harwood Panting, Story

UOMINI CONTRO 1970 d: Francesco Rosi. ITL/YGS., *Un Anno Sull'altopiano*, Emilio Lussu, Novel

UOMINI DAL PASSO PESANTE, GLI 1966 d: Alfredo Antonini, Mario Sequi. ITL., *Guns of North Texas*, Will Cook, New York 1958, Novel

UOMINI E NO 1979 d: Valentino Orsini. ITL., *Uomini E No*, Elio Vittorini, 1945, Novel

UOMINI E NOBILUOMINI 1959 d: Giorgio Bianchi. ITL., *L' Eredita Della Zio Nicola*, Emo Bistolfi, Play

UOMINI NON SONO INGRATI, GLI 1937 d: Guido Brignone. ITL., *Gli Uomini Non Sono Igrati*, Alessandro de Stefani, Play

UOMINI SENZA DONNE 1996 d: Angelo Longoni. ITL., *Uomini Senza Donne*, Angelo Longoni, Play

Uomo Che Non Seppe Tacere, L' *see* LE SILENCIEUX (1972).

UOMO CHE RIDE, L' 1966 d: Sergio Corbucci. ITL/FRN., *L' Homme Qui Rit*, Victor Hugo, 1869, Novel

UOMO CHE SORRIDE, L' 1936 d: Mario Mattoli. ITL., *L' Uomo Che Sorride*, Luigi Bonelli, Aldo de Benedetto, Play

Uomo Che Valeva Miliardi, L' *see* L' HOMME QUI VALAIT DES MILLIARDS (1967).

Uomo Dal Mantello Rosso, L' *see* MON ONCLE BENJAMIN (1969).

Uomo Dalla Maschera Di Ferro, L' *see* LE MASQUE DE FER (1962).

UOMO DALL'ARTIGLIO, L' 1931 d: Nunzio MalasommA. ITL., *L' Uomo Dall'Artiglio*, Egon Eis, Otto Eis, Rudolf Katscher, Novel

Uomo Dalle Due Ombre, L' *see* COLD SWEAT (1971).

Uomo Dall'Impermeabile, L' *see* L' HOMME A L'IMPERMEABLE (1957).

UOMO DALL'ORECCHIO MOZZATO, L' 1916 d: Ubaldo Maria Del Colle. ITL., *L' Homme a l'Oreille Cassee*, Edmond About, 1862, Short Story

UOMO DEL ROMANZO, L' 1941 d: Mario Bonnard. ITL., *L' Uomo Del Romanzo*, Guido Cantini, Play

Uomo Della C.I.a., The *see* GOODBYE & AMEN (1978).

UOMO DELLA GUERRA POSSIBILE, L' 1979 d: Romeo Costantini. ITL., *Il Diario Di un Provacatore*, Dario Paccino, Novel

Uomo Della Mancha, L' *see* MAN OF LA MANCHA (1972).

Uomo Di Casablanca, L' *see* L' HOMME DE MARRAKECH (1966).

999

Uomo Di Hong Kong, L' see **LES TRIBULATIONS D'UN CHINOIS EN CHINE** (1965).

UOMO DIFFICILE, L' 1978 d: Giancarlo Cobelli. ITL., *L' Uomo Difficile*, Hugo von Hofmannsthal, Play

Uomo E Il Diavolo, L' see **LE ROUGE ET LE NOIR** (1954).

UOMO FATALE, L' 1912 d: Mario Caserini. ITL., *L' Uomo Fatale*, Jean Willaume

Uomo, la Bestia E la Vertu, L' see **LA BESTIA, LA VIRTU, L' UOMO** (1953).

UOMO, LA BESTIA, LA VIRTU, L' 1953 d: Steno. ITL., *L' Uomo la Bestia la Virtu*, Luigi Pirandello, Play

UOMO, L'ORGOGLIO, LA VENDETTA, L' 1967 d: Luigi Bazzoni. ITL/GRM., *Carmen*, Prosper Merimee, Paris 1846, Novel

Uomo, Un see **IL GIORNO DEL FURORE** (1973).

UOMO UNA CITTA, UN 1974 d: Romolo Guerrieri. ITL., *Il Commissario Di Torino*, Marcato, Novelli, Novel

Uomo Venuto Da Chicago, L' see **UN CONDE** (1970).

Up and Up, The see **RECKLESS LIVING** (1931).

UP FROM THE BEACH 1965 d: Robert Parrish. USA., *Epitaph for an Enemy*, George Barr, New York 1959, Novel

UP FROM THE DEPTHS 1915 d: Paul Powell. USA., *Up from the Depths*, Charles B. Loomis, Robert Stodard, Play

UP FRONT 1951 d: Alexander Hall. USA., *Willie and Joe*, Bill Mauldin, 1945, Book

UP IN ARMS 1944 d: Elliott Nugent. USA., *The Nervous Wreck*, Owen Davis, New York 1926, Play

UP IN CENTRAL PARK 1948 d: William A. Seiter. USA., *Up in Central Park*, Dorothy Fields, Herbert Fields, Sigmund Romberg, New York 1945, Musical Play

UP IN MABEL'S ROOM 1926 d: E. Mason Hopper. USA., *Up in Mabel's Room*, Wilson Collison, Otto Harbach, New York 1919, Play

UP IN MABEL'S ROOM 1944 d: Allan Dwan. USA., *Up in Mabel's Room*, Wilson Collison, Otto Harbach, New York 1919, Play

UP IN THE CELLAR 1970 d: Theodore J. Flicker. USA., *The Late Boy Wonder*, Angus Hall, London 1969, Novel

UP 'N' UNDER 1998 d: John Godber. UKN., *Up 'N' Under*, John Godber, 1984, Play

UP PERISCOPE 1959 d: Gordon Douglas. USA., Robb White, Story

UP POPS THE DEVIL 1931 d: A. Edward Sutherland. USA., *Up Pops the Devil*, Frances Goodrich, Albert Hackett, New York 1930, Play

UP THE DOWN STAIRCASE 1967 d: Robert Mulligan. USA., *Up the Down Staircase*, Bel Kaufman, Englewood Cliffs 1965, Novel

UP THE JUNCTION 1965 d: Kenneth Loach. UKN., *Up the Junction*, Nell Dunn, London 1963, Novel

UP THE JUNCTION 1967 d: Peter Collinson. UKN., *Up the Junction*, Nell Dunn, London 1963, Novel

UP THE LADDER 1925 d: Edward Sloman. USA., *Up the Ladder*, Owen Davis, New York 1922, Play

UP THE ROAD WITH SALLIE 1918 d: William D. Taylor. USA., *Up the Road With Sallie*, Frances Roberta Sterrett, New York 1915, Novel

Up the Road With Sally see **UP THE ROAD WITH SALLIE** (1918).

UP THE SANDBOX 1972 d: Irvin Kershner. USA., *Up the Sandbox*, Anne Richardson Roipke, Novel

Up to His Ears see **LES TRIBULATIONS D'UN CHINOIS EN CHINE** (1965).

U.P. TRAIL, THE 1920 d: Jack Conway. USA., *The U.P. Trail*, Zane Grey, New York 1918, Novel

UPHEAVAL, THE 1916 d: Charles Horan. USA., *The Upheaval*, Lawrence McCloskey, Short Story

UPIR Z FERATU 1982 d: Juraj Herz. CZC., *Upir Z Feratu*, Josef Nesvadba, Short Story

UPLIFTERS, THE 1919 d: Herbert Blache. USA., *Free*, Wallace Irwin, 1918, Short Story

UPPDRAGET 1977 d: Mats Arehn. SWD., *Uppdraget*, Per Wahloo, Novel

UPPER CRUST, THE 1917 d: Rollin S. Sturgeon. USA., *The Upper Crust*, Charles Sherman, Indianapolis 1913, Novel

Upper Hand, The see **DU RIFIFI A PANAMA** (1966).

Uprising, The see **RASCOALA** (1965).

Uproar in the Baolin Temple see **HUANGJIANG NUXIA (PART 1)** (1930).

UPSIDE DOWN 1919 d: Lawrence C. Windom. USA., *Lovely Reason*, George Agnew Chamberlain, 1916, Serial Story

Upside Down see **VZHURU NOHAMA** (1938).

UPSTAIRS 1919 d: Victor Schertzinger. USA., *Upstairs*, Perley Poore Sheehan, Short Story

UPSTAIRS AND DOWN 1919 d: Charles Giblyn. USA., *Upstairs and Down*, Fanny Hatton, Frederic Hatton, New York 1916, Play

Up-Stairs and Down see **UPSTAIRS AND DOWN** (1919).

UPSTAIRS AND DOWNSTAIRS 1959 d: Ralph Thomas. UKN., *Upstairs and Downstairs*, Ronald Scott Thorne, Novel

UPSTART, THE 1916 d: Edwin Carewe. USA., *The Upstart*, Tom Barry, New York 1910, Play

UPSTREAM 1927 d: John Ford. USA., *The Snake's Wife*, Wallace Smith, 1926, Short Story

Upstream see **THE GATEWAY OF THE MOON** (1928).

UPTIGHT 1968 d: Jules Dassin. USA., *The Informer*, Liam O'Flaherty, London 1925, Novel

UPTOWN NEW YORK 1932 d: Victor Schertzinger. USA., *Angie - Uptown Woman*, Vina Delmar, 1929, Short Story

Uptown Woman see **UPTOWN NEW YORK** (1932).

URAGANO AI TROPICI 1939 d: Gino Talamo, Pier Luigi Faraldo. ITL., *Uragano Ai Tropici*, Anton Giulio Majano, Novel

Uragano Sul Po see **LIEBE** (1956).

Uranium Conspiracy, The see **A CHI TOCCA..TOCCA!** (1978).

Uranium-Verschworung, Die see **A CHI TOCCA..TOCCA!** (1978).

URANUS 1990 d: Claude Berri. FRN., *Uranus*, Marcel Ayme, 1948, Novel

URGE TO KILL 1960 d: Vernon Sewell. UKN., *Hand in Glove*, Charles Freeman, Gerald Savory, 1944, Play

URI MURI 1949 d: Frigyes Ban. HNG., *Uri Muri*, Zsigmond Moricz, 1928, Play

URLAUB AUF EHRENWORT 1937 d: Karl Ritter. GRM., *Urlaub Auf Ehrenwort*, Kilian Koll, Novel

URLAUB AUF EHRENWORT 1955 d: Wolfgang Liebeneiner. GRM., *Urlaub Auf Ehrenwort*, Kilian Koll, Novel

URNEBESNA TRAGEDIJA 1995 d: Goran Markovic. BUL/FRN., *Urnebesna Tragedija*, Dusan Kovacevic, Play

URODA ZYCIA 1921 d: Eugeniusz Modzelewski, William Wauer. PLN., *Uroda Zycia*, Stefan Zeromski, 1912, Novel

URODA ZYCIA 1930 d: Juliusz Gardan. PLN., *Uroda Zycia*, Stefan Zeromski, 1912, Novel

UROK FRANZUSKOVO 1978 d: Yevgyeni Tashkov. USS., Valentin Rasputin, Story

Urs Ad-Dam see **ORS AL-DAM** (1977).

URSULA 1978 d: Egon Gunther. GDR/SWT., *Ursula*, Gottfried Keller, Novel

URSULE MIROUET 1912. FRN., *Ursule Mirouet*, Honore de Balzac, 1843, Novel

Us see **BENEFIT OF THE DOUBT** (1967).

USERS, THE 1978 d: Joseph Hardy. USA., *The Users*, Joyce Haber, Novel

USKI ROTI 1969 d: Mani Kaul. IND., *Uski Roti*, Mohan Rakesh, Short Story

U.S.S. Teakettle see **YOU'RE IN THE NAVY NOW** (1951).

USTED TIENE OJOS DE MUJER FATAL 1962 d: Jose Maria ElorrietA. SPN., *Usted Tiene Ojos de Mujer Fatal*, Enrique Jardiel Poncela, 1926, Play

USURAIO, L' 1943 d: Harry Hasso. ITL., *L' Usuraio*, Hans Possendorff, Play

USURPER, THE 1919 d: Duncan MacRae. UKN., *The Usurper*, William J. Locke, Novel

USURPER, THE 1919 d: James Young. USA., *The Usurper*, I. N. Morris, New York 1904, Play

UTA ANDON 1943 d: Mikio Naruse. JPN., *Uta Andon*, Kyoka Izumi, 1910, Novel

UTA ANDON 1960 d: Teinosuke KinugasA. JPN., *Uta Andon*, Kyoka Izumi, 1910, Novel

UTAH BLAINE 1957 d: Fred F. Sears. USA., *Utah Blaine*, Louis L'Amour, Novel

Utamaro and His Five Women see **UTAMARO O MEGURU GONIN NO ONNA** (1946).

UTAMARO O MEGURU GONIN NO ONNA 1946 d: Kenji Mizoguchi. JPN., Kanji Kunieda, Story

UTAZAS A KOPONYAM KORUL 1970 d: Gyorgy Revesz. HNG., *Utazas a Koponyam Korul*, Frigyes Karinthy, 1937, Novel

UTBOROPPRORET 1997 d: Svein Andersen. NRW., Bjorn Niteberg, Novel

UTE BLASER SOMMARVIND 1955 d: Ake Ohberg. SWD/NRW., *Ute Blaser Sommarvind*, Per Bang, Novel

Ute Blaser Sommervind see **UTE BLASER SOMMARVIND** (1955).

UTEK 1967 d: Stepan Skalsky. CZC., *Utek*, Ota Hofman, Novel

UTOLSO KEZIRAT, AZ 1986 d: Karoly Makk. HNG., *Vidam Temetes*, Tibor Dery, 1963, Short Story

UTOLYENIYE ZHAZHDY 1968 d: Bulat Mansurov. USS., *Utolyeniye Zhazhdy*, Yuri Valentinovich Trifonov, 1963, Novel

Utrpeni Mlade Lasky see **WERTHER** (1926).

UTSAV 1983 d: Girish Karnad. IND., *Mrichchakatikam*, Sudraka, c400-500, Play

UTSUKUSHISA TO KANASHIMI TO 1965 d: Masahiro ShinodA. JPN., *Utsukushisa to Kanshim' to*, Yasunari Kawabata, 1961-64, Novel

U-TURN 1997 d: Oliver Stone. USA., *Stray Dogs*, John Ridley, Book

UTVANDRARNA 1970 d: Jan Troell. SWD., *Invandrarna*, Vilhelm Moberg, 1952, Novel, *Utvandrarna*, Vilhelm Moberg, 1949, Novel

UTZ 1992 d: George Sluizer. UKN/GRM/ITL., *Utz*, Bruce Chatwin, Novel

UZ ZASE SKACU PRES KALUZE 1970 d: Karel KachynA. CZC., *I'm Jumping Over Puddles Again*, Alan Marshall, Autobiography

UZNIK ZAM IF 1988 d: Georgy Jangvald-Khilkevitch. USS/FRN., *Le Comte de Monte-Cristo*, Alexandre Dumas (pere), Paris 1845, Novel

Uznik Zamka if see **UZNIK ZAM IF** (1988).

V 1 see **BATTLE OF THE V 1** (1958).

V GORODE "S" 1966 d: Josif Heifitz. USS., *Ionych*, Anton Chekhov, 1898, Short Story

V Lasurevoi Stepi see **V LAZOREVOY STEPI** (1970).

V LAZOREVOY STEPI 1970 d: Vitali Koltzov, Oleg Bondarev. USS., *Chervotochina*, Mikhail Sholokhov, 1925, Short Story

V LAZOREVOY STEPI 1970 d: Valery Lonskoj, Vladimir Shamshurin. USS., *Kolevert*, Mikhail Sholokhov, 1925, Short Story

V LAZOREVOY STEPI 1970 d: Vitali Koltzov, Oleg Bondarev. USS., *Prodkomissar*, Mikhail Sholokhov, 1925, Short Story

V LAZOREVOY STEPI 1970 d: Valery Lonskoj, Vladimir Shamshurin. USS., *Rodinka*, Mikhail Sholokhov, 1924, Short Story

V Ljudjah see **V LYUDKYAKH** (1939).

V LYUDKYAKH 1939 d: Mark Donskoi. USS., *V Lyudyakh*, Maxim Gorky, 1915, Autobiography

V Navecherieto see **NAKANUNYE** (1959).

V PANSKEM STAVU 1927 d: Vaclav Kubasek. CZC., *V Panskem Stavu*, Popelka Bilianova, Novel

V POISKACH RADOSTI 1939 d: Grigori Roshal, Vera StroyevA. USS., *Bruski*, Fyodor Panfyorov, 1928-37, Novel

V Poiskakh Radosti see **V POISKACH RADOSTI** (1939).

V POKUSENI 1938 d: Miroslav Cikan. CZC., *Velke Pokuseni*, Marie Krizova, Novel

V STEPJAH UKRAINY 1952 d: Timofey Levchuk. USS., *V Stepyakh Ukrayiny*, Aleksander Korniychuk, 1941, Play

V Stepyakh Ukrayiny see **V STEPJAH UKRAINY** (1952).

V Ticha Vetscher see **V TIHATA VECHER** (1959).

V Tiha Vecer see **V TIHATA VECHER** (1959).

V TIHATA VECHER 1959 d: Borislav Shariliev. BUL., *V Tikha Vecher*, Emilian Stanev, 1948, Novel

V Tikha Vecher see **V TIHATA VECHER** (1959).

V TOM DOMECKU POD EMAUZY 1933 d: Otto Kanturek. CZC., *Das Hauschen in Grinzing*, Joseph Lanner, Opera

V Zacetku Je Bil Greh see **AM ANFANG WAR ES SUNDE** (1954).

VA DOVE TI PORTA IL CUORE 1996 d: Cristina Comencini. ITL/FRN/GRM., *Va Dove Ti Porta Il Cuore*, Susanna Tamaro, Novel

VANISHING AMERICAN, THE 1925 d: George B. Seitz. USA., *The Vanishing American*, Zane Grey, New York 1925, Novel

VANISHING AMERICAN, THE 1955 d: Joseph Kane. USA., *The Vanishing American*, Zane Grey, New York 1925, Novel

Vanishing Body, The see **THE BLACK CAT** (1934).

Vanishing Corporal, The see **LE CAPORAL EPINGLE** (1961).

Vanishing Race, The see **THE VANISHING AMERICAN** (1925).

Vanishing Strain, The see **DANGEROUS LOVE** (1920).

VANISHING, THE 1993 d: George Sluizer. USA., *The Golden Egg*, Tim Krabbe, Novel

VANISHING VIRGINIAN, THE 1941 d: Frank Borzage. USA., *The Vanishing Virginian*, Rebecca Yancey Williams, Book

VANITA 1947 d: Giorgio PastinA. ITL., *La Gibigianna*, Carlo Bertolazzi, 1898, Play

VANITY 1935 d: Adrian Brunel. UKN., *Vanity*, Ernest Denny, London 1913, Play

Vanity see **VANITA** (1947).

VANITY AND SOME SABLES 1917 d: John S. Robertson. USA., *Vanity and Some Sables*, O. Henry, Short Story

VANITY FAIR 1911 d: Charles Kent. USA., *Vanity Fair*, William Makepeace Thackeray, London 1848, Novel

VANITY FAIR 1915 d: Charles J. Brabin, Eugene Nowland. USA., *Vanity Fair*, William Makepeace Thackeray, London 1848, Novel

VANITY FAIR 1922 d: W. C. Rowden. UKN., *Vanity Fair*, William Makepeace Thackeray, London 1848, Novel

VANITY FAIR 1923 d: Hugo Ballin. USA., *Vanity Fair*, William Makepeace Thackeray, London 1848, Novel

VANITY FAIR 1932 d: Chester M. Franklin. USA., *Vanity Fair*, William Makepeace Thackeray, London 1848, Novel

Vanity Fair of Today see **VANITY FAIR** (1932).

VANITY POOL, THE 1918 d: Ida May Park. USA., *The Vanity Pool*, Nalbro Bartley, Novel

VANKA 1960 d: Edvard Bocharov. USS., *Vanka*, Anton Chekhov, 1884, Short Story

VANKA ZHUKOV 1981 d: Leonid Zarubin. USS., *Vanka*, Anton Chekhov, 1884, Short Story

VANKANSYA 1981 d: Margarita Mikaelyan. USS., *Dokhodnoe Mesto*, Alexander Ostrovsky, 1857, Play

VANQUISHED, THE 1953 d: Edward Ludwig. USA., *Decision to Kill*, Karl Brown, Novel

VARIETE 1925 d: E. A. Dupont. GRM., Felix Hollander, Novel

Varietes see **VARIETE** (1925).

VARIETES 1935 d: Nicolas Farkas. FRN., *Der Eid Des Stephan Huller*, Felix Hollaender, Novel

Variety see **VARIETE** (1925).

Variety see **VARIETES** (1935).

VARLDENS BASTA KARLSSON 1974 d: Olle Hellbom. SWD., Astrid Lindgren, Story

VARMINT, THE 1917 d: William D. Taylor. USA., *The Varmint*, Owen Johnson, New York 1910, Novel

VARNATT 1976 d: Erik Solbakken. NRW., *Varnatt*, Tarjei Vesaas, 1954, Novel

Varsity Girl, The see **THE FAIR CO-ED** (1927).

Vaschi Della Bujosa, I see **IL DELITTO DI CASTEL GIUBILEO** (1918).

VASSA 1982 d: Gleb Panfilov. USS., *Vassa Zheleznova*, Maxim Gorky, 1910, Play

Vassa Zeleznova see **VASSA ZHELEZNOVA** (1953).

VASSA ZHELEZNOVA 1953 d: Leonid Lukov. USS., *Vassa Zheleznova*, Maxim Gorky, 1910, Play

Vassili Bortnikov's Return see **VOZVRASHCHENIE VASSILIYA BORTNIKOVA** (1953).

VATER SEIN DAGEGEN SEHR 1957 d: Kurt Meisel. GRM., *Vater Sein Dagegen Sehr*, Horst Biernath, Novel

Vater Und Sohn see **MARKURELLS I WADKOPING** (1930).

Vaudeville see **VARIETE** (1925).

VAUTRIN 1943 d: Pierre Billon. FRN., *Vautrin*, Honore de Balzac, 1840, Play

Vautrin the Thief see **VAUTRIN** (1943).

VAVASOUR BALL, THE 1914 d: Van Dyke Brooke. USA., *The Vavasour Ball*, Frances Livingstone, Story

VAVILON-XX 1980 d: Ivan Mikolaichuk. USS., *Swan Flock*, Vasil Zemljak, Novel

VCERA NEDELE BYLA 1938 d: Walter Schorsch. CZC., *Male Stesti*, Vaclav Skutecky, Play

VDAVALA SE JEDNA PANNA 1926 d: Josef Kokeisl. CZC., *Vdavala Se Jedna Panna*, Karel Hasler, Poem

VDAVKY NANYNKY KULICHOVY 1925 d: M. J. Krnansky. CZC., *Vdavky Nanynky Kulichovy*, Ignat Herrmann, Novel

VDAVKY NANYNKY KULICHOVY 1941 d: Vladimir Slavinsky. CZC., *Vdavky Nanynky Kulichovy*, Ignat Herrmann, Novel

Ve Sparech Hrisne Zeny see **KAINOVO ZNAMENI** (1928).

VEAU GRAS, LE 1939 d: Serge de Poligny. FRN., *Le Veau Gras*, Bernard Zimmer, Play

VECCHI E I GIOVANI, I 1978 d: Marco Leto. ITL., *I Vecchi E I Giovani*, Luigi Pirandello, 1909, Novel

VECHERA NA KHUTORE BLIZ DIKANKI 1961 d: Aleksandr Rou. USS., *Noch Pered Rozhdestvom*, Nikolay Gogol, 1832, Short Story

VED VEJEN 1988 d: Max von Sydow. SWD/DNM/UKN., *Ved Vejen*, Herman Bang, 1886, Novel

Vedam Puthithu see **VEDHAM PUDITHU** (1987).

VEDHAM PUDITHU 1987 d: BharathirajA. IND., *Jatikal*, B. Kannan, Play

Vedham Puthithu see **VEDHAM PUDITHU** (1987).

VEDMA 1956 d: Alexander Abramov. USS., *Vedma*, Anton Chekhov, 1886, Short Story

Vedova Elettrica, La see **LE SEPTIEME CIEL** (1957).

VEDOVA, LA 1939 d: Goffredo Alessandrini. ITL., *La Vedova*, Renato Simoni, Play

VEDOVA X, LA 1956 d: Lewis Milestone. ITL/FRN., *The Widow*, Susannah York, Novel

Veglione, La see **HER BELOVED VILLAIN** (1920).

Veil of Happiness, The see **LE VOILE DU BONHEUR** (1923).

VEILED ARISTOCRATS 1932 d: Oscar Micheaux. USA., *Veiled Aristocrats*, Charles Chestnutt, Novel

Veiled One, The see **INSPECTOR WEXFORD: THE VEILED ONE** (1989).

Veiled Prophet, The see **IL PROFETA VELATO** (1912).

VEILED WOMAN, THE 1917 d: Leedham Bantock. UKN., *The Veiled Woman*, Harold Simpson, Play

VEILED WOMAN, THE 1922 d: Lloyd Ingraham. USA., *A Spinner in the Sun*, Myrtle Reed, New York 1906, Novel

VEILLE D'ARMES 1925 d: Jacques de Baroncelli. FRN., *La Veille d'Armes*, Claude Farrere, Lucien Nepoty, Paris 1917, Play

VEILLE D'ARMES 1935 d: Marcel L'Herbier. FRN., *La Veille d'Armes*, Claude Farrere, Lucien Nepoty, Paris 1917, Play

VEINE, LA 1928 d: Rene Barberis. FRN., *La Veine*, Alfred Capus, Play

VELAIKKARI 1949 d: A. S. A. Sami. IND., *Velaikkari*, C. N. Annadurai, Play

VELBLOUD UCHEM JEHLY 1936 d: Hugo Haas, Otakar VavrA. CZC., *Velbloud Uchem Jehly*, Frantisek Langer, Play

Veliki Plavi Put see **LA GRANDE STRADA AZZURRA** (1957).

VELKA SYROVA SOUTEZ 1987 d: Vaclav Bedrich. CZC/GRM., Jan Van Leeuwen, Book

VELOCITY OF GARY, THE 1998 d: Dan Ireland. USA., *The Velocity of Gary*, James Still, Play

Vem Mordale Fru Skrof? see **KOMISARIO PALMU KAASUA** (1961).

VENA D'ORO, LA 1928 d: Guglielmo Zorzi. ITL., *La Vena d'Oro*, Guglielmo Zorzi, 1919, Play

VENA D'ORO, LA 1955 d: Mauro Bolognini. ITL., *La Vena d'Oro*, Guglielmo Zorzi, 1919, Play

VENCEDORES DE LA MUERTE, LOS 1927 d: Antonio Calvache. SPN., *Los Vencedores de la Muerte*, Alberto Insua, Novel

Venda En Los Ojos, La see **NADA MAS QUE UNA MUJER** (1934).

VENDETTA 1950 d: Mel Ferrer, Stuart Heisler (Uncredited). USA., *Colomba*, Prosper Merimee, 1841, Novel

Vendetta Dei Moschettieri, La see **LES TROIS MOUSQUETAIRES** (1961).

VENDETTA DEI TUGHS, LA 1955 d: Gian Paolo Callegari, Ralph Murphy. ITL., Emilio Salgari, Novel

Vendetta Della Maschera Di Ferro see **VENGEANCE DU MASQUE DE FER** (1962).

Vendetta Della Signora, La see **DER BESUCH** (1964).

VENDETTA DI UNA PAZZA, LA 1952 d: Pino Mercanti. ITL., *La Vendetta Di Una Pazza*, Carolina Invernizio, Novel

VENDETTA, LA 1961 d: Jean-A. Cherasse. FRN/ITL., *Le Candidat Lauriston*, Henri Omessa, Novel

VENDICATORE, IL 1959 d: William Dieterle. ITL/YGS., *Dubrovsky*, Alexander Pushkin, 1841, Short Story

Vendredi 13 Heures see **AN EINEM FREITAG UM HALB ZWOLF** (1961).

VENDREDI OU LA VIE SAUVAGE 1981 d: Gerard Vergez. FRN., *Robinson Crusoe*, Daniel Defoe, 1719, Novel

Veneer see **YOUNG BRIDE** (1932).

VENENOSA, LA 1928 d: Roger Lion. FRN., *El Caballero Audaz*, Jose-Maria Carretero, Novel

Venere Bruna see **UN CATTIVO SOGGETTO** (1933).

VENERE CREOLA 1961 d: Lorenzo Ricciardi. ITL., *Le Belle Creole Di Melchior de la Cruz*, Lorenzo Ricciardi, Short Story

VENERE D'ILLE, LA 1979 d: Mario Bava, Lamberto BavA. ITL., Prosper Merimee, Short Story

Venere Nuda see **LE MALIZIE DI VENERE** (1969).

VENETIAN AFFAIR, THE 1966 d: Jerry Thorpe. USA., *The Venetian Affair*, Helen MacInnes, New York 1963, Novel

Venetian Baker, The see **IL FORNARETTO DI VENEZIA** (1907).

VENETIAN BIRD 1952 d: Ralph Thomas. UKN., *Venetian Bird*, Victor Canning, Novel

Venetian Nights see **CARNIVAL** (1931).

VENETSIANSKIY MAVR 1961 d: Vakhtang Chabukiani. USS., *Othello*, William Shakespeare, c1604, Play

VENGA A PRENDERE IL CAFFE DA NOI 1970 d: Alberto LattuadA. ITL., *La Spartizione*, Piero Chiara, Novel

VENGANZA ISLENA 1923 d: Manuel NoriegA. SPN., *Venganza Islena*, Andres Perez de La Mota

Vengeance see **RANGE WARFARE** (1935).

Vengeance see **ALRAUNE** (1952).

Vengeance see **REVENGE** (1960).

VENGEANCE 1962 d: Freddie Francis. UKN/GRM., *Donovan's Brain*, Curt Siodmak, New York 1943, Novel

Vengeance see **SOLDATAMI NYE ROZHDAYUTSYA** (1968).

Vengeance see **EL PERRO** (1977).

VENGEANCE A RIO 1991 d: Murilo Salles. FRN/BRZ/GRM., *Vengeance a Rio*, Maxime Delamare, Novel

VENGEANCE DU MASQUE DE FER 1962 d: Francesco de Feo. FRN/ITL., *Le Vicomte de Bragelonne*, Alexandre Dumas (pere), Paris 1847, Novel

VENGEANCE D'UNE FEMME, LA 1989 d: Jacques Doillon. FRN., *Vechnyi Muzh*, Fyodor Dostoyevsky, 1870, Short Story

Vengeance in Timber Valley see **UND EWIG SINGEN DIE WALDER** (1959).

VENGEANCE IS MINE 1918 d: Frank H. Crane. USA., *Vengeance Is Mine*, John A. Moroso, Novel

VENGEANCE OF DURAND, THE 1919 d: Tom Terriss. USA., *The Vengeance of Durand*, Rex Beach, Novel

Vengeance of Gregory Walters, The see **FEUD OF THE WEST** (1936).

VENGEANCE OF RANNAH 1936 d: Bernard B. Ray. USA., James Oliver Curwood, Short Story

VENGEANCE OF RANNAH, THE 1915 d: Thomas Santschi. USA., James Oliver Curwood, Short Story

VENGEANCE OF SHE, THE 1968 d: Cliff Owen. UKN., *She*, H. Rider Haggard, London 1886, Novel

Vengeance of the Three Musketeers see **LES TROIS MOUSQUETAIRES** (1961).

VENGEANCE VALLEY 1950 d: Richard Thorpe. USA., *Vengeance Valley*, Luke Short, 1950, Novel

Vengeur, Le see **LE JUGEMENT DE MINUIT** (1932).

VENGEZ-MOI MON GENDRE!. 1916. FRN., *Octave*, Henri Geroule, Yves Mirande, Play

Venin, Le see **ORAGE** (1937).

VENNER 1960 d: Tancred Ibsen. NRW., *Venner*, Arnulf Overland, 1917, Play

VENOM 1981 d: Piers Haggard. UKN., *Venom*, Alan Scholefield, Novel

VENOUSEK A STAZICKA 1922 d: Svatopluk Innemann. CZC., *Venousek a Stazicka*, Josef Skruzny, Novel

VENOUSEK A STAZICKA 1939 d: Cenek Slegl. CZC., *Venousek a Stazicka*, Josef Skruzny, Novel

Venousek and Stazicka *see* **VENOUSEK A STAZICKA** (1922).

Venousek and Stazicka *see* **VENOUSEK A STAZICKA** (1939).

VENTESIMO DUCA, IL 1943 d: Lucio de Caro. ITL., *L' Ultimo Lord*, Ugo Falena, Play

VENTI GIORNI ALL'OMBRA 1918 d: Gennaro Righelli. ITL., *Vingt Jours a l'Ombre*, Maurice Hennequin, Pierre Veber, 1907, Play

Venticinquesima Ora, La *see* **LA VINGT-CINQUIEME HEURE** (1966).

Vento Caldo Di Battaglia *see* **CARILLONS SANS JOIE** (1962).

VENTO DI MILIONI 1940 d: Dino Falconi. ITL., *Money for Nothing*, Seymour Hicks, Play

Vento Di Montagna *see* **L' ULTIMO UOMO DELLA TERRA** (1964).

Vento Di Morte *see* **L' ULTIMO UOMO DELLA TERRA** (1964).

VENTRE DI PARIGI, IL 1917 d: Ubaldo Maria Del Colle. ITL., *Les Mysteres de Paris*, Eugene Sue, 1842-43, Novel

Ventre Di Parigi, Il *see* **PARIGI MISTERIOSA** (1917).

VENTURERS, THE 1917 d: Thomas R. Mills. USA., *The Venturers*, O. Henry, Short Story

VENUS 1929 d: Louis Mercanton. FRN., *Venus*, Jean Vignaud, Novel

VENUS D'ARLES, LA 1917 d: Georges DenolA. FRN., *Le Venus d'Arles*, Mery, Short Story

VENUS DE L'OR, LA 1938 d: Charles Mere, Jean Delannoy. FRN., *Business*, Pierre Sabatier, Play

Venus du Tivoli, La *see* **DIE VENUS VOM TIVOLI** (1953).

Venus Im Pelz *see* **LE MALIZIE DI VENERE** (1969).

Venus in Furs *see* **LE MALIZIE DI VENERE** (1969).

VENUS IN THE EAST 1919 d: Donald Crisp. USA., *Venus in the East*, Wallace Irwin, New York 1918, Novel

VENUS PETER 1989 d: Ian Sellar. UKN., *A Twelve-Month and a Day*, Christopher Rush, Book

VENUS VOM TIVOLI, DIE 1953 d: Leonard Steckel. SWT., *Die Venus Vom Tivoli*, Peter Haggenmacher, Aarau 1931, Novel

VERA LUKASOVA 1939 d: E. F. Burian. CZC., *Don Pablo Don Pedro a Vera Lukasova*, Bozena Benesova, Novel

Vera Mirzewa *see* **DER FALL DES STAATSANWALTS M..** (1928).

Vera Storia Della Signore Dalle Camelie, La *see* **LA DAME AUX CAMELIAS** (1981).

Vera the Lawyer *see* **ADVOKATKA VERA** (1937).

VERA THE MEDIUM 1916 d: G. M. Anderson. USA., *Vera the Medium*, Richard Harding Davis, New York 1908, Novel

VERANDA FOR EN TENOR 1998 d: Lisa Ohlin. SWD., Klas Ostergren, Short Story

Verano de Infierno, Un *see* **UN ETE D'ENFER** (1984).

Vera's Training *see* **ANGI VERA** (1979).

VERBENA DE LA PALOMA, LA 1921 d: Jose Buchs. SPN., *La Verbena de la Paloma*, Tomas Breton, Ricardo de La Vega, Opera

VERBORGEN LEVEN, HET 1920 d: Maurits H. Binger, B. E. Doxat-Pratt. NTH/UKN., *Hidden Lives*, Robert Hichens, John Knittell, Play

Verbrechen, Das *see* **ES GESCHAH AM HELLICHTEN TAG** (1958).

VERBRECHEN NACH SCHULSCHLUSS 1959 d: Alfred Vohrer. GRM., *Verbrechen Nach Schulschluss*, Walter Ebert, Baden-Baden 1956, Novel

VERBRECHEN NACH SCHULSCHLUSS 1975 d: Alfred Vohrer. GRM., *Verbrechen Nach Schulschluss*, Walter Ebert, Baden-Baden 1956, Novel

VERBRECHER AUS VERLORENER EHRE, DER 1913. GRM., *Wahren Geschichte*, Friedrich von Schiller, Play

VERDACHT AUF URSULA 1939 d: Karl Heinz Martin. GRM., *Ursula Schwebt Voruber*, Walther Harich, Novel

..VERDAMMT, ICH BIN ERWACHSEN. 1974 d: Rolf Losansky. GDR., *Verdammt Ich Bin Erwachsen*, Joachim Novotny, Novel

VERDAMMT ZUR SUNDE 1964 d: Alfred Weidenmann. GRM., *Verdammt Zur Sunde*, Henry Jaeger, Novel

Verdi *see* **GIUSEPPE VERDI** (1953).

Verdict *see* **LE VERDICT** (1974).

VERDICT, LE 1974 d: Andre Cayatte. FRN/ITL., *Le Verdict*, Henri Coupon, Novel

VERDICT OF THE HEART, THE 1915 d: Wilfred Noy. UKN., *The Verdict of the Heart*, Charles Garvice, Novel

VERDICT, THE 1946 d: Don Siegel. USA., *The Big Bow Mystery*, Israel Zangwill, London 1892, Novel

VERDICT, THE 1964 d: David Eady. UKN., *The Big Four*, Edgar Wallace, London 1929, Novel

VERDICT, THE 1982 d: Sidney Lumet. USA., *The Verdict*, Barry Reed, Novel

VEREDA DA SALVACAO 1965 d: Anselmo Duarte. BRZ., *Vereda Da Salvacao*, Jorge Andrade, 1965, Play

VERENA STADLER 1940 d: Hermann Haller. SWT., *Verena Stadler*, Ernst Zahn, Wiesbaden 1906, Short Story

VERESKOVYI MYOD 1974 d: Irina Gurvich. USS., *Heather Ale: a Galloway Legend*, Robert Louis Stevenson, 1890, Verse

VERFUHRUNG: DIE GRAUSAME FRAU 1984 d: Elfi Mikesch, Monika Treut. GRM., *Venus in Furs*, Leopold von Sacher-Masoch, Novel

VERGELOSE, DE 1939 d: Leif Sinding. NRW., *De Vergelose; Et Barns Historie*, Gabriel Scott, 1938, Novel

VERGESSENEN KINDER, DIE 1981 d: Kurt K. Hieber. GRM., Otto Uhlig, Books

Vergie Winters *see* **THE LIFE OF VERGIE WINTERS** (1934).

VERGINE DI NORIMBERGA, LA 1963 d: Antonio Margheriti. ITL., *The Virgin of Nuremberg*, Frank Bogart, Novel

VERGINE FOLLE, LA 1920 d: Gennaro Righelli. ITL., *La Vierge Folle*, Henry Bataille, 1910, Play

VERGINI DI ROMA, LE 1960 d: Vittorio Cottafavi, Carlo Ludovico BragagliA. ITL/FRN., *Le Vergini Di Roma*, Luigi Emmanuele, Gaetano Laffredo, Short Story

Vergini, Le *see* **LE TRE SORELLE** (1918).

VERGISS NICHT DEINE FRAU ZU KUSSEN 1967 d: Egil Kolsto. GRM/DNM., *Vergiss Nicht Deine Frau Zu Kussen*, Willy Breinholst, Novel

VERGISS, WENN DU KANNST 1956 d: Hans H. Konig. GRM/AUS., *Ein Weiter Weg*, Irmgard Wurmbrand, Novel

Verhor Um Mitternacht *see* **PARKSTRASSE 13** (1939).

Verite Sur Bebe Donge, La *see* **LA VERITE SUR LE BEBE DONGE** (1951).

VERITE SUR LE BEBE DONGE, LA 1951 d: Henri Decoin. FRN., *La Verite Sur Bebe Donge*, Georges Simenon, 1942, Novel

VERKAUFTE BRAUT, DIE 1932 d: Max Ophuls. GRM., *Prodana Nevesta*, Bedrich Smetana, Prague 1866, Opera

VERKLUNGENE TRAUME 1930 d: Martin Berger. GRM/RMN., *Ciuleandra*, Liviu Rebreanu, 1927, Novel

VERLEGENHEITSKIND, DAS 1938 d: Peter P. Brauer. GRM., *Schutt Die Sorgen in Ein Glaschen Wein*, Franz Streicher, Play

Verlieb' Dich Nicht in Sizilien *see* **FRUHLINGSMARCHEN** (1934).

Verliebte Herzen *see* **HEIRATEN - ABER WEN?** (1938).

VERLOBTE, DIE 1980 d: Gunther Rucker, Gunter Reisch. GDR., Eva Lippold, Books

VERLORENE, DER 1951 d: Peter Lorre. GRM., *Der Verlorene*, Peter Lorre, Novel

VERLORENE EHRE DER KATHERINA BLUM, DIE 1975 d: Volker Schlondorff, Margarethe von TrottA. GRM., *Die Verlorene Ehre Der Katharina Blum*, Heinrich Boll, 1974, Novel

VERLORENE TAL, DAS 1934 d: Edmund Heuberger. GRM/SWT., *Das Verlorene Tal. Ein Roman von Jagd Und Liebe*, Gustav Friedrich Renker, Basle 1931, Novel

Vermachtnis Des Inka, Das *see* **VIVA GRINGO** (1966).

Vermilon Mark, The *see* **DUNIYA NA MANE** (1937).

Veronica *see* **VERONICA CYBA** (1910).

Veronica Cibo *see* **VERONICA CYBA** (1910).

Veronica Cjbo *see* **VERONICA CYBA** (1910).

VERONICA CYBA 1910 d: Mario Caserini. ITL., *Veronica Cybo*, Riccardo Olivieri

VERONIQUE 1949 d: Robert Vernay. FRN., *Veronique*, Georges Duval, Albert Vanloo, Opera

Verrateror, Das *see* **TRAITOR'S GATE** (1964).

VERS L'ABIME 1934 d: Serge Veber, Hans Steinhoff. FRN., *Die Insel*, Harald Bratt, Play

VERS L'EXTASE 1960 d: Rene Wheeler. FRN., *Vers l'Extase*, Madeleine Alleins, Novel

Versailles Affair, The *see* **MONSIEUR SUZUKI** (1959).

Versailles No Bara *see* **BERUSAIYU NO BARA** (1978).

VERSCHWENDER, DER 1953 d: Leopold Hainisch. AUS., *Der Verschwender*, Ferdinand Raimund, 1868, Play

VERSCHWUNDENE FRAU, DIE 1937 d: E. W. Emo. AUS., *Die Verschwundene Frau*, Max Durr, Novel

VERSCHWUNDENE MINIATUR, DIE 1954 d: Carl-Heinz Schroth. GRM., *Die Verschwundene Miniatur*, Erich Kastner, 1935, Novel

VERSPRECHEN, DAS 1983 d: Alberto Negrin. ITL., *Das Versprechen*, Friedrich Durrenmatt, Zurich 1958, Novel

VERSPRICH MIR NICHTS 1937 d: Wolfgang Liebeneiner. GRM., *Versprich Mir Nichts*, Charlotte Rissmann, Play

Versteckt *see* **FORBIDDEN** (1986).

VERTA KASISSMAAME 1958 d: William Markus. FNL., *Ei Koskaan Huomispaivaa*, Mika Waltari, 1942, Novel

VERTAGTE HOCHZEITSNACHT, DIE 1953 d: Karl G. Kulb. GRM., *Die Vertagte Hochzeitsnacht*, Franz Robert Arnold, Ernst Bach, Play

VERTAUSCHTE GESICHTER 1929 d: Rolf Randolf. GRM., *Der Mann Den Niemand Sah*, Paul Rosenhayn, Novel

VERTE MOISSON, LA 1959 d: Francois Villiers. FRN., *La Verte Moisson*, Henri Brunel, Novel

Vertige d'un Soir *see* **LA PEUR** (1936).

VERTIGE, LE 1926 d: Marcel L'Herbier. FRN., *Le Vertige*, Charles Mere, Play

VERTIGE, LE 1935 d: Paul Schiller. FRN., *Le Vertige*, Charles Mere, Play

Vertiges *see* **PER LE ANTICHE SCALE** (1975).

VERTIGINE D'AMORE 1951 d: Luigi Capuano. ITL., *Le Pain Des Pauvres*, Thyde Monnier, Novel

VERTIGO 1958 d: Alfred Hitchcock. USA., *D'entre Les Morts*, Pierre Boileau, Thomas Narcejac, 1954, Novel

VERTRAUMTE TAGE 1951 d: Emile Edwin Reinert, Franz Zimmermann. GRM/FRN., *Das Joch*, Vicki Baum, Novel

Vertudieu! *see* **AH! SI MON MOINE VOULAIT.** (1973).

VERUNTREUTE HIMMEL, DER 1958 d: Ernst MarischkA. GRM., *Der Veruntreute Himmel*, Franz Werfel, 1948, Novel

VERWEHTE SPUREN 1938 d: Veit Harlan. GRM., *Verwehte Spuren*, Hans Rothe, Radio Play

VERY BRITISH COUP, A 1988 d: Mick Jackson. UKN., *A Very British Coup*, Chris Mullen, Novel

Very Busy Gentlemen *see* **PAN NA ROZTRHANI** (1934).

VERY GOOD YOUNG MAN, A 1919 d: Donald Crisp. USA., *A Very Good Young Man*, Martin Brown, Robert Housum, New York 1918, Play

Very Handy Man, A *see* **LIOLA** (1964).

Very Happy Alexander *see* **ALEXANDRE LE BIENHEUREUX** (1968).

VERY HONORABLE GUY, A 1934 d: Lloyd Bacon. USA., *A Very Honorable Guy*, Damon Runyon, 1929, Short Story

Very Honourable Man, A *see* **A VERY HONORABLE GUY** (1934).

VERY IDEA, THE 1920 d: Lawrence C. Windom. USA., *The Very Idea*, William le Baron, New York 1917, Play

VERY MISSING PERSON, A 1972 d: Russ Mayberry. USA., *Hildegarde Withers Makes the Scene*, Fletcher Flora, Stuart Palmer

Very Moral Night, A see EGY ERKOLCSOS EJSZAKA (1977).

Very Old Man With Enormous Wings, A see UN SENOR MUY VIEJO CON UNAS ALAS ENORMES (1988).

Very Practical Joke, A see INSIDE STORY (1938).

Very Rich Man, A see THAT WAY WITH WOMEN (1947).

VERY YOUNG LADY, A 1941 d: Harold Schuster. USA., Mature, Ladislaus Fodor, Play

VERZAUBERTE PRINZESSIN, DIE 1939 d: Aloys Alfons Zengerling. GRM., Der Rubin, Christian Friedrich Hebbel, 1851, Play

VERZAUBERTE TAG, DER 1944 d: Peter Pewas. GRM., Die Augen, Franz Nabl, Short Story

Veselye Rraspliuyevskie Dni see VESYOLYYE RASPLYUYEVSKIYE DNI (1966).

VESNA NA ODERYE 1968 d: Leon Saakov. USS., Vesna Na Odere, Emmanuil Kazakevich, 1950, Novel

VESSEL OF WRATH 1938 d: Erich Pommer. UKN., The Beachcomber, W. Somerset Maugham, 1931, Short Story

VESTALE DU GANGE, LA 1927 d: Andre Hugon. FRN., A l'Ombre Des Tombeaux, Jose Germain, Guerinon, Novel

VESTIDO COR DE FOGO, O 1984 d: Lauro Antonio. PRT., O Vestido Cor de Fogo, Jose Regio, 1946, Short Story

VESTIRE GLI IGNUDI 1954 d: Marcello Pagliero. ITL/FRN., Vestire Gli Ignudi, Luigi Pirandello, 1937, Play

VESTITO PER UN SAGGIO, UN 1979 d: Giuliana Berlinguer. ITL., The Last Mohican, Bernard Malamud, Novel

VESYOLYYE RASPLYUYEVSKIYE DNI 1966 d: Erast Garin. USS., Smert Tarelkina, Aleksandr Sukhovo-Kobylin, 1869, Play

VESZELYES JATEKOK 1979 d: Tamas Fejer. HNG/GDR., Heinrich Beginnt Den Kampf, Bela Balazs, 194-, Short Story

Vet in the Doghouse see IN THE DOGHOUSE (1961).

VETERAN OF WATERLOO, THE 1933 d: A. V. Bramble. UKN., A Story of Waterloo, Arthur Conan Doyle, London 1894, Play

VETERAN VOTRUBA 1928 d: Hans Otto Lowenstein. CZC/AUS., Spitzenhoschen Und Schusterpech, Rudolf Sturzer, Short Story

Vetir Ceux Qui Sont Nus see VESTIRE GLI IGNUDI (1954).

VETTER AUS DINGSDA, DER 1934 d: Georg Zoch. GRM., Der Vetter Aus Dingsda, Hermann Haller, Eduard Kunneke, Rideamus, Opera

VETTER AUS DINGSDA, DER 1953 d: Karl Anton. GRM., Der Vetter Aus Dingsda, Hermann Haller, Opera, Max Kempner-Hochstadt, Play, Der Vetter Aus Dingsda, Eduard Kunneke, Rideamus, Opera

VETTURALE DEL MONCENISIO, IL 1916 d: Leopoldo Carlucci. ITL., Jean le Coucher, Jean Bouchardy, 1852, Novel

VETTURALE DEL MONCENISIO, IL 1927 d: Baldassarre Negroni. ITL., Jean le Coucher, Jean Bouchardy, 1852, Novel

VETTURALE DEL MONCENISIO, IL 1956 d: Guido Brignone. ITL., Jean le Coucher, Jean Bouchardy, 1852, Novel

VEUVE COUDERC, LE 1971 d: Pierre Granier-Deferre. FRN/ITL., La Veuve Couderc, Georges Simenon, 1942, Novel

Veuve de Montiel, La see LA VIUDA DE MONTIEL (1979).

VEUVE JOYEUSE, LA 1934 d: Ernst Lubitsch. USA., La Veuve Joyeuse, Viktor Leon, Leo Stein, Book

Veuve, La see LA VEDOVA X (1956).

Veuves, Les see DU GRABUGE CHEZ LES VEUVES (1963).

VI ARME SYNDERE 1952 d: Erik Balling, Ole Palsbo. DNM., Vi Arme Syndere, Sigfrid Siwertz, Novel

Vi' Che M'ha Fatto Frateme! see TUTTO PER MIO FRATELLO (1911).

V.I. WARSHAWSKI 1991 d: Jeff Kanew. USA., Indemnity, Sara Paretsky, Novel

Via Del Rhum, La see BOULEVARD DU RHUM (1971).

VIA DELLA LUCE, LA 1917 d: Baldassarre Negroni. ITL., La Via Della Luce, Alfredo Bacchelli, Novel

VIA DELLE CINQUE LUNE 1942 d: Luigi Chiarini. ITL., O Giovannino O la Morte!, Matilde Serao, 1912, Novel

VIA MALA 1944 d: Josef von Baky. GRM., Via Mala, John Knittel, Novel

VIA MALA 1961 d: Paul May. GRM., Via Mala, John Knittel, Novel

VIA MALA 1985 d: Tom Toelle. GRM/FRN/AUS., Via Mala, John Knittel, Novel

VIA MARGUTTA 1960 d: Mario Camerini. ITL/FRN., Gente Al Babuino, Ugo Moretti, Florence 1957, Novel

VIA PIU LUNGA, LA 1918 d: Mario Caserini. ITL., Le Detour, Henri Bernstein, 1902, Play

VIA SATELLITE 1998 d: Anthony McCarten. NZL., Via Satellite, Anthony McCarten, Play

VIA WIRELESS 1915 d: George Fitzmaurice. USA., Via Wireless, Paul Armstrong, Winchell Smith, New York 1908, Play

VIACCIA, LA 1961 d: Mauro Bolognini. ITL/FRN., L' Eredita, Mario Pratesi, Florence 1889, Novel

VIAGEM AO FIM DO MUNDO 1968 d: Fernando Cony Campos. BRZ., Memorias Postumas de Bras Cubas, Joaquim Maria Machado de Assis, 1881, Novel

VIAGEM AOS SEIOS DE DUILIA 1963 d: Carlos Hugo Christensen. BRZ., Viagem Aos Seios de Duilia, Aribal Machado, 1959, Short Story

Viaggiatore Di Ognissanti, Il see LE VOYAGEUR DE LA TOUSSAINT (1942).

VIAGGIATORI DELLA SERA, I 1979 d: Ugo Tognazzi. ITL/SPN., I Viaggiatori Della Sera, Umberto Simonetta, Novel

VIAGGIO DEL SIGNOR PERRICHON, IL 1944 d: Paolo MoffA. ITL., Le Voyage de Monsieur Perrichon, Eugene Labiche, Edouard Martin, 1860, Play

VIAGGIO DI BERLURON, IL 1919 d: Camillo de Riso. ITL., Le Voyage de Berluron, E. Grenet-Dancourt, Maurice Ordonneau, 1893

VIAGGIO DI PIACERE, UN 1922 d: Ermanno Geymonat. ITL., Voyage d'Agrement, Alexandre Bisson, Edmond Gondinet, 1881, Play

VIAGGIO, IL 1921 d: Gennaro Righelli. ITL., Il Viaggio, Luigi Pirandello, 1910, Short Story

VIAGGIO, IL 1974 d: Vittorio de SicA. ITL/FRN., Il Viaggio, Luigi Pirandello, 1910, Short Story

VIAGGIO IN ITALIA 1953 d: Roberto Rossellini. ITL/FRN., Duo, Sidonie Gabrielle Colette, Short Story

VIAJE AL CENTRO DE LA TIERRA 1977 d: Piquer Simon. SPN., Voyage Au Centre de la Terre, Jules Verne, 1864, Novel

VIAJE DE NOVIOS, UN 1947 d: Gonzalo Delgras. SPN., Un Viaje de Novios, Emilia Pardo Bazan, 1881, Novel

Viaje de Placer see NO DEJES LA PUERTA ABIERTA (1933).

Viajeros Del Atardecer, Los see I VIAGGIATORI DELLA SERA (1979).

VIAJES DE GULLIVER, LOS 1983 d: Cruz Delgado, Antonio de Font. SPN., Gulliver's Travels, Jonathan Swift, London 1726, Novel

VIATA INVINGE 1951 d: Dinu Negreanu. RMN., Iarba Rea, Aurel Baranga, 1949, Play

VIATA NU IARTA 1957 d: Manole Marcus, Iulian Mihu. RMN., Intoarcerea Tatii Din Razboi, Alexandru Sahia, 1934, Short Story, Moartea Tinarului Cu Termen Redus, Alexandru Sahia, 1933, Short Story

VICAR OF BRAY, THE 1937 d: Henry Edwards. UKN., The Vicar of Bray, Anson Dyer, Story

Vicar of Vejlby, The see PRAESTEN I VEJLBY (1920).

VICAR OF WAKEFIELD, THE 1910 d: Theodore Marston. USA., The Vicar of Wakefield, Oliver Goldsmith, 1766, Novel

VICAR OF WAKEFIELD, THE 1912 d: Frank Powell. UKN., The Vicar of Wakefield, Oliver Goldsmith, 1766, Novel

VICAR OF WAKEFIELD, THE 1913 d: John Douglas. UKN., The Vicar of Wakefield, Oliver Goldsmith, 1766, Novel

VICAR OF WAKEFIELD, THE 1913 d: Frank Wilson. UKN., The Vicar of Wakefield, Oliver Goldsmith, 1766, Novel

VICAR OF WAKEFIELD, THE 1916 d: Fred Paul. UKN., The Vicar of Wakefield, Oliver Goldsmith, 1766, Novel

VICAR OF WAKEFIELD, THE 1917 d: Ernest C. Warde. USA., The Vicar of Wakefield, Oliver Goldsmith, 1766, Novel

Vice and Virtue see LE VICE ET LA VERTU (1963).

Vice Dolls see LES CLANDESTINES (1954).

VICE ET LA VERTU, LE 1963 d: Roger Vadim. FRN/ITL., Juliette, Donatien Sade, 1797, Novel, Justine; Ou Les Malheurs de la Vertu, Donatien Sade, 1791, Novel

VICE SQUAD 1953 d: Arnold Laven. USA., Harness Bull, Leslie T. White, 1937, Novel

VICE VERSA 1916 d: Maurice Elvey. UKN., Vice Versa, F. Anstey, 1882, Novel

VICE VERSA 1948 d: Peter Ustinov. UKN., Vice Versa, F. Anstey, 1882, Novel

Vicious Circle see HUIS-CLOS (1954).

Vicious Circle see CHAKRA (1979).

VICIOUS CIRCLE, THE 1948 d: W. Lee Wilder. USA., The Burning Bush, Heinz Herald, Geza Herczeg, Play

VICKI 1953 d: Harry Horner. USA., I Wake Up Screaming, Steve Fisher, Novel

Vicky Van see THE WOMAN NEXT DOOR (1919).

VICOMTE DE BRAGELONNE, LE 1954 d: Fernando Cerchio. FRN/ITL., Le Vicomte de Bragelonne, Alexandre Dumas (pere), Paris 1847, Novel

VICOMTE REGLE SES COMPTES, LE 1967 d: Maurice Cloche. FRN/ITL/SPN., Bonne Mesure, Jean Bruce, Paris 1953, Novel

Victim of Hate see VICTIMA DEL ODIO (1921).

Victim of Passion see UNE FEMME FATALE (1976).

VICTIM, THE 1917 d: Joseph Levering. USA., A Victim to the Seal of Confession, Rev. Joseph Spillman, St. Louis 1898, Novel

Victim, The see THE DAMNED DON'T CRY (1950).

VICTIM, THE 1972 d: Herschel Daugherty. USA., MacIntoch Malmar, Story

Victima de la Calumnia see VICTIMA DEL ODIO (1921).

Victima de la Seduccion see LA SEDUCCION (1980).

VICTIMA DEL ODIO 1921 d: Jose Buchs. SPN., Roger Larocque, Jules Mary, Novel

VICTIMES, LES 1996 d: Patrick Grandperret. FRN., Les Victimes, Pierre Boileau, Thomas Narcejac, Novel

Victims see LES VICTIMES (1996).

VICTIMS OF PERSECUTION 1933 d: Bud Pollard. USA., Victims of Persecution, David Leonard, Play

VICTOR 1951 d: Claude Heymann. FRN., Victor, Henri Bernstein, Play

VICTOR FRANKENSTEIN 1977 d: Calvin Floyd. IRL/SWD., Frankenstein; Or the Modern Prometheus, Mary Wollstonecraft Shelley, London 1818, Novel

VICTOR. PENDANT QU'IL EST TROP TARD 1998 d: Sandrine Veysset. FRN., Les Ailes de Julien, Denis Belloc, Novel

VICTOR, THE 1923 d: Edward Laemmle. USA., Two Bells for Pegasus, Gerald Beaumont, 1922, Short Story

Victor. While It's Too Late see VICTOR. PENDANT QU'IL EST TROP TARD (1998).

VICTORIA 1978 d: Bo Widerberg. SWD/GRM., Victoria, Knut Hamsun, 1898, Novel

Victoria and Her Hussar see VIKTORIA UND IHR HUSAR (1954).

VICTORIA THE GREAT 1937 d: Herbert Wilcox. UKN., Victoria Regina, Laurence Houseman, London 1937, Play

VICTORIAN CHAISE-LONGUE, THE 1962 d: James MacTaggart. UKN., The Victorian Chaise-Longue, Marghanita Laski, Short Story

VICTORINE 1915 d: Paul Powell. USA., The Goings on of Victorine, Julian Leonard Street, Story

VICTORS, THE 1963 d: Carl Foreman. UKN/USA., The Human Kind; a Sequence, Alexander Baron, New York 1953, Novel

VICTORY 1919 d: Maurice Tourneur. USA., Victory, Joseph Conrad, London 1915, Novel

VICTORY 1940 d: John Cromwell. USA., Victory, Joseph Conrad, London 1915, Novel

VICTORY 1997 d: Mark Peploe. UKN/FRN/GRM., Victory, Joseph Conrad, London 1915, Novel

Victory Boulevard, Or the Key of Dreams see CALEA VICTORIEI SAU CHEIA VISURILOR (1966).

Victory Song see HISSHOKA (1945).

VIDA BOHEMIA, LA 1938 d: Josef Berne. USA., La Vie de Boheme, Henri Murger, Paris 1848, Play

VIDA CONYUGAL, LA 1992 d: Carlos CarrerA. MXC., La Vida Conyugal, Sergio Pitol, Novel

Vida Criminal de Archibaldo de la Cruz, La *see* ENSAYO DE UN CRIMEN (1955).

VIDAS CRUZADAS 1942 d: Luis MarquinA. SPN., *Vidas Cruzadas*, Jacinto Benavente y Martinez, 1929, Play

VIDAS SECAS 1963 d: Nelson Pereira Dos Santos. BRZ., *Vidas Secas*, Graciliano Ramos, 1938, Novel

VIDOCQ 1923 d: Jean Kemm. FRN., *Vidocq*, Arthur Bernede, Novel

VIDOCQ 1938 d: Jacques Daroy. FRN., *Vidocq*, Francis Eugene Vidocq, Book

VIE A DEUX, LA 1958 d: Clement Duhour, Sacha Guitry (Uncredited). FRN., Sacha Guitry, Story

VIE DE BOHEME, LA 1916 d: Albert Capellani. USA., *La Vie de Boheme*, Henri Murger, Paris 1848, Play

VIE DE BOHEME, LA 1942 d: Marcel L'Herbier. FRN/ITL., *La Vie de Boheme*, Henri Murger, Paris 1848, Play

VIE DE CHIEN, UNE 1941 d: Maurice Cammage. FRN., *Une Vie de Chien*, Andre Mycho, Novel

VIE DEL CUORE, LE 1942 d: Camillo Mastrocinque. ITL., *Cause Ed Effetti*, Paolo Ferrari, 1871, Play

VIE DEL PECCATO, LE 1946 d: Giorgio PastinA. ITL., *Dramma*, Grazia Deledda, Short Story

VIE DEVANT SOI, LA 1977 d: Moshe Mizrahi. FRN., *Madame Rosa*, Emile Ajar, Novel

VIE EST MAGNIFIQUE, LA 1938 d: Maurice Cloche. FRN., *Belle Jeunesse*, Marcelle Vioux, Novel

VIE NORMAL, LA 1966 d: Andre Charpak. FRN., *La Vie Normale*, Micheline Morel, Novel

VIE PARISIENNE, LA 1977 d: Christian-Jaque. FRN/GRM/ITL., *La Vie Parisienne*, Ludovic Halevy, Henri Meilhac, Operetta

Vie, Un *see* ONNA NO ISSHO (1967).

Vie, Une *see* NAISKOHTALOITA (1948).

VIE, UNE 1958 d: Alexandre Astruc. FRN/ITL., *Une Vie: l'Humble Verite*, Guy de Maupassant, Paris 1883, Novel

VIEHJUD LEVI 1999 d: Didi Danquart. GRM/SWT/AUS., *Viehjud Levi*, Thomas Strittmatter, Play

VIEILLE DAME INDIGNE, LA 1964 d: Rene Allio. FRN., *Die Unwurdige Greisin*, Bertolt Brecht, Berlin 1948, Short Story

VIEILLE QUI MARCHAIT DANS LA MER, LA 1991 d: Laurent Heynemann. FRN., *La Vieille Qui Marchait Dans la Mer*, San Antonio, Novel

VIEL LARM UM NICHTS 1964 d: Martin Hellberg. GDR., *Much Ado About Nothing*, William Shakespeare, c1598, Play

Vielgeliebte, Der *see* OBERWACHTMEISTER SCHWENKE (1935).

Viennese Melody, The *see* THE GREATER GLORY (1926).

VIENT DE PARAITRE 1949 d: Jacques Houssin. FRN., *Vient de Paraitre*, Edouard Bourdet, 1928, Play

VIENTO DEL NORTE 1954 d: Antonio Momplet. SPN., *Viento Del Norte*, Elena Quiroga, 1951, Novel

VIENTO NEGRO 1964 d: Servando Gonzalez. MXC., *Viento Negro*, Mario Martini, Novel

VIER GESELLEN, DIE 1938 d: Carl Froelich. GRM., *Die Vier Gesellen*, Jochen Huth, Play

VIER MUSKETIERE, DIE 1935 d: Heinz Paul. GRM., *Die Vier Musketiere*, Sigmund Graff, Play

VIER SCHLUSSEL 1965 d: Jurgen Roland. GRM., *Vier Schlussel*, Max Pierre Schaeffer, Novel

Vier von Der Infanterie *see* WESTFRONT 1918 (1930).

VIERAS MIES 1958 d: Hannu Leminen. FNL., *Jalkinaytos*, Mika Waltari, 1938, Novel, *Vieras Mies Tuli Taloon*, Mika Waltari, 1937, Novel

VIERAS MIES TULI TALOON 1938 d: Wilho Ilmari. FNL., *Jalkinaytos*, Mika Waltari, 1938, Novel, *Vieras Mies Tuli Taloon*, Mika Waltari, 1937, Novel

Vieras Mies Tuli Taloon *see* VIERAS MIES (1958).

VIERDE MAN, DE 1983 d: Paul Verhoeven. NTH., *De Vierde Man*, Gerard Kornelius Van Het Reve, 1981, Novel

VIERGE DU RHIN, LA 1953 d: Gilles Grangier. FRN., *La Vierge du Rhin*, Pierre Nord, Novel

VIERGE FOLLE, LA 1913. FRN., *La Vierge Folle*, Henry Bataille, 1910, Play

VIERGE FOLLE, LA 1928 d: Luitz-Morat. FRN., *La Vierge Folle*, Henry Bataille, 1910, Play

VIERGE FOLLE, LA 1938 d: Henri Diamant-Berger. FRN., *La Vierge Folle*, Henry Bataille, 1910, Play

Vierges de Rome, Les *see* LE VERGINI DI ROMA (1960).

VIERTE GEBOT, DAS 1920 d: Richard Oswald. GRM., *Das Vierte Gebot*, Ludwig Anzengruber, 1891, Play

VIERTE GEBOT, DAS 1950 d: Eduard von Borsody. AUS., *Das Vierte Gebot*, Ludwig Anzengruber, 1891, Play

VIERTE ZEIT, DIE 1984 d: Klaus Andre. GRM., Leopold von Sacher-Masoch, Novel

Vietnam House *see* VIETNAM VEEDU (1970).

VIETNAM VEEDU 1970 d: P. Madhavan. IND., *Vietnam Veedu*, Sundaram, Play

VIEUX DE LA VIEILLE, LES 1960 d: Gilles Grangier. FRN/ITL., *Les Vieux de la Vieille*, Rene Fallet, Novel

VIEW FROM POMPEY'S HEAD, THE 1955 d: Philip Dunne. USA., *The View from Pompey's Head*, Hamilton Basso, 1954, Novel

View from the Bridge, A *see* VU DU PONT (1962).

View of America, A *see* AMERIKAI ANZIKSZ (1976).

VIGIL IN THE NIGHT 1940 d: George Stevens. USA., *Vigil in the Night*, A. J. Cronin, Cleveland 1941, Novel

Vigil, The *see* VEILLE D'ARMES (1935).

VIGNES DU SEIGNEUR, LES 1932 d: Rene Hervil. FRN., *Les Vignes du Seigneur*, Francis de Croisset, Robert de Flers, Play

VIGNES DU SEIGNEUR, LES 1958 d: Jean Boyer. FRN., *Les Vignes du Seigneur*, Francis de Croisset, Robert de Flers, Play

VIHREA KULTA 1939 d: Valentin VaalA. FNL., *Vihrea Kulta*, Hella Wuolijoki, 1938, Play

VIKING, THE 1929 d: R. William Neill. USA., *The Thrall of Leif the Lucky; a Story of Viking Days*, Ottilia Adelina Liljencrantz, Chicago 1902, Novel

VIKINGS, THE 1958 d: Richard Fleischer. USA., *The Viking*, Edison Marshall, 1951, Novel

VIKTORIA 1935 d: Carl Hoffmann. GRM., *Victoria*, Knut Hamsun, 1898, Novel

VIKTORIA UND IHR HUSAR 1954 d: Rudolf Schundler. GRM., *Viktoria Und Ihr Husar*, Paul Abraham, Opera

VIKTORKA 1935 d: Jan Kyzour. CZC., *Babicka*, Bozena Nemcova, 1846, Novel

VILDANDEN 1963 d: Tancred Ibsen. NRW., *Vildanden*, Henrik Ibsen, 1884, Play

VILLA DA VENDERE 1942 d: Ferruccio Cerio. ITL., *Villa Da Vendere*, Geza von Cziffra, Play

VILLA DEL VENERDI, LA 1992 d: Mauro Bolognini. ITL., *La Villa Del Venerdi*, Alberto Moravia, Novel

VILLA FALCONIERI 1929 d: Richard Oswald. ITL/GRM., *Villa Falconieri*, Richard Voss, Novel

VILLA RIDES 1968 d: Buzz Kulik. USA., *Pancho Villa*, William Douglas Lansford, Los Angeles 1965, Novel

VILLAFRANCA 1933 d: Giovacchino Forzano. ITL., *Villafranca*, Giovacchino Forzano, Benito Mussolini, Play

Village Bathtub, The *see* DAS BAD AUF DER TENNE (1943).

Village Bathtub, The *see* DAS BAD AUF DER TENNE (1956).

VILLAGE BLACKSMITH, THE 1905 d: Percy Stow. UKN., *The Village Blacksmith*, Henry Wadsworth Longfellow, 1841, Poem

VILLAGE BLACKSMITH, THE 1908 d: A. E. Coleby. UKN., *The Village Blacksmith*, Henry Wadsworth Longfellow, 1841, Poem

VILLAGE BLACKSMITH, THE 1913. USA., *The Village Blacksmith*, Henry Wadsworth Longfellow, 1841, Poem

VILLAGE BLACKSMITH, THE 1917 d: A. E. Coleby. Arthur Rooke. UKN., *The Village Blacksmith*, Henry Wadsworth Longfellow, 1841, Poem

VILLAGE BLACKSMITH, THE 1922 d: John Ford. USA., *The Village Blacksmith*, Henry Wadsworth Longfellow, 1841, Poem

Village Correspondent, The *see* SELCOR (1975).

Village Festival, The *see* FIDLOVACKA (1930).

Village Feud, The *see* LA TABLE AUX CREVES (1951).

Village in the Jungle, The *see* BEDDEGAMA (1980).

Village in Your Palm, The *see* MESTECKO NA DLANI (1942).

Village Near the Sky, The *see* DAS DORF UNTERM HIMMEL (1953).

VILLAGE OF THE DAMNED 1960 d: Wolf RillA. UKN., *The Midwich Cuckoos*, John Wyndham, 1957, Novel

VILLAGE OF THE DAMNED 1995 d: John Carpenter. USA., *The Midwich Cuckoos*, John Wyndham, 1957, Novel

VILLAGE OF THE GIANTS 1965 d: Bert I. Gordon. USA., *The Food of the Gods and How It Came to Earth*, H. G. Wells, London 1904, Novel

Village on the River *see* DORP AAN DE RIVIER (1958).

VILLAGE PERDU, LE 1947 d: Christian Stengel. FRN., *Le Village Perdu*, Gilbert Dupe, Novel

Village Priest, The *see* EL CURA DE ALDEA (1926).

Village Shoemakers, The *see* NUMMISUUTARIT (1923).

Village Shoemakers, The *see* NUMMISUUTARIT (1938).

Village Shoemakers, The *see* NUMMISUUTARIT (1957).

VILLAGE SQUIRE, THE 1935 d: Reginald Denham. UKN., *The Village Squire*, Arthur Jarvis Black, Play

Village Story, A *see* OKA OORIE KATHA (1977).

VILLAGE TALE 1935 d: John Cromwell. USA., *A Village Tale*, Philip Duffield Stong, New York 1934, Novel

VILLAIN 1971 d: Michael Tuchner. UKN., *The Burden of Proof*, James Barlow, Novel

Ville Des Mille Joies, La *see* DIE STADT DER TAUSEND FREUDEN (1927).

Ville Sans Pitie *see* STADT OHNE MITLEID (1961).

Vincent, Francois, Paul and the Others *see* FRANCOIS, PAUL. ET LES AUTRES VINCENT (1974).

VINCENT, FRANCOIS, PAUL. ET LES AUTRES 1974 d: Claude Sautet. FRN/ITL., *La Grande Marrade*, Claude Neron, Novel

Vindinge Waltz *see* VINDINGEVALS (1968).

VINDINGEVALS 1968 d: Ake Falck. SWD., *Vindingevals*, Nils Artur Lundkvist, 1956, Novel

Vine Bridge, The *see* LIANBRON (1965).

Vinegar Tree, The *see* SHOULD LADIES BEHAVE? (1933).

Vinetu *see* WINNETOU I (1963).

Vinetu II *see* WINNETOU II (1964).

Vinetu III *see* WINNETOU III (1965).

VINGT ANS APRES 1922 d: Henri Diamant-Berger. FRN., *Vingt Ans Apres; Suite de Trois Mousquetaires*, Alexandre Dumas (pere), 1845, Novel

VINGT MILLE LIEUES SOUS LES MERS 1918. FRN., *Vingt Mille Lieues Sous Les Mers*, Jules Verne, 1870, Novel

VINGT-CINQ ANS DE BONHEUR 1943 d: Rene Jayet. FRN., *Vingt-Cinq Ans de Bonheur*, Germaine Lefrancq, Play

VINGT-CINQUIEME HEURE, LA 1966 d: Henri Verneuil. FRN/ITL/YGS., *La Vingt-Cinquieme Heure*, Virgil Gheorghiu, Novel

VINGT-HUIT JOURS DE CLAIRETTE, LES 1933 d: Andre Hugon. FRN., *Les Vingt-Huit Jours de Clairette*, Antony Mars, Hippolyte Raymond, Roger, Opera

Vingt-Quatre Heures de la Vie d'une Femme *see* 24 HEURES DE LA VIE D'UNE FEMME (1968).

VINGT-SEPT RUE DE LA PAIX 1936 d: Richard Pottier. FRN., *La Chaine Des Peuves*, Thomas B. Forster, Play

VINTAGE, THE 1957 d: Jeffrey Hayden. USA., *The Vintage*, Ursula Keir, 1953, Novel

VINTAGE WINE 1935 d: Henry Edwards. UKN., *Der Ewige Jungeling*, Alexander Engel, Play

Vinterbjorn *see* VINTERBORN (1978).

VINTERBORN 1978 d: Astrid Henning-Jensen. DNM., *Vinterborn*, Dea Trier Morch, 1976, Novel

Viola and Sebastian *see* VIOLA UND SEBASTIAN (1971).

VIOLA UND SEBASTIAN 1971 d: Ottokar Runze. GRM., *Twelfth Night*, William Shakespeare, c1600, Play

VIOLANTA 1942 d: Paul May. GRM., *Der Schatten*, Ernst Zahn, 1904, Short Story

VIOLANTA 1978 d: Daniel Schmid. SWT., *Die Richterin*, Conrad Ferdinand Meyer, 1885, Short Story

VIOLANTHA 1927 d: Carl Froelich. GRM/SWT., *Der Schatten*, Ernst Zahn, 1904, Short Story

Violated *see* THE LADIES CLUB (1986).

VIOLATED PARADISE 1963 d: Marion Gering, Robert de Leonardis. ITL/JPN., *L' Isola Delle Pescatrici*, Fosco Maraini, Bari 1960, Novel

Violation of Justine, The *see* JUSTINE DE SADE (1970).

Violence at High Noon *see* HAKUCHU NO TORIMA (1966).

Violence at Noon *see* HAKUCHU NO TORIMA (1966).

VIOLENCE: THE LAST RESORT 1992 d: Rainer Kaufmann. GRM., Jan de Zanger, Novel

VIOLENT ENEMY, THE 1969 d: Don Sharp. UKN., *A Candle for the Dead*, Hugh Marlowe, Novel

Violent Journey, A *see* THE FOOL KILLER (1963).

Violent Land, The *see* SEARA VERMELHA (1963).

Violent Life, A *see* UNA VITA VIOLENTA (1962).

VIOLENT MEN, THE 1954 d: Rudolph Mate. USA., *Smoky Valley*, Donald Hamilton, Novel

Violent Patriot, The *see* GIOVANNI DALLE BANDE NERE (1957).

VIOLENT PLAYGROUND 1958 d: Basil Dearden. UKN., *Violent Playground*, James Kennaway, Novel

VIOLENT ROAD 1958 d: Howard W. Koch. USA., *Hell's Highway*, Don Martin, Story

VIOLENT SATURDAY 1955 d: Richard Fleischer. USA., *Violent Saturday*, William L. Heath, 1955, Novel

Violent Streets *see* THIEF (1981).

VIOLENTATA SULLA SABBIA 1971 d: Renzo Cerrato. ITL/FRN., *Violentata Sulla Sabbia*, Andre Peyre Mandargues, Novel

Violenti Di Rio Bravo, I *see* DER SCHATZ DER AZTEKEN (1965).

VIOLENZA: QUINTO POTERE, LA 1972 d: Florestano Vancini. ITL., *La Violenza*, Giuseppe Fava, Play

VIOLENZA SEGRETA 1963 d: Giorgio Moser. ITL., *Settimana Nera*, Enrico Emanuelli, Novel

VIOLER ER BLA 1974 d: Peter Refn. DNM., *Fri Os Fra Kaerligheden*, Suzanne Brogger, 1973, Novel

VIOLETA 1998 d: Alberto Cortes. CUB/MXC., *Violeta*, Nicolas Dorr, Play

Violets are Blue *see* VIOLER ER BLA (1974).

Violette *see* VIOLETTE NOZIERE (1978).

VIOLETTE NEI CAPELLI 1942 d: Carlo Ludovico BragagliA. ITL., *Violette Nei Capelli*, Luciana Peverelli, Novel

VIOLETTE NOZIERE 1978 d: Claude Chabrol. FRN/CND., *Violette Noziere*, Jean-Marie Fitere, Novel

VIOLIN MAKER OF CREMONA, THE 1909 d: D. W. Griffith. USA., *The Violin Maker of Cremona*, Francois Coppee, Story

Violin Maker of Mittenwald, The *see* DER GEIGENMACHER VON MITTENWALD (1950).

Viper Three *see* TWILIGHT'S LAST GLEAMING (1977).

VIRGEN DE CRISTAL, LA 1925 d: Jose Buchs, Saturio Luis Pineiro. SPN., *A Virxen Do Cristal*, Manuel Curros Enriquez, Poem

Virgin *see* 36 FILLETTE (1987).

Virgin - 36 Fillette *see* 36 FILLETTE (1987).

VIRGIN AND THE GYPSY, THE 1970 d: Christopher Miles. UKN., *The Virgin and the Gypsy*, D. H. Lawrence, London 1930, Novel

Virgin and the Soldier, The *see* LE PETIT MATIN (1971).

Virgin Campus *see* LEIDENSCHAFTLICHE BLUMCHEN (1978).

Virgin from Oyuki, The *see* MARIA NO OYUKI (1935).

VIRGIN ISLAND 1958 d: Pat Jackson. UKN., *Our Virgin Island*, Robb White, Book

Virgin of Cedar, The *see* A MADONA DE CEDRO (1968).

Virgin of Nuremburg, The *see* LA VERGINE DI NORIMBERGA (1963).

Virgin of Paris, The *see* THE VIRGIN OF PARIS SOPHY OF KRAVONIA; OR (1920).

Virgin Playboy, The *see* DER KEUSCHE LEBEMANN (1952).

Virgin Soil Upturned *see* PODNYATAYA TZELINA (1940).

Virgin Soil Upturned *see* PODNYATAYA TSELINA (1959-61).

VIRGIN SOLDIERS, THE 1969 d: John Dexter. UKN., *The Virgin Soldiers*, Leslie Thomas, London 1966, Novel

VIRGIN, THE 1924 d: Alvin J. Neitz. USA., *The Virgin of San Blas*, Julio Sabello, Story

Virgin, The *see* PANNA (1940).

Virgin, The *see* O PARTHENOS (1967).

VIRGIN WITCH 1970 d: Ray Austin. UKN., *Virgin Witch*, Klaus Vogel, Novel

Virgin Youth *see* LE GRAND DADAIS (1967).

Virginia *see* THE PATH SHE CHOSE (1920).

VIRGINIA FLY IS DROWNING 1982 d: Mark Cullingham. UKN., *Virginia Fly Is Drowning*, Angela Huth, Novel

VIRGINIAN, THE 1914 d: Cecil B. de Mille. USA., *The Virginian*, Owen Wister, New York 1902, Novel

VIRGINIAN, THE 1923 d: Tom Forman. USA., *The Virginian*, Owen Wister, New York 1902, Novel

VIRGINIAN, THE 1929 d: Victor Fleming. USA., *The Virginian*, Owen Wister, New York 1902, Novel

VIRGINIAN, THE 1946 d: Stuart Gilmore. USA., *The Virginian*, Owen Wister, New York 1902, Novel

VIRGINIA'S HUSBAND 1928 d: Harry Hughes. UKN., *Virginia's Husband*, Florence Kilpatrick, Play

VIRGINIA'S HUSBAND 1934 d: MacLean Rogers. UKN., *Virginia's Husband*, Florence Kilpatrick, Play

VIRGINIE 1962 d: Jean Boyer. FRN., Michel Andre, Play

Virginity *see* PANENSTVI (1937).

VIRGINIUS 1909 d: J. Stuart Blackton. USA., *Virginius*, James Sheridan Knowles, 1820, Play

VIRGINIUS 1912 d: Hal Reid. USA., *Virginius*, James Sheridan Knowles, 1820, Play

Virgin's Guild of Kutna Hora *see* CECH PANEN KUTNOHORSKYCH (1938).

Virgins of Rome, The *see* LE VERGINI DI ROMA (1960).

VIRTUE ITS OWN REWARD 1914 d: Joseph de Grasse. USA., *Virtue Its Own Reward*, John Barton Oxford, Short Story

Virtue Runs Wild *see* DYDEN GAR AMOK (1967).

VIRTUOSO 1989 d: Tony Smith. UKN., *Virtuoso*, Michael Kerr, Brenda Ogdon, Book

Virtuous Dames of Pardubice, The *see* POCESTNE PANI PARDUBICKE (1944).

Virtuous Fool, A *see* BROADWAY GOLD (1923).

VIRTUOUS HUSBAND, THE 1931 d: Vin Moore. USA., *Apron Strings*, Dorrance Davis, 1930, Play

Virtuous Isadore, The *see* LE ROSIER DE MADAME HUSSON (1931).

Virtuous Isadore, The *see* LE ROSIER DE MADAME HUSSON (1950).

VIRTUOUS MODEL, THE 1919 d: Albert Capellani. USA., *Le Ruisseau*, Pierre Wolff, Paris 1907, Play

VIRTUOUS SIN, THE 1930 d: George Cukor, Louis J. Gasnier. USA., *A Tabornok*, Lajos Zilahy, Budapest 1928, Play

Virtuous Tramps, The *see* THE DEVIL'S BROTHER (1933).

VIRTUOUS VAMP, A 1919 d: David Kirkland. USA., *The Bachelor*, Clyde Fitch, New York 1909, Play

Virtuous Wife, The *see* MEN ARE LIKE THAT (1930).

Virtuous Wife, The *see* ARIZONA (1931).

VIRTUOUS WIVES 1918 d: George Loane Tucker. USA., *Virtuous Wives*, Owen Johnson, Boston 1917, Novel

Virus *see* FUKKATSU NO HI (1979).

VISAGE D'AIEULE 1926 d: Gaston Roudes. FRN., *Visage d'Aieule*, Marie Thierry, Short Story

VISAGES DE FEMMES 1938 d: Rene Guissart. FRN., *Visages de Femmes*, A. Germain, Michel Trebor, Play

Visconte Di Bragelonne, Il *see* LE VICOMTE DE BRAGELONNE (1954).

Viscount of Bragelonne, The *see* LE VICOMTE DE BRAGELONNE (1954).

Viscount, The *see* LE VICOMTE REGLE SES COMPTES (1967).

VISHNEVYJ SAD 1993 d: Anna ChernakovA. RSS., *The Cherry Orchard*, Anton Chekhov, Play

VISION BEAUTIFUL, THE 1912. USA., *The Legend Beautiful*, Henry Wadsworth Longfellow, Poem

VISION QUEST 1985 d: Harold Becker. USA., *Vision Quest*, Terry Davis, Novel

Visioni Dell'inferno *see* L' INFERNO (1911).

Visit, A *see* VIZITA (1952).

Visit, The *see* LA VISITA (1963).

Visit, The *see* DER BESUCH (1964).

VISIT TO A CHIEF'S SON 1974 d: Lamont Johnson. USA., *Visit to a Chief's Son*, Robert Halmi, Book

VISIT TO A SMALL PLANET 1960 d: Norman Taurog. USA., *Visit to a Small Planet*, Gore Vidal, 1956, Play

VISITA, LA 1963 d: Antonio Pietrangeli. ITL/FRN., *La Visita*, Carlo Cassola, 1942, Short Story

Visita Que No Llamo Al Timbre, La *see* LA VISITA QUE NO TOCO EL TIMBRE (1964).

VISITA QUE NO TOCO EL TIMBRE, LA 1964 d: Mario Camus. SPN., *La Visita Que No Toco El Timbre*, Joaquin Calvo Sotelo, 1951, Play

VISITACIONES DEL DIABLO, LAS 1968 d: Alberto Isaac. MXC., *Las Visitaciones Del Diablo*, Emilio Carballido, 1965, Novel

Visitations of the Devil, The *see* LAS VISITACIONES DEL DIABLO (1968).

Visiteur de la Nuit, Le *see* JUSTE AVANT LA NUIT (1971).

Visitor, The *see* OF UNKNOWN ORIGIN (1983).

Visitor Who Did Not Ring the Bell, The *see* LA VISITA QUE NO TOCO EL TIMBRE (1964).

VISITORS 1987 d: Piers Haggard. UKN., *Sufficient Carbohydrate*, Dennis Potter, Play

Visitors to New York *see* ZUIHOUDE GUIZU (1989).

Vistrel *see* VYSTREL (1967).

VITA AGRA, LA 1964 d: Carlo Lizzani. ITL., *La Vita Agra*, Luciano Bianciardi, Novel

Vita Avventurosa Di Milady, La *see* IL BOIA DI LILLA (1953).

Vita Col Figlio *see* INCOMPRESO (1966).

Vita Di Ligabue, La *see* LIGABUE (1978).

Vita (Il Dramma Di Una Sposa), Una *see* UNE VIE (1958).

VITA KATTEN, DEN 1950 d: Hasse Ekman. SWD., *Nycklar Till Okant Rum*, Walter Ljungquist, 1950, Novel

Vita, Una *see* UNE VIE (1958).

VITA VENDUTA, UNA 1977 d: Aldo Florio. ITL., *L' Antimonio*, Leonardo Sciasia, 1958, Short Story

VITA VIOLENTA, UNA 1962 d: Paolo Heusch, Brunello Rondi. ITL/FRN., *Una Vita Violenta*, Pier Paolo Pasolini, 1959, Novel

Vite Vendute *see* LE SALAIRE DE LA PEUR (1953).

Vitriers, Les *see* IL PICCOLO VETRAIO (1955).

VIUDA DE MONTIEL, LA 1979 d: Miguel Littin. MXC/VNZ/CLM., *La Viuda de Montiel*, Gabriel Garcia Marquez, 1962, Short Story

VIUDA ROMANTICA, UNA 1933 d: Louis King. USA., *Sueno de Una Noche de Agosto*, Gregorio Martinez Sierra, Madrid 1918, Play

Viva El Presidente *see* EL RECURSO DEL METODO (1978).

VIVA GRINGO 1966 d: Georg MarischkA. ITL/SPN/GRM., Karl Friedrich May, Novel

VIVA LA MUERTE 1970 d: Fernando Arrabal. FRN/TNS., *Baal Babylone*, Fernando Arrabal, 1959, Novel

VIVA LO IMPOSIBLE! 1957 d: Rafael Gil. SPN., *Viva Lo Imposible!*, Joaquin Calvo Sotelo, 1951, Play

VIVA MAX! 1969 d: Jerry Paris. USA., *Viva Max!*, James Lehrer, New York 1966, Novel

VIVA VILLA! 1934 d: Jack Conway, Howard Hawks (Uncredited). USA., *Viva Villa*, Edgcumb Pinchon, O. B. Stade, New York 1933, Book

VIVACIOUS LADY 1938 d: George Stevens. USA., *Vivacious Lady*, I. A. R. Wylie, 1936, Short Story

VIVANTE EPINGLE, LA 1921 d: Jacques Robert. FRN., *La Vivante Epingle*, Jean-Joseph Renaud, Novel

Vive Monsieur Blaireau *see* NI CONNU. NI VU (1958).

VIVEMENT DIMANCHE 1983 d: Francois Truffaut. FRN., *The Long Saturday Night*, Charles Williams, Novel

VIVIETTE 1918 d: Walter Edwards. USA., *Viviette*, William J. Locke, 1910, Novel

VIVO PER LA TUA MORTE 1968 d: Camillo Bazzoni. ITL., *Judas Gun*, Gordon D. Shirreffs, New York 1964, Novel

VIVRE 1928 d: Robert Boudrioz. FRN/GRM., *Le Createur*, Hans Muller, Play

VIVRE AU PARADIS 1998 d: Bourlem Guerdjou. FRN/BLG/ALG., Brahim Benaicha, Book

Vixen, The see **LA LUPA** (1953).

VIY 1967 d: Alexander Ptushko. USS., *Viy*, Nikolay Gogol, 1835, Short Story

Vizietto, Il see **LA CAGE AUX FOLLES** (1978).

Vizio E la Virtu, Il see **LE VICE ET LA VERTU** (1963).

VIZITA 1952 d: Jean Georgescu. RMN., *Vizita*, Ion Luca Caragiale, 1901, Short Story

Vizita see **VIZITA! POZOR** (1981).

VLASCHAARD, DE 1983 d: Jan Gruyaert. BLG/NTH., *De Vlaschaard*, Frank Lateur, 1908, Novel

Vlashins' Leaving see **PLECAREA VLASINILOR** (1982).

Vlashins' Return see **INTOARCEREA VLASINILOR** (1983).

VLCI JAMA 1958 d: Jiri Weiss. CZC., *Vlci Jama*, Jarmila Glazarova, 1941, Novel

VLUCHT REGENWULPEN, EEN 1981 d: Ate de Jong. NTH., *Een Vlucht Regenwulpen*, Maarten 't Hart, Novel

VO IMYA RODINI 1943 d: V. I. Pudovkin, Dimitri Vasiliev. USS., *Russkiye Lyudi*, Konstantin Simonov, 1942, Play

VOCATION, LA 1928 d: Jean Bertin. FRN., *La Vocation*, Jean d'Avesne, Novel

VOCE DELLA LUNA, LA 1990 d: Federico Fellini. ITL/FRN., *La Voce Della Luna*, Ermanno Cavazzoni, Novel

VOCE 'E NOTTE 1919 d: Oreste Gherardini. ITL., *Voce 'E Notte*, G. B. de Curtis, Eduardo Nicolardi, Song

Voci Della Luna, Le see **LA VOCE DELLA LUNA** (1990).

VOGELHANDLER, DER 1953 d: Arthur M. Rabenalt. GRM., *Der Vogelhandler*, L. Held, M. West, Carl Zeller, Vienna 1891, Operetta

VOGELHANDLER, DER 1962 d: Geza von CziffrA. GRM., *Der Vogelhandler*, L. Held, M. West, Vienna 1891, Operetta

Vogelod Castle see **SCHLOSS VOGELOD** (1921).

Vogelod Castle see **SCHLOSS VOGELOD** (1936).

Vogelod: the Haunted Castle see **SCHLOSS VOGELOD** (1921).

VOGELVRIJ 1916 d: Maurits H. Binger. NTH/UKN., *Sparrows*, Horace W. C. Newte, 1909, Novel

VOGLIA MATTA, LA 1962 d: Luciano Salce. ITL., *Una Ragazza Di Nome Francesca*, Enrico Stella, Short Story

VOICE FROM THE FIREPLACE, A 1910. USA., *A Voice from the Fireplace*, Guy de Maupassant, Short Story

Voice from the Grave see **THE SIN OF NORA MORAN** (1933).

VOICE FROM THE MINARET, THE 1923 d: Frank Lloyd. USA., *The Voice from the Minaret*, Robert Hichens, London 1919, Play

VOICE IN THE DARK, A 1921 d: Frank Lloyd. USA., *A Voice in the Dark*, Ralph E. Dyar, New York 1919, Play

VOICE IN THE FOG, THE 1915 d: Frank Reicher. USA., *The Voice in the Fog*, Harold MacGrath, Indianapolis 1915, Novel

Voice in the Night, A see **WANTED FOR MURDER** (1946).

VOICE OF BUGLE ANN, THE 1936 d: Richard Thorpe. USA., *The Voice of Bugle Ann*, MacKinlay Kantor, New York 1935, Novel

Voice of Life, The see **TWO AGAINST THE WORLD** (1936).

Voice of Terror, The see **SHERLOCK HOLMES AND THE VOICE OF TERROR** (1942).

VOICE OF THE HEART 1989 d: Tony Wharmby. USA., *Voice of the Heart*, Barbara Taylor Bradford, Novel

VOICE OF THE HURRICANE 1964 d: George Fraser. USA., *The Hurricane*, Peter Howard, Alan Thornhill, London 1960, Novel

Voice of the Moon, The see **LA VOCE DELLA LUNA** (1990).

VOICE OF THE TURTLE, THE 1947 d: Irving Rapper. USA., *The Voice of the Turtle*, John Van Druten, New York 1943, Play

VOICES 1973 d: Kevin Billington. UKN., *Voices*, Richard Lortz, Play

VOICES IN THE GARDEN 1992 d: Pierre Boutron. UKN/FRN., *Voices in the Garden*, Dirk Bogarde, Short Story

Voices of the Moon see **LA VOCE DELLA LUNA** (1990).

Voices Within see **VOICES WITHIN: THE LIVES OF TRUDDI CHASE** (1990).

VOICES WITHIN: THE LIVES OF TRUDDI CHASE 1990 d: Lamont Johnson. USA., *When Rabbit Howls*, E. Jack Neuman, Book

VOIE SANS DISQUE, LA 1933 d: Leon Poirier. FRN., *La Voie Sans Disque*, Andre Armandy, Novel

VOILE DU BONHEUR, LE 1910 d: Albert Capellani. FRN., *Le Voile du Bonheur*, Georges Clemenceau, Play

VOILE DU BONHEUR, LE 1923 d: Edouard-Emile Violet. FRN., *Le Voile du Bonheur*, Georges Clemenceau, Play

VOINA I MIR 1967 d: Sergei Bondarchuk. USS., *Voyna I Mir*, Lev Nikolayevich Tolstoy, 1863-69, Novel

VOIR VENISE ET CREVER 1966 d: Andre Versini. FRN/GRM/ITL., *Mission to Venice*, James Hadley Chase, Novel

VOIX DE L'OCEAN, LA 1922 d: Gaston Roudes. FRN., *La Voix de l'Ocean*, Georges G. Toudouze, Novel

Voix Humaine, La see **AMORE** (1948).

VOJNARKA 1936 d: Vladimir Borsky. CZC., *Vojnarka*, Alois Jirasek, Play

VOL ETRANGE, UN 1919 d: Henri Desfontaines. FRN., *Un Vol Etrange*, H. Heywood, Novel

VOL, LE 1925 d: Robert Peguy. FRN., *L' Amour Qui Doute*, R. Florigny, Charles Veyre, Novel

VOL SUPREME, LE 1917 d: Rene Plaissetty. FRN., *La Vol Supreme*, Valentin Mandelstamm, Short Story

VOLATA, LA 1919 d: Gaston Ravel. ITL., *La Volata*, Dario Niccodemi, 1918, Play

VOLCANO 1926 d: William K. Howard. USA., *Martinique*, Laurence Eyre, New York 1920, Play

VOLEGENY 1982 d: Laszlo Vamos. HNG., *Volegeny*, Erno Szep, 1922, Play

VOLEUR DE FEMMES, LE 1936 d: Abel Gance. FRN., *Le Voleur de Femmes*, Pierre Frondaie, Novel

VOLEUR DE FEMMES, LE 1963 d: Willy Rozier. FRN., *Le Roi Des Montagnes*, Edmond About, 1857, Short Story

VOLEUR DE VIE 1998 d: Yves Angelo. FRN., *Voleur de Vie*, Steinunn Sigurdardottir, Novel

VOLEUR, LE 1914 d: Adrien Caillard. FRN., *Le Voleur*, Henri Bernstein, Paris 1907, Play

VOLEUR, LE 1933 d: Maurice Tourneur. FRN., *Le Voleur*, Henri Bernstein, Paris 1907, Play

VOLEUR, LE 1967 d: Louis Malle. FRN/ITL., *Le Voleur*, Georges Darien, Paris 1898, Novel

VOLEURS DE GLOIRE, LES 1926 d: Pierre Marodon. FRN., *Die Frau Des Kunstlers*, Frantz Kaver Kappus, Novel

VOLEUSE D'ENFANTS, LA 1912 d: Georges DenolA. FRN., *La Voleuse d'Enfants*, Eugene Grange, Lambert Thiboust, Play

VOLGA BOATMAN, THE 1926 d: Cecil B. de Mille. USA., *The Volga Boatman*, Konrad Bercovici, New York 1926, Novel

Volga En Feu see **VOLGA EN FLAMMES** (1933).

VOLGA EN FLAMMES 1933 d: Victor Tourjansky. FRN/CZC., Alexander Pushkin, Novel

Volha V Plamenech see **VOLGA EN FLAMMES** (1933).

VOLKI I OVSKY 1952 d: Vladimir Sukhobokov. USS., *Volki I Ovsty*, Alexander Ostrovsky, 1875, Play

VOLKSFEIND, EIN 1937 d: Hans Steinhoff. GRM., *En Folkefiende*, Henrik Ibsen, 1882, Play

Vollmacht Zum Mord see **PERMISSION TO KILL** (1975).

VOLONTE 1916 d: Henri Pouctal. FRN., *Volonte*, Georges Ohnet, Novel

VOLPONE 1940 d: Maurice Tourneur. FRN., *Volpone*, Ben Jonson, 1607, Play

VOLTAIRE 1933 d: John G. Adolfi. USA., E. Lawrence Dudley, George Gibbs, Novel

VOLUNTAD! 1928 d: Mario Roncoroni. SPN., *A Orillas Del Jucar*, Agustin Caballero, Story

VOLUNTEER ORGANIST, THE 1913?. USA., *The Volunteer Organist*, William B. Gray, New York 1902, Novel

VOLVORETA 1976 d: Jose Antonio Nieves Conde. SPN., *Volvoreta*, Wenceslao Fernandez Florez, 1917, Novel

VOM ANDEREN STERN 1982 d: Petra Haffter. GRM., Peter Carey, Short Story

VOM SCHICKSAL VERWEHT 1942 d: Nunzio MalasommA. GRM., *Dschungel*, Joseph Maria Franck, Play

VON DER LIEBE BESIEGT 1956 d: Luis Trenker. GRM., *Schicksal Am Matterhorn*, Luis Trenker, Novel

VON DER LIEBE REDEN WIR SPATER 1953 d: Karl Anton. GRM., *Von Der Liebe Reden Wir Spater*, Frank F. Braun, Novel

Von Der Wolke Zum Widerstand see **DALLA NUBE ALLA RESISTENZA** (1979).

Von Liebe Reden Wir Spater see **VON DER LIEBE REDEN WIR SPATER** (1953).

VON RYAN'S EXPRESS 1965 d: Mark Robson. USA., *Von Ryan's Express*, David Westheimer, New York 1964, Novel

Voodoo see **DRUMS O' VOODOO** (1934).

Voodoo Devil Drums see **DRUMS O' VOODOO** (1934).

Voodoo Drums see **DRUMS O' VOODOO** (1934).

Voodoo Mystery see **THE CARIBBEAN MYSTERY** (1945).

Voodoo Village see **THE SORCERER'S VILLAGE** (1958).

Voor Eer En Deugd see **LA RENZONI** (1916).

VOR DEN VATERN STERBEN DIE SOHNE 1981 d: Claudia Holldack. GRM., Thomas Brasch, Story

VOR SONNENAUFGANG 1976 d: Oswald Dopke. GRM., *Vor Sonnenaufgang*, Gerhart Hauptmann, 1889, Play

VOR SONNENUNTERGANG 1956 d: Gottfried Reinhardt. GRM., *Vor Sonnenuntergang*, Gerhart Hauptmann, Berlin 1932, Play

VORHANG FALLT, DER 1939 d: Georg Jacoby. GRM., *Schuss Im Rampenlicht*, Paul Vand Der Hurck, Play

VORSTADTKROKODILE 1978 d: Wolfgang Becker. GRM., *Vorstadtkrokodile*, Max von Der Grun, 1976, Novel

VORSTADTVARIETE 1934 d: Werner Hochbaum. AUS., *Vorstadtvariete*, Felix Salten, Play

VORTEX, THE 1927 d: Adrian Brunel. UKN., *The Vortex*, Noel Coward, London 1924, Play

VORUNTERSUCHUNG 1931 d: Robert Siodmak. GRM., *Voruntersuchung*, Max Alsberg, Ernst Hesse, Play

VOSEMNADCATYJ GOD 1958 d: Grigori Roshal. USS., *Khozhdeniye Po Mukam*, Alexsey Nikolayevich Tolstoy, 1922-45, Novel

Vosemnadtsaty God see **VOSEMNADCATYJ GOD** (1958).

VOSHOZDENIE NA FUDZIJAMU 1988 d: Bolotbek Shamshiev. USS., *Voskhozhdeniye Na Fudziyamu*, Chingiz Aimatov, Kaltai Mukhamedzhanov, 1978, Play

Voskohzhdeniye Na Fudziyama see **VOSHOZDENIE NA FUDZIJAMU** (1988).

VOSKRESENIE 1961 d: Mikhail Schweitzer. USS., *Voskreseniye*, Lev Nikolayevich Tolstoy, Moscow 1899, Novel

VOSTANIYE RYBAKOV 1934 d: Erwin Piscator. USS., *Der Aufstand Der Fischer von Santa Barbara*, Anna Seghers, 1928, Novel

Vote, The see **IL VOTO** (1951).

VOTO, IL 1907 d: Roberto Troncone. ITL., *'O Voto*, Salvatore Di Giacomo, 1889, Play

VOTO, IL 1918 d: Mario Gargiulo. ITL., *'O Voto*, Salvatore Di Giacomo, 1889, Play

VOTO, IL 1951 d: Mario Bonnard. ITL., *'O Voto*, Salvatore Di Giacomo, 1889, Play

VOTRE SOURIRE 1934 d: Pierre Caron, Monty Banks. FRN., *Votre Sourire*, Andre Birabeau, Georges Dolley, Play

VOUIVRE, LA 1988 d: Georges Wilson. FRN., *La Vouivre*, Marcel Ayme, Novel

VOULEZ-VOUS DANSER AVEC MOI? 1960 d: Michel Boisrond. FRN/ITL., *Valse Blonde*, Kelley Roos, Novel

Voulez-Vous Mourir Avec Moi? see **DER KUSS DES TIGERS** (1989).

VOUS INTERESSEZ-VOUS A LA CHOSE? 1973 d: Jacques Baratier. FRN/GRM., *Vous Interessez-Vous a la Chose?*, Claude Eymouche, Novel

VOUS N'AVEZ RIEN A DECLARER? 1916. FRN., *Vous N'avez Rien a Declarer?*, Maurice Hennequin, Pierre Veber, Play

VOUS N'AVEZ RIEN A DECLARER? 1936 d: Leo Joannon, Yves Allegret. FRN., *Vous N'avez Rien a Declarer?*, Maurice Hennequin, Pierre Veber, Play

VOUS N'AVEZ RIEN A DECLARER? 1959 d: Clement Duhour. FRN., *Vous N'avez Rien a Declarer?*, Maurice Hennequin, Pierre Veber, Play

WALL OF NOISE 1963 d: Richard Wilson. USA., *Wall of Noise*, Daniel Michael Stein, New York 1960, Novel

Wall, The *see* **LA MURALLA** (1958).

WALLABY JIM OF THE ISLANDS 1937 d: Charles Lamont. USA., *Albert Richard Wetjen*, Short Story

WALLENSTEIN 1962 d: Franz Peter Wirth. GRM., *Wallenstein*, Friedrich von Schiller, 1800, Play

Waller's Last Run *see* **WALLERS LETZTER GANG** (1988).

WALLERS LETZTER GANG 1988 d: Christian Wagner. GRM., *Wallers Letzter Gang*, Thomas Mauch, Novel

Wallet *see* **PI BAO** (1956).

WALLFLOWER 1948 d: Frederick de CordovA. USA., *Wallflower*, Reginald Denham, Mary Orr, New York 1944, Play

WALLFLOWERS 1928 d: James Leo Meehan. USA., *Wallflowers*, Temple Bailey, Philadelphia 1927, Novel

Wallnerbub, Der *see* **DAS JAHR DES HERRN** (1950).

WALLOP, THE 1921 d: John Ford. USA., *The Girl He Left Behind Him*, Eugene Manlove Rhodes, Story

WALLOPING WALLACE 1924 d: Richard Thorpe. USA., *A Man of Action*, Robert J. Horton, Short Story

WALLS 1984 d: Thomas Shandel. CND., *Walls*, Christian Bruyere, Play

WALLS CAME TUMBLING DOWN, THE 1946 d: Lothar Mendes. USA., *The Walks Came Tumbling Down*, Jo Eisinger, Novel

WALLS OF GOLD 1933 d: Kenneth MacKennA. USA., *Walls of Gold*, Kathleen Norris, New York 1933, Novel

WALLS OF JERICHO 1948 d: John M. Stahl. USA., *Walls of Jericho*, Paul I. Wellman, 1947, Novel

WALLS OF JERICHO, THE 1914 d: Lloyd B. Carleton. USA., *The Walls of Jericho*, Alfred Sutro, New York 1905, Play

WALLS OF PREJUDICE 1920 d: Charles Calvert. UKN., *Break Down the Walls*, Mrs. Alexander Grossman, Play

Wally and the Vultures *see* **DIE GEIERWALLY** (1940).

WALLY, LA 1932 d: Guido Brignone. ITL., *Die Geierwally*, Wilhelmine von Hillern, Novel

WALPURGIS NIGHT 1932 d: Howard Higgin. USA., *Faust*, Johann Wolfgang von Goethe, 1808-32, Play

WALSUNGENBLUT 1964 d: Rolf Thiele. GRM., *Ein Gluck*, Thomas Mann, 1904, Short Story, *Walsungenblut*, Thomas Mann, 1921, Short Story

WALTER 1982 d: Stephen Frears. UKN., *Winter Doves*, David Cook, Novel

Waltz of Sex *see* **VINDINGEVALS** (1968).

Waltz of the Gorilla, The *see* **LA VALSE DU GORILLE** (1959).

WALTZ OF THE TOREADORS 1962 d: John Guillermin. UKN., *La Valse Des Toreadors*, Jean Anouilh, Paris 1952, Play

WALTZ TIME 1933 d: Wilhelm Thiele. UKN., *Die Fledermaus*, Henri Meilhac, Johann Strauss, Vienna 1874, Operetta

WALTZES FROM VIENNA 1933 d: Alfred Hitchcock. UKN., *Walzerkreig*, Ernst Marischka, Heinz Reichart, Play

WAN SHUI-QIAN SHAN 1959 d: Cheng Yin, Hua Chun. CHN., *Wan Shui-Qian Shan*, Chen Qitong, Play

WANDA LA PECCATRICE 1952 d: Duilio Coletti. ITL/FRN., Aldo de Benedetti, Short Story

Wanda la Pecheresse *see* **WANDA LA PECCATRICE** (1952).

WANDA (THE SATANIC HYPNOTIST) 1969 d: Greg Corarito. USA., *The Sadistic Hypnotist*, Greg Corarito

WANDA WARENINE 1917 d: Riccardo Tolentino. ITL., *I Racconti Della Piccola Russia*, Alexander Pushkin

WANDERER OF THE WASTELAND 1924 d: Irvin V. Willat. USA., *The Wanderer of the Wasteland*, Zane Grey, New York 1923, Novel

WANDERER OF THE WASTELAND 1945 d: Edward Killy, Wallace A. Grissell. USA., *The Wanderer of the Wasteland*, Zane Grey, New York 1923, Novel

WANDERER OF THE WASTELAND, THE 1934 d: Otho Lovering. USA., *The Wanderer of the Wasteland*, Zane Grey, New York 1923, Novel

WANDERER, THE 1926 d: Raoul Walsh. USA., *The Wanderer*, Maurice V. Samuels, New York 1917, Play

Wanderer, The *see* **LE GRAND MEAULNES** (1967).

Wanderers *see* **ZBEHOVIA A PUTNICI** (1968).

Wanderers *see* **LANDSTRYKERE** (1988).

Wanderer's Notebook, A *see* **HOROKI** (1962).

Wanderers, The *see* **I GIROVAGHI** (1956).

WANDERERS, THE 1979 d: Philip Kaufman. USA., *The Wanderers*, Richard Price, Novel

WANDERING DAUGHTERS 1923 d: James Young. USA., *Wandering Daughters*, Dana Burnet, 1922, Short Story

WANDERING FOOTSTEPS 1925 d: Phil Rosen. USA., *A Wise Son*, Charles Sherman, Indianapolis 1914, Novel

WANDERING JEW, THE 1923 d: Maurice Elvey. UKN., *Le Juif Errant*, Eugene Sue, 1845, Novel

WANDERING JEW, THE 1933 d: Maurice Elvey. UKN., *Le Juif Errant*, Eugene Sue, 1845, Novel

Wandering Jew, The *see* **L' EBREO ERRANTE** (1947).

Wandering Soul, The *see* **ASHWATHAMA** (1979).

Wandering With the Moon *see* **VANDRING MED MANEN** (1945).

Wanderlust *see* **MARY JANE'S PA** (1935).

Wandsbek Axe, The *see* **DAS BEIL VON WANDSBEK** (1951).

WANG JIANG TING 1958 d: Zhou Feng. CHN., *Wang Jiang Ting*, Guan Hanqing, c1230, Play

WANG XIFENG DANAO NING-KUOFU 1939 d: Yueh Feng. CHN., *Hong Lou Meng*, Cao Zhan, c1750-92, Novel

WANING SEX, THE 1926 d: Robert Z. Leonard. USA., *The Waning Sex*, Fanny Hatton, Frederic Hatton, 1923, Play

WANREN QINGFU 1996 d: T'ao Shu-HuA. TWN., *Wanren Qingfu*, Yuan Ch'iung-Ch'iung, Novel

Wanted *see* **PURSUED** (1934).

WANTED 1937 d: George King. UKN., *Wanted*, Brock Williams, Play

Wanted *see* **FOUR FACES WEST** (1948).

WANTED - A HUSBAND 1919 d: Lawrence C. Windom. USA., *Enter d'Arcy*, Samuel Hopkins Adams, 1917, Short Story

Wanted -a Blemish *see* **AN AMATEUR DEVIL** (1920).

WANTED, A BOY 1924 d: Thomas Bentley. UKN., *Wanted - a Boy*, W. Pett Ridge, Short Story

Wanted a Wife *see* **THE ELDER MISS BLOSSOM** (1918).

WANTED AT HEADQUARTERS 1920 d: Stuart Paton. USA., *Kate Plus Ten*, Edgar Wallace, London 1919, Novel

Wanted By Scotland Yard *see* **DANGEROUS FINGERS** (1937).

WANTED FOR MURDER 1946 d: Lawrence Huntington. UKN., *Wanted for Murder*, Terence de Marney, Percy Robinson, London 1937, Play

Wanted Men *see* **WOLVES** (1930).

Wanted Men *see* **VALLEY OF WANTED MEN** (1935).

Wanted Men *see* **FIGHTING COWARD** (1935).

Wanting Weight, The *see* **DAS FALSCHE GEWICHT** (1970).

Wanton Contessa, The *see* **SENSO** (1954).

Wanton Countess, The *see* **SENSO** (1954).

Wanton Journey *see* **SHIN SANTO JUYAKU: TEISHU KYO IKU NO MAKI** (1961).

Wanton of Spain -la Celestina, The *see* **LA CELESTINA** (1968).

Wanton of Spain, The *see* **LA CELESTINA** (1968).

War Along the Stage Trail *see* **STAGECOACH WAR** (1940).

War and a Man, The *see* **NINGEN NO JOKEN I** (1959).

WAR AND LOVE 1985 d: Moshe Mizrahi. USA., *The Survivor*, Jack P. Eisner, Book

WAR AND PEACE 1956 d: King Vidor, Mario Soldati. USA/ITL., *Voyna I Mir*, Lev Nikolayevich Tolstoy, 1863-69, Novel

WAR AND PEACE 1963 d: Silvio Narizzano. UKN., *Voyna I Mir*, Lev Nikolayevich Tolstoy, 1863-69, Novel

War and Peace *see* **VOINA I MIR** (1967).

WAR AND PEACE 1972 d: John Howard Davies. UKN., *Voyna I Mir*, Lev Nikolayevich Tolstoy, 1863-69, Novel

War and Peace Season *see* **OH! WHAT A LOVELY WAR** (1969).

WAR AND REMEMBRANCE 1988 d: Dan Curtis. USA., *War and Remembrance*, Herman Wouk, Novel

WAR AT HOME, THE 1996 d: Emilio Estevez. USA., *Homefront*, James Duff, Play

WAR AT WALLAROO MANSIONS, THE 1922 d: Kenneth Graeme. UKN., Derwent Nicol, Short Story

War Begins in Cuba, The *see* **LA GUERRA EMPIEZA EN CUBA** (1957).

WAR BETWEEN MEN AND WOMEN, THE 1972 d: Melville Shavelson. USA., James Thurber, Story

WAR BETWEEN THE TATES, THE 1977 d: Lee Philips. USA., *The War Between the Tates*, Alison Lurie, Novel

WAR BRIDES 1916 d: Herbert Brenon. USA., *War Brides*, Marion Craig Wentworth, Play

War Correspondent *see* **THE STORY OF G.I. JOE** (1945).

WAR GAME, THE 1966 d: Peter Watkins. UKN., *The War Game*, Peter Watkins, 1967, Play

War Head *see* **ON THE FIDDLE** (1961).

War in the Dark *see* **THE MYSTERIOUS LADY** (1928).

War in the Highlands, The *see* **LA GUERRE DANS LE HAUT-PAYS** (1999).

War Lord *see* **WEST OF SHANGHAI** (1937).

WAR LORD, THE 1965 d: Franklin J. Schaffner. USA., *The Lovers*, Leslie Stevens, New York 1956, Play

WAR LOVER, THE 1962 d: Philip Leacock. UKN/USA., *The War Lover*, John Hersey, New York 1959, Novel

War of Insects *see* **KONCHU DAISENSO** (1968).

War of Oxen, The *see* **DER OCHSENKRIEG** (1920).

War of the Buttons *see* **LA GUERRE DES BOUTONS** (1961).

WAR OF THE BUTTONS, THE 1994 d: John Roberts. UKN/FRN/IRL., *La Guerre Des Boutons*, Louis Pergaud, Paris 1912, Novel

War of the Planets *see* **THIS ISLAND EARTH** (1955).

WAR OF THE ROSES 1989 d: Danny Devito. USA., *War of the Roses*, Warren Adler, Novel

War of the Trojans, The *see* **LA LEGGENDA DI ENEA** (1962).

WAR OF THE WILDCATS 1943 d: Albert S. Rogell. USA., *War of the Wildcats*, Thomas Burtis, Short Story

WAR OF THE WORLDS, THE 1953 d: Byron Haskin. USA., *War of the Worlds*, H. G. Wells, 1897, Novel

WAR OF WARS; OR, THE FRANCO-GERMAN INVASION, THE 1914 d: Will S. Davis. USA., *The Conquerors*, Paul M. Potter, New York 1898, Play

War of Wars, The *see* **THE FRANCO-GERMAN INVASION, THE WAR OF WARS; OR**, (1914).

War Starts in Cuba, The *see* **LA GUERRA EMPIEZA EN CUBA** (1957).

WAR WAGON, THE 1967 d: Burt Kennedy. USA., *Badman*, Clair Huffaker, New York 1957, Novel

WAR ZONE, THE 1999 d: Tim Roth. UKN., *The War Zone*, Alexander Stuart, 1989, Novel

Warbonnet *see* **THE SAVAGE** (1952).

WARE CASE, THE 1917 d: Walter West. UKN., *The Ware Case*, George Pleydell Bancroft, London 1915, Play

WARE CASE, THE 1928 d: Manning Haynes. UKN., *The Ware Case*, George Pleydell Bancroft, London 1915, Play

WARE CASE, THE 1938 d: Robert Stevenson. UKN., *The Ware Case*, George Pleydell Bancroft, London 1915, Play

Warehouse *see* **MOJU** (1969).

War-Gods of the Deep *see* **THE CITY UNDER THE SEA** (1965).

WARLOCK 1959 d: Edward Dmytryk. USA., *Warlock*, Oakley Hall, 1958, Novel

Warlords of the Deep *see* **THE CITY UNDER THE SEA** (1965).

WARM CORNER, A 1930 d: Victor Saville. UKN., *A Warm Corner*, Franz Robert Arnold, Ernst Bach, Play

WARM IN THE BUD 1969 d: Rudolph Caringi. USA., *Fruhlings Erwachen*, Frank Wedekind, 1891, Play

Warm Wind *see* **GARAM HAWA** (1973).

WARN LONDON 1934 d: T. Hayes Hunter. UKN., *Warn London*, Denison Clift, Novel

WARN THAT MAN 1943 d: Lawrence Huntington. UKN., *Warn That Man*, Vernon Sylvaine, Play

WARNED OFF 1928 d: Walter West. UKN., *Warned Off*, Robert Sevier, Novel

Warning from Space *see* **UCHUJIN TOKYO NI ARAWARU** (1956).

WARNING SHOT 1967 d: Buzz Kulik. USA., *711 - Officer Needs Help*, Whit Masterson, New York 1965, Novel

WARNING TO WANTONS 1949 d: Donald B. Wilson. UKN., *Warning to Wantons*, Mary Mitchell, Novel

WARREN CASE, THE 1934 d: Walter Summers. UKN., *The Last Chance*, Arnold Ridley, Play

WARRENS OF VIRGINIA 1915 d: Cecil B. de Mille. USA., *The Warrens of Virginia*, William C. de Mille, New York 1907, Play

WARRENS OF VIRGINIA, THE 1924 d: Elmer Clifton. USA., *The Warrens of Virginia*, William C. de Mille, New York 1907, Play

Warrior Children *see* KRIGERNES BORN (1979).

WARRIOR GAP 1925 d: Alvin J. Neitz. USA., *Warrior Gap; a Story of the Sioux Outbreak of '68*, Gen. Charles King, New York 1897, Novel

Warrior Women *see* LE VERGINI DI ROMA (1960).

WARRIOR'S HUSBAND, THE 1933 d: Walter Lang. USA., *The Warrior's Husband*, Julian Thompson, New York 1932, Play

Warriors of Faith *see* JAN ROHAC Z DUBE (1947).

Warrior's Rest *see* LE REPOS DU GUERRIER (1962).

WARRIORS, THE 1979 d: Walter Hill. USA., *The Warriors*, Sol Yurick, Novel

Warrior's Tragedy, The *see* BIAN CHENG LANG ZI (1993).

WARS, THE 1983 d: Robin Philips. CND/GRM., *The Wars*, Timothy Findley, Novel

WARSCHAUER ZITADELLE, DIE 1930 d: Jacob Fleck, Luise Fleck. GRM., *Tamten*, Gabriele Zapolska, Play

WARSCHAUER ZITADELLE, DIE 1938 d: Fritz Peter Buch. GRM., *Tamten*, Gabriele Zapolska, Play

WARTEZIMMER ZUM JENSEITS 1964 d: Alfred Vohrer. GRM., *James Hadley Chase*, Novel

Warum Bell Herr Bobikow? *see* CUORE DI CANE (1975).

WARUM LUGST DU, ELISABETH? 1944 d: Fritz Kirchhoff. GRM., *Sommerrausch*, J. Schneider-Foerstl, Novel

WARUM LUGT FRAULEIN KATHE? 1935 d: Georg Jacoby. GRM., *Warum Lugt Fraulein Kathe?*, Curt J. Braun, Novel

WAS DIE SCHWALBE SANG 1956 d: Geza von Bolvary. GRM., *Immensee*, Theodor Storm, 1852, Novel

Was Eine Frau Im Fruhling Traumt *see* LEICHTE MUSE (1941).

Was Eltern Nicht Fur Moglich Halten *see* SCHULMADCHEN-REPORT 1. TEIL - WAS ELTERN NICHT FUR MOGLICH HALTEN (1970).

WAS ISCH DENN I MYM HAREM LOS? 1937 d: Rene Guggenheim. SWT., *Die Flucht in Den Harem*, Paul Altheer, Zurich 1927, Play

WAS MACHT PAPA DENN IN ITALIEN? 1961 d: Hans D. Schwarze. GRM., *Was macht Papa Denn in Italien?*, Doris Eicke, Novel

WAS SHE A VAMPIRE? 1915 d: Albert W. Hale. USA., *Was She a Vampire?*, George Edwardes Hall, Story

WAS SHE GUILTY? 1922 d: George A. Beranger. UKN/NTH., *Haar Groote Dag*, D. Van Veen, Novel

WAS SHE JUSTIFIED? 1922 d: Walter West. UKN., *The Pruning Knife*, Andrew Soutar, Maud Williamson, Play

Was She to Blame? *see* SOULS THAT MEET IN THE DARK WAS SHE TO BLAME? OR (1915).

WAS SHE TO BLAME? OR, SOULS THAT MEET IN THE DARK 1915. USA., *Was She to Blame?; Or Souls That Meet in the Dark*, Eugen Illes, Book

WAS WILL BRIGITTE? 1940 d: Paul Martin. GRM., *Das Verzauberte Madchen*, Martin Doerhoff, Play

WASH, THE 1988 d: Michael Toshiyuki Uno. USA., *The Wash*, Philip Kan Gotanda, Play

WASHINGTON: BEHIND CLOSED DOORS 1977 d: Gary Nelson. USA., *The Company*, John Ehrlichman, Book

WASHINGTON MASQUERADE, THE 1932 d: Charles J. Brabin. USA., *La Griffe*, Henri Bernstein, Paris 1906, Play

WASHINGTON MELODRAMA 1941 d: S. Sylvan Simon. USA., *Washington Melodrama*, L. Du Rocher MacPherson, Play

WASHINGTON MERRY-GO-ROUND 1932 d: James Cruze. USA., *Washington Merry-Go-Round*, Robert Sharon Allen, Drew Pearson, New York 1931, Book

Washington Show, The *see* THE WASHINGTON MASQUERADE (1932).

WASHINGTON SQUARE 1997 d: Agnieszka Holland. USA., *Washington Square*, Henry James, 1881, Novel

Washington Whirlpool *see* THE WASHINGTON MASQUERADE (1932).

WASSER FUR CANITOGA 1939 d: Herbert Selpin. GRM., *Wasser Fur Canitoga*, Hans Rehfisch, Play

Wastrel, The *see* IL RELITTO (1961).

WAT EEUWIG BLIJFT 1920 d: Maurits H. Binger, B. E. Doxat-Pratt. NTH/UKN., *Oranges and Lemons*, Mrs. D. C. F. Harding, 1916, Novel

WAT ZIEN IK 1971 d: Paul Verhoeven. NTH., *Wat Zien Ik*, Albert Mol, Novel

WATASHI GA SUTETA ONNA 1969 d: Kirio UrayamA. JPN., *Watashi Ga Suteta Onna*, Shusaku Endo, Novel

Watch Beverley *see* WATCH BEVERLY (1932).

WATCH BEVERLY 1932 d: Arthur Maude. UKN., *Watch Beverly*, Cyril Campion, 1930, Play

WATCH IT SAILOR! 1961 d: Wolf RillA. UKN., *Watch It Sailor!*, Falkland Cary, Philip King, London 1960, Play

WATCH ON THE RHINE 1943 d: Herman Shumlin, Vincent Sherman. USA., *Watch on the Rhine*, Lillian Hellman, New York 1941, Play

Watch Out, the Doctors' Rounds *see* VIZITA! POZOR (1981).

Watch, The *see* BIAO (1949).

WATCH YOUR STERN 1960 d: Gerald Thomas. UKN., *Something About a Sailor*, Earle Couttie, Play

WATCH YOUR WIFE 1926 d: Svend Gade. USA., *Watch Your Wife*, Gosta Segercrantz, Story

WATCHER IN THE WOODS, THE 1980 d: John Hough. UKN/USA., *The Watcher in the Woods*, Florence Engel Randall, Novel

WATCHERS 1988 d: Jon Hess. CND/USA., *Watchers*, Dean R. Koontz, Novel

WATCHERS REBORN 1998 d: John Carl Buechler. USA., *Watchers Reborn*, Dean R. Koontz, Novel

Watchmaker of St. Paul, The *see* L' HORLOGER DE ST. PAUL (1973).

Watchman No.47 *see* HLIDAC C. 47 (1937).

WATER BABIES; OR, THE LITTLE CHIMNEY SWEEP, THE 1907 d: Percy Stow. UKN., *The Water Babies*, Charles Kingsley, 1863, Novel

WATER BABIES, THE 1979 d: Lionel Jeffries. UKN/PLN., *The Water Babies*, Charles Kingsley, 1863, Novel

Water for Canitoga *see* WASSER FUR CANITOGA (1939).

Water for Chocolate *see* COMO AGUA PARA CHOCOLATE (1991).

WATER GIPSIES, THE 1932 d: Maurice Elvey. UKN., *The Water Gipsies*, A. P. Herbert, London 1930, Novel

WATER HOLE, THE 1928 d: F. Richard Jones. USA., *The Water Hole*, Zane Grey, 1927, Serial Story

Water Magician, The *see* TAKI NO SHIRAITO (1933).

Water Nymph *see* MAN OF THE MOMENT (1935).

WATER, WATER, EVERYWHERE 1920 d: Clarence Badger. USA., *Billy Fortune and the Hard Proposition*, William Rheem Lighton, Englewood Cliffs, Nj.1912, Novel

WATERFRONT 1939 d: Terry O. Morse. USA., *Blindspot*, Kenyon Nicholson, Play

WATERFRONT 1950 d: Michael Anderson. UKN., *Waterfront*, John Brophy, Novel

Water-Front *see* THE PAINTED WOMAN (1932).

Waterfront Women *see* WATERFRONT (1950).

WATERLAND 1992 d: Stephen Gyllenhaal. UKN., *Waterland*, Graham Swift, Novel

WATERLOO BRIDGE 1931 d: James Whale. USA., *Waterloo Bridge*, R. E. Sherwood, New York 1930, Play

WATERLOO BRIDGE 1940 d: Mervyn Leroy. USA., *Waterloo Bridge*, R. E. Sherwood, New York 1930, Play

Waters Run Deep *see* LAS AGUAS BAJAN NEGRAS (1948).

WATERSHIP DOWN 1978 d: Martin Rosen. UKN., *Watership Down*, Richard Adams, Novel

WATUSI 1959 d: Kurt Neumann. USA., *King Solomon's Mines*, H. Rider Haggard, London 1885, Novel

Wave of Unrest, A *see* YI CHANG FENG BO (1954).

Waves, The *see* GOLVEN (1982).

WAX MODEL, THE 1917 d: E. Mason Hopper. USA., *The Wax Model*, George Vere Tyler, 1915, Short Story

WAY DOWN EAST 1920 d: D. W. Griffith. USA., *Annie Laurie*, Lottie Blair Parker, Chicago 1897, Play

WAY DOWN EAST 1935 d: Henry King. USA., *Annie Laurie*, Lottie Blair Parker, Chicago 1897, Play

WAY FOR A SAILOR 1930 d: Sam Wood. USA., *Way for a Sailor*, Albert Richard Wetjen, New York 1928, Novel

Way Men Love, The *see* BY DIVINE RIGHT (1924).

WAY OF A GAUCHO 1952 d: Jacques Tourneur. USA., *Way of a Gaucho*, Herbert Childs, 1948, Novel

WAY OF A GIRL, THE 1925 d: Robert G. VignolA. USA., *Summoned*, Katharine Newlin Burt, 1923, Short Story

Way of a Lancer *see* CYNARA (1932).

Way of a Man, The *see* MIEHEN TIE (1940).

WAY OF A MAN WITH A MAID, THE 1918 d: Donald Crisp. USA., *The Way of a Maid With a Man*, Ida M. Evans, 1918, Short Story

WAY OF A WOMAN, THE 1919 d: Robert Z. Leonard. USA., *Nancy Lee*, Eugene Walter, H. Crownin Wilson, New York 1918, Play

Way of a Woman, The *see* THE WONDERFUL WOOING (1925).

WAY OF ALL FLESH, THE 1927 d: Victor Fleming. USA., *The Way of All Flesh*, Perley Poore Sheehan, Story

WAY OF ALL FLESH, THE 1940 d: Louis King. USA., *The Way of All Flesh*, Perley Poore Sheehan, Story

WAY OF ALL MEN, THE 1930 d: Frank Lloyd. USA., *Syndafloden*, Henning Berger, Play

WAY OF AN EAGLE, THE 1918 d: G. B. Samuelson. UKN., *The Way of an Eagle*, Ethel M. Dell, Novel

Way of Life, The *see* THEY CALL IT SIN (1932).

Way of the Cross, The *see* CESTOU KRIZOVOU (1938).

WAY OF THE STRONG, THE 1919 d: Edwin Carewe. USA., *The Way of the Strong*, Ridgwell Cullum, London 1914, Novel

WAY OF THE WORLD, THE 1916 d: Lloyd B. Carleton. USA., *The Way of the World*, Clyde Fitch, New York 1901, Play

WAY OF YOUTH, THE 1934 d: Norman Walker. UKN., *Wayward Youth*, Amy Kennedy Gould, Ralph Neale, Play

Way of Youth, The *see* LE CHEMIN DES ECOLIERS (1959).

WAY OUT 1966 d: Irvin S. Yeaworth Jr. USA., *The Addict*, John Giminez, Play

Way Out, The *see* DIAL 999 (1955).

Way to Love, A *see* A BEDTIME STORY (1933).

Way to Paradise *see* PUT U RAJ (1971).

WAY TO THE GOLD, THE 1957 d: Robert D. Webb. USA., *The Way to the Gold*, Wilbur Daniel Steele, 1955, Novel

WAY UPSTREAM 1989 d: Terry Johnson. UKN., *Way Upstream*, Alan Ayckbourn, 1983, Play

WAY UPSTREAM 1991 d: Sandor Francken. NTH., *Way Upstream*, Alan Ayckbourn, 1983, Play

WAY WE LIVE NOW, THE 1970 d: Barry Brown. USA., *The Way We Live Now*, Warren Miller, Boston 1958, Novel

WAY WE WERE, THE 1973 d: Sydney Pollack. USA., *The Way We Were*, Arthur Laurents, 1972, Novel

WAY WEST, THE 1967 d: Andrew V. McLaglen. USA., *The Way West*, A. B. Guthrie Jr., New York 1949, Novel

Wayfarer, The *see* RAHI (1953).

Wayfarers *see* LANDSTRYKERE (1988).

Ways of Love *see* JOFROI (1933).

Ways of Love *see* AMORE (1948).

WAYWARD 1932 d: Edward Sloman. USA., *Wild Beauty*, Mateel Howe Farnham, New York 1930, Novel

WAYWARD BUS, THE 1957 d: Victor Vicas. USA., *The Wayward Bus*, John Steinbeck, 1947, Novel

Wayward Girl, The *see* UNG FLUKT (1959).

Wayward Wife, The *see* LA PROVINCIALE (1953).

Wayward Youth *see* RESTLESS YOUTH (1928).

We All Die Alone *see* JEDER STIRBT FUR SICH ALLEIN (1976).

We All Fall Down *see* TUTTI GIU PER TERRA (1997).

WE AMERICANS 1928 d: Edward Sloman. USA., *We Americans*, Milton Herbert Gropper, Max Siegel, New York 1926, Play

We are All Dead Demons *see* KLABAUTERMANDEN (1969).

We are All Demons see KLABAUTERMANDEN (1969).

We are French see THE BUGLER OF ALGIERS (1916).

We are in the Navy Now see WE JOINED THE NAVY (1962).

WE ARE NOT ALONE 1939 d: Edmund Goulding. USA., *We are Not Alone*, James Hilton, 1937, Novel

WE ARE SEVEN 1991 d: Ken Horn. UKN., *We are Seven*, Una Troy, New York 1957, Novel

WE CAN'T HAVE EVERYTHING 1918 d: Cecil B. de Mille. USA., *We Can't Have Everything*, Rupert Hughes, New York 1917, Novel

We Children from Bahnhof Zoo see CHRISTIANE F. WIR KINDER VOM BAHNHOF ZOO (1981).

We Die Alone see NI LIV (1957).

We Don't Bury on Sundays see ON N'ENTERRE PAS LE DIMANCHE (1959).

We Humans see YOUNG AMERICA (1932).

WE JOINED THE NAVY 1962 d: Wendy Toye. UKN., *We Joined the Navy*, John Winton, Novel

WE LIVE AGAIN 1934 d: Rouben Mamoulian. USA., *Voskreseniye*, Lev Nikolayevich Tolstoy, Moscow 1899, Novel

WE MODERNS 1925 d: John Francis Dillon. USA., *We Moderns*, Israel Zangwill, New York 1923, Play

WE OF THE NEVER NEVER 1982 d: Igor Auzins. ASL., *We of the Never Never*, Jeannie Gunn, Autobiography

We Shall Rise Again see UNCENSORED (1942).

WE SHALL SEE 1964 d: Quentin Lawrence. UKN., *We Shall See*, Edgar Wallace, London 1926, Novel

We Still Kill the Old Way see A CIASCUNO IL SUO (1967).

We, the Jury see WE'RE ON THE JURY (1937).

We the Living see NOI VIVI (1942).

We Thieves are Honest People see LOS LADRONES SOMOS GENTE HONRADA (1942).

WE THINK THE WORLD OF YOU 1989 d: Colin Gregg. UKN., *We Think the World of You*, J. R. Ackerley, Novel

We Three see COMPROMISED (1931).

We Two see NAM IRUVAR (1947).

WE WERE DANCING 1941 d: Robert Z. Leonard. USA., *Tonight at 8.30*, Noel Coward, Play

WE WERE STRANGERS 1949 d: John Huston. USA., *Rough Sketch*, Robert Sylvester, Novel

We Whiz Kids see WIR WUNDERKINDER (1958).

WE WHO ARE ABOUT TO DIE 1936 d: W. Christy Cabanne. USA., *We Who are About to Die*, David Lamson, New York 1936, Book

WE WOMEN 1925 d: W. P. Kellino. UKN., *We Women*, Countess Barcynska, Novel

WEAK AND THE WICKED, THE 1953 d: J. Lee Thompson. UKN., *Who Lie in Gaol*, Joan Henry, Novel

Weaker Sex see AH JONAN (1960).

Weaker Sex, The see THE WISER SEX (1932).

Weaker Sex, The see LE SEXE FAIBLE (1934).

WEAKER SEX, THE 1948 d: Roy Ward Baker. UKN., *No Medals*, Esther McCracken, London 1944, Play

WEAKNESS OF MAN, THE 1916 d: Barry O'Neil. USA., *Zhivoi Trup*, Lev Nikolayevich Tolstoy, Moscow 1911, Play

Weapons of Destruction see VYNALEZ ZKAZY (1958).

Weather Forecast see PROGNOZA POGODY (1982).

WEATHER IN THE STREETS, THE 1984 d: Gavin Millar. UKN., *The Weather in the Streets*, Rosamund Lehmann, 1936, Novel

WEAVER OF DREAMS, A 1918 d: John H. Collins. USA., *A Weaver of Dreams*, Myrtle Reed, New York 1911, Novel

Weavers, The see DIE WEBER (1927).

WEB OF CHANCE, THE 1919 d: Alfred E. Green. USA., *Right After Brown*, Edgar Franklin, Short Story

Web of Evidence see BEYOND THIS PLACE (1959).

Web of Fear see CONSTANCE AUX ENFERS (1964).

Web of Passion see A DOUBLE TOUR (1959).

Web of Violence see TRE NOTTI VIOLENTE (1966).

WEBER, DIE 1927 d: Friedrich Zelnik. GRM., *Die Weber*, Gerhart Hauptmann, Play

Wedding see SVADBA (1944).

WEDDING BELLS 1921 d: Chet Withey. USA., *Wedding Bells*, Edward Salisbury Field, Play

Wedding Breakfast see THE CATERED AFFAIR (1956).

Wedding Day, The see JOUR DE NOCES (1971).

Wedding for a Maiden, A see VDAVALA SE JEDNA PANNA (1926).

WEDDING GROUP 1936 d: Alex Bryce, Campbell Gullan. UKN., *Wedding Group*, Philip Wade, Radio Play

Wedding in the Hay see HOCHZEIT IM HEU (1951).

Wedding Night see NUIT DE NOCES (1949).

Wedding Night see EN BROLLOPSNATT (1959).

Wedding Night in Paradise see HOCHZEITSNACHT IM PARADIES (1950).

Wedding Night's Gift, The see DAR SVATEBNI NOCI (1926).

Wedding of Nanynka Kulichova, The see VDAVKY NANYNKY KULICHOVY (1925).

Wedding on the Road see HOCHZEIT AUF REISEN (1953).

WEDDING PRESENT 1936 d: Richard Wallace. USA., *Wedding Present*, Paul Gallico, 1935, Short Story

Wedding Ring, The see L' ALLIANCE (1970).

WEDDING RINGS 1929 d: William Beaudine. USA., *The Dark Swan*, Ernest Pascal, New York 1924, Novel

Wedding Shirt, The see SVATEBNI KOSILE (1925).

Wedding -Swedish Style see BROLLOPSBESVAR (1964).

Wedding, The see ZHENITBA (1937).

Wedding, The see WESELE (1972).

Wedding, The see SVADBA (1973).

Wedding, The see O CASAMENTO (1975).

Wedding With Erika see HOCHZEIT MIT ERIKA (1949).

WEDDINGS ARE WONDERFUL 1938 d: MacLean Rogers. UKN., *Peaches*, Sidney Blow, Douglas Hoare, 1915, Play

Wedle Wyrokow Twoich see RUTH (1983).

WEDNESDAY'S CHILD 1934 d: John S. Robertson. USA., *Wednesday's Child*, Leopold L. Atlas, New York 1934, Play

Wednesday's Child see FAMILY LIFE (1971).

Wee Geordie see GEORDIE (1955).

WEE MACGREGOR'S SWEETHEART, THE 1922 d: George Pearson. UKN., *Courting Christina*, J. J. Bell, Short Story, *Oh Christina*, J. J. Bell, Short Story

WEE WILLIE WINKIE 1937 d: John Ford. USA., *Wee Willie Winkie*, Rudyard Kipling, 1888, Short Story

WEEDS 1987 d: John Hancock. USA., *The Cage*, Rick Cluchey, Play

WEEK ENDS ONLY 1932 d: Alan Crosland. USA., *Week-End Girl*, Warner Fabian, New York 1932, Novel

WEEK-END A ZUYDCOOTE 1964 d: Henri Verneuil. FRN./ITL., *Week-End a Zuydcoote*, Robert Merle, Novel

Weekend at Dunkirk see WEEK-END A ZUYDCOOTE (1964).

WEEKEND AT THE WALDORF 1945 d: Robert Z. Leonard. USA., *Menschen Im Hotel*, Vicki Baum, Berlin 1929, Novel

Weekend Lives see WEEK-END MARRIAGE (1932).

Week-End Madness see AUGUST WEEK-END (1936).

WEEK-END MARRIAGE 1932 d: Thornton Freeland. USA., *Weekend Marriage*, Faith Baldwin, New York 1932, Novel

WEEKEND OF SHADOWS 1978 d: Tom Jeffrey. ASL., *The Reckoning*, Hugh Atkinson, Novel

WEEP NO MORE MY LADY 1994 d: Michel Andrieu. FRN/GRM., Mary Higgins Clark, Novel

Weg Abwarts, Der see DAS VIERTE GEBOT (1950).

WEG DURCH DIE NACHT, DER 1929 d: Robert Dinesen. GRM., *Der Weg Durch Die Nacht*, John Knittel, Novel

WEG IN DIE VERGANGENHEIT, DER 1954 d: Karl Hartl. AUS., *Die Forelle*, Wilfried Christensen, Novel

WEG ZU ISABEL, DER 1939 d: Erich Engel. GRM., *Weg Zu Isabell*, Frank Thiess, Novel

WEGEN VERFUHRUNG MINDERJAHRIGER 1960 d: Hermann Leitner. AUS., *Wegen Verfuhrung Minderjahriger*, Hans Wolfgang, Novel

WEHE, WENN ER LOSGELASSEN 1931 d: Martin Fric, Carl Lamac. GRM/CZC., *Unter Geschaftsaufsicht*, Franz Robert Arnold, Ernst Bach, Play

WEI HAI ZI MEN ZHU FU 1953 d: Zhao Dan. CHN., Qin Zhaoyang, Novel

WEIB IM DSCHUNGEL 1930 d: Dimitri Buchowetzki. FRN., *The Letter*, W. Somerset Maugham, 1925, Short Story

WEIB IN FLAMMEN 1928 d: Max Reichmann. GRM., *Weib in Flammen*, Georg Froschel, Novel

WEIBERKRIEG, DER 1928 d: Franz Seitz. GRM., *Die Kreuzelschreiber*, Ludwig Anzengruber, 1892, Play

WEIBSTEUFEL, DER 1951 d: Wolfgang Liebeneiner. AUS., *Der Weibsteufel*, Karl Schonherr, 1914, Play

WEIBSTEUFEL, DER 1966 d: Georg Tressler. AUS., *Der Weibsteufel*, Karl Schonherr, 1914, Play

WEIDENBAUM, DER 1984 d: Sohrab Shahid Saless. GRM/CZC., Anton Chekhov, Novel

WEIL DU ARM BIST, MUSST DU FRUHER STERBEN 1956 d: Paul May. GRM., *Weil du Arm Bist Musst du Fruher Sterben*, Hans Gustl Kernmayr, Novel

WEIRD NEMESIS, THE 1915 d: Jacques Jaccard. USA., *The Weird Nemesis*, G. E. Jenks, Story

Weird Tales see KWAIDAN (1964).

Weird Weirdo see LE GRAND CEREMONIAL (1968).

WEIRD WOMAN 1944 d: Reginald Le Borg. USA., *Conjure Wife*, Fritz Leiber, Story

Weisheit Des Blutes, Die see WISE BLOOD (1979).

WEISSBLAUE LOWE, DER 1952 d: Werner Jacobs, Olf Fischer. GRM., *Erster Klasse*, Ludwig Thoma, Play

Weisse Frau Des Maharadscha, Die see DIE LIEBE DES MAHARADSCHA (1936).

WEISSE SCHLEIER, DER 1912 d: Adolf Gartner. GRM., *Der Weisse Schleier*, Moritz Hartmann, Poem

WEISSE SKLAVEN 1936 d: Karl Anton. GRM., Charlie Roellinghoff, Book

WEISSE SPINNE, DIE 1963 d: Harald Reinl. GRM., *Die Weisse Spinne*, Louis Weinert-Wilton, Novel

WEISSE TEUFEL, DER 1930 d: Alexander Volkov. GRM., *Khadzh-Murat*, Lev Nikolayevich Tolstoy, 1911, Novel

WEISSE WOLKE CAROLIN 1984 d: Rolf Losansky. GDR., *Weisse Wolke Carolin*, Klaus Meyer, Novel

WEISSEN ROSEN VON RAVENSBERG, DIE 1919 d: Nils Chrisander. GRM., *Die Weissen Rosen von Ravensberg*, Adlersfeld-Ballestrem, Novel

WEISSEN ROSEN VON RAVENSBERG, DIE 1929 d: Rudolf Meinert. GRM., *Die Weissen Rosen von Ravensberg*, Adlersfeld-Ballestrem, Novel

WEITE LAND, DAS 1970 d: Peter Beauvais. AUS., *Das Weite Land*, Arthur Schnitzler, 1911, Play

WEITE LAND, DAS 1987 d: Luc Bondy. AUS/GRM/FRN., *Das Weite Land*, Arthur Schnitzler, 1911, Play

WEITE STRASSEN - STILLE LIEBE 1969 d: Hermann Zschoche. GDR., Hans-Georg Lietz, Story

Weite Weg, Der see SCHICKSAL IN KETTEN (1946).

Welcome Back, Mr. McDonald see RADIO NO JIKAN (1998).

WELCOME HOME 1925 d: James Cruze. USA., *Minick*, Edna Ferber, 1922, Short Story

Welcome Home see SNAFU (1945).

Welcome, Mr. Beddoes see A MAN COULD GET KILLED (1966).

WELCOME MR. WASHINGTON 1944 d: Leslie Hiscott. UKN., *Welcome Mr. Washington*, Noel Streatfeild, Story

WELCOME STRANGER 1924 d: James Young. USA., *Welcome Stranger*, Aaron Hoffman, New York 1920, Play

WELCOME TO HARD TIMES 1967 d: Burt Kennedy. USA., *Welcome to Hard Times*, E. L. Doctorow, New York 1960, Novel

WELCOME TO OUR CITY 1922 d: Robert H. Townley. USA., *Welcome to Our City*, George V. Hobart, New York 1910, Play

WELCOME TO SARAJEVO 1997 d: Michael Winterbottom. UKN/USA., *Natasha's Story*, Michael Nicholson, Book

WELCOME TO THE CLUB 1970 d: Walter Shenson. UKN/USA., *Welcome to the Club*, Clement Biddle Wood, Novel

Welcome to the Suicide Club see THE SUICIDE CLUB (1988).

WELCOME TO WOOP WOOP 1997 d: Stephan Elliott. ASL/UKN., *The Dead Heart*, Michael Thomas, Book

Welcome to Xanadu see SWEET HOSTAGE (1975).

Well Guarded Trains see OSTRE SLEDOVANE VLAKY (1966).

We'll Really Hurt You see LE FAREMO TANTO MALE (1998).

We'll Talk About Love Later see VON DER LIEBE REDEN WIR SPATER (1953).

WELL, THE 1997 d: Samantha Lang. ASL., *The Well*, Elizabeth Jolley, Novel

Well, Young Man? see FIATALEMBER? HOGY ALLUNK (1963).

WELSH SINGER, A 1915 d: Henry Edwards. UKN., *A Welsh Singer*, Allen Raine, Novel

WELT IN JENEM SOMMER, DIE 1979 d: Ilse Hofmann. GRM., *Die Welt in Jenem Sommer*, Robert Muller, Novel

Welt Und Halwelt see DER GOLDENE ABGRUND (1927).

Welt Und Theater see MACHTRAUSCH - ABER DIE LIEBE SIEGT (1942).

WELTREKORD IM SEITENSPRUNG 1940 d: Georg Zoch. GRM., *Weltrekord Im Seitensprung*, Josef Geissler, Play

Welttheater Einsiedeln - Geld Oder Glaube see MACHTRAUSCH - ABER DIE LIEBE SIEGT (1942).

WEN DIE GOTTER LIEBEN 1942 d: Karl Hartl. GRM., *Wen Die Gotter Lieben*, Richard Billinger, Novel

Wench, The see BAGARRES (1948).

WENN BEIDE SCHULDIG WERDEN 1962 d: Hermann Leitner. AUS., *Wenn Beide Schuldig Werden*, Hans Nogly, Novel

Wenn Dann Die Grun von Neuem Euch Erglanzt see DER TOD DES EMPEDOKLES (1986).

WENN DER HAHN KRAHT 1936 d: Carl Froelich. GRM., *Wenn Der Hahn Kraht*, August Hinrichs, Play

Wenn Die Geigen Klingen see IHR JUNGE (1931).

WENN DIE MUSIK NICHT WAR' 1935 d: Carmine Gallone. GRM., *Der Kraft-Mayr*, Ernst von Wolzogen, Novel

WENN DIE MUTTER UND DIE TOCHTER. 1928 d: Carl Boese. GRM., *Poker*, Edmund Edel, Novel

WENN DIE SONNE WIEDER SCHEINT 1943 d: Boleslav Barlog. GRM., *De Vlaschaard*, Frank Lateur, 1908, Novel

WENN DU EINMAL DEIN HERZ VERSCHENKST 1929 d: Johannes Guter. GRM., *Der Vagabund Vom Aquator*, Ludwig von Wohl, Novel

Wenn du Noch Ein Heim Hast see DER STROM (1942).

WENN EINE FRAU LIEBT 1950 d: Wolfgang Liebeneiner. GRM., *Versprich Mir Nichts*, Charlotte Rissmann, Play

WENN LUDWIG INS MANOVER ZIEHT 1967 d: Werner Jacobs. GRM., *Ludwig Thoma*, Play

WENN MENSCHEN REIF ZUR LIEBE WERDEN 1927 d: Jacob Fleck, Luise Fleck. GRM., *Die Haubenlerche*, Ernst von Wildenbruch, Play

WENN POLDI INS MANOVER ZIEHT 1956 d: Hans Quest. AUS., *Der Farber Und Sein Zwillingsbruder*, Johann Nestroy, 1890, Play

WENN SUSS DAS MONDLICHT AUF HUGELN SCHLAFT 1969 d: Wolfgang Liebeneiner. GRM., *Wenn Suss Das Mondlicht Auf Den Hugeln Schlaft*, Eric Malpass, Novel

WENN WIR ALLE ENGEL WAREN 1936 d: Carl Froelich. GRM., *Wenn Wir Alle Engel Waren*, Heinrich Spoerl, Novel

WENN WIR ALLE ENGEL WAREN 1956 d: Gunther Luders. GRM., *Wenn Wir Alle Engel Waren*, Heinrich Spoerl, Novel

WENT THE DAY WELL? 1942 d: Alberto Cavalcanti. UKN., *The Lieutenant Died Last*, Graham Greene, 1940, Short Story

WER BIST DU DEN ICH LIEBE? 1949 d: Geza von Bolvary. GRM., *Die Abenteuer Des Herrn von Barabas*, Hugo Maria Kritz, Novel

Wer Die Heimat Liebt see DIE SACHE MIT STYX (1942).

WER REISST DENN GLEICH VORM TEUFEL AUS? 1978 d: Egon Schlegel. GDR., *Der Teufel Mit Den Drei Goldenen Haaren*, Jacob Grimm, Wilhelm Grimm, Short Story

WER STIRBT SCHON GERNE UNTER PALMEN? 1974 d: Alfred Vohrer. GRM., *Wer Stirbt Schon Gerne Unter Palmen?*, Heinz G. Konsalik, Novel

Wera Mirzewa see DER FALL DES STAATSANWALTS M..** (1928).

WE'RE ALL GAMBLERS 1927 d: James Cruze. USA., *Lucky Sam McCarver*, Sidney Coe Howard, New York 1925, Play

WE'RE NO ANGELS 1955 d: Michael Curtiz. USA., *Les Cuisine de Anges*, Albert Husson, Play

WE'RE NO ANGELS 1989 d: Neil Jordan. USA., *Le Cuisine Des Anges*, Albert Husson, Play

WE'RE NOT DRESSING 1934 d: Norman Taurog. USA., *The Admirable Crichton*, J. M. Barrie, London 1902, Play

WE'RE ON THE JURY 1937 d: Ben Holmes. USA., *Ladies of the Jury*, John Frederick Ballard, New York 1929, Play

WE'RE ONLY HUMAN 1935 d: James Flood. USA., *Husk*, Thomas Walsh, 1935, Short Story

WE'RE RICH AGAIN 1934 d: William A. Seiter. USA., *And Let Who Will Be Clever*, Alden Nash, Hollywood 1934, Play

Werewolf, The see LE LOUP-GAROU (1923).

WERTHER 1910 d: Henri Pouctal. FRN., *Die Leiden Des Jungen Werthers*, Johann Wolfgang von Goethe, 1774, Novel

WERTHER 1926 d: Milos Hajsky. CZC., *Werther*, Jaroslav Maria, Novel

Werther see LE ROMAN DE WERTHER (1938).

Werther Und Lotte see BEGEGNUNG MIT WERTHER (1949).

WESELE 1972 d: Andrzej WajdA. PLN., *Wesele*, Stanislaw Wyspianski, 1901, Play

WEST 11 1963 d: Michael Winner. UKN., *The Furnished Room*, Laura Del Rivo, Novel

WEST CASE, THE 1923 d: A. E. Coleby. UKN., *The West Case*, Sax Rohmer, Short Story

West Eleven see WEST 11 (1963).

WEST OF BROADWAY 1926 d: Robert T. Thornby. USA., *New York West*, Wallace Smith, 1926, Short Story

West of Montana see MAIL ORDER BRIDE (1963).

WEST OF SHANGHAI 1937 d: John Farrow. USA., *The Bad Man*, Porter Emerson Browne, New York 1920, Play

West of the Badlands see THE BORDER LEGION (1940).

WEST OF THE PECOS 1934 d: Phil Rosen. USA., *West of the Pecos*, Zane Grey, New York 1937, Novel

WEST OF THE PECOS 1945 d: Edward Killy. USA., *West of the Pecos*, Zane Grey, New York 1937, Novel

WEST OF THE WATER TOWER 1924 d: Rollin S. Sturgeon. USA., *West of the Water Tower*, Homer Croy, New York 1923, Novel

WEST POINT STORY, THE 1950 d: Roy Del Ruth. USA., *Classmates*, Irving Wallace, Story

WEST POINT WIDOW 1941 d: Robert Siodmak. USA., *The Baby's Had a Hard Day*, Anne Wormser, Story

West Side Miracle see SECRETS OF A NURSE (1938).

WEST SIDE STORY 1961 d: Robert Wise, Jerome Robbins. USA., *West Side Story*, Leonard Bernstein, Arthur Laurents, New York 1957, Play

WESTERN GOLD 1937 d: Howard Bretherton. USA., *Helen of the Old House*, Harold Bell Wright, New York 1921, Novel

WESTERN PRINCE CHARMING, A 1912. USA., *A Chaparral Prince*, O. Henry, Short Story

WESTERN ROMANCE, A 1910 d: Edwin S. Porter. USA., *The Westerner*, Owen Whister, Story

WESTERN SPEED 1922 d: Scott R. Dunlap, C. R. Wallace. USA., *Lynch Lawyers*, William Patterson White, Boston 192O, Novel

WESTERN UNION 1941 d: Fritz Lang. USA., *Western Union*, Zane Grey, Novel

WESTERN WALLOP, THE 1924 d: Cliff Smith. USA., *On Parole*, Adolf Bannauer, Story

WESTERNER, THE 1934 d: David Selman. USA., *Burnt Ranch*, Walter J. Coburn, 1933, Short Story

WESTERNER, THE 1940 d: William Wyler. USA., *The Westerner*, Stuart N. Lake, Story

WESTERNERS, THE 1919 d: Edward Sloman. USA., *The Westerners*, Stewart Edward White, New York 1901, Novel

WESTFRONT 1918 1930 d: G. W. Pabst. GRM., *Vier von Der Infanterie*, Ernst Johannsen, Novel

WESTLAND CASE, THE 1937 d: W. Christy Cabanne. USA., *Headed for a Hearse*, Jonathan Latimer, New York 1935, Novel

WESTMINSTER PASSION PLAY - BEHOLD THE MAN, THE 1951 d: Walter RillA. UKN., *Ecce Homo*, Charles P. Carr, Walter Meyjes, Play

WESTWARD HO! 1919 d: Percy Nash. UKN., *Westward Ho!*, Charles Kingsley, 1855, Novel

WESTWARD HO THE WAGONS! 1957 d: William Beaudine. USA., *Children of the Covered Wagon*, Mary Jane Carr, 1934, Novel

WESTWARD PASSAGE 1932 d: Robert Milton. USA., *Westward Passage*, Margaret Ayer Barnes, Boston 1931, Novel

WET PARADE, THE 1932 d: Victor Fleming. USA., *The Wet Parade*, Upton Sinclair, New York 1931, Novel

WETTERLEUCHTEN AM DACHSTEIN 1952 d: Anton Kutter. GRM/AUS., *Die Kleine Passion*, Elmira Koref, Play

WETTERLEUCHTEN UM MARIA 1957 d: Luis Trenker. GRM., *Im Herbst Verbluhen Die Rosen*, Hans Ernst, Novel

We've Got a Bone to Pick With You see THE PACK (1977).

WHALE FOR THE KILLING, A 1980 d: Richard T. Heffron. USA/CND., *A Whale for the Killing*, Farley Mowat, Novel

WHALES OF AUGUST, THE 1987 d: Lindsay Anderson. USA., *The Whales of August*, David Berry, Play

WHARF ANGEL 1934 d: William Cameron Menzies, George Somnes. USA., *The Man Who Broke His Heart*, Frederick Schlick, Play

WHAT A CARVE UP! 1961 d: Pat Jackson. UKN., *The Ghoul*, Frank King, London 1928, Novel

WHAT A CRAZY WORLD 1963 d: Michael Carreras. UKN., *What a Crazy World*, Alan Klein, Play

What a Gang! see CHAVURA SHE'KA'ZOT (1962).

What a Life! see WHAT A LIFE (1939).

WHAT A LIFE 1939 d: Theodore Reed. USA., *What a Life*, Clifford Goldsmith, New York 1938, Play

WHAT A MAN! 1930 d: George J. Crone. USA., *They All Want Something*, Courtenay Savage, New York 1926, Play

WHAT A MOTHER-IN-LAW! 1934 d: Harry S. Brown. USA., *The Lunatic*, H. Kalmon, Play

What a Wonderful Life see FOLLOW THAT DREAM (1962).

WHAT BECAME OF JACK AND JILL? 1971 d: Bill Bain. UKN., *The Ruthless Ones*, Laurence Moody, Novel

WHAT DREAMS MAY COME 1998 d: Vincent Ward. USA/NZL., *What Dreams May Come*, Richard Matheson, Novel

WHAT EVER HAPPENED TO AUNT ALICE? 1969 d: Lee H. Katzin. USA., *The Forbidden Garden*, Ursula Curtiss, New York 1962, Novel

WHAT EVER HAPPENED TO BABY JANE? 1962 d: Robert Aldrich. USA., *What Ever Happened to Baby Jane Hudson?*, Henry Farrell, New York 1960, Novel

WHAT EVER HAPPENED TO BABY JANE? 1991 d: David Greene. USA., *What Ever Happened to Baby Jane Hudson?*, Henry Farrell, New York 1960, Novel

What Ever Happened to Cousin Charlotte? see SWEET CHARLOTTE HUSH. HUSH (1964).

WHAT EVERY WOMAN KNOWS 1917 d: Fred W. Durrant. UKN., *What Every Woman Knows*, J. M. Barrie, London 1908, Play

WHAT EVERY WOMAN KNOWS 1921 d: William C. de Mille. USA., *What Every Woman Knows*, J. M. Barrie, London 1908, Play

WHAT EVERY WOMAN KNOWS 1934 d: Gregory La CavA. USA., *What Every Woman Knows*, J. M. Barrie, London 1908, Play

WHAT EVERY WOMAN WANTS 1954 d: Maurice Elvey. UKN., *Relations are Best Apart*, Edwin Lewis, Play

WHAT FOOLS MEN 1925 d: George Archainbaud. USA., *Joseph Greer and His Daughter*, Henry Kitchell Webster, Indianapolis 1922, Novel

WHAT FOOLS MEN ARE 1922 d: George W. Terwilliger. USA., *The Flapper*, Eugene Walter, 1923, Play

WHAT HAPPENED AT 22 1916 d: George Irving. USA., *What Happened at 22*, Paul Wilstach, New York 1914, Play

What Happened, Caroline? see BETWEEN US GIRLS (1942).

WHAT HAPPENED THEN? 1934 d: Walter Summers. UKN., *What Happened Then?*, Lillian T. Bradley, Play

WHAT HAPPENED TO FATHER 1915 d: C. Jay Williams. USA., *What Happened to Father*, Mary Roberts Rinehart, 1909, Short Story

WHAT HAPPENED TO FATHER 1927 d: John G. Adolfi. USA., *What Happened to Father*, Mary Roberts Rinehart, 1909, Short Story

WHAT HAPPENED TO JONES 1915 d: Fred MacE. USA., *What Happened to Jones*, George Broadhurst, New York 1897, Play

WHAT HAPPENED TO JONES 1920 d: James Cruze. USA., *What Happened to Jones*, George Broadhurst, New York 1897, Play

WHAT HAPPENED TO JONES 1926 d: William A. Seiter. USA., *What Happened to Jones*, George Broadhurst, New York 1897, Play

What Happened to Polynin *see* CHTO SLUCHILOS S POLINIM? (1971).

WHAT HAPPENED TO ROSA 1920 d: Victor Schertzinger. USA., *Entrante Rosa Alvaro*, Pearl Lenore Curran, 1919, Short Story

What Ladies Dream *see* ONE EXCITING ADVENTURE (1934).

What Lola Wants *see* THE PAJAMA GAME (1957).

What Lola Wants *see* DAMN YANKEES (1958).

WHAT LOVE SEES 1996 d: Michael Switzer. USA., *What Love Sees*, Susan Vreeland, Book

WHAT MAD PURSUIT? 1985 d: Tony Smith. UKN., *What Mad Pursuit?*, Noel Coward, 1939, Short Story

WHAT MAISIE KNEW 1976 d: Babette Mangolte. USA., *What Maisie Knew*, Henry James, 1897, Novel

WHAT MEN LIVE BY 1939 d: Donald Taylor, Vernon Sewell. UKN., *Chem Liudi Zhivy*, Lev Nikolayevich Tolstoy, 1882, Short Story

WHAT MONEY CAN BUY 1928 d: Edwin Greenwood. UKN., *What Money Can Buy*, Ben Landeck, Arthur Shirley, Play

WHAT MONEY CAN'T BUY 1917 d: Lou Tellegen. USA., *What Money Can't Buy*, George Broadhurst, New York 1915, Play

WHAT PRICE DECENCY? 1933 d: Arthur Gregor. USA., Arthur Gregor, Play

WHAT PRICE GLORY 1926 d: Raoul Walsh. USA., *What Price Glory*, Maxwell Anderson, Laurence Stallings, New York 1924, Play

WHAT PRICE GLORY 1952 d: John Ford. USA., *What Price Glory*, Maxwell Anderson, Laurence Stallings, New York 1924, Play

What Price Melody? *see* LORD BYRON OF BROADWAY (1930).

What Price Murder *see* UNE MANCHE ET LA BELLE (1957).

What Remains Forever *see* WAT EEUWIG BLIJFT (1920).

What Shall It Profit *see* HARD STEEL (1942).

What Shall It Profit a Man *see* THE MONEY-CHANGERS (1920).

WHAT SHOULD A WOMAN DO TO PROMOTE YOUTH AND HAPPINESS? 1915?. USA., *What Should a Woman Do to Promote Youth and Happiness*, Mrs. Barry MacDonald, Novel

WHAT THE BUTLER SAW 1924 d: George Dewhurst. UKN., *What the Butler Saw*, Frederick Mouillot, Edward F. Parry, London 1905, Play

WHAT THE DEAF MAN HEARD 1997 d: John Kent Harrison. USA., *What the Deaf-Mute Heard*, G. D. Gearino, Novel

What the Hell, Jack! *see* JACK (1977).

What the Peeper Saw *see* NIGHT HAIR CHILD (1971).

WHAT THE RIVER FORETOLD 1915 d: William Franey, Joseph J. Franz. USA., *What the River Foretold*, Peter B. Kyne, Story

What the Swallow Sang *see* WAS DIE SCHWALBE SANG (1956).

What to Do With It? *see* KAM S NIM? (1922).

WHAT WILL PEOPLE SAY? 1915 d: Alice Blache. USA., *What Will People Say?*, Rupert Hughes, New York 1914, Novel

What Wives Don't Want *see* THE VIRTUOUS HUSBAND (1931).

What Women Give *see* MEN MUST FIGHT (1932).

WHAT WOULD A GENTLEMAN DO? 1918 d: Wilfred Noy. UKN., *What Would a Gentleman Do?*, Gilbert Daylis, Play

WHATEVER SHE WANTS 1921 d: C. R. Wallace. USA., *Whatever She Wants*, Edgar Franklin, 1921, Short Story

What's a Fixer for? *see* FIXER DUGAN (1939).

WHAT'S A NICE GIRL LIKE YOU..? 1971 d: Jerry Paris. USA., *Shirley*, Howard Fast, Novel

WHAT'S BRED. COMES OUT IN THE FLESH 1916 d: Sidney Morgan. UKN., *What's Bred in the Bone*, Grant Allen, Novel

WHAT'S EATING GILBERT GRAPE 1993 d: Lasse Hallstrom. USA., *What's Eating Gilbert Grape*, Peter Hedges, Novel

WHAT'S HIS NAME 1914 d: Cecil B. de Mille. USA., *What's-His-Name*, George Barr McCutcheon, New York 1911, Novel

WHAT'S LOVE GOT TO DO WITH IT 1993 d: Brian Gibson. USA., *I Tina*, Kurt Loder, Autobiography, *I - Tina*, Tina Turner, Autobiography

WHAT'S SO BAD ABOUT FEELING GOOD? 1968 d: George Seaton. USA., *I Am Thinking of My Darling*, Vincent McHugh, New York 1943, Novel

What's the Time, Mr. Clock? *see* VEKKER UR? HANY AZ ORA (1985).

WHAT'S YOUR HURRY? 1920 d: Sam Wood. USA., *The Hippopotamus Parade*, Byron Morgan, 1919, Short Story

Wheel *see* CHAKRA (1979).

WHEEL OF CHANCE 1928 d: Alfred Santell. USA., *Roulette*, Fannie Hurst, 1922, Short Story

WHEEL OF DESTINY, THE 1927 d: Duke Worne. USA., *The Man Without a Past*, Joseph Anthony, Short Story

WHEEL OF FATE 1953 d: Francis Searle. UKN., *Wheel of Fate*, Alex Atkinson, Play

WHEEL OF LIFE, THE 1929 d: Victor Schertzinger. USA., *The Wheel of Life*, James B. Fagan, New York 1923, Play

WHEEL, THE 1925 d: Victor Schertzinger. USA., *The Wheel*, Winchell Smith, New York 1921, Play

WHEELER DEALERS, THE 1963 d: Arthur Hiller. USA., *The Wheeler Dealers*, George J. W. Goodman, New York 1959, Novel

WHEELS 1976 d: Cathal Black. IRL., *Wheels*, John McGahern, 1970, Short Story

WHEELS OF CHANCE, THE 1922 d: Harold Shaw. UKN., *The Wheels of Chance*, H. G. Wells, Novel

WHEELS OF TERROR 1987 d: Gordon Hessler. USA/UKN., *Wheels of Terror*, Sven Hassel, Novel

WHEN A FELLER NEEDS A FRIEND 1932 d: Harry Pollard. USA., *Limpy: the Boy Who Felt Neglected*, William Andrew Johnston, Boston 1917, Novel

When a Fellow Needs a Friend *see* WHEN A FELLER NEEDS A FRIEND (1932).

When a Man Grows Old *see* SENILITA (1962).

WHEN A MAN LOVES 1927 d: Alan Crosland. USA., *L' Histoire du Chevalier Des Grieux Et de Manon Lescaut*, Antoine-Francois Prevost d'Exiles,, la Haye 1731, Novel

WHEN A MAN SEES RED 1917 d: Frank Lloyd. USA., *The Painted Lady*, Larry Evans, 1912, Short Story

WHEN A MAN'S A MAN 1924 d: Eddie Cline. USA., *When a Man's a Man*, Harold Bell Wright, New York 1916, Novel

WHEN A MAN'S A MAN 1935 d: Eddie Cline. USA., *When a Man's a Man*, Harold Bell Wright, New York 1916, Novel

When a Woman Gives Her Love *see* WENN EINE FRAU LIEBT (1950).

When a Woman in Love. *see* UNE FEMME FIDELE (1976).

When a Woman Is in Love *see* UNE FEMME FIDELE (1976).

When a Woman Meddles *see* QUAND LA FEMME S'EN MELE (1957).

WHEN BEARCAT WENT DRY 1919 d: Oliver L. Sellers. USA., *When Bear Cat Went Dry*, Charles Neville Buck, New York 1918, Novel

When Boys Leave Home *see* DOWNHILL (1927).

When Civilization Failed *see* IS DIVORCE A FAILURE? (1923).

When Destry Rides *see* DESTRY RIDES AGAIN (1932).

WHEN DREAMS COME TRUE 1929 d: Duke Worne. USA., *Sunburst Valley*, Victor Rousseau, Story

When Duty Calls *see* ARMY WIVES (1986).

WHEN EIGHT BELLS TOLL 1971 d: Etienne Perier. UKN., *When Eight Bells Toll*, Alistair MacLean, 1966, Novel

When Eve Came Back *see* THE RETURN OF EVE (1916).

WHEN FATE LEADS TRUMPS 1914 d: Harry Handworth. USA., *When Fate Leads Trumps*, Alice M. Roberts, Novel

When Girls Leave Home *see* CARELESS LADY (1932).

WHEN GREEK MEETS GREEK 1922 d: Walter West. UKN., *When Greek Meets Greek*, Paul Trent, Novel

WHEN HELL BROKE LOOSE 1958 d: Kenneth L. Crane. USA., Ib Melchior, Article

When I Fall in Love *see* EVERYBODY'S ALL-AMERICAN (1988).

WHEN IT WAS DARK 1919 d: Arrigo Bocchi. UKN., *When It Was Dark*, Guy Thorne, Novel

When Johnny Comes Marching Home *see* RIDERS UP (1924).

WHEN KNIGHTHOOD WAS IN FLOWER 1922 d: Robert G. VignolA. USA., *When Knighthood Was in Flower*, Charles Major, Indianapolis 1898, Novel

When Knighthood Was in Flower *see* THE SWORD AND THE ROSE (1953).

WHEN KNIGHTS WERE BOLD 1916 d: Maurice Elvey. UKN., *When Knights Were Bold*, Charles Marlowe, London 1907, Play

WHEN KNIGHTS WERE BOLD 1929 d: Tim Whelan. UKN., *When Knights Were Bold*, Charles Marlowe, London 1907, Play

WHEN KNIGHTS WERE BOLD 1936 d: Jack Raymond. UKN., *When Knights Were Bold*, Charles Marlowe, London 1907, Play

When Ladies Fly *see* LADIES COURAGEOUS (1944).

WHEN LADIES MEET 1933 d: Harry Beaumont. USA., *When Ladies Meet*, Rachel Crothers, New York 1932, Play

WHEN LADIES MEET 1941 d: Robert Z. Leonard. USA., *When Ladies Meet*, Rachel Crothers, New York 1932, Play

When Lights are Low *see* WHERE LIGHTS ARE LOW (1921).

When London Burned *see* OLD ST. PAUL'S (1914).

WHEN LONDON SLEEPS 1914 d: Ernest G. Batley. UKN., *When London Sleeps*, Charles Darrell, Play

WHEN LONDON SLEEPS 1932 d: Leslie Hiscott. UKN., *When London Sleeps*, Charles Darrell, Play

WHEN LOVE GROWS COLD 1925 d: Harry O. Hoyt. USA., *When Love Grows Cold*, Laura Jean Libbey, Story

WHEN LOVE IS YOUNG 1937 d: Hal Mohr. USA., *Class Prophecy*, Eleanore Griffin, 1935, Short Story

When Ludwig Goes on Manoeuvres *see* WENN LUDWIG INS MANOVER ZIEHT (1967).

When Meadows Bloom *see* NAR ANGARNA BLOMMAR (1946).

WHEN MEN ARE TEMPTED 1918 d: William Wolbert. USA., *John Burt*, Frederick Upham Adams, Philadelphia 1903, Novel

When Men Carried Clubs, Women Played Ding Dong! *see* QUANDO GLI UOMINI ARMARONO LA CLAVA. E CON LE DONNE FECERO DIN DON (1971).

When Mother Went on Strike *see* ALS MUTTER STREIKTE (1973).

WHEN MY BABY SMILES AT ME 1948 d: Walter Lang. USA., *Burlesque*, Arthur Hopkins, George Manker Watters, New York 1927, Play

WHEN MY SHIP COMES IN 1919 d: Robert T. Thornby. USA., *When My Ship Comes in*, Gouverneur Morris, New York 1915, Novel

WHEN PARIS SLEEPS 1917 d: A. V. Bramble. UKN., *When Paris Sleeps*, Charles Darrell, Play

When Peace Broke Out *see* LOS QUE NO FUIMOS A LA GUERRA (1961).

WHEN ROMANCE RIDES 1922 d: Eliot Howe, Charles O. Rush. USA., *Wildfire*, Zane Grey, New York 1916, Novel

WHEN STRANGERS MEET 1934 d: W. Christy Cabanne. USA., *The Way*, Zona Gale, Short Story

When Strangers Meet *see* EINER FRISST DEN ANDEREN (1964).

When Sugar Cookies are Broken *see* SATOGASHI GA KOWARERU TOKI (1967).

When Svante Disappeared *see* DA SVANTE FORSVANDT (1975).

WHEN THE BOUGH BREAKS 1986 d: Waris Hussein. USA., *When the Bough Breaks*, Jonathan Kellerman, Novel

WHEN THE BOYS MEET THE GIRLS 1965 d: Alvin Ganzer. USA., *Girl Crazy*, Guy Bolton, John McGowan, New York 1930, Musical Play

WHEN THE CALL CAME 1915 d: Sidney M. Goldin, De Villiers. USA., *The Song of Songs*, Bruno Lessing, Story

When the Cookie Crumbles *see* **SATOGASHI GA KOWARERU TOKI** (1967).

WHEN THE DALTONS RODE 1940 d: George Marshall. USA., *When the Daltons Rode*, Emmett Dalton, Jack Jungmeyer, New York 1931, Book

WHEN THE DESERT CALLS 1922 d: Ray C. Smallwood. USA., *When the Desert Calls*, Donald McGibney, 1920, Short Story

When the Devil Commands *see* **THE DEVIL COMMANDS** (1941).

WHEN THE DOOR OPENED 1925 d: Reginald Barker. USA., *When the Door Opened*, James Oliver Curwood, 1920, Short Story

When the Door Opened *see* **ESCAPE** (1940).

When the Future Began *see* **THE RIGHT STUFF** (1983).

When the Girls Meet the Boys *see* **GIRL CRAZY** (1943).

WHEN THE KISSING HAD TO STOP 1962 d: Bill Hitchcock. UKN., *When the Kissing Had to Stop*, Constantine Fitzgibbon, Novel

WHEN THE LEGENDS DIE 1972 d: Stuart Millar. USA., *When the Legends Die*, Hal Borland, Novel

WHEN THE LIGHT COMES 1999 d: Stijn Coninx. NTH/BLG/GRM., *Waar Blijft Het Licht (When the Light Comes)*, Heleen Van Der Laan, Novel

When the Light Vanished *see* **TOEN 'T LICHT VERDWEEN** (1918).

When the Mist Is Lifting *see* **VIATA NU IARTA** (1957).

When the Moonlight Sleeps Upon the Hills *see* **WENN SUSS DAS MONDLICHT AUF HUGELN SCHLAFT** (1969).

When the Night Comes *see* **CUANDO LLEGUE LA NOCHE** (1946).

When the Strings Wailed *see* **KDYZ STRUNY LKAJI** (1930).

When the Strings Weep *see* **KDYZ STRUNY LKAJI** (1930).

When the Sugar Cake Breaks *see* **SATOGASHI GA KOWARERU TOKI** (1967).

When the Sugar Cookie Crumbles *see* **SATOGASHI GA KOWARERU TOKI** (1967).

When the Sun Rises *see* **CELA S'APPELLE L'AURORE** (1955).

When the Violin Sighs *see* **KDYZ STRUNY LKAJI** (1930).

When the West Was Young *see* **HERITAGE OF THE DESERT** (1933).

WHEN THE WHALES CAME 1989 d: Clive Rees. UKN., *Why the Whales Came*, Michael Morpurgo, Novel

When the Wind Blows *see* **MAKE WAY FOR TOMORROW** (1937).

WHEN THE WIND BLOWS 1986 d: Jimmy T. Murakami. UKN., *When the Wind Blows*, Raymond Briggs, Book

When Thief Meets Thief *see* **JUMP FOR GLORY** (1937).

WHEN TIME RAN OUT. 1980 d: James Goldstone. USA., *The Day the World Ended*, Max Morgan-Witts, Gordon Thomas, Novel

When Tomorrow Comes *see* **DR. MONICA** (1934).

WHEN TOMORROW COMES 1939 d: John M. Stahl. USA., *Serenade*, James M. Cain, 1937, Novel

When Tomorrow Comes *see* **INTERLUDE** (1967).

When We are Married *see* **THE TRUTHFUL SEX** (1926).

WHEN WE ARE MARRIED 1943 d: Lance Comfort. UKN., *When We are Married*, J. B. Priestley, London 1938, Play

When We Were 21 *see* **THE TRUTH ABOUT YOUTH** (1930).

WHEN WE WERE TWENTY-ONE 1915 d: Edwin S. Porter, Hugh Ford. USA., *When We Were Twenty-One*, H. V. Esmond, New York 1900, Play

WHEN WE WERE TWENTY-ONE 1921 d: Henry King. USA., *When We Were Twenty-One*, H. V. Esmond, New York 1900, Play

WHEN WILLIE COMES MARCHING HOME 1950 d: John Ford. USA., *When Leo Comes Marching Home*, Sy Gomberg, Story

When Wolves Cry *see* **L' ARBRE DE NOEL** (1969).

WHEN WOMAN HATES 1916 d: Albert Ward. UKN., *When Woman Hates*, Fred Bulmer, Play

When Women Played Ding-Dong *see* **QUANDO GLI UOMINI ARMARONO LA CLAVA. E CON LE DONNE FECERO DIN DON** (1971).

WHEN WORLDS COLLIDE 1951 d: Rudolph Mate. USA., *When Worlds Collide*, Edwin Balmer, Philip Wylie, 1950, Novel

WHEN'S YOUR BIRTHDAY? 1937 d: Harry Beaumont. USA., *When's Your Birthday?*, John Frederick Ballard, 1935, Play

WHERE ANGELS FEAR TO TREAD 1966 d: Naomi Capon. UKN., *Where Angels Fear to Tread*, E. M. Forster, 1905, Novel

WHERE ANGELS FEAR TO TREAD 1991 d: Charles Sturridge. UKN., *Where Angels Fear to Tread*, E. M. Forster, 1905, Novel

WHERE ARE THE CHILDREN? 1986 d: Bruce Malmuth. USA., *Where are the Children*, Mary Higgins Clark, Novel

WHERE BONDS ARE LOOSED 1919 d: David G. Fischer. USA., *Where Bonds are Loosed*, E. L. Grant Watson, New York 1918, Novel

Where Chimneys are Seen *see* **ENTOTSU NO MIERU BASHO** (1953).

WHERE DOES IT HURT? 1972 d: Rod Amateau. USA/UKN., *The Operator*, Rod Amateau, Budd Robinson, Novel

WHERE EAGLES DARE 1968 d: Brian G. Hutton, Yakima Canutt. UKN/USA., *Where Eagles Dare*, Alistair MacLean, London 1966, Novel

WHERE IS MY CHILD? 1937 d: Abraham Leff. USA., *Forgotten Mothers*, William Siegal, Sam Steinberg, 1937, Play

WHERE IS MY FATHER? 1916 d: Joseph Adelman. USA., *The Story of a Dog Black*, Alexandre Dumas (pere), 1868, Short Story

WHERE IS MY WANDERING BOY TONIGHT? 1922 d: James P. Hogan, Millard Webb. USA., *Where Is My Wandering Boy Tonight?*, Robert Lowry, 1877, Song

WHERE IT'S AT 1969 d: Garson Kanin. USA., *Where It's at*, Garson Kanin, Play

WHERE LIGHTS ARE LOW 1921 d: Colin Campbell. USA., *East Is East*, Lloyd Osbourne, 1920, Short Story

WHERE LOVE HAS GONE 1964 d: Edward Dmytryk. USA., *Where Love Has Gone*, Harold Robbins, New York 1962, Novel

WHERE LOVE IS 1917. USA., *Where Love Is*, William J. Locke, New York 1903, Novel

WHERE LOVE IS, THERE GOD IS ALSO 1912 d: Oscar Eagle. USA., Lev Nikolayevich Tolstoy, Story

WHERE MEN ARE MEN 1921 d: William Duncan. USA., *The Princess of the Desert Dream*, Ralph Cummins, Story

WHERE PIGEONS GO TO DIE 1990 d: Michael Landon. USA., *Where Pigeons Go to Die*, R. Wright Campbell, Book

WHERE SINNERS MEET 1934 d: J. Walter Ruben. USA., *The Dover Road*, A. A. Milne, New York 1921, Play

WHERE THE BOYS ARE 1960 d: Henry Levin. USA., *Where the Boys are*, Glendon Swarthout, Novel

WHERE THE BOYS ARE '84 1984 d: Hy Averback. USA., *Where the Boys are*, Glendon Swarthout, Novel

WHERE THE FOREST ENDS 1915 d: Joseph de Grasse. USA., *Where the Forest Ends*, Olga Printzlau, Story

Where the Hot Wind Blows *see* **LA LOI** (1958).

WHERE THE LILIES BLOOM 1974 d: William A. Graham. USA., *Where the Lilies Bloom*, Bill Cleaver, Vera Cleaver, Book

WHERE THE PAVEMENT ENDS 1923 d: Rex Ingram. USA., *The Passion Vine*, John Russell, 1919, Short Story

WHERE THE RAINBOW ENDS 1921 d: H. Lisle Lucoque. UKN., *Where the Rainbow Ends*, Clifford Mills, John Ramsey, London 1911, Play

WHERE THE RED FERN GROWS 1974 d: Norman Tokar. USA., *Where the Red Fern Grows*, Wilson Rawls, Novel

Where the River Bends *see* **BEND OF THE RIVER** (1952).

WHERE THE RIVER RUNS BLACK 1986 d: Christopher Cain. USA., *Lazaro*, David Kendall, Book

WHERE THE RIVERS FLOW NORTH 1993 d: Jay Craven. USA., *Where the Rivers Flow North*, Howard Frank Mosher, Novel

WHERE THE SIDEWALK ENDS 1950 d: Otto Preminger. USA., *Night Cry*, William L. Stuart, 1948, Novel

WHERE THE SPIES ARE 1966 d: Val Guest. UKN/USA., *Passport to Oblivion*, James Leasor, London 1964, Novel

Where the Summer Wind Blows *see* **UTE BLASER SOMMARVIND** (1955).

WHERE THE TRAIL DIVIDES 1914 d: James Neill. USA., *Where the Trail Divides*, William Otis Lillibridge, New York 1907, Novel

Where the Truth Lies *see* **MALEFICES** (1961).

Where the Wind Blows *see* **THE HAUNTING OF JULIA** (1976).

Where the Winds Lead *see* **DIT VINDARNA BAR** (1948).

WHERE THE WORST BEGINS 1925 d: John McDermott. USA., *Out Where the Worst Begins*, George Frank Worts, 1924, Short Story

WHERE THERE'S A WILL 1955 d: Vernon Sewell. UKN., *Where There's a Will*, R. F. Delderfield, 1954, Play

Where Time Began *see* **VIAJE AL CENTRO DE LA TIERRA** (1977).

Where to Put It? *see* **KAM S NIM?** (1922).

WHERE WAS I? 1925 d: William A. Seiter. USA., *Where Was I?*, Edgar Franklin, 1924, Short Story

Where Was You Majesty Between 3 and 5? *see* **MIT CSINALT FELSEGED 3-TOL 5-IG?** (1964).

WHERE WERE YOU WHEN THE LIGHTS WENT OUT? 1968 d: Hy Averback. USA., *Monsieur Masure*, Claude Magnier, Paris 1956, Play

WHERE'S CHARLEY? 1952 d: David Butler. UKN/USA., *Charley's Aunt*, Brandon Thomas, London 1892, Play

WHERE'S POPPA? 1970 d: Carl Reiner. USA., *Where's Poppa?*, Robert Klane, Novel

Wherever Love Takes Me *see* **THE SEVENTH DAWN** (1964).

WHICH SHALL IT BE? 1924 d: Renaud Hoffman. USA., *No One to Spare Or Which Shall It Be?*, Ethel Lynn Beers, Story

WHICH WOMAN? 1918 d: Tod Browning, Harry Pollard. USA., *Nobody's Bride*, Evelyn Campbell, Novel

Whiff of Heliotrope, A *see* **HELIOTROPE** (1920).

WHILE I LIVE 1947 d: John Harlow. UKN., *This Same Garden*, Robert Bell, Play

WHILE PARENTS SLEEP 1935 d: Adrian Brunel. UKN., *While Parents Sleep*, Anthony Kimmins, London 1932, Play

WHILE PARIS SLEEPS 1923 d: Maurice Tourneur. USA., *The Glory of Love*, Pan, London 1919, Novel

WHILE SATAN SLEEPS 1922 d: Joseph Henabery. USA., *The Parson of Panamint*, Peter B. Kyne, 1915, Short Story

WHILE THE AUTO WAITS 1920 d: Joseph Byron Totten. USA., *While the Auto Waits*, O. Henry, Short Story

WHILE THE CITY SLEEPS 1956 d: Fritz Lang. USA., *The Bloody Spur*, Charles Einstein, 1953, Novel

WHILE THE PATIENT SLEPT 1935 d: Ray Enright. USA., *While the Patient Slept*, Mignon G. Eberhart, New York 1930, Novel

WHILE THE SUN SHINES 1947 d: Anthony Asquith. UKN., *While the Sun Shines*, Terence Rattigan, London 1943, Play

While You Have a Mother *see* **DOKUD MAS MAMINKU** (1934).

WHIP, THE 1917 d: Maurice Tourneur. USA., *The Whip*, Henry Hamilton, Cecil Raleigh, London 1909, Play

WHIP, THE 1928 d: Charles J. Brabin. USA., *The Whip*, Henry Hamilton, Cecil Raleigh, London 1909, Play

Whipped, The *see* **THE UNDERWORLD STORY** (1950).

WHIPSAW 1935 d: Sam Wood. USA., *The Whipsaw*, James Edward Grant, 1934, Short Story

Whirl, A *see* **WIR** (1983).

WHIRLIGIG OF LIFE, THE 1917 d: Floyd France. USA., *The Whirligig of Life*, O. Henry, Short Story

Whirlpool *see* **REMOUS** (1934).

WHIRLPOOL 1950 d: Otto Preminger. USA., *Methinks the Lady*, Guy Endore, Novel

WHIRLPOOL 1959 d: Lewis Allen. UKN., *The Lorelei*, Lawrence P. Bachmann, Novel

WHIRLPOOL, THE 1918 d: Alan Crosland. USA., *The Whirlpool*, Victoria Morton, New York 1916, Novel

Whirlpool, The *see* **LONDON LOVE** (1926).

Whirlwind *see* **DAI TATSUMAKI** (1964).

WHIRLWIND OF YOUTH, THE 1927 d: Rowland V. Lee. USA., *Soundings*, Arthur Hamilton Gibbs, Boston 1925, Novel

WHISKY A MEZZOGIORNO 1962 d: P. V. Oscar de FinA. ITL., *La Banda Del Sole*, Enzo Barbieri, Novel

WHISKY GALORE! 1948 d: Alexander MacKendrick. UKN., *Whisky Galore!*, Compton Mackenzie, 1947, Novel

Whisky, Wodka, Wienerin *see* **RENDEZ-VOUS IN WIEN** (1959).

WHISPERED NAME, THE 1924 d: King Baggot. USA., *The Co-Respondent*, Alice Leal Pollock, Rita Weiman, New York 1916, Play

WHISPERERS, THE 1966 d: Bryan Forbes. UKN., *Mrs. Ross*, Robert Nicolson, London 1961, Novel

WHISPERING CANYON 1926 d: Tom Forman. USA., *The Whispering Canyon*, John Mersereau, New York 1926, Novel

WHISPERING CHORUS, THE 1917 d: Cecil B. de Mille. USA., *The Whispering Chorus*, Perley Poore Sheehan, 1918, Short Story

WHISPERING CITY 1947 d: Fedor Ozep. CND., Michael Lennox, George Zuckerman, Story

WHISPERING DEATH 1975 d: Jurgen Goslar. SAF/GRM., *Whispering Death*, Daniel Carney, Novel

WHISPERING DEVILS 1920 d: Harry Garson. USA., *Michael and His Lost Angel*, Henry Arthur Jones, London 1896, Play

WHISPERING GABLES 1927 d: Edwin Greenwood. UKN., *Whispering Gables*, Agnes Platt, Short Story

WHISPERING SAGE 1927 d: Scott R. Dunlap. USA., *Whispering Sage*, Harry Sinclair Drago, Joseph Noel, New York 1922, Novel

WHISPERING SMITH 1916 d: J. P. McGowan. USA., *Whispering Smith*, Frank Hamilton Spearman, New York 1906, Novel

WHISPERING SMITH 1926 d: George Melford. USA., *Whispering Smith*, Frank Hamilton Spearman, New York 1906, Novel

WHISPERING SMITH 1948 d: Leslie Fenton. USA., *Whispering Smith*, Frank Hamilton Spearman, New York 1906, Novel

WHISPERING WIRES 1926 d: Albert Ray. USA., *Whispering Wires*, Henry Leverage, New York 1918, Novel

WHISPERS 1990 d: Douglas Jackson. CND., *Whispers*, Dean R. Koontz, Novel

WHISTLE BLOWER, THE 1987 d: Simon Langton. UKN., *The Whistle Blower*, John Hale, Novel

WHISTLE DOWN THE WIND 1961 d: Bryan Forbes. UKN., *Whistle Down the Wind*, Mary Hayley Bell, London 1958, Novel

WHISTLE STOP 1946 d: Leonide Moguy. USA., *Whistle Stop*, Maritta Martin Wolff, Novel

WHISTLING BULLETS 1937 d: John English. USA., *The Fifth Man*, James Oliver Curwood, Short Story

Whistling Dick *see* **AN UNWILLING HERO** (1921).

WHISTLING DICK'S CHRISTMAS STOCKING 1917 d: George Ridgwell. USA., *Whistling Dick's Christmas Stocking*, O. Henry, Short Story

WHISTLING IN THE DARK 1932 d: Elliott Nugent. USA., *Whistling in the Dark*, Edward Childs Carpenter, Laurence Gross, New York 1932, Play

WHISTLING IN THE DARK 1941 d: S. Sylvan Simon. USA., *Whistling in the Dark*, Edward Childs Carpenter, Laurence Gross, New York 1932, Play

Whistling in the Nose, The *see* **IL FISCHIO AL NASO** (1967).

WHITE AND UNMARRIED 1921 d: Tom Forman. USA., *Billy Kane - White and Unmarried*, John D. Swain, Story

White As Snow *see* **BLANC COMME NEIGE** (1931).

WHITE BANNERS 1938 d: Edmund Goulding. USA., *White Banners*, Lloyd C. Douglas, Boston 1936, Novel

White Bird *see* **RENDEZVOUS** (1935).

WHITE BIRD PASSES, THE 1980 d: Michael Radford. UKN., *The White Bird Passes*, Jessie Kesson, Autobiography

White Boat, The *see* **BYELI PAROKHOD** (1976).

WHITE BUFFALO, THE 1976 d: J. Lee Thompson. USA., *The White Buffalo*, Richard Sale, Novel

WHITE BUS, THE 1967 d: Lindsay Anderson. UKN., *White Bus*, Shelagh Delaney, Short Story

WHITE CARGO 1929 d: J. B. Williams, Arthur W. Barnes. UKN., *White Cargo*, Ida Vera Simonton, 1925, Novel

WHITE CARGO 1942 d: Richard Thorpe. USA., *Hell's Playground*, Ida Vera Simonton, 1925, Novel

WHITE CARGO 1974 d: Ray Selfe. UKN., *Albert's Follies*, Ray Selfe, Story

White Cat, The *see* **THE TWO-SOUL WOMAN** (1918).

White Cat, The *see* **THE UNTAMEABLE** (1923).

White Cat, The *see* **DEN VITA KATTEN** (1950).

WHITE CIRCLE, THE 1920 d: Maurice Tourneur. USA., *The Pavilion on the Links*, Robert Louis Stevenson, 1882, Short Story

WHITE CLIFFS OF DOVER, THE 1944 d: Clarence Brown. USA., *The White Cliffs*, Alice Duer Miller, Poem, Robert Nathan, Poems

White Cloud Caroline *see* **WEISSE WOLKE CAROLIN** (1984).

WHITE COCKATOO, THE 1935 d: Alan Crosland. USA., *The White Cockatoo*, Mignon G. Eberhart, New York 1933, Novel

White Collars *see* **POOR GIRL RICH MAN** (1938).

White Colt, The *see* **RUN FREE RUN WILD** (1969).

WHITE CORRIDORS 1951 d: Pat Jackson. UKN., *Yeoman's Hospital*, Helen Ashton, Novel

White Crow *see* **BILA VRANA** (1938).

WHITE DESERT, THE 1925 d: Reginald Barker. USA., *The White Desert*, Courtney Ryley Cooper, New York 1922, Novel

White Devil, The *see* **DER WEISSE TEUFEL** (1930).

White Disease, The *see* **BILA NEMOC** (1937).

WHITE DOG 1982 d: Samuel Fuller. USA., *White Dog*, Romain Gary, Novel

WHITE DOVE, THE 1920 d: Henry King. USA., *The White Dove*, William J. Locke, New York 1899, Novel

White Dragon, The *see* **MAD HOLIDAY** (1936).

White Eagle *see* **THE FLYING HORSEMAN** (1926).

WHITE FACE 1932 d: T. Hayes Hunter. UKN., *White Face*, Edgar Wallace, London 1930, Novel

WHITE FANG 1925 d: Larry Trimble. USA., *White Fang*, Jack London, New York 1905, Novel

WHITE FANG 1936 d: David Butler. USA., *White Fang*, Jack London, New York 1905, Novel

White Fang *see* **BELISCH KLYK** (1946).

White Fang *see* **ZANNA BIANCA** (1973).

WHITE FANG 1990 d: Randall Kleiser. USA., *White Fang*, Jack London, New York 1905, Novel

WHITE FEATHER 1955 d: Robert D. Webb. USA., *My Great-Aunt Appearing Day*, John Prebble, Story

WHITE FLANNELS 1927 d: Lloyd Bacon. USA., *White Flannels*, Lucian Cary, 1925, Short Story

White Flowers for the Dead *see* **AHASIN POLA WATHA** (1976).

White Frontier, The *see* **SLANDER THE WOMAN** (1923).

WHITE GOLD 1927 d: William K. Howard. USA., *White Gold*, J. Palmer Parsons, New York 1925, Play

WHITE GUARD, THE 1982 d: Don Taylor. UKN., *The White Guard*, Mikhail Bulgakov, Play

WHITE HEAT 1926 d: Thomas Bentley. UKN., *White Heat*, Pan, Novel

WHITE HEAT 1949 d: Raoul Walsh. USA., *White Heat*, Virginia Kellogg, Story

White Heather *see* **CIRCLE OF DANGER** (1951).

WHITE HEATHER, THE 1919 d: Maurice Tourneur. USA., *The White Heather*, Henry Hamilton, Cecil Raleigh, London 1897, Play

White Hell of Pitz Palu, The *see* **FOHN** (1950).

WHITE HEN, THE 1921 d: Frank Richardson. UKN., *The White Hen*, Phyllis Campbell, Novel

White Heron, The *see* **SHIRASAGI** (1958).

WHITE HOPE, THE 1915 d: Frank Wilson. UKN., *The White Hope*, W. H. R. Trowbridge, Novel

WHITE HOPE, THE 1922 d: Frank Wilson. UKN., *The White Hope*, W. H. R. Trowbridge, Novel

WHITE HUNTER, BLACK HEART 1990 d: Clint Eastwood. USA., *White Hunter, Black Heart*, Peter Viertel, Novel

White Illness, The *see* **BILA NEMOC** (1937).

WHITE LIES 1920 d: Edward J. Le Saint. USA., *White Lies*, Charles Reade, Boston 1857, Novel

WHITE LILAC 1935 d: Albert Parker. UKN., *White Lilac*, Ladislaus Fodor, Play

WHITE LIONS, THE 1979 d: Mel Stuart. USA., *Bwana*, Chris McBride, Novel

WHITE MAN 1924 d: Louis J. Gasnier. USA., *The White Man*, George Agnew Chamberlain, Indianapolis 1919, Novel

White Man, The *see* **THE SQUAW MAN** (1914).

White Man, The *see* **THE SQUAW MAN** (1918).

White Man, The *see* **THE SQUAW MAN** (1931).

WHITE MAN'S CHANCE, A 1919 d: Ernest C. Warde. USA., *A White Man's Chance*, Johnston McCulley, Short Story

WHITE MASKS, THE 1921 d: George Holt. USA., Ett Corr, Story

WHITE MICE 1926 d: Edward H. Griffith. USA., *White Mice*, Richard Harding Davis, New York 1909, Novel

WHITE MISCHIEF 1988 d: Michael Radford. UKN., *White Mischief*, James Fox, Book

WHITE MOLL, THE 1920 d: Harry Millarde. USA., *The White Moll*, Frank L. Packard, New York 1920, Novel

WHITE MONKEY, THE 1925 d: Phil Rosen. USA., *The White Monkey*, John Galsworthy, London 1924, Novel

White Moor *see* **DE-AS FI HARAP ALB** (1965).

White Moth, The *see* **CHRISTOPHER STRONG** (1933).

WHITE MOUSE, THE 1914 d: Colin Campbell. USA., *The White Mouse*, James Oliver Curwood, Story

White Nights *see* **LE NOTTI BIANCHE** (1957).

WHITE OF THE EYE 1987 d: Donald Cammell. UKN., *Mrs. White*, Margaret Tracy, Novel

White Outside, Pink Inside *see* **ROSA POR DENTRO BLANCA POR FUERA** (1971).

WHITE PALACE 1990 d: Luis Mandoki. USA., *White Palace*, Glenn Savan, Novel

WHITE PANTS WILLIE 1927 d: Charles Hines. USA., *White Pants Willie*, Elmer Holmes Davis, Novel

WHITE PARADE, THE 1934 d: Irving Cummings. USA., *The White Parade*, Rian James, New York 1934, Novel

WHITE PEARL, THE 1915 d: George Irving. USA., *The White Pearl*, Edith Barnard Delano, Story

WHITE RAT, THE 1922 d: George A. Cooper. UKN., *The White Rat*, K. R. G. Browne, Story

White Road Before Me, The *see* **TULAK** (1925).

White Rook, The *see* **HIS WIFE'S FRIEND** (1919).

WHITE ROSE OF THE WILDS, THE 1911 d: D. W. Griffith. USA., *The White Rose of the Wilds*, Bret Harte, Short Story

White Rose, The *see* **VALKOISET RUUSUT** (1944).

White Rose, The *see* **ROSA BLANCA** (1961).

White Roses *see* **DJAVOLJI RAJ - ONO LJETO BIJELIH RUZA** (1989).

White Roses, The *see* **VALKOISET RUUSUT** (1944).

WHITE SHADOW, THE 1924 d: Graham Cutts. UKN., *Children of Chance*, Michael Morton, Novel

White Shadows *see* **THE WHITE SHADOW** (1924).

WHITE SHADOWS IN THE SOUTH SEAS 1928 d: W. S. Van Dyke, Robert Flaherty. USA., *White Shadows in the South Seas*, Frederick O'Brien, New York 1919, Novel

WHITE SHEIK, THE 1928 d: Harley Knoles. UKN., *King's Mate*, Rosita Forbes, Novel

White Ship, The *see* **BYELI PAROKHOD** (1976).

WHITE SHOULDERS 1931 d: Melville Brown. USA., *Recoil*, Rex Beach, 1922, Short Story

White Sickness, The *see* **BILA NEMOC** (1937).

WHITE SISTER, THE 1915 d: Fred E. Wright. USA., *The White Sister*, F. Marion Crawford, New York 1909, Novel

WHITE SISTER, THE 1923 d: Henry King. USA., *The White Sister*, F. Marion Crawford, New York 1909, Novel

WHITE SISTER, THE 1933 d: Victor Fleming. USA., *The White Sister*, F. Marion Crawford, New York 1909, Novel

WHITE SLAVE, THE 1913. USA., *The White Slave*, Bartley Campbell, Play

WHITE SLIPPERS 1924 d: Sinclair Hill. UKN., *White Slippers*, Charles Edholm, Novel

White Spider, The *see* **DIE WEISSE SPINNE** (1963).

White Squadron, The *see* **SQUADRONE BIANCO** (1936).

WHITE SQUAW, THE 1956 d: Ray Nazarro. USA., *The Gun Witch of Wyoming*, Larabie Sutter, Story

White Steamer, The *see* **BYELI PAROKHOD** (1976).

WHITE STOCKING, THE 1967 d: Claude Whatham. UKN., *The White Stocking*, D. H. Lawrence, Short Story

White Threads of the Cascades *see* **TAKI NO SHIRAITO** (1933).

White Threads of the Waterfall *see* **TAKI NO SHIRAITO** (1933).

WHITE TIE AND TAILS 1946 d: Charles T. Barton. USA., *The Victoria Docks at Eight*, Charles Beahan, Rufus King, Novel

WHITE TOWER, THE 1950 d: Ted Tetzlaff. USA., *The White Tower*, James Ramsay Ullman, 1945, Novel

White Trial, The *see* **PROCESUL ALB** (1966).

WHITE UNICORN, THE 1947 d: Bernard Knowles. UKN., *The Milkwhite Unicorn*, Flora Sandstrom, Novel

White Warrior, The *see* **IL DIAVOLO BIANCO AGI MURAD** (1959).

WHITE WITCH DOCTOR 1953 d: Henry Hathaway. USA., *White Witch Doctor*, Louise A. Stinetorf, 1950, Novel

WHITE WOMAN 1933 d: Stuart Walker. USA., *Hangman's Whip*, Norman Reilly Raine, New York 1933, Play

White Yacht in Split, The *see* **BILA JACHTA VE SPLITU** (1939).

White-Haired Girl, The *see* **BAI MAO NU** (1950).

WHITEWASHED WALLS 1919 d: Park Frame. USA., *Whitewashed Walls*, Ethel Dorrance, James Dorrance, Short Story

Whither Mankind *see* **THINGS TO COME** (1936).

WHO? 1974 d: Jack Gold. UKN., *Who?*, Algis Budrys

WHO AM I? 1921 d: Henry Kolker. USA., *Who Am I?*, Max Brand, 1918, Short Story

WHO AM I THIS TIME? 1981 d: Jonathan Demme. USA., *Who Am I This Time?*, Kurt Vonnegut Jr., 1968, Short Story

WHO ARE MY PARENTS? 1922 d: J. Searle Dawley. USA., *The Divine Gift*, Merle Johnson, Story

Who Can Kill a Child? *see* **QUIEN PUEDE MATAR A UN NINO?** (1975).

WHO CARES? 1919 d: Walter Edwards. USA., *Who Cares? a Story of Adolescence*, Cosmo Hamilton, Boston 1919, Novel

WHO CARES 1925 d: David Kirkland. USA., *Who Cares? a Story of Adolescence*, Cosmo Hamilton, Boston 1919, Novel

WHO DARES WINS 1982 d: Ian Sharp. UKN., *The Tiptoe Boys*, George Markstein, Novel

WHO GOES NEXT? 1938 d: Maurice Elvey. UKN., *Who Goes Next?*, J. W. Drawbell, Reginald Simpson, Play

WHO GOES THERE? 1914 d: Ashley Miller. USA., *Who Goes There?*, Henry A. Du Souchet, Play

WHO GOES THERE! 1917 d: William P. S. Earle. USA., *Who Goes There*, Robert W. Chambers, New York 1915, Novel

WHO GOES THERE! 1952 d: Anthony Kimmins. UKN., *Who Goes There!*, John Dighton, London 1951, Play

WHO HAS SEEN THE WIND 1977 d: Allan King. CND., *Who Has Seen the Wind*, W. O. Mitchell, Novel

Who Is Guilty? *see* **I KILLED THE COUNT** (1938).

WHO IS HOPE SCHUYLER? 1942 d: Thomas Z. Loring. USA., *Hearses Don't Hurry*, Stephen Ransome, Novel

WHO IS JULIA? 1986 d: Walter Grauman. USA., *Who Is Julia?*, Barbara S. Harris, Novel

WHO IS KILLING THE GREAT CHEFS OF EUROPE? 1978 d: Ted Kotcheff. USA/GRM., *Who Is Killing the Great Chefs of Europe?*, Ivan Lyons, Nan Lyons, Novel

WHO IS THE MAN? 1924 d: Walter Summers. UKN., *Daniel*, Louis Verneuil, Play

Who Is This Person I Love? *see* **WER BIST DU DEN ICH LIEBE?** (1949).

WHO KILLED AUNT MAGGIE? 1940 d: Arthur Lubin. USA., *Who Killed Aunt Aggie?*, Medora Field, New York 1939, Novel

Who Killed Harry Field? *see* **INSPECTOR MORSE: WHO KILLED HARRY FIELD?** (1989).

WHO KILLED JOHN SAVAGE? 1937 d: Maurice Elvey. UKN., *Rynox*, Philip MacDonald, Novel

Who Killed Pixote? *see* **QUEM MATOU PIXOTE?** (1996).

WHO KILLED THE CAT? 1966 d: Montgomery Tully. UKN., *Tabitha*, Mary Cathcart Borer, Arnold Ridley, London 1956, Play

WHO KILLED WALTON? 1918 d: Thomas N. Heffron. USA., *The Veil*, Norman Sherbrooke, Story

WHO KNOWS? 1917 d: Jack Pratt. USA., *Who Knows?*, Ethel Dorrance, James Dorrance, 1916, Short Story

Who Rides With Kane? *see* **YOUNG BILLY YOUNG** (1969).

Who Shall Cast the First Stone *see* **WITHIN THE LAW** (1917).

Who Wants to Shoot Carlos? *see* **GEHEIMNISSE IN GOLDENEN NYLONS** (1966).

WHO WAS MADDOX? 1964 d: Geoffrey Nethercott. UKN., *The Undisclosed Client*, Edgar Wallace, Short Story

WHO WAS THAT LADY? 1960 d: George Sidney. USA., *Who Was That Lady?*, Norman Krasna, Play

Who Will Save Our Children? *see* **WHO'LL SAVE OUR CHILDREN?** (1978).

Whole Man, A *see* **TODO UN HOMBRE** (1943).

Whole River Bed, The *see* **MANJIANG HONG** (1933).

Whole Sky, The *see* **SARA AKASH** (1969).

WHOLE TOWN'S TALKING, THE 1926 d: Edward Laemmle. USA., *The Whole Town's Talking*, John Emerson, Anita Loos, New York 1923, Play

Whole Town's Talking, The *see* **EX-BAD BOY** (1931).

WHOLE TOWN'S TALKING, THE 1935 d: John Ford. USA., *Jail Breaker*, William Riley Burnett, 1932, Story

WHOLE TRUTH, THE 1958 d: John Guillermin. UKN., *The Whole Truth*, Philip MacKie, Television Play

WHO'LL SAVE OUR CHILDREN? 1978 d: George Schaefer. USA., *The Orchard Children*, Rachel Maddux, Book

WHO'LL STOP THE RAIN 1978 d: Karel Reisz. USA., *Dog Soldiers*, Robert Stone, 1974, Novel

Whom the Gods Destroy *see* **WHOM THE GODS WOULD DESTROY** (1919).

WHOM THE GODS DESTROY 1934 d: Walter Lang. USA., *The Hero*, Albert Payson Terhune, 1928, Short Story

WHOM THE GODS WOULD DESTROY 1919 d: Frank Borzage. USA., *Humanity*, Nan Blair, Charles R. Macauley, Short Story

WHOOPEE! 1930 d: Thornton Freeland. USA., *The Nervous Wreck*, Owen Davis, New York 1926, Play

WHOPPER-PUNCH 777 1988 d: Jurgen Troster. GRM., Maria Axt, Book

WHORE 1991 d: Ken Russell. USA., *Bondage*, David Hines, Play

WHO'S AFRAID OF VIRGINIA WOOLF? 1966 d: Mike Nichols. USA., *Who's Afraid of Virginia Wolf?*, Edward Albee, New York 1962, Play

WHO'S GOT THE ACTION? 1962 d: Daniel Mann. USA., *Four Horse-Players are Missing*, Alexander Rose, New York 1960, Novel

Who's Got the Black Box? *see* **LA ROUTE DE CORINTHE** (1967).

Who's Who? *see* **SOONER OR LATER** (1920).

WHO'S YOUR FATHER? 1935 d: Henry W. George. UKN., *Turned Up*, Mark Melford, London 1886, Play

WHO'S YOUR LADY FRIEND? 1937 d: Carol Reed. UKN., *Der Herr Ohne Wornung*, B. Jenbach, Osterreicher, Play

WHO'S YOUR SERVANT? 1920. USA., *Hari Kari*, Julian Johnson, New York 1913, Play

WHOSE LIFE IS IT ANYWAY? 1981 d: John Badham. USA., *Whose Life Is It Anyway?*, Brian Clark, 1978, Play

WHOSOEVER SHALL OFFEND 1919 d: Arrigo Bocchi. UKN., *Whosoever Shall Offend*, Marion Crawford, Novel

Why Anna? *see* **DIARIO DI UNA SCHIZOFRENICA** (1968).

Why are the Bells Ringing, Mitica? *see* **MITICA DE CE TRAG CLOPOTELE** (1981).

Why Bother to Knock? *see* **DON'T BOTHER TO KNOCK** (1961).

Why Change Your Husband? *see* **GOLD DUST GERTIE** (1931).

Why Do the Bells Toll, Mitica? *see* **MITICA DE CE TRAG CLOPOTELE** (1981).

Why Does Your Husband Cheat on You? *see* **POR QUE TE ENGANA TU MARIDO?** (1968).

WHY I AM HERE 1913 d: Ralph Ince. USA., *Why I Am Here*, James Oliver Curwood, Story

Why Is Mr. Bobikow Barking? *see* **CUORE DI CANE** (1975).

Why Is Your Husband Unfaithful? *see* **POR QUE TE ENGANA TU MARIDO?** (1968).

WHY LEAVE HOME? 1929 d: Raymond Cannon. USA., *Cradle Snatchers*, Russell G. Medcraft, Norma Mitchell, New York 1925, Play

WHY ME? 1990 d: Gene Quintano. USA., *Why Me?*, Donald E. Westlake, Novel

Why Men Forget *see* **DEMOS** (1921).

WHY MEN LEAVE HOME 1924 d: John M. Stahl. USA., *Why Men Leave Home*, Avery Hopwood, New York 1922, Play

WHY NOT STAY FOR BREAKFAST? 1979 d: Terry Marcel. UKN., *Why Not Stay for Breakfast?*, Ray Cooney, Gene Stone, Play

WHY ROCK THE BOAT? 1974 d: John Howe. CND., *Why Rock the Boat?*, William Weintraub, Novel

Why Saps Leave Home *see* **THE INNOCENTS OF CHICAGO** (1932).

WHY SHOOT THE TEACHER? 1976 d: Silvio Narizzano. CND., *Why Shoot the Teacher?*, Max Braithwaite, Novel

Why Should I Lie? *see* **WHY WOULD I LIE?** (1980).

WHY SMITH LEFT HOME 1919 d: Donald Crisp. USA., *Why Smith Left Home*, George Broadhurst, New York 1899, Play

Why the Whales Came *see* **WHEN THE WHALES CAME** (1989).

WHY WOMEN LOVE 1925 d: Edwin Carewe. USA., *The Sea Woman*, Willard Robertson, New York 1925, Play

WHY WOMEN SIN 1920 d: Burton L. King. USA., *Why Women Sin*, Will C. Murphy, New York 1903, Play

WHY WOULD I LIE? 1980 d: Larry Peerce. USA., *The Fabricator*, Hollis Hodges, Novel

Wiatr W Oczy *see* **NOCE I DNIE** (1975).

WICKED AS THEY COME 1956 d: Ken Hughes. UKN., *Portrait in Smoke*, William S. Ballinger, Novel

Wicked Carabel, The *see* **EL MALVADO CARABEL** (1934).

Wicked Carabel, The *see* **EL MALVADO CARABEL** (1955).

WICKED CITY 1993 d: Yoshiaki Kawajiri. JPN., Hideyuki Kikuchi, Novel

Wicked City, The *see* **HANS LE MARIN** (1948).

Wicked Duchess, The *see* **LA DUCHESSE DE LANGEAIS** (1942).

Wicked Go to Hell, The *see* **LES SALAUDS VONT EN ENFER** (1955).

WICKED LADY, THE 1945 d: Leslie Arliss. UKN., *The Life and Death of the Wicked Lady Skelton*, Magdalen King-Hall, Novel

WICKED LADY, THE 1983 d: Michael Winner. UKN., *The Life and Death of the Wicked Lady Skelton*, Magdalen King-Hall, Novel

Wicked Ones, The *see* **DIE HALBSTARKEN** (1956).

Wicked Wife *see* **GRAND NATIONAL NIGHT** (1953).

WICKED WOMAN, A 1934 d: Charles J. Brabin. USA., *Wicked Woman*, Anne Austin, New York 1933, Novel

WICKHAM MYSTERY, THE 1931 d: G. B. Samuelson. UKN., *The Paper Chase*, John McNally, Play

Widdicombe Fair *see* **WIDECOMBE FAIR** (1928).

Wide Blue Road, The *see* **LA GRANDE STRADA AZZURRA** (1957).

WIDE EYED AND LEGLESS 1993 d: Richard Loncraine. UKN., *Diana's Story*, Deric Longden, Book, *Lost for Words*, Deric Longden, Book

WIDE OPEN 1930 d: Archie Mayo. USA., *The Narrow Street*, Edwin Bateman Morris, Philadelphia 1924, Novel

Wide Roads - Quiet Love *see* **WEITE STRASSEN - STILLE LIEBE** (1969).

WIDE SARGASSO SEA, THE 1992 d: John Duigan. ASL., *Wide Sargasso Sea*, Jean Rhys, Novel

WIDECOMBE FAIR 1928 d: Norman Walker. UKN., *Widecombe Fair*, Eden Philpotts, Novel

WIDOW 1976 d: J. Lee Thompson. USA., *Widow*, Lynn Caine, Novel

Widow and the Gigolo, The *see* **THE ROMAN SPRING OF MRS. STONE** (1961).

WIDOW BY PROXY 1919 d: Walter Edwards. USA., *Widow By Proxy*, Catherine Chisholm Cushing, New York 1913, Play

Widow Couderc, The see LE VEUVE COUDERC (1971).

WIDOW FROM MONTE CARLO 1936 d: Arthur G. Collins. USA., *A Present from Margate*, Ian Hay, A. E. W. Mason, London 1933, Play

Widow Makers, The see SEE HOW THEY RUN (1965).

Widow, The see LA VEDOVA X (1956).

WIDOWING OF MRS. HOLROYD, THE 1961 d: Claude Whatham. UKN., *The Widowing of Mrs. Holroyd*, D. H. Lawrence, Play

Widow's Island see A ROMANCE IN FLANDERS (1937).

Widows Might see THE WIDOW'S MIGHT (1935).

Widow's Might see CARELESS LADY (1932).

WIDOW'S MIGHT, THE 1935 d: Cyril Gardner. UKN., *The Widow's Might*, Frederick Jackson, 1931, Play

Wie Anne Babi Haushaltet Und Wie Es. see ANNE BABI JOWAGER (1960).

Wie Bitte Werde Ich Ein Held? see A LA GUERRE COMME A LA GUERRE (1971).

Wie Der Sturmwind see WIE EIN STURMWIND (1957).

Wie Die Kleine Hexe Zaubern Lernte see MALA CARODEJNICE (1983).

WIE D'WARRET WURKT 1933 d: Walter Lesch, Richard Schweizer. SWT., *Wie d'Wahrheit Wurkt*, August Corrodi, Zurich 1886, Play

Wie d'Warret Wurkt see WIE D'WARRET WURKT (1933).

WIE EIN DIEB IN DER NACHT 1945 d: Hans Thimig. AUS., *Das Madchen Im Fenster*, Fritz Gottwald, Play

WIE EIN STURMWIND 1957 d: Falk Harnack. GRM., *Wie Ein Sturmwind*, Klaus Hellmer, Novel

WIE HEIRATET MAN EINEN KONIG 1968 d: Rainer Simon. GDR., *Die Kluge Bauerntochter*, Jacob Grimm, Wilhelm Grimm, 1812, Short Story

WIE ICH EIN NEGER WURDE 1970 d: Roland Gall. GRM., *Jugend Ohne Gott*, Odon von Horvath, 1938, Novel

Wiedergefundene Freund, Der see REUNION (1989).

Wiedersehen Mit Heidi see HEIDI UND PETER (1954).

WIENER BLUT 1942 d: Willi Forst. GRM., *Wiener Blut*, Johann Strauss, Operetta

WIERNA RZEKA 1936 d: Leonard Buczkowski. PLN., *Wierna Rzeka*, Stefan Zeromski, 1912, Novel

WIERNA RZEKA 1983 d: Tadeusz Chmielewski. PLN., *Wierna Rzeka*, Stefan Zeromski, 1912, Novel

Wife see TSUMA (1953).

WIFE AGAINST WIFE 1921 d: Whitman Bennett. USA., *The Price*, George Broadhurst, New York 1911, Play

Wife Be Like a Rose see TSUMA YO BARA NO YONI (1935).

Wife By Purchase, A see GOD'S LAW AND MAN'S (1917).

Wife for a Night see MOGLIE PER UNA NOTTE (1950).

WIFE FOR WIFE 1915 d: Kenean Buel. USA., *Wife for Wife*, John A. Stephens, Play

WIFE HE BOUGHT, THE 1918 d: Harry Salter. USA., *One Clear Call*, Larry Evans, Short Story

WIFE, HUSBAND AND FRIEND 1939 d: Gregory Ratoff. USA., *Career in C Major*, James M. Cain, 1938, Short Story

WIFE IN NAME ONLY 1923 d: George W. Terwilliger. USA., *Wife in Name Only*, Bertha M. Clay, Play

WIFE NUMBER TWO 1917 d: William Nigh. USA., *Madame Bovary*, Gustave Flaubert, Novel

Wife of Seishu Hanaoka, The see HANAOKA SEISHU NO TSUMA (1967).

WIFE OF THE CENTAUR 1924 d: King Vidor. USA., *Wife of the Centaur*, Cyril Hume, 1923, Novel

WIFE ON TRIAL, A 1917 d: Ruth Ann Baldwin. USA., *The Rose-Garden Husband*, Margaret Widdemer, Philadelphia 1915, Novel

WIFE OR TWO, A 1936 d: MacLean Rogers. UKN., *A Wife Or Two*, Roland Daniel, C. B. Poultney, Play

WIFE SAVERS 1928 d: Ralph Ceder. USA., *Louie the Fourteenth*, Frank Wilhelm, Julius Wilhelm, A. Wimperis, New York 1925, Play

Wife Smells a Rat, The see MANZELKA NECO TUSI (1938).

WIFE VS. SECRETARY 1936 d: Clarence Brown. USA., *Wife Versus Secretary*, Faith Baldwin, 1935, Short Story

WIFE WHO WASN'T WANTED, THE 1925 d: James Flood. USA., *The Wife Who Wasn't Wanted*, Gertie Wentworth-James, London 1923, Novel

WIFE WHOM GOD FORGOT, THE 1920 d: William J. Humphrey. UKN., *The Wife Whom God Forgot*, Cecil H. Bullivant, Novel

Wife's Devotion, A see AMORE SENZA STIMA (1914).

WIFE'S ROMANCE, A 1923 d: Thomas N. Heffron. USA., *La Rubia*, H. W. Roberts, Story

WILBY CONSPIRACY, THE 1975 d: Ralph Nelson. UKN/USA., *The Wilby Conspiracy*, Peter Driscoll, Novel

WILD AFFAIR, THE 1963 d: John Krish. UKN., *The Last Hours of Sandra Lee*, William Sansom, London 1961, Novel

Wild and the Wanton, The see MARIE DES ISLES (1959).

WILD AND THE WILLING, THE 1962 d: Ralph Thomas. UKN., *The Tinker*, Laurence Dobie, Robert Sloman, Stratford 1960, Play

WILD AND WONDERFUL 1964 d: Michael Anderson. USA., *I Married a Dog*, Dorothy Crider, Short Story

Wild Ass's Skin, The see LA PEAU DE CHAGRIN (1911).

WILD AT HEART 1990 d: David Lynch. USA., *Wild at Heart*, Barry Gifford, Novel

Wild Bird see TWO ALONE (1934).

Wild Birds see TWO ALONE (1934).

Wild Boy see LE GARCON SAUVAGE (1951).

Wild Boy, The see L' ENFANT SAUVAGE (1970).

WILD BRIAN KENT 1936 d: Howard Bretherton. USA., *The Re-Creation of Brian Kent*, Harold Bell Wright, Chicago 1919, Novel

WILD BULL'S LAIR, THE 1925 d: Del Andrews. USA., *The Wild Bull's Lair*, Frank M. Clifton, Story

WILD CARGO 1934 d: Armand Denis. USA., *Wild Cargo*, Edward S. Anthony, Frank Buck, New York 1932, Book

Wild Cat see WILDCAT TROOPER (1936).

Wild Cat Hetty see THE HELLCAT (1928).

Wild Cherry Trees see CHERYOMUSHKI (1963).

Wild Child, The see L' ENFANT SAUVAGE (1970).

WILD COMPANY 1930 d: Leo McCarey. USA., *Soft Shoulders*, Philip Hurn, Story

Wild Drifter see COCKFIGHTER (1974).

Wild Duck, The see VILDANDEN (1963).

Wild Duck, The see DIE WILDENTE (1976).

WILD DUCK, THE 1983 d: Henri Safran. ASL., *Vildanden*, Henrik Ibsen, 1884, Play

Wild Fawn, The see THE GOOD-BAD WIFE (1920).

Wild Fifties, The see DIE WILDEN FUNFZIGER (1982).

Wild Fruit see LES FRUITS SAUVAGES (1953).

Wild Game see WILDWECHSEL (1972).

Wild Games see COMBAT DE FAUVES (1997).

WILD GEESE 1927 d: Phil Stone. USA., *Wild Geese*, Martha Ostenso, New York 1925, Novel

Wild Geese see GAN (1953).

WILD GEESE CALLING 1941 d: John Brahm. USA., *Wild Geese Calling*, Stewart Edward White, Novel

WILD GEESE II 1985 d: Peter Hunt. UKN/USA., *The Square Circle*, Daniel Carney, Novel

WILD GEESE, THE 1978 d: Andrew V. McLaglen. UKN., *The Wild Geese*, Daniel Carney, Novel

WILD GIRL 1932 d: Raoul Walsh. USA., *Salomy Jane's Kiss*, Bret Harte, 1900, Short Story

Wild Girl see DIVOCH (1936).

Wild Girls at Puente San Gil, The see LOS SALVAJES EN PUENTE SAN GIL (1967).

WILD GOOSE CHASE, THE 1915 d: Cecil B. de Mille. USA., *The Wild Goose Chase*, William C. de Mille, Play

WILD GOOSE, THE 1921 d: Albert Capellani. USA., *The Wild Goose*, Gouverneur Morris, 1919, Short Story

WILD HARVEST 1947 d: Tay Garnett. USA., Houston Branch, Story

WILD HARVEST 1961 d: Jerry A. Baerwitz. USA., *Wild Harvest*, Stephen Longstreet, New York 1960, Novel

Wild Heart, The see GONE TO EARTH (1950).

WILD HEATHER 1921 d: Cecil M. Hepworth. UKN., *Wild Heather*, Dorothy Brandon, Play

WILD HERITAGE 1958 d: Charles Haas. USA., *Death Rides the Trail*, Steve Frazee, Short Story

WILD HONEY 1918 d: Francis J. Grandon. USA., *Wild Honey*, Vingie E. Roe, 1918, Short Story

WILD HONEY 1922 d: Wesley Ruggles. USA., *Wild Honey*, Cynthia Stockley, New York 1914, Novel

WILD HORSE 1930 d: Richard Thorpe, Sidney Algier. USA., Peter B. Kyne, Short Story

WILD HORSE HANK 1978 d: Eric Till. CND., *The Wild Horse Killers*, Mel Ellis, Novel

WILD HORSE MESA 1925 d: George B. Seitz. USA., *Wild Horse Mesa*, Zane Grey, Novel

WILD HORSE MESA 1932 d: Henry Hathaway. USA., *Wild Horse Mesa*, Zane Grey, Novel

Wild Horse Roundup see WILD HORSE ROUND-UP (1936).

WILD HORSE ROUND-UP 1936 d: Alan James. USA., James Oliver Curwood, Story

WILD HORSE STAMPEDE, THE 1926 d: Albert S. Rogell. USA., *Blind Trails*, W. C. Tuttle, Story

Wild Horses, The see VALDEZ IL MEZZOSANGUE (1974).

WILD IN THE COUNTRY 1961 d: Philip Dunne. USA., *The Lost Country*, J. R. Salamanca, New York 1958, Novel

WILD IN THE STREETS 1968 d: Barry Shear. USA., *Baby, the Day It All Happened*, Robert Thom, 1966, Short Story

WILD IS THE WIND 1957 d: George Cukor. USA., *Furia*, Vittorio Nino Novarese, Novel

Wild Kurdistan see DURCHS WILDE KURDISTAN (1965).

WILD MAN OF BORNEO, THE 1941 d: Robert B. Sinclair. USA., *The Wild Man of Borneo*, Marc Connelly, Herman J. Mankiewicz, New York 1927, Play

WILD MONEY 1937 d: Louis King. USA., *Tightwad*, Paul Gallico, 1936, Short Story

Wild Mountains see YE SHAN (1985).

WILD NORTH, THE 1952 d: Andrew Marton. USA., *When Terror Stalked Behind*, Walter W. Liggert, 1930, Story

WILD OATS LANE 1926 d: Marshall Neilan. USA., *Wild Oats Lane*, George Broadhurst, New York 1922, Play

WILD OLIVE, THE 1915 d: Oscar Apfel. USA., *The Wild Olive*, Basil King, New York 1910, Novel

WILD ONE, THE 1953 d: Laslo Benedek. USA., *The Cyclist's Raid*, Frank Rooney, 1951, Short Story

Wild Ones of San Gil Bridge, The see LOS SALVAJES EN PUENTE SAN GIL (1967).

WILD ORANGES 1924 d: King Vidor. USA., *Wild Oranges*, Joseph Hergesheimer, New York 1919, Novel

WILD PACK, THE 1971 d: Hall Bartlett. USA., *Capitaes Da Areia*, Jorge Amado, 1937, Novel

WILD PARTY, THE 1975 d: James Ivory. USA., *The Wild Party*, Joseph Moncure March, 1928, Verse

WILD RIVER 1960 d: Elia Kazan. USA., *Wild River*, William Bradford Huie, Novel

Wild Shore, The see NA DIKOM BEREGYE (1967).

WILD WEED 1949 d: Sam Newfield. USA., *Wild Weed*, Arthur Hoerl, Novel

WILD WEST DAYS 1937 d: Ford Beebe, Cliff Smith. USA., *Saint Johnson*, William Riley Burnett, New York 1930, Novel

WILD, WILD SUSAN 1925 d: A. Edward Sutherland. USA., *The Wild, Wild Child*, Steuart M. Emery, 1925, Short Story

WILD WOMEN 1970 d: Don Taylor. USA., *The Trailmakers*, Vincent Forte, Story

Wild Women in Puente San Gil, The see LOS SALVAJES EN PUENTE SAN GIL (1967).

WILD YOUTH 1918 d: George Melford. USA., *Wild Youth*, Gilbert Parker, Philadelphia 1919, Novel

WILDCAT TROOPER 1936 d: Elmer Clifton. USA., *The Midnight Call*, James Oliver Curwood, Story

WILDE 1997 d: Brian Gilbert. UKN., *Oscar Wilde*, Richard Ellman, Biography

WILDEN FUNFZIGER, DIE 1982 d: Peter Zadek. GRM., *Wir Leben Noch Hurra*, Johannes Mario Simmel, Novel

WILDENTE, DIE 1976 d: Hans W. Geissendorfer. AUS/GRM., *Vildanden*, Henrik Ibsen, 1884, Play

Wilder Urlaub see LA NUIT SANS PERMISSION (1943).

Wilderness see LOVE'S WILDERNESS (1924).

WILDERNESS 1996 d: Ben Bolt. UKN., *Wilderness*, Dennis Danvers, Novel

WILDERNESS MAIL 1935 d: Forrest Sheldon. USA., *The Wilderness Mail*, James Oliver Curwood, Short Story

WILDERNESS MAIL, THE 1914 d: Colin Campbell. USA., *The Wilderness Mail*, James Oliver Curwood, Short Story

WILDERNESS TRAIL, THE 1919 d: Edward J. Le Saint. USA., *The Wilderness Trail*, Francis William Sullivan, New York 1913, Novel

WILDERNESS WOMAN, THE 1926 d: Howard Higgin. USA., *The Wilderness Woman*, Arthur Stringer, 1926, Short Story

WILDFANG, DER 1936 d: Jan Svitak. GRM/CZC., *Divoch*, Milos Krenovsky, Novel

WILDFIRE 1915 d: Edwin Middleton. USA., *Wildfire*, George Broadhurst, George V. Hobart, New York 1908, Play

WILDFIRE 1925 d: T. Hayes Hunter. USA., *Wildfire*, George Broadhurst, George V. Hobart, New York 1908, Play

Wildfire see IT'S A DOG'S LIFE (1955).

WILDFLOWER 1914 d: Allan Dwan. USA., *Wildflower*, Mary Germaine, Story

WILDFLOWER 1991 d: Diane Keaton. USA., *Wildflower*, Sara Flanigan, Book

WILDSCHUT 1986 d: Bobby Eerhart. BLG/NTH., *Wildschut*, Felix Thijssen, Novel

Wildschutz von Tirol, Der see BERGKRISTALL (1949).

WILDTOTER, DER 1966 d: Richard Groschopp. GDR., James Fenimore Cooper, Novel

WILDWECHSEL 1972 d: R. W. Fassbinder. GRM., *Wildwechsel*, Franz Xaver Kroetz, 1968, Play

Wildwest Im Emmenthal see DIE KASEREI IN DER VEHFREUDE (1958).

WILFUL YOUTH 1927 d: Dallas M. Fitzgerald. USA., *Whispering Pines*, Edith Sessions Tupper, Story

Wilhelm Tell see GUILLAUME TELL (1912).

Wilhelm Tell see GUILLAUME TELL (1913).

WILHELM TELL 1921 d: Friedrich Genhardt. SWT., *Wilhelm Tell*, Friedrich von Schiller, 1804, Play

WILHELM TELL 1934 d: Heinz Paul. GRM/SWT., *Wilhelm Tell*, Friedrich von Schiller, 1804, Play

WILHELM TELL 1956 d: Alfred Stoger, Josef Gielen. AUS., *Wilhelm Tell*, Friedrich von Schiller, 1804, Play

WILHELM TELL - BERGEN IN FLAMMEN 1960 d: Michel Dickoff, Karl Hartl. SWT., *Wilhelm Tell*, Friedrich von Schiller, 1804, Play

Wilhelm Tell - Flammende Berge see WILHELM TELL - BERGEN IN FLAMMEN (1960).

Wilhelm Tell Oder Die Befreiung Der Schweiz see GUILLAUME TELL (1913).

Wilhelm Tells Kampf Um Die Freiheit see WILHELM TELL - BERGEN IN FLAMMEN (1960).

WILL AND A WAY, A 1922 d: Manning Haynes. UKN., *A Will and a Way*, W. W. Jacobs, Novel

WILL ANY GENTLEMAN? 1953 d: Michael Anderson. UKN., *Will Any Gentleman?*, Vernon Sylvaine, London 1950, Play

WILL JAMES' SAND 1949 d: Louis King. USA., *Sand*, Will James, Novel

Will O' the Wisp see DIE LIEBE DER BRUDER ROTT (1929).

Will O' the Wisp see LE FEU FOLLET (1963).

Will of His Grace, The see HANS NADS TESTAMENTE (1919).

Will O'The Wisp see FLACARI PE COMORI (1988).

WILL SUCCESS SPOIL ROCK HUNTER? 1957 d: Frank Tashlin. USA., *Will Success Spoil Rock Hunter?*, George Axelrod, New York 1955, Play

WILL, THE 1921 d: A. V. Bramble. UKN., *The Will*, J. M. Barrie, London 1913, Play

WILLARD 1971 d: Daniel Mann. USA., *Ratman's Notebooks*, Stephen Gilbert, Novel

William at the Circus see WILLIAM COMES TO TOWN (1948).

WILLIAM BALUCHET, ROI DES DETECTIVES 1920 d: Gaston Leprieur. FRN., *Roi Des Detectives William Baluchet*, Andre Bancey, Novel

WILLIAM COMES TO TOWN 1948 d: Val Guest. UKN., Richmal Crompton, Short Story

WILLIAM SHAKESPEARE'S ROMEO & JULIET 1996 d: Baz Luhrmann. USA., *Romeo and Juliet*, William Shakespeare, c1596, Play

William Tell see GUGLIELMO TELL (1911).

Willie Boy see TELL THEM WILLIE BOY IS HERE (1969).

Will-O'-the-Wisp see TY PETRINSKE STRANE (1922).

Will-O'-the-Wisp see HET DWAALLICHT (1973).

WILLOW 1988 d: Ron Howard. USA., George Lucas, Story

WILLOW TREE, THE 1920 d: Henry Otto. USA., *The Willow Tree*, J. H. Benrimo, Harrison Rhodes, New York 1917, Play

Willow Tree, The see DER WEIDENBAUM (1984).

WILLY 1963 d: Allan J. Buckhantz. GRM/USA., *The First Lesson*, Gunter Rudorf, Play

WILLY REILLY AND HIS COLLEEN 1918 d: Fred O'Donovan. IRL/UKN., *The Homes of Tipperary*, Charles Kickham, Play

WILT 1989 d: Michael Tuchner. UKN., *Wilt*, Tom Sharpe, Novel

WIN THAT GIRL 1928 d: David Butler. USA., *Father and Son*, James Hopper, 1924, Short Story

WINCHELL 1998 d: Paul Mazursky. USA., *Walter Winchell: His Life and Times*, Herman Klurfeld, Book

WINCHESTER '73 1950 d: Anthony Mann. USA., Stuart N. Lake, Story

WINCHESTER '73 1967 d: Herschel Daugherty. USA., Stuart N. Lake, Story

WINCHESTER WOMAN, THE 1919 d: Wesley Ruggles. USA., Charles Stokes Wayne, Story

WIND ACROSS THE EVERGLADES 1958 d: Nicholas Ray. USA., *Across the Everglades*, Budd Schulberg, Story

WIND CANNOT READ, THE 1958 d: Ralph Thomas. UKN., *The Wind Cannot Read*, Richard Mason, Novel

WIND IN THE WILLOWS 1949 d: James Algar, Jack Kinney. USA., *The Wind in the Willows*, Kenneth Grahame, 1908, Novel

WIND IN THE WILLOWS, THE 1983 d: Brian Cosgrove, Mark Hall. UKN., *The Wind in the Willows*, Kenneth Grahame, 1908, Novel

WIND IN THE WILLOWS, THE 1983 d: Arthur Rankin Jr., Jules Bass. USA., *The Wind in the Willows*, Kenneth Grahame, 1908, Novel

WIND IN THE WILLOWS, THE 1984 d: Jackie Cockle. UKN., *The Wind in the Willows*, Kenneth Grahame, 1908, Novel

WIND IN THE WILLOWS, THE 1996 d: Dave Unwin. UKN., *The Wind in the Willows*, Kenneth Grahame, 1908, Novel

WIND IN THE WILLOWS, THE 1996 d: Terry Jones. UKN., *The Wind in the Willows*, Kenneth Grahame, 1908, Novel

Wind of Death see L' ULTIMO UOMO DELLA TERRA (1964).

WIND, THE 1928 d: Victor Sjostrom. USA., *The Wind*, Dorothy Scarborough, New York 1925, Novel

WINDFALL 1935 d: George King. UKN., *Windfall*, R. C. Sherriff, London 1934, Play

WINDING STAIR, THE 1925 d: John Griffith Wray. USA., *The Winding Stair*, A. E. W. Mason, New York 1923, Novel

WINDJAMMER, THE 1930 d: John Orton. UKN., *By Way of Cape Horn*, A. J. Villiers, Novel

WINDMILL, THE 1937 d: Arthur Woods. UKN., *The Windmill*, John Drabble, Novel

WINDMILLS OF THE GODS 1988 d: Lee Philips. USA., *Windmills of the Gods*, Sidney Sheldon, Novel

WINDOM'S WAY 1957 d: Ronald Neame. UKN., *Windom's Way*, James Ramsay Ullman, Novel

WINDOW, THE 1949 d: Ted Tetzlaff. USA., *The Boy Cried Murder*, Cornell Woolrich, 1947, Short Story

Window to the Sky, A see THE OTHER SIDE OF THE MOUNTAIN (1975).

WINDS OF CHANCE 1925 d: Frank Lloyd. USA., *The Winds of Chance*, Rex Beach, New York 1918, Novel

Winds of Change see METAMORPHOSES (1978).

WINDS OF JARRAH, THE 1983 d: Mark Egerton. ASL., *The House in the Timberwoods*, Joyce Dingwell, Novel

WINDS OF THE PAMPAS 1927 d: Arthur Varney-Serrao. USA., *Wind of the Pampas*, Elynor Ewing, Story

WINDS OF WAR, THE 1983 d: Dan Curtis. USA., *The Winds of War*, Herman Wouk, Novel

WINDWALKER 1980 d: Kieth Merrill. USA., *Windwalker*, Blaine M. Yorgason, Novel

WINE 1924 d: Louis J. Gasnier. USA., *Wine*, William Briggs MacHarg, 1922, Short Story

Wine and the Music, The see PIECES OF DREAMS (1970).

Wine Cellar, The see LA BODEGA (1930).

Wine in the Blood see FRIENDS AND LOVERS (1931).

WINE OF LIFE, THE 1924 d: Arthur Rooke. UKN., *The Wine of Life*, Maude Annesley, Novel

WINE OF YOUTH 1924 d: King Vidor. USA., *Mary the Third*, Rachel Crothers, Boston 1923, Play

WINE, WOMEN AND HORSES 1937 d: Louis King. USA., *Dark Hazard*, William Riley Burnett, New York 1933, Novel

Winged Victory see SHINING VICTORY (1941).

WINGED VICTORY 1944 d: George Cukor. USA., *Winged Victory*, Moss Hart, New York 1943, Play

WINGLESS BIRD, THE 1996. UKN., *The Wingless Bird*, Catherine Cookson, Novel

WINGS FOR THE EAGLE 1942 d: Lloyd Bacon. USA., *Shadow of Their Wings*, Morgan Orkow, Story

WINGS OF CHANCE 1959 d: Edward Dew. CND., *Kirby's Gander*, John Patrick Gillese, Toronto 1957, Novel

WINGS OF DANGER 1952 d: Terence Fisher. UKN., *Dead on Course*, Elleston Trevor, Novel

WINGS OF EAGLES, THE 1956 d: John Ford. USA., *Wings of Men*, Frank Wead, Autobiography

WINGS OF PRIDE 1920 d: B. A. Rolfe. USA., *Wings of Pride*, Louise Kennedy Mabie, New York 1913, Novel

WINGS OF THE DOVE, THE 1997 d: Iain Softley. UKN/USA., *The Wings of the Dove*, Henry James, 1902, Novel

WINGS OF THE DOVE, THE 1997 d: John Gorrie. UKN., *The Wings of the Dove*, Henry James, 1902, Novel

WINGS OF THE HAWK 1953 d: Budd Boetticher. USA., *Wings of the Hawk*, Gerald Drayson Adams, Novel

WINGS OF THE MORNING 1919 d: J. Gordon Edwards. USA., *Wings of the Morning*, Louis Tracy, New York 1903, Novel

WINGS OF THE MORNING 1937 d: Harold Schuster. UKN/USA., *The Tale of a Gypsy Horse*, Donn Byrne, Short Story

WINGS OF THE STORM 1926 d: John G. Blystone. USA., *On the Wings of the Storm*, Lawrence William Pedrose, 1926, Short Story

WINGS OF YOUTH 1925 d: Emmett J. Flynn. USA., *Sisters of Jezebel*, Harold B. Montayne, 1924, Short Story

Wings of Youth see YOUNG SINNERS (1931).

WINGS OVER HONOLULU 1937 d: H. C. Potter. USA., Mildred Cram, Short Story

WINIFRED THE SHOP GIRL 1916 d: George D. Baker. USA., *The Shop Girl*, Alice Muriel Williamson, Charles Norris Williamson, New York 1916, Novel

WINNER TAKE ALL 1924 d: W. S. Van Dyke. USA., *Winner Take All*, Larry Evans, New York 1920, Novel

WINNER TAKE ALL 1932 d: Roy Del Ruth. USA., *133 at 3*, Gerald Beaumont, 1921, Short Story

WINNER TAKES ALL 1918 d: Elmer Clifton. USA., *The Rustler of Wind River*, George Washington Ogden, Chicago 1917, Novel

Winner Takes All see BOULEVARD DU RHUM (1971).

WINNER, THE 1996 d: Alex Cox. USA/ASL., *A Darker Purpose*, Wendy Riss, Play

Winner's Circle, The see RECKLESS LIVING (1938).

WINNETOU I 1963 d: Harald Reinl. GRM/ITL/YGS., *Winnetou Der Rote Gentleman*, Karl Friedrich May, Freiberg 1893, Novel

WINNETOU II 1964 d: Harald Reinl. GRM/FRN/ITL., *Winnetou Der Rote Gentleman*, Karl Friedrich May, Freiberg 1893, Novel

WINNETOU III 1965 d: Harald Reinl. GRM/YGS., *Winnetou Der Rote Gentleman*, Karl Friedrich May, Freiberg 1893, Novel

Winnetou: Last of the Renegades see WINNETOU II (1964).

Winnetou: the Desperado Trail see WINNETOU III (1965).

Winnetou the Warrior see **WINNETOU I** (1963).

WINNIE 1988 d: John Korty. USA., *Winnie: My Life in the Institution*, Paster Bolnick, Book

WINNIE'S DANCE 1912. USA., *That Winsome Winnie's Smile*, Carolyn Wells, Story

WINNING GIRL, THE 1919 d: Robert G. VignolA. USA., *Jem of the Old Rock*, George Weston, 1918, Short Story

WINNING GOAL, THE 1920 d: G. B. Samuelson. UKN., *The Winning Goal*, Harold Brighouse, Play

WINNING OF BARBARA WORTH, THE 1926 d: Henry King. USA., *The Winning of Barbara Worth*, Harold Bell Wright, Chicago 1911, Novel

WINNING OF SALLY TEMPLE, THE 1917 d: George Melford. USA., *The Heart of Sally Temple*, Rupert Sargent Holland, New York 1913, Novel

Winning Position, The see **NOBODY'S PERFECT** (1968).

Winning the West see **THE LIGHT OF WESTERN STARS** (1930).

WINNING WALLOP, THE 1926 d: Charles Hutchison. USA., *The Winning Wallop*, L. V. Jefferson, Story

Winning Way, The see **THE ALL-AMERICAN** (1953).

WINNING WITH WITS 1922 d: Howard M. Mitchell. USA., *The Girl Who Dared*, H. H. Van Loan, Story

WINSLOW BOY, THE 1948 d: Anthony Asquith. UKN., *The Winslow Boy*, Terence Rattigan, London 1946, Play

WINSLOW BOY, THE 1999 d: David Mamet. USA., *The Winslow Boy*, Terence Rattigan, London 1946, Play

WINSTANLEY 1975 d: Kevin Brownlow. UKN., *Comrade Jacob*, David Caute, 1961, Novel

Winston Affair, The see **MAN IN THE MIDDLE** (1963).

WINTER CARNIVAL 1939 d: Charles F. Reisner. USA., *Echoes That Old Refrain*, Corey Ford, 1937, Short Story

Winter Children see **VINTERBORN** (1978).

WINTER GUEST, THE 1997 d: Alan Rickman. UKN/USA., *The Winter Guest*, Sharman MacDonald, Play

WINTER KILLS 1979 d: William Richert. USA., *Winter Kills*, Richard Condon, 1974, Novel

WINTER MEETING 1948 d: Bretaigne Windust. USA., *Winter Meeting*, Ethel Vance, 1946, Novel

WINTER PEOPLE 1988 d: Ted Kotcheff. USA., *Winter People*, John Ehle, Novel

Winter Sirocco see **SIROKKO** (1969).

Winter Stories see **HISTOIRES D'HIVER** (1999).

WINTER TAN, A 1988 d: Jackie Burroughs, John Frizzell. CND., *A Winter Tan*, Maryse Holder, Novel

Winter Trip in the Olympic Stadium see **WINTERREISE IM OLYMPIASTADION** (1979).

Winter War, The see **TALVISOTA** (1989).

Winter Wind see **SIROKKO** (1969).

Winter-Born see **VINTERBORN** (1978).

Winterchildren see **VINTERBORN** (1978).

WINTERREISE IM OLYMPIASTADION 1979 d: Klaus Michael Gruber, Ellen Hammer. GRM., *Hyperion; Oder Der Eremit in Griechenland*, Friedrich Holderlin, 1797-99, Novel

Winter's Tale, A see **RACCONTI D'INVERNO** (1910).

WINTER'S TALE, THE 1910 d: Theodore Marston. USA., *The Winter's Tale*, William Shakespeare, c1611, Play

Winter's Tale, The see **RACCONTO D'INVERNO** (1913).

WINTER'S TALE, THE 1953 d: Charles Deane. UKN., *The Winter's Tale*, William Shakespeare, c1611, Play

WINTER'S TALE, THE 1968 d: Frank Dunlop. UKN., *The Winter's Tale*, William Shakespeare, c1611, Play

WINTER'S TALE, THE 1981 d: Jane Howell. UKN., *The Winter's Tale*, William Shakespeare, 1611, Play

WINTERSCHLAEFER 1997 d: Tom Tykwer. GRM., *Expense of Spirit*, Anne-Francoise Pyszora, Novel

WINTERSET 1936 d: Alfred Santell. USA., *Winterset*, Maxwell Anderson, New York 1935, Play

WINTERSET 1951. USA., *Winterset*, Maxwell Anderson, New York 1935, Play

WINTERSET 1959. USA., *Winterset*, Maxwell Anderson, New York 1935, Play

Wintersleepers see **WINTERSCHLAEFER** (1997).

Winterspelt see **WINTERSPELT 1944** (1977).

WINTERSPELT 1944 1977 d: Eberhard Fechner. GRM., *Winterspelt*, Alfred Andersch, 1974, Novel

Winton Wakes Up see **BRINGIN' HOME THE BACON** (1924).

Winzig Simule see **DE WINZIG SIMULIERT** (1942).

WINZIG SIMULIERT, DE 1942 d: Rudolf Bernhard. SWT., *Wem Gott Ein Amt Gibt*, Wilhelm Lichtenberg, Play

WIR 1983 d: Henryk Jacek Schoen. PLN., *Il Gorgo*, Luigi Pirandello, 1913, Short Story, *In Silenzio*, Luigi Pirandello, 1905, Short Story

WIR FAHREN MIT DER U-BAHN NACH ST. PAULI 1970 d: Claus Muras. GRM., *Wir Fahren Mit Der U-Bahn Nach St. Pauli*, Frank Boyss, Play

WIR MACHEN MUSIK 1942 d: Helmut Kautner. GRM., *Wir machen Musik*, Manfred Rossner, Play

WIR PFEIFEN AUF DEN GURKENKONIG 1974 d: Hark Bohm. GRM., *Wir Pfeifen Auf Den Gurkenkonig*, Christine Nostlinger, Novel

WIR WERDEN DAS KIND SCHON SCHAUKELN 1952 d: E. W. Emo. AUS., *Bubusch*, Gabor von Vaszary, Play

WIR WUNDERKINDER 1958 d: Kurt Hoffmann. GRM., *Wir Wunderkinder*, Hugo Hartung, Novel

Wirbel Um Irene see **IRENE IN NOTEN** (1953).

WIRED 1989 d: Larry Peerce. USA., *Wired*, Bob Woodward, Biography

WIRETAPPER 1956 d: Dick Ross. USA., *Why I Quit Syndicated Crime*, Jim Vaus, 1956, Book

Wiretappers see **WIRETAPPER** (1956).

WIRTIN AN DER LAHN, DIE 1955 d: J. A. Hubler-KahlA. GRM., *Meiseken*, Hans Alfred Kihn, Play

Wirtin Zum Roten Ochsen, Die see **DER FUNF-MINUTEN-VATER** (1951).

WIRTSHAUS IM SPESSART, DAS 1958 d: Kurt Hoffmann. GRM., *Das Wirthaus Im Spessart*, Wilhelm Hauff, 1828, Short Story

WIRTSHAUS VON DARTMOOR, DAS 1964 d: Rudolf Zehetgruber. GRM., Victor Gunn, Novel

Wise Baby see **FUGITIVES** (1929).

WISE BLOOD 1979 d: John Huston. USA/GRM., *Wise Blood*, Flannery O'Connor, 1955, Novel

WISE FOOL, A 1921 d: George Melford. USA., *The Money Master*, Gilbert Parker, New York 1915, Novel

WISE GIRLS 1929 d: E. Mason Hopper. USA., *Kempy*, Elliott Nugent, J. C. Nugent, New York 1922, Play

Wise Guys, The see **LES GRANDES GUEULES** (1965).

WISE WIFE, THE 1927 d: E. Mason Hopper. USA., *The Wise Wife*, Arthur Somers Roche, New York 1928, Novel

WISER SEX, THE 1932 d: Berthold Viertel. USA., *The Woman in the Case*, Clyde Fitch, New York 1905, Play

Wish machine, The see **STALKER** (1979).

WISHBONE, THE 1933 d: Arthur Maude. UKN., *One Crowded Hour*, W. Townend, Play

WISHING RING; AN IDYLL OF OLD ENGLAND, THE 1914 d: Maurice Tourneur. USA., *The Wishing Ring*, Owen Davis, New York 1910, Play

WISHING RING MAN, THE 1919 d: David Smith. USA., *The Wishing Ring Man*, Margaret Widdemer, New York 1917, Novel

Wishing Ring, The see **THE WISHING RING; AN IDYLL OF OLD ENGLAND** (1914).

Wishing Well see **THE HAPPINESS OF THREE WOMEN** (1954).

WISSELWACHTER, DE 1986 d: Jos Stelling. NTH., *De Wisselwachter*, Jean Paul Franssens, Novel

Wisteria see **LILA AKAC** (1934).

Wisteria Lodge see **THE RETURN OF SHERLOCK HOLMES: WISTERIA LODGE** (1986).

Witch Hunt see **HAJKA** (1977).

Witch in Love, The see **LA STREGA IN AMORE** (1966).

Witch Love see **EL AMOR BRUJO** (1967).

Witch of Timbuktoo, The see **THE DEVIL-DOLL** (1936).

Witch of Timbuktu, The see **THE DEVIL-DOLL** (1936).

Witch Reborn, The see **NOITA PALAA ELAMAAN** (1952).

Witch Returns to Life, The see **NOITA PALAA ELAMAAN** (1952).

WITCH, THE 1916 d: Frank Powell. USA., *La Sorciere*, Victorien Sardou, Paris 1903, Play

Witch, The see **NOITA PALAA ELAMAAN** (1952).

Witch, The see **DIE HEXE** (1954).

Witch, The see **VEDMA** (1956).

Witch, The see **LA STREGA IN AMORE** (1966).

Witch, The see **YOBA** (1976).

Witch, The see **SUPERSTITION** (1982).

Witchcraft see **MALIA** (1912).

Witchcraft see **SORTILEGES** (1944).

WITCHCRAFT 1992 d: Peter Sasdy. UKN., *Witchcraft*, Nigel Williams, Novel

WITCHES OF EASTWICK, THE 1987 d: George Miller. USA., *The Witches of Eastwick*, John Updike, 1984, Novel

Witches of Salem, The see **LES SORCIERES DE SALEM** (1957).

WITCHES, THE 1966 d: Cyril Frankel. UKN., *The Devil's Own*, Peter Curtis, London 1960, Novel

WITCHES, THE 1989 d: Nicolas Roeg. UKN/USA., *The Witches*, Roald Dahl, Novel

WITCHFINDER GENERAL 1968 d: Michael Reeves. UKN., *Witchfinder General*, Ronald Bassett, London 1966, Novel

Witchhammer see **KLADIVO NA CARODEJNICE** (1969).

WITCHING HOUR, THE 1916 d: George Irving. USA., *The Witching Hour*, Augustus Thomas, New York 1907, Play

WITCHING HOUR, THE 1921 d: William D. Taylor. USA., *The Witching Hour*, Augustus Thomas, New York 1907, Play

WITCHING HOUR, THE 1934 d: Henry Hathaway. USA., *The Witching Hour*, Augustus Thomas, New York 1907, Play

WITH ALL HER HEART 1920 d: Frank Wilson. UKN., *With All Her Heart*, Charles Garvice, Novel

With Banners Blowing see **VALIANT IS THE WORD FOR CARRIE** (1936).

With Bated Breath see **COL CUORE IN GOLA** (1967).

With Beauty and Sorrow see **UTSUKUSHISA TO KANASHIMI TO** (1965).

With Bound Eyes see **BEKOTOTT SZEMMEL** (1974).

WITH BRIDGES BURNED 1915 d: Ashley Miller. USA., *With Bridges Burned*, Rex Beach, Story

WITH FATHER'S HELP 1915 d: Al Christie. USA., *With Father's Help*, A. R. Lloyd, Story

With Fire and Sword see **COL FERRO E COL FUOCO** (1962).

WITH HARMFUL INTENT 1993 d: Richard Friedman. USA., *Somebody's Waiting*, Judith Kelman, Novel

With Heart in Mouth see **COL CUORE IN GOLA** (1967).

WITH HOOPS OF STEEL 1918 d: Eliot Howe. USA., *With Hoops of Steel*, Florence Finch Kelly, Indianapolis 1900, Novel

With Love see **Z LASKY** (1928).

WITH NEATNESS AND DISPATCH 1918 d: Will S. Davis. USA., *With Neatness and Dispatch*, Kenneth Lewis Roberts, 1918, Short Story

With the Hot Easterly Wind see **CON EL VIENTO SOLANO** (1968).

With the Next Man Everything Will Be Different see **BEIM NACHSTEN MANN WIRD ALLES ANDERS** (1988).

With the Subway to St. Paul's see **WIR FAHREN MIT DER U-BAHN NACH ST. PAULI** (1970).

With the Wind in Hot Sunlight see **CON EL VIENTO SOLANO** (1968).

WITH THIS RING 1925 d: Fred Windermere. USA., *With This Ring*, Fanny Heaslip Lea, New York 1925, Novel

Within and Without see **UN' ESTATE CON SENTIMENTO** (1970).

Within the Cloister see **INTERNO DI UN CONVENTO** (1977).

WITHIN THE ENEMY'S LINES 1913 d: Charles M. Seay. USA., *A Captured Santa Claus*, Thomas Nelson Page, Book

WITHIN THE LAW 1917 d: William P. S. Earle. USA., *Within the Law*, Bayard Veiller, New York 1912, Play

WITHIN THE LAW 1923 d: Frank Lloyd. USA., *Within the Law*, Bayard Veiller, New York 1912, Play

Within the Law see **PAID** (1930).

WITHIN THE LAW 1939 d: Gustav Machaty. USA., *Within the Law*, Bayard Veiller, New York 1912, Play

WITHIN THE ROCK 1935 d: Albert Ray. USA., *Within the Rock*, Marie Buxton Martin, New York 1925, Novel

Without a Dowry see BESPRIDANNITSA (1936).

Without a Net see CIRCUS GIRL (1937).

Without a Soul see LOLA (1914).

Without a Stitch see UDEN EN TRAEVL (1968).

WITHOUT A TRACE 1983 d: Stanley Jaffe. USA., *Without a Trace*, Beth Gutcheon, Novel

Without Apparent Motive see SANS MOBILE APPARENT (1971).

WITHOUT BENEFIT OF CLERGY 1921 d: James Young. USA., *Without Benefit of Clergy*, Rudyard Kipling, New York 1899, Novel

WITHOUT CHILDREN 1935 d: William Nigh. USA., *Eyes of Youth*, Mrs. Wilson Woodrow, Short Story

WITHOUT COMPROMISE 1922 d: Emmett J. Flynn. USA., *Without Compromise*, Lillian Bennett-Thompson, George Hubbard, New York 1922, Novel

Without Dowry see BESPRIDANNITSA (1936).

Without Honor see THE MACOMBER AFFAIR (1947).

WITHOUT LIMIT 1921 d: George D. Baker. USA., *Temple Dusk*, Calvin Johnston, 1920, Short Story

WITHOUT LOVE 1945 d: Harold S. Bucquet. USA., *Without Love*, Philip Barry, New York 1943, Play

WITHOUT MERCY 1925 d: George Melford. USA., *Without Mercy*, John Godwin, New York 1920, Novel

WITHOUT ORDERS 1936 d: Lew Landers. USA., *Without Orders*, Peter B. Kyne, 1936, Short Story

WITHOUT REGRET 1935 d: Harold Young. USA., *Interference*, Harold Dearden, Roland Pertwee, London 1927, Play

WITHOUT RESERVATIONS 1946 d: Mervyn Leroy. USA., *Thanks God I'll Take It from Here*, Jane Allen, Novel, *Thanks God - I'll Take It from Here*, Mae Livingston, Novel

Without Warning see THE STORY WITHOUT A NAME (1924).

Without Warning see FAIR WARNING (1937).

Without Warning see THE INVISIBLE MENACE (1938).

Without Witness see BEZ SVIDETELEI (1983).

Without Witnesses see BEZ SVIDETELEI (1983).

WITNESS CHAIR, THE 1936 d: George Nicholls Jr. USA., *The Witness Chair*, Rita Weiman, 1935, Novel

WITNESS FOR THE DEFENSE, THE 1919 d: George Fitzmaurice. USA., *The Witness for the Defence*, A. E. W. Mason, London 1911, Play

WITNESS FOR THE PROSECUTION 1957 d: Billy Wilder. USA., *Witness for the Prosecution*, Agatha Christie, London 1953, Play

WITNESS FOR THE PROSECUTION 1983 d: Alan Gibson. UKN., *Witness for the Prosecution*, Agatha Christie, London 1953, Play

Witness in Danger see TESTIMONE A RISCHIO (1997).

Witness of Mankind see NINGEN NO SHOMEI (1977).

Witness, The see LE TEMOIN (1977).

WITNESS VANISHES, THE 1939 d: Otis Garrett. USA., *They Can't Hang Me*, James Ronald, New York 1938, Novel

Witte, de see DE WITTE VAN SICHEM (1980).

WITTE VAN SICHEM, DE 1980 d: Robbe de Hert. BLG., Ernest Claes, Novel

WIVES AND LOVERS 1963 d: John Rich. USA., *The First Wife*, Jay Presson Allen, Play

Wives Beware see TWO WHITE ARMS (1932).

WIVES OF THE PROPHET, THE 1926 d: J. A. Fitzgerald. USA., *Teh Wives of the Prophet*, Opie Read, Chicago 1894, Novel

WIVES UNDER SUSPICION 1938 d: James Whale. USA., *Der Kuss Vor Dem Spiegel*, Ladislaus Fodor, Vienna 1932, Play

WIZ, THE 1978 d: Sidney Lumet. USA., *The Wonderful Wizard of Oz*, L. Frank Baum, Chicago 1900, Novel

WIZARD OF LONELINESS, THE 1988 d: Jenny Bowen. USA., *The Wizard of Loneliness*, John Nichols, Novel

WIZARD OF OZ 1910 d: Otis Turner. USA., *The Wonderful Wizard of Oz*, L. Frank Baum, Chicago 1900, Novel

WIZARD OF OZ, THE 1908. USA., *The Wonderful Wizard of Oz*, L. Frank Baum, Chicago 1900, Novel

WIZARD OF OZ, THE 1925 d: Larry Semon. USA., *The Wonderful Wizard of Oz*, L. Frank Baum, Chicago 1900, Novel

WIZARD OF OZ, THE 1939 d: Victor Fleming, King Vidor (Uncredited). USA., *The Wonderful Wizard of Oz*, L. Frank Baum, Chicago 1900, Novel

WIZARD OF OZ, THE 1982. USA., *The Wonderful Wizard of Oz*, L. Frank Baum, Chicago 1900, Novel

WIZARD, THE 1927 d: Richard Rosson. USA., *Balaoo*, Gaston Leroux, Paris 1912, Novel

Wizard, The see DAS ZAUBERMANNCHEN (1960).

Wizard, The see DER HEXER (1964).

WO AI CHUFANG 1997 d: Yim Ho. HKG/JPN., *Kitchen*, Banana Yoshimoto, Novel

WO DIE LERCHE SINGT 1936 d: Carl Lamac. GRM/HNG/SWT., *Wo Die Lerche Singt*, Franz Lehar, Operetta

WO DIE LERCHE SINGT 1956 d: Hans Wolff. AUS., *Wo Die Lerche Singt*, Franz Lehar, Operetta

WO SHI HI BA BA MA? 1995 d: Wang Shuo. CHN., *Wo Shi Ni Ba Ba Ma?*, Wang Shuo, Novel

WO YAO HUO XIA CHU 1995 d: Raymond Lee. CHN/HKG., *Wo Yao Huo XIa Chu*, Liang Fengyi, Novel

WO ZHE YIBEIZI 1950 d: Shi Hui. CHN., *Wo Zhe Yibeizi*, Shu Qingchun, 1949, Short Story

Wochenend Im Paradies see LIEBE IM FINANZAMT (1952).

WODZECK 1984 d: Oliver Herbrich. GRM., *Woyzeck*, Georg Buchner, 1879, Play

Wodzek see WODZECK (1984).

WOLF HUNTERS, THE 1926 d: Stuart Paton. USA., *The Wolf Hunters; a Tale of Adventure in the Wilderness*, James Oliver Curwood, Indianapolis 1908, Novel

WOLF HUNTERS, THE 1949 d: Budd Boetticher. USA., *The Wolf Hunters; a Tale of Adventure in the Wilderness*, James Oliver Curwood, Indianapolis 1908, Novel

WOLF LARSEN 1958 d: Harmon Jones. USA., *The Sea Wolf*, Jack London, New York 1904, Novel

Wolf Larsen see IL LUPO DEI MARI (1975).

WOLF LAW 1922 d: Stuart Paton. USA., *Wolf Law*, Hugh Pendexter, 1921, Short Story

Wolf of the Seven Seas see IL LUPO DEI MARI (1975).

WOLF SONG 1929 d: Victor Fleming. USA., *Wolf Song*, Harvey Fergusson, 1927, Short Story

WOLF, THE 1914 d: Barry O'Neil. USA., *The Wolf*, Eugene Walter, New York 1908, Play

WOLF, THE 1919 d: James Young. USA., *The Wolf*, Eugene Walter, New York 1908, Play

Wolf to the Slaughter see INSPECTOR WEXFORD: WOLF TO THE SLAUGHTER (1987).

Wolf Trap see VLCI JAMA (1958).

WOLFEN 1981 d: Michael Wadleigh. USA., *Wolfen*, Whitley Strieber, Novel

Wolfpack see DIE HALBSTARKEN (1956).

Wolfpack see THE MCKENZIE BREAK (1970).

WOLF'S CLOTHING 1927 d: Roy Del Ruth. USA., *Wolf's Clothing*, Arthur Somers Roche, 1926, Short Story

WOLF'S CLOTHING 1936 d: Andrew Marton. UKN., *The Emancipation of Ambrose*, Evadne Price, Play

WOLVERINE, THE 1921 d: William Bertram. USA., *The Ranch at the Wolverine*, B. M. Bower, Boston 1914, Novel

WOLVES 1930 d: Albert de Courville. UKN., *Wolves*, Georges G. Toudouze, Play

Wolves Cry Under the Moon see GUODAO FENGBI (1997).

Wolves of Catclaw see THE PRESCOTT KID (1934).

WOLVES OF KROMER, THE 1998 d: Will Gould. UKN., *The Wolves of Kromer*, Charles Lambert, Play

WOLVES OF WILLOUGHBY CHASE, THE 1989 d: Stuart Orme. UKN., *The Wolves of Willoughby Chase*, Joan Aiken, Novel

Woman see AMORE (1948).

WOMAN ACCUSED, THE 1933 d: Paul Sloane. USA., *The Woman Accused*, Polan Banks, Irvin S. Cobb, 1933, Story

Woman Against Woman see WHICH WOMAN? (1918).

WOMAN AGAINST WOMAN 1938 d: Robert B. Sinclair. USA., *Enemy Territory*, Margaret Culkin Banning, 1937, Short Story

Woman Alone, A see SABOTAGE (1936).

Woman Alone, The see SABOTAGE (1936).

WOMAN AND THE PUPPET, THE 1920 d: Reginald Barker. USA., *La Femme Et le Pantin*, Pierre Louys, Paris 1898, Novel

Woman and the Stranger, The see DIE FRAU UND DER FREMDE (1984).

Woman and the Wild River, The see WILD RIVER (1960).

WOMAN AND WIFE 1918 d: Edward Jose. USA., *Jane Eyre*, Charlotte Bronte, London 1847, Novel

Woman and Wife see THE LUCK OF GERALDINE LAIRD (1920).

Woman at Her Window, A see UNE FEMME A SA FENETRE (1976).

Woman at the Crossroads see ZENA NA ROZCESTI (1937).

Woman at the Dark Window, The see EINE FRAU AM DUNKLEN FENSTER (1960).

Woman at the Window see UNE FEMME A SA FENETRE (1976).

WOMAN AT WAR, A 1990 d: Edward Bennett. UKN., *Inside the Gestapo*, Helene Moskiewicz

Woman Bait see MAIGRET TEND UN PIEGE (1957).

Woman Below the Cross see ZENA POD KRIZEM (1937).

WOMAN BETWEEN FRIENDS, THE 1918 d: Tom Terriss. USA., *Between Friends*, Robert W. Chambers, New York 1914, Novel

WOMAN BETWEEN, THE 1931 d: Victor Schertzinger. USA., *Madame Julie*, Irving Kaye Davis, 1930, Play

WOMAN BETWEEN, THE 1931 d: Miles Mander. UKN., *Conflict*, Miles Malleson, London 1925, Play

Woman Between, The see THE WOMAN I LOVE (1937).

Woman Breaker, The see A HOUSE DIVIDED (1932).

WOMAN CALLED MOSES, A 1978 d: Paul Wendkos. USA., *A Woman Called Moses*, Marcy Heidish, Book

Woman Decides, The see THE WOMAN BETWEEN (1931).

Woman Disappeared, A see UNE FEMME DISPARAIT (1942).

WOMAN DISPUTED, THE 1928 d: Henry King, Sam Taylor. USA., *Boule de Suif*, Guy de Maupassant, 1880, Short Story

Woman Eternal, The see HER MAN (1918).

Woman, Flower see NUREN HUA (1994).

WOMAN FOR JOE, THE 1955 d: George M. O'Ferrall. UKN., *And Delilah*, Neil Paterson, Short Story

Woman for Men see MANS KVINNA (1945).

Woman for Two, A see CHUN TAO (1988).

Woman from Hell, The see QUEEN OF THE MOB (1940).

Woman from Lebanon, The see LA CHATELAINE DU LIBAN (1956).

WOMAN FROM MONTE CARLO, THE 1932 d: Michael Curtiz. USA., *La Veille d'Armes*, Claude Farrere, Lucien Nepoty, Paris 1917, Play

WOMAN FROM MOSCOW, THE 1928 d: Ludwig Berger. USA., *Fedora*, Victorien Sardou, Paris 1882, Play

Woman from the Mountain, The see LA DONNA DELLA MONTAGNA (1943).

WOMAN GIVES, THE 1920 d: R. William Neill. USA., *The Woman Gives*, Owen Johnson, Boston 1916, Novel

WOMAN GOD CHANGED, THE 1921 d: Robert G. VignolA. USA., *The Woman God Changed*, Brian Oswald Donn-Byrne, 1921, Short Story

Woman Hater, The see SOONER OR LATER (1920).

WOMAN HATER, THE 1925 d: James Flood. USA., *The Eleventh Virgin*, Dorothy Day, New York 1924, Novel

Woman He Chose, The see TOSEN FRAN STORMYRTORPET (1918).

WOMAN HUNGRY 1931 d: Clarence Badger. USA., *The Great Divide*, William Vaughn Moody, New York 1906, Play

WOMAN I LOVE, THE 1929 d: George Melford. USA., *The Woman I Love*, Irma Stormquist, Story

WOMAN I LOVE, THE 1937 d: Anatole Litvak. USA., *L' Equipage*, Joseph Kessel, Paris 1923, Novel

WOMAN I STOLE, THE 1933 d: Irving Cummings. USA., *Tampico*, Joseph Hergesheimer, New York 1926, Novel

WOMAN IN A DRESSING GOWN 1957 d: J. Lee Thompson. UKN., *Woman in a Dressing Gown*, Ted Willis, Television Play

WOMAN IN BLACK, THE 1914 d: Lawrence Marston. USA., *The Woman in Black*, H. Grattan Donnelly, New York 1897, Play

Woman in Bondage *see* THE IMPASSIVE FOOTMAN (1932).

Woman in Brown *see* THE VICIOUS CIRCLE (1948).

Woman in Chains *see* THE IMPASSIVE FOOTMAN (1932).

WOMAN IN CHAINS, THE 1923 d: William P. Burt. USA., *The Madonna in Chains*, Edward Owings Towne, Story

WOMAN IN GREEN, THE 1945 d: R. William Neill. USA., *Adventure of the Empty House*, Arthur Conan Doyle, 1903, Short Story

WOMAN IN HIDING 1949 d: Michael Gordon. USA., *Fugitive Form Terror*, James R. Webb, Serial Story

Woman in Hiding *see* MANTRAP (1953).

Woman in His House, The *see* THE ANIMAL KINGDOM (1932).

Woman in July, A *see* THE STRIPPER (1963).

WOMAN IN PAWN, A 1927 d: Victor Saville, Edwin Greenwood. UKN., *In Pawn*, Frank Stayton, Play

WOMAN IN RED, THE 1935 d: Robert Florey. USA., *North Shore*, Wallace Irwin, Boston 1932, Novel

WOMAN IN ROOM 13, THE 1920 d: Frank Lloyd. USA., *The Woman in Room 13*, Max Marcin, Samuel Shipman, Percival Wilde, New York 1919, Play

WOMAN IN ROOM 13, THE 1932 d: Henry King. USA., *The Woman in Room 13*, Max Marcin, Samuel Shipman, Percival Wilde, New York 1919, Play

WOMAN IN THE CASE, THE 1916 d: Hugh Ford. USA., *The Woman in the Case*, Clyde Fitch, New York 1905, Play

Woman in the Chair, The *see* THE SIN OF NORA MORAN (1933).

WOMAN IN THE DARK 1934 d: Phil Rosen. USA., *Woman in the Dark*, Dashiell Hammett, 1933, Short Story

Woman in the Dunes *see* SUNA NO ONNA (1964).

WOMAN IN THE HALL, THE 1947 d: Jack Lee. UKN., *The Woman in the Hall*, Gladys Bronwyn Stern, Novel

Woman in the Moon *see* DIE FRAU IM MOND (1929).

Woman in the Night, A *see* TESHA (1928).

Woman in the Sand *see* SUNA NO ONNA (1964).

WOMAN IN THE WINDOW, THE 1944 d: Fritz Lang. USA., *Once Off Guard*, J. H. Wallis, Novel

Woman in White, A *see* LE JOURNAL D'UNE FEMME EN BLANC (1964).

WOMAN IN WHITE, THE 1912. USA., *The Woman in White*, Wilkie Collins, London 1860, Novel

WOMAN IN WHITE, THE 1917 d: Ernest C. Warde. USA., *The Woman in White*, Wilkie Collins, London 1860, Novel

WOMAN IN WHITE, THE 1929 d: Herbert Wilcox. UKN., *The Woman in White*, Wilkie Collins, London 1860, Novel

WOMAN IN WHITE, THE 1948 d: Peter Godfrey. USA., *The Woman in White*, Wilkie Collins, London 1860, Novel

WOMAN JUROR, THE 1926 d: Milton Rosmer. UKN., *The Woman Juror*, E. F. Parr, Play

Woman Lies, A *see* THUNDER IN THE NIGHT (1935).

Woman Like Satan, A *see* LA FEMME ET LE PANTIN (1958).

Woman Melon Garden Guard *see* GUA PENG NU JIE (1985).

WOMAN MICHAEL MARRIED, THE 1919 d: Henry Kolker. USA., *The Woman Michael Married*, Du Vernet Rabell, 1918, Novel

WOMAN NEXT DOOR, THE 1915 d: Walter Edwin. USA., *The Woman Next Door*, Owen Davis, Play

WOMAN NEXT DOOR, THE 1919 d: Robert G. VignolA. USA., *Vicky Van*, Carolyn Wells, Philadelphia 1918, Novel

Woman Next Door, The *see* THE LAST CARD (1921).

WOMAN OBSESSED 1959 d: Henry Hathaway. USA., *The Snow Birch*, John Mantley, 1958, Novel

WOMAN OF AFFAIRS, A 1928 d: Clarence Brown. USA., *The Green Hat*, Michael Arlen, New York 1924, Novel

Woman of Antwerp *see* DEDEE D'ANVERS (1947).

WOMAN OF BRONZE, THE 1923 d: King Vidor. USA., *Woman of Bronze*, Henri Kistemaeckers, Play

Woman of Darkness *see* YNGSJOMORDET (1966).

Woman of Desire *see* THE MEN IN HER LIFE (1941).

Woman of Destiny *see* WITHIN THE ROCK (1935).

Woman of Evil, A *see* LA REINE MARGOT (1954).

WOMAN OF EXPERIENCE, A 1931 d: Harry J. Brown. USA., *The Registered Woman*, John Farrow, Play

Woman of Flame, The *see* THE MAN FROM YESTERDAY (1932).

WOMAN OF HIS DREAMS, THE 1921 d: Harold Shaw. UKN., *The Woman of His Dreams*, Ethel M. Dell, Novel

WOMAN OF IMPULSE, A 1918 d: Edward Jose. USA., *A Woman of Impulse*, Louis K. Anspacher, New York 1909, Play

Woman of Musashino *see* MUSASHINO FUJIN (1951).

Woman of My Own, A *see* DESIRE ME (1947).

WOMAN OF NO IMPORTANCE, A 1921 d: Denison Clift. UKN., *A Woman of No Importance*, Oscar Wilde, London 1893, Play

Woman of No Importance, A *see* EINE FRAU OHNE BEDEUTUNG (1936).

WOMAN OF NO IMPORTANCE, A 1960 d: Joan Kemp-Welch. UKN., *A Woman of No Importance*, Oscar Wilde, London 1893, Play

WOMAN OF PLEASURE, A 1919 d: Wallace Worsley. USA., *A Woman of Pleasure*, James Willard, Play

Woman of Rome *see* LA ROMANA (1954).

Woman of Sin *see* LA MOUCHARDE (1958).

WOMAN OF STRAW 1964 d: Basil Dearden. UKN., *La Femme de Paille*, Catherine Arley, Paris 1956, Novel

WOMAN OF SUBSTANCE, A 1984 d: Don Sharp. UKN/USA., *A Woman of Substance*, Barbara Taylor Bradford, Novel

Woman of Summer *see* THE STRIPPER (1963).

Woman of the Dunes *see* SUNA NO ONNA (1964).

WOMAN OF THE IRON BRACELETS, THE 1920 d: Sidney Morgan. UKN., *The Woman of the Iron Bracelets*, Frank Barrett, Novel

WOMAN OF THE WORLD, A 1925 d: Malcolm St. Clair. USA., *The Tattooed Countess*, Carl Van Vechten, New York 1924, Novel

Woman of the World, A *see* THE MALTESE FALCON (1931).

Woman of the World, A *see* OUTCAST LADY (1934).

Woman on Board, A *see* EN KVINNA OMBORD (1941).

WOMAN ON THE BEACH, THE 1946 d: Jean Renoir. USA., *None So Blind*, Mitchell Wilson, 1945, Novel

WOMAN ON THE INDEX, THE 1919 d: Hobart Henley. USA., *The Woman on the Index*, Lillian T. Bradley, George Broadhurst, New York 1918, Novel

WOMAN ON THE JURY, THE 1924 d: Harry O. Hoyt. USA., *The Woman on the Jury*, Bernard K. Burns, New York 1923, Play

WOMAN ON THE RUN 1950 d: Norman Foster. USA., *Woman on the Run*, Sylvia Tate, 1948, Short Story

WOMAN ON THE RUN: THE LAWRENCIA BEMBENEK STORY 1993 d: Sandor Stern. USA., *Woman on Trial*, Lawrencia Bembenek, Autobiography

WOMAN ON TRIAL, THE 1927 d: Mauritz Stiller. USA., *Confession*, Erno Vajda, Play

Woman Opposite *see* THAT WOMAN OPPOSITE (1957).

WOMAN PAYS, THE 1915 d: Edgar Jones. USA., *The Woman Pays*, Florence Gerald, Play

WOMAN RACKET, THE 1929 d: Robert Ober, Albert Kelley. USA., *The Night Hostess*, Frances Dunning, Philip Dunning, New York 1928, Play

WOMAN REBELS, A 1936 d: Mark Sandrich. USA., *Portrait of a Rebel*, Netta Syrett, New York 1936, Novel

WOMAN REDEEMED, A 1927 d: Sinclair Hill. UKN., *The Fining Pot Is for Silver*, F. Britten Austin, Novel

Woman Sees It Through, The *see* MOTHER (1927).

WOMAN TEMPTED, THE 1926 d: Maurice Elvey. UKN., *The Woman Tempted*, Countess Vera Cathcart, Novel

Woman That Sails Alone *see* DIE ALLEINSEGLERIN (1987).

WOMAN, THE 1915 d: George Melford. USA., *The Woman*, William C. de Mille, New York 1911, Play

WOMAN THERE WAS, A 1919 d: J. Gordon Edwards. USA., *Creation's Tears*, Neje Hopkins, Short Story

WOMAN THEY ALMOST LYNCHED, THE 1953 d: Allan Dwan. USA., *The Woman They Almost Lynched*, Michael Fessier, 1951, Short Story

WOMAN THOU GAVEST ME, THE 1919 d: Hugh Ford. USA., *The Woman Thou Gavest Me*, Hall Caine, London 1913, Novel

WOMAN TO WOMAN 1923 d: Graham Cutts. UKN., *Woman to Woman*, Michael Morton, London 1921, Play

WOMAN TO WOMAN 1929 d: Victor Saville. UKN., *Woman to Woman*, Michael Morton, London 1921, Play

WOMAN TO WOMAN 1946 d: MacLean Rogers. UKN., *Woman to Woman*, Michael Morton, London 1921, Play

Woman to Woman *see* DE MUJER A MUJER (1950).

WOMAN TRAP 1929 d: William A. Wellman. USA., *Brothers*, Edwin Burke, Play

WOMAN UNDER COVER, THE 1919 d: George Siegmann. USA., *Playing the Game*, Sada Cowan, Play

WOMAN WANTED 1935 d: George B. Seitz. USA., *Get That Girl*, Wilson Collison, Story

Woman Who Came Back, The *see* THE GIRL WHO CAME BACK (1918).

WOMAN WHO DARED, THE 1916 d: George E. Middleton. USA., *The Woman Who Dared*, Alice Muriel Williamson, London 1903, Novel

WOMAN WHO DID NOT CARE, THE 1927 d: Phil Rosen. USA., *The Woman Who Did Not Care*, Rida Johnson Young, Story

WOMAN WHO DID, THE 1915 d: Walter West. UKN., *The Woman Who Did*, Grant Allen, Novel

Woman Who Killed a Vulture, The *see* DIE GEIER-WALLY (1921).

Woman Who Knows What She Wants, A *see* KTERA VI CO CHCE ZENA (1934).

Woman Who Knows What She Wants, A *see* DIE WEISS, WAS SIE WILL, EINE FRAU (1958).

WOMAN WHO MARRIED CLARK GABLE, THE 1986 d: Thaddeus O'Sullivan. IRL/UKN., *The Woman Who Married Clark Gable*, Sean O'Faolain, 1948, Short Story

Woman Who Needed Killing, The *see* A DANGEROUS WOMAN (1929).

WOMAN WHO WALKED ALONE, THE 1922 d: George Melford. USA., *The Cat That Walked Alone*, John Colton, Story

WOMAN WHO WAS FORGOTTEN, THE 1930 d: Richard Thomas. USA., *The Woman Who Was Forgotten*, Bess Streeter Aldrich, 1926, Short Story

WOMAN WHO WAS NOTHING, THE 1917 d: Maurice Elvey. UKN., *The Woman Who Was Nothing*, Tom Gallon, Novel

Woman Who Wouldn't Die, The *see* CATACOMBS (1964).

WOMAN WINS, THE 1918 d: Frank Wilson. UKN., *The Woman Wins*, Cecil H. Bullivant, Play

WOMAN WITH FOUR FACES, THE 1923 d: Herbert Brenon. USA., *The Woman With Four Faces*, Bayard Veiller, Play

WOMAN WITH NO NAME, THE 1950 d: Ladislao Vajda, George M. O'Ferrall. UKN., *Happy Now I Go*, Theresa Charles, Novel

WOMAN WITH THE FAN, THE 1921 d: Rene Plaissetty. UKN., *The Woman With the Fan*, Robert Hichens, Novel

Woman Without a Face *see* MISTER BUDDWING (1965).

Woman Without Love, A *see* UNA MUJER SIN AMOR (1951).

Woman Without Pity, A *see* UNA MUJER SIN AMOR (1951).

WOMAN! WOMAN! 1919 d: Kenean Buel. USA., *On Desert Altars*, Norma Lorimer, New York 1915, Novel

WOMANHANDLED 1925 d: Gregory La CavA. USA., *Woman-Handled*, Arthur Stringer, 1925, Short Story

Womanlight *see* CLAIR DE FEMME (1979).

WOMANPOWER 1926 d: Harry Beaumont. USA., *You Can't Always Tell*, Harold MacGrath, 1925, Short Story

WOMAN'S ANGLE, THE 1952 d: Leslie Arliss. UKN., *Three Cups of Coffee*, Ruth Feiner, Novel

WOMAN'S BUSINESS, A 1920 d: B. A. Rolfe. USA., *Nothing a Year*, Charles Belmont Davis, New York 1915, Novel

Woman's Day *see* LIFE BEGINS (1932).

Woman's Destiny, A *see* YI GE NU REN DE MING YUN (1984).

WOMAN'S EXPERIENCE, A 1918 d: Perry N. Vekroff. USA., *Agnes*, Paul M. Potter, New York 1908, Play

Woman's Face, A *see* EN KVINNAS ANSIKTE (1938).

WOMAN'S FACE, A 1941 d: George Cukor. USA., *Il Etait une Fois*, Francis de Croisset, Play

WOMAN'S FAITH, A 1925 d: Edward Laemmle. USA., *Miracle*, Clarence Budington Kelland, New York 1925, Novel

WOMAN'S FOOL, A 1918 d: John Ford. USA., *Lin McLean*, Owen Wister, New York 1897, Novel

WOMAN'S GUIDE TO ADULTERY, A 1993 d: David Hayman. UKN., *A Woman's Guide to Adultery*, Carol Clewlow, Novel

WOMAN'S HEART, A 1926 d: Phil Rosen. USA., *The Revelations of a Woman's Heart*, Ruth d'Agostino, Novel

WOMAN'S HONOR, A 1916 d: Roland West. USA., *La Terribula*, George L. Knapp, 1915, Short Story

Woman's Law, A *see* THE TRAP (1919).

WOMAN'S LAW, THE 1916 d: Lawrence McGill. USA., *The Woman's Law*, Maravene Thompson, New York 1914, Novel

WOMAN'S MAN, A 1934 d: Edward Ludwig. USA., *The Great God Four Flush*, Adela Rogers St. Johns, Short Story

Woman's Paradise *see* DAS FRAUENPARADIES (1936).

WOMAN'S PAST, A 1915 d: Frank Powell. USA., *A Woman's Past*, Capt. John King, Play

WOMAN'S POWER, A 1916 d: Robert T. Thornby. USA., *The Code of the Mountains*, Charles Neville Buck, New York 1915, Novel

WOMAN'S RESURRECTION, A 1915 d: J. Gordon Edwards. USA., *Voskreseniye*, Lev Nikolayevich Tolstoy, Moscow 1899, Novel

Woman's Secret, A *see* SOUTHERN LOVE (1924).

WOMAN'S SECRET, A 1949 d: Nicholas Ray. USA., *Mortgage of Life*, Vicki Baum, Novel

Woman's Testament, A *see* JOKYO (1960).

WOMAN'S TRIUMPH, A 1914 d: J. Searle Dawley. USA., *The Heart of Midlothian*, Sir Walter Scott, 1818, Novel

WOMAN'S VENGEANCE, A 1947 d: Zoltan KordA. USA., *The Gioconda Smile*, Aldous Huxley, 1922, Short Story

WOMAN'S WAY, A 1916 d: Barry O'Neil. USA., *A Woman's Way*, Thompson Buchanan, New York 1909, Play

Woman's Way, A *see* A SONG OF SIXPENCE (1917).

WOMAN'S WOMAN, A 1922 d: Charles Giblyn. USA., *A Woman's Woman*, Nalbro Bartley, Boston 1919, Novel

WOMAN'S WORLD, A 1954 d: Jean Negulesco. USA., *May the Best Wife Win*, Mona Williams, Story

Womantrap *see* THE SHADOW STRIKES (1937).

WOMEN AND ROSES 1914 d: Wallace Reid. USA., *Women and Roses*, Robert Browning, Poem

Women and War *see* ARRETEZ LES TAMBOURS (1961).

Women and Wine *see* THE MODEL (1915).

Women are Born Newspapermen *see* FRONT PAGE WOMAN (1935).

Women are Dangerous *see* HUSBAND AND FRIEND WIFE (1939).

WOMEN ARE LIKE THAT 1938 d: Stanley Logan. USA., *Return from Limbo*, A. H. Z. Carr, 1936, Short Story

Women are Like That *see* COMMENT QU'ELLE EST? (1960).

Women are Talkative *see* LES FEMMES SONT MARRANTES (1958).

Women are Weak *see* FAIBLES FEMMES (1959).

WOMEN AREN'T ANGELS 1942 d: Lawrence Huntington. UKN., *Women Aren't Angels*, Vernon Sylvaine, Play

Women at the Petrol Station *see* ZENY U BENZINU (1939).

Women Behind Bars *see* WOMEN WITHOUT NAMES (1940).

Women Doctors *see* ARZTINNEN (1983).

Women Flowers *see* NUREN HUA (1994).

WOMEN GO ON FOREVER 1931 d: Walter Lang. USA., *Women Go on Forever*, Daniel N. Rubin, New York 1927, Play

Women in Chains, The *see* THE WOMAN IN CHAINS (1923).

Women in Hospital *see* FRAUENSTATION (1975).

Women in Love *see* SINNER'S HOLIDAY (1930).

WOMEN IN LOVE 1969 d: Ken Russell. UKN., *Women in Love*, D. H. Lawrence, 1920, Novel

WOMEN IN THE WIND 1939 d: John Farrow. USA., *Women in the Wind*, Francis Walton, New York 1935, Novel

Women in Waiting *see* CEKANKY (1940).

Women in War *see* ARRETEZ LES TAMBOURS (1961).

WOMEN LOVE ONCE 1931 d: Edward Goodman. USA., *Daddy's Gone a-Hunting*, Zoe Akins, New York 1921, Play

WOMEN MEN LOVE 1920 d: Samuel R. Bradley. USA., *Women Men Love*, Charles T. Dazey, Short Story

WOMEN OF BREWSTER PLACE, THE 1989 d: Donna Deitch. USA., *The Women of Brewster Place*, Gloria Naylor, Book

WOMEN OF GLAMOUR 1937 d: Gordon Wiles. USA., *Ladies of the Evening*, Milton Herbert Gropper, New York 1924, Play

Women of Glamour *see* WOMEN OF GLAMOUR (1937).

Women of Niskavuori *see* NISKAVUOREN NAISET (1938).

Women of Niskavuori *see* NISKAVUOREN NAISET (1958).

Women of the Jury *see* LADIES OF THE JURY (1932).

Women of the Lake *see* ONNA NO MISUMI (1966).

Women of the Night *see* YORU NO ONNATACHI (1948).

WOMEN OF TWILIGHT 1952 d: Gordon Parry. UKN., *Women of Twilight*, Sylvia Rayman, London 1951, Play

WOMEN, THE 1939 d: George Cukor. USA., *The Women*, Clare Boothe Luce, New York 1936, Play

WOMEN WHO GIVE 1924 d: Reginald Barker. USA., *Cape Cod Folks*, Sarah P. McLean Greene, Boston 1881, Novel

WOMEN WHO PLAY 1932 d: Arthur Rosson. UKN., *Spring Cleaning*, Frederick Lonsdale, New York 1923, Play

Women Who Wait *see* WOMEN WHO GIVE (1924).

WOMEN WHO WIN 1919 d: Percy Nash, Fred W. Durrant. UKN., *Women Who Win*, Mrs. E. Almez Stout, Novel

Women Without Men *see* DIRNENTRAGODIE (1927).

WOMEN WITHOUT NAMES 1940 d: Robert Florey. USA., *Ladies of the Big House*, Ernest Booth, 1931, Play

WOMEN'S ROOM, THE 1980 d: Glenn Jordan. USA., *The Women's Room*, Marilyn French, Novel

Women's Scroll *see* JOKYO (1960).

WON BY A HEAD 1920 d: Percy Nash. UKN., *Won By a Head*, John Gabriel, Novel

WONDER BAR 1934 d: Lloyd Bacon. USA., *Die Wunderbar*, Karl Farkas, Geza Herczeg, Robert Katscher, 1930, Play

Wonder of Love, The *see* OSWALT KOLLE: DAS WUNDER DER LIEBE -SEXUALITAT IN DER EHE (1968).

WONDER OF WOMEN 1929 d: Clarence Brown. USA., *Die Frau Des Steffen Tromholt*, Hermann Sudermann, Stuttgart 1927, Novel

WONDERFUL ADVENTURE, THE 1915 d: Frederick A. Thompson. USA., *The Wonderful Adventure*, Captain Wilbur Lawson, Play

Wonderful Adventures of Nils, The *see* NILS HOLGERSSONS UNDERBARA RESA (1962).

WONDERFUL COUNTRY, THE 1959 d: Robert Parrish. USA., *The Wonderful Country*, Tom Lea, 1952, Novel

WONDERFUL ICE CREAM SUIT, THE 1998 d: Stuart Gordon. USA., *The Magic White Suit*, Ray Bradbury, 1957, Short Story

WONDERFUL LAND OF OZ, THE 1969 d: Barry Mahon. USA., *The Marvelous Land of Oz*, L. Frank Baum, Chicago 1904, Novel

Wonderful November, A *see* UN BELLISSIMO NOVEMBRE (1968).

WONDERFUL ONE-HORSE SHAY, THE 1912. USA., *The Wonderful One-Horse Shay*, Oliver Wendell Holmes, Poem

WONDERFUL STORY, THE 1922 d: Graham Cutts. UKN., *The Wonderful Story*, I. A. R. Wylie, Novel

WONDERFUL STORY, THE 1932 d: Reginald Fogwell. UKN., *The Wonderful Story*, I. A. R. Wylie, Novel

Wonderful Summer, A *see* KINDER DER BERGE (1958).

WONDERFUL THING, THE 1921 d: Herbert Brenon. USA., *The Wonderful Thing*, Lillian T. Bradley, Forrest Halsey, New York 1920, Play

WONDERFUL WIFE, A 1922 d: Paul Scardon. USA., *The Rat Trap*, Dolf Wyllarde, New York 1904, Novel

WONDERFUL WOOING, THE 1925 d: Geoffrey H. Malins. UKN., *The Wonderful Wooing*, Douglas Walshe, Novel

WONDERFUL WORLD OF THE BROTHERS GRIMM, THE 1963 d: Henry Levin, George Pal. USA., *Die Bruder Grimm*, Hermann Gerstner, Munich 1952, Biography

WONDERFUL YEAR, THE 1921 d: Kenelm Foss. UKN., *The Wonderful Year*, William J. Locke, Novel

Wonderful Years of Lousy Loving, The *see* BAJECNA LETA POD PSA (1997).

Wonderful Years, The *see* THE RESTLESS YEARS (1958).

Wonderful Years, The *see* DIE WUNDERBAREN JAHRE (1979).

WOOD DEMON, THE 1974 d: Donald McWhinnie. UKN., *Leshii*, Anton Chekhov, 1890, Play

Wooden Anchors *see* SUBMARINE PATROL (1938).

Wooden Crosses *see* LES CROIX DE BOIS (1931).

Wooden Horse of Troy, The *see* LA GUERRA DI TROIA (1961).

WOODEN HORSE, THE 1950 d: Jack Lee. UKN., *The Wooden Horse*, Eric Williams, Book

WOODLANDERS, THE 1997 d: Phil Agland. UKN., *The Woodlanders*, Thomas Hardy, 1877, Novel

Word, The *see* ORDET (1943).

Word, The *see* ORDET (1954).

WORD, THE 1978 d: Richard Lang. USA., *The Word*, Irving Wallace, Novel

Words and Music *see* WORDS AND MUSIC BY. (1919).

WORDS AND MUSIC BY. 1919 d: Scott R. Dunlap. USA., *Words and Music By.*, William Charles Lengel, 1919, Story

Words to Say It *see* LES MOTS POUR LE DIRE (1983).

WORK IS A FOUR LETTER WORD 1967 d: Peter Hall. UKN., *Eh?*, Henry Livings, London 1964, Play

Work of Art, A *see* KHUDOZHESTVO (1960).

Work of Art: Satirical Shorts, A *see* KHUDOZHESTVO (1960).

WORKING GIRLS 1931 d: Dorothy Arzner. USA., *Blind Mice*, Vera Caspary, Winifred Lenihan, New York 1930, Play

WORKING MAN, THE 1933 d: John G. Adolfi. USA., *Adopted Father*, Edgar Franklin, 1916, Short Story

Working Wives *see* WEEK-END MARRIAGE (1932).

Working Women *see* VYDELECNE ZENY (1937).

Works of the Devil, The *see* PRAESTEN I VEJLBY (1972).

WORLD ACCORDING TO GARP, THE 1982 d: George Roy Hill. USA., *The World According to Garp*, John Irving, 1978, Novel

WORLD AND HIS WIFE, THE 1920 d: Robert G. VignolA. USA., *El Gran Galeoto*, Jose Echegaray, Madrid 1881, Play

World and His Wife, The *see* STATE OF THE UNION (1948).

WORLD AND THE FLESH, THE 1932 d: John Cromwell. USA., *On the Black Sea*, Ernst Spitz, Philipp Zeska, Play

WORLD AT HER FEET, THE 1927 d: Luther Reed. USA., *Maitre Bolbec Et Son Mari*, Georges Berr, Louis Verneuil, Play

World Belongs to Us, The *see* SVET PATRI NAM (1937).

WORLD FOR SALE, THE 1918 d: J. Stuart Blackton. USA., *The World for Sale*, Gilbert Parker, New York 1916, Novel

WORLD IN HIS ARMS, THE 1952 d: Raoul Walsh. USA., *The World in His Arms*, Rex Beach, 1946, Novel

World in My Pocket, The *see* AN EINEM FREITAG UM HALB ZWOLF (1961).

WORLD IS FULL OF MARRIED MEN, THE 1979 d: Robert Young. UKN., *The World Is Full of Married Men*, Jackie Collins, Novel

World Is Ours, The *see* CHANGE OF HEART (1934).

World Is Ours, The *see* SVET PATRI NAM (1937).

World Is Still in Order at Seven in the Morning, The *see* MORGENS UM 7 IST DIE WELT NOCH IN ORDNUNG (1968).

World of Apu, The *see* APU SANSAR (1958).

World of Beggars, The *see* SVET KDE SE ZEBRA (1938).

World of Buster, The *see* BUSTERS VERDEN (1984).

WORLD OF HENRY ORIENT, THE 1964 d: George Roy Hill. USA., *The World of Henry Orient*, Nora Johnson, Boston 1958, Novel

WORLD OF SIN, A 1915. UKN., *A World of Sin*, Walter Melville, Play

World of Strangers, A *see* DILEMMA (1962).

WORLD OF SUZIE WONG, THE 1960 d: Richard Quine. UKN/USA., *The World of Suzie Wong*, Richard Mason, Novel

WORLD OF WONDERFUL REALITY, THE 1924 d: Henry Edwards. UKN., *The City of Beautiful Nonsense*, E. Temple Thurston, 1909, Novel

WORLD OWES ME A LIVING, THE 1945 d: Vernon Sewell. UKN., *The World Owes Me a Living*, John Llewellyn-Rhys, Novel

World Song, The *see* LE CHANT DU MONDE (1965).

WORLD STRUGGLE FOR OIL, THE 1924 d: Hank E. Butler. USA., *The World Struggle for Oil*, Isaac Frederick Marcosson, 1924, Article

World That Summer, The *see* DIE WELT IN JENEM SOMMER (1979).

WORLD, THE FLESH AND THE DEVIL, THE 1914 d: F. Martin Thornton. UKN., *The World the Flesh and the Devil*, Lawrence Cowen, Play

WORLD, THE FLESH AND THE DEVIL, THE 1932 d: George A. Cooper. UKN., *The World the Flesh and the Devil*, Lawrence Cowen, Play

WORLD, THE FLESH AND THE DEVIL, THE 1959 d: Ranald MacDougall. USA., *The Purple Cloud*, Matthew Phipps Shiel, 1902, Novel

World Where One Goes Begging, The *see* SVET KDE SE ZEBRA (1938).

World Will Shake, The *see* LE MONDE TREMBLERA (1939).

World Without Frontiers *see* SVET BEZ HRANIC (1931).

WORLDLINGS, THE 1920 d: Eric Harrison. UKN., *The Worldlings*, Leonard Merrick, New York 1900, Novel

WORLDLY GOODS 1924 d: Paul Bern. USA., *Worldly Goods*, Sophie Kerr, 1924, Short Story

World's a Stage: a Midsummer Night's Dream, The *see* A MIDSUMMER NIGHT'S DREAM (1953).

World's a Stage: Julius Caesar, The *see* JULIUS CAESAR (1953).

World's a Stage: MacBeth, The *see* MACBETH (1953).

World's a Stage: Othello, The *see* OTHELLO (1953).

World's a Stage: the Winter's Tale, The *see* THE WINTER'S TALE (1953).

World's a Stage: Twelfth Night, The *see* TWELFTH NIGHT (1953).

WORLD'S CHAMPION, THE 1922 d: Phil Rosen. USA., *The Champion*, Thomas Louden, A. E. Thomas, New York 1921, Play

WORLD'S GREAT SNARE, THE 1916 d: Joseph Kaufman. USA., *The World's Great Snare*, E. Phillips Oppenheim, London 1896, Novel

WORM'S EYE VIEW 1951 d: Jack Raymond. UKN., *Worm's Eye View*, R. F. Delderfield, London 1945, Play

WORMWOOD 1915 d: Marshall Farnum. USA., *Wormwood: a Drama of Paris*, Marie Corelli, London 1890, Novel

Worries of Shanti Andia, The *see* LAS INQUIETUDES DE SHANTI ANDIA (1946).

WORTH WINNING 1989 d: Will MacKenzie. USA., *Worth Winning*, Dan Lewandowski, Novel

Would You Kill a Child? *see* QUIEN PUEDE MATAR A UN NINO? (1975).

Would-Be Gentleman, The *see* LE BOURGEOIS GENTILHOMME (1958).

Wound of Light, A *see* LA HERIDA LUMINOSA (1997).

Wounded Love *see* L' AMORE MOLESTO (1995).

WOUNDINGS 1998 d: Roberta Hanley. UKN., *Woundings*, Jeff Noon, Play

Woyzeck *see* WOZZECK (1947).

WOYZECK 1967 d: Rudolf Noelte. GRM., *Woyzeck*, Georg Buchner, 1879, Play

Woyzeck *see* WOZZECK (1979).

Woyzeck *see* WODZECK (1984).

WOZZECK 1947 d: Georg C. Klaren. GDR., *Woyzeck*, Georg Buchner, 1879, Play

WOZZECK 1979 d: Werner Herzog. GRM., *Woyzeck*, Georg Buchner, 1879, Play

WRATH OF GOD, THE 1972 d: Ralph Nelson. USA., *The Wrath of God*, James Graham, Novel

Wrath of Jealousy *see* WEDDING GROUP (1936).

Wrath of the Sea *see* CHEMMEEN (1965).

WRECK OF THE HESPERUS, THE 1926 d: Frank Tilley. UKN., *The Wreck of the Hesperus*, Henry Wadsworth Longfellow, 1841, Poem

WRECK OF THE HESPERUS, THE 1927 d: Elmer Clifton. USA., *The Wreck of the Hesperus*, Henry Wadsworth Longfellow, 1841, Poem

WRECK OF THE HESPERUS, THE 1948 d: John Hoffman. USA., *The Wreck of the Hesperus*, Henry Wadsworth Longfellow, 1841, Poem

WRECK OF THE MARY DEARE, THE 1959 d: Michael Anderson. USA/UKN., *The Wreck of the Mary Deare*, Hammond Innes, 1956, Novel

Wreck, The *see* GHOSTS (1915).

Wreck, The *see* TAINATA NA APOLONIA (1984).

WRECKAGE 1925 d: Scott R. Dunlap. USA., *Salvage*, Izola Forrester, 1924, Short Story

WRECKER, THE 1928 d: Geza von Bolvary. UKN., *The Wrecker*, Bernard Merivale, Arnold Ridley, London 1927, Play

Wrecker, The *see* SEVEN SINNERS (1936).

Wrecking Boss, The *see* THE CRASH (1928).

WRECKING CREW, THE 1968 d: Phil Karlson. USA., *The Wrecking Crew*, Donald Hamilton, Greenwich, Ct. 1963, Novel

WRITING ON THE WALL, THE 1916 d: Tefft Johnson. USA., *The Writing on the Wall*, Olga Nethersole, New York 1909, Play

Written on the Sand *see* PLAY DIRTY (1968).

WRITTEN ON THE WIND 1956 d: Douglas Sirk. USA., *Written on the Wind*, Robert Wilder, 1946, Novel

WRONG BOX, THE 1966 d: Bryan Forbes. UKN., *The Wrong Box*, Lloyd Osbourne, Robert Louis Stevenson, London 1889, Novel

Wrong Door, The *see* THROUGH THE WRONG DOOR (1919).

WRONG IS RIGHT 1982 d: Richard Brooks. USA., *The Better Angels*, Charles McCarry, Novel

Wrong Kind of Girl, The *see* BUS STOP (1956).

WRONG MAN, THE 1957 d: Alfred Hitchcock. USA., *The Story of Christopher Emmanuel Balestrero*, Maxwell Anderson, Book

Wrong Move, The *see* FALSCHE BEWEGUNG (1975).

Wrong Movement *see* FALSCHE BEWEGUNG (1975).

WRONG MR. WRIGHT, THE 1927 d: Scott Sidney. USA., *The Wrong Mr. Wright*, George Broadhurst, Play

WRONG NUMBER 1959 d: Vernon Sewell. UKN., *Wrong Number*, Norman Edwards, Play

WRONG WOMAN, THE 1915 d: Richard Ridgely. USA., *The Wrong Woman*, Fawcett Lomax, Play

WSROD NOCNEJ CISZY 1978 d: Tadeusz Chmielewski. PLN., *Pribeh Kriminalniho Rady*, Ladislav Fuks, 1971, Novel

WU LI CHANG 1930 d: Nick Grinde. USA., *Mr. Wu*, Harold Owen, Harry M. Vernon, London 1913, Play

WU MING YING XIONG 1958 d: Gao Heng. CHN., *Wu Ming Ying XIong*, Du Xuan, Play

WU SONG 1963 d: Ying Yunwei, Yu Zhongying. CHN., *Shuihu Zhuan*, Luo Guanzhong, Shi Naian, c1500, Novel

WU SONG AND PAN JINLIAN 1938 d: Wu Cun. CHN., *Shuihu Zhuan*, Luo Guanzhong, Shi Naian, c1500, Novel

Wuk, Der Fuchs *see* VUK (1982).

WUNDER DES MALACHIAS, DAS 1961 d: Bernhard Wicki. GRM., Bruce Marshall, Novel

WUNDERBAREN JAHRE, DIE 1979 d: Reiner Kunze. GRM., *Die Wunderbaren Jahre*, Reiner Kunze, Novel

Wunderbarer Sommer, Ein *see* KINDER DER BERGE (1958).

WUREN HECAI 1993 d: XIa Gang. CHN/HKG., *Wuren Hecai*, Wang Shuo, Novel

WURGER VON SCHLOSS BLACKMOOR, DER 1963 d: Harald Reinl. GRM., Bryan Edgar Wallace, Novel

WUSA 1970 d: Stuart Rosenberg. USA., *A Hall of Mirrors*, Robert Stone, Boston 1966, Novel

WUTHERING HEIGHTS 1920 d: A. V. Bramble. UKN., *Wuthering Heights*, Emily Jane Bronte, London 1847, Novel

WUTHERING HEIGHTS 1939 d: William Wyler. USA., *Wuthering Heights*, Emily Jane Bronte, London 1847, Novel

Wuthering Heights *see* CUMBRES BORRASCOSAS (1953).

WUTHERING HEIGHTS 1970 d: Robert Fuest. USA/UKN., *Wuthering Heights*, Emily Jane Bronte, London 1847, Novel

Wuthering Heights *see* HURLEVENT (1986).

WUTHERING HEIGHTS 1992 d: Peter Kosminsky. USA., *Wuthering Heights*, Emily Jane Bronte, London 1847, Novel

Wyatt Earp, Frontier Marshal *see* FRONTIER MARSHAL (1939).

WYNNE AND PENKOVSKY 1987 d: Paul Seed. UKN/USA., *The Man from Moscow*, Greville Wynne, Book

WYOMING MAIL 1950 d: Reginald Le Borg. USA., Robert Hardy Andrews, Story

Wyoming Wonder *see* A HOLY TERROR (1931).

XAFNIKOS EROTAS 1984 d: Yorgos Tseberopoulos. GRC., *Talgo*, Vassilis Alexakis, Novel

XALA 1974 d: Ousmane Sembene. SNL., *Xala*, Ousmane Sembene, 1973, Novel

XAOS 1984 d: Paolo Taviani, Vittorio Taviani. ITL., *L' Altro Figlio*, Luigi Pirandello, 1905, Short Story, *Male Di Luna*, Luigi Pirandello, 1925, Short Story, *Requiem Aeternam Dona Eis Domine!*, Luigi Pirandello, 1913, Short Story

XI XING PING YAO 1991 d: Zhang Che. CHN., *Xi You Ji*, Wu Chengen, 1592, Novel

XIANGNU XIAOXIAO 1987 d: XIe Fei, Wu Lan. CHN., *Xiao XIao*, Shen Congwen, 193-, Short Story

XIANGYANG YUAN DE GUSHI 1974 d: Yuan Naicheng. CHN., *Xiangyang de Gushi*, Xu Ying, Novel

XIAO BAI QI DE FENG BO 1956 d: Gao Heng. CHN., *Xiao Bai Qi de Feng Bo*, Ji Xuexu, Novel

XIAO ERHEI JIEHUN 1964 d: Gan Xuewei, Shi Yifu. CHN., *Xiao Erhei Jiehun*, Zhao Shuli, 1945, Short Story

XIAO FU GENG 1922 d: Ren Pengnian. CHN., *Shanhu*, Pu Songling, Short Story

XIAO HUO BAN 1956 d: Ge XIn. CHN., *Xiao Huo Ban*, Liu Zhen, Novel

XIAO PENGYOU 1925 d: Zhang Shichuan. CHN., *Ku'er Liulang Ji*, Bao Tianxiao, Novel

XIAO SHI DE NU REN 1992 d: He Qun, Liu Baolin. CHN., *Xiao Shi de Nu Ren*, Wang Shuo, Novel

Xiao XIao -a Girl from Hunan *see* XIANGNU XIAOXIAO (1987).

XIN ER NU YING XIONG ZHUAN 1951 d: Shi Dongshan, Lu Ban. CHN., *Xin Er Nu Ying XIong Zhuan*, Kong Jue, Yuan Jing, Novel

XIN JU ZHANG DAO LAI XHI QIAN 1956 d: Lu Ban. CHN., *Xin Ju Zhang Dao Lai Zhi*, He Qiu, Play

XIN LIAN XIN 1958 d: Wu Tian. CHN., *People Whose Hearts Link With Hearts*, Yang Runshen, Novel

XIU XIU: THE SENT-DOWN GIRL 1998 d: Joan Chen. USA., *Tian Yu*, Yan Geling, Novel

XUE JIAN HUA PING 1986 d: Zhang Qicang. CHN., *The Lacquer Screen*, Robert Van Gulick, Novel

XUESE QINGCHEN 1991 d: Li Shaohong. CHN., *Cronaca Di Una Morte Annunciata*, Gabriel Garcia Marquez, 1981, Novel

Xumao and His Daughters *see* XUMAO HE TA DE NU ER MEN (1981).

XUMAO HE TA DE NU ER MEN 1981 d: Wang Yan. CHN., *Xumao He Ta de Nu er Men*, Zhou Keqin, Novel

XUMAO HE TA DE NU ER MEN 1981 d: Li Jun. CHN., *Xumao He Ta de Nu Er Men*, Zhou Keqin, Novel

Y En a Marre *see* Y'EN A MARRE (1959).

YA QI 1948 d: Wu Renzhi. CHN., *La Comedie de Celui Qui Epousa une Femme Muette*, Anatole France, 1912, Play

Yacht of the Seven Sins *see* DIE JACHT DER SIEBEN SUNDEN (1928).

YAGYU BUGEICHO 1957 d: Hiroshi Inagaki. JPN., *Yagyu Bugeicho*, Kosuke Gomi, 1956-59, Novel

YI GE MING DE MING YI 1960 d: Li Enjie, Shi Daqian. CHN., *Lenin and the Second Generation*, Mi Shateluofu, Play

YI GE NU REN DE MING YUN 1984 d: Yuan Ye, Zhang Jinbiao. CHN., *Star*, Ye Zi, Novel

YI JIAN TIAN 1954 d: Li Enjie. CHN., *Yi Jian Tian*, Gu Yu, Novel

YIDDISH KING LEAR, THE 1935 d: Harry Thomashefsky. USA., *Der Yiddishe Kenigen Lear*, Jacob Gordin, 1889, Play

Yidishe Tochter *see* A DAUGHTER OF HER PEOPLE (1932).

YIELD TO THE NIGHT 1956 d: J. Lee Thompson. UKN.; *Yield to the Night*, Joan Henry, Novel

YIJIAN MEI 1931 d: Bu Wancang. CHN., *The Two Gentlemen of Verona*, William Shakespeare, c1592, Play

YINGXIONG BENSE 1993 d: Chen Huiyi. CHN/HKG., *Shuihu Zhuan*, Luo Guanzhong, Shi Naian, c1500, Novel

YINGXIONG ERNU 1964 d: Wu Zhaodi. CHN., *Tuan Yuan*, Li Feigan, 1956, Short Story

YINYANG JIE 1988 d: Wu Ziniu. CHN., *Stormy Tong River*, Sima Wensen, Novel

YISKOR 1932 d: George Roland. USA., *Yiskor*, Harry Seckler, c1923, Play

YNGSJOMORDET 1966 d: Arne Mattsson. SWD., *Yngsjomordet*, Yngve Lyttkens, Stockholm 1951, Novel

YO, LA PEOR DE TODAS 1990 d: Maria Luisa Bemberg. ARG., *Sor Juana; Her Life and World (the Traps of Faith)*, Octavio Paz, Book

Yo Soy Mia *see* IO SONO MIA (1978).

YO, TU Y ELLA 1933 d: John Reinhardt. USA., *Mujer*, Gregorio Martinez Sierra, Barcelona 1925, Play

YOBA 1976 d: Tadashi Imai. JPN., *Yoba*, Ryunosuke Akutagawa, Short Story

YOKE, THE 1915 d: James W. Vickers. UKN., *The Yoke*, Hubert Wales, Novel

YOKEL BOY 1942 d: Joseph Santley. USA., *Yokel Boy*, Lew Brown, Samuel Stept, Charles Tobias, New York 1939, Musical Play

Yokels *see* CHAM (1931).

YOLANDA 1924 d: Robert G. VignolA. USA., *Yolanda*, Charles Major, New York 1905, Novel

Yolanda *see* IOLANTA (1963).

YONG SHI WO AI 1994 d: Feng XIaogang. CHN., *Yong Shi Wo Ai*, Wang Shuo, Novel

YORK MYSTERY, THE 1924 d: Hugh Croise. UKN., *The York Mystery*, Baroness Orczy, Short Story

YORK STATE FOLKS 1915 d: Harry Jackson. USA., *York State Folks*, Fred E. Wright, New York 1905, Play

YORKSHIRE SCHOOL, A 1910. USA., *Nicholas Nickleby*, Charles Dickens, London 1870, Novel

YORU NO HADA 1960 d: Yuzo KawashimA. JPN., *Yoru No Hada*, Shigeko Yuki, Novel

YORU NO HENRIN 1964 d: Noboru NakamurA. JPN., Kyoko Ohta, Story

YORU NO ONNATACHI 1948 d: Kenji Mizoguchi. JPN., *Joseimatsuri*, Eijiro Hisaita, Novel

YOSEMITE TRAIL, THE 1922 d: Bernard J. Durning. USA., *The One Way Trail*, Ridgwell Cullum, London 1911, Novel

YOSHIWARA 1937 d: Max Ophuls. FRN., *Yoshiwara*, Maurice Dekobra, Novel

YOSHIWARA ENJO 1987 d: Hideo GoshA. JPN., *Yoshiwara Enjo*, Shinichi Saito, Book

Yotsuya Ghost Story, The *see* YOTSUYA KAIDAN (1949).

Yotsuya Ghost Story, The *see* YOTSUYA KAIDAN (1959).

Yotsuya Ghost Story, The *see* YOTSUYA KAIDAN (1965).

YOTSUYA KAIDAN 1949 d: Keisuke KinoshitA. JPN., *Tokaido Yotsuya Kaidan*, Nanboku Tsuruya, 1825, Play

YOTSUYA KAIDAN 1959 d: Kenji Misumi. JPN., *Tokaido Yotsuya Kaidan*, Nanboku Tsuruya, 1825, Play

YOTSUYA KAIDAN 1965 d: Shiro ToyodA. JPN., *Tokaido Yotsuya Kaidan*, Nanboku Tsuruya, 1825, Play

YOTSUYA KAIDAN -OIWA NO BOREI 1969 d: Issei Mori. JPN., *Yotsuya Kaidan*, Nanboku Tsuruya, Play

You and I *see* THE BARGAIN (1931).

You and I *see* ICH UND DU (1953).

You and Me are Three *see* TU Y YO SOMOS TRES (1961).

You are Like a Daisy *see* NOGIKU NO GOTOKI KIMI NARIKI (1955).

You are Musik *see* DU BIST MUSIK (1956).

YOU BELONG TO ME 1934 d: Alfred L. Werker. USA., *Fifty-Two Weeks for Florette*, Elizabeth Alexander, 1921, Short Story

You Can No Longer Remain Silent *see* DU DARFST NICHT LANGER SCHWEIGEN (1955).

You Can Rest Easy, Dear Fatherland *see* MAGST RUHIG SEIN LIEB VATERLAND (1976).

YOU CAN THANK ME LATER 1998 d: Shimon Dotan. CND., *Hyper-Aller-Genic*, Oren Safdie, Play

You Can't Always Tell *see* RIGHT TO THE HEART (1942).

YOU CAN'T BEAT LOVE 1937 d: W. Christy Cabanne. USA., *Quintuplets to You*, Olga Moore, 1936, Short Story

You Can't Beat the Irish *see* TALK OF A MILLION (1951).

YOU CAN'T BELIEVE EVERYTHING 1918 d: Jack Conway. USA., *Smoke*, Norman Sherbrooke, Short Story

YOU CAN'T ESCAPE 1956 d: Wilfred Eades. UKN., *She Died Young*, Alan Kennington, Novel

YOU CAN'T ESCAPE FOREVER 1942 d: Jo Graham. USA., *Hi Nellie*, Roy Chanslor, Story

You Can't Figure Women *see* THE SNOB (1921).

You Can't Fool Your Wife *see* THE NUTCRACKER (1926).

YOU CAN'T FOOL YOUR WIFE 1940 d: Ray McCarey. USA., *The Romantic Mr. Hinklin*, Richard Carroll, Ray McCarey, Story

You Can't Get Away With It *see* THE FALLEN ANGEL (1918).

YOU CAN'T GET AWAY WITH IT 1923 d: Rowland V. Lee. USA., *You Can't Get Away With It*, Gouverneur Morris, 1913, Short Story

YOU CAN'T GET AWAY WITH MURDER 1939 d: Lewis Seiler. USA., *Chalked Out*, Jonathan Finn, Lewis E. Lawes, 1937, Play

YOU CAN'T GO HOME AGAIN 1979 d: Ralph Nelson. USA., *You Can't Go Home Again*, Thomas Wolfe, 1940, Novel

YOU CAN'T RUN AWAY FROM IT 1956 d: Dick Powell. USA., *Night Bus*, Samuel Hopkins Adams, 1933, Short Story

YOU CAN'T TAKE IT WITH YOU 1938 d: Frank CaprA. USA., *You Can't Take It With You*, Moss Hart, George S. Kaufman, New York 1936, Play

YOU CAN'T TAKE IT WITH YOU 1979 d: Paul Bogart. USA., *You Can't Take It With You*, Moss Hart, George S. Kaufman, New York 1936, Play

You Can't Take Money *see* INTERNES CAN'T TAKE MONEY (1937).

You Can't Win Them All *see* ONCE YOU KISS A STRANGER (1969).

You Dig? *see* VOUS PIGEZ? (1955).

You Don't Know Hadimrska *see* TO NEZNATE HADIMRSKU (1931).

You Don't Play Around With Love *see* MAN SPIELT NICHT MIT DER LIEBE (1949).

YOU FIND IT EVERYWHERE 1921 d: Charles Horan. USA., *The Gibson Upright*, Booth Tarkington, Harry Leon Wilson, Play

You Get It? *see* VOUS PIGEZ? (1955).

YOU GOTTA STAY HAPPY 1948 d: H. C. Potter. USA., *You Gotta Stay Happy*, Robert Carson, Serial Story

You Have to Learn to Love *see* LIEBE WILL GELERNT SEIN (1963).

YOU HUA HAO HAO SHUO 1997 d: Zhang Yimou. CHN., *Evening News*, Shu Ping, Novel

You Just Can't Wait *see* THE HOME TOWN GIRL (1919).

YOU KNOW WHAT SAILORS ARE 1928 d: Maurice Elvey. UKN., *A Light for His Pipe*, W. Townend, Novel

YOU KNOW WHAT SAILORS ARE 1954 d: Ken Annakin. UKN., *Sylvester*, Edward Hyams, Novel

YOU LIVE AND LEARN 1937 d: Arthur Woods. UKN., *Have You Come for Me*, Norma Patterson, Novel

YOU MUST GET MARRIED 1936 d: A. Leslie Pearce. UKN., *You Must Get Married*, David Evans, Novel

YOU NEVER CAN TELL 1920 d: Chester M. Franklin. USA., *Class*, Grace Lovell Bryan, 1919, Short Story, *You Never Can Tell*, Grace Lovell Bryan, 1919, Short Story

You Never Can Tell *see* STRANDED IN PARIS (1926).

YOU NEVER KNOW YOUR LUCK 1919 d: Frank Powell. USA., *You Never Know Your Luck*, Gilbert Parker, London 1914, Novel

YOU NEVER SAW SUCH A GIRL 1919 d: Robert G. VignolA. USA., *You Never Saw Such a Girl*, George Weston, New York 1919, Novel

You Only Live Once *see* MAN LEBT NUR EINMAL (1952).

YOU ONLY LIVE TWICE 1967 d: Lewis Gilbert. UKN., *You Only Live Twice*, Ian Fleming, London 1964, Novel

YOU PAY YOUR MONEY 1957 d: MacLean Rogers. UKN., *You Pay Your Money*, Michael Cronin, Novel

YOU REMEMBER ELLEN 1912 d: Sidney Olcott. USA., *You Remember Ellen*, Thomas Moore, Poem

YOU SAN JIE 1963 d: Wu Yong-Gang. CHN., *Hong Lou Meng*, Cao Zhan, c1750-92, Novel

You Were a Prophet, My Dear *see* SZIVEM PROFETA VOLTAL (1968).

You Were Like a Wild Chrysanthemum *see* NOGIKU NO GOTOKI KIMI NARIKI (1955).

YOU WERE NEVER LOVELIER 1942 d: William A. Seiter. USA., *The Gay Senorita*, Carlos A. Olivari, Sixto Pondal Rios, Story

You'll Cry for Me Tomorrow *see* MORGEN WIRST DU UM MICH WEINEN (1959).

YOU'LL NEVER SEE ME AGAIN 1973 d: Jeannot Szwarc. USA., *You'll Never See Me Again*, Cornell Woolrich, Short Story

YOUNG AMERICA 1922 d: Arthur Berthelet. USA., *Young America*, John Frederick Ballard, New York 1915, Play

YOUNG AMERICA 1932 d: Frank Borzage. USA., *Young America*, John Frederick Ballard, New York 1915, Play

Young and Eager *see* CLAUDELLE INGLISH (1961).

YOUNG AND INNOCENT 1937 d: Alfred Hitchcock. UKN., *A Shilling for Candles*, Josephine Tey, Novel

YOUNG AND THE BRAVE, THE 1963 d: Francis D. Lyon. USA., *The Young and the Brave*, Ronald Davidson, Harry M. Slott, Novel

YOUNG AND THE GUILTY, THE 1958 d: Peter Cotes. UKN., *The Young and the Guilty*, Ted Willis, Television Play

Young and the Willing, The *see* THE WILD AND THE WILLING (1962).

YOUNG AND WILLING 1942 d: Edward H. Griffith. USA., *Out of the Frying Pan*, Francis Swann, Play

Young and Willing *see* THE WEAK AND THE WICKED (1953).

Young and Willing *see* THE WILD AND THE WILLING (1962).

Young Aphrodites *see* MIKRES APHRODITES (1962).

Young Apollo *see* MEN OF TOMORROW (1932).

YOUNG APRIL 1926 d: Donald Crisp. USA., *Young April*, Egerton Castle, New York 1899, Novel

YOUNG AS YOU FEEL 1931 d: Frank Borzage. USA., *Father and the Boys*, George Ade, New York 1908, Play

YOUNG AS YOU FEEL 1940 d: Malcolm St. Clair. USA., *Merry Andrew*, Lewis Beach, New York 1929, Play

YOUNG AT HEART 1954 d: Gordon Douglas. USA., *Sister Act*, Fannie Hurst, 1937, Short Story

Young Beast, The *see* WAKAI KEMONO (1958).

YOUNG BILLY YOUNG 1969 d: Burt Kennedy. USA., *Who Rides With Wyatt?*, Will Henry, New York 1955, Novel

YOUNG BRIDE 1932 d: William A. Seiter. USA., *Veneer*, Hugh Stange, New York 1929, Play

Young Caruso, The *see* ENRICO CARUSO (1951).

YOUNG CASSIDY 1965 d: Jack Cardiff, John Ford (Uncredited). UKN/USA., *Mirror in My House*, Sean O'Casey, 1956, Autobiography

Young Composer's Odyssey, A *see* PUTSCHESTWIE MOLODOGO KOMPOSITORA (1984).

Young Couple, A *see* UN JEUNE COUPLE (1968).

YOUNG DESIRE 1930 d: Lewis D. Collins. USA., *Carnival*, William R. Doyle, New York 1924, Play

YOUNG DIANA, THE 1922 d: Albert Capellani, Robert G. VignolA. USA., *The Young Diana*, Marie Corelli, 1918, Novel

YOUNG DOCTORS, THE 1961 d: Phil Karlson. USA., *The Final Diagnosis*, Arthur Hailey, New York 1959, Novel

YOUNG DONOVAN'S KID 1931 d: Fred Niblo. USA., *Big Brother*, Rex Beach, 1923, Short Story

YOUNG DON'T CRY, THE 1957 d: Alfred L. Werker. USA., *The Cunning and the Haunted*, Richard Jessup, 1954, Novel

YOUNG DYNAMITE 1937 d: Leslie Goodwins. USA., *State Trooper*, Arthur Durlam, Short Story, *The New Freedom*, Peter B. Kyne, Short Story

YOUNG EAGLES 1930 d: William A. Wellman. USA., *The One Who Was Clever*, Elliott White Springs, 1929, Short Story, *Sky High*, Elliott White Springs, 1929, Short Story

Young Englishman see **DER JUNGE ENGLANDER** (1958).

Young Erhei's Marriage see **XIAO ERHEI JIEHUN** (1964).

YOUNG EVE AND OLD ADAM 1920. UKN., *Young Eve and Old Adam*, Tom Gallon, Novel

Young Friend see **XIAO PENGYOU** (1925).

Young Generation see **WAKAI HITO** (1952).

Young Girls Beware see **FILLETTES MEFIEZ-VOUS** (1957).

Young Girl's Body, The see **IL CORPO DELLA RAGAZZA** (1979).

Young Girls of Wilko, The see **PANNY Z WILKO** (1979).

Young Go Wild, The see **VERBRECHEN NACH SCHULSCHLUSS** (1959).

YOUNG GOODMAN BROWN 1972 d: Donald Fox. USA., *Young Goodman Brown*, Nathaniel Hawthorne, 1846, Short Story

Young Guard, The see **MOLODAYA GVARDIYA** (1948).

Young Have No Time, The see **UNG LEG** (1956).

YOUNG IDEAS 1924 d: Robert F. Hill. USA., *Relative Values*, Sophie Kerr, 1923, Short Story

YOUNG IN HEART, THE 1938 d: Richard Wallace. USA., *The Gay Banditti*, I. A. R. Wylie, 1938, Novel

Young Invaders, The see **DARBY'S RANGERS** (1958).

YOUNG JOE, THE FORGOTTEN KENNEDY 1977 d: Richard T. Heffron. USA., *The Lost Prince: Young Joe the Forgotten Kennedy*, Henry Searls, Biography

Young Ladies in White see **THE WHITE PARADE** (1934).

Young Ladies of Wilko, The see **PANNY Z WILKO** (1979).

Young Lady see **GOSPODJICA** (1980).

Young Lady's Fan, The see **SHAO NAINAI DE SHANZI** (1938).

YOUNG LAND, THE 1959 d: Ted Tetzlaff. USA., *Frontier Frenzy*, John Reese, Serial Story

YOUNG LIONS, THE 1958 d: Edward Dmytryk. USA., *The Young Lions*, Irwin Shaw, 1948, Novel

YOUNG LOCHINVAR 1911. USA., *Marmion a Tale of Flodden Field*, Sir Walter Scott, 1808, Poem

YOUNG LOCHINVAR 1923 d: W. P. Kellino. UKN., *Marmion a Tale of Flodden Field*, Sir Walter Scott, 1808, Poem

Young Lord see **BONCHI** (1960).

Young Lord, The see **DER JUNGE LORD** (1965).

Young Love see **LIEBELEI** (1933).

YOUNG LOVERS, THE 1964 d: Samuel Goldwyn Jr. USA., *The Young Lovers*, Julian Halevy, New York 1955, Novel

YOUNG MAN OF MANHATTAN 1930 d: Monta Bell. USA., *Young Man of Manhattan*, Katharine Brush, New York 1930, Novel

Young Man of Music see **YOUNG MAN WITH A HORN** (1950).

Young Man, Who Can Do Anything see **DER ALLES KANN JUNGER MANN** (1957).

YOUNG MAN WITH A HORN 1950 d: Michael Curtiz. USA., *Young Man With a Horn*, Dorothy Baker, 1938, Novel

Young Master Octavio, The see **EL SENORITO OCTAVIO** (1950).

YOUNG MRS. WINTHROP 1915 d: Richard Ridgely. USA., *The Young Mrs. Winthrop*, Bronson Howard, New York 1882, Play

YOUNG MRS. WINTHROP 1920 d: Walter Edwards. USA., *The Young Mrs. Winthrop*, Bronson Howard, New York 1882, Play

YOUNG NOWHERES 1929 d: Frank Lloyd. USA., *Young Nowheres*, I. A. R. Wylie, 1927, Short Story

Young Nowheres see **SOME DAY** (1935).

YOUNG ONE, THE 1960 d: Luis Bunuel. MXC., *Travelin' Man*, Peter Matthiessen, 1957, Short Story

Young People see **NEW FACES OF 1937** (1937).

Young People see **WAKAI HITO** (1937).

Young People see **WAKAI HITO** (1952).

Young People in the City see **JUNGE LEUTE IN DER STADT** (1985).

Young Person in Pink, The see **THE GIRL WHO FORGOT** (1939).

YOUNG PHILADELPHIANS, THE 1959 d: Vincent Sherman. USA., *The Philadelphian*, Richard Powell, 1956, Novel

YOUNG PIONEERS 1976 d: Michael O'Herlihy. USA., *Let the Hurricane Roar*, Rose Wilder Lane, Novel, *Young Pioneers*, Rose Wilder Lane, Novel

YOUNG RAJAH, THE 1922 d: Phil Rosen. USA., *Amos Judd*, John Ames Mitchell, New York 1895, Novel

Young Rebel, The see **AKUTARO** (1963).

Young Rebel, The see **LE AVVENTURE E GLI AMORI DI MIGUEL CERVANTES** (1967).

YOUNG ROMANCE 1915 d: George Melford. USA., *Young Romance*, William C. de Mille, Play

Young Sanchez see **EL JOVEN SANCHEZ** (1963).

Young Scarface see **BRIGHTON ROCK** (1947).

YOUNG SINNERS 1931 d: John G. Blystone. USA., *Young Sinners*, Elmer Harris, New York 1929, Play

YOUNG STRANGER, THE 1957 d: John Frankenheimer. USA., *Deal a Blow*, Robert Dozier, 1955, Television Play

Young Summer see **UNG SOMMAR** (1954).

Young Torless see **DER JUNGE TORLESS** (1966).

YOUNG WARRIORS, THE 1967 d: John Peyser. USA., *The Beardless Warriors*, Richard Matheson, Boston 1960, Novel

YOUNG WIDOW 1946 d: Edwin L. Marin. USA., *Young Widow*, Clarissa Fairchild Cushman, Novel

YOUNG WINSTON 1972 d: Richard Attenborough. UKN., *My Early Life*, Winston Spencer Churchill, Autobiography

YOUNG WIVES' TALE 1951 d: Henry Cass. UKN., *Young Wives' Tale*, Ronald Jeans, London 1949, Play

Young Woman of 1914 see **JUNGE FRAU VON 1914** (1969).

YOUNG WOODLEY 1929 d: Thomas Bentley. UKN., *Young Woodley*, John Van Druten, London 1928, Play

YOUNG WOODLEY 1930 d: Thomas Bentley. UKN., *Young Woodley*, John Van Druten, London 1928, Play

YOUNGBLOOD HAWKE 1964 d: Delmer Daves. USA., *Youngblood Hawke*, Herman Wouk, New York 1962, Novel

Younger Brother see **OTOTO** (1960).

Younger Generation, The see **NIAN QING DE YI DAI** (1965).

Younger Generation, The see **NIAN QING DE YI DAI** (1976).

YOUNGEST PROFESSION, THE 1943 d: Edward Buzzell. USA., *The Youngest Profession*, Lillian Day, 1940, Book

Youngest Spy, The see **IVANOVO DETSTVO** (1962).

Younost Petra see **JUNOST PETRA** (1980).

YOUR FRIEND AND MINE 1923 d: Clarence Badger. USA., *Your Friend and Mine*, Willard Mack, Play

Your Good Name see **TRIFLING WITH HONOR** (1923).

YOUR MONEY OR YOUR WIFE 1972 d: Allen Reisner. USA., *If You Want to See Your Wife Again*, John Craig, Novel

Your Name Poisons My Dreams see **TU NOMBRE ENVENENA MIS SUENOS** (1996).

YOUR OBEDIENT SERVANT 1917 d: Edward H. Griffith. USA., *Black Beauty*, Anna Sewell, London 1877, Novel

Your Only Young Twice see **THE HAPPY YEARS** (1950).

Your Red Wagon see **THEY LIVE BY NIGHT** (1948).

YOUR TICKET IS NO LONGER VALID 1980 d: George Kaczender. CND., *Your Ticket Is No Longer Valid*, Romain Gary, Novel

Your Turn, Darling see **MIGNONNE A TOI DE FAIRE** (1963).

YOUR UNCLE DUDLEY 1935 d: Eugene J. Forde. USA., *Your Uncle Dudley*, Howard Lindsay, Bertrand Robinson, New York 1929, Play

YOU'RE A BIG BOY NOW 1966 d: Francis Ford Coppola. USA., *You're a Big Boy Now*, David Benedictus, London 1963, Novel

YOU'RE FIRED 1919 d: James Cruze. USA., *The Halberdier of the Little Rheinschloss*, O. Henry, 1907, Short Story

YOU'RE IN THE NAVY NOW 1951 d: Henry Hathaway. USA., *Flying Teakettle*, John W. Hazard, 1950, Article

You're Laughing see **TU RIDI** (1998).

YOU'RE MY EVERYTHING 1949 d: Walter Lang. USA., *George Jessel*, Story

YOU'RE NEVER TOO YOUNG 1955 d: Norman Taurog. USA., *Sunny Goes Home*, Fanny Kilbourne, Short Story

YOU'RE NOT SO TOUGH 1940 d: Joe May. USA., *Son of Mama Posita*, Maxwell Aley, Story

YOU'RE ONLY YOUNG TWICE! 1952 d: Terry Bishop. UKN., *What Say They?*, James Bridie, 1939, Play

YOU'RE TELLING ME 1934 d: Erle C. Kenton. USA., *Mr. Bisbee's Princess*, Julian Leonard Street, Short Story

YOURS, MINE AND OURS 1968 d: Melville Shavelson. USA., *Who Gets the Drumstick*, Helen Beardsley, New York 1965, Novel

Youth see **JUGEND** (1938).

Youth see **UNE JEUNESSE** (1983).

YOUTH FOR SALE 1924 d: W. Christy Cabanne. USA., *The Gray Path*, Izola Forrester, 1922, Short Story

Youth in Revolt see **ALTITUDE 3200** (1938).

Youth in the Flames of War see **ZHAN HUO ZHONG DE QING CHUN** (1959).

Youth March see **GIOVINEZZA GIOVINEZZA** (1969).

Youth of Japan, The see **NIHON NO SEISHUN** (1968).

Youth of the Beast see **YAJU NO SEISHUN** (1963).

Youth to Sell see **YOUTH FOR SALE** (1924).

Youth Triumphant see **ENEMIES OF CHILDREN** (1923).

Youth, Youth see **GIOVINEZZA GIOVINEZZA** (1969).

YOUTHFUL FOLLY 1934 d: Miles Mander. UKN., *Youthful Folly*, Josephine Tey, Play

YOUTH'S DESIRE 1920. USA., *The Aviator*, James Montgomery, New York 1910, Play

Youth's Ghost Story, The see **SEISHUN KAIDAN** (1955).

You've Been a Prophet, My Dear see **SZIVEM PROFETA VOLTAL** (1968).

YOU'VE GOT MAIL 1998 d: Nora Ephron. USA., *Parfumerie*, Miklos Laszlo, Play

YOUYI 1959 d: Li Jun. CHN., *Youyi*, Wang Ying, Play

Yovita see **JOWITA** (1967).

YU LI HUN 1924 d: Zhang Shichuan, Xu Hu. CHN., *Yu Li Hun*, Xu Zhenya, Novel

YUAN YE 1988 d: Ling Zi. CHN., *Yuan Ye*, Wan Jiabao, 1939, Play

YUE YAER 1986 d: Sun Yu. CHN., *Yue Yaer*, Shu Qingchun, 194-, Short Story

YUKI FUJIN EZU 1950 d: Kenji Mizoguchi. JPN., *Yuki Fujin Ezu*, Seiichi Funabashi, Novel

YUKIGUNI 1957 d: Shiro ToyodA. JPN., *Yukiguni*, Yasunari Kawabata, 1947, Novel

YUKIGUNI 1965 d: Hideo ObA. JPN., *Yukiguni*, Yasunari Kawabata, 1947, Novel

Yukionna see **KAIDAN YUKIJORO** (1968).

Yukionna, Woman of the Snow see **KAIDAN YUKIJORO** (1968).

YUKON FLIGHT 1940 d: Ralph Staub. USA., *Renfrew Rides North*, Laurie York Erskine, New York 1931, Novel

YUKON GOLD 1952 d: Frank McDonald. USA., *The Gold Hunters*, James Oliver Curwood, Indianapolis 1909, Novel

YUKON MANHUNT 1951 d: Frank McDonald. USA., James Oliver Curwood, Short Story

YUKON VENGEANCE 1954 d: William Beaudine. USA., James Oliver Curwood, Story

YUME NO GINGA 1997 d: Sogo Ishii. JPN., Kyusaku Yumeno, Novel

Yunost Petra see **JUNOST PETRA** (1980).

YUREISEN 1957 d: Teiji MatsudA. JPN., *Yurei-Sen*, Jiro Osaragi, Novel

Yusha Nomi *see* **NONE BUT THE BRAVE** (1965).

YVETTE 1927 d: Alberto Cavalcanti. FRN., *Yvette*, Guy de Maupassant, 1885, Short Story

YVETTE 1938 d: Wolfgang Liebeneiner. GRM., *Yvette*, Guy de Maupassant, 1885, Short Story

YVETTE 1990 d: Jean-Pierre Marchand. FRN., *Yvette*, Guy de Maupassant, 1885, Short Story

Z 1968 d: Costa-Gavras. FRN/ITL/ALG., *Z*, Vassilis Vassilikos, Athens 1966, Novel

Z CESKYCH MLYNU 1925 d: Svatopluk Innemann, Ferry Seidl. CZC., *Z Ceskych Mlynu*, Karel Tuma, Play

Z CESKYCH MLYNU 1929 d: M. J. Krnansky, Ferry Seidl. CZC., *Z Ceskych Mlynu*, Karel Tuma, Play

Z CESKYCH MLYNU 1941 d: Miroslav Cikan. CZC., Karel Fort, Play

Z LASKY 1928 d: Vladimir Slavinsky. CZC., *Z Lasky*, Marie Kyzlinkova, Novel

Z (L'orgia Del Potere) *see* **Z** (1968).

ZA DVUMYA ZAYTSAMI 1961 d: V. Ivanov. USS., *Za Dvoma Zaytsyami*, Mikhaylo Petrovich Staritsky, 1883, Play

ZA RANNICH CERVANKU 1934 d: Josef Rovensky. CZC., *Za Rannich Cervanku*, Alois Vojtech Smilovsky, Novel

ZA TICHYCH NOCI 1940 d: Gina Hasler. CZC., *Pisne Zavisovy*, Jan Cervenka, Verse

ZA VLAST SOVETOV 1956 d: Boris Buneyev. USS., *Za Vlast Sovetov*, Valentin Kataev, 1949, Novel

ZAAK VAN LEVEN OF DOOD, EEN 1983 d: George Schouten. NTH., *Zonder Dollen*, Hans Vervoort

Zabec *see* **TRNY A KVETY** (1921).

ZABEC 1939 d: Vladimir Slavinsky. CZC., *Zabec*, Josef Skruzny, Play

ZABICIE CIOTKI 1984 d: Grzegorz Krolikiewicz. PLN., *Zabicie Ciotki*, Andrzej Bursa, Novel

ZABRAVETE TOZI SLOUCHAI 1984 d: Krassimir Spassov. BUL., *Zabravete Tozi Slouchai*, Georgi Danailow, Play

ZADAH TELA 1983 d: Zivojin Pavlovic. YGS., *Zadah Tela*, Zivojin Pavlovic, 1982, Novel

ZAGANELLA E IL CAVALIERE 1932 d: Gustavo Serena, Giorgio Mannini. ITL., *Lu Cavalieri Pidagna*, Luigi Capuana, 1909, Play

ZAHADA HLAVOLAMU 1993 d: Petr Kotek. CZC., *Zahada Hlavolamu*, Jaroslav Foglar, Book

ZAHADNY PRIPAD GALGINUV 1923 d: Vaclav Kubasek. CZC., *Hrdina Lackmann*, Otomar Schafer, Book

Zahari Saap *see* **ZEHARI SAAP** (1933).

ZAIRA 1910. ITL., *Zaire*, Voltaire, 1739

ZAKOLDOVANNY MALCHIK 1956. USS., *Nils Holgerssons Underbara Resa*, Selma Lagerlof, 1906-07, Novel

ZAKON I DOLG 1927 d: Konstantin Mardzhanov. USS., *Amok*, Stefan Zweig, 1922, Short Story

ZALACAIN, EL AVENTURERO 1929 d: Francisco Camacho. SPN., *Zalacain El Aventurero*, Pio Baroja Y Nessi, 1909, Novel

ZALACAIN, EL AVENTURERO 1954 d: Juan de OrdunA. SPN., *Zalacain El Aventurero*, Pio Baroja Y Nessi, 1909, Novel

Zalacain the Adventurer *see* **EL AVENTURERO ZALACAIN** (1954).

ZAMBA 1949 d: William Berke. USA., *The Girl and the Gorilla*, Maurice Conn, Story

Zamba the Gorilla *see* **ZAMBA** (1949).

ZANDER THE GREAT 1925 d: George W. Hill. USA., *Zander the Great*, Edward Salisbury Field, New York 1923, Play

ZANNA BIANCA 1973 d: Lucio Fulci. ITL/FRN/SPN., *White Fang*, Jack London, New York 1905, Novel

ZANZIBAR 1940 d: Harold Schuster. USA., *Rigadoon*, Maurice Tombragel, Story, *River of Missing Men*, Maurice Wright, Story

Zanzibar *see* **SANSIBAR ODER DER LETZTE GRUND** (1986).

Zao Chun Er Yue *see* **ZAOCHUN ERYUE** (1963).

ZAOCHUN ERYUE 1963 d: XIe Tieli. CHN., *Er Yue*, Zhao Pingfu, 1956, Novel

ZAPADLI VLASTENCI 1932 d: M. J. Krnansky. CZC., *Zapadli Vlastenci*, Karel Vaclav Rais, Novel

ZAPOMENUTE SVETLO 1997 d: Vladimir Michalek. CZE., *Zapomenute Svetlo*, Jakub Demi, Novel

ZAPOROZETS ZA DUNAYEM 1938 d: Y. P. Kavaledge. USS., *Zaporozheta Za Dunayem*, Semen Artemowsky, St. Petersburg 1863, Opera

ZAPPLER, DER 1982 d: Wolfram Deutschmann. GRM., *Der Zappler*, Ernst Klee, Novel

ZAR UND ZIMMERMANN 1970 d: Joachim Hess. GRM., *Zar Und Zimmermann*, Albert Lortzing, Leipzig 1837, Opera

ZARAK 1957 d: Terence Young, Yakima Canutt. UKN., *The Story of Zarak Khan*, A. C. Bevan, Book

ZAREWITSCH, DER 1928 d: Jacob Fleck, Luise Fleck. GRM., *Der Zarewitsch*, Gabriele Zapolska, Play

ZAREWITSCH, DER 1933 d: Victor Janson. GRM., *Der Zarewitsch*, Franz Lehar, Berlin 1927, Operetta

ZAREWITSCH, DER 1954 d: Arthur M. Rabenalt. GRM/FRN., *Der Zarewitsch*, Franz Lehar, Berlin 1927, Operetta

ZARTE HAUT IN SCHWARZER SEIDE 1961 d: Max Pecas. GRM/FRN., Walter Ebert, Novel

Zartliche Cousinen *see* **TENDRES COUSINES** (1980).

ZARTLICHES GEHEIMNIS 1956 d: Wolfgang Schleif. GRM., *Was Am See Geschah*, Lisa Tetzner, Short Story

ZATO ICHI MONOGATARI 1962 d: Kenji Misumi. JPN., *Zato Ichi Monogatari*, Kan Shimosawa, Novel

Zatoichi Enters Again *see* **ZATO ICHI MONOGATARI** (1962).

Zatoulane Princezne, O *see* **O PRINCEZNE JULINCE** (1987).

ZAUBERBERG, DER 1981 d: Hans W. Geissendorfer. GRM/FRN/ITL., *Der Zauberberg*, Thomas Mann, 1924, Novel

ZAUBERGEIGE, DIE 1944 d: Herbert Maisch. GRM., *Die Zaubergeige*, Kurt Kluge, 1940, Novel

Zauberhafte Erbschaft, Eine *see* **CAROVNE DEDICTVI** (1985).

ZAUBERMANNCHEN, DAS 1960 d: Christoph Engel. GDR., *Das Zaubermannchen*, Gudrun Kaltofen, Play

Zavetat Na Inkata *see* **VIVA GRINGO** (1966).

ZAVTRAK U PREVODITELYA 1953 d: Anatoly Rybakov. USS., *Zavtrak U Predvoditelya*, Ivan Turgenev, 1856, Play

ZAZA 1910. ITL., *Zaza*, Pierre Berton, Charles Simon, Paris 1898, Play

ZAZA 1913 d: Adrien Caillard. FRN., *Zaza*, Pierre Berton, Charles Simon, Paris 1898, Play

ZAZA 1915 d: Edwin S. Porter, Hugh Ford. USA., *Zaza*, Pierre Berton, Charles Simon, Paris 1898, Play

ZAZA 1923 d: Allan Dwan. USA., *Zaza*, Pierre Berton, Charles Simon, Paris 1898, Play

ZAZA 1938 d: George Cukor. USA., *Zaza*, Pierre Berton, Charles Simon, Paris 1898, Play

ZAZA 1942 d: Renato Castellani. ITL., *Zaza*, Pierre Berton, Charles Simon, Paris 1898, Play

ZAZA 1955 d: Rene Gaveau. FRN., *Zaza*, Pierre Berton, Charles Simon, Paris 1898, Play

ZAZDROSC I MEDYCYNA 1973 d: Janusz Majewski. PLN., *Zazdrosc I Medycyna*, Michal Choromanski, 1932, Novel

Zazie *see* **ZAZIE DANS LE METRO** (1960).

ZAZIE DANS LE METRO 1960 d: Louis Malle. FRN., *Zazie Dans le Metro*, Raymond Queneau, Paris 1959, Novel

Zazie in the Underground *see* **ZAZIE DANS LE METRO** (1960).

ZBEHOVIA A PUTNICI 1968 d: Juraj Jakubisko. CZC/ITL., *Zbehove*, Ladislav Tazky

Zbehova a Tulaci *see* **ZBEHOVIA A PUTNICI** (1968).

ZDI MENJA 1943 d: Alexander Stolper, Boris Ivanov. USS., *Zhdi Menya*, Konstantin Simonov, 1941, Verse

ZE SVETA LESNICH SAMOT 1933 d: M. J. Krnansky. CZC., *Ze Sveta Lesnich Samot*, Karel Klostermann, Novel

ZEBRACKA OPERA 1991 d: Jiri Menzel. CZC., *The Beggar's Opera*, John Gay, London 1728, Play

ZEBRE, LE 1992 d: Jean Poiret. FRN., *Le Zebre*, Alexandre Jardin, Novel

ZEEMANSVROUWEN 1930 d: Henk Kleinmann. NTH., *Zeemansvrouwen*, Herman Bouber, 1928, Play

ZEHARI SAAP 1933 d: J. J. Madan. IND., *Zehari Saap*, Narayan Prasad Betaab, Play

ZEHN KLEINE NEGERLEIN 1954 d: Rolf von Sydow. GRM., Inka Kohler-Rechnitz, Story

Zeit Der Kirschen Ist Vorbei, Die *see* **LE GRAND DADAIS** (1967).

ZEIT DER SCHULDLOSEN, DIE 1964 d: Thomas Fantl. GRM., *Zeit de Schuldlosen*, Siegfried Lenz, 1962, Play

ZEIT DER STILLE 1986 d: Thorsten Nater. GRM., Nino Jacusso, Story

ZELENY AUTOMOBIL 1921 d: Svatopluk Innemann. CZC., *Zeleny Automobil*, Josef Skruzny, Novel

ZELLE, DIE 1971 d: Horst Bienek. GRM., *Die Zelle*, Horst Bienek, 1968, Novel

Zelmaide *see* **PASSI FURTIVI IN UNA NOTTE BOIA** (1976).

Zemja *see* **ZEMYA** (1957).

Zemma *see* **ZENMA** (1951).

ZEMSTA 1957 d: Antoni Bohdziewicz. PLN., *Zemsta*, Alexander Fredro, 1833, Play

ZEMYA 1957 d: Zahari Zhandov. BUL., *Zemya*, Pelin Elin, 1922, Novel

ZENA, KTERA SE SMEJE 1931 d: Jan Bor. CZC., Alfred Puter, Play

ZENA, KTERA VI CO CHCE 1934 d: Vaclav Binovec. CZC., *Eine Frau Die Weiss Was Sie Will*, Alfred Grunwald, Oscar Straus, Operetta

ZENA NA ROZCESTI 1937 d: Oldrich Kminek. CZC., *Zena Na Rozcesti Z Casopisu Prazanka*, Olga Fujerova, Novel

ZENA POD KRIZEM 1937 d: Vladimir Slavinsky. CZC., *Zena Pod Krizem*, Maryna Radomerska, Novel

ZENMA 1951 d: Keisuke KinoshitA. JPN., *Zenma*, Kunio Kishida, 1951, Novel

ZENOBIA 1939 d: Gordon Douglas. USA., *Zenobia's Infidelity*, Henry C. Bunner, 1925, Short Story

Zenobia's Infidelity *see* **ZENOBIA** (1939).

ZENY U BENZINU 1939 d: Vaclav Kubasek. CZC., *Zeny U Benzinu*, Vladimir Zika, Novel

ZEPPELIN 1981 d: Lasse Glomm. NRW., Tormod Haugen, Story

ZER TO PIDHAN JANI JANI 1972 d: Upendra Trivedi. IND., *Zer to Pidhan Jani Jani*, Manubhai Pancholi, Novel

ZERBROCHENE KRUG, DER 1937 d: Gustav Ucicky. GRM., *Der Zerbrochene Krug*, Heinrich von Kleist, 1811, Play

Zerebonok *see* **ZHEREBYONOK** (1960).

ZERO 1928 d: Jack Raymond. UKN., *Zero*, Collinson Owen, Novel

ZERO HOUR! 1957 d: Hall Bartlett. USA., *Flight Into Danger*, Arthur Hailey, Television Play

Zero in Amore *see* **E ARRIVATO L'ACCORDATORE** (1952).

Zero Murder Case, The *see* **THE STRANGE AFFAIR OF UNCLE HARRY** (1945).

Zero Pilot *see* **OZORA NO SAMURAI** (1976).

ZERT 1968 d: Jaromil Jires. CZC., *Zert*, Milan Kundera, 1967, Novel

ZESTOKIJ ROMANS 1984 d: Eldar Ryazanov. USS., *Bespridannitsa*, Alexander Ostrovsky, 1878, Play

Zex *see* **ESCAPEMENT** (1957).

Zex, the Electronic Fiend *see* **ESCAPEMENT** (1957).

ZEZOWATE SZCZESCIE 1960 d: Andrzej Munk. PLN., *Szesc Wcielen Jana Piszczyka*, Jerzy Stefan Stawicki, 1951, Short Story

ZHAN HUO ZHONG DE QING CHUN 1959 d: Wang Yan. CHN., *Zhan Huo Zhong de Qing Chun*, Lu Zhuguo, Novel

Zhdi Menya *see* **ZDI MENJA** (1943).

ZHELEZNAYA PYATA OLIGARKHIJ 1998 d: Alexander Bashirov. RSS., *The Iron Heel*, Jack London

Zheleznyi Potok *see* **ZHELYEZNY POTOK** (1967).

ZHELYEZNY POTOK 1967 d: Yefim Dzigan. USS., *Zheleznyi Potok*, Aleksandr Serafimovich, 1924, Short Story

ZHEN NU 1988 d: Huang Jianzhong. CHN., *Zhen Nu*, Gu Hua, Novel

ZHENG TU 1976 d: Yan Bili, Bao Qicheng. CHN., *Zheng Tu*, Guo XIanhong, Novel

ZHENITBA 1937 d: Erast Garin, Khessia LokshinA. USS., *Zhenitba*, Nikolay Gogol, 1841, Play

ZHENITBA BALZAMINOVA 1965 d: Konstantin Voinov. USS., *Prazdnichnyy Son - Do Obeda*, Alexander Ostrovsky, St. Petersburg 1857, Play

Zherebenok *see* **ZHEREBYONOK** (1960).